2013

JANUARY
M	T	W	T	F	S	S
	1	2	3	4	5	6
7	8	9	10	11	12	13
14	15	16	17	18	19	20
21	22	23	24	25	26	27
28	29	30	31			

FEBRUARY
M	T	W	T	F
				1
4	5	6	7	8
11	12	13	14	15
18	19	20	21	22
25	26	27	28	

APRIL
M	T	W	T	F	S	S
1	2	3	4	5	6	7
8	9	10	11	12	13	14
15	16	17	18	19	20	21
22	23	24	25	26	27	28
29	30					

MAY
M	T	W	T	F	S	S
		1	2	3	4	5
6	7	8	9	10	11	12
13	14	15	16	17	18	19
20	21	22	23	24	25	26
27	28	29	30	31		

JUNE
M	T	W	T	F	S	S
					1	2
3	4	5	6	7	8	9
10	11	12	13	14	15	16
17	18	19	20	21	22	23
24	25	26	27	28	29	30

JULY
M	T	W	T	F	S	S
1	2	3	4	5	6	7
8	9	10	11	12	13	14
15	16	17	18	19	20	21
22	23	24	25	26	27	28
29	30	31				

AUGUST
M	T	W	T	F	S	S
			1	2	3	4
5	6	7	8	9	10	11
12	13	14	15	16	17	18
19	20	21	22	23	24	25
26	27	28	29	30	31	

SEPTEMBER
M	T	W	T	F	S	S
						1
2	3	4	5	6	7	8
9	10	11	12	13	14	15
16	17	18	19	20	21	22
23	24	25	26	27	28	29
30						

OCTOBER
M	T	W	T	F	S	S
	1	2	3	4	5	6
7	8	9	10	11	12	13
14	15	16	17	18	19	20
21	22	23	24	25	26	27
28	29	30	31			

NOVEMBER
M	T	W	T	F	S	S
				1	2	3
4	5	6	7	8	9	10
11	12	13	14	15	16	17
18	19	20	21	22	23	24
25	26	27	28	29	30	

DECEMBER
M	T	W	T	F	S	S
						1
2	3	4	5	6	7	8
9	10	11	12	13	14	15
16	17	18	19	20	21	22
23	24	25	26	27	28	29
30	31					

2014

JANUARY
M	T	W	T	F	S	S
		1	2	3	4	5
6	7	8	9	10	11	12
13	14	15	16	17	18	19
20	21	22	23	24	25	26
27	28	29	30	31		

FEBRUARY
M	T	W	T	F	S	S
					1	2
3	4	5	6	7	8	9
10	11	12	13	14	15	16
17	18	19	20	21	22	23
24	25	26	27	28		

MARCH
M	T	W	T	F	S	S
					1	2
3	4	5	6	7	8	9
10	11	12	13	14	15	16
17	18	19	20	21	22	23
24	25	26	27	28	29	30
31						

APRIL
M	T	W	T	F	S	S
	1	2	3	4	5	6
7	8	9	10	11	12	13
14	15	16	17	18	19	20
21	22	23	24	25	26	27
28	29	30				

MAY
M	T	W	T	F	S	S
			1	2	3	4
5	6	7	8	9	10	11
12	13	14	15	16	17	18
19	20	21	22	23	24	25
26	27	28	29	30	31	

JUNE
M	T	W	T	F	S	S
						1
2	3	4	5	6	7	8
9	10	11	12	13	14	15
16	17	18	19	20	21	22
23	24	25	26	27	28	29
30						

JULY
M	T	W	T	F	S	S
	1	2	3	4	5	6
7	8	9	10	11	12	13
14	15	16	17	18	19	20
21	22	23	24	25	26	27
28	29	30	31			

AUGUST
M	T	W	T	F	S	S
				1	2	3
4	5	6	7	8	9	10
11	12	13	14	15	16	17
18	19	20	21	22	23	24
25	26	27	28	29	30	31

SEPTEMBER
M	T	W	T	F	S	S
					1	2
3	4	5	6	7	8	9
10	11	12	13	14	15	16
17	18	19	20	21	22	23
24	25	26	27	28	29	30

OCTOBER
M	T	W	T	F	S	S
	1	2	3	4	5	6
7	8	9	10	11	12	13
14	15	16	17	18	19	20
21	22	23	24	25	26	27
28	29	30	31			

NOVEMBER
M	T	W	T	F	S	S
					1	2
3	4	5	6	7	8	9
10	11	12	13	14	15	16
17	18	19	20	21	22	23
24	25	26	27	28	29	30

DECEMBER
M	T	W	T	F	S	S
1	2	3	4	5	6	7
8	9	10	11	12	13	14
15	16	17	18	19	20	21
22	23	24	25	26	27	28
29	30	31				

THE
FAMILY
COURT
PRACTICE
2013

CELEBRATING
150
YEARS

J O R D A N S

THE
FAMILY
COURT
PRACTICE
2013

Family Law

Family Law is a publishing imprint of

Jordan Publishing Limited
21 St Thomas Street
Bristol BS1 6JS

British Library Cataloguing-in-Publication Data
A catalogue record for this book is available from the British Library.

ISSN 1350–1860

ISBN 978 184661 6327

The publishers are grateful to the Secretariat of the Principal Registry of the Family Division for providing updated texts of a number of practice directions issued by the Division, which are set out in Part V of this work.

The kind permission of the President of the Family Division to reproduce certain materials from the *Handbook of Best Practice in Children Act Cases* is also gratefully acknowledged.

The kind permission of The Law Society to reproduce the *Legal Policy (Appointing a Solicitor for the Child in Specified Proceedings: Guidelines for Courts)* © The Law Society 2007 is also gratefully acknowledged.

This volume is typeset by Letterpart Ltd, Reigate, Surrey.

MAJOR WORKS MANAGER: Jonathan Cailes BA (Hons)

FAMILY LAW PSL: Amy Royce-Greensill, Solicitor
                Amy Sanders, Solicitor
                Hayley Trim MA, Solicitor

COMMISSIONING EDITOR: Gregory Woodgate LLB, LLM, Barrister

PUBLISHER: Will Ricketts BA (Hons)

The Index is researched and compiled by Josephine Joyce

Printed and bound by CPI Group (UK) Ltd, Croydon, CR0 4YY

Preface

When first published in 1993, *The Family Court Practice* was new and innovative, designed to meet the need for a definitive work of reference covering the entire range of family proceedings at every level of court. It was hoped then that it might stand alongside *The Supreme Court Practice* and *The County Court Practice* as the comprehensive and authoritative guide for practitioners.

Over the ensuing years the hope has become reality and as civil procedure has changed so *The Family Court Practice* has been updated annually to reflect developments in law and procedure. The work is now universally accepted as a standard book of reference for judges and practitioners throughout the jurisdiction.

Congratulations are due to the team of contributors who have achieved so much in just a few years.

The Hon Mrs Justice Bracewell
Family Division   **February 2001**

Foreword

It is a high honour for me to become the new Editor-in-Chief of *The Family Court Practice* but my pleasure is mixed with sadness that the position should have become vacant. For Mrs Justice Bracewell was the book's Editor-in-Chief for the first 14 years of its life and was far more than a distinguished figurehead. If she did not help to conceive the book, she was certainly its midwife at its birth in 1993; and she nursed it assiduously through its formative years. To my knowledge, she was very proud to be associated with its phenomenal success but typically she disclaimed any of the credit for it.

When in 1967 I began to practise family law, there was in effect only one text-book. And, being a creature of habit, I stuck almost exclusively to it for several years after 1993. It remains an admirable book which not infrequently I still use. But, like (I believe) almost all other family judges, I came to resolve that, in particular because of its ease of use, its compactness, its clarity of presentation, its reliability of text, and, above all, the accessibility of up-to-date material which only its annual format can readily provide, I would generally consult *The Family Court Practice*.

It has been clever of Jordan Publishing to insinuate *The Family Court Practice* so close to the hearts of the family judiciary. For advocates have been quick to realise that, faced with the judge's question "Where do I find it in the Red Book?", it runs counter to their need to have an answer to everything for them to admit that they have not brought a copy. Thus has the book's bandwagon rolled on.

For the last few months, since becoming associated with the book, I have begun to realise the degree of effort, initially on the part in particular of the General Editor, which results in the book's immediacy. All significant developments, whether in case-law or otherwise, are communicated to the team within hours of publication, often with apologetic directions to the relevant contributor to include reference to it within the imminent fresh edition. You, the subscribers, are the beneficiaries of this astonishing level of committed efficiency.

Nicholas Wilson
Rt Hon Lord Justice Wilson   **January 2008**

Introduction

The ill health of the President overshadowed 2012 and resulted in the post falling vacant in the latter part of the year. During his tenure, many helpful and practical initiatives were published – Sir Nicholas's bulletins remain pertinent and valuable – and his departure is a great loss. All is not gloom, however. In December, the appointment of Sir James Munby was announced. In the current troubled legal climate, the advent of our new President is a tonic.

The Department for Education announced in November 2012 that the Government intends to insert a new section 1(2A) into the Children Act 1989. Commentators have loosely described this insertion as "shared parenting". A superficial reading of the section (which imports a presumption that "involvement of [each] parent in the life of the child concerned will further the child's welfare") suggests that the good intentions espoused in the proposed legislation can only be helpful. But more thought is needed, given that the amendment stems from pressure from those who would assert that absent parents – usually fathers – are at a significant disadvantage in Children Act cases, this despite the introduction and recognition of the sharing of parental responsibility, enshrined for the first time in the 1989 Act.

The paramount consideration – the welfare of the child – was not a startling development in 1989. Statutory acknowledgement of that principle was articulated, for example, in the Guardianship of Infants Act 1925 and re-iterated in 1971. The Children Act 1989, however, bolted a menu on to the welfare declaration, found in section 1(3) – the now well-known "checklist".

One might be surprised by the assertion that, taken together, the best interests declaration and the checklist are not enough and that somehow they do not adequately promote the interests of the child. Except that on analysis, to many commentators, it is apparent that it is not the interest of the child that is promoted by the concept of "shared parenting", but that of the absent parent.

Of the substantial number of separations between parents, only a minority find themselves in conflict over the upbringing of their children (as low as 10%, according to the Parliamentary Justice Select Committee). Unhappily, the disputes that require judicial intervention usually arise out of multiple problems and it is unlikely that a declaration, or a statutory starting point, of shared "involvement" will lessen conflict. To the contrary, it is likely to encourage argument and promote control over the resident parent, adding yet another ingredient to the conflict.

Unhappily, a considerable number of contact and even residence disputes are accompanied by allegations of risk to the child. Analysis of risk is not assisted by, and is likely to be obscured by, the proposed presumption. Litigants in person (the term "self-represented litigants" flared briefly in 2012) will inevitably equate "sharing" with "equal". Pity the judges who, as well as nursing disputes through the management of introductory contact, interim arrangements and emotionally charged directions hearings, will have somehow to assist the parents in understanding that they do not have *rights* – he and she have *responsibilities* – and that those responsibilities are of equal weight; however, the rights to shared involvement are not, where they conflict with the needs of the child.

Rather than assisting the parents to reach a common goal – to help their child make the best of his fractured home – shared parenting is likely to herald more and lengthier litigation. Fathers who claim during proceedings that the odds are stacked against them, that judges are always on the side of the mother or that they are always marginalised, are fathers who cannot communicate with the other parent or listen to (let alone understand) what the court or Cafcass is saying. To add to this, to muddle the principles or welfare considerations with starting points that will be so easily misunderstood, is unhelpful to the process and damages any attempt to promote a civil, let alone cordial, relationship between the parents, which is so vital to the wellbeing of the child as he struggles to come to terms with the departure of one parent.

Flaws have been identified and expressed by the Nuffield Foundation and the Family Justice Review. The experience in Australia, whence we have often taken examples as a guide, is that litigation has increased, while willingness to compromise has reduced. Mediation is now a required filter before entry to private law disputes but, unhappily, combative parents are habitually less willing to negotiate and resolve arguments over their children outside the court arena and will hardly be encouraged to do so when their unrealistic definition of the term "shared" is challenged during the process. Coming at a time when those who cannot afford legal representation are denied access to legal advice by the removal of Legal Aid in family proceedings, the moment is hardly opportune.

A perfect storm brews: unrepresented litigants handicapped by ignorance of the system, probable bewilderment with the procedure and likely fear of each other; a new, fit for purpose but substantial core of Rules which are wholly alien to the lay person; and a rump of parents who are disadvantaged emotionally, are often angry, and are likely to misunderstand, intentionally or otherwise, the use of terms such as "rights" and "responsibilities". All this matched against static court resources, demoralised court listing personnel and harassed judges seeking to accommodate an ever-lengthening queue of private law litigants against a public law imprimatur that all public law cases should be concluded within 26 weeks. The warnings have been sounding for months, if not years. We can only pray that the forecasts are wrong or, if our worst fears are realised, that Government is watching.

Meanwhile, the Law Commission is consulting on Matrimonial Property, Needs and Agreements. There is inadequate space in this Introduction to rehearse the arguments for and against the section 25 menu, but it has to be recognised that the determination of the outcomes of applications under that section are led by advice which follows decisions of the Division and the Court of Appeal (and of course the Supreme Court), driven by cases which are litigated between spouses with access to eye-watering amounts of assets, the like of which are never seen in the vast majority of disputes litigated by family practitioners in the provinces. In times of a faltering economy, the good intentions of the section are likely to be unbalanced when there is inequality of arms and inadequacy of assets.

There is danger, however, in prescription. Rigidity of outcome might not be universally "fair". And that very word brings into focus the remarkable criticism by the Court of Appeal of the longstanding attempts at "fairness" practised by the family courts as reported in the litigation between Mr and Mrs Prest. Lord Justice Thorpe's compelling judgment was robustly overcome by the icy logic of his commercial colleagues in a decision which will, if not overturned by the Supreme Court, result in likely further subterfuge, costly enquiry and, no doubt, unfairness – issues which might remain outside the likely boundaries of the Law Commission report. The decision is expected shortly after publication of this Edition. It is keenly awaited.

Save where narratives have taken account of subsequent developments, the law is stated as at 1 February 2013.

Anthony Cleary   **March 2013**

Contents

PART I: Procedural Guides

SECTION A: APPLICATIONS FOR RELIEF OTHER THAN DIVORCE

SECTION B: APPLICATION FOR MATRIMONIAL AND CIVIL PARTNERSHIP PROCEEDINGS AND RELATED ORDERS

SECTION C: ENFORCEMENT OF ORDERS

SECTION E: JUDICIAL REVIEWS AND APPEALS

SECTION F: MISCELLANEOUS

PART II: Statutes

PART III: Procedure Rules

PART IV: Statutory Instruments

PART V: Practice Guidance

PART VI: European Material

Table of Statutes

References are to page numbers.

Table of Statutory Instruments

References are to page numbers.

A chronological list of statutory instruments referred to in this work appears at the end of the alphabetical list below.

Chronological List of Statutory Instruments

Table of Cases

References are to page numbers.

Table of Practice Directions

References are to page numbers.

Table of CPR, FPR and Supreme Court Practice Directions

References are to page numbers.

Abbreviations

AA 1976	Adoption Act 1976
ACA 2002	Adoption and Children Act 2002
AEA 1971	Attachment of Earnings Act 1971
AFER 2005	Adoptions with a Foreign Element Regulations 2005
AJA 1920/1960/1969/1970/1977/1982/1985	Administration of Justice Act 1920/1960/1969/1970/1977/1982/1985
AJA 1999	Access to Justice Act 1999
AJA 1999(DA)(FP)O 2009	Access to Justice Act 1999 (Destination of Appeals) (Family Proceedings) Order 2009
ATPO 2008	Allocation and Transfer of Proceedings Order 2008
CA 1989/2004	Children Act 1989/2004
CAA 2006	Children and Adoption Act 2006
CACA 1985	Child Abduction and Custody Act 1985
C(AP)O 1991	Children (Allocation of Proceedings) Order 1991
CCA 1981	Contempt of Court Act 1981
CCA 1984	County Courts Act 1984
CC(F)R 1982	County Court (Forms) Rules 1982
CC(IJD)O 1991	County Courts (Interest on Judgment Debts) Order 1991
CCR	County Court Rules 1981
CCRR 1991	County Court Remedies Regulations 1991
CJA 2003	Criminal Justice Act 2003
CJCSA 2000	Criminal Justice and Court Services Act 2000
CJJA 1991/1982	Civil Jurisdiction and Judgments Act 1991/1982
CJJ(M)R 2011	Civil Jurisdiction and Judgments (Maintenance) Regulations 2011
CLA(G)R 1989	Civil Legal Aid (General) Regulations 1989
CLSA 1990	Courts and Legal Services Act 1990
CLS(CP)R 2000	Community Legal Service (Cost Protection) Regulations 2000
CLS(C)R 2000	Community Legal Service (Costs) Regulations 2000
CLS(F)R 2000	Community Legal Service (Financial) Regulations 2000
CMOPA 2008	Child Maintenance and Other Payments Act 2008
COA 1979	Charging Orders Act 1979
CPA 2004	Civil Partnership Act 2004
CPFO 2008	Civil Proceedings Fees Order 2008
CPR 1998	Civil Procedure Rules 1998
CPR 1998, Sch 1, RSC	Rules taken from the Rules of the Supreme Court 1965 and set out (as amended) in Schedule 1 to CPR
CPR 1998, Sch 2, CCR	Rules taken from the County Court Rules 1981 and set out (as amended) in Schedule 2 to CPR
CRA 2005	Constitutional Reform Act 2005
CSA 1991	Child Support Act 1991
C(SA)R 1991	Children (Secure Accommodation) Regulations 1991
C(SA)(No 2)R 1991	Children (Secure Accommodation) (No 2) Regulations 1991
CS(CE)R 1992	Child Support (Collection and Enforcement) Regulations 1992
CSPSSA 2000	Child Support, Pensions and Social Security Act 2000
CSR	Court of Session Rules
CYPA 2008	Children and Young Persons Act 2008
DA 1869	Debtors Act 1869
DAP(RP)A 1968	Domestic and Appellate Proceedings (Restriction of Publicity) Act 1968
DMPA 1973	Domicile and Matrimonial Proceedings Act 1973
DPMCA 1978	Domestic Proceedings and Magistrates' Courts Act 1978

D(P)R 2000	Divorce etc (Pensions) Regulations 2000
ECHR 1950	European Convention for the Protection of Human Rights and Fundamental Freedoms 1950
ECtHR	European Court of Human Rights
FJ(RE)A 1933	Foreign Judgments (Reciprocal Enforcement) Act 1933
FLA 1986/1996	Family Law Act 1986/1996
FLA 1986(DT)O 1991	Family Law Act 1986 (Dependent Territories) Order 1991
FLA 1996(FM)(RTP)O 2009	Family Law Act 1996 (Forced Marriage) (Relevant Third Party) Order 2009
FLA 1996(Pt IV)(AP)O 1997	Family Law Act 1996 (Part IV) (Allocation of Proceedings) Order 1997
FLRA 1969/1987	Family Law Reform Act 1969/1987
FP(AJ)D 1999/2009	Family Proceedings (Allocation to Judiciary) Directions 1999/2009
FPC(CA 1989)R 1991	Family Proceedings Courts (Children Act 1989) Rules 1991
FPC(CSA 1991)R 1993	Family Proceedings Courts (Child Support Act 1991) Rules 1993
FPC(MP etc)R 1991	Family Proceedings Courts (Matrimonial Proceedings etc) Rules 1991
FPFO 2008	Family Proceedings Fees Order 2008
FP(A)R 2005	Family Procedure (Adoption) Rules 2005
FPR 1991	Family Proceedings Rules 1991
FPR 2010	Family Procedure Rules 2010
GRA 2004	Gender Recognition Act 2004
HCCCJO 1991	High Court and County Courts Jurisdiction Order 1991
HFEA 1990/2008	Human Fertilisation and Embryology Act 1990/2008
IA 1978	Interpretation Act 1978
I(PFD)A 1975	Inheritance (Provision for Family and Dependants) Act 1975
JA 1838	Judgments Act 1838
JCR 2005	Justices' Clerks Rules 2005
LASPOA 2012	Legal Aid, Sentencing and Punishment of Offenders Act 2012
LR(MP)A 1970	Law Reform (Miscellaneous Provisions) Act 1970
MA 1949	Marriage Act 1949
MCA 1973	Matrimonial Causes Act 1973
MCA 1980	Magistrates' Courts Act 1980
MCA 2005	Mental Capacity Act 2005
MC(AE)R 1971	Magistrates' Courts (Attachment of Earnings) Rules 1971
MC(CJJA 1982)R 1986	Magistrates' Courts (Civil Jurisdiction and Judgments Act 1982) Rules 1986
MC(EVOFP & MP)R 2011	Magistrates' Courts (Enforcement or Variation of Orders made in Family Proceedings and Miscellaneous Provisions) Rules 2011
MCFO 2008	Magistrates' Courts Fees Order 2008
MC(GM)R 1974	Magistrates' Courts (Guardianship of Minors) Rules 1974
MC(MOA 1958)R 1959	Magistrates' Courts (Maintenance Orders Act 1958) Rules 1959
MCR 1981	Magistrates' Courts Rules 1981
MC(RAM)R 1975	Magistrates' Courts (Recovery Abroad of Maintenance) Rules 1975
MC(REMO)(HCC)R 1980	Magistrates' Courts (Reciprocal Enforcement of Maintenance Orders) (Hague Convention Countries) Rules 1980
MC(REMO)(MA)R 2007	Magistrates' Courts (Reciprocal Enforcement of Maintenance Orders) (Miscellaneous Amendments) Rules 2007
MC(REMO)R 1974	Magistrates' Courts (Reciprocal Enforcement of Maintenance Orders) Rules 1974

MC(REMO)(RI)R 1975	Magistrates' Courts (Reciprocal Enforcement of Maintenance Orders) (Republic of Ireland) Rules 1975
MC(REMO)(USA)R 1995	Magistrates' Courts (Reciprocal Enforcement of Maintenance Orders) (United States of America) Rules 1995
MEA 1991	Maintenance Enforcement Act 1991
MFPA 1984	Matrimonial and Family Proceedings Act 1984
MOA 1950/1958	Maintenance Orders Act 1950/1958
MOA 1950(SJ)R 1950	Maintenance Orders Act 1950 (Summary Jurisdiction) Rules 1950
MO(FE)A 1920	Maintenance Orders (Facilities for Enforcement) Act 1920
MO(FE)R 1922	Maintenance Orders (Facilities for Enforcement) Rules 1922
MO(RE)A 1972/1992	Maintenance Orders (Reciprocal Enforcement) Act 1972/1992
MoJ	Ministry of Justice
MPPA 1970	Matrimonial Proceedings and Property Act 1970
MWPA 1882	Married Women's Property Act 1882
PACE 1984	Police and Criminal Evidence Act 1984
PD	Practice Direction, Registrar's Direction, Secretary's Circular etc
PD[number]	Practice Direction which supplements Part [number] of CPR 1998 or FPR 2010
PD(PI)R 2000	Pensions on Divorce etc (Provision of Information) Regulations 2000
PHA 1997	Protection from Harassment Act 1997
PO(HFE)R 1994	Parental Orders (Human Fertilisation and Embryology) Regulations 1994
REMO(HCC)O 1993	Reciprocal Enforcement of Maintenance Orders (Hague Convention Countries) Order 1993
REMO(RI)O 1993	Reciprocal Enforcement of Maintenance Orders (Republic of Ireland) Order 1993
REMO(USA)O 1995/2007	Reciprocal Enforcement of Maintenance Orders (United States of America) Order 1995/2007
RM(USA)O 1979	Recovery of Maintenance (United States of America) Order 1979
RRCOSC 1988	Act of Sederunt (Rules for the Registration of Custody Orders of the Sheriff Court) 1988
RSC	Rules of the Supreme Court 1965
SCA 1981	Senior Courts Act 1981
SCFO 2009	Supreme Court Fees Order 2009
SCR 2009	Supreme Court Rules 2009
SSAA 1992	Social Security Administration Act 1992
TCEA 2007	Tribunals, Courts and Enforcement Act 2007
TLATA 1996	Trusts of Land and Appointment of Trustees Act 1996
WRA 2009/2012	Welfare Reform Act 2009/2012
WRPA 1999	Welfare Reform and Pensions Act 1999
****	Some of the text from the statutory provision is not included in this work

PART I

Procedural Guides

PART I: Procedural Guides

Contents

SECTION D: CHILDREN

PART I

PART I

Notes to Procedural Guides

(1) Index

(2) Fees

Information concerning fees payable is included, where appropriate, in the Guides that follow. However, **no** fee is payable:

   (a)   in family proceedings in the High Court and county courts (ie as set out in the Family Proceedings Fees Order 2008) where the applicant:
          (i)   is acting in person and is receiving either income support, working tax credit (provided no child tax credit is being paid), income-based jobseeker's allowance, guarantee credit, or income-related employment and support allowance; or
          (ii)   is a child or, if over 18, seeks financial relief under CA 1989, Sch 1, para 2 or

      (iii)   is not a beneficiary of a trust fund in court of more than £50,000 and is under 18; or

      (iv)   has a gross annual income or a disposable monthly income which does not exceed that specified in FPFO, Sch 2, paras 3–6.

(b)   in the magistrates' court (ie as set out in the Magistrates' Courts Fees Order 2008) where the applicant: (i) is in receipt of income support, income-based jobseeker's allowance, working tax credit (provided that no child tax credit is being paid) or guarantee credit; or (ii) is a child or, if over 18, seeks financial relief under CA 1989, Sch 1, para 2; or (iii) is not a beneficiary of a trust fund in court of more than £50,000 and is under 18; or (iv) has a gross annual income or disposable monthly income not exceeding that set out in MCFO 2008, Sch 2, paras 3–6.

PART I

A1: Contribution Order

Legal background

Where a local authority is looking after a child, it has to consider whether it should recover contributions towards that child's maintenance from either of his parents (where he is under 16) or from the child himself (where he is 16 or over) (CA 1989, Sch 2, para 21). If the local authority decides that it is reasonable to recover a contribution, it will first serve a contribution notice on the proposed contributor specifying the weekly sum he should contribute and the arrangements for payment (CA 1989, Sch 2, para 22). An agreement may then be reached between the authority and the contributor, but if no agreement is reached within one month from the service of the contribution notice, or if the contributor subsequently serves a notice withdrawing his agreement, the authority may apply to the court for a contribution order (CA 1989, Sch 2, para 23). The court may make an order requiring the contributor to contribute a weekly sum towards the child's maintenance. In fixing the sum, the court must have regard to the contributor's means and must not specify a sum greater than that specified in the local authority's contribution notice. A contribution order may be varied or revoked by the court (CA 1989, Sch 2, para 23(8)). Alternatively, a subsequent contribution agreement between the local authority and the contributor in accordance with para 23(6) will have the effect of discharging the order.

Procedure

Who may apply	Local authority looking after child	CA 1989, Sch 2, para 23
Which court	Magistrates' court	ATPO 2008, art 5(1)(b)
	Proceedings can be transferred sideways but not upwards	ATPO 2008, arts 14, 15
Which proceedings	Freestanding application	
Variation or discharge of order by which court	Court by which original order made	
Application	*Initial application* On Form C1, with sufficient copies for each respondent	
	Copy of contribution notice	
	Copy of any contributor's notice under CA 1989, Sch 2, para 22(8) withdrawing agreement	FPR 2010, rr 12.5, 12.7, 12.8 and 12.16; PD12C, para 2.1(1)
	Variation/revocation application On Form C1, with sufficient copies for each respondent	
	Copy of contribution order	FPR 2010, rr 12.5, 12.7, 12.8 and 12.16
Respondents	*Initial application* Contributor	
	Variation/revocation application Where local authority is applicant, contributor	
	Where contributor is applicant, local authority	FPR 2010, r 12.3
Additional persons to whom notice in Form C6A is to be given	Local authority providing accommodation for child	
	Person caring for child at commencement of proceedings	FPR 2010, rr 12.3, 12.5, 12.7, 12.8 and 12.16; PD12C, para 3.1(1)
	Person providing a s 51 refuge for child	

PART I

Service	Copy of application, together with Form C6, to be served on respondents at least 14 days before date of hearing or directions appointment	FPR 2010, r 12.8; PD12C, paras 1.1, 2.1
	Form C6A to be served on additional persons at same time as application etc served on respondents	FPR 2010, r 12.8; PD12C, paras 1.1, 3.1
Ex parte	Not available	FPR 2010, r 12.16
Joinder or removal of parties	By court order, of its own motion or on written request	FPR 2010, rr 12.3(3), 16.2
Answer to application	No provision either forbidding or permitting an answer	
Directions	As to the powers of the justices' clerk or the court, see –	FPR 2010, rr 2.5, 2.6, 12.12 and Pt 4
Children's guardian	Not "specified proceedings"	CA 1989, s 41(6); FPR 2010, r 12.27
Who has power to make the order	A magistrates' court; however, justices' clerk or single justice has no such power	CA 1989, s 93(2)(i), Sch 2, para 23(2); FPR 2010, r 2.6
Order	Form C21	FPR 2010, Pt 5
Appeals	See Guide E2: note an appeal from a magistrates' court lies to a county court	CA 1989, s 94, Sch 2, para 23(11); FPR 2010, Pt 30

A2: Financial Relief for a Child under Children Act 1989, Sch 1

Legal background

Subject to the provisions of CSA 1991, which leave the court with a limited role in ordering maintenance or variation of maintenance agreements in respect of children, CA 1989, Sch 1 provides three forms of financial relief for a child: first, para 1 enables a maintenance order, settlement and transfer of property order to be made in favour of a child against either or both of its parents; secondly, para 2 enables a periodical payments order and lump sum order to be made in favour of a child who has reached 18 where (i) the child's parents are not living with each other, (ii) there was not in force a periodical payments order for the child immediately before he reached 16, and (iii) he is undergoing education or training or there are special circumstances (orders under both paras 1 and 2 may be varied or extended under para 6); and, thirdly, by paras 10 and 11, the court may vary a maintenance agreement containing financial arrangements for the child either during the lifetime of the parent or after the death of one of them. For the reasons set out under s 15, if a child's parents are married, the greater procedural powers that are available make it more advantageous for an application for financial relief against a parent by a child to be brought under MCA 1973, ss 23, 24 and 27 and for an alteration of a maintenance agreement to be brought under MCA 1973, ss 35 and 36; however, where the parents are not married, there is no jurisdiction apart from CA 1989, Sch 1.

An application under CA 1989, Sch 1 is defined as a financial remedy under FPR 2010, r 2.3. The procedure under Pt 9 applies. The application may be made to the High Court, designated county court or magistrates' court.

Where proceedings under Sch 1 or paras 4–7 or 9 of Sch A1 to CA 1989 are transferred to the county court, they must be transferred to a family hearing centre (ATPO 2008, art 20 and Sch 1).

Procedure

Who may apply	*Application for child under 18* Parent or guardian or special guardian of child or holder of residence order	CA 1989, Sch 1, para 1(1); FPR 2010, r 9.10
	The order will be made either on the application of the above or without an application on the making, varying or discharging of a residence order	CA 1989, Sch 1, para 1(6)
	Application by child over 18 The child who is over 18 and:	
	who is or will be undergoing education or training or where there are special circumstances	CA 1989, Sch 1, para 2(1)(a),(b)
	who has not had in force a periodical payments order immediately before he was 16	CA 1989, Sch 1, para 2(3),(6)
	whose parents are not living together	CA 1989, Sch 1, para 2(4)
	Variation application Any of the persons set out above, with, additionally on an application under CA 1989, Sch 1, para 1, the child himself if he has reached 16	CA 1989, Sch 1, para 6(4)
	Application to alter maintenance agreement Either party to the agreement or a personal representative	CA 1989, Sch 1, paras 10(2), 11(1)
Application	To the High Court, designated county court or magistrates' court	FPR 2010, r 9.5(2)
	The application is on Form A1 together with any documents stated to be required or referred to in the application. Proceedings start when a court officer issues an application, and are issued on that date	FPR 2010, rr 5.1–5.3, PD5A
Fee	£200	FPFO 2008, fee 2.1
Service in the High Court and county court	Within 4 days of the date on which the application was filed, a court officer will serve a copy of the application on the respondent and give notice of the date of the first hearing to both parties.	
	Alternatively, the applicant must serve the respondent within 4 days, beginning with the date on which the copy of the application was received from the court, and file a certificate of service on or before the first appointment	FPR 2010, r 9.12(1),(2)
Respondents	Any parent who is not an applicant, or both parents, where the holder of a residence order or special guardianship order applies	CA 1989, Sch 1, para 1(2)

Directions/Interim orders	The court may make an interim order for periodical payments. FPR 2010, Pt 18 procedure applies to applications for interim orders	CA 1989, Sch 1, para 9; FPR 2010, r 9.7(2)
Procedure in the High Court and the county court	The court will fix a first appointment not less than 12 weeks and not more than 16 weeks after the filing of the application	FPR 2010, r 9.12
	By 35 days before the first appointment, the parties must simultaneously exchange a financial statement on Form E1, accompanied by a limited category of documents. No disclosure or inspection of the parties' documents may be given between the filing of the application and the first appointment, save as laid down in FPR 2010, r 9.14(4)	FPR PD5A; FPR 2010, r 9.14(4)
	By 14 days before the first appointment, each party must file and serve a concise statement, a chronology, a questionnaire and a notice stating whether that party will be in a position to use the hearing as a FDR appointment. In addition, the parties should if possible exchange an agreed case summary, a schedule of assets and a draft of directions sought by the parties	FPR PD9A; FPR 2010, r 9.14(5)
	At the first appointment, the court in pursuance of the overriding objective in FPR 2010, Pt 1 will case manage the financial application in relation to defining the issues and saving costs. The court will approve the content of questionnaires and make directions in respect of replies, requests for documents and expert evidence. The next hearing, normally the FDR, will be timetabled. Both parties must attend in person. Costs will be considered. After the first appointment, there is no further provision for the disclosure of documents, save with the leave of the court	FPR 2010, rr 9.15–9.16
	At the FDR appointment, the parties are to meet for discussion and negotiation. 7 days before the FDR appointment, the applicant must file details of all offers and proposals and the responses to them. If the court cannot make a consent order, the court must give direction for final hearing. Both parties must personally attend the FDR hearing, unless the court directs otherwise	FPR PD9A; FPR 2010, r 9.17

Procedure in the magistrates' court	The court will fix a first-hearing date not less than 4 weeks and not more than 8 weeks after the filing of the application. Parties must exchange and file a financial statement. There is no provision in the magistrates' court for a FDR appointment	FPR 2010, rr 9.18–9.20
Order	*Application for child under 18* Periodical payments	
	Secured periodical payments	
	Lump sum	
	Settlement of property or transfer of property	
	Application by child over 18 Periodical payments	
	Lump sum	
	Application to alter maintenance agreement Varying or revoking any financial arrangements contained in the maintenance agreement, including inserting provision for periodical payments or for security for increasing or decreasing the level of periodical payments	
Appeals	See Guides E2 and E5	

A3: Financial Relief for a Child in a Magistrates' Court under Children Act 1989, Sch 1

Legal background

CA 1989, Sch 1 provides three forms of financial relief for a child in a magistrates' court: first, para 1 enables a periodical payments order or lump sum order to be made in favour of a child against either or both of its parents; second, para 2 enables a periodical payments order and lump sum order to be made in favour of a child who has reached 18 where (i) the child's parents are not living with each other, (ii) there was not in force a periodical payments order for the child immediately before he reached 16, and (iii) he is undergoing education or training or there are special circumstances; and, third, a limited power to vary maintenance agreements under para 10. Orders under paras 1 and 2 may be varied or extended under para 6.

With the exception of paras 2 and 15, the definition of parent in CA 1989, Sch 1, is extended to include any party to a marriage (whether subsisting or not) and any civil partner in a civil partnership (whether subsisting or not), in relation to whom the child concerned is a child of the family.

CA 1989, Sch 1 is governed by the FPR 2010. There is a concurrent jurisdiction with the High Court and county courts for the making of these orders, but the High Court and county courts have additional powers under Sch 1 to make secured periodical payments orders, orders for the settlement or transfer of property and wider powers to vary the terms of maintenance agreements (see Guide A2). Where proceedings under Sch 1 or paras 4–7 or 9 of Sch A1 of CA 1989 are transferred to the county court, they must be transferred to a family hearing centre (ATPO 2008, art 20 and Sch 1).

Where the parties are married to each other or have entered into a civil partnership, application for financial provision for a child may also be made under the DPMCA 1978 or CPA 2004, Sch 6. The magistrates' jurisdiction to make orders for financial relief in respect of a child under CA 1989, Sch 1 or DPMCA 1978 is limited by the provisions of CSA 1991. A claim for child maintenance against a step-parent or civil partner is unaffected by CSA 1991.

Procedure

Who may apply	*Application for child under 18* Parent or guardian of child or holder of residence order	CA 1989, Sch 1, para 1(1)
	The order may be made either on the application of the above or without an application on the making, varying or discharging of a residence order	CA 1989, Sch 1, para 1(6)
	Where the child is a ward of court, the court may exercise any of its powers under Sch 1, even if no application has been made	CA 1989, Sch 1, para 1(7)
	Application by child over 18 The child who is over 18 and:	
	who is or will be undergoing education or training or where there are special circumstances	CA 1989, Sch 1, para 2(1)(a),(b)
	who has not had in force a periodical payments order immediately before he was 16	CA 1989, Sch 1, para 2(3),(6)
	whose parents are not living together	CA 1989, Sch 1, para 2(4)
	Variation application Any of the persons set out above, with, additionally on an application under CA 1989, Sch 1, para 1, the child himself if he has reached 16	CA 1989, Sch 1, para 6(4)
	Application to alter maintenance agreement Either party to the agreement	CA 1989, Sch 1, para 10(2)
Application	To any magistrates' court, except in the case of an application under CA 1989, Sch 1, para 10 where the application must be made to a magistrates' court acting for the local justice area in which at least one of the parties to the agreement resides	CA 1989, Sch 1, para 10(6)
	The application must be made on Form A2, with financial statement on Form E2	FPR PD5A
Hearing date	The court will fix a first hearing date not less than 4 weeks and not more than 8 weeks after the date that the application was filed	
	Hearing dates may only be cancelled with the permission of the court and, if cancelled, a new date must immediately be fixed	FPR 2010, r 9.18(1)(a),(3)
Service	Within 4 days of the date on which the application was filed, the court will serve a copy of the application on the respondent, give notice of the date of first hearing to both parties and send a copy of a blank financial statement to the respondent and also to the applicant	FPR 2010, r 9.18(1)(b)

	Alternatively, the applicant may choose to serve the application on the respondent. In which case, the issued application will be returned to the applicant and, within 4 days of receipt, the applicant must serve the application, notice of first hearing and a blank financial statement on the respondent. The applicant must also file a certificate of service at or before the first hearing	FPR 2010, r 9.18(2)
Fee	£200	MCFO 2008, fee 8.1(v)
Respondent	The other parent	
Financial statements	Within 14 days of issue of the application, the parties must serve their financial statements on each other and file a copy with the court	
	The financial statement must be verified by statement of truth and be accompanied by any documents referred to in the statement or which clarify information contained in the statement. Any party unavoidably prevented from sending such documents must, at the earliest opportunity, serve a copy on the other party and file a copy with the court, together with an explanation	CA 1989, Sch 1 FPR 2010, r 9.19(1)–(3)
Directions/Interim orders	The court may make an interim order for periodical payments	CA 1989, Sch 1, para 9
	The court or justices' clerk can give directions for the conduct of proceedings, including the filing of further evidence	FPR 2010, r 9.20; JCR 2005
Order	*Application for financial relief* Periodical payments	CA 1989, Sch 1, paras 1–4
	Lump sum	CA 1989, Sch 1, para 5
	Application to alter maintenance agreement Where the agreement contains provision for periodical payments by either of the parties, an order varying or terminating those payments	CA 1989, Sch 1, para 10(6)
	All applications, once made, can only be withdrawn with leave	FPR 2010, r 29.4
	Reasons for the court's decision must be recorded and stated	FPR 2010, r 27.2; *S v S* [1993] 1 FLR 606
Appeals	See Guide E2	

A4: Declaration of Proprietary Rights under Married Women's Property Act 1882, s 17 or Civil Partnership Act 2004, s 66

Legal background

Both the High Court and county courts have jurisdiction on an application by a spouse, fiancé(e) to declare and enforce their proprietary rights in respect of any property that they possess or control at the time of the application or, as extended by s 7 of the Matrimonial Causes (Property and Maintenance) Act 1958, that they formerly possessed or controlled. The use of MWPA 1882, s 17 has been strongly disapproved when MCA 1973, ss 23 and 24 are available but it is useful in two circumstances: (i) where a declaration of beneficial ownership is needed if there are doubts about the solvency of one of the parties; (ii) as suggested in *Wicks v Wicks* [1998] 1 FLR 470 where an order for sale is required before the making of a financial order.

Where a claim for title or possession of property under MWPA 1882, s 17 or CPA 2004, s 66 is made in any proceedings for a financial order, the procedure under FPR 2010, Pt 18 applies. An application under MWPA 1882 or CPA 2004 is not a claim for a financial order or financial remedy.

Procedure

Who may apply	Spouse, civil partner, fiancé(e), provided application made within 3 years of decree absolute or termination of engagement	MPPA 1970, s 39; LR(MP)A 1970, s 2(2)
Application	The application may be made to the High Court or county court, or to the Principal Registry of the Family Division if matrimonial proceedings started or are intended to be started there	FPR 2010, r 8.14
	Application must be made using Pt 18 procedure if it is made in the course of existing proceedings. If there are no existing proceedings then Pt 19 applies	FPR 2010, r 8.13
	Application is by notice of application on Form D50, stating what order is sought and why, with a draft order attached. Application to transfer tenancy under MWPA 1882, s 17 is on Form D50B	FPR 2010, rr 18.14–18.7
Fee	£230	FPFO 2008, fee 1.1
Service	A copy of the application notice must be served in accordance with the provisions of FPR 2010, Pt 6, at least 7 days before the hearing, with any written evidence in support and the draft order sought	FPR 2010, r 18.8
	Where there is a mortgage, the applicant must serve the mortgagee	FPR 2010, r 8.15
Respondents	Spouses, fiancé(e)s, parties to concluded proceedings and any other person the court may direct	FPR 2010, r 18.3
	A mortgagee who requests joinder must be made a party	FPR 2010, r 8.15(2)

Procedure	Application may be dealt with without a hearing, if the court considers it appropriate and the parties agree. There is power to proceed in the absence of the parties	FPR 2010, rr 18.9, 18.11
	Order may be made without notice to the respondent, subject to his right to apply to set aside or vary	FPR 2010, r 18.10
Orders	The court may make interim orders, give directions, grant injunctions ancillary to the claim and make final orders	
	Power to grant injunctions ancillary to claim	FPR 2010, r 8.16
	Power to declare and enforce proprietary rights of both parties, including power to order sale; power to order lump sum equal in value to assessed interest	MC(PM)A 1958, s 7(7); *Bothe v Amos* [1976] Fam 46
Appeals	See Guides E2, E4 and E5	

A5: Order under Trusts of Land and Appointment of Trustees Act 1996, s 14

Legal background

TLATA 1996, s 14 entitles a trustee or a beneficiary of the proceeds of sale of land to apply for any order relating to the exercise by the trustees of any of their functions (including the power of exclusion and the power of sale), or declaring the nature and extent of a person's interest in a trust of land. Applications may be made by former cohabitees, family members or third parties such as trustees in bankruptcy wishing to establish a beneficial interest. By virtue of the HCCCJO 1991, the county court's jurisdiction is unlimited. Section 14 of the 1996 Act is to be read together with ss 13 and 15. An application under TLATA 1996 is governed by CPR 1998, Pt 7 or 8. See also CPR PD7A and CPR PD8A.

Procedure

Who may apply	A trustee, a joint legal or beneficial owner, or a judgment creditor holding a charging order	*Midland Bank v Pike* [1988] 2 All ER 434
Property	Legal title owned jointly by co-owners	
Application	For an order "declaring the nature or extent of a person's interest in [the] property"	TLATA 1996, s 14(2)(b)
Court	High Court: Chancery Division	
	County court: if issued in a county court the claim form must be marked "Chancery Business"	CPR PD7A, para 2.5
Fee	For recovery of land: in High Court: £465 in county court: £175	CPFO 2008, fee 1.4

Procedure	CPR 1998, Pt 7 – normally claims will be more appropriate for issue under this procedure	
	CPR 1998, Pt 8 – traditionally claims have often been issued under the Pt 8 procedure (formerly originating summons). Pt 8 only applies where there is "unlikely [to be] a dispute of fact". By definition most s 14 claims involve disputed questions of fact	CPR 1998, r 8.1(2)(a)
Issue of claim: Pt 7	Issue claim in Form N1 with particulars of claim (in the form or separately)	CPR 1998, r 7.1; r 7.4(1)(a)
Particulars of claim: served separately	Particulars of claim are likely to include the following: (1) the background facts; (2) reference to the facts which define the form of trust or equity claimed: (a) contributions; (b) any agreement with terms defined (if possible) and description of when formed; (c) detrimental reliance; (3) aspects of the claim that come within s 15(1); (4) aspects of the claim relevant to the check list at [69] of *Stack*	TLATA 1996, s 15; *Stack v Dowden* [2007] 1 FLR 1858 at [69]
Defendant	Other owner of the property	
Pt 8 claim: issue of claim	If there is little "dispute of fact" this procedure can be used Claim issued in Form 208 with specific requirements, eg: (1) statement that Pt 8 applies; (2) remedy sought by the claimant and the "legal basis" for it; (3) enactment for claim: ie, TLATA 1996 (shown in the heading to the claim)	CPR 1998, r 8.1(2)(a); CPR PD8A; CPR 1998, r 8.2
Pt 8 claim: evidence	(1) Claimant's evidence: served with claim form	CPR 1998, r 8.5(2)
	(2) Any "written evidence": filed with claim form	CPR 1998, r 8.5(1)
	(3) Any other written evidence: only with permission	CPR 1998, r 8.6(1)(b)
Defence	(1) Acknowledgement of service	CPR 1998, r 8.3
	(2) Service of defendant's evidence on claimant with acknowledgement of service	CPR 1998, r 8.5(3),(4)
Case management	Pt 8: treated as allocated to the multi-track	CPR 1998, r 8.9(c)
	Definition of issues:	
	(1) What are the issues of fact?	CPR 1998, r 1.4(2)(b)
	(2) Are there any issues of law?	CPR 1998, r 3.1(2)(i),(l)

| Order | Declaration as to the parties' respective holding of the beneficial interests | TLATA 1996, s 14(2)(b) |
| | Under TLATA 1996 the court may then go on to deal with other matters, such as sale of the property, provision for an occupation rent, etc | TLATA 1996TLATA 1996, s 14(2)(a) (see, for example, *Mortgage Corporation v Shaire* [2000] 1 FLR 973) |

A6: Financial Provision Order in a Case of Neglect under Matrimonial Causes Act 1973, s 27

Legal background

Subject to the effect of CSA 1991, s 27 enables a spouse to apply to the High Court or a county court for periodical payments, secured periodical payments and a lump sum (but not a transfer of property) for himself or herself and/or the children, without filing a petition for divorce, judicial separation or nullity. Once failure to provide reasonable maintenance is proved, the application is determined on the same principles as if such a petition had been filed, except there is no presumption that the marriage has broken down. The jurisdictional requirement as to domicile or habitual residence is the same as for a petition, except that under s 27 the applicant can establish jurisdiction on the additional ground that the respondent is resident in England and Wales at the date of the application.

An application under MCA 1973, s 27 is defined as a financial remedy under FPR 2010, r 2.3. The procedure under FPR 2010 Pt 9 applies. It is a freestanding application not requiring the issue of a petition. The application must be made at a divorce county court.

Procedure

Who may apply	Either spouse	MCA 1973, s 27(1),(2)
Application	To divorce county court of applicant's choice	FPR 2010, r 9.5(2)
	The application is on Form D50C, together with any documents stated to be required, or referred to in the application. Proceedings start when a court officer issues an application and are issued on that date	FPR 2010, rr 5.1–5.3; PD5A
Fee	£230	FPFO 2008, fee 1.1
Service	Within 4 days of the date on which the application was filed, a court officer will serve a copy of the application upon the respondent and give notice of the date of the first hearing to both parties	
	Alternatively, the applicant must serve the respondent within 4 days, beginning with the date on which the copy of the application was received from the court, and file a certificate of service on or before the first appointment	FPR 2010, r 9.12(1),(2)

Procedure	The court will fix a first appointment not less than 12 weeks and not more than 16 weeks after the filing of the application	FPR 2010, r 9.12
	By 35 days before the first appointment, the parties must simultaneously exchange a financial statement on Form E1, accompanied by a limited category of documents. No disclosure or inspection of the parties' documents may be given between the filing of the application and the first appointment, save as laid down in FPR 2010, r 9.14(4)	FPR PD5A; FPR 2010, r 9.14(4)
	By 14 days before the first appointment, each party must file and serve a concise statement, a chronology, a questionnaire and a notice stating whether that party will be in a position to use the hearing as a FDR appointment. In addition, the parties should if possible exchange an agreed case summary, a schedule of assets and a draft of directions sought by the parties	FPR PD9A; FPR 2010, r 9.14(5)
	At the first appointment, the court in pursuance of the overriding objective in FPR 2010, Pt 1 will case manage the financial application in relation to defining the issues and saving costs. The court will approve the content of questionnaires and make directions in respect of replies, requests for documents and expert evidence. The next hearing, normally the FDR, will be timetabled. Both parties must attend in person. Costs will be considered. After the first appointment, there is no further provision for the disclosure of documents, save with the leave of the court	FPR 2010, rr 9.15, 9.16
	At the FDR appointment, the parties are to meet for discussion and negotiation. 7 days before the FDR appointment, the applicant must file details of all offers and proposals and the responses to them. If the court cannot make a consent order, the court must give direction for final hearing. Both parties must personally attend the FDR hearing, unless the court directs otherwise	FPR 2010, r 9.17; PD9A
Interim orders	Power to make interim orders for periodical payments. No power to make an interim lump sum order, property adjustment order, order for sale or pension sharing order	MCA 1973, ss 23(1)(c), 24, 27(5); *Wicks v Wicks* [1998] 1 FLR 470
Appeals	See Guides E2, E4 and E5	

A7: Variation of a Maintenance Agreement under Matrimonial Causes Act 1973, s 35

Legal background

The court's power to vary a maintenance agreement during the lives of the parties (MCA 1973, s 35) is exercised by the High Court, a county court or a magistrates' court.

An application under s 35 is defined as a financial remedy under FPR 2010, r 2.3. The procedure under Pt 9 applies. For the procedure to vary a maintenance agreement on the death of one of the parties, see FPR 2010, rr 8 6–8.11.

Procedure

Who may apply	Either spouse	MCA 1973, s 35(1)
Application	The application is on Form D50H, together with any documents stated to be required, or referred to in the application. Proceedings start when a court officer issues an application and are issued on that date	FPR 2010, rr 5.1–5.3; PD5A
Fee	£230	FPFO 2008, fee 1.1
Service	Within 4 days of the date on which the application was filed, a court officer will serve a copy of the application on the respondent and give notice of the date of first hearing to both parties	
	Alternatively, the applicant must serve the respondent within 4 days, beginning with the date on which the copy of the application was received from the court, and file a certificate of service on or before the first appointment	FPR 2010, r 9.12(1),(2)
Procedure in the High Court and county court	The court will fix a first appointment not less than 12 weeks and not more than 16 weeks after the filing of the application	FPR 2010, r 9.12
	By 35 days before the first appointment, the parties must simultaneously exchange a financial statement on Form E1, accompanied by a limited category of documents. No disclosure or inspection of the parties' documents may be given between the filing of the application and the first appointment, save as laid down in FPR 2010, r 9.14(4)	FPR PD5A; FPR 2010, r 9.14(4)
	By 14 days before the first appointment, each party must file and serve a concise statement, a chronology, a questionnaire and a notice stating whether that party will be in a position to use the hearing as a FDR appointment. In addition, the parties should if possible exchange an agreed case summary, a schedule of assets and a draft of directions sought by the parties	FPR 2010, r 9.14(5); PD9A

	At the first appointment, the court in pursuance of the overriding objective in FPR 2010, Pt 1 will case manage the financial application in relation to defining the issues and saving costs. The court will approve the content of questionnaires and make directions in respect of replies, requests for documents and expert evidence. The next hearing, normally the FDR, will be timetabled. Both parties must attend in person. Costs will be considered. After the first appointment, there is no further provision for the disclosure of documents, save with the leave of the court	FPR 2010, rr 9.15, 9.16
	At the FDR appointment, the parties are to meet for discussion and negotiation. 7 days before the FDR appointment, the applicant must file details of all offers and proposals and the responses to them. If the court cannot make a consent order, the court must give direction for final hearing. Both parties must personally attend the FDR hearing, unless the court directs otherwise	FPR 2010, r 9.17; PD9A
Procedure in magistrates' court	The court will fix a first hearing date not less than 4 weeks and not more than 8 weeks after the filing of the application. Parties must exchange and file a financial statement. There is no provision in the magistrates' court for a FDR appointment	FPR 2010, rr 9.18–9.20
Order	Vary or revoke financial arrangements contained in the agreement, or insert new financial arrangements into the agreement for the benefit of spouse or child	MCA 1973, ss 34(2), 35(2)
	Statutory charge may be rolled over on MCA 1973, s 35	CLA(G)R 1989, reg 94(d)(i)
Appeals	See Guides E2, E4 and E5	

A8: Claim for Financial Provision under the Inheritance (Provision for Family and Dependants) Act 1975

Legal background

A claim may be made against the estate of a deceased person by certain members of the deceased's family and dependants categorised in the I(PFD)A 1975, s 1 and CPA 2004 (CPA 2005) for financial provision out of the net estate of the deceased, on the ground that the disposition of the deceased's estate effected by his will and/or under the laws of intestacy is not such as to make reasonable financial provision for the applicant. Unless the court gives permission extending the time limit, the application must be made within 6 months of the date on which representation is first granted (s 4).

The procedure for both the High Court and county court is governed by CPR 1998, Pt 57. See also CPR PD57 and CPR PD8A in Part III. Before issuing proceedings practitioners must comply with the CPR Protocol. Non-compliance could result in the court making an order for costs against the non-complying party (CPR 1998, r 44.2).

Procedure

Who may apply	The spouse of the deceased	I(PFD)A 1975, s 1(a)
	The registered civil partner of the deceased	I(PFD)A 1975, s 1(a); CPA 2004, s 71, Sch 4
	The former spouse of the deceased who has not remarried	I(PFD)A 1975, s 1(b)
	The former civil partner of the deceased who has not formed a subsequent civil partnership	I(PFD)A 1975, s 1(b); CPA 2004, s 71, Sch 4
	A cohabitant of the deceased	I(PFD)A 1975, ss 1(ba), 1A
	A person who lived in the same household as the deceased as his/her civil partner	I(PFD)A 1975, s 1(ba), s 1B; CPA 2004, s 71, Sch 4
	A child of the deceased	I(PFD)A 1975, s 1(c)
	Any person who was treated as a child of the family whether within a marriage or in a civil partnership	I(PFD)A 1975, s 1(d)
	Any other person who immediately before the death of the deceased was being maintained by him	I(PFD)A 1975, s 1; CPA 2004
Which court	High Court (Chancery or Family Division) or county court	CPR 1998, r 57.15; CCA 1984, s 25
	District judges (including district judges of the Principal Registry of the Family Division) have jurisdiction to hear such applications	CPR 1998, r 57.15; I(PFD)A 1975, s 22
Application	*High Court/county court* By Pt 8 claim form, which should be entitled "In the estate of . . . deceased" and "In the matter of I(PFD)A 1975" and set out the remedy sought and the grounds for the same	CPR 1998, rr 8.2, 57.16
Time limit	The claim must be issued within 6 months of the date on which representation is taken out (unless extended by the court). Application to extend the time limit must be included in the claim form	I(PFD)A 1975, s 4
Documents	The applicant must file with the claim form a witness statement/affidavit in support exhibiting an official copy of the grant of representation and of every testamentary document admitted to proof	CPR 1998, rr 8.5(1),(2), 57.16(3)

Defendants	Personal representatives Beneficiaries Other persons affected by the claim Any other person directed by the court to be added	CPR 1998, r 19.7
Service	The claim form must be served within 4 months after date of issue	
	Extension of time must be sought under CPR 1998, r 7.6	
	Acknowledgement of service must be filed within 21 days after service of the claim form and served on the claimant and other parties if served within the jurisdiction If served outside the jurisdiction extended period is permitted by CPR 1998, r 57.16(4A)	CPR 1998, rr 6.19, 6.22, 8.3(1), 10.3(1), 57.16(4)
	A personal representative who wishes to remain neutral and agrees to abide by the decision of the court should state this in section A of the acknowledgement of service	CPR 1998, rr 57.16(5); PD57, para 15
	For service on children and patients see CPR 1998, r 6.6	
	otherwise, in accordance with CPR 1998, r 10.3(2)	CPR 1998, r 10.3(2)
Statement/Affidavit in answer	Must be filed by the personal representatives within 21 days after service of the claim form (it should include the matters set out in CPR PD57, para 16)	CPR 1998, r 57.16(4),(5); PD57, para 16
	May be filed by other defendants within 21 days after service of the claim form	CPR 1998, r 57.16(4)
Service of answer	Every defendant who files any written evidence within 21 days in answer must serve a copy on the claimant and every other defendant who is not represented by the same solicitor	CPR 1998, r 57.16(4)
Reply	A claimant may serve a statement in reply on all other parties within 14 days of service of the defendant's evidence on him	CPR 1998, r 8.5(5),(6)
Directions/case management conference pre-trial hearing	At the same time as issuing the claim form a directions hearing may be requested The court will in any event give directions after the defendant has filed the acknowledgement of service or after the time for filing it has expired	CPR PD8A, para 4.1
	Parties must complete the listing questionnaire in Form N170 and provide an estimate of costs, following which the court will consider whether to hold a pre-trial review, set a timetable and fix the date for the trial	CPR PD8A, para 4.2 CPR 1998, rr 29.6–29.8

Fee	High Court: £465	CPFO 2008, fee 1.5
	County court: £175	CPFO 2008, fee 1.5
Order	Periodical payments	I(PFD)A 1975, s 2(1)(a)
	Lump sum	I(PFD)A 1975, s 2(1)(b)
	Transfer of property	I(PFD)A 1975, s 2(1)(c)
	Settlement of property	I(PFD)A 1975, s 2(1)(d)
	Acquisition, transfer and settlement of property	I(PFD)A 1975, s 2(1)(e)
	Variation of antenuptial and post-nuptial settlement	I(PFD)A 1975, s 2(1)(f)
	Variation or discharge of secured periodical payments	I(PFD)A 1975, s 16
	Variation or revocation of maintenance agreements	I(PFD)A 1975, s 17
	Order setting aside disposition intended to defeat a claim under the Act	I(PFD)A 1975, ss 10, 11
	Treatment of deceased's former beneficial interest in joint property as part of his estate and not passing by survivorship	I(PFD)A 1975, s 9
	Interim order	I(PFD)A 1975, s 5
	Consequential orders	I(PFD)A 1975, s 2(4)
Appeals	See Guides E2, E4 and E5	

PART I

A9: Financial Provision in the Magistrates' Court

Legal background

Three separate forms of application for financial provision may be made under DPMCA 1978: an application under DPMCA 1978, s 2 based on the grounds in s 1 (failure to provide reasonable maintenance for the applicant or for any child of the family, behaviour or desertion); an application under DPMCA 1978, s 6 based on agreed financial provision; or an application under DPMCA 1978, s 7 based on the level of maintenance paid in the 3 months preceding the date of the application while the parties have been living apart by agreement.

There is provision for the "conversion" of an application under DPMCA 1978, s 2 to an application under s 6, and for the "conversion" of an application under s 7 to an application under s 2.

Financial provision may be made for either party to the marriage and for any child of the family (as defined in DPMCA 1978, s 88). The court is required to have regard to the matters contained in DPMCA 1978, s 3 in assessing the amount of any order.

A lump sum order is available under DPMCA 1978, s 2(1)(b) for the benefit of a spouse and under s 2(1)(d) for the benefit of a child of the family. The amount of any lump sum order under s 2 is limited to £1000. Lump sum orders are also available under DPMCA 1978, s 6(2)(b) to a spouse and s 6(2)(d) for a child of the family. There is no limit to the amount of a lump sum order under s 6.

The term of a periodical payments order to a spouse is governed by DPMCA 1978, s 4; the term of an order to or for a child of the family is governed by DPMCA 1978, s 5. Financial provision for children is also available under CA 1989, Sch 1.

Periodical payments and lump sum orders payable by instalments may be ordered to be paid under MCA 1980, s 59 either directly between the parties, through the designated officer, by standing order or by an attachment of earnings order.

CPA 2004, s 72(3) and Sch 6 make provision for financial relief in connection with civil partnerships (civil partners and children of the family) in magistrates' courts corresponding to the provisions in DPMCA 1978.

DPMCA 1978 and CPA 2004 are governed by FPR 2010. However, the enforcement and variation of periodical payments orders do not automatically constitute family proceedings within the meaning of MCA 1980, s 65, although the court may treat them as such. FPR 2010 do not apply to such proceedings and the previous provisions in FPC(MP etc)R 1991 will continue to apply until further rules are made.

The magistrates' jurisdiction to make orders for financial relief in respect of a child under CA 1989, Sch 1 or DPMCA 1978 is limited by the provisions of CSA 1991. A claim for child maintenance against a step-parent or civil partner is unaffected by CSA 1991.

Procedure

Who may apply	Either party to a marriage	DPMCA 1978, ss 1, 6(1), 7(1)
	Either party to a civil partnership	CPA 2004, Sch 6, paras 1, 9, 15
Which court	A magistrates' court with jurisdiction for the local justice area in which the applicant or respondent ordinarily resides	DPMCA 1978, s 30; MCA 1980, s 52; CPA 2004, Sch 6, para 47; FPR 2010, r 9.5(2)
Application	The application must be made on Form A2 with financial statement on Form E2	FPR PD5A
Hearing date	The court will fix a first hearing date not less than 4 weeks and not more than 8 weeks after the date that the application was filed	
	Hearing dates may only be cancelled with the permission of the court and, if cancelled, a new date must immediately be fixed	FPR 2010, r 9.18(1)(a),(3)
	Fee: £200	MCFO 2008, fee 6.1
Respondent	The other party to the marriage	DPMCA 1978
	The other party to a civil partnership	CPA 2004
Service	Within 14 days of the date on which the application was filed, the court will serve a copy of the application on the respondent, give notice of the date of first hearing to both parties and send a copy of a blank financial statement to the respondent and also to the applicant	FPR 2010, r 9.18(1)(b)
	Alternatively, the applicant may choose to serve the application on the respondent. In which case, the issued application will be returned to the applicant and, within 4 days of receipt, the applicant must serve the application, notice of first hearing and a blank financial statement on the respondent. The applicant must also file a certificate of service at or before the first hearing	FPR 2010, r 9.18(2)
Financial statements	Within 14 days of issue of the application, the parties must serve their financial statements on each other and file a copy with the court	

	The financial statement must be verified by statement of truth and be accompanied by any documents referred to in the statement or that clarify information contained in the statement. Any party unavoidably prevented from sending such documents must, at the earliest opportunity, serve a copy on the other party and file a copy with the court, together with an explanation	FPR 2010, r 9.19(1)–(3)
Consent orders	Applicant files two copies of draft order endorsed with statement signed by respondent signifying agreement and each party files with the court and serves on the other a statement of information	FPR 2010, r 9.26
Directions	May be given by the justices' clerk or court, on a party's written request filed and served, or on written request by consent or (in an urgent case) orally without notice or on the court's own initiative	FPR 2010, rr 4.1, 4.3, 9.20; JCR 2005
	Directions for the conduct of the proceedings may include the timetable for the proceedings, variation of the time within which or by which an act is required to be done, the service of documents, the submission of evidence and attendance at a directions appointment or hearing	
Additional or alternative orders	Interim order	DPMCA 1978, s 19; CPA 2004, Sch 6, Pt 4; FPR 2010, r 9.7
	Financial provision for child	CA 1989, Sch 1
	Costs	FPR 2010, rr 28.1, 28.3
	Adjournment for reconciliation and report	DPMCA 1978, s 26
Variation, revival and revocation	Application may be made by either party, or by a child who has attained the age of 16 on Form A2 with financial statement on Form E2, following the procedure for the making of an order set out above	DPMCA 1978, ss 20, 20A, 20ZA, 20(12); CPA 2004, Sch 6, para 39; FPR 2010, as applied by MC(EVOFP & MP)R 2011, r 69
Fee	£20	MCFO 2008, fee 12.1
Appeals	See Guide E3	

A10: Non-molestation and/or Occupation Order under Family Law Act 1996, Pt IV

Legal background

An application under FLA 1996, Pt IV can be issued in a family hearing centre or the Principal Registry of the Family Division (ATPO 2008). Alternatively, subject to FLA 1996, s 59 and Sch 7, para 1, proceedings under Pt IV may be commenced in a family proceedings court. The application should be made to, or transferred to the lowest appropriate tier.

An application by a person under the age of 18, or for leave under s 43 (applications by children under 16) must be made in the county court and can be made to a district judge.

Where "family proceedings" (see FLA 1996, s 63) are pending in a county court or family proceedings court, an application under FLA 1996, Pt IV may be made in those proceedings.

Personal protection in the form of a "non-molestation order" is available to "associated persons", a term widely defined in s 62(3). "Molestation" is not defined in the Act. It includes violence and threats of violence but is not confined to such acts (see s 42). It includes controlling, coercive or threatening behaviour and all forms of abuse.

"Occupation orders" are available under ss 33, 35, 36, 37 and 38. Each section is self-contained, setting out who may apply and the court's powers. In practice, most applications will be under s 33. If an application is made under the wrong section, the court can make an order under another section (s 39). The court can include ancillary provisions (s 40).

Power of arrest may be attached to an occupation order. However, it is no longer possible to attach a power of arrest to a non-molestation order. Section 42A came into force on 1 July 2007 and a breach of a non-molestation made since then is a criminal offence.

Where injunctive relief from harassment within the meaning of PHA 1997 is sought, see Guide A12. Thus a person who is not an "associated person" within FLA 1996, Pt IV may need to sue under PHA 1997. Compensatory damages can be awarded under PHA 1997 and thus that Act (and/or proceedings in tort for, eg, assault) should be used where such a claim is pursued. Concurrent proceedings under FLA 1996 and PHA 1997 can be brought and should be consolidated (see *Lomas v Parle* [2004] 1 FLR 812).

Procedure

What is a "non-molestation" order?	An order prohibiting the respondent from molesting another person who is associated with the respondent and/or a relevant child	FLA 1996, s 42(1)
Who may apply for a "non-molestation" order?	An associated person; a person is associated with another person if: they are or have been married to each other	FLA 1996, s 62(3)
	they are or have been civil partners of each other	
	they are cohabitants or former cohabitants	
	they live or have lived in the same household, otherwise than merely by reason of one of them being the other's employee, tenant, lodger or boarder	
	they are relatives (as defined)	FLA 1996, s 63(1)
	they have agreed to marry one another (whether or not that agreement has been terminated)	
	they have entered into a civil partnership agreement (whether or not that agreement has been terminated)	CPA 2004, s 73

	they have or have had an intimate personal relationship with each other which is or was of significant duration	FLA 1996, s 62(3)
	in relation to a child both persons are parents or have or have had parental responsibility for the child	FLA 1996, s 62(4)
	they are parties to the same family proceedings	FLA 1996, s 63(1),(2)
Who may apply for an "occupation order" under s 33?	An applicant who is entitled to occupy a dwelling-house by virtue of a beneficial estate or interest or contract or by virtue of any enactment giving him the right to remain in occupation or who has home rights	FLA 1996, s 30
	The respondent is an "associated person"	FLA 1996, s 62(3)
	The dwelling-house must be, have been, or have been intended to be, the home of the applicant and respondent	FLA 1996, s 33
Who may apply for an "occupation order" under s 35?	An applicant former spouse or former civil partner who is not entitled to occupy; the respondent is entitled to occupy; the dwelling-house was or was intended to be their home	FLA 1996, s 35
Who may apply for an "occupation order" under s 36?	An applicant cohabitant or former cohabitant who is not entitled to occupy; the respondent is entitled to occupy; the dwelling-house is, was, or was intended to be the home where they live(d) together	FLA 1996, s 36
Who may apply for an "occupation order" under s 37?	An applicant spouse former spouse, civil partner or former civil partner where neither applicant nor respondent is entitled to occupy; the dwelling-house must be or have been their home	FLA 1996, s 37
Who may apply for an "occupation order" under s 38?	An applicant cohabitant or former cohabitant where neither applicant nor respondent is entitled to occupy. The dwelling-house must be or have been the home in which they live(d) together	FLA 1996, s 38
How is the application made?	In all cases, on Form FL401 supported by a witness statement (which must state the grounds)	FPR 2010, r 10.2
Which court?	County court that is a family hearing centre. The Principal Registry is treated as a county court	ATPO 2008
	Family proceedings court (subject to FLA 1996, s 59)	ATPO 2008
	County court, if the applicant is under 18 or seeks leave under s 43	ATPO 2008
Fee	£70	FPFO 2008, fee 1.3

Transfer of proceedings	Court may transfer proceedings to a more convenient court (including a higher or lower court)	FPR 2010, r 10.4; Form FL417
Ex parte applications	In any case where it considers it is "just and convenient" to do so the court can make a non-molestation order or an occupation order on an ex parte basis. The court must have regard to "all the circumstances", including the criteria in s 45(2)	FLA 1996, s 45(1),(2)
	The witness statement must state the reasons why notice was not given	FPR 2010, r 10.2(4)
	If an ex parte order is made there must be a "full hearing" as soon as just and convenient	FLA 1996, s 45(3)
Form of order	An occupation order is in Form FL404. A non-molestation order is in Form FL404a	
Service of ex parte order	Respondent must be personally served with: a copy of the order made a copy of the application in Form FL401 a copy of the witness statement in support of the application notice of the date of the full hearing in Form FL402	FPR 2010, r 10.6; FJC Protocol of November 2011: *Process Servers: Non-Molestation Orders*
Application on notice	Notice in Form FL402, together with a copy of the application in Form FL401 and the witness statement in support must be served on the respondent personally not less than 2 days before the application is to be heard	FPR 2010, r 10.3
	Before the application is served, the court can abridge time for service	FPR 2010, r 10.3(1)(b)(ii)
	If the application is for an occupation order under ss 33, 35 or 36 a copy of the application and notice in Form FL416 must be served by first class post on the mortgagee or landlord	FPR 2010, r 10.3(3)
Proof of service	After service, the applicant must file a statement in Form FL415	FPR 2010, r 6.37
Response	Respondent may, but is not required to, serve a statement in reply and/or make a cross-application	
Hearing	An application for a non-molestation order or an occupation order is dealt with in private unless the court otherwise directs	FPR 2010, r 10.5
	The application in the county court is heard by a district judge or circuit judge	FP(AJ)D 2009
	The court keeps a record of the hearing in Form FL405	

Orders available	*Non-molestation order*	
	An order may forbid molestation in general or particular acts of molestation or both	FLA 1996, s 42(6)
	The better modern practice is to make the order as specific as is appropriate whether or not it also contains a clause forbidding molestation in general. In particular, an order can require the respondent to "keep-away" from a specified address (but not to "get out", which needs to be part of an occupation order).	*Boness v R* [2005] EWCA Crim 2395
	Occupation order under s 33	
	An order may:	
	enforce the applicant's entitlement to remain in occupation as against the respondent	
	require the respondent to permit the applicant to enter and remain in the dwelling-house or part of the dwelling-house	
	regulate the occupation of the dwelling-house by either or both of the parties	
	if the respondent is entitled to occupy, prohibit, suspend or restrict the exercise by him of his right to occupy the dwelling-house	
	if the respondent has home rights in relation to the dwelling-house, restrict or terminate those rights	
	require the respondent to leave the dwelling-house or part of the dwelling-house	
	exclude the respondent from a defined area in which the dwelling-house is included	
	For additional provisions, see s 40	
	Occupation orders under ss 35, 36	
	Mandatory provisions are set out in ss 35(3), (4), 36(3), (4), and discretionary provisions in ss 35(5), 36(6)	
	For additional provisions, see s 40	
	Occupation orders under ss 37, 38	
	See ss 37(3), 38(3)	
Duration of non-molestation orders	For a specified period or until further order	
	Application for extension of the order is made in Form FL403	FLA 1996, s 42(7) FPR 2010, r 10.8
Duration of occupation orders	*Applicant with estate or interest etc or with home rights*	
	for a specified period	
	until the occurrence of a specified event	
	or until further order	FLA 1996, s 33(10)

	Application for extension of the order is made in Form FL403	FPR 2010, r 10.8
	Spouse, former spouse, civil partner or former civil partner not entitled to an interest for a maximum of 6 months, but can be renewed any number of times	FLA 1996, ss 35(10), 37(5)
	Application for extension of the order is made in Form FL403	FPR 2010, r 10.8
	Cohabitant or former cohabitant not entitled to an interest for a maximum of 6 months, but can be renewed only once	FLA 1996, ss 36(10), 38(6)
	Application for extension of the order is made in Form FL403	FPR 2010, r 10.8
Penal notice	A penal notice must be endorsed on an order before it can be enforced by committal	CPR 1998, Sch 2, CCR Ord 29, r 1(3), as modified by FPR 2010, r 10.12
	The prescribed forms of order (FL404 and FL404a) include an appropriately worded penal notice. Because the sanction for breach is different, the wording of the penal notice for breach of a non-molestation order is unique to that form of order. Thus two separate orders are required if the court makes both types of order	FPR 2010, rr 10.12, 33.7
Power of arrest	The court "*shall* attach a power of arrest to one or more provisions of an occupation order unless satisfied that ... the applicant ... will be adequately protected without [it]" if the respondent has used or threatened violence	FLA 1996, s 47(2)
	If the order is made ex parte, the court *may* attach a power of arrest to an occupation order if "the respondent has used or threatened violence" and "there is a risk of significant harm ... if the power of arrest is not attached"	FLA 1996, s 47(3)
	It is no longer possible to attach a power of arrest to a non-molestation order. Breach of such an order is a criminal offence	FLA 1996, s 42A
Undertakings	The court may accept an undertaking. The court "shall not accept an undertaking ... instead of making an occupation order in any case where ... a power of arrest would be attached" nor instead of making a non-molestation order where "it is necessary ... that any breach may be punishable under s 42A"	FLA 1996, s 46(1),(3), (3A)
	The court must deliver a copy of the undertaking to the party giving the undertaking	CPR 1998, Sch 2, CCR Ord 29, r 1A

	A warrant of arrest can be issued to enforce an undertaking	FLA 1996, s 46(4)
Damages	It is not possible to claim damages under FLA 1996. However, damages can be claimed under PHA 1997, s 3. If concurrent proceedings are brought they should be consolidated	*Lomas v Parle* [2004] 1 FLR 812
Service of injunction	Personal service of an order is required The applicant's solicitor should endeavour to effect service as soon as possible	FPR 2010, r 10.6; FJC Protocol of November 2011: *Process Servers: Non-Molestation Orders*
	An injunction directing an act to be done cannot be enforced unless it is served before the time within which the act is to be done has expired; an injunction cannot be enforced unless the respondent knows about it. Service should be effected in accordance with the terms of the Protocol	CPR 1998, Sch 2, CCR Ord 29, r 1(2); FJC Protocol of November 2011: *Process Servers: Non-Molestation Orders*
	Form 404a (non-molestation order) and/or Form FL406 (containing only those provisions of the occupation order to which a power of arrest has been attached) must be delivered to the officer in charge of any police station for the applicant's address or such other police station as the court may specify. The form must be served together with a statement showing that the respondent has been served with the order(s) or otherwise informed of its terms	FPR 2010, r 10.10
	A copy of an occupation order made under s 33, 35 or 36 must be served by the applicant by first class post on the mortgagee or landlord	FPR 2010, r 10.6(3)

A11: Order for Forced Marriage Protection Order under Family Law Act 1996, Pt 4A

Legal background

An application for a forced marriage protection order (FMPO) may be made as a freestanding application or in other family proceedings in the High Court, the Principal Registry of the Family Division, or in one of the 11 county courts specified to hear such applications. The definition of family proceedings has been extended to include applications under Pt 4A of FLA 1996. An order may also be made by the court of its own motion (FPR 2010, r 11.8) in circumstances set out in s 63C(6).

There is no age restriction for applicants for a forced marriage protection order. A child does not require leave of the court but the provisions of FPR 2010, rr 16.5 and 16.6 apply to applications for a FMPO. Procedure generally is governed by FPR 2010, r 11. For applications commenced before 6 April 2011, the transitional provisions in FPR PD36A apply.

The court is given a great deal of flexibility in relation to the terms which may be imposed within a FMPO. Any order which is appropriate to protect a person being forced into marriage, or to protect a person who has been forced into a marriage may be made. The terms of such an order may relate to conduct outside England and Wales, and persons who are or may be involved or become involved in the forced marriage or in any other respects (s 63B).

A power of arrest may be attached to a FMPO.

Procedure

Who may apply	The person who is to be protected by the order	
	A relevant third party, ie a local authority that is now specified as a relevant third party	FLA 1996, s 63C
	Any other person with permission of the court	FLA 1996 (FM)(RTP)O 2009
Application for permission to apply	Where permission to apply is required, the applicant must use the Pt 18 procedure and file (a) an application on Form FL430, setting out the reasons for the application, the applicant's connection with the person to be protected and the applicant's knowledge of the person's circumstances and of the person's wishes and feelings; and (b) a draft of the substantive application with sufficient copies for service on each respondent and the person to be protected	FLA 1996, s 63C; FPR 2010, r 11.3(1) and Pt 18; PD5A Table 2
	The application or the statement in support should be verified by statement of truth	FPR 2010, rr 17 and 18.7
	The application notice must have attached to it a draft of the order sought and must state: (a) what order the applicant is seeking; and (b) the reasons for seeking the order It must be verified by a statement of truth	
Substantive application	A draft of the substantive application in Form FL401A with sufficient copies for service	
	Sworn statement in support and documents as on without notice application	
Which court	The High Court The Principal Registry of the Family Division	
	A specified county court	FLA 1996, s 63M; FP(AJ)D 2009
Fee	£70	FPFO 2008

Respondent	Parents of the applicant or person to be protected The person to be protected Any person who is involved in forcing or is attempting to force a person to enter into a marriage Any person who is or may become involved in other respects Any other person as the court may direct	FLA 1996, s 63B See also FPR 2010, r 18.3(1)(b)(ii) and r 18.3(1)(c)
Without notice application	In any case where it is considered "just and convenient" to do so, the court may make a FMPO. The court must have regard to all the circumstances including the matters set out in s 63D	FLA 1996, s 63D; FPR 2010, r 18.4
Documents	Pt 18 application notice	
	A sworn statement in support must be made explaining why notice was not given. Where the application is made by an organisation, it must state the name and address of the person submitting the application and the position that person holds in the organisation	FPR 2010, rr 11.2(2),(3)
	The substantive application on Form 401A	FPR 2010, r 18.10(3)
	Draft of the order that must contain a statement of the respondent's right to make an application to set aside or vary the order within 7 days of service	
	If an order is made without notice the respondent must be given an opportunity to make representation at a hearing on notice as soon as "just and convenient"	FLA 1996, s 63D(3); FLA 1996, s 63D(4)
	Emergency legal aid certificate	
	Notice of legal aid certificate, if any, with a copy for service on the respondent(s)	
Service of without notice and on notice proceedings	Unless otherwise directed, the respondent, the person to be protected (if not the applicant) and any other person directed by the court must be personally served in accordance with the FJC's November 2011 Protocol on service (see Part V) with: • a copy of any order made; • a copy of the application in Form FL 401A; • a copy of any statement in support; • notice of the date of the next hearing in Form FL402A not less than 2 days before the next hearing	FPR 2010, rr 11.3(3), 11.4 and 18.5(10)(b)
	A sworn statement of service containing all the information set out in the FJC's Protocol must be prepared and filed	FJC Protocol of November 2011: *Process Servers: Non-Molestation Orders*

Service of order made on application without notice	An order made without notice must be served on all the parties and the person to be protected in accordance with the FJC's Protocol of November 2011. Note that the order must contain a statement of the right of the respondent and the person to be protected to make an application for the order to be set aside or to be varied within 7 days of service of the order The court may abridge time for service or make an order for substituted service	FPR 2010, rr 11.4(2),(3), 18.10(2),(3), 18.11 and Pt 6; FJC Protocol of November 2011: *Process Servers: Non-Molestation Orders*
Service on person to be protected of application on notice	Where the application is served on the person to be protected, it must be accompanied by a notice informing that person of how to apply to become a party to the proceedings and of that person's right to make representations in writing or orally at any hearing Where the person to be protected is not the applicant and is: a child; a person not being a party, who lacks capacity within the meaning of MCA 2005; or a protected person, the court should be asked to consider giving directions about the person(s) who is/are to be served with the application	FPR 2010, r 11.4(4),(5)
Documents to be served	A copy of the order Copy of Form 401A Copy of statement in support Notice of the hearing Copy of draft order sought at the next hearing where appropriate	FPR 2010, rr 11.4 and 18.8
Time for service of substantive application	The application in Form FL401A, sworn statement in support and notice of the hearing in Form FL402A must be served personally on the respondent/s unless otherwise directed by the court, not less than 2 days before the application is to be heard The court may abridge time for service The court may make an order for substituted service	FPR 2010, r 11.4(1)–(3)
Proof of service	Where the application is served by the applicant, the applicant must file a certificate of service on Form FL415 stating the date and time of personal service and details required under r 6.37	FPR 2010, rr 6.37, 11.4(6)
Hearing	An application for a FMPO is dealt with in private unless the court otherwise directs The court may deal with the application notwithstanding that the applicant or any respondent is absent from the hearing	FPR 2010, rr 11.7(1), 18.12

	The application in the specified county court is dealt with by: • a circuit judge or deputy circuit judge nominated for private or public family law proceedings; • a recorder nominated for private or public family law proceedings; • a district judge of the PRFD; • a district judge nominated for private or public family law proceedings	FP(AJ)D 2009
Form of order	Form 404B	FPR PD5A
Substantive orders	See Form FL404B for the precedent. The order may include: • prohibitions, restrictions and other requirements preventing a forced marriage taking place; • provision forbidding the named respondent/s from entering into any arrangement in relation to the engagement or marriage whether civil or religious of the person to be protected whether in this jurisdiction or overseas and from arranging or holding any celebration for such a marriage; • order prohibiting the removal of the person to be protected from the jurisdiction; • order prohibiting the named respondent from applying for a passport or other travel documents for the person to be protected; • order for surrender of passports; • non molestation orders; • disclosure of whereabouts order; • for the local authority where appropriate, the police and the legal representatives of the person to be protected to that person; • for the person to be protected to be interviewed by a member of the British High Commission in (a named country) (where the person to be protected is outside the jurisdiction); • order for the return of the person to be protected; • order for disclosure of the case papers to the Foreign and Commonwealth Office FMU; • any other order that may be appropriate, e g that the FMPO be served on the FMU and the UK Border Agency via the FMU	FLA 1996, s 63B; FPR 2010, r 11.7(3)

Interlocutory order	The court may direct non-disclosure of information to protect the person to be protected or any other person or for any good reason. Where such an order is made it may also list a further hearing to consider representations by the respondent, person to be protected or any other person. A copy of the order, record of the hearing and (if the order is made without notice) a copy of the application statement in support must be served personally on the respondent, the person to be protected (if neither the applicant nor a respondent) and any other person named in the order as soon as practicable	FPR 2010, rr 11.7 and 11.9 and 21.3(1)–(8)
Penal notice	A penal notice must be endorsed on the order. The prescribed forms of orders include an appropriate notice	CPR 1998, Sch 2, CCR Ord 29, r 1(3), FPR 2010, r 11.15
Power of arrest	The court must attach a power of arrest to one or more provisions of the order where it considers that the respondent has used or threatened violence towards the person to be protected or otherwise in connection with the matters being dealt with by the order unless it considers that in all the circumstances of the case, there will be adequate protection without such a power	FLA 1996, s 63H
	Where a power of arrest is attached to an order each provision must be set out in a separate paragraph in the order and a paragraph containing the relevant provision must not include a provision of the order to which the power of arrest is not attached. If the order is made on a without notice application, the terms of the order must be announced in open court when the court proceeds to hear cases in open court	FPR 2010, r 11.11; see FPR PD10A, para 3.1

	The following documents must be delivered to the officer for the time being in charge of any police station as the court may specify: • the power of arrest form; • a statement showing that the respondent/s and any other person directed by the court to be served with the order, have been served or informed of its terms whether by being present when the order was made or by telephone or otherwise. Service must be effected by the process server in accordance with the FJC's Protocol for process servers of November 2011 and the statement of service must be a sworn statement and contain the information set out in the Protocol. The documents must be served by the applicant if the applicant is responsible for service and by the court, if the court is responsible	FPR 2010, r 11.12; FJC Protocol of November 2011: *Process Servers: Non-Molestation Orders*
Undertakings	The court may accept an undertaking but not if a power of arrest would have been attached had it been an order	FLA 1996, s 63E; see FPR PD33A on form of undertaking
Duration of orders	A FMPO may be made for a specified period or until varied or discharged	FLA 1996, s 63F
Variation/Discharge of orders	The court may vary or discharge a FMPO on the application of: • any party to the proceedings; • the person being protected by the order if not a party to the proceedings; • any person affected by the order	FLA 1996, s 63G; see also FPR 2010, r 11.10
Application to vary extend or discharge FMPO	Must be made on Form FL403A setting out the facts relied on and if the application is not verified by a statement of truth A statement in support that is verified by a statement of truth must be filed Pt 18 procedure will apply to such an application	FPR PD5A
Warrant of arrest	In certain circumstances the court may issue a warrant for arrest of a person if there has been a breach of the order, but the application must be supported by a sworn statement and the court must have reasonable grounds for believing that the person to be arrested has failed to comply with the order or is otherwise in contempt of court The warrant must be in Form FL408	FLA 1996, s 63J(2); FPR 2010, r 11.13; FPR PD5A
Application for warrant of arrest	The application must be in Form FL407A accompanied by a sworn statement	FPR PD5A; FPR 2010, rr 10.9–10.16

A12: Claims under the Protection from Harassment Act 1997

Legal background

The High Court and county courts have jurisdiction to grant an injunction for personal protection by forbidding harassment under PHA 1997 or any conduct which amounts to a recognised form of tort (*Khorasandjian v Bush* [1993] 2 FLR 66). Such proceedings are not "family proceedings"; however, a warrant of arrest can be granted in respect of a breach (PHA 1997, s 3(3), (5)). Unlike FLA 1996, the court can award damages under PHA 1997 (see *Singh v Bhakar* [2007] 1 FLR 880, where damages of £35,000 were awarded). In *Burris v Azadani* [1996] 1 FLR 266, the Court of Appeal held that, where it is necessary to make the injunction effective for the protection of the applicant, an "exclusion zone" can be ordered forbidding the defendant to go within a specified area around the applicant's home. In *Silverton v Gravett* [2001] All ER (D) 282, the "exclusion zone" included also the claimant's place of work.

Where the victim and the perpetrator of harassment or molestation are "associated persons" within FLA 1996, s 62(3), the remedies under that Act are more comprehensive, particularly if occupation of the family home is an issue. See Guide A10.

For precedents, see *Emergency Remedies in the Family Courts* (Jordan Publishing Ltd).

Injunctions under Protection from Harassment Act 1997

An injunction can be granted in a county court (as in the High Court) without a claim for damages or other relief, by virtue of CCA 1984, s 38. Whereas an injunction under FLA 1996 is applied for by way of an application in Form FL401 under FPR 2010, Pt 10, an application for an injunction under PHA 1997 is governed by CPR 1998, Pt 65 which requires the claim to be brought under CPR, Pt 8.

Under the CPR, proceedings are commenced by "claim form". Claims under PHA 1997 must be brought under the Pt 8 procedure (see r 65.28 and CPR 1998, Pt 8). Generally, a Pt 8 claim form (N208) should not contain the same amount of detail as in a Pt 7 claim. A Pt 8 claim form should set out in summary form the issue which the claimant wants the court to decide and the remedy sought. If an interim remedy is also sought (e g a without notice injunction) see also CPR 1998, Pt 25 and in particular CPR PD25A (see Part III) which supplements Pt 25. Best practice for making a freestanding application is to file N208 incorporating short particulars of claim, which can, but need not, include a claim for damages, together with an application in Form N16A (county court) or Application Notice in Form N244 (High Court), provided that the evidence setting out the relevant facts is given in Form N16A or N244, or in witness statement(s), verified by a statement of truth (see para 3 of PD25A).

Assault and battery

If protection is required but is not available under the FLA 1996 (e g because the parties are not "associated persons") nor under the PHA 1997 (e g because there is no "course of conduct": in *Andreson v Lovell* [2009] EWHC 3397 (QB) a "one-off unwanted grope" was an isolated incident and not harassment, but it would be an assault) it may be possible to sue in tort and seek an injunction in those proceedings. Such actions are beyond the scope of this work.

Procedure

Who may apply	A person who is or may be the victim of a course of conduct prohibited by PHA 1997, s 1	PHA 1997, s 3(1)
	Application for an interim injunction may be made by the defendant to the claim	*Huntingdon Life Sciences v Stop Huntingdon Animal Cruelty* [2003] EWHC 1139 (QB); CPR 1998, rr 25.1(1)(a), 25.2(1)

Which court?	High Court or the county court for the district where the claimant or defendant resides A district judge has jurisdiction to deal with all claims under PHA 1997	PHA 1997, s 3(3); CPR 1998, r 65.28
Application	Claim Form N208 must be issued, unless the court allows the application to be made before proceedings are started because the matter is urgent or there are good reasons for not giving notice	
	A claimant must file any written evidence on which he intends to rely when he files his claim form. A claimant may rely on the matters set out in the claim form if it is verified by a statement of truth	CPR 1998, rr 65.28, 25.2(1),(2), 25.3(1); PD25A, para 4.4 CPR 1998, rr 8.5 and 8.6
	An urgent application for an injunction should be made as an interim application in pending proceedings by application notice in Form N16A (county court) or Form N244 (High Court)	CPR 1998, Pt 23; PD23A; CPR 1998, r 25.1(1)(a); PD25A, para 2.1
	A form of acknowledgement of service (N210) must be served with the claim form. The defendant must file an acknowledgement of service. If he does not do so, he may attend the hearing but may not take part unless the court gives permission	PD8, para 3; CPR 1998, rr 8.3 and 8.4
	Damages can be claimed, but need not be	PHA 1997, s 3; CCA 1984, s 38; CPR 1998; PD2, para 8.1(d)(ii)
	An application for an interim injunction must be supported by evidence, ie a witness statement, unless the court orders otherwise	CPR 1998, r 25.3(2)
Fee	High Court: £465 County court: £175 (non-money claim) payable on issue of application in Form N16A or N244 together with Claim Form N208	CPFO 2008, fee 1.5
Oral application without documents	The court can dispense with the requirement for an application notice and in cases of extreme urgency can grant an interim injunction by telephone. However, the court should be expected to require an undertaking to file evidence, verified by a statement of truth, notice of application and, if not yet done, to issue a claim form	CPR 1998, r 23.3(2)(b); PD25A, paras 4.2, 4.5, 5.1(2)
	Such an undertaking must be strictly complied with	*Re S (A Child) (Family Division: Without Notice Orders)* [2001] 1 All ER 362

PART I

Application begun without notice	An interim injunction can be granted without notice of the application having been given, where the matter is urgent and the court considers that there are good reasons for not giving notice	CPR 1998, rr 25.2(1),(2), 25.3(1)
	Any applicant without notice is under a duty to give full and frank disclosure of all relevant facts	W v H [2001] 1 All ER 300; B v A [2012] EWHC 3127 (Fam)
	In an urgent case informal notice, i e short notice, of application for a personal protection injunction is better practice than no notice, unless the circumstances require secrecy	CPR PD23A, para 4.2
	If a claim form has already been served, the applicant should take steps to tell the respondent that the application is being made without full notice unless secrecy is essential	CPR PD25A, para 4.3
	The reasons for not giving notice must be stated in the evidence in support	CPR 1998, r 25.3(3); PD25A, para 3.4
	If the application is made before the application notice has been issued, the notice and evidence in support and fee must be filed on the same or next working day (or as ordered by the court), as should the claim form and fee, if not already issued	CPR PD25A, paras 4.4(3), 5.1(4),(5)
	The respondent against whom an interim injunction is granted may apply to have it set aside or varied, but must apply within 7 days after it is served or at the return date provided in the order	CPR 1998, r 23.10(1),(2); PD25A, para 5.1(3)
Evidence	Applications for interim injunctions must be supported by evidence, i e set out in a document verified by a statement of truth, which may be in a witness statement or the statement of case or the application itself	CPR 1998, r 25.3(2); PD25, para 3.2
	The evidence must set out the facts on which the applicant relies for the claim including all material facts of which the court should be made aware	CPR PD25A, para 3.3
	The witness statement must be verified by a statement of truth	CPR 1998, rr 8.2 and 22.1(1)
Service of notice	The application and evidence in support must be served as soon as practicable after it is filed and at least 3 working days before the hearing to give valid notice, unless the court shortens the time	CPR 1998, rr 2.8, 3.1(2)(a), 23.7(1)(a); PD25A, para 2.2
	Informal notice (i e less than 3 days) is better than no notice	G v G [1990] 1 FLR 395
	Where proceedings have commenced, informal notice should be given unless secrecy is essential	CPR PD25A, para 4.3(3)

Response	The defendant must file an acknowledgment of service. A defendant who intends to rely on written evidence must file it when he files his acknowledgment of service. (A claimant may file further written evidence in reply). If the defendant fails to acknowledge service, he may attend the hearing but may not take part unless the court gives permission	CPR 1998, rr 8.3–8.5; PD8A, para 3,
	Respondent to application for injunction may: (i) elect not to oppose (ii) oppose in whole or in part by filing and serving evidence (iii) make his own application in like form	CPR 1998, r 23.11(1)
Hearing	CPR 1998 do not require the hearing of an interim application to be conducted in open court in public	CPR 1998, rr 23.8, 25.1, 25.2, 39.2(1)
	The applicant should submit a draft of the injunction in typescript (in Form N16 in a county court) and on disk (in a format compatible with the word processing format used by the court) if he has not filed one already	CPR 1998, r 23.7(3)(b); PD25A, paras 2.4, 4.3
	Breach of an order under PHA 1997, s 3 is both a crime and a contempt of court. The facts on which the order is obtained need to be proven to the civil standard	*Hipgrave and Hipgrave v Jones* [2005] 2 FLR 174
Orders available	The court may grant an injunction restraining the defendant from pursuing any conduct which amounts to harassment. The order may prohibit specific conduct and/ or harassment in general.	
	Where necessary for the protection of the applicant, an exclusion zone can be provided around her home or her place of work	*Burris v Azadani* [1996] 1 FLR 266; *Silverton v Gravett* [2001] All ER (D) 282
	Power of arrest is not available (though a warrant of arrest can be granted after the event)	PHA 1997, s 3(3),(4)
Order made without notice: duration and review	If an injunction is granted at a hearing of which the respondent has not been given notice:	
	a return date must (unless the court orders otherwise) be given for a hearing at which the respondent can be present	CPR PD25A, para 5.1(3)
	the respondent is in any event entitled within 7 days of service on him to apply to have the order set aside	CPR 1998, r 23.10; Form N16
	Where an injunction is granted without notice having been given, it is good practice for the court to order that it runs to a date later than the return date, so that there is no hiatus until an injunction granted on notice can be served	

Damages	The court can award damages under PHA 1997	PHA 1997, s 3, eg, *Singh v Bhakar* [2007] 1 FLR 880
	Concurrent proceedings under FLA 1996 and PHA 1997 should be consolidated and tried together	*Lomas v Parle* [2004] 1 FLR 812
Undertakings	An enforceable undertaking can be accepted by the court	*Hussain v Hussain* [1986] 2 FLR 271; CPR 1998, rr 81.4–81.11
Form of injunction order or undertaking: penal notice and clear instructions	To be enforceable, when served an injunction order must have prominently displayed on the front a warning notice of the consequences of disobedience	CPR PD81, paras 1, 2; Form N16A
	Any order for an injunction must set out clearly what the respondent must do or not do (in a county court the injunction should be issued in Form N138)	CPR PD25A, para 5.2
	An undertaking given to a county court must be recorded in Form N117	
Service of injunction or delivery of form of undertaking	Before an injunction can be enforced it must have been personally served on the respondent, before any alleged breach, unless the court has dispensed with service or he was present when the order was made or he has been notified of the terms of the order. Service should be effected in accordance with the Protocol (see "Introduction" in the Protocol, which extends it to "harassment")	CPR 1998, r 81.5; Family Justice Council *Protocol for Process Servers*, November 2011
	An undertaking becomes enforceable when and because it is given to the court; however, unless a record of it is given to the person who gave it, difficulties can arise on enforcement proceedings, and in county courts a copy is required to be delivered to the giver by the court or, failing that, served by the applicant	CPR 1998, r 81.7; *Hussain v Hussain* [1986] 2 FLR 271
Duration of interim injunction made on notice	An interim injunction granted on notice can be ordered to last until a fixed date or trial or further order	CPR PD25A, para 5.2
	If the claim is stayed other than by agreement between the parties, an interim injunction shall be set aside unless the court orders that it should continue to have effect	CPR 1998, r 25.10

| Warrant for arrest | Application for a warrant of arrest in respect of disobedience of an injunction prohibiting harassment should be made in the High Court if the order was made there or, if the order was made in a county court, the application may be made in any county court | PHA 1997, s 3(4),(5) |
| | The formal requirements upon making application for a warrant are provided by rules; see Guide C15 for practice | CPR 1998, r 65.29 |

A13: Transfer of a Tenancy under Family Law Act 1996, Pt IV, s 53 and Sch 7

Legal background

Since the coming into force of FLA 1996, Pt IV on 1 October 1997, the court is empowered to transfer tenancies, both contractual and statutory, between cohabitants who no longer live together as husband and wife, as well as between spouses and former spouses. As set out in FLA 1996, Sch 7, para 10, the person to whom the tenancy is transferred can be ordered to pay compensation to the other party. The power to transfer the tenancy to a former spouse arises on decree nisi; the order becomes effective on decree absolute; and there is a prohibition on applying if that former spouse has remarried. If there is a decree of judicial separation, the power to transfer arises after the decree is pronounced. A tenancy in the other spouse's name, or in joint names, can be destroyed by the unilateral surrender or giving of notice to quit by one tenant without consultation with the other (*Hammersmith and Fulham London Borough Council v Monk* [1992] 1 FLR 465). A party should ask for an undertaking that the tenancy will not be surrendered and then serve that undertaking on the landlord. If the undertaking is not given the applicant should apply for an injunction and serve the order on the landlord (*Bater v Greenwich London Borough Council* [1999] 2 FLR 993).

An application under FLA 1996, s 53 and Sch 7 is governed by the procedure in FPR 2010, rr 8.29–8.34.

Procedure

Who may apply	Either spouse, but a decree of judicial separation must be granted before the order is made	FLA 1996, Sch 7, para 2(2)
	Either former spouse, but a decree nisi must be granted before the order is made and the applicant must not have remarried; if application is for the transfer of a statutory tenancy or contractual tenancy containing a prohibition on assignment, it must be made before decree absolute	FLA 1996, Sch 7, para 13
	A cohabitant who is no longer living with the other cohabitant as husband and wife	FLA 1996, Sch 7, para 3
Application	To the High Court or a county court or to the court where there are pending divorce or civil partnership proceedings	FLA 1996, Sch 7, para 2(2); FPR 2010, r 8.30
Fee	£70	FPFO 2008, fee 1.3

Service	The court will serve the respondent and the landlord unless the applicant is directed to serve	FPR 2010, r 8.31
	A landlord may be made a party to proceedings	FPR 2010, r 8.32
Respondent	The other spouse or cohabitant	
Interlocutory injunction	The court may grant an injunction if ancillary or incidental to the assistance sought; an application for an injunction must be in accordance with procedure under FPR 2010, r 20.4	FPR 2010, r 8.34
Orders for disclosure	Any party may apply to the court under r 21.2 for any person to attend a production appointment to produce documents specified or described in the order	FPR 2010, r 8.33
Order	Transfer of tenancy or statutory tenancy	FLA 1996, Sch 7, paras 7–9
	Payment by the spouse or cohabitant to whom the tenancy is transferred, to the other; deferment of payment or payment by instalments if transferee's financial hardship greater than transferor's	FLA 1996, Sch 7, para 10
	Order that both liable to discharge obligations before date of transfer and indemnity	FLA 1996, Sch 7, para 11
Appeals	See Guides E2, E4 and E5	

A14: Parental Order under Human Fertilisation and Embryology Act 2008, s 54

Legal background

The HFEA 2008 (Commencement No 3) Order 2010 brought into force from 6 April 2010 the provisions of HFEA 2008, s 54. Section 30 of the 1990 Act has been repealed as from that date. The new provisions extend the categories of applicants who may make an application for a parental order to heterosexual married couples, civil partners who have entered into a civil partnership and unmarried heterosexual and same-sex couples who are living in an enduring relationship, thus bringing the eligibility of applicants in-line with applicants for an adoption order. The FPC(CA 1989) (Amendment) (No 2) Rules 2010 inserted rules 21A–21J and the FPR (Amendment) (No 2) Rules 2010 inserted Pt IVA. The procedure is governed by FPR 2010, Pt 13. For proceedings commenced before 6 April 2011 and in relation to existing proceedings under s 30 of the 1990 Act the transitional arrangements set out in FPR PD36A apply and reference should be made to *The Family Court Practice 2010* where necessary. The following Guide is provided as a guide but practitioners should refer to s 54 of the Act and FPR 2010 when making applications for a parental order. The ATPO 2008 has been amended by the HFE (Parental Orders) Consequential Transitional and Savings Provisions) Order 2010 to substitute s 54 of the 2008 Act for s 30 of the 1990 Act to provide that all applications under s 54 must be started in the FPC. The Schedule to the Order makes amendments to a number of Orders to take account of the repeal of s 30 of the 1990 Act and the revocation of the Parental Orders (HFE) Regulations 1994 and related regulations that apply to Scotland and Northern Ireland. HFE (Parental Orders) Regulations 2010 provides for many of the provisions of ACA 2002.

Procedure

Who may apply	Married heterosexual couples (ie husband and wife) Civil partners of each other Two persons who are living as partners in an enduring family relationship and are not within the prohibited degrees of relationship in relation to each other	See HFEA 2008, s 54; FPR 2010, r 13.3
Which court	The proceedings must be commenced in the family proceedings court unless certain conditions set out in the ATPO apply, when it may be commenced in the High Court or county court	ATPO 2008
	Proceedings may be transferred upwards, sideways or downwards	ATPO 2008
	If an application for a transfer to the county court is refused under r 12.9, application may be made to a county court for an order transferring the proceedings from the family proceedings court	FPR 2010, rr 12.10, 13.2
Application	Freestanding in Form C51 for each child (if more than one) with sufficient copies for each respondent	FPR PD5A
Documents to be filed with application	Marriage certificate if the applicants are married Civil partnership certificate if applicants are civil partners Child's birth certificate Any relevant orders Agreement (if any) to the making of a parental order in Form A101A	FPR PD5A; FPR 2010, rr 13.5(1)(b), 13.15(2)(a)
Grounds for application	Consent of the birth parent(s) in Form A101A or birth parent(s) cannot be found or birth parent(s) are incapable of giving consent	FPR PD5A; HFEA 2008, s 54
Respondent	The woman who carried the child The other parent (if any) Any person in whose favour there is provision for contact Any other person or body with parental responsibility for the child	FPR 2010, r 13.3(2)
	Any other person with parental responsibility on the direction of the court and on request by that person Any other person or body on the direction of the court	FPR 2010, r 13.3(3),(4)
Appointment of parental order reporter	As soon as is practicable after issue the court will consider the appointment of a parental order reporter	FPR 2010, r 13.5

Service	Respondent/s must be served with: • a copy of the application • notice of hearing and first direction hearing (Form C6) and • Form C52 must be served on each respondent within 14 days before the hearing or first directions hearing; notice of proceedings must be served on any local authority or voluntary organisation who has accommodated the child	FPR PD5A; FPR 2010, r 13.6
Acknowledgement	Each respondent must file and serve an acknowledgement of service within 7 days of service on all other parties	FPR 2010, r 13.7
First direction hearing	Must take place within 4 weeks of issue of the application unless the court otherwise directs	FPR 2010, r 13.8
Directions	(a) Fix a timetable for filing of: – parental order reporter's report and give directions relating to the report – statement of fact or amendment to it – any other evidence (b) Directions relating to the parental order reporter's report and other evidence (c) Consider whether any other person should be made a party and give appropriate directions in relation thereto (d) Consider the appointment of a litigation friend for a protected person unless one has already been appointed (e) Consider transfer of proceedings and if so give directions in relation thereto in accordance with the allocation order (f) Give direction for: tracing the other parent or the woman who carried the child; service of documents; disclosure; and final hearing Other directions may be given at any stage of the proceedings The parties or their legal representatives must attend the first hearing unless otherwise directed by the court	FPR 2010, r 13.9(1),(3),(4)
Consent of birth parent(s)	May be given on Form A101 or a form to like effect Any form of agreement executed in Scotland must be witnessed by a Justice of the Peace or sheriff Any form of agreement executed in Northern Ireland must be witnessed by a Justice of the Peace Any form of agreement executed outside the UK must be witnessed by:	

	(a) any person currently authorised by law in the place where the document is executed to administer an oath for any judicial or other legal process (b) a British Consular officer (c) a notary public (d) an officer holding a commission in any of the armed forces if the person executing the document is serving in the regular armed forces	FPR PD5A; FPR 2010, r 13.11
Disclosure of parental order reporter's report	Only on the direction of the court. Before giving such directions the court should consider whether the report needs redacting	FPR 2010, r 13.12
Notice of final hearing	Must be by the court on the parties and the parental order reporter, stating the date and place of the hearing	FPR 2010, r 13.13
Final hearing	Any person who has been given notice of the hearing may attend and be heard on the question of whether an order should be made The court may direct that any person may attend the hearing	FPR 2010, r 13.14(a),(b)
Order	A parental order takes effect on the date when it is made or such later date as the court may specify If the proceedings are in Wales a party may request the order to be drawn up in Welsh as well as in English	FPR 2010, rr 13.20(1),(2)
Service of order	Within 7 days of the order being made or such shorter time as the court may direct, the court must send a copy of the order to the persons and court referred to in FPR 2010, rr 13.3, 13.21	

B1: Declaration as to Marital Status

Legal background

FLA 1986, s 55 allows the court to make a declaration that a marriage: (a) was valid at its inception; (b) subsisted on a particular date; or (c) did not subsist on a particular date. If the truth of the proposition sought to be declared is established, the court is obliged to make the declaration, unless to do so would manifestly be contrary to public policy (FLA 1986, s 58(1)). If made, a declaration binds the world and not just the parties (FLA 1986, s 58(2)). Procedure for a declaration is at FPR 2010, Pt 8, Ch 5, by the Pt 19 procedure.

Procedure

Who may apply	A party to the marriage in question and any other person who has a sufficient interest	FLA 1986, s 55(1),(3); see also under FPR 2010, Pt 8, Ch 5

Which court	High Court or county court	FLA 1986, ss 55(1), 63; see also under FPR 2010, r 8.19
Pre-application requirement	The application must be served on Attorney-General at least 1 month before it is filed	FPR 2010, r 8.21
Application	By application on Form D70 Fee: £340	FPR PD5A FPFO 2008, fee 1.2
Documents to accompany petition	Any marriage certificate or divorce/annulment/legal separation decree where relevant (and with an authenticated English translation where relevant)	Per Form D70
Respondents	The parties (or other party) to the marriage in question	FPR 2010, r 8.20(1)
Other parties	The Attorney-General has the right to intervene in accordance with – Addition of other parties	FLA 1986, s 59(2) No specific provision: see, for example, FPR 2010, r 9.26B
Service		FPR 2010, Pt 6
Acknowledgment of service	14 days after service of the application	FPR 2010, r 19.5
Other interim procedures		FPR 2010, Pt 18
Hearing		FPR 2010, rr 27.10, 27.11
Order	A declaration that the marriage: was valid at its inception subsisted on a particular date did not subsist on a particular date	FLA 1986, s 55
Appeals	See Guide E5	

B2: Applications for Divorce, Judicial Separation or Nullity Orders and Equivalent Civil Partnership Orders on Undefended Case

Legal background

A marriage or civil partnership may be dissolved on the ground that it has broken down irretrievably (MCA 1973, s 1(1); CPA 2004, s 44(1)). Application is made to the court (by application form, formerly by petition) for a matrimonial or civil partnership order.

To prove that the marriage or civil partnership has broken down irretrievably, the applicant (petitioner) must prove one or more of five facts set out in MCA 1973, s 1(2) or, in the case of a civil partnership, four facts in CPA 2004, s 44(5). If satisfied on the fact(s), the court grants an order, which in the first instance is a decree nisi or conditional order. This cannot be made absolute/final for 6 weeks (MCA 1973, s 1(5), as varied by Matrimonial Causes (Decree Absolute) General Order 1972; CPA 2004, s 38(1)).

A marriage or civil partnership may be annulled on the ground that either it is void as set out in MCA 1973, s 11 or CPA 2004, s 49, or that it is voidable as set out in MCA 1973, s 12 or CPA 2004, s 50. Any order is a decree nisi or conditional order, which cannot be made absolute/final for 6 weeks (MCA 1973, s 15 which applies s 1(5) to nullity cases; CPA 2004, ss 37(2), 38(1)).

Parties to a marriage may be judicially separated on the ground that one or more of the facts set out in MCA 1973, s 1(2) or CPA 2004, s 44(5) is proved (MCA 1973, s 17(1); CPA 2004, s 56). The procedure is the same as for dissolution of a marriage or civil partnership, save that no final order is made: the marriage or civil partnership is not finally dissolved.

Procedure

Who may apply	Either party to the marriage or civil partnership	MCA 1973, s 1(1); CPA 2004, s 44(1)
Which court	Principal Registry of the Family Division or any divorce county court; or any civil partnership proceedings county court	FPR 2010, r 7.5
Application	By prescribed application form	FPR PD5A
	The application form must be accompanied by:	FPR 2010, r 7.8
	copies for service on all other parties	
	statement of arrangements for the children	
	marriage (civil partnership) certificate	
	reconciliation statement (if solicitor acting)	FPR 2010, r 7.6
	public funding certificate (if any) and notice thereof	Funding Code, Procedures, paras C16.2 and C16.3
	court fee or "fee exempt" form	FPFO 2008, Sch 2
	Fee: £340	FPFO 2008, fee 1.2
Filing without marriage certificate	Application (normally without notice) with explanation as to why no certificate	FPR PD7A, paras 3.2 and 3.3
	Proof of urgency (as indicated by PD7A) is not a prerequisite for an application	*G v M* [2011] EWHC 2651 (Fam)
Parties	As respondent, other party to the marriage	
	As co-respondent, anyone with whom respondent is alleged to have committed adultery or had improper association	FPR 2010, r 7.10
Service	The application and relevant documents (as above) are served personally or by post on respondent and co-respondent	FPR 2010, Pt 6, Ch 2
	Service may be by the court by post, DX or alternative service provider	FPR 2010, rr 6.8, 6.18; PD6A, para 3.1
	Alternatively, service may be:	
	bailiff service on application to the court	FPR 2010, r 6.9; PD6A, paras 11.1–13.2
	deemed	FPR 2010, rr 6.15, r 6.16

PART I

	substituted, including by advertisement	FPR 2010, r 6.19; PD6A, paras 6.1–6.4
	dispensed with by the court	FPR 2010, r 6.20; PD6A, para 7.1
Acknowledgement of service	A party served may: acknowledge service on Form M6 stating no intention to defend	FPR 2010, r 7.12
	Notice of intention to defend must be given within 7 days of service	FPR 2010, r 7.12(1)
Amendment petitions	Filed as of right before answer filed; thereafter, filing only with leave	FPR 2010, r 7.13(1)
	Fee: £90	FPFO 2008, fee 1.4
Directions for trial	Directions may be:	FPR 2010, r 7.20
	in the undefended list or	FPR 2010, r 7.20(2)(a)
	for cause to be treated as defended	FPR 2010, r 7.20(2)(b)
Decree, conditional order in undefended list		FPR 2010, r 7.18
Undefended application procedure	In the case of undefended petitions for divorce or judicial separation (or nullity where an interim gender recognition certificate has been issued post marriage), the applicant files an affidavit (FPR PD17A)	FPR 2010, r 7.19(4)
	The court (ie district judge) considers the evidence	FPR 2010, r 7.20(2)
	If satisfied on consideration of evidence filed, the court certifies satisfaction as to entitlement to decree nisi or conditional order	FPR 2010, r 7.20(2)(a)
	If not satisfied, court directs (1) further evidence or (2) listing for case management hearing	FPR 2010, r 7.20(2)(b)
	If entitlement to a decree/order certified, court fixes date for formal pronouncement	FPR 2010, r 7.18
Children	If no contested children application is pending, district judge considers evidence filed concerning children (if any) and:	MCA 1973, s 41(1); CPA 2004, s 63(1); FPR 2010, r 7.25(1),(2)
	certifies that there are no relevant children; or	FPR 2010, r 7.25(3)(a)
	certifies that there are relevant children but no need to exercise statutory powers; or	FPR 2010, r 7.25(3)(b)
	gives directions for the provision of further information	FPR 2010, r 7.25(4),(5)
Decree	In cases of divorce or nullity, the decree is initially a "decree nisi"	MCA 1973, ss 1(5), 15; CPA 2004, s 38

	Subject to MCA 1973, ss 10(2) and 41(1), application for the decree nisi to be made absolute can be made: by the applicant (petitioner) after 6 weeks	MCA 1973, s 1(5); CPA 2004, s 38(1); FPR 2010, r 7.32
	Fee: £45	FPFO 2008, fee 4.1
	by the respondent by application on notice 3 months after that 6-week period	MCA 1973, s 9(2); CPA 2004, s 40(2); FPR 2010, r 7.33
	Fee: £90	FPFO 2008, fee 4.3
	If application is made by applicant more than 12 months after decree nisi or conditional order, it must be supported by a letter or other document: (1) explaining the delay; (2) stating whether parties lived together since decree; and (3) stating whether another child has been born to the couple and (if so) whether it is a child of the family (if delay is substantially more than 12 months, see note under FPR 2010, r 7.32(3) as to the court's power to rescind a decree nisi)	FPR 2010, r 7.32(3)
Costs	The court may deal with costs when dealing with a FPR 2010, r 7.20(2) certificate	FPR 2010, r 7.20(3)
	If a party wishes to be heard on costs claimed against them notice should be given to the court;	FPR 2010, r 7.21(1)
	decided on family proceedings costs award principles	FPR 2010, r 28.2, applying CPR 1998, r 44.2
Case management hearing	If the court is not satisfied that an applicant is entitled to a decree or conditional order (per FPR 2010, r 7.20(2)(a)) it may list the application for a case management hearing	FPR 2010 rr 7.20(2)(b)(ii), 7.22(3)

B3: Staying Grant of Decree Absolute under Matrimonial Causes Act 1973, s 10A

Legal background

MCA 1973, s 10A provides that, where a couple were married in accordance with "the usages of the Jews" or other religious usages which prescribe final dissolution, the grant of a decree absolute can be stayed. No decree absolute will be granted until the court is satisfied by a declaration of both parties that the marriage is also dissolved in accordance with "those [Jewish or other] usages". FPR 2010, r 7.30 provides the regulatory framework for an application under s 10A.

Procedure

Who may apply	Either party to the marriage; though in Jewish marriages it is more likely to be the wife (whether respondent or petitioner)	MCA 1973, s 10A(2)
Time for application	After decree nisi, but before grant of decree absolute NB: Because of the time-frame from grant of decree nisi, prompt application is essential	MCA 1973, s 10A(1)
Application	On notice with affidavit in support setting out grounds of application	FPR 2010, r 7.30
Fee on application	£90	FPFO 2008, fee 4.3
Effect of order	Stay on grant of decree absolute until parties jointly declare that they have co-operated in arranging dissolution of their marriage in accordance with their religious usages	
Stay lifted	Upon filing declaration containing:	MCA 1973, s 10A(4)
	signature of both parties	FPR 2010, r 7.30(1)(a)
	particulars of MCA 1973 proceedings	FPR 2010, r 7.30(1)(b)
	confirmation of necessary religious steps being taken	FPR 2010, r 7.30(1)(c)
	Declaration should be accompanied by documents listed in FPR 2010, r 7.30(1)(d)	FPR 2010, r 7.30(1)(d)

B4: Applications for Divorce, Judicial Separation or Nullity Orders and Equivalent Civil Partnership Orders in Defended Case

Legal background

See Guide B2.

Procedure

Answer to petition	An answer to the divorce etc application must be filed by any respondent or co-respondent who: wishes to defend the application or to dispute any of the facts in it wishes to cross-pray (respondent only) wishes to oppose the grant of a decree under MCA 1973, s 5(1); CPA 2004, s 47	FPR 2010, r 7.12(8)

	The answer must be filed 7 days plus 21 days (note: this is not necessarily 28 days – see commentary to FPR 2010, r 2.9)	FPR 2010, r 7.12(8)
	Fee: £230	FPFO 2008, fee 1.5
Service of answer	There are no special rules for service of an answer as there are for a matrimonial and civil partnership proceedings application: normal service rules	FPR 2010, Pt 6, Chs 1, 3
Case management hearing	Case management hearing is listed by the court (ie district judge) as directed on application for a decree nisi or conditional order	FPR 2010, r 7.20(4)
	At the hearing the court decides:	
	place of hearing	FPR 2010, r 7.22(2)(a)
	timetable for filing and service of evidence; and for attendances of witnesses	FPR 2010, r 7.22(2)(b),(d)
	documents disclosure – as appropriate; and see FPR 2010, r 7.15 for further information	FPR 2010, r 7.22(2)(c) and Pt 21
Hearing	In public	FPR 2010, r 7.16
	Application for hearing in private:	FPR 2010, Pt 18 procedure
	Factors or decision as to publicity	FPR 2010, r 7.16(3)
	Witness statements and other requirements as to evidence	FPR 2010, Pts 22, 23, 25
Children	As for undefended cases, per Guide B2	
Decree	As for undefended cases, per Guide B2	
Costs	In the discretion of the court	CPR 1998, r 44.2
Appeals	See Guides E2, E4 and E5	FPR 2010, Pt 30

B5: Applications in the High Court and County Court under MCA 1973 for Orders for Maintenance Pending Suit (s 22), Financial Provision and Property Adjustment (ss 23–24), Pension Orders (ss 21B, 21C, 24B–24D and 24E–24G), Variation (s 31) and Consideration of Respondent's Financial Position (s 10(2)) and under CPA 2004, s 72 and Sch 5

Legal background

MCA 1973, s 10(2) enables the court to consider the financial position of a respondent to a petition based on 5 years' separation or 2 years' separation with consent before allowing the decree to be made absolute. MCA 1973, ss 22 (maintenance pending suit), 23 (periodical payments and lump sum for a party to the marriage and the children, including pension attachment under ss 23B and 23C and pension compensation attachment under s 25F), 24 (property adjustment), 21A and 24B–24D (pension sharing) and 21B, 21C and 24E–24G (pension compensation sharing) enable the court in a suit for divorce, judicial separation or nullity to make wide-ranging orders allocating the income and capital of both parties between themselves and in respect of any children. There are restrictions on the availability of pension sharing/attachment and pension compensation sharing/attachment (see further under MCA 1973, ss 24B, 24E, 25B, 25C and 25F). Further, neither pension sharing nor pension compensation sharing may be ordered on an application for judicial separation.

CPA 2004, s 72 and Sch 5 provides for financial relief for civil partners on dissolution, nullity or separation, which corresponds to the provision made for financial relief in connection with marriages under MCA 1973, Pt II.

The court's power to impose a clean break does not apply to judicial separation (MCA 1973, s 25A). The court has power to order the sale of property, when making a secured periodical payments order, a lump sum order or a property adjustment order (MCA 1973, s 24A), and will exercise its discretion in accordance with MCA 1973, ss 25 and 25A.

If a party remarries before making an application for a financial provision or property adjustment order (but not a pension sharing order), that party is barred by MCA 1973, s 28(3) from making the application for himself or herself (although an application for children is unaffected by the s 28(3) bar). The corresponding provision for civil partners is found in CPA 2004, Sch 5, para 48. Remarriage after an application is made but before it is heard is not a bar to jurisdiction, although a periodical payments or secured periodical payments order ends on the remarriage of the payee.

Orders that can be varied under MCA 1973, s 31 include those for maintenance pending suit, periodical payments, lump sum by instalments and deferred pension attachment lump sums. A pension sharing order may be varied where the order has not taken effect and the decree has not been made absolute. The court's powers under MCA 1973, s 31 are extensive and include the power to extend the term of a fixed term order in the absence of a s 28(1A) bar.

All of the applications to which this Guide relates are defined as "financial orders" with the exception of an order under MCA 1973, s 10(2), which is defined as a "financial remedy" (FPR 2010, r 2.3). A financial order is within the definition of a financial remedy (FPR 2010, r 2.3). The definition of "financial remedy" covers a wide range of other applications, including MCA 1973, ss 10(2), 27 and 35, and CA 1989, Sch 1. The procedure relating to all financial remedy applications, including financial orders, is governed by FPR 2010, Pt 9.

Procedure

Who may apply	*Under MCA 1973, s 10(2)* The respondent to a petition under MCA 1973, s 1(2)(d) or (e) in the court where the application is proceeding at any time after the petition is filed but before the decree is made absolute	
	Under MCA 1973, ss 22–24G Either spouse, provided (in the case of financial provision and property adjustment orders) the applicant is not remarried at the time of application	
Application	To appropriate court	FPR 2010, r 9.5(2)
	The application is on Form A, or Form B for an application under s 10(2), together with any documents stated to be required, or referred to in the application. Proceedings start when a court officer issues the application and are issued on that date	FPR 2010, rr 5.1–5.3; PD5A

	If claim omitted from petition or answer claiming relief, permission is needed to make claim. If application for permission is made before decree nisi, apply on notice to other party with supporting statement	FPR 2010, r 7.13, Pt 18 (Form D11)
Fee	On an application by consent: £45 On an application for a financial order: £240	FPFO 2008, fee 4.1 FPFO 2008, fee 4.4
Service	Within 4 days of the date on which the application was filed, a court officer will serve a copy of the application upon the respondent and give notice of the date of the first hearing to both parties	
	Alternatively, the applicant must serve the respondent within 4 days, beginning with the date on which the copy of the application was received from the court, and file a certificate of service on or before the first appointment	FPR 2010, r 9.12(2)
	Where an application is for a variation of settlement, an avoidance of disposition or an application relating to land, the relevant trustees, mortgagees etc must be served. A person so served may file a statement in answer within 14 days of service. A certificate of service must be filed on or before the first appointment	FPR 2010, r 9.13
Respondent	The other spouse	
Procedure in the High Court and county court	The court will fix a first appointment not less than 12 weeks and not more than 16 weeks after the filing of the application	FPR 2010, r 9.12
	By 35 days before the first appointment, the parties must simultaneously exchange a financial statement on Form E, or Form E1 for applications under s 10(2) and other financial remedies such as MCA 1973, ss 27 and 35, accompanied by a limited category of documents. No disclosure or inspection of the parties' documents may be given between the filing of the application and the first appointment, save as laid down in r 9.14(4)	FPR PD5A; FPR 2010, r 9.14(4)
	By 14 days before the first appointment, each party must file and serve a concise statement of issues, a chronology, a questionnaire and a notice stating whether that party will be in a position to use the hearing as a FDR appointment. In addition, the parties should (if possible) exchange an agreed case summary, a schedule of assets and a draft of directions sought by the parties	FPR PD9A, para 4; FPR 2010, r 9.14(5)

	At the first appointment, the court in pursuance of the overriding objective in Pt 1 will case manage the financial application in relation to defining the issues and saving costs. The court will approve the content of questionnaires and make direction in respect of replies, requests for documents and expert evidence. In applications for pension (compensation) sharing/attachment orders, the court may direct the filing and service of Form P (Pension Inquiry Form) or Form PPF (PPF Inquiry Form). Both parties must attend in person. The next hearing, normally the FDR (not magistrates' courts), will be timetabled. Alternatively, the court may list for further directions, the making of an interim order, a final hearing or treat the First Appointment as an FDR. Costs will be considered. After the first appointment, there is no further provision for the disclosure of documents, save with the permission of the court	FPR 2010, rr 9.15, 9.16
	At the FDR appointment, the parties are to meet for discussion and negotiation. 7 days before the FDR appointment, the applicant must file details of all offers and proposals and the responses to them. If the court cannot make a consent order, the court must give direction for a final hearing. Both parties must personally attend the FDR hearing, unless the court directs otherwise	FPR PD9A, para 6; FPR 2010, r 9.17
Interim orders	At any stage of the proceedings, a party may apply for orders for maintenance pending suit, maintenance pending outcome of proceedings, an order for interim periodical payments, a interim variation order or any other form of interim order. The application is governed by FPR 2010, Pt 18 procedure. Where an application is made before a financial statement is filed, written evidence in support must explain why the order is necessary and give up-to-date financial information	FPR 2010, r 9.7
	There is no power to make an interim lump sum order, property adjustment order, order for sale or pension (compensation) sharing order	MCA 1973, ss 23(1)(c), 24; *Wicks v Wicks* [1998] 1 FLR 470
Orders	Periodical payments and/or secured periodical payments for spouse and/or children (by standing order or by direct debit)	MCA 1973, s 23(1)(a), (b),(d),(e)
	Lump sum for spouse and/or children; for wording of roll-over of statutory charge, see –	MCA 1973, s 23(1)(c),(f); *PD of 19 August 1991*

Interest on lump sum before and after payment due	MCA 1973, s 23(6); JA 1838
Order for sale of property (where order also made for secured periodical payments, lump sum or property adjustment), with a direction that vacant possession be given	MCA 1973, s 24A; FPR 2010, r 9.24
If there is to be a complete, clean break (divorce or nullity only), a direction preventing an application to extend the term of the periodical payments order or to make any future application in relation to the marriage. A dismissal of Inheritance Act claims should also be made	I(PFD)A 1975, ss 2, 15; MCA 1973, ss 28(1A), 25A(3)
A pension sharing order (divorce or nullity only) is for a percentage of the Cash Equivalent	MCA 1973, s 21A; PD(PI)R 2000, reg 3; D(P)R 2000, reg 3; *H v H (Financial Relief: Pensions)* [2010] 2 FLR 173
A pension sharing order cannot take effect until the later of decree absolute and 7 days after the time for appealing has expired	D(P)R 2000, reg 9
A pension compensation sharing order (divorce or nullity only) is for a percentage of the Cash Equivalent of the PPF compensation	MCA 1973, s 21B(1); Pension Protection Fund (Pension Compensation Sharing and Attachment on Divorce etc) Regulations 2011, regs 3 and 4
A pension compensation sharing order cannot take effect until the later of decree absolute and 7 days after the time for appealing has expired	Divorce and Dissolution etc (Pension Protection Fund) Regulations 2011, reg 5
A pension attachment order is for a percentage of the benefit and, if the benefit is for a lump sum, the pension member can be required to commute, but he cannot be ordered to commute on any specific date	MCA 1973, s 25B(5),(7); *Field v Field* [2003] 1 FLR 376
A pension compensation attachment order is for a percentage of the payment that becomes due to the party with compensation rights and, where the party with compensation rights has a right to commute, he/she may be required to exercise that right to any extent	MCA 1973, s 25F(3),(5)
A pension (compensation) sharing or attachment order must contain appropriate annexes and should direct whether the court or one of the parties is to serve the order and accompanying documents on the pension arrangement/PPF	FPR 2010, rr 9.35, 9.36, 9.44 and 9.45

	Costs including payment on account and interest	CPR 1998, r 44.2; FPR 2010, r 28.3
Service and implementation of pension orders	Within 7 days of making the order or decree absolute, whichever is the later, the court or one of the parties (as directed) serves order for pension (compensation) sharing or attachment on pension provider together with copy of the decree absolute	FPR 2010, rr 9.36(5) and 9.45(2)
	Parties serve on the pension provider formal information	PD(PI)R 2000, reg 5; Pension Protection Fund (Pension Compensation Sharing and Attachment on Divorce etc) Regulations 2011, reg 9
	4-month period that the pension provider/PPF has to implement the order then starts. Within 3 weeks of receiving pension (compensation) sharing order pension provider/PPF gives notice of charges	PD(PI)R 2000, reg 7; Pension Protection Fund (Pension Compensation Sharing and Attachment on Divorce etc) Regulations 2011, reg 9
Pension provider's/PPF's obligations on pension (compensation) sharing	Percentage debited from member's share and transferred to applicant by way of pension credit either by internal or external transfer. Alternatively, percentage debited from member's rights to PPF compensation and transfer to applicant by way of pension credit by internal transfer. Pension arrangement/PPF then gives notice of completion of this process (notice of discharge)	PD(PI)R 2000, reg 8; Pension Protection Fund (Pension Compensation Sharing and Attachment on Divorce etc) Regulations 2011, reg 16
Appeals	See Guides E2, E4 and E5	

B6: Injunctions to Restrain Future Disposals and Avoidance of Disposition Orders under Matrimonial Causes Act 1973, s 37

Legal background

There are two separate jurisdictions enabling the court to grant injunctions to protect a claim for financial relief. The first is the statutory route specific to matrimonial financial proceedings under MCA 1973, s 37. This enables an applicant for a financial order in matrimonial proceedings to apply to the court under s 37(1) to restrain anticipated dealings that may defeat the applicant's financial claim. Under s 37(2)(b),(c), the court may set aside a reviewable disposition or order where there was a transaction for valuable consideration without notice to the applicant. This power may be exercised by the court at the final hearing of the financial applications under MCA 1973, under FPR 2010, Pt 9 procedure. Before this, injunction orders may be made to prevent a third party *disposing* of an asset acquired in such a way, under SCA 1981, s 37 and Civil Procedure Act 1997, s 7 (see below).

The second jurisdiction is the general framework that is available in all civil claims. It has two separate bases: (i) the court's inherent jurisdiction to freeze assets where the balance of convenience justifies such a course; (ii) under SCA 1981, s 37(1) as fortified by Civil Procedure Act 1997, s 7. Under these Acts the court can make injunctions, including freezing injunctions (formerly called *Mareva* injunctions) against assets in England and Wales or worldwide, and make search orders (formerly called *Anton Piller* orders) whereby a home or business premises is searched under the auspices of a supervising solicitor. Search orders may only be made in exceptional circumstances in family cases (*A v A* [1997] Fam Law 301) and must be made in the High Court. Other orders may be made in the county court.

An injunction may be applied for on notice. Where the applicant shows good grounds for no notice, the application may be made without notice. The application for an injunction without notice carries with it a strict obligation to give full disclosure of facts that may militate against an order being made (*Re W (Ex Parte Orders)* [2000] 2 FLR 927). The with notice hearing should be listed and the absent respondent is entitled to copies of the material presented to the court and a note of what was said at the hearing.

An application under MCA 1973, s 37 for the avoidance of a disposition is defined as a financial remedy under FPR 2010, r 2.3. By FPR 2010, r 9.6(1), the procedure under Pt 18 applies in an application for an order preventing a disposition.

Procedure

Who may apply	A spouse, where proceedings for financial relief under MCA 1973 have been brought	MCA 1973, s 37(1),(2)
Application	The application may be made to the High Court or county court, or to the Principle Registry of the Family Division if matrimonial proceedings started or are intended to be started there	
	Application may be made using FPR 2010, Pt 18 procedure in the course of existing matrimonial proceedings or in connection with concluded proceedings	FPR 2010, r 9.6(1)
	Application is by an application notice, stating what order is sought and why the applicant is seeking the order, with a draft order attached	FPR 2010, rr 18.4–18.7
Fee	On notice: £90 Without notice: £45	FPFO 2008, fee 4.3 FPFO 2008, fee 4.1
Service	A copy of the application notice must be served in accordance with the provisions of Pt 6 at least 7 days before the hearing, with any written evidence in support and the draft order	FPR 2010, r 18.8
Respondents	Spouses, parties to existing or concluded proceedings and any other person as the court may direct	FPR 2010, r 18.3
Procedure	The application may be made without notice to the respondent. The evidence in support of the application must state why notice has not been given. It is then usual to list a return date	FPR 2010, r 9.6(2)
	The order, application notice and evidence in support must normally be served on all parties. The order must state the respondent's right to apply to set aside or vary	FPR 2010, r 18.10

	Where a disposition has been made in favour of a third party, the third party may be joined to the proceedings and an order made under the court's inherent jurisdiction restraining any disposition by him of the property	
Orders	The injunction order must set out clearly what the respondent must and must not do. The court may make whatever order is necessary to protect the claim, including a freezing injunction and orders for the surrender of the respondent's passport and restraining him from leaving the jurisdiction	*Bayer AG v Winter* [1986] 1 WLR 497
	A respondent cannot be restrained from leaving the jurisdiction as a means of enforcement in its own right; the court may exercise the power to impound a respondent's passport	*B v B (Injunction: Restraint on Leaving Jurisdiction)* [1997] 2 FLR 148; *Young v Young* [2012] [2012] 2 FLR 470
	The applicant may be required to give an undertaking as to damages, if the order may affect third party rights	*Re W (Ex parte Orders)* [2000] 2 FLR 927
	On an application to set aside a disposition, the court may give consequential directions, including the making of payment or for the disposal of any property,	MCA 1973, s 37(3)
Appeals	See Guides E2, E4 and E5	

B7: Financial Relief after Overseas Proceedings under Matrimonial and Family Proceedings Act 1984, Pt III, Including Injunctions under s 24 to Restrain Anticipated Dealings

Legal background

MFPA 1984, ss 12–27 allow a party to a marriage that has been ended by overseas proceedings that are recognised in England and Wales to apply for financial relief in the same way as if the marriage had been ended here. FPR 2010 define the relief as "financial remedy". The court can make the same order available under MCA 1973/CPA 2004, subject to permission to proceed being granted. Jurisdiction to grant permission depends on domicile, habitual residence for 1 year or the existence of a matrimonial home within the jurisdiction: if this is the sole ground, the court can only make capital orders in respect of that property and cannot make income or other capital orders for the applicant or children.

At the permission stage, the application will be dealt with on a without notice basis following the Pt 18 procedure supplementing rr 8.23–8.28: see Lord Collins in *Agbaje v Agbaje* [2010] 1 FLR 1813 (at [33]) and Munby LJ in *Traversa v Freddi* [2011] 2 FLR 272 (at [49]–[58])).

Under MFPA 1984, s 24, the court may restrain anticipated dealings with property where the sole ground on which the applicant may claim jurisdiction is habitual residence for 1 year, and that year has not been completed. Once permission is granted, the applicant may apply to restrain anticipated dealings and set aside past dealings where the intention was to defeat the claim for financial relief.

When applying for permission to apply for a financial remedy after an overseas divorce, the procedure under FPR 2010, rr 8.23–8.28 applies. If permission is granted, the application proceeds as an application for a financial order under FPR 2010, Pt 9. When applying for an injunction under MFPA 1984, s 24, the procedures under FPR 2010, Pts 18 and 20 apply.

Procedure

Who may apply for leave	A party whose marriage has been ended by overseas proceedings (judicial or otherwise) recognised in England and Wales and who can establish domicile, 1 year's habitual residence or the existence of a matrimonial home within the jurisdiction. Remarriage bars an application	MFPA 1984, ss 12, 15
Application for permission (leave)	To the Principal Registry. If in relation to an application for a consent order, in a divorce county court	FPR 2010, r 8.24(1),(2)
	The application should be dealt with without notice in the first instance	FPR 2010, r 18.9; *Traversa v Freddi* [2011] 2 FLR 272
Issue of application	The application will be by Forms D50E (application for permission) and D50F (substantive application), accompanied by: (1) a statement (as outlined in Form D50F) by the applicant (2) a draft order (3) documents, including in relation to existing court proceedings and financial documents to the Principal Registry (r 8.24(12)) Where the application is by consent, Forms D50E and D50F should be filed (together with evidence of the respondent's consent) in the divorce county court (rr 8.24(2), 9.5(2), 9.26(6))	FPR 2010, r 8.24, read in conjunction with rr 18.4 and 18.7
Service	Issue and permission dealt with on notice; no rules are provided for service in that event	FPR 2010, rr 8.25 and 18.5(1); *Traversa v Freddi* [2011] 2 FLR 272 at [56]
Test for permission	"Substantial ground", not high, but higher than "serious issue to be tried". May be made if order made in another jurisdiction	MFPA 1984, s 13(1) and (2); *Agbaje v Agbaje* [2010] 1 FLR 1813 at [33]
Disposal of application	The application for leave should be listed ex parte for a hearing before a judge, time estimate: 30 mins	*Agbaje* (above) at [33]; *Traversa* (above) at [56]–[58] (for permission to appeal, see FPR PD30A, paras 4.10–4.13, 4.15 4.22–4.24)
Order made without notice		FPR 2010, r 8.25

Setting aside leave granted without notice	A person who was not served with a copy of the application notice before an order was made may apply within 7 days beginning with the date on which the order was served to have the order set aside or varied	
	An application to set aside leave, if not dismissed then and there, should be adjourned to be heard with the substantive application It will succeed only if compelling reason ("knock-out" blow: per Lord Collins; and see CPR 1998, r 52.9(2))	FPR 2010, r 18.11; *Agbaje* (above) at [33]; *Traversa* (above) at [58]
Order on leave application	Grant or refusal of leave, with or without conditions. A judge may direct that substantive application may be heard by a district judge at the Principal Registry	MFPA 1984, s 13; FPR 2010, rr 8.28, 9.5(3)
Costs	As for Court of Appeal permission, the respondent should not normally have costs, even on an attended permission hearing	FPR PD30A, paras 4.22, 4.23
Application	Once leave has been granted, application is to the Principal Registry. Application proceeds as a Pt 9 financial remedy application (save that a final hearing is before a judge unless released)	FPR 2010, rr 5.1–5.3, 9.5(2); PD5A
Fee	On an application by consent: £45 On an application to start proceedings where no other fee is specified: £230	FPFO 2008, fee 4.1; FPFO 2008, fee 1.1
Procedure	As in Guide B5 for a financial remedy	FPR 2010, Pt 9
Interim order	Where leave has been granted under MFPA 1984, s 13 and it appears that an applicant or child is in immediate need of financial assistance, the court may make an interim order for maintenance	MFPA 1984, s 14(1)
Application for interim order	Pt 18 procedure	FPR 2010, r 9.7
Injunctions	Applications to restrain the respondent from disposing of assets may be applied for before the conclusion of 1 year's habitual residence. Once leave is granted, the applicant can apply for an injunction to restrain anticipated dealings	MFPA 1984, s 24(1)(a),(b)
	The application for an injunction is governed by FPR 2010, Pt 18 and Pt 20 procedures	
	The without notice order, application notice and evidence in support must normally be served on all parties. The order must state the respondent's right to apply to set aside or vary	FPR 2010, r 20.3

Orders	Injunction restraining any disposition, transfer out of the jurisdiction or any other dealing with the property	MFPA 1984, s 24(a)
	Periodical payments, secured periodical payments and lump sum for the applicant and the children, but no power to award interest on lump sum	MFPA 1984, ss 17, 21
	Property adjustment order for the spouse and/or children, and an order for sale	MFPA 1984, ss 17, 21
	Transfer of a statutory or contractual tenancy	MFPA 1984, s 22
	Setting aside a disposition made with the intention of defeating a claim for financial relief	MFPA 1984, s 23
	If only fact establishing jurisdiction is existence of matrimonial home in England and Wales, the court can only make orders in relation to that asset and cannot make any income order for applicant or children	MFPA 1984, s 20
Appeals	See Guides E2, E4 and E5	

C1: Enforcement of an Order for Financial Provision in a Magistrates' Court

Legal background

The authority and procedure for the enforcement of magistrates' court maintenance orders are contained in MOA 1958, MC(EVOFP & MP)R 2011, Pt 4, MCA 1980 and MCR 1981.

The orders under the following provisions are enforceable as magistrates' court maintenance orders: MO(FE)A 1920; National Assistance Act 1948, s 43; MOA 1950, Pt II; Affiliation Proceedings Act 1957; MOA 1958; Matrimonial Proceedings (Magistrates' Courts) Act 1960; Guardianship of Minors Act 1971; MO(RE)A 1972; Guardianship Act 1973; Supplementary Benefits Act 1976, s 18; DPMCA 1978, Pt I; Child Care Act 1980; Social Security Act 1986, s 24; CA 1989, Sch 1; CPA 2004, Sch 6.

Procedure

Who may apply	The person entitled to payment including, where payment is made through the court, the designated officer	
Which court	The court which made the order (or the court where the order is registered) or, where it would be more convenient, the court acting for the area where the complainant or defendant resides. Venue to be decided by the person to whom the complaint is made, i e a justice of the peace or, if the complaint is not on oath, a justices' clerk	MCR 1981, r 59
Application	By way of complaint	MCA 1980, s 93; MCR 1981, r 4(1)

Fee	None	
Process	A summons may be issued or, if the complaint is in writing and on oath, a warrant with or without bail may be issued	MCR 1981, rr 59, 96, 98
Service	Service of a summons may be effected by personal service or by leaving it with some person at his last known or usual place of residence or (except in the case of HM Forces personnel) by post at his last known or usual place of residence	MCR 1981, r 99
Non-appearance	If the defendant fails to appear, the court may, if satisfied as to reasonable service, proceed in his absence or, if the complaint is substantiated on oath and the defendant has not already given evidence in the proceedings, issue a warrant	
	If the complainant fails to appear, the court may dismiss the complaint or, if evidence has been received on a previous occasion, proceed in the absence of the complainant	
	If neither party appears, the court may dismiss the complaint	MCA 1980, ss 55–57
Procedure at the hearing	The general procedure on the hearing of a complaint applies	MCA 1980, s 53
Orders available	Adjournment	MCA 1980, s 54
	Distress warrant (immediate or postponed)	MCA 1980, ss 76(1), 77; MCR 1981, r 54
	Warrant of commitment to prison (immediate or postponed), maximum period of committal being 6 weeks	MCA 1980, ss 76(1), (2), (3), 77, Sch 4
	For payment after imprisonment imposed, see –	MCA 1980, ss 79, 80(2); MCR 1981, rr 55, 64
	While a person is in custody under a warrant of commitment for arrears, further arrears under the order may not accrue, unless the court otherwise directs	MCA 1980, s 94
Alternative orders	The court may also order direct payments between the parties, payments through the designated officer, payments by standing order or payments under an attachment of earnings order	MCA 1980, ss 59, 95

	The court may remit all or part of the arrears, but it must, unless it considers it to be unnecessary or impracticable, give prior notice to the person in whose favour the order was made or, if a child, to the person with whom the child has its home	MCA 1980, s 95; MCR 1981, r 44
Appeals	See Guide E3	

C2: Enforcement of an Order other than for the Payment of Money in a Magistrates' Court

Legal background

An order for anything other than the payment of money or to abstain from doing anything may be enforced under MCA 1980, s 63(3), either by order on complaint or on the court's own motion. Where the court acts on its own motion, the relevant provisions of MCA 1980 have been amended by Contempt of Court Act 1981, s 17 and Sch 3.

Caution should be exercised when dealing with the person with whom a child has his residence for breach of a contact order. A variation of the contact order, if acceptable to both parents, will be preferable to punishment for breach of the order (*T v T* (1984) *The Times*, 19 July). See also *Re H (Contact: Enforcement)* [1996] 1 FLR 614. Separate provision is to be found in CA 1989, s 11J (inserted by CAA 2006) for the court, on application, to consider the making of an enforcement order (unpaid work) to secure compliance with a contact order.

Breach of a non-molestation order is a criminal offence (FLA 1996, s 42A). From 1 July 2007 a power of arrest can no longer be attached to such orders. The victim has the choice of contacting the police so that the respondent may be arrested with a view to prosecution or, alternatively, seeking to enforce the order as a civil contempt by means of the issue of a warrant of arrest or notice to show good reason why the respondent should not be committed to prison as a result of the exercise of the court's powers under s 63(3). Provisions for the enforcement of occupation orders remain unaffected. A power of arrest can still be attached to such orders and they are also capable of enforcement under s 63(3).

Section 63(3) is intended to be used only in the event of deliberate and wilful disobedience of an order of the court.

The proceedings attract the full protection of ECHR, Art 6 and, in particular, the minimum rights in Art 6(3).

FLA 1996, Pt IV is governed by FPR 2010, but enforcement of non-molestation or occupation orders in magistrates' courts do not automatically constitute family proceedings within the meaning of MCA 1980, s 65. However, MC(EVOFP & MP)R 2011, Pt 11 applies FPR 2010, with modifications, to the enforcement of Pt IV orders.

Procedure

Availability	The court may act of its own motion or by order on complaint	CCA 1981, s 17(1)
	Where the breach is of an occupation order made under FLA 1996, proceedings may be commenced by the exercise of a power of arrest attached to the relevant provisions of the order	FLA 1996, s 47(6)

	Where there is no power of arrest, either because the order is a non-molestation order made under FLA 1996 or there is no power of arrest attached to the relevant provisions of an occupation order, or the breach is of an undertaking, proceedings may be commenced by the issue of a warrant on an application substantiated on oath or by request for the issue of a notice warning the respondent that an application will be made for him to be committed to prison (notice to show cause)	FLA 1996, s 47(8),(9); FPR 2010, r 10.18(10),(11), as applied by MC(EVOFP & MP)R 2011, r 80
Which court	Any magistrates' court has jurisdiction to hear a complaint	MCA 1980, s 52
	Where enforcement proceedings have been commenced by the exercise of a power of arrest attached to an occupation order made under FLA 1996, the constable is required to bring the arrested person before any magistrates' court	FLA 1996, ss 47(7), 63
	Where enforcement proceedings are to be commenced by application for a warrant of arrest under FLA 1996, s 47(8), or by way of notice to show cause why the respondent should not be committed to prison, application may be made to any magistrates' court	FLA 1996, ss 47(8), 63
	There is power to transfer proceedings to another court once they have been commenced	ATPO 2008
Forms	Where enforcement proceedings have been commenced by way of complaint, no form is prescribed, but a summons should be issued which cites the disobedience of the order and requires the defendant to appear to show cause why an order requiring him to pay money or be committed to prison should not be made; clear details of the breach, including date, time and place must be given	*P v W (Access Order: Breach)* [1984] FLR 408
	Where proceedings are commenced by way of an application under FLA 1996, s 47(8), for a warrant of arrest the application must be made on Form FL407. Any warrant issued must be delivered by the court officer to the police	FPR PD5A; FPR 2010, r 10.18(5), as applied by MC(EVOFP & MP)R 2011, r 80

	Where proceedings are commenced by way of notice to show cause warning the respondent of an application for him to be committed to prison, the request for the issue of such notice is treated as a complaint. It must identify the provisions that it is alleged have been breached, the ways in which it is alleged that the order or undertaking has been breached and be supported by a signed statement	FPR 2010, r 10.18(11), as applied by MC(EVOFP & MP)R 2011, r 80
Fee	Upon the court treating the proceedings as family proceedings, no fee is payable	See MCFO 2008, fee 15
	Fee for warrant: £75 but no fee is payable if the court issues a warrant of its own initiative	MCFO 2008, fee 16.2
Service	If a summons has been issued, service may be effected on the respondent by leaving it with some person at his last known or usual place of residence or (except in the case of HM Forces personnel) by post at his usual or last known residence	MCR 1981, r 99
	Any notice to show cause issued in breach proceedings in respect of orders/undertakings under FLA 1996, Pt IV, must be served on the respondent personally together with a supporting statement unless service is dispensed with	FPR 2010, r 10.18(10),(14), as applied by MC(EVOFP & MP)R 2011, r 80
	The complainant is responsible for service	
	Proof of service by certificate is permissible	MCR 1981, r 67
Orders available	Where the order to be enforced was made in family proceedings, an order that the enforcement proceedings be treated as family proceedings	MCA 1980, s 65(2)
	An order to pay £50 for every day during which he is in default or a sum not exceeding £5000	
	Committal to prison for a period not exceeding 2 months or until he has remedied his default	MCA 1980, s 63(3)
	A hospital or guardianship order	FLA 1996, ss 50, 51
Imprisonment	Occupation/non-molestation orders under FLA 1996, Pt IV and exclusion orders under CA 1989, ss 38A, 44A are enforceable by way of suspended committal	FLA 1996, s 50
	Consecutive committal orders are not available	*Head v Head* (1983) 4 FLR 175

	A person in custody under warrant or order for breach of an order or undertaking under FLA 1996, Pt IV may apply in writing for discharge of the warrant or order. The court is responsible for serving notice on the other party not less than 1 day before the hearing on that application	FPR 2010, r 10.18(17), as applied by MC(EVOFP & MP)R 2011, r 80
	No procedure is prescribed for formally accepting that the default has been remedied and for ordering the defaulter's release from prison. A certificate of the justice of the peace who ordered committal, addressed to the governor of the prison, would appear to be appropriate	
Appeals	See Guide E3	

C3: Reciprocal Enforcement

Legal background

The provisions for enforcing in other countries judgments and orders (including maintenance orders) made in England and Wales, and vice versa, and for making in England and Wales claims for maintenance against persons resident in other countries, and vice versa, are complex. The Table and Procedural Guides that follow constitute an outline of the relevant procedures and their availability. However, reference should always be made to the text of the rules, statutes and, where appropriate, international conventions from which the remedies derive. Moreover, no attempt is made to provide a comprehensive account of the particular requirements of individual countries. Before expense is undertaken in attempting to pursue a remedy abroad, enquiry should be made of a local lawyer as to any requirements of a particular territory and, indeed, as to the likelihood of the remedy being effective, for example because of stringent exchange control regulation. For enforcement abroad of residence (custody) and contact (access) orders and recovery of children abducted abroad, see Guides D20–D22.

How to use the Table

Identify from the list below the activity to be undertaken. The letter (A to F) associated with it is the number of a vertical column in the Table. Locate the territory concerned on the left-hand side of the Table and note the number reference(s) given (1 to 16) in the chosen column beside it. Find the number reference(s) in the Guides (C3(1) to C3(16)) that follow the Table. Each Guide deals with the English (and Welsh) aspect of "outward" enforcement (i e an applicant in England pursuing a remedy abroad) and, so far as appropriate, "inward" enforcement (i e a foreign applicant pursuing the equivalent remedy in England).

The presence of more than one number reference indicates that alternative remedies may be available to the applicant. The absence of any indicates that no appropriate remedy has been discovered by the authors. However, the information has had to be gathered from a wide range of sources and international arrangements are constantly changing. It is always worth checking the up-to-date position: in the case of maintenance orders, assistance can usually be obtained from the REMO (Reciprocal Enforcement of Maintenance Orders) Unit, Official Solicitor & Public Trustee, 81 Chancery Lane, London WC2A 1DD, telephone 0845 345 5303 (UK only – calls charged at local rate) or +44 (0)20 7911 7016 (international), email remo@offsol.gsi.gov.uk. The website at *www.justice.gov.uk/guidance/protecting-the-vulnerable/official-solicitor/index.htm* offers useful guidance and a number of international links.

In the Table, lower case letters in parentheses refer to notes given at the foot of the Table.

The cases to which the Table refers

A   A maintenance order having been made in England or Wales, the payee seeks to enforce it abroad, and vice versa

B   Application in England and Wales for a provisional maintenance order against a respondent abroad, and vice versa

C   Applicant in England or Wales makes a maintenance claim for transmission abroad for determination there against a respondent there, and vice versa

D   Application to vary, discharge or revoke an order which has been registered or made under Case A, B or C

E   A money judgment having been given in England or Wales, the creditor seeks to enforce it abroad, and vice versa

F   A judgment or order including a non-monetary provision having been given or made in England or Wales, the person entitled to the benefit of that provision seeks to enforce it abroad, and vice versa

Table

CASE	A	B	C	D	E	F
Scotland and Northern Ireland	3			4	15	15
Akrotiri (Sovereign Base Area)					10	
Algeria			8	9		
Anguilla	5	6		7	10	
Antigua and Barbuda	1	2			10	
Antilles (n)						
Aruba (n)						
Australia	5(h)	6(h)	8	7(h),9	11	
Austria	12		8		13, 16(aa)	13
Bahamas	1	2			10	
Barbados	5	6	8	7,9	10	
Belgium	12		8		13, 16(aa)	13
Belize	1	2			10	
Bermuda	5	6		7	10	
Bosnia and Herzegovina			8	9		
Botswana	1	2			10	
Brazil			8	9		
British Indian Ocean Territory					10	
British Virgin Islands	1	2				
Brunei Darussalam	5(l)	6(l)		7(l)		
Bulgaria	12	6(h)	8		13, 16(aa)	
Burkina Faso			8	9		
Canada:						
Federal Court					11	
Alberta	5(ab)	6(abc)		7(ab)	11	
British Columbia	5	6		7	11	
Manitoba	5	6		7	11	
New Brunswick	5(abc)	6(abc)		7(abc)	11	

CASE	A	B	C	D	E	F
Newfoundland and Labrador	5	6		7	11	
Northwest Territories	5(abc)	6(abc)		7(abc)	11	
Nunavut	5(abc)	6(abc)		7(abc)	11	
Nova Scotia	5(ab)	6(ab)		7(ab)	11	
Ontario	5(b)	6(b)		7(b)	11	
Prince Edward Island	1	2			11	
Saskatchewan	5(b)	6(bc)		7(b)	11	
Yukon	1	2			11	
Cape Verde Islands			8	9		
Cayman Islands	1	2			10	
Central African Republic			8	9		
Chile			8	9		
Christmas Island	1	2			10	
Cocos (Keeling) Islands	1	2			10	
Comoro Archipelago			8	9		
Croatia			8	9		
Cyprus	12		8		10,13,16(aa)	
Czech Republic, The	12		8		13, 16(aa)	
Denmark	12		8		13	13
Dhekelia (Sovereign Base Area)					10	
Dominica	1	2			10	
Ecuador			8	9		
Estonia	12				13, 16(aa)	
Falkland Islands	5	6		7	10	
Fiji	5	6		7	10	
Finland	12		8		13, 16(aa)	13
France (f)	12		8		13, 16(aa)	13
French Guiana (f)			8	9		
French Polynesia			8	9		
Gambia	1	2			10	
Germany	12		8		13, 16(aa)	13
Ghana	5(bc)	6(bc)		7(bc)	10	
Gibraltar	5,12	6		7	13	13
Greece	12		8		13, 16(aa)	13
Grenada	1	2			10	
Guadeloupe (f)			8	9		
Guatemala			8	9		
Guernsey	1	2			11	
Guyana	1	2			10	
Haiti			8	9		
Holy See see Vatican						
Hong Kong	5	6		7	10	

CASE	A	B	C	D	E	F
Hungary	12		8		13, 16(aa)	
Iceland	12				13	13
India	5(abc)	6(abc)		7(abc)	10(z)	
Ireland, Republic of	12		8		13, 16(aa)	13
Isle of Man	5	6		7	11(d)	
Israel			8	9	11	
Italy	12		8		13, 16(aa)	13
Jamaica	1	2			10	
Jersey	5(bb)	6(bb)			11(e)	
Kenya	5(bc)	6(bc)		7(bc)	10	
Kiribati	1	2			10	
Latvia	12		8		13, 16(aa)	
Lesotho	1	2			10	
Lithuania	12				13, 16(aa)	
Luxembourg	12		8		13, 16(aa)	13
Macedonia (former Yugoslav republic)			8	9		
Malawi	1	2			10	
Malaysia	1	2			10	
Malta and Gozo (g)	12				10,13, 16(aa)	
Martinique (f)			8	9		
Mauritius	1	2			10	
Mexico			8	9		
Monaco			8	9		
Montserrat	1	2			10	
Morocco			8	9		
Nauru	5	6		7		
Netherlands (n)	12		8		13, 16(aa)	13
New Caledonia and Dependencies			8	9		
New Zealand	5	6	8	7,9	10	
Niger			8	9		
Nigeria	1	2			10	
Norfolk Island	5(a)	6(a)	8	7(a),9	10	
Norway	5(h),12	6(h)	8	7(h),9	13	13
Pakistan			8	9	11	
Papua New Guinea	5	6(c)		7	10	
Philippines			8	9		
Poland	12		8		13, 16(aa)	

Polynesia, French *see* French
    Polynesia

CASE	A	B	C	D	E	F
Portugal	12		8		13, 16(aa)	13
Réunion (f)			8	9		
Romania	12		8			
St Helena	5	6		7	10	
St Kitts and Nevis	1	2			10	
St Lucia	1	2			10	
St Pierre et Miquelon			8	9		
St Vincent and the Grenadines	1	2			10	
Serbia and Montenegro			8	9		
Seychelles	1	2			10	
Sierra Leone	1	2			10	
Singapore	5	6		7	10	
Slovakia	12		8		13, 16(aa)	
Slovenia	12		8		13, 16(aa)	
Solomon Islands	1	2			10	
South Africa	5(bc)	6(bc)		7(bc)		
Spain	12		8		13, 16(aa)	13
Sri Lanka	1	2	8	9	10	
Surinam			8	9	11	
Swaziland	1	2			10	
Sweden	12		8		13, 16(aa)	13
Switzerland	5(h),12	6(h)	8	7(h),9	13	13
Tanzania (except Zanzibar)	5(abc)	6(abc)		7(abc)	10	
Tonga					11	
Trinidad and Tobago	1	2			10	
Tunisia			8	9		
Turkey	5(h)	6(h)	8	7(h),9		
Turks and Caicos Islands	5(abc)	6(abc)		7(abc)	10	
Tuvalu	1	2			10	
Uganda	1	2			10	
USA	5		8	7,9		
Uruguay			8	9		
Vatican			8	9		
Virgin Islands (UK) see British Virgin Islands						
Zambia	1	2			10	
Zanzibar	1	2			10	
Zimbabwe	5(bc)	6(bc)		7(bc)	10	

Notes

(a) Other than orders obtained by or in favour of a public authority

(aa) An alternative procedure for the enforcement of uncontested claims is available, at the creditor's option, under Council Regulation (EU) No 805/2004

(b) Other than orders for the payment of birth and funeral expenses of child

(bb) MO(RE)A 1972, Pt I applies to Jersey since 19 June 2008 (SI 2008/1202)
(c)   Other than affiliation orders
(d)   County court judgments and orders must have first been transferred to the High Court
(e)   High Court judgments and orders only
(f)   For some purposes, France includes the overseas departments of Guadeloupe, Guiana, Martinique and Réunion
(g)   Malta is a "reciprocating country" for the purpose of MO(RE)A 1972, but the Maintenance Regulation (EC) No 4/2009 takes precedence
(h)   MO(RE)A 1972, Pt I applies to the Hague Convention countries as modified by SI 1993/593 and SI 1999/1318
(l)   Other than lump sum orders
(n)   For most purposes, the Netherlands include the Netherlands Antilles and Aruba
(z)   The territories named in SI 1958/425

C3(1): Maintenance Order having been Made in England or Wales, Payee Seeks to Enforce it Abroad, and Vice Versa

OUTWARD

Registration abroad of maintenance order made in England or Wales

Who may apply	The payee under a maintenance order made in England or Wales where the payer resides in a Commonwealth country which is not designated as a reciprocating country under MO(RE)A 1972, Pt I	MO(FE)A 1920, s 2
Which court	*High Court order* The Principal Registry or the district registry if the cause is proceeding there	FPR 2010, r 34.10(3),(4)
	County court order Although MO(FE)A 1920 refers to "a court in England" (Wales is included for the purposes of the Act), the rule under which application is made refers only to a maintenance order made in the High Court. If possible, it is prudent to seek to transfer to the High Court before the order is made; otherwise (ie if the maintenance order has already been made in the county court), the proceedings should be transferred to the High Court under MFPA 1984, s 39 as a preliminary step	
	Magistrates' court order The magistrates' court which made the order	MO(FE)A 1920, s 2
Documents required	*High Court (or transferred county court) order* A certified copy of the maintenance order	
	An affidavit stating the reason for believing that the payer is residing in the territory in question	

	So far as known, his address and occupation	
	Any other information required by the law of that territory for the purpose of enforcement of the order	
	It is therefore necessary to enquire in advance as to the particular requirements of the territory and to disclose the result in the affidavit	FPR 2010, r 34.10(6)
	In the case of Australia, Canada, New Zealand and South Africa, if the payer's address is unknown the court can cause enquiries to be made	FPR PD34B
	Magistrates' court order A certified copy of the order	
	Information sufficient to ascertain the whereabouts of the payer (including his last known address)	
	Information sufficient to identify the payer (including where possible a photograph)	
	A certificate of marriage	
	A certificate of the birth of the child (where maintenance is payable in respect of a child)	
	The name and address of the justices' chief executive	MO(FE)A 1920, ss 2, 8
Fee	High Court and county court: £40	FPFO 2008, fee 9.2
	Magistrates' court: none prescribed	
What happens next	If satisfied, the court sends the documents to the Lord Chancellor for transmission to the governor of that part of Her Majesty's dominions	MO(FE)A 1920, s 2
Variation or discharge	MO(FE)A 1920 contains no provisions affecting the court's power to vary or discharge a maintenance order, but enforcement will be subject to any equivalent powers which the corresponding legislation in the country of registration may accord to its courts	
Appeals	See relevant Guides in Appeals section	

INWARD

Registration in England of maintenance order made abroad

Who may apply	The Lord Chancellor, on receipt of a maintenance order made in a Commonwealth country which is not designated as a reciprocating country under MO(RE)A 1972, Pt I	MO(FE)A 1920, s 1

Which court	If the maintenance order was made by a court of superior jurisdiction, the Principal Registry of the Family Division; otherwise, the magistrates' court for the area where the defendant resides	FPR 2010, r 34.9; MO(FE)A 1920, s 1
Fee	High Court or magistrates' court: none	
What happens next	The senior district judge or justices' chief executive as the case may be enters the order in the register. In the magistrates' court, unless it is satisfied that it is undesirable to do so, the court will order payment to be made through an officer of the court or such other person as the court may specify	
	The order has full retrospective effect from the date specified in the order	
	Registration is an administrative act and the defendant cannot appeal against registration of the order	MO(FE)A 1920, s 1
Enforcement	*High Court* The order is enforceable as a High Court maintenance order and all proceedings may be taken on it as if it had been made by the High Court (including further registration in the magistrates' court)	MO(FE)A 1920, s 1(1)
	Magistrates' court The order is enforceable as a magistrates' court maintenance order	
	Monies collected are to be sent to the court which made the order or to such other person or authority as that court or the Lord Chancellor may from time to time direct	
	Enforcement proceedings are subject to the modifications of MCA 1980, ss 76 and 93, as specified in MOA 1950, s 18	MO(FE)A 1920, s 6

C3(2): Application in England and Wales for a Provisional Maintenance Order against a Respondent Abroad, and Vice Versa

OUTWARD

Confirmation abroad of provisional maintenance order made in England and Wales

Who may apply	An applicant for maintenance against a person who lives in one of the countries to which the Act is extended by Order in Council; there is no power under the Act to make a provisional affiliation order	MO(FE)A 1920, ss 3, 10

Which court	The magistrates' court acting for the area in which the applicant resides	*Collister v Collister* [1972] 1 WLR 54
What happens next	The court must hear an application for a maintenance order as if the respondent had received reasonable notice of the date of the hearing and the respondent had failed to appear; if satisfied of the justice of the application, the court must make a provisional maintenance order	
	The evidence of any witnesses must be taken down as a deposition	MO(FE)A 1920, s 3(1),(2)
Documents required	Where a provisional maintenance order is made, the court must send to the Lord Chancellor (in practice, the Reciprocal Enforcement of Maintenance Unit (REMO), Office of the Official Solicitor and Public Trustee, 81 Chancery Lane, London WC2A 1DD; tel: 0845 345 5303; fax: 020 7911 7030; email: remo@offsol.gsi.gov.uk), for transmission to the appropriate authority of the relevant country, the following documents:	
	the depositions	
	a certified copy of the order	
	a statement of possible grounds of opposition	
	information for facilitating the identification of the person and ascertaining his whereabouts	
	a photograph, where available	
	a marriage certificate	
	the birth certificate(s) of any child(ren) for whom maintenance has been ordered, where appropriate	
	There is provision for the taking of further evidence and for the rescission of the provisional order on the remittal of the case to the original court by the foreign court	MO(FE)A 1920, s 3(3),(4); FPR 2010, r 34.8
Fee	None prescribed	

INWARD

Confirmation in England and Wales of provisional maintenance order made abroad

Application	The application for confirmation is sent by the Lord Chancellor to the appropriate court on receipt of the relevant documents from the foreign court	MO(FE)A 1920, s 4
Which court	The documents are to be sent to the justices' chief executive acting for the area within which the respondent is alleged to be living	

Documents required	The following documents should be sent to the justices' chief executive:	
	the depositions	
	a certified copy of the order	
	a statement of possible grounds of opposition	
	information for facilitating the identification of the person and ascertaining his whereabouts	
	a photograph, where available	
	a marriage certificate	
	the birth certificate(s) of any child(ren) for whom maintenance has been ordered, where appropriate	
	a requisition for the notice to be served	MO(FE)A 1920, s 4(1)
Fee	None	
What happens next	A notice should be issued and served	FPR 2010, rr 6.23, 6.34
	At the hearing, it is open to the respondent only to oppose the confirmation of the order on any grounds on which he might have opposed the making of the original order	
	If the respondent does not appear, it is open to the court to confirm the order with or without modifications	
	If the respondent appears and the court is satisfied that it is necessary to obtain further evidence, it may adjourn the proceedings and/or remit the case to the court which made the original order	MO(FE)A 1920, s 4(2)–(5)
Enforcement	The order is enforceable as a magistrates' court maintenance order	
	Monies collected are to be sent to the court which made the order or to such other person or authority as that court or the Lord Chancellor may from time to time direct	
	Enforcement proceedings are subject to the modifications of MCA 1980, ss 76 and 93, as specified in MOA 1950, s 18	MO(FE)A 1920, s 6

C3(3): Maintenance Order having been Made in England or Wales, Payee Seeks to Enforce it in Scotland or Northern Ireland, and Vice Versa

OUTWARD

Registration in Scotland or Northern Ireland of maintenance order made in England or Wales

Who may apply	The person entitled to payments under the order or on that person's behalf	MOA 1950(SJ)R 1950, r 2
Which court	The appropriate court is the court which made the order or to which the proceedings have since been transferred	MOA 1950, s 17(1)
Application	*High Court or county court* The applicant files in the court or registry in which the cause or matter is proceeding a certified copy of the order, an affidavit and a copy of the affidavit. The affidavit must state:	
	the address and occupation of the payer	
	the date the order was served on him or the reason why service has not been effected	
	the reason why it is convenient that the order should be enforceable in Scotland or Northern Ireland	
	the amount of any arrears	
	that the order is not already registered	FPR 2010, r 32.3(1)
	Magistrates' court Applicant to make an oral or written application for the registration of the order	
	Unless the applicant appears in person, a statutory declaration must be lodged containing the following information:	
	the address of the person liable to make payments under the order	
	the reason why it is convenient that the order should be enforced in Scotland or Northern Ireland	
	unless a certificate of arrears is lodged, the amount of any arrears due under the order	
	a statement that the order is not already registered under Pt II of the Act	MOA 1950, s 17; MOA 1950(SJ)R 1950, r 2
Fee	High Court and county court: £40 Magistrates' court: none	FPFO 2008, fee 9.1

What happens next	*High Court or county court* If the district judge is satisfied, the court sends the certified copy order and the affidavit to (in the case of a High Court order) the Court of Session or the Court of Judicature of Northern Ireland or (in the case of a county court order) the Sheriff Court or the court of summary jurisdiction in whose area the payer resides, and the order is registered in that court	MOA 1950, s 17; FPR 2010, rr 32.3(2), (3)
	Magistrates' court If the justice is satisfied that the payer resides in Scotland or Northern Ireland and that it is convenient that the order should be enforced there, he requires the clerk to send to the sheriff-clerk (in Scotland) or the clerk of the court in Northern Ireland:	
	a certified copy of the order	
	the certificate of arrears (in Form 3 of MOA 1950(SJ)R 1950) or statutory declaration (if any)	
	if no statutory declaration has been lodged, written notice of the address of the person liable to make payments under the order	
	The court to which the documents are to be sent is the sheriff court or the court of summary jurisdiction having jurisdiction in the place where the person liable to make payments resides	
	The justices' chief executive of the original court must enter a memorandum of the proceedings in the register and, on receipt of notice of registration, must enter particulars in the register	MOA 1950, s 17; MOA 1950(SJ)R 1950, r 2(3),(4)
Transfer of registration	Once an order has been registered in the High Court in Northern Ireland or in a court of summary jurisdiction there, either party may apply to the court which made the order for its registration in a court of summary jurisdiction or the High Court in Northern Ireland instead	CJJA 1982, s 36
Enforcement	The order is enforceable as if it had been made in the court in which the order is registered. In Northern Ireland, enforcement is undertaken by the court. In Scotland, proceedings for enforcement must be taken in the payee's own name and legal representation is advisable	MOA 1950, ss 18, 20(3)
Appeals	See relevant Guides in Appeals section	

INWARD

Registration in England and Wales of maintenance order made in Scotland or Northern Ireland

Application	Application for registration is made by the original court sending prescribed documents to the court in England	MOA 1950, s 17(1)(b),(c); MOA 1950(SJ)R 1950, r 7
Which court	If the order was made by the Court of Session or the Court of Judicature of Northern Ireland, it is transmitted to the Principal Registry for registration; otherwise, the court of registration is the court of summary jurisdiction acting for the place in England in which the defendant appears to be	MOA 1950, s 17(3)(b); FPR 2010, r 32.7; MOA 1950(SJ)R 1950, r 7
Fee	High Court: none prescribed Magistrates' court: none prescribed	
What happens next	On receipt of the certified copy of the maintenance order, the proper officer of the Principal Registry or the justices' chief executive must cause the order to be registered in that court and gives written notice of the registration of the order to the original court	MOA 1950, s 17(4); FPR 2010, r 32.7; MOA 1950(SJ)R 1950, r 7
Enforcement	The order may be enforced in all respects as if it had been made by the court in which it is registered and as if that court had had jurisdiction to make it	
	A Scottish order which carries interest will continue to do so if registered in the High Court, but not if registered in a magistrates' court	
	The senior district judge of the Principal Registry may, on written application, order that an order registered there may be enforced in a district registry	
	The order is enforceable as a magistrates' court maintenance order subject to the amendment of MCA 1980, ss 76 and 93 (means of payments orders); see Guide C1	MOA 1950, s 18(1), (1A), (2), (2ZA), (2ZB)
Payment of money	On registration in the magistrates' court, the court orders payments to be made through the collecting officer of the court or through the collecting officer of some other court of summary jurisdiction	
	An alternative means of payment order may be made on enforcement of the order (see Guide C11).	

C3(4): Variation or Discharge of Registered Maintenance Orders and Cancellation of Registration (Scotland and Northern Ireland)

Variation or discharge	*Maintenance order made by or registered in the High Court* The court which made the order retains the exclusive jurisdiction to vary or discharge it. However, in the case of a Scottish order registered in the High Court, the payer on application may adduce in the High Court evidence for the purpose of variation or discharge proceedings in the original court. The application is made by lodging in the Principal Registry a request for an appointment before a district judge. Notice of the appointment is given by post to both parties	FPR 2010, r 32.8 and Pt 18; MOA 1950, s 21
	Any other case Application to vary the rate of payments must be made to the court in which the order is registered; however, application to vary it in any other respect or to discharge it must be made to the court that made it	
	Either party may, on application to the other court, adduce his evidence there for transmission to the court hearing the variation or discharge application	MOA 1950, s 22
	If the order is varied, notice of the variation is to be given to the prescribed officer of the court which made the order and any court in which the order is registered. The notice must consist of a certified copy of the order of variation	MOA 1950, s 23; MOA 1950(SJ)R 1950, r 10
Fee	High Court and county court: £90 Magistrates' court: none	FPFO 2008, fee 4.3
Cancellation	The payee may apply, using the Pt 18 procedure without notice to the payor, to the court where the order is registered to cancel the registration. The court of registration gives notice of the cancellation to the original court	FPR 2010, r 32.10 and Pt 18; MOA 1950, s 24; MOA 1950(SJ)R 1950, rr 11, 12, 12A
	The payer may apply to the original court if he has ceased to reside in the jurisdiction of the court where the order is registered; if satisfied, the court sends notice to the court of registration which cancels the registration	MOA 1950, s 24(2)
Fee	High Court and county court: £90 Magistrates' court: none	FPFO 2008, fee 4.3

C3(5): Maintenance Order having been Made in England or Wales, Payee Seeks to Enforce it Abroad, and Vice Versa

OUTWARD

Registration abroad of maintenance order made in England

Who may apply	The payee under the order	MO(RE)A 1972, s 2(1)
Which court	*High Court or county court* The court or registry in which the order was made *Magistrates' court* Application is to be made to the justices' chief executive of the magistrates' court which made the order	MO(RE)A 1972, s 2(1); FPR 2010, r 34.2(2)
Application	The following must be filed:	
	an affidavit stating the reasons for believing that the payer resides in the country in question, and the current arrears, the date to which they are calculated and the date the next payment falls due	
	a certified copy of the maintenance order	
	a statement giving all known information as to the payer's whereabouts	
	all known information to help identify the payer (including employer, occupation and date and place of issue of passport)	
	if possible, a photograph of the payer	FPR 2010, r 34.14; PD34A
	In the cases of Australia, Canada, New Zealand and South Africa, if the payer's address is unknown the court can cause enquiries to be made	FPR PD34B
	The court, if satisfied that the payer is residing in a reciprocating country, will send the relevant documents to the Lord Chancellor with a view to their being transmitted to the responsible authority in the reciprocating country	MO(RE)A 1972, s 2
	If the applicant relies on the alternative ground (added into MO(RE)A 1972 by CJJA 1982, Sch 11, Pt III, paras 8, 9(a)) that the payer has assets in the foreign country, the affidavit or application should also give reasons for believing that fact and set out the nature and location of the assets	
Fee	*High Court or county court:* £40 Magistrates' court: none	FPFO 2008, fee 9.2

PART I

Applicability to Hague Convention countries	MO(RE)A 1972, Pt I applies to Hague Convention countries as modified by SI 1993/593 and SI 1999/1318. In addition to the basic requirements, the affidavit must state whether the time for appealing against the order has expired and whether an appeal is pending. The applicant files in addition a statement as to whether the payer appeared in the proceedings and, if not, a document (or certified copy) establishing that notice of the proceedings including notice of the substance of the claim was served on him, a document which establishes that notice of the order was sent to him and a statement whether the payee had legal aid for those proceedings or the instant application with a certified copy of any such legal aid certificate	MO(RE)A 1972, s 2; FPR 2010, r 34.27; PD34A
	The procedure for registration on the basis of assets in the foreign country is not available in Hague Convention countries. In the case of the EU and EFTA countries, reference should be made to Guide C3(12)	
Applicability to USA	MO(RE)A 1972, Pt I, as modified by SI 2007/2005, applies to the USA. The application follows the procedure for Hague Convention countries, except that the information required from the applicant is to be in the form of a sworn statement, and that three certified copies of the maintenance order must be lodged	FPR 2010, r 34.28; PD34A, paras 4.10, 4.11
Restrictions	In the case of territories indicated (a), (b) or (c) in the Table, the facility does not exist to enforce respectively (a) orders obtained by or in favour of a public authority, (b) orders for the payment of birth or funeral expenses of a child, or (c) affiliation orders	
What happens next	If satisfied, the court sends the relevant documents to the Lord Chancellor with a view to their being transmitted to the responsible authority in the reciprocating country, provided the Lord Chancellor is satisfied that there is sufficient information. He has a discretion to transmit them or not	
	The relevant documents are:	
	a certified copy of the maintenance order (or, for the USA, three certified copies)	
	a certificate signed by the proper officer certifying that the order is enforceable in the UK	
	a certificate of arrears so signed	

	a statement giving such information as the officer possesses as to the whereabouts of the payer and the nature and location of his assets in that country	
	a statement giving such information as the officer possesses for facilitating the identification of the payer	
	where available, a photograph of the payer	
Appeals	See relevant Guides in Appeals section	

INWARD

Registration in England of maintenance order made abroad

Who may apply	Where the Lord Chancellor receives a certified copy of a maintenance order made by a court in a reciprocating country and it appears that the payer is residing or has assets in the UK, he must send it to the prescribed officer of the appropriate court	MO(RE)A 1972, s 6(2)
Which court	The appropriate court is the magistrates' court where the payer resides or where the payer has assets. If the justices' chief executive receives a certified order and, after taking such steps as he considers appropriate, is satisfied that the payer is not residing and has no assets within the jurisdiction of the court, he will return the order to the Lord Chancellor with a statement giving such information as he possesses as to the whereabouts of the payer and the nature and location of his assets	MO(RE)A 1972, s 6(4)
Fee	None prescribed	
What happens next	Unless the justices' chief executive returns the order to the Lord Chancellor under MO(RE)A 1972, s 6(4), he registers the order by means of a signed entry in his register and specifies the section of the Act under which the order is registered	MO(RE)A 1972, s 6(3); FPR 2010, r 34.3
Enforcement	The order is enforceable as a magistrates' court maintenance order. For the purposes of enforcement of the order, MCA 1980, ss 76 and 93 are modified in accordance with MO(RE)A 1972, ss 8(4A) and (4B) (see also Guide C1)	

	The justices' chief executive is under a duty, in any case where the order is in arrears to an amount equal to four weekly payments, to take enforcement proceedings in his own name. The justices' chief executive is also under a duty to take reasonable steps to notify the payee of the steps available for the enforcement of the order	MO(RE)A 1972, s 8; FPR 2010, r 34.24
Applicability to Hague Convention countries	The provisions outlined above apply equally to orders made in a Hague Convention country, except for the modifications made by REMO(HCC)O 1993 and REMO(HCC)(V)O 1999. The main differences are that:	
	registration may be refused if there was an error of jurisdiction in the court which made the order, if registration is manifestly contrary to public policy, if the order was obtained by fraud in connection with a matter of procedure, if there are similar proceedings pending between the same parties in the UK and those proceedings were the first to be instituted or if the order is incompatible with a similar order between the parties in the UK or in another country and the latter order fulfils the conditions necessary for registration	
	the justices' chief executive will refuse to register the order if the payer did not appear in the proceedings in which the order was made and there was a defect of service	
	an appeals procedure is prescribed and forms are prescribed for the purposes of giving notices under the modified Act and for the purposes of any appeal	MO(RE)A 1972, s 6, as modified by REMO(HCC)O 1993, REMO(HCC)(V)O 1999 and MC(RE-MO)(HCC)R 1980
Applicability to USA	The provisions outlined above apply equally to orders from the USA	MO(RE)A 1972, s 6, as modified by REMO(USA)O 2007, FPR 2010, r 34.28
Payment of money	The sum to be paid, if expressed in a foreign currency, is calculated on the basis of the rate of exchange prevailing at the date of registration of the order or the date of last variation. A written certificate of a bank officer in the UK is evidence of the rate of exchange prevailing at that time	

PART I

| | Payments under the order are to be made to the justices' chief executive of the registering court. The justices' chief executive is required to send the payments to the court which made the order or to such other person or authority as the Secretary of State may direct | |
| | If the court that made the order is in one of the countries listed in FPR PD34A any such sums must be sent to the Crown Agents for Overseas Governments and Administrations for transmission to the person to whom they are due | MO(RE)A 1972, s 16; FPR 2010, r 34.24; PD34A |

C3(6): Application in England and Wales for a Provisional Maintenance Order against a Respondent Abroad, and Vice Versa

OUTWARD

Confirmation abroad of provisional maintenance order made in England and Wales

Who may apply	Any person entitled to make an application for a maintenance order	
Which court	A magistrates' court has jurisdiction as if the respondent resided in England and Wales and as if notice of hearing had been duly served on him	MO(RE)A 1972, s 3(1)
Fee	None prescribed	
What happens next	The court hears the application and may make a provisional maintenance order For procedure, see –	FPR 2010, rr 2.5, 2.7, 22.2, 22.4, 22.5, 23.9, 27.2–27.4
	If a provisional maintenance order is made, the justices' chief executive sends the following documents to the Lord Chancellor (in practice, the Reciprocal Enforcement of Maintenance Unit (REMO), Office of the Official Solicitor and Public Trustee, 81 Chancery Lane, London WC2A 1DD; tel: 0845 345 5303; fax: 020 7911 7030; email: remo@offsol.gsi.gov.uk) for transmission to the responsible authority in the reciprocating country:	
	a certified copy of the maintenance order	
	a document authenticated in accordance with FPR 2010, r 34.15, setting out or summarising the evidence given in the proceedings	

a certificate signed by the justices' clerk of possible grounds of opposition

a statement giving such information as was available to the court as to the whereabouts of the payer

a statement giving such information as the justices' clerk possesses for facilitating the identification of the payer

where available, a photograph of the payer

Applicability to Hague Convention countries	A separate procedure exists for making maintenance orders against payers resident in a Hague Convention country to which the Maintenance Regulation (EC) No 4/2009 does not apply, namely Australia, Norway, Switzerland and Turkey	MO(RE)A 1972, s 3, as modified by REMO(HCC)O 1993 and REMO(HCC)(V)O 1999
	An applicant who is habitually resident in England and Wales may make application for a maintenance order	MO(RE)A 1972, s 3(1), as modified
	The application is made to the court which would have jurisdiction to make a maintenance order if the respondent were residing in England and Wales and a notice of hearing had been duly served on him	
	On hearing an application, the court may make a maintenance order	MO(RE)A 1972, s 3(1), (3), as modified
	For procedure, see –	FPR 2010, rr 2.5, 2.7, 22.2, 22.4, 22.5, 23.9, 27.2–27.4

On the making of an application the following documents must be sent to the Lord Chancellor (in practice, the Reciprocal Enforcement of Maintenance Unit (REMO), Office of the Official Solicitor and Public Trustee, 81 Chancery Lane, London WC2A 1DD; tel: 0845 345 5303; fax: 020 7911 7030; email: remo@offsol.gsi.gov.uk) for transmission to the appropriate authority in the Hague Convention country:

notice of the institution of the proceedings, including notice of the substance of the application

a statement signed by the justices' clerk giving such information as he possesses as to the whereabouts of the respondent

a statement giving such information as the officer possesses for facilitating the identification of the respondent

where available, a photograph of the respondent

The notice mentioned above must be served in accordance with the laws of the Hague Convention country or in such other manner as the Lord Chancellor may authorise at least 6 weeks before the hearing at which any order is made

MO(RE)A 1972, s 3(5), (6C), as modified

The court is obliged to take into account any representations made or evidence adduced by or on behalf of the respondent, and a copy of any representations or evidence must be served by the justices' clerk on the applicant before the hearing

MO(RE)A 1972, s 3(6), (6A), as modified

The justices' clerk must give the respondent notice in writing of the date fixed for the hearing

MO(RE)A 1972, s 3(6B), as modified

Where a maintenance order has been made, the justices' clerk must send the following documents to the Lord Chancellor for transmission to the appropriate authority in the Hague Convention country with a view to recognition and enforcement of the order:

a certified copy of the order

a certificate signed by the justices' clerk certifying that the order is enforceable and that it is no longer subject to the ordinary forms of review

a written statement signed by the justices' clerk as to whether the respondent appeared and, if not, the original or a certified copy of a document that establishes that the notice of the institution of the proceedings and substance of the application was duly served

a document that establishes that notice of the order was sent to the respondent

a written statement signed by the justices' clerk as to whether or not the applicant received legal aid in the proceedings

MO(RE)A 1972, s 3(6D), as modified

INWARD

Confirmation in England and Wales of maintenance order made abroad

Who may apply

Where the Lord Chancellor receives a certified copy of a provisional order from a reciprocating country and it appears that the payer under the order is residing in the UK, he must send the relevant documents to the justices' clerk of the appropriate court

MO(RE)A 1972, s 7(2)

Which court	The appropriate court is the magistrates' court having jurisdiction where the payer resides or where the payer has assets	MO(RE)A 1972, s 21
Documents required	The Lord Chancellor must send to the justices' clerk a certified copy of the order, a duly authenticated document setting out or summarising the evidence and a statement of possible grounds of opposition	MO(RE)A 1972, s 7(2)
Fee	None prescribed	
What happens next	A notice must be issued and served in accordance with FPR 2010, rr 6.23, 6.34. The court then proceeds as if an application for a maintenance order had been made against the payer	
	If the payer establishes any defence he might have raised in the proceedings in which the order was made, the court will refuse to confirm the order. In any other case, the court confirms the order either with or without such alteration as the court thinks reasonable	
	If the court confirms the order, the justices' clerk registers the order. At the same time as confirming the order, the court will make an order as to the method of payment (payment by standing order or otherwise to a clerk of a court or payment under an attachment of earnings order)	
	If the court refuses to confirm the order, the justices' clerk must return the documents to the Lord Chancellor. If the summons cannot be served, the justices' clerk returns the documents to the Lord Chancellor, together with a statement giving such information as he possesses as to the whereabouts of the payer	
Applicability to Hague Convention countries	A separate procedure exists for the registration in a UK court of an order made in a Hague Convention country to which the Maintenance Regulation (EC) No 4/2009 does not apply	MO(RE)A 1972, s 6, as modified by REMO(HCC)O 1993, REMO(HCC)(V)O 1999 and FPR 2010, r 34.27
	The following differences are of importance:	

registration may be refused if there was an error of jurisdiction in the court which made the order, if registration is manifestly contrary to public policy, if the order was obtained by fraud in connection with a matter of procedure, if there are similar proceedings pending between the same parties in the UK and those proceedings were the first to be instituted or if the order is incompatible with a similar order between the parties in the UK or in another country and the latter order fulfils the conditions necessary for registration

the justices' clerk will refuse to register the order if the payer did not appear in the proceedings in which the order was made and there was a defect in service

an appeals procedure is prescribed and forms are prescribed for the purposes of giving notices under the modified Act and for the purposes of any appeal

partial registration and enforcement, on request, is permissible

MO(RE)A 1972, s 6, as modified

Enforcement	The order is enforceable as a magistrates' court maintenance order. For the purposes of enforcement of the order, MCA 1980, ss 76 and 93 are modified in accordance with MO(RE)A 1972, s 8(4A),(4B)	
	The justices' clerk is under a duty, in any case where the order is in arrears to an amount equal to four weekly payments, to take enforcement proceedings in his own name. The justices' clerk is also under a duty to take reasonable steps to notify the payee of the steps available for the enforcement of the order	MO(RE)A 1972, s 8; FPR 2010, r 34.24
Payment of money	The sum to be paid, if expressed in a foreign currency, is calculated on the basis of the rate of exchange prevailing at the date of registration of the order or the date of last variation. A written certificate of a bank officer in the UK is evidence of the rate of exchange prevailing at that time	

Payments under the order are to be made to the justices' clerk of the registering court. The justices' clerk is required to send the payments to the court which made the order or to such other person or authority as the Lord Chancellor may direct	
If the court which made the order is in one of the countries listed in FPR PD34A, any such sums must be sent to the Crown Agents for Overseas Governments and Administrations for transmission to the person to whom they are due	MO(RE)A 1972, s 16; FPR 2010, r 34.24; FPR PD34A

C3(7): Application to Vary, Discharge or Revoke an Order Registered under Maintenance Orders (Reciprocal Enforcement) Act 1972, Pt I

Legal background

Where a maintenance order has been registered abroad under MO(RE)A 1972 for enforcement, the power to vary the order under the provision ordinarily applicable (e g MCA 1973, s 3(1)) is modified by MO(RE)A 1972, s 5.

Procedure

General position	In addition to its usual powers, the court may vary such a maintenance order by a provisional order. If the court proposes to increase the payments, the order varying *must* be a provisional order, unless both the payer and payee appear or the applicant appears and the process has been duly served on the other party	MO(RE)A 1972, s 5(3)
	For procedure, see –	FPR 2010, rr 2.5, 2.7, 22.2, 22.4, 22.5, 23.9, 27.2–27.4
	If the order is a provisional order, the court sends a certified copy of it and a note or a summary of the evidence taken, authenticated in accordance with the rules, to the foreign court for confirmation	MO(RE)A 1972, s 5(4); FPR 2010, rr 34.15, 34.22

	The court in the reciprocating country may, under powers given to it by its own laws, transmit to the original court in England and Wales which made the order a provisional order varying or revoking it, together with an authenticated note or summary of the evidence which it heard. The court must then proceed as if the application to vary or revoke had been made to it and may confirm or refuse to confirm the order. If it confirms a variation order, it may do so with or without alteration	MO(RE)A 1972, s 5(5), (6)
	The order, whether provisional or not, must state the date from which it takes effect; in the case of a provisional order, it does so in the form in which it is confirmed (i e subject to any alteration made by the confirming court)	MO(RE)A 1972, s 5(7)
	There is no right of appeal against the making of a provisional order	MO(RE)A 1972, s 12(1)
Fee	None prescribed	
Applicability to Hague Convention countries	Article 12 of the Hague Convention states: "There shall be no review by the authority of the State addressed of the merits of the decision" and the Permanent Bureau in the Hague has confirmed that the intention of Art 12 is to prevent receiving countries from varying orders except for the method of payment	REMO(HCC)(V)O 1999
	Any request by a payer living in the UK for variation of an order made by a Hague Convention country and registered in the UK should be sent to the Reciprocal Enforcement of Maintenance Orders (REMO) Section at the office of the Official Solicitor & Public Trustee, 81 Chancery Lane, London WC2A 1DD; tel: 0845 345 5303; fax: 020 7911 7030; email: remo@offsol.gsi.gov.uk for onward transmission to the overseas authority	

Applicability to USA

The provisional order procedure does not apply. When a maintenance order has been registered under MO(RE)A 1972 for enforcement and the payee applies for variation or revocation, the justices' clerk sends to the Lord Chancellor notice of the institution of proceedings, including notice of the substance of the application, with a view to its being transmitted to the appropriate authority in the specified State for service on the payer and also sends to the payer notice in writing of the date fixed for the hearing by post to his last known or usual place of abode

MO(RE)A 1972, s 5(4), as modified by REMO(USA)O 2007

The order may not be varied or revoked unless the notice is served by the appropriate authority, and any representations and evidence adduced by the payer must be served on the payee before the hearing and taken into account by the court

MO(RE)A 1972, s 5(5), as modified by REMO(USA)O 2007

Where the application is made by the payer, the justices' clerk is required to arrange for the service of notice of institution of the proceedings, including notice of the substance of the application, on the payee

MO(RE)A 1972, s 5(6), as modified by REMO(USA)O 2007

Where the order is varied or revoked, the justices' clerk must send to the Lord Chancellor three certified copies of the order and a written statement signed by the justices' clerk as to whether both parties appeared in the proceedings and, if only the applicant appeared, the original or certified copy of the document establishing proof of service of the notice of the proceedings upon the other party. The Lord Chancellor will send these documents to the appropriate authority in the specified State for registration and enforcement

MO(RE)A 1972, s 5(7), as modified by REMO(USA)O 2007

The variation or revocation takes effect as from the date of the order but, in the case of revocation, arrears continue to be enforceable

MO(RE)A 1972, s 5(8), (9), as modified by REMO(USA)O 2007

PART I

C3(8): Applicant in England or Wales Makes Maintenance Claim for Transmission Abroad for Determination There against Respondent, and Vice Versa

OUTWARD

Application by person in England or Wales for recovery etc of maintenance in a convention country

General position	A person in the UK who claims to be entitled to recover, in a convention country, maintenance from another person is required to make an application to the Lord Chancellor	
	The application must be made through the justices' clerk acting for the area in which the applicant resides and the clerk is under a duty to assist the applicant complete the relevant forms	
	The Lord Chancellor is under a duty to forward the application to the appropriate authority in the convention country unless he is satisfied that the application is not made in good faith or that it does not comply with the requirements of the law applied in that country. If the Lord Chancellor requires further information, he can request the justices' clerk to obtain the information from the court, and the court is under a duty to furnish the information	MO(RE)A 1972, s 26
Fee	None prescribed	
Applicability to USA	For the states specified in RM(USA)O 1993, there is an additional requirement for a certificate signed by a justice to the effect that the application sets out facts from which it may be determined that the respondent owes a duty to maintain the applicant and any other person named in the application, and that a court in the specified state may "obtain jurisdiction of the respondent" or his property must be registered in the court by the justices' clerk	MO(RE)A 1972, s 26(3A)

INWARD

Pursuit in England of a claim for maintenance made in a convention country

General position	Where the Lord Chancellor receives an application from the appropriate authority in a convention country for the recovery of maintenance, he sends the claim to the clerk of the magistrates' court for the area in which the respondent is residing. The claim is to be treated as an application for an appropriate order made at a time when the application was received by the Lord Chancellor	MO(RE)A 1972, ss 27A, 27B
	If a notice of hearing cannot be served, the justices' clerk of the court is required to return the application and documents to the Lord Chancellor, together with such information he may have as to the whereabouts of the respondent or, if the justices' clerk is satisfied that the respondent is residing in the area of another magistrates' court, he may send the documents to the justices' clerk of that court and notify the Lord Chancellor accordingly	MO(RE)A 1972, s 27B(3), (4)
	For procedure, see –	MC(RAM)R 1975, Sch 2
	If the court makes an order, the clerk must register the order and, at the time of making the order, the court orders payments to be made to a justices' clerk by standing order or otherwise, or by an attachment of earnings order	
	The justices' clerk must also notify the Lord Chancellor that the order has been registered	MO(RE)A 1972, s 27C; MC(RAM)R 1975, r 6
	Where the application is for an order under DPMCA 1978, s 2, the provisions of the 1978 Act are modified by MO(RE)A 1972, ss 28 and 28A. The order is, unless for the time being registered in the High Court, enforceable as a magistrates' court maintenance order as defined in MCA 1980, s 150(1). The power of the court to make orders for the method of payment under MCA 1980, ss 76 and 93 is modified	MO(RE)A 1972, s 33; see also MC(RAM)R 1975, r 7
	There is power to transfer the order to another magistrates' court if the payer moves to the jurisdiction of that court	MO(RE)A 1972, s 32
	Payments received by the justices' clerk under the order must be sent to the Lord Chancellor by post	MC(RAM)R 1975, r 7
Fee	None prescribed	

C3(9): Variation and Revocation of Orders Registered under Maintenance Orders (Reciprocal Enforcement) Act 1972, Pt II

General position	Jurisdiction to vary or revoke an order registered under MO(RE)A 1972, Pt II may only be exercised by the registering court and, where the registering court revokes an order, it must cancel the registration	MO(RE)A 1972, s 34(1), (2)
	Application is made through the appropriate authority in the convention country and transmitted to the Lord Chancellor (in practice, the Reciprocal Enforcement of Maintenance Unit (REMO), Office of the Official Solicitor and Public Trustee, 81 Chancery Lane, London WC2A 1DD; tel: 0845 345 5303; fax: 020 7911 7030; email: remo@offsol.gsi.gov.uk), who then sends it together with any accompanying documents (which may include evidence taken in the convention country and which is admissible under MO(RE)A 1972, s 36) to the justices' clerk of the registering court	MO(RE)A 1972, s 34(3)
	For procedure, see –	MC(RAM)R 1975, Sch 2
	On the variation of a registered order, if the court is satisfied that payment has not been made in accordance with the order, the court may also order that payments are made to the justices' clerk of that court or of any other magistrates' court, either directly or by standing order, or the court may order payment by attachment of earnings	MO(RE)A 1972, s 34A
	The application is treated as if an application for variation had been made, and the court must proceed as if the applicant were before the court	MO(RE)A 1972, s 35(3)
	Where the respondent does not appear, if the court is satisfied that the respondent is residing outside England and Wales and that notice of the proceedings has been given in the prescribed form, the court may nevertheless proceed	MO(RE)A 1972, s 35(3); MC(RAM)R 1975, r 8, Sch 2
	Where the court makes or refuses to make an order, any person has the same right of appeal as they would have if the registered order had been made by that court	MO(RE)A 1972, s 34(4)
Fee	None prescribed	

C3(10): Money Judgment or Order having been Made in England or Wales, Payee Seeks to Enforce it in Certain Commonwealth Countries, and Vice Versa

PART I

Legal background

A judgment of a foreign court cannot be directly enforced in England and Wales, but a judgment other than a maintenance order (*Harrop v Harrop* [1920] 3 KB 386) can be made the basis of an action in the English courts. Four pieces of legislation – AJA 1920, FJ(RE)A 1933 and CJJA 1982 and Council Regulation (EC) No 44/2001 on Jurisdiction and the Recognition and Enforcement of Judgments in Civil and Commercial Matters (the Judgments Regulation, herein JR) – allow foreign judgments to be registered in the High Court for enforcement, without the claimant needing to bring a fresh action. A fifth, Council Regulation (EC) No 805/2004, creating the European enforcement order, allows certain judgments from EU countries to be enforced in the High Court or the county court. Unless the case falls within the scope of one of them, there is no power to register a foreign judgment for enforcement and a fresh action is necessary.

OUTWARD

Enforcement in certain Commonwealth countries of a High Court judgment or order for payment of a sum of money

What countries	Countries to which the 1920 Act was applied by Order in Council before 1933	See notes to CPR 1998, r 74.1 for the full list
Who may apply	The judgment creditor under a judgment or order given or made by the High Court	AJA 1920, ss 10(1), 12(1)
To whom application made	A district judge of the Family Division presumably (PD74 is silent on the point) in the PRFD	CPR PD74A, para 4.2
Documents required	Application without notice under CPR 1998, Pt 23 supported by written evidence exhibiting copies of:	CPR 1998, rr 74.12, 74.13(1)
	the claim form;	
	evidence of service;	
	the statements of case;	
	where relevant, notice that the applicant was an assisted person or LSC funded client.	
	The written evidence must:	CPR 1998, r 74.13(2)
	(a) identify the grounds on which the judgment was obtained;	
	(b) state whether the defendant objected to the jurisdiction, and if so, on what grounds;	
	(c) show that the judgment has been served and is not subject to a stay of execution;	
	(d) give details of any possible appeal;	
	(e) state the amount in respect of which the judgment remains unsatisfied;	

	(f) give particulars of interest recoverable	
Fee	£60	FPFO 2008, fee 14.2
What happens next	The court issues a certified (office) copy of the judgment accompanied by a certificate signed by a district judge in Form 110	CPR PD74A, paras 7.1–7.3
	The creditor must transmit this to the country in question and attempt enforcement in accordance with that country's procedures	
Limitations	The 1920 Act only applies to High Court judgments. Not all countries will recognise a county court judgment which has been transferred to the High Court for enforcement, and advice should be sought in the country in which enforcement is desired	

INWARD

Enforcement in England and Wales of a money judgment or order of the courts of certain Commonwealth countries

What countries	As above	
Who may apply	A judgment creditor under a judgment or order obtained in a superior court in a country to which AJA 1920 applies	AJA 1920, ss 9(1), 12(1)
Which court	The Queen's Bench Division of the High Court (even in family-related cases). Application is made in the Action Department at the Royal Courts of Justice, not in a district registry	CPR PD74A, para 4.1(1)
Documents required	Application without notice under CPR 1998, Pt 23 to a master supported by written evidence exhibiting:	CPR 1998, r 74.3; PD74A, para 4.1
	(a) the judgment or a certified copy of it;	CPR 1998, r 74.4(1)
	(b) where the judgment is not in English, a certified translation	
	The written evidence must state:	
	the name and address of the judgment creditor and judgment debtor;	CPR 1998, r 74.4(2)
	the grounds on which the creditor is entitled to enforce the judgment;	
	the amount unsatisfied;	
	particulars of interest;	
	and confirm the creditor's entitlement to enforce the judgment or order, the amount outstanding under it and that it does not contravene AJA 1920, s 9(2) (see Limitations below) and verify that Protection of Trading Interests Act 1980, s 5 does not apply	

PART I

Fee	£230	FPFO 2008, fee 1.1
What happens next	A registration order must be drawn up by the judgment creditor and served on the debtor	CPR 1998, r 74.6
	It must state:	
	full particulars of the judgment registered;	
	the name of the judgment creditor and his address for service within the jurisdiction;	
	the right of the judgment debtor to apply to have the registration set aside;	
	the period within which such an application may be made;	
	that no enforcement measures (other than for preservation of property) will be taken before the end of that period	CPR 1998, r 74.9
Setting aside	The debtor may apply to set aside the registration within the period stated in the registration order, which may be extended	CPR 1998, r 74.7(1),(2)
	Application is made under CPR 1998, Pt 23 to a master	
	The court may order an issue to be tried. The registration may be set aside if the court finds that the judgment or order contravenes AJA 1920, s 9(2) (see Limitations below), that it is not just or convenient that it be enforced in England and Wales or that there is some other sufficient reason to set aside the registration	
	Fee: £90	FPFO 2008, fee 4.3
Limitations	The application must generally be made within 12 months of the date of the judgment or order, although the court has power to allow a later application	AJA 1920, s 9(1)
	A judgment or order cannot be registered for enforcement in England and Wales under this provision if:	
	the original court acted without jurisdiction	
	the debtor did not live or carry on business within that court's jurisdiction and did not appear or submit to the court's jurisdiction	
	the debtor (being the defendant) was not duly served with the court's process and did not appear	
	the judgment or order was obtained by fraud	
	the debtor satisfies the court that an appeal is pending or that he is entitled to, and intends to, appeal	

	the action would not have been entertained by the High Court for some public policy or similar reason	AJA 1920, s 9(2)
Security for costs	Note that the procedures under the 1920 and 1933 Acts effectively require the claimant to give security for costs	

C3(11): Enforcement in Certain Foreign Countries of an English or Welsh Judgment or Order for Payment of a Sum of Money, and Vice Versa

Legal background

CPR 1998 provides (see CPR PD74A, paras 4.2(2) and 4.3(2)) for the reciprocal enforcement of money judgments or orders arising in family proceedings, other than maintenance orders, as to which see the appropriate Guides elsewhere in this work.

OUTWARD

Enforcement in certain foreign countries of a judgment or order for payment of a sum of money

Which countries	Australia including the Australian Capital Territory, the Federal Court of Canada and courts of all provinces except Quebec, Island of Guernsey, Isle of Man, Bailiwick of Jersey, certain territories of the Republic of India named in the Schedule to the Reciprocal Enforcement of Judgments (India) Order 1958, Israel, Pakistan, Surinam and Tonga	
Who may apply	The judgment creditor under a judgment or order for payment or a sum of money given or made by a court in England or Wales in civil proceedings or, if for compensation or damages to an injured party, in criminal proceedings, but not taxes etc or a fine or other penalty	FJ(RE)A 1933, ss 10(2), 11(1)
Which court	A district judge of the Family Division in the case of a judgment in that Division; a district judge in the case of a county court judgment	CPR PD74A, para 4.2
Documents required	Application without notice under CPR 1998, Pt 23 supported by written evidence exhibiting copies of: the claim form; evidence of service; the statements of case;	CPR 1998, rr 74.12, 74.13(1)

where relevant, notice that the applicant was an assisted person or LSC funded client

The written evidence must:

(a) identify the grounds on which the judgment was obtained;

(b) state whether the defendant objected to the jurisdiction, and if so, on what grounds;

(c) show that the judgment has been served and is not subject to a stay of execution;

(d) give details of any possible appeal;

(e) state the amount in respect of which the judgment remains unsatisfied;

(f) give particulars of interest recoverable

As to county court judgments, note under Limitations below. There are no provisions applying the 1933 Act to the orders of magistrates' courts

CPR 1998, r 74.13(2)

| Fee | High Court: £60 | FPFO 2008, fee 14.2 |
| | County court: £45 | FPFO 2008, fee 4.1 |

What happens next

In the High Court or the county court, the creditor receives from the court a sealed copy of the judgment or order appropriately certified by the district judge and a sealed certificate signed by him setting out, in essence, the information required to be given in the affidavit and any other particulars which it may be necessary to give to the foreign court

The creditor must then apply to the relevant court or authority in the foreign state in accordance with its law and procedures for enforcement of the judgment there

Limitations

If the judgment or order was given or made by a court other than the High Court, its enforceability in a particular country depends on the terms of the individual arrangements made with that country. Reference to the Statutory Instrument enabling that country's judgments to be enforced here will give an indication, as the reciprocal arrangements will be equivalent. Further enquiry may be made of the Ministry of Justice, 102 Petty France, London SW1H 9AJ (Tel 020 3334 3555)

The foreign country's relevant provisions may impose conditions similar to those which the Act applies in the case of foreign judgments sought to be enforced in the UK (see INWARD section below)

INWARD

Enforcement in England and Wales of a judgment or order for payment of a sum of money given in certain foreign countries

Who may apply	The judgment creditor under a judgment or order	FJ(RE)A 1933, s 2(1)
Which court	The Queen's Bench Division of the High Court (even in family-related cases). Application is made in the Action Department at the Royal Courts of Justice, not in a district registry	CPR PD74A, para 4.1(1)
Documents required	Application without notice under CPR 1998, Pt 23 to a master supported by written evidence exhibiting:	CPR 1998, r 74.4(1)
	(a) the judgment or a certified copy of it;	
	(b) where the judgment is not in English, a certified translation	
	The written evidence must state:	CPR 1998, r 74.4(2)
	the name and address of the judgment creditor and judgment debtor;	
	the grounds on which the creditor is entitled to enforce the judgment;	
	the amount unsatisfied;	
	particulars of interest	
	It must also:	CPR 1998, r 74.4(4)
	state that the judgment is a money judgment, that it can be enforced by execution in the original country and that any registration is not liable to be set aside under FJ(RE)A 1933, s 4 (see Setting aside below)	
	specify the interest (if any) then due on it under the law of the original country and	
	verify that the Protection of Trading Interests Act 1980, s 5 does not apply	
	If there are several provisions in the judgment, it must be made clear which ones are to be registered	
	The Order in Council applying FJ(RE)A 1933 to the country may also require further evidence to be given as to the enforceability of the judgment or the accrual of interest	
Fee	£230	FPFO 2008, fee 1.1
Note	Security may be required for the costs of registration and of any application by the debtor to set the registration aside	
What happens next	A registration order must be drawn up by the judgment creditor and served on the debtor	CPR 1998, r 74.6
	It must state:	

full particulars of the judgment registered;

the name of the judgment creditor and his address for service within the jurisdiction;

the right of the judgment debtor to apply to have the registration set aside;

the period within which such an application may be made;

that no enforcement measures (other than for preservation of property) will be taken before the end of that period

CPR 1998, r 74.9

Setting aside

The debtor may apply to set aside the registration within the period stated in the registration order, which may be extended

Application is made under CPR 1998, Pt 23 to a master

The court may order an issue to be tried. The registration must be set aside if the court finds that:

the Act does not apply to the judgment, or was contravened in effecting the registration

the original court acted without jurisdiction

the debtor (being the defendant) had insufficient notice to enable him to defend and did not appear

the judgment was obtained by fraud

enforcement would be contrary to public policy or

the benefit of the judgment is not vested in the applicant

The registration *may* be set aside if, before the judgment, another court of competent jurisdiction had already decided the issue; it may also be set aside if there is an appeal pending against the judgment or if the debtor is entitled to and intends to appeal

FJ(RE)A 1933, s 4

Fee: £90

FPFO 2008, fee 4.3

Limitations

FJ(RE)A 1933 applies only to the judgments and orders of the courts identified in the Statutory Instruments applying it to the particular country. (Statutory Instruments made before the Act was amended, with effect from 1 January 1987, by CJJA 1982 applied the Act only to superior courts.) A judgment or order cannot be registered if it could not be enforced by execution in the original country, if it is fully paid (though if partly paid it can be registered as to the balance), or if it was given or made more than 6 years before the application for registration

FJ(RE)A 1933, ss 1(1)(c), 2(1)

	Enforcement more than 6 years after the judgment is registered will not be allowed except in a special case, notwithstanding that a longer limitation period applies in the country where the judgment was given	*Duer v Frazer* [2001] 1 WLR 919, QBD
Appeals	See relevant Guides in Appeals section	

C3(12): Enforcement in a European Union or EFTA Country of a Maintenance Order Made in England and Wales, and Vice Versa

OUTWARD

Enforcement in a European Union or EFTA country of a maintenance order

General position	In the cases of the High Court and county court, the procedure is substantially identical to that in respect of other judgments and orders (see Guide C3(13) but see also the Maintenance Regulation (EC) No 4/2009, Art 28)	FPR 2010, r 34.40
	If the order has been registered in the magistrates' court, a certificate as to the payments made and arrears accrued under it while it has been registered may be obtained from the designated officer of the court. Accordingly, the following description deals only with the position in the magistrates' court	FPR 2010, r 34.39
Who may apply	Any interested party	CJJA 1982, s 12
Which court	The court which made the order	FPR 2010, r 34.39
Application for a certified copy order	Application for a certified copy of the order is made in writing to the designated officer of the magistrates' court. The application must give:	FPR 2010, r 2.3; Courts Act 2007, s 37(1)
	the names of the parties to the proceedings in which the order was made	FPR 2010, rr 34.2(2), 34.39(3)
	the date or approximate date and the nature of those proceedings	
	The designated officer sends to the applicant a copy of the order with a certificate certifying that it is a true copy and giving particulars of the proceedings in which it was made and, where the Maintenance Regulation (Council Regulation (EC) No 4/2009) applies, a completed extract from the decision in the form of Annex II to that Regulation	FPR 2010, r 34.39(3)

Application for a certificate of payments made or arrears accrued under a registered order	Application for a certified copy of the order is made in writing to the designated officer for the registering court	FPR 2010, r 34.39(5),(6)
	The officer must send the applicant a certificate giving the information requested	FPR 2010, r 34.39(7)
What happens next	The applicant must then deliver these documents to the Lord Chancellor (in practice, the Reciprocal Enforcement of Maintenance Unit (REMO), Office of the Official Solicitor and Public Trustee, 81 Chancery Lane, London WC2A 1DD; tel: 0845 345 5303; fax: 020 7911 7030; email: remo@offsol.gsi.gov.uk) for transmission to the Central Authority in the State in question	FPR 2010, r 34.39
Alternative procedures	The procedures afforded by MO(RE)A 1972 (see Guides C3(5) and C3(8)) continue to be available in respect of the countries where they are indicated in the Table	

INWARD

Enforcement in England and Wales of a maintenance order made in a European Union or EFTA country

Who may apply	Any interested party	CJJA 1982, Sch 1, Art 31
Which court	The appropriate court is the magistrates' court	CJJ(M)R 2011, para 4(1)
	Jurisdiction is based on (a) the residence of the paying party, (b) the location of the paying party's assets or (c) where any other matter relevant to enforcement arises	CJJ(M)R 2011, para 4(3)
	If the order was made in Denmark, the justices' clerk must determine an application for enforceability, but given the mandatory nature of the Regulation this is a formality, provided that the requirements of Art 28 have been complied with. The paying party is not entitled to make any submissions at this stage; but see "Challenge by paying party" below	Council Regulation (EC) No 4/2009, Art 30; FPR 2010, r 34.29A; PD34C, para 3.1
	If the order was made in an EFTA country bound by the Lugano Convention, the order may be registered for enforcement and if registered is treated as having been declared enforceable	CJJ(M)R 2011, para 6(3)

	The designated officer of the court must consider whether the payer resides in the local justice area or has assets against which the order could be enforced	FPR 2010, r 34.30(3)
	If the payer is not resident but does have assets against which the order could be enforced, the court officer may either register or, if he believes that the payer is resident in another magistrates' court's area, refuse the application and return the documents to the Lord Chancellor (in practice, the Reciprocal Enforcement of Maintenance Unit (REMO), Office of the Official Solicitor and Public Trustee, 81 Chancery Lane, London WC2A 1DD; tel: 0845 345 5303; fax: 020 7911 7030; email: remo@offsol.gsi.gov.uk) with a view to registration in that court	FPR 2010, r 34.30(5)
	If the payer is not resident and does not have assets in that area against which the order could be enforced, the court officer must refuse the application	FPR 2010, r 34.30(6)
	If the court officer considers that it would be appropriate for the order to be registered in the High Court for enforcement, he must notify the applicant of his opinion and that further registration under MOA 1958 is possible	FPR 2010, r 34.30(9)
Application	The application (including the documents supplied by the foreign court) is forwarded by the Central Authority in the State in question to the Lord Chancellor (in practice, the Reciprocal Enforcement of Maintenance Unit (REMO), Office of the Official Solicitor and Public Trustee, 81 Chancery Lane, London WC2A 1DD; tel: 0845 345 5303; fax: 020 7911 7030; email: remo@offsol.gsi.gov.uk) for transmission to the appropriate court. Authenticated copy orders are deemed to be true copies, and other documents required to be produced are admissible in evidence	CJJA 1982, s 11, Sch 1, Art 32
What happens next	If the court officer refuses the application, he notifies the applicant. If he registers the order, he notifies the Lord Chancellor, the applicant and the payer	FPR 2010, rr 34.3, 34.30
Challenge by paying party	Where the Maintenance Regulation (EC) No 4/2009 applies, the decision may not be reviewed as to its substance in the enforcing court	Maintenance Regulation, Art 42

	It appears, however, that obvious arithmetical errors may be corrected	*Vogel v Lothschütz* [2012] EWHC 3411 (QB): a decision on a European Enforcement Order
	In addition to resisting enforcement on its merits, the paying party may challenge the registration only by:	
	applying for review in the State of origin. Note the strict time limit and that "no extension may granted on account of distance";	Art 19; Art 19(2)
	applying to the enforcing court for the refusal or suspension of enforcement on the grounds that:	
	enforcement is time-barred;	Art 21(2)
	enforcement would be inconsistent with another decision;	
	an application for review has been made in the State of origin	Art 21(3)
Enforcement	On registration, the order is enforceable as if it had been made by the magistrates' court, except that payments must be made only to the designated officer of the court and sent by him to the original court (or to such other person or authority as that court or the Lord Chancellor may direct);	CJJA 1982, s 5(4); FPR 2010, r 34.32(2)
	the court officer may, or, if at least 4 weeks' arrears accrue, must (unless it appears unreasonable to do so), take steps in his own name to enforce the order whether or not the payee so requests	FPR 2010, r 34.33(4)
	The court officer is also under a duty to take reasonable steps to notify the payee of the methods of enforcement available	FPR 2010, r 34.33(2)

C3(13): Enforcement in a European Union or EFTA Country of a Judgment or Order (other than a Maintenance Order) Made in England or Wales, and Vice Versa

Legal background

The CJJA 1982 gave effect to the Brussels Convention (to which the EEC countries were parties) and the similar Lugano Convention of 1988 signed by the Member States of EFTA. As with FJ(RE)A 1933, a registrable judgment cannot be made the subject of an action. The grounds on which registration may be set aside are very limited. The JR applies a uniform regime, similar though not identical to that under the Brussels Convention, to all the Member States of the European Union. It applies to Denmark from 1 July 2007. With effect from 1 January 2010 the 2007 Lugano Convention applies in relation to Norway, but the 1988 Convention remains in force in relation to Iceland and Switzerland for the time being.

OUTWARD

Enforcement in a European Union or EFTA country of any High Court or county court judgment or order

Who may apply	Any interested party	CJJA 1982, s 12; JR Art 33 para 2
To whom application made	A district judge of the Family Division in the case of a judgment in that Division; a district judge in the case of a county court judgment	CPR PD74A, para 4.2
Application	Application without notice under CPR 23 supported by written evidence exhibiting copies of:	CPR 1998, r 74.12
	the claim form; evidence of service; the statements of case; where relevant, notice that the applicant was an assisted person or LSC funded client	CPR 1998, r 74.13(1)
	The written evidence must:	CPR 1998, r 74.13(2)
	(a) identify the grounds on which the judgment was obtained;	
	(b) state whether the defendant objected to the jurisdiction, and if so, on what grounds;	
	(c) show that the judgment has been served and is not subject to a stay of execution;	
	(d) give details of any possible appeal;	
	(e) state the amount in respect of which the judgment remains unsatisfied;	
	(f) give particulars of interest recoverable	
Fee	High Court: £60 County court: £45	FPFO 2008, fee 14.2 FPFO 2008, fee 4.1
What happens next	If the district judge is satisfied, the court issues a certified copy of the judgment and a certificate in Form 110 prescribed by RSC, adapted as necessary and signed by the district judge. The applicant must apply to the relevant court or authority in the foreign State in accordance with its law and procedures for enforcement of the judgment there	
Recent EU members	The more recent members of the European Union may not yet have put in place the facilities for enforcement under this provision	
Appeals	See relevant Guides in Appeals section	

INWARD

Enforcement in England or Wales of a judgment or order (other than a maintenance order) made in a European Union or EFTA country

Who may apply	Any interested party	CJJA 1982, Sch 1, Art 31; JR Art 33 para 2
Which court	High Court, Queen's Bench Division. Application should be made to the Action Department of the Royal Courts of Justice, not a district registry	CPR 1998, r 74.3; PD74A, para 4.1(1)
Application	Ex parte application under CPR Pt 23 supported by written evidence which must exhibit an authenticated translation of the judgment, if not in English, and give particulars of interest due	CPR 1998, rr 74.4(1)(b), 74.4(6)
	The evidence in support of an application under the 1982 Act must exhibit:	
	the judgment or order or an authenticated copy;	CPR 1998, r 74.4(1)(a)
	documents to show that the judgment is enforceable in the country of origin and has been served;	CPR 1998, r 74.4(5)(a)
	if a default judgment, evidence that the proceedings were served;	CPR 1998, r 74.4(5)(b)
	where appropriate, evidence of the judgment creditor's legal aid	CPR 1998, r 74.4(5)(c)
	and must state:	CPR 1998, r 74.4(2)
	(a) the judgment creditor's name and address for service within England and Wales;	
	(b) the name and address (if known) of the judgment debtor;	
	(c) the grounds on which the judgment creditor is entitled to enforce the judgment;	
	(d) the amount unsatisfied;	
	(e) details of interest payable	
	An application under the JR must state the judgment creditor's address for service and be accompanied by an authentic copy of the judgment and the certificate at Annex V of the JR	CPR 1998, r 74.4(6); JR Art 40.2; JR Art 53
Fee	£230	FPFO 2008, fee 1.1
Order	Drawn up by the applicant, stating the period for appeal against it and that the judgment or order will not be enforced by execution until that period has expired	CPR 1998, r 74.6

Service	Notice of the registration of the judgment or order must be served on the debtor, stating full particulars of the judgment or order registered and of the order for registration, the name and address for service of the applicant, the right of the debtor to appeal against the registration and the time for such an appeal (1 month from service, or 2 months in the case of a debtor not domiciled within the jurisdiction) which may be extended in the case of a debtor not domiciled in a convention country on application made within 2 months after service	There is power to extend the time for appealing but the burden of showing that this should happen is heavy (*Citibank NA v Rafidian Bank* [2003] EWHC 1950 (QB)
Appeal by judgment debtor	The debtor has a right of appeal but, since the court is not permitted to review the foreign judgment as to its substance, the appeal may extend only to the grounds on which registration could have been refused, i e that the judgment is one which would not be recognised here for the reasons set out in CJJA 1982, Sch 1, Arts 27, 28, or JR Arts 34 and 35 as the case may be, principally:	CPR 1998, r 74.8 and see *Banco Nacional de Comercio Exterior v Empresa de Telecomunucaciones de Cuba SA* [2007] EWHC 2322 (Comm)
	if recognition of the judgment is manifestly contrary to public policy	
	in the case of a default judgment, if the defendant was not served and failed to challenge the judgment when it was possible for him to do so;	JR Art 45.2
	if it is irreconcilable with certain other judgments between the same parties. The appeal is by summons to a judge – an application to a master to set aside a registration under CJJA 1982 or the JR is a nullity	*Maronier v Larmer* [2003] QB 620, CA
Appeal by judgment creditor	Appeal from refusal to register, see relevant Guides in Appeals section	CPR 1998, r 74.8
Enforcement	Execution may not be issued, nor may the judgment or order be otherwise enforced, until the time for appeal (including any extension) has expired and any appeal has been disposed of. This does not prevent an application, for example, to prevent the disposal of assets	

Limitation	Enforcement more than 6 years after the judgment is registered will not be allowed except in a special case, notwithstanding that a longer limitation period applies in the country where the judgment was given	*Duer v Frazer* [2001] 1 WLR 919
Recent EU members	The more recent members of the European Union may not yet have put in place the facilities for enforcement under this provision	

C3(14): Applications for Recognition, Non-Recognition and Enforcement of Court Orders under the 1996 Convention

Legal background

The Hague Convention on Jurisdiction, Applicable Law, Recognition and Enforcement and Co-operation in Respect of Parental Responsibility and Measures for Protection of Children (the 1996 Convention; see Part VI) was signed on 19 October 1996. It was ratified by the UK on 27 July 2012, coming into force on 1 November 2012. Its aim is to improve the protection of children and their property in cross-border cases. Its objects are (a) to determine which country's authorities has jurisdiction to take protective measures; (b) to determine which country's laws are to be applied in exercising the jurisdiction; (c) to determine the applicable law in relation to parental responsibility; (d) to provide for recognition and enforcement of measures taken in one Contracting State to apply in all other Contracting States; and (e) to establish co-operation and to provide a framework for the exchange of information and collaboration between the authorities in the Contracting States.

The Convention sets out a non-exhaustive list of protective measures that are within its scope and also a list of issues to which it does not apply. Articles 23 and 25 deal with recognition and non-recognition by operation of Art 24 and set out the grounds on which recognition may be refused. Article 24 allows any interested party to ask for a declaration confirming whether or not a measure will be recognised in another State. The enforcement provisions are set out in Arts 26–28. The Parental Responsibility and Measures for the Protection of Children (International Obligations) (England and Wales and Northern Ireland) Regulations 2010 (see Part IV) facilitate the operation of the Convention.

The procedural rules for making an application under the Convention are set out in FPR 2010, Pt 31 and PD31A.

Note that although Belgium, Italy and the USA have signed the Convention, they have not ratified it.

Procedure

Who may apply	Any interested party	FPR 2010, r 31.4(1)
Which court	To a district judge of the Principal Registry	FPR 2010, r 31.3(1), 31.4(2)(a)
Form of application	Pt 19. If recognition of an order only is sought, the application must indicate that it does not extend to registration and enforcement	FPR PD31A, paras 1.1, 1.2
Fee	£230	FPFO 2008, fee 1.1

Evidence	All applications for recognition, registration and non-recognition must be supported by a sworn statement or an affidavit exhibiting the judgment or verified or certified or otherwise authenticated copy of the judgment	FPR PD31A, para 2.2
	Grounds for refusing recognition are set out in Art 23(2) of the Convention	
Documents in relation to an application for registration	(a) All documents necessary to show that the judgment is enforceable according to the law of the Contracting State;	FPR PD31A, para 4.2(a)
	(b) Description of the opportunities provided to the child by the authorities that gave the judgment, to be heard except where the judgment was given in an emergency;	FPR PD31A, para 4.2(b)
	(c) Where the judgment was given in a case of urgency, a statement as to the circumstances of the urgency that led to the child not being heard;	FPR PD31A, para 4.2(c)
	(d) Details of any measures taken in a non-Contracting State of the child's habitual residence, if applicable, specifying the nature and effect of the measure and the date on which it was taken;	FPR PD31A, para 4.2(d)
	(e) In so far as it is not apparent from the copy judgment provided, a statement of the grounds on which the judgment was based together with any documentary evidence to support that statement;	FPR PD31A, para 4.2(e)
	(f) Where appropriate, a statement regarding whether Art 33 of the 1996 Convention (where it is contemplated placing a child in a foster placement or institutional care or an analogous institution) had been complied with, and the identity and address of the authority or authorities from which consent has been obtained together with any evidence of that consent;	FPR PD31A, para 4.2(f) and Art 33
	(g) The information set out in FPR PD31A, para 3.2(c)–(e)	
Documents in applications for an order that a judgment should not be recognised	(a) A statement of the ground(s) under Art 23 of the 1996 Convention on which it is requested that the judgment be not recognised, the reasons why the applicant asserts that such ground(s) is/are made out and any documentary evidence on which the applicant relies;	FPR PD31A, para 4.3
	(b) An address within the jurisdiction for service on the applicant and stating in so far as is known to the applicant, the name and usual or last known address or place of business of the person in whose favour judgment was given.	FPR PD31A, para 4.4

Documents in support of an application for recognition only	All the documents referred to above under applications for registration with the exception of documents to show that the judgment is enforceable according to the law the of the Contracting State in which it was given	
Directions	As soon as practicable after an application is made, the court may give such directions as it considers appropriate, inter alia dealing with dispensation of service and other issues of service and filing of evidence and expedition of proceedings	FPR 2010, r 31.6
Respondent's answer	Upon receipt of an application for an order that the judgment should not be recognized, the person in whose favour the judgment was given must file an answer and serve it on the applicant within 1 month of service or within 2 months if that person is habitually resident in another Contracting State, unless the court has extended the time on account of distance. The answer may request recognition or registration of the judgment and in this event must be accompanied by the documents, information and evidence set out in FPR 2010, r 31.4(2) (above) insofar as these are not included in the application	FPR 2010, r 31.8(3)(b),(4),(5)
If no answer is filed	In a case where the 1996 Convention applies and the Service Regulation does not, if an answer is not filed the Court will apply Art 15 of the 1965 Hague Convention if applicable and if it does not, in all other cases the court will not consider the application unless – (a) it is proved to the satisfaction of the court that the person in whose favour judgment was given was served with the application within a reasonable period of time to arrange his or her response; or (b) the court is satisfied that the circumstances of the case justify proceeding with the application	
Directions if an application for non recognition is refused	The court may direct that the judgment be recognised or alternatively that it should be treated as an application for enforcement and order that the judgment be registered for enforcement provided that the requirement for the filing of the relevant documents and information has been satisfied	FPR 2010, r 31.10
Court orders	(1) Where the judgment is ordered to be registered, the court officer will serve a copy of the order on each party as soon as practicable	FPR 2010, r 31.14(2)

	(2) Where the court orders that the judgment should be registered for enforcement the court officer will:	FPR 2010, r 31.11(3)
	(a) register the judgment in the central index of judgments kept by the Principal Registry;	
	(b) confirm on the order that the judgment has been registered;	
	(c) serve on the parties the court's order endorsed with confirmation that the judgment has been registered	
	(3) Where the court refuses an application for registration for enforcement, the court officer must serve the order on the applicant and the person against whom the judgment was given in the state of origin	FPR 2010, r 31.11(2)
Contents of the notice of registration or a sealed copy of the order	Full particulars of the judgment registered and the order or registration or the full particulars of the judgment recognised;	FPR 2010, rr 31.11(5)(a), 31.14(4)(a)
	the name of the party making the application and his address for service within the jurisdiction;	FPR 2010, rr 31.11(5)(b), 31.14(4)(b)
	the right of the person against whom the judgment was given to appeal against the order for registration or recognition as the case may be;	FPR 2010, rr 31.11(5)(c), 31.14(4)(c)
	the period within which an appeal against the order for registration or recognition as the case may be made.	FPR 2010, rr 31.11(5)(d), 31.14(4)(d)
Appeal	Must be made to a judge of the High Court within 1 month or in the case of an appellant habitually resident in another Contracting State within 2 months of the date of service or notice of registration refusal to recognise or to register for enforcement	FPR 2010, r 31.15(1),(2)
	Time cannot be extended	
	Appeals from the High Court lie to the Court of Appeal and then to the Supreme Court, but permission to appeal is required	SCR 2009
Stay of proceedings	Stay of proceedings for recognition or non-recognition or enforcement of a registered order may be granted if an appeal is pending in the State of origin	FPR 2010, r 31.9

C3(15): Enforcement in Scotland or Northern Ireland of a Judgment or Order (other than a Maintenance Order) of an English or Welsh Court other than a Magistrates' Court, and Vice Versa

PART I

Legal background

CPR 1998 apply to the reciprocal enforcement of money judgments or orders arising in family proceedings, other than maintenance orders, as to which see the appropriate Guides in this volume.

OUTWARD

Enforcement in Scotland or Northern Ireland of an existing High Court or county court judgment or order (other than a maintenance order)

Who may apply	Any interested party	CJJA 1982, Sch 6, para 2(1), Sch 7, para 2(1)
Which court	The Principal Registry, district registry or county court in which the judgment or order was given or made	CPR 1998, rr 74.17, 74.18
	Application is made to a master or district judge	CPR PD74A, para 4.3
Documents required	*Money judgments* The judgment creditor may obtain a certificate to enable the money provisions of a judgment to be enforced in another part of the UK by filing written evidence stating:	CPR 1998, r 74.17
	the name and address of the judgment creditor and (if known) the debtor;	
	the sums payable and unsatisfied;	
	details of interest recoverable;	
	that the judgment is not stayed;	
	the date on which the time for appealing expired or will expire, and whether an appeal or application for permission to appeal is current (in practice, confirming that it is not)	
	Non-monetary provisions of a judgment or order The judgment creditor may obtain a certificate by filing written evidence which must:	
	give particulars of the judgment	
	confirm that the judgment is not stayed; the date on which the time for appealing expired or will expire, and whether an appeal or application for permission to appeal is current (in practice, confirming that it is not)	
	give the usual or last known addresses of the creditor and the debtor	CPR 1998, r 74.18

Fee	High Court: £60	FPFO 2008, fee 14.2
	County court: £45	FPFO 2008, fee 4.1
What happens next	*Monetary provisions* The certificate is completed by the proper officer and issued to the creditor, who uses it to found the appropriate steps in Scotland or Northern Ireland	CJJA 1982, Sch 6
	Non-monetary provisions The court provides a certified copy of the judgment and a certificate annexed to it in Form 112 prescribed by RSC adapted as necessary. The applicant uses these documents to found the appropriate application in Scotland or Northern Ireland	CJJA 1982, Sch 7
Appeals	Not applicable	

INWARD

Enforcement in England and Wales of a judgment or order (other than a maintenance order) of a Scottish or Northern Irish court other than a magistrates' court

Who may apply	Any interested party	CJJA 1982, Sch 6, para 2(1), Sch 7, para 2(1)
Which court	High Court. Applications to register Scottish or Northern Irish judgments are assigned to the Queen's Bench Division	CPR PD74A, para 4.1(2)
Application	*Monetary provisions* No application as such is made. The certificate issued by the Scottish or Northern Ireland court is filed in the Central Office of the Senior Courts	CPR 1998, r 74.15
	Non-monetary provisions Application is made without notice under CPR Pt 23	CPR 1998, r 74.16
Documents required	*Monetary provisions* A certificate of the judgment or order issued within the preceding 6 months by the Scottish or Northern Irish court, together with a copy certified by written evidence (usually that of the applicant's solicitor) to be a true copy	CPR 1998, r 74.15
	Non-monetary provisions A certified copy of the judgment or order and the prescribed form of certificate issued within the previous 6 months by the Scottish or Northern Irish court	CJJA 1982, Sch 7, para 5(3); CPR 1998, r 74.16
Fee	£230	FPFO 2008, fee 1.1

What happens next	*Monetary provisions* The certified copy is sealed by the court and returned as evidence of the registration of the judgment or order, which may then be enforced as a judgment or order of the High Court	CJJA 1982, Sch 6, paras 5, 6; PD74A, para 8.1
	Non-monetary provisions The judgment or order must not be registered if compliance would breach the law in England and Wales; otherwise, the court must order it to be registered. If the order is granted, the applicant must draw it up. The order must state the period within which an application may be made to set aside the order for registration and that execution will not be issued on the judgment or order until that period has expired. No period is in fact specified in the Act or Rules, but it seems likely that the court would apply by analogy the 1-month period applicable under CPR 1998, r 74.8 in the case of an order made in a convention country	CJJA 1982, Sch 7, para 5(4),(5); CPR 1998, rr 74.6, 74.7, 74.9, 74.16(4),(5)
Service	*Monetary provisions* There is no requirement for notice of the registration to be served	
	Non-monetary provisions Notice of the registration must be served on the person against whom the order was made, giving full particulars of the judgment or order registered and the order for registration, the name of the applicant and his address for service within England and Wales. It must state the right of that person to apply to set aside the registration and the period within which that application must be made. The order is then enforceable as if made by the High Court	CJJA 1982, Sch 7, para 6; CPR 1998, rr 74.6, 74.7, 74.16(4) and (5)
Costs and interest	*Monetary provisions* The costs of obtaining and registering the certificate are added to the judgment debt. Interest continues to accrue at the rate stated in the certificate, including interest from the date of registration on the added costs. No other interest is recoverable	CJJA 1982, Sch 6, paras 7, 8
	Non-monetary provisions The costs of obtaining the copy order and certificate and of registration are recoverable as if the original order included an order for their payment, but interest is recoverable on those costs as if, on registration, the High Court had ordered their payment	CJJA 1982, Sch 7, para 7

Stay and setting aside	If satisfied that the debtor is entitled to and intends to appeal against or apply to have set aside the judgment or order, the court may stay enforcement on such terms as it thinks fit and for such period as appears to be sufficient. On the application of any interested party, the court *must* set aside the registration if satisfied that registration was contrary to the provisions of the relevant Schedule, and it *may* set the registration aside if the issue in the original proceedings had previously been decided by another court of competent jurisdiction	CJJA 1982, Sch 6, paras 9, 10, Sch 7, paras 8, 9
	Any application to set aside the registration must be made under CPR Pt 23, supported by written evidence. The court may order an issue to be tried	CPR 1998, rr 74.7(3), 74.16(5)
	Fee: £90	FPFO 2008, fee 4.3
Appeals	Appeal against master's refusal; appeal from application to set aside	See relevant Guide in Appeals section

C3(16): Enforcement of an Uncontested Claim as a European Enforcement Order

Legal background

Regulation (EC) No 805/2004 of 21 April 2004 (see Part VI) introduces an optional procedure for the enforcement of uncontested claims within the European Union. The rules relating to this procedure are in CPR rr 74.28 and PD74B, to which the (lengthy) text of the Regulation is annexed. Whereas the Judgments Regulation applies to Denmark, the European Enforcement Order (EEO) does not.

Note that the EEO procedure also applies to "court settlements and authentic instruments".

OUTWARD

Registration of an Uncontested Judgment as an EEO

What claims	The EEO procedure does not apply to, inter alia, "rights in property arising out of a matrimonial relationship"	EC Reg 805/2004, Art 2(2)(b)
What judgments	Judgments on uncontested claims, ie where the debtor:	
	has expressly agreed to the claim; or	
	has failed to object to the claim; or	
	has failed to attend a hearing as a result of which judgment has been entered	
	If the creditor relies on default of defence or objection, it must be shown that the debtor was aware of the proceedings	Regulation 805/2004, Art 3

Service of proceedings	If the debtor's default of defence or objection is relied upon, the proceedings must have been served with proof of receipt by the debtor; or	Regulation 805/2004, Art 13
	served without proof of receipt eg by delivery to the debtor's address, but only if the debtor's address is known with certainty	Regulation 805/2004, Art 14(1)
	Postal service is only acceptable if the debtor's address is in England and Wales	Regulation 805/2004, Art 14(2) Regulation 805/2004, Art 14(1)(e)
Documents needed	The judgment;	
	Costs certificate (if debtor has not objected to the principle of bearing the costs);	CPR PD74B, para 2.1
	Document attesting service (if relevant);	
	Completed draft EEO Certificate;	Annex to CPR PD74B (not printed in this work – see *Civil Court Service* (Jordan Publishing Ltd)
	Practice Form N219 (express agreement) or N219A (default)	
Fee	High Court: £60 County court: £45	FPFO 2008, fee 14.2; FPFO 2008, fee 4.1
Which judge	In the county court, a district judge;	CPR PD74B, para 2.1
	in the Chancery or Queen's Bench Divisions of the High Court, or in a District Registry, a master or a district judge	
	No express provision is made for money judgments in the Family Division – it is submitted that application should be made to a district judge of the Principal Registry	See Regulation 805/2004, Art 4, para 1
What happens next	If the application is granted, the court will send the EEO certificate and a sealed copy of the judgment to the applicant. Enforcement proceedings may then be taken in another Regulation State	CPR PD74B, para 2.2

INWARD

Enforcement of an Uncontested Claim which has been registered as an EEO

Which court	High Court or county court; judgments in excess of £5000 may only be enforced by execution against goods in the High Court; judgments for less than £600 shall only be enforced in the county court	CPR r 74.31; HCCCJO 1991, art 8

From which country	Any Regulation State, i e any Member State other than Denmark	CPR 1998, r 74.27(d)
Documents required	Authentic copy of the judgment, court settlement or authentic instrument;	Regulation 805/2004, Arts 20, 24, 25
	Authentic copy of the EEO certificate issued by the foreign court;	CPR 1998, r 74.31(1)
	(An official copy issued by the court of the Member State of origin will be acceptable)	CPR PD74B, para 5.2
	Certified translation of each of the above documents into English	Form C20(2)(c)
Fee	High Court: £60	FPFO 2008, fee 14.2
	County court: £45	FPFO 2008, fee 4.1
What happens next	The EEO will be assigned a case number in the court in which it is lodged	
	Enforcement proceedings may be taken without further formality	CPR PD74B, para 5.1
Review of decision	Neither a judgment nor its certification as an EEO may be reviewed as to its substance	Regulation 805/2004, Art 21(2)
Refusal of enforcement	In the case of an EEO based on a judgment, the debtor may apply under Pt 23 to the court in which the EEO is being enforced for an order that the court should refuse to enforce an EEO but the only grounds on which this can be done are that the EEO is irreconcilable with an earlier judgment and that the irreconcilability was not, and could not have been, raised in the court proceedings in the Member State of origin	Regulation 805/2004, Art 21
	But a court settlement or authentic instrument that has been certified as an EEO in the Member State of origin shall be enforced "without any possibility of opposing its enforceability"	Regulation 805/2004, Arts 24(2), 25(2)
	Clerical errors (e g an authentic instrument being wrongly described as a judgment debt) are not a ground for setting aside registration. It appears that obvious errors of calculation may be corrected	*Vogel v Lothschütz* [2012] EWHC 3411 (QB)
Documents required	Application notice under CPR Pt 23	
	Official copy of earlier judgment;	
	Written evidence showing why the judgment is irreconcilable and why this could not have been raised in the proceedings in the court of origin	CPR 1998, r 74.32; PD74B, para 6.1
Stay or limitation of *enforcement*	Before the debtor can ask the court not to enforce an EEO based on a judgment he must first apply for a stay to the court of origin, unless the court otherwise orders	CPR PD74B, para 7.1; Regulation 805/2004, Art 23

Documents required	Application notice under CPR Pt 23;	
	Evidence of application in the court of origin;	
	Certified translation of that application;	
	Written evidence stating that an application has been made to the court of origin, the nature of that application and the grounds for it, and the date on which it was filed and the date by which it is believed it will be determined	CPR PD74B, paras 7.1, 7.2

C4: Registration in a Magistrates' Court of a Maintenance Order Made in the High Court or a County Court

Legal background

The person entitled to receive payment under a maintenance order made by the High Court or a county court may apply to that court for its registration in a magistrates' court and, provided that it remains registered, it is treated as a magistrates' court order for the purpose of enforcement and (broadly) variation.

Procedure

Availability	Only "maintenance orders" may be registered, but this expression includes lump sum orders. Although an application may be made and granted while enforcement process is outstanding in the original court, the registration will not be effected until that process has been completed	MOA 1958, s 1(1)
	The grant of the application will become void if the enforcement process is not completed within 14 days	MOA 1958, s 2(2); FPR 2010, rr 32.14, 32.15
Application	Two copies of the application form and a certified copy of the order are lodged in the court which made the order (or the court to which the cause has since been transferred)	
	If the application is granted, the order is registered in the magistrates' court for the place where the payer resides	FPR 2010, rr 32.14, 32.15
	The magistrates' court has no discretion to decline registration	MOA 1958, s 2(5)
Fee	£40	FPFO 2008, fee 9.1
Effect	Any attachment of earnings order ceases to have effect	AEA 1971, s 11(1)(a)

	Unless a means of payment order under MEA 1991 is in force, future payments must be ordered to be paid through the magistrates' clerk	MOA 1958, s 2(6ZA)(b)
	Where the payee is receiving income support, this enables the payee to divert the payments to the Department for Work and Pensions, enabling her (or him) to receive full benefit regardless of any irregularity in payment	
	The order is enforceable only as if it were an order made by the magistrates' court	MOA 1958, s 3
	Variation proceedings must be in the magistrates' court, unless there is an application to vary some provision (eg extension of the term of the order) other than merely the rate of payment or the payer is outside England and Wales; in either of those cases, the application is to the original court. In any event, the magistrates' court may remit a variation application made to it to the original court for hearing	MOA 1958, s 4
Cancellation	The person entitled to receive payment may simply give notice to the magistrates' court. The original court may give such a notice, but only where it varies or discharges the maintenance order	
	The notice has the effect of cancelling the registration as soon as any outstanding enforcement process or variation application has been concluded	MOA 1958, s 5
	Fee: none prescribed	
Form	Form D151	FPR PD5A
Appeals	See relevant Guide in Appeals section	

C5: Attachment of Earnings Order (High Court or County Court)

Legal background

Where the debtor is in employment, the court may order his employer to deduct periodic amounts from his earnings and remit them to the court against the amount(s) due under the order to be enforced. The position varies according to whether the attachment of earnings order is to secure (a) a qualifying periodical maintenance order (including some lump sum orders), (b) some other maintenance order (including a lump sum order) or (c) an order which is not a maintenance order.

Procedure

Availability	Leave is required if it is sought to enforce arrears more than 12 months old under a financial provision or similar order	MCA 1973, s 32; CPA 2004, Sch 5, para 63
	The application for leave is made to the district judge on notice to the debtor and may be issued with (and made returnable with) the attachment of earnings application itself	FPR 2010, rr 18.1–18.5, 18.7, 18.8
	The court has a discretion whether to make the attachment of earnings order or not. If the circumstances would require the creditor to obtain leave before issuing execution against goods, similar considerations apply as on an application for such leave	
	An attachment of earnings order cannot be made against a member of HM Forces, but a deduction from pay may be sought	Armed Forces (Forfeitures and Deductions) Regulations 2009
	Qualifying periodical maintenance order The person to whom the payments are to be made, the person (if different) who applied for the maintenance order or the debtor may apply at any time; otherwise, the court may make an order of its own motion on making the maintenance order or in the course of any proceedings relating to it	MEA 1991, s 1(1),(3)
	Other maintenance order The person to whom the payments are to be made may apply at any time	AEA 1971, s 3
	The debtor may apply on the making or variation of the maintenance order	CPR 1998, Sch 2, CCR Ord 27, r 17(4)
	Other order The person to whom the payments are to be made may apply if the debtor has defaulted under the order, but only if the amount due under the order is (or was when it was made) at least £50	AEA 1971, ss 1(2)(b), 3(3); CPR 1998, Sch 2, CCR Ord 27, r 17(9)
Application	*High Court* No rules currently exist. The county court procedure should be adapted (or the application may be made to the county court)	CPR 1998, Sch 2, CCR Ord 25, r 11
	The High Court has power to make an attachment of earnings order only to secure a High Court maintenance order, unless the proceedings in the Principal Registry are treated as pending in a divorce county court or civil partnership proceedings county court	AEA 1971, s 1(1); FPR 2010, r 33.19
	County court The application is filed in the court which made the order	CPR 1998, Sch 2, CCR Ord 27, r 17(2)

	The creditor must file a statement, verified by a statement of truth, showing how the amount due and any interest claimed are calculated	FPR 2010, r 33.3(1)
	If the application is to enforce a maintenance order, a return date is given before the district judge, which the applicant should attend	CPR 1998, Sch 2, CCR Ord 27, r 4(2)
	Notice of the hearing should be served not less than 21 days before the hearing, unless the debtor is "about to remove from his address for service"	CPR 1998, Sch 2, CCR Ord 27, r 17(3B)
	The debtor must file a reply in the form provided, giving particulars of his means, within 8 days of being served	CPR 1998, Sch 2, CCR Ord 27, r 5(2)
Fee	High Court: £90	FPFO 2008, fee 4.3
	County court: £100 for each person against whom the order is sought (NB it appears that no fee is payable if the order is made of the court's own motion, and it is not payable when an attachment of earnings order is made on the hearing of a judgment summons)	FPFO 2008, fee 12.4
Debtor's address	It is for the creditor to provide the address of the debtor. In case of difficulty, assistance may sometimes be obtained from certain Government departments	FPR PD6C
	However, it may be necessary to obtain a High Court order authorising the disclosure	*President's Office Guidance of November 2003*
Powers of the court	The court has wide powers to require the debtor to provide the information needed to deal with the application	AEA 1971, s 14
	Provision is also made for where a debtor fails to attend or provide information	AEA 1971, s 23; CPR 1998, Sch 2, CCR Ord 27, r 8
Order	The debtor's employer must make periodic deductions from his pay and remit them to CAPS (Central Attachment of Earnings Payment System), PO Box 464, Northampton NN1 2ZY, which passes them on to the creditor	
	Where the payee is receiving income support, this enables the payee to divert the payments to the Department for Work and Pensions enabling her (or him) to receive full benefit, regardless of any irregularity in payment	
Forms	Request for order N337 will need adaptation for a maintenance order case. The court prepares Notice to the debtor in Form N55 (debt) or N55(1) (maintenance)	

Appeals	See Guide E2	
	NB Appeal from a district judge's committal order under AEA 1971, s 23 also lies direct to the Court of Appeal but this route will rarely be appropriate	AJA 1960, s 13; *King v Read & Slack* [1999] 1 FLR 425, CA

C6: Charging Order

Legal background

The court may impose a charge on the debtor's interest in land, securities or a fund in court. The effect of this remedy is to provide security for the debt, rather than enforce it but, having made a charging order, the court may appoint a receiver of the income generated by the property charged, as to which see the relevant Guide in *Civil Court Service* (Jordan Publishing Ltd), and/or may order its sale.

There is a two-stage procedure, with an interim charging order made without notice to the debtor, followed by a hearing on notice at which the interim order may be made "final" (i e confirmed, with or without variation).

Procedure

Availability	Leave is required if it is sought to enforce arrears more than 12 months old under a financial provision or similar order	MCA 1973, s 32; CPA 2004, Sch 5, para 63
	The application for leave is made to the district judge on notice to the debtor	FPR 2010, rr 18.1–18.5, 18.7, 18.8
	Otherwise, the creditor may apply at any time. However, the court has a discretion whether to make the charging order or not; if the circumstances would require the creditor to obtain leave before issuing execution against goods, similar considerations apply as on an application for such leave; only in exceptional circumstances will an order be made if the debtor is not in default. The remedy will also not be granted if it would be oppressive, e g by reason of the small amount of the debt	
	An order may be made even if the debt is the subject of a county court instalment order that is up to date when the application is made, but that fact must be taken into account in deciding whether the interim order should be confirmed	COA 1979, s 1(7),(8)
Which court	*High Court order* In the case of a maintenance or lump sum order or an order for over £5000, the application may be made to the High Court (in the Principal Registry or the district registry in which the cause or matter is proceeding)	COA 1979, s 1(2)(b),(c)

	Otherwise, the application must be made in the county court; if the application must be made in the county court and relates to a High Court judgment the proceedings must first be transferred to the relevant county court	CPR 1998, r 73.3(1)
Which particular court	*High Court* The High Court or the district registry in which the judgment was entered or to which the proceedings have been transferred	CPR 1998, r 73.3(2)
	County court The county court in which the judgment was obtained or to which the proceedings have been transferred	CPR 1998, r 73.3(2)
	The debtor may request in writing that the hearing of the application is transferred to a more convenient court	CPR PD73, para 3
Application	The application is made by filing an application notice in Form N379, verified by a statement of truth. The application notice must contain the following information:	CPR 1998, r 73.3(1)
	(a) The name and address of the judgment debtor; (b) Details of the judgment or order sought to be enforced; (c) The amount of money remaining due; (d) If the judgment is payable by instalments, the amount of money remaining due; (e) The names and (if known) the addresses of any other creditors of the debtor of whom the judgment creditor is aware; (f) The asset or assets that it is sought to charge; (g) Details of the judgment debtor's interest in each asset; (h) The names and addresses of the persons on whom an interim order must be served under CPR 1998, r 73.5(1)	CPR PD73, para 1.2
	While the Practice Direction does not explicitly require this, it is good practice to set out how the amount remaining due is arrived at, by analogy with FPR 2010, r 33.3(1)(a)	
	If a charging order is sought over the judgment debtor's interest in registered land, an official copy of the entries on the Land Register should be filed with the application notice	

	If satisfied that the application notice contains the required information and that it is proper to make the order, the master or District Judge makes an interim charging order and fixes a date to consider whether a final order should be made	CPR 1998, r 73.4(2)
Fee	£100 in respect of each charging order applied for	FPFO 2008, fee 10.3
Debtor's address	It is for the creditor to provide the address of the debtor. In case of difficulty, assistance may sometimes be obtained from certain Government departments	FPR PD6C
	However, it may be necessary to obtain a High Court order authorising the disclosure	*President's Office Guidance of November 2003*
Service	A copy of the interim order, the application notice and the documents filed in support shall be served by the creditor not less than 21 days before the day fixed for the hearing	CPR 1998, r 73.5(1)
	If the judgment creditor serves, he must either file a certificate of service not less than 2 days before the hearing or produce the certificate at the hearing	CPR 1998, r 73.5(2)
	Persons to be served: (a) the judgment debtor;	CPR 1998, r 73.5(1)(a)
	(b) where the order relates to securities not in court, the keeper of the stock register;	CPR 1998, r 73.5(1)(d)
	(c) where the order relates to a fund in court, the Accountant General at the Court Funds Office;	CPR 1998, r 73.5(1)(e)
	(d) where the order relates to an interest under a trust, such of the trustees as the court may direct;	CPR 1998, r 73.5(1)(c)
	(e) any other creditor or interested person as the court may direct	CPR 1998, r 73.5(1)(b)
Objections to the order	Any person who wishes to object to the making of a final charging order must file and serve on the judgment creditor written evidence stating the grounds of his objection not less than 7 days before the hearing	CPR 1998, r 73.8(1)
	At the hearing the judge may make a final charging order confirming that the charge should remain in force with or without modifications. The order may be made subject to conditions, for example restricting enforcement	COA 1979, s 1(2)(c), CPR 1998, r 73.8(2)

	A charging order affecting an interest in land can and should be protected by registration at HM Land Registry or HM Land Charges Registry as appropriate as soon as an interim order is made. If it is discharged on the hearing, the registration must be removed by the creditor	
Order for sale	The judgment creditor holding a charging order may apply for an order for sale of the property charged. Although the charging order may have been made in family proceedings, an order for sale is applied for by fresh proceedings which are not themselves family proceedings.	
	If the debt secured does not exceed £30,000, the application may be made to the county court; in any case, the application may be made to the Chancery Division of the High Court	CCA 1984, s 23(c); CPR 1998, r 73.10; PD73, paras 4.1–4.5
	If the interest charged is merely a beneficial interest under a trust (e g if the property is in the joint names of the debtor and another), the creditor may apply (see Guide A5) for an order for sale of the trust property; in this case, the county court has jurisdiction irrespective of the amount of the debt or the value of the property	TLATA 1996, s 14; HCCCJO 1991, art 2(1)(a)
	The court will have regard to the relative values of the debt and the property charged, and will be reluctant to make an order where either is small	
	See the relevant Guide in *Civil Court Service* (Jordan Publishing Ltd)	
Appeals	See Guide E2	

C7: Writ or Warrant of Delivery

Legal background

In the High Court, a writ of delivery is issued to an enforcement officer (formerly the sheriff) and, in the county court, a delivery warrant is issued to the bailiff, requiring him physically to take the goods from the person against whom the order was made. If the order provides the alternative of payment of the value of the goods, the writ or warrant will require the enforcement officer or bailiff to levy execution for the value if the goods cannot be uplifted, unless the court has ordered otherwise.

Procedure

Availability	Permission is required to issue the writ or warrant if more than 6 years have elapsed since the order, if there has been a change of parties or (High Court only) if the order was conditional; otherwise, the person in whose favour the order is made may issue the writ or warrant as soon as it is made or, if it allows a time for compliance, as soon as that time has expired	CPR 1998, Sch 1, RSC Ord 46, r 2, Sch 2, CCR Ord 26, r 5
	Permission is required if the judgment was obtained in default against one of several defendants and judgment has not been obtained against all the defendants	CPR 1998, r 12.8(3)
	The High Court has a general power to stay execution of an order on the ground of matters that have occurred since it was made. The county court has a similar power in the case of monetary orders on the ground of inability to pay, whenever arising	CCA 1984, ss 38, 76; CPR 1998, Sch 1, RSC Ord 45, r 11
Issue	*High Court* The applicant files a praecipe together with the form of writ for sealing, and then sends the writ to the sheriffs' lodgement centre or other enforcement office of his choice	CPR 1998, Sch 1, RSC Ord 46, r 6
	County court The applicant files a form of request for the issue of the warrant	CPR 1998, Sch 2, CCR Ord 26, rr 1, 16
Fee	*High Court* £60 (NB a further fee is payable to the enforcement officer)	FPFO 2008, fee 14.1
	County court £110	FPFO 2008, fee 12.3
	No further court fee is payable if the writ or warrant is issued also to recover money	
Form	*High Court* Praecipe in Form PF90; writ in Form 64 or 65	
	County court Request in Form N324	
Appeals	See Guide E2	

C8: Execution against Goods

Legal background

In the High Court, a writ of fieri facias is issued, addressed to an "enforcement officer" (formerly the sheriff) and, in the county court, a warrant of execution is issued to the bailiff, requiring him to seize and sell the debtor's goods to produce the amount due under the order. The court may stay or suspend the execution if there are special circumstances or if the debtor is unable to pay.

Procedure

Availability	Permission is required if it is sought to enforce arrears more than 12 months old under a financial provision or similar order or where a variation application is pending	MCA 1973, s 32; CPA 2004, Sch 5, para 63; FPR 2010, r 33.20
	The application for permission is made to a district judge	FPR 2010, rr 18.1–18.5, 18.7, 18.8
	Permission is also required to issue the writ or warrant if more than 6 years have elapsed since the order, if there has been a change of parties, if the order was conditional (High Court only), in certain circumstances if the order was against the estate of a deceased person or if a receiver or sequestrator has been appointed. In these cases the application may be made either with or without notice according to circumstance	
	Otherwise, the person in whose favour the order is made may issue the writ or warrant as soon as it is made or, if it allows a time for compliance, then as soon as that time has expired	CPR 1998, Sch 1, RSC Ord 46, r 2, Sch 2, CCR Ord 26, r 5
	In the county court, if the debt is the subject of an instalment order, the warrant may not be issued so long as the payments are up to date	CCA 1984, s 86
	If the payments are in arrears, a warrant can be issued for all or part of the debt then unpaid	CPR 1998, Sch 2, CCR Ord 26, r 1(2)
	The High Court has a general power to stay execution of an order on the ground of matters which have occurred since it was made. The county court has a similar power in the case of monetary orders on the ground of inability to pay, whenever arising	CCA 1984, ss 38, 71(2), 76; CPR 1998, Sch 1, RSC Ord 45, r 11
	A county court order other than for periodical payments or arrears thereof may be transferred to the High Court and enforced as a High Court order. The application is made to the county court without notice, accompanied by a statement, verified by a statement of truth, of the amount due under the order and showing how that amount is arrived at. The transfer has immediate effect	FPR 2010, r 33.4

Issue	*High Court* The applicant files a statement, verified by a statement of truth, showing the amount due and how it is calculated and a praecipe together with the form of writ for sealing; he then sends the writ to the sheriffs' lodgement centre	FPR 2010, r 33.3; CPR 1998, Sch 1, RSC Ord 46, r 6
	County court The applicant files a statement, verified by a statement of truth, showing how the amount due and any interest claimed are calculated, together with a further copy of the interest calculation and a form of request for the issue of the warrant	FPR 2010, r 33.3; CPR 1998, Sch 2, CCR Ord 26, r 1
Fee	*High Court* £60 (NB a further fee is payable to the enforcement officer)	FPFO 2008, fee 14.1
	County court £100	FPFO 2008, fee 12.1
Debtor's address	It is for the creditor to provide the address of the debtor. In case of difficulty, assistance may sometimes be obtained from certain Government departments	FPR PD6C
	However, it may be necessary to obtain a High Court order authorising the disclosure	*President's Office Guidance of November 2003*
Form	*High Court* Praecipe in Form PF86; Writ in Form Nos 53 to 63	
	County court Request in Form N323	
Appeals	Application for leave or for stay, see Guide E2	

C9: Application for a Third Party Debt Order

Procedure

Availability	The judgment creditor must have a money judgment against the judgment debtor and money must be owed to the judgment debtor by a third party who is or carries on business within England and Wales. The money judgment must be immediately enforceable, i e one that has not been stayed; where the date for payment has passed; or at least one instalment has not been paid under any instalment order	CPR 1998, r 72.1(1)

	There is no longer a requirement that the amount due to the applicant must exceed £50, but the order is discretionary and may be refused, for example if the administrative costs to which the third party is entitled in complying with the order are out of proportion with the judgment debt. A third-party debt order may not be made against the Crown	
Which court	The application is made to the court in which the judgment was given or to which the case has since been transferred	CPR 1998, r 72.3(1)(b)
Application	By filing in the court office, an application notice in Form N349, verified by a statement of truth and containing the following information:	CPR 1998, r 72.3

(1) the name and address of the judgment debtor;

(2) details of the judgment or order sought to be enforced;

(3) the amount of money remaining due under the judgment or order;

(4) if the judgment debt is payable by instalments, the amount of any instalments that have fallen due and remain unpaid;

(5) the name and address of the third party;

(6) if the third party is a bank or building society –

(a) its name and the address of the branch at which the judgment debtor's account is believed to be held; and
(b) the account number;

(7) confirmation that to the best of the judgment creditor's knowledge or belief the third party –
(a) is within the jurisdiction; and
(b) owes money to or holds money to the credit of the judgment debtor

(8) if the judgment creditor knows or believes that any person other than the judgment debtor has any claim to the money owed by the third party –
(a) his name and (if known) his address; and
(b) such information as is known to the judgment creditor about his claim

(9) details of any other applications for third party debt orders issued by the judgment creditor in respect of the same judgment debt; and

	(10) the source or grounds of the judgment creditor's knowledge or belief of the matters referred to in (7), (8) and (9)	
	While the Practice Direction does not explicitly require this, it is good practice to set out how the amount remaining due is arrived at, by analogy with FPR 2010, r 33.3(1)(a)	
	The application is not normally served on the judgment debtor	CPR PD72, para 1.2
Interim third party debt order	The master or district judge may make an interim third party debt order: (a) fixing a hearing date, not less than 28 days ahead, to consider whether to make a final third party debt order ("the final hearing"); and	CPR 1998, r 72.4(2)(a),(5)
	(b) directing that until the hearing the third party must not make any payment that reduces the amount that he owes to the judgment debtor to less than the figure specified in the order	CPR 1998, r 72.4(2)(b)
	The amount specified will be the amount remaining due under the judgment, together with the fixed costs allowable to the judgment creditor for making the application	CPR PD72, para 2
	The order becomes binding on the third party when it is served on him	CPR 1998, r 72.4(4)
Service of the order	*On the third party* The order may be served by the court or by the judgment creditor (who might wish to deliver it immediately, rather than wait for the court to post it). It must be served not less than 21 days before the date of the hearing	CPR 1998, r 72.5(1)(a)
	On the judgment debtor The order may be served by the court or by the judgment creditor. It must be served not less than 7 days after service on the third party and not less than 7 days before the date of the hearing	CPR 1998, r 72.5(1)(b)
	The order must be served in accordance with CPR 1998, Pt 6	
	If served by the judgment creditor, he must file a certificate of service not less than 2 days before the hearing or produce the certificate at the hearing	CPR 1998, r 72.5(2)
	If the third party is a company, it may be served by posting it to the registered office	Companies Act 1985, s 725
	Banks or building societies If the third party is a bank or building society, it must carry out a search immediately to identify any accounts held with it by the judgment debtor	CPR 1998, r 72.6(1)

	Unless otherwise ordered, this will not include accounts where the judgment debtor is not the sole account holder	CPR PD72, paras 3.1, 3.2
	In respect of each account identified, the bank or building society must within 7 days of service inform the court and the judgment creditor:	
	(a) of the number of each account;	
	(b) whether it is in credit;	
	(c) if it is in credit, whether the balance is sufficient to cover the amount specified in the order; or, if the amount is insufficient, the credit balance at the date of service; and	
	(d) if the bank or building society claims to be entitled to retain the money, details of that claim	CPR 1998, r 72.6(2)
	Alternatively, the bank or building society must inform the court and the judgment creditor within 7 days of service:	
	(a) that the judgment debtor does not hold an account with the bank or building society; or	
	(b) that it is unable to comply with the order for any other reason, for example that the information given is insufficient positively to identify the judgment debtor as the holder of a particular account	CPR 1998, r 72.6(3)
	The rules do not require banks or building societies to give the information in writing	
	Other third parties	
	Third parties who are not banks or building societies must inform the court and the judgment creditor in writing if they claim –	
	(a) not to owe money to the judgment debtor; or	
	(b) to owe less than the amount specified in the order	CPR 1998, r 72.6(4)
Hardship order	Pending the final hearing, a judgment debtor may apply for a hardship payment order if the following conditions are satisfied:	
	(a) he is an individual;	
	(b) he is prevented from withdrawing money from his bank or building society as a result of an interim third party debt order; and	
	(c) as a result he or his family is suffering hardship in meeting ordinary living expenses	CPR 1998, r 72.7(1)
	A judgment debtor may only apply to one court for a hardship payment order	CPR 1998, r 72.7(3)

	If the interim order was made in the High Court, the application may be made either at the Royal Courts of Justice or at any district registry	CPR 1998, r 72.7(2)(a)
	If the interim order was made in a county court, the application may be made at *any* county court	CPR 1998, r 72.7(2)(b)
	Application is made by filing an application notice, quoting the case number and the court that made the interim order, verified by a statement of truth and setting out detailed evidence explaining why a hardship payment is needed. Documentary evidence, such as bank statements, wage slips, or mortgage statements should be included	CPR 1998, r 72.7(4)(a),(b); PD72, paras 5.1, 5.6
	The application will be dealt with at the court to which it is made	CPR PD72, paras 5.2, 5.3(1)
	The court in which the interim order has been made will send copies of the original application notice for the third party debt order and the interim order to the court dealing with the hardship application	CPR PD72, para 5.3(2)
	Unless the court otherwise orders, the judgment creditor must be given 2 days' notice of the hearing but the application need not be served on the third party	CPR 1998, r 72.7(5)
	In case of exceptional urgency the court may deal with the application without notice. If so, then wherever possible the judgment creditor will be informed of the application and given an opportunity to make representations by telephone, fax or other means of communication	CPR PD72, para 5.5
	A hardship payment order is directed to the third party and will permit one or more payments out of the account and may specify to whom those payments are to be made (for example by honouring standing order mandates)	CPR 1998, r 72.7(6)
Transfer at the debtor's request	If the judgment debtor wishes to oppose the application for a final order, he may apply for the application to be transferred to the court for the district in which he resides or carries on business, or another court	CPR PD72, para 4
Notice of objection etc	If either the third party or the judgment debtor wishes to object to the final order, he must file and serve written evidence setting out the grounds of his objection not less than 3 days before the hearing	CPR 1998, r 72.8(1),(4)

	If either the third party or the judgment debtor knows or believes that any other person has a claim to the money specified in the interim order, he must file and serve written evidence stating his knowledge of that matter not less than 3 days before the hearing	CPR 1998, r 72.8(4)
	If the judgment creditor wishes to dispute a claim by a third party other than a bank or building society, either that it does not owe money to the judgment debtor or that the amount owing is less than the amount specified in the order, he must file and serve written evidence setting out his grounds for disputing the third party's claim not less than 3 days before the hearing	CPR 1998, r 72.8(3),(4)
	If the court is notified that some other person may have a claim to the money specified in the interim order it will serve notice on that person of the application and the date of hearing	CPR 1998, r 72.8(5)
Hearing	The court may, if the third party does not attend or dispute his indebtedness to the debtor, make a final third party debt order	CPR 1998, r 72.8(6)(a)
	The court may discharge the interim third party debt order and dismiss the application	CPR 1998, r 72.8(6)(b)
	The court may dispose summarily of issues in dispute between the parties and any other person claiming the money specified in the order and either make a final third party debt order or discharge the interim third party debt order and dismiss the application	CPR 1998, r 72.8(6)(c)
	If it is unable to dispose of the issues summarily, the court may direct the trial of an issue and give further directions	CPR 1998, r 72.8(6)(d)
Effect of final order	The final third party debt order requires the third party to pay to the creditor the lesser of:	
	(a) the amount of the debt due from the garnishee to the debtor (except the last £1 in an account with a Building Society or Credit Union), less any costs allowed to the third party and expenses of £55 if it is a deposit-taking institution; or	CPR 1998, r 72.2(1); SCA 1981, s 40A
	(b) the amount of the debt due from the debtor to the creditor together with any costs allowed to the creditor	CCA 1984, s 109
	The order is enforceable against the third party as any other order for payment of money may be enforced	CPR 1998, r 72.9(1)

	To the extent of the payment made or enforced against him (but not enforcement costs) under the terms of the final third party debt order, the third party is discharged from his liability to the debtor	CPR 1998, r 72.9(2)
Fee	On application: High Court and county court – £100 for each third party against whom the order is sought	FPFO 2008, fee 10.2
Forms	Application for third party debt order – Form N349 Application for hardship payment order – Form N244	

C10: Committal by way of Judgment Summons

Legal background

The court's usual powers to commit for contempt of court a person who disobeys an order do not apply in the case of an order to pay money. Instead, the court may imprison for up to 6 weeks (and no longer: *Zuk v Zuk* [2012] EWCA Civ 1871) a person who has been ordered to pay maintenance (including a lump sum), who has or has had the means to pay it and who neglects or refuses or has neglected or refused to do so. However, this special procedure does not change the character of the disobedience as contempt of court. The contemnor may be subjected to appropriate conditions in relation to other proceedings between the parties (*Mubarak v Mubarik* [2007] 1 FLR 722).

FPR 2010 require the creditor to file and serve in advance his evidence to prove the debtor's means and neglect or refusal. Other procedural requirements reflect the view of judgment summons proceedings expressed in *Mubarak v Mubarak* [2001] 1 FLR 698, CA that they are penal in character.

Procedure

Availability	The remedy is only available in the case of a maintenance order (including a lump sum order)	AJA 1970, s 11, Sch 8
	Permission is required if it is sought to enforce arrears more than 12 months old under a financial provision or similar order. The application for permission may be combined with the summons, the prescribed forms including such an application for use if required	MCA 1973, s 32; CPA 2004, Sch 5, para 63
	Permission of the court is required before the summons is issued if the debtor is in default under a committal order made on an earlier judgment summons	FPR 2010, r 33.11
	A committal order will not be made unless refusal or neglect to pay, notwithstanding the means to pay, is proved	DA 1869, s 5; *Mubarak v Mubarik* [2007] 1 FLR 722 at [71]

Which court	The High Court may hear a judgment summons to enforce a High Court maintenance order; the county court may hear a judgment summons to enforce a High Court or a county court maintenance order	
	The specific court may be chosen by the judgment creditor having regard to the place where the debtor resides or carries on business and irrespective of the court in which the original order was made	FPR 2010, r 33.10(1)
Application	The application must be filed in the appropriate court together with a statement, verified by a statement of truth, which states the amount due under the order, shows how that amount is arrived at, and contains all the evidence on which the judgment creditor intends to rely	
	If interest is claimed, the statement should set out how it is calculated	FPR 2010, r 33.10(2)
Fee	High Court and county court: £100	FPFO 2008, fee 10.4
Service	The judgment summons is issued by the court and must be served, together with the statement referred to in r 33.10(2), not less than 14 days before the hearing; travelling expenses must be paid or tendered	FPR 2010, r 33.11
	It is for the creditor to provide the address of the debtor. In case of difficulty, assistance may sometimes be obtained from certain Government departments	FPR PD6C
	However, it may be necessary to obtain a High Court order authorising the disclosure	*President's Office Guidance of November 2003*
Evidence	The evidence adduced by the creditor must prove beyond reasonable doubt that the debtor has or has had the means to pay and that he has neglected or refused or is neglecting or refusing to pay	FPR 2010, r 33.14(1)(c)
Debtor's attendance	If the debtor fails to attend, the court may order him to attend an adjourned hearing and, if he disobeys, commit him for up to 14 days	CCA 1984, s 110; CPR 1998, Sch 2, CCR Ord 28, r 4
	However, as the proceedings are penal in character, the debtor cannot be compelled to give evidence	FPR 2010, r 33.14(2)
	If the judge is satisfied that the judgment summons and evidence have been duly served, he may be prepared to proceed in the debtor's absence	

Order	If satisfied of his neglect or refusal to pay, the judge may commit the debtor to prison for up to 6 weeks, but may and usually will suspend the order on condition that he makes payment (by instalments or otherwise)	DA 1869, s 5; FPR 2010, r 33.16(2)
	Alternatively, the judge may make a new order for payment	FPR 2010, r 33.16(1)
Form	Request in Form D62	
Appeals	See Guide E5	

PART I

C11: Means of Payment Order

Legal background

The court may order the debtor to make the required payments by standing order or by direct debit, and to open an account for the purpose.

Procedure

Availability	The order to be enforced must be a "qualifying periodical maintenance order", i e one made when the debtor was ordinarily resident in England and Wales; it includes a lump sum order if the sum is payable by instalments	MEA 1991, s 1(2),(10)
	Any interested party may apply. If the order is sought to enforce arrears more than 12 months old, permission must be obtained (but may be requested in the same application)	MCA 1973, s 32
	An order may be made when the maintenance order is made or at any time thereafter, on application or (in the course of any proceedings concerning the maintenance order) of the court's own initiative; similarly, the court may revoke, suspend, revive or vary such an order	MEA 1991, s 1(1),(3),(7)
	An order to open an account cannot be made until the debtor has been given an opportunity to do so voluntarily	MEA 1991, s 1(6)
Application	In the course of proceedings concerning the maintenance order, the court will generally consider an oral invitation to exercise its powers, but it must (if practicable) give every interested party the opportunity to make representations; if a party is absent, this may necessitate an adjournment so that notice can be given	MEA 1991, s 1(8)

	Otherwise, the application is to the district judge on notice and, if some other application is pending, may conveniently be made so as to be returnable on the same occasion	FPR 2010, rr 18.1–18.5, 18.7, 18.8
	The creditor must file a statement, verified by a statement of truth, of the amount due under the order and showing how that amount is arrived at	FPR 2010, r 33.3
Fee	£90 (NB it appears that no fee is payable if the order is made of the court's own initiative)	FPFO 2008, fee 4.3
Debtor's address	It is for the creditor to provide the address of the debtor. In case of difficulty, assistance may sometimes be obtained from certain Government departments	FPR PD6C
	However, it may be necessary to obtain a High Court order authorising the disclosure	*President's Office Guidance of November 2003*
Appeals	See Guides E2, E4 and E5	

C12: Obtaining Information from the Debtor and Seeking "Such Method of Enforcement as the Court Considers Appropriate"

Legal background

The court may order the debtor to attend and be cross-examined as to his means to pay the amount ordered or otherwise to comply with the order if it is not for payment of money. This procedure, while not itself an enforcement measure, is a valuable aid to enforcement.

CPR 1998, Pt 71, which applies to family proceedings, amalgamates and modifies provisions formerly contained in RSC Ord 48 and CCR Ord 25, r 3.

Under FPR 2010, r 33.3(2)(b), application may be made for "an order for such means of enforcement as the court may consider appropriate". If an application is made under that paragraph, an order to attend court will be issued and CPR 1998, r 71.2(6),(7) will apply. Accordingly, the provision is considered in this Procedural Guide.

Procedure

Availability	The person who obtained the order may apply for an order for the debtor to attend for questioning at any time after the judgment or order has become enforceable	CPR 1998, r 71.1
	He may also apply for an order for such means of enforcement as the court may consider appropriate	FPR 2010, r 33.3(2)(b)

	Either application is made to the court that made the order that it is sought to enforce, unless the proceedings have been transferred to another court, in which case the application is made to that court	CPR 1998, r 71.2(2)(b)(i)
Application	The application is made by filing an application notice without notice to the judgment debtor	CPR 1998, r 71.2(2)(a)
	The notice must:	
	state the name and address of the judgment debtor;	
	identify the order that it is sought to enforce;	
	be accompanied by a statement, verified by a statement of truth, of the amount due under the order and showing how that amount is arrived at;	FPR 2010, r 33.3(1)
	identify particular matters about which questions are to be asked;	
	if the judgment creditor wishes particular documents to be produced, identify them;	CPR PD71, para 1.2
	if the judgment creditor wishes the questioning to be before a judge, specify that request and the reasons for it. If an application has been made under FPR 2010, r 33.3(2)(b), the questioning should take place before a judge;	CPR 1998, r 71.6(2) ; PD71 para 2.2
	where the questioning is to be conducted by a court officer and the judgment creditor wishes specific questions to be asked, a list of them should be attached to the application notice	CPR PD71, para 4.2(2)
Fee	High Court and county court: £50	FPFO 2008, fee 10.1
Order	The order requires the debtor to attend at a court office on a specified appointment and to submit to cross-examination. Unless otherwise ordered by a judge, the debtor will be directed to attend the county court for the district in which he resides or carries on business	CPR PD71, para 2.1
Service	The order must be served personally on the debtor not less than 14 days before the hearing	CPR 1998, r 71.3
	Service may be effected by the creditor, by a High Court enforcement officer (at the creditor's expense) or by a county court bailiff (if the debtor is an individual litigant)	

	The court may order service by an alternative method but as failure to attend may render the debtor liable to imprisonment, convincing evidence will be required both that personal service is impracticable and that the debtor will become aware of the order in time to comply	CPR 1998, rr 6.15, 6.27
	Within 7 days of service the debtor may request the judgment creditor to pay him a reasonable sum to cover his travelling expenses; the judgment creditor must comply with any such request	CPR 1998, rr 71.4(1),(2)
Affidavits	Where the judgment creditor has been responsible for service an affidavit must be sworn and filed evidencing how and when the order was served	CPR 1998, r 71.4(1)(a),(b)
	In any event, affidavits must be sworn and filed:	CPR 1998, r 71.4(1)(c)
	evidencing that no request for travelling expenses has been received, or that if such a request has been received it has been complied with;	
	stating how much of the judgment debt remains unpaid	
	NB the amount unpaid must here be verified by affidavit, not a statement of truth	
Examination	Normally conducted by a senior member of the court staff, who will put standard questions to the debtor. This may not be appropriate in family proceedings; if the questioning is conducted by the district judge, the creditor or his representative must attend to question the debtor	CPR PD71, para 4.1; CPR 1998 r 71.6(3)(b)
Failure to attend	If the judgment debtor fails to attend; refuses to take the oath; refuses to answer any questions; otherwise fails to comply with the order, eg by failing to produce documents he has been ordered to produce the judge or court officer conducting the hearing will certify the manner in which the order has not been complied with	CPR PD71, para 6; CPR 1998 r 71.8(1)
	The matter will then be referred to a High Court or circuit judge	CPR 1998 r 71.8(2)
	The judge may make a suspended committal order against the debtor, but this should not be regarded as routine	*Broomleigh HA v Okonkwo* [2010] EWCA Civ 1113
	Any committal order will be suspended on terms that the person named in the order:	
	(a) attends court for a further appointment at the time and place specified;	CPR 1998 r 71.8(4)

(b) complies with the terms of the order and of the original order

If the suspended committal order has been duly served and the judgment debtor fails to attend on the further appointment, the judge or court officer conducting the hearing will certify in writing his failure to attend — CPR PD71, para 8.1

Similarly, if the judgment debtor attends but fails to comply (e g by refusing to be sworn or answer questions), the judge or court officer will so certify in writing — CPR PD71, para 8.2

In either case, on the basis of that certificate, the court will then issue a warrant for the arrest of the judgment debtor to be brought before a judge, who may be a master or district judge, and who will consider whether the committal order should be discharged or put into effect — CPR 1998 r 71.8(4); PD71, paras 8.3, 8.4

In practice, the person arrested will be offered the opportunity to purge his contempt by complying with the original order to provide information. If he complies, the suspended committal order will be discharged

If he declines the opportunity the court must proceed immediately to consider whether or not the committal order should be discharged or put into effect

At this point, to comply with HRA 1998 the person arrested must be given details in writing of his alleged contempt and be offered the opportunity both to have legal representation and to challenge the evidence against him. An adjournment may be essential, for example if the person arrested wishes to challenge the evidence of service either of the original order or the suspended committal order or the contents of a certificate of non-attendance — *Newman v Modern Bookbinders* [2000] 1 WLR 2559; *Hammerton v Hammerton* [2007] 2 FLR 1133

Further proceedings — Where an application has been made for "such method of enforcement as the court may consider appropriate" the judge who has conducted the questioning may proceed to make an appropriate order: see Guides C5, C6, C8, C9 and C11. Committal by way of judgment summons will not be appropriate because a debtor facing a judgment summons cannot be compelled to give evidence — FPR 2010, r 33.14(2)

Appeals — See Guide E2

C13: Writ or Warrant of Possession of Land

Legal background

In the High Court, a writ of possession is issued to an enforcement officer (formerly the sheriff) and, in the county court, a possession warrant is issued to the bailiff, requiring him physically to take possession of the land (and buildings) and give it to the person in whose favour the order was made.

Procedure

Availability	In the High Court, leave is generally required	CPR 1998, Sch 1, RSC Ord 45, r 3(2), Ord 46, r 2
	In the county court, leave is required if more than 6 years have elapsed since the order or if there has been a change of parties	CPR 1998, Sch 2, CCR Ord 26, r 5
	Otherwise, the person in whose favour the order is made may issue the writ or warrant as soon as it is made or, if it allows a time for compliance, as soon as that time has expired	
	The High Court has a general power to stay execution of an order on the ground of matters which have occurred since it was made. The county court has a similar power in the case of monetary orders on the ground of inability to pay, whenever arising	CCA 1984, ss 38, 76; CPR 1998, Sch 1, RSC Ord 45, r 11
Application for leave	In the High Court, the application for leave is made by summons to the district judge if the possession order was conditional, if 6 years have elapsed since it was made or if the person against whom it is to be enforced has changed; otherwise, ex parte by affidavit, which must give details of any occupiers other than the defendant and of any tenancies held by them	CPR 1998, Sch 1, RSC Ord 46, r 4
	In the county court, the application (when needed) is made ex parte by affidavit or witness statement, although the district judge may require notice to be given	CPR 1998, Sch 2, CCR Ord 26, rr 5(2), 17(6)
Issue	*High Court* The applicant files a praecipe together with the form of writ for sealing, and then sends the writ to a High Court Enforcement Officer	CPR 1998, Sch 1, RSC Ord 46, r 6
	County court The applicant files a form of request for the issue of the warrant	CPR 1998, Sch 2, CCR Ord 26, r 1
Fee	*High Court* £60 (NB a further fee is payable to the enforcement officer)	FPFO 2008, fee 14.1
	County court £110	FPFO 2008, fee 12.3

	No further court fee is payable if the writ or warrant is issued also to recover money	
Forms	*High Court* Praecipe in Form PF88 or 89; writ in Form No 66 *County court* Request in Form N325	
Appeals	Application for leave or for stay, see Guide E2	

C14: Writ of Sequestration

Legal background

In the High Court, the person in whose favour an order has been made may issue a writ of sequestration requiring the sequestrators named to take possession of all the assets of the person against whom it was made if he has not complied with it. The remedy is appropriate in circumstances where committal for contempt might be imposed, save that the restrictions on the court's power to commit for non-compliance with an order to pay money do not apply to sequestration. The county court also may exercise this remedy, but it is usually considered more appropriate to transfer a county court order to the High Court and make the application there.

Procedure

Availability	Leave is always required and is generally only granted in the largest cases, in view of the considerable expense involved	CPR 1998, r 81.26
Application	In the High Court, by application to a single judge of the relevant Division In any other case (e g in the county court), to a single judge of the Queen's Bench Division NB The application must be supported by an affidavit or affidavits	CPR 1998, r 81.26
Fee	£90	FPFO 2008, fee 4.3
Service	The application notice and a copy of the affidavit must usually be served personally	CPR 1998, r 81.26(4)
Form	No form is prescribed for the application notice or affidavit; writ of sequestration in Form No 67	CPR 1998, r 81.27
Appeals	See Guide E5	

C15: Committal and Arrest for Disobedience of an Injunctive Order or Breach of an Undertaking in the High Court, County Court or Magistrates' Court

Legal background

An injunctive order (including a non-molestation order or occupation order under FLA 1996, Pt IV; a CA 1989, s 8 order to which a penal notice has been attached; and an order under PHA 1997) directing a person to do an act at or within a specified time, or to abstain from doing an act, or an undertaking to like effect which incorporates a penal warning notice, may be enforced by committal proceedings initiated by the person entitled to the benefit of the direction or undertaking. Any undertaking for the payment of money that has effect as if it was an order made under Matrimonial Causes Act 1973, Pt II may be enforced as if it was an order and FPR 2010, Pt 33 applies (FPR PD33A). Some money orders may be enforceable by judgment summons under the Debtors Acts 1869 and 1878 (see Guide C10). Personal service of an injunctive order is required by CPR 1998, r 81.5 and FPR 2010, r 10.6. The court can dispense with service or provide for some other form of service, but an injunction cannot be enforced unless it can be proved that the person to whom it was directed knew about the order and, where an act is directed to be done, the order must have been served before the time set for the act to be done. "Any procedural defect in the commencement or conduct by the applicant of a committal application may be waived by the court if satisfied that no injustice has been caused to the respondent by the defect" (*Nicholls v Nicholls* [1997] 1 FLR 649; CPR PD81, para 16.2). However, grave procedural errors will result in the findings and sentences being quashed (*Hammerton v Hammerton* [2007] 2 FLR 1133).

Which rules of court?

Applications for committal in respect of injunctive orders are interlocutory in nature (*Savings and Investment Bank v Gasco Investments (Netherlands) BV (No 2)* [1988] Ch 422). Consequently, if the injunctive order was made in family proceedings an application for committal is made in family proceedings and is governed by FPR 2010. In civil proceedings, committal proceedings are now governed by CPR 1998, Pt 81. However, Pt 81 does not apply to family proceedings. If the injunctive order was made in non-family civil proceedings, e g under PHA 1997, then CPR 1998 apply.

Committal proceedings begun by notice to show good reason

The standard procedure for beginning proceedings for committal for enforcement of an injunction or an undertaking is by way of notice to show good reason why an order for committal should not be made, begun by application notice or Pt 8 claim form (High Court), Form N78 (county court) or FL418 (magistrates' court).

Committal proceedings begun by arrest under a power of arrest

The power to arrest, for breach of an occupation order granted under FLA 1996, s 47(3) or for breach of a forced marriage protection order granted under FLA 1996, s 63I(2), provides the police with authority to intervene and stop a breach while it is happening or where they have reason to believe that such a breach has occurred. A power of arrest can also be exercised after the disobedience has ended and after an arrest for a criminal offence (*Wheeldon v Wheeldon* [1998] 1 FLR 463). Where the police use the civil power of arrest the arrested person must be brought before the civil court within 24 hours (FLA 1996, s 47(7)). Breach of a non-molestation order in Form 404a made after 30 June 2007 is a criminal offence in respect of which the police may use their criminal powers of arrest.

There is no power to attach a power of arrest to an injunction under the PHA 1997 or at common law. Further, as from 1 July 2007, the power of arrest is abolished for non-molestation orders (see FLA 1996, s 42A).

Committal proceedings begun by arrest under a warrant of arrest

FLA 1996, s 47(8),(9) extended to the High Court and county courts a power previously available only in family proceedings courts. This power is available where no power of arrest was attached to the breached direction (s 47(8)). The court can issue a warrant for the arrest of a person where the court has reasonable grounds, substantiated on oath (s 47(9)), to believe that he has failed to comply with a non-molestation or occupation order made under FLA 1996, Pt IV.

PHA 1997, s 3(3)–(5) provides the High Court and county courts with the power to issue a warrant of arrest where the court has reasonable grounds, substantiated on oath (s 3(5)), to believe that the respondent has failed to comply with an injunction which forbids harassment.

Remand following arrest

Once an arrested respondent is before the court, the court can immediately deal with the breach for which he has been arrested or adjourn (whether or not upon enlarged injunctive provisions). If adjourning, the court may remand. In FLA 1996 cases the power to remand is given to the High Court and county courts by s 47(11) and Sch 5, and exists in a magistrates' court by virtue of MCA 1980, ss 128 and 129. The remand can be in custody or on bail. Under FLA 1996, s 48, the power to remand can be exercised to enable a medical report to be made on the respondent.

There is no power to remand under PHA 1997.

Conduct of committal proceedings where the respondent is before the court following an arrest – preliminaries

Where a respondent is before the court for an alleged breach of an injunction, in order to ensure a fair trial there are essential preliminaries which the judge will consider. Is the respondent before the court within 24 hours of the arrest and is a lawful arrest admitted or proved? Is there proof of service of the injunction? Have the alleged breaches been reduced to writing and is Form N78 required? Is the respondent represented and, if not, does he seek an adjournment to obtain it or require time to prepare? Does he appreciate that he may be entitled to legal aid? Is the applicant present or represented and, if not, is an adjournment required? If adjourning, what directions are required and should the respondent be remanded? If remanded, should it be on bail or in custody?

An arrest is effected on the basis of a particular alleged breach. Earlier breaches cannot be dealt with unless Form N78 is also served (see FPR 2010, r 10.11 and, in the case of PHA 1997, CPR 1998, r 65.29).

Conduct of committal proceedings when the respondent is before the court, whether on notice or following an arrest

Whether the respondent appears on notice in answer to a notice to show good reason, or following an arrest, the procedure to be followed for the determination of whether the respondent has disobeyed an order or breached an undertaking, and the disposal powers of the court, are the same. The breach must be proved to the criminal standard of proof. Thus, if not admitted, the applicant's evidence is heard first.

Absence of respondent

Provided that the court is satisfied that the respondent has been duly served, and has had the opportunity to obtain legal advice, the court can proceed in his absence. In *Begum v Anam* [2004] EWCA Civ 578 a committal order was set aside as the respondent had not had the opportunity to obtain legal representation nor to arrange a production warrant to secure his attendance from prison.

Penalties

The court can order imprisonment (immediate or suspended) and/or a fine, or adjourn consideration of penalty for a fixed period and/or extend or enlarge the injunction. The common disposal orders are set out in county court Form N79 and family proceedings court Form FL419.

Procedure

Preliminary matters	An injunctive order must be served personally on the person to whom it is directed, unless there has been an order for substituted service or dispensing with service	CPR 1998, r 81.5 (civil) Sch 2, CCR Ord 29, r 1(2) (family)
	However, pending service, if the respondent disobeys an injunctive order which requires him to abstain from doing an act, the court can impose a penalty if it is satisfied that he knew about the terms of the order	CPR 1998, r 81.8 (civil) Sch 2, CCR Ord 29, r 1(2)(a) (family)
	Proof of service of the order is required. In all courts this is usually by Form FL415. Service should be effected in accordance with the Protocol	Family Justice Council *Protocol for Process Servers*, November 2011
	A mandatory injunctive order directing a person to do an act cannot be enforced unless it was served before the time at or by which the act was directed to be done	CPR 1998, r 81.5 (civil) Sch 2, CCR Ord 29, r 1(2)(b) (family)
	An undertaking becomes enforceable on being given to and accepted by the court; however, the court can require the giver to sign a statement to the effect that he understands the terms of his undertaking and the consequences of failure to comply with it	*Hussain v Hussain* [1986] 2 FLR 271; CPR PD81, para 2.2
	A copy of the undertaking in Form N117 in a county court, D787 in the Principal Registry or FL422 in a family proceedings court, is required to be delivered to the giver of the undertaking, but the giver is bound even if he does not receive a copy	CPR 1998, r 81.7 (civil) Sch 2, CCR Ord 29, r 1A (family)
Who may apply for committal or enforcement?	Person in whose favour the injunctive order was granted or the undertaking was given	CPR 1998, r 81.3 (civil) Sch 2, CCR Ord 29, r 1(4) (family)
Which court?	The court which granted the injunctive order or undertaking	CPR PD81, para 10 (civil); CPR PDCommittal, paras 1.2, 1.3 (family)
	The powers of county courts to deal with disobedience or breach are the same as the High Court	Contempt of Court Act 1981; CCA 1984, s 38
	Magistrates' courts statutory powers to deal with disobedience or breach are limited to imposing immediate or suspended committal, fine or adjourning consideration of penalty	MCA 1980, s 63(3); FLA 1996, s 50(1)

Application by notice to show good reason (family proceedings)	In the High Court, by Pt 8 claim form supported by an affidavit In a county court, by application notice or request for notice, supported by affidavit, for issue of notice in Form N78. A draft Form N78 is usually accepted as the application In a magistrates' court, by request, supported by statement declaring the facts recited are true, for issue of notice in Form FL 418. The request is usually a draft Form N418 In every case, the summons or notice must "identify, separately and numerically, each alleged act of contempt"	FPR 2010, r 33.1; CPR 1998, Sch 1, RSC Ord 52, r 4; CPR PDCommittal, paras 2, 3; N244 CPR 1998, Sch 2, CCR Ord 29, r 1(4),(4A); CPR PDCommittal, paras 2.2, 2.5, 3.1 CPR PDCommittal, para 2.5(2)
Committal applications (civil proceedings)	Application under CPR 1998, Pt 23, supported by affidavit	CPR 1998, r 81.10
Committal applications (general)	The affidavit or statement in support should narrate the facts relied on, but the list of alleged breaches must be given in the summons, application notice, Pt 8 claim form or notice to show good reason, as appropriate Fee on application in family proceedings in High Court or county court: £90 No fee payable in magistrates' court	CPR 1998, r 81.10 (civil)· Sch 2, CCR Ord 29, r 1(4A) (family); *Harmsworth v Harmsworth* [1988] 1 FLR 349 at [354D]–[355B] FPFO 2008, fee 4.3
Application for warrant of arrest under FLA 1996, s 47(8) or s 63J	Application is made, without notice to the respondent, in Form FL408, to "the relevant judicial authority", ie the convenient court in whichever tier of court the injunctive order was granted The application must be substantiated on oath and the court must have reasonable grounds for believing that the respondent has failed to comply with an order, or part of an order to which no power of arrest had been attached Breach of a non-molestation order is a criminal offence. However, the respondent cannot be both punished for a criminal offence and a contempt of court for the same breach. An application for a warrant of arrest to a civil court should confirm that there is no conviction The warrant is executed in the High Court by the Tipstaff, in the county court by the bailiffs (or, in each case, by the police on request), and in the magistrates' court by the police	FLA 1996, ss 47(8), 63(1) and 63J FLA 1996, s 47(9), s 63J FLA 1996, s 42A(3),(4) Form FL408

PART I

	In the magistrates' court the justices' clerk is responsible for delivering the warrant to the police	
Application for warrant of arrest under PHA 1997, s 3(3)	Application must be made in accordance with CPR Pt 23 and may be made without notice	PHA 1997, s 3(4); CPR 1998, r 65.29
	The application must be supported by affidavit evidence setting out the grounds for the application and state whether the claimant has informed the police and whether criminal proceedings are being pursued	PHA 1997, s 3(5); CPR 1998, r 65.29
Production in court following arrest under FLA 1996, s 47 or s 63I	A person arrested under a power of arrest must be brought before the relevant judicial authority within 24 hours not including Sunday, Christmas Day or Good Friday	FLA 1996, s 47(7), s 63I
	Neither FLA 1996 nor the rules prescribe how soon a person arrested under a warrant of arrest must be brought before the court. Nevertheless it must be as soon as practicable	FLA 1996, s 47(8)–(10), s 63J
Procedures open to court under FLA 1996, ss 47, 48 when arrested person produced in court and under ss 63I–63M	The court may hear the facts upon which the arrest was based, and decide penalty or adjourn, in which case the respondent must be given not less than 2 days' notice of the adjourned hearing, or	FLA 1996, s 47(7)(b), (10); FPR 2010, r 10.11(3)
	remand in custody for a period not exceeding 8 days or	FLA 1996, ss 47(11), 63K, Sch 5 para 2(5)
	remand on bail on conditions and/or recognisances	FLA 1996, s 47(11),(12), Sch 5 para 2(5)
	where the court has reason to suspect mental illness or severe mental impairment, the court may remand, to enable a medical examination and report, for not more than 3 weeks if in custody or 4 weeks if on bail	FLA 1996, s 48, s 63L
Powers of court under PHA 1997, s 3(5) when arrested person produced in court	The court may hear the facts upon which the arrest was based, and decide penalty, or adjourn for not more than 28 days, in which case the defendant must be given not less than 2 days' notice of the adjourned hearing	CPR 1998, r 65.30
Hearing without notice to the respondent	In exceptional circumstances, the court may, without notice having been given to the respondent, deal with an application begun by notice to show good reason, by dispensing with service of the summons or notice	CPR 1998, rr 39.3, 81.28 (civil), Sch 1, RSC Ord 52, r 4(3); CPR 1998, Sch 2, CCR Ord 29, r 1(7) (family)

	It is not appropriate for a court to proceed without notice where arrest under a power or warrant can be achieved under FLA 1996, s 47, or under PHA 1997, s 3(5). However, where a power or warrant of arrest is not available, proceeding without notice may exceptionally be appropriate. When the court takes this exceptional step and imposes imprisonment, the court should fix a date and time for the contemnor to be brought before the court	CPR 1998, r 81.28 (civil), Sch 2, CCR Ord 29, r 1(8) (family)
Service of application (Form N78) or claim form	Personal service of the Form N78 (or claim form) and affidavit in support, is required at least 2 working days before the hearing	CPR 1998, Sch 1, RSC Ord 52, r 4(2), Sch 2, CCR Ord 29, r 1(4),(4A)
	In civil proceedings under CPR 1998 a period of 14 clear days after service is required unless the court directs otherwise by using its powers to abridge time for service	CPR PD81, para 15.2
	in exceptional cases, the court can dispense with service	see Hearing without notice to the respondent (above)
Service of notice of adjourned hearing	Where a hearing is adjourned, personal service of notice of the adjourned hearing is required, unless the respondent was present in court and was told when and where the adjourned hearing would resume and/or was remanded under FLA 1996, s 47(7),(10), Sch 5 or MCA 1980, ss 128, 129	*Chiltern DC v Keane* [1985] 1 WLR 619 at [622H]–[623C]
Case management	The court can make directions at any time as to service of evidence and conduct of the proceedings, or strike out an inappropriate application	CPR PD81, paras 15, 16 (civil) CPR PDCommittal, paras 4.3, 5 (family)
The hearing	District judges as well as High Court and circuit judges have power to hear committal proceedings under FLA 1996, Parts 4 and 4A	FLA 1996, ss 58, 63(1), 63O, 63S
	However district judges do not have power to hear committal proceedings under PHA 1997	PHA 1997, s 3(3), (4) only gives power to issue a warrant; CPR PDCommittal, para 11
	Normally held in open court, unless it relates to the welfare of a child or to a person suffering from mental disorder. A finding of contempt in private must be announced in public	CPR 1998, rr 39.2, 81.28 (civil), Sch 1, RSC Ord 52, r 6(1); CPR PDCommittal, para 9 (family)
	If it is just to do so, the court can proceed if the respondent, having been duly served, fails to attend	*Begum v Anam* [2004] EWCA Civ 578; CPR 1998, r 39.3

	Committal proceedings, although technically civil proceedings, are treated as criminal proceedings for the purposes of ECHR, Art 6. Consequently, persons in danger of losing their liberty are, subject to means, eligible for legal aid. (Contempt in the face of the court is separately dealt with in LASPOA 2012, s 14(g).)	LASPOA 2012, Schs 1 and 3. Also, Lord Chancellor's Guidance under s 4
	Procedure is akin to criminal trial. The criminal standard of proof ("beyond reasonable doubt") applies	*Dean v Dean* [1987] 1 FLR 517
	An application notice can be amended with the permission of the court but not otherwise	CPR PD81, paras 12(2), 13.2(2), (civil), CPR PDCommittal, para 2.6(3) (family)
	An alleged contemnor cannot be directed or compelled to give information	CPR 1998, r 81.28 (civil), CPR PDCommittal, paras 6, 7 (family); *Comet Products UK Ltd v Hawkex Plastics Ltd* [1971] 2 QB 67
	A deliberate act or failure to act (actus reus) with knowledge of the terms of the order (mens rea) must be proved	*DG of Fair Trading v Smiths Concrete* [1992] QB 213
Powers of court	The disposal must be proportionate to the seriousness of the contempt, reflect the court's disapproval and be designed to secure compliance in future. The principles of sentencing in the CJA 2003 apply. The judge cannot sentence again for matters already dealt with by the criminal court. The court should briefly explain its reasons for the choice of disposal	*Murray v Robinson* [2006] 1 FLR 365 *Hale v Tanner* [2000] 2 FLR 879; *Lomas v Parle* [2004] 1 FLR 812; *Slade v Slade* [2010] 1 FLR 160
	Committal to prison is appropriate only where no reasonable alternative exists	*Hale v Tanner* (above)
	Imprisonment is restricted to total of 2 years in the High Court or a county court, 2 months in a magistrates' court, and must be for a fixed term	CCA 1981, s 14; MCA 1980, s 63(3)
	Sentence can be suspended or adjourned on terms	FLA 1996, s 50(1); CPR 1998, r 81.29 (civil) Sch 1, RSC Ord 52, r 7(1) (family)
	Any time spent on remand in custody must be taken into account in the sentence	*Kerai v Patel* [2008] 2 FLR 2137
	Person under the age of 21 can be detained under Powers of Criminal Courts (Sentencing) Act 2000, s 96	*R v Selby Justices ex parte Frame* [1992] 1 QB 72
	Person under the age of 18 cannot be committed to any form of detention for contempt of court (but could be prosecuted for breach of a non-molestation order)	*R v Selby Justices* (above); FLA 1996, s 42A

	MHA powers are available	CCA 1981, s 14; MHA 1983, ss 35, 37, 38
	Fine can be imposed	*Hale v Tanner* [2000] 2 FLR 879
	A fresh injunction can be granted	*Coats v Chadwick* [1894] 1 Ch 347
	A power of arrest can be attached, if available, to the injunctive order	*Ansah v Ansah* (1976) FLR Rep 9; FLA 1996, s 47
	Sequestration is available only in the High Court	CPR 1998, rr 81.19–81.27, CPR PD81, paras 6, 7
Form of order	The order must specify "exact details" of each contempt found proved and specify the disposal ordered	*Nguyen v Phung* [1984] FLR 773 at [778C]; *Re C (A Minor) (Contempt)* [1986] 1 FLR 578 at [585A]
	Where sentence is suspended or adjourned, the period of suspension or adjournment and the precise terms for activation must be specified	*Pidduck v Molloy* [1992] 2 FLR 202; CPR 1998, r 81.29 (civil), Sch 1, RSC Ord 52, r 7(1) (family)
	In the High Court, the order is issued in Form A85 and warrant in Form PF303. In a county court, Form N79 and warrant in Form N80. In a magistrates' court, Form FL419 and warrant in Form FL420	
Service of order	Where immediate imprisonment or detention is imposed, the court serves the order	CPR 1998, rr 6.21(2), 81.30 (civil), Sch 2, CCR Ord 29, r 1(5) (family); *Clarke v Clarke* [1990] 2 FLR 115
	Where sentence is suspended, the applicant must serve the order, unless the court directs otherwise	CPR 1998, r 81.29(2) (civil), Sch 1, RSC Ord 52, r 7(2) (family)
Review by Official Solicitor	The court sends a copy of every committal order and relevant details to the Official Solicitor, who reviews the case and may apply or appeal of his own motion or at the contemnor's request	*Lord Chancellor's Direction of 29 May 1963; Secretary's Circular of 28 September 1981*
Discharge of contemnor	A contemnor is entitled to apply to purge his contempt and be discharged from prison	CPR 1998, r 81.31 (civil), Sch 1, RSC Ord 52, r 8(1), Sch 2, CCR Ord 29, r 3(1) (family)
	The application should be made in accordance with CPR 1998, Pt 23 but in practice a letter from the contemnor usually suffices	CPR 1998, Pt 23. See *CJ v Flintshire Borough Council* [2010] 2 FLR 1224

	If the committal was made in civil proceedings, the application notice must be served as soon as practicable after it is filed and at least 3 days before the hearing	CPR 1998, r 23.7(1)
	The contemnor should be in court	*PD of 25 July 1983*
	On an application to purge, the court can say "yes", "no" or "not yet" but may not suspend the remainder of the sentence	*Harris v Harris* [2002] 1 FLR 248
Appeals	See Guide E5	

D1: Consent to Marriage of a Minor

Legal background

MA 1949, s 3(1) and CPA 2004, Sch 2, paras 3, 4 and 10 set out a general rule that those under the age of 18, who are not widows or widowers, may not marry under a superintendent registrar's certificate or a common licence without the consent of the persons mentioned in MA 1949, s 3(1A) or CPA 2004, Sch 2, para 1 (usually the parents but with variations according to circumstances, eg where a residence order is in force or the child is in care). The child can apply to the court if no-one is available to give consent or to give consent instead of any person whose consent is required and who refuses that consent. Application is made under the Pt 19 procedure under FPR 2010, Pt 8, Ch 9.

Procedure

Who may apply	The child who needs the consent to marry	MA 1949, s 3; CPA 2004, Sch 2
Which court	High Court county court for the district in which any applicant or respondent resides or magistrates' court in a commission area in which any applicant or respondent resides	MA 1949, s 3(1)(b),(5); CPA 2004, Sch 2, paras 3.3(3), 4(3), 10(1)
Application	Pt 19 application in High Court, county court or magistrates' court	FPR 2010, rr 8.1, 19.3
	Application may be made without litigation friend	FPR 2010, r 8.42
Fee	High Court or county court: £230	FPFO 2008, fee 1.1
	Magistrates' court: None	MCFO 2008
Respondents	Those refusing consent in the case of an application under MA 1949, s 3(1)(b); CPA 2004, Sch 2, para 4(3)	FPR 2010, r 8.43

Service	Effected 7 days before the hearing (unless otherwise ordered) in a county court or the High Court	FPR 2010, Pt 6
Hearing	High Court and county courts: district judge Magistrates Hearing in private	FPR 2010, r 27.10(1)

D2: Emergency Protection Order

Legal background

An emergency protection order (EPO) may be sought under CA 1989, s 44, to ensure the short-term safety of a child where it appears that the child may be at risk. It can authorise the applicant to remove a child from where he is (e g from his home) to a safe place or to keep him in a safe place (e g a hospital). The maximum duration of an order is generally 8 days in the first instance but there can be one extension for a maximum of 7 days (see CA 1989, s 45). The grounds for making an order differ according to the status of the applicant. All applicants may rely on the ground that there is reasonable cause to believe that the child is likely to suffer significant harm if he is not removed to accommodation provided by or on behalf of the applicant, or does not remain where he is.

Where the applicant is a local authority which is making enquiries under CA 1989, s 47(1)(b), about a child in its area, it can obtain an order on the alternative ground that the enquiries are being frustrated by access to the child being unreasonably refused to a person authorised to seek access to the child and that it has reasonable cause to believe that access to the child is urgently required. Where the applicant is an authorised person, an order can be made on the ground that the applicant is making enquiries into the welfare of a child whom he has reasonable cause to suspect is suffering or is likely to suffer significant harm, that the enquiries are being frustrated by access being unreasonably refused to a person authorised to seek access and that the applicant has reasonable cause to believe that access to the child is urgently required.

Various directions may be given at the same time as an EPO is made (for example, as to medical, psychiatric or other assessment of the child and as to contact with him) and, under CA 1989, s 48, supplementary provisions can also be included in the order requiring another person to disclose information as to the child's whereabouts, authorising the applicant to enter specified premises to search for the child or for another child and authorising a constable to assist in the execution of the EPO.

Section 44A enables the court to include an exclusion requirement in an EPO and to attach a power of arrest to that provision. The purpose of an exclusion requirement is to safeguard a child by removing from the scene (whether from the child's home or from part of it or from the area in which it is situated) a person who poses a threat to the child.

An emergency protection order is a draconian measure and reference should be made to the guidance on the use of EPOs given in *X Council v B (Emergency Protection Orders)* [2005] 1 FLR 341 and *Re X (Emergency Protection Orders)* [2006] 2 FLR 701. There is no appeal against the grant of or refusal to grant an EPO, but, if an order is made, an application to discharge it may be possible.

Although the Public Law Outline (PLO) in FPR PD12A specifically applies to care and supervision proceedings, it also states that, insofar as practicable, it is to be applied to all other public law proceedings (para 1.1). See also FPR 2010, r 12.22. It will therefore be a decision for the court in each case as to how and when it is appropriate for the PLO to apply when an application commences by way of an EPO.

Procedure

Who may apply	Any person including a local authority or an authorised person such as the NSPCC or a designated police officer	CA 1989, ss 44(1), 46(7)

Which court	Magistrates' court, unless pending proceedings or application arises out of a CA 1989, s 37 investigation by local authority, in which case application is to the court where proceedings are pending or the court which required investigation	ATPO 2008, art 5
	Proceedings commenced in the magistrates' court can be transferred sideways but not upwards	ATPO 2008, arts 14, 15(2)
	Proceedings commenced in the county court or High Court can be transferred between county courts, and between High Court and county court and down to magistrates' court	ATPO 2008, arts 16–19
Which proceedings	Freestanding application	CA 1989, ss 44(1), 46(7)
	EPO can be made on application for child assessment order	CA 1989, s 43(3), (4)
Application	On Form C1 and Supplement C11, with copies for each respondent; see below for without notice applications	FPR PD5A, PD12A
	Fee: £170	FPFO 2008, fee 2.1(o); MCFO 2008, fee 8.1(o)
Respondents	Every person whom applicant believes has parental responsibility	
	Every person whom applicant believes had parental responsibility before care order	
	The child	FPR 2010, r 12.3
Additional persons to whom notice in Form C6A is to be given	Local authority providing accommodation for child	
	Persons caring for child at commencement of proceedings	
	Person providing a CA 1989, s 51 refuge for child	
	Every person whom applicant believes is a parent	FPR PD12C, para 3.1
Service	Copy of application, together with Form C6, to be served on respondents at least 1 day before date of hearing or directions appointment	FPR PD12C
	Form C6A to be served on additional persons at same time as application etc served on respondents	FPR PD12C, para 3.1
	At or before first directions appointment or hearing, applicant must file statement in Form C9 to prove that requirements for service have been complied with	FPR PD5A, PD12A
Without notice	Permitted (permission of justices' clerk required in magistrates' court)	
	High Court or county court Where application made by telephone, file Form C1 and Supplement C11 the next business day after application	

	Where made otherwise, file at time application made	
	Magistrates' court File Form C1 and Supplement C11 when emergency protection order application made or as directed by justices' clerk	
	Any court Serve copy of application on each respondent (see above) within 48 hours after making of order	FPR 2010, r 12.16; PD12E
Joinder or removal of parties	By court order, of its own initiative or on written request	FPR 2010, rr 4.3, 12.3(3)
Answer to application	Respondent may file an answer; serve on other parties	FPR PD12A
Directions	Powers of the justices' clerk or the court	FPR 2010, rr 12.12, 12.24
Children's guardian	Must normally be appointed	CA 1989, s 41(1)
Who has power to make the order	High Court or nominated county court judge, any district judge of the Principal Registry or nominated district judge outside the Principal Registry or nominated recorder	FP(AJ)D 2009, para 6 and Sch
	Magistrates' court	
	A single justice may grant an EPO without notice	CA 1989, s 93(2)(i); FPR 2010, r 2.6(1)(a)
	A justices' clerk has no such power	JCR 2005
Order	On Form C23 (naming child wherever reasonably practicable or describing him as clearly as possible)	CA 1989, s 44(14); FPR PD12A
	If without notice, applicant to serve copy within 48 hours after making of order on:	
	each party	
	any person with actual care of child or who had actual care immediately before order local authority in whose area child lives or is found	FPR 2010, r 12.16(5)
Additional or alternative orders	No order	CA 1989, s 1(5)
Procedure for exclusion requirements	Applicant for EPO prepares separate statement of evidence in support re: exclusion requirement	

	Applicant serves statement and copy of order containing exclusion requirement (and of any power of arrest attached) personally on relevant person (ie person who is excluded) and informs relevant person of right to apply to vary/discharge exclusion requirement. It is important when effecting service that the process server complies with the Family Justice Council *Protocol for Process Servers*	CA 1989, s 44A; FPR 2010, r 12.28(2); FJC Protocol of November 2011: *Process Servers: Non-Molestation Orders*
	If power of arrest attached, once relevant person served with order/informed of terms, copy of order shall be delivered to police together with statement showing relevant person served/informed of terms	FPR 2010, r 12.28(3); FJC Protocol of November 2011: *Process Servers: Non-Molestation Orders*
	Unless relevant person given notice and attended hearing, if power of arrest attached to exclusion order, court must announce in open court at earliest opportunity the name of person and fact that such order made	FPR PD12K
	Consent of person who is assuming care of child is required	CA 1989, s 44A(2); FPR 2010, r 12.29
Appeals	None possible	CA 1989, s 45(10)
Transitional arrangements	FPR 1991 to FPR 2010	FPR PD36A

D3: Discharge of an Emergency Protection Order

Legal background

CA 1989, s 45(8) enables an application to be made for the discharge of an emergency protection order (EPO). However, there are two exceptions where: (a) the person who wishes to apply for the discharge was given due notice of the hearing at which the original order was made and was present at the hearing, and (b) the period of the EPO has been extended (CA 1989, s 45(11)). The CYPA 2008 has repealed CA 1989, s 45(9), thereby removing the prohibition on applying to discharge the EPO before the expiry of 72 hours from the making of the original order.

Section 45(8A), (8B) deals with applications to vary or discharge an EPO insofar as it imposes an exclusion requirement, or to vary or discharge the attendant power of arrest. It is a decision for the court in each case as to how and when it is appropriate for the Public Law Outline (PLO) in FPR PD12A to apply when an application commences by way of an EPO; see also Guide D2 and FPR 2010, r 12.22.

Procedure

Who may apply	The child	
	A parent	
	Any person with parental responsibility	
	Any person with whom the child was living immediately before the emergency protection order was made	CA 1989, s 45(8)

Which court	The court which made the original order	C(AP)O 1991, art 4(1)
	Proceedings commenced in the magistrates' court can be transferred sideways but not upwards	ATPO 2008, arts 14, 15(2)
	Proceedings commenced in the county court or High Court can be transferred between county courts, and between High Court and county court and down to magistrates' court	ATPO 2008, arts 16–19
Which proceedings	Freestanding application	CA 1989, s 45(8)
Application	On Form C2, with copies for each respondent	FPR PD5A, PD12A
Fee	£170	FPFO 2008, fee 2.1(o); MCFO 2008, fee 8.1(o)
Respondents	Every person whom applicant believes has parental responsibility	
	Every person whom applicant believes had parental responsibility before care order	
	The child	
	The parties to the original proceedings	FPR 2010, r 12.3
Additional persons to whom notice in Form C6A is to be given	Local authority providing accommodation for child	
	Persons caring for child at commencement of proceedings	
	Person providing a CA 1989, s 51 refuge for child	FPR PD12C, para 3.1
Service	Copy of application, together with Form C6, to be served on respondents at least 1 day before date of hearing or directions appointment	FPR PD12C
	Form C6A to be served on additional persons at same time as application etc served on respondents	FPR PD12C, para 3.1
	At or before first directions appointment or hearing, applicant must file statement in Form C9 to prove that requirements for service have been complied with	FPR PD5A, PD12A
Without notice	Permitted (see definition of "emergency proceedings" in FPR 2010, r 12.2). Permission of justices' clerk required in magistrates' court	
	High Court or county court Where application made by telephone, file Form C1 and Supplement C11 the next business day after application Where made otherwise, file at time of application	
	Magistrates' court File Form C1 and Supplement C11 when application made or as directed by justices' clerk	

	Any court Serve copy of application on each respondent (see above) within 48 hours after making order	FPR 2010, r 12.16
Joinder or removal of parties	By court order, of its own initiative or on written request	FPR 2010, r 4.3, 12.3(3)
Answer to application	Respondent may file an answer; serve on other parties	FPR PD12A
Directions	Powers of the justices' clerk or the court	FPR 2010, rr 12.12, 12.24
Children's guardian	Must normally be appointed	CA 1989, s 41(1)
Special requirements	No application allowed where applicant had proper notice of original application and was present at the hearing or where EPO has already been extended	CA 1989, s 45(11)
Who has power to make the order	High Court or nominated county court judge, any district judge of the Principal Registry or nominated district judge outside the Principal Registry or nominated recorder	FP(AJ)D 2009, para 6 and Sch
	Magistrates' court; however, justices' clerk or single justice has no such power	JCR 2005; CA 1989, s 93(2)(i); FPR 2010, r 2.6
Order	Form C24	FPR PD12A
Procedure for variation/discharge of exclusion requirements and attendant power of arrest	Application for variation/discharge re: exclusion requirement or re: power of arrest by person to whom it applies, Form C2 suggested	CA 1989, s 45(8A),(8B)
	Applicant serves parties to the proceedings with application for variation/discharge	FPR 2010, r 12.28(5)
	Consider giving notice to person caring for child	FPR 2010, r 12.28(5)
	Steps to be taken on variation/discharge affecting exclusion requirement/power of arrest	FPR 2010, r 12.28 (4),(6)
Appeals	None possible	CA 1989, s 45(10)
Transitional arrangements	FPR 1991 to FPR 2010	FPR PD36A

D4: Extension of an Emergency Protection Order, Warrant under Children Act 1989, s 48(9) or Variation of Directions as to Contact or Assessment under Children Act 1989, s 44(9)(b)

PART I

Legal background

An emergency protection order (EPO) can be extended once for a period not exceeding 7 days if the court has reasonable cause to believe that the child concerned is likely to suffer significant harm if the order is not extended (CA 1989, s 45(4)–(6)). Where a person is attempting to exercise powers under an EPO and has been prevented from doing so by being refused entry to the premises concerned or access to the child concerned or is likely to be so prevented, the court may issue a warrant authorising a constable to give assistance, using reasonable force if necessary (CA 1989, s 48(9)).

When making an EPO or at any time while such an order is in force, the court may give directions under CA 1989, s 44(6) with respect to contact with the child concerned and as to medical or psychiatric examination or other assessment of him. Application may be made at any time under CA 1989, s 44(9) for such directions to be varied.

It is a decision for the court in each case as to how and when it is appropriate for the Public Law Outline in FPR PD12A to apply when an application commences by way of an EPO. See further under Guide D2.

Procedure

Who may apply	*Extension of EPO* Any person who has parental responsibility as a result of an EPO and is entitled to apply for a care order	CA 1989, s 45(4)
	CA 1989, s 48(9) warrant Any person	CA 1989, s 48(9)
	CA 1989, s 44(9)(b) variation Parties to original application	
	Children's guardian Local authority in whose area child is ordinarily resident Anyone named in the directions	CA 1989, s 44(9); FPR 2010, r 12.3
Which court	The court which made the original order	C(AP)O 1991, art 4(1); CA 1989, s 48
	Proceedings commenced in the magistrates' court can be transferred sideways but not upwards	ATPO 2008, arts 14, 15(2)
	Proceedings commenced in the county court or High Court can be transferred between county courts, and between High Court and county court and down to magistrates' court	ATPO 2008, arts 16–19
Which proceedings	Freestanding application	CA 1989, ss 44(9), 45(4), 48(9)
Application	*Extension of EPO* On Form C2, with copies for each respondent	FPR PD5A, PD12A
	Fee: £170	FPFO 2008, fee 2.1(o); MCFO 2008, fee 8.1(o)

	CA 1989, s 48(9) *warrant* On Form C2 and Supplement C12 (naming child wherever reasonably practicable or describing him as clearly as possible), with copies for each respondent Fee: £170	CA 1989, s 48(13); FPR PD5A, PD12A FPFO 2008, fee 2.1(p); MCFO 2008, fee 8.1(p)
	CA 1989, s 44(9)(b) variation On Form C2, with copies for each respondent Fee: £170	FPR PD5A, PD12A FPFO 2008, fee 2.1(o); MCFO 2008, fee 8.1(o)
Respondents	*In all cases* Every person whom applicant believes has parental responsibility Every person whom applicant believes had parental responsibility before care order The child AND *Extension of EPO or CA 1989, s 44(9)(b) variation* The parties to the original EPO proceedings *CA 1989, s 44(9)(b) variation* Any person who was caring for child before making of the order Any person whose contact with child is affected by the direction which is to be varied	FPR 2010, r 12.3
Additional persons to whom notice is to be given	*In all cases* Local authority providing accommodation for child Persons caring for child at commencement of proceedings Person providing a CA 1989, s 51 refuge for child AND *CA 1989, s 44(9)(b) variation* Local authority in whose area child is living Any person whom applicant believes is affected by the direction which is to be varied	FPR PD12C, para 3.1
Service	Copy of application, together with Form C6, to be served on respondents at least 1 day before date of hearing or directions appointment Form C6A to be served on additional persons at same time as application etc served on respondents	FPR PD12C, para 2.1 FPR PD12C

	At or before first directions appointment or hearing, applicant must file statement in Form C9 to prove that requirements for service have been complied with	FPR PD5A, PD12A
Without notice	*Extension of EPO or CA 1989, s 44(9)(b) variation* Permitted (see definition of "emergency proceedings" in FPR 2010, r 12.2) *CA 1989, s 48(9) warrant* In High Court or county court, Form C1 and Supplement C12 is filed next business day after application where made by telephone; otherwise, filed at time when application made In magistrates' court, application must be made with permission of justices' clerk; Form C1 and Supplement C12 is filed when application made or as directed by justices' clerk	FPR 2010, r 12.16; PD5A
Joinder or removal of parties	By court order, of its own initiative or on written request	FPR 2010, rr 4.3, 12.13(3)
Answer to application	Respondent may file an answer; serve on other parties	FPR PD12A
Directions	Powers of the justices' clerk or the court	FPR 2010, rr 12.12, 12.24
Children's guardian	Must normally be appointed	CA 1989, s 41(1)
Who has power to make the order	High Court or nominated county court judge, any district judge of the Principal Registry or nominated district judge outside the Principal Registry or nominated recorder	FP(AJ)D 2009, para 6 and Sch
	Magistrates' court A single justice may grant a without notice warrant under CA 1989, s 48(9) and variation under s 44(9)(b), but may not extend an EPO	CA 1989, s 93(2)(i); FPR 2010, r 2.6(1)(c)
	A justices' clerk has no such power	JCR 2005
Order	*Extension of EPO* Form C24 *CA 1989, s 48(9) warrant* Form C25 (naming child wherever reasonably practicable or describing him as clearly as possible). If without notice, applicant must serve copy, within 48 hours of making of order, on each party, on any person with actual care of child or who had actual care immediately before order and on the local authority in whose area the child lives or is found	CA 1989, s 48(13); FPR PD12A
	CA 1989, s 44(9)(b) variation Form C24	FPR PD12A

| Appeals | Extension of EPO or CA 1989, s 44(9)(b) variation
None permitted
CA 1989, s 48(9) warrant
See Guides E2, E4 and E5 | CA 1989, s 45(10) |
| Transitional arrangements | FPR 1991 to FPR 2010 | FPR PD36A |

D5: Recovery Order

Legal background

Where it appears to the court that there is reason to believe that a child who is in care or is the subject of an emergency protection order or is in police protection, is missing or has been unlawfully taken or kept away or has run away or is staying away from the person who has care of him under the care order etc, it may make a recovery order under CA 1989, s 50. The order has the following effects: (a) it operates as a direction to any person who is in a position to do so to produce the child to any authorised person on request; (b) it authorises any authorised person to remove the child; (c) it requires any person who has information as to the child's whereabouts to disclose that information, if asked to do so, to a constable or an officer of the court; and (d) it authorises a constable to enter any premises specified in the order and search for the child, using reasonable force if necessary. A recovery order is open-ended, remaining in force until it is discharged or until the child is recovered.

Procedure

Who may apply	Any person with parental responsibility for child by virtue of care order or emergency protection order Where child is in police protection, designated officer	CA 1989, s 50(4)
Which court	Magistrates' court, unless pending proceedings in which case apply to court where proceedings pending	ATPO 2008, art 5
	Proceedings may be transferable sideways, upwards or downwards, depending on circumstances	ATPO 2008, arts 14–19
Which proceedings	Freestanding application	CA 1989, s 50(4)
Application	On Form C1 and Supplement C18, with sufficient copies for each respondent; see below for without notice applications	FPR PD5A, PD12A
	Fee: £170	FPFO 2008, fee 2.1(q); MCFO 2008, fee 8.1(q)
Respondents	Every person whom applicant believes has parental responsibility Every person whom applicant believes had parental responsibility before care order	

	The child	
	Person whom applicant alleges to have effected, or to have been or to be responsible for, taking or keeping of child	FPR 2010, r 12.3
Additional persons to whom notice is to be given	Local authority providing accommodation for child Persons caring for child at commencement of proceedings Person providing a CA 1989, s 51 refuge for child	FPR PD12C, para 3.1
Service	Copy of application, together with Form C6, to be served on respondents at least 1 day before date of hearing or directions appointment	FPR PD12C
	Form C6A to be served on additional persons at same time as application etc served on respondents	FPR PD12C, para 3.1
	At or before first directions appointment or hearing, applicant must file statement in Form C9 to prove that requirements for service have been complied with	FPR PD5A, PD12A
Without notice	Permitted (permission of justices' clerk required in magistrates' court) *High court or county court* Where application is made by telephone, file Form C1 and Supplement C18 next business day after application	
	Where made otherwise, file at time application made	
	Magistrates' court File Form C1 and Supplement C18 when application made or as directed by justices' clerk	FPR 2010, r 12.16
Joinder or removal of parties	By court order, of its own initiative or on written request	FPR 2010, rr 4.3, 12.3(3)
Answer to application	Respondent may file answer; serve on other parties	FPR PD12A
Directions	Powers of the justices' clerk or the court	FPR 2010, rr 12.12, 12.24
Children's guardian	Must normally be appointed	CA 1989, s 41(1)
Who has power to make the order	High Court or nominated county court judge, any district judge of the Principal Registry or nominated district judge outside the Principal Registry or nominated recorder	FP(AJ)D 2009, para 6 and Sch
	Magistrates' court A single justice may grant a without notice order	CA 1989, s 93(2)(i); FPR 2010, r 2.6(1)(a)
	A justices' clerk has no such power	JCR 2005

Order	Form C29 (naming child and any person with parental responsibility by virtue of care order or emergency protection order or designated officer where child in police protection)	CA 1989, s 50(5); FPR PD12A
	If without notice, applicant to serve copy within 48 hours after making of order on:	FPR 2010, r 12.16
	every party	
	any person with actual care of child or who had actual care immediately before order	
	local authority in whose area child lives or is found	
Appeals	See Guides E2, E4 and E5	
Transitional arrangements	FPR 1991 to FPR 2010	FPR PD36A

D6: Parental Responsibility Order or Agreement (or Discharge of the Same)

Legal background

Parental responsibility comprises all the rights, duties, powers, responsibilities and authority which, by law, a parent has in relation to a child and his property, or which a guardian of a child's estate has in relation to his property (CA 1989, s 3).

A child's mother always has parental responsibility for the child; however, if she was not married to the child's father at the time of the birth, the father will only acquire parental responsibility by marrying the mother, by making a formal parental responsibility agreement with her (using Form C(PRA1)) or by obtaining an order from the court (CA 1989, s 4, to be read in conjunction with FLRA 1987, s 1(2)) or if his name is placed on the birth certificate at registration or re-registration of the birth under the Births and Deaths Registration Act 1953 (see CA 1989, s 4(1)(a)). A step-parent may acquire parental responsibility for a child of his spouse or civil partner by agreement (using Form C(PRA2)), or by order of the court (CA 1989, s 4A). A second female parent may acquire responsibility for a child by agreement (using Form C(PRA3)) or by order of the court (CA 1989, s 4ZA).The court must make such an order where it makes a residence order in favour of the father (CA 1989, s 12(1)) and care should therefore be taken to consider this requirement when making or opposing an interim residence application; otherwise, it is in the court's discretion whether to grant a specific application under CA 1989, s 4.

On making an application to the court, the applicant should also file a completed Form FM1 confirming attendance at a mediation information and assessment meeting or giving reasons for not attending (FPR PD3A, Annex A).

The court may subsequently discharge a parental responsibility order or a parental responsibility agreement (which may not be revoked merely by agreement).

Note that the 1996 Hague Convention came into force in the UK on 1 November 2012. Art 1 defines the meaning of "parental responsibility" in cases to which the Convention applies. The definition is purposively broad and should be given an autonomous Convention meaning rather than its purely domestic law meaning. Arts 16–18 cover the attribution, extinction and exercise of parental responsibility in such cases. See commentary under the Convention.

Procedure

Who may apply	Father without parental responsibility	CA 1989, s 4(1)(a)
	The spouse or civil partner of a parent with parental responsibility	CA 1989, s 4A
	The second female parent of a child	CA 1989, s 4ZA; HFEA 2008, s 43
	Discharge of parental responsibility order or agreement: Any person with parental responsibility The child (with permission)	CA 1989, ss 4(3), 4A
Which court	Magistrates' court (subject to certain exceptions)	CA 1989, ss 10(1); ATPO 2008, arts 5(2),(4)
	High Court judge, circuit judge, deputy circuit judge or recorder nominated for public family law proceedings, or Category B judge	FP(AJ)D 2009, para 6 and Sch
	Proceedings can be transferred sideways, upwards or downwards, using order in Form C49	ATPO 2008, arts 14–19
Which proceedings	Freestanding application	CA 1989, s 4(1)
	Court must make order on making residence order in favour of father without parental responsibility even if no specific application is made	CA 1989, s 12(1)
Application	On Form C1, together with Form FM1, with sufficient copies for each respondent. Where it is alleged that the child who is the subject of the application has suffered, or is at risk of suffering, any harm from (a) any form of domestic abuse; (b) violence within the household; (c) child abduction; or (d) other conduct or behaviour, supplemental Form C1A must also be completed	FPR PD3A, PD5A, PD12B
	Fee: £200	FPFO 2008, fee 2.1(a),(b); MCFO 2008, fee 8.1(a),(b)
	Where child applies for permission to apply for discharge, use Form C2	FPR 2010, rr 18.1–18.13; PD12B
Respondents	Notice to be served in Form C6 on every person with parental responsibility and on every person with parental responsibility before care order	FPR 2010, r 12.3
	Discharge of parental responsibility order or agreement: As above, and service on other parties to original proceedings	FPR 2010, r 12.3
Additional persons to be served with notice of the proceedings	Notice to be served in Form C6A on local authority, if providing accommodation, and on person caring for child or providing refuge	FPR PD12C, para 3.1

Service	Applicant must serve a copy of the application, together with Form C6 (endorsed with date fixed for hearing), on each respondent at least 14 days before the hearing; notice of the proceedings must be served in Form C6A (endorsed with date fixed for hearing) on other persons to be served at least 14 days before the hearing	FPR PD12C
	At or before first directions appointment or hearing, applicant must file statement in Form C9 to prove that requirements for service have been complied with	FPR PD5A, PD12B
Answer to application	Respondent to an application must file a written answer and serve it on the other parties to the proceedings within 14 days of the date on which the application is served	FPR 2010, r 12.32
Joinder or removal of parties	By court order, of its own initiative or on written request on Form C2 together with Form C1A if necessary (see under "Application" above)	FPR 2010, rr 4.3, 12.3(3)
Directions	As to applications for directions, see –	FPR 2010, r 12.12
	NB A written request for directions must be made on Form C2 and C1A if necessary (see under "Application" above)	
	Directions which may be given (e g timetable for the proceedings, submission of evidence or transfer of proceedings to another court)	FPR 2010, r 12.12
	Timing of proceedings	FPR 2010, r 12.13
	Attendance at the directions hearing	FPR 2010, r 12.14
Order	Conferring parental responsibility on the father, spouse, civil partner or second female parent, in Form C45	CA 1989, ss 4(1)(a), 12(1); FPR PD12B
	Terminating parental responsibility order or agreement, in Form C45	FPR PD12B
Appeals	See Guides E2, E4 and E5	
Transitional arrangements	FPR 1991 to FPR 2010	FPR PD36A

D7: Residence or Contact Order (or Discharge or Variation of the Same)

Legal background

A residence order under CA 1989, s 8 settles the arrangements as to the person with whom a child is to live (CA 1989, s 8(1)). Such an order automatically confers parental responsibility on any person in whose favour it is made for as long as the order is in force (CA 1989, s 12(2)).

A contact order under CA 1989, s 8 requires the person with whom a child lives, or is to live, to allow the child to visit or stay with the person named in the order, or for that person and the child otherwise to have contact with each other (CA 1989, s 8(1)).

An order for "no contact" does fall within the definition of "contact order" in CA 1989, s 8(1) (*Nottinghamshire County Council v P* [1993] 2 FLR 134 at [143G]).

On making an application to the court, the applicant should also file a completed Form FM1 confirming attendance at a mediation information and assessment meeting or giving reasons for not attending (FPR PD3A, Annex A).

Note that the 1996 Hague Convention came into force in the UK on 1 November 2012. It lays down rules in respect of measures directed to the protection of the person or property of the child in cases to which the Convention applies (Art 1). "Measures of protection" include the attribution, exercise, termination, restriction and delegation of parental responsibility, and of custody and access (Art 3). "Rights of custody" essentially include all measures relating to the care and upbringing of, and access, contact or visitation rights concerning the child (Art 3(b)). See further under the commentary to the Convention.

Contact activity directions and contact activity conditions

CA 1989, ss 11A–11P give the court power to enforce contact orders. When there is some dispute about contact and the court is considering whether or not to make, vary or discharge a contact order it may make a "contact activity direction" (a "CAD") (s 11A), directing a party to the proceedings to undertake activities promoting contact, for example information meetings about mediation, parenting information programmes and domestic violence prevention programmes (known as "contact activities").

Whenever a court makes or varies a contact order it may make a "contact activity condition" (a "CAC") requiring the person named to take part in a "contact activity" (s 11C). Those who may be subject to a CAC are the person with whom the child lives, the person in whose favour the contact order is made, or a person subject to a s 11(7) condition.

A court may ask a Cafcass officer to monitor compliance with CAD or CAC and to report to the court if there is a failure to comply (s 11G). Contact activity providers may also be asked to provide a report to the court about the attendance and participation of those required to undertake a contact activity.

Monitoring compliance with contact orders

A court may ask a Cafcass officer to monitor compliance with a contact order for a period of up to 1 year after the making of the order (s 11H). Those who can be subject to monitoring are: a person who is required to allow contact with a child; a person whose contact with the child is provided for; a person subject to s 11(7) condition. However, the general assumption is that this provision should not be used in "consent order" cases where proceedings have ended, but should be limited to those cases where the issue of contact has remained in dispute and where a trial and judicial determination of the contact issue has taken place.

Warning notices

Whenever a court makes or varies a contact order, it is to attach a notice warning of the consequences of failing to comply with the contact order (s 11I) ie an enforcement order (for unpaid work) (ss 11J–11N), an order for financial compensation (ss 11O, 11P), and sanctions for contempt of court. The warning notice must also make clear the person to whom it is addressed, and the exact provisions of the order to which it relates.

The wording of s 11I looks as though it is mandatory for a court to attach a warning notice when it makes or varies any contact order. It follows that judges will have to decide whether the contact order that they propose to make is to be made in terms that comply with s 8(1), in which case a warning notice will be added automatically, or simply in declaratory terms, in which case there is no need for a warning notice to be attached. Equally, it may be more appropriate for consent orders to set out the agreed regime as a recital or schedule to the order on the basis of which the court then applies the "no order" principle. Judges will need to make sure that orders set out in Form C45 accurately reflect what has actually been ordered.

See further the introduction to Guide D8.

Procedure

Who may apply	Parent or guardian	
	Residence order holder	
	Either party to marriage	
	Person with whom child has lived for 3 of the last 5 years and within the preceding 3	
	Person with consent of those with parental responsibility	
	Application to discharge or vary may be made by previous applicant or person named in order (in case of contact order only)	
	Any person with permission, except a local authority; special requirements apply to some foster-parents	CA 1989, ss 9(2)–(4), 10
Fee	Application to discharge or vary: £200	FPFO 2008, fee 2.1(d); MCFO 2008, fee 8.1(d)
	Application for permission: £200	FPFO 2008, fee 2.1(d); MCFO 2008, fee 8.1(d)
Which court	Any court (subject to certain exceptions) but should be transferred to magistrates' court if none of criteria in art 15(1)(b) to (i) apply	CA 1989, ss 10(1), 92(7); ATPO 2008, art 9; *PD: Allocation and Transfer of Proceedings (3 November 2008)*, para 9.2
	High Court judge, circuit judge, deputy circuit judge or recorder nominated for public family law proceedings, or Category B judge	FP(AJ)D 2009, para 6 and Sch
	Proceedings can be transferred sideways, upwards or downwards, using order in Form C49	ATPO 2008, art 14–19
Which proceedings	Freestanding application	CA 1989, s 10(2)
	Application made in family proceedings	CA 1989, s 10(1)(a)
	On court's own initiative in family proceedings	CA 1989, s 10(1)(b)
Application	On Form C100, together with Form FM1, with sufficient copies for each respondent. Where it is alleged that the child who is the subject of the application has suffered, or is at risk of suffering, any harm from (a) any form of domestic abuse; (b) violence within the household; (c) child abduction; or (d) other conduct or behaviour supplemental Form C1A must also be completed	FPR 2010, r 5.1; PD3A, PD5A, PD12B

Respondents	Notice to be served in Form C6 on every person with parental responsibility, every person with parental responsibility before care order, and (on application to discharge or vary) parties to proceedings where order was made	FPR 2010, r 12.3
Additional persons to whom notice in Form C6A is to be given	Local authority, if providing accommodation for child Person caring for child or providing refuge Person named in a court order (unless not relevant) Party to pending proceedings Person with whom the child has lived for 3 years	FPR PD12C, para 3.1
Service	Applicant must serve a copy of the application, together with Form C6 (endorsed with date fixed for hearing), on each respondent at least 14 days before the hearing, unless emergency (see Without notice procedure below) Notice of the proceedings must be served in Form C6A (endorsed with date fixed for hearing) on other persons to be served At or before first directions appointment or hearing, applicant must file statement in Form C9 to prove that requirements for service have been complied with	FPR PD12C FPR PD5A, PD12A
Power to abridge time-limits	In appropriate cases, court has power to abridge time-limits set by rules Court has power to abridge time for service	FPR 2010, rr 4.1(3)(a), 12.12 FPR 2010, rr 4.1(3)(a), 12.12
Without notice procedure	If without notice order obtained by telephone, file application by the next business day; otherwise, file at time application is made (NB without notice residence orders will be made only in exceptional circumstances) If an order is made, it must be served on respondents within 48 hours	*Re G* [1993] 1 FLR 910; *Re P* [1993] 1 FLR 915 FPR 2010, r 12.16
Joinder or removal of parties	By court order, of its own initiative or on written request on Form C2 together with Form C1A if necessary (see under "Application" above)	FPR 2010, rr 4.3, 12.3(3)
Acknowledgement of application	Respondent must file acknowledgement of application in Form C7 and serve it on the parties within 14 days of service of the application together with Form C1A if necessary (see under "Application" above)	FPR PD5A, PD12B

Answer to application	Respondent must file a written answer and serve it on the other parties to the proceedings within 14 days of the date on which the application is served	FPR 2010, r 12.32
Withdrawal of application	Permitted only with permission; application may be made orally if parties and welfare officer present; otherwise, by written request on Form C2 giving reasons, served on parties	FPR 2010, rr 18.1–18.13, 29.4
	If by consent, court may grant request without a hearing; otherwise, hearing on 7 days' notice	FPR 2010, rr 18.8, 29.4
Directions	Court may give directions of own initiative or on written (or oral, if urgent) request, subject to certain procedural requirements	FPR 2010, r 12.12
	NB A written request for directions must be made on Form C2 together with Form C1A if necessary (see under "Application" above)	
	Directions which may be given (eg as to timetable for the proceedings, submission of evidence or transfer of proceedings to another court)	FPR 2010, r 12.12
	Timing of proceedings	FPR 2010, r 12.13
	Attendance at the directions hearing	FPR 2010, r 12.14
	Contact activity direction	CA 1989, s 11A
Order	On Form C43, making, discharging or varying a residence order or contact order (including an order for "no contact"); order may contain directions and conditions	CA 1989, ss 8, 11(7); FPR PD12B
	Contact activity condition	CA 1989, s 11C
	Penal notice may be attached on specific application (High Court or county court only)	FPR 2010, r 33.7
	A warning notice *must* be added whenever court makes or varies a contact order	CA 1989, s 11I
Additional or alternative orders	Parental responsibility order (Form C45)	CA 1989, s 4(1)(a)
	Appointment of guardian (Form C46)	CA 1989, s 5(2)
	Family assistance order (but only with the consent of persons named) (Form C42)	CA 1989, s 16
	Financial provision order (Form C21)	CA 1989, Sch 1, para 1
	Supervision order (Form C35)	CA 1989, ss 31(1)(b), 35, 38
	Education supervision order (provided the application is made by a local education authority) (Form C37)	CA 1989, s 36(1)
Restrictions on court's powers	A contact order may not be made in respect of a child in care	CA 1989, s 9(1)

Appeals	See Guides E2, E4 and E5	
Transitional arrangements	FPR 1991 to FPR 2010	FPR PD36A

D8: Enforcement of Contact Orders

Legal background

CA 1989, ss 11I–11P make extra provision for the enforcement of contact orders.

Warning notices

Whenever a court makes or varies a contact order, it is to attach a notice warning of the consequences of failing to comply with the contact order (s 11I) ie an enforcement order (for unpaid work) (ss 11J–N), an order for financial compensation (ss 11O, 11P), and sanctions for contempt of court. The warning notice must also make clear the person to whom it is addressed, and the exact provisions of the order to which it relates. The procedure for applying for warning notices is set out in FPR 2010, r 12.33. The application is made using Form C78. Warning notices can be addressed to a much wider range of individuals than was the case previously, because applications for enforcement orders and financial compensation orders can be made not only by the person in whose favour the order is made, but also by the person with whom the child lives, or the child, or any other person subject to a s 11(7) condition or contact activity condition. Judges need to make sure that orders set out in Form C45 accurately reflect what has actually been ordered.

FPR 2010, r 12.33 provides for the application to be made without notice, but there is no provision in Form C78 for the applicant to specify the provisions of the order to which he wishes the warning notice attached, or any space for him to say why the application is being made. The without notice order has potential quasi-criminal consequences for the respondent, but does not give him a right to apply to set it aside. In these circumstances, it is respectfully submitted that the safer course would be for the judge to direct a hearing inviting the applicant to file a brief statement setting out the provisions of the order to which he wishes the warning notice to be attached and explaining why he is asking for a warning notice.

If the relevant order does not comply with s 8(1), then the application should be dismissed as misconceived. The applicant would have to apply using Form C100 to vary the existing order to a mandatory order to which a warning notice can be added (see Guide D7).

Transitional orders

Applications to attach a warning notice to an existing order must be made on Form C78. The application can be made to any court with family jurisdiction. When faced with a C78 application the judge should first obtain a copy of the original order, but in itself that may not be enough. Without the existing court file it may be impossible to discover whether the order is still in force. Furthermore, the relevant provisions may be contained in more than one order. The proper course may be to ask the court in which the order was made either to transfer the existing proceedings or to order transfer of the C78 application back to the court that made the existing order. For the transitional arrangements covering the replacement of FPR 1991 with FPR 2010, see FPR PD36A.

Enforcement Orders

Where the court is satisfied beyond reasonable doubt that a person has failed to comply with a contact order made under s 8 of CA 1989, the court may make an enforcement order, imposing on that person an "unpaid work requirement" (community service): s 11J(2). The application is made using Form C79. The court may not make an enforcement order if satisfied that the person in breach had a "reasonable excuse" for breaching the order: s 11J(3). The burden of proving a reasonable excuse is on the person in breach and the standard of proof is the balance of probabilities: s 11(4). The court may not make an enforcement order unless the person concerned has received a "warning notice" or has been otherwise informed of its terms: s 11K. The factors to be considered by the court before making an enforcement order are set out in s 11L and in Sch A1, Pt I. The maximum number of hours of unpaid work that may be required is 200, and the minimum is 40. The court has power to amend or revoke an enforcement order: Sch A1, Pt II. The court may ask a Cafcass officer to monitor, or arrange for the monitoring of, a person's compliance with an enforcement order, and to report to the court on failure to comply and on any unsuitability to undertake the unpaid work: s 11M. Where an enforcement order is made, the court must attach a warning notice setting out the consequences of breaching the order ie imposition of a further enforcement order; enhancement of the existing enforcement order; use of existing sanctions for contempt. If the terms of an enforcement order are breached, the court may (in certain circumstances) amend the original order to make it more onerous, or impose another enforcement order: Sch A1, Pt II. See also FPR 2010, PD12N.

Financial compensation orders

The court may require a person who has caused financial loss to another person as a result of breaching a contact order (including breaching a condition attached to a contact order), to pay compensation up to the amount of the loss: s 11O. Before making a compensation order the court must take into account the welfare of any child concerned, and the financial circumstances of the person in breach. The people who can apply for compensation are: the person with whom the child lives; the person whose contact with the child is provided for in the order; any individual subject to a contact activity condition or direction; the child concerned (with permission of the court). The court may not make an order for financial compensation where the person in breach did not receive a warning notice under s 11I and was not otherwise informed of its terms: s 11P.

Procedure

Note: The following procedure applies to cases where a warning notice has been attached properly to a contact order and it is alleged that the order has been breached so that enforcement of the order is required.

Who may apply	The person with whom the child lives; the person in whose favour the order is made; a person subject to a s 11(7) condition or contact activity condition; the child concerned (with permission)	CA 1989, s 11J(5), s 11O(6)
Fee	£200	FPFO 2008, fee 2.1(e); MCFO 2008, fee 8.1(e)
Which court	Any court, (subject to certain exceptions), but should be transferred to magistrates' court if none of criteria in art 15(1)(b)–(i) apply	CA 1989, ss 10(1), 92(7); ATPO 2008, art 9; PD: Allocation and Transfer of Proceedings (3 November 2008), para 9.2
	High Court judge, circuit judge, deputy circuit judge, recorder nominated for public law proceedings or Category B judge	FP(AJ)D 2009, para 6 and Schedule
	Proceedings can be transferred sideways, upwards or downwards, using order in Form C49	ATPO 2008, arts 14–19
Which proceedings	Freestanding application	CA 198 9, s 10(2)
	Application made in family proceedings	CA 1989, s 10(1)(a)
Application	On Form C79	FPR PD5A, PD12B
Respondents	Notice to be served in Form C6 on person the applicant alleges has failed to comply with the contact order	FPR 2010, r 12.3

Additional persons on whom notice is to be served in Form C6A	Any Cafcass officer monitoring compliance with contact order; where child was a party to contact proceedings, the children's guardian, guardian ad litem or child's next friend or child's legal representative	FPR PD12C, para 3.1
Service	Applicant must serve a copy of the application, together with Form C6 (endorsed with date fixed for hearing), on each respondent, at least 14 days before hearing date	FPR PD12C, para 2.1
	Notice of the proceedings must be served in Form C6A (endorsed with date fixed for hearing) on other persons to be served, at least 14 days before hearing date	FPR PD12C
Power to abridge time limits	In appropriate cases, court has power to abridge time limits	
	Court has power to abridge time for service	FPR 2010, rr 4.1(3)(a), 12.12
Joinder or removal of parties	By court order, of its own initiative or on written request in Form C2	FPR 2010, r 12.3
Acknowledgement of application	Respondent must file acknowledgement of application in Form C7 and serve it on parties within 14 days of service of application	FPR PD12B
Answer to application	Respondent must file a written answer and serve it on the other parties to the proceedings within 14 days of the date on which the application was served	
Withdrawal of application	Permitted only with permission; application may be made orally if parties and Cafcass officer present; otherwise by written request on Form C2 giving reasons, served on parties	FPR 2010, rr 18.1–18.13, 29.4
Directions	Court may give directions of own initiative or on written request in Form C2 (or oral request if urgent), subject to certain procedural requirements	FPR 2010, rr 4.3, 12.12
	Directions as to timetable, evidence, transfer	FPR 2010, r 12.12
	Directions as to timing of proceedings	FPR 2010, r 12.13
	Directions as to attendance at directions hearing	FPR 2010, r 12.14
Order	Enforcement order: Form C80	FPR PD12B
	Revocation or amendment of enforcement order: Form C81	CA 1989, Sch A1, Pt II, para 4; FPR PD12B
	Financial compensation order: Form C82	CA 1989, ss 11O, 11P; FPR PD12B
	Committal for breach of order or undertaking	CPR 1998, Sch 2, CCR Ord 29, r 1; FPR 2010, r 33.7

Service of enforcement order	Copy to be served as soon as practicable by proper officer on parties (except person against whom order is made), and Cafcass officer, and responsible officer	FPR 2010, r 12.35; for meaning of "responsible officer" see CA 1989, Sch A1, para 8(8)
	Applicant to serve copy personally on person against whom order is made	FPR 2010, r 12.35
Appeals	See Guides E2, E4 and E5	
Transitional arrangements	FPR 1991 to FPR 2010	FPR PD36A

D9: Specific Issue Order or Prohibited Steps Order (or Discharge or Variation of the Same)

Legal background

A specific issue order under CA 1989, s 8(1) gives directions for the purpose of determining a specific question which has arisen, or which may arise, in connection with any aspect of parental responsibility for a child. In effect it is used to settle ad hoc disputes where those who share parental responsibility cannot agree over the issue in question.

A prohibited steps order under CA 1989, s 8(1), specifies that no step that could be taken by a parent in meeting his or her parental responsibility for a child, and which is of a kind specified in the order, can be taken by any person without the consent of the court. This is a negative version of a specific issue order.

On making an application to the court, the applicant should also file a completed Form FM1 confirming attendance at a mediation information and assessment meeting or giving reasons for not attending (FPR PD3A, Annex A).

Note that the 1996 Hague Convention came into force in the UK on 1 November 2012. See introductions to Guides D6 and D7 and the commentary to the Convention.

Procedure

Who may apply	Parent or guardian	
	Residence order holder	
	Application to discharge or vary may be made by previous applicant	
	Any person with permission	CA 1989, s 10
Which court	Any court (subject to certain exceptions) but should be transferred to magistrates' court if none of the criteria in art 15(1)(b)–(i) apply	CA 1989, ss 10(1), 92(7); ATPO 2008, art 9; *PD: Allocation and Transfer of Proceedings (3 November 2008)*, para 9.2
	High Court judge, circuit judge, deputy circuit judge, recorder nominated for public law proceedings or Category B judge	FP(AJ)D 2009, para 6 and Sch
	Proceedings can be transferred sideways, upwards or downwards, using order in Form C49	ATPO 2008, arts 14–19

Which proceedings	Freestanding application	CA 1989, s 10(2)
	Application made in family proceedings	CA 1989, s 10(1)(a)
	On court's own initiative in family proceedings	CA 1989, s 10(1)(b)
Application	On Form C100, together with Form FM1, with sufficient copies for service on each respondent. Where it is alleged that the child who is the subject of the application has suffered, or is at risk of suffering, any harm from (a) any form of domestic abuse; (b) violence within the household; (c) child abduction; or (d) other conduct or behaviour, supplemental Form C1A must also be completed	FPR PD3A, PD5A, PD12B
	Fee payable on application: £200	FPFO 2008, fee 2.1(d); MCFO 2008, fee 8.1(d)
	Fee payable on application to discharge or vary order: £200	FPFO 2008, fee 2.1(d); MCFO 2008, fee 8.1(d)
Respondents	Notice to be served in Form C6 on every person with parental responsibility, every person with parental responsibility before care order, and (on application to discharge or vary) parties to proceedings where order was made	FPR 2010, r 12.3
Additional persons to whom notice in Form C6A is to be given	Local authority, if providing accommodation for child Person caring for child or providing refuge Person named in a court order (unless not relevant) Party to pending proceedings Person with whom the child has lived for 3 years	FPR PD12C, para 3.1
Service	At least 14 days, unless emergency (see Without notice procedure below)	
	Applicant must serve copy of application, together with Form C6 (endorsed with date fixed for hearing) on each respondent	
	Notice of the proceedings must be served in Form C6A (endorsed with date fixed for hearing) on other persons to be served	FPR PD12C
	At or before first directions appointment or hearing, applicant must file statement in Form C9 to prove that requirements for service have been complied with	FPR PD5A, PD12B
Power to abridge time-limits	In appropriate cases, court has power to abridge time-limits set by rules	
	Court has power to abridge time for service	FPR 2010, rr 4.1(3)(a), 12.12

Without notice procedure	If without notice order obtained by telephone, file application the next business day; otherwise, file at time application is made	
	If an order is made, it must be served on respondents within 48 hours	FPR 2010, r 12.16
Joinder or removal of parties	By court order, of its own initiative or on written request on Form C2 together with Form C1A if necessary (see under "Application" above)	FPR 2010, rr 4.3, 12.3(3)
Acknowledgement of application	Respondent must file acknowledgement of application in Form C7 and serve it on the parties within 14 days of service of the application together with Form C1A if necessary (see under "Application" above)	FPR PD5A, PD12B
Answer to application	Respondent must file a written answer and serve it on the other parties to the proceedings within 14 days of the date on which the application is served	FPR 2010, r 12.32
Directions	Applications for directions	FPR 2010, rr 5.1, 12.12; PD5A
	NB A written request for directions must be made on Form C2 together with Form C1A if necessary (see under "Application" above)	
	Directions which may be given (e g as to timetable for the proceedings, submission of evidence or transfer of proceedings to another court)	FPR 2010, r 12.12
	Timing of proceedings	FPR 2010, r 12.13
	Attendance at the directions hearing	FPR 2010, r 12.14
Order	On Form C43, making, discharging or varying a specific issue order or prohibited steps order; order may contain directions and conditions	CA 1989, ss 8, 11(7); FPR PD12B
	Penal notice may be attached on specific application	FPR 2010, r 33.7
Appeals	See Guides E2, E4 and E5	
Transitional arrangements	FPR 1991 to FPR 2010	FPR PD36A

D10: Special Guardianship Order (or Discharge or Variation of the Same)

Legal background

Special guardianship orders are private law orders which give the special guardian parental responsibility for the child concerned (CA 1989, ss 14A–14F). They provide permanence and security for those children for whom adoption is not suitable but who cannot live with their birth parents. The basic legal links between the child and his birth family are preserved. However, subject to any other existing CA 1989 order, a special guardian is entitled to exercise parental responsibility to the exclusion of any other person with parental responsibility (save for another special guardian) (CA 1989, s 14C(1)). It allows the special guardian to remove the child from the jurisdiction for up to 3 months without the consent of others with parental responsibility (however, he would need the consent of another guardian) (CA 1989, s 14C(4)). The order can be varied or discharged (unlike an adoption order) (CA 1989, s 14D). Where the child himself applies for permission, the court may only grant permission if it is satisfied that the child has sufficient understanding to make the proposed application for a special guardianship order (CA 1989, ss 14A(12) and 10(8)). The court may not make a special guardianship order unless it has first received a report from the local authority (CA 1989, s 14A(11)) or has received the required information about the case in some other acceptable form, for example in a parental assessment. The report must deal with the matters prescribed by the Schedule to the Special Guardianship Regulations 2005 (SGR 2005) and the matters required by CA 1989, s 10(9) (CA 1989, s 14A(12)). Once a special guardianship order has been made, the local authority is under a duty to make arrangements for the provision of a package of special guardian support services, including counselling, advice, information and financial support (CA 1989, s 14F; SGR 2005 (above)).

On making an application to the court, the applicant should also file a completed Form FM1 confirming attendance at a mediation information and assessment meeting or giving reasons for not attending (FPR PD3A, Annex A).

Procedure

Who may apply	Applicant must be 18 or over and *not* the parent of the child in question,	CA 1989, s 14A(2)
	Guardian,	
	Residence order holder,	
	Either party to marriage,	
	Any civil partner in a civil partnership in relation to whom child is a child of the family	
	Person with whom child has lived for 3 of the last 5 years and within the preceding 3 months	
	Person with consent of those with parental responsibility	
	Any person with permission, except a local authority, including the child (if sufficient understanding);	CA 1989, ss 14A(3)–(7), 14D(4), 10(5), (8)–(10)
	Foster parents with whom child has lived for 1 year before application	CA 1989, s 14A(5)(d)
	If placement order in force, special requirements apply	CA 1989, s 14A(13)
Fee	Application for permission: £160	FPFO 2008, fee 2.1(h); MCFO 2008, fee 8.1(h)
	Application to discharge or vary: £160	FPFO 2008, fee 2.1(h); MCFO 2008, fee 8.1(h)
Which court	Any court (subject to certain exceptions) but should be transferred to magistrates' court if none of the criteria in art 15(1)(b) to (i) apply	CA 1989, s 92(7); ATPO 2008, art 9; *PD: Allocation and Transfer of Proceedings (3 November 2008)*, para 9.2
	High Court judge, circuit judge, deputy circuit judge, recorder nominated for public law proceedings or Category B judge	FP(AJ)D 2009, para 6 and Sch

	Proceedings can be transferred sideways, upwards or downwards using order in Form C49	ATPO 2008, arts 14–19
	Where SGO in force and application is for permission to change name or remove from UK, commence in court which made SGO	CA 1989, s 14C(3), ATPO 2008, art 9
	Application which would vary or discharge SGO made by county court of its own initiative must be made to a family hearing centre	ATPO 2008, art 9
	Application for permission to apply for a residence order or SGO under CA 1989, ss 29(4)(b) or 29(5)(b) and any subsequent application for an order to be made to court in which adoption proceedings are pending	ATPO 2008, art 8(d)
Which proceedings	Freestanding application	CA 1989, s 14A(3)
	Application made in family proceedings	CA 1989, s 14A(3)
	On court's own initiative in family proceedings (e g in care or adoption proceedings)	CA 1989, s 14A(6)(b)
Application	On Forms C1 and C13A, together with Form FM1, with sufficient copies for each respondent	FPR PD3A, PD5A, PD12B
Respondents	The applicant must give the local authority 3 months' notice of the application in Form C6, so that the authority can prepare a report addressing the matters prescribed by regulations	SGR 2005, Sch; CA 1989, s 10(9)
	NB *Exception*: the requirement for 3 months' notice is waived where a placement order is in force and an application has been made for an adoption order and the applicant has obtained permission to apply for an SGO	ACA 2002, s 29(6); CA 1989, s 14A(13)
	Notice to be served in Form C6 on every person with parental responsibility, every person with parental responsibility before care order and (on application to vary or discharge) parties to proceedings where order was made	FPR 2010, r 12.3; FPR PD12C,
Additional persons to whom notice in Form C6A is to be given	If child not being accommodated, the authority in whose area applicant is ordinarily resident	
	Person named in a court order which remains in force	
	Person to be a party in pending proceedings in respect of child	
	Person with whom child has lived for at least 3 years before application	
	For application under s 14D, see below under "Variation or discharge"	FPR PD12C, para 3.1

Service	Applicant must serve a copy of application, together with Form C6 (endorsed with date fixed for hearing), on each respondent at least 14 days before the hearing	
	Notice of the proceedings must be served in Form C6A (endorsed with date of hearing) on other persons to be served	FPR PD12C
	At or before first directions hearing applicant must file statement in Form C9 to proved that requirements for service have been complied with	FPR PD5A, PD12B
Power to abridge time-limits	In appropriate cases, court has power to abridge time-limits set by rules	FPR 2010, rr 4.1(3)(a), 12.12
	Court has power to abridge time for service	FPR 2010, rr 4.1(3)(a), 12.12
Joinder or removal of parties	By court order, of its own initiative or on written request on Form C2	FPR 2010, rr 4.3, 12.3
Acknowledgement of application	Respondent must file acknowledgement of application in Form C7 and serve it on the parties within 14 days of service of the application	FPR PD12B
Answer to application	Respondent must file a written answer and serve it on the other parties to the proceedings within 14 days of the date on which the application is served	FPR 2010, r 12.32
Withdrawal of application	Permitted only with permission; application may be made orally if parties are present; otherwise, by written request on Form C2 giving reasons, served on the parties	
	If by consent, the court may grant request without a hearing; otherwise, hearing on 7 days' notice	FPR 2010, rr 18.1–18.13, 29.4; PD5A
Directions	Court may give directions of own initiative or on written (or oral, if urgent) request, subject to certain procedural requirements	CA 1989, s 14E(1); FPR 2010, rr 4.3, 12.12
	NB A written request for directions must be made on Form C2	
	Directions which may be given e g as to timetable, submission of evidence or transfer to another court	CA 1989, s 14E(1)–(3); FPR 2010, r 12.12
	Timing of proceedings	FPR 2010, r 12.13
	Attendance at the directions hearing	FPR 2010, r 12.14
Children's guardian	The child will not automatically be represented in the proceedings. The court may appoint a children's guardian if it considers it to be in the child's best interests to do so	FPR 2010, rr 16.2, 16.4

Order	On Form C43A making, discharging or varying a special guardianship order; order may contain directions or conditions	CA 1989, ss 14E(5), 11(7)
	SGO (or order varying one) may contain provisions which are to have effect for a specified period	CA 1989, s 14E(4)
	Before making an SGO court must consider whether a contact order should also be made with respect to the child, and whether any s 8 order in force with respect to the child should be varied or discharged	CA 1989, s 14B(1)
	On making an SGO the court may also give permission for the child to be known by a new surname; and grant permission to remove him from the UK	CA 1989, s 14B(2)–(4)
Variation or discharge	The court may vary or discharge an SGO on the application of:	
	The special guardian (or any of them if more than one)	
	Any parent or guardian of the child	
	Any residence order holder	
	Anyone else who has, or immediately before the making of the SGO, had parental responsibility	
	The child himself	
	A local authority designated in a care order with respect to the child	CA 1989, s 14D(1)
	The following must obtain permission before making an application to vary or discharge an SGO:	
	The child	
	Any parent or guardian of the child	
	Any step-parent of the child who has parental responsibility under s 4A	
	Anyone else who had parental responsibility for the child immediately before the making of the SGO	CA 1989, s 14D(3)–(5)
Appeals	See Guides E2, E4 and E5	
Transitional arrangements	FPR 1991 to FPR 2010	FPR PD36A

D11: Private Law Proceedings for the Disclosure of Information as to the Whereabouts of a Child

Legal background

FLA 1986, s 33, provides a power for any court, in any proceedings in relation to a child within Pt I of that Act brought in that court, to order "any person" to disclose information to the court as to the whereabouts of the child if his whereabouts are not sufficiently known. In the High Court, this adds nothing to the court's inherent powers, but a county court or family proceedings court can proceed in

this way only under s 33. The order directs that the information be given to the court, not to a party (*Chief Constable of West Yorkshire Police v S* [1998] 2 FLR 973).

Application without notice or with notice?

Where it is likely that the person who has the child may remove the child to frustrate the proceedings or order, an application may be made without notice; where the risk of the child being removed is negligible, it will usually be appropriate to apply with notice.

Procedure

Pre-condition	Missing child who is subject of proceedings or order within FLA 1986, Pt I	FLA 1986, s 33
	"Part I order" includes proceedings for or in relation to a CA 1989, s 8 order, or previous custody order, and similar orders made in Scotland, Northern Ireland and specified dependent territories; it does not include an order in proceedings for adoption or under CA 1989, Pt IV or V (public law)	FLA 1986, s 25
	Where application is made in relation to an order made in Scotland, Northern Ireland or a specified dependent territory, the order must have been registered in the High Court, and proceedings for enforcement must have been begun in that court	FLA 1986, ss 25(3), 27(1), 29(1), 32(1)
	Recovery order in public law proceedings under CA 1989	CA 1989, s 50
Who may apply	Any party with a legitimate interest in CA 1989, s 8 proceedings	
	A person who has registered an order made elsewhere in the UK or a specified dependent territory, being a person on whom rights are conferred by the order	FLA 1986, s 27(1)
Who may be directed to provide information	Any person can be so directed; see also Duty of person to whom order is directed, below	FLA 1986, s 33(1)
	Where a mother has taken a child to stay at a women's refuge, the police should not be directed to disclose the address other than to the Court manager	*Chief Constable of West Yorkshire Police v S* [1998] 2 FLR 973
Which court	Where made in pending proceedings or in relation to a subsisting s 8 order, the application should be made in the same court	FLA 1986, s 33(1)
	Where made in relation to an order registered in the High Court, the application must be made in the High Court	FLA 1986, ss 25(3), 29(1), 32(1)

	High Court judge, circuit judge, deputy circuit judge, recorder nominated for public law proceedings or Category B judge	FP(AJ)D 2009, para 6 and Sch
Form of application	On Form C4, which should be supported by evidence. Where the application is made in proceedings in the High Court or a county court under, or in relation to an order under, CA 1989, s 8 (or previous custody order), or is made in a family proceedings court, a statement that complies with FPR 2010, r 22.4 and PD22A should be ready for use at the hearing	FPR 2010, rr 16.4, 22.4; PD5A; PD12B; PD22A
	Where the application is made in the High Court otherwise than in relation to proceedings under CA 1989, s 8 (or previous custody order), an affidavit should be made in support	FPR 2010, rr 22.12, 22.13; PD22A
Fee	High Court or county court: £90 Magistrates' court: £75	FPFO 2008, fee 4.3; MCFO 2008, fee 16.2
Without notice procedure	Application may be made without notice; in an emergency, it may be made by telephone, in which case Form C4 must be (i) filed the next business day and (ii) served within 48 hours after the making of the order	FPR 2010, r 12.16
	In a magistrates' court, an application without notice by telephone is impractical, as there is no provision for the application to be heard by a single justice	FPR 2010, r 2.6
Service of application where made on notice	2 days' notice in a county court, or reasonable or adequate notice in a magistrates' court (NB FPR 2010 do not specify the period of notice required for an application made in pending proceedings)	CPR 1998, Sch 2, CCR Ord 13, r 1(2); MCA 1980, s 55(3),(4)
With notice response by respondent	The respondent should appear, and may prepare a statement that complies with FPR 2010, r 22.4 and PD22A, or affidavit, as appropriate	
Hearing	Judge or district judge in private, in High Court or county court; magistrates in family proceedings court	FP(AJ)D 2009; FPR 2010, r 27.10
	Permission needed to rely on statement of evidence in pending s 8 proceedings	FPR 2010, r 12.19
	Applicant should submit draft order, including formulation of the way in which the order should require information to be provided to the court; see –	Form C30
Form of order	C30 (note that C30 incorporates a penal notice)	FPR PD12B

Service of order	Personal service is advisable if penal enforcement may be needed	CPR 1998, Sch 2, CCR Ord 29, r 1A; MCA 1980, s 63(3)
Duty of person to whom order is directed	Person to whom order is directed must, forthwith after service, disclose to the court, in the way specified in the order, "all the information" he has about the whereabouts of the child; the court will decide what to do with the information	FLA 1986, s 33(1); see also *Re B* [1993] 1 FLR 191
	Refusal to comply cannot be excused on the basis that giving the information may tend to incriminate the giver (NB the statement or admission cannot be used in criminal proceedings other than for perjury)	FLA 1986, s 33(2)
	Legal professional privilege is no answer to the order; see under –	FLA 1986, s 33
Transitional arrangements	FPR 1991 to FPR 2010	FPR PD36A

D12: Private Law Proceedings for an Order Authorising the Taking Charge of, and Delivery of, a Child

Legal background

Under FLA 1986, s 34 any court may authorise "an officer of the court or a constable to take charge of [a] child and deliver him to" a person entitled, under an order within Pt I of that Act, to have the child given up to him. The authority under a s 34 order includes the power to "enter and search any premises where ... the child may be found, and to use such force as may be necessary". In the High Court, this power adds nothing to its inherent powers, but a county court or a family proceedings court can proceed in this way only under s 34. The powers under s 34 become available to the court only after "the child has not been given up in accordance with the order" which entitles a person to have the child given up to him: thus, unlike the inherent power of the High Court, this power cannot be used if there has been no disobedience of a previous order.

Suitability of order under s 34

An order which authorises the use of force to take charge of a child should not be granted, nor should the powers under a s 34 order be exercised, unless this is in the interests of the welfare of the child. Use of this power is more likely to be appropriate for achieving transfer of residence than for achieving contact.

Without notice or with notice?

Where it is likely that the party who has the child may remove the child to frustrate the order, an application without notice is appropriate. Where the risk is negligible, it will usually be appropriate to apply with notice.

Exercise of the power under a s 34 order

Only "an officer of the court or a constable" can exercise the power under a s 34 order. County court bailiffs are not trained for this work and do not undertake it. The police cannot be compelled to act:

R v Chief Constable of Cheshire [1990] 1 FLR 70. Although a solicitor is an officer of the Senior Courts (Solicitors Act 1974, s 50), he is not an officer of either a county court (CCA 1984, s 147) or a family proceedings court.

An order under s 34 authorises taking charge of the child, but it is not directive. Anyone seeking to exercise the authority should exercise discretion, having regard to the welfare of the child.

Procedure

Pre-condition	Failure to comply with an order (within FLA 1986, Pt I) to give up a child	FLA 1986, s 34
	"Part I order" includes a CA 1989, s 8 order, or previous custody order, and similar orders made in Scotland and Northern Ireland; it does not include an order in proceedings for adoption or under CA 1989, Pt IV or V (public law)	FLA 1986, s 25
	In a county court, a specific order to give up the child must have been ignored	FLA 1986, s 34; CPR 1998, Sch 2, CCR Ord 29, r 1(1)
	In a magistrates' court, failure to comply with a residence order which has been served is sufficient	CA 1989, s 14(1), (2)
	The order to give up the child may be in the form of a condition or direction under CA 1989, s 11(7) attached to a s 8 order, and may be attached when the s 8 order is first made, or later	
	Where the order was made elsewhere in the UK or in a specified dependent territory, it must have been registered in the High Court, and proceedings for enforcement must have been begun in that court	FLA 1986, ss 25(3), 27(1), 29(1), 32(1)
	Recovery order in public law proceedings under CA 1989	CA 1989, s 50
Who may apply	Any party with a legitimate interest in s 8 proceedings	FLA 1986, s 34
	A person who has registered an order made elsewhere in the UK or a specified dependent territory, being a person on whom rights have been conferred by the order	FLA 1986, s 27(1)
Which court	In respect of an order made in England and Wales, the court which made the order not complied with	FLA 1986, s 34(1)
	Where made in relation to an order registered in the High Court, the application must be made in the High Court	FLA 1986, ss 25(3), 29(1), 32(1)
	High Court judge, circuit judge, deputy circuit judge, recorder nominated for public law proceedings or Category B judge	FP(AJ)D 2009, para 6 and Sch

Form of application	On Form C3, which should be supported by evidence. Where the application is made in proceedings in the High Court or a county court in relation to an order under CA 1989, s 8 (or previous custody order), or is made in a magistrates' court, a statement that complies with FPR 2010, r 22.4 and PD22A should be ready for use at the hearing	FPR 2010, rr 16.4, 22.4; PD5A, PD12B, PD22A
	Where the application is made in the High Court or otherwise than in relation to proceedings under CA 1989, s 8 (or previous custody order), an affidavit should be made in support	FPR 2010, rr 22.12, 22.13; PD22A
Fee	High Court or county court: £90 Magistrates' court: £75	FPFO 2008, fee 4.3; MCFO 2008, fee 16.2
Without notice procedure	Application may be made without notice; in an emergency, it may be made by telephone, in which case Form C3 must be (i) filed the next business day and (ii) served within 48 hours after the making of the order	FPR 2010, r 12.16
	In a magistrates' court, an application without notice by telephone is impractical, as there is no provision for the application to be heard by a single justice	FPR 2010, r 2.16
Service of application where made on notice	2 days' notice in a county court, or reasonable or adequate notice in a magistrates' court (NB FPR 2010 do not specify the period of notice required for an application made in pending proceedings)	CPR 1998, Sch 2, CCR Ord 13, r 1(2); MCA 1980, s 55(3),(4)
	Personal service is advisable so that the court may be satisfied that the respondent is aware of the hearing	
With notice response by respondent	The respondent should appear, and may prepare a statement which complies with FPR 2010, r 22.4 and PD22A or affidavit, as appropriate	
Hearing	Judge or district judge in private, in High Court or a county court; magistrates in family proceedings court	FP(AJ)D 2009; FPR 2010, r 27.10
	Permission needed to rely on statement of evidence in pending s 8 proceedings	FPR 2010, r 12.19
	Applicant should submit draft order	Form C31
Form of order	C31	FPR PD12B

| "Unless" order | C31 may be adapted to state that, unless the respondent hands over the child at a specified time and place, the power may be exercised thereafter. This allows the respondent to save face by delivering the child | |
| Transitional arrangements | FPR 1991 to FPR 2010 | FPR PD36A |

D13: Care or Supervision Order

Legal background

By virtue of CA 1989, s 31, the court may only make an order placing a child in the care of a local authority or putting him under the supervision of a local authority or a probation officer if it is satisfied, that the child is suffering or is likely to suffer significant harm under the threshold criteria and that the harm or likelihood of harm is attributable to the care given to him (or likely to be given to him if an order were not made) falling below a reasonable standard or his being beyond parental control. If the court finds the threshold criteria proved, it must then decide whether or not to make an order and, if so, which sort of order would be appropriate. In so doing, it must take into account the CA 1989, s 1(1) welfare principle and the checklist of factors set out in CA 1989, s 1(3), bearing in mind the general principle that delay is likely to prejudice the welfare of the child (CA 1989, s 1(2)). It must not make an order unless it considers that to do so would be better for the child than to make no order at all (CA 1989, s 1(5)). Before making a care order, the court must consider the arrangements that the local authority have made, or propose to make, for affording any person contact with the child and invite the parties to comment on those arrangements (CA 1989, s 33(11)).

While a care order is in force, the designated local authority has a duty to receive the child into its care and to keep him in its care for the duration of the order (see CA 1989, s 33(1)). Subject to certain restrictions set out in CA 1989, s 33, the local authority has parental responsibility for the child and has the power to decide what role his parents or guardian may play in the child's life. The order can be discharged or a supervision order substituted on an application under CA 1989, s 39, or it may be discharged by the making of a residence order in respect of the child (CA 1989, s 91(1)).

A supervision order lasts for 1 year in the first instance (though it can subsequently be extended so as to run for a period of up to 3 years from the date on which it was originally made) and imposes a general duty on the supervisor to advise, assist and befriend the child (see CA 1989, s 35 and Sch 3, Pts I and II). The supervisor must take such steps as are reasonably necessary to give effect to the order and, where the order is not wholly complied with or where he considers that it may no longer be necessary, he must consider whether he should apply to the court for it to be varied or discharged. The order can be discharged or varied on an application under CA 1989, s 39. A subsequent care order also discharges a supervision order (CA 1989, s 91(3)).

Where the main care or supervision proceedings are adjourned or the court gives a direction to the local authority under CA 1989, s 37(1) to investigate the child's circumstances, CA 1989, s 38(1) permits the making of an interim care or supervision order, provided that the court is satisfied that there are reasonable grounds for believing that the grounds for a full order exist (CA 1989, s 38(2)). There are stringent restrictions on the duration of interim orders (see CA 1989, s 38(4)). Directions with regard to the medical or psychiatric examination or other assessment of the child can be given either at the time of making an interim care or supervision order or at any time while it is in force (CA 1989, s 38(6)–(8)) and can be varied on application. Section 38A enables the court to include an exclusion requirement in an interim care order and to attach a power of arrest to that provision. The purpose of an exclusion requirement is to safeguard a child by removing from the scene (whether from the child's home or from part of it or from the area in which it is situated) a person who poses a threat to the child. Application can be made to vary or discharge the exclusion requirement and attendant power of arrest (CA 1989, s 39).

All applications made under CA 1989, Pt IV (care and supervision orders) are subject to the Public Law Outline (PLO) in FPR PD12A. See **First appointment**, **Case management conference** and **Issues resolution hearing** *under FPR 2010, r 12.25.*

In August 2009, the MoJ issued a *Best Practice Guide: Preparing for Care and Supervision Proceedings* (see Part V), which is for use by all professionals involved with children and families pre-proceedings and in preparation for applications made under CA 1989, s 31. It complements the Statutory Guidance and the PLO (FPR PD12A) but is not intended to be prescriptive. In April 2011, the President of the Family Division issued *Listing and Hearing Care Cases* (see Part V), which outlines best practice in ensuring judicial continuity and proactive judicial case management in accordance with the PLO (FPR PD12A). In respect of cases proceeding in the Family Proceedings Court, this guidance should be read with the *President's Guidance in Relation to Allocation and Continuity of Case Managers in the Family Proceedings Courts* (see Part V) issued in July 2011.

Procedure

Who may apply	Any local authority or authorised person (ie officer of NSPCC or anyone authorised by the Secretary of State)	CA 1989, s 31(1),(9)
Which court	Magistrates' court unless pending proceedings or application arises out of a CA 1989, s 37 investigation by local authority, in which case apply to court where proceedings pending or court which requires investigation	ATPO 2008, arts 5, 9
	Proceedings may be transferable sideways, upwards or downwards, depending on circumstances	ATPO 2008, arts 14–19
Which proceedings	Freestanding application or application in other family proceedings	CA 1989, s 31(4)
	Court may make supervision order on application for care order or vice versa, but otherwise has no power to make full care or supervision order of its own initiative	CA 1989, s 31(1),(5)
Pre-proceedings checklist	Local authority must carry out specified work set out in checklist before filing an application	FPR PD12A
Application	On Form C110, with copies for each respondent	FPR PD12A; PD5A
	On filing Form C110 the timetable under the PLO starts at Day 1 and must be strictly adhered to until the conclusion of the case	FPR PD12A (PLO, stage 1)
	Cases commenced in or transferred to the Family Division at the Royal Courts of Justice will be allocated to a High Court judge and special procedures apply	FPR 2010, PD12A
Fees	On application: £2225	FPFO 2008, fee 2.2(a); MCFO 2008, fee 8.2(a)
	Where IRH or PHR listed, at least 14 days before hearing: £700	FPFO 2008, fee 2.2(b); MCFO 2008, fee 8.2(b)
	Where final hearing listed, at least 14 days before hearing: £1900	FPFO 2008, fee 2.2(c); MCFO 2008, fee 8.2(c)
	In certain circumstances part or all of the fee may be refunded	FPFO 2008, notes to fee 2.2; MCFO 2008, notes to fee 8.2
Respondents	Every person whom applicant believes has parental responsibility	
	The child	FPR 2010, r 12.3

Additional persons to whom notice in Form C6A is to be given	Local authority providing accommodation for child	
	Persons caring for child at commencement of proceedings	
	Person providing a CA 1989, s 51 refuge for child	
	Every person whom applicant believes is a party to pending relevant proceedings re same child	
	Every person whom applicant believes is a parent without parental responsibility for child	FPR PD12C
Service	Copy of application, together with Form C6, to be served on respondents at least 3 days before date of hearing or directions appointment (ie by Day 3 of PLO)	FPR PD12A (PLO, stage 1), PD12C
	Form C6A to be served on additional persons at same time as application etc served on respondents	FPR PD12C
	At or before first directions appointment or hearing (by Day 6 of PLO), applicant must file statement in Form C9 to prove that requirements for service have been complied with	FPR PD12A (PLO, stage 1)
Without notice	May not be available (but see below as to interim orders)	FPR 2010, r 12.16
Joinder or removal of parties	By court order, of its own initiative or on written request	FPR 2010, rr 4.3, 12.3(3)
Answer to application	Respondent may file answer; serve on other parties	FPR PD12A
Directions	Powers of the justices' clerk or the court	FPR 2010, rr 12.12, 12.24; PD12A (PLO, stage 1)
Children's guardian	Must normally be appointed	CA 1989, s 41(1); FPR PD12A (PLO, stage 1)
Interim orders	Unless permission given, interim application must be in writing on notice (can be included on Form C1)	FPR 2010, r 12.12
	With permission, interim order can be sought without formal written application or notice	
Who has power to make the order	High Court judge, circuit judge, deputy circuit judge, recorder nominated for public law proceedings or Category B judge	FP(AJ)D 2009, para 6 and Sch
	Magistrates' court	
	A justices' clerk or single justice has *limited* power to make interim orders by consent, but no power to make full care or supervision orders	JCR 2005; CA 1989, s 93(2)(i); FPR 2010, r 2.6

Order	*Interim care order* Form C33 *Care order* Form C32 *Supervision order (interim or full)* Form C35	FPR PD12A
Additional or alternative orders available without prior application	Interim care/supervision order with or without directions as to assessment Care order/supervision order Residence order (but not in favour of local authority and not with a care order)	CA 1989, s 38(1),(6) CA 1989, s 31(1),(5) CA 1989, ss 9(2), 10(1), 91(1)
	Prohibited steps order (but subject to s 9(5) and not with a care order)	CA 1989, ss 9(1), 10(1)
	Specific issue order (but subject to s 9(5) and not with a care order)	CA 1989, ss 9(1), 10(1)
	Section 8 contact order (but not in favour of local authority and not with a care order)	CA 1989, ss 9(1),(2), 10(1)
	Section 34 contact order (in conjunction with care order)	CA 1989, s 34(5)
	Family assistance order	CA 1989, s 16(1)
	Order appointing children's guardian	CA 1989, s 5(2)
	Order terminating appointment of guardian	CA 1989, s 6(7)(c)
	Order for financial relief (in certain limited circumstances only)	CA 1989, s 15, Sch 1
	No order	CA 1989, s 1(5)
	There is no reason why other orders (e g a parental responsibility order under s 4) should not be sought at the same time as a care or supervision order in an appropriate case, but a prior application would need to be made in accordance with the rules (FPR 2010)	
Procedure for exclusion requirements	Applicant for interim care order prepares separate statement of evidence in support re: exclusion requirement	
	Applicant serves statement and copy of order containing exclusion requirement (and of any power of arrest attached) personally on relevant person (i e person who is excluded) and informs relevant person of right to apply to vary/discharge exclusion requirement. It is important when effecting service that the process server complies with the Family Justice Council *Protocol for Process Servers*	CA 1989, s 38A; FPR 2010, r 12.28(2); FJC Protocol of November 2011: *Process Servers:* *Non-Molestation Orders*
	If power of arrest attached, once relevant person served with order/informed of terms, copy of order must be delivered to police together with statement showing relevant person served/informed of terms	FPR 2010, r 12.28(3); FJC Protocol of November 2011: *Process Servers:* *Non-Molestation Orders*

	Unless relevant person given notice and attended hearing, if power of arrest attached to exclusion order, court must announce in open court at earliest opportunity the name of person and fact that such order made	FPR PD12K
	Consent of person who is assuming care of child is required	CA 1989, s 38A(2); FPR 2010, r 12.29
Variation/discharge of exclusion requirement and attendant power of arrest	Application for variation/discharge re: exclusion requirement or re: power of arrest by person to whom it applies, Form C2 suggested	CA 1989, s 39(3A),(3B)
	Applicant serves parties to the proceedings with application for variation/discharge	FPR 2010, r 12.28(5)
	Consider giving notice to person caring for child	FPR PD12C
	Steps to be taken on variation/discharge affecting exclusion requirement/power of arrest	FPR 2010, r 12.18(4),(6)
Appeals	See Guides E2, E4 and E5	
Transitional arrangements	FPR 1991 to FPR 2010	FPR PD36A

D14: Discharge etc of a Care or Supervision Order, Substitution of a Supervision Order for a Care Order or Variation or Extension of a Supervision Order

Legal background

Under CA 1989, s 39, application may be made for the discharge of a care or supervision order or the variation of a supervision order. CA 1989, s 39(4) also empowers the court, on application, to substitute a supervision order for a care order, regardless of whether the threshold provisions set out in CA 1989, s 31(2) are satisfied at the time. In considering all s 39 applications, the court must apply the principle that the child's welfare is paramount (CA 1989, s 1(1)) and have regard to the checklist of factors in CA 1989, s 1(3) as well as to its duty not to make an order unless to do so would be more beneficial for the child than not to do so (CA 1989, s 1(5)).

Since the making of a residence order in relation to a child who is the subject of a care order discharges the care order (CA 1989, s 91(1)), an application for a residence order can, in an appropriate case, be an alternative to an application under s 39(1) for discharge.

An application to extend the length of a supervision order should be made by the supervisor under CA 1989, Sch 3, para 6(3) rather than in reliance on the more general power in s 39(2) to vary a supervision order.

All applications issued by local authorities under CA 1989, Pt IV are subject to the Public Law Outline (PLO) in FPR PD12A. See further in the introduction to Guide D13 and **First appointment, Case management conference** and **Issues resolution hearing** under FPR 2010, r 12.25.

Procedure

Who may apply	The child	
	Any person with parental responsibility for the child	
	Discharge of care order	
	Local authority designated in order	
	Discharge of supervision order	
	Supervisor and, where application is to vary a requirement affecting a person with whom child is living, that person	CA 1989, s 39(1)–(3)
	Extension of supervision order	CA 1989, Sch 3,
	Supervisor only	para 6(3)
Which court	The court which made the original order	ATPO 2008, art 5(3)
	Proceedings may be transferable sideways, upwards or downwards, depending on circumstances	ATPO 2008, arts 14–19
Which proceedings	Freestanding application	
Pre-proceedings checklist	Local authority must carry out specified work set out in checklist before filing an application	FPR PD12A
Application	On Form C110, with sufficient copies for each respondent	FPR PD5A, PD12A
	On filing Form C110 the timetable under the PLO starts at Day 1 and must be strictly adhered to until the conclusion of the case	FPR PD12A (PLO, stage 1)
	Fee: £170	FPFO 2008, fee 2.1(m); MCFO 2008, fee 8.1(m)
Respondents	Every person whom applicant believes has parental responsibility	
	Every person whom applicant believes had parental responsibility before care order	
	The child	
	The parties to the original proceedings	
	The supervisor (supervision order only)	FPR 2010, r 12.3
Additional persons to whom notice in Form C6A is to be given	Local authority providing accommodation for child	
	Persons caring for child at commencement of proceedings	
	Person providing a CA 1989, s 51 refuge for child	FPR PD12C
Service	Copy of application, together with Form C6, to be served on respondent by Day 3	FPR PD5A, PD12A (PLO, stage 1)
	Form C6A to be served on additional persons at same time as application etc served on respondents	FPR PD12C, para 3.1

	At or before first directions appointment or hearing (by Day 6 of PLO), applicant must file statement in Form C9 to prove that requirements for service have been complied with	PD12A (PLO, stage 1)
Without notice	Not available	FPR 2010, r 12.16
Joinder or removal of parties	By court order, of its own initiative or on written request	FPR 2010, rr 4.3, 12.3(3); FPR PD12A (PLO, stage 1)
Answer to application	Respondent may file answer; serve on other parties	FPR PD12A
Directions	Powers of the justices' clerk or the court	FPR 2010, rr 12.12, 12.24; PD12A (PLO, stage 1)
Children's guardian	Must normally be appointed	CA 1989, s 41(1); FPR PD12A (PLO, stage 1)
Special requirements	Following application for discharge of care order, supervision order, education supervision order, or for substitution of supervision order for care order or for child assessment order, bar on further application within 6 months from disposal of application, unless permission given	CA 1989, s 91(15)
Who has power to make the order	High Court judge, circuit judge, deputy circuit judge, recorder nominated for public law proceedings or Category B judge	FP(AJ)D 2009, para 6 and Sch
	Magistrates' court; however, justices' clerk or single justice has no such power	JCR 2005; CA 1989, s 93(2)(i); FPR 2010, r 2.6
Order	*Discharge of care order* Form C32 *Other applications* Form C36	FPR PD12A
Additional or alternative orders available on applications under CA 1989, s 39 without prior application	Section 8 order (residence, prohibited steps, specific issue or contact), but subject to certain restrictions Section 34 contact order (if care order is to continue)	CA 1989, ss 9(1), (2), 10(1), 91(1) CA 1989, s 34(5)
	Family assistance order	CA 1989, s 16(1)
	Order appointing children's guardian	CA 1989, s 5(2)
	Order terminating appointment of guardian	CA 1989, s 6(7)(c)
	Order for financial relief (in certain limited circumstances only)	CA 1989, s 15, Sch 1
	No order	CA 1989, s 1(5)

	There is no reason why other orders (e g a parental responsibility order under s 4) should not be sought in an appropriate case at the same time as an application for discharge or variation is made, but a prior application would need to be made in accordance with the rules (FPR 1991 and FPC(CA 1989)R 1991)	
Appeals	See Guides E2, E4 and E5	
Transitional arrangements	FPR 1991 to FPR 2010	
		FPR PD36A

D15: Regulating Contact with Children in Care

Legal background

The local authority has a duty to allow reasonable contact between a child in care and the child's parents, guardian, any person who had a residence order immediately before the care order was made and any person who had care of the child immediately before the care order by virtue of an order made under the High Court's inherent jurisdiction (CA 1989, s 34(1)). As a matter of urgency, the local authority may withhold contact for a period of up to 7 days if it is satisfied that it is necessary to do so to safeguard or promote the child's welfare (CA 1989, s 34(6)). If this is not sufficient to cover the situation, an order authorising the local authority to refuse contact to a named person can be obtained from the court under CA 1989, s 34(4) and is not limited in time.

The court also has a general power to make such an order (with or without conditions, CA 1989, s 34(7)) as it considers appropriate with respect to the contact that is to be allowed between the child and a named person (CA 1989, s 34(2), (3)), and this can be used to define contact where there is dissatisfaction with the level of contact the local authority has decided upon, to resolve a dispute with the local authority as to whether contact needs to be supervised etc. CA 1989, s 8 contact orders cannot co-exist with a care order and the position is therefore regulated exclusively by CA 1989, s 34. If a CA 1989, s 8 contact order existed before the making of the care order, the care order will automatically discharge it (CA 1989, s 91(2)), and no s 8 contact order can be made in relation to a child in care (CA 1989, s 9(1)).

All applications issued by local authorities under CA 1989, Pt IV are subject to the Public Law Outline (PLO) in FPR PD12A. See further in the introduction to Guide D13 and **First appointment**, **Case management conference** and **Issues resolution hearing** under FPR 2010, r 12.25.

Procedure

Who may apply	Local authority	
	Child	
	AND (unless application is for refusal of contact)	
	Parent	
	Children's guardian	
	Person who had residence order immediately before care order	
	Person who had care of child immediately before care order by virtue of High Court order under inherent jurisdiction	
	Any other person with permission	CA 1989, s 34(2)–(4)

Which court	Magistrates' court unless pending proceedings, in which case apply to court where proceedings pending	ATPO 2008, art 5(3)
	Proceedings may be transferable sideways, upwards or downwards, depending on circumstances	ATPO 2008, arts 14–19
Which proceedings	Freestanding application	CA 1989, s 34(2)–(4)
	When making care order or in any family proceedings in connection with child in care, even though no application has been made	CA 1989, s 34(5)
Pre-proceedings checklist	Local authority must carry out specified work set out in checklist before filing an application	FPR PD12A
Application	*Contact* Form C110 and Supplement C15, with sufficient copies for each respondent	
	Refusal of contact Form C110 and Supplement C14, with sufficient copies for each respondent	FPR PD5A, PD12A
	On filing Forms C110 and C15/C14 the Timetable under the PLO starts at Day 1 and must be strictly adhered to until the conclusion of the case	FPR PD12A (PLO, stage 1)
	Fee: £170	FPFO 2008, fee 2.1(k); MCFO 2008, fee 8.1(k)
Respondents	Every person whom applicant believes has parental responsibility	
	Every person whom applicant believes had parental responsibility before care order	
	The child The person whose contact with the child is the subject of the application	FPR 2010, r 12.3
Additional persons to whom notice in Form C6A is to be given	Local authority providing accommodation for child Persons caring for child at commencement of proceedings Person providing a s 51 refuge for child	FPR PD12C, para 3.1
Service	Copy of application, together with Form C6, to be served on respondents at least 3 days before date of hearing or directions appointment (ie by Day 3 of PLO)	FPR PD12A (PLO, stage 1), PD12C
	Form C6A to be served on additional persons at same time as application etc served on respondents	FPR PD12C
	At or before first directions appointment or hearing (by Day 6 of PLO), applicant must file statement in Form C9 to prove that requirements for service have been complied with	FPR PD5A, PD12A (PLO, stage 1)
Without notice	Not available	FPR 2010, r 12.16

Joinder or removal of parties	By court order, of its own initiative or on written request	FPR 2010, rr 4.3, 12.3(3); PD12A (PLO, stage 1)
Answer to application	Respondent may file answer; serve on other parties	FPR PD12A
Directions	As to the powers of the justices' clerk or the court, see –	FPR 2010, rr 12.12, 12.24; PD12A (PLO, stage 1)
Children's guardian	Must normally be appointed	CA 1989, s 41(1); FPR PD12A (PLO, stage 1)
Special requirements	Bar on further application within 6 months from refusal of application unless permission given	CA 1989, s 91(17)
Who has power to make the order	High Court judge, circuit judge, deputy circuit judge, recorder nominated for public law proceedings or Category B judge	FP(AJ)D 2009, para 6 and Sch
	Magistrates' court	
	A justices' clerk or single justice has no such power, although a single justice may grant permission to make the application	JCR 2005; FPR 2010, r 2.6
Order	Form C34	FPR PD12A
Additional or alternative orders	Residence order in favour of someone other than local authority (but subject to CA 1989, s 9 restrictions, and note that effect would be to discharge care order)	CA 1989, ss 9(1),(2), 10(1), 91(1)
	No order	CA 1989, s 1(5)
	Other orders which are theoretically possible but very unlikely to be appropriate:	
	family assistance order	CA 1989, s 16(1)
	order appointing children's guardian/terminating appointment	CA 1989, ss 5(2), 6(7)(c)
Appeals	See Guides E2, E4 and E5	
Transitional arrangements	FPR 1991 to FPR 2010	FPR PD36A

D16: Discharge or Variation of an Order Regulating Contact with Children in Care

Legal background

An order under CA 1989, s 34 may be varied or discharged by the court on an application under CA 1989, s 34(9); alternatively, the local authority and the person entitled to contact can agree a variation in accordance with the Contact with Children Regulations 1991.

All applications issued by local authorities under CA 1989, Pt IV are subject to the Public Law Outline (PLO) in FPR PD12A. See further in the introduction to Guide D13 and **First appointment**, **Case management conference** and **Issues resolution hearing** under FPR 2010, r 12.25.

Procedure

Who may apply	Local authority	
	The child	
	The person named in the order	CA 1989, s 34(9)
Which court	The court which made the original order	ATPO 2008, art 5(3)
	Proceedings may be transferable sideways, upwards or downwards, depending on circumstances	ATPO 2008, arts 14–19
Which proceedings	Freestanding application	CA 1989, s 34(9)
	In any family proceedings in connection with child in care, even though no application has been made	CA 1989, s 34(5)
Pre-proceedings checklist	Local authority must carry out specified work set out in checklist before filing an application	FPR PD12A
Application	On Form C110, with copies for each respondent	FPR PD5A, PD12A
	On filing Form C110 the timetable under the PLO starts at Day 1 and must be strictly adhered to until the conclusion of the case	FPR PD5A, PD12A (PLO, stage 1)
	Fee: £170	FPFO 2008, fee 2.1(k); MCFO 2008, fee 8.1(k)
Respondents	As for initial application, *plus* the parties to the original proceedings	FPR 2010, r 12.3
Additional persons to whom notice in Form C6A is to be given	Local authority providing accommodation for child Persons caring for child at commencement of proceedings Person providing a s 51 refuge for child	FPR PD12C, para 3.1
Service	Copy of application, together with Form C6, to be served on respondents at least 3 days before date of hearing or directions appointment (i e by Day 3 of PLO)	FPR PD12A (PLO, stage 1), PD12C
	Form C6A to be served on additional persons at same time as application etc served on respondents	FPR PD12C
	At or before first directions appointment or hearing (by Day 6 of PLO), applicant must file statement in Form C9 to prove that requirements for service have been complied with	FPR PD5A, PD12A
Without notice	Not available	FPR 2010, r 12.16
Joinder or removal of parties	By court order, of its own initiative or on written request	FPR 2010, rr 4.3, 12.3(3); PD12A (PLO, stage 1)

Answer to application	Under FPR 2010, respondent may file answer; serve on other parties	FPR PD12A
Directions	Powers of the justices' clerk or the court	FPR 2010, rr 12.12, 12.24; PD12A (PLO, stage 1)
Children's guardian	Must normally be appointed	CA 1989, s 41(1); FPR PD12A (PLO, stage 1)
Special requirements	Bar on further application within 6 months from refusal of application unless permission given	CA 1989, s 91(17)
Who has power to make the order	High Court judge, circuit judge, deputy circuit judge, recorder nominated for public law proceedings or Category B judge	FP(AJ)D 2009, para 6 and Sch
	A nominated district judge outside the Principal Registry, in relation to interlocutory matters, unopposed trials and opposed hearings where the application is for a contact order and the principle of contact is unopposed	FP(AJ)D 2009
	Magistrates' court; however, justices' clerk or single justice has no such power	JCR 2005; CA 1989, s 93(2)(i); FPR 2010, r 2.6
Order	Form C21	
Additional or alternative orders	Residence order in favour of someone other than local authority (but subject to CA 1989, s 9 restrictions, and note that effect would be to discharge care order)	CA 1989, ss 9(1), (2), 10(1), 91(1)
	No order	CA 1989, s 1(5)
	Other orders which are theoretically possible but very unlikely to be appropriate:	
	family assistance order	CA 1989, s 16(1)
	order appointing children's guardian/terminating appointment	CA 1989, ss 5(2), 6(7)(c)
Appeals	See Guides E2, E4 and E5	
Transitional arrangements	FPR 1991 to FPR 2010	FPR PD36A

D17: Secure Accommodation Order

Legal background

Restricting the liberty of a child is a serious step and is therefore strictly regulated by CA 1989, s 25 and by the Children (Secure Accommodation) Regulations 1991 and the Children (Secure Accommodation) (No 2) Regulations 1991. With certain exceptions, a child may not be placed or kept in secure accommodation unless either he has a history of absconding and is likely to abscond if kept in any other type of accommodation and, if he absconds, to suffer significant harm or he is likely to injure himself or others if kept in any other type of accommodation. Where either of these criteria is satisfied, a child may be kept in secure accommodation for a maximum of 72 hours without court authority but, if there is a need to detain him for longer, an application must be made to the court. If the court is satisfied that the relevant criteria are met, it will make an order authorising the child to be kept in secure accommodation for a specified maximum period of time (up to 3 months for a first application and up to 6 months on any further application).

A freestanding application for an *interim* secure accommodation order cannot be made. Where the court is satisfied it has all the information needed to determine the issues raised by the application and that it would be procedurally fair to proceed, it is unlikely there would be grounds upon which the court could properly adjourn the application. Prolonging secure accommodation proceedings, simply in order to keep a children's guardian involved for the purposes of assisting the child or overseeing the performance of the local authority's statutory duties is not a proper use of the court's power (*Birmingham City Council v M* [2008] 2 FLR 542).

Procedure

Who may apply	Where local authority looking after child, only the local authority	C(SA)R 1991, reg 8
	Where health authority, National Health Service trust or local education authority providing accommodation for child, only the health authority etc, unless local authority looking after child	C(SA)(No 2)R 1991, reg 2(1)
	Where child provided with accommodation in residential care home, nursing home or mental nursing home, only the person providing such accommodation, unless local authority looking after child	C(SA)(No 2)R 1991, reg 2(2)
Which court	Magistrates' court, unless pending proceedings, in which case apply to court where proceedings pending	ATPO 2008, art 5(2)(c)
	Proceedings may be transferable sideways, upwards or downwards, depending on circumstances	ATPO 2008, arts 14–18; *President's PD:* 3 November 2008
Which proceedings	Freestanding application for a final order but may not apply for an interim order	
Which court for variation, extension or discharge of order	Court by which original order made	
Application	On Form C1 and Supplement C20, with sufficient copies for each respondent	FPR 2010, rr 12.5, 12.7, 12.8 and 12.16; PD12C, para 2.1(1)
	Fee payable in High Court or county court: £170	FPFO 2008, art 2.1(i)
	Fee payable in magistrates' court: £170	MCFO 2008, fee 8.1(i)
Respondents	Every person whom applicant believes has parental responsibility	
	Every person whom applicant believes had parental responsibility before care order	
	The child	
	Where application is to vary etc, parties to original proceedings	FPR 2010, r 12.3

Additional persons to whom notice in Form C6A is to be given	Local authority providing accommodation for child Person caring for child at commencement of proceedings Person providing a CA 1989, s 51 refuge for child	FPR 2010, rr 12.3, 12.5, 12.7, 12.8 and 12.16; PD12C, para 3.1(1)
Additional persons to be notified of intention to apply	Where application relates to child already kept in secure accommodation in a community home: child's independent visitor, if appointed any other person whom local authority considers should be informed	C(SA)R 1991, reg 14
Service	Copy of application, together with Form C6, to be served on respondent at least 1 day before date of hearing or directions appointment	FPR 2010, r 12.8; PD12C, para 2.1(6)
	Form C6A to be served on additional persons at same time as application etc served on respondents	FPR 2010, r 12.8; PD12C, paras 1.1, 3.1
Ex parte	May not be available	FPR 2010, r 12.16
Joinder or removal of parties	By court order, of its own motion or on written request	FPR 2010, rr 12.3(3), 16.2
Answer to application	Respondent may file answer; serve on other parties	
Directions	Powers of the justices' clerk or the court	FPR 2010, rr 2.5, 2.6, 12.12 and Pt 4
Children's guardian	Must normally be appointed	CA 1989, s 41(1)
Special requirements	Order may not be made unless child is legally represented or has been told of the right to apply for CLS funding and given opportunity to do so and has refused or failed to apply	CA 1989, s 25(6)
Who has power to make the order	A High Court judge, a circuit judge, deputy circuit judge, recorder nominated for public law proceedings or a category B judge	FP(AJ)D 2009, para 6 and Sch
	A magistrates' court; however, justices' clerk or single justice has no such power	FPR 2010, rr 2.5, 2.6, 12.12 and Pt 4; PD2A
Order	Form C26	FPR 2010, r 5
Additional or alternative orders	No order Wide range of alternative orders may be available, e g s 8 orders, since CA 1989, s 25 proceedings in magistrates' courts are "family proceedings" by virtue of s 92(2)	CA 1989, s 1(5)
Appeals	See Guides E2 and E5: note an appeal from a magistrates' court lies to a county court	

D18: Education Supervision Order

Legal background

If the court is satisfied that a child of compulsory school age is not being properly educated it can make an education supervision order (ESO) putting him under the supervision of a designated local education authority (CA 1989, s 36). In making a decision whether or not to grant an ESO, the court must take into account the CA 1989, s 1(1) welfare principle and the checklist of factors set out in CA 1989, s 1(3), as well as bearing in mind the general principle that delay is likely to prejudice the welfare of the child (CA 1989, s 1(2)). It must not make an order unless it considers that to do so would be better for the child than to make no order at all (CA 1989, s 1(5)). An ESO cannot be made in respect of a child who is in the care of a local authority (CA 1989, s 36(6)), but there is no bar on the co-existence of an ESO and a supervision order, in which case the supervision order will take precedence (CA 1989, Sch 3, para 14).

An education supervision (ESO) order may be discharged by the court on application under CA 1989, Sch 3, para 17. On discharging an ESO, the court may direct the local authority within whose area the child lives, or will live, to investigate the child's circumstances (CA 1989, Sch 3, para 17(2)).

Detailed provisions as to the effect and duration etc of an ESO can be found in CA 1989, Sch 3, Pt III. In the first instance the order lasts for 1 year but can be extended subsequently. It imposes a general duty on the supervisor to advise, assist, befriend and give directions to the child and his parents to ensure that he is properly educated. A parent who persistently fails to comply with a direction given under an ESO can be guilty of an offence under CA 1989, Sch 3, para 18. Where the child persistently fails to comply with any directions given under an ESO, the local education authority must notify the appropriate local authority, which then has to investigate the child's circumstances and may see fit to apply for a care order (CA 1989, Sch 3, para 19).

All applications issued by local authorities under CA 1989, Pt IV are subject to the Public Law Outline (PLO) in FPR PD12A. See further in the introduction to Guide D13 and **First appointment, Case management conference** and **Issues resolution hearing** under FPR 2010, r 12.25.

Procedure

Who may apply	Any local education authority	CA 1989, s 36(1)
Which court	Magistrates' court, unless pending proceedings or application arises out of a s 37 investigation by local authority, in which case apply to court where proceedings pending or court which required investigation	ATPO 2008, art 5(3)
	Proceedings may be transferable sideways, upwards or downwards, depending on circumstances	ATPO 2008, arts 14–19
Which proceedings	Freestanding application	CA 1989, s 36(1)
Pre-proceedings checklist	Local authority must carry out specified work set out in checklist before filing an application	FPR PD12A (PLO)
Application	On Forms C110 and Supplement C17, with sufficient copies for each respondent	FPR PD5A, PD12A
	On filing Form C110 the timetable under the protocol starts at Day 1 and must be strictly adhered to until the conclusion of the case	FPR PD12A (PLO, stage 1)
	Fee: £170	FPFO 2008, fee 2.1(l); MCFO 2008, fee 8.1(l)

Respondents	Every person whom applicant believes has parental responsibility The child	FPR 2010, r 12.3
Additional persons to whom notice in Form C6A is to be given	Local authority providing accommodation for child Persons caring for child at commencement of proceedings Person providing a CA 1989, s 51 refuge for child	FPR PD12C, para 3.1
Service	Copy of application, together with a Notice of Proceedings, to be served on respondents at least 7 days before date of hearing or directions appointment (but NB under PLO all respondents must be served by Day 3)	FPR PD12A (PLO, stage 1), PD12C
	A Notice of Proceedings (non-parties) to be served on additional persons at same time as application etc served on respondents	FPR PD12C
	At or before first directions appointment or hearing (by Day 6 of the PLO), applicant must file statement in Form C9 to prove that requirements for service have been complied with	FPR PD5A, PD12A (PLO, stage 1)
Without notice	Not available	FPR 2010, r 12.16
Joinder or removal of parties	By court order, of its own initiative or on written request	FPR 2010, rr 4.3, 12.3(3)
Answer to application	Respondent may file answer; serve on other parties at least 2 days before date fixed for hearing of application	FPR PD12A
Directions	Powers of the justices' clerk or the court	FPR 2010, rr 12.12, 12.24; PD12A (PLO, stage 1)
Children's guardian	Not "specified proceedings"	CA 1989, s 41(1)
Special requirements	Local education authority must consult local authority social services committee before applying	CA 1989, s 36(8)
Who has power to make the order	High Court judge, circuit judge, deputy circuit judge, recorder nominated for public law proceedings or Category B judge	FP(AJ)D 2009, para 6 and Sch
	Magistrates' court; however, justices' clerk or single justice has no such power	JCR 2005; CA 1989, s 93(2)(i); FPR 2010, r 2.6
Order	Form C37	FPR PD12A
Additional or alternative orders	Direction requiring local authority to investigate with a view to care or supervision order	CA 1989, s 37(1)
	CA 1989, s 8 order (but subject to restrictions in CA 1989, s 9)	CA 1989, s 10(1)
	Family assistance order	CA 1989, s 16(1)

PART I

	Order appointing children's guardian or terminating appointment	CA 1989, ss 5(2), 6(7)(c)
	No order	CA 1989, s 1(5)
Appeals	See Guides E2, E4 and E5	
Transitional arrangements	FPR 1991 to FPR 2010	FPR PD36A

D19: Extension of an Education Supervision Order

Legal background

An education supervision order (ESO) may be extended by the court (CA 1989, Sch 3, para 15(2)). Application must be made during the currency of the order (para 15(2)) but may not be made earlier than 3 months before the date on which the order is due to expire (para 15(3)). There can be more than one extension, each extension being for not more than 3 years (para 15(4), (5)).

All applications issued by local authorities under CA 1989, Pt IV are subject to the Public Law Outline (PLO) in FPR PD12A. See further in the introduction to Guide D13 and **First appointment**, **Case management conference** and **Issues resolution hearing** under FPR 2010, r 12.25.

Procedure

Who may apply	Local education authority in whose favour order was made	CA 1989, Sch 3, para 15(2)
Which court	The court which made the original order	ATPO 2008, art 5(3)
	Proceedings may be transferable sideways, upwards or downwards, depending on circumstances	ATPO 2008, arts 14–19
Which proceedings	Freestanding application	CA 1989, Sch 3, para 15(2)
Pre-proceedings checklist	Local authority must carry out specified work set out in checklist before filing an application	FPR PD12A
Application	On Forms C110 and Supplement C17A	FPR PD5A, PD12A
	On filing Forms C110 and C17A the timetable under the PLO starts at Day 1 and must be strictly adhered to until the conclusion of the case	FPR PD12A (PLO, stage 1)
	Fee: £170	FPFO 2008, fee 2.1(x); MCFO 2008, fee 8.1(x)
Respondents	Every person whom applicant believes has parental responsibility	
	The child	
	The parties to the original application	FPR 2010, r 12.3
Additional persons to whom notice in Form C6A is to be given	Local authority providing accommodation for child	
	Persons caring for child at commencement of proceedings	
	Person providing a s 51 refuge for child	FPR PD12C, para 3.1

PART I

Service	Copy of application, together with Form C6, to be served on respondents at least 7 days before date of hearing or directions appointment (but NB under PLO all respondents must be served by Day 3)	FPR PD12A (PLO, stage 1), PD12C
	Form C6A to be served on additional persons at same time as application etc served on respondents	FPR PD12C
	At or before first directions appointment or hearing (by Day 6 of PLO), applicant must file statement in Form C9 to prove that requirements for service have been complied with	FPR PD5A, PD12A (PLO, stage 1)
Without notice	Not available	FPR 2010, r 12.16
Joinder or removal of parties	By court order, of its own initiative or on written request	FPR 2010, rr 4.3, 12.3(3); PD12A (PLO, stage 1)
Answer to application	Respondent may file answer; serve on other parties at least 2 days before date fixed for hearing of application	FPR PD12A
Directions	Powers of the justices' clerk or the court	FPR 2010, rr 12.12, 12.24; PD12A (PLO, stage 1)
Children's guardian	Not "specified proceedings"	CA 1989, s 41(1)
Special requirements	No application earlier than 3 months before expiry date of order	CA 1989, Sch 3, para 15(3)
Who has power to make the order	High Court judge, circuit judge, deputy circuit judge, recorder nominated for public law proceedings or Category B judge	FP(AJ)D 2009, para 6 and Sch
	A magistrates' court; however, justices' clerk or single justice has no such power	JCR 2005; CA 1989, s 93(2)(i); FPR 2010, r 2.6
Order	Form C38	FPR PD5A, PD12A
Additional or alternative orders	Direction requiring local authority to investigate with a view to care or supervision order	CA 1989, s 37(1)
	CA 1989, s 8 order (but subject to restrictions in CA 1989, s 9)	CA 1989, s 10(1)
	Family assistance order	CA 1989, s 16(1)
	Order appointing children's guardian or terminating appointment	CA 1989, ss 5(2), 6(7)(c)
	No order	CA 1989, s 1(5)
Appeals	See Guides E2, E4 and E5	
Transitional arrangements	FPR 1991 to FPR 2010	FPR PD36A

D20: Application in Respect of an Abducted Child under the Hague Convention 1980 or European Convention 1980

Legal background

CACA 1985 ratifies the Hague Convention of 25 October 1980 and the European Convention of 20 May 1980. Applications under the Hague Convention are made: (a) to secure the prompt return of children wrongfully removed to or retained in any Contracting State; or (b) to ensure that rights of custody and of access under the law of the Contracting State are effectively respected in the other Contracting State. Also note the application of Brussels IIA, which regulates which Contracting State should be seised of the matter in the event of competing applications and the 1996 Hague Convention on Jurisdiction, Applicable Law, Enforcement and Co-operation in Respect of Parental Responsibility and Measures for the Protection of Children.

Applications under the European Convention are made for: (a) recognition and enforcement of a custody order, including enforcement by means of returning the child to the person in whose favour the custody order was made; (b) recognition of a custody or contact order; or (c) recognition and enforcement of a contact order.

In relation to the Republic of Pakistan, see *Protocol of January 2003 (Child Abduction Cases Between the UK and Pakistan)* (see Part V) and *Re H (Child Abduction: Mother's Asylum)* [2003] 2 FLR 1105 where the principles of the Protocol were considered.

In relation to Egypt, see the *Cairo Declaration Resulting from Anglo-Egyptian Meetings on Judicial Co-operation in International Child Abduction Matters between Egypt and the United Kingdom* (see Part V) signed on 17 January 2005.

Procedure

Who may apply	*Hague Convention* Any person, institution or body who claims that a child has been removed or retained in breach of custody rights	CACA 1985, Sch 1, Art 8
	European Convention Any person who has a court order giving them rights of custody and contact	CACA 1985, Sch 2, Art 4
Which court	The High Court in England and Wales or Northern Ireland The Court of Session in Scotland	CACA 1985, s 4
	In England and Wales the application must be issued in the Principal Registry and heard by a judge of the High Court, unless the application is to join a party or dispense with service	FPR 2010, r 12.45
Fee	£230	FPFO 2008, fee 1.1
Conditions to be met	*Hague Convention* The child must be under 16	CACA 1985, Sch 1, Art 4
	If the child is aged 16–18 the application for the return of the child should be made under the inherent jurisdiction of the High Court	FPR PD12F, para 1.5
	The child must have been habitually resident in a Contracting State immediately before his removal or breach of contact rights	FPR PD12F, para 1.4

	The child must have been wrongfully taken or retained in breach of rights of custody after the date on which the Convention came into force between the two countries	FPR PD12F, Pt 2
	European Convention The child must be under 16	CACA 1985, Sch 2, Art 1
	At the time of removal the applicant must have a custody or contact order made in his favour	CACA 1985, Sch 2, Art 4
	The child must have been removed in breach of those custody or contact rights to another Contracting State	CACA 1985, Sch 1, Art 3
	If, at the time of removal, there is no custody order in force, the Convention may apply to an order made after the removal if it also contains a declaration that the removal was wrongful	CACA 1985, Sch 2, Art 12
Application procedure in England and Wales	In Form C67 it must be headed "in the matter of the CACA 1985" and "in the matter of Council Regulation (EC) 2201/2003" and must contain the information set out in PD12F, para 2.11 failing which the court may fix a time within which the document must be produced, accept equivalent documents or dispense with their production	FPR 2010, r 12.46
Documents	*Hague Convention* Authenticated copy of any relevant decision or agreement	
	Certificate or affidavit concerning the relevant law of the Contracting State	CACA 1985, Sch 1, Art 8
	A statement in support made by the applicant or on his behalf by the applicant's solicitor which must contain a statement of truth	FPR PD12F paras 2.12–2.13; PD17A
	Any other relevant document	
	European Convention Document of authorization	
	Copy court order	
	Evidence of service	
	Document establishing that the order is enforceable in the Contracting State	
	Statement indicating the whereabouts of the child	
	Proposals on how the custody of the child should be restored	CACA 1985, Sch 2, Art 13
Respondents	The abductor The harbourer The parent or guardian within the UK Any person in whose favour a custody order has been made Any other person who has an interest in the welfare of the child The child if directed by the court	FPR 2010, rr 12.3, 12.48(1)(g) and see r 16.2; see also FPR PD12F, para 2.24

PART I

Service of answer	The answer must be filed and served within 7 days of service of the application unless extended by the court	FPR 2010, r 12.49
Statement in support	A statement verified by a statement of truth together with any further evidence may be filed and served with the answer within 7 days of service of the application. The statement must disclose where the child is and particulars of any defence to the application. For defences that may be raised see Arts 12 and 13	FPR 2010, r 12.50(1); CACA 1985, Sch 1; FPR PD12F, paras 2.22, 2.23
Affidavit in reply	May be filed and served within 7 days of service of the affidavit in answer	FPR 2010, r 12.50(2)
Without notice applications	May be made for: – interim directions under ss 5 or 19 of CACA 1985; – disclosure of information about the child; his or her whereabouts; or – for a collection, location or passport order (FPR 2010, r 12.47)	
Directions hearing	May be listed to deal with, among others, the matters set out in FPR 2010, r 12.48(1) The court has a duty to set a timetable to complete the case within 6 weeks	FPR PD12F, para 2.14
Orders	All the orders under the inherent jurisdiction, including: collection and location orders in the prescribed form – see *Emergency Remedies in the Family Courts* disclosure of whereabouts disclosure of information from the Home Office attendance order surrender of passport port alert flight information publicity injunction prohibiting further removal and removal from UK injunction freezing assets return of the child dispensing with service stay of proceedings transfer of proceedings to Scotland or Northern Ireland	 CACA 1985, s 24A FPR PD12F, para 4.14 FPR PD12F, para 4.10 FPR PD12F, paras 4.2–4.8 for 24 hours service available from the police for assistance without a court order FPR PD12F, para 4.15 FPR PD12F, para 4.9 FPR 2010, r 12.48 FPR 2010, r 12.58 FPR 2010, r 12.54

	interim direction	FPR 2010, r 12.47; CACA 1985, s 5
	any other direction contact order where there is a breach a writ of sequestration may be issued under CPR 1998, r 81.19	CACA 1985, s 5
Appeals	See Guide E5	

Applications in non-Convention cases

Who may apply	Any person who claims that a child has been removed or retained in breach of custody rights	FPR PD12F, para 3.1
Which court	High Court under its inherent jurisdiction The application must be issued in the Principal Registry and heard by a Judge of the High Court	FPR PD12F, paras 3.1 and 3.2
Application	Must be in Form C66 and must include the information set out in PD12F, para 2.11	FPR PD12F, para 3.3
Documents	Statement in support verified by a statement of truth. The Statement must exhibit any relevant documents	FPR PD12F, para 3.4; PD17A
Timetable	Directions will be given to complete the case within 6 weeks except where exceptional circumstances make this impossible	FPR PD12F, paras 3.5 and 2.14
	See further above under application under the Hague Convention and the Inherent Jurisdiction	

D21: Application for Registration of an Order under the Family Law Act 1986 in Respect of an Abducted Child

Legal background

Application for the registration of a Pt I order may be made by any person in whose favour rights have been conferred by the order, in another part of the UK under FLA 1986, s 27, or in the Isle of Man under a corresponding provision. If the order was made in the family proceedings court, the procedure laid down in the Magistrates' Courts (Family Law Act 1986) Rules 1988 should be followed. In the case of an order made in the High Court in England and Wales and Northern Ireland, the Court of Session in Scotland and the High Court of Justice in the Isle of Man, the procedure set out in FPR 2010, r 32.23 applies. For applications commenced before 6 April 2011 the transitional arrangements in PD36A apply.

Procedure

Who may apply	Any person on whom rights are conferred by a Pt I order	FLA 1986, s 27
Which court	(a) Application in respect of High Court orders must be made to the court which made the order, that is:	FLA 1986, s 27
	(i) High Court in England and Wales and Northern Ireland	FPR 2010, r 32.23(1)
	(ii) The Court of Session in Scotland	FLA 1986(DT)O 1991
	(iii) High Court of Justice of the Isle of Man	FLA 1986(DT)O 1991
	(b) Applications in respect of an order made in the county court must be made to the county court which made the order	FLA 1986, s 27; FPR 2010, r 32.25(1)
Which department	In respect of High Court orders the application should be made as follows:	
	in the Principal Registry, to the family proceedings department manager	
	in the district registry, to the court manager	
	in Northern Ireland, to the master (care and protection) of the High Court	FPR 2010, r 32.23
	in Scotland, to the deputy principal clerk of session or the sheriff clerk, as the case may be	FPR 2010, r 32.23
	in the Isle of Man, the corresponding officer of the High Court of Justice of the Isle of Man	FPR 2010, r 32.23
	In respect of an order made by the county court, to the court manager	
Application	Request in Form D151 signed by or on behalf of the applicant	FPR 2010, r 32.25; FPR PD5A; Ord 90 (NI); CSR 260R (Scotland)
Documents	Copy of the letter of application	
	Statement by the applicant, with a copy, stating the matters set out in FPR 2010, r 32.25(1)(c) exhibiting any document relevant to the application	
	Certified copy of the order	FPR 2010, r 32.25(1);
	Certified copy of any order which has varied the original order	Ord 90 (NI); CSR 260R; RRCOSC 1988, r 3(2)
In the event of refusal to send documents	The applicant may apply to a judge for an order	FPR 2010, r 32.25(4),(5)(a)

D22: Application to Enforce a Registered Order in Respect of an Abducted Child under the Family Law Act 1986

Procedure

Which court	As under Guide D21, the court at which the order is registered	FLA 1986, s 27
Application	On Form D151, supported by statement In Scotland, by petition	FPR PD5A CSR 260V
Defendant	The abductor	
Service	No specific rules, but the court will give directions In Scotland, usually 21 days unless the court otherwise directs	FLA 1986, s 27; FPR 2010, r 32.29 CSR 260V(4)
Orders	All the orders under the inherent jurisdiction, including: collection and location orders (formerly known as find and return and search and locate orders)	For prescribed forms see *Emergency Remedies in the Family Courts*
	disclosure of whereabouts	CACA 1985, s 24A; FLA 1986, s 33
	attendance order	
	surrender of passport	FLA 1986, s 37
	port alert	
	flight information	
	publicity	
	injunction prohibiting further removal and removal from UK	
	injunction freezing assets	
	any other direction	
	contact order	CA 1989, s 8

D23: Applications under the Inherent Jurisdiction of the High Court, including Wardship

Legal background

The inherent jurisdiction of the High Court is generally unrestricted and unlimited, except insofar as restrictions have been imposed by statutes or by judicial decisions of the court itself. The most significant statutory restriction on the court's jurisdiction is that imposed on local authorities by CA 1989, s 100. A child who is the subject of a care order cannot be the subject of a wardship application. Wardship is just one of the ways in which the court exercises its inherent jurisdiction in relation to children; in such cases (save for the restrictions imposed) the court has powers to make such orders as are deemed necessary for the protection of the child. The High Court's inherent jurisdiction may be invoked to protect the interest of a vulnerable adult or a child, without the child being warded, e g where the court is asked to give directions on medical treatment to be given to, or withdrawn from, a child. The procedure in respect of wardship is set out in FPR 2010, rr 12.36–12.42

and in PD12D in all cases for applications under the court's inherent jurisdiction (including wardship) but other rules in Pt 12 are also applicable. In urgent cases, where possible, the application should be made within court hours and liaison should be made with the Clerk of the Rules who will attempt to accommodate such application in the Family Division applications court. If it is not possible to make an application during court hours contact should be made with the security officer at the RCJ: 020 7947 6000/6260. CAFCASS Cymru and members of the Official Solicitor's legal team should be given advance notice of urgent and out-of-hours applications and be provided with details of the circumstances (FPR PD12E, para 4.1) Note: all applications in relation to an adult who lacks capacity are dealt with in the Court of Protection and PD12E, para 4.4 specifically brings this to the attention of the practitioner and sets out to whom enquiries should be addressed in urgent cases.

Procedure

Who may apply	Local authority (subject to the restrictions imposed by CA 1989, s 100 and only with permission)	FPR 2010, r 12.3
	Any person with a genuine interest in the person who is the subject of the proceedings	FPR 2010, r 16.6(1)(c); see also *Re CT (A Minor)* [1993] 2 FLR 278
	The ward (wardship only)	
In medical treatment and press injunction cases where an interim declaration or order is required	Either the NHS Trust or A local authority; An interested adult (where necessary with permission of the court) or By the child with sufficient understanding	FPR PD12E, para 3.2
Respondents	Parent or guardian of the child; Any other person who has an interest in or relationship to the child;	FPR 2010, rr 12.3, 12.37 and Pt 16
	the child (wardship proceedings only) and with the court's permission as described in r 12.37. In medical treatment and press injunction cases it may be desirable for a child who is the subject of the proceedings to be made a party and represented by a children's guardian. A child of sufficient understanding to instruct his own solicitor should be made a party and given notice of the application	FPR PD12E para 3.1; see also *L v L* [1994] 1 FLR 156
	Where the child has formed an undesirable relationship the other party should not be made a party to the substantive proceedings- only a respondent to the application and must not be allowed to see the documents other than those directly relating to the application for injunction or committal	FPR PD12D, para 3.1
Which court	Family Division of the High Court (Principal Registry or district registry)	SCA 1981, Sch 1
	Proceedings may be transferred to an appropriate county court	MFPA 1984, s 38(2); FPR 2010, r 12.36(2); PD12D, para 2.1
Application	On Form C66 (including any supplementary forms) with written evidence in support, which must set out:	

	– the question that the applicant wants the court to decide or the order that is sought and the legal basis for the same;	
	– if the application is made under an enactment it must identify the enactment;	
	- if the applicant or the respondent is applying in a representative capacity what that capacity is	
	The statement of case must be verified by a statement of truth	FPR 2010, rr 5, 17.2; PD5A
	Fee: £160	FPFO 2008, fee 3.3
	On notice application: £90	FPFO 2008, fee 4.3
	Without notice application: £45	FPFO 2008, fee 4.1
Documents	Application on Form C66 and supplementary documents with copy for service Statement in support Notice of proceedings Certified copy of the child's birth certificate copy of entry in the Adopted Children Register	FPR PD12C; FPR 2010, r 19.7(1),(2)
Other applications in existing proceedings or proceedings that have been concluded, including without notice applications	By Pt 18 application, in Form C2. The procedure set out in Pt 18 and PD18A should be followed The application notice verified by a statement of truth must state: – what order is sought and – the reasons for seeking the order(s) A statement in support (if the evidence relied on is not set out in the application notice) must be verified by a statement of truth A draft order	FPR PD5A; FPR 2010, rr 18.1(1), 18.2, 18.7(2)
Service/ Acknowledgement of service	The general provisions for service under FPR 2010, r 6 apply. Notice of wardship must be served with the application	
Documents to be served	Copy of without notice order; Copy of application Copy of statement in support Notice of wardship Notice of return date/directions hearing	FPR 2010, r 18.8(3)
	Every respondent must file with the acknowledgement of service a notice stating the matters set out in r 12.39	FPR 2010, r 12.39(1)
	Unless the court otherwise directs, the acknowledgement of service must be filed within 14 days of service, if served within the jurisdiction	FPR PD5A
Time for service	If served in Scotland, Northern Ireland, a Member State or Hague Convention country, within 21 days of service If served outside Europe, within 31 days of service	FPR 2010, r 6.42(1)–(3)

Respondent's evidence in answer	The respondent must file: – the acknowledgement of service – notice setting out the information required under r 12.39 If respondent wishes to rely on written evidence the statement verified by a statement of truth must be filed with the acknowledgement of service	FPR 2010, r 19.7(4)
Applicant's reply	Written evidence must be filed and served within 14 days of service of the respondent's evidence	FPR 2010, r 19.7(5),(6)
Further evidence	No written evidence may be relied on unless it has been served in accordance with r 19.7 or with the court's permission	FPR 2010, r 19.8 and see r 22.1
Case management	When the court receives the acknowledgment of service it will give directions as to case management of the case, but an appointment should be sought within 21 days in any event to confirm the wardship or the wardship will lapse	SCA 1981, s 41(2); FPR 2010, r 12.5, see also r 12.13 and PD12B
	In the case of a without notice application, the time for the directions appointment will usually be abridged on the applicant's application	
	On the hearing for directions, if the case appears complex and uncertain in its outcome, the judge may give further directions, including directions for trial	*Re C* [1990] 2 FLR 527
Urgent out-of-hours telephone hearing	Should be by tape-recorded conference call arranged and paid for in the first instance by the applicant's solicitors. All parties, especially the judge, should be informed that the call is being recorded by the service provider	FPR PD12E, paras 1.4, 1.5
	The applicant's solicitors should order a transcript of the hearing from the service provider otherwise the applicant's legal representatives should prepare a note for approval by the judge	
Orders in urgent applications	In suitable cases applications may be made for directions for:	FPR PD12E, para 2.2
	Anonymity of the parties and others in any order or listing of the case;	
	Exceptionally for a reporting restriction order	
Orders	Any order, directions or declaration sought and consequential orders that may be necessary	
	Where appropriate, any of the following orders:	

	collection and location orders in the prescribed form – see *Emergency Remedies in the Family Courts* (Jordan Publishing Ltd)	
	disclosure of whereabouts	CACA 1985, s 24A; FLA 1986, s 33
	attendance order	
	surrender of passport	FLA 1986, s 37
	port alert	
	flight information	
	publicity	
	injunction prohibiting further removal and removal from UK	
	injunction freezing assets	
	any other direction	
	contact order	CA 1989, s 8
	Where appropriate, any order under CA 1989, s 8	
Appeals	See Guide E5	

D24: Placement Order

Legal background

Under ACA 2002, s 18 an adoption agency may only place a child for adoption if either each parent or guardian consents (s 19), or a court has made a placement order authorising a local authority to place the child for adoption (s 21). On the making of a placement order, parental responsibility for the child is given to the local authority and to the prospective adopters (while the child is placed with them) (s 25). Any parent or guardian retains parental responsibility, but the local authority may determine the extent of its use. Any previous care order is suspended during the placement order and any previous s 8 or supervision order ceases to have effect. Contact may be regulated by court order under s 26. Unless there has been a change of circumstances after a placement order, and the court gives leave to do so, a parent cannot oppose a subsequent application for adoption (s 47). A placement order may be revoked (s 24).

Placement order applications are conducted under FPR 2010, Pt 14.

Proceedings under ACA 2002 are "family proceedings" under CA 1989, s 8 and FLA 1996, Pt IV; therefore the court may make orders under CA 1989, Pt II or non-molestation orders within ACA 2002 proceedings.

Procedure

Who may apply	A local authority	ACA 2002, s 22
Who may be the subject of a placement order	A child (being a person under the age of 18 years)	ACA 2002, ss 21(1) and 144(1)
Which court	An application for a placement order may be commenced in:	
	– the High Court; or	
	– an adoption centre county court; or	
	– family proceedings court	ATPO 2008
	Proceedings can be transferred sideways, upwards or downwards	ATPO 2008

Application	Originating application in Form A50 A fee of £400 is normally payable	FPR 2010, Pt 5; PD5A FPFO 2008; MCFO 2008
Respondents	Each parent with PR or guardian of the child	FPR 2010, r 14.3(1)
	A person in whose favour there is a CA 1989 order in force relating to the child	
	Any adoption agency that has parental responsibility for, is looking after, or is caring for the child	
	The child; and	
	The parties or any persons who are or have been parties to proceedings for a care order in respect to the child where those proceedings have led to the application for the placement order	
	The court may direct that any other person be made (or removed as) a respondent	FPR 2010, r 14.3(2),(3)
Documents	The applicant must file:	Form A50
	– three copies of the completed application form;	
	– a certified copy of the full entry in the Register of Live Births that relates to the child or, where the child has been adopted, a certified copy of the entry in the Adopted Children Register;	
	– any written consent of the parent or guardian to the child being placed for adoption, and any notice of withdrawal of such consent;	
	– if the applicant is asking the court to dispense with the consent of any parent or guardian to the child being placed for adoption, a brief statement of the facts relied on in support of the request, and two copies of the statement;	
	– a copy of any final care order relating to the child;	
	– if available, a copy of any parental responsibility order or parental responsibility agreement relating to the child;	
	– if the authority was a party to the proceedings, a copy of any other final order relating to the child that is in force and, if available, a copy of any maintenance agreement or maintenance award relating to the child;	
	– if the authority was a party to the proceedings, a copy of any final order relating to a full, half or step brother or sister of the child that is in force	

	The applicant local authority (if directed to do so) must file a report on the child and birth family containing matters in PD14C, Annex B	FPR 2010, r 14.11
Parental consent	Court must be satisfied in the case of each parent with PR or guardian of the child that *either* he has consented to the child being placed for adoption and has not withdrawn consent *or* that his consent should be dispensed with under ACA 2002, s 52(1)	ACA 2002, ss 21(3) and 52
	Consent of mother is ineffective if given within 6 weeks of birth	ACA 2002, s 52(3)
Reporting officer	Appointed if parent appears willing to consent to placement for adoption and is in England and Wales	FPR 2010, r 16.30
Children's guardian	Appointed in every case, unless it is not necessary to do so to safeguard child's interests	CA 1989, s 41(6)(hh); FPR 2010, r 16.3
	Children's guardian must appoint a solicitor for the child	FPR PD16A, para 6.2
Children and Family Reporter	Court may ask a C and FR to report on welfare issue(s)	FPR 2010, r 16.33
Reports	Local authority may be ordered to report on reasons for placing for adoption	FPR 2010, r 14.6(3)
Hearing	Notice to be served on all parties, any reporting officer, children's guardian or children and family reporter	FPR 2010, r 14.6(1)(b)
	Proceedings under ACA 2002 are "family proceedings"	CA 1989, s 8(4); FLA 1996, Pt IV, s 63(2)
	First directions hearing must be within 4 weeks of application (unless court directs otherwise)	FPR 2010, r 14.7
	At first directions hearing court will consider matters listed at FPR 2010, r 14.8	
	No placement order can be made without the personal attendance of the child (unless court permits non-attendance) and attendance by a legal representative of the applicant	FPR 2010, r 14.16(6),(7),(9)
Order	A placement order authorises local authority to place the child for adoption and gives parental responsibility to the local authority and to any prospective adopters with whom child is placed. Parents with PR retain it, but local authority may restrict their exercise of PR	ACA 2002, ss 21 and 25
Appeals	See relevant Guide in Appeals section	

D25: Adoption Order

Legal background

An adoption order is an order giving parental responsibility for a child to the adopters made on their application (ACA 2002, s 46(1)). At the same time, the making of an adoption order operates to extinguish permanently the parental responsibility which any person had for the child immediately before the making of the order (s 46(2) – save in a single step-parent adoption, see s 46(3)(b)). Application may be by a single person, or by a couple (married, civil partners or partners (whether different or same sex) living in an enduring family relationship (s 144(4)–(6)). An adoption order is irrevocable, save in the very restricted circumstances of ACA 2002, s 55 (revocation on subsequent legitimation). The adopted child is deemed to be the adopter's legitimate child and, if adopted by a couple, is treated as the child of their relationship (s 67). Adoption is therefore the legal process by which a child becomes a permanent and full member of a new family. Adoption order applications are conducted under FPR 2010, Pt 14. Proceedings under ACA 2002 are "family proceedings" under CA 1989, s 8 and FLA 1996, Pt IV; therefore the court may make orders under CA 1989, Pt II or non-molestation orders within ACA 2002 proceedings.

Intercountry adoptions

Adoption of a child who is habitually resident abroad in a state that is a signatory to the Hague Convention on Intercountry Adoption will be under a Convention adoption order – see notes to ACA 2002, s 67. If the state is not a signatory, and if the adoption is not otherwise recognised in the UK as a valid "overseas adoption" (see notes to ACA 2002, s 87), an adoption application must be made in England and Wales. Strict limitations are imposed upon making arrangements for such an adoption, bringing the child into the country, preparing reports and making any payments (ACA 2002, ss 83, 92–96).

Procedure

Who may apply	*Joint applicants* Each applicant must be over 21 (save for the child's parent who must be over 18)	
	Each applicant must be married, in a civil partnership or in an enduring family relationship	ACA 2002, ss 50, 144
	One of the following conditions is met:	ACA 2002, s 49
	(1) At least one of the applicants must be domiciled in the British Isles, or	
	(2) Both have been habitually resident in a part of the British Isles for at least 1 year before application	
	Sole applicant Must be over 21	ACA 2002, s 51
	Either: Must not be married or a civil partner or must satisfy court that spouse or civil partner cannot be found, or is permanently separated, or is mentally/physically incapable of applying	ACA 2002, s 51(1); ACA 2002, s 51(3),(3A)
	Or: Is the partner of a parent of the person to be adopted	ACA 2002, s 51(2)
	May be the parent of the child provided that the other parent is dead or cannot be found or there is none or there is other good reason	ACA 2002, s 51(4)

	One of the following conditions is met:	ACA 2002, s 49(2),(3)
	(1) Applicant must be domiciled in the British Isles; or	
	(2) Applicant must have been habitually resident in a part of the British isles for at least 1 year before application	
	In all "non-agency" cases (joint or sole applications) proper notice of intention to apply to adopt must have been given to local authority	ACA 2002, s 44(2)
Who may be adopted	Adoption order may be made only in respect of a child (a person under the age of 18) on date of application and still under 19, who has never been married or in a civil partnership at date of order	ACA 2002, ss 49(4), 47(8),(9)
	Child must live with adopters for the relevant probationary period	ACA 2002, s 42
	The court must not be denied jurisdiction by ACA 2002, s 48	ACA 2002, s 48
Which court	An application to adopt must be commenced in a magistrates' court unless local authority will be a party, in which case it may be commenced in:	ATPO 2008
	– the High Court;	
	– county court adoption centre;	
	– family proceedings court	
	application for a Convention adoption order or if ACA 2002, s 83 applies need not be started in FPC; if started in county court must start at intercountry adoption centre	ATPO 2008
	Proceedings can be transferred sideways, upwards or downwards	ATPO 2008
Application	Form A58	FPR 2010, Pt 5; PD5A
	If the applicant wishes his identity to be kept confidential, he may apply for a serial number to be issued	FPR 2010, r 14.2
	A fee of £160 is normally payable	FPFO 2008, fee 3.1; MCFO 2008, fee 10.1
Respondents	Each parent with PR or guardian of the child (unless he has given notice of not wishing to be informed under ACA 2002, s 20(4)(a))	
	A person in whose favour there is provision for contact	
	Any adoption agency that has parental responsibility under a placement order	
	Any adoption agency involved in the adoption arrangements	
	Any local authority to whom notice has been given under ACA 2002, s 44	

	Any local authority or voluntary organisation which has parental responsibility for, or is looking after or caring for, the child	
	The child in specific circumstances	FPR 2010, r 14.3(1)
	The court may direct that the child or any other person be made (or removed as) a respondent	FPR 2010, r 14.3(2),(3)
Documents	The applicant must file three copies of the application form together with the documents listed on Form A58, in particular:	Form A58
	– a copy birth certificate	
	– a statement of facts (if applying for dispensation of consent) and two copies	
	– a copy of relevant order(s)	
	– a copy of relevant certificates or marriage, civil partnership, divorce, dissolution of civil partnership, death	
	– a medical report on each applicant and the child (not required in agency cases)	FPR 2010, r 14.12
	The relevant adoption agency or local authority (not the applicant) must file:	
	(a) a report on applicant's suitability;	
	(b) a report on child's placement for adoption,	
	that comply with FPR PD14C, Annex A	FPR 2010, r 14.11
Parental Consent or Placement Order	One of two conditions must be met: (1) In the case of each parent with PR or guardian of the child ("parent") that either he, with full understanding, agrees unconditionally to the making of an adoption order or that his consent should be dispensed with under ACA 2002, s 52(1); or	ACA 2002, s 4
	(2) An adoption agency placed child for adoption and either the placement was with consent of each parent, or it was under a placement order and no parent has leave to oppose the adoption (if leave is granted, condition (1) must be used)	
	Consent must be proved in compliance with rules	Forms A100–106
	Consent of mother to adoption is ineffective if given within 6 weeks of birth	ACA 2002, s 52(3)
Reporting officer	Appointed if parent appears willing to consent to adoption and is in England and Wales	FPR 2010, r 16.30
Children's guardian	Appointed if child is a party, unless it is not necessary to do so to safeguard child's interests	FPR 2010, r 16.3

	Children's guardian must appoint a solicitor for the child	FPR PD16A, para 6.2
Children and Family Reporter	Court may ask a C and FR to report on welfare issue(s)	FPR 2010, r 16.33
Hearing	Notice to be served on all parties, any reporting officer, children's guardian or children and family reporter	FPR 2010, r 14.6(1)(b)
	Proceedings under ACA 2002 are "family proceedings"	CA 1989, s 8(4); FLA 1996, Pt IV, s 63(2)
	First directions hearing must be within 4 weeks of application (unless court directs otherwise)	
	At first directions hearing the court will consider matters listed at FPR 2010, r 14.8	FPR 2010, r 14.8
	No order can be made without the personal attendance of the applicant(s) and the child (unless the court permits non-attendance)	FPR 2010, r 14.16(6)–(8)
Order	An adoption order gives parental responsibility to the adopters and extinguishes any previous parental responsibility and any earlier court orders. The child is treated as if he was born to the adopter(s) in marriage	ACA 2002, s 46
Appeals	See relevant Guide in Appeals section	

E1: Application for Judicial Review

Legal background

Judicial review is the process whereby the High Court exercises its supervisory jurisdiction to review the legality and validity of the actions and decisions of persons or bodies exercising administrative powers, whether of a legislative, executive, judicial or adjudicatory character. The jurisdiction is over the proceedings and decisions of inferior courts (such as magistrates' courts and county courts), tribunals and other bodies performing public acts and duties. It is not a system of appeal. The procedure must be used where the claimant is seeking a mandatory order (formerly known as an order of mandamus), a prohibiting order (formerly known as an order of prohibition) or a quashing order (formerly known as an order of certiorari). The procedure for an application for judicial review is prescribed by CPR 1998, Pt 54 and PD54A and SCA 1981, ss 29 to 31 (and CCA 1984, ss 83 and 84). Judicial review claims are dealt with in the Administrative Court (see further annotation under CPR 1998, r 54.1).

A *Pre-Action Protocol for Judicial Review* came into force on 4 March 2002. There is also a helpful booklet available from the Administrative Court Office entitled *Notes for Guidance on Applying for Judicial Review*.

For the interplay between judicial review and applications under the HRA 1998, see notes to CPR 1998, Pt 54 and to the 1998 Act.

All applications for judicial review must be made to the Administrative Court, either at The Royal Courts of Justice, The Strand, London WC2A 2LL, or at one of the regional centres, namely: Cardiff Civil Justice Centre, 2 Park Street, Cardiff, CF10 1ET; Birmingham Civil Justice Centre Priory Courts, 5th Floor, 33 Bull Street, Birmingham B4 6DS; Leeds Combined Court, 1 Oxford Row, Leeds LS1 3BG; or Manchester Civil Justice Centre, 12th Floor, 1 Bridge Street West, Manchester M3 3FX.

Procedure

Who may apply	Any person with sufficient interest in the matter subject to the proposed review	SCA 1981, s 31(3)
Application for permission	Made by filing a claim form (N461) promptly, and in any event within 3 months of the decision, in the Administrative Court in London or in one of the regional centres, namely Cardiff, Birmingham, Leeds or Manchester	CPR 1998, rr 54.1, 54.5
	The prospective claimant should write a detailed letter before action allowing 14 days for the prospective defendant to respond (unless the nature of the claim precludes this)	*Judicial Review Protocol*, paras 8–17, Annexes A and B
	Note the additional provisions where an application is made following the refusal by the Upper Tribunal for permission to appeal against a decision of the First-Tier Tribunal	CPR 1998, r 54.7A, PD54A, para 19
The claim form must include or be accompanied by	(i) a detailed statement of the claimant's grounds for bringing the claim for judicial review	CPR PD54A, para 5.6
	(ii) a statement of facts relied on	
	(iii) any application to extend the time limit for filing the claim form	
	(iv) any application for directions	
	(v) a time estimate for the hearing	
Additional documents to accompany the claim form	(i) written evidence in support of the claim (verified by a statement of truth) (ii) a copy of the order complained of (iii) where the decision complained of relates to a decision of a court or tribunal, an approved copy of the reasons for the decision	CPR PD54A, paras 5.7, 5.10
	(iv) copies of any documents on which the claimant proposes to rely	
	(v) copies of any statutory material	
	(vi) a list of essential documents for advance reading by the court (with page references to passages); and	
	if necessary, reasons why the documents cannot be filed and details of any person considered to be an interested party	
HRA 1998	Where the applicant seeks to raise any issue under HRA 1998, or seeks a remedy under that Act, the claim form must:	CPR PD16, para 15.1
	(a) state that there is a claim in respect of a HRA issue; and	
	(b) give details of the alleged convention right infringed	
	(c) specify the relief sought	

	(d) state if the relief sought includes a declaration of incompatibility or damages in respect of a judicial act	
	(e) where there is a claim for a declaration of incompatibility, provide details of the legislative provision	
	(f) where the claim relates to unlawfulness by another court or tribunal, give details of the finding	
	(g) where the claim relates to a judicial act, give details of the act complained of and the court or tribunal concerned	
Acknowledgment of service	Must be filed within 21 days of service of the claim form	CPR 1998, r 54.8(2)(a)
	and served within 7 days of filing	CPR 1998, r 54.8(2)(b)
	It should state whether the defendant contests the claim and, if so, summarise his grounds for doing so (see under "Response")	CPR 1998, r 54.8(4)
Determination of permission application	Usually determined without a hearing Reasons being provided (on Form JRJ)	CPR PD54A, para 8.4 CPR PD54A, para 9.1
	If refused without a hearing (or granted on terms), a request for reconsideration (at an oral hearing) must be filed within 7 days of the reasons given for refusal	CPR 1998, r 54.12
	If refused after a hearing, an application for permission may be made to the Court of Appeal within 7 days of the refusal	CPR 1998, r 52.15
	Fee: £60 (to HM Paymaster General)	CPFO 2008, art 1.9(a)
Application	The application must proceed on the claim form (see above) used to seek leave	CPR 1998, r 54.15
	Where the claimant seeks to rely on additional grounds he must give notice no later than 7 days before the hearing	CPFO 2008, art 1.9(b)
	Fee: £215	
Defendants	Where the claim relates to proceedings in a court or tribunal all parties to those proceedings must be named in the claim form as an interested party	CPR PD54A, para 5.1
	The claimant must serve all the parties within 7 days of the issue of the claim form	CPR 1998, r 54.7; PD54A, para 6.1
	The claimant must lodge a certificate of service in the Administrative Court within 7 days of service	
Additional persons to be served	The claim form must be served by the claimant upon any person the claimant considers to be an interested party within 7 days of the date of issue	CPR 1998, r 54.7

	Any person may apply for permission to file evidence or make representations at the hearing	CPR 1998, r 54.17
Response	A defendant or any other person served with the claim form who wishes to contest or support the claim must:	
	(a) file an acknowledgment of service (Form N462) within 21 days setting out a summary of the grounds for contesting the claim and the name and address of any person claiming to be an interested party;	
	(b) serve the acknowledgment of service on the claimant and interested persons within 7 days of filing (the court will do this if requested)	CPR 1998, r 54.8
	(c) file and serve detailed grounds and any written evidence within 35 days after service of the order giving permission	CPR 1998, r 54.14
Case management directions	Directions may be given as to service or evidence	
	The court may direct that the proceedings be heard by a Divisional Court	CPR 1998, r 54.10
	A court officer of the Administrative Court who is a barrister or solicitor may, with the consent of the President of the QBD, give incidental or non-contentious directions	CPR 1998, r 54.1A
	Where a claim is under HRA 1998 a direction may be made for giving notice to the Crown or joining the Crown as a party	CPR 1998, r 19.4A
	Case management directions may be sought	CPR 1998, Pt 23
	List of those to be served, see –	CPR PD66, Annex 1
Interim remedy	A range of interim orders may be sought (including an interim injunction or declaration)	CPR 1998, Pt 25
Documents	The claimant must file two copies of a paginated and indexed bundle which must include the documents of the other parties	CPR PD54A, para 5.9
	The claimant should also provide a paginated indexed bundle of statutory material	CPR PD54A, para 5.9
	Skeleton argument must be filed by the claimant not less than 21 working days before the hearing (or the warned date for hearing) and by the defendant or any other person wishing to make representations not less than 14 days before the hearing	CPR PD54A, para 15.1
	The skeleton argument must contain:	CPR PD54A, para 15.3

(a) a time estimate;

(b) a list of issues;

(c) a list of legal points with justification for citing more than one authority on any proposition of law

(d) a chronology;

(e) a list of essential reading (where only part of a page needs to be read, that part should be marked (not highlighted)) and;

(f) a list of persons referred to

Hearing	When an application is ready to be heard it will be entered in the Administrative Court Warned List and all involved will be notified. The case will usually be heard by a single judge in open court but may be heard by two or more judges sitting as the Divisional Court	
Order	The court may:	
	make a mandatory order, a prohibiting order or a quashing order	CPR 1998, rr 54.2, 54.3
	grant an injunction or declaration	SCA 1981, s 30
	award damages, order restitution or the recovery of a sum due	SCA 1981, s 31(4); CPR 1998, r 54.3
Appeals	If permission to apply for judicial review has been refused, an application for permission to appeal must be made to the Court of Appeal within 7 days of the decision (the Court of Appeal may either grant permission to appeal or grant permission to apply for judicial review). In all other cases permission to appeal is required, which must be sought either from the Administrative Court or from the Court of Appeal within 21 days of the decision or within such other period as the Administrative Court may direct	CPR 1998, rr 52.15(2) and 52.4

E2: Appeal from a Family Proceedings Court, a District Judge or a District Judge of the High Court

Introductory note

With effect from 6 April 2011, all appeals from magistrates' courts and from district judges are governed by FPR 2010, Pt 30 and PD30A.

All appeals are dealt with as a review (unless an enactment or practice direction provides otherwise or the court considers it in the interests of justice to hold a re-hearing: FPR 2010, r 30.12(1)). In *Piglowska v Piglowski* [1999] 2 FLR 763 guidance was given to the profession in respect of the conduct of appeals. The parties do not begin the appeal with a "clean sheet". Lord Hoffmann, at [783H]–[784H], stated that the appellate court must always bear in mind: (i) the advantage that the trial judge has of seeing and hearing the witnesses; (ii) that there is a discretion vested in the trial court and the appellate court should resist the temptation to substitute their own discretion for that of the trial judge on a narrow textual analysis of the judgment below; and (iii) that there must be a consideration of proportionality between the amount at stake and the legal resources to be expended. In *Re J (Child Returned Abroad: Convention Rights)* [2005] 2 FLR 802 at [12], Baroness Hale observed "[t]oo ready an interference by the appellate court, particularly if it always seems to be in the direction of one result rather than the other, risks robbing the trial judge of the discretion entrusted to him by law".

Legal background

An appeal from a magistrates' court or from a district judge in relation to a decision made in family proceedings is to a county court in accordance with the provisions of CA 1989, s 94. An appeal from a district judge of the High Court in relation to a decision made in such proceedings is to a judge of the High Court. The only exception is where the court has refused an application to transfer care proceedings in accordance with ATPO 2008, in which case a further application is made to a district judge of the appropriate care centre and not to the High Court. The appeals procedure is as set out in FPR 2010, Pt 30 and PD30A.

An appeal against the decision of a district judge in the county court or of a district judge of the High Court may only be made with the permission of the lower court or of the appeal court. Permission to appeal is not required against an order or decision of a magistrates' court (whether made by justices or by a district judge (magistrates' court)). Further, permission to appeal is not required where the appeal is against a committal order or a secure accommodation order (ie where the liberty of the subject is in issue). Other restrictions on an appeal relate to certain types of order: there is no appeal against the decision of the court to decline jurisdiction (CA 1989, s 94(2)); to make or refuse to make an emergency protection order (CA 1989, s 45(10)); or against an interim periodical payments order (CA 1989, s 94(3)). Special provisions apply to orders for the transfer of proceedings (see ATPO 2008).

In relation to the power for a judge to change his mind after delivering a judgment at the conclusion of a fact-finding hearing, see the notes to Guide E5.

On an application for permission to appeal, the appeal court has five options: (1) dismiss the application; (2) order a further without notice hearing; (3) order a hearing of the application on notice to the other parties; (4) order a hearing of the application on notice with the appeal to follow; (5) grant the application: *NLW v ARC* [2012] 2 FLR 129.

Mostyn J observed in *NLW v ARC* that "real prospect of success" means it is more likely than not that the appeal would be allowed at the substantive hearing; "anything less than a 50:50 threshold could only mean there was a real prospect of failure". Moor J, however, has held that a "real prospect of success" is one that is realistic rather than fanciful and does not mean a greater than 50:50 chance of success. He commented that a practice direction was required to clarify the procedure for applications for permission to appeal: *AV v RM (Appeal)* [2012] 2 FLR 709.

It is suggested that an appellate court should exercise caution before directing at a without notice permission to appeal hearing that a matter should be remitted for rehearing by the lower court when (a) the respondent to the application has not been heard by the court and (b) the court has not determined the full appeal: *Livock v Livock* [2012] 1 FLR 776.

A notice of appeal does not operate as a stay. The existence of an arguable appeal with reasonable prospects of success was the minimum requirement before a court could even consider granting a stay: *NB v Haringey LBC* [2012] 2 FLR 125.

Regarding transcripts of the hearing or of the evidence, where a party is considering obtaining transcripts for the purposes of an appeal, see the notes to Guide E5.

The Court of Appeal has observed that it would be "enormously helpful" if a chronology was provided in all family appeals as they are for most first instance hearings: *Re H (A Child)* [2013] EWCA Civ 72.

Where events change or develop after the making of an interim order, the appropriate course is to seek a variation of the order from the judge, rather than seek to appeal against the order: *Re H (A Child)* [2011] Fam Law 941.

The unlawful removal of a child from his usual place of residence called for a peremptory order to be sought for his return, rather than to seek to challenge the dismissal of an appeal for an interim residence order by way of a second appeal to the Court of Appeal: *Re R (Children: Peremptory Return)* [2011] 2 FLR 863.

Permission is required from the appeal court to instruct fresh experts for the purposes of an appeal: see the notes to Guide E5.

For the grounds on which an appeal against findings of fact may be allowed, see the notes to Guide E5.

For the approach that an appellate court should adopt to (a) appeals where the adequacy of a trial judge's reasoning is in issue and (b) appeals against the exercise of a discretion by a trial judge, see the notes to Guide E5.

For the new practice direction on the citation of authorities, see the notes to Guide E5.

Procedure

Who may appeal	Any party to the hearing against an order or refusal to make an order	CA 1989, s 94; FPR 2010, rr 30.1, 30.3
	except where the order was an interim periodical payments order	CA 1989, s 94(3)
Which court	From a magistrates' court to a county court	CA 1989, s 94; Access to Justice Act 1999 (Destination of Appeals) (Family Proceedings) Order 2011, paras 2, 3
	From a district judge to a circuit judge	
	From a district judge of the High Court to a High Court judge	
	Where the decision is a refusal to transfer care proceedings to a county court, further application may be made to the district judge of the care centre listed in ATPO 2008	ATPO 2008, art 25
Permission to appeal	Permission to appeal is required in any appeal against a decision of a district judge or a costs judge but permission to appeal is not required in an appeal against a committal order or a secure accommodation order or against an order or decision of a magistrates' court	FPR 2010, r 30.3(1),(2); PD30A, paras 4.1–4.24
Material omission	Where a party's advocate considers that there is a material omission from a judgment or written reasons of the lower court, the advocate should give the lower court the opportunity to consider whether there is an omission and should not immediately use the omission as a grounds for an application to appeal	PD30A, para 4.6
	The court must consider whether there is a material omission and, if so, to provide additions to the judgment	PD30A, paras 4.7–4.9
Filing of appeal	To be filed within:	
	(i) such period as may be directed by the lower court; or	
	(ii) if no such direction is made, 21 days after the date of the decision to be appealed;	
	except that in the case of an appeal against an order under CA 1989, s 38(1), within 7 days	FPR 2010, r 30.4(2),(3)
	The notice of appeal must be served on each respondent (and those specified in r 30.4(5)) as soon as practicable and in any event no later than 7 days after filing	FPR 2010, r 30.4(4)
Amendment of notice	An appeal notice cannot be amended without the permission of the appeal court	FPR 2010, r 30.9
	Fee: £200 (private law); £170 (public law); £160 (special guardianship)	FPFO 2008, fee 2.3

Respondents	Any party to the proceedings in the lower court who is affected by the appeal and any person who is permitted by the appeal court to be a party to the appeal	FPR 2010, r 30.1(3)
	The appellant's notice must be served on:	
	(i) any children's guardian, welfare officer or children and family reporter;	
	(ii) a local authority that prepared a report under CA 1989, s 14A(8) or (9);	
	(iii) an adoption agency or local authority that prepared a suitability report on the applicant to adopt;	
	(iv) a local authority that prepared a report on the placement of the child for adoption;	FPR 2010, r 30.4(5)
	(v) on appeal from the FPC, the court officer	FPR 2010, r 30.4(5)
Respondent's notice	A respondent's notice may be filed within (i) such period as directed by the lower court or (ii) where no direction is made, 14 days of (a) the date on which served with the appellant's notice (where no permission to appeal required or permission granted by lower court), or (b) the date of notification that the appeal court has granted permission to appeal or (c) the date of notification that the application for permission and the appeal itself are to be heard together. But note, where the appeal is under s 38(1), no respondent's notice may be filed and a respondent may not seek to appeal the order or invite the appeal court to uphold the order of the lower court for different or additional reasons to those given	FPR 2010, r 30.5; PD30A, paras 7.1–7.4
Documents	The appellant must file the following documents, together with an appeal bundle, with the appellant's notice:	
	(i) two additional copies of the appellant's notice for the appeal court;	
	(ii) one copy of the appellant's notice for each of the respondents;	
	(iii) one copy of the appellant's skeleton argument for each copy of the appellant's notice that is filed;	
	(iv) a sealed or stamped copy of the order being appealed or a copy of the notice of the making of an order;	
	(v) a copy of any order giving or refusing permission to appeal together with a copy of the court's reasons for allowing or refusing the same;	

(vi) any witness statements or affidavits in support of any application included in the appellant's notice.

Items (ii)–(vi) should be filed with the appellant's notice of appeal or as soon as practicable after filing of the appellant's notice

FPR PD30A, paras 5.8, 5.12

Appeal bundle

An appellant must include the following documents in the appeal bundle:

(i) a sealed or stamped copy of the appellant's notice;

(ii) a sealed or stamped copy of the order being appealed or a copy of the notice of the making of an order;

(iii) a copy of any order giving or refusing permission to appeal together with a copy of the court's reasons for allowing or refusing the same;

(iv) any witness statements or affidavits in support of any application included in the appellant's notice;

(v) where the appeal is against a consent order, a statement setting out the change in circumstances since the order was agreed or other circumstances justifying a review or re-hearing;

(vi) a copy of the appellant's skeleton argument;

(vii) a transcript or note of judgment or, in a magistrates' court, written reasons for the court's decision, and in cases where permission to appeal was given by the lower court or is not required those parts of any transcript of evidence that are directly relevant to any question or issue on the appeal;

(viii) the application form;

(ix) any application notice (or case management documentation) relevant to the subject of the appeal;

(x) any other documents that the appellant reasonably considers necessary to enable the appeal court to reach its decision on the hearing of the application or appeal; and

(xi) such other documents as the court may direct.

FPR PD30A, paras 5.9–5.12

If a respondent considers that additional documents should be included in the appeal bundle, any amendments should be agreed with the appellant if possible

If the parties are unable to reach an agreement, the respondent may prepare a supplemental bundle

FPR PD30A, paras 7.16, 7.17

Skeleton arguments	The skeleton argument may be included in the appellant's notice or filed and served with the notice	
	Where it is impracticable to do so, the skeleton argument must be filed and served within 14 days of the filing of the notice	
	A skeleton argument must contain "a numbered list of the points which the party wishes to make. These should both define and confine the areas of controversy. Each point should be stated as concisely as the nature of the case allows"	
	The skeleton argument must set out, in respect of each authority cited, the proposition of law that it demonstrates and identify the relevant page or paragraph. Where more than one authority is cited in support of a proposition, brief reasons must be given for doing so	
	A party who files a respondent's notice but does not include a skeleton argument must file one within 14 days of filing the notice	FPR PD30A, paras 5.13–5.22
	A party who does not file a respondent's notice but who proposes to file a skeleton argument must do so at least 7 days before the appeal hearing	
	The respondent's skeleton argument should, where appropriate, answer the arguments set out in the appellant's skeleton argument	FPR PD30A, paras 7.7–7.12, 7.14, 7.15
Directions	Applications to:	
	dismiss the appeal for want of prosecution	
	dismiss the appeal by consent or	
	seek leave to withdraw the appeal	
	may be made to the district judge	
	Unless the court otherwise directs any interlocutory application may be made to a district judge	FPR PD30A, para 9.8
Order	The order on appeal is treated as an order of the family proceedings court	CA 1989, s 94(9)
Stay	Unless the court otherwise directs, an appeal does not operate as a stay of the order or decision appealed against	FPR 2010, r 30.8
Hearing of appeal	The appeal is limited to a review of the decision of the court below unless statute provides otherwise or the appeal court considers that in the particular case it would be in the interests of justice to hold a re-hearing	

	Unless the appeal court orders otherwise the court will not receive oral evidence or evidence which was not before the court below	FPR 2010, r 30.12(1),(2)
Grounds of appeal	The appeal court will allow the appeal where the decision of the court below was: (i) wrong; or (ii) unjust because of a serious procedural or other irregularity	FPR 2010, r 30.12(3)
Powers of the court	The appeal court may: make such orders as may be necessary to give effect to the determination of the appeal make such incidental or consequential orders as appear just	CA 1989, s 94(4)
	The appeal court has all the powers of the court below and has the power to: (i) affirm, set aside or vary any order or judgment made; (ii) refer any application or issue for determination by the court below; (iii) order a new hearing (iv) make order for the payment of interest; (v) make a costs order; (vi) exercise its powers in relation to the whole of part of an order of the lower court	CA 1989, s 94(5); FPR 2010, r 30.11
Assignment to Court of Appeal	Where the lower court or appeal court considers the appeal raises an important point of principle or practice or there is some other compelling reason, it may direct the appeal be transferred to the Court of Appeal (Note: does not apply to proceedings in FPC)	FPR 2010, r 30.13
Re-opening final appeals	The High Court will not reopen a final determination of any appeal unless: (i) it is necessary to do so to avoid real injustice; (ii) the circumstances are exceptional; and (iii) there is no alternative effective remedy	FPR 2010, r 30.14
Appeals	To the Court of Appeal (with permission) and note the restrictions in respect of second appeals; or to the Supreme Court, if a certificate has been issued by the judge under AJA 1969, s 12	SCA 1981, s 16; CPR 1998, r 52.13; AJA 1999, s 55 AJA 1969, s 12; Supreme Court PD 1.2.17, 3.6.1 and 3.6.8–3.6.13

E3: Appeal from the Magistrates in Family Proceedings (other than the Children Act 1989)

Legal background

MCA 1980, s 111A provides for appeals from the magistrates' courts to a county court of orders in "family proceedings" as defined by MCA 1980, s 65. Section 65 is extended by MCA 1980, s 111A(5) by adding CSA 1991 appeals to the list of "family proceedings" (enforcement or variation proceedings are excluded from "family proceedings": MCA 1980, s 65(2)). Appeals are as of right (ie without permission) limited only to their being "wrong in law" or "in excess of jurisdiction" (s 111A(2)).

Procedure is governed by parts of FPR 2010, Pt 30 and PD30A, paras 9.2–9.12. Paragraph 9.4 applies r 30.1, r 30.2 (compliance with PD30A), r 30.4 (appellant's notice), r 30.6 (grounds of appeal), r 30.8 (stay) and r 30.9 (amendment of appeal notice).

Procedure

Who may appeal	Any party to the hearing	
Which court	County court	MCA 1980, s 111A(2)
Procedure on appeal	Filing of appellant's notice	FPR 2010, r 30.4; PD30A, para 9.2
	Appeal on question of law or procedural irregularity only	MCA 1980, s 111A(2)
Time for issue	21 days "after the day on which the decision of the magistrates" court was given	MCA 1980, s 111A(4)
Respondents	The parties to the original hearing directly affected by the appeal	
Service	By appellant at time of issue	FPR 2010, r 30.4(3)
Documents	The appellant must file and serve documents, including documents per para 9.9	FPR 2010, r 30.4; PD30A, para 9.9
Appeal notice	As for Pt 30 appeals: N161	PD5A
Powers of the court	(a) Affirm set aside or vary	
	(b) Refer back for re-determination or rehearing	
	(c) Orders for costs and interest	FPR 2010, r 30.11(2)
Stay of order	Filing appeal notice does not stay order	FPR 2010, r 30.8
	Apply to magistrates at time of hearing; or to circuit judge (application included in appeal notice (Form N161))	
Appeals	To the Court of Appeal subject to AJA 1999, s 55 limitations ("second appeals")	

E4: Appeal from a Judge of the High Court or from the Court of Appeal to the Supreme Court

Legal background

On 1 October 2009, the Supreme Court replaced the House of Lords as the final court of appeal in the UK.

An appeal from a decision of a judge of the High Court lies to the Court of Appeal, unless a certificate has been issued by that judge stating that the case merits a "leapfrog" appeal direct to the Supreme Court. Where such a certificate is granted, a prospective appellant must seek leave of the Supreme Court to appeal direct and, if such leave is refused, he may then appeal to the Court of Appeal (see AJA 1969, s 13). An appeal from a decision of the Court of Appeal must be made to the Supreme Court, but only with leave of the Court of Appeal or, if refused, from the Supreme Court. The procedure for all appeals to the Supreme Court is prescribed by the SCR 2009 and the 14 PDs (available at *www.supremecourt.gov.uk/procedures/practice-directions.html*).

The Supreme Court has decided that there must be compelling reasons for withdrawing public funding from a party who had been publicly funded in the court below, had been successful in that court and wished to resist an appeal to a higher court by the unsuccessful party: *R (E) v Governing Body of JFS and the Admissions Appeal Panel of JFS and others* [2009] UKSC 1.

Procedure

Who may appeal	If permission has been granted:	
	any party to a decision of the Court of Appeal	CRA 2005, s 40(2)
	any party to a decision of the High Court where a certificate under AJA 1969, s 12 has been granted	AJA 1969, s 12
Application for permission	*Appeal from Court of Appeal* Permission must be sought from the Court of Appeal or, if refused, from the Supreme Court:	SCR 2009, r 10
	28 days from the order or decision of the court below	SCR 2009, r 11(1)
	Appeal from High Court Permission must be sought from the Supreme Court:	Supreme Court PD 1.2.17, 3.6.1 and 3.6.8–3.6.13
	within 1 month of the grant of a certificate under AJA 1969, s 12 (unless extended by the Supreme Court) or	
	The application for permission will be heard by the Appeal Committee of the Supreme Court	
Documents for permission application	The appellant must file four copies of the following documents: (i) an application for permission to appeal	SCR 2009, rr 11, 14; Supreme Court PD 3.2.1 and PD 7 Form 1
	(ii) a copy of the order appealed from	
	(iii) a copy of the order refusing permission to appeal	
	and within 7 days after the filing of the application	
	(iv) a transcript of the judgment appealed	

(v) all other orders made by the courts
below

(vi) all other judgments given by the
courts below

(vii) transcripts of any unreported
authorities cited in the court below

(viii) a document setting out the history
of the matter

Notice of objection	A respondent who wishes to object to an application for permission must file a notice of objection within 14 days after service of the application for permission	SCR 2009, r 13; Supreme Court PD 3.1.8–3.1.10 and PD 7 Form 3
Intervention in application for permission	Any person may make written submissions to the Supreme Court in support of an application for permission to appeal and request the court takes them into account	SCR 2009, r 15; Supreme Court PD 3.3.17
	The submissions must be served on the appellant, every respondent and every intervenor in the court below before four copies are filed with the court	
Procedure on permission application	The application for permission will be considered on paper without a hearing by a panel of Justices who may:	SCR 2009, r 16; Supreme Court PD 3.3.1–3.4.8
	(i) grant or refuse permission	
	(ii) invite the parties to file written submissions within 14 days as to the grant of permission on terms; or	
	(iii) direct an oral hearing	
	Fee payable on filing an application for permission to appeal: £1000	SCFO 2009, fee 1.1
	Fee payable on filing notice of objection: £160	SCFO 2009, fee 1.2
Procedure on appeal	Where permission to appeal is granted	SCR 2009, r 18
	(i) the application for permission shall stand as the notice of appeal;	
	(ii) the grounds of appeal shall be limited to those on which permission has been granted; and	
	(iii) the appellant must within 14 days after the grant of permission file a notice of intention to proceed	
	Fee payable on filing a notice of intention to proceed: £800	SCFO 2009, fee 2.1
	Where permission is not required (i) a notice of appeal in the appropriate form must be filed within 42 days of the date of the order or decision;	SCR 2009, r 19; Supreme Court PD 4 and PD 7
	(ii) a copy of the order appealed from;	
	(iii) a copy of the order granting permission to appeal	
	Fee payable on filing a notice of appeal: £1600	SCFO 2009, fee 2.2

Respondents	The parties to the hearing in the court below	
	Each respondent who intends to participate in the appeal must within 14 days after service of a notice of intention to proceed or a rule 20 notice file a notice in the appropriate form	SCR 2009, r 21 and Supreme Court PD 7 Form 3
	Fee: £320	SCFO 2009, fee 2.4
	A respondent who wishes to argue that the decision of the court below should be upheld on different grounds from those relied on by the court below, must state that clearly in the written case but need not cross-appeal	SCR 2009, r 25(1)
Cross-appeals	A respondent who wishes to argue that the order appealed from should be varied must obtain permission to cross-appeal from the court and SCR, Pt 2 applies	SCR 2009, rr 25(2) and 10–17; Supreme Court PD 8.3.1–8.3.8
Lodgement of documents	The appellant must lodge within 112 days after the filing of the notice to proceed or the notice of appeal:	SCR 2009, r 22; Supreme Court PD 5.1.2–5.1.5
	(i) the original and seven copies of statement of facts and issues; and	
	(ii) eight copies of the appendix of the essential documents that were before or record the proceedings of the court below	
	both of which must be agreed with by every respondent before filing	
	Documents must be included in the appendix in the following order:	
	(a) the order appealed against;	
	(b) if separate from the order at (a) above, the order refusing permission to appeal to the Supreme Court;	
	(c) the official transcript of the judgment of the court below;	
	(d) the final order(s) of all other courts below;	
	(e) the official transcript of the final judgment(s) of all other courts below;	
	(f) (where they are necessary for understanding the legal issues and the argument) the relevant documents filed in the courts below;	
	(g) (where they are necessary for understanding the legal issues and the argument) the relevant documents and correspondence relating to the appeal	
	All documents must be numbered, and each part of the Appendix must include a list of its contents	
	Fee payable on filing a statement of relevant facts and issues and an appendix of relevant documents: £4820	SCFO 2009, fee 2.5

PART I

Intervenors to appeal	Any person who wishes to intervene in the appeal may apply for permission, which will be considered on paper by a panel of justices	SCR 2009, r 26
	No permission is required for intervention by the Crown under HRA 1998, s 5, or by the relevant officer when the court is exercising its devolution jurisdiction	
Appellants' and respondents' cases	The appellant and every respondent and every intervenor or advocate to the court must sequentially exchange and file their respective written cases	SCR 2009, r 22(4); Supreme Court PD 6.3.1–6.3.13
Core volumes	As soon as the parties' cases have been exchanged and in any event no later than 14 days after the date fixed for the hearing, the appellant must file 10 core volumes and 10 volumes of authorities	SCR 2009, rr 23 and 24; Supreme Court PD 6.4.1–6.4.4 and 6.5.1
	The core volume must contain in the following order:	
	(a) Form 1 – a copy of the notice of appeal or the re-sealed application for permission to appeal;	
	(b) notice of cross-appeal (if any);	
	(c) statement of facts and issues;	
	(d) appellants' and respondents' cases, with cross-references to the Appendix and authorities volume(s);	
	(e) case of the advocate to the court or intervener, if any;	
	(f) Pt 1 of the Appendix; and	
	(g) index to the authorities volume(s)	
	Form of core volumes	
	The core volumes:	
	(a) should be bound, preferably with plastic comb binding and with blue (or, for criminal appeals, red) card covers;	
	(b) should include tabs for each of the documents set out in paragraph 6.4.3, preferably with the name of the document on the tab;	
	(c) should show on the front cover a list of the contents and the names and addresses of the solicitors for all parties;	
	(d) must indicate (by e.g. a label (printed in landscape) attached to the plastic spine) the volume number (in roman numerals) and the short title of the appeal	
Hearing of the appeal	Every contested appeal shall be heard in open court unless it is necessary in the interests of justice or in the public interest to sit in private for part of the appeal hearing	SCR 2009, r 27

Judgment	A judgment may be given in open court or, if the court so directs, promulgated by the Registrar	SCR 2009, r 28
Powers of the court	The Supreme Court has all the powers of the court below and may: (i) affirm, set aside or vary the order or judgment; (ii) remit any issue for determination by the court below; (iii) order a new trial or hearing; (iv) make an order for the payment of interest; and (v) make a costs order	

PART I

E5: Appeal from a Judge of the County Court or the High Court to the Court of Appeal

Legal background

An appeal from a judge of either the High Court or a county court lies to the Court of Appeal (SCA 1981, s 16 and CCA 1984, s 77). The Court of Appeal is a superior court of record, and has all the authority and jurisdiction of the court from which the appeal is brought (SCA 1981, s 15). The procedure for all appeals to the Court of Appeal is prescribed by CPR 1998, Pt 52 as supplemented, as from 1 October 2012, by PDs 52A, 52C and 52D. Most decisions of the lower court require leave from that court or, if refused, from the Court of Appeal before an appeal may be made.

An appeal is against the order and not the judgment (*Vaughan v Vaughan* [2008] 1 FLR 1108, CA). It is not sufficient for a party to draw attention to an alleged deficiency in a judgment by way of an application for permission to appeal. It is incumbent on the party to point out the deficiency and to request clarification or a supplemental judgment on the issue (*Re S (Children) (Contact: Fact-finding Hearing)* [2007] EWCA Civ 694), but practitioners should proceed with caution: this practice should only be adopted as a prelude to an application for permission to appeal and should not be routinely used to invite the judge to reconsider a point of substance (*Egan v Motor Services (Bath) Ltd* [2008] 1 FLR 1346 CA). "Before launching an application for permission to appeal, it is incumbent on the applicant to seek clarification of the judgment or amplification of the findings from the trial judge." *Re A (Child Abuse)* [2008] 1 FLR 1423, CA. Where an alleged lack of reasons in the judgment had not been drawn to the attention of the trial judge or the judge had subsequently failed to elaborate his reasons, the normal procedure was remittal to the judge at first instance with a list of specific questions: *Re A & L (Appeal: Fact-Finding)* [2012] 1 FLR 134.

In care proceedings, a judge is entitled to change his mind – and thus his findings of fact – after delivering judgment, written or oral, at a fact-finding hearing even in the absence of an intervening change of circumstances. In *Re L and B (Children)* [2013] UKSC 8, the Supreme Court has held that a court should not be required to make welfare decisions concerning a child on a false factual basis. It declined to offer even a provisional view on whether the power was available after the order made at the conclusion of the fact-finding hearing had been perfected (i e sealed by the court): it was said the arguments either way were finely balanced. The power must be exercised "judicially and not capriciously". "The best safeguard against having to do so is a fully and properly reasoned judgment in the first place."

In *Re W, Re A, Re B (Change of Name)* [1999] 2 FLR 930 the Court of Appeal held that the test to be applied by the appellate court in children cases, whether that be the High Court, county court or Court of Appeal, should be the same – i e in accordance with the principles established by *G v G (Minors: Custody Appeal)* [1985] FLR 894. The House of Lords in *Piglowska v Piglowski* [1999] 2 FLR 763 gave guidance to the profession in respect of the conduct of appeals. The parties do not begin the appeal with a "clean sheet". Lord Hoffmann, at [783H]–[784H], stated the appellate court must always bear in mind: (i) the advantage that the trial judge has of seeing and hearing the witnesses; (ii) that there is a discretion vested in the trial court and the appellate court should resist the temptation to substitute their own discretion for that of the trial judge on a narrow textual analysis of the judgment below; and (iii) that there must be a consideration of proportionality between the amount at stake and the legal resources to be expended. In *Re J (Child Returned Abroad: Convention Rights)* [2005] 2 FLR 802 at [12], Baroness Hale observed "[t]oo ready an interference by the appellate court, particularly if it always seems to be in the direction of one result rather than the other, risks robbing the trial judge of the discretion entrusted to him by law". The President has reiterated that appellate courts should respect brave discretionary decisions made at first instance and must be on "secure ground" if they are to reverse the exercise of a discretion: *Re W (Relocation: Removal Outside Jurisdiction)* [2011] 2 FLR 409.

The Court of Appeal has given guidance on the limited grounds on which the court may grant an application for permission to appeal and to allow an appeal (particularly for the benefit of litigants in person) (*Re W (Permission to Appeal)* [2008] 1 FLR 406).

For further guidance on the approach that an appellate court should adopt to (a) appeals where the adequacy of a trial judge's reasoning is in issue and (b) appeals against the exercise of a discretion by a trial judge, see the notes to CPR 1998, Pt 52.

Applications for permission to appeal in children's cases, especially those with an international element, have to be brought on for hearing swiftly. The filing of the notice of appeal should not be delayed until the applicant has received a copy of the approved judgment under appeal (*Re A (Children: Split Hearing)* [2007] 1 FLR 905 (CA); *Re EC (Child Abduction: Stayed Proceedings)* [2007] 1 FLR 57).

It is suggested that an appellate court should exercise caution before directing at a without notice permission to appeal hearing that a matter should be remitted for rehearing by the first instance court when (a) the respondent to the application has not been heard by the court and (b) the court has not determined the full appeal: *Livock v Livock* [2012] 1 FLR 776.

In urgent cases where the judge has refused a stay of the order pending the application for permission to appeal, the prospective appellant may telephone the Court of Appeal to apply for a stay (during office hours the telephone number is 0207 947 6000 and out of hours contact is made to the security office at the RCJ on 0207 947 6260 who will refer the matter to the duty deputy master): PD52C, para 26. A deputy master will refer the matter to a Lord Justice who may grant the stay or list the matter urgently for consideration of the application for a stay (*Re S (Child Proceedings: Urgent Appeals)* [2007] 2 FLR 1044 (CA); *Re A (A Child)* [2007] EWCA Civ 899).

The Court of Appeal has emphasised that there is an obligation on an applicant seeking permission to appeal, or on an appellant who had obtained permission, to seek the Court of Appeal's leave before instructing a fresh expert and releasing court papers to him: see the notes to CPR 1998, r 52.11 (*Re McC (Care Proceedings: Fresh Evidence of Foreign Expert)* [2012] 2 FLR 121 and the Family Justice Council Guidelines of December 2011, *Instruction of Medical Experts from Overseas in Family Cases* (see Part V)).

Where an appeal is against findings of fact, Mostyn J has observed that "an appellate court would only be able to say that a fact-finder has plainly got the wrong answer if:

(i)   His conclusion was demonstrably contrary to the weight of the evidence, or
(ii)   The decision-making process can be identified as being plainly defective so that it can be said that the findings in question are unsafe.

I would include in the second category errors of principle as to, say, the burden or standard of proof, or a failure to take into account well-established principles as to the weight to be given to proven lies or litigation misconduct in reaching the factual findings." (*NG v SG (Appeal: Non-Disclosure)* [2012] 1 FLR 1211).

Where a single Lord Justice makes observations on Form 269C1, when granting permission to appeal or directing an oral hearing on notice with the appeal to follow immediately if permission was granted, they are to be obeyed. Primary responsibility for a failure to comply will usually lie with the party who brings the appeal/application: *Re M-W (Care Proceedings: Expert Evidence)* [2010] 2 FLR 46 (CA).

When considering ordering a transcript of the whole, or a part, of the evidence or hearing in the court below, practitioners should bear in mind the following:

(i)   The preparation of and authorisation of the payment for a transcript might take time, therefore practitioners should consider whether a transcript is an essential prerequisite before filing of a notice of appeal or before an application for permission to appeal is sought.
(ii)   Practitioners should consider filing a notice of appeal even though a transcript might not be available.
(iii) The judge of the lower court could be contacted if necessary to speed up the process.
(iv)   Pursuit of a transcript, which might be peripheral, should not affect the consideration of an application for permission to appeal: *Re GB (Children)* [2013] EWCA Civ 164.

The Court of Appeal has observed that it would be "enormously helpful" if a chronology was provided in all family appeals as they are for most first instance hearings: *Re H (A Child)* [2013] EWCA Civ 72.

While the period in which the notice of appeal has to be lodged in the Court of Appeal has been increased from 14 to 21 days, such an extension might not generally be appropriate for family cases involving children where time is of the essence. CPR 1998, r 52.4(2)(a) permits the judge in the lower court to have regard to what time limit should be imposed for the issue of a notice of appeal (*Re M & H* [2006] EWCA Civ 499).

The Court of Appeal will only permit fresh evidence to be adduced in an appeal if the three *Ladd v Marshall* (1954) FLR Rep 422 conditions are satisfied, namely:

(i)   first, it must be shown that the evidence could not have been obtained with reasonable diligence for use at the trial;

(ii)   the evidence must be such that, if given, it would probably have an important influence on the result of the case, although it need not be decisive;

(iii)   the evidence must be such as was presumably to be believed, or in other words, it must be apparently credible, although it need not be incontrovertible.

Where events changed or developed after the making of an interim order, the appropriate course was to seek a variation of the order from the judge, rather than seek to appeal against the order: *Re H (A Child)* [2011] Fam Law 941.

The unlawful removal of a child from his usual place of residence called for a peremptory order to be sought for his return, rather than to seek to challenge the dismissal of an appeal for an interim residence order by way of a second appeal to the Court of Appeal: *Re R (Children: Peremptory Return)* [2011] 2 FLR 863.

In those cases where it is plain that whatever the professionals' assessment of the prospects of success, the litigants cannot rest until they have exhausted their legal remedies, the court should consider imposing tight time limits on the filing of an application for permission to appeal and contact the Civil Appeals office to seek an early listing, so that finality may be achieved as soon as ever possible (*Re P (Residence: Appeal)* [2008] 1 FLR 198, [2008] 1 FLR 1346 (CA)).

The Supreme Court has criticised the imposition by the Court of Appeal of conditions to the grant of a stay pending determination of an application for permission to appeal by the Supreme Court. "As a general rule, conditions such as were imposed by the Court of Appeal in this case should not be made where a party seeks permission to appeal, not least because these might be seen as an unwarranted disincentive to the pursuit of what proved in this case to be a fully merited application," per Lord Kerr: *Re B (A Child)* [2010] 1 FLR 551. The Court of Appeal had approved the decision of the court below to transfer residence from the maternal grandmother to the father: in granting a stay of the transfer of residence the court imposed a provision for extensive overnight staying contact to the father.

The Court of Appeal may impose conditions on the grant of permission if compelling reasons were found to exist (unlike r 52.9, r 52.3(7) does not specify the need for compelling reasons, but the court has held that the latter should be read as if those words were included in the rule). Thus, where a party had attempted to evade enforcement and was in gross breach of court orders, it was appropriate that conditions were attached to the grant of permission to appeal, including the transfer of a lump sum into this jurisdiction in a secure environment and a requirement to comply with existing court orders: *Radmacher v Granatino* [2009] 1 FLR 1566.

The Master of the Rolls has emphasised "in the strongest possible terms that it is only where it is clear that there is an unavoidable conflict of interest, as a matter of law, between two parties in the same interest that they should have separate legal representation, especially where public money is involved. The fact that the parties may have different factual points, or that one party's case may be seen as stronger than the other's, or that the parties' legal advisers may see the legal arguments or the prospects somewhat differently, are not good reasons for their incurring the expense and the court time of separate representation": *Oxfordshire County Council v X, Y and J* [2011] 1 FLR 272.

There are detailed provisions in PDs 52A and 52C for the preparation of case bundles and appeal bundles and the revised provisions governing the content of skeleton arguments and the citing of authorities – PD52A, paras 5.1–5.3 and PD52C, paras 9, 13, 14, 16, 17, 21–24, 27, 29, 31 and 32.

On 24 March 2012, the Lord Chief Justice issued a new practice direction entitled *Citation of Authorities*. In summary, the principal requirements are that:

(a)   where a judgment is reported in the Official Law Reports, that report must be cited;

(b)   if a judgment is not reported in the Official Law Reports but is reported in the WLR or All ER, that report should be cited;

(c)   if a judgment is not reported in any of the above, but is reported in one of the authoritative specialist series of reports, that report should be cited if it contains a headnote and is made by an individual holding a Senior Courts qualification;

(d)   if a judgment is not reported in any of the above but is reported in other reports, they may be cited; and

(e)   if a judgment is not reported, reference may be made to the official transcript if that is available.

The bundle of authorities should comply with the requirements of Practice Direction of 24 March 2012: *Citation of Authorities* (PD52C, paras 29(2),(4)) and in general:

(a)   have the relevant passages of the authorities marked;

(b)   not include authorities for propositions not in dispute; and

(c)   not contain more than 10 authorities unless the scale of the appeal warrants more extensive citation.

For appeals against case management decisions and discretionary decisions by first instance trial judges, see *President's Guidance No 2 December 2010* in Part V and *Re W (Relocation: Removal Outside Jurisdiction)* [2011] 2 FLR 409, at [7]–[12].

   Appeal notices may be filed by email (www.justice.gov.uk/courts). The guidelines on the use of email are as follows: there is "a ceiling of 2Mb on attachments to e-mails, and the Civil Appeals Office cannot accept documents which exceed this limit. The Civil Appeals Office will not take responsibility for printing documents which exceed twenty pages or contain colour content. These should be provided in hard copy. Only documents in Word or PDF/Adobe Acrobat format will be acceptable. E-mail submissions will be checked twice daily at 9.30am and 2.00pm. For the purpose of adherence to time limits prescribed by the rules of procedure, e-mails received later than 4.30pm will be treated as having been received on the following working day."

   Note: when a draft judgment is provided to the parties pursuant to CPR 1998, PD40E it must remain confidential. Solicitors ought not to disclose a draft judgment to other members of their firms or organisations, save to the extent necessary for the taking of instructions in respect of the immediate conduct of the case and allowing for a junior solicitor to consult with a senior supervising solicitor. If any solicitor is in doubt as to the propriety of a particular disclosure, he should request permission from the judge concerned by emailing the judge's clerk (*Director of Public Prosecutions v P* [2007] EWHC 1144 (Admin)).

Procedure

Who may appeal	With permission, any party aggrieved by the decision	SCA 1981, s 16; CCA 1984, s 77
Permission to appeal	Required for all cases apart from where the appeal is against:	CPR 1998, r 52.3
	(a) a committal order	
	(b) a refusal to grant habeas corpus	
	(c) a secure accommodation order; or	
	(d) otherwise as provided by PD	
	Application should be made to the judge if possible (if not to the Court of Appeal) or, if refused, to the Court of Appeal	CPR 1998, r 52.3(2),(3); PD52A, para 4.1 and PD52C, paras 15 and 16
	Consideration of permission is without a hearing unless a hearing is requested	CPR PD52C, para 15
	Respondents will be notified, but do not attend, unless requested by the Court of Appeal	CPR PD52C, paras 16, 19, 20
	For the permission hearing the proposed appellant should lodge a Notice and an appeal bundle with as many documents as are available (see below)	
	Permission may be subject to conditions or may limit the issues	CPR 1998, r 52.3(7)
	Fee: £235	CPFO 2008, fee 13.1(a)

	But if permission to appeal is not required or permission was granted by the court below, fee: £465	CPFO 2008, fee 13.1(b)
Procedure on appeal	The Notice of Appeal (Form N161) must be filed within such period as directed by the lower court (which should not exceed 35 days) and where the lower court makes no direction, then within 21 days of the date of the order and it must be served not later than 7 days after filing	CPR 1998, r 52.4, PD52C, paras 3, 4
	A skeleton argument should be served with it	CPR PD52C, paras 3, 31
	The appellant must serve the Notice and any skeleton argument upon the respondents within 7 days of filing the Notice of Appeal. Once permission is granted by the lower court or the Court of Appeal or the permission hearing will be listed with the appeal to follow, the appellant must serve on each respondent an index of the proposed bundle of documents 7 days after the date of the listing window notification and file and serve a bundle of documents no later than 42 days before the appeal hearing	CPR 1998, r 52.4(3), PD52C, paras 21 and 27
	The appellant must complete the appeal questionnaire sent by the Court of Appeal 14 days after the listing window notification	CPR PD52C, para 23
	Fee: £465 (unless the appellant paid the fee required by 13.1(b))	CPFO 2008, fee 13.1(c)
Respondents	All parties to the proceedings who are affected by the appeal and anyone allowed to become a party	CPR 1998, r 52.1(3)
Lodgement of documents	The appellant must file (at the Civil Appeals Registry: RCJ Room E307) with his notice:	
	(a) a copy of his notice for each respondent and three additional copies for the court;	
	(b) one copy of his skeleton argument for each notice filed;	
	(c) a sealed copy of the order being appealed and any order giving or refusing permission to appeal together with any reasons;	
	(d) witness statements and affidavits;	
	(e) a transcript or note of the judgment	CPR PD52C, para 3
	A bundle of authorities must be filed 7 days before the hearing which must comply with PD	CPR PD52C, paras 21 and 29
Respondent's notice	May be filed but *must* be filed where the respondent seeks to appeal or seeks to uphold the decision for different reasons	

	Unless otherwise directed, must be filed within 14 days of (i) service of the notice of appeal if permission has been given by the lower court or is not needed, (ii) notification that permission has been granted by the CoA or (iii) notification that the permission application will be listed with the appeal to follow	
	The respondent must file two additional copies of the notice for the court and one for each party	
	A skeleton argument must be filed within 14 days of filing the notice and a copy served on each party	CPR 1998, r 52.5; PD52C, paras 8–10 and 21
	Fee: £235	CPFO 2008, fee 13.2
Appeal bundle	No later than 42 days before the appeal hearing the appellant must file and serve a bundle of documents. The bundle must be paginated and in chronological order and contain an index at the front. Subject to the order of the court, the bundle must contain:	
	(a) a copy of the appellant's notice;	
	(b) a copy of any respondent's notice;	
	(c) a copy of the skeleton arguments;	
	(d) a copy of the order under appeal;	
	(e) a copy of the order granting or refusing permission to appeal, with reasons given, if any;	
	(f) the approved transcript	
	The bundle may contain, where relevant to the appeal, statements of case, application notices, other orders, a chronology, witness statements and other documents but no original documents should be included	CPR PD52C, paras 21 and 27
Powers of the Court of Appeal	To receive fresh evidence	
	To give any judgment and make any order that could have been made by the lower court	CPR 1998, r 52.11(2) CPR 1998, r 52.10(1)
	To order a new trial or hearing	CPR 1998, r 52.10(2)
Appeals	To the Supreme Court with leave of either the Court of Appeal or, if refused, the Supreme Court	CRA 2005, s 40(2); SCR 2009, r 11(1)

E6: Applications Based on Supervening Events

Legal background

The law seeks finality in its orders (eg in *Ampthill Peerage* [1977] 1 AC 547 at [569]). Truly exceptional circumstances may occur later that justify reconsideration of the original order. This may be because events come to light (eg non-disclosure, fraud or mistake) that were not known by the court when its order was made. Alternatively, where an assumption on which the original order was based changes fundamentally (*Barder v Barder* [1987] 2 FLR 480) it may be appropriate to seek permission out of time to appeal against the order.

SCA 1981, s 17 prevents application to the High Court to set aside an original order, save where rules provide for this (e g CPR 1998, r 52.17 and FPR 2010, r 30.14, considered below). The Court of Appeal has nevertheless assumed inherent jurisdiction in the High Court to set aside its own orders (*Robinson v Robinson (Disclosure)* (1983) 4 FLR 102; *Judge v Judge* [2009] 1 FLR 1287 at [44]) and in *R (ota AM (Cameroon)) v Asylum and Immigration Tribunal* [2008] 1 WLR 2062 at [25] the jurisdiction of the High Court to set aside its own orders was explained as "an inherent power to see that it does not become the instrument of injustice". SCA 1981, s 17 does not seem to have been considered by the court in terms in any of these cases.

In their civil jurisdiction, magistrates have no jurisdiction to review or set aside their own orders (*R (ota Mathialagan) v London Borough of Southwark* [2004] EWCA Civ 1689), save by consent of the parties; it can only be done by judicial review.

The Supreme Court has power "in appropriate cases to rescind or vary an earlier order" that it made (*R v Bow Street Metropolitan Stipendiary Magistrate, ex p Pinochet Ugarte (No 2)* [2000] 1 AC 119).

The Court of Appeal and High Court may re-open final appeals "to avoid real injustice" (CPR 1998, r 52.17; FPR 2010, r 30.14; and see *Taylor v Lawrence* [2003] QB 528; *Jaffray v Society of Lloyd's* [2008] 1 WLR 75).

County court re-opening of appeals is expressly excluded by CPR 1998, r 52.17(3) and FPR 2010, r 30.14(3), perhaps because when r 52.17 came into force (October 2003) CCR 1981, Ord 37, r 1 was still part of CPR 1998, Sch 2 and enabled applications for rehearing to go to a county court judge. Order 37 has now been removed from Sch 2 and since April 2011 (when FPR 2010 came into force) it has not applied directly to family proceedings.

If the High Court does have an inherent jurisdiction to set aside its first instance decisions then so too does the county court (CCA 1984, s 38).

Terminology

(1) *Set aside* This term is defined in the Glossary (in both sets of rules) as "Cancelling a judgment or order or a step taken by a party in proceedings". To set aside an order is one of the powers of an appellate court (CPR 1998, r 52.10(2)(a); FPR 2010, r 30.11(2)(a)). An application to set aside (normally, and if possible, to the judge who made the order) can be made in respect of: (a) an interim order (e g FPR 2010, r 18.11(1)); (b) a final order following a first instance hearing; or (c) a final appeal order (e g where an order is challenged on grounds of fraud (*de Lasala v de Lasala* (1979) FLR Rep 223), material non-disclosure or mistake (*Richardson v Richardson* [2011] 2 FLR 244) or that the judge below was said to be biased (*Taylor v Lawrence* (above)). The court made no error on the original facts as it heard them. Facts have been discovered since. It is applications under (b) and (c) above that will be considered here.

(2) *Barder permission to appeal* If after the final order, a fundamental assumption on which the order was made alters in such a way as materially to invalidate the order, it may be possible (exceptionally) to seek permission to appeal out of time against the original order.

(3) *Taylor v Lawrence appellate court jurisdiction* Where a final appeal order is made by the Court of Appeal or High Court it may be re-opened, provided the stringent conditions in CPR 1998, r 52.17(1) (FPR 2010, r 30.14(1): family proceedings in the High Court) apply and that permission to apply is given (CPR 1998, r 52.17(4); FPR 2010, r 30.14(4)).

This guide does not deal with the "slip rule" (CPR 1998, r 40.12; FPR 2010, r 29.16) or the power of the court to correct its own decision before the order is drawn (*Re Barrell Enterprises* [1973] 1 WLR 19; *Paulin v Paulin* [2009] 2 FLR 354).

Route of the application

(1) A set aside application is in the proceedings in which the impugned order was made: CPR 1998, Pt 23 or the FPR 2010, Pt 18 procedure (and see *Re C (Financial Provision: Leave to Appeal)* [1993] 2 FLR 799; FPR 2010, r 18.1(2)(c) (for which there is no CPR 1998 equivalent)).

(2) *Barder* appeal: Proceed as for a conventional appeal (CPR 1998, Pt 52 or FPR 2010, Pt 30), with accompanying application to appeal out of time. Form N161 (appellant's notice) at Section 8, Part C prompts what amounts to a CPR Pt 23/FPR Pt 18 application in the court appealed to.

(3) Appellate court re-opening CPR Pt 23/FPR Pt 18 application in the original appeal proceedings that led to the impugned order.

If in family proceedings it is considered that a separate originating application is necessary (in *de Lasala v de Lasala* (above) Lord Diplock referred to "a fresh action to set [the order] aside"), then it should be by FPR 2010, Pt 19 application.

Both sets of rules have exemption provisions: CPR 1998, r 3.10 and FPR 2010, r 4.7 each enable the court to correct procedural errors.

Permission to proceed

Permission is required for a *Barder* appeal and to re-open appeal orders:

(1) *Barder appeals*   In *O v O (Procedure for Listing Applications for Permission to Appeal to the High Court)* [2011] EWHC 14 July 2011 (reported), Baron J suggested that applications for permission to appeal to a judge from a district judge should replicate FPR 2010, Pt 30 appellate procedures (and see also Munby LJ's comments on the FPR 2010, Pt 18 procedure in relation to an application for permission under MFPA 1984, Pt III under FPR 2010, r 8.23: *Traversa v Freddi* [2011] 2 FLR 272 (at [56])):

    (a) Application for permission is on paper: if the judge considers that the appeal has real prospects of success, the judge can grant permission on paper (and see FPR 2010, r 18.9(1)(a)).

    (b) If permission is refused on paper, the appellant has the right to ask for an oral hearing (FPR 2010, r 18.11).

    (c) The permission application may be listed for hearing, normally of the applicant only (save where the judge says that there should be a hearing of both parties (e g with the appeal to follow if permission is given)).

(2) *Re-opening of appeal orders*   Procedure for the application for permission under CPR 1998, r 52.17 and FPR 2010, r 30.14 is prescribed by rules (CPR 1998, r 52.17(4), FPR 2010, r 30.14(4)) and practice directions (CPR PD52A, para 7.1 and FPR PD30A, para 18.3).

There is no reason why similar procedures should not apply for *Barder* appeal permission in the county court, but re-opening of appeal orders in the county court is not available under CPR 1998, r 52.17 and FPR 2010, r 30.14.

E6(1): Application in the High Court and County Court in Family Proceedings to Set Aside an Order

Procedure

Who may apply	Any party to the hearing that led to the original order	
Application	To the judge who made the original order (if available)	*Robinson v Robinson (Disclosure)* (1983) 4 FLR 102; *Judge v Judge* [2009] 1 FLR 1287
	Application is on notice to all parties to the original order	FPR 2010, Pt 18; CPR 1998, Pt 23
Grounds	Grounds for an application are not closed: grounds will depend on, for example, non-disclosure by one spouse, discovery of material new evidence, mistake, fraud	FPR 2010, r 18.7(1)(b); CPR 1998, r 23.6(b); *de Lasala v de Lasala* (1979) FLR Rep 223; *Judge v Judge* (above)
Draft order	The draft order will recite the terms of the basis for set aside and the disposal sought by the applicant: normally full directions for evidence to cure the error; for a fresh trial; and costs	FPR 2010, r 18.7(1)(a); CPR 1998, r 23.6(b)

Procedure	FPR 2010, Pt 18 (or possibly Pt 19); CPR 1998, Pt 23	FPR 2010, r 18.1(2)(c); but see *de Lasala* (above)
Time for application	No time is specified by the rules: delay may be a factor in the court considering any application	See, for example, the comments of Wilson LJ in *Judge v Judge* (above) on the pre-FPR 2010 procedure
Respondent	Parties to original proceedings	FPR 2010, r 18.3
Documents	No documents or other procedural matters are prescribed by the rules. Documents with the application should include: (1) The original court order; (2) Relevant pleadings (sparingly) in the original proceedings; (3) Statement(s) as to the fresh circumstances giving rise to the claim; (4) Any documents in support of (3)	
Reply/answer	The respondent (and any other parties) can reply by affidavit or sworn statement	
Application without hearing	The court can deal with applications without a hearing (eg where merit of claim appears clear)	FPR 2010, r 18.9(1)
Right to vary order made without hearing	If an order is made without a hearing, application can be made to set that order aside or vary it	FPR 2010, r 18.11(1); CPR 1998, r 23.10(1)
	Time for application: 7 days	FPR 2010, r 18.11(2); CPR 1998, r 23.10(2)
Case management of set aside application	(i) Disclosure: for example, all information as to the mistake pleaded (ii) Preliminary issues: materiality of non-disclosure (iii) Fraud: all appropriate notice given (iv) Joinder of third parties: any affected	FPR 2010, r 4.1(3); CPR 1998, r 3.1(2)
Disposal available on application	(i) Setting aside of order under application and order for rehearing, with directions for trial, including: adducing evidence of facts giving rise to application; permission to call oral evidence (ii) Dismissal (iii) Costs	
Case management of re-opened hearing	If the application is granted, the judge is likely immediately to move to case management of any further process to lead to a fresh order	FPR 2010, r 4.1; CPR 1998, r 3.1

PART I

E6(2): Application for Permission to Appeal Out of Time (*Barder* Appeal)

Procedure

Who may apply	Any party to the hearing that led to the order appealed against	
Application for permission on paper	District judge to judge, or judge to the Court of Appeal	FPR 2010, Pt 30; and see note on *O v O* (2011) Baron J (unreported), above, for district judge appeals
Grounds	Grounds for an application are: (i) Events have occurred that invalidate the basis, or a fundamental assumption, on which the original order was made and, if permission be given, the appeal would very likely succeed (ii) New events have occurred within a short time of the original order (probably not more than a year) (iii) Application must be made promptly (iv) Grant of permission must not prejudice third parties who have acquired property involved in the proceedings	*Barder v Barder* [1987] 2 FLR 480
Procedure	By appellant's notice (Form N161) at appropriate level, with application attached to Section 8, Part C	FPR 2010, Pt 30, suitably amended to reflect change of circumstances and any delay
Procedure and documents	Procedure and documents will be as required by FPR 2010, Pt 30 or CPR 1998, Pt 52, for example: (1) Grounds of appeal; (2) Evidence and documents in support of application (ie new events); (3) Skeleton argument; (4) Relevant documents from original proceedings including: (a) The original court order; (b) Relevant court orders, documents and reports (sparingly) in the original proceedings	FPR 2010, Pt 30; PD30A; and see Guides E4, E5
Permission	Application for permission will depend on level of judge who made the order: (1) District judge to circuit judge; (2) Circuit judge to High Court judge; (3) High Court judge to Court of Appeal	

Dealing with permission	Suggested procedure as per *O v O* (2011) (above): (1) List before appellate judge on paper; (2) Refusal on paper: appellant can apply to rehear: proceed to appeal if allowed; (3) Application allowed: proceed to appeal, unless respondent has "killer point" in reply	See analogy with *Traversa v Freddi* [2011] 2 FLR 272
Permission granted	Proceed with appeal as per FPR 2010, Pt 30 or CPR 1998, Pt 52 (as appropriate) and according to relevant PDs	
Disposal available on application	If appeal allowed, set aside or vary original order and rehearing (based on facts as they are at the time of the rehearing): (a) by appellate court; or (b) upon referral back to first instance court	FPR 2010, r 30.11(2); *Smith v Smith (Smith and ors intervening)* [1991] 2 FLR 432, CA

PART I

E6(3): Application to Re-Open a Final Appeal

Procedure

Who may apply	Any party to the appeal that led to the original order	
Application	For permission to a judge of the court that made the original order	CPR 1998, r 52.17(4); FPR 2010, r 30.14(4); CPR PD52A, para 7.1; FPR PD30A, para 18.3; *Taylor v Lawrence* [2003] QB 528
	Application in the first instance is not on notice to any parties: it must be considered by a judge on a preliminary basis first	CPR PD52A, para 7.2; FPR PD30A, para 18.5
Grounds	The rules state the grounds as follows: (1) It is necessary to avoid real injustice (eg material non-disclosure, mistake, fraud, bias (including of the judge below)) (2) Exceptional circumstances and it is appropriate to re-open (3) There is no alternative effective remedy	CPR 1998, r 52.17(1); FPR 2010, r 30.14(1)
Procedure	Application is made by "application notice"(ie CPR 1998, Pt 23 or FPR 2010, Pt 18 procedure), supported by written evidence verified by a statement of truth	CPR PD52A, para 7.2; FPR PD30A, para 18.4

Service of application	Only if directed by the court	CPR PD52A, para 7.2; FPR PD30A, para 18.5
Response	If the application is directed to be served "on another party" and thereby is able to proceed, that party may file and serve a written reply Time for reply: 14 days	CPR 1998, r 52.17(6); FPR 2010, r 30.14(6); CPR PD52A, para 7.3; FPR PD30A, para 18.6
Consideration by single judge of appellate court	The application and documents in support and in reply will be considered on paper	CPR PD52A, para 7.4; FPR PD30A, para 18.7
	The application only proceeds to a hearing if "exceptionally the judge so directs"	CPR 1998, r 52.17(5); FPR 2010, r 30.14(5)
Hearing of application	No right to an oral hearing, unless the judge directs	CPR 1998, r 52.17(5); FPR 2010, r 30.14(5)

F1: Proceedings involving a Protected Party

Legal background

Court rules have in the past defined the circumstances in which a person was to be treated as being "under a disability" in relation to proceedings and the procedure then to be adopted. A person under disability was a person under the age of 18 years (variously described as a "minor" or an "infant") or a "patient" (as defined). The terms "child" and "protected party" are now used and the expression "under a disability" is no longer appropriate.

It has long been the case that a person under disability may not:

(i)   bring or make a claim in any proceedings;
(ii) acknowledge service, defend, make a counterclaim or intervene in any proceedings; or
(iii) appear in any proceedings under a judgment or order, notice of which has been served on him;

other than by an appointed representative. This has traditionally been a next friend for the person bringing proceedings or a guardian ad litem for the person defending or responding but the term "litigation friend" was introduced for both categories in civil proceedings by CPR 1998 and in family proceedings by FPR 2010.

Proceedings commenced or conducted in breach of these requirements will be of no effect unless the court orders otherwise and a solicitor who purports to act on the record for such a party might become personally liable for the costs of opposing parties.

F1(1): Family Proceedings involving a Protected Party

Procedure

Who is a protected party	A party, or an intended party, who lacks capacity (within the meaning of MCA 2005) to conduct the proceedings	FPR 2010, r 2.3

Who "lacks capacity"	A person lacks capacity in relation to a matter if at the material time he is unable to make a decision for himself in relation to the matter because of an impairment of, or a disturbance in the functioning of, the mind or brain	MCA 2005, s 2(1)
When is a person unable to make a decision for himself	If unable to: – understand the information relevant to the decision; – retain that information; – use or weigh that information as part of the process of making the decision; or – communicate his decision (whether by talking, using sign language or any other means)	MCA 2005, s 3(1)
Requirement for litigation friend	A protected party must have a litigation friend to conduct proceedings on his behalf	FPR 2010, r 15.2; PD15A, para 1.1
Title to proceedings	"A.B. (by C.D. his/her litigation friend)"	FPR PD15A, para 1.2
When must litigation friend be appointed	Before take any step in proceedings (unless court grants permission) except: – filing an application form; – applying for the appointment of a litigation friend Also if party becomes incapable of continuing proceedings	FPR 2010, r 15.3
What if litigation friend not appointed	Any step taken before a protected party has a litigation friend has no effect unless the court orders otherwise	FPR 2010, 15.3(3)
Who is appointed	Person authorised by the Court of Protection as a deputy to conduct the proceedings in the name of protected party or on his behalf, or – suitable person; or – Official Solicitor	FPR 2010, r 15.4(2) FPR 2010, r 15.4(3) FPR 2010, r 15.4(4)
Who is a suitable person?	Person who: – can fairly and competently conduct proceedings on behalf of protected party; – has no adverse interest; and – undertakes to pay any costs awarded	FPR 2010, r 15.4(3)
Duties of litigation friend	Fairly and competently to conduct proceedings on behalf of protected party	FPR PD15A, para 2.1
Is a solicitor required to act	Failure to instruct may cause suitability to be questioned in a significant case	
Appointment without a court order	May be made on filing: – authority of deputy; or – a certificate of suitability Not by the Official Solicitor	FPR PD15A, para 3.1 FPR 2010, r 15.5

Certificate of suitability	States that the proposed litigation friend: consents to act;	FPR 2010, r 15.4(3)
	believes the party to be a protected party (with reasons/medical evidence);	
	can fairly and competently conduct proceedings on behalf of the party;	
	has no adverse interest;	
	undertakes to pay any costs which party may be ordered to pay (applicant or respondent)	Form FP9 Certificate of suitability of litigation friend
Appointment by court order	On court's own initiative or on the application of:	FPR PD15A, para 4
	– person wishing to be litigation friend; or	
	– a party	
	Any application must be supported by evidence	
	Person appointed must be a suitable person (as above) or Official Solicitor	FPR 2010, r 15.6
Change of litigation friend	Court may: – direct that person may not act;	FPR PD15A, para 5
	– terminate an appointment; or	
	– appoint a substitute	
	Any application must be supported by evidence	
	Person appointed must be (as above)	FPR 2010, r 15.7
Ceasing to be protected party	Appointment continues until brought to end by court order	FPR PD15A, para 6
	Application made by:	
	– former protected party;	
	– litigation friend; or	
	– a party	FPR 2010, r 15.9
Service before appointment of litigation friend	Service upon a protected party is effected on: – attorney (EPA or LPA);	
	– deputy; or	
	– adult with whom the protected party resides or in whose care he is	FPR 2010, rr 6.28, 6.14(2)
Service of application	Application under r 15.6 or 15.7 must be sent by court to protected party (unless otherwise orders)	FPR 2010, r 15.8(1)
	Application under r 15.7 must be sent by court to former and proposed litigation friend	FPR 2010, r 15.8(2)
Service after appointment of litigation friend	Service is upon the litigation friend	FPR 2010, r 6.29
Withdrawal of claim	Permission of court required	FPR 2010, r 29.4
Compromise or settlement	No specific provision	

Control of money recovered	Court of Protection may need to be involved in absence of attorney or deputy	MCA 2005
	In ancillary relief proceedings court may order transfer of property or payments (including lump sum) to another person where party lacks capacity	MCA 1973, s 40

PART I

F1(2): Family Proceedings involving a Child

Procedure

Who is a child	A person who is under the age of 18	FLRA 1969, ss 1, 12
Requirement for litigation friend	A child must have a litigation friend to conduct proceedings on his behalf	FPR 2010, r 16.5
	A child who is a party but is not the subject of the proceedings can bring or defend certain proceedings without a representative	FPR 2010, r 16.6(1),(2)
Title to proceedings	"A.B. (a child by C.D. his/her litigation friend)"	FPR PD16A, para 1.1
When must litigation friend be appointed	Eefore take any step in proceedings (unless court grants permission) except: – filing an application form; – applying for the appointment of a litigation friend	FPR 2010, r 16.8
What if litigation friend not appointed	Any step taken before a protected party has a litigation friend has no effect unless the court orders otherwise	FPR 2010, r 16.8(3)
Who is appointed	– suitable person; or – Official Solicitor	FPR 2010, r 16.9(2),(3)
Who is a suitable person?	Person who: – can fairly and competently conduct proceedings on behalf of child; – has no adverse interest; and – undertakes to pay any costs awarded	FPR 2010, r 16.9(2)
Duties of litigation friend	Fairly and competently to conduct proceedings on behalf of protected party	FPR PD16A, para 2.1
Is a solicitor required to act	Failure to instruct may cause suitability to be questioned in a significant case	
Appointment without a court order	May be made on filing a certificate of suitability This rule does not apply to Official Solicitor	FPR 2010, r 16.10(1),(4); PD16A, para 3
Certificate of suitability	States that the proposed litigation friend: – consents to act	FPR 2010, r 16.9(2)

	– believes the party to be a child	
	– can fairly and competently conduct proceedings on behalf of the party	
	– has no adverse interest	
	– undertakes to pay any costs which child may be ordered to pay (applicant and respondent)	Form FP9 Certificate of suitability of litigation friend
Appointment by court order	On court's own initiative or on the application of:	FPR PD16A, para 4
	– person wishing to be litigation friend; or	
	– a party	
	Any application must be supported by evidence	
	Person appointed must be a suitable person (as above) or (with consent):	
	– Official Solicitor; or	
	– Officer as defined	FPR 2010, r 16.11
Change of litigation friend	Court may:	FPR PD16A, para 5
	– direct that person may not act;	
	– terminate an appointment; or	
	– appoint a substitute	
	Any application must be supported by evidence	
	Person appointed must be (as above)	FPR 2010, r 16.12
Ceasing to be a child	When a child who is not a protected party attains 18 the appointment ends	
	Court gives notice to the other parties	FPR 2010, r 16.15
Service before appointment of litigation friend	Service upon a child is effected on:	
	– a parent or guardian, or, if none	
	– adult with whom child resides or in whose care he is	FPR 2010, rr 6.14(1), 6.28
Service of application	Application under r 16.11 or 16.12 must be sent by court to person to be served (as above)	FPR 2010, r 16.13(1)
	Application under r 16.12 must be sent by court to former and proposed litigation friend	FPR 2010, r 15.13(2)
Service after appointment of litigation friend	Service is upon the litigation friend	FPR 2010, r 6.29
Withdrawal of claim	Permission of court required	FPR 2010, r 29.4
Compromise or settlement	No specific provision	
Control of money recovered	No specific provision	

F1(3): Non-family Proceedings involving a Child or a Protected Party

Issue

When dealing with proceedings that are *not* family proceedings it is necessary to comply with CPR 1998. Pt 21 contains special provisions that apply in proceedings involving children and protected parties. These are supplemented by CPR PD21 (Children and Protected Parties). Unless the court orders otherwise (in the case of a child) it is necessary for the child or protected party to be represented by a litigation friend. The term "under disability" is no longer used and under the Civil Procedure (Amendment) Rules 2007 the old term "patient" was replaced by "protected party" and a new definition applies. This became necessary because of the implementation on 1 October 2007 of MCA 2005.

The following is an abbreviated version of Guide 17 in *Civil Court Service* (Jordan Publishing Ltd).

Procedure

Who is a child	A person under 18	CPR 1998, r 21.1(2)(a)
Who is a protected party	A party, or an intended party, who lacks capacity (within the meaning of MCA 2005) to conduct the proceedings	CPR 1998, r 21.1(2)(d)
Who "lacks capacity"	A person lacks capacity in relation to a matter if at the material time he is unable to make a decision for himself in relation to the matter because of an impairment of, or a disturbance in the functioning of, the mind or brain	MCA 2005, s 2(1)
When is a person unable to make a decision for himself	if unable to: – understand the information relevant to the decision; – retain that information; – use or weigh that information as part of the process of making the decision; or – communicate his decision (whether by talking, using sign language or any other means)	MCA 2005, s 3(1)
Requirement for a litigation friend (protected party)	A protected party must have a litigation friend to conduct proceedings on his behalf	CPR 1998, r 21.2(1)
Requirement for a litigation friend (child)	A child must have a litigation friend to conduct proceedings on his behalf unless the court orders otherwise	CPR 1998, r 21.2(2)
	the court may permit child to conduct proceedings without a litigation friend (for procedure see r 21.2(4))	CPR 1998, rr 21.2(3),(4)
	if it subsequently appears desirable for there to be a litigation friend court may so appoint	CPR 1998, r 21.2(5)

When must a litigation friend be appointed	A person may not, without permission of the court:	
	(a) make an application against a child or protected party before proceedings have started; or	
	(b) take any step in proceedings except –	
	(i) issuing/serving a claim form; or	
	(ii) applying for the appointment of a litigation friend under r 21.6,	
	until the child or protected party has a litigation friend	CPR 1998, r 21.3(2)
	If a party becomes a protected party during proceedings, no party may take any step in the proceedings without the permission of the court until the protected party has a litigation friend	CPR 1998, r 21.3(3)
	Any step taken before a child or protected party has a litigation friend is of no effect, unless the court otherwise orders	CPR 1998, r 21.3(4)
Title to proceedings	"A. B. (a child by . . . his litigation friend)" or, if a litigation friend is dispensed with, "C. D. (a child)"	CPR PD21, para 1.2
	"A.B. (a protected party by . . . his litigation friend)"	CPR PD21, para 1.1
Who is appointed (without court order)	A deputy appointed by the Court of Protection under MCA 2005, with power to conduct proceedings on the protected party's behalf, is entitled to be the litigation friend of the protected party in any proceedings to which his power extends	CPR 1998, r 21.4(2)
	If nobody has been appointed by the court (or appointed as a deputy), a person may act as a litigation friend if he:	
	can fairly and competently conduct proceedings on behalf of the child or protected party; and	
	has no interest adverse to that of the child or protected party; and	
	(claim or counterclaim) undertakes to pay any costs that the child or protected party may be ordered to pay	CPR 1998, r 21.4(3)
Appointment (without court order)	A person wishing to act as a litigation friend must:	
	(if empowered by the Court of Protection) file an official copy of the order conferring the power;	
	(otherwise) file a certificate of suitability –	
	(claimant) when making the claim;	

	(defendant) when first taking a step in the proceedings	CPR 1998, r 21.5
Certificate of suitability	States that proposed litigation friend:	
	consents to act;	
	believes the person to be a child or protected party (with reasons/medical evidence);	
	can fairly and competently conduct proceedings on behalf of the person;	
	has no adverse interest;	
	(claimant) undertakes to pay any costs which claimant may be ordered to pay in the proceedings	Form N235; CPR 1998, r 21.4(3); CPR PD21, para 2.2
	A counterclaim is treated like a claim for the purpose of the costs undertaking	CPR 1998, r 20.3(1)
Service of certificate	The litigation friend must: serve the certificate of suitability on every person on whom the claim form should be served (it is good practice to serve the patient unless obviously unable to respond); and	CPR 1998, rr 21.5(4)(a)
	fi e a certificate of service when filing the certificate of suitability	CPR 1998, rr 6.13, 21.5(4)(b)
Certificate of service	Must set out required details of method o service	CPR 1998, r 6.17
Application for appointment by court	Application for an order appointing a litigation friend is made by person wishing to be appointed or a party	
	Claimant must apply where claim against child or protected party with no litigation friend and either (i) someone who is not entitled files a defence or (ii) claimant wishes to take some step in the proceedings	CPR 1998, r 21.6; CPR PD21, paras 3.1–3.4
	Application must be supported by evidence; court to be satisfied that the person appointed is "suitable"	CPR 1998, rr 21.6(4),(5), 21.4(3)
Change of litigation friend	The court may: direct that a person may not act as a litigation friend;	
	te minate the appointment; or appoint a substitute	
	Application to be supported by evidence; court may not appoint a litigation friend unless satisfied that the person is suitable	CPR 1998, rr 21.4(3), 21.7
Who is appointed (by court)	On an application court may appoint: person proposed, or	
	any other person who complies with the conditions in r 21.4(3)	CPR 1998, r 21.8(4)

Official Solicitor	May be appointed provided he consents and provision is made for payment of his costs	CPR PD21, para 3.4
Appointment ceasing (child/protected party)	When a child who is not a protected party reaches 18 a litigation friend's appointment ceases	CPR 1998, r 21.9(1); CPR PD21, paras 4.2–4.4
	When a protected party acquires capacity, appointment continues until ended by a court order	CPR 1998, r 21.9(2); CPR PD21, paras 4.5, 4.6
Service of claim form (child)	Service of claim form is upon: a parent or guardian or (if none) the person with whom the child resides or in whose care he is	CPR 1998, r 6.13(1)
Service of claim form (protected party)	Service of the claim form is upon: (i) the attorney under a registered enduring power of attorney, (ii) the donee of a lasting power of attorney, (iii) the deputy appointed by the Court of Protection; or (if none) the person with whom the protected party resides or in whose care he is	CPR 1998, r 6.13(2)
Service of claim form – general	The court may by order: permit the claim form to be served on the child or protected party, or on a person other than as specified;	CPR 1998, r 6.13(4)
	treat a document as if it had been properly served although it has been served on someone other than as specified	CPR 1998, r 6.13(6)
Service generally	On litigation friend once appointed (or child allowed to conduct proceedings)	CPR 1998, r 25(2)
	The court may by order: permit service on child or protected party, or on a specified person; or	CPR 1998, r 6.25(3)
	treat a document as if it had been properly served	CPR 1998, r 6.25(5)
Service of application	Application for order appointing or changing litigation friend served on: every person on whom claim form should be served; and	CPR 1998, r 21.8(1)
	(if appointing) the protected party, unless court otherwise orders; or	CPR 1998, r 21.8(2)
	(if changing) the existing and proposed litigation friend	CPR 1998, r 21.8(3)
Compromise or settlement	On a claim or counterclaim by or on behalf of, or against, a child or protected party, no settlement, compromise or payment and no acceptance of money paid into court is valid without court approval	CPR 1998, r 21.10(1)

	Procedures are available where the sole purpose of proceedings is to obtain the approval of the court	CPR 1998, r 21.10(2); CPR PD21, paras 5.1–5.3; Form N292
Who is a protected beneficiary	A protected party who lacks capacity to manage and control any money recovered by him or on his behalf or for his benefit in the proceedings	CPR 1998, r 21.1(2)(e)
Control of money recovered	Money recovered on behalf of or for the benefit of a child or protected beneficiary is dealt with under directions of the court	CPR 1998, r 21.11(1); CPR PD21, paras 8.1–8.4
	These may provide that the money shall be wholly or partly paid into court and invested; or otherwise dealt with	CPR 1998, r 21.11(2); CPR PD21, paras 9.1–9.8, 10.1–10.7
	Applications may be made relating to payment out or investment	CPR PD21, paras 12.2, 13
Guardian of child's estate	The court may appoint the Official Solicitor as a guardian of a child's estate	CPR 1998, r 21.13; CPR PD21, para 12
Deputy for a protected beneficiary	The Court of Protection may appoint a financial deputy for the estate of a protected beneficiary	CPR PD21, paras 10.1–10.7
	money of a protected beneficiary will be transferred	Form CFO 200
	applications for payment out of funds are to the Court of Protection	CPR PD21, para 13.4
Costs	Costs of solicitor for child or protected party must be approved by court	CPR 1998, r 46.4
	Liability of litigation friend continues until:	
	appointment ceases; and	
	former child or protected party (or litigation friend) serves notice on other parties	CPR 1998, r 21.9(6); CPR PD21, para 5.5
Forms	Certificate of Suitability of Litigation Friend	N235
	Order approving terms of a settlement or compromise	N292

F1(4): Resolving Doubt about Capacity

Issue

A problem arises when there is a significant doubt as to whether a party lacks capacity because the proceedings should not continue until this doubt has been resolved. There is no simple solution but this Guide sets out some of the options available to the parties and the court in both family and civil proceedings.

Procedure

The procedural problem

Why is "capacity" relevant	Special provisions apply to parties who lack capacity – see generally Guides F1(1) and F1(3)	FPR 2010, Pt 15 and PD15A; CPR 1998, Pt 21 and PD21; MCA 2005, Pt 1
What aspects of capacity are relevant	Capacity to: – conduct the proceedings; – manage any monies recovered; – obey court orders; – make personal welfare decisions	See generally MCA 2005
What are the implications	*Family and civil:* A party who lacks capacity to conduct the proceedings is a protected party *Civil only:* A party who lacks capacity to manage and control any monies recovered is a protected beneficiary	FPR 2010, r 2.3; CPR 1998, r 21.1(2)(d) CPR 1998, r 21.1(2)(e)
What are the consequences	A protected party will normally require a representative to be appointed, known as a litigation friend *Civil:* A protected party will normally require a *litigation friend* to be appointed *Civil only:* A protected beneficiary will not be permitted to receive money	FPR 2010, r 15.2; CPR 1998, r 21.2(1) CPR 1998, r 21.2(1) CPR 1998, r 21.11(3)
Who may raise doubts as to the capacity of a party	The solicitors for the party, another party or the court The court should investigate question of capacity whenever there is reason to suppose it may be absent	*Masterman-Lister* [2003] 1 WLR 1511
What should be done when doubts are raised	The doubts should be resolved and any proceedings stayed until this has been done	FPR 2010, r 15.3(1); CPR 1998, r 21.3
What discretion does the court have	Steps may not be taken without the permission of the court The court can thus allow steps to be taken that are needed at that stage and may do so if these will not prejudice the party who may lack capacity	FPR 2010, r 15.3(1); CPR 1998, r 21.3(2),(3)
What if a party is found to lack capacity during proceedings	Any step taken before a protected party has a litigation friend has no effect *unless the court orders otherwise* The court may thus waive the procedural irregularity and give consequential directions if this will not prejudice the party who lacked capacity and there has been no abuse of process	FPR 2010, r 15.3(3); CPR 1998, r 21.3(4)

How will the court know if there has been prejudice	A representative will have been appointed and can make submissions as to the future conduct of the proceedings	

Resolving doubt as to capacity

What help do the FPR and CPR provide	The Rules assume that it is known whether a party lacks capacity so any doubt must be addressed as an issue in the proceedings and a finding of fact made	
What is required	– Expert evidence – Factual evidence	
The expert evidence	Medical evidence as to an impairment of, or a disturbance in the functioning of, the mind or brain (the diagnostic threshold)	MCA 2005, s 2(1)
The factual evidence	Evidence of expert and lay witnesses as to whether the party is unable to make a decision in the matter for himself according to the statutory criteria	MCA 2005, s 3(1)
Are both types of evidence required	In practice the medical evidence may extend to ability to make and communicate decisions – unless challenged it will be all that is required	
What is the standard of proof	There is a presumption of capacity but lack of capacity may be proved on the balance of probability	MCA 2005, ss 1(2), 2(4)
Petitioner/ Applicant *or* Claimant	Where significant doubt arises, the court will expect this party to produce evidence to dispel that doubt Proceedings may be stayed until the party submits to a medical examination	
Respondent *or* Defendant	The court will expect the party bringing the proceedings to produce evidence if the Defendant/Respondent does not respond Not appropriate to make a default order that a defendant/respondent who fails to submit to an examination be treated as capable	

What if a respondent *or* defendant will not co-operate
The following options may be available to the claimant

Certificate of suitability	A suitable adult may be prepared to complete the required *Certificate of suitability* which states a belief that the person is a protected party and includes evidence in support	FPR 2010, r 15.5(3); Form FP9; CPR 1998, rr 21.4(3), 21.5; Form N235

Evidence	Medical evidence may already exist that establishes the diagnostic threshold Evidence of conduct may be available (e g as to how the party has responded to the claim) – this may in itself create doubts as to capacity	
Lack of medical evidence	The court has no power to force the party to submit to an examination A default order would not be appropriate because an actual finding of lack of capacity is required	
Involve social services	A recital in a court order that there is an appearance of need for community care services coupled with a request for an indication as to whether such assessment has been or will be carried out may produce information. A social worker may be invited to attend the next directions hearing	NHS and Community Care Act 1990, s 47
Official Solicitor	Cannot act for party in the absence of a finding of lack of capacity The court can direct the Official Solicitor to make inquiries and report: The Official Solicitor, 81 Chancery Lane, London WC2A 1DD; tel 020 7911 7127; fax 020 7911 7105	*Harbin v Masterman* [1896] 1 Ch 351, CA
Court of Protection	See below	

Who will be the representative
The following options may be available

Person already involved	*Attorney* (under registered enduring or lasting power)	FPR 2010, r 15.4(2)
	Deputy appointed by Court of Protection	CPR 1998, r 21.4(2)
	Appointee for social security benefits	MCA 2005
Concerned person	Relative, partner, friend, carer or personal advocate	FPR 2010, r 15.4(3); CPR 1998, r 21.4(3)
Solicitor for party	Not usually appropriate – conflict of roles	
Official Solicitor	Representative of last resort if consents May also act as solicitor Requires provision for costs	

Involving the Court of Protection

What can this Court do	– Make declaration as to capacity – Make decisions on behalf of a person who lacks capacity – Appoint a deputy to do so – Nominate a person to conduct proceedings	MCA 2005, ss 15, 16
Why involve this Court	– Resolve capacity issues – Find someone to be litigation friend – Clarify whether the Court of Protection needs to be involved	MCA 2005

Advantages	– Expertise in this area – Power to give directions even before finding of incapacity – Additional powers to obtain reports	MCA 2005, ss 48, 49
What reports can be obtained	– Local authority (e g social services) – NHS body (health authority or trust) – Court of Protection general visitor – Court of Protection special visitor – Public Guardian	MCA 2005, s 49
Disadvantages	– Cost and delay – Someone must apply to this Court (but that may become necessary anyway)	

PART I

F2: Scientific Test Direction

Legal background

In any civil proceedings in which an issue as to parentage arises, a party may apply to the court for a direction for the use of scientific tests or bodily samples to determine the issue, or the court may, on its own initiative, issue such a direction (FLRA 1969, s 20(1)). An application cannot be made on a freestanding basis but only in existing proceedings (e g FLA 1986, s 55A, CA 1989, s 9 or CSA 1991, s 27, TLATA 1996, s 14 or under I(PFD)A 1975). The court issues a direction (see also *Re H (Paternity: Blood Test)* [1996] 2 FLR 65, CA). No sample can be taken without consent (FLRA 1969, s 21(1)) or by direction of the court where a person having care and control of a child refuses consent (FLRA 1969, s 21(3)): failure to comply with a direction enables the court to draw such inferences as appear proper in the circumstances of the particular case (FLRA 1969, s 23(1)). Procedure is governed by CPR PD23B (as applied by para 2.1 of FPR PD on Practice Directions Relating to Family Proceedings In Force Before 6 April 2011 which Support the Family Procedure Rules 2010) and application is by the FPR 2010, Pt 18 procedure.

A child under 16 or who lacks capacity acts by a "responsible adult" as defined in CPR PD23B, para 1.1(3).

Procedure

Who may apply	Any party to the proceedings; or the court on own initiative	FLRA 1969, s 20(1)
The proceedings	Any civil (including family) proceedings in which parentage is in issue	FLRA 1969, s 20(1)
The application	By FPR 2010, Pt 18 procedure application notice (Form D11)	FPR 2010, r 18.1(2)(a)
	The application must specify who is to carry out the tests	FLRA 1969, s 20(1A)
	If application is regarding (1) a person under 16 or (2) who is a protected party (per FPR 2010, Pt 15), the name and address of the responsible adult must be given	CPR PD23B, para 1.2
Respondent/ Other parties	(1) All other parties to the existing proceedings (2) Anyone else from whom samples may be required	See, for example, FPR 2010, r 8.20 for declarations under r 8.18

Notice	(1) FPR 2010 proceedings: 7 days before hearing	FPR 2010, r 18.8(1)(b)(ii)
	(2) CPR 1998 proceedings: 3 days before hearing	CPR 1998, r 23.7(1)(b)
Direction	Court gives a direction in form proposed in *Re H*	*Re H* [1996] 2 FLR 65 at [83]
	The name of the tester must be included in the direction	
Service of direction	By the court (1) on parties to proceedings	CPR PD23B, para 1.4(1)
	(2) anyone from whom sample is to be taken	CPR PD23B, para 1.4(2)
Report	Made to the court by the tester	FLRA 1969, s 20(2)
	Report in form prescribed by Blood Tests (Evidence of Paternity) Regs 1971	FLRA 1969, ss 20(3), 22
	Served by the court on (1) parties to proceedings, (2) responsible adult (as applicable) and (3) anyone from whom sample to be taken	CPR PD23B, para 1.5
Fees and costs	Fee for report payable by applicant for direction; but treated as costs in the main proceedings	FLRA 1969, s 20(6)

F3: Withdrawal of Treatment in Persistent Vegetative State etc Cases where the Patient is an Adult

See MCA 2005. All cases dealt with by the Court of Protection. See *Court of Protection Practice* and *Urgent Applications in the Court of Protection* (Jordan Publishing Ltd).

F4: Costs in Family Proceedings (High Court and County Court)

Legal background

Costs may only be recovered by order of the court (SCA 1981, s 51(3)), save by consent as between the parties. In all family proceedings, the factors that affect the award of costs, and the procedure to be followed, are governed by FPR 2010, rr 28.2 and 28.3, which apply to family proceedings CPR 1998, Pts 44 (except rr 44.2(2),(3) and 44.10(2),(3)), 46 and 47 and r 45.8.

Orders for costs are entirely in the discretion of the court (SCA 1981, s 51(1), which covers the Court of Appeal, the High Court and county courts), subject to "any other enactment and to rules of court". However, there are factors which the court is required to take into account when exercising its discretion whether to award costs (CPR 1998, r 44.2(4),(5)).

Costs awarded to the "successful party"

CPR 1998, r 44.2(2) provides that where the court decides to make an order as to costs, the general rule is that the "unsuccessful party" should pay the costs of the "successful party", but the court may make a different order (r 44.2(2)(b)). This rule does not apply in family proceedings: FPR 2010, r 28.2(1) disapplies CPR 1998 r 44.2(2) from family proceedings. However, in family courts the judge must have some starting-point, which may be that costs should be awarded to the "successful party" (*Gojkovic v Gojkovic (No 2)* [1991] 2 FLR 233, CA; and see for example *Baker v Rowe* (below)). See further Guide F4(1).

Costs may be awarded against a third party (ie who was not a party to the proceedings: *Symphony Group plc v Hodgson* [1994] QB 179, and see CPR 1998, r 46.2) or as between intervenors in, for example, financial remedy proceedings (*Baker v Rowe* [2010] 1 FLR 761).

Costs and children cases

Costs orders will be rare in children cases (*Keller v Keller and Legal Aid Board* [1995] 1 FLR 259, CA), although costs orders are always entirely in the discretion of the court. In *R v R (Costs: Child Case)* [1997] 2 FLR 95, CA, that a criterion for an order for costs in children cases might be whether or not a party has been guilty of unreasonable conduct in connection with a case. See further Guide F4(1).

In care proceedings, where the local authority is the applicant, they should not be inhibited from carrying out their statutory duties by the threat of costs orders "in the absence of reprehensible behaviour or an unreasonable stance" on their part (*Re T (Children)* [2013] 1 FLR 133.

In proceedings involving the Official Solicitor the "general rule" is that the Official Solicitor should have half his costs in the absence of special features that override this "rule" (*Re D (Costs)* [2012] COPLR 499).

Costs in financial remedy proceedings

Under FPR 2010, r 28.3, costs orders may not be made in "financial remedy proceedings" (as defined by r 28.3(4)(b): ie the majority of matrimonial and civil partnership proceedings), save in cases of litigation misconduct. The remaining proceedings for a financial remedy (eg interim hearings, preliminary issue hearings, enforcement of orders, appeals etc) will be dealt with on the basis of a "clean sheet" principle (as explained in the commentary to r 28.3 and *Judge v Judge* [2009] 1 FLR 1287.

Costs awarded to person acting in a fiduciary capacity

CPR 1998, r 46.3 provides the court with power to award costs to a trustee, personal representative or other person acting in a fiduciary capacity, from the fund held by him. Where there is any doubt whatsoever in the mind of the trustee or his adviser as to whether the action should be continued on behalf of the beneficiaries of the fund, an application should be made to the court for a *Beddoe* order (*Re Beddoe* [1893] 1 Ch 547; for analogical position of trustee in bankruptcy see *Brook v Reed* [2011] EWCA Civ 331). See further Guide F4(2).

Wasted costs

Where a legal representative behaves in a manner which is held to be "improper, unreasonable or negligent" (SCA 1981, s 51(7)), a wasted costs order may be made against him or her. These words bear their ordinary meaning, as explained in *Ridehalgh v Horsefield and ors* [1994] 2 FLR 194, CA: (i) "improper" means behaviour which amounts to a significant breach of professional conduct; (ii) "unreasonable" means conduct which does not permit of a reasonable explanation; and (iii) "negligent" means failure to act with the competence to be expected of ordinary members of the profession. Conduct of a hopeless or difficult case does not, of itself, justify a finding under s 51(7). See further Guide F4(3).

Funded (legal aid) cases

An order for costs may be made against a funded (legally aided) client as against any other party to proceedings; but the amount he can be ordered to pay cannot exceed the amount which it is reasonable for him to pay (LASPOA 2012, s 29).

Assessment of costs

The court must consider whether to order summary assessment (ie assessment on the day, which will be much more common than hitherto) or detailed assessment (formerly taxation of costs), in which case assessment will be delayed. Detailed assessment will always occur in a CLS funded case. When assessing the amount of any possible award of costs (either on the indemnity or standard basis) the court should have regard to the various factors set out in CPR 1998, rr 44.3, 44.4. See further Guides F4(4)–F4(5).

F4(1): Order for Costs Against Another Party to the Proceedings

Procedure

Who may apply	Any party to the proceedings. In appropriate circumstances application may be against a third party	SCA 1981, s 51(3)
Time for application	At any stage in the case; and in particular when the court is dealing with an application or makes an order	CPR PD44, para 4.1
Principles on which orders made	Costs are in the discretion of the court (ie whether, when and how much is to be paid), subject to "any other enactment and to rules of court"	SCA 1981, s 51(1); CPR 1998, r 44.2(1)
Orders for costs	Costs orders may include: (a) a proportion of another party's costs; (b) a stated amount of those costs; (c) costs from or until a certain date; (d) costs incurred before issue of proceedings; (e) costs relating to particular steps; (f) costs relating only to one part of the proceedings; and (g) interest on costs from or until a certain date	CPR 1998, r 44.2(6)
	Types of order include: Costs in any event Costs in the case/application Costs reserved (NB means that if no later order is made, costs are in the application) Applicant's/respondent's costs in the application No order as to costs	CPR PD44, para 4.2
	If a party is not present when an order is made his solicitor must notify him of the order made within 7 days	CPR 1998, r 44.8
When to comply with order for costs	Within 14 days of: (a) date of judgment or order (if amount of costs fixed thereby); or (b) date of certificate following detailed assessment (see Guide F4(3))	CPR 1998, r 44.7

Factors in deciding the order for costs: general	All the circumstances of the case, including: (a) the conduct of all the parties; (b) whether a party has succeeded in only part of his case; and (c) any admissible (e g *Calderbank*) offer to settle made by a party which is drawn to the court's attention	CPR 1998, r 44.2(4)
"The conduct of the parties"	Conduct under CPR 1998, r 44.2(4) includes (non-exhaustive list): (a) conduct before, as well as during, the proceedings, and in particular the extent to which the parties followed any relevant pre-action protocol; (b) whether it was reasonable for a party to raise, pursue or contest a particular allegation or issue; (c) the manner in which a party has pursued or defended his case or a particular allegation or issue; and (d) whether a claimant who has succeeded in his claim, in whole or in part, exaggerated his claim	CPR 1998, r 44.2(5)
Factors in deciding the order for costs: "financial remedy proceedings" (as defined by FPR 2010, r 28.3(4)(b))	The "general rule" is that there is no order for costs, save where there has been "conduct" relating to the proceedings and before or after they were commenced	FPR 2010, r 28.3(5),(6)
	Note (1) No Calderbank letter is admissible on the issue of costs	FPR 2010, r 28.3(8)
	(2) If the court chooses to ignore the "general rule" for financial order proceedings, then SCA 1981, s 51 applies; in no circumstances can r 44.3(1)–(5) apply	FPR 2010, r 28.3(2)
"Conduct"	"Conduct" in relation to financial remedy proceedings is the following exhaustive list: (a) failure by a party to comply with FPR 2010, a court order or a relevant PD; (b) any open offer to settle made by a party; (c) whether it was reasonable for a party to raise, pursue or contest a particular allegation or issue; (d) the manner of response to the application or a particular issue; (e) any other relevant aspect of a party's conduct in relation to the proceedings; and (f) the financial effect on the parties of any costs order	FPR 2010, r 28.3(7)

Payment on account	The court must make an order for payment of costs on account pending detailed assessment	CPR 1998, r 44.2(8)
Assessment of costs	Summary assessment (see Guide F4(4)) Detailed assessment (see Guide F4(5))	
Basis of assessment	*Standard* (i) Costs assessed on a standard basis are only costs which are proportionate to the matters in issue (ii) Any doubt which the court may have as to whether costs were reasonably incurred or reasonable and proportionate in amount are resolved in favour of the paying party (iii) If no basis for assessment is stated, costs are assessed on the standard basis	CPR 1998, rr 44.3(1)(a), (2),(4), 44.4(1)(a)
	Indemnity Any doubt as to whether costs were reasonably incurred is resolved in favour of the receiving party	CPR 1998, rr 44.3(1)(b), (3), 44.4(1)(b)
Factors in defining amount of costs on assessment	(a) the conduct of all parties, including in particular: (i) conduct before, and during, the proceedings; and (ii) attempts at mediation (if any) made before and during the proceedings; (b) the monetary value of the claim; (c) the importance of the case to all parties; (d) the complexity of the case or difficulty or novelty of the issues raised; (e) the skill, effort, specialised knowledge and responsibility involved; (f) the time spent on the case; and (g) the place where and circumstances in which work (or part of it) was done	CPR 1998, r 44.4(3)

F4(2): Application for a *Beddoe* Order

Procedure

Who may apply	Trustee, personal representative or person in other fiduciary relationship	*Re Beddoe* [1893] 1 Ch 547
Costs and personal representatives, trustees etc	General rule: costs paid to the trustee etc on an indemnity basis but not if he is held to have acted other than for the benefit of the fund	CPR 1998, r 46.3(2),(3)

Time for application	At any time in proceedings; but in any event where there is a risk of a trustee being criticised by the court for expending the trust fund in costs	
Mode of application	*All types of proceedings* By application in the proceedings [*quaere*: "without serving a copy of the application notice" (i e ex parte)] *Family proceedings* (i) as above; or (ii) on ex parte application interlocutory to the proceedings in question	CPR 1998, r 23.4(2) FPR 2010, Pt 18 procedure
Order	That the [trustee etc] be indemnified in any event in respect of costs from [fund concerned; e g name of trust fund/pension fund/bankrupt's estate] in the event of no order being made against another party to the proceedings	

F4(3): Order for Wasted Costs

Procedure

Who may apply	Any party to the proceedings The court on its own initiative	SCA 1981, s 51(6); CPR PD46, para 5.3
Time for application	At any stage in proceedings where an order for costs can be made but normally at the end of "the trial" or final hearing of an application	CPR PD46, para 5.2
Application	(i) By notice of application. The application should be accompanied by evidence of what the legal representative is alleged to have done and specify the costs sought	CPR PD46, paras 5.4, 5.9; application: by FPR 2010, Pt 18 procedure
	(ii) By making application in the course of hearing (as with any other application for costs)	CPR PD46, para 5.4
Order	Against legal or other representative, that they pay costs incurred and wasted by another party to the proceedings	SCA 1981, s 51(6), (7); CPR 1998, r 46.8
Factors in making the order	Has the legal representative behaved in a way which is "improper, unreasonable or negligent"; or	SCA 1981, s 51(6)(a); c f *Ridehalgh v Horsefield* [1994] 2 FLR 194, CA
	is there expenditure caused by the legal representative that the court considers the other party should not have to pay?	SCA 1981, s 51(6)(b)

Procedure	No order can be made unless the legal representative has had a reasonable opportunity to show cause why an order should not be made	CPR 1998, r 46.8; *Ridehalgh v Horsfield* (above)
Court's directions	The court gives directions as it sees fit for disposal of the application. Directions may include the following:	CPR PD46, para 5.6; *Ridehalgh v Horsfield* (above)
	(i) Court may direct that privileged documents be disclosed to both itself and to the applicant for wasted costs	CPR 1998, r 46.8
	(ii) Before making an order the court can seek an enquiry from a costs judge or district judge	CPR 1998, r 46.8
	(iii) The court can refer the decision on the issue of an order to a costs judge or district judge	CPR 1998, r 46.8
Court's considerations	(i) Has the lawyer acted improperly, unreasonably or negligently? (ii) If so, has the applicant incurred unnecessary costs as a result? (iii) If so, is it just to require the lawyer to pay the applicant's relevant costs?	*Re A Barrister (Wasted Costs Order)* (above) (approved in *Ridehalgh v Horsefield* at [203H])
	If the court makes an order: it must specify the amount to be paid; or	CPR 1998, r 46.8
	it may ask a costs judge/district judge to report on the amount to be paid	CPR 1998, r 46.8

F4(4): Summary Assessment of Costs

Procedure

Stage in proceedings	When a party is ordered to pay costs (for detailed assessment see Guide F4(5))	CPR 1998, r 44.6
Application	Form N260 should be followed "as closely as possible"	CPR PD44, paras 1.2, 9.5
Time for summary assessment	Whenever an order for costs is made the court should consider whether to make a summary assessment	CPR PD44, para 9.1
	NB no summary assessment can be made for a receiving party who is:	
	(i) a legally assisted party or LSC funded party	CPR PD44, para 9.8
	(ii) a child or patient, unless the child's solicitor waives the right to further costs	CPR PD44, para 9.9
Factors in deciding on summary assessment	The court should make a summary assessment at the conclusion of a hearing:	
	(i) of less than one day	CPR PD44, para 9.2

	(iii) certain hearings in the Court of Appeal unless there is good reason not to do so, e g a substantial dispute as to amount due from the paying party which cannot be resolved immediately; or there is insufficient time	CPR PD44, para 9.2
Duty of legal representatives	Legal representatives who intend to seek an order for costs must prepare a statement of costs following Form N206 and setting out the detail required by PDCosts, para 13.5(2)	CPR PD44 para 9.5
Time for filing	The statement of costs should be filed and served not later than "24 hours before the date fixed for the hearing"	CPR PD44, para 9.5
Failure to comply	Failure ("without reasonable excuse") to comply with PD44, para 9.5 may be taken into account by the court in considering what order to make, e g no order for costs, costs in claim etc	CPR PD44, para 9.6; and see *Macdonald v Taree Hldgs Ltd* [2001] CPLR 439, CA
Factors in deciding basis of award and amount of assessment	See Guide F4(1)	CPR 1998, rr 44.2, 44.3

F4(5): Detailed Assessment of Costs

Procedure

Order for detailed assessment	On ordering a party to pay costs the court may order detailed assessment of costs, instead of making a summary assessment (see Guide F4(4))	CPR 1998, r 44.6
Time for order	(i) At the conclusion of proceedings (ii) At any other time when the court makes an order for detailed assessment; or (iii) When the parties agree	CPR 1998, r 47.1; CPR PD47, paras 1.1–1.4 CPR PD47, paras 1.1–1.4
	NB An order for detailed assessment is not stayed pending appeal, save where so ordered by the court appealed from, or to which appeal is made	CPR 1998, r 47.2; CPR PD47, para 2
Parties	(i) receiving party (ii) paying party (iii) other parties ("relevant persons")	CPR 1998, r 44.1 CPR 1998, r 44.1 CPR 1998, r 47.6(2); CPR PD47, para 5.5
Notice of commencement of proceedings	Commencement of detailed assessment proceedings occurs upon service by receiving party of the following:	

	(i) notice of commencement (N252)	
	(ii) a copy of the bill of costs	
	(iii) fee notes of counsel, experts etc	
	(iv) evidence of disbursements over £250	
	(v) addresses of persons to be served	CPR PD47, para 5.2
Service of notice of commencement and other documents	Notice of commencement etc served on: (i) paying party (ii) other parties ("relevant persons")	CPR 1998, r 47.6(1) CPR 1998, r 47.6(2)
Time for commencement of detailed assessment proceedings	(i) 3 months from date of judgment, direction or order (ii) If order stayed pending appeal, 3 months from lifting of stay	CPR 1998, r 47.7
	(iii) Other period: as agreed by parties or ordered by the court	CPR PD47, para 6.1
	NB There is no need for permission to commence out of time (but see CPR 1998, r 47.8 for sanctions for delay in commencement)	CPR PD47, para 5.2
Costs agreed	Where costs are agreed, the parties may apply (under CPR 1998, r 40.6) for a consent order setting out the amount to be paid and any terms for such payment	CPR 1998, r 47.10
Points of dispute	Served by paying party and any other party on receiving party and any other party	CPR 1998, r 47.9(1)
	Points of dispute should be succinct and should follow Precedent G	CPR PD47, para 8.2
	Service: 21 days after receipt of notice of commencement	CPR 1998, r 47.9(2)
	Upon receipt, receiving party can: (i) apply for detailed assessment hearing	CPR 1998, r 47.14(1)
	(ii) serve reply to points of dispute	CPR 1998, r 47.13
Default costs certificate	Receiving party can request if no points of dispute are served within 21 days	CPR 1998, r 47.9(4)
Setting aside a default costs certificate	Where receiving party is not entitled to certificate, court must set aside	CPR 1998, r 47.12(1)
	The court has a discretion to set aside if there is some good reason for detailed assessment proceedings to continue	CPR 1998, r 47.12(2)
	If the notice of commencement is not received by the paying party within 21 days and a default costs certificate is issued, the receiving party must apply to set it aside or seek court directions	CPR 1998, r 47.12(3)
Detailed assessment hearing: application	Upon service of points of dispute the receiving party files a request for a detailed assessment hearing	CPR 1998, r 47.14(1)

	Time for application	
	(i) by receiving party: within 3 months of the expiry of the period for commencement of detailed assessment (see above) or as directed	CPR 1998, r 47.14(2)
	(ii) by paying party: on application to the court to request receiving party to request a hearing	CPR 1998, r 47.14(3),(4)
Procedure for detailed assessment	Request for a detailed assessment must be in Form N258 and must be accompanied by the documents listed in PD47, para 13.2	CPR PD47, para 13.2
Parties to detailed assessment	The receiving party, the paying party and any party who has served points of dispute	CPR 1998, r 47.14(6)
Notice of hearing	Notice of hearing is given by the court	CPR PD47, paras 13.4, 13.6
Interim costs certificate	After the receiving party has applied for a detailed assessment hearing the court may, on a Pt 23 application, issue an interim costs certificate (Form N257):	CPR 1998, r 47.16; CPR PD47, para 15
	(i) for costs to be paid; or	
	(ii) for costs to be paid into court	
	NB Where a party is ordered to pay costs he may be required to pay an amount on account before costs are assessed	CPR 1998, r 44.2
Detailed assessment hearing	Only items raised in points of dispute can be raised at the detailed assessment hearing	CPR 1998, r 47.14(7)
Final costs certificate	14 days from the end of the detailed assessment hearing a completed bill of costs must be filed	CPR 1998, r 47.17; CPR PD47, paras 16.3–16.8
	The court then:	
	(i) issues a final costs certificate (Form N256); and	
	(ii) serves it on all parties to the detailed assessment hearing	CPR 1998, r 47.17
Time for payment of costs	Costs are payable 14 days from the date of the costs certificate	CPR 1998, r 44.7
Offers to settle	"Without prejudice offers" to settle the detailed assessment proceedings may be taken into account in ordering costs of assessment	
Costs of detailed assessment	Receiving party is entitled to the costs of the detailed assessment in the absence of any order, rule, PD etc which provides otherwise	CPR 1998, r 47.20
Appeals		CPR 1998, rr 47.21–47.24

F5: Application in Respect of the Human Rights Act 1998

Legal background

From 2 October 2000 by virtue of HRA 1998, s 3, all primary and subordinate legislation must be read and given effect in a way which is compatible with the European Convention of Human Rights (as prescribed in HRA 1998, s 1). The provisions of HRA 1998 are not retrospective (*R (on the Application of Wright) v Secretary of State of the Home Department* [2006] EWCA Civ 67). Where it is not possible to read legislation in this way, an application may be made for a declaration of incompatibility (under s 4). Otherwise, a complaint that there has been a decision by a public authority (court, tribunal, local authority or any person whose functions are of a public nature) which is incompatible with a convention right (under s 6) may be the subject of separate proceedings (pursuant to s 7(1)(a)) or brought within existing proceedings (pursuant to s 7(1)(b)). For consideration of the definitions of "a public authority" and "functions of a public nature" see *YL v Birmingham City Council* [2008] 1 AC 95. A claim pursuant to HRA 1998, s 7(1)(a) should be made to the Administrative Court as an application for judicial review (see Guide E1). Although the ECtHR generally favours an award of damages in cases in which local authorities have infringed the rights of parents under Art 8 as a result of shortcomings in the procedures by which they have taken or kept children in care, there is a spectrum of ECHR 1950 violations. Where the breach has been purely procedural and not significant, an award of damages may be inappropriate: in such cases the declaration of a violation of Art 8 may afford the parent just satisfaction (*Re C (Breach of Human Rights: Damages)* [2007] 1 FLR 1957 (CA) per Wilson LJ at [64]-[71]). However, contrast the decision in *Re V (Care: Pre Birth Actions)* [2005] 1 FLR 627 where the Court of Appeal took a much more restrictive approach to the concept of awarding damages for breach of ECHR 1950 rights in public law proceedings.

Procedure

Who may apply	Any person who is a victim of the action which is the subject of the complaint	HRA 1998, s 7(1)
	A claim under HRA 1998, s 7(1)(a) may only be brought within 12 months of the act complained of or such longer period as the court considers equitable	HRA 1998, s 7(5)
Which court	A claim under HRA 1998, s 7(1) (other than in respect of a judicial act) may be brought in any court in existing or ongoing proceedings	HRA 1998, s 9(1)
	A claim under HRA 1998, s 7(1)(a) in respect of a judicial act may only be brought in the High Court (in relation to the actions of an inferior court or tribunal)	CPR 1998, r 7.11; HRA 1998, s 9(1)
	A claim under HRA 1998, s 4 for a declaration of incompatibility must be brought in or transferred to the High Court	HRA 1998, s 4
Application	A claim made in existing or continuing proceedings should specify the details in the originating documentation or amend the documentation accordingly setting out:	FPR 2010, r 29.5
	(a) the precise details of the Convention right claimed to have been infringed and details;	
	(b) specify the relief sought; and	

	(c) state whether a declaration of incompatibility is claimed	
	Any application to amend documentation to make a claim should be made as soon as possible any in any event within 28 days, unless otherwise ordered	
	A separate claim (not one made in existing or ongoing proceedings) should be made by issuing proceedings under CPR 1998, Pt 8. Such a claim may be brought in the High Court or county court	CPR 1998, r 7.11
	Where the claim is for damages in respect of a judicial act, the claim must be set out in the statement of case	
Defendants	The parties to the existing or ongoing proceedings, if the claim is made within those proceedings	
Additional persons to be served	Where a claim is in respect of damages for a judicial act notice must be given to the Crown	CPR 1998, r 19.4A; FPR 2010, r 29.5(5); PD29A
	Where a claim for a declaration of incompatibility is made pursuant to HRA 1998, s 4 notice must be given to the Crown, and the Crown or a Minister shall be joined as a party	HRA 1998, s 5; CPR 1998, r 19.4A; FPR 2010, r 29.5(3),(4) (Family Proceedings); CPR PD19A, para 6.1 (Non-Family Proceedings including judicial review and appeals to the Court of Appeal); Annex 1 to CPR PD66
Procedure	The claim form (N208) must state that Pt 8 applies; the question which the claimant wants the court to decide, or remedy sought and legal basis	CPR 1998, r 8.2
	The court will then give directions as to the filing of an acknowledgment of service, date for hearing and filing of evidence	CPR 1998, r 8.9
Order	The court may make such order as is within its power. Damages or compensation may be awarded only by a court that has power to make such an award	HRA 1998, s 8
	On an application pursuant to HRA 1998, s 4 the court may make a declaration of incompatibility	

PART II

Statutes

PART II: Statutes

Contents

All relevant provisions in the following legislation, as amended and fully
annotated, and the principal core substantive provisions:

PART II

Access to Justice Act 1999
****

PART IV
APPEALS, COURTS, JUDGES AND COURT PROCEEDINGS

Appeals

54 Permission to appeal

(1) Rules of court may provide that any right of appeal to –

    (a) a county court,
    (b) the High Court, or
    (c) the Court of Appeal,

may be exercised only with permission.

(2) This section does not apply to a right of appeal in a criminal cause or matter.

(3) For the purposes of subsection (1) rules of court may make provision as to –

    (a) the classes of case in which a right of appeal may be exercised only with permission,
    (b) the court or courts which may give permission for the purposes of this section,
    (c) any considerations to be taken into account in deciding whether permission should be given, and
    (d) any requirements to be satisfied before permission may be given,

and may make different provision for different circumstances.

(4) No appeal may be made against a decision of a court under this section to give or refuse permission (but this subsection does not affect any right under rules of court to make a further application for permission to the same or another court).

(5) For the purposes of this section a right to make an application to have a case stated for the opinion of the High Court constitutes a right of appeal.

(6) For the purposes of this section a right of appeal to the Court of Appeal includes –

    (a) the right to make an application for a new trial, and
    (b) the right to make an application to set aside a verdict, finding or judgment in any cause or matter in the High Court which has been tried, or in which any issue has been tried, by a jury.

Scope—This section provides the rule making power in relation to the requirement of permission to appeal to the Court of Appeal. CPR 1998, r 52.3 provides that permission to appeal is required in all cases (save for the limited exceptions set out there). While there can be no appeal against the refusal of permission to appeal, r 52.3(3) provides that where the lower court (the court which made the order which is the subject of the proposed appeal) refuses permission to appeal, a further application for permission to appeal may be made to the appeal court. This does not mean that permission to appeal is sought in relation to the refusal to grant permission to appeal, but in relation to the substantive order (see *Bulled v Khayat and Another* [2002] EWCA Civ 804). Procedure for the application for permission to appeal is contained within CPR PDs52A–52E (see Part III).

55 Second appeals

(1) Where an appeal is made to a county court or the High Court in relation to any matter, and on hearing the appeal the court makes a decision in relation to that matter, no appeal may be made to the Court of Appeal from that decision unless the Court of Appeal considers that –

(a)   the appeal would raise an important point of principle or practice, or

(b)   there is some other compelling reason for the Court of Appeal to hear it.

(2) This section does not apply in relation to an appeal in a criminal cause or matter.

Scope—This section imposes a further hurdle in relation to a proposed appeal where the appeal to the Court of Appeal would be a second tier appeal. This further hurdle is in addition to the requirement of permission to appeal (CPR 1998, r 52.13); see *McFarlane v McFarlane* [2004] 2 FLR 893, CA. An application for permission to adduce fresh evidence is an application preliminary to the appellate process and does not constitute the appellate process itself. Accordingly, it is not caught by s 55: *Kaur v Matharu* [2011] 1 FLR 698 (CA).

****

57 Assignment of appeals to Court of Appeal

(1) Where in any proceedings in a county court or the High Court a person appeals, or seeks permission to appeal, to a court other than the Court of Appeal or the Supreme Court –

(a)   the Master of the Rolls, or

(b)   the court from which or to which the appeal is made, or from which permission to appeal is sought,

may direct that the appeal shall be heard instead by the Court of Appeal.

(2) The power conferred by subsection (1)(b) shall be subject to rules of court.

Amendments—CRA 2005, Sch 9, para 68(2).

Scope—Where the county court or High Court is to hear an appeal which would raise an important point of principle or practice or there is some other compelling reason for it to be transferred, that court, or the Master of the Rolls may direct that the appeal be heard by the Court of Appeal. If transferred up in accordance with this provision, the Court of Appeal or the Master of the Rolls may transfer it back for hearing by the original court (CPR 1998, r 52.14(2)).

****

Administration of Justice Act 1960

****

12 Publication of information relating to proceedings in private

(1) The publication of information relating to proceedings before any court sitting in private shall not of itself be contempt of court except in the following cases, that is to say –

(a)   where the proceedings –

    (i)   relate to the exercise of the inherent jurisdiction of the High Court with respect to minors;

    (ii)   are brought under the Children Act 1989 or the Adoption and Children Act 2002; or

    (iii) otherwise relate wholly or mainly to the maintenance or upbringing of a minor;

(b)–(e)   ...

(2) Without prejudice to the foregoing subsection, the publication of the text or a summary of the whole or part of an order made by a court sitting in private shall not of itself be contempt of court except where the court (having power to do so) expressly prohibits the publication.

(3) In this section references to a court include references to a judge and to a tribunal and to any person exercising the functions of a court, a judge or a tribunal; and references to a court sitting in private include references to a court sitting in camera or in chambers.

(4) Nothing in this section shall be construed as implying that any publication is punishable as contempt of court which would not be so punishable apart from this section (and in particular where the publication is not so punishable by reason of being authorised by rules of court).

Amendments—CA 1989, s 103, Sch 13, para 14; CA 2004, s 62(2); SI 2005/2213.

Scope—See also under CA 1989, s 97, CYPA 1933, s 39 set out under **The use of the inherent jurisdiction to prohibit publication** below. A useful review of the use of these sections was carried out by the CA in *Clayton v Clayton* [2007] 1 FLR 11 and it should be noted that although the prohibition on identification under CA 1989, s 97 comes to an end once the proceedings are concluded, the limitation upon reporting information relating to the proceedings themselves under s 12 will remain. This section has the effect of abrogating the strict liability rule of contempt of court, except in certain types of proceedings (ie those mentioned in s 12(1)(a), which relate to most types of family proceedings in which children are the focal point). For an exposition of the strict liability rule, reference should be made to specialist works on contempt of court. Section 12 is designed to prevent the publication of information in respect of child law cases which are heard in private. Section 12 does not apply solely to wardship proceedings but includes proceedings under CA 1989 and ACA 2002 (*Her Majesty's Attorney-General v Pelling* [2006] 1 FLR 93). In *Re B (A Child) (Disclosure)* [2004] 2 FLR 142, Munby J reviewed many of the authorities and made the following observations on the ambit of s 12:

"(i) Section 12(1)(a) of the Administration of Justice Act 1960 has the effect of prohibiting the publication of:

'information relating to proceedings before any court sitting in private ... where the proceedings
    (i) relate to the exercise of the inherent jurisdiction of the High Court with respect to minors;
    (ii) are brought under Children Act 1989; or (iii) otherwise relate wholly or mainly to the ... upbringing of a minor.'

(ii) Subject only to proof of knowledge that the proceedings in question are of the type referred to in s 12(1)(a), the publication of such information is a contempt of court.

(iii) There is a 'publication' for this purpose whenever the law of defamation would treat there as being a publication. This means that most forms of dissemination, whether oral or written, will constitute a publication. The only exception is where there is a communication of information by someone to a professional, each acting in furtherance of the protection of children.
...
(v) Section 12 does not of itself prohibit the publication of:
    (a) the fact, if it be the case, that a child is a ward of court and is the subject of wardship proceedings or that a child is the subject of residence or other proceedings under the Children Act 1989 or of proceedings relating wholly or mainly to his maintenance or upbringing;
    (b) the name, address or photograph of such a child;
    (c) the name, address or photograph of the parties (or, if the child is a party, the other parties) to such proceedings;
    (d) the date, time or place of a past or future hearing of such proceedings;
    (e) the nature of the dispute in such proceedings;
    (f) anything which has been seen or heard by a person conducting himself lawfully in the public corridor or other public precincts outside the court in which the hearing in private is taking place;
    (g) the name, address or photograph of the witnesses who have given evidence in such proceedings;
    (h) the party on whose behalf such a witness has given evidence; and
    (i) the text or summary of the whole or part of any order made in such proceedings.
(vi) Section 12 prohibits the publication of:
    (a) accounts of what has gone on in front of the judge sitting in private;
    (b) documents such as affidavits, witness statements, reports, position statements, skeleton arguments or other documents filed in the proceedings, transcripts or notes of the evidence or submissions, and transcripts or notes of the judgment (this list is not necessarily exhaustive);
    (c) extracts or quotations from such documents;
    (d) summaries of such documents.
These prohibitions apply whether or not the information or the document being published has been anonymised." at [82].

This section does not prevent the identification of witnesses (*British Broadcasting Corporation v Rochdale Metropolitan Borough Council & X & Y* [2007] 1 FLR 101). However, in the cases of *Norfolk County Council v Webster & ors* [2007] 2 FLR 415 and *British Broadcasting Corporation v CAFCASS Legal & Ors* [2007] 2 FLR 765, the court granted anonymity to both domestic and foreign experts.

Disclosure and restraint jurisdiction—*A v Ward* [2010] 1 FLR 1497 concerns two fundamental questions, first the meaning and effect of s 12(1)(a) and second the anonymity of professional witnesses in care proceedings under Pt IV of CA 1989. In relation to the first question, "What brings a document within the scope of s 12 depends not on whether it is otherwise or already confidential but whether it is 'information relating to [the] proceedings.'" at [110]. What is and what is not included within the statutory prohibition? Further to his observations in *Re B (A Child) (Disclosure)* (see above):

"(i) 'information relating to [the] proceedings' includes:
  (a) documents prepared for the purpose of the proceedings; and
  (b) information, even if not reduced to writing, which has emerged during the course of information gathering for the purpose of proceedings already on foot.
(ii) In contrast, 'information relating to [the] proceedings' does *not* include:
  (a) documents (or the information contained in documents) not prepared for the purpose of the proceedings, even if the documents are lodged with the court or referred to in or annexed to a witness statement or report; or
  (b) information (even if contained in documents falling within paragraph (i)(a)) which does not fall within paragraph (i)(b);

unless the document or information is published in such a way as to link it with the proceedings so that it can sensibly be said that what is published is 'information relating to [the] proceedings'." at [112].

In the instant case the care proceedings, in which the local authority had failed to prove the threshold criteria of s 31(2), had come to an end and the child had been restored to his parents' care. They wished to "go public" about the case, which the judge found was a decision solely and entirely for the parents to take. The judge held that on the facts of the case the balance between, on the one hand, the private interests of the family and the various public interests they prayed in aid and, on the other hand, the other private and public interests involved came down on favour of "lifting" s 12 and allowing the parents to make use of and publish those documents that would otherwise be subject to the restriction of s 12 (at [138]).

In relation to the second question, some of the medical expert witnesses involved in the care proceedings, the treating clinicians and the social workers (by their employer local authority) each sought contra mundum injunctions to prevent the parents disclosing their identities. The judge considered the applications by each group of witnesses separately but reached the same conclusion in each case, namely that they were not entitled to the orders sought. "When all is said and done, it seems to me to be a very strong thing to say that the identities of expert witnesses giving evidence in care cases – cases where the consequences for both child and parent are potentially so serious – should be concealed from the public. And ... does not the public in this context have an interest not merely in knowing what is being done in its name but also in knowing who the experts are whose evidence may have led (though not of course in this case) to a child being removed from his parents and placed for adoption?" at [157]. The judge questioned why experts who give evidence in the family courts should be treated differently from experts who give evidence in the Crown Court in public.

The starting point is the same, namely that witnesses (experts, treating clinicians or social workers) are not afforded anonymity either by the general law or by section 12, and accordingly they need to be able to demonstrate that the balancing exercise tips in their favour (at [179]). "The question, at the end of the day, is whether having regard to all the evidence and other material before the court, the balance comes down in favour of conferring anonymity. And the fact is that in the case of the treating clinicians, as in the case of both the expert witnesses and the social workers, the claim for injunctive relief here is not being put by reference to the particular circumstances or particular vulnerabilities of specific individuals ... The claim in all three cases is, in reality, a 'class' claim, that is, a claim that any professional who falls into a certain class ... is, for that reason, and, truth be told, for that reason alone, entitled in current circumstances to have their identity protected, in plain language to have their identity concealed from the public." (at [181]). The answer was a resounding "no". The judge found that in the case of each group the applications for anonymity did not counter-balance the arguments in favour of openness and did not establish a "pressing need" for the protection sought. Nevertheless the judge recognised that there may be cases where there was clear and specific evidence in respect of a particular witness that did justify the need for the protection of his/her identity and the granting of a contra mundum injunction.

In relation to the treating clinicians, the parents had earlier entered into a contractual agreement with the NHS Trust, one term of which was that the parents agreed not to disclose the identities of the treating clinicians. The judge held that the parents were bound by the terms of that agreement.

Routine disclosure of experts' reports—The President has observed that he would like to see a practice develop in which expert reports would be routinely disclosed: the practice would aid the need for the family justice system to be as transparent as possible and encourage informed debate about the quality and content of expert evidence: *Re X, Y and Z (Expert Witness)* [2011] 2 FLR 1437.

Publication—In *Re B* above, Munby J held that, subject to the exception where there is communication of information by someone to a professional, each acting in furtherance of the protection of children, there is a "publication" for the purposes of s 12 whenever the law of defamation would treat such communication as amounting to publication. This must be read in conjunction with CA 1989, s 97(2) which prevents publication of material "to the public at large or any section of the public". Furthermore reference should be made to FPR 2010, rr 12.72–12.75 and PD12G, which permits parties and other specified people to disclose certain information from family proceedings heard in private involving children, to other specified people for specific purposes without needing permission of the court and without being in contempt of court. These rules are not applicable to disclosure in adoption proceedings where different rules apply. For guidance, see *http://hmctsformfinder.justice.gov.uk/courtfinder/forms/ex710-eng.pdf.*

The use of the inherent jurisdiction to prohibit publication—The High Court can use its inherent jurisdiction both to relax and increase the restrictions imposed by s 12. However, in *Harris v Harris; Attorney-General v Harris* [2001] 2 FLR 895 Munby J stated that the court should only exercise its powers to restrain publicity under the inherent jurisdiction if the automatic restraints under s 12 of the 1960 Act, CCA 1981, s 2 and CA 1989, s 97(2) were inadequate to protect the child from harm and if the interests of the child could not be adequately protected under CYPA 1933, s 39 which provides as follows:

"(1) In relation to any proceedings in any court, the court may direct that –
  (a) no newspaper report of the proceedings shall reveal the name, address, or school, or include particulars calculated to lead to the identification, of any child or young person concerned with the proceedings, either as being the person by or against whom or in respect of whom the proceedings are taken, or as being a witness therein;
  (b) no picture shall be published in any newspaper as being or including a picture of any child or young person so concerned in the proceedings as aforesaid;
except in so far (if at all) as may be permitted by the direction of the court.
(2) Any person who publishes any matter in contravention of any such direction shall on summary conviction be liable in respect of each offence to a fine not exceeding level 5 on the standard scale."

In *Re S (Identification: Restrictions on Publication)* [2005] 1 FLR 591 the House of Lords was of the view that the foundation of the jurisdiction to restrain publicity was derived from rights under ECHR 1950 and that since HRA 1998 came into force, the earlier case-law concerning the existence and scope of the inherent jurisdiction need not be considered. The court needs to balance the Art 8 rights of the child and the Art 10 rights of the proposed publisher and to consider the proportionality of the potential interference with each right. In *British Broadcasting Corporation v Rochdale Metropolitan Borough Council and X and Y* [2007] 1 FLR 101, Ryder J conducted an extensive analysis of the relevant domestic and ECHR 1950 case-law and an illustration of the balancing exercise required. See also *Practice Note (Official Solicitor: Deputy Director of Legal Services: Cafcass; Applications for Reporting Restriction Orders)* [2005] 2 FLR 111 (see Part V).

Matters to be considered when prohibiting the publication of information relating to proceedings in private—The proper approach is for the court to identify the various rights that are engaged and then to conduct the necessary balancing exercise between the competing rights, considering the proportionality of the potential interference with each right considered independently – see *Re B* above; *A Local Authority v W, L, W, T and R (by the Children's Guardian)* [2006] 1 FLR 1. In *Re S* above, the House of Lords indicated that it was not helpful to provide a court with detailed analysis of past case-law. In *Norfolk County Council v Webster, BBC, Associated Newspapers Ltd and Archant Group; Re Webster* [2007] 1 FLR 1146 four factors, namely (i) that the case was alleged to involve a miscarriage of justice; (ii) that the parents themselves wished for publicity; (iii) that the case had already been extensively publicised; and (iv) that, very importantly, there was a need for the full facts to emerge in a way which would command public confidence in the judicial system, led to Munby J finding that an order restricting access by the media to an interim hearing within care proceedings would be too wide and would interfere disproportionately with the freedom of expression of the parents whose child was the subject of proceedings. See also the *Practice Note* at [2005] 2 FLR 111 above. In *Norfolk County Council v Webster & ors* [2007] 2 FLR 415 Munby J allowed publication of counsel's position statement in view of the current practice of significant advocacy being in written form, which is pre-read by the judge and not dealt with orally in court; such written material should be disclosed to allow the media to report in a fully informed way. However, Munby J declined to approve a draft press release prepared on behalf of the parents: it is not the function of the judge to give advice. In *Re LM (Reporting Restrictions: Coroner's Inquest)* [2008] 1 FLR 1360 the court was not satisfied that there would be lasting harm to a child arising from the reporting of a coroner's inquest relating to the death of a sibling. However, the court placed an embargo on publication of the name or existence of the surviving child or any information that was likely to lead to her identification.

Proceedings restraining freedom of press to be heard in the High Court—Where an injunction is sought to impose a restraint on the freedom of the press and the media generally, the case should be transferred to the High Court – see *Practice Note* at [2005] 2 FLR 111 and *President's PD* at [2005] 2 FLR 120 (above).

Power of court to allow disclosure—See also FPR 2010, rr 12.73–12.75 and PD12G. The court has power to allow disclosure of information that would otherwise be subject to a prohibition on publication. However, now that FPR 2010, rr 12.73–12.75 and PD12G allow parties and other specified people to disclose certain information from family proceedings heard in private to other specified people for specific purposes without needing the permission of the court, it remains to be seen how often the additional power of the court to order disclosure will be called upon.

Power of court to restrict publicity relating to the identity of a ward in criminal proceedings—A judge in wardship proceedings may have power to restrict publicity relating to the identity of a ward in criminal proceedings but, even if he does have such a power, he should not exercise it; any decision as to restraining the publicity relating to the identity of persons concerned in criminal proceedings should be a matter for the discretion of the criminal trial judge (*Re R (Wardship: Restrictions on Publication)* [1994] 2 FLR 637; *R v Central Criminal Court ex parte Godwin and Crook* [1995] 1 FLR 132 – power of criminal court under CYPA 1933, s 39 to restrict the reporting of information relating to the identification of a child involved in criminal proceedings). However, Munby J, in care proceedings concerning unusually and exceptionally vulnerable children, made injunctive orders preventing the media reporting details about the children and their family which might lead to the identification of the children. The injunction did not prevent the media from reporting the criminal proceedings against the father but importantly, he did prohibit the media from reporting the father's home address where the children lived, even if the same was referred to in the course of the criminal proceedings (*Re X (Children)* [2008] 1 FLR 589).

Duration of prohibition on publication (s 12(1)(a)(i))—The prohibition on publication is not limited in time, and it thus remains a contempt to publish such information even if wardship proceedings are discharged (*Re E (A Minor) (Child Abuse: Evidence)* [1991] 1 FLR 420). Presumably, the same principle applies to the prohibition in s 12(1)(a)(ii) and (iii).

Publication of court order and judgment (s 12(2))—In *Re G (Celebrities: Publicity)* [1999] 1 FLR 409, the Court of Appeal indicated that it was hard to conceive of circumstances which would justify preventing the media from publishing the bare outcome of a hearing; the court should issue a terse statement approved by the judge and agreed between the parties. In *Pelling v Bruce-Williams (Secretary of State for Constitutional Affairs Intervening)* [2004] 2 FLR 823, Dame Elizabeth Butler-Sloss P stated that it may be worth giving consideration to increasing the frequency in which anonymised family court judgments in general are made public, not just in cases where there are principles of law involved. In view of the current climate, and increasing complaints of "secrecy" in the family justice system, a broader approach to making judgments public may be desirable. In *Re H (Freeing Orders: Publicity)* [2006] 1 FLR 815 the Court of Appeal stated that there was a strong argument for judges in controversial cases, or cases that attracted media attention, to accompany delivery of their judgements with a short written summary of their conclusions and reasons, which could be made publicly available. The publication of a judgment, which in the interests of the child the court had determined should be kept private, is an interference with the interests of justice and is punishable as criminal contempt (*Her Majesty's Attorney-General v Pelling* [2006] 1 FLR 93).

When publicity involving the mother of children who had been the subject of care proceedings, gave an inaccurate and/or misleading account of those proceedings, and the reasons why the children were removed from the mother (including criticisms of the secrecy of the family courts), the president authorized the release of an agreed summary of the facts of the case to the media (*Medway Council v G and ors* [2008] 2 FLR 1687).

Where most unusually, the court had granted permission for care proceedings to be heard in public subject to a schedule of anonymisations, and the family had been the subject of a documentary, Hedley J. refused to the mother's later application, to relax some of the anonymisations provisions, because to do so would have been highly likely to lead to the identification of the child who lived in a rural community and was therefore more likely to be identifiable than if he lived in a massive conurbation (*Z County Council v TS, DES, ES and A* [2008] 2 FLR 1800.

Attendance of media—Accredited representatives of the media may attend family hearings held in private (but not hearings held for the purpose of judicially assisted conciliation or negotiation). The framework is set out in:

(a) FPR 2010, r 27.11;
(b) *President's Guidance in Relation to Applications Consequent Upon the Attendance of the Media in Family Proceedings* (22 April 2009) (see Part V);
(c) FPR PD27B; and
(d) FPR PD27C.

The provisions give accredited media representatives the right to attend private hearings in family proceedings but at any stage of the proceedings the court may direct that the media may not attend all or any part of the proceedings. The court may make such a direction of its own motion or at the request of a party, a witness in the proceedings, a children's guardian, a Cafcass officer or the child (if of sufficient age and understanding). The media representatives present must be given an opportunity to make representations.

A decision to exclude the media is not discretionary and may only be made if one of the four grounds set out in r 10.28(4) is satisfied: the burden of proof rests on the party seeking to exclude the media. The President considered the court's approach to an application to exclude in *Re Child X (Residence and Contact: Rights of Media Attendance – FPR r 10.28(4))* [2009] 2 FLR 1467: see the notes to FPR 2010, r 27.11.

Court of Protection and the media—The general rule in the Court of Protection is that hearings are held in private, The court may, however, direct part or all of a hearing to be held in public or may direct that representatives of the media may attend all or part of the hearing if there is good reason to do so: COPR 2007, rr 90–93. The burden of establishing good reason rests on the party applying for a public hearing or for the media to attend. A finding of good reason does not automatically trigger a public hearing but does engage Art 10 and requires the court to conduct a balancing exercise between the respective Art 8 and Art 10 rights engaged: *Independent News Media Ltd & Ors v A (by the Official Solicitor)* [2009] COPLR Con Vol 702.

Waiver of anonymity—Long after the conclusion of the care proceedings and at a time when there was no State involvement with the family, the mother and the children (10 and 15 respectively), sought permission to waive their anonymity and thus identify themselves to the media, as the subjects of the anonymised judgment. Munby J gave permission while observing that the wisdom of the decision to waive anonymity was not a matter for the court (*Re B; X Council v B (No 2)* [2008] 1 FLR 1460).

Release of information—In exceptional cases, the court may permit the disclosure of information into the public domain about the proceedings to correct inaccurate or false versions of events given by a party to the proceedings: *Doncaster MBC v Haigh, Tune and X (by the Children's Guardian)* [2012] 1 FLR 577.

Concurrent care and criminal proceedings—Baron J gave guidance on the duties of experts instructed in both care and concurrent criminal proceedings. It was preferable for different experts to be instructed in each set of proceedings, but where this was not practicable, it was important that the experts were clear about the boundaries and limits of their role in each set of proceedings, to avoid a breach of s 12. The judge urged the relevant medical colleges to issue very clear guidelines as a matter of urgency: the colleges have yet to respond or to issue any formal guidance (*Re M (Care Disclosure to Police)* [2008] 2 FLR 390).

13 Appeal in cases of contempt of court

(1) Subject to the provisions of this section, an appeal shall lie under this section from any order or decision of a court in the exercise of jurisdiction to punish for contempt of court (including criminal contempt); and in relation to any such order or decision the provisions of this section shall have effect in substitution for any other enactment relating to appeals in civil or criminal proceedings.

(2) An appeal under this section shall lie in any case at the instance of the defendant and, in the case of an application for committal or attachment, at the instance of the applicant; and the appeal shall lie –

(a) from an order or decision of any inferior court not referred to in the next following paragraph, to the High Court;
(b) from an order or decision of a county court or any other inferior court from which appeals generally lie to the Court of Appeal, and from an order or decision (other than a decision on an appeal under this section) of a single judge

of the High Court, or of any court having the powers of the High Court or of a judge of that court, to the Court of Appeal;

(bb) from an order or decision of the Crown Court to the Court of Appeal;

(c)   from a decision of a single judge of the High Court on an appeal under this section, from an order or decision of a Divisional Court or the Court of Appeal (including a decision of either of those courts on an appeal under this section), and from an order or decision of the Court of Criminal Appeal or the Courts-Martial Appeal Court, to the Supreme Court.

(3) The court to which an appeal is brought under this section may reverse or vary the order or decision of the court below, and make such other orders as may be just; and without prejudice to the inherent powers of any court referred to in subsection (2) of this section, provision may be made by rules of court for authorising the release on bail of an appellant under this section.

(4) Subsections (2) to (4) of section one and section two of this Act shall apply to an appeal to the Supreme Court under this section as they apply to an appeal to the Supreme Court under the said section one, except that so much of the said subsection (2) as restricts the grant of leave to appeal shall apply only where the decision of the court below is a decision on appeal to that court under this section.

(5) In this section "court" includes any tribunal or person having power to punish for contempt; and references in this section to an order or decision of a court in the exercise of jurisdiction to punish for contempt of court include references –

(a)   to an order or decision of the High Court, the Crown Court or a county court under any enactment enabling that court to deal with an offence as if it were contempt of court;

(b)   to an order or decision of a county court, or of any court having the powers of a county court, under section 14, 92 or 118 of the County Courts Act 1984;

(c)   to an order or decision of a magistrates' court under subsection (3) of section 63 of the Magistrates' Courts Act 1980,

but do not include references to orders under section five of the Debtors Act 1869, or under any provision of the Magistrates' Courts Act 1980 or the County Courts Act 1984, except those referred to in paragraphs (b) and (c) of this subsection and except sections 38 and 142 of the last-mentioned Act so far as those sections confer jurisdiction in respect of contempt of court.

(6) This section does not apply to a conviction or sentence in respect of which an appeal lies under Part I of the Criminal Appeal Act 1968, or to a decision of the criminal division of the Court of Appeal under that Part of that Act.

Amendments—Criminal Appeal Act 1968, s 52(1), Sch 5, Pt I; Courts Act 1971, s 56(1),(4), Sch 8, Pt II, para 40(1),(2), Sch 11, Pt II; MCA 1980, s 154, Sch 7, para 37; SCA 1981, s 152(4), Sch 7; CCA 1984, s 148(1), Sch 2, para 25; AJA 1999, ss 64, 106, Sch 15; CRA 2005, Sch 9, para 13(7).

Scope—Proceedings on appeal under this section from an order or decision under MCA 1980, s 63(3) (the power to punish for breach of a court order) are assigned to the Family Division of the High Court by SCA 1981, s 61(1),(3), Sch 1, para 3(d), and the procedure on such appeal is prescribed by FPR 2010, Pt 30 and PD30A. The court has power to punish for an assault on an officer of the court (CCA 1984, s 14), for the rescue of goods seized in execution of process of a county court (CCA 1984, s 92) and for contempt (CCA 1984, s 118).

Committal by district judge—A committal order may be made in the county court by a district judge (see AEA 1971, s 23(11) and CCA 1984, s 118(3)), and an appeal from such a decision appears to be to the judge (see *Marya v Marya* [1995] 2 FLR 911; *King v Read & Slack* [1999] 1 FLR 425, CA).

****

Administration of Justice Act 1970

****

SCHEDULE 8

MAINTENANCE ORDERS FOR PURPOSES OF 1958 ACT AND PART II OF THIS ACT

1 An order for alimony, maintenance or other payments made, or having effect as if made, under Part II of the Matrimonial Causes Act 1965 (ancillary relief in actions for divorce etc).

2 An order for payments to or in respect of a child being an order made, or having effect as if made, under Part III of the said Act of 1965 (maintenance of children following divorce, etc).

2A An order for periodical or other payments made, or having effect as if made, under Part II of the Matrimonial Causes Act 1973.

3 An order for maintenance or other payments to or in respect of a spouse or child being an order made under Part I of the Domestic Proceedings and Magistrates' Courts Act 1978.

4 An order for periodical or other payments made or having effect as if made under Schedule 1 to the Children Act 1989.

5 (*repealed*)

6 An order –

    (a)   made or having effect as if made under paragraph 23 of Schedule 2 to the Children Act 1989; or

    (b)   made under section 23 of the Ministry of Social Security Act 1966, section 18 of the Supplementary Benefits Act 1976, section 24 of the Social Security Act 1986 or section 106 of the Social Security Administration Act 1992 (various provisions for obtaining contributions from a person whose dependants are assisted or maintained out of public funds).

7 (*repealed*)

8 An order to which section 16 of the Maintenance Orders Act 1950 applies by virtue of subsection (2)(b) or (c) of that section (that is to say an order made by a court in Scotland or Northern Ireland and corresponding to one of those specified in the foregoing paragraphs) and which has been registered in a court in England and Wales under Part II of that Act.

9 A maintenance order within the meaning of the Maintenance Orders (Facilities for Enforcement) Act 1920 (Commonwealth orders enforceable in the United Kingdom) registered in, or confirmed by, a court in England and Wales under that Act.

10 An order for periodical or other payments made under Part I of the Matrimonial Proceedings and Property Act 1970.

11 A maintenance order within the meaning of Part I of the Maintenance Orders (Reciprocal Enforcement) Act 1972 registered in a magistrates' court under the said Part I.

12 (*repealed*)

13 A maintenance order within the meaning of Part I of the Civil Jurisdiction and Judgments Act 1982, which is registered in a magistrates' court under that Part.

13A A maintenance judgment within the meaning of Council Regulation (EC) No 44/2001 of 22 December 2000 on jurisdiction and the recognition and enforcement of judgments in civil and commercial matters, as amended from time to time and as applied by the Agreement made on 19th October 2005 between the European Community and the Kingdom of Denmark on jurisdiction and the recognition and enforcement of judgments in civil and commercial matters (OJ No. L 299 16.11.2005 at p 62), which is registered in a magistrates' court under that Regulation.

13B (1) A decision, court settlement or authentic instrument which falls to be enforced by a magistrates' court by virtue of the Maintenance Regulation and the Civil Jurisdiction and Judgments (Maintenance) Regulations 2011.

(2) In this paragraph –

"the Maintenance Regulation" means Council Regulation (EC) No 4/2009 including as applied in relation to Denmark by virtue of the Agreement made on 19 October 2005 between the European Community and the Kingdom of Denmark;

"decision", "court settlement" and "authentic instrument" have the meanings given by Article 2 of the Maintenance Regulation.

14 An order for periodical or other payments made under Part III of the Matrimonial and Family Proceedings Act 1984.

15 An order for periodical or other payments made under Schedule 5, 6 or 7 to the Civil Partnership Act 2004.

Amendments—MPPA 1970, s 42(1), Sch 2, para 5; MO(RE)A 1972, s 22(1), Sch, para 6; MCA 1973, s 54(1), Sch 2, para 10(2); Supplementary Benefits Act 1976, s 35(2), Sch 7, para 17; DPMCA 1978, s 89, Sch 2, para 26; CJJA 1982, s 15(4), Sch 12, para 5; MFPA 1984, s 46(1), Sch 1, para 8; Social Security Act 1986, s 86, Sch 10, para 42; FLRA 1987, s 33(1), Sch 2, para 27, Sch 4; CLSA 1990, s 116, Sch 16, paras 6, 37; Social Security (Consequential Provisions) Act 1992, s 4, Sch 2, para 7; SI 2001/3929; CPA 2004, s 261(1), Sch 27, para 34, SI 2007/1655; Health and Social Care Act 2008, Sch 15; SI 2011/1484.

Adoption and Children Act 2002

ARRANGEMENT OF SECTIONS

PART 1
ADOPTION

Chapter 1
Introductory

Chapter 7
Miscellaneous

Restrictions

Information

Proceedings

The Children and Family Court Advisory and Support Service

Evidence

General

PART 3
MISCELLANEOUS AND FINAL PROVISIONS

Chapter 1
Miscellaneous

Advertisements in the United Kingdom

Chapter 2
Final provisions

PART II

PART 1
ADOPTION

Chapter 1
Introductory

1 Considerations applying to the exercise of powers

(1) This section applies whenever a court or adoption agency is coming to a decision relating to the adoption of a child.

(2) The paramount consideration of the court or adoption agency must be the child's welfare, throughout his life.

(3) The court or adoption agency must at all times bear in mind that, in general, any delay in coming to the decision is likely to prejudice the child's welfare.

(4) The court or adoption agency must have regard to the following matters (among others) –

    (a)   the child's ascertainable wishes and feelings regarding the decision (considered in the light of the child's age and understanding),

    (b)   the child's particular needs,

    (c)   the likely effect on the child (throughout his life) of having ceased to be a member of the original family and become an adopted person,

    (d)   the child's age, sex, background and any of the child's characteristics which the court or agency considers relevant,

    (e)   any harm (within the meaning of the Children Act 1989) which the child has suffered or is at risk of suffering,

    (f)   the relationship which the child has with relatives, and with any other person in relation to whom the court or agency considers the relationship to be relevant, including –

        (i)   the likelihood of any such relationship continuing and the value to the child of its doing so,

        (ii)   the ability and willingness of any of the child's relatives, or of any such person, to provide the child with a secure environment in which the child can develop, and otherwise to meet the child's needs,

        (iii)   the wishes and feelings of any of the child's relatives, or of any such person, regarding the child.

(5) In placing the child for adoption, the adoption agency must give due consideration to the child's religious persuasion, racial origin and cultural and linguistic background.

(6) The court or adoption agency must always consider the whole range of powers available to it in the child's case (whether under this Act or the Children Act 1989); and the court must not make any order under this Act unless it considers that making the order would be better for the child than not doing so.

(7) In this section, "coming to a decision relating to the adoption of a child", in relation to a court, includes –

    (a)   coming to a decision in any proceedings where the orders that might be made by the court include an adoption order (or the revocation of such an order), a placement order (or the revocation of such an order) or an order under section 26 (or the revocation or variation of such an order),

(b) coming to a decision about granting leave in respect of any action (other than the initiation of proceedings in any court) which may be taken by an adoption agency or individual under this Act,

but does not include coming to a decision about granting leave in any other circumstances.

(8) For the purposes of this section –

(a) references to relationships are not confined to legal relationships,
(b) references to a relative, in relation to a child, include the child's mother and father.

Defined terms—"adoption agency": s 2(1); "child": ss 49(5), 144; "harm": CA 1989, s 31(9); "relative": ss 1(8), 144; "adoption (in relation to Chapter 4 of Part 1)": s 66; "adoption order": s 46(1); "court": s 144; "placement order": s 21: "placing, or placed, for adoption": s 18(5), 19(4).

"welfare throughout his life" (s 1(2))—Paramount consideration must be given to the child's welfare "throughout his life" when coming to a decision relating to adoption. Under the earlier law, a benefit arising from adoption which might accrue to the child after the age of 18 was a relevant factor to be taken into account in deciding whether to make an adoption order (*Re D (A Minor) (Adoption Order: Validity)* [1991] 2 FLR 66). The ECtHR has held that in identifying where a child's best interests lie, two considerations must be borne in mind: first, it is in the child's best interests that his ties with his family be maintained except in cases where the family has proved particularly unfit; and second, it is in the child's best interests to ensure his development in a safe and secure environment (*YC v United Kingdom* (Application No 4547/10) [2012] 2 FLR 332).

"delay ... is likely to prejudice child's welfare" (s 1(3))—See notes to CA 1989, s 1.

Ceasing to be a member of the original family and becoming an adopted person (s 1(4)(c))—This element of the checklist has a twofold focus: (a) ceasing to be a member of the original family; and (b) becoming an adopted person.

On adoption the cessation of membership of the original family is total and intended to be so for all time. The original parents' parental responsibility is extinguished and there is a complete severing of all legal ties with the family. The cut off from his family of origin may have a potentially damaging impact on the child's sense of identity and emotional wellbeing. "Becoming an adopted person" provides for the child a permanent substitute family, where the adopters are legally responsible and, therefore, fully committed to fulfilling their parental responsibilities.

In focusing upon the likely effect on the child of these changes, the court or adoption agency will be focusing upon the degree of interference with the child's ECHR 1950, Art 8 rights to family life that would be consequent upon an adoption. This will have to be balanced against the family life that the child is, or will be, enjoying with the adoptive family.

Relationship which the child has with relatives (s 1(4)(f))—A court or adoption agency is required to consider the child's existing family relationships to a degree and in a manner which is not expressly required by CA 1989, s 1(3).

A "relative" in relation to a child means a grandparent, brother, sister, uncle or aunt, whether of the full blood or half-blood or by marriage or civil partnership and includes the child's mother and father (ss 1(8) and 144). The pool of relationships is not confined to relatives, but will include any de facto relationships considered to be of importance; on the facts of a particular case this might include foster parents.

Consideration must be given to: (i) the value to the child of a continuing relationship with his relatives (and any other person who is important to the child); and (ii) the wishes and feelings of those relatives. Particular importance is likely to be given to relationships between siblings. Any "skewing" of family relationships must be considered (*Re S (Adoption Order or Special Guardianship Order)* [2007] 1 FLR 819).

Choice between adoption and special guardianship—In *Re AJ (Adoption Order or Special Guardianship Order)* [2007] 1 FLR 507 the Court of Appeal expressly endorsed a detailed schedule of the main differences between special guardianship orders and adoption orders.

Religious persuasion (s 1(5))—A parent's religious beliefs can never be determinative when considering the totality of a child's welfare; a parent's rights under ECHR 1950, Art 9 are qualified by the child's right to family life under Art 8 (*Re S; Newcastle City Council v Z* [2007] 1 FLR 861).

Dispensing with parental consent—The circumstances in which the paramountcy principle applies include those where the issue is whether or not to dispense with parental consent to placement and/or adoption (s 1(7)).

PART II

****

Chapter 3
Placement for Adoption and Adoption Orders

Placement of children by adoption agency for adoption

18   Placement for adoption by agencies

(1) An adoption agency may –

    (a)   place a child for adoption with prospective adopters, or

    (b)   where it has placed a child with any persons (whether under this Part or not), leave the child with them as prospective adopters,

but, except in the case of a child who is less than six weeks old, may only do so under section 19 or a placement order.

(2) An adoption agency may only place a child for adoption with prospective adopters if the agency is satisfied that the child ought to be placed for adoption.

(3) A child who is placed or authorised to be placed for adoption with prospective adopters by a local authority is looked after by the authority.

(4) If an application for an adoption order has been made by any persons in respect of a child and has not been disposed of –

    (a)   an adoption agency which placed the child with those persons may leave the child with them until the application is disposed of, but

    (b)   apart from that, the child may not be placed for adoption with any prospective adopters.

"Adoption order" includes a Scottish or Northern Irish adoption order.

(5) References in this Act (apart from this section) to an adoption agency placing a child for adoption –

    (a)   are to its placing a child for adoption with prospective adopters, and

    (b)   include, where it has placed a child with any persons (whether under this Act or not), leaving the child with them as prospective adopters;

and references in this Act (apart from this section) to a child who is placed for adoption by an adoption agency are to be interpreted accordingly.

(6) References in this Chapter to an adoption agency being, or not being, authorised to place a child for adoption are to the agency being or (as the case may be) not being authorised to do so under section 19 or a placement order.

(7) This section is subject to sections 30 to 35 (removal of children placed by adoption agencies).

Defined terms—"adoption agency": s 2(1); "child": ss 49(5), 144; "adoption (in relation to Chapter 4 of Part 1)": s 66; "adoption agency placing a child for adoption": s 18(5); "adoption order": s 46(1); "local authority": s 144; "Northern Irish adoption order": s 144; "placement order": s 21; "placing, or placed, for adoption": s 18(5), 19(4).

Placement—Before ACA 2002, the placing of a child for adoption was largely an administrative process conducted by a local authority or adoption agency either with the agreement of the parent(s) or under the authority provided by a care order (interim or full) or an order freeing a child for adoption. ACA 2002, ss 18–41 establish a statutory code regulating the circumstances in which a child can be placed for adoption and the consequences once such a placement is made. There is provision for substantial court involvement in the process.

    The general effect of the placement provisions in ACA 2002, Chapter 3 is twofold. First, before a placement for adoption can be made, a parent must be fully engaged in the decision making process, either by giving express consent or by having the opportunity to contest the issue in court proceedings. Secondly, if either a parent consents to placement for adoption, or the court makes a "placement order", and an adoptive placement is then made the parent's options for later overturning the move towards adoption or challenging any eventual adoption application are significantly restricted.

A central aim of ACA 2002, Chapter 3 provisions is to bring the parent's opportunity to challenge the crucial adoption decision forward to a stage before any adoptive placement is made. A feature of the earlier law was that in many cases the first opportunity a parent had to challenge a placement in court might be months or years after the placement had been made.

In contrast to the repealed provisions "freeing" a child for adoption, where a child is placed for adoption (by agreement or order) the birth parents remain the child's parents until any final adoption order but they will be required to share parental responsibility with the prospective adopters and the adoption agency. There is also some (albeit limited) ability to reverse a placement order or withdraw consent whereas a freeing order could only be reversed on appeal or revoked in very circumscribed circumstances.

"Placement for adoption"—"Placing a child for adoption" by an adoption agency is defined as "placing a child for adoption with prospective adopters" and includes "where it has placed a child with any persons (whether under ACA 2002 or not), leaving the child with them as prospective adopters" (s 18(5)).

A child who is placed or authorised to be placed for adoption by a local authority is a *"looked after"* child under the provisions of CA 1989, Pt III (s 18(3)). All adoption agencies, whether a local authority or voluntary agency, must comply with the requirements imposed by Adoption Agency Regulations 2005, Pt 6 regarding placement for adoption and conducting statutory reviews.

Two routes to placement for adoption—The ACA 2002 establishes two routes by which an adoption agency may be authorised to place a child for adoption:

(i)   Placement with parental consent (s 19); or
(ii) Placement under a placement order (s 21).

19 Placing children with parental consent

(1) Where an adoption agency is satisfied that each parent or guardian of a child has consented to the child –

(a)   being placed for adoption with prospective adopters identified in the consent, or
(b)   being placed for adoption with any prospective adopters who may be chosen by the agency,

and has not withdrawn the consent, the agency is authorised to place the child for adoption accordingly.

(2) Consent to a child being placed for adoption with prospective adopters identified in the consent may be combined with consent to the child subsequently being placed for adoption with any prospective adopters who may be chosen by the agency in circumstances where the child is removed from or returned by the identified prospective adopters.

(3) Subsection (1) does not apply where –

(a)   an application has been made on which a care order might be made and the application has not been disposed of, or
(b)   a care order or placement order has been made after the consent was given.

(4) References in this Act to a child placed for adoption under this section include a child who was placed under this section with prospective adopters and continues to be placed with them, whether or not consent to the placement has been withdrawn.

(5) This section is subject to section 52 (parental etc consent).

Defined terms—"adoption agency": s 2(1); "care order": Sch 6 and CA 1989, s 105(1); "child": ss 49(5), 144; "consent": s 52; "parent": s 52(6); "adoption (in relation to Chapter 4 of Part 1)": s 66; "guardian": s 144; "placement order": s 21; "placing, or placed, for adoption": ss 18(5), 19(4).

Placement with parental consent (s 19(1))—An adoption agency may place a child for adoption where it is satisfied that each parent or guardian of the child has consented (and has not withdrawn the consent) to the child either: (a) being placed for adoption with prospective adopters identified in the consent; or

(b) being placed for adoption with any prospective adopters who may be chosen by the agency. Where the question of parental consent is in doubt, a local authority may apply to the court for a declaration to clarify the issue (*A Local Authority v GC* [2009] 1 FLR 299).

Once a child has been placed for adoption pursuant to a consent given under ACA 2002, s 19, he will continue to be regarded as placed there under that provision notwithstanding that a parent may have withdrawn their consent at a later stage (s 19(4)).

Consequences of parental consent to placement for adoption—The following important and potentially irrevocable consequences flow from a parent giving consent to the placement of a child for adoption:

- The parent may only oppose any adoption application with the leave of the court (s 47);
- The parent's ability to apply for a residence order is restricted (s 28(1));
- The parent's ability to have contact with the child will be determined by the adoption agency or subject to a court order under ACA 2002, s 26;
- Parental responsibility is given to the adoption agency (and in due course to prospective adopters with whom the child is placed) (s 25);
- There are restrictions on a parent's ability to require removal/return of the child (ss 30–35).

"Consent" (s 19(1))—This means consent given unconditionally and with full understanding of what is involved (s 52(5)). Consent to a child being placed for adoption with prospective adopters identified in the consent (under s 19(1)(a)) may be combined with consent to the child subsequently being placed for adoption with any prospective adopters chosen by the agency (under s 19(1)(b)) if the child were to be removed from or returned by the identified adopters (s 19(2)). A child may be placed for adoption with maternal consent at under 6 weeks old, but that consent is not valid for any subsequent adoption (see s 47(4)(b)(i)).

Consent to placement for adoption may be withdrawn; however any purported withdrawal will be ineffective if it occurs after an adoption application has been made (s 52(4)).

Form of consent—Consent to placement for adoption and advance consent to adoption must be given using the relevant statutory form, or a form to like effect (ACA 2002, s 52(7); FPR 2010, r 14.10(1)(a))). The appropriate forms are:

- Consent to placement for adoption with any prospective adopters (Form A100);
- Consent to placement for adoption with identified prospective adopters (Form A101);
- Consent to placement for adoption with identified prospective adopters and, if the placement breaks down, with any prospective adopters (Form A102);
- Advance consent to adoption (Form A103);
- Form A106 for withdrawal of consent.

In England and Wales, any consent form must be witnessed by a Cafcass officer or by a Welsh family proceedings officer (Adoption Agency Regulations 2005, reg 20). In Scotland it should be witnessed by a Justice of the Peace or a Sheriff, and in Northern Ireland by a Justice of the Peace (see notes on relevant form). Outside the UK, the form should be witnessed by a person who is authorised by law in the place where the document is signed to administer an oath for any judicial or legal purpose, a British Consular Officer, a notary public, or, if the person executing the document is serving in the regular armed forces of the Crown, an officer holding a commission in any of those forces.

"Parent" (s 19(1))—This refers to a parent who has parental responsibility for the child (s 52(6)). Each such parent or guardian must consent before an agency is authorised to make an adoption placement under s 19.

Consensual route not available in care proceedings—The consensual route cannot be used where an application for a care or supervision order has been made under CA 1989, s 31 and that application has not been disposed of (s 19(3)). Also, where a care order has been made after parental consent to placement has been given, the consent does not give the agency authority to place the child for adoption. In such circumstances, if the appropriate local authority is satisfied that the child ought to be placed for adoption, it must apply for a placement order (s 22(2); see annotation to s 22 **Local authority required to apply for placement order** below).

Once a placement order has been made, it is that order, and not any earlier s 19 parental consent, that provides authority for an agency to place the child for adoption (s 19(3)).

Placing a child under 6 weeks old—Any consent "to the making of an adoption order" given by a mother is ineffective if given less than 6 weeks after the child's birth (s 52(3); *A Local Authority v GC and Others* [2009] 1 FLR 299). An adoption agency may not place a child who is less than 6 weeks old for adoption unless the parent or guardian of the child has agreed in writing with the agency that the child may be placed for adoption (Adoption Agencies Regulations 2005, reg 35(4)).

Limit on change of surname or removal from UK—Where a child is placed for adoption pursuant to parental consent under ACA 2002, s 19, or a placement order has been made, no person may:

- cause the child to be known by a new surname, or
- remove the child from the UK

unless the court gives leave to do so or each parent or guardian of the child gives written consent (s 28(2),(3)). A person who provides the child's home may however remove the child from the UK for a period of less than 1 month without the need to obtain parental consent or court leave (s 28(4)).

Discharge of CA 1989 contact orders—On an agency being authorised to place a child for adoption pursuant to parental consent given under ACA 2002, s 19, any existing contact orders under CA 1989 (s 8 or s 34) will cease to have effect and no application may be made for a contact order (save where a s 8 contact application is to be heard together with the application to adopt) (s 26). However, an application for contact may be made during the currency of an agency's authorisation to place for adoption under ACA 2002, s 26.

20 Advance consent to adoption

(1) A parent or guardian of a child who consents to the child being placed for adoption by an adoption agency under section 19 may, at the same or any subsequent time, consent to the making of a future adoption order.

(2) Consent under this section –

    (a) where the parent or guardian has consented to the child being placed for adoption with prospective adopters identified in the consent, may be consent to adoption by them, or

    (b) may be consent to adoption by any prospective adopters who may be chosen by the agency.

(3) A person may withdraw any consent given under this section.

(4) A person who gives consent under this section may, at the same or any subsequent time, by notice given to the adoption agency –

    (a) state that he does not wish to be informed of any application for an adoption order, or

    (b) withdraw such a statement.

(5) A notice under subsection (4) has effect from the time when it is received by the adoption agency but has no effect if the person concerned has withdrawn his consent.

(6) This section is subject to section 52 (parental etc consent).

Defined terms—"adoption agency": s 2(1); "child": ss 49(5), 144; "consent": s 52; "parent": s 52(6); "adoption (in relation to Chapter 4 of Part 1)": s 66; "adoption order": s 46(1); "guardian", "notice": s 144; "placing, or placed, for adoption": ss 18(5) and 19(4).

Advance consent to adoption—A parent or guardian of a child who consents to the child being placed for adoption under ACA 2002, s 19 may, at the same time or any subsequent time, consent to the making of a future adoption order. In this context, where the placement consent is for placement with identified prospective adopters the additional consent may be advance consent to adoption by them, or it may be consent to adoption by any prospective adopters who may be chosen by the adoption agency (s 20(2)). Advance consent to adoption may be withdrawn (s 20(3)), but any such withdrawal is ineffective if it takes place after an application for an adoption order has been made (s 52(4)).

A parent who gives advance consent to adoption may, at the same time or any subsequent time, give notice to the adoption agency stating that he does not wish to be informed of any application for an adoption order. Such a notice, once given, may subsequently be withdrawn (s 20(4)).

"Consent" and form of consent (s 20(1))—See note to s 19.

21 Placement orders

(1) A placement order is an order made by the court authorising a local authority to place a child for adoption with any prospective adopters who may be chosen by the authority.

(2) The court may not make a placement order in respect of a child unless –

    (a) the child is subject to a care order,

    (b) the court is satisfied that the conditions in section 31(2) of the 1989 Act (conditions for making a care order) are met, or

    (c) the child has no parent or guardian.

(3) The court may only make a placement order if, in the case of each parent or guardian of the child, the court is satisfied –

    (a) that the parent or guardian has consented to the child being placed for adoption with any prospective adopters who may be chosen by the local authority and has not withdrawn the consent, or

    (b) that the parent's or guardian's consent should be dispensed with.

This subsection is subject to section 52 (parental etc consent).

(4) A placement order continues in force until –

    (a) it is revoked under section 24,

    (b) an adoption order is made in respect of the child, or

    (c) the child marries, forms a civil partnership or attains the age of 18 years.

"Adoption order" includes a Scottish or Northern Irish adoption order.

Amendments—CPA 2004, s 79(1),(2).

Defined terms—"child": ss 49(5), 144; "care order": Sch 6 and CA 1989, s 105(1); "civil partnership": CPA 2004, s 1; "consent": s 52; "parent": s 52(6); "the 1989 Act": s 2(5); "adoption (in relation to Chapter 4 of Part 1)": s 66; "adoption order": s 46(1); "court", "guardian", "local authority", "Northern Irish adoption order": s 144; "placement order": s 21; "placing, or placed, for adoption": ss 18(5), 19(4).

Placement orders—A "placement order" is "an order made by the court authorising a local authority to place a child for adoption with any prospective adopters who may be chosen by the authority" (s 21(1)). While a placement order is in force, parental responsibility for the child is given to the local authority and, while the child is with prospective adopters, also to them (s 25).

Conditions for making a placement order (s 21(2),(3))—The court may not make a placement order unless:

– the child is subject to a care order, or
– the court is satisfied that the threshold conditions in CA 1989, s 31(2) are met, or
– the child has no parent or guardian

and

– each parent or guardian has consented to the child being placed for adoption with any prospective adopters who may be chosen by the local authority and has not withdrawn consent, or the parent's consent should be dispensed with under ACA 2002, s 52.

In addition to these conditions, a court will only make a placement order if that is justified having given paramount consideration to the child's welfare throughout his life and having regard to the other matters set out in ACA 2002, s 1. The drastic step of making a placement order should only be sanctioned when all avenues to rehabilitation have been reasonably explored, but, whereas the court must avoid infringement of ECHR, Art 8, there is no requirement for express analysis of Art 8 in every judgment (*D McG v Neath Talbot County Borough Council* [2010] 2 FLR 1827). It is an insufficient foundation for a placement order that the long-term aim of the court is that the child should be adopted. The necessary foundation is that – broadly speaking – the child is presently in a condition to be adopted and is ready to be adopted (*Re T (Placement Order)* [2008] 1 FLR 1721; *NS-H v Kingston upon Hull City Council and MC* [2008] 2 FLR 918). Conversely, where the aim is for an adoptive placement, but the local authority realistically takes the view that such a placement may be impossible to find, the court is nevertheless justified in endorsing a dual (adoption/fostering) plan by making a placement order (*Re P (Placement Orders: Parental Consent)* [2008] 2 FLR 625).

The statutory definition of the phrase "care order" includes an interim care order (Sch 6 and CA 1989, ss 31(11) and 105(1)); whether proof of the lower CA 1989, s 38 threshold conditions is sufficient to support the making of a placement order must await judicial clarification.

Consequences of a placement order—Where a placement order has been made to a local authority and is in force the following consequences flow:

– The regime for the regulation of contact under s 26 applies;
– A parent or guardian may not apply for a residence order (and no guardian may apply for a special guardianship order) unless an application for an adoption order has been made and the parent or guardian has obtained the court's leave to oppose the adoption application (s 28(1));
– Unless the court gives leave or each parent or guardian gives written consent, no person may:
  (i) cause the child to be known by a new surname;
  (ii) remove the child from the UK (save for a period of less than one month by a person who provides the child's home) (s 28(2),(3));
– Any existing care order on the child does not have effect at any time when the placement order is in force (s 29(1));
– Any pre-existing CA 1989, s 8 order or supervision order will cease to have effect on the making of a placement order (s 29(2));
– No prohibited steps, specific issue or residence order and no supervision or child assessment orders may be made in respect of the child (s 29(3));
– No special guardianship order may be made (unless an adoption application has been made and the court has given leave to a person to apply for a special guardianship order or a guardian has been given leave to oppose the adoption) (s 29(5)).

Advertising child for adoption—Publications that advertise children as available for adoption are unlikely to advertise a child unless the adoption agency is authorised to place for adoption or a court has given leave for such advertising; *Re K (Adoption: Permission to Advertise)* [2007] 2 FLR 326 describes the court's approach when asked to give leave to advertise.

22 Applications for placement orders

(1) A local authority must apply to the court for a placement order in respect of a child if –

(a) the child is placed for adoption by them or is being provided with accommodation by them,
(b) no adoption agency is authorised to place the child for adoption,
(c) the child has no parent or guardian or the authority consider that the conditions in section 31(2) of the 1989 Act are met, and
(d) the authority are satisfied that the child ought to be placed for adoption.

(2) If –

(a) an application has been made (and has not been disposed of) on which a care order might be made in respect of a child, or
(b) a child is subject to a care order and the appropriate local authority are not authorised to place the child for adoption,

the appropriate local authority must apply to the court for a placement order if they are satisfied that the child ought to be placed for adoption.

(3) If –

(a) a child is subject to a care order, and
(b) the appropriate local authority are authorised to place the child for adoption under section 19,

the authority may apply to the court for a placement order.

(4) If a local authority –

(a) are under a duty to apply to the court for a placement order in respect of a child, or

   (b) have applied for a placement order in respect of a child and the application has not been disposed of,

the child is looked after by the authority.

(5) Subsections (1) to (3) do not apply in respect of a child –

   (a) if any persons have given notice of intention to adopt, unless the period of four months beginning with the giving of the notice has expired without them applying for an adoption order or their application for such an order has been withdrawn or refused, or

   (b) if an application for an adoption order has been made and has not been disposed of.

"Adoption order" includes a Scottish or Northern Irish adoption order.

(6) Where –

   (a) an application for a placement order in respect of a child has been made and has not been disposed of, and

   (b) no interim care order is in force,

the court may give any directions it considers appropriate for the medical or psychiatric examination or other assessment of the child; but a child who is of sufficient understanding to make an informed decision may refuse to submit to the examination or other assessment.

(7) The appropriate local authority –

   (a) in relation to a care order, is the local authority in whose care the child is placed by the order, and

   (b) in relation to an application on which a care order might be made, is the local authority which makes the application.

Defined terms—"the 1989 Act": s 2(5); "adoption (in relation to Chapter 4 of Part 1)": s 66; "adoption agency": s 2(1); "adoption order": s 46(1); "care order": s 105(1) of the 1989 Act; "child": ss 49(5), 144; "court", "guardian": s 144; "interim care order": s 38 of the 1989 Act; "local authority": s 144; "Northern Irish adoption order", "notice": s 144; "notice of intention to adopt": s 44(2); "placement order": s 21; "placing, or placed, for adoption": ss 18(5), 19(4).

Local authority required to apply for a placement order—Section 22 places a mandatory requirement upon a local authority to apply for a placement order in the following circumstances:

(1) Where a child is placed for adoption by them or is being provided with accommodation by them, and
   – no adoption agency is authorised to place the child for adoption, and
   – they consider that the threshold conditions in CA 1989, s 31(2) are met (or that the child has no parent or guardian); and
   – they are satisfied that the child ought to be placed for adoption.

(2) Where
   – there is a pending application for a care or supervision order (which has not been disposed of) or
   – the child is the subject of a care order and the appropriate local authority are not authorised to place, and
   – they are satisfied that the child ought to be placed for adoption.

A local authority cannot be "satisfied that the child ought to be placed for adoption" (s 22(1),(2)) until it has made a decision to that effect under Adoption Agencies Regulations 2005, reg 19; such a decision is not to be referred to an adoption panel but is to be taken by a decision maker within the local authority, who must consider the child's "permanence report" and medical reports on the child and his parents (AAR 2005, reg 19, as amended).

In addition, a local authority has discretion whether to apply for a placement order where a child is subject to a care order and they are the appropriate authority authorised to place the child for adoption with parental consent under ACA 2002, s 19.

The provisions of ACA 2002, s 22(1)–(3) do not apply in respect of a child if any person has given notice of intention to adopt the child, unless more than four months have gone by since the notice and no adoption application has been made (or it has been withdrawn or dismissed), or if an adoption application has been made and not disposed of.

Procedure—An application for a placement order is governed by FPR 2010, Pt 14. The application must be in Form A50 or a form to like effect (FPR 2010, r 5.1). There is no restriction upon the level of court in which an application relating to a placement order may be made.

The respondents to an application for a placement order will be (FPR 2010, r 14.3):

- Each parent who has parental responsibility for the child or guardian of the child;
- Any person in whose favour a CA 1989 order is in force with respect to the child;
- Any adoption agency or voluntary organisation which has parental responsibility for, or is looking after, or is caring for, the child;
- The child; and
- The parties, or any persons who are or have been parties to proceedings for a care order with respect to the child where those proceedings have led to the application for the placement order.

The court may at any time direct that a child, who is not already a respondent to proceedings, be made a respondent where the child wishes to make an application or has evidence to give to the court, or a legal submission to make, which has not been given or made by any other party, or there are other special circumstances. The court may at any time direct that a person or body be made a respondent or be removed as a respondent.

In addition to any respondents, a copy of the application form for a placement order must be sent to any appointed children's guardian, children and family reporter or reporting officer and to any other person directed by the court to receive a copy (PD, Pt 5).

The application must be accompanied by the documents referred to in Form A50, namely:

- Three copies of the completed application form;
- A certified copy of the full entry in the Register of Live Births that relates to the child or, where the child has been adopted, a certified copy of the entry in the Adopted Children Register;
- Any written consent of the parent or guardian to the child being placed for adoption, and any notice of withdrawal of such consent;
- If the applicant is asking the court to dispense with the consent of any parent or guardian to the child being placed for adoption, a brief statement of the facts relied on in support of the request, and two copies of the statement;
- A copy of any final care order relating to the child;
- If available, a copy of any parental responsibility order or parental responsibility agreement relating to the child;
- If the authority was a party to the proceedings, a copy of any other final order relating to the child that has effect and, if available, a copy of any maintenance agreement;
- If the authority was a party to the proceedings, a copy of any final order relating to a full, half or step brother or sister of the child that has effect.

Preliminary steps to be taken by court—As soon as practicable after an application for a placement order has been issued, the court must take the steps set out in FPR 2010, r 14.6(1),(3). If the court considers it appropriate to do so, instead of setting a date for a first directions hearing, the court may simply give the directions that would otherwise be considered at such a hearing (FPR 2010, r 14.6(4)).

Children's guardian—An application for the making or revocation of a placement order constitutes "specified proceedings" under CA 1989, s 41 and there is a presumption that a children's guardian will be appointed for the child. The child is automatically a respondent to any application for a placement order and a children's guardian will be appointed unless it is not necessary to do so to safeguard the interests of the child (FPR 2010, rr 14.3, 16.3). The children's guardian must appoint a solicitor for the child unless a solicitor has already been appointed (FPR PD16A).

The first directions hearing—The parties or their legal representatives must attend the first directions hearing unless the court directs otherwise (FPR 2010, r 14.8(4)). The hearing must be held within 4 weeks of the application being issued, unless the court otherwise directs (FPR 2010, r 14.7). At the first directions hearing the matters listed at FPR 2010, r 14.8(1) must be considered.

Request to dispense with parental consent—Where the applicant applies for the court to dispense with the consent of a parent or guardian to the child being placed for adoption, the applicant must (FPR 2010, r 14.9):

- give notice of the request in the application form (or at a later stage by filing a written request);
- file a statement of facts setting out a summary of the history of the case and any other facts to satisfy the court of the ground(s) relied upon to dispense with consent.

The final hearing (FPR 2010, r 14.16)—Any person who has been given notice of the final hearing may attend the hearing and be heard on the question of whether a placement order should be made. The court may direct any other person to attend the final hearing. Any member or employee of a party which is a local authority, adoption agency or other body may address the court if he is authorised to do so.

The court cannot make a placement order unless a legal representative of the applicant and also the child personally attend the final hearing. The court may, however, direct that the child need not attend the hearing.

Placement order application consolidated with care proceedings—A placement order application may be made during the currency of ongoing proceedings under CA 1989, Pt IV for a care or supervision order. In such circumstances the same court will consider both applications.

FPR 2010 do not make any reference to consolidated care and placement order proceedings. The implication is that the provisions of FPR 2010, both Pts 12 and 14 will apply. In particular, care must be taken to ensure that, when a placement order application is issued during the currency of CA 1989 proceedings, the additional requirements of FPR 2010, Pt 14 as to parties, documentation and reports are adhered to. Where the issue of adoption is already before the court in care proceedings, it is not necessarily unfair for a placement application to be issued and heard after the start of the final hearing (*Re P-B (Placement Order)* [2007] 1 FLR 1106).

Where CA 1989 proceedings are pending in, or transferred to, a county court any related placement order application must be heard by a county court that is an adoption centre (C(AP)O 1991, art 17).

Form of order—FPR 2010 do not establish a standard form of order for a placement order.

Duration of a placement order (s 21(4))—A placement order remains in force until the first of the following takes place:

–   the placement order is revoked by a court order made under ACA 2002, s 24; or
–   an adoption order is made; or
–   the child marries or forms a civil partnership; or
–   the child attains 18.

Directions for assessment of child (s 22(6))—See notes to CA 1989, s 38(6).

23 Varying placement orders

(1) The court may vary a placement order so as to substitute another local authority for the local authority authorised by the order to place the child for adoption.

(2) The variation may only be made on the joint application of both authorities.

Defined terms—"adoption (in relation to Chapter 4 of Part 1)": s 66; "child": ss 49(5), 144; "court", "local authority": s 144; "placement order": s 21.

Application for change of local authority—Another local authority may be substituted for the local authority named in a placement order on a joint application made by both authorities. The application must be made to a family proceedings court (C(AP)O 1991, Art 3(1)(r)) and is governed by FPR 2010, Pt 18.

24 Revoking placement orders

(1) The court may revoke a placement order on the application of any person.

(2) But an application may not be made by a person other than the child or the local authority authorised by the order to place the child for adoption unless –

(a)   the court has given leave to apply, and
(b)   the child is not placed for adoption by the authority.

(3) The court cannot give leave under subsection (2)(a) unless satisfied that there has been a change in circumstances since the order was made.

(4) If the court determines, on an application for an adoption order, not to make the order, it may revoke any placement order in respect of the child.

(5) Where –

(a)   an application for the revocation of a placement order has been made and has not been disposed of, and
(b)   the child is not placed for adoption by the authority,

the child may not without the court's leave be placed for adoption under the order.

Defined terms—"adoption (in relation to Chapter 4 of Part 1)": s 66; "adoption order": s 46(1); "child": ss 49(5), 144; "court", "local authority": s 144; "placement order": s 21; "placing, or placed, for adoption": ss 18(5), 19(4).

Revocation of a placement order—The child or local authority may apply to revoke a placement order at any time; however other persons (including the parents) may not apply to revoke the order unless they meet each of the following pre-conditions:

– the court gives leave, which it cannot do unless it is satisfied that there has been a change of circumstances since the order was made, and
– the child is not yet placed for adoption by the authority.

Where an application for revocation is pending and the child is not placed for adoption, the child may not be placed for adoption by the authority without the court's leave.

At the final adoption hearing, if the court decides not to make an adoption order and further considers that the child should not even be placed for adoption, it has the discretion to revoke the placement order. If, however, the court decides that the child should still be placed for a future adoption, then it may order the placement order to continue.

"Placed for adoption" (s 24(2)(b))—A child is not "placed for adoption" merely because the current foster carer may be interested in adopting him. There are three stages that are required before a child can be said to be "placed for adoption" with a prospective adopter, namely:

(a) adoption panel recommend child suitable for adoption;
(b) obtaining a placement order; and
(c) adoption panel recommend that the child is adopted by identified prospective adopters (who have been approved as adopters) (*Re S (Placement Order: Revocation)* [2009] 1 FLR 503).

A child will be "placed for adoption" once all of the above formalities have been completed and introductory meetings between the child and the prospective adopters have commenced (*R (W) v Brent LBC* [2010] 1 FLR 1914).

"Change in circumstances" (s 24(3))—The phrase "change of circumstances" appears throughout ACA 2002 as the threshold justifying reopening an issue that has previously been determined by consent or court order. While the statute does not require that the change is "significant", the Court of Appeal in *Re P (Adoption: Leave Provisions)* [2007] 2 FLR 1069 held that any such change must be of a nature and degree sufficient to reopen consideration of the issue. In the absence of a decision on appeal or by the first instance court that reopens previously determined factual issues, the production of "fresh evidence" is not capable of amounting to a "change in circumstances" within the meaning of s 47 (*Re M (Adoption: Leave to Oppose)* [2010] 1 FLR 238).

Grant of leave to apply to revoke placement order (s 24(2)(a))—The grant of leave is a two-stage process:

(a) has there been a change in circumstances?
(b) if so, should leave to apply be granted?

When exercising discretion at the second stage under s 24(3), the child's welfare is not the paramount consideration (in contrast to where a parent seeks leave to oppose an adoption – see **Leave to oppose adoption** under s 47(5)), and the court must consider whether the proposed application has "a real prospect of success". In considering the prospects of success the court will almost always include an analysis of the child's welfare (*M v Warwickshire County Council* [2008] 1 FLR 1093). The question that the court should ask is "whether in all the circumstances, including the parent's prospects of success in securing revocation of the placement order and the child's interests, leave should be given" (*NS-H v Kingston upon Hull City Council and MC* [2008] 2 FLR 918). The prospects of success relate to achieving revocation of the placement order and not necessarily the return of the child to the parent's care (*NS-H v Kingston*, above).

Procedure—The respondents to an application to revoke a placement order will be the parties to the proceedings leading to the placement order which it is sought to have revoked and any person in whose favour there is provision for contact (FPR 2010, r 14.3). The application will be governed by FPR 2010, Pt 14. The application should be made to the court which made the placement order (C(AP)O 1991, art 3C(2)).

Embargo on placement where revocation application pending (s 24(5))—The embargo upon placement only applies where a substantive revocation application is pending, and does not apply to a preliminary application for leave to apply (*Re F (Placement Order)* [2008] 2 FLR 550). In *Re F* (above) the Court of Appeal stressed that it is the court (not the local authority) that should control arrangements and held that good practice required that:

(1) the parent should request that the local authority undertake not to take any steps to place the child with prospective adopters, pending the hearing of his ACA 2002, s 24 leave application; and
(2) the local authority should explain if its plans are at an advanced stage and about to be implemented. The LA could then apply to the Court, on short notice, for leave to place the child for adoption under s 24(5).

25 Parental responsibility

(1) This section applies while –
  (a) a child is placed for adoption under section 19 or an adoption agency is authorised to place a child for adoption under that section, or
  (b) a placement order is in force in respect of a child.

(2) Parental responsibility for the child is given to the agency concerned.

(3) While the child is placed with prospective adopters, parental responsibility is given to them.

(4) The agency may determine that the parental responsibility of any parent or guardian, or of prospective adopters, is to be restricted to the extent specified in the determination.

Defined terms—"adoption (in relation to Chapter 4 of Part 1)": s 66; "adoption agency": s 2(1); "child": ss 49(5), 144; "guardian": s 144; "parental responsibility": s 3 of the 1989 Act; "placement order": s 21; "placing, or placed, for adoption": ss 18(5), 19(4).

26 Contact

(1) On an adoption agency being authorised to place a child for adoption, or placing a child for adoption who is less than six weeks old, any provision for contact under the 1989 Act ceases to have effect and any contact activity direction relating to contact with the child is discharged.

(2) While an adoption agency is so authorised or a child is placed for adoption –
  (a) no application may be made for any provision for contact under that Act, but
  (b) the court may make an order under this section requiring the person with whom the child lives, or is to live, to allow the child to visit or stay with the person named in the order, or for the person named in the order and the child otherwise to have contact with each other.

(3) An application for an order under this section may be made by –
  (a) the child or the agency,
  (b) any parent, guardian or relative,
  (c) any person in whose favour there was provision for contact under the 1989 Act which ceased to have effect by virtue of subsection (1),
  (d) if a residence order was in force immediately before the adoption agency was authorised to place the child for adoption or (as the case may be) placed the child for adoption at a time when he was less than six weeks old, the person in whose favour the order was made,
  (e) if a person had care of the child immediately before that time by virtue of an order made in the exercise of the High Court's inherent jurisdiction with respect to children, that person,
  (f) any person who has obtained the court's leave to make the application.

(4) When making a placement order, the court may on its own initiative make an order under this section.

(5) This section does not prevent an application for a contact order under section 8 of the 1989 Act being made where the application is to be heard together with an application for an adoption order in respect of the child.

(6) In this section, "contact activity direction" has the meaning given by section 11A of the 1989 Act and "provision for contact under the 1989 Act" means a contact order under section 8 of that Act or an order under section 34 of that Act (parental contact with children in care).

Amendments—CAA 2006, s 15(1), Sch 2, paras 13, 14.

Defined terms—"the 1989 Act": s 2(5); "adoption (in relation to Chapter 4 of Part 1)": s 66; "adoption agency": s 2(1); "adoption order": s 46(1); "by virtue of": s 144; "child": ss 49(5), 144; "court", "guardian": s 144; "placement order": s 21; "placing, or placed, for adoption": ss 18(5), 19(4); "relative": s 144, read with s 1(8); "residence order": s 8(1) of the 1989 Act.

Contact where an adoption agency is authorised to place a child for adoption—Upon an adoption agency being authorised to place a child for adoption, any contact order under CA 1989, s 8 or s 34 ceases to have effect (s 26(1)). Further, no application for a contact order under CA 1989 can be made while an agency is authorised to place for adoption (save where the contact application is to be heard with an application for adoption) (s 26(2),(5)). These provisions apply whether the placement is authorised as a result of parental consent or under a placement order.

Before making a placement order, the court is under a duty to consider the arrangements made or proposed by the agency for allowing contact with the child and to invite the parties to the proceedings to comment on those arrangements (s 27(4)). The agency must take into account the wishes and feelings of the parent (and, if appropriate, a father without parental responsibility), the advice of the adoption panel and the adoption welfare check list in ACA 2002, s 1 before making a decision on contact (Adoption Agency Regulations 2005, reg 46).

While an agency is authorised to place for adoption, or a child is so placed, the court may make an order under ACA 2002, s 26, requiring the person with whom the child lives, or is to live, to allow the child to visit or stay with the person named in the order, or for the person named in the order and the child otherwise to have contact with each other. When making the placement order, the court may of its own initiative make an order for contact (s 26(4)).

When considering whether to make a s 26 order the court must afford paramount consideration to the child's welfare in accordance with ACA 2002, s 1. A s 26 contact order has effect while the adoption agency is authorised to place the child for adoption but may be varied or revoked by the court on an application by the child, the agency or the person named in the order (s 27(1)).

In *Re P (Placement Orders: Parental Consent)* [2008] 2 FLR 625 the Court of Appeal held that the previous case-law relating to post-adoption contact needs to be revisited in the context of the court's jurisdiction to control contact under ACA 2002, s 26; issues of contact will be a matter for the court, rather than for the local authority with or without the prospective adopters.

The terms of any s 26 order may be departed from by agreement between the agency and any person for whose contact with the child the order provides, provided that the child (if of sufficient age and understanding) agrees, the prospective adopters agree and relevant persons have been informed of the change (Adoption Agency Regulations 2005, reg 47(2)).

Where the court is satisfied that the local authority is committed to the level of contact endorsed by the court, an order for contact is unnecessary (*Re C (Contact)* [2008] 1 FLR 1151).

Adoption agency power to refuse to allow contact—Unlike the position that applies under a care order, there is no requirement upon an adoption agency to allow contact between the child and any person unless such contact is stipulated in an order under ACA 2002, s 26. Consequently, unless to do so would be in conflict with provision in a s 26 order, the agency may refuse contact without having to seek the court's approval.

In addition, an adoption agency is permitted to refuse to allow contact that would otherwise be required by virtue of a s 26 order, without first obtaining a court order, if it is satisfied that it is necessary to do so in order to safeguard or promote the child's welfare and the refusal is decided upon as a matter of urgency and does not last for more than seven days (s 27(2)). The agency is under a duty to inform relevant individuals as soon as any decision to refuse contact is made (Adoption Agency Regulations 2005, reg 47).

Application for contact when placement for adoption authorised (s 26(3))—An application for a s 26 contact order may be made by (FPR 2010, r 14.3):

- the child;
- the agency;
- any parent or guardian or relative;
- any person in whose favour there was a CA contact order (which ceased to have effect under s 26(1));

–   the person with a residence order in force immediately before the adoption agency was authorised to place;
–   the person who had care of the child by an order under the High Court's inherent jurisdiction before the agency was authorised to place;
–   any person with the court's permission.

The procedure is governed by FPR 2010, Pt 14. An application for contact should be made to the court which made the placement order (C(AP)O 1991, art 3C(2)).

The respondents to an application for a s 26 contact order will be (FPR 2010, r 14.3):

–   The adoption agency authorised to place the child (or which has placed the child) for adoption;
–   The person with whom the child lives or is to live;
–   Each parent with parental responsibility for the child or guardian of the child;
–   The child where:
    (i)   the agency or a parent with parental responsibility order opposes the making of the contact order;
    (ii) he opposes the making of the contact order;
    (iii) existing provision for contact is to be revoked;
    (iv) relatives of the child do not agree to the arrangements for contact;
    (v)   he is suffering or is at risk of suffering "harm" within the meaning of CA 1989, s 31(9).

The court may at any time direct that a child, who is not already a respondent to proceedings be made a respondent where the child wishes to make an application or has evidence to give to the court, or a legal submission to make, which has not been given or made by any other party, or there are other special circumstances. The court may at any time direct that a person or body be made a respondent or be removed as a respondent (FPR 2010, r 14.3(2),(3)).

27   Contact: supplementary

(1) An order under section 26 –

(a) has effect while the adoption agency is authorised to place the child for adoption or the child is placed for adoption, but

(b) may be varied or revoked by the court on an application by the child, the agency or a person named in the order.

(2) The agency may refuse to allow the contact that would otherwise be required by virtue of an order under that section if –

(a) it is satisfied that it is necessary to do so in order to safeguard or promote the child's welfare, and

(b) the refusal is decided upon as a matter of urgency and does not last for more than seven days.

(3) Regulations may make provision as to –

(a) the steps to be taken by an agency which has exercised its power under subsection (2),

(b) the circumstances in which, and conditions subject to which, the terms of any order under section 26 may be departed from by agreement between the agency and any person for whose contact with the child the order provides,

(c) notification by an agency of any variation or suspension of arrangements made (otherwise than under an order under that section) with a view to allowing any person contact with the child.

(4) Before making a placement order the court must –

(a) consider the arrangements which the adoption agency has made, or proposes to make, for allowing any person contact with the child, and

(b) invite the parties to the proceedings to comment on those arrangements.

(5) An order under section 26 may provide for contact on any conditions the court considers appropriate.

Defined terms—"adoption (in relation to Chapter 4 of Part 1)": s 66; "adoption agency": s 2(1); "by virtue of": s 144; "child": ss 49(5), 144; "court": s 144; "placement order": s 21; "placing, or placed, for adoption": ss 18(5), 19(4); "regulations": s 144.

28 Further consequences of placement

(1) Where a child is placed for adoption under section 19 or an adoption agency is authorised to place a child for adoption under that section –

    (a) a parent or guardian of the child may not apply for a residence order unless an application for an adoption order has been made and the parent or guardian has obtained the court's leave under subsection (3) or (5) of section 47,

    (b) if an application has been made for an adoption order, a guardian of the child may not apply for a special guardianship order unless he has obtained the court's leave under subsection (3) or (5) of that section.

(2) Where –

    (a) a child is placed for adoption under section 19 or an adoption agency is authorised to place a child for adoption under that section, or

    (b) a placement order is in force in respect of a child,

then (whether or not the child is in England and Wales) a person may not do either of the following things, unless the court gives leave or each parent or guardian of the child gives written consent.

(3) Those things are –

    (a) causing the child to be known by a new surname, or

    (b) removing the child from the United Kingdom.

(4) Subsection (3) does not prevent the removal of a child from the United Kingdom for a period of less than one month by a person who provides the child's home.

Defined terms—"adoption (in relation to Chapter 4 of Part 1)": s 66; "adoption agency": s 2(1); "adoption order": s 46(1); "child": ss 49(5), 144; "consent (in relation to making adoption orders or placing for adoption)": s 52; "court", "guardian": s 144; "placement order": s 21; "placing, or placed, for adoption": ss 18(5) and 19(4); "residence order": s 8(1) of the 1989 Act.

Application to court that made placement order (C(AP)O 1991, art 3C(2))—An application to change a child's surname or remove him from the UK should be made to the court which made the placement order.

29 Further consequences of placement orders

(1) Where a placement order is made in respect of a child and either –

    (a) the child is subject to a care order, or

    (b) the court at the same time makes a care order in respect of the child,

the care order does not have effect at any time when the placement order is in force.

(2) On the making of a placement order in respect of a child, any order mentioned in section 8(1) of the 1989 Act, and any supervision order in respect of the child, ceases to have effect.

(3) Where a placement order is in force –

    (a) no prohibited steps order, residence order or specific issue order, and

    (b) no supervision order or child assessment order,

may be made in respect of the child.

(4) Subsection (3)(a) does not apply in respect of a residence order if –

    (a) an application for an adoption order has been made in respect of the child, and

    (b) the residence order is applied for by a parent or guardian who has obtained the court's leave under subsection (3) or (5) of section 47 or by any other person who has obtained the court's leave under this subsection.

(5) Where a placement order is in force, no special guardianship order may be made in respect of the child unless –

(a)   an application has been made for an adoption order, and

(b)   the person applying for the special guardianship order has obtained the court's leave under this subsection or, if he is a guardian of the child, has obtained the court's leave under section 47(5).

(6) Section 14A(7) of the 1989 Act applies in respect of an application for a special guardianship order for which leave has been given as mentioned in subsection (5)(b) with the omission of the words "the beginning of the period of three months ending with".

(7) Where a placement order is in force –

(a)   section 14C(1)(b) of the 1989 Act (special guardianship: parental responsibility) has effect subject to any determination under section 25(4) of this Act,

(b)   section 14C(3) and (4) of the 1989 Act (special guardianship: removal of child from UK etc) does not apply.

Defined terms—"the 1989 Act": s 2(5); "adoption (in relation to Chapter 4 of Part 1)": s 66; "adoption order": s 46(1); "care order": s 105(1) of the 1989 Act; "child": ss 49(5) and 144; "child assessment order": s 43(2) of the 1989 Act; "court", "guardian": s 144; "parental responsibility": s 3 of the 1989 Act; "placement order": s 21; "prohibited steps order": s 8(1) of the 1989 Act; "residence order": s 8(1) of the 1989 Act; "specific issue order": s 8(1) of the 1989 Act; "supervision order": s 31(11) of the 1989 Act.

Removal of children who are or may be placed by adoption agencies

30   General prohibitions on removal

(1) Where –

(a)   a child is placed for adoption by an adoption agency under section 19, or

(b)   a child is placed for adoption by an adoption agency and either the child is less than six weeks old or the agency has at no time been authorised to place the child for adoption,

a person (other than the agency) must not remove the child from the prospective adopters.

(2) Where –

(a)   a child who is not for the time being placed for adoption is being provided with accommodation by a local authority, and

(b)   the authority have applied to the court for a placement order and the application has not been disposed of,

only a person who has the court's leave (or the authority) may remove the child from the accommodation.

(3) Where subsection (2) does not apply, but –

(a)   a child who is not for the time being placed for adoption is being provided with accommodation by an adoption agency, and

(b)   the agency is authorised to place the child for adoption under section 19 or *would be so authorised* if any consent to placement under that section had not been withdrawn,

a person (other than the agency) must not remove the child from the accommodation.

(4) This section is subject to sections 31 to 33 but those sections do not apply if the child is subject to a care order.

(5) This group of sections (that is, this section and those sections) apply whether or not the child in question is in England and Wales.

(6) This group of sections does not affect the exercise by any local authority or other person of any power conferred by any enactment, other than section 20(8) of the 1989 Act (removal of children from local authority accommodation).

(7) This group of sections does not prevent the removal of a child who is arrested.

(8) A person who removes a child in contravention of this section is guilty of an offence and liable on summary conviction to imprisonment for a term not exceeding three months, or a fine not exceeding level 5 on the standard scale, or both.

Defined terms—"the 1989 Act": s 2(5); "adoption (in relation to Chapter 4 of Part 1)": s 66; "adoption agency": s 2(1); "care order": s 105(1) of the 1989 Act; "child": ss 49(5), 144; "consent (in relation to making adoption orders or placing for adoption)": s 52; "court", "enactment", "local authority": s 144; "placement order": s 21; "placing, or placed, for adoption": ss 18(5), 19(4).

Application in pending placement proceedings—Where an application for a placement order is pending, proceedings for leave to remove a child under ACA 2002, s 30(2)(b) must be started in the court where the placement order application is pending (ATPO 2008, art 8(2)).

31 Recovery by parent etc where child not placed or is a baby

(1) Subsection (2) applies where –

  (a) a child who is not for the time being placed for adoption is being provided with accommodation by an adoption agency, and

  (b) the agency would be authorised to place the child for adoption under section 19 if consent to placement under that section had not been withdrawn.

(2) If any parent or guardian of the child informs the agency that he wishes the child to be returned to him, the agency must return the child to him within the period of seven days beginning with the request unless an application is, or has been, made for a placement order and the application has not been disposed of.

(3) Subsection (4) applies where –

  (a) a child is placed for adoption by an adoption agency and either the child is less than six weeks old or the agency has at no time been authorised to place the child for adoption, and

  (b) any parent or guardian of the child informs the agency that he wishes the child to be returned to him,

unless an application is, or has been, made for a placement order and the application has not been disposed of.

(4) The agency must give notice of the parent's or guardian's wish to the prospective adopters who must return the child to the agency within the period of seven days beginning with the day on which the notice is given.

(5) A prospective adopter who fails to comply with subsection (4) is guilty of an offence and liable on summary conviction to imprisonment for a term not exceeding three months, or a fine not exceeding level 5 on the standard scale, or both.

(6) As soon as a child is returned to an adoption agency under subsection (4), the agency must return the child to the parent or guardian in question.

Defined terms—"adoption (in relation to Chapter 4 of Part 1)": s 66; "adoption agency": s 2(1); "child": ss 49(5), 144; "consent (in relation to making adoption orders or placing for adoption)": s 52; "guardian", "notice": s 144; "placement order": s 21; "placing, or placed, for adoption": ss 18(5), 19(4).

PART II

32 Recovery by parent etc where child placed and consent withdrawn

(1) This section applies where –

- (a) a child is placed for adoption by an adoption agency under section 19, and
- (b) consent to placement under that section has been withdrawn,

unless an application is, or has been, made for a placement order and the application has not been disposed of.

(2) If a parent or guardian of the child informs the agency that he wishes the child to be returned to him –

- (a) the agency must give notice of the parent's or guardian's wish to the prospective adopters, and
- (b) the prospective adopters must return the child to the agency within the period of 14 days beginning with the day on which the notice is given.

(3) A prospective adopter who fails to comply with subsection (2)(b) is guilty of an offence and liable on summary conviction to imprisonment for a term not exceeding three months, or a fine not exceeding level 5 on the standard scale, or both.

(4) As soon as a child is returned to an adoption agency under this section, the agency must return the child to the parent or guardian in question.

(5) Where a notice under subsection (2) is given, but –

- (a) before the notice was given, an application for an adoption order (including a Scottish or Northern Irish adoption order), special guardianship order or residence order, or for leave to apply for a special guardianship order or residence order, was made in respect of the child, and
- (b) the application (and, in a case where leave is given on an application to apply for a special guardianship order or residence order, the application for the order) has not been disposed of,

the prospective adopters are not required by virtue of the notice to return the child to the agency unless the court so orders.

Defined terms—"adoption (in relation to Chapter 4 of Part 1)": s 66; "adoption agency": s 2(1); "adoption order": s 46(1); "by virtue of": s 144; "child": ss 49(5), 144; "consent (in relation to making adoption orders or placing for adoption)": s 52; "court", "guardian", "Northern Irish adoption order", "notice": s 144; "placement order": s 21; "placing, or placed, for adoption": ss 18(5), 19(4); "residence order": s 8(1) of the 1989 Act.

33 Recovery by parent etc where child placed and placement order refused

(1) This section applies where –

- (a) a child is placed for adoption by a local authority under section 19,
- (b) the authority have applied for a placement order and the application has been refused, and
- (c) any parent or guardian of the child informs the authority that he wishes the child to be returned to him.

(2) The prospective adopters must return the child to the authority on a date determined by the court.

(3) A prospective adopter who fails to comply with subsection (2) is guilty of an offence and liable on summary conviction to imprisonment for a term not exceeding three months, or a fine not exceeding level 5 on the standard scale, or both.

(4) As soon as a child is returned to the authority, they must return the child to the parent or guardian in question.

Defined terms—"adoption (in relation to Chapter 4 of Part 1)": s 66; "child": ss 49(5), 144; "court", "guardian", "local authority": s 144; "placement order": s 21; "placing, or placed, for adoption": ss 18(5), 19(4).

34 Placement orders: prohibition on removal

(1) Where a placement order in respect of a child –

  (a) is in force, or

  (b) has been revoked, but the child has not been returned by the prospective adopters or remains in any accommodation provided by the local authority,

a person (other than the local authority) may not remove the child from the prospective adopters or from accommodation provided by the authority.

(2) A person who removes a child in contravention of subsection (1) is guilty of an offence.

(3) Where a court revoking a placement order in respect of a child determines that the child is not to remain with any former prospective adopters with whom the child is placed, they must return the child to the local authority within the period determined by the court for the purpose; and a person who fails to do so is guilty of an offence.

(4) Where a court revoking a placement order in respect of a child determines that the child is to be returned to a parent or guardian, the local authority must return the child to the parent or guardian as soon as the child is returned to the authority or, where the child is in accommodation provided by the authority, at once.

(5) A person guilty of an offence under this section is liable on summary conviction to imprisonment for a term not exceeding three months, or a fine not exceeding level 5 on the standard scale, or both.

(6) This section does not affect the exercise by any local authority or other person of a power conferred by any enactment, other than section 20(8) of the 1989 Act.

(7) This section does not prevent the removal of a child who is arrested.

(8) This section applies whether or not the child in question is in England and Wales.

Defined terms—"the 1989 Act": s 2(5); "child": ss 49(5), 144; "court", "enactment", "guardian", "local authority": s 144; "placement order": s 21; "placing, or placed, for adoption": ss 18(5), 19(4).

35 Return of child in other cases

(1) Where a child is placed for adoption by an adoption agency and the prospective adopters give notice to the agency of their wish to return the child, the agency must –

  (a) receive the child from the prospective adopters before the end of the period of seven days beginning with the giving of the notice, and

  (b) give notice to any parent or guardian of the child of the prospective adopters' wish to return the child.

(2) Where a child is placed for adoption by an adoption agency, and the agency –

  (a) is of the opinion that the child should not remain with the prospective adopters, and

  (b) gives notice to them of its opinion,

the prospective adopters must, not later than the end of the period of seven days beginning with the giving of the notice, return the child to the agency.

(3) If the agency gives notice under subsection (2)(b), it must give notice to any parent or guardian of the child of the obligation to return the child to the agency.

(4) A prospective adopter who fails to comply with subsection (2) is guilty of an offence and liable on summary conviction to imprisonment for a term not exceeding three months, or a fine not exceeding level 5 on the standard scale, or both.

(5) Where –

    (a)   an adoption agency gives notice under subsection (2) in respect of a child,

    (b)   before the notice was given, an application for an adoption order (including a Scottish or Northern Irish adoption order), special guardianship order or residence order, or for leave to apply for a special guardianship order or residence order, was made in respect of the child, and

    (c)   the application (and, in a case where leave is given on an application to apply for a special guardianship order or residence order, the application for the order) has not been disposed of,

prospective adopters are not required by virtue of the notice to return the child to the agency unless the court so orders.

(6) This section applies whether or not the child in question is in England and Wales.

Defined terms—"adoption (in relation to Chapter 4 of Part 1)": s 66; "adoption agency": s 2(1); "adoption order": s 46(1); "by virtue of": s 144; "child": ss 49(5), 144; "court", "guardian", "Northern Irish adoption order", "notice": s 144; "placing, or placed, for adoption": ss 18(5), 19(4); "residence order": s 8(1) of the 1989 Act.

Return of child in emergency—Where a local authority seek the urgent return of the child (in a period shorter than the 7-day notice required by s 35(1)) or a return without any notice, the proper course is for the matter to come before the family court via an application for an emergency protection order or an interim care order (*DL and ML v Newham London Borough Council and Secretary of State for Education* [2011] 2 FLR 1033).

Removal of children in non-agency cases

36 Restrictions on removal

(1) At any time when a child's home is with any persons ("the people concerned") with whom the child is not placed by an adoption agency, but the people concerned –

    (a)   have applied for an adoption order in respect of the child and the application has not been disposed of,

    (b)   have given notice of intention to adopt, or

    (c)   have applied for leave to apply for an adoption order under section 42(6) and the application has not been disposed of,

a person may remove the child only in accordance with the provisions of this group of sections (that is, this section and sections 37 to 40).

The reference to a child placed by an adoption agency includes a child placed by a Scottish or Northern Irish adoption agency.

(2) For the purposes of this group of sections, a notice of intention to adopt is to be disregarded if –

    (a)   the period of four months beginning with the giving of the notice has expired without the people concerned applying for an adoption order, or

    (b)   the notice is a second or subsequent notice of intention to adopt and was given during the period of five months beginning with the giving of the preceding notice.

(3) For the purposes of this group of sections, if the people concerned apply for leave to apply for an adoption order under section 42(6) and the leave is granted, the application for leave is not to be treated as disposed of until the period of three days beginning with the granting of the leave has expired.

(4) This section does not prevent the removal of a child who is arrested.

(5) Where a parent or guardian may remove a child from the people concerned in accordance with the provisions of this group of sections, the people concerned must at the request of the parent or guardian return the child to the parent or guardian at once.

(6) A person who –

    (a)   fails to comply with subsection (5), or

    (b)   removes a child in contravention of this section,

is guilty of an offence and liable on summary conviction to imprisonment for a term not exceeding three months, or a fine not exceeding level 5 on the standard scale, or both.

(7) This group of sections applies whether or not the child in question is in England and Wales.

PART II

Defined terms—"adoption agency": s 2(1); "adoption order": s 46(1); "child": ss 49(5), 144; "guardian", "Northern Irish adoption agency", "notice": s 144; "notice of intention to adopt": s 44(2); "placing, or placed, for adoption": ss 18(5), 19(4).

37 Applicants for adoption

If section 36(1)(a) applies, the following persons may remove the child –

    (a)   a person who has the court's leave,

    (b)   a local authority or other person in the exercise of a power conferred by any enactment, other than section 20(8) of the 1989 Act.

Defined terms—"the 1989 Act": s 2(5); "adoption (in relation to Chapter 4 of Part 1)": s 66; "child": ss 49(5), 144; "court", "enactment", "local authority": s 144.

38 Local authority foster parents

(1) This section applies if the child's home is with local authority foster parents.

(2) If –

    (a)   the child has had his home with the foster parents at all times during the period of five years ending with the removal and the foster parents have given notice of intention to adopt, or

    (b)   an application has been made for leave under section 42(6) and has not been disposed of,

the following persons may remove the child.

(3) They are –

    (a)   a person who has the court's leave,

    (b)   a local authority or other person in the exercise of a power conferred by any enactment, other than section 20(8) of the 1989 Act.

(4) If subsection (2) does not apply but –

    (a)   the child has had his home with the foster parents at all times during the period of one year ending with the removal, and

    (b)   the foster parents have given notice of intention to adopt,

the following persons may remove the child.

(5) They are –

    (a)   a person with parental responsibility for the child who is exercising the power in section 20(8) of the 1989 Act,

    (b)   a person who has the court's leave,

    (c)   a local authority or other person in the exercise of a power conferred by any enactment, other than section 20(8) of the 1989 Act.

39 Partners of parents

(1) This section applies if a child's home is with a partner of a parent and the partner has given notice of intention to adopt.

(2) If the child's home has been with the partner for not less than three years (whether continuous or not) during the period of five years ending with the removal, the following persons may remove the child –

(a) a person who has the court's leave,

(b) a local authority or other person in the exercise of a power conferred by any enactment, other than section 20(8) of the 1989 Act.

(3) If subsection (2) does not apply, the following persons may remove the child –

(a) a parent or guardian,

(b) a person who has the court's leave,

(c) a local authority or other person in the exercise of a power conferred by any enactment, other than section 20(8) of the 1989 Act.

40 Other non-agency cases

(1) In any case where sections 37 to 39 do not apply but –

(a) the people concerned have given notice of intention to adopt, or

(b) the people concerned have applied for leave under section 42(6) and the application has not been disposed of,

the following persons may remove the child.

(2) They are –

(a) a person who has the court's leave,

(b) a local authority or other person in the exercise of a power conferred by any enactment, other than section 20(8) of the 1989 Act.

Breach of restrictions on removal

41 Recovery orders

(1) This section applies where it appears to the court –

(a) that a child has been removed in contravention of any of the preceding provisions of this Chapter or that there are reasonable grounds for believing that a person intends to remove a child in contravention of those provisions, or

(b) that a person has failed to comply with section 31(4), 32(2), 33(2), 34(3) or 35(2).

(2) The court may, on the application of any person, by an order –

(a) direct any person who is in a position to do so to produce the child on request to any person mentioned in subsection (4),

(b) authorise the removal of the child by any person mentioned in that subsection,

  (c) require any person who has information as to the child's whereabouts to disclose that information on request to any constable or officer of the court,

  (d) authorise a constable to enter any premises specified in the order and search for the child, using reasonable force if necessary.

(3) Premises may only be specified under subsection (2)(d) if it appears to the court that there are reasonable grounds for believing the child to be on them.

(4) The persons referred to in subsection (2) are –

  (a) any person named by the court,

  (b) any constable,

  (c) any person who, after the order is made under that subsection, is authorised to exercise any power under the order by an adoption agency which is authorised to place the child for adoption.

(5) A person who intentionally obstructs a person exercising a power of removal conferred by the order is guilty of an offence and liable on summary conviction to a fine not exceeding level 3 on the standard scale.

(6) A person must comply with a request to disclose information as required by the order even if the information sought might constitute evidence that he had committed an offence.

(7) But in criminal proceedings in which the person is charged with an offence (other than one mentioned in subsection (8)) –

  (a) no evidence relating to the information provided may be adduced, and

  (b) no question relating to the information may be asked,

by or on behalf of the prosecution, unless evidence relating to it is adduced, or a question relating to it is asked, in the proceedings by or on behalf of the person.

(8) The offences excluded from subsection (7) are –

  (a) an offence under section 2 or 5 of the Perjury Act 1911 (false statements made on oath otherwise than in judicial proceedings or made otherwise than on oath),

  (b) an offence under section 44(1) or (2) of the Criminal Law (Consolidation) (Scotland) Act 1995 (false statements made on oath or otherwise than on oath).

(9) An order under this section has effect in relation to Scotland as if it were an order made by the Court of Session which that court had jurisdiction to make.

Defined terms—"adoption (in relation to Chapter 4 of Part 1)": s 66; "adoption agency": s 2(1); "child": ss 49(5), 144; "court", "information": s 144.

Scope—Sections 30–40 make provision with regard to the ability of those connected with a child to remove him from an adoption placement in various circumstances. By s 41 the court may make a recovery order in the event that a child has been removed in contravention of those provisions, or there are reasonable grounds for believing that a person intends to do so or a person has failed to comply with a request to return the child. A recovery order may direct that a person produce the child, or authorise a person to remove the child, or require information about the child's whereabouts or authorise a constable to enter premises to search for the child. It is a criminal offence to obstruct a person acting under a recovery order.

Preliminaries to adoption

42 Child to live with adopters before application

(1) An application for an adoption order may not be made unless –

  (a) if subsection (2) applies, the condition in that subsection is met,

  (b) if that subsection does not apply, the condition in whichever is applicable of subsections (3) to (5) applies.

(2) If –

   (a) the child was placed for adoption with the applicant or applicants by an adoption agency or in pursuance of an order of the High Court, or

   (b) the applicant is a parent of the child,

the condition is that the child must have had his home with the applicant or, in the case of an application by a couple, with one or both of them at all times during the period of ten weeks preceding the application.

(3) If the applicant or one of the applicants is the partner of a parent of the child, the condition is that the child must have had his home with the applicant or, as the case may be, applicants at all times during the period of six months preceding the application.

(4) If the applicants are local authority foster parents, the condition is that the child must have had his home with the applicants at all times during the period of one year preceding the application.

(5) In any other case, the condition is that the child must have had his home with the applicant or, in the case of an application by a couple, with one or both of them for not less than three years (whether continuous or not) during the period of five years preceding the application.

(6) But subsections (4) and (5) do not prevent an application being made if the court gives leave to make it.

(7) An adoption order may not be made unless the court is satisfied that sufficient opportunities to see the child with the applicant or, in the case of an application by a couple, both of them together in the home environment have been given –

   (a) where the child was placed for adoption with the applicant or applicants by an adoption agency, to that agency,

   (b) in any other case, to the local authority within whose area the home is.

(8) In this section and sections 43 and 44(1) –

   (a) references to an adoption agency include a Scottish or Northern Irish adoption agency,

   (b) references to a child placed for adoption by an adoption agency are to be read accordingly.

Defined terms—"adoption (in relation to Chapter 4 of Part 1)": s 66; "adoption agency": s 2(1); "adoption order": s 46(1); "child": ss 49(5), 144; "child placed for adoption by an adoption agency": s 18(5); "couple": s 144(4); "court", "local authority": s 144; "local authority foster parent": s 23(3) of the 1989 Act; "Northern Irish adoption agency": s 144; "partner, in relation to a parent of a child": s 144(7); "placing, or placed, for adoption": ss 18(5), 19(4).

"had his home with applicant" (s 42(2)–(5))—The question of where a child has had his home is one of fact. (*ECC v M* [2008] EWHC 332 (Fam)). For whether the "home" should be in England or Wales, see s 42(7). Even if the child is physically absent, he may still be held to have his home with the applicant(s) if they remain in effective parental control of him (*Re CSC (An Infant)* [1960] 1 WLR 304; *Re KT (Adoption Application)* (1993) Fam Law 567). There is no longer a statutory disregard for time in boarding school or hospital. Where s 42(7)(b) applies the "home" must be within a local authority area in England and Wales. Where, however, s 42(7)(a) applies (either to an adoption or an order under ACA 2002, s 84) there is no territorial restriction and the "home environment" may be outside England and Wales (*Re A (A Child)* [2009] 2 FLR 597 – on appeal from *Haringey London Borough Council v MA, JN, IA* [2008] 2 FLR 1857).

"application ... if court gives leave" (s 42(6))—When determining a leave application under ACA 2002, s 42(6) the child's welfare is not the paramount consideration and the court must consider whether the proposed application has "a real prospect of success"; this test applies to all categories of applicant. In considering the prospects of success, the court will almost always include an analysis of the child's welfare (*Re A; Coventry City Council v CC and A* [2008] 1 FLR 959, applying *M v Warwickshire County Council* [2008] 1 FLR 1093).

"sufficient opportunities to see the child ... in the home environment" (s 42(7))—This requirement, coupled with s 44, means that, where the child has not been placed for adoption by an adoption agency, the applicant must have a "home" within England and Wales (ie within the area of a local authority (as defined by s 144(1); *Re SL (Adoption: Home in Jurisdiction)* [2005] 1 FLR 118). In intercountry adoptions the court requires the child to have been resident in the UK for 12 months before it will entertain an application – see **Intercountry adoptions** under s 47 below.

43 Reports where child placed by agency

Where an application for an adoption order relates to a child placed for adoption by an adoption agency, the agency must –

(a) submit to the court a report on the suitability of the applicants and on any other matters relevant to the operation of section 1, and

(b) assist the court in any manner the court directs.

Defined terms—"adoption (in relation to Chapter 4 of Part 1)": s 66; "adoption agency": s 2(1); "child": ss 49(5), 144; "child placed for adoption by an adoption agency": s 18(5); "court": s 144; "placing, or placed, for adoption": ss 18(5), 19(4).

Adoption reports—The adoption agency or local authority must file a report on the suitability of the applicant to adopt a child within the timetable fixed by the court (FPR 2010, r 14.11(1),(2)). The reports must contain the matters set out in FPR PD14C. Any such report will be confidential (r 14.11(6)). The court may at any stage request a further report (r 14.11(4)).

44 Notice of intention to adopt

(1) This section applies where persons (referred to in this section as "proposed adopters") wish to adopt a child who is not placed for adoption with them by an adoption agency.

(2) An adoption order may not be made in respect of the child unless the proposed adopters have given notice to the appropriate local authority of their intention to apply for the adoption order (referred to in this Act as a "notice of intention to adopt").

(3) The notice must be given not more than two years, or less than three months, before the date on which the application for the adoption order is made.

(4) Where –

(a) if a person were seeking to apply for an adoption order, subsection (4) or (5) of section 42 would apply, but

(b) the condition in the subsection in question is not met,

the person may not give notice of intention to adopt unless he has the court's leave to apply for an adoption order.

(5) On receipt of a notice of intention to adopt, the local authority must arrange for the investigation of the matter and submit to the court a report of the investigation.

(6) In particular, the investigation must, so far as practicable, include the suitability of the proposed adopters and any other matters relevant to the operation of section 1 in relation to the application.

(7) If a local authority receive a notice of intention to adopt in respect of a child whom they know was (immediately before the notice was given) looked after by another local authority, they must, not more than seven days after the receipt of the notice, inform the other local authority in writing that they have received the notice.

(8) Where –

(a) a local authority have placed a child with any persons otherwise than as prospective adopters, and

(b) the persons give notice of intention to adopt,

the authority are not to be treated as leaving the child with them as prospective adopters for the purposes of section 18(1)(b).

(9) In this section, references to the appropriate local authority, in relation to any proposed adopters, are –

    (a)   in prescribed cases, references to the prescribed local authority,

    (b)   in any other case, references to the local authority for the area in which, at the time of giving the notice of intention to adopt, they have their home,

and "prescribed" means prescribed by regulations.

Defined terms—"adoption (in relation to Chapter 4 of Part 1)": s 66; "adoption agency": s 2(1); "adoption order": s 46(1); "child": ss 49(5), 144; "court", "local authority", "notice": s 144; "notice of intention to adopt": s 44(2); "placing, or placed, for adoption": ss 18(5), 19(4); "regulations": s 144.

"notice to the ... local authority" (s 44(2))—The relevant local authority is the one in whose area the applicant has his home at the time of giving notice. The applicant must therefore have a home within England and Wales at the time of giving notice (*Re SL (Adoption: Home in Jurisdiction)* [2005] 1 FLR 118). Notice, which must be in writing (s 144(1)), may be given by post (s 110). When notice has been given, the ability to remove the child from the home is governed by ss 36–40. Upon receipt of a s 44 notice in relation to a child from abroad living with non-agency prospective adopters, the local authority should immediately inform the DfE and clarify whether the intention to adopt was disclosed to an immigration officer. If it was not, or if the applicants are not able to produce written evidence of parental consent, or the applicants have not previously obtained a home study report, then any adoption application should be transferred to the High Court and listed for urgent directions before a judge (*Re R (Inter-Country Adoptions: Practice)* [1999] 1 FLR 1042).

"appropriate local authority" (s 44(2))—The "appropriate local authority" for the purpose of a s 44 notice either, where the applicant(s) no longer have a home in England or Wales, the authority where they last had such a home, or (in any other case) the authority for the area in which the applicants are living at the time that the notice is given (The Local Authority (Adoption) (Miscellaneous Provisions) Regulations 2005, reg 3 and The Local Authority (Non-agency Adoptions) (Wales) Regulations 2005, reg 3).

45 Suitability of adopters

(1) Regulations under section 9 may make provision as to the matters to be taken into account by an adoption agency in determining, or making any report in respect of, the suitability of any persons to adopt a child.

(2) In particular, the regulations may make provision for the purpose of securing that, in determining the suitability of a couple to adopt a child, proper regard is had to the need for stability and permanence in their relationship.

Defined terms—"adoption agency": s 2(1); "child": ss 49(5), 144; "couple": s 144(4); "regulations": s 144.

Adoption reports—See note to s 43.

The making of adoption orders

46 Adoption orders

(1) An adoption order is an order made by the court on an application under section 50 or 51 giving parental responsibility for a child to the adopters or adopter.

(2) The making of an adoption order operates to extinguish –

    (a)   the parental responsibility which any person other than the adopters or adopter has for the adopted child immediately before the making of the order,

    (b)   any order under the 1989 Act or the Children (Northern Ireland) Order 1995 (SI 1995/755 (NI 2)),

(c)   any order under the Children (Scotland) Act 1995 other than an excepted order, and

(d)   any duty arising by virtue of an agreement or an order of a court to make payments, so far as the payments are in respect of the adopted child's maintenance cr upbringing for any period after the making of the adoption order.

"Excepted order" means an order under section 9, 11(1)(d) or 13 of the Children (Scotland) Act 1995 or an exclusion order within the meaning of section 76(1) of that Act.

(3)   An adoption order –

(a)   does not affect parental responsibility so far as it relates to any period before the making of the order, and

(b)   in the case of an order made on an application under section 51(2) by the partner of a parent of the adopted child, does not affect the parental responsibility of that parent or any duties of that parent within subsection (2)(d).

(4)   Subsection (2)(d) does not apply to a duty arising by virtue of an agreement –

(a)   which constitutes a trust, or

(b)   which expressly provides that the duty is not to be extinguished by the making of an adoption order.

(5)   An adoption order may be made even if the child to be adopted is already an adopted child.

(6)   Before making an adoption order, the court must consider whether there should be arrangements for allowing any person contact with the child; and for that purpose the court must consider any existing or proposed arrangements and obtain any views of the parties to the proceedings.

Defined terms—"the 1989 Act": s 2(5); "adoption order": s 46(1); "by virtue of": s 144; "child": ss 49(5), 144; "child to be adopted, adopted child": s 49(5); "court": s 144; "parental responsibility": s 3 of the 1989 Act; "partner, in relation to a parent of a child": s 144(7).

Scope—This section describes the legal consequences of the making of an adoption order and makes it clear that a child may be adopted more than once. Once made, an adoption order is irrevocable save in wholly exceptional circumstances (*Re M (Minors) (Adoption)* [1991] 1 FLR 458) or on the child's subsequent legitimation (s 55).

Procedure for making an adoption application—The relevant procedure is contained in FPR 2010, Pt 14. Adoption proceedings are subject to ATPO 2008; for international adoptions, see ATPO 2008, arts 6(c),(d) and 11(2), *President's Guidance: Adoption Proceedings: Intercountry Adoption Centres* (24 November 2008) (see Part V) and *PD: Allocation and Transfer of Proceedings* (3 November 2008).

"extinguish" (s 46(2))—One effect of this provision is that a natural parent ceases to be regarded as a parent under CA 1989, and can only apply for subsequent s 8 orders with the leave of the court (see CA 1989, ss 9, 10; *M v C and Calderdale Metropolitan Borough Council* [1993] 1 FLR 505). A natural parent will require leave to apply for a contact order post-adoption (see **Meaning of parent** under CA 1989, s 10).

"any order under the 1989 Act" (s 46(2)(b))—If it is intended that a pre-adoption CA 1989 order (e g a s 8 contact order) is to continue after adoption, a fresh order will have to be made after the adoption order.

Arrangements for contact (s 46(6))—Before making an adoption order the court must consider whether there should be arrangements for allowing any person contact with the child. Where adopters are willing to agree to contact, it is unnecessary to make an order that binds the adopters to their agreement (*Re T (Adoption: Contact)* [1995] 2 FLR 251). A contact order made in relation to an adopted child is made under CA 1989, s 8 and is governed by the welfare checklist in CA 1989, s 1(3). In consequence, *Re P (Placement Orders: Parental Consent)* [2008] 2 FLR 625 relating to contact under a placement order does not affect the application and the approach described in *Re R (Adoption: Contact)* [2006] 1 FLR 373 should be followed to the effect that it is "extremely unusual" to impose on adoptive parents some obligation that they were unwilling, voluntarily, to assume (*Oxfordshire County Council v X, Y and J* [2011] 1 FLR 272).

Adoption orders and any arrangements for contact are intended to be permanent and final; it is therefore incompatible with that intention for known potential issues for contact to be left unresolved when making an adoption order (*X and Y v A Local Authority (Adoption: Procedure)* [2009] 2 FLR 984).

In *Re G (Adoption: Contact)* [2003] 1 FLR 270, Ward LJ summarised the modern approach to contact and adoption:

"the benefit [of contact] ... comes from the children simply knowing who the natural parental figures are. It is to remove the sense of ogre, as they reach adolescence and begin to search for their own identity, with the double crisis not only of adolescence itself but of coming to grips with the fact that they are adopted. That is why current research is in favour of some contact in adoption."

In *Down Lisburn Health and Social Services Trust v H* [2007] 1 FLR 121 the House of Lords reviewed the approach to post-adoption contact.

Once an adoption order has been made, a fundamental question such as contact, even if confined to indirect contact, should only be subsequently reopened if there is some fundamental change in circumstances (*Re C (A Minor) (Adopted Child: Contact)* [1993] 2 FLR 431). In some cases, it may be necessary to transfer the case to the High Court, but that should not be the general rule; an application for leave to apply for contact should be served on the adoption agency (*Re T (Adopted Children: Contact)* [1995] 2 FLR 792). A natural family member, in order to obtain leave to apply for contact, must satisfy the court that any decision of the adopters to oppose contact is sufficiently contrary to the best interests of the child, or sufficiently unreasonable, to warrant the court overriding the discretion concerning contact conferred on the adopters by the adoption order (*Re T (Adoption: Contact)* [2011] 1 FLR 1805). Leave to apply is likely to be granted where adopters totally resile from an earlier agreement on contact (*Re R (Adoption: Contact)* [2006] 1 FLR 373).

Effect of adoption—See ss 66–76. The court does not have an inherent power to set aside an adoption order, but an appeal may be allowed in an exceptional case where there has been a breach of natural justice against a natural parent (*Re K (Adoption and Wardship)* [1997] 2 FLR 221; *Re B (Adoption: Jurisdiction to Set Aside)* [1995] 2 FLR 1). The effect of setting aside an adoption order is that the legal position in respect of parental responsibility reverts to the status immediately preceding the adoption order (*Re W (Adoption Order: Set Aside and Leave to Oppose)* [2011] 1 FLR 2153).

47 Conditions for making adoption orders

(1) An adoption order may not be made if the child has a parent or guardian unless one of the following three conditions is met; but this section is subject to section 52 (parental etc consent).

(2) The first condition is that, in the case of each parent or guardian of the child, the court is satisfied –

    (a)   that the parent or guardian consents to the making of the adoption order,

    (b)   that the parent or guardian has consented under section 20 (and has not withdrawn the consent) and does not oppose the making of the adoption order, or

    (c)   that the parent's or guardian's consent should be dispensed with.

(3) A parent or guardian may not oppose the making of an adoption order under subsection (2)(b) without the court's leave.

(4) The second condition is that –

    (a)   the child has been placed for adoption by an adoption agency with the prospective adopters in whose favour the order is proposed to be made,

    (b)   either –

        (i)   the child was placed for adoption with the consent of each parent or guardian and the consent of the mother was given when the child was at least six weeks old, or

        (ii)   the child was placed for adoption under a placement order, and

    (c)   no parent or guardian opposes the making of the adoption order.

(5) A parent or guardian may not oppose the making of an adoption order under the second condition without the court's leave.

(6) (*applies to Scotland and Northern Ireland only*)

(7) The court cannot give leave under subsection (3) or (5) unless satisfied that there has been a change in circumstances since the consent of the parent or guardian was given or, as the case may be, the placement order was made.

(8) An adoption order may not be made in relation to a person who is or has been married.

(8A) An adoption order may not be made in relation to a person who is or has been a civil partner.

(9) An adoption order may not be made in relation to a person who has attained the age of 19 years.

(10) (*applies to Scotland only*)

Amendments—CPA 2004, s 79(1),(3); SI 2011/1740.

Modifications—Section 47(6) modified for certain purposes (SI 2010/2469).

Defined terms—"adoption (in relation to Chapter 4 of Part 1)": s 66; "adoption agency": s 2(1); "adoption order": s 46(1); "by virtue of": s 144; "child": ss 49(5), 144; "consent (in relation to making adoption orders or placing for adoption)": s 52; "court", "guardian": s 144; "placement order": s 21; "placing, or placed, for adoption": ss 18(5), 19(4).

Scope—If the child has a parent or guardian, an adoption order may only be made if one of three conditions is met. The first condition is based upon parental consent to adoption being either given or dispensed with. The second condition is based upon the fact that the child has been placed for adoption. The third condition relates to the child being free for adoption in Scotland or N Ireland or under an AA 1976 freezing order (ACA 2002, Sch 4). Where a parent has given an earlier consent to placement or to adoption (which has not been validly withdrawn), or there has been a placement order, the parent may only oppose the making of an adoption order if there has been a subsequent change of circumstances and the court gives leave to oppose (s 47(7)).

First condition: parental consent (s 47(2))—The court has jurisdiction to make an adoption order if it is satisfied in the case of each parent or guardian of the child:

(a) that the parent or guardian consents to the making of the adoption order:
  – unconditionally; and
  – with full understanding of what is involved; or
(b) that the parent or guardian has given advance consent to adoption under ACA 2002, s 20 (and has not withdrawn that consent) and does not oppose the making of the adoption order; or
(c) that the parent or guardian's consent should be dispensed with under one of the two statutory grounds in s 52.

A parent who has given advance consent to adoption may only oppose the adoption order if a court is satisfied that there has been a change of circumstances and has given leave to oppose (s 47(3),(7)).

It should be noted that, in the case of an application for an adoption order, the consent of the parent or guardian is required to the particular adoption order which the court is being asked to make (even if the identity of the applicants is not known to the parent).

The provisions of ACA 2002, s 1, which require the court to give paramount consideration to the welfare of the child throughout his life, apply to a decision upon whether consent should be dispensed with (s 1(7)).

Second condition: placed for adoption (s 47(4))—The court has jurisdiction to make an adoption order if it is satisfied that the child has been placed for adoption by an adoption agency and either:

(a) the child was placed for adoption with the consent of each parent or guardian and the consent of the mother was given when the child was at least 6 weeks old; or
(b) the child was placed for adoption under a placement order;

and no parent or guardian opposes the making of the adoption order.

Leave to oppose adoption (s 47(5))—Where the second condition applies, a parent may only oppose the adoption order if a court is satisfied that there has been a change of circumstances and has granted leave to oppose (s 47(5),(7)). For **"change in circumstances"** see note to s 24(3). Where a change of circumstances is established, the child's welfare must be the paramount consideration when deciding whether to grant leave under s 47(5) (*Re P (Adoption: Leave Provisions)* [2007] 2 FLR 1069; as clarified in *M v Warwickshire County Council* [2008] 1 FLR 1093). The test is stringent and is not based upon there merely being "a real possibility" that the court may be persuaded not to grant an adoption (*Re W (Adoption Order: Set Aside and Leave to Oppose)* [2011] 1 FLR 2153). Due process must be observed and documents relevant to the leave to oppose issue must be disclosed to the applicant parent (*Re T (Adoption Order)* [2013] 1 FLR 360). If leave to oppose is given, the case can only be proved using the first condition.

Parent—Section 52(6) defines the term "parent" as meaning, in relation to a child, "a parent having parental responsibility for the child under the CA 1989". The following people are therefore included within the meaning of "parent" for the purposes of the Act:

– the child's natural mother (unless parental responsibility has been removed by order of a foreign court or a previous adoption order);
– the child's natural father:
    (i) if he was married to the child's mother at the time of the child's birth;
    (ii) if he subsequently married the child's mother (Legitimacy Act 1976, s 2; FLRA 1987);
    (iii) if after 1 December 2003 he is registered as the child's father on the birth certificate (CA 1989, s 4);
    (iv) if he has obtained an order granting him parental responsibility with respect to the child (CA 1989, ss 4(1), 11(1));
    (v) if, before the commencement of CA 1989, he has obtained an order granting him parental rights and duties in respect of the child as that order will be deemed to be an order under CA 1989, s 4 granting him parental responsibility for the child;
    (vi) if he has acquired parental responsibility for the child under a parental responsibility agreement made with the mother (CA 1989, s 4);
– the child's adoptive parent if he has been the subject of a previous adoption. (In those circumstances, the child's natural parents' consent would not be relevant).

Firm evidence is required to prove that a parent has died (*Re K (Adoption and Wardship)* [1997] 2 FLR 221).

Where an order made in a foreign jurisdiction purports to remove the parental rights of a parent (including a mother), it will be for the court in England and Wales to determine whether the consequence of the order is that the parent no longer has parental responsibility for the child (the court will require expert evidence relating to the foreign jurisdiction) (*Re AMR (Adoption: Procedure)* [1999] 2 FLR 807. See also *Re AGN (Adoption: Foreign Adoption)* [2000] 2 FLR 431).

Father without parental responsibility—The consent of the father of a child, who was not married to the child's mother, or deemed to be so married, at the time of the child's birth is not required within adoption proceedings, unless he has obtained parental responsibility for the child. The term "parent" within ACA 2002 means, in relation to a child, "a parent having parental responsibility" for the child under CA 1989 (ACA 2002, s 52(6)).

A father without parental responsibility may be made a respondent to the adoption application (FPR 2010, r 14.3(3). See also *Re L (A Minor) (Adoption: Procedure)* [1991] 1 FLR 171).

Where the father of the child does not have parental responsibility for the child and the father's identity is known to the adoption agency and the agency is satisfied it is appropriate to do so, the agency must (Adoption Agency Regulations 2005, reg 14) –

(a) carry out in respect of the father the requirements of Adoption Agency Regulations 2005, reg 14(1)(a),(b)(i) and (iii) and (c) as if they applied to him, unless the agency is satisfied that the requirements have been carried out in respect of the father by another agency; and
(b) ascertain so far as possible whether the father –
    (i) wishes to acquire parental responsibility for the child under CA 1989, s 4; or
    (ii) intends to apply for a residence order or contact order with respect to the child under CA 1989, s 8 or, where the child is subject to a care order, an order under CA 1989, s 34.

Where there is doubt about the appropriateness of contacting the father, a direction from the court may be sought. In any event the court may direct that the father be given notice of any court proceedings; such a direction may be sought before issuing any proceedings (*Re C (Adoption: Disclosure to Father)* [2006] 2 FLR 589; FPR 2010, r 14.21); such an application can be made under FPR 2010, Pt 19 rather than issuing care proceedings (*Re C (A Child) v XYZ County Council* [2008] 1 FLR 1294). Where a mother, who alone knows his identity, continues to refuse to identify the father then there is in reality nothing more that can or should be done (*Re C (A Child) v XYZ County Council*, above).

As a matter of practice, where the father has established "family life" with respect to the child (ECHR 1950, Art 8), the court is likely to give him notice of the proceedings unless there are strong reasons to the contrary (*Re H; Re G (Adoption: Consultation of Unmarried Fathers)* [2001] 1 FLR 646; *Keegan v Ireland* (No 16969/90) (1994) 18 EHRR 342, ECtHR).

Guardian—A child's "guardian", for the purpose of adoption proceedings, has the same meaning as in CA 1989, and includes a special guardian (s 144(1)). The definition of "guardian" does not automatically include the father without parental responsibility.

Where a person, or institution, has been appointed to be the child's guardian by an order made in a foreign jurisdiction, it is for the court in England and Wales to determine whether the "guardian" is a guardian within the meaning of the adoption legislation and the court will require expert evidence relating to the foreign jurisdiction (*Re AMR (Adoption: Procedure)* [1999] 2 FLR 807; *Re AGN (Adoption: Foreign Adoption)* [2000] 2 FLR 431).

When considering whether a person or authority in another jurisdiction is or is not to be treated as a guardian under ACA 2002, ss 47 and 52, the court should consider (per *Re J (Adoption: Consent of Foreign Public Authority)* [2002] 2 FLR 618):

- the extent to which that person's duties, rights and responsibilities equated to those of a person (a) who had parental responsibility in English Law; and (b) whose consent to an adoption order had to be given or dispensed with;
- having particular regard to the purposes of ss 47 and 52, whether in all the circumstances that person's consent to an adoption order should be given or dispensed with before an adoption order was made.

Form and proof of consent—The relevant consent of a parent or guardian must be given in the relevant form required by FPR PD5A (Forms A100–A106) or a form to like effect (FPR 2010, r 14.10(1)). A document signifying consent that is witnessed in accordance with the rules is admissible as proof of the signature of the person giving consent without further proof (ACA 2002, s 104(1)).

Intercountry adoptions—For detailed guidance on inter-country adoptions, go to *www.education.gov.uk/childrenandyoungpeople/families/intercountryadoption*. On being notified of a foreign child's presence a local authority should immediately attempt to contact the natural parents to ascertain their views; if it appears that natural parents do not consent, the local authority should immediately inform the DfE and the Home Office; where the applicants cannot produce written parental consent to adoption (and a certified English translation), the application should be transferred to the High Court for urgent directions; there should be personal service on the natural parents (if necessary via the relevant British Embassy); the children's guardian should make early contact with the natural parents; where it appears that the natural parents oppose the adoption the court should consider dismissing the application summarily at an early directions hearing.

Dispensing with consent (s 47(2)(c))—See notes to s 52.

Adoption order not available over the age of 19 years (s 47(9))—An adoption application must be made before the person to be adopted's 18th birthday (s 49(4)) but the order may be made after that date but before the 19th birthday. See **"attained the age of"** under s 50.

Child under 6 weeks (s 47(4)(b)(i))—It is possible validly to place a child for adoption with maternal consent at under 6 weeks old, but s 47(4)(b)(i) expressly provides that such consent is not sufficient to satisfy the second ("placed for adoption") condition; consequently the adoption application will be under the first condition (with parental consent being determined at the time of that hearing) (*Local Authority v GC* [2009] 1 FLR 299).

48 Restrictions on making adoption orders

(1) The court may not hear an application for an adoption order in relation to a child, where a previous application to which subsection (2) applies made in relation to the child by the same persons was refused by any court, unless it appears to the court that, because of a change in circumstances or for any other reason, it is proper to hear the application.

(2) This subsection applies to any application –

(a)   for an adoption order or a Scottish or Northern Irish adoption order, or
(b)   for an order for adoption made in the Isle of Man or any of the Channel Islands.

Defined terms—"adoption (in relation to Chapter 4 of Part 1)": s 66; "adoption order": s 46(1); "child": ss 49(5), 144; "court", "Northern Irish adoption order": s 144.

Procedure in respect of ACA 2002, s 48—If s 48 applies, as soon as practicable after an adoption application has been issued, the court must consider whether it is proper to hear the application (FPR 2010, r 14.6(1)(a)(i)).

49 Applications for adoption

(1) An application for an adoption order may be made by –

    (a) a couple, or
    (b) one person,

but only if it is made under section 50 or 51 and one of the following conditions is met.

(2) The first condition is that at least one of the couple (in the case of an application under section 50) or the applicant (in the case of an application under section 51) is domiciled in a part of the British Islands.

(3) The second condition is that both of the couple (in the case of an application under section 50) or the applicant (in the case of an application under section 51) have been habitually resident in a part of the British Islands for a period of not less than one year ending with the date of the application.

(4) An application for an adoption order may only be made if the person to be adopted has not attained the age of 18 years on the date of the application.

(5) References in this Act to a child, in connection with any proceedings (whether or not concluded) for adoption, (such as "child to be adopted" or "adopted child") include a person who has attained the age of 18 years before the proceedings are concluded.

Defined terms—"British Islands": Interpretation Act 1978, Sch 1; "adoption (in relation to Chapter 4 of Part 1)": s 66; "adoption order": s 46(1); "child": ss 49(5), 144; "child to be adopted, adopted child": s 49(5); "couple": s 144(4).

Conditions precedent to making an adoption application (s 49)—An adoption order may only be made if the circumstances comply with either s 50 (adoption by couple) or s 51 (adoption by one person) and one of the two conditions in this section relating to domicile or habitual residence is met. For discussion of "domicile", see under DMPA 1973, s 5 below.

First condition: domicile (s 49(2))—At least one of the couple, or the single applicant, must be domiciled in a part of the British Islands.

Second condition: habitual residence (s 49(3))—As an alternative to the first condition, both of the couple, or the single applicant, must have been habitually resident in a part of the British Islands for a period of not less than 1 year before making the application. For "**habitual residence**", see under CACA 1985, Sch 1, Art 4, below.

Adoption of a person aged over 18 years (s 49(4) and (5))—An adoption application must be made before the person to be adopted's 18th birthday (s 49(4)) but the order may be made after that date but before the 19th birthday. See "**attained the age of**" under s 50.

50 Adoption by couple

(1) An adoption order may be made on the application of a couple where both of them have attained the age of 21 years.

(2) An adoption order may be made on the application of a couple where –

    (a) one of the couple is the mother or the father of the person to be adopted and has attained the age of 18 years, and
    (b) the other has attained the age of 21 years.

Defined terms—"adoption (in relation to Chapter 4 of Part 1)": s 66; "adoption order": s 46(1); "couple": s 144(4).

"a couple" (s 50)—In ACA 2002 "a couple" means a married couple, or civil partners or two people (whether of differing sexes or the same sex) living as partners in an enduring family relationship (s 144(4)). Two people, one of whom is the other's parent, grandparent, sister, brother, aunt or uncle, are not "a couple" for these purposes (s 144(5),(6)). Potential adopters require assessment in accordance with the Suitability of Adopters Regulations 2005.

"attained the age of ..." (s 50(1),(2))—Age is attained at the commencement of the relevant anniversary of the person's date of birth (FLRA 1969, s 9(1)).

"father" (s 50(2)(a))—The term "parent" is restricted to a parent with parental responsibility for the limited purpose of the consent provisions (s 52(3),(6)); it therefore seems that the term "father" in s 50 includes a father without parental responsibility.

Validity of the marriage or civil partnership—The validity of the applicant's marriage is a factor which the court will consider. Documentary evidence of their marriage must be filed with the application (FPR PD5A, Form A58). The adoption agency is required to report on the applicant's marital status and the stability of their relationship, together with details of any previous marriages (FPR PD14C). The court may make an adoption order in favour of married applicants even where the couple have separated after the adoption application has been issued (*Re WM (Adoption: Non-patrial)* [1997] 1 FLR 132). If an adoption order is made in favour of a couple whose marriage is later found to be bigamous, the adoption order will be regarded as valid until the court makes an order setting it aside (*Re F (Infants) (Adoption Order: Validity)* [1977] Fam 165).

Step-parents—Provision in AA 1976, s 14(3) requiring a specific approach to step-parent applications was repealed in 1991. However, this repeal does not imply that earlier cautionary dicta concerning step-parent adoptions no longer apply (*Re PJ (Adoption: Practice on Appeal)* [1998] 2 FLR 252; see also *Re G (Adoption Order)* [1999] 1 FLR 400). It is still considered comparatively unusual for an adoption order to be made in favour of a step-parent in a contested case, particularly where the parents have been married, even where the child consents (*Re B (Adoption: Father's Objections)* [1999] 2 FLR 215). Although a step-parent adoption does amount to an interference with a father's right to family life, the decision falls within the state's margin of appreciation and the adverse affects on the father are not disproportionate to protecting the child's interests. There is no breach of ECHR 1950, Art 8 (*Söderbäck v Sweden* [1999] 1 FLR 250). This approach is likely to continue under ACA 2002, with the court looking to other ways in which a step-parent may acquire parental responsibility for the child. For "step-parent as sole applicant" see note to s 51.

51 Adoption by one person

(1) An adoption order may be made on the application of one person who has attained the age of 21 years and is not married or a civil partner.

(2) An adoption order may be made on the application of one person who has attained the age of 21 years if the court is satisfied that the person is the partner of a parent of the person to be adopted.

(3) An adoption order may be made on the application of one person who has attained the age of 21 years and is married if the court is satisfied that –

(a) the person's spouse cannot be found,
(b) the spouses have separated and are living apart, and the separation is likely to be permanent, or
(c) the person's spouse is by reason of ill-health, whether physical or mental, incapable of making an application for an adoption order.

(3A) An adoption order may be made on the application of one person who has attained the age of 21 years and is a civil partner if the court is satisfied that –

(a) the person's civil partner cannot be found,
(b) the civil partners have separated and are living apart, and the separation is likely to be permanent, or
(c) the person's civil partner is by reason of ill-health, whether physical or mental, incapable of making an application for an adoption order.

(4) An adoption order may not be made on an application under this section by the mother or the father of the person to be adopted unless the court is satisfied that –

(a) the other natural parent is dead or cannot be found,

    (b)   by virtue of the provisions specified in subsection (5), there is no other parent, or

    (c)   there is some other reason justifying the child's being adopted by the applicant alone,

and, where the court makes an adoption order on such an application, the court must record that it is satisfied as to the fact mentioned in paragraph (a) or (b) or, in the case of paragraph (c), record the reason.

(5) The provisions referred to in subsection (4)(b) are –

    (a)   section 28 of the Human Fertilisation and Embryology Act 1990 (disregarding subsections (5A) to (5I) of that section), or

    (b)   sections 34 to 47 of the Human Fertilisation and Embryology Act 2008 (disregarding sections 39, 40 and 46 of that Act).

Amendments—CPA 2004, s 79(1),(4),(5); Human Fertilisation and Embryology (Deceased Fathers) Act 2003, s 2(1), Sch, para 18; HFEA 2008, Sch 6, para 39.

Defined terms: "partner", s 144(7); "adoption (in relation to Chapter 4 of Part 1)": s 66; "adoption order": s 46(1); "by virtue of": s 144; "child": ss 49(5), 144; "court": s 144.

Adoption by one person (s 51)—A sole applicant may obtain an adoption order if he is over 21 years old and if:

(a) he is neither married nor a civil partner; or
(b) he is the partner of a parent of one of the child's parent (in which case he is the sole adopter, but that parent's status and parental responsibility is not affected by the adoption (ss 46(3)(b), 67(2)); or
(c) he is married or a civil partner but the spouse or partner cannot be found or is for health reasons incapable of applying, or the couple are permanently separated.

"attained the age of ..." (s 51)—See note to s 50. The age limit of 21 years applies to all sole applicants, even if they are the child's mother or father.

Adoption by parent (s 51(4))—Where the applicant relies upon "some other reason justifying the child's being adopted by the applicant alone", that reason must be sufficient to outweigh the adverse consequences an adoption order may have by reason of the exclusion of the other parent from the child's life. The other reason, which is likely to be exceptional, and which will depend on the circumstances of each case, does not have to be comparable with the death or disappearance of the other parent. Before making an order, the court must consider alternative orders under CA 1989; an adoption order is not to be used simply to prevent inappropriate intervention by the other parent (*Re B (Adoption: Natural Parent)* [2002] 1 FLR 196). For entitlement to property on such an adoption, see s 67(4).

Placement and adoption: general

52 Parental etc consent

(1) The court cannot dispense with the consent of any parent or guardian of a child to the child being placed for adoption or to the making of an adoption order in respect of the child unless the court is satisfied that –

    (a)   the parent or guardian cannot be found or lacks capacity (within the meaning of the Mental Capacity Act 2005) to give consent, or

    (b)   the welfare of the child requires the consent to be dispensed with.

(2) The following provisions apply to references in this Chapter to any parent or guardian of a child giving or withdrawing –

    (a)   consent to the placement of a child for adoption, or

    (b)   consent to the making of an adoption order (including a future adoption order).

(3) Any consent given by the mother to the making of an adoption order is ineffective if it is given less than six weeks after the child's birth.

(4) The withdrawal of any consent to the placement of a child for adoption, or of any consent given under section 20, is ineffective if it is given after an application for an adoption order is made.

(5) "Consent" means consent given unconditionally and with full understanding of what is involved; but a person may consent to adoption without knowing the identity of the persons in whose favour the order will be made.

(6) "Parent" (except in subsections (9) and (10) below) means a parent having parental responsibility.

(7) Consent under section 19 or 20 must be given in the form prescribed by rules, and the rules may prescribe forms in which a person giving consent under any other provision of this Part may do so (if he wishes).

(8) Consent given under section 19 or 20 must be withdrawn –

    (a)   in the form prescribed by rules, or

    (b)   by notice given to the agency.

(9) Subsection (10) applies if –

    (a)   an agency has placed a child for adoption under section 19 in pursuance of consent given by a parent of the child, and

    (b)   at a later time, the other parent of the child acquires parental responsibility for the child.

(10) The other parent is to be treated as having at that time given consent in accordance with this section in the same terms as those in which the first parent gave consent.

Amendments—MCA 2005, s 67(1), Sch 6, para 45.

Defined terms—"adoption (in relation to Chapter 4 of Part 1)": s 66; "adoption order": s 46(1); "child": ss 49(5), 144; "consent (in relation to making adoption orders or placing for adoption)": s 52; "court", "guardian", "notice": s 144; "parental responsibility": s 3 of the 1989 Act; "placing, or placed, for adoption": ss 18(5), 19(4); "rules": s 144; "lacks capacity": MCA 2005, s 2.

Dispensing with consent (s 52(1))—Dispensing with agreement involves the court in a two stage process:

(a) is adoption in the best interests of the child?

(b) If so, is a ground for dispensing with agreement established?

Parent—See note to s 47.

Father without parental responsibility—See note to s 47.

Guardian—See note to s 47.

"welfare of the child requires the consent to be dispensed with" (s 52(1)(b))—The question for the court on this point is not "is adoption in the child's best interests?", but "does the child's welfare require consent to adoption to be dispensed with?". In *Re P (Placement Orders: Parental Consent)* [2008] 2 FLR 625 the Court of Appeal held that the word "requires" has a connotation of the imperative (ie what is demanded rather than what is merely optional or reasonable or desirable). What has to be shown is that the child's welfare throughout his life "requires" adoption as opposed to something short of adoption. A child's circumstances may "require" statutory intervention, perhaps may even "require" the indefinite or long-term removal of the child from the family and his or her placement with strangers, but that is not to say that the same circumstances will necessarily "require" that the child be adopted. The question, at the end of the day, is whether what is "required" is adoption. But this does not mean that there is some enhanced welfare test to be applied in cases of adoption. The vital difference is simply that between s 1 of the 1989 Act and s 1 of the 2002 Act. *Re P* has been endorsed by the Supreme Court in *ANS v ML (Scotland)* [2012] UKSC 30 in relation to identical Scottish legislation. The Supreme Court held that for an outcome to be "required" meant that it was "necessary", that is that "there is an overriding requirement that the adoption proceed for the sake of the child's welfare"; on such an interpretation the statutory provision is compatible with the ECHR.

Form and proof of consent—See note to s 47.

Intercountry adoption—See note to s 47.

Procedure for dispensing with consent (FPR 2010, r 14.9)—Where the applicant is asking the court to dispense with the consent of any parent or guardian of a child to:

-   the child being placed for adoption;
-   the making of an adoption order (except a Convention adoption order); or
-   the making of an order facilitating the adoption of the child abroad (ACA 2002, s 84)

the applicant must:

(a)   give notice of the request in the application form or at any later stage by filing a written request setting out the reasons for the request; and
(b)   file a statement of facts file setting out a summary of the history of the case and any other facts to satisfy the court of the ground(s) relied upon to dispense with consent.

On receipt of the notice a court officer will inform the parent or guardian of the request and send a copy of the statement of facts to them and to any children's guardian, reporting officer or children and family reporter.

If the application relates to the parent being incapable of giving consent, the court must consider whether to appoint a litigation friend for the parent or guardian under FPR 2010, Pt 15.

53 Modification of 1989 Act in relation to adoption

(1) Where –

(a)   a local authority are authorised to place a child for adoption, or
(b)   a child who has been placed for adoption by a local authority is less than six weeks old,

regulations may provide for the following provisions of the 1989 Act to apply with modifications, or not to apply, in relation to the child.

(2) The provisions are –

(a)   section 22(4)(b), (c) and (d) and (5)(b) (duty to ascertain wishes and feelings of certain persons),
(b)   paragraphs 15 and 21 of Schedule 2 (promoting contact with parents and parents' obligation to contribute towards maintenance).

(3) Where a registered adoption society is authorised to place a child for adoption or a child who has been placed for adoption by a registered adoption society is less than six weeks old, regulations may provide –

(a)   for section 61 of that Act to have effect in relation to the child whether or not he is accommodated by or on behalf of the society,
(b)   for subsections (2)(b) to (d) and (3)(b) of that section (duty to ascertain wishes and feelings of certain persons) to apply with modifications, or not to apply, in relation to the child.

(4) Where a child's home is with persons who have given notice of intention to adopt, no contribution is payable (whether under a contribution order or otherwise) under Part 3 of Schedule 2 to that Act (contributions towards maintenance of children looked after by local authorities) in respect of the period referred to in subsection (5).

(5) That period begins when the notice of intention to adopt is given and ends if –

(a)   the period of four months beginning with the giving of the notice expires without the prospective adopters applying for an adoption order, or
(b)   an application for such an order is withdrawn or refused.

(6) In this section, "notice of intention to adopt" includes notice of intention to apply for a Scottish or Northern Irish adoption order.

Defined terms—"the 1989 Act": s 2(5); "adoption (in relation to Chapter 4 of Part 1)": s 66; "adoption order": s 46(1); "adoption society": s 2(5); "child": ss 49(5), 144; "local authority", "Northern Irish adoption order", "notice": s 144; "notice of intention to adopt": s 44(2); "placing, or placed, for adoption": ss 18(5), 19(4); "registered adoption society": s 2(2); "regulations": s 144.

54 Disclosing information during adoption process

Regulations under section 9 may require adoption agencies in prescribed circumstances to disclose in accordance with the regulations prescribed information to prospective adopters.

Defined terms—"adoption (in relation to Chapter 4 of Part 1)": s 66; "information", "regulations": s 144.

55 Revocation of adoptions on legitimation

(1) Where any child adopted by one natural parent as sole adoptive parent subsequently becomes a legitimated person on the marriage of the natural parents, the court by which the adoption order was made may, on the application of any of the parties concerned, revoke the order.

(2) In relation to an adoption order made by a magistrates' court, the reference in subsection (1) to the court by which the order was made includes a court acting for the same local justice area.

Amendments—Courts Act 2003, s 109(1), Sch 8, para 412.

Defined terms—"adoption (in relation to Chapter 4 of Part 1)": s 66; "adoption order": s 46(1); "child": ss 49(5), 144; "court": s 144.

Procedure—An application to revoke an adoption order under s 55 is governed by FPR 2010, Pt 18.

****

Chapter 4
Status of Adopted Children

66 Meaning of adoption in Chapter 4

(1) In this Chapter "adoption" means –

    (a)   adoption by an adoption order or a Scottish or Northern Irish adoption order,

    (b)   adoption by an order made in the Isle of Man or any of the Channel Islands,

    (c)   an adoption effected under the law of a Convention country outside the British Islands, and certified in pursuance of Article 23(1) of the Convention (referred to in this Act as a "Convention adoption"),

    (d)   an overseas adoption, or

    (e)   an adoption recognised by the law of England and Wales and effected under the law of any other country;

and related expressions are to be interpreted accordingly.

(2) But references in this Chapter to adoption do not include an adoption effected before the day on which this Chapter comes into force (referred to in this Chapter as "the appointed day").

(3) Any reference in an enactment to an adopted person within the meaning of this Chapter includes a reference to an adopted child within the meaning of Part 4 of the Adoption Act 1976.

Defined terms—"adoption (in relation to Chapter 4 of Part 1)": s 66; "adoption order": s 46(1); "appointed day (in relation to Chapter 4 of Part 1)": s 66(2); "child": ss 49(5), 144; "child to be adopted, adopted child": s 49(5); "the Convention": s 144; "Convention adoption": s 66(1)(c); "Convention country", "enactment", "Northern Irish adoption order": s 144; "overseas adoption": s 87.

Pre-30 December 2005 adoptions—For adoptions effected before 30 December 2005, AA 1976, Pt IV remains in force (ACA 2002, Sch 5).

"Convention adoption" (s 66(1)(c))—A Convention adoption is an adoption within the terms of the 1993 Hague Convention on Protection of Children and Cooperation with respect to Intercountry

Adoption. The Convention is essentially a framework setting out minimum standards for the control and regulation of the flow of children between States for adoption. It has been signed by 52 States and ratified, or acceded to, by a further 10 States (for an up-to-date list of Convention States, see *www.hcch.net/index*). The Hague Convention aims to ensure that intercountry adoption takes place in the best interests of the child, puts in place a system of co-operation between those States that have implemented the Convention, and ensures that adoption orders made under the Convention are recognised in all Hague Convention countries. Anyone wishing to adopt under the Hague Convention in the UK must comply with AFER 2005, Pt 3, Ch 1.

The UK Government has issued advisory guidance on Convention adoptions (available at *www.education.gov.uk/childrenandyoungpeople/families/intercountryadoption*).

For a full discussion of Convention adoptions, see *Children: Law and Practice* Division D, Section 6 (Jordan Publishing Ltd).

"overseas adoption" (s 66(1)(d))—An "overseas adoption" ranks automatically as an adoption order, without the need to institute court proceedings. Specification of overseas adoptions has been made by the Adoption (Designation of Overseas Adoptions) Order 1973. The Order covers adoptions made by statute law (and not customary or common law) in any of 39 Commonwealth countries and UK dependent territories or 23 other countries named in the Schedule (not set out here).

"an adoption recognised by the law of England and Wales ..." (s 66(1)(e))—The effect of recognition is that the foreign adoption will rank as an adoption, so far as it relates to the status of the child, as if it had been made by an adoption order in England and Wales. Certain adoptions made in a jurisdiction outside England and Wales are recognised automatically as being adoption orders, without the need to initiate court proceedings either to obtain an adoption order or to establish the status of the adoption order made abroad.

The following are automatically recognised adoption orders:

(a) adoption orders made in Scotland, Northern Ireland, Isle of Man or the Channel Islands;
(b) "overseas adoptions";
(c) Convention adoption orders.

Any other adoption order made abroad will only be recognised as valid in England and Wales if it satisfies the criteria for recognition at common law. The key questions when considering whether or not to recognise a foreign adoption under common law are:

(a) Was the adoption obtained wholly lawfully in the foreign jurisdiction?
(b) If so, did the concept of adoption in that jurisdiction substantially conform with the English concept? and
(c) If so, was there any public policy consideration that should mitigate against recognition?

(*Re T and M (Adoption)* [2011] 1 FLR 1487; see also *Re N (Recognition of Foreign Adoption Order)* [2010] 1 FLR 1102.)

"Overseas adoptions" or Convention adoptions may be registered as adoptions by application to the Registrar General under Adopted Children and Adoption Contact Registers Regulations 2005 (ACA 2002, Sch 1, para 3(5)).

A foreign adoption which is neither automatically recognised, nor recognised at common law, will not be treated as a valid adoption. In those circumstances, it will be necessary for an application for an adoption order to be made in England and Wales.

Application to court for declaration as to status of adopted child—Any person whose status as an adopted child of any person depends on whether he has been validly adopted by that person by either a Convention adoption, an overseas adoption or an adoption recognised at common law may apply to the court for a declaration that the applicant either is or is not, for the purposes of ACA 2002, s 66, the adopted child of that person (FLA 1986, s 57(1),(2)). The application is made under the FPR 2010, Pt 19 procedure in the High Court or a county court (FPR 2010, rr 8.18–8.21) (see also under those rules)). The fact that the "child" has been adopted and is now an adult, does not prevent a court making a declaration of parentage with regard to the adopted person's natural father; indeed, the modern approach to adoption would support an adopted person having full and sound information about their background (*M v W (Declaration of Parentage)* [2007] 2 FLR 270).

67 Status conferred by adoption

(1) An adopted person is to be treated in law as if born as the child of the adopters or adopter.

(2) An adopted person is the legitimate child of the adopters or adopter and, if adopted by –

(a) a couple, or

(b) one of a couple under section 51(2),

is to be treated as the child of the relationship of the couple in question.

(3) An adopted person –

(a) if adopted by one of a couple under section 51(2), is to be treated in law as not being the child of any person other than the adopter and the other one of the couple, and

(b) in any other case, is to be treated in law, subject to subsection (4), as not being the child of any person other than the adopters or adopter;

but this subsection does not affect any reference in this Act to a person's natural parent or to any other natural relationship.

(4) In the case of a person adopted by one of the person's natural parents as sole adoptive parent, subsection (3)(b) has no effect as respects entitlement to property depending on relationship to that parent, or as respects anything else depending on that relationship.

(5) This section has effect from the date of the adoption.

(6) Subject to the provisions of this Chapter and Schedule 4, this section –

(a) applies for the interpretation of enactments or instruments passed or made before as well as after the adoption, and so applies subject to any contrary indication, and

(b) has effect as respects things done, or events occurring, on or after the adoption.

Defined terms—"adoption (in relation to Chapter 4 of Part 1)": s 66; "child": ss 49(5), 144; "couple": s 144(4); "enactment": s 144.

Status conferred by adoption—The effect of this section combined with s 46 is that upon the making of an adoption order, the adopters are given parental responsibility for the child, with the order effectively extinguishing the parental responsibility of any other person (together with any existing orders regarding the child) and the child is treated in law as if born as the child of the adopter(s) and of no other person.

The only exception to this effect is where the partner of one of the child's parents adopts as a sole applicant under s 51(2) (or an equivalent foreign adoption – *Re N (Recognition of Foreign Adoption Order)* [2010] 1 FLR 1102). In such circumstances the said parent retains parental responsibility and the status of parent (ss 46(3)(b), 67(2),(3)), while the other parent loses parental responsibility and parental status as in a normal adoption. References to a child's "natural parent" are unaffected (s 67(3)).

Convention adoptions that are not "full" adoptions—Section 88 modifies the effect of s 67(3) (eradication of parental status) in relation to certain Convention adoptions. A UK adoption order achieves total severance of the legal tie between a child and his natural family and is a "full" adoption. Adoption orders made in some Convention states do not necessarily achieve a complete severance of all ties with the natural family; such adoptions are referred to as "simple" adoptions.

In order to be able to reflect the differences between a full or simple adoption in a Convention case the High Court may direct that ACA 2002, s 67(3), which provides that the child shall be treated in law as if he were not the child of any person other than the adopter(s), shall not apply, or shall not apply to such extent as may be specified by the court. Under ACA 2002, s 88 such a direction may be given where the court is satisfied:

– that under the law of the country in which the adoption was effected the adoption was not a full adoption;

– that the consents of the child and other persons or institutions whose consent is necessary for adoption referred to in Arts 4(c) and (d) of the Hague Convention have not been given for a full adoption, or that the UK is not the receiving State (within the meaning of Art 2 of the Convention); and

– that it would be more favourable to the adopted child for such a direction to be given.

An application for a s 88 direction may be made by the adopted child, the adopters, any parent or any other parent and is governed by FPR 2010, Pt 14. Form A62 (or one to like effect) must be used and the respondents will be the adopters, the parents, the adoption agency, local authority and the Attorney-General (FPR 2010, r 14.3).

68 Adoptive relatives

(1) A relationship existing by virtue of section 67 may be referred to as an adoptive relationship, and –

    (a)   an adopter may be referred to as an adoptive parent or (as the case may be) as an adoptive father or adoptive mother,

    (b)   any other relative of any degree under an adoptive relationship may be referred to as an adoptive relative of that degree.

(2) Subsection (1) does not affect the interpretation of any reference, not qualified by the word "adoptive", to a relationship.

(3) A reference (however expressed) to the adoptive mother and father of a child adopted by –

    (a)   a couple of the same sex, or

    (b)   a partner of the child's parent, where the couple are of the same sex,

is to be read as a reference to the child's adoptive parents.

Defined terms—"by virtue of": s 144; "child": ss 49(5), 144; "couple": s 144(4); "partner, in relation to a parent of a child": s 144(7); "relative": s 144, read with s 1(8).

69 Rules of interpretation for instruments concerning property

(1) The rules of interpretation contained in this section apply (subject to any contrary indication and to Schedule 4) to any instrument so far as it contains a disposition of property.

(2) In applying section 67(1) and (2) to a disposition which depends on the date of birth of a child or children of the adoptive parent or parents, the disposition is to be interpreted as if –

    (a)   the adopted person had been born on the date of adoption,

    (b)   two or more people adopted on the same date had been born on that date in the order of their actual births;

but this does not affect any reference to a person's age.

(3) Examples of phrases in wills on which subsection (2) can operate are –

    1.   Children of A "living at my death or born afterwards".

    2.   Children of A "living at my death or born afterwards before any one of such children for the time being in existence attains a vested interest and who attain the age of 21 years".

    3.   As in example 1 or 2, but referring to grandchildren of A instead of children of A.

    4.   A for life "until he has a child", and then to his child or children.

Note. Subsection (2) will not affect the reference to the age of 21 years in example 2.

(4) Section 67(3) does not prejudice –

    (a)   any qualifying interest, or

    (b)   any interest expectant (whether immediately or not) upon a qualifying interest.

"Qualifying interest" means an interest vested in possession in the adopted person before the adoption.

(5) Where it is necessary to determine for the purposes of a disposition of property effected by an instrument whether a woman can have a child –

  (a)   it must be presumed that once a woman has attained the age of 55 years she will not adopt a person after execution of the instrument, and

  (b)   if she does so. then (in spite of section 67) that person is not to be treated as her child or (if she does so as one of a couple) as the child of the other one of the couple for the purposes of the instrument.

(6) In this section, "instrument" includes a private Act settling property, but not any other enactment.

Defined terms—"adoption (in relation to Chapter 4 of Part 1)": s 66; "child": ss 49(5), 144; "couple": s 144(4); "disposition (in relation to Chapter 4 of Part 1)": s 73; "enactment", "rules": s 144.

70 Dispositions depending on date of birth

(1) Where a disposition depends on the date of birth of a person who was born illegitimate and who is adopted by one of the natural parents as sole adoptive parent, section 69(2) does not affect entitlement by virtue of Part 3 of the Family Law Reform Act 1987 (dispositions of property).

(2) Subsection (1) applies for example where –

  (a)   a testator dies in 2001 bequeathing a legacy to his eldest grandchild living at a specified time,

  (b)   his unmarried daughter has a child in 2002 who is the first grandchild,

  (c)   his married son has a child in 2003,

  (d)   subsequently his unmarried daughter adopts her child as sole adoptive parent.

In that example the status of the daughter's child as the eldest grandchild of the testator is not affected by the events described in paragraphs (c) and (d).

Defined terms—"by virtue of": s 144; "child": ss 49(5), 144; "disposition (in relation to Chapter 4 of Part 1)": s 73.

71 Property devolving with peerages etc

(1) An adoption does not affect the descent of any peerage or dignity or title of honour.

(2) An adoption does not affect the devolution of any property limited (expressly or not) to devolve (as nearly as the law permits) along with any peerage or dignity or title of honour.

(3) Subsection (2) applies only if and so far as a contrary intention is not expressed in the instrument, and has effect subject to the terms of the instrument.

Defined terms—"adoption (in relation to Chapter 4 of Part 1)": s 66.

72 Protection of trustees and personal representatives

(1) A trustee or personal representative is not under a duty, by virtue of the law relating to trusts or the administration of estates, to enquire, before conveying or distributing any property, whether any adoption has been effected or revoked if that fact could affect entitlement to the property.

(2) A trustee or personal representative is not liable to any person by reason of a conveyance or distribution of the property made without regard to any such fact if he has not received notice of the fact before the conveyance or distribution.

(3) This section does not prejudice the right of a person to follow the property, or any property representing it, into the hands of another person, other than a purchaser, who has received it.

Defined terms—"adoption (in relation to Chapter 4 of Part 1)": s 66; "by virtue of", "notice": s 144.

73 Meaning of disposition

(1) This section applies for the purposes of this Chapter.

(2) A disposition includes the conferring of a power of appointment and any other disposition of an interest in or right over property; and in this subsection a power of appointment includes any discretionary power to transfer a beneficial interest in property without the furnishing of valuable consideration.

(3) This Chapter applies to an oral disposition as if contained in an instrument made when the disposition was made.

(4) The date of death of a testator is the date at which a will or codicil is to be regarded as made.

(5) The provisions of the law of intestate succession applicable to the estate of a deceased person are to be treated as if contained in an instrument executed by him (while of full capacity) immediately before his death.

Defined terms—"disposition (in relation to Chapter 4 of Part 1)": s 73.

74 Miscellaneous enactments

(1) Section 67 does not apply for the purposes of –

  (a) section 1 of and Schedule 1 to the Marriage Act 1949 or Schedule 1 to the Civil Partnership Act 2004 (prohibited degrees of kindred and affinity),
  (b) sections 64 and 65 of the Sexual Offences Act 2003 (sex with an adult relative).

(2) Section 67 does not apply for the purposes of any provision of –

  (a) the British Nationality Act 1981,
  (b) the Immigration Act 1971,
  (c) any instrument having effect under an enactment within paragraph (a) or (b), or
  (d) any other provision of the law for the time being in force which determines British citizenship, British overseas territories citizenship, the status of a British National (Overseas) or British Overseas citizenship.

Amendments—CPA 2004, s 79(1),(7); Sexual Offences Act 2003, s 139, Sch 6, para 47.

Defined terms—"enactment": s 144.

75 Pensions

Section 67(3) does not affect entitlement to a pension which is payable to or for the benefit of a person and is in payment at the time of the person's adoption.

Defined terms—"adoption (in relation to Chapter 4 of Part 1)": s 66.

76 Insurance

(1) Where a child is adopted whose natural parent has effected an insurance with a friendly society or a collecting society or an industrial insurance company for the payment on the death of the child of money for funeral expenses, then –

  (a) the rights and liabilities under the policy are by virtue of the adoption transferred to the adoptive parents, and

(b)   for the purposes of the enactments relating to such societies and companies, the adoptive parents are to be treated as the person who took out the policy.

(2) Where the adoption is effected by an order made by virtue of section 51(2), the references in subsection (1) to the adoptive parents are to be read as references to the adopter and the other one of the couple.

Defined terms—"by virtue of": s 144; "child": ss 49(5), 144; "couple", "enactment": s 144.

Chapter 5
The Registers

Adopted Children Register etc

77 Adopted Children Register

(1) The Registrar General must continue to maintain in the General Register Office a register, to be called the Adopted Children Register.

(2) The Adopted Children Register is not to be open to public inspection or search.

(3) No entries may be made in the Adopted Children Register other than entries –

(a)   directed to be made in it by adoption orders, or
(b)   required to be made under Schedule 1.

(4) A certified copy of an entry in the Adopted Children Register, if purporting to be sealed or stamped with the seal of the General Register Office, is to be received as evidence of the adoption to which it relates without further or other proof.

(5) Where an entry in the Adopted Children Register contains a record –

(a)   of the date of birth of the adopted person, or
(b)   of the country, or the district and sub-district, of the birth of the adopted person,

a certified copy of the entry is also to be received, without further or other proof, as evidence of that date, or country or district and sub-district, (as the case may be) in all respects as if the copy were a certified copy of an entry in the registers of live-births.

(6) Schedule 1 (registration of adoptions and the amendment of adoption orders) is to have effect.

Defined terms—"Adopted Children Register": s 77; "adoption (in relation to Chapter 4 of Part 1)": s 66; "adoption order": s 46(1); "registers of live-births (in relation to Chapter 5 of Part 1)": s 82.

Scope—Every domestic adoption must be registered in the Adopted Children Register by the Registrar General in the prescribed form (see ACA 2002, Sch 1 and The Adopted Children and Adoption Contact Registers Regulations 2005). The child's entry in the Register of Births must also be marked "adopted". Where a foreign adoption satisfies the requirements for registration it must also be entered in the Register. A certified copy of an entry in the Adopted Children Register, if sealed and stamped with the Registrar General's seal, is, without further proof, to be received as evidence of the adoption as if it were a birth certificate.

General Register Office—Smedley Hydro, Trafalgar Road, Birkdale, Southport PR8 2HH.

Foreign adoptions (s 77(3)(b) and Sch 1, para 3)—A foreign adoption which is either a Convention adoption or an "overseas adoption" (see note to s 66), and which satisfies the requirement of the Adopted Children and Adoption Contact Registers Regulations 2005, must be entered in the Adopted Children Register (ACA 2002, Sch 1, para 3). Such adoptions are automatically recognised in English law as a valid adoption; the effect of registration is to provide domestic documentary proof of adopted status.

78 Searches and copies

(1) The Registrar General must continue to maintain at the General Register Office an index of the Adopted Children Register.

(2) Any person may –

   (a) search the index,
   (b) have a certified copy of any entry in the Adopted Children Register.

(3) But a person is not entitled to have a certified copy of an entry in the Adopted Children Register relating to an adopted person who has not attained the age of 18 years unless the applicant has provided the Registrar General with the prescribed particulars.

   "Prescribed" means prescribed by regulations made by the Registrar General with the approval of the Secretary of State.

(4) The terms, conditions and regulations as to payment of fees, and otherwise, applicable under the Births and Deaths Registration Act 1953, and the Registration Service Act 1953, in respect of –

   (a) searches in the index kept in the General Register Office of certified copies of entries in the registers of live-births,
   (b) the supply from that office of certified copies of entries in those certified copies,

also apply in respect of searches, and supplies of certified copies, under subsection (2).

Amendments—SI 2008/678.

Defined terms—"Adopted Children Register": s 77; "fee": s 144; "registers of live-births (in relation to Chapter 5 of Part 1)": s 82; "regulations": s 144.

High Court power to restrict disclosure from records—The Registrar General can refuse to allow access to the birth records on grounds of public policy (see *R v Registrar General ex parte Smith* [1990] 2 FLR 79, QBD). The High Court may, under its inherent jurisdiction, attach to an adoption order an order that the Registrar General should not reveal details of an adoption which are recorded in the Adopted Children Register without the leave of the court (*Re X (A Minor) (Adoption Details: Disclosure)* [1994] 2 FLR 450; *Re W (Adoption Details: Disclosure)* [1998] 2 FLR 625). A local authority is required to obtain leave to make such an application (under CA 1989, s 100(3)) and any application for an order restricting disclosure must be made in, or transferred to, the High Court (*President's Direction of 17 December 1998*).

79 Connections between the register and birth records

(1) The Registrar General must make traceable the connection between any entry in the registers of live-births or other records which has been marked "Adopted" and any corresponding entry in the Adopted Children Register.

(2) Information kept by the Registrar General for the purposes of subsection (1) is not to be open to public inspection or search.

(3) Any such information, and any other information which would enable an adopted person to obtain a certified copy of the record of his birth, may only be disclosed by the Registrar General in accordance with this section.

(4) In relation to a person adopted before the appointed day the court may, in exceptional circumstances, order the Registrar General to give any information mentioned in subsection (3) to a person.

(5) On an application made in the prescribed manner by the appropriate adoption agency in respect of an adopted person a record of whose birth is kept by the Registrar General, the Registrar General must give the agency any information relating to the adopted person which is mentioned in subsection (3).

   "Appropriate adoption agency" has the same meaning as in section 65.

(6) In relation to a person adopted before the appointed day, Schedule 2 applies instead of subsection (5).

(7) On an application made in the prescribed manner by an adopted person a record of whose birth is kept by the Registrar General and who –

(a) is under the age of 18 years, and

(b) intends to be married or form a civil partnership,

the Registrar General must inform the applicant whether or not it appears from information contained in the registers of live-births or other records that the applicant and the intended spouse or civil partner may be within the prohibited degrees of relationship for the purposes of the Marriage Act 1949 or for the purposes of the Civil Partnership Act 2004.

(8) Before the Registrar General gives any information by virtue of this section, any prescribed fee which he has demanded must be paid.

(9) In this section –

"appointed day" means the day appointed for the commencement of sections 56 to 65,

"prescribed" means prescribed by regulations made by the Registrar General with the approval of the Secretary of State.

Amendments—CPA 2004, s 79(1),(8); SI 2005/3542; SI 2008/678.

Defined terms—"Adopted Children Register": s 77; "adoption agency": s 2(1); "appointed day (in relation to Chapter 4 of Part 1)": s 66(2); "by virtue of", "court", "fee", "information": s 144; "records (in relation to Chapter 5 of Part 1)": s 82; "registers of live-births (in relation to Chapter 5 of Part 1)": s 82; "regulations": s 144.

Adoption Contact Register

80 Adoption Contact Register

(1) The Registrar General must continue to maintain at the General Register Office in accordance with regulations a register in two Parts to be called the Adoption Contact Register.

(2) Part 1 of the register is to contain the prescribed information about adopted persons who have given the prescribed notice expressing their wishes as to making contact with their relatives.

(3) The Registrar General may only make an entry in Part 1 of the register for an adopted person –

(a) a record of whose birth is kept by the Registrar General,

(b) who has attained the age of 18 years, and

(c) who the Registrar General is satisfied has such information as is necessary to enable him to obtain a certified copy of the record of his birth.

(4) Part 2 of the register is to contain the prescribed information about persons who have given the prescribed notice expressing their wishes, as relatives of adopted persons, as to making contact with those persons.

(5) The Registrar General may only make an entry in Part 2 of the register for a person –

(a) who has attained the age of 18 years, and

(b) who the Registrar General is satisfied is a relative of an adopted person and has such information as is necessary to enable him to obtain a certified copy of the record of the adopted person's birth.

(6) Regulations may provide for –

(a) the disclosure of information contained in one Part of the register to persons for whom there is an entry in the other Part,

PART II

(b)   the payment of prescribed fees in respect of the making or alteration of entries in the register and the disclosure of information contained in the register.

Defined terms—"Adoption Contact Register": s 80; "fee", "information", "notice", "regulations", "relative": s 144, read with s 1(8).

Adoption Contact Register—The Adoption Contact Register is divided into two parts: in Pt I are details relating to the adopted person; in Pt II are details of any relative of the adoptee, by blood, half-blood or marriage (but not adoption), who wishes to make contact with the adoptee. The system operates by the Registrar General transmitting, to the adopted person whose name appears in Pt I, the name and address of any relative entered in Pt II. A fee is payable for entry on the register (Adopted Children and Adoption Contact Registers Regulations 2005, reg 9). The Register is held at OPCS, Smedley Hydro, Trafalgar Road, Birkdale, Southport PR8 2HH.

81 Adoption Contact Register: supplementary

(1) The Adoption Contact Register is not to be open to public inspection or search.

(2) In section 80, "relative", in relation to an adopted person, means any person who (but for his adoption) would be related to him by blood (including half-blood), marriage or civil partnership.

(3) The Registrar General must not give any information entered in the register to any person except in accordance with subsection (6)(a) of that section or regulations made by virtue of section 64(4)(b).

(4) In section 80, "regulations" means regulations made by the Registrar General with the approval of the Secretary of State, and "prescribed" means prescribed by such regulations.

Amendments—CPA 2004, s 79(1),(9); SI 2008/678.

Defined terms—"adoption (in relation to Chapter 4 of Part 1)": s 66; "adoption agency placing a child for adoption": s 80; "by virtue of", "information", "regulations", "relative": s 144, read with s 1(8).

General

82 Interpretation

(1) In this Chapter –

"records" includes certified copies kept by the Registrar General of entries in any register of births,

"registers of live-births" means the registers of live-births made under the Births and Deaths Registration Act 1953.

(2) Any register, record or index maintained under this Chapter may be maintained in any form the Registrar General considers appropriate; and references (however expressed) to entries in such a register, or to their amendment, marking or cancellation, are to be read accordingly.

Defined terms—"records (in relation to Chapter 5 of Part 1)", "registers of live-births (in relation to Chapter 5 of Part 1)": s 82.

Chapter 6
Adoptions with a Foreign Element

Bringing children into and out of the United Kingdom

83 Restriction on bringing children in

(1) This section applies where a person who is habitually resident in the British Islands (the "British resident") –

    (a)   brings, or causes another to bring, a child who is habitually resident outside the British Islands into the United Kingdom for the purpose of adoption by the British resident, or

    (b)   at any time brings, or causes another to bring, into the United Kingdom a child adopted by the British resident under an external adoption effected within the period of twelve months ending with that time.

The references to adoption, or to a child adopted, by the British resident include a reference to adoption, or to a child adopted, by the British resident and another person.

(2) But this section does not apply if the child is intended to be adopted under a Convention adoption order.

(3) An external adoption means an adoption, other than a Convention adoption, of a child effected under the law of any country or territory outside the British Islands, whether or not the adoption is –

    (a)   an adoption within the meaning of Chapter 4, or

    (b)   a full adoption (within the meaning of section 88(3)).

(4) Regulations may require a person intending to bring, or to cause another to bring, a child into the United Kingdom in circumstances where this section applies –

    (a)   to apply to an adoption agency (including a Scottish or Northern Irish adoption agency) in the prescribed manner for an assessment of his suitability to adopt the child, and

    (b)   to give the agency any information it may require for the purpose of the assessment.

(5) Regulations may require prescribed conditions to be met in respect of a child brought into the United Kingdom in circumstances where this section applies.

(6) In relation to a child brought into the United Kingdom for adoption in circumstances where this section applies, regulations may –

    (a)   provide for any provision of Chapter 3 to apply with modifications or not to apply,

    (b)   if notice of intention to adopt has been given, impose functions in respect of the child on the local authority to which the notice was given.

(7) If a person brings, or causes another to bring, a child into the United Kingdom at any time in circumstances where this section applies, he is guilty of an offence if –

    (a)   he has not complied with any requirement imposed by virtue of subsection (4), or

    (b)   any condition required to be met by virtue of subsection (5) is not met,

before that time, or before any later time which may be prescribed.

(8) A person guilty of an offence under this section is liable –

    (a)   on summary conviction to imprisonment for a term not exceeding six months, or a fine not exceeding the statutory maximum, or both,

PART II

(b)   on conviction on indictment, to imprisonment for a term not exceeding twelve months, or a fine, or both.

(9) In this section, "prescribed" means prescribed by regulations and "regulations" means regulations made by the Secretary of State, after consultation with the Assembly.

Amendments—CAA 2006, s 14(1).

Defined terms—"adoption (in relation to Chapter 4 of Part 1)": s 66; "adoption agency": s 2(1); "adoption order": s 46(1); "Assembly", "by virtue of": s 144; "child": ss 49(5) and 144; "Convention adoption": s 66(1)(c); "Convention adoption order", "information", "local authority", "Northern Irish adoption agency", "notice": s 144; "notice of intention to adopt": s 44(2); "regulations": s 144.

Bringing in a child from a "restricted country"—Under CAA 2006, s 9 the Secretary of State may, by order, declare that special restrictions set out in CAA 2006, Pt 2 are to apply to bringing a child into the UK from certain named states (currently Cambodia and Guatemala are named as "restricted countries" (for further discussion see Hershman & McFarlane, *Children: Law and Practice* at para D[783] (Jordan Publishing Ltd)).

Bringing in a child for adoption (s 83(1)(a))—It is a criminal offence, punishable with up to 12 months' imprisonment and/or a fine, for a person who is habitually resident in the British Isles to bring a child, who is habitually resident outside the British Isles, into the UK for the purpose of adoption, unless the requirements of the AFER 2005 have been satisfied (ACA 2002, s 83(7),(8)).

Before the child enters the UK it will be necessary to obtain permission for him to enter. Permission is available on two general bases:

–   where there has been a formal legal or de facto (customary) adoption before entry, by adoptive parents who have a right to enter the UK (see **Bringing in an adopted child** below);
–   in any event, the Home Secretary has a discretion to permit entry or extend a temporary visa so that adoption proceedings may be heard.

To avoid uncertainty, practitioners are recommended to advise prospective adopters to apply for prior entry clearance. The procedure is fully described in the comprehensive guidance from the DfES and the Home Office: *Adoption Guidance: Adoption and Children Act 2002* (DfES 2005), Annex C (available at *www.education.gov.uk/childrenandyoungpeople/families/adoption*) and Annexes Q–U (regarding children) to the Immigration Directorates Instructions, Chapter 8 "Family Members" (available at *www.ukba.homeoffice.gov.uk/*).

"twelve months" (s 83(1)(b))—The period of 12 months applies only in relation to a child adopted under an external adoption effected after 1 October 2007; in all other cases the period is 6 months (CAA 2006, s 14(2)).

Statutory requirements—AFER 2005, reg 3, provides that a prospective adopter must satisfy the following requirements before bringing a child into the UK for adoption:

–   apply in writing to an adoption agency for an assessment of his suitability to adopt; and
–   give the adoption agency any information it may require for the purposes of the assessment.

Before the child's entry into the UK, in order to comply with AFER 2005, reg 5, the person bringing the child into the UK must receive written notification from the Secretary of State that he has issued a certificate confirming to the relevant foreign authority (which performs the functions of an adoption agency or of the Government with respect to foreign adoptions) the following:

–   that the person has been assessed and approved as eligible and suitable to be an adoptive parent; and
–   if entry clearance and leave to enter and remain, as may be necessary, is granted and not revoked or curtailed, and an adoption order is made or an overseas adoption is effected, that the child will be authorised to enter and reside permanently in the UK.

Before bringing a child into the UK, each prospective adopter must visit the child in the state of origin (and before doing so have given required information to the relevant local authority). On return to the UK, the adopter must confirm that the visit has taken place and inform the local authority of the expected date of the child's arrival in the UK. Unless there has been prior agreement that only one adopter will accompany the child, each adopter must travel into the UK with the child.

A prospective adopter must also, within a period of 14 days beginning with the date on which he brings the child into the UK, give notice to the local authority within whose area he has his home of his intention to apply for an adoption order in accordance with ACA 2002, s 44 or his intention not to give the child a home.

Bringing in an adopted child—If a child who has been adopted abroad is brought into the UK, and that adoption is recognised in England and Wales, there will normally be no need for a subsequent adoption order.

A child who has been genuinely adopted abroad has a right of entry into the UK if one of the adoptive parents has such a right. Reference should be made to paragraphs 310–313 of the Immigration Rules (see *www.ukba.homeoffice.gov.uk*). The immigration authorities will need to be satisfied that (i) the child's adoption has been due to the inability of the original parents or current carers to care for the child, and (ii) there has been a genuine transfer of parental responsibility.

Where natural parents lack neither the skill, ability nor opportunity to care for their child, but simply have chosen not to do so, there is no "inability" sufficient to satisfy the immigration requirements (*RS v Entry Clearance Officer (New Delhi)* [2005] 2 FLR 219).

Where there is doubt about the validity of a foreign adoption order, the local authority should at once seek information from the relevant embassy or consulate; any delay may affect the quality of a later court decision (*Re An Adoption Application* [1992] 1 FLR 341).

84 Giving parental responsibility prior to adoption abroad

(1) The High Court may, on an application by persons who the court is satisfied intend to adopt a child under the law of a country or territory outside the British Islands, make an order giving parental responsibility for the child to them.

(2) An order under this section may not give parental responsibility to persons who the court is satisfied meet those requirements as to domicile, or habitual residence, in England and Wales which have to be met if an adoption order is to be made in favour of those persons.

(3) An order under this section may not be made unless any requirements prescribed by regulations are satisfied.

(4) An application for an order under this section may not be made unless at all times during the preceding ten weeks the child's home was with the applicant or, in the case of an application by two people, both of them.

(5) Section 46(2) to (4) has effect in relation to an order under this section as it has effect in relation to adoption orders.

(6) Regulations may provide for any provision of this Act which refers to adoption orders to apply, with or without modifications, to orders under this section.

(7) In this section, "regulations" means regulations made by the Secretary of State, after consultation with the Assembly.

Defined terms—"adoption (in relation to Chapter 4 of Part 1)": s 66; "adoption order": s 46(1); "Assembly": s 144; "child": ss 49(5), 144; "court": s 144; "parental responsibility": s 3 of the 1989 Act; "regulations": s 144.

Section 84 application treated as adoption application—A s 84 application is treated in relation to key parts of ACA 2002 exactly as if it were an application for an adoption order (AFER 2005, reg 11(1)). The paramount consideration when determining whether an order should be made will be the welfare of the child throughout his life (reg 11(1)(a)). A s 84 order may only be made if either the first or second condition required before an adoption order can be made (i e parental consent or placed for adoption by an agency) is satisfied (ACA 2002, s 47). It follows that a s 84 order may only be made if the consent of each parent or guardian with parental responsibility has either been given or dispensed with.

"the preceding ten weeks the child's home was with the applicant" (s 84(4))—This statutory requirement (which, coupled with ss 42(7) and 44) seeks to enable the local adoption agency to see the child with the applicant in a home environment, to ensure that a relationship between the adopters and the child has begun, to assess the applicants and to assess the relationship. The word "home" in s 84(4) is not geographically defined; where prospective adopters live abroad, the phrase in s 84(4) "the child's home was with the applicants" is applicable to the child being in the applicants' home abroad and there is no requirement that the 10-week period is to be spent somewhere in England and Wales (*Re A (Adoption: Removal)* [2009] 2 FLR 597 (on appeal from *Haringey London Borough Council v MA, JN, IA* [2008] 2 FLR 1857)). Where s 42(7)(b) applies the "home" must be within a local authority area in England and Wales. Where, however, s 42(7)(a) applies there is no territorial restriction and the "home environment" may be outside England and Wales (*Re A (Adoption: Removal)* above). CA 1989, Sch 2, para 19, which permits a local authority in certain circumstances to make arrangements for a child to live abroad, does not apply "to a local authority placing a child for adoption with prospective adopters" (CA 1989, Sch 2, para 19(9)). Arrangements that fall short of actually "placing the child for adoption" (e g for assessment) are permissible under Sch 2, para 19 (*Re A (Adoption: Removal)* above).

"regulations" (s 84(7))—See AFER 2005 in Part IV. Regulation 10(b) requires that "the relevant foreign authority" has counselled the prospective adopter, prepared a report, confirmed his eligibility to adopt and confirmed that the child will be allowed entry and permanent residence. The "authority" is to be taken as the foreign equivalent of the English adoption agency; a government body is not required and the confirmation does not have to be in absolute terms (*Re G* above).

85 Restriction on taking children out

(1) A child who –

    (a) is a Commonwealth citizen, or

    (b) is habitually resident in the United Kingdom,

must not be removed from the United Kingdom to a place outside the British Islands for the purpose of adoption unless the condition in subsection (2) is met.

(2) The condition is that –

    (a) the prospective adopters have parental responsibility for the child by virtue of an order under section 84, or

    (b) *(applies to Scotland and Northern Ireland only)*

(3) Removing a child from the United Kingdom includes arranging to do so; and the circumstances in which a person arranges to remove a child from the United Kingdom include those where he –

    (a) enters into an arrangement for the purpose of facilitating such a removal of the child,

    (b) initiates or takes part in any negotiations of which the purpose is the conclusion of an arrangement within paragraph (a), or

    (c) causes another person to take any step mentioned in paragraph (a) or (b).

An arrangement includes an agreement (whether or not enforceable).

(4) A person who removes a child from the United Kingdom in contravention of subsection (1) is guilty of an offence.

(5) A person is not guilty of an offence under subsection (4) of causing a person to take any step mentioned in paragraph (a) or (b) of subsection (3) unless it is proved that he knew or had reason to suspect that the step taken would contravene subsection (1).

But this subsection only applies if sufficient evidence is adduced to raise an issue as to whether the person had the knowledge or reason mentioned.

(6) A person guilty of an offence under this section is liable –

    (a) on summary conviction to imprisonment for a term not exceeding six months, or a fine not exceeding the statutory maximum, or both,

    (b) on conviction on indictment, to imprisonment for a term not exceeding twelve months, or a fine, or both.

(7) In any proceedings under this section –

    (a) a report by a British consular officer or a deposition made before a British consular officer and authenticated under the signature of that officer is admissible, upon proof that the officer or the deponent cannot be found in the United Kingdom, as evidence of the matters stated in it, and

    (b) it is not necessary to prove the signature or official character of the person who appears to have signed any such report or deposition.

Defined terms—"adoption (in relation to Chapter 4 of Part 1)": s 66; "by virtue of": s 144; "child": ss 49(5), 144; "parental responsibility": s 3 of the 1989 Act.

Scope—This section creates a blanket ban upon the removal of any child out of the UK for the purpose of adoption unless (in the case of England and Wales) the prospective adopters have parental responsibility for the child under ACA 2002, s 84 (in order to facilitate adoption abroad). A local authority must comply with ss 84 and 85 if contemplating placing a child abroad for adoption (CA 1989, Sch 2, Para 19 does not apply to arrangements for adoption). There may be no breach of s 85 where removal abroad is for the purpose of assessment of a prospective placement with a view to an adoption order subsequently being made here (*ECC (The Local Authority) v SM* [2011] 1 FLR 234).

86 Power to modify sections 83 and 85

(1) Regulations may provide for section 83 not to apply if –

(a) the adopters or (as the case may be) prospective adopters are natural parents, natural relatives or guardians of the child in question (or one of them is), or

(b) the British resident in question is a partner of a parent of the child,

and any prescribed conditions are met.

(2) Regulations may provide for section 85(1) to apply with modifications, or not to apply, if –

(a) the prospective adopters are parents, relatives or guardians of the child in question (or one of them is), or

(b) the prospective adopter is a partner of a parent of the child,

and any prescribed conditions are met.

(3) On the occasion of the first exercise of the power to make regulations under this section –

(a) the statutory instrument containing the regulations is not to be made unless a draft of the instrument has been laid before, and approved by a resolution of, each House of Parliament, and

(b) accordingly section 140(2) does not apply to the instrument.

(4) In this section, "prescribed" means prescribed by regulations and "regulations" means regulations made by the Secretary of State after consultation with the Assembly.

Defined terms—"Assembly": s 144; "child": ss 49(5), 144; "guardian": s 144; "partner, in relation to a parent of a child": s 144(7); "regulations": s 144; "relative": s 144, read with s 1(8).

Overseas adoptions

87 Overseas adoptions

(1) In this Act, "overseas adoption" –

(a) means an adoption of a description specified in an order made by the Secretary of State, being a description of adoptions effected under the law of any country or territory outside the British Islands, but

(b) does not include a Convention adoption.

(2) Regulations may prescribe the requirements that ought to be met by an adoption of any description effected after the commencement of the regulations for it to be an overseas adoption for the purposes of this Act.

(3) At any time when such regulations have effect, the Secretary of State must exercise his powers under this section so as to secure that subsequently effected adoptions of any description are not overseas adoptions for the purposes of this Act if he considers that they are not likely within a reasonable time to meet the prescribed requirements.

(4) In this section references to this Act include the Adoption Act 1976.

(5) An order under this section may contain provision as to the manner in which evidence of any overseas adoption may be given.

(6) In this section –

"adoption" means an adoption of a child or of a person who was a child at the time the adoption was applied for,

"regulations" means regulations made by the Secretary of State after consultation with the Assembly.

Defined terms—"adoption (in relation to Chapter 4 of Part 1)": s 66; "Assembly": s 144; "child": ss 49(5), 144; "Convention adoption": s 66(1)(c); "overseas adoption": s 87; "regulations": s 144.

Miscellaneous

88 Modification of section 67 for Hague Convention adoptions

(1) If the High Court is satisfied, on an application under this section, that each of the following conditions is met in the case of a Convention adoption, it may direct that section 67(3) does not apply, or does not apply to any extent specified in the direction.

(2) The conditions are –

(a)   that under the law of the country in which the adoption was effected, the adoption is not a full adoption,

(b)   that the consents referred to in Article 4(c) and (d) of the Convention have not been given for a full adoption or that the United Kingdom is not the receiving State (within the meaning of Article 2 of the Convention),

(c)   that it would be more favourable to the adopted child for a direction to be given under subsection (1).

(3) A full adoption is an adoption by virtue of which the child is to be treated in law as not being the child of any person other than the adopters or adopter.

(4) In relation to a direction under this section and an application for it, sections 59 and 60 of the Family Law Act 1986 (declarations under Part 3 of that Act as to marital status) apply as they apply in relation to a direction under that Part and an application for such a direction.

Defined terms—"adoption (in relation to Chapter 4 of Part 1)": s 66; "by virtue of": s 144; "child": ss 49(5), 144; "child to be adopted, adopted child": s 49(5); "consent (in relation to making adoption orders or placing for adoption)": s 52; "the Convention": s 144; "Convention adoption": s 66(1)(c).

89 Annulment etc of overseas or Hague Convention adoptions

(1) The High Court may, on an application under this subsection, by order annul a Convention adoption or Convention adoption order on the ground that the adoption is contrary to public policy.

(2) The High Court may, on an application under this subsection –

(a)   by order provide for an overseas adoption or a determination under section 91 to cease to be valid on the ground that the adoption or determination is contrary to public policy or that the authority which purported to authorise the adoption or make the determination was not competent to entertain the case, or

(b)   decide the extent, if any, to which a determination under section 91 has been affected by a subsequent determination under that section.

(3) The High Court may, in any proceedings in that court, decide that an overseas adoption or a determination under section 91 is to be treated, for the purposes of those proceedings, as invalid on either of the grounds mentioned in subsection (2)(a).

(4) Subject to the preceding provisions, the validity of a Convention adoption, Convention adoption order or overseas adoption or a determination under section 91 cannot be called in question in proceedings in any court in England and Wales.

Defined terms—"adoption (in relation to Chapter 4 of Part 1)": s 66; "adoption order": s 46(1); "Convention adoption": s 66(1)(c); "Convention adoption order", "court": s 144; "overseas adoption": s 87.

Procedure—An application under s 89 is governed by FPR 2010, Pt 14 and must be made in Form A63 (or a form to like effect).

90 Section 89: supplementary

(1) Any application for an order under section 89 or a decision under subsection (2)(b) or (3) of that section must be made in the prescribed manner and within any prescribed period.

"Prescribed" means prescribed by rules.

(2) No application may be made under section 89(1) in respect of an adoption unless immediately before the application is made –

    (a)   the person adopted, or
    (b)   the adopters or adopter,

habitually reside in England and Wales.

(3) In deciding in pursuance of section 89 whether such an authority as is mentioned in section 91 was competent to entertain a particular case, a court is bound by any finding of fact made by the authority and stated by the authority to be so made for the purpose of determining whether the authority was competent to entertain the case.

Defined terms—"adoption (in relation to Chapter 4 of Part 1)": s 66; "court", "rules": s 144.

91 Overseas determinations and orders

(1) Subsection (2) applies where any authority of a Convention country (other than the United Kingdom) or of the Channel Islands, the Isle of Man or any British overseas territory has power under the law of that country or territory –

    (a)   to authorise, or review the authorisation of, an adoption order made in that country or territory, or
    (b)   to give or review a decision revoking or annulling such an order or a Convention adoption.

(2) If the authority makes a determination in the exercise of that power, the determination is to have effect for the purpose of effecting, confirming or terminating the adoption in question or, as the case may be, confirming its termination.

(3) Subsection (2) is subject to section 89 and to any subsequent determination having effect under that subsection.

Defined terms—"adoption (in relation to Chapter 4 of Part 1)": s 66; "adoption order": s 46(1); "Convention adoption": s 66(1)(c); "Convention country": s 144.

91A Power to charge

(1) This section applies to adoptions to which –

    (a)   section 83 applies, or
    (b)   regulations made under section 1 of the Adoption (Intercountry Aspects) Act 1999 apply.

(2) The Secretary of State may charge a fee to adopters for services provided or to be provided by him in relation to adoptions to which this section applies.

(3) The Assembly may charge a fee to adopters for services provided or to be provided by it as the Central Authority in relation to adoptions to which this section applies by virtue of subsection (1)(b).

(4) The Secretary of State and the Assembly may determine the level of fee as he or it sees fit, and may in particular –

(a) charge a flat fee or charge different fees in different cases or descriptions of case, and

(b) in any case or description of case, waive a fee.

(5) But the Secretary of State and the Assembly must each secure that, taking one financial year with another, the income from fees under this section does not exceed the total cost to him or, as the case may be, to it of providing the services in relation to which the fees are imposed.

(6) In this section –

references to adoptions and adopters include prospective adoptions and prospective adopters,

"Central Authority" is to be construed in accordance with section 2 of the Adoption (Intercountry Aspects) Act 1999,

"financial year" means a period of twelve months ending with 31 March.

Amendments—Inserted by CAA 2006, s 13.

Chapter 7
Miscellaneous

Restrictions

92   Restriction on arranging adoptions etc

(1) A person who is neither an adoption agency nor acting in pursuance of an order of the High Court must not take any of the steps mentioned in subsection (2).

(2) The steps are –

(a) asking a person other than an adoption agency to provide a child for adoption,

(b) asking a person other than an adoption agency to provide prospective adopters for a child,

(c) offering to find a child for adoption,

(d) offering a child for adoption to a person other than an adoption agency,

(e) handing over a child to any person other than an adoption agency with a view to the child's adoption by that or another person,

(f) receiving a child handed over to him in contravention of paragraph (e),

(g) entering into an agreement with any person for the adoption of a child, or for the purpose of facilitating the adoption of a child, where no adoption agency is acting on behalf of the child in the adoption,

(h) initiating or taking part in negotiations of which the purpose is the conclusion of an agreement within paragraph (g),

(i) causing another person to take any of the steps mentioned in paragraphs (a) to (h).

(3) Subsection (1) does not apply to a person taking any of the steps mentioned in paragraphs (d), (e), (g), (h) and (i) of subsection (2) if the following condition is met.

(4) The condition is that –

(a) the prospective adopters are parents, relatives or guardians of the child (or one of them is), or

(b)   the prospective adopter is the partner of a parent of the child.

(5) References to an adoption agency in subsection (2) include a prescribed person outside the United Kingdom exercising functions corresponding to those of an adoption agency, if the functions are being exercised in prescribed circumstances in respect of the child in question.

(6) The Secretary of State may, after consultation with the Assembly, by order make any amendments of subsections (1) to (4), and any consequential amendments of this Act, which he considers necessary or expedient.

(7) In this section –

(a)   "agreement" includes an arrangement (whether or not enforceable),
(b)   "prescribed" means prescribed by regulations made by the Secretary of State after consultation with the Assembly.

Defined terms—"adoption (in relation to Chapter 4 of Part 1)": s 66; "adoption agency": s 2(1); "Assembly": s 144; "child": ss 49(5), 144; "guardian": s 144; "partner, in relation to a parent of a child": s 144(7); "regulations": s 144; "relative": s 144, read with s 1(8).

Restrictions upon arranging adoptions—Section 92(2) sets out a list of steps relating to adoption that are illegal, unless taken by an adoption agency or a person acting in pursuance of a High Court order. While the prohibited steps apply to domestic as much as to intercountry adoptions, s 92 extends to the adoption of persons wherever they may be habitually resident, effected under the law of any country or territory, within or outside the British Isles (s 97(c)). The steps itemised in s 92(3) are permitted if the prospective adopters are parents, relatives, or guardians of the child (or the sole adopter is a parent's partner). Breach of s 92(1) is a criminal offence under s 93.

Restrictions on advertisements—Specific restrictions upon advertising in relation to adoption are made by s 123.

93 Offence of breaching restrictions under section 92

(1) If a person contravenes section 92(1), he is guilty of an offence; and, if that person is an adoption society, the person who manages the society is also guilty of the offence.

(2) A person is not guilty of an offence under subsection (1) of taking the step mentioned in paragraph (f) of section 92(2) unless it is proved that he knew or had reason to suspect that the child was handed over to him in contravention of paragraph (e) of that subsection.

(3) A person is not guilty of an offence under subsection (1) of causing a person to take any of the steps mentioned in paragraphs (a) to (h) of section 92(2) unless it is proved that he knew or had reason to suspect that the step taken would contravene the paragraph in question.

(4) But subsections (2) and (3) only apply if sufficient evidence is adduced to raise an issue as to whether the person had the knowledge or reason mentioned.

(5) A person guilty of an offence under this section is liable on summary conviction to imprisonment for a term not exceeding six months, or a fine not exceeding £10,000, or both.

Defined terms—"adoption society": s 2(5); "child": ss 49(5), 144.

94 Restriction on reports

(1) A person who is not within a prescribed description may not, in any prescribed circumstances, prepare a report for any person about the suitability of a child for adoption or of a person to adopt a child or about the adoption, or placement for adoption, of a child.

"Prescribed" means prescribed by regulations made by the Secretary of State after consultation with the Assembly.

(2) If a person –

(a) contravenes subsection (1), or

(b) causes a person to prepare a report, or submits to any person a report which has been prepared, in contravention of that subsection,

he is guilty of an offence.

(3) If a person who works for an adoption society –

(a) contravenes subsection (1), or

(b) causes a person to prepare a report, or submits to any person a report which has been prepared, in contravention of that subsection,

the person who manages the society is also guilty of the offence.

(4) A person is not guilty of an offence under subsection (2)(b) unless it is proved that he knew or had reason to suspect that the report would be, or had been, prepared in contravention of subsection (1).

But this subsection only applies if sufficient evidence is adduced to raise an issue as to whether the person had the knowledge or reason mentioned.

(5) A person guilty of an offence under this section is liable on summary conviction to imprisonment for a term not exceeding six months, or a fine not exceeding level 5 on the standard scale, or both.

Defined terms—"adoption (in relation to Chapter 4 of Part 1)": s 66; "adoption society": s 2(5); "Assembly": s 144; "child": ss 49(5), 144; "regulations": s 144.

Restriction on reports—Section 94 and the Preparation of Adoption Reports Regulations 2005 establish tight parameters, outside which it is illegal for a person to prepare a report in connection with a proposed adoption or adoptive placement. The prohibition extends to the adoption of persons wherever they may be habitually resident, effected under the law of any country or territory, within or outside the British Isles (s 97(c)). Contravention of these provisions constitutes a criminal offence (s 94(2)).

95 Prohibition of certain payments

(1) This section applies to any payment (other than an excepted payment) which is made for or in consideration of –

(a) the adoption of a child,

(b) giving any consent required in connection with the adoption of a child,

(c) removing from the United Kingdom a child who is a Commonwealth citizen, or is habitually resident in the United Kingdom, to a place outside the British Islands for the purpose of adoption,

(d) a person (who is neither an adoption agency nor acting in pursuance of an order of the High Court) taking any step mentioned in section 92(2),

(e) preparing, causing to be prepared or submitting a report the preparation of which contravenes section 94(1).

(2) In this section and section 96, removing a child from the United Kingdom has the same meaning as in section 85.

(3) Any person who –

(a) makes any payment to which this section applies,

(b) agrees or offers to make any such payment, or

(c) receives or agrees to receive or attempts to obtain any such payment,

is guilty of an offence.

(4) A person guilty of an offence under this section is liable on summary conviction to imprisonment for a term not exceeding six months, or a fine not exceeding £10,000, or both.

Defined terms—"adoption (in relation to Chapter 4 of Part 1)": s 66; "adoption agency": s 2(1); "child": ss 49(5), 144; "consent (in relation to making adoption orders or placing for adoption)": s 52.

Prohibition on certain payments—Section 95 renders any payment which is made for, or in consideration of, the adoption of a child or any of the other steps listed in s 95(1) unless the payment is an "excepted payment" within s 96. "Payment" includes reward (s 97(b)). The prohibition extends to the adoption of persons wherever they may be habitually resident, effected under the law of any country or territory, within or outside the British Isles (s 97(c)). Breach of these provisions constitutes a criminal offence (s 95(3)).

96 Excepted payments

(1) A payment is an excepted payment if it is made by virtue of, or in accordance with provision made by or under, this Act, the Adoption (Scotland) Act 1978, the Adoption and Children (Scotland) Act 2007 or the Adoption (Northern Ireland) Order 1987 (SI 1987/2203 (NI 22)).

(2) A payment is an excepted payment if it is made to a registered adoption society by –

    (a)   a parent or guardian of a child, or

    (b)   a person who adopts or proposes to adopt a child,

in respect of expenses reasonably incurred by the society in connection with the adoption or proposed adoption of the child.

(3) A payment is an excepted payment if it is made in respect of any legal or medical expenses incurred or to be incurred by any person in connection with an application to a court which he has made or proposes to make for an adoption order, a placement order, or an order under section 26 or 84.

(4) A payment made as mentioned in section 95(1)(c) is an excepted payment if –

    (a)   the condition in section 85(2) is met, and

    (b)   the payment is made in respect of the travel and accommodation expenses reasonably incurred in removing the child from the United Kingdom for the purpose of adoption.

Amendments—SI 2011/1740.

Defined terms—"adoption (in relation to Chapter 4 of Part 1)": s 66; "adoption order": s 46(1); "adoption society": s 2(5); "by virtue of": s 144; "child": ss 49(5), 144; "court", "guardian": s 144; "placement order": s 21; "registered adoption society": s 2(2).

97 Sections 92 to 96: interpretation

In sections 92 to 96 –

    (a)   "adoption agency" includes a Scottish or Northern Irish adoption agency,

    (b)   "payment" includes reward,

    (c)   references to adoption are to the adoption of persons, wherever they may be habitually resident, effected under the law of any country or territory, whether within or outside the British Islands.

Defined terms—"adoption (in relation to Chapter 4 of Part 1)": s 66; "adoption agency": s 2(1); "Northern Irish adoption agency": s 144.

Information

98 Pre-commencement adoptions: information

(1) Regulations under section 9 may make provision for the purpose of –

   (a) assisting persons adopted before the appointed day who have attained the age of 18 to obtain information in relation to their adoption, and
   (b) facilitating contact between such persons and their relatives.

(2) For that purpose the regulations may confer functions on –

   (a) registered adoption support agencies,
   (b) the Registrar General,
   (c) adoption agencies.

(3) For that purpose the regulations may –

   (a) authorise or require any person mentioned in subsection (2) to disclose information,
   (b) authorise or require the disclosure of information contained in records kept under section 8 of the Public Records Act 1958 (court records),

and may impose conditions on the disclosure of information, including conditions restricting its further disclosure.

(4) The regulations may authorise the charging of prescribed fees by any person mentioned in subsection (2) or in respect of the disclosure of information under subsection (3)(b).

(5) An authorisation or requirement to disclose information by virtue of subsection (3)(a) has effect in spite of any restriction on the disclosure of information in Chapter 5.

(6) The making of regulations by virtue of subsections (2) to (4) which relate to the Registrar General requires the approval of the Secretary of State.

(7) In this section –

   "appointed day" means the day appointed for the commencement of sections 56 to 65,
   "registered adoption support agency" means an adoption support agency in respect of which a person is registered under Part 2 of the Care Standards Act 2000,
   "relative", in relation to an adopted person, means any person who (but for his adoption) would be related to him by blood (including half-blood), marriage or civil partnership.

Amendments—CPA 2004, s 79(1),(10); SI 2008/678.

Defined terms—"adoption (in relation to Chapter 4 of Part 1)": s 66; "adoption support agency": s 8; "appointed day (in relation to Chapter 4 of Part 1)": s 66(2); "by virtue of", "court", "fee", "information": s 144; "records (in relation to Chapter 5 of Part 1)": s 82; "regulations": s 144; "relative": s 144, read with s 1(8).

Proceedings

99 Proceedings for offences

Proceedings for an offence by virtue of section 9 or 59 may not, without the written consent of the Attorney General, be taken by any person other than Her Majesty's Chief Inspector of Education, Children's Services and Skills or the Assembly.

Amendments—Health and Social Care (Community Health and Standards) Act 2003, s 147, Sch 9, para 32; Education and Inspections Act 2006, Sch 14, para 76.

Defined terms—"Assembly", "by virtue of": s 144.

****

101 Privacy

(1) Proceedings under this Act in the High Court or a County Court may be heard and determined in private.

(2)–(3) ...

The Children and Family Court Advisory and Support Service

102 Officers of the Service

(1) For the purposes of –

    (a) any relevant application,

    (b) the signification by any person of any consent to placement or adoption,

rules must provide for the appointment in prescribed cases of an officer of the Children and Family Court Advisory and Support Service ("the Service") or a Welsh Family proceedings officer.

(2) The rules may provide for the appointment of such an officer in other circumstances in which it appears to the Lord Chancellor to be necessary or expedient to do so.

(3) The rules may provide for the officer –

    (a) to act on behalf of the child upon the hearing of any relevant application, with the duty of safeguarding the interests of the child in the prescribed manner,

    (b) where the court so requests, to prepare a report on matters relating to the welfare of the child in question,

    (c) to witness documents which signify consent to placement or adoption,

    (d) to perform prescribed functions.

(4) A report prepared in pursuance of the rules on matters relating to the welfare of a child must –

    (a) deal with prescribed matters (unless the court orders otherwise), and

    (b) be made in the manner required by the court.

(5) A person who –

    (a) in the case of an application for the making, varying or revocation of a placement order, is employed by the local authority which made the application,

    (b) in the case of an application for an adoption order in respect of a child who was placed for adoption, is employed by the adoption agency which placed him, or

    (c) is within a prescribed description,

is not to be appointed under subsection (1) or (2).

(6) In this section, "relevant application" means an application for –

    (a) the making, varying or revocation of a placement order,

    (b) the making of an order under section 26, or the varying or revocation of such an order,

    (c) the making of an adoption order, or

    (d) the making of an order under section 84.

PART II

(7) Rules may make provision as to the assistance which the court may require an officer of the Service to give to it.

(8) In this section and section 103 "Welsh family proceedings officer" has the meaning given to it by section 35 of the Children Act 2004.

Amendments—CA 2004, s 40, Sch 3, paras 15, 16.

Defined terms—"adoption (in relation to Chapter 4 of Part 1)": s 66; "adoption agency": s 2(1); "adoption order": s 46(1); "child": ss 49(5), 144; "consent (in relation to making adoption orders or placing for adoption)": s 52; "court", "local authority": s 144; "placement order": s 21; "placing, or placed, for adoption": ss 18(5), 19(4); "rules": s 144.

103 Right of officers of the Service to have access to adoption agency records

(1) Where an officer of the Service or a Welsh family proceedings officer has been appointed to act under section 102(1), he has the right at all reasonable times to examine and take copies of any records of, or held by, an adoption agency which were compiled in connection with the making, or proposed making, by any person of any application under this Part in respect of the child concerned.

(2) Where an officer of the Service or a Welsh family proceedings officer takes a copy of any record which he is entitled to examine under this section, that copy or any part of it is admissible as evidence of any matter referred to in any –

    (a) report which he makes to the court in the proceedings in question, or

    (b) evidence which he gives in those proceedings.

(3) Subsection (2) has effect regardless of any enactment or rule of law which would otherwise prevent the record in question being admissible in evidence.

Amendments—CA 2004, s 40, Sch 3, paras 15, 17.

Defined terms—"adoption agency": s 2(1); "child": ss 49(5), 144; "court", "enactment": s 144; "records (in relation to Chapter 5 of Part 1)": s 82.

Evidence

104 Evidence of consent

(1) If a document signifying any consent which is required by this Part to be given is witnessed in accordance with rules, it is to be admissible in evidence without further proof of the signature of the person by whom it was executed.

(2) A document signifying any such consent which purports to be witnessed in accordance with rules is to be presumed to be so witnessed, and to have been executed and witnessed on the date and at the place specified in the document, unless the contrary is proved.

Defined terms—"consent (in relation to making adoption orders or placing for adoption)": s 52; "rules": s 144.

****

General

109 Avoiding delay

(1) In proceedings in which a question may arise as to whether an adoption order or placement order should be made, or any other question with respect to such an order, the court must (in the light of any rules made by virtue of subsection (2)) –

(a)   draw up a timetable with a view to determining such a question without delay, and

(b)   give such directions as it considers appropriate for the purpose of ensuring that the timetable is adhered to.

(2) Rules may –

(a)   prescribe periods within which prescribed steps must be taken in relation to such proceedings, and

(b)   make other provision with respect to such proceedings for the purpose of ensuring that such questions are determined without delay.

Defined terms—"adoption order": s 46(1); "by virtue of", "court": s 144; "placement order": s 21.

110 Service of notices etc

Any notice or information required to be given by virtue of this Act may be given by post.

Defined terms—"by virtue of", "information", "notice": s 144.

****

PART 3
MISCELLANEOUS AND FINAL PROVISIONS

Chapter 1
Miscellaneous

Advertisements in the United Kingdom

123 Restriction on advertisements etc

(1) A person must not –

(a)   publish or distribute an advertisement or information to which this section applies, or

(b)   cause such an advertisement or information to be published or distributed.

(2) This section applies to an advertisement indicating that –

(a)   the parent or guardian of a child wants the child to be adopted,

(b)   a person wants to adopt a child,

(c)   a person other than an adoption agency is willing to take any step mentioned in paragraphs (a) to (e), (g) and (h) and (so far as relating to those paragraphs) (i) of section 92(2),

(d)   a person other than an adoption agency is willing to receive a child handed over to him with a view to the child's adoption by him or another, or

(e)   a person is willing to remove a child from the United Kingdom for the purposes of adoption.

(3) This section applies to –

(a)   information about how to do anything which, if done, would constitute an offence under section 85 or 93, Article 11 or 58 of the Adoption (Northern Ireland) Order 1987 (SI 1987/2203 (NI 22)) or section 60 or 75 of the Adoption and Children (Scotland) Act 2007 (whether or not the information includes a warning that doing the thing in question may constitute an offence),

(b)   information about a particular child as a child available for adoption.

PART II

(4) For the purposes of this section and section 124 –

(a) publishing or distributing an advertisement or information means publishing it or distributing it to the public and includes doing so by electronic means (for example, by means of the internet),

(b) the public includes selected members of the public as well as the public generally or any section of the public.

(5) Subsection (1) does not apply to publication or distribution by or on behalf of an adoption agency.

(6) The Secretary of State may by order make any amendments of this section which he considers necessary or expedient in consequence of any developments in technology relating to publishing or distributing advertisements or other information by electronic or electro-magnetic means.

(7) References to an adoption agency in this section include a prescribed person outside the United Kingdom exercising functions corresponding to those of an adoption agency, if the functions are being exercised in prescribed circumstances.

"Prescribed" means prescribed by regulations made by the Secretary of State.

(8) Before exercising the power conferred by subsection (6) or (7), the Secretary of State must consult the Scottish Ministers, the Department of Health, Social Services and Public Safety and the Assembly.

(9) In this section –

(a) "adoption agency" includes a Scottish or Northern Irish adoption agency,

(b) references to adoption are to the adoption of persons, wherever they may be habitually resident, effected under the law of any country or territory, whether within or outside the British Islands.

Amendments—SI 2011/1740.

Defined terms—"adoption (in relation to Chapter 4 of Part 1)": s 66; "adoption agency": s 2(1); "Assembly": s 144; "child": ss 49(5), 144; "child to be adopted, adopted child": s 49(5); "guardian", "information", "Northern Irish adoption agency", "regulations": s 144.

124 Offence of breaching restriction under section 123

(1) A person who contravenes section 123(1) is guilty of an offence.

(2) A person is not guilty of an offence under this section unless it is proved that he knew or had reason to suspect that section 123 applied to the advertisement or information.

But this subsection only applies if sufficient evidence is adduced to raise an issue as to whether the person had the knowledge or reason mentioned.

(3) A person guilty of an offence under this section is liable on summary conviction to imprisonment for a term not exceeding three months, or a fine not exceeding level 5 on the standard scale, or both.

Defined terms—"information": s 144.

****

Chapter 2
Final provisions

140 Orders, rules and regulations

(1) Any power to make subordinate legislation conferred by this Act on the Lord Chancellor, the Secretary of State, the Scottish Ministers, the Assembly or the Registrar General is exercisable by statutory instrument.

(2) A statutory instrument containing subordinate legislation made under any provision of this Act (other than section 14 or 148 or an instrument to which subsection (3) applies) is to be subject to annulment in pursuance of a resolution of either House of Parliament.

(3) A statutory instrument containing subordinate legislation –

(a) under section 9 which includes provision made by virtue of section 45(2),
(b) under section 92(6), 94 or 123(6), or
(c) which adds to, replaces or omits any part of the text of an Act,

is not to be made unless a draft of the instrument has been laid before, and approved by resolution of, each House of Parliament.

(4) Subsections (2) and (3) do not apply to an Order in Council or to subordinate legislation made –

(a) by the Scottish Ministers, or
(b) by the Assembly, unless made jointly by the Secretary of State and the Assembly.

(5) A statutory instrument containing regulations under section 63(2) made by the Scottish Ministers is to be subject to annulment in pursuance of a resolution of the Scottish Parliament.

(6) The power of the Department of Health, Social Services and Public Safety to make regulations under section 63(2) is to be exercisable by statutory rule for the purposes of the Statutory Rules (Northern Ireland) Order 1979 (SI 1979/1573 (NI 12)); and any such regulations are to be subject to negative resolution within the meaning of section 41(6) of the Interpretation Act (Northern Ireland) 1954 as if they were statutory instruments within the meaning of that Act.

(7) Subordinate legislation made under this Act may make different provision for different purposes.

(8) A power to make subordinate legislation under this Act (as well as being exercisable in relation to all cases to which it extends) may be exercised in relation to –

(a) those cases subject to specified exceptions, or
(b) a particular case or class of case.

(9) In this section, "subordinate legislation" does not include a direction.

Defined terms—"Assembly", "by virtue of", "regulations", "rules", "subordinate legislation": s 144.

141 Rules of procedure

(1) Family Procedure Rules may make provision in respect of any matter to be prescribed by rules made by virtue of this Act and dealing generally with all matters of procedure.

(2) (*repealed*)

(3) In the case of an application for a placement order, for the variation or revocation of such an order, or for an adoption order, the rules must require any person mentioned in subsection (4) to be notified –

    (a)   of the date and place where the application will be heard, and

    (b)   of the fact that, unless the person wishes or the court requires, the person need not attend.

(4) The persons referred to in subsection (3) are –

    (a)   in the case of a placement order, every person who can be found whose consent to the making of the order is required under subsection (3)(a) of section 21 (or would be required but for subsection (3)(b) of that section) or, if no such person can be found, any relative prescribed by rules who can be found,

    (b)   in the case of a variation or revocation of a placement order, every person who can be found whose consent to the making of the placement order was required under subsection (3)(a) of section 21 (or would have been required but for subsection (3)(b) of that section),

    (c)   in the case of an adoption order –

        (i)   every person who can be found whose consent to the making of the order is required under subsection (2)(a) of section 47 (or would be required but for subsection (2)(c) of that section) or, if no such person can be found, any relative prescribed by rules who can be found,

        (ii) every person who has consented to the making of the order under section 20 (and has not withdrawn the consent) unless he has given a notice under subsection (4)(a) of that section which has effect,

        (iii) every person who, if leave were given under section 47(5), would be entitled to oppose the making of the order.

(5) Rules made in respect of magistrates' courts may provide –

    (a)   for enabling any fact tending to establish the identity of a child with a child to whom a document relates to be proved by affidavit, and

    (b)   for excluding or restricting in relation to any facts that may be so proved the power of a justice of the peace to compel the attendance of witnesses.

(6) Rules may, for the purposes of the law relating to contempt of court, authorise the publication in such circumstances as may be specified of information relating to proceedings held in private involving children.

Amendments—Courts Act 2003, s 109(1), Sch 8, para 413, Sch 10; CA 2004, s 62(6).

Defined terms—"adoption order": s 46(1); "by virtue of": s 144; "child": ss 49(5), 144; "consent (in relation to making adoption orders or placing for adoption)": s 52; "court", "information", "notice": s 144; "placement order": s 21; "relative": s 144, read with s 1(8); "rules": s 144.

142 Supplementary and consequential provision

(1) The appropriate Minister may by order make –

    (a)   any supplementary, incidental or consequential provision,

    (b)   any transitory, transitional or saving provision,

which he considers necessary or expedient for the purposes of, in consequence of or for giving full effect to any provision of this Act.

(2) For the purposes of subsection (1), where any provision of an order extends to England and Wales, and Scotland or Northern Ireland, the appropriate Minister in relation to the order is the Secretary of State.

(3) Before making an order under subsection (1) containing provision which would, if included in an Act of the Scottish Parliament, be within the legislative competence of that Parliament, the appropriate Minister must consult the Scottish Ministers.

(4) Subsection (5) applies to any power of the Lord Chancellor, the Secretary of State or the Assembly to make regulations, rules or an order by virtue of any other provision of this Act or of Her Majesty to make an Order in Council by virtue of section 125.

(5) The power may be exercised so as to make –

    (a)   any supplementary, incidental or consequential provision,

    (b)   any transitory, transitional or saving provision,

which the person exercising the power considers necessary or expedient.

(6) The provision which may be made under subsection (1) or (5) includes provision modifying Schedule 4 or amending or repealing any enactment or instrument.

In relation to an Order in Council, "enactment" in this subsection includes an enactment comprised in, or in an instrument made under, an Act of the Scottish Parliament.

(7) The power of the Registrar General to make regulations under Chapter 5 of Part 1 may, with the approval of the Secretary of State, be exercised so as to make –

    (a)   any supplementary, incidental or consequential provision,

    (b)   any transitory, transitional or saving provision,

which the Registrar General considers necessary or expedient.

Amendments—SI 2008/678.

Defined terms—"appropriate Minister", "Assembly", "by virtue of", "enactment", "regulations", "rules": s 144.

143 Offences by bodies corporate and unincorporated bodies

(1) Where an offence under this Act committed by a body corporate is proved to have been committed with the consent or connivance of, or to be attributable to any neglect on the part of, any director, manager, secretary or other similar officer of the body, or a person purporting to act in any such capacity, that person as well as the body is guilty of the offence and liable to be proceeded against and punished accordingly.

(2) Where the affairs of a body corporate are managed by its members, subsection (1) applies in relation to the acts and defaults of a member in connection with his functions of management as it applies to a director of a body corporate.

(3) Proceedings for an offence alleged to have been committed under this Act by an unincorporated body are to be brought in the name of that body (and not in that of any of its members) and, for the purposes of any such proceedings in England and Wales or Northern Ireland, any rules of court relating to the service of documents have effect as if that body were a corporation.

(4) A fine imposed on an unincorporated body on its conviction of an offence under this Act is to be paid out of the funds of that body.

(5) If an unincorporated body is charged with an offence under this Act –

    (a)   in England and Wales, section 33 of the Criminal Justice Act 1925 and Schedule 3 to the Magistrates' Courts Act 1980 (procedure on charge of an offence against a corporation),

    (b)   in Northern Ireland, section 18 of the Criminal Justice Act (Northern Ireland) 1945 and Schedule 4 to the Magistrates' Courts (Northern Ireland) Order 1981 (SI 1981/1675 (NI 26)) (procedure on charge of an offence against a corporation),

have effect in like manner as in the case of a corporation so charged.

(6) Where an offence under this Act committed by an unincorporated body (other than a partnership) is proved to have been committed with the consent or connivance of, or to

be attributable to any neglect on the part of, any officer of the body or any member of its governing body, he as well as the body is guilty of the offence and liable to be proceeded against and punished accordingly.

(7) Where an offence under this Act committed by a partnership is proved to have been committed with the consent or connivance of, or to be attributable to any neglect on the part of, a partner, he as well as the partnership is guilty of the offence and liable to be proceeded against and punished accordingly.

Defined terms—"body", "court", "rules": s 144.

144 General interpretation etc

(1) In this Act –

"appropriate Minister" means –
- (a)   in relation to England, Scotland or Northern Ireland, the Secretary of State,
- (b)   in relation to Wales, the Assembly,
and in relation to England and Wales means the Secretary of State and the Assembly acting jointly,

"the Assembly" means the National Assembly for Wales,

"body" includes an unincorporated body,

"by virtue of" includes "by" and "under",

"child", except where used to express a relationship, means a person who has not attained the age of 18 years,

"the Convention" means the Convention on Protection of Children and Co-operation in respect of Intercountry Adoption, concluded at the Hague on 29th May 1993,

"Convention adoption order" means an adoption order which, by virtue of regulations under section 1 of the Adoption (Intercountry Aspects) Act 1999 (regulations giving effect to the Convention), is made as a Convention adoption order,

"Convention country" means a country or territory in which the Convention is in force,

"court" means, subject to any provision made by virtue of Part 1 of Schedule 11 to the 1989 Act, the High Court, a county court or a magistrates' court,

"enactment" includes an enactment comprised in subordinate legislation,

"fee" includes expenses,

"guardian" has the same meaning as in the 1989 Act and includes a special guardian within the meaning of that Act,

"information" means information recorded in any form,

"local authority" means any unitary authority, or any county council so far as they are not a unitary authority,

"Northern Irish adoption agency" means an adoption agency within the meaning of Article 3 of the Adoption (Northern Ireland) Order 1987 (SI 1987/2203 (NI 22)),

"Northern Irish adoption order" means an order made, or having effect as if made, under Article 12 of the Adoption (Northern Ireland) Order 1987,

"notice" means a notice in writing,

"registration authority" (in Part 1) has the same meaning as in the Care Standards Act 2000,

"regulations" means regulations made by the appropriate Minister, unless they are required to be made by the Lord Chancellor, the Secretary of State or the Registrar General,

"relative", in relation to a child, means a grandparent, brother, sister, uncle or aunt, whether of the full blood or half-blood or by marriage or civil partnership,

"rules" means Family Procedure Rules made by virtue of section 141(1),

...

"subordinate legislation" has the same meaning as in the Interpretation Act 1978,
"unitary authority" means –

    (a)   the council of any county so far as they are the council for an area for which there are no district councils,

    (b)   the council of any district comprised in an area for which there is no county council,

    (c)   the council of a county borough,

    (d)   the council of a London borough,

    (e)   the Common Council of the City of London.

(2) Any power conferred by this Act to prescribe a fee by Order in Council or regulations includes power to prescribe –

    (a)   a fee not exceeding a prescribed amount,

    (b)   a fee calculated in accordance with the Order or, as the case may be, regulations,

    (c)   a fee determined by the person to whom it is payable, being a fee of a reasonable amount.

(3) In this Act, "Scottish adoption agency" means –

    (a)   a local authority, or

    (b)   a voluntary organisation providing a registered adoption service;

but in relation to the provision of any particular service, references to a Scottish adoption agency do not include a voluntary organisation unless it is registered in respect of that service or a service which, in Scotland, corresponds to that service.

Expressions used in this subsection have the same meaning as in the Regulation of Care (Scotland) Act 2001 and "registered" means registered under Part 1 of that Act.

(4) In this Act, a couple means –

    (a)   a married couple, or

    (aa) two people who are civil partners of each other, or

    (b)   two people (whether of different sexes or the same sex) living as partners in an enduring family relationship.

(5) Subsection (4)(b) does not include two people one of whom is the other's parent, grandparent, sister, brother, aunt or uncle.

(6) References to relationships in subsection (5) –

    (a)   are to relationships of the full blood or half blood or, in the case of an adopted person, such of those relationships as would exist but for adoption, and

    (b)   include the relationship of a child with his adoptive, or former adoptive, parents,

but do not include any other adoptive relationships.

(7) For the purposes of this Act, a person is the partner of a child's parent if the person and the parent are a couple but the person is not the child's parent.

Amendments—Courts Act 2003, s 109(1), Sch 8, para 414; CPA 2004, s 79(1),(11),(12).

Defined terms—"the 1989 Act": s 2(5); "adoption (in relation to Chapter 4 of Part 1)": s 66; "adoption agency": s 2(1); "adoption order": s 46(1); "Adoption Service": s 2(1); "appropriate Minister", "Assembly", "body", "by virtue of": s 144; "child": ss 49(5), 144; "the Convention", "Convention adoption order", "Convention country": s 144; "couple": s 144(4); "court", "enactment", "fee", "guardian", "information", "local authority", "Northern Irish adoption agency", "Northern Irish adoption order", "notice": s 144; "partner, in relation to a parent of a child": s 144(7); "registration authority (in Part 1)", "regulations" and "relative": s 144, read with s 1(8); "rules": s 144; "Scottish adoption agency": s 144(3); "Scottish adoption order", "subordinate legislation", "unitary authority": s 144; "voluntary organisation": s 2(5).

"relative" (s 144(1))—The definition is in precise terms – a great-uncle does not come within the definition (*Re C (Minors) (Wardship: Adoption)* [1989] 1 FLR 222); however, a step-grandparent *is* within the definition (for example, see *Re U (Application to Free for Adoption)* [1993] 2 FLR 992).

"couple" (s 144(4))—To establish that a couple are "living as partners in an enduring family relationship", there must first be an unambiguous intention to create and maintain family life and, second, a factual matrix consistent with that intention. Both matters are a question of fact and degree in each case. There is no requirement that both partners should reside in the same property (*Re T and M (Adoption)* [2011] 1 FLR 1487).

145 Devolution: Wales

(1) The references to the Adoption Act 1976 and to the 1989 Act in Schedule 1 to the National Assembly for Wales (Transfer of Functions) Order 1999 (SI 1999/672) are to be treated as referring to those Acts as amended by virtue of this Act.

(2) This section does not affect the power to make further Orders varying or omitting those references.

(3) In Schedule 1 to that Order, in the entry for the Adoption Act 1976, "9" is omitted.

(4) The functions exercisable by the Assembly under sections 9 and 9A of the Adoption Act 1976 (by virtue of paragraphs 4 and 5 of Schedule 4 to this Act) are to be treated for the purposes of section 44 of the Government of Wales Act 1998 (parliamentary procedures for subordinate legislation) as if made exercisable by the Assembly by an Order in Council under section 22 of that Act.

Defined terms—"the 1989 Act": s 2(5); "Assembly", "by virtue of", "subordinate legislation": s 144.

146 Expenses

There shall be paid out of money provided by Parliament –

(a)   any expenditure incurred by a Minister of the Crown by virtue of this Act,
(b)   any increase attributable to this Act in the sums payable out of money so provided under any other enactment.

Defined terms—"by virtue of", "enactment": s 144.

147 Glossary

Schedule 6 (glossary) is to have effect.

148 Commencement

(1) This Act (except sections 116 and 136, this Chapter and the provisions mentioned in subsections (5) and (6)) is to come into force on such day as the Secretary of State may by order appoint.

(2) Before making an order under subsection (1) (other than an order bringing paragraph 53 of Schedule 3 into force) the Secretary of State must consult the Assembly.

(3) Before making an order under subsection (1) bringing sections 123 and 124 into force, the Secretary of State must also consult the Scottish Ministers and the Department of Health, Social Services and Public Safety.

(4) Before making an order under subsection (1) bringing sections 125 to 131 into force, the Secretary of State must also consult the Scottish Ministers.

(5) The following are to come into force on such day as the Scottish Ministers may by order appoint –

(a)   section 41(5) to (9), so far as relating to Scotland,
(b)   sections 132 to 134,

(c) paragraphs 21 to 35 and 82 to 84 of Schedule 3,

(d) paragraphs 15 and 23 of Schedule 4,

(e) the entries in Schedule 5, so far as relating to the provisions mentioned in paragraphs (c) and (d),

(f) section 139, so far as relating to the provisions mentioned in the preceding paragraphs.

(6) Sections 2(6), 3(3) and (4), 4 to 17, 27(3), 53(1) to (3), 54, 56 to 65 and 98, paragraphs 13, 65, 66 and 111 to 113 of Schedule 3 and paragraphs 3 and 5 of Schedule 4 are to come into force on such day as the appropriate Minister may by order appoint.

Defined terms—"appropriate Minister", "Assembly": s 144.

149 Extent

(1) The amendment or repeal of an enactment has the same extent as the enactment to which it relates.

(2) Subject to that and to the following provisions, this Act except section 137 extends to England and Wales only.

(3) The following extend also to Scotland and Northern Ireland –

(a) sections 63(2) to (5), 65(2)(a) and (b) and (3), 123 and 124,

(b) this Chapter, except sections 141 and 145.

(4) The following extend also to Scotland –

(a) section 41(5) to (9),

(b) sections 125 to 131,

(c) section 138,

(d) section 139, so far as relating to provisions extending to Scotland.

(5) In Schedule 4, paragraph 23 extends only to Scotland.

Defined terms—"enactment": s 144.

150 Short title

This Act may be cited as the Adoption and Children Act 2002.

SCHEDULE 1

REGISTRATION OF ADOPTIONS

1 Registration of adoption orders

(1) Every adoption order must contain a direction to the Registrar General to make in the Adopted Children Register an entry in the form prescribed by regulations made by the Registrar General with the approval of the Secretary of State.

(2) Where, on an application to a court for an adoption order in respect of a child, the identity of the child with a child to whom an entry in the registers of live-births or other records relates is proved to the satisfaction of the court, any adoption order made in pursuance of the application must contain a direction to the Registrar General to secure that the entry in the register or, as the case may be, record in question is marked with the word "Adopted".

(3) Where an adoption order is made in respect of a child who has previously been the subject of an adoption order made by a court in England or Wales under Part 1 of this Act or any other enactment –

(a)   sub-paragraph (2) does not apply, and

(b)   the order must contain a direction to the Registrar General to mark the previous entry in the Adopted Children Register with the word "Re-adopted".

(4) Where an adoption order is made, the prescribed officer of the court which made the order must communicate the order to the Registrar General in the prescribed manner; and the Registrar General must then comply with the directions contained in the order.

"Prescribed" means prescribed by rules.

Amendments—SI 2008/678.

Defined terms—"Adopted Children Register": s 77; "adoption order": s 46(1); "child": ss 49(5), 144; "court", "enactment": s 144; "records (in relation to Chapter 5 of Part 1)": s 82; "registers of live-births (in relation to Chapter 5 of Part 1)": s 82; "regulations", "rules": s 144.

2 Registration of adoptions in Scotland, Northern Ireland, the Isle of Man and the Channel Islands

(1) Sub-paragraphs (2) and (3) apply where the Registrar General is notified by the authority maintaining a register of adoptions in a part of the British Islands outside England and Wales that an order has been made in that part authorising the adoption of a child.

(2) If an entry in the registers of live-births or other records (and no entry in the Adopted Children Register) relates to the child, the Registrar General must secure that the entry is marked with –

(a)   the word "Adopted", followed by

(b)   the name, in brackets, of the part in which the order was made.

(3) If an entry in the Adopted Children Register relates to the child, the Registrar General must mark the entry with –

(a)   the word "Re-adopted", followed by

(b)   the name, in brackets, of the part in which the order was made.

(4) Where, after an entry in either of the registers or other records mentioned in sub-paragraphs (2) and (3) has been so marked, the Registrar General is notified by the authority concerned that –

(a)   the order has been quashed,

(b)   an appeal against the order has been allowed, or

(c)   the order has been revoked,

the Registrar General must secure that the marking is cancelled.

(5) A copy or extract of an entry in any register or other record, being an entry the marking of which is cancelled under sub-paragraph (4), is not to be treated as an accurate copy unless both the marking and the cancellation are omitted from it.

Defined terms—"Adopted Children Register": s 77; "adoption (in relation to Chapter 4 of Part 1)": s 66; "child": ss 49(5), 144; "records (in relation to Chapter 5 of Part 1)": s 82; "registers of live-births (in relation to Chapter 5 of Part 1)": s 82.

3 Registration of other adoptions

(1) If the Registrar General is satisfied, on an application under this paragraph, that he has sufficient particulars relating to a child adopted under a registrable foreign adoption to enable an entry to be made in the Adopted Children Register for the child he must make the entry accordingly.

(2) If he is also satisfied that an entry in the registers of live-births or other records relates to the child, he must –

(a) secure that the entry is marked "Adopted", followed by the name, in brackets, of the country in which the adoption was effected, or

(b) where appropriate, secure that the overseas registers of births are so marked.

(3) An application under this paragraph must be made, in the prescribed manner, by a prescribed person and the applicant must provide the prescribed documents and other information.

(4) An entry made in the Adopted Children Register by virtue of this paragraph must be made in the prescribed form.

(5) In this Schedule "registrable foreign adoption" means an adoption which satisfies prescribed requirements and is either –

(a) adoption under a Convention adoption, or

(b) adoption under an overseas adoption.

(6) In this paragraph –

(a) "prescribed" means prescribed by regulations made by the Registrar General with the approval of the Secretary of State,

(b) "overseas register of births" includes –

   (i) a register made under regulations made by the Secretary of State under section 41(1)(g), (h) or (i) of the British Nationality Act 1981,

   (ii) a record kept under an Order in Council made under section 1 of the Registration of Births, Deaths and Marriages (Special Provisions) Act 1957 (other than a certified copy kept by the Registrar General).

Amendments—SI 2008/678.

Defined terms—"Adopted Children Register": s 77; "adoption (in relation to Chapter 4 of Part 1)": s 66; "by virtue of": s 144; "child": ss 49(5), 144; "Convention adoption": s 66(1)(c); "information": s 144; "overseas adoption": s 87; "records (in relation to Chapter 5 of Part 1)": s 82; "registers of live-births (in relation to Chapter 5 of Part 1)": s 82; "regulations": s 144.

4 Amendment of orders and rectification of Registers and other records

(1) The court by which an adoption order has been made may, on the application of the adopter or the adopted person, amend the order by the correction of any error in the particulars contained in it.

(2) The court by which an adoption order has been made may, if satisfied on the application of the adopter or the adopted person that within the period of one year beginning with the date of the order any new name –

(a) has been given to the adopted person (whether in baptism or otherwise), or

(b) has been taken by the adopted person,

either in place of or in addition to a name specified in the particulars required to be entered in the Adopted Children Register in pursuance of the order, amend the order by substituting or, as the case may be, adding that name in those particulars.

(3) The court by which an adoption order has been made may, if satisfied on the application of any person concerned that a direction for the marking of an entry in the registers of live-births, the Adopted Children Register or other records included in the order in pursuance of paragraph 1(2) or (3) was wrongly so included, revoke that direction.

(4) Where an adoption order is amended or a direction revoked under sub-paragraphs (1) to (3), the prescribed officer of the court must communicate the amendment in the prescribed manner to the Registrar General.

"Prescribed" means prescribed by rules.

(5) The Registrar General must then –

(a) amend the entry in the Adopted Children Register accordingly, or

(b) secure that the marking of the entry in the registers of live-births, the Adopted Children Register or other records is cancelled,

as the case may be.

(6) Where an adoption order is quashed or an appeal against an adoption order allowed by any court, the court must give directions to the Registrar General to secure that –

(a) any entry in the Adopted Children Register, and

(b) any marking of an entry in that Register, the registers of live-births or other records as the case may be, which was effected in pursuance of the order,

is cancelled.

(7) Where an adoption order has been amended, any certified copy of the relevant entry in the Adopted Children Register which may be issued pursuant to section 78(2)(b) must be a copy of the entry as amended, without the reproduction of –

(a) any note or marking relating to the amendment, or

(b) any matter cancelled in pursuance of it.

(8) A copy or extract of an entry in any register or other record, being an entry the marking of which has been cancelled, is not to be treated as an accurate copy unless both the marking and the cancellation are omitted from it.

(9) If the Registrar General is satisfied –

(a) that a registrable foreign adoption has ceased to have effect, whether on annulment or otherwise, or

(b) that any entry or mark was erroneously made in pursuance of paragraph 3 in the Adopted Children Register, the registers of live-births, the overseas registers of births or other records,

he may secure that such alterations are made in those registers or other records as he considers are required in consequence of the adoption ceasing to have effect or to correct the error.

"Overseas register of births" has the same meaning as in paragraph 3.

(10) Where an entry in such a register is amended in pursuance of sub-paragraph (9), any copy or extract of the entry is not to be treated as accurate unless it shows the entry as amended but without indicating that it has been amended.

Defined terms—"Adopted Children Register": s 77; "adoption (in relation to Chapter 4 of Part 1)": s 66; "adoption order": s 46(1); "court": s 144; "records (in relation to Chapter 5 of Part 1)": s 82; "registers of live-births (in relation to Chapter 5 of Part 1)": s 82; "rules": s 144.

5 Marking of entries on re-registration of birth on legitimation

(1) Without prejudice to paragraphs 2(4) and 4(5), where, after an entry in the registers of live-births or other records has been marked in accordance with paragraph 1 or 2, the birth is re-registered under section 14 of the Births and Deaths Registration Act 1953 (re-registration of births of legitimated persons), the entry made on the re-registration must be marked in the like manner.

(2) Without prejudice to paragraph 4(9), where an entry in the registers of live-births or other records is marked in pursuance of paragraph 3 and the birth in question is subsequently re-registered under section 14 of that Act, the entry made on re-registration must be marked in the like manner.

Defined terms—"records (in relation to Chapter 5 of Part 1)", "registers of live-births (in relation to Chapter 5 of Part 1)": s 82.

6 Cancellations in registers on legitimation

(1) This paragraph applies where an adoption order is revoked under section 55(1).

(2) The prescribed officer of the court must communicate the revocation in the prescribed manner to the Registrar General who must then cancel or secure the cancellation of –

    (a)   the entry in the Adopted Children Register relating to the adopted person, and

    (b)   the marking with the word "Adopted" of any entry relating to the adopted person in the registers of live-births or other records.

"Prescribed" means prescribed by rules.

(3) A copy or extract of an entry in any register or other record, being an entry the marking of which is cancelled under this paragraph, is not to be treated as an accurate copy unless both the marking and the cancellation are omitted from it.

Defined terms—"Adopted Children Register": s 77; "court": s 144; "records (in relation to Chapter 5 of Part 1)" and "registers of live-births (in relation to Chapter 5 of Part 1)": s 82; "rules": s 144.

SCHEDULE 2

DISCLOSURE OF BIRTH RECORDS BY REGISTRAR GENERAL

1 On an application made in the prescribed manner by an adopted person –

    (a)   a record of whose birth is kept by the Registrar General, and

    (b)   who has attained the age of 18 years,

the Registrar General must give the applicant any information necessary to enable the applicant to obtain a certified copy of the record of his birth.

       "Prescribed" means prescribed by regulations made by the Registrar General with the approval of the Secretary of State.

Amendments—SI 2008/678.

Defined terms—"information", "regulations": s 144.

2 (1) Before giving any information to an applicant under paragraph 1, the Registrar General must inform the applicant that counselling services are available to the applicant –

    (a)   from a registered adoption society, an organisation within section 144(3)(b) or an adoption society which is registered under Article 4 of the Adoption (Northern Ireland) Order 1987 (SI 1987/2203 (NI 22)),

    (b)   if the applicant is in England and Wales, at the General Register Office or from any local authority or registered adoption support agency,

    (c)   if the applicant is in Scotland, from any council constituted under section 2 of the Local Government etc (Scotland) Act 1994,

    (d)   if the applicant is in Northern Ireland, from any Board.

(2) In sub-paragraph (1)(b), "registered adoption support agency" means an adoption support agency in respect of which a person is registered under Part 2 of the Care Standards Act 2000.

(3) In sub-paragraph (1)(d), "Board" means a Health and Social Services Board established under Article 16 of the Health and Personal Social Services (Northern Ireland) Order 1972 (SI 1972/1265 (NI 14)); but where the functions of a Board are exercisable by a Health and Social Services Trust, references in that sub-paragraph to a Board are to be read as references to the Health and Social Services Trust.

(4) If the applicant chooses to receive counselling from a person or body within sub-paragraph (1), the Registrar General must send to the person or body the information to which the applicant is entitled under paragraph 1.

Defined terms—"adoption society": s 2(5); "adoption support agency": s 8; "body", "information", "local authority": s 144; "registered adoption society": s 2(2).

3 (1) Where an adopted person who is in England and Wales –

  (a) applies for information under paragraph 1 or Article 54 of the Adoption (Northern Ireland) Order 1987, or

  (b) is supplied with information under section 55(4)(b) of the Adoption and Children (Scotland) Act 2007,

the persons and bodies mentioned in sub-paragraph (2) must, if asked by the applicant to do so, provide counselling for the applicant.

(2) Those persons and bodies are –

  (a) the Registrar General,

  (b) any local authority,

  (c) a registered adoption society, an organisation within section 144(3)(b) or an adoption society which is registered under Article 4 of the Adoption (Northern Ireland) Order 1987.

Amendments—SI 2011/1740.

Defined terms—"adoption society": s 2(5); "information", "local authority": s 144; "registered adoption society": s 2(2).

4 (1) Where a person –

  (a) was adopted before 12th November 1975, and

  (b) applies for information under paragraph 1,

the Registrar General must not give the information to the applicant unless the applicant has attended an interview with a counsellor arranged by a person or body from whom counselling services are available as mentioned in paragraph 2.

(2) Where the Registrar General is prevented by sub-paragraph (1) from giving information to a person who is not living in the United Kingdom, the Registrar General may give the information to any body which –

  (a) the Registrar General is satisfied is suitable to provide counselling to that person, and

  (b) has notified the Registrar General that it is prepared to provide such counselling.

Defined terms—"body", "information": s 144.

****

SCHEDULE 4

TRANSITIONAL AND TRANSITORY PROVISIONS AND SAVINGS

1 General rules for continuity

(1) Any reference (express or implied) in Part 1 or any other enactment, instrument or document to –

  (a) any provision of Part 1, or

(b)   things done or falling to be done under or for the purposes of any provision of Part 1,

must, so far as the nature of the reference permits, be construed as including, in relation to the times, circumstances or purposes in relation to which the corresponding provision repealed by this Act had effect, a reference to that corresponding provision or (as the case may be) to things done or falling to be done under or for the purposes of that corresponding provision.

(2)   Any reference (express or implied) in any enactment, instrument or document to –

(a)   a provision repealed by this Act, or

(b)   things done or falling to be done under or for the purposes of such a provision,

must, so far as the nature of the reference permits, be construed as including, in relation to the times, circumstances or purposes in relation to which the corresponding provision of Part 1 has effect, a reference to that corresponding provision or (as the case may be) to things done or falling to be done under or for the purposes of that corresponding provision.

2 General rule for old savings

(1)   The repeal by this Act of an enactment previously repealed subject to savings does not affect the continued operation of those savings.

(2)   The repeal by this Act of a saving made on the previous repeal of an enactment does not affect the operation of the saving in so far as it is not specifically reproduced in this Act but remains capable of having effect.

3–5 *(repealed)*

6 Pending applications for freeing orders

Nothing in this Act affects any application for an order under section 18 of the Adoption Act 1976 (freeing for adoption) where –

(a)   the application has been made and has not been disposed of immediately before the repeal of that section, and

(b)   the child in relation to whom the application is made has his home immediately before that repeal with a person with whom he has been placed for adoption by an adoption agency.

7 Freeing orders

(1)   Nothing in this Act affects any order made under section 18 of the Adoption Act 1976 and –

(a)   sections 19 to 21 of that Act are to continue to have effect in relation to such an order, and

(b)   Part 1 of Schedule 6 to the Magistrates' Courts Act 1980 is to continue to have effect for the purposes of an application under section 21 of the Adoption Act 1976 in relation to such an order.

(2)   Section 20 of that Act, as it has effect by virtue of this paragraph, is to apply as if, in subsection (3)(c) after "1989" there were inserted –

"(iia)   any care order, within the meaning of that Act".

(3)   Where a child is free for adoption by virtue of an order made under section 18 of that Act, the third condition in section 47(6) is to be treated as satisfied.

8 Pending applications for adoption orders

Nothing in this Act affects any application for an adoption order under section 12 of the Adoption Act 1976 where –

(a) the application has been made and has not been disposed of immediately before the repeal of that section, and

(b) the child in relation to whom the application is made has his home immediately before that repeal with a person with whom he has been placed for adoption by an adoption agency.

9 Notification of adoption applications

Where a notice given in respect of a child by the prospective adopters under section 22(1) of the Adoption Act 1976 is treated by virtue of paragraph 1(1) as having been given for the purposes of section 44(2) in respect of an application to adopt the child, section 42(3) has effect in relation to their application for an adoption order as if for "six months" there were substituted "twelve months".

10–16 (repealed)

17 Status

(1) Section 67 –

(a) does not apply to a pre-1976 instrument or enactment in so far as it contains a disposition of property, and

(b) does not apply to any public general Act in its application to any disposition of property in a pre-1976 instrument or enactment.

(2) Section 73 applies in relation to this paragraph as if this paragraph were contained in Chapter 4 of Part 1; and an instrument or enactment is a pre-1976 instrument or enactment for the purposes of this Schedule if it was passed or made at any time before 1 January 1976.

18 Section 69 does not apply to a pre-1976 instrument.

19 In section 70(1), the reference to Part 3 of the Family Law Reform Act 1987 includes Part 2 of the Family Law Reform Act 1969.

20 Registration of adoptions

(1) The power of the court under paragraph 4(1) of Schedule 1 to amend an order on the application of the adopter or adopted person includes, in relation to an order made before 1 April 1959, power to make any amendment of the particulars contained in the order which appears to be required to bring the order into the form in which it would have been made if paragraph 1 of that Schedule had applied to the order.

(2) In relation to an adoption order made before the commencement of the Adoption Act 1976, the reference in paragraph 4(3) of that Schedule to paragraph 1(2) or (3) is to be read –

(a) in the case of an order under the Adoption of Children Act 1926, as a reference to section 12(3) and (4) of the Adoption of Children Act 1949,

(b) in the case of an order under the Adoption Act 1950, as a reference to section 18(3) and (4) of that Act,

(c) in the case of an order under the Adoption Act 1958, as a reference to section 21(4) and (5) of that Act.

21 The Child Abduction Act 1984

Paragraph 43 of Schedule 3 does not affect the Schedule to the Child Abduction Act 1984 in its application to a child who is the subject of –

  (a) an order under section 18 of the Adoption Act 1976 freeing the child for adoption,
  (b) a pending application for such an order, or
  (c) a pending application for an order under section 12 of that Act.

22 The Courts and Legal Services Act 1990

Paragraph 80 of Schedule 3 does not affect section 58A(2)(b) of the Courts and Legal Services Act 1990 in its application to proceedings under the Adoption Act 1976.
****

PART II

SCHEDULE 6

GLOSSARY

In this Act, the expressions listed in the left-hand column below have the meaning given by, or are to be interpreted in accordance with, the provisions of this Act or (where stated) of the 1989 Act listed in the right-hand column.

Expression	Provision
the 1989 Act	section 2(5)
Adopted Children Register	section 77
Adoption and Children Act Register	section 125
adoption (in relation to Chapter 4 of Part 1)	section 66
adoption agency	section 2(1)
adoption agency placing a child for adoption	section 18(5)
Adoption Contact Register	section 80
adoption order	section 46(1)
Adoption Service	section 2(1)
adoption society	section 2(5)
adoption support agency	section 8
adoption support services	section 2(6)
appointed day (in relation to Chapter 4 of Part 1)	section 66(2)
appropriate Minister	section 144
Assembly	section 144
Body	section 144
by virtue of	section 144
care order	section 105(1) of the 1989 Act
Child	sections 49(5) and 144
child assessment order	section 43(2) of the 1989 Act
child in the care of a local authority	section 105(1) of the 1989 Act
child looked after by a local authority	section 22 of the 1989 Act
child placed for adoption by an adoption agency	section 18(5)
child to be adopted, adopted child	section 49(5)

Expression	Provision
consent (in relation to making adoption orders or placing for adoption)	section 52
the Convention	section 144
Convention adoption	section 66(1)(c)
Convention adoption order	section 144
Convention country	section 144
Couple	section 144(4)
Court	section 144
disposition (in relation to Chapter 4 of Part 1)	section 73
Enactment	section 144
Fee	section 144
Guardian	section 144
Information	section 144
interim care order	section 38 of the 1989 Act
local authority	section 144
local authority foster parent	section 22C(12) of the 1989 Act
Northern Irish adoption agency	section 144
Northern Irish adoption order	section 144
Notice	section 144
notice of intention to adopt	section 44(2)
overseas adoption	section 87
parental responsibility	section 3 of the 1989 Act
partner, in relation to a parent of a child	section 144(7)
placement order	section 21
placing, or placed, for adoption	sections 18(5) and 19(4)
prohibited steps order	section 8(1) of the 1989 Act
records (in relation to Chapter 5 of Part 1)	section 82
registered adoption society	section 2(2)
registers of live-births (in relation to Chapter 5 of Part 1)	section 82
registration authority (in Part 1)	section 144
Regulations	section 144
Relative	section 144, read with section 1(8)
residence order	section 8(1) of the 1989 Act
Rules	section 144
Scottish adoption agency	section 144(3)
Scottish adoption order	section 144
specific issue order	section 8(1) of the 1989 Act
subordinate legislation	section 144
supervision order	section 31(11) of the 1989 Act
unitary authority	section 144
voluntary organisation	section 2(5)

Amendments—CYPA 2008, s 8(3), Sch 1, para 14.

Defined terms—"the 1989 Act": s 2(5); "Adoption and Children Act Register": s 125; "adoption (in relation to Chapter 4 of Part 1)": s 66; "adoption agency": s 2(1); "adoption order": s 46(1); "Adoption Service": s 2(1); "adoption society": s 2(5); "adoption support agency": s 8; "adoption support services": s 2(6); "appointed day (in relation to Chapter 4 of Part 1)": s 66(2); "appropriate Minister", "Assembly", "body", "by virtue of": s 144; "care order": s 105(1) of the 1989 Act; "child": ss 49(5) and 144; "child assessment order": s 43(2) of the 1989 Act; "child in the care of a local authority": s 105(1) of the 1989 Act; "child looked after by a local authority": s 22 of the 1989 Act; "child placed for adoption by an adoption agency": s 18(5); "child to be adopted, adopted child": s 49(5); "consent (in relation to making adoption orders or placing for adoption)": s 52; "the Convention": s 144; "Convention adoption": s 66(1)(c); "Convention adoption order", "Convention country": s 144; "couple": s 144(4); "court": s 144; "disposition (in relation to Chapter 4 of Part 1)": s 73; "enactment": s 144; "fee", "guardian", "information": s 144; "interim care order": s 38 of the 1989 Act; "local authority": s 144; "local authority foster parent": s 23(3) of the 1989 Act; "Northern Irish adoption agency", "Northern Irish adoption order", "notice": s 144; "notice of intention to adopt": s 44(2); "overseas adoption": s 87; "parental responsibility": s 3 of the 1989 Act; "partner, in relation to a parent of a child": s 144(7); "placement order": s 21; "placing, or placed, for adoption": ss 18(5), 19(4); "prohibited steps order": s 8(1) of the 1989 Act; "records (in relation to Chapter 5 of Part 1)": s 82; "registered adoption society": s 2(2); "registers of live-births (in relation to Chapter 5 of Part 1)": s 82; "registration authority (in Part 1)", "regulations", "relative": s 144, read with s 1(8); "residence order": s 8(1) of the 1989 Act; "rules": s 144; "Scottish adoption agency": s 144(3); "Scottish adoption order": s 144; "specific issue order": s 8(1) of the 1989 Act; "subordinate legislation": s 144; "supervision order": s 31(11) of the 1989 Act; "unitary authority": s 144; "voluntary organisation": s 2(5).

Adoption (Intercountry Aspects) Act 1999

Guidance—Comprehensive guidance on intercountry adoption is published by the DOH – *Intercountry Adoption Guide* – which is available at *www.education.gov.uk/childrenandyoungpeople/families/ intercountryadoption*. For an up-to-date list of Convention States go to *www.hcch.net/index_en.php?act= conventions.status&cid=69*.

Liaison judge—In February [2008] Fam Law at [105] Lord Justice Thorpe offered the following information as to his role:

"… In trans-national cases there is a high chance of contemporaneous proceedings in both the involved jurisdictions. Unless the two responsible judges communicate, there is an obvious risk of conflict, legal complexity, delay and wasted costs. Each jurisdiction needs a co-ordinator, a liaison judge available to facilitate the essential communication. In this jurisdiction I am responsible for that service. My office is well equipped to initiate the process that results in judge communicating with judge."

The preferred route for contact is via Edward Bennett, lawyer to Thorpe LJ, International Family Justice Office. His office is in room C101 at the Royal Courts of Justice; tel: 0207 947 7906; email: edward.bennett@judiciary.gsi.gov.uk. He is supported by Karen Wheller.

Implementation of Convention

1 Regulations giving effect to Convention

(1) Subject to the provisions of this Act, regulations made by the Secretary of State may make provision for giving effect to the Convention on Protection of Children and Co-operation in respect of Intercountry Adoption, concluded at the Hague on 29th May 1993 ("the Convention").

(2) The text of the Convention (so far as material) is set out in Schedule 1 to this Act.

(3) Regulations under this section may –

    (a) apply, with or without modifications, any provision of the enactments relating to adoption;

    (b) provide that any person who contravenes or fails to comply with any provision of the regulations is to be guilty of an offence and liable on summary conviction to imprisonment for a term not exceeding three months, or a fine not exceeding level 5 on the standard scale, or both;

(c)   make different provision for different purposes or areas; and

(d)   make such incidental, supplementary, consequential or transitional provision as appears to the Secretary of State to be expedient.

(4) Regulations under this section shall be made by statutory instrument which shall be subject to annulment in pursuance of a resolution of either House of Parliament.

(5) Subject to subsection (6), any power to make subordinate legislation under or for the purposes of the enactments relating to adoption includes power to do so with a view to giving effect to the provisions of the Convention.

(6) Subsection (5) does not apply in relation to any power which is exercisable by the National Assembly for Wales.

(7) References in this section to enactments include references to Acts of the Scottish Parliament.

Amendments—SI 2011/1740.

Regulations giving effect to the Convention—For procedure see the Intercountry Adoption (Hague Convention) Regulations 2003.

2   Central Authorities and accredited bodies

(1) The functions under the Convention of the Central Authority are to be discharged –

(a)   separately in relation to England and Scotland by the Secretary of State; and

(b)   in relation to Wales by the National Assembly for Wales.

(2) A communication may be sent to the Central Authority in relation to any part of Great Britain by sending it (for forwarding if necessary) to the Central Authority in relation to England.

(2A) A registered adoption society is an accredited body for the purposes of the Convention if, in accordance with the conditions of the registration, the society may provide facilities in respect of Convention adoptions and adoptions effected by Convention adoption orders.

(2B) *(applies to Scotland only)*

(3) An approved adoption society is an accredited body for the purposes of the Convention if the approval extends to the provision of facilities in respect of Convention adoptions and adoptions effected by Convention adoption orders.

(4) The functions under Article 9(a) to (c) of the Convention are to be discharged by local authorities and accredited bodies on behalf of the Central Authority.

(5) In this section, 'registered adoption society' has the same meaning as in section 2 of the Adoption and Children Act 2002 (basic definitions); and expressions used in this section in its application to England and Wales which are also used in that Act have the same meanings as in that Act.

(6) *(applies to Scotland only)*

Amendments—Care Standards Act 2000, s 116, Sch 4, para 27; ACA 2002, s 139(1), Sch 3, paras 96, 97(a).

****

SCHEDULE 1
CONVENTION ON PROTECTION OF CHILDREN AND CO-OPERATION IN RESPECT OF INTERCOUNTRY ADOPTION

The States signatory to the present Convention.

Recognizing that the child, for the full and harmonious development of his or her personality, should grow up in a family environment, in an atmosphere of happiness, love and understanding,

Recalling that each State should take, as a matter of priority, appropriate measures to enable the child to remain in the care of his or her family of origin,

Recognizing that intercountry adoption may offer the advantage of a permanent family to a child for whom a suitable family cannot be found in his or her State of origin,

Convinced of the necessity to take measures to ensure that intercountry adoptions are made in the best interests of the child and with respect for his or her fundamental rights, and to prevent the abduction, the sale of, or traffic in children,

Desiring to establish common provisions to this effect, taking into account the principles set forth in international instruments, in particular the United Nations Convention on the Rights of the Child, of 20 November 1989, and the United Nations Declaration on Social and Legal Principles relating to the Protection and Welfare of Children, with Special Reference to Foster Placement and Adoption Nationally and Internationally (General Assembly Resolution 41/85, of 3 December 1986),

Have agreed upon the following provisions –

CHAPTER I
SCOPE OF THE CONVENTION

Article 1

The objects of the present Convention are –

(a) to establish safeguards to ensure that intercountry adoptions take place in the best interests of the child and with respect for his or her fundamental rights as recognised in international law;

(b) to establish a system of co-operation amongst Contracting States to ensure that those safeguards are respected and thereby prevent the abduction, the sale of, or traffic in children;

(c) to secure the recognition in Contracting States of adoptions made in accordance with the Convention.

Article 2

1 The Convention shall apply where a child habitually resident in one Contracting State ("the State of origin") has been, is being, or is to be moved to another Contracting State ("the receiving State") either after his or her adoption in the State of origin by spouses or a person habitually resident in the receiving State, or for the purposes of such an adoption in the receiving State or in the State of origin.

2 The Convention covers only adoptions which create a permanent parent-child relationship.

Article 3

The Convention ceases to apply if the agreements mentioned in Article 17, sub-paragraph (c), have not been given before the child attains the age of eighteen years.

CHAPTER II
REQUIREMENTS FOR INTERCOUNTRY ADOPTIONS

Article 4

An adoption within the scope of the Convention shall take place only if the competent authorities of the State of origin –

(a) have established that the child is adoptable;

(b) have determined, after possibilities for placement of the child within the State of origin have been given due consideration, that an intercountry adoption is in the child's best interests;

(c) have ensured that –

    (i) the persons, institutions and authorities whose consent is necessary for adoption, have been counselled as may be necessary and duly informed of the effects of their consent, in particular whether or not an adoption will result in the termination of the legal relationship between the child and his or her family of origin,

    (ii) such persons, institutions and authorities have given their consent freely, in the required legal form, and expressed or evidenced in writing,

    (iii) the consents have not been induced by payment or compensation of any kind and have not been withdrawn, and

    (iv) the consent of the mother, where required, has been given only after the birth of the child; and

(d) have ensured, having regard to the age and degree of maturity of the child, that –

    (i) he or she has been counselled and duly informed of the effects of the adoption and of his or her consent to the adoption, where such consent is required,

    (ii) consideration has been given to the child's wishes and opinions,

    (iii) the child's consent to the adoption, where such consent is required, has been given freely, in the required legal form, and expressed or evidenced in writing, and

    (iv) such consent has not been induced by payment or compensation of any kind.

Article 5

An adoption within the scope of the Convention shall take place only if the competent authorities of the receiving State –

(a) have determined that the prospective adoptive parents are eligible and suited to adopt;

(b) have ensured that the prospective adoptive parents have been counselled as may be necessary; and

(c) have determined that the child is or will be authorised to enter and reside permanently in that State.

CHAPTER III
CENTRAL AUTHORITIES AND ACCREDITED BODIES

Article 6

(1) A Contracting State shall designate a Central Authority to discharge the duties which are imposed by the Convention upon such authorities.

(2) Federal States, States with more than one system of law or States having autonomous territorial units shall be free to appoint more than one Central Authority and to specify the territorial or personal extent of their functions. Where a State has appointed more than one Central Authority, it shall designate the Central Authority to which any communication may be addressed for transmission to the appropriate Central Authority within that State.

Article 7

(1) Central Authorities shall co-operate with each other and promote co-operation amongst the competent authorities in their States to protect children and to achieve the other objects of the Convention.

(2) They shall take directly all appropriate measures to –

    (a)   provide information as to the laws of their States concerning adoption and other general information, such as statistics and standard forms;

    (b)   keep one another informed about the operation of the Convention and, as far as possible, eliminate any obstacles to its application.

Article 8

Central Authorities shall take, directly or through public authorities, all appropriate measures to prevent improper financial or other gain in connection with an adoption and to deter all practices contrary to the objects of the Convention.

Article 9

Central Authorities shall take, directly or through public authorities or other bodies duly accredited in their State, all appropriate measures, in particular to –

    (a)   collect, preserve and exchange information about the situation of the child and the prospective adoptive parents, so far as is necessary to complete the adoption;

    (b)   facilitate, follow and expedite proceedings with a view to obtaining the adoption;

    (c)   promote the development of adoption counselling and post-adoption services in their States;

    (d)   provide each other with general evaluation reports about experience with intercountry adoption;

    (e)   reply, in so far as is permitted by the law of their State, to justified requests from other Central Authorities or public authorities for information about a particular adoption situation.

Article 10

Accreditation shall only be granted to and maintained by bodies demonstrating their competence to carry out properly the tasks with which they may be entrusted.

Article 11

An accredited body shall –

    (a)   pursue only non-profit objectives according to such conditions and within such limits as may be established by the competent authorities of the State of accreditation;

    (b)   be directed and staffed by persons qualified by their ethical standards and by training or experience to work in the field of intercountry adoption; and

PART II

(c) be subject to supervision by competent authorities of that State as to its composition, operation and financial situation.

Article 12

A body accredited in one Contracting State may act in another Contracting State only if the competent authorities of both States have authorised it to do so.

Article 13

The designation of the Central Authorities and, where appropriate, the extent of their functions, as well as the names and addresses of the accredited bodies shall be communicated by each Contracting State to the Permanent Bureau of the Hague Conference on Private International Law.

CHAPTER IV
PROCEDURAL REQUIREMENTS IN INTERCOUNTRY ADOPTION

Article 14

Persons habitually resident in a Contracting State, who wish to adopt a child habitually resident in another Contracting State, shall apply to the Central Authority in the State of their habitual residence.

Article 15

(1) If the Central Authority of the receiving State is satisfied that the applicants are eligible and suited to adopt, it shall prepare a report including information about their identity, eligibility and suitability to adopt, background, family and medical history, social environment, reasons for adoption, ability to undertake an intercountry adoption, as well as the characteristics of the children for whom they would be qualified to care.

(2) It shall transmit the report to the Central Authority of the State of origin.

Article 16

(1) If the Central Authority of the State of origin is satisfied that the child is adoptable, it shall –

(a) prepare a report including information about his or her identity, adoptability, background, social environment, family history, medical history including that of the child's family, and any special needs of the child;

(b) give due consideration to the child's upbringing and to his or her ethnic, religious and cultural background;

(c) ensure that consents have been obtained in accordance with Article 4; and

(d) determine, on the basis in particular of the reports relating to the child and the prospective adoptive parents, whether the envisaged placement is in the best interests of the child.

(2) It shall transmit to the Central Authority of the receiving State its report on the child, proof that the necessary consents have been obtained and the reasons for its determination on the placement, taking care not to reveal the identity of the mother and the father if, in the State of origin, these identities may not be disclosed.

Article 17

Any decision in the State of origin that a child should be entrusted to prospective adoptive parents may only be made if –

  (a) the Central Authority of that State has ensured that the prospective adoptive parents agree;

  (b) the Central Authority of the receiving State has approved such decision, where such approval is required by the law of that State or by the Central Authority of the State of origin;

  (c) the Central Authorities of both States have agreed that the adoption may proceed; and

  (d) it has been determined, in accordance with Article 5, that the prospective adoptive parents are eligible and suited to adopt and that the child is or will be authorised to enter and reside permanently in the receiving State.

Article 18

The Central Authorities of both States shall take all necessary steps to obtain permission for the child to leave the State of origin and to enter and reside permanently in the receiving State.

Article 19

(1) The transfer of the child to the receiving State may only be carried out if the requirements of Article 17 have been satisfied.

(2) The Central Authorities of both States shall ensure that this transfer takes place in secure and appropriate circumstances and, if possible, in the company of the adoptive or prospective adoptive parents.

(3) If the transfer of the child does not take place, the reports referred to in Articles 15 and 16 are to be sent back to the authorities who forwarded them.

Article 20

The Central Authorities shall keep each other informed about the adoption process and the measures taken to complete it, as well as about the progress of the placement if a probationary period is required.

Article 21

(1) Where the adoption is to take place after the transfer of the child to the receiving State and it appears to the Central Authority of that State that the continued placement of the child with the prospective adoptive parents is not in the child's best interests, such Central Authority shall take the measures necessary to protect the child, in particular –

  (a) to cause the child to be withdrawn from the prospective adoptive parents and to arrange temporary care;

  (b) in consultation with the Central Authority of the State of origin, to arrange without delay a new placement of the child with a view to adoption or, if this is not appropriate, to arrange alternative long-term care; an adoption shall not take place until the Central Authority of the State of origin has been duly informed concerning the new prospective adoptive parents;

  (c) as a last resort, to arrange the return of the child, if his or her interests so require.

(2) Having regard in particular to the age and degree of maturity of the child, he or she shall be consulted and, where appropriate, his or her consent obtained in relation to measures to be taken under this Article.

Article 22

(1) The functions of a Central Authority under this Chapter may be performed by public authorities or by bodies accredited under Chapter III, to the extent permitted by the law of its State.

(2) Any Contracting State may declare to the depositary of the Convention that the functions of the Central Authority under Articles 15 to 21 may be performed in that State, to the extent permitted by the law and subject to the supervision of the competent authorities of that State, also by bodies or persons who –

(a) meet the requirements of integrity, professional competence, experience and accountability of that State; and

(b) are qualified by their ethical standards and by training or experience to work in the field of intercountry adoption.

(3) A Contracting State which makes the declaration provided for in paragraph 2 shall keep the Permanent Bureau of the Hague Conference on Private International Law informed of the names and addresses of these bodies and persons.

(4) Any Contracting State may declare to the depositary of the Convention that adoptions of children habitually resident in its territory may only take place if the functions of the Central Authorities are performed in accordance with paragraph 1.

(5) Notwithstanding any declaration made under paragraph 2, the reports provided for in Articles 15 and 16 shall, in every case, be prepared under the responsibility of the Central Authority or other authorities or bodies in accordance with paragraph 1.

CHAPTER V
RECOGNITION AND EFFECTS OF THE ADOPTION

Article 23

(1) An adoption certified by the competent authority of the State of the adoption as having been made in accordance with the Convention shall be recognised by operation of law in the other Contracting States. The certificate shall specify when and by whom the agreements under Article 17, sub-paragraph (c), were given.

(2) Each Contracting State shall, at the time of signature, ratification, acceptance, approval or accession, notify the depositary of the Convention of the identity and the functions of the authority or the authorities which, in that State, are competent to make the certification. It shall also notify the depositary of any modification in the designation of these authorities.

Article 24

The recognition of an adoption may be refused in a contracting State only if the adoption is manifestly contrary to its public policy, taking into account the best interests of the child.

Article 25

Any Contracting State may declare to the depositary of the convention that it will not be bound under this Convention to recognise adoptions made in accordance with an agreement concluded by application of Article 39, paragraph 2.

Article 26

(1) The recognition of an adoption includes recognition of –

  (a) the legal parent-child relationship between the child and his or her adoptive parents;
  (b) parental responsibility of the adoptive parents for the child;
  (c) the termination of a pre-existing legal relationship between the child and his or her mother and father, if the adoption has this effect in the Contracting State where it was made.

(2) In the case of an adoption having the effect of terminating a pre-existing legal parent-child relationship, the child shall enjoy in the receiving State, and in any other Contracting State where the adoption is recognised, rights equivalent to those resulting from adoptions having this effect in each such State.

(3) The preceding paragraphs shall not prejudice the application of any provision more favourable for the child, in force in the Contracting State which recognises the adoption.

Article 27

(1) Where an adoption granted in the State of origin does not have the effect of terminating a pre-existing legal parent-child relationship, it may, in the receiving State which recognises the adoption under the Convention, be converted into an adoption having such an effect –

  (a) if the law of the receiving State so permits; and
  (b) if the consents referred to in Article 4, sub-paragraphs (c) and (d), have been or are given for the purpose of such an adoption.

(2) Article 23 applies to the decision converting the adoption.

CHAPTER VI
GENERAL PROVISIONS

Article 28

The Convention does not affect any law of a State of origin which requires that the adoption of a child habitually resident within that State take place in that State or which prohibits the child's placement in, or transfer to, the receiving State prior to adoption.

Article 29

There shall be no contact between the prospective adoptive parents and the child's parents or any other person who has care of the child until the requirements of Article 4, sub-paragraphs (a) to (c), and Article 5, sub-paragraph (a), have been met, unless the adoption takes place within a family or unless the contact is in compliance with the conditions established by the competent authority of the State of origin.

Article 30

(1) The competent authorities of a Contracting State shall ensure that information held by them concerning the child's origin, in particular information concerning the identity of his or her parents, as well as the medical history, is preserved.

(2) They shall ensure that the child or his or her representative has access to such information, under appropriate guidance, in so far as is permitted by the law of that State.

Article 31

Without prejudice to Article 30, personal data gathered or transmitted under the Convention, especially data referred to in Articles 15 and 16, shall be used only for the purposes for which they were gathered or transmitted.

Article 32

(1) No one shall derive improper financial or other gain from an activity related to an intercountry adoption.

(2) Only costs and expenses, including reasonable professional fees of persons involved in the adoption, may be charged or paid.

(3) The directors, administrators and employees of bodies involved in an adoption shall not receive remuneration which is unreasonably high in relation to services rendered.

Article 33

A competent authority which finds that any provision of the Convention has not been respected or that there is a serious risk that it may not be respected, shall immediately inform the Central Authority of its State. This Central Authority shall be responsible for ensuring that appropriate measures are taken.

Article 34

If the competent authority of the State of destination of a document so requests, a translation certified as being in conformity with the original must be furnished. Unless otherwise provided, the costs of such translation are to be borne by the prospective adoptive parents.

Article 35

The competent authorities of the contracting States shall act expeditiously in the process of adoption.

Article 36

In relation to a State which has two or more systems of law with regard to adoption applicable in different territorial units –

   (a) any reference to habitual residence in that State shall be construed as referring to habitual residence in a territorial unit of that State;

   (b) any reference to the law of that State shall be construed as referring to the law in force in the relevant territorial unit;

   (c) any reference to the competent authorities or to the public authorities of that State shall be construed as referring to those authorised to act in the relevant territorial unit;

(d) any reference to the accredited bodies of that State shall be construed as referring to bodies accredited in the relevant territorial unit.

Article 37

In relation to a State which with regard to adoption has two or more systems of law applicable to different categories of persons, any reference to the law of that State shall be construed as referring to the legal system specified by the law of that State.

Article 38

A State within which different territorial units have their own rules of law in respect of adoption shall not be bound to apply the Convention where a State with a unified system of law would not be bound to do so.

Article 39

(1) The convention does not affect any international instrument to which Contracting States are Parties and which contains provisions on matters governed by the Convention, unless a contrary declaration is made by the States parties to such instrument.

(2) Any Contracting State may enter into agreements with one or more other Contracting States, with a view to improving the application of the Convention in their mutual relations. These agreements may derogate only from the provisions of Articles 14 to 16 and 18 to 21. The States which have concluded such an agreement shall transmit a copy to the depositary of the Convention.

Article 40

No reservation to the Convention shall be permitted.

Article 41

The Convention shall apply in every case where an application pursuant to Article 14 has been received after the Convention has entered into force in the receiving State and the State of origin.

Article 42

The Secretary General of the Hague Conference on Private International Law shall at regular intervals convene a Special Commission in order to review the practical operation of the Convention.

****

Attachment of Earnings Act 1971

ARRANGEMENT OF SECTIONS

Cases in which attachment is available

Cases in which attachment is available

1 Courts with power to attach earnings

(1) The High Court may make an attachment of earnings order to secure payments under a High Court maintenance order.

(2) A county court may make an attachment of earnings order to secure –

(a) payments under a High Court or a county court maintenance order;

(b) the payment of a judgment debt, other than a debt of less than £5 or such other sum as may be prescribed by county court rules; or

(c) payments under an administration order.

(3) A magistrates' court may make an attachment of earnings order to secure –

(a) payments under a magistrates' court maintenance order; or

(b) (*repealed*)

(c) the payment of any sum required to be paid under regulations under section 23 or 24 of the Legal Aid, Sentencing and Punishment of Offenders Act 2012.

(4) (*repealed*)

(5) Any power conferred by this Act to make an attachment of earnings order includes a power to make such an order to secure the discharge of liabilities arising before the coming into force of this Act.

Amendments—AJA 1999, s 24, Sch 4, para 8; Criminal Defence Service Act 2006, s 4(1); SI 2006/1737; LASPOA 2012, s 39, Sch 5, para 6.

Defined terms—"administration order": s 25(1); "judgment debt": s 2(c); "maintenance order": s 2(a).

Rules—If an application is to be made to the High Court, the county court procedure should be followed with the appropriate modifications; alternatively, advantage may be taken of the county court's power to make an attachment of earnings order to secure a High Court maintenance order.

In county courts, the provisions governing attachment of earnings are contained in CPR 1998, Sch 2, CCR Ord 27.

In magistrates' courts, the procedure is governed by MC(AE)R 1971.

"maintenance order"—The Act contains many provisions special to maintenance orders (including, for example, lump sum orders – see **"maintenance order"** under s 2 below). It is always necessary to bear in mind whether a particular attachment of earnings application or order secures a maintenance order. The same considerations apply equally to CPR 1998, Sch 2, CCR Ord 27.

"£5 or such other sum" (s 1(2)(b))—The minimum (in the case of a county court judgment debt) is now £50 or the balance under a judgment which was for £50 or more (CPR 1998, Sch 2, CCR Ord 27, r 7(9)).

1A Orders to which this Act applies

The following provisions of this Act apply, except where otherwise stated, to attachment of earnings orders made, or to be made, by any court under this Act or under Schedule 5 to the Courts Act 2003. or by a fines officer under that Schedule.

Amendments—Inserted by SI 2006/1737.

2 Principal definitions

In this Act –

(a)   "maintenance order" means any order, decision, settlement or instrument specified in Schedule 1 to this Act and includes one which has been discharged or has otherwise ceased to operate if any arrears are recoverable thereunder;

(b)   "High Court maintenance order", "county court maintenance order" and "magistrates' court maintenance order" mean respectively a maintenance order enforceable by the High Court, a county court and a magistrates' court;

(c)   "judgment debt" means a sum payable under –
  (i)   a judgment or order enforceable by a court in England and Wales (not being a magistrates' court);
  (ii) an order of a magistrates' court for the payment of money recoverable summarily as a civil debt; or
  (iii) an order of any court which is enforceable as if it were for the payment of money so recoverable;
  but does not include any sum payable under a maintenance order or an administration order;

(d)   "the relevant adjudication", in relation to any payment secured or to be secured by an attachment of earnings order, means the conviction, judgment, order or other adjudication from which there arises the liability to make the payment; and

(e)   "the debtor", in relation to an attachment of earnings order, or to proceedings in which a court has power to make an attachment of earnings order, or to proceedings arising out of such an order, means the person by whom payment is required by the relevant adjudication to be made.

Amendments—SI 2011/1484.

Defined terms—"administration order": s 25(1).

Scope—This section contains the definitions of the expressions which are fundamental to the Act. Other definitions are set out in ss 24 and 25.

"maintenance order" (s 2(a))—In addition to periodical payments, the definitions in Sch 1 include "other payments made or having effect as if made under" the provisions referred to, including, for example, MCA 1973, Pt II, which makes provision for lump sum orders and other orders for payment of money which would not normally be thought of as maintenance orders.

"judgment debt" (s 2(c))—In family proceedings, the most common judgment debt is an order for costs.

3 Application for order and conditions of court's power to make it

(A1) This section shall not apply to an attachment of earnings order to be made under Schedule 5 to the Courts Act 2003.

(1) The following persons may apply for an attachment of earnings order –

    (a)   the person to whom payment under the relevant adjudication is required to be made (whether directly or through an officer of any court);

    (b)   where the relevant adjudication is an administration order, any one of the creditors scheduled to the order;

    (c)   without prejudice to paragraph (a) above, where the application is to a magistrates' court for an order to secure maintenance payments, and there is in force an order under section 59 of the Magistrates' Courts Act 1980, or section 19(2) of the Maintenance Orders Act 1950, that those payments be made to the designated officer for a magistrates' court, that officer;

    (d)   in the following cases the debtor –

        (i)   where the application is to a magistrates' court; or

        (ii)   where the application is to the High Court or a county court for an order to secure maintenance payments.

(2) *(repealed)*

(3) Subject to subsection (3A) below for an attachment of earnings order to be made on the application of any person other than the debtor it must appear to the court that the debtor has failed to make one or more payments required by the relevant adjudication.

(3A) Subsection (3) above shall not apply when the relevant adjudication is a maintenance order.

(3B), (3C) *(repealed)*

(4) Where proceedings are brought –

    (a)   in the High Court or a county court for the enforcement of a maintenance order by committal under section 5 of the Debtors Act 1869; or

    (b)   in a magistrates' court for the enforcement of a maintenance order under section 76 of the Magistrates' Courts Act 1980 (distress or committal),

then the court may make an attachment of earnings order to secure payments under the maintenance order, instead of dealing with the case under section 5 of the said Act of 1869 or, as the case may be, section 76 of the said Act of 1980.

(5) *(repealed)*

(6) ...

(7) A county court shall not make an attachment of earnings order to secure the payment of a judgment debt if there is in force an order or warrant for the debtor's committal, under section 5 of the Debtors Act 1869, in respect of that debt; but in any such case the court may discharge the order or warrant with a view to making an attachment of earnings order instead.

Amendments—MCA 1980, s 154, Sch 7, para 97; MEA 1991, s 11(1), Sch 2, para 1; Criminal Procedure and Investigations Act 1996, s 53; AJA 1999, s 90, Sch 13, para 65; Powers of Criminal Courts (Sentencing) Act 2000, s 165, Sch 9, para 44; SI 2006/1737; Courts Act 2003, s 109(1), Sch 8, para 141.

Defined terms—"administration order": s 25(1); "debtor": s 2(e); "maintenance order": s 2(a); "maintenance payments": s 25(1); "relevant adjudication": s 2(d).

Application by the debtor (s 3(1)(d))—In the High Court or county courts, the debtor may apply only in the case of a maintenance order (on its being made or varied: CPR 1998, Sch 2, CCR Ord 27, r 17(4)).

Restriction on order (s 3(3))—No attachment of earnings order may be made (unless it is applied for by the debtor) if the debtor has not defaulted under the judgment or order. This restriction does not apply in the case of a maintenance order (s 3(3A)).

"subsection (3) above shall not apply" (s 3(3A))—Section 3(3) is disapplied from all maintenance orders as defined by s 2(e). Where the relevant adjudication is a "qualifying periodical maintenance order" within the meaning of MEA 1991, s 1 (one where money is to be paid periodically (including a lump sum order payable by instalments) and where the payer at the time the order is made is ordinarily resident in England and Wales), wider powers to make an attachment of earnings order exist. In such a case, the High Court and county courts may make an attachment of earnings order on making the relevant maintenance order and, subsequently, on application or of the court's own motion in the course of any proceedings concerning the order (MEA 1991, s 1). In magistrates' courts an attachment of earnings order may be made on the making of the maintenance order, in any enforcement proceedings or, where the court is satisfied that payment has not been made in accordance with the order, on variation (MCA 1980, ss 59, 60, 76).

Jurisdiction—The magistrates' court having jurisdiction to make an attachment of earnings order will be the court which enforces payment of the maintenance order (MC(AE)R 1971, r 4).

Own motion powers (s 3(4))—The court can make an attachment of earnings order, without an application, in lieu of committal or (in magistrates' courts) distress when hearing applications for those remedies, even where the extended powers under MEA 1991, s 1 do not apply.

****

Consequences of attachment order

6 Effect and contents of order

(1) An attachment of earnings order shall be an order directed to a person who appears to the court, or as the case may be the fines officer, making the order to have the debtor in his employment and shall operate as an instruction to that person –

    (a) to make periodical deductions from the debtor's earnings in accordance with Part I of Schedule 3 to this Act; and

    (b) at such times as the order may require, or as the court, or where the order is made under Schedule 5 to the Courts Act 2003, as the court or the fines officer as the case may be, may allow, to pay the amounts deducted to the collecting officer of the court, as specified in the order.

(2) For the purposes of this Act, the relationship of employer and employee shall be treated as subsisting between two persons if one of them, as a principal and not as a servant or agent, pays to the other any sums defined as earnings by section 24 of this Act.

(3) An attachment of earnings order shall contain prescribed particulars enabling the debtor to be identified by the employer.

(4) Except where it is made to secure maintenance payments, the order shall specify the whole amount payable under the relevant adjudication (or so much of that amount as remains unpaid), including any relevant costs.

(5) Subject to subsection (5A) below, the order shall specify –

    (a) the normal deduction rate, that is to say, the rate (expressed as a sum of money per week, month or other period) at which the court thinks it reasonable for the debtor's earnings to be applied to meeting his liability under the relevant adjudication; and

(b) the protected earnings rate, that is to say the rate (so expressed) below which, having regard to the debtor's resources and needs, the court thinks it reasonable that the earnings actually paid to him should not be reduced.

(5A) If the order is made under Schedule 5 to the Courts Act 2003 then it shall specify the percentage deduction rate in accordance with fines collection regulations made under that Schedule.

(6) In the case of an order made to secure payments under a maintenance order (not being an order for the payment of a lump sum), the normal deduction rate –

(a) shall be determined after taking account of any right or liability of the debtor to deduct income tax when making the payments; and

(b) shall not exceed the rate which appears to the court necessary for the purpose of –

(i) securing payment of the sums falling due from time to time under the maintenance order, and

(ii) securing payment within a reasonable period of any sums already due and unpaid under the maintenance order.

(7) For the purposes of an attachment of earnings order, the collecting officer of the court shall be (subject to later variation of the order under section 9 of this Act) –

(a) in the case of an order made by the High Court, either –

(i) the proper officer of the High Court, or

(ii) the appropriate officer of such county court as the order may specify;

(b) in the case of an order made by a county court, the appropriate officer of that court; and

(c) in the case of an order made by a magistrates' court, the designated officer for that court or for another magistrates' court specified in the order.

(8) In subsection (7) above "appropriate officer" means an officer designated by the Lord Chancellor.

(9)–(12) ...

Amendments—AJA 1977, s 19(5); (not in force) – see **Subsections (9)–(12)** below; AJA 1999, s 90, Sch 13, para 66; SI 2006/1737; Courts Act 2003, s 109(1), Sch 8, para 142.

Defined terms—"the debtor": s 2(e); "earnings": s 24; "maintenance order": s 2(a); "maintenance payments": s 25(1); "the relevant adjudication": s 2(d); "relevant costs": s 25(2).

Employer (s 6(2))—The relationship of employer/employee, for the purposes of this Act, is determined solely by the nature of the payments made by one to the other. If they fall within the definition in s 24 (and the payer is not merely a servant or agent of another) then the payer is the employer notwithstanding that no other attribute of employment exists.

"prescribed particulars" (s 6(3))—For the prescribed particulars see CPR 1998, Sch 2, CCR Ord 27, r 10 and MC(AE)R 1971, r 7 (see Part IV).

"normal deduction rate" (s 6(5)(a),(6))—In establishing the normal deduction rate, regard may be had only to the debtor's actual earnings, not to his earning potential, even though this may result in the normal deduction rate being less than the rate of the relevant periodical payments order, on the making of which unrealised earning capacity may have been taken into account (*Pepper v Pepper* [1960] 1 WLR 131).

"protected earnings rate" (s 6(5)(b))—The rate set will not normally be below the income support threshold, though this is not impossible in an appropriate case (*Billington v Billington* [1974] Fam 24). In practice it will usually be set a little above that threshold so that the debtor is not discouraged from continuing in employment. The debtor's needs include those of his dependants (s 25(3)).

"right or liability of the debtor to deduct income tax" (s 6(6)(a))—Maintenance orders are now paid gross of tax.

PART II

Insolvency—The fact that the debtor may become bankrupt does not (if he retains his employment) stay an attachment of earnings application or prevent an attachment of earnings order from being made or continuing to have effect to enforce a judgment or order made in family proceedings. There may be a hiatus in the payments received under an existing attachment of earnings order, since it was held in *Re Green; Official Receiver v Cutting* [1979] 1 WLR 1211, that deductions made by the employer which have not reached the court when the bankruptcy commences fall into the bankrupt's estate. However, that case was decided under the Bankruptcy Act 1914 and the changed status of periodical payments orders in relation to bankruptcy by virtue of the Insolvency Act 1986 and Insolvency Rules 1986, r 12.3 might lead a court to reach a different conclusion today.

Forms—Form 1 in the Schedule to MC(AE)R 1971 sets out the form of order to be used by magistrates' courts. In the county court, Form N60 is used.

7 Compliance with order by employer

(1) Where an attachment of earnings order has been made, the employer shall, if he has been served with the order, comply with it; but he shall be under no liability for non-compliance before seven days have elapsed since the service.

(2) Where a person is served with an attachment of earnings order directed to him and he has not the debtor in his employment, or the debtor subsequently ceases to be in his employment, he shall (in either case), within ten days from the date of service or, as the case may be, the cesser, give notice of that fact to the court.

(3) Part II of Schedule 3 to this Act shall have effect with respect to the priority to be accorded as between two or more attachment of earnings orders directed to a person in respect of the same debtor.

(4) On any occasion when the employer makes, in compliance with the order, a deduction from the debtor's earnings –

    (a)   he shall be entitled to deduct, in addition, five new pence, or such other sum as may be prescribed by order made by the Lord Chancellor, towards his clerical and administrative costs; and

    (b)   he shall give to the debtor a statement in writing of the total amount of the deduction.

(5) An order of the Lord Chancellor under subsection (4)(a) above –

    (a)   may prescribe different sums in relation to different classes of cases;

    (b)   may be varied or revoked by a subsequent order made under that paragraph; and

    (c)   shall be made by statutory instrument subject to annulment by resolution of either House of Parliament.

Defined terms—"the debtor": s 2(e); "the employer": s 25(2).

"seven days" (s 7(1))—The employer is given a period of grace to give effect to the order.

Priority of orders (s 7(3))—There are two categories of attachment of earnings order – those which secure judgment debts and administration orders and those which secure other liabilities (including maintenance orders). The latter are usually termed "priority orders" and must be applied to the debtor's earnings first. Within each category, priority follows the dates the orders were made.

Prescribed deduction (s 7(4)(a))—The current figure is £1 (prescribed by Attachment of Earnings (Employer's Deduction) Order 1991, SI 1991/356).

8 Interrelation with alternative remedies open to creditor

(1) Where an attachment of earnings order has been made to secure maintenance payments, no order or warrant of commitment shall be issued in consequence of any proceedings for the enforcement of the related maintenance order begun before the making of the attachment of earnings order.

(2) Where a county court has made an attachment of earnings order to secure the payment of a judgment debt –

    (a)   no order or warrant of commitment shall be issued in consequence of any proceedings for the enforcement of the debt begun before the making of the attachment of earnings order; and

    (b)   so long as the order is in force, no execution for the recovery of the debt shall issue against any property of the debtor without the leave of the county court.

(3) An attachment of earnings order made to secure maintenance payments shall cease to have effect upon the making of an order of commitment or the issue of a warrant of commitment for the enforcement of the related maintenance order, or upon the exercise for that purpose of the power conferred on a magistrates' court by section 77(2) of the Magistrates' Courts Act 1980 to postpone the issue of such a warrant.

(4) An attachment of earnings order made to secure the payment of a judgment debt shall cease to have effect on the making of an order of commitment or the issue of a warrant of commitment for the enforcement of the debt.

(5) An attachment of earnings order made to secure –

    (a)   any payment mentioned in section 1(3)(c) of this Act; or

    (b)   the payment of any sum mentioned in paragraph 1 of Schedule 5 to the Courts Act 2003,

shall cease to have effect on the issue of a warrant committing the debtor to prison for default in making that payment.

Amendments—MCA 1980, s 154, Sch 7, para 98; SI 2006/1737.

Defined terms—"judgment debt": s 2(c); "maintenance order": s 2(a); "maintenance payments": s 25(2).

Subsequent proceedings

9 Variation, lapse and discharge of orders

(1) The court, or where an attachment of earnings order is made under Schedule 5 to the Courts Act 2003, the court or the fines officer as the case may be, may make an order discharging or varying an attachment of earnings order.

(2) Where an order is varied, the employer shall, if he has been served with notice of the variation, comply with the order as varied; but he shall be under no liability for non-compliance before seven days have elapsed since the service.

(3) Rules of court may make provision –

    (a)   as to the circumstances in which an attachment of earnings order made under this Act may be varied or discharged by the court of its own motion:

    (aa) as to the circumstances in which an attachment of earnings order made under Schedule 5 to the Courts Act 2003 may be varied or discharged by the court or the fines officer of its or his own motion;

    (b)   in the case of an attachment of earnings order made by a magistrates' court, for enabling a single justice, on an application made by the debtor on the ground of a material change in his resources and needs since the order was made or last varied, to vary the order for a period of not more than four weeks by an increase of the protected earnings rate.

(4) Where an attachment of earnings order has been made and the person to whom it is directed ceases to have the debtor in his employment, the order shall lapse (except as respects deduction from earnings paid after the cesser and payment to the collecting officer of amounts deducted at any time) and be of no effect unless and until the court, or where the order was made under Schedule 5 to the Courts Act 2003, unless and until the

court or the fines officer as the case may be, again directs it to a person (whether the same as before or another) who appears to the court or the fines officer (as the case may be) to have the debtor in his employment.

(5) The lapse of an order under subsection (4) above shall not prevent its being treated as remaining in force for other purposes.

Amendments—SI 2006/1737.

Defined terms—"the debtor": s 2(e); "the employer": s 25(1); "protected earnings rate": s 6(5)(b).

"seven days" (s 9(2))—The employer is given a period of grace to give effect to the variation.

"Rules of court" (s 9(3))—For the relevant rules see CPR 1998, Sch 2, CCR Ord 27, r 13 and MC(AE)R 1971, rr 12–14 (see Part IV).

"resources and needs" (s 9(3)(b))—See **"normal deduction rate"** and **"protected earnings rate"** under s 6.

Lapse of order (s 9(4),(5))—If the debtor loses or changes his employment, this creates a temporary hiatus. As soon as the court learns of a new employer, the order will be redirected, and varied as appropriate (CPR 1998, Sch 2, CCR Ord 27, r 13(3); MC(AE)R 1971, r 12).

10 Normal deduction rate to be reduced in certain cases

(1) The following provisions shall have effect, in the case of an attachment of earnings order made to secure maintenance payments, where it appears to the collecting officer of the court that –

  (a) the aggregate of the payments made for the purposes of the related maintenance order by the debtor (whether under the attachment of earnings order or otherwise) exceeds the aggregate of the payments required up to that time by the maintenance order; and

  (b) the normal deduction rate specified by the attachment of earnings order (or, where two or more such orders are in force in relation to the maintenance order, the aggregate of the normal deduction rates specified by those orders) exceeds the rate of payments required by the maintenance order; and

  (c) no proceedings for the variation or discharge of the attachment of earnings order are pending.

(2) In the case of an order made by the High Court or a county court, the collecting officer shall give the prescribed notice to the person to whom he is required to pay sums received under the attachment of earnings order, and to the debtor; and the court shall make the appropriate variation order, unless the debtor requests it to discharge the attachment of earnings order, or to vary it in some other way, and the court thinks fit to comply with the request.

(3) In the case of an order made by a magistrates' court, the collecting officer shall apply to the court for the appropriate variation order; and the court shall grant the application unless the debtor appears at the hearing and requests the court to discharge the attachment of earnings order, or to vary it in some other way, and the court thinks fit to comply with the request.

(4) In this section, "the appropriate variation order" means an order varying the attachment of earnings order in question by reducing the normal deduction rate specified thereby so as to secure that that rate (or, in the case mentioned in subsection (1)(b) above, the aggregate of the rates therein mentioned) –

  (a) is the same as the rate of payments required by the maintenance order; or

  (b) is such lower rate as the court thinks fit having regard to the amount of the excess mentioned in subsection (1)(a).

Defined terms—"collecting officer": s 6(7); "the debtor": s 2(e); "maintenance order": s 2(a); "maintenance payments": s 25(1); "normal deduction rate": s 6(5)(a).

Restriction (s 10(1)(c))—This section does not apply if an application to vary or discharge the maintenance order is pending.

Variation—Arrears having been cleared, the court is likely to vary the normal deduction rate to the level of the maintenance order, but the debtor may apply for another variation or for the attachment of earnings order to be discharged.

"prescribed notice" (s 10(2))—In the county court Practice Form N341 is used. The debtor's application for the discharge or other variation of the order must be made within 14 days after the date of this notice (CPR 1998, Sch 2, CCR Ord 27, r 17(9)). There is no provision for any application or objection by the creditor.

"the collecting officer shall apply" (s 10(3))—See s 19(4) for service of summons and MC(AE)R 1971, r 8 (see Part IV) for service of notice of the hearing. Any application made by the collecting officer in the magistrates' court is deemed to be made on the request of the person in whose favour the order was made (s 18(3)).

11 Attachment order in respect of maintenance payments to cease to have effect on the occurrence of certain events

(1) An attachment of earnings order made to secure maintenance payments shall cease to have effect –

(a) upon the grant of an application for registration of the related maintenance order under section 2 of the Maintenance Orders Act 1958 (which provides for the registration in a magistrates' court of a High Court or county court maintenance order, and for registration in the High Court of a magistrates' court maintenance order);

(b) where the related maintenance order is registered under Part I of the said Act of 1958, upon the giving of notice with respect thereto under section 5 of that Act (notice with view to cancellation of registration);

(c) subject to subsection (3) below, upon the discharge of the related maintenance order while it is not registered under Part I of the said Act of 1958;

(d) upon the related maintenance order ceasing to be registered in a court in England or Wales, or becoming registered in a court in Scotland or Northern Ireland, under Part II of the Maintenance Orders Act 1950.

(2) Subsection (1)(a) above shall have effect, in the case of an application for registration under section 2(1) of the said Act of 1958, notwithstanding that the grant of the application may subsequently become void under subsection (2) of that section.

(3) Where the related maintenance order is discharged as mentioned in subsection (1)(c) above and it appears to the court discharging the order that arrears thereunder will remain to be recovered after the discharge, that court may, if it thinks fit, direct that subsection (1) shall not apply.

Defined terms—"maintenance order": s 2(a); "maintenance payments": s 25(1).

Registration and cancellation of registration—If the function of enforcement of the order later passes to another English or Welsh court, a fresh application for an attachment of earnings order may be made.

12 Termination of employer's liability to make deductions

(1) Where an attachment of earnings order ceases to have effect under section 8 or 11 of this Act, the proper officer of the prescribed court shall give notice of the cesser to the person to whom the order was directed.

(2) Where, in the case of an attachment of earnings order made otherwise than to secure maintenance payments, the whole amount payable under the relevant adjudication has

been paid, and also any relevant costs, the court shall give notice to the employer that no further compliance with the order is required.

(3) Where an attachment of earnings order –

(a) ceases to have effect under section 8 or 11 of this Act; or

(b) is discharged under section 9,

the person to whom the order has been directed shall be under no liability in consequence of his treating the order as still in force at any time before the expiration of seven days from the date on which the notice required by subsection (1) above or, as the case may be, a copy of the discharging order is served on him.

Defined terms—"employer", "maintenance payments": s 25(1); "relevant adjudication": s 2(d); "relevant costs": s 25(2).

"seven days" (s 12(3))—The employer is under no liability for a period of grace if he continues to treat the order as in force after service of the relevant notice or copy order.

Administrative provisions

13 Application of sums received by collecting officer

(1) Subject to subsection (3) below, the collecting officer to whom a person makes payments in compliance with an attachment of earnings order shall, after deducting such court fees, if any, in respect of proceedings for or arising out of the order, as are deductible from those payments, deal with the sums paid in the same way as he would if they had been paid by the debtor to satisfy the relevant adjudication.

(2) Any sums paid to the collecting officer under an attachment of earnings order made to secure maintenance payments shall, when paid to the person entitled to receive those payments, be deemed to be payments made by the debtor (with such deductions, if any, in respect of income tax as the debtor is entitled or required to make) so as to discharge –

(a) first, any sums for the time being due and unpaid under the related maintenance order (a sum due at an earlier date being discharged before a sum due at a later date); and

(b) secondly, any costs incurred in proceedings relating to the related maintenance order which were payable by the debtor when the attachment of earnings order was made or last varied.

(3) When a county court makes an attachment of earnings order to secure the payment of a judgment debt and also, under section 4(1) of this Act, orders the debtor to furnish to the court a list of his creditors, sums paid to the collecting officer in compliance with the attachment of earnings order shall not be dealt with by him as mentioned in subsection (1) above, but shall be retained by him pending the decision of the court whether or not to make an administration order and shall then be dealt with by him as the court may direct.

Defined terms—"administration order": s 25(1); "collecting officer": s 6(7); "the debtor": s 2(e); "maintenance order": s 2(a); "maintenance payments" s 25(1); "relevant adjudication": s 2(d).

Income tax (s 13(2))—Maintenance orders are now paid gross of tax.

14 Power of court to obtain statement of earnings etc

(1) Where in any proceedings a court has the power under this Act or under Schedule 5 to the Courts Act 2003, or a fines officer has power under that Schedule, to make an attachment of earnings order, the court or the fines officer, as the case may be, may –

(a) order the debtor to give to the court or the fines officer, as the case may be, within a specified period, a statement signed by him of –

PART II

    (i) the name and address of any person by whom earnings are paid to him;

    (ii) specified particulars as to his earnings and anticipated earnings, and as to his resources and needs; and

    (iii) specified particulars for the purpose of enabling the debtor to be identified by any employer of his;

  (b) order any person appearing to the court or the fines officer, as the case may be, to have the debtor in his employment to give to the court or the fines officer, as the case may be, within a specified period, a statement signed by him or on his behalf of specified particulars of the debtor's earnings and anticipated earnings.

(2) Where an attachment of earnings has been made, the court or the fines officer, as the case may be, may at any time thereafter while the order is in force –

  (a) make such an order as is described in subsection (1)(a) or (b) above; and

  (b) order the debtor to attend before the court on a day and at a time specified in the order to give the information described in subsection (1)(a) above.

(3) In the case of an application to a magistrates' court for an attachment of earnings order, or for the variation or discharge of such an order, the power to make an order under subsection (1) or (2) above shall be exercisable also, before the hearing of the application, by a single justice.

(4) Without prejudice to subsections (1) to (3) above, rules of court may provide that where notice of application for an attachment of earnings order is served on the debtor it shall include a requirement that he shall give to the court, within such period and in such manner as may be prescribed, a statement in writing of the matters specified in subsection (1)(a) above and of any other prescribed matters which are, or may be, relevant under section 6 of this Act to the determination of the normal deduction rate and the protected earnings rate to be specified in any order made on the application.

This subsection does not apply to an attachment of earnings order to be made under Schedule 5 to the Courts Act 2003.

(5) In any proceedings in which a court has the power under this Act or under Schedule 5 to the Courts Act 2003, or a fines officer has power under that Schedule, to make an attachment of earnings order, and in any proceedings for the making, variation or discharge of such an order, a document purporting to be a statement given to the court or the fines officer, as the case may be, in compliance with an order under subsection (1)(a) or (b) above, or with any such requirement of a notice of application for an attachment of earnings order as is mentioned in subsection (4) above, shall, in the absence of proof to the contrary, be deemed to be a statement so given and shall be evidence of the facts stated therein.

Amendments—AJA 1982, s 53(1); SI 2006/1737.

Defined terms—"the debtor": s 2(e); "earnings": s 24; "employer": s 25(1); "normal deduction rate": s 6(5)(a); "protected earnings rate": s 6(5)(b).

"in any proceedings" (s 14(1))—The power to order the debtor and apparent employer to provide information may be exercised, for example, in judgment summons proceedings or proceedings in the magistrates court for distress or committal (see s 3(4)) or in any High Court or county court proceedings concerning a qualifying periodical maintenance order within the meaning of MEA 1991, s 1 or enforcement or variation proceedings in the magistrates' court (see **"subsection (3) above shall not apply"** under s 3).

"resources and needs" (s 14(1)(a)(ii))—The debtor's needs include those of his dependants (s 25(3)).

"order the debtor to attend" (s 14(2)(b))—Unlike a failure to comply with an order to provide information by signed statement made under s 14(1), failure to attend pursuant to an order is not an offence under s 23 and the consequence of non-compliance is *not* committal but a further order to attend under s 23(1), breach of which may lead to committal.

"**exercisable ... by a single justice**" (s 14(3))—The power may also be exercised by a justices' clerk (MC(AE)R 1971, r 22).

15 Obligation of debtor and his employers to notify changes of employment and earnings

(1) While an attachment of earnings order is in force –

(a) the debtor shall from time to time notify the court in writing of every occasion on which he leaves any employment, or becomes employed or re-employed, not later (in each case) than seven days from the date on which he did so;

(b) the debtor shall, on any occasion when he becomes employed or re-employed, include in his notification under paragraph (a) above particulars of his earnings and anticipated earnings from the relevant employment; and

(c) any person who becomes the debtor's employer and knows that the order is in force and by, or (if the order was made by a fines officer) for, which court it was made shall, within seven days of his becoming the debtor's employer or of acquiring that knowledge (whichever is the later) notify that court in writing that he is the debtor's employer, and include in his notification a statement of the debtor's earnings and anticipated earnings.

(2) In the case of an attachment of earnings order made by a fines officer, the reference to "the court" in subsection (1)(a) above shall mean the court for which that order was made.

Amendments—SI 2006/1737.

Defined terms—"the debtor": s 2(e); "earnings": s 24; "employer": s 25(1).

16 Power of court to determine whether particular payments are earnings

(1) Where an attachment of earnings order is in force, the court shall, on application of a person specified in subsection (2) below, determine whether payments to the debtor of a particular class or description specified by the application are earnings for the purposes of the order; and the employer shall be entitled to give effect to any determination for the time being in force under this section.

(2) The persons referred to in subsection (1) above are –

(a) the employer;

(b) the debtor;

(c) the person to whom payment under the relevant adjudication is required to be made (whether directly or through the officer of any court); and

(d) without prejudice to paragraph (c) above, where the application is in respect of an attachment of earnings order made to secure payments under a magistrates' court maintenance order, the collecting officer.

(3) Where an application under this section is made by the employer, he shall not incur any liability for non-compliance with the order as respects any payments of the class or description specified by the application which are made by him to the debtor while the application, or any appeal in consequence thereof, is pending; but this subsection shall not, unless the court otherwise orders, apply as respects such payments if the employer subsequently withdraws the application or, as the case may be, abandons the appeal.

Defined terms—"collecting officer": s 6(7); "the debtor": s 2(e); "earnings": s 24; "the employer": s 25(1); "magistrates' court maintenance order": s 2(b); "the relevant adjudication": s 2(d).

Applicant (s 16(2))—An application to determine whether payments are "earnings" may be made by the debtor, the creditor, the employer or in the case of a magistrates' court maintenance order, the collecting officer. In magistrates' courts the application is made by way of complaint (s 19(3)). See s 21 as to the costs of such applications in magistrates' courts.

****

Special provisions with respect to magistrates' courts

18 Certain action not to be taken by collecting officer except on request

(1) A designated officer for a magistrates' court who is entitled to receive payments under a maintenance order for transmission to another person shall not –

    (a) apply for an attachment of earnings order to secure payments under the maintenance order; or

    (b) except as provided by section 10(3) of this Act, apply for an order discharging or varying such an attachment of earnings order; or

    (c) apply for a determination under section 16 of this Act,

unless he is requested in writing to do so by a person entitled to receive the payments through him.

(2) Where the designated officer for a magistrates' court is so requested –

    (a) he shall comply with the request unless it appears to him unreasonable in the circumstances to do so; and

    (b) the person by whom the request was made shall have the same liabilities for all the costs properly incurred in or about any proceedings taken in pursuance of the request as if the proceedings had been taken by that person.

(3) For the purposes of subsection (2)(b) above, any application made by the designated officer for a magistrates' court as required by section 10(3) of this Act shall be deemed to be made on the request of the person in whose favour the attachment of earnings order in question was made.

Amendments—AJA 1999, s 90, Sch 13, para 68; Courts Act 2003, s 109(1), Sch 8, para 143.

19 Procedure on applications

(1) Subject to rules of court made by virtue of the following subsection, an application to a magistrates' court for an attachment of earnings order, or an order discharging or varying an attachment of earnings order, shall be made by complaint.

(2) Rules of court may make provision excluding subsection (1) in the case of such an application as is referred to in section 9(3)(b) of this Act.

(3) An application to a magistrates' court for a determination under section 16 of this Act shall be made by complaint.

(4) For the purposes of section 51 of the Magistrates' Courts Act 1980 (which provides for the issue of a summons directed to the person against whom an order may be made in pursuance of a complaint) –

    (a) the power to make an order in pursuance of a complaint by the debtor for an attachment of earnings order, or the discharge or variation of such an order, shall be deemed to be a power to make an order against the person to whom payment under the relevant adjudication is required to be made (whether directly or through an officer of any court); and

    (b) the power to make an attachment of earnings order, or an order discharging or varying an attachment of earnings order, in pursuance of a complaint by any other person (including a complaint in proceedings to which section 3(4)(b) of this Act applies) shall be deemed to be a power to make an order against the debtor.

(5) A complaint for an attachment of earnings order may be heard notwithstanding that it was made within the six months allowed by section 127(1) of the Magistrates' Courts Act 1980.

Amendments—MCA 1980, s 154, Sch 7, para 100.

20 Jurisdiction in respect of persons residing outside England and Wales

(1) It is hereby declared that a magistrates' court has jurisdiction to hear a complaint by or against a person residing outside England and Wales for the discharge or variation of an attachment of earnings order made by a magistrates' court to secure maintenance payments; and where such a complaint is made, the following provisions shall have effect.

(2) If the person resides in Scotland or Northern Ireland, section 15 of the Maintenance Orders Act 1950 (which relates to the service of process on persons residing in those countries) shall have effect in relation to the complaint as it has effect in relation to the proceedings therein mentioned.

(3) Subject to the following subsection, if the person resides outside the United Kingdom and does not appear at the time and place appointed for the hearing of the complaint, the court may, if it thinks it reasonable in all the circumstances to do so, proceed to hear and determine the complaint at the time and place appointed for the hearing, or for any adjourned hearing, in like manner as if the person had then appeared.

(4) Subsection (3) above shall apply only if it is proved to the satisfaction of the court, on oath or in such other manner as may be prescribed, that the complainant has taken such steps as may be prescribed to give to the said person notice of the complaint and of the time and place appointed for the hearing of it.

Defined terms—"maintenance payments": s 25(1).

"such steps as may be prescribed" (s 20(4))—The relevant steps are prescribed by MC(AE)R 1971, rr 10, 11.

21 Costs on application under s 16

(1) On making a determination under section 16 of this Act, a magistrates' court may in its discretion make such order as it thinks just and reasonable for payment by any of the persons mentioned in subsection (2) of that section of the whole or any part of the costs of the determination (but subject to section 18(2)(b) of this Act).

(2) Costs ordered to be paid under this section shall –

(a) in the case of costs to be paid by the debtor to the person in whose favour the attachment of earnings order in question was made, be deemed –
   (i) if the attachment of earnings order was made to secure maintenance payments, to be a sum due under the related maintenance order, and
   (ii) otherwise, to be a sum due to the designated officer for the magistrates' court; and
(b) in any other case, be enforceable as a civil debt.

Amendments—AJA 1999, s 90, Sch 13, para 69; Courts Act 2003, s 109(1), Sch 8, para 144.

Defined terms—"maintenance order": s 2(a); "the debtor": s 2(e).

Miscellaneous provisions

22 Persons employed under the Crown

(1) The fact that an attachment of earnings order is made at the suit of the Crown shall not prevent its operation at any time when the debtor is in the employment of the Crown.

(2) Where a debtor is in the employment of the Crown and an attachment of earnings order is made in respect of him, then for the purposes of this Act –

(a) the chief officer for the time being of the department, office or other body in which the debtor is employed shall be treated as having the debtor in his employment (any transfer of the debtor from one department, office or body to another being treated as a change of employment); and

(b) any earnings paid by the Crown or a Minister of the Crown, or out of the public revenue of the United Kingdom, shall be treated as paid by the said chief officer.

(3) If any question arises, in the proceedings for or arising out of an attachment of earnings order, as to what department, office or other body is concerned for the purposes of this section, or as to who for those purposes is the chief officer thereof, the question shall be referred to and determined by the Minister for the Civil Service; but that Minister shall not be under any obligation to consider a reference under this subsection unless it is made by the court.

(4) A document purporting to set out a determination of the said Minister under subsection (3) above and to be signed by an official of the Office of Public Service shall, in any such proceedings as are mentioned in that subsection, be admissible in evidence and be deemed to contain an accurate statement of such a determination unless the contrary is shown.

(5) This Act shall have effect notwithstanding any enactment passed before 29 May 1970 and preventing or avoiding the attachment or diversion of sums due to a person in respect of service under the Crown, whether by way of remuneration, pension or otherwise.

Amendments—SI 1992/1296; SI 1995/2985.

Defined terms—"the debtor": s 2(e).

"notwithstanding any enactment" (s 22(5))—The protection formerly given to e g the pensions of ex-servicemen is removed; as to servicemen's pay, see s 24(2)(b).

23 Enforcement provisions

(1) If, after being served with notice of an application to a county court for an attachment of earnings order or for the variation of such an order or with an order made under section 14(2)(b) above, the debtor fails to attend on the day and at the time specified for any hearing of the application or specified in the order, the court may adjourn the hearing and order him to attend at a specified time on another day; and if the debtor –

(a) fails to attend at that time on that day; or

(b) attends, but refuses to be sworn or give evidence,

he may be ordered by the judge to be imprisoned for not more than fourteen days.

(1A) In any case where the judge has the power to make an order of imprisonment under subsection (1) for failure to attend, he may, in lieu of or in addition to making that order, order the debtor to be arrested and brought to the court either forthwith or at such time as the judge may direct.

(2) Subject to this section, a person commits an offence if –

(a)   being required by section 7(1) or 9(2) of this Act to comply with an attachment of earnings order, he fails to do so; or

(b)   being required by section 7(2) of this Act to give a notice for the purposes of that subsection, he fails to give it, or fails to give it within the time required by that subsection; or

(c)   he fails to comply with an order under section 14(1) of this Act or with any such requirement of a notice of application for an attachment of earnings order as is mentioned in section 14(4), or fails (in either case) to comply within the time required by the order or notice; or

(d)   he fails to comply with section 15 of this Act; or

(e)   he gives notice for the purposes of section 7(2) of this Act, or a notification for the purposes of section 15, which he knows to be false in a material particular, or recklessly gives such a notice or notification which is false in a material particular, or

(f)   in purported compliance with section 7(2) or 15 of this Act, or with an order under section 14(1), or with any such requirement of a notice of application for an attachment of earnings order as is mentioned in section 14(4), he makes any statement which he knows to be false in a material particular, or recklessly makes any statement which is false in a material particular.

(3) Where a person commits an offence under subsection (2) above in relation to proceedings in, or to an attachment of earnings order made by, the High Court or a county court, he shall be liable on summary conviction to a fine of not more than level 2 on the standard scale or he may be ordered by a judge of the High Court or the county court judge (as to the case may be) to pay a fine of not more than £250 or, in the case of an offence specified in subsection (4) below, to be imprisoned for not more than fourteen days; and where a person commits an offence under subsection (2) otherwise than as mentioned above in this subsection, he shall be liable on summary conviction to a fine of not more than level 2 on the standard scale.

(4) The offences referred to above in the case of which a judge may impose imprisonment are –

(a)   an offence under subsection (2)(c) or (d), if committed by the debtor; and

(b)   an offence under subsection (2)(e) or (f), whether committed by the debtor or any other person.

(5) It shall be a defence –

(a)   for a person charged with an offence under subsection (2)(a) above to prove that he took all reasonable steps to comply with the attachment of earnings order in question;

(b)   for a person charged with an offence under subsection (2)(b) to prove that he did not know, and could not reasonably be expected to know, that the debtor was not in his employment, or (as the case may be) had ceased to be so, and that he gave the required notice as soon as reasonably practicable after the fact came to his knowledge.

(6) Where a person is convicted or dealt with for an offence under subsection (2)(a), the court may order him to pay, to whoever is the collecting officer of the court for the purposes of the attachment of earnings order in question, any sums deducted by that person from the debtor's earnings and not already paid to the collecting officer.

(7) Where under this section a person is ordered by a judge of the High Court or a county court judge to be imprisoned, the judge may at any time revoke the order and, if the person is already in custody, order his discharge.

(8) Any fine imposed by a judge of the High Court under subsection (3) above and any sums ordered by the High Court to be paid under subsection (6) above shall be

recoverable in the same way as a fine imposed by that court in the exercise of its jurisdiction to punish for contempt of court; section 129 of the County Courts Act 1984 (enforcement of fines) shall apply to payment of a fine imposed by a county court judge under subsection (3) and of any sums ordered by a county court judge to be paid under subsection (6); and any sum ordered by a magistrates' court to be paid under subsection (6) shall be recoverable as a sum adjudged to be paid on a conviction by that court.

(9) For the purposes of section 13 of the Administration of Justice Act 1960 (appeal in cases of contempt of court), subsection (3) above shall be treated as an enactment enabling the High Court or a county court to deal with an offence under subsection (2) above as if it were contempt of court.

(10) In this section references to proceedings in a court are to proceedings in which that court has power to make an attachment of earnings order or has made such an order.

(11) A district judge, assistant district judge or deputy district judge shall have the same powers under this section as a judge of a county court.

Amendments—CCA 1981, s 41(5), Sch 2; AJA 1982, s 53(2); Criminal Justice Act 1982, ss 37, 38, 46; CCA 1984, s 148(1), Sch 2, para 41; CLSA 1990, s 125(2), Sch 17; Criminal Justice Act 1991, s 17, Sch 4, Pt I.

Defined terms—"the debtor": s 2(e).

Offences and penalties—Section 23(2) creates a number of offences which are punishable on summary conviction by a fine. Section 23(1) and (1A) empowers the county court to order the attendance of a debtor who has failed to attend the hearing of an application or pursuant to an order under s 14(2)(b); and if he again fails to attend or refuses to be sworn or give evidence then to order either his imprisonment for up to 14 days or his arrest and production to the court or both. Further, s 23(3) empowers the High Court or the county court, in proceedings before it, when one of the offences has been committed, directly to order payment of a fine or, in the cases identified in s 23(4), to order that the offender be imprisoned for up to 14 days. Imprisonment should not be regarded as routine: *Broomleigh HA v Okonkwo* [2010] EWCA Civ 1113.

"level 2 on the standard scale" (s 23(3))—Currently £500 (Criminal Justice Act 1982, s 37(2), as substituted).

Appeal (s 23(9))—An appeal from "any order or decision of a court in the exercise of jurisdiction to punish for contempt of court" lies under AJA 1960, s 13 to the Court of Appeal; orders under s 23(1) or (1A) clearly fall within this description. Section 23(9) applies the same provision to orders dealing with the offences created by s 23(2).

District judge (s 23(11))—The district judge has the same powers in county courts under this section as the circuit judge. Although an appeal from his order will lie direct to the Court of Appeal under AJA 1960, s 13, this does not remove the right of appeal to the circuit judge under FPR 2010, r 30.3 and that procedure is to be preferred (*King v Read & Slack* [1999] 1 FLR 425, CA).

24 Meaning of "earnings"

(1) For the purposes of this Act, but subject to the following subsection, "earnings" are any sums payable to a person –

(a) by way of wages or salary (including any fees, bonus, commission, overtime pay or other emoluments payable in addition to wages or salary or payable under a contract of service);

(b) by way of pension (including an annuity in respect of past services, whether or not rendered to the person paying the annuity, and including periodical payments by way of compensation for the loss, abolition or relinquishment, or diminution in emoluments, of any office or employment);

(c) by way of statutory sick pay.

(2) The following shall not be treated as earnings –

(a) sums payable by any department of the Government of Northern Ireland or of a territory outside the United Kingdom;

(b) pay or allowances payable to the debtor as a member of Her Majesty's forces other than pay or allowances payable by his employer to him as a special member of a reserve force (within the meaning of the Reserve Forces Act 1996);

(ba) a tax credit (within the meaning of the Tax Credits Act 2002);

(c) pension, allowances or benefit payable under any enactment relating to social security;

(d) pension or allowances payable in respect of disablement or disability;

(e) except in relation to a maintenance order wages payable to a person as a seaman, other than wages payable to him as a seaman of a fishing boat;

(f) guaranteed minimum pension within the meaning of the Social Security Pensions Act 1975.

(3) In subsection (2)(e) above –

"fishing boat" means a vessel of whatever size, and in whatever way propelled, which is for the time being employed in sea fishing or in the sea-fishing service;

"seaman" includes every person (except masters and pilots) employed or engaged in any capacity on board any ship; and

"wages" includes emoluments.

Amendments—Social Security Pensions Act 1975, s 65(1), Sch 4, para 15; Merchant Shipping Act 1979, s 39(1); Social Security Act 1985, s 21, Sch 4, para 1; Social Security Act 1986, s 86(1), Sch 10, Pt VI, para 102; Merchant Shipping Act 1995, s 314(2), Sch 13, para 46; SI 1998/3086; Tax Credits Act 2002, s 47, Sch 3, para 1.

Defined terms—"maintenance order": s 2(a).

Scope—This section defines earnings to include pensions and sick pay but subject to significant exceptions.

Holiday pay (s 24(1)(a))—Although holiday pay is not "wages" (*London County Council v Henry Boot & Sons Ltd* [1959] 1 WLR 1609), it would seem to be caught by "other emoluments payable in addition to wages ... or payable under a contract of service".

Pension (s 24(1)(b))—A pension may be attachable under the Act, but the making of the order may breach a prohibition against diversion of the pension contained in the relevant trust deed and so terminate entitlement to pension (see e g *Edmonds v Edmonds* [1965] 1 WLR 58).

Her Majesty's forces (s 24(2)(b))—This exception protects the pay or allowances of a serviceman (but not the pension of an ex-serviceman, as to which see **"notwithstanding any enactment"** under s 22). However, arrangements exist (see Armed Forces (Forfeitures and Deductions) Regulations 2009) under which relevant authorities may order deductions from the serviceman's pay to meet maintenance orders (and judgment debts) if the serviceman will not comply voluntarily with the judgment or order. The amount of such a deduction is in the discretion of the relevant authority, which is not bound to follow the rate indicated in any order of the court. Any request for such an order should set out the efforts made to secure voluntary compliance, enclose a copy of the judgment or order and set out the state of account under it. The appropriate authorities are:

(a) *Navy* All ranks: The Director of Naval Pay and Pensions (Accounts), Ministry of Defence, Room 1045, HMS Centurion, Grange Road, Gosport, Hants. PO13 9AX.

(b) *Army* *Officers*: Ministry of Defence, PF 2d (Army), Lansdowne House, Berkeley Square, London W1X 6AA; other ranks: the appropriate regimental pay office.

(c) *RAF* *Officers*: Ministry of Defence, DPS2 (RAF), Adastral House, Theobalds Road, London WC1X 8RU; other ranks: Ministry of Defence, DGPM (RAF), Eastern Avenue, Barnwood, Gloucester.

"pension or allowances payable in respect of disablement or disability" (s 24(2)(d))—This exception does not extend to a pension taken on early retirement due to ill-health (*Miles v Miles* [1979] 1 WLR 371).

"seaman" (s 24(2)(e))—See Home Office Circular No 124/1979 for advice on obtaining information regarding the address of a seaman's employer or a seaman's whereabouts.

25 General interpretation

(1) In this Act, except where the context otherwise requires –

"administration order" means an order made under, and so referred to in, Part VI of the County Courts Act 1984;

"the court", in relation to an attachment of earnings order, means the court which made the order, subject to rules of court as to the venue for, and the transfer of, proceedings in county courts and magistrates' courts;

"debtor" and "relevant adjudication" have the meanings given by section 2 of this Act;

"the employer", in relation to the attachment of earnings order, means the person who is required by the order to make deductions from earnings paid by him to the debtor;

"the fines officer", in relation to a debtor who is subject to a collection order made under Schedule 5 to the Courts Act 2003, means any fines officer working at the fines office specified in that order;

"judgment debt" has the meaning given by section 2 of this Act;

"maintenance order" has the meaning given by section 2 of this Act;

"maintenance payments" means payments required under a maintenance order;

"prescribed" means prescribed by rules of court.

(2) Any reference in this Act to sums payable under a judgment or order, or to the payment of such sums, includes a reference to costs and the payment of them; and the references in sections 6(4) and 12(2) to relevant costs are to any costs of the proceedings in which the attachment of earnings order in question was made, being costs which the debtor is liable to pay.

(3) References in sections 6(5)(b), 9(3)(b) and 14(1)(a) of this Act to the debtor's needs include references to the needs of any person for whom he must, or reasonably may, provide.

(4) (repealed)

(5) Any power to make rules which is conferred by this Act is without prejudice to any other power to make rules of court.

(6) This Act, so far as it relates to magistrates' courts, and Part III of the Magistrates' Courts Act 1980 shall be construed as if this Act were contained in that Part.

(7) References in this Act to any enactment include references to that enactment amended by or under any other enactment, including this Act.

Amendments—MCA 1980, s 154, Sch 7, para 101; CCA 1984, s 148(1), Sch 2, para 42; Legal Aid Act 1988, Sch 5, para 3; Dock Work Act 1989, Sch 1, Pt I; AJA 1999, s 106, Sch 15; Courts Act 2003, s 109(1), Sch 8, para 145; SI 2006/1737.

****

SCHEDULE 1

MAINTENANCE ORDERS TO WHICH THIS ACT APPLIES

1 An order for alimony, maintenance or other payments made, or having effect as if made, under Part II of the Matrimonial Causes Act 1965 (ancillary relief in actions for divorce etc).

2 An order for payments to or in respect of a child, being an order made, or having effect as if made, under Part III of the said Act of 1965 (maintenance of children following divorce etc).

3 An order for periodical or other payments made or having effect as if made under Part II of the Matrimonial Causes Act 1973.

4 An order for maintenance or other payments to or in respect of a spouse or child, being an order made under Part I of the Domestic Proceedings and Magistrates' Courts Act 1978.

5 An order for periodical or other payments made or having effect as if made under Schedule 1 to the Children Act 1989.

6 (*repealed*)

7 An order under paragraph 23 of Schedule 2 to the Children Act 1989, section 23 of the Ministry of Social Security Act 1966, section 18 of the Supplementary Benefits Act 1976, section 24 of the Social Security Act 1986, or section 106 of the Social Security Administration Act 1992 (various provisions for obtaining contributions from a person whose dependants are assisted or maintained out of public funds).

8 (*repealed*)

9 An order to which section 16 of the Maintenance Orders Act 1950 applies by virtue of subsection (2)(b) or (c) of that section (that is to say an order made by a court in Scotland or Northern Ireland and corresponding to one of those specified in the foregoing paragraphs) and which has been registered in a court in England and Wales under Part II of that Act.

10 A maintenance order within the meaning of the Maintenance Orders (Facilities for Enforcement) Act 1920 (Commonwealth orders enforceable in the United Kingdom) registered in, or confirmed in England and Wales under that Act.

11 A maintenance order within the meaning of Part I of the Maintenance Orders (Reciprocal Enforcement) Act 1972 registered in a magistrates' court under the said Part I.

12 An order under section 34(1)(b) of the Children Act 1975 (payments of maintenance in respect of a child to his custodian).

13 A maintenance order within the meaning of Part I of the Civil Jurisdiction and Judgments Act 1982 which is registered in a magistrates' court under that Part.

14 A maintenance judgment within the meaning of Council Regulation (EC) No 44/2001 of 22 December 2000 on jurisdiction and the recognition and enforcement of judgments in civil and commercial matters, as amended from time to time and as applied by the Agreement made on 19th October 2005 between the European Community and the Kingdom of Denmark on jurisdiction and the recognition and enforcement of judgments in civil and commercial matters (OJ No. L 299 16.11.2005 at p 62), which is registered in a magistrates' court under that Regulation.

14A (1) A decision, court settlement or authentic instrument which falls to be enforced by a magistrates' court by virtue of the Maintenance Regulation and the Civil Jurisdiction and Judgments (Maintenance) Regulations 2011.

(2) In this paragraph –

"the Maintenance Regulation" means Council Regulation (EC) No 4/2009 including as applied in relation to Denmark by virtue of the Agreement made on 19 October 2005 between the European Community and the Kingdom of Denmark;

"decision", "court settlement" and "authentic instrument" have the meanings given by Article 2 of that Regulation.

15 An order made under Schedule 5 to the Civil Partnership Act 2004 (financial relief in the High Court or a county court etc), for periodical or other payments.

16 An order made under Schedule 6 to the 2004 Act (financial relief in magistrates' courts etc), for maintenance or other payments to or in respect of a civil partner or child.

Amendments—MO(RE)A 1972, s 22(1), Sch, para 7; Guardianship Act 1973, s 9; MCA 1973, s 53, Sch 2, para 13; Children Act 1975, Sch 3, para 76; Supplementary Benefits Act 1976, s 35(2), Sch 7, para 20; DPMCA 1978, Sch 2, para 32; CJJA 1982, s 15(4), Sch 12, para 6; Social Security Act 1986, s 86(1), Sch 10, para 43; FLRA 1987, Schs 2, 3; CA 1989, s 108(5), Sch 13, para 29; CLSA 1990, s 116, Sch 16, para 38; Social Security (Consequential Provisions) Act 1992, s 4, Sch 2, para 7; SI 2001/3929; CPA 2004, s 261(1), Sch 27, para 35; SI 2007/1655; Health and Social Care Act 2008, Sch 15; SI 2011/1484.

Scope—This schedule provides the specific definition of maintenance orders for the purposes of the Act; the definition is not confined to orders for periodical maintenance payments.

****

SCHEDULE 3
DEDUCTIONS BY EMPLOYER UNDER ATTACHMENT OF EARNINGS ORDER

PART I
SCHEME OF DEDUCTIONS

Preliminary definitions

1 The following three paragraphs have effect for defining and explaining, for purposes of this Schedule, expressions used therein.

2 "Pay-day", in relation to earnings paid to a debtor, means an occasion on which they are paid.

3 "Attachable earnings", in relation to a pay-day, are the earnings which remain payable to the debtor on that day after deduction by the employer of –

(a) income tax;

(b) *(repealed)*

(bb) Primary Class I contributions under Part I of the Social Security Act 1975;

(c) amounts deductible under any enactment, or in pursuance of a request in writing by the debtor, for the purposes of a superannuation scheme, namely any enactment, rules, deed or other instrument providing for the payment of annuities or lump sums –

    (i)   to the persons with respect to whom the instrument has effect on their retirement at a specified age or on becoming incapacitated at some earlier age, or

    (ii)   to the personal representatives or the widows, relatives or dependants of such persons on their death or otherwise,

whether with or without any further or other benefits.

4 (1) On any pay-day –

    (a)   "the normal deduction" is arrived at by applying the normal deduction rate (as specified in the relevant attachment of earnings order) with respect to the relevant period; and

    (b)   "the protected earnings" are arrived at by applying the protected earnings rate (as so specified) with respect to the relevant period.

(2) For the purposes of this paragraph the relevant period in relation to any pay-day is the period beginning –

    (a)   if it is the first pay-day of the debtor's employment with the employer, with the first day of employment; or

    (b)   if on the last pay-day earnings were paid in respect of a period falling wholly or partly after that pay-day, with the first day after the end of that period; or

    (c)   in any other case, with the first day after the last pay-day, and ending –

        (i)   where earnings are paid in respect of a period falling wholly or partly after the pay-day, with the last day of that period; or

        (ii)   in any other case, with the pay-day.

5 Employer's deduction (judgment debts and administration orders)

In the case of an attachment of earnings order made to secure the payment of a judgment debt or payments under an administration order, the employer shall on any pay-day –

    (a)   if the attachable earnings exceed the protected earnings, deduct from the attachable earnings the amount of the excess or the normal deduction, whichever is the less;

    (b)   make no deduction if the attachable earnings are equal to, or less than, the protected earnings.

6 Employer's deduction (other cases)

(1) The following provision shall have effect in the case of an attachment of earnings order to which paragraph 5 above and paragraph 6A below do not apply.

(2) If on a pay-day the attachable earnings exceed the sum of –

    (a)   the protected earnings; and

    (b)   so much of any amount by which the attachable earnings on any previous pay-day fell short of the protected earnings as has not been made good by virtue of this sub-paragraph on another previous pay-day,

then, in so far as the excess allows, the employer shall deduct from the attachable earnings the amount specified in the following sub-paragraph.

(3) The said amount is the sum of –

    (a)   the normal deduction; and

    (b) so much of the normal deduction on any previous pay-day as was not deducted on that day and has not been paid by virtue of this sub-paragraph on any other previous pay-day.

(4) No deduction shall be made on any pay-day when the attachable earnings are equal to, or less than, the protected earnings.

Amendments—SI 2006/1737.

6A In the case of an attachment of earnings order made under Schedule 5 to the Courts Act 2003, the employer shall make deductions from the debtor's earnings in accordance with fines collection regulations made under that Schedule.

Amendments—SI 2006/1737.

PART II
PRIORITY AS BETWEEN ORDERS

7 Where the employer is required to comply with two or more attachment of earnings orders in respect of the same debtor, all or none of which orders are made to secure either the payment of judgment debts or payments under an administration order, then on any pay-day the employer shall, for the purpose of complying with Part I of this Schedule, –

    (a) deal with the orders according to the respective dates on which they were made, disregarding any later order until an earlier one has been dealt with;

    (b) deal with any later order as if the earnings to which it relates were the residue of the debtor's earnings after the making of deduction to comply with any earlier order.

8 Where the employer is required to comply with two or more attachment of earnings orders, and one or more (but not all) of those orders are made to secure either the payment of judgment debts or payments under an administration order, then on any pay-day the employer shall, for the purpose of complying with Part I of this Schedule –

    (a) deal first with any order which is not made to secure the payment of a judgment debt or payments under an administration order (complying with paragraph 7 above if there are two or more such orders); and

    (b) deal thereafter with any order which is made to secure the payment of a judgment debt or payments under an administration order as if the earnings to which it relates were the residue of the debtor's earnings after the making of any deduction to comply with an order having priority by virtue of sub-paragraph (a) above; and

    (c) if there are two or more orders to which sub-paragraph (b) above applies, comply with paragraph 7 above in respect of those orders.

Amendments—Social Security Pensions Act 1975, s 65(3), Sch 5; Social Security (Consequential Provisions) Act 1975, s 1(3), Sch 2, para 43; AJA 1982, s 54; Wages Act 1986, s 32(1), Sch 4, para 4; Employment Rights Act 1996, s 240, Sch 1, para 3; SI 2006/1737.

Priority orders—These are the orders which the employer must deal with first (para 8). If the net pay does not exceed the protected earnings rate sufficiently to allow the entire normal deduction to be made, the shortfall is carried forward and added to the normal deduction on the next pay-day. The shortfall may thus accumulate from pay-day to pay-day (para 6(3)). If in any pay period the net pay is less than the protected earnings rate, the unused protected earnings are similarly carried forward and "rolled up" (para 6(2)).

Other orders—The net pay is the amount left after any deductions have been made for priority orders (para 8(b)). The "roll-up" provisions do not apply. Deductions are made whenever the debtor's net pay exceeds the protected earnings rate and are limited to the normal deduction rate without regard to any shortfall (para 5). The result can be surprising: for example, if a debtor, having a priority order and another order against him, through absence has little or no pay for a time, on his return no deductions will be made under the priority order until his accumulated protected earnings have been used up; thereafter, all of the excess of his pay over the protected earnings rate will be deducted under the priority order until his accumulated normal deductions have been used up. In the meantime, deductions under the other order will recommence as soon as his pay exceeds the protected earnings rate but are likely to cease once the priority order takes effect and resume only after it has been caught up.

****

Charging Orders Act 1979

1 Charging orders

(1) Where, under a judgment or order of the High Court or a county court, a person (the "debtor") is required to pay a sum of money to another person (the "creditor") then, for the purpose of enforcing that judgment or order, the appropriate court may make an order in accordance with the provisions of this Act imposing on any such property of the debtor as may be specified in the order a charge for securing the payment of any money due or to become due under the judgment or order.

(2) The appropriate court is –

    (a)   in a case where the property to be charged is a fund in court, the court in which that fund is lodged;

    (b)   in a case where paragraph (a) above does not apply and the order to be enforced is a maintenance order of the High Court, the High Court or a county court;

    (c)   in a case where neither paragraph (a) nor paragraph (b) above applies and the judgment or order to be enforced is a judgment or order of the High Court for a sum exceeding the county court limit, the High Court or a county court; and

    (d)   in any other case, a county court.

In this section "county court limit" means the county court limit for the time being specified in an Order in Council under section 145 of the County Courts Act 1984 as the county court limit for the purposes of this section and "maintenance order" has the same meaning as in section 2(a) of the Attachment of Earnings Act 1971.

(3) An order under subsection (1) above is referred to in this Act as a "charging order".

(4) Where a person applies to the High Court for a charging order to enforce more than one judgment or order, that court shall be the appropriate court in relation to the application if it would be the appropriate court, apart from this subsection, on an application relating to one or more of the judgments or orders concerned.

(5) In deciding whether to make a charging order the court shall consider all the circumstances of the case and, in particular, any evidence before it as to –

    (a)   the personal circumstances of the debtor, and

    (b)   whether any other creditor of the debtor would be likely to be unduly prejudiced by the making of the order.

(6) Subsections (7) and (8) apply where, under a judgment or order of the High Court or a county court, a debtor is required to pay a sum of money by instalments.

(7) The fact that there has been no default in payment of the instalments does not prevent a charging order from being made in respect of that sum.

(8) But if there has been no default, the court must take that into account when considering the circumstances of the case under subsection (5).

Amendments—AJA 1982, s 34(3); TCEA 2007, s 93(2).

"required to pay a sum of money" (s 1(1))—There is no power to make a charging order until the sum is ascertained. Thus, an order for costs to be determined by detailed assessment will not found a charging order until after assessment (*A & M Records Inc v Darakjian* [1975] 1 WLR 1610).

"to another person" (s 1(1))—A charging order cannot be made to secure an order to pay into court (*Ward v Shakeshaft* [1860] 1 Dr & Sm 269) or an order to settle a sum of money for the benefit of a child (*Re N (a child) (payments for the benefit of child)* [2009] 1 FLR 1442 – although in that case the court achieved virtually the same result by granting an injunction.

"due or to become due" (s 1(1))—A charging order may secure amounts which have not yet fallen due for payment under the judgment, but the court may exercise its discretion not to include such payments in an order (see **"consider all the circumstances"** below). A charging order may be made to secure *arrears* under a periodical payments order; in view of the specific provision in MCA 1973, s 23(1)(b),(e), it is doubtful that a charging order may secure future payments under such an order.

"maintenance order" (s 1(2)(b))—As to the extended meaning of this expression, see AEA 1971, Sch 1 above and **"expressions used"** under CPR 1998, Sch 2, CCR Ord 27, r 1.

County court limit (s 1(2))—The relevant limit is currently £5000, notwithstanding the increase in the jurisdiction of the county court which took place on 1 July 1991.

"consider all the circumstances" (s 1(5))—The court has a general discretion. A charging order will not lightly be made where the costs of and consequent on doing so (including the costs of discharging the charge in due course) would be disproportionate in comparison with the judgment debt. A charging order will not be made where the creditor would gain security in the face of a pending liquidation (*Roberts Petroleum Ltd v Bernard Kenny Ltd* [1983] AC 192). In the absence of a pending bankruptcy of which the court is aware, the fact that the debtor may actually be insolvent is immaterial (*Nationwide Building Society v Wright* [2009] BPIR 1047).

The position of the debtor's spouse must be considered. In the absence of divorce proceedings, her interests will not prevent the order being made as her beneficial interest is not affected and the creditor will be in no better position than the debtor would be (on, for example, an application under TLATA 1996, s 14); however, the interests of the debtor's resident family must be taken into account (*Lloyds Bank plc v Byrne* [1993] 1 FLR 369). Where a divorce petition has been issued, the spouse's expectation of financial provision and of security of accommodation must be balanced against the creditor's expectation of payment so that it may be appropriate to hear the applications for ancillary relief and for the charging order together (*Harman v Glencross* [1986] 2 FLR 241; *Austin-Fell v Austin-Fell and Midland Bank* [1989] 2 FLR 497).

If the judgment debt is subject to an instalment order, a charging order may now be made even though the payments are up to date when the application is made (reversing *Mercantile Credit Co Ltd v Ellis* (1987) *The Times*, 1 April), but the fact that the instalments are up to date is a factor for the court to take into account in deciding whether to make the order final (c f *Ropaigealach v Allied Irish Bank plc* [2001] EWCA Civ 1790, CA). Similar considerations would no doubt apply to an instalment agreement.

2 Property which may be charged

(1) Subject to subsection (3) below, a charge may be imposed by a charging order only on –

    (a)   any interest held by the debtor beneficially –
        (i)   in any asset of a kind mentioned in subsection (2) below, or
        (ii) under any trust; or
    (b)   any interest held by a person as trustee of a trust ("the trust"), if the interest is in such an asset or is an interest under another trust and –
        (i)   the judgment or order in respect of which a charge is to be imposed was made against that person as trustee of the trust, or
        (ii) the whole beneficial interest under the trust is held by the debtor unencumbered and for his own benefit, or
        (iii) in a case where there are two or more debtors all of whom are liable to the creditor for the same debt, they together hold the whole beneficial interest under the trust unencumbered and for their own benefit.

(2) The assets referred to in subsection (1) above are –

    (a)   land,

(b) securities of any of the following kinds –
   (i) government stock,
   (ii) stock of any body (other than a building society) incorporated within England and Wales,
   (iii) stock of any body incorporated outside England and Wales or of any state or territory outside the United Kingdom, being stock registered in a register kept at any place within England and Wales, or
(c) funds in court.

(3) In any case where a charge is imposed by a charging order on any interest in an asset of a kind mentioned in paragraph (b) or (c) of subsection (2) above, the court making the order may provide for the charge to extend to any interest or dividend payable in respect of the asset.

Defined terms—"building society": s 6(1); "charging order", "debtor": s 1; "dividend", "stock": s 6(1).

Partnerships—A debtor's share in a partnership may also be made the subject of a charging order by virtue of Partnership Act 1890, s 23.

3 Provisions supplementing sections 1 and 2

(1) A charging order may be made absolutely or subject to conditions as to notifying the debtor or as to the time when the charge is to become enforceable, or as to other matters.

(2) The Land Charges Act 1972 and the Land Registration Act 2002 shall apply in relation to charging orders as they apply in relation to other orders or writs issued or made for the purpose of enforcing judgments.

(3) *(repealed)*

(4) Subject to the provisions of this Act, a charge imposed by a charging order shall have the like effect and shall be enforceable in the same courts and in the same manner as an equitable charge created by the debtor by writing under his hand.

(4A) Subsections (4C) to (4E) apply where –
   (a) a debtor is required to pay a sum of money in instalments under a judgment or order of the High Court or a county court (an "instalments order"), and
   (b) a charge has been imposed by a charging order in respect of that sum.

(4B) In subsections (4C) to (4E) references to the enforcement of a charge are to the making of an order for the enforcement of the charge.

(4C) The charge may not be enforced unless there has been default in payment of an instalment under the instalments order.

(4D) Rules of court may –
   (a) provide that, if there has been default in payment of an instalment, the charge may be enforced only in prescribed cases, and
   (b) limit the amounts for which, and the times at which, the charge may be enforced.

(4E) Except so far as otherwise provided by rules of court under subsection (4D) –
   (a) the charge may be enforced, if there has been default in payment of an instalment, for the whole of the sum of money secured by the charge and the costs then remaining unpaid, or for such part as the court may order, but
   (b) the charge may not be enforced unless, at the time of enforcement, the whole or part of an instalment which has become due under the instalments order remains unpaid.

(5) The court by which a charging order was made may at any time, on the application of the debtor or of any person interested in any property to which the order relates, make an order discharging or varying the charging order.

(6) Where a charging order has been protected by an entry registered under the Land Charges Act 1972 or the Land Registration Act 2002, an order under subsection (5) above discharging the charging order may direct that the entry be cancelled.

(7) The Lord Chancellor may by order made by statutory instrument amend section 2(2) of this Act by adding to, or removing from, the kinds of asset for the time being referred to there, any asset of a kind which in his opinion ought to be so added or removed.

(8) Any order under subsection (7) above shall be subject to annulment in pursuance of a resolution of either House of Parliament.

Amendments—Land Registration Act 2002, s 133, Schs 11, 13; TCEA 2007, s 93(3).

Defined terms—"charging order", "debtor": s 1.

"enforceable" (s 3(4))—An application for an order for sale to enforce the charge must be brought by separate proceedings. See CPR, r 73.10.

"person interested" (s 3(5))—The interest need not be a beneficial interest in the property charged (*Harman v Glencross* [1986] 2 FLR 241).

3A Power to set financial thresholds

(1) The Lord Chancellor may by regulations provide that a charge may not be imposed by a charging order for securing the payment of money of an amount below that determined in accordance with the regulations.

(2) The Lord Chancellor may by regulations provide that a charge imposed by a charging order may not be enforced by way of order for sale to recover money of an amount below that determined in accordance with the regulations.

(3) Regulations under this section may –

   (a) make different provision for different cases;
   (b) include such transitional provision as the Lord Chancellor thinks fit.

(4)–(6) …

Amendments—Inserted by TCEA 2007, s 94.

"may not be enforced by way of order for sale" (s 3A(2))—The Coalition Agreement of 2010 proposed that there should be no enforcement of charging orders by way of sale where the sum secured was under £25,000. At the time of writing, no regulations have been made but the Government now proposes a minimum figure of just £1000 and that only in relation to consumer credit debts. Courts are likely to remain ready to enforce debts arising in family proceedings or from failure to pay child support.

****

5 Stop orders and notices

(1) In this section –

   "stop order" means an order of the court prohibiting the taking, in respect of any of the securities specified in the order, of any of the steps mentioned in subsection (5) below;

   "stop notice" means a notice requiring any person or body on whom it is duly served to refrain from taking, in respect of any of the securities specified in the notice, any of those steps without first notifying the person by whom, or on whose behalf, the notice was served; and

   "prescribed securities" means securities (including funds in court) of a kind prescribed by rules of court made under this section.

(2) The power to make rules of court under section 1 of, and Schedule 1 to, the Civil Procedure Act 1997 shall include power by any such rules to make provision –

    (a)   for the High Court to make a stop order on the application of any person claiming to be entitled to an interest in prescribed securities; and

    (b)   for the service of a stop notice by any person claiming to be entitled to an interest in prescribed securities.

(3) (*repealed*)

(4) Rules of court made by virtue of subsection (2) above shall prescribe the person or body on whom a copy of any stop order or a stop notice is to be served.

(5) The steps mentioned in subsection (1) above are –

    (a)   the registration of any transfer of the securities;

    (b)   in the case of funds in court, the transfer, sale, delivery out, payment or other dealing with the funds, or of the income thereon;

    (c)   the making of any payment by way of dividend, interest or otherwise in respect of the securities; and

    (d)   in the case of a unit trust, any acquisition of or other dealing with the units by any person or body exercising functions under the trust.

(6) Any rules of court made by virtue of this section may include such incidental, supplemental and consequential provisions as the authority making them consider necessary or expedient, and may make different provision in relation to different cases or classes of case.

Amendments—SCA 1981, s 152(1), Sch 5; CCA 1984, s 148(1), Sch 2, para 72; SI 2002/439.

6 Interpretation

(1) In this Act –

    "building society" has the same meaning as in the Building Societies Act 1986;

    "charging order" means an order made under section 1(1) of this Act;

    "debtor" and "creditor" have the meanings given by section 1(1) of this Act;

    "dividend" includes any distribution in respect of any unit of a unit trust;

    "government stock" means any stock issued by Her Majesty's government in the United Kingdom or any funds of, or annuity granted by, that government;

    "stock" includes shares, debentures and any securities of the body concerned, whether or not constituting a charge on the assets of that body;

    "unit trust" means any trust established for the purpose, or having the effect, of providing, for persons having funds available for investment, facilities for the participation by them, as beneficiaries under the trust, in any profits or income arising from the acquisition, holding, management or disposal of any property whatsoever.

(2) For the purposes of sections 1 and 3 of this Act references to a judgment or order of the High Court or a county court shall be taken to include references to a judgment, order, decree or award (however called) of any court or arbitrator (including any foreign court or arbitrator) which is or has become enforceable (whether wholly or to a limited extent) as if it were a judgment or order of the High Court or a county court.

(3) References in section 2 of this Act to any securities include references to any such securities standing in the name of the Accountant General.

Amendments—Building Societies Act 1986, s 120(1), Sch 18, Pt I, para 14; TCEA 2007, s 93(4).

****

Child Abduction and Custody Act 1985

ARRANGEMENT OF SECTIONS

PART I
INTERNATIONAL CHILD ABDUCTION

PART II
RECOGNITION AND ENFORCEMENT OF CUSTODY DECISIONS

PART III
SUPPLEMENTARY

PART I
INTERNATIONAL CHILD ABDUCTION

1 The Hague Convention

(1) In this Part of this Act "the Convention" means the Convention on the Civil Aspects of International Child Abduction which was signed at The Hague on 25 October 1980.

(2) Subject to the provisions of this Part of this Act, the provisions of that Convention set out in Schedule 1 to this Act shall have the force of law in the United Kingdom.

(3) But –

- (a) those provisions of the Convention,
- (b) this Part of this Act, and
- (c) rules of court under section 10 of this Act,

are subject to Article 60 of the Council Regulation (by virtue of which the Regulation takes precedence over the Hague Convention, in so far as it concerns matters governed by the Regulation).

(4) "The Council Regulation" means Council Regulation (EC) No 2201/2003 of 27 November 2003 concerning jurisdiction and the recognition and enforcement of judgments in matrimonial matters and matters of parental responsibility.

Amendments—SI 2005/265.

Scope—The 1980 Hague Convention is concerned with the abduction of children and provides a mechanism for the return of a child who has been wrongfully removed or retained, but its provisions are superseded by Brussels IIA, as between Member States, insofar as its provisions deal with matters that are also governed by the Convention. As from 1 November 2012, the impact of the 1996 Convention on Jurisdiction, Applicable Law, Recognition, Enforcement and Co-operation in Respect of Parental Responsibility and Measures for the Protection of Children (see Part VI) must also be considered where appropriate in child abduction cases. Brussels IIA strengthens the application of the Hague Convention: *Re D (Abduction: Rights of Custody)* [2007] 1 FLR 961, HL and in many respects so will the 1996 Convention.

Object of the Convention—The Hague Convention seeks to protect rights of custody and access and to provide through legal process the expeditious return of any child who is under the age of 16 who has been wrongfully removed or retained in another Contracting State (Sch 1, Arts 3, 4) to the country of his habitual residence. Its first objective is to provide an effective mechanism for the prompt return of children through administrative and judicial procedures so that parents do not resort to self-help and secondary abduction. The second is to ensure that rights of custody and access under the law of one contracting state are effectively respected in the other contracting states. Since this is an international convention to be applied under a variety of systems of law, it must be given a "purposive construction in order to make as effective as possible the machinery set up under it" (see *Re H (Abduction: Rights of Custody)* [2000] 1 FLR 374). In a case where the child is between 16 and 18 years of age, as from 1 November 2012 the 1996 Convention may be relied on to obtain the appropriate relief, provided the respective States are Contracting States under that Convention.

Subject to Article 60 of the Council Regulation—The provisions of the Hague Convention 1980 do not automatically apply as Brussels IIA, Art 60 specifically provides that Brussels IIA takes precedence over the 1980 Convention. The 1996 Convention, Art 50 is also relevant after 1 November 2012 as it also provides that nothing precludes its provisions from being invoked for the purposes of obtaining the return of an abducted child. Thus, also of relevance are the provisions of the "applicable law" in Art 15 and the parental responsibility provisions in Arts 16–18. There will also be other instances when the inter-relationship between the two Conventions will need to be considered (see Part VI).

2 Contracting States

(1) For the purposes of the Convention as it has effect under this Part of this Act the Contracting States other than the United Kingdom shall be those for the time being specified by an Order in Council under this section.

(2) An Order in Council under this section shall specify the date of the coming into force of the Convention as between the United Kingdom and any State specified in the Order; and except where the Order otherwise provides, the Convention shall apply as between the United Kingdom and that State only in relation to wrongful removals or retentions occurring on or after that date.

(3) Where the Convention applies, or applies only, to a particular territory or particular territories specified in a declaration made by a Contracting State under Article 39 or 40 of the Convention references to that State in subsections (1) and (2) above shall be construed as references to that territory or those territories.

Defined terms—"the Convention": s 1(1).

"specified by an Order in Council under this section"—See the Child Abduction and Custody (Parties to Conventions) Order 1986 in Part IV for the Contracting States and the website of the permanent Bureau of the Hague Conference on Private International Law at *www.hcch.net*. To facilitate the goal of uniform interpretation the Bureau has set up a database (INCADAT) of decisions taken under the Convention, which can be accessed at *www.incadat.com*.

3 Central Authorities

(1) Subject to subsection (2) below, the functions under the Convention of a Central Authority shall be discharged –

    (a)   in England and Wales by the Lord Chancellor; and

    (b)   in Scotland by the Secretary of State; and

    (c)   in Northern Ireland by the Department of Justice in Northern Ireland.

(2) Any application made under the Convention by or on behalf of a person outside the United Kingdom may be addressed to the Lord Chancellor as the Central Authority in the United Kingdom.

(3) Where any such application relates to a function to be discharged under subsection (1) above by an authority ("the responsible authority") other than the authority to which the application is addressed, the authority to which the application is addressed shall transmit it to the responsible authority.

Amendments—SI 2010/976.

Defined terms—"the Convention": s 1(1); "Central Authority in relation to England and Wales": FPR 2010, r 12.44.

Central Authority for England and Wales—The authority is the Lord Chancellor. Application should be made to the International Child Abduction and Contact Unit, 81 Chancery Lane, London WC2A 1DD; Tel: 020 7911 7045/7047; Fax: 020 7911 7248; Email: enquiries@offsol.gsi.gov.uk.

Scottish Central Authority—The Authority should be contacted at: Scottish Government Justice Directorate, EU and International Law Branch, St Andrew's House, Regent Road, Edinburgh EH1 3DG. Contacts: Alan Finlayson, Tel: 0131 244 2417, Email: alan.finlayson@scotland.gsi.gov.uk; Martin McPheely, Tel: 0131 244 4827, Email: martin.mcpheely@scotland.gsi.gov.uk; Elizabeth Mathison, Tel: 0131 244 4825, Email: elizabeth.mathison@scotland.gsi.gov.uk. Fax: 0131 244 4848. Web: *www.scotland.gov.uk/Topics/Justice/law/17867/fm-children-root/18533/13589*.

NI Central Authority—NI Courts and Tribunals Service, Civil Policy and Tribunal Reform Division, 3rd Floor Laganside House, 23–27 Oxford Street, Belfast BT1 3LA. Tel: 02890 328 594; Fax: 02890 728 944; Web: *www.northernireland.gov.uk* or *www.courtsni.gov.uk/en-GB/Services/ChildAbduction/* (cf the appropriate Central Authority under the 1996 Convention in Part VI and the Parental Responsibility and Measures for the Protection of Children (International Obligations) (England and Wales and Northern Ireland) Regulations 2010 in Part IV).

"functions ... of a Central Authority"—These are specified by Arts 7–11, 15, 21, 26–28 of the Convention.

4 Judicial authorities

The courts having jurisdiction to entertain applications under this Convention shall be –

   (a)   in England and Wales or in Northern Ireland the High Court; and

   (b)   in Scotland the Court of Session.

Defined terms—"the Convention": s 1(1); "courts": FPR 2010, rr 12.45 and 12.54(4).

"applications under this Convention"—For procedure, see FPR 2010, r 12.43. On receiving the application, the ICACU may apply on behalf of the applicant to the Central Authority in the Contracting State. Where a child has been brought to England and Wales, the Central Authority in the Contracting State which is the country of the child's habitual residence should apply to the ICACU for assistance in securing the return of the child. The ICACU may then apply to the High Court as the judicial and administrative authority for the purposes of the Convention for assistance in ascertaining the whereabouts of the child and securing its return. It is also open to the applicant to apply directly to the High Court under Art 29. For contact details, see under s 3. In an emergency, including out of normal working hours, contact the RCJ on 020 7947 6000/6260. See further FPR PD12F.

5 Interim powers

Where an application has been made to a court in the United Kingdom under the Convention, the court may, at any time before the application is determined, give such interim directions as it thinks fit for the purpose of securing the welfare of the child concerned or of preventing changes in the circumstances relevant to the determination of the application.

Defined terms—"the Convention": s 1(1).

Application for interim directions—See FPR 2010, r 12.47.

Extent of court's power on interim direction—The court has very wide powers under this section to deal with all interlocutory matters, including taking all appropriate steps to ascertain the whereabouts of the child, to safeguard his interests, to order disclosure of information under s 24A and to ensure his return (Sch 1, Arts 7 and 10; FPR 2010, r 12.47). The court can exercise jurisdiction even before a child's arrival within England and Wales (*A v A (Abduction: Jurisdiction)* [1995] 1 FLR 341). It may make a collection and location order and passport order (FPR 2010 r 12.47; for the prescribed forms see *Emergency Remedies in the Family Courts* (Jordan Publishing Ltd)). A solicitor representing the abductor may be ordered to disclose the whereabouts of the abductor and all documents in his possession relating to the abductor's whereabouts until the order is served or comes to the knowledge of the abductor; but thereafter it would be inappropriate to adopt such a course as it is unlikely to assist in the recovery of the child (*Re H (Abduction: Whereabouts Order to Solicitors)* [2000] 1 FLR 766). The court also has powers to grant injunctions, to order a Cafcass reporter to prepare a report (s 9), to give specific directions for trial (see FPR PD12F) and to order publicity (FPR PD12F, para 4.15; *Re D (A Minor) (Child Abduction)* [1989] 1 FLR 97). The court may dispense with service (FPR 2010, r 12.48), adjourn the hearing for up to 21 days (FPR 2010, r 12.51) and stay the proceedings (FPR 2010, r 12.52). The court has power to give directions concerning the manner in which a child's welfare and whereabouts are to be managed, if removal from an abducting parent to temporary placement is necessary. In exceptional circumstances, to protect and safeguard the child's welfare, particularly if the child has special needs, or to prevent further harm to the child or prejudice to an interested party (Art 7(b)), the court may direct a local authority to accommodate the child and the abducting parent. If such an order is contemplated, the appropriate authority should be given notice, supported by evidence. In the event that it is not clear which local authority should bear the burden of accommodation, the court has a discretion to identify the local authority having regard to the welfare of the child. "Domestic statutory provisions designed to deal with transition from one local authority to another are not engaged" (*Re A (Abduction: Interim Directions: Accommodation by Local Authority)* [2011] 1 FLR 1). A direction may also be made for the abducting parent to undergo electronic tagging as part of the package of protective measures to secure the welfare of the child and/or to prevent changes in the circumstances. Where tagging is under consideration, the representatives of the parties should contact the Office of the President to assist in making inquiries and arrangements (*Re C (Abduction: Interim Directions: Accommodation by Local Authority)* [2004] 1 FLR 653). Additionally, in cases where Brussels IIA applies, Art 20 enables courts of Member States in urgent cases to take "such provisional, including protective, measures in respect of persons or assets in that State as may be available under the law of that Member State, even if, under this Regulation, the court of another Member State has jurisdiction" (see further Council Regulation (EC) No 2201/2003) in Part VI).

Art 11 of the 1996 Convention also authorises the authorities of any Contracting State in whose territory the child or property belonging to the child is present to take any necessary measures of protection in cases of urgency. Although the Article does not define "urgency", it is envisaged that it includes a situation where irreparable harm might be caused to the child, or the protection of the child or interests of the child might be compromised if protective measures are not taken to protect the child until the authorities with general jurisdiction can take the necessary protective steps (see the *Handbook* on the operation of the 1996 Convention, where examples are given of what constitutes a situation of urgency). Although the 1996 Convention also empowers the authorities of a Contracting State to take provisional (non-urgent) measures for the protection of the person and property of a child, provided such measures are not incompatible with those taken by authorities within the jurisdiction of the child's habitual residence, Art 7(3) excludes the exercise of such powers in cases where the child has been wrongfully removed or retained. In *Re Y (A Child)* [2013] All ER (D) 133 (Jan), the Court of Appeal ruled that pursuant to art 23 of the 1996 Convention undertakings given by a parent to facilitate the return of an abducted child, where a defence under Art 13(b) of the Hague Convention 1980 is raised amounts to "protective measures" within Art 11(4) of BIIR as they were capable of recognition and enforcement by other Contracting States under the 1996 Convention. It was not necessary for the protective measures to be in the form of a court order.

The court also has powers to adjourn the application to enable the parties to be involved in a mediation process where appropriate. Where there are very exceptional circumstances, the court may endorse the parties' agreement to a non-binding arbitration process to resolve all their matrimonial disputes but if it includes decisions relating to a child, this will be only be approved if it is in line with English legal principles and the welfare of the child (ie the paramountcy principle: *AI v MT* [2013] EWHC 100 (Fam)).

6 Reports

Where the Lord Chancellor, the Department of Justice in Northern Ireland or the Secretary of State is requested to provide information relating to a child under Article 7(d) of the Convention he may –

(a) request a local authority or an officer of the Service or a Welsh family proceedings officer to make a report to him in writing with respect to any matter which appears to him to be relevant;

(b) request the Department of Health and Social Services for Northern Ireland to arrange for a suitably qualified person to make such a report to him;

(c) request any court to which a written report relating to the child has been made to send him a copy of the report;

and such a request shall be duly complied with.

Amendments—CJCSA 2000 s 74, Sch 7, para 80; CA 2004, Sch 3, para 3; SI 2010/976.

Defined terms—"the Convention": s 1(1); "local authority": s 27(3).

7 Proof of documents and evidence

(1) For the purposes of Article 14 of the Convention a decision or determination of a judicial or administrative authority outside the United Kingdom may be proved by a duly authenticated copy of the decision or determination; and any document purporting to be such a copy shall be deemed to be a true copy unless the contrary is shown.

(2) For the purposes of subsection (1) above a copy is duly authenticated if it bears the seal, or is signed by a judge or officer, of the authority in question.

(3) For the purposes of Articles 14 and 30 of the Convention any such document as is mentioned in Article 8 of the Convention, or a certified copy of any such document, shall be sufficient evidence of anything stated in it.

Defined terms—"the Convention": s 1(1).

8 Declarations by United Kingdom courts

The High Court or Court of Session may, on an application made for the purposes of Article 15 of the Convention by any person appearing to the court to have an interest in the matter, make a declaration or declarator that the removal of any child from, or his retention outside, the United Kingdom was wrongful within the meaning of Article 3 of the Convention.

Defined terms—"the Convention": s 1(1).

Scope—The declaration is often necessary to enable the applicant in proceedings outside the UK to obtain an order for the return of a child who has been wrongly removed or retained. Applications for such a declaration should be made to the High Court (FPR PD12F, para 2.15). This section contemplates applications being made for the purposes of Art 15 by *any person* appearing to the court to have an interest in the matter and is not limited to the applicant or to the circumstances within the narrow definition of Art 15. See *Re G (Abduction: Rights of Custody)* [2002] 2 FLR 703, where an unmarried father and his mother were regarded as having an interest in the child within the terms of Art 8. When determining whether to grant the declaration, the court will consider, inter alia, whether the applicant parent had rights of custody according to English law at the time of removal and possible issues of habitual residence and any breach (*A v B (Abduction: Declaration)* [2009] 1 FLR 1253).

"wrongful"—See **Wrongful removal or retention** under Sch 1, Art 3.

9 Suspension of court's powers in cases of wrongful removal

The reference in Article 16 of the Convention to deciding on the merits of rights of custody shall be construed as a reference to –

(a) making, varying or revoking a custody order, or a supervision order under section 31 of the Children Act 1989 or Article 50 of the Children (Northern Ireland) Order 1995;

(aa) enforcing under section 29 of the Family Law Act 1986 a custody order within the meaning of Chapter V of Part I of that Act;

(b) registering or enforcing a decision under Part II of this Act;

(ba) registering or enforcing a decision under the Convention on Jurisdiction, Applicable Law, Recognition, Enforcement and Co-Operation in respect of Parental Responsibility and Measures for the Protection of Children that was signed at The Hague on 19 October 1996 ("the 1996 Convention"), except where provisions of the 1996 Convention are invoked in accordance with Article 50 of the 1996 Convention;

(c)–(e) ...

Amendments—FLA 1986, s 68(1), Sch 1, para 28; CA 1989, s 108(5), Sch 13, para 57(1), Sch 15; Children (Scotland) Act 1995, s 105(4), Sch 4, para 37; SI 1995/756; SI 2010/1898.

Defined terms—"the Convention": s 1(1); "custody order": s 27(1), Sch 3; "rights of custody": Sch 1, Art 5.

Scope—This section supports Art 16 of the Hague Convention (see Sch 1, Art 16) which prevents the court from deciding on the merits of rights of custody until it has determined that a child is not to be returned or unless an application under the Convention is not lodged within a reasonable time after notice of wrongful removal or retention of the child. FPR 2010, rr 12.52 and 12.53 provide a procedure that inter alia guards against any court proceeding to determine rights of custody in ignorance of an application under the Convention and to stay all proceedings before it until the proceedings under the 1980 Hague Convention have been disposed of.

10 Rules of court

(1) An authority having power to make rules of court may make such provision for giving effect to this Part of this Act as appears to that authority to be necessary or expedient.

(2) Without prejudice to the generality of subsection (1) above, rules of court may make provision –

(a) with respect to the procedure on applications for the return of a child and with respect to the documents and information to be furnished and the notices to be given in connection with any such application;

(b) for the transfer of any such application between the appropriate courts in the different parts of the United Kingdom;

(c) for the giving of notices by or to a court for the purposes of the provisions of Article 16 of the Convention and section 9 above and generally as respects proceedings to which those provisions apply;

(d) for enabling a person who wishes to make an application under the Convention in a Contracting State other than the United Kingdom to obtain from any court in the United Kingdom an authenticated copy of any decision of that court relating to the child to whom the application is to relate.

Defined terms—"appropriate court": s 27(2); "the Convention": s 1(1); "part of the United Kingdom": s 27(2).

Rules of court—FPR 2010, Pt 12 (in particular Ch 6, rr 12.51–12.57 and PDs 12D, 12E and 12F) applies to this Part.

11 Cost of applications

The United Kingdom having made such a reservation as is mentioned in the third paragraph of Article 26 of the Convention, the costs mentioned in that paragraph shall not be borne by any Minister or other authority in the United Kingdom except so far as they fall to be so borne by virtue of –

(a) the provision of any civil legal services (within the meaning of Part 1 of the Legal Aid, Sentencing and Punishment of Offenders Act 2012) under arrangements made for the purposes of that Part of that Act, or

(b) the grant of legal aid or legal advice and assistance under the Legal Aid (Scotland) Act 1967, Part I of the Legal Advice and Assistance Act 1972 or the Legal Aid Advice and Assistance (Northern Ireland) Order 1981.

Amendments—Legal Aid Act 1988, s 45(1),(3), Sch 5, para 16; AJA 1999, s 24, Sch 4, para 31; LASPOA 2012, s 39, Sch 5, para 26.

Defined terms—"the Convention": s 1(1).

Reservation on costs—The UK is not bound to meet any costs other than those that may be covered by the Legal Aid Agency (which replaced the Legal Services Commission on 1 April 2013). Article 26 (see Sch 1, Art 26) permits a Contracting State to require the payment of expenses incurred in the return of the child (eg air fare).

Power to order payment of costs and expenses—The court's powers include the payment of travel expenses, any costs incurred or payment made for locating the child, the costs of legal representation of the applicant and those of returning the child.

PART II
RECOGNITION AND ENFORCEMENT OF CUSTODY DECISIONS

12 The European Convention

(1) In this Part of this Act "the Convention" means the European Convention on Recognition and Enforcement of Decisions concerning Custody of Children and on the Restoration of Custody of Children which was signed in Luxembourg on 20 May 1980.

(2) Subject to the provisions of this Part of this Act, the provisions of that Convention set out in Schedule 2 to this Act (which include Articles 9 and 10 as they have effect in consequence of a reservation made by the United Kingdom under Article 17) shall have the force of law in the United Kingdom.

(3) But –

  (a) those provisions of the Convention,
  (b) this Part of this Act, and
  (c) rules of court under section 24 of this Act,

are subject to Article 60 of the Council Regulation (by virtue of which the Regulation takes precedence over the European Convention, in so far as it concerns matters governed by the Regulation).

(4) "The Council Regulation" means Council Regulation (EC) No 2201/2003 of 27 November 2003 concerning jurisdiction and the recognition and enforcement of judgments in matrimonial matters and matters of parental responsibility.

Amendments—SI 2001/310; SI 2005/265.

Object of the Convention—The European Convention provides for the registration, recognition and enforcement of decisions relating to custody where there has been an improper removal of a child in breach of such a decision. Note, however, that where Brussels IIA applies, its provisions take precedence over both the Hague Convention 1980 and the European Convention 1980 (see Procedural Guide C3(14) and FPR 2010, Pt 31 for procedure for registration etc where Brussels IIA and the 1996 Convention apply). Where the matter is not governed by Brussels IIA, the Convention will continue to apply in relations between States (*Purrucker v Vallés Pérez (No 1)* Case C-256/09 [2012] 1 FLR 903).

13 Contracting States

(1) For the purposes of the Convention as it has effect under this Part of this Act the Contracting States other than the United Kingdom shall be those for the time being specified by an Order in Council under this section.

(2) An Order in Council under this section shall specify the date of the coming into force of the Convention as between the United Kingdom and any State specified in the Order.

(3) Where the Convention applies, or applies only, to a particular territory or particular territories specified by a Contracting State under Article 24 or 25 of the Convention references to that State in subsections (1) and (2) above shall be construed as references to that territory or those territories.

Amendments—SI 2010/976.

Defined terms—"the Convention": s 12(1).

"specified by an Order in Council under this section"—See the Child Abduction and Custody (Parties to Conventions) Order 1986, which specifies the Contracting States for this purpose.

14 Central Authorities

(1) Subject to subsection (2) below, the functions under the Convention of a Central Authority shall be discharged –

  (a) in England and Wales by the Lord Chancellor; and
  (b) in Scotland by the Secretary of State; and
  (c) in Northern Ireland by the Department of Justice in Northern Ireland.

(2) Any application made under the Convention by or on behalf of a person outside the United Kingdom may be addressed to the Lord Chancellor as the Central Authority in the United Kingdom.

(3) Where any such application relates to a function to be discharged under subsection (1) above by an authority ("the responsible authority") other than the authority to which the application is addressed, the authority to which the application is addressed shall transmit it to the responsible authority.

Amendments—SI 2010/976.

Defined terms—"the Convention": s 12(1).

"functions of a Central Authority"—These are specified in Arts 7–11, 15, 21, 26–28 of the Convention.

15 Recognition of decisions

(1) Articles 7 and 12 of the Convention shall have effect in accordance with this section.

(2) A decision to which either of those Articles applies which was made in a Contracting State other than the United Kingdom shall be recognised in each part of the United Kingdom as if made by a court having jurisdiction to make it in that part but –

    (a) the appropriate court in any part of the United Kingdom may, on the application of any person appearing to it to have an interest in the matter, declare on any of the grounds specified in Article 9 or 10 of the Convention that the decision is not to be recognised in any part of the United Kingdom; and

    (b) the decision shall be enforceable in any part of the United Kingdom unless registered in the appropriate court under section 16 below.

(3) The references in Article 9(1)(c) of the Convention to the removal of the child are to his improper removal within the meaning of the Convention.

Defined terms—"appropriate court": s 27(2); "child": Sch 2, Art 1(a); "the Convention": s 12(1); "improper removal": Sch 2, Art 1(d); "part of the United Kingdom": s 27(2).

16 Registration of decisions

(1) A person on whom any rights are conferred by a decision relating to custody made by an authority in a Contracting State other than the United Kingdom may make an application for the registration of the decision in an appropriate court in the United Kingdom.

(2) The Central Authority in the United Kingdom shall assist a person in making such an application if a request for such assistance is made by him or on his behalf by the Central Authority of the Contracting State in question.

(3) An application under subsection (1) above or a request under subsection (2) above shall be treated as a request for enforcement for the purposes of Articles 10 and 13 of the Convention.

(4) The High Court or Court of Session shall refuse to register a decision if –

    (a) the court is of the opinion that on any of the grounds specified in Article 9 or 10 of the Convention the decision should not be recognised in any part of the United Kingdom;

    (b) the court is of the opinion that the decision is not enforceable in the Contracting State where it was made and is not a decision to which Article 12 of the Convention applies;

    (c) an application in respect of the child under Part I of this Act is pending.

(5) Where an authority mentioned in subsection (1) of section 14 above is requested to assist in making an application under this section to the appropriate court in a part of the United Kingdom ("the relevant part of the United Kingdom") other than the part in

relation to which the authority has functions under that subsection, the authority shall transmit the request to the authority which has functions under that subsection in relation to the relevant part of the United Kingdom.

(6) In this section "decision relating to custody" has the same meaning as in the Convention.

Amendments—SI 2010/976.

Defined terms—"appropriate court": s 27(2); "authority": Sch 2, Art 1(b); "Central Authority in the United Kingdom": s 14; "child": Sch 2, Art 1(a); "the Convention": s 12(1); "Contracting State": s 13(1); "decision relating to custody": Sch 2, Art 1(c).

Procedure on application—The procedure on application is set out in Sch 2, Arts 4 and 13 and FPR 2010, Pt 12, Ch 6 and PD12F. In the majority of cases the matters are dealt with under the provisions of Brussels IIA (see Part VI), under which there has been a proliferation of case-law on practice and decisions of the ECtHR (FPR PD12F, paras 2.20, 5.1–5.6). See also the commentary under FPR 2010, rr 12.58–12.71.

Shall refuse to register—Although the language of s 16(4) is mandatory, see Art 10 of the European Convention (Sch 2) which is permissive and thus gives the court a discretion.

17 Variation and revocation of registered decisions

(1) Where a decision which has been registered under section 16 above is varied or revoked by an authority in the Contracting State in which it was made, the person on whose behalf the application for registration of the decision was made shall notify the court in which the decision is registered of the variation or revocation.

(2) Where a court is notified under subsection (1) above of the revocation of a decision, it shall –

(a)   cancel the registration, and
(b)   notify such persons as may be prescribed by rules of court of the cancellation.

(3) Where a court is notified under subsection (1) above of the variation of a decision, it shall –

(a)   notify such persons as may be prescribed by rules of court of the variation; and
(b)   subject to any conditions which may be so prescribed, vary the registration.

(4) The court in which a decision is registered under section 16 above may also, on the application of any person appearing to the court to have an interest in the matter, cancel or vary the registration if it is satisfied that the decision has been revoked or, as the case may be, varied by an authority in the Contracting State in which it was made.

Defined terms—"authority": Sch 2, Art 1(b); "Contracting State": s 13(1).

Procedure—See under FPR 2010, r 12.55.

18 Enforcement of decisions

Where a decision relating to custody has been registered under section 16 above, the court in which it is registered shall have the same powers for the purpose of enforcing the decision as if it had been made by that court; and proceedings for or with respect to enforcement may be taken accordingly.

19 Interim powers

Where an application has been made to a court for the registration of a decision under section 16 above or for the enforcement of such a decision, the court may, at any time before the application is determined, give such interim directions as it thinks fit for the purpose of securing the welfare of the child concerned or of preventing changes in the circumstances relevant to the determination of the application or, in the case of an application for registration, to the determination of any subsequent application for the enforcement of the decision.

Defined terms—"child": Sch 2, Art 1(a).

Application for interim directions—For procedure see FPR 2010, r 12.47.

Extent of court's power on interim directions—The court has broadly similar powers to those described under s 5. See also *T v R* [2002] 2 FLR 544.

20 Suspension of court's powers

(1) Where it appears to any court in which such proceedings as are mentioned in subsection (2) below are pending in respect of a child that –

   (a)   an application has been made for the registration of a decision in respect of the child under section 16 above (other than a decision mentioned in subsection (3) below) or that such a decision is registered; and

   (b)   the decision was made in proceedings commenced before the proceedings which are pending,

the powers of the court with respect to the child in those proceedings shall be restricted as mentioned in subsection (2) below unless, in the case of an application for registration, the application is refused.

(2) Where subsection (1) above applies the court shall not –

   (a)   in the case of custody proceedings, make, vary or revoke any custody order, or a supervision order under section 31 of the Children Act 1989 or Article 50 of the Children (Northern Ireland) Order 1995;

   (aa) in the case of proceedings under section 29 of the Family Law Act 1986 for the enforcement of a custody order within the meaning of Chapter V or Part I of that Act, enforce that order; or

   (b)–(e)   ...

(2A) Where it appears to the Secretary of State –

   (a)   that an application has been made for the registration of a decision in respect of a child under section 16 above (other than a decision mentioned in subsection (3) below); or

   (b)   that such a decision is registered;

the Secretary of State shall not make, vary or revoke any custody order in respect of the child unless, in the case of an application for registration, the application is refused.

(3) The decision referred to in subsection (1) or (2A) above is a decision which is only a decision relating to custody within the meaning of section 16 of this Act by virtue of being a decision relating to rights of access.

(4) Paragraph (b) of Article 10(2) of the Convention shall be construed as referring to custody proceedings within the meaning of this Act.

(5) This section shall apply to a children's hearing (as defined in section 93(1) of the Children (Scotland) Act 1995) as it does to a court.

Amendments—FLA 1986, ss 67(2),(3), 68(1), Sch 1, para 29; CA 1989, s 108(5), Sch 13, para 57(1), Sch 15; Children (Scotland) Act 1995, s 105(4), Sch 4, para 37; SI 1995/756.

Defined terms—"child": Sch 2, Art 1(a); "the Convention": s 12(1); "custody order", "custody proceedings": s 27(1), Sch 3.

Scope—See annotation under s 9.

21 Reports

Where the Lord Chancellor, the Department of Justice in Northern Ireland or the Secretary of State is requested to make enquiries about a child under Article 15(1)(b) of the Convention he may –

(a) request a local authority or an officer of the Service to make a report to him in writing with respect to any matter relating to the child concerned which appears to him to be relevant;

(b) request the Department of Health and Social Services for Northern Ireland to arrange for a suitably qualified person to make such a report to him;

(c) request any court to which a written report relating to the child has been made to send him a copy of the report;

and any such request shall be duly complied with.

Amendments—CJCSA 2000 s 74, Sch 7, para 80; SI 2010/976.

Defined terms—"child": Sch 2, Art 1(a); "the Convention": s 12(1); "local authority": s 27(3).

22 Proof of documents and evidence

(1) In any proceedings under this Part of this Act a decision of an authority outside the United Kingdom may be proved by a duly authenticated copy of the decision; and any document purporting to be such a copy shall be deemed to be a true copy unless the contrary is shown.

(2) For the purpose of subsection (1) above a copy is duly authenticated if it bears the seal, or is signed by a judge or officer, of the authority in question.

(3) In any proceedings under this Part of this Act any such document as is mentioned in Article 13 of the Convention, or a certified copy of any such document, shall be sufficient evidence of anything stated in it.

Defined terms—"authority": Sch 2, Art 1(b); "the Convention": s 12(1).

23 Decisions of United Kingdom courts

(1) Where a person on whom any rights are conferred by a decision relating to custody made by a court in the United Kingdom makes an application to the Lord Chancellor, the Department of Justice in Northern Ireland or the Secretary of State under Article 4 of the Convention with a view to securing its recognition or enforcement in another Contracting State, the Lord Chancellor, the Department of Justice in Northern Ireland or the Secretary of State may require the court which made the decision to furnish him with all or any of the documents referred to in Article 13(1)(b), (c) and (d) of the Convention.

(2) Where in any custody proceedings a court in the United Kingdom makes a decision relating to a child who has been removed from the United Kingdom, the court may also, on an application made by any person for the purposes of Article 12 of the Convention, declare the removal to have been unlawful if it is satisfied that the applicant has an interest in the matter and that the child has been taken from or sent or kept out of the United Kingdom without the consent of the person (or, if more than one, all the persons) having the right to determine the child's place of residence under the law of the part of the United Kingdom in which the child was habitually resident.

(3) In this section "decision relating to custody" has the same meaning as in the Convention.

Amendments—SI 2010/976.

Defined terms—"child": Sch 2, Art 1(a); "Contracting State": s 13(1); "the Convention": s 12(1); "decision relating to custody": Sch 2, Art 1(c); "part of the United Kingdom": s 27(2).

Decision of UK court relating to custody—Where a court makes a without notice order in proceedings under CA 1989, s 8 of which the abducting parent has notice, the order is both recognised and enforceable for the purposes of Art 9, and the court has jurisdiction to declare the removal unlawful even though the applicant did not possess the appropriate "rights" when the child was removed (*Re S (Abduction: Hague and European Convention)* [1996] 1 FLR 660).

"Article 12 of the Convention"—In cases where the provisions of both Conventions may apply, if a custody order existed, for example to a mother whose child has been abducted to France, it would be advisable to obtain a declaration under s 23(2) so that both Conventions may be relied on.

"unlawful"—Where a removal is declared unlawful then the removal is an improper removal (Sch 2, Art 1(d)).

24 Rules of court

(1) An authority having power to make rules of court may make such provision for giving effect to this Part of this Act as appears to that authority to be necessary or expedient.

(2) Without prejudice to the generality of subsection (1) above, rules of court may make provision –

   (a) with respect to the procedure on application to a court under any provision of this Part of this Act and with respect to the documents and information to be furnished and the notices to be given in connection with any such application;
   (b) for the transfer of any such application between the appropriate courts in the different parts of the United Kingdom;
   (c) for the giving of directions requiring the disclosure of information about any child who is the subject of proceedings under this Part of this Act and for safeguarding its welfare.

Defined terms—"appropriate court": s 27(2); "authority": Sch 2, Art 1(b); "child": Sch 2, Art 1(a); "part of the United Kingdom": s 27(2).

Rules of court—FPR 2010, rr 12.44–12.57 apply to this Part, along with PD12F.

PART III
SUPPLEMENTARY

24A Power to order disclosure of child's whereabouts

(1) Where –

   (a) in proceedings for the return of a child under Part I of this Act; or
   (b) on an application for the recognition, registration or enforcement of a decision in respect of a child under Part II of this Act,

there is not available to the court adequate information as to where the child is, the court may order any person who it has reason to believe may have relevant information to disclose it to the court.

(2) A person shall not be excused from complying with an order under subsection (1) above by reason that to do so may incriminate him or his spouse or civil partner of an offence; but a statement or admission made in compliance with such an order shall not be admissible in evidence against either of them in proceedings for any offence other than perjury.

Amendments—Inserted by FLA 1986, s 67(4); amended by CPA 2004, s 261(1), Sch 27, para 110.

Defined terms—"child": Sch 2, Art 1(a).

Scope—This section supplements the court's wide powers under its inherent jurisdiction (see *Re D (A Minor) (Child Abduction)* [1989] 1 FLR 97).

Self-incrimination—See under CA 1989, s 98.

Rules—FPR 2010, r 12.57 makes further provision as to orders for disclosure of information on applications under the European Convention.

25 Termination of existing custody orders etc

(1) Where –

    (a) an order is made for the return of a child under Part I of this Act; or

    (b) a decision with respect to a child (other than a decision mentioned in subsection (2) below) is registered under section 16 of this Act,

any custody order relating to him shall cease to have effect.

(2) The decision referred to in subsection (1)(b) above is a decision which is only a decision relating to custody within the meaning of section 16 of this Act by virtue of being a decision relating to rights of access.

(3)–(7) (*repealed*)

Amendments—CA 1989, s 108(7), Sch 15; Children (Scotland) Act 1995, s 105(4), Sch 4, para 37(1),(4); SI 1995/756.

Defined terms—"child": Sch 2, Art 1(a).

26 Expenses

There shall be paid out of money provided by Parliament –

    (a) any expenses incurred by the Lord Chancellor or the Secretary of State by virtue of this Act; and

    (b) any increase attributable to this Act in the sums so payable under any other Act.

27 Interpretation

(1) In this Act "custody order" means (unless contrary intention appears) any such order as is mentioned in Schedule 3 to this Act and "custody proceedings" means proceedings in which an order within paragraphs 1, 2, 5, 6, 8 or 9 of that Schedule may be made, varied or revoked.

(2) For the purposes of this Act "part of the United Kingdom" means England and Wales, Scotland or Northern Ireland and "the appropriate court", in relation to England and Wales or Northern Ireland means the High Court and, in relation to Scotland, the Court of Session.

(3) In this Act "local authority" means –

    (a) in relation to England and Wales, the council of a non-metropolitan county, a metropolitan district, a London borough or the Common Council of the City of London; and

    (b) in relation to Scotland, a council constituted under section 2 of the Local Government etc (Scotland) Act 1994.

(4) In this Act a decision relating to rights of access in England and Wales or Scotland or Northern Ireland means a decision as to the contact which a child may, or may not, have with any person.

(5) In this Act "officer of the Service" has the same meaning as in the Criminal Justice and Court Services Act 2000.

(5A) In this Act "Welsh family proceedings officer" has the meaning given by section 35 of the Children Act 2004.

Amendments—FLA 1986, ss 67(5), 68(1), Sch 1, para 30; CA 1989, s 108(5), Sch 13, para 57(2); Local Government etc (Scotland) Act 1994, s 180(1), Sch 13, para 139; Children (Scotland) Act 1995, s 105(4), Sch 4, para 37(5); SI 1995/756; CJCSA 2000 s 74, Sch 7, para 81; CA 2004, Sch 3, para 4.

28 Application as respects British Islands and colonies

(1) Her Majesty may by Order in Council direct that any of the provisions of this Act specified in the Order shall extend, subject to such modifications as may be specified in the Order, to –

    (a) the Isle of Man,
    (b) any of the Channel Islands, and
    (c) any colony.

(2) Her Majesty may by Order in Council direct that this Act shall have effect in the United Kingdom as if any reference in this Act, or in any amendment made by this Act, to any order which may be made, or any proceedings which may be brought or any other thing which may be done in, or in any part of, the United Kingdom included a reference to any corresponding order which may be made or, as the case may be, proceedings which may be brought or other thing which may be done in any of the territories mentioned in subsection (1) above.

(3) An Order in Council under this section may make such consequential, incidental and supplementary provision as Her Majesty considers appropriate.

(4) An Order in Council under this section shall be subject to annulment in pursuance of a resolution of either House of Parliament.

Orders under this section—With effect from 6 December 1994, the Child Abduction and Custody Act 1985 (Isle of Man) Order 1994 extends the provisions of this Act to the Isle of Man.

With effect from 2 December 1997, the Child Abduction and Custody (Cayman Islands) Order 1997 extends ss 1–24A, 25(1),(2), 27 and Schs 1–3 of this Act (as modified in the Schedule thereto) to the Cayman Islands.

29 Short title, commencement and extent

(1) This Act may be cited as the Child Abduction and Custody Act 1985.

(2) This Act shall come into force on such day as may be appointed by an order made by statutory instrument by the Lord Chancellor and the Lord Advocate; and different days may be so appointed for different provisions.

(3) This Act extends to Northern Ireland.

SCHEDULE 1
CONVENTION ON THE CIVIL ASPECTS OF INTERNATIONAL CHILD ABDUCTION

Liaison judge—Thorpe LJ is the Liaison Judge for England and Wales. His role is to communicate and liaise with the appropriate judge in the Requested State. See further February [2008] Fam Law at p 105. (See also Brussels IIA, Art 8 in Part VI.)

The preferred route for contact is via Edward Bennett, lawyer to Thorpe LJ, International Family Justice Office. His office is in room C101 at the Royal Courts of Justice; tel: 0207 947 7906; email: edward.bennett@judiciary.gsi.gov.uk. He is supported by Karen Wheller.

Article 3

The removal or the retention of a child is to be considered wrongful where –

    (a) it is in breach of rights of custody attributed to a person, an institution or any

other body, either jointly or alone, under the law of the State in which the child was habitually resident immediately before the removal or retention; and
(b)   at the time of removal or retention those rights were actually exercised, either jointly or alone, or would have been so exercised but for the removal or retention.

The rights of custody mentioned in sub-paragraph (a) above, may arise in particular by operation of law or by reason of a judicial or administrative decision, or by reason of an agreement having legal effect under the law of that State.

Defined terms—"rights of custody": Art 5; see also FPR PD12F, paras 2.16–2.19. Similar definitions are given under Brussels IIA, Art 2(9) and the 1996 Convention, Art 3(b) (see Part VI).

Custody rights—Where the applicant's rights of custody are in issue, the question should not be determined by the English court unless it is unavoidable (see *A v B (Abduction: Declaration)* [2009] 1 FLR 1253, where a declaration was granted to correct an inaccurate and incomplete opinion of English law on which the French court had made its decision). It should be adjudicated upon by the foreign court at the highest level, but in order to avoid delay, a balance should be struck if the matter can be dealt with more speedily by a court at a lower level (*Re T (Abduction: Rights of Custody)* [2008] 2 FLR 1794; *Re D (Abduction: Rights of Custody)* [2007] 1 FLR 961, HL). Reliance on experts rather than the decision of the foreign court (*Re JB (Child Abduction) (Rights of Custody: Spain)* [2004] 1 FLR 796) was criticised by the House of Lords in *Re D*, but in *Re F (Abduction: Rights of Custody)* [2008] 2 FLR 1239, despite the lack of evidence on Polish law, with the consent of the parties and the particular facts of the case, the court considered that a decision as to rights of custody could be reached with reasonable confidence. With the 1996 Convention in force as of 1 November 2012, the provisions set out in Art 1(2) and Ch III of that Convention relating to parental responsibility will be relevant when determining whether the applicant has "custody rights" (see further the narrative in Part VI).
A person with whom a child is placed on a long-term placement with the authority to make decisions may acquire "custody rights", as will an unmarried father with no parental responsibility if he lives in the same household and exercises parental rights for a period of time (*Re G (Abduction: Rights of Custody)* [2002] 2 FLR 703), or where his rights have been confirmed (*Re E (Abduction: Rights of Custody)* [2005] 2 FLR 759) (see ACA 2002, s 111). Where a mother has custody rights and then agrees that the child should reside with the father, the agreement is simply a continuing exercise of the mother's custody rights; the agreement does not revoke her rights nor does it enable the father to acquire custody rights (*Re W (Abduction: Procedure)* [1995] 1 FLR 878; *Re J (Abduction: Acquiring Custody Rights by Caring For Child)* [2005] 2 FLR 791)
The issue of whether the removal of a child was in contravention of custody rights should be resolved by reference to the Convention law as applied by the English courts, so that where the father had been awarded the right to "decide vital problems" with the mother (*Re F (Abduction: Rights of Custody)* [2008] 2 FLR 1239) and where a father had enjoyed equal and separate rights the removal of the child by the mother was found to be in breach of those rights (*Re F (Child Abduction: Risk if Returned)* [1995] 2 FLR 31, applied in *S v H (Abduction: Access Rights)* [1997] 1 FLR 971 and see *Re P (Abduction: Declaration)* [1995] 1 FLR 831). See also **"rights of custody"** under Art 5 and *Practice Note of 14 October 1997* (see *The Family Court Practice 2011*).

Wrongful removal or retention—Removal is usually wrongful when it is in breach of someone else's rights (*C v S (A Minor) (Abduction)* [1990] 2 FLR 442, HL). Removal can be wrongful where it is in breach of the defendant's own rights of custody (*Re H (A Minor) (Abduction)* [1990] 2 FLR 439) or where it is in breach of an express court order (*Re E (Abduction: Rights of Custody)* [2005] 2 FLR 759). Removal is also wrongful within the terms of the Convention where it is in breach of an implied prohibition established on case-law, but not by reason of a court order (*C v C (Minors) (Child Abduction)* [1992] 1 FLR 163). See also *Re H (Minors) (Abduction: Custody Rights), Re S (Minors) (Abduction: Custody Rights)* [1991] 2 FLR 262 and **Scope** under Art 8. See the identical definition in Art 7(2) of the 1996 Convention and also the wider definition set out in Brussels IIA, Art 2(11) (see Part VI).

"Retention" for the purposes of the Convention is "an event which occurs on a specific occasion rather than enjoying its usual and wider connotation of a continuous state of affairs. It occurs when a child who has previously been for a limited period of time outside the state of habitual residence is not returned to that state on the expiry of that period" but see *De L v H* [2010] 1 FLR 1229, where although the initial non-return was held not to be wrongful the father's later conduct was found to constitute retention. Removal and retention has to be mutually exclusive (*Re H (Abduction: Custody Rights)* [1991] 2 FLR 262) but see *RS v KS (Abduction: Wrongful Retention)* [2009] EWHC 1494 (Fam), [2009] 2 FLR 1231, where on the facts the court departed from the decision in *Re H* and, in holding that wrongful retention could subsume a wrongful removal, preferred Lord Slynn's view in *Re S (A Minor) (Custody: Habitual*

Residence) [1998] 1 FLR 122 that although the two are mutually exclusive both can occur on the facts in relation to the same child at different times. A lawful removal can become a wrongful retention if a return order is made by the court of the child (*Mercredi v Chaffe* [2011] 1 FLR 1293).Where the evidence is confused or uncertain as to the agreement between the parties the court will determine the date of retention after a proper analysis of the evidence (*Re G (Abduction: Withdrawal of Proceedings)* [2008] 2 FLR 351). "Retention" includes not only acts of physical restraint but also court orders obtained on the initiative of the offending parent "which have the effect of frustrating the child's return to the jurisdiction of its habitual residence" (*Re G* (above); *Re AZ (A Minor) (Abduction: Acquiescence)* [1993] 1 FLR 682).

A unilateral decision by one parent not to return a child to the country of the child's habitual residence may constitute wrongful retention (*Re S (Minors) (Abduction: Wrongful Retention)* [1994] 1 FLR 82; *H v H (Child Abduction: Stay of Domestic Proceedings)* [1994] 1 FLR 530 where, on the basis that there were exceptional circumstances, the court decided to deal with the merits of the application). Where the retention by one parent has been equivocal pending a determination by the court of the place from where the child has been abducted, a clear finding in that court requiring the return of the child would be sufficient to convert an equivocal retention into an unlawful one (*Re R (Minors) (Abduction)* [1994] 1 FLR 190). On the interpretation of Art 3 in the context of Art 5, see *B v B (Abduction: Custody Rights)* [1993] 1 FLR 238. A removal which is not in breach of domestic law may nevertheless be wrongful for the purposes of the Convention (*Re F (Child Abduction: Risk if Returned)* [1995] 2 FLR 31 and *Practice Note of 14 October 1997* in *The Family Court Practice 2011*). See also *Re S (Custody: Habitual Residence)* [1998] 1 FLR 122, HL where, although the initial removal and retention of the child was not wrongful because the unmarried father had no rights of custody capable of being breached, once he had acquired such rights by virtue of an order giving him care and control, the retention of the child thereafter, contrary to the order and his wishes, became wrongful (notwithstanding the fact that the abductors had obtained an order from the foreign court).

Article 4

The Convention shall apply to any child who was habitually resident in a Contracting State immediately before any breach of custody or access rights. The Convention shall cease to apply when the child attains the age of sixteen years.

Age of the child—The Convention does not apply to a child who is 16 when the application is heard. In such cases, however, the court may consider dealing with the application for the return of the child under its inherent jurisdiction (*Re H (Abduction: Child of 16)* [2000] 2 FLR 51) but since the 1996 Convention applies until the child is 18 years of age, an application for recognition, registration and enforcement of measures taken in a Contracting State under this Convention is an option and should be considered.

Habitual residence—The concept of habitual residence is central to the Hague Convention 1980, Brussels IIA and the 1996 Convention, but there is no uniform approach to its meaning. The term is not defined in the Act or the Conventions, but this may be because it is an issue dependant on the particular facts of the case. Difficulty arises because the English courts have applied the European test of "centre of interests" with the focus on the country with which a person has the closest connection, when dealing with issues under Brussels IIA, and the traditional English principles to cases under the Hague Convention 1980 (see also Part VI). For a review of the applicable principles and main authorities, see *Re G (Abduction: Withdrawal of proceedings)* [2008] 2 FLR 351 *Re P-J (Abduction: Habitual Residence: Consent)* [2009] 2 FLR 1051 and *Re A (Removal Outside Jurisdiction: Habitual Residence)* [2011] 1 FLR 2025, where the CA upheld the decision of the first instance court, which having considered two different versions of events identified a third version on the facts; and *A v P (Habitual Residence)* [2012] 1 FLR 125). Although reference is made to the terms "ordinarily resident" and "habitually resident" in other statutory provisions relating to the fields of family, revenue and welfare law, these provisions do not identify any specific criteria which need to be satisfied before habitual residence is established. Habitual residence and the concept of ordinary residence are not always synonymous (*Nessa v Chief Adjudication Officer* [1999] 2 FLR 1116). It has been established that there are two features which must be proved to establish "habitual residence"; namely, that the person was present in a place or country (i) voluntarily and (ii) for settled purposes and with a settled intention (*Al Habtoor v Fotheringham* [2001] 1 FLR 951; *Re D (Abduction: Habitual Residence)* [2005] 2 FLR 403 and *Re M (Abduction: Habitual Residence: Relocation)* [2005] Fam Law 441). A person must be taken to have acted voluntarily in adopting their habitual residence in a country unless it can be established that the person's presence there was the result of force. Domestic violence, even if extreme, without more will be insufficient to establish that the presence was enforced (*DT v LBT* [2011] 1 FLR 1215, which confirms that the decision in *Neulinger and Shuruk v Switzerland* [2011] 1 FLR 122 has not relaxed or lowered the threshold or brought about any "sea change" or "seismic shift" in the way that the courts will in future deal with abduction cases. This decision has been confirmed by the Court of Appeal in *Re E (Children); sub nom (1) KE (2) TB*

Appellants v SE Respondent & others [2011] EWCA Civ 361). The need to establish residence in a place for "an appreciable period of time" was not specifically considered as a necessary ingredient until the decision in *C v S (A Minor) (Abduction)* [1990] 2 FLR 442, HL. Although the reference to the need to establish an elapse of "an appreciable period of time" was obiter, in subsequent cases emphasis has been placed on this requirement as an additional ingredient. On what would constitute appreciable time, see *Re P(GE) (An Infant)* [1965] Ch 568; *Re E (Child: Abduction)* [1992] 1 FCR 541; *Re R (Wardship: Child Abduction)* [1992] 2 FLR 481; *Re F (A Minor) (Child Abduction)* [1992] 1 FLR 548; *Re R (Wardship: Child Abduction) (No 2)* [1993] 1 FLR 249; *Re B-M (Wardship: Jurisdiction)* [1993] 1 FLR 979; *Re M (Minors) (Residence Order: Jurisdiction)* [1993] 1 FLR 495 and *Re M v M (Abduction: England and Scotland)* [1997] 2 FLR 263. A period of 1 day, or even 7–8 days, is insufficient if an intention to settle is not established (*A v A (Child Abduction)* [1993] 2 FLR 225; *Re A (Abduction: Habitual Residence)* [2007] 2 FLR 129; but see *Re S (Habitual Residence)* [2010] 1 FLR 1146, where on the facts, 7–8 weeks residence was considered sufficient). A short period of time spent in another country with a view to effecting a reconciliation that fails would be insufficient (*Re B (Child Abduction: Habitual Residence)* [1994] 2 FLR 915); see also *Re W (Abduction: Acquiescence: Children's Objections)* [2010] 2 FLR 1150). The mere fact of taking a child out of the country is not enough to establish habitual residence (*Re M (Abduction: Habitual Residence)* [1996] 1 FLR 887). A stay in a country for a holiday or children sent abroad for education does not lead to a change of the child's habitual residence (*Re O* [1995] 2 FCR 649; *B v D (Abduction: Inherent Jurisdiction)* [2009] 1 FLR 1015). In *Hunt v Hunt* [2012] All ER (D) 217 (Oct), where the father, on having taken proceedings under the Convention and warded the child who had been retained by the mother in Mexico, entered into an agreement that the child should remain with the mother and the father should have access. The father then failed to return the child. In Convention proceedings issued by the mother, it was held that even if the father had consented to a change of residence, an appreciable period of settled residence was needed to establish habitual residence. See also *ZA & PA v NA* [2012] EWCA Civ 1396, where reference was made to the need for an appreciable period of time to elapse before habitual residence became complete. A move in connection with the father's employment on a short and temporary basis, notwithstanding the fact that the family maintained a constant principal home in another country, has been held to be the family's residence for settled purposes (*Re S (Habitual Residence)* [2010] 1 FLR 1146, where it was also held that the concept of "centre of interests" test, which applies to decisions under Brussels IIA, Art 3, does not apply to Convention cases). A mother who moved to the US, with a clear intention of settling there with the father and the child, could acquire residence in the US during that period, though she was not entitled to remain in the US for longer than 90 days: *Re A (Abduction: Habitual Residence: Consent)* [2006] 2 FLR 1. In *Re H-K (Habitual Residence)* [2012] 1 FLR 436, an intended stay in England by an Australian couple for a year with the family retaining their home and possessions in Australia was held to result in a change of habitual residence. The court applied the traditional English test rather than the European one. By contrast, in a number of cases the court has rejected a claim of change of habitual residence (e g where the move was for a period of a scholarship or a child's education). The inconsistency of approach leads to uncertainty and confusion, especially when the concept of habitual residence often involves the application of different international provisions. Habitual residence cannot be acquired by a child who is not present in the country concerned (*Re M* (above)), nor can an unborn child acquire habitual residence during his/her mother's pregnancy and before his/her birth (*Re F (Abduction: Unborn Child)* [2007] 1 FLR 627). Where a family has two homes, and part of the year is spent in one country and part in another, there is continuity of residence for habitual residence to arise in both countries, but in Convention cases there cannot be habitual residence in more than one place at the same time. In such cases, the child's habitual residence will be where the child was living at the moment when the wrongful retention or removal occurred (*Re V (Abduction: Habitual Residence)* [1995] 2 FLR 992). An alternative would be to apply the European test of "centre of interests" and the country with which there is the closest connection.

Since habitual residence is a question of fact to be decided on the date when the determination has to be made and in the light of the circumstances of each case (see *Re J (A Minor) (Abduction: Custody Rights)* [1990] 2 FLR 442 applied in *ES v AJ* [2010] 2 FLR 1257), facts such as whether the person has: (i) brought possessions; (ii) a right of abode; (iii) sought to bring family; and (iv) "durable ties" with the country of residence or intended residence are relevant. The requisite period is not a fixed one. It will depend on the facts of each case (*Re S (Custody: Habitual Residence)* [1998] 1 FLR 122, HL). Fraud or mistake may prevent the acquisition or retention of habitual residence. Whether a move agreed to be of limited period prevents the acquisition of habitual residence will depend on the facts of the case (see *Re Z (Abduction)* [2009] 2 FLR 298 in which the court rejected the mother's argument that it does not). Going to a country for a trial period does not establish habitual residence (*E v E* above), nor is it established from the mere fact of ownership of property; it will be a question of fact and degree in each case (*High Tech International AG & Ors v Deripaska* [2006] EWHC 3276 (QB), [2007] EMLR 449).

FLA 1986, s 41 does not apply to conflicts on the issue of habitual residence under the Hague Convention (*Re S (A Child: Abduction)* [2003] 1 FLR 1008). It is for the applicant initially to satisfy the court that it has jurisdiction (*Re R (Wardship: Child Abduction) (No 2)* [1993] 1 FLR 249). In deciding the issue of habitual residence the court does not need to make a searching and microscopic inquiry. Generally it will suffice for the court to stand back and take a general panoramic view of the evidence (*Re B (Minors) (Abduction) (No 1)* [1993] 1 FLR 988). Once habitual residence is established, the burden shifts on to the defendant to show otherwise or that a change has occurred (*Re R (Wardship: Child Abduction)* [1992] 2 FLR 481). As to the residence of a child, a child aged four who is in the sole custody of the mother will necessarily have the same habitual residence as the mother (*Re J* (above)). Where parents separate, the child's habitual residence follows that of the parent who has the day-to-day care of the child and with whom the child lives. Uncommunicated reservations and a subsequent change of mind by one party which is not communicated to the other party will not be a relevant consideration (*Re A (Abduction: Habitual Residence)* [1998] 1 FLR 497). Similarly, where the mother alone has parental responsibility for her child, the child will take on the habitual residence of its mother (*Re G (Abduction: Withdrawal of Proceedings, Acquiescence)* [2008] 2 FLR 351; she alone can determine where they should live and change the habitual residence of her child (*Re M (Minors) (Residence Order: Jurisdiction)* [1993] 1 FLR 495). Where parents are living together, the child is habitually resident with both, and where one parent becomes habitually resident elsewhere, the child does not lose its original habitual residence (*Re N (Abduction: Habitual Residence)* [2000] 2 FLR 899). When the parents separate the child's habitual residence will follow that of its principal carer. Where the parents are habitually resident in different places at the time of the child's birth the issue will depend on the circumstances of the individual case (see *Re G* above). In the case of a married couple, it is not possible for one parent unilaterally to terminate the habitual residence of a child by removing the child from one jurisdiction to another wrongfully and in breach of the other parent's rights (*Re A (Abduction: Habitual Residence: Consent)* [2006] 2 FLR 1; *A v P (Habitual Residence)* [2012] 1 FLR 125). Similarly, where both parents have parental responsibility, neither parent can unilaterally change a child's habitual residence without the consent or acquiescence of the other (*ES v AJ* [2010] 2 FLR 1257, above). In *B v H (Habitual Residence: Wardship)* [2002] 1 FLR 388 it was held that a father could not unilaterally change the habitual residence of his children who had been taken from England to Bangladesh, along with the mother, on the pretext of a holiday and then detained there. However, although in *B v H* it was held that the habitual residence of a newborn baby will be that of the parent who has parental responsibility for and the day-to-day care of the child and that the fact that the child is born abroad does not of itself lead to the conclusion that the child is not habitually resident in England, in *ZA & PA v NA* [2012] EWCA Civ 1396 the Court of Appeal overruled this concept. The Court held that in relation to a child born to parents outside the jurisdiction, to establish that the child was habitually resident in England and Wales it was necessary for the child to have been physically present within the jurisdiction. To adopt a special rule for a newly born child would lead to derogating from a purely factual analysis of where a child was resident; see also *Re F (Abduction: Unborn Child)* (above). For a change to take effect, the child must be actually transferred into the care of the parent who seeks to establish habitual residence (*Re O (A Minor) (Abduction: Habitual Residence)* [1993] 2 FLR 594). Where the mother has been the sole carer of the child, her death will not immediately strip the child of the habitual residence acquired from her. Nor will the clandestine removal of the child, without a court order or the consent of any interested party, immediately clothe the child with the habitual residence of the person removing him. The longer the child lives in the new jurisdiction without challenge, the more likely it is that the child will be said to acquire the habitual residence of those who continue to care for him without opposition (*Re G (Abduction: Rights of Custody)* [2002] 2 FLR 703; *Re S (Custody: Habitual Residence)* [1998] 1 FLR 122, HL; and see *H v H (Jurisdiction to Grant Wardship)* [2012] 1 FLR 23 on the issues of jurisdiction under Brussels IIA and habitual residence). In *Re S* it was held that a period of 2 days was not sufficient, of itself, to result in the child's existing habitual residence being lost and a new one being acquired. Nor could habitual residence be altered by the courts of the country where the child was retained. Contrast with *Mercredi v Chaffe* [2011] 1 FLR 1293, where a child born to a French mother was removed by her to France shortly after the child's birth without informing the father, who did not have parental responsibility. On her return to France she commenced proceedings there. The father invoked the Hague Convention and later wardship proceedings. The Court of Appeal ruled that since the father did not have parental responsibility and had not exercised any custody rights the mother was entitled to exercise her rights of freedom of movement when she returned with her child to France, the country of her birth. The removal was not wrongful. In any case given that the French court had already embarked on a welfare inquiry following the mother's application it was wrong to proceed in England. See also *Re A (Removal Outside Jurisdiction: Habitual Residence)* [2011] 1 FLR 2025 where it was held that there was no need to be able to identify a specific point in time at which the children ceased to be habitually resident in England, because the loss of one habitual residence, and the acquisition of another, was gradual.

Where a parent abducts a baby, fails to comply with any court order for the child's return and successfully goes to ground for many years, there is a powerful argument that it would be an affront to common sense to hold, perhaps 10–12 years later, that the habitual residence of the child was other than the country in which he had spent virtually the whole of his life (*Re B (Abduction: Children's Objection)* [1998] 1 FLR 667). On the issue of the habitual residence of a child born to a surrogate mother with whom she has no biological connection see *W and B v H (Child Abduction: Surrogacy)* [2002] 1 FLR 1008 and *W and W v H (Child Abduction: Surrogacy) No 2* [2002] 2 FLR 252. It is clear from these two decisions that, in appropriate cases, where there is any doubt about proving the habitual residence of a child it would be advisable to seek relief under the Convention and, alternatively under the inherent jurisdiction, to enable the court to exercise the full range of powers available to it.

The habitual residence of a child in England before the abduction will give the High Court inherent jurisdiction to entertain an application in respect of the child. The issue of wardship proceedings, and any orders made by the English court giving interim care and control, will stand, and give both the court and the parent in whose favour the order is made "custody rights" within Art 3 of the Convention, even though an order may have been obtained by the abductors from the foreign court (*Re S* above). The habitual residence of a child of a US serviceman who is posted to a non-Convention country is that country and not the US (*Re A (Abduction: Habitual Residence)* [1996] 1 FLR 1).

It should be noted that Art 4 does not require that, at the time of the application, the child should be habitually resident in the state under which the rights of custody or access arose; it does require, however, that the child should be habitually resident in "a Contracting State" (*Re G (A Minor) (Hague Convention: Access)* [1993] 1 FLR 669; see also *A v A (Child Abduction)* [1993] 2 FLR 225).

Article 5

For the purposes of this Convention –

   (a) "rights of custody" shall include rights relating to the care of the person of the child and, in particular, the right to determine the child's place of residence;

   (b) "rights of access" shall include the right to take a child for a limited period of time to a place other than the child's habitual residence.

"rights of custody"—See also the notes under Art 3. A parent of a child who is serving a sentence retains "custody rights". Such rights are not suspended but are merely curtailed (*Re A (Abduction: Rights of Custody: Imprisonment)* [2004] 1 FLR 1 and *Re L (A Child)* [2006] 1 FLR 843). A provision in an order that a child is not to be removed from the jurisdiction of a State without the prior approval of the court or the written agreement of the parties, confers "rights of custody" for Convention purposes on the non-custodial parent (*Re P (Abduction: Consent)* [2004] 2 FLR 1057) as does an implied prohibition on such removal (*C v C (Child Abduction)* [1992] 1 FLR 163). Rights of custody include rights relating to the care of the child and, in particular, the right to determine the child's place of residence but not the right to be informed about a decision to change the residence of the child (*Re V-B (Abduction: Custody Rights)* [1999] 2 FLR 192, CA) or his education. A potential right of veto, or to "watch over" the child's upbringing, education or to be consulted on any change in the child's status, does not amount to "rights of custody" but a "right to veto" to a removal does amount to "custody rights" (*Re D (Abduction: Rights of Custody)* [2007] 1 FLR 961). See also *S v H (Abduction: Access Rights)* [1997] 1 FLR 971; *Re B (A Minor) (Abduction)* [1994] 2 FLR 249 and the dissenting judgment of Peter Gibson LJ. A father who gives his consent to the children travelling to the mother continues to exercise custody rights (*W v W (Child Abduction: Acquiescence)* [1993] 2 FLR 211). The right of custody may arise by operation of law or by reason of a judicial or administrative decision or by reason of an agreement having legal effect under the law of that state. A court itself may have a right of custody at the relevant time in the sense that it has a right to determine the child's place of residence, provided that it has acquired "custody rights" (see *Re E (Abduction: Rights of Custody)* [2005] 2 FLR 759). It acquires custody rights when its jurisdiction is invoked in respect of matters within the meaning of the Convention. The date on which the court's jurisdiction is invoked is at the latest when the proceedings are served, or in special cases where an order is made or direction given on a without notice application and before the application or order is served (*A v B (Abduction: Declaration)* [2009] 1 FLR 1253; *X County Council v B (Abduction: Rights of Custody in the Court)* [2010] 1 FLR 1197; *Re H (Abduction: Rights of Custody)* [2000] 1 FLR 374, HL) and in any event once it has made an interim order (*Re W; Re B (Child Abduction: Unmarried Father)* [1998] 2 FLR 146); or where the court is actively seised of the proceedings to determine custody rights (*Re J (Abduction: Declaration of Wrongful Removal)* [1999] 2 FLR 653 applied in *A v B* above); or it has adjourned the hearing for the issue to be resolved by agreement (*Re C (Abduction: Wrongful Removal)* [1999] 2 FLR 859); or where wardship proceedings have been issued (*Re S (Custody: Habitual Residence)* [1998] 1 FLR 122). Where Brussels IIA, Art 16 applies, the court is deemed to be seised only where a document instituting proceedings or an equivalent document is lodged with the court. Hence an application made by telephone does not operate to confer those rights in the court until the formal application is made: *Mercredi v Chaffe* [2011] 1 FLR 1293.

Where an issue is raised regarding whether the foreign law gives the applicant custody rights or not, the court will normally be bound by the decision of the court of the Requesting State as to the applicant's rights and the legality of the child's removal from that State (*Re D (Abduction: Rights of Custody)* (above)). The court may determine the issue on expert evidence adduced before it (see *Re JB (Child Abduction) (Rights of Custody: Spain)* [2004] 1 FLR 796) but where a foreign court has made a decision, that should be relied on (*Re D (Abduction: Rights of Custody),* above). (See also ante under Art 3.) The court should resist the temptation to make its own findings as to the foreign laws applicable and should be reluctant to allow rights of access to a child to metamorphose into rights of custody (*Re F (Abduction: Rights of Custody)* [2008] 2 FLR 1239). Where the court is faced with conflicting expert evidence, it is for the applicant to prove his rights under the relevant foreign law.

Custody rights and unmarried fathers—As from 1 November 2012, the parental responsibility and applicable law provisions of the 1996 Convention affect how an unmarried father's custody rights are viewed under the Hague Convention 1980. An unmarried father has parental responsibility if he is registered as the child's father (ACA 2002, s 111) but for such registration to be valid and effective to confer parental responsibility, s 10 of the Births and Deaths Registration Act 1953 must be strictly complied with (*AAA v ASH, Registrar-General for England and Wales and The Secretary for Justice Intervening* [2010] 1 FLR 1). Where the issue relates to an unmarried father's rights under a foreign law the usual procedure is to make a referral pursuant to Art 15 for the foreign court to determine the issue, but see: *Re K (Rights of Custody: Spain)* [2010] 1 FLR 57; *Kennedy v Kennedy* [2010] 1 FLR 782. The rights within Art 3 may extend to "inchoate rights of those who are carrying out duties and enjoying privileges of a custodial or parental character which, though not yet formally recognised or granted by law, a court would nevertheless be likely to uphold in the interests of the child" (*Re B (A Minor) (Abduction)* [1994] 2 FLR 249). In *Re F (Abduction: Unmarried Father: Sole Carer)* [2003] 1 FLR 839 this principle was extended to a father to whom the primary care of his children and a child of whom he was not the father had been delegated by the mother; but cf *Re C (Child Abduction) (Unmarried Father: Rights of Custody)* [2003] 1 FLR 252. Confirmation in solicitors' correspondence, in which the offending party confirms that there is no intention to remove the child from the jurisdiction and in consequence thereof immediate steps are not taken to issue proceedings to prevent removal, has been held to attribute "custody rights" (*Re H (Child Abduction) (Unmarried Father: Rights of Custody)* [2003] 2 FLR 153). See also *Re C (Abduction: Wrongful Removal)* [1999] 2 FLR 859 and *Re S (Custody: Habitual Residence)* [1998] 1 FLR 122, HL. In *JMcB v Le* C-400/10 [2011] 1 FLR 518, the Court of Justice of the European Union held that Brussels IIA, pursuant to Art 7 of Charter of Fundamental Rights of the European Union or otherwise, does not preclude a Member State from requiring by its law that the father of a child who is not married to the mother shall have obtained an order of a court of competent jurisdiction granting him custody in order to qualify as having "custody rights" that render the removal of that child from its country of habitual residence wrongful for the purposes of Art 2(1) of Brussels IIA. Brussels IIA must, therefore, be interpreted to mean that whether a child's removal is wrongful is entirely dependent on the existence of custody rights conferred by the national law in breach of which the child was removed. It is the law of the Member State that determines the conditions under which the natural father acquires rights of custody in respect of his child within the meaning of Art 2(9) and that may provide that his acquisition of such rights is dependent upon his obtaining an order from a national court awarding such rights to him. The fact that the national law provides for the mother to have parental responsibility alone would not be contrary to Art 8 of the ECHR, provided that it permitted the child's father to apply to the national court to grant him parental responsibility. (See further FPR PD12F, para 2.17 in Part III and *Practice Note of 14 October 1997,* which is set out in *The Family Court Practice 2011.*)

Custody rights of same-sex female partners where a child is born as result of assisted reproduction—See HFEA 2008.

Orders made after removal—The view expressed in *Practice Note of 14 October 1997* that an application for parental responsibility does not involve an exercise by the court of "rights of custody" was challenged in *Re C* (above).

"rights of access"—The definition in the 1996 Convention, Art 3(b) is in identical terms and in similar terms in Brussels IIA, Art 2(10). Under Art 21, an application to make arrangements for organising or securing the effective exercise of rights of access may be presented to the Central Authority of a Contracting State in the same way as an application for the return of a child. Article 21 also provides that Central Authorities are bound by the obligations of co-operation in Art 7 to promote the peaceful enjoyment of access rights and the fulfilment of any conditions to which the exercise of those rights may be subject.

****

Article 8

Any person, institution or other body claiming that a child has been removed or retained in breach of custody rights may apply either to the Central Authority of the child's habitual residence or to the Central Authority of any other Contracting State for assistance in securing the return of the child. The application shall contain –

(a) information concerning the identity of the applicant, of the child and of the person alleged to have removed or retained the child;
(b) where available, the date of birth of the child;
(c) the grounds on which the applicant's claim for return of the child is based;
(d) all available information relating to the whereabouts of the child and the identity of the person with whom the child is presumed to be.

The application may be accompanied or supplemented by –

(e) an authenticated copy of any relevant decision or agreement;
(f) a certificate or an affidavit emanating from a Central Authority or other competent authority of the State of the child's habitual residence, or from a qualified person, concerning the relevant law of that State:
(g) any other relevant document.

Scope—See **"rights of custody"** under Art 5.

Procedure on application—See FPR 2010, rr 12.44–12.57 and PD12F.

****

Article 11

The judicial or administrative authorities of Contracting States shall act expeditiously in proceedings for the return of children.

If the judicial or administrative authority concerned has not reached a decision within six weeks from the date of commencement of the proceedings, the applicant or the Central Authority of the requested State, on its own initiative or if asked by the Central Authority of the requested State, shall have the right to request a statement of the reasons for the delay. If a reply is received by the Central Authority of the requested State, that Authority shall transmit the reply to the Central Authority of the requesting State, or to the applicant, as the case may be.

"act expeditiously"—The State has an obligation to take positive and effective measures to enforce the right of a parent to be re-united with his/her child and to deal swiftly with the abduction proceedings (ECHR 1950, Art 8; *Caras v Romania* (Application No 7198/04)). This includes taking adequate sanctions against the offending parent (*Maire v Portugal* (Application No 48206/99) ECtHR [2004] 2 FLR 653; *Re C (Abduction: Interim Directions: Accommodation by Local Authority)* [2004] 1 FLR 653; and *Karadzic v Croatia* [2006] 1 FCR 36). In *Deak v Romania and UK* (Application No 19055/05) ECtHR it was held that the UK's court's insistence on expert evidence had unreasonably delayed the proceedings and that the delay of nine months by the Romanian court was also a cause for concern. In Hague Convention proceedings and where Brussels IIA applies there is a six-week time limit. FPR PD12F, para 2.14 specifically refers to the need for expedition and confirmed the procedure set out in *Vigreux v Michel* [2006] 2 FLR 1180.Attention is drawn to the cases of *Klentzeris v Klentzeris* [2007] 2 FLR 996 and *Re F (Abduction: Child's Wishes)* [2007] 2 FLR 697 for the procedure to be followed where an appeal is contemplated. In *Re K (Rights of Custody: Spain)* [2010] 1 FLR 57 the court dealt with the issues without reference to the foreign court pursuant to Art 15 to avoid delay (see also below under Art 12 **"Brussels IIA"**). Also note that, in contrast, the 1996 Hague Convention does not make any reference to time limits.

Article 12

Where a child has been wrongfully removed or retained in terms of Article 3 and, at the date of the commencement of the proceedings before the judicial or administrative

authority of the Contracting State where the child is, a period of less than one year has
elapsed from the date of the wrongful removal or retention, the authority concerned shall
order the return of the child forthwith.

The judicial or administrative authority, even where the proceedings have been
commenced after the expiration of the period of one year referred to in the preceding
paragraph, shall also order the return of the child, unless it is demonstrated that the child
is now settled in its new environment.

Where the judicial or administrative authority in the requested state has reason to believe
that the child has been taken to another State, it may stay the proceedings or dismiss the
application for the return of the child.

"a period of less than one year"—Under similar provisions in Brussels IIA and the 1996 Convention,
the relevant date when time begins to run is not "from the date of the wrongful removal or retention", but
the date when the holder of the rights of custody has or should have had knowledge of the whereabouts of
the child. For the purposes of establishing the 1-year period, where the parties have agreed the date of the
child's return, in the absence of any communication of the change of intention or decision not to return
the child, the relevant date at which a wrongful retention takes place is the date on which the child should
have been returned. An uncommunicated decision to retain the child does not constitute retention
(*RS v KS (Abduction: Wrongful Retention)* [2009] 2 FLR 1231.

"shall order the return of the child"—This is a mandatory provision where less than 1 year has elapsed
and discretionary when the period is in excess of 1 year. For examples of the inter-relationship between
these provisions and the jurisdiction of the home court or where the court's involvement preceded the
non-return order by a Contracting State on a Convention application under Brussels IIA, see *Re AJ
(Brussels II Revised)* [2012] 2 FLR 689 and the final determination as *Re AJ (Contact: Brussels II
Revised)* [2012] 2 FLR 1065, where the English court held that it had retained jurisdiction as it had been
seised of the case before the Polish court.

"now settled in its new environment"—Contrast with the additional conditions required under
Brussels IIA, Art 10(b). For meaning of and what constitutes settlement, see *Re H and L (Abduction:
Acquiescence)* [2010] 2 FLR 1277. Where there has been significant delay in issuing proceedings or
where proceedings have not been conducted expeditiously and where, as a result of the delay, the children
have become settled, the court in appropriate circumstances may regard the continuance of the
proceedings as an abuse of the process of the court and strike out the application (*Re G (Abduction:
Striking Out Application)* [1995] 2 FLR 410) but that case was distinguished in *RS v KS (Abduction:
Wrongful Retention)* [2009] 2 FLR 1231, where the father was found not to be at fault for the delay and
had actively sought to pursue his application). See: *Re O (Abduction: Settlement)* [2011] 2 FLR 1307,
where the father's immoderate and underhand activities since 2009 were a factor that was taken into
account; *Re C (Child Abduction: Settlement)* [2006] 2 FLR 797 (*Re F (Abduction: Rights of Custody)*
[2008] 2 FLR 1239), where the applicant's unexplained delay was a factor in the court exercising its
discretion not to return the children but in *F v M and N (Abduction: Acquiescence: Settlement)* [2008]
2 FLR 1270, although almost 2 years had elapsed, the court held that the father had not acquiesced in her
retention as he had actively pursued proceedings in Poland and sought the return of the child and the
Polish court had been seised of the matter before the mother abducted the child and had gone a long way
into its determination of what arrangements should be in her best interests. A return order was made but
suspended to enable the mother to pursue an application before the Polish court and also to apply for
permission to remove the child to England. In *Re E (Abduction: Intolerable Situation)* [2009] 2 FLR 485
the court refused to return the child as the child was settled in England and there was a grave risk that the
child would be exposed to psychological harm if returned. The court also considered the impact of
separation of the child from its half-sibling (see also *RS v KS (Abduction: Wrongful Retention)* above.

"now settled"—This refers to the date when the proceedings were commenced as otherwise any delay in
hearing the case might affect the outcome (*Re N (Minors) (Abduction)* [1991] 1 FLR 413).

The word "settlement" has two constituents: (i) it involves a physical element of relating to, being
established in, a community and an environment; (ii) it has an emotional constituent denoting security
and stability in the sense of permanence. The word "new" encompasses place, home, school, people,
friends, activities and opportunities, but not, per se, the relationship with the mother (see *Re H and L*,
above).

**Duty to order the return of the child and protection of human rights and fundamental
freedoms**—In *Re O (Abduction: Settlement)* [2011] 2 FLR 1307, the Supreme Court confirmed that when
exercising its discretion whether or not to order the return of a child, the principles set out in *Re M
(Abduction: Zimbabwe)* [2008] 1 FLR 251 apply. Hague policy considerations, while relevant in

exercising discretion in settlement cases, are not to be given more importance than other welfare considerations and their relevance is only part of the whole picture. In assessing the adaptability of a child to a return order, the court should consider the individual circumstances of each child and examine and weigh this in the balance when exercising its discretion under the Hague Convention. The Court approved the approach adopted in *RS v XS (Abduction: Wrongful Retention)* [2009] 2 FLR 1231 that the disruption of living arrangements of a young child "would have more far reaching consequences and adverse impact than in the case of an older and less sensitive child able to comprehend a sudden departure from one routine and community and the prospect of the next". Article 20 of the Hague Convention provides that the return of the child under the provisions of Art 12 may be refused if this would not be permitted by the fundamental principles of the requested State relating to the protection of human rights and fundamental freedoms. This Article has not been included in Sch 1 to this Act and does not therefore have the force of law in England and Wales. However, in *Re K (Abduction: Psychological Harm)* [1995] 2 FLR 550, it was raised as an aid to establish that, in considering the issue of whether the return of the child should be ordered under Art 12 and the provisions of Art 13(b), the court can and should have regard to the provisions of Art 20 relating to the "protection of human rights", which includes the respondent being given adequate notice of the hearing and of the case which that parent has to meet and an opportunity to participate in the proceedings. In *Re J (Abduction: Wrongful Removal)* [2000] 1 FLR 78 breach of ECHR 1950, Art 6 was raised where orders had been made without notice, but in *Caras v Romania* (Application No 7198/04) [2007] 1 FLR 661 and *Sylvester v Austria* (Application Nos 36812/97 and 40114/98) [2003] 2 FLR 210 the ECtHR held that, if there is a risk that contact between a child and his parent may be threatened, there is an obligation on the national authority, under ECHR 1950, Art 8, to take immediate and all necessary steps to facilitate an abducted child's return to the jurisdiction of its habitual residence in order to avoid the effect of delay adversely affecting the future relationship between the child and his parent and the determination of that issue by the passage of time (see *Maire v Portugal* (Application No 48206/99) ECHR [2004] 2 FLR 653 where Article 8 was raised to establish breach of a father's rights to family life by reason of the failure by a State Authority to take active and effective action to locate the child and enforce the return of the child for 4 years). It may be appropriate for the court to delay the return for a limited period to enable the offending parent to settle his/her affairs before the return: *R v K (Abduction: Return Order)* [2010] 1 FLR 1456. See also *Gill and Aui v Spain* [2005] 1 FLR 190. In *Re H (Child Abduction: Mother's Asylum)* [2003] 2 FLR 1105 the principles of the *Protocol of January 2003 (Child Abduction Cases Between the UK and Pakistan)* (see Part V) were considered, as was the mother's asylum status, but the court did not regard itself as inhibited by her status in ordering the return of the child. For the application of ECHR 1950 in non-Convention abduction cases, see *Re J (Child Returned Abroad: Human Rights)* [2004] 2 FLR 85 and *Re R (Abduction: Immigration Concerns)* [2005] 1 FLR 33 and *Re E* above where there is a conflict between immigration and welfare concerns. The principle that the court of the State of the child's habitual residence is best placed to deal with issues relating to the child is reinforced by Art 7.1 of the 1996 Convention, which confirms that where a child has been wrongfully removed or retained, the authorities of the Contracting State in which the child was habitually resident immediately before the removal or retention keep their jurisdiction until the child has acquired habitual residence in another State and the person/s having rights of custody has acquiesced in the removal or retention or the child has resided in that other State for a period of at least 1 year after the person with rights of custody has or should have had knowledge of the child's whereabouts, and no request for a return lodged within that period is pending and the child is settled in his or her new environment. Owing to the differences in the provisions relating to when time begins to run, in some cases reliance on this provision may be a better option.

Brussels IIA—For the application of Brussels IIA in child abduction cases see *Povse v Alpago* (C-211/10) [2010] 2 FLR 1343, ECJ and earlier cases of *F v M (Abduction: Grave Risk of Harm)* [2008] 2 FLR 1263; *Vigreux v Michel* [2006] 2 FLR 1180 and *Re A (Custody Decision After Maltese Non-Return Order)* [2007] 1 FLR 1923. For the issue of "rights of custody" of an unmarried father without parental responsibility under Brussels IIA, Art 2(9), see *JMcB v Le* C-400/10 [2011] 1 FLR 518. For the inter-relationship between Brussels IIA, the Hague Convention and domestic law see *Re RC and BC (Child Abduction: Brussels II Revised: Article 11(7))* [2009] 1 FLR 574; *Re RD (Child Abduction: Brussels II Revised: Articles 11(7) and 19)* [2009] 1 FLR 586; *Re H (Abduction)* [2009] 2 FLR 1513; and *Re S (Habitual Residence)* [2010] 1 FLR 1146 and see *Re F (Abduction: Refusal to Return)* [2009] 2 FLR 1023, which recommends that the procedure under Art 11 of the Regulation should be followed when the court refuses to make a return order instead of pursuing the matter by way of appeal. Where an application under Brussels IIA, Art 11(7) is issued the following procedure is recommended: (a) a directions appointment should be sought for the court to consider whether the case should be determined on a summary basis and/or whether there should be a welfare inquiry and if so, the extent of such an inquiry; (b) Cafcass Legal and its High Court Team should be notified as soon as such an application is made and at the first directions hearing the court should be asked to consider whether or not to join the child as a party and whether Cafcass Legal or its High Court Team should be invited to make representations; (c) if the child is joined and Cafcass is directed to take an active role directions must be given on the nature and extent of their role; (d) at an early stage issues relating to interim contact should be considered; and (e) the court should set a timetable for the final hearing with a timescale that complies with the provisions of Art 11 and the need for urgency (*M v T (Abduction: Brussels IIR Art (7))* [2010] 2 FLR 1685. In *Vigreux v Michel* it was also directed with the President's approval that where an application is governed by Art 13 of the Hague Convention it should be headed under both CACA 1985 and Brussels IIA. On issue, the outside the court file should be clearly marked to draw attention to the nature of the application and should state the date on which the 6-week period will expire; this will draw to the court administration's attention the "hear-by" date which stringent compliance with Brussels IIA would require. (This procedure has been incorporated in FPR PD12F, para 2.14 and applies to both the 1980 Convention and Brussels IIA.) In *Re A, HA v MB (Brussels II Revised: Article 11(7) Application)* [2008] 1 FLR 289, Singer J, with the approval of the President, set out the following steps that should be taken by a parent who has not secured the return of a child under the Hague Convention: (1) where a non return order is made before the commencement of proceedings in England the application should be commenced by Pt 18 application issued out of the High Court in London (or if issued in a District Registry transferred to London forthwith) and should be headed "in the Matter of an application pursuant to the Brussels Revised Regulation Article 11(7) for the return of the child from [The Member State in question]"; (2) where English proceedings have already been issued, a Hague Convention non-return order is made and the home parent wishes to pursue an application for a return of a child, an application should be made in the existing proceedings; the terms of the application should be for "Directions in light of the Order made in the [Member State] on [date] declining in reliance of Art 13 of the Hague Convention on Child Abduction to order the return of the child[ren] to England and Wales" and the proceedings should be transferred to the Family Division in London, if not already proceeding there. The case also raises other issues, which should be considered by practitioners, where a non-return order is made. Attention is also drawn to the provisions set out in FPR 2010, rr 12.58–12.71, which deals with procedural issues when a non-return order is made and to the Council Regulations set out in Part VI of this work. See also the commentary under FPR 2010, rr 12.58–12.71 and *Re F (Abduction: Child Wishes)* [2007] 2 FLR 697 for the procedure to be followed in other cases where Brussels IIA applies.

The following guidance on the operation of Brussels IIA, Art 11(7) and the effect of a non-return order by a Member State was given in *D v N and D (by her Guardian ad Litem)* [2011] 2 FLR 464: (a) proceedings under Art 11(7) should be determined as soon as possible; (b) in determining a return order, the court is exercising a welfare jurisdiction and it has the whole range of orders that would normally be available to a judge if the child had not been abducted; but (c) the issue of an Art 42(2) certificate should be considered only where the conditions set out in Art 42(2) are satisfied. In *AF v T and Another (Brussels II Revised: Art 11(7) Application)* [2011] 2 FLR 891, following a non-return order, notwithstanding the lapse of time since that order was made, the court dealt with the father's application and made orders for residence and contact on the ground that the maintenance of the child's relationship with the parent left behind formed an intrinsic purpose of both the Hague Convention and Brussels IIA (see further under Art 13). For the operation of Brussels IIA, Art 20, see *Detiček v Sgueglia* (Case C–403/09) [2010] 1 FLR 1381.

Duty to return in non-Convention cases—The Hague Convention principles are not applicable to non-Convention countries (*Re J (Child Returned Abroad: Convention Rights)* [2005] 2 FLR 802, HL). In all such cases, the court must act in accordance with the welfare of the child. Within those principles, the court has jurisdiction to order the return of the child without a full investigation of the merits (*Re J* applied in *Re U (Abduction: Nigeria)* [2011] 1 FLR 354 and see FPR PD12F, para 3.1). Relevant factors are the child's connection with the country, including nationality, residence, language, race, ethnicity; religion, culture and education. The effect of such an order on the primary carer, although not decisive, is relevant, as is the sincerity of the refusal to return the child and its effect on the child. The relevance and extent of the difference between the legal system in England and the foreign country would depend upon the particular facts of each case. The court did not go so far as to say that the future of a child should be decided in every case according to the concept of child welfare which exactly corresponds to that in England and Wales, but see *Re H (Abduction: Non-Convention Application)* [2006] 2 FLR 314 where the child was not returned by reason of the local court's unwillingness to apply international standards. The provision of Art 20 of the Hague Convention, which provides that the return of a child under Art 12 may be refused if this would not be permitted by reason of human rights principles in the requesting state, is also relevant. However, the decision in *Re H (Abduction: Dominica: Corporal Punishment)* [2007] 1 FLR 72 seems to suggest that in non-Hague Convention cases a full investigation on the merits and a welfare inquiry should be undertaken unless the children's return could be safeguarded by appropriate undertakings and a full inquiry in the country of the children's habitual residence.

Duty to order the return of the child after the expiration of 12 months—Where more than 12 months have elapsed, the court has jurisdiction to entertain the application and a discretion to return the child notwithstanding that settlement has been established. In *Re M (Abduction: Zimbabwe)* [2008] 1 FLR 251

it was held that in such cases when exercising its discretion, the court is required to have regard to the overriding objectives of the Convention as well as the consideration of the welfare of the child and its rights. However, there is no principle which requires that the Convention policies should always outweigh other considerations save in exceptional cases. It would be "wrong to import any test of exceptionality into the exercise of discretion under the Hague Convention. The circumstances in which return may be refused are themselves exceptions to the general rule. That in itself is sufficient exceptionality. It is neither necessary nor desirable to import an additional gloss into the Convention". It was impressed by the House of Lords that in settlement cases it must be borne in mind that the major objective of the Convention, namely that of swift return, could not be achieved and therefore it could no longer be assumed that the country of origin is the best forum for the resolution of the dispute. Other considerations, such as the child's objections and its integration into the community, were relevant factors to be taken into account. However, it was made clear that the policy of the Convention does not yield identical results in all cases, and has to be weighed together with the circumstances which produced the exception and such pointers as there are towards the welfare of the particular child (applied in *F v M and N (Abduction: Acquiescence: Settlement)* [2008] 2 FLR 1270, *Re S (Abduction: Children's Representation)* [2008] 2 FLR 1918 and *Re H and L (Abduction: Acquiescence)* [2010] 2 FLR 1277. The approach to be adopted in non-Convention cases remains as set out by the House of Lords in *Re J (A Child) (Custody Rights: Jurisdiction)* [2005] 2 FLR 802. In *M v M* [2008] 2 FLR 1884 the court applied Thorpe LJ's interpretation of settlement in *Cannon v Cannon* [2005] 1 FLR 169 when ordering the return of the children to Poland. Any delay in the making of the application (see *Re F (Abduction: Rights of Custody)* [2008] 2 FLR 1239) will be relevant. Where there has been significant delay in instituting the proceedings, and the proceedings have not been conducted expeditiously, the court may regard the application as an abuse of the process of the court (*Re G (Abduction: Striking Out Application)* [1995] 2 FLR 410). The court will similarly refuse an application for an adjournment in such cases. Delay will also be a relevant factor when weighing up the child's objections against the whole policy of the Convention (*Re C (Abduction: Residence and Contact)* [2006] 2 FLR 277; *Re S (Child Abduction: Delay)* [1998] 1 FLR 651). The reason for the delay in bringing the proceedings and the parties' conduct, particularly that of the abducting parent in concealing the child's whereabouts are relevant factors in determining the issue of settlement and the exercise of the discretion (*Re C (Abduction: Settlement)* [2005] 1 FLR 127 and *Re C (Child Abduction: Settlement)* [2006] 2 FLR 797 – for an exceptional and extreme case of concealment). See *D v S (Abduction: Acquiescence)* [2008] 2 FLR 293 where delay was considered but where on balance the court ruled that a return was justified on welfare grounds and the fact that the issues between the parties were likely to be easier to manage in Mexico.

Separate representation for the child—Brussels IIA, Art 11 provides that when applying Hague Convention, Arts 12 and 13, the court should ensure that the child is given the opportunity to be heard during the proceedings unless this appears to be inappropriate having regard to the child's age or maturity. The need to hear the child is reinforced by the provision in the 1996 Convention, Art 23.2, under which the failure of the child being given the opportunity to be heard is one of the grounds for refusing to recognise measures taken in a Contracting State. Generally, the child's views and the strength of his or her objections will be adequately represented by one of the parties assisted by the appointment of a Cafcass officer to report on the child's degree of maturity and wishes. In *De L v H* [2010] 1 FLR 1229, the judge saw the child aged 12 in the presence of a Cafcass officer to ascertain the child's maturity and the strength and basis for his objections and strong feelings in not wishing to return to the State of his habitual residence.

Initially, the views only of children approaching adolescence were considered to be appropriate. More recently the child's voice is heard far more frequently in Hague Convention cases even where the child has been much younger more particularly where the defence of a child's objections is raised. The practice has developed and is encouraged to ascertain the child's views by arranging a meeting between the judge and the child. In *Re G (Abduction: Children's Objections)* [2011] 1 FLR 1645 Thorpe LJ pointed out that the fact that neither mediation nor a meeting between the judge and the child had been considered were matters of concern, particularly in a case where the child was an articulate, determined and courageous adolescent. He referred to the practice of hearing the voice of the child through the Cafcass officer but stated that "that tradition was now under scrutiny debate and revision". He expressed the view that judges should be meeting with children and hearing their wishes directly. In *B v B (Abduction: Child with Learning Difficulties)* [2012] 1 FLR 881, the child who had Asperger's syndrome was seen by the judge and despite his psychological difficulties his objections were given significant weight, especially since they were in line with the expert's evidence of the risk of significant harm to him. If this process is intended to be followed, reference should be made to Practice Note of April 2010: *Guidelines for Judges Meeting Children who are Subject to Family Proceedings*, but note that the guidance states that a meeting with the child is not to be used for evidence-gathering but for the child to be heard, understood and to be reassured. In most cases, it will not be necessary to join the child as a party to the proceedings but the court is required to consider this issue when giving directions. In *WF v FJ, BF and RF (Abduction:*

PART II

Child's Objections) [2011] 1 FLR 1153, Baker J when dealing with the issue relating to party status being given to a child said (i) that "in view of the recent developments in the law, it is now even more important that the voice of the child is heard in proceedings under the Hague Convention" and that without laying down any rigid rules, it was clearly preferable where time and resources permitted, for the child to be seen by Cafcass High Court Team before the decision is taken to give a child party status; and (ii) that FPR 1991, r 9.2A, which had made provisions for a child to conduct proceedings without a litigation friend in proceedings under CA 1989 and FLA 1996, Pt 4A, did not apply to proceedings under the Hague Convention and that in "the light of the great emphasis now being given to children's objections under Art 13" it was hoped that the FPR Committee would find time to review this lacuna (which in that case was overcome by the appointment of a child's solicitor to act as litigation friend with the agreement of all parties). FPR PD16A, paras 7.1–7.5 set out the circumstances when a child may be made a party to proceedings but para 7.4 provides that where a child is made a party a guardian should be appointed. FPR 2010, r 16.6 sets out the circumstances in which a child may conduct proceedings without a guardian or litigation friend but these do not include proceedings under the Hague Convention or Brussels IIA.

If the child is made a party, the appointment of a guardian and/or representation for the child and attendance of the child should be dealt with (*D v N and D (by her Guardian ad Litem)* [2011] 2 FLR 464, where a guardian ad litem was appointed to ascertain the child's views). If the child is not made a party, the court should consider the manner in which the child's wishes and feelings are to be ascertained (FPR 2010, r 12.48).

It is only in exceptional circumstances, and where there has been State intervention in the affairs of the family, or where the facts disclose that it would be inappropriate for Cafcass to be invited to report, that the court will consider joining the child as a party to the application and ordering separate representation (*Re D (Abduction: Rights of Custody)* [2007] 1 FLR 961; *Re F (Abduction: Joinder of Child as Party)* [2007] 2 FLR 313; and *Re H (Abduction)* [2007] 1 FLR 242). There must also be an arguable case that the discretion under Art 13 should be exercised (*Re S (Abduction: Children: Separate Representation)* [1997] 1 FLR 486).

The House of Lords in *Re M (Abduction: Zimbabwe)* (above), however, observed that children must not be given an exaggerated impression of the relevance and importance of their views in child abduction cases and it might send children the wrong message. However, in cases where settlement is argued under Art 12 the separate point of view of the children is particularly important and should not be lost in the competing claims of the adults. If this were routine in such cases there would be no additional delay. In all other cases the question for the directions judge is whether separate representation of the child will add enough to the court's understanding of the issues that arise under the Hague Convention to justify the intrusion, the expense and the delay that may result. In the general run of cases it will not be justified. However, in *Re C (Abduction: Separate Representation of Children)* [2008] 2 FLR 6 the children's application to be separately represented was allowed because of their ages, understanding and experiences and because it was felt that it was more likely to cause them harm if they were not allowed to voice their views. This case also confirmed that in non-Convention cases the test of best interest should be applied on the issue of whether a child should be made a party to proceedings and the test in *Mabon v Mabon* [2005] 2 FLR 1011 was applied. This case was unusual not only because it related to four children who were actively objecting to removal but also because the court was dealing with the issue of returning the oldest child, who was over 16 and not subject to the Convention, under its inherent jurisdiction, where different welfare issues apply to those under the Convention.

Enforcement of order to return—Article 12 places a duty on the court to order the return of the child forthwith. In exercising that duty, the court has jurisdiction to enforce the order for return by issuing a writ of sequestration against the property of a third party, provided it is satisfied so that it is sure that the third party knew of the order requiring the return of the child and that he nevertheless deliberately frustrated the order or aided and abetted the abducting parent in avoiding compliance with the order (*Re S (Abduction: Sequestration)* [1995] 1 FLR 858).

Article 13

Notwithstanding the provisions of the preceding Article, the judicial or administrative authority of the requested State is not bound to order the return of the child if the person, institution or other body which opposes its return establishes that –

    (a)   the person, institution or other body having the care of the person of the child was not actually exercising the custody rights at the time of removal or retention, or had consented to or subsequently acquiesced in the removal or retention; or

(b) there is a grave risk that his or her return would expose the child to physical or psychological harm or otherwise place the child in an intolerable situation.

The judicial or administrative authority may also refuse to order the return of the child if it finds that the child objects to being returned and has attained an age and degree of maturity at which it is appropriate to take account of its views.

In considering the circumstances referred to in this Article, the judicial and administrative authorities shall take into account the information relating to the social background of the child provided by the Central Authority or other competent authority of the child's habitual residence.

Consent or acquiescence—The leading case on the meaning of consent or acquiescence is *Re H (Abduction: Acquiescence)* [1997] 1 FLR 872, in which the House of Lords laid down the following principles to be adopted when considering the meaning of "acquiescence" within Art 13 of the Convention:

(a) The English law concept of acquiescence, which was normally viewed objectively, had no direct application to the proper construction of Art 13. Under the Convention, it must have the same meaning and effect throughout the laws of all the Contracting States. Acquiescence in Art 13 means looking to the subjective state of mind of the wronged parent and asking has he in fact consented to the continued presence of the children in the jurisdiction to which they have been abducted. It is a question of the actual subjective intention of the wronged parent, not the outside world's perception of his intention.

(b) Acquiescence is a pure question of fact to be determined by the trial judge on the material before him. In the process of the fact-finding operation to ascertain the subjective intention, the court is more likely to attach weight to the contemporaneous express words and actions of the wronged party than to his subsequent bare assertions in evidence of his intention.

(c) The burden of proving that the wronged party has consented to, or acquiesced in, the abduction is on the abducting parent (See *Re P (Abduction: Consent)* [2004] 2 FLR 1057, CA).

(d) Judges should be slow to infer an intention to acquiesce from attempts by the wronged parent to effect a reconciliation, or agree a voluntary return of the abducted child.

(e) There is only one exception to this general principle. Where the words or actions of the wronged parent clearly and unequivocally lead the other parent to believe that the wronged parent is not asserting or going to assert his right to the summary return of the child and are inconsistent with such return, justice requires that the wronged parent be held to have acquiesced (for a recent example see *D v S* [2008] 2 FLR 293).

For recent cases on the application of this guidance and the issue of "subjective" and "non subjective" acquiescence see *Re G (Abduction: Withdrawal of Proceedings, Acquiescence and Habitual Residence)* [2008] 2 FLR 351; *D v S* (above); *B-G v B-G* [2008] 2 FLR 965; *Re E (Abduction: Intolerable Situation)* [2009] 2 FLR 485; and *Re H and L (Abduction: Acquiescence)* [2010] 2 FLR 1277.

The evidence to establish consent must be clear, compelling and unequivocal (*D v S (Abduction: Acquiescence)* [2008] 2 FLR 293; *Re R (Child Abduction: Acquiescence)* [1995] 1 FLR 716). Evidence of consent may be in writing or in documentary form but it is not necessary to provide the court with unequivocal written material to establish consent. It can be deduced from the words and conduct of the wronged parent; (*Re M (Abduction) (Consent: Acquiescence)* [1999] 1 FLR 171). It cannot be passive, but must be positive consent to the removal of the child (*Re W (Abduction: Procedure)* [1995] 1 FLR 878). A third party cannot give consent on behalf of the parent even if under the law of the foreign State such consent is permissible (*C v H (Abduction: Consent)* [2010] 1 FLR 225). In *Re P-J (Abduction: Habitual Residence)* [2009] 2 FLR 1051 and *K v K (Abduction) (No 1)* [2010] 1 FLR 1295 the suggestion that "consent" could be given after removal was rejected. An effective consent to removal can be given in advance provided it subsisted at the time of removal (*Re L (Abduction: Future Consent)* [2008] 1 FLR 914). A refusal by a custodial parent to assist the non-custodial parent in returning the child is unlikely to amount to acquiescence (*De L v H* [2010] 1 FLR 1229). The means of proof will vary according to the circumstances of the case, and may include the court receiving oral evidence from the parties (*Re C (Abduction: Consent)* [1996] 1 FLR 414).

The question of whether a purported consent to the child's removal is a valid consent will depend on the circumstances of the case (*Re S (A Child: Abduction)* [2003] 1 FLR 1008). Consent to the removal of a child may be valid even if it is dependent on a future event provided it is not too vague, uncertain or subjective and the facts at the time are not wholly or manifestly different to those prevailing at the time of removal (*Re L (Abduction: Future Consent)* [2008] 1 FLR 914) and may be conditional (*BT v JRT (Abduction: Conditional Acquiescence and Consent)* [2008] 2 FLR 972). A consent obtained by fraud or deception is unlikely to be regarded as valid (see *M v T (Abduction)* [2009] 1 FLR 1309; *Re B (Abduction:*

PART II

Art 13 Defence) [1997] 2 FLR 573, *Re B (A Minor) (Abduction)* [1994] 2 FLR 249 and *BT v JRT* (above)). The court should be slow to infer an intention to acquiesce from attempts by the wronged parent to effect a reconciliation or to reach an agreed voluntary return of the child (Arts 7(c), 10; *Re I (Abduction: Acquiescence)* [1999] 1 FLR 778; and *Re G (Abduction: Withdrawal of Proceedings, Acquiescence, Habitual Residence)* [2008] 2 FLR 351 – where a consent order had been made expressly on the basis that the parties were attempting a reconciliation). A similar approach applies to discussions between the parents after separation with a view to possible reconciliation (*M v M* [2007] 2 FLR 1010). Following *Re S (Abduction: Acquiescence)* [1998] 2 FLR 115, it was considered that reliance by the wronged parent on incorrect advice could not be regarded as acquiescence to a child's removal, but acting on "adequate and realistic advice" could. However, this issue has become confused as in *D v S* (above), Charles J appears to have held that it is not necessary to have received correct advice nor does the advice need to be "adequate or realistic". It is difficult to understand how "incorrect" advice can be adequate. In *B-G v B-G* [2008] 2 FLR 965 Coleridge J appears to have taken the view that full legal advice or knowledge is not necessary to conclude that the wronged parent has acquiesced. The only common factor which emerges from these cases is the fact that once a person becomes aware of the Convention and the process for the return of the child and fails to act expeditiously, he may be considered to have acquiesced.

Once acquiescence has been established, it is not necessary for the court to consider grave harm. The court can go on to consider what is in the child's best interest and how it should exercise its discretion on whether the child's return should be ordered (see *Re A (Minors) (Abduction: Acquiescence) (No 2)* [1993] 1 FLR 396) but in *D v S* (above) the court entered into a full inquiry on the evidence and made findings and expressed its views on the issue of welfare.

"grave risk"—As to the meaning of "grave risk", see *Re A (A Minor) (Abduction)* [1988] 1 FLR 365, CA: there must be a weighty risk of substantial harm (*C v B (Abduction: Grave Risk)* [2006] 1 FLR 1095). The Art 13(b) defence "is likely to apply in the most extreme cases, where evidence of the exposure to physical or psychological harm or otherwise place the child in an intolerable situation" (*Re D (A Minor) (Child Abduction) Note* [1989] 1 FLR 97). Following the decision in *Neulinger and Shuruk v Switzerland* [2011] 1 FLR 122 and the subsequent ruling in *Raban v Romania* (App No 25437/08) [2011] 1 FLR 1130, it was assumed that a return order could not be made under the Hague Convention unless the court had carried out an "in-depth investigation of the entire family situation". The Supreme Court ruled in *Re E (Children) (Abduction: Custody Appeal)* [2011] 2 FLR 758 that the Hague Convention is designed for the benefit of the children and not the adults and with the children's best interests as a primary consideration. In this respect, the best interests of a child are the need to be reunited with his/her parents as soon as possible so that one does not gain an unfair advantage over another through the passage of time and to be brought up in a sound environment; if a fair balance is struck between these two interests it is unlikely to raise any issue concerning any breach of Art 8. It also confirmed that the provision of Art 13(b) needed no gloss or elaboration and that the decision in *Neulinger* did not suggest any change in the principle of a summary process provided that the decision was not arbitrary or mechanical. Where allegations and counter-allegations were made, the court was required to consider what protective measures could be put in place in the Requesting State for the protection of the children. (See *Re Y (A Child)* [2013] All ER (D) 133 (Jan), where undertakings were considered to come within "protective measures" under Brussels IIA and the 1996 Convention. See also under s 5, above.) The court will require clear, compelling and substantial evidence of the grave risk or other intolerable situation, that is "a situation which this particular child in these particular circumstances should not be expected to tolerate", but contrast with *Re S (A Child) (Abduction: Rights of Custody)* [2012] 2 FLR 442 where the Supreme Court, while confirming its earlier decision, nevertheless concluded that if it is established that the mother would suffer such anxiety as to affect her mental health such that it would create an intolerable situation for the child, a return should not be ordered irrespective of whether on an objective basis her anxieties were reasonable or not. Subjective perceptions could found the defence under Art 13 and if there was a grave risk to the child, the source of the mother's anxieties are irrelevant. Although the court reaffirmed its decision in *Re E* (above), the non-return order in this case may have been fact-specific. Such risks were confirmed in *Re E* and *RS v KS (Abduction: Wrongful Retention)* above. See *Re S (Abduction: Custody Rights)* [2002] 2 FLR 815 – where the court considered the risk of harm posed by reason of terrorist attacks and held that the issue was whether there was a risk of specific harm to the particular child and not whether there was a general risk of harm (c f *Re D (Article 13(B): Non-Return)* [2006] 2 FLR 305 where the risk was specific and targeted and involved extreme violence and danger). The burden of proof lies on the person who opposes the peremptory return of a child on the grounds set out in Art 13(b) on the civil standard of proof to show exceptional circumstances for the court to justify exercising its discretion. It will rarely be appropriate to hear oral evidence (*Re E*, above). Such exceptional circumstances may include a situation that demonstrates the risk in the jurisdiction of the habitual residence of persecution, discrimination or some other overt harm, for example that the respondent would be subjected to criminal process or otherwise denied justice, or real fear for the safety of the mother and children: *Re D (Article 13(B): Non-Return)* [2006] 2 FLR 305.

To establish such exceptional circumstances, the court may permit expert evidence to be called as to the law and practice in the state of habitual residence, provided it does not lead to undue delay (*B v El-B (Abduction: Sharia Law: Welfare of Child)* [2003] 1 FLR 811). Domestic violence, even if proved in itself, will not be considered sufficient; it is only in exceptional circumstances that the court will be justified in making a non-return order. Where the facts establish an exceptional degree of violence on the mother, the court will consider its effect on the child and his/her needs and welfare and take these factors and other factors relevant to the mother into account to determine whether the threshold of grave harm is crossed (*DT v LBT* [2011] 1 FLR 1215, further confirmed by the Court of Appeal in *Re E (Children)* [2011] 2 FLR 724 and approved by the Supreme Court). However, see *Klentzeris v Klentzeris* [2007] 2 FLR 996 – where despite the provision of Brussels IIA, Art 11(4) the court did not consider it appropriate to return the children on the strength of the evidence of the Cafcass officer and *Re M (Abduction: Child's Objections)* [2007] 2 FLR 72 – where the exceptional welfare considerations were said to outweigh Convention considerations (cf *JPC v SLW and SMW (Abduction)* [2007] 2 FLR 900 – where a return was ordered to enable the Irish courts to determine the welfare issues). Where it is alleged that the applicant has breached conditions attached to an order made by a court in the requesting state, the proper course should be to return the children for that court to consider the issues raised on a renewed application: *C v B (Abduction: Grave Risk)* [2006] 1 FLR 1095. The evidence will be considered objectively. It has been held that the approach taken will be equivalent to that adopted when considering the hostility of a mother to contact (*Re M (Abduction: Intolerable Situation)* [2000] 1 FLR 930). See also *Re J (A Minor) (Abduction: Ward of Court)* [1990] 1 FLR 276; *Re N (Minors) (Abduction)* [1991] 1 FLR 413; *Re L (Child Abduction: Psychological Harm)* [1993] 2 FLR 401. In *Re M (Abduction: Acquiescence)* [1996] 1 FLR 315, the court found that a fuller investigation of the issue of risk, and the consequent need for protection, needed to be established. In *Re HB (Abduction: Children's Objections)* [1997] 1 FLR 392 complaints by the children of ill-treatment by their stepfather and mother were held not to be sufficiently serious to constitute deliberate ill-treatment so as to bring the case within Art 13. Having regard to the report by the Children Act Sub-Committee, which underlined the need for awareness of the effect of domestic violence on children, it remains to be seen whether in future the courts will consider the matters raised in that report, the joint report of Drs Sturge and Glaser ([2000] Fam Law 615) and the guidance given by the Court of Appeal in *Re L (Contact: Domestic Violence)*; *Re V (Contact: Domestic Violence)*; *Re M (Contact: Domestic Violence)*; *Re H (Contact: Domestic Violence)* [2000] 2 FLR 334, applied in *Re H (Contact: Domestic Violence)* [2006] 1 FLR 943, as relevant in reaching their rulings in cases under the Convention. In *Re W (Abduction: Domestic Violence)* [2005] 1 FLR 727, CA it was held that domestic violence was not by itself enough and the child was returned with protective measures by way of undertakings put in place (*F v M (Abduction: Grave Risk of Harm)* [2008] 2 FLR 1263). It may be helpful to utilise the arrangements for international co-operation between the liaison judges. See also *R v K (Abduction: Return Order)* [2010] 1 FLR 1456 for the use of undertakings and the article of Professor Bates "The Child Abduction Convention: Troubles in Australia" March [2007] *International Family Law*, 24).

The burden of proof on the defendant to establish that the exception should apply is a very heavy one (*Re E (A Minor) (Abduction)* [1989] 1 FLR 135). The court will require clear and compelling evidence (see *Re M (Child Abduction: Existence of Undertakings)* [2000] 3 FCR 693 and the cases cited therein). The court should not make findings on the basis of contested and untested allegations (*Re H (Abduction: Grave Risk)* [2003] 2 FLR 141). For the degree of intolerability that must be established, see *B v B (Abduction: Custody Rights)* [1993] 1 FLR 238; see also *C v C (Abduction: Jurisdiction)* [1994] 1 FCR 6, [1993] Fam Law 185, where a delay of 12 months for the proceedings to be heard in the foreign jurisdiction was held to fall within Art 13(b). Problems which arise from the fact of abduction and are self-induced will not generally suffice (*M v T (Abduction)* [2009] 1 FLR 1309). Evidence of a grave risk to the children of psychological harm if they are returned is likely to be more significant than the importance of the court marking its disapproval of the abducting parent's behaviour because the child's welfare will be the primary concern in Hague Convention proceedings (the UKSC's decision in *Re S (A Child) (Abduction: Rights of Custody)* [2012] 2 FLR 442).

The defence of grave risk of exposing the child to physical or psychological harm must be weighed both in the light of the immediate past and in comparative terms. As to the latter, the court is entitled to weigh the risk of psychological harm of return against the psychological consequences of refusing to order the return of the child. Where both risks are substantial, the court must, in exercising its discretion, give due weight to the primary purpose of the Convention, ie to ensure the swift return of abducted children (*N v N (Abduction: Article 13 Defence)* [1995] 1 FLR 107). See *DT v LBT* [2011] 1 FLR 1215, where the impact on one of the children who suffered from an autistic-spectrum disorder and the lack of any protective measures from the father's abusive behaviour led the court to conclude that the children would be at risk of psychological harm if returned (see also *B v B (Abduction: Child with Learning Difficulties)* [2012] 1 FLR 881, where the child suffered from Asperger's syndrome). However, the court confirmed that the decision in *Neulinger and Shuruk v Switzerland* [2011] 1 FLR 122 has not relaxed or lowered the threshold or brought about any "sea change" or "seismic shift" in the way the courts will in future deal with abduction cases. This decision has been confirmed by the Supreme Court in *Re E (Children) (Abduction: Custody Appeal)* [2011] 2 FLR 758. The judgments in *Re E* by the Court of Appeal ([2011] 2 FLR 724) and the Supreme Court ([2011] 2 FLR 758) should be read in full as they assess fully the effect of the decision in *Neulinger* and a number of other cases.

The child's objections—When this defence is raised, the court will need to carry out three discrete inquiries: (i) whether the objections are made out; (ii) whether the child is of sufficient age and maturity for the court to take account of its objections and whether in the circumstances it is appropriate to take account of his views; and (iii) whether the court should exercise its discretion. (See *M v T (Abduction)* above in which the children's views were influenced by the mother; and *Re E (Abduction: Intolerable Situation)* [2009] 2 FLR 485 where the child's objections were weighed against other relevant specific facts in the case when refusing a summary return; *Re M (Abduction: Child's Objections)* [2007] 2 FLR 72 and *Re C (Abduction: Separate Representation of Children)* [2008] 2 FLR 6). Where Brussels IIA, Art 11(2) applies the procedure to be followed has been set out in *Re F (Abduction: Child's Wishes)* [2007] 2 FLR 697, see *Re T (Abduction: Child's Objection to Return)* [2000] 2 FLR 192, CA for factors that may need to be considered when determining what, if any, weight should be attached to the child's views. In exercising the discretion, the conduct of both parties will be relevant, particularly where such conduct has led to delay (*Re L (Abduction: Child's Objections to Return)* [2002] 2 FLR 1042; *Re R (A Minor) (Abduction)* [1992] 1 FLR 105). For recent cases where these principles were applied, see *Re J (Abduction: Child's Objection to Return)* [2004] 2 FLR 64; *Re J and K (Abduction: Objections of Child)* [2005] 1 FLR 273 and *Zaffino v Zaffino (Abduction: Children's Views)* [2006] 1 FLR 410. In *Re M (Abduction: Habitual Residence: Relocation)* [2005] Fam Law 441, an 11 year old's preference was not directed to be further investigated by a Cafcass reporter on the ground that there was a likelihood that he had been influenced by his father; in *Re G (Abduction)* [2009] 1 FLR 760 an 11-year-old child's objections were considered to be objections to return to her father rather than Lithuania and she was returned in the care of her mother.

Expressed views of the children must be carefully and cautiously assessed, bearing in mind that the wishes and feelings which children express may vary according to mood, adult influence and/or their reaction to the person carrying out the assessment. There is no absolute threshold below which a child is not considered sufficiently mature to voice his objection. It is for the court to determine the attributes of the child and the nature of his objections to the return (*Re W (Abduction: Acquiescence: Children's Objections)* [2010] 2 FLR 1150 and upheld on appeal: *Re W (Abduction: Child's Objections)* [2010] 2 FLR 1165, where the views of children who were 8 and 6 years of age were taken into account). In *De L v H* [2010] 1 FLR 1229 the judge saw the child who was 13 in the presence of a Cafcass officer and was satisfied of the child's maturity and his strong, rational and sound objections and strong feelings about not wishing to return to the State of his habitual residence and exercised his discretion to refuse the child's return on the grounds that it would cause disruption, distress and feelings of disillusion. In *WF v FJ* [2011] 1 FLR 1153, the views of the older child aged 13 was considered to be strong enough to justify a non-return order in respect of the younger child, and it was also held that to split the siblings would result in placing them in an intolerable situation. see also *Re G (Abduction: Children's Objections)* [2011] 1 FLR 1645, *DT v LBT* [2011] 1 FLR 1215, *Re E (Children)* [2011] 2 FLR 724 and *B v B (Abduction: Child with Learning Difficulties)* [2012] 1 FLR 881.

In general, the younger the child is, the less likely it is that the child would have the maturity which would make it appropriate to take his views into account. Even where the child's views are taken into account, the court is not obliged to give effect to that preference. The decision whether to give effect to it must turn on the particular circumstances of each case (*Re R (Abduction: Hague and European Conventions)* [1997] 1 FLR 663 where the wishes of a 10-year-old were taken into account; *Re R (Child Abduction: Acquiescence)* [1995] 1 FLR 716). See also *Re F (Child Abduction: Risk if Returned)* [1995] 2 FLR 31, where the court declined to order the return of the child. In *Re M (Abduction: Child's Objections)* (above) due to the exceptional circumstances the child was returned, but in *JPC v SLW and SLW* [2007] 2 FLR 900 the court declined to make an order.

Where a child's objection to returning arises from a desire to remain with the abducting parent, little or no weight is given to the child's views (*A v A (Child Abduction)* [1993] 2 FLR 225). In *S v S (Child Abduction)* [1992] 2 FLR 31, a child aged nine but with a mental age of 12 put forward her views which were found to be mature and rational and based on genuine and cogent reasons. At first instance, the court refused to order her return; on appeal ([1992] 2 FLR 492), while confirming the decision, the court said that the scheme of the Convention was that in normal circumstances it is considered to be in the interest of children generally that they should be promptly returned to the country from which they have been wrongfully removed. It was only in exceptional circumstances that the court should have a discretion to refuse to order the child's immediate return. It was a question of fact for the judge whether the child's objections were genuine and whether the child had reached an age and maturity at which it was appropriate to take account of his or her views. See *Re H (Abduction)* [2007] 1 FLR 242 – where the exceptional circumstance test was found not to have been met although the child was 15 years of age and it was held that the test for grant of party status to children in abduction cases should not be relaxed.

The court's approach where there are siblings who express different views and are of a varying degree of maturity and understanding has varied. Cases contain seemingly conflicting decisions. In *Re HB (Abduction: Children's Objections)* [1997] 1 FLR 392 the older child's objections were not regarded as sufficient to outweigh the policy of the Convention that summary return should be ordered. In *The Ontario Court v M and M (Abduction: Children's Objections)* [1997] 1 FLR 475 the children were aged 2 and 10. The older child raised strong objections to returning to Canada to be cared for by her grandmother whom she disliked and feared. The court considered that to return her would place her in an intolerable situation within Art 13. See also *Zaffino v Zaffino (Abduction: Children's Views)* [2006] 1 FLR 410, *S v B (Abduction: Human Rights)* [2005] 2 FLR 878, and *WF v FJ, BF and RF (Abduction: Child's Objections)* [2011] 1 FLR 1153 the views of the older child aged 13 was considered to be strong enough to justify a non-return order in respect of the younger child, and it was also held that to split the siblings would result in placing them in an intolerable situation. See also *Re G (Abduction: Children's Objections)* [2011] 1 FLR 1645. The apparent conflict between these decisions can be rationalised on the basis that each case turned on its own facts. However, in *WF v FJ, BF and RF (Abduction: Child's Objections)* [2011] 1 FLR 1153 guidance is given on how to approach the issue of a child's objection to return and it was emphasised that the position of sibling groups should be considered "in the round".

Separate representation of children—See under Art 12, above.

Intolerable situation—In relation to a child, "intolerable" must mean "a situation which this particular child in these particular circumstances should not be expected to tolerate" (*Re D (Abduction: Rights of Custody)* [2007] 1 FLR 961, HL; see also *Re E (Children) (Abduction: Custody Appeal)* [2011] 2 FLR 758) and *Re S (A Child) (Abduction: Rights of Custody)* [2012] 2 FLR 442. It will be necessary to establish a high degree of intolerability (*E v E (Child Abduction: Intolerable Situation)* [1998] 2 FLR 980) – hardship or discomfort or the application of the religious laws or dual system of justice to a parent is insufficient (*Re S (Abduction: Intolerable Situation: Beth Din)* [2000] 1 FLR 454; *B v B (Abduction: Custody Rights)* [1993] 1 FLR 238, CA). The intolerability complained of must relate to the child. Litigation in a country and language foreign to both parents, resulting in financial chaos could render an order to return intolerable: *Re J (Abduction: Acquiring Custody Rights by Caring for Child)* [2005] 2 FLR 791. Problems created by the offending party's conduct (*Re C (Abduction: Grave Risk of Psychological Harm)* [1999] 1 FLR 1145) and dependence on welfare benefits (*Re M (Abduction: Undertakings)* [1995] 1 FLR 1021; *Re A (Minors) (Abduction: Acquiescence)* [1992] 2 FLR 14) are insufficient. Delay in the determination of the issues in the country of habitual residence may be considered as placing the child in an intolerable position (*C v C (Abduction: Jurisdiction)* [1994] 1 FCR 6). For the effect of Art 20 on the provisions of Art 13 and, in particular, Art 13(b) and the use of undertakings see *Re K (Abduction: Psychological Harm)* [1995] 2 FLR 550 and **Duty to order the return of the child and protection of human rights and fundamental freedoms** under Art 12. Note also the provisions of Brussels IIA, Art 11(4), which states that a court cannot refuse to return a child on the basis of the Hague Convention, Art 13(b) if it is "established that adequate arrangements have been made to secure the protection of the child after his return".

Abduction and the claim for asylum—The court's jurisdiction to order the return of an abducted child is not restricted by the provisions of the Immigration and Asylum Act 1999 and, in particular, the prohibition on removal under s 15 of the 1999 Act is directed at the immigration authorities. It is not intended to circumscribe the duty and discretion of a judge exercising the wardship, Convention or family jurisdiction (*Re S (Child Abduction: Asylum Appeal)* [2002] 2 FLR 465).

Art 13 and the welfare test—The welfare of the child in CACA 1985 cases is not the paramount consideration but a primary consideration (see **"grave risk"**, above). The court will apply a two-stage process when considering the application of Art 13, namely: (i) establish whether a prima facie case under the Article is made out; and (ii) consider whether or not to order the return of the children. The Art 13 threshold is strictly applied and it is only in exceptional circumstances that the court will consider not returning the children. See *Re S (A Child) (Abduction: Rights of Custody)* [2012] 2 FLR 442, *Re M (Abduction: Child's Objections)* [2007] 2 FLR 72 and *Klentzeris v Klentzeris* [2007] 2 FLR 996 where due to the exceptional circumstances welfare considerations outweighed Hague Convention considerations. *Re D (Abduction: Discretionary Return)* [2000] 1 FLR 24 is an example of the robust attitude adopted by the English courts. However, it could also be argued that the decision turned on the particular facts of the case. See also *Re M (Abduction: Conflict of Jurisdiction)* [2000] 2 FLR 372 for an example of how the High Court seeks to resolve conflicts between the application of two jurisdictions.

Article 14

In ascertaining whether there has been a wrongful removal or retention within the meaning of Article 3, the judicial or administrative authorities of the requested State may take notice directly of the law of, and of judicial or administrative decisions, formally recognised or not in the State of the habitual residence of the child, without recourse to the specific procedures for the proof of that law or for the recognition of foreign decisions which would otherwise be applicable.

Article 15

The judicial or administrative authorities of a Contracting State may, prior to the making of an order for the return of the child, request that the applicant obtain from the authorities of the State of the habitual residence of the child a decision or other determination that the removal or retention was wrongful within the meaning of Article 3 of the Convention, where such a decision or determination may be obtained in that State. The Central Authorities of the Contracting States shall so far as practicable assist applicants to obtain such a decision or determination.

Request by the judicial or administrative authorities of a Contracting State—The provisions of this Article should be read with those of s 8 which contemplates applications for the purposes of Art 15 to be made by any person who appears to have an interest in the matter. Its terms are broader than the limited ones set out in this Article. See *Re P (Abduction: Declaration)* [1995] 1 FLR 831 for an example of where the court applied the provisions of s 8, and proceeded to make a declaration although it involved making a preliminary decision on the issues of habitual residence and breach which were to be decided by the court in the requested State. It is, however, not appropriate to seek a declaration on a matter of interpretation of the Convention from the foreign court. This task falls to be determined by the Court seised of the application. Whether it would be right to seek an Article 15 determination would depend on the nature of the dispute, whether the parties intended to adduce expert evidence and the delay that would be caused (*Hunter v Murrow (Abduction: Rights of Custody)* [2005] 2 FLR 1119). In any event, an Article 15 determination made in another country is not binding on the English court (*Re J (A Minor)* [1990] 2 FLR 442).

Article 16

After receiving notice of a wrongful removal or retention of a child in the sense of Article 3, the judicial or administrative authorities of the Contracting State to which the child has been removed or in which it has been retained shall not decide on the merits of rights of custody until it has been determined that the child is not to be returned under this Convention or unless an application under this Convention is not lodged within a reasonable time following receipt of the notice.

"notice"—This reference is not restricted to notice from any particular source or in any particular form (*R v R (Residence Order: Child Abduction)* [1995] 2 FLR 625). As soon as the court learns that it is concerned with a child who has formerly lived abroad in a Convention country and one parent wishes, or may wish, to return to that country, a possible case under the Hague Convention may arise. If there is any doubt, the matter should be transferred to the High Court. It is the duty of the practitioners involved to draw the attention of the court to the possibility that the Hague Convention may apply (*Re H (Abduction: Habitual Residence: Consent)* [2000] 2 FLR 294).

Application—The machinery of the Convention contemplates a summary procedure, to be operated only once. There cannot be second or subsequent applications under the Convention. This principle also applies where the application has been made and the summary procedure has taken place in another Contracting State (*Re O (Child Abduction: Re-Abduction)* [1997] 2 FLR 712).

Lodging of application within a reasonable time—The question of what is reasonable time must be considered objectively but, unless the court makes a finding that no application has been lodged within a reasonable time, it should refrain from deciding the merits of right of custody and making a residence order including one which is interim (*R v R* (above)).

Procedural steps to be taken by the court—Where the court becomes seised of a matter relating to a child, and it becomes apparent that there has been wrongful removal or retention within the meaning of the Convention, the court has a duty to take steps to secure that the parent in the other State is informed of his rights under the Convention. The English central authority should be requested to inform the central authority of the State from which the child has been removed of the circumstances of the case. The court should also communicate with the parent in that State by means of directions to the effect that he should seek legal advice expeditiously as to his rights, and communicate with the central authority of his State, of which he should be given the name and address.

****

SCHEDULE 2
EUROPEAN CONVENTION ON RECOGNITION AND ENFORCEMENT OF DECISIONS CONCERNING CUSTODY OF CHILDREN

Liaison judge—See under Sch 1.

Article 1

For the purposes of this Convention:

(a) "child" means a person of any nationality, so long as he is under 16 years of age and has not the right to decide on his own place of residence under the law of his habitual residence, the law of his nationality or the internal law of the State addressed;

(b) "authority" means a judicial or administrative authority;

(c) "decision relating to custody" means a decision of an authority in so far as it relates to the care of the person of the child, including the right to decide on the place of his residence, or to the right of access to him;

(d) "improper removal" means the removal of a child across an international frontier in breach of a decision relating to his custody which has been given in a Contracting State and which is enforceable in such a State; "improper removal" also includes:

  (i) the failure to return a child across an international frontier at the end of a period of the exercise of the right of access to this child or at the end of any other temporary stay in a territory other than that where the custody is exercised;

  (ii) a removal which is subsequently declared unlawful within the meaning of Article 12.

Scope—Although this Convention provides for the recognition and enforcement of custody orders of Contracting Member States, it has been superseded by Brussels IIA and as from 1 November 2012 by the 1996 Hague Convention, as both these instruments take precedence over the European Convention. Thus, its provisions, save insofar as they relate to Denmark, are almost redundant.

****

Article 4

(1) Any person who has obtained in a Contracting State a decision relating to the custody of a child and who wishes to have that decision recognised or enforced in another Contracting State may submit an application for this purpose to the central authority in any Contracting State.

(2) The application shall be accompanied by the documents mentioned in Article 13.

(3) The central authority receiving the application, if it is not the central authority in the State addressed, shall send the documents directly and without delay to that central authority.

(4) The central authority receiving the application may refuse to intervene where it is manifestly clear that the conditions laid down by this Convention are not satisfied.

(5) The central authority receiving the application shall keep the applicant informed without delay of the progress of his application.

Procedure on application—See FPR 2010, rr 12.44–12.57 and FPR PD12F, para 20, but note that it is recognised that the European Convention has been superseded to a very great extent by the Council Regulations.

Determination of application—Determination of the application under the European Convention should not be made while Hague Convention proceedings are pending (*Re R (Abduction: Hague and European Conventions)* [1997] 1 FLR 663).

"decision relating to the custody of a child"—This term refers to a decision of an authority insofar as it relates to the care of the person of the child, including the right to decide on the place of his residence, or to the right of access to him (Art 1(c)). Where there is a subsisting order, it is irrelevant that the order was made before the ratification of the European Convention between England and the other Contracting party and, by virtue of Art 7, it is required to be recognised and enforced (*Re L (Child Abduction: European Convention)* [1992] 2 FLR 178). Where a final order has been made in matrimonial proceedings, permitting the mother to remove the children to England where they remain habitually resident, enforcement of any order for contact should be sought under Brussels IIA and not under the Convention (*Re G (Foreign Contact Order: Enforcement)* [2004] 1 FLR 378), and for a recent decision where Brussels IIA applied and the court assumed jurisdiction, see *Re S (Brussels II Revised: Enforcement of Contact Order)* [2008] 2 FLR 1358.

****

Article 7

A decision relating to custody given in a Contracting State shall be recognised and, where it is enforceable in the State of origin, made enforceable in every other Contracting State.

"decision relating to custody"—Where the abducting parent had notice of the proceedings for a residence and parental responsibility order, an ex parte residence order and an order requiring the abductor to return the child to England are enforceable in other Contracting States, because the recognition and enforcement of such an order could not be refused under the provisions of Art 9 (*Re S (Custody: Habitual Residence)* [1998] 1 FLR 122).

****

Article 9

(1) Recognition and enforcement may be refused if:

(a) in the case of a decision given in the absence of the defendant or his legal representative, the defendant was not duly served with the document which instituted the proceedings or an equivalent document in sufficient time to enable him to arrange his defence; but such a failure to effect service cannot constitute a ground for refusing recognition or enforcement where service was not effected because the defendant had concealed his whereabouts from the person who instituted the proceedings in the State of origin;

(b) in the case of a decision given in the absence of the defendant or his legal representative, the competence of the authority giving the decision was not founded:

   (i)   on the habitual residence of the defendant; or

   (ii) on the last common habitual residence of the child's parents, at least one parent being still habitually resident there, or

   (iii) on the habitual residence of the child;

(c) the decision is incompatible with a decision relating to custody which became enforceable in the State addressed before the removal of the child, unless the child has had his habitual residence in the territory of the requesting State for one year before his removal.

(3) In no circumstances may the foreign decision be reviewed as to its substance.

Scope—This Article provides for the court to refuse recognition and enforcement on procedural grounds; see *Re G (A Minor) (Child Abduction: Enforcement)* [1990] 2 FLR 325.

Recognition and enforcement—This should be construed disjunctively; thus, a court is entitled to refuse an order which has been registered, e g where it is found that, by reason of changes in the circumstances including the passage of time, the effects of the original decision are manifestly no longer in the interests of the child (*Re H (A Minor) (Foreign Custody Order: Enforcement)* [1994] 1 FLR 512). The provisions of this Article are discretionary, since the court *may* refuse to recognise and enforce the order (*Re G (A Minor) (Child Abduction: Enforcement)* [1990] 2 FLR 325).

"decision is incompatible with a decision ... enforceable in the State addressed" (Art 9(1)(c))—Recognition and enforcement was refused in *Re M (Child Abduction) (European Convention)* [1994] 1 FLR 551.

Review of foreign decision—Under no circumstances may the foreign decision be reviewed as to its substance; see also *Re A (Foreign Access Order: Enforcement)* [1996] 1 FLR 561 and *Re G (Foreign Contact Order: Enforcement)* [2004] 1 FLR 378.

Article 10

(1) Recognition and enforcement may also be refused on any of the following grounds –

    (a) if it is found that the effects of the decision are manifestly incompatible with the fundamental principles of the law relating to the family and children in the State addressed;

    (b) if it is found that by reason of a change in the circumstances including the passage of time but not including a mere change in the residence of the child after an improper removal, the effects of the original decision are manifestly no longer in accordance with the welfare of the child;

    (c) if at the time when the proceedings were instituted in the State of origin:

        (i) the child was a national of the State addressed or was habitually resident there and no such connection existed with the State of origin;

        (ii) the child was a national both of the State of origin and of the State addressed and was habitually resident in the State addressed;

    (d) if the decision is incompatible with a decision in the State addressed or enforceable in that State after being given in a third State, pursuant to proceedings begun before the submission of the request for recognition or enforcement, and if the refusal is in accordance with the welfare of the child.

(2) Proceedings for recognition or enforcement may be adjourned on any of the following grounds:

    (a) if an ordinary form of review of the original decision has been commenced;

    (b) if proceedings relating to the custody of the child, commenced before the proceedings in the State of origin were instituted, are pending in the State addressed;

    (c) if another decision concerning the custody of the child is the subject of proceedings for enforcement or of any other proceedings concerning the recognition of the decision.

Scope—This Article sets out the substantive ground for refusal of recognition and enforcement. See *Re G (A Minor) (Abduction: Enforcement)* [1990] 2 FLR 325; *Re F (Minors) (Custody: Foreign Order: Enforcement)* [1989] 1 FLR 335; *Re K (A Minor) (Abduction)* [1990] 1 FLR 387. Notwithstanding the mandatory terms of s 16(4), the use of the word "may" in the Article gives the court a discretion, but in *Re A (Foreign Contact Order: Jurisdiction)* [2004] 1 FLR 641 it was held that the Article should be construed and applied stringently. When Brussels IIA (Council Regulation (EC) No 2201/2003) applies, it takes precedence over the European Convention. However, if the court permits registration, in view of the provisions of Art 9(3) which prohibit a review of the foreign order, enforcement of that order must follow. Therefore, in exercising its discretion on whether to allow registration, the court will also necessarily have to consider the effect on the child of enforcing the order.

"effects of the original decision"—This refers to the effects of the enforcement of the decision, in particular in relation to the welfare of the child, at the date of the determination of the application by the requested State without delay, review or alteration. It does not refer to the effects of taking steps towards its enforcement or the return of the child to the State of origin to enable the original order to be enforced. This flows from:

"(a) the language of the phrase;
  (b) the underlying purpose of the European Convention which is concerned with the enforcement of existing orders made in the State of origin by the courts of the State addresses;
  (c) the terms of Art 7;
  (d) the terms of Art 5(1)(d);
  (e) Art 9(3) which precludes the State addressed from reviewing the substance of the original order; and
  (f) Art 10(2)(a) which provides for the possibility of adjournment if an ordinary review has been commenced". (*T v R* [2002] 2 FLR 544.)

Change in the circumstances and the child's views are relevant in respect of any dispute under Art 10(1)(b), unless this is impracticable having regard to the child's age and understanding (Art 15(1)(a)). A report by a Cafcass reporter may be ordered to ascertain the child's feelings and views (see also *Re T (Abduction: Appointment of Guardian ad Litem)* below).

"Incompatible with the fundamental principles of family law"—Foreign law relating to the importance of contact and its conclusion that the residence of a child should be changed when a custodial parent opposes and refuses contact with the other parent (which does not reasonably warrant such opposition), is not incompatible with the approach to residence and contact in England having regard to the welfare principle and the application of the welfare check list (see *T v R* (above) and *Re M (Child Abduction) (European Convention)* [1994] 1 FLR 551).

"improper removal"—For definition see Art 1(c) and note that the phrase "decisions relating to custody" includes access. Any action which thwarts such access by the removal of the child to another jurisdiction amounts to improper removal (see *T v R* (above)).

Issues to be determined—The essential tasks of the court under this Article are: to establish what the circumstances were at the time of the original decision; to ascertain whether any or all of the grounds set out in the Article have been proved; and whether the original decision can no longer be sustained because it does not accord with the welfare of the child (*Re R (Abduction: Hague and European Conventions)* [1997] 1 FLR 663).

"manifestly no longer in accordance with the welfare of the child"—It is only in circumstances where it is clear that a return of the child would be manifestly against the interest of the child, and that the original decision is manifestly no longer in accordance with the welfare of the child, that the court should exercise its discretion not to comply with the spirit and terms of the Act and Convention. The party who seeks to persuade the court as to this bears a very high burden of proof (*Re L (Child Abduction: European Convention)* [1992] 2 FLR 178). See also *Re A (Foreign Access Order: Enforcement)* [1996] 1 FLR 561, where the decision was found not to come within the exceptions provided by Art 10(2). In appropriate cases a child may be joined as a party to the proceedings and represented by a children's guardian (*Re T (Abduction: Appointment of Guardian Ad Litem)* [1999] 2 FLR 796). Although recognition and enforcement may be refused, the court under its inherent jurisdiction may go on to consider what is the appropriate forum for determining the welfare of the child and any dispute relating to the child's residence and contact and whether, in the circumstances, it would be in the interests of the child to order his/her return while the dispute is resolved in the appropriate forum.

Article 11

(1) Decisions on rights of access and provisions of decisions relating to custody which deal with the rights of access shall be recognised and enforced subject to the same conditions as other decisions relating to custody.

(2) However, the competent authority of the State addressed may fix the conditions for the implementation and exercise of the right of access taking into account, in particular, undertakings given by the parties on this matter.

(3) Where no decision on the right of access has been taken or where recognition or enforcement of the decision relating to custody is refused, the central authority of the State addressed may apply to its competent authorities for a decision on the right of access if the person claiming a right of access so requests.

Discretion to fix condition—Conditions may be imposed to implement and to exercise right of access. This discretion must be exercised in the light of Art 9(3), which provides that under no circumstances may a foreign decision be reviewed as to its substance (*Re A (Foreign Access Order: Enforcement)* [1996] 1 FLR 561). See *Re G (Foreign Contact Order: Enforcement)* [2004] 1 FLR 378, where the court directed that the father should have preliminary visiting contact as a condition of implementation of the original order.

Article 12

Where, at the time of the removal of a child across an international frontier, there is no enforceable decision given in a Contracting State relating to his custody, the provisions of this Convention shall apply to any subsequent decision, relating to the custody of that child and declaring the removal to be unlawful, given in a Contracting State at the request of any interested person.

Declaration of unlawful removal—Art 12 prohibits the continued retention of a child when an enforceable decision relating to his custody has been made in a Contracting State. Once the court has found that the child has been wrongfully removed or retained under Art 3 of the Hague Convention, it can give a declaration that he has been unlawfully removed from the jurisdiction contrary to Art 12 (*Re S (Custody: Habitual Residence)* [1998] 1 FLR 122, HL).

"any subsequent decision"—Where the father of an illegitimate child did not have any custody or parental responsibility order in his favour relating to his child who had been unlawfully removed to Denmark, but obtained an ex parte residence order and an order requiring the mother to return the child to the father in England, it was held that the removal of the child was covered by the provisions of s 23(2) and thereby entitled the court to make a declaration under Art 12 that the removal of the child was unlawful (*Re S (Custody: Habitual Residence)* [1998] 1 FLR 122).

Article 13

(1) A request for recognition or enforcement in another Contracting State of a decision relating to custody shall be accompanied by:

    (a) a document authorising the central authority of the State addressed to act on behalf of the applicant or to designate another representative for that purpose;

    (b) a copy of the decision which satisfies the necessary conditions of authenticity;

    (c) in the case of a decision given in the absence of the defendant or his legal representative, a document which establishes that the defendant was duly served with the document which instituted the proceedings or an equivalent document;

    (d) if applicable, any document which establishes that, in accordance with the law of the State of origin, the decision is enforceable;

    (e) if possible, a statement indicating the whereabouts or likely whereabouts of the child in the State addressed;

    (f) proposals as to how the custody of the child should be restored.

****

Article 15

(1) Before reaching a decision under paragraph (1)(b) of Article 10, the authority concerned in the State addressed:

    (a) shall ascertain the child's views unless this is impracticable having regard in particular to his age and understanding; and

(b)   may request that any appropriate enquiries be carried out.

(2) The cost of enquiries in any Contracting State shall be met by the authorities of the State where they are carried out.

Requests for enquiries and the results of enquiries may be sent to the authority concerned through the central authorities.

****

Article 26

(1) In relation to a State which has in matters of custody two or more systems of law of territorial application:

(a)   reference of the law of a person's habitual residence or to the law of a person's nationality shall be construed as referring to the system of law determined by the rules in force in that State or, if there are no such rules, to the system of law with which the person concerned is most closely connected;

(b)   reference to the State of origin or to the State addressed shall be construed as referring, as the case may be, to the territorial unit where the decision was given or to the territorial unit where recognition or enforcement of the decision or restoration of custody is requested.

(2) Paragraph (1)(a) of this Article also applies mutatis mutandis to States which have in matters of custody two or more systems of law of personal application.

SCHEDULE 3

CUSTODY ORDERS

PART I
ENGLAND AND WALES

1 The following are the orders referred to in section 27(1) of this Act –

(a)   a care order under the Children Act 1989 (as defined by section 31(11) of that Act, read with section 105(1) and Schedule 14);

(b)   a residence order (as defined by section 8 of the Act of 1989);

(bb)   a special guardianship order (within the meaning of the Act of 1989); and

(c)   any order made by a court in England and Wales under any of the following enactments –

(i)   section 9(1), 10(1)(a) of the Guardianship of Minors Act 1971;

(ii)   section 42(1) or (2) or 43(1) of the Matrimonial Causes Act 1973;

(iii)   section 2(2)(b), (4)(b) or (5) of the Guardianship Act 1973 as applied by section 34(5) of the Children Act 1975;

(iv)   section 8(2)(a), 10(1) or 19(1)(ii) of the Domestic Proceedings and Magistrates' Courts Act 1978.

Amendments—CA 1989, s 108(5), Sch 13, para 57(3); ACA 2002, Sch 3, para 45.

2 An order made by the High Court in the exercise of its jurisdiction relating to wardship so far as it gives the care and control of a child to any person.

3 (*repealed*)

4 An authorisation given by the Secretary of State under section 26(2) of the Children and Young Persons Act 1969 (except where the relevant order, within the meaning of that section, was made by virtue of the court which made it being satisfied that the child was guilty of an offence).

PART II
SCOTLAND

5 An order made by a court of civil jurisdiction in Scotland under any enactment or rule of law with respect to the residence, custody, care or control of a child or contact with or access to a child, excluding –

    (i)   an order placing a child under the supervision of a local authority;

    (ii), (iia)   (*repealed*)

    (iii)   an order relating to the guardianship of a child;

    (iv)   an order made under section 86 of the Children (Scotland) Act 1995;

    (v)   an order made, or warrant or authorisation granted, under or by virtue of Chapter 2 or 3 of Part II of the Children (Scotland) Act 1995 to remove the child to a place of safety or to secure accommodation, to keep him at such a place or in such accommodation, or to prevent his removal from a place where he is being accommodated (or an order varying or discharging any order, warrant or authorisation so made or granted);

    (vi)   an order made in proceedings under this Act;

    (vii)   an adoption order (as defined in section 28(1) of the Adoption and Children (Scotland) Act 2007);

    (viii)   a permanence order (as defined in subsection (2) of section 80 of that Act) which includes provision such as is mentioned in paragraph (c) of that subsection.

Amendments—FLA 1986, s 68(1), Sch 1, para 31; Children (Scotland) Act 1995, s 105(4), Sch 4, para 37(6)(a); SI 2011/1740.

5A The reference in paragraph 5(viii) to a permanence order includes a deemed permanence order having effect by virtue of article 13(1), 14(2), 17(1) or 19(2) of the Adoption and Children (Scotland) Act 2007 (Commencement No 4, Transitional and Savings Provisions) Order 2009.

Amendments—Inserted by SI 2011/1740.

6 A supervision requirement made by a children's hearing under section 70 of the Children (Scotland) Act 1995 (whether or not continued under section 73 of that Act) or made by the sheriff under section 51(5)(c)(iii) of that Act and any order made by a court in England and Wales or in Northern Ireland if it is an order which, by virtue of section 33(1) of that Act, has effect as if it were such a supervision requirement.

Amendments—Substituted by Children (Scotland) Act 1995, s 105(4), Sch 4, para 37(6)(b).

7 (*repealed*)

PART III
NORTHERN IRELAND

8 The following orders –

(a) a care order under the Children (Northern Ireland) Order 1995 (as defined by Article 49(1) of that Order read with Article 2(2) and Schedule 8);

(b) a residence order (as defined by Article 8 of that Order);

(c) any order made by a court in Northern Ireland under any of the following enactments –

    (i) section 5 of the Guardianship of Infants Act 1886 (except so far as it relates to costs);

    (ii) section 49 of the Mental Health Act (Northern Ireland) 1961;

    (iii) Article 45(1) or (2) or 46 of the Matrimonial Causes (Northern Ireland) Order 1978;

    (iv) Article 10(2)(a), 12(1) or 20(1)(ii) of the Domestic Proceedings (Northern Ireland) Order 1980;

    (v) Article 27(1)(b) of the Adoption (Northern Ireland) Order 1987.

Amendments—Substituted by SI 1995/756.

9 An order made by the High Court in the exercise of its jurisdiction relating to wardship so far as it gives the care and control of a child to any person.

10 (*repealed*)

Child Support Act 1991

ARRANGEMENT OF SECTIONS
The basic principles

The basic principles

General note—CSA 1991 has been extensively amended by four later substantive sets of legislation: by the Child Support Act 1995, the Social Security Act 1998, the Child Support, Pensions and Social Security Act 2000 and by the CMOPA 2008. Under the 2008 Act, the Secretary of State for Work and Pensions retains responsibility for the scheme (released until August 2012 to the Child Maintenance and Enforcement Commission).

The earlier 2000 Act introduced the enabling legislation for a new system of calculation of child support maintenance which came into operation on 3 March 2003 in respect of calculations made *on or after* that date (although pre-3 March 2003 assessments continue under the old rules).

Court action under and in relation to the Act can proceed in seven different courts and tribunals, as set out below. The tribunal structure for appeals against decisions under the scheme has been extensively amended by the Tribunals Courts and Enforcement Act 2007 ("TCEA 2007"): appeals under CSA 1991, s 20 lie to the First-tier Tribunal (formerly an appeal tribunal) and then ("on a question of law, and with permission": CSA 1991, s 24) to the Upper Tribunal. These appeals are outside the scope of *The Family Court Practice*.

Child support and Income Support—The link between child support and state benefits (latterly only Income Support) ended with the repeal of CSA 1991, s 6, with effect from 14 July 2008 (SI 2008/1476).

The Child Support Act 1991 – procedural overview

The seven judicial systems with jurisdiction

Court	Types of application covered	CSA 1991 reference	Procedure
1 Magistrates' courts	(1) Liability order	s 33	MCR 1981
	(2) Committal/ disqualification	ss 39A, 40	MCR 1981
	(3) Deduction from earnings order appeal	C&E Regs, reg 22	MCR 1981
	(4) Declaration of parentage (FLA 1986, s 55A)	s 27	FPR 2010, rr 8.18(b), 8.19
	(5) Parentage appeals from Secretary of State decisions	CSA 1991, s 20	FPC(CSA 1991)R 1993
2 County courts	(1) Declaration of parentage (FLA 1986, s 55A)	s 27	FPR 2010, r 8.18(b)
	(2) Charging order	s 36	FPR 2010, Pt 33, Ch 8
	(3) Third party debt order	s 36	FPR 2010, Pt 33, Ch 7

Court	Types of application covered	CSA 1991 reference	Procedure
	(4) Appeals from magistrates at 1 above	Magistrates' Courts Act 1980 s 111A	FPR 2010, Pt 30
	(5) Appeals from deduction orders	CSA 1991, ss 32A, 32E and 32G	CS(CE)R 1992 (SI 1992/1989), reg 25B
3A High Court – Family Division	Declaration of parentage (FLA 1986, s 55A)	s 27	FPR 2010, r 8.18(b)
3B High Court	Judicial Review	SCA 1981, s 29	CPR 1998, Pt 54
4 First–tier Tribunal	Appeals from CSA ss 11, 16 and 17	s 20	(Outside scope of FCP)
5 Upper Tribunal	Appeals on a point of law from appeal tribunal	s 24, TCEA 2007, s 11	(Outside scope of FCP)
6 Court of Appeal	Appeals on a point of law from the Commissioners	TCEA 2007, s 13	CPR 1998, Pt 52
7 Supreme Court	Appeal from Court of Appeal	N/a	SCPD

1 The duty to maintain

(1) For the purposes of this Act, each parent of a qualifying child is responsible for maintaining him.

(2) For the purposes of this Act, a non-resident parent shall be taken to have met his responsibility to maintain any qualifying child of his by making periodical payments of maintenance with respect to the child of such amount, and at such intervals, as may be determined in accordance with the provisions of this Act.

(3) Where a maintenance calculation made under this Act requires the making of periodical payments, it shall be the duty of the non-resident parent with respect to whom the calculation was made to make those payments.

Amendments—CSPSSA 2000, ss 1(2), 26, Sch 3, para 11(1),(2).

Defined terms—"non-resident parent": s 3(2); "child": s 55(1); "maintenance calculation", "parent": s 54; "periodical payments": s 3(6); "qualifying child": s 3(1).

"parent" (s 1(1))—The term is defined narrowly at s 54 to comprise only those "in law the mother or father of the child". Adoptive parents are included, but step-parents are not.

"child" (s 1(2))—The term is extensively defined at s 55 in markedly different terms from, for example, "child of the family" in MCA 1973, s 52(1) and CA 1989, s 105(1) and "child" in CA 1989, s 105(1).

"periodical payments" and "maintenance" (s 1(2),(3))—The scheme uses these terms more or less interchangeably; but the term most used is "child support maintenance" (s 3(6)).

"calculation" (s 1(3))—This term has replaced "assessment" throughout CSA 1991 for all cases started from 3 March 2003. It reflects the fact that the original assessment process has been simplified in the amended Act. Calculation is carried out by the Secretary of State in accordance with s 11 and Sch 1.

2 Welfare of children: the general principle

Where, in any case which falls to be dealt with under this Act, the Secretary of State is considering the exercise of any discretionary power conferred by this Act, the Secretary of State shall have regard to the welfare of any child likely to be affected by the decision.

Amendments—Social Security Act 1998, s 86, Sch 7, para 18, Sch 8; CMOPA 2008, s 13(4), Sch 3, paras 1, 2; SI 2012/2007.

Defined terms—"child": s 55(1).

Judicial review: discretion—Only decisions under CSA 1991 (mostly as to calculation under s 11 or revision or supersession) can be appealed against under CSA 1991. Where a decision-maker exercises a discretion (e g as to whether to enforce arrears of child support maintenance or quantification of arrears) there is no statutory appeal under the 1991 Act. Such a decision can only be challenged by means of judicial review (see e g *R v Secretary of State for Social Security ex parte Biggin* [1995] 1 FLR 851). To succeed in an application for judicial review the applicant must show that factors, including the following, apply in relation to the decision:

(a) that the decision-maker has failed to act in accordance with the rules of natural justice (breach of his duty to act fairly);

(b) that the *Wednesbury* principle applies (*Associated Provincial Picture Houses Limited v Wednesbury Corporation* (1947) FLR Rep 44, CA). Is the decision such that the decision-maker in the performance of his duties, properly directing himself on the relevant law and acting reasonably, could have reached the decision in question?

(c) that the decision-maker has acted in a way that is procedurally incorrect (e g considered s 2; given notice to appropriate parties etc).

Procedure for judicial review—Procedure for judicial review is covered by CPR 1998, Pt 54 (and see Procedural Guide E1). The Upper Tribunal is intended also to have judicial review powers (TCEA 2007, ss 15–19); for judicial review procedure in the Upper Tribunal, see Tribunal Procedure (Upper Tribunal) Rules 2008/2698, Pt 4.

"he shall have regard"—That is to say, the welfare of the child is only one of the factors, not the paramount consideration, for the Secretary of State, but it is a factor for which the Secretary of State has a statutory duty to have regard (*Brookes v Secretary of State for Work and Pensions* [2010] 2 FLR 1038).

"any child"—The reference to "*any* child likely to be affected" (emphasis supplied) makes it clear that it is not only qualifying children who are entitled to be considered; though in practice their welfare may weigh more heavily with the decision-maker than that of other children. The definition would include children living with the person with care in her household, but it could also include children in the non-resident parent's household who might, for example, be affected by his committal to prison (*Brookes*, above, provides an example of this: none of the children in the case were qualifying children).

3 Meaning of certain terms used in this Act

(1) A child is a "qualifying child" if –

    (a) one of his parents is, in relation to him, a non-resident parent; or

    (b) both of his parents are, in relation to him, non-resident parents.

(2) The parent of any child is a "non-resident parent", in relation to him, if –

    (a) that parent is not living in the same household with the child; and

    (b) the child has his home with a person who is, in relation to him, a person with care.

(3) A person is a "person with care", in relation to any child, if he is a person –

    (a) with whom the child has his home;

    (b) who usually provides a day to day care for the child (whether exclusively or in conjunction with any other person); and

    (c) who does not fall within a prescribed category of person.

(4) The Secretary of State shall not, under subsection (3)(c), prescribe as a category –

    (a) parents;

    (b) guardians;

    (c)   persons in whose favour residence orders under section 8 of the Children Act 1989 are in force;

    (d)   in Scotland, persons with whom a child is to live by virtue of a residence order under section 11 of the Children (Scotland) Act 1995.

(5) For the purposes of this Act there may be more than one person with care in relation to the same qualifying child.

(6) Periodical payments which are required to be paid in accordance with a maintenance calculation are referred to in this Act as "child support maintenance".

(7) Expressions are defined in this section only for the purposes of this Act.

Amendments—Children (Scotland) Act 1995, s 105(4), Sch 4, para 52; CSPSSA 2000, ss 1(2)(a), 26, Sch 3, para 11(1),(2).

Defined terms—"child": s 55(1); "guardian": CA 1989, s 5.

"person with care" (s 3(3))—The person who has care of the child and is therefore entitled to seek a maintenance calculation against the non-resident parent(s). The person with care need not be a parent of the child, nor need they have parental responsibility (within the terms of CA 1989, s 3) for the child. There may be more than one person with care (s 3(5); and see *C v Secretary of State for Work and Pensions and B* [2003] 1 FLR 829, CA).

"prescribed category of person" (s 3(3)(c))—Child Support (Maintenance Calculation Procedure) Regulations 2001, reg 21 prescribes, for the purposes of s 3(3)(c), local authorities and foster parents with whom a child is placed when looked after by the local authority under CA 1989, s 22, who cannot therefore be a person with care.

4 Child support maintenance

(1) A person who is, in relation to any qualifying child or any qualifying children, either the person with care or the non-resident parent may apply to the Secretary of State for a maintenance calculation to be made under this Act with respect to that child, or any of those children.

(2) Where a maintenance calculation has been made in response to an application under this section the Secretary of State may, if the person with care or non-resident parent with respect to whom the calculation was made applies to the Secretary of State under this subsection, arrange for –

    (a)   the collection of the child support maintenance payable in accordance with the calculation;

    (b)   the enforcement of the obligation to pay child support maintenance in accordance with the calculation.

(3) Where an application under subsection (2) for the enforcement of the obligation mentioned in subsection (2)(a) authorises the Secretary of State to take steps to enforce that obligation whenever the Secretary of State considers it necessary to do so, the Secretary of State may act accordingly.

(4) A person who applies to the Secretary of State under this section shall, so far as that person reasonably can, comply with such regulations as may be made by the Secretary of State with a view to the Secretary of State being provided with the information which is required to enable –

    (a)   the non-resident parent to be identified or traced (where that is necessary);

    (b)   the amount of child support maintenance payable by the non-resident parent to be calculated; and

    (c)   that amount to be recovered from the non-resident parent.

(5) Any person who has applied to the Secretary of State under this section may at any time request the Secretary of State to cease acting under this section.

(6) It shall be the duty of the Secretary of State to comply with any request made under subsection (5) (but subject to any regulations made under subsection (8)).

(7) The obligation to provide information which is imposed by subsection (4) –

(a) shall not apply in such circumstances as may be prescribed; and
(b) may, in such circumstances as may be prescribed, be waived by the Secretary of State.

(8) The Secretary of State may by regulations make such incidental, supplemental or transitional provision as he thinks appropriate with respect to cases in which he is requested to cease to act under this under this section.

(9) (*repealed*)

(10) No application may be made at any time under this section with respect to a qualifying child or any qualifying children if –

(a) there is in force a written maintenance agreement made before 5 April 1993, or a maintenance order made before a prescribed date, in respect of that child or those children and the person who is, at that time, the non-resident parent; or
(aa) a maintenance order made on or after the date prescribed for the purposes of paragraph (a) is in force in respect of them, but has been so for less than the period of one year beginning with the date on which it was made; or
(ab) a maintenance agreement –
  (i) made on or after the date prescribed for the purposes of paragraph (a); and
  (ii) registered for execution in the Books of Council and Session or the sheriff court books,
  is in force in respect of them, but has been so for less than the period of one year beginning with the date on which it was made.

(11) (*repealed*)

Amendments—Child Support Act 1995, s 18; Social Security Act 1998, s 86, Sch 7, para 19, Sch 8; CSPSSA 2000, s 2(1),(2); CMOPA 2008, ss 1(2), s 2(1),(3), ss 13(4), 26, 35(1), s 58, Sch 3, paras 1, 3, 11(1)–(3)(a), Sch 8; SI 2012/2007.

Defined terms—"non-resident parent": s 3(2); "child": s 55(1); "child support maintenance": s 3(6); "maintenance calculation", "parent": s 54; "periodical payments": s 3(6); "qualifying child": s 3(1).

Outline of child support calculation—There are now three schemes running in parallel:
- Original scheme under CSA 1991 (April 1993 – 2 March 2003): **CS1**
- Scheme under CSPSSA 2000 from 3 March 2003 (**CS2**)
- Gross income scheme under CMOPA 2008 (**CS3**) starting 12 December 2012 for cases on a "pathfinder" (ie pilot scheme) basis

Calculation and effective date

Under CS2 and CS3, the calculation goes through up to four stages: (1) calculation based on earned income and number of qualifying children; adjustment for (2) "relevant other children" and (3) "shared care"; and (4) revision/supersession to take account of any variation direction. Figures below are weekly amounts. For CS3, the sources for the new gross income calculations are:
- CSA 1991, s 11 and Sch 1 (inserted by CMOPA 2008)
- Child Support Maintenance Calculation Regulations 2012 (CSMCR 2012)

Stage 1

The first stage is to assess whether the payer is a "basic", "reduced", "flat" or "nil" rate payer, as follows.

Basic rate
CS2 – net earned income of £200–£2,000 a week
- 15% for one qualifying child
- 20% for two qualifying children
- 25% for three or more qualifying children

CS3 – (1) Gross income of £200–£800 a week

- 12% for one qualifying child
- 16% for two qualifying children
- 19% for three or more qualifying children

(2) Gross income of £800–£3,000 a week

- 9% for one qualifying child
- 12% for two qualifying children
- 15% for three qualifying children and more

Reduced rate—Takes the calculation on a straight-line graph from £7 where payments are required at the flat rate to payments at the basic rate on an income of £200 or more, achieved by reference to a formula in CSA 1991, Sch 1.

Flat rate—Income less than £100 a week and certain prescribed benefits: £7 a week is the fixed amount of child support maintenance.

Stage 2

Relevant other children—Where the non-resident parent is living in a household where there are other dependent children, his income is reduced proportionately before the Stage 1 calculation is carried out, as follows:

For CS2

- 12% where the non-resident parent has one relevant other child;
- 16% where the non-resident parent has two relevant other children;
- 19% where the non-resident parent has three or more relevant other children

For CS3

- 12% where the non-resident parent has one relevant other child;
- 16% where the non-resident parent has two relevant other children;
- 19% where the non-resident parent has three or more relevant other children

Stage 3 – shared care

If the non-resident parent has "shared care" for an average of one night a week or more, there is a proportionate reduction to the calculation: $\frac{1}{7}$ for 52 days and more a year, $\frac{2}{7}$ for 104, etc (CSA 1991, Sch 1 para 7).

Stage 4 – variation directions

CSA 1991 (as amended), ss 28A–28F, Schs 4A and 4B and Child Support (Variations) Regulations 2000 (CS3 variation regulations are in CSMCR 2012).

"either the person with care or the non-resident parent may apply" (s 4(1))—Either the person with care or the non-resident parent of the qualifying children may apply. There may be circumstances where the payment under the pre-March 2003 scheme would have been less than under the new. Broadly, the non-resident parent whose gross income exceeds £75,000 will pay more under the new scheme than the old.

Request to Secretary of State to "cease acting" (s 4(5),(6))—In respect of a current assessment (old scheme), or a maintenance calculation, the parent with care may request the Secretary of State to "cease acting" (s 4(5)) in collection and recovery of child support maintenance (e g where private arrangements are made between the parties concerning payments and repayment of any arrears). The assessment or calculation then terminates. There may then remain a live issue as to whether arrears due to the Secretary of State will be pursued by him (and this must be borne in mind in connection with any case settled under this provision).

"a maintenance order made on or after the date prescribed" (s 4(10)(aa))—As a result of s 4(10(aa)) no application for child support maintenance under s 4 can be made within 1 year of a court-ordered child periodical payments order, where that original order post-dates the "prescribed" date (i e 3 March 2003 (see SI 2003/194)). The order ceases to have effect on the effective date of the application (see below). Either parent may apply to the Secretary of State under s 4 after the s 4(10(aa) 1-year period. This provision does not apply to pre-March 2003 orders, which are immune from application under s 4 (and also under s 6, which is repealed with effect from 14 July 2008 (SI 2008/1476)).

Effective date—In the case of a new calculation made where there is an existing court order, the order "ceases to have effect on the effective date of the maintenance calculation" (CS(MAJ)R 1992, reg 3(2)).

That effective date – when the new maintenance arrangements start to run – is "two months and two days after the application [for a calculation] is made". Until that date payments under the order will continue to run.

Variation of periodical payments orders—So long as the order remains effective either parent may apply to the originating court for a variation of child periodical payments (CSA 1991, s 8(3A); MCA 1973, s 31(1)).

****

8 Role of the courts with respect to maintenance for children

(1) This subsection applies in any case where the Secretary of State would have jurisdiction to make a maintenance calculation with respect to a qualifying child and a non-resident parent of his on an application duly made by a person entitled to apply for such a calculation with respect to that child.

(2) Subsection (1) applies even though the circumstances of the case are such that the Secretary of State would not make a calculation if it were applied for.

(3) Except as provided in subsection (3A), in any case where subsection (1) applies, no court shall exercise any power which it would otherwise have to make, vary or revive any maintenance order in relation to the child and non-resident parent concerned.

(3A) In any case in which section 4(10) or 7(10) prevents the making of an application for a maintenance calculation, and –

    (a) no application has been made for a maintenance calculation under section 6, or

    (b) such an application has been made but no maintenance calculation has been made in response to it, subsection (3) shall have effect with the omission of the word 'vary'.

(3A) Unless a maintenance calculation has been made with respect to the child concerned, subsection (3) does not prevent a court from varying a maintenance order in relation to that child and the non-resident parent concerned –

    (a) if the maintenance order was made on or after the date prescribed for the purposes of section 4(10)(a) or 7(10)(a); or

    (b) where the order was made before then, in any case in which section 4(10) or 7(10) prevents the making of an application for a maintenance calculation with respect to or by that child.

(4) Subsection (3) does not prevent a court from revoking a maintenance order.

(5) The Lord Chancellor or in relation to Scotland the Lord Advocate may by order provide that, in such circumstances as may be specified by the order, this section shall not prevent a court from exercising any power which it has to make a maintenance order in relation to a child if –

    (a) a written agreement (whether or not enforceable) provides for the making, or securing, by a non-resident parent of the child of periodical payments to or for the benefit of the child; and

    (b) the maintenance order which the court makes is, in all material respects, in the same terms as that agreement.

(5A) The Lord Chancellor may make an order under subsection (5) only with the concurrence of the Lord Chief Justice.

(6) This section shall not prevent a court from exercising any power which it has to make a maintenance order in relation to a child if –

    (a) a maintenance calculation is in force with respect to the child;

    (b) the non-resident parent's gross weekly income exceeds the figure referred to in paragraph 10(3) of Schedule 1 (as it has effect from time to time pursuant to regulations made under paragraph 10A(1)(b)); and

(c) the court is satisfied that the circumstances of the case make it appropriate for the non-resident parent to make or secure the making of periodical payments under a maintenance order in addition to the child support maintenance payable by him in accordance with the maintenance calculation.

(7) This section shall not prevent a court from exercising any power which it has to make a maintenance order in relation to a child if –

(a) the child is, will be or (if the order were to be made) would be receiving instruction at an educational establishment or undergoing training for a trade, profession or vocation (whether or not while in gainful employment); and

(b) the order is made solely for the purposes of requiring the person making or securing the making of periodical payments fixed by the order to meet some or all of the expenses incurred in connection with the provision of the instruction or training.

(8) This section shall not prevent a court from exercising any power which it has to make a maintenance order in relation to a child if –

(a) an allowance under Part 4 of the Welfare Reform Act 2012 (personal independence payment) or a disability living allowance is paid to or in respect of him; or

(b) no such allowance is paid but he is disabled,

and the order is made solely for the purpose of requiring the person making or securing the making of periodical payments fixed by the order to meet some or all of any expenses attributable to the child's disability.

(9) For the purposes of subsection (8), a child is disabled if he is blind, deaf or dumb or is substantially and permanently handicapped by illness, injury, mental disorder or congenital deformity or such other disability as may be prescribed.

(10) This section shall not prevent a court from exercising any power which it has to make a maintenance order in relation to a child if the order is made against a person with care of the child.

(11) In this Act "maintenance order", in relation to any child, means an order which requires the making or securing of periodical payments to or for the benefit of the child and which is made under –

(a) Part II of the Matrimonial Causes Act 1973;
(b) the Domestic Proceedings and Magistrates' Courts Act 1978;
(c) Part III of the Matrimonial and Family Proceedings Act 1984;
(d) the Family Law (Scotland) Act 1985;
(e) Schedule 1 to the Children Act 1989;
(ea) Schedule 5, 6 or 7 to the Civil Partnership Act 2004; or
(f) any other prescribed enactment,

and includes any order varying or reviving such an order.

(12) The Lord Chief Justice may nominate a judicial office holder (as defined in section 109(4) of the Constitutional Reform Act 2005) to exercise his functions under this section.

Amendments—Child Support Act 1995, s 18; Social Security Act 1998, s 86(1), Sch 7, para 22; CSPSSA 2000, s 1(2), s 26, Sch 3, para 11(1),(2); CPA 2004, ss 254(1), 261(4), Sch 24, para 1, Sch 30; CRA 2005, s 15(1), Sch 4, paras 218, 219; CMOPA 2008, ss 13(4), 57(1), 58, Sch 3, paras 1, 6, Sch 7, para 1(2), Sch 8; SI 2012/2007; WRA 2012, s 91, Sch 9, para 2.

Defined terms—"non-resident parent": s 3(2); "child": s 55(1); "child support maintenance": s 3(6); "maintenance calculation", "parent": s 54; "periodical payments": s 3(6); "person with care": s 3(3); "qualifying child": s 3(1).

"jurisdiction to make a maintenance calculation" (s 8(1))—The jurisdiction of the Secretary of State to make a calculation depends upon:

(a)   one or both of a child's parents not being resident with the child (s 3);
(b)   the child coming within the definition of "child" (s 55 as amended by CMOPA 2008, s 42 (not yet in force); and
(c)   each of the non-resident parent, the person with care and the qualifying child being habitually resident in the UK (s 44).

Cohabitation—A child support calculation terminates after cohabitation for more than 6 months (CSA 1991, Sch 1, para 16(1)(d); *Brough v Law* [2012] 1 FLR 375; c f payments under CA 1989, Sch 1, para 3(4), where an order ceases upon the parents living together for more than 6 months. During the period of resumption of cohabitation for less than 3 months, the surviving duty to pay child support maintenance would be "suspended ... and cease at the expiry of six months" (*Brough v Law* (above) at [58]).

"no court shall exercise any power" (s 8(3))—Provided that the Secretary of State has jurisdiction, and even though no application is made to him, the court has no jurisdiction to hear a contested application for child periodical payments. This is subject to the following exceptions and the court having power to make an order:

(i)   *Applications for top up orders*   Where s 8(5)–(10) applies, application can be made to the court for one or more of the top-up orders therein referred to (see *Re P (Child: Financial Provision)* [2003] 2 FLR 865, CA).
(ii)   *Variations of existing periodical payments orders* (s 8(3A))   *V v V (Child Maintenance)* [2001] 2 FLR 799, at [804], clarifies that it remains possible for the court to vary existing orders, whether made before or after April 1993, subject to (where the parent with care is on benefit) there being no application for a child support calculation.
(iii)   *"Segal" orders*   The court can make an order for periodical payments for a parent which will later absorb any subsequent child support maintenance calculation (a "Segal" order); but only where the order contains a substantial amount of spousal maintenance (*Dorney-Kingdom v Dorney-Kingdom* [2000] 2 FLR 855, CA).
(iv)   *Lump sums for children*   The court has power in proceedings under MCA 1973, s 23(1)(f) and CA 1989, Sch 1, para 1(2)(c) to make lump sum orders (in the narrow circumstances where this may be appropriate) including interim orders for expenses reasonably incurred (MCA 1973, s 23(3)(b); CA 1989, Sch 1, para 5(1); and see *Askew-Page v Page* [2001] Fam Law 794, HH Judge Meston QC). A lump sum order can be made for children where the husband withdraws his consent to varying an agreed order (*V v V (Child Maintenance)* [2001] 2 FLR 799).
(v)   *Costs allowances*   It may be possible to obtain a costs allowance for the financially disadvantaged parent in top-up child maintenance proceedings (*MT v OT (Financial provision: costs)* [2008] 2 FLR 1311; and see CA 1989, Sch 1, para 5(1) (MCA 1973, ss 22ZA and 22ZB and CPA 2004, ss 38A and 38B (LASPOA 2012, ss 49, 50) for matrimonial and civil partnership (only) financial proceedings).
(vi)   *Consent orders*   See under **Written Agreements and consent orders**, below.

Maintenance Regulation: Council Regulation (EC) No 4/2009—For purposes of enforcement of child support maintenance in Europe, an enforceable "decision" includes all "matters relating to maintenance obligations given in a third state" (Council Regulation (EC) No 4/2009, Art 2(1)(1)). Art 64(1) provides that enforcement of decisions applies in respect of public bodies acting in place of individuals to whom maintenance is owed. These provisions may enable a parent with care to enforce maintenance obligations abroad (if the non-resident parent leaves the jurisdiction) where she cannot do so in the UK (*R (Kehoe) v Secretary of State for Work and Pensions* [2005] 2 FLR 1249).

Application for a top-up order—Application is made for a top-up order in FPR 2010 financial remedies proceedings under MCA 1973, CPA 2004 proceedings by Form A, alongside existing proceedings (eg, for a school fees order: s 8(7)(a)); or as a freestanding application in proceedings under CA 1989, Sch 1, where there are (or have been) no MCA 1973/CPA 2004 proceedings or the couple were not married. In all cases, procedure is governed by FPR 2010, Pt 9. Applications for a top-up order where the maximum calculation has been reached (s 8(6)) should generally be transferred to be heard before a judge of the Family Division (*Re P (Child: Financial Provision)* (above)).

Interim applications—Interim application for orders and a costs allowance can be made (*CF v KM* [2011] 1 FLR 208) and such applications will still be necessary (e g under CA 1989, Sch 1). It will be important to define the applicant's budget and her costs requirements before any interim hearing:

(i) *MCA 1973/CPA 2004* The court has its general powers to award interim financial provision on
   Pt 18 procedure application being made in existing proceedings in accordance with FPR 2010, r 9.7;
(ii) *CA 1969, Sch 1* Provision for interim provision is set out in Sch 1, para 9. The applicant proceeds
   by Pt 18 procedure in accordance with FPR 2010, r 9.7; and see *CF v KM*, above.

Backdating of orders—Backdating of any final top-up order will depend upon when the application for
the top-up order (the application) is made and the date (the effective date) from which the child support
maintenance calculation is effective (MCA 1973, s 29(5) and (6); CA 1989, Sch 1, para 3(5) and (6); and
as explained in *Re P (Child: Financial Provision)* (above): the provisions of s 29 and CA 1989, Sch 1,
para 3 are identical). The order, and thus any provision for arrears, runs from the "earliest permitted date"
(s 29(6); para 3(5)), namely the later of 6 months before the application (s 29(6)(a); para 3(5)(a)) or the
"effective date" of the original calculation that led to the maximum assessment calculation that enables
the top-up application to be made (s 29(6)(b); para 3(5)(b)).

Date for application for a top-up order—There is no reason why application cannot be made (including
for interim financial provision) where a maximum assessment has not yet been made (*CF v KM* [2011]
1 FLR 208) and, because of the effects of CA 1989, Sch 1, para 3(5) (see above) in unmarried couples'
cases, every reason why an application should be made. (For an example of this and of back-dating
arrears see e g *H v C* [2009] 2 FLR 1540, where the appeals process to reach a maximum assessment took
more than 3 years: but for an early application the children's arrears would have been back-dated to any
later application as the "later" of the two "earliest dates".)

Effective date—The effective date of a maintenance calculation is:

(1) New calculation – the date on which the application is made, including any revision of that
   calculation (Child Support (Maintenance Calculation Procedure) Regulations 2001, Pt VII);
(2) Supersession (CSA 1991, s 17) – the date on which any application for a decision to supersede is
   made (CSA 1991, s 17(4)).

Effect of calculation and ceasing of a maintenance order—See under s 10 below.

Termination of child periodical payments order—See annotation to s 4(10)(aa) above.

FPR 2010—To ensure that applications in respect of qualifying children are not wrongly pursued in the
courts, there are procedures in FPR 2010, r 29.8, which requires the court to give notice to the applicant
concerning possible rejection of such applications.

Written agreements and consent orders (s 8(5))—Child Maintenance (Written Agreements)
Order 1993, art 2 gives effect to s 8(5) and provides:
   "Section 8 shall not prevent a court from exercising any power which it has to make a maintenance
   order in relation to a child in any circumstances in which paragraphs (a) and (b) of section 8(5) apply."
Thus the court retains its powers, subject to the provisions of s 4(10)(aa), to make orders by consent of the
parties, even though the Secretary of State would have had jurisdiction were application to be made to the
Agency.

"mental disorder" (s 8(9))—By virtue of MHA 1983, s 1(2), this means "mental illness, arrested or
incomplete development of mind, psychopathic disorder and any other disorder or disability of mind and
'mentally disordered' shall be construed accordingly".

"any other prescribed enactment" (s 8(11)(f))—Child Support (Maintenance Arrangements and
Jurisdiction) Regulations 1992, reg 2 adds a number of further enactments under which maintenance
orders are covered for the purposes of s 8.

Voluntary payments—The treatment of voluntary payments is dealt with in CSA 1991, s 28J. The
Secretary of State has a discretion to allow payments and for them to be set against child support
maintenance arrears (and see CSA 1991, s 41C: power to treat liability as satisfied). In
R (Green) v Secretary of State for Work and Pensions [2010] EWHC 1278 (Admin) Black J found that a
decision-maker had a discretion to permit school fees to be offset against child support. The
decision-maker must consider its internal guidance and document the exercise. Where school fees have
been dealt with by court order (by consent or otherwise under s 8(7)), this is not "voluntary payments" in
terms of s 28J nor a component in agreement to a variation direction under s 28D (*DB v CMEC* [2010]
UKUT 356).

9 Agreements about maintenance

(1) In this section "maintenance agreement" means any agreement for the making, or for securing the making, of periodical payments by way of maintenance, or in Scotland aliment, to or for the benefit of any child.

(2) Nothing in this Act shall be taken to prevent any person from entering into a maintenance agreement.

(3) Subject to section 4(10)(a) and (ab) and section 7(10), the existence of a maintenance agreement shall not prevent any party to the agreement, or any other person, from applying for a maintenance calculation with respect to any child to or for whose benefit periodical payments are to be made or secured under the agreement.

(4) Where any agreement contains a provision which purports to restrict the right of any person to apply for a maintenance calculation, that provision shall be void.

(5) Where section 8 would prevent any court from making a maintenance order in relation to a child and a non-resident parent of his, no court shall exercise any power that it has to vary any agreement so as –

(a) to insert a provision requiring that non-resident parent to make or secure the making of periodical payments by way of maintenance, or in Scotland aliment, to or for the benefit of that child; or

(b) to increase the amount payable under such a provision.

(6) In any case in which section 4(10) or 7(10) prevents the making of an application for a maintenance calculation, subsection (5) shall have effect with the omission of paragraph (b).

Amendments—Child Support Act 1995, s 18; CSPSSA 2000, s 1(2), 26, Sch 3, para 11(2),(6), CMOPA 2008, ss 35(3), 58, Sch 8.

Defined terms—"non-resident parent": s 3(2); "child": s 55(1); "maintenance calculation", "parent": s 54; "periodical payments": s 3(6).

"maintenance agreement" (s 9(1))—This definition can be contrasted with that in MCA 1973, s 34(2) and CSA 1991, s 8(5)(a), which state that the agreement must be in writing; however, s 9(1) contemplates the existence of agreements other than in writing (which must raise questions, beyond the scope of this note, as to their enforceability). In any event, whatever the nature of the agreement and the extent of its enforceability, s 9(3) ensures that its existence cannot prevent application being made for a maintenance calculation in respect of the child concerned.

"any child" (s 9(1),(3))—Although the section uses the term "any child", the context – applications for a maintenance calculation, which can only be for qualifying children (ss 4(1) and 6(1)) – makes it clear that it can only apply to qualifying children.

Restriction on the right to apply for maintenance calculation (s 9(4))—Any restriction on the right to apply for a maintenance calculation recorded in a consent order would also fail under s 9(4) within the terms of the definition in s 9(1): it may be assumed that the term "maintenance agreement" includes the consent application which would have led to the order.

Alteration of maintenance agreements (s 9(5))—MCA 1973, s 35 and CA 1989, Sch 1, para 10 enable a party to a maintenance agreement to apply to the court for its variation. Section 9(5) prevents this where application is in respect of a qualifying child, save for the following: (i) existing agreements to which s 9(6) applies; and (ii) where the variation is by agreement, in which case it could be made the subject of a *consent application to the court*, either where matrimonial proceedings are contemplated or are under way (MCA 1973, s 7) or under DPMCA 1978, s 6. The difference between this arrangement and MCA 1973, s 35 is that the new "agreement" becomes a court order totally separate from the original agreement; whereas under s 35 and CA 1989, Sch 1, para 10 the whole agreement stands subject only as varied by the court order. See *Morgan v Hill* [2007] 1 FLR 1480 on the court's powers to vary agreements between parents not married to one another.

Written agreements and consent orders—The Child Maintenance (Written Agreements) Order 1993 gives effect to s 8(5), whereby the court retains its powers to make orders in accordance with a written agreement. This is so even though the Secretary of State would have had jurisdiction and whether or not the written agreement on which the order is to be based postdates the coming into operation of the Act.

10   Relationship between maintenance calculations and certain court orders and related matters

(1) Where an order of a kind prescribed for the purposes of this subsection is in force with respect to any qualifying child with respect to whom a maintenance calculation is made, the order –

    (a)   shall, so far as it relates to the making or securing of periodical payments, cease to have effect to such extent as may be determined in accordance with regulations made by the Secretary of State; or

    (b)   where the regulations so provide, shall, so far as it so relates, have effect subject to such modifications as may be so determined.

(2) Where an agreement of a kind prescribed for the purposes of this subsection is in force with respect to any qualifying child with respect to whom a maintenance calculation is made, the agreement –

    (a)   shall, so far as it relates to the making or securing of periodical payments, be unenforceable to such extent as may be determined in accordance with regulations made by the Secretary of State; or

    (b)   where the regulations so provide, shall, so far as it so relates, have effect subject to such modifications as may be so determined.

(3) Any regulations under this section may, in particular, make such provision with respect to –

    (a)   any case where any person with respect to whom an order or agreement of a kind prescribed for the purposes of subsection (1) or (2) has effect applies to the prescribed court, before the end of the prescribed period, for the order or agreement to be varied in the light of the maintenance calculation and of the provisions of this Act;

    (b)   the recovery of any arrears under the order or agreement which fell due before the coming into force of the maintenance calculation,

as the Secretary of State considers appropriate and may provide that, in prescribed circumstances, an application to any court which is made with respect to an order of a prescribed kind relating to the making or securing of periodical payments to or for the benefit of a child shall be treated by the court as an application for the order to be revoked.

(4) The Secretary of State may by regulations make provision for –

    (a)   notification to be given by the Secretary of State concerned to the prescribed person in any case where the Secretary of State considers that the making of a maintenance calculation has affected, or is likely to affect, any order of a kind prescribed for the purposes of this subsection;

    (b)   notification to be given by the prescribed person to the Secretary of State in any case where a court makes an order which it considers has affected, or is likely to affect, a maintenance calculation.

(5) Rules may be made under section 144 of the Magistrates' Courts Act 1980 (rules of procedure) requiring any person who, in prescribed circumstances, makes an application to a magistrates' court for a maintenance order to furnish the court with a statement in a prescribed form, and signed by an officer of the Secretary of State, as to whether or not, at the time when the statement is made, there is a maintenance calculation in force with respect to that person or the child concerned.

In this subsection –

    "maintenance order" means an order of a prescribed kind for the making or securing of periodical payments to or for the benefit of a child; and

    "prescribed" means prescribed by the rules.

Amendments—Social Security Act 1998, s 86(1), Sch 7, para 23; CSPSSA 2000, s 1(2); CMOPA 2008, s 13(4), Sch 3, paras 1, 7; SI 2012/2007.

Defined terms—"child": s 55(1); "child support maintenance": s 3(6); "maintenance calculation", "parent": s 54; "periodical payments": s 3(6); "qualifying child": s 3(1).

"an order of a kind prescribed" (s 10(1))—The orders prescribed under s 10(1) are the same as those listed in s 8(11) with the addition of an order under the Affiliation Proceedings Act 1957 (Child Support (Maintenance Arrangements and Jurisdiction) Regulations 1992, reg 3(1)).

"an agreement of a kind prescribed" (s 10(2),(3)(a))—Maintenance agreements as defined in s 9(1) are those which are prescribed for this subsection (Child Support (Maintenance Arrangements and Jurisdiction) Regulations 1992, reg 4(1)).

Effect of calculation (s 10(1)(a),(2)(a))—Orders or agreements in respect of any children affected by the maintenance calculation cease to be effective or are unenforceable from the effective date of the calculation (as explained under Child Support (Maintenance Arrangements and Jurisdiction) Regulations 1992, regs 3(2), 4(2)).

****

Reviews and appeals
****

26 Disputes about parentage

(1) Where a person who is alleged to be a parent of the child with respect to whom an application for a maintenance assessment has been made ("the alleged parent") denies that he is one of the child's parents, the Secretary of State shall not make a maintenance assessment on the assumption that the alleged parent is one of the child's parents unless the case falls within one of those set out in subsection (2).

****

Amendments—SI 1995/756; Social Security Act 1998, s 86(1), Sch 7, para 31(1); CMOPA 2008, ss 13(4), 58, Sch 3, paras 1, 18, Sch 8; SI 2012/2007.

Defined terms—"child": s 55(1); "maintenance calculation", "parent": s 54.

Denial of parentage (s 26(_))—This section provides for an alleged parent's entitlement to deny parentage which brings the application for a calculation to an end, unless one of the presumptions called "Cases" set out in s 26(2) apply, when the onus shifts to the putative male parent to prove that he is not the parent. The cases set out in s 26(2) include:

– where the person was married to the mother at some time in the period "beginning with conception" and ending with the birth of the child (Case A1);
– registration of the father on the birth certificate (Case A2);
– the alleged parent refuses to take a "scientific test" (a paternity test, normally by DNA samples); or a test shows that he is the parent (Case A3);
– a parent has adopted the child (Case A);
– where there is a previous parentage declaration under FLA 1986, s 55A (Case C);
– the parent has already been adjudged to be the father in other relevant court proceedings (Case F).

Inference of parentage—Where a married woman gives birth to a child, the husband is presumed to be the father (Case A1). However, where a man who has been clearly identified by the mother as the father refuses to undergo scientific tests, the magistrates may draw appropriate inferences from such a refusal (FLRA 1969, s 23; *Secretary of State for Work and Pensions v Jones* [2004] 1 FLR 282, Dame Elizabeth Butler-Sloss P; and see *Re A (A Minor) (Paternity: Refusal of Blood Test)* [1994] 2 FLR 463, CA).

27 Applications for declaration of parentage under Family Law Act 1986

(1) This section applies where –

  (a) an application for a maintenance calculation has been made or a maintenance calculation is in force, with respect to a person ("the alleged parent") who denies that he is a parent of a child with respect to whom the application or calculation was made,

  (b) the Secretary of State is not satisfied that the case falls within one of those set out in section 26(2); and

  (c) the Secretary of State or the person with care makes an application for a declaration under section 55A of the Family Law Act 1986 as to whether or not the alleged parent is one of the child's parents.

(2) Where this section applies –

  (a) if it is the person with care who makes the application, she shall be treated as having a sufficient personal interest for the purposes of subsection (3) of that section; and

  (b) if it is the Secretary of State who makes the application, that subsection shall not apply.

(3) This section does not apply to Scotland.

Amendments—Substituted by CSPSSA 2000, s 83(5), Sch 8, para 13; CMOPA 2008, ss 13(4), 58, Sch 3, paras 1, 19, Sch 8; SI 2012/2007.

Defined terms—"alleged parent": s 26(1); "child": s 55(1); "maintenance calculation", "parent": s 54; "person with care": s 3(3).

Parentage applications—Parentage applications may come before the family courts in the context of CSA 1991 in one of two ways:

(1) *Under FLA 1986, s 55A* On application to the courts as a freestanding declaration application (FPR 2010, Pt 8, Ch 5, and see FLA 1986, s 55A procedure, below).

(2) *On appeal by a parent to first-tier tribunal* Under CSA 1991, s 20 (see below).

"sufficient personal interest" (s 27(2)(a))—Where the applicant is a person with care she does not have to go through the s 55A(3) filter of establishing whether she has a sufficient personal interest in the application. As a parent she will automatically have sufficient personal interest (s 55A(4)), so this section can apply only to persons with care who are not also parents.

Scientific tests—The issue of parentage is likely to turn on the outcome of scientific testing (under FLRA 1969, s 20, see below), which, if the court does not direct of its own initiative, one of the parties will require the court to direct.

Appeals under CSA 1991, s 20 to first-tier tribunal on parentage—On an appeal under CSA 1991, s 20 to the first-tier tribunal, where an appellant parent raises an issue as to parentage, following a calculation decision, that appeal is heard in the magistrates' court, rather than in the First-tier Tribunal (Child Support Appeals (Jurisdiction of Courts) Order 2002). The appeal may be transferred by the justices to the High Court or to a county court.

27A Recovery of fees for scientific tests

(1) This section applies in any case where –

  (a) an application for a maintenance calculation has been made or a maintenance calculation is in force;

  (b) scientific tests have been carried out (otherwise than under a direction or in response to a request) in relation to bodily samples obtained from a person who is alleged to be a parent of a child with respect to whom the application or calculation is made;

  (c) the results of the tests do not exclude the alleged parent from being one of the child's parents; and

  (d) one of the conditions set out in subsection (2) is satisfied.

(2) The conditions are that –

  (a) the alleged parent does not deny that he is one of the child's parents;

(b) in proceedings under section 55A of the Family Law Act 1986, a court has
made a declaration that the alleged parent is a parent of the child in question; or
(c) (*applies to Scotland only*)

(3) In any case to which this section applies, any fee paid by the Secretary of State in
connection with scientific tests may be recovered by the Secretary of State from the
alleged parent as a debt due to the Crown.

(4) In this section –
"bodily sample" means a sample of bodily fluid or bodily tissue taken for the
purpose of scientific tests;
"direction" means a direction given by a court under section 20 of the Family Law
Reform Act 1969 (tests to determine paternity);
"request" means a request made by a court under section 70 of the Law Reform
(Miscellaneous Provisions) (Scotland) Act 1990 (blood and other samples in
civil proceedings); and
"scientific tests" means scientific tests made with the object of ascertaining the
inheritable characteristics of bodily fluids or bodily tissue.

(5) Any sum recovered by the Secretary of State under this section shall be paid by the
Secretary of State into the Consolidated Fund.

Amendments—Inserted by Child Support Act 1995, s 21; amended by CSPSSA 2000, ss 1(2), 83(5),
Sch 3, para 11(9), Sch 8, para 14; CMOPA 2008, ss 13(4), Sch 3, Pt 1, paras 1, 20, Sch 8; SI 2012/2007.

Defined terms—"maintenance calculation", "parent": s 54.

Costs of application for declaration of parentage—Only the fee for the test is covered by s 27A(3),
since the court costs of any application for a declaration of parentage are provided for by FLRA 1969,
s 20(6).

****

Collection and enforcement

Introductory note

Enforcement under CSA 1991—The scheme of enforcement under CSA 1991 (as amended, and yet to
be further amended, by CMOPA 2008) currently contains two categories of means of enforcement. Both
involve the family courts at different levels:

(1) Administrative direction (ss 31–32K)—Known as "orders" these provisions enable the Secretary of
State to impose a direction upon the liable parent and his employer (deduction from earnings orders:
s 31) and "deposit-takers" and other creditors of the liable parent (regular deduction orders: s 32A;
lump sum deduction orders: s 32E). Appeals from a deduction from earnings order lie to the
magistrates' courts in the restricted circumstances of CS(CE)R 1992, reg 22, and to the county courts
for ss 32A and 32E orders.
(2) Enforcement following a liability order—A liability order under s 33 provides the Secretary of State
with the means of enforcement set out in s 34 (distress: bailiffs), s 36 (enforcement in the county
court by charging order or third-party debt order) and s 39A (committal and disqualification from
driving). Court involvement is built into the enforcement procedures (CS(CE)R 1992, Pt IV) under
ss 33 and 39A. Appeal lies to the county court (MCA 1980, s 111A; FPR 2010, Pt 30) and there is an
appeal in connection with distress (which requires no court involvement beyond the liability order)
under CS(CE)R 1992, reg 31.

"welfare of any child affected" (s 2)—Each means of enforcement involves an exercise of a
decision-maker's discretion, thus engaging CSA 1991, s 2, and an assessment of whether "any" child is
likely to be affected by his/her decision (*Brookes v Secretary of State for Work and Pensions* [2010]
2 FLR 1038). This decision must be taken in accordance with the principles summarised by Wyn Wilson J
in *R (Equality & Human Rights Commission) v Secretary of State for Justice and anor* [2010] EWHC 147
(Admin) at [45–46]: has the decision-maker had regard to the relevant statutory duty, the "relevant
statutory need" demanded by that duty and discharged his/her duty with an open mind. The judgment
at [46] contains a helpful decision analysis of recent case-law on decision-making duties.

Judicial review—Where there is no statutory means under CSA 1991, s 20 to challenge the decision of the Secretary of State, the route for challenge of the decision-maker may be by judicial review.

Further enforcement powers under CMOPA 2008—CMOPA 2008 gave the Secretary of State further powers to enforce, by amendment to CSA 1991. The following have so far been introduced:

(1) *Regular and lump sum deduction orders* These "orders" provide the Secretary of State with administrative powers over a liable parent's funds. Appeal from a deduction order decision is direct to the county court.

(2) *Avoidance of disposition by parent* Application by the Secretary of State to the High Court to restrain disposal (s 32L(1)) or to avoid a disposition (s 32L(2)).

****

31 Deduction from earnings orders

(1) This section applies where any person ("the liable person") is liable to make payments of child support maintenance.

(2) The Secretary of State may make an order ("a deduction from earnings order") against a liable person to secure the payment of any amount due under the maintenance calculation in question.

(3) A deduction from earnings order may be made so as to secure the payment of –

(a) arrears of child support maintenance payable under the calculation;

(b) amounts of child support maintenance which will become due under the calculation; or

(c) both such arrears and such future amounts.

(4) A deduction from earnings order –

(a) shall be expressed to be directed at a person ("the employer") who has the liable person in his employment; and

(b) shall have effect from such date as may be specified in the order.

(5) A deduction from earnings order shall operate as an instruction to the employer to –

(a) make deductions from the liable person's earnings; and

(b) pay the amounts deducted to the Secretary of State.

(6) The Secretary of State shall serve a copy of any deduction from earnings order made under this section on –

(a) the person who appears to the Secretary of State to have the liable person in question in his employment; and

(b) the liable person.

(7) Where –

(a) a deduction from earnings order has been made; and

(b) a copy of the order has been served on the liable person's employer,

it shall be the duty of that employer to comply with the order; but he shall not be under any liability for non-compliance before the end of the period of 7 days beginning with the date on which the copy was served on him.

(8) In this section and in section 32 "earnings" has such meaning as may be prescribed.

Amendments—CSPSSA 2000, s 1(2); CMOPA 2008, s 13(4), Sch 3, paras 1, 34; SI 2012/2007.

Defined terms—"child support maintenance": s 3(6); "earnings": s 31(8), CS(CE)R 1992, reg 8(3),(4); "maintenance calculation": s 54.

Challenging the order

(a) *Appeals to the magistrates' courts* Under CS(CE)R 1992, reg 22 limited grounds for appeal against the making of a deduction from earnings order exist: (i) that the order is defective; or (ii) that the payments concerned are not earnings (as defined in reg 8(3)). The magistrates' powers on appeal are limited to quashing the order or stating that the payments in question are not earnings. (*R v Secretary of State for Social Security ex parte Biggin* [1995] 1 FLR 851.

(b) *Judicial review* As an administrative decision involving the exercise of discretion, the making of a deduction from earnings order may be susceptible to judicial review in exceptional circumstances and subject to any appeal (where grounds existed) under reg 22 (above); for example, where the liable person's employment may be affected by the order (especially if a child might suffer where he is to lose his job: and see s 2); or if the Secretary of State can be shown to have acted unreasonably or maliciously in imposing the order where other forms of enforcement or collection were available and had been proposed by the liable person.

Procedure on appeal—Appeal is by complaint for an order to the magistrates' courts in accordance with MCR 1981 (for forms of summons and complaint see Magistrates' Courts (Forms) Rules 1981). The complaint must be issued within 28 days of "the date on which the matter complained against arose" (reg 22). The procedure for judicial review is covered by CPR 1998, Pt 54.

****

32A Orders for regular deductions from accounts

(1) If in relation to any person it appears to the Secretary of State –

(a)   that the person has failed to pay an amount of child support maintenance; and

(b)   that the person holds an account with a deposit-taker;

the Secretary of State may make an order against that person to secure the payment of any amount due under the maintenance calculation in question by means of regular deductions from the account.

(2) An order under this section may be made so as to secure the payment of –

(a)   arrears of child support maintenance payable under the calculation;

(b)   amounts of child support maintenance which will become payable under the calculation; or

(c)   both such arrears and such future amounts.

(3) An order under this section may be made in respect of amounts due under a maintenance calculation which is the subject of an appeal only if it appears to the Secretary of State –

(a)   that liability for the amounts would not be affected were the appeal to succeed; or

(b)   where paragraph (a) does not apply, that the making of an order under this section in respect of the amounts would nonetheless be fair in all the circumstances.

(4) An order under this section –

(a)   may not be made in respect of an account of a prescribed description; and

(b)   may be made in respect of a joint account which is held by the person against whom the order is made and one or more other persons, and which is not of a description prescribed under paragraph (a), if (but only if) regulations made by the Secretary of State so provide.

(5) An order under this section –

(a)   shall specify the account in respect of which it is made;

(b)   shall be expressed to be directed at the deposit-taker with which the account is held; and

(c)   shall have effect from such date as may be specified in the order.

(6) An order under this section shall operate as an instruction to the deposit-taker at which it is directed to –

(a)   make deductions from the amount (if any) standing to the credit of the account specified in the order; and

PART II

(b) pay the amount deducted to the Secretary of State.

(7) The Secretary of State shall serve a copy of any order made under this section on –

(a) the deposit-taker at which it is directed;

(b) the person against whom it is made; and

(c) if the order is made in respect of a joint account, the other account-holders.

(8) Where –

(a) an order under this section has been made; and

(b) a copy of the order has been served on the deposit-taker at which it is directed,

it shall be the duty of that deposit-taker to comply with the order; but the deposit-taker shall not be under any liability for non-compliance before the end of the period of 7 days beginning with the day on which the copy was served on the deposit-taker.

(9) Where regulations have been made under section 29(3)(a), a person liable to pay an amount of child support maintenance is to be taken for the purposes of this section to have failed to pay an amount of child support maintenance unless it is paid to or through the person specified in, or by virtue of, the regulations for the case in question.

Amendments—Inserted by CMOPA 2008, s 22; SI 2012/2007.

****

32E Lump sum deductions: interim orders

(1) The Secretary of State may make an order under this section if it appears to the Secretary of State that a person (referred to in this section and sections 32F to 32J as "the liable person") has failed to pay an amount of child support maintenance and –

(a) an amount stands to the credit of an account held by the liable person with a deposit-taker; or

(b) an amount not within paragraph (a) that is of a prescribed description is due or accruing to the liable person from another person (referred to in this section and sections 32F to 32J as the "third party").

(2) An order under this section –

(a) may not be made by virtue of subsection (1)(a) in respect of an account of a prescribed description; and

(b) may be made by virtue of subsection (1)(a) in respect of a joint account which is held by the liable person and one or more other persons, and which is not of a description prescribed under paragraph (a) of this subsection, if (but only if) regulations made by the Secretary of State so provide.

(3) The Secretary of State may by regulations make provision as to conditions that are to be disregarded in determining whether an amount is due or accruing to the liable person for the purposes of subsection (1)(b).

(4) An order under this section –

(a) shall be expressed to be directed at the deposit-taker or third party in question;

(b) if made by virtue of subsection (1)(a), shall specify the account in respect of which it is made; and

(c) shall specify the amount of arrears of child support maintenance in respect of which the Secretary of State proposes to make an order under section 32F.

(5) An order under this section may specify an amount of arrears due under a maintenance calculation which is the subject of an appeal only if it appears to the Secretary of State –

(a) that liability for the amount would not be affected were the appeal to succeed; or

(b) where paragraph (a) does not apply, that the making of an order under section 32F in respect of the amount would nonetheless be fair in all the circumstances.

(6) The Secretary of State shall serve a copy of any order made under this section on –

(a) the deposit-taker or third party at which it is directed;

(b) the liable person: and

(c) if the order is made in respect of a joint account, the other account-holders.

(7) An order under this section shall come into force at the time at which it is served on the deposit-taker or third party at which it is directed.

(8) An order under this section shall cease to be in force at the earliest of the following –

(a) the time at which the prescribed period ends;

(b) the time at which the order under this section lapses or is discharged; and

(c) the time at which an order under section 32F made in pursuance of the proposal specified in the order under this section is served on the deposit-taker or third party at which that order is directed.

(9) Where regulations have been made under section 29(3)(a), a person liable to pay an amount of child support maintenance is to be taken for the purposes of this section to have failed to pay the amount unless it is paid to or through the person specified in, or by virtue of, the regulations for the case in question.

Amendments—Inserted by CMOPA 2008, s 23; SI 2012/2007.

32F Lump sum deductions: final orders

(1) The Secretary of State may make an order under this section in pursuance of a proposal specified in an order under section 32E if –

(a) the order in which the proposal was specified ("the interim order") is in force;

(b) the period prescribed for the making of representations to the Secretary of State in respect of the proposal specified in the interim order has expired; and

(c) the Secretary of State has considered any representations made to the Secretary of State during that period.

(2) An order under this section –

(a) shall be expressed to be directed at the deposit-taker or third party at which the interim order was directed;

(b) if the interim order was made by virtue of section 32E(1)(a), shall specify the account specified in the interim order; and

(c) shall specify the amount of arrears of child support maintenance in respect of which it is made.

(3) The amount so specified –

(a) shall not exceed the amount of arrears specified in the interim order which remain unpaid at the time at which the order under this section is made; and

(b) if the order is made in respect of a joint account, shall not exceed the amount that appears to the Commission to be fair in all the circumstances.

(4) In determining the amount to be specified in an order made in respect of a joint account the Secretary of State shall have particular regard –

(a) to the amount contributed to the account by each of the account-holders; and

(b) to such other matters as may be prescribed.

(5) An order under this section may specify an amount of arrears due under a maintenance calculation which is the subject of an appeal only if it appears to the Secretary of State –

(a) that liability for the amount would not be affected were the appeal to succeed; or

(b) where paragraph (a) does not apply, that the making of an order under this section in respect of the amount would nonetheless be fair in all the circumstances.

(6) The Secretary of State shall serve a copy of any order made under this section on –

(a) the deposit-taker or third party at which it is directed;

(b) the liable person; and

(c) if the order is made in respect of a joint account, the other account-holders.

Amendments—Inserted by CMOPA 2008, s 23; SI 2012/2007.

"the Commission" (s 32F(3)(b))—By virtue of SI 2012/2007, art 5(3), this should be read as "the Secretary of State".

****

32L Orders preventing avoidance

(1) The Secretary of State may apply to the court, on the grounds that a person –

(a) has failed to pay an amount of child support maintenance, and

(b) with the intention of avoiding payment of child support maintenance, is about to make a disposition or to transfer out of the jurisdiction or otherwise deal with any property, for an order restraining or, in Scotland, interdicting the person from doing so.

(2) The Secretary of State may apply to the court, on the grounds that a person –

(a) has failed to pay an amount of child support maintenance, and

(b) with the intention of avoiding payment of child support maintenance, has at any time made a reviewable disposition, for an order setting aside or, in Scotland, reducing the disposition.

(3) If the court is satisfied of the grounds mentioned in subsection (1) or (2) it may make an order under that subsection.

(4) Where the court makes an order under subsection (1) or (2) it may make such consequential provision by order or directions as it thinks fit for giving effect to the order (including provision requiring the making of any payments or the disposal of any property).

(5) Any disposition is a reviewable disposition for the purposes of subsection (2), unless it was made for valuable or, in Scotland, adequate consideration (other than marriage) to a person who, at the time of the disposition, acted in relation to it in good faith and without notice of an intention to avoid payment of child support maintenance.

(6) Subsection (7) applies where an application is made under this section with respect to –

(a) a disposition or other dealing with property which is about to take place, or

(b) a disposition which took place after the making of the application on which the maintenance calculation concerned was made.

(7) If the court is satisfied –

(a) in a case falling within subsection (1), that the disposition or other dealing would (apart from this section) have the consequence of making ineffective a step that has been or may be taken to recover the amount outstanding, or

(b) in a case falling within subsection (2), that the disposition has had that consequence, it is to be presumed, unless the contrary is shown, that the person who disposed of or is about to dispose of or deal with the property did so or, as the case may be, is about to do so, with the intention of avoiding payment of child support maintenance.

(8) In this section "disposition" does not include any provision contained in a will or codicil but, with that exception, includes any conveyance, assurance or gift of property of any description, whether made by an instrument or otherwise.

(9) This section does not apply to a disposition made before the coming into force of section 24 of the Child Maintenance and Other Payments Act 2008.

(10) In this section "the court" means –

(a)   in relation to England and Wales, the High Court;

(b)   in relation to Scotland, the Court of Session or the sheriff.

(11) An order under this section interdicting a person –

(a)   is effective for such period (including an indefinite period) as the order may specify;

(b)   may, on application to the court, be varied or recalled.

Amendments—Inserted by CMOPA 2008, s 24; SI 2012/2007.

Defined terms—"court": s 32L(1).

Coming into effect—Section 32L came into effect on 6 April 2010 (SI 2010/697).

Preventing avoidance—The terminology of s 32L(1)(b) is taken directly from insolvency law and from MCA 1973, s 37(2)(a) (avoidance of dispositions intended to defeat an ancillary relief claim), save that here application for the order is triggered by the avoidance of payment of child support, and s 32L(2)(b) replicates MCA 1973, s 37(2)(b). This provision partially reverses *Department of Social Security v Butler* [1996] 1 FLR 65, CA (which established that, as the law then stood, the Secretary of State had no means of freezing a liable persons assets (under CPA 1997, s 7)).

Procedure for application for an order—Application must be made in the High Court (s 31L(10)). The application can only be made by the Secretary of State (ie not by a parent with care). Application is by FPR 2010, Pt 19 procedure (FPR 2010, rr 8.1 and 8.35–8.40).

Grounds for the application—The Secretary of State must establish each of the following:

1   that there are arrears ("an amount" is outstanding (s 32L(1)(a) and (2)(a));
2   that the liable person "has the intention of avoiding payment of child support maintenance"; and
3   that either:
(a)   that person "is about to make a disposition" as provided for in s 32L(1)(b); or
(b)   that person has made a reviewable disposition (s 32L(2)(b)).
   The burden of proving each ground is on the Secretary of State. Proof of intent to avoid may not be easy to prove.

The order–Any order must define its period (s 32L(11)(a)). It may be varied or "recalled" (s 32L(11)(b)), presumably on application by the liable person or Secretary of State (but probably not the person for whose benefit the order is obtained: the carer parent).

Inherent jurisdiction—The order – whether to restrain disposal or to set aside a disposition – is made in the discretion of the High Court judge (s 32L(3)). It is not as wide as a CPA 1997, s 7 freezing order, which can deal with property abroad; or a *Shipman* order (*Shipman v Shipman* [1991] 1 FLR 250), which enables the court to make an order even though no intent is proved. It remains to be seen whether the *Butler* (see above) approach lives on (it is not possible, in a statutory scheme, to make an order not prescribed in the statute) to prevent a High Court judge, in effect, doing as did Anthony Lincoln J in *Shipman* and making an order in his inherent jurisdiction.

Presumed evasive disposal (s 32L(7))—This provision is intended to be akin to MCA, s 37(5). It is intended to leave a wide door open to the Secretary of State to argue a presumption of evasion of liability. For example, more or less any movement of cash could be caught by s 32L(7)(a).

****

33 Liability orders

(1) This section applies where –

    (a) a person who is liable to make payments of child support maintenance ("the liable person") fails to make one or more of those payments; and

    (b) it appears to the Secretary of State that –

        (i) it is inappropriate to make a deduction from earnings order against him (because, for example, he is not employed); or

        (ii) although such an order has been made against him, it has proved ineffective as a means of securing that payments are made in accordance with the maintenance calculation in question.

(2) The Secretary of State may apply to a magistrates' court or, in Scotland, to the sheriff for an order ("a liability order") against the liable person.

(3) Where the Secretary of State applies for a liability order, the magistrates' court or (as the case may be) sheriff shall make the order if satisfied that the payments in question have become payable by the liable person and have not been paid.

(4) On an application under subsection (2), the court or (as the case may be) the sheriff shall not question the maintenance calculation under which the payments of child support maintenance fell to be made.

(5) If the Secretary of State designates a liability order for the purposes of this subsection it shall be treated as a judgment entered in a county court for the purposes of section 98 of the Courts Act 2003 (register of judgments and orders etc).

(6) Where regulations have been made under section 29(3)(a) –

    (a) the liable person fails to make a payment (for the purposes of subsection (1)(a) of this section); and

    (b) a payment is not paid (for the purposes of subsection (3)),

unless the payment is made to, or through, the person specified in or by virtue of those regulations for the case of the liable person in question.

Amendments—Child Support Act 1995, s 30, Sch 3, para 10; CSPSSA 2000, s 26, Sch 3, para 11(1), (17); SI 2006/1001; CMOPA 2008, s 13(4), Sch 3, Pt 1, paras 1, 36; SI 2012/2007.

Defined terms—"child support maintenance": s 3(6); "deduction from earnings order": s 31(2); "maintenance calculation": s 54.

Discretion of the Secretary of State—All decisions to enforce are discretionary and must therefore be exercised subject to considerations under s 2 (welfare of any child affected: e g what would the effect be of any enforcement of arrears on "any" child concerned and affected by the decision?). The discretion must be exercised fairly and without irrationality. If it is not so exercised, the only challenge to the Secretary of State is by judicial review (see CPR 1998, Pt 54).

Magistrates "shall not question the maintenance calculation" (s 33(4))—The magistrates are not able to question the underlying calculation on which the calculation decision is based. (If there is an appeal pending that goes to the question of the amount of the calculation or the Secretary of State's jurisdiction, the magistrates may wish to consider adjourning the application for an order (*Farley v Secretary of State for Department of Work and Pensions and Another* [2006] 2 FLR 1243, HL).)

Function of the magistrates: "payments in question" (s 33(3))—The magistrates must be satisfied that payments in question remain payable: for example if paid by the liable person, although not specifically by a method dictated by the Secretary of State (e g direct on a voluntary basis to the other parent) (*Bird v Secretary of State for Work and Pensions* [2009] 2 FLR 660).

Appeals—An appeal against a liability order is by MCA 1980, s 111A.

****

36 Enforcement in county courts

(1) Where a liability order has been made against a person, the amount in respect of which the order was made, to the extent that it remains unpaid, shall, if a county court so orders, be recoverable by means of a third party debt order or a charging order, as if it were payable under a county court order.

(2) (*repealed*)

Amendments—CMOPA 2008. Sch 7, para 1(10), Sch 8.

Defined terms—"liability order": s 33(2).

"if a county court so orders" (s 36(1))—While the magistrates' court has little discretion but to make a liability order (see s 33(1)), the wording of s 36(1) reflects the wording of COA 1979, s 1(1) which give the county court a discretion as to whether or not the orders should be made.

Application in the county court—Whereas application for the other means of enforcement (distress or commitment) is by the Secretary of State, s 36 is silent as to who should make the application in the county court. It may therefore be open to the person with care to make her own application. (This point does not appear to have been considered in *R (Kehoe) v Secretary of State for Work and Pensions* [2005] 2 FLR 1249, HL which stated that only the Secretary of State can enforce arrears.)

Jurisdiction of the county court—Applications under s 36(1) are to the county court. Application is by CPR 1998, Pt 73.

****

39A Commitment to prison and disqualification from driving

(1) Where the Secretary of State has sought –

    (a)   in England and Wales to levy an amount by distress under this Act; or
    (b)   to recover an amount by virtue of section 36 or 38,

and that amount, or any portion of it, remains unpaid the Secretary of State may apply to the court under this section.

(2) An application under this section is for whichever the court considers appropriate in all the circumstances of –

    (a)   the issue of a warrant committing the liable person to prison; or
    (b)   an order for him to be disqualified from holding or obtaining a driving licence.

(3) On any such application the court shall (in the presence of the liable person) inquire as to –

    (a)   whether he needs a driving licence to earn his living;
    (b)   his means; and
    (c)   whether there has been wilful refusal or culpable neglect on his part.

(4) The Secretary of State may make representations to the court as to whether the Secretary of State thinks it more appropriate to commit the liable person to prison or to disqualify him from holding or obtaining a driving licence; and the liable person may reply to those representations.

(5) In this section and section 40B, "driving licence" means a licence to drive a motor vehicle granted under Part III of the Road Traffic Act 1988.

(6) In this section "the court" means –

    (a)   in England and Wales, a magistrates' court;
    (b)   in Scotland, the sheriff.

Amendments—Inserted by CSPSSA 2000, s 16(1); amended by CMOPA 2008, s 13(4), Sch 3, Pt 1, paras 1, 41; SI 2012/2007.

Defined terms—"the court": s 39A(6); "driving licence": s 39A(5); "liable person": s 33(1).

"wilful refusal or culpable neglect"—In *R v Luton Magistrates' Courts* (above) Waite J defined the meaning of this term as: "blameworthiness ... at a very high level. It is not just a matter of improvidence or dilatoriness. Something in the nature of a deliberate defiance or reckless disregard of the court's order is required". Magistrates should ensure that a liable person's refusal or neglect comes within this ambit before he or she is punished under s 39A or s 40.

Public funding—This is made to the magistrates' court by legal aid forms provided by the Criminal Defence Service (e g Forms CDS 1 and CDS 14).

****

40 Commitment to prison

(1), (2) (*repealed*)

(3) If, but only if, the court is of the opinion that there has been wilful refusal or culpable neglect on the part of the liable person it may –

(a) issue a warrant of commitment against him; or

(b) fix a term of imprisonment and postpone the issue of the warrant until such time and on such conditions (if any) as it thinks just.

(4) Any such warrant –

(a) shall be made in respect of an amount equal to the aggregate of –
(i) the amount mentioned in section 35(1) or so much of it as remains outstanding; and
(ii) an amount (determined in accordance with regulations made by the Secretary of State) in respect of the costs of commitment; and

(b) shall state that amount.

(5) No warrant may be issued under this section against a person who is under the age of 18.

(6) A warrant issued under this section shall order the liable person –

(a) to be imprisoned for a specific period; but

(b) to be released (unless he is in custody for some other reason) on payment of the amount stated in the warrant.

(7) The maximum period of imprisonment which may be imposed by virtue of subsection (6) shall be calculated in accordance with Schedule 4 to the Magistrates' Courts Act 1980 (maximum periods of imprisonment in default of payment) but shall not exceed six weeks.

(8) The Secretary of State may by regulations make provision for the period of imprisonment specified in any warrant issued under this section to be reduced where there is part payment of the amount in respect of which the warrant was issued.

(9) A warrant issued under this section may be directed to such person or persons as the court issuing it thinks fit.

(10) Section 80 of the Magistrates' Courts Act 1980 (application of money found on defaulter) shall apply in relation to a warrant issued under this section against a liable person as it applies in relation to the enforcement of a sum mentioned in subsection (1) of that section.

(11) The Secretary of State may by regulations make provision –

(a) as to the form of any warrant issued under this section;

(b) allowing an application under this section to be renewed where no warrant is issued or term of imprisonment is fixed;

(c) that a statement in writing to the effect that wages of any amount have been paid to the liable person during any period, purporting to be signed by or on behalf of his employer, shall be evidence of the facts stated;

(d) that, for the purposes of enabling an inquiry to be made as to the liable person's conduct and means, a justice of the peace may issue a summons to him to appear before a magistrates' court and (if he does not obey) may issue a warrant for his arrest;

(e) that for the purpose of enabling such an inquiry, a justice of the peace may issue a warrant for the liable person's arrest without issuing a summons;

(f) as to the execution of a warrant for arrest.

(12) This section does not apply to Scotland.

Amendments—CSPSSA 2000, ss 16(2), 17(1), 85, Sch 9, Pt I.

Defined terms—"employer": s 31(4)(a); "liable person": s 33(1).

Warrant of commitment or imprisonment (s 40(3))—The powers of the magistrates' courts to commit for breach of their own order are provided for by MCA 1980, s 76, and their power to postpone issue of a warrant by MCA 1980, s 77 (the terminology of which resembles s 40(3)). The justices must make a judgment concerning the conduct of the liable person over his failure to pay and whether that failure constitutes wilful refusal or culpable neglect. If they do so find, and having had regard to his means, they have a discretion as to whether or not to commit to prison immediately. Alternatively they can fix a term of imprisonment but suspend issue of the warrant of commitment to prison on "such conditions as [the court] thinks just".

"such conditions (if any) as [the court] thinks just" (s 40(3)(b))—This provision will enable the magistrates, for example, to suspend the warrant on terms that the liable person maintains payments due and pays off the arrears and costs (the amount stated on the warrant: s 40(4)) by fixed periodic instalments (*Fowler v Fowler* (1981) 2 FLR 141).

Delay in enforcement of liability order—All enforcement process must comply with ECHR 1950, Art 6(1), that application to the court must be within a "reasonable" time (and see *Lloyd v Bow Street Magistrates' Court* [2003] EWHC 2294 (Admin)). Applications under s 39A are not proceedings to recover money and therefore cannot be caught by any limitation periods under Limitation Act 1980, s 9 (*Child Maintenance and Enforcement Commission v Mitchell* [2010] 2 FLR 622).

Execution of the warrant (s 40(9),(11)(f))—CS(CE)R 1992, reg 34(3),(4) deals with execution of the warrant by the person to whom it is addressed or by the police constable within his area.

Further regulations (s 40(11))—The CS(CE)R 1992 make further provision in accordance with s 40(11):

(a) A warrant for commitment is in the form in Sch 3 to the regulations (s 40(11)(a); reg 34(1)).

(b) Regulation 33(3) is narrower than s 40(11)(b); for the regulation provides that, where the magistrates refuse an application to commit, reapplication can only be made where there is a change in the liable person's circumstances. Such change would not be restricted to financial circumstances.

(c) Provision for a statement of income from the liable person's employer is in reg 33(2) (s 40(11)(c)).

(d) To enable an enquiry into the liable person's means to be undertaken reg 33(1) provides for issue of a summons or warrant (s 40(11)(d),(e)).

Appeals—An appeal against a committal application is by MCA 1980, s 111A.

****

40B Disqualification from driving: further provision

(1) If, but only if, the court is of the opinion that there has been wilful refusal or culpable neglect on the part of the liable person, it may –

(a) order him to be disqualified, for such period specified in the order but not exceeding two years as it thinks fit, from holding or obtaining a driving licence (a "disqualification order"); or

(b) make a disqualification order but suspend its operation until such time and on such conditions (if any) as it thinks just.

(2) The court may not take action under both section 40 and this section.

(3) A disqualification order must state the amount in respect of which it is made, which is to be the aggregate of –

(a) the amount mentioned in section 35(1), or so much of it as remains outstanding; and

(b) an amount (determined in accordance with regulations made by the Secretary of State) in respect of the costs of the application under section 39A.

(4) A court which makes a disqualification order shall require the person to whom it relates to produce any driving licence held by him, and its counterpart (within the meaning of section 108(1) of the Road Traffic Act 1988).

(5) On an application by the Secretary of State or the liable person, the court –

(a) may make an order substituting a shorter period of disqualification, or make an order revoking the disqualification order, if part of the amount referred to in subsection (3) (the "amount due") is paid to any person authorised to receive it; and

(b) must make an order revoking the disqualification order if all of the amount due is so paid.

(6) The Secretary of State may make representations to the court as to the amount which should be paid before it would be appropriate to make an order revoking the disqualification order under subsection (5)(a), and the person liable may reply to those representations.

(7) The Secretary of State may make a further application under section 39A if the amount due has not been paid in full when the period of disqualification specified in the disqualification order expires.

(8) Where a court –

(a) makes a disqualification order;

(b) makes an order under subsection (5); or

(c) allows an appeal against a disqualification order,

it shall send notice of that fact to the Secretary of State; and the notice shall contain such particulars and be sent in such manner and to such address as the Secretary of State may determine.

(9) Where a court makes a disqualification order, it shall also send any driving licence and its counterpart, on their being produced to the court, to the Secretary of State at such address as the Secretary of State may determine.

(10) Section 80 of the Magistrates' Courts Act 1980 (application of money found on defaulter) shall apply in relation to a disqualification order under this section in relation to a liable person as it applies in relation to the enforcement of a sum mentioned in subsection (1) of that section.

(11) The Secretary of State may by regulations make provision in relation to disqualification orders corresponding to the provision he may make under section 40(11).

(12) *(applies to Scotland only)*

Amendments—Inserted by CSPSSA 2000, s 16(3); amended by CMOPA 2000, s 13(4), Sch 3, paras 1, 42; Road Safety Act 2006, s 9(6), Sch 2, para 33; SI 2012/2007.

****

Jurisdiction

44 Jurisdiction

(1) The Secretary of State shall have jurisdiction to make a maintenance calculation with respect to a person who is –

(a) a person with care;
(b) a non-resident parent; or
(c) a qualifying child,

only if that person is habitually resident in the United Kingdom, except in the case of a non-resident parent who falls within subsection (2A).

(2) Where the person with care is not an individual, subsection (1) shall have effect as if paragraph (a) were omitted.

(2A) A non-resident parent falls within this subsection if he is not habitually resident in the United Kingdom, but is –

(a) employed in the civil service of the Crown, including Her Majesty's Diplomatic Service and Her Majesty's Overseas Civil Service;
(b) a member of the naval, military or air forces of the Crown, including any person employed by an association established for the purposes of Part XI of the Reserve Forces Act 1996;
(c) employed by a company of a prescribed description registered under the Companies Act 2006; or
(d) employed by a body of a prescribed description.

(3) (*repealed*)

(4) The Secretary of State does not have jurisdiction under this section if the exercise of jurisdiction would be contrary to the jurisdictional requirements of the Maintenance Regulation.

(5) In subsection (4) "the Maintenance Regulation" means Council Regulation (EC) No 4/2009 including as applied in relation to Denmark by virtue of the Agreement made on 19 October 2005 between the European Community and the Kingdom of Denmark.

Amendments—Social Security Act 1998, s 86(1), Sch 7, para 41; CSPSSA 2000, ss 1(2), 22, 26, 85, Sch 3, para 11, Sch 9, Pt I; CMOPA 2008, s 13(4), Sch 3, paras 1, 46; SI 2009/1941; SI 2011/1484; SI 2012/2007.

Defined terms—"child": s 55(1); "maintenance calculation": s 54; "maintenance order": s 8(11); "Maintenance Regulation": s 44(5); "parent": s 54; "qualifying child": s 3(1).

Habitual residence (s 44(1))—The term "habitual residence" is not defined in the Act, nor has it been authoritatively considered under the Act. Reference may be made to authorities where the applicant seeks to invoke the jurisdiction of the English courts (e g DMPA, s 5(2)(b) or under **Habitual residence** in CACA 1985, Sch 1, Art 4), where the term was authoritatively considered by Lord Brandon of Oakbrook in *C v S (A Minor) (Abduction: Illegitimate Child)* [1990] 2 FLR 442 at [454] (affirmed by Baker J in the child maintenance context in *O v P (Jurisdiction under Children Act 1989 Sch 1)* [2012] 1 FLR 329).

Non-resident parent treated as habitually resident (s 44(1),(2A))—The effect of the riders at the end of s 44(1) and (2A) (both added by the 2000 Act) is to bring a number of previously exempt non-resident parents into the Child Support Agency net by providing that those listed in s 44(2A) are comprised within the term "habitually resident" in s 44(1), so as to enable the Secretary of State to assume jurisdiction to make a calculation in respect of them.

Want of residential jurisdiction

(i) If any of: (a) the person with care, (b) the qualifying children or (c) the non-resident parent are not habitually resident, or treated as habitually resident, no calculation can be made under CSA 1991.
(ii) If any of: (a) the person with care; (b) non-resident parent; or (c) qualifying child cease to be habitually resident while a calculation is in force, then an application is made to the Secretary of State for the calculation to be superseded (CSA 1991, s 17) and terminated with effect from the date habitual residence ceased.

If the Secretary of State does not have jurisdiction or it is terminated, application for periodical payments will then be to the court under MCA 1973 or CPA 2004 (if parents were married) or under CA 1989, Sch 1 (subject to any other jurisdictional requirements arising from actual residence of any of the parties).

****

Miscellaneous and supplemental

****

54 Interpretation

(1) In this Act –

"non-resident parent", has the meaning given in section 3(2);

"application for a variation" means an application under section 28A or 28G;

"benefit Acts" means the Social Security Contributions and Benefits Act 1992 and the Social Security Administration Act 1992;

"charging order" has the same meaning as in section 1 of the Charging Orders Act 1979;

"Chief Adjudication Officer" has the same meaning as in the benefit Acts;

"child benefit" has the same meaning as in the Child Benefit Act 1975;

"child support maintenance" has the meaning given in section 3(6);

...

"deduction from earnings order" has the meaning given in section 31(2);

"default maintenance decision" has the meaning given in section 12;

"deposit-taker" means a person who, in the course of a business, may lawfully accept deposits in the United Kingdom;

"disability living allowance" has the same meaning as in the benefit Acts;

...

"income support" has the same meaning as in the benefit Acts;

"income-based jobseeker's allowance" has the same meaning as in the Jobseekers Act 1995;

"income-related employment and support allowance" means an income-related allowance under Part 1 of the Welfare Reform Act 2007 (employment and support allowance);

"interim maintenance decision" has the meaning given in section 12;

"liability order" has the meaning given in section 33(2);

"maintenance agreement" has the meaning given in section 9(1);

"maintenance calculation" means a calculation of maintenance made under this Act and, except in prescribed circumstances, includes a default maintenance decision and an interim maintenance decision;

"maintenance order" has the meaning given in section 8(11);

"parent", in relation to any child, means any person who is in law the mother or father of the child;

"parent with care" means a person who is, in relation to a child, both a parent and a person with care;

"parental responsibility", in the application of this Act –

(a)   to England and Wales, has the same meaning as in the Children Act 1989; and

(b)   to Scotland, shall be construed as a reference to "parental responsibilities" within the meaning given by section 1(3) of the Children (Scotland) Act 1995;

...

"person with care" has the meaning given in section 3(3);

"prescribed" means prescribed by regulations made by the Secretary of State;

"qualifying child" has the meaning given in section 3(1);

"voluntary payment" has the meaning given in section 28J;

(2) The definition of "deposit-taker" in subsection (1) is to be read with –

(a)   section 22 of the Financial Services and Markets Act 2000;

(b) any relevant order under that section; and

(c) Schedule 2 to that Act.

Amendments—Social Security (Consequential Provisions) Act 1992, s 4, Sch 2, para 114; Child Support Act 1995, s 30, Sch 3, para 16; Children (Scotland) Act 1995, s 105(4), Sch 4, para 52, Sch 5; Jobseekers Act 1995, s 41, Sch 2, para 20; Social Security Act 1998, s 86(1),(2) Sch 7, para 47, Sch 8; Tax Credits Act 1999, s 1(2), Sch 1, paras 1, 6(f)(ii); CSPSSA 2000, ss 1(2), 26, 85, Sch 3, para 11(1),(2),(20), Sch 9, Pt I; Tax Credits Act 2002, s 60, Sch 6, with savings and transitional provisions; Tribunals, Courts and Enforcement Act 2007, s 146, Sch 23, Pt 2; Welfare Reform Act 2007, s 28(1), Sch 3, para 7(1),(7); CMOPA 2008, s 57, Sch 7, para 1(1),(25),(26); SI 2008/2833; WRA 2009, ss 9(3)(b), 58(1), Sch 7, Pt I; SI 2012/2007.

55 Meaning of "child"

(1) In this Act, "child" means (subject to subsection (2)) a person who –

(a) has not attained the age of 16, or

(b) has not attained the age of 20 and satisfies such conditions as may be prescribed.

(2) A person who is or has been party to a marriage or civil partnership is not a child for the purposes of this Act.

(3) For the purposes of subsection (2), "marriage" and "civil partnership" include a void marriage and a void civil partnership respectively.

Amendments—CPA 2004, s 254(1), Sch 24, para 3; CMOPA 2008, s 42.

"not attained the age of 20"—This gives effect to the reforms outlined in CMOPA 2008, s 42, so that the upper age for child support increases.

Regulations and the meaning of "child"—Child Support (Maintenance Calculation Procedure) Regulations 2001, Sch 1 elaborates the definition of "child" under s 55 to include the following:

(a) para 1 defines conditions which apply to children under 18 who are to be treated as children within the terms of s 55(1)(c), i e where they are registered for work or for training under youth training for a number of specified employers or where they are not in remunerative employment (save of a temporary nature);

(b) the meaning of "advanced education", in accordance with s 55(3), is defined by para 2 to include degree and other tertiary level courses and "any other course which is of a standard above that of an ordinary national diploma";

(c) for persons under 19, the circumstances in which education is to be treated as full-time for the purposes of s 55(5), and thus bringing them within s 55(1), are defined in terms of time spent in instruction, supervised study, examination and other activities within the course curriculum, where such education exceeds 12 hours per week (para 3);

(d) interruptions in education of up to 6 months, where reasonable, are permitted (s 55(6) and para 4);

(e) circumstances in which a person who has ceased full-time education, but remains under 19, may be treated as coming within the terms of s 55(1), and therefore being treated as a "child", are set out in para 5 for the purposes of s 55(7); but where a person is in employment, he cannot be a "child" under s 55(1) (para 5(5)).

****

Children Act 1989

ARRANGEMENT OF SECTIONS

PART I
INTRODUCTORY

PART II
ORDERS WITH RESPECT TO CHILDREN IN FAMILY PROCEEDINGS

General

Special guardianship

Financial relief

PART II

PART VI
COMMUNITY HOMES

PART VII
VOLUNTARY HOMES AND VOLUNTARY ORGANISATIONS

PART VIII
REGISTERED CHILDREN'S HOMES

PART IX
PRIVATE ARRANGEMENTS FOR FOSTERING CHILDREN

PART XA
CHILD MINDING AND DAY CARE FOR CHILDREN IN WALES

Introductory

Regulations

Registration

PART II

PART I
INTRODUCTORY

1 Welfare of the child

(1) When a court determines any question with respect to –

    (a) the upbringing of a child; or

    (b) the administration of a child's property or the application of any income arising from it,

the child's welfare shall be the court's paramount consideration.

(2) In any proceedings in which any question with respect to the upbringing of a child arises, the court shall have regard to the general principle that any delay in determining the question is likely to prejudice the welfare of the child.

(3) In the circumstances mentioned in subsection (4), a court shall have regard in particular to –

    (a) the ascertainable wishes and feelings of the child concerned (considered in the light of his age and understanding);

    (b) his physical, emotional and educational needs;

    (c) the likely effect on him of any change in his circumstances;

    (d) his age, sex, background and any characteristics of his which the court considers relevant;

    (e) any harm which he has suffered or is at risk of suffering;

    (f) how capable each of his parents, and any other person in relation to whom the court considers the question to be relevant, is of meeting his needs;

    (g) the range of powers available to the court under this Act in the proceedings in question.

(4) The circumstances are that –

(a)   the court is considering whether to make, vary or discharge a section 8 order, and the making, variation or discharge of the order is opposed by any party to the proceedings; or

(b)   the court is considering whether to make, vary or discharge a special guardianship order or an order under Part IV.

(5) Where a court is considering whether or not to make one or more orders under this Act with respect to a child, it shall not make the order or any of the orders unless it considers that doing so would be better for the child than making no order at all.

Amendments—ACA 2002, s 115.

Defined terms—"child", "upbringing": s 105(1).

Delay generally (s 1(2))—The general principle that delay is harmful applies to any proceedings concerning "the upbringing" of a child, but does not apply where the question at issue is the child's maintenance. Both practitioners and courts have a duty to avoid delay in children cases. A children's guardian has a duty to review the file regularly and, if the case is not making satisfactory progress, should apply for directions (*B v B (Minors) (Interviews and Listing Arrangements)* [1994] 2 FLR 489, CA, *Re A and B (Minors) (No 2)* [1995] 1 FLR 351, FD, and *B v B (Child Abuse: Contact)* [1994] 2 FLR 713). The possibility of avoiding delay by arranging for a split hearing should be borne in mind (*Re S (Care Proceedings: Split Hearing)* [1996] 2 FLR 773, FD, considered further under s 31), but a split hearing should not be ordered unless the case cannot properly be decided without one. See further **Split hearings** under s 31 and FPR 2010, r 12.12.

   However, it is the welfare of the child that is the court's paramount consideration (s 1(1)) and there are bound to be cases in which planned and purposeful delay will improve the chances of meeting the child's needs satisfactorily (for example, where a parent needs time to resolve housing difficulties, or where it is felt that the court would benefit from a full investigation and report from a psychiatrist, or where, as in *C v Solihull MBC* [1993] 1 FLR 290 and *Hounslow LBC v A* [1993] 1 FLR 702, an investigation by the local authority is not yet complete, or where, as in *Re W (Welfare Reports)* [1995] 2 FLR 142, CA, the need to ensure that the court is as fully informed and advised as possible outweighs the disadvantage of delay caused by ordering a court welfare report). See also **Delay occasioned by obtaining welfare report** and **Court differing with recommendations in welfare report** under s 7. For consideration of the difficult problem of when the court should cease to be involved in the case and should hand over to the local authority by making a full care order, see under s 38.

Public Law Outline (PLO)—The PLO is contained in PD12A and applies to all courts hearing applications issued by local authorities under CA 1989, Pt IV (care and supervision orders). In August 2009 the MoJ issued a *Best Practice Guide: Preparing for Care and Supervision Proceedings* (see Part V), which is for use by all professionals involved with children and families pre-proceedings, and in preparation for applications made under CA 1989, s 31. It complements the *Statutory Guidance* and the PLO (FPR PD12A), but is not intended to be prescriptive. There is a revised statutory guidance for local authorities in *The Children Act 1989 Guidance and Regulations, Volume 1* (Department for Children, Schools and Families). Annex 1 to the *Guidance* contains a useful flow chart showing the way in which the pre-proceedings checklist and subsequent court proceedings will work. The *Guidance* aims to: ensure that families and children understand proceedings and are as far as possible enabled positively to engage with the system; ensure that applications are only made after all safe and appropriate alternatives have been explored; improve the quality and consistency of applications under CA 1989, s 31; and encourage closer working relationships between agencies in the system. See further **PLO** under FPR 2010, r 12.24 and **First appointment**, **Case management conference** and **Issues resolution hearing** under FPR 2010, r 12.25.

Private Law Programme—The framework for private law cases is contained in the Private Law Programme (FPR PD12B).

Delay and pending criminal proceedings—The fact that criminal proceedings are pending does not prevent the court exercising its discretion to proceed to hear a related children's case in order to avoid undesirable delay. The court must balance all the factors involved, taking into account any risk of prejudice to the accused and any risk so far as the child is concerned (*Re TB (Care Proceedings: Criminal Trial)* [1995] 2 FLR 801). Each case must be decided on its merits. The welfare of the child has to take precedence over the detriment to the family facing criminal proceedings.

Related provisions—The provision as to delay is related to other provisions of the Act, namely s 11 (duty of the court in s 8 proceedings to draw up a timetable and to give appropriate directions) and s 32(1) (corresponding duty in proceedings under s 31 for a care or supervision order). See also the provisions as to timing contained in FPR 2010, rr 12.12 (Directions) and 12.13 (Timetables).

Status of s 1(3) checklist factors—The s 1(3) checklist sets out a range of factors to be taken into account and the weight of each factor will vary from case to case. The wishes and feelings of a mature child do not carry any presumption of precedence over any other factors (*Re P-S (Children)* [2013] EWCA Civ 223).

No order (s 1(5))—Section 1(5) does not create a presumption one way or the other. All it demands is that before the court makes any order it must ask the question: "Will it be better for the child to make the order than making no order at all?" (*Re G (Children)* [2006] 1 FLR 771). For an example of the approach being adopted by the courts in relation to the "no order" principle see *Re J (Refusal of Contact)* [2012] EWCA Civ 720. Where the court makes no order, there should still be a written order to that effect (*S v R (Parental Responsibility)* [1993] 1 FCR 331). If appropriate, it is possible for the order to recite the intention of the parties at the time of the order, as a preliminary to stating that the court considered an order unnecessary (*M v M (Defined Contact Application)* [1998] 2 FLR 244 in which there was an order of "no order as to defined contact" but with the parents' joint wishes and expectations set out in the preamble).

Shared parenting—The Children and Families Bill: the Justice Select Committee is engaged in pre-legislative scrutiny of draft clauses on shared parenting that are expected to be published in the autumn.

2 Parental responsibility for children

(1) Where a child's father and mother were married to each other at the time of his birth, they shall each have parental responsibility for the child.

(1A) Where a child –

    (a)   has a parent by virtue of section 42 of the Human Fertilisation and Embryology Act 2008; or

    (b)   has a parent by virtue of section 43 of that Act and is a person to whom section 1(3) of the Family Law Reform Act 1987 applies,

the child's mother and the other parent shall each have parental responsibility for the child.

(2) Where a child's father and mother were not married to each other at the time of his birth –

    (a)   the mother shall have parental responsibility for the child;

    (b)   the father shall have parental responsibility for the child if he has acquired it (and has not ceased to have it) in accordance with the provisions of this Act.

(2A) Where a child has a parent by virtue of section 43 of the Human Fertilisation and Embryology Act 2008 and is not a person to whom section 1(3) of the Family Law Reform Act 1987 applies –

    (a)   the mother shall have parental responsibility for the child;

    (b)   the other parent shall have parental responsibility for the child if she has acquired it (and has not ceased to have it) in accordance with the provisions of this Act.

(3) References in this Act to a child whose father and mother were, or (as the case may be) were not, married to each other at the time of his birth must be read with section 1 of the Family Law Reform Act 1987 (which extends their meaning).

(4) The rule of law that a father is the natural guardian of his legitimate child is abolished.

(5) More than one person may have parental responsibility for the same child at the same time.

(6) A person who has parental responsibility for a child at any time shall not cease to have that responsibility solely because some other person subsequently acquires parental responsibility for the child.

(7) Where more than one person has parental responsibility for a child, each of them may act alone and without the other (or others) in meeting that responsibility; but nothing in this Part shall be taken to affect the operation of any enactment which requires the consent of more than one person in a matter affecting the child.

(8) The fact that a person has parental responsibility for a child shall not entitle him to act in any way which would be incompatible with any order made with respect to the child under this Act.

(9) A person who has parental responsibility for a child may not surrender or transfer any part of that responsibility to another but may arrange for some or all of it to be met by one or more persons acting on his behalf.

(10) The person with whom any such arrangement is made may himself be a person who already has parental responsibility for the child concerned.

(11) The making of any such arrangement shall not affect any liability of the person making it which may arise from any failure to meet any part of his parental responsibility for the child concerned.

Amendments—ACA 2002, s 111; HFEA 2008, s 56, Sch 6, Pt 1, para 26(1)–(3).

3 Meaning of "parental responsibility"

(1) In this Act "parental responsibility" means all the rights, duties, powers, responsibilities and authority which by law a parent of a child has in relation to the child and his property.

(2) It also includes the rights, powers and duties which a guardian of the child's estate (appointed, before the commencement of section 5, to act generally) would have had in relation to the child and his property.

(3) The rights referred to in subsection (2) include, in particular, the right of the guardian to receive or recover in his own name, for the benefit of the child, property of whatever description and wherever situated which the child is entitled to receive or recover.

(4) The fact that a person has, or does not have, parental responsibility for a child shall not affect –

    (a)   any obligation which he may have in relation to the child (such as a statutory duty to maintain the child); or

    (b)   any rights which, in the event of the child's death, he (or any other person) may have in relation to the child's property.

(5) A person who –

    (a)   does not have parental responsibility for a particular child; but

    (b)   has care of the child,

may (subject to the provisions of this Act) do what is reasonable in all the circumstances of the case for the purpose of safeguarding or promoting the child's welfare.

Hague Convention 1996—The Hague Convention 1996 came into force in the UK on 1 November 2012. Art 1 defines the meaning of "parental responsibility" in cases to which the Convention applies. The definition is purposively broad and should be given an autonomous Convention meaning rather than its purely domestic law meaning. Arts 16-18 cover the attribution, extinction and exercise of parental responsibility in such cases. See commentary under the Convention in Part VI.

4 Acquisition of parental responsibility by father

(1) Where a child's father and mother were not married to each other at the time of his birth, the father shall acquire parental responsibility for the child if –

(a) he becomes registered as the child's father under any of the enactments specified in subsection (1A);

(b) he and the child's mother make an agreement (a "parental responsibility agreement") providing for him to have parental responsibility for the child; or

(c) the court, on his application, orders that he shall have parental responsibility for the child.

(1A) The enactments referred to in subsection (1)(a) are –

(a) paragraphs (a), (b) and (c) of section 10(1) and of section 10A(1) of the Births and Deaths Registration Act 1953;

(b) paragraphs (a), (b)(i) and (c) of section 18(1), and sections 18(2)(b) and 20(1)(a) of the Registration of Births, Deaths and Marriages (Scotland) Act 1965; and

(c) sub-paragraphs (a), (b) and (c) of Article 14(3) of the Births and Deaths Registration (Northern Ireland) Order 1976.

(1B) The Secretary of State may by order amend subsection (1A) so as to add further enactments to the list in that subsection.

(2) No parental responsibility agreement shall have effect for the purposes of this Act unless –

(a) it is made in the form prescribed by regulations made by the Lord Chancellor; and

(b) where regulations are made by the Lord Chancellor prescribing the manner in which such agreements must be recorded, it is recorded in the prescribed manner.

(2A) A person who has acquired parental responsibility under subsection (1) shall cease to have that responsibility only if the court so orders.

(3) The court may make an order under subsection (2A) on the application –

(a) of any person who has parental responsibility for the child; or

(b) with leave of the court, of the child himself,

subject, in the case of parental responsibility acquired under subsection (1)(c), to section 12(4).

(4) The court may only grant leave under subsection (3)(b) if it is satisfied that the child has sufficient understanding to make the proposed application.

Amendments—ACA 2002, s 111; SI 2003/3191.

Defined terms—"child": s 105(1); "parental responsibility": s 3.

Duty on parents to work to put aside differences—It is an integral aspect of parental responsibility that parents should work to put aside differences and ensure that their children have relationships with both parents (*Re W (Direct Contact)* [2013] 1 FLR 494).

Father and mother not married to each other at time of child's birth (s 4(1))—Section 2(3) provides that references in the Act to a child whose father and mother were not married to each other at the time of his birth must be read with FLRA 1987, s 1. Consequently, where the child in question is treated as legitimate by virtue of Legitimacy Act 1976, s 1 (legitimacy of children of certain void marriages), is a legitimated person under s 10 of that Act (legitimation in various circumstances such as by subsequent marriage of the child's parents), has been adopted by the parents within the meaning of AA 1976, Pt IV, or is otherwise treated in law as legitimate, the case does not fall within the provisions of s 4(1) (FLRA 1987, s 1(2), (3)). The time of a person's birth must be taken to include any time during the period beginning with the insemination resulting in his birth or, where there was no such insemination, his conception, and ending with his actual birth (FLRA 1987, s 1(4)). As to the parents of a child born of in vitro fertilisation, artificial insemination etc see HFEA 1990, ss 33–48.

Unmarried father acquires parental responsibility on registration or re-registration of birth—A father who was not married to the mother at the time of the child's birth has parental responsibility if his name is placed on the birth certificate at registration or re-registration of the birth under the Births and Deaths Registration Act 1953. However, in reality, the unmarried father will not be able to register his name without the consent of the mother. Once the unmarried father acquires parental responsibility by such registration then parental responsibility can only be removed by order of court, on application by any person with parental responsibility for the child or, with permission, on the application of the child himself (provided he has sufficient understanding).

Parental responsibility order on application of father (s 4(1)(a))—Where the parents agree that the father should have parental responsibility, they may enter into a parental responsibility agreement. Where the mother is not prepared to do this or cannot be found, the father will have to apply to the court for a parental responsibility order (see Procedural Guide D6). The mother cannot apply under s 4 for an order against the father but, if she felt the father was not pulling his weight with regard to the child's upbringing, she would have other remedies open to her, for example a s 8 application or an application under Sch 1 for financial relief for the child. A father is entitled to ask the court to recognise his position as the father of the child irrespective of any question of residence or contact. The order confers on the committed father the status of parenthood for which nature has already ordained he must bear responsibility (*Re S (Parental Responsibility)* [1995] 2 FLR 648, CA, which contains a helpful review of the authorities). The court considers the degree of commitment the father has shown towards the child, the degree of attachment between him and the child and the reasons why he is applying for the order but these three requirements, though a starting point, are not intended to be exhaustive and the court must take into account all the relevant circumstances, bearing in mind that CA 1989, s 1 applies and the welfare of the child is therefore paramount (*Re H (Parental Responsibility)* [1998] 1 FLR 855, CA). The leading case on the proper approach to determine parental responsibility is *Re C and V (Minors) (Contact: Parental Responsibility Order)* [1998] 1 FLR 392 and this indicates that such applications are to be considered wholly separately. In *Re W (A Child)* [2013] All ER (D) 243 (Feb), although a court had been entitled to refuse a father's application for direct contact with his son on the basis that the mother's fears from his playing any role in the child's life put his future stability and well-being at risk, it was wrong to refuse to grant the father parental responsibility for that same reason; the application should have been considered separately and not refused because of the mother's speculative anxiety. Where a father is unable to exercise such responsibility his application will be refused (*M v M (Parental Responsibility)* [1999] 2 FLR 737).

Parental responsibility subject to conditions—When a parental responsibility order has been granted but it is necessary to limit the practical impact of the order so as to protect the integrity of the child's family, the court may impose certain conditions when making the accompanying contact order (*Re D (Contact and PR: Lesbian Mothers and Known Father) (No 2)* [2006] EWHC 2 (Fam)).

Parental responsibility order not susceptible to suspension—Where the court decides to make a parental responsibility order it has no power under s 4 to suspend its operation, but it can adjourn the application with liberty to restore it if circumstances change (*Re G (Parental Responsibility Order)* [2006] 2 FLR 1092).

Where natural unmarried father has not signed Birth Register but wishes to be acknowledged as the parent—In these circumstances, the father may make an application, either himself or jointly with the mother, to have the birth re-registered so as to show him as the father (Births and Deaths Registration Act 1953, s 10A). This may be done in one of several ways, by presenting the court with the appropriate declaration, statutory declaration of parentage (as to which see **Statutory declaration of parentage** below), parental responsibility agreement or parental responsibility order in the prescribed form. Where he does so, he will acquire parental responsibility for the child (CA 1989, s 4(1)).

Statutory declaration of parentage—FLA 1986, s 55A provides for declarations of parentage and enables a person to apply to the High Court, a county court or a magistrates' court for a declaration of parentage to confirm whether or not a person named in the application is or was the parent of another person so named (s 55A(1)). This remedies defects in the pre-existing law whereby, for example, a person could seek a declaration that someone else was his parent, but he could not seek confirmation of his own claim that he was a parent. Furthermore, previously it was not possible to obtain a declaration that a named person was *not* the parent of a particular child. There are various restrictions on applications made under s 55A (s 55A(2)), but the general rule is that the applicant must have a sufficient personal interest in the determination of the application (s 55A(3); see further s 55A). The procedure to be followed is set out in FPR 2010, rr 8.18–8.22.

Parental responsibility where a care order is in force—As to the granting of a parental responsibility order where a care order is in force, see *Re G (A Minor) (Parental Responsibility Order)* [1994] 1 FLR 504 and *Re CB (A Minor) (Parental Responsibility Order)* [1993] 1 FLR 920). Where a care order and a parental responsibility order co-exist, the local authority will also have parental responsibility for the child (s 33(3)(a)) and will have the power, subject to the provisions of s 33, to determine the extent to which the father may meet his parental responsibility (s 33(3)(b)). A local authority responsible for a child under a care order has no power to prevent the child from entering into a parental responsibility agreement with the child's unmarried father (*Re X (Parental Responsibility Agreement: Children in Care)* [2000] 1 FLR 517 – where the court held that the facility under s 4(1)(b) for parents of a non-marital child to enter into a parental responsibility agreement is self-contained and does not depend on the exercise of such responsibility. The local authority's argument, that where a care order is in force it shares parental responsibility by virtue of s 33 and therefore has power to determine the extent to which a parent of a child might meet that responsibility, was rejected because the entry into the agreement by the mother did not amount to an exercise by her of parental responsibility).

Parental responsibility where child is accommodated by local authority—Where a child is simply accommodated by a local authority parental responsibility remains vested in the child's parents (i e not shared by the local authority, as would be the case if a care order or interim care order were in force) and the local authority has no right to move the child from residential care to the home of foster parents without the consent of the child's parents, since parental responsibility includes the right to decide where the child lives (*R v Tameside Metropolitan Borough Council ex parte J* [2000] 1 FLR 942).

Jurisdiction—The jurisdiction of the court to make a parental responsibility order is not limited by the FLA 1986 and can be exercised in relation to a child who is permanently out of the jurisdiction, even if that child was also born out of the jurisdiction (*Re S (Parental Responsibility: Jurisdiction)* [1998] 2 FLR 921, CA).

Parental responsibility – ECHR 1950—The fact that English law treats unmarried fathers differently from married fathers in relation to the automatic acquisition of parental rights in relation to their children does not amount to a breach of Article 8 of the Convention (*B v UK* [2000] 1 FLR 1).

Automatic parental responsibility order—Where the court makes a residence order in favour of an unmarried father it must also, if he would not otherwise have parental responsibility for the child, make a parental responsibility order (s 12(1)). There may, therefore, be no need for a separate parental responsibility application to be filed if the father is confident of obtaining a residence order. In *Re A (Joint Residence: Parental Responsibility)* [2008] 2 FLR 1593 the mother's former partner was not the biological parent of her child, but he brought up the child while they cohabited. The court made a joint residence order to ensure that the ex-partner would acquire parental responsibility and so prevent the mother from marginalising him in the future upbringing of the child.

Parental responsibility agreement to be in prescribed form (s 4(2)(a))—The form of agreement is prescribed by Parental Responsibility Agreement Regulations 1991, reg 2 and is set out in the Schedule thereto. It must be signed by both parents and witnessed.

Agreement to be recorded in the prescribed manner (s 4(2)(b))—Parental Responsibility Agreement Regulations 1991, reg 3 prescribes the manner in which such agreements must be recorded.

Application to terminate parental responsibility order or agreement (s 4(3))—Anyone with parental responsibility may apply as of right (see Procedural Guide D6). A child who wishes to apply must first seek permission (in accordance with FPR 2010, rr 8.1–8.13.

Section 1(1) applies when the court is considering whether to terminate parental responsibility (*Re P (Terminating Parental Responsibility)* [1995] 1 FLR 1048, FD). Section 12(4) prevents the court bringing to an end a parental responsibility order made as a consequence of s 12(1) (see **Automatic parental responsibility order** above) at any time while the residence order to which it is linked remains in force.

Leave under s 4(3)(b) not to be given unless child of sufficient understanding (s 4(4))—Although there are no reported authorities considering the question of the child's understanding in the context of an application for permission to seek the discharge of a parental responsibility order, assistance may be gained from authorities in relation to the child's understanding in other contexts within CA 1989. These are gathered together in the annotation **"able ... to give such instructions on his own behalf"** under FPR 2010, r 16.29. The understanding of the child is the factor to which the court's attention is specifically directed, but it is unlikely to be the only relevant factor. Although the checklist of factors in s 1(3) does not apply specifically (see s 1(4)), it indicates the sort of matters that the court might want to consider in an appropriate case. By analogy with permission and other similar applications under other provisions of the Act and rules, the court will no doubt take into account the likelihood of success of the proposed application (see further under s 10). Whether the welfare of the child is paramount on the

PART II

permission application seems to be a moot point and one which has not yet been considered in the context of s 4(3). See further under **Application for leave by child** under s 10.

Procedure where leave is given—If permission is given, the application proceeds in the normal way save that there is no need for an application form to be filed because the court will already have received a draft with the appropriate number of copies as part of the permission application (FPR 2010, rr 18.1–18.13).

Family proceedings—Any application under this section is classified as "family proceedings" (s 8(3),(4)).

Hague Convention 1996—See notes to s 3.

4ZA   Acquisition of parental responsibility by second female parent

(1) Where a child has a parent by virtue of section 43 of the Human Fertilisation and Embryology Act 2008 and is not a person to whom section 1(3) of the Family Law Reform Act 1987 applies, that parent shall acquire parental responsibility for the child if –

  (a)   she becomes registered as a parent of the child under any of the enactments specified in subsection (2);

  (b)   she and the child's mother make an agreement providing for her to have parental responsibility for the child; or

  (c)   the court, on her application, orders that she shall have parental responsibility for the child.

(2) The enactments referred to in subsection (1)(a) are –

  (a)   paragraphs (a), (b) and (c) of section 10(1B) and of section 10A(1B) of the Births and Deaths Registration Act 1953;

  (b)   paragraphs (a), (b) and (d) of section 18B(1) and sections 18B(3)(a) and 20(1)(a) of the Registration of Births, Deaths and Marriages (Scotland) Act 1965; and

  (c)   sub-paragraphs (a), (b) and (c) of Article 14ZA(3) of the Births and Deaths Registration (Northern Ireland) Order 1976.

(3) The Secretary of State may by order amend subsection (2) so as to add further enactments to the list in that subsection.

(4) An agreement under subsection (1)(b) is also a "parental responsibility agreement", and section 4(2) applies in relation to such an agreement as it applies in relation to parental responsibility agreements under section 4.

(5) A person who has acquired parental responsibility under subsection (1) shall cease to have that responsibility only if the court so orders.

(6) The court may make an order under subsection (5) on the application –

  (a)   of any person who has parental responsibility for the child; or

  (b)   with the leave of the court, of the child himself,

subject, in the case of parental responsibility acquired under subsection (1)(c), to section 12(4).

(7) The court may only grant leave under subsection (6)(b) if it is satisfied that the child has sufficient understanding to make the proposed application.

Amendments—Inserted by HFEA 2008, s 56, Sch 6, Pt 1, para 27.

Scope—This provision enables a second female parent to acquire parental responsibility for a child where she becomes registered as a parent of the child under the statutory provisions set out in subsection (2), or enters into an agreement with the child's mother or by order of the court. An agreement will be a "parental responsibility agreement" within the definition of CA 1989, s 4(2) and will only be terminated by the court on application by anyone with parental responsibility for the child or, with permission, on application by the child himself.

Procedure—The procedure for applying for a parental responsibility order under s 4ZA, and for applying to discharge a parental responsibility or agreement, is the same as for s 4: see Procedural Guide D6.

Prescribed form for parental responsibility agreement—See under s 4.

Application to terminate parental responsibility order or agreement—See under s 4.

Leave under s 4ZA(7) not to be given unless child of sufficient understanding—See under s 4.

Procedure where leave is given—See under s 4.

Hague Convention 1996—See notes to s 3.

4A Acquisition of parental responsibility by step-parent

(1) Where a child's parent ("parent A") who has parental responsibility for the child is married to, or a civil partner of, a person who is not the child's parent ("the step-parent") –

  (a) parent A or, if the other parent of the child also has parental responsibility for the child, both parents may by agreement with the step-parent provide for the step-parent to have parental responsibility for the child; or

  (b) the court may, on the application of the step-parent, order that the step-parent shall have parental responsibility for the child.

(2) An agreement under subsection (1)(a) is also a "parental responsibility agreement", and section 4(2) applies in relation to such agreements as it applies in relation to parental responsibility agreements under section 4.

(3) A parental responsibility agreement under subsection (1)(a), or an order under subsection (1)(b), may only be brought to an end by an order of the court made on the application –

  (a) of any person who has parental responsibility for the child; or

  (b) with the leave of the court, of the child himself.

(4) The court may only grant leave under subsection (3)(b) if it is satisfied that the child has sufficient understanding to make the proposed application.

Amendments—Inserted by ACA 2002, s 112; amended by CPA 2004, s 75(1),(2).

Scope—This provision enables a step-parent to acquire parental responsibility for a child of his spouse by agreement between the step-parent and the parents who have parental responsibility for the child, or by order of the court. This will be a "parental responsibility agreement" within the definition of CA 1989, s 4(2) and will only be terminated by the court on application by any person with parental responsibility for the child, or, with permission, on application by the child himself.

Procedure—The procedure for applying for a parental responsibility order under s 4A, and for applying to discharge a parental responsibility order or agreement, is the same as that for s 4: see Procedural Guide D6.

Extent of court's power under s 4A—Where the husband is married to the mother of the child but is not the biological parent, s 4A is the only available route by which he can seek parental responsibility. The fact that he has become the psychological parent of the child is significant but will not necessarily be sufficient to invest him with an ongoing major role in the child's life (*Re R (Parental Responsibility)* [2011] 2 FLR 1132).

Parental responsibility agreement to be in prescribed form—See under s 4.

Agreement to be recorded in the prescribed manner—See under s 4.

Application to terminate parental responsibility order or agreement—See under s 4.

Leave under s 4A(3)(b) not to be given unless child of sufficient understanding (s 4A(4))—See under s 4.

Procedure where leave is given—See under s 4.

Hague Convention 1996—See notes to s 3.

5 Appointment of guardians

(1) Where an application with respect to a child is made to the court by any individual, the court may by order appoint that individual to be the child's guardian or special guardian if –

   (a)   the child has no parent with parental responsibility for him; or
   (b)   a residence order has been made with respect to the child in favour of a parent, guardian or special guardian of his who has died while the order was in force; or
   (c)   paragraph (b) does not apply, and the child's only or last surviving special guardian dies.

(2) The power conferred by subsection (1) may also be exercised in any family proceedings if the court considers that the order should be made even though no application has been made for it.

(3) A parent who has parental responsibility for his child may appoint another individual to be the child's guardian in the event of his death.

(4) A guardian of a child may appoint another individual to take his place as the child's guardian in the event of his death; and a special guardian of a child may appoint another individual to be the child's guardian in the event of his death.

(5) An appointment under subsection (3) or (4) shall not have effect unless it is made in writing, is dated and is signed by the person making the appointment or –

   (a)   in the case of an appointment made by a will which is not signed by the testator, is signed at the direction of the testator in accordance with the requirements of section 9 of the Wills Act 1837; or
   (b)   in any other case, is signed at the direction of the person making the appointment, in his presence and in the presence of two witnesses who each attest the signature.

(6) A person appointed as a child's guardian under this section shall have parental responsibility for the child concerned.

(7) Where –

   (a)   on the death of any person making an appointment under subsection (3) or (4), the child concerned has no parent with parental responsibility for him; or
   (b)   immediately before the death of any person making such an appointment, a residence order in his favour was in force with respect to the child or he was the child's only (or last surviving) special guardian,

the appointment shall take effect on the death of that person.

(8) Where, on the death of any person making an appointment under subsection (3) or (4) –

   (a)   the child concerned has a parent with parental responsibility for him; and
   (b)   subsection (7)(b) does not apply,

the appointment shall take effect when the child no longer has a parent who has parental responsibility for him.

(9) Subsections (1) and (7) do not apply if the residence order referred to in paragraph (b) of those subsections was also made in favour of a surviving parent of the child.

(10) Nothing in this section shall be taken to prevent an appointment under subsection (3) or (4) being made by two or more persons acting jointly.

(11) Subject to any provision made by rules of court, no court shall exercise the High Court's inherent jurisdiction to appoint a guardian of the estate of any child.

(12) Where the rules of court are made under subsection (11) they may prescribe the circumstances in which, and conditions subject to which, an appointment of such a guardian may be made.

(13) A guardian of a child may only be appointed in accordance with the provisions of this section.

Amendments—ACA 2002, s 115.

Defined terms—"child": s 105(1); "family proceedings": s 8(3); "parental responsibility": s 3; "residence order": s 8(1).

Scope—A guardian appointed under this section will generally take over parental responsibility for the child after the death of a parent and must, of course, be distinguished from a guardian ad litem appointed for the purposes of legal proceedings.

Application by any individual (s 5(1))—Application must be made by the person who wishes to be appointed as guardian. "Individual" is not defined in the Act; it clearly does not include a company or a local authority, or even an "artificial individual" within the local authority such as the director of social services (*Re SH (Care Order: Orphan)* [1995] 1 FLR 746, FD). However, there is nothing to prevent a number of individuals each launching separate applications and this could lead to the appointment of a couple, for example, an aunt and uncle. Although there does not seem to be any bar on an application by a minor, good sense suggests that the court would be unlikely to grant an application by one child to be appointed to act as guardian for another.

"power ... may also be exercised in any family proceedings" (s 5(2))—If it thinks fit, the court may, in any family proceedings, make an order appointing a guardian of its own initiative without any formal application having been filed. No doubt such an order will most frequently be prompted at the suggestion of a party to the proceedings or of an interested friend or relative who has been allowed to address the court, or even of the child himself, but there is nothing to prevent the court itself taking the lead in appropriate circumstances.

Date from which the appointment is effective—There may be a delay between a guardian being named (e g in a will or in a court order) and the time when he actually acquires parental responsibility for the child concerned. Although the Act makes no specific provision, it is apparent that the guardian is not regarded as having been appointed in accordance with the provisions of this section until the later stage.

Family proceedings—Any application under this section is classified as "family proceedings" (s 8(3),(4)).

Procedure—A guardian may be appointed in writing by a parent with parental responsibility, the appointment to take effect when he dies (if he has a residence order) or when the last surviving parent with parental responsibility dies. In default (or in addition), the court has a concurrent right of appointment. The court may also terminate the appointment of a guardian, whether he had been appointed by the court or a parent (CA 1989, s 6(7)). On making an application to the court, the applicant should also file a completed Form FM1 confirming attendance at a mediation information and assessment meeting or giving reasons for not attending (FPR PD3A, Annex A).

Hague Convention 1996—The Hague Convention 1996 came into force in the UK on 1 November 2012. It lays down rules in respect of measures directed to the protection of the person or property of the child in cases to which the Convention applies (Art 1). "Measures of protection" include guardianship, curatorship or analogous institutions (Art 3). They are intended to include systems of protection, representation or assistance that are established in favour of a child when his parents are deceased or are no longer authorised to represent him (*Handbook*, para 3.23; *Lagarde Report*, para 21). See further under the Convention in Part VI.

6 Guardians: revocation and disclaimer

(1) An appointment under section 5(3) or (4) revokes an earlier such appointment (including one made in an unrevoked will or codicil) made by the same person in respect of the same child, unless it is clear (whether as the result of an express provision in the later appointment or by any necessary implication) that the purpose of the later appointment is to appoint an additional guardian.

(2) An appointment under section 5(3) or (4) (including one made in an unrevoked will or codicil) is revoked if the person who made the appointment revokes it by a written and dated instrument which is signed –

(a) by him; or

(b) at his direction, in his presence and in the presence of two witnesses who each attest the signature.

(3) An appointment under section 5(3) or (4) (other than one made in a will or codicil) is revoked if, with the intention of revoking the appointment, the person who made it –

(a) destroys the instrument by which it was made; or

(b) has some other person destroy that instrument in his presence.

(3A) An appointment under section 5(3) or (4) (including one made in an unrevoked will or codicil) is revoked if the person appointed is the spouse of the person who made the appointment and either –

(a) a decree of a court of civil jurisdiction in England and Wales dissolves or annuls the marriage, or

(b) the marriage is dissolved or annulled and the divorce or annulment is entitled to recognition in England and Wales by virtue of Part II of the Family Law Act 1986,

unless a contrary intention appears by the appointment.

(3B) An appointment under section 5(3) or (4) (including one made in an unrevoked will or codicil) is revoked if the person appointed is the civil partner of the person who made the appointment and either –

(a) an order of a court of civil jurisdiction in England and Wales dissolves or annuls the civil partnership, or

(b) the civil partnership is dissolved or annulled and the dissolution or annulment is entitled to recognition in England and Wales by virtue of Chapter 3 of Part 5 of the Civil Partnership Act 2004,

unless a contrary intention appears by the appointment.

(4) For the avoidance of doubt, an appointment under section 5(3) or (4) made in a will or codicil is revoked if the will or codicil is revoked.

(5) A person who is appointed as a guardian under section 5(3) or (4) may disclaim his appointment by an instrument in writing signed by him and made within a reasonable time of his first knowing that the appointment has taken effect.

(6) Where regulations are made by the Lord Chancellor prescribing the manner in which such disclaimers must be recorded, no such disclaimer shall have effect unless it is recorded in the prescribed manner.

(7) Any appointment of a guardian under section 5 may be brought to an end at any time by order of the court –

(a) on the application of any person who has parental responsibility for the child;

(b) on the application of the child concerned, with leave of the court; or

(c) in any family proceedings, if the court considers that it should be brought to an end even though no application has been made.

Amendments—Law Reform (Succession) Act 1995, s 4; CPA 2004, s 76.

Defined terms—"child": s 105(1); "family proceedings": s 8(3); "parental responsibility": s 3.

Scope—This section deals with the ways in which the appointment of a guardian may be brought to an end (ie by revocation, disclaimer or court order). It has been extended to provide for the revocation of appointment of a guardian, in the absence of any express contrary intention, in the case of an appointment of a former spouse or civil partner as guardian in the will of a testator dying after 1 January 1996 by dissolution or annulment of the marriage or civil partnership. In practical terms, this will affect appointments made by a testator in favour of his or her former spouse or civil partner in respect of a child who is not the child of the former spouse or civil partner. Where the child is the child of both parties, the revocation will not have any practical effect since the former spouse or civil partner will continue to have parental responsibility for the child.

"Where regulations are made" (s 6(6))—No such regulations have yet been made.

"on the application of any person who has parental responsibility for the child" (s 6(7)(a))—As the guardian himself will have acquired parental responsibility for the child under s 5(6), he could apply for an order terminating his own appointment if the circumstances made it inappropriate for him to disclaim under s 6(5).

"on the application of the child concerned, with leave" (s 6(7)(b))—Permission must be sought in accordance with FPR 2010, rr 18.1–18.13. As to the circumstances in which leave should be given, see **Leave under s 4(3)(b) not to be given unless child of sufficient understanding** under s 4. As is the case with s 4, the checklist of factors in s 1(3) does not apply specifically but gives examples of factors that may be relevant. The position is also likely to be the same under s 4 and s 6 with regard to the relevance of the chances of success of the proposed application, and there is similar uncertainty with regard to the applicability of s 1(1). One difference between the two provisions is that the court is not, under s 6(7), expressly directed to consider whether the child is of sufficient understanding to make the proposed application, but it will no doubt bear this factor in mind.

Once permission has been given, the application proceeds in the normal way save that there is no need for an application form to be filed because the court will already have received a draft with the appropriate number of copies as part of the permission application (FPR 2010, rr 18.1–18.13).

"in any family proceedings ... even though no application has been made" (s 6(7)(c))—If it thinks fit, the court may, in any family proceedings, make an order terminating the appointment of a guardian even though no formal application has been filed. No doubt such an order will most frequently be prompted at the suggestion of a party to the proceedings or of an interested friend or relative who has been allowed to address the court, or even of the child himself, but there is nothing to prevent the court itself taking the lead in appropriate circumstances. Section 6(7)(c) could be used by an individual who seeks to replace an existing guardian but who does not have parental responsibility and therefore cannot apply directly for the termination of the existing guardian's appointment. Where such an individual launches an application under s 5(1) for his own appointment (which application is classified as family proceedings), he could then invite the court in the course of that application not only to appoint him as guardian for the child but also to terminate the appointment of the existing guardian.

Hague Convention 1996—See notes to s 5.

7 Welfare reports

(1) A court considering any question with respect to a child under this Act may –

    (a)   ask an officer of the Service or a Welsh family proceedings officer; or
    (b)   ask a local authority to arrange for –
        (i)   an officer of the authority; or
        (ii)   such other person (other than an officer of the Service or a Welsh family proceedings officer) as the authority considers appropriate,

to report to the court on such matters relating to the welfare of that child as are required to be dealt with in the report.

(2) The Lord Chancellor may, after consulting the Lord Chief Justice, make regulations specifying matters which, unless the court orders otherwise, must be dealt with in any report under this section.

(3) The report may be made in writing, or orally, as the court requires.

(4) Regardless of any enactment or rule of law which would otherwise prevent it from doing so, the court may take account of –

    (a)   any statement contained in the report; and
    (b)   any evidence given in respect of the matters referred to in the report,

in so far as the statement or evidence is, in the opinion of the court, relevant to the question which it is considering.

(5) It shall be the duty of the authority or officer of the Service or a Welsh family proceedings officer to comply with any request for a report under this section.

(6) The Lord Chief Justice may nominate a judicial office holder (as defined in section 109(4) of the Constitutional Reform Act 2005) to exercise his functions under subsection (2).

Amendments—CJCSA 2000 s 74, Sch 7, para 88; CA 2004, s 40, Sch 3, paras 5, 6; CRA 2005, s 15(1), Sch 4, Pt 1, paras 203, 204.

Defined terms—"child", "local authority": s 105(1); "officer of the Service": CJCSA 2000, s 11(3).

Cafcass (Children and Family Court Advisory and Support Service)—Cafcass combines the family court welfare function provided by the Guardian ad litem and Reporting Officer Service, the Family Court Welfare Service and the Children's Branch of the Official Solicitor's Office within one unified service under the responsibility of the Secretary of State for Children, Schools and Families. The central functions of Cafcass are (i) to safeguard and promote the welfare of children; (ii) to give advice to any court about any application made to it in such proceedings; (iii) to make provision for children to be represented in such proceedings; and (iv) to provide information, advice and other support for children and their families.

References to guardians ad litem, reporting officers and probation officers are subsumed within CJCSA 2000 as "officers of the service". For details of the terminology see annotations to CJCSA 2000, s 11.

FPR 2010, rr 16.33, 16.38 and PD16A, respectively, set out the principal functions of officers of the service in relation to court proceedings. The rules include section 7 reporting by officers of Cafcass and certain children cases formerly handled by the Official Solicitor. The rules do not generally extend to cover local authority officers reporting under section 7. However, the one exception is that the power of courts to request reports under CA 1989, s 7(1)(b) from the local authority is unaffected by the Cafcass provisions and officers so instructed will still be referred to as "welfare officers".

The Cafcass *Safeguarding Framework 2010* (see *www.cafcass.gov.uk*) sets out Cafcass policy in line with changes to legislation and guidance, in particular as to child protection, domestic violence and information sharing with other agencies. It reinforces the *Domestic Violence Toolkit* (see *Improving Safety, Reducing Harm* (September 2009) *www.dh.gov.uk*) by setting out the minimum standards that are expected in working with families where domestic violence may have been an issue.

A protocol has been agreed between Cafcass and the National Youth Advocacy Service (NYAS) with respect to children made parties in private law proceedings under FPR 2010, 16.4 (*Protocol of December 2005 Between the National Youth Advocacy Service and the Children and Family Court Advisory and Support Service* (see Part V)). The protocol states that Cafcass should be approached first and will usually provide a guardian. However, in certain cases NYAS may be asked by the court to provide a guardian, for example, where despite the best efforts of Cafcass, one or more members of the family can no longer work with the organisation.

Role of National Youth Advocacy Service (NYAS)—Where there is an intractable contact dispute, the court may give permission for NYAS to be approached and shown the court papers in order that they might provide advice and a voice for the children (*Re A-H (Contact Order)* [2008] 2 FLR 1188). For examples of such cases see *Re S (Unco-operative Mother)* [2004] 2 FLR 710, *Re H (National Youth Advocacy Service)* [2007] 1 FLR 1028, *Re C (A Child)* [2005] EWCA Civ 300 and *Re B (A Child)* [2006] EWCA Civ 716. In *Re C (Contact: Moratorium: Change of Gender)* [2007] 1 FLR 1642, NYAS were invited to represent two children who had not seen their father since he began to live as a woman and had no idea that he had undergone gender reassignment surgery. On the recommendation of the expert instructed in the case NYAS were also to be involved in informing the children of the truth about their father's gender.

International social services—Where the assistance of international social services, now called Children and Families Across Borders (CFAB) is required contact may be made on their UK advice and information hotline on 0207 735 8941. The line is open to all statutory and voluntary agencies as well as to private individuals in the UK. Their website is at *www.cfab.uk.net* and they also provide a secure online enquiry system which may be accessed from the website. Common subjects for inquiry include: children who are taken abroad where there are child protection concerns; assessing the capacity of relatives overseas to care for a child in an out of home placement; tracing and re-establishing contacts with family members abroad when a child presents unaccompanied; living and contact arrangements of children whose parents' have separated and live in different countries; and information about adoption.

National Standards for the Children and Family Court Advisory and Support Service (Cafcass)—The most recent document is dated June 2007 and sets out the framework of service principles and standards, including a rigorous complaints procedure to ensure that issues regarding the service are reviewed and resolved efficiently. They are available on the Cafcass website at *www.cafcass.gov.uk.*

President's Interim Guidance to address backlog of work for Cafcass—On 1 October 2010, the President of the Family Division issued *Agreement to Assist Cafcass Pending Implementation of the Family Justice Review*, which was to be read alongside the *Public Law Outline* (PLO) in FPR PD12A. It urged full and effective implementation of the PLO and aimed to enhance interagency working, reduce backlogs in the allocation of public law guardians, assist guardians to make the best use of their time and minimise the use of Cafcass "duty advisers". Particular emphasis was given to the need for judicial continuity and active case management (para 2). Although the Agreement expired on 30 September 2011, it was felt that the good practice generated by it is now so well established that it would continue without the need for any formal agreement. A joint message to this effect was published by the President of the Family Division and the Chief Executive of Cafcass on 29 July 2011 (see Part V).

Rules as to children and family reporter's duties—See FPR 2010, r 16.33 and PD16A.

"A court considering any question with respect to a child under this Act" (s 7(1))—The court's power is a very wide one and can be used not only in the traditional way in residence/contact proceedings under s 8 but also, for example, in connection with parental responsibility applications, applications for specific issue orders, applications by children for permission to commence proceedings under the Act, and emergency protection order applications.

Where children's guardian acting—Although there is power both at first instance (CA 1989, s 7) and on appeal to the High Court from the magistrates' court (CA 1989, ss 7 and 94(5)) to appoint a children and family reporter in public law proceedings, only in exceptional circumstances will a welfare report be sought when a children's guardian is already involved (*Re S (A Minor) (Guardian ad litem/Welfare Officer)* [1993] 1 FLR 110). The roles of the children and family reporter and the children's guardian are not identical, in that a children's guardian has an extra duty to represent the child in court and to instruct legal representation for him if necessary, but they are similar in many respects. Therefore, it will usually be a duplication of effort and expense to appoint both in the same proceedings. The general principle in *Re S* was confirmed by the Court of Appeal in *L v L (Minors) (Separate Representation)* [1994] 1 FLR 156 (s 8 case), but the court expressed the hope that the welfare officer (children and family reporter) who had already begun investigations would report despite the subsequent appointment of a guardian ad litem (children's guardian) in that particular difficult case.

Conciliation as an alternative—At the First Hearing Dispute Resolution Appointment (see FPR 2010, r 12.31, and PD12B) the district judge is attended by a children and family reporter, and it is essential that both parties and their legal advisers attend. There is an opportunity for the parties to attempt to reach agreement with the assistance of the children and family reporter. If they are able to do so, the district judge will make the appropriate orders; if not, he will give directions for hearing. That district judge and children and family reporter then take no further part in that application. Outside the Principal Registry, before ordering an inquiry and report by a children and family reporter, a judge or district judge should, where local conciliation facilities exist, consider whether the case is suitable for conciliation; if so, a direction should be given to that effect. If conciliation fails, any report which is ordered must be by a children and family reporter who did not act as a conciliator (see also *Re H (Conciliation: Welfare Reports)* [1986] 1 FLR 476).

When a children and family reporter is reporting as opposed to acting as conciliator, he must investigate and report on the situation, but it is not his role to attempt conciliation although he may encourage the parties to settle their differences if the likelihood of a settlement arises during the course of his enquiries.

Statements made by parties in conciliation meetings are not admissible in evidence, except where the statement clearly indicates that the maker has in the past caused, or is likely in the future to cause, serious harm to the well-being of a child. Even in such a case, the judge has a discretion whether to admit the evidence and should do so only if the public interest in protecting the child outweighs the public interest in the confidentiality of attempted conciliation (*Re D (Minors) (Conciliation: Privilege)* [1993] 1 FLR 932, CA).

Officer of the Service—Historically, children and family reporters have usually been officers of the Service; however, the court has power to invite a report from the local authority. In this context, the old terminology "welfare officer" remains, since the welfare officer is appointed to report under CA 1989, s 7(1)(b) (see under **Children and Family Court Advisory and Support Service (Cafcass)** (above) and under FPR 2010, r 16.33 and PD16A). *Re W (Welfare Reports)* [1995] 2 FLR 142, CA, highlights the different expertise that can be expected from the two classes of reporter. Welfare officers are accustomed to the court process, to interviewing the child and relevant adults, to attending court, to making recommendations orally or in writing and to submitting to questioning by the parties. Social workers are familiar with the reporting routine in the context of preparing reports for use at case conferences and for placing on file for the assistance of other social workers etc. Their knowledge of the court process may be much more limited, and their role will frequently be confined to fact-finding reports and will not involve the making of any recommendations at all.

Despite the fact that paras (a) and (b) of s 7(1) are expressed as alternatives, it appears that it can be right to order a report from the children and family reporter as well as a report from a social worker (see *Re W (Welfare Reports)* (above) and *Re A and B (Minors) (No 2)* [1995] 1 FLR 351). When there has been a referral to or involvement by Social Services, it is sensible that the local authority be directed to provide a s 7 report rather than Cafcass to ease the burden placed on Cafcass. Once the report is received, the court will consider the conduct of the case further in the light of it at a directions hearing. The local authority will be expected to make the social worker who writes the s 7 report available to give evidence (which will be at the invitation of the court rather than as a witness for any party) and to be cross-examined at the substantive hearing or at any interim hearing where oral evidence is required and to agree to discovery of relevant documentation underlying the report (as to this, see also *W v Wakefield City Council* [1995] 1 FLR 170). Wall J clearly contemplates that, having received the local authority's report, the court might direct that a further report be prepared, this time by a children and family reporter.

In deciding whether to direct a local authority report under s 7, the alternative of s 37 must, of course, be kept in mind. This entitles the court to direct the local authority to investigate the child's circumstances, provided that it appears that it may be appropriate for a care or supervision order to be made in respect of him. However, Wall J points out in *Re A and B (Minors) (No 2)* (above) that, in most cases, s 37 does not apply and that, in any event, it does not appear appropriate in circumstances where the court is requesting the local authority to provide information about an investigation that has already been undertaken rather than requiring it to embark on an investigation.

For further guidance as to whether a children and family reporter or a local authority should be used, see **Best practice guidance on s 37(1) directions** under CA 1989, s 37, which also provides guidance on the communication to a local authority of a s 7(1) referral and draws attention to the need to fix a hearing at the time of referral. See **PLO** under FPR 2010, r 12.24, and PD12A.

"such other person ... as the authority considers appropriate" (s 7(1)(b)(ii))—It is not appropriate to use s 7(1)(b)(ii) to make an order requiring the local authority to appoint an officer to obtain a report from a child psychiatrist (*Re K (Contact: Psychiatric Report)* [1995] 2 FLR 432, CA). Section 7(1)(b)(ii) confers on the local authority discretion as to the other person appointed, and the court has no power to control that appointment or to require the local authority to pay for expert advice. In specified proceedings, a psychiatric report can be obtained independently through a s 41 children's guardian but there can be no such guardian appointed in private law proceedings. Section 41(6A) includes within the category of proceedings which may be "specified for the time being ... by rules of court" any proceedings for the making, varying or discharging of an order under CA 1989, s 8 (ie residence, contact, specific issue and prohibited steps orders). This potential to widen the definition of "specified proceedings" reflects the growing pressure for the appointment of children's guardians in certain private law children cases, for example bitterly contested residence or contact disputes, where children frequently have particular needs and interests that do not coincide with or cannot be adequately represented by the parents (*Re H (Contact Order) (No 2)* [2002] 1 FLR 22; *Re M (Intractable Contact Dispute: Interim Care Order)* [2003] 2 FLR 636). The use of expert evidence and the instruction of experts in family proceedings is governed by FPR Pt 25 and PD25A–PD25F.

Delay occasioned by obtaining a welfare report—Obtaining a welfare report will normally take some weeks or months and will not infrequently cause delay in achieving a final resolution of the issues between the parties. In deciding whether to order a report, the court will therefore have to have in mind s 1(2) (the delay principle) and balance any prejudice that there is likely to be to the child through delay against the desirability of obtaining a report, the child's welfare being the paramount consideration (see *Re H (Minors) (Welfare Reports)* [1990] 2 FLR 172, CA). For the position where delay may be occasioned through the need to adjourn proceedings for the children and family reporter to attend to give oral evidence, see **Court differing with recommendations in welfare report** below.

"such matters relating to the welfare of that child as are required" (s 7(1))—Although there is nothing to prevent the court issuing a general request for a report on the child's welfare (in which case, the children and family reporter must simply comply with any regulations in force under s 7(2) and be guided by the National Standards for Cafcass), it will usually be more efficient for it to indicate which matters should be addressed. This could be a broad request, for example to produce a report relevant to the issue of residence, or a very specific request, for example to visit premises where the child is living to investigate whether or not they present a health risk or to interview the child's teacher with a view to ascertaining his school attendance record and progress. If the children and family reporter becomes concerned about other matters in the course of preparing his report, it would, of course, be entirely proper for him to bring these (and any other relevant factors) to the attention of the court. By virtue of

FPR PD12J *Residence and Contact Orders: Domestic Violence and Harm*, and the Cafcass Safeguarding Framework, copies of all applications for residence and contact are sent to Cafcass to enable them to undertake initial screening of the parties, including seeking information from the police about any previous convictions and information from the local authority about any previous referrals concerning them. Before the first hearing, Cafcass notifies the court of the results of their searches (see the *Private Law Programme* in FPR PD12B). There are circulars governing the obtaining of details of previous convictions of parties, spouses etc from the police: Home Office Circulars 88/1982, 105/1982, 47/1993. As to the desirability of the court knowing of previous convictions of a party, see *Re R (Minors) (Custody)* [1986] 1 FLR 6. See also the *Police/Family Disclosure Protocol* of July 2007 in Part V.

"regulations specifying matters which ... must be dealt with" (s 7(2))—No regulations have yet been made in this respect. The reporter must therefore pay careful attention to any specific directions given by the commissioning court about the scope of the report and derive guidance from authorities and from the National Standards for Cafcass (see note above). Subject to any limitations expressly imposed by the court it will generally be appropriate to visit the child's home (and, where a change of accommodation is proposed, any proposed new home), to interview the protagonists (mother, father and grandparents if closely involved), local authority social workers with knowledge of the family and anyone else whose view might be of assistance (for example, playgroup leader, teacher or health visitor) and to meet the child (alone and/or in company with parents or carers as appropriate to the application before the court) so as to ascertain, where possible, his wishes and feelings. In *Re R (A Minor) (Court Welfare Report)* [1993] Fam Law 722 the court emphasised the duty to see all relevant parties and, whenever possible, the child with each of the protagonists.

Duty of local authority or officer of the Service to comply (s 7(5))—In theory, there is no room for argument once the court has made its request for a report; the officer of the Service or local authority chosen has a duty to report as requested. The time for representations about who should be responsible for the report and what it is feasible for it to cover is therefore before the report is commissioned. The problem is that this depends upon a representative of Cafcass or the local authority being on hand at the relevant time which will not always be the case. In the event that the court's request does cause difficulties, contact should be made with the court explaining the nature of the obstacle and asking for directions to be given under FPR 2010, r 12.12. If the difficulty is an inability to meet the time-limits set down by the court or, in default of any time-limit set by the court, by the rules (see FPR 2010, r 16.33 and PD16A), the court will have to balance the prejudice that there is likely to be to the welfare of the child (see s 1(2)) against the desirability of obtaining a relevant report, the child's welfare being the paramount consideration (*Re H (Minors) (Welfare Reports)* [1990] 2 FLR 172). The power to vary time-limits derives from FPR 2010, rr 4.1(3), 12.12(2) and 12.13. Normally, the appropriate course is to find out from Cafcass how long is required for the report and to fix a date in the light of that information so that the report will be available for the fixed hearing (*B v B (Minors) (Interviews and Listing Arrangements)* [1994] 2 FLR 489, CA; *Re A and B (Minors) (No 2)* [1995] 1 FLR 351). In a case which is clearly going to be contested, it is desirable that the direction for a welfare report should, as was pointed out in *Re A and B (Minors) (No 2)*, be given in the context of overall directions for the filing of evidence and a fixed date for final determination.

Statements and evidence otherwise inadmissible (s 7(4))—The welfare report and the children and family reporter's evidence will often contain reports of conversations that he has had with third parties (e g relatives, neighbours and teachers) and with the child, and may also contain other statements traditionally viewed as inadmissible. Section 7(4) is a very broad provision enabling the court to disregard all rules of evidence and to take into account any statement or evidence which is relevant to the question in issue. Plainly certain statements or evidence will be more influential than others and the court must decide what weight is appropriate to attach to each (*R v B County Council ex parte P* [1991] 1 FLR 470; see also the Children (Admissibility of Hearsay Evidence) Order 1993 in Part IV). Where the children and family reporter includes hearsay in his report, he should identify it as such, give the source of it and give any reasons he has for agreeing with any opinions he passes on (*Thompson v Thompson* [1986] 1 FLR 212). Although it is always difficult for a party to deal with hearsay evidence that is prejudicial to him, this practice will at least alert the court to the deficiencies of the evidence and enable the party who feels himself prejudiced to interview the original author of the statement or opinion with a view to calling him to give evidence if he has been inaccurately reported. It appears that, in accordance with s 7(4)(b), once a particular matter has found its way into the welfare report, the court may entertain any relevant evidence with regard to it from any witness (not just the parties and the children and family reporter) with no restrictions as to hearsay.

Guarantees of confidentiality not appropriate—A children and family reporter cannot guarantee confidentiality to a person who makes allegations to him while he is investigating the circumstances of the case. It is for the judge to decide whether or not evidence must be disclosed to the parties (*Re G (Minors) (Welfare Report: Disclosure)* [1993] 2 FLR 293). The principles applicable are set out in **Submission of evidence** under FPR 2010, r 12.12.

Court differing with recommendation in welfare report—The final decision as to any question in issue rests with the court, but the welfare report and any recommendations that the children and family reporter makes must be taken into account (*Re P (Custody of Children: Split Custody Order)* [1991] 1 FLR 337). If the court decides not to follow the recommendation of the children and family reporter, it should give its reasons (*Re J (Children) (Residence: Expert Evidence)* [2001] 2 FCR 44). In *Re R (Residence Order)* [2010] 1 FLR 509, the Court of Appeal held that the judge had erred in setting on one side the firm evidence of the child's own wishes (a boy aged 9) and in rejecting the Cafcass officer's clear recommendation, together with the reasons for both, without any new evidence or any reasoned challenge to either, and without having heard the officer's oral evidence. There should have been a short adjournment to allow for the attendance of the officer.

Clearly, it will usually be desirable to set out *in terms* the reasons for differing from the children and family reporter's recommendations, but *Re V (Residence: Review)* [1995] 2 FLR 1010, CA, shows that failure to do so will not necessarily vitiate the decision, provided that the reasons for the decision were sound and either explained or constituted a sound basis for dissenting from the children and family reporter. In *Re CB (Access: Attendance of Court Welfare Officer)* [1995] 1 FLR 622, CA (a case concerning the risk of sexual abuse of a child by a Sch 1 offender), it was said to be a defective exercise of discretion for a judge to reject clear-cut recommendations and warnings in a children and family reporter's report without availing himself of the opportunity of receiving further assistance from the officer by way of oral evidence. The court suggested that where, as in *Re CB*, the children and family reporter is not available in person for some reason, it is open to the judge to adjourn the case and demand his or her presence. He can then put to the children and family reporter the reasons why he, the judge, does not agree with him and obtain from the officer an explanation of the officer's views. However, in *Re C (Section 8 Order: Court Welfare Officer)* [1995] 1 FLR 617, the Court of Appeal pointed out that *Re CB* is not a hard and fast rule of law. Whether to adjourn a case so that the children and family reporter can attend is a matter for the judge's discretion and he must carry out the balancing act which is required by the paramount consideration of the child's welfare and the provisions as to delay in s 1(2). Many factors will have to be taken into account, including how much further assistance the children and family reporter can give, what his attendance is likely to change and the extent to which it would be safe and proper to depart from any recommendations made. Whereas in *Re CB*, the children and family reporter had made clear recommendations and warnings of the most serious kind and it was not proper to reject these in his absence, in *Re C* the report was in reality an account of the interviews that the children and family reporter had had with both parents and with the child and reached conclusions which set out the arguments and considerations very fairly and did not make firm recommendations in any particular directions, although the tenor of the considerations was in favour of the status quo (residence with the mother). In these circumstances, the judge had been entitled to exercise his discretion by refusing the father's application for an adjournment for the children and family reporter to attend.

Position of children and family reporter in court—See under CJCSA 2000, s 16 below.

Independent welfare reports—The *Family Justice Review Final Report* recommends that independent social workers should only be used exceptionally (paras 3.131, 3.132).

PART II
ORDERS WITH RESPECT TO CHILDREN IN FAMILY PROCEEDINGS

General

8 Residence, contact and other orders with respect to children

(1) In this Act –

"a contact order" means an order requiring the person with whom a child lives, or is to live, to allow the child to visit or stay with the person named in the order, or for that person and the child otherwise to have contact with each other;

"a prohibited steps order" means an order that no step which could be taken by a parent in meeting his parental responsibility for a child, and which is of a kind specified in the order, shall be taken by any person without the consent of the court;

"a residence order" means an order settling the arrangements to be made as to the person with whom a child is to live; and

"a specific issue order" means an order giving directions for the purpose of determining a specific question which has arisen, or which may arise, in connection with any aspect of parental responsibility for a child.

(2) In this Act "a section 8 order" means any of the orders mentioned in subsection (1) and any order varying or discharging such an order.

(3) For the purposes of this Act "family proceedings" means any proceedings –

    (a) under the inherent jurisdiction of the High Court in relation to children; and

    (b) under the enactments mentioned in subsection (4),

but does not include proceedings on an application for leave under section 100(3).

(4) The enactments are –

    (a) Parts I, II and IV of this Act;

    (b) the Matrimonial Causes Act 1973;

    (ba) Schedule 5 to the Civil Partnership Act 2004;

    (c) (*repealed*)

    (d) the Adoption Act and Children Act 2002;

    (e) the Domestic Proceedings and Magistrates' Courts Act 1978;

    (ea) Schedule 6 to the Civil Partnership Act 2004;

    (f) (*repealed*)

    (g) Part III of the Matrimonial and Family Proceedings Act 1984;

    (h) the Family Law Act 1996.

    (i) sections 11 and 12 of the Crime and Disorder Act 1998.

Amendments—FLA 1996, s 66(1), (3), Sch 8, para 60(1), Sch 10; Crime and Disorder Act 1998, s 119, Sch 8, para 68; ACA 2002, Sch 3, para 55; CPA 2004, s 261(1), Sch 27, para 129(1)–(3).

Defined terms—"child": s 105(1); "parental responsibility": s 3.

Scope—The Act seeks to set up a flexible system which enables the court to have as wide a choice of orders as possible so that any question which arises with regard to the welfare of a child can be resolved, whatever the nature of the proceedings before the court. The wide definition of "family proceedings" that is contained in the section facilitates this.

Jurisdiction—See FLA 1986, Pt I.

Duty on parents to work to put aside differences—It is an integral aspect of parental responsibility that parents should work to put aside differences and ensure that their children have relationships with both parents (*Re W (Direct Contact)* [2013] 1 FLR 494; *Re W (Contact: Permission to Appeal)* [2013] 1 FLR 609).

Residence of and contact with adult child—Where the local authority felt that an adult child of 17 with a mental age of between 5 and 8 years was at risk of significant harm if she lived at home with her mother, but was too old to be made the subject of a care order, the court held that it had inherent declaratory jurisdiction to keep the "child" in local authority accommodation and to restrict and supervise the child's contact with her family (*Re F (Adult: Court's Jurisdiction)* [2000] 2 FLR 512). The doctrine of necessity could be invoked in such circumstances and the inherent jurisdiction was not excluded by the statutory framework. There is no presumption of a right to contact between a parent and an adult child. Where the adult child is under a disability and is not in a position to consent to contact, the question is whether it is in the adult child's best interests to have contact with her parents (*Re D-R (Adult: Contact)* [1999] 1 FLR 1161). The jurisdictional basis for such an application is unclear, but would not appear to fall within s 8, where the definition of "child" for the purposes of a contact application refers to a child under the age of 18 (s 105(1)). Furthermore, the court is required by CA 1989, s 9(6) not to make any s 8 order which is to have effect for a period that will end after the child has reached the age of 16, unless the circumstances of the case are exceptional. The MCA 2005 contains remedies in respect of welfare, finance and health issues for those persons over 16 years of age who lack capacity.

Residence and contact – importance of biological parentage—Where an applicant for a residence order is both the biological and psychological parent of the child, this is an important and significant factor in determining what would be best for the children in the short term and in the long term (*Re G*

(Children) [2006] 2 FLR 629, HL). In *Re B (A Child)* [2010] 1 FLR 551, the Supreme Court held that consideration of the importance of parenthood in private law disputes about residence must be firmly rooted in an examination of what is in the child's best interests. This is the paramount consideration. It is only as a contributor to the child's welfare that parenthood assumes any significance. In common with all other factors bearing on what is in the best interests of the child, it must be examined for its potential to fulfil that aim. To talk in terms of a child's rights – as opposed to his or her best interests – diverts from the focus that the child's welfare should occupy in the minds of those called on to make decisions as to residence. Furthermore, in decisions about residence there is no place for the question whether the proposed placement would be "good enough" or a supposedly adequate alternative. Where a father donates his sperm to a lesbian couple so that they can have a child but then wishes to have a relationship with the child, it is wrong to class him as a "secondary" parent because it has the danger of demeaning him and his potential future role in the child's life; his application for contact must be considered in terms of the paramountcy of the child's welfare (*A v B and C (Lesbian Co-Parents: Role of Father)* [2012] 2 FLR 607).

Contact orders cannot be made without first determining with whom a child lives—CA 1989 does not require that in every case there should be a residence order in relation to which a contact order exists but simply that there should be a person defined or capable of definition with whom the child lived. If one parent is the primary carer but does not trouble to obtain a residence order enshrining her role, a contact order can still be made against her as the person with whom the child lives (*Re H (Contact: Adverse Findings of Fact)* [2011] 2 FLR 1201).

Enforcement of contact orders—The court has specific powers to impose directions and conditions on contact orders (ss 11A, 11B). The court can impose contact activities (ss 11D–11G) and require Cafcass officers to monitor a person's compliance (s 11G). When the court makes a contact order it may order a Cafcass officer to facilitate and monitor compliance for up to 12 months and report to the court (s 11H). Courts have additional tools for enforcement where contact orders are breached, including curfews, tagging and unpaid work: ss 11J–11N. Financial compensation may be ordered for losses sustained by failure, without reasonable excuse, to comply with an order (ss 11O–11P). However, none of these provisions apply to children who are subject to an application for an adoption order (s 11B(4)). See also FPR PD12N *Enforcement of Children Act 1989 Contact orders: Disclosure of Information to Officers of the National Probation Service.*

Warning notices on contact orders—All contact orders made or varied after 8 December 2008 must have a warning notice on them, setting out the consequences of not complying with the order. It is no longer necessary to make a separate application for a penal notice to be attached. Transitional provisions allow parties to apply to have a warning notice attached to an existing contact order (CAA 2006, s 8). The application must be made on Form C78 by a person who falls within the criteria set down by CA 1989, s 11J(5)(a)–(d). See further s 11I.

Care required when drafting contact orders to which warning notices are to be attached—It is *mandatory* for a court to attach a warning notice when it makes or varies *any* contact order. It follows that a contact order must be made in terms that comply with s 8(1), whereas a recital in declaratory terms does not require a warning notice to be attached. Thus, it may be more appropriate for consent orders to set out the agreed regime as a recital or schedule to the order on the basis of which the court then applies the "no order" principle. See further under s 11I.

Revised protocol for referrals of families to Supported Child Contact Centres by Judges and Magistrates—See Protocol on the NACC website at *www.naccc.org.uk* (tel 0845 4500 280).

Contact – ECHR 1950—The ECHR 1950 was implemented in this jurisdiction on the coming into force of HRA 1998. There are a number of cases in which unmarried fathers have complained that the refusal of the court to grant them contact with their children constitutes a breach of their right to family life, which right is protected by ECHR 1950, Art 8. The ECtHR upheld such complaints by unmarried fathers in *Elsholz v Germany* [2000] 2 FLR 486; *Ciliz v The Netherlands* [2000] 2 FLR 469; *Elsholz v Italy* [2000] Fam Law 680, but rejected the father's complaint in *Glaser v UK* (Case No 32346/96) [2001] 1 FLR 153. In *S and G v Italy* [2000] 2 FLR 771 a mother's complaint that the authorities had prevented her having contact with her children was upheld and found to constitute a breach of Art 8. In three cases the ECtHR considered the approach of the German courts to contact applications by unmarried fathers and held that consideration of what lies in the best interests of the child is of crucial importance in every case of this kind. A fair balance has to be struck between the interests of each parent and those of the child and in doing so particular importance must be attached to the best interests of the child which, depending on their nature and seriousness, may override those of the parent. A parent's rights are secondary to the child's health and development (*Sahin v Germany; Sommerfeld v Germany; Hoffmann v Germany* [2002] 1 FLR 119). However, it is going too far to say that domestic courts should always hear evidence from a child in court on the issue of access or that a psychological expert should be involved (see Grand Chamber decision, *Sahin v Germany; Sommerfeld v Germany* [2003] 2 FLR 671). There will be no violation of Art 8 where a reduction in contact is justified in the child's interests (*Hoppe v Germany* [2003] 1 FLR 384). Where the court makes a private law order there is a positive obligation on public authorities under Art 8 to take measures to enforce a parent's right to be reunited with his child, although the obligation is not absolute and the interests and freedoms of all parties must be taken into account (*Sylvester v Austria* [2003] 2 FLR 210; *Hansen v Turkey* (Application No 36141/97) [2004] 1 FLR 142; *Kosmopoulou v Greece* [2004] 1 FLR 800). In *Bove v Italy* [2005] Fam Law 752, the failure of the court to enforce the father's access rights had infringed his Art 8 rights to respect for his family life. The key question to be asked is whether the national authority has taken all steps that are reasonable in the circumstances (*Zawadka v Poland* [2005] 2 FLR 897). These include ensuring that the parent concerned can exercise effective contact at a time compatible with his work and on suitable premises (*Gluhakovic v Croatia* [2011] 2 FLR 294). For a succinct recital of the principles to be derived from case-law both from the ECtHR and the domestic courts, see the judgment of Munby LJ in *Re C (Direct Contact: Suspension)* [2011] 2 FLR 912 at [47].

For the procedure to be followed in making a claim under HRA 1998, see annotation thereto and FPR 2010, r 29.5.

Contact – domestic violence—A new cross-government definition of domestic violence has been recognised and applies to any incidents of controlling, coercive or threatening behaviour, violence or abuse between those aged 16 or over who are or have been intimate partners or family members regardless of gender, sexuality or ethnic group. This definition, which is not a legal definition, includes, but is not limited to, psychological, physical, sexual, financial and emotional abuse, so-called "honour"-based violence, female genital mutilation and forced marriage. The Court of Appeal in *Re L (Contact: Domestic Violence). Re V (Contact: Domestic Violence). Re M (Contact: Domestic Violence)* and *Re H (Contact: Domestic Violence)* [2000] 2 FLR 334 laid down useful guidelines as to the way in which courts should approach the hearing of contact applications in which allegations of domestic violence are raised. Their lordships referred to the joint report of Drs Sturge and Glaser ([2000] Fam Law 615) and it is recommended that practitioners read it in full. FPR PD12J *Residence and Contact Orders: Domestic Violence and Harm* places a duty on the court at all stages of the proceedings to consider whether domestic violence is an issue and, if so, to identify the factual and welfare issues involved. The PD represents good practice and judges are not entitled to take short-cuts that either run the risk of compromising the welfare of the children or that fail to follow accepted practice (*Re Z (Unsupervised Contact: Allegations of Domestic Violence)* [2009] EWCA Civ 430). However, FPR PD12J does not prevent a judge from making an order for contact without making findings of fact in relation to disputed allegations of domestic violence. Para 13 does not dictate that there must be a fact-finding hearing; it simply requires the court to determine as soon as possible whether it is necessary to conduct such a hearing before it can proceed to consider any final order for residence or contact (*Re H (A Child)* [2013] EWCA Civ 72). Once findings of fact of domestic violence have been made, the judge must ensure that he considers all the evidence necessary to determine the children's best interests (*Re W (Children: Domestic Violence)* [2012] EWCA Civ 528). See further under **Fact-finding hearings** (below).

The Domestic Violence, Crime and Victims Act 2004 makes breach of a non-molestation order a criminal offence as from 1 July 2007. Consequently, it is no longer possible to attach a power of arrest to a non-molestation order. However, breach of a non-molestation order automatically becomes an arrestable offence under PACE 1984, s 24(1). See further under Procedural Guide A10.

Where there is a conflict between the rights and interests of a child and those of a parent, the interests of the child must prevail under ECHR 1950, Art 8(2) (*Re L* etc (above)). See further **Contact – ECHR 1950** (above).

Fact-finding hearings—The *President's Guidance in Relation to Split Hearings*, issued in May 2010 (see Part V) makes it clear that a split hearing should not be ordered unless the case cannot properly be decided without one. Allegations of violence do not automatically justify a preliminary fact-finding hearing. FPR PD12J, para 15 contemplates a two-stage process of fact-finding and welfare hearing, but it does not require two separate hearings. PD12J should be read as imposing an obligation on the court to determine whether findings need to be made about factual issues at all and whether, and if so, that should be done in a separate fact-finding hearing or as part of a composite fact-finding and welfare hearing. If the court decides that a separate fact-finding hearing is necessary then it must give directions for it and fix a date for the welfare hearing there and then (*Re (H (A Child)* [2013] EWCA Civ 72 and see annotation **Contact – Domestic Violence** (above)). The court must consider the nature of the allegations and the extent to which, if admitted or proved, they would be relevant in making its decision. If they are unlikely to have any impact on the court's order, there is no need for a separate fact-finding hearing. Where there is a multiplicity of allegations and counter-allegations the court must be careful to establish whether or not a fact-finding hearing has a true purpose and whether the scale of the inquiry is proportionate to the nature of the allegations made; see the guidance given in *AA v NA and KAB* [2010] 2 FLR 1173. However, a judge must be very cautious before reversing the decision of another judge that a fact-finding hearing is necessary (*Re F-H (Dispensing With Fact-Finding Hearing)* [2009] 1 FLR 349). Only when he has heard all the evidence and made findings of fact can he determine where the best interests of the child really lie (*Re Z (Unsupervised Contact: Allegations of Domestic Violence)* [2009] 2 FLR 877). It is not appropriate for the judge to accept a submission of no case to answer because of the quasi-inquisitorial nature of his enquiry and the objective of identifying and resolving issues of fact relevant to the best interests of the child (*Re R (Fact-Finding Hearing)* [2009] 2 FLR 83). The judicial task is to lay the foundation for subsequent hearings and in the interim to inform professionals who have to make assessments and report to the court. Where a fact-finding hearing is adjourned part-heard it is unusual for the court to order interim contact. However, in *S v S (Interim Contact)* [2009] 2 FLR 1586, the district judge ordered one hour of interim supervised contact a fortnight when he was forced to adjourn the hearing part-heard for several months. In upholding his decision on appeal, Hedley J observed that an interim contact order raises the very question at issue in the proceedings, namely whether there should be contact at all. On the other hand, the longer the delay, if it be that contact should be ordered, the more inimical for the child.

Risk assessments—The CA 1989, s 16A requires a Cafcass officer carrying out any function in private law CA 1989 proceedings to carry out a risk assessment if he has cause to suspect that the child concerned is at risk of harm, and to provide that assessment to the court. See further under s 16A and FPR 2010, rr 16.33 and 12.34, and see PD16A, paras 11.1–11.7 and the amended Form 42. See also FPR PD12L *Risk Assessments under Section 16A*.

Contact disputes – separate representation of children—As a matter of principle where the court is faced with difficult contact issues, consideration may be given to the children being separately represented (*Re H (Contact Order) (No 2)* [2002] 1 FLR 22; *Re W (Contact: Joining Child as Party)* [2003] 1 FLR 681; *Re M (Intractable Contact Dispute: Interim Care Order)* [2003] 2 FLR 636). In difficult private law cases where the child does need separate representation, the appropriate course will be to invite Cafcass Legal to provide a guardian to represent the child and take over the child's case (*Re W (A Child)* [2001] All ER (D) 348 (Nov); and see further under FPR 2010, r 16.4 and PD16A). General guidance in relation to the appointment of a children's guardian is to be found under CA 1989, s 7 **Cafcass Practice Note**.

   See annotation **Role of National Youth Advocacy Service (NYAS)** under CA 1989, s 7 for details of the increased importance of NYAS in the separate representation of children, particularly in acrimonious contact disputes.

Electronic tagging in family proceedings—The availability of electronic tagging arrangements in family proceedings was established in *Re C (Abduction: Interim Directions: Accommodation by Local Authority)* [2004] 1 FLR 653. The President confirmed this and devised a process whereby tagging could be arranged through the Tagging Team of the National Office for the Management of Offenders. The decision in *Re A (Family Proceedings: Electronic Tagging)* [2009] 2 FLR 891 sets out the procedure to be adopted, including a Specimen Electronic Tagging Order.

Transfer of residence—There have been a number of reported cases in which the court has ordered the transfer of residence from the primary carer to a parent with whom contact has been frustrated or sabotaged. However, this is a judicial weapon of last resort (*Re A (Residence Order)* [2010] 1 FLR 1083, CA – where the judge had been wrong to make an order transferring residence of three children to their father, following the mother's refusal to allow contact, as no clear contact order had been made by the court). Nevertheless, in *Re C (Residence Order)* [2008] 1 FLR 211, the court did transfer residence from the mother to the father as a result of the mother's implacable hostility to contact. The draconian step of an immediate order for transfer, without giving time for a relationship to develop between the child and father, had been necessary because of the mother's intractability. There is no consensus in the research as to the approach that should be taken in a case involving an alienated child. In *Re S (Transfer of Residence)* [2011] 1 FLR 1789 the court considered three approaches to effecting the transfer of residence: (a) a stepping-stone process involving a period in foster care before transfer; (b) a therapeutic approach; and (c) use of the tipstaff. In *Re S* (above) the judge said, per curiam, that when determining any high-conflict case involving an alienated child, it is essential that the court has the benefit of professional evidence from an expert. See also *Re M (Contact)* [2012] EWHC 1948 in note **Section 11(7)** under s 11.

Suspended transfer of residence—Where a parent persists in disobeying a contact order the court may order the transfer of residence of the children, but suspend the operation of the transfer upon the obdurate parent complying with the order (*Re D (Children)* [2009] EWCA Civ 1467).

"shall be taken by any person" (s 8(1))—In the definition of a prohibited steps order, "any person" includes someone who is not a party to the proceedings (*Re H (Prohibited Steps Order)* [1995] 1 FLR 638, CA – prohibited steps order requiring mother's former cohabitee, who was not a party, not to have or to seek contact with the children, liberty being given to him to apply on notice to vary or discharge the order under s 11(7)(d)).

Change of surname—At birth, a child must be registered in accordance with the Births and Deaths Registration Act 1953. Where the parents are married, the duty to register lies on both the mother and father; where they are not married at the time of the birth, the duty is the mother's alone. The surname entered is to be the one by which at the date of the registration it is intended that the child shall be known. However, it is possible either for the parents jointly or for the mother alone to apply for the name of the father to be entered into the Register of Births, on the production of Statutory Declarations (see Births and Deaths Registration Act 1953, s 10A). See further **Where natural unmarried father has not signed Birth Register but wishes to be acknowledged as the parent** under s 4. Once the surname has been registered, there is nothing in BDRA 1953 to permit it to be changed in the register (see the consideration of BDRA 1953 in *Dawson v Wearmouth* [1997] 2 FLR 629, CA and [1999] 1 FLR 1167, HL; *Re C (Change of Surname)* [1998] 2 FLR 656, CA and *Re W, Re A, Re B (Change of Name)* [1999] 2 FLR 930). Accordingly, the courts' powers are limited to regulating the name by which a child should be known. However, there is a requirement that the parents of a child who is legitimated by their subsequent marriage must re-register the child's birth within 3 months of the date of the marriage by virtue of which he was legitimated (Legitimacy Act 1976, s 9).

A change of the name by which a child is known can be evidenced by deed poll or, in practice, can be achieved more informally, by a parent simply arranging for a child to be known on a day-to-day basis by a new surname (for example at school). In each case, there are important pre-conditions for the change of name. The general principle that must be observed is that "the registration or change of a child's surname is a profound and not a merely formal issue, whatever the age of the child. Any dispute on such an issue must be referred to the court for determination whether or not there is a residence order in force and whoever has or has not parental responsibility. No disputed registration or change should be made unilaterally." (*Dawson v Wearmouth* (above); *Re T (Change of Surname)* [1998] 2 FLR 620). Note the reconsideration by the House of Lords (reported at [1999] 1 FLR 1167, HL) of some aspects of the Court of Appeal's decision in *Dawson v Wearmouth*. The House of Lords reviewed the principles to be applied to a change of name application (including the question of what weight is to be given to the name in which the child has been duly registered) but the procedural aspects of such an application were not the subject of an appeal and were not considered.

It appears that the proper course in all cases in which a change of name is contemplated will be as follows:

(1) There should first be consultation with anyone who has parental responsibility. This should happen whether or not there is a residence order in force (*Re PC (Change of Surname)* [1997] 2 FLR 730, FD).

(2) There remains uncertainty about the extent to which consent of a father who does not have parental responsibility is material to a change of name. Thorpe LJ in *Re T* (above) remarked at p 623B when speaking of the decision in *Re PC* that it was "persuasively indicative of the clear principle that children's names are important and in any situation of dispute, either the consent of the other parent or the permission of the court is an essential pre-requisite, *certainly where both parents have parental responsibility*" (author's emphasis) thus begging the question. Holman J in *Re PC* had, in fact, held (p 739) that where a child is born of parents who are not married to each other and there is no order or agreement for parental responsibility, the mother can lawfully change the child's surname without any other permission or consent. Furthermore, it will be noted that CA 1989, s 13 (which applies where there is a residence order) only refers to the consent of those with parental responsibility and it may be reasonable to infer from this a more general view that a father without parental responsibility should not be entitled to prior consultation about name changes. On the other hand, if a father without parental responsibility learns of, and disagrees with, plans to change his child's name (or wishes to contest a fait accompli), he is entitled to bring the matter before the court under s 8 (*Dawson v Wearmouth*, see further below), despite the absence of a right to prior consultation. The Court of Appeal in *Re C (Change of Surname)* (above), considering the action of a mother who effected a change of name by deed poll at a time when the father did not have parental responsibility but had made his opposition to the name change known, commented that at the first signs of dispute about a child's name the court should be involved, but expressly left to one side whether that arose as a matter of wisdom, common decency or binding obligation.

(3) If consent is forthcoming, it would be prudent in all cases to have it put in writing. Written consent of everyone with parental responsibility is, in any event, a statutory requirement by virtue of CA 1989, s 13(1) where there is a residence order (or a deemed residence order dating from before CA 1989, see *Re B (Change of Surname)* [1996] 1 FLR 791). Written consent will also generally be required if a deed poll is to be enrolled (see below).

(4) If the change of name is disputed, the matter must be referred to the court for determination.
 (a) Where a residence order (or deemed residence order) is in force, a freestanding application for permission should be made under CA 1989, s 13. An application under s 8 is not appropriate (*Re B (Change of Surname)* (above) as explained in *Dawson v Wearmouth* [1997] 2 FLR 629, CA, undisturbed by the House of Lords decision at [1999] 1 FLR 1167).

(b) Where there is no residence order, application should be made under CA 1989, s 8. An application under s 13 is not appropriate (*Dawson v Wearmouth* (above)). Whether the application will be for a specific issue order or for a prohibited steps order may depend upon the circumstances. In both *Dawson v Wearmouth* and *Re T (Change of Surname)* (above), the order sought was a specific issue order; in *Re PC* both specific issue and prohibited steps orders were made.

There looks, technically, to be a difference in the way in which a court should approach s 8 and s 13 applications. Section 1(1) applies in both cases to make the child's welfare the court's paramount consideration but s 1(3) (welfare check list), while applicable to s 8 applications, is not applicable to s 13 applications (see s 1(4)). However, as the Court of Appeal pointed out in *Dawson v Wearmouth*, the distinction is more theoretical than real because the judge entertaining an application under s 13 will invariably have regard, in fact, to the considerations identified in s 1(3) in his search for welfare as the paramount consideration even if under no specific statutory duty so to do. It is anticipated that the review by the House of Lords in *Dawson v Wearmouth* of the approach that should be taken with a s 8 application will accordingly be influential also in s 13 applications. The present position in cases which deal with changing the name of a child is helpfully summarised by Butler-Sloss LJ in *Re W, Re A, Re B (Change of Name)* [1999] 2 FLR 930, with the caveat that the summary only lays down guidelines and does not purport to be exhaustive. Each case must be decided on its own facts, with the welfare of the child the paramount consideration and all the relevant factors weighed in the balance by the court at the time of the hearing. The factors are set out at page 933F of the judgment.

A deed poll evidences a change of name in a formal way. It is first executed then enrolled with the Central Office of the High Court. Enrolment will not be permitted unless certain conditions are complied with. Reference should be made to the Enrolment of Deeds (Change of Name) Regulations 1994 and CPR PD5A, para 6.1 and its Appendix.

Re PC (above) raises (but does not rule upon) the possibility that the position as to name change may be different for an older child, in particular a child of over 16, where the consent of the child *may* be necessary and sufficient. See also *Re S (Change of Surname)* [1999] 1 FLR 672 (annotated under CA 1989, s 33).

It may be appropriate in certain cases for a child to use the surnames of both his mother and father (*Re R (Surname: Using Both Parents')* [2001] 2 FLR 1358 – where the child was to move to Spain with his mother and the parents were urged to follow the Spanish practice of using both parents' surnames in order to ease the child's adjustment to a life in that culture and to encourage transparency as to his parentage).

Although a change of surname should not be permitted without evidence that it would improve the children's welfare, in certain circumstances the court may find that it is justified and give permission accordingly (*Re F (Contact)* [2008] 1 FLR 1163 – where a change of surname for the children gave them some extra protection against the possibility of abduction by their father).

Statutory declaration of parentage—See **Statutory Declaration of Parentage** under CA 1989, s 4.

Revealing the identity of the child's father; revealing the fact of the existence of the child—There have been a number of cases concerning the circumstances in which it may be in the child's interests to be informed of the identity of his father, and whether the child's family have a right to know of his existence. It is difficult to draw any consistent principles from these cases as each appears to turn upon its own facts (*Re L (Adoption: Contacting Natural Father)* [2008] 1 FLR 1079; *Re C v X Y Z County Council* [2008 1 FLR 1294; *Birmingham City Council v S, R and A* [2007] 1 FLR 1223; *Re F (Paternity Jurisdiction)* [2008] 1 FLR 225; *Re J (Paternity: Welfare of Child)* [2007] 1 FLR 1064; *Re D (Paternity)* [2007] 2 FLR 26). However, what is clear is that the courts will not sanction the withholding of information about the existence of a child from his parent, or dispense with service on that parent of proceedings relating to the child, in anything other than exceptional circumstances (*Re A (Father: Knowledge of Child's Birth)* [2011] 2 FLR 123).

Where there is an unduly long delay in proceedings relating to the establishment of a child's paternity this may amount to a violation of ECHR 1950, Arts 6, 8, 10 and 13 because of the resulting uncertainty for the child as to his or her personal identity (*Jevremović v Serbia* (Application No 3150/05) [2008] 1 FLR 550).

Change of forenames—The forename(s) given to a child at the registration of his birth are less concrete than the surname, since it is commonplace for a child to receive a statutory registered name and also to receive different given names during the course of family life (*Re H (Child's Name: First Name)* [2002] 1 FLR 973, CA – where the father and mother, who were separated, had each registered the child with different forenames; although the father's registration was first in time the mother should be permitted to use the forename she had chosen for the child both at home and when dealing with external authorities).

Sterilisation applications—The question of sterilisation of a minor can be raised under s 8 (specific issue order); however it may be preferable to apply under the inherent jurisdiction of the court because of the procedural and administrative difficulties attached to such an application. The representation of children in family proceedings is governed by FPR 2010, Pt 16, and PD16A.

"the inherent jurisdiction of the High Court" (s 8(3)(a))—The inherent jurisdiction of the High Court was, before CA 1989, most commonly exercised in wardship proceedings. The Act has put an end to the majority of wardship applications, but applications are still made under the inherent jurisdiction of the court; see, in particular, under s 100.

"application for leave under section 100(3)" (s 8(3))—This is a reference to an application by a local authority for permission to apply for the exercise of the court's inherent jurisdiction with respect to children.

"Parts I, II and IV of this Act" (s 8(4))—Broadly speaking, this means that most proceedings under the Act are classed as family proceedings but those relating to the protection of children (under Pt V), such as applications for emergency protection orders etc, are not so classified.

Enforcement of s 8 orders—For implementing order, see s 11(7) directions and conditions and ss 11A–11P for enforcement of contact orders; for enforcement under MCA 1980, s 63(3), see s 14; for penal notices, see FPR 2010, r 33.7; and for orders for recovery of a child, see FLA 1986, s 34. See Procedural Guide D8 for enforcement of contact orders.

Costs orders in children cases—FPR 2010 disapply that part of CPR 1998 that provides a starting point that the unsuccessful party pays the costs of the successful party so that in family cases the court has a broad discretion to make such order as it thinks just. However, on an application for permission to appeal, the court may take the view that although the appeal has a real prospect of success it must be refused because it lacks any proportionality to the amount at stake (*HH v BLW (Appeal: Costs: Proportionality)* [2013] 1 FLR 420). See further under FPR 2010, Pt 28 and r 30.11.

Hague Convention 1996—The Hague Convention 1996 came into force in the UK on 1 November 2012. It lays down rules in respect of measures directed to the protection of the person or property of the child in cases to which the Convention applies (Art 1). "Measures of protection" include the attribution, exercise, termination, restriction and delegation of parental responsibility, and of custody and access (Art 3). "Rights of custody" essentially include all measures relating to the care and upbringing of, and access, contact or visitation rights concerning the child (Art 3(b)). See also the commentary to the Convention in Part VI.

Draft Legislation on Family Justice—In September 2012, draft legislation was presented to Parliament in response to David Norgrove's Family Justice Review. Clause 2(2) proposes to remove the current definitions of residence and contact orders and clause 2(3) would replace them with a "child arrangements order". However, specific issue orders and prohibited steps orders would continue as before.

9 Restrictions on making section 8 orders

(1) No court shall make any section 8 order, other than a residence order, with respect to a child who is in the care of a local authority.

(2) No application may be made by a local authority for a residence order or contact order and no court shall make such an order in favour of a local authority.

(3) A person who is, or was at any time within the last six months, a local authority foster parent of a child may not apply for leave to apply for a section 8 order with respect to the child unless –

    (a)   he has the consent of the authority;

    (b)   he is a relative of the child; or

    (c)   the child has lived with him for at least one year preceding the application.

(4) (*repealed*)

(5) No court shall exercise its powers to make a specific issue order or prohibited steps order –

    (a)   with a view to achieving a result which could be achieved by making a residence or contact order; or

    (b)   in any way which is denied to the High Court (by section 100(2)) in the exercise of its inherent jurisdiction with respect to children.

(6) No court shall make a specific issue order, contact order or prohibited steps order which is to have effect for a period which will end after the child has reached the age of sixteen unless it is satisfied that the circumstances of the case are exceptional.

(7) No court shall make any section 8 order, other than one varying or discharging such an order, with respect to a child who has reached the age of sixteen unless it is satisfied that the circumstances of the case are exceptional.

Amendments—ACA 2002, ss 113, 114(2); CYPA 2008, s 37(1).

Defined terms—"child": s 105(1); "contact order": s 8(1); "local authority": s 105(1); "local authority foster parent": s 23(3); "relative": s 105(1); "residence order": s 8(1); "section 8 order": s 8(2).

"child who is in the care of a local authority" (s 9(1))—A child who is the subject of a care order as defined in ss 31(11) and 105(1). There is power to make an order under s 34 (parental contact with child in care) as this is not a contact order within the meaning of s 8(1). An order made under s 8 on the application of a child in care for him to have contact with his siblings would be an order in respect of the siblings rather than in respect of the child in care and would not, therefore, fall foul of s 9(1) (*Re F (Contact: Child in Care)* [1995] 1 FLR 510, FD).

No application by a local authority for residence or contact order (s 9(2))—See, for example, *Re C (Contact: Jurisdiction)* [1995] 1 FLR 777, CA (local authority could not apply for contact or variation of contact in relation to children who had been freed for adoption).

"local authority foster parent of a child" (s 9(3))—The mere fact that a person is a local authority foster parent does not bring him within the section. His right to seek permission will be restricted only if he is or has been the foster parent of the particular child who would be the subject of the s 8 application. A person with whom a local authority places a child for adoption is a "local authority foster parent" and therefore precluded by s 9(3) from applying for permission (*Re C (Adoption: Notice)* [1999] 1 FLR 384, FD). For applications by local authority foster parents, see *JR v Merton London Borough* [1992] 2 FCR 174 reversed on appeal as *Re A and W (Minors) (Residence Order: Leave to Apply)* [1992] 2 FLR 154 and *C v Salford City Council and Others* [1994] 2 FLR 926. The court cannot make a s 8 order in favour of a local authority foster parent of its own initiative if s 9(3) would debar that foster parent from applying for permission to apply for such an order. The power to make orders of the court's own initiative is subject to the restrictions in s 9 (see CA 1989, s 10(3), but note the exception in *Gloucestershire County Council v P* [1999] 2 FLR 61 which is referred to in **When the court may make a s 8 order** under s 10).

Leave to apply (s 9(3))—Certain people may apply as of right for a s 8 order (see s 10(4),(5),(7)) and a foster parent is not prevented by s 9(3) from making such an application should he fall into any of these categories. For example, he may apply for a residence order where the child is in care and the local authority for whom he fosters gives its consent (s 10(5)(c)(ii)) or where the child has been living with him for at least 1 year (s 10(5A)(b)). In all other situations, permission must be obtained before an application is launched (see s 10(1)–(3)) and s 9(3) restricts the foster parents who may seek permission, as s 10 is expressed to be subject to the restrictions imposed by s 9.

"consent of the authority" (s 9(3)(a))—It is the consent of the social services authority accommodating the child that is required where the child is simply accommodated rather than being the subject of a care order (*C v Salford City Council and Others* [1994] 2 FLR 926, FD), just as it appears that it will be the authority that is responsible for the placement of the child with the foster parents that will have to consent where a care order is in force. It is ambiguous whether it is enough for the authority to consent to the foster parent making a permission application or whether the consent must be to the making of the full s 8 application or indeed to the granting of the s 8 order that the foster parent wishes to seek. There is no requirement as to the form of the consent but it would be prudent for it to be given in writing.

Restrictions on specific issue and prohibited steps orders (s 9(5))—*Nottinghamshire County Council v P* [1993] 2 FLR 134, CA, is an example of an attempt by a local authority to obtain a prohibited steps order (instead of proceeding by way of the public law provisions of CA 1989, Pt IV) which failed because it contravened s 9(5). Supervision orders with an order restraining the mother from removing the children from their foster homes are also contrary to ss 9(5) and 100(2)(b) (*Re S and D (Children: Powers of Court)* [1995] 2 FLR 456, CA). For further examples of contravention of s 9(5), see *M v C (Children Orders: Reasons)* [1993] 2 FLR 584 (without notice specific issue order for the return of children to their mother from their father) and *Re H (Prohibited Steps Order)* [1995] 1 FLR 638, CA (prohibited steps order requiring mother to prevent contact between children and former cohabitee contravened s 9(5), but prohibited steps order against former cohabitee requiring him not to have contact was acceptable). *Re M (Care: Leave to Interview Child)* [1995] 1 FLR 825, FD, also illustrates the limitations imposed by s 9(5) (not possible to use specific issue order to deal with question of whether father's solicitor could interview his two sons who were in care for purposes of preparing his defence to criminal charges; inherent jurisdiction of court used instead).

10 Power of court to make section 8 orders

(1) In any family proceedings in which a question arises with respect to the welfare of any child, the court may make a section 8 order with respect to the child if –

    (a) an application for the order has been made by a person who –
        (i) is entitled to apply for a section 8 order with respect to the child; or
        (ii) has obtained the leave of the court to make the application; or
    (b) the court considers that the order should be made even though no such application has been made.

(2) The court may also make a section 8 order with respect to any child on the application of a person who –

    (a) is entitled to apply for a section 8 order with respect to the child; or
    (b) has obtained the leave of the court to make the application.

(3) This section is subject to the restrictions imposed by section 9.

(4) The following persons are entitled to apply to the court for any section 8 order with respect to a child –

    (a) any parent, guardian or special guardian of the child;
    (aa) any person who by virtue of section 4A has parental responsibility for the child;
    (b) any person in whose favour a residence order is in force with respect to the child.

(5) The following persons are entitled to apply for a residence or contact order with respect to a child –

    (a) any party to a marriage (whether or not subsisting) in relation to whom the child is a child of the family;
    (aa) any civil partner in a civil partnership (whether or not subsisting) in relation to whom the child is a child of the family;
    (b) any person with whom the child has lived for a period of at least three years;
    (c) any person who –
        (i) in any case where a residence order is in force with respect to the child, has the consent of each of the persons in whose favour the order was made;
        (ii) in any case where the child is in the care of a local authority, has the consent of that authority; or
        (iii) in any other case, has the consent of each of those (if any) who have parental responsibility for the child.

(5A) A local authority foster parent is entitled to apply for a residence order with respect to a child if the child has lived with him for a period of at least one year immediately preceding the application.

(5B) A relative of a child is entitled to apply for a residence order with respect to the child if the child has lived with the relative for a period of at least one year immediately preceding the application.

(6) A person who would not otherwise be entitled (under the previous provisions of this section) to apply for the variation or discharge of a section 8 order shall be entitled to do so if –

    (a) the order was made on his application; or
    (b) in the case of a contact order, he is named in the order.

(7) Any person who falls within a category of person prescribed by rules of court is entitled to apply for any such section 8 order as may be prescribed in relation to that category of person.

(7A) If a special guardianship order is in force with respect to a child, an application for a residence order may only be made with respect to him, if apart from this subsection the leave of the court is not required, with such leave.

(8) Where the person applying for leave to make an application for a section 8 order is the child concerned, the court may only grant leave if it is satisfied that he has sufficient understanding to make the proposed application for the section 8 order.

(9) Where the person applying for leave to make an application for a section 8 order is not the child concerned, the court shall, in deciding whether or not to grant leave, have particular regard to –

    (a)   the nature of the proposed application for the section 8 order;

    (b)   the applicant's connection with the child;

    (c)   any risk there might be of that proposed application disrupting the child's life to such an extent that he would be harmed by it; and

    (d)   where the child is being looked after by a local authority –

        (i)   the authority's plans for the child's future; and

        (ii) the wishes and feelings of the child's parents.

(10) The period of three years mentioned in subsection (5)(b) need not be continuous but must not have begun more than five years before, or ended more than three months before, the making of the application.

Amendments—ACA 2002, s 139(1), Sch 3, paras 54, 56; CPA 2004, s 77; CYPA 2008, s 36.

Defined terms—"child", "child of the family": s 105(1); "contact order": s 8(1); "family proceedings": s 8(3); "guardian", "local authority": s 105(1); "parental responsibility": s 3; "residence order": s 8(1); "section 8 order": s 8(2).

When the court may make a s 8 order—The net effect of s 10(1)–(4) is that (subject to the restrictions set out in s 9) the court may make a s 8 order either:

(a) on the application of a person who is entitled to apply as of right, or on the application of a person who can apply with permission and has obtained permission; any such application may be an independent application (s 10(2)) or may be made in the course of existing family proceedings in which a question arises with respect to the welfare of the child (s 10(1)(a)); or

(b) in any family proceedings in which a question arises with respect to the welfare of a child, where it considers that a s 8 order should be made in respect of the child despite the fact that no application has actually been made (s 10(1)(b)).

    No doubt the court will normally be prompted to make an order under s 10(1)(b) at the suggestion of one of the parties to the proceedings or of an interested friend or relative who has been allowed to address the court, or even at the suggestion of the child himself, but there is nothing to prevent the court itself taking the lead in appropriate circumstances (see e g *Re H (A Minor) (Contact)* [1994] 2 FLR 969). The power to make orders of the court's own initiative is subject to the restrictions in s 9 (see s 10(3)). However, in *Gloucestershire County Council v P* [1999] 2 FLR 61, the Court of Appeal (Thorpe LJ dissenting) held that although s 10(3) stated that s 10 is subject to the restrictions in s 9, it did not clearly refer to the restriction in s 9(3) which is purely procedural in nature. Therefore, the court did have power under s 10(1)(b), on the exceptional facts of the case, to make an order of its own initiative, in the interests of the child, unlimited by s 9(3); this meant that the court could grant a residence order to foster-parents even where they were not entitled themselves to seek leave to apply for residence. As to the court's power to make a s 8 order even though it is not in a position to dispose finally of the proceedings before it, see s 11(3).

Application for a s 8 order—For the procedure on an application for a s 8 order, see FPR 2010, r 5.1, PD5A, PD12B and Procedural Guide D7. Where an application for permission has already been made, there is no need for an application form to be filed because the court will already have received a draft with the appropriate number of copies as part of the permission application (FPR 2010, rr 18.1–18.13), but the procedure is otherwise the same as for applications without permission.

"In any family proceedings" (s 10(1))—Where orders of a "final" nature have already been made, care must be taken to ensure that there are extant family proceedings for the purposes of s 10(1); see, for example, *Re C (Contact: Jurisdiction)* [1995] 1 FLR 777, CA.

"a person who ... is entitled to apply for a section 8 order" (s 10(1)(a))—Those persons who are entitled to apply for a s 8 order without permission are specified in s 10(4) (those entitled to apply for any s 8 order), s 10(5) (those entitled to apply for a residence or contact order) and s 10(7) (those entitled to apply by virtue of rules of court). Where the child is in care or the proposed applicant is a local authority or a local authority foster parent, the restrictions imposed by s 9 apply (s 10(3)).

Meaning of "parent" (s 10(4))—This term is not defined in the Act. A child's natural mother and father (including, by virtue of FLRA 1987, s 1, an unmarried father whether or not he has parental responsibility) are his parents unless he has been adopted, in which case his adoptive mother and father are his parents (ACA 2002, s 57). A child's natural parents are not parents within the meaning of s 10 once an adoption order has been made in respect of the child (*Re C (A Minor) (Adopted Child: Contact)* [1993] 2 FLR 431). A step parent is not a parent but may nevertheless be entitled to apply as of right for a s 8 order by virtue of s 10(5)(a). Where a child's mother cohabits with but does not marry a man who is not the child's natural father, that man cannot be classed as a parent of the child (*J v J (A Minor: Property Transfer)* [1993] 2 FLR 56). As to the parents of children born of in vitro fertilisation, artificial insemination etc, see HFEA 1990, ss 33–48.

Guardians (s 10(4)(a))—There may be a delay between a guardian being named (for example, in a will or in a court order) and the time when he actually acquires parental responsibility for the child concerned (see **Date from which the appointment is effective** under s 5). See also s 6 as to the circumstances in which an appointment can be disclaimed or revoked.

"a residence order is in force" (s 10(4)(b))—Although most residence orders are open-ended, a residence order can be made for a specified period of time (s 11(7)), in which case it will cease to be in force at the end of that period. A residence order will also cease to have effect where the court makes a further order to that effect, in certain circumstances where the parents resume cohabitation (see s 11(5)). The person in whose favour a residence order is in force is the person named in the order as the person with whom the child is to live (s 105(13)).

"person with whom the child has lived" (s 10(5)(b))—It is usually obvious where a child has been living, but it is less clear to whom the provision applies in cases where he has had more than one base, for example where he has spent weekdays with his aunt and stayed with his grandmother from Friday teatime to Monday morning. In such circumstances, it is submitted that both parties may qualify under s 10(5)(b).

"child is in the care of a local authority" (s 10(5)(c)(ii))—This refers to a child who is the subject of a care order as defined in ss 31(11) and 105(1).

Form of consent (s 10(5)(c)(iii))—Although neither the Act nor any rules stipulate the form in which consent must be expressed, it would be prudent for written consent to be obtained wherever possible and for this to be filed with the application. This will prevent difficulties arising if consent is subsequently withdrawn or the person concerned denies that it was ever given.

Persons not otherwise entitled to apply for variation or discharge (s 10(6))—An order varying or discharging a s 8 order is itself a s 8 order (s 8(2)). Consequently, anyone who may apply for a s 8 order may apply for a variation or discharge as well, with permission where appropriate. Section 10(6) adds two extra categories of person who can apply for variation or discharge, namely the original applicant for the order and, where the application concerns a contact order, any person named in that order. A person who has obtained an order for indirect contact with a child is entitled, by virtue of s 10(6), subsequently to apply for face-to-face contact without permission (*Re W (Application for Leave)* [1996] Fam Law 665, FD).

Procedure on application for variation or discharge— The procedure for variation or discharge of a s 8 order is the same as for the original application. See FPR 2010, Pt 12 and Procedural Guides D7 and D9.

Rules of court entitling persons to apply for a s 8 order (s 10(7))—No rules specifically list additional persons who may apply for a s 8 order; however, *Re HG (Specific Issue Order: Sterilisation)* [1993] 1 FLR 587 held that FPR 1991, r 9.2 (see FPR 2010, r 16.14 and PD16A, para 2.1) does make such a prescription in relation to a child's next friend.

Application by a person requiring leave—If a proposed applicant is not one of those specifically listed in s 10, he will require permission of the court before he can apply. Such applicants could include the child himself, a local authority wishing to apply for a specific issue or prohibited steps order (though note the restrictions on local authority applications imposed by s 9), past carers and relatives other than parents who cannot establish the requisite period of residence.

Application for leave by child (s 10(8))—Where the child is seeking permission, the only factor to which the court is specifically directed is that in s 10(8). However, the fact that the child has sufficient understanding does not mean that the court is bound to grant permission; it has a discretion, and his welfare is not paramount (*M v Warwickshire County Council* [2008] 1 FLR 1093. Nor is it paramount where the permission application is by anyone other than the child concerned (*Re A and W (Minors) (Residence Order: Leave to Apply)* [1992] 2 FLR 154, CA). Such applications should be approached cautiously; once a child is a party to proceedings between warring parents, he will be exposed to hearing evidence of the parents which it might be better for him not to hear and may have to be cross-examined (*Re N (Contact: Minor Seeking Leave to Defend and Removal of Guardian)* [2003] 1 FLR 652 – where the 11-year-old child did not have sufficient understanding to participate as a party in contact proceedings or give instructions that would be fully considered in their implications). For guidance as to the role that a child applicant is likely to play in the proceedings, see the notes to FPR 2010, r 12.12.

The court should also have regard to the likelihood of success of the proposed application (*Re C (Residence: Child's Application for Leave)* and *Re SC (A Minor) (Leave to Seek Residence Order)* [1994] 1 FLR 96, FD). *Re M (Care: Contact: Grandmother's Application for Leave)* [1995] 2 FLR 86, CA, although a case where permission was sought under CA 1989, s 34, has been taken to provide the most authoritative guidance as to the appropriate test with regard to the prospects of success, see further under **Application for leave by person other than child concerned**. *Re M (Care: Contact: Grandmother's Application)* is fully annotated at CA 1989, s 34 and is helpful also in demonstrating the correct approach to permission applications.

While the checklist in s 1(3) probably does not strictly apply, the matters listed there may be relevant to the court's consideration of whether to grant permission. The court will also consider why the child is seeking to apply for an order to be made in favour of someone else rather than the application being made by that person directly (*Re SC (A Minor) (Leave to Seek Residence Order)* (above) – girl of 14 sought permission to apply for residence order in favour of family friend). As to assessing the understanding of a child, see the annotation **"able ... to give such instructions on his own behalf"** to FPR 2010, r 16.29. As to the possibility of a s 8 application by a child through his next friend when the child does not have sufficient understanding to satisfy s 10(8), see *Re HG (Specific Issue Order: Sterilisation)* [1993] 1 FLR 587 and the comment thereon at [1993] Fam Law 403.

Applications for permission by children should be made in the High Court using the procedure in FPR 2010, rr 18.1–18.13.

Section 10(8) does not make provision for children to be joined as additional respondents to applications; application for that purpose is properly made under FPR 2010, rr 12.3 and 16.2 (*Re N (A Minor)* (unreported) 25 September 1997, CA).

Application for leave by person other than child concerned (s 10(9))—Section 10(9) applies to any case in which the applicant for permission is not the child who would be the subject of the substantive application, notwithstanding that the permission applicant is himself a child (*Re S (Contact: Application by Sibling)* [1998] 2 FLR 897. An order granting leave to apply for orders under s 8 of the Children Act is a case management order. It is not a "final" order in the sense of an order that determines the substantive outcome of the proceedings. The court is obliged under the rules to exercise its case management powers in accordance with the overriding objective (*Re G (A minor); Re Z (A minor)* [2013] EWHC 134 (Fam), at [58]).

Section 10(9) lists the factors to which the court should have particular regard in deciding an application for permission by someone other than the child himself, but other factors may also be relevant. The case-law relating to these factors was re-examined thoroughly by Black LJ in *Re B (Paternal Grandmother: Joinder as Party)* [2012] 2 FLR 1358 at [63–65]. The s 1(3) checklist does not apply here, nor does s 1(1) (*Re S (Contact: Application by Sibling)* (above)). The same test should be applied to applications for party status in public and private law proceedings; the test is also the same where an applicant seeks party status without making, or intending to make, any application for a specific order (*Re W (Care Proceedings: Leave to Apply)* [2005] 2 FLR 468).

It is well accepted that the court must have regard to the merits of the proposed application (see *Re S (Contact: Application by Sibling)* and the *Warwickshire* case (above)). *Re M (Care: Contact: Grandmother's Application)* [1995] 2 FLR 86, CA, although a case where permission was sought under CA 1989, s 34, has been taken to provide the most authoritative guidance as to the appropriate test with regard to the prospects of success. It is essential, however, that the court gives proper weight to the statutory criterion and does not place too great an emphasis on the factors in *Re M* (above) (*Re J (Leave to Issue Application for Residence Order)* [2003] 1 FLR 114 – where the judge erred in dismissing an application by the maternal grandmother to join contested care proceedings and apply for a residence order in relation to her granddaughter).

In considering the risk of disruption (s 10(9)(c)), it is not only the risk of disruption from the making of the substantive application that is relevant but also the disruption that there may be to the child's life if the application succeeds (*Re M (Care: Contact: Grandmother's Application)* (above) at [95H]). In *Re M* it was emphasised that the risk of disruption which is primarily contemplated in the subsection is the risk of disruption to the extent that the child would be harmed. By virtue of s 105(1), harm is defined in s 31(9). Ward LJ identified disruption as a factor of crucial significance, a fortiori for a child in care. *Re M (Prohibited Steps Order: Application for Leave)* [1993] 1 FLR 275 exemplifies the application of s 10(9)(d)(ii) which specifically requires the court to have regard to the local authority's plans for the child's future (former guardian ad litem of child in emergency protection order proceedings sought permission to apply for a s 8 order). *Re S (Contact: Application by Sibling)* (above) deals with disruption in the context of an adopted child.

The difficulty that natural parents will experience in obtaining permission to seek a s 8 order where their child has been adopted or freed for adoption is illustrated by *Re E (Adopted Child: Contact: Leave)* [1995] 1 FLR 57. See also the *Warwickshire* case (above), which concerned an application under ACA 2002, s 24(3) for permission to apply to revoke a placement order and in which the Court of Appeal suggested that when deciding whether or not to grant permission the court might usefully borrow the language of the test set out in CPR 1998, r 52.3(6) and ask whether the applicant would have a real prospect of success. Applications in relation to siblings who have been adopted will also be subject to special considerations (*Re S (Contact: Application by Sibling)*, above).

The fact that permission has been granted does not create a presumption in favour of a substantive order (*Re A (Section 8 Order: Grandparent Application)* [1995] 2 FLR 153, CA; *G v F (Contact and Shared Residence: Applications for Leave)* (above)) or elevate a person who is not a natural parent to the position of a natural parent (*Re W (Contact: Application by Grandparent)* [1997] 1 FLR 793, FD). Decisions in disputes between two female parents and a biological father are so fact-specific that "this is an area of law in which generalised guidance is not possible" (per Black LJ in *A v B and C (Lesbian Co-Parents: Role of Father)* [2012] 2 FLR 607. As part of the analysis, the court will consider the rights of legal parents to family life, including the right to make decisions about their children. Those rights are widely recognised both as a long-standing principle of English law and under ECHR 1950, Art 8. In this regard, the position of a lesbian couple who have been granted the status of legal parents by the HFEA 2008 is exactly the same as any other legal parent. Having taken those rights into account, however, it is still open to the court, after considering all relevant factors, to grant leave to other persons to apply for s 8 orders. In this regard, the position of biological fathers who have been deprived of the status of legal parent by the 2008 Act is the same as any other person (*Re G (A minor); Re Z (A minor)* (above), at [115]). However, where the lesbian couple, who are vested with legal parenthood, encourage and enable the biological father to become a psychological parent by involving him in the child's life and where the facts establish that the relationship that has developed between him and the child amounts to, or is capable of amounting to, "family life" within Art 8, those are also important facts to be taken into consideration. (See further under HFEA 2008, ss 42, 45 and 48.

"the applicant's connection with the child" (s 10(9)(b))—It is right for half siblings to be brought up together wherever possible. In *Re H (Leave to Apply for Residence Order)* [2008] 2 FLR 848 the applicants applied for permission to apply for a residence order. Their connection with the child was an "indirect" one as they were the adopters of his older half-brother. However, the court considered their connection to be of crucial importance in this case since the applicants were the older child's legal parents and the two boys were half brothers and aware of each other's existence.

"child ... being looked after by a local authority" (s 10(9)(d))—See s 22(1),(2).

Procedure on application for leave—Permission must be sought in accordance with FPR 2010, rr 18.1–18.13.

11 General principles and supplementary provisions

(1) In proceedings in which any question of making a section 8 order, or any other question with respect to such an order, arises, the court shall (in the light of any rules made by virtue of subsection (2)) –

    (a)   draw up a timetable with a view to determining the question without delay; and

    (b)   give such directions as it considers appropriate for the purpose of ensuring, so far as is reasonably practicable, that that timetable is adhered to.

(2) Rules of court may –

    (a)   specify periods within which specified steps must be taken in relation to proceedings in which such questions arise; and

(b) make other provision with respect to such proceedings for the purpose of ensuring, so far as is reasonably practicable, that such questions are determined without delay.

(3) Where a court has power to make a section 8 order, it may do so at any time during the course of the proceedings in question even though it is not in a position to dispose finally of those proceedings.

(4) Where a residence order is made in favour of two or more persons who do not themselves all live together, the order may specify the periods during which the child is to live in the different households concerned.

(5) Where –

(a) a residence order has been made with respect to a child; and
(b) as a result of the order the child lives, or is to live, with one of two parents who each have parental responsibility for him,

the residence order shall cease to have effect if the parents live together for a continuous period of more than six months.

(6) A contact order which requires the parent with whom a child lives to allow the child to visit, or otherwise have contact with, his other parent shall cease to have effect if the parents live together for a continuous period of more than six months.

(7) A section 8 order may –

(a) contain directions about how it is to be carried into effect;
(b) impose conditions which must be complied with by any person –
    (i)   in whose favour the order is made;
    (ii) who is a parent of the child concerned;
    (iii) who is not a parent of his but who has parental responsibility for him; or
    (iv) with whom the child is living,
    and to whom the conditions are expressed to apply;
(c) be made to have effect for a specified period, or contain provisions which are to have effect for a specified period;
(d) make such incidental, supplemental or consequential provision as the court thinks fit.

Defined terms—"section 8 order": s 8(2).

Scope—This section contains provisions designed to ensure that any question that arises with regard to a s 8 order is determined without delay (s 11(1) and (2)) and enabling the court to make a s 8 order at any stage during proceedings even where it is not yet ready finally to dispose of the proceedings (s 11(3)). It also contains miscellaneous provisions as to the content and duration of s 8 orders.

Avoidance of delay—Section 11(1) forces the court to take a firm hold of the reins and to lay down a procedural timetable and give appropriate directions (under FPR 2010, rr 12.12 and 12.13) to ensure that any material question is determined without delay. Both practitioners and courts have a duty to avoid delay in children cases. The Public Law Outline (PLO) in PD12A applies to all applications issued by local authorities under CA 1989, Pt IV in any court (see annotations **PLO** under FPR 2010, r 12.24 and **First hearing**, **Case management conference** and **Issues resolution hearing** under FPR 2010, r 12.25). In private law cases the *Private Law Programme* in PD12B applies to any application issued under CA 1989, Pt II.

   The non-adversarial approach to children's litigation means that the solicitors for the parties have a duty, irrespective of whether delay might be tactically advantageous to their client, to ensure that a case does not drift and is resolved with the minimum of delay. Courts have a duty to be proactive in ensuring (through the giving of precise directions) that applications, once launched, are not allowed to moulder but are brought into court in a fully prepared state at the earliest opportunity. A children's guardian, be he the Official Solicitor or an officer of Cafcass, has a duty to review the file regularly and, if the case is not making satisfactory progress, should apply to the court for further directions (see *B v B (Minors) (Interviews and Listing Arrangements)* [1994] 2 FLR 489, CA). It is good practice to avoid the delay that might otherwise be occasioned by awaiting a court welfare report by finding out in advance from Cafcass how long is required for the report and fixing a date in the light of that information. Where an assessment is in progress, it may be right to timetable the proceedings to enable them to be concluded as soon as possible once the assessment is completed; the fact that the timetable might need to be revised is not of itself a reason not to timetable (*E v Humberside County Council and S* [1996] Fam Law 444, FD). Although the general principle stated in s 1(2) is that delay is likely to be prejudicial, speed should not be the only consideration in making arrangements for the determination of an issue. The welfare of the child is the paramount consideration when a court determines any question with respect to the upbringing of a child (s 1(1)) and certain cases benefit from the passage of time which can allow tempers to cool, housing arrangements to be sorted out, medical investigations to take place etc. For cases approving planned and purposeful delay in the public law sphere, see *C v Solihull MBC* [1993] 1 FLR 290 and *Hounslow LBC v A* [1993] 1 FLR 702, and see also *Re W (Welfare Reports)* [1995] 2 FLR 142, CA, a private law case in which it was proper to call for a welfare report despite the delay that would thereby be occasioned. For the position where there are criminal proceedings pending, see **Delay** under s 1. As Wall J pointed out in *Re A and B (Minors) (No 2)*, above, in such a case the family court will need to be made aware of the current state of the criminal investigation and criminal process (if there is a prosecution) at every stage so that it can make a fully informed decision about the extent to which the duty under s 11 can be fulfilled.

"proceedings in which any question of making a section 8 order ... arises" (s 11(1))—The court's duty with regard to timetabling and the giving of directions applies whenever any question of making a s 8 order or any other question with respect to such an order arises. It is not therefore confined to applications specifically for a s 8 order.

Shared residence orders (s 11(4))—It is not necessary to show that exceptional circumstances exist before a shared residence order may be granted (*D v D (Shared Residence Order)* [2001] 1 FLR 495; *Re F (Shared Residence Order)* [2003] 2 FLR 397). Nor is it probably necessary to show a positive benefit to the child. What is required is a demonstration that the order is in the interests of the child in accordance with the requirements of s 1(1) (*D v D* (above)). It is not open to a judge to make a shared residence order as a means of ensuring that there is no resistance to a contact order (*Re W (Children)* [2003] EWCA Civ 116, CA). In *A v A (Shared Residence)* [2004] 1 FLR 1195 there was a history of acrimony and failed contact between the father and children. Eventually, the children were separately represented by the National Youth Advocacy Service and Wall J made a shared residence order based on the time spent in each home and the need for the importance of each parent to be recognised. The failure of the parents to co-operate is not a bar to the making of a joint residence order where this would in all other respects be the right order; *Re R (Residence: Shared Care: Children's Views)* [2006] 1 FLR 491; *Re W (Shared Residence Order)* [2009] 2 FLR 436. Because a shared residence order may serve the interests of the child even where the division of time between the two homes is not equal, the two aspects of the application, (1) an equal division of time and (2) a shared residence order, do not stand or fall together. They must be considered separately, with the court considering the issues together but ruling first on the optimum division of the child's time and then considering whether that division should be expressed as a shared residence order or a contact order (*Re K (Shared Residence Order)* [2008] 2 FLR 380; *Re W (Shared Residence Order)* (above)). Where the facts dictate that a shared care arrangement is in the interests of the child, equality of time with each parent is the starting point (*Re M (Residence Order)* [2008] 1 FLR 1087). However, in *Re P (Shared Residence Order)* [2006] 2 FLR 347 the children spent 55% of their time with the mother and 45% of their time with the father and the court held that this was a plain case for a shared residence order that would reflect the reality that the parents had established for the child. Where a mother's former partner is not the biological parent of her child, but the child was brought up by him while they cohabited, a joint residence order may be made so that he acquires parental responsibility (*Re A (A Child: Joint Residence: Parental Responsibility)* [2008] 2 FLR 1593 – where such an order was made so as to prevent the mother from marginalising the role of her ex-partner in the upbringing of her child).

Practical difficulties may arise where parents with shared care both claim that they are "in priority need" of council accommodation. In such cases, the Housing Act 1996, s 189(1)(b) requires the authority to consider whether the applicant is a person with whom dependent children reside or might reasonably be expected to reside. In *Holmes-Moorhouse v Richmond-upon-Thames London Borough Council* [2009] 1 FLR 904, the House of Lords gave guidance on the approach to be followed by local authorities in determining whether an applicant for council housing who has been granted a shared residence order was a person with whom dependent children "might reasonably be expected to reside", pursuant to Housing Act 1996, s 189(1)(b). Their Lordships warned that family courts should not use residence orders to try to exert pressure on housing authorities to allocate their resources in a particular way. Only in exceptional circumstances would it be reasonable to expect children who had a home with one parent to be provided by the housing authority with another so that they could also reside with the other parent. Housing is a scarce resource and the procedures for deciding how it is to be allocated should not be entangled with the procedures for deciding children's welfare.

Shared residence – relocation—The approach for the court where the question of relocation arises in the context of a shared residence order is to look at the underlying factual substratum in welfare terms, bearing in mind the tension that may well exist between a parent's freedom to relocate and the welfare of the child, which may militate against relocation. The balance is critical and, as a matter of law, the danger of distinguishing the case from the authorities because it involves a shared as opposed to sole residence order is that the court might either lose sight of, or give insufficient weight to, the former consideration (*Re L (Shared Residence: Relocation)* [2009] 1 FLR 1157 – where the judge refused the mother's application for internal relocation from London to Somerset as he reached the conclusion that she sought to undermine shared residence). A shared residence order must not be seen as an automatic bar to relocation. It may well be in the child's best interests to relocate notwithstanding the existence of such an order. The question of relocation abroad was considered in *Re D (Leave to Remove: Shared Residence)* [2006] Fam Law 1006, where the court allowed the mother to remove the children permanently from the UK to the USA, but made an order for shared residence with the father because the children would spend significant time with each parent in each jurisdiction. In *Re F (Relocation)* [2013] 1 FLR 645, the court granted a shared residence order but granted the mother permission permanently to remove the child from the jurisdiction, allowing for certain holidays to be spent with the father in the UK. In *Re AR (A Child: Relocation)* [2010] 2 FLR 1577, Mostyn J held that shared residence orders should be normative for they avoid the psychological baggage of right, power and control that attends a sole residence order; they were not inapt even where permission to relocate was granted (see further under CA 1989, s 13, below).

"Joint residence" orders—The phrase 'joint residence' as opposed to 'shared residence' is to be reserved for situations in which a residence order is invested in two people living together (per curiam in *Re K (Shared Residence Order)* [2008] 2 FLR 380).

Making a s 8 order before final disposal of proceedings (s 11(3))—Section 11(3) is equivalent to the power to make interim orders. It applies whenever the court has power to make a s 8 order (see s 10 and, as to the restrictions on that power, s 9). It can, of course, be used in the traditional way, for example to grant one parent a temporary residence order pending the final determination of an issue as to residence or to regulate contact pending determination of such an issue. However, given that the court has power to make a s 8 order of its own initiative in any family proceedings in which a question arises as to the welfare of a child (see FPR 2010, r 4.3), and given the wide definition of family proceedings in s 8(3), it could be used in a much wider variety of circumstances as well, for example where an issue arises over the children in the course of pending proceedings under FLA 1996 or financial proceedings under MCA 1973. For a case in which the father's residence order was left in force to run alongside an interim order placing the children with their mother pending a fuller hearing of the question of residence, see *Re M (Minors) (Interim Residence Order)* [1997] 2 FCR 28, CA.

The object of an interim order should normally be to hold the balance so as to cause the least possible harm to the child; see e g *B v B (Interim Contact with Grandparents)* [1993] Fam Law 393. By analogy with *Re L (Interim Care Order: Power of Court)* [1996] 2 FLR 742, CA, it should not be treated as an indication of how the matter will finally be disposed of; it is not an irreversible decision. Some useful guidance as to the approach to be taken to interim hearings (much of it equally applicable to both the magistrates' courts and the county courts, *Re W (A Minor) (Interim Care Order)* [1994] 2 FLR 892) can be found in *Hampshire County Council v S* [1993] 1 FLR 559, albeit a public law case (see further under FPR 2010, r 12.21: interim hearings). When a court hears an application for an interim residence order it is not necessary for it to give elaborate consideration to the welfare check list under CA 1989, s 1(3) (*Re C (A Child)* [2001] EWCA Civ 718). As to the difficulties that may be encountered in persuading the court to make without notice interim orders, particularly in residence cases, see **Power to make without notice orders** under FPR 2010, r 12.16 and PD12E (*Urgent Business*). As to the situation in which it may be appropriate to make a residence order on an interim application in pending care proceedings, see *Re RJ (Fostering: Person Disqualified)* [1999] 1 FLR 605, CA (noted under s 38).

When events develop following the making of an interim residence order—When events develop following the making of an interim residence order, the appropriate course is to seek a variation from the judge, rather than apply to the Court of Appeal (*Re H (A Child)* [2011] EWCA Civ 762).

Section 11(7)—Section 11(7)(d) can be used to afford liberty to a non-party to apply to vary or discharge a s 8 order (*Re H (Prohibited Steps Order)* [1995] 1 FLR 638, CA – prohibited steps order against mother's former cohabitee, J, requiring him not to have or to seek contact with the children, with liberty to J to apply on notice to vary or discharge the order). However, the section must not be used to regulate occupation of the former family home for the purpose of facilitating contact (*Re K (Contact Order: Condition Ousting Parent from Family Home)* [2012] 2 FLR 635).

Section 11(7) should not be used to restrict a parent to an area of residence within the UK save in exceptional circumstances. In *Re H (Children) (Residence Order: Condition)* [2001] 2 FLR 1277 the facts justified a different approach to the general rule, as the medical evidence showed that the effect of the father moving the children away from the area where the mother lived would be devastating and therefore a condition attached to the residence order was justified. Exceptional circumstances justified a similar order in *Re S (A Child) (Residence Order: Condition) (No 2)* [2003] 1 FCR 138, where the court imposed a condition on a residence order to prevent the mother from moving her 9-year-old Down's Syndrome child to Cornwall. In *B v B (Residence: Condition Limiting Geographical Area)* [2004] 2 FLR 979 the court attached to the mother's residence order a condition that she reside in a defined area of Southern England as she had no good reasons for her proposed move to Newcastle other than to be distanced further from the father. See further **Relocation within the UK** under CA 1989, s 13. The court has jurisdiction under s 11(7) to impose any condition that secures the paramountcy of the welfare of the child, but the greater the restriction on the freedom of the parent subject to the condition, the more exceptional the case must be to justify it (*Re H (A Child)* [2002] EWCA Civ 2005 – discussed further under **Shared residence orders** (above)). For example, in *Re M (Contact)* [2012] EWHC 1948, the court made a conditional residence order, ordering that staying contact take place and that if it did not there would be a transfer of residence from the mother to the father. The court has no power in private law proceedings concerning the residence of a child to use s 11(7) to order a residential assessment of one parent with the child against the wishes of the other parent (*R v R (Private Law Proceedings: Residential Assessment)* [2002] 2 FLR 953; *Birmingham City Council v H* [1992] 2 FLR 323).

Enforcement of s 11(7) directions and conditions—For enforcement under MCA 1980, s 63(3), see s 14; for penal notices, see FPR 2010, r 33.7; and for orders for recovery of a child, see FLA 1986, s 34.

Enforcement of contact orders—CA 1989, ss 11A–11P give the court specific powers to impose directions and conditions on contact orders and to improve enforcement. See further annotation **Enforcement of contact orders** under s 8, and ss 11A–11P below, and see Procedural Guide D8.

11A Contact activity directions

(1) This section applies in proceedings in which the court is considering whether to make provision about contact with a child by making –

(a) a contact order with respect to the child, or

(b) an order varying or discharging a contact order with respect to the child.

(2) The court may make a contact activity direction in connection with that provision about contact.

(3) A contact activity direction is a direction requiring an individual who is a party to the proceedings to take part in an activity that promotes contact with the child concerned.

(4) The direction is to specify the activity and the person providing the activity.

(5) The activities that may be so required include, in particular –

(a) programmes, classes and counselling or guidance sessions of a kind that –
   (i) may assist a person as regards establishing, maintaining or improving contact with a child;
   (ii) may, by addressing a person's violent behaviour, enable or facilitate contact with a child;

(b) sessions in which information or advice is given as regards making or operating arrangements for contact with a child, including making arrangements by means of mediation.

(6) No individual may be required by a contact activity direction –

(a) to undergo medical or psychiatric examination, assessment or treatment;

(b) to take part in mediation.

(7) A court may not on the same occasion –

(a) make a contact activity direction, and

(b) dispose finally of the proceedings as they relate to contact with the child concerned.

(8) Subsection (2) has effect subject to the restrictions in sections 11B and 11E.

(9) In considering whether to make a contact activity direction, the welfare of the child concerned is to be the court's paramount consideration.

Amendments—Inserted by CAA 2006, s 1.

Contact activity directions—When there is some dispute (s 11B(1)) about contact and the court is considering whether or not to make, vary or discharge a contact order it may make a "contact activity direction": s 11A. This allows the court to direct a *party* to undertake activities promoting contact ("contact activities").

Cafcass Guidance—The provisions place a number of specific new duties on Cafcass officers and the President of the Family Division endorsed *Guidance to Cafcass practitioners on their roles in supporting the courts in their use of the s 11A–P provisions* ("Cafcass Guidance"). The Cafcass Guidance (para 2.2) refers to three types of "contact activity": (1) Information meetings about mediation – provided by LSC-approved providers on a one-off basis, free of charge to both parties if either party is publicly funded. Both parties will be required to participate, but can initially be seen separately; (2) Separated parents information programmes – provided by Cafcass-commissioned providers, typically involving group sessions lasting for a total of 4 hours, free of charge to all. Generally, both parties are required to participate, though the programmes will be delivered to them separately; (3) Domestic violence prevention programmes – run by Cafcass-commissioned providers, involving an intensive programme of 60 hours' intervention. The Cafcass Guidance (paras 2.4, 2.5) observes that in practice the Cafcass officer is likely to have suggested to the court that participation in a contact activity might be beneficial. Much will depend on the attitude of the parties towards the activity. This will be an important factor to be addressed in any oral or written report to the court.

Draft Legislation on Family Justice—In September 2012, draft legislation was presented to Parliament in response to David Norgrove's Family Justice Review. Clause 2(2) proposes to remove the current definitions of residence and contact orders and clause 2(3) would replace them with a "child arrangements order". Consequently, "contact activity directions" and "contact activity conditions" would be replaced by "activity directions" and "activity conditions", respectively. Amendments proposed to ss 11A–11E will mean that the activities directed or imposed will be able to relate to more than just promoting the contact provided for in the child arrangements order. Instead, the activities will be about helping to establish, maintain or improve the involvement of a person in a child's life. The shift in focus is to recognise that where the child lives with more than one person, or lives with one person and spends time or otherwise has contact with another person, there may be issues that relate to the time spent by the child with the person with whom he lives that affect the smooth operation of the arrangements for his care. In some circumstances, these issues could be addressed by an activity direction or the court would still be limited by s 11B, so that an activity direction could not be made where there is no dispute about the provision that the court is making.

11B   Contact activity directions: further provision

(1) A court may not make a contact activity direction in any proceedings unless there is a dispute as regards the provision about contact that the court is considering whether to make in the proceedings.

(2) A court may not make a contact activity direction requiring an individual who is a child to take part in an activity unless the individual is a parent of the child in relation to whom the court is considering provision about contact.

(3) A court may not make a contact activity direction in connection with the making, variation or discharge of a contact order, if the contact order is, or would if made be, an excepted order.

(4) A contact order with respect to a child is an excepted order if –

   (a)   it is made in proceedings that include proceedings on an application for a relevant adoption order in respect of the child; or
   (b)   it makes provision as regards contact between the child and a person who would be a parent or relative of the child but for the child's adoption by an order falling within subsection (5).

(5) An order falls within this subsection if it is –

   (a)   a relevant adoption order;
   (b)   an adoption order, within the meaning of section 72(1) of the Adoption

Act 1976, other than an order made by virtue of section 14 of that Act on the application of a married couple one of whom is the mother or the father of the child;

(c) a Scottish adoption order, within the meaning of the Adoption and Children Act 2002, other than an order made –

  (i) by virtue of section 14 of the Adoption (Scotland) Act 1978 on the application of a married couple one of whom is the mother or the father of the child, or

  (ii) by virtue of section 15(1)(aa) of that Act; or

  (iii) (*applies to Scotland only*)

(d) a Northern Irish adoption order, within the meaning of the Adoption and Children Act 2002, other than an order made by virtue of Article 14 of the Adoption (Northern Ireland) Order 1987 on the application of a married couple one of whom is the mother or the father of the child.

(6) A relevant adoption order is an adoption order, within the meaning of section 46(1) of the Adoption and Children Act 2002, other than an order made –

(a) on an application under section 50 of that Act by a couple (within the meaning of that Act) one of whom is the mother or the father of the person to be adopted, or

(b) on an application under section 51(2) of that Act.

(7) A court may not make a contact activity direction in relation to an individual unless the individual is habitually resident in England and Wales; and a direction ceases to have effect if the individual subject to the direction ceases to be habitually resident in England and Wales.

Amendments—Inserted by CAA 2006, s 1; amended by SI 2011/1740.

11C Contact activity conditions

(1) This section applies if in any family proceedings the court makes –

(a) a contact order with respect to a child, or

(b) an order varying a contact order with respect to a child.

(2) The contact order may impose, or the contact order may be varied so as to impose, a condition (a "contact activity condition") requiring an individual falling within subsection (3) to take part in an activity that promotes contact with the child concerned.

(3) An individual falls within this subsection if he is –

(a) for the purposes of the contact order so made or varied, the person with whom the child concerned lives or is to live;

(b) the person whose contact with the child concerned is provided for in that order; or

(c) a person upon whom that order imposes a condition under section 11(7)(b).

(4) The condition is to specify the activity and the person providing the activity.

(5) Subsections (5) and (6) of section 11A have effect as regards the activities that may be required by a contact activity condition as they have effect as regards the activities that may be required by a contact activity direction.

(6) Subsection (2) has effect subject to the restrictions in sections 11D and 11E.

Amendments—Inserted by CAA 2006, s 1.

Contact activity condition—Whenever the court makes or varies a contact order it may make a "contact activity condition" requiring the person named to take part in a "contact activity"; the activities are the same as those for a "contact activity direction" – see annotation **Cafcass Guidance** under s 11A, above.

11D Contact activity conditions: further provision

(1) A contact order may not impose a contact activity condition on an individual who is a child unless the individual is a parent of the child concerned.

(2) If a contact order is an excepted order (within the meaning given by section 11B(4)), it may not impose (and it may not be varied so as to impose) a contact activity condition.

(3) A contact order may not impose a contact activity condition on an individual unless the individual is habitually resident in England and Wales; and a condition ceases to have effect if the individual subject to the condition ceases to be habitually resident in England and Wales.

Amendments—Inserted by CAA 2006, s 1.

11E Contact activity directions and conditions: making

(1) Before making a contact activity direction (or imposing a contact activity condition by means of a contact order), the court must satisfy itself as to the matters falling within subsections (2) to (4).

(2) The first matter is that the activity proposed to be specified is appropriate in the circumstances of the case.

(3) The second matter is that the person proposed to be specified as the provider of the activity is suitable to provide the activity.

(4) The third matter is that the activity proposed to be specified is provided in a place to which the individual who would be subject to the direction (or the condition) can reasonably be expected to travel.

(5) Before making such a direction (or such an order), the court must obtain and consider information about the individual who would be subject to the direction (or the condition) and the likely effect of the direction (or the condition) on him.

(6) Information about the likely effect of the direction (or the condition) may, in particular, include information as to –

    (a)   any conflict with the individual's religious beliefs;

    (b)   any interference with the times (if any) at which he normally works or attends an educational establishment.

(7) The court may ask an officer of the Service or a Welsh family proceedings officer to provide the court with information as to the matters in subsections (2) to (5); and it shall be the duty of the officer of the Service or Welsh family proceedings officer to comply with any such request.

(8) In this section "specified" means specified in a contact activity direction (or in a contact activity condition).

Amendments—Inserted by CAA 2006, s 1.

Factors to be taken into account when making contact activity directions (CAD) or contact activity conditions (CAC)—Before the court makes a CAD or CAC it must first be satisfied that the activity is appropriate in the circumstances of the case, that the provider of the activity is suitable to provide it, and that the activity is available in a place to which it is reasonable to expect the person in question to travel. The court must also consider the likely *effect* of the contact activity on the person required to undertake it, e g any conflict with the person's religious beliefs, the times when he works, and the times when he attends an educational establishment. The court may ask a Cafcass officer to provide information about these matters (s 11E(7)).

11F Contact activity directions and conditions: financial assistance

(1) The Secretary of State may by regulations make provision authorising him to make payments to assist individuals falling within subsection (2) in paying relevant charges or fees.

(2) An individual falls within this subsection if he is required by a contact activity direction or condition to take part in an activity that promotes contact with a child, not being a child ordinarily resident in Wales.

(3) The National Assembly for Wales may by regulations make provision authorising it to make payments to assist individuals falling within subsection (4) in paying relevant charges or fees.

(4) An individual falls within this subsection if he is required by a contact activity direction or condition to take part in an activity that promotes contact with a child who is ordinarily resident in Wales.

(5) A relevant charge or fee, in relation to an activity required by a contact activity direction or condition, is a charge or fee in respect of the activity payable to the person providing the activity.

(6) Regulations under this section may provide that no assistance is available to an individual unless –

(a) the individual satisfies such conditions as regards his financial resources as may be set out in the regulations;

(b) the activity in which the individual is required by a contact activity direction or condition to take part is provided to him in England or Wales;

(c) where the activity in which the individual is required to take part is provided to him in England, it is provided by a person who is for the time being approved by the Secretary of State as a provider of activities required by a contact activity direction or condition;

(d) where the activity in which the individual is required to take part is provided to him in Wales, it is provided by a person who is for the time being approved by the National Assembly for Wales as a provider of activities required by a contact activity direction or condition.

(7) Regulations under this section may make provision –

(a) as to the maximum amount of assistance that may be paid to or in respect of an individual as regards an activity in which he is required by a contact activity direction or condition to take part;

(b) where the amount may vary according to an individual's financial resources, as to the method by which the amount is to be determined;

(c) authorising payments by way of assistance to be made directly to persons providing activities required by a contact activity direction or condition.

Amendments—Inserted by CAA 2006, s 1.

11G Contact activity directions and conditions: monitoring

(1) This section applies if in any family proceedings the court –

(a) makes a contact activity direction in relation to an individual, or

(b) makes a contact order that imposes, or varies a contact order so as to impose, a contact activity condition on an individual.

(2) The court may on making the direction (or imposing the condition by means of a contact order) ask an officer of the Service or a Welsh family proceedings officer –

(a) to monitor, or arrange for the monitoring of, the individual's compliance with the direction (or the condition);

(b)   to report to the court on any failure by the individual to comply with the direction (or the condition).

(3) It shall be the duty of the officer of the Service or Welsh family proceedings officer to comply with any request under subsection (2).

Amendments—Inserted by CAA 2006, s 1.

Monitoring compliance with a contact activity direction (CAD) or contact activity condition (CAC)—A court may ask a Cafcass officer to monitor compliance with a CAD or CAC and to report to the court if there is a failure to comply. The Cafcass Guidance (para 2.6) (see further under s 11A, above) observes that the court may also ask Cafcass to provide information about the impact, beneficial or otherwise, of attendance, in terms of helping to address the issues in the case. Both elements require there to be liaison with the provider, information from which should be reported to the court, together with any additional Cafcass analysis and recommendations. In some cases, the Cafcass officer will have been asked by the court to have other forms of involvement with the parties and/ or child during the period of participation in the contact activities, the outcome of which should also be reported to the court. Contact activity providers may also be asked to provide a report to the court, not just to Cafcass, about the attendance, participation etc of parties. However the content of any such report has not yet been defined.

11H Monitoring contact

(1) This section applies if in any family proceedings the court makes –

(a)   a contact order with respect to a child in favour of a person, or

(b)   an order varying such a contact order.

(2) The court may ask an officer of the Service or a Welsh family proceedings officer –

(a)   to monitor whether an individual falling within subsection (3) complies with the contact order (or the contact order as varied);

(b)   to report to the court on such matters relating to the individual's compliance as the court may specify in the request.

(3) An individual falls within this subsection if the contact order so made (or the contact order as so varied) –

(a)   requires the individual to allow contact with the child concerned;

(b)   names the individual as having contact with the child concerned; or

(c)   imposes a condition under section 11(7)(b) on the individual.

(4) If the contact order (or the contact order as varied) includes a contact activity condition, a request under subsection (2) is to be treated as relating to the provisions of the order other than the contact activity condition.

(5) The court may make a request under subsection (2) –

(a)   on making the contact order (or the order varying the contact order), or

(b)   at any time during the subsequent course of the proceedings as they relate to contact with the child concerned.

(6) In making a request under subsection (2), the court is to specify the period for which the officer of the Service or Welsh family proceedings officer is to monitor compliance with the order; and the period specified may not exceed twelve months.

(7) It shall be the duty of the officer of the Service or Welsh family proceedings officer to comply with any request under subsection (2).

(8) The court may order any individual falling within subsection (3) to take such steps as may be specified in the order with a view to enabling the officer of the Service or Welsh family proceedings officer to comply with the court's request under subsection (2).

(9) But the court may not make an order under subsection (8) with respect to an individual who is a child unless he is a parent of the child with respect to whom the order falling within subsection (1) was made.

(10) A court may not make a request under subsection (subsection (2) in relation to a contact order that is an excepted order (within the meaning given by section 11B(4)).

Amendments—Inserted by CAA 2006, s 1.

Monitoring compliance with contact order—A court may ask a Cafcass officer to monitor compliance with a contact order, and to report to the court on such matters relating to compliance as the court may specify. The court may ask the Cafcass officer to carry out this role for up to 1 year. The people who can be subject to monitoring are: a person who is required to allow contact with a child; a person whose contact with the child is provided for; and, a person who is subject to a condition under s 11(7)(b). The Cafcass Guidance (paras 3.2, 3.3) (see further under s 11A, above) observes that with nearly 40,000 contact orders having been made in 2007, this provision has major resource implications for Cafcass. It has been agreed with the President of the Family Division that the general assumption is that the provision should not be used in "consent order" cases where proceedings have ended. Instead, consideration of its use should be limited to those cases where the issue of contact has remained in dispute during the proceedings and where a trial and judicial determination of the contact issue has taken place. Eg, where there is a strong feeling of dissatisfaction on the part of one or both parties, the court may consider that the imposition of a monitoring requirement is appropriate. The consent of the parties is *not* required (unlike Family Assistance Orders).

The court may end the proceedings, having made a contact order with a monitoring requirement, or it may set a further date for a review hearing (usually before the same judge). In either event, it is essential that timely monitoring takes place in the immediate aftermath of the contact order being made. This is likely primarily to take the form of telephone contact with both parties and, where the children are of sufficient age and understanding, also with the children.

The court may request that it be notified in writing about the outcome of the monitoring, either at the end of the monitoring period if compliance has been adequate, or at an earlier stage if the Cafcass officer deems it to have been inadequate. Non-compliance can range from outright refusal to allow contact, to a chronic series of more minor failures to observe the terms of the contact order. Chronic cases should not be allowed to "drag on" and the Cafcass officer should notify the court and ask for guidance as to how to proceed (para 3.4).

On receipt of such notification from Cafcass, the court may, if a review date has been set, choose to bring forward the hearing. Alternatively, if proceedings have ended, the court will have to await the making of an application for enforcement by a party. Once non-compliance has been notified to the court, the parties and, in the most appropriate way, the children, monitoring should continue while guidance of the court is awaited (para 3.5).

Draft Legislation on Family Justice—In September 2012, draft legislation was presented to Parliament in response to David Norgrove's Family Justice Review. Clause 2(2) proposes to remove the current definitions of residence and contact orders and clause 2(3) would replace them with a "child arrangements order" (CAO). There will be amendments to ss 11H–11P to ensure that where a CAO is in force with respect to a child and the provisions setting out the living arrangements (not just arrangements about contact) are sufficiently precise so that it is clear when a person is in breach of the order, the sanctions currently available to the court by virtue of ss 11H–11P will be available in relation to breaches of a CAO by any person with whom the child is to live.

11I Contact orders: warning notices

Where the court makes (or varies) a contact order, it is to attach to the contact order (or the order varying the contact order) a notice warning of the consequences of failing to comply with the contact order.

Amendments—Inserted by CAA 2006, s 1.

Consequences of failing to comply with contact order—The consequences of failure to comply with a contact order may be an enforcement order, an order for financial compensation, or the use of the courts' sanctions for contempt.

Care required when drafting contact orders to which warning notices are to be attached—Whenever a court makes or varies a contact order, it is to attach a notice warning of the consequences of failing to comply with the contact order (s 11I) ie an enforcement order (for unpaid work) (ss 11J–N), an order for financial compensation (ss 11 O–P), and sanctions for contempt of court. The wording of s 11I looks as though it is *mandatory* for a court to attach a warning notice when it makes or varies *any* contact order. It follows that judges have to decide whether the contact order which they propose to make is to be made in terms that comply with s 8(1), in which case a warning notice will be added automatically, or whether it would be more appropriate for consent orders to set out the agreed regime as a recital or schedule to the order on the basis of which the court then applies the "no order" principle. Judges will need to make sure that orders that go out in Form C45 accurately reflect what has actually been ordered.

Procedure for applying for a warning notice to be attached—The procedure for applying for warning notices is set out in FPR 2010, r 12.33. The application is made using Form C78. Warning notices can be addressed to a much wider range of individuals than was the case previously, because applications for enforcement orders and financial compensation orders can be made not only by the person in whose favour the order is made, but also by the person with whom the child lives, or the child, or any other person subject to a s 11(7) condition or contact activity condition.

FPR 2010, r 12.33 requires that an application for a warning notice to be attached to a contact order should be made to the High Court or a county court without notice, but there is no provision in Form C78 for the applicant to specify the provisions of the order to which he wishes the warning notice attached, or any space for him to say why the application is being made. The without notice order has potential quasi-criminal consequences for the respondent, but does not give him a right to apply to set it aside. In these circumstances, it is respectfully submitted that the safer course would be for the judge to direct a hearing inviting the applicant to file a brief statement setting out the provisions of the order to which he wishes the warning notice to be attached and explaining why he is asking for a warning notice.

If the relevant order does not comply with s 8(1), then the application should be dismissed as misconceived. The applicant would have to apply using Form C100 to vary the existing order to a mandatory order to which a warning notice can be added (see Procedural Guide D7.

Transitional orders—Applications to attach a warning notice to an existing order must be made on Form C78. The application can be made to any court with family jurisdiction. When faced with a C78 application the judge should first obtain a copy of the original order, but in itself that may not be enough. Without the existing court file it may be impossible to discover whether the order is still in force. Furthermore, the relevant provisions may be contained in more than one order. The proper course may be to ask the court in which the order was made either to transfer the existing proceedings or to order transfer of the C78 application back to the court that made the existing order.

11J Enforcement orders

(1) This section applies if a contact order with respect to a child has been made.

(2) If the court is satisfied beyond reasonable doubt that a person has failed to comply with the contact order, it may make an order (an "enforcement order") imposing on the person an unpaid work requirement.

(3) But the court may not make an enforcement order if it is satisfied that the person had a reasonable excuse for failing to comply with the contact order.

(4) The burden of proof as to the matter mentioned in subsection (3) lies on the person claiming to have had a reasonable excuse, and the standard of proof is the balance of probabilities.

(5) The court may make an enforcement order in relation to the contact order only on the application of –

    (a)   the person who is, for the purposes of the contact order, the person with whom the child concerned lives or is to live;

    (b)   the person whose contact with the child concerned is provided for in the contact order;

    (c)   any individual subject to a condition under section 11(7)(b) or a contact activity condition imposed by the contact order; or

    (d)   the child concerned.

(6) Where the person proposing to apply for an enforcement order in relation to a contact order is the child concerned, the child must obtain the leave of the court before making such an application.

(7) The court may grant leave to the child concerned only if it is satisfied that he has sufficient understanding to make the proposed application.

(8) Subsection (2) has effect subject to the restrictions in sections 11K and 11L.

(9) The court may suspend an enforcement order for such period as it thinks fit.

(10) Nothing in this section prevents a court from making more than one enforcement order in relation to the same person on the same occasion.

(11) Proceedings in which any question of making an enforcement order, or any other question with respect to such an order, arises are to be regarded for the purposes of section 11(1) and (2) as proceedings in which a question arises with respect to a section 8 order.

(12) In Schedule A1 –

   (a) Part 1 makes provision as regards an unpaid work requirement;
   (b) Part 2 makes provision in relation to the revocation and amendment of enforcement orders and failure to comply with such orders.

(13) This section is without prejudice to section 63(3) of the Magistrates' Courts Act 1980 as it applies in relation to contact orders.

Amendments—Inserted by CAA 2006, s 1.

Enforcement orders—Where the court is satisfied beyond reasonable doubt that a person has failed to comply with a contact order made under CA 1989, s 8, it may make an enforcement order, imposing on that person an "unpaid work requirement" (community service): s 11J(2). The court may not make an enforcement order if satisfied that the person in breach had a "reasonable excuse" for breaching the order: s 11J(3). The burden of proving a reasonable excuse is on the person in breach and the standard of proof is the balance of probabilities: s 11(4). The court may not make an enforcement order unless the person concerned has received a "warning notice" or has been otherwise informed of its terms: s 11K. The court has a discretion as to whether to join the child as a party and may ask the Cafcass officer to consider this and report to the court with his opinion (FPR 2010, r 16.39). The factors to be considered by the court before making an enforcement order are set out in s 11L and in Sch A1, Pt I. The maximum number of hours of unpaid work that may be required is 200, and the minimum is 40. The court has power to amend or revoke an enforcement order: Sch A1, Pt II. The court may ask a Cafcass officer to monitor, or arrange for the monitoring of, a person's compliance with an enforcement order, and to report to the court on failure to comply and on any unsuitability to undertake the unpaid work: s 11M. Where an enforcement order is made, the court must attach a warning notice setting out the consequences of breaching the order i e imposition of a further enforcement order; enhancement of the existing enforcement order; use of existing sanctions for contempt. If the terms of an enforcement order are breached, the court may (in certain circumstances) amend the original order to make it more onerous, or impose another enforcement order: Sch A1, Pt II.

Committal to prison for contempt—The court will take a robust approach to the question of committal to prison for contempt in family proceedings (*Re W (Family Proceedings: Applications)* [2011] 1 FLR 2163; *Doncaster MBC v Watson and Haigh* [2012] 1 FLR 599). In committal proceedings it is vital to ensure that the evidential and procedural rules are obeyed, and extra vigilance is required when the respondent to such proceedings is a litigant in person (*Hammerton v Hammerton* [2007] 2 FLR 1133). Where the respondent's breach is an active breach that directly strikes at the heart of what the court ordered, it may be appropriate to impose a custodial sentence (*Re X (A Child by His Litigation Friend)* [2011] 2 FLR 793) and an appellate court is unlikely to interfere unless the sentence passed is manifestly disproportionate or excessive (*Slade v Slade* [2010] 1 FLR 160). The length of any sentence for committal for contempt must bear some reasonable relationship to the statutory maximum of 2 years (*Hale v Tanner* [2000] 2 FLR 879). A sentence for contempt in civil proceedings can be the subject of an application for early discharge (*CJ v Flintshire Borough Council* [2010] 2 FLR 1224; *Doncaster Metropolitan District Council v Watson* [2012] 1 FLR 613). However, where the court allows an application to purge contempt it cannot then suspend the relevant term of imprisonment. The court has three choices when dealing with an application to purge contempt: (1) grant the application and order the immediate release of the contemnor; (2) defer the contemnor's release until a stated future date; or (3) refuse the application (*Doncaster Metropolitan Borough Council v Watson (No 2)* [2012] 1 FLR 619). See further under CCA 1981, s 14.

Enforcement of contact orders when child does not wish to go—Where the parent's obligation is to "allow" contact and to "make [the child] available" for contact, that wording does not place him in breach of the order if the child refuses to co-operate (*Re L-W (Enforcement and Committal: Contact); CPL v CH-W and Others* [2011] 1 FLR 1095). Neither is the father under a legally enforceable obligation to take such steps in the exercise of his parental discipline, guidance and encouragement as are reasonable in all of the circumstances to ensure that contact takes place. Before deciding that a parent is the author of a child's resistance to contact so that he can be made the subject of a coercive order, the court must be sure that the parent can still reverse the child's attitude. Even then, a court (despite the affront to its dignity) might have to be prepared, if it comes to the point of committal, to accept that the predictive premise on which it initially acted has turned out to be wrong: for example, where the child has internalised the residential parent's hostility so that punishing that parent could no longer produce the intended outcome and might produce the opposite. See also **Transfer of residence** and **Suspended transfer of residence** under s 8.

Procedure for applying for an enforcement order—An application for an enforcement order must be made on Form C79 by a person who falls within the criteria set out in s 11J (5)(a)–(d). See Procedural Guide D8.

Draft Legislation on Family Justice—See under ss 11A and 11H.

11K Enforcement orders: further provision

(1) A court may not make an enforcement order against a person in respect of a failure to comply with a contact order unless it is satisfied that before the failure occurred the person had been given (in accordance with rules of court) a copy of, or otherwise informed of the terms of –

  (a) in the case of a failure to comply with a contact order that was varied before the failure occurred, a notice under section 11I relating to the order varying the contact order or, where more than one such order has been made, the last order preceding the failure in question;

  (b) in any other case, a notice under section 11I relating to the contact order.

(2) A court may not make an enforcement order against a person in respect of any failure to comply with a contact order occurring before the person attained the age of 18.

(3) A court may not make an enforcement order against a person in respect of a failure to comply with a contact order that is an excepted order (within the meaning given by section 11B(4)).

(4) A court may not make an enforcement order against a person unless the person is habitually resident in England and Wales; and an enforcement order ceases to have effect if the person subject to the order ceases to be habitually resident in England and Wales.

Amendments—Inserted by CAA 2006, s 1.

11L Enforcement orders: making

(1) Before making an enforcement order as regards a person in breach of a contact order, the court must be satisfied that –

  (a) making the enforcement order proposed is necessary to secure the person's compliance with the contact order or any contact order that has effect in its place;

  (b) the likely effect on the person of the enforcement order proposed to be made is proportionate to the seriousness of the breach of the contact order.

(2) Before making an enforcement order, the court must satisfy itself that provision for the person to work under an unpaid work requirement imposed by an enforcement order can be made in the local justice area in which the person in breach resides or will reside.

(3) Before making an enforcement order as regards a person in breach of a contact order, the court must obtain and consider information about the person and the likely effect of the enforcement order on him.

(4) Information about the likely effect of the enforcement order may, in particular, include information as to –

(a)   any conflict with the person's religious beliefs;

(b)   any interference with the times (if any) at which he normally works or attends an educational establishment.

(5) A court that proposes to make an enforcement order may ask an officer of the Service or a Welsh family proceedings officer to provide the court with information as to the matters in subsections (2) and (3).

(6) It shall be the duty of the officer of the Service or Welsh family proceedings officer to comply with any request under this section.

(7) In making an enforcement order in relation to a contact order, a court must take into account the welfare of the child who is the subject of the contact order.

Amendments—Inserted by CAA 2006, s 1.

Factors to be considered by the court before making an enforcement order—In deciding whether to make an enforcement order, the court must be satisfied that doing so is necessary to secure compliance with the contact order, and that the order is proportionate to the seriousness of the breach. Before making an enforcement order the court must obtain and consider information about the person on whom the order would be imposed, and the likely effect of the order on him e g any conflict with the person's religious beliefs, the times when he works, and the times when he attends an educational establishment. The court may ask a Cafcass officer to provide information about these matters. The Cafcass Guidance (para 4.1) (see further under s 11A, above) observes that where an enforcement order imposing an unpaid work requirement (of between 40 and 200 hours) is made, Cafcass will be sent a copy of each C79 enforcement application, to enable it to undertake updating screening checks with the relevant local authority and the police. The outcome of these checks must be promptly notified to the court, together with any other requested information. The court has a discretion to join the child as a party to enforcement proceedings. The child is not automatically a party even where he was a party to the original proceedings. In practice, it will rarely be necessary, and Cafcass Legal will advise in cases of difficulty. The court must also take into account the welfare of the child concerned, but this is *not* its paramount consideration (see Cafcass Guidance, para 4.2). The Cafcass Guidance (para 4.2) observes that in order to inform the court about the local availability of unpaid work, it will be necessary to liaise with the local National Probation Service (NPS), which stands ready to provide unpaid work to those ordered by the court to undertake it. When making the order, the court should give leave to the officer to disclose to NPS such information in relation to the proceedings as necessary (see FPR PD12N *Enforcement of Children Act 1989 Contact Orders: Disclosure of Information to Officers of the National Probation Service*).

11M Enforcement orders: monitoring

(1) On making an enforcement order in relation to a person, the court is to ask an officer of the Service or a Welsh family proceedings officer –

(a)   to monitor, or arrange for the monitoring of, the person's compliance with the unpaid work requirement imposed by the order;

(b)   to report to the court if a report under paragraph 8 of Schedule A1 is made in relation to the person;

(c)   to report to the court on such other matters relating to the person's compliance as may be specified in the request;

(d)   to report to the court if the person is, or becomes, unsuitable to perform work under the requirement.

(2) It shall be the duty of the officer of the Service or Welsh family proceedings officer to comply with any request under this section.

Amendments—Inserted by CAA 2006, s 1.

Monitoring enforcement orders—The court may ask a Cafcass officer to monitor, or arrange for the monitoring of, a person's compliance with an enforcement order, and to report to the court on failure to comply and on any unsuitability to undertake the unpaid work. The Cafcass Guidance (para 4.3) (see further under s 11A, above) observes that the monitoring of individuals' compliance with unpaid work requirements will be undertaken by the National Probation Service (NPS), which in turn will report to Cafcass. When making the order, the court should give leave to the officer to disclose to NPS such information in relation to the proceedings as necessary (see FPR PD12N *Enforcement of Children*

Act 1989 Contact Orders: Disclosure of Information to Officers of the National Probation Service). Where NPS determines there has been non-compliance without reasonable excuse, this will be reported to Cafcass. Similarly, if an individual is or becomes unsuitable to perform unpaid work, NPS will notify Cafcass of this. In both instances, Cafcass must report such matters to the court. There may be other matters that should be reported to the court eg where someone moves from their address without providing a new address.

11N Enforcement orders: warning notices

Where the court makes an enforcement order, it is to attach to the order a notice warning of the consequences of failing to comply with the order.

Amendments—Inserted by CAA 2006, s 1.

Attaching a warning notice to an enforcement order—Where an enforcement order is made, the court must attach a warning notice setting out the consequences of breaching the order ie the imposition of a further enforcement order, the enhancement of the existing enforcement order, and the use of existing sanctions for contempt. Schedule A1 makes further provision about enforcement orders: the maximum number of hours of unpaid work that may be required is 200 and the minimum is 40; the court has power to amend or revoke an enforcement order; if terms of an enforcement order are breached, the court may (in certain circumstances) amend the original order to make it more onerous, or impose another enforcement order.

11O Compensation for financial loss

(1) This section applies if a contact order with respect to a child has been made.

(2) If the court is satisfied that –

    (a)   an individual has failed to comply with the contact order, and

    (b)   a person falling within subsection (6) has suffered financial loss by reason of the breach,

it may make an order requiring the individual in breach to pay the person compensation in respect of his financial loss.

(3) But the court may not make an order under subsection (2) if it is satisfied that the individual in breach had a reasonable excuse for failing to comply with the contact order.

(4) The burden of proof as to the matter mentioned in subsection (3) lies on the individual claiming to have had a reasonable excuse.

(5) An order under subsection (2) may be made only on an application by the person who claims to have suffered financial loss.

(6) A person falls within this subsection if he is –

    (a)   the person who is, for the purposes of the contact order, the person with whom the child concerned lives or is to live;

    (b)   the person whose contact with the child concerned is provided for in the contact order;

    (c)   an individual subject to a condition under section 11(7)(b) or a contact activity condition imposed by the contact order; or

    (d)   the child concerned.

(7) Where the person proposing to apply for an order under subsection (2) is the child concerned, the child must obtain the leave of the court before making such an application.

(8) The court may grant leave to the child concerned only if it is satisfied that he has sufficient understanding to make the proposed application.

(9) The amount of compensation is to be determined by the court, but may not exceed the amount of the applicant's financial loss.

(10) In determining the amount of compensation payable by the individual in breach, the court must take into account the individual's financial circumstances.

(11) An amount ordered to be paid as compensation may be recovered by the applicant as a civil debt due to him.

(12) Subsection (2) has effect subject to the restrictions in section 11P.

(13) Proceedings in which any question of making an order under subsection (2) arises are to be regarded for the purposes of section 11(1) and (2) as proceedings in which a question arises with respect to a section 8 order.

(14) In exercising its powers under this section, a court is to take into account the welfare of the child concerned.

Amendments—Inserted by CAA 2006, s 1.

Financial compensation orders—The court may require a person who has caused financial loss to another person as a result of breaching a contact order (including breaching a condition attached to a contact order), to pay compensation up to the amount of the loss: s 11O. Before making a compensation order the court must take into account the welfare of any child concerned, and the financial circumstances of the person in breach. The applicant must fall within the criteria set down by s 11O(6)(a)–(d). The court may not make an order for financial compensation where the person in breach did not receive a warning notice under s 11I and was not otherwise informed of its terms: s 11P. The Cafcass Guidance (para 5.1) (see further under s 11A, above) observes that while Cafcass is unlikely to be aware of applications being made for compensation, it is possible that the court may seek information from Cafcass about the welfare of the child. Cafcass should respond in accordance with the specific request made by the court. The court has a discretion as to whether to join the child as a party (see para 4.1) and may ask the Cafcass officer to consider this and report to the court with his opinion (FPR 2010, r 16.39 and PD16A). Section 11P provides for circumstances in which a court may not make an order for financial compensation; these include: where a person did not receive a warning notice under s 11I; where he was not otherwise informed of the terms; or where the order is a excepted order (see s 11B(4) for meaning of "excepted" orders).

Procedure for applying for a financial compensation order—See Procedural Guide D8.

Draft Legislation on Family Justice—See under ss 11A and 11H.

11P Orders under section 11O(2): further provision

(1) A court may not make an order under section 11O(2) requiring an individual to pay compensation in respect of a failure by him to comply with a contact order unless it is satisfied that before the failure occurred the individual had been given (in accordance with rules of court) a copy of, or otherwise informed of the terms of –

   (a) in the case of a failure to comply with a contact order that was varied before the failure occurred, a notice under section 11I relating to the order varying the contact order or, where more than one such order has been made, the last order preceding the failure in question;

   (b) in any other case, a notice under section 11I relating to the contact order.

(2) A court may not make an order under section 11O(2) requiring an individual to pay compensation in respect of a failure by him to comply with a contact order where the failure occurred before the individual attained the age of 18.

(3) A court may not make an order under section 11O(2) requiring an individual to pay compensation in respect of a failure by him to comply with a contact order that is an excepted order (within the meaning given by section 11B(4)).

Amendments—Inserted by CAA 2006, s 1.

12 Residence orders and parental responsibility

(1) Where the court makes a residence order in favour of the father of a child it shall, if the father would not otherwise have parental responsibility for the child, also make an order under section 4 giving him that responsibility.

(1A) Where the court makes a residence order in favour of a woman who is a parent of a child by virtue of section 43 of the Human Fertilisation and Embryology Act 2008 it shall, if that woman would not otherwise have parental responsibility for the child, also make an order under section 4ZA giving her that responsibility.

(2) Where the court makes a residence order in favour of any person who is not the parent or guardian of the child concerned that person shall have parental responsibility for the child while the residence order remains in force.

(3) Where a person has parental responsibility for a child as a result of subsection (2), he shall not have the right –

  (a) (repealed)
  (b) to agree, or refuse to agree, to the making of an adoption order, or an order under section 84 of the Adoption and Children Act 2002, with respect to the child; or
  (c) to appoint a guardian for the child.

(4) Where subsection (1) or 1A requires the court to make an order under section 4 or 4ZA in respect of the parent of a child, the court shall not bring that order to an end at any time while the residence order concerned remains in force.

(5), (6) (repealed)

Amendments—ACA 2002, ss 114, 139, Sch 3, paras 54, 57; CYPA 2008, s 37(2); HFEA 2008, s 56, Sch 6, Pt 1, para 28(1),(2).

Draft Legislation on Family Justice—In September 2012, draft legislation was presented to Parliament in response to David Norgrove's Family Justice Review. Clause 2(2) proposes to remove the current definitions of residence and contact orders and clause 2(3) would replace them with a "child arrangements order" (CAO). Sch 1, para 21 proposes to substitute a new s 12(1) so that when making a CAO the court would be required to give parental responsibility to the father of the child concerned, or to the child's second female parent (by virtue of HFEA 2008, s 43), in cases where he or she is named in the order as a person with whom the child is to live. This would only apply in cases in which the father or second female parent would not otherwise have parental responsibility. The proposed new s 12(1A) would give the court the power to give parental responsibility to the child's father or second female parent in cases where he or she is named in the order as a person with whom the child is to spend time or otherwise have contact. It would be for the court to determine whether it is appropriate for him or her to be given parental responsibility in the light of the specific provisions of the order and, if the court considers it appropriate, it must give parental responsibility to him or her. In cases where a court gives parental responsibility in either of these circumstances, it would do so by means of an order under s 4 or 4ZA. The proposed new s 12(2) provides that where a CAO makes provision for a child to live with a person who is not his parent or guardian, that person would be given parental responsibility. The proposed s 12(2A) would enable the court to give parental responsibility to a person who is not a child's parent or guardian in cases where a CAO provides for the child to spend time with or otherwise have contact (but not live) with that person (although it is envisaged that this power would be exercised rarely). In relation to both ss 12(2) and 12(2A), respectively, parental responsibility would be for the duration of the relevant provision.

13 Change of child's name or removal from jurisdiction

(1) Where a residence order is in force with respect to a child, no person may –

  (a) cause the child to be known by a new surname; or
  (b) remove him from the United Kingdom;

without either the written consent of every person who has parental responsibility for the child or the leave of the court.

(2) Subsection (1)(b) does not prevent the removal of a child, for a period of less than one month, by the person in whose favour the residence order is made.

(3) In making a residence order with respect to a child the court may grant the leave required by subsection (1)(b), either generally or for specified purposes.

Defined terms—"child": s 105(1); "parental responsibility": s 3; "residence order": s 8(1).

Change of surname (s 13(1)(a))—See annotations to s 8.

Method of application for leave (s 13(1)(a),(b))—The permission application is a freestanding application and not a species of s 8 application (*Re B (Change of Surname)* [1996] 1 FLR 791, CA). It is made in accordance with FPR 2010, rr 18.1–18.13, which deal only with applications for permission to commence proceedings. Although the application can be made in any court, where it is for permission to remove a child permanently from the jurisdiction, it should not be heard by magistrates but should be transferred for determination either in a county court or the High Court, depending on the complexity and difficulty of the decision (*MH v GP (Child: Emigration)* [1995] 2 FLR 106, FD).

Removal from jurisdiction (s 13(1)(b))—The Court of Appeal in *Payne v Payne* [2001] 1 FLR 1052 has laid down useful guidelines for cases in which permission is sought to remove a child permanently from the jurisdiction. These are set out by Butler-Sloss P at p 1079 of the judgment. It is not essential to have a Cafcass investigation into the circumstances; ordering a report may not always be helpful to the court in reaching its decision, and it is a matter for the judge's discretion (*Re R (Leave to Remove: Contact)* [2011] 1 FLR 1336). The judge is entitled to depart from the recommendations of the Cafcass officer where the report is not balanced and the judge has to look at the case in the round (*Re E* [2012] EWCA Civ 1893). In *Re R* Wilson LJ stated his firm view that contact orders should not be made when granting leave to relocate, as they are contrary to principle and the court must recognize that it is relinquishing jurisdiction to the courts of the State to which the parent is moving. For a classic example of the application of *Payne*, see *Re Z (Relocation)* [2012] 2 FLR 653.

There are a number of cases in which non-residential parents have argued that the permanent removal of their child from the jurisdiction by the residential parent constitutes a breach of Art 8, which guarantees the right to family life. In *Re D (Children)* [2010] 2 FLR 1605 it was stated that *Payne* ignored the harm to children caused by a breach of the relationship that they had with the "left behind" parent. However, in *Re W (Relocation: Removal Outside Jurisdiction)* [2011] 2 FLR 409, the Court of Appeal held that too much prominence had been given to *Re D*. The task for the court under ECHR 1950, Art 8(2) is to balance the right of the non-residential parent to family life (guaranteed by Art 8(1)) against the right of the residential parent to their own right to private life when the two rights are in conflict (*Re A (Permission to Remove Child from Jurisdiction: Human Rights)* [2000] 2 FLR 225; *Payne v Payne* (above); *Re C (Permission to Remove from Jurisdiction)* [2003] 1 FLR 1066). Where there is a shared care arrangement in place, the approach in *Payne* may need to be modified because it is based on the premise that the applicant is the primary carer (*K v K (Relocation: Shared Care Arrangement)* [2012] 2 FLR 880; *Re F (Relocation)* [2013] 1 FLR 645; *Re Y (Leave to Remove from Jurisdiction)* [2004] 2 FLR 330; *C v C (International Relocation: Shared Care Arrangement)* [2011] 2 FLR 701). In *K v K*, the Court of Appeal held that, given the shared care arrangement, the court should apply *Re Y* rather than *Payne*. The only principle to be extracted from *Payne* is that the child's welfare is the court's paramount consideration; all the rest is guidance as to the factors to be weighed when making that decision. Where there is more than one child involved, the court must consider separately the interests of each child in the light of their ages, stages of development and the nature of their needs (*Re S (Relocation: Interests of Siblings)* [2011] 2 FLR 678).

In *Re B (Removal from Jurisdiction); Re S (Removal from Jurisdiction)* [2003] 2 FLR 1043, the Court of Appeal emphasised that where a mother cared for the children within a new family, the impact of refusal on the new family and the stepfather must also be carefully evaluated. It was acknowledged that *Payne v Payne* (above) did not of itself sufficiently alert the judge to the weight to be given to the relationship between the mother and her new partner and its natural consequences. However, where removal from the jurisdiction will cause a significant loss to the child in relation to emotional and educational issues permission may be refused (*Re Y*, above). For a recent case applying the relevant test see *Re W (Relocation: Removal Outside Jurisdiction)* [2011] 2 FLR 409. For examples of the court refusing permission to relocate, see *Re AR (A Child: Relocation)* [2010] 2 FLR 1577 and *C v C* (above).

Note that where there is a residence order in place, the removal of a child from England and Wales to Scotland does not require an application for permission to remove the child from the jurisdiction, since Scotland is part of the UK (*Re T (A Child)* [2001] EWCA Civ 1067).

Temporary removal from jurisdiction—Where it is intended that the removal of a child from the jurisdiction is only temporary, then different considerations will apply to those relating to permanent removal (*Re A (Temporary Removal from Jurisdiction)* [2005] 1 FLR 639 – where the court had to balance the mother's desire to move abroad for 2 years for her career development against the need for the child to have contact with the father). The more temporary the removal, the less regard should be paid to the principles in *Payne v Payne* [2001] 1 FLR 1052. In *Re S and O (Temporary Removal from Jurisdiction)* [2009] Fam Law 114 the court granted the father temporary permission to take the children to Barbados, on giving various undertakings. For a suggested menu of undertakings and declarations in holiday applications to a non-Convention country, see *Re DS (Removal from Jurisdiction)* [2010] 1 FLR 576.

Relocation within the UK—Relocation within the UK can present problems because while the primary carer might not have an obligation to apply under s 13(1)(b) he may still have to defeat the challenge of an application for a prohibited steps order under s 8 or for the imposition of a condition to the residence order under s 11(7). In making such decisions, the welfare of the child is always paramount (*Re H (Children) (Residence Order: Condition)* [2001] 2 FLR 1277 – the court made a residence order in favour of the father but attached a condition prohibiting him from removing the children to Northern Ireland). The Court of Appeal in *Re H* (above) held that the test to be applied for external or internal relocation is that laid down in *Payne v Payne* [2001] 1 FLR 1052 (see **Removal from jurisdiction** (above)) and has not been affected by HRA 1998. However, the test is less stringent in cases of internal relocation than for cases of external relocation (*Re H* (above); *Re S (A Child) (Residence Order: Condition)* [2001] 3 FCR 154; *E v E (Shared Residence: Financial Relief: Yardstick of Equality)* [2006] 2 FLR 1228). In *Re B (Prohibited Steps Order)* [2008] 1 FLR 613, the Court of Appeal emphasised that the imposition of a condition on a residence order restricting the primary carer's right to choose his or her place of residence is a truly exceptional order and confirmed that the case of *Re E (Residence: Imposition of Conditions)* [1997] 2 FLR 638 governs consideration of cases involving a move within the UK. However, in *Re F (Children)* [2011] 1 FLR 1382 the Court of Appeal held that the test of "exceptionality" places an impermissible gloss on the exercise of CA 1989, s 1 by which the child's welfare is paramount. It is wrong in principle to apply different criteria if a shared residence order is in place as opposed to a sole residence order; the correct approach is to examine the underlying facts and decide in all of the circumstances whether it is in the child's interests to relocate with the parent who wishes to move (*Re L (Shared Residence Order)* [2009] 1 FLR 1157).

14 Enforcement of residence orders

(1) Where –

    (a)   a residence order is in force with respect to a child in favour of any person; and

    (b)   any other person (including one in whose favour the order is also in force) is in breach of the arrangements settled by that order,

the person mentioned in paragraph (a) may, as soon as the requirement in subsection (2) is complied with, enforce the order under section 63(3) of the Magistrates' Courts Act 1980 as if it were an order requiring the other person to produce the child to him.

(2) The requirement is that a copy of the residence order has been served on the other person.

(3) Subsection (1) is without prejudice to any other remedy open to the person in whose favour the residence order is in force.

Defined terms—"residence order": s 8(1).

Scope—This section is intended to allow enforcement of residence orders under the penal procedures of MCA 1980 in addition to any other available procedure for enforcement, e g under FLA 1986, s 34(3). Unlike the High Court or county court, the additional directive requirement under CA 1989, s 11 (for example, to deliver the child to the residential parent) is not required because it may be enforced under MCA 1980, s 63(3) "as if it were an order requiring the other person to produce the child" to the person in whose favour the order was made. There is no need for a specific order requiring when the child should be given up – contrast with FLA 1986, s 34(3).

"section 63(3) of the Magistrates' Courts Act 1980"—MCA 1980, s 63(3) is the penal procedure in magistrates' courts for the enforcement of its orders, and empowers the court to punish for breach of its order. The court may order the contemnor to pay a sum not exceeding £50 for every day during which he is in default or a sum not exceeding £5000 or to commit him to prison until he has remedied the breach or for a period not exceeding 2 months.

Procedure—Proceedings under MCA 1980, s 63(3) are commenced by complaint (CCA 1981, s 17(2)).

Special guardianship

14A Special guardianship orders

(1) A "special guardianship order" is an order appointing one or more individuals to be a child's "special guardian" (or special guardians).

(2) A special guardian –

(a)   must be aged eighteen or over; and
(b)   must not be a parent of the child in question,

and subsections (3) to (6) are to be read in that light.

(3) The court may make a special guardianship order with respect to any child on the application of an individual who –

(a)   is entitled to make such an application with respect to the child; or
(b)   has obtained the leave of the court to make the application,

or on the joint application of more than one such individual.

(4) Section 9(3) applies in relation to an application for leave to apply for a special guardianship order as it applies in relation to an application for leave to apply for a section 8 order.

(5) The individuals who are entitled to apply for a special guardianship order with respect to a child are –

(a)   any guardian of the child;
(b)   any individual in whose favour a residence order is in force with respect to the child;
(c)   any individual listed in subsection (5)(b) or (c) of section 10 (as read with subsection (10) of that section);
(d)   a local authority foster parent with whom the child has lived for a period of at least one year immediately preceding the application;
(e)   a relative with whom the child has lived for a period of at least one year immediately preceding the application.

(6) The court may also make a special guardianship order with respect to a child in any family proceedings in which a question arises with respect to the welfare of the child if –

(a)   an application for the order has been made by an individual who falls within subsection (3)(a) or (b) (or more than one such individual jointly); or
(b)   the court considers that a special guardianship order should be made even though no such application has been made.

(7) No individual may make an application under subsection (3) or (6)(a) unless, before the beginning of the period of three months ending with the date of the application, he has given written notice of his intention to make the application –

(a)   if the child in question is being looked after by a local authority, to that local authority, or
(b)   otherwise, to the local authority in whose area the individual is ordinarily resident.

(8) On receipt of such a notice, the local authority must investigate the matter and prepare a report for the court dealing with –

(a)   the suitability of the applicant to be a special guardian;
(b)   such matters (if any) as may be prescribed by the Secretary of State; and
(c)   any other matter which the local authority consider to be relevant.

(9) The court may itself ask a local authority to conduct such an investigation and prepare such a report, and the local authority must do so.

(10) The local authority may make such arrangements as they see fit for any person to act on their behalf in connection with conducting an investigation or preparing a report referred to in subsection (8) or (9).

(11) The court may not make a special guardianship order unless it has received a report dealing with the matters referred to in subsection (8).

(12) Subsections (8) and (9) of section 10 apply in relation to special guardianship orders as they apply in relation to section 8 orders.

(13) This section is subject to section 29(5) and (6) of the Adoption and Children Act 2002.

Amendments—Inserted by ACA 2002, s 115; amended by CYPA 2008, s 38.

Scope—Special guardianship orders (SGOs) are private law orders which give the special guardian parental responsibility for the child concerned. They provide permanence and security for those children for whom adoption is not suitable but who cannot live with their birth parents. The basic legal links between the child and his birth family are preserved. Where the child himself applies for permission, the court may only grant permission if it is satisfied that the child has sufficient understanding to make the proposed application for an SGO: ss 14A(12) and 10(8). The court may not make an SGO unless it has received a report from the local authority: s 14A(11). The report must deal with the matters prescribed by the Schedule to the Special Guardianship Regulations 2005 and the matters required by s 10(9): s 14A(12).

Procedure—The procedure for applying for a special guardianship order (SGO) is set out in Procedural Guide D10.

Guidance on making special guardianship orders—In *Re S (Adoption Order or Special Guardianship Order)* [2007] 1 FLR 819 the Court of Appeal gave detailed guidance at [40]–[77] as to the statutory framework, the making of special guardianship orders (SGOs) within pre-existing family relationships and the need under a SGO for permission for a parent to apply for a s 8 order. This guidance has been endorsed by the President of the Family Division. See also *Re M-J (Adoption Order or Special Guardianship Order)* [2007] 1 FLR 691 and *Re AJ (Adoption Order or Special Guardianship Order)* [2007] 1 FLR 507, which should be read together with *Re S* (above). In *A Local Authority v Y, Z and Others* [2006] 2 FLR 41 the court approved SGOs in respect of three older children who had been in settled wider family placements for around 2 years. The court also made an order for defined contact to the mother. In *S v B and Newport City Council; Re K* [2007] 1 FLR 1116 a SGO was made in favour of the maternal grandparents, together with a prohibited steps order preventing the parents from having direct contact with the child, a s 91(14) order preventing the parents from making further applications without permission from the court and a specific issue order authorising a change of name. In *Re L (Special Guardianship: Surname)* [2007] 2 FLR 50 the court refused to allow the child's surname to be changed as it was important that as she grew up she knew that she was being raised by her grandparents rather than her parents.

Special Guardianship Regulations 2005—The Special Guardianship Regulations 2005 form part of the legislative framework for special guardianship orders. They relate mainly to the special guardianship support services (SGSS), which local authorities are required to provide by virtue of section 14F. They prescribe the services which are SGSS and state which bodies other than local authorities can provide services on the local authority's behalf and which local authority should be responsible for providing SGSS in cross-border arrangements (regs 3–5). The Regulations set out the circumstances in which financial support is payable and the considerations to which an authority must have regard when deciding on the amount of that financial support (regs 6–10). They set out the procedure for an assessment of special guardianship support needs, identifying those entitled to an assessment and how those assessments should be carried out (regs 11–16). They specify the steps an authority must take following an assessment to notify the relevant persons of the outcome and they require the authority to plan and review their service provision where appropriate (regs 17–18). The Regulations prescribe the matters that local authorities are required to include in the report that the court must receive before it can make a special guardianship order (reg 21 and Schedule). They also specify which local authority is to be the relevant local authority where the child becomes entitled to advice and assistance under the provisions relating to care leavers (reg 22).

Special Guardianship Guidance—Special Guardianship Guidance has been issued under the Local Authority Social Services Act 1970, s 7, by the Department for Education and Skills. While the Guidance does not have the full force of statute, it should be complied with unless exceptional circumstances justify departure from it (*B v Lewisham Borough Council* [2008] 2 FLR 523).

Guidance where more than one local authority is involved—In *Suffolk County Council v Nottinghamshire County Council* [2012] EWCA Civ 1640, the court held that where more than one local authority is involved in an out-of-area placement in special guardianship proceedings, the key question in determining which authority is responsible is whether a child is "looked after" by one of them within the meaning of s 22(1); if so, then that authority is responsible. If the child is not a "looked after" child, the responsible authority is the one in whose area the child is living. A child ceases to be "looked after" as soon as parental responsibility becomes vested in another by, for example, the making of a residence order or a special guardianship order. In such a situation, local authorities are bound by Special Guardianship Regulations 2005, reg 5 to co-operate with one another in the discharge of functions. Every authority will be both a sender and a receiver over time and there ought to be self-regulation in respect of who would fund the statutory duties.

Special guardianship not confined to kinship cases—In *Re I (Adoption: Appeal: Special Guardianship)* [2012] Fam Law 1461, McFarlane LJ emphasised that where the issue is whether to dispense with parental consent for the purposes of an adoption or placement order, the test in s 52(1)(b) is that the court must be satisfied that "the welfare of the child requires the consent to be dispensed with" and it will be difficult – or indeed impossible – for the judge to be satisfied of this, unless relevant alternatives have been considered. Here, where the foster carers would continue to be the carers of the child and where the paternal family would continue to have contact with the child, special guardianship should have been properly considered. The judgment is, therefore, also a helpful reminder that special guardianship is by no means intended to be confined to cases of kinship care.

Leave to apply (s 14A(4))—The factors governing an application for permission to apply for a SGO are the same as those for other s 8 orders: see under CA 1989, s 9(3). Where the person applying for permission is the child concerned, the court may only grant permission if it is satisfied that the child has sufficient understanding to make the proposed application for the special guardianship order (see s 14A(12) and **Application for leave by child** under s 10(8)). Where the person applying for permission is not the child concerned, the court must have regard to the factors in s 10(9) in just the same way as it does when considering an application for permission to apply for a s 8 order (see s 14A(12) and **Application for leave by person other than child concerned** under s 10(9)).

Orders can be made of court's own motion (s 14A(6))—The court can make a SGO in an appropriate case, even where no application has been made.

Need for a local authority report before order can be made (s 14A(7),(8),(11))—Anyone wishing to apply for a SGO must give 3 months' notice to the relevant local authority so that a report can be prepared as to his suitability and any other relevant matters (but see below for those cases in which the requirement for 3 months' notice will be waived: ACA 2002, s 29(5), (6)). The court may not make a SGO unless it has received the prescribed report (s 14A (11); *Re S (Adoption Order or Special Guardianship Order) (No 2)*) [2007] 1 FLR 855)). In *Birmingham City Council v R* [2007] 1 FLR 564 the Court of Appeal held that a person who requires the permission of the court to make an application for a SGO cannot either make an application for such an order or give notice of an intention to do so unless and until he has obtained the court's permission to make an application. Section 14A(8), which requires the authority to investigate and prepare a report, is not triggered when a person who requires the court's permission to make an application but has not obtained it, purports to give notice of an intention to make an application for a SGO. The matters that the local authority must include in their report to the court are set out in the Special Guardianship Regulations, reg 21, and in the Schedule thereto.

"subject to section 29(5) and (6) of the Adoption and Children Act 2002" (s 14A(13))—ACA 2002, s 29(5) states that where a placement order is in force, no SGO may be made in respect of the child unless: (a) an application has been made for an adoption order; and (b) the person applying for the SGO has obtained the court's permission, or if he is a guardian of the child, has obtained the court's permission under s 47(5). Where permission has been given in these circumstances, the applicant must still give written notice of his application to the relevant local authority but the requirement for 3 months' notice is waived (ACA 2002, s 29(6)).

Hague Convention 1996—The Hague Convention 1996 came into force in the UK on 1 November 2012. It lays down rules in respect of measures directed to the protection of the person or property of the child in cases to which the Convention applies (Art 1). "Measures of protection" include guardianship, curatorship or analogous institutions (Art 3). They are intended to include systems of protection, representation or assistance that are established in favour of a child when his parents are deceased or are no longer authorised to represent him (*Handbook*, para 3.23; *Lagarde Report*, para 21). See further under the Convention in Part VI.

14B Special guardianship orders: making

(1) Before making a special guardianship order, the court must consider whether, if the order were made –

    (a)   a contact order should also be made with respect to the child,

    (b)   any section 8 order in force with respect to the child should be varied or discharged,

    (c)   where a contact order made with respect to the child is not discharged, any enforcement order relating to that contact order should be revoked, and

    (d)   where a contact activity direction has been made as regards contact with the child and is in force, that contact activity direction should be discharged.

(2) On making a special guardianship order, the court may also –

    (a)   give leave for the child to be known by a new surname;

    (b)   grant the leave required by section 14C(3)(b), either generally or for specified purposes.

Amendments—Inserted by ACA 2002, s 115; amended by CAA 2006, s 15, Sch 2, paras 7, 8, Sch 3.

14C Special guardianship orders: effect

(1) The effect of a special guardianship order is that while the order remains in force –

    (a)   a special guardian appointed by the order has parental responsibility for the child in respect of whom it is made; and

    (b)   subject to any other order in force with respect to the child under this Act, a special guardian is entitled to exercise parental responsibility to the exclusion of any other person with parental responsibility for the child (apart from another special guardian).

(2) Subsection (1) does not affect –

    (a)   the operation of any enactment or rule of law which requires the consent of more than one person with parental responsibility in a matter affecting the child; or

    (b)   any rights which a parent of the child has in relation to the child's adoption or placement for adoption.

(3) While a special guardianship order is in force with respect to a child, no person may –

    (a)   cause the child to be known by a new surname; or

    (b)   remove him from the United Kingdom,

without either the written consent of every person who has parental responsibility for the child or the leave of the court.

(4) Subsection (3)(b) does not prevent the removal of a child, for a period of less than three months, by a special guardian of his.

(5) If the child with respect to whom a special guardianship order is in force dies, his special guardian must take reasonable steps to give notice of that fact to –

    (a)   each parent of the child with parental responsibility; and

    (b)   each guardian of the child,

but if the child has more than one special guardian, and one of them has taken such steps in relation to a particular parent or guardian, any other special guardian need not do so as respects that parent or guardian.

(6) This section is subject to section 29(7) of the Adoption and Children Act 2002.

Amendments—Inserted by ACA 2002, s 115.

Scope—Subject to any other existing CA 1989 order, a special guardian is entitled to exercise parental responsibility to the exclusion of any other person with parental responsibility (save for another special guardian): s 14C(1). It allows the special guardian to remove the child from the jurisdiction for up to 3 months without the consent of others with parental responsibility (but he would need the consent of another special guardian): s 14C(4).

"subject to section 29(7) of the Adoption and Children Act 2002" (s 14C(6))—ACA 2002, s 29(7) states that, where a placement order is in force, s 14C(1)(b) has effect subject to any determination made by the adoption agency under ACA 2002, s 25(4), to restrict the exercise of parental responsibility. CA 1989, s 14C(3) and (4) do not apply.

14D Special guardianship orders: variation and discharge

(1) The court may vary or discharge a special guardianship order on the application of –

(a)   the special guardian (or any of them, if there are more than one);

(b)   any parent or guardian of the child concerned;

(c)   any individual in whose favour a residence order is in force with respect to the child;

(d)   any individual not falling within any of paragraphs (a) to (c) who has, or immediately before the making of the special guardianship order had, parental responsibility for the child;

(e)   the child himself; or

(f)   a local authority designated in a care order with respect to the child.

(2) In any family proceedings in which a question arises with respect to the welfare of a child with respect to whom a special guardianship order is in force, the court may also vary or discharge the special guardianship order if it considers that the order should be varied or discharged, even though no application has been made under subsection (1).

(3) The following must obtain the leave of the court before making an application under subsection (1) –

(a)   the child;

(b)   any parent or guardian of his;

(c)   any step-parent of his who has acquired, and has not lost, parental responsibility for him by virtue of section 4A;

(d)   any individual falling within subsection (1)(d) who immediately before the making of the special guardianship order had, but no longer has, parental responsibility for him.

(4) Where the person applying for leave to make an application under subsection (1) is the child, the court may only grant leave if it is satisfied that he has sufficient understanding to make the proposed application under subsection (1).

(5) The court may not grant leave to a person falling within subsection (3)(b),(c) or (d) unless it is satisfied that there has been a significant change in circumstances since the making of the special guardianship order.

Amendments—Inserted by ACA 2002, s 115.

Scope—A special guardianship order can be varied or discharged (unlike an adoption order).

Application for leave by child (s 14D(4))—See **Application for leave by child** under s 10(9).

Leave to apply to discharge special guardianship order (s 14D(5))—In *Re G (A Child) (Special Guardianship Order)* [2010] 2 FLR 696 the court gave guidance as to the construction of s 14D(5) and the correct approach to applications for permission to apply to discharge special guardianship orders (SGOs). In *Re G*, the judge observed that whereas permission to apply for revocation of a placement order under ACA 2002, s 24 required "a change in circumstances", permission to apply for the discharge of an SGO under CA 1989, s 14D(5) required "a significant change in circumstances". For the time being, the Court of Appeal takes the view that there is no relevant difference between the two. Until the emergence of further guidance, the proper approach should be that commended in *M v Warwickshire County Council* [2008] 1 FLR 1093, ie that the approach to permission to apply for revocation of a placement order should also apply to permission to apply for the discharge of an SGO. CA 1989, s 10(9), is not the right approach because that section applies to those who need to apply for permission to apply for a s 8 order and there appears to be no ground for considering that the matters specified there should be formally weighed upon an application to discharge an SGO.

14E Special guardianship orders: supplementary

(1) In proceedings in which any question of making, varying or discharging a special guardianship order arises, the court shall (in the light of any rules made by virtue of subsection (3)) –

    (a)   draw up a timetable with a view to determining the question without delay; and

    (b)   give such directions as it considers appropriate for the purpose of ensuring, so far as is reasonably practicable, that the timetable is adhered to.

(2) Subsection (1) applies also in relation to proceedings in which any other question with respect to a special guardianship order arises.

(3) The power to make rules in subsection (2) of section 11 applies for the purposes of this section as it applies for the purposes of that.

(4) A special guardianship order, or an order varying one, may contain provisions which are to have effect for a specified period.

(5) Section 11(7) (apart from paragraph (c)) applies in relation to special guardianship orders and orders varying them as it applies in relation to section 8 orders.

Amendments—Inserted by ACA 2002, s 115.

"Section 11(7)" (s 14E(5))—Section 11(7) permits the court to attach to the special guardianship order directions as to how it is to be carried into effect and to impose conditions which must be complied with.

14F Special guardianship support services

(1) Each local authority must make arrangements for the provision within their area of special guardianship support services, which means –

    (a)   counselling, advice and information; and

    (b)   such other services as are prescribed,

in relation to special guardianship.

(2) The power to make regulations under subsection (1)(b) is to be exercised so as to secure that local authorities provide financial support.

(3) At the request of any of the following persons –

    (a)   a child with respect to whom a special guardianship order is in force;

    (b)   a special guardian;

    (c)   a parent;

    (d)   any other person who falls within a prescribed description,

a local authority may carry out an assessment of that person's needs for special guardianship support services (but, if the Secretary of State so provides in regulations, they must do so if he is a person of a prescribed description, or if his case falls within a prescribed description, or if both he and his case fall within prescribed descriptions).

(4) A local authority may, at the request of any other person, carry out an assessment of that person's needs for special guardianship support services.

(5) Where, as a result of an assessment, a local authority decide that a person has needs for special guardianship support services, they must then decide whether to provide any such services to that person.

(6) If –

   (a)   a local authority decide to provide any special guardianship support services to a person, and

   (b)   the circumstances fall within a prescribed description,

the local authority must prepare a plan in accordance with which special guardianship support services are to be provided to him, and keep the plan under review.

(7) The Secretary of State may by regulations make provision about assessments, preparing and reviewing plans, the provision of special guardianship support services in accordance with plans and reviewing the provision of special guardianship support services.

(8) The regulations may in particular make provision –

   (a)   about the type of assessment which is to be carried out, or the way in which an assessment is to be carried out;

   (b)   about the way in which a plan is to be prepared;

   (c)   about the way in which, and the time at which, a plan or the provision of special guardianship support services is to be reviewed;

   (d)   about the considerations to which a local authority are to have regard in carrying out an assessment or review or preparing a plan;

   (e)   as to the circumstances in which a local authority may provide special guardianship support services subject to conditions (including conditions as to payment for the support or the repayment of financial support);

   (f)   as to the consequences of conditions imposed by virtue of paragraph (e) not being met (including the recovery of any financial support provided);

   (g)   as to the circumstances in which this section may apply to a local authority in respect of persons who are outside that local authority's area;

   (h)   as to the circumstances in which a local authority may recover from another local authority the expenses of providing special guardianship support services to any person.

(9) A local authority may provide special guardianship support services (or any part of them) by securing their provision by –

   (a)   another local authority; or

   (b)   a person within a description prescribed in regulations of persons who may provide special guardianship support services,

and may also arrange with any such authority or person for that other authority or that person to carry out the local authority's functions in relation to assessments under this section.

(10) A local authority may carry out an assessment of the needs of any person for the purposes of this section at the same time as an assessment of his needs is made under any other provision of this Act or under any other enactment.

(11) Section 27 (co-operation between authorities) applies in relation to the exercise of functions of a local authority under this section as it applies in relation to the exercise of functions of a local authority under Part 3.

Amendments—Inserted by ACA 2002, s 115.

Scope—Once a special guardianship order has been made, the local authority is under a duty to make arrangements for the provision of a package of special guardian support services, including counselling, advice, information and financial support. The Special Guardianship Regulations 2005 set out the details of those support services.

Financial support for special guardians—Under the Special Guardianship Regulations 2005, the local authority must make appropriate financial support available to special guardians (regs 6–10) and must make an assessment of their relevant needs (regs 12–13). In doing so it must comply with the Special

Guardianship Guidance issued under the Local Authority Social Services Act 1970, s 7, by the Department for Education and Skills. While the Guidance does not have the full force of statute, it should be complied with by local authorities unless exceptional circumstances justify departure from it (*B v Lewisham Borough Council* [2008] 2 FLR 523 – it was unlawful for the authority to make a rigid link with adoption allowances rather than focusing on fostering allowances). In *B v Kirklees Metropolitan Council* [2010] 2 FLR 405, the authority's decision that the SGO allowance should be two-thirds of the core fostering allowance was unlawful. It had deviated substantially from the Ministerial Guidance without justification. The authority is expected to consider the fostering allowance as a starting point and then to make appropriate adjustments to it (*R (TT) v London Borough of Merton* [2012] EWCA 2055 (Admin)).

Guidance where more than one local authority is involved—In *Suffolk County Council v Nottinghamshire County Council* [2012] EWCA Civ 1640, the court held that where more than one local authority is involved in an out-of-area placement in special guardianship proceedings, the key question in determining which authority is responsible is whether a child is "looked after" by one of them within the meaning of s 22(1); if so, then that authority is responsible. If the child is not a "looked after" child, the responsible authority is the one in whose area the child is living. A child ceases to be "looked after" as soon as parental responsibility becomes vested in another by, for example, the making of a residence order or a special guardianship order. In such a situation, local authorities are bound by the Special Guardianship Regulations 2005, reg 5 to cooperate with one another in the discharge of functions. Every authority will be both a sender and a receiver over time and there ought to be self-regulation in respect of who would fund the statutory duties. It is, therefore, of critical importance when a child is placed out of area to have regard as to whether a child should or will remain looked after (ie under an interim care order or accommodated) or not (ie under a residence order). At the same time, the local authorities involved should cooperate from the earliest stage in deciding who will in fact execute the statutory duties that arise and who will fund that work. Local authorities have powers to make sensible arrangements between themselves wherever primary legal responsibility may in fact lie. The role of the court should also be carefully considered. Section 14F imposes duties on a local authority but it does not empower the family court to direct how or (in some aspects) even whether such duties are to be performed. Moreover, the statute gives the court no power to make directions as to payment of money or provision of services. Of course, judges may properly express views to local authorities and are entitled no doubt to expect that they will receive serious consideration (just as judges can and do express views about adoption and care plans) and of course it is only the judge who in the end can make the SGO.

14G   *(repealed)*

Financial relief

15   Orders for financial relief with respect to children

(1) Schedule 1 (which consists primarily of the re-enactment, with consequential amendments and minor modifications, of provisions of section 6 of the Family Law Reform Act 1969, the Guardianship of Minors Acts 1971 and 1973, the Children Act 1975 and of sections 15 and 16 of the Family Law Reform Act 1987) makes provision in relation to financial relief for children.

(2) The powers of a magistrates' court under section 60 of the Magistrates' Courts Act 1980 to revoke, revive or vary an order for the periodical payment of money and the power of a clerk of a magistrates' court to vary such an order shall not apply in relation to an order made under Schedule 1.

Amendments—CLSA 1990, s 116, Sch 16, para 10(1); MEA 1991, s 11(1), Sch 2, para 10.

Scope—This section introduces Sch 1 which contains the court's powers to make financial orders for children. Subject to CSA 1991, which restricts the court's power to order child maintenance (see Procedural Guide A2), Sch 1 covers three situations, namely:

(a)   orders that a parent pay maintenance or a lump sum or transfer property to children when the first application for such an order is made while the child is under the age of 18 (although an order for periodical payments can subsequently be extended if the child is continuing in education or there are special circumstances);

(b) orders for periodical payments or a lump sum where the first time an application is made is when the child is aged over 18;

(c) alteration, either during the joint lives of the parents or after the death of one of them, of maintenance agreements containing financial provision for a child.

Orders for financial relief against parents—Schedule 1, para 1 essentially re-enacts Guardianship of Minors Act 1971, ss 11B and 11C. An order under para 1 is made either on application or without application at the time a residence order is made, varied or discharged. If the child's parents are married, an alternative way of applying for financial relief for the child is MCA 1973, ss 23 and 24, if there are divorce proceedings, or if there are no such proceedings, under s 27. By applying for relief for the child under those sections, the practitioner is able to take advantage of the power under MCA 1973, s 37 to restrain anticipated disposals of assets and to set aside past disposals where the intention is to defeat the claim. If, however, the child's parents are not married, that alternative jurisdiction is not available and the application has to be brought under Sch 1, para 1.

Orders for financial relief for persons aged over 18—Schedule 1, para 2 re-enacts Guardianship of Minors Act 1971, s 11D. It enables a child who has reached 18 and who is continuing in education or to whom special circumstances apply to obtain from his parents an order for periodical payments or a lump sum where his parents are not living with each other in the same household and there was no periodical payments order in force in respect of him before he reached the age of 16. This is the only provision in the Act which permits an original application for relief by a child aged over 18. Paragraph 16(1) of Sch 1 provides that, for this purpose, a person who has reached the age of 18 falls within the meaning of "child". If there was a periodical payments order in force before the child reached the age of 16, the child's remedy is to apply in the proceedings in which that order was made to extend that order. If, however, there was no such order and the applicant's parents are living with each other in the same household, then the applicant has no remedy against his parents. Thus, for instance, the adult child whose parents are living together and for no valid reason are refusing to support him or her through university is in a markedly worse situation than an adult child whose parents have separated.

Alteration of maintenance agreements containing financial provision for a child—Schedule 1, paras 10 and 11 re-enact the powers contained in FLRA 1987, ss 15 and 16 to alter agreements made between parents for the maintenance of a child. The jurisdiction is similar to that contained in MCA 1973, ss 35 (lifetime variations) and 36 (variation after death), except that ss 35 and 36 apply only where the parents are married. Where the parents are married, the more sophisticated procedural provisions of ss 35 and 36 (including the power to restrain dealings under s 37) make it sensible to bring the application under those sections; where the parents are not married, there is no alternative but to bring the application under Sch 1.

Restriction of magistrates' powers—Section 15(2) prohibits magistrates' courts from revoking or varying an order for periodical payments made under Sch 1.

Procedure—Applications under Sch 1 are governed by FPR 2010 (Pt 9 applies). The hearings progress through first appointment and FDR hearing to final order: see Procedural Guide A2. Where a father's resources are subject to a criminal restraint order under the Proceeds of Crime Act 2002, a mother seeking relief including the disclosure of the father's means should apply to the Crown Court that made the order, on notice: *T v B and Revenue and Customs Prosecutions Office* [2009] 1 FLR 1231.

Costs—Applications under CA 1989, s 15 and Sch 1 are financial remedy proceedings under FPR 2010, r 2.3. However, they are not included within the application provided for in r 28.3(4)(b), so the costs rule in r 28.3 does not apply to s 15 and Sch 1 applications. The court may exercise its discretion as to costs in the light of CPR 1998, r 44.2. See FPR PD28A.

Family assistance orders

16 Family assistance orders

(1) Where, in any family proceedings, the court has power to make an order under this Part with respect to any child, it may (whether or not it makes such an order) make an order requiring –

    (a) an officer of the Service or a Welsh family proceedings officer to be made available; or

    (b) a local authority to make an officer of the authority available,

to advise, assist and (where appropriate) befriend any person named in the order.

(2) The persons who may be named in an order under this section ("a family assistance order") are –

(a) any parent, guardian or special guardian of the child;

(b) any person with whom the child is living or in whose favour a contact order is in force with respect to the child;

(c) the child himself.

(3) No court may make a family assistance order unless –

(a) (*repealed*)

(b) it has obtained the consent of every person to be named in the order other than the child.

(4) A family assistance order may direct –

(a) the person named in the order; or

(b) such of the persons named in the order as may be specified in the order,

to take such steps as may be so specified with a view to enabling the officer concerned to be kept informed of the address of any person named in the order and to be allowed to visit any such person.

(4A) If the court makes a family assistance order with respect to a child and the order is to be in force at the same time as a contact order made with respect to the child, the family assistance order may direct the officer concerned to give advice and assistance as regards establishing, improving and maintaining contact to such of the persons named in the order as may be specified in the order.

(5) Unless it specifies a shorter period, a family assistance order shall have effect for a period of twelve months beginning with the day on which it is made.

(6) If the court makes a family assistance order with respect to a child and the order is to be in force at the same time as a section 8 order made with respect to the child, the family assistance order may direct the officer concerned to report to the court on such matters relating to the section 8 order as the court may require (including the question whether the section 8 order ought to be varied or discharged).

(7) A family assistance order shall not be made so as to require a local authority to make an officer of theirs available unless –

(a) the authority agree; or

(b) the child concerned lives or will live within their area.

(8), (9) (*repealed*)

Amendments—CJCSA 2000 ss 74, 75, Sch 7, Pt II, paras 87, 89, Sch 8; CA 2004, s 40, Sch 3, paras 5, 7; ACA 2002, Sch 3, para 58; CAA 2006, s 6(1)–(5).

Defined terms—"child": s 105(1); "family proceedings": s 8(3); "local authority": s 105(1); "officer of the Service": CJCSA 2000, s 11(3).

Scope—A family assistance order (FAO) is a short-term order lasting for no more than 12 months which obliges an officer of the Service or local authority officer to advise, assist and (where appropriate) befriend a named person or persons. Any of the following may be named in the order: a parent, guardian or special guardian of the child, anyone with whom the child is living or who has a contact order with respect to the child and the child himself (s 16(2)). An order is to be made only where every person who is to be named in the order (other than the child) has given consent (s 16(3)). Normally the court will make a family assistance order of its own initiative, but although the rules and the Act do not specifically prescribe any procedure for applying for a s 16 order neither do they prohibit such an application and therefore presumably one can be made.

Where a FAO is to be in force at the same time as a contact order, the officer may give advice and assistance to establish, improve and maintain contact to the persons named in the contact order (s 16(4A)). Where a FAO is in force at the same time as a s 8 order in relation to the child, the officer may be directed to report to the court on such matters relating to the s 8 order as the court may require, including variation and discharge (s 16(6)).

PART II

Practice Direction—FPR PD12M *Family Assistance Orders: Consultation* requires that, before making a Family Assistance Order (FAO) the court must have obtained the opinion (verbally or in writing) of the appropriate officer about whether it would be in the best interests of the child for a FAO to be made and, if so, how the order could operate and for what period. Furthermore, before making a FAO, the court must give any person whom it proposes be named in the order an opportunity to comment upon any opinion given by the officer.

Risk assessments—CA 1989, s 16A requires a Cafcass officer carrying out any function in private law CA 1989 proceedings to carry out a risk assessment if he has cause to suspect that the child concerned is at risk of harm and to provide that assessment to the court. See further under s 16A below and **Contact and Domestic Violence** under CA 1989, s 1.

"order under this Part" (s 16(1))—The orders available under Pt II are: a contact order, a prohibited steps order, a residence order and a specific issue order (all under s 8). It would also seem that an order for financial relief under Sch 1 may be classified as an order under Pt II as Sch 1 derives from s 15. The power to make a family assistance order (FAO) is not limited to applications for s 8 orders; it may be exercised in any family proceedings where there is power to make an order under Pt II and "family proceedings" is widely defined by s 8(3). It follows that a FAO could, for example, be made on an application for a care or supervision order.

Enforcement of family assistance order—In *Re C (Family Assistance Order)* [1996] 1 FLR 424, FD, a family assistance order (FAO) had been made directed to a local authority. The local authority did not have the resources to implement it and restored the matter before the court. There being no remedy provided in CA 1989 for such a circumstance, the judge supposed that one might make an order directed to the director of social services, endorsed with a penal notice, so that enforcement proceedings could ensue, but commented that that would be totally contrary to the best interests of the child concerned and the child care system as a whole. See also *Re E (Family Assistance Order)* [1999] 2 FLR 512 in which an FAO was made against a local authority in spite of the authority's reluctance to submit to it; on the exceptional facts of the case supervised contact between the child and his mother could not have taken place without such an order.

Children and Adoption Act 2006—CAA 2006, s 6(2), removed the requirement for family assistance orders (FAOs) to be made only in exceptional circumstances. It inserted s 16(4A) to provide that where a FAO is to be in force at the same time as a contact order, the officer may give advice and assistance to establish, improve and maintain contact to the persons named in the contact order (CAA 2006, s 6(3)). It increased the maximum duration of a FAO from 6 to 12 months (CAA 2006, s 6(4)). It substituted s 16(6) to provide that if the FAO is in force at the same time as a s 8 order in relation to the child, the officer may be directed to report to the court on such matters relating to the s 8 order as the court may require (including variation or discharge) (CAA 2006, s 6(5)).

Draft Legislation on Family Justice—In September 2012, draft legislation was presented to Parliament in response to David Norgrove's Family Justice Review. Clause 2(2) proposes to remove the current definitions of residence and contact orders and clause 2(3) would replace them with a "child arrangements order" (CAO). Sch 1, para 28 proposes to make certain changes to the terminology of s 16 to ensure that a family assistance order can be made in relation to a CAO.

16A Risk assessments

(1) This section applies to the following functions of officers of the Service or Welsh family proceedings officers –

    (a)   any function in connection with family proceedings in which the court has power to make an order under this Part with respect to a child or in which a question with respect to such an order arises;

    (b)   any function in connection with an order made by the court in such proceedings.

(2) If, in carrying out any function to which this section applies, an officer of the Service or a Welsh family proceedings officer is given cause to suspect that the child concerned is at risk of harm, he must –

    (a)   make a risk assessment in relation to the child, and

    (b)   provide the risk assessment to the court.

(3) A risk assessment, in relation to a child who is at risk of suffering harm of a particular sort, is an assessment of the risk of that harm being suffered by the child.

Amendments—Inserted by CAA 2006, s 7.

Scope—CA 1989, s 16A requires a Cafcass officer carrying out any function in private law CA 1989 proceedings to carry out a risk assessment if he has cause to suspect that the child concerned is at risk of harm and to provide that assessment to the court.

Practice direction—FPR PD12L *Risk Assessments under Section 16A* applies to any family proceedings in the High Court, a county court or a magistrates' court in which a risk assessment is made under s 16A. Where an officer of the service makes a risk assessment he must provide it to the court irrespective of the outcome of the assessment and even if he reaches the conclusion that there is no risk of harm to the child. In reporting the outcome, the officer should make clear the factors that triggered the decision to carry out the assessment.

Duty arising even where there are no pending proceedings—It is possible that the duty to make a risk assessment could arise even where there are no pending proceedings. For example, if the court makes a final s 8 order and an associated family assistance order (FAO) the proceedings would be concluded but the officer would still be exercising his functions for the life of the FAO. If the officer perceives a risk to the child he must make a risk assessment and provide it to the court (s 16A(2)). See FPR 2010, r 16.38 and PD16A, paras 11.1–11.7 and the amended Form 42.

Cafcass protocol for information sharing with the police—There is a joint protocol between Cafcass and the Association of Chief Police Officers (ACPO) for disclosure of information from the police, which sets out the principles of information sharing between Cafcass and all local police forces in England and Wales. It includes a standard request form that Cafcass will use to highlight the areas of risk (as set out in *Working Together to Safeguard Children* (2010)) that they have already identified. The guiding principle is that evidence of one risk or from one incident will act as a key to allowing the police to provide information about all risks and incidents. The protocol can be accessed online at *www.cafcass.gov.uk*. Pursuant to the Protocol, Cafcass is under a duty to comply with the Data Protection Act 1998 whenever it processes sensitive personal information in carrying out its safeguarding checks. It is therefore unable to reproduce in its reports information received from the police if it is not relevant to the child or children with whom Cafcass is concerned (*G v B* [2010] EWHC 2639 (Fam)).

PART III
LOCAL AUTHORITY SUPPORT FOR CHILDREN AND FAMILIES

Provision of services for children and their families

17 Provision of services for children in need, their families and others

(1) It shall be the general duty of every local authority (in addition to the other duties imposed on them by this Part) –

   (a) to safeguard and promote the welfare of children within their area who are in need; and

   (b) so far as is consistent with that duty, to promote the upbringing of such children by their families,

by providing a range and level of services appropriate to those children's needs.

(2) For the purpose principally of facilitating the discharge of their general duty under this section, every local authority shall have the specific duties and powers set out in Part I of Schedule 2.

(3) Any service provided by an authority in the exercise of functions conferred on them by this section may be provided for the family of a particular child in need or for any member of his family, if it is provided with a view to safeguarding or promoting the child's welfare.

(4) The appropriate national authority may by order amend any provision of Part I of Schedule 2 or add any further duty or power to those for the time being mentioned there.

(4A) Before determining what (if any) services to provide for a particular child in need in the exercise of functions conferred on them by this section, a local authority shall, so far as is reasonably practicable and consistent with the child's welfare –

    (a) ascertain the child's wishes and feelings regarding the provision of those services; and

    (b) give due consideration (having regard to his age and understanding) to such wishes and feelings of the child as they have been able to ascertain.

(5) Every local authority –

    (a) shall facilitate the provision by others (including in particular voluntary organisations) of services which it is a function of the authority to provide by virtue of this section, or section 18, 20, 22A to 22C, 23B to 23D, 24A or 24B; and

    (b) may make such arrangements as they see fit for any person to act on their behalf in the provision of any such service.

(6) The services provided by a local authority in the exercise of functions conferred on them by this section may include providing accommodation and giving assistance in kind or in cash.

(7) Assistance may be unconditional or subject to conditions as to the repayment of the assistance or of its value (in whole or in part).

(8) Before giving any assistance or imposing any conditions, a local authority shall have regard to the means of the child concerned and of each of his parents.

(9) No person shall be liable to make any repayment of assistance or of its value at any time when he is in receipt of income support under Part VII of the Social Security Contributions and Benefits Act 1992, of any element of child tax credit other than the family element, of working tax credit, of an income-based jobseeker's allowance or of an income-related employment and support allowance.

(10) For the purposes of this Part a child shall be taken to be in need if –

    (a) he is unlikely to achieve or maintain, or to have the opportunity of achieving or maintaining, a reasonable standard of health or development without the provision for him of services by a local authority under this Part;

    (b) his health or development is likely to be significantly impaired, or further impaired, without the provision for him of such services; or

    (c) he is disabled,

and "family," in relation to such a child, includes any person who has parental responsibility for the child and any other person with whom he has been living.

(11) For the purposes of this Part, a child is disabled if he is blind, deaf or dumb or suffers from mental disorder of any kind or is substantially and permanently handicapped by illness, injury or congenital deformity or such other disability as may be prescribed; and in this Part –

"development" means physical, intellectual, emotional, social or behavioural development; and

"health" means physical or mental health.

(12) The Treasury may by regulations prescribe circumstances in which a person is to be treated for the purposes of this Part (or for such of those purposes as are prescribed) as in receipt of any element of child tax credit other than the family element or of working tax credit.

Amendments—Disability Living Allowance and Disability Working Allowance Act 1991, s 7(2), Sch 3, para 13; Social Security (Consequential Provisions) Act 1992, s 4, Sch 2, para 108; Jobseekers Act 1995, s 41, Sch 2, para 19; Children (Leaving Care) Act 2000, s 7(2); ACA 2002, s 116(1); Tax Credits

Act 2002, s 47, Sch 3, paras 15, 16; CA 2004, s 53; Welfare Reform Act 2007, s 28(1), Sch 3, para 6(1),(2); CYPA 2008, ss 8(3), 24, 39, Sch 1, para 1, Sch 3, paras 1, 2.

Extent of local authorities' duties (s 17(1))—Section 17(1) imposes a general and overriding duty on local authorities to maintain a level and range of services in their area sufficient to enable them to discharge their functions under CA 1989, Pt III for the benefit of children in need. The other specific duties which follow must be performed in each individual case by reference to the general duty in s 17(1). However, s 17(1) does not itself impose a duty to meet the assessed needs of a child (*R (G) v Barnet London Borough Council; R (W) v Lambeth London Borough Council; R (A) v Lambeth London Borough Council* [2004] 1 FLR 454, HL – where the question at the heart of each appeal was whether s 17(1) required the local authority to meet every need that had been identified by an assessment of the needs of each "child in need" in its area; in both G's case and W's case the question was whether s 17(1) imposed a mandatory duty on a local authority to provide housing to the parent of a child in need so as to enable the child to live with his parents, regardless of the cost or the financial resources of the local authority). The principle that there is no duty under s 17(1) to meet the assessed needs of a particular child applies even where it can be demonstrated that the delivery of the assessed services is feasible having regard to the local authority's available resources (*R (VC) v Newcastle City Council and Secretary of State for the Home Department* [2012] 1 FLR 944). The adequacy of a risk assessment under CA 1989, s 17 may be the subject of judicial review. However, the ambit of the judicial review process, and any subsequent appeal, is limited to determining whether the assessment can stand. Where the assessment cannot stand and a fresh assessment is thus required, the Administrative court cannot dictate how the local authority should go about that further assessment. (*ET, BT, CT v Islington London Borough Council* [2013] EWCA Civ 323). In *R (TG) v Lambeth Borough Council* [2011] 2 FLR 1007, Wilson LJ observed that whereas the failure of a local authority to discharge its duties under CA 1989, Pt III may lead to an infringement of a person's rights under ECHR, Art 3, the consequences of such a failure are likely to be far too nebulous, speculative or slight to lead to the conclusion that there has been a breach of ECHR, Art 8.

Assessing the age of a "child" (s 17(1))—A local authority has a duty to safeguard and promote the welfare of children within their area who are in need. The definition of "child" means a person under the age of 18. Where there is difficulty in assessing the exact age of the claimant, the test to be applied is described in *R (B) v Merton London Borough Council* [2003] 2 FLR 888 (where the claimant was an asylum seeker asserting that he was 17 years of age but the local authority believed he was over 18). The phrase "child in need" in s 17 is a composite phrase and is not a limiting condition stated in wholly objective terms. In other words, there can be a range of reasonable conclusions about the matter, which are therefore subjective. It is not enough for the operation of s 20 for there just to be a child; the threshold to cross is constituted by there being a "child in need". In *R (A) v London Borough of Croydon; R (M) v London Borough of Lambeth* [2010] 1 FLR 959 the Supreme Court held that where social workers dispute a person's claim to be under the age of 18 for the purposes of s 20(1), the question of age is an objective fact that is subject, in the event of challenge, to determination by the court rather than by other kinds of decision-makers. The Act draws clear distinction between different types of questions. The question whether a child is in need involves a number of different value-judgments, such as what would be a reasonable standard of health or development for a particular child. Where the issue is what service the local authority should provide, it is reasonable to assume that Parliament intended such evaluative questions to be determined by the authority, subject to control by the courts on the ordinary principles of judicial review. However, the question of whether a person is a child is a different kind of question, to which there is a right and a wrong answer, as was found by the Supreme Court.

In *R (F) v Lewisham London Borough Council; R (D) v Manchester City Council; Secretary of State (Interested Party) and Others* [2010] 1 FLR 1463, Thorpe LJ set out useful guidance to assist courts having to manage proceedings where the issue of age is to be determined for the purposes of CA 1989 and to indicate to those representing the parties what steps can and cannot be taken in preparing for the hearing.

Where the local authority receives an expert's report about the age of a child it is not entitled to disregard the report unless there is evidence to show that the report is unreliable; it must give such reports proper consideration (*R (A) v London Borough of Croydon* [2009] 2 FLR 173 – where the decision of the authority was quashed).

Children of failed asylum seekers (s 17(1))—In *R (VC) v Newcastle City Council and Secretary of State for the Home Department* [2012] 1 FLR 944, Munby LJ held (in circumstances where children of failed asylum seekers retain eligibility for support under s 17) that where Immigration and Asylum Act 1999, s 4 (asylum support for failed asylum seekers) and CA 1989, s 17 are both engaged, the more advantageous regime under s 17 will apply. A local authority will not be able to justify the non-provision of assessed services under s 17 on the ground that s 4 support is available unless it can be shown that the Secretary of State is able and willing (or if not willing, can be compelled) to provide such services and that those services are sufficient to meet the child's needs. Munby LJ considered that, given the residual nature of the Secretary of State's functions under s 4 and the likely very significant difference between the services available under s 4 and the services assessed as required under s 17, in the general run of cases a local authority is very unlikely to be able to justify non-intervention under CA 1989, s 17 by reliance on Immigration and Asylum Act 1999, s 4.

"within their area" (s 17(2) and Sch 2, Pt I, para 1(1))—Sch 2, Pt I, para 1(1) requires that "every local authority shall take reasonable steps to identify the extent to which there are children in need within their area". The definition of "within their area" requires physical presence within the relevant area (*R v Wandsworth London Borough Council, Hammersmith & Fulham London Borough Council and Lambeth London Borough Council ex parte Stewart* [2002] 1 FLR 469; *R v London Borough of Barking & Dagenham ex parte Bilkisu Mohammed* [2002] EWHC 2663 (Admin)). Crane J emphasised that since there are no formal guidelines to assist local authorities in cases where more than one authority may be involved, it is vital, particularly in cases involving children, that the needs of the children are considered and that, as far as possible, arguments about who considers and meets those needs do not hold up the provision of services to those children; the needs should be met first and the redistribution of resources should, if necessary, take place afterwards.

"mental disorder" (s 17(11))—The definition of "mental disorder" in MHA 1983, s 1(2) has been amended by MHA 2007, s 1(2) to "any disorder or disability of the mind" (for details of the representation of children suffering from a disability see FPR 2010, r 16.2 and PD16A).

****

Provision of accommodation for children

20 Provision of accommodation for children: general

(1) Every local authority shall provide accommodation for any child in need within their area who appears to them to require accommodation as a result of –

    (a)   there being no person who has parental responsibility for him;

    (b)   his being lost or having been abandoned; or

    (c)   the person who has been caring for him being prevented (whether or not permanently, and for whatever reason) from providing him with suitable accommodation or care.

(2) Where a local authority provide accommodation under subsection (1) for a child who is ordinarily resident in the area of another local authority, that other local authority may take over the provision of accommodation for the child within –

    (a)   three months of being notified in writing that the child is being provided with accommodation; or

    (b)   such other longer period as may be prescribed.

(3) Every local authority shall provide accommodation for any child in need within their area who has reached the age of sixteen and whose welfare the authority consider is likely to be seriously prejudiced if they do not provide him with accommodation.

(4) A local authority may provide accommodation for any child within their area (even though a person who has parental responsibility for him is able to provide him with accommodation) if they consider that to do so would safeguard or promote the child's welfare.

(5) A local authority may provide accommodation for any person who has reached the age of sixteen but is under twenty-one in any community home which takes children who have reached the age of sixteen if they consider that to do so would safeguard or promote his welfare.

(6) Before providing accommodation under this section, a local authority shall, so far as is reasonably practicable and consistent with the child's welfare –

    (a)   ascertain the child's wishes and feelings regarding the provision of accommodation; and

(b)   give due consideration (having regard to his age and understanding) to such wishes and feelings of the child as they have been able to ascertain.

(7) A local authority may not provide accommodation under this section for any child if any person who –

    (a)   has parental responsibility for him; and

    (b)   is willing and able to –

        (i)   provide accommodation for him; or

        (ii)   arrange for accommodation to be provided for him,

objects.

(8) Any person who has parental responsibility for a child may at any time remove the child from accommodation provided by or on behalf of the local authority under this section.

(9) Subsections (7) and (8) do not apply while any person –

    (a)   in whose favour a residence order is in force with respect to the child;

    (aa) who is a special guardian of the child; or

    (b)   who has care of the child by virtue of an order made in the exercise of the High Court's inherent jurisdiction with respect to children,

agrees to the child being looked after in accommodation provided by or on behalf of the local authority.

(10) Where there is more than one such person as is mentioned in subsection (9), all of them must agree.

(11) Subsections (7) and (8) do not apply where a child who has reached the age of sixteen agrees to being provided with accommodation under this section.

Amendments—ACA 2002, s 139(1),(3), Sch 3, paras 54, 59, Sch 5; CA 2004, s 53.

Local authority has no power to transfer accommodated child out of residential care and into foster care without permission of natural parents—Where a child is being accommodated by a local authority under a voluntary arrangement with her natural parents the local authority has no power to arrange a transfer of the child from a residential institution to foster care without the permission of her natural parents; parental responsibility includes the right to decide where a child lives (*R v Tameside Metropolitan Borough Council ex parte J* [2000] 1 FLR 942).

Definition of children who are eligible for accommodation—A child who had been looked after by a local authority and placed with foster parents when he was aged 14 (under CA 1989, s 20) and then, at the age of 16, had been provided by the local authority with accommodation or housing (CA 1989, s 17) was an "eligible child" for the purposes of CA 1989, a "relevant child" when he ceased to be looked after and, once he attained 18 years, would be a "former relevant child" to whom after-care code duties are owed under CA 1989 (*R v Essex County Council ex parte W* [2003] EWHC 3175 (Admin)). For the definitions of "looked after" child see CA 1989, s 22(1); for "relevant child" see CA 1989, s 23A(2); for "eligible child" see CA 1989, s 23A(2) and Sch 2, para 19B. In *R (G) v Southwark London Borough Council* [2009] 2 FLR 380 the House of Lords held that if a child meets the criteria in s 20 then he is entitled to support under that section. The discharge of the s 20 duty may be assisted by a housing authority but it cannot simply be passed over to the housing authority. The accommodation of a child pursuant to CA 1989, s 20 does not act as a bar to that child being made a ward of court in an appropriate case (*Re E (A Child)* [2012] EWCA Civ 1773).

A local authority cannot determine or specify that they provided accommodation under s 17 when, on the facts of the case, they were also under a duty to do so under s 20(1). They cannot "finesse away" their specific duty under s 20(1), claiming merely to act under their general s 17 duty (*H, Barhanu & B v London Borough of Wandsworth, London Borough of Hackney, London Borough of Islington & Secretary of State for Education & Skills (Interested Party)* [2007] 2 FLR 822; *R (W) v North Lincolnshire Council* [2008] 2 FLR 2150). Where the local authority asked the mother of the boyfriend of a 14 year old girl to look after her on a long-term basis because she was a child in need whose step-father was "prevented" from providing her with suitable care, they had a duty to provide her with accommodation under s 20, and to provide the appropriate weekly foster allowance to the foster mother until the girl's 18th birthday (*R (C) v Knowsley Metropolitan Borough Council* [2009] 1 FLR 493). Where the authority has led a foster parent to believe that she will receive financial support from it, rather than having to fund the cost of keeping the child herself, it may be concluded that the authority was exercising its functions under CA 1989, ss 20 and 23, and was not simply facilitating a private fostering arrangement (*R (A) v Coventry City Council* [2009] 1 FLR 1202).

The Court of Appeal applied a similar analysis in *R (O) v East Riding of Yorkshire County Council (Secretary of State for Education Intervening)* [2011] 2 FLR 207 when considering the position of a looked-after child who required residential schooling because of a diagnosis of autism. In examining the interrelationship between CA 1989, s 20 and the special educational needs regime of the Education Act 1996, Rix LJ accepted that where a residential placement is provided wholly or mainly to meet the child's special educational needs, it might be reasonable for that placement to be provided solely by exercising the local authority's powers under Pt IV of the 1996 Act but that, even in such circumstances, the child might still require accommodation within CA 1989, s 20(1) or be provided with accommodation under CA 1989, s 20(4). Where, however, the placement was not provided wholly or mainly to meet the child's special educational needs and the child was within CA 1989, s 20(1), or s 20(4) applied, then the local authority could not side-step its duties under CA 1989, s 20 and the placement should be provided under either CA 1989 alone or under both Acts.

Meaning of "prevented" (s 20(1)(c))—Under s 20(1)(c) "prevention" involves an objective test. It is not satisfied if the facts are only that the child does not want to live with someone who is willing to provide suitable accommodation (*R (M) v London Borough of Barnet* [2009] 2 FLR 725); circumstances can arise where people are so incompatible that they simply cannot live together (*R (S) v Sutton London Borough Council* [2007] 2 FLR 849).

Consent and CA 1989, s 20 (s 20(7))—Care should be taken when concluding voluntary arrangements under s 20 to ensure that consent has been validly given by the parent to the accommodation of the child. In *Coventry City Council v C, B, CA and CH* [2012] COPLR 658, Hedley J gave the following guidance applicable where a local authority seeks agreement to remove a child immediately or soon after birth, emphasising that the guidance is not intended to cast doubt on the use of s 20 in those circumstances where it is proper to seek agreement to accommodation:

(a) every parent has a right, if he or she is capacitous, to exercise his or her parental responsibility to give consent under s 20 to have their child accommodated by the local authority;

(b) every local authority has the power under s 20(4) so to accommodate, provided that it is consistent with the child's welfare;

(c) every social worker obtaining consent from a parent is under a personal duty to be satisfied that the person giving consent does not lack the required capacity;

(d) the social worker must actively address the issue of capacity, take into account all the prevailing circumstances and must consider the questions raised by MCA 2005, s 3 and in particular the mother's capacity to use and weigh all the relevant information;

(e) if the social worker has doubts about capacity, no further attempt should be made to obtain consent on that occasion. Advice should be sought from the social work team leader or management;

(f) if the social worker is satisfied that the person does not lack capacity, they then have to be satisfied that the consent is fully informed. Being satisfied that the consent is fully informed involves (i) questioning whether the parent understands fully the consequences of giving such a consent, (ii) whether they appreciate fully the range of choices available and the consequences of refusal and (iii) whether the parent is in possession of all the facts and issues material to the giving of consent;

(g) if not satisfied that the answers to the questions at (f) are all "yes", once again, no further attempt should be made to obtain consent on that occasion. Advice should be sought and the social work team should further consider taking legal advice if thought necessary;

(h) if satisfied that the consent is fully informed, the social worker must then be satisfied that the giving of such consent and the subsequent removal is both fair and proportionate;

(i) in considering whether the giving of consent is both fair and proportionate, it might be necessary to ask (i) what the current physical and psychological state of the parent is, (ii) whether they have a solicitor, (iii) whether they have been encouraged to seek legal advice and/or advice from family or friends, (iv) whether it is necessary for the safety of the child for the child to be removed at that time and (v) whether it would be fairer for the matter to be the subject of a court order rather than an agreement;

(j) if, having taken all of these steps and, if necessary, having taken further advice, including where necessary legal advice, the social worker considers that a fully informed consent had been received from a capacitous mother in circumstances where removal was necessary and proportionate, that fully informed consent may be acted upon by the social worker;

(k) in the context of newborn children, local authorities may wish to approach with great care the obtaining of s 20 consent from mothers in the aftermath of birth, especially where there is no immediate danger to the child and where it is probable that no order would be made by the court.

PART II

21   Provision of accommodation for children in police protection or detention or on remand etc

(1) Every local authority shall make provision for the reception and accommodation of children who are removed or kept away from home under Part V.

(2) Every local authority shall receive, and provide accommodation for, children –

    (a)   in police protection whom they are requested to receive under section 46(3)(f);

    (b)   whom they are requested to receive under section 38(6) of the Police and Criminal Evidence Act 1984;

    (c)   who are –

        (i)   ...

        (ia) remanded to accommodation provided by or on behalf of a local authority by virtue of paragraph 4 of Schedule 1 or paragraph 6 of Schedule 8 to the Powers of Criminal Courts (Sentencing) Act 2000 (breach etc. of referral orders and reparation orders);

        (ii) remanded to accommodation provided by or on behalf of a local authority by virtue of paragraph 21 of Schedule 2 to the Criminal Justice and Immigration Act 2008 (breach etc. of youth rehabilitation orders);

        (iia) remanded to accommodation provided by or on behalf of a local authority by virtue of paragraph 10 of the Schedule to the Street Offences Act 1959 (breach of orders under section 1(2A) of that Act);

        (iii) the subject of a youth rehabilitation order imposing a local authority residence requirement or a youth rehabilitation order with fostering,

and with respect to whom they are the designated authority.

(2A) In subsection (2)(c)(iii), the following terms have the same meanings as in Part 1 of the Criminal Justice and Immigration Act 2008 (see section 7 of that Act) –

"local authority residence requirement";

"youth rehabilitation order";

"youth rehabilitation order with fostering".

(3) Where a child has been –

    (a)   removed under Part V; or

    (b)   detained under section 38 of the Police and Criminal Evidence Act 1984,

and he is not being provided with accommodation by a local authority or in a hospital vested in the Secretary of State or the Welsh Ministers or otherwise made available pursuant to arrangements made by the Secretary of State, the National Health Service Commissioning Board or a clinical commissioning group under the National Health Service Act 2006 or a Local Health Board, any reasonable expenses of accommodating him shall be recoverable from the local authority in whose area he is ordinarily resident.

Amendments—CLSA 1990, s 116, Sch 16, para 11; National Health Service and Community Care Act 1990, s 66(1), Sch 9, para 36; Health Authorities Act 1995, s 2, Sch 1, para 118; SI 2000/90; Powers of Criminal Courts (Sentencing) Act 2000, s 165, Sch 9, para 126; Anti-social Behaviour Act 2003, s 88, Sch 2, para 5; SI 2007/961; CYPA 2008, s 39, Sch 3, paras 1, 5; Criminal Justice and Immigration Act 2008, ss 6(2), 6(3), 149, Sch 4, paras 34 and 105, Sch 28, Pt 1; Policing and Crime Act 2009, s 112, Sch 7, para 21; LASPOA 2012, s 105, Sch 12, para 24 (subject to savings in certain cases); Health and Social Care Act 2012, s 55(2), Sch 5, para 48.

Geographic extent of local authorities' duties (s 21(2)(a),(b))—The duty on every local authority under CA 1989, s 22(2)(a),(b) to receive, and provide accommodation for, children in police protection whom they are requested to receive under s 46(3)(f) or whom they are requested to receive under PACE 1984, s 38(6) falls on the authority receiving the request, irrespective of the area from which the child comes (*R (M) v Gateshead Council* [2006] 2 FLR 379).

Secure accommodation—Although s 21(2)(b) imposes a duty on the local authority to receive and accommodate children when requested to do so under PACE 1984, s 38(6), it does not impose a duty to provide secure accommodation where such is requested (*R (M) v Gateshead Council* [2006] 2 FLR 379).

The local authority has a discretionary power to provide secure accommodation when requested to do so, in so far as it is practicable in order to further the policy objective of preventing children from being detained in police cells.

Police Protection Guidance—Government circular *The Duties and Powers of the Police under the Children Act 1989* (number 017/2008) explains when and how police protection powers should be used under CA 1989. It can be found at *www.gov.uk/government/organisations/home-office*. Paragraph 25 sets out the meaning of "suitable accommodation"; this would normally be local authority accommodation, a registered children's home or foster care. If appropriate, the child may be placed with relatives provided that the relevant police checks as to their suitability are carried out beforehand (para 30). A police station is not deemed suitable accommodation and the child should not be taken there unless the circumstances are exceptional (para 28).

Duties of local authorities in relation to children looked after by them

22 General duty of local authority in relation to children looked after by them

(1) In this Act, any reference to a child who is looked after by a local authority is a reference to a child who is –

    (a)   in their care; or

    (b)   provided with accommodation by the authority in the exercise of any functions (in particular those under this Act) which are social services functions within the meaning of the Local Authority Social Services Act 1970, apart from functions under sections 17, 23B and 24B.

(2) In subsection (1) "accommodation" means accommodation which is provided for a continuous period of more than 24 hours.

(3) It shall be the duty of a local authority looking after any child –

    (a)   to safeguard and promote his welfare; and

    (b)   to make such use of services available for children cared for by their own parents as appears to the authority reasonable in his case.

(3A) The duty of a local authority under subsection (3)(a) to safeguard and promote the welfare of a child looked after by them includes in particular a duty to promote the child's educational achievement.

(4) Before making any decision with respect to a child whom they are looking after, or proposing to look after, a local authority shall, so far as is reasonably practicable, ascertain the wishes and feelings of –

    (a)   the child;

    (b)   his parents;

    (c)   any person who is not a parent of his but who has parental responsibility for him; and

    (d)   any other person whose wishes and feelings the authority consider to be relevant,

regarding the matter to be decided.

(5) In making any such decision a local authority shall give due consideration –

    (a)   having regard to his age and understanding, to such wishes and feelings of the child as they have been able to ascertain;

    (b)   to such wishes and feelings of any person mentioned in subsection (4)(b) to (d) as they have been able to ascertain; and

    (c)   to the child's religious persuasion, racial origin and cultural and linguistic background.

PART II

(6) If it appears to a local authority that it is necessary, for the purposes of protecting members of the public from serious injury, to exercise their powers with respect to a child whom they are looking after in a manner which may not be consistent with their duties under this section, they may do so.

(7) If the appropriate national authority considers it necessary, for the purpose of protecting members of the public from serious injury, to give directions to a local authority with respect to the exercise of their powers with respect to a child whom they are looking after, the appropriate national authority may give such directions to the local authority.

(8) Where any such directions are given to an authority they shall comply with them even though doing so is inconsistent with their duties under this section.

Amendments—Children (Leaving Care) Act 2000, s 2(1), (2); Local Government Act 2000, s 107(1), Sch 5, para 19; ACA 2002, s 116(2); CA 2004, s 52; CYPA 2008, s 39, Sch 3, paras 1, 6.

Meaning of "a child who is looked after by a local authority" (s 22(1))—The local authority have a duty when assessing the needs of homeless 16 and 17 year olds to consider whether the criteria of CA 1989, s 20, are met. If they are met, then social services (and not the housing department) should take long-term responsibility for the child, including the additional responsibilities involved in helping and supporting their transition to independent adult life. Social services are not able to avoid those responsibilities by looking to the housing authority to accommodate the child *(R (M) v Hammersmith and Fulham London Borough Council* [2008] 1 FLR 1384).

Care Planning, Placement and Case Review (England) Regulations 2010—These Regulations, set out in Part IV, make provision, inter alia, for care planning for looked-after children. A revised edition of Vol 2 of the *Children Act 1989 Guidance and Regulations* entitled *Care Planning, Placement and Case Review* accompanies the Regulations. Part 2 of the Regulations requires that in respect of a child who is to become looked after (but who is not the subject of a care order) the local authority must assess the child's need for services to achieve or maintain a reasonable standard of health or development, and prepare a care plan if one has not been prepared already. The assessment of the child's needs for the purposes of preparing the plan must include an assessment of whether the child's placement meets the requirements under CA 1989, Pt III. The plan must be prepared before the child is accommodated or, if this is not practicable, within 10 working days of the start of the first placement. As far as is reasonably practicable, the plan should be agreed by the local authority with the child's parent, any person holding parental responsibility for the child and, if there is no such person, the person who was caring for the child immediately before the placement being arranged. Where the child is aged 16 or over and agrees to be provided with accommodation under CA 1989, s 20, the care plan should be agreed with the child. The care plan must be kept under review by the local authority in accordance with Pt 6 of the Regulations.

The Children Act 1989 Guidance and Regulation Volume 4: Fostering Services—This guidance sets out the functions and responsibilities of local authorities and their partner agencies in relation to fostering services under CA 1989, Pts 3, 7 and 8. It also sets out the responsibilities arising from the Children Act 2004 and the Children and Young Persons Act 2008 in relation to fostering services. It is issued as guidance under Local Authority Social Services Act 1970, s 7, which requires local authorities in exercising their social services functions, to act under the general guidance of the Secretary of State.

Fostering Services (England) Regulations 2011—These regulations provide a regulatory framework for fostering agencies and local authority fostering services by placing duties on the "fostering service provider". Pt 2 requires each fostering service provider to have, and keep under review, a statement of purpose setting out the aims, objectives, services and facilities provided by the fostering service, and a children's guide to the service. Pt 3 makes provision about the management of fostering services: the fitness of the provider and the appointment and fitness of the manager. Pt 4 concerns the conduct of the fostering service, including safeguarding duties, the promotion of contact between foster children and their families, promoting the health and development of foster children, providing support and information for foster parents, and ensuring that there is an effective complaints procedure. Pt 5 concerns the approval of foster parents by the fostering service provider, and reviews of approval. Pt 6 relates only to fostering agencies; it makes provision about fostering agencies that cease to carry out the functions of fostering agencies. Pt 7 provides for the regulations to apply to "short breaks" with certain modifications.

Arrangements for Placement of Children by Voluntary Organisations and others (England) Regulations 2011—These regulations make provision for children who are not looked after by a local authority but are provided with accommodation by voluntary organisations or in private children's homes. Pt 2 contains general provisions about placements, including the placement plan to be prepared by the voluntary organisation or the private children's home, the assessment of the child's health, the persons who must be notified of the arrangements and the arrangements for contact. Pt 3 makes provisions about the placement of children by voluntary organisations with foster parents and imposes general requirements on responsible authorities as to the making and supervision of placements. Pt 4 makes prelates to other duties, including the circumstances in which responsible authorities or local authorities must terminate placements, and prohibiting the placement of a child by a voluntary organisation outside the British Islands. It also places a duty on local authorities to visit children who are placed with voluntary organisations or in children's homes and requires the authority to report concerns to the Chief Inspector Pt 5 prescribes the manner in which children's cases must be reviewed. Pt 6 makes provision in respect of short-term placements.

Duty to ascertain wishes and feelings of the parents (s 22(4)(b))—The duty of the local authority to ascertain the wishes and feelings of the parents before making any decision with respect to a looked-after child is directory and not mandatory; the result of any non-compliance with the provisions should be treated as an irregularity (*Re P (Children Act 1989, ss 22 and 26: Local Authority Compliance)* [2000] 2 FLR 910). In exceptional circumstances the court has power to make a declaration that the local authority be absolved from the duty to provide information to a parent and from the duty to consult them in any way about the child (*Re C (Care: Consultation with Parents Not in Child's Best Interests)* [2006] 2 FLR 787).

Duty to ascertain wishes and feelings of any other person (s 22(4)(d))—There is no general duty on a local authority to consult foster parents in every case where it is proposed to move a child (*R v Hereford and Worcester County Council ex p D* [1992] 1 FLR 448). However, in *R (Bewry) v Norfolk County Council* [2011] 1 FLR 945, the local authority should clearly have consulted the foster carer with whom the children had been placed for an indefinite period of time, before deciding to terminate the placement of the children with him. Although each matter will be fact-specific, in this case no local authority could reasonably have considered that his wishes and feelings were other than relevant.

The Adoption Agencies Regulations 2005—These Regulations state that where: (a) a local authority is authorised to place a child for adoption; or (b) a child who has been placed for adoption by a local authority is less than 6 weeks old, s 22(4)(b) does not apply (reg 45(2)(a)). Section 22(4)(c) will apply as if there were instead inserted "(c) any prospective adopter with whom the local authority has placed the child for adoption" (reg 45(2)(b)). Section 22(5)(b) applies as if for the words "(4)(b) to (d)" there were inserted "(4)(c) and (d)" (reg 45(2)(c)). Schedule 2, paras 15 and 21 do not apply (reg 45(2)(d)).

22A Provision of accommodation for children in care

When a child is in the care of a local authority, it is their duty to provide the child with accommodation.

Amendments—Inserted by CYPA 2008, s 8(1), in relation to England.

Wales—Sections 22A–22F come into force for Wales on a date to be appointed by the Welsh Ministers. Until such date, s 23 (set out below) remains in force for Wales:

"**23 Provision of accommodation and maintenance by local authority for children whom they are looking after**

(1) It shall be the duty of any local authority looking after a child –
    (a) when he is in their care, to provide accommodation for him; and
    (b) to maintain him in other respects apart from providing accommodation for him.

(2) A local authority shall provide accommodation and maintenance for any child whom they are looking after by –
    (a) placing him (subject to subsection (5) and any regulations made by the appropriate national authority) with –
        (i) a family;
        (ii) a relative of his; or
        (iii) any other suitable person,
on such terms as to payment by the authority and otherwise as the authority may determine (subject to section 49 of the Children Act 2004);
    (aa) maintaining him in an appropriate children's home;
    (b)–(e)(*repealed*)
    (f) making such other arrangements as –
        (i) seem appropriate to them; and
        (ii) comply with any regulations made by the appropriate national authority.

PART II

(2A) Where under subsection (2)(aa) a local authority maintains a child in a home provided, equipped and maintained by an appropriate national authority under section 82(5), it shall do so on such terms as that national authority may from time to time determine.
(3) Any person with whom a child has been placed under subsection (2)(a) is referred to in this Act as a local authority foster parent unless he falls within subsection (4).
(4) A person falls within this subsection if he is –
    (a) a parent of the child;
    (b) a person who is not a parent of the child but who has parental responsibility for him; or
    (c) where the child is in care and there was a residence order in force with respect to him immediately before the care order was made, a person in whose favour the residence order was made.
(5) Where a child is in the care of a local authority, the authority may only allow him to live with a person who falls within subsection (4) in accordance with regulations made by the appropriate national authority.
(5A) For the purposes of subsection (5) a child shall be regarded as living with a person if he stays with that person for a continuous period of more than 24 hours.
(6) Subject to any regulations made by the appropriate national authority for the purposes of this subsection, any local authority looking after a child shall make arrangements to enable him to live with –
    (a) a person falling within subsection (4); or
    (b) a relative, friend or other person connected with him,
unless that would not be reasonably practicable or consistent with his welfare.
(7) Where a local authority provide accommodation for a child whom they are looking after, they shall, subject to the provisions of this Part and so far as is reasonably practicable and consistent with his welfare, secure that –
    (a) the accommodation is near his home; and
    (b) where the authority are also providing accommodation for a sibling of his, they are accommodated together.
(8) Where a local authority provide accommodation for a child whom they are looking after and who is disabled, they shall, so far as is reasonably practicable, secure that the accommodation is not unsuitable to his particular needs.
(9) Part II of Schedule 2 shall have effect for the purposes of making further provision as to children looked after by local authorities and in particular as to the regulations that may be made under subsections (2)(a) and (f) and (5).
(10) In this Act –
    "appropriate children's home" means a children's home in respect of which a person is registered under Part II of the Care Standards Act 2000; and
    "children's home" has the same meaning as in that Act."

22B Maintenance of looked after children

It is the duty of a local authority to maintain a child they are looking after in other respects apart from the provision of accommodation.

Amendments—Inserted by CYPA 2008, s 8(1) in relation to England. For Wales, see notes to s 22A.

Payment of foster allowances—It is unlawful and in breach of ECHR 1950, Arts 8 and 14 for a local authority to have a policy whereby it pays its short-term foster carers who are friends or relatives of the child concerned at a different and significantly lower rate than it pays other such foster carers (*The Queen OTA L and Others v Manchester City Council; The Queen OTA of R and another v Manchester City Council* [2002] 1 FLR 43).

Recovery of contributions towards child's maintenance—The parents of a child who is looked after by the local authority or, where the child has reached the age of 16, the child himself, can be required to contribute towards the child's maintenance (CA 1989, s 29(6) and Sch 2, Pt III).

22C Ways in which looked after children are to be accommodated and maintained

(1) This section applies where a local authority are looking after a child ("C").

(2) The local authority must make arrangements for C to live with a person who falls within subsection (3) (but subject to subsection (4)).

(3) A person ("P") falls within this subsection if –

    (a)   P is a parent of C;

    (b)   P is not a parent of C but has parental responsibility for C; or

    (c)   in a case where C is in the care of the local authority and there was a residence order in force with respect to C immediately before the care order was made, P was a person in whose favour the residence order was made.

(4) Subsection (2) does not require the local authority to make arrangements of the kind mentioned in that subsection if doing so –

    (a)   would not be consistent with C's welfare; or

    (b)   would not be reasonably practicable.

(5) If the local authority are unable to make arrangements under subsection (2), they must place C in the placement which is, in their opinion, the most appropriate placement available.

(6) In subsection (5) "placement" means –

    (a)   placement with an individual who is a relative, friend or other person connected with C and who is also a local authority foster parent;

    (b)   placement with a local authority foster parent who does not fall within paragraph (a);

    (c)   placement in a children's home in respect of which a person is registered under Part 2 of the Care Standards Act 2000; or

    (d)   subject to section 22D, placement in accordance with other arrangements which comply with any regulations made for the purposes of this section.

(7) In determining the most appropriate placement for C, the local authority must, subject to the other provisions of this Part (in particular, to their duties under section 22) –

    (a)   give preference to a placement falling within paragraph (a) of subsection (6) over placements falling within the other paragraphs of that subsection;

    (b)   comply, so far as is reasonably practicable in all the circumstances of C's case, with the requirements of subsection (8); and

    (c)   comply with subsection (9) unless that is not reasonably practicable.

(8) The local authority must ensure that the placement is such that –

    (a)   it allows C to live near C's home;

    (b)   it does not disrupt C's education or training;

    (c)   if C has a sibling for whom the local authority are also providing accommodation, it enables C and the sibling to live together;

    (d)   if C is disabled, the accommodation provided is suitable to C's particular needs.

(9) The placement must be such that C is provided with accommodation within the local authority's area.

(10) The local authority may determine –

    (a)   the terms of any arrangements they make under subsection (2) in relation to C (including terms as to payment); and

    (b)   the terms on which they place C with a local authority foster parent (including terms as to payment but subject to any order made under section 49 of the Children Act 2004).

(11) The appropriate national authority may make regulations for, and in connection with, the purposes of this section.

PART II

(12) In this Act "local authority foster parent" means a person who is approved as a local authority foster parent in accordance with regulations made by virtue of paragraph 12F of Schedule 2.

Amendments—Inserted by CYPA 2008, s 8(1) in relation to England. For Wales, see notes to s 22A.

22D Review of child's case before making alternative arrangements for accommodation

(1) Where a local authority are providing accommodation for a child ("C") other than by arrangements under section 22C(6)(d), they must not make such arrangements for C unless they have decided to do so in consequence of a review of C's case carried out in accordance with regulations made under section 26.

(2) But subsection (1) does not prevent a local authority making arrangements for C under section 22C(6)(d) if they are satisfied that in order to safeguard C's welfare it is necessary –

(a) to make such arrangements; and
(b) to do so as a matter of urgency.

Amendments—Inserted by CYPA 2008, s 8(1) in relation to England. For Wales, see notes to s 22A.

Regulations—Care Planning, Placement and Case Review (England) Regulations 2010, Pt 6 governs the review of a looked-after child's case.

22E Children's homes provided by appropriate national authority

Where a local authority place a child they are looking after in a children's home provided, equipped and maintained by an appropriate national authority under section 82(5), they must do so on such terms as that national authority may from time to time determine.

Amendments—Inserted by CYPA 2008, s 8(1) in relation to England. For Wales, see notes to s 22A.

22F Regulations as to children looked after by local authorities

Part 2 of Schedule 2 has effect for the purposes of making further provision as to children looked after by local authorities and in particular as to the regulations which may be made under section 22C(11).

Amendments—Inserted by CYPA 2008, s 8(1) in relation to England. For Wales, see notes to s 22A.

22G General duty of local authority to secure sufficient accommodation for looked after children

(1) It is the general duty of a local authority to take steps that secure, so far as reasonably practicable, the outcome in subsection (2).

(2) The outcome is that the local authority are able to provide the children mentioned in subsection (3) with accommodation that –

(a) is within the authority's area; and
(b) meets the needs of those children.

(3) The children referred to in subsection (2) are those –

(a) that the local authority are looking after,
(b) in respect of whom the authority are unable to make arrangements under section 22C(2), and
(c) whose circumstances are such that it would be consistent with their welfare for them to be provided with accommodation that is in the authority's area.

(4) In taking steps to secure the outcome in subsection (2), the local authority must have regard to the benefit of having –

    (a)   a number of accommodation providers in their area that is, in their opinion, sufficient to secure that outcome; and

    (b)   a range of accommodation in their area capable of meeting different needs that is, in their opinion, sufficient to secure that outcome.

(5) In this section "accommodation providers" means –

    local authority foster parents; and

    children's homes in respect of which a person is registered under Part 2 of the Care Standards Act 2000.

Amendments—Inserted by CYPA 2008, s 9 in relation to England.

Care Planning, Placement and Case Review (England) Regulations 2010 (s 23(4),(5))—These regulations are set out in Part IV. Where the local authority plans to place a child in care with his parents, regs 14–20 will apply. See further under CA 1989, s 33. A revised edition of Vol 2 of the *Children Act 1989 Guidance and Regulations* entitled *Care Planning, Placement and Case Review* accompanies the Regulations, replacing some existing volumes and integrating guidance issued since 1991. It covers each of the elements of care planning required throughout the child's journey in the care system. Further guidance, *Sufficiency: statutory guidance securing sufficient accommodation* (see *www.media.education. gov.uk*) seeks to improve outcomes for looked after children and young people by providing guidance on the implementation of section 22G. This section requires local authorities to take steps that secure, so far as reasonably practicable, sufficient accommodation within the authority's area that meets the needs of children that the local authority are looking after, and whose circumstances are such that it would be consistent with their welfare for them to be provided with accommodation that is in the local authority's area ("the sufficiency duty").

****

Visiting

23ZA Duty of local authority to ensure visits to, and contact with, looked after children and others

(1) This section applies to –

    (a)   a child looked after by a local authority;

    (b)   a child who was looked after by a local authority but who has ceased to be looked after by them as a result of prescribed circumstances.

(2) It is the duty of the local authority –

    (a)   to ensure that a person to whom this section applies is visited by a representative of the authority ("a representative");

    (b)   to arrange for appropriate advice, support and assistance to be available to a person to whom this section applies who seeks it from them.

(3) The duties imposed by subsection (2) –

    (a)   are to be discharged in accordance with any regulations made for the purposes of this section by the appropriate national authority;

    (b)   are subject to any requirement imposed by or under an enactment applicable to the place in which the person to whom this section applies is accommodated.

(4) Regulations under this section for the purposes of subsection (3)(a) may make provision about –

    (a)   the frequency of visits;

    (b)   circumstances in which a person to whom this section applies must be visited by a representative; and

    (c)   the functions of a representative.

(5) In choosing a representative a local authority must satisfy themselves that the person chosen has the necessary skills and experience to perform the functions of a representative.

Amendments—Inserted by CYPA 2008, s 15.

Regulations—Care Planning, Placement and Case Review (England) Regulations 2010, Pt 5 governs visits to and contact with a looked-after child.

23ZB Independent visitors for children looked after by a local authority

(1) A local authority looking after a child must appoint an independent person to be the child's visitor if –

(a)   the child falls within a description prescribed in regulations made by the appropriate national authority; or

(b)   in any other case, it appears to them that it would be in the child's interests to do so.

(2) A person appointed under this section must visit, befriend and advise the child.

(3) A person appointed under this section is entitled to recover from the appointing authority any reasonable expenses incurred by that person for the purposes of that person's functions under this section.

(4) A person's appointment as a visitor in pursuance of this section comes to an end if –

(a)   the child ceases to be looked after by the local authority;

(b)   the person resigns the appointment by giving notice in writing to the appointing authority; or

(c)   the authority give him notice in writing that they have terminated it.

(5) The ending of such an appointment does not affect any duty under this section to make a further appointment.

(6) Where a local authority propose to appoint a visitor for a child under this section, the appointment shall not be made if –

(a)   the child objects to it; and

(b)   the authority are satisfied that the child has sufficient understanding to make an informed decision.

(7) Where a visitor has been appointed for a child under this section, the local authority shall terminate the appointment if –

(a)   the child objects to its continuing; and

(b)   the authority are satisfied that the child has sufficient understanding to make an informed decision.

(8) If the local authority give effect to a child's objection under subsection (6) or (7) and the objection is to having anyone as the child's visitor, the authority does not have to propose to appoint another person under subsection (1) until the objection is withdrawn.

(9) The appropriate national authority may make regulations as to the circumstances in which a person is to be regarded for the purposes of this section as independent of the appointing authority.

Amendments—Inserted by CYPA 2008, s 16.

Regulations—Care Planning, Placement and Case Review (England) Regulations 2010, Pt 8 governs the provision of independent visitors for children looked after by a local authority.

Advice and assistance for certain children and young persons

23A The responsible authority and relevant children

(1) The responsible local authority shall have the functions set out in section 23B in respect of a relevant child.

(2) In subsection (1) "relevant child" means (subject to subsection (3)) a child who –

(a) is not being looked after by any local authority;

(b) was, before last ceasing to be looked after, an eligible child for the purposes of paragraph 19B of Schedule 2; and

(c) is aged sixteen or seventeen.

(3) The appropriate national authority may prescribe –

(a) additional categories of relevant children; and

(b) categories of children who are not to be relevant children despite falling within subsection (2).

(4) In subsection (1) the "responsible local authority" is the one which last looked after the child.

(5) If under subsection (3)(a) the appropriate national authority prescribes a category of relevant children which includes children who do not fall within subsection (2)(b) (for example, because they were being looked after by a local authority in Scotland), the appropriate national authority may in the regulations also provide for which local authority is to be the responsible local authority for those children.

Amendments—Inserted by Children (Leaving Care) Act 2000, s 2(1),(4); amended by CYPA 2008, s 39, Sch 3, paras 1, 8.

Care Leavers (England) Regulations 2010—These Regulations revoke, and in part replace, the Children (Leaving Care) (England) Regulations 2001. They make provision about support to be provided to "relevant children" (as defined in CA 1989, s 23A(2) and reg 3) and to "former relevant children" (as defined in CA 1989, s 23C; the position of "eligible" children as defined by CA 1989, Sch 2, para 19B is dealt with under the Care Planning, Placement and Case Review (England) Regulations 2010). The Care Leavers (England) Regulations 2010 make provision about the way in which the local authority must carry out an assessment of the needs of relevant and former relevant children, about the preparation and review of pathway plans for such children, about the functions of personal advisers appointed for relevant and former relevant children and also about other support, the suitability of accommodation and the provision of vacation accommodation.

Meaning of "relevant child" (s 23A(2))—In determining whether a child is a "relevant child" for the purposes of s 23A(2), reference must also be made to Care Leavers (England) Regulations 2010, reg 3, which prescribes additional categories of relevant children to whom local authorities will or, as the case may be, will not, owe additional duties as provided for CA 1989, Pt III.

23B Additional functions of the responsible authority in respect of relevant children

(1) It is the duty of each local authority to take reasonable steps to keep in touch with a relevant child for whom they are the responsible authority, whether he is within their area or not.

(2) It is the duty of each local authority to appoint a personal adviser for each relevant child (if they have not already done so under paragraph 19C of Schedule 2).

(3) It is the duty of each local authority, in relation to any relevant child who does not already have a pathway plan prepared for the purposes of paragraph 19B of Schedule 2 –

(a) to carry out an assessment of his needs with a view to determining what advice, assistance and support it would be appropriate for them to provide him under this Part; and

(b) to prepare a pathway plan for him.

(4)–(7) (*repealed*)

(8) The responsible local authority shall safeguard and promote the child's welfare and, unless they are satisfied that his welfare does not require it, support him by –

(a) maintaining him;

(b) providing him with or maintaining him in suitable accommodation; and

(c) providing support of such other descriptions as may be prescribed.

(9) Support under subsection (8) may be in cash.

(10) The appropriate national authority may by regulations make provision about the meaning of "suitable accommodation" and in particular about the suitability of landlords or other providers of accommodation.

(11) If the local authority have lost touch with a relevant child, despite taking reasonable steps to keep in touch, they must without delay –

(a) consider how to re-establish contact; and

(b) take reasonable steps to do so,

and while the child is still a relevant child must continue to take such steps until they succeed.

(12) Subsections (7) to (9) of section 17 apply in relation to support given under this section as they apply in relation to assistance given under that section.

(13) Subsections (4) and (5) of section 22 apply in relation to any decision by a local authority for the purposes of this section as they apply in relation to the decisions referred to in that section.

Amendments—Inserted by Children (Leaving Care) Act 2000, s 2(1),(4); amended by CYPA 2008, ss 22, 39, Sch 3, paras 1, 9.

Functions of personal advisers (s 23B(2))—The functions of a personal adviser are set out in Care Leavers (England) Regulations 2010, reg 8.

Duty to carry out an assessment (s 23B(3)(a))—Pursuant to Care Leavers (England) Regulations 2010, reg 4, in carrying out an assessment of the relevant child's, or former relevant child's, needs the local authority must, unless it is not reasonably practicable, seek and have regard to the views of the child and take all reasonable steps to enable the child to attend and participate in any meetings at which their case is to be considered. The assessment itself must take account of the matters set out in Care Leavers (England) Regulations 2010, reg 5.

Meaning of "suitable accommodation" (s 23B(8)(b),(10))—Reg 9(2) and Sch 2 of the Care Leavers (England) Regulations 2010 prescribe the meaning of "suitable accommodation" for the purposes of CA 1989, s 23B.

23C Continuing functions in respect of former relevant children

(1) Each local authority shall have the duties provided for in this section towards –

(a) a person who has been a relevant child for the purposes of section 23A (and would be one if he were under eighteen), and in relation to whom they were the last responsible authority; and

(b) a person who was being looked after by them when he attained the age of eighteen, and immediately before ceasing to be looked after was an eligible child,

and in this section such a person is referred to as a "former relevant child".

(2) It is the duty of the local authority to take reasonable steps –

(a) to keep in touch with a former relevant child whether he is within their area or not; and

(b)   if they lose touch with him, to re-establish contact.

(3)   It is the duty of the local authority –

   (a)   to continue the appointment of a personal adviser for a former relevant child; and

   (b)   to continue to keep his pathway plan under regular review.

(4)   It is the duty of the local authority to give a former relevant child –

   (a)   assistance of the kind referred to in section 24B(1), to the extent that his welfare requires it;

   (b)   assistance of the kind referred to in section 24B(2), to the extent that his welfare and his educational or training needs require it;

   (c)   other assistance, to the extent that his welfare requires it.

(5)   The assistance given under subsection (4)(c) may be in kind or, in exceptional circumstances, in cash.

(5A)   It is the duty of the local authority to pay the relevant amount to a former relevant child who pursues higher education in accordance with a pathway plan prepared for that person.

(5B)   The appropriate national authority may by regulations –

   (a)   prescribe the relevant amount for the purposes of subsection (5A);

   (b)   prescribe the meaning of "higher education" for those purposes;

   (c)   make provision as to the payment of the relevant amount;

   (d)   make provision as to the circumstances in which the relevant amount (or any part of it) may be recovered by the local authority from a former relevant child to whom a payment has been made.

(5C)   The duty set out in subsection (5A) is without prejudice to that set out in subsection (4)(b).

(6)   Subject to subsection (7), the duties set out in subsections (2), (3) and (4) subsist until the former relevant child reaches the age of twenty-one.

(7)   If the former relevant child's pathway plan sets out a programme of education or training which extends beyond his twenty-first birthday –

   (a)   the duty set out in subsection (4)(b) continues to subsist for so long as the former relevant child continues to pursue that programme; and

   (b)   the duties set out in subsections (2) and (3) continue to subsist concurrently with that duty.

(8)   For the purposes of subsection (7)(a) there shall be disregarded any interruption in a former relevant child's pursuance of a programme of education or training if the local authority are satisfied that he will resume it as soon as is reasonably practicable.

(9)   Section 24B(5) applies in relation to a person being given assistance under subsection (4)(b) or who is in receipt of a payment under subsection (5A) as it applies in relation to a person to whom section 24B(3) applies.

(10)   Subsections (7) to (9) of section 17 apply in relation to assistance given under this section as they apply in relation to assistance given under that section.

Amendments—Inserted by Children (Leaving Care) Act 2000, s 2(1),(4); amended by CYPA 2008, s 21.

Meaning of "other assistance" (s 23C(4)(c))—In *R (O) v London Borough of Barking and Dagenham (SSHD and the Children's Society Intervening)* [2011] 1 FLR 734, the Court of Appeal held that the words "other assistance" can include the provision of accommodation for the former relevant child.

23CA Further assistance to pursue education or training

(1) This section applies to a person if –

    (a)   he is under the age of twenty-five or of such lesser age as may be prescribed by the appropriate national authority;

    (b)   he is a former relevant child (within the meaning of section 23C) towards whom the duties imposed by subsections (2), (3) and (4) of that section no longer subsist; and

    (c)   he has informed the responsible local authority that he is pursuing, or wishes to pursue, a programme of education or training.

(2) It is the duty of the responsible local authority to appoint a personal adviser for a person to whom this section applies.

(3) It is the duty of the responsible local authority –

    (a)   to carry out an assessment of the needs of a person to whom this section applies with a view to determining what assistance (if any) it would be appropriate for them to provide to him under this section; and

    (b)   to prepare a pathway plan for him.

(4) It is the duty of the responsible local authority to give assistance of a kind referred to subsection (5) to a person to whom this section applies to the extent that his educational or training needs require it.

(5) The kinds of assistance are –

    (a)   contributing to expenses incurred by him in living near the place where he is, or will be, receiving education or training; or

    (b)   making a grant to enable him to meet expenses connected with his education and training.

(6) If a person to whom this section applies pursues a programme of education or training in accordance with the pathway plan prepared for him, the duties of the local authority under this section (and under any provision applicable to the pathway plan prepared under this section for that person) subsist for as long as he continues to pursue that programme.

(7) For the purposes of subsection (6), the local authority may disregard any interruption in the person's pursuance of a programme of education or training if they are satisfied that he will resume it as soon as is reasonably practicable.

(8) Subsections (7) to (9) of section 17 apply to assistance given to a person under this section as they apply to assistance given to or in respect of a child under that section, but with the omission in subsection (8) of the words "and of each of his parents".

(9) Subsection (5) of section 24B applies to a person to whom this section applies as it applies to a person to whom subsection (3) of that section applies.

(10) Nothing in this section affects the duty imposed by subsection (5A) of section 23C to the extent that it subsists in relation to a person to whom this section applies; but the duty to make a payment under that subsection may be taken into account in the assessment of the person's needs under subsection (3)(a).

(11) In this section "the responsible local authority" means, in relation to a person to whom this section applies, the local authority which had the duties provided for in section 23C towards him.

Amendments—Inserted by CYPA 2008, s 22.

Personal advisers and pathway plans

23D Personal advisers

(1) The appropriate national authority may by regulations require local authorities to appoint a personal adviser for children or young persons of a prescribed description who have reached the age of sixteen but not the age of twenty-five who are not –

    (a)   children who are relevant children for the purposes of section 23A;
    (b)   the young persons referred to in section 23C;
    (c)   the children referred to in paragraph 19C of Schedule 2; or
    (d)   persons to whom section 23CA applies.

(2) Personal advisers appointed under or by virtue of this Part shall (in addition to any other functions) have such functions as the Secretary of State prescribes.

Amendments—Inserted by Children (Leaving Care) Act 2000, s 3; amended by CYPA 2008, ss 23(1), 39, Sch 3, paras 1, 10.

Functions of personal adviser—These are set out in Care Planning, Placement and Case Review (England) Regulations 2010, reg 44 (see Part IV) and Care Leavers (England) Regulations 2010, reg 8(1).

23E Pathway plans

(1) In this Part, a reference to a "pathway plan" is to a plan setting out –

    (a)   in the case of a plan prepared under paragraph 19B of Schedule 2 –
        (i)   the advice, assistance and support which the local authority intend to provide a child under this Part, both while they are looking after him and later; and
        (ii)   when they might cease to look after him; and
    (b)   in the case of a plan prepared under section 23B or 23CA, the advice, assistance and support which the local authority intend to provide under this Part,

and dealing with such other matters (if any) as may be prescribed.

(1A) A local authority may carry out an assessment under section 23B(3) or 23CA(3) of a person's needs at the same time as any assessment of his needs is made under –

    (a)   the Chronically Sick and Disabled Persons Act 1970;
    (b)   Part 4 of the Education Act 1996 (in the case of an assessment under section 23B(3));
    (c)   the Disabled Persons (Services, Consultation and Representation) Act 1986; or
    (d)   any other enactment.

(1B) The appropriate national authority may by regulations make provision as to assessments for the purposes of section 23B(3) or 23CA.

(1C) Regulations under subsection (1B) may in particular make provision about –

    (a)   who is to be consulted in relation to an assessment;
    (b)   the way in which an assessment is to be carried out, by whom and when;
    (c)   the recording of the results of an assessment;
    (d)   the considerations to which a local authority are to have regard in carrying out an assessment.

(1D) A local authority shall keep each pathway plan prepared by them under section 23B or 23CA under review.

(2) The appropriate national authority may by regulations make provision about pathway plans and their review.

Amendments—Inserted by Children (Leaving Care) Act 2000, s 3; amended by CYPA 2008, ss 22, 39, Sch 3, paras 1, 11.

PART II

Care Planning, Placement and Case Review (England) Regulations 2010—These regulations came into force on 1 April 2011 (see Part IV). Pt 7 sets out arrangements to be made by the local authority for ceasing to look after a child. It is a re-enactment of provisions in the Children (Leaving Care) (England) Regulations 2001 (above) relating to "eligible" children, as defined in CA 1989, Sch 2, para 19B. It provides for the assessment of needs, the preparation and review of pathway plans, the keeping of records, assistance with education and training, and accommodation. Regulation 44 prescribes the functions of a personal adviser. In *R (G) v Nottingham City Council and Nottingham University Hospital* [2008] 1 FLR 1668 the authority acted unlawfully by failing to conduct a lawful assessment or produce a lawful pathway plan. The statutory scheme in CA 1989, ss 23A–23C and Sch 2, and the Regulations envisage two separate stages:

(1) the assessment, culminating in the preparation of a written record, and
(2) the preparation of a pathway plan. There was a serious failure by the authority to comply with its statutory duties and to heed judicial authority. The plan lacked specificity and the mother's personal adviser had been involved in its preparation, which was impermissible (*R (J) v Caerphilly County Borough Council* [2005] 2 FLR 860).

Care Leavers (England) Regulations 2010—Reg 6 governs the preparation and contents of pathway plans for relevant children and former relevant children. Reg 7 prescribes the duties on the local authority concerning review of the pathway plans of relevant and former relevant children.

Advice and assistance for certain children and young persons

24 Persons qualifying for advice and assistance

(1) In this Part "a person qualifying for advice and assistance" means a person to whom subsection (1A) or (1B) applies.

(1A) This subsection applies to a person –

(a) who has reached the age of sixteen but not the age of twenty-one;
(b) with respect to whom a special guardianship order is in force (or, if he has reached the age of eighteen, was in force when he reached that age); and
(c) who was, immediately before the making of that order, looked after by a local authority.

(1B) This subsection applies to a person to whom subsection (1A) does not apply, and who –

(a) is under twenty-one; and
(b) at any time after reaching the age of sixteen but while still a child was, but is no longer, looked after, accommodated or fostered.

(2) In subsection (1B)(b), "looked after, accommodated or fostered" means –

(a) looked after by a local authority;
(b) accommodated by or on behalf of a voluntary organisation;
(c) accommodated in a registered children's home;
(d) accommodated for a consecutive period of at least three months –
   (i) by any Local Health Board, Special Health Authority or by a local authority in the exercise of education functions, or
   (ii) in any residential care home, nursing home or mental nursing home or in any accommodation provided pursuant to arrangements made by the Secretary of State, the National Health Service Commissioning Board or a clinical commissioning group under the National Health Service Act 2006 or by a National Health Service trust or an NHS foundation trust; or
(e) privately fostered.

(3) Subsection (2)(d) applies even if the period of three months mentioned there began before the child reached the age of sixteen.

(4) In the case of a person qualifying for advice and assistance by virtue of subsection (2)(a), it is the duty of the local authority which last looked after him to take

such steps as they think appropriate to contact him at such times as they think appropriate with a view to discharging their functions under sections 24A and 24B.

(5) In each of sections 24A and 24B, the local authority under the duty or having the power mentioned there ("the relevant authority") is –

(za) in the case of a person to whom subsection (1A) applies, a local authority determined in accordance with regulations made by the appropriate national authority;

(a) in the case of a person qualifying for advice and assistance by virtue of subsection (2)(a), the local authority which last looked after him; or

(b) in the case of any other person qualifying for advice and assistance, the local authority within whose area the person is (if he has asked for help of a kind which can be given under section 24A or 24B).

Amendments—Substituted by Children (Leaving Care) Act 2000, s 4(1); amended by Health and Social Care (Community Health and Standards) Act 2003, s 34, Sch 4, paras 75, 76; ACA 2002, s 139(1), Sch 3, paras 54, 60; SI 2007/961; CYPA 2008, s 39, Sch 3, paras 1, 12- SI 2010/1158; Health and Social Care Act 2012, s 55(2), Sch 5, para 49.

24A Advice and assistance

(1) The relevant authority shall consider whether the conditions in subsection (2) are satisfied in relation to a person qualifying for advice and assistance.

(2) The conditions are that –

(a) he needs help of a kind which they can give under this section or section 24B; and

(b) in the case of a person to whom section 24(1A) applies, or to whom section 24(1B) applies and who was not being looked after by any local authority, they are satisfied that the person by whom he was being looked after does not have the necessary facilities for advising or befriending him.

(3) If the conditions are satisfied –

(a) they shall advise and befriend him if he is a person to whom section 24(1A) applies, or he is a person to whom section 24(1B) applies and he was being looked after by a local authority or was accommodated by or on behalf of a voluntary organisation; and

(b) in any other case they may do so.

(4) Where as a result of this section a local authority are under a duty, or are empowered, to advise and befriend a person, they may also give him assistance.

(5) The assistance may be in kind and, in exceptional circumstances, assistance may be given –

(a) by providing accommodation, if in the circumstances assistance may not be given in respect of the accommodation under section 24B, or

(b) in cash.

(6) Subsections (7) to (9) of section 17 apply in relation to assistance given under this section or section 24B as they apply in relation to assistance given under that section.

Amendments—Inserted by Children (Leaving Care) Act 2000, s 4(1); amended by ACA 2002, ss 116(3), 139(1), Sch 3, paras 54, 61.

Care Planning, Placement and Case Review (England) Regulations 2010—These regulations are set out in Part IV. Regulations 28–31 set out the arrangements that a local authority should make to visit the child and to provide him with advice, support and assistance.

24B Employment, education and training

(1) The relevant local authority may give assistance to any person who qualifies for advice and assistance by virtue of section 24(1A) or section 24(2)(a) by contributing to expenses incurred by him in living near the place where he is, or will be, employed or seeking employment.

(2) The relevant local authority may give assistance to a person to whom subsection (3) applies by –

    (a)   contributing to expenses incurred by the person in question in living near the place where he is, or will be, receiving education or training; or

    (b)   making a grant to enable him to meet expenses connected with his education or training.

(3) This subsection applies to any person who –

    (a)   is under twenty-five; and

    (b)   qualifies for advice and assistance by virtue of section 24(1A) or section 24(2)(a), or would have done so if he were under twenty-one.

(4) Where a local authority are assisting a person under subsection (2) they may disregard any interruption in his attendance on the course if he resumes it as soon as is reasonably practicable.

(5) Where the local authority are satisfied that a person to whom subsection (3) applies who is in full-time further or higher education needs accommodation during a vacation because his term-time accommodation is not available to him then, they shall give him assistance by –

    (a)   providing him with suitable accommodation during the vacation; or

    (b)   paying him enough to enable him to secure such accommodation himself.

(6) The appropriate national authority may prescribe the meaning of "full-time", "further education", "higher education" and "vacation" for the purposes of subsection (5).

Amendments—Inserted by Children (Leaving Care) Act 2000, s 4(1); amended by ACA 2002, s 139(1), Sch 3, paras 54, 62; CYPA 2008, ss 22, 39, Sch 3, paras 1, 13.

24C Information

(1) Where it appears to a local authority that a person –

    (a)   with whom they are under a duty to keep in touch under section 23B, 23C or 24; or

    (b)   whom they have been advising and befriending under section 24A; or

    (c)   to whom they have been giving assistance under section 24B,

proposes to live, or is living, in the area of another local authority, they must inform that other authority.

(2) Where a child who is accommodated –

    (a)   by a voluntary organisation or in a registered children's home;

    (b)   by any Local Health Board or Special Health Authority or by a local authority in the exercise of education functions; or

    (c)   in any residential care home, nursing home or mental nursing home or any accommodation provided pursuant to arrangements made by the Secretary of State, the National Health Service Commissioning Board or a clinical commissioning group under the National Health Service Act 2006 or by a National Health Service trust or an NHS foundation trust, ceases to be so accommodated, after reaching the age of sixteen, the organisation, authority or (as the case may be) person carrying on the home shall inform the local authority within whose area the child proposes to live.

(3) Subsection (2) only applies, by virtue of paragraph (b) or (c), if the accommodation has been provided for a consecutive period of at least three months.

(4) In a case where a child was accommodated by a local authority in the exercise of education functions, subsection (2) applies only if the local authority who accommodated the child are different from the local authority within whose area the child proposes to live.

Amendments—Inserted by Children (Leaving Care) Act 2000, s 4(1); amended by Health and Social Care (Community Health and Standards) Act 2003, s 34, Sch 4, paras 75, 77; SI 2007/961; SI 2010/1158; Health and Social Care Act 2012, s 55(2), Sch 5, para 50.

24D Representations: sections 23A to 24B

(1) Every local authority shall establish a procedure for considering representations (including complaints) made to them by –

   (a)   a relevant child for the purposes of section 23A or a young person falling within section 23C;
   (b)   a person qualifying for advice and assistance; or
   (c)   a person falling within section 24B(2),

about the discharge of their functions under this Part in relation to him.

(1A) Regulations may be made by the appropriate national authority imposing time limits on the making of representations under subsection (1).

(2) In considering representations under subsection (1), a local authority shall comply with regulations (if any) made by the appropriate national authority for the purposes of this subsection.

Amendments—Inserted by Children (Leaving Care) Act 2000, s 5; amended by ACA 2002, s 117; CYPA 2008, s 39, Sch 3, paras 1, 14.

Secure accommodation

25 Use of accommodation for restricting liberty

(1) Subject to the following provisions of this section, a child who is being looked after by a local authority may not be placed, and, if placed, may not be kept, in accommodation provided for the purpose of restricting liberty ("secure accommodation") unless it appears –

   (a)   that –
        (i)   he has a history of absconding and is likely to abscond from any other description of accommodation; and
        (ii) if he absconds, he is likely to suffer significant harm, or
   (b)   that if he is kept in any other description of accommodation he is likely to injure himself or other persons.

(2) The appropriate national authority may by regulations –

   (a)   specify a maximum period –
        (i)   beyond which a child may not be kept in secure accommodation without the authority of the court; and
        (ii) for which the court may authorise a child to be kept in secure accommodation;

(b) empower the court from time to time to authorise a child to be kept in secure accommodation for such further period as the regulations may specify; and

(c) provide that applications to the court under this section shall be made only by local authorities.

(3) It shall be the duty of a court hearing an application under this section to determine whether any relevant criteria for keeping a child in secure accommodation are satisfied in his case.

(4) If a court determines that any such criteria are satisfied, it shall make an order authorising the child to be kept in secure accommodation and specifying the maximum period for which he may be so kept.

(5) On any adjournment of the hearing of an application under this section, a court may make an interim order permitting the child to be kept during the period of the adjournment in secure accommodation.

(6) No court shall exercise the powers conferred by this section in respect of a child who is not legally represented in that court unless, having been informed of his right to apply for the provision of representation under Part 1 of the Legal Aid, Sentencing and Punishment of Offenders Act 2012 and having had the opportunity to do so, he refused or failed to apply.

(7) The appropriate national authority may by regulations provide that –

(a) this section shall or shall not apply to any description of children specified in the regulations;

(b) this section shall have effect in relation to children of a description specified in the regulations subject to such modifications as may be so specified;

(c) such other provisions as may be so specified shall have effect for the purpose of determining whether a child of a description specified in the regulations may be placed or kept in secure accommodation.

(8) The giving of an authorisation under this section shall not prejudice any power of any court in England and Wales or Scotland to give directions relating to the child to whom the authorisation relates.

(9) This section is subject to section 20(8).

Amendments—AJA 1999, s 24, Sch 4, para 45; CYPA 2008, s 39, Sch 3, paras 1, 15; LASPOA 2012, s 39, Sch 5, para 38.

Defined terms—"child": s 105(1).

Scope—The C(SA)R 1991 and the C(SA)(No 2)R 1991 have been made under this section and reference should also be made to these.

"secure accommodation"—To constitute "secure accommodation" a place does not have to be so designated; each case will depend on its own facts. It is the restriction of liberty which is the essential factor in determining what is secure accommodation, see *A Metropolitan Borough Council v DB* [1997] 1 FLR 767, in which Cazalet J held that a maternity ward was secure accommodation where entrance was only by way of a key or pass. The 17-year-old mother had not been given a key or pass and staff were instructed not to let her leave. However, contrast *Re C (Detention: Medical Treatment)* [1997] 2 FLR 180, where Wall J, while agreeing that premises which are not designed as secure accommodation may become such by virtue of the use to which they are put in the particular circumstances of individual cases, held that the more natural meaning of the words "provided for the purpose of restricting liberty" in s 25(1) is "designed for, or having as its primary purpose the restriction of liberty". In *Re C* a clinic for the treatment of anorexia nervosa was held not to be secure accommodation because the primary purpose of the clinic was to achieve treatment, and the restriction of liberty was only incidental to that end. However, a similar result was achieved by invoking the inherent jurisdiction under CA 1989, s 100 to direct that the minor remain an in-patient at the clinic. A secure accommodation order is a deprivation of liberty within the meaning of Art 5 of the ECHR, but is not incompatible with the Convention where it is justified under one of the exceptions in Art 5(1), for example where the order is for the purposes of educational supervision (*Re K (Secure Accommodation Order: Right to Liberty)* [2001] 1 FLR 526, CA).

Maximum periods—The maximum period that a child may be held in secure accommodation without a court order is 72 hours per 28 days: C(SA)R 1991, reg 10. The initial maximum period for which a court may authorise a child to be held in secure accommodation is 3 months and thereafter for periods of up to 6 months: C(SA)R 1991, regs 11, 12.

"being looked after by a local authority" (s 25(1))—See CA 1989, s 22(1) and, as to a child who is bailed with a condition of residence to the local authority, see *Re C (Secure Accommodation: Bail)* [1994] 2 FLR 922.

"may not be placed, and, if placed, may not be kept" (s 25(1))—The legislation does not specify that a child should already have been placed in secure accommodation before an order is sought. The court's authority is not required for the first 72 hours that a child is placed in secure accommodation. While in ordinary cases a child ought to be in secure accommodation at the time of the application, having satisfied either the absconding or injury criterion, exceptional circumstances can justify the making of an application where a child is not already so placed. Neither knowing that the child is absconding nor the lack of suitable accommodation amount to exceptional circumstances (*Re AK (Secure Accommodation Order)* [2000] 1 FLR 317).

Criteria for order (s 25(1)(a),(b))—The two limbs of s 25(1) should be read disjunctively and not conjunctively. Therefore, the court does not have to find both s 25(1)(a) and (b) satisfied before making an order, since either is sufficient (*Re D (Secure Accommodation Order) (No 1)* [1997] 1 FLR 197). It is essential that there should be a clear record of facts as found by the court and for which sworn evidence was necessary (*Re AS (Secure Accommodation Order)* [1999] 1 FLR 103). The phrase "likely to abscond" in s 25(1)(a)(i) should be construed in the same way as the threshold criteria in s 31. "Likely" is used in the sense of a real possibility, a possibility that cannot be sensibly ignored having regard to the nature and gravity of the feared harm in the particular case (*S v Knowsley Borough Council* [2004] 2 FLR 716).

"child who is not legally represented" (s 25(6))—A child who is instructing a solicitor himself (in accordance with FPR 2010, r 16.29(2)) is obviously legally represented within the meaning of this section. From the wording of the Act and the rules, it is clear that a child is also legally represented where it is his children's guardian who is actually giving instructions to the solicitor (the more normal case since a children's guardian *will* normally be appointed by virtue of s 41(1)). It is implicit that in order for legal representation to be effective it must involve the taking of instructions (*Re AS (Secure Accommodation Order)* [1999] 1 FLR 103 – where an application for a s 25 order was held to be procedurally flawed because the child was not informed of the hearing and a guardian was not appointed). However, where the local authority have complied with the service requirements by serving the application on the parents and the solicitor appointed on behalf of the guardian it may still be fair to allow the application to proceed where the child and her own solicitor have only a short time to consult; although in such circumstances it may be preferable to make an interim order and adjourn for a few days to allow the child to respond to the application (*Re C (Secure Accommodation Order: Representation)* [2001] 2 FLR 169).

Attendance of child at hearing—While the court can allow the child who is the subject of the application to attend court, it must always bear in mind that attendance is likely to be harmful to the child and should only permit it if satisfied that it is in the interests of the child (*Re W (Secure Accommodation Order: Attendance at Court)* [1994] 2 FLR 1092, and see further **Use of the power to exclude** under FPR 2010, rr 12.14 and see also r 27.4(1),(3). However, the ordinary practice in relation to children attending court hearings has evolved since the decision in *Re W* (see *A City Council v T, J and K* [2011] 2 FLR 803). There is no in-built presumption against a child attending a hearing. The starting point should be an open evaluation of the consequences of attendance or non-attendance in terms of the child's welfare and the court's ability to manage its proceedings fairly. The following factors were relevant: (a) the age and level of understanding of the child; (b) the nature and strength of the child's wishes; (c) the child's emotional and psychological state; (d) the effect of influence from others; (e) the matters to be discussed; (f) the evidence to be given; (g) the child's behaviour; (h) practical and logistical considerations; and (i) the integrity of the proceedings.

The fact that the child would need to be physically restrained during the hearing in order to control him (as in *Re W* above) would, in itself, be sufficient ground for refusing to allow the child to be in court. Further examples given in *Re W* of situations in which the court would not allow a child to be present are where there is a prospect of disturbance or unruliness in court or the possibility of the child being educationally subnormal or where the child is much younger than the 10-year-old boy in that case. But see *J v Merthyr Tydfil County Borough Council* [1997] Fam Law 522 where a 15-year-old girl successfully appealed the magistrates' decision to exclude her from a hearing, on the grounds that: (i) they failed to balance her interests against the risk of her behaving in an unruly manner; (ii) reached the decision to exclude her without hearing from her guardian or solicitor; and (iii) refused to allow her solicitor an opportunity of seeing her before the hearing.

Role of children's guardian in secure accommodation proceedings—The welfare of the child is not the paramount consideration, and although it remains relevant, CA 1989, s 1 does not apply. The guardian has to adapt his general duties to the specific requirements of the application before the court and recommend what he believes to be in the best interests of the child (*Re M (Secure Accommodation Order)* [1995] 1 FLR 418, CA).

Duration of order—A s 25 order runs from the date of the court order and not from the date when the child is actually placed in secure accommodation (*Re B (A Minor) (Secure Accommodation)* [1994] 2 FLR 707, CA). The power to make an interim order is confined to circumstances when the application is adjourned. That power is commonly used where the court lacks sufficient information to justify a finding on the s 25(1) criteria (*Re A (Secure Accommodation Order)* [2001] Fam Law 806). A free–standing application for an *interim* secure accommodation order cannot be made. Where the court is satisfied it has all the information needed to determine the issues raised by the application, and that it would be procedurally fair to proceed, it is unlikely there would be grounds upon which the court could properly adjourn the application. Prolonging secure accommodation proceedings simply in order to keep a children's guardian involved for the purposes of assisting the child or overseeing the performance of the local authority's statutory duties, was not a proper use of the court's power (*Birmingham City Council v M* [2008] 2 FLR 542).

Where an interim order is made, the court, at the adjourned hearing, is still seised of the original application and must take into account the interim period as part of the maximum period of secure accommodation permitted by the regulations (*C v Humberside County Council* [1994] 2 FLR 759, FD). A local authority cannot lawfully keep a child in secure accommodation within the maximum period specified in an order under s 25(4), or the maximum period permitted without the authority of the court, at a time when the local authority itself does not consider the criteria in s 25(1) continue to be met (*LM v Essex County Council* [1999] 1 FLR 988). It is unclear whether the authority can lawfully keep the child in secure accommodation for some further period (provided it is within the maximum period specified in the order) while suitable alternative arrangements are made. There is no provision for discharge of secure accommodation orders within s 25. Once a s 25 order has been made, the family proceedings court cannot discharge or set the order aside if the facts subsequently change, nor can a higher court do so under CA 1989, s 94, unless the order has been incorrectly made. Where the local authority themselves no longer considered that the criteria were satisfied, the proper remedy was a writ of habeas corpus under CPR 1998, Pt 50, Sch 1 and PDRSC54 (*LM v Essex County Council* (above)). Where there is disagreement as to whether the criteria are still satisfied, the role of the local authority is susceptible to judicial review and that is likely to be the most appropriate remedy (see *S v Knowsley Borough Council* [2004] 2 FLR 716). The court does not have power to make an order under s 25 in respect of someone who is already 16 and being accommodated under s 20(5), but does have power to make an order in respect of a child who is not yet 16, and therefore not yet accommodated under s 20(5), even if the period of the order extends beyond the child's sixteenth birthday and thereafter the child's accommodation will fall under s 20(5) (*Re G (Secure Accommodation)* [2000] 2 FLR 259).

Appropriate court—Where a child has been remanded to local authority accommodation by a youth court pursuant to Criminal Justice Act 1991, s 60(3), any application by the local authority under CA 1989, s 25 should be made to the appropriate youth court rather than the appropriate family court (*Liverpool City Council v B* [1995] 2 FLR 84; *Re G (Secure Accommodation Order)* [2001] 1 FLR 884; and see C(SA)R 1991, reg 6 in Part IV).

Relationship between secure accommodation orders and refusal of bail—Where magistrates decide that bail is inappropriate in relation to children charged with criminal offences, it does not follow that the court is bound in principle to make a secure accommodation order; it is open to the court to consider other methods of disposal, such as remanding the children to local authority accommodation and imposing conditions on them (*Re W and D (Secure Accommodation)* [1995] 2 FLR 807; and see C(SA)R 1991, reg 6 in Part IV).

Independent reviewing officers

25A Appointment of independent reviewing officer

(1) If a local authority are looking after a child, they must appoint an individual as the independent reviewing officer for that child's case.

(2) The initial appointment under subsection (1) must be made before the child's case is first reviewed in accordance with regulations made under section 26.

(3) If a vacancy arises in respect of a child's case, the local authority must make another appointment under subsection (1) as soon as is practicable.

(4) An appointee must be of a description prescribed in regulations made by the appropriate national authority.

Amendments—Inserted by CYPA 2008, s 10.

25B Functions of the independent reviewing officer

(1) The independent reviewing officer must –

    (a)   monitor the performance by the local authority of their functions in relation to the child's case;

    (b)   participate, in accordance with regulations made by the appropriate national authority, in any review of the child's case;

    (c)   ensure that any ascertained wishes and feelings of the child concerning the case are given due consideration by the local authority;

    (d)   perform any other function which is prescribed in regulations made by the appropriate national authority.

(2) An independent reviewing officer's functions must be performed –

    (a)   in such manner (if any) as may be prescribed in regulations made by the appropriate national authority; and

    (b)   having regard to such guidance as that authority may issue in relation to the discharge of those functions.

(3) If the independent reviewing officer considers it appropriate to do so, the child's case may be referred by that officer to –

    (a)   an officer of the Children and Family Court Advisory and Support Service; or

    (b)   a Welsh family proceedings officer.

(4) If the independent reviewing officer is not an officer of the local authority, it is the duty of the authority –

    (a)   to co-operate with that individual; and

    (b)   to take all such reasonable steps as that individual may require of them to enable that individual's functions under this section to be performed satisfactorily.

Amendments—Inserted by CYPA 2008, s 10.

Independent Reviewing Officers (IROs)—The *IRO Handbook* (see *www.education.gov.uk*) provides guidance to independent reviewing officers about how they should discharge their distinct responsibilities to looked after children. It also provides guidance to local authorities on their strategic and managerial responsibilities in establishing an effective IRO service. The Care Planning, Placement and Case Review (England) Regulations 2010, which came into force on 1 April 2011 (see Part IV), set out the requirements for the qualifications and experience of IROs (reg 46). Reg 45 sets out their additional functions, including the duty to: ensure that the child has been informed of his right to apply, with leave, for a CA 1989, s 8 order and, where he is in the care of the local authority, to apply for the discharge of the care order; ensure that the child has been informed about the procedure for making representations and complaints to the authority; and ensure that if the child wishes to take legal proceedings under CA 1989 he has access to legal advice. In the circumstances defined in reg 45(3), the IRO must consider whether it would be appropriate to refer the child's case to a Cafcass officer. Where appropriate, the IRO must ensure that the authority has given due consideration to the child's wishes and feelings, and must consider whether to request a review of his case (reg 45(4)). In *A and S v Lancashire County Council* [2012] EWHC 1689 (Fam), Jackson J considered the case of two brothers who had been the subject of freeing orders for 11 years and who had during that time moved between placements 77 and 96 times, respectively. They were subjected to sexual and physical abuse in two foster placements. Notwithstanding that their respective care plans changed from adoption to long-term fostering no steps were taken to discharge the freeing orders, rendering the brothers "statutory orphans". During the relevant period, the case had been the subject of 35 Looked After Children Reviews, 16 chaired by the same IRO. In declaring that the local authority and the IRO acted in a manner incompatible with the children's rights under Arts 8, 6 and 3 of ECHR 1950, Jackson J gave a detailed description of the proper role of Independent Reviewing Officers and the steps needed to ensure the effectiveness of that role (see also *S (A Child Acting by the Official Solicitor) v Rochdale Metropolitan Borough Council and the Independent Reviewing Officer* [2009] 1 FLR 1090).

25C Referred cases

(1) In relation to children whose cases are referred to officers under section 25B(3), the Lord Chancellor may by regulations –

    (a)   extend any functions of the officers in respect of family proceedings (within the meaning of section 12 of the Criminal Justice and Court Services Act 2000) to other proceedings;

    (b)   require any functions of the officers to be performed in the manner prescribed by the regulations.

(2) The power to make regulations in this section is exercisable in relation to functions of Welsh family proceedings officers only with the consent of the Welsh Ministers.

Amendments—Inserted by CYPA 2008, s 10.

Supplemental

26 Review of cases and inquiries into representations

(1) The appropriate national authority may make regulations requiring the case of each child who is being looked after by a local authority to be reviewed in accordance with the provisions of the regulations.

(2) The regulations may, in particular, make provision –

    (a)   as to the manner in which each case is to be reviewed;

    (b)   as to the considerations to which the local authority are to have regard in reviewing each case;

    (c)   as to the time when each case is first to be reviewed and the frequency of subsequent reviews;

    (d)   requiring the authority, before conducting any review, to seek the views of –

        (i)   the child;

        (ii)   his parents;

        (iii)   any person who is not a parent of his but who has parental responsibility for him; and

        (iv)   any other person whose views the authority consider to be relevant, including, in particular, the views of those persons in relation to any particular matter which is to be considered in the course of the review;

    (e)   requiring the authority, in the case of a child who is in their care –

        (i)   to keep the section 31A plan for the child under review and, if they are of the opinion that some change is required, to revise the plan, or make a new plan, accordingly,

        (ii)   to consider whether an application should be made to discharge the care order;

    (f)   requiring the authority, in the case of a child in accommodation provided by the authority –

        (i)   if there is no plan for the future care of the child, to prepare one,

        (ii)   if there is such a plan for the child, to keep it under review and, if they are of the opinion that some change is required, to revise the plan or make a new plan, accordingly,

      (iii) to consider whether the accommodation accords with the requirements of this Part;

  (g) requiring the authority to inform the child, so far as is reasonably practicable, of any steps he may take under this Act;

  (h) requiring the authority to make arrangements, including arrangements with such other bodies providing services as it considers appropriate, to implement any decision which they propose to make in the course, or as a result, of the review;

  (i) requiring the authority to notify details of the result of the review and of any decision taken by them in consequence of the review to –

      (i) the child;

      (ii) his parents;

      (iii) any person who is not a parent of his but who has had parental responsibility for him; and

      (iv) any other person whom they consider ought to be notified;

  (j) requiring the authority to monitor the arrangements which they have made with a view to ensuring that they comply with the regulations;

  (k) for the authority to appoint a person in respect of each case to carry out in the prescribed manner the functions mentioned in subsection (2A) and any prescribed function.

(2A) The functions referred to in subsection (2)(k) are –

  (a) participating in the review of the case in question,

  (b) monitoring the performance of the authority's functions in respect of the review,

  (c) referring the case to an officer of the Children and Family Court Advisory and Support Service or a Welsh family proceedings officer, if the person appointed under subsection (2)(k) considers it appropriate to do so.

(2B) A person appointed under subsection (2)(k) must be a person of a prescribed description.

(2C) In relation to children whose cases are referred to officers under subsection (2A)(c), the Lord Chancellor may by regulations –

  (a) extend any functions of the officers in respect of family proceedings (within the meaning of section 12 of the Criminal Justice and Court Services Act 2000) to other proceedings,

  (b) require any functions of the officers to be performed in the manner prescribed by the regulations.

(2D) The power to make regulations in subsection (2C) is exercisable in relation to functions of Welsh family proceedings officers only with the consent of the Welsh Ministers.

(3) Every local authority shall establish a procedure for considering any representations (including any complaint) made to them by –

  (a) any child who is being looked after by them or who is not being looked after by them but is in need;

  (b) a parent of his;

  (c) any person who is not a parent of his but who has parental responsibility for him;

  (d) any local authority foster parent;

  (e) such other person as the authority consider has a sufficient interest in the child's welfare to warrant his representations being considered by them,

about the discharge of the authority of any of their qualifying functions in relation to the child.

(3A) The following are qualifying functions for the purposes of subsection (3) –

    (a)   functions under this Part,

    (b)   such functions under Part 4 or 5 as are specified by the appropriate national authority in regulations.

(3B) The duty under subsection (3) extends to representations (including complaints) made to the authority by –

    (a)   any person mentioned in section 3(1) of the Adoption and Children Act 2002 (persons for whose needs provision is made by the Adoption Service) and any other person to whom arrangements for the provision of adoption support services (within the meaning of that Act) extend,

    (b)   such other person as the authority consider has sufficient interest in a child who is or may be adopted to warrant his representations being considered by them,

about the discharge by the authority of such functions under the Adoption and Children Act 2002 as are specified by the appropriate national authority in regulations.

(3C) The duty under subsection (3) extends to any representations (including complaints) which are made to the authority by –

    (a)   a child with respect to whom a special guardianship order is in force,

    (b)   a special guardian or a parent of such a child,

    (c)   any other person the authority consider has a sufficient interest in the welfare of such a child to warrant his representations being considered by them, or

    (d)   any person who has applied for an assessment under section 14F(3) or (4), about the discharge by the authority of such functions under section 14F as may be specified by the appropriate national authority in regulations.

(4) The procedure shall ensure that at least one person who is not a member or officer of the authority takes part in –

    (a)   the consideration; and

    (b)   any discussions which are held by the authority about the action (if any) to be taken in relation to the child in the light of the consideration

but this subsection is subject to subsection (5A).

(4A) Regulations may be made by the appropriate national authority imposing time limits on the making of representations under this section.

(5) In carrying out any consideration of representations under this section a local authority shall comply with any regulations made by the appropriate national authority for the purpose of regulating the procedure to be followed.

(5A) Regulations under subsection (5) may provide that subsection (4) does not apply in relation to any consideration or discussion which takes place as part of a procedure for which provision is made by the regulations for the purpose of resolving informally the matters raised in the representations.

(6) The appropriate national authority may make regulations requiring local authorities to monitor the arrangements that they have made with a view to ensuring that they comply with any regulations made for the purposes of subsection (5).

(7) Where any representation has been considered under the procedure established by a local authority under this section, the authority shall –

    (a)   have due regard to the findings of those considering the representation; and

    (b)   take such steps as are reasonably practicable to notify (in writing) –

        (i)   the person making the representation;

        (ii) the child (if the authority consider that he has sufficient understanding); and

(iii) such other persons (if any) as appear to the authority to be likely to be affected,

of the authority's decision in the matter and their reasons for taking that decision and of any action which they have taken, or propose to take.

(8) Every local authority shall give such publicity to their procedure for considering representations under this section as they consider appropriate.

Amendments—ACA 2002, ss 117, 118, 139; Health and Social Care (Community Health and Standards) Act 2003, s 117; CA 2004, s 40, Sch 3, paras 5, 8(1)–(3); CYPA 2008, s 39, Sch 3, paras 1, 16.

Section 26 and judicial review—For the potential relevance of the s 26 representation procedure in judicial review proceedings, see under CA 1989, s 84 and see Children Act 1989 Representations Procedure (England) Regulations 2006, reg 8(1).

Scope of complaints procedure—In deciding not to apply for a care order, the local authority is exercising a function under CA 1989, Pt III and the complaints procedure is applicable to such a decision (*R v East Sussex CC ex parte W* [1998] 2 FLR 1082, QBD).

Duty to consider representations made by a parent – (s 26(3)(b))—The duty of the local authority to establish a procedure to consider any representations made to them by the persons named in s 26(3) is directory and not mandatory; the result of any non-compliance with the provisions should be treated as an irregularity (*Re P (Children Act 1989, ss 22 and 26: Local Authority Compliance)* [2000] 2 FLR 910). In exceptional circumstances the court has power to make a declaration that the local authority be absolved from the duty to provide information to a parent and from the duty to consult them in any way about the child (*Re C (Care: Consultation with Parents Not in Child's Best Interests)* [2006] 2 FLR 787).

Adoption and Children Act 2002 – review of cases of looked-after children—ACA 2002, s 118 created the role of independent reviewing officer (IRO) and amended CA 1989, s 26(2)(e) (requirement to consider the discharge of a care order) to encompass a review of the care plan and revision of it as necessary. Once a care order has been made, the responsibility for the child is transferred to the local authority, removing it from the control of the court even in cases where a judge feels that it is necessary for the court to monitor the progress of the child in care.

The ACA 2002 amendment of CA 1989, s 26(2)(e) requires the local authority to appoint an IRO whose functions are to participate in the review process, chair the review meeting, monitor the local authority's functions in respect of the review and refer the case to Cafcass if the IRO considers it appropriate to do so. The detailed provisions are contained in the Review of Children's Cases (Amendment) (England) Regulations 2004. IROs have power to refer cases they are unable to resolve to their satisfaction to Cafcass Legal, who may start court proceedings against the local authority seeking an order requiring it to put right its failings in relation to the care plan. The Care Planning, Placement and Case Review (England) Regulations 2010 (see Part IV), which came into force on 1 April 2011, set out the additional functions, qualifications and experience of IROs (see Pt 8, regs 45, 46). Reg 36 sets out the manner in which the IRO should ensure that the review is conducted. They are accompanied by the *IRO Handbook: Statutory Guidance for Local Authorities and Independent Reviewing Officers on Reviewing Arrangements for Looked After Children*, which provides statutory guidance for IROs about their distinct responsibilities in relation to looked-after children under the 1989 Act and the regulations, and replaces the 2004 *Independent Reviewing Officers Guidance*.

Concerns have been expressed about the independence of IROs. They may be wholly independent of, or employed by, the local authority. If the latter, then they should not be subject to the same line management that is responsible for the decision-making in relation to the care plan. It is intended that all looked-after children will have an IRO. Cafcass Legal will only be able to accept referrals from IROs and their options would be to: reject the referral; attempt to resolve the matter by mediation; refer the matter to another agency; or bring civil proceedings against the local authority. If further proceedings under CA 1989 are required, Cafcass Legal will refer the case back to the children's guardian from the care proceedings: see the Children and Family Court Advisory and Support Service (Reviewed Case Referral) Regulations 2004, which empower officers of Cafcass Legal to bring civil actions against local authorities. If a civil action is brought against the local authority, one of the social work practitioners in Cafcass Legal will act as the child's litigation friend. The options for civil action are: judicial review proceedings; a compensation claim; or, a freestanding HRA 1998 application (for the latter see *A and S v Lancashire County Council* [2012] EWHC 1689 (Fam)). See further **Procedure for raising issues under the Human Rights Act 1998** under CA 1989, s 31, and annotation to HRA 1998.

26ZB Representations: further consideration (Wales)

(1) The Welsh Ministers may by regulations make provision for the further consideration of representations which have been considered by a local authority in Wales under section 24D or section 26.

(2) The regulations may in particular make provision –

   (a) for the further consideration of a representation by an independent panel established under the regulations;

   (b) about the procedure to be followed on the further consideration of a representation;

   (c) for the making of recommendations about the action to be taken as the result of a representation;

   (d) about the making of reports about a representation;

   (e) about the action to be taken by the local authority concerned as a result of the further consideration of a representation;

   (f) for a representation to be referred back to the local authority concerned for reconsideration by the authority.

(3) The regulations may require –

   (a) the making of a payment, in relation to the further consideration of a representation under this section, by any local authority in respect of whose functions the representation is made;

   (b) any such payment to be –

     (i) made to such person or body as may be specified in the regulations;

     (ii) of such amount as may be specified in, or calculated or determined under, the regulations; and

   (c) for an independent panel to review the amount chargeable under paragraph (a) in any particular case and, if the panel thinks fit, to substitute a lesser amount.

(4) The regulations may also –

   (a) provide for different parts or aspects of a representation to be treated differently;

   (b) require the production of information or documents in order to enable a representation to be properly considered;

   (c) authorise the disclosure of information or documents relevant to a representation to a person or body who is further considering a representation under the regulations;

and any such disclosure may be authorised notwithstanding any rule of common law that would otherwise prohibit or restrict the disclosure.

Amendments—Inserted by Health and Social Care (Community Health and Standards) Act 2003, s 116(2); amended by CYPA 2008, s 39, Sch 3, paras 1, 17.

26A Advocacy services

(1) Every local authority shall make arrangements for the provision of assistance to –

   (a) persons who make or intend to make representations under section 24D; and

   (b) children who make or intend to make representations under section 26.

(2) The assistance provided under the arrangements shall include assistance by way of representation.

(3) The arrangements –

   (a) shall secure that a person may not provide assistance if he is a person who is prevented from doing so by regulations made by the appropriate national authority; and

(b)   shall comply with any other provision made by the regulations in relation to the arrangements.

(4) The appropriate national authority may make regulations requiring local authorities to monitor the steps that they have taken with a view to ensuring that they comply with regulations made for the purposes of subsection (3).

(5) Every local authority shall give such publicity to their arrangements for the provision of assistance under this section as they consider appropriate.

Amendments—Inserted by ACA 2002, s 119; amended by CYPA 2008, s 39, Sch 3, paras 1, 18.

27 Co-operation between authorities

(1) Where it appears to a local authority that any authority mentioned in subsection (3) could, by taking any specified action, help in the exercise of any of their functions under this Part, they may request the help of that other authority, specifying the action in question.

(2) An authority whose help is so requested shall comply with the request if it is compatible with their own statutory or other duties and obligations and does not unduly prejudice the discharge of any of their functions.

(3) The authorities are –

    (a)   any local authority;
    (b)   (*repealed*)
    (c)   any local housing authority;
    (ca) the National Health Service Commissioning Board;
    (d)   any clinical commissioning group, Local Health Board, Special Health Authority, National Health Service trust or NHS foundation trust; and
    (e)   any person authorised by the appropriate national authority for the purposes of this section.

(4) (*repealed*)

Amendments—CLSA 1990, ss 116, 125(7), Sch 16, para 14, Sch 20; Education Act 1993, s 307, Sch 19, para 147, Sch 21, Pt II; Health Authorities Act 1995, s 2, Sch 1, para 118; SI 2000/90; Health and Social Care (Community Health and Standards) Act 2003, s 34, Sch 4, para 78; SI 2007/961; CYPA 2008, s 39, Sch 3, paras 1, 19; SI 2010/1158; Health and Social Care Act 2012, s 55(2), Sch 5, para 51.

28 (*repealed*)

29 Recoupment of cost of providing services etc

(1) Where a local authority provide any service under section 17 or 18, other than advice, guidance or counselling, they may recover from a person specified in subsection (4) such charge for the service as they consider reasonable.

(2) Where the authority are satisfied that that person's means are insufficient for it to be reasonably practicable for him to pay the charge, they shall not require him to pay more than he can reasonably be expected to pay.

(3) No person shall be liable to pay any charge under subsection (1) for a service provided under section 17 or section 18(1) or (5) at any time when he is in receipt of income support under Part VII of the Social Security Contributions and Benefits Act 1992, of any element of child tax credit other than the family element, of working tax credit, of an income-based jobseeker's allowance or of an income-related employment and support allowance.

(3A) No person shall be liable to pay any charge under subsection (1) for a service provided under section 18(2) or (6) at any time when he is in receipt of income support under Part VII of the Social Security and Benefits Act 1992, of an income-based jobseeker's allowance or of an income-related employment and support allowance.

(3B) No person shall be liable to pay any charge under subsection (1) for a service provided under section 18(2) or (6) at any time when –

    (a)   he is in receipt of guarantee state pension credit under section 1(3)(a) of the State Pension Credit Act 2002, or

    (b)   he is a member of a couple (within the meaning of that Act) the other member of which is in receipt of guarantee state pension credit.

(4) The persons are –

    (a)   where the service is provided for a child under sixteen, each of his parents;

    (b)   where it is provided for a child who has reached the age of sixteen, the child himself; and

    (c)   where it is provided for a member of the child's family, that member.

(5) Any charge under subsection (1) may, without prejudice to any other method of recovery, be recovered summarily as a civil debt.

(6) Part III of Schedule 2 makes provision in connection with contributions towards the maintenance of children who are being looked after by local authorities and consists of the re-enactment with modifications of provisions in Part V of the Child Care Act 1980.

(7) Where a local authority provide any accommodation under section 20(1) for a child who was (immediately before they began to look after him) ordinarily resident within the area of another local authority, they may recover from that other authority any reasonable expenses incurred by them in providing the accommodation and maintaining him.

(8) Where a local authority provide accommodation under section 21(1) or (2)(a) or (b) for a child who is ordinarily resident within the area of another local authority and they are not maintaining him in –

    (a)   a community home provided by them;

    (b)   a controlled community home; or

    (c)   a hospital vested in the Secretary of State or the Welsh Ministers, or any other hospital made available pursuant to arrangements made by the Secretary of State, the National Health Service Commissioning Board or a clinical commissioning group under the National Health Service Act 2006 or by Local Health Board,

they may recover from that other authority any reasonable expenses incurred by them in providing the accommodation and maintaining him.

(9) Except where subsection (10) applies, where a local authority comply with any request under section 27(2) in relation to a child or other person who is not ordinarily resident within their area, they may recover from the local authority in whose area the child or person is ordinarily resident any reasonable expenses incurred by them in respect of that person.

(10) Where a local authority ("authority A") comply with any request under section 27(2) from another local authority ("authority B") in relation to a child or other person –

    (a)   whose responsible authority is authority B for the purposes of section 23B or 23C; or

    (b)   whom authority B are advising or befriending or to whom they are giving assistance by virtue of section 24(5)(a),

authority A may recover from authority B any reasonable expenses incurred by them in respect of that person.

Amendments—CLSA 1990, s 116, Sch 16, para 15; National Health Service and Community Care Act 1990, s 66(1), Sch 9, para 36(3); Disability Living Allowance and Disability Working Allowance Act 1991, s 7(2), Sch 3, para 14; Social Security (Consequential Provisions) Act 1992, s 4, Sch 2, para 108; Health Authorities Act 1995, s 2, Sch 1, para 118; Jobseekers Act 1995, s 41, Sch 2, para 19; Tax Credits Act 1999, s 1(2), Sch 1, paras 1, 6(d)(ii); Children (Leaving Care) Act 2000, s 7; Local Government Act 2000, s 103; SI 2000/90; Tax Credits Act 2002, s 47, Sch 3, paras 15, 18; SI 2002/2469; State Pension Credit Act 2002, s 14, Sch 2, Pt 3, para 30; SI 2005/3129; SI 2007/961; Welfare Reform Act 2007, s 28(1), Sch 3, para 6; CYPA 2008, s 39, Sch 3, paras 1, 20; Health and Social Care Act 2012, s 55(2), Sch 5, para 52.

30 Miscellaneous

(1) Nothing in this Part shall affect any duty imposed on a local authority by or under any other enactment.

(2) Any question arising under section 20(2), 21(3) or 29(7) to (9) as to the ordinary residence of a child shall be determined by agreement between the local authorities concerned or, in default of agreement, by the determining authority.

(2A) For the purposes of subsection (2) "the determining authority" is –

(a) in a case where all the local authorities concerned are in Wales, the Welsh Ministers;

(b) in any other case, the Secretary of State.

(2B) In a case where –

(a) the determining authority is the Secretary of State, and

(b) one or more of the local authorities concerned are in Wales,

the Secretary of State must consult the Welsh Ministers before making a determination for the purposes of subsection (2).

(3) (*repealed*)

(4) The appropriate national authority may make regulations for determining, as respects any education functions specified in the regulations, whether a child who is being looked after by a local authority is to be treated, for purposes so specified, as a child of parents of sufficient resources or as a child of parents without resources.

Amendments—CYPA 2008, s 39, Sch 3, paras 1, 21; SI 2010/1158.

30A Meaning of appropriate national authority

In this Part "the appropriate national authority" means –

(a) in relation to England, the Secretary of State; and

(b) in relation to Wales, the Welsh Ministers.

Amendments—Inserted by CYPA 2008, s 39, Sch 3, paras 1, 22.

PART IV
CARE AND SUPERVISION

General

31 Care and supervision orders

(1) On the application of any local authority or authorised person, the court may make an order –

(a) placing the child with respect to whom the application is made in the care of a designated local authority; or

(b) putting him under the supervision of a designated local authority.

(2) A court may only make a care order or supervision order if it is satisfied –

    (a)   that the child concerned is suffering, or is likely to suffer, significant harm; and

    (b)   that the harm, or likelihood of harm, is attributable to –

        (i)   the care given to the child, or likely to be given to him if the order were not made, not being what it would be reasonable to expect a parent to give to him; or

        (ii)   the child's being beyond parental control.

(3) No care order or supervision order may be made with respect to a child who has reached the age of seventeen (or sixteen, in the case of a child who is married).

(3A) No care order may be made with respect to a child until the court has considered a section 31A plan.

(4) An application under this section may be made on its own or in any other family proceedings.

(5) The court may –

    (a)   on an application for a care order, make a supervision order;

    (b)   on an application for a supervision order, make a care order.

(6) Where an authorised person proposes to make an application under this section he shall –

    (a)   if it is reasonably practicable to do so; and

    (b)   before making the application,

consult the local authority appearing to him to be the authority in whose area the child concerned is ordinarily resident.

(7) An application made by an authorised person shall not be entertained by the court if, at the time when it is made, the child concerned is –

    (a)   the subject of an earlier application for a care order, or supervision order, which has not been disposed of; or

    (b)   subject to –

        (i)   a care order or supervision order;

        (ii)   a youth rehabilitation order within the meaning of Part 1 of the Criminal Justice and Immigration Act 2008; or

        (iii)   a supervision requirement within the meaning of Part II of the Children (Scotland) Act 1995.

(8) The local authority designated in a care order must be –

    (a)   the authority within whose area the child is ordinarily resident; or

    (b)   where the child does not reside in the area of a local authority, the authority within whose area any circumstances arose in consequence of which the order is being made.

(9) In this section –

    "authorised person" means –

        (a)   the National Society for the Prevention of Cruelty to Children and any of its officers; and

        (b)   any person authorised by order of the Secretary of State to bring proceedings under this section and any officer of a body which is so authorised;

    "harm" means ill-treatment or the impairment of health or development including, for example, impairment suffered from seeing or hearing the ill-treatment of another;

    "development" means physical, intellectual, emotional, social or behavioural development;

"health" means physical or mental health; and
"ill-treatment" includes sexual abuse and forms of ill-treatment which are not
physical.

(10) Where the question of whether harm suffered by a child is significant turns on the
child's health or development, his health or development shall be compared with that
which could reasonably be expected of a similar child.

(11) In this Act –

"a care order" means (subject to section 105(1)) an order under subsection (1)(a) and
(except where express provision to the contrary is made) includes an interim care
order made under section 38; and

"a supervision order" means an order under subsection (1)(b) and (except where
express provision to the contrary is made) includes an interim supervision order
made under section 38.

Amendments—Children (Scotland) Act 1995, s 105(4), Sch 4, para 48(1),(2); CJCSA 2000 ss 74, 75,
Sch 7, Pt II, paras 87, 90; Powers of Criminal Courts (Sentencing) Act 2000, s 165, Sch 9, para 127;
ACA 2002, ss 120, 121; Criminal Justice and Immigration Act 2008, ss 6(2), 149, Sch 4, para 35.

Modifications—Section 31 is modified for certain purposes by SI 2010/1898, reg 5(3).

Defined terms—"authorised person": s 31(9); "care order": ss 31(11), 105(1); "child"; s 105(1); "family
proceedings": s 8(3); "local authority": s 105(1); "supervision order": s 31(11).

Jurisdiction—The jurisdictional basis for an application under CA 1989, Pt IV, is effectively the same as
that established by FLA 1986 in relation to s 8 orders, namely that the child concerned is either habitually
resident in England and Wales, or present in England and Wales when the application is made (*Re R (Care
Orders: Jurisdiction)* [1995] 1 FLR 711). As to the meaning of "habitual residence", see further under
CA 1989, s 105(6) and CACA 1985, Sch 1, Art 4. The widest permissible approach should be adopted for
the jurisdictional basis for an application under CA 1989, Pt IV. Where a child living in England at the
time of the application is habitually resident in Scotland, the child's presence at the time of the
application will give the English court jurisdiction throughout the currency of the proceedings (*Re M
(Care Orders: Jurisdiction)* [1997] 1 FLR 456). A parent or child's diplomatic immunity does not act to
oust jurisdiction under CA 1989, s 31 (*Re B (Care Proceedings: Diplomatic Immunity)* [2003] 1 FLR
241.

European Council Regulation (EC) No 2201/2003 concerning Jurisdiction and the Recognition and
Enforcement in Judgments in Matrimonial Matters and Matters of Parental Responsibility (Brussels IIA)
(see Part VI) applies to care proceedings under CA 1989, Pt IV (*Re A (Area of Freedom, Security and
Justice)* (C-532/01) [2009] 2 FLR 1, ECJ and *Re C* (C-435/06) [2008] 1 FLR 490, ECJ). Pursuant to
Art 20(1) of BIIA, the courts of a Member State may in an urgent case take provisional, including
protective, measures notwithstanding that another Member State has jurisdiction as to the substance of the
proceedings (*Detiček v Sgueglia* (Case C–403/09) [2010] 1 FLR 1381, ECJ). Such measures include the
power to make interim orders, including interim care orders, in public law proceedings in respect of a
child who is habitually resident in another Member State where the child is present in the Member State
making the order (*Re A (Area of Freedom, Security and Justice)*, above; *Re S (Care: Jurisdiction)* [2009]
2 FLR 550). Where the child is habitually resident in a State that is not a Member State of the European
Union but is a Contracting State of the Hague Convention on Jurisdiction, Applicable Law, Recognition,
Enforcement and Co-Operation in Respect of Parental Responsibility and Measures for the Protection of
Children 1996, the latter Convention will apply (see Part IV). Thus, in what will be the vast majority of
cases, where the child who is subject to proceedings under CA 1989, Pt IV is habitually resident in the
European Union, in respect of matters falling within its scope, Brussels IIA must be applied. In a smaller
number of cases where the child is habitually resident in a State that is not subject to Brussels IIA but is
a party to the 1996 Convention, the 1996 Convention will apply. Where Brussels IIA is or may be
engaged in care proceedings, the following procedure should be adopted at an early case management
hearing: (a) the local authority should make a prompt assessment of the needs and risks to the child to
determine an action plan; (b) the local authority should immediately notify both parents and any adult
involved with the child to tell them what has happened, to inform them of their rights (including under the
Hague Conventions where appropriate) and obtain their wishes and feelings about the placement sought
for the child; (c) the local authority should give notice to the consulate of the relevant country to inform
them of the situation and, where they have not been located, seek assistance in finding the parents, with
care being taken to recognise the relevant jurisdictional points and thus the roles of the respective national
authorities; and (d) the local authority should apply for a prompt hearing, on notice if possible, at which
hearing should be considered (i) the circumstances of the case and the local authority's proposals for the

child, (ii) the possibility of transfer to the High Court, (iii) the interim arrangements, (iv) the international obligations and any relevant Convention rights and (v) the issues requiring resolution (*S v Slough Borough Council and others* [2009] All ER (D) 182 (Apr); *Re S (Care: Jurisdiction)* (above) and *Tower Hamlets LBC v MK and others* [2012] 2 FLR 762. See also *HSE Ireland v SF (A Minor)* [2012] 2 FLR 1131). It is likely that the foregoing procedure is applicable in cases to which the Hague Convention 1996 applies. The return of the child to his or her country of origin should be sought without unreasonable delay unless a risk and security assessment determines that such a move is not in the best interests of the child. Note that Art 56(1),(2) of Brussels IIA requires only (i) that a court that is considering authorising the placement of a child in institutional or foster care in another Member State consults the competent authority responsible for child placement in that Member State and (ii) that a court that is considering authorising the placement of a child in institutional or foster care in another Member State does not decide on any such placement without first obtaining that competent authority's consent (*Re AB (BIIR: Care Proceedings)* [2013] 1 FLR 168; *Health Service Executive v SC and AC (Case C-92/12)* [2012] Fam Law 1085). Art 56(1),(2) does not give a Member State an entitlement to call for the placement of the child within its jurisdiction (*Re AB (BIIR: Care Proceedings)*, above).

Under Brussels IIA, Art 15(1)(b) the court of another jurisdiction may request that the English or Welsh court accept jurisdiction over care proceedings begun in the foreign jurisdiction. The Art 15 transfer request should be made promptly through the International Judicial Network and should be accompanied by a request pursuant to Brussels IIA, Art 56 that the relevant competent English or Welsh authority consent to the placement of the child in the domestic jurisdiction. Where the English or Welsh court receives a transfer request from the court of another jurisdiction, the English or Welsh court should determine whether to accept that request by reference to the child's best interests rather than a wider review of all of the criteria for transfer set out in Art 15. Where the English or Welsh court accepts that it is in the child's best interests for proceedings to be transferred, FPR 2010, r 12.66(2) permits the English or Welsh court to take preparatory steps to give effect to the imminent receipt of the proceedings. The provisions of Pt V of CA 1989 will apply in their entirety to the future management of the proceedings once the jurisdiction of the English or Welsh court has been engaged. In such cases, the applicant local authority will be the authority that is likely to become the designated authority under CA 1989, s 31(8) if a care or supervision order is granted (*Re LM (A Child)* [2013] EWHC 646).

Objective nature of threshold test—The nature of the test prescribed by s 31(2) to determine whether a court may make a care or supervision order is, and has to be, objective (*Re D (Care Order: Evidence)* [2011] 1 FLR 447).

Case management and the Public Law Outline (PLO)—The PLO is contained in PD12A. The court should adopt a robust but fair approach to case management in public law cases. The task of the case management judge is to arrange a trial that is fair by reference to domestic standards and Arts 6 and 8 of the ECHR. In case managing the proceedings, the court should aim to achieve the overriding objective set out in FPR 2010, r 1.1 (*Re TG (A Child)* [2013] EWCA Civ 5). In *Re TG*, the President emphasised that the circumstances in which the Court of Appeal will interfere with a case management decision are limited. The Court of Appeal will only interfere if it is satisfied that the case management judge erred in principle, took account of irrelevant matters, failed to take account of relevant matters or came to a decision that is so plainly wrong that it must be regarded as outside the generous ambit of the discretion entrusted to the judge. There are however limits to robust case management (see for example *Re B* [2012] EWCA Civ 1742, where the judge's decision to refuse to permit certain witnesses to be called deprived him of the evidence necessary to make safe findings of fact). See also **First appointment, Case management conference** and **Issues resolution hearing** under FPR 2010, r 12.25.

Care orders – ECHR 1950—Under HRA 1998, a parent may complain that his right to respect for his family life, protected by ECHR 1950, Art 8(1), has been violated by the making of a care order. In dealing with such a claim the court must consider whether, if there has been such an interference with the right, that interference was justified under Art 8(2) as being necessary in a democratic society for the protection of the health and morals and of the rights and freedoms of others. If such interference is justified the court must also consider whether it is proportionate to the aim of protecting the rights of the child concerned (*Re B (Care: Interference with Family Life)* [2003] 2 FLR 813). The task of the domestic court when faced with such a complaint under Art 8(1) is to review under ECHR 1950 decisions taken by other public authorities in the exercise of their similar powers and to compare them with the case currently before the court. The width of the discretion allowed to a public authority in each case will vary according to the issues and the interests at stake. While the public authority will have a wide discretion in relation to the actual decision to take a child into care, a stricter scrutiny will be applied to any further steps proposed by the authority which might have the effect of restricting even more tightly the family relations between parents and a young child, for example limits on the amount and/or frequency of contact between the parents and the child in care (*Scott v UK* [2000] 1 FLR 958 – where the child was ultimately freed for adoption since the mother had been unable to overcome a chronic dependence on alcohol; *HK v Finland*

(Application No 36065/97) [2007] 1 FLR 633 – where the father was wrongfully accused of sexual abuse and his child was removed from him for 4 years, during which time he was given no opportunity to contest the restrictions on his contact with the child). In judicial decisions where the Art 8 rights of parents and those of a child are at stake, the domestic courts, relying on the decision of the ECtHR in *Yousef v The Netherlands* [2003] 1 FLR 210, have held that the child's interests remain the paramount consideration, so that if any balancing of interests is necessary as between the parents and the child, the child's interests must prevail (*Dawson v Wearmouth* [1997] 2 FLR 629, CA and [1999] 1 FLR 1167; *Payne v Payne* [2001] 1 FLR 1052; *CF v Secretary of State for the Home Department* [2004] 2 FLR 517 and *Re S (Contact: Promoting Relationship with Absent Parent)* [2004] 1 FLR 1279). However, it should be noted that the judgment in *Yousef v The Netherlands* constitutes only one decision within a long line of European authority, beginning with *Johansen v Norway* [1996] ECHR 31, which stipulates that the correct approach under Art 8 is to strike a fair balance between the interests of the child and those of the parent, attaching particular importance to the best interest of the child, which interests, depending on their nature and seriousness, may override those of the parent. Since its decision in *Yousef v The Netherlands*, the ECtHR has repeatedly cited the test in *Johansen v Norway* rather than relying on the formulation adopted in *Yousef v The Netherlands* (*C v Finland* [2006] 2 FLR 597; *HK v Finland*, above; *Dolhamre v Sweden* [2010] 2 FLR 912 and *Neulinger and Shuruk v Switzerland* [2011] 1 FLR 122). The Draconian step of removing a baby from its mother shortly after birth must be supported by relevant and sufficient reasons and must be regarded as necessary in a democratic society (*R (G) v Nottingham City Council and Nottingham University Hospital* [2008] 1 FLR 1668 – where the authority acted unlawfully by separating the mother and baby without lawful authority; *CF v Secretary of State for the Home Department* (above) – where Munby J held that the policy in Prison Service Order 4801 (that the interests of a child generally are best served by having an upper age limit of 18 months for living with his mother in prison) is lawful under Art 8, but that the child's interests had not been properly represented at the separation care planning meeting so that the decision of the Secretary of State based on the meeting had to be quashed. See further under **Removal of babies at birth** (below).

Article 6 of the Convention guarantees the right to a fair hearing and in *L v Finland* [2000] 2 FLR 118, it was successfully argued that there was a violation of Art 6 because no oral hearing had been held before the decision to take the children concerned into care. The need to take emergency action and to limit the notice given to the parents must be balanced with the circumstances of the case (*KA v Finland* [2003] 1 FLR 696 – where the social services had not made any serious effort to reunite the family). In *Re GB (Children)* [2013] EWCA Civ 164), the Court of Appeal held that a refusal to grant an adjournment during the final hearing so that a parent can obtain alternative representation does not constitute a breach of Art 6 where the Court has given a prior indication that there would be no such adjournment and has thereafter conducted the trial so as to ensure that the party who has dispensed with her legal representation is on an equal footing in accordance with FPR 2010, r 1.1(2)(c). Emergency measures to take children into care must be justified and there will be a breach of Arts 6 and 8 if parents are not given sufficient opportunity to participate in proceedings which will potentially disrupt their family life (*Venema v The Netherlands* [2003] 1 FLR 552 – where doctors suspected that the mother was suffering from Munchausen's Syndrome by Proxy and the Child Welfare Board took the child into care without first expressing these concerns to the parents, resulting in a breach of Art 8; *Haase v Germany* [2004] 2 FLR 39 – where the emergency removal of eight children from the applicants, including a 7-day-old baby, was not proportionate to the circumstances, failed to allow the applicants to participate in the decision-making process and was in breach of Art 8). In *G v N County Council* [2009] 1 FLR 774 the court made a declaration that the local authority acted unlawfully by removing children from the mother without first involving or consulting with the parents, and without giving them due notice of their intention to remove the children; their actions were not proportionate to the level of concern in the case.

The local authority, when seeking to take a child into care, is under a heavy obligation to ensure that the procedure at all stages is transparent and fair, both in and out of court. Article 8 requires the local authority to involve parents fully in the decision-making process, at all stages of the child protection procedure, whether before, during or after the making of a care order (*Re G (Care: Challenge to Local Authority's Decision)* [2003] 2 FLR 42 – where the local authority planned to remove children who were subject to care orders from their parents and re-admit them to care but failed to invite the parents to a planning meeting to discuss this, resulting in a breach of Art 8; *Haase v Germany* (above); *Moser v Austria* (Application No 12643/02) [2007] 1 FLR 702 – where there had been a failure to explore arrangements to allow mother and child to remain in contact while proceedings were pending, the mother had not been allowed to challenge reports and the appeal proceedings had been conducted without holding any hearing). In *Jucius and Juciuvienè v Lithuania* [2009] 1 FLR 403, the court had determined the appeal of the children's uncle and his wife by way of written procedure. The ECHR held that questions of fact could not be resolved adequately in this way and there should have been a hearing to ensure that the best interests of the children were considered. In particular, it is vital that a litigant has a proper opportunity in care proceedings to examine and comment on experts' reports and other documents being considered by the court and to cross-examine witnesses interviewed and relied on therein (*Re L*

(Care: Assessment: Fair Trial) [2002] 2 FLR 730). PD25A–PD25F regulate the use of expert evidence and the instruction of experts in family proceedings.

Procedure for raising issues under the Human Rights Act 1998—For the procedure to be followed when raising an issue under HRA 1998, see the annotation thereto and FPR 2010, r 29.5 and PD29B. Where care proceedings have come to an end the appropriate remedy may well be a freestanding application under HRA 1998, s 7(1)(a). Where the proceedings are still ongoing s 7(1)(b) provides an appropriate remedy within the care proceedings themselves. Therefore, where a HRA 1998 complaint arises before the making of a final care order, it should normally be dealt with within the context of the care proceedings and by the court dealing with those proceedings (*Re L (Care Proceedings: Human Rights Claims)* [2003] 2 FLR 160; *Re L (Care: Assessment: Fair Trial)* [2002] 2 FLR 730). Only in a wholly exceptional case would it be appropriate to treat human rights arguments as raising a discrete issue to be heard in the High Court, while care proceedings continued in the family proceedings court. If a case really requires transfer, then the whole case should be transferred (*Re L* [2003], above). However, it is not necessary or desirable to transfer care proceedings under CA 1989, Pt IV, from the county court to the High Court merely because a breach of human rights under ECHR 1950 is alleged (*Re V (Care Proceedings: Human Rights Claim)* [2004] 1 FLR 944).

Need to file a care plan (s 31(3A))—See under s 31A.

Requirement to keep parents properly involved in the planning process—It is essential that the local authority keeps the parents properly involved in the planning process when care proceedings are initiated and the care plan is being formulated (*Re S (Minors) (Care Order: Implementation of Care Plan)*; *Re W (Minors) (Care Order: Adequacy of Care Plan)* [2002] 1 FLR 815). Likewise, it is essential to ensure that children are given the appropriate opportunity to participate in the decisions being made. A failure to do so may leave it open for the parents of the child concerned, or the child himself, to bring an application under HRA 1998, ss 6, 7 and 8 for breaches of ECHR 1950, Art 6 (right to a fair trial) and Art 8 (right to respect for private and family life) (*Re C (Care Plan: Human Rights Challenge)* [2002] Fam Law 790; *Re G (Care: Challenge to Local Authority's Decision)* [2003] 2 FLR 42; *Venema v The Netherlands* [2003] 1 FLR 552). See further **Procedure for raising issues under the Human Rights Act 1998** above and annotation to HRA 1998. *Re L (Care: Assessment: Fair Trial)* [2002] 2 FLR 730 sets out useful guidelines for local authorities and all professionals concerned in care proceedings as to the proper conduct and recording of meetings and the provision of documents. In January 2013, the Children Act Sub-Committee of the Law Society has published guidance entitled *Attendance of Solicitors at Local Authority Children Act Meetings*, which provides guidance on the role and professional conduct of solicitors representing all parties at such meetings.

Removal of babies at birth—The separation of a newborn baby from his mother is unlawful where there is no prior judicial sanction, no suggestion that the mother poses a risk of exposing him to immediate physical attack or physical harm and no medical justification for the intervention (*R (G) v Nottingham City Council and Nottingham University Hospital* [2008] 1 FLR 1668). However, in an appropriate case the court may, in the public interest and for the proper protection of a public authority, grant anticipatory relief that a proposed course of conduct is lawful or unlawful. In *Re D (Unborn Baby)* [2009] 2 FLR 313, the court granted a declaration that the authority was acting lawfully and in accordance with ECHR 1950 in not engaging the parents in the planning process in the way that Art 8 would normally require. The circumstances of the case were exceptional in that the experts considered that the mother posed a severe risk to the child, herself and others and was likely to react adversely and harm both herself and the baby immediately after birth. The authority therefore sought a declaration that it was lawful to conceal the nature of their birth plan from the mother before the point at which, immediately following the birth, the child was removed. The court has jurisdiction to injunct a local authority from separating mother and child under HRA 1998, s 8(1) (*Re H (Care Plan: Human Rights)* [2012] 1 FLR 191).

Intervention by court after making of care order—Once a care order has been made the responsibility for the child is transferred to the local authority, removing it from the control of the court even in cases where, for example, a judge feels that it is necessary for the court to monitor the progress of the child in care, or where a care plan goes wrong at an early stage (see *A Local Authority v K and others* [2012] 1 FLR 765). ACA 2002, s 118, has amended CA 1989, s 26(2)(e) (requirement to consider the discharge of a care order) to encompass a requirement for the authority to review the care plan and revise it as necessary, together with a route for returning it to the court through the intervention of a Cafcass officer where appropriate. See further **Adoption and Children Act 2002 – review of cases of looked-after children** under CA 1989, s 26. A remedy also exists under HRA 1998, ss 6, 7 and 8 on the basis that the process adopted by the authority is incompatible with ECHR 1950, Art 8 (the right to respect for family life), and Art 6 (right to a fair trial) (*Re S (Minors) (Care Order: Implementation of Care Plan)*; *Re W (Minors) (Care Order: Adequacy of Care Plan)* [2002] 1 FLR 815; *Re C (Care Plan: Human Rights*

Challenge) [2002] Fam Law 790). See further **Procedure for raising issues under the Human Rights Act 1998** above, annotation to HRA 1998 and FPR 2010, r 29.5.

Where adoption is the preferred option—Local authorities must follow the Local Authority Circular of 28 August 1998 (LAC(98)20) *"Adoption – Achieving the Right Balance"*, paragraphs 28–33 of which were reissued in an amended form in *Chief Inspector Letter* of June 1999 (CI(99)6). Where adoption is the probable option, the courts will need to be advised of the likely steps and time-scales required to implement the plan. Paragraph 29 of the amended Circular provides that where the choice of placement depends significantly on findings of fact then, even though it may be difficult to effect much preparatory work concerning possible adoptive placement before the final hearing, it should still be possible to explain within the care plan the key steps that would need to be taken before an adoptive placement could be made and give estimated time-scales for each of these steps. Even where the facts of the care application are not disputed and the preferred option is adoption, paragraph 30 makes it clear that local authorities must have satisfied themselves that sufficient assessment has taken place in order to rule out rehabilitation or placement with relatives, for example, under a s 8 residence order. In those cases in which the local authority has ruled out rehabilitation or placement with relatives and has confirmed adoption as the preferred option, paragraph 31 sets out the steps which should always have been addressed before the final care hearing, including:

(a) the co-ordination of information between the team responsible for the care proceedings application and those responsible for family finding;
(b) the completion, as far as possible, of the BAAF Form E giving details about the child;
(c) consideration of the case by the adoption panel with a view to making a recommendation on whether adoption is in the child's best interests;
(d) the identification by the local authority of the key steps and timetable which would lead to an adoptive placement if the court made a care order;
(e) a contingency plan to be used if the preferred option for adoption cannot be achieved.

Procedure for adoption—The ACA 2002 governs the legal process for placing a child for adoption. A placement order authorises the local authority to place a child with prospective adopters (ACA 2002, ss 18–29). The ACA 2002, s 1(2) makes the child's welfare the court's paramount concern in all decisions relating to adoption, bringing the law into line with the guiding principle in CA 1989, s 1(1). Thus a court hearing applications for care and placement orders at the same time is able to hear all the evidence needed for both orders in the course of one hearing, adopting the paramountcy principle for both issues.

Linked care and placement orders—On 7 July 2008, the Safeguarding Committee of the Family Justice Council issued further guidance for "Linked Care and Placement Order Applications", building on the guidance of 29 January 2007. which addressed the practical difficulties that arise where an authority has issued care proceedings but is unable/unwilling to issue an application for a placement order until all of the relevant assessments are concluded (see *www.judiciary.gov.uk/about-the-judiciary/advisory-bodies/fjc*). The updated guidance accepts that the emphasis within the PLO on a speedier and more focused process places greater strains on the local authority panel process. However, it emphasises that there will be some cases (perhaps only a few) where, even before the local authority commences care proceedings, it has a clear plan for adoption. In these cases the local authority must ensure that a placement order application is issued simultaneously with, or as soon as possible after, the issue of care proceedings so that the court can determine the placement order application at the same hearing as the care case without any undue delay. Guidance is given about judicial case management, local authority procedures, the duties of local authority solicitors, the duties of parents' legal advisors and the duties of the child's guardian to ensure that both care and placement order applications are kept "on track" and that appropriate and timely directions are given and implemented.

Concurrent planning—"Concurrent planning" describes a scheme whereby the local authority choose foster parents who are trained and willing to foster children on the basis that they work with the natural family towards rehabilitation, but who in the event that rehabilitation is ruled out wish to adopt the children. The aim is to reduce the number of moves a child experiences while in care and to reduce temporary placements so that children can achieve permanence, whether rehabilitated with their family or with the foster family, with minimum disruption. Bracewell J explained in *Re D and K (Care Plan: Twin Track Planning)* [1999] 2 FLR 872, at [875C], that "contact between carers and birth children is encouraged and there is openness between the parties, about the primary aim of rehabilitation with the alternative secondary plan of permanent placement". Therefore, in cases in which concurrent planning takes place it is vital that the two options are clearly explained to the natural family from the outset and that they are reassured that it in no way pre-empts the outcome of the care proceedings. Her Ladyship emphasised (at [875D]): "Not every case will be suitable for such placement. Generally it is likely to apply to babies or young children where there are some but by no means optimistic prospects in relation to rehabilitation to the natural family." There are currently five projects in the UK offering concurrent

planning. Of these, two are provided in the voluntary sector and three are local authority projects. There
are concerns among those who are resistant to concurrent planning that unless it is implemented very
carefully, and appropriately resourced, the very fact of being within the process runs the risk of having a
negative impact on the prospects of the child returning to the birth family. Research into these projects has
been conducted by the Coram charitable foundation (see *www.coram.org.uk*). For an example of the
application of concurrent planning in relation to a 15-year-old mother and her baby see *B Metropolitan
Borough Council v H (Goodman Project: Concurrent Planning)* [2000] Fam Law 237.

See also **Where adoption is the preferred option** and **Procedure for adoption** (above).

Teenage mothers and their children—The case of *Re R (Child of a Teenage Mother)* [2000] 2 FLR 660
sets out guidelines to be followed by local authorities in the very difficult cases dealing with teenage
mothers and their babies.

Social work practice—In *Re E (Care Proceedings: Social Work Practice)* [2000] 2 FLR 254, Bracewell J
set out guidance in relation to social work practice in the light of lessons learned in the case, which
covered a 20-year period of social work intervention with a highly dysfunctional family.

Working Together to Safeguard Children (2010) sets out how individuals and organisations should
work together to safeguard and promote the welfare of children, and *Information Sharing: Practitioners'
Guide* and *Information Sharing: Further Guidance on Legal Issues*. These documents can be found on the
Department for Education website at *www.education.gov.uk/publications*. Pt I of *Working Together 2010*
is issued as statutory guidance and although it does not have the force of statute, generally speaking it
must be followed (*R v London Borough of Islington ex parte Rixon* [1997] ELR 66; *R v Cornwall County
Council ex parte LH* [2000] 1 FLR 236). However, whereas a local authority is bound by the guidance in
Working Together, a judge may proceed without a core assessment or similar social work document where
there is other evidence available to the court that makes it clear that no matter how favourable the social
work assessment may be there are obstacles in the way that prevent the parent caring for his or her child.
Where there are gaps in the material provided by a core assessment, the judge is entitled to disregard them
in the light of the entirety of the evidence that is available (*Re D O'H (Parenting Assessment)* [2012]
2 FLR 713). Where assessments are incomplete at the date of the final hearing, the court will have to look
again at the evidence available and determine afresh whether further assessment is required having
regard, inter alia, to developments since the assessment was ordered, the impact of delay and the totality
of the evidence available. It may transpire that other evidence is available that covers the ground intended
to be covered by the assessment (*Re K (Special Guardianship Order)* [2012] 1 FLR 1265).

Whereas it is inevitable and quite proper for there to be discussions between the members of the local
authority and officers of Cafcass during the currency of a case, such discussions should be (i) rare,
(ii) strictly necessary for the progress of the case, (iii) minuted and (iv) disclosed to all other parties to the
proceedings and available, if necessary, to the court (*A County Council v K, T and C* [2011] 2 FLR 817).

Preparation of public law cases—The PLO is contained in FPR PD12A. See also **First Appointment,
Case management conference** and **Issues Resolution Hearing** under FPR 2010, r 12.25. Important
guidance as to the preparation of public law cases by local authorities and other parties is contained in
Re R (Care: Disclosure: Nature of Proceedings) [2002] 1 FLR 755 and in *Re L (Care: Assessment: Fair
Trial)* [2002] 2 FLR 730. The principles underpinning the duty of disclosure on local authorities in public
law cases are clearly and comprehensively summarised by Baker J in *Kent County Council v A Mother, F
and X, X and Z (IR Intervener)* [2011] EWHC 402 (Fam) at [153]–[158]. Whereas it is possible to make
an application for disclosure against a local authority under the provisions of the Data Protection
Act 1998, applications for disclosure against the local authority in family proceedings are best made by
reference to the general common law principles governing disclosure in such proceedings. In
SM v A Local Authority [2012] 1 FLR 974, Admin Wyn-Williams J dealt with an application by a mother
seeking an order compelling the local authority to disclose material concerning the children into ongoing
public and private family proceedings pursuant to the provisions of the Data Protection Act 1998.
Wyn-Williams J held that, while he had jurisdiction to deal with the mother's application under Data
Protection Act 1998, ss 7 and 35, the application would be more appropriately determined by the family
judge, preferably in accordance with the rules of disclosure that govern private and public law family
proceedings.

Basic Guidance to Good Practice in Care Proceedings across London—This guidance highlights the
basic requirements of good practice during the currency of care proceedings in London. It was issued by
DJ Richard Harper and HHJ John Altman and came into effect in October 2010.

Care Monitoring System—The Care Monitoring System (CMS) is a judicially led management
information programme intended to provide accurate ongoing information about case volumes, case
progress and allocation. The programme is intended to assist judges, legal advisers and magistrates to
focus on avoiding delay for children and to help identify the real causes of delay. The system has been
piloted nationwide since 2 April 2012, from which date all new care and supervision cases are entered

onto the system and orders are required to contain information that is monitored by the system, in particular the timetable for the child expressed as the expected number of weeks necessary to conclude the proceedings. In preparation for the reforms contemplated by the family modernisation programme, all cases are given a standard 26-week timetable on issue.

"suffering " and "is likely to suffer" (s 31(2)(a))—The first limb of s 31(2)(a) (suffering significant harm) predicates an existing state of affairs: that the child is suffering significant harm. The relevant time for this purpose is the date of the care order application or, if temporary protective arrangements have been continuously in place from an earlier date, the date when those arrangements were initiated (*Re M (A Minor) (Care Order: Threshold Conditions)* [1994] 2 FLR 577). However, the local authority does not have to be in possession of all the information it wishes to rely upon at the date of the application. Evidence-gathering continues after proceedings have begun and later acquired information as to the state of affairs at the relevant date can be taken into account (*Re G (Care Proceedings: Threshold Conditions)* [2001] 2 FLR 1111). In *Re G*, Hale LJ identified three different sets of circumstances where this issue might arise: (i) where information is discovered after the relevant date that throws light on what the facts were at the relevant date; (ii) entirely new events may indicate a completely different risk that did not exist at the relevant date; and (iii) where there are new events that may or may not be capable of proving that there was a risk of significant harm at the relevant time. The relevant time for the second limb (likely to suffer significant harm) is the same (*Southwark LBC v B* [1998] 2 FLR 1095, FD).

"designated local authority" (s 31(8))—The construction of s 31(8) and s 105(6) was considered by the Court of Appeal in *Northamptonshire CC v Islington LBC* [1999] 2 FLR 881, which held that the two sections should be construed so as to provide a simple mechanism for designation. To ensure that s 31(8) provided a test applicable in all cases it was legitimate to construe s 31(8)(b) as though it read "where the child does not ordinarily reside" in a local authority area, inserting the word "ordinarily". The preferred approach to periods which had to be disregarded under s 105(6) was notionally to extend the child's residence in the authority area where he or she had been ordinarily resident immediately before the commencement of the disregard period. By virtue of ss 31(8)(a) and 105(6), this simple test will identify the local authority to be designated in the care order. If there are exceptional circumstances, such as developments affecting the family during the period to be disregarded (e g the movement of the entire family into a different authority area) then these could be considered. If the child has no ordinary residence, the designated local authority will be the one for the principal area in which the primary circumstances that led to the care order being made occurred. Thorpe LJ emphasised that the function of the judge was limited to carrying out a rapid and not over-sophisticated review of the history in order to make a purely factual determination of the child's place of ordinary residence or, if there was no place of ordinary residence, of the place where the case was carried over the s 31 threshold, and to designate a local authority accordingly. It is open to the court to hold that a newborn baby is incapable of ordinary residence apart from the mother, so that the baby's ordinary residence is the same as that of the mother (*C (A Child) v Plymouth County Council* [2000] 1 FLR 875). For the purpose of designation, the time to consider a child's ordinary residence is at the time the matter is being considered by the court and not, for example, at the time of commencement of proceedings (*London Borough of Redbridge v Newport City Council* [2004] 2 FLR 226). A designation of a local authority at an interim hearing is subject to reconsideration and possible variation at a later date. In *Sheffield County Council v Bradford MBC* [2013] Fam Law 32, Bodey J held that the repeal of CA 1989, s 23 meant that the decision of the Court of Appeal in *Re H (Care Order: Appropriate Local Authority)* [2004] 1 FLR 534 that a child placed with relatives ceases to be "provided with accommodation by or on behalf of a local authority" within the meaning of CA 1989, s 105(6) could no longer be considered correct. Under CA 1989, s 22C, a child placed with a relative is "provided with accommodation by the local authority" for the purposes of s 105(6) and the disregard period has to be applied. For the principles governing the designation of local authorities in the context of special guardianship support services, see CA 1989, s 14F and *Re D (Local Authority Responsibility)* [2012] EWCA Civ 627 and *Suffolk County Council v Nottinghamshire County Council* [2012] EWCA Civ 1640.

Where it is clear that a care order, if made, would designate a local authority other than the applicant authority, full and early liaison needs to take place between the authorities and the care plan must be prepared in co-operation between them. Even if the second authority is not present or represented throughout the hearing, proper arrangements should be made in advance for a representative of the authority to attend court to deal with any issues that might arise and to assure the court and the parents of the authority's commitment to the care plan and its capacity to implement it (*L v London Borough of Bexley* [1996] 2 FLR 595, FD and see *Suffolk County Council v Nottinghamshire County Council* (above) *on the need for local authorities to cooperate in respect of special guardianship support services under the* CA 1989). The arrangements for contact which the court has to consider under s 34(11) before making a care order are the arrangements proposed by the authority into whose care the child would be placed. *Re C (Care Order: Appropriate Local Authority)* [1997] 1 FLR 544 endorsed *L v London Borough of Bexley*. See further under s 105 and **Habitual residence** under CACA 1985, Sch 1, Art 4.

"ordinarily resident" (s 31(6),(8))—See under s 105(6) and **Habitual residence** under CACA 1985, Sch 1, Art 4.

"any person authorised by order of the Secretary of State" (s 31(9))—No person has yet been so authorised.

Degree of "significant harm" to be proved (s 31(2),(9))—CA 1989, s 31 defines the nature of the harm that may be suffered, but does not indicate the necessary degree of that harm. In the original guidance to CA 1989 issued by the Department of Health *The Children Act 1989: Guidance and Regulations (Volume 1, Court Orders)* (HMSO 1991) at para 3.21 it was stated that: "Minor shortcomings in health care or minor deficits in physical, psychological or social development should not require compulsory intervention unless cumulatively they are having, or are likely to have, serious and lasting effects on the child". The Court of Appeal in *Re MA (Care Threshold)* [2010] 1 FLR 431 considered the dividing line between "harm" and "significant harm" and held that the harm must be significant enough to justify the intervention of the State and disturb the autonomy of the parents to bring up their children by themselves in the way they choose. It must be significant enough to enable the court to make a care or supervision order if the welfare of the child so demands. Although ECHR, Art 8 has more relevance at the disposal stage, it nonetheless informs the meaning of "significant" and serves to emphasise that there must be a "relevant and sufficient" reason for crossing the threshold, and the interference itself has to be proportionate to the need (see *K and T v Finland* [2001] 2 FLR 707; and *Scozzari and Giunta v Italy* (2002) 35 EHRR 243; *Kutzner v Germany* (2002) 35 EHRR 653). In *Re L (Care: Threshold Criteria)* [2007] 1 FLR 2050 the court had been wrong to suggest that the threshold for establishing significant harm was comparatively low. Ward LJ gave a useful analysis of the meaning of "significant", citing the dictionary definition of "considerable, noteworthy or important" and reviewing the evolution of the concept within CA 1989. He also analysed the House of Lords decision in *Re H and R (Minors) (Child Sexual Abuse: Standard of Proof)* [1996] 1 FLR 80 and concluded that where the issue was whether or not there was a likelihood of harm Lord Nicholls had made it clear that there still had to be a "real possibility of significant harm". See also the speech of Baroness Hale in *Re B (Children) (Care Proceedings: Standard of Proof)* [2008] 2 FLR 141 where she referred to the "unacceptable risk of harm".

Extended definition of "harm" (s 31(9))—The definition has been extended by ACA 2002, s 120 to include "impairment suffered from seeing or hearing the ill-treatment of another". As a consequence, the court forms for applications in respect of a child have been amended to include questions relating to harm.

Agreed orders—The agreement of the parties cannot deprive the court of its duty to satisfy itself by evidence that the strict criteria for a care order have been fulfilled, but the degree of investigation required of the court will vary from case to case, and the factors relevant to the exercise of that discretion are set out in *A County Council v DP, RS, BS by his Children's Guardian* [2005] 2 FLR 1031. Where the parties are agreed on a care order and also as to the factual substratum underlying the fulfilment of the threshold criteria, the court's duty may be discharged by perusing the documents and approving the agreed order (*Devon County Council v S* [1992] 2 FLR 244).

In some cases parents are prepared to make concessions in relation to the threshold criteria and do not seek to argue as to the disposal of the case, but other parties do not agree that the concessions reflect the nature of the case appropriately. It is a matter for the discretion of the judge as to whether the concessions are sufficient to meet the justice of the matter and the best interests of the children (*Re B (Agreed Findings of Fact)* [1998] 2 FLR 968 – concessions accepted as sufficient; *Re M (Threshold Criteria: Parental Concessions)* [1999] 2 FLR 728 – parents only made anodyne concessions and it was necessary for a finding of fact hearing to be held to determine the true factual basis on which the threshold criteria were satisfied; *Re W (Children) (Threshold Criteria: Parental Concessions)* [2001] 1 FCR 139 – parental concessions held to be inadequate because they had not accepted any responsibility for the children's sexualised behaviour and therefore there was no firm basis upon which to deal with future applications by the parents for contact with the children). Where parents agree with the local authority to make concessions, this in no way ties the hands of the judge and arguments by the parents of "issue estoppel" are wholly inappropriate (*Re D (Child: Threshold Criteria)* [2001] 1 FLR 274 – where the experts were unable to advise on issues of child protection without a preliminary judicial determination of the core factual issue). In *Re T (Care Order)* [2009] 2 FLR 574 the Court of Appeal held that there must be strong and cogent reasons to force upon a local authority a more draconian order than that for which they had asked, particularly when the guardian supports a less draconian order as appropriate to the child's needs. No such strong and cogent reasons were demonstrated in this case. That said, the power to make a care order where the application had been for a supervision order was not "neutered by an agreement reached between the parties outside the court". What is important is that the court examines the background facts and reasons underlying the agreement and justifies the order made, particularly where this involves departing from professional assessment and guidance.

In determining whether further investigation is appropriate and deciding upon the extent of that investigation, the court will take into account the circumstances of the case including the interests of the children, whether there is likely to be future litigation in which the disputed facts would be relevant, the relevance of the disputed allegations to the local authority's care plan and management of the case, the time likely to be spent investigating any given issue and the cost to public funds of the investigation, the likely evidential result of the investigation and the emotional toll of the court hearing. See also *Re K (Supervision Orders)* [1999] 2 FLR 303.

In *Re C (A Minor) (Care Order: Appeal)* [1996] 1 FCR 332, FD, it was pointed out that it was unhelpful to have no findings as to the facts underlying the s 31 conditions and that, where the parties agree that the threshold criteria are met, they should at the very least be invited by the court to agree the factual basis for this and to acknowledge it by the signature of the parties or of the legal representatives. Similarly, in *Oxfordshire County Council v L* [1998] 1 FLR 70, it was observed that, even where the s 31 threshold was conceded, it was the court's duty to be satisfied that the circumstances under s 31(2) were met and therefore generally appropriate for the court to record the basis upon which this was so. Sometimes it may do so by making its own findings of fact upon the agreed evidence. Sometimes it may do so by reference to an agreed statement of facts. Without such a statement, it was difficult to know what the basis for making an order had been. In *Stockport MBC v D* [1995] 1 FLR 873, Thorpe J expressed the view that, where orders were made without judicial investigation on oral evidence, it would be inappropriate for the court to make findings of fact; he chose to deal with the matter by simply accepting the formal admissions made by the parents and pronouncing the orders sought.

Summary disposal by judge may not be appropriate—In care proceedings where there are issues that require a full investigation and are likely to have a direct impact on the case it is inappropriate for the judge to summarily dismiss them (*Re H (Children)* [2002] EWCA Civ 1692).

Split hearings—In May 2010 the President of the Family Division issued *Guidance in Relation to Split Hearings* (see Part V). This applies to both private and public law proceedings and warns that split hearings are taking place when they need not do so. Judges are reminded that a fact-finding hearing should only be ordered if the court takes the view that the case cannot properly be decided without one (para 7). Practitioners will also find it useful to refer to *Re S (Care Proceedings: Split Hearing)* [1996] 2 FLR 773, FD, *Re P (Care Proceedings: Split Hearings)* [2007] EWCA Civ 1265, *Re C (Domestic Violence: Fact-finding Hearing)* [2010] 1 FLR 1728 and *A Local Authority v K and N* [2011] 2 FLR 1165. All public law applications issued by local authorities under CA 1989, Pt IV (care and supervision orders) are subject to the time limits contained in the PLO (PD12A); see and **First appointment, Case management conference** and **Issues resolution hearing** under FPR 2010, r 12.25. The outcome of a fact-finding hearing provides an essential foundation for resolving welfare issues and determining the future care of the children (*Re B and H (Children)* [2012] EWCA Civ 1359).

In preparing for a split hearing it is essential that the local authority defines precisely what facts it is inviting the court to find (*CL v East Riding Yorkshire Council, MB and BL (A Child)* [2006] 2 FLR 24). Once findings of fact are made, any further assessments that are necessary can be timetabled.

Where the local authority's schedule of proposed findings has been prepared with care and the hearing itself has been the subject of a directions appointment, it requires very good reasons for the judge to depart from the schedule of proposed findings. Where the judge wishes to make findings of fact not contained within the schedule or sought by the authority, he must ensure that those findings are securely founded in evidence and that the fairness of the fact-finding process is not compromised (*Re G and B (Fact-Finding Hearing)* [2009] 1 FLR 1145 and see *Re J-L* [2012] EWCA Civ 1832). Nonetheless, a judge is not limited to expert evidence; he or she can, for example, include their own assessment of credibility. Furthermore, issues that have not been known to exist can emerge during oral evidence and in these cases it would be absurd if such matters had to be ignored. Judges need to apply a rigorous intellectual discipline to fact-finding hearings to ensure that they do not overstep the mark and address questions more fitted to the welfare stage of the proceedings, when the judge considers the best, or least worst, outcome for the child in the light of the findings made and the assessments undertaken by others consequent upon them (*Re L 'Care Proceedings: Risk Assessment)* [2010] 1 FLR 790). The difficulties created by the fact that a parent has learning difficulties is not a valid reason for abandoning a fact-finding hearing (*Re B and H (Children)* [2012] EWCA Civ 1359). However, where a parent has learning difficulties or limited cognitive abilities, the court should consider the use of special measures during the fact-finding hearing in order to facilitate that parent giving evidence. A failure to follow recommendations for such measures may breach the parent's right to a fair trial under Art 6 (*Re M (A Child)* [2012] EWCA Civ 1905). The court should make the appropriate findings without regard to the gravity of the consequences of doing so (*Re D (Children)* [2012] EWCA Civ 1584).

Where there is a split hearing there is nothing wrong in the court determining at the preliminary hearing, in advance of the local authority's final care plan, that a particular individual will not be in a position to care for a child safely within the timescale that the child needs, provided, of course, that the evidence substantiates this conclusion. The split hearing and the subsequent disposal hearing is a single process (*North Yorkshire County Council v B* [2008] 1 FLR 1645). However, the judge should not prejudge the outcome of the care proceedings, however clear that outcome might appear to be (see *Re L*, above), and there will be some cases where the true abilities of an individual to care for a child can only be assessed reliably by a process carried out by relevant professionals outside the court room (*Re S-L* [2011] EWCA Civ 1022).

The court has jurisdiction to hear an appeal from a fact-finding hearing even if there is no order (*Re A (A Child)* [2010] EWCA Civ 1413). Where findings are made at a preliminary hearing but subsequent evidence casts doubts upon them, the judge is entitled to reconsider his findings at the disposal hearing in the light of that new evidence (*Re B and H (Children)* [2003] EWCA Civ 1818). The judge must be astute to express at the preliminary hearing such views as he is able to, in order to assist social workers and psychiatrists in making their assessments and drafting the care plan. To that end, transcripts of judgments given at the preliminary hearing should always be made available when required so that reliance does not have to be placed on summaries or even bare statements of conclusions (*Re O and N: Re B* [2003] 1 FLR 1169, at [35]). After a judge has given judgment, counsel have a positive duty to raise with the judge not just any alleged deficiency in the judge's reasoning process but also any genuine query or ambiguity that arises in relation to the judgment (*Re M (Fact-Finding Hearing: Burden of Proof)* [2009] 1 FLR 1177).

The requirement for judicial continuity in all care cases is a core element of the PLO (FPR PD12A). However, there may be exceptions to judicial continuity, for example, where a judge has died or is ill and it is unlikely to be proportionate or in the interests of the child or in conformity with the overriding objective for the court to start again from scratch. Similar considerations apply where a litigant has legitimately lost confidence in the judge or where there could be an appearance of bias (*Re G and B (Fact-Finding Hearing)* [2009] 1 FLR 1145). Furthermore, where an expert is asked to express an opinion, he must have all the relevant information, including a copy of any judgment given in the case; the summary of a judgment is not sufficient (*Re G (Care Proceedings: Split Trials)* [2001] 1 FLR 872).

Parents can be compelled to give evidence in care proceedings—Parents can be compelled to give evidence in any care proceedings. They have no right to refuse to do so, nor to refuse to answer questions which may incriminate them (*per curiam* in *Re Y and K (Split Hearing: Evidence)* [2003] 2 FLR 273; *R v B County Council ex parte P* [1991] 1 FLR 470) and if they decline to answer questions or to give evidence, the court should usually draw the inference that the allegations made against them are true (*Re O (Care Proceedings: Evidence)* [2004] 1 FLR 161). See further under s 98.

Legal professional privilege—In *Re D (Care Proceedings: Legal Privilege)* [2011] 2 FLR 1183, the Court of Appeal held that where a parent has, when viewed objectively, waived legal professional privilege, then the application of the principle of fairness may demand further disclosure to meet the risk that the parties might otherwise have only a partial and potentially misleading understanding of the material disclosed as a result of the waiver. The undesirability of breaching confidentiality between the parent and his or her legal representatives had to be balanced against the unfairness to the other parties if it was not. Counsel and solicitors ought to be aware of the fact that advice might have been given to prompt a change of attitude by their client and they should be on guard to protect their client from revealing that advice either in written or oral evidence. Judges need to be astute to anticipate an unintentional observation that might result in privilege being waived and should be ready to warn witnesses of any such danger.

Burden and standard of proof—The legal burden of establishing the existence of the threshold conditions in s 31(2) rests on the applicant for a care order. In cases of alleged non-accidental injury, the court should be careful not inadvertently to reverse the burden of proof by requiring a parent to prove that the injuries in question have an innocent explanation as opposed to requiring the local authority to prove that they do not (see *Re M (Children)* [2012] EWCA Civ 1580).

The standard of proof is the ordinary civil standard of balance of probabilities (*Re B (Care Proceedings: Standard of Proof)* [2008] 2 FLR 141; *Re H and Others (Minors) (Sexual Abuse: Standard of Proof)* [1996] 1 FLR 80; *Re M and R (Child Abuse: Expert Evidence)* [1996] 2 FLR 195). If a judge finds it more likely than not that something has taken place, then it is treated as having taken place; if he finds it more likely than not that it has not taken place, then it is treated as not having taken place.

In *Re B (Care Proceedings: Standard of Proof)* [2008] 2 FLR 141, the House of Lords noted that neither the seriousness of the allegation nor the seriousness of the consequences should make any difference to the standard of proof to be applied in determining the facts. There is no "heightened standard" and no legal rule that "the more serious the allegation, the more cogent the evidence needed to prove it". Baroness Hale emphasised that there is no logical or necessary connection between seriousness and probability. In the context of care proceedings this point applies with particular force to the identification of the perpetrator. It may be unlikely that any person looking after a baby would take him by the wrist and swing him against a wall, causing multiple fractures and other injuries. But once the evidence is clear that that is indeed what happened, it ceases to be improbable. Someone looking after the child at the relevant time must have done it. The inherent improbability of the event has no relevance to deciding who that was. The simple balance of probabilities test should be applied.

It is in the public interest that those who cause non-accidental injuries be identified (*Re K (Non-accidental Injuries: Perpetrator: New Evidence)* [2005] 1 FLR 285). The court should not, however, "strain" the evidence before it to identify on the simple balance of probabilities the individual who inflicted the injuries. If it is clear that identification of the perpetrator is not possible and the judge remains genuinely uncertain, then the judge should reach that conclusion (*Re D (Care Proceedings: Preliminary Hearing)* [2009] 2 FLR 668). The Supreme Court in *Re S-B (Children)* [2010] 1 FLR 1161 emphasised that if the judge cannot identify a perpetrator or perpetrators, it is still important to identify the pool of possible perpetrators (para 40) by asking whether the evidence establishes that there is a "likelihood or real possibility" that a given person perpetrated the injuries in question (*North Yorkshire CC v SA* [2003] 2 FLR 849). However, it is not helpful for the judge to give an indication of percentages as to the likelihood that one or other of the pool of possible perpetrators was responsible and judges should be cautious about amplifying a judgment in which they have been unable to identify a specific perpetrator (para 44).

Where the court is satisfied that the child has suffered significant harm, the threshold conditions under CA 1989, s 31(2)(b)(i) will be met in relation to that child even though the court is unable to identify who within the pool of possible perpetrators inflicted the harm: *Lancashire County Council v B* [2000] 1 FLR 583, in which helpful guidance is given as to how evidence needs to be tested to establish the threshold criteria for the purposes of s 31 where the perpetrator is uncertain. In determining whether a person is properly included in the pool of potential perpetrators, it is essential that the court weighs any lies told by that person against any evidence that points away from them having been responsible for the injuries (*H v City and Council of Swansea and Others* [2011] EWCA Civ 195). In these "uncertain perpetrator" cases, the correct approach is for the case to proceed at the welfare stage on the basis that each of the possible perpetrators is treated as such (*Re O and N: Re B* [2003] 1 FLR 1169). The House of Lords held in that case that it would be grotesque if, because neither parent had been proved to be the perpetrator, the court had to proceed at the welfare stage as though the child were not at risk from either parent, even though one or other of them was the perpetrator of significant harm. The judge conducting the welfare hearing should have regard to the facts found at the preliminary hearing when they leave open the possibility that a parent or carer was a perpetrator of proved harm and that conclusion should not be excluded from consideration.

Whether either limb of s 31(2)(a) is satisfied is an issue to be decided by the court on the basis of the facts admitted or proved on the balance of probability before it; suspicion is not sufficient (*Re M and R (Child Abuse: Evidence)* [1996] 2 FLR 195; *Re B and W (Threshold Criteria)* [1999] 2 FLR 833). The range of facts that may properly be taken into account is infinite (see *Re H and Others (Minors) (Sexual Abuse: Standard of Proof)* [1996] 1 FLR 80 at [101B] for examples) and facts that are minor or even trivial if considered in isolation, when taken together may suffice to satisfy the court of harm or the likelihood of future harm. In *Re S-B (Children)* [2010] 1 FLR 1161, the first instance judge had found that the threshold had been crossed in relation to the younger of the two children on the basis that there was a real possibility that the mother had injured the older child. Lady Hale said that this was not a permissible approach to a finding of likelihood of future harm. A prediction of future harm has to be based on findings of actual fact made on the balance of probabilities, since it is only once those facts have been found that the degree of likelihood of future events becomes the "real possibility" required by the test adopted in *Re H* (above). Lady Hale noted that it might have been open to the judge to find the threshold crossed in relation to child B on a different basis, but she did not do so.

The Supreme Court reiterated these principles in *Re J (Children)* [2013] UKSC 9, holding that because a previous finding that a person was within the "pool" of possible perpetrators of established injuries occurring in a prior family unit is a finding made on the basis of a "real possibility" (as opposed to the balance of probabilities), such a finding is not capable by itself of supporting a finding of likelihood of future harm in subsequent proceedings concerning a new family unit. Lady Hale made clear that there must be a clearly established objective basis for interference by the State in family life and, accordingly, that while reasonable suspicion is a sufficient basis for the local authority to investigate and to take interim protective measures, it cannot be a sufficient basis for long-term intervention. Within this context, Lady Hale reiterated that only a finding of fact made on the balance of probabilities is sufficient to ground a finding of likelihood of future harm. The requirement of proven factual foundations on which to base a finding of likelihood of future harm has been described as a precious bulwark against the removal by the State of a child from his or her family (*Re F (Interim Care Order)* [2011] 2 FLR 856 and *Re J*). Lady Hale pointed out in *Re J* that the inability to identify a past perpetrator on the balance of probabilities does not preclude a finding of likelihood of future harm where there are other facts established on the balance of probabilities from which such likelihood could itself be established. In this regard, when the case was before the Court of Appeal, McFarlane LJ stated that in determining whether the threshold criteria are satisfied in relation to children in the new family unit, a judge is under a duty to become acquainted with all of the available evidence and then bring it to bear on the ultimate question of whether, in the context of the particular case, each or any of the children can be said to be "likely to suffer significant harm" attributable to failures in parental care likely to be given to him as at that date. The court is also under a duty to ensure that it has before it not only evidence of what may have happened in one of the parent's lives years before, but also some account of the events in that parent's life during the following years and the current circumstances in the family unit that is now before the court (*Re J (Care Proceedings: Past Possible Perpetrators in a New Family Unit)* [2012] 2 FLR 842). Note in this context that Lady Hale, Lord Hope and Lord Reed suggest that, whereas a person's consignment to the "pool" of possible perpetrators on the basis of a real possibility cannot on its own constitute a factual foundation for the prediction of likelihood of future harm, in combination with other established facts and circumstances it may figure as part of the requisite factual foundation. In partly dissenting judgments in *Re J*, Lord Wilson and Lord Sumption reject this approach as illogical, holding that if, for the purpose of establishing the factual foundation of likelihood of future harm, a person's consignment to the "pool" of possible perpetrators on the basis of a real possibility has a value of zero on its own, it can for that purpose have no greater value in the company of facts established on the balance of probabilities.

It is important for the court to hear proper evidence before making a finding of sexual abuse in the face of a complete and consistent denial by the alleged perpetrator (see *Re D (Sexual Abuse Allegations: Evidence of Adult Victim)* [2002] 1 FLR 723, where the findings of the magistrates were not supported by direct evidence and were overturned on appeal).

"Lucas direction"—Charles J held in *A County Council v K, D and L* [2005] 1 FLR 851 that, in determining the facts in a family case, the court should have regard to the guidance given in *R v Lucas* [1981] QB 720 to the effect that a conclusion that a person is lying or telling the truth about point A does not mean that he is lying or telling the truth about point B (known in criminal proceedings as a *Lucas* direction).

Fabricated or induced illness (FII) in care proceedings—In *Coventry City Council v X, Y and Z (Care Proceedings: Costs)* [2011] 1 FLR 1045, HHJ Bellamy, sitting as a deputy judge of the High Court, drew up a list of points that he considered to be of particular importance where allegations of FII were concerned. These included: (a) before making an allegation of FII a local authority had to be rigorous in satisfying itself that the evidence was capable of establishing the fact of the FII to the requisite standard; (b) in a case of suspected FII, the letter of instruction to the expert should make it clear that he or she should have regard to *Fabricated or Induced Illness by Carers (FII): A Practical Guide for Paediatricians* (Royal College of Paediatricians and Child Health 2009); (c) In reaching the decision to allege FII the authority should normally seek the views of the health professionals involved in the children's care rather than relying on the report of one independent expert; and (d) all of those involved should consider and review the expert's report and raise any relevant points with the expert. In reaching his determination, the judge drew assistance from *LB of Southwark v B* [1993] 2 FLR 559, *Re X (Emergency Protection Orders)* [2006] 2 FLR 701, *Re N (Leave to Withdraw Care Proceedings)* [2000] 1 FLR 134, *Re M (Local Authority's Costs)* [1995] 1 FLR 533 and *Re R (Care: Disclosure: Nature of Proceedings)* [2002] 1 FLR 755 alongside *Fabricated or Induced Illness by Carers* (2002; the report of a working party of the Royal College of Paediatrics and Child Health).

Guidance where one parent has been killed by the other—Cases where one parent has been killed by the other are relatively rare but raise particularly difficult issues. In *Re A and B (One Parent Killed by the Other: Guidance)* [2011] 1 FLR 783 Hogg J gave the following guidance to provide a framework to avoid compounding the very significant harm that the children involved in such cases have already suffered by poor management and unnecessary delay: (1) In all cases where one parent has been killed by the other the threshold criteria will be met; (2) The local authority should give immediate consideration to the issue of proceedings and, whether it considers it appropriate or inappropriate to issue proceedings immediately, it should appoint a social worker specifically for the affected sibling group who should offer immediate practical help and keep the decision under constant review in conjunction with the local authority's legal department; (3) In the majority of cases the surviving parent with parental responsibility will be in custody or otherwise unable to exercise parental responsibility. In the aftermath of the killing there will be strong emotions on both sides of the extended family. It is critical therefore that the local authority is able to undertake that function. Any dispute regarding the responsible designated authority should be resolved at an early stage and should not cause initial assessments to be delayed. It is not appropriate to leave the extended family to attempt to resolve matters through private law proceedings. In the event that the case comes before the court as private law proceedings in the first instance then the court should direct that a Section 37 report is prepared by the relevant local authority; (4) In the event that proceedings are commenced Children's Guardian should be appointed at the earliest available opportunity. (5) Following issue the case should be transferred to the High Court for urgent consideration by a High Court Judge at the first appointment. There should be early and effective consideration of interim placement and contact arrangements by the local authority. Emergency arrangements made in the immediate aftermath of the killing should not be allowed to drift into becoming long term due to a lack of planning. (6) Consideration should be given to the effect of any press coverage on the children. (7) Where there are concurrent criminal proceedings there should be liaison between the local authority solicitor and the CPS case manager. In areas where there is a protocol in place for the joint listing of Criminal and Care Directions that should be utilised. Where there is not, consideration should be given to joint criminal and care case management hearings. Joint case management hearings have been strongly recommended by the Court of Appeal, Criminal Division, in the case of *R v Levey* [2007] 1 FLR 462. Those involved in the case should give consideration to the *Good Practice Guidance Related Family and Criminal Proceedings: A Good Practice Guide* (Editor Ananda Hall). (8) Professionals involved with the family should familiarise themselves with the issues involved in cases where one parent has killed the other and seek specialist guidance and advice from an appropriate Child and Family Psychiatrist or clinical psychologist. It is important that the backdrop of the tragedy against which the decisions are made does not paralyse the professionals involved. (9) The children may be traumatised whether or not they have witnessed the killing. They are likely to require therapeutic help. Carers, whether they are local authority carers or family carers, will require specialist help in managing the children's reaction and a referral to CAMHS for support for the children and the carers should be made expeditiously. If specialist therapeutic input is not available through local services then a referral should be made to an outside service. Where a child is a potential witness in the criminal proceedings there may be an issue as to whether therapy should commence before the child has given evidence. In certain circumstances therapy may be regarded as potentially compromising the child's evidence. There should be careful liaison between those involved in the criminal process and the local authority in those circumstances to ensure that any delay in the provision of therapy to the child is kept to the shortest possible period. (10) If the children are of school age the school should be kept informed of their situation. Consistency of personnel and the regular provision of support and appropriate information to all members of the family and the school by the social work team are particularly important. (11) If the killing has taken place in the family home it will be a crime scene and there may be difficulties for the carers in securing access to the children's belongings. The local authority should liaise with the police in respect of recovery of some of the children's familiar toys and clothes. Immediate financial and practical support for carers should be put in place by the local authority. (12) Contact is the right of the child and expert advice should be sought regarding the planning of contact between the children and other key relatives, particularly in relation to visits to prisons and hospitals. Where there is conflict within the extended family decisions in relation to contact should be made by the court. Communication between the family members can be difficult particularly in the immediate aftermath of the killing, during the criminal trial and when the killer is released from prison. Consideration should be given by the local authority to family group conferencing and help should be offered to members of the family in facilitating communication. (13) Each case should be considered on its own individual facts and the merits of each placement looked at individually. It would be a misreading of the otherwise helpful research in this area (Hendricks/Black et al) to assume that there is a presumption that the family of the perpetrator should be discounted as carers for the child(ren). The research does not advance such a proposition rather it emphasises that it is important to consider each case individually. Assessment of family members who wish to care for children in these circumstances should include not just child psychiatric assessment but consideration should also be given to adult psychological or psychiatric assessment. (14) Where appropriate professionals involved in the assessment should receive a copy of the Judgment so that they are able to reflect on the work that they have done in a particular case.

Multi-agency risk assessment conferences (MARACs)—MARAC meetings collate information about high-risk cases of domestic abuse with a view to creating a coordinated safety plan for the victim and children (if any). The work is case-specific and all relevant agencies will attend or contribute to the conference. MARACs may be a valuable source of information in public law proceedings where domestic abuse towards an adult or a child may be an issue. However, it should be noted that the information shared at MARACs is confidential and will invariably be sensitive in nature. Accordingly, any disclosure of such information should be dealt with by way of an application for disclosure within the proceedings. For the principles governing the disclosure of documents or other information generated by MARACs, see **Multi-agency risk assessment conferences (MARACs) – disclosure in public law and private law proceedings** under FPR 2010 r 12.12.

Care order or supervision order (s 31(5))—Whereas the court has no jurisdiction to compel a local authority to issue an application for an order under s 31 (s 31(1); *Nottinghamshire County Council v P* [1993] 2 FLR 134), once the local authority has issued its application and satisfied the court that the threshold criteria under s 31(2) are met, it is for the court to decide which out of a supervision order or a care order is the more appropriate order to make, if satisfied that an order is in the child's best interests. Thus, if the threshold criteria are satisfied, the court may make a care order where such an order is in the child's best interests even if the applicant local authority does not seek the same (*Re K (Care Order or Residence Order)* [1995] 1 FLR 675; *Re C (Care or Supervision Order)* [1999] 2 FLR 621). It is for the court to decide which order is the more appropriate, but the court should nonetheless satisfy itself that

PART II

very cogent reasons exist before it imposes on a local authority an order that the local authority does not seek (*Oxfordshire County Council v L* [1998] 1 FLR 70; *Re T (Care Order)* [2009] 2 FLR 574).

The protection of the child is the decisive factor when the court is deciding whether to make a care order or a supervision order (*Re D (A Minor) (Care or Supervision Order)* [1993] 2 FLR 423; *Re K (Care Order or Residence Order)* [1995] 1 FLR 675). When determining which of a care order or a supervision order is appropriate, the court should first make a careful assessment of the likelihood of future harm to the child and then weigh that harm against the harm that would follow the child being removed from his parents under a care order (*Re S (Care or Supervision Order)* [1996] 1 FLR 753; *Re V (Care or Supervision Order)* [1996] 1 FLR 776). A care order rather than a supervision order should be made only if the stronger order is necessary for the protection of the child (*Re B (Care or Supervision Order)* [1996] 2 FLR 693). In deciding whether to make a care order or a supervision order in a particular case where the balance between the two is equal, the court should adopt the least interventionist approach (*Re D (Care or Supervision Order)* [2000] Fam Law 600).

The choice between a care order and a supervision order has also to be considered in the light of HRA 1998 and ECHR 1950. The key in each case is to decide whether a supervision order is proportionate as a response to the risk presented (*Re O (Supervision Order)* [2001] 1 FLR 923; *Re C (Care Order or Supervision Order)* [2001] 2 FLR 466). There must be strong and cogent reasons to force upon a local authority a more draconian order than that for which they had asked, particularly when the guardian supported a less draconian order as appropriate to the child's needs (*Re T (Care Order)*, above – in which no such strong and cogent reasons were demonstrated). See further under **Care Orders – ECHR 1950** (above).

Children's guardian has no continuing role after making of care order—Following the repeal of CJCSA 2000, s 12(5)(b) by ACA 2002, there is no longer jurisdiction for a court to provide for a continuing role for a children's guardian following the making of a care order. Therefore, *Re MH (A Child); Re SB and MB (Children)* [2001] 2 FLR 1334, which was based on s 12(5)(b), is no longer a correct statement of the law.

Undertakings and injunctions—The county court has no jurisdiction to grant injunctions in relation to the exercise by local authorities of their statutory powers in public law proceedings (*D v D (County Court: Jurisdiction: Injunctions)* [1993] 2 FLR 802, CA (no jurisdiction to grant order restraining local authority and police from investigating alleged abuse), *Re S and D (Children: Powers of Court)* [1995] 2 FLR 456, CA (no power to add to a supervision order a provision prohibiting the mother from removing the children from foster parents) and *Devon County Council v B* [1997] 1 FLR 591, CA (no jurisdiction to grant an injunction restraining the mother from entering the town where her child who was in care was living)). The High Court's inherent jurisdiction can only be invoked once permission of that court has been obtained under s 100. For further discussion, see the notes to s 100. However, the powers conferred on the High Court by SCA 1981, s 37 are available in support of the rights conferred by CA 1989, s 33, and in particular s 33(3) (the right of the local authority to determine the extent to which a parent may meet his parental responsibility for a child in care) after a care order has been made. Section 100 does not apply to the general statutory power to make injunctions and therefore it is not necessary for the local authority to have permission to apply for such injunctive relief (*Re P (Care Orders: Injunctive Relief)* [2000] 2 FLR 385 – where the local authority sought injunctions ancillary to a care order requiring the parents to allow the child to attend college without interference, and permitting the local authority to monitor the family).

The county court has a statutory jurisdiction under CCA 1984, s 38 to grant injunctions in care proceedings where a care order is made to protect local authority employees from violence and intimidation by the parents (*Tameside Metropolitan Borough Council v M (Injunctive Relief: County Courts: Jurisdiction)* [2001] Fam Law 873; see also *D v D (County Court Jurisdiction: Injunctions)* [1993] 2 FLR 802). The court does not have inherent jurisdiction to accept undertakings in care proceedings. Where appropriate, the agreement or acknowledgements of a party to do or refrain from doing any act may be recorded in a preamble to the order made (*Re B (Supervision Order: Parental Undertaking)* [1996] 1 FLR 676).

As to the partial change that FLA 1996 introduces with regard to undertakings, see under CA 1989, s 38B.

Orders for anonymity of social workers only made in exceptional cases—It has to be recognized that social workers receive threats and actual violence from adults engaged in bitterly contested public law cases at the end of which they face a forced and permanent separation from their children. This is part of their job and it will not generally be possible to obtain an order for anonymity of a social worker involved in such proceedings unless the circumstances are exceptional (*Re W (Care Proceedings: Witness Anonymity)* [2003] 1 FLR 329).

Withdrawal of care proceedings—Care proceedings may only be withdrawn with the permission of the court (FPR 2010, r 29.4). The applicant must file a written request for permission setting out his reasons

(FPR 2010, r 29.4(3)). The court may deal with the written request without a hearing if the other parties have had an opportunity to make written representations to the court about it (FPR 2010, r 29.4(6)). The request may be made orally to the court if the parties are present (FPR 2010, r 29.4(4)). Where the local authority is unable to satisfy the threshold criteria under CA 1989, s 31(2) the application for permission to withdraw will succeed. However, where the threshold could be established, the granting of permission to withdraw depends on the court concluding under CA 1989, s 1(5) that no order is required because withdrawal is consistent with the child's welfare (*Redbridge LBC v B and C and A (Through his Children's Guardian)* [2011] 2 FLR 117). In such circumstances, CA 1989, s 1(1) is engaged in the giving of permission, the use of the welfare checklist in s 1(3) is not mandatory; the application to withdraw care proceedings falls outside s 1(4) and therefore s 1(3) is not engaged. In *WSCC v M, F, W, X, Y and Z* [2011] 1 FLR 188, the court held that in such an application the court should take into account the principles set out in CPR 1998, Pt 1 as to the 'overriding objective' (which has been included in the FPR 2010, r 1.1). A refusal of permission to withdraw in this case would commit the parties to the listed 15-day hearing and, while proportionality could not be allowed to trump welfare, it nonetheless remained a factor to which the court should give proper consideration. Where an application is made to withdraw public law child care proceedings on the basis that to continue them would amount to an interference with the right of the parents of the child concerned under Art 8(1) of the Convention to respect for their private and family life, the court must assess whether such interference is necessary to protect one of the interests set out in Art 8(2) (*Re N (Leave to Withdraw Care Proceedings)* [2000] 1 FLR 134). Where there is a serious conflict between the interests of the child and one of its parents which can only be resolved to the disadvantage of one of them, the interests of the child must prevail under Art 8(2) (*Hendriks v The Netherlands* (1982) 5 EHRR 223).

An application for permission to withdraw care proceedings is made in the course of existing proceedings and, therefore, should be made using the procedure in FPR 2010, rr 18.1–18.13.

31A Care orders: care plans

(1) Where an application is made on which a care order might be made with respect to a child, the appropriate local authority must, within such time as the court may direct, prepare a plan ("a care plan") for the future care of the child.

(2) While the application is pending, the authority must keep any care plan prepared by them under review and, if they are of the opinion some change is required, revise the plan, or make a new plan, accordingly.

(3) A care plan must give any prescribed information and do so in the prescribed manner.

(4) For the purposes of this section, the appropriate local authority, in relation to a child in respect of whom a care order might be made, is the local authority proposed to be designated in the order.

(5) In section 31(3A) and this section, references to a care order do not include an interim care order.

(6) A plan prepared, or treated as prepared, under this section is referred to in this Act as a "section 31A plan".

Amendments—Inserted by ACA 2002, s 121.

Modifications—Section 31A is modified for certain purposes by SI 2010/1898, reg 5(3).

Need to file a care plan—Section 31A places a statutory duty on the local authority to prepare a care plan (known as a "s 31A care plan") in every case in which it seeks a care order. However, the statutory duty does not apply where the authority seeks only an interim care order. The local authority is required by statute to keep the care plan under review and to make changes as and when necessary. The amendment of the care plan during the course of proceedings does not need the consent or permission of the judge; once the amendment has been made the revised plan should be presented to the judge (*Re A (Care Plan)* [2008] 2 FLR 1183).

The care plan must accord with the Care Planning, Placement and Case Review (England) Regulations 2010 (see Part IV), which came into force on 1 April 2011. Part 2 of the Regulations prescribes the contents of the care plan. The care plan must include the long-term plans for the child, must state the arrangements made to meet the child's needs in respect of health, education, emotional and behavioural development, identity, family and social relationships, social presentation and self-care skills and must set out the wishes and feelings of those persons specified in CA 1989, s 22(4). The care plan should contain the name of the Independent Reviewing Officer (IRO) and the IRO should be given a copy of the care plan. The Regulations are accompanied by four sets of statutory guidance, as follows: (1) a revised edition of Vol 2 of the *Children Act 1989 Guidance and Regulations* entitled *Care Planning, Placement and Case Review*, which is statutory guidance in relation to the relevant provisions in the 1989 Act and the 2010 Regulations. It covers each of the elements of care planning required throughout the child's journey in the care system; (2) *IRO Handbook: Statutory Guidance For Local Authorities and Independent Reviewing Officers on Reviewing Arrangements for Looked After Children*, which provides statutory guidance for independent reviewing officers about their distinct responsibilities in relation to looked after children under CA 1989 and the 2010 Regulations, and replaces the 2004 *Independent Reviewing Officers Guidance*; (3) *Statutory Guidance: Securing Sufficient Accommodation for Looked After Children*, which provides guidance for local authorities and their partners about the local authority's duty under CA 1989, s 22G to take steps that secure, so far as reasonably practicable, sufficient accommodation for looked after children within the local authority area; (4) *Short Breaks Statutory Guidance: How to Safeguard and Promote the Welfare of Disabled Children Using Short Breaks,* which sets out how the legal requirements on short break services and support for children in need apply for different settings and arrangements. See also the Public Law Outline (PLO) in PD12A and **First appointment**, **Case management conference** and **Issues resolution hearing** under FPR 2010, r 12.25. Wherever possible, evidence in support of material parts of the care plan should be available and form part of it (for example, where the plan involves a particular foster placement for the child, it should contain a description of the placement and of the foster carers by a worker who has interviewed them and knows them sufficiently to satisfy the court that the placement is suitable – *Re J (Minors) (Care: Care Plan)* [1994] 1 FLR 253, in which much further guidance as to the making of a care plan is also to be found). The court will scrutinise the care plan rigorously and if it is not satisfied that it is in the best interests of the child it can refuse to make a care order (*Re J (Minors) (Care: Care Plan)*, above, *Re T (A Minor) (Care Order: Conditions)* [1994] 2 FLR 423, *Re C (Care Order: Appropriate Local Authority)* [1997] 1 FLR 544). In *Re X; Barnet London Borough Council v Y and X* [2006] 2 FLR 998 Munby J sets out important recommendations concerning the operation of placement panels and the reasoning behind care plans. The difficult issue of when the court relinquishes control of the case to the local authority by making a full care order as opposed to an interim order is dealt with further under s 38 **Interim care order or full care order?**. Where the care order will designate a local authority other than the applicant local authority, the care plan must be prepared in co-operation between the two authorities (*L v London Borough of Bexley* [1996] 2 FLR 595, FD). Reference should be made to the *Handbook of Best Practice in Children Act cases* produced by the Children Act Advisory Committee (see Part V, *Best Practice Guidance of June 1997*) for advice as to the care plan (see paras 7–12).

32 Period within which application for order under this Part must be disposed of

(1) A court hearing an application for an order under this Part shall (in the light of any rules made by virtue of subsection (2)) –

   (a) draw up a timetable with a view to disposing of the application without delay; and

   (b) give such directions as it considers appropriate for the purpose of ensuring, so far as is reasonably practicable, that that timetable is adhered to.

(2) Rules of court may –

   (a) specify periods within which specified steps must be taken in relation to such proceedings; and

   (b) make other provision with respect to such proceedings for the purpose of ensuring, so far as is reasonably practicable, that they are disposed of without delay.

Avoidance of delay—This section forces the court to take a firm hold of the case, to lay down a procedural timetable and give appropriate directions (under FPR 2010, r 12.12) to ensure that the application in question is determined without delay. Both practitioners and courts have a duty to avoid delay in children cases. All public law applications issued by local authorities under CA 1989, Pt IV (care and supervision orders) are subject to the time limits contained in the PLO in PD12A, and the court will direct the parties to monitor compliance with the court's directions and tell the court about any failure to comply with a direction by the court and any other delay in the proceedings (FPR 2010, r 12.24). For details see annotations **First appointment**, **Case management conference**, **Issues resolution hearing** under FPR 2010, r 12.25. See further the notes on continuity of judge and legal representatives and on the timetable for proceedings under FPR 2010, r 12.12. A children's guardian has a duty to review the file regularly and, if the case is not making satisfactory progress, should apply for further directions (*Re A and B (Minors) (No 2)* [1995] 1 FLR 351; *Re O (Care: Delay)* [2001] Fam Law 339). Where an assessment is in progress, it may be right to timetable the proceedings to enable them to be concluded as soon as possible once the assessment is completed; the fact that the timetable might need to be revised is not of itself a reason not to timetable (*E v Humberside County Council and S* [1996] Fam Law 444, FD). In *Re JC (Care Proceedings: Procedure)* [1995] 2 FLR 77, FD, it was stressed that all those who wish to participate in caring for a child need to make their position clear as soon as possible; otherwise, delay can result, for example because the local authority has not been able to assess the suitability of potential carers. The benefits of split hearings in reducing delay must be borne in mind, see **Split hearings** under s 31. Where there are criminal proceedings pending the family court will need to be made aware of the current state of the criminal investigation and criminal process (if there is a prosecution) at every stage so that it can make a fully informed decision about the extent to which the duty with regard to timetabling can be fulfilled (see *Re A and B (Minors) (No 2)*, above, and the annotation on delay, under s 1). See **Concurrent planning** under CA 1989, s 31 for discussion of twin track planning as a strategy for reducing delay and **Care monitoring system** under CA 1989, s 31 for discussion of the judicially led CMS management information programme intended to provide accurate ongoing information about case volumes, case progress and allocation.

Care orders

33 Effect of care order

(1) Where a care order is made with respect to a child it shall be the duty of the local authority designated by the order to receive the child into their care and to keep him in their care while the order remains in force.

(2) Where –

(a) a care order has been made with respect to a child on the application of an authorised person; but

(b) the local authority designated by the order was not informed that that person proposed to make the application,

the child may be kept in the care of that person until received into the care of the authority.

(3) While a care order is in force with respect to a child, the local authority designated by the order shall –

(a) have parental responsibility for the child; and

(b) have the power (subject to the following provisions of this section) to determine the extent to which

(i) a parent, guardian or special guardian of the child; or

(ii) a person who by virtue of section 4A has parental responsibility for the child

may meet his parental responsibility for him.

(4) The authority may not exercise the power in subsection (3)(b) unless they are satisfied that it is necessary to do so in order to safeguard or promote the child's welfare.

(5) Nothing in subsection (3)(b) shall prevent a person mentioned in that provision who has care of the child from doing what is reasonable in all the circumstances of the case for the purpose of safeguarding or promoting his welfare.

(6) While a care order is in force with respect to a child, the local authority designated by the order shall not –

(a) cause the child to be brought up in any religious persuasion other than that in which he would have been brought up if the order had not been made; or

(b) have the right –

(i) (*repealed*)

      (ii)   to agree or refuse to agree to the making of an adoption order, or an order under section 84 of the Adoption and Children Act 2002, with respect to the child; or

     (iii)   to appoint a guardian for the child.

(7) While a care order is in force with respect to a child, no person may –

    (a)   cause the child to be known by a new surname; or

    (b)   remove him from the United Kingdom,

without either the written consent of every person who has parental responsibility for the child or the leave of the court.

(8) Subsection (7)(b) does not –

    (a)   prevent the removal of such a child, for a period of less than one month, by the authority in whose care he is; or

    (b)   apply to arrangements for such a child to live outside England and Wales (which are governed by paragraph 19 of Schedule 2).

(9) The power in subsection (3)(b) is subject (in addition to being subject to the provisions of this section) to any right, duty, power, responsibility or authority which a person mentioned in that provision has in relation to the child and his property by virtue of any other enactment.

Amendments—ACA 2002, s 139(1), Sch 3, paras 54, 63, Sch 5.

Defined terms—"authorised person": s 31(9); "care order": ss 31(11), 105(1); "child", "guardian", "local authority": s 105(1); "parental responsibility": ss 3, 105(1).

Effect of s 33(3)—The effect of s 33(3) is to prevent the exercise of parental responsibility adverse to the views of the local authority, subject to the provisions of s 33(4)–(9) (see *A Local Authority v A, B and E* [2012] 2 FLR 601). A local authority does not have the power to prevent a mother entering into a parental responsibility agreement with the father under CA 1989, s 4(1)(b) because that facility to enter an agreement is self-contained and does not depend on the exercise of parental responsibility (*Re X (Parental Responsibility Agreement: Children in Care)* [2000] 1 FLR 517).

The Care Planning, Placement and Case Review (England) Regulations 2010 (see Part IV)—These Regulations came into force on 1 April 2011 and they revoke, inter alia, the Placement of Children with Parents etc Regulations 1991. They make provision about care planning for looked-after children, whether or not they are in the care of the local authority by virtue of care order, and associated matters. Pt 4 concerns particular types of placement, with parents, with local authority foster parents and other arrangements.

Religious upbringing (s 33(6)(a))—Section 33(6)(a) must be construed in a subtle and careful way. The local authority is bound to ensure that the child is brought up in the religious persuasion of the parents, but it is also bound to have regard to any change of religion, even if only one parent changes (*Re A and D (Local Authority: Religious Upbringing)* [2011] 1 FLR 615).

New surname (s 33(7))—In *Re J (A Minor) (Change of Name)* [1993] 1 FLR 699, an application under s 33(7)(a) was dealt with without notice and without the appointment of a children's guardian, as would normally be required in accordance with s 41.

In *Re M, T, P, K and B (Care: Change of Name)* [2000] 2 FLR 645 the court held that a similar approach should be adopted for public law and private law cases and the principles established in private law change of name cases should not be ignored. On any application to change a child's surname the welfare of the children concerned was paramount. In addition to the welfare check list factors the court should give very careful consideration to: (i) the wishes, feelings, needs and objectives of the applicant; (ii) the motives and stated objections of the respondents; and (iii) the opinion of the children's guardian. If a foster carer wishes to change a child's name (forename or surname) he should consult the local authority and the parents' views should be sought. If necessary, an application should be made to the court (*Re D, L and LA (Care: Change of Forename)* [2003] 1 FLR 339). See **Change of surname** under s 8, for details of the private law approach to a change of name.

Method of application for permission under s 33(7)—An application for permission to cause a child to be known by a new surname or to remove him from the UK should be commenced in a magistrates' court (ATPO 2008, art 5(2)(e), subject to the exceptions set out in that article and in art 15(1)(i)). In *MH v GP (Child: Emigration)* [1995] 2 FLR 106, FD, it was held, however, that a private law application for permission to remove a child permanently from the jurisdiction should not be heard by magistrates but should be transferred for determination either in a county court or the High Court, depending on the complexity and difficulty of the decision; a similar course should no doubt be considered in public law cases. The application for permission should be commenced in accordance with FPR 2010, rr 18.1–18.13.

34 Parental contact etc with children in care

(1) Where a child is in the care of a local authority, the authority shall (subject to the provisions of this section) allow the child reasonable contact with –

    (a)   his parents;

    (b)   any guardian or special guardian of his;

    (ba) any person who by virtue of section 4A has parental responsibility for him;

    (c)   where there was a residence order in force with respect to the child immediately before the care order was made, the person in whose favour the order was made; and

    (d)   where, immediately before the care order was made, a person had care of the child by virtue of an order made in the exercise of the High Court's inherent jurisdiction with respect to children, that person.

(2) On an application made by the authority or the child, the court may make such order as it considers appropriate with respect to the contact which is to be allowed between the child and any named person.

(3) On an application made by –

    (a)   any person mentioned in paragraph (a) to (d) of subsection (1); or

    (b)   any person who has obtained the leave of the court to make the application,

the court may make such order as it considers appropriate with respect to the contact which is to be allowed between the child and that person.

(4) On an application made by the authority or the child, the court may make an order authorising the authority to refuse to allow contact between the child and any person who is mentioned in paragraphs (a) to (d) of subsection (1) and named in the order.

(5) When making a care order with respect to a child, or in any family proceedings in connection with a child who is in the care of a local authority, the court may make an order under this section, even though no application for such an order has been made with respect to the child, if it considers that the order should be made.

(6) An authority may refuse to allow the contact that would otherwise be required by virtue of subsection (1) or an order under this section if –

    (a)   they are satisfied that it is necessary to do so in order to safeguard or promote the child's welfare; and

    (b)   the refusal –

        (i)   is decided upon as a matter of urgency; and

        (ii) does not last for more than seven days.

(7) An order under this section may impose such conditions as the court considers appropriate.

(8) The Secretary of State may by regulations make provision as to –

    (a)   the steps to be taken by a local authority who have exercised their power under subsection (6);

    (b)   the circumstances in which, and conditions subject to which, the terms of any order under this section may be departed from by agreement between the local authority and the person in relation to whom the order is made;

    (c)   notification by a local authority of any variation or suspension of arrangements made (otherwise than under an order under this section) with a view to affording any person contact with a child to whom this section applies.

(9) The court may vary or discharge any order made under this section on the application of the authority, the child concerned or the person named in the order.

(10) An order under this section may be made either at the same time as the care order itself or later.

(11) Before making a care order with respect to any child the court shall –

- (a) consider the arrangements which the authority have made, or propose to make, for affording any person contact with a child to whom this section applies; and
- (b) invite the parties to the proceedings to comment on those arrangements.

Amendments—ACA 2002, s 139(1), Sch 3, paras 54, 64.

Defined terms—"care order": ss 31(11), 105(1); "child": s 105(1); "family proceedings": s 8(3); "guardian", "local authority": s 105(1); "residence order": s 8(1).

"parents" (s 34(1)(a))—See **Meaning of "parent"** under s 10. See the Care Planning, Placement and Case Review (England) Regulations 2010 in Part IV, which are referred to under s 33.

"person in whose favour the residence order was made" (s 34(1)(c))—This refers to the person named in the order as the person with whom the child is to live.

High Court's inherent jurisdiction (s 34(1)(d))—The inherent jurisdiction of the High Court was, before CA 1989, most commonly exercised in wardship proceedings. The Act has put an end to the majority of wardship applications, but applications are still made under the inherent jurisdiction of the court; see, in particular, under s 100.

Leave to make an application (s 34(3))—An application for permission to make an application should be made using the procedure in FPR 2010, rr 18.1–18.13. In determining the application for permission under s 34 the court should consider the criteria set out in s 10(9) of the Act. It must have regard to all of the circumstances of the case and have particular regard to the following factors: (a) the nature of the contact sought; (b) the applicant's connection to the child; (c) the risk of the child's life being disrupted by the proposed application to such an extent that the child would be harmed by it; and (d) the wishes of the parents and local authority. In weighing up these factors, the following approach should be adopted: (a) if the application is frivolous, vexatious or an abuse of process, it will fail; (b) if the permission application fails to disclose any real prospect of eventual success (or the prospect is remote so that the application is obviously unsustainable), it must be dismissed; and (c) the applicant must satisfy the court that there is a serious issue to try and must present a good arguable case – is there a real issue that the applicant may reasonably ask the court to try and has he a case that is better than merely arguable yet not necessarily one that is shown to have a better-than-even chance, a fair chance, of success? Over-analysis of these "tests" should be avoided and the matter approached "in the loosest way possible, looking at the matter in the round", because it is important that the exercise of discretion by the court is unfettered. The court should also consider whether the person seeking to be made a party has an independent or separate point of view, or is putting forward an interest identical to that of another party. If there is no independent or separate point of view or different interest, then it is unlikely that the court will permit that person to become a party (*Re W (Care Proceedings: Leave to Apply)* [2005] 2 FLR 468).

Because contact between a child and his family will be assumed to be beneficial by virtue of CA 1989, Sch 2, para 15, a local authority which considers that it is not reasonably practicable or consistent with the child's welfare to promote that contact will need to file evidence to justify its stance (*Re M (Care: Contact: Grandmother's Application for Leave)* [1995] 2 FLR 86).

Interim contact hearing—See *West Glamorgan County Council v P (No 1)* [1992] 2 FLR 369. For the approach to be adopted by the court see *Hampshire County Council v S* [1993] 1 FLR 559 and *Re W (A Minor) (Interim Care Order)* [1994] 2 FLR 892, CA (discussed under FPR 2010, r 12.21); and in relation to a final order under s 34 during interim care see *A v M and Walsall MBC* [1993] 2 FLR 244. In cases of emergency, where the court is not satisfied that adequate safeguards can be put in place to ensure the safety of the child, the court may make a short order under s 34(4) authorising the local authority to refuse contact prior to the court having time to fully consider the matter (*Re W (A Child)* [2013] EWCA Civ 314. See also **No order as to contact/no contact order** below.

Review of contact by the court—It is not open to the court to retain control over the issue of contact with a child in care by providing for a general review of the progress of the care plan and of contact arrangements at some date after the making of a care order (*Re B (A Minor) (Care Order: Review)* [1993] 1 FLR 421). See also *Kent County Council v C* [1993] 1 FLR 308 in which Ewbank J held that the court cannot fetter the local authority's plans by adding a direction to a care order that the guardian ad litem (children's guardian) remain involved with the child. What the court *can* do, according to *Re B* (above), is to make what is in effect an interim contact order with a specific provision for a further hearing with a view to making more enduring provision for contact at the subsequent hearing. It may be, however, that *Re S (A Minor) (Care: Contact Order)* [1994] 2 FLR 222 casts doubt on this approach: the Court of Appeal there held that, where the nature and extent of the contact was an integral part of the local authority's care plan, it was not for the court to decide precisely what contact was reasonable. The judge had made a care order, but adjourned the issue of contact for further directions and this was, in effect, providing for a review of the implementation of the care plan which would lead the judge into the forbidden territory of supervising the administration of the local authority's arrangements for rehabilitation. The court has no jurisdiction under s 34 to prohibit a local authority, into whose care a child has been placed, from permitting parental contact with the child; if the court did make such an order it would be unenforceable because, by virtue of the Care Planning, Placement and Case Review (England) Regulations 2010, reg 8 (see Part IV), a local authority can, with the parents' agreement, depart from the terms of any order made under s 34 (*Re W (Section 34(2) Orders)* [2000] 1 FLR 502, CA). The whole question of the court relinquishing control of a child's case to the local authority is considered further under s 38 **Interim care order or full care order?**. See also **Adoption and Children Act 2002 – review of cases of looked-after children** under CA 1989, s 26, for a summary of the role of the independent reviewing officer in relation to the review of care orders under the amendments made to s 26(2)(e) by ACA 2002, s 118.

Contact at the discretion of the local authority—Orders for contact at the discretion of the local authority must be interpreted in accordance with CA 1989, s 34(1) and Sch 2, para 15(1). It is inappropriate for the court to indicate the frequency of such contact. Notwithstanding the no order principle in s 1(5), in many cases it is beneficial that when contact with a child is to be within the discretion of the local authority the court should spell it out (*L v London Borough of Bromley* [1998] 1 FLR 709; *Re P (Minors) (Contact with Children in Care)* [1993] 2 FLR 156, where the judge distinguished between an order for contact with a parent at the discretion of the local authority and an order for reasonable contact).

Contact – ECHR 1950—Where care orders have been made together with orders under s 34(4) authorising the local authority to terminate contact with the parents of the child concerned, the Convention should not be used routinely as a make-weight ground of appeal, nor should there be extensive citation of authorities from the ECtHR, particularly where such authorities pre-dated CA 1989 (see *Re F (Care Proceedings: Contact)* [2000] Fam Law 708, where the mother's argument that the decision to terminate contact was an essentially administrative rather than judicial decision failed, and her reliance on *W v UK* (1988) 10 EHHR 29 was found to be misplaced).

Contact with father is just as important as contact with mother—Where a care order was made in relation to children who had suffered serious injuries caused by one of the parents, although the court was unable to say which, and the mother was to continue to have contact, there was no reason to terminate the father's contact. The benefit of keeping the family link alive by way of contact operates just as much for the father as for the mother (*Re G (Adoption: Contact)* [2003] 1 FLR 270). In *A Local Authority v A, B and E* [2012] 2 FLR 601, the court considered the merits of indirect contact between the child and his violent father, who was serving a prison sentence. Hedley J determined that contact was in the best interests of the child unless the risk posed made any form of contact unacceptably unsafe, observing that while the preeminent concern was one of risk, there were other important issues to take into account, including the identity of parenthood, which, if at all feasible, should not be a closed book to the child.

Contact – domestic violence—See the guidance given in *Re L (Contact: Domestic Violence); Re V (Contact: Domestic Violence); Re M (Contact: Domestic Violence); Re H (Contact: Domestic Violence)* [2000] 2 FLR 334 and the principles embodied in FPR PD12J *Residence and Contact Orders: Domestic Violence and Harm*, which apply to any application for residence or contact and in which domestic violence or risk of it is alleged. The principles are equally applicable to public law cases (*Re G (Domestic Violence: Direct Contact)* [2000] 2 FLR 865). The outcome of any Multi-agency risk assessment conferences (MARACs), which collate information about high-risk cases of domestic abuse with a view to creating a coordinated safety plan for the victim and any children, may be relevant in determining applications for contact under s 34 where alleged domestic violence is an issue. For the principles governing the disclosure of documents or other information generated by MARACs, see **Multi-agency risk assessment conferences (MARACs) – disclosure in public law and private law proceedings** under FPR 2010, r 12.12. See also **Contact – Domestic violence** under s 8.

No order as to contact/no contact order—The court has power to make an order for no contact between a parent and child (*Kent County Council v C* [1993] 1 FLR 308,) but in the light of the provisions of the Care Planning, Placement and Case Review (England) Regulations 2010 (see Part IV), where the court thinks there should be no contact, it should make such an order and care must be taken in drafting it to avoid any misunderstanding in relation to the local authority's duty to allow contact (*Re SW (A Minor)*

[1993] 2 FLR 609). Although *Re S (A Minor) (Care: Contact Order)* [1994] 2 FLR 222 suggests that such an order, or an order providing for reasonable contact, is not necessary, *L v London Borough of Bromley* [1998] 1 FLR 709 recognises that there can be a benefit in spelling things out in certain circumstances; see **Contact at the discretion of the local authority** (above). A s 34(4) order should not be made merely against the possibility that circumstances might change to justify the termination of contact (*Re S (Care: Parental Contact)* [2005] 1 FLR 469). In the early stages of care proceedings extraordinarily compelling reasons must be shown to justify a s 34(4) order (*Re K (Contact)* [2008] 2 FLR 581 – where the baby's safety demanded such an order, although it would be too drastic for it to last until the final hearing; at the case management conference it would be for the mother to show that carefully supervised contact should resume).

Discharge of a s 34(4) "no contact" order—There must be some material change of circumstances between the making of the order and the application to discharge it (*Re T (Termination of Contact: Discharge of Order)* [1997] 1 FLR 517). In determining such an application the court should consider (i) the extent to which circumstances have changed since the original order, and (ii) bearing those changes in mind, the extent to which it is appropriate to reinvestigate the central question and apply the paramountcy principle. The greater the change in circumstances, the more intensively the court would be prepared to reconsider the desirability of leaving the s 34(4) order in place. As to the power of local authorities to override no contact orders without having further recourse to the court, see Care Planning, Placement and Case Review (England) Regulations 2010, reg 8 (in Part IV).

Disclosure of information concerning prospective adopters—For disclosure to parents where a s 34(4) application is running concurrently with an adoption application, see *Re S (A Minor) (Adoption)* [1993] 2 FLR 204.

Contact arrangements (s 34(11))—This applies to the arrangements proposed in the care plan. Where the arrangements will be made by a local authority other than the applicant authority, directions should be given for that authority to be represented to deal with any issues that might arise and to assure the court and the parents of the authority's commitment to the care plan and its capacity to implement it (*L v London Borough of Bexley* [1996] 2 FLR 595).

Enforcement of public law contact orders—A public law contact order made under CA 1989 can be enforced by committal. A circuit judge sitting in the county court has the power to attach a penal notice to such an order and does not need to sit as a High Court judge pursuant to SCA 1981, s 9 to do so (*Re P-B (Contact: Committal)* [2009] 2 FLR 66). Pursuant to FPR 2010, r 33.1(2), the CCR and RSC continue to apply to family proceedings, subject to FPR 2010; CCR Ord 29.1 covers orders made under CA 1989, s 34. However, many s 34 orders will be made in the family proceedings courts (FPC) and the enforcement of orders in the FPC are not "family proceedings" for the purposes of FPR 2010.

Supervision orders

35 Supervision orders

(1) While a supervision order is in force it shall be the duty of the supervisor –

    (a) to advise, assist and befriend the supervised child;

    (b) to take such steps as are reasonably necessary to give effect to the order; and

    (c) where –

        (i) the order is not wholly complied with; or

        (ii) the supervisor considers that the order may no longer be necessary,

    to consider whether or not to apply to the court for its variation or discharge.

(2) Parts I and II of Schedule 3 make further provision with respect to supervision orders.

36 Education supervision orders

(1) On the application of any local authority, the court may make an order putting the child with respect to whom the application is made under the supervision of a designated local authority.

(2) In this Act "an education supervision order" means an order under subsection (1).

(3) A court may only make an education supervision order if it is satisfied that the child concerned is of compulsory school age and is not being properly educated.

(4) For the purposes of this section, a child is being properly educated only if he is receiving efficient full-time education suitable to his age, ability and aptitude and any special educational needs he may have.

(5) Where a child is –

   (a)   the subject of a school attendance order which is in force under section 437 of the Education Act 1996 and which has not been complied with; or

   (b)   is not attending regularly within the meaning of section 444 of that Act –
      (i)   a school at which he is a registered pupil,
      (ii) any place at which education is provided for him in the circumstances mentioned in subsection (1) of section 444ZA of that Act, or
      (iii) any place which he is required to attend in the circumstances mentioned in subsection (2) of that section,

then, unless it is proved that he is being properly educated, it shall be assumed that he is not.

(6) An education supervision order may not be made with respect to a child who is in the care of a local authority.

(7) The local authority designated in an education supervision order must be –

   (a)   the authority within whose area the child concerned is living or will live; or

   (b)   where –
      (i)   the child is a registered pupil at a school; and
      (ii) the authority mentioned in paragraph (a) and the authority within whose area the school is situated agree,
      the latter authority.

(8) Where a local authority propose to make an application for an education supervision order they shall, before making the application, consult the appropriate local authority if different.

(9) The appropriate local authority is –

   (a)   in the case of a child who is being provided with accommodation by, or on behalf of, a local authority, that authority; and

   (b)   in any other case, the local authority within whose area the child concerned lives, or will live

(10) Part III of Schedule 3 makes further provision with respect to education supervision orders.

Amendments—Education Act 1993, s 307(1),(3), Sch 19, para 149, Sch 21, Pt II; Education Act 1996, s 582(1), Sch 37, Pt I, para 85; Education Act 2005, s 117, Sch 18, para 1; SI 2010/1158.

Defined terms—"appropriate local authority": s 36(9); "child": s 105(1); "education supervision order": s 36(2); "local authority": s 105(1).

"local authority"—Section 36(7) specifies which authority must be designated.

"in the care of the local authority" (s 36(6))—This refers to a child who is in the care of a local authority by virtue of a care order (see ss 31(11) and 105(1)).

Powers of court

37 Powers of court in certain family proceedings

(1) Where, in any family proceedings in which a question arises with respect to the welfare of any child, it appears to the court that it may be appropriate for a care or

supervision order to be made with respect to him, the court may direct the appropriate authority to undertake an investigation of the child's circumstances.

(2) Where the court gives a direction under this section the local authority concerned shall, when undertaking the investigation, consider whether they should –

    (a)   apply for a care order or for a supervision order with respect to the child;

    (b)   provide services or assistance for the child or his family; or

    (c)   take any other action with respect to the child.

(3) Where a local authority undertake an investigation under this section, and decide not to apply for a care order or supervision order with respect to the child concerned, they shall inform the court of –

    (a)   their reasons for so deciding;

    (b)   any service or assistance which they have provided, or to intend to provide, for the child and his family; and

    (c)   any other action which they have taken, or propose to take, with respect to the child.

(4) The information shall be given to the court before the end of the period of eight weeks beginning with the date of the direction, unless the court otherwise directs.

(5) The local authority named in a direction under subsection (1) must be –

    (a)   the authority in whose area the child is ordinarily resident; or

    (b)   where the child is not ordinarily resident in the area of a local authority, the authority within whose area any circumstances arose in consequence of which the direction is being given.

(6) If, on the conclusion of any investigation or review under this section, the authority decide not to apply for a care order or supervision order with respect to the child –

    (a)   they shall consider whether it would be appropriate to review the case at a later date; and

    (b)   if they decide that it would be, they shall determine the date on which that review is to begin.

Amendments—CLSA 1990, s 116, Sch 16, para 16.

Defined terms—"care order": ss 31(11), 105(1); "child": s 105(1); "family proceedings": s 8(3); "local authority": s 105(1); "supervision order": s 31(11).

Scope—This section empowers the court, of its own initiative, to direct the local authority to look into the circumstances of a child with a view to the possibility of taking action with respect to the child and to report to the court about what, if any, action it intends to take, including the matters referred to in s 37(4)–(6). The court is not limited to one s 37 direction for each set of proceedings. Where a judge is satisfied that the local authority has either not complied with a direction under s 37 or failed to conduct an investigation that met the court's concerns, the court may extend or renew its direction under s 37 (*Re K (Children)* [2012] EWCA Civ 1549). An interim order may be made pending the results of the investigation (s 38(1)). If the local authority decides not to issue proceedings the court has no power to make a care or supervision order of its own initiative (see e g *Nottinghamshire County Council v P* [1993] 2 FLR 134). In *Re L (A Child)* [2013] EWCA Civ 179, the Court of Appeal declined, in the particular circumstances of the case, to criticise the judge's use of s 37 to direct the local authority to undertake an investigation of the child's situation and to grant an interim care order in circumstances where the local authority had already provided a report under CA 1989, s 7 and made the decision to issue an application for a care order.

"appropriate authority" (s 37(1))—See **"designated local authority"** under s 31.

"ordinarily resident" (s 37(5))—See under s 31.

Procedure—For the procedure where a direction is given under s 37 by a county court or the High Court, see FPR 2010, r 12.17. All public law applications issued by local authorities under CA 1989, Pt IV, including cases in which a s 37(1) direction is made, are subject to the procedure in the revised Public Law Outline in PD12A. For details see annotations **First appointment, Case management conference**

and **Issues resolution hearing** under FPR 2010, r 12.25. Note that there may be a new protocol for s 37(1) applications in due course. It is a requirement of the Revised Private Law Programme (FPR PD12B) that the need for a s 37 investigation be considered at the first hearing dispute resolution appointment in private law proceedings.

Best Practice Guidance on s 37(1) directions—This Guidance was issued by the Children Act Advisory Committee (before its abolition) in its *Annual Report 1992/93* to deal with the unjustified and overuse of s 37(1) provisions. The text is as follows:

(1) A direction under s 37(1) is appropriate where the court desires an investigation because "it appears to the court that it may be appropriate for a care or supervision order to be made" (s 37(1)).

(2) A direction under s 37(1) is not lawful unless it appears to the court that a care or supervision order may be appropriate. Thus, in private law proceedings, a direction under s 37(1) should not be used as a device for the purpose of enabling the court to appoint a guardian ad litem. Unless "it appears to the court that it may be appropriate for a care or supervision order to be made", any referral for a welfare investigation should be made under s 7.

(3) The purpose of a s 37(1) direction is to enable the court to cause the local authority to assess whether a care or supervision order is needed. It is not to obtain a general welfare report. However, the making of a s 37(1) direction will also cause the local authority to consider whether and which child welfare support services should be provided by the local authority, or other action taken, as well as or instead of a care or supervision order: s 37(2), and note the details of the duty of the local authority to report to the court under s 37(3).

(4) Upon a direction under s 37, the local authority must report back within 8 weeks unless the court otherwise directs: s 37(4). The date for the next hearing must be fixed: FPR 2010, r 12.13(1). The date for the report should also be specified under FPR 2010, r 12.12(2).

(5) When a county court that is not a care centre makes a direction under s 37(1), it will facilitate expedition of any proceedings begun by the local authority if the court makes a direction under Art 20(2) of ATPO 2008.

Appointment of a panel guardian ad litem

(6) When a court has made a direction under s 37(1), and "has made, or is considering whether to make, an interim care order" (s 41(6)(b)), "the court shall appoint an officer of the Service or a Welsh family proceedings officer for the child concerned unless satisfied that it is not necessary to do so in order to safeguard his interests": s 41(1).

(7) The court cannot appoint a panel guardian unless the proceedings are "specified" within s 41(6). Section 41 does not authorise the court to appoint a guardian ad litem, upon making a s 37(1) direction, if the court has not made and is not considering whether to make an interim care order: s 41(6)(b).

Section 7(1) referrals

(8) Section 7(1) is for cases where the court desires a welfare investigation and report. This might include a child protection issue, for example, abusive interference with a child by a parent or other person who does not have care of the child: in such a case an injunction may be the appropriate remedy.

(9) The reporter under a s 7(1) order is the eyes and ears of the court and is required to investigate and to report to the court on the welfare of the child. The reporter is an independent agent of the court, is not a party to the proceedings and is not legally represented.

(10) Whether an order under s 7(1) should be directed to the court welfare service or the local authority may be affected by:
(i) previous involvement with and knowledge of the family by the local authority, in which case the local authority is likely to be appropriate, particularly if the involvement is recent or continuing;
(ii) local arrangements between the court welfare service and the local authority for distribution or sharing of investigation work.

(11) When considering whether to make a s 7(1) referral or a s 37(1) direction, the court should as far as practicable obtain the available relevant information from any social worker or court welfare officer who is currently involved with the child, or a duty court welfare officer.

(12) Upon making a s 7(1) referral, the date for the next hearing must be fixed: FPR 2010, r 12.13(1). The date for the report should also be specified under FPR 2010, r 12.12(2).

Communication to local authority of s 37(1) direction or s 7(1) referral

(13) It is important that whenever a court makes a s 37(1) direction or a s 7(1) referral to a local authority, the authority should be informed as quickly as possible. An immediate telephone notification should be confirmed in writing. FPR 2010, r 12.17(4)(a) require that a copy of a s 37(1) direction shall be

PART II

served on the local authority as soon as practicable. FPR 2010, r 12.17(4)(b) provides for the court to direct which parts of the documentary evidence should be served on the local authority where a s 37(1) direction has been made.

Practical considerations—The court must spell out the reasons for making the s 37 order very carefully and a transcript (or very full note) of the judgment should be made available to the local authority at the earliest opportunity (*Re M (Intractable Contact Dispute: Interim Care Order)* [2003] 2 FLR 636). It is not sufficient for the local authority simply to be told that the judge has ordered a s 37 report. The court should be clear about how, and by whom, the order is going to be communicated to the local authority (*Re M* (above), at [14], for example, by facsimile to an identified officer of the authority). See *Re H (A Minor) (Section 37 Direction)* [1993] 2 FLR 541 ("child's circumstances" under s 37(1) to be widely construed and should include any situation which might have a bearing on the child being likely to suffer significant harm in the future; judge's s 37 order went into detail with regard to investigations to be carried out, and included a time-scale for the investigation). The judge must not, however, seek to fetter the local authority in the execution of its statutory function under s 37 (*Re M (Official Solicitor's Role)* [1998] 2 FLR 815, CA in which the judge wrongly sought to use the Official Solicitor to regulate the s 37 enquiry). In *Re A and B (Minors) (No 2)* [1995] 1 FLR 351, Wall J questioned whether s 37 was appropriate where the local authority had already carried out an investigation and what the court wanted was information about this; he saw s 7 as the better choice (see **Officer of the Service** under s 7). In *Re D (Residence: Imposition of Conditions)* [1996] 2 FLR 281, CA, a children and family reporter was ordered to investigate the issue of residence, and the local authority (which had recently been involved in the matter) was also invited to report pursuant to s 37. A s 37 investigation is not to be ordered in private law proceedings unless it appears that a public law order might be appropriate (*Re F (Family Proceedings: Section 37 Investigation)* [2006] 1 FLR 1122; *Re L (Section 37 Direction)* [1999] 1 FLR 984).

Section 37 can be utilised in intractable contact disputes to remove children who are being denied all contact with their non-resident parent and are suffering significant harm because of the residential parent's false and distorted belief system about the non-residential parent (*Re M (Intractable Contact Dispute: Interim Care Order)* (above) – where the children were removed from their mother under an interim care order and residence orders were subsequently made in favour of the father, with 2-year supervision orders to the local authority). However, in *Re M* (above) Wall J was careful to point out that this procedure is not a panacea and must only be used when the circumstances truly justify it.

Duty of local authority—Where the court makes an unopposed direction to a local authority under s 37(1) there can be no appeal against that direction by the authority. Section 37 sets out three threshold requirements for the exercise of the court's power, namely that: (1) there is a child; (2) there are family proceedings; and (3) that a question has arisen with respect to the child's welfare. It is for the court to determine whether those criteria are satisfied or not, e.g. the age of the child. Where an issue arises, a fact-finding hearing should be directed to determine it (*Lambeth London Borough Council v TK and KK* [2008] 1 FLR 1229).

Position of children's guardian—Proceedings which become specified by virtue of s 41(6)(b) following the making of a s 37 order cease to be specified if the local authority, as a result of its investigation (albeit as yet incomplete), decides not to apply for a care order or supervision order and so informs the court (*Re CE (Section 37 Direction)* [1995] 1 FLR 26). In that case, however, it was in the child's interests for the children's guardian, who had been appointed on the proceedings originally becoming specified, to remain involved until the local authority's final assessment was in place and a final resolution could be ordered or sanctioned by the court. The guardian had consented to her continuing involvement and could be funded as an expert on the child's legal aid certificate, so the court invoked its jurisdiction under FPR 1991, r 9.5 (FPR 2010, r 16.4) to appoint a guardian in private law proceedings.

When considering whether to make an interim care order and appoint a guardian on the making of a direction under s 37, regard should be had to the considerations set out in *Re CE (Section 37 Direction)*, above, and in s 41. Where all contact has ceased and the issue of contact has become intractable the child should be separately represented (*Re M (Intractable Contact Dispute: Interim Care Order)* [2003] 2 FLR 636, where the court made a s 37 direction as a result of the mother's denial of all contact to the father because of her false and distorted belief system about him and ordered that the children be separately represented).

Local authority as party—In *F v Cambridgeshire County Council* [1995] 1 FLR 516, FD, it was held that it had been an error to permit a local authority which had carried out a s 37 investigation and decided not to seek a care or supervision order to become a party in private law proceedings by a father against a mother for contact, given the restrictions on local authorities seeking private law orders.

38 Interim orders

(1) Where –

    (a) in any proceedings on an application for a care order or supervision order, the proceedings are adjourned; or

    (b) the court gives a direction under section 37(1),

the court may make an interim care order or an interim supervision order with respect to the child concerned.

(2) A court shall not make an interim care order or interim supervision order under this section unless it is satisfied that there are reasonable grounds for believing that circumstances with respect to the child are as mentioned in section 31(2).

(3) Where, in any proceedings on an application for a care order or supervision order, a court makes a residence order with respect to the child concerned, it shall also make an interim supervision order with respect to him unless satisfied that his welfare will be satisfactorily safeguarded without an interim order being made.

(4) An interim order made under or by virtue of this section shall have effect for such period as may be specified in the order, but shall in any event cease to have effect on whichever of the following events first occurs –

    (a) the expiry of the period of eight weeks beginning with the date on which the order is made;

    (b) if the order is the second or subsequent such order made with respect to the same child in the same proceedings, the expiry of the relevant period;

    (c) in a case which falls within subsection (1)(a), the disposal of the application;

    (d) in a case which falls within subsection (1)(b), the disposal of an application for a care order or a supervision order made by the authority with respect to the child;

    (e) in a case which falls within subsection (1)(b) and in which –

        (i) the court has given a direction under section 37(4), but

        (ii) no application for a care order or supervision order has been made with respect to the child,

    the expiry of the period fixed by that direction.

(5) In subsection (4)(b) "the relevant period" means –

    (a) the period of four weeks beginning with the date on which the order in question is made; or

    (b) the period of eight weeks beginning with the date on which the first order was made if that period ends later than the period mentioned in paragraph (a).

(6) Where the court makes an interim care order, or interim supervision order, it may give such directions (if any) as it considers appropriate with regard to the medical or psychiatric examination or other assessment of the child; but if the child is of sufficient understanding to make an informed decision he may refuse to submit to the examination or other assessment.

(7) A direction under subsection (6) may be to the effect that there is to be –

    (a) no such examination or assessment; or

    (b) no such examination or assessment unless the court directs otherwise.

(8) A direction under subsection (6) may be –

    (a) given when the interim order is made or at any time while it is in force; and

    (b) varied at any time on the application of any person falling within any class of person prescribed by rules of court for the purposes of this subsection.

(9) Paragraphs 4 and 5 of Schedule 3 shall not apply in relation to an interim supervision order.

(10) Where a court makes an order under or by virtue of this section it shall, in determining the period for which the order is to be in force, consider whether any party who was, or might have been, opposed to the making of the order was in a position to argue his case against the order in full.

Modifications—Section 38 is modified for certain purposes by SI 2010/1898, reg 5(2).

Defined terms—"care order": ss 31(11), 105(1); "child": s 105(1); "relevant period": s 38(5); "residence order": s 8(1); "supervision order": s 31(11).

Public Law Outline (PLO)—The PLO in FPR PD12A applies to all applications for care and supervision orders made under CA 1989, Pt II. See also annotations **First appointment**, **Case management conference** and **Issues resolution hearing** under FPR 2010, r 12.25.

Nature of interim orders—The object of an interim order should normally be to hold the balance so as to cause the least possible harm to the child; see e g *B v B (Interim Contact with Grandparents)* [1993] Fam Law 393 (s 8 contact case), *Hampshire County Council v S* [1993] 1 FLR 559 (interim order re contact with child in care). An interim care order is not a step involving any advance judgment of the final issue on the part of the court (see *Re H (A Child)* (2002) Lawtel, 12 December – where the Court of Appeal held that an interim hearing could not be a substitute for a full trial of a local authority's concerns about the safety of a child). In circumstances where the court should refrain from making findings of fact at an interim stage in the proceedings, it is open to the court to refuse to hear oral evidence at an interim hearing (*Re W (Interim Care Order)* [2012] 2 FLR 240, in which the Court of the Appeal held that the judge at first instance had not fallen into error in refusing to hear oral evidence on an application for an interim care order in circumstances where the judge would not have gained a radically different insight into the fathers case had he done so). However, while there is a spectrum of procedure for interim hearings there is also a line beyond which it is impermissible for the court to go in abbreviating that procedure. The court should be careful not to truncate procedure to a point where the hearing becomes unfair (see *Re N (A Child)* [2012] EWCA Civ 1563). An interim care order can be a neutral and effective way of preserving the status quo, an essentially impartial step favouring neither one side nor the other and affording to no-one, least of all the local authority in whose favour it is made, an opportunity for tactical or adventitious advantage. An interim care order may be used as a temporary measure to safeguard the child's welfare while sufficient information is gathered to inform a final decision by the court as to whether or not a care order should be made; the information gathering process is intended to be completed speedily (*Re G (Interim Care Order: Residential Assessment)* [2006] 1 FLR 601). Where the children have been removed from the jurisdiction, the court should not automatically equate the need for a recovery order with the need to make an interim care order. The merits of each order should be considered separately and there is no presumption that the making of a recovery order also requires the making of an interim care order (*Re O-C (Children)* [2013] EWCA Civ 162). An interim care order may be made solely to vest the local authority with the power to transmit sensitive information to a child. In *Re M (Child Abuse: Disclosure)* [2012] 1 FLR 205, the Court of Appeal upheld the decision of the first instance judge to grant an interim care order to the local authority for the sole purpose of informing the children of the fact that their father had pleaded guilty to sexual assault on his daughters by a previous marriage when they were still children.

Removal under an interim order—The court should not equate satisfaction of the interim threshold criteria with satisfaction of the case for removing the child from a parent. The test to be applied in considering the question of removal is set out in no less than eight Court of Appeal authorities. *Re H (A Child) (Interim Care Order)* [2003] 1 FCR 350, at [38] and [39] states two propositions: (1) that the decision taken by the court on an interim care order application must necessarily be limited to issues that cannot await the final hearing and must not extend to issues that are being prepared for determination at that hearing; and (2) that separation is only to be ordered if the child's safety demands immediate separation. In *Re M (Interim Care Order: Removal)* [2006] 1 FLR 1043, at [27], Thorpe LJ stated that a local authority in seeking to justify the continuing removal of a child from home necessarily must meet a very high standard. In *Re K and H* [2007] 1 FLR 2043, at [16], the court held that "at an interim stage the removal of children from their parents is not to be sanctioned unless the child's safety requires interim protection". In *Re L-A (Care: Chronic Neglect)* [2010] 1 FLR 80, the Court of Appeal reviewed these authorities and made it clear that the words of Ryder J in *Re L (Care Proceedings: Removal of Child)* [2008] 1 FLR 575 requiring "an imminent risk of really serious harm" were not intended to "raise the bar" for a new standard to be reached before the making of an interim care order, but were simply intended to restate the test defined in the appellate cases. In *Re B (Care Proceedings: Interim Care Order)* [2010] 1 FLR 1211, Wall LJ asked whether the child's safety, using that word in a broad sense to include psychological welfare, required interim protection (see also *Re GR (Care Order)* [2011] 1 FLR 669). In *Re B (Interim Care Order)* [2010] 2 FLR 283, Wall LJ reviewed the jurisprudence and held that the continued removal of a child must be proportionate to the risk of harm to which she would be exposed if she were allowed to return to the parent's care, cited with approval in *Re S (Care Proceedings: Human Rights)* [2012] 2 FLR 209. In *Re G (Interim Care Order)* [2011] 2 FLR 955, the President summarised the authorities on removal as requiring the court to ask itself (i) whether the children's safety (using that term to include both psychological and physical elements) requires removal and (ii) whether removal is proportionate in the light of the risks posed by leaving the children where they are. See also *Dolhamre v Sweden* [2010] 2 FLR 912, in which the European Court of Human Rights held that a fair balance had to be struck between the interests of the child remaining in care and those of the parent in being reunited with the child, attaching particular importance to the best interests of the child, which, depending on their nature and seriousness, might override those of the parent. In *Re F (Care Proceedings: Interim Care Order)* [2010] 2 FLR 1455, Thorpe LJ held that the judge's elevation of emotional harm to satisfy the making of an interim care order for separation of parents and children did not begin to meet the high threshold set by the authorities on removal at an interim stage.

In *R (G) v Nottingham City Council* [2008] 1 FLR 1660, Munby J emphasised that no local authority and no social worker has any power to remove a child from its parent, or, without the agreement of the parent, to take a child into care, unless they have first obtained a court order authorizing that step, whether that be an emergency protection order, an interim care order, or, in an exceptional case, a wardship order. For useful guidance as to the nature of interim care orders see *Re S (Minors) (Care Order: Implementation of Care Plan); Re W (Minors) (Care Order: Adequacy of Care Plan)* [2002] 1 FLR 815, at [89]–[102]. When making an interim care order in relation to a young child, where it is impossible to fix the final hearing for several months, the court must balance the effect of long-term removal on the child with the risk of short-term harm if left with the parents (*Re M (Interim Care Order: Removal)* (above)). Parliament intended the regime of an interim care order to operate as a tightly run procedure, closely monitored by the court and affording to all parties an opportunity of frequent review as events unfold during the currency of the order. Therefore, renewals of interim care orders should not be sought routinely by local authorities without any attempt to keep the court up to date with progress, nor should they be granted by the court perfunctorily without the making of any inquiries necessary to eliminate the risk of essential disclosure being lost through administrative lethargy (*Re G (Minors) (Interim Care Order)* [1993] 2 FLR 839). An interim care order is not irreversible either in law or in fact (*Re L (Interim Care Order: Power of Court)* [1996] 2 FLR 742, CA). It does not follow that an interim care order will be made automatically upon the threshold criteria having been met in a particular case (*Re A (Children) (Interim Care Order)* [2001] 3 FCR 402 – although in that case interim care orders were made). Where an application for an interim care order has been made, in anything other than wholly exceptional circumstances, the rule must be that it is for the court to make the decision to remove the child (*Re S (Care Proceedings: Human Rights)* [2012] 2 FLR 209, in which the local authority had decided to arrange for the baby to be separated from the mother under police protection despite an application for an interim care order having been made and being listed before the court the next day). The circumstances that demand removal without notice to the parents will be rare. Where this is necessary, the matter must be listed as a matter of extreme urgency to allow the parent(s) to challenge the removal (*Re S (Authorising Children's Immediate Removal)* [2010] 2 FLR 873).

Interim care order or full care order?—In *Re S (Minors) (Care Order: Implementation of Care Plan); Re W (Minors) (Care Order: Adequacy of Care Plan)* [2002] 1 FLR 815, at [89]–[102], Lord Nicholls gives useful guidance as to the nature of interim care orders and sets out examples of cases that fall either side of the line. See also *Re G (Interim Care Order: Residential Assessment)* [2006] 1 FLR 601, at [55]. The court must go through a two-stage process before making a care order, namely: (i) it must be satisfied that the threshold criteria have been met; and (ii) it must consider whether the making of a care order is better than no order. The court must carefully scrutinise the care plan and satisfy itself that it is in the child's best interests. If the court is not satisfied of this or is not satisfied by any material aspect of the care plan it may refuse to make the care order. The court should only pass responsibility to the local authority by a final care order when all of the facts are as clearly known as can be hoped. On the other hand, the court should be alert to the danger of (wrongly) using an interim care order as a means of exercising the defunct supervisory role of the court (*Re J (Minors) (Care: Care Plan)* [1994] 1 FLR 253, approved by the Court of Appeal in *Re CH (Care or Interim Care Order)* [1998] 1 FLR 402; *Re L (Sexual Abuse: Standard of Proof)* [1996] 1 FLR 116). As the Court of Appeal held in *Re P (Minors) (Interim Order)* [1993] 2 FLR 742, when current issues regarding care have been determined, it can seldom, if ever, be right for the court to continue to adjourn a case, making interim orders. On the other hand, the fact that a care order is the inevitable eventual outcome should not deflect the judge from using the litigation process to its maximum effect (*Re CH*). In deciding whether to grant interim or final care orders the essential question is whether the court has a sufficiently clear picture of the way forward. The child's well-being demands that the court be satisfied by the local authority's proposals and it is primarily for the trial judge to decide when a sufficiently clear position has been reached (*Re H (Children)* [2011] EWCA Civ 1218). It is open to the court to use an interim care order, rather than a full care order, at the disposal or second stage of care proceedings where the circumstances are exceptional (*Re F (Interim Care Order)* [2007] 2 FLR 891 – where the court considered that the mother deserved a further chance to prove her parenting abilities). The court may, in appropriate cases, use a combination of other orders under CA 1989 to allow a parent the chance to further prove his or her parenting abilities (see *Re H (A Child)* [2012] EWCA Civ 1700). It is not, however, permissible for the court to treat the hearing as final while only making interim care orders (*Re G (Interim Care Order)* [2011] 2 FLR 955).

The point at which the court withdraws from further control over the child and passes responsibility to the local authority is a matter of the exercise of discretion by the court and will vary with each set of circumstances (*Re L (Sexual Abuse: Standard of Proof)* above). Where the care plan does not contain any proposals for direct post-adoption contact when it is appropriate the court should approve the care plan, save in relation to contact; it should make a care order and then proceed to deal with the question of contact there and then or by giving directions for future determination of the issue, or by leaving the mother or the guardian to make an appropriate application (*Re K (Care Proceedings: Care Plan)* [2008] 1 FLR 1).

Subject to s 38(6), the court cannot on the making of an interim care order impose conditions on the local authority as to the manner in which a child is cared for. Where the care plan is unacceptable, the judge has to decide whether to make an interim residence order subject to supervision instead (*Re L (Interim Care Order: Power of Court)* [1996] 2 FLR 742, CA). Where a care order is made a case may be returned to court in certain circumstances (e g where the care plan has not been properly implemented) under s 26(2)(e), which encompasses a requirement for the authority to review the care plan and revise it as necessary, together with a route for returning it to the court through the intervention of a Cafcass officer where appropriate. See further **Adoption and Children Act 2002 – review of cases of looked-after children** under CA 1989, s 26.

Residence order on interim application in pending care proceedings—There is jurisdiction to make a residence order on an interim application in pending care proceedings (see s 38(3)) but the view was expressed in *Re RJ (Fostering: Disqualified Person)* [1999] 1 FLR 605, CA that where the effect of the interim order would be to alter the status quo, the jurisdiction should only be used in those exceptional cases in which, at the time of the interim application, the court can be confident that, following a substantive hearing, a long-term residence order will be made in favour of the same persons. It is wrong for the court to make residence orders rather than interim care orders pending the final hearing (*Re B (Children)* [2002] 3 FCR 562 – where there was strong evidence that returning the children to their mother was plainly exposing them to severe risk of emotional abuse and distorted development, but see also *Re H (A Child)* [2012] EWCA Civ 1700).

Repeated interim orders (s 38(4),(5))—In theory, provided the time-limits in s 38(4) are observed for each individual interim care order, any number of interim orders can be made until such time as the case is ready for effective hearing; the court's power to make interim orders does not expire eight weeks after the original interim order is made (*Gateshead MBC v N* [1993] 1 FLR 811). Each interim application has to be considered independently on its merits in the light of the circumstances existing at the time. It is not right for the court in granting an interim order to attempt to lay down a policy which would or might fetter the discretion of any future sitting to grant or refuse a further interim order (*Re P (Minors) (Interim Order)* [1993] 2 FLR 742). A court considering a renewal application for an interim care order has a discretion to limit the scope of the hearing to changes in circumstances since the last hearing (*Re B (Interim Care Orders: Renewal)* [2001] 2 FLR 1217). The renewal of interim care orders is tightly controlled by the time limits laid down in the Public Law Outline (see further PD12A and **First appointment, Case management conference** and **Issues resolution hearing** under FPR 2010, r 12.25).

Interim orders and split hearings—Where the court conducts a split hearing, it appears to be assumed, in practice, that the period between the preliminary or fact-finding hearing and the final hearing can appropriately be regulated by an interim order.

Directions under s 38(6)—In *Re C (Interim Care Order: Residential Assessment)* [1997] 1 FLR 1, HL, a direction under s 38(6) for a residential assessment of the child and his parents was upheld, the House of Lords holding that s 38(6) and (7) enables the court to order or prohibit any assessment (whether of a type similar to a medical or psychiatric assessment or not) which involves the participation of the child and is directed to providing the court with material which, in the view of the court, is required to enable it to reach a proper decision at the final hearing of the application for a full care order (*Re B (Interim Care Order: Directions)* [2002] 1 FLR 545). The local authority assumes control of the child once an interim care order has been made, save in specified cases where the court has power to intervene under s 38(6) (*Re B* (above) – it was within the court's jurisdiction to make a direction for residency at a mother and baby unit under s 38(6) even though the local authority objected, since the residential placement was important for assessment purposes). The giving of directions for therapeutic treatment for a parent is not within the court's s 38(6) powers. What is directed under s 38(6) must clearly be an examination or assessment of the child, including where appropriate, his relationship with his parents, the risk that his parents may present to him and the ways in which those risks may be avoided or managed, all with a view to enabling the court to make the decisions which it has to make under the Act with the minimum of delay. Any services which are provided for the child and his family must be ancillary to that end. They must not be an end in themselves (*Re G (Interim Care Order: Residential Assessment)* [2006] 1 FLR 601 – where the House of Lords held that the court had no power to make an order for a s 38(6) "assessment" if the main purpose of the order was to provide a continuing course of psychotherapy to the mother with a view to giving her the opportunity to change sufficiently so as to become a safe and acceptable carer for her child). Before taking the step of removing children permanently from their natural families and placing them for adoption with strangers, the court must be satisfied that the threshold criteria for a care order are met and that care orders with care plans for adoption are in the best interests of the children concerned. This requires the court to be astute to ensure that the case has been fully investigated and that all the relevant evidence necessary for the decision is in place (*Re L and H (Residential Assessment)* [2007] 1 FLR 1370 – where the court held that any final hearing which followed a denial to these parents of the opportunity to take part in a residential assessment of the child would be unfair; *Re M (Assessment: Official Solicitor)* [2009] 2 FLR 950 – where the Court of Appeal held that a judge should be slow to refuse an independent psychiatric assessment on the mother when the immediate and foreseeable consequence would be to deprive an incapacitated litigant of any prospect of averting the care and placement orders sought by the local authority). However, in *Re T (Residential Parenting Assessment)* [2012] 2 FLR 308, Black LJ made clear, having comprehensively reviewed the authorities, that insofar as earlier Court of Appeal decisions might be taken to suggest that a parent facing the permanent removal of their child has a right in all cases to an assessment of their choice rather than one carried out or commissioned by the local authority, this is not what the court intended. Still less do those authorities establish a principle that parents must be given the chance to put forward a positive case to the judge determining the issue of whether a care order should be made. Referring to the case of *Re G*, Black LJ reiterated that further or other assessments should only be commissioned if they can bring something important to the case that neither the local authority nor the guardian is able to bring. Care proceedings must be fair, but it is not necessary for the purposes of ECHR, Art 6 to continue to assess parents if the process is not going to contribute anything to the information that is needed for the ultimate decision.

In *Re W (Assessment of Child)* [1998] 2 FLR 130, CA, it was held that the court had jurisdiction to direct a particular social worker, as a named employee of the local authority, to carry out a s 38(6) assessment but that applications naming social workers were not to be encouraged. An individual could not be directed to carry out the assessment if unwilling or unable to do so and it should be ascertained in advance that the person concerned was willing and able to act. Account ought to be taken of the resources of the local authority employing the social worker and any difficulties with regard to the authority's responsibility for and duty to supervise him. The court commented that a better direction might be that given in *Berkshire CC v C and Others* [1993] 1 FLR 569 (ie that assessment should be carried out by a "suitably qualified social worker").

In exercising its discretion whether to order any particular examination or assessment, the court has to take into account the cost of the proposed assessment and the limits on local authority resources. It is important in determining whether to order a local authority to provide residential assessment to give proper weight to the benefits to the children from such an assessment, compared with the wider responsibility of the authority generally (*Re C (Children) (Residential Assessment)* [2001] 3 FCR 164 – where the authority was ordered to provide a residential assessment in spite of the fact that the cost was so high that it would allegedly absorb most of the authority's remaining budget; *B County Council v L and Others* [2002] EWHC 2327 (Fam) – where the local authority was criticised for terminating an assessment early because of staff commitments and funding problems and a further assessment was ordered before a full care order could be considered). There are useful guidelines in *Sheffield City Council v V (Legal Services Commission Intervening)* [2007] 1 FLR 279: (i) s 38(6) directions should not be made until the court has had an opportunity to examine the details of the proposed assessment; (ii) the assessment provider should be told in advance what it is proposed that the assessment should cover; (iii) the parties should obtain from the assessment provider clear information as to the nature, timing and cost of the work it expects to undertake; (iv) if the work includes elements of therapy, training or treatment then that element of the work should be separately stated by the provider; (v) upon receipt of this information all parties should endeavour to agree whether and how the costs are to be apportioned; (vi) if the court does have to rule on a contested funding issue it should take a common-sense view; (vii) when an assessment is genuinely of a mixed nature the court should identify the work that is outside s 38(6) and which, therefore, cannot be ordered or paid for; and (viii) the issue of funding should be determined at the same hearing as the application for permission to commission the assessment. Since 1 October 2007 the Legal Services Commission Funding Code has been amended so that where a party is publicly funded the court can no longer direct the LSC to make a contribution to the costs, thus leaving the local authority to bear the entire bill. In *A Local Authority v M (Funding of Residential Assessments)* [2008] 1 FLR 1579 the already financially over-stretched local authority was ordered to pay for the mother to participate in a shortened residential assessment period of 7 weeks (rather than the recommended 12 weeks) with a report and prognosis at the end; if things went well then a further period of assessment may be ordered.

Re O (Minors) (Medical Examination) [1993] 1 FLR 860 establishes that directions made under s 38(6) can be appealed under s 94(1). Magistrates are not precluded from granting an application by the children's guardian for a psychological assessment of the child by the fact that an earlier bench had refused a similar application (*Re F (A Minor) (Care Proceedings: Directions)* [1995] 3 FCR 601). In *Re T (Residential Parenting Assessment)* [2012] 2 FLR 308, Black LJ (recognising that a hearing for the purposes of determining whether to make a direction under s 38(6) is inevitably shorter and more focused than a full hearing at which the threshold criteria are considered and/or a final welfare decision is taken) made clear that it is a matter for the individual judge to regulate the nature and extent of the material upon which the s 38(6) decision is taken and the format of the s 38(6) hearing, and that this aspect of the judge's case management will, like most case management, be highly dependent on the facts of the individual case.

President's Guidance: *Case Management Decisions and Appeals Therefrom*—In December 2010, the President issued guidance concerning appeals in respect of case management decisions, entitled *Case Management Decisions and Appeals Therefrom*. It states that its genesis was based in part on concern expressed by judges and magistrates that they must order an expert's report or an additional assessment by an independent social worker for fear that if they do not they will be appealed and criticised on appeal for not having done so. Within this context, the guidance summarises and reiterates the principles that the court should apply in determining an application under CA 1989, s 38(6).

"class of person prescribed by rules of court" (s 38(8))—See FPR 2010, r 12.27(2), which refers the practitioner to the table in r 12.3, for a list of the appropriate applicants and respondents.

38A   Power to include exclusion requirement in interim care order

(1) Where –

(a) on being satisfied that there are reasonable grounds for believing that the circumstances with respect to a child are as mentioned in section 31(2)(a) and (b)(i), the court makes an interim care order with respect to a child, and

(b) the conditions mentioned in subsection (2) are satisfied,

the court may include an exclusion requirement in the interim care order.

(2) The conditions are –

(a) that there is reasonable cause to believe that, if a person ("the relevant person") is excluded from a dwelling-house in which the child lives, the child will cease to suffer, or cease to be likely to suffer, significant harm, and

(b) that another person living in the dwelling-house (whether a parent of the child or some other person) –

(i) is able and willing to give to the child the care which it would be reasonable to expect a parent to give him, and

(ii) consents to the inclusion of the exclusion requirement.

(3) For the purposes of this section an exclusion requirement is any one or more of the following –

(a) a provision requiring the relevant person to leave a dwelling-house in which he is living with the child,

(b) a provision prohibiting the relevant person from entering a dwelling-house in which the child lives, and

(c) a provision excluding the relevant person from a defined area in which a dwelling-house in which the child lives is situated.

(4) The court may provide that the exclusion requirement is to have effect for a shorter period than the other provisions of the interim care order.

(5) Where the court makes an interim care order containing an exclusion requirement, the court may attach a power of arrest to the exclusion requirement.

(6) Where the court attaches a power of arrest to an exclusion requirement of an interim care order, it may provide that the power of arrest is to have effect for a shorter period than the exclusion requirement.

(7) Any period specified for the purposes of subsection (4) or (6) may be extended by the court (on one or more occasions) on an application to vary or discharge the interim care order.

(8) Where a power of arrest is attached to an exclusion requirement of an interim care order by virtue of subsection (5), a constable may arrest without warrant any person whom he has reasonable cause to believe to be in breach of the requirement.

(9) Sections 47(7), (11) and (12) and 48 of, and Schedule 5 to, the Family Law Act 1996 shall have effect in relation to a person arrested under subsection (8) of this section as they have effect in relation to a person arrested under section 47(6) of that Act.

(10) If, while an interim care order containing an exclusion requirement is in force, the local authority have removed the child from the dwelling-house from which the relevant person is excluded to other accommodation for a continuous period of more than 24 hours, the interim care order shall cease to have effect in so far as it imposes the exclusion requirement.

Amendments—Inserted by FLA 1996, s 52, Sch 6, para 1.

Defined terms—"child": s 105(1); "relevant person": s 38A(2)(a).

Scope—Providing the conditions in s 38A(2) are satisfied, the court can safeguard a child by granting an interim care order including a provision excluding from the home the person ("the relevant person") who is putting the child at risk. A power of arrest can be attached to the exclusion requirement. Note the requirement under s 38A(2)(b)(ii) that another person living in the house, whether a parent of the child or some other person, must consent to the exclusion requirement.

Interim care order—See s 38.

Power of arrest (s 38A(5))—Under s 38A(5) and s 44A(5) the court may attach a power of arrest to an exclusion requirement included in an interim care order or an emergency protection order. Where a power of arrest is attached, once the relevant person has been served with the order/informed of its terms, a copy of the order must be delivered to police together with a statement showing that the relevant person has been served with the order/informed of its terms. In serving the relevant person and delivering a copy of the order to the police, it is important to comply with the guidance set out in the Family Justice Council *Protocol for Process Servers* of November 2011 (see Part V). In cases where an order is made which includes an exclusion requirement, FPR PD12K *Children Act 1989: Exclusion Requirement*, sets out requirements to ensure that unless the person to whom the exclusion requirement refers was given notice of the hearing and attended, the name of that person and that an order has been made must be announced in open court at the earliest opportunity (PD12K, para 1). Paragraph 2 sets out the arrangements for bringing the person arrested before the relevant judicial authority, and para 3 requires that any order of committal made otherwise than in public must be announced in open court at the earliest opportunity.

Procedure—See FPR 2010, r 12.28.

38B Undertakings relating to interim care orders

(1) In any case where the court has power to include an exclusion requirement in an interim care order, the court may accept an undertaking from the relevant person.

(2) No power of arrest may be attached to any undertaking given under subsection (1).

(3) An undertaking given to a court under subsection (1) –

    (a) shall be enforceable as if it were an order of the court, and

    (b) shall cease to have effect if, while it is in force, the local authority have removed the child from the dwelling-house from which the relevant person is excluded to other accommodation for a continuous period of more than 24 hours.

(4) This section has effect without prejudice to the powers of the High Court and county court apart from this section.

(5) In this section "exclusion requirement" and "relevant person" have the same meaning as in section 38A.

Amendments—Inserted by FLA 1996, s 52, Sch 6, para 1.

Defined terms—"child": s 105(1); "exclusion requirement": s 38A(3); "relevant person": s 38A(2)(a).

Procedure—See under FLA 1996, s 46 for assistance as to procedure which will be the same, albeit that the context is different.

Powers of High Court and county court apart from s 38B (s 38B(4))—As to the question of the county court accepting undertakings in public law proceedings, see **Undertakings and injunctions** under CA 1989, s 31. As to the inherent jurisdiction of the High Court, see CA 1989, s 100.

39 Discharge and variation etc of care orders and supervision orders

(1) A care order may be discharged by the court on the application of –

  (a)   any person who has parental responsibility for the child;
  (b)   the child himself; or
  (c)   the local authority designated by the order.

(2) A supervision order may be varied or discharged by the court on the application of –

  (a)   any person who has parental responsibility for the child;
  (b)   the child himself; or
  (c)   the supervisor.

(3) On the application of a person who is not entitled to apply for the order to be discharged, but who is a person with whom the child is living, a supervision order may be varied by the court in so far as it imposes a requirement which affects that person.

(3A) On the application of a person who is not entitled to apply for the order to be discharged, but who is a person to whom an exclusion requirement contained in the order applies, an interim care order may be varied or discharged by the court in so far as it imposes the exclusion requirement.

(3B) Where a power of arrest has been attached to an exclusion requirement of an interim care order, the court may, on the application of any person entitled to apply for the discharge of the order so far as it imposes the exclusion requirement, vary or discharge the order in so far as it confers a power of arrest (whether or not any application has been made to vary or discharge any other provision of the order).

(4) Where a care order is in force with respect to a child the court may, on the application of any person entitled to apply for the order to be discharged, substitute a supervision order for the care order.

(5) When a court is considering whether to substitute one order for another under subsection (4) any provision of this Act which would otherwise require section 31(2) to be satisfied at the time when the proposed order is substituted or made shall be disregarded.

Amendments—FLA 1996, s 52, Sch 6, para 2.

Defined terms—"care order": ss 31(11), 105(1); "child", "exclusion requirement": s 38A(3); "local authority": s 105(1); "parental responsibility": s 3; "relevant person": s 38A(2)(a); "supervision order": s 31(11); "supervisor": s 105(1).

"any person who has parental responsibility" (s 39(1),(2))—Parental responsibility may be acquired (and lost) in a number of ways, for example by virtue of being the child's mother or married father (s 2(1)), by a parental responsibility agreement or order under s 4, or by being appointed a child's guardian under s 5(6).

"the child himself" (s 39(1)(b))—The child does not require permission to make his application (*Re A (Care: Discharge Application by Child)* [1995] 1 FLR 599, FD). For guidance as to the role that a child applicant should play in the proceedings, see *Re A* (above) and the notes to FPR 2010, r 12.14.

Supervision orders imposing a requirement (s 39(3))—The requirements that may be imposed under a supervision order are set out in Sch 3, which applies by virtue of s 35(2).

Applicants for variation/discharge of an exclusion requirement—Section 39(1) establishes three categories of applicant for the discharge of a care order. Section 39(3A) speaks of the discharge of a care order in so far as it imposes an exclusion requirement. It is therefore submitted that s 39(1) entitles a person with parental responsibility, the child himself or the local authority designated in the interim care order to apply for an exclusion requirement to be discharged. Whether an application can be made under s 39(1) for the variation of an exclusion requirement, however, is a moot point. Section 39(3A) appears to draw a distinction between discharge of that part of the interim order which imposes the exclusion requirement and variation of it. A similar distinction between discharge and variation can be found in s 39(2) concerning supervision orders. No doubt the reason that the Act, as originally drafted, was silent as to variation of care orders was that care orders were a bald transfer of responsibility to a local authority and could not, under the statutory scheme, stipulate any particular requirements whereas, in accordance with CA 1989, Sch 3, supervision orders could impose specified obligations. This has, of course, changed with the introduction of the concept of exclusion requirements and it may be that, in the amendment process, the need to extend s 39(1) to provide a right to local authorities etc to apply for a variation of an exclusion requirement, as well as for its discharge, was overlooked. The only person who is secure in his right to apply for a variation of the exclusion requirement is the person to whom it applies (s 39(3A)). This must mean the "relevant person" who has been excluded in accordance with s 38A(1) and (2). Certainly the s 39(3A) right cannot extend to local authorities, the child or those with parental responsibility because they are all entitled to apply for discharge of the order, and therefore expressly excluded by the opening words of the subsection. To what extent the limitation on the categories of applicant really matters in practice remains to be seen. How each case develops will naturally depend on its own particular circumstances. Where the local authority fear for the welfare of the child who is the subject of the interim care order, they can remove him forthwith without further recourse to the court and, if the removal persists for more than 24 hours, s 38A(10) provides that the exclusion requirement ceases to be effective automatically. At the other end of the scale, if time is not of the essence and an application to the court is the most appropriate way forward, the matter can be raised at the next renewal of the interim care order when the court can reconsider the whole picture. Should an earlier application about the exclusion requirement be needed, it seems extremely likely that, whatever the strict technicalities of s 39, an application could legitimately be launched by an interested party (whether for variation or discharge) and that the court would proceed to review the matter broadly.

Applicants for variation or discharge of power of arrest (s 39(3B))—This provision is slightly less unhappily drafted than s 39(3A) and may entitle all those listed in s 39(1), plus the person excluded by the exclusion requirement, to apply for an attendant power of arrest to be varied or discharged.

Burden of proving application—The criterion for deciding on discharge of a care order is the welfare test in CA 1989, s 1(1) and it is the person applying for the care order to be discharged who has the burden of showing that the child's welfare requires the revocation of the order (*Re MD and TD (Minors) (No 2)* [1994] Fam Law 489, and see *Re S (Discharge of Care Order)* [1995] 2 FLR 639, CA).

40 Orders pending appeals in cases about care or supervision orders

(1) Where –

    (a)   a court dismisses an application for a care order; and

    (b)   at the time when the court dismisses the application, the child concerned is the subject of an interim care order,

the court may make a care order with respect to the child to have effect subject to such directions (if any) as the court may see fit to include in the order.

(2) Where –

    (a)   a court dismisses an application for a care order, or an application for a supervision order; and

    (b)   at the time when the court dismisses the application, the child concerned is the subject of an interim supervision order, the court may make a supervision order with respect to the child to have effect subject to such directions (if any) as the court sees fit to include in the order.

(3) Where a court grants an application to discharge a care order or supervision order, it may order that –

(a)   its decision is not to have effect; or

(b)   the care order, or supervision order, is to continue to have effect but subject to such directions as the court sees fit to include in the order.

(4) An order made under this section shall only have effect for such a period, not exceeding the appeal period, as may be specified in the order.

(5) Where –

(a)   an appeal is made against any decision of a court under this section; or

(b)   any application is made to the appellate court in connection with a proposed appeal against that decision,

the appellate court may extend the period for which the order in question is to have effect, but not so as to extend it beyond the end of the appeal period.

(6) In this section "the appeal period" means –

(a)   where an appeal is made against the decision in question, the period between the making of that decision and the determination of the appeal; and

(b)   otherwise, the period during which an appeal may be made against the decision.

Defined terms—"care order": s 31(11); "child": s 105(1); "the court": s 92(7).

Scope—This section provides the court with power to make a care or supervision order pending an appeal. The power may be exercised when dismissing an application for such an order or granting an application to discharge such an order (if there was an interim order in force beforehand) or on an application to discharge such an order. If the original court refused to make a care order pending appeal, the appeal court has no power to make such an order. The appeal court can only make an interim order pending appeal (*Croydon London Borough Council v A (No 2)* [1992] 2 FLR 348).

Appeal period—Where the appeal relates to an order (or refusal to make an order) in a family proceedings court or by a district judge, the appeal must be lodged within 21 days, or 7 days if appealing the making of an interim care order or an interim supervision order (FPR 2010, r 30.4(2),(3)). Where the appeal lies to the Court of Appeal, the appeal should be lodged within the time directed by the lower court and within 21 days in the absence of a direction by the lower court (CPR 1998, r 52.4). As a general rule in children's cases, courts should direct a period of less than 21 days within which to lodge a notice of appeal and the appeal should be brought on swiftly (*Re M-H (Children)* [2006] EWCA Civ 499; *Re A (Children: Split Hearing)* [2007] 1 FLR 905). To extend the time in which to lodge the appeal an application must be made to the appeal court (FPR 2010, r 30.7(1)).

In those cases where it is plain that whatever the professionals' assessment of the prospects of success the litigants cannot rest until they have exhausted their legal remedies, the court should consider imposing tight time limits on the filing of an application for permission to appeal, and contact the Civil Appeals office to seek an early listing so that finality may be achieved as soon as ever possible (*Re P (Residence: Appeal)* [2008] 1 FLR 198 (CA)).

Directions—When making an order under this section pending appeal, the court has wide powers to make the order subject to such directions "as the court sees fit". An order under this section is governed by the principles contained in CA 1989, s 1.

Stay—This section does not give the court power to grant a stay of the operation of a care or supervision order pending appeal. A family proceedings court has no power to grant a stay in any event (*Re O (A Minor) (Care Order: Education: Procedure)* [1992] 2 FLR 7) but can give directions pursuant to s 11 as to when the order should come into force (*Re J (A Minor) (Residence)* [1993] 2 FCR 636). Once an appeal has been filed, the appeal court has the power to grant a stay (FPR 2010, r 30.8). The lower court has the power to grant a stay and any application should first be made to that court and thereafter to the appeal court (FPR 2010, r 30.8; CPR 1998, r 52.7). If the appeal is against the making of an adoption order, an application should be made immediately for a stay of the order (together with an application for an expedited hearing). The existence of an arguable appeal with reasonable prospects of success is the minimum requirement before a court can even consider granting a stay: *NB v Haringey LBC* [2012] 2 FLR 125.

Imposition of conditions to grant of stay—The Supreme Court has criticised the imposition by the Court of Appeal of conditions to the grant of a stay pending determination of an application for permission to appeal by the Supreme Court. "As a general rule, conditions such as were imposed by the Court of Appeal in this case should not be made where a party seeks permission to appeal, not least because these might be seen as an unwarranted disincentive to the pursuit of what proved in this case to be a fully merited application," per Lord Kerr: *Re B (A Child)* [2010] 1 FLR 551. The Court of Appeal had approved the decision of the court below to transfer residence from the maternal grandmother to the father: in granting a stay of the transfer of residence the court imposed a provision for extensive overnight staying contact to the father.

Urgent appeals—In urgent cases where the judge has refused a stay of the order pending the application for permission to appeal, the prospective appellant may telephone the Court of Appeal to apply for a stay (during office hours the telephone number is 0207 947 6000 and out of hours contact is made to the security office at the RCJ on 0207 947 6260 who will refer the matter to the duty deputy master): see CPR PD52C, para 26. A deputy master will refer the matter to a Lord Justice who may grant the stay or list the matter urgently for consideration of the application for a stay (*Re S (Child Proceedings: Urgent Appeals)* [2007] 2 FLR 1044).

"appellate court may extend the period" (s 40(5))—In *Re M (A Minor) (Appeal: Interim Order)* [1994] 1 FLR 54, the Court of Appeal held that, where there was an appeal against the refusal to make a care order, an order under this section should be extended by the Court of Appeal unless the appeal is utterly hopeless, so as to preserve the position of the child pending appeal.

Representation of child

41 Representation of child and of his interests in certain proceedings

(1) For the purpose of any specified proceedings, the court shall appoint an officer of the Service or a Welsh family proceedings officer for the child concerned unless satisfied that it is not necessary to do so in order to safeguard his interests.

(2) The officer of the Service or a Welsh family proceedings officer shall –

    (a)   be appointed in accordance with rules of court; and

    (b)   be under a duty to safeguard the interests of the child in the manner prescribed by such rules.

(3) Where –

    (a)   the child concerned is not represented by a solicitor; and

    (b)   any of the conditions mentioned in subsection (4) is satisfied,

the court may appoint a solicitor to represent him.

(4) The conditions are that –

    (a)   no officer of the Service or Welsh family proceedings officer has been appointed for the child;

    (b)   the child has sufficient understanding to instruct a solicitor and wishes to do so;

    (c)   it appears to the court that it would be in the child's best interests for him to be represented by a solicitor.

(5) Any solicitor appointed under or by virtue of this section shall be appointed, and shall represent the child, in accordance with rules of court.

(6) In this section "specified proceedings" means any proceedings –

    (a)   on an application for a care order or supervision order;

    (b)   in which the court has given a direction under section 37(1) and has made, or is considering whether to make, an interim care order;

    (c)   on an application for the discharge of a care order or the variation or discharge of a supervision order;

    (d)   on an application under section 39(4);

(e) in which the court is considering whether to make a residence order with respect to a child who is the subject of a care order;

(f) with respect to contact between a child who is the subject of a care order and any other person;

(g) under Part V;

(h) on an appeal against –
  (i) the making of, or refusal to make, a care order, supervision order or any order under section 34;
  (ii) the making of, or refusal to make, a residence order with respect to a child who is the subject of a care order; or
  (iii) the variation or discharge of, or refusal of an application to vary or discharge, an order of a kind mentioned in sub-paragraph (i) or (ii);
  (iv) the refusal of an application under section 39(4);
  (v) the making of, or refusal to make, an order under Part V;

(hh) on an application for the making or revocation of a placement order (within the meaning of section 21 of the Adoption and Children Act 2002); or

(i) which are specified for the time being, for the purposes of this section, by rules of court.

(6A) The proceedings which may be specified under subsection (6)(i) include (for example) proceedings for the making, varying or discharging of a section 8 order.

(7)–(9) (*repealed*)

(10) Rules of court may make this provision as to –

(a) the assistance which any officer of the Service or Welsh family proceedings officer may be required by the court to give to it;

(b) the consideration to be given by any officer of the Service or Welsh family proceedings officer, where an order of a specified kind has been made in the proceedings in question, as to whether to apply for the variation or discharge of the order;

(c) the participation of officers of the Service or Welsh family proceedings officers in reviews, of a kind specified in the rules, which are conducted by the court.

(11) Regardless of any enactment or rule of law which would otherwise prevent it from doing so, the court may take account of –

(a) any statement contained in a report made by an officer of the Service or a Welsh family proceedings officer who is appointed under this section for the purpose of the proceedings in question; and

(b) any evidence given in respect of the matters referred to in the report,

in so far as the statement or evidence is, in the opinion of the court, relevant to the question which the court is considering.

(12) (*repealed*)

Amendments—CLSA 1990, s 116, Sch 16, para 17; CJCSA 2000, ss 74, 75, Sch 7, Pt II, paras 87, 91, Sch 8; ACA 2002, s 122(1); CA 2004, s 40, Sch 3, paras 5, 9.

Modifications—Section 41(3)–(5) is modified for certain purposes by SI 2011/2866, Art 8(1), Sch 2. Section 41(6) is modified for certain purposes by SI 2010/1898, reg 5(3).

Defined terms—"care order": ss 31(11), 105(1); "child": s 105(1); "supervision order": s 31(11).

Public Law Outline (PLO)—The PLO *Public Law Proceedings Guide to Case Management* (FPR PD12A) applies to all courts, including the Family Proceedings Court, hearing applications issued by local authorities under CA 1989, Pt IV. Under the PLO there will be an early analysis by a Cafcass officer to be made available at the first appointment, within 6 days of issue of the application. Thereafter, there is to be a Cafcass analysis at each stage of the proceedings to help identify issues from a welfare perspective.

"the child concerned" (s 4 (1))—This would appear to mean the child who is the subject of the proceedings and not any other children who may happen to be parties to them (for example, if the mother of a baby in respect of whom a care order was being sought was herself a minor, a children's guardian could not be appointed under s 41 although, in the High Court and county courts, a children's guardian with different powers and duties may be constituted for her under FPR 2010, Pt 16).

"unless satisfied that it is not necessary to do so" (s 41(1))—In *Re J (A Minor) (Change of Name)* [1993] 1 FLR 699, an ex parte application was made by the local authority for leave to change the name of a child in its care. Booth J was satisfied that, although the application fell within CA 1989, s 41, it was not necessary to appoint a guardian ad litem (children's guardian) in order to safeguard the interests of the child. In this particular case, the guardian could not have said any more than counsel for the local authority, and there was no conflict of interest. See also under **"direction under s 37(1)"** below.

Appointment of Official Solicitor—The Official Solicitor no longer represents children who are the subject of family proceedings (other than in very exceptional circumstances and after liaison with Cafcass) see further PD16A, which governs the representation of children in family proceedings.

Appointment of Official Solicitor as amicus curiae (advocate to the court)—There may arise cases in which the Official Solicitor has initially been appointed to act as guardian ad litem to the child who is subject to the proceedings, but is then removed from his position as guardian ad litem as a result of an application made by the child under FPR 2010, r 16.6(5). In such circumstances, it is likely that the Official Solicitor will be invited to remain involved in the case as amicus curiae (advocate to the court) – see *Re H (A Minor) (Role of Official Solicitor)* [1993] 2 FLR 552, FD; see also PD16A, which governs the representation of children in family proceedings. For further discussion of recent case-law, see under FPR 2010, r 16.6(5).

"appointed in accordance with rules of court" (s 41(2)(a))—The relevant rules are FPR 2010, rr 12.6, 12.7, 14.6 and 16.3.

Duration of appointment—See under See FPR 2010, r 16.19.

"safeguard the interests of the child in the manner prescribed by such rules" (s 41(2)(b))—The relevant rules are set out in PD16A, Pts 3 and 4.

"court may appoint a solicitor to represent him" (s 41(3))—The power to appoint a solicitor under this section relates only to "specified proceedings" as defined in s 41(6); it does not apply, for example, to proceedings brought under CA 1989, s 8 (*Re W (A Minor) (Contact)* [1994] 1 FLR 843). The conditions in s 41(4) relating to the appointment of a solicitor are not confined to a situation where the court has decided that the appointment of a guardian is not necessary to safeguard the interests of the child, but include the situation where there are practical difficulties leading to delay in appointing a guardian (*R v Children and Family Court Advisory and Support Service* [2003] 1 FLR 953). The Law Society has produced the guidance *Appointing a Solicitor for the Child in Specified Proceedings: Guidelines for Courts* (see Part V) intended for use nationally throughout England and Wales from April 2007 and a practice note *Acting in the Absence of a Children's Guardian* 25 August 2009.

"child has sufficient understanding" (s 41(4)(b))—See **"able ... to give such instructions on his own behalf"** under FPR 2010, r 16.29.

Appointment of solicitor (s 41(5))—The appointment, removal and role of a solicitor under this section is regulated by FPR 2010, r 15.29.

"specified proceedings" (s 41(6))—ACA 2002, s 122 inserts in CA 1989, s 41(6A) so as to include within the category of proceedings which may be "specified for the time being ... by rules of court" (s 41(6)(i)) any proceedings for the making, varying or discharging of an order under CA 1989, s 8. This extension of the definition of 'specified proceedings" reflects the growing pressure for the appointment of children's guardians in certain private law children cases, for example bitterly contested residence or contact disputes, where children frequently have particular needs and interests which do not coincide with or cannot be adequately represented by the parents (*Re M (Intractable Contact Dispute: Interim Care Order)* [2003] 2 FLR 636). Proceedings for an education supervision order are *not* specified proceedings within the meaning of s 41(6) and so the court in such proceedings cannot appoint a guardian for the child under that section (*Essex County Council v B* [1993] 1 FLR 866). However, in a case where applications were made by the police for disclosure of documents, and by parents for the variation of injunctions restricting publicity in respect of care proceedings which had terminated the day before those applications were made, the court allowed the guardian to continue to represent the child's interests despite the fact that, strictly speaking, the proceedings were no longer specified under s 41(6) (*Oxfordshire County Council v L and F* [1997] 1 FLR 235). Following the repeal of CJCSA 2000, s 12(5)(b) by ACA 2002, as from 28 November 2003 there is no longer jurisdiction for a court to provide for a continuing role for a children's guardian following the making of a supervision order, and therefore *Re MH (A Child) and Re SB and MB (Children)* [2001] 2 FLR 1334 is no longer a correct statement of the law. Provision is made in FPR 2010, rr 16.2, 16.4, 16.24 and 16.27 for the appointment in the High Court or the county court of the Official Solicitor or some other person where it appears to the court that the child should be separately represented. See FPR 2010, Pt 16 and PD16A, which govern the representation of children in family proceedings.

Hybrid proceedings—In hybrid proceedings, or in any straightforward adoption proceedings, where the wishes and feelings of the child are in conflict with the guardian's assessment of welfare and disposal, it may be necessary to give the child an independent voice through his own legal representation (*Re O (Transracial Adoption: Contact)* [1995] 2 FLR 597 – where the court considered an application for adoption of a child in the care of the local authority together with applications by the mother for discharge of the care order and the making of a residence order in her favour).

"direction under section 37(1)" (s 41(6)(b))—See also annotations under s 37. In *Re CE (Section 37 Direction)* [1995] 1 FLR 26 Wall J gave guidance as to the approach that should be taken by the court when considering the appointment of a guardian in such cases. A guardian should not be appointed automatically when a s 37 direction is made; the purpose for which a s 37 report is required should be carefully considered. The following matters should be borne in mind although the list was not said to be definitive:

(a) Is the court actually making an interim care order, or merely considering whether to do so? If so, the circumstances are likely to be serious and it may well be appropriate to appoint a guardian immediately.
(b) If an interim order is only being considered, what factors require an appointment to be made?
(c) Will there be sufficient time for the guardian to be informed of the issues and play a useful role?
(d) Is there any specific role to be played by the guardian in the s 37 investigation itself?
(e) If there is no appointment, will the child's interests be properly safeguarded in the interim and during the course of the investigation?
(f) Does the child have a solicitor?

Sections 37 and 41 should not be used to avoid the restrictions on appointing a guardian in private law proceedings.

The proceedings cease to be "specified proceedings" if the local authority, having investigated, decides not to apply for an order. Once a guardian has been appointed, the appointment subsists until terminated by the court (unless the terms of the appointment specify when it otherwise comes to an end). This remains so even where the proceedings cease to be "specified". It is good practice for the order making the appointment to contain a direction that the guardian's continuing involvement should be reviewed on completion of the s 37 report. The appointment has to be terminated by order of the court following the procedure set out in FPR 2010, r 16.19 (*Re CE* above).

Discharge of a care order and discharge or variation of a supervision order (s 41(6)(c))—Discharge and variation of such orders are dealt with in s 39.

"application under section 39(4)" (s 41(6)(d),(h)(iv))—Section 39(4) provides for an application to substitute a supervision order for a care order which is in force.

"proceedings in which the court is considering whether to make a residence order" (s 41(6)(e))—The court may consider making such an order on a specific application for a residence order or in any family proceedings (see s 10(1),(2)).

Contact with a child in care (s 41(6)(f))—Applications for contact with a child who is the subject of a care order are made under s 34.

Part V (s 41(6)(g),(h)(v))—Pt V (ss 43–52) provides for proceedings for the protection of children, such as emergency protection orders, child assessment orders and recovery orders.

"specified ... by rules of court" (s 41(6)(i))—See FPR 2010, rr 2.3, 12.27.

"regardless of any enactment or rule of law which would otherwise prevent it from doing so" (s 41(11))—Section 41(11) is aimed at the hearsay rule, which would otherwise render a report inadmissible save where the cumbersome procedures laid down under the Civil Evidence Acts are followed. It makes it clear that the court may take account of the contents of a guardian's written report regardless of whether it is otherwise technically admissible as evidence.

42 Right of officer of the Service to have access to local authority records

(1) Where an officer of the Service or Welsh family proceedings officer has been appointed under section 41 he shall have the right at all reasonable times to examine and take copies of –

(a) any records of, or held by, a local authority or an authorised person which were compiled in connection with the making, or proposed making, by any person of any application under this Act with respect to the child concerned;

(b) any records of, or held by, a local authority which were compiled in connection with any functions which are social services functions within the meaning of the Local Authority Social Services Act 1970, so far as those records relate to that child; or

(c) any records of, or held by, an authorised person which were compiled in connection with the activities of that person, so far as those records relate to that child.

(2) Where an officer of the Service or Welsh family proceedings officer takes a copy of any record which he is entitled to examine under this section, that copy or any part of it shall be admissible as evidence of any matter referred to in any –

(a) report which he makes to the court in the proceedings in question; or

(b) evidence which he gives in those proceedings.

(3) Subsection (2) has effect regardless of any enactment or rule of law which would otherwise prevent the record in question being admissible in evidence.

(4) In this section "authorised person" has the same meaning as in section 31.

Amendments—CLSA 1990, ss 116, 125(7), Sch 16, para 18, Sch 20; CJCSA 2000 s 74, Sch 7, Pt II, paras 87, 92; Local Government Act 2000, s 107(1), Sch 5, para 20; CA 2004, s 40, Sch 3, paras 5, 10.

Defined terms—"authorised person": s 31(9); "child", "local authority": s 105(1).

Public interest immunity—Where an issue arises as to whether, because of public interest immunity, certain material (often material in the possession of the local authority) should or should not be disclosed, guidance as to the procedure to be followed can be derived from *Re C (Expert Evidence: Disclosure: Practice)* [1995] 1 FLR 204 and *Re R (Care: Disclosure: Nature of Proceedings)* [2002] 1 FLR 755.

"officer of the Service ... appointed under section 41" (s 42(1))—The rights granted by this section are available only to guardians appointed under s 41 and not those appointed under FPR 2010, Pt 16 in non-specified proceedings or for minors who are parties to specified proceedings other than as the subject of those proceedings. For example, the guardian ad litem of a minor mother of a child in respect of whom a care order is being sought will not have a right to inspect the records covered by this section, but the guardian ad litem for her child will have that right.

Local Authority Social Services Act 1970 (s 42(1)(b))—Section 2(1) of that Act requires every local authority to establish a social services committee and provides for certain things to stand referred to it. These include all the local authority's functions under the enactments mentioned in Sch 1 to the Act and such other functions as may be designated by the Secretary of State by order. A report of an area child protection committee into a half-brother's death is a document held by the local authority and is compiled in connection with its functions under the Local Authority Social Services Act 1970. The guardian therefore has a right to see such a report in order to ascertain if there is any material relevant to a child (who is the subject of subsequent proceedings) which may help him to give the appropriate advice and provide the appropriate report to the court. Once the guardian has seen the report, he ought to be very careful as to how the information is further disseminated and, if there are particular concerns, the agency can alert the guardian to its sensitivity or request that the information should not be further disseminated (*Re R (Care Proceedings: Disclosure)* [2000] 2 FLR 751). The same applies to the report of an independent inquiry by a senior member of a neighbouring local authority (*Re J (Care Proceedings: Disclosure)* [2003] 2 FLR 522).

Adoption records—In care proceedings, s 42(1)(b) entitles a guardian ad litem of the child to see Form F (a case record prepared by the local authority giving detailed information concerning the prospective adopters with whom it is intended to place the child if a care order is granted), and s 42(2)(a) entitles him to include the relevant information derived from it in his report in the care proceedings (*Re T (A Minor) (Guardian ad Litem: Case Record)* [1994] 1 FLR 632).

"any enactment or rule of law which would otherwise prevent" (s 42(3))—Section 42(3) is aimed at the hearsay rule, which would otherwise often make a copy of a record inadmissible save where the cumbersome procedures laid down under the Civil Evidence Acts are followed. It has also been held to override the Adoption Agencies Regulations 1983, reg 14 which makes a local authority's Form F concerning prospective adopters a confidential record (see *Re T* above).

Limitations of s 42—Section 42 does not entitle a guardian ad litem to see witness statements and similar documents disclosed by the Crown Prosecution Service or the police to the local authority, although their existence is likely to be reflected in the social work records so that, if the guardian feels they are likely to be of particular importance to the parents' case, steps would be taken to determine whether they should be disclosed to the parents (*Nottinghamshire County Council v H* [1995] 1 FLR 115, FD).

Furthermore, s 42 does not entitle a guardian to disclose documents which are covered by public interest immunity – see **Public interest immunity** above.

Access to materials held by the prosecution authorities in Scotland—See *Cheshire County Council v C* [1995] 2 FLR 862.

PART V
PROTECTION OF CHILDREN

43 Child assessment orders

(1) On the application of a local authority or authorised person for an order to be made under this section with respect to a child, the court may make the order if, but only if, it is satisfied that –

(a) the applicant has reasonable cause to suspect that the child is suffering, or is likely to suffer, significant harm;

(b) an assessment of the state of the child's health or development, or of the way in which he has been treated, is required to enable the applicant to determine whether or not the child is suffering, or is likely to suffer, significant harm; and

(c) it is unlikely that such an assessment will be made, or be satisfactory, in the absence of an order under this section.

(2) In this Act "a child assessment order" means an order under this section.

(3) A court may treat an application under this section as an application for an emergency protection order.

(4) No court shall make a child assessment order if it is satisfied –

(a) that there are grounds for making an emergency protection order with respect to the child; and

(b) that it ought to make such an order rather than a child assessment order.

(5) A child assessment order shall –

(a) specify a date by which the assessment is to begin; and

(b) have effect for such period, not exceeding 7 days beginning with that date, as may be specified in the order.

(6) Where a child assessment order is in force with respect to a child it shall be the duty of any person who is in a position to produce the child –

(a) to produce him to such person as may be named in the order; and

(b) to comply with such directions relating to the assessment of the child as the court thinks fit to specify in the order.

(7) A child assessment order authorises any person carrying out the assessment, or any part of the assessment, to do so in accordance with the terms of the order.

(8) Regardless of subsection (7), if the child is of sufficient understanding to make an informed decision he may refuse to submit to a medical or psychiatric examination or other assessment.

(9) The child may only be kept away from home –

(a) in accordance with directions specified in the order;
(b) if it is necessary for the purposes of the assessment; and
(c) for such period or periods as may be specified in the order.

(10) Where the child is to be kept away from home, the order shall contain such directions as the court thinks fit with regard to the contact that he must be allowed to have with other persons while away from home.

(11) Any person making an application for a child assessment order shall take such steps as are reasonably practicable to ensure that notice of the application is given to –

(a) the child's parents;
(b) any person who is not a parent of his but who has parental responsibility for him;
(c) any other person caring for the child;
(d) any person in whose favour a contact order is in force with respect to the child;
(e) any person who is allowed to have contact with the child by virtue of an order under section 34; and
(f) the child,

before the hearing of the application.

(12) Rules of court may make provision as to the circumstances in which –

(a) any of the persons mentioned in subsection (11); or
(b) such other person as may be specified in the rules,

may apply to the court for a child assessment order to be varied or discharged.

(13) In this section "authorised person" means a person who is an authorised person for the purposes of section 31.

Defined terms—"authorised person": s 43(13); "child": s 105(1); "child assessment order": s 43(2); "contact order": s 8(1); "emergency protection order": s 44(4); "local authority": s 105(1); "parental responsibility": s 3; "significant harm": s 31(10).

"authorised person" (s 43(1))—An authorised person is, according to s 43(13), a person who is authorised for the purposes of s 31, ie the National Society for the Prevention of Cruelty to Children and any of its officers. Any person authorised by order of the Secretary of State to bring proceedings under s 31 would also be an "authorised person" (s 31(9)), but no such order has yet been made.

Persons who are to be given notice of application (s 43(11))—The table set out in FPR 2010, r 12.3(2) sets out the persons who should be made respondents to a s 43 application or should be given notice of it.

"the child's parents" (s 43(11)(a))—The term "parent" is not defined in the Act (see **Meaning of "parent"** under s 10).

"any person ... who has parental responsibility" (s 43(11)(b))—Parental responsibility may be acquired in a variety of ways, for example automatically (see s 2), by order or agreement under s 4, or by virtue of being appointed a guardian of the child under s 5(6).

"order under section 34" (s 43(11)(e))—An order under s 34 is an order for contact with a child in care.

44 Orders for emergency protection of children

(1) Where any person ("the applicant") applies to the court for an order to be made under this section with respect to a child, the court may make the order if, but only if, it is satisfied that –

(a) there is reasonable cause to believe that the child is likely to suffer significant harm if –

(i)   he is not removed to accommodation provided by or on behalf of the applicant; or

(ii)   he does not remain in the place in which he is then being accommodated;

(b)   in the case of an application made by the local authority –

    (i)   enquiries are being made with respect to the child under section 47(1)(b); and

    (ii)   those enquiries are being frustrated by access to the child being unreasonably refused to a person authorised to seek access and that the applicant has reasonable cause to believe that access to the child is required as a matter of urgency; or

(c)   in the case of an application made by an authorised person –

    (i)   the applicant has reasonable cause to suspect that a child is suffering, or is likely to suffer, significant harm;

    (ii)   the applicant is making enquiries with respect to the child's welfare; and

    (iii)   those enquiries are being frustrated by access to the child being unreasonably refused to a person authorised to seek access and the applicant has reasonable cause to believe that access to the child is required as a matter of urgency.

(2) In this section –

(a)   "authorised person" means a person who is an authorised person for the purposes of section 31; and

(b)   "a person authorised to seek access" means –

    (i)   in the case of an application by a local authority, an officer of the local authority or a person authorised by the local authority to act on their behalf in connection with the enquiries; or

    (ii)   in the case of an application by an authorised person, that person.

(3) Any person –

(a)   seeking access to a child in connection with enquiries of a kind mentioned in subsection (1); and

(b)   purporting to be a person authorised to do so,

shall, on being asked to do so, produce some duly authenticated document as evidence that he is such a person.

(4) While an order under this section ("an emergency protection order") is in force it –

(a)   operates as a direction to any person who is in a position to do so to comply with any request to produce the child to the applicant;

(b)   authorises –

    (i)   the removal of the child at any time to accommodation provided by or on behalf of the applicant and his being kept there; or

    (ii)   the prevention of the child's removal from any hospital, or other place, in which he was being accommodated immediately before the making of the order; and

(c)   gives the applicant parental responsibility for the child.

(5) Where an emergency protection order is in force with respect to a child, the applicant –

(a)   shall only exercise the power given by virtue of subsection (4)(b) in order to safeguard the welfare of the child;

(b)   shall take, and shall only take, such action in meeting his parental responsibility for the child as is reasonably required to safeguard or promote the welfare of the child (having regard in particular to the duration of the order); and

(c)   shall comply with the requirements of any regulations made by the Secretary of State for the purposes of this subsection.

(6) Where the court makes an emergency protection order, it may give such directions (if any) as it considers appropriate with respect to –

(a) the contact which is, or is not, to be allowed between the child and any named person;

(b) the medical or psychiatric examination or other assessment of the child.

(7) Where any direction is given under subsection (6)(b), the child may, if he is of sufficient understanding to make an informed decision, refuse to submit to the examination or other assessment.

(8) A direction under subsection (6)(a) may impose conditions and one under subsection (6)(b) may be to the effect that there is to be –

(a) no such examination or assessment; or

(b) no such examination or assessment unless the court directs otherwise.

(9) A direction under subsection (6) may be –

(a) given when the emergency protection order is made or at any time while it is in force; and

(b) varied at any time on the application of any person falling within any class of person prescribed by rules of court for the purposes of this subsection.

(10) Where an emergency protection order is in force with respect to a child and –

(a) the applicant has exercised the power given by subsection (4)(b)(i) but it appears to him that it is safe for the child to be returned; or

(b) the applicant has exercised the power given by subsection (4)(b)(ii) but it appears to him that it is safe for the child to be allowed to be removed from the place in question,

he shall return the child or (as the case may be) allow him to be removed.

(11) Where he is required by subsection (10) to return the child the applicant shall –

(a) return him to the care of the person from whose care he was removed; or

(b) if that is not reasonably practicable, return him to the care of –

   (i) a parent of his;

   (ii) any person who is not a parent of his but who has parental responsibility for him; or

   (iii) such other person as the applicant (with the agreement of the court) considers appropriate.

(12) Where the applicant has been required by subsection (10) to return the child, or to allow him to be removed, he may again exercise his powers with respect to the child (at any time while the emergency protection order remains in force) if it appears to him that a change in the circumstances of the case makes it necessary for him to do so.

(13) Where an emergency protection order has been made with respect to a child, the applicant shall, subject to any direction given under subsection (6), allow the child reasonable contact with –

(a) his parents;

(b) any person who is not a parent of his but who has parental responsibility for him;

(c) any person with whom he was living immediately before the making of the order;

(d) any person in whose favour a contact order is in force with respect to him;

(e) any person who is allowed to have contact with the child by virtue of an order under section 34; and

(f) any person acting on behalf of any of those persons.

(14) Wherever it is reasonably practicable to do so, an emergency protection order shall name the child; and where it does not name him it shall describe him as clearly as possible.

(15) A person shall be guilty of an offence if he intentionally obstructs any person exercising the power under subsection (4)(b) to remove, or prevent the removal of, a child.

(16) A person guilty of an offence under subsection (15) shall be liable on summary conviction to a fine not exceeding level 3 on the standard scale.

Defined terms—"authorised person": s 44(2)(a); "child", "contact order", "harm", "local authority": s 105(1); "parental responsibility": s 3; "person authorised to seek access": s 44(2)(b).

"any person falling within any class of person prescribed by rules of court" (s 44(9))—See FPR 2010, r 12.27(3).

Procedure for application for an emergency protection order—An emergency protection order is a draconian measure and in *X Council v B (Emergency Protection Orders)* [2005] 1 FLR 341, Munby J gave guidance as to the way in which such applications should be approached. A guardian must be appointed immediately on issue of the proceedings. There are unusual and exceptional cases (of which this was an example) in which a without notice application is appropriate, but adequate evidence must be presented and a proper note of the hearing prepared by the local authority and made available to the parents. In this case, it was not clear that the removal of the children had been justified in view of both of the requirements of CA 1989, s 44(5),(10) and Art 8. Even in emergency situations, it is desirable that, where possible, the local authority works in partnership with parents and that the least interventionist approach is taken (*A v East Sussex County Council and Chief Constable of Sussex* [2010] 2 FLR 1596). Further detailed guidance on the use of EPOs can be found in *Re X (Emergency Protection Orders)* [2006] 2 FLR 701.

Public Law Outline (PLO)—Although the PLO in FPR PD12A specifically applies to care and supervision proceedings, it states that, in so far as practicable, it is to be applied to all other public law proceedings (para 1.1). See further **Public Law Outline (PLO)** under FPR 2010, r 12.22. It will therefore be a decision for the court in each case as to how and when it is appropriate for the PLO to apply when an application commences by way of an EPO.

44A Power to include exclusion requirement in emergency protection order

(1) Where –
- (a) on being satisfied as mentioned in section 44(1)(a), (b) or (c), the court makes an emergency protection order with respect to a child, and
- (b) the conditions mentioned in subsection (2) are satisfied,

the court may include an exclusion requirement in the emergency protection order.

(2) The conditions are –
- (a) that there is reasonable cause to believe that, if a person ("the relevant person") is excluded from a dwelling-house in which the child lives, then –
  - (i) in the case of an order made on the ground mentioned in section 44(1)(a), the child will not be likely to suffer significant harm, even though the child is not removed as mentioned in section 44(1)(a)(i) or does not remain as mentioned in section 44(1)(a)(ii), or
  - (ii) in the case of an order made on the ground mentioned in paragraph (b) or (c) of section 44(1), the enquiries referred to in that paragraph will cease to be frustrated, and
- (b) that another person living in the dwelling-house (whether a parent of the child or some other person) –
  - (i) is able and willing to give to the child the care which it would be reasonable to expect a parent to give him, and
  - (ii) consents to the inclusion of the exclusion requirement.

(3) For the purposes of this section an exclusion requirement is any one or more of the following –

   (a) a provision requiring the relevant person to leave a dwelling-house in which he is living with the child,

   (b) a provision prohibiting the relevant person from entering a dwelling-house in which the child lives, and

   (c) a provision excluding the relevant person from a defined area in which a dwelling-house in which the child lives is situated.

(4) The court may provide that the exclusion requirement is to have effect for a shorter period than the other provisions of the order.

(5) Where the court makes an emergency protection order containing an exclusion requirement, the court may attach a power of arrest to the exclusion requirement.

(6) Where the court attaches a power of arrest to an exclusion requirement of an emergency protection order, it may provide that the power of arrest is to have effect for a shorter period than the exclusion requirement.

(7) Any period specified for the purposes of subsection (4) or (6) may be extended by the court (on one or more occasions) on an application to vary or discharge the emergency protection order.

(8) Where a power of arrest is attached to an exclusion requirement of an emergency protection order by virtue of subsection (5), a constable may arrest without warrant any person whom he has reasonable cause to believe to be in breach of the requirement.

(9) Sections 47(7), (11) and (12) and 48 of, and Schedule 5 to, the Family Law Act 1996 shall have effect in relation to a person arrested under subsection (8) of this section as they have effect in relation to a person arrested under section 47(6) of that Act.

(10) If, while an emergency protection order containing an exclusion requirement is in force, the applicant has removed the child from the dwelling-house from which the relevant person is excluded to other accommodation for a continuous period of more than 24 hours, the order shall cease to have effect in so far as it imposes the exclusion requirement.

Amendments—Inserted by FLA 1996, s 52, Sch 6, para 3.

Defined terms—"child": s 105(1); "emergency protection order": s 44(4); "relevant person": s 44A(2)(a).

Procedure—See FPR 2010, r 12.28.

Power of arrest (s 44A(5))—See under s 38A(5).

44B Undertakings relating to emergency protection orders

(1) In any case where the court has power to include an exclusion requirement in an emergency protection order, the court may accept an undertaking from the relevant person.

(2) No power of arrest may be attached to any undertaking given under subsection (1).

(3) An undertaking given to a court under subsection (1) –

   (a) shall be enforceable as if it were an order of the court, and

   (b) shall cease to have effect if, while it is in force, the applicant has removed the child from the dwelling-house from which the relevant person is excluded to other accommodation for a continuous period of more than 24 hours.

(4) This section has effect without prejudice to the powers of the High Court and county court apart from this section.

(5) In this section "exclusion requirement" and "relevant person" have the same meaning as in section 44A.

Amendments—Inserted by FLA 1996, s 52, Sch 6, para 3.

Defined terms—"child": s 105(1); "emergency protection order": s 44(4); "exclusion requirement": s 44A(3); "relevant person": s 44A(2)(a).

Procedure—See under FLA 1996, s 46 for assistance as to procedure which will be the same, albeit that the context is different.

Powers of High Court and county court apart from s 44B (s 44B(4))—As to the question of the county court accepting undertakings in public law proceedings, see **Undertakings and injunctions** under CA 1989, s 31. As to the inherent jurisdiction of the High Court, see CA 1989, s 100.

45 Duration of emergency protection orders and other supplemental provisions

(1) An emergency protection order shall have effect for such period, not exceeding eight days, as may be specified in the order.

(2) Where –

    (a)   the court making an emergency protection order would, but for this subsection, specify a period of eight days as the period for which the order is to have effect; but

    (b)   the last of those eight days is a public holiday (that is to say, Christmas Day, Good Friday, a bank holiday or a Sunday),

the court may specify a period which ends at noon on the first later day which is not such a holiday.

(3) Where an emergency protection order is made on an application under section 46(7), the period of eight days mentioned in subsection (1) shall begin with the first day on which the child was taken into police protection under section 46.

(4) Any person who –

    (a)   has parental responsibility for a child as the result of an emergency protection order; and

    (b)   is entitled to apply for a care order with respect to the child,

may apply to the court for the period during which the emergency protection order is to have effect to be extended.

(5) On an application under subsection (4) the court may extend the period during which the order is to have effect by such period, not exceeding seven days, as it thinks fit, but may do so only if it has reasonable cause to believe that the child concerned is likely to suffer significant harm if the order is not extended.

(6) An emergency protection order may only be extended once.

(7) Regardless of any enactment or rule of law which would otherwise prevent it from doing so, a court hearing an application for, or with respect to, an emergency protection order may take account of –

    (a)   any statement contained in any report made to the court in the course of, or in connection with, the hearing; or

    (b)   any evidence given during the hearing,

which is, in the opinion of the court, relevant to the application.

(8) Any of the following may apply to the court for an emergency protection order to be discharged –

    (a)   the child;

    (b)   a parent of his;

(c) any person who is not a parent of his but who has parental responsibility for him; or

(d) any person with whom he was living immediately before the making of the order.

(8A) On the application of a person who is not entitled to apply for the order to be discharged, but who is a person to whom an exclusion requirement contained in the order applies, an emergency protection order may be varied or discharged by the court in so far as it imposes the exclusion requirement.

(8B) Where a power of arrest has been attached to an exclusion requirement of an emergency protection order, the court may, on the application of any person entitled to apply for the discharge of the order so far as it imposes the exclusion requirement, vary or discharge the order in so far as it confers a power of arrest (whether or not any application has been made to vary or discharge any other provision of the order).

(9) (*repealed*)

(10) No appeal may be made against –

(a) the making of, or refusal to make, an emergency protection order;

(b) the extension of, or refusal to extend, the period during which such an order is to have effect;

(c) the discharge of, or refusal to discharge, such an order; or

(d) the giving of, or refusal to give, any direction in connection with such an order.

(11) Subsection (8) does not apply –

(a) where the person who would otherwise be entitled to apply for the emergency protection order to be discharged –

(i) was given notice (in accordance with rules of court) of the hearing at which the order was made; and

(ii) was present at that hearing; or

(b) to any emergency protection order the effective period of which has been extended under subsection (5).

(12) A court making an emergency protection order may direct that the applicant may, in exercising any powers which he has by virtue of the order, be accompanied by a registered medical practitioner, registered nurse or registered midwife, if he so chooses.

(13) The reference in subsection (12) to a registered midwife is to such a midwife who is also registered in the Specialist Community Public Health Nurses' Part of the register maintained under article 5 of the Nursing and Midwifery Order 2001.

Amendments—CLSA 1990, s 116, Sch 16, para 19; FLA 1996, s 52, Sch 6, para 4; SI 2002/253; SI 2004/1771; CYPA 2008, s 30.

Defined terms—"care order": s 31(11); "child": s 105(1); "emergency protection order": s 44(4); "parental responsibility": s 3.

Police Protection Guidance—Government circular *The Duties and Powers of the Police under the Children Act 1989* (number 017/2008) explains when and how police protection powers should be used under CA 1989. It can be found at *http://old.homeoffice.gov.uk/about-us/corporate-publications-strategy/home-office-circulars/circulars-2008/017-2008/*.

"Person with parental responsibility" (s 45(4),(8))—Parental responsibility may be acquired in a variety of ways, for example automatically (see s 2), by order or agreement under s 4, or by virtue of being appointed a guardian under s 5(6). Section s 45(8) encompasses anyone who has parental responsibility whereas s 45(4)(a) is restricted to anyone who has parental responsibility as a result of an emergency protection order (ie by virtue of s 44(4)(c)). See also Emergency Protection Order (Transfer of Responsibilities) Regulations 1991, which apply where the original applicant for the emergency protection order was not the local authority in whose area the child is ordinarily resident.

"any person who ... is entitled to apply for a care order" (s 45(4)(b))—As to who is entitled to apply for a care order, see s 31(1).

"parent" (s 45(8)(b))—This term is not defined in the Act (see **Meaning of "parent"** under s 10).

Variation/discharge of exclusion requirement and power of arrest (s 45(8A),(8B))—Section 45(8) lists those who may apply for an emergency protection order to be discharged. Discharge of the order itself would discharge any exclusion requirement or power of arrest attached to it. In addition, by virtue of s 45(8A), discharge/variation of the exclusion requirement element of the order can be sought by the person to whom it applies. That person is also entitled to apply, under s 45(8B), for any attendant power of arrest to be varied or discharged. It is far from clear whether the combined effect of s 45(8) and ss 45(8A),(8B) permits anyone other than the person to whom the exclusion requirement applies to seek a limited order from the court discharging/varying the exclusion requirement or power of arrest, or whether the only application open to these other interested parties (local authority, parent etc) is one for complete discharge (see also **Applicants for variation/discharge of an exclusion requirement** under CA 1989, s 39).

Restrictions on appeal generally (s 45(10))—Magistrates, who adjourned an emergency protection order application on the basis that the mother had not had one clear day's notice of the proceedings and refused to grant an without notice emergency protection order, had refused to make an order within the meaning of s 45(10) and there was no appeal from their decision (*Essex County Council v F* [1993] 1 FLR 847). If the magistrates had acted unreasonably, the only remedy lay with judicial review proceedings. *Re P (Emergency Protection Order)* [1996] 1 FLR 482, FD, illustrates the dangers of the lack of any appeal procedure, and various devices were there suggested in order to get round the problem (see at [484G]).

Prohibition on appeal relating to direction (s 45(10)(d))—It is assumed that s 45(10)(d) also prohibits an appeal against the outcome of an application under s 44(9)(b) for the variation of a s 44(6) direction as to contact with or assessment of the child.

"notice (in accordance with rules of court) of the hearing" (s 45(11)(a))—As to the rules concerning notice, see FPR 2010, r 12.3(1).

"was present at the hearing" (s 45(11)(a))—A person who attends through his legal representative but not in person may nevertheless have been present (see MCA 1980, s 122). However, the position in this context is far from clear. See, for example, *Re AS (Secure Accommodation Order)* [1999] 1 FLR 103, FD (annotated under FPR 2010, r 12.14).

46 Removal and accommodation of children by police in cases of emergency

(1) Where a constable has reasonable cause to believe that a child would otherwise be likely to suffer significant harm, he may –

    (a)   remove the child to suitable accommodation and keep him there; or

    (b)   take such steps as are reasonable to ensure that the child's removal from any hospital, or other place, in which he is then being accommodated is prevented.

(2) For the purposes of this Act, a child with respect to whom a constable has exercised his powers under this section is referred to as having been taken into police protection.

(3) As soon as is reasonably practicable after taking a child into police protection, the constable concerned shall –

    (a)   inform the local authority within whose area the child was found of the steps that have been, and are proposed to be, taken with respect to the child under this section and the reasons for taking them;

    (b)   give details to the authority within whose area the child is ordinarily resident ("the appropriate authority") of the place at which the child is being accommodated;

    (c)   inform the child (if he appears capable of understanding) –

        (i)   of the steps that have been taken with respect to him under this section and of the reasons for taking them; and

        (ii) of the further steps that may be taken with respect to him under this section;

(d)   take such steps as are reasonably practicable to discover the wishes and feelings of the child;

(e)   secure that the case is inquired into by an officer designated for the purposes of this section by the chief officer of the police area concerned; and

(f)   where the child was taken into police protection by being removed to accommodation which is not provided –

(i)   by or on behalf of a local authority; or

(ii)   as a refuge, in compliance with the requirements of section 51,

secure that he is moved to accommodation which is so provided.

(4)   As soon as is reasonably practicable after taking a child into police protection, the constable concerned shall take such steps as are reasonably practicable to inform –

(a)   the child's parents;

(b)   every person who is not a parent of his but who has parental responsibility for him; and

(c)   any other person with whom the child was living immediately before being taken into police protection,

of the steps that he has taken under this section with respect to the child, the reasons for taking them and the further steps that may be taken with respect to him under this section.

(5)   On completing any inquiry under subsection (3)(e), the officer conducting it shall release the child from police protection unless he considers that there is still reasonable cause for believing that the child would be likely to suffer significant harm if released.

(6)   No child may be kept in police protection for more than 72 hours.

(7)   While a child is being kept in police protection, the designated officer may apply on behalf of the appropriate authority for an emergency protection order to be made under section 44 with respect to the child.

(8)   An application may be made under subsection (7) whether or not the authority know of it or agree to its being made.

(9)   While a child is being kept in police protection –

(a)   neither the constable concerned nor the designated officer shall have parental responsibility for him; but

(b)   the designated officer shall do what is reasonable in all the circumstances of the case for the purpose of safeguarding or promoting the child's welfare (having regard in particular to the length of the period during which the child will be so protected).

(10)   Where a child has been taken into police protection, the designated officer shall allow –

(a)   the child's parents;

(b)   any person who is not a parent of the child but who has parental responsibility for him;

(c)   any person with whom the child was living immediately before he was taken into police protection;

(d)   any person in whose favour a contact order is in force with respect to the child;

(e)   any person who is allowed to have contact with the child by virtue of an order under section 34; and

(f)   any person acting on behalf of any of those persons,

to have such contact (if any) with the child as, in the opinion of the designated officer, is both reasonable and in the child's best interests.

(11) Where a child who has been taken into police protection is in accommodation provided by, or on behalf of, the appropriate authority, subsection (10) shall have effect as if it referred to the authority rather than to the designated officer.

Defined terms—"appropriate authority": s 46(3)(b); "child", "contact order": s 105(1); "designated officer": s 46(3)(e); "emergency protection order": s 44(4); "police protection": s 46(2).

Removal where an emergency protection order is in force—The s 46 power to remove a child can be exercised even where an emergency protection order (EPO) is in force in respect of the child. However, where a police officer knows that an EPO is in force, he should not exercise the s 46 power unless there are compelling reasons to do so (*Langley v Liverpool City Council* [2006] 1 FLR 342 and see *Lumba (Congo) v SSHD; Mighty (Jamaica) v SSHD* [2012] AC 245, per Lord Dyson SCJ, at [80]–[82]).

Court of Appeal guidance as to the use of s 46—Even in an emergency it is desirable, where possible, to work in partnership with a parent. Where parents have access to a solicitor, the solicitor should be apprised of the local authority's concerns and proposals and then be invited, if the solicitor thinks it proper to do so, to advise the parent. Even where emergency powers are obtained under s 44 or exercised under s 46, the least amount of intervention is best. Removal of a child to a known destination is to be preferred to removal to a stranger. However, if there is to be removal to a stranger, the parent should, in the absence of a good reason, be informed of the fact and allowed to pass relevant information to the carer and speedy arrangements should be made for contact. If a court order has not been obtained, or has been obtained without notice, a with-notice hearing should be arranged as soon as possible. A hearing in 2 days should be normal. Where practicable, a court order should be sought in preference to the use of the s 46 powers (*A v East Sussex County Council and Chief Constable of Sussex* [2010] 2 FLR 1596).

Designated officer—It is the responsibility of the chief officer of each police area to designate an officer for the purposes of this section (s 46(3)(e)).

"on behalf of the appropriate authority" (s 46(7))—The appropriate authority is the local authority within whose area the child is ordinarily resident (s 46(3)(b)). For assistance in identifying which local authority this is, see the annotations to s 31. Although only the designated police officer may make an application on behalf of the local authority, any police officer is entitled to apply for an emergency protection order in his own right by virtue of the wide terms of s 44(1).

47 Local authority's duty to investigate

(1) Where a local authority –

  (a) are informed that a child who lives, or is found, in their area –
    (i) is the subject of an emergency protection order; or
    (ii) is in police protection; or
    (iii) has contravened a ban imposed by a curfew notice within the meaning of Chapter I of Part I of the Crime and Disorder Act 1998; or
  (b) have reasonable cause to suspect that a child who lives, or is found, in their area is suffering, or is likely to suffer, significant harm,

the authority shall make, or cause to be made, such enquiries as they consider necessary to enable them to decide whether they should take any action to safeguard or promote the child's welfare.

In the case of a child falling within paragraph (a)(iii) above, the enquiries shall be commenced as soon as practicable and, in any event, within 48 hours of the authority receiving the information.

(2) Where a local authority have obtained an emergency protection order with respect to a child, they shall make, or cause to be made, such enquiries as they consider necessary to enable them to decide what action they should take to safeguard or promote the child's welfare.

(3) The enquiries shall, in particular, be directed towards establishing –

  (a) whether the authority should make any application to the court, or exercise any of their other powers under this Act or section 11 of the Crime and Disorder Act 1998 (child safety orders), with respect to the child;

    (b)   whether, in the case of a child –
        (i)   with respect to whom an emergency protection order has been made; and
        (ii) who is not in accommodation provided by or on behalf of the authority,
        it would be in the child's best interests (while an emergency protection order remains in force) for him to be in such accommodation; and
    (c)   whether, in the case of a child who has been taken into police protection, it would be in the child's best interests for the authority to ask for an application to be made under section 46(7).

(4) Where enquiries are being made under subsection (1) with respect to a child, the local authority concerned shall (with a view to enabling them to determine what action, if any, to take with respect to him) take such steps as are reasonably practicable –

    (a)   to obtain access to him; or
    (b)   to ensure that access to him is obtained, on their behalf, by a person authorised by them for the purpose,

unless they are satisfied that they already have sufficient information with respect to him.

(5) Where, as a result of any such enquiries, it appears to the authority that there are matters connected with the child's education which should be investigated, they shall consult the local authority (as defined in section 579(1) of the Education 1996), if different, specified in subsection (5ZA).

(5ZA) The local authority referred to in subsection (5) is –

    (a)   the local authority who –
        (i)   maintain any school at which the child is a pupil, or
        (ii) make arrangements for the provision of education for the child otherwise than at school pursuant to section 19 of the Education Act 1996, or
    (b)   in a case where the child is a pupil at a school which is not maintained by a local authority, the local authority in whose area the school is situated.

(5A) For the purposes of making a determination under this section as to the action to be taken with respect to a child, a local authority shall, so far as is reasonably practicable and consistent with the child's welfare –

    (a)   ascertain the child's wishes and feelings regarding the action to be taken with respect to him; and
    (b)   give due consideration (having regard to his age and understanding) to such wishes and feelings of the child as they have been able to ascertain.

(6) Where, in the course of enquiries made under this section –

    (a)   any officer of the local authority concerned; or
    (b)   any person authorised by the authority to act on their behalf in connection with those enquiries –
        (i)   is refused access to the child concerned; or
        (ii) is denied information as to his whereabouts,

the authority shall apply for an emergency protection order, a child assessment order, a care order or a supervision order with respect to the child unless they are satisfied that his welfare can be satisfactorily safeguarded without their doing so.

(7) If, on the conclusion of any enquiries or review made under this section, the authority decide not to apply for an emergency protection order, a care order, a child assessment order or a supervision order they shall –

    (a)   consider whether it would be appropriate to review the case at a later date; and
    (b)   if they decide that it would be, determine the date on which that review is to begin.

PART II

(8) Where, as a result of complying with this section, a local authority conclude that they should take action to safeguard or promote the child's welfare they shall take that action (so far as it is both within their power and reasonably practicable for them to do so).

(9) Where a local authority are conducting enquiries under this section, it shall be the duty of any person mentioned in subsection (11) to assist them with those enquiries (in particular by providing relevant information and advice) if called upon by the authority to do so.

(10) Subsection (9) does not oblige any person to assist a local authority where doing so would be unreasonable in all the circumstances of the case.

(11) The persons are –

    (a) any local authority;
    (b) *(repealed)*
    (c) any local housing authority;
    (ca) the National Health Service Commissioning Board;
    (d) any clinical commissioning group, Local Health Board, Special Health Authority, National Health Service trust or NHS foundation trust; and
    (e) any person authorised by the Secretary of State for the purposes of this section.

(12) Where a local authority are making enquiries under this section with respect to a child who appears to them to be ordinarily resident within the area of another authority, they shall consult that other authority, who may undertake the necessary enquiries in their place.

Amendments—CLSA 1990, s 116, Sch 16, para 20; Health Authorities Act 1995, s 2, Sch 1, para 118; Crime and Disorder Act 1998, ss 15(4), 119, Sch 8, para 69; SI 2000/90; Health and Social Care (Community Health and Standards) Act 2003, s 34, Sch 4, para 79; CA 2004, s 53; SI 2007/961; SI 2010/1158; Health and Social Care Act 2012, s 55(2), Sch 5, para 53.

"reasonable cause to suspect" (s 47(1)(b))—The threshold contained in s 47 is clearly and deliberately lower than that of "reasonable cause to believe" contained in ss 38, 44 and 46, which all involve a compulsory intervention in the lives of both the child and the family and constitute an interference with family life under ECHR 1950, Art 6, incorporated into domestic law by HRA 1998. By contrast, a s 47 investigation does not generally infringe rights, but merely imposes a duty to conduct investigations necessary for decisions about the child's welfare (*G v Hertfordshire County Council* [2000] Fam Law 883). The adequacy of a risk assessment under CA 1989, s 47 may be the subject of judicial review. However, the ambit of the judicial review process, and any subsequent appeal, is limited to determining whether the assessment can stand. Where the assessment cannot stand and a fresh assessment is thus required, the Administrative court cannot dictate how the local authority should go about that further assessment (*ET, BT, CT v Islington London Borough Council* [2013] EWCA Civ 323).

48 Powers to assist in discovery of children who may be in need of emergency protection

(1) Where it appears to a court making an emergency protection order that adequate information as to the child's whereabouts –

    (a) is not available to the applicant for the order; but
    (b) is available to another person,

it may include in the order a provision requiring that other person to disclose, if asked to do so by the applicant, any information that he may have as to the child's whereabouts.

(2) No person shall be excused from complying with such a requirement on the ground that complying might incriminate him or his spouse or civil partner of an offence; but a statement of admission made in complying shall not be admissible in evidence against either of them in proceedings for any offence other than perjury.

(3) An emergency protection order may authorise the applicant to enter premises specified by the order and search for the child with respect to whom the order is made.

(4) Where the court is satisfied that there is reasonable cause to believe that there may be another child on those premises with respect to whom an emergency protection order ought to be made, it may make an order authorising the applicant to search for that other child on those premises.

(5) Where –

    (a)   an order has been made under subsection (4);

    (b)   the child concerned has been found on the premises; and

    (c)   the applicant is satisfied that the grounds for making an emergency protection order exist with respect to him,

the order shall have effect as if it were an emergency protection order.

(6) Where an order has been made under subsection (4), the applicant shall notify the court of its effect.

(7) A person shall be guilty of an offence if he intentionally obstructs any person exercising the power of entry and search under subsection (3) or (4).

(8) A person guilty of an offence under subsection (7) shall be liable on summary conviction to a fine not exceeding level 3 on the standard scale.

(9) Where, on an application made by any person for a warrant under this section, it appears to the court –

    (a)   that a person attempting to exercise powers under an emergency protection order has been prevented from doing so by being refused entry to the premises concerned or access to the child concerned; or

    (b)   that any such person is likely to be so prevented from exercising any such powers,

it may issue a warrant authorising any constable to assist the person mentioned in paragraph (a) or (b) in the exercise of those powers, using reasonable force if necessary.

(10) Every warrant issued under this section shall be addressed to, and executed by, a constable who shall be accompanied by the person applying for the warrant if –

    (a)   that person so desires; and

    (b)   the court by whom the warrant is issued does not direct otherwise.

(11) A court granting an application for a warrant under this section may direct that the constable concerned may, in executing the warrant, be accompanied by a registered medical practitioner, registered nurse or registered midwife if he so chooses.

(11A) The reference in subsection (11) to a registered midwife is to such a midwife who is also registered in the Specialist Community Public Health Nurses' Part of the register maintained under article 5 of the Nursing and Midwifery Order 2001.

(12) An application for a warrant under this section shall be made in the manner and form prescribed by rules of court.

(13) Wherever it is reasonably practicable to do so, an order under subsection (4), an application for a warrant under this section and any such warrant shall name the child; and where it does not name him it shall describe him as clearly as possible.

Amendments—SI 2002/253; CPA 2004, s 261(1), Sch 27, para 130; SI 2004/1771.

Defined terms—"child": s 105(1); "emergency protection order": s 44(4).

Authority to search for another child (s 48(4))—The order giving authority should be in Form C27.

Issue of warrants—A warrant may be issued under s 48(9) to authorise a constable to assist in the enforcement of an emergency protection order.

PART II

"prescribed by rules of court" (s 48(12))—See FPR 2010, Pt 5 and PD5A. The application for a warrant should be made on Form C1 with the prescribed supplement Form C12. The warrant should be in Form C25.

49 Abduction of children in care etc

(1) A person shall be guilty of an offence if, knowingly and without lawful authority or reasonable excuse, he –

   (a)   takes a child to whom this section applies away from the responsible person;

   (b)   keeps such a child away from the responsible person; or

   (c)   induces, assists or incites such a child to run away or stay away from the responsible person.

(2) This section applies in relation to a child who is –

   (a)   in care;

   (b)   the subject of an emergency protection order; or

   (c)   in police protection,

and in this section "the responsible person" means any person who for the time being has care of him by virtue of the care order, the emergency protection order, or section 46, as the case may be.

(3) A person guilty of an offence under this section shall be liable on summary conviction to imprisonment for a term not exceeding six months, or to a fine not exceeding level 5 on the standard scale, or to both.

50 Recovery of abducted children etc

(1) Where it appears to the court that there is reason to believe that a child to whom this section applies –

   (a)   has been unlawfully taken away or is being unlawfully kept away from the responsible person;

   (b)   has run away or is staying away from the responsible person; or

   (c)   is missing,

the court may make an order under this section ("a recovery order").

(2) This section applies to the same children to whom section 49 applies and in this section "the responsible person" has the same meaning as in section 49.

(3) A recovery order –

   (a)   operates as a direction to any person who is in a position to do so to produce the child on request to any authorised person;

   (b)   authorises the removal of the child by any authorised person;

   (c)   requires any person who has information as to the child's whereabouts to disclose that information, if asked to do so, to a constable or an officer of the court;

   (d)   authorises a constable to enter any premises specified in the order and search for the child, using reasonable force if necessary.

(4) The court may make a recovery order on the application of –

   (a)   any person who has parental responsibility for the child by virtue of a care order or emergency protection order; or

   (b)   where the child is in police protection, the designated officer.

(5) A recovery order shall name the child and –

   (a)   any person who has parental responsibility for the child by virtue of a care order or emergency protection order; or

(b) where the child is in police protection, the designated officer.

(6) Premises may only be specified under subsection (3)(d) if it appears to the court that there are reasonable grounds for believing the child to be on them.

(7) In this section –

"an authorised person" means –

(a) any person specified by the court;

(b) any constable;

(c) any person who is authorised –

(i) after the recovery order is made; and

(ii) by a person who has parental responsibility for the child by virtue of a care order or an emergency protection order,

to exercise any power under a recovery order; and

"the designated officer" means the officer designated for the purposes of section 46.

(8) Where a person is authorised as mentioned in subsection (7)(c) –

(a) the authorisation shall identify the recovery order; and

(b) any person claiming to be so authorised shall, if asked to do so, produce some duly authenticated document showing that he is so authorised.

(9) A person shall be guilty of an offence if he intentionally obstructs an authorised person exercising the power under subsection (3)(b) to remove a child.

(10) A person guilty of an offence under this section shall be liable on summary conviction to a fine not exceeding level 3 on the standard scale.

(11) No person shall be excused from complying with any request made under subsection (3)(c) on the ground that complying with it might incriminate him or his spouse or civil partner of an offence; but a statement or admission made in complying shall not be admissible in evidence against either of them in proceedings for an offence other than perjury.

(12)–(14) ...

Amendments—CPA 2004, s 261(1), Sch 27, para 131.

Defined terms—"care order": ss 31(11), 105(1); "child": s 105(1); "designated officer": s 50(7); "emergency protection order": s 44(4); "parental responsibility": s 3; "police protection": s 46(2); "recovery order": s 50(1).

"child to whom this section applies" (s 50(1))—See ss 50(2) and 49(2).

"responsible person" (s 50(1))—See ss 50(2) and 49(2). See also *Re R (Recovery Orders)* [1998] 2 FLR 401, FD.

"any person who has parental responsibility" (s 50(4),(5))—In the case of a care order, the local authority designated by the order (see s 33(3)) will have parental responsibility and, in the case of an emergency protection order, the applicant for the emergency protection order (see s 44(4)(c)) will have parental responsibility. Where either the applicant was a designated police officer applying by virtue of s 46(7) on behalf of the local authority or the local authority has taken over the emergency protection order from the original applicant in accordance with the Emergency Protection Order (Transfer of Responsibilities) Regulations 1991, the local authority has parental responsibility.

"designated officer" (s 50(4)(b),(5)(b))—It is the responsibility of the chief officer for each police area to designate an officer for the purpose of the police protection provisions contained in s 46 (s 46(3)(e)).

Procedure—For consideration of the proper procedure where a local authority has replaced a parent or carer as a "responsible person" shortly before seeking a recovery order, see *Re R (Recovery Orders)* [1998] 2 FLR 401, FD which also deals with the role the child should play in the proceedings (13-year-old boy's wishes and feelings as to his schooling were properly taken into account even though he was not separately represented at the recovery order hearing).

51 Refuges for children at risk

(1) Where it is proposed to use a voluntary home or private children's home to provide a refuge for children who appear to be at risk of harm, the Secretary of State may issue a certificate under this section with respect to that home.

(2) Where a local authority or voluntary organisation arrange for a foster parent to provide such a refuge, the Secretary of State may issue a certificate under this section with respect to that foster parent.

(3) In subsection (2) "foster parent" means a person who is, or who from time to time is, a local authority foster parent or a foster parent with whom children are placed by a voluntary organisation.

(4) The Secretary of State may by regulations –

    (a) make provision as to the manner in which certificates may be issued;

    (b) impose requirements which must be complied with while any certificate is in force; and

    (c) provide for the withdrawal of certificates in prescribed circumstances.

(5) Where a certificate is in force with respect to a home, none of the provisions mentioned in subsection (7) shall apply in relation to any person providing a refuge for any child in that home.

(6) Where a certificate is in force with respect to a foster parent, none of those provisions shall apply in relation to the provision by him of a refuge for any child in accordance with arrangements made by the local authority or voluntary organisation.

(7) The provisions are –

    (a) section 49;

    (b) sections 82 (recovery of certain fugitive children) and 83 (harbouring) of the Children (Scotland) Act 1995, so far as they apply in relation to anything done in England and Wales;

    (c) section 32(3) of the Children and Young Persons Act 1969 (compelling, persuading, inciting or assisting any person to be absent from detention etc), so far as it applies in relation to anything done in England and Wales;

    (d) section 2 of the Child Abduction Act 1984.

Amendments—Children (Scotland) Act 1995, s 105(4), Sch 4, para 48(1),(3); Care Standards Act 2000, s 116, Sch 4, para 14(1),(7).

52 Rules and regulations

(1) Without prejudice to section 93 or any other power to make such rules, rules of court may be made with respect to the procedure to be followed in connection with proceedings under this Part.

(2) The rules may in particular make provision –

    (a) as to the form in which any application is to be made or direction is to be given;

    (b) prescribing the persons who are to be notified of –

        (i) the making, or extension, of an emergency protection order; or

        (ii) the making of an application under section 45(4) or (8) or 46(7); and

    (c) as to the content of any such notification and the manner in which, and person by whom, it is to be given.

(3) The Secretary of State may by regulations provide that, where –

    (a) an emergency protection order has been made with respect to a child;

    (b) the applicant for the order was not the local authority within whose area the child is ordinarily resident; and

(c) that local authority are of the opinion that it would be in the child's best interests for the applicant's responsibilities under the order to be transferred to them,

that authority shall (subject to their having complied with any requirements imposed by the regulations) be treated, for the purposes of this Act, as though they and not the original applicant had applied for, and been granted, the order.

(4) Regulations made under subsection (3) may, in particular, make provision as to –

(a) the considerations to which the local authority shall have regard in forming an opinion as mentioned in subsection (3)(c); and

(b) the time at which responsibility under any emergency protection order is to be treated as having been transferred to a local authority.

PART VI
COMMUNITY HOMES

53 Provision of community homes by local authorities

(1) Every local authority shall make such arrangements as they consider appropriate for securing that homes ("community homes") are available –

(a) for the care and accommodation of children looked after by them; and

(b) for purposes connected with the welfare of children (whether or not looked after by them),

and may do so jointly with one or more other local authorities.

(2) In making such arrangements, a local authority shall have regard to the need for ensuring the availability of accommodation –

(a) of different descriptions; and

(b) which is suitable for different purposes and the requirements of different descriptions of children.

(3) A community home may be a home –

(a) provided, equipped, maintained and (subject to subsection (3A)) managed by a local authority; or

(b) provided by a voluntary organisation but in respect of which a local authority and the organisation –

(i)   propose that, in accordance with an instrument of management, the equipment, maintenance and (subject to subsection (3B)) management of the home shall be the responsibility of the local authority; or

(ii) so propose that the management, equipment and maintenance of the home shall be the responsibility of the voluntary organisation.

(3A) A local authority may make arrangements for the management by another person of accommodation provided by the local authority for the purpose of restricting the liberty of children.

(3B) Where a local authority are to be responsible for the management of a community home provided by a voluntary organisation, the local authority may, with the consent of the body of managers constituted by the instrument of management for the home, make arrangements for the management by another person of accommodation provided for the purpose of restricting the liberty of children.

(4) Where a local authority are to be responsible for the management of a community home provided by a voluntary organisation, the authority shall designate the home as a controlled community home.

(5) Where a voluntary organisation are to be responsible for the management of a community home provided by the organisation, the local authority shall designate the home as an assisted community home.

(6) Schedule 4 shall have effect for the purpose of supplementing the provisions of this Part.

Amendments—Criminal Justice and Public Order Act 1994, s 22.

54 (repealed)

55 Determination of disputes relating to controlled and assisted community homes

(1) Where any dispute relating to a controlled community home arises between the local authority specified in the home's instrument of management and –

  (a)   the voluntary organisation by which the home is provided; or
  (b)   any other local authority who have placed, or desire or are required to place, in the home a child who is looked after by them,

the dispute may be referred by either party to the Secretary of State for his determination.

(2) Where any dispute relating to an assisted community home arises between the voluntary organisation by which the home is provided and any local authority who have placed, or desire to place, in the home a child who is looked after by them, the dispute may be referred by either party to the Secretary of State for his determination.

(3) Where a dispute is referred to the Secretary of State under this section he may, in order to give effect to his determination of the dispute, give such directions as he thinks fit to the local authority or voluntary organisation concerned.

(4) This section applies even though the matter in dispute may be one which, under or by virtue of Part II of Schedule 4, is reserved for the decision, or is the responsibility, of –

  (a)   the local authority specified in the home's instrument of management; or
  (b)   (as the case may be) the voluntary organisation by which the home is provided.

(5) Where any trust deed relating to a controlled or assisted community home contains provision whereby a bishop or any other ecclesiastical or denominational authority has power to decide questions relating to religious instruction given in the home, no dispute which is capable of being dealt with in accordance with that provision shall be referred to the Secretary of State under this section.

(6) In this Part "trust deed", in relation to a voluntary home, means any instrument (other than an instrument of management) regulating –

  (a)   the maintenance, management or conduct of the home; or
  (b)   the constitution of a body of managers or trustees of the home.

56 Discontinuance by voluntary organisation of controlled or assisted community home

(1) The voluntary organisation by which a controlled or assisted community home is provided shall not cease to provide the home except after giving to the Secretary of State and the local authority specified in the home's instrument of management not less than two years' notice in writing of their intention to do so.

(2) A notice under subsection (1) shall specify the date from which the voluntary organisation intend to cease to provide the home as a community home.

(3) Where such a notice is given and is not withdrawn before the date specified in it, the home's instrument of management shall cease to have effect on that date and the home shall then cease to be a controlled or assisted community home.

(4) Where a notice is given under subsection (1) and the home's managers give notice in writing to the Secretary of State that they are unable or unwilling to continue as its managers until the date specified in the subsection (1) notice, the Secretary of State may by order –

    (a) revoke the home's instrument of management; and

    (b) require the local authority who were specified in that instrument to conduct the home until –

        (i) the date specified in the subsection (1) notice; or

        (ii) such earlier date (if any) as may be specified for the purposes of this paragraph in the order,

as if it were a community home provided by the local authority.

(5) Where the Secretary of State imposes a requirement under subsection (4)(b) –

    (a) nothing in the trust deed for the home shall affect the conduct of the home by the local authority;

    (b) the Secretary of State may by order direct that for the purposes of any provision specified in the direction and made by or under any enactment relating to community homes (other than this section) the home shall, until the date or earlier date specified as mentioned in subsection (4)(b), be treated as a controlled or assisted community home;

    (c) except in so far as the Secretary of State so directs, the home shall until that date be treated for the purposes of any such enactment as a community home provided by the local authority; and

    (d) on the date or earlier date specified as mentioned in subsection (4)(b) the home shall cease to a community home.

57 Closure by local authority of controlled or assisted community home

(1) The local authority specified in the instrument of management for a controlled or assisted community home may give –

    (a) the Secretary of State; and

    (b) the voluntary organisation by which the home is provided,

not less than two years' notice in writing of their intention to withdraw their designation of the home as a controlled or assisted community home.

(2) A notice under subsection (1) shall specify the date ("the specified date") on which the designation is to be withdrawn.

(3) Where –

    (a) a notice is given under subsection (1) in respect of a controlled or assisted community home;

    (b) the home's managers give notice in writing to the Secretary of State that they are unable or unwilling to continue as managers until the specified date; and

    (c) the managers' notice is not withdrawn,

the Secretary of State may by order revoke the home's instrument of management from such date earlier than the specified date as may be specified in the order.

(4) Before making an order under subsection (3), the Secretary of State shall consult the local authority and the voluntary organisation.

(5) Where a notice has been given under subsection (1) and is not withdrawn, the home's instrument of management shall cease to have effect on –

(a)   the specified date; or

(b)   where an earlier date has been specified under subsection (3), that earlier date,

and the home shall then cease to be a community home.

58 Financial provisions applicable on cessation of controlled or assisted community home or disposal etc of premises

(1) Where –

(a)   the instrument of management for a controlled or assisted community home is revoked or otherwise ceases to have effect under section 56(3) or (4)(a) or 57(3) or (5); or

(b)   any premises used for the purposes of such a home are (at any time after 13 January 1987) disposed of, or put to use otherwise than for those purposes,

the proprietor shall become liable to pay compensation ("the appropriate compensation") in accordance with this section.

(2) Where the instrument of management in force at the relevant time relates –

(a)   to a controlled community home; or

(b)   to an assisted community home which, at any time before the instrument came into force, was a controlled community home,

the appropriate compensation is a sum equal to that part of the value of any premises which is attributable to expenditure incurred in relation to the premises, while the home was a controlled community home, by the authority who were then the responsible authority.

(3) Where the instrument of management in force at the relevant time relates –

(a)   to an assisted community home; or

(b)   to a controlled community home which, at any time before the instrument came into force, was an assisted community home,

the appropriate compensation is a sum equal to that part of the value of the premises which is attributable to the expenditure of money provided by way of grant under section 82, section 65 of the Children and Young Persons Act 1969 or section 82 of the Child Care Act 1980.

(4) Where the home is, at the relevant time, conducted in premises which formerly were used as an approved school or were an approved probation hostel or home, the appropriate compensation is a sum equal to that part of the value of the premises which is attributable to the expenditure –

(a)   of sums paid towards the expenses of the managers of an approved school under section 104 of the Children and Young Persons Act 1933;

(b)   of sums paid under section 51(3)(c) of the Powers of Criminal Courts Act 1973 or section 20(1)(c) of the Probation Service Act 1993 in relation to expenditure on approved probation hostels or homes; or

(c)   of sums paid under section 3, 5 or 9 of the Criminal Justice and Court Services Act 2000 in relation to expenditure on approved premises (within the meaning of Part I of that Act).

(5) The appropriate compensation shall be paid –

(a)   in the case of compensation payable under subsection (2), to the authority who were the responsible authority at the relevant time; and

(b)   in any other case, to the Secretary of State.

(6) In this section –

"disposal" includes the grant of a tenancy and any other conveyance, assignment, transfer, grant, variation or extinguishment of an interest in or right over land, whether made by instrument or otherwise;

"premises" means any premises or part of premises (including land) used for the purposes of the home and belonging to the proprietor;

"the proprietor" means –

    (a) the voluntary organisation by which the home is, at the relevant time, provided; or

    (b) if the premises are not, at the relevant time, vested in that organisation, the persons in whom they are vested;

"the relevant time" means the time immediately before the liability to pay arises under subsection (1); and

"the responsible authority" means the local authority specified in the instrument of management in question.

(7) For the purposes of this section an event of a kind mentioned in subsection (1)(b) shall be taken to have occurred –

    (a) in the case of a disposal, on the date on which the disposal was completed or, in the case of a disposal which is effected by a series of transactions, the date on which the last of those transactions was completed;

    (b) in the case of premises which are put to different use, on the date on which they first begin to be put to their new use.

(8) The amount of any sum payable under this section shall be determined in accordance with such arrangements –

    (a) as may be agreed between the voluntary organisation by which the home is, at the relevant time, provided and the responsible authority or (as the case may be) the Secretary of State; or

    (b) in default of agreement, as may be determined by the Secretary of State.

(9) With the agreement of the responsible authority or (as the case may be) the Secretary of State, the liability to pay any sum under this section may be discharged, in whole or in part, by the transfer of any premises.

(10) This section has effect regardless of –

    (a) anything in any trust deed for a controlled or assisted community home;

    (b) the provisions of any enactment or instrument governing the disposition of the property of a voluntary organisation.

Amendments—Probation Service Act 1993, s 32, Sch 3, para 9; CJCSA 2000, ss 74, 75, Sch 7, Pt II, paras 87, 93, Sch 8; Care Standards Act 2000, s 117, Sch 6.

PART VII
VOLUNTARY HOMES AND VOLUNTARY ORGANISATIONS

59 Provision of accommodation by voluntary organisations

(1) Where a voluntary organisation provide accommodation for a child, they shall do so by –

    (a) placing him (subject to subsection (2)) with –
      (i) a family;
      (ii) a relative of his; or
      (iii) any other suitable person,
    on such terms as to payment by the organisation and otherwise as the organisation may determine (subject to section 49 of the Children Act 2004);

(aa)   maintaining him in a children's home in respect of which a person is registered under Part 2 of the Care Standards Act 2000;

(b)–(e)   *(repealed)*

(f)   making such other arrangements (subject to subsection (3)) as seem appropriate to them.

(1A) Where under subsection (1)(aa) a voluntary organisation maintains a child in a home provided, equipped and maintained by an appropriate national authority under section 82(5), it shall do so on such terms as the that national authority may from time to time determine.

(2) The appropriate national authority may make regulations as to the placing of children with foster parents by voluntary organisations.

(3) The appropriate national authority may make regulations as to the arrangements which may be made under subsection (1)(f).

(3A) Regulations under subsection (2) or (3) may in particular make provision which (with any necessary modifications) is similar to that which may be made under section 22C by virtue of any of paragraphs 12B, 12E and 12F of Schedule 2.

(4) The appropriate national authority may make regulations requiring any voluntary organisation who are providing accommodation for a child –

(a)   to review his case; and

(b)   to consider any representations (including any complaint) made to them by any person falling within a prescribed class of person,

in accordance with the provisions of the regulations.

(5A) Regulations under subsection (4) may, in particular –

(a)   apply with modifications any provision of section 25A or 25B;

(b)   make provision which (with any necessary modifications) is similar to any provision which may be made under section 25A, 25B or 26.

(6) Regulations under subsections (2) to (4) may provide that any person who, without reasonable excuse, contravenes or fails to comply with a regulation shall be guilty of an offence and liable on summary conviction to a fine not exceeding level 4 on the standard scale.

(7) In this Part "appropriate national authority" means –

(a)   in relation to England, the Secretary of State; and

(b)   in relation to Wales, the Welsh Ministers.

Amendments—Care Standards Act 2000, s 116, Sch 4, para 14(1), (8); CA 2004, s 49(4); CYPA 2008, ss 8· 39, Sch 1, para 2, Sch 3, paras 1, 23.

60 Voluntary homes

(1), (2) *(repealed)*

(3) In this Act "voluntary home" means a children's home which is carried on by a voluntary organisation but does not include a community home.

(4) Schedule 5 shall have effect for the purpose of supplementing the provisions of this Part.

Amendments—Registered Homes (Amendment) Act 1991, s 2(6); Care Standards Act 2000, s 116, Sch 4, para 14(1), (9), Sch 6.

61 Duties of voluntary organisations

(1) Where a child is accommodated by or on behalf of a voluntary organisation, it shall be the duty of the organisation –

(a) to safeguard and promote his welfare;

(b) to make such use of the services and facilities available for children cared for by their own parents as appears to the organisation reasonable in his case; and

(c) to advise, assist and befriend him with a view to promoting his welfare when he ceases to be so accommodated.

(2) Before making any decision with respect to any such child the organisation shall, so far as is reasonably practicable, ascertain the wishes and feelings of –

(a) the child;

(b) his parents;

(c) any person who is not a parent of his but who has parental responsibility for him; and

(d) any other person whose wishes and feelings the organisation consider to be relevant,

regarding the matter to be decided.

(3) In making any such decision the organisation shall give due consideration –

(a) having regard to the child's age and understanding, to such wishes and feelings of his as they have been able to ascertain;

(b) to such other wishes and feelings mentioned in subsection (2) as they have been able to ascertain; and

(c) to the child's religious persuasion, racial origin and cultural and linguistic background.

The Adoption Agencies Regulations 2005—The Adoption Agencies Regulations 2005, came into force on 30 December 2005. They state that where a registered adoption society is authorised to place a child for adoption, or a child who has been so placed for adoption is less than 6 weeks old, s 61(2)(a) has effect in relation to the child whether or not he is accommodated by or on behalf of the society (reg 45(4)(a)). Furthermore, s 61(2)(b) does not apply, and s 61(2)(c) applies as if there were instead inserted "(c) any prospective adopter with whom the registered adoption society has placed the child for adoption" (reg 45(4)(b) and (c)).

62 Duties of local authorities

(1) Every local authority shall satisfy themselves that any voluntary organisation providing accommodation –

(a) within the authority's area for any child; or

(b) outside that area for any child on behalf of the authority,

are satisfactorily safeguarding and promoting the welfare of the children so provided with accommodation.

(2) Every local authority shall arrange for children who are accommodated within their area by or on behalf of voluntary organisations to be visited, from time to time, in the interests of their welfare

(3) The appropriate national authority may make regulations –

(a) requiring every child who is accommodated within a local authority's area, by or on behalf of a voluntary organisation, to be visited by an officer of the authority –

(i) in prescribed circumstances; and

(ii) on specified occasions or within specified periods; and

(b) imposing requirements which must be met by any local authority, or officer of a local authority, carrying out functions under this section.

(4) Subsection (2) does not apply in relation to community homes.

(5) Where a local authority are not satisfied that the welfare of any child who is accommodated by or on behalf of a voluntary organisation is being satisfactorily safeguarded or promoted they shall –

    (a) unless they consider that it would not be in the best interests of the child, take such steps as are reasonably practicable to secure that the care and accommodation of the child is undertaken by –

        (i) a parent of his;

        (ii) any person who is not a parent of his but who has parental responsibility for him; or

        (iii) a relative of his; and

    (b) consider the extent to which (if at all) they should exercise any of their functions with respect to the child.

(6) Any person authorised by a local authority may, for the purpose of enabling the authority to discharge their duties under this section –

    (a) enter, at any reasonable time, and inspect any premises in which children are being accommodated as mentioned in subsection (1) or (2);

    (b) inspect any children there;

    (c) require any person to furnish him with such records of a kind required to be kept by regulations made under section 22 of the Care Standards Act 2000 (in whatever form they are held), or allow him to inspect such records, as he may at any time direct.

(7) Any person exercising the power conferred by subsection (6) shall, if asked to do so, produce some duly authenticated document showing his authority to do so.

(8) Any person authorised to exercise the power to inspect records conferred by subsection (6) –

    (a) shall be entitled at any reasonable time to have access to, and inspect and check the operation of, any computer and any associated apparatus or material which is or has been in use in connection with the records in question; and

    (b) may require –

        (i) the person by whom or on whose behalf the computer is or has been so used; or

        (ii) any person having charge of, or otherwise concerned with the operation of, the computer, apparatus or material,

    to afford him such assistance as he may reasonably require.

(9) Any person who intentionally obstructs another in the exercise of any power conferred by subsection (6) or (8) shall be guilty of an offence and liable on summary conviction to a fine not exceeding level 3 on the standard scale.

(10) This section does not apply in relation to any voluntary organisation which is an institution within the further education sector, as defined in section 91 of the Further and Higher Education Act 1992, a 16 to 19 Academy or a school.

Amendments—Care Standards Act 2000, ss 105(5), 116, Sch 4, para 14(1), (10); CYPA 2008, s 39, Sch 3, paras 1, 24; Education Act 2011, s 54, Sch 13, para 6.

PART VIII
REGISTERED CHILDREN'S HOMES

63 Private children's homes etc

(1)–(10) (*repealed*)

(11) Schedule 6 shall have effect with respect to private children's homes.

(12) Schedule 7 shall have effect for the purpose of setting out the circumstances in which a person may foster more than three children without being treated, for the purposes of this Act and the Care Standards Act 2000, as carrying on a children's home.

Amendments—Registered Homes (Amendment) Act 1991, s 2(6); Education Act 1996, s 582(1), Sch 37, Pt I, para 86; Care Standards Act 2000, ss 116, 117, Sch 4, para 14(1),(11), Sch 6.

64 Welfare of children in children's homes

(1) Where a child is accommodated in a private children's home, it shall be the duty of the person carrying on the home to –

    (a) safeguard and promote the child's welfare;

    (b) make such use of the services and facilities available for children cared for by their own parents as appears to that person reasonable in the case of the child; and

    (c) advise, assist and befriend him with a view to promoting his welfare when he ceases to be so accommodated.

(2) Before making any decision with respect to any such child the person carrying on the home shall, so far as is reasonably practicable, ascertain the wishes and feelings of –

    (a) the child;

    (b) his parents;

    (c) any other person who is not a parent of his but who has parental responsibility for him; and

    (d) any person whose wishes and feelings the person carrying on the home considers to be relevant,

regarding the matter to be decided.

(3) In making any such decision the person concerned shall give due consideration –

    (a) having regard to the child's age and understanding, to such wishes and feelings of his as he has been able to ascertain;

    (b) to such other wishes and feelings mentioned in subsection (2) as he has been able to ascertain; and

    (c) to the child's religious persuasion, racial origin and cultural and linguistic background.

(4) Section 62, except subsection (4), shall apply in relation to any person who is carrying on a private children's home as it applies in relation to any voluntary organisation.

Amendments—Care Standards Act 2000, s 116, Sch 4, para 14(1), (12).

65 Persons disqualified from carrying on, or being employed in, children's homes

(1) A person who is disqualified (under section 68) from fostering a child privately shall not carry on, or be otherwise concerned in the management of, or have any financial interest in, a children's home unless he has –

    (a) disclosed to the appropriate authority the fact that he is so disqualified; and

(b)   obtained its written consent.

(2) No person shall employ a person who is so disqualified in a children's home unless he has –

(a)   disclosed to the appropriate authority the fact that that person is so disqualified; and

(b)   obtained its written consent.

(3) Where the appropriate authority refuses to give its consent under this section, it shall inform the applicant by a written notice which states –

(a)   the reason for the refusal;

(b)   the applicant's right to appeal under section 65A against the refusal to the First-tier Tribunal; and

(c)   the time within which he may do so.

(4) Any person who contravenes subsection (1) or (2) shall be guilty of an offence and liable on summary conviction to imprisonment for a term not exceeding six months or to a fine not exceeding level 5 on the standard scale or to both.

(5) Where a person contravenes subsection (2) he shall not be guilty of an offence if he proves that he did not know, and had no reasonable grounds for believing, that the person whom he was employing was disqualified under section 68.

(6) In this section and section 65A "appropriate authority" means –

(a)   in relation to England, Her Majesty's Chief Inspector of Education, Children's Services and Skills; and

(b)   in relation to Wales, the National Assembly for Wales.

Amendments—Care Standards Act 2000, s 116, Sch 4, para 14(1), (13); Health and Social Care (Community Health and Standards) Act 2003, s 147, Sch 9, para 10; Education and Inspections Act 2006, Sch 14, para 12; SI 2008/2833.

65A Appeal against refusal of authority to give consent under section 65

(1) An appeal against a decision of an appropriate authority under section 65 shall lie to the First-tier Tribunal.

(2) On an appeal the Tribunal may confirm the authority's decision or direct it to give the consent in question.

Amendments—Inserted by Care Standards Act 2000, s 116, Sch 4, para 14(1),(14); amended by SI 2008/2833.

PART IX
PRIVATE ARRANGEMENTS FOR FOSTERING CHILDREN

66 Privately fostered children

(1) In this Part –

(a)   "a privately fostered child" means a child who is under the age of sixteen and who is cared for, and provided with accommodation in their own home by, someone other than –

(i)   a parent of his;

(ii)   a person who is not a parent of his but who has parental responsibility for him; or

(iii) a relative of his; and

(b)   "to foster a child privately" means to look after the child in circumstances in which he is a privately fostered child as defined by this section.

(2) A child is not a privately fostered child if the person caring for and accommodating him –

    (a) has done so for a period of less than 28 days; and
    (b) does not intend to do so for any longer period.

(3) Subsection (1) is subject to –

    (a) the provisions of section 63; and
    (b) the exceptions made by paragraphs 1 to 5 of Schedule 8.

(4) In the case of a child who is disabled, subsection (1)(a) shall have effect as if for "sixteen" there were substituted "eighteen".

(4A) The Secretary of State may by regulations make provision as to the circumstances in which a person who provides accommodation to a child is, or is not, to be treated as providing him with accommodation in the person's own home.

(5) Schedule 8 shall have effect for the purposes of supplementing the provision made by this Part.

Amendments—Care Standards Act 2000, s 116, Sch 4, para 14(1),(15).

67 Welfare of privately fostered children

(1) It shall be the duty of every local authority to satisfy themselves that the welfare of children who are or are proposed to be privately fostered within their area is being or will be satisfactorily safeguarded and promoted and to secure that such advice is given to those concerned with them as appears to the authority to be needed.

(2) The Secretary of State may make regulations –

    (a) requiring every child who is privately fostered within a local authority's area to be visited by an officer of the authority –
        (i) in prescribed circumstances; and
        (ii) on specified occasions or within specified periods; and
    (b) imposing requirements which are to be met by any local authority, or officer of a local authority, in carrying out functions under this section.

(2A) Regulations under subsection (2)(b) may impose requirements as to the action to be taken by a local authority for the purposes of discharging their duty under subsection (1) where they have received notification of a proposal that a child be privately fostered.

(3) Where any person who is authorised by a local authority for the purpose has reasonable cause to believe that –

    (a) any privately fostered child is being accommodated in premises within the authority's area; or
    (b) it is proposed to accommodate any such child in any such premises,

he may at any reasonable time inspect those premises and any children there.

(4) Any person exercising the power under subsection (3) shall, if so required, produce some duly authenticated document showing his authority to do so.

(5) Where a local authority are not satisfied that the welfare of any child who is or is proposed to be privately fostered within their area is being or will be satisfactorily safeguarded or promoted they shall –

    (a) unless they consider that it would not be in the best interests of the child, take such steps as are reasonably practicable to secure that the care and accommodation of the child is undertaken by –
        (i) a parent of his;
        (ii) any person who is not a parent of his but who has parental responsibility for him; or

(iii) a relative of his; and
(b) consider the extent to which (if at all) they should exercise any of their functions under this Act with respect to the child.

(6) The Secretary of State may make regulations requiring a local authority to monitor the way in which the authority discharge their functions under this Part (and the regulations may in particular require the authority to appoint an officer for that purpose).

Amendments—CA 2004, s 44.

68 Persons disqualified from being private foster parents

(1) Unless he has disclosed the fact to the appropriate local authority and obtained their written consent, a person shall not foster a child privately if he is disqualified from doing so by regulations made by the Secretary of State for the purposes of this section.

(2) The regulations may, in particular, provide for a person to be so disqualified where –
(a) an order of a kind specified in the regulations has been made at any time with respect to him;
(b) an order of a kind so specified has been made at any time with respect to any child who has been in his care;
(c) a requirement of a kind so specified has been imposed at any time with respect to any such child, under or by virtue of any enactment;
(d) he has been convicted of any offence of a kind so specified, or discharged absolutely or conditionally for any such offence;
(e) a prohibition has been imposed on him at any time under section 69 or under any other specified enactment;
(f) his rights and powers with respect to a child have at any time been vested in a specified authority under a specified enactment.

(2A) A conviction in respect of which a probation order was made before 1 October 1992 (which would not otherwise be treated as a conviction) is to be treated as a conviction for the purposes of subsection (2)(d).

(3) Unless he has disclosed the fact to the appropriate local authority and obtained their written consent, a person shall not foster a child privately if –
(a) he lives in the same household as a person who is himself prevented from fostering a child by subsection (1); or
(b) he lives in a household at which any such person is employed.

(4) Where an authority refuse to give their consent under this section, they shall inform the applicant by a written notice which states –
(a) the reason for the refusal;
(b) the applicant's right under paragraph 8 of Schedule 8 to appeal against the refusal; and
(c) the time within which he may do so.

(5) In this section –
"the appropriate authority" means the local authority within whose area it is proposed to foster the child in question; and
"enactment" means any enactment having effect, at any time, in any part of the United Kingdom.

Amendments—CJCSA 2000 s 74, Sch 7, para 94; CJA 2003, ss 304, 332, Sch 32, Pt 1, paras 59, 60, Sch 37, Pt 7.

69 Power to prohibit private fostering

(1) This section applies where a person –

    (a)   proposes to foster a child privately; or

    (b)   is fostering a child privately.

(2) Where the local authority for the area within which the child is proposed to be, or is being, fostered are of the opinion that –

    (a)   he is not a suitable person to foster a child;

    (b)   the premises in which the child will be, or is being, accommodated are not suitable; or

    (c)   it would be prejudicial to the welfare of the child for him to be, or continue to be, accommodated by that person in those premises,

the authority may impose a prohibition on him under subsection (3).

(3) A prohibition imposed on any person under this subsection may prohibit him from fostering privately –

    (a)   any child in any premises within the area of the local authority; or

    (b)   any child in premises specified in the prohibition;

    (c)   a child identified in the prohibition, in premises specified in the prohibition.

(4) A local authority who have imposed a prohibition on any person under subsection (3) may, if they think fit, cancel the prohibition –

    (a)   of their own motion; or

    (b)   on an application made by that person,

if they are satisfied that the prohibition is no longer justified.

(5) Where a local authority impose a requirement on any person under paragraph 6 of Schedule 8, they may also impose a prohibition on him under subsection (3).

(6) Any prohibition imposed by virtue of subsection (5) shall not have effect unless –

    (a)   the time specified for compliance with the requirement has expired; and

    (b)   the requirement has not been complied with.

(7) A prohibition imposed under this section shall be imposed by notice in writing addressed to the person on whom it is imposed and informing him of –

    (a)   the reason for imposing the prohibition;

    (b)   his right under paragraph 8 of Schedule 8 to appeal against the prohibition; and

    (c)   the time within which he may do so.

70 Offences

(1) A person shall be guilty of an offence if –

    (a)   being required, under any provision made by or under this Part, to give any notice or information –

        (i)   he fails without reasonable excuse to give the notice within the time specified in that provision; or

        (ii)   he fails without reasonable excuse to give the information within a reasonable time; or

        (iii)   he makes, or causes or procures another person to make, any statement in the notice or information which he knows to be false or misleading in a material particular;

    (b)   he refuses to allow a privately fostered child to be visited by a duly authorised officer of a local authority;

    (c)   he intentionally obstructs another in the exercise of the power conferred by section 67(3);

(d) he contravenes section 68;

(e) he fails without reasonable excuse to comply with any requirement imposed by a local authority under this Part;

(f) he accommodates a privately fostered child in any premises in contravention of a prohibition imposed by a local authority under this Part;

(g) he knowingly causes to be published, or publishes, an advertisement which he knows contravenes paragraph 10 of Schedule 8.

(2) Where a person contravenes section 68(3), he shall not be guilty of an offence under this section if he proves that he did not know, and had no reasonable ground for believing, that any person to whom section 68(1) applied was living or employed in the premises in question.

(3) A person guilty of an offence under subsection (1)(a) shall be liable on summary conviction to a fine not exceeding level 5 on the standard scale.

(4) A person guilty of an offence under subsection (1)(b), (c) or (g) shall be liable on summary conviction to a fine not exceeding level 3 on the standard scale.

(5) A person guilty of an offence under subsection (1)(d) or (f) shall be liable on summary conviction to imprisonment for a term not exceeding six months, or to a fine not exceeding level 5 on the standard scale, or to both.

(6) A person guilty of an offence under subsection (1)(e) shall be liable on summary conviction to a fine not exceeding level 4 on the standard scale.

(7) If any person who is required, under any provision of this Part, to give a notice fails to give the notice within the time specified in that provision, proceedings for the offence may be brought at any time within six months from the date when evidence of the offence came to the knowledge of the local authority.

(8) Subsection (7) is not affected by anything in section 127(1) of the Magistrates' Courts Act 1980 (time limit for proceedings).

****

PART XA
CHILD MINDING AND DAY CARE FOR CHILDREN IN WALES

Introductory

79A Child minders and day care providers

(1) This section and section 79B apply for the purposes of this Part.

(2) "Act as a child minder" means (subject to the following subsections) look after one or more children under the age of eight on domestic premises for reward; and "child minding" shall be interpreted accordingly.

(3) A person who –

(a) is the parent, or a relative, of a child;

(b) has parental responsibility for a child;

(c) is a local authority foster parent in relation to a child;

(d) is a foster parent with whom a child has been placed by a voluntary organisation; or

(e) fosters a child privately,

does not act as a child minder when looking after that child.

(4) Where a person –

(a) looks after a child for the parents ("P1"), or

(b)   in addition to that work, looks after another child for different parents ("P2"),

and the work consists (in a case within paragraph (a)) of looking after the child wholly or mainly in P1's home or (in a case within paragraph (b)) of looking after the children wholly or mainly in P1's home or P2's home or both, the work is not to be treated as child minding.

(5) In subsection (4), "parent", in relation to a child, includes –

    (a)   a person who is not a parent of the child but who has parental responsibility for the child;

    (b)   a person who is a relative of the child.

(6) "Day care" means care provided at any time for children under the age of eight on premises other than domestic premises.

(7) This Part does not apply in relation to a person who acts as a child minder, or provides day care on any premises, unless the period, or the total of the periods, in any day which he spends looking after children or (as the case may be) during which the children are looked after on the premises exceeds two hours.

(8) In determining whether a person is required to register under this Part for child minding, any day on which he does not act as a child minder at any time between 2 am and 6 pm is to be disregarded.

Amendments—Inserted by Care Standards Act 2000, s 79(1). Part heading amended by Childcare Act 2006, s 103, Sch 2, para 5, Sch 3, Pt 2.

79B Other definitions, etc

(1) (*repealed*)

(2) In this Act "the Assembly" means the National Assembly for Wales.

(3) A person is qualified for registration for child minding if –

    (a)   he, and every other person looking after children on any premises on which he is or is likely to be child minding, is suitable to look after children under the age of eight;

    (b)   every person living or employed on the premises in question is suitable to be in regular contact with children under the age of eight;

    (c)   the premises in question are suitable to be used for looking after children under the age of eight, having regard to their condition and the condition and appropriateness of any equipment on the premises and to any other factor connected with the situation, construction or size of the premises; and

    (d)   he is complying with regulations under section 79C and with any conditions imposed under this Part.

(4) A person is qualified for registration for providing day care on particular premises if –

    (a)   he has made adequate arrangements to ensure that –

       (i)   every person (other than himself and the responsible individual) looking after children on the premises is suitable to look after children under the age of eight; and

       (ii)   every person (other than himself and the responsible individual) living or working on the premises is suitable to be in regular contact with children under the age of eight;

    (b)   the responsible individual –

       (i)   is suitable to look after children under the age of eight, or

       (ii)   if he is not looking after such children, is suitable to be in regular contact with them;

   (c)   the premises are suitable to be used for looking after children under the age of eight, having regard to their condition and the condition and appropriateness of any equipment on the premises and to any other factor connected with the situation, construction or size of the premises; and

   (d)   he is complying with regulations under section 79C and with any conditions imposed under this Part.

(5) For the purposes of subsection (4)(a) a person is not treated as working on the premises in question if –

   (a)   none of his work is done in the part of the premises in which children are looked after; or

   (b)   he does not work on the premises at times when children are looked after there.

(5ZA) For the purposes of subsection (4), "the responsible individual" means –

   (a)   in a case of one individual working on the premises in the provision of day care, that person;

   (b)   in a case of two or more individuals so working, the individual so working who is in charge.

(5A) Where, for the purposes of determining a person's qualification for registration under this Part –

   (a)   the Assembly requests any person ("A") to consent to the disclosure to the authority by another person ("B") of any information relating to A which is held by B and is of a prescribed description, and

   (b)   A does not give his consent (or withdraws it after having given it),

the Assembly may, if regulations so provide and it thinks it appropriate to do so, regard A as not suitable to look after children under the age of eight, or not suitable to be in regular contact with such children.

(6) "Domestic premises" means any premises which are wholly or mainly used as a private dwelling and "premises" includes any area and any vehicle.

(7) "Regulations" means regulations made by the Assembly.

(8) (*repealed*)

(9) Schedule 9A (which supplements the provisions of this Part) shall have effect.

Amendments—Inserted by Care Standards Act 2000, s 79(1); amended by Education Act 2002, s 152, Sch 13, para 1; CA 2004, s 48, Sch 4, paras 1, 2, 6; Education and Inspections Act 2006, Sch 14, para 13; Childcare Act 2006, s 103, Sch 2, paras 6, 7, Sch 3, Pt 2; SI 2008/2833.

Regulations

79C Regulations etc governing child minders and day care providers

(1) (*repealed*)

(2) The Assembly may make regulations governing the activities of registered persons who act as child minders, or provide day care, on premises in Wales.

(3) The regulations under this section may deal with the following matters (among others) –

   (a)   the welfare and development of the children concerned;

   (b)   suitability to look after, or be in regular contact with, children under the age of eight;

   (c)   qualifications and training;

   (d)   the maximum number of children who may be looked after and the number of persons required to assist in looking after them;

(e)   the maintenance, safety and suitability of premises and equipment;
(f)   the keeping of records;
(g)   the provision of information.

(4), (5) (*repealed*)

(6) If the regulations require any person (other than the Assembly) to have regard to or meet factors, standards and other matters prescribed by or referred to in the regulations, they may also provide for any allegation that the person has failed to do so to be taken into account –

(a)   by the registration authority in the exercise of its functions under this Part, or
(b)   in any proceedings under this Part.

(7) Regulations may provide –

(a)   that a registered person who without reasonable excuse contravenes, or otherwise fails to comply with, any requirement of the regulations shall be guilty of an offence; and
(b)   that a person guilty of the offence shall be liable on summary conviction to a fine not exceeding level 5 on the standard scale.

Amendments—Inserted by Care Standards Act 2000, s 79(1); amended by Childcare Act 2006, s 103, Sch 2, paras 6, 8, Sch 3, Pt 2.

Registration

79D   Requirement to register

(1) No person shall act as a child minder in Wales unless he is registered under this Part for child minding by the Assembly.

(2) Where it appears to the Assembly that a person has contravened subsection (1), the authority may serve a notice ("an enforcement notice") on him.

(3) An enforcement notice shall have effect for a period of one year beginning with the date on which it is served.

(4) If a person in respect of whom an enforcement notice has effect contravenes subsection (1) without reasonable excuse, he shall be guilty of an offence.

(5) No person shall provide day care on any premises in Wales unless he is registered under this Part for providing day care on those premises by the Assembly.

(6) If any person contravenes subsection (5) without reasonable excuse, he shall be guilty of an offence.

(7) A person guilty of an offence under this section shall be liable on summary conviction to a fine not exceeding level 5 on the standard scale.

Amendments—Inserted by Care Standards Act 2000, s 79(1); amended by Childcare Act 2006, s 103, Sch 2, paras 6, 9, Sch 3, Pt 2

79E   Applications for registration

(1) A person who wishes to be registered under this Part shall make an application to the Assembly.

(2) The application shall –

(a)   give prescribed information about prescribed matters;
(b)   give any other information which the Assembly reasonably requires the applicant to give;
(c)   be accompanied by the prescribed fee.

(3) Where a person provides, or proposes to provide, day care on different premises, he shall make a separate application in respect of each of them.

(4) Where the Assembly has sent the applicant notice under section 79L(1) of its intention to refuse an application under this section, the application may not be withdrawn without the consent of the authority.

(5) A person who, in an application under this section, knowingly makes a statement which is false or misleading in a material particular shall be guilty of an offence and liable, on summary conviction, to a fine not exceeding level 5 on the standard scale.

Amendments—Inserted by Care Standards Act 2000, s 79(1); amended by CA 2004, s 48, Sch 4, paras 1, 3(1); Childcare Act 2006, s 103, Sch 2, para 6.

79F Grant or refusal of registration

(1) If, on an application under section 79E by a person for registration for child minding –

    (a)   the Assembly is of the opinion that the applicant is, and will continue to be, qualified for registration for child minding (so far as the conditions of section 79B(3) are applicable);

    (b)   (*repealed*)

the Assembly shall grant the application; otherwise, it shall refuse it.

(2) If, on an application under section 79E by any person for registration for providing day care on any premises –

    (a)   the Assembly is of the opinion that the applicant is, and will continue to be, qualified for registration for providing day care on those premises (so far as the conditions of section 79B(4) are applicable);

    (b)   (*repealed*)

the Assembly shall grant the application; otherwise, it shall refuse it.

(3) An application may, as well as being granted subject to any conditions the Assembly thinks necessary or expedient for the purpose of giving effect to regulations under section 79C, be granted subject to any other conditions the authority thinks fit to impose.

(4) The Assembly may as it thinks fit vary or remove any condition to which the registration is subject or impose a new condition.

(5) Any register kept by the Assembly of persons who act as child minders or provide day care shall be open to inspection by any person at all reasonable times.

(6) A registered person who without reasonable excuse contravenes, or otherwise fails to comply with, any condition imposed on his registration shall be guilty of an offence.

(7) A person guilty of an offence under subsection (6) shall be liable on summary conviction to a fine not exceeding level 5 on the standard scale.

Amendments—Inserted by Care Standards Act 2000, s 79(1); amended by CA 2004, ss 48, 64, Sch 4, paras 1, 3(2), Sch 5; Childcare Act 2006, s 103, Sch 2, para 6.

79G Cancellation of registration

(1) The Assembly may cancel the registration of any person if –

    (a)   in the case of a person registered for child minding, the Assembly is of the opinion that the person has ceased or will cease to be qualified for registration for child minding;

(b) in the case of a person registered for providing day care on any premises, the Assembly is of the opinion that the person has ceased or will cease to be qualified for registration for providing day care on those premises,

or if a fee which is due from the person has not been paid.

(2) Where a requirement to make any changes or additions to any services, equipment or premises has been imposed on a registered person, his registration shall not be cancelled on the ground of any defect or insufficiency in the services, equipment or premises if –

(a) the time set for complying with the requirements has not expired; and

(b) it is shown that the defect or insufficiency is due to the changes or additions not having been made.

(3) Any cancellation under this section must be in writing.

Amendments—Inserted by Care Standards Act 2000, s 79(1); amended by CA 2004, ss 48, 64, Sch 4, paras 1, 2(2), 4, Sch 5; Childcare Act 2006, s 103, Sch 2, para 6.

79H Suspension of registration

(1) Regulations may provide for the registration of any person for acting as a child minder or providing day care to be suspended for a prescribed period by the Assembly in prescribed circumstances.

(2) Any regulations made under this section shall include provision conferring on the person concerned a right of appeal to the First-tier Tribunal against suspension.

(3)–(6) ...

Amendments—Inserted by Care Standards Act 2000, s 79(1); amended by Childcare Act 2006, s 103, Sch 2, para 6; SI 2008/2833.

79J Resignation of registration

(1) A person who is registered for acting as a child minder or providing day care may by notice in writing to the Assembly resign his registration.

(2) But a person may not give a notice under subsection (1) –

(a) if the Assembly has sent him a notice under section 79L(1) of its intention to cancel the registration, unless the authority has decided not to take that step; or

(b) if the Assembly has sent him a notice under section 79L(5) of its decision to cancel the registration and the time within which an appeal may be brought has not expired or, if an appeal has been brought, it has not been determined.

Amendments—Inserted by Care Standards Act 2000, s 79(1); amended by Childcare Act 2006, s 103, Sch 2, para 6.

79K Protection of children in an emergency

(1) If, in the case of any person registered under this Part for acting as a child minder or providing day care –

(a) the Assembly applies to a justice of the peace for an order –
    (i) cancelling the registration;
    (ii) varying or removing any condition to which the registration is subject; or
    (iii) imposing a new condition; and

(b) it appears to the justice that a child who is being, or may be, looked after by that person, or (as the case may be) in accordance with the provision for day care made by that person, is suffering, or is likely to suffer, significant harm,

the justice may make the order.

PART II

(2) The cancellation, variation, removal or imposition shall have effect from the time when the order is made.

(3) An application under subsection (1) may be made without notice.

(4) An order under subsection (1) shall be made in writing.

(5) Where an order is made under this section, the Assembly shall serve on the registered person, as soon as is reasonably practicable after the making of the order –

    (a)   a copy of the order;

    (b)   a copy of any written statement of the Assembly's reasons for making the application for the order which supported that application; and

    (c)   notice of any right of appeal conferred by section 79M.

(6) Where an order has been so made, the Assembly shall, as soon as is reasonably practicable after the making of the order, notify the local authority in whose area the person concerned acts or acted as a child minder, or provides or provided day care, of the making of the order.

Amendments—Inserted by Care Standards Act 2000, s 79(1); amended by Childcare Act 2006, s 103, Sch 2, para 6.

Procedure – applications without notice—Section 79K authorises without notice applications and where the justice of the peace accedes to such an application he or she must make the order in writing. The with notice procedure in s 79L (below) obviously does not apply to such applications, but it should be used when circumstances permit. It is suggested that it would nevertheless be sensible for the authority, in without notice applications to the court, to follow the procedure in FPR 2010, rr 12.5, 5.1–5.3 and PD5A and to use Form C5 so as to give a written statement of their reasons, indicating at para 2 "About the Respondent" that the application will be made without notice. The order should be on Form C41.

There appears, however, to be no requirement for an order made without notice to be served on the person registered; it only has to be served on the registration authority who, in turn, notify the local authority in whose area the person concerned acts as child minder or as a provider of day care. Section 79M provides a right of appeal to the Tribunal against any order made under s 79K.

Under the repealed s 75 there was provision for notice of the order, and a copy of the authority's reasons supporting the application, to be served on the person registered as soon as possible after the making of the order. However, it is suggested that it would constitute good practice for the authority to continue to serve a copy of the order and a copy of the authority's reasons supporting the application for the order on the person registered, as previously required by s 75(4), since the person registered will need this information in order to decide whether to appeal to the Tribunal or, alternatively, whether it is appropriate to pursue redress through judicial review (see *R v St Albans Magistrates' Court ex parte J* [1993] Fam Law 518 for the principles applied under the pre-existing law).

79L Notice of intention to take steps

(1) Not less than 14 days before –

    (a)   refusing an application for registration;

    (b)   cancelling a registration;

    (c)   removing or varying any condition to which a registration is subject or imposing a new condition; or

    (d)   refusing to grant an application for the removal or variation of any condition to which a registration is subject,

the Assembly shall send to the applicant, or (as the case may be) registered person, notice in writing of its intention to take the step in question.

(2) Every such notice shall –

    (a)   give the Assembly's reasons for proposing to take the step; and

    (b)   inform the person concerned of his rights under this section.

(3) Where the recipient of such a notice informs the Assembly in writing of his desire to object to the step being taken, the Assembly shall afford him an opportunity to do so.

(4) Any objection made under subsection (3) may be made orally or in writing, by the recipient of the notice or a representative.

(5) If the Assembly, after giving the person concerned an opportunity to object to the step being taken, decides nevertheless to take it, it shall send him written notice of its decision.

(6) A step of a kind mentioned in subsection (1)(b) or (c) shall not take effect until the expiry of the time within which an appeal may be brought under section 79M or, where such an appeal is brought, before its determination.

(7) Subsection (6) does not prevent a step from taking effect before the expiry of the time within which an appeal may be brought under section 79M if the person concerned notifies the Assembly in writing that he does not intend to appeal.

Amendments—Inserted by Care Standards Act 2000, s 79(1); amended by Childcare Act 2006, s 103, Sch 2, para 6.

Procedure – applications with notice—Although s 79K(3) (above) permits an application to be made without notice to the person registered, the with notice procedure in this section should be used when circumstances permit. It would appear that the registration authority alone has the power to grant or refuse the application. Section 79M provides a right of appeal to the Tribunal against any step mentioned in s 79L(1). On an appeal, the Tribunal will be able to (a) confirm the taking of the step or the making of the order or direct that it shall not have, or shall cease to have, effect; and (b) impose, vary or cancel any condition.

79M Appeals

(1) An appeal against –

    (a)   the taking of any step mentioned in section 79L(1);

    (b)   an order under section 79K; or

    (c)   a determination made by the Assembly under this Part (other than one falling within paragraph (a) or (b)) which is of a prescribed description

shall lie to the First-tier Tribunal.

(2) On an appeal, the First-tier Tribunal may –

    (a)   confirm the taking of the step or the making of the order or determination or direct that it shall not have, or shall cease to have, effect; and

    (b)   impose, vary or cancel any condition.

Amendments—Inserted by Care Standards Act 2000, s 79(1); amended by Education Act 2002, ss 148, 155, 215, Sch 13, para 3, Sch 14, para 3, Sch 22, Pt 3; Childcare Act 2006, s 103, Sch 2, para 6; SI 2008/2833.

Procedure—It is likely that the procedure to be followed by the Care Standards Tribunal will be a rehearing rather than a review of the decision which is the subject of appeal (*Tameside Metropolitan Borough Council v Grant* [2002] 1 FLR 318: a decision on the repealed CA 1989, s 71). Where there is a right of appeal to the Care Standards Tribunal, judicial review is not appropriate (*R (M) v London Borough of Bromley* [2002] 2 FLR 802).

79N–79R *(repealed)*

****

Supplementary

79U Rights of entry etc

(1) Any person authorised for the purposes of this subsection by the Assembly may at any reasonable time enter any premises in Wales on which child minding or day care is at any time provided.

(2) Where a person who is authorised for the purposes of this subsection by the Assembly has reasonable cause to believe that a child is being looked after on any premises in contravention of this Part, he may enter those premises at any reasonable time.

(2A) Authorisation under subsection (1) or (2) –

    (a) may be given for a particular occasion or period;

    (b) may be given subject to conditions.

(3) A person entering premises under this section may (subject to any conditions imposed under subsection (2A)(b)) –

    (a) inspect the premises;

    (b) inspect, and take copies of –

        (i) any records kept by the person providing the child minding or day care; and

        (ii) any other documents containing information relating to its provision;

    (c) seize and remove any document or other material or thing found there which he has reasonable grounds to believe may be evidence of a failure to comply with any condition or requirement imposed by or under this Part;

    (d) require any person to afford him such facilities and assistance with respect to matters within the person's control as are necessary to enable him to exercise his powers under this section;

    (e) take measurements and photographs or make recordings;

    (f) inspect any children being looked after there, and the arrangements made for their welfare;

    (g) interview in private the person providing the child minding or day care; and

    (h) interview in private any person looking after children, or living or working, there who consents to be interviewed.

(4) Section 58 of the Education Act 2005 (inspection of computer records for purposes of Part I of that Act) shall apply for the purposes of subsection (3) as it applies for the purposes of Part I of that Act.

(5) (*repealed*)

(6) A person exercising any power conferred by this section shall, if so required, produce some duly authenticated document showing his authority to do so.

(7) It shall be an offence wilfully to obstruct a person exercising any such power.

(8) Any person guilty of an offence under subsection (7) shall be liable on summary conviction to a fine not exceeding level 4 on the standard scale.

(9) In this section –

    "documents" and "records" each include information recorded in any form.

Amendments—Inserted by Care Standards Act 2000, s 79(1); amended by Education Act 2002, ss 152, 215(2), Sch 13, para 5, Sch 22, Pt 3; Education Act 2005, s 53, Sch 7, Pt 1, para 6; Childcare Act 2006, s 103, Sch 2, paras 6, 14, Sch 3, Pt 2.

79V Function of local authorities

Each local authority in Wales shall, in accordance with regulations, secure the provision –

    (a) of information and advice about child minding and day care; and

    (b) of training for persons who provide or assist in providing child minding or day care.

Amendments—Inserted by Care Standards Act 2000, s 79(1), amended by Childcare Act 2006, s 103, Sch 2, para 15.

Checks on suitability of persons working with children over the age of seven

79W Requirement for certificate of suitability

(1) This section applies to any person not required to register under this Part who looks after, or provides care for, children in Wales and meets the following conditions.

References in this section to children are to those under the age of 15 or (in the case of disabled children) 17.

(2) The first condition is that the period, or the total of the periods, in any week which he spends looking after children or (as the case may be) during which the children are looked after exceeds five hours.

(3) The second condition is that he would be required to register under this Part (or, as the case may be, this Part if it were subject to prescribed modifications) if the children were under the age of eight.

(4) Regulations may require a person to whom this section applies to hold a certificate issued by the Assembly as to his suitability, and the suitability of each prescribed person, to look after children.

(5) The regulations may make provision about –

    (a)   applications for certificates;

    (b)   the matters to be taken into account by the Assembly in determining whether to issue certificates;

    (c)   the information to be contained in certificates;

    (d)   the period of their validity.

(6) The regulations may provide that a person to whom this section applies shall be guilty of an offence –

    (a)   if he does not hold a certificate as required by the regulations; or

    (b)   if, being a person who holds such a certificate, he fails to produce it when reasonably required to do so by a prescribed person.

(7) The regulations may provide that a person who, for the purpose of obtaining such a certificate, knowingly makes a statement which is false or misleading in a material particular shall be guilty of an offence.

(8) The regulations may provide that a person guilty of an offence under the regulations shall be liable on summary conviction to a fine not exceeding level 5 on the standard scale.

Amendments—Inserted by Care Standards Act 2000, s 79(1); amended by Childcare Act 2006, s 103, Sch 2, paras 6, 16.

Time limit for proceedings

79X Time limit for proceedings

Proceedings for an offence under this Part or regulations made under it may be brought within a period of six months from the date on which evidence sufficient in the opinion of the prosecutor to warrant the proceedings came to his knowledge; but no such proceedings shall be brought by virtue of this section more than three years after the commission of the offence.

Amendments—Inserted by Care Standards Act 2000, s 79(1).

PART XI
SECRETARY OF STATE'S SUPERVISORY FUNCTIONS AND
RESPONSIBILITIES

80 Inspection of children's homes etc by persons authorised by Secretary of State

(1) The Secretary of State may cause to be inspected from time to time any –

   (a) private children's home;
   (b) premises in which a child who is being looked after by a local authority is living;
   (c) premises in which a child who is being accommodated by or on behalf of a local authority in the exercise of education functions or a or voluntary organisation is living;
   (d) premises in which a child who is being accommodated by or on behalf of a Local Health Board, Special Health Authority, National Health Service trust or NHS foundation trust or pursuant to arrangements made by the Secretary of State, the National Health Service Commissioning Board or a clinical commissioning group under the National Health Service Act 2006 is living;
   (e)–(f) (*repealed*)
   (g) premises in which a privately fostered child, or child who is treated as a foster child by virtue of paragraph 9 of Schedule 8, is living or in which it is proposed that he will live;
   (h) premises on which any person is acting as a child minder;
   (i) premises with respect to which a person is registered under section 71(1)(b) or with respect to which a person is registered for providing day care under Part XA;
   (j) care home or independent hospital used to accommodate children;
   (k) premises which are provided by a local authority and in which any service is provided by that authority under Part III;
   (l) school or college providing accommodation for any child.

(2) An inspection under this section shall be conducted by a person authorised to do so by the Secretary of State.

(3) An officer of a local authority shall not be authorised except with the consent of that authority.

(4) The Secretary of State may require any person of a kind mentioned in subsection (5) to furnish him with such information, or allow him to inspect such records (in whatever form they are held), relating to –

   (a) any premises to which subsection (1) or, in relation to Scotland, subsection (1)(h) or (i) applies;
   (b) any child who is living in any such premises;
   (c) the discharge by the Secretary of State of any of his functions under this Act;
   (d) the discharge by any local authority of any of their functions under this Act,

as the Secretary of State may at any time direct.

(5) The persons are any –

   (a) local authority;
   (b) voluntary organisation;
   (c) person carrying on a private children's home;
   (d) proprietor of an independent school or governing body of any other school;
   (da) governing body of an institution designated under section 28 of the Further and Higher Education Act 1992;
   (db) further education corporation;

(dc) sixth form college corporation;

(dd) proprietor of a 16 to 19 Academy;

(e) person fostering any privately fostered child or providing accommodation for a child on behalf of a local authority, Health Authority, Special Local Health Board, National Health Service trust, NHS foundation trust or voluntary organisation;

(ea) person providing accommodation for a child pursuant to arrangements made by the Secretary of State, the National Health Service Commissioning Board or a clinical commissioning group under the National Health Service Act 2006;

(f) (*repealed*)

(g) person employed in a teaching or administrative capacity at any educational establishment (whether or not maintained by a local authority) at which a child is accommodated on behalf of a local authority;

(h) person who is the occupier of any premises in which any person acts as a child minder (within the meaning of Part X) or provides day care for young children (within the meaning of that Part);

(hh) person who is the occupier of any premises –

    (i) in which any person required to be registered for child minding under Part XA acts as a child minder (within the meaning of that Part); or

    (ii) with respect to which a person is required to be registered under that Part for providing day care;

(i) person carrying on any home of a kind mentioned in subsection (1)(j);

(j) person carrying on a fostering agency.

(6) Any person inspecting any home or other premises under this section may –

(a) inspect the children there; and

(b) make such examination into the state and management of the home or premises and the treatment of the children there as he thinks fit.

(7) Any person authorised by the Secretary of State to exercise the power to inspect records conferred by subsection (4) –

(a) shall be entitled at any reasonable time to have access to, and inspect and check the operation of, any computer and any associated apparatus or material which is or has been in use in connection with the records in question; and

(b) may require –

    (i) the person by whom or on whose behalf the computer is or has been so used; or

    (ii) any person having charge of, or otherwise concerned with the operation of, the computer, apparatus or material,

    to afford him such reasonable assistance as he may require.

(8) A person authorised to inspect any premises under this section shall have a right to enter the premises for that purpose, and for any purpose specified in subsection (4), at any reasonable time.

(9) Any person exercising that power shall, if so required, produce some duly authenticated document showing his authority to do so.

(10) Any person who intentionally obstructs another in the exercise of that power shall be guilty of an offence and liable on summary conviction to a fine not exceeding level 3 on the standard scale.

(11) The Secretary of State may by order provide for subsections (1), (4) and (6) not to apply in relation to such homes, or other premises, as may be specified in the order.

(12) Without prejudice to section 104, any such order may make different provision with respect to each of those subsections.

PART II

(13) In this section –

"college" means an institution within the further education sector as defined in
section 91 of the Further and Higher Education Act 1992 or a 16 to 19 Academy;
"fostering agency" has the same meaning as in the Care Standards Act 2000;
"further education corporation" has the same meaning as in the Further and Higher
Education Act 1992;
"sixth form college corporation" has the same meaning as in that Act;
"proprietor" has the same meaning as in the Education Act 1996.

Amendments—National Health Service and Community Care Act 1990, s 66(1), Sch 9, para 36(4);
Health Authorities Act 1995, s 2, Sch 1, para 118; Care Standards Act 2000, ss 109, 116, 117, Sch 4,
para 14(1),(16), Sch 6; SI 2000/90; Health and Social Care (Community Health and Standards) Act 2003,
s 34, Sch 4, paras 75, 80; ACA 2002, Sch 3, para 65; SI 2007/961; SI 2010/1080, SI 2010/1185;
Education Act 2011, s 54, Sch 13, para 6; Health and Social Care Act 2012, s 55(2), Sch 5, para 54.

81 (*repealed*)

82 Financial support by Secretary of State

(1) The Secretary of State may (with the consent of the Treasury) defray or contribute
towards –

  (a) any fees or expenses incurred by any person undergoing approved child care
       training;
  (b) any fees charged, or expenses incurred, by any person providing approved child
       care training or preparing material for use in connection with such training; or
  (c) the cost of maintaining any person undergoing such training.

(2) The Secretary of State may make grants to local authorities in respect of expenditure
incurred by them in providing secure accommodation in community homes other than
assisted community homes.

(3) Where –

  (a) a grant has been made under subsection (2) with respect to any secure
       accommodation; but
  (b) the grant is not used for the purpose for which it was made or the
       accommodation is not used as, or ceases to be used as, secure accommodation,

the Secretary of State may (with the consent of the Treasury) require the authority
concerned to repay the grant, in whole or in part.

(4) The Secretary of State may make grants to voluntary organisations towards –

  (a) expenditure incurred by them in connection with the establishment,
       maintenance or improvement of voluntary homes which, at the time when the
       expenditure was incurred –
       (i)   were assisted community homes; or
       (ii) were designated as such; or
  (b) expenses incurred in respect of the borrowing of money to defray any such
       expenditure.

(5) The Secretary of State may arrange for the provision, equipment and maintenance of
homes for the accommodation of children who are in need of particular facilities and
services which –

  (a) are or will be provided in those homes; and
  (b) in the opinion of the Secretary of State, are unlikely to be readily available in
       community homes.

(6) In this Part –

"child care training" means training undergone by any person with a view to, or in the course of –

   (a) his employment for the purposes of any of the functions mentioned in section 83(9) or in connection with the adoption of children or with the accommodation of children in a care home or independent hospital; or

   (b) his employment by a voluntary organisation for similar purposes;

"approved child care training" means child care training which is approved by the Secretary of State; and

"secure accommodation" means accommodation provided for the purpose of restricting the liberty of children.

(7) Any grant made under this section shall be of such amount, and shall be subject to such conditions, as the Secretary of State may (with the consent of the Treasury) determine.

Amendments—Care Standards Act 2000, s 116, Sch 4, para 14(1),(18).

83 Research and returns of information

(1) The Secretary of State may conduct, or assist other persons in conducting, research into any matter connected with –

   (a) his functions, or the functions of local authorities, under the enactments mentioned in subsection (9);

   (aa) the functions of Local Safeguarding Children Boards;

   (b) the adoption of children; or

   (c) the accommodation of children in a care home or independent hospital.

(2) Any local authority may conduct, or assist other persons in conducting, research into any matter connected with –

   (a) their functions under the enactments mentioned in subsection (9);

   (aa) the functions of Local Safeguarding Children Boards;

   (b) the adoption of children; or

   (c) the accommodation of children in a care home or independent hospital.

(3) Every local authority shall, at such times and in such form as the Secretary of State may direct, transmit to him such particulars as he may require with respect to –

   (a) the performance by the local authority of all or any of their functions –

      (i) under the enactments mentioned in subsection (9); or

      (ii) in connection with the accommodation of children in a care home or independent hospital; and

   (b) the children in relation to whom the authority have exercised those functions; and

   (c) the performance by the Local Safeguarding Children Board established by them under the Children Act 2004 of all or any of its functions.

(4) Every voluntary organisation shall, at such times and in such form as the Secretary of State may direct, transmit to him such particulars as he may require with respect to children accommodated by them or on their behalf.

(4A) Particulars required to be transmitted under subsection (3) or (4) may include particulars relating to and identifying individual children.

(5) The Secretary of State may direct the designated officer for each magistrates' court to which the direction is expressed to relate to transmit –

   (a) to such person as may be specified in the direction; and

   (b) at such times and in such form as he may direct,

such particulars as he may require with respect to proceedings of the court which relate to children.

(6) The Secretary of State shall in each year lay before Parliament a consolidated and classified abstract of the information transmitted to him under subsections (3) to (5).

(7) The Secretary of State may institute research designed to provide information on which requests for information under this section may be based.

(8) The Secretary of State shall keep under review the adequacy of the provision of child care training and for that purpose shall receive and consider any information from or representations made by –

    (a)   the Central Council for Education and Training in Social Work;

    (b)   such representatives of local authorities as appear to him to be appropriate; or

    (c)   such other persons or organisations as appear to him to be appropriate,

concerning the provision of such training.

(9) The enactments are –

    (a)   this Act;

    (b)   the Children and Young Persons Acts 1933 to 1969;

    (c)   section 116 of the Mental Health Act 1983 (so far as it relates to children looked after by local authorities);

    (ca) Part 1 of the Adoption and Children Act 2002;

    (cb) the Children Act 2004;

    (cc) the Children and Young Persons Act 2008.

    (d)   *(repealed)*

Amendments—AJA 1999, s 90, Sch 13, para 160; Care Standards Act 2000, s 116, Sch 4, para 14(1),(19); Courts Act 2003, s 109(1), Sch 8, para 336; CA 2004, s 54; SI 2005/2078; CYPA 2008, s 33.

84 Local authority failure to comply with statutory duty: default power of Secretary of State

(1) If the Secretary of State is satisfied that any local authority has failed, without reasonable excuse, to comply with any of the duties imposed on them by or under this Act he may make an order declaring that authority to be in default with respect to that duty.

(2) An order under subsection (1) shall give the Secretary of State's reasons for making it.

(3) An order under subsection (1) may contain such directions for the purpose of ensuring that the duty is complied with, within such period as may be specified in the order, as appear to the Secretary of State to be necessary.

(4) Any such direction shall, on the application of the Secretary of State, be enforceable by mandamus.

Defined terms—"local authority": s 105(1).

Scope—This section does not confer either an express or an implied right on any individual to appeal from a decision by a local authority by which he is aggrieved and, although the existence of a default power such as s 84 can be taken into consideration by the court as an avenue of redress alternative to judicial review, it can be wrong, in view of the particular features of s 84, to treat it as a more suitable remedy for an individual than judicial review (*R v London Borough of Brent ex parte S* [1994] 1 FLR 203, CA).

There exists under s 26(3) a representation procedure which can be used by a person aggrieved by the way in which a local authority has exercised its functions, and this may have relevance as to whether relief will be granted in judicial review proceedings (*R v East Sussex CC ex parte W* [1998] 2 FLR 1082, QBD).

In *R v Hampshire CC ex parte H* [1999] 2 FLR 359, CA, judicial review was held to be appropriate in relation to a decision of a local authority case conference.

Declaration absolving local authority from duty to consult and provide information—In exceptional circumstances the court has power to make a declaration that the local authority be absolved from the duty to provide information to a parent and from the duty to consult him or her in any way about the child (*Re C (Care: Consultation with Parents not in Child's Best Interests)* [2006] 2 FLR 787).

PART XII
MISCELLANEOUS AND GENERAL

Notification of children accommodated in certain establishments

85 Children accommodated by health authorities and local education authorities

(1) Where a child is provided with accommodation by any Local Health Board, Special Health Authority, National Health Service trust or NHS foundation trust or by a local authority in the exercise of education functions ("the accommodating authority") –

   (a) for a consecutive period of at least three months; or
   (b) with the intention, on the part of that authority, of accommodating him for such a period,

the accommodating authority shall notify the appropriate officer of the responsible authority.

(2) Where subsection (1) applies with respect to a child, the accommodating authority shall also notify the appropriate officer of the responsible authority when they cease to accommodate the child.

(2ZA) Where a child is provided with accommodation –

   (a) by a body which is not mentioned in subsection (1), and
   (b) pursuant to arrangements made by the Secretary of State, the National Health Service Commissioning Board or a clinical commissioning group under the National Health Service Act 2006,

subsections (1) and (2) apply in relation to the Secretary of State, the Board or (as the case may be) the clinical commissioning group as if it were the accommodating authority.

(2A) In a case where the child is provided with accommodation by a local authority in the exercise of education functions, subsections (1) and (2) apply only if the local authority providing the accommodation is different from the responsible authority.

(3) In this section "the responsible authority" means –

   (a) the local authority appearing to the accommodating authority to be the authority within whose area the child was ordinarily resident immediately before being accommodated; or
   (b) where it appears to the accommodating authority that a child was not ordinarily resident within the area of any local authority, the local authority within whose area the accommodation is situated.

(3A) In this section and sections 86 and 86A "the appropriate officer" means –

   (a) in relation to a local authority in England, their director of children's services; and.
   (b) in relation to a local authority in Wales, their lead director for children and young people's services."

(4) Where the appropriate officer of a local authority has been notified under this section, the local authority shall –

(a) take such steps as are reasonably practicable to enable them to determine whether the child's welfare is adequately safeguarded and promoted while he is accommodated by the accommodating authority; and

(b) consider the extent to which (if at all) they should exercise any of their functions under this Act with respect to the child.

(5) For the purposes of subsection 4)(b), if the child is not in the area of the local authority, they must treat him as if he were in that area.

Amendments—National Health Service and Community Care Act 1990, s 66(1), Sch 9, para 36; Health Authorities Act 1995, s 2, Sch 1, para 118; SI 2000/90; Health and Social Care (Community Health and Standards) Act 2003, s 34, Sch 4, paras 75, 81; SI 2007/961; SI 2010/1185; CYPA 2008, s 17; Health and Social Care Act 2012, s 55(2), Sch 5, para 55.

86 Children accommodated in care homes or independent hospitals

(1) Where a child is provided with accommodation in any care home or independent hospital –

(a) for a consecutive period of at least three months; or

(b) with the intention, on the part of the person taking the decision to accommodate him, of accommodating him for such period,

the person carrying on the establishment in question shall notify the appropriate officer of the local authority within whose area the establishment is carried on.

(2) Where subsection (1) applies with respect to a child, the person carrying on the establishment shall also notify the appropriate officer of that authority when he ceases to accommodate the child in the establishment.

(3) Where the appropriate officer of a local authority has been notified under this section, the local authority shall –

(a) take such steps as are reasonably practicable to enable them to determine whether the child's welfare is adequately safeguarded and promoted while he is accommodated in the establishment in question; and

(b) consider the extent to which (if at all) they should exercise any of their functions under this Act with respect to the child.

(4) If the person carrying on any care home or independent hospital fails, without reasonable excuse, to comply with this section he shall be guilty of an offence.

(5) A person authorised by a local authority may enter any care home or independent hospital within the authority's area for the purpose of establishing whether the requirements of this section have been complied with.

(6) Any person who intentionally obstructs another in the exercise of the power of entry shall be guilty of an offence.

(7) Any person exercising the power of entry shall, if so required, produce some duly authenticated document showing his authority to do so.

(8) Any person committing an offence under this section shall be liable on summary conviction to a fine not exceeding level 3 on the standard scale.

Amendments—Care Standards Act 2000, s 116, Sch 4, para 14(1),(20); CYPA 2008, s 17.

86A Visitors for children notified to local authority under section 85 or 86

(1) This section applies if the appropriate officer of a local authority –

(a) has been notified with respect to a child under section 85(1) or 86(1); and

(b) has not been notified with respect to that child under section 85(2) or, as the case may be, 86(2).

(2) The local authority must, in accordance with regulations made under this section, make arrangements for the child to be visited by a representative of the authority ("a representative").

(3) It is the function of a representative to provide advice and assistance to the local authority on the performance of their duties under section 85(4) or, as the case may be, 86(3).

(4) Regulations under this section may make provision about –

(a) the frequency of visits under visiting arrangements;
(b) circumstances in which visiting arrangements must require a child to be visited; and
(c) additional functions of a representative.

(5) Regulations under this section are to be made by the Secretary of State and the Welsh Ministers acting jointly.

(6) In choosing a representative a local authority must satisfy themselves that the person chosen has the necessary skills and experience to perform the functions of a representative.

(7) In this section "visiting arrangements" means arrangements made under subsection (2).

Amendments—Inserted by CYPA 2008, s 18.

87 Welfare of children in boarding schools and colleges

(1) Where a school or college provides accommodation for any child, it shall be the duty of the relevant person to safeguard and promote the child's welfare.

(1A) For the purposes of this section and sections 87A to 87D, a school or college provides accommodation for a child if –

(a) it provides accommodation for the child on its own premises, or
(b) it arranges for accommodation for the child to be provided elsewhere (other than in connection with a residential trip away from the school).

(2) Subsection (1) does not apply in relation to a school or college which is a children's home or care home.

(3) Where accommodation is provided for a child by any school or college the appropriate authority shall take such steps as are reasonably practicable to enable them to determine whether the child's welfare is adequately safeguarded and promoted while accommodation for the child is provided by the school or college.

(3A) Where accommodation is provided for a child by a school or college in England, the Secretary of State may at any time (including a time when the duty under subsection (3) is suspended by virtue of section 87A) direct the Chief Inspector for England to take the steps referred to in subsection (3).

(3B) Where accommodation is provided for a child by a school or college in Wales, the Welsh Ministers may, at any time when the duty under subsection (3) is suspended by virtue of section 87A, take the steps referred to in subsection (3).

(4) Where the Chief Inspector for England is of the opinion that there has been a failure to comply with subsection (1) in relation to a child provided with accommodation by a school or college in England, he shall –

(a) in the case of a school other than an independent school or a special school, notify the local authority for the area in which the school is situated;

(b)   in the case of a special school which is maintained by a local authority, notify that authority;

(c)   in any other case, notify the Secretary of State.

(4A) Where the National Assembly for Wales are of the opinion that there has been a failure to comply with subsection (1) in relation to a child provided with accommodation by a school or college in Wales, they shall –

(a)   in the case of a school other than an independent school or a special school, notify the local authority for the area in which the school is situated;

(b)   in the case of a special school which is maintained by a local authority, notify that authority;

(5) Where accommodation is, or is to be, provided for a child by any school or college, a person authorised by the appropriate authority may, for the purpose of enabling that authority to discharge any of its functions under this section, enter at any time premises which are, or are to be, premises of the school or college.

(6) Any person exercising the power conferred by subsection (5) may carry out such inspection of premises, children and records as is prescribed by regulations made by the Secretary of State for the purposes of this section.

(7) Any person exercising that power shall, if asked to do so, produce some duly authenticated document showing his authority to do so.

(8) Any person authorised by the regulations to inspect records –

(a)   shall be entitled at any reasonable time to have access to, and inspect and check the operation of, any computer and any associated apparatus or material which is or has been in use in connection with the records in question; and

(b)   may require –
(i)   the person by whom or on whose behalf the computer is or has been so used; or
(ii)   any person having charge of, or otherwise concerned with the operation of, the computer, apparatus or material,
to afford him such assistance as he may reasonably require.

(9) Any person who intentionally obstructs another in the exercise of any power conferred by this section or the regulations shall be guilty of an offence and liable on summary conviction to a fine not exceeding level 3 on the standard scale.

(9A)–(9C) ...

(10) In this section and sections 87A to 87D –
"the 1992 Act" means the Further and Higher Education Act 1992;
"appropriate authority" means –
(a)   in relation to England, the Chief Inspector for England;
(b)   in relation to Wales, the National Assembly for Wales;
"the Chief Inspector for England" means Her Majesty's Chief Inspector of Education, Children's Services and Skills;
"college" means an institution within the further education sector as defined in section 91 of the 1992 Act or a 16 to 19 Academy;
"further education corporation" has the same meaning as in the 1992 Act;
"local authority" and "proprietor" have the same meanings as in the Education Act 1996;
"sixth form college corporation" has the same meaning as in the 1992 Act.

(11) In this section and sections 87A and 87D "relevant person" means –
(a)   in relation to an independent school, the proprietor of the school;
(b)   in relation to any other school, or an institution designated under section 28 of the 1992 Act, the governing body of the school or institution;

(c)   in relation to an institution conducted by a further education corporation or sixth form college corporation, the corporation;

(d)   in relation to a 16 to 19 Academy, the proprietor of the Academy.

(12) Where a person other than the proprietor of an independent school is responsible for conducting the school, references in this section to the relevant person include references to the person so responsible.

Amendments—Registered Homes (Amendment) Act 1991, s 2(6); Education Act 1996, s 582(1), Sch 37, Pt I, para 87; Care Standards Act 2000, s 105; Health and Social Care (Community Health and Standards) Act 2003, s 147, Sch 9, para 10: Education and Inspections Act 2006, s 184, Sch 14, para 16, Sch 18, Pt 5; SI 2010/1080; SI 2010/1185; Education Act 2011, ss 43, 54, Sch 13, para 6.

PART II

87A   Suspension of duty under section 87(3)

(1) The Secretary of State may appoint a person to be an inspector for the purposes of this section if –

(a)   that person already acts as an inspector for other purposes in relation to schools or colleges to which section 87(1) applies, and

(b)   the Secretary of State is satisfied that the person is an appropriate person to determine whether the welfare of children provided with accommodation by such schools or colleges is adequately safeguarded and promoted while accommodation for the children is provided by them.

(2) Where –

(a)   the relevant person enters into an agreement in writing with a person appointed under subsection (1),

(b)   the agreement provides for the person so appointed to have in relation to the school or college the function of determining whether section 87(1) is being complied with, and

(c)   the appropriate authority receive from the person mentioned in paragraph (b) ("the inspector") notice in writing that the agreement has come into effect,

the authority's duty under section 87(3) in relation to the school or college shall be suspended.

(3) Where the appropriate authority's duty under section 87(3) in relation to any school or college is suspended under this section, it shall cease to be so suspended if the appropriate authority receive –

(a)   a notice under subsection (4) relating to the inspector, or

(b)   a notice under subsection (5) relating to the relevant agreement.

(4) The Secretary of State shall terminate a person's appointment under subsection (1) if –

(a)   that person so requests, or

(b)   the Secretary of State ceases, in relation to that person, to be satisfied that he is such a person as is mentioned in paragraph (b) of that subsection,

and shall give notice of the termination of that person's appointment to the appropriate authority.

(4A) The Secretary of State may by regulations specify matters that must be taken into account in deciding whether to appoint a person to be an inspector for the purposes of this section in relation to schools or colleges in England, or to terminate the appointment of such a person under subsection (4)(b).

(5) Where –

(a)   the appropriate authority's duty under section 87(3) in relation to any school or college is suspended under this section, and

(b)   the relevant agreement ceases to have effect,

the inspector shall give to the appropriate authority notice in writing of the fact that it has ceased to have effect.

(6) In this section references to the relevant agreement, in relation to the suspension of the appropriate authority's duty under section 87(3) as regards any school or college, are to the agreement by virtue of which the appropriate authority's duty under that provision as regards that school or college is suspended.

Amendments—Substituted by Care Standards Act 2000, s 106(1); amended by Education Act 2011, s 43.

87B   Duties of inspectors under section 87A

(1) The Secretary of State may impose on a person appointed under section 87A(1) ("an authorised inspector") such requirements relating to, or in connection with, the carrying out under substitution agreements of the function mentioned in section 87A(2)(b) as the Secretary of State thinks fit.

(2) Where, in the course of carrying out under a substitution agreement the function mentioned in section 87A(2)(b), it appears to an authorised inspector that there has been a failure to comply with section 87(1) in the case of a child provided with accommodation by the school or college to which the agreement relates, the inspector shall give notice of that fact –

(a)   in the case of a school other than an independent school or a special school, to the local authority for the area in which the school is situated;

(b)   in the case of a special school which is maintained by a local authority, to that authority;

(c)   in any other case, to the Secretary of State.

(3) Where, in the course of carrying out under a substitution agreement the function mentioned in section 87A(2)(b), it appears to an authorised inspector that a child provided with accommodation by the school or college to which the agreement relates is suffering, or is likely to suffer, significant harm, the inspector shall –

(a)   give notice of the fact to the local authority in whose area the school or college is situated, and

(b)   where the inspector is required to make inspection reports to the Secretary of State, supply that local authority with a copy of the latest inspection report to have been made by the inspector to the Secretary of State in relation to the school or college.

(4) In this section "substitution agreement" means an agreement by virtue of which the duty of the appropriate authority under section 87(3) in relation to a school or college is suspended.

Amendments—Inserted by Deregulation and Contracting Out Act 1994, s 38; amended by Education Act 1996, s 582(1), Sch 37, Pt I, para 89; Care Standards Act 2000, s 106(2); SI 2010/1185.

87BA   Quality assurance of inspectors under section 87A.

(1) The Chief Inspector for England must, at intervals of no more than a year, prepare and send to the Secretary of State a report about inspectors who are appointed under section 87A in relation to schools or colleges in England.

(2) In preparing a report under this section the Chief Inspector for England must have regard to such matters as the Secretary of State may direct.

(3) The Secretary of State may in particular give directions about –

(a) matters to be taken into account in preparing a report, and

(b) the form and contents of a report.

Amendments—Inserted by Education Act 2011, s 43.

87C Boarding schools: national minimum standards

(1) The Secretary of State may prepare and publish statements of national minimum standards for safeguarding and promoting the welfare of children for whom accommodation is provided by a school or college.

(2) The Secretary of State shall keep the standards set out in the statements under review and may publish amended statements whenever he considers it appropriate to do so.

(3) Before issuing a statement, or an amended statement which in the opinion of the Secretary of State effects a substantial change in the standards, the Secretary of State shall consult any persons he considers appropriate.

(4) The standards shall be taken into account –

(a) in the making by the appropriate authority of any determination under section 87(4) or (4A);

(b) in the making by a person appointed under section 87A(1) of any determination under section 87B(2); and

(c) in any proceedings under any other enactment in which it is alleged that the person has failed to comply with section 87(1).

Amendments—Inserted by Care Standards Act 2000, s 107; amended by Education Act 2011, s 43.

87D Annual fee for boarding school inspections

(1) Regulations under subsection (2) may be made in relation to any school or college in respect of which the appropriate authority is required to take steps under section 87(3).

(2) The Secretary of State may by regulations require the relevant person to pay the appropriate authority an annual fee of such amount, and within such time, as the regulations may specify.

(3) A fee payable by virtue of this section may, without prejudice to any other method of recovery, be recovered summarily as a civil debt.

Amendments—Inserted by Care Standards Act 2000, s 108.

****

Criminal care and supervision orders

90 Care and supervision orders in criminal proceedings

(1) The power of a court to make an order under subsection (2) of section 1 of the Children and Young Persons Act 1969 (care proceedings in youth courts) where it is of the opinion that the condition mentioned in paragraph (f) of that subsection ("the offence condition") is satisfied is hereby abolished.

(2) The powers of the court to make care orders –

(a) under section 7(7)(a) of the Children and Young Persons Act 1969 (alteration in treatment of young offenders etc); and

(b) under section 15(1) of that Act, on discharging a supervision order made under section 7(7)(b) of that Act,

are hereby abolished.

(3) The powers given by that Act to include requirements in supervision orders shall have effect subject to amendments made by Schedule 12.

Amendments—Criminal Justice Act 1991, s 100, Sch 11, para 40.

Effect and duration of orders etc

91 Effect and duration of orders etc

(1) The making of a residence order with respect to a child who is the subject of a care order discharges the care order.

(2) The making of a care order with respect to a child who is the subject of any section 8 order discharges that order.

(2A) Where a contact activity direction has been made as regards contact with a child, the making of a care order with respect to the child discharges the direction.

(3) The making of a care order with respect to a child who is the subject of a supervision order discharges that other order.

(4) The making of a care order with respect to a child who is a ward of court brings that wardship to an end.

(5) The making of a care order with respect to a child who is the subject of a school attendance order made under section 437 of the Education Act 1996 discharges the school attendance order.

(5A) The making of a special guardianship order with respect to a child who is the subject of –

  (a)   a care order; or
  (b)   an order under section 34,

discharges that order.

(6) Where an emergency protection order is made with respect to a child who is in care, the care order shall have effect subject to the emergency protection order.

(7) Any order made under section 4(1), 4ZA(1), 4A(1) or 5(1) shall continue in force until the child reaches the age of eighteen, unless it is brought to an end earlier.

(8) Any –

  (a)   agreement under section 4, 4ZA or 4A; or
  (b)   appointment under section 5(3) or (4),

shall continue in force until the child reaches the age of eighteen, unless it is brought to an end earlier.

(9) An order under Schedule 1 has effect as specified in that Schedule.

(10) A section 8 order other than a residence order shall, if it would otherwise still be in force, cease to have effect when the child reaches the age of sixteen, unless it is to have effect beyond that age by virtue of section 9(6).

(11) Where a section 8 order has effect with respect to a child who has reached the age of sixteen, it shall, if it would otherwise still be in force, cease to have effect when he reaches the age of eighteen.

(12) Any care order, other than an interim care order, shall continue in force until the child reaches the age of eighteen, unless it is brought to an end earlier.

(13) Any order made under any other provision of this Act in relation to a child shall, if it would otherwise still be in force, cease to have effect when he reaches the age of eighteen.

(14) On disposing of any application for an order under this Act, the court may (whether or not it makes any other order in response to the application) order that no application for an order under this Act of any specified kind may be made with respect to the child concerned by any person named in the order without leave of the court.

(15) Where an application ("the previous application") has been made for –

(a) the discharge of a care order;
(b) the discharge of a supervision order;
(c) the discharge of an education supervision order;
(d) the substitution of a supervision order for a care order; or
(e) a child assessment order,

no further application of a kind mentioned in paragraphs (a) to (e) may be made with respect to the child concerned, without leave of the court, unless the period between the disposal of the previous application and the making of the further application exceeds six months.

(16) Subsection (15) does not apply to applications made in relation to interim orders.

(17) Where –

(a) a person has made an application for an order under section 34;
(b) the application has been refused; and
(c) a period of less than six months has elapsed since the refusal,

that person may not make a further application for such an order with respect to the same child, unless he has obtained the leave of the court.

Amendments—Education Act 1996, s 582(1), Sch 37, Pt I, para 90; ACA 2002, ss 114(5), 139(1), Sch 3, paras 54 and 68; CAA 2006, s 15(1), Sch 2, paras 7, 9; CYPA 2008, s 37(3); HFEA 2008, s 56, Sch 6, para 31.

Defined terms—"care order": ss 31(11), 105(1); "child": s 105(1); "child assessment order": s 43(2); "education supervision order": s 36(2); "supervision order": s 31(11).

Care order discharges s 8 order (s 91(2))—Where an English court made a care order it had the effect of discharging a Dutch custody order, just as it would discharge a s 8 order (*Oxfordshire County Council v S* [2000] Fam Law 20). The making of a care order also discharges any current contact activity direction (s 91(2A)).

"The making of a care order ... brings that wardship to an end" (s 91(4))—Although an injunction made within wardship proceedings would ordinarily end on the discharge of the wardship, the court has power to order that such an injunction is to continue after the discharge of those proceedings (*Re E (A Minor) (Child Abuse: Evidence)* [1991] 1 FLR 420 at [455F]). It is probable that the injunction does not subsist beyond the date when the minor achieves majority (*Re D (A Minor) (Adoption Order: Validity)* [1991] 2 FLR 66, at [76E]) or the death of the minor during his minority.

"no application ... without leave of the court" (s 91(14))—This subsection has produced many reported decisions concerning the circumstances in which an order restricting future applications should be made. In *Re P (Section 91(14) Guidelines) (Residence and Religious Heritage)* [1999] 2 FLR 573 Butler-Sloss LJ drew up a number of guidelines from the reported cases, while indicating that the court always has to carry out a balancing exercise between the welfare of the child and the right of unrestricted access of the litigant to the court. The guidelines are as follows:

1 Section 91(14) should be read in conjunction with s 1(1) which makes the welfare of the child the paramount consideration.
2 The power to restrict applications to the court is discretionary and in the exercise of its discretion the court must weigh in the balance all the relevant circumstances.
3 An important consideration is that to impose a restriction is a statutory intrusion into the right of a party to bring proceedings before the court and to be heard in matters affecting his/her child.
4 The power is therefore to be used with great care and sparingly, the exception and not the rule.
5 It is generally to be seen as a weapon of last resort in cases of repeated and unreasonable applications.
6 In suitable circumstances (and on clear evidence), a court may impose the leave restriction in cases

where the welfare of the child requires it, although there is no past history of making unreasonable applications (see also *Re P (Children Act 1989, ss 22 and 26: Local Authority Compliance)* [2000] 2 FLR 910).

7   In cases under para 6 above, the court will need to be satisfied first that the facts go beyond the commonly encountered need for a time to settle to a regime ordered by the court and the all too common situation where there is animosity between the adults in dispute or between the local authority and the family; and secondly that there is a serious risk that, without the imposition of the restriction, the child or the primary carers will be subject to unacceptable strain (see also *Re S (Contact: Promoting Relationship with Absent Parent)* [2004] 1 FLR 1279). The Court of Appeal has reiterated the principle that a need for time to settle to the regime ordered is not sufficient to justify a s 91(14) order: the purpose of the order could and should have been achieved by giving the order time to work itself out: *Re G (Residence: Restrictions on Further Applications)* [2009] 1 FLR 894.

8   A court may impose the restriction on making applications in the absence of a request from any of the parties, subject, of course, to the rules of natural justice such as an opportunity for the parties to be heard on the point. In particular it is wrong in principle, except in exceptional circumstances, to put a litigant in person in the position, at short notice, of having to contest a s 91(14) order (*Re C (Prohibition on Further Applications)* [2002] 1 FLR 1136).

9   A restriction may be imposed with or without limitation of time. In *Re B (Section 91(14) Order: Duration)* [2004] 1 FLR 871, it was said that where the mother was determined to excise the father from a child's life the court should never abandon endeavours to right the wrongs within the family dynamics. A s 91(14) order which was to last during the child's minority and was without limitation to specific applications gave the wrong message in a case in which the father had not abused the family justice system nor undermined the mother's primary care. An order which is indeterminate or is to last until a child is 16 should be an exceptional step because it is, in effect, an acknowledgement that nothing more can be done. If such an order is made the court must spell out why and what needs to be done to make a successful application in the future (*Re S (Permission to Seek Relief)* [2007] 1 FLR 482). In *S v B & Newport City Council: Re K* [2007] 1 FLR 1116 a special guardianship order and a s 91(14) order were made preventing the natural parents making any application for contact without limitation of time because the child's needs required that order to be made and failure to do so, in the light of the parents volatile behaviour, would impose an unacceptable strain on the carers.

10   The degree of restriction should be proportionate to the harm it is intended to avoid. Therefore the court imposing the restriction should carefully consider the extent of the restriction to be imposed and specify, where appropriate, the type of application to be restrained and the type of order (see also *Re G (Contempt: Committal)* [2003] 2 FLR 58).

11   It would be undesirable in other than the most exceptional cases to make the order ex parte.

Furthermore, Butler-Sloss LJ stated that in her view an absolute prohibition on making any application to the court could not be made under s 91(14). Additionally, a s 91(14) order did not infringe the HRA 1998 or ECHR 1950, Art 6(1) because it did not deny access to the court, only access to an immediate inter partes hearing. An order imposing an absolute prohibition would have to be made under the inherent jurisdiction of the court (see *Re R (Residence: Contact: Restricting Applications)* [1998] 1 FLR 749); where an order is made under the principles of *Grepe v Loam* (1887) 37 Ch D 168 preventing applications by any party without leave, and ordering that any application is to be filed with the court only and dealt with on paper, the guidelines in *Re P* above should apply (*Harris v Harris; Attorney-General v Harris* [2001] 2 FLR 895). It is not appropriate to make a s 91(14) order in contempt proceedings unless there is a contact application before the court (*Heathcote v Crackles* (2002) Lawtel, 19 February).

General principles:

(i)   Orders without limit of time should only be made in outstandingly bad cases, which merit the strongest degree of forensic protection for the child from ill-founded conflict (*Re J (A Child) (Restriction on Applications)* [2008] 1 FLR 369 (CA) and *Re G (Residence: restrictions on Further Applications)* [2009] 1 FLR 894). Wilson LJ has repeated that s 91(14) orders are to be used with great care, sparingly and as a weapon of last resort in cases of repeated and unreasonable applications. A court was not entitled to take the view that there was no undue hardship in requiring a parent to show an arguable case in support of a proposed application. The Court of Appeal spent a surprising and unfortunate amount of its time in reversing orders made on an inappropriately summary basis: *Re A (Contact: Section 91(14))* [2010] 2 FLR 151.

(ii) It is not permissible to impose conditions on a s 91(14) order (*Re S (Permission to Seek Relief)* [2007] 1 FLR 482). However, it is permissible for a judge imposing a s 91(14) order to identify a particular issue and to suggest to the litigant that unless he could show that that particular issue had been addressed any future application for permission to apply to the court for further relief was unlikely to be successful (*Stringer v Stringer* [2007] 1 FLR 1532).

(iii) Once a prohibition under s 91(14) has been made, any further applications for leave to bring proceedings should generally be heard inter partes rather than ex parte; this enables the court to investigate fully whether or not there is a genuine need for further proceedings (*Re N (Section 91(14) Order)* [1996] 1 FLR 356, but c f *Re S (Permission to Seek Relief)*). It is open to a judge making a s 91(14) order to direct that any permission to apply during its operation shall not in the first instance be served on the respondent, but should be considered by the judge on paper. However, an applicant should not be denied an oral hearing if that is sought (*Re Bradford; Re O'Connell* [2007] 1 FLR 530). The test for granting such leave once a s 91(14) order has been made is whether there is an arguable case.

Loss of self-control—Where a party loses their temper in court and/or walks out of the hearing it is wrong, on this ground alone, to make a s 91(14) order against that party. The appropriate course is to allow the party time to repent and come to his/her senses by adjourning the matter for a minimum of 24 hours to "draw the party back into the proceedings and not to put a further barrier on his further engagement with the system": *Re M (Section 91(14) Order)* [2012] 2 FLR 758.

Litigants in person—The Court of Appeal has handed down guidance on the approach to be taken when considering making an order under s 91(14). It is of utmost importance that the party, parties or other persons affected by the order, particularly if they are in person: (a) understand that such an application is being made, or that consideration is being given to making a s 91(14) order; (b) understand the meaning and effect of such an order; and (c) have a proper opportunity to make submissions to the court. A request for a short adjournment to consider the position should normally be granted: *Re C (Litigant in Person: s 91(14) Order)* [2009] 2 FLR 1461 at [13].

"order under section 34" (s 91(17)(a))—Section 34 provides for various types of order regulating the contact of children in care with their parents and others.

Leave of the court—Where any of the provisions of s 91(14)–(17) requires the leave of the court to be obtained before a particular application under the Act may be made, leave should be sought in accordance with FPR 2010, Pt 18. The application for leave should be made in Form C2 (see FPR 2010, r 5 and PD5A, Table 1). If leave is granted, the applicant will proceed to issue an application for an order in Form C1.

Jurisdiction and procedure etc

92 Jurisdiction of courts

(1) The name "domestic proceedings", given to certain proceedings in magistrates' courts, is hereby changed to "family proceedings" and the names "domestic court" and "domestic court panel" are hereby changed to "family proceedings court" and "family panel", respectively.

(2) Proceedings under this Act shall be treated as family proceedings in relation to magistrates' courts.

(3) Subsection (2) is subject to the provisions of section 65(1) and (2) of the Magistrates' Courts Act 1980 (proceedings which may be treated as not being family proceedings), as amended by this Act.

(4) A magistrates' court shall not be competent to entertain any application, or make any order, involving the administration or application of –

    (a)   any property belonging to or held in trust for a child; or

    (b)   the income of any such property.

(5) The powers of a magistrates' court under section 63(2) of the Act of 1980 to suspend or rescind orders shall not apply in relation to any order made under this Act.

(6) Part I of Schedule 11 makes provision, including provision for the Lord Chancellor to make orders, with respect to the jurisdiction of courts and justices of the peace in relation to –

    (a)   proceedings under this Act; and

    (b)   proceedings under certain other enactments.

(7) For the purposes of this Act "the court" means the High Court, a county court or a magistrates' court.

(8) Subsection (7) is subject to the provision made by or under Part I of Schedule 11 and to any express provision as to the jurisdiction of any court made by any other provision of this Act.

(9) The Lord Chancellor may, after consulting the Lord Chief Justice, by order make provision for the principal registry of the Family Division of the High Court to be treated as if it were a county court for such purposes of this Act, or of any provision made under this Act, as may be specified in the order.

(10) Any order under subsection (9) may make such provision as the Lord Chancellor thinks expedient, after consulting the Lord Chief Justice, for the purpose of applying (with or without modifications) provisions which apply in relation to the procedure in county courts to the principal registry when it acts as if it were a county court.

(10A) The Lord Chief Justice may nominate a judicial office holder (as defined in section 109(4) of the Constitutional Reform Act 2005) to exercise his functions under subsection (9) or (10).

(11) Part II of Schedule 11 makes amendments consequential on this section.

Amendments—CRA 2005, s 15(1), Sch 4, Pt 1, paras 203, 205.

Defined terms—"child": s 105(1).

Jurisdiction under the Act generally—The general scheme of the Act is to give courts as much flexibility as possible so, broadly speaking, most orders may be made by any court. Section 92(4) prevents magistrates' courts from dealing with the administration or application of any property belonging to or held in trust for a child or the income of any such property. They are also limited in the financial orders which they may make by the provisions of Sch 1, paras 1 and 5. ATPO 2008, art 5 introduces stricter criteria for commencement and transfer of proceedings and lists those proceedings which must be started in the FPC subject to certain exceptions. The High Court has full jurisdiction to hear all cases regarding children. In the county courts, ATPO 2008, Sch 1 ensures the competence of the tribunal by establishing a tier system. In addition, FP(AJ)D 2009 establish different categories of judges and district judges (nominated care judges, nominated family judges etc). In the magistrates' courts, competence is ensured by confining family proceedings (which include the majority of cases under the Act) to family proceedings courts. The magistrates in these courts are all drawn from the family panel, made up of specially trained justices and stipendiary magistrates.

"family proceedings" (s 92(2))—CA 1989, s 25 (secure accommodation) proceedings are, by virtue of s 92(2), treated as family proceedings notwithstanding that they are not included in the definition of family proceedings in s 8(3) (*Oxfordshire County Council v R* [1992] 1 FLR 648). Accordingly, hearsay evidence is admissible in accordance with the Children (Admissibility of Hearsay Evidence) Order 1993. It seems extremely unlikely, however, that the s 92(2) provision is intended to override the specific definition of "family proceedings" in s 8(3) when it comes to determining the powers of magistrates' courts to make orders. If it were, magistrates' courts would have wider powers than the High Court or a county court since a wider range of orders is available to a court in family proceedings than in non-family proceedings. Thus, by way of example, with an extended application of s 92(2), a magistrates' court entertaining an application for an emergency protection order would be seised of family proceedings and would be able to make, say, a residence order of its own motion under s 10(1); however, a county court or High Court, limited by the definition of family proceedings in s 8(3) which does not include any proceedings under Pt V of the Act, would not.

"section 65(1) and (2) of the Magistrates' Courts Act 1980" (s 92(3))—MCA 1980, s 65(1) and (2) lists the proceedings which are generally classed as family proceedings (which list expressly includes proceedings under CA 1989) and creates certain exceptions to the general list (for example, proceedings for the enforcement of an order made under one of the listed enactments). MCA 1980, s 65(2) reduces the impact of the exceptions created by s 65(1) by providing the court with a discretion to order that certain proceedings (for example, proceedings for the enforcement of an order under CA 1989) be treated as family proceedings notwithstanding that they would otherwise be excepted.

"powers of a magistrates' court under s 63(2) of the Act of 1980" (s 92(5))—MCA 1980, s 63(2) enables a magistrates' court, by order made on complaint, to suspend or rescind any order requiring either the doing of anything other than the payment of money or prohibiting the doing of anything.

Generally, CA 1989 contains its own powers for the variation, suspension and discharge of orders where appropriate, and the procedure provided by FPR 2010, r 12 should be followed.

"provision made by or under Part I of Schedule 11" (s 92(8))—The ATPO 2008 sets out the proceedings which must be commenced in the magistrates court subject to certain exceptions.

Principal registry treated as a county court (s 92(9))—C(AP)O 1991, art 19 has been made under this provision.

93 Rules of court

(1) An authority having power to make rules of court may make such provision for giving effect to –

    (a) this Act;

    (b) the provisions of any statutory instrument made under this Act; or

    (c) any amendment made by this Act in any other enactment,

as appears to that authority to be necessary or expedient.

(2) The rules may, in particular, make provision –

    (a) with respect to the procedure to be followed in any relevant proceedings (including the manner in which any application is to be made or other proceedings commenced);

    (b) as to the persons entitled to participate in any relevant proceedings, whether as parties to the proceedings or by being given the opportunity to make representations to the court;

    (bb) for children to be separately represented in relevant proceedings,

    (c) with respect to the documents and information to be furnished, and notices to be given, in connection with any relevant proceedings;

    (d) applying (with or without modification) enactments which govern the procedure to be followed with respect to proceedings brought on a complaint made to a magistrates' court to relevant proceedings in such a court brought otherwise than on a complaint;

    (e) with respect to preliminary hearings;

    (f) for the service outside England and Wales, in such circumstances and in such manner as may be prescribed, of any notice of proceedings in a magistrates' court;

    (g) for the exercise by magistrates' courts, in such circumstances as may be prescribed, of such powers as may be prescribed (even though a party to the proceedings in question is or resides outside England and Wales);

    (h) enabling the court, in such circumstances as may be prescribed, to proceed on any application even though the respondent has not been given notice of the proceedings;

    (i) authorising a single justice to discharge the functions of a magistrates' court with respect to such relevant proceedings as may be prescribed;

    (j) authorising a magistrates' court to order any of the parties to such relevant proceedings as may be prescribed, in such circumstances as may be prescribed, to pay the whole or part of the costs of all or any of the other parties.

(3) In subsection (2) –

    "notice of proceedings" means a summons or such other notice of proceedings as is required; and "given", in relation to a summons, means "served",

    "prescribed" means prescribed by the rules; and

    "relevant proceedings" means any application made, or proceedings brought, under any of the provisions mentioned in paragraphs (a) to (c) of subsection (1) and any part of such proceedings.

(4) This section and any other power in this Act to make rules of court are not to be taken as in any way limiting any other power of the authority in question to make rules of court.

(5) When making any rules under this section an authority shall be subject to the same requirements as to consultation (if any) as apply when the authority makes rules under its general rule making power.

Amendments—CLSA 1990, s 116, Sch 16, para 22; ACA 2002, s 122(2).

94 Appeals

(1) Subject to any express provisions to the contrary made by or under this Act, an appeal shall lie to a county court against –

    (a)   the making by a magistrates' court of any order under this Act or the Adoption and Children Act 2002; or

    (b)   any refusal by a magistrates' court to make such an order.

(2) Where a magistrates' court has power, in relation to any proceedings under this Act or the Adoption and Children Act 2002, to decline jurisdiction because it considers that the case can more conveniently be dealt with by another court, no appeal shall lie against any exercise by that magistrates' court of that power.

(3) Subsection (1) does not apply in relation to an interim order for periodical payments made under Schedule 1.

(4) On an appeal under this section, a county court may make such orders as may be necessary to give effect to its determination of the appeal.

(5) Where an order is made under subsection (4) a county court may also make such incidental or consequential orders as appears to it to be just.

(6) Where an appeal from a magistrates' court relates to an order for the making of periodical payments, a county court may order that its determination of the appeal shall have effect from such date as it thinks fit to specify in the order.

(7) The date so specified must not be earlier than the earliest date allowed in accordance with rules of court made for the purposes of this section.

(8) Where, on an appeal under this section in respect of an order requiring a person to make periodical payments, a county court reduces the amount of those payments or discharges the order –

    (a)   it may order the person entitled to the payments to pay to the person making them such sum in respect of payments already made as the county court thinks fit; and

    (b)   if any arrears are due under the order for periodical payments, it may remit payment of the whole, or part, of those arrears.

(9) Any order of a county court made on an appeal under this section (other than one directing that an application be re-heard by a magistrates' court) shall, for the purposes –

    (a)   of the enforcement of the order; and

    (b)   of any power to vary, revive or discharge orders,

be treated as if it were an order of the magistrates' court from which the appeal was brought and not an order of a county court.

(10) The Lord Chancellor may, after consulting the Lord Chief Justice, by order make provision as to the circumstances in which appeals may be made against decisions taken by courts on questions arising in connection with the transfer, or proposed transfer, of proceedings by virtue of any order under paragraph 2 of Schedule 11.

(11) Except to the extent provided for in any order made under subsection (10), no appeal may be made against any decision of a kind mentioned in that subsection.

(12) The Lord Chief Justice may nominate a judicial office holder (as defined in section 109(4) of the Constitutional Reform Act 2005) to exercise his functions under subsection (10).

Amendments—CLSA 1990, s 116, Sch 16, para 23; ACA 2002, s 100; CRA 2005, s 15(1), Sch 4, Pt 1, paras 203, 206; SI 2009/871.

New procedure—All appeals from a magistrates' court in relation to family proceedings lie to a county court and not to the High Court (AJA 1999(DA)(FP)O 2009). A party is not required to seek permission to appeal against a decision of a magistrates' court (FPR 2010, r 30.3(1)).

Scope—This section provides the machinery for all appeals under CA 1989 from family proceedings courts. The exceptions are that there can be no appeal against a decision to decline jurisdiction (s 94(2)), the making of or refusal to make an emergency protection order or any direction given in connection with such an order (s 45(10), and see *Essex County Council v F* [1993] 1 FLR 847), or an order for interim periodical payments (s 94(3)). On hearing an appeal under this section, the county court may make any such order as may be necessary to determine the appeal (s 94(4)), and any incidental or consequential orders as appears just (s 94(5)).

Appeals relating to transfer between courts—For appeals against a decision of a magistrates' court to refuse to transfer a case to the county court see ATPO 2008, art 25. For appeals against the order of a district judge to re-transfer a case to the magistrates' court, see ATPO 2008, art 26.

Notes of evidence and reasons—The notice of appeal must be filed and served together with the notes of evidence and reasons. In relation to appeals from magistrates' courts, the justices' legal advisor must keep a note of the substance of the oral evidence given (FPR 2010, r 23.9) and, before making any order, the legal advisor must record the reasons for the decision and any findings of fact (FPR 2010, r 27.2(6)). These notes should be in legible typescript in order to assist in the disposal of an appeal (*Re W and S* [1992] 2 FCR 665). In *Re U'T) (A Minor) (Care Order Contact)* [1993] 2 FCR 565, Douglas Brown J held that, in addition to filing notes of evidence and reasons, FPR 1991, r 4.22 should be read to include a requirement that reports and witness statements filed for the original hearing should also be filed with the documents on appeal. Although the court should make its decision as soon as practicable (under FPR 2010, r 27.2(2)), the court must be careful to consider its reasons and not make them under pressure of time (see *Oxfordshire County Council v R* [1992] 1 FLR 648). Only those findings of fact and reasons given can be considered on appeal, and they cannot be supplemented later (*Hillingdon London Borough Council v H* [1992] 2 FLR 372). In *Leicestershire County Council v G* [1994] 2 FLR 329, Stuart-White J said that it would be helpful if the legal advisor's notes were to include a list identifying any written statements before the magistrates and considered by them, and it would also be helpful if the notes could include information as to which parties were present and whether they were legally represented.

Hearing—The appeal is limited to a review of the decision of the court below unless statute provides otherwise or the appeal court considers that in the particular case it would be in the interests of justice to hold a re-hearing. Unless the appeal court orders otherwise the court will not receive oral evidence or evidence which was not before the court below (FPR 2010, r 30.12 and PD30A).

Procedure—The procedure for appeals is set out in FPR 2010, Pt 30 and PD30A: see Procedural Guide E2.

95 Attendance of child at hearing under Part IV or V

(1) In any proceedings in which a court is hearing an application for an order under Part IV or V, or is considering whether to make any such order, the court may order the child concerned to attend such stage or stages of the proceedings as may be specified in the order.

(2) The power conferred by subsection (1) shall be exercised in accordance with rules of court.

(3) Subsections (4) to (6) apply where –

    (a) an order under subsection (1) has not been complied with; or

    (b) the court has reasonable cause to believe that it will not be complied with.

(4) The court may make an order authorising a constable, or such person as may be specified in the order –

    (a)   to take charge of the child and to bring him to the court; and

    (b)   to enter and search any premises specified in the order if he has reasonable cause to believe that the child may be found on the premises.

(5) The court may order any person who is in a position to do so to bring the child to the court.

(6) Where the court has reason to believe that a person has information about the whereabouts of the child it may order him to disclose it to the court.

Defined terms—"child": s 105(1).

"Part IV or V" (s 95(1))—Parts IV and V concern public law orders, such as care and supervision orders, emergency protection orders and child assessment orders.

Court hearing an application or considering making an order (s 95(1))—The court's power to require the attendance of the child is not confined to cases in which there has been an original application for an order under Pt IV or V but may also be exercised where the court is considering making an order of its own initiative (for example, where it is entertaining family proceedings and considering making a s 34 contact order of its own initiative under s 34(5)).

Use of s 95(1) to compel attendance of child as witness—It is suggested that it may be inappropriate to use the power in s 95(1) to compel the attendance of a child to give evidence and that it would be more appropriate, in the very few instances in which the child's attendance for this reason should be compelled, to use those provisions expressly designed for the purpose (see **Children as witnesses in family proceedings** under s 96).

Rules of court (s 95(2))—The relevant rules of court are FPR 2010, r 12.14. The provisions as to the representations of the children's guardian, the child's solicitor and, in certain circumstances, the child where the court is considering who should be present or absent are contained in FPR 2010, rr 16.20, 16.29 and PD16A, para 6.6.

General position as to attendance of child—The application of CA 1989, s 95 and FPR 2010, r 12.14 was comprehensively considered by Jackson J in *A City Council v T, J and K* [2011] 2 FLR 803 and guidance provided. See **Child at court** under FPR 2010, r 12.14.

"reasonable cause to believe" (s 95(3)(b),(4)(b))—This phrase appears twice in this section and contrasts with the phrase "reason to believe" used in s 95(6). In s 95(3), it is the court which has to have reasonable cause to believe that its s 95(1) order will not be complied with whereas, in s 95(4), it is the constable or other specified person who has to have reasonable cause to believe that the child may be found on any premises before he enters and searches them.

"enter and search any premises specified in the order" (s 95(4))—The court will have to be given some idea of where the child may be because it is not empowered to grant a general authority to enter premises and look for him, only an authority in relation to specified premises. Furthermore, even when authorised to enter and search, the constable or other authorised person will not be able to do so unless *he* has reasonable cause to believe that the child may be found on the premises. He cannot therefore simply rely on the court's order but must give the matter independent thought and satisfy himself, presumably at the time when he is about to enter, that he is entitled to do so.

"reason to believe" (s 95(6))—It is submitted that the phrase "reason to believe" used in s 95(6) denotes a rather lower standard than the phrase "reasonable cause to believe" which is used elsewhere in this section; the s 95(6) terminology mirrors that used in FLA 1986, s 33, which provides for the court to order disclosure of information about the whereabouts of a child in various private law proceedings.

Application for an order under s 95—Although the general tenor of this section suggests that orders will normally be made of the court's own initiative, there does not appear to be anything preventing a party applying for such an order in an appropriate case.

96 Evidence given by, or with respect to, children

(1) Subsection (2) applies in any civil proceedings where a child who is called as a witness in any civil proceedings does not, in the opinion of the court, understand the nature of an oath.

(2) The child's evidence may be heard by the court if, in its opinion –

    (a)   he understands that it is his duty to speak the truth; and

    (b)   he has sufficient understanding to justify his evidence being heard.

(3) The Lord Chancellor may, with the concurrence of the Lord Chief Justice, by order make provision for the admissibility of evidence which would otherwise be inadmissible under any rule of law relating to hearsay.

(4) An order under subsection (3) may only be made with respect to –

    (a)   civil proceedings in general or such civil proceedings, or class of civil proceedings, as may be prescribed; and

    (b)   evidence in connection with the upbringing, maintenance or welfare of a child.

(5) An order under subsection (3) –

    (a)   may, in particular, provide for the admissibility of statements which are made orally or in a prescribed form or which are recorded by any prescribed method of recording;

    (b)   may make different provision for different purposes and in relation to different descriptions of court; and

    (c)   may make such amendments and repeals in any enactment relating to evidence (other than in this Act) as the Lord Chancellor considers necessary or expedient in consequence of the provision made by the order.

(6) Subsection (5)(b) is without prejudice to section 104(4):

(7) In this section –

"civil proceedings" means civil proceedings, before any tribunal, in relation to which the strict rules of evidence apply, whether as a matter of law or by agreement of the parties, and references to "the court" shall be construed accordingly;

"prescribed" means prescribed by an order under subsection (3).

Amendments—Civil Evidence Act 1995, s 15(1), Sch 1, para 16; CRA 2005, s 15(1), Sch 4, Pt 1, paras 203, 207.

Defined terms—"child": s 105(1).

Scope—Section 96(1) and (2) allows a child who does not understand the oath to give unsworn evidence providing he understands his duty to speak the truth and has sufficient understanding to justify his evidence being heard; s 96(3)–(6) are enabling provisions facilitating the making of orders by the Lord Chancellor as to the admissibility of hearsay evidence (see Children (Admissibility of Hearsay Evidence) Order 1993 in Part IV.

Children as witnesses in family proceedings—A child can give sworn evidence or, if he does not understand the nature of the oath but comes within s 96(2), unsworn evidence. In *Re W (Children)* [2010] 1 FLR 1485, the Supreme Court held that the presumption against a child giving evidence in family proceedings cannot be reconciled with the approach of the ECtHR, which always aims to strike a fair balance between competing convention rights under ECHR 1950 (*LM (by her Guardian) v Medway Council* [2007] 1 FLR 1698; *R v BCC ex parte P* [1991] 1 FLR 470; *Re P (Witness Summons)* [1997] 2 FLR 447; and *Re W (Care Order: Sexual Abuse)* [2009] 2 FLR 1106 overruled). Following *Re W*, the Working Party of the Family Justice Council issued *Guidelines in Relation to Children Giving Evidence in Family Proceedings* (see Part V) to be used when the court is considering the possible advantages that the child being called will bring to the determination of truth, as balanced against the possible damage to the child's welfare from giving evidence (paras 8–11). It lists the practical matters that should be considered before a hearing at which a child is to give evidence (paras 13–17) and the practical steps to be taken at the hearing itself (para 18). Paragraph 19 sets out the ground rules for the examination of the child, taking into account the matters set out in *R v Barker* [2010] EWCA Crim 4 (at [42]), which called for advocacy to be adapted "to enable the child to give the best evidence of which her or she is capable". The guidelines will be reviewed periodically.

    Although the United Nations Convention on the Rights of the Child 1989 has not been made part of English law, the court is obliged to have regard to it when considering matters to which it relates. Article 12 of the Convention recognises that a child who is capable of forming his own views has the right to express those views freely in all matters affecting him, and that the voice of the child might be conveyed either directly or through a representative or appropriate body. Accordingly, while children have a right to be heard in proceedings, that right does not specify how they are to be heard. It does not seem to be essential that it must be the judge who hears directly from the child; it may be enough that a social worker, that is to say the Cafcass officer or guardian, hears their views. So, while the child must be listened to, there is nothing in the Convention that entitles him to a "right" to give evidence (*Re P-S (Children)* [2013] EWCA Civ 223, at [28], [32], [35]–[36]). In *Re P-S*, the Court of Appeal reminded judges that they must be very cautious when they see children in the absence of the other parties. Ward LJ said by way of footnote that he would encourage the judge to do so to explain the judgment he is about to give, or has just or recently given, in order to reassure the child that his wishes have been given proper weight and respect by the court. If the judge cannot accede to the child's wishes, the judge can take that useful opportunity to explain why. However, that meeting should not be used to take evidence from the child because if that evidence is given in the absence of the other parties, they could legitimately claim that their right to a fair trial has been invaded because a part of it was not undertaken in public (at [42]).

Article 6 of the EHCR requires that the proceedings be fair, and this normally entails an opportunity to challenge evidence presented by the other side. However, account must be taken of the Article 8 rights of the perceived victim. Striking that balance in care proceedings may mean that the child is not called in the great majority of cases, but this will be the result of the balancing exercise and not a presumption. The Supreme Court in *Re W* held that the approach in private family proceedings between parents is the same in principle, although there are specific risks. In such cases the allegations of abuse are made by a parent seeking to gain advantage, not by a neutral local authority. This does not mean that the allegations are false, but it does increase the risk of fabrication or exaggeration. Furthermore, the child would not routinely have the protection of a Cafcass guardian, and there are many more litigants in person in private law proceedings, meaning that the court would have to take very careful precautions to ensure that the child was not harmed. The first reported decision to apply the guidance in *Re W* is *Re J (Child Giving Evidence)* [2010] 2 FLR 1080. However, in *Re M (Sexual Abuse: Evidence)* [2010] Fam Law 1270, Hughes LJ, sitting as a single judge in the Court of Appeal, held that there should not, even now, be any question of young children giving oral evidence, at least in a family court. The child's welfare is very important, albeit not the paramount consideration. It will be rare for an unwilling child to be compelled to give evidence, although unwillingness is not of itself determinative (*SMBC v PR (SR Intervening) (Care Proceedings: Children's Evidence) (No 1)* [2012] 1 FLR 842). In *SMBC v PR (SR Intervening) (Care Proceedings: Children's Evidence) (No 2)* [2012] 1 FLR 852, the court pointed out that there is little authority on the compellability of an alleged perpetrator who is also a minor (in this case, SR, aged 17) and who is not a party to the care proceedings, but is merely an intervener, and did not wish to give evidence. *R v B County Council ex parte P* [1991] 1 FLR 470 (which has not subsequently been overruled) indicated that such a minor was compellable. However, there was no direct authority as to whether SR should, in the circumstances of that case, be so compelled. Balancing the relevant considerations, the court decided that it would not be appropriate to force him to give evidence.

Section 95(1) enables the court to require the attendance of the child concerned in a Pt IV or Pt V application. It is suggested (and this suggestion derives some support from comments in *R v B County Council* (above) at [475], [479]) that this procedure may not, however, be appropriate where the attendance of the child *as a witness* is required and that, in such cases, recourse should be had to provisions expressly designed for the purpose. The rules setting out the power of the court to control evidence are set out in FPR 2010, rr 22.1–22.17 and PD22A.

Where a parent wishes to call a willing child to give evidence, he may apparently be prevented from doing so in an appropriate case by means of a specific issue order (see Cousins, "Child's Evidence: Specific Issue Order" [1992] Fam Law 278).

Child understanding the nature of the oath—See *R v Hayes* [1977] 1 WLR 234, where it was held that a child could give evidence on oath if he has a sufficient appreciation of the solemnity of the occasion and the added responsibility to tell the truth which is involved in taking the oath, over and above the duty to tell the truth which is an ordinary duty of normal social conduct. The court in *R v Hayes* thought that the dividing line between children who are competent to give sworn evidence and those who are not is normally between the ages of eight and ten. However, under Criminal Justice Act 1988, s 33A, which governs the competence of children to give evidence in criminal proceedings, the general rule is that under-14s give unsworn evidence and children of 14 and over give sworn evidence.

Intermediaries—It is important that questions that challenge the child's account are fairly put to the child so that the child may answer them. This could be done through an early videoed cross-examination or through cross-examination via video-link. However, another way might be through use of an intermediary – the intermediary could be the court itself, as would be common in continental Europe (*Re W (Children)* [2010] 1 FLR 1485 at [28]). The Public Law Outline of April 2010 makes no mention of intermediaries, although it does make two references to the court needing to consider "special measures" (see FPR PD12A, paras 8.4 and 15.3(7)). The Family Justice Council Guidelines of December 2011 in relation to children giving evidence in family proceedings (see Part V) require specifically that if "live" cross-examination is appropriate, there should be early consideration of the need for and use of a registered intermediary or other communication specialist to facilitate the communication of others with the child or relay questions directly, if indicated by the needs of the child (para 14). Intermediaries are a "special measure", but a relatively new one. The use of intermediaries in England and Wales came about as a result of the Youth Justice and Criminal Evidence Act 1999, s 29. They operate in the criminal courts and are recruited and regulated by the MoJ. They are known as Registered Intermediaries (RIs) and their remit is to facilitate communication with vulnerable witnesses in the criminal justice system. The MoJ's Better Trials Unit (BTU) is responsible for RI policy and regulation, and its records show that since August 2009 there have been no RI appointments in family cases. The current policy of the BTU is that it will agree to assist in the provision of a RI for family court proceedings only where there is a direct link with a criminal case in which the witness is involved and where a RI has already been used and provided for that witness. In addition, assistance will only be provided where the RI used in the criminal trial is available and doing so does not affect the provision of RIs under the 1999 Act. There is currently no intermediary scheme for family courts and no obvious source of funding in place to provide a RI for family cases, even on an ad hoc basis. See the two articles by Penny Cooper "Child Witnesses in Family Proceedings: Should Intermediaries be Showing Us the Way?" [2011] Fam Law 397 and "Intermediaries and vulnerable witnesses: what do we do now?" [2012] Fam Law 868. The Final Report of the Family Justice Review, chaired by David Norgrove, recommended (at para 4.151) that the government and judiciary should actively consider how children and young witnesses may be protected when giving evidence in family proceedings. In relation to the factors to be considered when deciding whether or not to use an intermediary for a person who lacks capacity and is a vulnerable person, see the implications of *Re X (A Child)* [2012] 2 FLR 456 under FPR 2010, rr 11.4 and 15.1.

"sufficient understanding" (s 96(2)(b))—See **"able ... to give such instructions on his own behalf"** under FPR 2010, r 16.29.

Child giving unsworn evidence under s 96(2)—A child who gives unsworn evidence is still liable to be cross-examined.

Compelling attendance of a party to give evidence—A subpoena or witness summons can be issued to compel the attendance of a party to the proceedings to give evidence, irrespective of whether that party is a child or an adult (*R v B County Council ex parte P* [1991] 1 FLR 470).

Judge seeing child privately—See under FPR 2010, r 12.21.

97 Privacy for children involved in certain proceedings

(1) Family Procedure Rules may make provision for a magistrates' court to sit in private in proceedings in which any powers under this Act or the Adoption and Children Act 2002 may be exercised by the court with respect to any child.

(2) No person shall publish to the public at large or any section of the public any material which is intended, or likely, to identify –

    (a)   any child as being involved in any proceedings before the High Court, a county court or a magistrates' court in which any power under this Act or the Adoption and Children Act 2002 may be exercised by the court with respect to that or any other child; or

    (b)   an address or school as being that of a child involved in any such proceedings.

(3) In any proceedings for an offence under this section it shall be a defence for the accused to prove that he did not know, and had no reason to suspect, that the published material was intended, or likely, to identify the child.

(4) The court or the Lord Chancellor may, if satisfied that the welfare of the child requires it and, in the case of the Lord Chancellor, if the Lord Chief Justice agrees, by order dispense with the requirements of subsection (2) to such extent as may be specified in the order.

(5) For the purposes of this section –

    "publish" includes –

        (a)   include in a programme service (within the meaning of the Broadcasting Act 1990); or

     (b)   cause to be published; and

"material" includes any picture or representation.

(6) Any person who contravenes this section shall be guilty of an offence and liable, on summary conviction, to a fine not exceeding level 4 on the standard scale.

(7) Subsection (1) is without prejudice to –

     (a) ...
     (b)   any other power of a magistrates' court to sit in private.

(8) Sections 69 (sittings of magistrates' courts for family proceedings) and 71 (newspaper reports of certain proceedings) of the Act of 1980 shall apply in relation to any proceedings (before a magistrates' court) to which this section applies subject to the provisions of this section.

(9) The Lord Chief Justice may nominate a judicial office holder (as defined in section 109(4) of the Constitutional Reform Act 2005) to exercise his functions under subsection (4).

Amendments—Broadcasting Act 1990, s 203(1), Sch 20, para 53; CLSA 1990, s 116, Sch 16, para 24; SI 1992/709; AJA 1999, s 72; ACA 2002, s 101(2),(3); Courts Act 2003, s 109(1), Sch 8, para 337; CA 2004, s 62(1); CRA 2005, s 15(1), Sch 4, Pt 1, paras 203, 208.

Defined terms—"child", "school"; s 105(1).

Scope—This section makes provision to ensure that court proceedings in which powers under the Act may be exercised remain confidential. See also MCA 1980 and AJA 1960 (contempt by way of publishing information relating to children proceedings).

"Rules made under section 144 of the Magistrates' Courts Act 1980" (s 97(1))—FPR 2010, r 27.10 provides for proceedings to which FPR 2010 apply to be held in private, except where the rules provide otherwise or, subject to any enactment, where the court directs otherwise. "In private" means that the general public have no right to be present (r 27.10(2)). Attendance at private hearings is regulated by FPR 2010, r 27.11.

"publish" (s 97(2),(5))—The word "publish" in s 97 should be given its ordinary meaning. It does not extend to the situation where a children and family reporter communicates concerns to the relevant statutory authority charged with the collection and investigation of material suggestive of child abuse (*Re M (Disclosure: Children and Family Reporter)* [2002] 2 FLR 893 – where the children and family reporter in the course of his enquiries encounters suspicion of child abuse he has an unfettered independent discretion as to whether to make an immediate report to social services or the police; he must, however, inform the judge of any such steps he has taken at the earliest convenient opportunity).

Material which is intended or likely to identify a child (s 97(2))—The prohibition is not an absolute prohibition against publishing material about a child. In *Clayton v Clayton* [2007] 1 FLR 11 the court held that although the s 97(2) prohibition ends once the proceedings have been concluded, the provisions of AJA 1960, s 12 remain. Furthermore, in the course of the proceedings the judge may make an injunction or order prohibiting identification for a period beyond the proceedings in the welfare interests of the child, or in order to protect privacy under ECHR 1950, Art 8. However, in deciding to make a long-term injunction aimed at restricting the reporting and publication of proceedings, the court is obliged to conduct a balancing exercise between the Art 8 rights of the child and the Art 10 (freedom of expression) rights of a parent asserting such a right. In *Clayton* the court held that the father was free to discuss or communicate matters about the case, but the making of a film and the taking of the child back to Portugal for that purpose related to her upbringing and thus engaged her welfare interests and infringed her Art 8 rights. Consequently, the court made a prohibited steps order pursuant to CA 1989, ss 8 and 10(1)(b) to restrain him in that regard. In *Re R (Secure Editing of Documents)* [2007] 2 FLR 759 in contact proceedings the court made an order permitting omission of the mother's address and contact details from any evidence and documents filed and served in the course of the proceedings in order to protect her and the children from the father. Due to inadequate editing of the documents by the various solicitors involved, the father discovered the mother's new name and he contacted her. The court held that this amounted to a gross breach of the mother's rights under ECHR 1950, Art 8. In order to avoid repetition of such instances, the court issued detailed guidelines with the approval of the President of the Family Division and these are set out in the judgment.

Power to dispense with restrictions on publicity (s 97(4))—This power might be used by the court where, for example, a child is missing and press publicity may help in tracing him. It would appear that an order may be made of the court's own initiative or on application. If an application is to be made, it may be appropriate to use the directions procedure under FPR 2010, r 12.12. The Government's recent decision to allow attendance of the media at hearings in family proceedings has been implemented by a change to FPR 2010, r 27.11(2). See further under FPR 2010, r 27.11.

The court has moved towards the lifting of reporting restrictions in certain circumstances, see *Re Webster; Norfolk County Council v Webster and Ors* [2007] 1 FLR 1146, where Munby J analysed publicity issues both in principle and in relation to detailed statutory provisions and rights under ECHR 1950; *Re LM (Reporting Restrictions: Coroner's Inquest)* [2008] 1 FLR 1360, where the Press were permitted to report certain details at an inquest into the death of the child's sister; *Re B; X Council v B* [2008] 1 FLR 482 – an order enabling the local authority to be named; *Re B; X Council v B (No 2)* [2008] 1 FLR 1460 – an order allowing the mother and two of the children to waive their anonymity should they so wish; *Re H (Care Plan)* [2008] 2 FLR 21 – an order allowing a short summary of the judicial criticism of the social workers involved and of the local authority's response; *Z County Council v TS, DS, ES and A* [2008] 2 FLR 1800 – the judge allowed the care proceedings to be held in public, subject to a schedule of anonymisation covering all parties and witnesses; *Medway Council v G and Others* [2008] 2 FLR 1687 – in the course of care proceedings, the court gave permission for a newspaper to interview the stepfather about related criminal proceedings on the basis of an agreed statement of facts prepared by the parties, provided that the child was not identified. However, in *Re R (Identification: Restrictions on Publication)* [2008] 1 FLR 1252, the court made injunctions restraining the parents from seeking to identify the prospective adopters and stopping them from contacting the children, and restraining publication of any details identifying the children. In *S (A Child Acting by the Official Solicitor) v Rochdale Metropolitan Borough Council and the Independent Reviewing Officer* [2009] 1 FLR 1090, the court approved a confidentiality clause reached by agreement between the child and the authority as part of a compromise approved by the court.

Courts should take great care when imposing orders restricting the reporting of criminal proceedings, and before doing so should carry out a balancing exercise with regard to the public interest under ECHR 1950, Arts 8 and 10. Members of the press should be asked whether they wished to make submissions (*Crawford v Director of Public Prosecutions* [2008] *The Times*, 20 February – where the court heard representations by the media and then lifted reporting restrictions in a case where the appellant had been convicted of harassing his former wife and her partner; there was no evidence of any particular harm being caused to his children by so doing, other than the obvious embarrassment of their father having been convicted of a criminal offence).

In *Re K (Adoption: Permission to Advertise)* [2007] 2 FLR 326, the local authority applied under s 97(4) for permission to advertise a child for adoption by placing potentially identifying details about him in national and local publications. The Family Proceedings Court (FPC) gave permission to advertise in relevant publications, provided that it was anonymous. These restrictions were upheld on appeal. It was not open to a local authority to place a full identifying advertisement for the adoption of a particular child until they had obtained the necessary recommendation from the adoption panel and had decided that the child ought to be placed for adoption. When such an application is made before a final care hearing and where the care plan for adoption has yet to be endorsed, the court is unlikely to give permission to advertise unless the adoption plan is unopposed or there is some exceptional feature to the case justifying advertising.

"without prejudice to ... any other power of a magistrates' court to sit in private" (s 97(7)(b))—See MCA 1980, s 69, which continues to apply, subject to this section.

Magistrates' Courts Act 1980, ss 69 and 71 (s 97(8))—MCA 1980, s 69(2) ensures a certain minimum degree of privacy in family proceedings in a magistrates' court by providing that no person shall be present during the hearing and determination of most such proceedings except officers of the court, the parties and their legal representatives, witnesses and other people directly concerned in the case, representatives of the press and news agencies and anyone else whom the court permits. As to provisions for the attendance of the media at hearings in family proceedings, see FPR 2010, r 27.11. Section 69(4) enables the court, if it thinks it necessary in the interest of the administration of justice or public decency, to exclude anyone who is not an officer of the court, a party or his legal representative or otherwise directly concerned in the case where "indecent evidence" is being taken. Section 69(6) ensures that the court can exclude witnesses until they are called for examination. All the provisions of s 69 are, however, subject to the provisions of FPR 2010, rr 27.10 and 27.11, which enables the court to restrict attendance at court even further.

Section 71 makes it an offence to publish particulars of family proceedings except as expressly permitted by the section (which, depending on the type of case involved, normally permits publication of such information as names, addresses and occupations of parties and witnesses, submissions on any point of law, the decision of the court etc). It is less restrictive than s 97(2) but, by virtue of s 97(8), s 97(2) prevails wherever it applies.

98 Self-incrimination

(1) In any proceedings in which a court is hearing an application for an order under Part IV or V, no person shall be excused from –

(a) giving evidence on any matter; or

(b) answering any question put to him in the course of his giving evidence,

on the ground that doing so might incriminate him or his spouse or civil partner of an offence.

(2) A statement or admission made in such proceedings shall not be admissible in evidence against the person making it or his spouse or civil partner in proceedings for an offence other than perjury.

Amendments—CPA 2004, s 261(1), Sch 27, para 132.

Self-incrimination—The general rule, to which this section creates an exception, is that a person is not bound to answer any question if his answer would, in the opinion of the court, tend to expose him to any criminal charge or penalty which the court regards as reasonably likely to be preferred or sued for (*Blunt v Park Lane Hotels* [1942] 2 KB 253).

"Part IV or V" (s 98(1))—Parts IV and V concern public law orders, such as care and supervision orders, emergency protection orders, and child assessment orders.

Ambit of s 98—Ultimately, it will be the criminal court which decides the degree of protection afforded by s 98(2) in any given case. However, there have been a number of views expressed, in the context of family proceedings, about its extent.

(a) *Meaning of "statement or admission made in such proceedings"* (s 98(2))   In *Oxfordshire County Council v P* [1995] 1 FLR 552, Ward J considered that s 98(2) provided protection with regard to oral admissions made in advance of care proceedings to a children's guardian. In *Cleveland County Council v F* [1995] 1 FLR 797, Hale J agreed with him and added her view that it extends also to statements made to social workers investigating in a child protection case, at least once the proceedings have begun. *Oxfordshire County Council v P* was referred to without demur in *Oxfordshire County Council v L and F* [1997] 1 FLR 235, FD. In *Re K and Others (Minors) (Disclosure)* [1994] 1 FLR 377, Booth J (albeit in a different context) may have been expressing a narrower view when she said that it provided "protection to a witness who is required to give evidence in relation to a child when such evidence could incriminate him or his spouse". In *Re G (Social Worker: Disclosure)* [1996] 1 FLR 276, Butler-Sloss LJ, obiter, doubted that s 98(2) could be extended as far as Ward and Hale JJ had suggested.

(b) *Meaning of "admissible in evidence"* (s 98(2))   In *Re EC (Disclosure of Material)* [1996] 2 FLR 725, the Court of Appeal decided inter alia that transcripts of an admission made by the father when giving evidence should be disclosed to the police, who would then be free to use it when questioning him. The content of any further interview may, of course, be the subject of submissions as to admissibility in criminal proceedings by virtue of PACE 1984, and that would be a matter for the discretion of the trial judge in those proceedings. According to *Re EC* (above), s 98(2) gives protection only against statements being admissible in evidence in criminal proceedings except for an offence of perjury, and does not protect against their use in a police inquiry into the commission of an offence (see also *Re X (Children)* [2008] 1 FLR 589; *Re X (Disclosure for Purposes of Criminal Proceedings)* [2008] 2 FLR 944); *Re M (Care: Disclosure to Police)* [2008] 2 FLR 390). A judge cannot give a witness in family proceedings any absolute guarantee as to confidentiality, since there is power to order disclosure even of material falling within s 98(2). In *Re EC*, before they gave evidence, the judge had told all members of the child's family who were suspected of causing her injuries that anything they said from the witness-box could not be used in any criminal trial against them relating to the death of the child. The Court of Appeal said that judges may well like to point out to witnesses to whom such a statement is made that guarantees of confidentiality cannot be given; almost certainly legal advisers should do so. As to applications for disclosure of Children Act material for the purposes of criminal proceedings/investigation, by virtue of the Criminal Justice Act 2003, s 119, a previous inconsistent statement by a witness that is put to him in criminal proceedings is admissible as evidence of any matter stated of which oral evidence by him would be admissible (subject to the discretion of the court to exclude it under PACE 1984). Note that this statutory provision supersedes the decision in *Re L (Care: Confidentiality)* [1999] 1 FLR 165. In *Re O (Care Proceedings: Evidence)* [2004] 1 FLR 161 Johnson J held that where a parent declines to answer questions or to give oral evidence, the court should usually draw the inference that the allegations made against him or her are true. The provisions of s 98(2) do apply to any statement or admission which a parent gives to an expert witness (*Re AB (Care Proceedings: Disclosure of Medical Evidence to Police)* [2003] 1 FLR 579 – where Wall J held (at [134]) that the position of expert witnesses is analogous for these purposes with that of the guardian and therefore a statement made to an expert witness is a statement made in the proceedings and thus entitled to the protection of s 98(2)). Before being interviewed by an expert witness, parents should have the terms and purpose of s 98(2) explained to them by their lawyers (*Re AB* (above) at [134]).

Legal professional privilege—See notes under s 31, above.

****

100 Restrictions on use of wardship jurisdiction

(1) Section 7 of the Family Law Reform Act 1969 (which gives the High Court power to place a ward of court in the care, or under the supervision, of a local authority) shall cease to have effect.

(2) No court shall exercise the High Court's inherent jurisdiction with respect to children –

(a) so as to require a child to be placed in the care, or put under the supervision, of a local authority;

(b) so as to require a child to be accommodated by or on behalf of a local authority;

(c) so as to make a child who is the subject of a care order a ward of court; or

(d) for the purpose of conferring on any local authority power to determine any question which has arisen, or which may arise, in connection with any aspect of parental responsibility for a child.

(3) No application for any exercise of the court's inherent jurisdiction with respect to children may be made by a local authority unless the authority have obtained the leave of the court.

(4) The court may only grant leave if it is satisfied that –

(a) the result which the authority wish to achieve could not be achieved through the making of any order of a kind to which subsection (5) applies; and

(b) there is reasonable cause to believe that if the court's inherent jurisdiction is not exercised with respect to the child he is likely to suffer significant harm.

(5) This subsection applies to any order –

(a) made otherwise than in the exercise of the court's inherent jurisdiction; and

(b) which the local authority is entitled to apply for (assuming, in the case of any application which may only be made with leave, that leave is granted).

Scope—This section prevents a child from being both in care and a ward of court, and restricts any application by the local authority for the exercise of the court's inherent jurisdiction without leave; see further s 91(4), Sch 14, para 16A and FPR 2010, rr 12.36–12.42 and FPR PD12D; FPR 2010, Pt 18 appears to be the appropriate procedure for applying for permission. While the effect of s 100(2) is to prevent orders in wardship being used to require a child to be placed in the care or under the supervision of the local authority, the provisions of this section do not (either explicitly or implicitly) preclude the court from making a child a ward of court where the child has been accommodated voluntarily by the local authority under CA 1939, s 20 with the consent of the parent(s) and that consent has not been withdrawn (*Re E (A Child)* [2012] EWCA Civ 1773). In *W and X (Wardship: Relatives Rejected as Foster Carers)* [2004] 1 FLR 415 the court used its inherent jurisdiction, when the Fostering Services Regulations 2002 prevented the placement of children with their grandparents, by making the children wards of court and placing them with the grandparents in conjunction with a supervision order. In *Re F (Mental Health Act: Guardianship)* [2000] 1 FLR 192 wardship was considered by the Court of Appeal to be the preferred option to an application for guardianship under MHA 1983. Where the circumstances are unusual, the court will consider warding a child within care proceedings to maintain control over decisions relating to a child where the court considers that a "unique solution for a unique case" is required. Such a situation arose in *Re K (Children with Disabilities: Wardship)* [2012] 2 FLR 745: when granting permission to withdraw the care proceedings, Hedley J took the view that "given the conflicted history of the case it was desirable that some legal structure should remain in place, to ensure equality between the parties" and so that "it reminds all that they remain accountable to the court for making the necessary arrangements for the care, education and nurturing of these three children and it confirms the court's powers over the control and delegation of parental responsibility. It provides a reference point for disputes, although not one that will be easily engaged". To facilitate a working relationship between the parents and the professionals, the court also took the unusual course of directing the use of an independent case manager.

There have, however, been conflicting decisions on the correct procedure to be followed when the need arises for the court to authorise the administration or withdrawal of medical treatment. In *Re T (Wardship: Medical Treatment)* [1997] 1 FLR 502 the local authority was granted leave under s 100(3) to commence proceedings where the issue before the court was whether it was in the best interests of a baby to undergo liver transplant surgery. In *Re S (A Minor) (Medical Treatment)* [1993] 1 FLR 376, *Re O (A Minor) (Medical Treatment)* [1993] 2 FLR 149 and *South Glamorgan County Council v W and B* [1993] 1 FLR 574, the court considered that the appropriate procedure was to invoke the inherent jurisdiction of the court. In *A Local Authority v SB, AB & MB* [2010] 2 FLR 1203 the specific issue route was rejected as an appropriate procedure where the medical treatment initially proposed was for surgery for a child who suffered from a rare and progressive brain disease. However, in *Re R (A Minor) (Blood Transfusion)* [1993] 2 FLR 757, an application for a specific issue order under s 8 was considered to be appropriate where the application related to blood transfusion. It is submitted that, in cases involving children, a distinction may need to be made between cases where the dispute is between parents, and relates to the administration of ordinary medical treatment which is neither life threatening nor controversial, and those cases which raise issues of public policy. In the former category of cases, an application for a specific issue order may be appropriate, provided the child is not in care and the local authority is not seeking to acquire parental responsibility of the child. In the latter case the inherent jurisdiction of the court should be invoked. In *Devon County Council v S and Another* [1994] 1 FLR 355 it was held that in such cases the court's approach should not be too restrictive.

The inherent jurisdiction is available to exclude a parent from his property indefinitely if there is reasonable cause to believe that the child otherwise would suffer significant harm. Wall J laid down the following propositions in *C v K (Inherent Powers: Exclusion Order)* [1996] 2 FLR 506:

"(1) Where judicial interference with the rights of occupation of property, as between spouses, cohabitees or former cohabitees, is specifically governed by statute, the relevant statutory provisions apply.

(2) Leaving on one side the parens patriae jurisdiction of the High Court over children who are specifically its wards, there exists an inherent jurisdiction in both the High Court and the county court to protect children from harm which is exercisable irrespective of the proceedings in which the issue of the need to protect the children arises.

(3) There is a co-existing jurisdiction given in the High Court by s 37 of the Senior Courts Act and in the county court by s 38 of the County Courts Act to grant injunctive relief in support of legal and equitable rights.

(4) The powers exercisable under ss 37 and 38 of the respective statutes may be invoked in support of the rights and duties conferred on a person by a residence order. Thus, in cases where neither the Matrimonial Homes Act 1983 nor the Domestic Violence and Matrimonial Proceedings Act 1976 applies, a non-residential parent may be restrained from interfering with the residential parent's exercise of parental responsibility. The powers of the court in this context extend to orders against molestation and to ouster injunctions.

(5) The powers exercisable by the court under ss 37 and 38 extend to the grant of injunctions against third parties. Thus, a person who is not a parent of the child may be restrained from interfering with the exercise of parental responsibility by a person who has a residence order in relation to the child. The powers of the court to grant injunctive relief include the power to exclude the stranger from property in which he has a beneficial interest.

(6) There is no reported case in which the inherent jurisdiction, unaffected by ss 37 and 38, has been used to exclude anybody who is not a parent from the occupation of property in which he has a proprietary interest. While the power to make such an order may exist, the better course, in my judgment, is to invoke the jurisdiction under ss 37 and 38, since the need to protect the child is then bolstered by the need to protect the rights of the party with parental responsibility to exercise that parental responsibility appropriately.

(7) The powers of the court to exclude a person from property in which he has a proprietary interest should be exercised with extreme caution. By analogy with s 100(4) of the Children Act the jurisdiction is likely only to be exercised where the court is satisfied that if the jurisdiction is not exercised the child is likely to suffer significant harm. In reaching any conclusion the court must look at all the circumstances of the case, including of course the circumstances of each of the parties and the conduct of the parties towards each other and the child. The court must make findings of fact upon which the assessment of likely future harm can be made.

(8) While the jurisdiction exists to make a final order excluding a person from occupation of property in which he has a proprietary interest, without limitation of time, the court cannot by these means vary

proprietary interests and must in every such case consider whether an indefinite order is required in order to protect the child from the likelihood of significant harm, and to achieve a result which is just."

The county court has no inherent jurisdiction to grant injunctions in relation to the exercise of its statutory powers in children cases, whether under CA 1989 or ACA 2002 (*D v D (County Court Jurisdiction: Injunctions)* [1993] 2 FLR 802; applied in *Devon County Council v B* [1997] 1 FLR 591, CA). It may thus be argued that, in view of these decisions and particularly the Court of Appeal case, the decision in *C v K* cannot stand. However, it is submitted that *C v K* is distinguishable since, although reference was made in that case to the inherent jurisdiction of the court to protect children, the decision to grant injunctive relief was not made under the inherent jurisdiction of the court. It was based on the court's jurisdiction to grant such relief under SCA 1981, s 37 and CCA 1984, s 38 to protect the rights of the party with parental responsibility to exercise appropriately that parental responsibility, and the rights and duties which that legal responsibility entails.

Where a care order is made in favour of a local authority, the authority has parental responsibility for the child, and it can be argued that the jurisdiction under SCA 1981, s 37 and CCA 1984, s 38 may be invoked to protect its rights to exercise that parental responsibility appropriately and, in particular, to protect the child. Therefore, in an appropriate case, where a care order or interim care order is made in favour of a local authority, application may be made for injunctive relief by the local authority against a parent or a third party, pursuant to the power conferred by SCA 1981, s 37 or CCA 1984, s 38 instead of invoking the court's inherent jurisdiction, provided that it can be shown that, if the jurisdiction is not exercised, the child is likely to suffer significant harm. It is also submitted that *C v K* provides a remedy where injunctive relief under any other provision proves impossible, provided it is necessary to protect the child from significant harm, and it is needed to enable the party with parental responsibility to exercise that legal right appropriately and effectively. This view has been confirmed by the decision in *Re P (Care Orders: Injunctive Relief)* [2000] 2 FLR 385.

The court has the power to include an exclusion order and accept an undertaking, in appropriate cases, when an interim care order or emergency protection order is made under ss 38 and 44, respectively. However, the remedy available under ss 38A and 38B, and ss 44A and 44B of the CA, is limited in its nature and extent and is subject to the conditions set out in those sections. It is, therefore, submitted that the decision in *C v K* will continue to be of importance to cover both private and public law cases, which do not come within any statutory provisions, to provide relief where it is required to enable a person or body with parental responsibility to exercise those rights and duties.

Inherent jurisdiction and forced marriages—The Forced Marriage (Civil Protection) Act 2007 is in force (see FLA 1996, s 63B).

101 Effect of orders as between England and Wales and Northern Ireland, the Channel Islands or the Isle of Man

(1) The Secretary of State may make regulations providing –

    (a)   for prescribed orders which –
        (i)   are made by a court in Northern Ireland; and
        (ii) appear to the Secretary of State to correspond in their effect to orders which may be made under any provision of this Act,
    to have effect in prescribed circumstances, for prescribed purposes of this Act, as if they were orders of a prescribed kind made under this Act;

    (b)   for prescribed orders which –
        (i)   are made by a court in England and Wales; and
        (ii) appear to the Secretary of State to correspond in their effect to orders which may be made under any provision in force in Northern Ireland,
    to have effect in prescribed circumstances, for prescribed purposes of the law of Northern Ireland, as if they were orders of a prescribed kind made in Northern Ireland.

(2) Regulations under subsection (1) may provide for the order concerned to cease to have effect for the purposes of the law of Northern Ireland, or (as the case may be) the law of England and Wales, if prescribed conditions are satisfied.

(3) The Secretary of State may make regulations providing for prescribed orders which –

(a) are made by a court in the Isle of Man or in any of the Channel Islands; and

(b) appear to the Secretary of State to correspond in their effect to orders which may be made under this Act,

to have effect in prescribed circumstances for prescribed purposes of this Act, as if they were orders of a prescribed kind made under this Act.

(4) Where a child who is in the care of a local authority is lawfully taken to live in Northern Ireland, the Isle of Man or in any of the Channel Islands, the care order in question shall cease to have effect if the conditions prescribed in regulations by the Secretary of State are satisfied.

(5) Any regulations made under this section may –

(a) make such consequential amendments (including repeals) in –

(i) section 25 of the Children and Young Persons Act 1969 (transfers between England and Wales and Northern Ireland); or

(ii) section 26 (transfers between England and Wales and Channel Islands or Isle of Man) of that Act,

as the Secretary of State considers necessary or expedient; and

(b) modify any provision of this Act, in its application (by virtue of the regulations) in relation to an order made otherwise than in England and Wales.

Defined terms—"prescribed": s 105(1).

Scope—This section is intended to give reciprocal effect to orders as between England, Northern Ireland, the Channel Islands and the Isle of Man. It complements the provisions under Sch 2, para 19(2),(3)(d), which permit the local authority to arrange for a child in its care to live outside England and Wales. If a child who is the subject of a care order is moved to live in Northern Ireland, the Channel Islands or the Isle of Man, the care order may be transferred in accordance with regulations to the public authority there (see s 101(4) and Children (Prescribed Orders – Northern Ireland, Guernsey and Isle of Man) Regulations 1991). Where a child is lawfully moved, the care order ceases to have effect if the conditions prescribed in the regulations are satisfied.

Search warrants

102 Power of constable to assist in exercise of certain powers to search for children or inspect premises

(1) Where, on an application made by any person for a warrant under this section, it appears to the court –

(a) that a person attempting to exercise powers under any enactment mentioned in subsection (6) has been prevented from doing so by being refused entry to the premises concerned or refused access to the child concerned; or

(b) that any such person is likely to be so prevented from exercising any such powers,

it may issue a warrant authorising any constable to assist that person in the exercise of those powers, using reasonable force if necessary.

(2) Every warrant issued under this section shall be addressed to, and executed by, a constable who shall be accompanied by the person applying for the warrant if –

(a) that person so desires; and

(b) the court by whom the warrant is issued does not direct otherwise.

(3) A court granting an application for a warrant under this section may direct that the constable concerned may, in executing the warrant, be accompanied by a registered medical practitioner, registered nurse or registered midwife if he so chooses.

(3A) The reference in subsection (3) to a registered midwife is to such a midwife who is also registered in the Specialist Community Public Health Nurses' Part of the register maintained under article 5 of the Nursing and Midwifery Order 2001.

(4) An application for a warrant under this section shall be made in the manner and form prescribed by rules of court.

(5) Where –

  (a) an application for a warrant under this section relates to a particular child; and
  (b) it is reasonably practicable to do so,

the application and any warrant granted on the application shall name the child; and where it does not name him it shall describe him as clearly as possible.

(6) The enactments are –

  (a) sections 62, 64, 67, 76, 80, 86 and 87;
  (b) paragraph 8(1)(b) and (2)(b) of Schedule 3;
  (c) (*repealed*)

Amendments—ACA 2002, s 139(1),(3), Sch 3, paras 54, 69; SI 2002/253; SI 2004/1771.

Defined terms—"child": s 105(1).

Jurisdiction—ATPO 2008, art 5(2) requires proceedings under this section to be commenced in a magistrates' court unless the child concerned is the subject of proceedings in a county court or the High Court or the application arises out of the same circumstances as ongoing proceedings, in which case the application may be started in that court (art 5(3)).

"manner and form prescribed by rules of court" (s 102(4))—FPR 2010, r 12.16 allows an application under this section to be made without notice, in which case r 2.6(1)(a) empowers a single justice to determine it. The proceedings are not "specified proceedings" for the purposes of s 41(6). Form C19 in FPR 2010, r 5 and PD5A is the form prescribed (under the 2010 Rules the format of orders and warrants is no longer prescribed – for an example of the format of the warrant see the former FPC(CA 1989)R 1991, Sch 1, Form 28).

General

103 Offences by bodies corporate

(1) This section applies where any offence under this Act is committed by a body corporate.

(2) If the offence is proved to have been committed with the consent or connivance of or to be attributable to any neglect on the part of any director, manager, secretary or other similar officer of the body corporate, or any person who was purporting to act in any such capacity, he (as well as the body corporate) shall be guilty of the offence and shall be liable to be proceeded against and punished accordingly.

104 Regulations and orders

(1) Any power of the Lord Chancellor, the Treasury, the Secretary of State or the National Assembly for Wales under this Act to make an order, regulations, or rules, except an order under section 56(4)(a), 57(3), 84 or 97(4) or paragraph 1(1) of Schedule 4, shall be exercisable by statutory instrument.

(2) Any such statutory instrument, except one made under section 4(1B), 4ZA(3), 17(4), 107 or 108(2) or one containing regulations which fall within subsection (3B) or (3C), shall be subject to annulment in pursuance of a resolution of either House of Parliament.

(2A) (*repealed*)

(3A) An order under section 4(1B), 4ZA(3) or 17(4) or regulations which fall within subsection (3B) or (3C) shall not be made by the Secretary of State unless a draft of the statutory instrument containing the order or regulations has been laid before, and approved by a resolution of, each House of Parliament.

(3B) Regulations fall within this subsection if they are the first regulations to be made by the Secretary of State in the exercise of the power conferred by section 23C(5B)(b).

(3C) Regulations fall within this subsection if they are the first regulations to be made by the Secretary of State in the exercise of the power conferred by paragraph 6(2) of Schedule 2.

(4) Any statutory instrument made under this Act may –

    (a)   make different provision for different cases;

    (b)   provide for exemptions from any of its provisions; and

    (c)   contain incidental, supplemental and transitional provisions.

Amendments—Care Standards Act 2000, s 117, Sch 6; ACA 2002, s 111; Tax Credits Act 2002, s 47, Sch 3; CAA 2006, s 15(1), Sch 2, paras 7, 10; HFEA 2008, s 56, Sch 6, para 30; CYPA 2008, ss 39, 42, Sch 3, paras 1, 25, Sch 4, SI 2009/1892.

104A Regulations and orders made by the Welsh Ministers under Part 3 etc

(1) Any power of the Welsh Ministers under Part 3, Part 7 or section 86A to make an order or regulations shall be exercisable by statutory instrument.

(2) Any such statutory instrument, except one made under section 17(4) or one containing regulations which fall within subsection (4) or (5), shall be subject to annulment in pursuance of a resolution of the National Assembly for Wales.

(3) An order under section 17(4) or regulations which fall within subsection (4) or (5) shall not be made by the Welsh Ministers unless a draft of the statutory instrument containing the order or regulations has been laid before and approved by a resolution of the National Assembly for Wales.

(4) Regulations fall within this subsection if they are the first regulations to be made by the Welsh Ministers in the exercise of the power conferred by section 23C(5B)(b).

(5) Regulations fall within this subsection if they are the first regulations to be made by the Welsh Ministers in the exercise of the power conferred by paragraph 6(2) of Schedule 2.

Amendments—Inserted by CYPA 2008, s 39, Sch 3, paras 1, 26.

105 Interpretation

(1) In this Act –

    "adoption agency" means a body which may be referred to as an adoption agency by virtue of section 2 of the Adoption and Children Act 2002;

    "bank holiday" means a day which is a bank holiday under the Banking and Financial Dealings Act 1971;

    "care home" has the same meaning as in the Care Standards Act 2000;

    "care order" has the meaning given by section 31(11) and also includes any order which by or under any enactment has the effect of, or is deemed to be, a care order for the purposes of this Act; and any reference to a child who is in the care of an authority is a reference to a child who is in their care by virtue of a care order;

    "child" means, subject to paragraph 16 of Schedule 1, a person under the age of eighteen;

"child assessment order" has the meaning given by section 43(2);

"child minder" has the meaning given by section 71;

"child of the family", in relation to parties to a marriage, or to two people who are civil partners of each other, means –
  (a)   a child of both of them, and
  (b)   any other child, other than a child placed with them as foster parents by a local authority or voluntary organisation, who has been treated by both of them as a child of their family;

"children's home" has the same meaning as it has for the purposes of the Care Standards Act 2000 (see section 1 of that Act);

"clinical commissioning group" means a body established under section 14D of the National Health Service Act 2006;

"community home" has the meaning given by section 53;

"contact activity condition" has the meaning given by section 11C;

"contact activity direction" has the meaning given by section 11A;

"contact order" has the meaning given by section 8(1);

"day care" (except in Part XA) has the same meaning as in section 18;

"disabled", in relation to a child, has the same meaning as in section 17(11);

"domestic premises" has the meaning given by section 71(12);

"dwelling-house" includes –
  (a)   any building or part of a building which is occupied as a dwelling;
  (b)   any caravan, house-boat or structure which is occupied as a dwelling;
and any yard, garden, garage or outhouse belonging to it and occupied with it;

"education functions" has the meaning given by section 579(1) of the Education Act 1996;

"education supervision order" has the meaning given in section 36;

"emergency protection order" means an order under section 44;

"enforcement order" has the meaning given by section 11J;

"family assistance order" has the meaning given in section 16(2);

"family proceedings" has the meaning given by section 8(3);

"functions" includes powers and duties;

"guardian of a child" means a guardian (other than a guardian of the estate of a child) appointed in accordance with the provisions of section 5;

"harm" has the same meaning as in section 31(9) and the question of whether harm is significant shall be determined in accordance with section 31(10);

"Health Authority" means a Health Authority established under section 8 of the National Health Service Act 1977;

"health service hospital" has the same meaning as in the National Health Service Act 1977;

"hospital" (except in Schedule 9A) has the same meaning as in the Mental Health Act 1983, except that it does not include a hospital at which high security psychiatric services within the meaning of that Act are provided;

"ill-treatment" has the same meaning as in section 31(9);

"income-based jobseeker's allowance" has the same meaning as in the Jobseekers Act 1995;

"income-related employment and support allowance" means an income-related allowance under Part 1 of the Welfare Reform Act 2007 (employment and support allowance);

"independent hospital" has the same meaning as in the Care Standards Act 2000;

"independent school" has the same meaning as in the Education Act 1996;

"local authority" means, in relation to England, the council of a county, a metropolitan district, a London Borough or the Common Council of the City of

London, in relation to Wales, the council of a county or a county borough and, in
relation to Scotland, a local authority within the meaning of section 1(2) of the
Social Work (Scotland) Act 1968;

"local authority foster parent" has the meaning given in section 22C(12);

    "Local Health Board" means a Local Health Board established under section 11
of the National Health Service (Wales) Act 2006;

"local housing authority" has the same meaning as in the Housing Act 1985;

"officer of the Service" has the same meaning as in the Criminal Justice and Court
Services Act 2000;

"parental responsibility" has the meaning given in section 3;

"parental responsibility agreement" has the meaning given in sections 4(1), 4ZA(4)
and 4A(2);

"prescribed" means prescribed by regulations made under this Act;

...

"private children's home" means a children's home in respect of which a person is
registered under Part II of the Care Standards Act 2000 which is not a
community home or a voluntary home;

"privately fostered child" and "to foster a child privately" have the same meaning as
in section 66;

"prohibited steps order" has the meaning given by section 8(1);

"registered pupil" has the same meaning as in the Education Act 1996;

"relative", in relation to a child, means a grandparent, brother, sister, uncle or aunt
(whether of the full blood or half blood or by marriage or civil partnership) or
step-parent;

"residence order" has the meaning given by section 8(1);

"responsible person", in relation to a child who is the subject of a supervision order,
has the meaning given in paragraph 1 of Schedule 3;

"school" has the same meaning as in the Education Act 1996 or, in relation to
Scotland, in the Education (Scotland) Act 1980;

"section 31A plan" has the meaning given by section 31A(6);

"service", in relation to any provision made under Part III, includes any facility;

"signed", in relation to any person, includes the making by that person of his mark;

"special educational needs" has the same meaning as in the Education Act 1996;

"special guardian" and "special guardianship order" have the meaning given by
section 14A;

"Special Health Authority" means a Special Health Authority established under
section 11 of the National Health Service Act 1977;

"specific issue order" has the meaning given by section 8(1);

...

"supervision order" has the meaning given by section 31(11);

"supervised child" and "supervisor", in relation to a supervision order or an
education supervision order, mean respectively the child who is (or is to be)
under supervision and the person under whose supervision he is (or is to be) by
virtue of the order;

"upbringing", in relation to any child, includes the care of the child but not his
maintenance;

"voluntary home" has the meaning given by section 60;

"voluntary organisation" means a body (other than a public or local authority) whose
activities are not carried on for profit;

"Welsh family proceedings officer" has the meaning given by section 35 of the
Children Act 2004.

(2) References in this Act to a child whose father and mother were, or (as the case may
be) were not, married to each other at the time of his birth must be read with section 1 of
the Family Law Reform Act 1987 (which extends the meaning of such references).

(3) References in this Act to –

    (a)   a person with whom a child lives, or is to live, as the result of a residence order; or

    (b)   a person in whose favour a residence order is in force,

shall be construed as references to the person named in the order as the person with whom the child is to live.

(4) References in this Act to a child who is looked after by a local authority have the same meaning as they have (by virtue of section 22) in Part III.

(5) References in this Act to accommodation provided by or on behalf of a local authority are references to accommodation so provided in the exercise of functions of that or any other local authority which are social services functions within the meaning of the Local Authority Social Services Act 1970.

(5A) References in this Act to a child minder shall be construed –

    (a)   *(repealed)*

    (b)   in relation to Wales, in accordance with section 79A.

(5B) References in this Act to acting as a child minder and to a child minder shall be construed, in relation to Scotland, in accordance with section 2(17) of the Regulation of Care (Scotland) Act 2001.

(6) In determining the "ordinary residence" of a child for any purpose of this Act, there shall be disregarded any period in which he lives in any place –

    (a)   which is a school or other institution;

    (b)   in accordance with the requirements of a supervision order under this Act;

    (ba) in accordance with the requirements of a youth rehabilitation order under Part 1 of the Criminal Justice and Immigration Act 2008; or

    (c)   while he is being provided with accommodation by or on behalf of a local authority.

(7) References in this Act to children who are in need shall be construed in accordance with section 17.

(7A) References in this Act to a hospital or accommodation made available or provided pursuant to arrangements made by the Secretary of State under the National Health Service Act 2006 are references to a hospital or accommodation made available or provided pursuant to arrangements so made in the exercise of the public health functions of the Secretary of State (within the meaning of that Act).

(7B) References in this Act to arrangements made by the National Health Service Commissioning Board or a clinical commissioning group under the National Health Service Act 2006 include references to arrangements so made by virtue of section 7A of that Act.

(8) Any notice or other document required under this Act to be served on any person may be served on him by being delivered personally to him, or being sent by post to him in a registered letter or by the recorded delivery service at his proper address.

(9) Any such notice or other document required to be served on a body corporate or a firm shall be duly served if it is served on the secretary or clerk of that body or a partner of that firm.

(10) For the purposes of this section, and of section 7 of the Interpretation Act 1978 in its application to this section, the proper address of a person –

    (a)   in the case of a secretary or clerk of a body corporate, shall be that of the registered or principal office of that body;

PART II

(b)   in the case of a partner of a firm, shall be that of the principal office of the firm; and

(c)   in any other case, shall be the last known address of the person to be served.

Amendments—Registered Homes (Amendment) Act 1991, s 2(6); Local Government (Wales) Act 1994, ss 22, 66, Sch 10, para 13, Sch 18; Health Authorities Act 1995, ss 2, 5 Sch 1, para 118, Sch 3; Jobseekers Act 1995, s 41, Sch 2, para 19; Education Act 1996, s 582(1), Sch 37, Pt I, para 91; FLA 1996, s 52, Sch 6, para 5; Care Standards Act 2000, s 116, Sch 4, para 14(23); CJCSA 2000 s 74, Sch 7, para 95; Local Government Act 2000, s 107(1), Sch 5, para 22; Powers of Criminal Courts (Sentencing) Act 2000, s 165, Sch 9, para 129; SI 2000/90; Regulation of Care (Scotland) Act 2001, s 79, Sch 3, paras 15;SI 2002/2469; CA 2004, s 40, Sch 3, paras 5, 11; ACA 2002, Sch 3, para 70; CPA 2004, s 75(1),(3),(4); Childcare Act 2006, s 103, Sch 2, para 17, Sch 3, Pt 2; CAA 2006, s 15(1), Sch 2, paras 7, 11; SI 2007/961; Welfare Reform Act 2007, s 28(1), Sch 3, para 6(1),(5); CYPA 2008, s 8(3), Sch 1,para 3; HFEA 2008, s 56, Sch 6, para 31; Criminal Justice and Immigration Act 2008, ss 6(2), 149, Sch 4, para 36; SI 2010/1185; Health and Social Care Act 2012, s 55(2), Sch 5, para 56.

"ordinary residence" (s 105(6))—A young child who cannot decide for himself where to live is ordinarily resident in his parents' matrimonial home, and this ordinary residence cannot be changed by one parent without the consent of the other (*Re P (GE) (An Infant)* [1965] Ch 568). If a child's parents are living apart and they have agreed that the child is to live with one of them, he is ordinarily resident in the home of that one and his ordinary residence is not changed just because the other parent removes the child from that home (*Re P* (above)). In *London Borough of Southwark v B* [1993] 2 FLR 559, a young child, in respect of whom the local authority was about to issue care proceedings, was removed from England to Algeria by her mother. It was held that the local authority still had locus standi to apply for a return order. The precipitate way in which she was removed, and the very limited information available as to the nature or permanence of the arrangements for her accommodation in Algeria, gave the judge ample justification for treating the child as being "ordinarily resident" in the area of the authority at the date of the application for the return order.

Subsection 105(6) is closely allied to s 31(8) and the interrelationship between the provisions was considered by the Court of Appeal in *Northamptonshire County Council v Islington County Council* [1999] 2 FLR 881 where Thorpe LJ held that s 31(8) and s 105(6) are to be construed in a way which provides a simple mechanism to determine the question of administration. The subsections are not about child protection or the promotion of child welfare. They are to be read as a simple test to determine which local authority is to be responsible for the care plan and its implementation. It is not appropriate to apply the s 1(3) checklist to this determination. In *C (A Child) v Plymouth County Council* [2000] 1 FLR 875 the Court of Appeal reiterated that the *Northamptonshire* case was not meant to give judges a discretionary exit from the plain application of the statutory mechanisms of ss 31 and 105, but only to indicate that the simple rules of construction should be sufficient to determine all but the most exceptional cases. Where the child is not accommodated by the local authority, because the local authority permits the child to reside with (i) a parent, (ii) a person with parental responsibility or (iii) a person who was the holder of a residence order before the care proceedings commenced under an interim care order, s 105(6)(c) does not apply and the court is free to apply conventional principles to the definition of "ordinary residence", see *Re C (Care Order: Appropriate Local Authority)* [1997] 1 FLR 544. The decision in *Re H (Care Order: Appropriate Local Authority)* [2004] 1 FLR 534, where the Court of Appeal applied the same principle to a placement with grandparents, does not survive amendments to the 1989 Act and the provisions of s 22. Accordingly, placement with a relative who does not satisfy condition (i), (ii) or (iii) above is caught by the provisions of s 105(6) and the "disregard" has to be applied: *Sheffield County Council v Bradford MBC* [2013] Fam Law 32. See also *Kirklees MBC v London Borough of Brent* [2004] 2 FLR 800. A useful list of the principles to be applied when considering the application of ss 31(8) and 105(6) is set out at [24] of *London Borough of Redbridge v Newport City Council* [2004] 2 FLR 226. See also **"designated local authority"** under s 31(8). Where the mother is herself a child in the care of a local authority but resides with her child in the area of another local authority, the provisions of s 105(6) do not apply for the purpose of determining the child's ordinary residence. It is a question of fact: *Re D (Local Authority Responsibility)* [2012] EWCA Civ 627.

106 Financial provisions

(1) Any –

(a)   grants made by the Secretary of State under this Act; and

(b)   any other expenses incurred by the Secretary of State under this Act,

shall be payable out of money provided by Parliament.

(2) Any sums received by the Secretary of State under section 58, or by way of the repayment of any grant made under section 82(2) or (4) shall be paid into the Consolidated Fund.

107 Application to Channel Islands

Her Majesty may by Order in Council direct that any of the provisions of this Act shall extend to any of the Channel Islands with such exceptions and modifications as may be specified in the Order.

108 Short title, commencement, extent etc

(1) This Act may be cited as the Children Act 1989.

(2) Sections 89 and 96(3) to (7), and paragraph 35 of Schedule 12, shall come into force on the passing of this Act and paragraph 36 of Schedule 12 shall come into force at the end of the period of two months beginning with the day on which this Act is passed but otherwise this Act shall come into force on such date as may be appointed by order made by the Lord Chancellor or the Secretary of State, or by both acting jointly.

(3) Different dates may be appointed for different provisions of this Act in relation to different cases.

(4) The minor amendments set out in Schedule 12 shall have effect.

(5) The consequential amendments set out in Schedule 13 shall have effect.

(6) The transitional provisions and savings set out in Schedule 14 shall have effect.

(7) The repeals set out in Schedule 15 shall have effect.

(8) An order under subsection (2) may make such transitional provisions or savings as appear to the person making the order to be necessary or expedient in connection with the provisions brought into force by the order, including –

  (a) provisions adding to or modifying the provisions of Schedule 14; and
  (b) such adaptations –
    (i) of the provisions brought into force by the order; and
    (ii) of any provisions of this Act then in force,
    as appear to him necessary or expedient in consequence of the partial operation of this Act.

(9) The Lord Chancellor may by order make such amendments or repeals, in such enactments as may be specified in the order, as appear to him to be necessary or expedient in consequence of any provision of this Act.

(10) This Act shall, in its application to the Isles of Scilly, have effect subject to such exceptions, adaptations and modifications as the Secretary of State may by order prescribe.

(11) The following provisions of this Act extend to Scotland –

  section 19;
  section 25(8);
  section 50(13);
  Part X;
  section 80(1)(h) and (i), (2) to (4), (5)(a), (b) and (h) and (6) to (12);
  section 88;
  section 104 (so far as necessary);
  section 105 (so far as necessary);
  subsections (1) to (3). (8) and (9) and this subsection;
  in Schedule 2, paragraph 24;

in Schedule 12, paragraphs 1, 7 to 10, 18, 27, 30(a) and 41 to 44;
in Schedule 13, paragraphs 18 to 23, 32, 46, 47, 50, 57, 62, 63, 68(a), (b) and 71;
in Schedule 14, paragraphs 1, 33 and 34;
in Schedule 15, the entries relating to –
  (a) the Custody of Children Act 1891;
  (b) the Nurseries and Child Minders Regulation Act 1948;
  (c) section 53(3) of the Children and Young Persons Act 1963;
  (d) section 60 of the Health Services and Public Health Act 1968;
  (e) the Social Work (Scotland) Act 1968;
  (f) the Adoption (Scotland) Act 1978;
  (g) the Child Care Act 1980;
  (h) the Foster Children (Scotland) Act 1984;
  (i) the Child Abduction and Custody Act 1985; and
  (j) the Family Law Act 1986.

(12) The following provisions of this Act extend to Northern Ireland –
section 101(1)(b), (2) and (5)(a)(i);
subsections (1) to (3), (8) and (9) and this subsection;
in Schedule 2, paragraph 24;
in Schedule 12, paragraphs 7 to 10, 18 and 27;
in Schedule 13, paragraphs 21, 22, 46, 47, 57, 62, 63, 68(c) to (e) and 69 to 71;
in Schedule 14, paragraphs 28 to 30 and 38(a); and
in Schedule 15, the entries relating to the Guardianship of Minors Act 1971, the Children Act 1975, the Child Care Act 1980, and the Family Law Act 1986.

Amendments—CLSA 1990, ss 116, 125(7), Sch 16, para 25, Sch 20.

SCHEDULE A1
ENFORCEMENT ORDERS

PART I
UNPAID WORK REQUIREMENT

1 General

Subject to the modifications in paragraphs 2 and 3, Chapter 4 of Part 12 of the Criminal Justice Act 2003 has effect in relation to an enforcement order as it has effect in relation to a community order (within the meaning of Part 12 of that Act).

2 References to an offender

Subject to paragraph 3, references in Chapter 4 of Part 12 of the Criminal Justice Act 2003 to an offender are to be treated as including references to a person subject to an enforcement order.

3 Specific modifications

(1) The power of the Secretary of State by order under section 197(3) to amend the definition of "responsible officer" and to make consequential amendments includes power to make any amendments of this Part (including further modifications of Chapter 4 of Part 12 of the Criminal Justice Act 2003) that appear to the Secretary of State to be necessary or expedient in consequence of any amendment made by virtue of section 197(3)(a) or (b).

(2) In section 198 (duties of responsible officer) –

    (a) in subsection (1) –
        (i) at the end of paragraph (a) insert "and", and
        (ii) omit paragraph (c) and the word "and" immediately preceding it, and
    (b) after subsection (1) insert –

"(1A) Subsection (1B) applies where –

    (a) an enforcement order is in force, and
    (b) an officer of the Children and Family Court Advisory and Support Service or a Welsh family proceedings officer (as defined in section 35 of the Children Act 2004) is required under section 11M of the Children Act 1989 to report on matters relating to the order.

(1B) The officer of the Service or the Welsh family proceedings officer may request the responsible officer to report to him on such matters relating to the order as he may require for the purpose of making a report under section 11M(1)(c) or (d); and it shall be the duty of the responsible officer to comply with such a request."

(3) In section 199 (unpaid work requirement) –

    (a) in subsection (2) (minimum and maximum hours of unpaid work) for paragraph (b) substitute –
      "(b) not more than 200.",
    (b) omit subsections (3) and (4), and
    (c) in subsection (5) for the words from the beginning to "of them" substitute "Where on the same occasion and in relation to the same person the court makes more than one enforcement order imposing an unpaid work requirement".

(4) In section 200 (obligations of person subject to unpaid work requirement), for subsection (2) substitute –

"(2) Subject to paragraphs 7 and 9 of Schedule A1 to the Children Act 1989, the work required to be performed under an unpaid work requirement imposed by an enforcement order must be performed during a period of twelve months.

(2A) But the period of twelve months is not to run while the enforcement order is suspended under section 11J(9) of the Children Act 1989."

(5) Section 217 (requirement to avoid conflict with religious beliefs, etc) is omitted.

(6) In section 218 (availability of arrangements in local area), subsection (1) (condition for imposition of unpaid work requirement) is omitted.

(7) Section 219 (provision of copies of relevant order) is omitted.

(8) The power of the Secretary of State to make rules under section 222 in relation to persons subject to relevant orders may also be exercised in relation to persons subject to enforcement orders.

(9) The power of the Secretary of State by order under section 223(1) to amend the provision mentioned in section 223(1)(a) includes power to amend this Part so as to make such modifications of Chapter 4 of Part 12 of the Criminal Justice Act 2003 as appear to the Secretary of State to be necessary or expedient in consequence of any amendment of the provision mentioned in section 223(1)(a).

PART II
REVOCATION, AMENDMENT OR BREACH OF ENFORCEMENT ORDER

4 Power to revoke

(1) This paragraph applies where a court has made an enforcement order in respect of a person's failure to comply with a contact order and the enforcement order is in force.

(2) The court may revoke the enforcement order if it appears to the court that –

    (a)   in all the circumstances no enforcement order should have been made,

    (b)   having regard to circumstances which have arisen since the enforcement order was made, it would be appropriate for the enforcement order to be revoked, or

    (c)   having regard to the person's satisfactory compliance with the contact order or any contact order that has effect in its place, it would be appropriate for the enforcement order to be revoked.

(3) The enforcement order may be revoked by the court under sub-paragraph (2) of its own motion or on an application by the person subject to the enforcement order.

(4) In deciding whether to revoke the enforcement order under sub-paragraph (paragraph (2)(b), the court is to take into account –

    (a)   the extent to which the person subject to the enforcement order has complied with it, and

    (b)   the likelihood that the person will comply with the contact order or any contact order that has effect in its place in the absence of an enforcement order.

(5) In deciding whether to revoke the enforcement order under sub-paragraph (2)(c), the court is to take into account the likelihood that the person will comply with the contact order or any contact order that has effect in its place in the absence of an enforcement order.

5 Amendment by reason of change of residence

(1) This paragraph applies where a court has made an enforcement order in respect of a person's failure to comply with a contact order and the enforcement order is in force.

(2) If the court is satisfied that the person has changed, or proposes to change, his residence from the local justice area specified in the order to another local justice area, the court may amend the order by substituting the other area for the area specified.

(3) The enforcement order may be amended by the court under sub-paragraph (2) of its own motion or on an application by the person subject to the enforcement order.

6 Amendment of hours specified under unpaid work requirement

(1) This paragraph applies where a court has made an enforcement order in respect of a person's failure to comply with a contact order and the enforcement order is in force.

(2) If it appears to the court that, having regard to circumstances that have arisen since the enforcement order was made, it would be appropriate to do so, the court may reduce the number of hours specified in the order (but not below the minimum specified in section 199(2)(a) of the Criminal Justice Act 2003).

(3) In amending the enforcement order under sub-paragraph (2), the court must be satisfied that the effect on the person of the enforcement order as proposed to be amended is no more than is required to secure his compliance with the contact order or any contact order that has effect in its place.

(4) The enforcement order may be amended by the court under sub-paragraph (2) of its own motion or on an application by the person subject to the enforcement order.

7 Amendment to extend unpaid work requirement

(1) This paragraph applies where a court has made an enforcement order in respect of a person's failure to comply with a contact order and the enforcement order is in force.

(2) If it appears to the court that, having regard to circumstances that have arisen since the enforcement order was made, it would be appropriate to do so, the court may, in relation to the order, extend the period of twelve months specified in section 200(2) of the Criminal Justice Act 2003 (as substituted by paragraph 3).

(3) The period may be extended by the court under sub-paragraph (2) of its own motion or on an application by the person subject to the enforcement order.

8 Warning and report following breach

(1) This paragraph applies where a court has made an enforcement order in respect of a person's failure to comply with a contact order.

(2) If the responsible officer is of the opinion that the person has failed without reasonable excuse to comply with the unpaid work requirement imposed by the enforcement order, the officer must give the person a warning under this paragraph unless –

(a) the person has within the previous twelve months been given a warning under this paragraph in relation to a failure to comply with the unpaid work requirement, or

(b) the responsible officer reports the failure to the appropriate person.

(3) A warning under this paragraph must –

(a) describe the circumstances of the failure,

(b) state that the failure is unacceptable, and

(c) inform the person that, if within the next twelve months he again fails to comply with the unpaid work requirement, the warning and the subsequent failure will be reported to the appropriate person.

(4) The responsible officer must, as soon as practicable after the warning has been given, record that fact.

(5) If –

(a) the responsible officer has given a warning under this paragraph to a person subject to an enforcement order, and

(b) at any time within the twelve months beginning with the date on which the warning was given, the responsible officer is of the opinion that the person has since that date failed without reasonable excuse to comply with the unpaid work requirement imposed by the enforcement order,

the officer must report the failure to the appropriate person.

(6) A report under sub-paragraph (5) must include a report of the warning given to the person subject to the enforcement order.

(7) The appropriate person, in relation to an enforcement order, is the officer of the Service or the Welsh family proceedings officer who is required under section 11M to report on matters relating to the enforcement order.

(8) "Responsible officer", in relation to a person subject to an enforcement order, has the same meaning as in section 197 of the Criminal Justice Act 2003 (as modified by paragraph 2).

9 Breach of an enforcement order

(1) This paragraph applies where a court has made an enforcement order ("the first order") in respect of a person's failure to comply with a contact order.

(2) If the court is satisfied beyond reasonable doubt that the person has failed to comply with the unpaid work requirement imposed by the first order, the court may –

  (a) amend the first order so as to make the requirement more onerous, or
  (b) make an enforcement order ("the second order") in relation to the person and (if the first order is still in force) provide for the second order to have effect either in addition to or in substitution for the first order.

(3) But the court may not exercise its powers under sub-paragraph (2) if it is satisfied that the person had a reasonable excuse for failing to comply with the unpaid work requirement imposed by the first order.

(4) The burden of proof as to the matter mentioned in sub-paragraph (3) lies on the person claiming to have had a reasonable excuse, and the standard of proof is the balance of probabilities.

(5) The court may exercise its powers under sub-paragraph (2) in relation to the first order only on the application of a person who would be able to apply under section 11J for an enforcement order if the failure to comply with the first order were a failure to comply with the contact order to which the first order relates.

(6) Where the person proposing to apply to the court is the child with respect to whom the contact order was made, subsections (6) and (7) of section 11J have effect in relation to the application as they have effect in relation to an application for an enforcement order.

(7) An application to the court to exercise its powers under sub-paragraph (2) may only be made while the first order is in force.

(8) The court may not exercise its powers under sub-paragraph (2) in respect of a failure by the person to comply with the unpaid work requirement imposed by the first order unless it is satisfied that before the failure occurred the person had been given (in accordance with rules of court) a copy of, or otherwise informed of the terms of, a notice under section 11N relating to the first order.

(9) In dealing with the person under sub-paragraph (2)(a), the court may –

  (a) increase the number of hours specified in the first order (but not above the maximum specified in section 199(2)(b) of the Criminal Justice Act 2003, as substituted by paragraph 3);
  (b) in relation to the order, extend the period of twelve months specified in section 200(2) of the Criminal Justice Act 2003 (as substituted by paragraph 3).

(10) In exercising its powers under sub-paragraph (2), the court must be satisfied that, taking into account the extent to which the person has complied with the unpaid work requirement imposed by the first order, the effect on the person of the proposed exercise of those powers –

  (a) is no more than is required to secure his compliance with the contact order or any contact order that has effect in its place, and
  (b) is no more than is proportionate to the seriousness of his failures to comply with the contact order and the first order.

(11) Where the court exercises its powers under sub-paragraph (2) by making an enforcement order in relation to a person who has failed to comply with another enforcement order –

  (a) sections 11K(4), 11L(2) to (7), 11M and 11N have effect as regards the making of the order in relation to the person as they have effect as regards the making of an enforcement order in relation to a person who has failed to comply with a contact order;

(b) this Part of this Schedule has effect in relation to the order so made as if it were an enforcement order made in respect of the failure for which the other order was made.

(12) Sub-paragraph (2) is without prejudice to section 63(3) of the Magistrates' Courts Act 1980 as it applies in relation to enforcement orders.

10 Provision relating to amendment of enforcement orders

Sections 11L(2) to (7) and 11M have effect in relation to the making of an order under paragraph 6(2), 7(2) or 9(2)(a) amending an enforcement order as they have effect in relation to the making of an enforcement order; and references in sections 11L(2) to (7) and 11M to an enforcement order are to be read accordingly.

Amendments—Schedule inserted by CAA 2006, s 4(2), Sch 1.

SCHEDULE 1

FINANCIAL PROVISION FOR CHILDREN

1 Orders for financial relief against parents

(1) On an application made by a parent, guardian or special guardian of a child, or by any person in whose favour a residence order is in force with respect to a child, the court may –

(a) in the case of an application to the High Court or a county court, make one or more of the orders mentioned in sub-paragraph (2);

(b) in the case of an application to a magistrates' court, make one or both of the orders mentioned in paragraphs (a) and (c) of that sub-paragraph.

(2) The orders referred to in sub-paragraph (1) are –

(a) an order requiring either or both parents of a child –
    (i) to make to the applicant for the benefit of the child; or
    (ii) to make to the child himself,
    such periodical payments, for such term, as may be specified in the order;

(b) an order requiring either or both parents of a child –
    (i) to secure to the applicant for the benefit of the child; or
    (ii) to secure to the child himself,
    such periodical payments, for such term, as may be so specified;

(c) an order requiring either or both parents of a child –
    (i) to pay to the applicant for the benefit of the child; or
    (ii) to pay to the child himself,
    such lump sum as may be so specified;

(d) an order requiring a settlement to be made for the benefit of the child, and to the satisfaction of the court, of property –
    (i) to which either parent is entitled (either in possession or in reversion); and
    (ii) which is specified in the order;

(e) an order requiring either or both parents of a child –
    (i) to transfer to the applicant, for the benefit of the child; or
    (ii) to transfer to the child himself,
    such property to which the parent is, or the parents are, entitled (either in possession or in reversion) as may be specified in the order.

(3) The powers conferred by this paragraph may be exercised at any time.

(4) An order under sub-paragraph (2)(a) or (b) may be varied or discharged by a subsequent order made on the application of any person by or to whom payments were required to be made under the previous order.

(5) Where a court makes an order under this paragraph –

   (a) it may at any time make a further such order under sub-paragraph (2)(a), (b) or (c) with respect to the child concerned if he has not reached the age of eighteen;

   (b) it may not make more than one order under sub-paragraph (2)(d) or (e) against the same person in respect of the same child.

(6) On making, varying or discharging a residence order or a special guardianship order the court may exercise any of its powers under this Schedule even though no application has been made to it under this Schedule.

(7) Where a child is a ward of court, the court may exercise any of its powers under this Schedule even though no application has been made to it.

Amendments—CLSA 1990, s 116, Sch 16, para 10(2); ACA 2002, Sch 3, para 71.

Scope—Subject to CSA 1991, which restricts the court's power to order child maintenance (see Procedural Guide A2), this provision enables the High Court and county courts to make orders for periodical payments, secured periodical payments, a lump sum, settlement of property or transfer of property. Magistrates' courts may make periodical payments, secured periodical payments or a lump sum order. The power is irrespective of whether the parents are married. The court may make an order without an application being made where a residence order is made, varied or discharged, or on application by a parent, guardian or holder of a residence order. The child must be aged under 18, but para 3 allows a periodical payments order to be extended for a child over 18 in tertiary education or where special circumstances apply. There is no jurisdiction to make an order against a father for the benefit of the mother's children by a different partner: *Morgan v Hill* [2007] 1 FLR 1480.

   The words "for the benefit of the child" in para 1(2) include financial and welfare benefit. The power of the court is construed widely, where a benefit to the mother also benefits the child. In *Re S (Child: Financial Provision)* [2005] 2 FLR 94, CA, the court made a financial order to include the costs of the mother's travel to the Sudan to see the child and to pursue contact: the court has the power to make an order against a parent who is out of the jurisdiction with the child. A parent bringing a Sch 1 application is acting in a quasi-representative capacity for the benefit of the child and may be entitled to an interim costs order to pursue the application: see *M-T v T* [2007] 2 FLR 925, disapproving *W v J (Child: variation of financial provision)* [2004] 2 FLR 300, where the court had declined to make a costs order because it was held to benefit the mother, not the child. The width of the court's jurisdiction is shown in *MB v KB* [2007] 2 FLR 586, where a mother who had secured periodical payments and the right to reside in a house owned by the husband's family under MCA 1973 was permitted to apply for a settlement of property and a lump sum under Sch 1: the application of estoppel was disapproved in cases involving children and a change of circumstances and the child's needs entitled the mother to make her Sch 1 application. The mother may have concluded her own claims for housing, but not the right to claim on behalf of her child. See *PK v BC (Financial Remedies: Schedule 1)* [2012] 2 FLR 1426: jurisdiction to consider a further lump sum existed after a clean break in divorce proceedings, but circumstances had to be exceptional. There was a very high hurdle to be overcome to achieve a further award as to housing, and no jurisdiction to award a car, where there had been a consent order for financial provision in divorce.

Power to order lump sum—There is jurisdiction to order a lump sum, which may be used for the applicant's costs. A lump sum is not precluded by CSA 1991, s 8, which prohibits maintenance awards by the court for a child.

Power to transfer property—There is power to transfer property to the applicant for the benefit of the child, or directly to the child, or to settle property upon a child. Property is usually a house for the mother and child to live in; it may include a joint tenancy: *K v K (Minors: Property Transfer)* [1992] 2 FLR 220.

Power to enforce lump sum and transfer of property orders—Where a reluctant father had not complied with orders for the payment of a lump sum to enable the purchase of a property for a child for more than 5 years, the court had the power to order a binding obligation to pay by a fixed date, and in default to consider orders under TLATA 1996 or the inherent jurisdiction to direct the performance of the trust. There was no need for a separate trust deed in straightforward cases where the court order served to set out the terms of the trust arising out of capital provision: *G v A (Financial Remedy: Enforcement) (No 1)* [2012] 1 FLR 389. There was power to order the disclosure of the father's assets to assist the mother in enforcing the order: *G v A (Financial Remedy: Enforcement) (No 2)* [2012] 1 FLR 402. Where there is conflict over the operation of the trust, the court may override or supersede the trust deed and a transfer to the Chancery division is not required: *G v A (Financial Remedy: Enforcement) (No 3)* [2012] 1 FLR 415. Such powers may include the discharge of one party's trustee: *G v A (Financial Remedy: Enforcement) (No 4)* [2012] 1 FLR 427.

Interim orders—Paragraph 1 gives the court the jurisdiction to make more than one order for a lump sum and to order a lump sum 'at any time", although there is no specific reference to interim lump sum payments: *CF v KM* [2011] 1 FLR 208. There is also jurisdiction to award interim maintenance by way of periodical payments, which may be used for legal costs: *G v G (Child Maintenance: Interim Costs Provision)* [2010] 2 FLR 1264.

Power to order a review—The court may order a review of payments, expressed as "subject to further order of the court", where the father's capital and income is in transition: *FG v MBW (Financial Remedy for Child)* [2012] 1 FLR 152.

Costs orders in Sch 1 applications—The jurisdiction to make such orders is discretionary: there is a risk of unfairness to the payer who funds both sides and then may not be able to recoup his costs. By analogy with matrimonial jurisdiction, the approach to costs orders in *Currey v Currey (No 2)* [2007] 1 FLR 946, CA, is commended in Sch 1 proceedings. The applicant must demonstrate that she could not reasonably procure legal advice and representation at the appropriate level of expertise by any other means. The court must then have regard to all other relevant circumstances, including the reasonableness of the mother's stance in the proceedings and the merits of her claim: *G v G (Child Maintenance: Interim Costs Provision)* [2010] 2 FLR 1264. There are advantages flowing from competent representation and equality of arms, which would be of benefit ultimately to the child: see *CF v KM* [2011] 1 FLR 208, following *M-T v T* [2007] 2 FLR 925. The court should conduct a broad-brush approach to avoid a full-blown contested financial hearing, which would not be proportionate. A Sch 1 application in relation to costs should be issued without delay: *R v F (Schedule One: Child Maintenance: Mother's Costs of Contact Proceedings)* [2011] 2 FLR 991.

By analogy with MCA 1973, long-term capital provision to endure after the end of dependency should be made only in "special circumstances" (see para 3). Where a settlement has previously been made by a parent for a child, a subsequent transfer of property is precluded by para 1(5)(b). In *Phillips v Peace* [2005] 2 FLR 1212, where a mother applied a second time for a capital payment to provide a larger home for the child, a lump sum subject to conditions of repayment was akin to a settlement and thus impermissible. Therefore the provision of a home should be large enough to meet the child's needs until maturity.

2 Orders for financial relief for persons over eighteen

(1) If, on an application by a person who has reached the age of eighteen, it appears to the court –

    (a) that the applicant is, will be or (if an order were made under this paragraph) would be receiving instruction at an educational establishment or undergoing training for a trade, profession or vocation, whether or not while in gainful employment; or

    (b) that there are special circumstances which justify the making of an order under this paragraph,

the court may make one or both of the orders mentioned in sub-paragraph (2).

(2) The orders are –

    (a) an order requiring either or both of the applicant's parents to pay to the applicant such periodical payments, for such term, as may be specified in the order;

    (b) an order requiring either or both of the applicant's parents to pay to the applicant such lump sum as may be so specified.

(3) An application may not be made under this paragraph by any person if, immediately before he reached the age of sixteen, a periodical payments order was in force with respect to him.

(4) No order shall be made under this paragraph at a time when the parents of the applicant are living with each other in the same household.

(5) An order under sub-paragraph (2)(a) may be varied or discharged by a subsequent order made on the application of any person by or to whom payments were required to be made under the previous order.

(6) In sub-paragraph (3) "periodical payments order" means an order made under –

(a)   this Schedule;

(b)   (repealed)

(c)   section 23 or 27 of the Matrimonial Causes Act 1973;

(d)   Part I of the Domestic Proceedings and Magistrates' Courts Act 1978, for the making or securing of periodical payments;

(e)   Part 1 or 9 of Schedule 5 to the Civil Partnership Act 2004 (financial relief in the High Court or a county court etc);

(f)   Schedule 6 to the 2004 Act (financial relief in the magistrates' courts etc).

(7) The powers conferred by this paragraph shall be exercisable at any time.

(8) Where the court makes an order under this paragraph it may from time to time while that order remains in force make a further such order.

Amendments—CSA 1991, s 58(14); CPA 2004, s 78(1),(2).

Scope—Subject to CSA 1991 (see Procedural Guide A2), this paragraph enables an adult child, whose parents are not living with each other in the same household and in respect of whom there was no periodical payments order in force before he reached the age of 16, to apply for periodical payments or a lump sum if either he is receiving further education or training or there are special circumstances.

"periodical payments order" (para 2(3),(6))—The term "periodical payments order" as defined by para 2(6) means an order under (i) this Schedule, (ii) MCA 1973, s 23, which provides maintenance in divorce, nullity or judicial separation proceedings, (iii) s 27 of that Act, which provides maintenance on an application for wilful neglect to maintain in the High Court or county court, or (iv) DPMCA 1978, Pt I in the magistrates' court, on the same ground as in (iii).

3 Duration of orders for financial relief

(1) The term to be specified in an order for periodical payments made under paragraph 1(2)(a) or (b) in favour of a child may begin with the date of the making of an application for the order in question or any later date or a date ascertained in accordance with sub-paragraph (5) or (6) but –

(a)   shall not in the first instance extend beyond the child's seventeenth birthday unless the court thinks it right in the circumstances of the case to specify a later date; and

(b)   shall not in any event extend beyond the child's eighteenth birthday.

(2) Paragraph (b) of sub-paragraph (1) shall not apply in the case of a child if it appears to the court that –

(a)   the child is, or will be or (if an order were made without complying with that paragraph) would be receiving instruction at an educational establishment or undergoing training for a trade, profession or vocation, whether or not while in gainful employment; or

(b)   there are special circumstances which justify the making of an order without complying with that paragraph.

(3) An order for periodical payments made under paragraph 1(2)(a) or 2(2)(a) shall, notwithstanding anything in the order, cease to have effect on the death of the person liable to make payments under the order.

(4) Where an order is made under paragraph 1(2)(a) or (b) requiring periodical payments to be made or secured to the parent of a child, the order shall cease to have effect if –

    (a)   any parent making or securing the payments; and

    (b)   any parent to whom the payments are made or secured,

live together for a period of more than six months.

(5) Where –

    (a)   a maintenance calculation ("the current calculation") is in force with respect to a child; and

    (b)   an application is made for an order under paragraph 1(2)(a) or (b) of this Schedule for periodical payments in favour of that child –

        (i)   in accordance with section 8 of the Child Support Act 1991; and

        (ii) before the end of the period of 6 months beginning with the making of the current calculation,

the term to be specified in any such order made on that application may be expressed to begin on, or at any time after, the earliest permitted date.

(6) For the purposes of subsection (5) above, "the earliest permitted date" is whichever is the later of –

    (a)   the date 6 months before the application is made; or

    (b)   the date on which the current calculation took effect or, where successive maintenance calculations have been continuously in force with respect to a child, on which the first of those calculations took effect.

(7) Where –

    (a)   a maintenance calculation ceases to have effect by or under any provision of the Child Support Act 1991, and

    (b)   an application is made, before the end of the period of 6 months beginning with the relevant date, for an order for periodical payments under paragraph 1(2)(a) or (b) in favour of a child with respect to whom that maintenance calculation was in force immediately before it ceases to have effect,

the term to be specified in any such order, or in any interim order under paragraph 9, made on that application may begin with the date on which that maintenance calculation ceased to have effect, or any later date.

(8) In sub-paragraph (7)(b) –

    (a)   where the maintenance calculation ceased to have effect, the relevant date is the date on which it so ceased; and

    (b)   *(repealed)*

Amendments—SI 1993/623; CSPSSA 2000, ss 26, 85, Sch 3, para 10, Sch 9.

Scope—This paragraph is equivalent to MCA 1973, s 29(2)–(4) and provides the upper limit for the duration of a periodical payments order. It also provides that any order ceases to have effect if the child's parents live together for more than 6 months.

"special circumstances" (para 3(2)(b))—Compare MCA 1973, s 29(3)(b). Where there are special circumstances the order can continue beyond 18 years despite CSA 1991, ss 8 and 55. Special circumstances may include physical or other disability, and the expenses attributed to the child's disability should be in the broadest sense (*C v F (Disabled Child: Maintenance Orders)* [1998] 2 FLR 1). Paragraph 3 allows a periodical payments order to be extended for a child over 18, who is or will be undergoing education, or where there are special circumstances which must be identified: they may include physical or other disability and the expenses attributed to the child's disability taken into account in the broadest sense (*C v F (Disabled Child: Maintenance Orders)* [1998] 2 FLR 1). Special circumstances have been held not to include the extreme wealth of the father or the possibility that the child might not inherit upon his death: *MT v OT (Financial Provision: Costs)* [2008] 2 FLR 1311. The tendency of adult children to remain living at home with a parent is not a special circumstance: however, payment for a gap year before or after tertiary education may be permissible: see *Re N (Payments for Benefit of Child)* [2009] 1 FLR 1442, following *A v A (A Minor: Financial Provision)* [1994] 1 FLR 657; *Phillips v Peace* [1996] 2 FLR 230. In the absence of "special circumstances", any capital settlement under Sch 1 should be expressed as terminating when the child attains 18 or completes tertiary education.

Orders for financial relief shall not in any event extend beyond the child's 18th birthday, unless the child is receiving tertiary education or training or where "special circumstances" apply; the exception is despite CSA 1991, ss 8 and 55.

4 Matters to which court is to have regard in making orders for financial relief

(1) In deciding whether to exercise its powers under paragraph 1 or 2, and if so in what manner, the court shall have regard to all the circumstances including –

  (a) the income, earning capacity, property and other financial resources which each person mentioned in sub-paragraph (4) has or is likely to have in the foreseeable future;
  (b) the financial needs, obligations and responsibilities which each person mentioned in sub-paragraph (4) has or is likely to have in the foreseeable future;
  (c) the financial needs of the child;
  (d) the income, earning capacity (if any), property and other financial resources of the child;
  (e) any physical or mental disability of the child;
  (f) the manner in which the child was being, or was expected to be, educated or trained.

(2) In deciding whether to exercise its powers under paragraph 1 against a person who is not the mother or father of the child, and if so in what manner, the court shall in addition have regard to –

  (a) whether that person had assumed responsibility for the maintenance of the child, and, if so, the extent to which and basis on which he assumed that responsibility and the length of the period during which he met that responsibility;
  (b) whether he did so knowing that the child was not his child;
  (c) the liability of any other person to maintain the child.

(3) Where the court makes an order under paragraph 1 against a person who is not the father of the child, it shall record in the order that the order is made on the basis that the person against whom the order is made is not the child's father.

(4) The persons mentioned in sub-paragraph (1) are –

  (a) in relation to a decision whether to exercise its powers under paragraph 1, any parent of the child;
  (b) in relation to a decision whether to exercise its powers under paragraph 2, the mother and father of the child;
  (c) the applicant for the order;
  (d) any other person in whose favour the court proposes to make the order.

(5) In the case of a child who has a parent by virtue of section 42 or 43 of the Human Fertilisation and Embryology Act 2008, any reference in sub-paragraph (2), (3) or (4) to the child's father is a reference to the woman who is a parent of the child by virtue of that section.

Amendments—HFEA 2008, s 56, Sch 6, Pt 1, para 32(1),(2).

Scope—The court is directed to have regard to "all the circumstances", and there is therefore a wide discretion under Schedule I. This falls short of the wider discretion in MCA 1973, s 25, in that there is no statutory duty to consider the parties conduct or the duration of their relationship. However, a long relationship may be relevant in that it has accustomed a child to a particular standard of living – the effect of a 17-year cohabitation was considered in *N v D* [2008] 1 FLR 1629.

The court will consider the welfare of the child. Strictly, welfare is not the court's paramount consideration, as questions about the upbringing of a child, which trigger considerations of paramountcy, specifically exclude maintenance (CA 1989, ss 1(1)(a) and105(1)). However, the Court of Appeal in *Re P (Child: Financial Provision)* [2003] 2 FLR 865 puts welfare not just as a relevant circumstance, but "in most cases a constant influence on the discretionary outcome", an approach followed in *N v D*.

Large awards have been secured in cases with wealthy fathers. In *Re P* (above) £1m was awarded for a home in central London, plus £70,000 in periodical payments. The child may be entitled to be brought up in circumstances which bear some relation to the father's resources and standard of living (*J v C (Child: Financial Provision)* [1999] 1 FLR 152; *F v G (Child: Financial Provision)* [2005] 1 FLR 261; *MT v OT (Financial Provision: Costs)* [2008] 2 FLR 1311; *H v C* [2009] 2 FLR 1540). The court will consider as a starting point what home must be provided, and normally settle upon the mother until the child's majority, and then the size of any lump sum required to equip the home and to provide a car. Secondly, the mother may be entitled to a carer's allowance for looking after the child if she has to give up work, a principle developed in *Haroutunian v Jennings* (1980) 1 FLR 62. Thirdly, the court will consider periodical payments for the maintenance of the child, in line with the mother's budget, on the basis of a "broad common-sense assessment" (*Re P*).

In *Re P*, it was suggested that although the mother has control of the budget, the father may receive an account of what is spent and deduct state benefits. In *Re C (Financial Provision)* [2007] 2 FLR 13, the notion of the mother producing detailed accounts for the father's scrutiny would "almost always be unhelpful and counterproductive". However, in *Re N (Payments for Benefit of Child)* [2009] 1 FLR 1442, where there had been difficulties about the setting up of the trust, the court suggested ground rules to be followed: the mother was to account to the father for moneys not used for the intended purpose, including receipts for items over £10, and the mother in turn was entitled to interest from the father on unpaid sums. The case deals with the procedure for the appointment of trustees and the entitlement of the mother to buy out the father's interest. Where a father failed to settle a sum upon the mother for the benefit of the child, no judgment debt arose and therefore no charging order could be made; however, the mother could be protected by an injunction preventing the father from dealing with the property.

The needs of the individual child in the light of the available resource are likely to be the determining factor. The court should be wary of taking *Re P* as a benchmark and scaling up or down from it. The economic circumstances of the payer will be scrutinised: where a father could not pay maintenance out of income but used capital and borrowing to provide himself with a good lifestyle, maintenance could be paid from capital resources: *SW v RC* [2008] 1 FLR 1703. The focus must be on the real needs of the child, not the aspirations of the mother for an enhanced lifestyle. It has been suggested that in some cases the child should have separate representation (*Re S (Unmarried Parents: Financial Provision)* [2006] 2 FLR 950).

5 Provisions relating to lump sums

(1) Without prejudice to the generality of paragraph 1, an order under that paragraph for the payment of a lump sum may be made for the purpose of enabling any liabilities or expenses –

(a) incurred in connection with the birth of the child or in maintaining the child; and

(b) reasonably incurred before the making of the order,

to be met.

(2) The amount of any lump sum required to be paid by an order made by a magistrates' court under paragraph 1 or 2 shall not exceed £1,000 or such larger amount as the Lord Chancellor may, after consulting the Lord Chief Justice, from time to time by order fix for the purposes of this sub-paragraph.

(3) The power of the court under paragraph 1 or 2 to vary or discharge an order for the making or securing of periodical payments by a parent shall include power to make an order under that provision for the payment of a lump sum by that parent.

(4) The amount of any lump sum which a parent may be required to pay by virtue of sub-paragraph (3) shall not, in the case of an order made by a magistrates' court, exceed the maximum amount that may at the time of the making of the order be required to be paid under sub-paragraph (2), but a magistrates' court may make an order for the

payment of a lump sum not exceeding that amount even though the parent was required to pay a lump sum by a previous order under this Act.

(5) An order made under paragraph 1 or 2 for the payment of a lump sum may provide for the payment of that sum by instalments.

(6) Where the court provides for the payment of a lump sum by instalments the court, on an application made either by the person liable to pay or the person entitled to receive that sum, shall have power to vary that order by varying –

    (a)   the number of instalments payable;

    (b)   the amount of any instalment payable;

    (c)   the date on which any instalment becomes payable.

(7) The Lord Chief Justice may nominate a judicial office holder (as defined in section 109(4) of the Constitutional Reform Act 2005) to exercise his functions under this paragraph.

Amendments—SI 1992/709; CRA 2005, s 15(1), Sch 4, Pt 1, paras 203, 209.

6 Variation etc of orders for periodical payments

(1) In exercising its powers under paragraph 1 or 2 to vary or discharge an order for the making or securing of periodical payments the court shall have regard to all the circumstances of the case, including any change in any of the matters to which the court was required to have regard when making the order.

(2) The power of the court under paragraph 1 or 2 to vary an order for the making or securing of periodical payments shall include power to suspend any provision of the order temporarily and to revive any provision so suspended.

(3) Where on an application under paragraph 1 or 2 for the variation or discharge of an order for the making or securing of periodical payments the court varies the payments required to be made under that order, the court may provide that the payments as so varied shall be made from such date as the court may specify except that, subject to sub-paragraph (9), the date shall not be earlier than the date of the making of the application.

(4) An application for the variation of an order made under paragraph 1 for the making or securing of periodical payments to or for the benefit of a child may, if the child has reached the age of sixteen, be made by the child himself.

(5) Where an order for the making or securing of periodical payments made under paragraph 1 ceases to have effect on the date on which the child reaches the age of sixteen, or at any time after that date but before or on the date on which he reaches the age of eighteen, the child may apply to the court which made the order for an order for its revival.

(6) If on such an application it appears to the court that –

    (a)   the child is, will be or (if an order were made under this sub-paragraph) would be receiving instruction at an educational establishment or undergoing training for a trade, profession or vocation, whether or not while in gainful employment; or

    (b)   there are special circumstances which justify the making of an order under this paragraph,

the court shall have power by order to revive the order from such date as the court may specify, not being earlier than the date of the making of the application.

(7) Any order which is revived by an order under sub-paragraph (5) may be varied or discharged under that provision, on the application of any person by whom or to whom payments are required to be made under the revived order.

(8) An order for the making or securing of periodical payments made under paragraph 1 may be varied or discharged, after the death of either parent, on the application of a guardian or special guardian of the child concerned.

(9) Where –

(a) an order under paragraph 1(2)(a) or (b) for the making or securing of periodical payments in favour of more than one child ("the order") is in force;

(b) the order requires payments specified in it to be made to or for the benefit of more than one child without apportioning those payments between them;

(c) a maintenance calculation ("the calculation") is made with respect to one or more, but not all, of the children with respect to whom those payments are to be made; and

(d) an application is made, before the end of the period of 6 months beginning with the date on which the calculation was made, for the variation or discharge of the order,

the court may, in exercise of its powers under paragraph 1 to vary or discharge the order, direct that the variation or discharge shall take effect from the date on which the calculation took effect or any later date.

Amendments—SI 1993/623, CSPSSA 2000, s 26, Sch 3, para 10; ACA 2002, Sch 3, para 71.

Scope—Subject to CSA 1991 (see **Outline of new bases for child support calculation** under CSA 1991, s 4), this paragraph contains the court's powers to vary orders made either under para 1 (order for financial relief for a child against parents) or para 2 (order for financial relief against parents where the child is applying for the first time when the child is over 18).

6A Variation of orders for periodical payments etc made by magistrates' courts

(1) Subject to sub-paragraphs (7) and (8), the power of a magistrates' court –

(a) under paragraph 1 or 2 to vary an order for the making of periodical payments, or

(b) under paragraph 5(6) to vary an order for the payment of a lump sum by instalments,

shall include power, if the court is satisfied that payment has not been made in accordance with the order, to exercise one of its powers under paragraphs (a) to (d) of section 59(3) of the Magistrates' Courts Act 1980.

(2) In any case where –

(a) a magistrates' court has made an order under this Schedule for the making of periodical payments or for the payment of a lump sum by instalments, and

(b) payments under the order are required to be made by any method of payment falling within section 59(6) of the Magistrates' Courts Act 1980 (standing order, etc),

any person entitled to make an application under this Schedule for the variation of the order (in this paragraph referred to as "the applicant") may apply to a magistrates' court acting in the same local justice area as the court which made the order for the order to be varied as mentioned in sub-paragraph (3).

(3) Subject to sub-paragraph (5), where an application is made under sub-paragraph (2), a justices clerk, after giving written notice (by post or otherwise) of the application to any interested party and allowing that party, within the period of 14 days beginning with the date of the giving of that notice, an opportunity to make written representations, may vary the order to provide that payments under the order shall be made to the designated officer for the court.

(4) The clerk may proceed with an application under sub-paragraph (2) notwithstanding that any such interested party as is referred to in sub-paragraph (3) has not received written notice of the application.

(5) Where an application has been made under sub-paragraph (2), the clerk may, if he considers it inappropriate to exercise his power under sub-paragraph (3), refer the matter to the court which, subject to sub-paragraphs (7) and (8), may vary the order by exercising one of its powers under paragraphs (a) to (d) of section 59(3) of the Magistrates' Courts Act 1980.

(6) Subsection (4) of section 59 of the Magistrates' Courts Act 1980 (power of court to order that account be opened) shall apply for the purposes of sub-paragraphs (1) and (5) as it applies for the purposes of that section.

(7) Before varying the order by exercising one of its powers under paragraphs (a) to (d) of section 59(3) of the Magistrates' Courts Act 1980, the court shall have regard to any representations made by the parties to the application.

(8) If the court does not propose to exercise its power under paragraph (c), (cc) or (d) of subsection (3) of section 59 of the Magistrates' Courts Act 1980, the court shall, unless upon representations expressly made in that behalf by the applicant for the order it is satisfied that it is undesirable to do so, exercise its power under paragraph (b) of that subsection.

(9) None of the powers of the court, or of a justices clerk, conferred by this paragraph shall be exercisable in relation to an order under this Schedule for the making of periodical payments, or for the payment of a lump sum by instalments, which is not a qualifying maintenance order (within the meaning of section 59 of the Magistrates' Courts Act 1980).

(10) In sub-paragraphs (3) and (4) "interested party", in relation to an application made by the applicant under sub-paragraph (2), means a person who would be entitled to be a party to an application for the variation of the order made by the applicant under any other provision of this Schedule if such an application were made.

Amendments—Inserted by MEA 1991, s 6; amended by SI 1994/731; AJA 1999, s 90, Sch 13, para 161; Courts Act 2003, s 109(1), Sch 8, para 338(1)–(4).

Scope—This paragraph gives to the court the same power to determine method of payment on an application to vary as it has on the making of a new order. In *B v B (Periodical Payments: Transitional Provisions)* [1995] 1 FLR 459, it was held that the court had power to grant an application to vary or discharge a financial provision order made under the Guardianship of Minors Act 1971, despite the repeal of that Act by CA 1989.

7 Variation of orders for secured periodical payments after death of parent

(1) Where the parent liable to make payments under a secured periodical payments order has died, the persons who may apply for the variation or discharge of the order shall include the personal representatives of the deceased parent.

(2) No application for the variation of the order shall, except with the permission of the court, be made after the end of the period of six months from the date on which representation in regard to the estate of that parent is first taken out.

(3) The personal representatives of a deceased person against whom a secured periodical payments order was made shall not be liable for having distributed any part of the estate of the deceased after the end of the period of six months referred to in sub-paragraph (2) on the ground that they ought to have taken into account the possibility that the court might permit an application for variation to be made after that period by the person entitled to payments under the order.

(4) Sub-paragraph (3) shall not prejudice any power to recover any part of the estate so distributed arising by virtue of the variation of an order in accordance with this paragraph.

(5) Where an application to vary a secured periodical payments order is made after the death of the parent liable to make payments under the order, the circumstances to which the court is required to have regard under paragraph 6(1) shall include the changed circumstances resulting from the death of the parent.

(6) In considering for the purposes of sub-paragraph (2) the question when representation was first taken out, a grant limited to settled land or to trust property shall be left out of account and a grant limited to real estate or to personal estate shall be left out of account unless a grant limited to the remainder of the estate has previously been made or is made at the same time.

(7) In this paragraph "secured periodical payments order" means an order for secured periodical payments under paragraph 1(2)(b).

8 Financial relief under other enactments

(1) This paragraph applies where a residence order or a special guardianship order is made with respect to a child at a time when there is in force an order ("the financial relief order") made under any enactment other than this Act and requiring a person to contribute to the child's maintenance.

(2) Where this paragraph applies, the court may, on the application of –

    (a)   any person required by the financial relief order to contribute to the child's maintenance; or

    (b)   any person in whose favour a residence order or a special guardianship order with respect to the child is in force,

make an order revoking the financial relief order, or varying it by altering the amount of any sum payable under that order or by substituting the applicant for the person to whom any such sum is otherwise payable under that order.

Amendments—ACA 2002, s 139(1), Sch 3, para 71.

Defined terms—"child": s 105(1), Sch 1, para 16(1); "residence order": s 8(1).

Scope—Where an order for periodical payments or secured periodical payments for the support of a child made outside Sch 1 (for instance in a divorce suit) already exists and a residence order is then made, this paragraph enables the court to vary that original order by varying the sum payable or the person to whom payment is to be made.

9 Interim orders

(1) Where an application is made under paragraph 1 or 2 the court may, at any time before it disposes of the application, make an interim order –

    (a)   requiring either or both parents to make such periodical payments, at such times and for such term as the court thinks fit; and

    (b)   giving any direction which the court thinks fit.

(2) An interim order made under this paragraph may provide for payments to be made from such date as the court may specify except that, subject to paragraph 3(5) and (6), the date shall not be earlier than the date of the making of the application under paragraph 1 or 2.

(3) An interim order made under this paragraph shall cease to have effect when the application is disposed of or, if earlier, on the date specified for the purposes of this paragraph in the interim order.

(4) An interim order in which a date has been specified for the purposes of sub-paragraph (3) may be varied by substituting a later date.

Amendments—SI 1993/623.

Scope—This paragraph enables the court to make interim orders.

10 Alteration of maintenance agreements

(1) In this paragraph and in paragraph 11 "maintenance agreement" means any agreement in writing made with respect to a child, whether before or after the commencement of this paragraph, which –

   (a) is or was made between the father and mother of the child; and
   (b) contains provision with respect to the making or securing of payments, or the disposition or use of any property, for the maintenance or education of the child,

and any such provisions are in this paragraph, and paragraph 11, referred to as "financial arrangements".

(2) Subject to sub-paragraph (2A), where a maintenance agreement is for the time being subsisting and each of the parties to the agreement is for the time being either domiciled or resident in England and Wales, then, either party may apply for an order under this paragraph.

(2A) If an application or part of an application relates to a matter where jurisdiction falls to be determined by reference to the jurisdictional requirements of the Maintenance Regulation and Schedule 6 to the Civil Jurisdiction and Judgments (Maintenance) Regulations 2011 –

   (a) the requirement as to domicile or residence in sub-paragraph (2) does not apply to the application or that part of it, but
   (b) the court may not entertain the application or that part of it unless it has jurisdiction to do so by virtue of that Regulation and that Schedule.

(2B) In sub-paragraph (2A), "the Maintenance Regulation" means Council Regulation (EC) No 4/2009 including as applied in relation to Denmark by virtue of the Agreement made on 19 October 2005 between the European Community and the Kingdom of Denmark.

(3) If the court to which the application is made is satisfied either –

   (a) that, by reason of a change in the circumstances in the light of which any financial arrangements contained in the agreement were made (including a change foreseen by the parties when making the agreement), the agreement should be altered so as to make different financial arrangements; or
   (b) that the agreement does not contain proper financial arrangements with respect to the child,

then that court may by order make such alterations in the agreement by varying or revoking any financial arrangements contained in it as may appear to it to be just having regard to all the circumstances.

(4) If the maintenance agreement is altered by an order under this paragraph, the agreement shall have effect thereafter as if the alteration had been made by agreement between the parties and for valuable consideration.

(5) Where a court decides to make an order under this paragraph altering the maintenance agreement –

   (a) by inserting provision for the making or securing by one of the parties to the agreement of periodical payments for the maintenance of the child; or

(b)   by increasing the rate of periodical payments required to be made or secured by one of the parties for the maintenance of the child,

then, in deciding the term for which under the agreement as altered by the order the payments or (as the case may be) the additional payments attributable to the increase are to be made or secured for the benefit of the child, the court shall apply the provisions of sub-paragraphs (1) and (2) of paragraph 3 as if the order were an order under paragraph 1(2)(a) or (b).

(6)   A magistrates' court shall not entertain an application under sub-paragraph (2) unless both the parties to the agreement are resident in England and Wales and the court acts in, or is authorised by the Lord Chancellor to act for, a local justice area in which at least one of the parties is resident, and shall not have power to make any order on such an application except –

(a)   in a case where the agreement contains no provision for periodical payments by either of the parties, an order inserting provision for the making by one of the parties of periodical payments for the maintenance of the child;

(b)   in a case where the agreement includes provision for the making by one of the parties of periodical payments, an order increasing or reducing the rate of, or terminating, any of those payments.

(7)   For the avoidance of doubt it is hereby declared that nothing in this paragraph affects any power of a court before which any proceedings between the parties to a maintenance agreement are brought under any other enactment to make an order containing financial arrangements or any right of either party to apply for such an order in such proceedings.

(8)   In the case of a child who has a parent by virtue of section 42 or 43 of the Human Fertilisation and Embryology Act 2008, the reference in sub-paragraph (1)(a) to the child's father is a reference to the woman who is a parent of the child by virtue of that section.

Amendments—Justices of the Peace Act 1997, s 73(2), Sch 5, para 27; AJA 1999, s 106, Sch 15; Courts Act 2003, s 109(1), Sch 8, para 339; HFEA 2008, s 56, Sch 6, Pt 1, para 32(1),(3); SI 2011/1484.

Defined terms—"child": s 105(1), Sch 1, para 16(1).

Scope—Subject to CSA 1991 (see Procedural Guides A2 and A7), this paragraph is equivalent to MCA 1973, s 35 and sets out the code for altering maintenance agreements during the lives of the parents. The major difference between this paragraph and MCA 1973, s 35 is that jurisdiction under s 35 depends on the parents being married. By para 10(6), the power of magistrates' courts is limited to inserting provision for periodical payments where none has been made in the maintenance agreement, or, where the agreement does include provision for periodical payments, increasing, reducing or terminating those payments. Previous agreements between parents for financial provision for their child cannot oust the duty of the court under s 15 and Sch 1. The court is free to depart from an agreement unless satisfied that the agreement makes appropriate financial provision for the child: see *Morgan v Hill* [2007] 1 FLR 1480, where the court set aside the agreement and made more substantial financial provision for the child. Such agreements are given less weight than in MCA 1973 applications.

11   (1)   Where a maintenance agreement provides for the continuation, after the death of one of the parties, of payments for the maintenance of a child and that party dies domiciled in England and Wales, the surviving party or the personal representatives of the deceased party may apply to the High Court or a county court for an order under paragraph 10.

(2)   If a maintenance agreement is altered by a court on an application under this paragraph, the agreement shall have effect thereafter as if the alteration had been made, immediately before the death, by agreement between the parties and for valuable consideration.

(3) An application under this paragraph shall not, except with leave of the High Court or a county court, be made after the end of the period of six months beginning with the day on which representation in regard to the estate of the deceased is first taken out.

(4) In considering for the purposes of sub-paragraph (3) the question when representation was first taken out, a grant limited to settled land or to trust property shall be left out of account and a grant limited to real estate or to personal estate shall be left out of account unless a grant limited to the remainder of the estate has previously been made or is made at the same time.

(5) A county court shall not entertain an application under this paragraph, or an application for leave to make an application under this paragraph, unless it would have jurisdiction to hear and determine proceedings for an order under section 2 of the Inheritance (Provision for Family and Dependants) Act 1975 in relation to the deceased's estate by virtue of section 25 of the County Courts Act 1984 (jurisdiction under the Act of 1975).

(6) The provisions of this paragraph shall not render the personal representatives of the deceased liable for having distributed any part of the estate of the deceased after the expiry of the period of six months referred to in sub-paragraph (3) on the ground that they ought to have taken into account the possibility that a court might grant leave for an application by virtue of this paragraph to be made by the surviving party after that period.

(7) Sub-paragraph (6) shall not prejudice any power to recover any part of the estate so distributed arising by virtue of the making of an order in pursuance of this paragraph.

Defined terms—"child": s 105(1), Sch 1, para 16(1); "financial arrangements", "maintenance agreement": para 10(1).

Scope—This paragraph is equivalent to MCA 1973, s 36 and enables a maintenance agreement containing provision for a child to be varied on the death of one of the parties to that agreement. MCA 1973, s 36 confers jurisdiction only if the parents are married; this paragraph applies irrespective of whether the parents have been married. The application must be made to the High Court, designated county court or a magistrates' court: FPR 2010, r 9.5(2).

12 Enforcement of orders for maintenance

(1) Any person for the time being under an obligation to make payments in pursuance of any order for the payment of money made by a magistrates' court under this Act shall give notice of any change of address to such person (if any) as may be specified in the order.

(2) Any person failing without reasonable excuse to give such a notice shall be guilty of an offence and liable on summary conviction to a fine not exceeding level 2 on the standard scale.

(3) An order for the payment of money made by a magistrates' court under this Act shall be enforceable as a magistrates' court maintenance order within the meaning of section 150(1) of the Magistrates' Courts Act 1980.

13 Direction for settlement of instrument by conveyancing counsel

Where the High Court or a county court decides to make an order under this Act for the securing of periodical payments or for the transfer or settlement of property, it may direct that the matter be referred to one of the conveyancing counsel of the court to settle a proper instrument to be executed by all necessary parties.

14 Jurisdiction in relation to matters relating to maintenance

(1) If an application under paragraph 1 or 2, or part of such an application, relates to a matter where jurisdiction falls to be determined by reference to the jurisdictional requirements of the Maintenance Regulation and Schedule 6 to the Civil Jurisdiction and Judgments (Maintenance) Regulations 2011, the court may not entertain the application or that part of it unless it has jurisdiction to do so by virtue of that Regulation and that Schedule.

(2) In sub-paragraph (1), "the Maintenance Regulation" means Council Regulation (EC) No 4/2009 including as applied in relation to Denmark by virtue of the Agreement made on 19 October 2005 between the European Community and the Kingdom of Denmark.

Amendments—Substituted by SI 2011/1484; amended by SI 2012/2814.

Scope—The restriction on the power to make financial provision against a parent in England and Wales where a child resides outside the jurisdiction (previously limited to periodical payments and secured periodical payments) is now abolished. By the operation of the Maintenance Regulation and CJJ(M)R 2011, in force from 18 June 2011, where an application relates to a matter where jurisdiction falls to be determined by reference to the Maintenance Regulation, then those jurisdictional provisions apply. The types of financial relief sought under this paragraph are no longer restricted to periodical payments and secured periodical payments.

15 Local authority contribution to child's maintenance

(1) Where a child lives, or is to live, with a person as the result of a residence order, a local authority may make contributions to that person towards the cost of the accommodation and maintenance of the child.

(2) Sub-paragraph (1) does not apply where the person with whom the child lives, or is to live, is a parent of the child or the husband or wife or civil partner of a parent of the child.

Amendments—CPA 2004, s 78(1), (3).

Defined terms—"child": s 105(1), Sch 1, para 16(1); "local authority": s 105(1); "residence order": s 8(1).

"may make contributions"—A local authority's contribution to a child's maintenance under this provision is discretionary, and will not apply where the child lives with a parent, or the parent's spouse or civil partner: *R (M) v Birmingham City Council* [2009] 1 FLR 1068.

16 Interpretation

(1) In this Schedule "child" includes, in any case where an application is made under paragraph 2 or 6 in relation to a person who has reached the age of eighteen, that person.

(2) In this Schedule except paragraphs 2 and 15, "parent" includes –

    (a)   any party to a marriage (whether or not subsisting) in relation to whom the child concerned is a child of the family, and

    (b)   any civil partner in a civil partnership (whether or not subsisting) in relation to whom the child concerned is a child of the family;

and for this purpose any reference to either parent or both parents shall be read as a reference to any parent of his and to all of his parents.

(3) In this Schedule, "maintenance calculation" has the same meaning as it has in the Child Support Act 1991 by virtue of section 54 of that Act as read with any regulations in force under that section.

Amendments—SI 1993/623; CSPSSA 2000, s 26, Sch 3, para 10; CPA 2004, s 78(1),(4).

PART II

Defined terms—"child of the family": s 105(1); "parent" means (in the strict legal sense) any party to a marriage or civil partnership. An order cannot be made against a same-sex former partner where there is no biological relationship or civil partnership: *T v B* [2010] 2 FLR 1966.

SCHEDULE 2
LOCAL AUTHORITY SUPPORT FOR CHILDREN AND FAMILIES

PART I
PROVISION OF SERVICES FOR FAMILIES

1 Identification of children in need and provision of information

(1) Every local authority shall take reasonable steps to identify the extent to which there are children in need within their area.

(2) Every local authority shall –

   (a) publish information –
       (i) about services provided by them under sections 17, 18, 20, 23B to 23D, 24A and 24B; and
       (ii) where they consider it appropriate, about the provision by others (including, in particular, voluntary organisations) of services which the authority have power to provide under those sections; and
   (b) take such steps as are reasonably practicable to ensure that those who might benefit from the services receive the information relevant to them.

Amendments—Children (Leaving Care) Act 2000, s 7(4).

1A *(repealed)*

2 Maintenance of a register of disabled children

(1) Every local authority shall open and maintain a register of disabled children within their area.

(2) The register may be kept by means of a computer.

3 Assessment of children's needs

Where it appears to a local authority that a child within their area is in need, the authority may assess his needs for the purposes of this Act at the same time as any assessment of his needs is made under –

   (a) the Chronically Sick and Disabled Persons Act 1970;
   (b) Part IV of the Education Act 1996;
   (c) the Disabled Persons (Services, Consultation and Representation) Act 1986; or
   (d) any other enactment.

Amendments—Education Act 1996, s 582(1), Sch 37, Pt I, para 92.

Court's function—In *R (LH and MH) v London Borough of Lambeth* [2006] 2 FLR 1275 the claimants sought judicial review of a core assessment relating to a 10-year-old child with moderate learning disabilities, autism and certain physical conditions. It was not the function of the court to decide what was best for a child; its function was one of review and to decide whether there had been a failure to fulfil the legal obligations of the local authority.

Age of child—Where it is in dispute whether an individual who is said to be in need is a child or not, the resolution of that issue is for the court to determine and not for the local authority to decide subject only to challenge by judicial review: *R (ota A) (FC) v London Borough of Croydon & Others* [2010] 1 FLR 959. A local authority undertaking age assessments for the purposes of CA 1989 is not bound by age assessments undertaken by the Secretary of State for the Home Department in discharging her immigration functions, nor is it bound by age assessments made by the First Tier Tribunal (Immigration and Asylum Chamber) on appeal: *R (Kadri) v Birmingham City Council & Othrs* [2012] EWCA Civ 1432.

4 Prevention of neglect and abuse

(1) Every local authority shall take reasonable steps, through the provision of services under Part III of this Act, to prevent children within their area suffering ill-treatment or neglect.

(2) Where a local authority believe that a child who is at any time within their area –

   (a)   is likely to suffer harm; but
   (b)   lives or proposes to live in the area of another local authority they shall inform that other local authority.

(3) When informing that other local authority they shall specify –

   (a)   the harm that they believe he is likely to suffer; and
   (b)   (if they can) where the child lives or proposes to live.

5 Provision of accommodation in order to protect child

(1) Where –

   (a)   it appears to a local authority that a child who is living on particular premises is suffering, or is likely to suffer, ill treatment at the hands of another person who is living on those premises; and
   (b)   that other person proposes to move from the premises,

the authority may assist that other person to obtain alternative accommodation.

(2) Assistance given under this paragraph may be in cash.

(3) Subsections (7) to (9) of section 17 shall apply in relation to assistance given under this paragraph as they apply in relation to assistance given under that section.

6 Provision for disabled children

(1) Every local authority shall provide services designed –

   (a)   to minimise the effect on disabled children within their area of their disabilities;
   (b)   to give such children the opportunity to lead lives which are as normal as possible; and
   (c)   to assist individuals who provide care for such children to continue to do so, or to do so more effectively, by giving them breaks from caring.

(2) The duty imposed by sub-paragraph (1)(c) shall be performed in accordance with regulations made by the appropriate national authority.

Amendments—CYPA 2008, s 25.

7 Provision to reduce need for care proceedings etc

Every local authority shall take reasonable steps designed –

   (a)   to reduce the need to bring –
      (i)   proceedings for care or supervision orders with respect to children within their area;
      (ii)   criminal proceedings against such children;
      (iii) any family or other proceedings with respect to such children which might lead to them being placed in the authority's care; or

(iv) proceedings under the inherent jurisdiction of the High Court with respect to children;
(b) to encourage children within their area not to commit criminal offences; and
(c) to avoid the need for children within their area to be placed in secure accommodation.

"reasonable steps" (para 7)—The duty to take "reasonable steps" in relation to the housing needs of an autistic child accommodated by the local authority meant that the council must do its best within the bounds of what is reasonably practicable to secure "not unsuitable" accommodation for the child; the accommodation to be secured was not required to be suitable to the particular needs of the child, only to be "not unsuitable" (*R v London Borough of Brent ex parte S* [1994] 1 FLR 203).

8 Provision for children living with their families

Every local authority shall make such provision as they consider appropriate for the following services to be available with respect to children in need within their area while they are living with their families –

(a) advice, guidance and counselling;
(b) occupational, social, cultural or recreational activities;
(c) home help (which may include laundry facilities);
(d) facilities for, or assistance with, travelling to and from home for the purpose of taking advantage of any other service provided under this Act or of any similar service;
(e) assistance to enable the child concerned and his family to have a holiday.

8A Provision for accommodated children

(1) Every local authority shall make provision for such services as they consider appropriate to be available with respect to accommodated children.

(2) "Accommodated children" are those children in respect of whose accommodation the local authority have been notified under section 85 or 86.

(3) The services shall be provided with a view to promoting contact between each accommodated child and that child's family.

(4) The services may, in particular, include –

(a) advice, guidance and counselling;
(b) services necessary to enable the child to visit, or to be visited by, members of the family;
(c) assistance to enable the child and members of the family to have a holiday together.

(5) Nothing in this paragraph affects the duty imposed by paragraph 10.

Amendments—Inserted by CYPA 2008, s 19.

9 Family centres

(1) Every local authority shall provide such family centres as they consider appropriate in relation to children within their area.

(2) "Family centre" means a centre at which any of the persons mentioned in sub-paragraph (3) may –

(a) attend for occupational, social, cultural or recreational activities;
(b) attend for advice, guidance or counselling; or
(c) be provided with accommodation while he is receiving advice, guidance or counselling.

(3) The persons are –

    (a)   a child;

    (b)   his parents;

    (c)   any person who is not a parent of his but who has parental responsibility for him;

    (d)   any other person who is looking after him.

10 Maintenance of the family home

Every local authority shall take such steps as are reasonably practicable, where any child within their area who is in need and whom they are not looking after is living apart from his family –

    (a)   to enable him to live with his family; or

    (b)   to promote contact between him and his family,

if, in their opinion, it is necessary to do so in order to safeguard or promote his welfare.

"such steps as are reasonably practicable"—A local authority is not required to contact extended family where a mother wants a child adopted without them being so informed (*Z County Council v R* [2001] 1 FLR 365 and *Re C (A Child) v XYZ County Council* [2008] 1 FLR 1294 (CA)).

11 Duty to consider racial groups to which children in need belong

Every local authority shall, in making any arrangements –

    (a)   for the provision of day care within their area; or

    (b)   designed to encourage persons to act as local authority foster parents,

have regard to the different racial groups to which children within their area who are in need belong.

PART II
CHILDREN LOOKED AFTER BY LOCAL AUTHORITIES

12A Regulations as to conditions under which child in care is allowed to live with parent, etc

Regulations under section 22C may, in particular, impose requirements on a local authority as to –

    (a)   the making of any decision by a local authority to allow a child in their care to live with any person falling within section 22C(3) (including requirements as to those who must be consulted before the decision is made and those who must be notified when it has been made);

    (b)   the supervision or medical examination of the child concerned;

    (c)   the removal of the child, in such circumstances as may be prescribed, from the care of the person with whom the child has been allowed to live;

    (d)   the records to be kept by local authorities.

12B Regulations as to placements of a kind specified in section 22C(6)(d)

Regulations under section 22C as to placements of the kind specified in section 22C(6)(d) may, in particular, make provision as to –

    (a)   the persons to be notified of any proposed arrangements;

    (b)   the opportunities such persons are to have to make representations in relation to the arrangements proposed;

    (c)   the persons to be notified of any proposed changes in arrangements;

(d)   the records to be kept by local authorities;

(e)   the supervision by local authorities of any arrangements made.

12C Placements out of area

Regulations under section 22C may, in particular, impose requirements which a local authority must comply with –

(a)   before a child looked after by them is provided with accommodation at a place outside the area of the authority; or

(b)   if the child's welfare requires the immediate provision of such accommodation, within such period of the accommodation being provided as may be prescribed.

12D Avoidance of disruption in education

(1) Regulations under section 22C may, in particular, impose requirements which a local authority must comply with before making any decision concerning a child's placement if he is in the fourth key stage.

(2) A child is "in the fourth key stage" if he is a pupil in the fourth key stage for the purposes of Part 6 or 7 of the Education 2002 (see section 82 and 103 of that Act).

12E Regulations as to placing of children with local authority foster parents

Regulations under section 22C may, in particular, make provision –

(a)   with regard to the welfare of children placed with local authority foster parents;

(b)   as to the arrangements to be made by local authorities in connection with the health and education of such children;

(c)   as to the records to be kept by local authorities;

(d)   for securing that where possible the local authority foster parent with whom a child is to be placed is –

(i)   of the same religious persuasion as the child; or

(ii)   gives an undertaking that the child will be brought up in that religious persuasion;

(e)   for securing the children placed with local authority foster parents, and the premises in which they are accommodated, will be supervised and inspected by a local authority and that the children will be removed from those premises if their welfare appears to require it.

12F (1) Regulations under section 22C may, in particular, also make provision –

(a)   for securing that a child is not placed with a local authority foster parent unless that person is for the time being approved as a local authority foster parent by such local authority as may be prescribed;

(b)   establishing a procedure under which any person in respect of whom a qualifying determination has been made may apply to the appropriate national authority for a review of that determination by a panel constituted by that national authority.

(2) A determination is a qualifying determination if –

(a)   it relates to the issue of whether a person should be approved, or should continue to be approved, as a local authority foster parent; and

(b)   it is of a prescribed description.

(3) Regulations made by virtue of sub-paragraph (1)(b) may include provision as to –

(a)   the duties and powers of a panel;

(b)   the administration and procedures of a panel;

(c)   the appointment of members of a panel (including the number, or any limit on the number, of members who may be appointed and any conditions for appointment);

(d)   the payment of fees to members of a panel;

(e)   the duties of any person in connection with a review conducted under the regulations;

(f)   the monitoring of any such reviews.

(4) Regulations made by virtue of sub-paragraph (3)(e) may impose a duty to pay to the appropriate national authority such sum as that national authority may determine; but such a duty may not be imposed upon a person who has applied for a review of a qualifying determination.

(5) The appropriate national authority must secure that, taking one financial year with another, the aggregate of the sums which become payable to it under regulations made by virtue of subparagraph (4) does not exceed the cost to it of performing its independent review functions.

(6) The appropriate national authority may make an arrangement with an organisation under which independent review functions are performed by the organisation on the national authority's behalf.

(7) If the appropriate national authority makes such an arrangement with an organisation, the organisation is to perform its functions under the arrangement in accordance with any general or special directions given by that national authority.

(8) The arrangement may include provision for payments to be made to the organisation by the appropriate national authority.

(9) Payments made by the appropriate national authority in accordance with such provision shall be taken into account in determining (for the purpose of sub-paragraph (5)) the cost to that national authority of performing its independent review functions.

(10) Where the Welsh Ministers are the appropriate national authority, sub-paragraphs (6) and (8) also apply as if references to an organisation included references to the Secretary of State.

(11) In this paragraph –

"financial year" means a period of twelve months ending with 31 March;

"independent review function" means a function conferred or imposed on a national authority by regulations made by virtue of sub-paragraph (1)(b);

"organisation" includes a public body and a private or voluntary organisation.

12G Regulations under section 22C may, in particular, also make provision as to the circumstances in which local authorities may make arrangements for duties imposed on them by the regulations to be discharged on their behalf.

Amendments—CLSA 1990, s 116, Sch 16, para 26; CYPA 2008, s 8(2), Sch 1, para 4.

15   Promotion and maintenance of contact between child and family

(1) Where a child is being looked after by a local authority, the authority shall, unless it is not reasonably practicable or consistent with his welfare, endeavour to promote contact between the child and –

(a)   his parents;

(b)   any person who is not a parent of his but who has parental responsibility for him; and

(c)   any relative, friend or other person connected with him.

(2) Where a child is being looked after by a local authority –

    (a)   the authority shall take such steps as are reasonably practicable to secure that
        (i)   his parents; and
        (ii)   any person who is not a parent of his but who has parental responsibility
            for him,
       are kept informed of where he is being accommodated; and
    (b)   every such person shall secure that the authority are kept informed of his or her
       address.

(3) Where a local authority ("the receiving authority") take over the provision of accommodation for a child from another local authority ("the transferring authority") under section 20(2) –

    (a)   the receiving authority shall (where reasonably practicable) inform
        (i)   the child's parents; and
        (ii)   any person who is not a parent of his but who has parental responsibility
            for him;
    (b)   sub-paragraph (2)(a) shall apply to the transferring authority, as well as the
       receiving authority, until at least one such person has been informed of the
       change; and
    (c)   sub-paragraph (2)(b) shall not require any person to inform the receiving
       authority of his address until he has been so informed.

(4) Nothing in this paragraph requires a local authority to inform any person of the whereabouts of a child if –

    (a)   the child is in the care of the authority; and
    (b)   the authority has reasonable cause to believe that informing the person would
       prejudice the child's welfare.

(5) Any person who fails (without reasonable excuse) to comply with sub-paragraph (2)(b) shall be guilty of an offence and liable on summary conviction to a fine not exceeding level 2 on the standard scale.

(6) It shall be a defence in any proceedings under sub-paragraph (5) to prove that the defendant was residing at the same address as another person who was the child's parent or had parental responsibility for the child and had reasonable cause to believe that the other person had informed the appropriate authority that both of them were residing at that address.

"local authority shall ... endeavour to promote contact" (para 15(1))—In *Re P (Minors) (Contact with Children in Care)* [1993] 2 FLR 156 it was observed that: "The previous practice of access at the discretion of the local authority should not be the regular practice as s 34 provides that reasonable contact should be the norm, not contact at the local authority's discretion which is not the same". Bearing in mind that, even in cases of urgent necessity, s 34(6) only permits refusal of contact for up to 7 days, reasonable contact should not be unduly restricted, unless by agreement or pursuant to a court order applied for by the local authority itself under s 34(2) (*Re T (Termination of Contact)* [1997] 1 FLR 517).

"any relative, friend or other person connected with him" (para 15(1)(c))—A person who for a period of time occupies the status of stepfather falls within the ambit of this paragraph, as do half-siblings (*L v London Borough of Bromley*) [1998] 1 FLR 709).

16 Visits to or by children: expenses

(1) This paragraph applies where –

    (a)   a child is being looked after by a local authority; and
    (b)   the conditions mentioned in sub-paragraph (3) are satisfied.

(2) The authority may –

    (a)   make payments to –
- (i) a parent of the child;
- (ii) any person who is not a parent of his but who has parental responsibility for him; or
- (iii) any relative, friend or other person connected with him,

        in respect of travelling, subsistence or other expenses incurred by that person in visiting the child; or

    (b)   make payments to the child, or to any person his behalf, in respect of travelling, subsistence or other expenses incurred by or on behalf of the child in his visiting –
- (i) a parent of his;
- (ii) any person who has parental responsibility for him; or
- (iii) any relative, friend or other person connected with him.

(3) The conditions are that –

    (a)   it appears to the authority that the visit in question could not otherwise be made without undue financial hardship; and

    (b)   the circumstances warrant the making of the payments.

17 (*repealed*)

18 Power to guarantee apprenticeship deeds etc

(1) While a child is being looked after by a local authority, or is a person qualifying for advice and assistance, the authority may undertake any obligation by way of guarantee under any deed of apprenticeship or articles of clerkship which he enters into.

(2) Where a local authority have undertaken any such obligation under any deed or articles they may at any time (whether or not they are still looking after the person concerned) undertake the like obligation under any supplemental deed or articles.

19 Arrangements to assist children to live abroad

(1) A local authority may only arrange for, or assist in arranging for, any child in their care to live outside England and Wales with the approval of the court.

(2) A local authority may, with the approval of every person who has parental responsibility for the child arrange for, or assist in arranging for, any other child looked after by them to live outside England and Wales.

(3) The court shall not give its approval under sub-paragraph (1) unless it is satisfied that –

    (a)   living outside England and Wales would be in the child's best interests;

    (b)   suitable arrangements have been, or will be, made for his reception and welfare in the country in which he will live;

    (c)   the child has consented to living in that country; and

    (d)   every person who has parental responsibility for the child has consented to his living in that country.

(4) Where the court is satisfied that the child does not have sufficient understanding to give or withhold his consent, it may disregard sub-paragraph (3)(c) and give its approval if the child is to live in the country concerned with a parent, guardian, special guardian or other suitable person.

(5) Where a person whose consent is required by sub-paragraph (3)(d) fails to give his consent, the court may disregard that provision and give its approval if it is satisfied that that person –

    (a) cannot be found;

    (b) is incapable of consenting; or

    (c) is withholding his consent unreasonably.

(6) Section 85 of the Adoption and Children Act 2002 (which imposes restrictions on taking children out of the United Kingdom) shall not apply in the case of any child who is to live outside England and Wales with the approval of the court given under this paragraph.

(7) Where a court decides to give its approval under this paragraph it may order that its decision is not to have effect during the appeal period.

(8) In sub-paragraph (7) "the appeal period" means –

    (a) where an appeal is made against the decision, the period between the making of the decision and the determination of the appeal; and

    (b) otherwise, the period during which an appeal may be made against the decision.

(9) This paragraph does not apply to a local authority placing a child for adoption with prospective adopters.

Amendments—ACA 2002, s 139(1), Sch 3, paras 54, 72.

"with the approval of the court" (para 19(1))—An application by a local authority to move children in its care to Northern Ireland was considered in *Re P (Minors) (Interim Order)* [1993] 2 FLR 742. In *Re G (Leave to Appeal: Jurisdiction)* [1999] 1 FLR 771 approval was not necessary because, on an application under Sch 2, para 19, the judge had decided that the best interests of the child were met by making an interim residence order in favour of her father in Scotland. The Court of Appeal held that the court was entitled to dispense with unnecessary procedural difficulties in order to achieve what was in the best interests of the child. In the circumstances of *Flintshire County Council v K* [2001] 2 FLR 476 it was found to be appropriate to order the return of children to the USA under a care order rather than the inherent jurisdiction as it enabled the local authority to manage the arrangements. The court approved a placement of a child abroad with the father pursuant to this provision rather than adopt the artificial exercise of permitting the local authority to withdraw the care proceedings, make the child a ward of court and place the child with the father in Turkey: *Islington LBC v EV & Othrs* [2011] 1 FLR 1681.

Paragraph 19 and adoption abroad—An assessment of potential carers for a child who lives abroad, and who may be approved as prospective adopters, may be undertaken in their country of residence and does not have to take place in the UK. A local authority was entitled to use this provision to place a child out of the country with the potential carers for an assessment which may lead to adoption, but may not do so: *Re A (Adoption: Removal)* [2009] 2 FLR 597.

"in the child's best interests" (para 19(3)(a))—The child's best interests are not paramount in this context; they are merely one of the four specific factors which the court must consider (*Re G (Minors) (Care: Leave to Place Outside Jurisdiction)* [1994] 2 FLR 301).

"is withholding his consent unreasonably" (para 19(5)(c))—In determining whether the parent's refusal is within the broad band of reasonable decisions which a responsible parent might take, the court should apply the test set out in *Re G* (above). It is surprising that this provision was not amended to reflect the "welfare" test contained in s 52 of ACA 2002 when considering the issue of the dispensation of parental consent.

Preparation for ceasing to be looked after

19A It is the duty of the local authority looking after a child to advise, assist and befriend him with a view to promoting his welfare when they have ceased to look after him.

Amendments—Inserted by Children (Leaving Care) Act 2000, s 1.

19B (1) A local authority shall have the following additional functions in relation to an eligible child whom they are looking after.

(2) In sub-paragraph (1) "eligible child" means, subject to sub-paragraph (3), a child who –

    (a)   is aged sixteen or seventeen; and

    (b)   has been looked after by a local authority for a prescribed period, or periods amounting in all to a prescribed period, which began after he reached a prescribed age and ended after he reached the age of sixteen.

(3) The appropriate national authority may prescribe –

    (a)   additional categories of eligible children; and

    (b)   categories of children who are not to be eligible children despite falling within sub-paragraph (2).

(4) For each eligible child, the local authority shall carry out an assessment of his needs with a view to determining what advice, assistance and support it would be appropriate for them to provide him under this Act –

    (a)   while they are still looking after him; and

    (b)   after they cease to look after him,

and shall then prepare a pathway plan for him.

(5) The local authority shall keep the pathway plan under regular review.

(6) Any such review may be carried out at the same time as a review of the child's case carried out by virtue of section 26.

(7) The appropriate national authority may by regulations make provision as to assessments for the purposes of sub-paragraph (4).

(8) The regulations may in particular provide for the matters set out in section 23B(6).

Amendments—Inserted by Children (Leaving Care) Act 2000, s 1; amended by CYPA 2008, s 39, Sch 3, paras 1, 27.

Pathway plans (para 19B(4),(5))—The statutory scheme envisages two quite separate stages: the assessment, culminating in the preparation of a written record; and the preparation of a pathway plan. The assessment of needs is to go beyond mere identification of needs: it involves analysis and evaluation of the nature, extent and severity of the child's needs, a process that has to go far enough to enable a pathway plan to be prepared, setting out in sufficiently precise detail the "manner in which" those needs are to be met (*R (G) v Nottingham City Council & Nottingham University Hospital* [2008] 1 FLR 1668; see also *R (S) v Sutton London Borough Council* [2007] 2 FLR 849).

19C Personal advisers

A local authority shall arrange for each child whom they are looking after who is an eligible child for the purposes of paragraph 19B to have a personal adviser.

Amendments—Inserted by Children (Leaving Care) Act 2000, s 1.

"Personal advisers"—See *R (J)* (above) for guidance as to who should be a personal adviser and what their role should be as between the local authority and the child.

20 Death of children being looked after by local authorities

(1) If a child who is being looked after by a local authority dies, the authority –

    (a)   shall notify the appropriate national authority and (in the case of a local authority in England) Her Majesty's Chief Inspector of Education, Children's Services and Skills;

    (b)   shall, so far as is reasonably practicable, notify the child's parents and every person who is not a parent of his but who has parental responsibility for him;

(c)   may, with the consent (so far as it is reasonably practicable to obtain it) of every person who has parental responsibility for the child, arrange for the child's body to be buried or cremated; and

(d)   may, if the conditions mentioned in sub-paragraph (2) are satisfied, make payments to any person who has parental responsibility for the child, or any relative, friend or other person connected with the child, in respect of travelling, subsistence or other expenses incurred by that person in attending the child's funeral.

(2) The conditions are that –

(a)   it appears to the authority that the person concerned could not otherwise attend the child's funeral without undue financial hardship; and

(b)   that the circumstances warrant the making of the payments.

(3) Sub-paragraph (1) does not authorise cremation where it does not accord with the practice of the child's religious persuasion.

(4) Where a local authority have exercised their power under sub-paragraph (1)(c) with respect to a child who was under sixteen when he died, they may recover from any parent of the child any expenses incurred by them.

(5) Any sums so recoverable shall, without prejudice to any other method of recovery, be recoverable summarily as a civil debt.

(6) Nothing in this paragraph affects any enactment regulating or authorising the burial, cremation or anatomical examination of the body of a deceased person.

Amendments—Health and Social Care (Community Health and Standards) Act 2003, s 147, Sch 9, para 10; Education and Inspection Act 2006, Sch 14, para 17; CYPA 2008, s 39, Sch 3, paras 1, 27.

PART III
CONTRIBUTIONS TOWARDS MAINTENANCE OF CHILDREN LOOKED AFTER BY LOCAL AUTHORITIES

21 Liability to contribute

(1) Where a local authority are looking after a child (other than in the cases mentioned in sub-paragraph (7)) they shall consider whether they should recover contributions towards the child's maintenance from any person liable to contribute ("a contributor").

(2) An authority may only recover contributions from a contributor if they consider it reasonable to do so.

(3) The persons liable to contribute are –

(a)   where the child is under sixteen, each of his parents;

(b)   where he has reached the age of sixteen, the child himself.

(4) A parent is not liable to contribute during any period when he is in receipt of income support under Part VII of the Social Security Contributions and Benefits Act 1992, of any element of child tax credit other than the family element, of working tax credit of an income-based jobseeker's allowance or of an income-related employment and support allowance.

(5) A person is not liable to contribute towards the maintenance of a child in the care of a local authority in respect of any period during which the child is living with, under arrangements made by the authority in accordance with section 22C, a parent of his.

(6) A contributor is not obliged to make any contribution towards a child's maintenance except as agreed or determined in accordance with this Part of this Schedule.

(7) The cases are where the child is looked after by a local authority under –

(a) section 21;

(b) an interim care order;

(c) section 92 of the Powers of Criminal Courts (Sentencing) Act 2000.

Amendments—Disability Living Allowance and Disability Working Allowance Act 1991, s 7(2), Sch 3, para 15; Social Security (Consequential Provisions) Act 1992, s 4, Sch 2, para 108; Jobseekers Act 1995, s 41, Sch 2, para 19; Tax Credits Act 1999, s 1(2), Sch 1, paras 1, 6(d)(iii); Powers of Criminal Courts (Sentencing) Act 2000, s 165, Sch 9, para 130; Tax Credits Act 2002, s 47, Sch 3, paras 15, 20; Welfare Reform Act 2007, s 28(1), Sch 3, para 6(1),(6); CYPA 2008, s 8(3), Sch 1, para 5.

22 Agreed contributions

(1) Contributions towards a child's maintenance may only be recovered if the local authority have served a notice ("a contribution notice") on the contributor specifying –

    (a) the weekly sum which they consider that he should contribute; and

    (b) arrangements for payment.

(2) The contribution notice must be in writing and dated.

(3) Arrangements for payment shall, in particular, include –

    (a) the date on which liability to contribute begins (which must not be earlier than the date of the notice);

    (b) the date on which liability under the notice will end (if the child has not before that date ceased to be looked after by the authority); and

    (c) the date on which the first payment is to be made.

(4) The authority may specify in a contribution notice a weekly sum which is a standard contribution determined by them for all children looked after by them.

(5) The authority may not specify in a contribution notice a weekly sum greater than that which they consider –

    (a) they would normally be prepared to pay if they had placed a similar child with local authority foster parents; and

    (b) it is reasonably practicable for the contributor to pay (having regard to his means).

(6) An authority may at any time withdraw a contribution notice (without prejudice to their power to serve another).

(7) Where the authority and the contributor agree –

    (a) the sum which the contributor is to contribute; and

    (b) arrangements for payment,

(whether as specified in the contribution notice or otherwise) and the contributor notifies the authority in writing that he so agrees, the authority may recover summarily as a civil debt any contribution which is overdue and unpaid.

(8) A contributor may, by serving a notice in writing on the authority, withdraw his agreement in relation to any period of liability falling after the date of service of the notice.

(9) Sub-paragraph (7) is without prejudice to any other method of recovery.

"reasonably practicable for the contributor to pay (having regard to his means)" (para 22(5)(a))—See **"A contribution order ... shall be made with due regard to the contributor's means"** under para 23.

23 Contribution orders

(1) Where a contributor has been served with a contribution notice and has –

    (a) failed to reach any agreement with the local authority as mentioned in paragraph 22(7) within the period of one month beginning with the day on which the contribution notice was served; or

(b)   served a notice under paragraph 22(8) withdrawing his agreement,

the authority may apply to the court for an order under this paragraph.

(2) On such an application the court may make an order ("a contribution order") requiring the contributor to contribute a weekly sum towards the child's maintenance in accordance with arrangements for payment specified by the court.

(3) A contribution order –

(a)   shall not specify a weekly sum greater than that specified in the contribution notice; and

(b)   shall be made with due regard to the contributor's means.

(4) A contribution order shall not –

(a)   take effect before the date specified in the contribution notice; or

(b)   have effect while the contributor is not liable to contribute (by virtue of paragraph 21); or

(c)   remain in force after the child has ceased to be looked after by the authority who obtained the order.

(5) An authority may not apply to the court under sub-paragraph (1) in relation to a contribution notice which they have withdrawn.

(6) Where –

(a)   a contribution order is in force;

(b)   the authority serve another contribution notice; and

(c)   the contributor and the authority reach an agreement under paragraph 22(7) in respect of that other contribution notice,

the effect of the agreement shall be to discharge the order from the date on which it is agreed that the agreement shall take effect.

(7) Where an agreement is reached under sub-paragraph (6) the authority shall notify the court –

(a)   of the agreement; and

(b)   of the date on which it took effect.

(8) A contribution order may be varied or revoked on the application of the contributor or the authority.

(9) In proceedings for the variation of a contribution order, the authority shall specify –

(a)   the weekly sum which, having regard to paragraph 22, they propose that the contributor should contribute under the order as varied; and

(b)   the proposed arrangements for payment.

(10) Where a contribution order is varied, the order –

(a)   shall not specify a weekly sum greater than that specified by the authority in the proceedings for variation; and

(b)   shall be made with due regard to the contributor's means.

(11) An appeal shall lie in accordance with rules of court from any order made under this paragraph.

Defined terms—"contribution notice": para 22(1); "contributor": para 21(1).

Jurisdiction—C(AP)O 1991, art 3 requires proceedings under this paragraph to be commenced in a magistrates' court. Articles 5 and 7(2) have the effect of preventing proceedings so commenced from being transferred to a county court; jurisdiction is therefore restricted, in effect, to magistrates' courts.

"A contribution order ... shall be made with due regard to the contributor's means"
(para 23(3)(b))—The criteria to be applied in assessing the contribution to be made by a parent in respect
of a child who is being accommodated by a local authority are different to those applied when assessing
maintenance for a child. The court must assess the contributor's means by reference to the sources of
income available to him and to the manner in which he has expended that income; so long as the money
was reasonably expended, the court cannot superimpose a value judgment as to priorities for family
spending (*Re C (A Minor) (Contribution Notice)* [1994] 1 FLR 111).

24 Enforcement of contribution orders etc

(1) A contribution order made by a magistrates' court shall be enforceable as a
magistrates' court maintenance order (within the meaning of section 150(1) of the
Magistrates' Courts Act 1980).

(2) Where a contributor has agreed, or has been ordered, to make contributions to a local
authority, any other local authority within whose area the contributor is for the time
being living may –

    (a)   at the request of the local authority who served the contribution notice; and
    (b)   subject to agreement as to any sum to be deducted in respect of services
          rendered,

collect from the contributor any contributions due on behalf of the authority who served
the notice.

(3) In sub-paragraph (2) the reference to any other local authority includes a reference
to –

    (a)   a local authority within the meaning of section 1(2) of the Social Work
          (Scotland) Act 1968; and
    (b)   a Health and Social Services Board established under Article 16 of the Health
          and Personal Social Services (Northern Ireland) Order 1972.

(4) The power to collect sums under sub-paragraph (2) includes the power to –

    (a)   receive and give a discharge for any contributions due; and
    (b)   (if necessary) enforce payment of any contributions,

even though those contributions may have fallen due at a time when the contributor was
living elsewhere.

(5) Any contributions collected under sub-paragraph (2) shall be paid (subject to any
agreed deduction) to the local authority who served the contribution notice.

(6) In any proceedings under this paragraph, a document which purports to be –

    (a)   a copy of an order made by a court under or by virtue of paragraph 23; and
    (b)   certified as a true copy by the designated officer for the court,

shall be evidence of the order.

(7) In any proceedings under this paragraph, a certificate which –

    (a)   purports to be signed by the clerk or some other duly authorised officer of the
          local authority who obtained the contribution order; and
    (b)   states that any sum due to the authority under the order is overdue and unpaid,

shall be evidence that the sum is overdue and unpaid.

Amendments—AJA 1999, s 90, Sch 13, para 162; Courts Act 2003, s 109(1), Sch 8, para 340.

Defined terms—"contribution notice": para 22(1); "contribution order": para 23(2); "contributor":
para 21(1); "local authority": s 105(1).

25 Regulations

The appropriate national authority may make regulations –

(a)   as to the considerations which a local authority must take into account in
      deciding –
      (i)   whether it is reasonable to recover contributions; and
      (ii)   what the arrangements for payment should be;
(b)   as to the procedures a local authority must follow in reaching agreements with –
      (i)   contributors (under paragraphs 22 and 23); and
      (ii)   any other local authority (under paragraph 23).

Amendments—CYPA 2008, s 39, Sch 3, paras 1, 27.

SCHEDULE 3

SUPERVISION ORDERS

PART I
GENERAL

1 Meaning of "responsible person"

In this Schedule, "the responsible person", in relation to a supervised child, means –

(a)   any person who has parental responsibility for the child; and
(b)   any other person with whom the child is living.

2 Power of supervisor to give directions to supervised child

(1) A supervision order may require the supervised child to comply with any directions
given from time to time by the supervisor which require him to do all or any of the
following things –

(a)   to live at a place or places specified in the directions for a period or periods so
      specified;
(b)   to present himself to a person or persons specified in the directions at a place or
      places and on a day or days so specified;
(c)   to participate in activities specified in the directions on a day or days so
      specified.

(2) It shall be for the supervisor to decide whether, and to what extent, he exercises his
power to give directions and to decide the form of any directions which he gives.

(3) Sub-paragraph (1) does not confer on a supervisor power to give directions in respect
of any medical or psychiatric examination or treatment (which are matters dealt with in
paragraphs 4 and 5).

Court specifying directions for supervisor to give—See under para 3 below.

3 Imposition of obligations on responsible person

(1) With the consent of any responsible person, a supervision order may include a
requirement –

(a)   that he take all reasonable steps to ensure that the supervised child complies
      with any direction given by the supervisor under paragraph 2;
(b)   that he take all reasonable steps to ensure that the supervised child complies
      with any requirement included in the order under paragraph 4 or 5;
(c)   that he comply with any directions given by the supervisor requiring him to
      attend at a place specified in the directions for the purpose of taking part in
      activities so specified.

(2) A direction given under sub-paragraph (1)(c) may specify the time at which the responsible person is to attend and whether or not the supervised child is required to attend with him.

(3) A supervision order may require any person who is a responsible person in relation to the supervised child to keep the supervisor informed of his address, if it differs from the child's.

Court cannot specify directions to be given—In *Re V (Care or Supervision Order)* [1996] 1 FLR 776, a supervision order cannot have conditions attached (in that case, the judge had wrongly made a supervision order subject to a condition that the child continue as a weekly boarder at a particular school). Sch 3 deals only with:

(a) directions given by the supervisor (see Sch 3, para 2);
(b) requirements which the court can impose with the consent of any responsible person (see Sch 3, para 3); and
(c) a detailed regime for psychiatric and medical examination of the child (see Sch 3, paras 4 and 5).

The only sanction for infringement of the terms of a supervision order, or of any directions given under it, is for the supervisor to return to court for the order to be varied or discharged; the ultimate sanction would be the substitution of a care order.

Re V was followed in *Re S (Care or Supervision Order)* [1996] 1 FLR 753, CA; *Re H (Supervision Order)* [1994] 2 FLR 979, FD (no power in court under para 3 to specify that supervisor should impose a particular direction on a responsible person); *Re H (Prohibited Steps Order)* [1995] 1 FLR 638, CA (court cannot impose on supervision order a condition of no contact with mother's former cohabitee); and *Re B (Supervision Order: Parental Undertaking)* [1996] 1 FLR 676, CA. The cases of *Croydon London Borough Council v A (No 3)* [1992] 2 FLR 350, FD, and *Re T (A Minor) (Care Order: Conditions)* [1994] 2 FLR 423, CA, which appear to suggest that conditions (e g of residence in a particular place) *can* be attached to a supervision order by the court, would seem to be wrong. Even though the county court has no inherent jurisdiction to accept undertakings in care proceedings or as part of a supervision order, a parent's agreement to behave in a particular way (in that case, to undergo medical treatment) could be recorded in a preamble to the order, and any failure to honour this agreement could be brought to the attention of the court in due course *Re B (Supervision Order: Parental Undertaking)*.

4 Psychiatric and medical examinations

(1) A supervision order may require the supervised child –

(a) to submit to a medical or psychiatric examination; or
(b) to submit to any such examination from time to time as directed by the supervisor.

(2) Any such examination shall be required to be conducted –

(a) by, or under the direction of, such registered medical practitioner as may be specified in the order;
(b) at a place specified in the order and at which the supervised child is to attend as a non-resident patient; or
(c) at –
    (i) a health service hospital; or
    (ii) in the case of a psychiatric examination, a hospital, independent hospital or care home,
at which the supervised child is, or is to attend as, a resident patient.

(3) A *requirement of a kind* mentioned in sub-paragraph (2)(c) shall not be included unless the court is satisfied, on the evidence of a registered medical practitioner, that –

(a) the child may be suffering from a physical or mental condition that requires, and may be susceptible to, treatment; and
(b) a period as a resident patient is necessary if the examination is to be carried out properly.

(4) No court shall include a requirement under this paragraph in a supervision order unless it is satisfied that –

(a)   where the child has sufficient understanding to make an informed decision, he
consents to its inclusion; and

(b)   satisfactory arrangements have been, or can be, made for the examination.

Amendments—Care Standards Act 2000, s 116, Sch 4, para 14(24).

5 Psychiatric and medical treatment

(1) Where a court which proposes to make or vary a supervision order is satisfied, on the
evidence of a registered medical practitioner approved for the purposes of section 12 of
the Mental Health Act 1983, that the mental condition of the supervised child –

(a)   is such as requires, and may be susceptible to, treatment; but

(b)   is not such as to warrant his detention in pursuance of a hospital order under
Part III of that Act,

the court may include in the order a requirement that the supervised child shall, for a
period specified in the order, submit to such treatment as is so specified.

(2) The treatment specified in accordance with sub-paragraph (1) must be –

(a)   by, or under the direction of, such registered medical practitioner as may be
specified in the order;

(b)   as a non-resident patient at such a place as may be so specified; or

(c)   as a resident patient in a hospital, independent hospital or care home.

(3) Where a court which proposes to make or vary a supervision order is satisfied, on the
evidence of a registered medical practitioner, that the physical condition of the
supervised child is such as requires, and may be susceptible to, treatment, the court may
include in the order a requirement that the supervised child shall, for a period specified in
the order, submit to such treatment as is so specified.

(4) The treatment specified in accordance with sub-paragraph (3) must be –

(a)   by, or under the direction of, such registered medical practitioner as may be
specified in the order;

(b)   as a non-resident patient at such place as may be so specified; or

(c)   as a resident patient in a health service hospital.

(5) No court shall include a requirement under this paragraph in a supervision order
unless it is satisfied –

(a)   where the child has sufficient understanding to make an informed decision, that
he consents to its inclusion; and

(b)   that satisfactory arrangements have been, or can be, made for the treatment.

(6) If a medical practitioner by whom or under whose direction a supervised person is
being treated in pursuance of a requirement included in a supervision order by virtue of
this paragraph is unwilling to continue to treat or direct the treatment of the supervised
child or is of the opinion that –

(a)   the treatment should be continued beyond the period specified in the order;

(b)   the supervised child needs different treatment;

(c)   he is not susceptible to treatment; or

(d)   he does not require further treatment,

the practitioner shall make a report in writing to that effect to the supervisor.

(7) On receiving a report under this paragraph the supervisor shall refer it to the court,
and on such a reference the court may make an order cancelling or varying the
requirement.

Amendments—Care Standards Act 2000, s 116, Sch 4, para 14(24).

PART II
MISCELLANEOUS

6 Life of supervision order

(1) Subject to sub-paragraph (2) and section 91, a supervision order shall cease to have effect at the end of the period of one year beginning with the date on which it was made.

(2) A supervision order shall also cease to have effect if an event mentioned in section 25(1)(a) or (b) of the Child Abduction and Custody Act 1985 (termination of existing orders) occurs with respect to the child.

(3) Where the supervisor applies to the court to extend, or further extend, a supervision order the court may extend the order for such period as it may specify.

(4) A supervision order may not be extended so as to run beyond the end of the period of three years beginning with the date on which it was made.

Defined terms—"supervision order": s 31(11); "supervisor": s 105(1).

Duration of supervision orders—Normally (subject to s 91 and to Sch 3, para 6(2)), a supervision order lasts for a maximum of 1 year in the first instance (para 6(1)) and there is no jurisdiction in the court to allow the making of an extended supervision order for 3 years from the outset (*Wakefield Metropolitan District Council v T* [2008] 1 FLR 1569); there is nothing to preclude an order for less than 1 year (*M v Warwickshire County Council* [1994] 2 FLR 593). Although para 6(3) facilitates the extension of this period, on more than one occasion if necessary, it nonetheless appears that the effect of para 6(4) is that the longest that the extended order can run is 3 years from the date of the original order (*Re A (Supervision Order: Extension)* [1995] 1 FLR 335, CA). Thereafter, there would have to be a fresh application under CA 1989, s 31, and the threshold criteria would have to be satisfied.

Test on extension application—To obtain an extension, the applicant must satisfy the court that the welfare of the child requires the supervision order to continue; the s 31 threshold test need not be satisfied again (*Re A (Supervision Order: Extension)* [1995] 1 FLR 335, CA).

CA 1989, s 38 not applicable—CA 1989, s 38 has no application to extension orders. If an application for an extension is made within time and is opposed, and the hearing date will be after the expiry of the original order, the court can make one or more short extension orders pending final determination (*Re A (Supervision Order: Extension)*, above). The court cannot make either a care order or an interim care order on an extension application (ibid).

Procedure—The supervisor must apply for an extension to the court which made the original order (C(AP)O 1991, art 4(1)) though by virtue of art 4(2) the court has power subsequently to transfer the proceedings in accordance with arts 5–13. See FPR 2010, rr 5.1–5.3 and PD5A, PD12A. For respondents to the application and other persons who must be given written notice, see the table set out in FPR 2010, r 12.3. As proceedings relating to an extension are "specified proceedings" within the meaning of s 41(6) (s 41(6)(i), and FPR 2010, r 12.27(1)(d)), a children's guardian will normally be appointed. In *Wakefield Metropolitan District Council v T* [2008] 1 FLR 1569, the Court of Appeal gave general guidance as to the procedure for applying for the extension of a supervision order.

Alternative applications—The court has a general power under s 39(2) and (3) to vary or discharge a supervision order.

7 (*repealed*)

8 Information to be given to supervisor etc

(1) A supervision order may require the supervised child –

    (a)   to keep the supervisor informed of any change in his address; and

    (b)   to allow the supervisor to visit him at the place where he is living.

(2) The responsible person in relation to any child with respect to whom a supervision order is made shall –

    (a)   if asked by the supervisor, inform him of the child's address (if it is known to him); and

(b) if he is living with the child, allow the supervisor reasonable contact with the child.

9 Selection of supervisor

(1) A supervision order shall not designate a local authority as the supervisor unless –

(a) the authority agree; or
(b) the supervised child lives or will live within their area.

(2)–(5) (repealed)

Amendments—Probation Service Act 1993, s 32, Sch 3, para 9; CJCSA 2000 ss 74, 75, Sch 7, Pt II, paras 87, 96, Sch 8.

10 Effect of supervision order on earlier orders

The making of a supervision order with respect to any child brings to an end any earlier care or supervision order which –

(a) was made with respect to that child; and
(b) would otherwise continue in force.

11 Local authority functions and expenditure

(1) The Secretary of State may make regulations with respect to the exercise by a local authority of their functions where a child has been placed under their supervision by a supervision order.

(2) Where a supervision order requires compliance with directions given by virtue of this section, any expenditure incurred by the supervisor for the purposes of the directions shall be defrayed by the local authority designated in the order.

PART III
EDUCATION SUPERVISION ORDERS

Effect of orders

12 (1) Where an education supervision order is in force with respect to a child, it shall be the duty of the supervisor –

(a) to advise, assist and befriend, and give directions to –
   (i)   the supervised child; and
   (ii) his parents;
   in such a way as will, in the opinion of the supervisor, secure that he is properly educated;
(b) where any such directions given to
   (i)   the supervised child; or
   (ii) a parent of his,
   have not been complied with, to consider what further steps to take in the exercise of the supervisor's powers under this Act.

(2) Before giving any directions under sub-paragraph (1) the supervisor shall, so far as is reasonably practicable, ascertain the wishes and feelings of –

(a) the child; and
(b) his parents;

including, in particular, their wishes as to the place at which the child should be educated.

(3) When settling the terms of any such directions, the supervisor shall give due consideration –

(a) having regard to the child's age and understanding, to such wishes and feelings of his as the supervisor has been able to ascertain; and

(b) to such wishes and feelings of the child's parents as he has been able to ascertain.

(4) Directions may be given under this paragraph at any time while the education supervision order is in force.

13 (1) Where an education supervision order is in force with respect to a child, the duties of the child's parents under sections 7 and 444 of the Education Act 1996 (duties to secure education of children and to secure regular attendance of registered pupils) shall be superseded by their duty to comply with any directions in force under the education supervision order.

(2) Where an education supervision order is made with respect to a child –

(a) any school attendance order –

(i)   made under section 437 of the Education Act 1996 with respect to the child; and

(ii) in force immediately before the making of the education supervision order,

shall cease to have effect; and

(b) while the education supervision order remains in force, the following provisions shall not apply with respect to the child –

(i)   section 437 of that Act (school attendance orders);

(ii) section 9 of that Act (pupils to be educated in accordance with wishes of their parents);

(iii) sections 411 and 423 of that Act (parental preference and appeals against admission decisions);

(c) a youth rehabilitation order made under Part 1 of the Criminal Justice and Immigration Act 2008 with respect to the child, while the education supervision order is in force, may not include an education requirement (within the meaning of that Part);

(d) any education requirement of a kind mentioned in paragraph (c), which was in force with respect to the child immediately before the making of the education supervision order, shall cease to have effect.

Amendments—Education Act 1996, s 582(1), Sch 37, Pt I, para 93; Powers of Criminal Courts (Sentencing) Act 2000, s 165, Sch 9, para 131; Criminal Justice and Immigration Act 2008, ss 6(2), 149, Sch 4, para 37.

14 Effect where child also subject to supervision order

(1) This paragraph applies where an education supervision order and a supervision order, or youth rehabilitation order (within the meaning of Part 1 of the Criminal Justice and Immigration Act 2008), are in force at the same time with respect to the same child.

(2) Any failure to comply with a direction given by the supervisor under the education supervision order shall be disregarded if it would not have been reasonably practicable to comply with it without failing to comply with a direction or instruction given under the other order.

Amendments—Powers of Criminal Courts (Sentencing) Act 2000, s 165, Sch 9, para 131; Criminal Justice and Immigration Act 2008, ss 6(2), 149, Sch 4, para 37.

15 Duration of orders

(1) An education supervision order shall have effect for a period of one year, beginning with the date on which it is made.

(2) An education supervision order shall not expire if, before it would otherwise have expired, the court has (on the application of the authority in whose favour the order was made) extended the period during which it is in force.

(3) Such an application may not be made earlier than three months before the date on which the order would otherwise expire.

(4) The period during which an education supervision order is in force may be extended under sub-paragraph (2) on more than one occasion.

(5) No one extension may be for a period of more than three years.

(6) An education supervision order shall cease to have effect on –

    (a)   the child's ceasing to be of compulsory school age; or

    (b)   the making of a care order with respect to the child;

and sub-paragraphs (1) to (4) are subject to this sub-paragraph.

Defined terms—"education supervision order": s 36(2).

Duration of education supervision orders—Normally (subject to para 15(6)) an education supervision order lasts for a maximum of 1 year in the first instance (para 15(1)). In contrast with para 6(2) and (3), which allow an ordinary supervision order to be extended for no more than 3 years from the original order, an ESO may be extended for any number of 3-year periods until the child ceases to be of compulsory school age or a care order is made and the order expires in accordance with para 15(6). For cases on duration and extension of ordinary supervision orders which may assist with education supervision orders by analogy, see **Duration of supervision orders** under para 6.

"authority in whose favour the order was made" (para 15(2))—Under s 36(1), the designated local education authority is the authority in whose favour the order was made.

16 Information to be given to supervisor etc

(1) An education supervision order may require the child –

    (a)   to keep the supervisor informed of any change in his address; and

    (b)   to allow the supervisor to visit him at the place where he is living.

(2) A person who is the parent of a child with respect to whom an education supervision order has been made shall –

    (a)   if asked by the supervisor, inform him of the child's address (if it is known to him); and

    (b)   if he is living with the child, allow the supervisor reasonable contact with the child.

17 Discharge of orders

(1) The court may discharge any education supervision order on the application of –

    (a)   the child concerned;

    (b)   a parent of his; or

    (c)   the local authority designated in the order.

(2) On discharging an education supervision order, the court may direct the local authority within whose area the child lives, or will live, to investigate the circumstances of the child.

Defined terms—"child": s 105(1); "education supervision order": s 36(2); "local authority": s 105(1).

Scope—This paragraph gives the court the option, if it does discharge the order, to require the local authority to investigate the circumstances of the child, no doubt with a view to the local authority seeking a care or supervision order if it considers such action appropriate.

"parent" (para 17(1)(a))—By virtue of para 21, for the purposes of Sch 3, Pt III (which includes para 17), "parent" has the same meaning as in the Education Act 1996, ie it includes any person who is not a parent of a child but who has parental responsibility for him or care of him (see Education Act 1996, s 576).

"local authority" (para 17(1)(c))—This refers to the local authority designated in the order under s 36(1).

Directing local authority investigation (para 17(2))—The wording of para 17(2) contrasts with that of s 37, which is of wider application and empowers the court to direct an investigation in family proceedings. However, a direction under s 37 can only be given where it appears to the court that it may be appropriate for a care or supervision order to be made in respect of the child whereas there is no such restriction under para 17(2). For further detail as to s 37 directions see that section and the annotation **Best Practice Guidance on s 37(1) directions** thereunder.

18 Offences

(1) If a parent of a child with respect to whom an education supervision order is in force persistently fails to comply with a direction given under the order he shall be guilty of an offence.

(2) It shall be a defence for any person charged with such an offence to prove that –

    (a)   he took all reasonable steps to ensure that the direction was complied with;

    (b)   the direction was unreasonable; or

    (c)   he had complied with –

        (i)   a requirement included in a supervision order made with respect to the child; or

        (ii) directions given under such a requirement,

and that it was not reasonably practicable to comply both with the direction and with the requirement or directions mentioned in this paragraph.

(3) A person guilty of an offence under this paragraph shall be liable on summary conviction to a fine not exceeding level 3 on the standard scale.

19 Persistent failure of child to comply with directions

(1) Where a child with respect to whom an education supervision order is in force persistently fails to comply with any direction given under the order, the local authority designated in the order shall notify the appropriate local authority, if different.

(2) Where a local authority have been notified under sub-paragraph (1) they shall investigate the circumstances of the child.

(3) In this paragraph "the appropriate local authority" has the same meaning as in section 36.

20 Miscellaneous

The Secretary of State may by regulations make provision modifying, or displacing, the provisions of any enactment about education in relation to any child with respect to whom an education supervision order is in force to such extent as appears to the Secretary of State to be necessary or expedient in consequence of the provision made by this Act with respect to such orders.

21 Interpretation

In this part of this Schedule "parent" has the same meaning as in the Education Act 1996.

Amendments—Education Act 1996, s 582(1), Sch 37, Pt I, para 93; SI 2010/1185.

****

SCHEDULE 7

FOSTER PARENTS: LIMITS ON NUMBER OF FOSTER CHILDREN

1 Interpretation

For the purposes of this Schedule, a person fosters a child if –

    (a) he is a local authority foster parent in relation to the child;

    (b) he is a foster parent with whom the child has been placed by a voluntary organisation; or

    (c) he fosters the child privately.

2 The usual fostering limit

Subject to what follows, a person may not foster more than three children ("the usual fostering limit").

3 Siblings

A person may exceed the usual fostering limit if the children concerned are all siblings with respect to each other.

4 Exemption by local authority

(1) A person may exceed the usual fostering limit if he is exempted from it by the local authority within whose area he lives.

(2) In considering whether to exempt a person, a local authority shall have regard, in particular, to –

    (a) the number of children whom the person proposes to foster;

    (b) the arrangements which the person proposes for the care and accommodation of the fostered children;

    (c) the intended and likely relationship between the person and the fostered children;

    (d) the period of time for which he proposes to foster the children; and

    (e) whether the welfare of the fostered children (and of any other children who are or will be living in the accommodation) will be safeguarded and promoted.

(3) Where a local authority exempt a person, they shall inform him by notice in writing –

    (a) that he is so exempted;

    (b) of the children, described by name, whom he may foster; and

    (c) of any condition to which the exemption is subject.

(4) A local authority may at any time by notice in writing –

    (a) vary or cancel an exemption; or

    (b) impose, vary or cancel a condition to which the exemption is subject,

and, in considering whether to do so, they shall have regard in particular to the considerations mentioned in sub-paragraph (2).

(5) The Secretary of State may make regulations amplifying or modifying the provisions of this paragraph in order to provide for cases where children need to be placed with foster parents as a matter of urgency.

5 Effect of exceeding fostering limit

(1) A person shall cease to be treated, for the purposes of this Act and the Care Standards Act 2000 as fostering and shall be treated as carrying on a children's home if –

    (a)   he exceeds the usual fostering limit; or

    (b)   where he is exempted under paragraph 4, –

        (i)   he fosters any child not named in the exemption; and

        (ii) in so doing, he exceeds the usual fostering limit.

(2) Sub-paragraph (1) does not apply if the children concerned are all siblings in respect of each other.

Amendments—Care Standards Act 2000, s 116, Sch 4, para 14(25).

6 Complaints etc

(1) Every local authority shall establish a procedure for considering any representations (including any complaint) made to them about the discharge of their functions under paragraph 4 by a person exempted or seeking to be exempted under that paragraph.

(2) In carrying out any consideration of representations under subparagraph (1), a local authority shall comply with any regulations made by the Secretary of State for the purposes of this paragraph.

SCHEDULE 8

PRIVATELY FOSTERED CHILDREN

Exemptions

1 A child is not a privately fostered child while he is being looked after by a local authority.

2 (1) A child is not a privately fostered child while he is in the care of any person –

    (a)   in premises in which any –

        (i)   parent of his;

        (ii) person who is not a parent of his but who has parental responsibility for him; or

        (iii) person who is a relative of his and who has assumed responsibility for his care,

        is for the time being living;

    (b)   (*repealed*)

    (c)   in accommodation provided by or on behalf of any voluntary organisation;

    (d)   in any school in which he is receiving full-time education;

    (e)   in any health service hospital;

    (f)   in any care home or independent hospital;

    (g)   in any home or institution not specified in this paragraph but provided, equipped and maintained by the Secretary of State.

(2) Sub-paragraph (1)(c) to (g) does not apply where the person caring for the child is doing so in his personal capacity and not in the course of carrying out his duties in relation to the establishment mentioned in the paragraph in question.

Amendments—Registered Homes (Amendment) Act 1991, s 2(6); Care Standards Act 2000, s 116, Sch 4, para 14(27),(28).

3 A child is not a privately fostered child while he is in the care of any person in compliance with –

  (a) a youth rehabilitation order made under section 1 of the Criminal Justice and Immigration Act 2008; or
  (b) a supervision requirement within the meaning of Part II of the Children (Scotland) Act 1995.

Amendments—Children (Scotland) Act 1995, s 105(4), Sch 4, para 48(1),(5); Powers of Criminal Courts (Sentencing) Act 2000, s 165, Sch 9, para 132; Criminal Justice and Immigration Act 2008, ss 6(2), 149, Sch 4, para 38.

4 A child is not a privately fostered child while he is liable to be detained, or subject to guardianship, under the Mental Health Act 1983.

5 A child is not a privately fostered child while he is placed in the care of a person who proposes to adopt him under arrangements made by an adoption agency within the meaning of –

  (a) section 2 of the Adoption and Children Act 2002;
  (b), (c)   ...

or while he is a child in respect of whom a local authority have functions by virtue of regulations under section 83(6)(b) of the Adoption and Children Act 2002 (which relates to children brought into the United Kingdom for adoption), or corresponding functions by virtue of regulations under section 1 of the Adoption (Intercountry Aspects) Act 1999 (regulations to give effect to Hague Convention on Protection of Children and Co-operation in respect of Intercountry Adoption).

Amendments—ACA 2002, Sch 3, para 73; CAA 2006, s 14(3).

6 Power of local authority to impose requirements

(1) Where a person is fostering any child privately, or proposes to foster any child privately, the appropriate local authority may impose on him requirements as to –

  (a) the number, age and sex of the children who may be privately fostered by him;
  (b) the standard of the accommodation and equipment to be provided for them;
  (c) the arrangements to be made with respect to their health and safety; and
  (d) particular arrangements which must be made with respect to the provision of care for them,

and it shall be his duty to comply with any such requirement before the end of such period as the authority may specify unless, in the case of a proposal, the proposal is not carried out.

(2) A requirement may be limited to a particular child, or class of child.

(3) A requirement (other than one imposed under sub-paragraph (1)(a)) may be limited by the authority so as to apply only when the number of children fostered by the person exceeds a specified number.

(4) A requirement shall be imposed by notice in writing addressed to the person on whom it is imposed and informing him of –

(a)   the reason for imposing the requirement;

(b)   his right under paragraph 8 to appeal against it; and

(c)   the time within which he may do so.

(5) A local authority may at any time vary any requirement, impose any additional requirement or remove any requirement.

(6) In this Schedule –

  (a)   "the appropriate local authority" means –

    (i)   the local authority within whose area the child is being fostered; or

    (ii)   in the case of a proposal to foster a child, the local authority within whose area it is proposed that he will be fostered; and

  (b)   "requirement", in relation to any person, means a requirement imposed on him under this paragraph.

7 Regulations requiring notification of fostering etc

(1) The Secretary of State may by regulations make provision as to –

  (a)   the circumstances in which notification is required to be given in connection with children who are, have been or are proposed to be fostered privately; and

  (b)   the manner and form in which such notification is to be given.

(2) The regulations may, in particular –

  (a)   require any person who is, or proposes to be, involved (whether or not directly) in arranging for a child to be fostered privately to notify the appropriate authority;

  (b)   require any person who is –

    (i)   a parent of a child; or

    (ii)   a person who is not a parent of his but who has parental responsibility for a child,

  and who knows that it is proposed that the child should be fostered privately, to notify the appropriate authority;

  (c)   require any parent of a privately fostered child, or person who is not a parent of such a child but who has parental responsibility for him, to notify the appropriate authority of any change in his address;

  (d)   require any person who proposes to foster a child privately, to notify the appropriate authority of his proposal;

  (e)   require any person who is fostering a child privately, or proposes to do so, to notify the appropriate authority of –

    (i)   any offence of which he has been convicted;

    (ii)   any disqualification imposed on him under section 68; or

    (iii)   any prohibition imposed on him under section 69;

  (f)   require any person who is fostering a child privately, to notify the appropriate authority of any change in his address;

  (g)   require any person who is fostering a child privately to notify the appropriate authority in writing of any person who begins, or ceases, to be part of his household;

  (h)   require any person who has been fostering a child privately, but has ceased to do so, to notify the appropriate authority (indicating, where the child has died, that that is the reason).

7A Every local authority must promote public awareness in their area of requirements as to notification for which provision is made under paragraph 7.

Amendments—CA 2004, s 44.

8 Appeals

(1) A person aggrieved by –

   (a) a requirement imposed under paragraph 6;

   (b) a refusal of consent under section 68;

   (c) a prohibition imposed under section 69;

   (d) a refusal to cancel such a prohibition;

   (e) a refusal to make an exemption under paragraph 4 of Schedule 7;

   (f) a condition imposed in such an exemption; or

   (g) a variation or cancellation of such an exemption,

may appeal to the court.

(2) The appeal must be made within fourteen days from the date on which the person appealing is notified of the requirement, refusal, prohibition, condition, variation or cancellation.

(3) Where the appeal is against –

   (a) a requirement imposed under paragraph 6;

   (b) a condition of an exemption imposed under paragraph 4 of Schedule 7; or

   (c) a variation or cancellation of such an exemption,

the requirement, condition, variation or cancellation shall not have effect while the appeal is pending.

(4) Where it allows an appeal against a requirement or prohibition, the court may, instead of cancelling the requirement or prohibition –

   (a) vary the requirement, or allow more time for compliance with it; or

   (b) if an absolute prohibition has been imposed, substitute for it a prohibition on using the premises after such time as the court may specify unless such specified requirements as the local authority had power to impose under paragraph 6 are complied with.

(5) Any requirement or prohibition specified or substituted by a court under this paragraph shall be deemed for the purposes of Part IX (other than this paragraph) to have been imposed by the local authority under paragraph 6 or (as the case may be) section 69.

(6) Where it allows an appeal against a refusal to make an exemption, a condition imposed in such an exemption or a variation or cancellation of such an exemption, the court may –

   (a) make an exemption;

   (b) impose a condition; or

   (c) vary the exemption.

(7) Any exemption made or varied under sub-paragraph (6), or any condition imposed under that sub-paragraph, shall be deemed for the purposes of Schedule 7 (but not for the purpose of this paragraph) to have been made, varied or imposed under that Schedule.

(8) Nothing in sub-paragraph (1)(e) to (g) confers any right of appeal on –

   (a) a person who is, or would be if exempted under Schedule 7, a local authority foster parent; or

   (b) a person who is, or would be if so exempted, a person with whom a child is placed by a voluntary organisation.

Jurisdiction—ATPO 2008, art 5(1)(c) requires proceedings under Sch 8, para 8 to be commenced in a magistrates' court. Article 15(2) has the effect of preventing proceedings so commenced from being transferred to a county court; jurisdiction is therefore restricted, in effect, to magistrates' courts.

"person aggrieved" (para 8(1))—Despite the apparently wide category of potential appellants, the restrictions contained in para 8(8) apply.

"**section 68**" (para 8(1)(b))—Section 68 relates to the need to obtain the consent of the local authority to foster a child privately.

"**section 69**" (para 8(1)(c))—Section 69 empowers a local authority to prohibit private fostering.

"**paragraph 4 of Schedule 7**" (para 8(1)(e))—Schedule 7, para 4 allows a local authority to provide an exemption from the usual fostering limit.

9 Extension of Part IX to certain school children during holidays

(1) Where a child under sixteen who is a pupil at a school lives at the school during school holidays for a period of more than two weeks, Part IX shall apply in relation to the child as if –

    (a)   while living at the school, he were a privately fostered child; and

    (b)   paragraphs 2(1)(c) and (d) and 6 were omitted.

But this sub-paragraph does not apply to a school which is a children's home in respect of which a person is registered under Part 2 of the Care Standards Act 2000.

(2) Sub-paragraph (3) applies to any person who proposes to care for and accommodate one or more children at a school in circumstances in which some or all of them will be treated as private foster children by virtue of this paragraph.

(3) That person shall, not less than two weeks before the first of those children is treated as a private foster child by virtue of this paragraph during the holiday in question, give written notice of his proposal to the local authority within whose area the child is ordinarily resident ("the appropriate authority"), stating the estimated number of the children.

(4) A local authority may exempt any person from the duty of giving notice under sub-paragraph (3).

(5) Any such exemption may be granted for a special period or indefinitely and may be revoked at any time by notice in writing given to the person exempted.

(6) Where a child who is treated as a private foster child by virtue of this paragraph dies, the person caring for him at the school shall, not later than 48 hours after the death, give written notice of it –

    (a)   to the appropriate local authority; and

    (b)   where reasonably practicable, to each parent of the child and to every person who is not a parent of his but who has parental responsibility for him.

(7) Where a child who is treated as a foster child by virtue of this paragraph ceases for any other reason to be such a child, the person caring for him at the school shall give written notice of the fact to the appropriate local authority.

Amendments—Care Standards Act 2000, ss 110, 116, Sch 4, para 14(27); CYAP 2008, s 8(3), Sch 1, para 6.

10 Prohibition of advertisements relating to fostering

No advertisement indicating that a person will undertake, or will arrange for, a child to be privately fostered shall be published, unless it states that person's name and address.

11 Avoidance of insurances on lives of privately fostered children

A person who fosters a child privately and for reward shall be deemed for the purposes of the Life Assurance Act 1774 to have no interest in the life of the child.

****

SCHEDULE 9A
CHILD MINDING AND DAY CARE FOR YOUNG CHILDREN IN WALES

1 Exemption of certain schools

(1) Except in prescribed circumstances, Part XA does not apply to provision of day care within sub-paragraph (2) for any child looked after in –

    (a)   a maintained school;

    (b)   a school assisted by a local authority;

    (c)   a school in respect of which payments are made by the Assembly under section 485 of the Education Act 1996;

    (d)   an independent school.

(2) The provision mentioned in sub-paragraph (1) is provision of day care made by –

    (a)   the person carrying on the establishment in question as part of the establishment's activities; or

    (b)   a person employed to work at that establishment and authorised to make that provision as part of the establishment's activities.

(3) In sub-paragraph (1) –

"assisted" has the same meaning as in the Education Act 1996;

"maintained school" has the meaning given by section 20(7) of the School Standards and Framework Act 1998.

Amendments—Childcare Act 2006, s 103, Sch 2, paras 6, 18, Sch 3, Pt 2; SI 2010/1185.

2 Exemption for other establishments

(1) Part XA does not apply to provision of day care within sub-paragraph (2) for any child looked after –

    (a)   in a children's home in respect of which a person is registered under Part 2 of the Care Standards Act 2000;

    (b)   in a care home;

    (c)   as a patient in a hospital (within the meaning of the Care Standards Act 2000);

    (d)   in a residential family centre.

(2) The provision mentioned in sub-paragraph (1) is provision of day care made by –

    (a)   the department, authority or other person carrying on the establishment in question as part of the establishment's activities; or

    (b)   a person employed to work at that establishment and authorised to make that provision as part of the establishment's activities.

Amendments—CYAP 2008, s 8(3), Sch 1, para 7.

2A (1) Part XA does not apply to provision of day care in a hotel, guest house or other similar establishment for children staying in that establishment where –

    (a)   the provision takes place only between 6pm and 2am; and

    (b)   the person providing the care is doing so for no more than two different clients at the same time.

(2) For the purposes of sub-paragraph (1)(b), a "client" is a person at whose request (or persons at whose joint request) day care is provided for a child.

Amendments—CA 2004, s 48, Sch 4, paras 1, 7.

3 Exemption for occasional facilities

(1) Where day care is provided on particular premises on less than six days in any year, that provision shall be disregarded for the purposes of Part XA if the person making it has notified the Assembly in writing before the first occasion on which the premises concerned are so used in that year.

(2) In sub-paragraph (1) "year" means the year beginning with the day (after the commencement of paragraph 5 of Schedule 9) on which the day care in question was or is first provided on the premises concerned and any subsequent year.

Amendments—Childcare Act 2006, s 103, Sch 2, para 6.

4 Disqualification for registration

(1) Regulations may provide for a person to be disqualified for registration for child minding or providing day care in Wales.

(2) The regulations may, in particular, provide for a person to be disqualified where –

- (a)   he is included in the list kept under section 1 of the Protection of Children Act 1999;
- (b)   he is subject to a direction under section 142 of the Education Act 2002, given on the grounds that he is unsuitable to work with children or on grounds relating to his health;
- (c)   an order of a prescribed kind has been made at any time with respect to him;
- (d)   an order of a prescribed kind has been made at any time with respect to any child who has been in his care;
- (e)   a requirement of a prescribed kind has been imposed at any time with respect to such a child, under or by virtue of any enactment;
- (f)   he has at any time been refused registration under Part X or Part XA, or Part 3 of the Childcare Act 2006, or any prescribed enactment or had any such registration cancelled;
- (g)   he has been convicted of any offence of a prescribed kind, or has been discharged absolutely or conditionally for any such offence;
- (ga) he has been given a caution in respect of any offence of a prescribed kind;
- (h)   he has at any time been disqualified from fostering a child privately;
- (j)   a prohibition has been imposed on him at any time under section 69, section 10 of the Foster Children (Scotland) Act 1984 or any prescribed enactment;
- (k)   his rights and powers with respect to a child have at any time been vested in a prescribed authority under a prescribed enactment.

(3) Regulations may provide for a person who lives –

- (a)   in the same household as a person who is himself disqualified for registration for child minding or providing day care in Wales; or
- (b)   in a household at which any such person is employed,

to be disqualified for registration for child minding or providing day care in Wales.

(3A) ...

(4) A person who is disqualified for registration for providing day care in Wales shall not provide day care in Wales, or be directly concerned in the management of any provision of day care in Wales.

(5) No person shall employ, in connection with the provision of day care in Wales, a person who is disqualified for registration for providing day care in Wales.

(6) In this paragraph –

"caution" includes a reprimand or warning within the meaning of section 65 of the Crime and Disorder Act 1998;

"enactment" means any enactment having effect, at any time, in any part of the United Kingdom.

(7) A conviction in respect of which a probation order was made before 1 October 1992 (which would not otherwise be treated as a conviction) is to be treated as a conviction for the purposes of this paragraph.

Amendments—Criminal Justice Act 2003, Sch 32, Pt 1, para 61; CA 2004, s 48, Sch 4, paras 1, 8; Childcare Act 2006, ss 102(1),(2)(a),(b), 103, Sch 2, paras 6, 18.

5 (1) If any person –

(a) acts as a child minder in Wales at any time when he is disqualified for registration for child minding in Wales; or

(b) contravenes any of sub-paragraphs (3) to (5) of paragraph 4,

he shall be guilty of an offence.

(2) Where a person contravenes sub-paragraph (3) of paragraph 4, he shall not be guilty of an offence under this paragraph if he proves that he did not know, and had no reasonable grounds for believing, that the person in question was living or employed in the household.

(3) Where a person contravenes sub-paragraph (5) of paragraph 4, he shall not be guilty of an offence under this paragraph if he proves that he did not know, and had no reasonable grounds for believing, that the person whom he was employing was disqualified.

(4) A person guilty of an offence under this paragraph shall be liable on summary conviction to imprisonment for a term not exceeding six months, or to a fine not exceeding level 5 on the standard scale, or to both.

5A (1) References in Part XA to a person, so far as relating to the provision of day care, include an unincorporated association.

(2) Proceedings for an offence under Part XA which is alleged to have been committed by an unincorporated association must be brought in the name of the association (and not in that of any of its members).

(3) For the purpose of any such proceedings, rules of court relating to the service of documents are to have effect as if the association were a body corporate.

(4) In proceedings for an offence under Part XA brought against an unincorporated association, section 33 of the Criminal Justice Act 1925 and Schedule 3 to the Magistrates' Courts Act 1980 (procedure) apply as they do in relation to a body corporate.

(5) A fine imposed on an unincorporated association on its conviction of an offence under Part XA is to be paid out of the funds of the association.

(6) If an offence under Part XA committed by an unincorporated association is shown–

(a) to have been committed with the consent or connivance of an officer of the association or a member of its governing body, or

(b) to be attributable to any neglect on the part of such an officer or member,

the officer or member as well as the association is guilty of the offence and liable to proceeded against and punished accordingly.

Amendments—Inserted by CA 2004, s 48, Sch 4, paras 1, 9.

6 Certificates of registration

(1) If an application for registration is granted, the Assembly shall give the applicant a certificate of registration.

(2) A certificate of registration shall give prescribed information about prescribed matters.

(3) Where, due to a change of circumstances, any part of the certificate requires to be amended, the Assembly shall issue an amended certificate.

(4) Where the Assembly is satisfied that the certificate has been lost or destroyed, the Assembly shall issue a copy, on payment by the registered person of any prescribed fee.

(5) For the purposes of Part XA, a person is –

    (a)   registered for providing child minding in Wales; or
    (b)   registered for providing day care on any premises in Wales,

if a certificate of registration to that effect is in force in respect of him.

Amendments—Childcare Act 2006, s 103, Sch 2, paras 6, 18.

7 Fees

Regulations may require registered persons to pay to the Assembly, at or by the prescribed times, fees of the prescribed amounts in respect of the discharge by the Assembly of its functions under Part XA.

Amendments—CA 2004, ss 48, 64, Sch 4, paras 1, 4(2)(b), Sch 5, Pt 2; Childcare Act 2006, s 103, Sch 2, para 6.

8 Co-operation between authorities

(1) *(repealed)*

(2) Where it appears to the Assembly that any local authority in Wales could, by taking any specified action, help in the exercise of any of its functions under Part XA, the Assembly may request the help of that authority specifying the action in question.

(3) An authority whose help is so requested shall comply with the request if it is compatible with their own statutory or other duties and obligations and does not unduly prejudice the discharge of any of their functions.

Amendments—Schedule inserted by Care Standards Act 2000, s 79(2), Sch 3; amended by Education Act 2002, s 215(1), Sch 21; Childcare Act 2006, s 103, Sch 2, para 18, Sch 3, Pt 2.

****

Civil Jurisdiction and Judgments Act 1982

ARRANGEMENT OF SECTIONS

PART I
IMPLEMENTATION OF THE CONVENTIONS

Main implementing provisions

PART IV
MISCELLANEOUS PROVISIONS

Provisions relating to jurisdiction

PART I
IMPLEMENTATION OF THE CONVENTIONS

Main implementing provisions

1 Interpretation of references to the Conventions and Contracting States

(1) In this Act –

"the 1968 Convention" means the Convention on jurisdiction and the enforcement of
judgments in civil and commercial matters (including the Protocol annexed to
that Convention), signed at Brussels on 27 September 1968;

...

"the 2007 Hague Convention" means the Convention on the International Recovery
of Child Support and other forms of Family Maintenance done at The Hague on
23 November 2007;

PART II

"the Brussels Conventions" means the 1968 Convention, the 1971 Protocol, the Accession Convention, the 1982 Accession Convention, the 1989 Accession Convention and the 1996 Accession Convention;

"the Lugano Convention" means the Convention on jurisdiction and the recognition and enforcement of judgments in civil and commercial matters, between the European Community and the Republic of Iceland, the Kingdom of Norway, the Swiss Confederation and the Kingdom of Denmark signed on behalf of the European Community on 30 October 2007;

"the Maintenance Regulation" means Council Regulation (EC) No 4/2009 including as applied in relation to Denmark by virtue of the Agreement made on 19 October 2005 between the European Community and the Kingdom of Denmark;

"the Regulation" means Council Regulation (EC) No. 44/2001 of 22 December 2000 on jurisdiction and the recognition and enforcement of judgments in civil and commercial matters, as amended from time to time and as applied by the Agreement made on 19 October 2005 between the European Community and the Kingdom of Denmark on jurisdiction and the recognition and enforcement of judgments in civil and commercial matters (OJ No. L 299 16.11.2005 at p 62).

(2) ...

(3) In this Act –

"2007 Hague Convention State", in any provision, in the application of that provision in relation to the 2007 Hague Convention, means a State bound by that Convention;

"Contracting State", without more, in any provision means –

(a) in the application of the provision in relation to the Brussels Convention, a Brussels Contracting State; and

(b) in the application of the provision in relation to the Lugano Convention, a State bound by the Lugano Convention;

"Brussels Contracting State" means a state which is one of the original parties to the 1968 Convention or one of the parties acceding to that Convention under the Accession Convention, or under the 1982 Accession Convention, or under the 1989 Accession Convention, but only with respect to any territory –

(a) to which the Brussels Conventions apply; and

(b) which is excluded from the scope of the Regulation pursuant to Articles 349 and 355 of the Treaty on the Functioning of the European Union;

"Maintenance Regulation State", in any provision, in the application of that provision in relation to the Maintenance Regulation means a Member State;

"State bound by the Lugano Convention" in any provision, in the application of that provision in relation to the Lugano Convention has the same meaning as in Article 1(3) of that Convention;

"Regulation State" in any provision, in the application of that provision in relation to the Regulation, means a Member State.

(4) ...

Amendments—SI 1989/1346; SI 1990/2591; CJJA 1991, s 2; SI 2000/1824; SI 2001/3929; SI 2007/1655; SI 2009/3131; SI 2011/1215; SI 2012/1770; SI 2012/1809.

2 The Brussels Conventions to have the force of law

(1) The Brussels Conventions shall have the force of law in the United Kingdom, and judicial notice shall be taken of them.

(2) ...

Defined terms—"The Brussels Conventions": s 1(1).

****

Supplementary provisions as to recognition and enforcement of judgments
****

5 Recognition and enforcement of maintenance orders

(1) The function of transmitting to the appropriate court an application under Article 31 of the 1968 Convention for the recognition or enforcement in the United Kingdom of a maintenance order shall be discharged –

   (a)   as respects England and Wales, by the Lord Chancellor;

   (b)   as respects Scotland, by the Secretary of State; and

   (c)   as respects Northern Ireland, by the Department of Justice in Northern Ireland.

In this subsection "the appropriate court" means the magistrates' court or sheriff court having jurisdiction in the matter in accordance with the second paragraph of Article 32.

(2) Such an application shall be determined in the first instance by the prescribed officer of that court.

(3) Where on such an application the enforcement of the order is authorised to any extent, the order shall to that extent be registered in the prescribed manner in that court.

(4) A maintenance order registered under this section shall, for the purposes of its enforcement, be of the same force and effect, the registering court shall have in relation to its enforcement the same powers, and proceedings for or with respect to its enforcement may be taken, as if the order had been originally made by the registering court.

(5) Subsection (4) is subject to Article 39 (restriction on enforcement where appeal pending or time for appeal unexpired), to section 7 and to any provision made by rules of court as to the manner in which and conditions subject to which an order registered under this section may be enforced.

(5A) A maintenance order which by virtue of this section is enforceable by a magistrates' court in England and Wales shall, subject to the modifications of sections 76 and 93 of the Magistrates' Courts Act 1980 specified in subsections (5B) and (5C) below, be enforceable in the same manner as a magistrates' court maintenance order made by that court.

In this subsection "magistrates' court maintenance order" has the same meaning as in section 150(1) of the Magistrates' Courts Act 1980.

(5B) Section 76 (enforcement of sums adjudged to be paid) shall have effect as if for subsections (4) to (6) there were substituted the following subsections –

   "(4) Where proceedings are brought for the enforcement of a magistrates' court maintenance order under this section, the court may vary the order by exercising one of its powers under subsection (5) below.

   (5) The powers of the court are –

      (a)   the power to order that payments under the order be made directly to the designated officer for the court or for any other magistrates' court;

      (b)   the power to order that payments under the order be made to the designated officer for the court or for any other magistrates' court, by such method of payment falling within section 59(6) above (standing order, etc) as may be specified;

(c)   the power to make an attachment of earnings order under the Attachment of Earnings Act 1971 to secure payments under the order.

(6) In deciding which of the powers under subsection (5) above it is to exercise, the court shall have regard to any representations made by the debtor (within the meaning of section 59 above).

(7) Subsection (4) of section 59 above (power of court to require debtor to open account) shall apply for the purposes of subsection (5) above as it applies for the purposes of that section but as if for paragraph (a) there were substituted –

'(a)   the court proposes to exercise its power under paragraph (b) of section 76(5) below, and'."

(5C) In section 93 (complaint for arrears), subsection (6) (court not to impose imprisonment in certain circumstances) shall have effect as if for paragraph (b) there were substituted –

"(b)   if the court is of the opinion that it is appropriate –
  (i)   to make an attachment of earnings order, or
  (ii)   to exercise its power under paragraph (b) of section 76(5) above."

(6) A maintenance order which by virtue of this section is enforceable by a magistrates' court in Northern Ireland shall, subject to the modifications of Article 98 of the Magistrates' Courts (Northern Ireland) Order 1981 specified in subsection (6A) below, be enforceable as an order made by that court to which that Article applies.

(6A) …

(7) The payer under a maintenance order registered under this section in a magistrates' court in England and Wales or Northern Ireland shall give notice of any change of address to the clerk of that court.

A person who without reasonable excuse fails to comply with this subsection shall be guilty of an offence and liable on summary conviction to a fine not exceeding level 2 on the standard scale.

Amendments—Criminal Justice Act 1982, s 46; FLRA 1987, s 33(1), Sch 2, para 89; CJJA 1991, s 3, Sch 2, para 2; MEA 1991, s 10, Sch 1, para 21; SI 1992/709; SI 1993/1576; SI 1995/755; Courts Act 2003, Sch 8, para 268; SI 2009/3131; SI 2010/976.

Defined terms—"maintenance order": s 15(1).

"level 2 on the standard scale" (s 5(7))—Currently £500 (Criminal Justice Act 1982, s 37(2), as substituted).

5A Recognition and enforcement of maintenance orders under the Lugano Convention

(1) The Secretary of State's function (under Article 39 and Annex II of the Lugano Convention) of transmitting to the appropriate court an application for the recognition or enforcement in the United Kingdom of a maintenance order (made under Article 38 of the Lugano Convention) shall be discharged –

(a)   as respects England and Wales by the Lord Chancellor; and
(b)   as respects Scotland, by the Scottish Ministers; and
(c)   as respects Northern Ireland, by the Department of Justice in Northern Ireland.

In this subsection "the appropriate court" means the magistrates' court or sheriff court having jurisdiction in the matter in accordance with the second paragraph of Article 39.

(2) Such an application shall be determined in the first instance by the prescribed officer of the court having jurisdiction in the matter.

(3) A maintenance order registered under the Lugano Convention shall, for the purposes of its enforcement, be of the same force and effect, the registering court shall have in relation to its enforcement the same powers, and proceedings for or with respect to its enforcement may be taken, as if the order had been made by the registering court.

(4) Subsection (3) is subject to Article 47 of the Lugano Convention (restriction on enforcement where appeal pending or time for appeal unexpired), to subsection (6) and to any provision made by rules of court as to the manner in which and conditions subject to which an order registered under the Lugano Convention may be enforced.

(5) A maintenance order which by virtue of the Lugano Convention is enforceable by a magistrates' court in England and Wales shall, subject to the modifications of sections 76 and 93 of the Magistrates' Courts Act 1980 specified in sections 5(5B) and 5(5C) of the Act, be enforceable in the same manner as a magistrates' court maintenance order made by that court.

In this subsection "magistrates' court maintenance order" has the same meaning as in section 150(1) of the Magistrates' Courts Act 1980.

(6) A maintenance order which by virtue of the Lugano Convention is enforceable by a magistrates' court in Northern Ireland shall, subject to the modifications of Article 98 of the Magistrates' Courts (Northern Ireland) Order 1981 specified in section 5(6A) of this Act, be enforceable as an order made by that court to which that Article applies.

(7) The payer under a maintenance order registered under the Lugano Convention in a magistrates' court in England and Wales or Northern Ireland shall give notice of any change of address to the proper officer of that court.

(8) A person who without reasonable excuse fails to comply with subsection (7) shall be guilty of an offence and liable on summary conviction to a fine not exceeding level 2 on the standard scale.

(9) In subsection (7) "proper officer" means –

    (a)   in relation to a magistrates' court in England and Wales, the designated officer; and

    (b)   in relation to a magistrates' court in Northern Ireland, the clerk of the court.

Amendments—Inserted by SI 2009/3131; amended by SI 2010/976.

6 Appeals under Article 37, second paragraph and Article 41

(1) The single further appeal on a point of law referred to in the 1968 Convention in Article 37, second paragraph and Article 41 in relation to the recognition or enforcement of a judgment other than a maintenance order lies –

    (a)   in England and Wales or Northern Ireland, to the Court of Appeal or to the Supreme Court in accordance with Part II of the Administration of Justice Act 1969 (appeals direct from the High Court to the Supreme Court);

    (b)   *(applies to Scotland only)*

(2) Paragraph (a) of subsection (1) has effect notwithstanding section 15(2) of the Administration of Justice Act 1969 (exclusion of direct appeal to the Supreme Court in cases where no appeal to the Supreme Court lies from a decision of the Court of Appeal).

(3) The single further appeal on a point of law referred to in the 1968 Convention in Article 37, second paragraph and Article 41 in relation to the recognition or enforcement of a maintenance order lies –

    (a)   in England and Wales, to a county court in accordance with section 111A of the Magistrates' Courts Act 1980;

    (b)   *(applies to Scotland only)*

    (c)   in Northern Ireland, to the Court of Appeal.

Amendments—CJJA 1991, s 3, Sch 2, para 3; SI 2009/871; CRA 2005, Sch 9, para 39; SI 2009/3131.

Defined terms—"1968 Convention", "the Lugano Convention": s 1(1); "maintenance order": s 15(1).

6A Appeals under Article 44 and Annex IV of the Lugano Convention

(1) The single further appeal on a point of law referred to in Article 44 and Annex IV of the Lugano Convention in relation to the recognition or enforcement of a judgment other than a maintenance order lies –

    (a)   in England and Wales or Northern Ireland, to the Court of Appeal or to the Supreme Court in accordance with Part II of the Administration of Justice Act 1969 (appeals direct from the High Court to the Supreme Court);

    (b)   in Scotland, to the Inner House of the Court of Session.

(2) Paragraph (a) of subsection (1) has effect notwithstanding section 15(2) of the Administration of Justice Act 1969 (exclusion of direct appeal to the Supreme Court in cases where no appeal to that House lies from a decision of the Court of Appeal).

(3) The single further appeal on a point of law referred to in Article 44 and Annex IV of the Lugano Convention in relation to the recognition or enforcement of a maintenance order lies –

    (a)   in England and Wales, to a county court in accordance with section 111A of the Magistrates' Courts Act 1980;

    (b)   in Scotland, to the Inner House of the Court of Session;

    (c)   in Northern Ireland, to the Court of Appeal.

Amendments—Inserted by SI 2009/3131.

7 Interest on registered judgments

(1) Subject to subsection (4), where in connection with an application for registration of a judgment under section 4, 4A, 5 or 5A the applicant shows –

    (a)   that the judgment provides for the payment of a sum of money; and

    (b)   that in accordance with the law of the Contracting State in which the judgment was given interest on that sum is recoverable under the judgment from a particular date or time,

the rate of interest and the date or time from which it is so recoverable shall be registered with the judgment and, subject to any provision made under subsection (2), the debt resulting, apart from section 4(2), from the registration of the judgment shall carry interest in accordance with the registered particulars.

(2) Provision may be made by rules of court as to the manner in which and the periods by reference to which any interest payable by virtue of subsection (1) is to be calculated and paid, including provision for such interest to cease to accrue as from a prescribed date.

(3) Costs or expenses recoverable by virtue of section 4(2) shall carry interest as if they were the subject of an order for the payment of costs or expenses made by the registering court on the date of registration.

(4) Interest on arrears of sums payable under a maintenance order registered under section 5 in a magistrates' court in England and Wales or Northern Ireland shall not be recoverable in that court, but without prejudice to the operation in relation to any such order of section 2A of the Maintenance Orders Act 1958 or section 11A of the Maintenance and Affiliation Orders Act (Northern Ireland) 1966 (which enable interest to be recovered if the order is re-registered for enforcement in the High Court).

(5) Except as mentioned in subsection (4), debts under judgments registered under section 4, 4A, 5 or 5A shall carry interest only as provided by this section.

Amendments—SI 2009/3131.

Defined terms—"Contracting State": s 1(3); "judgment", "maintenance order": s 15(1).

Scope—This section makes limited provision for the enforcement of interest on registered orders. Interest may only be enforced if the original judgment provided for the payment of interest (no more than 6 years' interest may be recovered (*Lowsley and another v Forbes* [1998] 3 All ER 897, HL)).

"shall not be recoverable" (s 7(4))—Interest may not be recovered in a magistrates' court, although re-registration for enforcement in the High Court is possible.

8 Currency of payment under registered maintenance orders

(1) Sums payable in the United Kingdom under a maintenance order by virtue of its registration under section 5 or 5A, including any arrears so payable, shall be paid in the currency of the United Kingdom.

(2) Where the order is expressed in any other currency, the amounts shall be converted on the basis of the exchange rate prevailing on the date of registration of the order.

(3) For the purposes of this section, a written certificate purporting to be signed by an officer of any bank in the United Kingdom and stating the exchange rate prevailing on a specified date shall be evidence, and in Scotland sufficient evidence, of the facts stated.

Amendments—SI 2009/3131.

Defined terms—"maintenance order": s 15(1).

****

Other supplementary provisions
****

11 Proof of admissibility of certain judgments and related documents

(1) For the purposes of the 1968 Convention –

    (a)   a document, duly authenticated, which purports to be a copy of a judgment given by a court of a Contracting State other than the United Kingdom shall without further proof be deemed to be a true copy, unless the contrary is shown; and

    (b)   the original or a copy of any such document as is mentioned in Article 46(2) or 47 (supporting documents to be produced by a party seeking recognition or enforcement of a judgment) shall be evidence, and in Scotland sufficient evidence, of any matter to which it relates.

(2) A document purporting to be a copy of a judgment given by any such court as is mentioned in subsection (1)(a) is duly authenticated for the purposes of this section if it purports –

    (a)   to bear the seal of that court; or

    (b)   to be certified by any person in his capacity as a judge or officer of that court to be a true copy of a judgement given by that court.

(3) Nothing in this section shall prejudice the admission in evidence of any document which is admissible apart from this section.

Amendments—CJJA 1991, s 3, Sch 2, para 6; SI 2009/3131.

Defined terms—"Contracting State": s 1(3); "judgment": s 15(1); "the 1968 Convention", "the Lugano Convention": s 1(1).

11A Proof and admissibility of certain judgments and related documents for the purposes of the Lugano Convention

(1) For the purposes of the Lugano Convention –

(a) a document, duly authenticated, which purports to be a copy of a judgment given by a court of a State bound by the Lugano Convention other than the United Kingdom shall without further proof be deemed to be a true copy, unless the contrary is shown; and

(b) a certificate obtained in accordance with Article 54 and Annex V shall be evidence, and in Scotland sufficient evidence, that the judgment is enforceable in the State of origin which is bound by the Lugano Convention.

(2) A document purporting to be a copy of a judgment given by any such court as is mentioned in subsection (1)(a) is duly authenticated for the purposes of this section if it purports –

(a) to bear the seal of that court; or

(b) to be certified by any person in his capacity as a judge or officer of that court to be a true copy of a judgment given by that court.

(3) Nothing in this section shall prejudice the admission in evidence of any document which is admissible apart from this section.

Amendments—Inserted by SI 2009/3131.

12 Provision for issue of copies of, and certificates in connection with, UK judgments

Rules of court may make provision for enabling any interested party wishing to secure under the 1968 Convention or the Lugano Convention the recognition or enforcement in another Contracting State of a judgment given by a court in the United Kingdom to obtain, subject to any conditions specified in the rules –

(a) a copy of the judgment; and

(b) a certificate giving particulars relating to the judgment and the proceedings in which it was given.

Amendments—CJJA 1991, s 3, Sch 2, para 7.

Defined terms—"Contracting State": s 1(3); "judgment": s 15(1), "the 1968 Convention", "the Lugano Convention": s 1(1).

Scope—This section provides for rules to be made concerning the issue of copies of, and certificates in connection with, maintenance orders: see FPR 2010, r 34.39.

****

15 Interpretation of Part I and consequential amendments

(1) In this Part, unless the context otherwise requires –

"judgment" has the meaning given by Article 25 of the 1968 Convention or, as the case may be, Article 32 of the Lugano Convention;

"maintenance order" means a maintenance judgment within the meaning of the 1968 Convention or, as the case may be, the Lugano Convention;

"payer", in relation to a maintenance order, means the person liable to make the payments for which the order provides;

"prescribed" means prescribed by rules of court.

(2) References in this Part to a judgment registered under section 4, 4A, 5 or 5A include, to the extent of its registration, references to a judgment so registered to a limited extent only.

(3) Anything authorised or required by the 1968 Convention, the Lugano Convention or this Part to be done by, to or before a particular magistrates' court may be done by, to or before any magistrates' court acting in the same local justice area (or, in Northern Ireland, for the same, petty sessions district) as that court.

(4) The enactments specified in Part I of Schedule 12 shall have effect with the amendments specified there, being amendments consequential on this Part.

Amendments—CJJA 1991, s 3, Sch 2, para 10; Courts Act 2003, Sch 8, para 269; SI 2009/3131.

****

PART IV
MISCELLANEOUS PROVISIONS

Provisions relating to jurisdiction

****

25 Interim relief in England and Wales and Northern Ireland in the absence of substantive proceedings

(1) The High Court in England and Wales or Northern Ireland shall have power to grant interim relief where –

    (a) proceedings have been or are to be commenced in a Brussels Contracting State or a State bound by the Lugano Convention or a Regulation State or a Maintenance Regulation State other than the United Kingdom or in a part of the United Kingdom other than that in which the High Court in question exercises jurisdiction; and

    (b) they are or will be proceedings whose subject-matter is either within the scope of the Regulation as determined by Article 1 of the Regulation, within the scope of the Maintenance Regulation as determined by Article 1 of that Regulation or within the scope of the Lugano Convention as determined by Article 1 of the Lugano Convention (whether or not the Regulation, the Maintenance Regulation or the Lugano Convention has effect in relation to the proceedings).

(2) On an application for any interim relief under subsection (1) the court may refuse to grant that relief if, in the opinion of the court, the fact that the court has no jurisdiction apart from this section in relation to the subject-matter of the proceedings in question makes it inexpedient for the court to grant it.

(3) Her Majesty may by Order in Council extend the power to grant interim relief conferred by subsection (1) so as to make it exercisable in relation to proceedings of any of the following descriptions, namely –

    (a) proceedings commenced or to be commenced otherwise than in a Brussels Contracting State or a State bound by the Lugano Convention or Regulation State or a Maintenance Regulation State;

    (b) proceedings whose subject-matter is not within the scope of the Regulation as determined by Article 1 of the Regulation, the Maintenance Regulation as determined by Article 1 of that Regulation or the Lugano Convention as determined by Article 1 of the Lugano Convention.

    (c) *(repealed)*

(4) An Order in Council under subsection (3) –

    (a) may confer power to grant only specified descriptions of interim relief;

    (b) may make different provision for different classes of proceedings, for proceedings pending in different countries or courts outside the United Kingdom or in different parts of the United Kingdom, and for other different circumstances; and

    (c)   may impose conditions or restrictions on the exercise of any power conferred by the Order.

(5) *(repealed)*

(6) Any Order in Council under subsection (3) shall be subject to annulment in pursuance of a resolution of either House of Parliament.

(7) In this section "interim relief", in relation to the High Court in England and Wales or Northern Ireland, means interim relief of any kind which that court has power to grant in proceedings relating to matters within its jurisdiction, other than –

    (a)   a warrant for the arrest of property; or

    (b)   provision for obtaining evidence.

Amendments—CJJA 1991, s 3, Sch 2, para 12; Arbitration Act 1996, s 107(2), Sch 4; SI 2001/3929; SI 2009/3131; SI 2011/1484.

Scope—Where there are proceedings for financial relief outside the UK, this section enables the court, by injunction or other interim orders, to preserve the assets which are the subject of that overseas litigation. *Credit Suisse Fides Trust SA v Cuoghi* [1998] QB 818 and *Ryan v Friction Dynamics* [2001] CP Rep 75 set out the principles governing the court's jurisdiction to grant interim relief.

****

Provisions relating to recognition and enforcement of judgments
****

36 Registration of maintenance orders in Northern Ireland

(1) Where –

    (a)   a High Court order or a Court of Session order has been registered in the High Court of Justice in Northern Ireland ("the Northern Ireland High Court") under Part II of the Maintenance Orders Act 1950; or

    (b)   a county court order, a magistrates' court order or a sheriff court order has been registered in a court of summary jurisdiction in Northern Ireland under that Part,

an application may be made to the original court for the registration of the order in, respectively, a court of summary jurisdiction in Northern Ireland or the Northern Ireland High Court.

(2) In subsection (1) "the original court", in relation to an order, means the court by which the order was made.

(3) Section 2 (except subsection (6A)) and section 2A of the Maintenance Orders Act 1958 shall have effect for the purposes of an application under subsection (1), and subsections (2), (3), (4) and (4A) of section 5 of that Act shall have effect for the purposes of the cancellation of a registration made on such an application, as if –

    (a)   "registration" in those provisions included registration in the appropriate Northern Ireland court ("registered" being construed accordingly);

    (b)   any reference in those provisions to a High Court order or a magistrates' court order included, respectively, a Court of Session order or a sheriff court order; and

(c)   any other reference in those provisions to the High Court or a magistrates' court included the Northern Ireland High Court or a court of summary jurisdiction in Northern Ireland.

(d)   for section 2(6), there were substituted the following subsections –

"(6)   Where a magistrates' court order is registered under this Part of this Act in the High Court, then –

(a)   if payments under the magistrates' court order are required to be made (otherwise than to a collecting officer) by any method of payment falling within Article 85(7) of the Magistrates' Courts (Northern Ireland) Order 1981 (standing order, etc), any order requiring payment by that method shall continue to have effect after registration;

(b)   any order by virtue of which sums payable under the magistrates' court order are required to be paid to the collecting officer (whether or not by any method of payment falling within Article 85(7) of that Order) on behalf of the person entitled thereto shall cease to have effect.

(6ZA)   Where a High Court or county court order is registered under this Part of this Act in a magistrates' court, then –

(a)   if a means of payment order (within the meaning of Article 96A(7) of the Judgments Enforcement (Northern Ireland) Order 1981) has effect in relation to the order in question, it shall continue to have effect after registration; and

(b)   in any other case, the magistrates' court shall order that all payments to be made under the order in question (including any arrears accrued before registration) shall be made to the collecting officer.

(6ZB)   Any such order as to payment –

(a)   as is referred to in paragraph (a) of subsection (6) of this section may be revoked, suspended, revived or varied by an exercise of the powers conferred by section 13A of the Maintenance and Affiliation Orders Act (Northern Ireland) 1966; and

(b)   as is referred to in paragraph (a) or (b) of subsection (6ZA) of this section may be varied or revoked by an exercise of the powers conferred by section 12(2) or 13(2A) or (5A) of that Act of 1966.

(6ZC)   Where by virtue of the provisions of this section or any order under subsection (6ZA)(b) of this section payments under an order cease to be or become payable to the collecting officer, the person liable to make the payments shall, until he is given the prescribed notice to that effect, be deemed to comply with the order if he makes payments in accordance with the order and any order under subsection (6ZA)(b) of this section of which he has received such notice.

(6ZD)   In subsections (6), (6ZA) and (6ZC) of this section "collecting officer" means the officer mentioned in Article 85(4) of the Magistrates' Courts (Northern Ireland) Order 1981."

(4) Where an order is registered in Northern Ireland under this section, Part II of the Maintenance and Affiliation Orders Act (Northern Ireland) 1966, except sections 11, 11A and 14(2) and (3), shall apply as if the order had been registered in accordance with the provisions of that Part, as if –

(a)   in section 12(2), for modifications of Article 98(8B) to (8D) of the Magistrates' Court (Northern Ireland) Order 1981 specified in that subsection there were substituted the modifications specified in section 18(3ZA) of the Maintenance Orders Act 1950 (enforcement of registered orders); and

(b)   for section 13(5A), there were substituted the following subsection –

"(5A) Subject to the following provisions of this section, paragraphs (4) to (11) of Article 86 of the Magistrates' Courts (Northern Ireland) Order 1981 (power of clerk and court to vary maintenance orders) shall apply in relation to a registered order as they apply in relation to a maintenance order made by a court of summary jurisdiction (disregarding Article 25(2) of the Domestic Proceedings (Northern Ireland) Order 1980) but –

(a)   as if for paragraph (4)(b) there were substituted –
   '(b) payments under the order are required to be made to the collecting officer, by any method of payment falling within Article 85(7) (standing order, etc)';
and as if after the words 'petty sessions' there were inserted 'for the petty sessions district for which the court which made the order acts';

(b)   as if in paragraph (5) for the words 'to the collecting officer' there were substituted 'in accordance with sub-paragraph (a) of paragraph (9)';

(c)   as if in paragraph (7), sub-paragraph (c) and the word 'and' immediately preceding it were omitted;

(d)   as if in paragraph (8) for the words 'sub-paragraphs (a) to (d) of Article 85(3)' there were substituted 'paragraph (9)';

(e)   as if for paragraphs (9) and (10) there were substituted the following paragraphs –

'(9) The powers of the court are –

(a)   the power to order that payments under the order be made directly to the collecting officer;

(b)   the power to order that payments under the order be made to the collecting officer, by such method of payment falling within Article 85(7) (standing order, etc) as may be specified;

(c)   the power to make an attachment of earnings order under Part IX to secure payments under the order.

(10) In deciding which of the powers under paragraph (9) above it is to exercise, the court shall have regard to any representations made by the debtor.

(10A) Paragraph (5) of Article 85 (power of court to require debtor to open account) shall apply for the purposes of paragraph (9) as it applies for the purposes of that Article but as if for sub-paragraph (a) there were substituted –

"(a) the court proposes to exercise its power under sub-paragraph (b) of Article 86(9)".'.".

(5) A court of summary jurisdiction in Northern Ireland shall have jurisdiction to hear an application by or against a person residing outside Northern Ireland for the discharge or variation of an order registered in Northern Ireland under this section; and where such an application is made against a person residing outside Northern Ireland, then, if he resides in England and Wales or Scotland, section 15 of the Maintenance Orders Act 1950 (which relates to the service of process on persons residing in those countries) shall have effect in relation to the application as it has effect in relation to the proceedings therein mentioned.

(5A) Article 165 of the Children (Northern Ireland) Order 1995 (provision which may be made by magistrates' courts rules, etc) shall apply for the purpose of giving effect to subsection (5) above as it applies for the purpose of giving effect to that Order, except that in the application of that Article by virtue of this subsection "relevant proceedings" means any application made, or proceedings brought, by virtue of that subsection and any part of such proceedings.

(6) The enactments specified in Part III of Schedule 12 shall have effect with the amendments specified there, being amendments consequential on this section.

Amendments—SI 1993/1576; SI 1995/755.

****

Civil Partnership Act 2004

ARRANGEMENT OF SECTIONS

PART 1
INTRODUCTION

PART 2
CIVIL PARTNERSHIP: ENGLAND AND WALES

Introduction

Dissolution of civil partnership

Nullity

Presumption of death orders

Separation orders

Declarations

PART II

PART 5
CIVIL PARTNERSHIP FORMED OR DISSOLVED ABROAD ETC

Scope of Act—The Act came into force on 5 December 2005. There are 8 Parts, 264 sections and 30 Schedules. The purpose of the Act is to enable same-sex couples to obtain legal recognition of their relationship by registration of a civil partnership, given that same-sex partners (unlike heterosexual cohabitants) do not have the option of marriage. Given that a same-sex couple is unable to marry and a heterosexual couple unable to register a civil partnership, an application has been made to the European Court of Human Rights claiming that s 3(1)(a) of the Act, which requires those seeking to register a civil partnership to be of the same sex, constitutes discrimination contrary to ECHR, Art 14 (in conjunction with Arts 8 and 12) or, alternatively, amounts to a violation of the right to marry (Art 12) and the right to private and family life (Art 8) (*Ferguson and others v United Kingdom* (2011) ECtHR Ref 8254/11). In the meantime, the Marriage (Same Sex Couples) Bill has been introduced into Parliament, which will (if enacted) extend marriage to same-sex couples. Under a civil partnership, civil partners assume legal rights and responsibilities with regard to each other and to third parties including the State. Same-sex couples acquire many of the legal rights and benefits currently enjoyed by married couples. The Act does not, however, purport to create same-sex marriage. Civil partnership is a distinct institution with specific statutory rights and responsibilities. Nevertheless, in terms of the conditions of entering into and dissolving a civil partnership, and the legal consequences flowing from it, the Act adopts a model based closely on marriage which is closer to that of marriage than the registered partnership models in other EU Member States, while falling short of same-sex marriage as permitted in, e g the Netherlands and Belgium. Only certain county courts (in addition to the Principal Registry of the Family Division) are designated as civil partnership proceedings county courts; these are: Birmingham, Brighton, Bristol, Cardiff, Chester, Exeter, Leeds, Manchester and Newcastle (Civil Courts (Amendment) Order 2005).

The commentary below summarises the provisions not reproduced in this work.

Registration of civil partnerships—This is provided for by Ch 1 of Pt 2 of the Act. In much the same way as for marriage, each party to the partnership must under the standard procedure give notice to their relevant registration authority of their intention to form the partnership and also must have resided in the same registration authority in England and Wales for 7 days immediately before the notice is given (s 8). There is then a waiting period of 15 days (s 11), which may be shortened (s 12), before which the registration authority may issue a civil partnership schedule (s 14). Specified relevant information must be publicised during the waiting period (s 10). The couple then have 12 months from the date the notice is registered in which to form and register their civil partnership (s 17).

To form a civil partnership, a civil partnership document (s 7) must be signed by both parties in the presence of each other and in the presence of a civil partnership registrar and two witnesses (s 2). No religious service is to be used while a civil partnership registrar is officiating (s 2(5)). However, a ceremony may take place on religious premises in certain circumstances (ss 6 and 6A; Marriages and Civil Partnerships (Approved Premises) (Amendment) Regulations 2011).

In the same way as for married couples, there are prohibited degrees of relationship. Other prohibitions include parties who are not of the same sex, parties who are already married or in a civil partnership and if either party is under the age of 16 (s 3). Parental consent will be required for any party under the age of 18 in normal circumstances (s 4).

Modified procedures apply to partners who are housebound (s 18), detained (s 19) and non-resident (s 20). There is also a special procedure for those who are seriously ill and not expected to recover (ss 21–27).

Children (Chapter 5 of Pt 2)—Chapter 5 makes various amendments to CA 1989 and ACA 2002 to reflect the creation of the status of civil partnership. The Act enables a civil partner to acquire parental responsibility for their civil partner's child (in the same way as a step-parent) by agreement between the parent (and any other parent who also has parental responsibility) and the civil partner, or by court order on the application of the civil partner (CA 1989, s 4A, as amended by s 75(1),(2)). As to the acquisition of parental responsibility by civil partners in cases of assisted conception, see CA 1989, ss 2(1A),(2A) and 4ZA and HFEA 2008, ss 42–45. As to disputes over parental responsibility and contact involving lesbian mothers and a known father, see: *Re D (Contact and Parental Responsibility: Lesbian Mothers and Known Father) (No 2)* [2006] 1 FCR 556; *Re B (Role of Biological Father)* [2008] 1 FLR 1015; *R v E and F (Female Parents: Known Father)* [2010] 2 FLR 383; *T v T* [2010] EWCA Civ 1366; and *A v B and C (Lesbian Co-Parents: Role of Father)* [2012] 2 FLR 607, which rejected the concept of primary and secondary parenting roles developed in *MA v RS (Contact: Parenting Roles)* [2012] 1 FLR 1056 and *Re P and L (Contact)* [2012] 1 FLR 1068). While there is no presumption in favour of a biological parent when determining a dispute between same-sex partners, the fact of parentage is still an important and significant factor in determining the child's best interests (*Re G (Residence: Same-Sex Partner)* [2006] 2 FLR 629, HL). The definition of "child of the family" in CA 1989 is amended to include civil partners as well as parties to a marriage (s 75(3)). A civil partner is also entitled to make an application for a residence or contact order (s 77). The right to apply for financial provision for children under CA 1989, Sch 1 is extended to civil partners (s 78). ACA 2002 is amended to ensure that civil partners are recognised for the purposes of adoption (s 79), e g by restricting adoption of a person who is or has been a civil partner, generally, by substituting "marriage or civil partnership" for "marriage", and by adding "two people who are civil partners of each other" to the definition of "couple" in s 144(4) of the 2002 Act.

Miscellaneous (Chapter 6 of Pt 2 and Pt 7)—Section 81 and Sch 8 amend certain enactments relating to housing and tenancies. Section 82 and Sch 9 amend FLA 1996, Pt IV to allow civil partners the same rights to occupy the civil partnership home as married persons have to occupy the matrimonial home and to apply for non-molestation and occupation orders. Section 83 amends the Fatal Accidents Act 1976 to include a civil partner as a dependant.

Pt 7 includes other miscellaneous amendments. The Sex Discrimination Act 1975 is amended so that civil partners have the right not to be discriminated against on the grounds of their civil partnership just as married persons have the right not to be discriminated against on the grounds of their marriage (s 251).

Amendments are made to social security, child support and tax credits legislation with the intention that, in general, civil partners are treated in the same way as married persons and that same-sex couples who are living together are treated in the same way as opposite sex unmarried couples who are living together as husband and wife (s 254 and Sch 24).

Pensions—Section 255 gives Ministers power to amend the Act and other enactments in relation to pensions by order to make provision with respect to pensions, allowances or gratuities for the surviving civil partners or dependants of deceased civil partners. Reference should be made to the Civil Partnership (Contracted-out Occupational and Appropriate Personal Pension Schemes) (Surviving Civil Partners) Order 2005, the Civil Partnership (Pensions and Benefit Payments) (Consequential, etc Provisions) Order 2005, the Civil Partnership (Miscellaneous and Consequential Provisions) Order 2005 and the Tax and Civil Partnership Regulations 2007.

Amendments to the Social Security Contributions and Benefits Act 1992 ensure that state pension rights are extended to civil partners (s 254 and Sch 24, Pt 3) (see Civil Partnership (Pensions and Benefit Payments) (Consequential, etc Provisions) Order 2005; Civil Partnership (Pensions, Social Security and Child Support) (Consequential, etc Provisions) Order 2005; Civil Partnership Act 2004 (Tax Credits, etc) (Consequential Amendments) Order 2005). Sch 24, paras 23–33 and 51 extend state pension rights to civil partners. Female civil partners are now able to claim a basic state pension using their civil partner's NI contribution record, where the contributing civil partner was born on or after 6 April 1950 and has attained state pension age. However, because of the difference in state pension ages, male civil partners will only qualify from 2015. A civil partner may also, in the same circumstances as surviving spouses,

PART II

become entitled to widowed parents' allowance, bereavement allowance and bereavement payment. The formation of a new civil partnership or same-sex cohabitation has the same effect as remarriage (Sch 41, paras 16–22).

Surviving civil partners of members of contracted-out schemes are eligible for survivors' benefits based on contracted-out rights earned by service from 6 April 1988. Additionally, they are eligible for survivors' benefits based upon pensionable service from 5 December 2005. In summary, civil partners do not enjoy full equality in relation to survivors' benefits: survivors' benefits in respect of pre-5 December 2005 non-contracted-out service depend upon an amendment to the relevant scheme rules (Equality Act 2010, Sch 9, para 18(1)).

Widows'/widowers' rights are extended to certain surviving civil partners by ss 256 and 257 and Schs 25 and 26 (statutory pensions).

Wills, administration of estates and family provision (Sch 4)—Section 71 and Sch 4 amend the Wills Act 1837, Public Trustee Act 1906, Administration of Estates Act 1925, Intestates' Estates Act 1952, Family Provision Act 1966 and I(PFD)A 1975 so that civil partners are given the same rights as those that exist for married couples.

A will is revoked, as upon marriage, when a testator forms a civil partnership, unless it is expressed to be made in expectation of registration (Wills Act 1837, s 18B(1) (as inserted); *Court v Despallieres; Re Ikin (Deceased)* [2010] 1 FLR 1734) and once a civil partnership is dissolved, annulled or there is a presumption of death order, former civil partners, where named as executors and beneficiaries, are prevented from becoming such unless the will provides otherwise (Wills Act 1837, s 18C (as inserted)).

Civil partners are entitled to inherit the estate of their deceased civil partners under the intestacy rules in the same way as surviving spouses and to acquire the home that they have shared with the deceased civil partners.

Civil partners have been added to the class of person entitled to make an application for reasonable financial provision from the estate of their deceased civil partner.

PART 1
INTRODUCTION

1 Civil partnership

(1) A civil partnership is a relationship between two people of the same sex ('civil partners') –

    (a) which is formed when they register as civil partners of each other –
        (i) in England or Wales (under Part 2),
        (ii) in Scotland (under Part 3),
        (iii) in Northern Ireland (under Part 4), or
        (iv) outside the United Kingdom under an Order in Council made under Chapter 1 of Part 5 (registration at British consulates etc or by armed forces personnel), or
    (b) which they are treated under Chapter 2 of Part 5 as having formed (at the time determined under that Chapter) by virtue of having registered an overseas relationship.

(2) Subsection (1) is subject to the provisions of this Act under or by virtue of which a civil partnership is void.

(3) A civil partnership ends only on death, dissolution or annulment.

(4) The references in subsection (3) to dissolution and annulment are to dissolution and annulment having effect under or recognised in accordance with this Act.

(5) References in this Act to an overseas relationship are to be read in accordance with Chapter 2 of Part 5.

PART 2
CIVIL PARTNERSHIP: ENGLAND AND WALES
****

Introduction

37 Powers to make orders and effect of orders

(1) The court may, in accordance with this Chapter –

(a) make an order (a 'dissolution order') which dissolves a civil partnership on the ground that it has broken down irretrievably;

(b) make an order (a 'nullity order') which annuls a civil partnership which is void or voidable;

(c) make an order (a 'presumption of death order') which dissolves a civil partnership on the ground that one of the civil partners is presumed to be dead;

(d) make an order (a 'separation order') which provides for the separation of the civil partners.

(2) Every dissolution, nullity or presumption of death order –

(a) is, in the first instance, a conditional order, and

(b) may not be made final before the end of the prescribed period (see section 38);

and any reference in this Chapter to a conditional order is to be read accordingly.

(3) A nullity order made where a civil partnership is voidable annuls the civil partnership only as respects any time after the order has been made final, and the civil partnership is to be treated (despite the order) as if it had existed up to that time.

(4) In this Chapter, other than in sections 58 to 61, 'the court' means –

(a) the High Court, or

(b) if a county court has jurisdiction by virtue of Part 5 of the Matrimonial and Family Proceedings Act 1984, a county court.

(5) This Chapter is subject to sections 219 to 224 (jurisdiction of the court).

Defined term—"civil partners": s 1(1).

Scope—This section provides for four types of orders which may be made in relation to a civil partnership: a dissolution order (s 44), a nullity order (ss 49–50), a presumption of death order (s 55) and a separation order (s 56). Irretrievable breakdown is the sole ground for the court to grant a dissolution order (ss 37(1)(a) and 44). Dissolution, nullity and presumption of death orders are granted in two stages and are initially conditional for a period of 6 weeks (ss 37(2) and 38). Jurisdiction to entertain proceedings is provided for by s 221 (dissolution, separation or nullity) and s 222 (presumption of death).

38 The period before conditional orders may be made final

(1) Subject to subsections (2) to (4), the prescribed period for the purposes of section 37(2)(b) is –

(a) 6 weeks from the making of the conditional order, or

(b) if the 6 week period would end on a day on which the office or registry of the court dealing with the case is closed, the period of 6 weeks extended to the end of the first day on which the office or registry is next open.

(2) The Lord Chancellor may by order amend this section so as to substitute a different definition of the prescribed period for the purposes of section 37(2)(b).

(3) But the Lord Chancellor may not under subsection (2) provide for a period longer than 6 months to be the prescribed period.

(4) In a particular case the court dealing with the case may by order shorten the prescribed period.

(5) The power to make an order under subsection (2) is exercisable by statutory instrument.

(6) An instrument containing such an order is subject to annulment in pursuance of a resolution of either House of Parliament.

Defined terms—"conditional order": s 37(2); "the court" s 37(4).

39 Intervention of the Queen's Proctor

(1) This section applies if an application has been made for a dissolution, nullity or presumption of death order.

(2) The court may, if it thinks fit, direct that all necessary papers in the matter are to be sent to the Queen's Proctor who must under the directions of the Attorney General instruct counsel to argue before the court any question in relation to the matter which the court considers it necessary or expedient to have fully argued.

(3) If any person at any time –

    (a)   during the progress of the proceedings, or

    (b)   before the conditional order is made final,

gives information to the Queen's Proctor on any matter material to the due decision of the case, the Queen's Proctor may take such steps as the Attorney General considers necessary or expedient.

(4) If the Queen's Proctor intervenes or shows cause against the making of the conditional order in any proceedings relating to its making, the court may make such order as may be just as to –

    (a)   the payment by other parties to the proceedings of the costs incurred by him in doing so, or

    (b)   the payment by the Queen's Proctor of any costs incurred by any of those parties because of his doing so.

(5) The Queen's Proctor is entitled to charge as part of the expenses of his office –

    (a)   the costs of any proceedings under subsection (2);

    (b)   if his reasonable costs of intervening or showing cause as mentioned in subsection (4) are not fully satisfied by an order under subsection (4)(a), the amount of the difference;

    (c)   if the Treasury so directs, any costs which he pays to any parties under an order made under subsection (4)(b).

Defined terms—"conditional order": s 37(2); "the court": s 37(4); "dissolution order": s 37(1)(a); "nullity order": s 37(1)(b); "presumption of death order": s 37(1)(c).

Procedure—The rules relating to an application by the Queen's Proctor are found in FPR 2010, r 7.31(6).

40 Proceedings before order has been made final

(1) This section applies if –

    (a)   a conditional order has been made, and

    (b)   the Queen's Proctor, or any person who has not been a party to proceedings in which the order was made, shows cause why the order should not be made final on the ground that material facts have not been brought before the court.

(2) This section also applies if –

    (a)   a conditional order has been made,

(b)   3 months have elapsed since the earliest date on which an application could have been made for the order to be made final,

(c)   no such application has been made by the civil partner who applied for the conditional order, and

(d)   the other civil partner makes an application to the court under this subsection.

(3) The court may –

(a)   make the order final,

(b)   rescind the order,

(c)   require further inquiry, or

(d)   otherwise deal with the case as it thinks fit.

(4) Subsection (3)(a) –

(a)   applies despite section 37(2) (period before conditional orders may be made final), but

(b)   is subject to section 48(4) (protection for respondent in separation cases) and section 63 (restrictions on making of orders affecting children).

Defined terms—"civil partner": s 1(1); "conditional order": s 37(2); "the court": s 37(4).

Procedure—The procedure for showing cause why a conditional order should not be made final is set out in FPR 2010, r 7.31.

41 Time bar on applications for dissolution orders

(1) No application for a dissolution order may be made to the court before the end of the period of 1 year from the date of the formation of the civil partnership.

(2) Nothing in this section prevents the making of an application based on matters which occurred before the end of the 1 year period.

Defined terms—"the court": s 37(4); "dissolution order": s 37(1)(a).

42 Attempts at reconciliation of civil partners

(1) This section applies in relation to cases where an application is made for a dissolution or separation order.

(2) Rules of court must make provision for requiring the legal representative acting for the applicant to certify whether he has –

(a)   discussed with the applicant the possibility of a reconciliation with the other civil partner, and

(b)   given the applicant the names and addresses of persons qualified to help effect a reconciliation between civil partners who have become estranged.

(3) If at any stage of proceedings for the order it appears to the court that there is a reasonable possibility of a reconciliation between the civil partners, the court may adjourn the proceedings for such period as it thinks fit to enable attempts to be made to effect a reconciliation between them.

(4) The power to adjourn under subsection (3) is additional to any other power of adjournment.

Amendments—Legal Services Act 2007, s 208(1), Sch 21, para 150.

Defined terms—"civil partners": s 1(1); "the court": s 37(4); "dissolution order": s 37(1)(a); "separation order": s 37(1)(d).

Scope—This section provides for any solicitor for a petitioner to certify that reconciliation has been discussed with his client and enables the court to adjourn the proceedings if reconciliation appears to be a possibility.

"Rules of court must make provision" (s 42(2))—Such provision is made by FPR 2010, r 7.6 and PD5A, which require the solicitor acting for the petitioner in dissolution or separation proceedings to file a certificate concerning reconciliation.

43 Consideration by the court of certain agreements or arrangements

(1) This section applies in relation to cases where –

    (a) proceedings for a dissolution or separation order are contemplated or have begun, and

    (b) an agreement or arrangement is made or proposed to be made between the civil partners which relates to, arises out of, or is connected with, the proceedings.

(2) Rules of court may make provision for enabling –

    (a) the civil partners, or either of them, to refer the agreement or arrangement to the court, and

    (b) the court –

        (i) to express an opinion, if it thinks it desirable to do so, as to the reasonableness of the agreement or arrangement, and

        (ii) to give such directions, if any, in the matter as it thinks fit.

Defined terms—"civil partners": s 1(1); "the court": s 37(4); "dissolution order": s 37(1)(a); "separation order": s 37(1)(d).

Scope—This section is a curious perpetuation of MCA 1973, s 7 described in *Brockwell v Brockwell* (1975) 6 Fam Law 46 as "an almost vestigial provision, not unlike the human appendix". At the time of writing, no rules have been made under s 43(2).

Dissolution of civil partnership

44 Dissolution of civil partnership which has broken down irretrievably

(1) Subject to section 41, an application for a dissolution order may be made to the court by either civil partner on the ground that the civil partnership has broken down irretrievably.

(2) On an application for a dissolution order the court must inquire, so far as it reasonably can, into –

    (a) the facts alleged by the applicant, and

    (b) any facts alleged by the respondent.

(3) The court hearing an application for a dissolution order must not hold that the civil partnership has broken down irretrievably unless the applicant satisfies the court of one or more of the facts described in subsection (5)(a), (b), (c) or (d).

(4) But if the court is satisfied of any of those facts, it must make a dissolution order unless it is satisfied on all the evidence that the civil partnership has not broken down irretrievably.

(5) The facts referred to in subsections (3) and (4) are –

    (a) that the respondent has behaved in such a way that the applicant cannot reasonably be expected to live with the respondent;

    (b) that –

        (i) the applicant and the respondent have lived apart for a continuous period of at least 2 years immediately preceding the making of the application ('2 years' separation'), and

        (ii) the respondent consents to a dissolution order being made;

(c)   that the applicant and the respondent have lived apart for a continuous period of at least 5 years immediately preceding the making of the application ('5 years' separation');

(d)   that the respondent has deserted the applicant for a continuous period of at least 2 years immediately preceding the making of the application.

Defined terms—"civil partner": s 1(1); "the court": s 37(4); "dissolution order": s 37(1)(a).

Scope—Subject to the 1-year time bar (s 41), the sole ground for the dissolution of a civil partnership is that it has irretrievably broken down, as evidenced by one of the four facts in s 44(5). Adultery is not included as a separate fact. Infidelity which leads to an irretrievable breakdown of a civil partnership may be regarded as unreasonable behaviour within s 44(5)(a).

45 Supplemental provisions as to facts raising presumption of breakdown

(1) Subsection (2) applies if –

(a)   in any proceedings for a dissolution order the applicant alleges, in reliance on section 44(5)(a), that the respondent has behaved in such a way that the applicant cannot reasonably be expected to live with the respondent, but

(b)   after the date of the occurrence of the final incident relied on by the applicant and held by the court to support his allegation, the applicant and the respondent have lived together for a period (or periods) which does not, or which taken together do not, exceed 6 months.

(2) The fact that the applicant and respondent have lived together as mentioned in subsection (1)(b) must be disregarded in determining, for the purposes of section 44(5)(a), whether the applicant cannot reasonably be expected to live with the respondent.

(3) Subsection (4) applies in relation to cases where the applicant alleges, in reliance on section 44(5)(b), that the respondent consents to a dissolution order being made.

(4) Rules of court must make provision for the purpose of ensuring that the respondent has been given such information as will enable him to understand –

(a)   the consequences to him of consenting to the making of the order, and

(b)   the steps which he must take to indicate his consent.

(5) For the purposes of section 44(5)(d) the court may treat a period of desertion as having continued at a time when the deserting civil partner was incapable of continuing the necessary intention, if the evidence before the court is such that, had he not been so incapable, the court would have inferred that the desertion continued at that time.

(6) In considering for the purposes of section 44(5) whether the period for which the civil partners have lived apart or the period for which the respondent has deserted the applicant has been continuous, no account is to be taken of –

(a)   any one period not exceeding 6 months, or

(b)   any two or more periods not exceeding 6 months in all,

during which the civil partners resumed living with each other.

(7) But no period during which the civil partners have lived with each other counts as part of the period during which the civil partners have lived apart or as part of the period of desertion.

(8) For the purposes of section 44(5)(b) and (c) and this section civil partners are to be treated as living apart unless they are living with each other in the same household, and references in this section to civil partners living with each other are to be read as references to their living with each other in the same household.

Defined terms—"civil partners": s 1(1); "the court": s 37(4); "dissolution order": s 37(1)(a).

Rules of court to ensure respondent's consent under s 44(5)(b) (s 45(4))—See FPR 2010, r 7.12(4),(6) and (12).

46 Dissolution order not precluded by previous separation order etc

(1) Subsections (2) and (3) apply if any of the following orders has been made in relation to a civil partnership –

    (a)   a separation order;

    (b)   an order under Schedule 6 (financial relief in magistrates' courts etc);

    (c)   an order under section 33 of the Family Law Act 1996 (occupation orders);

    (d)   an order under section 37 of the 1996 Act (orders where neither civil partner entitled to occupy the home).

(2) Nothing prevents –

    (a)   either civil partner from applying for a dissolution order, or

    (b)   the court from making a dissolution order,

on the same facts, or substantially the same facts, as those proved in support of the making of the order referred to in subsection (1).

(3) On the application for the dissolution order, the court –

    (a)   may treat the order referred to in subsection (1) as sufficient proof of any desertion or other fact by reference to which it was made, but

    (b)   must not make the dissolution order without receiving evidence from the applicant.

(4) If –

    (a)   the application for the dissolution order follows a separation order or any order requiring the civil partners to live apart,

    (b)   there was a period of desertion immediately preceding the institution of the proceedings for the separation order, and

    (c)   the civil partners have not resumed living together and the separation order has been continuously in force since it was made,

the period of desertion is to be treated for the purposes of the application for the dissolution order as if it had immediately preceded the making of the application.

(5) For the purposes of section 44(5)(d) the court may treat as a period during which the respondent has deserted the applicant any period during which there is in force –

    (a)   an injunction granted by the High Court or a county court which excludes the respondent from the civil partnership home, or

    (b)   an order under section 33 or 37 of the 1996 Act which prohibits the respondent from occupying a dwelling-house in which the applicant and the respondent have, or at any time have had, a civil partnership home.

Defined terms—"civil partners": s 1(1); "the court": s 37(4); "dissolution order": s 37(1)(a); "separation order": s 37(1)(d).

Scope—This section replicates the provisions of MCA 1973, s 4, the commentary to which reference should be made.

47 Refusal of dissolution in 5 year separation cases on ground of grave hardship

(1) The respondent to an application for a dissolution order in which the applicant alleges 5 years' separation may oppose the making of an order on the ground that –

    (a)   the dissolution of the civil partnership will result in grave financial or other hardship to him, and

(b)   it would in all the circumstances be wrong to dissolve the civil partnership.

(2) Subsection (3) applies if –

(a)   the making of a dissolution order is opposed under this section,

(b)   the court finds that the applicant is entitled to rely in support of his application on the fact of 5 years' separation and makes no such finding as to any other fact mentioned in section 44(5), and

(c)   apart from this section, the court would make a dissolution order.

(3) The court must –

(a)   consider all the circumstances, including the conduct of the civil partners and the interests of the civil partners and of any children or other persons concerned, and

(b)   if it is of the opinion that the ground mentioned in subsection (1) is made out, dismiss the application for the dissolution order.

(4) 'Hardship' includes the loss of the chance of acquiring any benefit which the respondent might acquire if the civil partnership were not dissolved.

Defined terms—"civil partners": s 1(1); "the court": s 37(4); "dissolution order": s 37(1)(a).

Scope—This section replicates the provisions of MCA 1973, s 5, the commentary to which reference should be made.

48   Proceedings before order made final: protection for respondent in separation cases

(1) The court may, on an application made by the respondent, rescind a conditional dissolution order if –

(a)   it made the order on the basis of a finding that the applicant was entitled to rely on the fact of 2 years' separation coupled with the respondent's consent to a dissolution order being made,

(b)   it made no such finding as to any other fact mentioned in section 44(5), and

(c)   it is satisfied that the applicant misled the respondent (whether intentionally or unintentionally) about any matter which the respondent took into account in deciding to give his consent.

(2) Subsections (3) to (5) apply if –

(a)   the respondent to an application for a dissolution order in which the applicant alleged –

(i)   2 years' separation coupled with the respondent's consent to a dissolution order being made, or

(ii)   5 years' separation,

has applied to the court for consideration under subsection (3) of his financial position after the dissolution of the civil partnership, and

(b)   the court –

(i)   has made a conditional dissolution order on the basis of a finding that the applicant was entitled to rely in support of his application on the fact of 2 years' or 5 years' separation, and

(ii)   has made no such finding as to any other fact mentioned in section 44(5).

(3) The court hearing an application by the respondent under subsection (2) must consider all the circumstances, including –

(a)   the age, health, conduct, earning capacity, financial resources and financial obligations of each of the parties, and

PART II

    (b)   the financial position of the respondent as, having regard to the dissolution, it is likely to be after the death of the applicant should the applicant die first.

(4) Subject to subsection (5), the court must not make the order final unless it is satisfied that –

    (a)   the applicant should not be required to make any financial provision for the respondent, or

    (b)   the financial provision made by the applicant for the respondent is –
        (i)   reasonable and fair, or
        (ii) the best that can be made in the circumstances.

(5) The court may if it thinks fit make the order final if –

    (a)   it appears that there are circumstances making it desirable that the order should be made final without delay, and

    (b)   it has obtained a satisfactory undertaking from the applicant that he will make such financial provision for the respondent as it may approve.

Defined terms—"the court": s 37(4); "conditional order": s 37(2); "dissolution order": s 37(1)(a).

Scope—This section replicates the provisions of MCA 1973, s 10, the commentary to which reference should be made.

Nullity

49 Grounds on which civil partnership is void

Where two people register as civil partners of each other in England and Wales, the civil partnership is void if –

    (a)   at the time when they do so, they are not eligible to register as civil partners of each other under Chapter 1 (see section 3),

    (b)   at the time when they do so they both know –
        (i)   that due notice of proposed civil partnership has not been given,
        (ii) that the civil partnership document has not been duly issued,
        (iii) that the civil partnership document is void under section 17(3) or 27(2) (registration after end of time allowed for registering),
        (iv) that the place of registration is a place other than that specified in the notices (or notice) of proposed civil partnership and the civil partnership document,
        (v) that a civil partnership registrar is not present, or
        (vi) that the place of registration is on premises that are not approved premises although the registration is purportedly in accordance with section 6(3A)(a), or

    (c)   the civil partnership document is void under paragraph 6(5) of Schedule 2 (civil partnership between child and another person forbidden).

Amendments—SI 2005/2000.

Defined terms—"civil partners": s 1(1); "civil partnership document": s 7; "civil partnership registrar": s 29.

Scope—A nullity order annuls a civil partnership which is either void or voidable (s 37(1)(b)). This section sets out the circumstances in which a civil partnership is void, i e invalid from the outset.

50 Grounds on which civil partnership is voidable

(1) Where two people register as civil partners of each other in England and Wales, the civil partnership is voidable if –

(a)   either of them did not validly consent to its formation (whether as a result of duress, mistake, unsoundness of mind or otherwise);

(b)   at the time of its formation either of them, though capable of giving a valid consent, was suffering (whether continuously or intermittently) from mental disorder of such a kind or to such an extent as to be unfitted for civil partnership;

(c)   at the time of its formation, the respondent was pregnant by some person other than the applicant;

(d)   an interim gender recognition certificate under the GRA 2004 has, after the time of its formation, been issued to either civil partner;

(e)   the respondent is a person whose gender at the time of its formation had become the acquired gender under the 2004 Act.

(2) In this section and section 51 'mental disorder' has the same meaning as in the Mental Health Act 1983.

Defined terms—"civil partners": s 1(1); "the acquired gender": GRA 2004, ss 1(2), 25.

Scope—A nullity order annuls a civil partnership which is either void or voidable (s 37(1)(b)). This section sets out the grounds for obtaining a nullity order where the civil partnership is voidable, i e invalid from the date of the final order (s 37(3)). The bars to relief where a civil partnership is voidable are contained in s 51. In particular, the application for a nullity order must be made within 3 years of registration, unless the court gives leave for the institution of proceedings after that period (s 51(2)). There is no requirement for a civil partnership to be consummated. The provisions of s 50(1)(c) appear to be a replication of MCA 1973, s 12(f). There is, however, no corresponding provision to MCA 1973, s 12(e) that "the respondent was suffering from venereal disease in a communicable form".

51 Bars to relief where civil partnership is voidable

(1) The court must not make a nullity order on the ground that a civil partnership is voidable if the respondent satisfies the court –

(a)   that the applicant, with knowledge that it was open to him to obtain a nullity order, conducted himself in relation to the respondent in such a way as to lead the respondent reasonably to believe that he would not seek to do so, and

(b)   that it would be unjust to the respondent to make the order.

(2) Without prejudice to subsection (1), the court must not make a nullity order by virtue of section 50(1)(a), (b), (c) or (e) unless –

(a)   it is satisfied that proceedings were instituted within 3 years from the date of the formation of the civil partnership, or

(b)   leave for the institution of proceedings after the end of that 3 year period has been granted under subsection (3).

(3) A judge of the court may, on an application made to him, grant leave for the institution of proceedings if he –

(a)   is satisfied that the applicant has at some time during the 3 year period suffered from mental disorder, and

(b)   considers that in all the circumstances of the case it would be just to grant leave for the institution of proceedings.

(4) An application for leave under subsection (3) may be made after the end of the 3 year period.

(5) Without prejudice to subsection (1), the court must not make a nullity order by virtue of section 50(1)(d) unless it is satisfied that proceedings were instituted within the period of 6 months from the date of issue of the interim gender recognition certificate.

(6) Without prejudice to subsections (1) and (2), the court must not make a nullity order by virtue of section 50(1)(c) or (e) unless it is satisfied that the applicant was at the time of the formation of the civil partnership ignorant of the facts alleged.

Defined terms—"the court": s 37(4); "nullity order": s 37(1)(b); "mental disorder": s 50(2).

52 Proof of certain matters not necessary to validity of civil partnership

(1) Where two people have registered as civil partners of each other in England and Wales, it is not necessary in support of the civil partnership to give any proof –

    (a)   that any person whose consent to the civil partnership was required by section 4 (parental etc consent) had given his consent, or

    (aa) that before the registration either of the civil partners resided, or resided for any period, in the area stated in the notices of proposed civil partnership to be the area of that person's place of residence;

    (b)   (*repealed*)

and no evidence is to be given to prove the contrary in any proceedings touching the validity of the civil partnership.

(2) Subsection (1)(a) is subject to section 49(c) (civil partnership void if forbidden).

Amendments—SI 2005/2000.

Defined terms—"civil partners": s 1(1); "civil partnership registrar": s 29; "registration authority": s 28.

53 Power to validate civil partnership

(1) Where two people have registered as civil partners of each other in England and Wales, the Lord Chancellor may by order validate the civil partnership if it appears to him that it is or may be void under section 49(b).

(2) An order under subsection (1) may include provisions for relieving a person from any liability under section 31(2), 32(2) or 33(5) or (7).

(3) The draft of an order under subsection (1) must be advertised, in such manner as the Lord Chancellor thinks fit, not less than one month before the order is made.

(4) The Lord Chancellor must –

    (a)   consider all objections to the order sent to him in writing during that month, and

    (b)   if it appears to him necessary, direct a local inquiry into the validity of any such objections.

(5) An order under subsection (1) is subject to special parliamentary procedure.

Defined terms—"civil partners": s 1(1).

54 Validity of civil partnerships registered outside England and Wales

(1) Where two people register as civil partners of each other in Scotland, the civil partnership is –

    (a)   void, if it would be void in Scotland under section 123, and

    (b)   voidable, if the circumstances fall within section 50(1)(d).

(2) Where two people register as civil partners of each other in Northern Ireland, the civil partnership is –

    (a)   void, if it would be void in Northern Ireland under section 173, and

    (b)   voidable, if the circumstances fall within any paragraph of section 50(1).

(3) Subsection (4) applies where two people register as civil partners of each other under an Order in Council under –

(a)   section 210 (registration at British consulates etc), or

(b)   section 211 (registration by armed forces personnel),

('the relevant section').

(4) The civil partnership is –

(a)   void, if –

(i)   the condition in subsection (2)(a) or (b) of the relevant section is not met, or

(ii)   a requirement prescribed for the purposes of this paragraph by an Order in Council under the relevant section is not complied with, and

(b)   voidable, if –

(i)   the appropriate part of the United Kingdom is England and Wales or Northern Ireland and the circumstances fall within any paragraph of section 50(1), or

(ii)   the appropriate part of the United Kingdom is Scotland and the circumstances fall within section 50(1)(d).

(5) The appropriate part of the United Kingdom is the part by reference to which the condition in subsection (2)(b) of the relevant section is met.

(6) Subsections (7) and (8) apply where two people have registered an apparent or alleged overseas relationship.

(7) The civil partnership is void if –

(a)   the relationship is not an overseas relationship, or

(b)   (even though the relationship is an overseas relationship) the parties are not treated under Chapter 2 of Part 5 as having formed a civil partnership.

(8) The civil partnership is voidable if –

(a)   the overseas relationship is voidable under the relevant law,

(b)   the circumstances fall within section 50(1)(d), or

(c)   where either of the parties was domiciled in England and Wales or Northern Ireland at the time when the overseas relationship was registered, the circumstances fall within section 50(1)(a), (b), (c) or (e).

(9) Section 51 applies for the purposes of –

(a)   subsections (1)(b), (2)(b) and (4)(b),

(b)   subsection (8)(a), in so far as applicable in accordance with the relevant law, and

(c)   subsection (8)(b) and (c).

(10) In subsections (8)(a) and (9)(b) 'the relevant law' means the law of the country or territory where the overseas relationship was registered (including its rules of private international law).

(11) For the purposes of subsections (8) and (9)(b) and (c), references in sections 50 and 51 to the formation of the civil partnership are to be read as references to the registration of the overseas relationship.

Defined terms—"civil partners": s 1(1); "overseas relationship": s 212(1).

Presumption of death orders

55 Presumption of death orders

(1) The court may, on an application made by a civil partner, make a presumption of death order if it is satisfied that reasonable grounds exist for supposing that the other civil partner is dead.

(2) In any proceedings under this section the fact that –

    (a)   for a period of 7 years or more the other civil partner has been continually absent from the applicant, and

    (b)   the applicant has no reason to believe that the other civil partner has been living within that time,

is evidence that the other civil partner is dead until the contrary is proved.

Defined terms—"civil partner": s 1(1); "the court": s 37(4); "presumption of death order": s 37(1)(c).

Scope—The fact that a civil partner has been continually absent for 7 years and the applicant has no reason to believe him to be alive during that time creates a rebuttable presumption of the death of that civil partner. This section is the counterpart of MCA 1973, s 19, the commentary to which reference should be made. A presumption of death order is granted in two stages and is initially conditional for a period of 6 weeks (ss 37(2) and 38).

Separation orders

56 Separation orders

(1) An application for a separation order may be made to the court by either civil partner on the ground that any such fact as is mentioned in section 44(5)(a), (b), (c) or (d) exists.

(2) On an application for a separation order the court must inquire, so far as it reasonably can, into –

    (a)   the facts alleged by the applicant, and

    (b)   any facts alleged by the respondent,

but whether the civil partnership has broken down irretrievably is irrelevant.

(3) If the court is satisfied on the evidence of any such fact as is mentioned in section 44(5)(a), (b), (c) or (d) it must, subject to section 63, make a separation order.

(4) Section 45 (supplemental provisions as to facts raising presumption of breakdown) applies for the purposes of an application for a separation order alleging any such fact as it applies in relation to an application for a dissolution order alleging that fact.

Defined terms—"civil partner": s 1(1); "the court": s 37(4); "separation order": s 37(1)(d).

Scope—A separation order provides for the separation of the civil partners. The grounds are as for dissolution (s 56(1)). If either party dies intestate, while a separation order is in effect, his or her property would devolve as though the other civil partner were dead (s 57).

57 Effect of separation order

If either civil partner dies intestate as respects all or any of his or her real or personal property while –

    (a)   a separation order is in force, and

    (b)   the separation is continuing,

the property as respects which he or she died intestate devolves as if the other civil partner had then been dead.

Defined terms —"civil partner": s 1(1); "separation order": s 37(1)(d).

Declarations

58 Declarations

(1) Any person may apply to the High Court or a county court for one or more of the following declarations in relation to a civil partnership specified in the application –

(a)   a declaration that the civil partnership was at its inception a valid civil partnership;

(b)   a declaration that the civil partnership subsisted on a date specified in the application;

(c)   a declaration that the civil partnership did not subsist on a date so specified;

(d)   a declaration that the validity of a dissolution, annulment or legal separation obtained outside England and Wales in respect of the civil partnership is entitled to recognition in England and Wales;

(e)   a declaration that the validity of a dissolution, annulment or legal separation so obtained in respect of the civil partnership is not entitled to recognition in England and Wales.

(2) Where an application under subsection (1) is made to a court by a person other than a civil partner in the civil partnership to which the application relates, the court must refuse to hear the application if it considers that the applicant does not have a sufficient interest in the determination of that application.

Defined term —"civil partner": s 1(1).

Scope—Sections 58–61 contain provisions enabling the court to make declarations in relation to a civil partnership, e g that a civil partnership was at its inception a valid civil partnership or that a civil partnership subsisted or did not subsist on a specified date, which are akin to the provisions relating to declarations as to marital status in FLA 1986, s 55. The procedure is to be found in FPR 2010, Pt 8, Ch 5. Jurisdiction to entertain an application under this section is provided for by s 224. Applications under this section are assigned to the Family Division of the High Court (SCA 1981, s 61(1)(iii), Sch 1, para 3).

59 General provisions as to making and effect of declarations

(1) Where on an application for a declaration under section 58 the truth of the proposition to be declared is proved to the satisfaction of the court, the court must make the declaration unless to do so would be manifestly contrary to public policy.

(2) Any declaration under section 58 binds Her Majesty and all other persons.

(3) The court, on the dismissal of an application for a declaration under section 58, may not make any declaration for which an application has not been made.

(4) No declaration which may be applied for under section 58 may be made otherwise than under section 58 by any court.

(5) No declaration may be made by any court, whether under section 58 or otherwise, that a civil partnership was at its inception void.

(6) Nothing in this section affects the powers of any court to make a nullity order in respect of a civil partnership.

Defined term—"nullity order": s 37(1)(b).

60 The Attorney General and proceedings for declarations

(1) On an application for a declaration under section 58 the court may at any stage of the proceedings, of its own motion or on the application of any party to the proceedings, direct that all necessary papers in the matter be sent to the Attorney General.

(2) The Attorney General, whether or not he is sent papers in relation to an application for a declaration under section 58, may –

(a)   intervene in the proceedings on that application in such manner as he thinks necessary or expedient, and

(b)   argue before the court dealing with the application any question in relation to the application which the court considers it necessary to have fully argued.

(3) Where any costs are incurred by the Attorney General in connection with any application for a declaration under section 58, the court may make such order as it considers just as to the payment of those costs by parties to the proceedings.

61 Supplementary provisions as to declarations

(1) Any declaration made under section 58, and any application for such a declaration, must be in the form prescribed by rules of court.

(2) Rules of court may make provision –

    (a)   as to the information required to be given by any applicant for a declaration under section 58;

    (b)   requiring notice of an application under section 58 to be served on the Attorney General and on persons who may be affected by any declaration applied for.

(3) No proceedings under section 58 affect any final judgment or order already pronounced or made by any court of competent jurisdiction.

(4) The court hearing an application under section 58 may direct that the whole or any part of the proceedings must be heard in private.

(5) An application for a direction under subsection (4) must be heard in private unless the court otherwise directs.

General provisions

62 Relief for respondent in dissolution proceedings

(1) If in any proceedings for a dissolution order the respondent alleges and proves any such fact as is mentioned in section 44(5)(a), (b), (c) or (d) the court may give to the respondent the relief to which he would have been entitled if he had made an application seeking that relief.

(2) When applying subsection (1), treat –

    (a)   the respondent as the applicant, and

    (b)   the applicant as the respondent,

for the purposes of section 44(5).

Defined terms—"the court": s 37(4); "dissolution order": s 37(1)(a).

Scope—This section is the counterpart of MCA 1973, s 20, the commentary to which reference should be made.

63 Restrictions on making of orders affecting children

(1) In any proceedings for a dissolution, nullity or separation order, the court must consider –

    (a)   whether there are any children of the family to whom this section applies, and

    (b)   if there are any such children, whether (in the light of the arrangements which have been, or are proposed to be, made for their upbringing and welfare) it should exercise any of its powers under the Children Act 1989 with respect to any of them.

(2) If, in the case of any child to whom this section applies, it appears to the court that –

    (a)   the circumstances of the case require it, or are likely to require it, to exercise any of its powers under the 1989 Act with respect to any such child,

    (b)   it is not in a position to exercise the power or (as the case may be) those powers without giving further consideration to the case, and

(c)   there are exceptional circumstances which make it desirable in the interests of the child that the court should give a direction under this section,

it may direct that the order is not to be made final, or (in the case of a separation order) is not to be made, until the court orders otherwise.

(3) This section applies to –

(a)   any child of the family who has not reached 16 at the date when the court considers the case in accordance with the requirements of this section, and

(b)   any child of the family who has reached 16 at that date and in relation to whom the court directs that this section shall apply.

Defined terms—"the court": s 37(4); "dissolution order": s 37(1)(a); "nullity order": s 37(1)(b); "separation order": s 37(1)(d).

Scope—Where there are children (as defined by s 63(3)) involved in proceedings for dissolution, nullity or separation relating to a civil partnership, the court is required to consider whether it should exercise any of its powers under CA 1989. This provision is designed to safeguard their welfare and provide for their upbringing and, if necessary, the court may direct that the dissolution, nullity or separation order is not to be made final until it is considered whether or not to exercise its powers under the 1989 Act (s 63(2)). This section is the counterpart to MCA 1973, s 41, the commentary to which reference should be made.

64 Parties to proceedings under this Chapter

(1) Rules of court may make provision with respect to –

(a)   the joinder as parties to proceedings under sections 37 to 56 of persons involved in allegations of improper conduct made in those proceedings,

(b)   the dismissal from such proceedings of any parties so joined, and

(c)   the persons who are to be parties to proceedings on an application under section 58.

(2) Rules of court made under this section may make different provision for different cases.

(3) In every case in which the court considers, in the interest of a person not already a party to the proceedings, that the person should be made a party, the court may if it thinks fit allow the person to intervene upon such terms, if any, as the court thinks just.

Defined terms—"the court": s 37(4).

Scope—This section is the counterpart to MCA 1973, s 49.

65 Contribution by civil partner to property improvement

(1) This section applies if –

(a)   a civil partner contributes in money or money's worth to the improvement of real or personal property in which or in the proceeds of sale of which either or both of the civil partners has or have a beneficial interest, and

(b)   the contribution is of a substantial nature.

(2) The contributing partner is to be treated as having acquired by virtue of the contribution a share or an enlarged share (as the case may be) in the beneficial interest of such an extent –

(a)   as may have been then agreed, or

(b)   in default of such agreement, as may seem in all the circumstances just to any court before which the question of the existence or extent of the beneficial interest of either of the civil partners arises (whether in proceedings between them or in any other proceedings).

(3) Subsection (2) is subject to any agreement (express or implied) between the civil partners to the contrary.

Defined terms—"civil partners": s 1(1).

Scope—This section provides that substantial contributions in money or money's worth to the improvement of property in which either or both civil partners have an interest entitles that contributing civil partner to a share or enlarged share in the property as may have been agreed or, in default of agreement, as may seem in all the circumstances just (subject to any agreement, express or implied, to the contrary) (s 65). This mirrors MPPA 1970, s 37. This section also applies where a civil partnership agreement is terminated (s 74(2)).

66 Disputes between civil partners about property

(1) In any question between the civil partners in a civil partnership as to title to or possession of property, either civil partner may apply to –

    (a)   the High Court, or
    (b)   such county court as may be prescribed by rules of court.

(2) On such an application, the court may make such order with respect to the property as it thinks fit (including an order for the sale of the property).

(3) Rules of court made for the purposes of this section may confer jurisdiction on county courts whatever the situation or value of the property in dispute.

Defined term—"civil partners": s 1(1).

Scope—Civil partners may apply to the court where there is a dispute as to the title or possession of property and the court may make an order as it sees fit including an order for sale (s 66) (corresponding to MWPA 1882, s 17) subject to a limitation period of 3 years from the date of dissolution or annulment (s 68). This section also applies where a civil partnership agreement is terminated (s 66(3)). The procedure is found in FPR 2010, Pt 8, Ch 4.

67 Applications under section 66 where property not in possession etc

(1) The right of a civil partner ('A') to make an application under section 66 includes the right to make such an application where A claims that the other civil partner ('B') has had in his possession or under his control –

    (a)   money to which, or to a share of which, A was beneficially entitled, or
    (b)   property (other than money) to which, or to an interest in which, A was beneficially entitled,

and that either the money or other property has ceased to be in B's possession or under B's control or that A does not know whether it is still in B's possession or under B's control.

(2) For the purposes of subsection (1)(a) it does not matter whether A is beneficially entitled to the money or share –

    (a)   because it represents the proceeds of property to which, or to an interest in which, A was beneficially entitled, or
    (b)   for any other reason.

(3) Subsections (4) and (5) apply if, on such an application being made, the court is satisfied that B –

    (a)   has had in his possession or under his control money or other property as mentioned in subsection (1)(a) or (b), and
    (b)   has not made to A, in respect of that money or other property, such payment or disposition as would have been appropriate in the circumstances.

(4) The power of the court to make orders under section 66 includes power to order B to pay to A –

(a) in a case falling within subsection (1)(a), such sum in respect of the money to which the application relates, or A's s share of it, as the court considers appropriate, or

(b) in a case falling within subsection (1)(b), such sum in respect of the value of the property to which the application relates, or A's interest in it, as the court considers appropriate.

(5) If it appears to the court that there is any property which –

(a) represents the whole or part of the money or property, and

(b) is property in respect of which an order could (apart from this section) have been made under section 66,

the court may (either instead of or as well as making an order in accordance with subsection (4)) make any order which it could (apart from this section) have made under section 66.

(6) Any power of the court which is exercisable on an application under section 66 is exercisable in relation to an application made under that section as extended by this section.

Defined term—"civil partner": s 1(1).

Scope—This section replicates the provisions of the Matrimonial Causes (Property and Maintenance) Act 1958, s 7 and extends s 66 to enable the court to make orders where money or property has ceased to be in the possession or under the control of one of the civil partners.

68 Applications under section 66 by former civil partners

(1) This section applies where a civil partnership has been dissolved or annulled.

(2) Subject to subsection (3), an application may be made under section 66 (including that section as extended by section 67) by either former civil partner despite the dissolution or annulment (and references in those sections to a civil partner are to be read accordingly).

(3) The application must be made within the period of 3 years beginning with the date of the dissolution or annulment.

69 Actions in tort between civil partners

(1) This section applies if an action in tort is brought by one civil partner against the other during the subsistence of the civil partnership.

(2) The court may stay the proceedings if it appears –

(a) that no substantial benefit would accrue to either civil partner from the continuation of the proceedings, or

(b) that the question or questions in issue could more conveniently be disposed of on an application under section 66.

(3) Without prejudice to subsection (2)(b), the court may in such an action –

(a) exercise any power which could be exercised on an application under section 66, or

(b) give such directions as it thinks fit for the disposal under that section of any question arising in the proceedings.

Defined term—"civil partner": s 1(1).

70 Assurance policy by civil partner for benefit of other civil partner etc

Section 11 of the Married Women's Property Act 1882 (money payable under policy of assurance not to form part of the estate of the insured) applies in relation to a policy of assurance –

(a) effected by a civil partner on his own life, and

(b) expressed to be for the benefit of his civil partner, or of his children, or of his civil partner and children, or any of them,

as it applies in relation to a policy of assurance effected by a husband and expressed to be for the benefit of his wife, or of his children, or of his wife and children, or of any of them.

Defined term—"civil partner": s 1(1).

Scope—If a civil partner takes out a life insurance policy to provide for his or her civil partner or children, the application of MWPA 1882, s 11 is extended so that the money payable under the policy is not to form part of the estate of the insured. While this section deals with assurance policies effected by a civil partner on his own life, a civil partner is presumed for the purposes of the Life Assurance Act 1774, s 1 to have an unlimited insurable interest in the life of his civil partner (s 253).

****

72 Financial relief for civil partners and children of family

(1) Schedule 5 makes provision for financial relief in connection with civil partnerships that corresponds to provision made for financial relief in connection with marriages by Part 2 of the Matrimonial Causes Act 1973.

(2) Any rule of law under which any provision of Part 2 of the 1973 Act is interpreted as applying to dissolution of a marriage on the ground of presumed death is to be treated as applying (with any necessary modifications) in relation to the corresponding provision of Schedule 5.

(3) Schedule 6 makes provision for financial relief in connection with civil partnerships that corresponds to provision made for financial relief in connection with marriages by the Domestic Proceedings and Magistrates' Courts Act 1978.

(4) Schedule 7 makes provision for financial relief in England and Wales after a civil partnership has been dissolved or annulled, or civil partners have been legally separated, in a country outside the British Islands.

Defined term—"civil partners": s 1(1).

Scope—This section makes provision for financial relief for civil partners corresponding to Pt II of MCA 1973 (Sch 5), corresponding with the DPMCA 1978 (Sch 6) and corresponding to the MFPA 1984, Pt III after a civil partnership has been dissolved or annulled, or civil partners have been legally separated, in a country outside the British Isles (Sch 7). Reference should be made to the commentary in Schs 5–7.

73 Civil partnership agreements unenforceable

(1) A civil partnership agreement does not under the law of England and Wales have effect as a contract giving rise to legal rights.

(2) No action lies in England and Wales for breach of a civil partnership agreement, whatever the law applicable to the agreement.

(3) In this section and section 74 'civil partnership agreement' means an agreement between two people –

(a) to register as civil partners of each other –

(i) in England and Wales (under this Part),

(ii) in Scotland (under Part 3),

     (iii) in Northern Ireland (under Part 4), or
     (iv) outside the United Kingdom under an Order in Council made under Chapter 1 of Part 5 (registration at British consulates etc or by armed forces personnel), or
  (b) to enter into an overseas relationship.

(4) This section applies in relation to civil partnership agreements whether entered into before or after this section comes into force, but does not affect any action commenced before it comes into force.

Defined terms—"civil partners": s 1(1); "overseas relationship": s 212.

Scope—A civil partnership agreement is an agreement between two people to register as the civil partners of each other (ie the counterpart of an engagement) (s 73(3)). Such an agreement does not give rise to legal rights (s 73(1),(2)). A person is associated with another person if they have entered into a civil partnership agreement (FLA 1996, s 62(3)(eza)) and may thus be entitled to apply for an occupation order or a non-molestation order under ss 33 and 42 respectively of the 1996 Act.

74 Property where civil partnership agreement is terminated

(1) This section applies if a civil partnership agreement is terminated.

(2) Section 65 (contributions by civil partner to property improvement) applies, in relation to any property in which either or both of the parties to the agreement had a beneficial interest while the agreement was in force, as it applies in relation to property in which a civil partner has a beneficial interest.

(3) Sections 66 and 67 (disputes between civil partners about property) apply to any dispute between or claim by one of the parties in relation to property in which either or both had a beneficial interest while the agreement was in force, as if the parties were civil partners of each other.

(4) An application made under section 66 or 67 by virtue of subsection (3) must be made within 3 years of the termination of the agreement.

(5) A party to a civil partnership agreement who makes a gift of property to the other party on the condition (express or implied) that it is to be returned if the agreement is terminated is not prevented from recovering the property merely because of his having terminated the agreement.

Defined terms—"civil partners": s 1(1); "civil partnership agreement": s 73(3).

Scope—Although a civil partnership agreement does not give rise to legal rights (s 73(1),(2)), the provisions of the Act in respect of contributions to property (s 65) and disputes as to title or possession (ss 66 and 67) apply when a civil partnership agreement is terminated provided an application under ss 66 and 67 is made within 3 years of the termination of the agreement (s 74(4)).

****

84 Evidence

(1) Any enactment or rule of law relating to the giving of evidence by a spouse applies in relation to a civil partner as it applies in relation to the spouse.

(2) Subsection (1) is subject to any specific amendment made by or under this Act which relates to the giving of evidence by a civil partner.

(3) For the avoidance of doubt, in any such amendment, references to a person's civil partner do not include a former civil partner.

(4) References in subsections (1) and (2) to giving evidence are to giving evidence in any way (whether by supplying information, making discovery, producing documents or otherwise).

(5) Any rule of law –

   (a)   which is preserved by section 7(3) of the Civil Evidence Act 1995 or section 118(1) of the Criminal Justice Act 2003, and

   (b)   under which in any proceedings evidence of reputation or family tradition is admissible for the purpose of proving or disproving the existence of a marriage,

is to be treated as applying in an equivalent way for the purpose of proving or disproving the existence of a civil partnership.

Defined term—"civil partner": s 1(1).

****

PART 5
CIVIL PARTNERSHIP FORMED OR DISSOLVED ABROAD ETC
****

212 Meaning of 'overseas relationship'

(1) For the purposes of this Act an overseas relationship is a relationship which –

   (a)   is either a specified relationship or a relationship which meets the general conditions, and

   (b)   is registered (whether before or after the passing of this Act) with a responsible authority in a country or territory outside the United Kingdom, by two people –

      (i)   who under the relevant law are of the same sex at the time when they do so, and

      (ii)   neither of whom is already a civil partner or lawfully married.

(2) In this Chapter, 'the relevant law' means the law of the country or territory where the relationship is registered (including its rules of private international law).

Defined terms—"civil partner": s 1(1); "specified relationship": s 213 and Sch 20; "general conditions": s 214.

Scope—It is possible for overseas relationships to be treated as civil partnerships (even though entered into before the Act came into force) providing the requirements of Pt 5 are met (ss 212–218 and Sch 20). Pt 5 of the Act also permits registration abroad at a British Consulate (s 210) or by armed forces personnel (s 211). An overseas relationship, which is either a specified relationship (s 213) or a relationship meeting the general conditions (s 214) will be treated as a civil partnership providing the requirements of s 215 are met. The same-sex requirement (s 216) is relaxed where a full gender recognition certificate has been issued under GRA 2004. These provisions may give rise to applications, as some forms of foreign civil partnership give fewer rights and responsibilities than a civil partnership in England and Wales. Conversely, marriage between same-sex couples in eg, Belgium, The Netherlands or British Columbia is only afforded civil partnership status under the Act (*Wilkinson v Kitzinger and Her Majesty's Attorney-General (the Lord Chancellor Intervening)* [2006] 2 FLR 397 (preliminary costs issue) and *Wilkinson v Kitzinger* [2007] 1 FLR 295 (substantive hearing)).

213 Specified relationships

(1) A specified relationship is a relationship which is specified for the purposes of section 212 by Schedule 20.

(2) The Secretary of State may by order amend Schedule 20 by –

   (a)   adding a relationship,

   (b)   amending the description of a relationship, or

   (c)   omitting a relationship.

(3) No order may be made under this section without the consent of the Scottish Ministers and the Department of Finance and Personnel.

(4) The power to make an order under this section is exercisable by statutory instrument.

(5) An order which contains any provision (whether alone or with other provisions) amending Schedule 20 by –

(a)   amending the description of a relationship, or
(b)   omitting a relationship,

may not be made unless a draft of the statutory instrument containing the order is laid before, and approved by a resolution of, each House of Parliament.

(6) A statutory instrument containing any other order under this section is subject to annulment in pursuance of a resolution of either House of Parliament.

Amendments—SI 2007/2914; SI 2010/1839.

Subordinate legislation—The orders made under this section are the Civil Partnership Act 2004 (Overseas Relationships and Consequential, etc Amendments) Order 2005 and the Civil Partnership Act 2004 (Overseas Relationships) Order 2005.

214 The general conditions

The general conditions are that, under the relevant law –

(a)   the relationship may not be entered into if either of the parties is already a party to a relationship of that kind or lawfully married,
(b)   the relationship is of indeterminate duration, and
(c)   the effect of entering into it is that the parties are –
(i)   treated as a couple either generally or for specified purposes, or
(ii)   treated as married.

Defined terms—"relevant law": s 212(2).

215 Overseas relationships treated as civil partnerships: the general rule

(1) Two people are to be treated as having formed a civil partnership as a result of having registered an overseas relationship if, under the relevant law, they –

(a)   had capacity to enter into the relationship, and
(b)   met all requirements necessary to ensure the formal validity of the relationship.

(2) Subject to subsection (3), the time when they are to be treated as having formed the civil partnership is the time when the overseas relationship is registered (under the relevant law) as having been entered into.

(3) If the overseas relationship is registered (under the relevant law) as having been entered into before this section comes into force, the time when they are to be treated as having formed a civil partnership is the time when this section comes into force.

(4) But if –

(a)   before this section comes into force, a dissolution or annulment of the overseas relationship was obtained outside the United Kingdom, and
(b)   the dissolution or annulment would be recognised under Chapter 3 if the overseas relationship had been treated as a civil partnership at the time of the dissolution or annulment,

subsection (3) does not apply and subsections (1) and (2) have effect subject to subsection (5).

(5) The overseas relationship is not to be treated as having been a civil partnership for the purposes of any provisions except –

(a)   Schedules 7, 11 and 17 (financial relief in United Kingdom after dissolution or annulment obtained outside the United Kingdom);

(b)   such provisions as are specified (with or without modifications) in an order under section 259;

(c)   Chapter 3 (so far as necessary for the purposes of paragraphs (a) and (b)).

(6) This section is subject to sections 216, 217 and 218.

Defined terms—"overseas relationship": s 212(1); "relevant law": s 212(2).

"such provisions as are specified" (s 215(5)(b))—The relevant provisions are Civil Partnership (Treatment of Overseas Relationships) Order 2005 and Civil Partnership (Treatment of Overseas Relationships) (No 2) Order 2005.

216 The same-sex requirement

(1) Two people are not to be treated as having formed a civil partnership as a result of having registered an overseas relationship if, at the critical time, they were not of the same sex under United Kingdom law.

(2) But if a full gender recognition certificate is issued under the 2004 Act to a person who has registered an overseas relationship which is within subsection (4), after the issue of the certificate the relationship is no longer prevented from being treated as a civil partnership on the ground that, at the critical time, the parties were not of the same sex.

(3) However, subsection (2) does not apply to an overseas relationship which is within subsection (4) if either of the parties has formed a subsequent civil partnership or lawful marriage.

(4) An overseas relationship is within this subsection if (and only if), at the time mentioned in section 215(2) –

(a)   one of the parties ('A') was regarded under the relevant law as having changed gender (but was not regarded under United Kingdom law as having done so), and

(b)   the other party was (under United Kingdom law) of the gender to which A had changed under the relevant law.

(5) In this section –

"the critical time" means the time determined in accordance with section 215(2) or (as the case may be) (3);

"the 2004 Act" means the GRA 2004;

"United Kingdom law" means any enactment or rule of law applying in England and Wales, Scotland and Northern Ireland.

(6) Nothing in this section prevents the exercise of any enforceable Community right.

Defined terms—"overseas relationship": s 212(1).

217 Person domiciled in a part of the United Kingdom

(1) Subsection (2) applies if an overseas relationship has been registered by a person who was at the time mentioned in section 215(2) domiciled in England and Wales.

(2) The two people concerned are not to be treated as having formed a civil partnership if, at the time mentioned in section 215(2) –

(a)   either of them was under 16, or

(b)   they would have been within prohibited degrees of relationship under Part 1 of Schedule 1 if they had been registering as civil partners of each other in England and Wales.

(3) Subsection (4) applies if an overseas relationship has been registered by a person who at the time mentioned in section 215(2) was domiciled in Scotland.

(4) The two people concerned are not to be treated as having formed a civil partnership if, at the time mentioned in section 215(2), they were not eligible by virtue of paragraph (b), (c) or (e) of section 86(1) to register in Scotland as civil partners of each other.

(5) Subsection (6) applies if an overseas relationship has been registered by a person who at the time mentioned in section 215(2) was domiciled in Northern Ireland.

(6) The two people concerned are not to be treated as having formed a civil partnership if, at the time mentioned in section 215(2) –

(a) either of them was under 16, or
(b) they would have been within prohibited degrees of relationship under Schedule 12 if they had been registering as civil partners of each other in Northern Ireland.

Defined terms—"civil partners": s 1(1); "overseas relationship": s 212(1).

Scope—Where one of the parties was domiciled in England and Wales when the overseas relationship was registered, it will not be recognised as a civil partnership if either of the parties was under 16 or they would have been within the prohibited degrees of relationship if they had been registering in England and Wales (s 217(1),(2)).

218 The public policy exception

Two people are not to be treated as having formed a civil partnership as a result of having entered into an overseas relationship if it would be manifestly contrary to public policy to recognise the capacity, under the relevant law, of one or both of them to enter into the relationship.

Defined terms—"overseas relationship": s 212(1); "relevant law": s 212(2).

Introduction

219 Power to make provision corresponding to EC Regulation 2201/2003

(1) The Lord Chancellor may by regulations make provision –

(a) as to the jurisdiction of courts in England and Wales in proceedings for the dissolution or annulment of a civil partnership or for legal separation of the civil partners in cases where a civil partner –
   (i) is or has been habitually resident in a member State,
   (ii) is a national of a member State, or
   (iii) is domiciled in a part of the United Kingdom or the Republic of Ireland, and
(b) as to the recognition in England and Wales of any judgment of a court of another member State which orders the dissolution or annulment of a civil partnership or the legal separation of the civil partners.

(1A) The Department of Justice in Northern Ireland may by regulations make provision –

(a) as to the jurisdiction of courts in Northern Ireland in proceedings for the dissolution or annulment of a civil partnership or for legal separation of the civil partners in such cases as are mentioned in subsection (1)(a), and
(b) as to the recognition in Northern Ireland of any such judgment as is mentioned in subsection (1)(b).

(2) The Scottish Ministers may by regulations make provision –

(a) as to the jurisdiction of courts in Scotland in proceedings for the dissolution or annulment of a civil partnership or for legal separation of the civil partners in such cases as are mentioned in subsection (1)(a), and

(b)   as to the recognition in Scotland of any such judgment as is mentioned in subsection (1)(b).

(3) The regulations may in particular make provision corresponding to that made by Council Regulation (EC) No 2201/2003 of 27 November 2003 in relation to jurisdiction and the recognition and enforcement of judgments in matrimonial matters.

(4) The regulations may provide that for the purposes of this Part and the regulations 'member State' means –

(a)   all member States with the exception of such member States as are specified in the regulations, or

(b)   such member States as are specified in the regulations.

(5) The regulations may make provision under subsections (1)(b), (1A)(b) and (2)(b) which applies even if the date of the dissolution, annulment or legal separation is earlier than the date on which this section comes into force.

(6) Regulations under subsection (1) are to be made by statutory instrument and may only be made if a draft has been laid before and approved by resolution of each House of Parliament.

(6A) Regulations under subsection (1A) are to be made by statutory rule for the purposes of the Statutory Rules (Northern Ireland) Order 1979.

(6B) No regulations shall be made under subsection (1A) unless a draft has been laid before and approved by resolution of the Northern Ireland Assembly.

(6C) Section 41(3) of the Interpretation Act (Northern Ireland) 1954 applies for the purposes of subsection (6B) in relation to the laying of a draft as it applies in relation to the laying of a statutory document under an enactment.

(7) Regulations under subsection (2) are to be made by statutory instrument and may only be made if a draft has been laid before and approved by resolution of the Scottish Parliament.

(8) In this Part 'section 219 regulations' means regulations made under this section.

Amendments—SI 2010/976.

Defined term—"civil partners": s 1(1).

Scope—This section provides the basis of jurisdiction in England and Wales for proceedings for dissolution, separation or annulment of a civil partnership, or the recognition of the termination of a civil partnership by another EU Member State. Jurisdiction for the termination of a civil partnership is as on divorce adopting Brussels IIa criteria. Reference should also be made to Civil Partnership (Jurisdiction and Recognition of Judgments) Regulations 2005.

Jurisdiction of courts in England and Wales

220 Meaning of 'the court'

In sections 221 to 224 'the court' means –

(a)   the High Court, or

(b)   if a county court has jurisdiction by virtue of Part 5 of the Matrimonial and Family Proceedings Act 1984, a county court.

County court (s 220(b))—By Civil Courts (Amendment) Order 2005, the following county courts have been designated as a "civil partnership proceedings county court": Birmingham, Brighton, Bristol, Cardiff, Chester, Exeter, Leeds, Manchester and Newcastle.

221 Proceedings for dissolution, separation or nullity order

(1) The court has jurisdiction to entertain proceedings for a dissolution order or a separation order if (and only if) –

    (a) the court has jurisdiction under section 219 regulations,

    (b) no court has, or is recognised as having, jurisdiction under section 219 regulations and either civil partner is domiciled in England and Wales on the date when the proceedings are begun, or

    (c) the following conditions are met –

        (i) the two people concerned registered as civil partners of each other in England or Wales,

        (ii) no court has, or is recognised as having, jurisdiction under section 219 regulations, and

        (iii) it appears to the court to be in the interests of justice to assume jurisdiction in the case.

(2) The court has jurisdiction to entertain proceedings for a nullity order if (and only if) –

    (a) the court has jurisdiction under section 219 regulations,

    (b) no court has, or is recognised as having, jurisdiction under section 219 regulations and either civil partner –

        (i) is domiciled in England and Wales on the date when the proceedings are begun, or

        (ii) died before that date and either was at death domiciled in England and Wales or had been habitually resident in England and Wales throughout the period of 1 year ending with the date of death, or

    (c) the following conditions are met –

        (i) the two people concerned registered as civil partners of each other in England or Wales,

        (ii) no court has, or is recognised as having, jurisdiction under section 219 regulations, and

        (iii) it appears to the court to be in the interests of justice to assume jurisdiction in the case.

(3) At any time when proceedings are pending in respect of which the court has jurisdiction by virtue of subsection (1) or (2) (or this subsection), the court also has jurisdiction to entertain other proceedings, in respect of the same civil partnership, for a dissolution, separation or nullity order, even though that jurisdiction would not be exercisable under subsection (1) or (2).

Defined terms—"civil partners": s 1(1); "the court": s 220; "dissolution order": s 37(1)(a); "nullity order": s 37(1)(b); "section 219 regulations": s 219(8); "separation order": s 37(1)(d).

Scope—This section sets out the basis of jurisdiction in England and Wales for dissolution, nullity and separation orders on the basis of Brussels IIa criteria and, where no court has jurisdiction under the s 219 regulations, on the ground that either party is domiciled in England and Wales. The provisions of s 221(1)(c) and (2)(c) are intended to meet the situation where a civil partnership has been registered in England or Wales, but the civil partners are unable to obtain a termination of the partnership in the jurisdiction in which they are resident as a result of which one or both of them would have otherwise to return to England or Wales in order to establish jurisdiction.

222 Proceedings for presumption of death order

The court has jurisdiction to entertain proceedings for a presumption of death order if (and only if) –

    (a) the applicant is domiciled in England and Wales on the date when the proceedings are begun,

(b)   the applicant was habitually resident in England and Wales throughout the period of 1 year ending with that date, or

(c)   the two people concerned registered as civil partners of each other in England and Wales and it appears to the court to be in the interests of justice to assume jurisdiction in the case.

Defined terms—"civil partners": s 1(1); "the court": s 220; "presumption of death order": s 37(1)(c).

223 Proceedings for dissolution, nullity or separation order: supplementary

(1) Rules of court may make provision in relation to civil partnerships corresponding to the provision made in relation to marriages by Schedule 1 to the Domicile and Matrimonial Proceedings Act 1973.

(2) The rules may in particular make provision –

(a)   for the provision of information by applicants and respondents in proceedings for dissolution, nullity or separation orders where proceedings relating to the same civil partnership are continuing in another jurisdiction, and

(b)   for proceedings before the court to be stayed by the court where there are concurrent proceedings elsewhere in respect of the same civil partnership.

Defined terms—"the court": s 220; "dissolution order": s 37(1)(a); "nullity order": s 37(1)(b); "separation order": s 37(1)(d).

"Rules of court" (s 223(1))—The relevant rules are Family Procedure (Civil Partnership: Staying of Proceedings) Rules 2010, which make provision in relation to civil partnerships corresponding to the DMPA 1973, Sch 1. The procedure is contained in FPR 2010, r 7.27.

224 Applications for declarations as to validity etc

The court has jurisdiction to entertain an application under section 58 if (and only if) –

(a)   either of the civil partners in the civil partnership to which the application relates –

(i)   is domiciled in England and Wales on the date of the application,

(ii)   has been habitually resident in England and Wales throughout the period of 1 year ending with that date, or

(iii)   died before that date and either was at death domiciled in England and Wales or had been habitually resident in England and Wales throughout the period of 1 year ending with the date of death, or

(b)   the two people concerned registered as civil partners of each other in England and Wales and it appears to the court to be in the interests of justice to assume jurisdiction in the case.

Defined terms—"civil partners": s 1(1); "the court": s 220.

****

Recognition of dissolution, annulment and separation

233 Effect of dissolution, annulment or separation obtained in the UK

(1) No dissolution or annulment of a civil partnership obtained in one part of the United Kingdom is effective in any part of the United Kingdom unless obtained from a court of civil jurisdiction.

(2) Subject to subsections (3) and (4), the validity of a dissolution or annulment of a civil partnership or a legal separation of civil partners which has been obtained from a court of civil jurisdiction in one part of the United Kingdom is to be recognised throughout the United Kingdom.

(3) Recognition of the validity of a dissolution, annulment or legal separation obtained from a court of civil jurisdiction in one part of the United Kingdom may be refused in any other part if the dissolution, annulment or separation was obtained at a time when it was irreconcilable with a decision determining the question of the subsistence or validity of the civil partnership –

(a) previously given by a court of civil jurisdiction in the other part, or
(b) previously given by a court elsewhere and recognised or entitled to be recognised in the other part.

(4) Recognition of the validity of a dissolution or legal separation obtained from a court of civil jurisdiction in one part of the United Kingdom may be refused in any other part if the dissolution or separation was obtained at a time when, according to the law of the other part, there was no subsisting civil partnership.

Defined terms—"annulment": s 237(5); "civil partners": s 1(1); "part of the United Kingdom": s 237(5).

Scope—This section provides for the recognition of dissolution, annulment and legal separation in one part of the UK in another part of the UK.

234 Recognition in the UK of overseas dissolution, annulment or separation

(1) Subject to subsection (2), the validity of an overseas dissolution, annulment or legal separation is to be recognised in the United Kingdom if, and only if, it is entitled to recognition by virtue of sections 235 to 237.

(2) This section and sections 235 to 237 do not apply to an overseas dissolution, annulment or legal separation as regards which provision as to recognition is made by section 219 regulations.

(3) For the purposes of subsections (1) and (2) and sections 235 to 237, an overseas dissolution, annulment or legal separation is a dissolution or annulment of a civil partnership or a legal separation of civil partners which has been obtained outside the United Kingdom (whether before or after this section comes into force).

Defined terms—"annulment": s 237(5); "civil partners": s 1(1); "section 219 regulations": s 219(8).

Scope—This section, along with ss 235–7, provides for the recognition in the UK of overseas dissolution, annulment or legal separation other than those granted in another EU Member State (other than Denmark) (s 219). Reference should also be made to Civil Partnership (Supplementary Provisions relating to the Recognition of Overseas Dissolutions, Annulments or Legal Separations) (England and Wales and Northern Ireland) Regulations 2005.

235 Grounds for recognition

(1) The validity of an overseas dissolution, annulment or legal separation obtained by means of proceedings is to be recognised if –

(a) the dissolution, annulment or legal separation is effective under the law of the territory in which it was obtained, and at the relevant date either civil partner was habitually resident or domiciled in that territory, or
(b) the dissolution, annulment or legal separation is effective throughout the country in which it was obtained and at the relevant date either civil partner was a national of that country.

(1A) The validity of an overseas dissolution, annulment or legal separation obtained by means of proceedings is also to be recognised if –

    (a)   the dissolution, annulment or legal separation is effective under the law of the country in which it was obtained, and

    (b)   at the relevant date neither civil partner –

        (i)   was habitually resident in the country in which the dissolution, annulment or legal separation was obtained,

        (ii) was domiciled in that country, or

        (iii) was a national of that country.

    (c)   at the relevant date the party seeking the dissolution, annulment or legal separation was either habitually resident or domiciled in a country whose law does not recognise legal relationships between people of the same sex and does not provide for dissolution, annulment or legal separation as regards such relationships.

(1B) References in paragraph (1A) to "country" shall, where appropriate, include a territory which comprises part of a country in which different systems of law are in force in matters relating to the dissolution or annulment of a civil partnership or the legal separation of civil partners.

(2) The validity of an overseas dissolution, annulment or legal separation obtained otherwise than by means of proceedings is to be recognised if –

    (a)   the dissolution, annulment or legal separation is effective under the law of the territory in which it was obtained,

    (b)   at the relevant date –

        (i)   each civil partner was domiciled in that territory, or

        (ii) either civil partner was domiciled in that territory and the other was domiciled in a country or territory under whose law the dissolution, annulment or legal separation is recognised as valid, and

    (c)   neither civil partner was habitually resident in the United Kingdom throughout the period of 1 year immediately preceding that date.

(2A) The validity of an overseas dissolution, annulment or legal separation obtained otherwise than by means of proceedings is also to be recognised if –

    (a)   the dissolution, annulment or legal separation is effective under the law of the country in which it was obtained,

    (b)   at the relevant date one civil partner was domiciled in that country and the other was domiciled in a country whose law does not recognise legal relationships between people of the same sex and does not provide for recognition of the validity of dissolutions, annulments or legal separations as regards such relationships, and

    (c)   neither civil partner was habitually resident in the United Kingdom throughout the period of 1 year immediately preceding that date.

(2B) References in paragraph (2A) to "country" shall include a territory which comprises part of a country in which different systems of law are in force in matters relating to the dissolution or annulment of a civil partnership or the legal separation of civil partners.

(3) In this section 'the relevant date' means –

    (a)   in the case of an overseas dissolution, annulment or legal separation obtained by means of proceedings, the date of the commencement of the proceedings;

    (b)   in the case of an overseas dissolution, annulment or legal separation obtained otherwise than by means of proceedings, the date on which it was obtained.

(4) Where in the case of an overseas annulment the relevant date fell after the death of either civil partner, any reference in subsection (1) or (2) to that date is to be read in relation to that civil partner as a reference to the date of death.

Amendments—SI 2005/3104.

Defined terms—"annulment": s 237(5); "civil partner": s 1(1); "proceedings": s 237(5).

Scope—This section provides, under s 234, the grounds for recognition in the UK of an overseas dissolution, annulment or legal separation other than one granted in another EU Member State (other than Denmark).

236 Refusal of recognition

(1) Recognition of the validity of an overseas dissolution, annulment or legal separation may be refused in any part of the United Kingdom if the dissolution, annulment or separation was obtained at a time when it was irreconcilable with a decision determining the question of the subsistence or validity of the civil partnership –

(a) previously given by a court of civil jurisdiction in that part of the United Kingdom, or

(b) previously given by a court elsewhere and recognised or entitled to be recognised in that part of the United Kingdom.

(2) Recognition of the validity of an overseas dissolution or legal separation may be refused in any part of the United Kingdom if the dissolution or separation was obtained at a time when, according to the law of that part of the United Kingdom, there was no subsisting civil partnership.

(3) Recognition of the validity of an overseas dissolution, annulment or legal separation may be refused if –

(a) in the case of a dissolution, annulment or legal separation obtained by means of proceedings, it was obtained –
  (i) without such steps having been taken for giving notice of the proceedings to a civil partner as, having regard to the nature of the proceedings and all the circumstances, should reasonably have been taken, or
  (ii) without a civil partner having been given (for any reason other than lack of notice) such opportunity to take part in the proceedings as, having regard to those matters, he should reasonably have been given, or

(b) in the case of a dissolution, annulment or legal separation obtained otherwise than by means of proceedings –
  (i) there is no official document certifying that the dissolution, annulment or legal separation is effective under the law of the territory in which it was obtained, or
  (ii) where either civil partner was domiciled in another country or territory at the relevant date, there is no official document certifying that the dissolution, annulment or legal separation is recognised as valid under the law of that other country or territory, or

(c) in either case, recognition of the dissolution, annulment or legal separation would be manifestly contrary to public policy.

(4) In this section –

"official", in relation to a document certifying that a dissolution, annulment or legal separation is effective, or is recognised as valid, under the law of any country or territory, means issued by a person or body appointed or recognised for the purpose under that law;

"the relevant date" has the same meaning as in section 235.

Amendments—SI 2005/3104.

Defined terms—"annulment": s 237(5); "civil partner": s 1(1); "part of the United Kingdom", "proceedings": s 237(5).

Scope—This section provides for the grounds upon which recognition of the validity of an overseas dissolution, annulment or legal separation may be refused under s 234, where granted in jurisdiction other than another EU Member State (apart from Denmark).

237 Supplementary provisions relating to recognition of dissolution etc

(1) For the purposes of sections 235 and 236,

    (a) where a civil partner has obtained an overseas dissolution, annulment or legal separation in a territory, he is to be treated as domiciled in that territory if he was domiciled there –

        (i) according to the law of that territory in family matters, or

        (ii) the law of the part of the United Kingdom in which the question of recognition arises,

    (b) in all other cases a civil partner is to be treated as domiciled in a country or territory if he was domiciled in that country or territory –

        (i) according to the law of that country or territory in family matters, or

        (ii) according to the law of the part of the United Kingdom in which the question of recognition arises.

(2) The Lord Chancellor or the Scottish Ministers may by regulations make provision –

    (a) applying sections 235 and 236 and subsection (1) with modifications in relation to any country whose territories have different systems of law in force in matters of dissolution, annulment or legal separation;

    (b) applying sections 235 and 236 with modifications in relation to –

        (i) an overseas dissolution, annulment or legal separation in the case of an overseas relationship (or an apparent or alleged overseas relationship);

        (ii) any case where a civil partner is domiciled in a country or territory whose law does not recognise legal relationships between two people of the same sex;

    (c) with respect to recognition of the validity of an overseas dissolution, annulment or legal separation in cases where there are cross-proceedings;

    (d) with respect to cases where a legal separation is converted under the law of the country or territory in which it is obtained into a dissolution which is effective under the law of that country or territory;

    (e) with respect to proof of findings of fact made in proceedings in any country or territory outside the United Kingdom.

(3) The power to make regulations under subsection (2) is exercisable by statutory instrument.

(4) A statutory instrument containing such regulations –

    (a) if made by the Lord Chancellor, is subject to annulment in pursuance of a resolution of either House of Parliament;

    (b) if made by the Scottish Ministers, is subject to annulment in pursuance of a resolution of the Scottish Parliament.

(5) In this section (except subsection (4)) and sections 233 to 236 and 238 –

"annulment" includes any order annulling a civil partnership, however expressed;

"part of the United Kingdom" means England and Wales, Scotland or Northern Ireland;

"proceedings" means judicial or other proceedings.

(6) Nothing in this Chapter is to be read as requiring the recognition of any finding of fault made in proceedings for dissolution, annulment or legal separation or of any maintenance, custody or other ancillary order made in any such proceedings.

Amendments—SI 2005/3104.

Defined term—"civil partner": s 1(1).

Regulations—The regulations made under this section are the Civil Partnership (Supplementary Provisions relating to the Recognition of Overseas Dissolutions, Annulments or Legal Separations) (England and Wales and Northern Ireland) Regulations 2005.

Scope—This section provides supplementary provisions relating to the recognition in the UK under s 234 of an overseas dissolution, annulment or legal separation granted other than in another EU Member State (apart from Denmark).

238 Non-recognition elsewhere of dissolution or annulment

(1) This section applies where, in any part of the United Kingdom –

    (a)   a dissolution or annulment of a civil partnership has been granted by a court of civil jurisdiction, or

    (b)   the validity of a dissolution or annulment of a civil partnership is recognised by virtue of this Chapter.

(2) The fact that the dissolution or annulment would not be recognised outside the United Kingdom does not –

    (a)   preclude either party from forming a subsequent civil partnership or marriage in that part of the United Kingdom, or

    (b)   cause the subsequent civil partnership or marriage of either party (wherever it takes place) to be treated as invalid in that part.

Defined terms—"annulment", "part of the United Kingdom": s 237(5).

Scope—Where an overseas dissolution, annulment or legal separation is recognised under Pt 5 (s 219: other EU Member States apart from Denmark; s 233: other parts of the UK; s 234: other jurisdictions), a party is not precluded from forming a subsequent civil partnership or divorce in the UK because the dissolution or annulment would not be recognised outside the UK nor will the subsequent civil partnership or divorce be treated as invalid.

****

SCHEDULE 5
FINANCIAL RELIEF IN THE HIGH COURT OR A COUNTY COURT ETC

Scope—Section 72(1) and Sch 5 make provision for financial relief for civil partners on dissolution, nullity or separation. It should be noted that the provision corresponds to the provision made for financial relief in connection with marriages by Pt II of MCA 1973, thus indicating that the purpose of the civil partnership regime is to extend, so far as financial remedies are concerned, all the rights and responsibilities of married couples to civil partners (*Lawrence v Gallagher* [2012] 2 FLR 643). Pt 1 of Sch 5 relates to financial provision; Pt 2 to property adjustment; Pt 3 to sale of property orders; Pt 4 to pension sharing; and Pt 4A to pension compensation sharing. The matters to which the court is to have regard under Pts 1–4A are provided for by Pt 5. The court must take into account all the circumstances of the case, giving first consideration to the welfare of any child of the family who is under 18 (para 20). More specifically, when exercising its powers under Parts 1–4A in relation to civil partners, the court must take into account the factors contained in para 21(2) which mirror the checklist in MCA 1973, s 25(2). Where the court is asked to exercise its powers under Parts 1–3 in relation to a child of the family, it must have particular regard to the factors contained in para 22(2), which mirror MCA 1973, s 25(3). Further, unless an adoption order has been made in favour of the non-biological parent, a child of the family will not be a child of those civil partners and, therefore, the additional factors in para 22(3), which mirror MCA 1973, s 25(4), will come into operation where the court is asked to exercise its powers in relation to a child of the family who is not that civil partner's child. Paragraph 23 provides for the termination of financial obligations and translates to the principle of the clean break from MCA 1973, s 25A into civil partnerships. Pt 6 makes provision for pension attachment orders made under Pt 1. Pt 7 makes provision for the Pension Protection Fund in a manner comparable to MCA 1973, s 25E (see annotations), including pension compensation attachment (paras 34A and 34B) (cf MCA 1973, ss 21C, 25F and 25G). Pt 8 (para 38) makes provision for maintenance pending outcome in dissolution, nullity or separation proceedings, which is the counterpart of maintenance pending suit under MCA 1973, s 22. Pt 9 makes provision for financial provision on failure to maintain in a manner comparable to MCA 1973, s 27. Pt 10 provides for the commencement of proceedings and duration of orders mirror-imaging MCA 1973, ss 26, 28 and 29. It should be noted that para 48 replicates the lacuna in MCA 1973, s 28(3) in that a subsequent civil partnership or marriage does not bar an application for a pension sharing order. Pt 11 provides for the variation, discharge, suspension or revival of certain orders for financial relief comparable to MCA 1973, s 31. Pt 12 provides for arrears and repayments in a manner comparable to MCA 1973, ss 32, 33. Pt 14 makes provision for consent orders and maintenance agreements in a manner comparable to MCA 1973, ss 33A–36. Pt 14 contains miscellaneous and supplementary provisions dealing with avoidance of transactions intended to prevent or reduce financial relief (para 74: the counterpart of MCA 1973, s 37), the direction for a settlement of an instrument (para 76: the counterpart of the MCA 1973, s 30), bankruptcy (para 77: the counterpart of MCA 1973, s 39), payments in favour of persons suffering from mental disorder (para 78: the counterpart of MCA 1973, s 40), appeals relating to pension sharing orders (para 79: the counterpart of MCA 1973, s 40A) and appeals relating to pension compensation sharing orders (para 79A: the counterpart of MCA 1937, s 40B).

PART 1
FINANCIAL PROVISION IN CONNECTION WITH DISSOLUTION, NULLITY OR SEPARATION

1 Circumstances in which orders under this Part may be made

(1) The court may make any one or more of the orders set out in paragraph 2(1) –

    (a)   on making a dissolution, nullity or separation order, or

    (b)   at any time afterwards.

(2) The court may make any one or more of the orders set out in paragraph 2(1)(d), (e) and (f) –

    (a)   in proceedings for a dissolution, nullity or separation order, before making the order;

    (b)   if proceedings for a dissolution, nullity or separation order are dismissed after the beginning of the trial, either straightaway or within a reasonable period after the dismissal.

(3) The power of the court to make an order under sub-paragraph (1) or (2)(a) in favour of a child of the family is exercisable from time to time.

(4) If the court makes an order in favour of a child under sub-paragraph (2)(b), it may from time to time make a further order in the child's favour of any of the kinds set out in paragraph 2(1)(d), (e) or (f).

2 The orders: periodical and secured periodical payments and lump sums

(1) The orders are –

    (a)   an order that either civil partner must make to the other such periodical payments for such term as may be specified;

    (b)   an order that either civil partner must secure to the other, to the satisfaction of the court, such periodical payments for such term as may be specified;

    (c)   an order that either civil partner must pay to the other such lump sum or sums as may be specified;

    (d)   an order that one of the civil partners must make –

        (i)   to such person as may be specified for the benefit of a child of the family, or

   (ii) to a child of the family,
  such periodical payments for such term as may be specified;
 (e) an order that one of the civil partners must secure –
   (i) to such person as may be specified for the benefit of a child of the family,
    or
   (ii) to a child of the family,
  to the satisfaction of the court, such periodical payments for such term as may
  be specified;
 (f) an order that one of the civil partners must pay such lump sum as may be
  specified –
   (i) to such person as may be specified for the benefit of a child of the family,
    or
   (ii) to a child of the family.

(2) 'Specified' means specified in the order.

3 Particular provision that may be made by lump sum orders

(1) An order under this Part requiring one civil partner to pay the other a lump sum may be made for the purpose of enabling the other civil partner to meet any liabilities or expenses reasonably incurred by the other in maintaining –

 (a) himself or herself, or
 (b) a child of the family,

before making an application for an order under this Part in his or her favour.

(2) An order under this Part requiring a lump sum to be paid to or for the benefit of a child of the family may be made for the purpose of enabling any liabilities or expenses reasonably incurred by or for the benefit of the child before making an application for an order under this Part to be met.

(3) An order under this Part for the payment of a lump sum may –

 (a) provide for its payment by instalments of such amount as may be specified, and
 (b) require the payment of the instalments to be secured to the satisfaction of the
  court.

(4) Sub-paragraphs (1) to (3) do not restrict the powers to make the orders set out in paragraph 2(1)(c) and (f).

(5) If the court –

 (a) makes an order under this Part for the payment of a lump sum, and
 (b) directs that –
   (i) payment of the sum or any part of it is to be deferred, or
   (ii) the sum or any part of it is to be paid by instalments,

it may provide for the deferred amount or the instalments to carry interest at such rate as may be specified from such date as may be specified until the date when payment of it is due.

(6) A date specified under sub-paragraph (5) must not be earlier than the date of the order.

(7) 'Specified' means specified in the order.

4 When orders under this Part may take effect

(1) If an order is made under paragraph 2(1)(a), (b) or (c) on or after making a dissolution or nullity order, neither the order nor any settlement made in pursuance of it takes effect unless the dissolution or nullity order has been made final.

PART II

(2) This paragraph does not affect the power of the court to give a direction under paragraph 76 (settlement of instrument by conveyancing counsel).

5 Restrictions on making of orders under this Part

The power to make an order under paragraph 2(1)(d), (e) or (f) is subject to paragraph 49(1) and (5) (restrictions on orders in favour of children who have reached 18).

PART 2
PROPERTY ADJUSTMENT ON OR AFTER DISSOLUTION, NULLITY OR SEPARATION

6 Circumstances in which property adjustment orders may be made

(1) The court may make one or more property adjustment orders –

    (a)   on making a dissolution, nullity or separation order, or

    (b)   at any time afterwards.

(2) In this Schedule 'property adjustment order' means a property adjustment order under this Part.

7 Property adjustment orders

(1) The property adjustment orders are –

    (a)   an order that one of the civil partners must transfer such property as may be specified, being property to which he is entitled –
        (i)   to the other civil partner,
        (ii)   to a child of the family, or
        (iii)   to such person as may be specified for the benefit of a child of the family;

    (b)   an order that a settlement of such property as may be specified, being property to which one of the civil partners is entitled, be made to the satisfaction of the court for the benefit of –
        (i)   the other civil partner and the children of the family, or
        (ii)   either or any of them;

    (c)   an order varying for the benefit of –
        (i)   the civil partners and the children of the family, or
        (ii)   either or any of them,
        a relevant settlement;

    (d)   an order extinguishing or reducing the interest of either of the civil partners under a relevant settlement.

(2) The court may make a property adjustment order under sub-paragraph (1)(c) even though there are no children of the family.

(3) In this paragraph –

"entitled" means entitled in possession or reversion,

"relevant settlement" means, in relation to a civil partnership, a settlement made, during its subsistence or in anticipation of its formation, on the civil partners including one made by will or codicil, but not including one in the form of a pension arrangement (within the meaning of Part 4), and

"specified" means specified in the order.

8 When property adjustment orders may take effect

(1) If a property adjustment order is made on or after making a dissolution or nullity order, neither the property adjustment order nor any settlement made under it takes effect unless the dissolution or nullity order has been made final.

(2) This paragraph does not affect the power to give a direction under paragraph 76 (settlement of instrument by conveyancing counsel).

9 Restrictions on making property adjustment orders

The power to make a property adjustment order under paragraph 7(1)(a) is subject to paragraph 49(1) and (5) (restrictions on making orders in favour of children who have reached 18).

PART 3
SALE OF PROPERTY ORDERS

10 Circumstances in which sale of property orders may be made

(1) The court may make a sale of property order –

    (a)   on making –
        (i)   under Part 1, a secured periodical payments order or an order for the payment of a lump sum,
        (ii)   a property adjustment order, or
        (iii)   an order under paragraph 38A for a payment in respect of legal services, or
    (b)   at any time afterwards.

(2) In this Schedule 'sale of property order' means a sale of property order under this Part.

Amendments—LASPOA 2012, s 54.

11 Sale of property orders

(1) A sale of property order is an order for the sale of such property as may be specified, being property in which, or in the proceeds of sale of which, either or both of the civil partners has or have a beneficial interest, either in possession or reversion.

(2) A sale of property order may contain such consequential or supplementary provisions as the court thinks fit.

(3) A sale of property order may in particular include –

    (a)   provision requiring the making of a payment out of the proceeds of sale of the property to which the order relates, and
    (b)   provision requiring any property to which the order relates to be offered for sale to a specified person, or class of persons.

(4) 'Specified' means specified in the order.

12 When sale of property orders may take effect

(1) If a sale of property order is made on or after the making of a dissolution or nullity order, it does not take effect unless the dissolution or nullity order has been made final.

(2) Where a sale of property order is made, the court may direct that –

    (a)   the order, or
    (b)   such provision of it as the court may specify,

is not to take effect until the occurrence of an event specified by the court or the end of a period so specified.

13 When sale of property orders cease to have effect

If a sale of property order contains a provision requiring the proceeds of sale of the property to which the order relates to be used to secure periodical payments to a civil partner, the order ceases to have effect –

(a)   on the death of the civil partner, or

(b)   on the formation of a subsequent civil partnership or marriage by the civil partner.

14 Protection of third parties

(1) Sub-paragraphs (2) and (3) apply if –

(a)   a civil partner has a beneficial interest in any property, or in the proceeds of sale of any property, and

(b)   another person ('A') who is not the other civil partner also has a beneficial interest in the property or the proceeds.

(2) Before deciding whether to make a sale of property order in relation to the property, the court must give A an opportunity to make representations with respect to the order.

(3) Any representations made by A are included among the circumstances to which the court is required to have regard under paragraph 20.

PART 4
PENSION SHARING ORDERS ON OR AFTER DISSOLUTION OR NULLITY ORDER

Scope—The Parts of Sch 5 that make provision for pensions are explained in the table below.

Pensions on making of dissolution, nullity or separation orders in relation to civil partnerships

Remedy	CPA 2004, Sch 5	MCA 1973 counterpart (see annotations)	Relevant SIs	Availability
Pension sharing order	Part 4	Sections 21A, 24B–24D	Dissolution etc (Pensions) Regulations 2005, SI 2005/2920	Dissolution or nullity
Pension compensation sharing orders	Part 4A	Sections 21B, 21C, 24E–24G and 25G	Pension Protection Fund (Pension Compensation Sharing and Attachment on Divorce etc) Regulations 2011, SI 2011/731; Divorce and Dissolution etc (Pension Protection Fund) Regulations 2011, SI 2011/780	Dissolution or nullity

Remedy	CPA 2004, Sch 5	MCA 1973 counterpart (see annotations)	Relevant SIs	Availability
Pension attachment orders	Part 6	Sections 25B–25D	Dissolution etc (Pensions Regulations) 2005, SI 2005/2920	Dissolution, nullity or separation
Pension compensation attachment orders	Part 7, paras 34A and 34B	Sections 21C, 25F and 25G	Pension Protection Fund (Pension Compensation Sharing and Attachment on Divorce etc) Regulations 2011, SI 2011/731; Divorce and Dissolution etc (Pension Protection Fund) Regulations 2011, SI 2011/780	Dissolution, nullity or separation
Pension sharing orders: subsequent assumption of responsibility by Pension Protection Fund	Pensions Act 2004, s 220, Sch 7	Sections 25E(1), 25E(7) and 25E(9) Pensions Act 2004, s 220, Sch 7	Pension Protection Fund (Pension Sharing) Regulations 2006, SI 2006/1690	Dissolution or nullity
Pension attachment orders: subsequent assumption of responsibility by Pension Protection Fund	Part 7, paras 31–34 and 35–37	Section 25E	Dissolution etc (Pension Protection Fund) Regulations 2006, SI 2006/1934	Dissolution, nullity or separation

15 Circumstances in which pension sharing orders may be made

(1) The court may make a pension sharing order –

    (a)   on making a dissolution or nullity order, or

    (b)   at any time afterwards.

(2) In this Schedule 'pension sharing order' means a pension sharing order under this Part.

16 Pension sharing orders

(1) A pension sharing order is an order which –

    (a)   provides that one civil partner's –

        (i)   shareable rights under a specified pension arrangement, or

        (ii)   shareable state scheme rights,

        are to be subject to pension sharing for the benefit of the other civil partner, and

    (b)   specifies the percentage value to be transferred.

(2) Shareable rights under a pension arrangement are rights in relation to which pension sharing is available under –

    (a)   Chapter 1 of Part 4 of the Welfare Reform and Pensions Act 1999, or

    (b)   corresponding Northern Ireland legislation.

(3) Shareable state scheme rights are rights in relation to which pension sharing is available under –

    (a)   Chapter 2 of Part 4 of the 1999 Act, or

    (b)   corresponding Northern Ireland legislation.

(4) In this Part 'pension arrangement' means –

    (a)   an occupational pension scheme,

    (b)   a personal pension scheme,

    (c)   a retirement annuity contract,

    (d)   an annuity or insurance policy purchased, or transferred, for the purpose of giving effect to rights under –

        (i)   an occupational pension scheme, or

        (ii) a personal pension scheme, and

    (e)   an annuity purchased, or entered into, for the purpose of discharging liability in respect of a pension credit under –

        (i)   section 29(1)(b) of the 1999 Act, or

        (ii) corresponding Northern Ireland legislation.

(5) In sub-paragraph (4) –

"occupational pension scheme" has the same meaning as in the Pension Schemes Act 1993;

"personal pension scheme" has the same meaning as in the 1993 Act;

"retirement annuity contract" means a contract or scheme approved under Chapter 3 of Part 14 of the Income and Corporation Taxes Act 1988.

17 Pension sharing orders: apportionment of charges

If a pension sharing order relates to rights under a pension arrangement, the court may include in the order provision about the apportionment between the civil partners of any charge under –

    (a)   section 41 of the 1999 Act (charges in respect of pension sharing costs), or

    (b)   corresponding Northern Ireland legislation.

18 Restrictions on making of pension sharing orders

(1) A pension sharing order may not be made in relation to a pension arrangement which –

    (a)   is the subject of a pension sharing order in relation to the civil partnership, or

    (b)   has been the subject of pension sharing between the civil partners.

(2) A pension sharing order may not be made in relation to shareable state scheme rights if –

    (a)   such rights are the subject of a pension sharing order in relation to the civil partnership, or

    (b)   such rights have been the subject of pension sharing between the civil partners.

(3) A pension sharing order may not be made in relation to the rights of a person under a pension arrangement if there is in force a requirement imposed by virtue of Part 6 which relates to benefits or future benefits to which that person is entitled under the pension arrangement.

19 When pension sharing orders may take effect

(1) A pension sharing order is not to take effect unless the dissolution or nullity order on or after which it is made has been made final.

(2) No pension sharing order may be made so as to take effect before the end of such period after the making of the order as may be prescribed by regulations made by the Lord Chancellor.

(3) The power to make regulations under sub-paragraph (2) is exercisable by statutory instrument which is subject to annulment in pursuance of a resolution of either House of Parliament.

PART 4A
PENSION COMPENSATION SHARING ORDERS ON OR AFTER DISSOLUTION OR NULLITY ORDER

Scope—See annotations to Pt 4.

19A Circumstances in which pension compensation sharing orders may be made

(1) The court may make a pension compensation sharing order –

(a) on making a dissolution or nullity order, or

(b) at any time afterwards.

(2) In this Schedule "pension compensation sharing order" means a pension compensation sharing order under this Part.

Amendments—Inserted by Pensions Act 2008, Sch 6, Pt 3.

19B Pension compensation sharing orders

(1) A pension compensation sharing order is an order which –

(a) provides that one civil partner's shareable rights to PPF compensation that derive from rights under a specified pension scheme are to be subject to pension compensation sharing for the benefit of the other civil partner, and

(b) specifies the percentage value to be transferred.

(2) Shareable rights to PPF compensation are rights in relation to which pension compensation sharing is available under –

(a) Chapter 1 of Part 3 of the Pensions Act 2008, or

(b) corresponding Northern Ireland legislation.

(3) In sub-paragraph (1) "specified" means specified in the order.

Amendments—Inserted by Pensions Act 2008, Sch 6, Pt 3.

19C Pension compensation sharing orders: apportionment of charges

The court may include in a pension compensation sharing order provision about the apportionment between the civil partners of any charge under –

(a)   section 117 of the Pensions Act 2008 (charges in respect of pension compensation sharing costs), or

(b)   corresponding Northern Ireland legislation.

Amendments—Inserted by Pensions Act 2008, Sch 6, Pt 3.

19D Restrictions on making pension compensation sharing orders

(1) A pension compensation sharing order may not be made in relation to rights to PPF compensation that –

(a)   are the subject of pension attachment,

(b)   derive from rights under a pension scheme that were the subject of pension sharing between the civil partners,

(c)   are the subject of pension compensation attachment, or

(d)   are or have been the subject of pension compensation sharing between the civil partners.

(2) For the purposes of sub-paragraph (1)(a), rights to PPF compensation "are the subject of pension attachment" if any of the following three conditions is met.

(3) The first condition is that –

(a)   the rights derive from rights under a pension scheme in relation to which an order was made under Part 1 imposing a requirement by virtue of paragraph 25(2), and

(b)   that order, as modified under paragraph 31, remains in force.

(4) The second condition is that –

(a)   the rights derive from rights under a pension scheme in relation to which an order was made under Part 1 imposing a requirement by virtue of paragraph 25(5), and

(b)   that order –

(i)   has been complied with, or

(ii)   has not been complied with and, as modified under paragraph 32, remains in force.

(5) The third condition is that –

(a)   the rights derive from rights under a pension scheme in relation to which an order was made under Part 1 imposing a requirement by virtue of paragraph 26, and

(b)   that order remains in force.

(6) For the purposes of sub-paragraph (1)(b), rights under a pension scheme "were the subject of pension sharing between the civil partners" if the rights were at any time the subject of a pension sharing order in relation to the civil partnership or a previous civil partnership between the same parties.

(7) For the purposes of sub-paragraph (1)(c), rights to PPF compensation "are the subject of pension compensation attachment" if there is in force a requirement imposed by virtue of Part 6 relating to them.

(8) For the purposes of sub-paragraph (1)(d), rights to PPF compensation "are or have been the subject of pension compensation sharing between the civil partners" if they are or have ever been the subject of a pension compensation sharing order in relation to the civil partnership or a previous civil partnership between the same parties.

Amendments—Inserted by Pensions Act 2008, Sch 6, Pt 3.

19E When pension compensation sharing orders may take effect

(1) A pension compensation sharing order is not to take effect unless the dissolution or nullity order on or after which it is made has been made final.

(2) No pension compensation sharing order may be made so as to take effect before the end of such period after the making of the order as may be prescribed by regulations made by the Lord Chancellor.

(3) The power to make regulations under sub-paragraph (2) is exercisable by statutory instrument which is subject to annulment in pursuance of a resolution of either House of Parliament.

Amendments—Inserted by Pensions Act 2008, Sch 6, Pt 3.

19F Interpretation

In this Schedule –

"PPF compensation" means compensation payable under the pension compensation provisions;

"the pension compensation provisions" means –

    (a)   Chapter 3 of Part 2 of the Pensions Act 2004 (pension protection) and any regulations or order made under it,

    (b)   Chapter 1 of Part 3 of the Pensions Act 2008 (pension compensation sharing) and any regulations or order made under it, and

    (c)   any provision corresponding to the provisions mentioned in paragraph (a) or (b) in force in Northern Ireland.

Amendments—Inserted by Pensions Act 2008, Sch 6, Pt 3.

PART 5
MATTERS TO WHICH COURT IS TO HAVE REGARD UNDER PARTS 1 TO 4A

20 General

The court in deciding –

    (a)   whether to exercise its powers under –

        (i)   Part 1 (financial provision on dissolution etc),

        (ii)   Part 2 (property adjustment orders),

        (iii)   Part 3 (sale of property orders),

        (iv)   any provision of Part 4 (pension sharing orders) other than paragraph 17 (apportionment of charges), or

        (v)   any provision of Part 4A (pension compensation sharing orders) other than paragraph 19C (apportionment of charges), and

    (b)   if so, in what way,

must have regard to all the circumstances of the case, giving first consideration to the welfare, while under 18, of any child of the family who has not reached 18.

Amendments—Pensions Act 2008, Sch 6, Pt 3.

21 Particular matters to be taken into account when exercising powers in relation to civil partners

(1) This paragraph applies to the exercise by the court in relation to a civil partner of its powers under –

(a) Part 1 (financial provision on dissolution etc) by virtue of paragraph 2(1)(a), (b) or (c),

(b) Part 2 (property adjustment orders),

(c) Part 3 (sale of property orders),

(d) Part 4 (pension sharing orders), or

(e) Part 4A (pension compensation sharing orders).

(2) The court must in particular have regard to –

(a) the income, earning capacity, property and other financial resources which each civil partner –
   (i)   has, or
   (ii) is likely to have in the foreseeable future,
   including, in the case of earning capacity, any increase in that capacity which it would in the opinion of the court be reasonable to expect a civil partner in the civil partnership to take steps to acquire;

(b) the financial needs, obligations and responsibilities which each civil partner has or is likely to have in the foreseeable future;

(c) the standard of living enjoyed by the family before the breakdown of the civil partnership;

(d) the age of each civil partner and the duration of the civil partnership;

(e) any physical or mental disability of either of the civil partners;

(f) the contributions which each civil partner has made or is likely in the foreseeable future to make to the welfare of the family, including any contribution by looking after the home or caring for the family;

(g) the conduct of each civil partner, if that conduct is such that it would in the opinion of the court be inequitable to disregard it;

(h) in the case of proceedings for a dissolution or nullity order, the value to each civil partner of any benefit which, because of the dissolution or annulment of the civil partnership, that civil partner will lose the chance of acquiring.

Amendments—Pensions Act 2008, Sch 6, Pt 3.

22 Particular matters to be taken into account when exercising powers in relation to children

(1) This paragraph applies to the exercise by the court in relation to a child of the family of its powers under –

(a) Part 1 (financial provision on dissolution etc) by virtue of paragraph 2(1)(d), (e) or (f)),

(b) Part 2 (property adjustment orders), or

(c) Part 3 (sale of property orders).

(2) The court must in particular have regard to –

(a) the financial needs of the child;

(b) the income, earning capacity (if any), property and other financial resources of the child;

(c) any physical or mental disability of the child;

(d) the way in which the child was being and in which the civil partners expected the child to be educated or trained;

(e) the considerations mentioned in relation to the civil partners in paragraph 21(2)(a), (b), (c) and (e).

(3) In relation to the exercise of any of those powers against a civil partner ('A') in favour of a child of the family who is not A's child, the court must also have regard to –

(a) whether A has assumed any responsibility for the child's maintenance;

(b) if so, the extent to which, and the basis upon which, A assumed such responsibility and the length of time for which A discharged such responsibility;

(c) whether in assuming and discharging such responsibility A did so knowing that the child was not A's child;

(d) the liability of any other person to maintain the child.

23 Terminating financial obligations

(1) Sub-paragraphs (2) and (3) apply if, on or after the making of a dissolution or nullity order, the court decides to exercise its powers under –

(a) Part 1 (financial provision on dissolution etc) by virtue of paragraph 2(1)(a), (b) or (c),

(b) Part 2 (property adjustment orders),

(c) Part 3 (sale of property orders),

(d) Part 4 (pension sharing orders), or

(e) Part 4A (pension compensation sharing orders),

in favour of one of the civil partners.

(2) The court must consider whether it would be appropriate to exercise those powers in such a way that the financial obligations of each civil partner towards the other will be terminated as soon after the making of the dissolution or nullity order as the court considers just and reasonable.

(3) If the court decides to make –

(a) a periodical payments order, or

(b) a secured periodical payments order,

in favour of one of the civil partners ('A'), it must in particular consider whether it would be appropriate to require the payments to be made or secured only for such term as would in its opinion be sufficient to enable A to adjust without undue hardship to the termination of A's financial dependence on the other civil partner.

(4) If –

(a) on or after the making of a dissolution or nullity order, an application is made by one of the civil partners for a periodical payments or secured periodical payments order in that civil partner's favour, but

(b) the court considers that no continuing obligation should be imposed on either civil partner to make or secure periodical payments in favour of the other,

the court may dismiss the application with a direction that the applicant is not entitled to make any future application in relation to that civil partnership for an order under Part 1 by virtue of paragraph 2(1)(a) or (b).

Amendments—Pensions Act 2008, Sch 6, Pt 3.

PART 6
MAKING OF PART 1 ORDERS HAVING REGARD TO PENSION BENEFITS

Scope—See annotations to Pt 4.

24 Pension benefits to be included in matters to which court is to have regard

(1) The matters to which the court is to have regard under paragraph 21(2)(a) include any pension benefits under a pension arrangement or by way of pension which a civil

PART II

partner has or is likely to have; and, accordingly, in relation to any pension benefits paragraph 21(2)(a)(ii) has effect as if 'in the foreseeable future' were omitted.

(2) The matters to which the court is to have regard under paragraph 21(2)(h) include any pension benefits which, because of the making of a dissolution or nullity order, a civil partner will lose the chance of acquiring.

(3) 'Pension benefits' means –

    (a)   benefits under a pension arrangement, or

    (b)   benefits by way of pension (whether under a pension arrangement or not).

25 Provisions applying where pension benefits taken into account in decision to make Part 1 order

(1) This paragraph applies if, having regard to any benefits under a pension arrangement, the court decides to make an order under Part 1.

(2) To the extent to which the Part 1 order is made having regard to any benefits under a pension arrangement, it may require the person responsible for the pension arrangement, if at any time any payment in respect of any benefits under the arrangement becomes due to the civil partner with pension rights, to make a payment for the benefit of the other civil partner.

(3) The Part 1 order must express the amount of any payment required to be made by virtue of sub-paragraph (2) as a percentage of the payment which becomes due to the civil partner with pension rights.

(4) Any such payment by the person responsible for the arrangement –

    (a)   discharges so much of his liability to the civil partner with pension rights as corresponds to the amount of the payment, and

    (b)   is to be treated for all purposes as a payment made by the civil partner with pension rights in or towards the discharge of that civil partner's liability under the order.

(5) If the civil partner with pension rights has a right of commutation under the arrangement, the Part 1 order may require that civil partner to exercise it to any extent.

(6) This paragraph applies to any payment due in consequence of commutation in pursuance of the Part 1 order as it applies to other payments in respect of benefits under the arrangement.

(7) The power conferred by sub-paragraph (5) may not be exercised for the purpose of commuting a benefit payable to the civil partner with pension rights to a benefit payable to the other civil partner.

(8) The powers conferred by sub-paragraphs (2) and (5) may not be exercised in relation to a pension arrangement which –

    (a)   is the subject of a pension sharing order in relation to the civil partnership, or

    (b)   has been the subject of pension sharing between the civil partners.

Pension Protection Fund—Paragraph 25 is modified for certain purposes when the Pension Protection Fund has assumed responsibility for the pension arrangement in question by Pt 7, paras 31 and 32 and the Divorce etc (Pension Protection Fund) Regulations 2006.

26 Pensions: lump sums

(1) This paragraph applies if the benefits which the civil partner with pension rights has or is likely to have under a pension arrangement include any lump sum payable in respect of that civil partner's death.

(2) The court's power under Part 1 to order a civil partner to pay a lump sum to the other civil partner includes the power to make by the order any provision in sub-paragraph (3) to (5).

(3) If the person responsible for the pension arrangement has power to determine the person to whom the sum, or any part of it, is to be paid, the court may require him to pay the whole or part of that sum, when it becomes due, to the other civil partner.

(4) If the civil partner with pension rights has power to nominate the person to whom the sum, or any part of it, is to be paid, the court may require the civil partner with pension rights to nominate the other civil partner in respect of the whole or part of that sum.

(5) In any other case, the court may require the person responsible for the pension arrangement in question to pay the whole or part of that sum, when it becomes due, for the benefit of the other civil partner instead of to the person to whom, apart from the order, it would be paid.

(6) Any payment by the person responsible for the arrangement under an order made under Part 1 made by virtue of this paragraph discharges so much of his liability in respect of the civil partner with pension rights as corresponds to the amount of the payment.

(7) The powers conferred by this paragraph may not be exercised in relation to a pension arrangement which –

(a) is the subject of a pension sharing order in relation to the civil partnership, or
(b) has been the subject of pension sharing between the civil partners.

27 Pensions: supplementary

If –

(a) a Part 1 order made by virtue of paragraph 25 or 26 imposes any requirement on the person responsible for a pension arrangement ('the first arrangement'),
(b) the civil partner with pension rights acquires rights under another pension arrangement ('the new arrangement') which are derived (directly or indirectly) from the whole of that civil partner's rights under the first arrangement, and
(c) the person responsible for the new arrangement has been given notice in accordance with regulations made by the Lord Chancellor,

the Part 1 order has effect as if it had been made instead in respect of the person responsible for the new arrangement.

28 Regulations

(1) The Lord Chancellor may by regulations –

(a) make provision, in relation to any provision of paragraph 25 or 26 which authorises the court making a Part 1 order to require the person responsible for a pension arrangement to make a payment for the benefit of the other civil partner, as to –
(i) the person to whom, and
(ii) the terms on which,
the payment is to be made;
(b) make provision, in relation to payment under a mistaken belief as to the continuation in force of a provision included by virtue of paragraph 25 or 26 in a Part 1 order, about the rights or liabilities of the payer, the payee or the person to whom the payment was due;
(c) require notices to be given in respect of changes of circumstances relevant to Part 1 orders which include provision made by virtue of paragraphs 25 and 26;

(d) make provision for the person responsible for a pension arrangement to be discharged in prescribed circumstances from a requirement imposed by virtue of paragraph 25 or 26;

(e) make provision about calculation and verification in relation to the valuation of –
(i) benefits under a pension arrangement, or
(ii) shareable state scheme rights (within the meaning of paragraph 16(3)), for the purposes of the court's functions in connection with the exercise of any of its powers under this Schedule.

(2) Regulations under sub-paragraph (1)(e) may include –

(a) provision for calculation or verification in accordance with guidance from time to time prepared by a prescribed person, and

(b) provision by reference to regulations under section 30 or 49(4) of the 1999 Act.

(3) The power to make regulations under paragraph 27 or this paragraph is exercisable by statutory instrument which is subject to annulment in pursuance of a resolution of either House of Parliament.

(4) 'Prescribed' means prescribed by regulations.

Subordinate legislation—Dissolution etc (Pensions) Regulations 2005.

29 Interpretation of provisions relating to pensions

(1) In this Part 'the civil partner with pension rights' means the civil partner who has or is likely to have benefits under a pension arrangement.

(2) In this Part 'pension arrangement' has the same meaning as in Part 4.

(3) In this Part, references to the person responsible for a pension arrangement are to be read in accordance with section 26 of the Welfare Reform and Pensions Act 1999.

PART 7
PENSION PROTECTION FUND COMPENSATION ETC

Scope—See annotations to Pt 4.

30 PPF compensation to be included in matters to which court is to have regard

(1) The matters to which a court is to have regard under paragraph 21(2)(a) include any PPF compensation to which a civil partner is or is likely to be entitled; and, accordingly, in relation to any PPF compensation paragraph 21(2)(a)(ii) has effect as if 'in the foreseeable future' were omitted.

(2) The matters to which a court is to have regard under paragraph 21(2)(h) include any PPF compensation which, because of the making of a dissolution or nullity order, a civil partner will lose the chance of acquiring entitlement to.

Amendments—Pensions Act 2008, Sch 6, Pt 3.

31 Assumption of responsibility by PPF Board in paragraph 25(2) cases

(1) This paragraph applies to an order under Part 1 so far as it includes provision made by virtue of paragraph 25(2) which –

(a) imposed requirements on the trustees or managers of an occupational pension scheme for which the Board has assumed responsibility, and

(b) was made before the trustees or managers received the transfer notice.

(2) From the time the trustees or managers of the scheme receive the transfer notice, the order has effect –

    (a)   except in descriptions of case prescribed by regulations, with the modifications set out in sub-paragraph (3), and

    (b)   with such other modifications as may be prescribed by regulations.

(3) The modifications are that –

    (a)   references in the order to the trustees or managers of the scheme have effect as references to the Board, and

    (b)   references in the order to any pension or lump sum to which the civil partner with pension rights is or may become entitled under the scheme have effect as references to any PPF compensation to which that person is or may become entitled in respect of the pension or lump sum.

32 Assumption of responsibility by PPF Board in paragraph 25(5) cases

(1) This paragraph applies to an order under Part 1 if –

    (a)   it includes provision made by virtue of paragraph 25(5) which requires the civil partner with pension rights to exercise his right of commutation under an occupational pension scheme to any extent, and

    (b)   before the requirement is complied with the Board has assumed responsibility for the scheme.

(2) From the time the trustees or managers of the scheme receive the transfer notice, the order has effect with such modifications as may be prescribed by regulations.

33 Lump sums: power to modify paragraph 26 in respect of assessment period

Regulations may modify paragraph 26 in its application to an occupational pension scheme during an assessment period in relation to the scheme.

34 Assumption of responsibility by the Board not to affect power of court to vary order etc

(1) This paragraph applies where the court makes, in relation to an occupational pension scheme –

    (a)   a pension sharing order, or

    (b)   an order including provision made by virtue of paragraph 25(2) or (5).

(2) If the Board subsequently assumes responsibility for the scheme, that does not affect –

    (a)   the powers of the court under paragraph 51 to vary or discharge the order or to suspend or revive any provision of it;

    (b)   on an appeal, the powers of the appeal court to affirm, reinstate, set aside or vary the order.

34A Attachment of PPF compensation

(1) This paragraph applies if, having regard to any PPF compensation to which a civil partner is or is likely to be entitled, the court decides to make an order under Part 1.

(2) To the extent to which the Part 1 order is made having regard to such compensation, it may require the Board, if at any time any payment in respect of PPF compensation becomes due to the civil partner with compensation rights, to make a payment for the benefit of the other civil partner.

(3) The Part 1 order must express the amount of any payment required to be made by virtue of sub-paragraph (2) as a percentage of the payment which becomes due to the civil partner with compensation rights.

(4) Any such payment by the Board –

(a) discharges so much of its liability to the civil partner with compensation rights as corresponds to the amount of the payment, and

(b) is to be treated for all purposes as a payment made by the civil partner with compensation rights in or towards the discharge of that civil partner's liability under the order.

(5) If the civil partner with compensation rights has a right to commute any PPF compensation, the Part 1 order may require that civil partner to exercise it to any extent.

(6) This paragraph applies to any payment due in consequence of commutation in pursuance of the Part 1 order as it applies to other payments in respect of PPF compensation.

(7) The power conferred by sub-paragraph (5) may not be exercised for the purpose of commuting a benefit payable to the civil partner with compensation rights to a benefit payable to the other civil partner.

(8) The powers conferred by sub-paragraphs (2) and (5) may not be exercised in relation to rights to PPF compensation that –

(a) derive from rights under a pension scheme that were at any time the subject of a pension sharing order in relation to the civil partnership or a previous civil partnership between the same parties, or.

(b) are or have ever been the subject of a pension compensation sharing order in relation to the civil partnership or a previous civil partnership between the same parties.

Amendments—Pensions Act 2008, Sch 6, Pt 3.

34B (1) Regulations may –

(a) make provision, in relation to any provision of paragraph 34A which authorises the court making a Part 1 order to require the Board to make a payment for the benefit of the other civil partner, as to the person to whom, and the terms on which, the payment is to be made;

(b) make provision, in relation to payment under a mistaken belief as to the continuation in force of a provision included by virtue of paragraph 34A in a Part 1 order, about the rights or liabilities of the payer, the payee or the person to whom the payment was due;

(c) require notices to be given in respect of changes of circumstances relevant to Part 1 orders which include provision made by virtue of paragraph 34A;

(d) make provision for the Board to be discharged in prescribed circumstances from a requirement imposed by virtue of paragraph 34A;

(e) make provision about calculation and verification in relation to the valuation of PPF compensation for the purposes of the court's functions in connection with the exercise of any of its powers under this Schedule.

(2) Regulations under sub-paragraph (1)(e) may include –

(a) provision for calculation or verification in accordance with guidance from time to time prepared by a prescribed person;

(b) provision by reference to regulations under section 112 of the Pensions Act 2008.

Amendments—Pensions Act 2008, Sch 6, Pt 3.

35 Regulations

Regulations may make such consequential modifications of any provision of, or made by virtue of, this Schedule as appear to the Lord Chancellor necessary or expedient to give effect to the provisions of this Part.

36 (1) In this Part 'regulations' means regulations made by the Lord Chancellor.

(2) A power to make regulations under this Part is exercisable by statutory instrument which is subject to annulment in pursuance of a resolution of either House of Parliament.

37 Interpretation

(1) In this Part –
"assessment period" means –
(a) an assessment period within the meaning of Part 2 of the Pensions Act 2004 (pension protection), or
(b) an equivalent period under corresponding Northern Ireland legislation;
"the Board" means the Board of the Pension Protection Fund;
"the civil partner with compensation rights" means the civil partner who is or is likely to be entitled to PPF compensation;
"the civil partner with pension rights" has the meaning given by paragraph 29(1);
"occupational pension scheme" has the same meaning as in the Pension Schemes Act 1993;
"prescribed" means prescribed by regulations;
"transfer notice" has the same meaning as in –
(a) Chapter 3 of Part 2 of the 2004 Act, or
(b) corresponding Northern Ireland legislation.

(2) References in this Part to the Board assuming responsibility for a scheme are to the Board assuming responsibility for the scheme in accordance with –

(a) Chapter 3 of Part 2 of the 2004 Act (pension protection), or
(b) corresponding Northern Ireland legislation.

Amendments—Pensions Act 2008, Sch 6, Pt 3.

PART 8
MAINTENANCE AND OTHER PAYMENTS PENDING OUTCOME OF DISSOLUTION, NULLITY OR SEPARATION PROCEEDINGS

Amendments—LASPOA 2012, s 52.

38 Maintenance orders

(1) On an application for a dissolution, nullity or separation order, the court may make an order requiring either civil partner to make to the other for the other's maintenance such periodical payments for such term –

(a) beginning no earlier than the date on which the application was made, and
(b) ending with the date on which the proceedings are determined,

as the court thinks reasonable.

(2) An order under this paragraph may not require one civil partner to pay to the other any amount in respect of legal services for the purposes of the proceedings.

(3) In sub-paragraph (2) "legal services" has the same meaning as in paragraph 38A.

Amendments—LASPOA 2012, s 52.

38A Orders in respect of legal services

(1) In proceedings for a dissolution, nullity or separation order, the court may make an order or orders requiring one civil partner to pay to the other ("the applicant") an amount for the purpose of enabling the applicant to obtain legal services for the purposes of the proceedings.

(2) The court may also make such an order or orders in proceedings under this Schedule for financial relief in connection with proceedings for a dissolution, nullity or separation order.

(3) The court must not make an order under this paragraph unless it is satisfied that, without the amount, the applicant would not reasonably be able to obtain appropriate legal services for the purposes of the proceedings or any part of the proceedings.

(4) For the purposes of sub-paragraph (3), the court must be satisfied, in particular, that –

   (a) the applicant is not reasonably able to secure a loan to pay for the services, and
   (b) the applicant is unlikely to be able to obtain the services by granting a charge over any assets recovered in the proceedings.

(5) An order under this paragraph may be made for the purpose of enabling the applicant to obtain legal services of a specified description, including legal services provided in a specified period or for the purposes of a specified part of the proceedings.

(6) An order under this paragraph may –

   (a) provide for the payment of all or part of the amount by instalments of specified amounts, and
   (b) require the instalments to be secured to the satisfaction of the court.

(7) An order under this paragraph may direct that payment of all or part of the amount is to be deferred.

(8) The court may at any time in the proceedings vary an order made under this paragraph if it considers that there has been a material change of circumstances since the order was made.

(9) For the purposes of the assessment of costs in the proceedings, the applicant's costs are to be treated as reduced by any amount paid to the applicant pursuant to an order under this section for the purposes of those proceedings.

(10) In this paragraph "legal services", in relation to proceedings, means the following types of services –

   (a) providing advice as to how the law applies in the particular circumstances,
   (b) providing advice and assistance in relation to the proceedings,
   (c) providing other advice and assistance in relation to the settlement or other resolution of the dispute that is the subject of the proceedings, and
   (d) providing advice and assistance in relation to the enforcement of decisions in the proceedings or as part of the settlement or resolution of the dispute,

and they include, in particular, advice and assistance in the form of representation and any form of dispute resolution, including mediation.

(11) In sub-paragraphs (5) and (6) "specified" means specified in the order concerned.

Amendments—Inserted by LASPOA 2012, s 52.

38B (1) When considering whether to make or vary an order under paragraph 38A, the court must have regard to –

    (a)   the income, earning capacity, property and other financial resources which each of the applicant and the paying party has or is likely to have in the foreseeable future,

    (b)   the financial needs, obligations and responsibilities which each of the applicant and the paying party has or is likely to have in the foreseeable future,

    (c)   the subject matter of the proceedings, including the matters in issue in them,

    (d)   whether the paying party is legally represented in the proceedings,

    (e)   any steps taken by the applicant to avoid all or part of the proceedings, whether by proposing or considering mediation or otherwise,

    (f)   the applicant's conduct in relation to the proceedings,

    (g)   any amount owed by the applicant to the paying party in respect of costs in the proceedings or other proceedings to which both the applicant and the paying party are or were party, and

    (h)   the effect of the order or variation on the paying party.

(2) In sub-paragraph (1)(a) "earning capacity", in relation to the applicant or the paying party, includes any increase in earning capacity which, in the opinion of the court, it would be reasonable to expect the applicant or the paying party to take steps to acquire.

(3) For the purposes of sub-paragraph (1)(h), the court must have regard, in particular, to whether the making or variation of the order is likely to –

    (a)   cause undue hardship to the paying party, or

    (b)   prevent the paying party from obtaining legal services for the purposes of the proceedings.

(4) The Lord Chancellor may by order amend this paragraph by adding to, omitting or varying the matters mentioned in sub-paragraphs (1) to (3).

(5) An order under sub-paragraph (4) must be made by statutory instrument.

(6) A statutory instrument containing an order under sub-paragraph (4) may not be made unless a draft of the instrument has been laid before, and approved by a resolution of, each House of Parliament.

(7) In this paragraph "legal services" has the same meaning as in paragraph B38A.

Amendments—Inserted by LASPOA 2012, s 53.

PART 9
FAILURE TO MAINTAIN: FINANCIAL PROVISION (AND INTERIM ORDERS)

39 Circumstances in which orders under this Part may be made

(1) Either civil partner in a subsisting civil partnership may apply to the court for an order under this Part on the ground that the other civil partner ('the respondent') –

    (a)   has failed to provide reasonable maintenance for the applicant, or

    (b)   has failed to provide, or to make a proper contribution towards, reasonable maintenance for any child of the family.

(2) The court must not entertain an application under this paragraph unless it has jurisdiction to do so by virtue of the Maintenance Regulation and Schedule 6 to the Civil Jurisdiction and Judgments (Maintenance) Regulations 2011.

(3) If, on an application under this paragraph, it appears to the court that –

    (a) the applicant or any child of the family to whom the application relates is in immediate need of financial assistance, but

    (b) it is not yet possible to determine what order, if any, should be made on the application,

the court may make an interim order.

(4) If, on an application under this paragraph, the applicant satisfies the court of a ground mentioned in sub-paragraph (1), the court may make one or more of the orders set out in paragraph 41.

(5) In this paragraph, "the Maintenance Regulation" means Council Regulation (EC) No 4/2009 including as applied in relation to Denmark by virtue of the Agreement made on 19 October 2005 between the European Community and the Kingdom of Denmark.

Amendments—SI 2011/1484.

40 Interim orders

An interim order is an order requiring the respondent to make to the applicant, until the determination of the application, such periodical payments as the court thinks reasonable.

41 Orders that may be made where failure to maintain established

(1) The orders are –

    (a) an order that the respondent must make to the applicant such periodical payments for such term as may be specified;

    (b) an order that the respondent must secure to the applicant, to the satisfaction of the court, such periodical payments for such term as may be specified;

    (c) an order that the respondent must pay to the applicant such lump sum as may be specified;

    (d) an order that the respondent must make such periodical payments for such term as may be specified –

        (i) to such person as may be specified, for the benefit of the child to whom the application relates, or

        (ii) to the child to whom the application relates;

    (e) an order that the respondent must secure –

        (i) to such person as may be specified for the benefit of the child to whom the application relates, or

        (ii) to the child to whom the application relates,

    to the satisfaction of the court, such periodical payments for such term as may be specified;

    (f) an order that the respondent must pay such lump sum as may be specified –

        (i) to such person as may be specified for the benefit of the child to whom the application relates, or

        (ii) to the child to whom the application relates.

(2) In this Part 'specified' means specified in the order.

42 Particular provision that may be made by lump sum orders

(1) An order under this Part for the payment of a lump sum may be made for the purpose of enabling any liabilities or expenses reasonably incurred in maintaining the applicant or any child of the family to whom the application relates before the making of the application to be met.

(2) An order under this Part for the payment of a lump sum may –

   (a)   provide for its payment by instalments of such amount as may be specified, and
   (b)   require the payment of the instalments to be secured to the satisfaction of the court.

(3) Sub-paragraphs (1) and (2) do not restrict the power to make an order by virtue of paragraph 41(1)(c) or (f).

43 Matters to which the court is to have regard on application under paragraph 39(1)(a)

(1) This paragraph applies if an application under paragraph 39 is made on the ground mentioned in paragraph 39(1)(a).

(2) In deciding –

   (a)   whether the respondent has failed to provide reasonable maintenance for the applicant, and
   (b)   what order, if any, to make under this Part in favour of the applicant,

the court must have regard to all the circumstances of the case including the matters mentioned in paragraph 21(2).

(3) If an application is also made under paragraph 39 in respect of a child of the family who has not reached 18, the court must give first consideration to the welfare of the child while under 18.

(4) Paragraph 21(2)(c) has effect as if for the reference in it to the breakdown of the civil partnership there were substituted a reference to the failure to provide reasonable maintenance for the applicant.

44 Matters to which the court is to have regard on application under paragraph 39(1)(b)

(1) This paragraph applies if an application under paragraph 39 is made on the ground mentioned in paragraph 39(1)(b).

(2) In deciding –

   (a)   whether the respondent has failed to provide, or to make a proper contribution towards, reasonable maintenance for the child of the family to whom the application relates, and
   (b)   what order, if any, to make under this Part in favour of the child,

the court must have regard to all the circumstances of the case.

(3) Those circumstances include –

   (a)   the matters mentioned in paragraph 22(2)(a) to (e), and
   (b)   if the child of the family to whom the application relates is not the child of the respondent, the matters mentioned in paragraph 22(3).

(4) Paragraph 21(2)(c) (as it applies by virtue of paragraph 22(2)(e)) has effect as if for the reference in it to the breakdown of the civil partnership there were substituted a reference to –

   (a)   the failure to provide, or
   (b)   the failure to make a proper contribution towards,

reasonable maintenance for the child of the family to whom the application relates.

45 Restrictions on making orders under this Part

The power to make an order under paragraph 41(1)(d), (e) or (f) is subject to paragraph 49(1) and (5) (restrictions on orders in favour of children who have reached 18).

PART 10
COMMENCEMENT OF CERTAIN PROCEEDINGS AND DURATION OF CERTAIN ORDERS

46 Commencement of proceedings for ancillary relief, etc

(1) Sub-paragraph (2) applies if an application for a dissolution, nullity or separation order has been made.

(2) Subject to sub-paragraph (3), proceedings for –

  (a) an order under Part 1 (financial provision on dissolution etc),
  (b) a property adjustment order, or
  (c) an order under Part 8 (maintenance pending outcome of dissolution, nullity or separation proceedings),

may be begun (subject to and in accordance with rules of court) at any time after the presentation of the application.

(3) Rules of court may provide, in such cases as may be prescribed by the rules, that –

  (a) an application for any such relief as is mentioned in sub-paragraph (2) must be made in the application or response, and
  (b) an application for any such relief which –
    (i)   is not so made, or
    (ii) is not made until after the end of such period following the presentation of the application or filing of the response as may be so prescribed,

may be made only with the leave of the court.

47 Duration of periodical and secured periodical payments orders for a civil partner

(1) The court may specify in a periodical payments or secured periodical payments order in favour of a civil partner such term as it thinks fit, except that the term must not –

  (a) begin before the date of the making of an application for the order, or
  (b) extend beyond the limits given in sub-paragraphs (2) and (3).

(2) The limits in the case of a periodical payments order are –

  (a) the death of either civil partner;
  (b) where the order is made on or after the making of a dissolution or nullity order, the formation of a subsequent civil partnership or marriage by the civil partner in whose favour the order is made.

(3) The limits in the case of a secured periodical payments order are –

  (a) the death of the civil partner in whose favour the order is made;
  (b) where the order is made on or after the making of a dissolution or nullity order, the formation of a subsequent civil partnership or marriage by the civil partner in whose favour the order is made.

(4) In the case of an order made on or after the making of a dissolution or nullity order, sub-paragraphs (1) to (3) are subject to paragraphs 23(3) and 59(4).

(5) If a periodical payments or secured periodical payments order in favour of a civil partner is made on or after the making of a dissolution or nullity order, the court may direct that that civil partner is not entitled to apply under paragraph 51 for the extension of the term specified in the order.

(6) If –

(a) a periodical payments or secured periodical payments order in favour of a civil partner is made otherwise than on or after the making of a dissolution or nullity order, and

(b) the civil partnership is subsequently dissolved or annulled but the order continues in force,

the order ceases to have effect (regardless of anything in it) on the formation of a subsequent civil partnership or marriage by that civil partner, except in relation to any arrears due under it on the date of its formation.

PART II

48 Subsequent civil partnership or marriage

If after the making of a dissolution or nullity order one of the civil partners forms a subsequent civil partnership or marriage, that civil partner is not entitled to apply, by reference to the dissolution or nullity order, for –

(a) an order under Part 1 in that civil partner's favour, or
(b) a property adjustment order,

against the other civil partner in the dissolved or annulled civil partnership.

49 Duration of continuing orders in favour of children, and age limit on making certain orders in their favour

(1) Subject to sub-paragraph (5) –

(a) no order under Part 1,
(b) no property adjustment order made by virtue of paragraph 7(1)(a) (transfer of property), and
(c) no order made under Part 9 (failure to maintain) by virtue of paragraph 41,

is to be made in favour of a child who has reached 18.

(2) The term to be specified in a periodical payments or secured periodical payments order in favour of a child may begin with –

(a) the date of the making of an application for the order or a later date, or
(b) a date ascertained in accordance with sub-paragraph (7) or (8).

(3) The term to be specified in such an order –

(a) must not in the first instance extend beyond the date of the birthday of the child next following the child's reaching the upper limit of the compulsory school age unless the court considers that in the circumstances of the case the welfare of the child requires that it should extend to a later date, and

(b) must not in any event, subject to sub-paragraph (5), extend beyond the date of the child's 18th birthday.

(4) Sub-paragraph (3)(a) must be read with section 8 of the Education Act 1996 (which applies to determine for the purposes of any enactment whether a person is of compulsory school age).

(5) Sub-paragraphs (1) and (3)(b) do not apply in the case of a child if it appears to the court that –

(a) the child is, or will be, or, if an order were made without complying with either or both of those provisions, would be –

> > > (i)   receiving instruction at an educational establishment, or
> > > (ii)   undergoing training for a trade, profession or vocation,
>
> whether or not the child also is, will be or would be in gainful employment, or
>
> > (b)   there are special circumstances which justify the making of an order without complying with either or both of sub-paragraphs (1) and (3)(b).

(6) A periodical payments order in favour of a child, regardless of anything in the order, ceases to have effect on the death of the person liable to make payments under the order, except in relation to any arrears due under the order on the date of the death.

(7) If –

> (a)   a maintenance calculation ('the current calculation') is in force with respect to a child, and
> (b)   an application is made under this Schedule for a periodical payments or secured periodical payments order in favour of that child –
> > (i)   in accordance with section 8 of the Child Support Act 1991, and
> > (ii)   before the end of 6 months beginning with the making of the current calculation,

the term to be specified in any such order made on that application may be expressed to begin on, or at any time after, the earliest permitted date.

(8) 'The earliest permitted date' is whichever is the later of –

> (a)   the date 6 months before the application is made, or
> (b)   the date on which the current calculation took effect or, where successive maintenance calculations have been continuously in force with respect to a child, on which the first of those calculations took effect.

(9) If –

> (a)   a maintenance calculation ceases to have effect by or under any provision of the 1991 Act, and
> (b)   an application is made, before the end of 6 months beginning with the relevant date, for a periodical payments or secured periodical payments order in favour of a child with respect to whom that maintenance calculation was in force immediately before it ceased to have effect,

the term to be specified in any such order made on that application may begin with the date on which that maintenance calculation ceased to have effect or any later date.

(10) 'The relevant date' means the date on which the maintenance calculation ceased to have effect.

(11) In this paragraph 'maintenance calculation' has the same meaning as it has in the 1991 Act by virtue of section 54 of the 1991 Act as read with any regulations in force under that section.

Child support—Civil Partnership (Pensions, Social Security and Child Support) (Consequential, etc Provisions) Order 2005, art 2(5), Sch 5, paras 1, 2(1),(2) provide that, in relation to old scheme cases, para 49 is to apply with certain prescribed amendments.

PART 11
VARIATION, DISCHARGE ETC OF CERTAIN ORDERS FOR FINANCIAL RELIEF

50 Orders etc to which this Part applies

(1) This Part applies to the following orders –

- (a) a periodical payments order under Part 1 (financial provision on dissolution etc) or Part 9 (failure to maintain);
- (b) a secured periodical payments order under Part 1 or 9;
- (c) an order under Part 8 (maintenance pending outcome of dissolution proceedings etc);
- (d) an interim order under Part 9;
- (e) an order made under Part 1 by virtue of paragraph 3(3) or under Part 9 by virtue of paragraph 42(2) (lump sum by instalments);
- (f) a deferred order made under Part 1 by virtue of paragraph 2(1)(c) (lump sum for civil partner) which includes provision made by virtue of –
  - (i) paragraph 25(2),
  - (ii) paragraph 26, or
  - (iii) paragraph 34A(2),
  (provision in respect of pension rights or pension compensation rights);
- (g) a property adjustment order made on or after the making of a separation order by virtue of paragraph 7(1)(b), (c) or (d) (order for settlement or variation of settlement);
- (h) a sale of property order;
- (i) a pension sharing order, or a pension compensation sharing order, made before the dissolution or nullity order has been made final.

(2) If the court has made an order referred to in sub-paragraph (1)(f)(ii), this Part ceases to apply to the order on the death of either of the civil partners.

(3) The powers exercisable by the court under this Part in relation to an order are also exercisable in relation to any instrument executed in pursuance of the order.

Amendments—Pensions Act 2008, Sch 6, Pt 3.

51 Powers to vary, discharge, suspend or revive order

(1) If the court has made an order to which this Part applies, it may –

- (a) vary or discharge the order,
- (b) suspend any provision of it temporarily, or
- (c) revive the operation of any provision so suspended.

(2) Sub-paragraph (1) is subject to the provisions of this Part and paragraph 47(5).

52 Power to remit arrears

(1) If the court has made an order referred to in paragraph 50(1)(a), (b), (c) or (d), it may remit the payment of any arrears due under the order or under any part of the order.

(2) Sub-paragraph (1) is subject to the provisions of this Part.

53 Additional powers on discharging or varying a periodical or secured periodical payments order after dissolution of civil partnership

(1) Sub-paragraph (2) applies if, after the dissolution of a civil partnership, the court –

(a)   discharges a periodical payments order or secured periodical payments order made in favour of a civil partner, or

(b)   varies such an order so that payments under the order are required to be made or secured only for such further period as is determined by the court.

(2) The court may make supplemental provision consisting of any of the following –

(a)   an order for the payment of a lump sum in favour of one of the civil partners;

(b)   one or more property adjustment orders in favour of one of the civil partners;

(c)   one or more pension sharing orders;

(ca)   a pension compensation sharing order;

(d)   a direction that the civil partner in whose favour the original order discharged or varied was made is not entitled to make any further application for –

  (i)   a periodical payments or secured periodical payments order, or

  (ii)   an extension of the period to which the original order is limited by any variation made by the court.

(3) The power under sub-paragraph (2) is in addition to any power the court has apart from that sub-paragraph.

Amendments—Pensions Act 2008, Sch 6, Pt 3.

54 (1) An order for the payment of a lump sum under paragraph 53 may –

(a)   provide for the payment of it by instalments of such amount as may be specified, and

(b)   require the payment of the instalments to be secured to the satisfaction of the court.

(2) Sub-paragraphs (5) and (6) of paragraph 3 (interest on deferred instalments) apply where the court makes an order for the payment of a lump sum under paragraph 53 as they apply where it makes such an order under Part 1.

(3) If under paragraph 53 the court makes more than one property adjustment order in favour of the same civil partner, each of those orders must fall within a different paragraph of paragraph 7(1) (types of property adjustment orders).

(4) Part 3 (orders for the sale of property) and paragraph 76 (direction for settlement of instrument) apply where the court makes a property adjustment order under paragraph 53 as they apply where it makes any other property adjustment order.

(5) Paragraph 18 (restrictions on making of pension sharing order) applies in relation to a pension sharing order under paragraph 53 as it applies in relation to any other pension sharing order.

(6) Paragraph 19D (restrictions on making pension compensation sharing orders) applies in relation to a pension compensation sharing order under paragraph 53 as it applies in relation to any other pension compensation sharing order.

Amendments—Pensions Act 2008, Sch 6, Pt 3.

55 Variation etc of periodical or secured periodical payments orders made in cases of failure to maintain

(1) An application for the variation under paragraph 51 of a periodical payments order or secured periodical payments order made under Part 9 in favour of a child may, if the child has reached 16, be made by the child himself.

(2) Sub-paragraph (3) applies if a periodical payments order made in favour of a child under Part 9 ceases to have effect –

(a)   on the date on which the child reaches 16, or

(b)   at any time after that date but before or on the date on which the child reaches 18.

(3) If, on an application made to the court for an order under this sub-paragraph, it appears to the court that –

(a)   the child is, will be or, if an order were made under this sub-paragraph, would be –

(i)   receiving instruction at an educational establishment, or

(ii)   undergoing training for a trade, profession or vocation,

whether or not the child also is, will be or would be in gainful employment, or

(b)   there are special circumstances which justify the making of an order under this sub-paragraph,

the court may by order revive the order mentioned in sub-paragraph (2) from such date as it may specify.

(4) A date specified under sub-paragraph (3) must not be earlier than the date of the application under that sub-paragraph.

(5) If under sub-paragraph (3) the court revives an order it may exercise its power under paragraph 51 in relation to the revived order.

56 Variation etc of property adjustment, pension sharing and pension compensation sharing orders

The court must not exercise the powers conferred by this Part in relation to a property adjustment order falling within paragraph 7(1)(b), (c) or (d) (order for settlement or for variation of settlement) except on an application made in proceedings –

(a)   for the rescission of the separation order by reference to which the property adjustment order was made, or

(b)   for a dissolution order in relation to the civil partnership.

Amendments—Pensions Act 2008, Sch 6, Pt 3.

57 (1) In relation to a pension sharing order or pension compensation sharing order which is made at a time before the dissolution or nullity order has been made final –

(a)   the powers conferred by this Part (by virtue of paragraph 50(1)(i)) may be exercised –

(i)   only on an application made before the pension sharing order or pension compensation sharing order has or, but for paragraph (b), would have taken effect, and

(ii)   only if, at the time when the application is made, the dissolution or nullity order has not been made final, and

(b)   an application made in accordance with paragraph (a) prevents the pension sharing order or pension compensation sharing order from taking effect before the application has been dealt with.

(2) No variation of a pension sharing order or pension compensation sharing order is to be made so as to take effect before the order is made final.

(3) The variation of a pension sharing order or pension compensation sharing order prevents the order taking effect before the end of such period after the making of the variation as may be prescribed by regulations made by the Lord Chancellor.

PART II

(4) The power to make regulations under sub-paragraph (3) is exercisable by statutory instrument which is subject to annulment in pursuance of a resolution of either House of Parliament.

Amendments—Pensions Act 2008, Sch 6, Pt 3.

58 (1) Sub-paragraphs (2) and (3) –

    (a)   are subject to paragraphs 53 and 54, and

    (b)   do not affect any power exercisable by virtue of paragraph 50(e), (f), (g) or (i) or otherwise than by virtue of this Part.

(2) No property adjustment order, pension sharing order or pension compensation sharing order may be made on an application for the variation of a periodical payments or secured periodical payments order made (whether in favour of a civil partner or in favour of a child of the family) under Part 1.

(3) No order for the payment of a lump sum may be made on an application for the variation of a periodical payments or secured periodical payments order in favour of a civil partner (whether made under Part 1 or 9).

Amendments—Pensions Act 2008, Sch 6, Pt 3.

59 Matters to which court is to have regard in exercising powers under this Part

(1) In exercising the powers conferred by this Part the court must have regard to all the circumstances of the case, giving first consideration to the welfare, while under 18, of any child of the family who has not reached 18.

(2) The circumstances of the case include, in particular, any change in any of the matters to which the court was required to have regard when making the order to which the application relates.

(3) Sub-paragraph (4) applies in the case of –

    (a)   a periodical payments order, or

    (b)   a secured periodical payments order,

made on or after the making of a dissolution or nullity order.

(4) The court must consider whether in all the circumstances, and after having regard to any such change, it would be appropriate to vary the order so that payments under the order are required –

    (a)   to be made, or

    (b)   to be secured,

only for such further period as will in the opinion of the court be sufficient to enable the civil partner in whose favour the order was made to adjust without undue hardship to the termination of those payments.

(5) In considering what further period will be sufficient, the court must, if the civil partnership has been dissolved, take into account any proposed exercise by it of its powers under paragraph 53.

(6) If the civil partner against whom the order was made has died, the circumstances of the case also include the changed circumstances resulting from that civil partner's death.

60 Variation of secured periodical payments order where person liable has died

(1) This paragraph applies if the person liable to make payments under a secured periodical payments order has died.

(2) Subject to sub-paragraph (3), an application under this Part relating to the order (and to any sale of property order which requires the proceeds of sale of property to be used for securing those payments) may be made by –

  (a)   the person entitled to payments under the periodical payments order, or
  (b)   the personal representatives of the deceased person.

(3) No such application may be made without the leave of the court after the end of 6 months from the date on which representation in regard to the estate of that person is first taken out.

(4) The personal representatives of the person who has died are not liable for having distributed any part of the estate of the deceased after the end of the 6 month period on the ground that they ought to have taken into account the possibility that the court might allow an application under this paragraph to be made after that period by the person entitled to payments under the order.

(5) Sub-paragraph (4) does not affect any power to recover any part of the estate so distributed arising by virtue of the making of an order in pursuance of this paragraph.

(6) In considering for the purposes of sub-paragraph (3) the question when representation was first taken out –

  (a)   a grant limited to settled land or to trust property is to be disregarded, and
  (b)   a grant limited to real estate or to personal estate is to be disregarded unless a grant limited to the remainder of the estate has previously been made or is made at the same time.

61 Power to direct when variation etc is to take effect

(1) If the court, in exercise of its powers under this Part, decides –

  (a)   to vary, or
  (b)   to discharge,

a periodical payments or secured periodical payments order, it may direct that the variation or discharge is not to take effect until the end of such period as may be specified in the order.

(2) Sub-paragraph (1) is subject to paragraph 47(1) and (6).

62 (1) If –

  (a)   a periodical payments or secured periodical payments order in favour of more than one child ('the order') is in force,
  (b)   the order requires payments specified in it to be made to or for the benefit of more than one child without apportioning those payments between them,
  (c)   a maintenance calculation ('the calculation') is made with respect to one or more, but not all, of the children with respect to whom those payments are to be made, and
  (d)   an application is made, before the end of the period of 6 months beginning with the date on which the calculation was made, for the variation or discharge of the order,

the court may, in exercise of its powers under this Part to vary or discharge the order, direct that the variation or discharge is to take effect from the date on which the calculation took effect or any later date.

(2) If –

- (a) an order ('the child order') of a kind prescribed for the purposes of section 10(1) of the Child Support Act 1991 is affected by a maintenance calculation,
- (b) on the date on which the child order became so affected there was in force a periodical payments or secured periodical payments order ('the civil partner's order') in favour of a civil partner having the care of the child in whose favour the child order was made, and
- (c) an application is made, before the end of the period of 6 months beginning with the date on which the maintenance calculation was made, for the civil partner's order to be varied or discharged,

the court may, in exercise of its powers under this Part to vary or discharge the civil partner's order, direct that the variation or discharge is to take effect from the date on which the child order became so affected or any later date.

(3) For the purposes of sub-paragraph (2), an order is affected if it ceases to have effect or is modified by or under section 10 of the 1991 Act.

(4) Sub-paragraphs (1) and (2) do not affect any other power of the court to direct that the variation of discharge of an order under this Part is to take effect from a date earlier than that on which the order for variation or discharge was made.

(5) In this paragraph 'maintenance calculation' has the same meaning as it has in the 1991 Act by virtue of section 54 of the 1991 Act as read with any regulations in force under that section.

Child support—Civil Partnership (Pensions, Social Security and Child Support) (Consequential, etc Provisions) Order 2005, art 2(5), Sch 5, paras 1, 2(1), (3) provide that, in relation to old scheme cases, para 62 is to apply with certain prescribed amendments.

PART 12
ARREARS AND REPAYMENTS

63 Payment of certain arrears unenforceable without the leave of the court

(1) This paragraph applies if any arrears are due under –

- (a) an order under Part 1 (financial provision on dissolution etc),
- (b) an order under Part 8 (maintenance pending outcome of dissolution, nullity or separation proceedings), or
- (c) an order under Part 9 (failure to maintain),

and the arrears became due more than 12 months before proceedings to enforce the payment of them are begun.

(2) A person is not entitled to enforce through the High Court or any county court the payment of the arrears without the leave of that court.

(3) The court hearing an application for the grant of leave under this paragraph may –

- (a) refuse leave,
- (b) grant leave subject to such restrictions and conditions (including conditions as to the allowing of time for payment or the making of payment by instalments) as that court thinks proper, or
- (c) remit the payment of the arrears or of any part of them.

(4) An application for the grant of leave under this paragraph must be made in such manner as may be prescribed by rules of court.

64 Orders for repayment in certain cases of sums paid under certain orders

(1) This paragraph applies if –

(a) a person ('R') is entitled to receive payments under an order listed in sub-paragraph (2), and

(b) R's circumstances or the circumstances of the person ('P') liable to make payments under the order have changed since the order was made, or the circumstances have changed as a result of P's death.

(2) The orders are –

(a) any order under Part 8 (maintenance pending outcome of dissolution, nullity or separation proceedings);

(b) any interim order under Part 9;

(c) any periodical payments order;

(d) any secured periodical payments order.

(3) P or P's personal representatives may (subject to sub-paragraph (7)) apply for an order under this paragraph against R or R's personal representatives.

(4) If it appears to the court that, because of the changed circumstances or P's death, the amount received by R in respect of a relevant period exceeds the amount which P or P's personal representatives should have been required to pay, it may order the respondent to the application to pay to the applicant such sum, not exceeding the amount of the excess, as it thinks just.

(5) 'Relevant period' means a period after the circumstances changed or (as the case may be) after P's death.

(6) An order under this paragraph for the payment of any sum may provide for the payment of that sum by instalments of such amount as may be specified in the order.

(7) An application under this paragraph –

(a) may be made in proceedings in the High Court or a county court for –

(i) the variation or discharge of the order listed in sub-paragraph (2), or

(ii) leave to enforce, or the enforcement of, the payment of arrears under that order, but

(b) if not made in such proceedings, must be made to a county court;

and accordingly references in this paragraph to the court are references to the High Court or a county court, as the circumstances require.

(8) The jurisdiction conferred on a county court by this paragraph is exercisable even though, because of the amount claimed in the application, the jurisdiction would not but for this sub-paragraph be exercisable by a county court.

65 Orders for repayment after cessation of order because of subsequent civil partnership etc

(1) Sub-paragraphs (3) and (4) apply if –

(a) a periodical payments or secured periodical payments order in favour of a civil partner ('R') has ceased to have effect because of the formation of a subsequent civil partnership or marriage by R, and

(b) the person liable to make payments under the order ('P') (or P's personal representatives) has made payments in accordance with it in respect of a relevant period in the mistaken belief that the order was still subsisting.

(2) 'Relevant period' means a period after the date of the formation of the subsequent civil partnership or marriage.

(3) P (or P's personal representatives) is not entitled to bring proceedings in respect of a cause of action arising out of the circumstances mentioned in sub-paragraph (1)(a) and (b) against R (or R's personal representatives).

(4) But, on an application under this paragraph by P (or P's personal representatives) against R (or R's personal representatives), the court –

    (a)   may order the respondent to pay to the applicant a sum equal to the amount of the payments made in respect of the relevant period, or

    (b)   if it appears to the court that it would be unjust to make that order, may –

        (i)   order the respondent to pay to the applicant such lesser sum as it thinks fit, or

        (ii) dismiss the application.

(5) An order under this paragraph for the payment of any sum may provide for the payment of that sum by instalments of such amount as may be specified in the order.

(6) An application under this paragraph –

    (a)   may be made in proceedings in the High Court or a county court for leave to enforce, or the enforcement of, payment of arrears under the order in question, but

    (b)   if not made in such proceedings, must be made to a county court;

and accordingly references in this paragraph to the court are references to the High Court or a county court, as the circumstances require.

(7) The jurisdiction conferred on a county court by this paragraph is exercisable even though, because of the amount claimed in the application, the jurisdiction would not but for this sub-paragraph be exercisable by a county court.

(8) Subject to sub-paragraph (9) –

    (a)   the designated officer for a magistrates' court to whom any payments under a payments order are required to be made is not liable for any act done by him in pursuance of the payments order after the date on which that order ceased to have effect because of the formation of a subsequent civil partnership or marriage by the person entitled to payments under it, and

    (b)   the collecting officer under an attachment of earnings order made to secure payments under a payments order is not liable for any act done by him after that date in accordance with any enactment or rule of court specifying how payments made to him in compliance with the attachment of earnings order are to be dealt with.

(9) Sub-paragraph (8) applies if (and only if) the act –

    (a)   was one which the officer would have been under a duty to do had the payments order not ceased to have effect, and

    (b)   was done before notice in writing of the formation of the subsequent civil partnership or marriage was given to him by or on behalf of –

        (i)   the person entitled to payments under the payments order,

        (ii) the person liable to make payments under it, or

        (iii) the personal representatives of either of them.

(10) In sub-paragraphs (8) and (9) 'payments order' means a periodical payments order or secured periodical payments order and 'collecting officer', in relation to an attachment of earnings order, means –

(a)   the officer of the High Court,

(b)   the district judge of a county court, or

(c)   the designated officer for a magistrates' court,

to whom a person makes payments in compliance with the order.

PART 13
CONSENT ORDERS AND MAINTENANCE AGREEMENTS

66 Consent orders for financial relief

(1) Regardless of anything in the preceding provisions of this Schedule, on an application for a consent order for financial relief, the court may, unless it has reason to think that there are other circumstances into which it ought to inquire, make an order in the terms agreed on the basis only of such information supplied with the application as is required by rules of court.

(2) Sub-paragraph (1) applies to an application for a consent order varying or discharging an order for financial relief as it applies to an application for an order for financial relief.

(3) In this paragraph –

"consent order", in relation to an application for an order, means an order in the terms applied for to which the respondent agrees;

"order for financial relief" means an order under any of Parts 1, 2, 3, 4 and 9.

67 Meaning of 'maintenance agreement' and 'financial arrangements'

(1) In this Part 'maintenance agreement' means any agreement in writing between the civil partners in a civil partnership which –

(a)   is made during the continuance or after the dissolution or annulment of the civil partnership and contains financial arrangements, or

(b)   is a separation agreement which contains no financial arrangements but is made in a case where no other agreement in writing between the civil partners contains financial arrangements.

(2) In this Part 'financial arrangements' means provisions governing the rights and liabilities towards one another when living separately of the civil partners in a civil partnership (including a civil partnership which has been dissolved or annulled) in respect of –

(a)   the making or securing of payments, or

(b)   the disposition or use of any property,

including such rights and liabilities with respect to the maintenance or education of a child (whether or not a child of the family).

(3) 'Education' includes training.

68 Validity of maintenance agreements

If a maintenance agreement includes a provision purporting to restrict any right to apply to a court for an order containing financial arrangements –

(a)   that provision is void, but

(b)   any other financial arrangements contained in the agreement –

(i)   are not void or unenforceable as a result, and

(ii)   unless void or unenforceable for any other reason, are (subject to paragraphs 69 and 73) binding on the parties to the agreement.

69 Alteration of agreements by court during lives of parties

(1) Subject to sub-paragraph (1A), either party to a maintenance agreement may apply to the court or, subject to sub-paragraph (6), to a magistrates' court for an order under this paragraph if –

(a)   the maintenance agreement is for the time being subsisting, and
(b)   each of the parties to the agreement is for the time being domiciled or resident in England and Wales.

(1A) If an application or part of an application relates to a matter where jurisdiction falls to be determined by reference to the jurisdictional requirements of the Maintenance Regulation and Schedule 6 to the Civil Jurisdiction and Judgments (Maintenance) Regulations 2011 –

(a)   the requirement as to domicile or residence in sub-paragraph (1)(b) does not apply to the application or that part of it, but
(b)   the court may not entertain the application or that part of it unless it has jurisdiction to do so by virtue of that Regulation and that Schedule.

(2) The court may make an order under this paragraph if it is satisfied that –

(a)   because of a change in the circumstances in the light of which –
(i)   any financial arrangements contained in the agreement were made, or
(ii)   financial arrangements were omitted from it,
the agreement should be altered so as to make different financial arrangements or so as to contain financial arrangements, or
(b)   that the agreement does not contain proper financial arrangements with respect to any child of the family.

(3) In sub-paragraph (2)(a) the reference to a change in the circumstances includes a change foreseen by the parties when making the agreement.

(4) An order under this paragraph may make such alterations in the agreement –

(a)   by varying or revoking any financial arrangements contained in it, or
(b)   by inserting in it financial arrangements for the benefit of one of the parties to the agreement or of a child of the family,

as appear to the court to be just having regard to all the circumstances, including, if relevant, the matters mentioned in paragraph 22(3).

(5) The effect of the order is that the agreement is to be treated as if any alteration made by the order had been made by agreement between the partners and for valuable consideration.

(6) The power to make an order under this paragraph is subject to paragraphs 70 and 71.

(7) In this paragraph, "the Maintenance Regulation" means Council Regulation (EC) No 4/2009 including as applied in relation to Denmark by virtue of the Agreement made on 19 October 2005 between the European Community and the Kingdom of Denmark.

Amendments—SI 2011/1484.

70 Restrictions on applications to and orders by magistrates' courts under paragraph 69

(1) A magistrates' court must not entertain an application under paragraph 69(1) unless –

(a)   both the parties to the agreement are resident in England and Wales, and
(b)   the court acts in, or is authorised by the Lord Chancellor to act for, a local justice area in which at least one of the parties is resident.

(2) A magistrates' court must not make any order on such an application other than –

(a) if the agreement includes no provision for periodical payments by either of the parties, an order inserting provision for the making by one of the parties of periodical payments for the maintenance of –
    (i) the other party, or
    (ii) any child of the family;
(b) if the agreement includes provision for the making by one of the parties of periodical payments, an order increasing or reducing the rate of, or terminating, any of those payments.

71 Provisions relating to periodical and secured periodical payments: duration

(1) If a court decides to make an order under paragraph 69 altering an agreement –

    (a) by inserting provision for the making or securing by one of the parties to the agreement of periodical payments for the maintenance of the other party, or
    (b) by increasing the rate of the periodical payments which the agreement provides shall be made by one of the parties for the maintenance of the other,

it may specify such term as it thinks fit as the term for which the payments or, as the case may be, the additional payments attributable to the increase are to be made under the altered agreement, except that the term must not extend beyond the limits in sub-paragraphs (2) and (3).

(2) The limits if the payments are not to be secured are –

    (a) the death of either of the parties to the agreement, or
    (b) the formation of a subsequent civil partnership or marriage by the party to whom the payments are to be made.

(3) The limits if the payments are to be secured are –

    (a) the death of the party to whom the payments are to be made, or
    (b) the formation of a subsequent civil partnership or marriage by that party.

(4) Sub-paragraph (5) applies if a court decides to make an order under paragraph 69 altering an agreement by –

    (a) inserting provision for the making or securing by one of the parties to the agreement of periodical payments for the maintenance of a child of the family, or
    (b) increasing the rate of the periodical payments which the agreement provides shall be made or secured by one of the parties for the maintenance of such a child.

(5) The court, in deciding the term for which under the agreement as altered by the order –

    (a) the payments are to be made or secured for the benefit of the child, or
    (b) the additional payments attributable to the increase are to be made or secured for the benefit of the child,

must apply paragraph 49(2) to (5) (age limits) as if the order in question were a periodical payments or secured periodical payments order in favour of the child.

72 Saving

Nothing in paragraphs 68 to 71 affects –

    (a) any power of a court before which any proceedings between the parties to a maintenance agreement are brought under any other enactment (including a provision of this Schedule) to make an order containing financial arrangements, or

(b)   any right of either party to apply for such an order in such proceedings.

73 Alteration of agreements by court after death of one party

(1) This paragraph applies if –

(a)   a maintenance agreement provides for the continuation of payments under the agreement after the death of one of the parties, and

(b)   that party ('A') dies domiciled in England and Wales.

(2) Subject to sub-paragraph (4), the surviving party or A's personal representatives may apply to the High Court or a county court for an order under paragraph 69.

(3) If a maintenance agreement is altered by a court on an application made under sub-paragraph (2), the same consequences follow as if the alteration had been made immediately before the death by agreement between the parties and for valuable consideration.

(4) An application under this paragraph may not, without the leave of the High Court or a county court, be made after the end of 6 months from the date on which representation in regard to A's estate is first taken out.

(5) A's personal representatives are not liable for having distributed any part of A's estate after the end of the 6 month period on the ground that they ought to have taken into account the possibility that a court might allow an application by virtue of this paragraph to be made by the surviving party after that period.

(6) Sub-paragraph (5) does not affect any power to recover any part of the estate so distributed arising by virtue of the making of an order in pursuance of this paragraph.

(7) Paragraph 60(6) applies for the purposes of sub-paragraph (4) as it applies for the purposes of paragraph 60(3).

PART 14
MISCELLANEOUS AND SUPPLEMENTARY

74 Avoidance of transactions intended to prevent or reduce financial relief

(1) This paragraph applies if proceedings for relief ('financial relief') are brought by one person ('A') against another ('B') under Part 1, 2, 4, 8, 9, or 11 (other than paragraph 60(2)), or paragraph 69.

(2) If the court is satisfied, on an application by A, that B is, with the intention of defeating A's claim for financial relief, about to –

(a)   make any disposition, or

(b)   transfer out of the jurisdiction or otherwise deal with any property,

it may make such order as it thinks fit for restraining B from doing so or otherwise for protecting the claim.

(3) If the court is satisfied, on an application by A, that –

(a)   B has, with the intention of defeating A's claim for financial relief, made a reviewable disposition, and

(b)   if the disposition were set aside, financial relief or different financial relief would be granted to A,

it make an order setting aside the disposition.

(4) If the court is satisfied, on an application by A in a case where an order has been obtained by A against B under any of the provisions mentioned in sub-paragraph (1), that B has, with the intention of defeating A's claim for financial relief, made a reviewable disposition, it may make an order setting aside the disposition.

(5) An application for the purposes of sub-paragraph (3) must be made in the proceedings for the financial relief in question.

(6) If the court makes an order under sub-paragraph (3) or (4) setting aside a disposition it must give such consequential directions as it thinks fit for giving effect to the order (including directions requiring the making of any payments or the disposal of any property).

75 (1) Any reference in paragraph 74 to defeating A's claim for financial relief is to –

    (a)   preventing financial relief from being granted to A, or to A for the benefit of a child of the family,

    (b)   reducing the amount of any financial relief which might be so granted, or

    (c)   frustrating or impeding the enforcement of any order which might be or has been made at A's instance under any of those provisions.

(2) In paragraph 74 and this paragraph 'disposition' –

    (a)   does not include any provision contained in a will or codicil, but

    (b)   subject to paragraph (a), includes any conveyance, assurance or gift of property of any description (whether made by an instrument or otherwise).

(3) Any disposition made by B (whether before or after the commencement of the proceedings for financial relief) is a reviewable disposition for the purposes of paragraphs 74(3) and (4) unless it was made –

    (a)   for valuable consideration (other than formation of a civil partnership), and

    (b)   to a person who, at the time of the disposition, acted in relation to it in good faith and without notice of any intention on B's part to defeat A's claim for financial relief.

(4) If an application is made under paragraph 74 with respect to a disposition which took place less than 3 years before the date of the application or with respect to a disposition or other dealing with property which is about to take place and the court is satisfied –

    (a)   in a case falling within paragraph 74(2) or (3), that the disposition or other dealing would (apart from paragraph 74) have the consequence of defeating A's claim for financial relief, or

    (b)   in a case falling within paragraph 74(4), that the disposition has had the consequence of defeating A's claim for financial relief,

it is presumed, unless the contrary is shown, that the person who disposed of or is about to dispose of or deal with the property did so or, as the case may be, is about to do so, with the intention of defeating A's claim for financial relief.

76 Direction for settlement of instrument for securing payments or effecting property adjustment

(1) This paragraph applies if the court decides to make –

    (a)   an order under Part 1 or 9 requiring any payments to be secured, or

    (b)   a property adjustment order.

(2) The court may direct that the matter be referred to one of the conveyancing counsel of the court for him to settle a proper instrument to be executed by all necessary parties.

(3) If the order referred to in sub-paragraph (1) is to be made in proceedings for a dissolution, nullity or separation order, the court may, if it thinks fit, defer the making of the dissolution, nullity or separation order until the instrument has been duly executed.

77 Settlement, etc, made in compliance with a property adjustment order may be avoided on bankruptcy of settlor

The fact that –

(a)   a settlement, or

(b)   a transfer of property,

had to be made in order to comply with a property adjustment order does not prevent the settlement or transfer from being a transaction in respect of which an order may be made under section 339 or 340 of the Insolvency Act 1986 (transfers at an undervalue and preferences).

78 Payments, etc, under order made in favour of person suffering from mental disorder

(1) This paragraph applies if –

(a)   the court makes an order under this Schedule requiring –

(i)   payments (including a lump sum payment) to be made, or

(ii)   property to be transferred,

to a civil partner, and

(b)   the court is satisfied that the person in whose favour the order is made is incapable, because of mental disorder, of managing and administering his or her property and affairs.

(2) 'Mental disorder' has the same meaning as in the Mental Health Act 1983.

(3) Subject to any order, direction or authority made or given in relation to that person under Part 8 of the 1983 Act, the court may order the payments to be made or, as the case may be, the property to be transferred to such persons having charge of that person as the court may direct.

79 Appeals relating to pension sharing orders which have taken effect

(1) Sub-paragraphs (2) and (3) apply if an appeal against a pension sharing order is begun on or after the day on which the order takes effect.

(2) If the pension sharing order relates to a person's rights under a pension arrangement, the appeal court may not set aside or vary the order if the person responsible for the pension arrangement has acted to his detriment in reliance on the order taking effect.

(3) If the pension sharing order relates to a person's shareable state scheme rights, the appeal court may not set aside or vary the order if the Secretary of State has acted to his detriment in reliance on the taking effect of the order.

(4) In determining for the purposes of sub-paragraph (2) or (3) whether a person has acted to his detriment in reliance on the taking effect of the order, the appeal court may disregard any detriment which in its opinion is insignificant.

(5) Where sub-paragraph (2) or (3) applies, the appeal court may make such further orders (including one or more pension sharing orders) as it thinks fit for the purpose of putting the parties in the position it considers appropriate.

(6) Paragraph 19 only applies to a pension sharing order under this paragraph if the decision of the appeal court can itself be the subject of an appeal.

(7) In sub-paragraph (2), the reference to the person responsible for the pension arrangement is to be read in accordance with paragraph 29(3).

79A Appeals relating to pension compensation sharing orders which have taken effect

(1) This paragraph applies where an appeal against a pension compensation sharing order is begun on or after the day on which the order takes effect.

(2) If the Board of the Pension Protection Fund has acted to its detriment in reliance on the taking effect of the order the appeal court –

  (a)   may not set aside or vary the order;
  (b)   may make such further orders (including a pension compensation sharing order) as it thinks fit for the purpose of putting the parties in the position it considers appropriate.

(3) In determining for the purposes of sub-paragraph (2) whether the Board has acted to its detriment the appeal court may disregard any detriment which in the court's opinion is insignificant.

(4) Paragraph 19E only applies to a pension compensation sharing order under this paragraph if the decision of the appeal court can itself be the subject of an appeal.

Amendments—Inserted by Pensions Act 2008, Sch 6, Pt 3.

80 Interpretation

(1) References in this Schedule to –

  (a)   periodical payments orders,
  (b)   secured periodical payments orders, and
  (c)   orders for the payment of a lump sum,

are references to such of the orders that may be made under Parts 1 and 9 (other than interim orders) as are relevant in the context of the reference in question.

(2) In this Schedule 'child of the family', in relation to two people who are civil partners of each other, means –

  (a)   a child of both of them, and
  (b)   any other child, other than a child placed with them as foster parents by a local authority or voluntary organisation, who has been treated by both the civil partners as a child of their family.

(3) In this Schedule 'the court' (except where the context otherwise requires) means –

  (a)   the High Court, or
  (b)   where a county court has jurisdiction by virtue of Part 5 of the Matrimonial and Family Proceedings Act 1984, a county court.

(4) References in this Schedule to a subsequent civil partnership include a civil partnership which is by law void or voidable.

(5) References in this Schedule to a subsequent marriage include a marriage which is by law void or voidable.

SCHEDULE 6
FINANCIAL RELIEF IN MAGISTRATES' COURTS ETC

Scope—Section 72(3) and Sch 6 make provision for financial relief in connection with civil partnerships in magistrates' courts corresponding to the DPMCA 1978. It should be noted that s 72(3) provides in terms that Sch 6 corresponds to the provision made by the 1978 Act, thus offering an important guide to the construction of Sch 6.

PART 1
FAILURE TO MAINTAIN ETC: FINANCIAL PROVISION

1 Circumstances in which orders under this Part may be made

(1) On an application to it by one of the civil partners, a magistrates' court may make any one or more of the orders set out in paragraph 2 if it is satisfied that the other civil partner –

    (a) has failed to provide reasonable maintenance for the applicant,

    (b) has failed to provide, or to make a proper contribution towards, reasonable maintenance for any child of the family,

    (c) has behaved in such a way that the applicant cannot reasonably be expected to live with the respondent, or

    (d) has deserted the applicant.

(2) The power of the court under sub-paragraph (1) is subject to the following provisions of this Schedule.

2 The orders: periodical and secured periodical payments and lump sums

(1) The orders are –

    (a) an order that the respondent must make to the applicant such periodical payments for such term as may be specified;

    (b) an order that the respondent must pay to the applicant such lump sum as may be specified;

    (c) an order that the respondent must make –

        (i) to the applicant for the benefit of a child of the family to whom the application relates, or

        (ii) to a child of the family to whom the application relates;

    such periodical payments for such term as may be specified;

    (d) an order that the respondent must pay such lump sum as may be specified –

        (i) to the applicant for the benefit of a child of the family to whom the application relates, or

        (ii) to such a child of the family to whom the application relates.

(2) The amount of a lump sum required to be paid under sub-paragraph (1)(b) or (d) must not exceed –

    (a) £1,000, or

    (b) such larger amount as the Lord Chancellor may from time to time by order fix for the purposes of this sub-paragraph.

(3) The power to make an order under sub-paragraph (2) is exercisable by statutory instrument which is subject to annulment in pursuance of a resolution of either House of Parliament.

(4) 'Specified' means specified in the order.

3 Particular provision that may be made by lump sum orders

(1) An order under this Part for the payment of a lump sum may be made for the purpose of enabling any liability or expenses reasonably incurred in maintaining the applicant or any child of the family to whom the application relates before the making of the order to be met.

(2) Sub-paragraph (1) does not restrict the power to make the orders set out in paragraph 2(1)(b) and (d).

4 Matters to which court is to have regard in exercising its powers under this Part – general

If an application is made for an order under this Part, the court, in deciding –

    (a)   whether to exercise its powers under this Part, and
    (b)   if so, in what way,

must have regard to all the circumstances of the case, giving first consideration to the welfare while under 18 of any child of the family who has not reached 18.

5 Particular matters to be taken into account when exercising powers in relation to civil partners

(1) This paragraph applies in relation to the exercise by the court of its power to make an order by virtue of paragraph 2(1)(a) or (b).

(2) The court must in particular have regard to –

    (a)   the income, earning capacity, property and other financial resources which each civil partner –
        (i)   has, or
        (ii) is likely to have in the foreseeable future,
        including, in the case of earning capacity, any increase in that capacity which it would in the opinion of the court be reasonable to expect a civil partner in the civil partnership to take steps to acquire;
    (b)   the financial needs, obligations and responsibilities which each civil partner has or is likely to have in the foreseeable future;
    (c)   the standard of living enjoyed by the civil partners before the occurrence of the conduct which is alleged as the ground of the application;
    (d)   the age of each civil partner and the duration of the civil partnership;
    (e)   any physical or mental disability of either civil partner;
    (f)   the contributions which each civil partner has made or is likely in the foreseeable future to make to the welfare of the family, including any contribution by looking after the home or caring for the family;
    (g)   the conduct of each civil partner, if that conduct is such that it would in the opinion of the court be inequitable to disregard it.

6 Particular matters to be taken into account when exercising powers in relation to children

(1) This paragraph applies in relation to the exercise by the court of its power to make an order by virtue of paragraph 2(1)(c) or (d).

(2) The court must in particular have regard to –

    (a)   the financial needs of the child;
    (b)   the income, earning capacity (if any), property and other financial resources of the child;

PART II

  (c) any physical or mental disability of the child;
  (d) the standard of living enjoyed by the family before the occurrence of the
       conduct which is alleged as the ground of the application;
  (e) the way in which the child was being and in which the civil partners expected
       the child to be educated or trained;
  (f) the considerations mentioned in relation to the civil partners in
       paragraph 5(2)(a) and (b).

(3) In relation to the exercise of its power to make an order in favour of a child of the
family who is not the respondent's child, the court must also have regard to –

  (a) whether the respondent has assumed any responsibility for the child's
       maintenance;
  (b) if so, the extent to which, and the basis on which, the respondent assumed that
       responsibility and the length of time during which the respondent discharged
       that responsibility;
  (c) whether in assuming and discharging that responsibility the respondent did so
       knowing that the child was not the respondent's child;
  (d) the liability of any other person to maintain the child.

7 Reconciliation

(1) If an application is made for an order under this Part –

  (a) the court, before deciding whether to exercise its powers under this Part, must
       consider whether there is any possibility of reconciliation between the civil
       partners, and
  (b) if at any stage of the proceedings on that application it appears to the court that
       there is a reasonable possibility of such a reconciliation, the court may adjourn
       the proceedings for such period as it thinks fit to enable attempts to be made to
       effect a reconciliation.

(2) If the court adjourns any proceedings under sub-paragraph (1), it may request –

  (a) an officer of the Children and Family Court Advisory and Support Service, or
  (b) any other person,

to attempt to effect a reconciliation between the civil partners.

(3) If any such request is made, the officer or other person –

  (a) must report in writing to the court whether the attempt has been successful, but
  (b) must not include in the report any other information.

8 Refusal of order in case more suitable for High Court

(1) If on hearing an application for an order under this Part a magistrates' court is of the
opinion that any of the matters in question between the civil partners would be more
conveniently dealt with by the High Court, the magistrates' court must refuse to make
any order on the application.

(2) No appeal lies from a refusal under sub-paragraph (1).

(3) But, in any proceedings in the High Court relating to or comprising the same subject
matter as an application in respect of which a magistrates' court has refused to make any
order, the High Court may order the application to be reheard and determined by a
magistrates' court acting for the same local justice area as the court which refused to
make any order.

PART 2
ORDERS FOR AGREED FINANCIAL PROVISION

9 Orders for payments which have been agreed by the parties

(1) Either civil partner may apply to a magistrates' court for an order under this Part on the ground that that civil partner or the other civil partner has agreed to make such financial provision as may be specified in the application.

(2) On such an application, the court may order that the applicant or the respondent (as the case may be) is to make the financial provision specified in the application, if –

    (a) it is satisfied that the applicant or the respondent (as the case may be) has agreed to make that provision, and

    (b) it has no reason to think that it would be contrary to the interests of justice to do so.

(3) Sub-paragraph (2) is subject to paragraph 12.

10 Meaning of 'financial provision' and of references to specified financial provision

(1) In this Part 'financial provision' means any one or more of the following –

    (a) the making of periodical payments by one civil partner to the other;

    (b) the payment of a lump sum by one civil partner to the other;

    (c) the making of periodical payments by one civil partner to a child of the family or to the other civil partner for the benefit of such a child;

    (d) the payment by one party of a lump sum to a child of the family or to the other civil partner for the benefit of such a child.

(2) Any reference in this Part to the financial provision specified in an application or specified by the court is a reference –

    (a) to the type of provision specified in the application or by the court,

    (b) to the amount so specified as the amount of any payment to be made under the application or order, and

    (c) in the case of periodical payments, to the term so specified as the term for which the payments are to be made.

11 Evidence to be produced where respondent not present etc

(1) This paragraph applies if –

    (a) the respondent is not present, or

    (b) is not represented by counsel or a solicitor,

at the hearing of an application for an order under this Part.

(2) The court must not make an order under this Part unless there is produced to it such evidence as may be prescribed by rules of court of –

    (a) the consent of the respondent to the making of the order,

    (b) the financial resources of the respondent, and

    (c) if the financial provision specified in the application includes or consists of provision in respect of a child of the family to be made by the applicant to the respondent for the benefit of the child or to the child, the financial resources of the child.

12 Exercise of powers in relation to children

(1) This paragraph applies if the financial provision specified in an application under this Part –

    (a)   includes, or

    (b)   consists of,

provision in respect of a child of the family.

(2) The court must not make an order under this Part unless it considers that the provision which the applicant or the respondent (as the case may be) has agreed to make in respect of the child provides for, or makes a proper contribution towards, the financial needs of the child.

13 Power to make alternative orders

(1) This paragraph applies if on an application under this Part the court decides –

    (a)   that it would be contrary to the interests of justice to make an order for the making of the financial provision specified in the application, or

    (b)   that any financial provision which the applicant or the respondent (as the case may be) has agreed to make in respect of a child of the family does not provide for, or make a proper contribution towards, the financial needs of that child.

(2) If the court is of the opinion –

    (a)   that it would not be contrary to the interests of justice to make an order for the making of some other financial provision specified by the court, and

    (b)   that, in so far as that other financial provision contains any provision for a child of the family, it provides for, or makes a proper contribution towards, the financial needs of that child,

then, if both the civil partners agree, the court may order that the applicant or the respondent (as the case may be) is to make that other financial provision.

14 Relationship between this Part and Part 1

(1) A civil partner who has applied for an order under Part 1 is not precluded at any time before the determination of the application from applying for an order under this Part.

(2) If –

    (a)   an order is made under this Part on the application of either civil partner, and

    (b)   either of them has also made an application for a Part 1 order,

the application for the Part 1 order is to be treated as if it had been withdrawn.

PART 3
ORDERS OF COURT WHERE CIVIL PARTNERS LIVING APART BY AGREEMENT

15 Powers of court where civil partners are living apart by agreement

(1) If –

    (a)   the civil partners have been living apart for a continuous period exceeding 3 months, neither civil partner having deserted the other, and

    (b)   one of the civil partners has been making periodical payments for the benefit of the other civil partner or of a child of the family,

the other civil partner may apply to a magistrates' court for an order under this Part.

(2) An application made under sub-paragraph (1) must specify the total amount of the payments made by the respondent during the period of 3 months immediately preceding the date of the making of the application.

(3) If on an application for an order under this Part the court is satisfied that the respondent has made the payments specified in the application, the court may make one or both of the orders set out in paragraph 16.

(4) Sub-paragraph (3) is subject to the provisions of this Schedule.

16 The orders that may be made under this Part

(1) The orders are –

- (a) an order that the respondent is to make to the applicant such periodical payments for such term as may be specified;
- (b) an order that the respondent is to make –
  - (i) to the applicant for the benefit of a child of the family to whom the application relates, or
  - (ii) to a child of the family to whom the application relates.

such periodical payments for such term as may be specified.

(2) 'Specified' means specified in the order.

17 Restrictions on orders under this Part

The court in the exercise of its powers under this Part must not require –

- (a) the respondent to make payments whose total amount during any period of 3 months exceeds the total amount paid by him for the benefit of –
  - (i) the applicant, or
  - (ii) a child of the family,
  during the period of 3 months immediately preceding the date of the making of the application;
- (b) the respondent to make payments to or for the benefit of any person which exceed in amount the payments which the court considers that it would have required the respondent to make to or for the benefit of that person on an application under Part 1;
- (c) payments to be made to or for the benefit of a child of the family who is not the respondent's child, unless the court considers that it would have made an order in favour of that child on an application under Part 1.

18 Relationship with powers under Part 1

(1) Sub-paragraph (2) applies if on an application under this Part the court considers that the orders which it has the power to make under this Part –

- (a) would not provide reasonable maintenance for the applicant, or
- (b) if the application relates to a child of the family, would not provide, or make a proper contribution towards, reasonable maintenance for that child.

(2) The court –

- (a) must refuse to make an order under this Part, but
- (b) may treat the application as if it were an application for an order under Part 1.

19 Matters to be taken into consideration

Paragraphs 4 to 6 apply in relation to an application for an order under this Part as they apply in relation to an application for an order under Part 1, subject to the modification that for the reference in paragraph 5(2)(c) to the occurrence of the conduct which is alleged as the ground of the application substitute a reference to the living apart of the civil partners.

PART 4
INTERIM ORDERS

20 Circumstances in which interim orders may be made

(1) This paragraph applies if an application has been made for an order under Part 1, 2 or 3.

(2) A magistrates' court may make an interim order –

    (a)   at any time before making a final order on, or dismissing, the application, or

    (b)   on refusing (under paragraph 8) to make on order on the application.

(3) The High Court may make an interim order on ordering the application to be reheard by a magistrates' court (either after the refusal of an order under paragraph 8 or on an appeal made by virtue of paragraph 46).

(4) Not more than one interim order may be made with respect to an application for an order under Part 1, 2 or 3.

(5) Sub-paragraph (4) does not affect the power of a court to make an interim order on a further application under Part 1, 2 or 3.

21 Meaning of interim order

(1) An interim order is an order requiring the respondent to make such periodical payments as the court thinks reasonable –

    (a)   to the applicant,

    (b)   to any child of the family who is under 18, or

    (c)   to the applicant for the benefit of such a child.

(2) In relation to an interim order in respect of an application for an order under Part 2 by the civil partner who has agreed to make the financial provision specified in the application, sub-paragraph (1) applies as if –

    (a)   the reference to the respondent were a reference to the applicant, and

    (b)   the references to the applicant were references to the respondent.

22 When interim order may start

(1) An interim order may provide for payments to be made from such date as the court may specify, except that the date must not be earlier than the date of the making of the application for an order under Part 1, 2 or 3.

(2) Sub-paragraph (1) is subject to paragraph 27(7) and (8).

23 Payments which can be treated as having been paid on account

(1) If an interim order made by the High Court on an appeal made by virtue of paragraph 46 provides for payments to be made from a date earlier than the date of the making of the order, the interim order may provide that payments made by the respondent under an order made by a magistrates' court are to be treated, to such extent and in such manner as may be provided by the interim order, as having been paid on account of any payment provided for by the interim order.

(2) In relation to an interim order in respect of an application for an order under Part 2 by the civil partner who has agreed to make the financial provision specified in the application, sub-paragraph (1) applies as if the reference to the respondent were a reference to the applicant.

24 When interim order ceases to have effect

(1) Subject to sub-paragraphs (2) and (3), an interim order made on an application for an order under Part 1, 2 or 3 ceases to have effect on the earliest of the following dates –

  (a) the date, if any, specified for the purpose in the interim order;
  (b) the date on which the period of 3 months beginning with the date of the making of the interim order ends;
  (c) the date on which a magistrates' court either makes a final order on, or dismisses, the application.

(2) If an interim order made under this Part would, but for this sub-paragraph, cease to have effect under sub-paragraph (1)(a) or (b) –

  (a) the magistrates' court which made the order, or
  (b) in the case of an interim order made by the High Court, the magistrates' court by which the application for an order under Part 1, 2 or 3 is to be reheard,

may by order provide that the interim order is to continue in force for a further period.

(3) An order continued in force under sub-paragraph (2) ceases to have effect on the earliest of the following dates –

  (a) the date, if any, specified for the purpose in the order continuing it;
  (b) the date on which ends the period of 3 months beginning with –
    (i)   the date of the making of the order continuing it, or
    (ii) if more than one such order has been made with respect to the application, the date of the making of the first such order;
  (c) the date on which the court either makes a final order on, or dismisses, the application.

25 Supplementary

(1) An interim order made by the High Court under paragraph 20(3) on ordering an application to be reheard by a magistrates' court is to be treated for the purposes of –

  (a) its enforcement, and
  (b) Part 6 (variation etc of orders),

as if it were an order of that magistrates' court (and not of the High Court).

(2) No appeal lies from the making of or refusal to make, the variation of or refusal to vary, or the revocation of or refusal to revoke, an interim order.

PART 5
COMMENCEMENT AND DURATION OF ORDERS UNDER PARTS 1, 2 AND 3

26 Duration of periodical payments order for a civil partner

(1) The court may specify in a periodical payments order made under paragraph 2(1)(a) or Part 3 in favour of a civil partner such term as it thinks fit, except that the term must not –

  (a) begin before the date of the making of the application for the order, or
  (b) extend beyond the death of either of the civil partners.

(2) If –

 (a) a periodical payments order is made under paragraph 2(1)(a) or Part 3 in favour of one of the civil partners, and

 (b) the civil partnership is subsequently dissolved or annulled but the order continues in force,

the periodical payments order ceases to have effect (regardless of anything in it) on the formation of a subsequent civil partnership or marriage by that civil partner, except in relation to any arrears due under the order on the date of that event.

27 Age limit on making orders for financial provision for children and duration of such orders

(1) Subject to sub-paragraph (5), no order is to be made under paragraph 2(1)(c) or (d) or Part 3 in favour of a child who has reached 18.

(2) The term to be specified in a periodical payments order made under paragraph 2(1)(c) or Part 3 in favour of a child may begin with –

 (a) the date of the making of an application for the order or a later date, or

 (b) a date ascertained in accordance with sub-paragraph (7) or (8).

(3) The term to be specified in such an order –

 (a) must not in the first instance extend beyond the date of the birthday of the child next following his reaching the upper limit of the compulsory school age unless the court considers that in the circumstances of the case the welfare of the child requires that it should extend to a later date, and

 (b) must not in any event, subject to sub-paragraph (5), extend beyond the date of the child's 18th birthday.

(4) Sub-paragraph (3)(a) must be read with section 8 of the Education Act 1996 (which applies to determine for the purposes of any enactment whether a person is of compulsory school age).

(5) Sub-paragraphs (1) and (3)(b) do not apply in the case of a child if it appears to the court that –

 (a) the child is, or will be, or, if such an order were made without complying with either or both of those provisions, would be –

  (i) receiving instruction at an educational establishment, or

  (ii) undergoing training for a trade, profession or vocation,

  whether or not also the child is, will be or would be, in gainful employment, or

 (b) there are special circumstances which justify the making of the order without complying with either or both of sub-paragraphs (1) and (3)(b).

(6) Any order made under paragraph 2(1)(c) or Part 3 in favour of a child, regardless of anything in the order, ceases to have effect on the death of the person liable to make payments under the order.

(7) If –

 (a) a maintenance calculation ('current calculation') is in force with respect to a child, and

 (b) an application is made for an order under paragraph 2(1)(c) or Part 3 –

  (i) in accordance with section 8 of the Child Support Act 1991, and

  (ii) before the end of 6 months beginning with the making of the current calculation,

the term to be specified in any such order made on that application may be expressed to begin on, or at any time after, the earliest permitted date.

(8) 'The earliest permitted date' is whichever is the later of –

    (a)   the date 6 months before the application is made, or

    (b)   the date on which the current calculation took effect or, where successive maintenance calculations have been continuously in force with respect to a child, on which the first of those calculations took effect.

(9) If –

    (a)   a maintenance calculation ceases to have effect by or under any provision of the 1991 Act, and

    (b)   an application is made, before the end of 6 months beginning with the relevant date, for a periodical payments order under paragraph 2(1)(c) or Part 3 in favour of a child with respect to whom that maintenance calculation was in force immediately before it ceased to have effect,

the term to be specified in any such order, or in any interim order under Part 4, made on that application, may begin with the date on which that maintenance calculation ceased to have effect or any later date.

(10) 'The relevant date' means the date on which the maintenance calculation ceased to have effect.

(11) In this Schedule 'maintenance calculation' has the same meaning as it has in the 1991 Act by virtue of section 54 of the 1991 Act as read with any regulations in force under that section.

28 Application of paragraphs 26 and 27 to Part 2 orders

(1) Subject to sub-paragraph (3), paragraph 26 applies in relation to an order under Part 2 which requires periodical payments to be made to a civil partner for his own benefit as it applies in relation to an order under paragraph 2(1)(a).

(2) Subject to sub-paragraph (3), paragraph 27 applies in relation to an order under Part 2 for the making of financial provision in respect of a child of the family as it applies in relation to an order under paragraph 2(1)(c) or (d).

(3) If –

    (a)   the court makes an order under Part 2 which contains provision for the making of periodical payments, and

    (b)   by virtue of paragraph 14, an application for an order under Part 1 is treated as if it had been withdrawn,

the term which may be specified under Part 2 as the term for which the payments are to be made may begin with the date of the making of the application for the order under Part 1 or any later date.

Child support—Civil Partnership (Pensions, Social Security and Child Support) (Consequential, etc Provisions) Order 2005, art 2(5), Sch 5, paras 1, 2(1),(4) provide that, in relation to old scheme cases, para 27 is to apply with certain prescribed amendments.

29 Effect on certain orders of parties living together

(1) Sub-paragraph (2) applies if periodical payments are required to be made to a civil partner (whether for the civil partner's own benefit or for the benefit of a child of the family) –

    (a)   by an order made under Part 1 or 2, or

    (b)   by an interim order made under Part 4 (otherwise than on an application under Part 3).

(2) The order is enforceable even though –

(a) the civil partners are living with each other at the date of the making of the order, or

(b) if they are not living with each other at that date, they subsequently resume living with each other;

but the order ceases to have effect if after that date the parties continue to live with each other, or resume living with each other, for a continuous period exceeding 6 months.

(3) Sub-paragraph (4) applies if –

(a) an order is made under Part 1 or 2 which requires periodical payments to be made to a child of the family, or

(b) an interim order is made under Part 4 (otherwise than on an application under Part 3) which requires periodical payments to be made to a child of the family.

(4) Unless the court otherwise directs, the order continues to have effect and is enforceable even if –

(a) the civil partners are living with each other at the date of the making of the order, or

(b) if they are not living with each other at that date, they subsequently resume living with each other.

(5) An order made under Part 3, and any interim order made on an application for an order under that Part, ceases to have effect if the civil partners resume living with each other.

(6) If an order made under this Schedule ceases to have effect under –

(a) sub-paragraph (2) or (5), or

(b) a direction given under sub-paragraph (4),

a magistrates' court may, on an application made by either civil partner, make an order declaring that the order ceased to have effect from such date as the court may specify.

PART 6
VARIATION ETC OF ORDERS

30 Power to vary, revoke, suspend or revive order

(1) If a magistrates' court has made an order for the making of periodical payments under Part 1, 2 or 3, the court may, on an application made under this Part –

(a) vary or revoke the order,

(b) suspend any provision of it temporarily, or

(c) revive any provision so suspended.

(2) If a magistrates' court has made an interim order under Part 4, the court may, on an application made under this Part –

(a) vary or revoke the order,

(b) suspend any provision of it temporarily, or

(c) revive any provision so suspended,

except that it may not by virtue of this sub-paragraph extend the period for which the order is in force.

31 Powers to order lump sum on variation

(1) If a magistrates' court has made an order under paragraph 2(1)(a) or (c) for the making of periodical payments, the court may, on an application made under this Part, make an order for the payment of a lump sum under paragraph 2(1)(b) or (d).

(2) If a magistrates' court has made an order under Part 2 for the making of periodical payments by a civil partner the court may, on an application made under this Part, make an order for the payment of a lump sum by that civil partner –

    (a)   to the other civil partner, or

    (b)   to a child of the family or to that other civil partner for the benefit of that child.

(3) Where the court has power by virtue of this paragraph to make an order for the payment of a lump sum –

    (a)   the amount of the lump sum must not exceed the maximum amount that may at that time be required to be paid under Part 1, but

    (b)   the court may make an order for the payment of a lump sum not exceeding that amount even if the person required to pay it was required to pay a lump sum by a previous order under this Schedule.

(4) Where –

    (a)   the court has power by virtue of this paragraph to make an order for the payment of a lump sum, and

    (b)   the respondent or the applicant (as the case may be) has agreed to pay a lump sum of an amount exceeding the maximum amount that may at that time be required to be paid under Part 1,

the court may, regardless of sub-paragraph (3), make an order for the payment of a lump sum of that amount.

32 Power to specify when order as varied is to take effect

An order made under this Part which varies an order for the making of periodical payments may provide that the payments as so varied are to be made from such date as the court may specify, except that, subject to paragraph 33, the date must not be earlier than the date of the making of the application under this Part.

33 (1) If –

    (a)   there is in force an order ('the order') –

        (i)   under paragraph 2(1)(c),

        (ii)   under Part 2 making provision of a kind set out in paragraph 10(1)(c) (regardless of whether it makes provision of any other kind mentioned in paragraph 10(1)(c)),

        (iii)   under paragraph 16(1)(b), or

        (iv)   which is an interim order under Part 4 under which the payments are to be made to a child or to the applicant for the benefit of a child,

    (b)   the order requires payments specified in it to be made to or for the benefit of *more than one child* without apportioning those payments between them,

    (c)   a maintenance calculation ('the calculation') is made with respect to one or more, but not all, of the children with respect to whom those payments are to be made, and

    (d)   an application is made, before the end of 6 months beginning with the date on which the calculation was made, for the variation or revocation of the order, the court may, in exercise of its powers under this Part to vary or revoke the order, direct that the variation or revocation is to take effect from the date on which the calculation took effect or any later date.

(2) If –

    (a) an order ('the child order') of a kind prescribed for the purposes of section 10(1) of the Child Support Act 1991 is affected by a maintenance calculation,

    (b) on the date on which the child order became so affected there was in force an order ('the civil partner's order') –

        (i) under paragraph 2(1)(a),

        (ii) under Part 2 making provision of a kind set out in paragraph 10(1)(a) (regardless of whether it makes provision of any other kind mentioned in paragraph 10(1)(a)),

        (iii) under paragraph 16(1)(a), or

        (iv) which is an interim order under Part 4 under which the payments are to be made to the applicant (otherwise than for the benefit of a child), and

    (c) an application is made, before the end of 6 months beginning with the date on which the maintenance calculation was made, for the civil partner's order to be varied or revoked,

the court may, in exercise of its powers under this Part to vary or revoke the civil partner's order, direct that the variation or revocation is to take effect from the date on which the child order became so affected or any later date.

(3) For the purposes of sub-paragraph (2), an order is affected if it ceases to have effect or is modified by or under section 10 of the 1991 Act.

Child support—Civil Partnership (Pensions, Social Security and Child Support) (Consequential, etc Provisions) Order 2005, art 2(5), Sch 5, paras 1, 2(1),(5) provide that, in relation to old scheme cases, para 33 is to apply with certain prescribed amendments.

34 Matters to which court is to have regard in exercising powers under this Part

(1) In exercising the powers conferred by this Part the court must, so far as it appears to the court just to do so, give effect to any agreement which has been reached between the civil partners in relation to the application.

(2) If –

    (a) there is no such agreement, or

    (b) if the court decides not to give effect to the agreement,

the court must have regard to all the circumstances of the case, giving first consideration to the welfare while under 18 of any child of the family who has not reached 18.

(3) Those circumstances include any change in any of the matters –

    (a) to which the court was required to have regard when making the order to which the application relates, or

    (b) in the case of an application for the variation or revocation of an order made under Part 2 or on an appeal made by virtue of paragraph 46, to which the court would have been required to have regard if that order had been made under Part 1.

35 Variation of orders for periodical payments: further provisions

(1) The power of the court under paragraphs 30 to 34 to vary an order for the making of periodical payments includes power, if the court is satisfied that payment has not been made in accordance with the order, to exercise one of its powers under section 59(3)(a) to (d) of the Magistrates' Courts Act 1980.

(2) Sub-paragraph (1) is subject to paragraph 37.

36 (1) If –

    (a)   a magistrates' court has made an order under this Schedule for the making of periodical payments, and

    (b)   payments under the order are required to be made by any method of payment falling within section 59(6) of the 1980 Act (standing order, etc),

an application may be made under this sub-paragraph to the court for the order to be varied as mentioned in sub-paragraph (2).

(2) Subject to sub-paragraph (4), if an application is made under sub-paragraph (1), a justices' clerk, after –

    (a)   giving written notice (by post or otherwise) of the application to the respondent, and

    (b)   allowing the respondent, within the period of 14 days beginning with the date of the giving of that notice, an opportunity to make written representations,

may vary the order to provide that payments under the order are to be made to the designated officer for the court.

(3) The clerk may proceed with an application under sub-paragraph (1) even if the respondent has not received written notice of the application.

(4) If an application has been made under sub-paragraph (1), the clerk may, if he considers it inappropriate to exercise his power under sub-paragraph (2), refer the matter to the court which, subject to paragraph 37, may vary the order by exercising one of its powers under section 59(3)(a) to (d) of the 1980 Act.

37 (1) Before varying the order by exercising one of its powers under section 59(3)(a) to (d) of the 1980 Act, the court must have regard to any representations made by the parties to the application.

(2) If the court does not propose to exercise its power under section 59(3)(c), (cc) or (d) of the 1980 Act, the court must, unless upon representations expressly made in that behalf by the person to whom payments under the order are required to be made it is satisfied that it is undesirable to do so, exercise its power under section 59(3)(b).

38 (1) Section 59(4) of the 1980 Act (power of court to order that account be opened) applies for the purposes of paragraphs 35 and 36(4) as it applies for the purposes of section 59.

(2) None of the powers of the court, or of a justices' clerk, conferred by paragraphs 35 to 37 and sub-paragraph (1) is exercisable in relation to an order under this Schedule for the making of periodical payments which is not a qualifying maintenance order (within the meaning of section 59 of the 1980 Act).

PART II

39 Persons who may apply under this Part

An application under paragraph 30, 31 or 36 may be made –

    (a)   if it is for the variation or revocation of an order under Part 1, 2, 3 or 4 for periodical payments, by either civil partner, and

    (b)   if it is for the variation of an order under paragraph 2(1)(c) or Part 2 or 3 for periodical payments to or in respect of a child, also by the child himself, if he has reached 16.

40 Revival of orders for periodical payments

(1) If an order made by a magistrates' court under this Schedule for the making of periodical payments to or in respect of a child (other than an interim order) ceases to have effect –

    (a)   on the date on which the child reaches 16, or

    (b)   at any time after that date but before or on the date on which he reaches 18,

the child may apply to the court which made the order for an order for its revival.

(2) If on such an application it appears to the court that –

    (a)   the child is, will be or (if an order were made under this sub-paragraph) would be receiving instruction at an educational establishment or undergoing training for a trade, profession or vocation, whether or not while in gainful employment, or

    (b)   there are special circumstances which justify the making of an order under this sub-paragraph,

the court may by order revive the order from such date as the court may specify, not being earlier than the date of the making of the application.

(3) Any order revived under this paragraph may be varied or revoked under paragraphs 30 to 34 in the same way as it could have been varied or revoked had it continued in being.

41 Variation of instalments of lump sum

If in the exercise of its powers under section 75 of the 1980 Act a magistrates' court orders that a lump sum required to be paid under this Schedule is to be paid by instalments, the court, on an application made by either the person liable to pay or the person entitled to receive that sum, may vary that order by varying –

    (a)   the number of instalments payable,

    (b)   the amount of any instalment payable, and

    (c)   the date on which any instalment becomes payable.

42 Supplementary provisions with respect to variation and revocation of orders

None of the following powers apply in relation to an order made under this Schedule –

    (a)   the powers of a magistrates' court to revoke, revive or vary an order for the periodical payment of money and the power of a justices' clerk to vary such an order under section 60 of the 1980 Act;

    (b)   the power of a magistrates' court to suspend or rescind certain other orders under section 63(2) of the 1980 Act.

PART 7
ARREARS AND REPAYMENTS

43 Enforcement etc of orders for payment of money

Section 32 of the Domestic Proceedings and Magistrates' Courts Act 1978 applies in relation to orders under this Schedule as it applies in relation to orders under Part 1 of that Act.

44 Orders for repayment after cessation of order because of subsequent civil partnership etc

(1) Sub-paragraphs (3) and (4) apply if –

    (a) an order made under paragraph 2(1)(a) or Part 2 or 3 has, under paragraph 26(2), ceased to have effect because of the formation of a subsequent civil partnership or marriage by the party ('R') in whose favour it was made, and

    (b) the person liable to make payments under the order ('P') made payments in accordance with it in respect of a relevant period in the mistaken belief that the order was still subsisting.

(2) 'Relevant period' means a period after the date of the formation of the subsequent civil partnership or marriage.

(3) No proceedings in respect of a cause of action arising out of the circumstances mentioned in sub-paragraph (1)(a) and (b) is maintainable by P (or P's personal representatives) against R (or R's personal representatives).

(4) But on an application made under this paragraph by P (or P's personal representatives) against R (or R's personal representatives) the court –

    (a) may order the respondent to pay to the applicant a sum equal to the amount of the payments made in respect of the relevant period, or

    (b) if it appears to the court that it would be unjust to make that order, may –

        (i) order the respondent to pay to the applicant such lesser sum as it thinks fit, or

        (ii) dismiss the application.

(5) An order under this paragraph for the payment of any sum may provide for the payment of that sum by instalments of such amount as may be specified in the order.

(6) An application under this paragraph –

    (a) may be made in proceedings in the High Court or a county court for leave to enforce, or the enforcement of, the payment of arrears under an order made under paragraph 2(1)(a) or Part 2 or 3, but

    (b) if not made in such proceedings, must be made to a county court,

and accordingly references in this paragraph to the court are references to the High Court or a county court, as the circumstances require.

(7) The jurisdiction conferred on a county court by this paragraph is exercisable by a county court even though, because of the amount claimed in an application under this paragraph, the jurisdiction would not but for this sub-paragraph be exercisable by a county court.

(8) Subject to sub-paragraph (9) –

    (a) the designated officer for a magistrates' court to whom any payments under an order made under paragraph 2(1)(a), or Part 2 or 3, are required to be made is not liable for any act done by him in pursuance of the order after the date on which that order ceased to have effect because of the formation of a subsequent civil partnership or marriage by the person entitled to payments under it, and

(b) the collecting officer under an attachment of earnings order made to secure payments under the order under paragraph 2(1)(a), or Part 2 or 3, is not liable for any act done by him after that date in accordance with any enactment or rule of court specifying how payments made to him in compliance with the attachment of earnings order are to be dealt with.

(9) Sub-paragraph (8) applies if (but only if) the act –

(a) was one which he would have been under a duty to do had the order under paragraph 2(1)(a) or Part 2 or 3 not ceased to have effect, and

(b) was done before notice in writing of the formation of the subsequent civil partnership or marriage was given to him by or on behalf of –

    (i) the person entitled to payments under the order,

    (ii) the person liable to make payments under it, or

    (iii) the personal representatives of either of them.

(10) In this paragraph 'collecting officer', in relation to an attachment of earnings order, means –

(a) the officer of the High Court, or

(b) the officer designated by the Lord Chancellor,

to whom a person makes payments in compliance with the order.

PART 8
SUPPLEMENTARY

45 Restrictions on making of orders under this Schedule: welfare of children

If –

(a) an application is made by a civil partner for an order under Part 1, 2 or 3, and

(b) there is a child of the family who is under 18,

the court must not dismiss or make a final order on the application until it has decided whether to exercise any of its powers under the Children Act 1989 with respect to the child.

46 Constitution of courts, powers of High Court and county court in relation to orders and appeals

The following provisions of the Domestic Proceedings and Magistrates' Courts Act 1978 apply in relation to an order under this Schedule relating to a civil partnership as they apply in relation to an order under Part 1 of that Act relating to a marriage –

(a) section 28 (powers of the High Court and a county court in relation to certain orders),

(b) section 29 (appeals), and

(c) section 31 (constitution of courts).

47 Provisions as to jurisdiction and procedure

(1) Subject to sub-paragraph (1A) and to section 2 of the Family Law Act 1986 and section 70 of the Magistrates' Courts Act 1980 and any determination of the Lord Chancellor, a magistrates' court has jurisdiction to hear an application for an order

under this Schedule if it acts in, or is authorised by the Lord Chancellor to act for, a local justice area in which either the applicant or the respondent ordinarily resides at the date of the making of the application.

(1A) If an application or part of an application for an order under this Schedule relates to a matter where jurisdiction falls to be determined by reference to the jurisdictional requirements of the Maintenance Regulation and Schedule 6 to the Civil Jurisdiction and Judgments (Maintenance) Regulations 2011, a magistrates' court may not entertain that application or that part of it unless it has jurisdiction to do so by virtue of that Regulation and that Schedule.

(2) Any jurisdiction conferred on a magistrates' court by this Schedule is exercisable even if any party to the proceedings is not domiciled in England and Wales.

(3) The Lord Chancellor may make a determination for the purposes of sub-paragraph (1) only with the concurrence of the Lord Chief Justice.

(4) The Lord Chief Justice may nominate a judicial office holder (as defined in section 109(4) of the Constitutional Reform Act 2005) to exercise his functions under this paragraph.

(5) In this paragraph "the Maintenance Regulation" means Council Regulation (EC) No 4/2009 including as applied in relation to Denmark by virtue of the Agreement made on 19 October 2005 between the European Community and the Kingdom of Denmark.

Amendments—SI 2006/1016; SI 2011/1484.

48 Meaning of 'child of the family'

In this Schedule 'child of the family', in relation to two people who are civil partners of each other, means –

(a) a child of both of them, and
(b) any other child, other than a child placed with them as foster parents by a local authority or voluntary organisation, who has been treated by both the civil partners as a child of their family.

SCHEDULE 7
FINANCIAL RELIEF IN ENGLAND AND WALES AFTER OVERSEAS DISSOLUTION ETC OF A CIVIL PARTNERSHIP

Scope—When a civil partnership has been dissolved or annulled or there has been a legal separation by means of judicial or other proceedings outside the British Isles, and the dissolution, annulment or legal separation is entitled to be recognised as valid in England and Wales (ss 219 and 234), such recognition confers on either of the civil partners the right to make an application to the court in England and Wales for financial relief (para 2) including financial provision, property adjustment, pension sharing and pension compensation sharing (para 9) and transfers of tenancies (para 13). However, any such application will be barred if either of the civil partners has formed a subsequent civil partnership or marriage (para 3). Further, the leave of the court is required in order to make an application (para 4). Where leave is granted, the court may make an interim order for maintenance (para 5). The jurisdictional requirements are set out in para 7. Before deciding an application for financial relief, the court must consider whether England and Wales is the appropriate venue (para 8). Sch 7 is the counterpart to Pt III in MFPA 1984 which provides for financial relief in England and Wales after an overseas divorce, annulment or legal separation. Reference should be made to the commentary on the comparable provisions in the 1984 Act. The relevant procedure is found in FPR 2010, Pt 8, Ch 6.

PART 1
FINANCIAL RELIEF

1 Part applies where civil partnership has been dissolved etc overseas

(1) This Part of this Schedule applies where –

    (a)   a civil partnership has been dissolved or annulled, or the civil partners have been legally separated, by means of judicial or other proceedings in an overseas country, and

    (b)   the dissolution, annulment or legal separation is entitled to be recognised as valid in England and Wales.

(2) This Part of this Schedule applies even if the date of the dissolution, annulment or legal separation is earlier than the date on which the Part comes into force.

(3) In this Schedule 'overseas country' means a country or territory outside the British Islands.

(4) In this Part of this Schedule 'child of the family' means –

    (a)   a child of both of the civil partners, and

    (b)   any other child, other than a child placed with them as foster parents or by a local authority or voluntary organisation, who has been treated by both the civil partners as a child of their family.

2 Either civil partner may make application for financial relief

(1) Either of the civil partners may make an application to the court for an order under paragraph 9 or 13.

(2) The rights conferred by sub-paragraph (1) are subject to –

    (a)   paragraph 3 (civil partner may not apply after forming subsequent civil partnership etc), and

    (b)   paragraph 4 (application may not be made until leave to make it has been granted).

(3) An application for an order under paragraph 9 or 13 must be made in a manner prescribed by rules of court.

3 No application after formation of subsequent civil partnership or marriage

(1) If –

    (a)   the civil partnership has been dissolved or annulled, and

    (b)   after the dissolution or annulment, one of the civil partners forms a subsequent civil partnership or marriage,

that civil partner shall not be entitled to make, in relation to the civil partnership, an application for an order under paragraph 9 or 13.

(2) The reference in sub-paragraph (1) to the forming of a subsequent civil partnership or marriage includes a reference to the forming of a civil partnership or marriage which is by law void or voidable.

4 Leave of court required for making of application

(1) No application for an order under paragraph 9 or 13 shall be made unless the leave of the court has been obtained in accordance with rules of court.

(2) The court shall not grant leave under this paragraph unless it considers that there is substantial ground for the making of an application for such an order.

(3) The court may grant leave under this paragraph notwithstanding that an order has been made by a court in a country outside England and Wales requiring the other civil partner to make any payment, or transfer any property, to the applicant or to a child of the family.

(4) Leave under this paragraph may be granted subject to such conditions as the court thinks fit.

5 Interim orders for maintenance

(1) Where –

    (a)   leave is granted under paragraph 4, and

    (b)   it appears to the court that the civil partner who applied for leave, or any child of the family, is in immediate need of financial assistance,

the court may, subject to sub-paragraph (4), make an interim order for maintenance.

(2) An interim order for maintenance is one requiring the other civil partner to make –

    (a)   to the applicant, or

    (b)   to the child,

such periodical payments as the court thinks reasonable for such term as the court thinks reasonable.

(3) The term must be one –

    (a)   beginning not earlier than the date of the grant of leave, and

    (b)   ending with the date of the determination of the application made under the leave.

(4) If it appears to the court that the court will, in the event of an application being made under the leave, have jurisdiction to entertain the application only under paragraph 7(4), the court shall not make an interim order under this paragraph.

(5) An interim order under this paragraph may be made subject to such conditions as the court thinks fit.

6 Paragraphs 7 and 8 apply where application made for relief under paragraph 9 or 13

Paragraphs 7 and 8 apply where –

    (a)   one of the civil partners has been granted leave under paragraph 4, and

    (b)   acting under the leave, that civil partner makes an application for an order under paragraph 9 or 13.

7 Jurisdiction of the court

(1) Subject to sub-paragraph (6), the court shall have jurisdiction to entertain the application only if one or more of the following jurisdictional requirements is satisfied.

(2) The first requirement is that either of the civil partners –

    (a)   was domiciled in England and Wales on the date when the leave was applied for, or

    (b)   was domiciled in England and Wales on the date when the dissolution, annulment or legal separation took effect in the overseas country in which it was obtained.

(3) The second is that either of the civil partners –

   (a) was habitually resident in England and Wales throughout the period of one year ending with the date when the leave was applied for, or

   (b) was habitually resident in England and Wales throughout the period of one year ending with the date on which the dissolution, annulment or legal separation took effect in the overseas country in which it was obtained.

(4) The third is that either or both of the civil partners had, at the date when the leave was applied for, a beneficial interest in possession in a dwelling-house situated in England or Wales which was at some time during the civil partnership a civil partnership home of the civil partners.

(5) In sub-paragraph (4) 'possession' includes receipt of, or the right to receive, rents and profits, but here 'rent' does not include mortgage interest.

(6) If an application or part of an application relates to a matter where jurisdiction falls to be determined by the jurisdictional requirements of the Maintenance Regulation and Schedule 6 to the Civil Jurisdiction and Judgments (Maintenance) Regulations 2011, those requirements are to determine whether the court has jurisdiction to entertain the application or that part of it.

(7) In sub-paragraph (6) "the Maintenance Regulation" means Council Regulation (EC) No 4/2009 including as applied in relation to Denmark by virtue of the Agreement made on 19 October 2005 between the European Community and the Kingdom of Denmark.

Amendments—SI 2011/1484.

8 Duty of the court to consider whether England and Wales is appropriate venue for application

(1) Before deciding the application, the court must consider whether in all the circumstances of the case it would be appropriate for an order of the kind applied for to be made by a court in England and Wales.

(2) Subject to sub-paragraph (4), if the court is not satisfied that it would be appropriate, the court shall dismiss the application.

(3) The court must, in particular, have regard to the following matters –

   (a) the connection which the civil partners have with England and Wales;

   (b) the connection which the civil partners have with the country in which the civil partnership was dissolved or annulled or in which they were legally separated;

   (c) the connection which the civil partners have with any other country outside England and Wales;

   (d) any financial benefit which, in consequence of the dissolution, annulment or legal separation –

      (i) the applicant, or

      (ii) a child of the family,

     has received, or is likely to receive, by virtue of any agreement or the operation of the law of a country outside England and Wales;

   (e) in a case where an order has been made by a court in a country outside England and Wales requiring the other civil partner –

      (i) to make any payment, or

      (ii) to transfer any property,

     for the benefit of the applicant or a child of the family, the financial relief given by the order and the extent to which the order has been complied with or is likely to be complied with;

   (f) any right which the applicant has, or has had, to apply for financial relief from the other civil partner under the law of any country outside England and Wales and, if the applicant has omitted to exercise that right, the reason for that omission;

(g)   the availability in England and Wales of any property in respect of which an order under this Schedule in favour of the applicant could be made;

(h)   the extent to which any order made under this Schedule is likely to be enforceable;

(i)   the length of time which has elapsed since the date of the dissolution, annulment or legal separation.

(4) If the court has jurisdiction in relation to the application or part of it by virtue of the Maintenance Regulation and Schedule 6 to the Civil Jurisdiction and Judgments (Maintenance) Regulations 2011, the court may not dismiss the application or that part of it on the ground mentioned in sub-paragraph (2) if to do so would be inconsistent with the jurisdictional requirements of that Regulation and that Schedule.

(5) In sub-paragraph (4) "the Maintenance Regulation" means Council Regulation (EC) No 4/2009 including as applied in relation to Denmark by virtue of the Agreement made on 19 October 2005 between the European Community and the Kingdom of Denmark.

Amendments—SI 2011/1484.

9 Orders for financial provision, property adjustment, pension sharing and pension compensation sharing

(1) Sub-paragraphs (2) and (3) apply where one of the civil partners has made an application for an order under this paragraph.

(2) If the civil partnership has been dissolved or annulled, the court may on the application make any one or more of the orders which it could make under Part 1, 2, 4 or 4A of Schedule 5 (financial provision, property adjustment, pension sharing and pension compensation sharing) if a dissolution order or nullity order had been made in respect of the civil partnership under Chapter 2 of Part 2 of this Act.

(3) If the civil partners have been legally separated, the court may on the application make any one or more of the orders which it could make under Part 1 or 2 of Schedule 5 (financial provision and property adjustment) if a separation order had been made in respect of the civil partners under Chapter 2 of Part 2 of this Act.

(4) Where under sub-paragraph (2) or (3) the court makes –

(a)   an order which, if made under Schedule 5, would be a secured periodical payments order,

(b)   an order for the payment of a lump sum, or

(c)   an order which, if made under that Schedule, would be a property adjustment order,

then, on making that order or at any time afterwards, the court may make any order which it could make under Part 3 of Schedule 5 (sale of property) if the order under sub-paragraph (2) or (3) had been made under that Schedule.

(5) The powers under sub-paragraphs (2) to (4) are subject to paragraph 11.

Amendments—Pensions Act 2008, Sch 6, Pt 3.

10 Matters to which court is to have regard in exercising its powers under paragraph 9

(1) The court, in deciding –

(a)   whether to exercise its powers under paragraph 9, and

   (b)   if so, in what way,

must act in accordance with this paragraph.

(2) The court must have regard to all the circumstances of the case, giving first consideration to the welfare, while under 18, of any child of the family who has not reached 18.

(3) The court, in exercising its powers under paragraph 9 in relation to one of the civil partners –

   (a)   must in particular have regard to the matters mentioned in paragraph 21(2) of Schedule 5, and

   (b)   shall be under duties corresponding to those imposed by sub-paragraphs (2) and (3) of paragraph 23 of that Schedule (duties to consider termination of financial obligations) where it decides to exercise under paragraph 9 powers corresponding to the powers referred to in those sub-paragraphs.

(4) The matters to which the court is to have regard under sub-paragraph (3)(a), so far as relating to paragraph 21(2)(a) of Schedule 5 (regard to be had to financial resources), include –

   (a)   any benefits under a pension arrangement which either of the civil partners has or is likely to have, and

   (b)   any PPF compensation to which a civil partner is or is likely to be entitled,

(whether or not in the foreseeable future).

(5) The matters to which the court is to have regard under sub-paragraph (3)(a), so far as relating to paragraph 21(2)(h) of Schedule 5 (regard to be had to benefits that cease to be acquirable), include –

   (a)   any benefits under a pension arrangement which, because of the dissolution or annulment of the civil partnership, one of the civil partners will lose the chance of acquiring, and

   (b)   any PPF compensation which, because of the making of the dissolution or nullity order, a civil partner will lose the chance of acquiring entitlement to.

(6) The court, in exercising its powers under paragraph 9 in relation to a child of the family, must in particular have regard to the matters mentioned in paragraph 22(2) of Schedule 5.

(7) The court, in exercising its powers under paragraph 9 against a civil partner ('A') in favour of a child of the family who is not A's child, must also have regard to the matters mentioned in paragraph 22(3) of Schedule 5.

(8) Where an order has been made by a court outside England and Wales for –

   (a)   the making of payments, or

   (b)   the transfer of property,

by one of the civil partners, the court in considering in accordance with this paragraph the financial resources of the other civil partner, or of a child of the family, shall have regard to the extent to which that order has been complied with or is likely to be complied with.

(9) In this paragraph –

   (a)   'pension arrangement' has the same meaning as in Part 4 of Schedule 5,

   (b)   references to benefits under a pension arrangement include any benefits by way of pension, whether under a pension arrangement or not, and

   (c)   'PPF compensation' has the same meaning as in Schedule 5.

Amendments—Pensions Act 2008, Sch 6, Pt 3.

11 Restriction of powers under paragraph 9 where jurisdiction depends on civil partnership home in England or Wales

(1) Sub-paragraphs (2) to (4) apply where the court has jurisdiction to entertain an application for an order under paragraph 9 only because a dwelling-house which was a civil partnership home of the civil partners is situated in England or Wales.

(2) The court may make under paragraph 9 any one or more of the following orders (but no other) –

    (a) an order that one of the civil partners shall pay to the other a specified lump sum;

    (b) an order that one of the civil partners shall pay to a child of the family, or to a specified person for the benefit of a child of the family, a specified lump sum;

    (c) an order that one of the civil partners shall transfer that civil partner's interest in the dwelling-house, or a specified part of that interest –

        (i) to the other,

        (ii) to a child of the family, or

        (iii) to a specified person for the benefit of a child of the family;

    (d) an order that a settlement of the interest of one of the civil partners in the dwelling-house, or a specified part of that interest, be made to the satisfaction of the court for the benefit of any one or more of –

        (i) the other civil partner and the children of the family, or

        (ii) either or any of them;

    (e) an order varying for the benefit of any one or more of –

        (i) the civil partners and the children of the family, or

        (ii) either or any of them,

    a relevant settlement so far as that settlement relates to an interest in the dwelling-house;

    (f) an order extinguishing or reducing the interest of either of the civil partners under a relevant settlement so far as that interest is an interest in the dwelling-house;

    (g) an order for the sale of the interest of one of the civil partners in the dwelling-house.

(3) Where under paragraph 9 the court makes just one order for the payment of a lump sum by one of the civil partners, the amount of the lump sum must not exceed the amount specified in sub-paragraph (5).

(4) Where under paragraph 9 the court makes two or more orders each of which is an order for the payment of a lump sum by the same civil partner, the total of the amounts of the lump sums must not exceed the amount specified in sub-paragraph (5).

(5) That amount is –

    (a) if the interest of the paying civil partner in the dwelling-house is sold in pursuance of an order made under sub-paragraph (2)(g), the amount of the proceeds of sale of that interest after deducting from those proceeds any costs incurred in the sale of that interest;

    (b) if that interest is not so sold, the amount which in the opinion of the court represents the value of that interest.

(6) Where the interest of one of the civil partners in the dwelling-house is held jointly or in common with any other person or persons –

    (a) the reference in sub-paragraph (2)(g) to the interest of one of the civil partners shall be construed as including a reference to the interest of that other person, or the interest of those other persons, in the dwelling-house, and

    (b) the reference in sub-paragraph (5)(a) to the amount of the proceeds of a sale

PART II

ordered under sub-paragraph (2)(g) shall be construed as a reference to that part of those proceeds which is attributable to the interest of that civil partner in the dwelling-house.

(7) In sub-paragraph (2) –

"relevant settlement" means a settlement made, during the subsistence of the civil partnership or in anticipation of its formation, on the civil partners, including one made by will or codicil;

"specified" means specified in the order.

12 Consent orders under paragraph 9

(1) On an application for a consent order under paragraph 9, the court may make an order in the terms agreed on the basis only of the prescribed information furnished with the application.

(2) Sub-paragraph (1) does not apply if the court has reason to think that there are other circumstances into which it ought to inquire.

(3) Sub-paragraph (1) applies to an application for a consent order varying or discharging an order under paragraph 9 as it applies to an application for such an order.

(4) Sub-paragraph (1) applies despite paragraph 10.

(5) In this paragraph –

"consent order", in relation to an application for an order, means an order in the terms applied for to which the respondent agrees;

"prescribed" means prescribed by rules of court.

13 Orders for transfers of tenancies of dwelling-houses

(1) This paragraph applies if –

(a) an application is made by one of the civil partners for an order under this paragraph, and

(b) one of the civil partners is entitled, either in his own right or jointly with the other civil partner, to occupy a dwelling-house in England or Wales by virtue of a tenancy which is a relevant tenancy within the meaning of Schedule 7 to the Family Law Act 1996.

(2) The court may make in relation to that dwelling-house any order which it could make under Part 2 of that Schedule (order transferring tenancy or switching statutory tenants) if it had power to make a property adjustment order under Part 2 of Schedule 5 to this Act with respect to the civil partnership.

(3) The provisions of paragraphs 10, 11 and 14(1) of Schedule 7 to the Family Law Act 1996 (payments by transferee, pre-transfer liabilities and right of landlord to be heard) apply in relation to any order under this paragraph as they apply to any order under Part 2 of that Schedule.

14 Application to orders under paragraphs 5 and 9 of provisions of Schedule 5

(1) The following provisions of Schedule 5 apply in relation to an order made under paragraph 5 or 9 of this Schedule as they apply in relation to a like order made under that Schedule –

(a) paragraph 3(1) to (3) and (7) (lump sums);

(b) paragraph 11(2) to (4), 12(2), 13 and 14 (orders for sale);

(c) paragraphs 17, 18 and 19(2) and (3) (pension sharing);

(ca) paragraphs 19C, 19D and 19E(2) and (3) (pension compensation sharing);

(d) paragraphs 25 and 26 (orders under Part 1 relating to pensions);

(e) paragraphs 31 to 34 and 35 to 37 (orders under Part 1 relating to pensions where Board has assumed responsibility for scheme);

(ea) paragraph 34A (orders under Part 1 relating to pension compensation attachment);

(f) paragraphs 47(1) to (4) and (6) and 49 (duration of orders);

(g) paragraphs 50 to 54 and 57 to 62, except paragraph 50(1)(g) (variation etc of orders);

(h) paragraphs 63 to 65 (arrears and repayments);

(i) paragraphs 76 to 79A (drafting of instruments, bankruptcy, mental disorder, pension-sharing appeals and pension compensation-sharing appeals).

(2) Sub-paragraph (1)(d) and (ea) does not apply where the court has jurisdiction to entertain an application for an order under paragraph 9 only because a dwelling-house which was a civil partnership home of the civil partners is situated in England or Wales.

(3) Paragraph 27 of Schedule 5 (change of pension arrangement under which rights are shared) applies in relation to an order made under paragraph 9 of this Schedule by virtue of sub-paragraph (1)(d) above as it applies to an order made under Part 1 of Schedule 5 by virtue of paragraph 25 or 26 of that Schedule.

(4) The Lord Chancellor may by regulations make for the purposes of this Schedule provision corresponding to any provision which may be made by him under paragraph 28(1) to (3) of Schedule 5 (supplementary provision about orders relating to pensions under Part 1 of that Schedule) or under paragraphs 34B to 36 of that Schedule (supplementary provision about orders relating to pension compensation).

(5) The power to make regulations under this paragraph is exercisable by statutory instrument which is subject to annulment in pursuance of a resolution of either House of Parliament.

Amendments—Pensions Act 2008, Sch 6, Pt 3.

Subordinate legislation—See annotations to Pt 4.

15 Avoidance of transactions designed to defeat claims under paragraphs 5 and 9

(1) Sub-paragraphs (2) and (3) apply where one of the civil partners ('A') is granted leave under paragraph 4 to make an application for an order under paragraph 9.

(2) If the court is satisfied, on application by A, that the other civil partner ('B') is, with the intention of defeating a claim by A, about to –

(a) make any disposition, or

(b) transfer out of the jurisdiction, or otherwise deal with, any property,

it may make such order as it thinks fit for restraining B from doing so or otherwise for protecting the claim.

(3) If the court is satisfied, on application by A –

(a) that the other civil partner ('B') has, with the intention of defeating a claim by A, made a reviewable disposition, and

(b) that, if the disposition were set aside –

(i) financial relief under paragraph 5 or 9, or

(ii) different financial relief under paragraph 5 or 9,

would be granted to A,

it may make an order setting aside the disposition.

(4) If –

    (a)   an order under paragraph 5 or 9 has been made by the court at the instance of one of the civil partners ('A'), and

    (b)   the court is satisfied, on application by A, that the other civil partner ('B') has, with the intention of defeating a claim by A, made a reviewable disposition,

the court may make an order setting aside the disposition.

(5) Where the court has jurisdiction to entertain an application for an order under paragraph 9 only under paragraph 7(4), it shall not make any order under sub-paragraph (2), (3) or (4) in respect of any property other than the dwelling-house concerned.

(6) Where the court makes an order under sub-paragraph (3) or (4) setting aside a disposition, it shall give such consequential directions as it thinks fit for giving effect to the order (including directions requiring the making of any payments or the disposal of any property).

(7) For the purposes of sub-paragraphs (3) and (4), but subject to sub-paragraph (8), any disposition made by B is a 'reviewable disposition' (whether made before or after the commencement of A's application under that sub-paragraph).

(8) A disposition made by B is not a reviewable disposition for those purposes if made for valuable consideration (other than formation of a civil partnership) to a person who, at the time of the disposition, acted in relation to it in good faith and without notice of any intention on the part of B to defeat A's claim.

(9) A reference in this paragraph to defeating a claim by one of the civil partners is a reference to –

    (a)   preventing financial relief being granted, or reducing the amount of financial relief which might be granted, under paragraph 5 or 9 at the instance of that civil partner, or

    (b)   frustrating or impeding the enforcement of any order which might be, or has been, made under paragraph 5 or 9 at the instance of that civil partner.

16   Presumptions for the purposes of paragraph 15

(1) Sub-paragraph (3) applies where –

    (a)   an application is made under paragraph 15(2) or (3) by one of the civil partners with respect to –

        (i)   a disposition which took place less than 3 years before the date of the application, or

        (ii)   a disposition or other dealing with property which is about to take place, and

    (b)   the court is satisfied that the disposition or other dealing would (apart from paragraph 15 and this paragraph of this Schedule) have the consequence of defeating a claim by the applicant.

(2) Sub-paragraph (3) also applies where –

    (a)   an application is made under paragraph 15(4) by one of the civil partners with respect to a disposition which took place less than 3 years before the date of the application, and

    (b)   the court is satisfied that the disposition has had the consequence of defeating a claim by the applicant.

(3) It shall be presumed, unless the contrary is shown, that the person who –

    (a)   disposed of, or

    (b)   is about to dispose of or deal with the property,

did so, or (as the case may be) is about to do so, with the intention of defeating the applicant's claim.

(4) A reference in this paragraph to defeating a claim by one of the civil partners has the meaning given by paragraph 15(9).

PART 2
STEPS TO PREVENT AVOIDANCE PRIOR TO APPLICATION FOR LEAVE UNDER PARAGRAPH 4

17 Prevention of transactions intended to defeat prospective claims under paragraphs 5 and 9

(1) If it appears to the court, on application by one of the persons ('A') who formed a civil partnership –

    (a)   that the civil partnership has been dissolved or annulled, or that the civil partners have been legally separated, by means of judicial or other proceedings in an overseas country,

    (b)   that A intends to apply for leave to make an application for an order under paragraph 9 as soon as he or she has been habitually resident in England and Wales for the period of one year, and

    (c)   that the other civil partner ('B') is, with the intention of defeating A's claim, about to –

        (i)   make any disposition, or

        (ii)   transfer out of the jurisdiction, or otherwise deal with, any property,

the court may make such order as it thinks fit for restraining B from taking such action as is mentioned in paragraph (c).

(2) Sub-paragraph (1) applies even if the date of the dissolution, annulment or legal separation is earlier than the date on which that sub-paragraph comes into force.

(3) Sub-paragraph (4) applies where –

    (a)   an application is made under sub-paragraph (1) with respect to –

        (i)   a disposition which took place less than 3 years before the date of the application, or

        (ii)   a disposition or other dealing with property which is about to take place, and

    (b)   the court is satisfied that the disposition or other dealing would (apart from this paragraph of this Schedule) have the consequence of defeating a claim by the applicant.

(4) It shall be presumed, unless the contrary is shown, that the person who –

    (a)   disposed of, or

    (b)   is about to dispose of or deal with the property,

did so, or (as the case may be) is about to do so, with the intention of defeating the applicant's claim.

(5) A reference in this paragraph to defeating a person's claim is a reference to preventing financial relief being granted, or reducing the amount of financial relief which might be granted, under paragraph 5 or 9 at the instance of that person.

PART 3
SUPPLEMENTARY

18 Paragraphs 15 to 17: meaning of 'disposition' and saving

(1) In paragraphs 15 to 17 'disposition' does not include any provision contained in a will or codicil but, with that exception, includes any conveyance, assurance or gift of property of any description, whether made by an instrument or otherwise.

(2) The provisions of paragraphs 15 to 17 are without prejudice to any power of the High Court to grant injunctions under section 37 of the Senior Courts Act 1981.

Amendments—CRA 2005, Sch 11, para 1(2).

19 Interpretation of Schedule

In this Schedule –

"the court" means the High Court or, where a county court has jurisdiction by virtue of Part 5 of the Matrimonial and Family Proceedings Act 1984, a county court;

"dwelling-house" includes –

(a)   any building, or part of a building, which is occupied as a dwelling, and

(b)   any yard, garden, garage or outhouse belonging to, and occupied with, the dwelling-house;

"overseas country" has the meaning given by paragraph 1(3).

****

SCHEDULE 20
MEANING OF OVERSEAS RELATIONSHIP: SPECIFIED RELATIONSHIPS

A relationship is specified for the purposes of section 213 (meaning of 'overseas relationship') if it is registered in a country or territory given in the first column of the table and fits the description given in relation to that country or territory in the second column –

Country or territory	Description
Andorra	unio estable de parella
Argentina	marriage
Argentina: Autonomous City of Buenos Aires	unión civil
Australia: Australian Capital Territory	civil partnership
Australia: New South Wales	a relationship registered under the Relationships Register Act 2010
Australia: Queensland	civil partnership
Australia: Tasmania	significant relationship
Australia: Victoria	registered domestic relationship
Austria	eingetragene Partnerschaft
Belgium	the relationship referred to as cohabitation légale, wettelijke samenwoning or gesetzliches zusammenwohnen
Belgium	marriage
Brazil	marriage
Brazil	união estável

Country or territory	Description
Canada	marriage
Canada: Manitoba	the relationship referred to as common-law relationship or as union de fait
Canada: Nova Scotia	domestic partnership
Canada: Quebec	the relationship referred to as union civile or as civil union
Colombia	unión de hecho
Czech Republic	registrované partnertsví
Denmark	marriage
Denmark	registreret partnerskab
Ecuador	unión civil
Finland	the relationship referred to as rekisteröity parisuhde or as registrerad partnerskap
France	pacte civil de solidarité
Germany	Lebenspartnerschaft
Greenland	the relationship referred to as nalunaarsukkamik inooqatigiinneq or as registreret partnerskab
Hungary	bejegyzett élettársi kapcsolat
Iceland	marriage
Iceland	staðfesta samvist
Ireland	civil partnership
Isle of Man	civil partnership
Jersey	civil partnership
Liechtenstein	eingetragene Partnerschaft
Luxembourg	the relationship referred to as partenariat enregistré or eingetragene partnerschaft
Mexico: Coahuila	pacto civil de solidaridad
Mexico: Mexico City Federal District	marriage
Mexico: Mexico City Federal District	sociedad de convivencia
Netherlands	geregistreerd partnerschap
Netherlands	marriage
New Zealand	civil union
Norway	marriage
Norway	registrert partnerskap
Portugal	marriage
Slovenia	zakon o registraciji istospolne partnerske skupnosti
South Africa	civil partnership
South Africa	marriage
Spain	marriage
Sweden	registrerat partnerskap
Switzerland	the relationship referred to as eingetragene Partnerschaft, as partnenariat enregistré or as unione domestica registrata
United States of America: California	domestic partnership

PART II

Country or territory	Description
United States of America: California	marriage
United States of America: Colorado	the relationship between designated beneficiaries
United States of America: Connecticut	civil union
United States of America: Connecticut	marriage
United States of America: Delaware	civil union
United States of America: District of Columbia	marriage
United States of America: Hawaii	civil union
United States of America: Hawaii	reciprocal beneficiary relationship
United States of America: Illinois	civil union
United States of America: Iowa	marriage
United States of America: Maine	domestic partnership
United States of America: Massachusetts	marriage
United States of America: Nevada	domestic partnership
United States of America: New Hampshire	marriage
United States of America: New Jersey	civil union
United States of America: New Jersey	domestic partnership
United States of America: New York	marriage
United States of America: Oregon	domestic partnership
United States of America: Rhode Island	civil union
United States of America: Vermont	civil union
United States of America: Vermont	marriage
United States of America: Washington	state registered domestic partnership
United States of America: Wisconsin	domestic partnership
Uruguay	unión concubinaria

Amendments—SI 2005/3129; SI 2005/3135; SI 2012/2976.

****

Civil Procedure Act 1997

****

7 Power of courts to make orders for preserving evidence, etc

(1) The court may make an order under this section for the purpose of securing, in the case of any existing or proposed proceedings in the court –

   (a)   the preservation of evidence which is or may be relevant, or

(b) the preservation of property which is or may be the subject-matter of the proceedings or as to which any question arises or may arise in the proceedings.

(2) A person who is, or appears to the court likely to be, a party to proceedings in the court may make an application for such an order.

(3) Such an order may direct any person to permit any person described in the order, or secure that any person so described is permitted –

(a) to enter premises in England and Wales, and
(b) while on the premises, to take in accordance with the terms of the order any of the following steps.

(4) Those steps are –

(a) to carry out a search for or inspection of anything described in the order, and
(b) to make or obtain a copy, photograph, sample or other record of anything so described.

(5) The order may also direct the person concerned –

(a) to provide any person described in the order, or secure that any person so described is provided, with any information or article described in the order, and
(b) to allow any person described in the order, or secure that any person so described is allowed, to retain for safe keeping anything described in the order.

(6) An order under this section is to have effect subject to such conditions as are specified in the order.

(7) This section does not affect any right of a person to refuse to do anything on the ground that to do so might tend to expose him or his spouse or civil partner to proceedings for an offence or for the recovery of a penalty.

(8) In this section –

"court" means the High Court, and
"premises" includes any vehicle;

and an order under this section may describe anything generally, whether by reference to a class or otherwise.

Amendments—CPA 2004, s 261(1), Sch 27, para 154.

"Search orders" and "Preservation orders"—This section (and see SCA 1981, s 37) clarifies the statutory basis of the court's power to grant the remedies described in CPR 1998, Pt 25.

****

Contempt of Court Act 1981

****

11 Publication of matters exempted from disclosure in court

In any case where a court (having power to do so) allows a name or other matter to be withheld from the public in proceedings before the court, the court may give such directions prohibiting the publication of that name or matter in connection with the proceedings as appear to the court to be necessary for the purpose for which it was so withheld.

Directions by the court to protect the position of witnesses and parties in public hearings—The general rule is that hearings are in public (ECHR 1950, Art 6) and that evidence put before the court should be put in public (*Attorney-General v Leveller Magazine* [1979] AC 440). In exceptional cases, which are necessarily rare, s 11 allows the court to give directions which are designed to protect the position of witnesses and parties who are involved in hearings conducted in open court (*Re G (Adult Patient: Publicity)* [1995] 2 FLR 528 – where the court decided that, although the application by the hospital for permission to discontinue life-sustaining treatment for a patient who was in a persistent vegetative state should take place in open court, the very greatest of care should be taken to protect the positions and anonymity of the wife and mother of the patient and the doctors and nurses caring for him). However, the power must be carefully exercised and cannot be used simply to protect privacy or avoid embarrassment (*Attorney-General v Leveller Magazine*, above). The applicant must be able to establish that the failure to grant anonymity would render the attainment of justice really doubtful or impracticable (*Scott v Scott* (1913) FLR Rep 657; *R v Westminster City Council ex parte Castelli; R v Same ex parte Tristran-Garcia* [1996] 1 FLR 534 – where the identity of applicants who were HIV positive had already been revealed at an earlier stage of the proceedings, the court refused to allow their subsequent application that identifying information need not be revealed in the hearing of their later substantive applications for judicial review). The court has power to consider at any stage of the hearing whether any particular evidence ought to be given in private (see *Re G (Adult Patient: Publicity)* [1995] 2 FLR 528 at [533A]). Ideally, applications for anonymity and orders under s 11 should be made at the same time as the application for leave. These applications can be heard ex parte and, where appropriate, in camera (*R v Westminster City Council ex parte Castelli; R v Same ex parte Tristran-Garcia* (above)). See also reporting restrictions under Children and Young Persons Act 1933, s 39. Any order needs to be precisely worded (*Briffett v DPP* [2001] EWHC Admin 841).

The obtaining of so-called "super-injunctions" by celebrities and others in the public eye to protect "privacy" has become a controversial issue in the press and Parliament. As a first step to considering the whole issue, the Master of the Rolls has issued CPR PD51F (*Non-Disclosure Injunctions Information Collection Pilot Scheme*), which is set out in *Civil Court Service* (Jordan Publishing Ltd). The PD does not apply to cases governed by FPR 2010.

Section 11 applies whether the proceedings are heard in public or in private. As to the court sitting in private, see generally CPR 1998, r 39.2 and PD39B.

****

14 Proceedings in England and Wales

(1) In any case where a court has power to commit a person to prison for contempt of court and (apart from this provision) no limitation applies to the period of committal, the committal shall (without prejudice to the power of the court to order his earlier discharge) be for a fixed term, and that term shall not on any occasion exceed two years in the case of committal by a superior court, or one month in the case of committal by an inferior court.

(2) In any case where an inferior court has power to fine a person for contempt of court and (apart from this provision) no limit applies to the amount of the fine, the fine shall not on any occasion exceed £2,500.

(2A) In the exercise of jurisdiction to commit for contempt of court or any kindred offence the court shall not deal with the offender by making an order under section 60 of the Powers of Criminal Courts (Sentencing) Act 2000 (an attendance centre order) if it appears to the court after considering any available evidence, that he is under 17 years of age.

(2A) A fine imposed under subsection (2) above shall be deemed, for the purposes of any enactment, to be a sum adjudged to be paid by a conviction.

(3) (*repealed*)

(4) Each of the superior courts shall have the like power to make a hospital order or guardianship order under section 37 of the Mental Health Act 1983 or an interim hospital order under section 38 of that Act in the case of a person suffering from mental disorder within the meaning of that Act who could otherwise be committed to prison for contempt of court as the Crown Court has under that section in the case of a person convicted of an offence.

(4A) Each of the superior courts shall have the like power to make an order under section 35 of the said Act of 1983 (remand for report on accused's mental condition) where there is reason to suspect that a person who could be committed to prison for contempt of court is suffering from mental disorder within the meaning of that Act as the Crown Court has under that section in the case of an accused person within the meaning of that section.

(4A) For the purposes of the preceding provisions of this section a county court shall be treated as a superior court and not as an inferior court.

(5) The enactments specified in Part III of Schedule 2 shall have effect subject to the amendments set out in that Part, being amendments relating to the penalties and procedure in respect of certain offences of contempt in coroners' courts, county courts and magistrates' courts.

Amendments—Criminal Justice Act 1982, ss 77, 78, Sch 14, para 60, Sch 16; Mental Health (Amendment) Act 1982, s 65(1), Sch 3, paras 59, 60; MHA 1983, s 148, Sch 4, para 57; County Courts (Penalties for Contempt) Act 1983, s 1; SI 1984/447; Criminal Justice Act 1991, s 17, Sch 4, Pt I, Pt V, para 4; Criminal Justice Act 1993, s 65(3), Sch 3, para 6(5); Powers of Criminal Courts (Sentencing) Act 2000, s 165, Sch 9, para 84. Due to an error in drafting, two subsections have been numbered (2A) and (4A) respectively, MHA 2007, s 1(4), Sch 1, Pt 2, para 19.

Defined terms—"court", "superior court": s 19.

Sentencing—The guideline case on sentencing is *Hale v Tanner* [2000] 2 FLR 879 as supplemented by *Lomas v Parle* [2004] 1 FLR 812 and *Murray v Robinson* [2006] 1 FLR 365. On a committal application the court has to direct itself whether committal to prison is appropriate. The full range of sentencing options available to the criminal courts is not available but there is still a range of options. If prison is appropriate, the length of sentence and whether it should be suspended are separate questions. The length of sentence depends on the court's objectives: one objective is to mark disapproval of disobedience of its order; another is to secure future compliance. The length needs to bear some reasonable relationship to the 2 years' maximum. The power to suspend is wider than in criminal cases and its length requires separate consideration. The context of the breach may be aggravating or mitigating. The court should explain the choices it has made in a particular case. On the facts of *Hale v Tanner*, a sentence of 6 months for abusive and threatening telephone calls was reduced to 28 days. See also *Wilson v Webster* [1998] 1 FLR 1097 (14 days increased on appeal to 3 months); *Neil v Ryan* [1998] 2 FLR 1068 (suspended sentence replaced by one of immediate committal) and *Lomas v Parle* [2004] 1 FLR 812 (4 months increased to 8 months). If there are parallel criminal proceedings there is no need to adjourn or anticipate the outcome: it is for the second court to reflect the prior sentence in its judgment (see *Lomas v Parle*, above). In cases involving a second breach, it is necessary to impose a sentence no longer than is required to mark the gravity of the breach (*Bartley (t/a Lundy) v Wilson* [2004] EWCA Civ 1338). Generally the civil court should follow the criminal court guidelines (see *Murray v Robinson* [2006] 1 FLR 365). In *Wood v Collins* [2006] EWCA Civ 743 an "unduly lenient" suspended sentence of 28 days was increased to 3 months (though still suspended). Where there is a continuing breach, a fresh order and a further committal order can be made (*Re W (Abduction: Committal)* [2012] 2 FLR 133). In *Re C (Children)* [2011] EWCA Civ 1230, breaches of an injunction restraining a mother from approaching within 200 metres of her children's foster home were serious enough to justify an immediate sentence of imprisonment. In *W v W* [2011] 2 FLR 1268, Baron J imposed a 1-year sentence for breach of an undertaking suspended on terms including the immediate payment of a lump sum.

Sentence must be for a fixed term—Once a contemnor has been found guilty of having breached an undertaking or an order, the court has no power to detain him in custody pending consideration of the appropriate sentence to be imposed upon him (*Delaney v Delaney* [1996] 1 FLR 458).

Non-payment—Failure to comply with an order to pay money (e g a lump sum) can be a contempt of court. However, the maximum sentence is the 6 weeks prescribed by DA 1869, s 5, not the 2 years under the 1981 Act (*Zuk v Zuk* [2012] EWCA Civ 1871). See further Procedural Guide C10.

Contempt in the face of the court—A High Court judge has power to order overnight detention of the alleged contemnor to allow both for a period of reflection and for arrangements to be made for legal representation. If the case cannot be dealt with the next day, detention until the next working day is "the very limit of what could be either lawful or acceptable" (see *Wilkinson v S & anor* [2003] 1 WLR 1254). In the county court, see CCA 1984, s 118. No breach of ECHR 1950, Art 6 is involved if the judge invokes the summary procedure and deals with the case himself (see *Wilkinson* (above)). The procedure to be followed by a judge faced with such a contempt is set out in CPR 1998, r 81.16 and CPR PD81, para 4.

"shall not on any occasion exceed two years in the case of committal by a superior court" (s 14(1))—A court may not, on any single occasion, impose on a contemnor a sentence of imprisonment which exceeds 2 years, even where it activates a sentence which was previously suspended (*Villiers v Villiers* [1994] 1 FLR 647). Where a contemnor acknowledges his breaches of the relevant order, apologises to the court and thus avoids the need for witnesses to give oral evidence substantiating the breaches, he is entitled to some credit to reduce the length of his total sentence to a period below the maximum of 2 years' imprisonment (*Re R (A Minor) (Contempt)* [1994] 2 FLR 185).

Early release—A person sentenced to imprisonment for contempt of court does not serve the full sentence imposed by the court. As soon as he has served one-half "it shall be the duty of the Secretary of State to release him unconditionally" (see CJA 2003, s 258). As release is unconditional, he is not on licence ("parole") and not subject to re-call. The early release provisions of CJA 2003 impose an obligation on the Secretary of State which cannot be overreached by a sentencing judge. It is therefore not lawful to sentence until a specified date (*Thomson v Mitchell* [2004] EWCA Civ 1271). The sentence must be for a fixed term.

Further, a contemnor may apply at any time to purge his contempt. Any such application is best heard by the sentencing judge. See **Purging of contempt**, below.

County court to be treated as superior court (s 14(4A))—County courts may equally impose prison sentences and fines and make hospital orders and guardianship orders.

Powers of inferior courts (s 14(1),(2))—This section imposes a general limit on the powers of inferior courts to punish for contempt, namely one month's imprisonment or a fine of £2500 or both.

Breach of non-molestation order—See commentary on FLA 1996 and FPR 2010, Pt 10.

Power of court to order earlier discharge—A court may release a contemnor before the end of his term of imprisonment whether he has purged his contempt or not (*Enfield London Borough Council v Mahoney* [1983] 1 WLR 749). However, the court does not have power to suspend the remainder of a part-served sentence (*Harris v Harris* [2002] 1 FLR 248, CA).

Purging of contempt—As part of the admission to prison process it is explained to a contemnor that he can apply to purge his contempt. Unfortunately, this results in applications that are premature and without genuine remorse. In *CJ v Flintshire Borough Council* [2010] 2 FLR 1224, when dismissing an appeal against refusal to release, the Court of Appeal asked eight non-exhaustive questions to be considered on an application to purge: (i) Could the court conclude that the contemnor had suffered punishment proportionate to his contempt? (ii) Would the interest of the State significantly be prejudiced by early discharge? (iii) How genuine was any expression of contrition? (iv) Had the contemnor demonstrated a resolve and ability not to commit a further breach? (v) Had he done all that he reasonably could to minimise the risk of committing a further breach if discharged? (vi) Had any specific proposal been made to augment the protection of those that the order was designed to protect against a further breach? (vii) How long had been served, taking account of the full term imposed and the early release provision of CJA 2003, s 258(2)? (viii) Were there any special factors impinging on the exercise of discretion either way? A successful application does not depend on affirmative answers to all eight questions.

Review of sentence—The court sends a copy of every committal order and relevant details to the Official Solicitor, who reviews the case and may apply or appeal of his own motion or at the contemnor's request.

Age (s 14(2A))—A person attains a particular age expressed in years at the commencement of the relevant anniversary of the date of his birth (FLRA 1969, s 9). Where a contemnor is aged under 18, there is no power at all to commit to any form of detention (*R v Selby Justices ex parte Frame* [1992] 1 QB 72). A person under the age of 21 cannot be sent to prison for contempt but, if he is aged 18 years or more, he can be detained under Powers of Criminal Courts (Sentencing) Act 2000, s 96 (see *R v Selby Justices ex parte Frame* (above); see also *Mason v Lawton* [1991] 2 FLR 50). Now that breach of a non-molestation order is a criminal offence arguably any person who has attained the age of criminal responsibility can (through a litigation friend) be made subject to such an order as it would be possible to prosecute for a breach even though not for a civil contempt.

Treatment of contempt prisoners—A person sentenced to imprisonment for contempt of court is not a "convicted prisoner" within the meaning of the Prison Rules 1999. Accordingly, he has the same rights and privileges as an "unconvicted prisoner". Note also the role of the Official Solicitor in contempt cases (see **Review of sentence** above).

Time on remand—If a contemnor has been remanded in custody (e g under FLA 1996, Sch 5) before sentence, time spent in custody is not automatically taken into account as part of the sentence. The sentencing judge must take this into consideration when passing sentence and should make it clear in sentencing remarks that he has done so. *Kerai v Patel* [2008] 2 FLR 2137 explains how this should be done bearing in mind the early release provisions (see above). If a judge say activates a 3-month suspended sentence and imposes a further sentence of 12 months but the contemnor has served 3 months on remand, then the sentence to be imposed is one of 9 months (of which four and a half will be served), the 3 months on remand in custody being the equivalent of a 6-month sentence.

Power of court to order contemnor to attend at attendance centre (s 14(2A))—This section, by implication, contemplates that a contemnor aged at least 17, but less than 21, may be ordered to attend at an attendance centre. However, see arguments to the contrary in *R v Selby Justices ex parte Frame* [1991] 2 All ER 344, where the Divisional Court upheld a submission by counsel as amicus curiae that, since a person found guilty of contempt had not been "convicted of an offence", it followed that no other means of disposal provided by criminal justice legislation, such as an attendance centre order, was available.

Mentally disordered contemnors (s 14(4),(4A))—Under MHA 1983, the court has power to remand a person to a hospital for a report on his mental condition (s 35), to authorise his admission to and detention in hospital, or to place him under the guardianship of a local social services authority or other approved person (s 37), and, where two registered medical practitioners certify that he is suffering from mental illness and that there is reason to suppose that it may be appropriate to make a hospital order, to make an *interim* hospital order (s 38). However, these powers cannot be exercised until the person has been found guilty of contempt. This is clear from the use in s 14(4) and (4A) of the words "a person who could be committed to prison for contempt of court".

Once a person has been found guilty of contempt of court, the High Court or county court has power:

(a) if there is reason to suspect that he is suffering from mental illness or severe mental impairment, to remand him in custody for reports under s 35 for not more than 28 days at a time or 12 weeks in all; and

(b) if satisfied that he is suffering from mental illness or severe mental impairment, to make either (i) an interim hospital order under s 38 for not more than 12 weeks initially or six months in all, or (ii) a hospital order under s 37.

However, none of these powers can be exercised unless the court has before it the required evidence of the relevant medical practitioner(s) as to the matters set out in MHA 1983, ss 35, 37 and 38. There is no general power to remand a contemnor before sentence, so the court may have to adjourn until the medical evidence is available. In FLA 1996, Pt IV cases, there is specific power to remand for a medical examination and report (see FLA 1996, s 48).

Appeal—Either the applicant or respondent can appeal to the Court of Appeal any order made in exercise of jurisdiction to punish for contempt of court. The contemnor does not need permission to appeal a committal order (CPR 1998, r 52.3) but the applicant does (*Poole BC v Hambridge* [2007] EWCA Civ 990). A fine is not a "committal order", so a respondent appealing a fine does require permission to appeal and is not within the exception in CPR 1998, r 52.3(1)(a).

****

16 Enforcement of fines imposed by certain superior courts

(1) Payment of a fine for contempt of court imposed by a superior court, other than the Crown Court or one of the courts specified in subsection (4) below, may be enforced upon the order of the court –

(a) in like manner as a judgment of the High Court for the payment of money; or
(b) in like manner as a fine imposed by the Crown Court.

(2) Where payment of a fine imposed by any court falls to be enforced as mentioned in paragraph (a) of subsection (1) –

(a) the court shall, if the fine is not paid in full forthwith or within such time as the court may allow, certify to Her Majesty's Remembrancer the sum payable;
(b) Her Majesty's Remembrancer shall thereupon proceed to enforce payment of that sum as if it were due to him as a judgment debt;
(c) (*repealed*)

(3) Where payment of a fine imposed by any court falls to be enforced as mentioned in paragraph (b) of subsection (1), the provisions of sections 139 and 140 of the Powers of Criminal Courts (Sentencing) Act 2000 shall apply as they apply to a fine imposed by the Crown Court.

(4) Subsection (1) of this section does not apply to fines imposed by the criminal division of the Court of Appeal or by the Supreme Court on appeal from that division.

(5) The Fines Act 1833 shall not apply to a fine to which subsection (1) of this section applies.

(6) *(repealed)*

Amendments—SCA 1981, s 152(4), Sch 7; Industrial Tribunals Act 1996, s 45, Sch 3, Pt I; Powers of Criminal Courts (Sentencing) Act 2000, s 165, Sch 9, para 85; CRA 2005, Sch 9, para 35(2).

Defined terms—"court", "superior court": s 19.

17 Disobedience to certain orders of magistrates' courts

(1) The powers of a magistrates' court under subsection (3) of section 63 of the Magistrates' Courts Act 1980 (punishment by fine or committal for disobeying an order to do anything other than the payment of money or to abstain from doing anything) may be exercised either of the court's own motion or by order on complaint.

(2) In relation to the exercise of those powers the provisions of the Magistrates' Courts Act 1980 shall apply subject to the modifications set out in Schedule 3 of this Act.

****

19 Interpretation

In this Act –

"court" includes any tribunal or body exercising the judicial power of the State, and "legal proceedings" shall be construed accordingly;

"publication" has the meaning assigned by subsection (1) of section 2, and "publish" (except in section 9) shall be construed accordingly;

"Scottish proceeding" means proceedings before any court, including the Courts-Martial Appeal Court and the Employment Appeal Tribunal, sitting in Scotland, and includes proceedings before the Supreme Court in the exercise of any appellate jurisdiction over proceedings in such a court;

"the strict liability rule" has the meaning assigned by section 1;

"superior court" means the Supreme Court, the Court of Appeal, the High Court, the Crown Court, the Courts-Martial Appeal Court, the Employment Appeal Tribunal and any other court exercising in relation to its proceedings powers equivalent to those of the High Court.

Amendments—Cable and Broadcasting Act 1984, s 57(1), Sch 5, para 39(2); Broadcasting Act 1990, s 203(1),(3), Sch 20, para 31, Sch 21; CRA 2005, Sch 9, para 35(3); SI 2013/294.

****

SCHEDULE 3

APPLICATION OF MAGISTRATES' COURTS ACT 1980 TO CIVIL CONTEMPT PROCEEDINGS UNDER SECTION 63(3)

1 (1) Where the proceedings are taken of the court's own motion the provisions of the Act listed in this sub-paragraph shall apply as if a complaint had been made against the person against whom the proceedings are taken, and subject to the modifications specified in sub-paragraphs (2) and (3) below. The enactments so applied are –

     section 51 (issue of summons)
     section 53(1) and (2) (procedure on hearing)
     section 54 (adjournment)

section 55 (non-appearance of defendant)
section 97(1) (summons to witness)
section 101 (onus of proving exceptions etc)
section 121(1) and (3)(a) (constitution and place of sitting of court)
section 123 (defect in process).

(2) In section 55, in subsection (1) for the words "the complainant appears but the defendant does not" there shall be substituted the words "the defendant does not appear", and in subsection (2) the words "if the complaint has been substantiated on oath, and" shall be omitted.

(3) In section 123, in subsections (1) and (2) the words "adduced on behalf of the prosecutor or complainant" shall be omitted.

2 Where the proceedings are taken by way of complaint for an order, section 127 of the Act (limitation of time) shall not apply to the complaint.

3 Whether the proceedings are taken of the court's own motion or by way of complaint for an order, subsection (3) of section 55 shall apply as if the following words were added at the end of the subsection –

> "or, having been arrested under section 47 of the Family Law Act 1996 in connection with the matter of the complaint, is at large after being remanded under subsection (7)(b) or (10) of that section.".

Amendments—FLA 1996, s 66(1), Sch 8, para 50.

"as if a complaint had been made" (para 1(1))—The court acts by order on complaint or as if on complaint. An order for costs in the proceedings appears permissible.

****

County Courts Act 1984

ARRANGEMENT OF SECTIONS

PART I
CONSTITUTION AND ADMINISTRATION

PART II
JURISDICTION AND TRANSFER OF PROCEEDINGS

PART IV
APPEALS ETC

Appeals

PART I
CONSTITUTION AND ADMINISTRATION
****

14 Penalty for assaulting officers

(1) If any person assaults an officer of a court while in the execution of his duty, he shall be liable –

(a) on summary conviction, to imprisonment for a term not exceeding 3 months or to a fine of an amount not exceeding level 5 on the standard scale, or both; or

(b) on an order made by the judge in that behalf, to be committed for a specified period not exceeding 3 months to prison or to such a fine as aforesaid, or to be so committed and to such a fine,

and a bailiff of the court may take the offender into custody, with or without warrant, and bring him before the judge.

(2) The judge may at any time revoke an order committing a person to prison under this section and, if he is already in custody, order his discharge.

(3) A district judge, assistant district judge or deputy district judge shall have the same powers under this section as a judge.

Amendments—Statute Law (Repeals) Act 1986; CLSA 1990, s 74(4).

"in the execution of his duty" (s 14(1))—An honest mistake as to whether the person assaulted was "an officer of the court" and/or was "in the execution of his duty" may be a defence (*Blackburn v Bowering* [1994] 1 WLR 1324).

"fine of an amount not exceeding level 5" (s 14(1)(a))—The current figure is £5000.

Procedure—See CPR 1998, Pt 81, S 9.

Standard of proof—Contempt proceedings are "criminal proceedings" for the purposes of ECHR 1950, Art 6. Thus proof to the criminal standard ("beyond reasonable doubt") is required: the judge must be sure that the case is proved.

Public funding—Persons in danger of losing their liberty (as is possible under s 14) are, subject to means, eligible for legal aid under LASPOA 2012.

Appeal—See AJA 1960, s 13.

****

PART II
JURISDICTION AND TRANSFER OF PROCEEDINGS
****

25 Jurisdiction under Inheritance (Provision for Family and Dependants) Act 1975

A county court shall have jurisdiction to hear and determine any application for an order under section 2 of the Inheritance (Provision for Family and Dependants) Act 1975 (including any application for permission to apply for such an order and any application made, in the proceedings on an application for such an order, for an order under any other provision of that Act).

Amendments—SI 1991/724.

Transfer of proceedings—CPR 1998, r 30.6 empowers the court to specify the particular court where the trial or some other hearing in the proceedings will take place, without an order for such transfer.
****

38 Remedies available in county courts

(1) Subject to what follows, in any proceedings in a county court the court may make any order which could be made by the High Court if the proceedings were in the High Court.

(2) Any order made by a county court may be –

    (a)   absolute or conditional;

    (b)   final or interlocutory.

(3) A county court shall not have power –

    (a)   to order mandamus, certiorari or prohibition; or

    (b)   to make any order of a prescribed kind.

(4) Regulations under subsection (3) –

    (a)   may provide for any of their provisions not to apply in such circumstances or descriptions of case as may be specified in the regulations;

    (b)   may provide for the transfer of the proceedings to the High Court for the purpose of enabling an order of a kind prescribed under subsection (3) to be made;

(c) *(repealed)*

(d) may make provision amending or repealing any provision made by or under any enactment, so far as may be necessary or expedient in consequence of the regulations.

(4A) If regulations are made under subsection (3), rules may be made in accordance with Part 1 of Schedule 1 to the Constitutional Reform Act 2005 about procedure relevant to the matters prescribed in the regulations.

(5) In this section "prescribed" means prescribed by regulations made under this section by the Lord Chancellor after consulting the Lord Chief Justice.

(6) The power to make regulations under this section shall be exercised by statutory instrument.

(7) No such statutory instrument shall be made unless a draft of the instrument has been approved by both Houses of Parliament.

Amendments—CLSA 1990, s 3; CRA 2005, ss 12(2), 15(1), 146, Sch 1, Pt 2, para 17, Sch 4, Pt 1, paras 160, 167, Sch 18, Pt 1.

Scope—This section provides county courts with the same powers as the High Court, subject to certain exceptions. Thus a county court may, like the High Court, grant a "freestanding" injunction, ie an injunction in support of a legal right, even though no other remedy is claimed in the proceedings. The power to commit for disobedience of an injunction, or breach of an undertaking, is a power of the High Court which is devolved on the county court by virtue of CCA 1984, s 38. The county court has no inherent jurisdiction to grant injunctions to restrain either a local authority from exercising its statutory powers in relation to children or the police from exercising their statutory or common law powers (*D v D (County Court Jurisdiction: Injunctions)* [1993] 2 FLR 802).

Regulations restricting county courts' powers—The CCRR 1991 have been made in exercise of the power under s 38(3)(b) and (4).

Personal protection injunctions—At common law, "harassment" or "molestation" can be prohibited in proceedings founded in the law of tort, if the conduct complained of amounts to a tort (*Burris v Azadani* [1996] 1 FLR 266). This usually involves proceedings for trespass to the person or trespass to land. However, PHA 1997, s 3 (below) has, in effect, created a statutory tort of harassment, and proceedings based on that Act will invariably be a better way of restraining harassment (see notes to that Act). See also FLA 1996, Pt IV and notes thereon.

Form of non-molestation injunction—It is vital, when submitting a draft injunction or undertaking, to use precise and explicit wording. It must be clear to the respondent what he must do or not do, as the case may be. Only an order requiring a person to do an act within a specified time, or to abstain from doing an act, can be enforced by committal proceedings (CPR 1998, r 81.4; *Parsons v Nasar* [1990] 2 FLR 103).

Power of arrest—There is no power at common law to attach a "power of arrest" to an injunction. A power of arrest can be attached only where authorised by statute, e g FLA 1996, s 47; Housing Act 1996, s 153C. There is no "power of arrest" available under the Protection from Harassment Act 1997, but see s 3(3) of that Act which provides for a "warrant of arrest".

Penal notice—Before an order can be enforced by committal proceedings, it must be endorsed with a "penal notice": CPR 1998, r 81.9, CPR PD81, para 1 and Form N77. (Different wording is prescribed for orders under FLA 1996.)

Enforcement of injunctions and undertakings—Injunctions and undertakings cannot be enforced by committal proceedings unless the direction or promise is to do or refrain from doing a specific act or acts. An undertaking to pay money is not enforceable by committal, save as permitted by Debtors Act 1869, s 5 (*Symmons v Symmons* [1993] 1 FLR 317). See also *Mubarak v Mubarak* [2007] 1 FLR 722, where Bodey J held that non-payment of a matrimonial order was itself contempt of court and the husband was placed under strict terms. In most cases where an order to pay money is made, or an undertaking to pay money is given, the appropriate remedy is by way of judgment summons. For the procedure to be adopted for breach of injunctions and undertakings, see Procedural Guide C15.

Undertakings—A formal undertaking given by the parties and recorded in court is equivalent to an injunction (*Gandolfo v Gandolfo (Standard Chartered Bank, Garnishee)* [1981] QB 359), save that an undertaking to pay money can only be enforced by committal in very limited circumstances (see

Enforcement of injunctions and undertakings, above). A power of arrest cannot be attached to an undertaking (*Carpenter v Carpenter* [1988] 1 FLR 121; FLA 1996, s 46(2)).

Injunction under MWPA 1882—In order to restrain a sale or disposal of property which is the subject matter of a dispute under MWPA 1882, s 17, an injunction may be sought. The injunction must be ancillary or incidental to any relief sought in the s 17 proceedings, which are governed by FPR 2010, Pt 8, Ch 4.

Injunction under MCA 1973, s 37—When proceedings for financial relief have been brought by one person against another under MCA 1973, the court may, pursuant to s 37(2)(a), grant an injunction to restrain disposal of property. The injunction may be granted by a district judge (FPR 2010, r 2.5). "Property" includes real and personal property and that situated outside the jurisdiction (*Hamlin v Hamlin* [1986] 1 FLR 61). However a court will not exercise its discretion so as to make an order under s 37 concerning foreign property if such an order cannot be enforced.

Freezing injunctions—Although CCRR 1991 removed the power of county courts, other than the patents county court, to grant freezing injunctions, reg 3(3)(a) preserves the power for family proceedings. The freezing injunction may be useful in two situations in which an injunction under MCA 1973, s 37 is not available:

(a) Where a party is not involved in a disposition to a third party, but is just putting obstacles in the way of the other party from recovering any sum awarded, or is making it difficult for the court to deal with the case, or where there is no evidence of intent to defeat a claim for ancillary relief (see *Shipman v Shipman* [1991] 1 FLR 250, where an injunction was used to restrain the husband from transferring his assets abroad notwithstanding the absence of any intention to avoid his obligations).
(b) Where the property is not yet in existence (e g award of damages in a civil action; redundancy payment; maturing insurance policy) but is to be paid at some future date. In the case of *Ghoth v Ghoth* [1992] 2 FLR 300, the Court of Appeal held that there is jurisdiction to grant freezing injunctions in matrimonial cases, but that the court should be cautious about granting such an injunction in respect of property outside the jurisdiction. The court can only act because it has personal jurisdiction over the respondent. Therefore the order should be limited to restraining the respondent from disposing of those foreign assets, or at least be limited to the extent in which an injunction would be enforced in that foreign court (*Babanaft International Co SA v Bassatne and Another* [1990] Ch 13). The injunction should not extend beyond the size of the fund necessary to achieve the maximum which the applicant is likely to be awarded in divorce proceedings.

For further detail as to the procedures to be followed and the law and practice involved, see *Emergency Remedies in the Family Courts* (Jordan Publishing Ltd). As to the forms and procedures, see **Freezing injunctions** et seq under SCA 1981, s 37.

Land Registration Act 2002, section 46—This section enables the court to make an order requiring a restriction to be entered in the register for the purpose of protecting a right or claim in relation to a registered estate or charge. The order may include a direction that the entry is to have overriding priority. The order may be made, for example, ancillary to a freezing order.

****

70 Finality of judgments and orders

Every judgment and order of a county court shall, except as provided by this or any other Act or as may be prescribed, be final and conclusive between the parties.

Scope—A judgment or order of the county court is final and cannot be altered by the court, except by consent (*Irving v Askew* (1870) LR 5 QB 208), although the court is entitled to amend the judgment to explain the sense of an ambiguous phrase which might be misunderstood (*Lowery v Walker* [1911] AC 10), and accidental slips and errors may be corrected (*Chessum & Sons v Gordon* [1901] 1 KB 694). A judgment or order may be set aside on appeal to the Court of Appeal (see s 77). CPR 1998, Sch 2, CCR Ord 37, r 1 allows a county court to review its own decision where no error of the court is alleged. If an error of the court is alleged, an appeal must be pursued to the Court of Appeal (see **Scope** under s 77).

****

PART IV
APPEALS ETC

Appeals

77 Appeals: general provisions

(1) Subject to the provisions of this section and the following provisions of this Part of this Act and to any order made by the Lord Chancellor under section 56(1) of the Access to Justice Act 1999, if any party to any proceedings in a county court is dissatisfied with the determination of the judge or jury, he may appeal from it to the Court of Appeal in such manner and subject to such conditions as may be provided by Civil Procedure Rules.

(1A) Without prejudice to the generality of the power to make rules of court under section 75, such rules may make provision for any appeal from the exercise by a district judge, assistant district judge or deputy district judge of any power given to him by virtue of any enactment to be to a judge of a county court.

(2)–(4) *(repealed)*

(5) Subject to the provisions of this section and the following provisions of this Part of this Act, where an appeal is brought under subsection (1) in any action, an appeal may be brought under that subsection in respect of any claim or counterclaim in the action notwithstanding that there could have been no such appeal if that claim had been the subject of a separate action.

(6) In proceedings in which either the plaintiff or the defendant is claiming possession of any premises this section shall not confer any right of appeal on any question of fact if by virtue of –

    (a)   section 13(4) of the Landlord and Tenant Act 1954; or

    (b)   Cases III to IX in Schedule 4 to the Rent (Agriculture) Act 1976; or

    (c)   section 98 of the Rent Act 1977, as it applies to Cases 1 to 6 and 8 and 9 in Schedule 15 to that Act, or that section as extended or applied by any other enactment; or

    (d)   section 99 of the Rent Act 1977, as it applies to Cases 1 to 6 and 9 in Schedule 15 to that Act; or

    (e)   section 84(2)(a) of the Housing Act 1985; or

    (ee) section 7 of the Housing Act 1988, as it applies to the grounds in Part II of Schedule 2 to that Act; or

    (f)   any other enactment,

the court can only grant possession on being satisfied that it is reasonable to do so.

(7) This section shall not –

    (a)   confer any right of appeal from any judgment or order where a right of appeal is conferred by some other enactment; or

    (b)   take away any right of appeal from any judgment or order where a right of appeal is so conferred,

and shall have effect subject to any enactment other than this Act.

(8) In this section –

"enactment" means an enactment whenever passed.

Amendments—Housing (Consequential Provisions) Act 1985, s 4, Sch 2, para 57(3); Housing Act 1988, s 140(1), Sch 17, para 35(2); CLSA 1990, s 125(2), Sch 17, para 15; Civil Procedure Act 1997, s 10, Sch 2, para 2(1),(2),(7); AJA 1999, s 106, Sch 15; SI 2000/1071.

Scope—Appeals from the decision of the county court judge lie to the Court of Appeal, in accordance with CPR 1998, Pt 52. Appeals from the decision of the district judge lie to the judge of the county court in accordance with FPR 2010, Pt 30 and PD30A: see Procedural Guide E2.

Permission to appeal—Permission to appeal to the Court of Appeal is required in all cases save for a few limited exceptions as prescribed by CPR 1998, r 52.3 and FPR 2010, r 30.3(2).

****

79 Agreement not to appeal

(1) No appeal shall lie from any judgment, direction, decision or order of a judge of county courts if, before the judgment, direction, decision or order is given or made, the parties agree, in writing signed by themselves or their legal representatives or agents, that it shall be final.

(2) (*repealed*)

Amendments—Statute Law (Repeals) Act 1986; CLSA 1990, s 125(3), Sch 18, para 49(3).

80 Judge's note on appeal

(1) At the hearing of any proceedings in a county court in which there is a right of appeal or from which an appeal may be brought with leave, the judge shall, at the request of any party, make a note –

    (a)   of any question of law raised at the hearing; and

    (b)   of the facts in evidence in relation to any such question; and

    (c)   of the decision on any such question and of his determination of the proceedings.

(2) Where such a note has been taken, the judge shall (whether notice of appeal has been served or not), on the application of any party to the proceedings, and on payment by that party of such fee as may be prescribed by the fees orders, furnish him with a copy of the note, and shall sign the copy, and the copy so signed shall be used at the hearing of the appeal.

Scope—If the judge refuses to supply a note he may be ordered to do so (*R v Sheffield County Court Judge* (1889) 5 TLR 303). In practice the parties may submit to the judge a note agreed by them for his approval. If an appeal alleges misconduct of the judge the notes should be submitted to the judge with any appeal notes and the judge may comment and communicate those comments to the Court of Appeal and to the parties (*Re R (A Minor) (Adoption: Parental Agreement)* [1987] 1 FLR 391).

"at the request of any party" (s 80(1))—Strictly this means that the request should be made direct to the judge (*Re Lock ex parte Poppleton (No 1)* (1891) 8 Morr 44), but in practice the application is made to the court clerk.

Approved transcripts for appeal—It is the duty of the appellant to include in his bundle of documents for the Court of Appeal the approved transcript of the judgment (CPR PD52C, para 3.3(h)).

81 Powers of Court of Appeal on appeal from county court

(1) On the hearing of an appeal, the Court of Appeal may draw any inference of fact and either –

    (a)   order a new trial on such terms as the court thinks just; or

    (b)   order judgment to be entered for any party; or

    (c)   make a final or other order on such terms as the court thinks proper to ensure the determination on the merits of the real question in controversy between the parties.

(2) Subject to Civil Procedure Rules, on any appeal from a county court the Court of Appeal may reverse or vary, in favour of a party seeking to support the judgment or order

of the county court in whole or in part, any determinations made in the county court on
questions of fact, notwithstanding that the appeal is an appeal on a point of law only, or
any such determinations on points of law, notwithstanding that the appeal is an appeal on
a question of fact only.

(3) Subsection (2) shall not enable the Court of Appeal to reverse or vary any
determination, unless the party dissatisfied with the determination would have been
entitled to appeal in respect of it if aggrieved by the judgment or order.

Amendments—Civil Procedure Act 1997, s 10, Sch 2, para 2(1),(8).

Scope—The Court of Appeal has power to order a new trial (see CPR 1998, r 52.10(2)). It also has power
to make or substitute a final order, and, under CPR 1998, r 52.11(2), to admit fresh evidence, where
special grounds exist, as to matters that have arisen since the hearing in the court below.

****

Certiorari and prohibition

83 Stay of proceedings in case of certiorari or prohibition

(1) The grant by the High Court of leave to make an application for an order of certiorari
or prohibition to a county court shall, if the High Court so directs, operate as a stay of the
proceedings in question until the determination of the application, or until the High
Court otherwise orders.

(2) Where any proceedings are so stayed, the judge of the county court shall from time
to time adjourn the hearing of the proceedings to such day as he thinks fit.

Scope—Where an application is made either to quash a decision of the county court by a quashing order
(formerly "certiorari") or to require a county court to make a certain order, by a mandatory order
(formerly "mandamus"), the High Court may stay the proceedings which are the subject of judicial
review (or relevant to them) until the application for judicial review is determined. This provision is to
avoid the effects of an order taking place, possibly undermining the judicial review proceedings, until
such an application is determined. An application to quash a decision of the county court is likely to be
rare. Where the complaint is against the decision or order, the usual course is to appeal under CCA 1984,
s 77. Where it is desired to move the proceedings to the High Court, the application will usually be under
CCA 1984, ss 41, 42 or ATPO 2008, art 18 (relating to proceedings under CA 1989 or AA 1976).

84 Prohibition

(1) Where an application is made to the High Court for an order of prohibition
addressed to any county court, the matter shall be finally disposed of by order.

(2) Upon any such application, the judge of the county court shall not be served with
notice of it, and shall not, except by the order of a judge of the High Court –

(a)   be required to appear or be heard; or
(b)   be liable to any order for the payment of the costs of the application;

but the application shall be proceeded with and heard in the same manner in all respects
as an appeal duly brought from a decision of the judge, and notice of the application
shall be given to or served upon the same parties as in the case of an order made or
refused by a judge in a matter within his jurisdiction.

Scope—Applications for mandatory orders (formerly "mandamus"), quashing orders (formerly
"certiorari") and prohibiting orders (formerly "prohibition") are made by way of application for judicial
review under CPR 1998, Pt 54. Permission to make such application is required (CPR 1998, r 54.4). A
mandatory order is appropriate where a judge, district judge or officer of the county court has improperly
refused or declined to perform his ordinary duty under CCA 1984, but not where he has erred in
performing it. Where the complaint is against the decision, the usual course will be an appeal under
CCA 1984, s 77 (see *R v Sir Donald Hurst, ex parte Smith* [1960] 2 QB 133). A prohibiting or quashing

order may be granted if a county court acts without jurisdiction or in excess of it. Such orders are rare, and an appeal is more usual; see also CCA 1984, s 83.

PART V
ENFORCEMENT OF JUDGMENTS AND ORDERS

Execution against goods

85 Execution of judgments or orders for payment of money

(1) Subject to article 8 of the High Court and County Courts Jurisdiction Order 1991, any sum of money payable under a judgment or order of a county court may be recovered, in case of default or failure of payment, forthwith or at the time or times and in the manner thereby directed, by execution against the goods of the party against whom the judgment or order was obtained.

(2) The district judge, on the application of the party prosecuting any such judgment or order, shall issue a warrant of execution in the nature of a writ of fieri facias whereby the district judge shall be empowered to levy or cause to be levied by distress and sale of the goods, wherever they may be found within the district of the court, the money payable under the judgment or order and the costs of the execution.

(3) The precise time of the making of the application to the district judge to issue such a warrant shall be entered by him in the record prescribed for the purpose under section 12 and on the warrant.

(4) It shall be the duty of every constable within his jurisdiction to assist in the execution of every such warrant.

Amendments—SI 1991/724.

"Subject to article 8" (s 85(1))—The HCCCJO 1991 does not apply to family proceedings (art 12(a)).

"application of the party" (s 85(2))—The procedure is contained in CPR 1998, Sch 2, CCR Ord 26.

"The precise time" (s 85(3))—It is necessary for the court to record the date and time of issue of execution so that if several warrants are issued against a debtor their relative priority can be determined. See CPR 1998, Sch 2, CCR Ord 26, r 1 and annotation **Considerations affecting issue of warrant**, (a) *Priority*. Where the debtor's goods are in the district of a court other than the court issuing the warrant, the warrant is sent to that court and the district judge there notes the date and time of receipt for the same purpose (s 103(3)).

86 Execution of orders for payment by instalments

(1) Where the court has made an order for payment of any sum of money by instalments, execution on the order shall not be issued until after default in payment of some instalment according to the order.

(2) Rules of court may prescribe the cases in which execution is to issue if there is any such default and limit the amounts for which and the times at which execution may issue.

(3) Except so far as may be otherwise provided by rules of court made for those purposes, execution or successive executions may issue if there is any such default for the whole of the said sum of money and costs then remaining unpaid or for such part as the court may order either at the time of the original order or at any subsequent time; but except so far as may be otherwise provided by such rules, no execution shall issue unless at the time when it issues the whole or some part of an instalment which has already become due remains unpaid.

Amendments—Civil Procedure Act 1997, s 10, Sch 2, para 2(1),(2).

"execution on the order" (s 86(1))—In *Mercantile Credit Co Ltd v Ellis* (1987) *The Times*, 1 April, the Court of Appeal considered that this provision applied by analogy to an application for a charging order against land. See **"consider all the circumstances"** under COA 1979, s 1.

"rules of court" (s 86(2),(3))—See CPR 1998, Sch 2, CCR Ord 26, rr 1(2),(3), 11.

87 Execution to be superseded on payment

(1) In or upon every warrant of execution issued from a county court against the goods of any person, the district judge shall cause to be inserted or indorsed the total amount to be levied, inclusive of the fee for issuing the warrant but exclusive of the fees for its execution.

(2) If the person against whom the execution is issued, before the actual sale of the goods, pays or causes to be paid or tendered to the district judge of the court from which the warrant is issued, or to the bailiff holding the warrant, the amount inserted in, or indorsed upon, the warrant under subsection (1), or such part as the person entitled agrees to accept in full satisfaction, together with the amount stated by the officer of the court to whom the payment or tender is made to be the amount of the fees for the execution of the warrant, the execution shall be superseded, and the goods shall be discharged and set at liberty.

"the total amount to be levied" (s 87(1))—Where the creditor is represented by a solicitor and the warrant is issued for more than £25, a fixed sum of costs (currently £2.25 – CPR 1998, r 45.8) is endorsed on the warrant in addition to the issue fee.

88 Power to stay execution

If at any time it appears to the satisfaction of the court that any party to any proceedings is unable from any cause to pay any sum recovered against him (whether by way of satisfaction of the claim or counterclaim in the proceedings or by way of costs or otherwise), or any instalment of such a sum, the court may, in its discretion, stay any execution issued in the proceedings for such time and on such terms as the court thinks fit, and so from time to time until it appears that the cause of inability has ceased.

Similar powers—The court may for similar reasons stay the judgment or order itself, s 71(2). Enforcement of a judgment or order may be stayed pending an appeal (CPR 1998, r 52.7; FPR 2010, r 30.8) or application to set aside an order (FPR 2010, r 18.11). The High Court's power under CPR 1998, Sch 1, RSC Ord 47, r 1(1)(a) to stay execution against goods on the ground that there are special circumstances which render it inexpedient to enforce the judgment or order may be exercised by the county court by virtue of ss 38 and 76.

****

Receivers and attachment of debts

107 Receivers

(1) The power of the county court to appoint a receiver by way of equitable execution shall operate in relation to all legal estates and interests in land.

(2) The said power may be exercised in relation to an estate or interest in land whether or not a charge has been imposed on that land under section 1 of the Charging Orders Act 1979 for the purpose of enforcing the judgment, decree, order or award in question, and the said power shall be in addition to and not in derogation of any power of any court to appoint a receiver in proceedings for enforcing such a charge.

(3) Where an order under section 1 of the Charging Orders Act 1979 imposing a charge for the purpose of enforcing a judgment, decree, order or award has been registered under section 6 of the Land Charges Act 1972, subsection (4) of that section (which

provides that, amongst other things, an order appointing a receiver and any proceedings pursuant to the order or in obedience to it, shall be void against a purchaser unless the order is for the time being registered under that section) shall not apply to an order appointing a receiver made either in proceedings for enforcing the charge or by way of equitable execution of the judgment, decree, order or award or, as the case may be, of so much of it as requires payment of moneys secured by the charge.

Procedure—As to the appointment of receivers, both under this section and generally, see CPR 1998, Pt 69 in *Civil Court Service* (Jordan Publishing Ltd).

108 Attachment of debts

(1) Subject to any order for the time being in force under subsection (4), this section applies to any deposit account, and any withdrawable share account, with a deposit-taker.

(2) In determining whether, for the purposes of the jurisdiction of the county court to attach debts for the purpose of satisfying judgments or orders for the payment of money, a sum standing to the credit of a person in an account to which this section applies is a sum due or accruing to that person and, as such, attachable in accordance with rules of court, any condition mentioned in subsection (3) which applies to the account shall be disregarded.

(3) Those conditions are –

(a) any condition that notice is required before any money or share is withdrawn;

(b) any condition that a personal application must be made before any money or share is withdrawn;

(c) any condition that a deposit book or share-account book must be produced before any money or share is withdrawn; or

(d) any other prescribed condition.

(4) The Lord Chancellor may by order make such provision as he thinks fit, by way of amendment of this section or otherwise, for all or any of the following purposes, namely –

(a) including in, or excluding from, the accounts to which this section applies accounts of any description specified in the order;

(b) excluding from the accounts to which this section applies all accounts with any particular deposit-taker so specified or with any deposit-taker of a description so specified.

(5) An order under subsection (4) shall be made by statutory instrument subject to annulment in pursuance of a resolution of either House of Parliament.

Amendments—Civil Procedure Act 1997, s 10, Sch 2, para 2(1),(2); SI 2001/3649.

"order" (s 108(1),(4),(5))—No such order has been made.

"rules of court" (s 108(2))—As to third party debt orders, see CPR Pt 72 as modified for family proceedings by FPR 2010, r 33.24.

109 Administrative and clerical expenses of garnishees

(1) Where an interim third party debt order made in the exercise of the jurisdiction mentioned in subsection (2) of the preceding section is served on a deposit-taker, it may, subject to the provisions of this section, deduct from the relevant debt or debts an amount not exceeding the prescribed sum towards its administrative and clerical expenses in complying with the order; and the right to make a deduction under this subsection shall be exercisable as from the time the interim third party debt order is served on it.

(1A) In subsection (1) "the relevant debt or debts", in relation to an interim third party debt order served on a deposit-taker, means the amount, as at the time the order is served on it, of the debt or debts of which the whole or a part is expressed to be attached by the order.

(1B) A deduction may be made under subsection (1) in a case where the amount referred to in subsection (1A) is insufficient to cover both the amount of the deduction and the amount of the judgment debt and costs in respect of which the attachment was made, notwithstanding that the benefit of the attachment to the creditor is reduced as a result of the deduction.

(2) An amount may not in pursuance of subsection (1) be deducted or, as the case may be, retained in a case where by virtue of section 346 of the Insolvency Act 1986 or section 325 of the Companies Act 1948 or otherwise, the creditor is not entitled to retain the benefit of the attachment.

(3) In this section "prescribed" means prescribed by an order made by the Lord Chancellor.

(4) An order under this section –

    (a)   may make different provision for different cases;

    (b)   without prejudice to the generality of paragraph (a) may prescribe sums differing according to the amount due under the judgment or order to be satisfied.

    (c)   may provide for this section not to apply to deposit-takers of any prescribed description.

(5) Any such order shall be made by statutory instrument subject to annulment in pursuance of a resolution of either House of Parliament.

Amendments—AJA 1985, ss 52, 67(2), Sch 8, Pt II; Insolvency Act 1986, s 439(2), Sch 14; SI 2001/3649; SI 2002/439.

"prescribed sum" (s 109(1))—The current sum is £55: SI 1996/3098.

Miscellaneous provisions as to enforcement of judgments and orders

110 Penalty for non-attendance on judgment summons

(1) If a debtor summoned to attend a county court by a judgment summons fails to attend on the day and at the time fixed for any hearing of the summons, the judge may adjourn or further adjourn the summons to a specified time on a specified day and order the debtor to attend at that time on that day.

(2) If –

    (a)   a debtor, having been ordered under subsection (1) to attend at a specified time on a specified day, fails to do so;

    (b)   *(repealed)*

the judge may make an order committing him to prison for a period not exceeding 14 days in respect of the failure or refusal.

(3) In any case where the judge has power to make an order of committal under subsection (2) for failure to attend, he may in lieu of or in addition to making that order, order the debtor to be arrested and brought before the court either forthwith or at such time as the judge may direct.

(4) A debtor shall not be committed to prison under subsection (2) for having failed to attend as required by an order under subsection (1) unless there was paid to him at the

time of the service of the judgment summons, or paid or tendered to him at the time of the service of the order, such sum in respect of his expenses as may be prescribed for the purposes of this section.

(5) The judge may at any time revoke an order committing a person to prison under this section and, if he is already in custody, order his discharge.

Amendments—SI 2002/439.

Defined terms—"judgment summons": s 147.

"prescribed sum" (s 110(4))—This is "a sum reasonably sufficient to cover his expenses in travelling to and from the court": CPR 1998, Sch 2, CCR Ord 28, r 4(2).

****

PART VII
COMMITTALS

118 Power to commit for contempt

(1) If any person –

    (a) wilfully insults the judge of a county court, or any juror or witness, or any officer of the court during his sitting or attendance in court, or in going to or returning from the court; or

    (b) wilfully interrupts the proceedings of a county court or otherwise misbehaves in court;

any officer of the court, with or without the assistance of any other person, may, by order of the judge, take the offender into custody and detain him until the rising of the court, and the judge may, if he thinks fit, –

    (i) make an order committing the offender for a specified period not exceeding one month to prison; or

    (ii) impose upon the offender, for every offence, a fine of an amount not exceeding £2,500,

or may both make such an order and impose such a fine.

(2) The judge may at any time revoke an order committing a person to prison under this section and, if he is already in custody, order his discharge.

(3) A district judge, assistant district judge or deputy district judge shall have the same powers under this section in relation to proceedings before him as a judge.

Amendments—Statute Law (Repeals) Act 1986; CLSA 1990, s 74(6); Criminal Justice Act 1991, s 17(3)(a), Sch 4.

Procedure by judge upon a contempt in the face of the court—The procedure to be followed upon a contempt in the face of the court is set out in CPR 1998, r 81.16 and CPR PD81, para 4. The procedure in the PD is distilled from a series of cases, including *King v Read and Slack* [1999] 1 FLR 425 and *Newman (t/a Mantella Publishing) v Modern Bookbinders Ltd* [2000] 1 WLR 2559.

There are two important principles: first the need to protect the administration of justice and preserve the authority of the court (*Chapman v Honig* [1963] 2 QB 502); and second the need to preserve the alleged contemnor's right to a fair trial. Contempt proceedings are criminal proceedings within the meaning of ECHR 1950, Art 6. Adopting a summary procedure to deal with a contempt in the face of the court is not, of itself, unfair or a breach of Art 6 (*Wilkinson v S* [2003] 1 WLR 1254).

Invariably, it is better for the judge to deal with any disruption/contempt immediately following the procedure in CPR PD81. The judge does have the option of referring the incident to another judge (in which case a witness statement will be required; see CPR PD81, para 4.5). However, if the judge can restore order and continue (if necessary after an adjournment) it is usually better to do so. It is crucial that the right to a fair trial is preserved (*Amberley Construction Ltd v Beamish* [2003] EWCA Civ 1267).

Contempt of Court Act 1981—See commentary to that Act.

Summons procedure—See CPR 1998, r 81.34, which permits the issue of a summons for an alleged breach of s 118 in line with the procedure under CCA 1984, ss 14 and 92.

Sentence—The maximum sentence is limited by s 118(1)(b) to 1 month and/or a fine of £2500. In contrast, the High Court deals with contempt in the face of the court under its inherent jurisdiction and its maximum sentence, formerly unlimited, is that prescribed by CCA 1981 (2 years).

119 Issue and execution of orders of committal

(1) Whenever any order or warrant for the committal of any person to prison is made or issued by a county court (whether in pursuance of this or any other Act or of rules of court), the order or warrant shall be directed to the district judge of the court, who shall thereby be empowered to take the body of the person against whom the order is made or warrant issued.

(2) It shall be the duty of every constable within his jurisdiction to assist in the execution of every such order or warrant.

(3) The governor of the prison mentioned in any such order or warrant shall be bound to receive and keep the person mentioned in it until he is lawfully discharged.

Amendments—Civil Procedure Act 1997, s 10, Sch 2, para 2(1),(2).

****

121 Power of judge to order discharge

If at any time it appears to the satisfaction of a judge of a county court that any debtor arrested or confined in prison by order of the court is unable from any cause to pay any sum recovered against him (whether by way of satisfaction of a claim or counterclaim or by way of costs or otherwise), or any instalment thereof, and ought to be discharged, the judge may order his discharge upon such terms (including liability to re-arrest if the terms are not complied with) as the judge thinks fit.

"unable from any cause to pay"—A debtor will not have been committed unless it was proved that he had the means but neglected or refused to pay (Debtors Act 1869, s 5). Any inability to pay apparent at the time of hearing the judgment summons will have been taken into account in the order made. This section allows the judge to deal with the case where further information comes to light subsequently, for example, where the debtor failed to attend the hearing and the judge proceeded in his absence.

"and ought to be discharged"—There must be some factor in addition to mere inability to pay.

****

PART IX
MISCELLANEOUS AND GENERAL
****

147 Interpretation

(1) In this Act, unless the context otherwise requires –
"action" means any proceedings in a county court which may be commenced as prescribed by plaint;
"Admiralty county court" means a county court appointed to have Admiralty jurisdiction by order under this Act;
"Admiralty proceedings" means proceedings in which the claim would not be within the jurisdiction of a county court but for sections 26 and 27;
"bailiff" includes a district judge;
"the county court limit" means –

PART II

(a) in relation to any enactment contained in this Act for which a limit is for the time being specified by an Order under section 145, that limit,

(b) *(repealed)*

(c) in relation to any enactment contained in this Act and not within paragraph (a), the county court limit for the time being specified by any other Order in Council or order defining the limit of county court jurisdiction for the purposes of that enactment;

"court" and "county court" mean a court held for a district under this Act;

"deposit-taking institution" means a person who may, in the course of his business, lawfully accept deposits in the United Kingdom;

"district" and "county district" mean a district for which a court is to be held under section 2;

"district judge" and "district judge of a county court" mean a district judge appointed for a district under this Act, or, in a case where two or more district judges are appointed jointly, either or any of those district judges;

"hearing" includes trial, and "hear" and "heard" shall be construed accordingly;

"hereditament" includes both a corporeal and an incorporeal hereditament;

"judge", in relation to a county court, means a judge assigned to the district of that court under subsection (1) of section 5 and any person sitting as a judge for that district under subsection (3) or (4) of that section;

"judgment summons" means a summons issued on the application of a person entitled to enforce a judgment or order under section 5 of the Debtors Act 1869 requiring a person, or, where two or more persons are liable under the judgment or order, requiring any one or more of them, to attend court;

"landlord", in relation to any land, means the person entitled to the immediate reversion or, if the property therein is held in joint tenancy, any of the persons entitled to the immediate reversion;

"legal representative" means a person who, for the purposes of the Legal Services Act 2007, is an authorised person in relation to an activity which constitutes the exercise of a right of audience or the conduct of litigation (within the meaning of that Act);

"matter" means every proceeding in a county court which may be commenced as prescribed otherwise than by plaint;

"officer", in relation to a court, means any district judge or deputy district judge assigned to that court and any clerk, bailiff, usher or messenger in the service of that court;

"part-time district judge" and "part-time assistant district judge" have the meaning assigned to them by section 10(3);

"party" includes every person served with notice of, or attending, any proceeding, whether named as a party to that proceeding or not;

"prescribed" means prescribed by rules of court;

"probate proceedings" means proceedings brought in a county court by virtue of section 32 or transferred to that court under section 40;

"proceedings" includes both actions and matters;

"return day" means the day appointed in any summons or proceeding for the appearance of the defendant or any other day fixed for the hearing of any proceedings;

"rules of court" means rules made under section 75;

"ship" includes any description of vessel used in navigation;

"solicitor" means solicitor of the Senior Courts.

(1A) The definition of "deposit-taking institution" in subsection (1) must be read with –

(a) section 22 of the Financial Services and Markets Act 2000;

(b) any relevant order under that section; and

(c)   Schedule 2 to that Act.

(2), (3) *(repealed)*

Amendments—MFPA 1984, s 46(3), Sch 3; Banking Act 1987, s 108(1), Sch 6, para 15; CLSA 1990, s 125(3), Sch 18, para 49(1); SI 1990/776; SI 1991/724; Statute Law (Repeals) Act 1993; Civil Procedure Act 1997, s 10, Sch 2, para 2(1),(2),(9); SI 2001/3649; SI 2002/439; Courts Act 2003, s 109, Sch 10; CRA 2005, Sch 11, para 4(1); Legal Services Act 2007, s 208(1), Sch 21, para 61.

****

Courts Act 1971
****

52 Award of costs where information or complaint is not proceeded with

(1), (2) *(repealed)*

(3) Where –

    (a)   *(repealed)*

    (b)   a complaint is made to a justice of the peace acting in any local justice area but the complaint is not proceeded with,

a magistrates' court acting in that area may make such order as to costs to be paid by the complainant to the defendant as it thinks just and reasonable.

(3A) Subsection (3) does not apply to family proceedings (within the meaning of section 65 of the Magistrates' Courts Act 1980).

(4) An order under subsection (3) above shall specify the amount of the costs ordered to be paid.

(5) For the purpose of enforcement an order under subsection (3) above made in relation to a complaint which is not proceeded with shall be treated as if it were an order made under section 64 of the Magistrates' Courts Act 1980 (power to award, and enforcement of, costs in civil proceedings).

Amendments—Costs in Criminal Cases Act 1973, s 21, Sch 2; MCA 1980, s 154, Sch 7, para 96; Courts Act 2003, Sch 8, para 140; SI 2011/1045.

"not proceeded with" (s 52(3))—For power to order costs where the complaint is proceeded with, see MCA 1980, s 64.

****

Courts and Legal Services Act 1990
****

9 Allocation of family proceedings which are within the jurisdiction of county courts

(1) The President of the Family Division may, after consulting the Lord Chancellor, give directions that, in such circumstances as may be specified –

    (a)   any family proceedings which are within the jurisdiction of county courts; or

(b)   any specified description of such proceedings,

shall be allocated to specified judges or to specified descriptions of judge.

(2) Any such direction shall have effect regardless of any rules of court.

(3) Where any directions have been given under this section allocating any proceedings to specified judges, the validity of anything done by a judge in, or in relation to, the proceedings shall not be called into question by reason only of the fact that he was not a specified judge.

(4) For the purposes of subsection (1) "county court" includes the principal registry of the Family Division of the High Court in so far as it is treated as a county court.

(5) In this section –

"family proceedings" has the same meaning as in the Matrimonial and Family Proceedings Act 1984 and also includes any other proceedings which are family proceedings for the purposes of the Children Act 1989;

"judge" means any person who –

(a)   is capable of sitting as a judge for a county court district;

(b)   is a district judge, an assistant district judge or a deputy district judge; or

(c)   is a district judge of the principal registry of the Family Division of the High Court; and

"specified" means specified in the directions.

Amendments—CRA 2005, s 15(1), Sch 4, Pt 1, paras 211, 213.

10 Family proceedings in magistrates' courts and related matters

(1) In subsection (2) "family proceedings" means proceedings under Part I of the Domestic Proceedings and Magistrates' Courts Act 1978 or Schedule 6 to the Civil Partnership Act 2004.

(2) Family Procedure Rules may make, in relation to any family proceedings, any provision which –

(a)   falls within subsection (2) of section 93 of the Children Act 1989 (rules of court); and

(b)   may be made in relation to relevant proceedings under section 93 of the Act of 1989.

(3)–(5) *(repealed)*

Amendments—MEA 1991, s 11(1), Sch 2, para 11; Police and Magistrates' Courts Act 1994, s 93, Sch 9, Pt II; Courts Act 2003, s 109(1), Sch 8, para 349; CPA 2004, s 261(1), Sch 27, para 137.

****

Criminal Justice and Court Services Act 2000
****

Chapter II
Children and Family Court Advisory and Support Service

11 Establishment of the Service

(1) There shall be a body corporate to be known as the Children and Family Court Advisory and Support Service (referred to in this Part as the Service) which is to exercise the functions conferred on it by virtue of this Act and any other enactment.

(2) Schedule 2 (which makes provision about the constitution of the Service, its powers and other matters relating to it) is to have effect.

(3) References in this Act or any other enactment to an officer of the Service are references to –

- (a) any member of the staff of the Service appointed under paragraph 5(1)(a) of that Schedule, and
- (b) any other individual exercising functions of an officer of the Service by virtue of section 13(2) or (4).

Status of Cafcass—Cafcass vested as a non-departmental public body, answerable to Parliament through the Department for Constitutional Affairs, on 1 April 2001.

"officer of the Service"—An officer of the Service is a person appointed by the Service under CJCSA 2000, Sch 2, para 5(1)(a) or authorised by the Service under s 13(2) or (4) to undertake one or more of the following functions:

- (i) As a "children and family reporter", to investigate and provide a welfare report under CA 1989, s 7(1)(a);
- (ii) As an "officer of the Service" or as a "local authority officer", to implement a family assistance order made under CA 1989, s 16(1)(a);
- (iii) As a "children's guardian" under CA 1989, s 41(1),(2), to take appropriate steps to safeguard the interests of a child in specified proceedings;
- (iv) As a "children's guardian" under Adoption Act 1976, s 65(1) and Adoption Rules 1984, r 6(1) or (2) or r 18(1) or (2), to investigate and report in relation to safeguarding the interests of a child who is the subject of freeing or adoption proceedings;
- (v) As a "reporting officer" under AA 1976, s 65(2) and AR 1984, r 5(1) or r 17(1), to investigate and report on the attitude of a parent or guardian of a child who is the subject of freeing or adoption proceedings;
- (vi) As a "parental order reporter" under FPR 2010, rr 13.1 and 13.9 to investigate and report on the circumstances relevant under HFEA 1990 and to carry out duties under FPR 2010, r 16.35 and PD16A.

12 Principal functions of the Service

(1) In respect of family proceedings in which the welfare of children other than children ordinarily resident in Wales is or may be in question, it is a function of the Service to –

- (a) safeguard and promote the welfare of the children,
- (b) give advice to any court about any application made to it in such proceedings,
- (c) make provision for the children to be represented in such proceedings,
- (d) provide information, advice and other support for the children and their families.

(2) The Service must also make provision for the performance of any functions conferred on officers of the Service by virtue of this Act or any other enactment (whether or not they are exercisable for the purposes of the functions conferred on the Service by subsection (1)).

(3) Regulations may provide for grants to be paid by the Service to any person for the purpose of furthering the performance of any of the Service's functions.

(4) The regulations may provide for the grants to be paid on conditions, including conditions –

- (a) regulating the purposes for which the grant or any part of it may be used,
- (b) requiring repayment to the Service in specified circumstances.

(5) In this section, "family proceedings" has the same meaning as in the Matrimonial and Family Proceedings Act 1984 and also includes any other proceedings which are family proceedings for the purposes of the Children Act 1989, but –

- (a) references to family proceedings include (where the context allows) family proceedings which are proposed or have been concluded,

(b)   (*repealed*)

Amendments—ACA 2002, s 139(1), Sch 3, para 118; CA 2004, s 40, Sch 3, paras 5, 12, 13.

"functions of the Service"—The Service is responsible for fulfilling the requirements of courts in respect of investigations and reporting, and implementing family assistance orders – see annotation to s 11 above.

The Service inherited the functions of the Official Solicitor where he was appointed to act in wardship or other proceedings under the inherent jurisdiction of the High Court; also where he accepted an invitation to investigate and report in a county court. The representation of children in family proceedings is governed by FPR 2010, Pt 16 and PD16A.

The Service also inherited involvement of local Probation Services in additional services such as mediation or pre-court advice for families. The Service is seeking to sustain these for the time being, subject to constraints of budget and to assessment of future viability of such services. Budgetary constraints inhibit significant development of additional services.

Duty to provide guardian as soon as practicable—Section 12 does not impose on Cafcass a specific duty to individual children to allocate a guardian and does not spell out any specific timescale within which to do so. The duty is to appoint a guardian as soon as reasonably practicable, having regard to the resources of Cafcass (*R and Others v Cafcass* [2012] 2 FLR 1432). See further under FPR 2010, rr 16.3 and 16.18.

****

15   Right to conduct litigation and right of audience

(1) The Service may authorise an officer of the Service of a prescribed description –

    (a)   to conduct litigation in relation to any proceedings in any court,

    (b)   to exercise a right of audience in any proceedings before any court,

in the exercise of his functions.

(2) An officer of the Service exercising a right to conduct litigation by virtue of subsection (1)(a) who would otherwise have such a right by virtue of the fact that he is a person who, for the purposes of the Legal Services Act 2007, is an authorised person in relation to that activity is to be treated as having acquired that right solely by virtue of this section.

(3) An officer of the Service exercising a right of audience by virtue of subsection (1)(b) who would otherwise have such a right by virtue of the fact that he is a person who, for the purposes of the Legal Services Act 2007, is an authorised person in relation to that activity is to be treated as having acquired that right solely by virtue of this section.

(4) In this section and section 16, "right to conduct litigation" and "right of audience" have the same meanings as in section 119 of the Courts and Legal Services Act 1990.

Amendments—Legal Services Act 2007, s 208(1), Sch 21, para 133.

"conduct litigation" and "exercise a right of audience"—The legal profession has expressed concern that the power to authorise an officer of the Service to conduct litigation or exercise a right of audience might be used to supplant lawyers by officers of the Service. The Government has disavowed this and stated that the intention was to allow functions previously undertaken by staff of the Official Solicitor to continue to be performed by appropriate officers of the Service.

16   Cross-examination of officers of the Service

(1) An officer of the Service may, subject to rules of court, be cross-examined in any proceedings to the same extent as any witness.

(2) But an officer of the Service may not be cross-examined merely because he is exercising a right to conduct litigation or a right of audience granted in accordance with section 15.

"officer of the Service – witness"—This provision settles the question raised by erroneous dicta in the Court of Appeal that a family court welfare officer was an officer of the court who could not be required to give sworn evidence. An officer of Cafcass is not an officer of the court. The officer prepares the report and gives evidence as an investigating expert, albeit with authority to perform statutory responsibilities bestowed by the court under the appointment to act in the individual case. Hence, an officer of Cafcass who exercises a right to conduct litigation or a right of audience under CJCSA 2000, s 15, but does not submit evidence as a reporter, under CJCSA 2000, s 16(2) cannot be cross-examined. This may happen when a representative of the Director of Legal Services of Cafcass exercises legal service functions which used to be exercised by the Official Solicitor's Office.

A children and family reporter appointed to report under CA 1989, s 16(1)(a) and FPR 2010, r 16.33 must attend court as directed by the court under PD16A, para 9.4(a). A children and family reporter who does attend should give evidence as soon as possible after the case has opened (and in any event on the first day) and be released after giving evidence.

****

Domestic and Appellate Proceedings (Restriction of Publicity) Act 1968

1 Power of court hearing certain appeals and applications to sit in private

(1) Where an appeal is brought against a decision of any of the courts mentioned in subsection (4) below, or an application is made for leave to appeal against a decision of any of those courts, and that court had power to sit in private during the whole or any part of the proceedings in which the decision was given, then, subject to subsections (2) and (3) below, the court hearing the appeal or application shall have power to sit in private during the whole or any part of the proceedings on the appeal or application.

(2) Without prejudice to the next following subsection, the court hearing the appeal or application shall give its decision and the reason for its decision in public unless there are good and sufficient grounds for giving them in private and in that case the court shall state those grounds in public.

(3) Where the decision of any of the courts mentioned in subsection (4) below against which an appeal is brought –

  (a) is a conviction, or a sentence or other order made on conviction, or
  (b) was given in the exercise of jurisdiction to punish for contempt of court,

the court hearing the appeal or any further appeal arising out of the same proceedings shall, notwithstanding that it sat in private during the whole of any part of the proceedings on the appeal, state in open court the order made by it on the appeal.

(4) The courts referred to in subsections (1) and (3) above are the Court of Appeal, the High Court, the Crown Court, a county court and a magistrates' court.

(5) An application to a court to sit in private during the whole of any part of the proceedings on such an appeal or application as is mentioned in subsection (1) above shall be heard in private unless the court otherwise directs.

(6) The powers conferred on a court by this section shall be in addition to any other power of the court to sit in private.

(7) In this section references to a power to sit in private are references to a power to sit in camera or in chambers, but the power conferred by this section on a court which has no power to sit in chambers is a power to sit in camera only.

(8) In this section "appeal" includes appeal by case stated, and references to a court include references to a judge exercising the powers of a court.

Amendments—Courts Act 1971, s 56, Sch 8, para 58, Sch 11, Pt IV; SI 2013/294.

2 Restriction of publicity for legitimacy proceedings etc and certain proceedings by a wife for maintenance

(1) The following provisions of this section shall have effect with a view to preventing or restricting publicity for –

   (a) *(repealed)*

   (b) proceedings under section 22 of that Act (which relates to proceedings by a wife against her husband for maintenance), including any proceedings begun before the said commencement and carried on under that section and any proceedings for the discharge or variation of an order made or deemed to have been made under that section or for the temporary suspension of any provision of any such order or the revival of the operation of any provision so suspended;

   (c) proceedings under section 27 of the Matrimonial Causes Act 1973 (which relates to proceedings by a wife against her husband, or by a husband against his wife, for financial provision) and any proceedings for the discharge or variation of an order made under that section or for the temporary suspension of any provision of any such order or the revival of the operation of any provision so suspended;

   (d) proceedings under Part III of the Family Law Act 1986;

   (da) proceedings under Part 9 of Schedule 5 to the Civil Partnership Act 2004 (provision corresponding to the provision referred to in paragraph (c) above);

   (db) proceedings under section 58 of the 2004 Act (declarations as to subsistence etc. of civil partnership).

   (e) *(repealed)*

(2) *(repealed)*

(3) Section 1(1)(b) of the Judicial Proceedings (Regulation of Reports) Act 1926 (which restricts the reporting of matrimonial causes) shall extend to any such proceedings as are mentioned in subsection (1) above subject, in the case of the proceedings mentioned in subsection (1)(d) or (db) to the modification that the matters allowed to be printed or published by virtue of sub-paragraph (ii) of the said section 1(1)(b) shall be particulars of the declaration sought by a petition (instead of a concise statement of the charges, defences and counter-charges in support of which evidence has been given).

Amendments—MPPA 1970, s 42(1), Sch 2, para 3; MCA 1973, ss 53, 54, Sch 1, Sch 2, para 7(1), Sch 3; FLA 1986, s 68, Sch 1, para 9, Sch 2; FLRA 1987, s 33, Sch 2, para 19, Sch 4; CSPSSA 2000, s 85, Sch 9; CPA 2004, s 261(1), Sch 27, para 29.

****

Domestic Proceedings and Magistrates' Courts Act 1978

ARRANGEMENT OF SECTIONS

PART I
MATRIMONIAL PROCEEDINGS IN MAGISTRATES' COURTS

Powers of court to make orders for financial provision for parties to a marriage and children of the family

PART I
MATRIMONIAL PROCEEDINGS IN MAGISTRATES' COURTS

Powers of court to make orders for financial provision for parties to a marriage and children of the family

1 Grounds of application for financial provision

Either party to a marriage may apply to a magistrates' court for an order under section 2 of this Act on the ground that the other party to the marriage –

(a) has failed to provide reasonable maintenance for the applicant; or
(b) has failed to provide, or to make a proper contribution towards, reasonable maintenance for any child of the family; or

(c) has behaved in such a way that the applicant cannot reasonably be expected to live with the respondent; or

(d) has deserted the applicant.

Amendments—MFPA 1984, s 46(1), Sch 1, para 21.

Defined terms—"child", "child of the family": s 88(1); "live with": s 88(2).

Procedure on application—For the procedure to be followed, see FPR 2010, Pt 9 and PD9A in Part III.

"behaved" (s 1(c))—The date of the behaviour may be relevant (see MCA 1980, s 127 (time limits)).

Fee payable—See MCFO 2008, fee 6.1.

2 Powers of court to make orders for financial provision

(1) Where on an application for an order under this section the applicant satisfies the court of any ground mentioned in section 1 of this Act, the court may, subject to the provisions of this Part of this Act, make any one or more of the following orders, that is to say –

(a) an order that the respondent shall make to the applicant such periodical payments, and for such term, as may be specified in the order;

(b) an order that the respondent shall pay to the applicant such lump sum as may be so specified;

(c) an order that the respondent shall make to the applicant for the benefit of a child of the family to whom the application relates, or to such a child, such periodical payments, and for such term, as may be so specified;

(d) an order that the respondent shall pay to the applicant for the benefit of a child of the family to whom the application relates, or to such a child, such lump sum as may be so specified.

(2) Without prejudice to the generality of subsection (1)(b) or (d) above, an order under this section for the payment of a lump sum may be made for the purpose of enabling any liability or expenses reasonably incurred in maintaining the applicant, or any child of the family to whom the application relates, before the making of the order to be met.

(3) The amount of any lump sum required to be paid by an order under this section shall not exceed £1,000 or such larger amount as the Lord Chancellor may from time to time by order fix for the purposes of this subsection.

(4) An order made by the Lord Chancellor under this section –

(a) shall be made only after consultation with the Lord Chief Justice;

(b) shall be made by statutory instrument and be subject to annulment in pursuance of a resolution of either House of Parliament.

(5) The Lord Chief Justice may nominate a judicial office holder (as defined in section 109(4) of the Constitutional Reform Act 2005) to exercise his functions under this section.

Amendments—SI 1988/1069; SI 1992/709; CRA 2005, ss 15(1), 146, Sch 4, Pt 1, para 96, Sch 18, Pt 2.

Defined terms—"child", "child of the family": s 88(1).

Scope—This section defines the powers of magistrates' courts to order periodical payments and lump sum payments to either party or to a child of the family. Separate but complementary provision for orders for financial provision for children is contained in CA 1989, Sch 1. The courts' powers in respect of child maintenance under this Act and under CA 1989 are subject to the radical restrictions imposed by CSA 1991.

"the applicant satisfies the court" (s 2(1))—For the procedure where the respondent fails to appear see MCA 1980, s 55. The court is entitled to consider written details of the respondent's means where the respondent does not appear and the applicant agrees the details but, if the applicant does not agree with the information supplied in this way, the case should be adjourned and the respondent required to attend

(*Whittingstall v Whittingstall* [1990] 2 FLR 368). For power to change the application to an agreed application, see s 6(4). Note the effect of an employer's statement of wages: MCA 1980, s 100.

"the court may … make any one or more of the following orders" (s 2(1))—Although an apparent discretion is given to the court, it has been held that there is a duty to exercise this power where the applicant has proved his case (*Hill v Hill* (1972) 116 Sol Jo 565). Before making an order, the court is obliged under s 26 to consider the possibility of reconciliation.

Form of order—If an order is made, it should include a statement that the ground of the application is found to be true (*Wilcox v Wilcox* (1902) 66 JP 166; *Dodd v Dodd* [1906] P 189). If there is a finding of desertion, the date of commencement of desertion should be included in the order (*Fengl v Fengl* [1914] P 274). Where the person against whom an order is to be made is a member of Her Majesty's forces, see the Army Act 1955, ss 144 and 150–152, the Air Force Act 1955, ss 144 and 150–152 and *Barnish v Barnish* (1976) Fam Law 174. Further guidance is given in Home Office Circulars 251/1970, 12/1982 (Royal Navy and Royal Marines) and 25/1986.

Lump sums (s 2(1)(b))—The general power to order payments by instalments appears to apply equally to lump sums (MCA 1980, s 75; see s 22 for the power to vary the instalments). Even though a payer does not have capital resources, the court may order a lump sum payment provided it has had regard to the payer's ability to pay from income (or potential income).

"a child of the family to whom the application relates" (s 2(1)(c))—These words seem to indicate that financial provision for children under this Act is dependent upon an application being made in respect of them and may not be awarded where the application relates only to the applicant spouse.

Method of payment—See MCA 1980, s 59 for the requirement for payment to be ordered directly between the parties, through the designated officer, by standing order (or similar method) or by attachment of earnings.

Court's duty to assist unrepresented party—For the duty of the court to assist an unrepresented party who is unable effectively to examine or cross-examine a witness, see MCA 1980, s 73.

3 Matters to which the court is to have regard in exercising its powers under s 2

(1) Where an application is made for an order under section 2 of this Act, it shall be the duty of the court, in deciding whether to exercise its powers under that section and, if so, in what manner, to have regard to all the circumstances of the case, first consideration being given to the welfare while a minor of any child of the family who has not attained the age of eighteen.

(2) As regards the exercise of its powers under subsection (1)(a) or (b) of section 2, the court shall in particular have regard to the following matters –

(a) the income, earning capacity, property and other financial resources which each of the parties to the marriage has or is likely to have in the foreseeable future, including in the case of earning capacity any increase in that capacity which it would in the opinion of the court be reasonable to expect a party to the marriage to take steps to acquire;

(b) the financial needs, obligations and responsibilities which each of the parties to the marriage has or is likely to have in the foreseeable future;

(c) the standard of living enjoyed by the parties to the marriage before the occurrence of the conduct which is alleged as the ground of the application;

(d) the age of each party to the marriage and the duration of the marriage;

(e) any physical or mental disability of either of the parties to the marriage;

(f) the contributions which each of the parties has made or is likely in the foreseeable future to make to the welfare of the family, including any contribution by looking after the home or caring for the family;

(g) the conduct of each of the parties, if that conduct is such that it would in the opinion of the court be inequitable to disregard it.

(3) As regards the exercise of its power under subsection (1)(c) or (d) of section 2, the court shall in particular have regard to the following matters –

(a)   the financial needs of the child;

(b)   the income, earning capacity (if any), property and other financial resources of the child;

(c)   any physical or mental disability of the child;

(d)   the standard of living enjoyed by the family before the occurrence of the conduct which is alleged as the ground of the application;

(e)   the manner in which the child was being and in which the parties to the marriage expected him to be educated or trained;

(f)   the matters mentioned in relation to the parties to the marriage in paragraphs (a) and (b) of subsection (2) above.

(4) As regards the exercise of its power under section 2 in favour of a child of the family who is not the child of the respondent, the court shall also have regard –

(a)   to whether the respondent has assumed any responsibility for the child's maintenance and, if he did, to the extent to which, and the basis on which, he assumed that responsibility and to the length of time during which he discharged that responsibility;

(b)   to whether in assuming and discharging that responsibility the respondent did so knowing that the child was not his own child;

(c)   to the liability of any other person to maintain the child.

Amendments—MFPA 1984, s 9.

Defined terms—"child of the family": s 88(1).

Scope—This section outlines the matters to which the court is to have regard in making an order under s 2. It follows (with only minor modifications) the guidelines set out in MCA 1973 (particularly s 25) and so the principles followed in divorce courts are of equal application in magistrates' courts (*Macey v Macey* (1982) 3 FLR 7).

   For those cases where jurisdiction is retained by the courts, there is no express duty to apply CSA 1991 formula to establish a starting-point for maintenance but the likely amount of child support maintenance which would be payable may provide the court with useful and "strongly persuasive" information (*E v C (Child Maintenance)* [1996] 1 FLR 472). There are three "ranging shots": the prescribed figures set out in the National Foster Care Allowance, in the DWP allowances, and the CSA calculation. The court finds it helpful to know all three figures. Good reasons must exist for any substantial differences between maintenance calculations and maintenance orders.

"shall in particular have regard" (s 3(2))—The procedure to be adopted should be for the court to make a finding upon each of the factors contained in the section. Each of the factors should then be balanced in order to arrive at a just and reasonable order (*Vasey v Vasey* [1985] FLR 596).

4 Duration of orders for financial provision for a party to a marriage

(1) The term to be specified in any order made under section 2(1)(a) of this Act shall be such term as the court thinks fit except that the term shall not begin earlier than the date of the making of the application for the order and shall not extend beyond the death of either of the parties to the marriage.

(2) Where the order is made under the said section 2(1)(a) and the marriage of the parties affected by the order is subsequently dissolved or annulled but the order continues in force, the order shall, notwithstanding anything in it, cease to have effect on the remarriage of, or formation of a civil partnership by, the party in whose favour it was made, except in relation to any arrears due under the order on the date of the remarriage or formation of the civil partnership.

Amendments—CPA 2004, s 261(1), Sch 27, para 57.

Revival of orders—The power to revive an order under s 20(6) is restricted to orders that have been temporarily suspended. An expired term order cannot be revived.

5 Age limit on making orders for financial provision for children and duration of such orders

(1) Subject to subsection (3) below, no order shall be made under section 2(1)(c) or (d) of this Act in favour of a child who has attained the age of eighteen.

(2) The term to be specified in an order made under section 2(1)(c) of this Act in favour of a child may begin with the date of the making of an application for the order in question or any later date or a date ascertained in accordance with subsection (5) or (6) below but –

(a) shall not in the first instance extend beyond the date of the birthday of the child next following his attaining the upper limit of the compulsory school age (construed in accordance with section 8 of the Education Act 1996) unless the court considers that in the circumstances of the case the welfare of the child requires that it should extend to a later date; and

(b) shall not in any event, subject to subsection (3) below, extend beyond the date of the child's eighteenth birthday.

(3) The court –

(a) may make an order under section 2(1)(c) or (d) of this Act in favour of a child who has attained the age of eighteen, and

(b) may include in an order made under section 2(1)(c) of this Act in relation to a child who has attained that age a provision for extending beyond the date when the child will attain that age the term for which by virtue of the order any payments are to be made to or for the benefit of that child,

if it appears to the court –

(i) that the child is, or will be, or if such an order or provision were made would be receiving instruction at an educational establishment or undergoing training for a trade, profession or vocation, whether or not he is also, or will also be, in gainful employment; or

(ii) that there are special circumstances which justify the making of the order or provision.

(4) Any order made under section 2(1)(c) of this Act in favour of a child shall, notwithstanding anything in the order, cease to have effect on the death of the person liable to make payments under the order.

(5) Where –

(a) a maintenance calculation ("the current calculation") is in force with respect to a child; and

(b) an application is made for an order under section 2(1)(c) of this Act –

(i) in accordance with section 8 of the Child Support Act 1991; and

(ii) before the end of the period of 6 months beginning with the making of the current calculation,

the term to be specified in any such order made on that application may be expressed to begin on, or at any time after, the earliest permitted date.

(6) For the purposes of subsection (5) above, "the earliest permitted date" is whichever is the later of –

(a) the date 6 months before the application is made; or

(b) the date on which the current calculation took effect or, where successive maintenance calculations have been continuously in force with respect to a child, on which the first of those calculations took effect.

(7) Where –

    (a)   a maintenance calculation ceases to have effect by or under any provision of the Child Support Act 1991; and

    (b)   an application is made, before the end of the period of 6 months beginning with the relevant date, for an order under section 2(1)(c) of this Act in relation to a child with respect to whom that maintenance calculation was in force immediately before it ceased to have effect,

the term to be specified in any such order, or in any interim order under section 19 of this Act, made on that application, may begin with the date on which that maintenance calculation ceased to have effect, or any later date.

(8) In subsection (7)(b) above –

    (a)   where the maintenance calculation ceased to have effect, the relevant date is the date on which it so ceased

    (b)   *(repealed)*

Amendments—MFPA 1984, s 9(2); SI 1993/623; Education Act 1996, s 582(1), Sch 37, Pt II, para 138; CSPSSA 2000, ss 26, 85, Sch 3, para 4, Sch 9.

Defined terms—"child": s 88(1).

Scope—This section sets out the permissible duration of an order for financial provision for a child. An existing maintenance calculation terminates when the child ceases to be a "child" under CSA 1991, s 55. A calculation will be cancelled by the Secretary of State in the event that one or more of the person with care, the non-resident parent or the child leaves the jurisdiction (Child Support (Maintenance Arrangements and Jurisdiction) Regulations 1992, reg 7). For power to backdate to the termination or cancellation of the order, see DPMCA 1978, s 5(7). For power to backdate a "top-up" order under CSA 1991, s 8(6), see DPMCA 1978, s 5(5).

Revival of orders—There are limited powers to revive an expired order (see s 20A).

6 Orders for payments which have been agreed by the parties

(1) Either party to a marriage may apply to a magistrates' court for an order under this section on the ground that either the party making the application or the other party to the marriage has agreed to make such financial provision as may be specified in the application and, subject to subsection (3) below, the court on such an application may, if –

    (a)   it is satisfied that the applicant or the respondent, as the case may be, has agreed to make that provision, and

    (b)   it has no reason to think that it would be contrary to the interests of justice to exercise its powers hereunder,

order that the applicant or the respondent, as the case may be, shall make the financial provisions specified in the application.

(2) In this section "financial provision" means the provision mentioned in any one or more of the following paragraphs, that is to say –

    (a)   the making of periodical payments by one party to the other,

    (b)   the payment of a lump sum by one party to the other,

    (c)   the making of periodical payments by one party to a child of the family or to the other party for the benefit of such a child,

    (d)   the payment by one party of a lump sum to a child of the family or to the other party for the benefit of such a child,

and any reference in this section to the financial provision specified in an application made under subsection (1) above or specified by the court under subsection (5) below is a reference to the type of provision specified in the application or by the court, as the case may be, to the amount so specified as the amount of any payment to be made thereunder and, in the case of periodical payments, to the term so specified as the term for which the payments are to be made.

(3) Where the financial provision specified in an application under subsection (1) above includes or consists of provision in respect of a child of the family, the court shall not make an order under that subsection unless it considers that the provision which the applicant or the respondent, as the case may be, has agreed to make in respect of that child provides for, or makes a proper contribution towards, the financial needs of the child.

(4) A party to a marriage who has applied for an order under section 2 of this Act shall not be precluded at any time before the determination of that application from applying for an order under this section; but if an order is made under this section on the application of either party and either of them has also made an application for an order under section 2 of this Act, the application made for the order under section 2 shall be treated as if it had been withdrawn.

(5) Where on an application under subsection (1) above the court decides –

    (a)   that it would be contrary to the interests of justice to make an order for the making of the financial provision specified in the application, or

    (b)   that any financial provision which the applicant or the respondent, as the case may be, has agreed to make in respect of a child of the family does not provide for, or make a proper contribution towards, the financial needs of that child,

but it is of the opinion –

    (i)   that it would not be contrary to the interests of justice to make an order for the making of some other financial provision specified by the court, and

    (ii)   that, in so far as that other financial provision contains any provision for a child of the family, it provides for, or makes a proper contribution towards, the financial needs of that child,

then if both the parties agree, the court may order that the applicant or the respondent, as the case may be, shall make that other financial provision.

(6) Subject to subsection (8) below, the provisions of section 4 of this Act shall apply in relation to an order under this section which requires periodical payments to be made to a party to a marriage for his own benefit as they apply in relation to an order under section 2(1)(a) of this Act.

(7) Subject to subsection (8) below, the provisions of section 5 of this Act shall apply in relation to an order under this section for the making of financial provision in respect of a child of the family as they apply in relation to an order under section 2(1)(c) or (d) of this Act.

(8) Where the court makes an order under this section which contains provision for the making of periodical payments and, by virtue of subsection (4) above, an application for an order under section 2 of this Act is treated as if it had been withdrawn, then the term which may be specified as the term for which the payments are to be made may begin with the date of the making of the application for the order under section 2 or any later date.

(9) Where the respondent is not present or represented by counsel or solicitor at the hearing of an application for an order under subsection (1) above, the court shall not make an order under this section unless there is produced to the court such evidence as may be prescribed by rules of court of –

    (a)   the consent of the respondent to the making of the order,

    (b)   the financial resources of the respondent, and

    (c)   in a case where the financial provision specified in the application includes or consists of provision in respect of a child of the family to be made by the applicant to the respondent for the benefit of the child or to the child, the financial resources of the child.

Amendments—MFPA 1984, s 10; Courts Act 2003, Sch 8, para 191.

Defined terms—"child", "child of the family": s 88(1).

Form of application—The form of application and the procedure on application is prescribed by the FPR 2010.

Method of payment—See under s 2.

Lump sums (s 6(2)(b))—The amount of any agreed lump sum is not limited by this section. Contrast the limitation imposed under s 2. The general power to order payment by instalments appears to apply to payment of lump sums under this section (MCA 1980, s 75); for the power to vary instalments see s 22.

Relationship with applications under s 2 (s 6(4))—It is possible to make an application under this section while an application under s 2 is outstanding; s 6(4) prescribes the procedure to be adopted in such circumstances.

"such evidence as may be prescribed" (s 6(9))—FPR 2010, r 9.26 prescribes the evidence that must be produced.

Fee payable—See MCFO 2008, fee 6.1.

7 Powers of court where parties are living apart by agreement

(1) Where the parties to a marriage have been living apart for a continuous period exceeding three months, neither party having deserted the other, and one of the parties has been making periodical payments for the benefit of the other party or of a child of the family, that other party may apply to a magistrates' court for an order under this section, and any application made under this subsection shall specify the aggregate amount of the payments so made during the period of three months immediately preceding the date of the making of the application.

(2) Where on an application for an order under this section the court is satisfied that the respondent has made the payments specified in the application, the court may, subject to the provisions of this Part of this Act, make one or both of the following orders, that is to say –

(a) an order that the respondent shall make to the applicant such periodical payments, and for such term, as may be specified in the order;

(b) an order that the respondent shall make to the applicant for the benefit of a child of the family to whom the application relates, or to such a child, such periodical payments, and for such term, as may be so specified.

(3) The court in the exercise of its powers under this section –

(a) shall not require the respondent to make payments which exceed in aggregate during any period of three months the aggregate amount paid by him for the benefit of the applicant or a child of the family during the period of three months immediately preceding the date of the making of the application;

(b) shall not require the respondent to make payments to or for the benefit of any person which exceed in amount the payments which the court considers that it would have required the respondent to make to or for the benefit of that person on an application under section 1 of this Act;

(c) shall not require payments to be made to or for the benefit of a child of the family who is not a child of the respondent unless the court considers that it would have made an order in favour of that child on an application under section 1 of this Act.

(4) Where on an application under this section the court considers that the orders which it has the power to make under this section –

(a)   would not provide reasonable maintenance for the applicant, or

(b)   if the application relates to a child of the family, would not provide, or make a proper contribution towards reasonable maintenance for that child,

the court shall refuse to make an order under this section, but the court may treat the application as if it were an application for an order under section 2 of this Act.

(5) The provisions of section 3 of this Act shall apply in relation to an application for an order under this section as they apply in relation to an application for an order under section 2 of this Act subject to the modification that for the reference in subsection (2)(c) of the said section 3 to the occurrence of the conduct which is alleged as the ground of the application there shall be substituted a reference to the living apart of the parties to the marriage.

(6) The provisions of section 4 of this Act shall apply in relation to an order under this section which requires periodical payments to be made to the applicant for his own benefit as they apply in relation to an order under section 2(1)(a) of this Act.

(7) The provisions of section 5 of this Act shall apply in relation to an order under this section for the making of periodical payments in respect of a child of the family as they apply in relation to an order under section 2(1)(c) of this Act.

Amendments—MFPA 1984, s 46(1), Sch 1, para 22.

Defined terms—"child of the family": s 88(1); "marriage": s 88(3).

Method of payment—See under s 2.

Fee payable—See MCFO 2008, fee 6.1.

Powers of court as to the custody etc of children

8 Restrictions on making of orders under this Act: welfare of children

Where an application is made by a party to a marriage for an order under section 2, 6 or 7 of this Act, then, if there is a child of the family who is under the age of eighteen, the court shall not dismiss or make a final order on the application until it has decided whether to exercise any of its powers under the Children Act 1989 with respect to the child.

Amendments—CA 1989, s 108(5), Sch 13, para 36.

Defined terms—"child", "child of the family": s 88(1).

"dismiss or make a final order"—An interim order under s 19 is not prohibited.

****

Interim orders

19 Interim orders

(1) Where an application is made for an order under section 2, 6 or 7 of this Act –

(a)   the magistrates' court at any time before making a final order on, or dismissing the application or on refusing to make an order on the application by virtue of section 27 of this Act,

(b)   the High Court on ordering the application to be reheard by a magistrates' court after the refusal of an order under section 27 of this Act, and

(c)   a county court on ordering the application to be reheard by a magistrates' court on an appeal under section 29 of this Act,

shall, subject to the provisions of this Part of this Act, have the

(i)   power to make an order (in this Part of this Act referred to as an "interim maintenance order") which requires the respondent to make to the applicant or to any child of the family who is under the age of eighteen, or to the applicant for the benefit of such a child, such periodical payments as the court thinks reasonable;

(ii)   (*repealed*)

(2) (*repealed*)

(3) An interim maintenance order may provide for payments to be made from such date as the court may specify, except that, subject to section 5(5) and (6) of this Act, the date shall not be earlier than the date of the making of the application for an order under section 2, 6 or 7 of this Act; and where such an order made by a county court on an appeal under section 29 of this Act provides for payments to be made from a date earlier than the date of the making of the order, the interim order may provide that payments made by the respondent under an order made by a magistrates' court shall, to such extent and in such manner as may be provided by the interim order, be treated as having been paid on account of any payment provided for by the interim order.

(3A) Where an application is made for an order under section 6 of this Act by the party to the marriage who has agreed to make the financial provision specified in the application –

(a)   subsection (1) shall apply as if the reference in paragraph (i) to the respondent were a reference to the applicant and the references to the applicant were references to the respondent; and

(b)   subsection (3) shall apply accordingly.

(4) (*repealed*)

(5) Subject to subsection (6) below, an interim order made on an application for an order under section 2, 6 or 7 of this Act shall cease to have effect on whichever of the following dates occurs first, that is to say –

(a)   the date, if any, specified for the purpose in the interim order;

(b)   the date of the expiration of the period of three months beginning with the date of the making of the interim order;

(c)   the date on which a magistrates' court either makes a final order on or dismisses the application.

(6) Where an interim order made under subsection (1) above would, but for this subsection, cease to have effect by virtue of subsection (5)(a) or (b) above, the magistrates' court which made the order or, in the case of an interim order made by the High Court or a county court, the magistrates' court by which the application for an order under section 2, 6 or 7 of this Act is to be reheard, shall have power by order to provide that the interim order shall continue in force for a further period, and any order continued in force under this subsection shall cease to have effect on whichever of the following dates occurs first, that is to say –

(a)   the date, if any specified for the purpose in the order made under this subsection;

(b)   the date of the expiration of the period of three months beginning with the date of the making of the order under this subsection or, if more than one order has been made under this subsection with respect to the application, beginning with the date of the making of the first of those orders;

(c)   the date on which the court either makes a final order on, or dismisses, the application.

(7) Not more than one interim maintenance order may be made with respect to any application for an order under section 2, 6 or 7 of this Act, but without prejudice to the powers of the court under this section on any further such application.

(8) No appeal shall lie from the making of or refusal to make, the variation of or refusal to vary, or the revocation of or refusal to revoke, an interim maintenance order.

(9) An interim order made by the High Court or a county court under this section on ordering that an application be reheard by a magistrates' court shall for the purpose of its enforcement and for the purposes of section 20 of this Act, be treated as if it were an order of that magistrates' court and not of the High Court or a county court.

Amendments—MFPA 1984, s 46(1), Sch 1, para 24; CA 1989, s 108(5),(7), Sch 13, para 37, Sch 15; SI 1993/623; SI 2009/871.

Defined terms—"child", "child of the family": s 88(1).

"an order" (s 19(1))—Only one interim order may be made with respect to an application (s 19(7)) but there is power under s 19(6) to extend the original interim order for up to a further 3 months.

"if more than one order has been made" (s 19(6)(b))—While only one interim order may be made, a number of extension orders is permissible provided that the aggregate period of extension orders does not exceed 3 months.

Variation, revocation and cessation of orders etc

20 Variation, revival and revocation of orders for periodical payments

(1) Where a magistrates' court has made an order under section 2(1)(a) or (c) of this Act for the making of periodical payments the court shall have power, on an application made under this section, to vary or revoke that order and also to make an order under section 2(1)(b) or (d) of this Act.

(2) Where a magistrates' court has made an order under section 6 of this Act for the making of periodical payments by a party to a marriage the court shall have power, on an application made under this section, to vary or revoke that order and also to make an order for the payment of a lump sum by that party either –

   (a)   to the other party to the marriage, or
   (b)   to a child of the family or to that other party for the benefit of that child.

(3) Where a magistrates' court has made an order under section 7 of this Act for the making of periodical payments, the court shall have power, on an application made under this section, to vary or revoke that order.

(4) *(repealed)*

(5) Where a magistrates' court has made an interim maintenance order under section 19 of this Act, the court, on an application made under this section, shall have power to vary or revoke that order, except that the court shall not by virtue of this subsection extend the period for which the order is in force.

(6) The power of the court under this section to vary an order for the making of periodical payments shall include power to suspend any provisions thereof temporarily and to revive any provision so suspended.

(7) Where the court has power by virtue of this section to make an order for the payment of a lump sum, the amount of the lump sum shall not exceed the maximum amount that may at that time be required to be paid under section 2(3) of this Act, but the court may make an order for the payment of a lump sum not exceeding that amount notwithstanding that the person required to pay the lump sum was required to pay a lump sum by a previous order under this Part of this Act.

(8) Where the court has power by virtue of subsection (2) above to make an order for the payment of a lump sum and the respondent or the applicant, as the case may be, has agreed to pay a lump sum of an amount exceeding the maximum amount that may at that

time be required to be paid under section 2(3) of this Act, the court may, notwithstanding anything in subsection (7) above, make an order for the payment of a lump sum of that amount.

(9) An order made by virtue of this section which varies an order for the making of periodical payments may provide that the payments as so varied shall be made from such date as the court may specify, except that, subject to subsections (9A) and (9B) below, the date shall not be earlier than the date of the making of the application under this section.

(9A) Where –

    (a)   there is in force an order ("the order") –

        (i)   under section 2(1)(c) of this Act,

        (ii)   under section 6(1) of this Act making provision of a kind mentioned in paragraph (c) of section 6(2) of this Act (regardless of whether it makes provision of any other kind mentioned in that paragraph),

        (iii)   under section 7(2)(b) of this Act, or

        (iv)   which is an interim maintenance order under which the payments are to be made to a child or to the applicant for the benefit of a child;

    (b)   the order requires payments specified in it to be made to or for the benefit of more than one child without apportioning those payments between them;

    (c)   a maintenance calculation ("the calculation") is made with respect to one or more, but not all, of the children with respect to whom those payments are to be made; and

    (d)   an application is made, before the end of the period of 6 months beginning with the date on which the calculation was made, for the variation or revocation of the order,

the court may, in exercise of its powers under this section to vary or revoke the order, direct that the variation or revocation shall take effect from the date on which the calculation took effect or any later date.

(9B) Where –

    (a)   an order ("the child order") of a kind prescribed for the purposes of section 10(1) of the Child Support Act 1991 is affected by a maintenance calculation;

    (b)   on the date on which the child order became so affected there was in force an order ("the spousal order") –

        (i)   under section 2(1)(a) of this Act,

        (ii)   under section 6(1) of this Act making provision of a kind mentioned in section 6(2)(a) of this Act (regardless of whether it makes provision of any other kind mentioned in that paragraph),

        (iii)   under section 7(2)(a) of this Act, or

        (iv)   which is an interim maintenance order under which the payments are to be made to the applicant (otherwise than for the benefit of a child); and

    (c)   an application is made, before the end of the period of 6 months beginning with the date on which the maintenance calculation was made, for the spousal order to be varied or revoked,

the court may, in exercise of its powers under this section to vary or revoke the spousal order, direct that the variation or revocation shall take effect from the date on which the child order became so affected or any later date.

(9C) For the purposes of subsection (9B) above, an order is affected if it ceases to have effect or is modified by or under section 10 of the Child Support Act 1991.

(10) (*repealed*)

(11) In exercising the powers conferred by this section the court shall, so far as it appears to the court just to do so, give effect to an agreement which has been reached between the parties in relation to the application and, if there is no such agreement or if the court decides not to give effect to the agreement, the court shall have regard to all the circumstances of the case, first consideration being given to the welfare while a minor of any child of the family who has not attained the age of eighteen, and the circumstances of the case shall include any change in any of the matters to which the court was required to have regard when making the order to which the application relates or, in the case of an application for the variation or revocation of an order made under section 6 of this Act or on an appeal under section 29 of this Act, to which the court would have been required to have regard if that order had been made under section 2 of this Act.

(12) An application under this section may be made –

(a) where it is for the variation or revocation of an order under section 2, 6, 7 or 19 of this Act for periodical payments, by either party to the marriage in question; and

(b) where it is for the variation of an order under section 2(1)(c), 6 or 7 of this Act for periodical payments to or in respect of a child, also by the child himself, if he has attained the age of sixteen.

(13) (*repealed*)

Amendments—MFPA 1984, ss 9(3), 11, 46(1), Sch 1, para 25; FLRA 1987, s 33, Sch 4; CA 1989, s 108(5),(7), Sch 13, para 38, Sch 15; SI 1993/623; CSPSSA 2000, s 26, Sch 3, para 4.

Defined terms—"child", "child of the family": s 88(1).

Variation—The court is required to have regard to all relevant factors under s 3 on an application to vary an order (s 20(11)). The factors must be considered afresh (*Riley v Riley* [1986] 2 FLR 429). The order may not be varied to include periodical payments or a lump sum payment unless the original order contained provision for periodical payments. Section 20(9B) permits an additional power to backdate an order for the variation of a spouse's payment following a child maintenance calculation under CSA 1991. As to the effect of CSA 1991 on existing orders for child maintenance, see further **Scope** under DPMCA 1978, s 2.

"give effect to any agreement" (s 20(11))—Consent may be given in writing by the party or through the party's solicitor. The court should interfere with an agreement only if a question of injustice to the parties arises (*Whitton v Devizes Justices* [1985] Fam Law 125). For procedure relating to applications for consent orders see FPR 2010, r 9.26. MC(EVOFP & MP)R 2011, r 69 applies FPR 2010, with modifications, to variation applications under this section.

Fee payable—See MCFO 2008, fee 12.1.

20ZA Variation of orders for periodical payments: further provisions

(1) Subject to subsections (7) and (8) below, the power of the court under section 20 of this Act to vary an order for the making of periodical payments shall include power, if the court is satisfied that payment has not been made in accordance with the order, to exercise one of its powers under paragraph (a) to (d) of section 59(3) of the Magistrates' Courts Act 1980.

(2) In any case where –

(a) a magistrates' court has made an order under this Part of this Act for the making of periodical payments, and

(b) payments under the order are required to be made by any method of payment falling within section 59(6) of the Magistrates' Courts Act 1980 (standing order, etc),

an application may be made under this subsection to court for the order to be varied as mentioned in subsection (3) below.

(3) Subject to subsection (5) below, where an application is made under subsection (2) above, a justices' clerk, after giving written notice (by post or otherwise) of the application to the respondent and allowing the respondent, within the period of 14 days beginning with the date of the giving of that notice, an opportunity to make written representations, may vary the order to provide that payments under the order shall be made to the designated officer for the court.

(4) The clerk may proceed with an application under subsection (2) above notwithstanding that the respondent has not received written notice of the application.

(5) Where an application has been made under subsection (2) above, the clerk may, if he considers it inappropriate to exercise his power under subsection (3) above, refer the matter to the court which, subject to subsections (7) and (8) below, may vary the order by exercising one of its powers under paragraphs (a) to (d) of section 59(3) of the Magistrates' Courts Act 1980.

(6) Subsection (4) of section 59 of the Magistrates' Courts Act 1980 (power of court to order that account be opened) shall apply for the purposes of subsections (1) and (5) above as it applies for the purposes of that section.

(7) Before varying the order by exercising one of its powers under paragraphs (a) to (d) of section 59(3) of the Magistrates' Courts Act 1980, the court shall have regard to any representation made by the parties to the application.

(8) If the court does not propose to exercise its power under paragraph (c), (cc) or (d) of subsection (3) of section 59 of the Magistrates' Courts Act 1980, the court shall, unless upon representations expressly made in that behalf by the person to whom payments under the order are required to be made it is satisfied that it is undesirable to do so, exercise its power under paragraph (b) of that subsection.

(9) Subsection (12) of section 20 of this Act shall have effect for the purposes of applications under subsection (2) above as it has effect for the purposes of applications under that section.

(10) None of the powers of the court, or of a justices' clerk, conferred by this section shall be exercisable in relation to an order under this Part of this Act for the making of periodical payments which is not a qualifying maintenance order (within the meaning of section 59 of the Magistrates' Courts Act 1980).

Amendments—Inserted by MEA 1991, s 5; amended by SI 1994/731; AJA 1999, s 90, Sch 13, para 91; Courts Act 2003, Sch 8, para 192.

"paragraph (a) to (d) of section 59(3) of the Magistrates' Courts Act 1980" (s 20ZA(1))—This subsection permits orders for payments direct between the parties, through the designated officer, by standing order (or similar method) or by attachment of earnings.

"paragraph (b) of that subsection" (s 20ZA(8))—This subsection appears to give the payee the right to veto an order for payments direct between the parties.

"qualifying maintenance order" (s 20ZA(10))—A maintenance order will qualify if, at the time the order was made, the debtor was ordinarily resident in England and Wales (MCA 1980, s 59(2)).

20A Revival of orders for periodical payments

(1) Where an order made by a magistrates' court under this Part of this Act for the making of periodical payments to or in respect of a child (other than an interim maintenance order) ceases to have effect –

(a) on the date on which the child attains the age of sixteen, or
(b) at any time after that date but before or on the date on which he attains the age of eighteen,

the child may apply to the court which made the order for an order for its revival.

(2) If on such an application it appears to the court that –

   (a)   the child is, will be or (if an order were made under this subsection) would be receiving instruction at an educational establishment or undergoing training for a trade, profession or vocation, whether or not while in gainful employment, or

   (b)   there are special circumstances which justify the making of an order under this subsection,

the court shall have power by order to revive the order from such date as the court may specify, not being earlier than the date of the making of the application.

(3) Any order revived under this section may be varied or revoked under section 20 in the same way as it could have been varied or revoked had it continued in being.

Amendments—Inserted by FLRA 1987, s 33(1), Sch 2, para 69; amended by CA 1989, s 108(5), Sch 13, para 39.

****

22 Variation of instalments of lump sum

Where in the exercise of its powers under section 75 of the Magistrates' Courts Act 1980 a magistrates' court orders that a lump sum required to be paid under Part of this Act shall be paid by instalments, the court, on an application made by either the person liable to pay or the person entitled to receive that sum, shall have power to vary that order by varying the number of instalments payable, the amount of any instalment payable and the date on which any instalment becomes payable.

Amendments—MCA 1980, s 154, Sch 7, para 160.

Payment—See MCR 1981, r 48 for the person to whom payments are to be ordered to be paid.

23 Supplementary provisions with respect to variation and revocation of orders

(1) (*repealed*)

(2) The powers of a magistrates' court to revoke, revive or vary an order for the periodical payment of money and the power of the clerk of a magistrates' court to vary such an order under section 60 of the Magistrates' Courts Act 1980 and the power of a magistrates' court to suspend or rescind certain other orders under section 63(2) of that Act shall not apply in relation to an order made under this Part of this Act.

Amendments—MCA 1980, s 154, Sch 7, para 161; CLSA 1990, s 125(7), Sch 20; MEA 1991, s 11(1), Sch 2, para 2.

24 (*repealed*)

25 Effect on certain orders of parties living together

(1) Where –

   (a)   periodical payments are required to be made to one of the parties to a marriage (whether for his own benefit or for the benefit of a child of the family) by an order made under section 2 or 6 of this Act or by an interim maintenance order made under section 19 of this Act (otherwise than on an application under section 7 of this Act),

   (b)   (*repealed*)

the order shall be enforceable notwithstanding that the parties to the marriage are living with each other at the date of the making of the order or that, although they are not living with each other at that date, they subsequently resume living with each other; but the order shall cease to have effect if after that date the parties continue to live with each other, or resume living with each other, for a continuous period exceeding 6 months.

(2) Where any of the following orders is made under this Part of this Act, that is to say –

    (a) an order under section 2 or 6 of this Act which requires periodical payments to be made to a child of the family, or

    (b) an interim maintenance order under section 19 of this Act (otherwise than on an application under section 7 of this Act) which requires periodical payments to be made to a child of the family,

    (c)–(d) *(repealed)*

then, unless the court otherwise directs, the order shall continue to have effect and be enforceable notwithstanding that the parties to the marriage in question are living with each other at the date of the making of the order or that, although they are not living with each other at that date, they subsequently resume living with each other.

(3) Any order made under section 7 of this Act, and any interim maintenance order made on an application for an order under that section, shall cease to have effect if the parties to the marriage resume living with each other.

(4) Where an order made under this Part of this Act ceases to have effect by virtue of subsection (1) or (3) above or by virtue of a direction given under subsection (2) above, a magistrates' court may, on an application made by either party to the marriage, make an order declaring that the first mentioned order ceased to have effect from such date as the court may specify.

Amendments—CA 1989, s 108(5),(7), Sch 13, para 41, Sch 15.

Defined terms—"child", "child of the family": s 88(1); "living with each other": s 88(2).

Reconciliation

26 Reconciliation

(1) Where an application is made for an order under section 2 of this Act the court, before deciding whether to exercise its powers under that section, shall consider whether there is any possibility of reconciliation between the parties to the marriage in question; and if at any stage of the proceedings on that application it appears to the court that there is a reasonable possibility of such a reconciliation, the court may adjourn the proceedings for such period as it thinks fit to enable attempts to be made to effect a reconciliation.

(2) Where the court adjourns any proceedings under subsection (1) above, it may request an officer of the Service (within the meaning of the Criminal Justice and Court Services Act 2000), a Welsh family proceedings officer (within the meaning given by section 35 of the Children Act 2004) or any other person to attempt to effect a reconciliation between the parties to the marriage, and where any such request is made, that officer or other person shall report in writing to the court whether the attempt has been successful or not, but shall not include in that report any other information.

Amendments—CJCSA 2000, s 74, Sch 7, para 57; CA 2004, s 40, Sch 3, para 1.

"an officer of the Service" (s 26(2))—That is an officer of the Children and Family Court Advisory and Support Service (Cafcass).

"shall not include in that report any other information" (s 26(2))—The content of the report is restricted to the outcome of the attempt at reconciliation.

Provisions relating to the High Court and county court

27 Refusal of order in case more suitable for High Court

Where on hearing an application for an order under section 2 of this Act a magistrates' court is of the opinion that any of the matters in question between the parties would be more conveniently dealt with by the High Court, the magistrates' court shall refuse to make any order on the application, and no appeal shall lie from that refusal; but if in any proceedings in the High Court relating to or comprising the same subject matter as that application the High Court so orders, the application shall be reheard and determined by a magistrates' court acting in the same local justice area as the first mentioned court.

Amendments—Courts Act 2003, Sch 8, para 193.

Scope—The power to refuse to deal with an application cannot be exercised in cases where the High Court does not have jurisdiction (*Perks v Perks* [1946] P 1; *Smyth v Smyth* [1956] P 427; *Davies v Davies* [1957] P 357).

"shall refuse to make any order"—The court may nevertheless exercise its power to make an interim order under s 19.

"no appeal shall lie"—This does not exclude a right of appeal on the issue of the High Court's jurisdiction (*Davies v Davies*, above).

28 Powers of High Court and county court in relation to certain orders under Part I

(1) Where after the making by a magistrates' court of an order under this Part of this Act proceedings between, and relating to the marriage of, the parties to the proceedings in which that order was made have been commenced in the High Court or a county court, then, except in the case of an order for the payment of a lump sum, the court in which the proceedings or any application made therein are or is pending may, if it thinks fit, direct that the order made by a magistrates' court shall cease to have effect on such date as may be specified in the direction.

(2) (*repealed*)

(3) Nothing in this section shall be taken as prejudicing the effect of any order made by the High Court or a county court so far as it implicitly supersedes or revokes an order or part of an order made by a magistrates' court.

Amendments—FLA 1996, s 66(3), Sch 10.

Scope—The court is required to send a copy of the High Court or county court order to the clerk to the magistrates' court that made the original order (Home Office Circular 78/1974; *Registrar's Direction of 11 March 1974*).

29 Appeals

(1) Subject to section 27 of this Act, where a magistrates' court makes or refuses to make, varies or refuses to vary, revokes or refuses to revoke an order (other than an interim maintenance order) under this Part of this Act, an appeal shall lie to a county court.

(2) On an appeal under this section a county court shall have power to make such orders as may be necessary to give effect to its determination of the appeal, including such incidental or consequential orders as appear to the court to be just, and, in the case of an appeal from a decision of a magistrates' court made on an application for or in respect of an order for the making of periodical payments, a county court shall have power to order that its determination of the appeal shall have effect from such date as the court thinks fit, not being earlier than the date of the making of the application to the magistrates' court or, in a case where there was made to the magistrates' court an application for an order

under section 2 and an application under section 6 and the term of the periodical payments was or might have been ordered to begin on the date of the making of the application for an order under section 2, the date of the making of that application.

(3) Without prejudice to the generality of subsection (2) above, where, on an appeal under this section in respect of an order of a magistrates' court requiring any person to make periodical payments, a county court reduces the amount of those payments or discharges the order, a county court shall have power to order the person entitled to payments under the order of the magistrates' court to pay to the person liable to make payments under that order such sum in respect of payments already made in compliance with the order as the courts thinks fit and, if any arrears are due under the order of the magistrates' court, a county court shall have power to remit the payment of those arrears or any part thereof.

(4) *(repealed)*

(5) Any order of a county court made on an appeal under this section (other than an order directing that an application shall be reheard by a magistrates' court) shall for the purposes of the enforcement of the order and for the purposes of section 20 of this Act be treated as if it were an order of the magistrates' court from which the appeal was brought and not of a county court.

Amendments—MFPA 1984, s 46(1), Sch 1, para 26; CA 1989, s 108(5),(7), Sch 13, para 42, Sch 15; SI 2009/871.

Scope—This section is to be construed narrowly and decisions not covered by s 29(1) cannot be appealed against under this section (see for example, *Berry v Berry* [1987] 1 FLR 105 where an appeal against remission of arrears was held to be excluded). The right of appeal to a county court on grounds of error of law or excess of jurisdiction is available under MCA 1980, s 111A for matters excluded from this section. In *P v P (Periodical Payments: Appeals)* [1995] 1 FLR 563, the Divisional Court held that the procedures for appealing under CA 1989, s 94 and this section were entirely different and not interchangeable.

Provisions relating to procedure, jurisdiction and enforcement

30 Provisions as to jurisdiction and procedure

(1) A magistrates' court shall, subject to subsection (1A) and to section 2 of the Family Law Act 1986 and section 70 of the Magistrates' Courts Act 1980 and any determination of the Lord Chancellor thereunder, have jurisdiction to hear an application for an order under this Part of this Act if it acts in, or is authorised by the Lord Chancellor to act for, a local justice area in which either the applicant or the respondent ordinarily resides at the date of the making of the application.

(1A) If an application or part of an application for an order under this Part relates to a matter where jurisdiction falls to be determined by reference to the jurisdictional requirements of the Maintenance Regulation and Schedule 6 to the Civil Jurisdiction and Judgments (Maintenance) Regulations 2011, a magistrates' court may not entertain that application or that part of it unless it has jurisdiction to do so by virtue of that Regulation and that Schedule.

(2)–(4) *(repealed)*

(5) It is hereby declared that any jurisdiction conferred on a magistrates' court by this Part of this Act is exercisable notwithstanding that any party to the proceedings is not domiciled in England.

(6) In this section "the Maintenance Regulation" means Council Regulation (EC) No 4/2009 including as applied in relation to Denmark by virtue of the Agreement made on 19 October 2005 between the European Community and the Kingdom of Denmark.

Amendments—MCA 1980, s 154, Sch 7, para 163; FLA 1986, s 68(1), Sch 1, para 24; CLSA 1990, s 125(7), Sch 20; Police and Magistrates' Courts Act 1994, s 91, Sch 8, para 29; Courts Act 2003, Sch 8, para 194; SI 2011/1484.

"ordinarily resides" (s 30(1))—Ordinary residence is established by a person's intention to make a place his or her home for an indefinite period (*Macrae v Macrae* [1949] P 397; *Stransky v Stransky* [1954] P 428; *Lewis v Lewis* [1956] 1 WLR 200).

"Maintenance Regulation and Schedule 6" (s 30(1A))—If one of the parties resides in another Member State of the EU, jurisdiction is determined by reference to the Maintenance Regulation and Sch 6 to the relevant 2011 Regulations, which take precedence over any other statutory provision or reciprocal arrangements.

Respondent in Scotland or Northern Ireland (s 30(3))—Where the respondent resides in Scotland or Northern Ireland, see MOA 1950, s 15 for endorsement and service of the summons.

31 Constitution of courts

(1) Where the hearing of an application under section 1 of this Act is adjourned after the court has decided that it is satisfied of any ground mentioned in that section, the court which resumes the hearing of that application may include justices who were not sitting when the hearing began if –

    (a) the parties to the proceedings agree; and

    (b) at least one of the justices composing the court which resumes the hearing was sitting when the hearing of the application began.

(2) Where, by virtue of subsection (1) above, among the justices composing the court which resumes the hearing of an application under section 1 of this Act there are any justices who were not sitting when the hearing of the application began, the court which resumes the hearing shall before making any order on the application make such inquiry into the facts and circumstances of the case as will enable the justices who were not sitting when the hearing began to be fully acquainted with those facts and circumstances.

32 Enforcement etc of orders for payment of money

(1) An order for the payment of money made by a magistrates' court under this Part of this Act shall be enforceable as a magistrates' court maintenance order.

(2) Without prejudice to section 59 of the Magistrates' Courts Act 1980 (which relates to the power of a magistrates' court to direct periodical payments to be made through the designated officer for a magistrates' court), a magistrates' court making an order under this Part of this Act for the making of a periodical payment by one person to another may direct that it shall be made to some third party on that other person's behalf instead of directly to that other person; and, for the purposes of any order made under this Part of this Act, the said section 59 shall have effect as if, in subsection (7) thereof, for the words "the person who applied for the maintenance order" there were substituted the words "the person to whom the payments under the order fall to be made".

(3) Any person for the time being under an obligation to make payments in pursuance of any order for the payment of money made under this Part of this Act shall give notice of any change of address to such person, if any, as may be specified in the order; and any person who without reasonable excuse fails to give such a notice shall be liable on summary conviction to a fine not exceeding level 2 on the standard scale.

(4) A person shall not be entitled to enforce through the High Court or any county court the payment of any arrears due under an order made by virtue of this Part of this Act without the leave of that court if those arrears became due more than twelve months before proceedings to enforce the payment of them are begun.

(5) The court hearing an application for the grant of leave under subsection (4) above may refuse leave, or may grant leave subject to such restrictions and conditions

(including conditions as to the allowing of time for payment or the making of payment by instalments) as that court thinks proper, or may remit the payment of such arrears or any part thereof.

(6) An application for the grant of leave under subsection (4) above shall be made in such manner as may be prescribed by rules of court.

Amendments—MCA 1980, s 154, Sch 7, para 164; Criminal Justice Act 1982, s 46; FLRA 1987, s 33(1), Sch 2, para 70; MEA 1991, s 11(1), Sch 2, para 3; AJA 1999, s 90, Sch 13, para 92; Courts Act 2003, Sch 8, para 195.

"An order" (s 32(1))—This includes a county court order made on appeal; see s 29(5) above.

"address" (s 32(3))—See FPR PD6C for disclosure of addresses by government departments.

"level 2 on the standard scale" (s 32(3))—Currently £500 (Criminal Justice Act 1982, s 37(2), as substituted).

****

35 Orders for repayment in certain cases of sums paid after cessation of order by reason of remarriage or formation of civil partnership

(1) Where –

    (a) an order made under section 2(1)(a), 6 or 7 of this Act has, by virtue of section 4(2) of this Act, ceased to have effect by reason of the remarriage of, or formation of a civil partnership by, the party in whose favour it was made, and

    (b) the person liable to make payments under the order made payments in accordance with it in respect of a period after the date of that remarriage or the formation of that civil partnership in the mistaken belief that the order was still subsisting,

no proceedings in respect of a cause of action arising out of the circumstances mentioned in paragraphs (a) and (b) above shall be maintainable by the person so liable or his personal representatives against the person so entitled or his personal representatives, but on an application made under this section the court may exercise the powers conferred on it by subsection (2) below.

(2) the court may order the respondent to an application made under this section to pay to the applicant a sum equal to the amount of the payments made in respect of the period mentioned in subsection (1)(b) above or, if it appears to the court that it would be unjust to make that order, it may either order the respondent to pay to the applicant such lesser sum as it thinks fit or dismiss the application.

(3) An application under this section may be made by the person liable to make payments under the order made under section 2(1)(a), 6 or 7 of this Act or his personal representatives and may be made against the person entitled to payments under that order or his personal representatives.

(4) An application under this section shall be made to a county court, except that such an application may be made in proceedings in the High Court or a county court for leave to enforce, or the enforcement of, the payment of arrears under an order made under section 2(1)(a), 6 or 7 of this Act; and accordingly references in this section to the court are references to the High Court or a county court, as the circumstances require.

(5) An order under this section for the payment of any sum may provide for the payment of that sum by instalments of such amount as may be specified in the order.

(6) The jurisdiction conferred on a county court by this section shall be exercisable by a county court notwithstanding that by reason of the amount claimed in an application under this section the jurisdiction would not but for this subsection be exercisable by a county court.

(7) The designated officer for a magistrates' court to whom any payments under an order made under section 2(1)(a), 6 or 7 of this Act are required to be made, and the collecting officer under an attachment of earnings order made to secure payments under the first mentioned order, shall not be liable –

(a) in the case of the designated officer, for any act done by him in pursuance of the first mentioned order after the date on which that order ceased to have effect by reason of the remarriage of, or formation of a civil partnership by, the person entitled to payments under it, and

(b) in the case of the collecting officer, for any act done by him after that date in accordance with any enactment or rule of court specifying how payments made to him in compliance with the attachment of earnings order are to be dealt with,

if, but only if, the act was one which he would have been under a duty to do had the first mentioned order not ceased to have effect by reason of the remarriage or the formation of that civil partnership and the act was done before notice in writing of the fact that the person so entitled had remarried or formed a civil partnership was given to him by or on behalf of that person, the person liable to make payments under the first mentioned order or the personal representatives of either of those persons.

(8) In this section "collecting officer", in relation to an attachment of earnings order, means the officer of the High Court or the officer designated by the Lord Chancellor to whom a person makes payments in compliance with the order.

Amendments—AJA 1999, s 90, Sch 13, para 93; CPA 2004, s 261(1), Sch 27, para 58(1); Courts Act 2003, Sch 8, para 196.

****

PART V
SUPPLEMENTARY PROVISIONS
****

88 Interpretation

(1) In this Act –

...

"child", in relation to one or both of the parties to a marriage, includes a child whose father and mother were not married to each other at the time of his birth;

"child of the family", in relation to the parties to a marriage, means –

(a) a child of both of those parties; and

(b) any other child, not being a child who is placed with those parties as foster parents by a local authority or voluntary organisation, who has been treated by both of those parties as a child of their family;

"family proceedings" has the meaning assigned to it by section 65 of the Magistrates' Courts Act 1980;

"local authority" means the council of a county (other than a metropolitan county), of a metropolitan district or of a London borough, or the Common Council of the City of London;

"magistrates' court maintenance order" has the same meaning as in section 150(1) of the Magistrates' Courts Act 1980;

"maintenance calculation has the same meaning as it has in the Child Support Act 1991 by virtue of section 54 of that Act as read with any regulations in force under that section.

(2) References in this Act to the parties to a marriage living with each other shall be construed as references to their living with each other in the same household.

(3) For the avoidance of doubt it is hereby declared that references in this Act to remarriage include references to a marriage which is by law void or voidable.

(4) Anything authorised or required by this Act to be done by, to or before the magistrates' court by, to or before which any other thing was done, or is to be done, may be done by, to or before any magistrates' court acting in the same local justice area as that court.

(5) Any reference in this Act to an enactment shall be construed as a reference to that enactment as amended or extended by or under any subsequent enactment, including this Act.

Amendments—MCA 1980, s 154, Sch 7, para 167; Local Government Act 1985, s 12; FLRA 1987, Sch 2; CA 1989, ss 92, 108(5), (7), Sch 11, para 6, Sch 13, para 43, Sch 15; SI 1993/623; Justices of the Peace Act 1997, s 73(2), Sch 5, para 18; AJA 1999, s 106, Sch 15; CSPSSA 2000, s 26, Sch 3, para 4; Courts Act 2003, Sch 8, para 197.

****

Domicile and Matrimonial Proceedings Act 1973

1 Abolition of wife's dependent domicile

(1) Subject to subsection (2) below, the domicile of a married woman as at any time after the coming into force of this section shall, instead of being the same as her husband's by virtue only of marriage, be ascertained by reference to the same factors as in the case of any other individual capable of having an independent domicile.

(2) Where immediately before this section came into force a woman was married and then had her husband's domicile by dependence, she is to be treated as retaining that domicile (as a domicile of choice, if it is not also her domicile of origin) unless and until it is changed by acquisition or revival of another domicile either on or after the coming into force of this section.

(3) This section extends to England and Wales, Scotland and Northern Ireland.

Scope—A court's matrimonial jurisdiction is founded on "habitual residence" and "domicile" (s 5(2)). Originally, a wife shared the domicile of her husband, and domicile alone (as distinct from habitual residence) determined jurisdiction. This position was eased in 1937 and 1949, and, with effect from 1 January 1974, this section ensures that a wife's domicile is decided independently of that of her husband. At the time of the coming into operation of the Act, a woman's domicile of dependence (on her husband) was retained as her domicile of choice (if not also her domicile of origin) until her domicile was changed (s 1(2); *IRC v Duchess of Portland* (1982) 3 FLR 293; *Plummer v IRC* [1988] 1 WLR 292; see also **Domicile** under s 5).

Domicile—This term is used in the UK and the Republic of Ireland. Elsewhere, jurisdiction depends, where applicable, on a person being a national of the Member State (Council Regulation (EC) No 2201/2003 (Brussels IIA) – see Part VI).

****

3 Age at which independent domicile can be acquired

(1) The time at which a person first becomes capable of having an independent domicile shall be when he attains the age of sixteen or marries under that age; and in the case of a person who immediately before 1 January 1974 was incapable of having an independent domicile, but had then attained the age of sixteen or been married, it shall be that date.

(2) This section extends to England and Wales and Northern Ireland (but not to Scotland).

Scope—A child is attributed a domicile of origin at birth. However, a child's domicile of origin may be replaced by a domicile of dependence until the child first becomes capable of having an independent domicile at the age of 16 or by marrying under that age. The domicile of a legitimate, legitimated or adopted dependent child follows any change in the domicile of his father (*Henderson v Henderson* [1967] P 77; AA 1976, s 39; ACA 2002: s 67(1)). After the father's death, a child's domicile will generally follow any change in the mother's domicile (*Re Beaumont* [1893] 3 Ch 490). An illegitimate child is regarded as having a domicile of dependence being that of his mother (s 4(4)).

4 Dependent domicile of child not living with his father

(1) Subsection (2) of this section shall have effect with respect to the dependent domicile of a child as at any time after the coming into force of this section when his father and mother are alive but living apart.

(2) The child's domicile as at that time shall be that of his mother if –

    (a)   he then has his home with her and has no home with his father; or

    (b)   he has at any time had her domicile by virtue of paragraph (a) above and has not since had a home with his father.

(3) As at any time after the coming into force of this section, the domicile of a child whose mother is dead shall be that which she last had before she died if at her death he had her domicile by virtue of subsection (2) above and he has not since had a home with his father.

(4) Nothing in this section prejudices any existing rule of law as to the cases in which a child's domicile is regarded as being, by dependence, that of his mother.

(5) In this section, "child" means a person incapable of having an independent domicile.

(6) This section extends to England and Wales, Scotland and Northern Ireland.

Amendments—Children Act 1975, s 108(1)(b), Sch 4, Pt I.

Scope—Where the parents of a legitimate, legitimated or adopted child are living apart, the child's domicile will be that of his mother if he has his home with his mother and has no home with his father or if, having once acquired his mother's domicile in this way, he has not since had his home with his father (s 4(1),(2)). Where a dependent child has his mother's domicile under s 4 and she then dies, he retains his last domicile until he has a home with his father (in which case he takes his father's domicile) or acquires an independent domicile of choice (s 4(3)). The provisions of s 4 do not affect the position of an illegitimate child who is regarded as having the domicile of his mother by dependence (s 4(4)).

5 Jurisdiction of High Court and county courts

(1) Subsections (2) to (5) below shall have effect, subject to section 6(3) and (4) of this Act, with respect to the jurisdiction of the court to entertain –

    (a)   proceedings for divorce, judicial separation or nullity of marriage; and

    (b)   proceedings for death to be presumed and a marriage to be dissolved in pursuance of section 19 of the Matrimonial Causes Act 1973.

(1A) In this Part of this Act –

"the Council Regulation" means Council Regulation (EC) No 2201/2003 of 27 November 2003 concerning jurisdiction and the recognition and enforcement of judgments in matrimonial matters and matters of parental responsibility;

"Contracting State" means –

    (a)   a party to the Council Regulation, that is to say, Belgium, Cyprus, Czech Republic, Germany, Greece, Spain, Estonia, France, Hungary, Ireland, Italy, Latvia, Lithuania, Luxembourg, Malta, Netherlands, Austria, Poland, Portugal, Slovakia, Slovenia, Finland, Sweden and the United Kingdom, and

    (b)   a party which has subsequently adopted the Council Regulation; and "the court" means the High Court and a divorce county court within the meaning of Part V of the Matrimonial and Family Proceedings Act 1984.

(2) The court shall have jurisdiction to entertain proceedings for divorce or judicial separation if (and only if) –

    (a)   the court has jurisdiction under the Council Regulation; or

    (b)   no court of a Contracting State has jurisdiction under the Council Regulation and either of the parties to the marriage is domiciled in England and Wales on the date when the proceedings are begun.

(3) The court shall have jurisdiction to entertain proceedings for nullity of marriage if (and only if) –

    (a)   the court has jurisdiction under the Council Regulation; or

    (b)   no court of a Contracting State has jurisdiction under the Council Regulation and either of the parties to the marriage –

        (i)   is domiciled in England and Wales on the date when the proceedings are begun; or

        (ii)   died before that date and either was at death domiciled in England and Wales or had been habitually resident in England and Wales throughout the period of one year ending with the date of death.

(3A) *(repealed)*

(4) The court shall have jurisdiction to entertain proceedings for death to be presumed and a marriage to be dissolved if (and only if) the petitioner –

    (a)   is domiciled in England and Wales on the date when the proceedings are begun; or

    (b)   was habitually resident in England and Wales throughout the period of one year ending with that date.

(5) The court shall, at any time when proceedings are pending in respect of which it has jurisdiction by virtue of subsection (2) or (3) above (or of this subsection), also have jurisdiction to entertain other proceedings, in respect of the same marriage, for divorce, judicial separation or nullity of marriage, notwithstanding that jurisdiction would not be exercisable under subsection (2) or (3).

(6) Schedule 1 to this Act shall have effect as to the cases in which matrimonial proceedings in England and Wales are to be, or may be, stayed by the court where there are concurrent proceedings elsewhere in respect of the same marriage, and as to the other matters dealt with in that Schedule; but nothing in the Schedule –

    (a)   requires or authorises a stay of proceedings which are pending when this section comes into force; or

    (b)   prejudices any power to stay proceedings which is exercisable by the court apart from the Schedule.

(6A) Subsection (6) and Schedule 1, and any power as mentioned in subsection (6)(b), are subject to Article 19 of the Council Regulation.

Amendments—MFPA 1984, s 46(1), Sch 1, para 17; SI 2001/310; SI 2005/265.

Scope—This section provides the basis for jurisdiction in England and Wales for divorce, judicial separation, nullity and a decree of presumption of death and dissolution. In the case of divorce, judicial separation or nullity, jurisdiction is based primarily on Brussels IIA, Art 3 (ie by reference to the parties' habitual residence or joint domicile in England and Wales). The sole domicile of either party is not available as a basis for jurisdiction, unless no other EU Member State has jurisdiction (s 5(1)–(5)). In the case of a divorce petition issued after 18 June 2011 on the basis of the sole domicile of one party, the English/Welsh court will not have jurisdiction to hear a claim for "maintenance", unless the Maintenance Regulation, Art 3(a) or (b) can be relied upon (Maintenance Regulation, Art 3). The section also sets out the circumstances in which proceedings should be stayed where there are concurrent matrimonial

PART II

proceedings in another jurisdiction (s 5(6),(6A)). For the counterpart jurisdictional provisions relating to civil partnerships, see CPA 2004, ss 219–223 and the Civil Partnership (Jurisdiction and Recognition of Judgments) Regulations 2005, SI 2005/3334.

Domicile—Domicile may be "of origin", "of choice" or "of dependence". Domicile of origin is acquired at birth and from parents. Domicile of dependence is considered under ss 3 and 4. Domicile of choice places a burden of proof on the applicant, and involves persuading the court that a person's domicile has changed: "The burden of establishing a change of domicile – from a domicile of origin to a domicile of choice – is … a heavy one", per Stephen Brown LJ in *Cramer v Cramer* [1987] 1 FLR 116 at [120]. For further discussion of the law relating to domicile, see *The International Family Law Practice (2nd edn)* (Hodson; Jordan Publishing Ltd).

Habitual residence—This term is not defined by the Act. The leading decision in relation to the forum for divorce and finance is *Marinos v Marinos* [2007] 2 FLR 1018, in which Munby J (as he then was) held that habitual residence must be defined in accordance with EC law rather than domestic law. Habitual residence is defined differently for the purposes of Brussels IIA, Arts 8 and 10. *Marinos* was followed in *V v V (Divorce: Jurisdiction)* [2011] 2 FLR 778 in preference to *Munro v Munro* [2008] 1 FLR 1613. Habitual residence is more directed to a person's fixed centre of interest rather than length of residency. A person can have only one habitual residence at any one time, although a person can be resident in more than one country at any one time. Habitual residence can be lost and gained (akin to domicile) contemporaneously or virtually contemporaneously in the case of a planned, purposeful and permanent relocation from one country to another, especially where there is already existing simple residency (*Marinos*). The previous English case-law on residency and habitual residency still applies in non-EU cases. See, further, annotations to Brussels IIA, Art 3 (in Part VI) and *The International Family Law Practice (2nd edn)* (Hodson; Jordan Publishing Ltd), 6.3.

Stay of proceedings (s 5(6),(6A) and Form D8N (Notes))—A petitioner is obliged to state in her petition if there are proceedings in another jurisdiction and whether they concern the marriage or are capable of affecting its validity or subsistence (Sch 1, para 7). In the event of reference being made to such proceedings, the court gives consideration to staying the proceedings as follows:

(a) *Obligatory (Sch 1, para 8) (another UK jurisdiction)*   Where there are divorce/nullity proceedings within a "related jurisdiction" (Sch 1, para 3(2)) and where certain residence conditions apply, the court in divorce proceedings *must* stay any further proceedings on application by either party to the marriage; or

(b) *Discretionary (Sch 1, para 9; s 5(6A)) (non-UK, non-EU proceedings)*   Where there are matrimonial proceedings in another jurisdiction (other than another EU Member State), the question of a stay is discretionary. As to the balance of fairness test, see *Shemshadford v Shemshadford* [1981] 1 All ER 726; *Spiliada Maritime Corporation v Cansulex* [1997] AC 460, HL; *De Dampierre v De Dampierre* [1987] 2 FLR 300, HL; *Gadd v Gadd* [1985] FLR 220, CA; *Butler v Butler (Nos 1 and 2)* [1997] 2 FLR 311; *Otobo v Otobo* [2003] 1 FLR 192; *Ella v Ella* [2007] 2 FLR 35; *JKN v JCN (Divorce: Forum)* [2011] 1 FLR 826 (discretionary stays after Brussels IIA).

(c) *Mandatory (Brussels IIA), Art 19(1)) (proceedings in another EU Member State)*   Where there are proceedings relating to divorce, separation or nullity between the same parties in another EU Member State, the court second seised must of its own initiative stay proceedings until such time as the jurisdiction of the court first seised is established. See annotation to Brussels IIA, Arts 3 and 19.

While the stay subsists, the court still has powers to make certain financial relief orders and orders under CA 1989, s 8 (Sch 1, para 11). The stay may be discharged if it appears that the other proceedings are stayed or concluded or they have been unreasonably delayed by the party pursuing them (Sch 1, para 10).

See, generally, *The International Family Law Practice (2nd edn)* (Hodson; Jordan Publishing Ltd), Ch 5.

Applications for stay: procedure—An application for an obligatory or discretionary stay may be made with or without notice adopting the FPR 2010, Pt 18 procedure (see FPR 2010, r 7.27 and annotations thereto). The application is made initially to a district judge who may either deal with it himself or transfer to the High Court. An application for a stay should be made at the outset and before other significant steps have been taken in the proceedings (*Mansour v Mansour* [1989] 1 FLR 418). A delay carries a real risk that a stay will not be granted (*Krenge v Krenge* [1999] 1 FLR 969). The court may also order a discretionary stay on its own initiative under its inherent jurisdiction where there are proceedings in a concurrent jurisdiction. This power has not been abrogated by DMPA 1973 (s 5(6)(b)).

****

SCHEDULE 1
STAYING OF MATRIMONIAL PROCEEDINGS (ENGLAND AND WALES)

Interpretation

Corresponding stay provision for civil partnerships—The Family Procedure (Civil Partnership: Staying of Proceedings) Rules 2010 make corresponding provision for stay of civil partnership proceedings.

1 The following five paragraphs have effect for the interpretation of this Schedule.

2 "Matrimonial proceedings" means any proceedings so far as they are one or more of the five following kinds, namely, proceedings for –

divorce,
judicial separation,
nullity of marriage,
a declaration as to the validity of a marriage of the petitioner, and
a declaration as to the subsistence of such a marriage.

3 (1) "Another jurisdiction" means any country outside England and Wales.

(2) "Related jurisdiction" means any of the following countries, namely, Scotland, Northern Ireland, Jersey, Guernsey and the Isle of Man (the reference to Guernsey being treated as including Alderney and Sark).

4 (1) References to the trial or first trial in any proceedings do not include references to the separate trial of an issue as to jurisdiction only.

(2) For purposes of this Schedule, proceedings in the court are continuing if they are pending and not stayed.

5 Any reference in this Schedule to proceedings in another jurisdiction is to proceedings in a court of that jurisdiction, and to any other proceedings in that jurisdiction, which are of a description prescribed for the purposes of this paragraph; and provision may be made by rules of court as to when proceedings of any description in another jurisdiction are continuing for the purposes of this Schedule.

6 "Prescribed" means prescribed by rules of court.

7 Duty to furnish particulars of concurrent proceedings in another jurisdiction

While matrimonial proceedings are pending in the court in respect of a marriage and the trial or first trial in those proceedings has not begun, it shall be the duty of any person who is a petitioner in the proceedings, or is a respondent and has in his answer included a prayer for relief to furnish, in such manner and to such persons and on such occasions as may be prescribed, such particulars as may be prescribed of any proceedings which –

(a) he knows to be continuing in another jurisdiction; and
(b) are in respect of that marriage or capable of affecting its validity or subsistence.

8 Obligatory stays

(1) Where before the beginning of the trial or first trial in any proceedings for divorce which are continuing in the court it appears to the court on the application of a party to the marriage –

    (a)   that in respect of the same marriage proceedings for divorce or nullity of marriage are continuing in a related jurisdiction; and

    (b)   that the parties to the marriage have resided together after its celebration; and

    (c)   that the place where they resided together when the proceedings in the court were begun or, if they did not then reside together, where they last resided together before those proceedings were begun, is in that jurisdiction; and

    (d)   that either of the said parties was habitually resident in that jurisdiction throughout the year ending with the date on which they last resided together before the date on which the proceedings in the court were begun,

it shall be the duty of the court, subject to paragraph 10(2) below, to order that the proceedings in the court be stayed.

(2) References in sub-paragraph (1) above to the proceedings in the court are, in the case of proceedings which are not only proceedings for divorce, to the proceedings so far as they are proceedings for divorce.

Defined term—"related jurisdiction": para 3(2).

Note—See annotation to s 5.

9 Discretionary stays

(1) Where before the beginning of the trial or first trial in any matrimonial proceedings, other than proceedings governed by the Council Regulation, which are continuing in the court it appears to the court –

    (a)   that any proceedings in respect of the marriage in question, or capable of affecting its validity or subsistence, are continuing in another jurisdiction; and

    (b)   that the balance of fairness (including convenience) as between the parties to the marriage is such that it is appropriate for the proceedings in that jurisdiction to be disposed of before further steps are taken in the proceedings in the court or in those proceedings so far as they consist of a particular kind of matrimonial proceedings,

the court may then, if it thinks fit, order that the proceedings in the court be stayed or, as the case may be, that those proceedings be stayed so far as they consist of proceedings of that kind.

(2) In considering the balance of fairness and convenience for the purposes of sub-paragraph (1)(b) above, the court shall have regard to all factors appearing to be relevant, including the convenience of witnesses and any delay or expense which may result from the proceedings being stayed, or not being stayed.

(3) In the case of any proceedings so far as they are proceeding for divorce, the court shall not exercise the power conferred on it by sub-paragraph (1) above while an application under paragraph 8 above in respect of the proceedings is pending.

(4) If, at any time after the beginning of the trial or first trial in any matrimonial proceedings which are pending in the court, the court declares by order that it is satisfied that a person has failed to perform the duty imposed on him in respect of the proceedings by paragraph 7 above, sub-paragraph (1) above shall have effect in relation to those proceedings and, to the other proceedings by reference to which the declaration is made, as if the words "before the beginning of the trial or first trial" were omitted; but no action shall lie in respect of the failure of a person to perform such a duty.

Amendments—SI 2001/310.

Defined term—"another jurisdiction": para 3(1).

Note—See annotation to s 5.

10 Supplementary

(1) Where an order staying any proceedings is in force in pursuance of paragraph 8 or 9 above, the court may, if it thanks fit, on the application of a party to the proceedings, discharge the order if it appears to the court that the other proceedings by reference to which the order was made are stayed or concluded, or that a party to those other proceedings has delayed unreasonably in prosecuting them.

(2) If the court discharges an order staying any proceedings and made in pursuance of paragraph 8 above, the court shall not again stay those proceedings in pursuance of that paragraph.

11 (1) The provisions of sub-paragraphs (2) and (3) below shall apply (subject to sub-paragraph (4)) where proceedings for divorce, judicial separation or nullity of marriage are stayed by reference to proceedings in a related jurisdiction for divorce, judicial separation of nullity of marriage; and in this paragraph –

"lump sum order" means such an order as is mentioned in paragraph (f) of section 23(1) of the Matrimonial Causes Act 1973 (lump sum payment for children), being an order made under section 23(1) or (2)(a) or an order made in equivalent circumstances under Schedule 1 to the Children Act 1989 and of a kind mentioned in paragraph 1(2)(c) of that Schedule;

"the other proceedings", in relation to any stayed proceedings, means the proceedings in another jurisdiction by reference to which the stay was imposed; "relevant order" means –

    (a)   an order under section 22 of the Matrimonial Causes Act 1973 (maintenance for spouse pending suit),

    (b)   such an order as is mentioned in paragraph (d) or (e) of section 23(1) of that Act (periodical payments for children) being an order made under section 23(1) or (2)(a) or an order in equivalent circumstances under Schedule 1 to the Children Act 1989 and of a kind mentioned in paragraph 1(2)(a) or (b) of that Schedule,

    (c)   an order under section 42(1)(a) of that Act (orders for the custody and education of children) or a section 8 order under the Children Act 1989, and

    (d)   except for the purposes of sub-paragraph (3) below, any order restraining a person removing a child out of England and Wales or out of the care of another person; and

"stayed" means stayed in pursuance of this Schedule.

(2) Where any proceedings are stayed, then, without prejudice to the effect of the stay apart from this paragraph –

(a)   the court shall not have power to make a relevant order or a lump sum order in connection with the stayed proceedings except in pursuance of paragraph (c) below; and

(b)   subject to paragraph (c) below, any relevant order made in connection with the stayed proceedings shall, unless the stay is previously removed or the order previously discharged, cease to have effect on the expiration of the period of three months beginning with the date on which the stay was imposed; but

(c)   if the court considers that, for the purpose of dealing with circumstances needing to be dealt with urgently, it is necessary during or after that period to make a relevant order or a lump sum order in connection with the stayed proceedings or to extend or further extend the duration of a relevant order made in connection with the stayed proceedings, the court may do so and the order shall not cease to have effect by virtue of paragraph (b) above.

(3) Where any proceedings are stayed and at the time when the stay is imposed an order is in force, or at a subsequent time an order comes into force, which was made in connection with the other proceedings and provides for any of the following matters, namely, periodical payments for a spouse of the marriage in question, periodical payments for a child, or any provision which could be made by a section 8 order under the Children Act 1989 then, on the imposition of the stay in a case where the order is in force when the stay is imposed and on the coming into force of the order in any other case –

(a)   any relevant order made in connection with the stayed proceedings shall cease to have effect in so far as it makes for a spouse or child any provision for any of those matters as respects which the same or different provision for that spouse or child is made by the other order;

(b)   the court shall not have power in connection with the stayed proceedings to make a relevant order containing for a spouse or child provision for any of those matters as respects which any provision for that spouse or child is made by the other order; and

(c)   if the other order contains provision for periodical payments for a child, the court shall not have power in connection with the stayed proceedings to make a lump sum order for that child.

(3A) Where any such order as is mentioned in paragraph (e) of section 23(1) of the Matrimonial Causes Act 1973, being an order made under section 23(1) or (2)(a) of that Act, ceases to have effect by virtue of sub-paragraph (2) or (3) above, any order made under section 24A(1) of the Act which requires the proceeds of sale of property to be used for securing periodical payments under the first mentioned order shall also cease to have effect.

(4) If any proceedings are stayed so far as they consist of matrimonial proceedings of a particular kind but are not stayed so far as they consist of matrimonial proceedings of a different kind, sub-paragraphs (2) and (3) above shall not apply to the proceedings but, without prejudice to the effect of the stay apart from this paragraph, the court shall not have power to make a relevant order or a lump sum order in connection with the proceedings so far as they are stayed; and in this sub-paragraph references to matrimonial proceedings do not include proceedings for a declaration.

(4A) Sub-paragraph (4B) applies where –

(a)   proceedings are stayed as described in sub-paragraph (1), and

(b)   at the time when the stay is imposed, a contact order (within the meaning of the Children Act 1989) made in connection with the stayed proceedings is in force.

(4B) While the stay applies to the proceedings, the court may not –

(a) make an enforcement order (within the meaning of the Children Act 1989) in relation to the contact order, or

(b) as regards an enforcement order already made in relation to the contact order, exercise its powers under paragraph 9(2) of Schedule A1 to the Children Act 1989 in relation to the enforcement order.

(5) Except as provided in sub-paragraph (4B), nothing in this paragraph affects any power of the court –

(a) to vary or discharge a relevant order so far as the order is for the time being in force; or

(b) to enforce a relevant order as respects any period when it is or was in force; or

(c) to make a relevant order or a lump sum order in connection with proceedings which were but are no longer stayed.

Amendments—Matrimonial Homes and Property Act 1981, s 8(3); CA 1989, s 108(5),(7), Sch 13, para 33, Sch 15; CAA 2006, s 15(1), Sch 2, paras 1, 12.

Family Law Act 1986

ARRANGEMENT OF SECTIONS

PART I
CHILD CUSTODY

Chapter I
Preliminary

PART II
RECOGNITION OF DIVORCES, ANNULMENTS AND LEGAL SEPARATIONS

Divorces, annulments and judicial separations granted in the British Islands

Overseas divorces, annulments and legal separations

Supplemental

PART I
CHILD CUSTODY

Chapter I
Preliminary

1 Orders to which Part I applies

(1) Subject to the following provisions of this section, in this Part "Part I order" means –

    (a)   a section 8 order made by a court in England and Wales under the Children Act 1989, other than an order varying or discharging such an order;

    (aa) a special guardianship order made by a court in England and Wales under the Children Act 1989;

    (ab) an order made under section 26 of the Adoption and Children Act 2002 (contact), other than an order varying or revoking such an order;

    (b)   an order made by a court of civil jurisdiction in Scotland under any enactment or rule of law with respect to the residence, custody, care or control of a child, contact with or access to a child or the education or upbringing of a child, excluding –

        (i)   an order committing the care of a child to a local authority or placing a child under the supervision of a local authority;

        (ii), (iii) *(repealed)*

        (iv) an order giving parental responsibilities and parental rights in relation to a child made in the course of proceedings for the adoption of the child (other than an order made following the making of a direction under section 53(1) of the Children Act 1975);

        (v)   an order made under the Education (Scotland) Act 1980;

        (vi) an order made under Part II and III of the Social Work (Scotland) Act 1968;

        (vii) an order made under the Child Abduction and Custody Act 1985;

        (viii) an order for the delivery of a child or other order for the enforcement of a Part I order;

        (ix) an order relating to the guardianship of a child;

        (x)   an adoption order (as defined in section 28(1) of the Adoption and Children (Scotland) Act 2007);

        (xi) a permanence order (as defined in subsection (2) of section 80 of that Act) which includes provision such as is mentioned in paragraph (c) of that subsection.

    (c)   an Article 8 order made by a court in Northern Ireland under the Children (Northern Ireland) Order 1995, other than an order varying or discharging such an order;

    (d)   an order made by a court in England and Wales in the exercise of the inherent jurisdiction of the High Court with respect to children –

> > (i)   so far as it gives care of a child to any person or provides for contact with, or the education of, a child; but
> > (ii) excluding an order varying or revoking such an order;
> (e) an order made by the High Court in Northern Ireland in the exercise of its inherent jurisdiction with respect to children –
> > (i)   so far as it gives care of a child to any person or provides for contact with, or the education of, a child; but
> > (ii) excluding an order varying or discharging such an order;
> (f) an order made by a court in a specified dependent territory corresponding to an order within paragraphs (a) to (e) above.

(2) In this Part "Part I order" does not include –

> (a)–(c)   (repealed)

(3) In this Part, "Part I order" –

> (a) includes any order which would have been a custody order by virtue of this section in any form in which it was in force at any time before its amendment by the Children Act 1989 or the Children (Northern Ireland) Order 1995, as the case may be; and
> (b) (subject to sections 32 and 40 of this Act) excludes any order which would have been excluded from being a custody order by virtue of this section in any such form, and
> (c) excludes any order falling within subsection (1)(f) above made before the date specified opposite the name of the territory concerned in Column 2 of Schedule 1 to the Family Law Act 1986 (Dependent Territories) Order 1991, as from time to time in force.

(3A) In subsection (1)(b)(xi) "permanence order" includes a deemed permanence order having effect by virtue of article 13(1), 14(2), 17(1) or 19(2) of the Adoption and Children (Scotland) Act 2007 (Commencement No 4, Transitional and Savings Provisions) Order 2009.

(6) Provision may be made by act of sederunt prescribing, in relation to orders within subsection (1)(b) above, what constitutes an application for the purposes of this Part.

Amendments—CA 1989, s 108, Sch 13, paras 62, 63, Sch 15; Age of Legal Capacity (Scotland) Act 1991, s 10(1), Sch 1, para 44; SI 1991/1723; Children (Scotland) Act 1995, s 105(4), Sch 4, para 41; SI 1995/756; ACA 2002, Sch 3, para 47; SI 2011/1740.

"order made by a court in a specified dependent territory" (s 1(1)(f))—See FLA 1986(DT)O 1991, Sch 3. See also FPR 2010, r 32.23.

"date specified ... Family Law Act 1986 (Dependent Territories) Order 1991" (s 1(3)(c))—The only territory currently named in Schedule 1 to that Order is the Isle of Man, and the relevant date specified is 14 October 1991.

Care orders and supervision orders under CA 1989, Pt IV—See under s 2.

Chapter II
Jurisdiction of Courts in England and Wales

2 Jurisdiction: general

(1) A court in England and Wales shall not make a section 1(1)(a) order with respect to a child unless –

> (a) it has jurisdiction under the Council Regulation or the Hague Convention, or
> (b) neither the Council Regulation nor the Hague Convention applies but –
> > (i)   the question of making the order arises in or in connection with

matrimonial proceedings or civil partnership proceedings and the condition in section 2A of this Act is satisfied, or

    (ii)   the condition in section 3 of this Act is satisfied.

(2) (*repealed*)

(2A) A court in England and Wales shall not have jurisdiction to make a special guardianship order under the Children Act 1989 unless the condition in section 3 of this Act is satisfied.

(2B) A court in England and Wales shall not have jurisdiction to make an order under section 26 of the Adoption and Children Act 2002 unless the condition in section 3 of this Act is satisfied.

(3) A court in England and Wales shall not make a section 1(1)(d) order unless –

    (a)   it has jurisdiction under the Council Regulation or the Hague Convention, or

    (b)   neither the Council Regulation nor the Hague Convention applies but –

        (i)   the condition in section 3 of this Act is satisfied, or

        (ii)   the child concerned is present in England and Wales on the relevant date and the court considers that the immediate exercise of its powers is necessary for his protection.

Amendments—CA 1989, s 108(5), Sch 13, para 64; SI 2001/310; SI 2005/165; ACA 2002, Sch 3, para 47; SI 2005/3336; SI 2010/1898.

Defined terms—"child": ss 7, 42(4); "corresponding dependent territory order": s 42(1); "the Council Regulation": s 42(1); "matrimonial proceedings", "relevant date": s 7; "specified dependent territory": s 42(1).

Matrimonial proceedings (s 2(1))—In matrimonial proceedings, a court in England and Wales only has jurisdiction to make an order under CA 1989, s 8 (other than an order varying or discharging a s 8 order) where the conditions in FLA 1986, s 2A are satisfied. The mere fact that a court in England and Wales had jurisdiction in respect of the parents' divorce proceedings did not establish jurisdiction in relation to issues of parental responsibility, concerning children who were habitually resident in another EU country in the absence of the unequivocal consent of both parents to the same. The scheme of Brussels IIA, was to ensure that jurisdiction rested with the courts of the child's habitual residence (*Bush v Bush* [2008] 2 FLR 1437, CA).

Non-matrimonial proceedings (s 2(2))—In non-matrimonial proceedings, a court in England and Wales has jurisdiction to make orders under CA 1989, s 8 (other than an order varying or discharging a s 8 order) only where the child is either habitually resident in England and Wales, or is present in England and Wales and is not habitually resident in any part of the UK or a specified territory, and the court's jurisdiction is not excluded by FLA 1986, s 3(2). The court has no jurisdiction derived simply from the fact that the child is a British National (*Al Habtoor v Fotheringham* [2001] 1 FLR 951). In *Re S (Residence Order: Forum Conveniens)* [1995] 1 FLR 314, an English court had no jurisdiction to entertain an application for a residence order in respect of a child who was habitually resident in Holland and who had not been present in England and Wales at the date of issue of the application; however, in that case, the court retained jurisdiction to specify or define conditions in a residence order which had been granted before the child moving to Holland. See also *D v D (Custody: Jurisdiction)* [1996] 1 FLR 574, which was held to be a non-matrimonial case because, at the relevant date as defined in s 7(c) (ie the date on which the s 8 application was made), there were no divorce proceedings in existence anywhere. A court in England and Wales is not excluded from making parental responsibility orders under CA 1989, s 4 in respect of children who are not born in and do not live in the jurisdiction (*Re S (Parental Responsibility: Jurisdiction)* [1998] 2 FLR 921).

Care orders and supervision orders under CA 1989, Pt IV—The legislation is silent as to the jurisdictional basis for the making of applications for care orders and supervision orders. However, in *Re R (Care Orders: Jurisdiction)* [1995] 1 FLR 711, Singer J held that the jurisdictional basis for an application under CA 1989, Pt IV was the same as that in relation to applications under CA 1989, s 8, namely that, for the court to have jurisdiction to entertain a local authority's application under Pt IV, the child concerned should either be habitually resident in England and Wales or present in England and Wales at the relevant time (see FLA 1986, s 3). Singer J's approach was followed in *Re M (Care Orders: Jurisdiction)* [1997] 1 FLR 456 and *Lewisham London Borough Council v D (Criteria for Territorial Jurisdiction in Public Law Proceedings)* [2008] 2 FLR 1449.

Proceedings under the inherent jurisdiction (s 2(3))—See also s 3 and *B v B (Scottish Contact Order: Jurisdiction to Vary)* [1996] 1 FLR 688. The inclusion of the exercise of the inherent jurisdiction within the orders which can be made in s 1(1)(d) gives the English court the jurisdiction to make orders in respect of a child, provided he is habitually resident in England and Wales, even if he is an alien and not physically within the jurisdiction at the start of the proceedings (*Re S (Custody: Habitual Residence)* [1998] 1 FLR 122). However, in *Re BRB v FB and MA (Forced Marriage: Wardship: Jurisdiction)* [2008] 2 FLR 1624, Hogg J made a 15 year old a ward of court and made orders for her to come to the UK, even though she was not present in the jurisdiction at the time of the order nor habitually resident in the UK. Her only connection to the UK was that her deceased father had been a British national. The judge held that the very dire circumstances in which the child found herself, namely the victim of a proposed forced marriage, justified the making of the order when the child wanted to leave Pakistan to join her half brother in the UK and the FCO had indicated its willingness to assist provided there were court orders in place. Where the child is not present in the UK and jurisdiction is claimed solely on the basis of the child's British nationality, the Court of Appeal held that, although the limits of the jurisdiction are not definitely set down, if such jurisdiction exists, it is only in extreme circumstances: *Re N (Abduction: Appeal)* [2013] 1 FLR 457.

Section 2(3)(b) has been used to make mirror orders required for the implementation of orders made in a USA court, in respect of a child resident in the USA, allowing contact to take place in England – see *Re P (A Child: Mirror Orders)* [2000] 1 FLR 435 where Singer J held that it was a very small step from the wording of s 2(3)(b) to make an order which expressly only had currency as far as the English courts were concerned while the child was present in the jurisdiction for the purposes of contact. In that context, assistance was to be derived from the general power of the court to make orders in anticipation of the institution of formal process. Singer J indicated that the jurisdiction should be invoked economically, and after appropriate investigation, and should be reserved to judges of the Family Division.

Brussels IIA—Jurisdiction primarily depended on whether Brussels IIA applied and only if it did not did the court's jurisdiction depend on either habitual residence or physical presence: *Re A (Removal Outside Jurisdiction: Habitual Residence)* [2011] 1 FLR 2025.

Child resident outside EU—In appropriate circumstances the UK courts may have jurisdiction under Brussels IIA to determine the future of a child who is habitually outside the EU where the parties have unequivocally accepted the jurisdiction of the UK courts at the date the court is seised of the matter: *Re I (A Child)* [2010] 1 FLR 361; see the notes to Article 12 of the Convention.

2A Jurisdiction in or in connection with matrimonial proceedings or civil partnership proceedings

(1) The condition referred to in section 2(1) of this Act is that the proceedings are proceedings in respect of the marriage or civil partnership of the parents of the child concerned and –

    (a)   the proceedings –
        (i)   are proceedings for divorce or nullity of marriage or dissolution or annulment of a civil partnership, and
        (ii) are continuing;
    (b)   the proceedings –
        (i)   are proceedings for judicial separation or legal separation of civil partner,
        (ii) are continuing,
    and the jurisdiction of the court is not excluded by subsection (2) below; or
    (c)   the proceedings have been dismissed after the beginning of the trial but –
        (i)   the section 1(1)(a) order is being made forthwith, or
        (ii) the application for the order was made on or before the dismissal.

(2) For the purposes of subsection (1)(b) above, the jurisdiction of the court is excluded if –

    (a)   after the grant of a decree of judicial separation, on the relevant date, proceedings for divorce or nullity in respect of the marriage, or
    (b)   after the making of a separation order, on the relevant date, proceedings for the dissolution or annulment in respect of the civil partnership,

are continuing in Scotland or Northern Ireland.

(3) Subsection (2) above shall not apply if the court in which the other proceedings there referred to are continuing has made –

(a) an order under section 13(6) or 19A(4) of this Act (not being an order made by virtue of section 13(6)(a)(i)), or a corresponding dependent territory order, or

(b) an order under section 14(2) or 22(2) of this Act, or a corresponding dependent territory order, which is recorded as being made for the purpose of enabling Part I proceedings to be taken in England and Wales with respect to the child concerned.

(4) Where a court –

(a) has jurisdiction to make a section 1(1)(a) order by virtue of section 2(1)(b)(i) of this Act, but

(b) considers that it would be more appropriate for Part I matters relating to the child to be determined outside England and Wales,

the court may by order direct that, while the order under this subsection is in force, no section 1(1)(a) order shall be made by any court by virtue of section 2(1)(b)(i) of this Act.

Amendments—Inserted by CA 1989, s 108(5), Sch 13, para 64; amended by SI 1991/1723; SI 1995/756; SI 2005/265; SI 2005/3336.

Defined terms—"child": ss 7, 42(4); "corresponding dependent territory order": s 42(1) (and see notes to s 42); "matrimonial proceedings": s 7; "Part I proceedings", "Part I matters": s 42(7); "relevant date": s 7; "specified dependent territory": s 42(1) (and see notes to s 42).

General interpretation—See s 42 in the case of Pt I of the Act.

"proceedings ... are continuing"—Although proceedings may be continuing and the decree absolute not yet pronounced, the court would decline jurisdiction if the continuance would not impinge on the children because the children's issues had already been decided. Where that was the case and international considerations arose, no encouragement should be given to reopening that issue within a comparatively short time. Nevertheless, the court would have jurisdiction if an urgent and serious issue arose over child protection (*Re L (Residence: Jurisdiction)* [2007] 1 FLR 1686).

"dependent territory" (s 2A(3))—Within the meaning of the British Nationality Act 1981, this term is to be read as a reference to "British overseas territory" (see British Overseas Territories Act 2002, s 1(2))

Discretion to make order under s 2A(4)—Where the English court in principle has jurisdiction over the living arrangements for a child by reason of current divorce proceedings between the child's parents, which fact would normally deprive courts in Scotland of jurisdiction, the English court nevertheless has a discretion contained in s 2A(4) to order that it would be more appropriate for matters relating to that child to be decided in Scotland (*Re S (Jurisdiction to Stay Application)* [1995] 1 FLR 1093 – where in reality the child had been looked after in Scotland for many years by her maternal grandmother).

Residual jurisdiction—To fall within the "residual jurisdiction" of ss 2 and 2A as a question connected with matrimonial or civil partnership proceedings, there must be a proximity between the divorce proceedings and the court being asked to determine a question of making an order in relation to children: *AP v TD (Relocation: Retention of Jurisdiction)* [2011] 1 FLR 1851.

3 Habitual residence or presence of child

(1) The condition referred to in section 2(1)(b)(ii) of this Act is that on the relevant date the child concerned –

(a) is habitually resident in England and Wales, or

(b) is present in England and Wales and is not habitually resident in any part of the United Kingdom or a specified dependent territory,

and, in either case, the jurisdiction of the court is not excluded by subsection (2) below.

(2) For the purposes of subsection (1) above, the jurisdiction of the court is excluded if, on the relevant date, matrimonial proceedings or civil partnership proceedings are

continuing in a court in Scotland, Northern Ireland or a specified dependent territory in respect of the marriage or civil partnership of the parents of the child concerned.

(3) Subsection (2) above shall not apply if the court in which the other proceedings there referred to are continuing has made –

    (a) an order under section 13(6) or 19A(4) of this Act (not being an order made by virtue of section 13(6)(a)(i)), or a corresponding dependent territory order, or

    (b) an order under section 14(2) or 22(2) of this Act, or a corresponding dependent territory order, which is recorded as made for the purpose of enabling Part I proceedings with respect to the child concerned to be taken in England and Wales,

and that order is in force.

(4)–(6) *(repealed)*

Amendments—CA 1989, s 108(5),(7) Sch 13, paras 62, 65, Sch 15; SI 1991/1723; SI 1995/756; SI 2005/265; SI 2005/3336.

Defined terms—"child": ss 7, 42(4); "corresponding dependent territory order": s 42(1); "matrimonial proceedings": s 7; "Part I proceedings", "Part I matters": s 42(7); "relevant date": s 7; "specified dependent territory": s 42(1).

General interpretation—See s 42.

"proceedings are continuing"—Section 3(2) proceedings are not continuing if they have been stayed (*Re B (Court's Jurisdiction)* [2004] 2 FLR 741).

"habitually resident" (s 3(1)(a))—There is no statutory definition of habitual residence, and its meaning is essentially a question of fact to be determined by reference to all the circumstances of a particular case. See **Habitual residence** under CACA 1985, Sch 1, Art 4. The Court of Appeal has clearly and helpfully summarised the firmly established principles in relation to the issue of habitual residence: *Re P-J (Abduction: Habitual Residence: Consent)* [2009] 2 FLR 1051, at [26]. Habitual residence could not be founded, in respect of a child who had never been to England, on the grounds that her father was a British national and at the time of her birth her mother had a settled intention to live and become habitually resident in England: *H v H (Jurisdiction to Grant Wardship)* [2012] 1 FLR 23. Habitual residence required the child to have been physically present within the jurisdiction at some point: *ZA & PA v NA* [2012] EWCA Civ 1396.

****

5 Power of court to refuse application or stay proceedings

(1) A court in England and Wales which has jurisdiction to make a Part I order may refuse an application for the order in any case where the matter in question has already been determined in proceedings outside England and Wales.

(2) Where, at any stage of the proceedings on an application made to a court in England and Wales for a Part I order, or for the variation of a Part I order, it appears to the court –

    (a) that proceedings with respect to the matters to which the application relates are continuing outside England and Wales,

    (b) that it would be more appropriate for those matters to be determined in proceedings to be taken outside England and Wales,

    (c) that it should exercise its powers under Article 15 of the Council Regulation (transfer to a court better placed to hear the case), or

    (d) that it should exercise its powers under Article 8 of the Hague Convention (request to authority in another Contracting State to assume jurisdiction),

the court may stay the proceedings on the application or (as the case may be) exercise its powers under Article 15 of the Council Regulation or Article 8 of the Hague Convention.

(2A) If the proceedings on the application are proceedings in which a contact activity direction has been made under section 11A of the Children Act 1989 (or an enforcement order has been made under section 11J of that Act), the court may when granting a stay under or by virtue of subsection (2) also suspend the contact activity direction (or the enforcement order).

(3) The court may remove a stay granted by virtue of subsection (2)(a) or (b) above if it appears to the court that there has been unreasonable delay in the taking or prosecution of the other proceedings referred to in that subsection, or that those proceedings are stayed, sisted or concluded.

(3A) The court may remove a stay granted under Article 15 of the Council Regulation only in accordance with that Article.

(3AA) The court may remove a stay granted in order for it to exercise its powers under Article 8 of the Hague Convention, and withdraw any request made by it to an authority in another Contracting State to assume jurisdiction, if –

    (a) the authority in the other Contracting State does not assume jurisdiction within the period for which the court granted the stay, or

    (b) the parties do not, within the period specified by the court, request the authority in the other Contracting State to assume jurisdiction.

(3B) If the stay removed under subsection (3), (3A) or (3AA) is a stay in relation to which the court suspended a contact activity direction made under section 11A of the Children Act 1989 (or an enforcement order made under section 11J of that Act), the court may when removing the stay under subsection (3) or (3A) also bring the suspension to an end.

(4) Nothing in this section so far as it relates to proceedings not governed by the Council Regulation shall affect any power exercisable apart from this section to refuse an application or to grant or remove a stay.

Amendments—CA 1989, s 108(5), Sch 13, para 62; SI 2001/310; SI 2005/265; CAA 2006, s 15(1), Sch 2, paras 2, 3; SI 2010/1898.

Defined terms—"Part I order": ss 1(2),(3), 42(5),(6).

General interpretation—See s 42.

"the court may stay the proceedings" (s 5(2))—In *H v H (Minors) (Forum Conveniens) (Nos 1 and 2)* [1993] 1 FLR 958, an application was made under s 5(2). In *Re V (Forum Conveniens)* [2005] 1 FLR 718 the court reviewed many of the authorities and held that: (a) the principles to be applied were those set out in *Spiliada Maritime Corporation v Cansulex* [1997] AC 460; and (b) the child's interests were not paramount (but were nonetheless very important), because a choice between international jurisdictions was not "a question with respect to the upbringing of a child" within the meaning of CA 1989 s 1(1)(a). Where an application for a stay coincided with an application to return to South Africa, in which interests of the child were paramount, the two applications stood or fell together and the correct approach was to apply the paramountcy principle and decide whether it was in the child's best interests to return to South Africa; and then, if so, to cross-check whether the criteria for a stay were satisfied: *M v M (Stay of Proceedings: Return of Children)* [2006] 1 FLR 138.

In *Re S (A Minor) (Stay of Proceedings)* [1993] 2 FLR 912, the Court of Appeal upheld a decision to grant a stay of English proceedings instituted by the father for residence and contact orders because similar proceedings were already in existence in Scotland. Furthermore, the Court of Appeal approved his decision to allow the father's application for a parental responsibility order to proceed in England. A parental responsibility order was not within the definition of "Part I order" under FLA 1986 and the statutory provisions did not apply. However, the court still retained an inherent power to stay proceedings in appropriate cases. In *H v H (A Minor) (No 2) (Forum Conveniens)* [1997] 1 FCR 603 Bracewell J held that the court could act of its own volition, irrespective of whether or not a party had applied for a stay. A stay should not be granted unless it is demonstrated that a more appropriate forum is available elsewhere (*M v B (Residence)* [1994] 2 FLR 819). Where the application for a Pt I order is in the context of matrimonial proceedings, see also DMPA 1973, Sch 1, paras 8 and 9, above. By virtue of FLA 1986, s 5(2) and DMPA 1973, Sch 1, para 9 the court *may* stay proceedings if either FLA 1986, s 5(2)(a) or (b) is satisfied. However, under DMPA 1973, Sch 1, para 8 the court is obliged to stay proceedings if the parties resided in a related jurisdiction and either of them was habitually resident there for 1 year before they separated. For further guidance, see *M v M (Abduction: England and Scotland)* [1997] 2 FLR 263, where it was held that the same jurisdiction should deal both with the dissolution of the marriage and the consequential decisions regarding the welfare of the children. In relation to the applicability of Art 15, see *A v B (Jurisdiction)* [2012] 1 FLR 768.

The Inner House of the Court of Session has recently held that the test for forum non conveniens was not the practical convenience of the witnesses, but whether the alternative forum contended for was one in which the case may be tried more suitably for the interests of all of the parties and the ends of justice. It concluded that the Scottish courts had jurisdiction as of right which jurisdiction could be abdicated only in exceptional circumstances (*RAB v MIB* [2009] 1 FLR 602).

6 Duration and variation of custody orders

(1) If a Part I order made by a court in Scotland, Northern Ireland or a specified dependent territory (or a variation of such an order) comes into force with respect to child at a time when a Part I order made by a court in England and Wales has effect with respect to him, the latter order shall cease to have effect so far as it makes provision for any matter for which the same or different provision is made by (or by the variation of) the order made by the court in Scotland, Northern Ireland or the territory.

(2) Where by virtue of subsection (1) above a Part I order has ceased to have effect so far as it makes provision for any matter, a court in England or Wales shall not have jurisdiction to vary that order so as to make provision for that matter.

(3) A court in England and Wales shall not have jurisdiction to vary a Part I order if, on the relevant date, matrimonial proceedings or civil partnership proceedings are continuing in Scotland, Northern Ireland or a specified dependent territory in respect of the marriage or civil partnership of the parents of the child concerned.

(3A) Subsection (3) above shall not apply if –

    (a) the Part I order was made in or in connection with proceedings –
        (i) for divorce or nullity in England and Wales in respect of the marriage of the parents of the child concerned; or
        (ii) for dissolution or annulment in England and Wales in respect of the civil partnership of the parents of the child concerned; and
    (b) those proceedings are continuing.

(3B) Subsection (3) above shall not apply if –

    (a) the Part I order was made in or in connection with proceedings –
        (i) for judicial separation in England and Wales; or
        (ii) for a separation order in England and Wales; and
    (b) those proceedings are continuing; and
    (c) as the case may be, the decree of judicial separation has not yet been granted or the separation order has not yet been made.

(4) Subsection (3) above shall not apply if the court in which the proceedings there referred to are continuing has made –

    (a) an order under section 13(6) or 19A(4) of this Act (not being an order made by virtue of section 13(6)(a)(i)), or a corresponding dependent territory order, or
    (b) an order under section 14(2) or 22(2) of this Act, or a corresponding dependent territory order, which is recorded as made for the purpose of enabling Part I proceedings with respect to the child concerned to be taken in England and Wales,

and that order is in force.

(5) Subsection (3) above shall not apply in the case of a variation of section 1(1)(d) order if the child concerned is present in England and Wales on the relevant date and the court considers that the immediate exercise of its powers is necessary for his protection.

(6) Subsection (7) below applies where a Part I order which is –

(a) a residence order (within the meaning of the Children Act 1989) in favour of a person with respect to a child,

(b) an order made in the exercise of the High Court's inherent jurisdiction with respect to children by virtue of which a person has care of a child, or

(c) an order –

(i) of a kind mentioned in section 1(3)(a) of this Act,

(ii) under which a person is entitled to the actual possession of a child,

ceases to have effect in relation to that person by virtue of subsection (1) above.

(7) Where this subsection applies, any family assistance order made under section 16 of the Children Act 1989 with respect to the child shall also cease to have effect.

(8) For the purposes of subsection (7) above the references to a family assistance order under section 16 of the Children Act 1989 shall be deemed to include a reference to an order for the supervision of a child made under –

(a) section 7(4) of the Family Law Reform Act 1969,

(b) section 44 of the Matrimonial Causes Act 1973,

(c) section 2(2)(a) of the Guardianship Act 1973,

(d) section 34(5) or 36(3)(b) of the Children Act 1975, or

(e) section 9 of the Domestic Proceedings and Magistrates' Courts Act 1978;

but this subsection shall cease to have effect once all such orders for the supervision of children have ceased to have effect in accordance with Schedule 14 to the Children Act 1989.

Amendments—CA 1989, s 108(5), Sch 13, paras 62, 66; SI 1991/1723; SI 1995/756; SI 2005/3336.

Defined terms—"child": ss 7, 42(4); "corresponding dependent territory order": s 42(1); "matrimonial proceedings": s 7; "Part I order": ss 1(2),(3), 42(5),(6); "Part I proceedings", "Part I matters": s 42(7); "relevant date": s 7; "specified dependent territory": s 42(1).

General interpretation—See s 42.

7 Interpretation of Chapter II

In this Chapter –

(a) "child" means a person who has not attained the age of eighteen;

(aa) "civil partnership proceedings" means proceedings for the dissolution or annulment of a civil partnership or for legal separation of the civil partners;

(b) "matrimonial proceedings" means proceedings for divorce, nullity of marriage or judicial separation;

(c) "the relevant date" means in relation to the making or variation of an order –

(i) where an application is made for an order to be made or varied, the date of the application (or first application, if two or more are determined together), and

(ii) where no such application is made, the date on which the court is considering whether to make or, as the case may be, vary the order; and

(d) "section 1(1)(a) order" and "section 1(1)(d) order" mean orders falling within section 1(1)(a) and (d) of this Act respectively.

Amendments—CA 1989, s 108(5), Sch 13, para 67; SI 2005/3336.

"the relevant date" (s 7(c))—Presence in the jurisdiction on the "relevant date", for any reason and brought about in any way, is sufficient to give jurisdiction to make a "Part I order" under the Act (ie a s 8 order "other than an order varying or discharging such an order") (*Re F (Residence Order: Jurisdiction)* [1995] 2 FLR 518, but see *Re S (Residence Order: Forum Conveniens)* [1995] 1 FLR 314, where Thorpe J expressed concern at the possibility of jurisdiction turning on "what might be either chance or strategic manoeuvre" resulting in the child's presence on the date of issue of proceedings). In *Re H (Residence Order: Placement Out of Jurisdiction)* [2006] 1 FLR 1140 it was agreed that the court had jurisdiction, where at the date of the hearing, the children were living in the UAE under an interim care order. The local authority were entitled at any time to recall them to England and thus they were still habitually resident in England and Wales and had not acquired habitual residence in the UAE. Where no application has been made, the relevant date under s 7(c)(ii) is that on which the court is considering whether to make or vary the order (*Re F (Residence Order: Jurisdiction)*, above – where the relevant date was the date of the directions hearing and not the date of the substantive hearing of the abduction issue). Similarly where an application has been made, the relevant date is when the court first addresses its mind to the application and makes directions, even if the order ultimately made is different in terms to that originally sought (*Re J (Abduction: Declaration of Wrongful Removal)* [1999] 2 FLR 653).

Chapter III
Jurisdiction of Courts in Scotland

8 Jurisdiction in independent proceedings

A court in Scotland may entertain an application for a Part I order otherwise than in matrimonial proceedings only if it has jurisdiction under section 9, 10, 12 or 15(2) of this Act.

9 Habitual residence

Subject to section 11 of this Act, an application for a Part I order otherwise than in matrimonial proceedings may be entertained by –

    (a) the Court of Session if, on the date of the application, the child concerned is habitually resident in Scotland;

    (b) the sheriff if, on the date of the application, the child concerned is habitually resident in the sheriffdom.

Amendments—CA 1989, s 108, Sch 13, para 62.

10 Presence of child

Subject to section 11 of this Act, an application for a Part I order otherwise than in matrimonial proceedings may be entertained by –

    (a) the Court of Session if, on the date of the application, the child concerned –
        (i) is present in Scotland; and
        (ii) is not habitually resident in any part of the United Kingdom or a specified dependent territory;

    (b) the sheriff if, on the date of the application, –
        (i) the child is present in Scotland;
        (ii) the child is not habitually resident in any part of the United Kingdom or a specified dependent territory; and
        (iii) either the pursuer or the defender in the application is habitually resident in the sheriffdom.

Amendments—CA 1989, s 108, Sch 13, para 62; SI 1991/1723.

11 Provisions supplementary to sections 9 and 10

(1) Subject to subsection (2) below, the jurisdiction of the court to entertain an application for a Part I order with respect to a child by virtue of section 9, 10 or 15(2) of this Act is excluded if, on the date of the application, matrimonial proceedings are continuing in a court in any part of the United Kingdom or a specified dependent territory in respect of the marriage of the parents of the child.

(2) Subsection (1) above shall not apply in relation to an application for a Part I order if the court in which the matrimonial proceedings are continuing has made one of the following orders, that is to say –

(a) an order under section 2A(4), 13(6) or 19A(4) of the Act (not being an order made by virtue of section 13(6)(a)(ii) or a corresponding dependent territory order; or

(b) an order under section 5(2), 14(2) or 22(2) of this Act, or a corresponding dependent territory order, which is recorded as made for the purpose of enabling Part I proceedings with respect to the child concerned to be taken in Scotland or, as the case may be, in another court in Scotland,

and that order is in force.

Amendments—CA 1989, s 108, Sch 13, paras 62, 68; SI 1991/1723; SI 1995/756.

12 Emergency jurisdiction

Notwithstanding that any other court, whether within or outside Scotland, has jurisdiction to entertain an application for a Part I order, the Court of Session or the sheriff shall have jurisdiction to entertain such an application if –

(a) the child concerned is present in Scotland or, as the case may be, in the sheriffdom on the date of the application; and

(b) the Court of Session or sheriff considers that, for the protection of the child, it is necessary to make such order immediately.

Amendments—CA 1989, s 108, Sch 13, para 62.

13 Jurisdiction ancillary to matrimonial proceedings

(1) The jurisdiction of a court in Scotland to entertain an application for a Part I order in matrimonial proceedings shall be modified by the following provisions of this section.

(2) A court in Scotland shall not have jurisdiction, after the dismissal of matrimonial proceedings or after decree of absolvitor is granted therein, to entertain an application for a Part I order under section 9(1) of the Matrimonial Proceedings (Children) Act 1958 unless the application therefore was made on or before such dismissal or the granting of the decree of absolvitor.

(3) Where, after a decree of separation has been granted, an application is made in the separation process for a Part I order, the court in Scotland shall not have jurisdiction to entertain that application if, on the date of the application, proceedings for divorce or nullity of marriage in respect of the marriage concerned are continuing in another court in the United Kingdom or a specified dependent territory.

(4) A court in Scotland shall not have jurisdiction to entertain an application for the variation of a Part I order made under section 9(1) of the Matrimonial Proceedings (Children) Act 1958 if, on the date of the application, matrimonial proceedings in respect of the marriage concerned are continuing in another court in the United Kingdom or a specified dependent territory.

(5) Subsections (3) and (4) above shall not apply if the court in which the other proceedings there referred to are continuing has made –

(a) an order under section 2A(4) or 19A(4) of this Act or under subsection (6) below (not being an order made by virtue of paragraph (a)(ii) of that subsection), or a corresponding dependent territory order, or

(b) an order under section 5(2), 14(2) or 22(2) of this Act, or a corresponding dependent territory order, which is recorded as made for the purpose of enabling Part I proceedings with respect to the child concerned to be taken in Scotland or, as the case may be, in another court in Scotland, and that order is in force.

(6) A court in Scotland which has jurisdiction in matrimonial proceedings to entertain an application for a Part I order with respect to a child may make an order declining such jurisdiction if –

    (a)   it appears to the court with respect to that child that –

        (i)   but for section 11(1) of this Act, another court in Scotland would have jurisdiction to entertain an application for a Part I order, or

        (ii)   but for section 3(2), 6(3), 20(2) or 23(3) of this Act or a corresponding territory provision, a court in another part of the United Kingdom or a specified dependent territory would have jurisdiction to make a Part I order or an order varying a Part I order; and

    (b)   the court considers that it would be more appropriate for Part I matters relating to that child to be determined in that other court or part.

(7) The court may recall an order made under subsection (6) above.

Amendments—CA 1989, s 108, Sch 13, paras 62, 68; SI 1991/1723; SI 1995/756.

14 Power of court to refuse application or sist proceedings

(1) A court in Scotland which has jurisdiction to entertain an application for a Part I order may refuse the application in any case where the matter in question has already been determined in other proceedings.

(2) Where, at any stage of the proceedings on an application made to a court in Scotland for a Part I order, it appears to the court –

    (a)   that proceedings with respect to the matter to which the application relates are continuing outside Scotland or in another court in Scotland; or

    (b)   that it would be more appropriate for those matters to be determined in proceedings outside Scotland or in another court in Scotland and that such proceedings are likely to be taken there.

the court may sist the proceedings on that application.

Amendments—CA 1989, s 108, Sch 13, para 62.

15 Duration, variation and recall of orders

(1) Where, after the making by a court in Scotland of a Part I order ("the existing order") with respect to a child, –

    (a)   a Part I order, or an order varying a Part I order, competently made by another court in any part of the United Kingdom or in a specified dependent territory with respect to that child; or

    (b)   an order for the custody of that child which is made outside the United Kingdom and any specified dependent territory and recognised in Scotland by virtue of section 26 of this Act,

comes into force, the existing order shall cease to have effect so far as it makes provision for any matter for which the same or different provision is made by the order of the other court in the United Kingdom or in the specified dependent territory or, as the case be, the order so recognised.

(2) Subject to sections 11(1) and 13(3) and (4) of this Act, a court in Scotland which has made a Part I order ("the original order") may, notwithstanding that it would no longer have jurisdiction to make the original order, make an order varying or recalling the original order; but if the original order has by virtue of subsection (1) above ceased to have effect so far as it makes provision for any matter, the court shall not have power to vary that order under this subsection so as to make provision for that matter.

(3) In subsection (2) above, an order varying an original order means any Part I order made with respect to the same child as the original order was made.

(4) Where any person who is entitled to the custody of a child under a Part I order made by a court in Scotland ceases to be so entitled by virtue of subsection (1) above, then, if there is in force an order made by a court in Scotland providing for the supervision of that child by a local authority, that order shall cease to have effect.

Amendments—CA 1989, s 108, Sch 13, para 62; SI 1991/1723; Children (Scotland) Act 1995, s 105(5), Sch 5.

Effect in relation to "interim" residence orders (s 15(1))—An "interim" residence order is no different in principle from a residence order, particularly since CA 1989 does not recognise that there is such an order as an interim residence order; instead, the court has power to make a residence order limited in time. Therefore, by the operation of s 15(1), the making of an "interim" residence order by an English court has the consequence that any order previously made by a Scottish court as to the living arrangements for a child no longer has any effect in law, since it makes "provision for any matter for which the same or different provision is made by the order of the other court in the United Kingdom" (*S v S (Custody: Jurisdiction)* [1995] 1 FLR 155; *T v T (Custody: Jurisdiction)* [1992] 1 FLR 43).

16 Tutory and curatory

(1) Subject to subsections (2) and (3) below, an application made after the commencement of this Part for an order relating to the guardianship of a child may be entertained by –

    (a) the Court of Session if, on the date of the application, the pupil or minor is habitually resident in Scotland;

    (b) the sheriff if, on the date of the application, the pupil or minor is habitually resident in the sheriffdom.

(2) Subsection (1) above shall not apply to an application for the appointment or removal of a judicial factor or of a curator bonis or any application made by such factor or curator.

(3) Subsection (1) above is without prejudice to any other ground of jurisdiction on which the Court of Session or the sheriff may entertain an application mentioned therein.

(4) Provision may be made by act of sederunt prescribing, in relation to orders relating to the guardianship of a child, what constitutes an application for the purposes of this Chapter.

Amendments—Age of Legal Capacity (Scotland) Act 1991, s 10, Sch 1, para 45.

17 Orders for delivery of child

(1) An application by one parent of a child for an order for the delivery of the child from the other parent, where the order is not sought to implement a Part I order, may be entertained by the Court of Session or a sheriff if, but only if, the Court of Session or, as the case may be, the sheriff would have jurisdiction under this Chapter to make a Part I order with respect to the child concerned.

(2) *(repealed)*

(3) Subsection (1) above shall apply to an application by one party to a marriage for an order for the delivery of the child concerned from the other party where the child is the child of one of the parties and has been accepted as one of the family by the other party as it applies to an application by one parent of a child for an order for the delivery of the child from the other parent.

Amendments—CA 1989, s 108, Sch 13, para 62; Children (Scotland) Act 1995, s 105(5), Sch 5.

18 Interpretation of Chapter III

(1) In this Chapter –

"child" means a person who has not attained the age of sixteen;

"matrimonial proceedings" means proceedings for divorce, nullity of marriage or judicial separation.

(2) In this Chapter, "the date of the application" means, where two or more applications are pending, the date of the first of those applications; and, for the purposes of this subsection, an application is pending until a Part I order or, in the case of an application mentioned in section 16(1) of this Act, an order relating to the guardianship of a child, has been granted in pursuance of the application or the court has refused to grant such an order.

Amendments—CA 1989, s 108, Sch 13, para 62; Age of Legal Capacity (Scotland) Act 1991, s 10, Sch 1, para 46.

Chapter IV
Jurisdiction of Courts in Northern Ireland

19 Northern Ireland: jurisdiction in cases other than divorce, dissolution of a civil partnership, etc

(1) A court in Northern Ireland shall not make a section 1(1)(c) order with respect to a child unless –

    (a)   it has jurisdiction under the Council Regulation or the Hague Convention, or

    (b)   neither the Council Regulation nor the Hague Convention applies but –

        (i)   the question of making the order arises in or in connection with matrimonial proceedings or civil partnership proceedings and the condition in section 19A of this Act is satisfied, or

        (ii) the condition in section 20 of this Act is satisfied.

(2) (*repealed*)

(3) A court in Northern Ireland shall not make a section 1(1)(e) order unless –

    (a)   it has jurisdiction under the Council Regulation or the Hague Convention, or

    (b)   neither the Council Regulation nor the Hague Convention applies but –

        (i)   the condition in section 20 of this Act is satisfied, or

        (ii) the child concerned is present in Northern Ireland on the relevant date and the court considers that the immediate exercise of its powers is necessary for his protection.

Amendments—Substituted by SI 1995/755; amended by SI 2001/660; SI 2005/265; SI 2005/3336; SI 2010/1898.

19A Jurisdiction in or in connection with matrimonial proceedings or civil partnership proceedings

(1) The condition referred to in section 19(1) of this Act is that the proceedings are proceedings in respect of the marriage or civil partnership of the parents of the child concerned and –

    (a)   the proceedings –

        (i)   are proceedings for divorce or nullity of marriage, or dissolution or annulment of a civil partnership, and

        (ii) are continuing;

(b)   the proceedings –

  (i)   are proceedings for judicial separation or legal separation of civil partners, and

  (ii)   are continuing;

and the jurisdiction of the court is not excluded by subsection (2) below; or

(c)   the proceedings have been dismissed after the beginning of the trial but –

  (i)   the section 1(1)(c) order is being made forthwith, or

  (ii)   the application for the order was made on or before the dismissal.

(2) For the purposes of subsection (1)(b) above, the jurisdiction of the court is excluded if –

(a)   after the grant of a decree of judicial separation, on the relevant date, proceedings for divorce or nullity in respect of the marriage, or

(b)   after the making of a separation order, on the relevant date, proceedings for dissolution or annulment in respect of the civil partnership,

are continuing in England and Wales or Scotland.

(3) Subsection (2) above shall not apply if the court in which the other proceedings there referred to are continuing has made –

(a)   an order under section 2A(4) or 13(6) of this Act (not being an order made by virtue of section 13(6)(a)(i)), or

(b)   an order under section 5(2) or 14(2) of this Act which is recorded as being made for the purpose of enabling Part I proceedings to be taken in Northern Ireland with respect to the child concerned.

(4) Where a court –

(a)   has jurisdiction to make a section 1(1)(c) order by virtue of section 19(1)(b)(i) of this Act, but

(b)   considers that it would be more appropriate for Part I matters relating to the child to be determined outside Northern Ireland,

the court may by order direct that, while the order under this subsection is in force, no section 1(1)(c) order shall be made by any court by virtue of section 19(1)(b)(i) of this Act.

Amendments—Inserted by SI 1995/755; amended by SI 2005/265; SI 2005/3336.

20 Habitual residence or presence of child

(1) The condition referred to in section 19(1)(b)(ii) of this Act is that on the relevant date the child concerned –

(a)   is habitually resident in Northern Ireland, or

(b)   is present in Northern Ireland and is not habitually resident in any part of the United Kingdom or in a specified dependent territory

and, in either case, the jurisdiction of the court is not excluded by subsection (2) below.

(2) For the purposes of subsection (1) above, the jurisdiction of the court is excluded if, on the relevant date, matrimonial proceedings or civil partnership proceedings are continuing in a court in England and Wales, Scotland or a specified dependent territory in respect of the marriage or civil partnership of the parents of the child concerned.

(3) Subsection (2) above shall not apply if the court in which the other proceedings there referred to are continuing has made –

(a)   an order under section 2A(4) or 13(6) of this Act (not being an order made by virtue of section 13(6)(a)(i)), or a corresponding dependent territory order, or

(b)   an order under section 5(2) or 14(2) of this Act, or a corresponding dependent territory order, which is recorded as made for the purpose of enabling Part I proceedings with respect to the child concerned to be taken in Northern Ireland,

and that order is in force.

(4)–(6) (*repealed*)

Amendments—CA 1989, s 108, Sch 13, paras 62, 68, 69; SI 1991/1723; SI 1995/755; SI 2005/265; SI 2005/3443.

21 (*repealed*)

22 Power of court to refuse application or stay proceedings

(1) A court in Northern Ireland which has jurisdiction to make a Part I order may refuse an application for the order in any case where the matter in question has already been determined in proceedings outside Northern Ireland.

(2) Where, at any stage of the proceedings on an application made to a court in Northern Ireland for a Part I order, or for the variation of a Part I order, it appears to the court –

(a)   that proceedings with respect to the matters to which the application relates are continuing outside Northern Ireland;

(b)   that it would be more appropriate for those matters to be determined in proceedings to be taken outside Northern Ireland,

(c)   that it should exercise its powers under Article 15 of the Council Regulation (transfer to a court better placed to hear the case), or

(d)   that it should exercise its powers under Article 8 of the Hague Convention (request to authority in another Contracting State to assume jurisdiction),

the court may stay the proceedings on the application or (as the case may be) exercise its powers under Article 15 of the Council Regulation or Article 8 of the Hague Convention.

(3) The court may remove a stay granted by virtue of subsection (2)(a) or (b) above if it appears to the court that there has been unreasonable delay in the taking or prosecution of the other proceedings referred to in that subsection, or that those proceedings are stayed, sisted or concluded.

(3A) The court may remove a stay granted under Article 15 of the Council Regulation only in accordance with that Article.

(3B) The court may remove a stay granted in order for it to exercise its powers under Article 8 of the Hague Convention, and withdraw any request made by it to an authority in another Contracting State to assume jurisdiction, if –

(a)   the authority in the other Contracting State does not assume jurisdiction within the period for which the court granted the stay, or

(b)   the parties do not, within the period specified by the court, request the authority in the other Contracting State to assume jurisdiction.

(4) Nothing in this section so far as it relates to proceedings not governed by the Council Regulation shall affect any power exercisable apart from this section to refuse an application or to grant or remove a stay.

Amendments—CA 1989, s 108, Sch 13, para 62; SI 2001/660; SI 2005/265; SI 2010/1898.

23 Duration and variation of custody orders

(1) If a Part I order made by a court in England and Wales, Scotland or a specified dependent territory (or a variation of such an order) comes into force with respect to a child at a time when a Part I order made by a court in Northern Ireland has effect with

respect to him, the latter order shall cease to have effect so far as it makes provision for any matter for which the same or different provision is made by (or by the variation of) the order made by the court in England and Wales, Scotland or the territory.

(2) Where by virtue of subsection (1) above a Part I order has ceased to have effect so far as it makes provision for any matter, a court in Northern Ireland shall not have jurisdiction to vary that order so as to make provision for that matter.

(3) A court in Northern Ireland shall not have jurisdiction to vary a Part I order if, on the relevant date, matrimonial proceedings or civil partnership proceedings are continuing in England and Wales or Scotland in respect of the marriage or civil partnership of the parents of the child concerned.

(3A) Subsection (3) above shall not apply if –

  (a) the Part I order was made in or in connection with proceedings –
    (i) for divorce or nullity in Northern Ireland in respect of the marriage of the parents of the child concerned; or
    (ii) for dissolution or annulment in Northern Ireland in respect of the civil partnership of the parents of the child concerned; and
  (b) those proceedings are continuing.

(3B) Subsection (3) above shall not apply if –

  (a) the Part I order was made in or in connection with proceedings –
    (i) for judicial separation in Northern Ireland; or
    (ii) for a separation order in Northern Ireland; and
  (b) those proceedings are continuing; and
  (c) as the case may be, the decree of judicial separation has not yet been granted or the separation order has not yet been made.

(4) Subsection (3) above shall not apply if the court in which the proceedings there referred to are continuing has made –

  (a) an order under section 2A(4) or 13(6) of this Act (not being an order made by virtue of section 13(6)(a)(i), or a corresponding dependent territory order, or
  (b) an order under section 5(2) or 14(2) of this Act, or a corresponding dependent territory order, which is recorded as made for the purpose of enabling Part I proceedings with respect to the child concerned to be taken in Northern Ireland,

and that order is in force.

(5) Subsection (3) above shall not apply in the case of a variation of a section 1(1)(e) order if the child concerned is present in Northern Ireland on the relevant date and the court considers that the immediate exercise of its powers is necessary for his protection.

(6) Subsection (7) below applies where a Part I order which is –

  (a) a residence order (within the meaning of the Children (Northern Ireland) Order 1995) in favour of a person with respect to a child,
  (b) an order made in the exercise of the High Court's inherent jurisdiction with respect to children by virtue of which a person has care of a child, or
  (c) an order –
    (i) of a kind mentioned in section 1(3)(a) of this Act,
    (ii) under which a person is entitled to the actual possession of a child,

ceases to have effect in relation to that person by virtue of subsection (1) above.

(7) Where this subsection applies, any family assistance order made under Article 16 of the Children (Northern Ireland) Order 1995 with respect to a child shall also cease to have effect.

(8) For the purposes of subsection (7) above the reference to a family assistance order under Article 16 of the Children (Northern Ireland) Order 1995 shall be deemed to include a reference to an order for the supervision of a child made under –

  (a)   Article 47 of the Matrimonial Causes (Northern Ireland) Order 1978, or
  (b)   Article 11 of the Domestic Proceedings (Northern Ireland) Order 1980;

but this subsection shall cease to have effect once all such orders for the supervision of children have ceased to have effect in accordance with Schedule 8 to the Children (Northern Ireland) Order 1995.

Amendments—CA 1989, s 108, Sch 13, paras 62, 68, 69; SI 1991/1723; SI 1995/755; SI 2005/3336.

24 Interpretation of Chapter IV

In this Chapter –

  (a)   "child" means a person who has not attained the age of 18;
  (aa) "civil partnership proceedings" means proceedings for the dissolution or annulment of a civil partnership or for legal separation of the civil partners;
  (b)   "matrimonial proceedings" means proceedings for divorce, nullity of marriage or judicial separation;
  (c)   "the relevant date" means, in relation to the making or variation of an order –
        (i)   where an application is made for an order to be made or varied, the date of the application (or first application, if two or more are determined together), and
        (ii) where no such application is made, the date on which the court is considering whether to make or, as the case may be, vary the order; and
  (d)   "section 1(1)(c) order" and "section 1(1)(e) order" mean orders falling within section 1(1)(c) and (e) of this Act respectively.

Amendments—Substituted by SI 1995/755; amended by SI 2005/3336.

Chapter V
Recognition and Enforcement

25 Recognition of custody orders: general

(1) Where a Part I order made by a court in any part of the United Kingdom or in a specified dependent territory is in force with respect to a child who has not attained the age of sixteen, then, subject to subsection (2) below, the order shall be recognised in any other part or, in the case of a dependent territory order, any part of the United Kingdom as having the same effect in that part as if it had been made by the appropriate court in that part and as if that court had had jurisdiction to make it.

(2) Where a Part I order includes provision as to the means by which rights conferred by the order are to be enforced, subsection (1) above shall not apply to that provision.

(3) A court in a part of the United Kingdom in which a Part I order is recognised in accordance with subsection (1) above shall not enforce the order unless it has been registered in that part of the United Kingdom under section 27 of this Act and proceedings for enforcement are taken in accordance with section 29 of this Act.

Amendments—CA 1989, s 108(5), Sch 13, para 62; SI 1991/1723.

Defined terms—"appropriate court": s 32(1) (and see notes to s 32); "part of the United Kingdom": s 42(1).

Scope—Recognition and enforcement are not automatic. The initiative and responsibility for pursuing enforcement proceedings lies with the aggrieved party, not with the court (*Glaser v United Kingdom*

(Case No 32346/96) ECtHR [2001] 1 FLR 153). An order may be enforced only if it has been registered under s 27 and proceedings for enforcement are taken in accordance with s 29.

"Part I order"—By virtue of ss 1, 32 and 42(5), Pt I orders include those set out in s 1(a)–(f). FLA 1986 is not retrospective and it does not affect any orders made before the Act came into force, and orders which vary or revoke previous orders are excluded.

"specified dependent territory" (s 25(1))—See FLA 1986 (DT)O 1991, art 2 and FPR 2010, r 32.23.

****

27 Registration

(1) Any person on whom any rights are conferred by a Part I order may apply to the court which made it for the order to be registered in another part of the United Kingdom under this section, or in a specified dependent territory under a corresponding provision.

(2) An application under this section shall be made in the prescribed manner and shall contain the prescribed information and be accompanied by such documents as may be prescribed.

(3) On receiving an application under this section the court which made the Part I order shall, unless it appears to the court that the order is no longer in force, cause the following documents to be sent to the appropriate court in the part of the United Kingdom or dependent territory specified in the application, namely –

(a) a certified copy of the order, and
(b) where the order has been varied, prescribed particulars of any variation which is in force, and
(c) a copy of the application and of any accompanying documents.

(4) Where the prescribed officer of the appropriate court in any part of the United Kingdom receives a certified copy of a Part I order under subsection (3) above or under a corresponding dependent territory provision, he shall forthwith cause the order, together with particulars of any variation, to be registered in that court in the prescribed manner.

(5) An order shall not be registered under this section in respect of a child who has attained the age of sixteen, and the registration of an order in respect of a child who has not attained the age of sixteen shall cease to have effect on the attainment by the child of that age.

Amendments—CA 1989, s 108(5), Sch 13, para 62; SI 1991/1723.

Defined terms—"appropriate court": s 32(1) (and see notes to s 32 and FPR 2010, r 32.23); "certified copy", "corresponding dependent territory provision", "corresponding provision", "part of the UK", "prescribed": s 42(1).

General note—The mere act of registering is not sufficient to cause the enforcement of the order. A separate application must be made to the registering court to enforce the order.

"Part I order"—See under s 25.

"specified dependent territory" (s 27(1))—See FLA 1986(DT)O 1991, art 2 and FPR 2010, r 32.23.

Application (s 27(2))—Applications made in the High Court and county court must be made in the prescribed manner as set out in FPR 2010, r 32.26. For application to the family proceedings court, see the Magistrates' Courts (Family Law Act 1986) Rules 1988 (see Part IV).

Documents (s 27(3))—A certified copy and a copy of the original order, any order which has varied any of the terms of the original order and any further orders obtained (e g an additional order under s 33 or 34), together with a statement in support and a copy must be filed (FPR 2010, r 32.25).

"appropriate court in the part of the United Kingdom specified" (s 27(3))—An order may be registered in any part of the UK to where the child has been or is likely to be abducted and where the order is sought to be enforced. A decision will need to be taken as to the jurisdiction in which the order is required to be registered. In most cases, registration in one jurisdiction will suffice; there may, however, be cases where it is desirable to have the order registered in more than one jurisdiction, particularly where there is a fear that the child may be moved about in order to avoid being traced.

"forthwith" (s 27(4))—The order must be registered as soon as practicable having regard to the circumstances and nature of the act to be done (see *Re Southam ex parte Lamb* (1881) 19 Ch D 169, [1881–5] All ER Rep 391; *Re Muscovitch ex parte M* [1939] Ch 694).

"in the prescribed manner" (s 27(4))—Registration in the appropriate court is to be in the prescribed manner. The following rules apply: in England and Wales, FPR 2010, rr 32.23–32.32. Magistrates' Courts (Family Law Act 1986) Rules 1988, as amended; in Northern Ireland, RSC (Northern Ireland) Ord 90, rr 26–35, CCR (Northern Ireland) 1991, Ord 51, rr 6–11, and the Magistrates' Courts (Family Law Act 1986) Rules (Northern Ireland) 1988; in Scotland, Court of Session Rules of Court, Act of Sederunt (Rules for the Registration of Custody Orders of the Sheriff Court) 1988.

28 Cancellation and variation of registration

(1) A court which revokes, recalls or varies an order registered under section 27 of this Act shall cause notice of the revocation, recall or variation to be given in the prescribed manner to the prescribed officer of the court in which it is registered and, on receiving the notice, the prescribed officer –

   (a)   in the case of the revocation or recall of the order, shall cancel the registration, and

   (b)   in the case of the variation of the order, shall cause particulars of the variation to be registered in the prescribed manner.

(2) Where –

   (a)   an order registered under section 27 of this Act ceases (in whole or in part) to have effect in the part of the United Kingdom or in a specified dependent territory in which it was made, otherwise than because of its revocation, recall or variation, or

   (b)   an order registered under section 27 of this Act in Scotland ceases (in whole or in part) to have effect there as a result of the making of an order in proceedings outside the United Kingdom and any specified dependent territory,

the court in which the order is registered may, of its own motion or on the application of any person who appears to the court to have an interest in the matter, cancel the registration (or, if the order has ceased to have effect in part, cancel the registration so far as it relates to the provisions which have ceased to have effect).

Amendments—SI 1991/1723.

Defined terms—"part of the United Kingdom", "prescribed": s 42(1).

Scope—FPR 2010, rr 32.27 and 32.28 make procedural provision with regard to such an application. The alteration in the register is made by the prescribed officer. Where however the order ceases to have effect otherwise than by revocation or variation, e g by lapse of time or by continued cohabitation or by resumption of cohabitation, or in the case of an order registered in Scotland, as a result of the making of an order in proceedings outside the UK, the cancellation may take place only where the court acts of its own motion or on an application of any person who has an interest in the matter.

"in the prescribed manner" (s 28(1)(b))—See under s 27 and FPR 2010, rr 32.23–32.32.

"specified dependent territory" (s 28(2))—See FLA 1986(DT)O 1991, art 2 and FPR 2010, r 32.23.

29 Enforcement

(1) Where a Part I order has been registered under section 27 of this Act, the court in which it is registered shall have the same powers for the purpose of enforcing the order (including, where an order with respect to contact is registered in England and Wales, the powers under section 11O of the Children Act 1989) as it would have if it had itself made the order and had jurisdiction to make it; and proceedings for or with respect to enforcement may be taken accordingly.

(2) Where an application has been made to any court for the enforcement of an order registered in that court under section 27 of this Act, the court may, at any time before the application is determined, give such interim directions as it thinks fit for the purpose of securing the welfare of the child concerned or of preventing changes in the circumstances relevant to the determination of the application.

(3) The references in subsection (1) above to a Part I order do not include references to any provision of the order as to the means by which rights conferred by the order are to be enforced.

Amendments—CA 1989, s 108(5), Sch 13, para 62; CAA 2006, s 15(1), Sch 2, paras 2, 4.

Court's powers to make orders (s 29(1))—Since the court has the same powers for the purposes of enforcement of a registered order as it would if it had itself made the order the court has the power:

(a) to order disclosure of the child's whereabouts under s 33 and the discovery of information held by Government departments;
(b) to order the recovery of the child under s 34;
(c) to order surrender of passports under s 37;
(d) to direct that wardship proceedings be commenced (subject to restrictions on jurisdiction);
(e) to grant injunctions and in particular restrain the further removal of the child from the country or from his present address;
(f) to order welfare reports and to give directions regarding evidence to be filed;
(g) to order the return of the child to the applicant and to his country of origin.

Interim directions (s 29(2))—FPR 2010, r 32.29 provides inter alia that all parties to the proceedings for enforcement, and the applicant for the Pt I order if he is not a party, must be made parties to the application for interim directions.

"Part I order"—See under s 25.

Matters to be considered—When considering an application to enforce a custody order made in another part of the UK, an English court is bound to have regard to the principle of comity and not, in effect, purport to act as a court of appeal from the court having jurisdiction in another part of the UK. The English judge should not question the correctness of the procedures and orders of the Scottish court (*Re M (Minors) (Custody: Jurisdiction)* [1992] 2 FLR 382).

30 Staying or sisting of enforcement proceedings

(1) Where in accordance with section 29 of this Act proceedings are taken in any court for the enforcement of an order registered in that court, any person who appears to the court to have an interest in the matter may apply for the proceedings to be stayed or sisted on the ground that he has taken or intends to take other proceedings (in the United Kingdom or elsewhere) as a result of which the order may cease to have effect, or may have a different effect, in the part of the United Kingdom in which it is registered.

(1A) No application may be made under subsection (1) for proceedings to be stayed or sisted if the proceedings are proceedings on an application for an order under section 11O(2) of the Children Act 1989.

(2) If after considering an application under subsection (1) above the court considers that the proceedings for enforcement should be stayed or sisted in order that other proceedings may be taken or concluded, it shall stay or sist the proceedings for enforcement accordingly.

(3) The court may remove a stay or recall a sist granted in accordance with subsection (2) above if it appears to the court –

(a) that there has been unreasonable delay in the taking or prosecution of the other proceedings referred to in that subsection, or
(b) that those other proceedings are concluded and that the registered order, or a relevant part of it, is still in force.

(4) Nothing in this section shall affect any power exercisable apart from this section to grant, remove or recall a stay or sist.

Amendments—CAA 2006, s 15(1), Sch 2, paras 2, 5.

Defined terms—"part of the United Kingdom": s 42(1).

Procedure—FPR 2010, r 32.30 makes provision for the procedure on an application under this section.

Grounds of application—In addition to the grounds mentioned in this section, where the enforcement proceedings are in Scotland, application may also be made that the court should deal with the application on its merits under s 12.

Stay by reason of other proceedings—See *Re M (Minors) (Custody: Jurisdiction)* [1992] 2 FLR 382 and the effect of DMPA 1973, Sch 3, para 8. For an example of proceedings being sisted/stayed see *P v G* [2010] 2 FLR 1888 and *Emergency Remedies in the Family Courts* (Jordan Publishing Ltd).

31 Dismissal of enforcement proceedings

(1) Where in accordance with section 29 of this Act proceedings are taken in any court for the enforcement of an order registered in that court, any person who appears to the court to have an interest in the matter may apply for those proceedings to be dismissed on the ground that the order has (in whole or in part) ceased to have effect in the part of the United Kingdom or specified dependent territory in which it was made.

(1A) No application may be made under subsection (1) for proceedings to be dismissed if the proceedings are proceedings on an application for an order under section 11O(2) of the Children Act 1989.

(2) Where in accordance with section 29 of this Act proceedings are taken in the Court of Session for the enforcement of an order registered in that court, any person who appears to the court to have an interest in the matter may apply for those proceedings to be dismissed on the ground that the order has (in whole or in part) ceased to have effect in Scotland as a result of the making of an order in proceedings outside the United Kingdom and any specified dependent territory.

(3) If, after considering an application under subsection (1) or (2) above, the court is satisfied that the registered order has ceased to have effect, it shall dismiss the proceedings for enforcement (or, if it is satisfied that the order has ceased to have effect in part, it shall dismiss the proceedings so far as they relate to the enforcement of provisions which have ceased to have effect).

Amendments—SI 1991/1723; CAA 2006, s 15(1), Sch 2, paras 2, 6.

Defined terms—"part of the United Kingdom": s 42(1).

Procedure—FPR 2010, r 32.30 makes provision as to the procedure on an application under this section.

Grounds of application—See annotation under s 30.

32 Interpretation of Chapter V

(1) In this Chapter –

"the appropriate court", in relation to England and Wales or Northern Ireland, means the High Court and, in relation to Scotland, means the Court of Session and, in relation to a specified dependent territory, means the corresponding court in that territory;

"Part I order" includes (except where the context otherwise requires) any order within section 1(3) of this Act which, on the assumptions mentioned in subsection (3) below –

   (a)   could have been made notwithstanding the provisions of this Part or the corresponding dependent territory provisions;

   (b)   would have been a Part I order for the purpose of this Part; and

(c)   would not have ceased to have effect by virtue of section 6, 15 or 23 of this Act.

(2) In the application of this Chapter to Scotland, "Part I order" also includes (except where the context otherwise requires) any order within section 1(3) of this Act which, on the assumptions mentioned in subsection (3) below –

(a)   would have been a Part I order for the purpose of this Part; and
(b)   would not have ceased to have effect by virtue of section 6 or 23 of this Act,

and which, but for the provisions of this Part, would be recognised in Scotland under any rule of law.

(3) The said assumptions are –

(a)   that this Part or the corresponding dependent territory provisions, as the case may be, had been in force at all material times; and
(b)   that any reference in section 1 of this Act to any enactment included a reference to any corresponding enactment previously in force.

Amendments—CA 1989, s 108(5), Sch 13, para 62; SI 1991/1723.

Defined terms—"corresponding dependent territory provisions", "specified dependent territory": s 42(1) (and see notes to s 42 and FPR 2010, r 32.23).

"appropriate court", "corresponding court" (s 32(1))—See FPR 2010, r 32.23.

"Part I order"—See under s 25.

Chapter VI
Miscellaneous and Supplemental

33 Power to order disclosure of child's whereabouts

(1) Where in proceedings for or relating to a Part I order in respect of a child there is not available to the court adequate information as to where the child is, the court may order any person who it has reason to believe may have relevant information to disclose it to the court.

(2) A person shall not be excused from complying with an order under subsection (1) above by reason that to do so may incriminate him or his spouse of an offence; but a statement or admission made in compliance with such an order shall not be admissible in evidence against either of them in proceedings for any offence other than perjury.

(3) A court in Scotland before which proceedings are pending for the enforcement of an order relating to parental responsibilities or parental rights in relation to a child made outside the United Kingdom and any specified dependent territory which is recognised in Scotland shall have the same powers as it would have under subsection (1) above if the order were its own.

Amendments—CA 1989, s 108(5), Sch 13, para 62; SI 1991/1723; Children (Scotland) Act 1995, s 105(4), Sch 4, para 41(1),(7).

Scope—This section provides a power to county courts and family proceedings courts in private law proceedings, as well as to the High Court, similar to an inherent power of the High Court in relation to children. This section also provides for an order for the purpose of giving effect to an order, akin to a CA 1989, s 8 order, made elsewhere in the UK or in a specified dependent territory, which has been registered in the High Court.

An order under this section may be directed to persons who are not parties to the proceedings, including a legal adviser, the manager of a women's refuge or the police, as well as relatives or friends of a person who may be keeping the child. However, where a mother has taken a child to stay at a women's refuge, the police should not be directed to disclose the address (*Chief Constable of West Yorkshire Police v S* [1998] 2 FLR 973). An order under the inherent jurisdiction of the High Court must be obeyed by a legal adviser and "privilege" is overridden (*Burton v Earl of Darnley* (1869) LR 8 Eq 576; *Ramsbotham v Senior* (1869) FLR Rep 591). The power given by s 33(1) is unqualified and, it is submitted, also overrides privilege.

"Part I order"—See under s 25.

Application for s 33 order—An application for an order under s 33 comes within the definition of "emergency proceedings" (FPR 2010, r 12.2). The application may be made at any time during CA 1989, s 8 proceedings and will usually be made without notice using the procedure in FPR 2010, r 12.16. The application is made in Form C4 (FPR 2010, r 5.1 and PD5A). If made without notice by telephone, as permitted by the rules, the Form C4 must be filed the next business day after making the application (FPR 2010, r 12.16(2),(3)). Where the court makes an order without notice, the rules provide that a copy of the application must be served on each respondent within 48 hours after the making of the order (FPR 2010, r 12.16(4),(5)). It is impractical to make an application without notice by telephone to a family proceedings court as there is no provision for the application to be heard by a single justice (FPR 2010, r 2.6). PD12E (*Urgent Business*) provides further details of the procedure for out of hours applications. See also PD12D (*Inherent Jurisdiction (including Wardship) Proceedings*).

Evidence in support of application—The application should be supported by evidence. When the application is made in pending CA 1989, s 8 proceedings, the evidence should be by a statement which complies with FPR 2010, r 12.19. When the application is made without notice, permission under FPR 2010, r 12.12 for the statement to be adduced may be sought at the hearing. See also FPR 2010, r 22.1 and PD22A, which deal with the power of the court to control evidence.

Form of order and enforcement—The order is issued in Form C30 (FPR 2010, r 5.1 and PD5A). Note that the order directs the person to disclose the information to the court. The order should not purport to direct disclosure to a party to the proceedings (*Chief Constable of West Yorkshire Police v S* [1998] 2 FLR 973). The court will decide what to do with the information. Form C30 incorporates a penal (warning) notice and may be enforced in a county court by application under CPR 1998, Sch 2, CCR Ord 29, r 1, or in a family proceedings court under MCA 1980, s 63(3). See also FPR PD6C.

34 Power to order recovery of child

(1) Where –

    (a)   a person is required by a Part I order, or an order for the enforcement of a Part I order, to give up a child to another person ("the person concerned"), and

    (b)   the court which made the order imposing the requirement is satisfied that the child has not been given up in accordance with the order,

the court may make an order authorising an officer of the court or a constable to take charge of the child and deliver him to the person concerned.

(2) The authority conferred by subsection (1) above includes authority –

    (a)   to enter and search any premises where the person acting in pursuance of the order has reason to believe the child may be found, and

    (b)   to use such force as may be necessary to give effect to the purpose of the order.

(3) Where by virtue of –

    (a)   section 14 of the Children Act 1989, or

    (b)   Article 14 (enforcement of residence orders) of the Children (Northern Ireland) Order 1995,

a Part I order (or a provision of a Part I order) may be enforced as if it were an order requiring a person to give up a child to another person, subsection (1) above shall apply as if the Part I order had included such a requirement.

(4) This section is without prejudice to any power conferred on a court by or under any other enactment or rule of law.

Amendments—CA 1989, s 108(5), Sch 13, paras 62, 70; SI 1995/755.

Scope—This section empowers a county court or a family proceedings court in private law proceedings, as well as the High Court, to authorise the physical taking charge of a child, with the use of such force as may be necessary, and delivery of the child to the person entitled, when a child has not been given up in accordance with an order of the same court. This section also provides for such a power in the High Court in respect of an order, akin to a CA 1989, s 8 order, made elsewhere in the UK or in a specified dependent territory, which has been registered in the High Court. The power given to county courts and family proceedings courts is similar to, but more restricted than, an inherent power of the High Court in relation to children. Unlike the power of the High Court to direct the tipstaff to take charge of a child even though no previous order has been disobeyed, the power under s 34 cannot be exercised unless the court is satisfied that an order requiring the giving up of the child has been disobeyed. Therefore, on an application for a s 34 order, proof is required that the order to give up the child has been served on, or effectively communicated to, the person bound by the order.

A residence order made in a family proceedings court, by virtue of CA 1989, s 14(1), can be enforced, under MCA 1980, s 63(3), against a person on whom the order has been served and who is in breach of the arrangements settled by the order, as if it were an order requiring that person to produce the child. Thus, s 34(3) enables a Pt I order made by a family proceedings court to be enforced under s 34(1), even though it does not specifically require the person concerned to give up the child or specify when the child should be given up.

"officer of the court" (s 34(1))—County courts do not have any person who is trained to undertake the functions of the tipstaff of the High Court, and county court bailiffs do not undertake this function.

"Part I order"—See under s 25.

Procedure on application for s 34 order—An application for an order under s 34 comes within the definition of "emergency proceedings" (FPR 2010, r 12.2). The application is made in Form C3 (FPR 2010, r 5.1 and PD5A). When the application is made to the High Court or a county court which made a CA 1989, s 8 order that has not been complied with, or to the High Court in respect of an order made elsewhere but registered in the High Court, it is submitted that the application may be made within the proceedings in which the order was made or the registration proceedings; the court can make injunctive orders to give effect to a judgment after the trial has concluded, in matrimonial proceedings (*Webb v Webb* [1986] 1 FLR 541, *Lucas v Lucas* [1992] 2 FLR 53) and in civil actions (*Zeeland Navigation Company Ltd v Banque Worms* (1995) *The Times*, 26 December). Where the order was made by a family proceedings court and the proceedings are no longer in motion, a fresh application may be required.

An application should not be made in respect of a county court order unless the order explicitly requires the person bound to "give up" the child, preferably specifying when or by when (c f CPR 1998, Sch 2, CCR Ord 29, r 1(2)(b)), and where, the child is to be given up. If a county court order does not so specify, an order to give up the child (which may be applied for without notice) should be obtained and served and have been disobeyed, before an application can be made for a s 34 order.

Without notice or with notice—Application should be made with notice unless there is reason to suppose that the child has been, or is likely to be, removed or hidden, or is likely to suffer significant harm. Proceedings under s 34 come within the definition of "emergency proceedings" (FPR 2010, r 12.2). If made without notice by telephone, as permitted by the rules (FPR 2010, r 12.16(2)), the Form C3 must be filed the next business day within 24 hours after making the application. It is impractical to make an application without notice by telephone to a family proceedings court as there is no provision for the application to be heard by a single justice (FPR 2010, r 2.6). Where the court makes an order without notice, the rules provide that a copy of the application must be served on each respondent within 48 hours after the making of the order (FPR 2010, r 12.16(4),(5)). PD12E (*Urgent Business*) provides further details of the procedure for out of hours applications. See also PD12D (*Inherent Jurisdiction (including Wardship) Proceedings*).

Evidence in support of application—The application should be supported by evidence. When the application is made to the court which made a CA 1989, s 8 order, the statement should comply with FPR 2010, r 12.19. When an application is made in the High Court in relation to an order made elsewhere in the UK or in a specified dependent territory, which has been registered in the High Court, the application should be supported by affidavit. When the application is made without notice, permission under r 12.12 for the statement to be adduced may be sought at the hearing. See also FPR 2010, r 22.1 and PD22A, which deal with the power of the court to control evidence.

Form of order—The order is issued in Form C31 (FPR 2010, r 5.1 and PD5A).

Execution of order—An order under s 34(1) gives authority to an officer of the court or a constable, but it does not direct them to act. Execution of an order under s 34(1) needs to be conducted with discretion, in order to avoid harmful distress to the child. The police are not obliged to assist and may refuse (*R v Chief Constable of Cheshire ex parte K* [1990] 1 FLR 70). Although a solicitor is an officer of the Senior Courts (Solicitors Act 1974, s 50), he is not an officer of either a county court (CCA 1984, s 147) or a family proceedings court.

****

36 Effect of orders restricting removal

(1) This section applies to any order made by a court in the United Kingdom or any specified dependent territory prohibiting the removal of a child from the United Kingdom or from any specified part of it or from any such territory.

(2) An order to which this section applies, made by a court in one part of the United Kingdom or in a specified dependent territory, shall have effect in each other part, or, in the case of an order made in a dependent territory, each part of the United Kingdom –

(a) as if it had been made by the appropriate court in that part, and

(b) in the case of an order which has the effect of prohibiting the child's removal to that part, as if it had included a prohibition on his further removal to any place except one to which he could be removed consistently with the order.

(3) The references in subsections (1) and (2) above to prohibitions on a child's removal include references to prohibitions subject to exceptions; and in a case where removal is prohibited except with the consent of the court, nothing in subsection (2) above shall be construed as affecting the identity of the court whose consent is required.

(4) In this section "child" means a person who has not attained the age of sixteen; and this section shall cease to apply to an order relating to a child when he attains the age of sixteen.

Amendments—SI 1991/1723.

Defined terms—"appropriate court": ss 40, 32(1) (and see below); "specified dependent territory": s 42(1).

"appropriate court" (s 36(2)(a))—In England and Wales, the High Court.

General interpretation—See s 42.

37 Surrender of passports

(1) Where there is in force an order prohibiting or otherwise restricting the removal of a child from the United Kingdom or from any specified part of it or from a specified dependent territory, the court by which the order was in fact made, or by which it is treated under section 36 of this Act as having been made, may require any person to surrender any United Kingdom passport which has been issued to, or contains particulars of, the child.

(2) In this section "United Kingdom passport" means a current passport issued by the Government of the United Kingdom.

Amendments—SI 1991/1723.

Defined terms—"specified dependent territory": s 42(1).

General interpretation—See ss 42, 40, 32(1).

Power to order the surrender of passports—This provision can only be invoked if the court makes an order prohibiting or otherwise restricting the removal of a child from the UK. Its scope is further restricted in that the court can only require the surrender of *any UK passport* which has been issued *to a child* or contains particulars *of a child*. It does not apply to non-UK passports and passports that do not contain particulars of the child concerned.

"the court ... by which [the order] is treated under section 36 as having been made"—Section 36 enables the appropriate court in each part of the UK to make an order under s 37 as though it had made the prohibitory order in fact made in another part of the UK or a specified dependent territory. Note that the "appropriate court" in England and Wales which can exercise the power under s 37 is the High Court.

Other remedies for prevention of removal of a child from the jurisdiction—For arrangements for police to institute a port alert, and for giving notice to the Passport Office that passport facilities should not be provided without the permission of the court, see FPR PD12P.

Application for s 37 order—The application may be made by making an application in the court which made, or under s 36 is treated as having made, the order. Where the order was made by a family proceedings court, and the proceedings are no longer in motion, a fresh complaint may be required. The application may be made without notice where removal is thought to be imminent. The parties to the proceedings are set out in the table in FPR 2010, r 12.3(1). There is no prescribed form of notice for an application.

38 Automatic restriction on removal of wards of court

(1) The rule of law which (without any order of the court) restricts the removal of a ward of court from the jurisdiction of the court shall, in a case to which this section applies, have effects subject to the modifications in subsection (3) below.

(2) This section applies in relation to a ward of court if –

(a) proceedings for divorce, nullity or judicial separation in respect of the marriage of his parents are continuing in a court in another part of the United Kingdom (that is to say, in a part of the United Kingdom outside the jurisdiction of the court of which he is a ward), or in a specified dependent territory, or

(aa) proceedings for dissolution or annulment or legal separation in respect of the civil partnership of his parents are continuing in a court in another part of the United Kingdom (that is to say, in a part of the United Kingdom outside the jurisdiction of the court of which he is a ward), or

(b) he is habitually resident in another part of the United Kingdom or in a specified dependent territory,

except where that other part is Scotland and he has attained the age of sixteen.

(3) Where this section applies, the rule referred to in subsection (1) above shall not prevent –

(a) the removal of the ward of court, without the consent of any court, to the other part of the United Kingdom or the specified dependent territory mentioned in subsection (2) above, or

(b) his removal to any other place with the consent of either the appropriate court in that other part of the United Kingdom or the specified dependent territory or the court mentioned in subsection (2)(a) or (aa) above.

Amendments—SI 1991/1723; SI 2005/3336.

Defined terms—"appropriate court": ss 40, 32(1); "specified dependent territory": s 42(1).

General interpretation—See s 42.

"habitually resident" (s 38(2)(b))—See under s 3 and **Habitual residence** under CSA 1991, s 44.

39 Duty to furnish particulars of other proceedings

Parties to proceedings for or relating to a Part I order shall, to such extent and in such manner as may be prescribed, give particulars of other proceedings known to them which relate to the child concerned (including proceedings instituted abroad and proceedings which are no longer continuing).

Amendments—CA 1989, s 108(5), Sch 13, para 62.

Defined terms—"Part I order": ss 1(2),(3), 42(5),(6); "prescribed": s 42(1).

General interpretation—See s 42.

"Part I order"—See under s 25.

"to such extent and in such manner as may be prescribed"—Section 42(1) defines "prescribed" in relation to England and Wales as meaning prescribed by rules of court.

40 Interpretation of Chapter VI

(1) In this Chapter –

"the appropriate court" has the same meaning as in Chapter V;

"Part I order" includes (except where the context otherwise requires) any such order as is mentioned in section 32(1) of this Act.

(2) In the application of this Chapter to Scotland, "Part I order" also includes (except where the context otherwise requires) any such order as is mentioned in section 32(2) of this Act.

Amendments—CA 1989, s 108(5), Sch 13, para 62.

41 Habitual residence after removal without consent etc

(1) Where a child who –

  (a) has not attained the age of sixteen, and
  (b) is habitually resident in a part of the United Kingdom or in a specified dependent territory,

becomes habitually resident outside that part of the United Kingdom or that territory in consequence of circumstances of the kind specified in subsection (2) below, he shall be treated for the purposes of this Part as continuing to be habitually resident in that part of the United Kingdom or that territory for the period of one year beginning with the date on which those circumstances arise.

(2) The circumstances referred to in subsection (1) above exist where the child is removed from or retained outside, or himself leaves or remains outside, the part of the United Kingdom or the territory in which he was habitually resident before his change of residence –

  (a) without the agreement of the person or all the persons having, under the law of that part of the United Kingdom or that territory, the right to determine where he is to reside, or
  (b) in contravention of an order made by a court in any part of the United Kingdom or in a specified dependent territory.

(3) A child shall cease to be treated by virtue of subsection (1) above as habitually resident in a part of the United Kingdom or a specified dependent territory if, during the period there mentioned –

  (a) he attains the age of sixteen, or
  (b) he becomes habitually resident outside that part of the United Kingdom or that territory with the agreement of the person or persons mentioned in subsection (2)(a) above and not in contravention of an order made by a court in any part of the United Kingdom or in any specified dependent territory.

Amendments—SI 1991/1723.

Defined terms—"specified dependent territory": s 42(1).

Scope—Section 41 has no application to the determination of questions of habitual residence under Art 3 of the Hague Convention. Section 41(1) is a deeming provision that applies only to Pt I of the 1986 Act. It regulates any jurisdictional or enforcement conflict between the constituent jurisdictions of the UK, but has no application to conflicts between UK jurisdictions and any jurisdiction that is not a constituent part of the UK. Questions of habitual residence in relation to Art 3 of the Hague Convention are to be determined by reference to international jurisprudence (*Re S (A Child: Abduction)* [2003] 1 FLR 1008).

General interpretation—See s 42.

"habitually resident" (s 41(1))—See under s 3 and **Habitual residence** under CSA 1991, s 44.

"one year period" (s 41(1))—When an order was made without jurisdiction in the 12-month period following a move from Scotland where the child had been habitually resident, the order remained in force until it was discharged. Where no application was made to discharge such an order in the 12-month period the English court had jurisdiction and it mattered not that the original order had been made unlawfully (*Re B (Court's Jurisdiction)* [2004] 2 FLR 741).

"agreement of the person or persons mentioned in subsection (2)(a)" (s 41(3)(b))—A parent's preliminary or interim views expressed during the course of legal proceedings taken to determine the child's future residence cannot be taken as consent to a change of habitual residence; a parent's participation in such legal proceedings is a sensible course of action and should not be held against the parent (*D v D (Custody: Jurisdiction)* [1996] 1 FLR 574).

42 General interpretation of Part I

(1) In this Part –

"certified copy", in relation to an order of any court, means a copy certified by the prescribed officer of the court to be a true copy of the order or of the official record of the order;

"corresponding dependent territory order", "corresponding dependent territory provision" and similar expressions, in relation to a specified dependent territory, shall be construed in accordance with Schedule 3 to the Family Law Act 1986 (Dependent Territories) Order 1991 as from time to time in force: "dependent territory" has the meaning given by section 43(2) of this Act;

"parental responsibilities" and "parental rights" have the meanings respectively given by sections 1(3) and 2(4) of the Children (Scotland) Act 1995;

"part of the United Kingdom" means England and Wales, Scotland or Northern Ireland;

"prescribed" means prescribed by rules of court or act of sederunt;

"specified dependent territory" means a dependent territory for the time being specified in Schedule 1 to the said order of 1991.

"the Council Regulation" means Council Regulation (EC) No 2201/2003 of 27 November 2003 concerning jurisdiction and the recognition and enforcement of judgments in matrimonial matters and matters of parental responsibility.

"the Hague Convention" means the Convention on Jurisdiction, Applicable Law, Recognition, Enforcement and Co-Operation in respect of Parental Responsibility and Measures for the Protection of Children that was signed at The Hague on 19 October 1996.

(2) For the purposes of this Part proceedings in England and Wales, Northern Ireland or a specified dependent territory for divorce, nullity or judicial separation in respect of the marriage of the parents of a child shall, unless they have been dismissed, be treated as continuing until the child concerned attains the age of eighteen (whether or not a decree has been granted and whether or not, in the case of a decree of divorce or nullity of marriage, that decree has been made absolute).

(2A) For the purposes of this Part proceedings in England and Wales or in Northern Ireland for dissolution, annulment or legal separation in respect of the civil partnership of the parents of the child shall, unless they have been dismissed, be treated as continuing until the child concerned attains the age of eighteen (whether or not a dissolution, nullity or separation order has been made and whether or not, in the case of a dissolution or nullity order, that order has been made final).

(3) For the purposes of this Part, matrimonial proceedings or civil partnership proceedings in a court in Scotland which has jurisdiction in those proceedings to make a Part I order with respect to a child shall, unless they have been dismissed or decree of absolvitor has been granted therein, be treated as continuing until the child concerned attains the age of sixteen.

(4) Any reference in this Part to proceedings in respect of the marriage of the parents of a child shall, in relation to a child who, although not a child of both parties to the marriage, is a child of the family of those parties, be construed as a reference to proceedings in respect of that marriage; and for this purpose "child of the family" –

    (a)   if the proceedings are in England and Wales, means any child who has been treated by both parties as a child of their family, except a child who is placed with those parties as foster parents by a local authority or a voluntary organisation;

    (b)   if the proceedings are in Scotland, means any child who has been treated by both parties as a child of their family, except a child who has been placed with those parties as foster parents by a local authority or a voluntary organisation;

    (c)   if the proceedings are in Northern Ireland, means any child who has been treated by both parties as a child of their family, except a child who is placed with those parties as foster parents by an authority within the meaning of the Children (Northern Ireland) Order 1995;

    (d)   if the proceedings are in a specified dependent territory, means any child who has been treated by both parties as a child of their family, except a child who has been placed with those parties as foster parents by a public authority in that territory.

(4A) Any reference in this Part to proceedings in respect of the civil partnership of the parents of a child shall, in relation to a child who, although not a child of the civil partners, is a child of the family of the civil partners, be construed as a reference to proceedings in respect of that civil partnership; and for this purpose "child of the family" has the meaning given in paragraphs (a) to (c) of subsection (4) (but substituting references to the civil partners for references to the parties to the marriage).

(5) References in this Part to Part I orders include (except where the context otherwise requires) references to Part I orders as varied.

(6) For the purposes of this Part each of the following orders shall be treated as varying the Part I order to which it relates –

    (a)   an order which provides for a person to be allowed contact with or to be given access to a child who is the subject of a Part I order, or which makes provision for the education of such a child,

    (b)–(e)   *(repealed)*

(7) In this Part –

    (a)   references to Part I proceedings in respect of a child are references to any proceedings for a Part I order or an order corresponding to a Part I order and include, in relation to proceedings outside the United Kingdom and any specified dependent territory, references to proceedings before a tribunal or other authority having power under the law having effect there to determine Part I matters; and

    (b)   references to Part I matters are references to matters that might be determined by a Part I order or an order corresponding to a Part I order.

Amendments—CA 1989, s 108(5), (7), Sch 13, paras 62, 71, Sch 15; SI 1991/1723; Children (Scotland) Act 1995, s 105(4), Sch 4, para 41(1),(9); SI 1995/756; SI 2001/310; SI 2001/660; SI 2005/265; SI 2005/3336; SI 2010/1898.

"dependent territory"—Within the meaning of the British Nationality Act 1981, this term is to be read as a reference to "British overseas territory" (see British Overseas Territories Act 2002, s 1(2)).

"corresponding dependent territory order" etc—In relation to the Isle of Man, see FLA 1986(DT)O 1991, Sch 3 for specific interpretation.

"specified dependent territory"—See also Family Law Act 1986 (Dependent Territories) (Amendment) Order 1994 and FPR 2010, r 32.23.

****

PART II
RECOGNITION OF DIVORCES, ANNULMENTS AND LEGAL SEPARATIONS

Divorces, annulments and judicial separations granted in the British Islands

44 Recognition in United Kingdom of divorces, annulments and judicial separations granted in the British Islands

(1) Subject to section 52(4) and (5)(a) of this Act, no divorce or annulment obtained in any part of the British Islands shall be regarded as effective in any part of the United Kingdom unless granted by a court of civil jurisdiction.

(2) Subject to section 51 of this Act, the validity of any divorce, annulment or judicial separation granted by a court of civil jurisdiction in any part of the British Islands shall be recognised throughout the United Kingdom.

Defined terms—"annulment", "part of the United Kingdom": s 54(1).

Overseas divorces, annulments and legal separations

45 Recognition in the United Kingdom of overseas divorces, annulments and legal separations

(1) Subject to subsection (2) of this section and to sections 51 and 52 of this Act, the validity of a divorce, annulment or legal separation obtained in a country outside the British Islands (in this Part referred to as an overseas divorce, annulment or legal separation) shall be recognised in the United Kingdom if, and only if, it is entitled to recognition –

(a) by virtue of sections 46 to 49 of this Act, or

(b) by virtue of any enactment other than this Part.

(2) Subsection (1) and the following provisions of this Part do not apply to an overseas divorce, annulment or legal separation as regards which provision as to recognition is made by Articles 21 to 27, 41(1) and 42(1) of the Council Regulation.

Amendments—SI 2001/310; SI 2005/265.

Defined terms—"annulment": s 54(1); "country": s 54(2).

46 Grounds for recognition

(1) The validity of an overseas divorce, annulment or legal separation obtained by means of proceedings shall be recognised if –

(a) the divorce, annulment or legal separation is effective under the law of the country in which it was obtained; and

(b) at the relevant date either party to the marriage –

(i) was habitually resident in the country in which the divorce, annulment or legal separation was obtained; or

(ii) was domiciled in that country; or

(iii) was a national of that country.

(2) The validity of an overseas divorce, annulment or legal separation obtained otherwise than by means of proceedings shall be recognised if –

(a) the divorce, annulment or legal separation is effective under the law of the country in which it was obtained;

(b)   at the relevant date –
    (i)   each party to the marriage was domiciled in that country; or
    (ii) either party to the marriage was domiciled in that country and the other party was domiciled in a country under whose law the divorce, annulment or legal separation is recognised as valid; and
(c)   neither party to the marriage was habitually resident in the United Kingdom throughout the period of one year immediately preceding that date.

(3) In this section "the relevant date" means –
    (a)   in the case of an overseas divorce, annulment or legal separation obtained by means of proceedings, the date of the commencement of the proceedings;
    (b)   in the case of an overseas divorce, annulment or legal separation obtained otherwise than by means of proceedings, the date on which it was obtained.

(4) Where in the case of an overseas annulment, the relevant date fell after the death of either party to the marriage, any reference in subsection (1) or (2) above to that date shall be construed in relation to that party as a reference to the date of death.

(5) For the purpose of this section, a party to a marriage shall be treated as domiciled in a country if he was domiciled in that country either according to the law of that country in family matters or according to the law of the part of the United Kingdom in which the question of recognition arises.

Defined terms—"annulment": s 54(1); "country": s 54(2); "part of the United Kingdom", "proceedings" s 54(1).

"effective under the law of the country in which it was obtained" (s 46(1)(a))—Where a husband had applied for a divorce to a tribunal in Ghana and had made his wife's mother a defendant to the proceedings, but where his wife had no knowledge of the proceedings and there was no evidence that her mother had voluntarily submitted to the jurisdiction of the tribunal, or that the tribunal had made adequate efforts by adjourning the case to hear the wife's side of the case, Wall J held that the order dissolving the marriage was not effective since the High Court in Ghana would not have upheld the decree on a judicial review. Even if this were not the case, FLA 1986, s 51(3)(a)(i) gives the court a wide discretion to refuse what would otherwise be mandatory recognition afforded under s 46 by applying the English concept of what would constitute "reasonable steps" to give notice of the proceedings to the wife (*D v D (Recognition of Foreign Divorce)* [1994] 1 FLR 38). See further under s 51(3)(a)(i). For an example of a case under s 46(2)(a) see *Wicken v Wicken* [1999] 1 FLR 293 where expert evidence called by both parties established that a divorce letter was, as a matter of substantive law, effective under the law of The Gambia to dissolve the marriage. There was a requirement that in the event of a dispute in The Gambia the authenticity of the document be proved by the testimony of two righteous male witnesses. However, that requirement was a matter of evidence and not substantive law, and as the dispute as to authenticity arose in England, the rules of evidence of England and Wales applied. Applying those rules, the letter was held to be authentic and therefore valid under Gambian law.
    Ordinarily, a talaq is not the product of judicial or other proceedings but is the product of a simple pronouncement. However, where Lebanese law required a talaq to be recorded with the Sharia court, that registration process was properly described as "proceedings" for the purposes of s 46(1), even though no judicial decision was required (*El Fadl v El Fadl* [2000] 1 FLR 175). In *H v H (Talaq Divorce)* [2008] 2 FLR 857 although a unilateral process that might offend English sensibilities, the talaq divorce (on the facts of this case) would be recognised; it was important that marriages and divorces recognised in one country be recognised in another. However, a bare talaq pronounced in England between nationals of Saudi Arabia did not dissolve a marriage, even if it was subsequently registered with the Sharia court in Saudi Arabia, because divorces obtained in the UK other than by proceedings in a court of civil jurisdiction are not recognised (s 44(1)). Furthermore, neither was it an overseas divorce within the meaning of s 45 (1)(a) as it was obtained in the UK not Saudi Arabia (*Sulaiman v Juffali* [2002] 1 FLR 479). A Japanese kyogi rikon was held to be a divorce obtained by a means of proceedings; it is a divorce agreed between the parties and registered with the State. The registration by the State is fundamental and not merely probative (*H v H (The Queen's Proctor Intervening)* [2007] 1 FLR 1318).
    "Effective" connotes a less rigorous standard than "valid". "Effective" can mean a decree which, although invalid per se in the granting state, is none the less to be treated as valid by virtue of some supervening legal decision or equitable principle such as estoppel (*Kellman v Kellman* [2000] 1 FLR 785).

"habitually resident" (s 46(1)(b)(i),(2)(c))—See under s 3 and **Habitual residence** under CSA 1991, s 44.

Transnational divorces (s 46(3))—FLA 1986 contemplates that the proceedings by which the "overseas divorce" has been obtained should have been commenced and concluded in the same place. The mere fact that a divorce was pronounced or finalised in one country does not entitle the court to overlook the fact that part of the proceedings has been conducted elsewhere. The word "obtained" connotes a process rather than a single act. Where an important step in the proceedings leading to the divorce has taken place in England rather than in the jurisdiction in which the divorce was pronounced, that divorce is properly to be regarded not as an "overseas divorce" but rather as a transnational divorce. If the divorce has not been terminated by means of "overseas proceedings", it cannot be recognised in England and Wales under FLA 1986 (*Berkovits v Grinberg (Attorney-General Intervening)* [1995] 1 FLR 477).

47 Cross-proceedings and divorces following legal separations

(1) Where there have been cross-proceedings, the validity of an overseas divorce, annulment or legal separation obtained either in the original proceedings or in the cross-proceedings shall be recognised if –

    (a)   the requirements of section 46(1)(b)(i), (ii) or (iii) of this Act are satisfied in relation to the date of the commencement either of the original proceedings or of the cross-proceedings, and

    (b)   the validity of the divorce, annulment or legal separation is otherwise entitled to recognition by virtue of the provisions of this Part.

(2) Where a legal separation, the validity of which is entitled to recognition by virtue of the provisions of section 46 of this Act or of subsection (1) above is converted, in the country in which it was obtained, into a divorce which is effective under the law of that country, the validity of the divorce shall be recognised whether or not it would itself be entitled to recognition by virtue of those provisions.

Defined terms—"annulment": s 54(1); "country": s 54(2); "proceedings": s 54(1).

48 Proof of facts relevant to recognition

(1) For the purpose of deciding whether an overseas divorce, annulment or legal separation obtained by means of proceedings is entitled to recognition by virtue of section 46 and 47 of this Act, any finding of fact made (whether expressly or by implication) in the proceedings and on the basis of which jurisdiction was assumed in the proceedings shall –

    (a)   if both parties to the marriage took part in the proceedings, be conclusive evidence of the fact found; and

    (b)   in any other case, be sufficient proof of that fact unless the contrary is shown.

(2) In this section "finding of fact" includes a finding that either party to the marriage –

    (a)   was habitually resident in the country in which the divorce, annulment or legal separation was obtained; or

    (b)   was under the law of that country domiciled there; or

    (c)   was a national of that country.

(3) For the purposes of subsection (1)(a) above, a party to the marriage who has appeared in judicial proceedings shall be treated as having taken part in them.

Defined terms—"annulment": s 54(1); "country": s 54(2); "proceedings": s 54(1).

"habitually resident" (s 48(2)(a))—See under s 3 and **Habitual residence** under CSA 1991, s 44.

Supplemental

49 Modifications of Part II in relation to countries comprising territories having different systems of law

(1) In relation to a country comprising territories in which different systems of law are in force in matters of divorce, annulment or legal separation, the provisions of this Part mentioned in subsections (2) to (5) below shall have effect subject to the modifications there specified.

(2) In the case of a divorce, annulment or legal separation the recognition of the validity of which depends on whether the requirements of subsection (1)(b)(i) or (ii) of section 46 of this Act are satisfied, that section and, in the case of a legal separation, section 47(2) of this Act shall have effect as if each territory were a separate country.

(3) In the case of a divorce, annulment or legal separation the recognition of the validity of which depends on whether the requirements of subsection (1)(b)(iii) of section 46 of this Act are satisfied –

   (a)   that section shall have effect as if for paragraph (a) of subsection (1) there were substituted the following paragraph –
         "(a) the divorce, annulment or legal separation is effective throughout the country in which it was obtained;"; and
   (b)   in the case of a legal separation, section 47(2) of this Act shall have effect as if for the words "is effective under the law of that country" there were substituted the words "is effective throughout that country".

(4) In the case of a divorce, annulment or legal separation the recognition of the validity of which depends on whether the requirements of subsection (2)(b) of section 46 of this Act are satisfied, that section and section 52(3) and (4) of this Act and, in the case of a legal separation, section 47(2) of this Act shall have effect as if each territory were a separate country.

(5) Paragraphs (a) and (b) of section 48(2) of this Act shall each have effect as if each territory were a separate country.

Defined terms—"annulment": s 54(1); "country": s 54(2).

50 Non-recognition of divorce or annulment in another jurisdiction no bar to remarriage

Where, in any part of the United Kingdom –

   (a)   a divorce or annulment has been granted by a court of civil jurisdiction, or
   (b)   the validity of a divorce or annulment is recognised by virtue of this Part,

the fact that the divorce or annulment would not be recognised elsewhere shall not preclude either party to the marriage from forming a subsequent marriage or civil partnership in that part of the United Kingdom or cause the subsequent marriage or civil partnership of either party (wherever it takes place) to be treated as invalid in that part.

Defined terms—"annulment", "part of the United Kingdom": s 54(1); CPA 2004, s 261(1), Sch 27, para 125.

51 Refusal of recognition

(1) Subject to section 52 of this Act, recognition of the validity of –

   (a)   a divorce, annulment or judicial separation granted by a court of civil jurisdiction in any part of the British Islands, or
   (b)   an overseas divorce, annulment or legal separation,

may be refused in any part of the United Kingdom if the divorce, annulment or separation was granted or obtained at a time when it was irreconcilable with a decision determining the question of the subsistence or validity of the marriage of the parties previously given (whether before or after the commencement of this Part) by a court of civil jurisdiction in that part of the United Kingdom or by a court elsewhere and recognised or entitled to be recognised in that part of the United Kingdom.

(2) Subject to section 52 of this Act, recognition of the validity of –

    (a) a divorce or judicial separation granted by a court of civil jurisdiction in any part of the British Islands, or

    (b) an overseas divorce or legal separation,

may be refused in any part of the United Kingdom if the divorce or separation was granted or obtained at a time when, according to the law of that part of the United Kingdom (including its rules of private international law and the provisions of this Part), there was no subsisting marriage between the parties.

(3) Subject to section 52 of this Act, recognition by virtue of section 45 of this Act of the validity of an overseas divorce, annulment or legal separation may be refused if –

    (a) in the case of a divorce, annulment or legal separation obtained by means of proceedings, it was obtained –

        (i) without such steps having been taken for giving notice of the proceedings to a party to the marriage as, having regard to the nature of the proceedings and all the circumstances, should reasonably have been taken; or

        (ii) without a party to the marriage having been given (for any reason other than lack of notice) such opportunity to take part in the proceedings as, having regard to those matters, he should reasonably have been given; or

    (b) in the case of a divorce, annulment or legal separation obtained otherwise than by means of proceedings –

        (i) there is no official document certifying that the divorce, annulment or legal separation is effective under the law of the country in which it was obtained; or

        (ii) where either party to the marriage was domiciled in another country at the relevant date, there is no official document certifying that the divorce, annulment or legal separation is recognised as valid under the law of that other country; or

    (c) in either case, recognition of the divorce, annulment or legal separation would be manifestly contrary to public policy.

(4) In this section –

    "official", in relation to a document certifying that a divorce, annulment or legal separation is effective, or is recognised as valid, under the law of any country, means issued by a person or body appointed or recognised for the purpose under that law;

    "the relevant date" has the same meaning as in section 46 of this Act;

and subsection (5) of that section shall apply for the purposes of this section as it applies for the purposes of that section.

(5) Nothing in this Part shall be construed as requiring the recognition of any finding of fault made in any proceedings for divorce, annulment or separation or of any maintenance, custody or other ancillary order made in any such proceedings.

Defined terms—"annulment": s 54(1); "country": s 54(2); "part of the United Kingdom", "proceedings": s 54(1).

"without such steps having been taken for giving notice of the proceedings to a party to the marriage" (s 51(3)(a)(i))—A foreign divorce may be refused even where the requirements of FLA 1986, s 46 are satisfied if it was obtained "without such steps being taken for giving notice of the proceedings to a party to the marriage as, having regard to the nature of the proceedings and all the circumstances, should reasonably have been taken" – see *Duhur-Johnson v Duhur-Johnson (Attorney-General intervening)* [2005] 2 FLR 1042 for an analysis of previous authorities and the approach that the court should take. See also **"effective under the law of the country in which it was obtained"** under s 46.

"manifestly contrary to public policy" (s 51(3)(c))—The discretion to refuse recognition on the grounds that it would be manifestly contrary to public policy is one to be exercised sparingly – see *El Fadl v El Fadl* [2000] 1 FLR 175 and *Kellman v Kellman* [2000] 1 FLR 785. The motive for the divorce is generally irrelevant to the exercise of that discretion. While fraud is not a ground for refusal of recognition, there may be exceptional circumstances where one party may have deceived the other and the foreign court which may be relevant to the exercise of the discretion. In *Eroglu v Eroglu* [1994] 2 FLR 287, where the petitioner participated with the respondent in a ruse to obtain a Turkish divorce which was designed to achieve material advantage for the respondent, and which material advantage was enjoyed and shared by the petitioner, the petitioner fell far short of persuading the court that the recognition of the Turkish divorce would be manifestly contrary to public policy. A divorce granted by a state that is not recognised by the UK Government can be recognised, provided that it was obtained in accordance with the relevant conditions applicable within the area and that the provisions under ss 46–54 have been complied with. However, such recognition must never be inconsistent with foreign policy or the diplomatic stance of the government and therefore when the court is asked to recognise the acts of an unrecognised state or its courts, it should, where possible, be assisted by representations on behalf of the Attorney-General (*Emin v Yeldag (Attorney-General and Secretary of State for Foreign and Commonwealth Affairs Intervening)* [2002] 1 FLR 956).

52 Provisions as to divorces, annulments etc obtained before commencement of Part II

(1) The provisions of this Part shall apply –

    (a) to a divorce, annulment or judicial separation granted by a court of civil jurisdiction in the British Islands before the date of the commencement of this Part, and

    (b) to an overseas divorce, annulment or legal separation obtained before that date,

as well as to one granted or obtained on or after that date.

(2) In the case of such a divorce, annulment or separation as is mentioned in subsection (1)(a) or (b) above, the provisions of this Part shall require or, as the case may be, preclude the recognition of its validity in relation to any time before that date as well as in relation to any subsequent time, but those provisions shall not –

    (a) affect any property to which any person became entitled before that date, or

    (b) affect the recognition of the validity of the divorce, annulment or separation if that matter has been decided by any competent court in the British Islands before that date.

(3) Subsections (1) and (2) above shall apply in relation to any divorce or judicial separation granted by a court of civil jurisdiction in the British Islands before the date of the commencement of this Part whether granted before or after the commencement of section 1 of the Recognition of Divorces and Legal Separations Act 1971.

(4) The validity of any divorce, annulment or legal separation mentioned in subsection (5) below shall be recognised in the United Kingdom whether or not it is entitled to recognition by virtue of any of the foregoing provisions of this Part.

(5) The divorces, annulments and legal separations referred to in subsection (4) above are –

    (a) a divorce which was obtained in the British Islands before 1 January 1974 and was recognised as valid under rules of law applicable before that date;

    (b) an overseas divorce which was recognised as valid under the Recognition of Divorces and Legal Separations Act 1971 and was not affected by section 16(2) of the Domicile and Matrimonial Proceedings Act 1973 (proceedings otherwise than in a court of law where both parties resident in the United Kingdom);

(c) a divorce of which the decree was registered under section 1 of the Indian and Colonial Divorce Jurisdiction Act 1926;

(d) a divorce or annulment which was recognised as valid under section 4 of the Matrimonial Causes (War Marriages) Act 1944; and

(e) an overseas legal separation which was recognised as valid under the Recognition of Divorces and Legal Separations Act 1971.

Defined terms—"annulment": s 54(1).

****

54 Interpretation of Part II

(1) In this Part –

"annulment" includes any decree or declarator of nullity of marriage, however expressed;

"the Council Regulation" means Council Regulation (EC) No 2201/2003 of 27 November 2003 concerning jurisdiction and the recognition and enforcement of judgments in matrimonial matters and matters of parental responsibility;

"part of the United Kingdom" means England and Wales, Scotland or Northern Ireland;

"proceedings" means judicial or other proceedings.

(2) In this Part "country" includes a colony or other dependent territory of the United Kingdom but for the purposes of this Part a person shall be treated as a national of such a territory only if it has a law of citizenship or nationality separate from that of the United Kingdom and he is a citizen or national of that territory under that law.

Amendments—SI 2001/310; SI 2005/265.

"dependent territory" (s 54(2))—Within the meaning of the British Nationality Act 1981, this term is to be read as a reference to "British overseas territory" (see British Overseas Territories Act 2002, s 1(2)).

PART III
DECLARATIONS OF STATUS

55 Declarations as to marital status

(1) Subject to the following provisions of this section, any person may apply to the High Court or a county court for one or more of the following declarations in relation to a marriage specified in the application, that is to say –

(a) a declaration that the marriage was at its inception a valid marriage;

(b) a declaration that the marriage subsisted on a date specified in the application;

(c) a declaration that the marriage did not subsist on a date so specified;

(d) a declaration that the validity of a divorce, annulment or legal separation obtained in any country outside England and Wales in respect of the marriage is entitled to recognition in England and Wales;

(e) a declaration that the validity of a divorce, annulment or legal separation so obtained in respect of the marriage is not entitled to recognition in England and Wales.

(2) A court shall have jurisdiction to entertain an application under subsection (1) above if, and only if, either of the parties to the marriage to which the application relates –

(a) is domiciled in England and Wales on the date of the application, or

    (b)   has been habitually resident in England and Wales throughout the period of one
          year ending with that date, or

    (c)   died before that date and either –

          (i)   was at death domiciled in England and Wales, or

          (ii)   had been habitually resident in England and Wales throughout the period
              of one year ending with the date of death.

(3) Where an application under subsection (1) above is made to a court by any person
other than a party to the marriage to which the application relates, the court shall refuse
to hear the application if it considers that the applicant does not have a sufficient interest
in the determination of that application.

Amendments—CSPSSA 2000, s 83, Sch 8, para 4.

"Deferral to court in another jurisdiction"—In *Abassi v Abassi and another* [2006] 2 FLR 415 the
Court of Appeal indicated that it was within the discretion of a judge to defer an issue of the validity of a
marriage to a court in another jurisdiction. Each case turned on its own facts. In family proceedings with
an international dimension it was becoming increasingly common to have regard to the sensible transfer
by the court acting on its own motion. It would be appropriate to use a liaison judge to facilitate
collaboration.

Overseas same-sex relationship—In *Wilkinson v Kitzinger* [2007] 1 FLR 295 the President refused to
declare a valid marriage between two women, domiciled in England and Wales who went through a
ceremony of marriage in British Columbia which was a valid marriage there.

Marriage not subsisting—In the case of couples who have a second "marriage" in the UK, they should
no longer need to apply for a declaration of non-marriage (s 55(1)(c)), suggests Mostyn J, on production
of his judgment in *Galloway v Goldstein* [2012] 1 FLR 1254 (at [15]).

"habitually resident" (s 55(2)(b),(c)(i))—See under s 3 and **Habitual residence** under CSA 1991, s 44.

Procedure—See Procedural Guide B1.

55A Declarations of parentage

(1) Subject to the following provisions of this section, any person may apply to the High
Court, a county court or a magistrates' court for a declaration as to whether or not a
person named in the application is or was the parent of another person so named.

(2) A court shall have jurisdiction to entertain an application under subsection (1) above
if, and only if, either of the persons named in it for the purposes of that subsection –

    (a)   is domiciled in England and Wales on the date of the application, or

    (b)   has been habitually resident in England and Wales throughout the period of one
          year ending with that date, or

    (c)   died before that date and either –

          (i)   was at death domiciled in England and Wales, or

          (ii)   had been habitually resident in England and Wales throughout the period
              of one year ending with the date of death.

(3) Except in a case falling within subsection (4) below, the court shall refuse to hear an
application under subsection (1) above unless it considers that the applicant has a
sufficient personal interest in the determination of the application (but this is subject to
section 27 of the Child Support Act 1991).

(4) The excepted cases are where the declaration sought is as to whether or not –

    (a)   the applicant is the parent of a named person;

    (b)   a named person is the parent of the applicant; or

    (c)   a named person is the other parent of a named child of the applicant.

(5) Where an application under subsection (1) above is made and one of the persons named in it for the purposes of that subsection is a child, the court may refuse to hear the application if it considers that the determination of the application would not be in the best interests of the child.

(6) Where a court refuses to hear an application under subsection (1) above it may order that the applicant may not apply again for the same declaration without leave of the court.

(7) Where a declaration is made by a court on an application under subsection (1) above, the prescribed officer of the court shall notify the Registrar General, in such a manner and within such period as may be prescribed, of the making of that declaration.

Amendments—Inserted by CSPSSA 2000, s 83(1),(2).

Procedure—Application is made by (1) FPR 2010, Pt 19 and rr 8.18–8.22 as a freestanding application or (2) alongside existing proceedings where an issue of parentage arises in those proceedings.

Child Support Act 1991, s 27—Application for a declaration by non-resident parent, parent with care or the Secretary of State for Work and Pensions (under CSA 1991, s 27, see above) where needed to prove parentage under the 1991 Act is under s 55A, that is where a parent or the Secretary of State disagree with a decision as to parentage.

Scientific tests direction—The court may direct scientific tests (FLRA 1969, s 20) to determine whether a person is the parent of the child. Application for a scientific tests direction can only be made in existing civil (including family) proceedings in which the issue of parentage arises, including in proceedings under FLA 1986, s 55A).

Appeal in family proceedings court—Where the issue of parentage arises on an appeal under CSA 1991, s 20, the appeal is transferred for hearing from the first-tier tribunal to the family proceedings court. A family proceedings court hearing an appeal under CSA 1991, s 20 cannot make a declaration under s 55A where no application has been made for such a declaration and the child in question has not been made a party (*Re L (Family Proceedings Court) (Appeal: Jurisdiction)* [2005] 1 FLR 210).

"parent" (s 55A(1))—Includes a person who is to be treated as a parent by virtue of HFEA 1990, s 27 or 28 (*Re R (IVF: Paternity of Child)* [2003] 1 FLR 1183).

"habitually resident" (s 55A(2))—See under s 3 and **Habitual residence** under CSA 1991, s 44.

Notification to the Registrar General (s 55A(7))—If a declaration is granted, the birth may be re-registered accordingly (Births and Deaths Registration Act 1953, s 14A). Registration of a declaration is prescribed by FPR 2010, r 8.22 as 21 days, although this period may be diverged from in exceptional circumstances (*Re F (Children)* [2011] EWCA Civ 1765: 4 months is permissible; 4 years was plainly too long).

56 Declarations as to legitimacy or legitimation

(1) Any person may apply to the High Court or a county court for a declaration –

    (a)   (*repealed*)

    (b)   that he is the legitimate child of his parents.

(2) Any person may apply to the High Court or a county court for one (or for one or, in the alternative, the other) of the following declarations, that is to say –

    (a)   a declaration that he has become a legitimated person;

    (b)   a declaration that he has not become a legitimated person.

(3) A court shall have jurisdiction to entertain an application under this section if, and only if, the applicant –

    (a)   is domiciled in England and Wales on the date of the application, or

    (b)   has been habitually resident in England and Wales throughout the period of one year ending with that date.

(4) Where a declaration is made by a court on an application under subsection (1) above, the prescribed officer of the court shall notify the Registrar General, in such a manner and within such period as may be prescribed, of the making of that declaration.

(5) In this section "legitimated person" means a person legitimated or recognised as legitimated –

- (a)   under section 2, 2A or 3 of the Legitimacy Act 1976; or
- (b)   under section 1 or 8 of the Legitimacy Act 1926; or
- (c)   by a legitimation (whether or not by virtue of the subsequent marriage of his parents) recognised by the law of England and Wales and effected under the law of another country.

Amendments—Substituted by FLRA 1987, s 22; CSPSSA 2000, s 83, Sch 8, para 5, Sch 9; HFEA 2008, s 56, Sch 6, Pt 1, para 23.

"habitually resident" (s 56(3)(b))—See under s 3 and **Habitual residence** under CSA 1991, s 44.

57   Declarations as to adoptions effected overseas

(1) Any person whose status as an adopted child of any person depends on whether he has been adopted by that person by either –

- (a)   a Convention adoption, or an overseas adoption, within the meaning of the Adoption and Children Act 2002, or
- (b)   an adoption recognised by the law of England and Wales and effected under the law of any country outside the British Islands,

may apply to the High Court or a county court for one (or for one or, in the alternative, the other) of the declarations mentioned in subsection (2) below.

(2) The said declarations are –

- (a)   a declaration that the applicant is for the purposes of section 39 of the Adoption Act 1976 or section 67 of the Adoption and Children Act 2002 the adopted child of that person;
- (b)   a declaration that the applicant is not for the purposes of that section the adopted child of that person.

(3) A court shall have jurisdiction to entertain an application under subsection (1) above if, and only if, the applicant –

- (a)   is domiciled in England and Wales on the date of the application, or
- (b)   has been habitually resident in England and Wales throughout the period of one year ending with that date.

(4) ...

Amendments—Adoption (Intercountry Aspects) Act 1999, s 15(1), Sch 2, para 5; CSPSSA 2000, s 83, Sch 8, para 6; ACA 2002, Sch 3, para 49.

58   General provisions as to the making and effect of declarations

(1) Where on an application to a court for a declaration under this Part the truth of the proposition to be declared is proved to the satisfaction of the court, the court shall make that declaration unless to do so would manifestly be contrary to public policy.

(2) Any declarations made under this Part shall be binding on Her Majesty and all other persons.

(3) A court, on the dismissal of an application for a declaration under this Part, shall not have power to make any declaration for which an application has not been made.

(4) No declaration which may be applied for under this Part may be made otherwise than under this Part by any court.

(5) No declaration may be made by any court, whether under this Part or otherwise –
- (a) that a marriage was at its inception void;
- (b) (*repealed*)

(6) Nothing in this section shall affect the powers of any court to grant a decree of nullity of marriage.

Amendments—CSPSSA 2000, s 83(3), Sch 8, para 7, Sch 9.

59 Provisions relating to the Attorney-General

(1) On an application to a court for a declaration under this Part the court may at any stage of the proceedings, of its own motion or on the application of any party to the proceedings, direct that all necessary papers in the matter be sent to the Attorney-General.

(2) The Attorney-General, whether or not he is sent papers in relation to an application to a court for a declaration under this Part, may –
- (a) intervene in the proceedings on that application in such manner as he thinks necessary or expedient, and
- (b) argue before the court any question in relation to the application which the court considers it necessary to have fully argued.

(3) Where any costs are incurred by the Attorney-General in connection with any application to a court for a declaration under this Part, the court may make such order as it considers just as to the payment of those costs by parties to the proceedings.

Amendments—CSPSSA 2000, s 83(3), Sch 8, para 8.

The Attorney-General's role—There are two main reasons for these provisions. First, to minimise the risk of success of unopposed, or collusive, proceedings which have been brought fraudulently to obtain a declaration. Section 58(2) provides that "Any declaration made under this Part shall be binding on Her Majesty and all other persons"; this creates scope for collusive proceedings to be brought for the purpose of obtaining some collateral result in relation to the state or other third parties, such as British citizenship. The role of the Attorney-General is therefore not dissimilar to that which the Queen's Proctor may play in undefended divorce proceedings. Secondly, quite apart from this aspect, s 58(1) provides that "Where on an application to a court for a declaration under this Part the truth of the proposition to be declared is proved to the satisfaction of the court, the court shall make that declaration unless to do so would manifestly be contrary to public policy". The Attorney-General may wish to express a view on the requirements of public policy in a particular case.

****

60 Supplementary provisions as to declarations

(1)–(4) ...

(5) An appeal shall lie to a county court against –
- (a) the making by a magistrates' court of a declaration under section 55A above,
- (b) any refusal by a magistrates' court to make such a declaration, or
- (c) any order under subsection (6) of that section made on such a refusal.

Amendments—Inserted by CSPSSA 2000, s 83(1),(4); amended by SI 2009/871.

****

Family Law Act 1996

ARRANGEMENT OF SECTIONS

PART IV
FAMILY HOMES AND DOMESTIC VIOLENCE

Rights to occupy matrimonial home

****

PART IV
FAMILY HOMES AND DOMESTIC VIOLENCE

Rights to occupy matrimonial home

30 Rights concerning matrimonial home where one spouse has no estate etc

(1) This section applies if –

    (a) one spouse or civil partner ("A") is entitled to occupy a dwelling-house by virtue of –

> (i)   a beneficial estate or interest or contract; or
>
> (ii)   any enactment giving "A" the right to remain in occupation; and

   (b)   the other spouse or civil partner ("B") is not so entitled.

(2)   Subject to the provisions of this Part, "B" has the following rights ("home rights") –

   (a)   if in occupation, a right not to be evicted or excluded from the dwelling-house or any part of it by "A" except with the leave of the court given by an order under section 33;

   (b)   if not in occupation, a right with the leave of the court so given to enter into and occupy the dwelling-house.

(3)   If "B" is entitled under this section to occupy a dwelling-house or any part of a dwelling-house, any payment or tender made or other thing done by "B" in or towards satisfaction of any liability of "A" in respect of rent, mortgage payments or other outgoings affecting the dwelling-house shall, whether or not it is made or done in pursuance of an order under section 40, be as good as if made or done by "A".

(4)   "B's" occupation by virtue of this section –

   (a)   is to be treated, for the purposes of the Rent (Agriculture) Act 1976 and the Rent Act 1977 (other than Part V and sections 103 to 106 of that Act), as occupation by A as A's residence, and

   (b)   if B occupies the dwelling-house as B's only or principal home, is to be treated, for the purposes of the Housing Act 1985, Part I of the Housing Act 1988 and Chapter I of Part V of the Housing Act 1996, as occupation by A as A's only or principal home.

(5)   If B –

   (a)   is entitled under this section to occupy a dwelling-house or any part of a dwelling-house, and

   (b)   makes any payment in or towards satisfaction of any liability of A in respect of mortgage payments affecting the dwelling-house,

the person to whom the payment is made may treat it as having been made by A, but the fact that that person has treated any such payment as having been so made does not affect any claim of B against A to an interest in the dwelling-house by virtue of the payment.

(6)   If B is entitled under this section to occupy a dwelling-house or part of a dwelling-house by reason of an interest of A under a trust, all the provisions of subsections (3) to (5) apply in relation to the trustees as they apply in relation to A.

(7)   This section does not apply to a dwelling-house which –

   (a)   in the case of spouses, has at no time been, and was at no time intended by them to be, a matrimonial home of theirs; and

   (b)   in the case of civil partners, has at no time been, and was at no time intended by them to be, a civil partnership home of theirs.

(8)   B's home rights continue –

   (a)   only so long as the marriage or civil partnership subsists, except to the extent that an order under section 33(5) otherwise provides; and

   (b)   only so long as A is entitled as mentioned in subsection (1) to occupy the dwelling-house, except where provision is made by section 31 for those rights to be a charge on an estate or interest in the dwelling-house.

(9)   It is hereby declared that a person –

   (a)   who has an equitable interest in a dwelling-house or in its proceeds of sale, but

   (b)   is not a person in whom there is vested (whether solely or as joint tenant) a legal estate in fee simple or a legal term of years absolute in the dwelling-house, is to be treated, only for the purpose of determining whether he has home rights, as not being entitled to occupy the dwelling-house by virtue of that interest.

Amendments—SI 1997/74; CPA 2004, s 82, Sch 9, para 1(1)–(11).

Scope—This section provides that where one spouse or civil partner has the right to occupy a dwelling-house, either because he owns it or has a contractual tenancy or is a statutory tenant of it, the other party has home rights. Those rights are, if in occupation, not to be evicted without leave of the court or, if not in occupation, the right, with leave of the court, to return. The provision mirrors Matrimonial Homes Act 1983, s 1 but is different in three respects: first, the rights are known as "home rights" instead of rights of occupation; secondly, by virtue of s 63(1), a "dwelling-house" includes a caravan or houseboat; and thirdly, under ss 30(7) and 33(1)(b), a dwelling-house which has not yet been, but is intended to be, a home is included (*Gull v Gull* [2008] 1 FLR 232). There are limitations to the right of a co-owner to go into property occupied by an estranged spouse. A husband, who is a co-owner with wife of a matrimonial property, in which he did not reside but had not been formally excluded and who used violence to gain entry, is not a protected occupier under Criminal Law Act 1977, s 12A and could be convicted of the use of violence to gain entry under s 6 of that Act: *Wakolo v DPP* [2012] EWHC 611 (Admin).

Duration of matrimonial home rights (s 30(8))—Matrimonial home rights subsist only for the duration of the marriage unless an order is made under s 33(5) before the marriage is ended by death or decree of divorce or nullity.

Treatment of one spouse's rights and obligations as those of the other spouse (s 30(3)–(5))—These subsections provide that payment of rent or mortgage by the spouse who does not have an interest or tenancy in the property is as good as payment by the other, and that the occupation of one spouse is to be treated as occupation by the other. Thus, if there is a statutory tenancy, even though the statutory tenant has left, the remaining spouse's occupation is as good as that of the statutory tenant. This protection lasts only so long as the status of the spouse is not ended by decree absolute. In s 30(4)(b) the references to the Housing Act 1985, the Housing Act 1988, Pt I and Housing Act 1996 are respectively to occupation by virtue of a secure tenancy, an assured tenancy/assured shorthold tenancy and an introductory tenancy (in effect a shorthold tenancy in the private sector).

Prevention of unilateral termination of tenancy—As set out in Procedural Guide A13, a tenancy in the other spouse's name or in joint names can be destroyed unilaterally by surrender or notice to quit. Consideration should therefore be given to applying for an injunction to prevent such action.

"matrimonial home" (s 30(7))—There is no definition of this term, although it includes a dwelling-house which has not yet been but is intended to be a matrimonial home, and a caravan or houseboat (see **Scope** above). However, for the purpose of certain sections, a caravan and a houseboat are *not* within the definition of dwelling-house (see s 63(4)). Whether a dwelling-house is or is intended to be a matrimonial home is a question of fact, having regard to any periods of time spent living there and any agreement between the parties as to whether a property is to be treated as their present or intended matrimonial home (*King v King* [1941] 2 All ER 103).

31 Effect of home rights as charge on dwelling-house

(1) Subsections (2) and (3) apply if, at any time during a marriage or civil partnership, A is entitled to occupy a dwelling-house by virtue of a beneficial estate or interest.

(2) B's home rights are a charge on the estate or interest.

(3) The charge created by subsection (2) has the same priority as if it were an equitable interest created at whichever is the latest of the following dates –

    (a)   the date on which A acquires the estate or interest;

    (b)   the date of the marriage or of the formation of the civil partnership; and

    (c)   1 January 1968 (the commencement date of the Matrimonial Homes Act 1967).

(4) Subsections (5) and (6) apply if, at any time when B's home rights are a charge on an interest of A under a trust, there are, apart from A or B, no persons, living or unborn, who are or could become beneficiaries under the trust.

(5) The rights are a charge also on the estate or interest of the trustees for A.

(6) The charge created by subsection (5) has the same priority as if it were an equitable interest created (under powers overriding the trusts) on the date when it arises.

(7) In determining for the purposes of subsection (4) whether there are any persons who are not, but could become, beneficiaries under the trust, there is to be disregarded any potential exercise of a general power of appointment exercisable by either or both of A and B alone (whether or not the exercise of it requires the consent of another person).

(8) Even though B's home rights are a charge on an estate or interest in the dwelling-house, those rights are brought to an end by –

(a)   the death of A, or

(b)   the termination (otherwise than by death) of the marriage or civil partnership,

unless the court directs otherwise by an order made under section 33(5).

(9) If –

(a)   B's home rights are a charge on an estate or interest in the dwelling-house, and

(b)   that estate or interest is surrendered to merge in some other estate or interest expectant on it in such circumstances that, but for the merger, the person taking the estate or interest would be bound by the charge,

the surrender has effect subject to the charge and the persons thereafter entitled to the other estate or interest are, for so long as the estate or interest surrendered would have endured if not so surrendered, to be treated for all purposes of this Part as deriving title to the other estate or interest under A or, as the case may be, under the trustees for A, by virtue of the surrender.

(10) If the title to the legal estate by virtue of which A is entitled to occupy a dwelling-house (including any legal estate held by trustees for A) is registered under the Land Registration Act 2002 or any enactment replaced by that Act –

(a)   registration of a land charge affecting the dwelling-house by virtue of this Part is to be effected by registering a notice under that Act; and

(b)   B's home rights are not to be capable of falling within paragraph 2 of Schedule 1 or 3 to that Act.

(11) (repealed)

(12) If –

(a)   B's home rights are a charge on the estate of A or of trustees of A, and

(b)   that estate is the subject of a mortgage,

then if, after the date of the creation of the mortgage ("the first mortgage"), the charge is registered under section 2 of the Land Charges Act 1972, the charge is, for the purposes of section 94 of the Law of Property Act 1925 (which regulates the rights of mortgagees to make further advances ranking in priority to subsequent mortgages), to be deemed to be a mortgage subsequent in date to the first mortgage.

(13) It is hereby declared that a charge under subsection (2) or (5) is not registrable under subsection 10 or under section 2 of the Land Charges Act 1972 unless it is a charge on a legal estate.

Amendments—CPA 2004, s 82, Sch 9, para 2(1)–(12); Land Registration Act 2002, s 34(2)(a),(b), Sch 13.

Protecting the charge—No protection under FLA 1996 is required in cases where the home is held jointly, both legally and beneficially, by the spouse or civil partner and the other spouse or the other civil partner. To give protection against third parties such as mortgagees or purchasers, in cases of sole ownership, it is essential that the charge is registered under either the Land Registration Act 2002 (agreed notice) or the Land Charges Act 1972 (Class F land charge), as appropriate. For the purpose of the Land Registration Act 2002, home rights are not an overriding interest, but constitute a charge on the home that can be protected in the register by an agreed notice (Land Registration Rules 2003, r 82). If the spouse or civil partner has home rights in relation to the other spouse's or civil partner's interest under a trust, notice of the charge can only be registered if there are no persons, living or unborn, who are or could become beneficiaries under the trust (s 31(4),(5),(13)). The charge should be registered as soon as the legal adviser is informed that the marriage or civil partnership is in difficulty (*Miles v Bull* [1969] 1 QB 258). The Land Registration Rules 2003 provide that notice of the charge is automatically given to the owner. Protection ends with the termination of the marriage or civil partnership subject to the power of the court, during the subsistence of the marriage or civil partnership, to direct that the home rights shall continue even though the marriage or civil partnership may have come to an end (FLA 1996, s 33(5)). Therefore, where no order is made under FLA 1996, s 33(5), immediately before final decree, an application should be made for a financial order or remedy, including a claim for a property adjustment order. The Class F land charge (unregistered land)/agreed notice (registered land) must be replaced with a pending action land charge (unregistered land)/notice or restriction (registered land) in respect of the pending application for a property adjustment order (see *Perez-Adamson v Perez-Rivas* [1987] 2 FLR 472 for applications in relation to unregistered land). A spouse's or civil partner's rights of occupation may only be protected in respect of one home at any one time, whether the other spouse's or civil partner's estate or interest in the home is held under a registered or unregistered title (FLA 1996, Sch 4, para 2).

For further procedural information on applications under FLA 1996, see Land Registry Practice Guide 20. See also, Land Registry Practice Guide 19 – Notices, Restrictions and the Protection of Third Party Interests in the Register. Consideration should also be given to the procedures available under Land Registration Act 2002, ss 42 (power of registrar to enter a restriction) and 46 (power of court to enter a restriction).

Cessation of rights—A spouse's or civil partner's rights of occupation may be brought to an end in the following ways:

- by the death of either spouse or civil partner (s 31(8)(a));
- by the ending of the marriage or civil partnership otherwise than by death (s 1(8)(b));
- by an order of the court (FLA 1996, Sch 4, para 4(1));
- by the spouse or civil partner voluntarily releasing the rights in writing (FLA 1996, Sch 4, para 5(1)).

If the charge under s 31 has been improperly registered, for example where the applicant is not in occupation of home and does not wish to enter (*Barnett v Hassett* [1982] 1 WLR 1385), the court can set aside the charge or injunct its removal. It is submitted, by analogy with *Poon v Poon* [1994] 2 FLR 857 (where it was held that a matrimonial court rather than a companies court should deal with the future of a company, by injunction if need be), that where a respondent is caused severe prejudice by registration of the charge, by for instance a bank refusing further borrowing, and the merits justify his application, the matrimonial court can set aside the charge.

Criminal liability—An individual who is freeholder of a matrimonial property, from which he is not formally excluded and which is occupied by his estranged wife, is not a protected intending occupier under the Criminal Law Act 1977, s 12A and thus cannot avail himself of the defence under s 6(1A) of that Act and can be convicted of the use of violence to gain entry to a property (*Wakolo v DPP* [2012] EWHC 611 (Admin)).

32 Further provisions relating to home rights

Schedule 4 (provisions supplementary to sections 30 and 31) has effect.

Amendments—Substituted by CPA 2004, s 82, Sch 9, para 3.

Occupation orders

33 Occupation orders where applicant has estate or interest etc or has home rights

(1) If –

    (a) a person ("the person entitled") –

        (i) is entitled to occupy a dwelling-house by virtue of a beneficial estate or interest or contract or by virtue of any enactment giving him the right to remain in occupation, or

        (ii) has home rights in relation to a dwelling-house, and

PART II

(b)   the dwelling-house –
>   (i)   is or at any time has been the home of the person entitled and of another person with whom he is associated, or
>   (ii)   was at any time intended by the person entitled and any such other person to be their home,

the person entitled may apply to the court for an order containing any of the provisions specified in subsections (3), (4) and (5).

(2) If an agreement to marry is terminated, no application under this section may be made by virtue of section 62(3)(e) by reference to that agreement after the end of the period of three years beginning with the date on which it is terminated.

(2A) If a civil partnership agreement (as defined by section 73 of the Civil Partnership Act 2004) is terminated, no application under this section may be made by virtue of section 62(3)(eza) by reference to that agreement after the end of the period of three years beginning with the day on which it is terminated.

(3) An order under this section may –
>   (a)   enforce the applicant's entitlement to remain in occupation as against the other person ("the respondent");
>   (b)   require the respondent to permit the applicant to enter and remain in the dwelling-house or part of the dwelling-house;
>   (c)   regulate the occupation of the dwelling-house by either or both parties;
>   (d)   if the respondent is entitled as mentioned in subsection (1)(a)(i), prohibit, suspend or restrict the exercise by him of his right to occupy the dwelling-house;
>   (e)   if the respondent has home rights in relation to the dwelling-house and the applicant is the other spouse or civil partner, restrict or terminate those rights;
>   (f)   require the respondent to leave the dwelling-house or part of the dwelling-house; or
>   (g)   exclude the respondent from a defined area in which the dwelling-house is included.

(4) An order under this section may declare that the applicant is entitled as mentioned in subsection (1)(a)(i) or has home rights.

(5) If the applicant has home rights and the respondent is the other spouse or civil partner, an order under this section made during the marriage or civil partnership may provide that those rights are not brought to an end by –
>   (a)   the death of the other spouse or civil partner; or
>   (b)   the termination (otherwise than by death) of the marriage or civil partnership.

(6) In deciding whether to exercise its powers under subsection (3) and (if so) in what manner, the court shall have regard to all the circumstances including –
>   (a)   the housing needs and housing resources of each of the parties and of any relevant child;
>   (b)   the financial resources of each of the parties;
>   (c)   the likely effect of any order, or of any decision by the court not to exercise its powers under subsection (3), on the health, safety or well-being of the parties and of any relevant child; and
>   (d)   the conduct of the parties in relation to each other and otherwise.

(7) If it appears to the court that the applicant or any relevant child is likely to suffer significant harm attributable to conduct of the respondent if an order under this section containing one or more of the provisions mentioned in subsection (3) is not made, the court shall make the order unless it appears to the court that –

(a)   the respondent or any relevant child is likely to suffer significant harm if the order is made; and

(b)   the harm likely to be suffered by the respondent or child in that event is as great as, or greater than, the harm attributable to conduct of the respondent which is likely to be suffered by the applicant or child if the order is not made.

(8) The court may exercise its powers under subsection (5) in any case where it considers that in all the circumstances it is just and reasonable to do so.

(9) An order under this section –

(a)   may not be made after the death of either of the parties mentioned in subsection (1); and

(b)   except in the case of an order made by virtue of subsection (5)(a), ceases to have effect on the death of either party.

(10) An order under this section may, in so far as it has continuing effect, be made for a specified period, until the occurrence of a specified event or until further order.

Amendments—CPA 2004, s 82, Sch 9, para 4(1)–(7).

Defined terms—"associated": s 62(3); "relevant child": s 62(2).

Occupation orders – general—Sections 33–41 deal with occupation orders. Occupation orders can be made under five different sections, namely ss 33, 35, 36, 37 and 38. Under each section the court can make orders to regulate occupation of the home, to exclude the respondent from the home and the vicinity of the home and to prohibit, terminate or restrict the exercise of the respondent's occupation rights, as appropriate. The court's powers, the factors to which regard is to be had in deciding what, if any, order to make, and the maximum duration of orders, differ from section to section, each representing a self-contained code. It is therefore important that the order is made under the correct section. (See also Sch 7 for transfer of tenancies.)

Scope—Section 33 is much wider in scope than the other sections dealing with occupation orders. Applications can be made under this section if the three conditions in s 33(1) are satisfied, namely that the applicant "is entitled to occupy"; the respondent is "associated"; and the house is, was, or was intended to be their home. Thus, most applications by spouses will be made under this section as the majority of spouses are entitled to occupy by virtue of their interest in the property or have home rights. Further, the section is wide enough to include an application by, for example, an owning parent seeking to exclude an adult child. Many cohabitants too will be "entitled to occupy" and can apply under s 33 rather than under s 36.

"home rights"—See s 30.

Court's powers—These are set out in s 33(3) and include the power in s 33(3)(f) to require the respondent to leave the dwelling-house. There is no maximum duration for an order under s 33 (s 33(10)).

Criteria—The criteria to be applied by the court in deciding whether to exercise its powers are prescribed in s 33(6). In *Lake v Lake* [2007] 1 FLR 427 the Court of Appeal included the conduct of the parties in the balancing exercise. The balance of harm test in s 33(7) must also be considered. In *Re K (A Child)* [2012] 1 FCR 89, the judge had acted outside his jurisdiction in ordering a father to vacate his home so that the mother could remain there while having contact. However, in *Re L (Occupation Order)* [2012] 2 FLR 1417, a father was excluded for 3 months after a finding that the children would suffer serious harm if the parents lived together.

The "balance of harm" test—Making or not making an order under s 33(3) inevitably causes some harm, and s 33(7) requires the court to balance the harm caused by not making an order against the harm that would be caused by making one. The wording of the section is important: in summary, if it appears that the applicant or any relevant child is likely to suffer significant harm, attributable to conduct of the respondent, if an order is not made, then the court *shall* make the order unless it appears that the respondent or any relevant child is likely to suffer significant harm if the order is made and that harm is as great as, or greater than, the harm likely to be suffered by the applicant or child if the order is not made. The balance of harm test may well prove decisive in many cases and require the court to make the order in the applicant's favour. Even if the test is not decisive (because, for example, the harm would be equal) the court still could make the order having regard to the criteria in s 33(6). The court must consider s 33(7) before s 33(6) (*Chalmers v Johns* [1999] 1 FLR 392).

Extension of home rights—The court has power to issue declarations under s 33(4) and to extend home rights beyond death or dissolution (s 33(5), subject to s 33(8)). Save where a declaration has been made under s 33(5)(a), an order ceases to have effect on the death of either party (s 33(9)).

34 Effect of order under s 33 where rights are charge on dwelling-house

(1) If B's home rights are a charge on the estate or interest of A or of trustees for the other spouse –

- (a) any order under section 33 against the other spouse has, except so far as a contrary intention appears, the same effect against persons deriving title under the other spouse or under the trustees and affected by the charge, and
- (b) subsections 33(1), (3), (4) and (10) and 30(3) to (6) apply in relation to any person deriving title under the other spouse or under the trustees and affected by the charge as they apply in relation to the other spouse.

(2) The court may make an order under section 33 by virtue of subsection (1)(b) if it considers that in all the circumstances it is just and reasonable to do so.

Amendments—CPA 2004, s 82, Sch 9, para 5.

35 One former spouse or former civil partner with no existing right to occupy

(1) This section applies if –

- (a) one former spouse or former civil partner is entitled to occupy a dwelling-house by virtue of a beneficial estate or interest or contract, or by virtue of any enactment giving him the right to remain in occupation;
- (b) the other former spouse or former civil partner is not so entitled; and
- (c) the dwelling-house –
  - (i)   in the case of former spouses, was at any time their matrimonial home or was at any time intended by them to be their matrimonial home, or
  - (ii) in the case of former civil partners, was at any time their civil partnership home or was at any time intended by them to be their civil partnership home.

(2) The former spouse or former civil partner not so entitled may apply to the court for an order under this section against the other former spouse or former civil partner ("the respondent").

(3) If the applicant is in occupation, an order under this section must contain provision –

- (a) giving the applicant the right not to be evicted or excluded from the dwelling-house or any part of it by the respondent for the period specified in the order; and
- (b) prohibiting the respondent from evicting or excluding the applicant during that period.

(4) If the applicant is not in occupation, an order under this section must contain provision –

- (a) giving the applicant the right to enter into and occupy the dwelling-house for the period specified in the order; and
- (b) requiring the respondent to permit the exercise of that right.

(5) An order under this section may also –

- (a) regulate the occupation of the dwelling-house by either or both of the parties;
- (b) prohibit, suspend or restrict the exercise by the respondent of his right to occupy the dwelling-house;

(c) require the respondent to leave the dwelling-house or part of the dwelling-house; or

(d) exclude the respondent from a defined area in which the dwelling-house is included.

(6) In deciding whether to make an order under this section containing provision of the kind mentioned in subsection (3) or (4) and (if so) in what manner, the court shall have regard to all the circumstances including –

(a) the housing needs and housing resources of each of the parties and of any relevant child;

(b) the financial resources of each of the parties;

(c) the likely effect of any order, or of any decision by the court not to exercise its powers under subsection (3) or (4), on the health, safety or well-being of the parties and of any relevant child;

(d) the conduct of the parties in relation to each other and otherwise;

(e) the length of time that has elapsed since the parties ceased to live together;

(f) the length of time that has elapsed since the marriage or civil partnership was dissolved or annulled; and

(g) the existence of any pending proceedings between the parties –

(i) for an order under section 23A or 24 of the Matrimonial Causes Act 1973 (property adjustment orders in connection with divorce proceedings etc);

(ia) for a property adjustment order under Part 2 of Schedule 5 to the Civil Partnership Act 2004;

(ii) for an order under paragraph 1(2)(d) or (e) of Schedule 1 to the Children Act 1989 (orders for financial relief against parents); or

(iii) relating to the legal or beneficial ownership of the dwelling-house.

(7) In deciding whether to exercise its power to include one or more of the provisions referred to in subsection (5) ("a subsection (5) provision") and (if so) in what manner, the court shall have regard to all the circumstances including the matters mentioned in subsection (6)(a) to (e).

(8) If the court decides to make an order under this section and it appears to it that, if the order does not include a subsection (5) provision, the applicant or any relevant child is likely to suffer significant harm attributable to conduct of the respondent, the court shall include the subsection (5) provision in the order unless it appears to the court that –

(a) the respondent or any relevant child is likely to suffer significant harm if the provision is included in the order; and

(b) the harm likely to be suffered by the respondent or child in that event is as great as or greater than the harm attributable to conduct of the respondent which is likely to be suffered by the applicant or child if the provision is not included.

(9) An order under this section –

(a) may not be made after the death of either of the former spouses or former civil partners; and

(b) ceases to have effect on the death of either of them.

(10) An order under this section must be limited so as to have effect for a specified period not exceeding six months, but may be extended on one or more occasions for a further specified period not exceeding six months.

(11) A former spouse or former civil partner who has an equitable interest in the dwelling-house or in the proceeds of sale of the dwelling-house but in whom there is not vested (whether solely or as joint tenant) a legal estate in fee simple or a legal term of years absolute in the dwelling-house is to be treated (but only for the purpose of determining whether he is eligible to apply under this section) as not being entitled to occupy the dwelling-house by virtue of that interest.

(12) Subsection (11) does not prejudice any right of such a former spouse or former civil partner to apply for an order under section 33.

(13) So long as an order under this section remains in force, subsections (3) to (6) of section 30 apply in relation to the applicant –

(a)   as if he were B (the person entitled to occupy the dwelling-house by virtue of that section); and

(b)   as if the respondent were A (the person entitled as mentioned in subsection (1)(a) of that section).

Amendments—CPA 2004, s 82, Sch 9, para 6(1)–(10).

Occupation orders – general—See under s 33.

Scope—Section 35 applies only to former spouses or former civil partners. There are three conditions (s 35(1),(2)): the applicant is not entitled to occupy; the respondent is entitled to occupy; and the dwelling-house in question was, or was intended to be, their home.

Declarations—An order under s 35 must contain a declaration pursuant to s 35(3) or s 35(4), as appropriate.

Subsection (5) provisions—In addition to the appropriate declaration, an order may also contain any of the provisions referred to in s 35(5). This includes a provision requiring the respondent to leave the dwelling-house.

Criteria—The criteria are prescribed in subsections (6),(7) and (8). Section 35(6)(a),(b),(c) and (d) are the same as s 33(6)(a),(b),(c) and (d) but s 35(6)(e),(f) and (g) are additional factors. Section 35(7) limits the factors to be considered in deciding whether or not to include a "subsection (5) provision".

The "balance of harm" test—The "balance of harm" test in s 35(8) differs from the "balance of harm" test in s 33(7). For s 35(8) to apply, the court must first decide to make an order but is then required to "include a subsection (5) provision" if (in summary) not doing so would cause greater harm attributable to conduct of the respondent than doing so.

Duration—Section 35 orders can only be for a specified period not exceeding 6 months (s 35(10)) but can be extended on one or more occasions for a maximum of 6 months each time.

36 One cohabitant or former cohabitant with no existing right to occupy

(1) This section applies if –

(a)   one cohabitant or former cohabitant is entitled to occupy a dwelling-house by virtue of a beneficial estate or interest or contract or by virtue of any enactment giving him the right to remain in occupation;

(b)   the other cohabitant or former cohabitant is not so entitled; and

(c)   that dwelling-house is the home in which they cohabit or a home in which they at any time cohabited or intended to cohabit.

(2) The cohabitant or former cohabitant not so entitled may apply to the court for an order under this section against the other cohabitant or former cohabitant ("the respondent").

(3) If the applicant is in occupation, an order under this section must contain provision –

(a)   giving the applicant the right not to be evicted or excluded from the dwelling-house or any part of it by the respondent for the period specified in the order, and

(b)   prohibiting the respondent from evicting or excluding the applicant during that period.

(4) If the applicant is not in occupation, an order under this section must contain provision –

(a)   giving the applicant the right to enter into and occupy the dwelling-house for the period specified in the order; and

(b)   requiring the respondent to permit the exercise of that right.

(5) An order under this section may also –

    (a)   regulate the occupation of the dwelling-house by either or both of the parties;

    (b)   prohibit, suspend or restrict the exercise by the respondent of his right to occupy the dwelling-house;

    (c)   require the respondent to leave the dwelling-house or part of the dwelling-house; or

    (d)   exclude the respondent from a defined area in which the dwelling-house is included.

(6) In deciding whether to make an order under this section containing provision of the kind mentioned in subsection (3) or (4) and (if so) in what manner, the court shall have regard to all the circumstances including –

    (a)   the housing needs and housing resources of each of the parties and of any relevant child;

    (b)   the financial resources of each of the parties;

    (c)   the likely effect of any order, or of any decision by the court not to exercise its powers under subsection (3) or (4), on the health, safety or well-being of the parties and of any relevant child;

    (d)   the conduct of the parties in relation to each other and otherwise;

    (e)   the nature of the parties' relationship and in particular the level of commitment involved in it;

    (f)   the length of time during which they have cohabited;

    (g)   whether there are or have been any children who are children of both parties or for whom both parties have or have had parental responsibility;

    (h)   the length of time that has elapsed since the parties ceased to live together; and

    (i)   the existence of any pending proceedings between the parties –

        (i)   for an order under paragraph 1(2)(d) or (e) of Schedule 1 to the Children Act 1989 (orders for financial relief against parents), or

        (ii)   relating to the legal or beneficial ownership of the dwelling-house.

(7) In deciding whether to exercise its powers to include one or more of the provisions referred to in subsection (5) ("a subsection (5) provision") and (if so) in what manner, the court shall have regard to all the circumstances including –

    (a)   the matters mentioned in subsection (6)(a) to (d); and

    (b)   the questions mentioned in subsection (8).

(8) The questions are –

    (a)   whether the applicant or any relevant child is likely to suffer significant harm attributable to conduct of the respondent if the subsection (5) provision is not included in the order; and

    (b)   whether the harm likely to be suffered by the respondent or child if the provision is included is as great as or greater than the harm attributable to conduct of the respondent which is likely to be suffered by the applicant or child if the provision is not included.

(9) An order under this section –

    (a)   may not be made after the death of either of the parties; and

    (b)   ceases to have effect on the death of either of them.

(10) An order under this section must be limited so as to have effect for a specified period not exceeding six months, but may be extended on one occasion for a further specified period not exceeding six months.

(11) A person who has an equitable interest in the dwelling-house or in the proceeds of sale of the dwelling-house but in whom there is not vested (whether solely or as joint

PART II

tenant) a legal estate in fee simple or a legal term of years absolute in the dwelling-house is to be treated (but only for the purpose of determining whether he is eligible to apply under this section) as not being entitled to occupy the dwelling-house by virtue of that interest.

(12) Subsection (11) does not prejudice any right of such a person to apply for an order under section 33.

(13) So long as the order remains in force, subsections (3) to (6) of section 30 apply in relation to the applicant –

> (a)   as if he were B (the person entitled to occupy the dwelling-house by virtue of that section); and
> (b)   as if the respondent were A (the person entitled as mentioned in subsection (1)(a) of that section).

Amendments—CPA 2004, s 82, Sch 9, para 7; Domestic Violence, Crime and Victims Act 2004, s 2(2), Sch 10, para 34.

Occupation orders – general—See under s 33.

Scope—Section 36 applies only to cohabitants and former cohabitants. (Applicants should first consider if they are eligible to apply under s 33.) There are three conditions for an application under s 36: namely that the applicant cohabitant, or former cohabitant, is not entitled to occupy; the respondent cohabitant, or former cohabitant, is entitled to occupy; and the dwelling-house in question is the home in which they live, did live or intended to live (s 36(1)).

Mandatory provisions—If the court does make an order under s 36 it must contain a provision under s 36(3) or s 36(4), as appropriate.

Discretionary provisions—The order may also contain any of the provisions in s 36(5). This includes requiring the respondent to leave the dwelling-house.

Criteria—The criteria are prescribed in s 36(6)–(8).

The "balance of harm" test—Note that the "balance of harm" test in s 36(8) is quite different from that in s 33(7) and s 35(8) as it imposes no duty on the court to make the order but merely requires the court to consider the questions posed.

Duration—A s 36 order is limited in time to 6 months and can be extended once only for a further period not exceeding 6 months (s 36(10)).

37 Neither spouse or civil partner entitled to occupy

(1) This section applies if –

> (a)   one spouse or former spouse and the other spouse or former spouse occupy a dwelling-house which is or was the matrimonial home; but
> (b)   neither of them is entitled to remain in occupation –
>> (i)   by virtue of a beneficial estate or interest or contract; or
>> (ii)   by virtue of any enactment giving him the right to remain in occupation.

(1A) This section also applies if –

> (a)   one civil partner or former civil partner and the other civil partner or former civil partner occupy a dwelling-house which is or was the civil partnership home; but
> (b)   neither of them is entitled to remain in occupation –
>> (i)   by virtue of a beneficial estate or interest or contract; or
>> (ii)   by virtue of any enactment giving him the right to remain in occupation.

(2) Either of the parties may apply to the court for an order against the other under this section.

(3) An order under this section may –

- (a) require the respondent to permit the applicant to enter and remain in the dwelling-house or part of the dwelling-house;
- (b) regulate the occupation of the dwelling-house by either or both of the parties;
- (c) require the respondent to leave the dwelling-house or part of the dwelling-house; or
- (d) exclude the respondent from a defined area in which the dwelling-house is included.

(4) Subsections (6) and (7) of section 33 apply to the exercise by the court of its powers under this section as they apply to the exercise by the court of its powers under subsection (3) of that section.

(5) An order under this section must be limited so as to have effect for a specified period not exceeding six months, but may be extended on one or more occasions for a further specified period not exceeding six months.

Amendments—CPA 2004, s 82, Sch 9, para 8(1)–(4).

Occupation orders – general—See under s 33.

Scope—An application under s 37 can be made if three conditions are satisfied: namely that the applicant is a spouse, former spouse, civil partner or former civil partner; the respondent is the spouse, former spouse, civil partner or formal civil partner; and neither of them is entitled to occupy the dwelling-house which is or was their home. Applications under s 37 will be relatively rare but can be made, for example, where the parties occupy under a bare licence and the property is owned by trustees, or even where applicant and respondent are squatters.

Court's powers—The orders which the court can make are specified in s 37(3). This includes power to require the respondent to leave the dwelling-house.

Criteria—The criteria are the same as those set out in s 33(6).

The "balance of harm" test—The balance of harm test in s 33(7) applies (s 37(4)).

Duration—Orders can be for a maximum period of 6 months but can be extended on one or more occasions each for 6 months (s 37(5)).

38 Neither cohabitant or former cohabitant entitled to occupy

(1) This section applies if –

- (a) one cohabitant or former cohabitant and the other cohabitant or former cohabitant occupy a dwelling-house which is the home in which they cohabit or cohabited; but
- (b) neither of them is entitled to remain in occupation –
  - (i) by virtue of a beneficial estate or interest or contract; or
  - (ii) by virtue of any enactment giving him the right to remain in occupation.

(2) Either of the parties may apply to the court for an order against the other under this section.

(3) An order under this section may –

- (a) require the respondent to permit the applicant to enter and remain in the dwelling-house or part of the dwelling-house;
- (b) regulate the occupation of the dwelling-house by either or both of the parties;
- (c) require the respondent to leave the dwelling-house or part of the dwelling-house; or
- (d) exclude the respondent from a defined area in which the dwelling-house is included.

(4) In deciding whether to exercise its powers to include one or more of the provisions referred to in subsection (3) ("a subsection (3) provision") and (if so) in what manner, the court shall have regard to all the circumstances including –

    (a)   the housing needs and housing resources of each of the parties and of any relevant child;

    (b)   the financial resources of each of the parties;

    (c)   the likely effect of any order, or of any decision by the court not to exercise its powers under subsection (3), on the health, safety or well-being of the parties and of any relevant child;

    (d)   the conduct of the parties in relation to each other and otherwise; and

    (e)   the questions mentioned in subsection (5).

(5) The questions are –

    (a)   whether the applicant or any relevant child is likely to suffer significant harm attributable to conduct of the respondent if the subsection (3) provision is not included in the order; and

    (b)   whether the harm likely to be suffered by the respondent or child if the provision is included is as great as or greater than the harm attributable to conduct of the respondent which is likely to be suffered by the applicant or child if the provision is not included.

(6) An order under this section shall be limited so as to have effect for a specified period not exceeding six months, but may be extended on one occasion for a further specified period not exceeding six months.

Amendments—Domestic Violence, Crime and Victims Act 2004, s 58(1), Sch 10, para 35.

Occupation orders – general—See under s 33.

Scope—An application can be made under s 38 if the applicant is a cohabitant or former cohabitant, the respondent is the other cohabitant or former cohabitant and neither of them is entitled to occupy the dwelling-house which is the home in which they live or lived together.

Court's powers—The court's powers are in s 38(3). This includes power to require the respondent to leave the dwelling-house.

Criteria—The criteria to be applied are in s 38(4) and (5).

The "balance of harm" test—The "balance of harm" test in s 38(5) imposes no duty on the court to make the order (unlike s 33(7) and s 35(8)) and the balancing of the harm caused by making or not making the order is merely a factor to be considered.

Duration—Orders under s 38 can be for a maximum duration of 6 months only and can be extended once only (s 38(6)).

39 Supplementary provisions

(1) In this Part an "occupation order" means an order under section 33, 35, 36, 37 or 38.

(2) An application for an occupation order may be made in other family proceedings or without any other family proceedings being instituted.

(3) If –

    (a)   an application for an occupation order is made under section 33, 35, 36, 37 or 38, and

    (b)   the court considers that it has no power to make the order under the section concerned, but that it has power to make an order under one of the other sections,

the court may make an order under that other section.

(4) The fact that a person has applied for an occupation order under sections 35 to 38, or that an occupation order has been made, does not affect the right of any person to claim a legal or equitable interest in any property in any subsequent proceedings (including subsequent proceedings under this Part).

Scope—Applications for occupation orders can be freestanding or ancillary to other family proceedings (s 39(2)). In either case the procedure is the same. Form FL401 is used to make the application (see Procedural Guide A10). Occupation orders often have to be sought at short notice where solicitors have to act on prima facie instructions, often given when the client is under emotional stress. It is inevitable, therefore, that despite every effort to proceed under the correct section, it may transpire at the hearing that the application has in fact been made under the wrong section. Section 39(3) prevents the court having to dismiss the application and gives it power to make the order as if the application had been made under the correct section.

Section 39(4) avoids an applicant being estopped from asserting an interest in the property. A misinformed applicant claiming a legal or beneficial interest will not be prejudiced by the fact that an application for an occupation order initially stated that the applicant had no interest in the property.

40 Additional provisions that may be included in certain occupation orders

(1) The court may on, or at any time after, making an occupation order under section 33, 35 or 36 –

    (a) impose on either party obligations as to –
        (i) the repair and maintenance of the dwelling-house; or
        (ii) the discharge of rent, mortgage payments or other outgoings affecting the dwelling-house;
    (b) order a party occupying the dwelling-house or any part of it (including a party who is entitled to do so by virtue of a beneficial estate or interest or contract or by virtue of any enactment giving him the right to remain in occupation) to make periodical payments to the other party in respect of the accommodation, if the other party would (but for the order) be entitled to occupy the dwelling-house by virtue of a beneficial estate or interest or contract or by virtue of any such enactment;
    (c) grant either party possession or use of furniture or other contents of the dwelling-house;
    (d) order either party to take reasonable care of any furniture or other contents of the dwelling-house;
    (e) order either party to take reasonable steps to keep the dwelling-house and any furniture or other contents secure.

(2) In deciding whether and, if so, how to exercise its powers under this section, the court shall have regard to all the circumstances of the case including –

    (a) the financial needs and financial resources of the parties; and
    (b) the financial obligations which they have, or are likely to have in the foreseeable future, including financial obligations to each other and to any relevant child.

(3) An order under this section ceases to have effect when the occupation order to which it relates ceases to have effect.

Scope—This section contains ancillary provisions which need to be considered in every case where an occupation order is sought under s 33, 35 or 36. Section 40(1)(a)(ii) enables the court, at the initial or a subsequent application, to order that rent or mortgage payments should be paid. It will sometimes be better, and certainly quicker, to obtain an order under this provision rather than, for example, making a separate application for maintenance pending suit. Under s 40(3) the additional provision cannot last longer than the occupation order itself. See **Duration** in the commentary to the relevant section. Unfortunately s 40 is seriously defective in that there is no procedure for enforcing compliance: "it was clear that orders under s 40 ... were unenforceable and of no value to the spouse or cohabitee remaining in occupation. That was a serious omission which required urgent alteration" (per Butler-Sloss P in *(Nwogbe v Nwogbe* [2000] 2 FLR 744). Thus s 40 is only of value if the respondent is likely to comply without the need for enforcement.

41 *(repealed)*

Non-molestation orders

42 Non-molestation orders

(1) In this Part a "non-molestation order" means an order containing either or both of the following provisions –

    (a)   provision prohibiting a person ("the respondent") from molesting another person who is associated with the respondent;

    (b)   provision prohibiting the respondent from molesting a relevant child.

(2) The court may make a non-molestation order –

    (a)   if an application for the order has been made (whether in other family proceedings or without any other family proceedings being instituted) by a person who is associated with the respondent; or

    (b)   if in any family proceedings to which the respondent is a party the court considers that the order should be made for the benefit of any other party to the proceedings or any relevant child even though no such application has been made.

(3) In subsection (2) "family proceedings" includes proceedings in which the court has made an emergency protection order under section 44 of the Children Act 1989 which includes an exclusion requirement (as defined in section 44A(3) of that Act).

(4) Where an agreement to marry is terminated, no application under subsection (2)(a) may be made by virtue of section 62(3)(e) by reference to that agreement after the end of the period of three years beginning with the day on which it is terminated.

(4ZA) If a civil partnership agreement (as defined by section 73 of the Civil Partnership Act 2004) is terminated, no application under this section may be made by virtue of section 62(3)(eza) by reference to that agreement after the end of the period of three years beginning with the day on which it is terminated.

(4A) A court considering whether to make an occupation order shall also consider whether to exercise the power conferred by subsection (2)(b).

(4B) In this Part "the applicant", in relation to a non-molestation order, includes (where the context permits) the person for whose benefit such an order would be or is made in exercise of the power conferred by subsection (2)(b).

(5) In deciding whether to exercise its powers under this section and, if so, in what manner, the court shall have regard to all the circumstances including the need to secure the health, safety and well-being –

    (a)   of the applicant; and

    (b)   of any relevant child.

(6) A non-molestation order may be expressed so as to refer to molestation in general, to particular acts of molestation, or to both.

(7) A non-molestation order may be made for a specified period or until further order.

(8) A non-molestation order which is made in other family proceedings ceases to have effect if those proceedings are withdrawn or dismissed.

Amendments—CPA 2004, s 82, Sch 9, para 9; Domestic Violence, Crime and Victims Act 2004, s 58(1),(2) , Sch 10, para 36(1)–(3), Sch 11.

Defined terms—"associated": s 62(3); "relevant child": s 62(2).

Scope—All non-molestation orders are made under s 42.

"Molesting"—The term "molesting" is not defined in FLA 1996. "Molest" has been considered synonymous with "pester" (*Vaughan v Vaughan* [1973] 1 WLR 1159) where the court considered the definition of molestation in the *Shorter Oxford Dictionary*, namely "to cause trouble; to vex; to annoy; to put to inconvenience". It includes conduct which does not amount to violent behaviour (*Davis v Johnson* [1979] AC 264, 334) and applies to any conduct which can properly be regarded as constituting such a degree of harassment as to call for the intervention of the court (*Horner v Horner* (1983) 4 FLR 50; *C v C* [2001] EWCA Civ 1625). The Home Office definition of domestic violence and abuse is: "Any incident or pattern of incidents of controlling, coercive or threatening behaviour, violence or abuse between those aged 16 or over who are or have been intimate partners or family members regardless of gender or sexuality. This can encompass, but is not limited to, the following types of abuse: psychological, physical, sexual, financial, emotional. Controlling behaviour is: a range of acts designed to make a person subordinate and/or dependent by isolating them from sources of support, exploiting their resources and capacities for personal gain, depriving them of the means needed for independence, resistance and escape and regulating their everyday behaviour. Coercive behaviour is: an act or a pattern of acts of assault, threats, humiliation and intimidation or other abuse that is used to harm, punish, or frighten their victim." This definition, although not a legal or statutory definition, is used by all government departments. It is submitted that any applicant who comes within it qualifies for a non-molestation order.

Wording of non-molestation orders—In *R v Shane Tony P* [2004] EWCA Crim 287 and *Boness v R* [2005] EWCA Crim 2395 (both cases concerning ASBOs) the Court of Appeal emphasised that the terms of an order must be precise and capable of being understood; the findings of fact giving rise to the order must be recorded; the order must be explained and that the exact terms of the order must be pronounced in open court and the written order must accurately reflect the order as pronounced. It is suggested that these points, particularly the first, apply with equal force to non-molestation orders. Thus, for example, a respondent may be forbidden to:

1 use or threaten any violence towards [applicant];
2 come within [25] metres of [address];
3 communicate with [applicant] whether by letter, text message telephone or other means except through her solicitors [name and address];
4 threaten [applicant].

Although such an order will necessarily contain more paragraphs, each paragraph of itself is clear and meets modern standards.

A "stay away" clause could be expressed as part of an occupation order but in our view is better expressed as part of a non-molestation order. In contrast, a "get-out" order should not form part of a non-molestation order and must be made as part of an occupation order. If the court makes both types of order each must be drawn up separately.

Criteria—The criteria for the making of a non-molestation order are in s 42(5), namely "all the circumstances including the need to secure the health, safety and well-being of the applicant or of any relevant child". The following three principles should be considered when deciding whether to grant a non-molestation injunction:

(a) there must be evidence of molestation (*C v C (Non-Molestation Order: Jurisdiction)* [1998] 1 FLR 554);
(b) the applicant (or child) must need protection; and
(c) the judge must be satisfied on the balance of probabilities that judicial intervention is required to control the behaviour which is the subject of the complaint (see for example *C v C* [2001] EWCA Civ 1625).

Ex parte ("without notice") applications—See notes to s 45.

Duration—By virtue of s 42(7) the order can be for a specified period or until further order. An injunction made "until further order" will last until such time as either the applicant or respondent applies to discharge it (see s 49): such orders are made only in exceptional cases, e g where there is a history of expired injunctions. It is established practice to stipulate a time-limit in the majority of cases. Obsolete Practice Notes issued under the old law suggested that "a period of up to 3 months is likely to suffice". Three months should be regarded as a minimum but experience shows that an order as short as this is often insufficient (see e g *Research Findings No 46 – Home Office Research and Statistics Directorate*). Orders are frequently made for 6 months, a year or longer duration where the case so requires (see e g *Galan v Galan* [1985] FLR 905; *Horgan v Horgan* [2002] EWCA Civ 1371). Application can be made to vary, extend, or discharge an order (see FPR 2010, Pt 10).

Forms—The form of application is Form FL401, and the order is in Form FL404.

Power of arrest—It is no longer possible to attach a power of arrest to a non-molestation order: see further ss 42A and 47.

Undertakings—See notes to s 46.

Service of application—Not less than 2 clear days before the hearing date unless otherwise ordered (FPR 2010, r 10.3).

Service of order—Both orders made ex parte and at an inter partes hearing must be served on the respondent personally (FPR 2010, r 10.6).

Multi-agency risk assessment conferences—See the notes on MARACs under FPR 2010, r 12.12 and the FJC Guidance of December 2011: *MARACS and Disclosure into Court Proceedings* in Part V.

42A Offence of breaching non-molestation order

(1) A person who without reasonable excuse does anything that he is prohibited from doing by a non-molestation order is guilty of an offence.

(2) In the case of a non-molestation order made by virtue of section 45(1), a person can be guilty of an offence under this section only in respect of conduct engaged in at a time when he was aware of the existence of the order.

(3) Where a person is convicted of an offence under this section in respect of any conduct, that conduct is not punishable as a contempt of court.

(4) A person cannot be convicted of an offence under this section in respect of any conduct which has been punished as a contempt of court.

(5) A person guilty of an offence under this section is liable –

    (a)   on conviction on indictment, to imprisonment for a term not exceeding five years, or a fine, or both;

    (b)   on summary conviction, to imprisonment for a term not exceeding 12 months, or a fine not exceeding the statutory maximum, or both.

(6) A reference in any enactment to proceedings under this Part, or to an order under this Part, does not include a reference to proceedings for an offence under this section or to an order made in such proceedings.

"Enactment" includes an enactment contained in subordinate legislation within the meaning of the Interpretation Act 1978.

Amendments—Inserted by Domestic Violence, Crime and Victims Act 2004, s 1.

Scope—The section makes breach of a non-molestation order a criminal offence if the defendant is aware of the existence of the order and, without reasonable excuse, does anything prohibited by the non-molestation order. A defendant cannot be both punished for a contempt of court and convicted under s 42A. Generally, it is the policy of the Crown Prosecution Service to prosecute all cases of domestic violence referred to it where it considers that there is a sufficient evidence to secure a conviction.

Section 42A came into force on 1 July 2007 and thus, the power to attach a "power of arrest" to a non-molestation order is abolished (Domestic Violence, Crime and Victims Act 2004, Sch 10, para 38). The power to issue a warrant of arrest under s 47(8) remains (but note ss 42A(3) and (4) above) and a power of arrest can still be attached to an occupation order.

Further provisions relating to occupation and non-molestation orders

43 Leave of court required for applications by children under sixteen

(1) A child under the age of sixteen may not apply for an occupation order or a non-molestation order except with the leave of the court.

(2) The court may grant leave for the purposes of subsection (1) only if it is satisfied that the child has sufficient understanding to make the proposed application for the occupation order or non-molestation order.

Scope—Applications for leave under this section need no longer be made to a High Court judge but must, by virtue of the ATPO 2008, be made in the county court (art 6). They can be dealt with by any judge, including a deputy district judge, as they fall within the category B(iii) of FP(AJ)D 2009. Application is made in the usual way in Form FL401 and is treated in the first instance as an application for leave. A litigation friend is not required for an application under this section (see FPR 2010, r 16.6).

44 Evidence of agreement to marry or form a civil partnership

(1) Subject to subsection (2) the court shall not make an order under section 33 or 42 by virtue of section 62(3)(e) unless there is produced to it evidence in writing of the existence of the agreement to marry.

(2) Subsection (1) does not apply if the court is satisfied that the agreement to marry was evidenced by –

(a) the gift of an engagement ring by one party to the agreement to the other in contemplation of their marriage, or

(b) a ceremony entered into by the parties in the presence of one or more other persons assembled for the purpose of witnessing the ceremony.

(3) Subject to subsection (4), the court shall not make an order under section 33 or 42 by virtue of section 62(3)(eza) unless there is produced to it evidence in writing of the existence of the civil partnership agreement (as defined by section 73 of the Civil Partnership Act 2004).

(4) Subsection (3) does not apply if the court is satisfied that the civil partnership agreement was evidenced by –

(a) a gift by one party to the agreement to the other as a token of the agreement, or

(b) a ceremony entered into by the parties in the presence of one or more other persons assembled for the purpose of witnessing the ceremony.

Amendments—CPA 2004, s 82, Sch 9, para 10(1)–(4).

45 Ex parte orders

(1) The court may, in any case where it considers that it is just and convenient to do so, make an occupation order or a non-molestation order even though the respondent has not been given such notice of the proceedings as would otherwise be required by rules of court.

(2) In determining whether to exercise its powers under subsection (1), the court shall have regard to all the circumstances including –

(a) any risk of significant harm to the applicant or a relevant child, attributable to conduct of the respondent, if the order is not made immediately;

(b) whether it is likely that the applicant will be deterred or prevented from pursuing the application if an order is not made immediately; and

(c) whether there is reason to believe that the respondent is aware of the proceedings but is deliberately evading service and that the applicant or a relevant child will be seriously prejudiced by the delay involved –

   (i) where the court is a magistrates' court, in effecting service of proceedings; or

   (ii) in any other case, in effecting substituted service.

(3) If the court makes an order by virtue of subsection (1) it must afford the respondent an opportunity to make representations relating to the order as soon as just and convenient at a full hearing.

(4) If, at a full hearing, the court makes an occupation order ("the full order"), then –

    (a)   for the purposes of calculating the maximum period for which the full order may be made to have effect, the relevant section is to apply as if the period for which the full order will have effect began on the date on which the initial order first had effect; and

    (b)   the provisions of section 36(10) or 38(6) as to the extension of orders are to apply as if the full order and the initial order were a single order.

(5) In this section –

    "full hearing" means a hearing of which notice has been given to all the parties in accordance with rules of court;

    "initial order" means an occupation order made by virtue of subsection (1); and

    "relevant section" means section 33(10), 35(10), 36(10), 37(5) or 38(6).

Scope—It has long been established practice to make orders on an ex parte basis where the circumstances of the case so justify. Under s 45 the court can only make an ex parte order where it is "just and convenient" and, although s 45(1) enables the court to make either an occupation order or a non-molestation order even though the respondent has not been served, there is an important difference of approach between these two different types of order. It is recognised that victims of domestic violence often need immediate protection which can be effectively granted only on an ex parte basis. As the respondent has no legal right to inflict or threaten violence, it follows that his legal rights are not infringed by a non-molestation order. This may be quite different in the case of an occupation order and it will be extremely unusual to deprive a respondent of his home on an ex parte basis. Unlike non-molestation orders, occupation orders override proprietary rights (*Chalmers v Johns* [1999] 1 FLR 392). In *G v G (Ouster: Ex parte application)* [1990] 1 FLR 395 and *Masich v Masich* (1977) Fam Law 245 it was stated that exclusion orders should seldom be granted ex parte. This still applies to occupation orders, and although the court clearly has power under s 45(1) to make an ex parte occupation order, this is reserved for exceptional cases only. An application on notice requires only 2 days' notice and the court has power to abridge time (FPR 2010, r 10.3). Even though the court may not feel able to grant an ex parte occupation order, it will very often grant an ex parte non-molestation order pending the hearing of the application for an occupation order on notice.

Without notice—FPR 2010 follow CPR 1998 in referring to applications being made "without notice" rather than using "ex parte". However, the Act is unamended and still says "ex parte".

Full hearing—Whenever an order has been made ex parte there must be a full hearing as soon as just and convenient thereafter. There are no circumstances in English law in which it is appropriate to make an ex parte order without provision for review once the order has been served. Any such order would be unlawful. It is the duty of the court to list for a full hearing as required by s 45.

Duration—The Act does not in fact require the ex parte order to be limited in time. Most judges take the view that an ex parte order should be for a period of (say) 12 months provided that the order is reconsidered promptly at a full inter partes hearing. This practice has the advantage that, if no change is required in the terms of the order (as often proves to be the case), no further order needs to be made, drawn up and served, thus saving time and costs. It is submitted that this practice is preferable to making an order for, say, just 28 days. However, if such a short order is made the ex parte order should at least extend beyond the date of the full hearing, as otherwise there is a risk of the applicant being left without protection during the gap between expiry of the ex parte order and service of the inter partes order. In *Horgan v Horgan* [2002] EWCA Civ 1371, the Court of Appeal, commenting on an ex parte order, stated that it was just to make the order run for 1 year.

Transfer to the Family Proceedings Court—In practice it is invariably quicker and simpler to obtain an ex parte order from a county court rather than the FPC. Pressure of work has resulted in many courts, including the PRFD, granting an ex parte order and then transferring a suitable case to the FPC for full hearing. Such transfers have increased now that a power of arrest can no longer be attached to a non-molestation order and any breach is likely to result in prosecution before magistrates. Transfer to the lowest appropriate tier is one aim of ATPO 2008.

46 Undertakings

(1) In any case where the court has power to make an occupation order or non-molestation order, the court may accept an undertaking from any party to the proceedings.

(2) No power of arrest may be attached to any undertaking given under subsection (1).

(3) The court shall not accept an undertaking under subsection (1) instead of making an occupation order in any case where apart from this section a power of arrest would be attached to the order.

(3A) The court shall not accept an undertaking under subsection (1) instead of making a non-molestation order in any case where it appears to the court that –

(a) the respondent has used or threatened violence against the applicant or a relevant child; and

(b) for the protection of the applicant or child it is necessary to make a non-molestation order so that any breach may be punishable under section 42A.

(4) An undertaking given to a court under subsection (1) is enforceable as if the court had made an occupation order or a non-molestation order in terms corresponding to those of the undertaking.

(5) This section has effect without prejudice to the powers of the High Court and the county court apart from this section.

Amendments—Domestic Violence, Crime and Victims Act 2004, s 58(1), Sch 10, para 37(1)–(4).

Scope—Where an undertaking is given it may be enforced as if it were an injunction (s 46(4)), ie as a contempt of court punishable by committal proceedings. An undertaking is a promise by the respondent to the court, not to the other party. Powers of arrest cannot be attached to undertakings (s 46(2)).

Procedure—The following procedural points arise in connection with undertakings:

(a) *Recording of undertaking* The undertaking should be in Form N117. It should be explained to the respondent by the judge and the respondent asked to sign it.

(b) *Mutual undertakings* Where both parties give undertakings, two separate forms must be used.

(c) *Service of undertakings* The court must provide a copy of the undertaking to the person who has given it. This may be effected by handing a copy to him before he leaves the court building, by posting him a copy, through his solicitor or, if none of these is practical, by personal service (CPR 1998, Sch 2, CCR Ord 29, r 1A). The better practice is for a copy of the undertaking to be given to both parties before they leave the court building. In any event the court clerk must record the way in which delivery was effected in the relevant box on the back of Form N117.

(d) *Judge's responsibility* Where an undertaking is to be given, the judge has the following responsibilities:

(i) to approve the terms of the proposed promises.

(ii) to ensure that the giver of the undertaking understands what has been promised and the consequences of breach.

(iii) to consider whether the signature of the giver should be included in the box on the back of Form N117 in order to avoid argument about what happened when the undertaking was given; and

(iv) where an undertaking is given in the absence of the giver through his advocate, to ensure that the advocate has been given specific instructions to give the undertaking and that the giver understands the consequences of breach. (In practice it is rare for undertakings to be taken in the absence of the giver.)

Restriction on undertakings (s 46(3))—By virtue of s 46(3) the court is prohibited from accepting an undertaking in any case where a power of arrest would be attached to the order. In fact the requirement to impose a power of arrest is "almost mandatory" (per Butler-Sloss LJ in *Chechi v Bashier* [1999] 2 FLR 489 at [495], commenting on s 47). The power of arrest is confined to occupation orders, as a breach of a non-molestation order is a criminal offence. Breach of an undertaking is not a crime, but s 46(3A) prohibits the court from accepting an undertaking where the respondent has used or threatened violence and, for the protection of the applicant or relevant child, it is necessary to make a non-molestation order so that any breach is punishable under s 42A.

Warrant of arrest—The effect of the amendment to s 46(4), effected by the 2004 Act, is to enable a warrant of arrest (see s 47(8)) to be applied for to enforce an undertaking.

47 Arrest for breach of order

(1) (*repealed*)

(2) If –

    (a)   the court makes an occupation order; and

    (b)   it appears to the court that the respondent has used or threatened violence against the applicant or a relevant child,

it shall attach a power of arrest to one or more provisions of the order unless the court is satisfied that in all the circumstances of the case the applicant or child will be adequately protected without such a power of arrest.

(3) Subsection (2) does not apply in any case where the occupation order is made by virtue of section 45(1), but in such a case the court may attach a power of arrest to one or more provisions of the order if it appears to it –

    (a)   that the respondent has used or threatened violence against the applicant or a relevant child; and

    (b)   that there is a risk of significant harm to the applicant or child, attributable to conduct of the respondent, if the power of arrest is not attached to those provisions immediately.

(4) If, by virtue of subsection (3), the court attaches a power of arrest to any provisions of an occupation order, it may provide that the power of arrest is to have effect for a shorter period than the other provisions of the order.

(5) Any period specified for the purposes of subsection (4) may be extended by the court (on one or more occasions) on an application to vary or discharge the occupation order.

(6) If, by virtue of subsection (2) or (3), a power of arrest is attached to certain provisions of an order, a constable may arrest without warrant a person whom he has reasonable cause for suspecting to be in breach of any such provision.

(7) If a power of arrest is attached under subsection (2) or (3) to certain provisions of the order and the respondent is arrested under subsection (6) –

    (a)   he must be brought before the relevant judicial authority within the period of 24 hours beginning at the time of his arrest; and

    (b)   if the matter is not then disposed of forthwith, the relevant judicial authority before whom he is brought may remand him.

In reckoning for the purposes of this subsection any period of 24 hours, no account is to be taken of Christmas Day, Good Friday or any Sunday.

(8) If the court –

    (a)   has made a non-molestation order, or

    (b)   has made an occupation order but has not attached a power of arrest under subsection (2) or (3) to any provision of the order, or has attached that power only to certain provisions of the order,

then, if at any time the applicant considers that the respondent has failed to comply with the order, he may apply to the relevant judicial authority for the issue of a warrant for the arrest of the respondent.

(9) The relevant judicial authority shall not issue a warrant on an application under subsection (8) unless –

    (a)   the application is substantiated on oath; and

(b) the relevant judicial authority has reasonable grounds for believing that the respondent has failed to comply with the order.

(10) If a person is brought before a court by virtue of a warrant issued under subsection (9) and the court does not dispose of the matter forthwith, the court may remand him.

(11) Schedule 5 (which makes provision corresponding to that applying in magistrates' courts in civil cases under sections 128 and 129 of the Magistrates' Courts Act 1980) has effect in relation to the powers of the High Court and a county court to remand a person by virtue of this section.

(12) If a person remanded under this section is granted bail (whether in the High Court or a county court under Schedule 5 or in a magistrates' court under section 128 or 129 of the Magistrates' Courts Act 1980), he may be required by the relevant judicial authority to comply, before release on bail or later, with such requirements as appear to that authority to be necessary to secure that he does not interfere with witnesses or otherwise obstruct the course of justice.

Amendments—Domestic Violence, Crime and Victims Act 2004, s 58(1), Sch 10, para 38(1)–(5).

Note—Section 42A (see above) makes breach of a non-molestation order an arrestable offence and the repeal of the power of arrest for such orders is a clear indication that the police are expected to use their new powers instead.

Powers of arrest—There is no inherent power to attach a power of arrest. The power of arrest was initially introduced in a restrictive way by Domestic Violence and Matrimonial Proceedings Act 1976. In its original form s 47 was much wider; attaching a power of arrest was "almost mandatory" (per Butler-Sloss LJ in *Chechi v Bashier* [1999] 2 FLR 489 at [495]). However, the power of arrest is confined to occupation orders, having been abolished for non-molestation orders (see s 42A).

Ex parte orders—A power of arrest can be attached to an ex parte order. The criteria are set out in s 47(3). The court has to be satisfied that the respondent has used or threatened violence and that there is a risk of significant harm if a power of arrest is not attached. The power of arrest must be announced in open court.

Order—Non-molestation orders and occupation orders must be drawn up as separate orders (FL404a and FL404 respectively) and not as part of one order. If a power of arrest is attached to the occupation order the clauses to which the power is attached (and only those clauses) must be set out on Form FL406. An order requiring the respondent to "keep away" from a stated address can be made either as part of an occupation order or a non-molestation order, whereas an order requiring the respondent to leave a stated address can be made only as part of an occupation order.

Penal notice—A penal notice, warning of the consequences of disobedience, must appear on the face of every order in the nature of an injunction. Although it is the court's task to endorse the order appropriately it is the solicitor's duty to ensure that this has been done. The penal notice on an occupation order is in the standard form but the penal notice on a non-molestation order reads: "If, without reasonable excuse, you do anything which you are forbidden from doing, you will be committing a criminal offence and liable on conviction to a term of imprisonment not exceeding 5 years or to a fine or to both. Alternatively, if you do not obey this order you will be guilty of contempt of court and may be sent to prison".

Duration—Section 47(4) expressly enables the court when attaching a power of arrest to an ex parte order to provide that the power of arrest is to have effect for a shorter period than the other provisions of the order. This provision is rarely used although the Court of Appeal has held that s 47(2) permits a similar order in the case of final orders (see *Re B-J (Power of Arrest)* [2000] 2 FLR 443).

Delivery to police station—By virtue of FPR 2010, Pt 10, a copy of Form FL406a (non-molestation order) and/or FL406 (the provisions of the occupation order to which a power of arrest is attached) must be delivered to the officer for the time being in charge of any police station for the applicant's address or of such other police station as the court may specify. The form must be accompanied by a statement showing that the respondent has been served with the order or informed of its terms (whether by being present when the order was made or by telephone or otherwise). Thus the police must only be notified of the non-molestation order and/or those provisions (only) of an occupation order to which the power of arrest is attached after the respondent has been notified. Where the relevant police authority has a Domestic Violence Unit which deals with all domestic violence cases within its area, it may be sensible to specify the address of the police station where the unit is located as the appropriate police station to be served, rather than the police station for the applicant's address. Service should be effected in compliance with the FJC Protocol of November 2011: *Process Servers: Non-Molestation Orders* (see Part V).

Arrest without warrant—The significance of a power of arrest is that, pursuant to s 47(6), a constable may arrest without warrant any person whom he has reasonable cause for suspecting to be in breach of the order to which the power has been attached. Any person arrested must then be brought before the relevant judicial authority within 24 hours. Where a person arrested under a power of arrest cannot conveniently be brought to a courtroom, he may be brought before the relevant judicial authority at any convenient place. If the person arrested is not dealt with immediately the court has power to remand. Remand can be on bail or in custody.

Warrant of arrest—Section 47(8) provides a procedure which involves the police even in cases where no power of arrest has been attached. As an alternative to applying for an order for committal under CPR 1998, Sch 2, CCR Ord 29 the applicant can apply to the court for a warrant for arrest. The police will then arrest the respondent and bring him before the court. Section 46(4) has been amended to make it clear that a warrant can be applied for to enforce an undertaking.

Remand—Magistrates' courts have power to remand in civil cases under MCA 1980, ss 128, 129. FLA 1996, Sch 5 gives a similar power to the High Court and county courts.

48 Remand for medical examination and report

(1) If the relevant judicial authority has reason to consider that a medical report will be required, any power to remand a person under section 47(7)(b) or (10) may be exercised for the purpose of enabling a medical examination and report to be made.

(2) If such a power is so exercised, the adjournment must not be for more than 4 weeks at a time unless the relevant judicial authority remands the accused in custody.

(3) If the relevant judicial authority so remands the accused, the adjournment must not be for more than 3 weeks at a time.

(4) If there is reason to suspect that a person who has been arrested –

(a)   under section 47(6), or

(b)   under a warrant issued on an application made under section 47(8),

is suffering from mental disorder within the meaning of the Mental Health Act 1983, the relevant judicial authority has the same power to make an order under section 35 of that Act (remand for report on accused's mental condition) as the Crown Court has under that section in the case of an accused person within the meaning of that section.

Amendments—MHA 2007, s 1(4), Sch 1, Pt 2, para 20.

Remand—Remands in custody are normally limited to 8 days (Sch 5, para 2(5)). Section 48 enables remands in custody to be for up to 3 weeks if the remand is for the purpose of a medical report. The section is silent on the question of who is to pay for the medical report. If the person to be medically examined is publicly funded, the Legal Aid Agency (which replaced the Legal Services Commission on 1 April 2013) will pay pursuant to the order of the court. If he is not publicly funded, no doubt, in an appropriate case, a party can be ordered to pay but quaere whether the prison to which he is remanded can be required to obtain the medical report and/or Her Majesty's Court Service be required to fund it.

For the powers of the court to make a hospital order once the medical report has been obtained see CCA 1981, s 14 and the sections of MHA 1983 there referred to, and FPR 2010, r 10.15.

49 Variation and discharge of orders

(1) An occupation order or non-molestation order may be varied or discharged by the court on an application by –

(a)   the respondent, or

(b)   the person on whose application the order was made.

(2) In the case of a non-molestation order made by virtue of section 42(2)(b), the order may be varied or discharged by the court even though no such application has been made.

(3) If B's home rights are, under section 31, a charge on the estate or interest of the other spouse or of trustees for A, an order under section 33 against A may also be varied or discharged by the court on an application by any person deriving title under the other spouse or under the trustees and affected by the charge.

(4) If, by virtue of section 47(3), a power of arrest has been attached to certain provisions of an occupation order, the court may vary or discharge the order under subsection (1) in so far as it confers a power of arrest (whether or not any application has been made to vary or discharge any other provision of the order).

Amendments—CPA 2004, s 82, Sch 9, para 11; Domestic Violence, Crime and Victims Act 2004, s 58(1), Sch 10, para 39.

Enforcement powers of magistrates' courts

50 Power of magistrates' court to suspend execution of committal order

(1) If, under section 63(3) of the Magistrates' Courts Act 1980, a magistrates' court has power to commit a person to custody for breach of a relevant requirement, the court may by order direct that the execution of the order of committal is to be suspended for such period or on such terms and conditions as it may specify.

(2) In subsection (1) "a relevant requirement" means –

   (a)   an occupation order or non-molestation order;
   (b)   an exclusion requirement included by virtue of section 38A of the Children Act 1989 in an interim care order made under section 38 of that Act; or
   (c)   an exclusion requirement included by virtue of section 44A of the Children Act 1989 in an emergency protection order under section 44 of that Act.

51 Power of magistrates' court to order hospital admission or guardianship

(1) A magistrates' court shall have the same power to make a hospital order or guardianship order under section 37 of the Mental Health Act 1983 or an interim hospital order under section 38 of that Act in the case of a person suffering from mental disorder within the meaning of that Act who could otherwise be committed to custody for breach of a relevant requirement as a magistrates' court has under those sections in the case of a person convicted of an offence punishable on summary conviction with imprisonment.

(2) In subsection (1) "a relevant requirement" has the meaning given by section 50(2).

Amendments—MHA 2007, s 1(4), Sch 1, Pt 2, para 20.

****

Transfer of tenancies

53 Transfer of certain tenancies

Schedule 7 makes provision in relation to the transfer of certain tenancies on divorce etc or on separation of cohabitants.

Procedure—Applications for a transfer of a tenancy under s 53 and Sch 7 are governed by FPR 2010, rr 8.29–8.34. See Procedural Guide A13.

Scope—This section and FLA 1996, Sch 7 (which re-enact Matrimonial Homes Act 1983, s 7 and Sch 1) provide the court with the power to transfer tenancies, including statutory tenancies. By virtue of MCA 1973, s 24, the court has jurisdiction to transfer a contractual tenancy where there is no covenant against assignment, but it has no power to transfer a statutory tenancy because that is not within the definition of property. Under Sch 7 the court has jurisdiction to transfer a contractual tenancy and may do so even where there is a covenant against assignment (although whether the court will, in its discretion, exercise its jurisdiction to transfer when there is such a covenant remains to be seen). It also has jurisdiction under Sch 7 to transfer a statutory tenancy. However, in contrast to the old provisions of MHA 1983, Sch 1, Sch 7 contains two new powers: first, tenancies of cohabitants can be transferred; and secondly, the party to whom the tenancy is being transferred can be ordered to make a payment to the other.

Prevention of unilateral termination of tenancy—As set out in Procedural Guide A13, a tenancy in the other spouse's or partner's name or in joint names can be destroyed unilaterally by surrender or notice to quit. Once the tenancy is surrendered it is lost and therefore a party should ask the other tenant for an undertaking not to surrender it. If the undertaking is given, it should be served on the landlord. If it is not given, application should be made for an injunction to prevent the tenancy being surrendered and, once made, the injunction order should be served on the landlord (*Bater v Greenwich London Borough Council* [1999] 2 FLR 993).

Dwelling-house subject to mortgage

54 Dwelling-house subject to mortgage

(1) In determining for the purposes of this Part whether a person is entitled to occupy a dwelling-house by virtue of an estate or interest, any right to possession of the dwelling-house conferred on a mortgagee of the dwelling-house under or by virtue of his mortgage is to be disregarded.

(2) Subsection (1) applies whether or not the mortgagee is in possession.

(3) Where a person ("A") is entitled to occupy a dwelling-house by virtue of an estate or interest, a connected person does not by virtue of –

    (a)   any home rights conferred by section 30, or

    (b)   any rights conferred by an order under section 35 or 36,

have any larger right against the mortgagee to occupy the dwelling-house than A has by virtue of his estate or interest and of any contract with the mortgagee.

(4) Subsection (3) does not apply, in the case of home rights, if under section 31 those rights are a charge, affecting the mortgagee, on the estate or interest mortgaged.

(5) In this section "connected person", in relation to any person, means that person's spouse, former spouse, civil partner, former civil partner, cohabitant or former cohabitant.

Amendments—CPA 2004, s 82, Sch 9, para 12.

55 Actions by mortgagees: joining connected persons as parties

(1) This section applies if a mortgagee of land which consists of or includes a dwelling-house brings an action in any court for the enforcement of his security.

(2) A connected person who is not already a party to the action is entitled to be made a party in the circumstances mentioned in subsection (3).

(3) The circumstances are that –

    (a)   the connected person is enabled by section 30(3) or (6) (or by section 30(3) or (6) as applied by section 35(13) or 36(13)), to meet the mortgagor's liabilities under the mortgage;

    (b)   he has applied to the court before the action is finally disposed of in that court; and

    (c)   the court sees no special reason against his being made a party to the action and is satisfied –

        (i)   that he may be expected to make such payments or do such other things in or towards satisfaction of the mortgagor's liabilities or obligations as might affect the outcome of the proceedings; or

    (ii)   that the expectation of it should be considered under section 36 of the Administration of Justice Act 1970.

(4) In this section "connected person" has the same meaning as in section 54.

Scope—This section which is based on Matrimonial Homes Act 1983, s 8(2) entitles the spouse, civil partner, cohabitant, former spouse, former civil partner or former cohabitant to be made a party in mortgage possession proceedings.

56 Actions by mortgagees: service of notice on certain persons

(1) This section applies if a mortgagee of land which consists, or substantially consists, of a dwelling-house brings an action for the enforcement of his security, and at the relevant time there is –

    (a)   in the case of unregistered land, a land charge of Class F registered against the person who is the estate owner at the relevant time or any person who, where the estate owner is a trustee, preceded him as trustee during the subsistence of the mortgage; or

    (b)   in the case of registered land, a subsisting registration of –

        (i)   a notice under section 31(10);

        (ii)   a notice under section 2(8) of the Matrimonial Homes Act 1983; or

        (iii)   a notice or caution under section 2(7) of the Matrimonial Homes Act 1967.

(2) If the person on whose behalf –

    (a)   the land charge is registered, or

    (b)   the notice or caution is entered,

is not a party to the action, the mortgagee must serve notice of the action on him.

(3) If –

    (a)   an official search has been made on behalf of the mortgagee which would disclose any land charge of Class F, notice or caution within subsection (1)(a) or (b),

    (b)   a certificate of the result of the search has been issued, and

    (c)   the action is commenced within the priority period,

the relevant time is the date of the certificate.

(4) In any other case the relevant time is the time when the action is commenced.

(5) The priority period is, for both registered and unregistered land, the period for which, in accordance with section 11(5) and (6) of the Land Charges Act 1972, a certificate on an official search operates in favour of a purchaser.

Defined terms—"dwelling-house": s 63(1),(4); "mortgage": s 63(1).

Jurisdiction and procedure etc

57 Jurisdiction of courts

(1) For the purposes of this Act "the court" means the High Court, a county court or a magistrates' court.

(2) Subsection (1) above is subject to the provision made by or under the following provisions of this section, to section 59 and to any express provision as to the jurisdiction of any court made by any other provision of this Part.

(3) The Lord Chancellor may, after consulting the Lord Chief Justice, by order specify proceedings under this Act which may only be commenced in –

    (a)   a specified level of court;

    (b)   a court which falls within a specified class of court; or

    (c)   a particular court determined in accordance with, or specified in, the order.

(4) The Lord Chancellor may, after consulting the Lord Chief Justice, by order specify circumstances in which specified proceedings under this Part may only be commenced in –

    (a)   a specified level of court;

    (b)   a court which falls within a specified class of court; or

    (c)   a particular court determined in accordance with, or specified in, the order.

(5) The Lord Chancellor may, after consulting the Lord Chief Justice, by order provide that in specified circumstances the whole, or any specified part of any specified proceedings under this Part shall be transferred to –

    (a)   a specified level of court;

    (b)   a court which falls within a specified class of court; or

    (c)   a particular court determined in accordance with, or specified in, the order.

(6) An order under subsection (5) may provide for the transfer to be made at any stage, or specified stage, of the proceedings and whether or not the proceedings, or any part of them, have already been transferred.

(7) An order under subsection (5) may make provision as the Lord Chancellor thinks appropriate, after consulting the Lord Chief Justice, for excluding specified proceedings from the operation of section 38 or 39 of the Matrimonial and Family Proceedings Act 1984 (transfer of family proceedings) or any other enactment which would otherwise govern the transfer of those proceedings, or any part of them.

(8) For the purposes of subsections (3), (4) and (5), there are three levels of court –

    (a)   the High Court;

    (b)   any county court; and

    (c)   any magistrates' court.

(9) The Lord Chancellor may, after consulting the Lord Chief Justice, by order make provision for the principal registry of the Family Division of the High Court to be treated as if it were a county court for specified purposes of this Part, or of any provision made under this Part.

(10) Any order under subsection (9) may make such provision as the Lord Chancellor thinks expedient, after consulting the Lord Chief Justice, for the purpose of applying (with or without modifications) provisions which apply in relation to the procedure in county courts to the principal registry when it acts as if it were a county court.

(11) In this section "specified" means specified by an order under this section.

(12) The Lord Chief Justice may nominate a judicial office holder (as defined in section 109(4) of the Constitutional Reform Act 2005) to exercise his functions under this section.

Amendments—CRA 2005, s 15(1), Sch 4, Pt 1, paras 252, 253.

Allocation and Transfer of Proceedings Order 2008—This Order (see Part IV), supplemented by *PD: Allocation and Transfer of Proceedings* (see Part V), replaces FLA(Pt IV)(AP)O 1997.

58 Contempt proceedings

The powers of the court in relation to contempt of court arising out of a person's failure to comply with an order under this Part may be exercised by the relevant judicial authority.

Defined terms—"relevant judicial authority": s 63.

"contempt of court"—The term has been in use since at least the 13th century. The court's powers to punish for contempt of court are in the CCA 1981. Committal must be for a specified (not sine die) period not exceeding 2 years. Proceedings for committal for contempt of court in a civil action are civil proceedings. Nevertheless the appropriate standard of proof to be applied in committal proceedings is the criminal standard of proof (*Dean v Dean* [1987] 1 FLR 517). An order of committal must be made in a courtroom open to the public or announced in open court at the earliest opportunity. See CCA 1981 and commentary thereon.

59 Magistrates' courts

(1) A magistrates' court shall not be competent to entertain any application, or make any order, involving any disputed question as to a party's entitlement to occupy any property by virtue of a beneficial estate or interest or contract or by virtue of any enactment giving him the right to remain in occupation, unless it is unnecessary to determine the question in order to deal with the application or make the order.

(2) A magistrates' court may decline jurisdiction in any proceedings under this Part if it considers that the case can more conveniently be dealt with by another court.

(3) The powers of a magistrates' court under section 63(2) of the Magistrates' Courts Act 1980 to suspend or rescind orders shall not apply in relation to any order made under this Part.

****

61 Appeals

(1) An appeal shall lie to a county court against –

    (a)   the making by a magistrates' court of any order under this Part, or

    (b)   any refusal by a magistrates' court to make such an order,

but no appeal shall lie against any exercise by a magistrates' court of the power conferred by section 59(2) of this Act.

(2) On an appeal under this section, a county court may make such orders as may be necessary to give effect to its determination of the appeal.

(3) Where an order is made under subsection (2), a county court may also make such incidental or consequential orders as appear to it to be just.

(4) Any order of a county court made on an appeal under this section (other than one directing that an application be re-heard by a magistrates' court) shall, for the purposes –

    (a)   of the enforcement of the order, and

    (b)   of any power to vary, revive or discharge orders,

be treated as if it were an order of the magistrates' court from which the appeal was brought and not an order of a county court.

(5) The Lord Chancellor may, after consulting the Lord Chief Justice, by order make provision as to the circumstances in which appeals may be made against decisions taken by courts on questions arising in connection with the transfer, or proposed transfer, of proceedings by virtue of any order under section 57(5).

(6) Except to the extent provided for in any order made under subsection (5), no appeal may be made against any decision of a kind mentioned in that subsection.

PART II

(7) The Lord Chief Justice may nominate a judicial office holder (as defined in section 109(4) of the Constitutional Reform Act 2005) to exercise his functions under this section.

Amendments—CRA 2005, s 15(1), Sch 4, Pt 1, paras 252, 254; SI 2009/871.

New procedure—All appeals from a magistrates' court in relation to proceedings under CA 1989 or FLA 1996, Pts IV and 4A lie to a county court and not to the High Court (AJA 1999(DA)(FP)O 2009). A party is not required to seek permission to appeal against a decision of a magistrates' court (FPR 2010, r 30.3(1)).

Scope—This section provides the machinery for all appeals in relation to non-molestation and occupation orders. The procedure is contained in FPR 2010, Pt 30 and PD30A. The exception is that there can be no appeal against a decision of magistrates to decline jurisdiction on the basis that the matter should be dealt with by another court (ss 61(1)(b), 59(2)). Decisions concerning the transfer of proceedings between courts are regulated by ATPO 2008 and not by way of appeal under this section (s 61(6)).

Procedure—The procedure for appeals under this section is governed by FPR 2010, Pt 30 and PD30A.

Hearing—The appeal is limited to a review of the decision of the court below unless statute provides otherwise or the appeal court considers that in the particular case it would be in the interests of justice to hold a re-hearing. Unless the appeal court orders otherwise the court will not receive oral evidence or evidence which was not before the court below (FPR 2010, r 30.12).

General

62 Meaning of "cohabitants", "relevant child" and "associated persons"

(1) For the purposes of this Part –
   (a) "cohabitants" are two persons who are neither married to each other nor civil partners of each other but are living together as husband and wife or as if they were civil partners; and
   (b) "cohabit" and former cohabitants" is to be read accordingly, but the latter expression does not include cohabitants who have subsequently married each other or become civil partners of each other.

(2) In this Part, "relevant child", in relation to any proceedings under this Part, means –
   (a) any child who is living with or might reasonably be expected to live with either party to the proceedings;
   (b) any child in relation to whom an order under the Adoption Act 1976, the Adoption and Children Act 2002, or the Children Act 1989 is in question in the proceedings; and
   (c) any other child whose interests the court considers relevant.

(3) For the purposes of this Part, a person is associated with another person if –
   (a) they are or have been married to each other;
   (aa) they are or have been civil partners of each other;
   (b) they are cohabitants or former cohabitants;
   (c) they live or have lived in the same household, otherwise than merely by reason of one of them being the other's employee, tenant, lodger or boarder;
   (d) they are relatives;
   (e) they have agreed to marry one another (whether or not that agreement has been terminated);
   (eza) they have entered into a civil partnership agreement (as defined by section 73 of the Civil Partnership Act 2004) (whether or not that agreement has been terminated);
   (ea) they have or have had an intimate personal relationship with each other which is or was of significant duration;
   (f) in relation to any child, they are both persons falling within subsection (4); or

(g)   they are parties to the same family proceedings (other than proceedings under this Part).

(4)   A person falls within this subsection in relation to a child if –

(a)   he is a parent of the child; or

(b)   he has or has had parental responsibility for the child.

(5)   If a child has been adopted or falls within subsection (7), two persons are also associated with each other for the purpose of this Part if –

(a)   one is a natural parent of the child or a parent of such a natural parent, and

(b)   the other is the child or any person –

(i)   who had become a parent of the child by virtue of an adoption order or has applied for an adoption order, or

(ii)   with whom the child has at any time been placed for adoption.

(6)   A body corporate and another person are not, by virtue of subsection (3)(f) or (g), to be regarded for the purposes of this Part as associated with each other.

(7)   A child falls within this subsection if –

(a)   an adoption agency, within the meaning of section 2 of the Adoption and Children Act 2002, has power to place him for adoption under section 19 of that Act (placing children with parental consent) or he has become the subject of an order under section 21 of that Act (placement orders), or

(b)   he is freed for adoption by virtue of an order made –

(i)   in England and Wales, under section 18 of the Adoption Act 1976,

…

Amendments—ACA 2002, Sch 3, para 86, 87; Domestic Violence, Crime and Victims Act 2004, ss 3, 58(1), Sch 10, para 40; CPA 2004, s 82, Sch 9, para 13(1)–(4).

Defined terms—"relative": s 63.

Associated persons (s 62(3))—Only "associated persons" and "a relevant child" can apply for a non-molestation order under s 42. To obtain an occupation order under s 33, the respondent must be associated with the applicant. The policy of the 1996 Act is to extend protection from domestic violence to "associated persons" (ie to virtually all family members). However, if the family relationship is merely incidental, eg to a dispute over land to be resolved by other civil proceedings, an order under FLA 1996 may be refused (*Chechi v Bashir* [1999] 2 FLR 489). The definition of "associated persons" is extended by Domestic Violence, Crime and Victims Act 2004 which inserts para (ea) in s 62(3). Section 62(3)(a) and (b) enables former spouses and cohabitants to seek the court's protection under FLA 1996 irrespective of when the relationship ended (*G v F (Non-molestation Order: Jurisdiction)* [2000] 2 FLR 533). An omission from the definition is, as the equivalent US statute states, "persons who are or have been dating". Such persons, if they do not fall within s 62(3)(ea) (or any other paragraph), will need to sue under PHA 1997 (see Procedural Guide A12, the Act and the commentary) or in tort (eg for assault).

63 Interpretation of Part IV

(1)   In this Part –

"adoption order" means an adoption order within the meaning of section 72(1) of the Adoption Act 1976 or section 46(1) of the Adoption and Children Act 2002;

"associated", in relation to a person, is to be read with section 62(3) to (6);

"child" means a person under the age of eighteen years;

"cohabit", cohabitant" and "former cohabitant" have the meaning given by section 62(1);

"the court" is to be read with section 57;

"development" means physical, intellectual, emotional, social or behavioural development;

"dwelling-house" includes (subject to subsection (4)) –

(a)   any building or part of a building which is occupied as a dwelling,

   (b)   any caravan, house-boat or structure which is occupied as a dwelling,

and any yard, garden, garage or outhouse belonging to it and occupied with it;

"family proceedings" means any proceedings –

   (a)   under the inherent jurisdiction of the High Court in relation to children; or

   (b)   under the enactments mentioned in subsection (2),

"harm" –

   (a)   in relation to a person who has reached the age of eighteen years, means ill-treatment or the impairment of health; and

   (b)   in relation to a child, means ill-treatment or the impairment of health or development;

"health" includes physical or mental health;

"home rights" has the meaning given by section 30;

"ill-treatment" includes forms of ill-treatment which are not physical and, in relation to a child, includes sexual abuse;

"mortgage", "mortgagor" and "mortgagee" have the same meaning as in the Law of Property Act 1925;

"mortgage payments" includes any payments which, under the terms of the mortgage, the mortgagor is required to make to any person;

"non-molestation order" has the meaning given by section 42(1);

"occupation order" has the meaning given by section 39;

"parental responsibility" has the same meaning as in the Children Act 1989;

"relative", in relation to a person, means –

   (a)   the father, mother, stepfather, stepmother, son, daughter, stepson, stepdaughter, grandmother, grandfather, grandson or granddaughter of that person or of that person's spouse, former spouse, civil partner or former civil partner, or

   (b)   the brother, sister, uncle, aunt, niece nephew or first cousin (whether of the full blood or of the half blood or by marriage or civil partnership) of that person or of that person's spouse or former spouse,

and includes, in relation to a person who is cohabiting or has cohabited with another person, any person who would fall within paragraph (a) or (b) if the parties were married to each other or were civil partners of each other;

"relevant child", in relation to any proceedings under this Part, has the meaning given by section 62(2);

"the relevant judicial authority", in relation to any order under this Part, means –

   (a)   where the order was made by the High Court, a judge of that court;

   (b)   where the order was made by a county court, a judge or district judge of that or any other county court; or

   (c)   where the order was made by a magistrates' court, any magistrates' court.

(2)   The enactments referred to in the definition of "family proceedings" are –

   (a)   Part II;

   (b)   this Part;

   (ba) Part 4A;

   (c)   the Matrimonial Causes Act 1973;

   (d)   the Adoption Act 1976;

   (e)   the Domestic Proceedings and Magistrates' Court Act 1978;

   (f)   Part III of the Matrimonial and Family Proceedings Act 1984;

   (g)   Parts I, II and IV of the Children Act 1989;

   (h)   section 30 of the Human Fertilisation and Embryology Act 1990;

   (i)   the Adoption and Children Act 2002;

   (j)   Schedules 5 to 7 to the CPA 2004.

(3) Where the question of whether harm suffered by a child is significant turns on the child's health or development, his health or development shall be compared with that which could reasonably be expected of a similar child.

(4) For the purposes of sections 31, 32, 53 and 54 and such other provisions of this Part (if any) as may be prescribed, this Part is to have effect as if paragraph (b) of the definition of "dwelling-house" were omitted.

(5) It is hereby declared that this Part applies as between the parties to a marriage even though either of them is, or has at any time during the marriage been, married to more than one person.

Amendments—ACA 2002, s 139(1), Sch 3, paras 85, 88; Domestic Violence, Crime and Victims Act 2004, s 58(1), Sch 10, para 41; CPA 2004, ss 82, 261(4), Sch 9, para 13(1)–(5), and Sch 30; Forced Marriage (Civil Protection) Act 2007, s 3(1), Sch 2, para 3.

PART 4A
FORCED MARRIAGE

Amendments—Inserted by Forced Marriage (Civil Protection) Act 2007, s 1.

Forced marriage protection orders

63A Forced marriage protection orders

(1) The court may make an order for the purposes of protecting –

    (a)   a person from being forced into a marriage or from any attempt to be forced into a marriage; or

    (b)   a person who has been forced into a marriage.

(2) In deciding whether to exercise its powers under this section and, if so, in what manner, the court must have regard to all the circumstances including the need to secure the health, safety and well-being of the person to be protected.

(3) In ascertaining that person's well-being, the court must, in particular, have such regard to the person's wishes and feelings (so far as they are reasonably ascertainable) as the court considers appropriate in the light of the person's age and understanding.

(4) For the purposes of this Part a person ("A") is forced into a marriage if another person ("B") forces A to enter into a marriage (whether with B or another person) without A's free and full consent.

(5) For the purposes of subsection (4) it does not matter whether the conduct of B which forces A to enter into a marriage is directed against A, B or another person.

(6) In this Part –

    "force" includes coerce by threats or other psychological means (and related expressions are to be read accordingly); and

    "forced marriage protection order" means an order under this section.

Amendments—Inserted by Forced Marriage (Civil Protection) Act 2007, s 1.

Scope—This provision defines the term "forced marriage" which must be distinguished from an "arranged marriage". It gives certain specified county courts (see below) the jurisdiction to make a forced marriage protection order (FMPO) with a view to protecting a person (the person to be protected)from being forced into marriage or one who has been forced into such a marriage. The force or threatened use of force may be directed at the potential victim or the perpetrator or another.

Defined terms—"court": s 63M and the Family Proceedings (Allocation to Judiciary) (Amendment) Directions 2008.

Forced marriage—This is defined in s 1(4),(5),(6). Where a marriage has taken place, the relief available is not only a FMPO but the annulment of the marriage. Where annulment is not available (e g by reason of lapse of time), relief may be sought for a declaration under the inherent jurisdiction of the court and under FLA 1996, Pt 4A for a declaration of non-marriage as in *XCC v AA and Others* [2012] COPLR 730, or that the marriage entered into was invalid because no proper free and full consent was given by the party in respect of that ceremony and it is the duty of the court to protect the individual from abuse or potential abuse. In such cases, it will be necessary to establish that "the threats, pressure, or whatever it is, is such as to destroy the reality of consent and overbears the will of the individual" (see *Re P (Forced Marriage)* [2011] 1 FLR 2060 and the earlier cases referred to and applied in that case).

Evidence and disclosure of all the circumstances of the case—The evidence relied upon by the applicant when seeking the order may include information that was shared in a multi-agency risk assessment conference (MARAC) and which is confidential. The perpetrator may either suspect that such a conference has taken place or wish to know whether it has and may wish to seek disclosure of the information by making an application under FPR 2010, r 21.2. When dealing with such an application, the FJC Guidance *MARACs and Disclosure into Court Proceedings* (see Part V) should be followed. However, it should be noted that the information shared at these risk-assessment conferences will invariably be sensitive and if disclosed is most likely to place the person to be protected and others (e g informants) in danger, particularly as many police authorities and local authorities use MARACs to handle forced marriage cases, to share information and to assess the risks to the person to be protected, who may be a minor. It is, therefore, important where such disclosure is applied for that the application is heard on notice. If it is heard without notice, it is essential to include a statement in the order that the person to whom it is addressed has a right to object to the disclosure of all or part of it and to apply to the court to have the order varied or discharged; the person to whom the order is addressed should be directed to the Guidance. In any event, to protect the person in question and others and safeguard their interests, the order should in the first instance direct that the disclosure of the information should be to the court and/or the local authority or, where appropriate, to Cafcass or a litigation friend only. The matter can then be determined under the court's powers under FPR 2010, r 21.3 and the cases cited under s 63D. See also the notes to FPR 2010, rr 12.12, 21.2 and 21.3.

63B Contents of orders

(1) A forced marriage protection order may contain –

    (a)   such prohibitions, restrictions or requirements; and

    (b)   such other terms;

as the court considers appropriate for the purposes of the order.

(2) The terms of such orders may, in particular, relate to –

    (a)   conduct outside England and Wales as well as (or instead of) conduct within England and Wales;

    (b)   respondents who are, or may become, involved in other respects as well as (or instead of) respondents who force or attempt to force, or may force or attempt to force, a person to enter into a marriage;

    (c)   other persons who are, or may become, involved in other respects as well as respondents of any kind.

(3) For the purposes of subsection (2) examples of involvement in other respects are –

    (a)   aiding, abetting, counselling, procuring, encouraging or assisting another person to force, or to attempt to force, a person to enter into a marriage; or

    (b)   conspiring to force, or to attempt to force, a person to enter into a marriage.

Amendments—Inserted by Forced Marriage (Civil Protection) Act 2007, s 1.

Contents of the order—The court is given a wide discretion in relation to the terms which it may include within an FMPO. (For precedent, see *Emergency Remedies in the Family Court* (Jordan Publishing Ltd.)) It gives the court the jurisdiction to make orders which relate to conduct within and outside the jurisdiction and any other orders which may be appropriate to protect the potential victim or a person who has been forced into a marriage. The order may be directed at a wide range of persons whose identity may not be known and thus reflects the High Court's power under its inherent jurisdiction and extends this jurisdiction to the specified county courts which are: Birmingham, Blackburn, Bradford, Bristol, Cardiff, Derby, Leeds, Leicester, Luton, Manchester, Middlesbrough, Newcastle-upon-Tyne, Romford and

Willesden. The Principal Registry (Family Div) is also included (ATPO 2008). There may still, however, be cases (particularly those that relate to and are to be enforced in a foreign jurisdiction with the involvement of the Foreign and Commonwealth Office and the International Family Justice Office) when it would be more appropriate to commence proceedings in the High Court or if proceedings have been commenced in the county to court to apply for the case to be transferred to the High Court.

63C Applications and other occasions for making orders

(1) The court may make a forced marriage protection order –

    (a)   on an application being made to it; or

    (b)   without an application being made to it but in the circumstances mentioned in subsection (6).

(2) An application may be made by –

    (a)   the person who is to be protected by the order; or

    (b)   a relevant third party.

(3) An application may be made by any other person with the leave of the court.

(4) In deciding whether to grant leave, the court must have regard to all the circumstances including –

    (a)   the applicant's connection with the person to be protected;

    (b)   the applicant's knowledge of the circumstances of the person to be protected; and

    (c)   the wishes and feelings of the person to be protected so far as they are reasonably ascertainable and so far as the court considers it appropriate, in the light of the person's age and understanding, to have regard to them.

(5) An application under this section may be made in other family proceedings or without any other family proceedings being instituted.

(6) The circumstances in which the court may make an order without an application being made are where –

    (a)   any other family proceedings are before the court ("the current proceedings");

    (b)   the court considers that a forced marriage protection order should be made to protect a person (whether or not a party to the current proceedings); and

    (c)   a person who would be a respondent to any such proceedings for a forced marriage protection order is a party to the current proceedings.

(7) In this section –

    "family proceedings" has the same meaning as in Part 4 (see section 63(1) and (2)) but also includes –

        (a)   proceedings under the inherent jurisdiction of the High Court in relation to adults;

        (b)   proceedings in which the court has made an emergency protection order under section 44 of the Children Act 1989 which includes an exclusion requirement (as defined in section 44A(3) of that Act); and

        (c)   proceedings in which the court has made an order under section 50 of the Act of 1989 (recovery of abducted children etc.); and

    "relevant third party" means a person specified, or falling within a description of persons specified, by order of the Lord Chancellor.

(8) An order of the Lord Chancellor under subsection (7) may, in particular, specify the Secretary of State.

Amendments—Inserted by Forced Marriage (Civil Protection) Act 2007, s 1.

Defined terms—"family proceedings", "relevant third party": s 63C(7).

Who may apply—"the person to be protected": there is no age restriction for applicants for an FMPO. A child applicant does not require the leave of the court but FPR 2010, rr 16.6(1),(3) apply to such applications. Thus a child may apply without a guardian or next friend if the court grants leave or a solicitor considers that the child has the capacity to give instructions. The court may provide that the child is separately represented. For representation of children see FPR 2010, r 16.

Relevant third party—Pursuant to FLA 1996(FM)(RTP)O 2009, as from 1 November 2009 the local authority is identified as a relevant third party in respect of both adults and children. See also the Guidance issued to the local authority by the MoJ.

In the case of an adult applicant it is essential to establish as soon as practicable whether the person has mental capacity within the meaning of MCA 2005 to enter into the marriage (see *Re E (An Alleged Patient); Sheffield City Council v E and S* [2005] 1 FLR 965) and also to conduct the proceedings. The guidance set out in the PLO, paras 7.1–7.4 should be considered in such cases. Consideration should be given to the appointment of a guardian (see FPR 2010, rr 16.6(2),(3) and see *Forced Marriage and Learning Disabilities: Multi-Agency Practice Guidelines* at *www.fco.gov.uk*).

The relevant third party may apply without seeking leave of the court and without the consent or knowledge of the potential victim but in deciding whether to grant the order the court will apply the criteria set out in s 63A(2) and (3). In the case of an application by a third party, leave of the court must be obtained and the court must be satisfied that the criteria set out in s 63C(4) have been met.

Application/order—The application may be freestanding or an order may be made without an application within other family proceedings if considered necessary to protect a person. An order may also be made of the court's own motion under s 63C but it must set out in the order a summary of its reasons for making the order and the names of the persons who are to be served with the order. It may also give directions on who is to be served and how service should be effected (FPR 2010, r 11.8).

Further provision about orders

63D Ex parte orders: Part 4A

(1) The court may, in any case where it considers that it is just and convenient to do so, make a forced marriage protection order even though the respondent has not been given such notice of the proceedings as would otherwise be required by rules of court.

(2) In deciding whether to exercise its powers under subsection (1), the court must have regard to all the circumstances including –

    (a)   any risk of significant harm to the person to be protected or another person if the order is not made immediately;

    (b)   whether it is likely that an applicant will be deterred or prevented from pursuing an application if an order is not made immediately; and

    (c)   whether there is reason to believe that –

        (i)   the respondent is aware of the proceedings but is deliberately evading service; and

        (ii) the delay involved in effecting substituted service will cause serious prejudice to the person to be protected or (if a different person) an applicant.

(3) The court must give the respondent an opportunity to make representations about any order made by virtue of subsection (1).

(4) The opportunity must be –

    (a)   as soon as just and convenient; and

    (b)   at a hearing of which notice has been given to all the parties in accordance with rules of court.

Amendments—Inserted by Forced Marriage (Civil Protection) Act 2007, s 1.

Without notice orders—The criteria set out in subsection (2) must be met before a without notice order is granted. The court has a discretion to withhold any submission made or any evidence adduced for or at any hearing in the proceedings to protect the person to be protected or any other person or for any good reason (FPR 2010, r 11.7(2)). The court may also withhold disclosure of any other information under

FPR 2010, r 21.3 on the ground that disclosure would damage the public interest. If such an order is made, the applicant must as soon as reasonably practicable serve personally a copy of the order, a record of the hearing and a copy of the application with any statement in support on the respondent and the person to be protected with a notice that the person affected by the order has a right to make representations to the court (FPR 2010, r 11.7). Service of orders made with or without notice must be effected in accordance with the FJC Protocol of November 2011: *Process Servers: Non-Molestation Orders* (see Part V). The statement of service must be a sworn statement and contain the information set out in the Protocol. See also *A Chief Constable v YK and Others* [2011] 1 FLR 1493 and *A County Council v SB, MA and AA* [2011] 1 FLR 651 on the circumstances when the withholding of information may be justified and on the issue of the use of special advocates. See also *BCC v FZ, AZ, HZ and TVP* [2012] EWHC 1154 (Fam) and *A (A Child) v Chief Constable of Dorset Police* [2011] 1 FLR 11, which although not a forced marriage case deals with the way in which the issue of sensitive information should be dealt with and the circumstances when it would be appropriate to appoint a special advocate.

"full hearing"—Where a without notice order is made, the court must list the case on notice as soon as is "just and convenient", to enable the parties against whom the order is made, to make representation. Hence, Art 6 rights are preserved. FPR 2010, r 18.11 provides that the order must contain a statement of the right of the respondent and the person to be protected to make an application for the order to be set aside or to be varied within 7 days of service of the order. FPR 2010, r 11.4 provides that personal service must be effected not less than 2 clear days before the hearing but the court may abridge time for service.

63E Undertakings instead of orders

(1) The court may, subject to subsection (3), accept an undertaking from the respondent to proceedings for a forced marriage protection order if it has power to make such an order.

(2) No power of arrest may be attached to an undertaking given under subsection (1).

(3) The court may not accept an undertaking under subsection (1) instead of making an order if a power of arrest would otherwise have been attached to the order.

(4) An undertaking given to the court under subsection (1) is enforceable as if the court had made the order in terms corresponding to those of the undertaking.

(5) This section is without prejudice to the powers of the court apart from this section.

Amendments—Inserted by Forced Marriage (Civil Protection) Act 2007, s 1.

Undertakings—Undertakings may not be accepted where a power of arrest would otherwise have been attached, had an order been made. It is submitted that in the majority of cases an undertaking would not be appropriate. A power of arrest may not be attached to an undertaking. For enforcement of undertakings in a county court see FPR 2010, r 10.13 and in the magistrates' courts see Magistrates Courts Act 1980, s 144 (for undertakings generally and the form of undertakings see FPR 2010, r 33 and PD33A, paras 1.4–1.6).

63F Duration of orders

A forced marriage protection order may be made for a specified period or until varied or discharged.

Amendments—Inserted by Forced Marriage (Civil Protection) Act 2007, s 1.

63G Variation of orders and their discharge

(1) The court may vary or discharge a forced marriage protection order on an application by –

    (a)   any party to the proceedings for the order;

    (b)   the person being protected by the order (if not a party to the proceedings for the order); or

    (c)   any person affected by the order.

(2) In addition, the court may vary or discharge a forced marriage protection order made by virtue of section 63C(1)(b) even though no application under subsection (1) above has been made to the court.

(3) Section 63D applies to a variation of a forced marriage protection order as it applies to the making of such an order.

(4) Section 63E applies to proceedings for a variation of a forced marriage protection order as it applies to proceedings for the making of such an order.

(5) Accordingly, references in sections 63D and 63E to making a forced marriage protection order are to be read for the purposes of subsections (3) and (4) above as references to varying such an order.

(6) Subsection (7) applies if a power of arrest has been attached to provisions of a forced marriage protection order by virtue of section 63H.

(7) The court may vary or discharge the order under this section so far as it confers a power of arrest (whether or not there is a variation or discharge of any other provision of the order).

Amendments—Inserted by Forced Marriage (Civil Protection) Act 2007, s 1.

Arrest for breach of orders

63H Attachment of powers of arrest to orders

(1) Subsection (2) applies if the court–

  (a) intends to make a forced marriage protection order otherwise than by virtue of section 63D; and
  (b) considers that the respondent has used or threatened violence against the person being protected or otherwise in connection with the matters being dealt with by the order.

(2) The court must attach a power of arrest to one or more provisions of the order unless it considers that, in all the circumstances of the case, there will be adequate protection without such a power.

(3) Subsection (4) applies if the court –

  (a) intends to make a forced marriage protection order by virtue of section 63D; and
  (b) considers that the respondent has used or threatened violence against the person being protected or otherwise in connection with the matters being dealt with by the order.

(4) The court may attach a power of arrest to one or more provisions of the order if it considers that there is a risk of significant harm to a person, attributable to conduct of the respondent, if the power of arrest is not attached to the provisions immediately.

(5) The court may provide for a power of arrest attached to any provisions of an order under subsection (4) to have effect for a shorter period than the other provisions of the order.

(6) Any period specified for the purposes of subsection (5) may be extended by the court (on one or more occasions) on an application to vary or discharge the order.

(7) In this section "respondent" includes any person who is not a respondent but to whom an order is directed.

Amendments—Inserted by Forced Marriage (Civil Protection) Act 2007, s 1.

Power of arrest—A power of arrest may be attached to all or some of the terms of the FMPO where the court considers that the respondent has used or threatened violence. This reflects the other provisions of the FLA. Subsection (2) is mandatory in its terms unless the court is satisfied that in all the circumstances of the case there will be adequate protection. It is difficult to envisage any circumstances where violence or the threat of violence has been used when it could be considered that the person to be protected would be adequately protected without a power of arrest being attached. If a power of arrest has been attached to the order the applicant must deliver Form FL406A and a statement showing that the respondent and any other person directed by the court to be served with the order, have been served or informed of its terms (whether by being present when the order was made or by telephone or otherwise). Service must be effected in accordance with the FJC Protocol of November 2011: *Process Servers: Non-Molestation Orders* (see Part V). The statement by the process server must be a sworn statement and must contain the information set out in the Protocol. Where the court makes an order containing one or more provisions to which a power of arrest is attached, each of such provisions must not include any provision to which the power is not attached (FPR 2010, r 10.9). If an order is made to which a power of arrest is attached without notice to the person to whom it is addressed, the terms of the order should be announced in open court at the earliest opportunity (FPR PD10A, para 3.2).

63I Arrest under attached powers

(1) Subsection Subsection (2) applies if a power of arrest is attached to provisions of a forced marriage protection order under section 63H.

(2) A constable may arrest without warrant a person whom the constable has reasonable cause for suspecting to be in breach of any such provision or otherwise in contempt of court in relation to the order.

(3) A person arrested under subsection (2) must be brought before the relevant judge within the period of 24 hours beginning at the time of the person's arrest.

(4) In calculating any period of 24 hours for the purposes of subsection (3), Christmas Day, Good Friday and any Sunday are to be ignored.

Amendments—Inserted by Forced Marriage (Civil Protection) Act 2007, s 1.

Breach of order—Unlike a breach of a non-molestation order under FLA 1996, Pt IV, a breach of a FMPO is not a criminal offence. This issue has raised considerable debate. Following a consultation process, the government announced its intention to make forced marriage a criminal offence and for a breach of a FMPO also to be criminalised. However, a draft Bill has not as yet been presented to Parliament.

63J Arrest under warrant

(1) Subsection (2) applies if the court has made a forced marriage protection order but –

  (a) no power of arrest is attached to any provision of the order under section 63H;
  (b) such a power is attached only to certain provisions of the order; or
  (c) such a power was attached for a shorter period than other provisions of the order and that period has expired.

(2) An interested party may apply to the relevant judge for the issue of a warrant for the arrest of a person if the interested party considers that the person has failed to comply with the order or is otherwise in contempt of court in relation to the order.

(3) The relevant judge must not issue a warrant on an application under subsection (2) unless –

  (a) the application is substantiated on oath; and
  (b) the relevant judge has reasonable grounds for believing that the person to be arrested has failed to comply with the order or is otherwise in contempt of court in relation to the order.

(4) In this section "interested party", in relation to a forced marriage protection order, means –

  (a) the person being protected by the order;
  (b) (if a different person) the person who applied for the order; or

(c)   any other person;

but no application may be made under subsection (2) by a person falling within paragraph (c) without the leave of the relevant judge.

Amendments—Inserted by Forced Marriage (Civil Protection) Act 2007, s 1.

Application for a warrant of arrest—This must be made in Form FL407A and must be accompanied by a sworn statement. If the application is made by a person other than the person to be protected or the person who applied for the order, the application will be treated as an application for leave to apply. In this case the court will either grant the application or list the application for a hearing. Notice of the court's decision will be given by the court to the person applying for the warrant, the person to be protected and any other person directed by the court (FPR 2010, r 11.13).

63K Remand: general

(1) The court before which an arrested person is brought under section 63I(3) or by virtue of a warrant issued under section 63J may, if the matter is not then disposed of immediately, remand the person concerned.

(2) Schedule 5 has effect in relation to the powers of the court to remand a person by virtue of this section but as if the following modifications were made to the Schedule.

(3) The modifications are that –

(a)   in paragraph 2(1) of Schedule 5, the reference to section 47 is to be read as a reference to this section; and

(b)   in paragraph 2(5)(b) of the Schedule, the reference to section 48(1) is to be read as a reference to section 63L(1).

(4) Subsection (5) applies if a person remanded under this section is granted bail under Schedule 5 as modified above.

(5) The person may be required by the relevant judge to comply, before release on bail or later, with such requirements as appear to the relevant judge to be necessary to secure that the person does not interfere with witnesses or otherwise obstruct the course of justice.

Amendments—Inserted by Forced Marriage (Civil Protection) Act 2007, s 1.

Remand—Schedule 5 of FLA 1996 applies to this provision as it does to "occupation orders" under FLA 1996 (see further the notes under FLA 1996, Sch 5).

Release on bail—For application for bail, see FPR PD10A, para 6 for the information to support the application. The application may be made in writing or orally. If made in writing it must be served on the person who obtained the injunction. Where a person who is arrested cannot be brought before a relevant judicial authority sitting in a court room within 24 hours after his arrest, that person may be brought before the judicial authority at any convenient place. As the liberty of the subject is involved, the press and the public should be permitted to be present unless security needs makes this impracticable.

63L Remand: medical examination and report

(1) Any power to remand a person under section 63K(1) may be exercised for the purpose of enabling a medical examination and report to be made if the relevant judge has reason to consider that a medical report will be required.

(2) If such a power is so exercised, the adjournment must not be for more than 4 weeks at a time unless the relevant judge remands the accused in custody.

(3) If the relevant judge remands the accused in custody, the adjournment must not be for more than 3 weeks at a time.

(4) Subsection (5) applies if there is reason to suspect that a person who has been arrested–

(a)   under section 63I(2); or

(b) under a warrant issued on an application made under section 63J(2);

is suffering from mental illness or severe mental impairment.

(5) The relevant judge has the same power to make an order under section 35 of the Mental Health Act 1983 (remand for report on accused's mental condition) as the Crown Court has under section 35 of that Act in the case of an accused person within the meaning of that section.

Amendments—Inserted by Forced Marriage (Civil Protection) Act 2007, s 1.

Power under the Mental Health Act 1983—Attention is drawn to the provisions of FPR PD10A, para 7.1.

Jurisdiction and procedure

63M Jurisdiction of courts: Part 4A

(1) For the purposes of this Part "the court" means the High Court or a county court.

(2) Subsection (1) is subject to any provision made by virtue of subsections (3) and (4).

(3) Section 57(3) to (12) (allocation of proceedings to courts etc.) apply for the purposes of this Part as they apply for the purposes of Part 4 but as if the following modification were made.

(4) The modification is that section 57(8) is to be read as if there were substituted for it –

"(8) For the purposes of subsections (3), (4) and (5), there are two levels of court –

(a) the High Court; and

(b) any county court."

Amendments—Inserted by Forced Marriage (Civil Protection) Act 2007, s 1.

63N Power to extend jurisdiction to magistrates' courts

(1) The Lord Chancellor may, after consulting the Lord Chief Justice, by order provide for magistrates' courts to be included among the courts who may hear proceedings under this Part.

(2) An order under subsection (1) may, in particular, make any provision in relation to magistrates' courts which corresponds to provision made in relation to such courts by or under Part 4.

(3) Any power to make an order under this section (including that power as extended by section 65(2)) may, in particular, be exercised by amending, repealing, revoking or otherwise modifying any provision made by or under this Part or any other enactment.

(4) The Lord Chief Justice may nominate a judicial office holder (as defined in section 109(4) of the Constitutional Reform Act 2005) to exercise the Lord Chief Justice's functions under this section.

Amendments—Inserted by Forced Marriage (Civil Protection) Act 2007, s 1.

63O Contempt proceedings: Part 4A

The powers of the court in relation to contempt of court arising out of a person's failure to comply with a forced marriage protection order or otherwise in connection with such an order may be exercised by the relevant judge.

Amendments—Inserted by Forced Marriage (Civil Protection) Act 2007, s 1.

Contempt of court—The court's powers to commit for contempt of court are set out in CCA 1981. See also FPR 2010, r 11.15 for the provisions of the RSC and CCR, which apply to the enforcement of FMPO.

63P Appeals: Part 4A

(1) The Lord Chancellor may, after consulting the Lord Chief Justice, by order make provision as to the circumstances in which appeals may be made against decisions taken by courts on questions arising in connection with the transfer, or proposed transfer, of proceedings by virtue of an order made under section 57(5) as applied by section 63M(3) and (4).

(2) Except so far as provided for in any order made under subsection (1), no appeal may be made against any decision of a kind mentioned in that subsection.

(3) The Lord Chief Justice may nominate a judicial office holder (as defined in section 109(4) of the Constitutional Reform Act 2005) to exercise the Lord Chief Justice's functions under this section.

Amendments—Inserted by Forced Marriage (Civil Protection) Act 2007, s 1.

Supplementary

63Q Guidance

(1) The Secretary of State may from time to time prepare and publish guidance to such descriptions of persons as the Secretary of State considers appropriate about –

    (a) the effect of this Part or any provision of this Part; or
    (b) other matters relating to forced marriages.

(2) A person exercising public functions to whom guidance is given under this section must have regard to it in the exercise of those functions.

(3) Nothing in this section permits the Secretary of State to give guidance to any court or tribunal.

Amendments—Inserted by Forced Marriage (Civil Protection) Act 2007, s 1.

63R Other protection or assistance against forced marriage

(1) This Part does not affect any other protection or assistance available to a person who –

    (a) is being, or may be, forced into a marriage or subjected to an attempt to be forced into a marriage; or
    (b) has been forced into a marriage.

(2) In particular, it does not affect –

    (a) the inherent jurisdiction of the High Court;
    (b) any criminal liability;
    (c) any civil remedies under the Protection from Harassment Act 1997;
    (d) any right to an occupation order or a non-molestation order under Part 4 of this Act;
    (e) any protection or assistance under the Children Act 1989;
    (f) any claim in tort; or
    (g) the law of marriage.

Amendments—Inserted by Forced Marriage (Civil Protection) Act 2007, s 1.

63S Interpretation of Part 4A

In this Part –
    "the court" is to be read with section 63M;

"force" (and related expressions), in relation to a marriage, are to be read in accordance with section 63A(4) to (6);

"forced marriage protection order" has the meaning given by section 63A(6);

"marriage" means any religious or civil ceremony of marriage (whether or not legally binding); and

"the relevant judge", in relation to any order under this Part, means –

(a) where the order was made by the High Court, a judge of that court; and

(b) where the order was made by a county court, a judge or district judge of that or any other county court.

Amendments—Inserted by Forced Marriage (Civil Protection) Act 2007, s 1.

****

SCHEDULE 4
PROVISIONS SUPPLEMENTARY TO SECTIONS 30 AND 31

1 Interpretation

In this Schedule "legal representative" means a person who, for the purposes of the Legal Services Act 2007, is an authorised person in relation to an activity which constitutes a reserved instrument activity (within the meaning of that Act).

Amendments—Substituted by Legal Services Act 2007, s 208(1), Sch 21, para 121.

2 Restriction on registration where spouse entitled to more than one charge

Where one spouse or civil partner is entitled by virtue of section 31 to a registrable charge in respect of each of two or more dwelling-houses, only one of the charges to which that spouse or civil partner is so entitled shall be registered under section 31(10) or under section 2 of the Land Charges Act 1972 at any one time, and if any of those charges is registered under either of those provisions the Chief Land Registrar, on being satisfied that any other of them is so registered, shall cancel the registration of the charge first registered.

Amendments—CPA 2004, s 82, Sch 9, para 15(1),(2).

3 Contract for sale of house affected by registered charge to include term requiring cancellation of registration before completion

(1) Where one spouse or civil partner is entitled by virtue of section 31 to a charge on an estate in a dwelling-house and the charge is registered under section 31(10) or section 2 of the Land Charges Act 1972, it shall be a term of any contract for the sale of that estate whereby the vendor agrees to give vacant possession of the dwelling-house on completion of the contract that the vendor will before such completion procure the cancellation of the registration of the charge at his expense.

(2) Sub-paragraph (1) shall not apply to any such contract made by a vendor who is entitled to sell the estate in the dwelling-house freed from any such charge.

(3) If, on the completion of such a contract as is referred to in sub-paragraph (1), there is delivered to the purchaser or his legal representative an application by the spouse or civil partner entitled to the charge for the cancellation of the registration of that charge, the term of the contract for which sub-paragraph (1) provides shall be deemed to have been performed.

(4) This paragraph applies only if and so far as a contrary intention is not expressed in the contract.

(5) This paragraph shall apply to a contract for exchange as it applies to a contract for sale.

(6) This paragraph shall, with the necessary modifications, apply to a contract for the grant of a lease or underlease of a dwelling-house as it applies to a contract for the sale of an estate in a dwelling-house.

Amendments—CPA 2004, s 82, Sch 9, para 15(1),(3); Legal Services Act 2007, s 208(1), Sch 21, para 121.

4 Cancellation of registration after termination of marriage or civil partnership etc

(1) Where a spouse's or civil partner's home rights are a charge on an estate in the dwelling-house and the charge is registered under section 31(10) or under section 2 of the Land Charges Act 1972, the Chief Land Registrar shall, subject to sub-paragraph (2), cancel the registration of the charge if he is satisfied –

    (a) in the case of a marriage –
        (i) by the production of a certificate or other sufficient evidence, that either spouse is dead,
        (ii) by the production of an official copy of a decree or order of a court, that the marriage has been terminated otherwise than by death, or
        (iii) by the production of an order of the court, that the spouse's home rights constituting the charge have been terminated by the order, and
    (b) in the case of a civil partnership –
        (i) by the production of a certificate or other sufficient evidence, that either civil partner is dead,
        (ii) by the production of an official copy of an order or decree of a court, that the civil partnership has been terminated otherwise than by death, or
        (iii) by the production of an order of the court, that the civil partner's home rights constituting the charge have been terminated by the order.

(2) Where –
    (a) the marriage or civil partnership in question has been terminated by the death of the spouse or civil partner entitled to an estate in the dwelling-house or otherwise than by death, and
    (b) an order affecting the charge of the spouse or civil partner not so entitled had been made under section 35(5),

then if, after the making of the order, registration of the charge was renewed or the charge registered in pursuance of sub-paragraph (3), the Chief Land Registrar shall not cancel the registration of the charge in accordance with sub-paragraph (1) unless he is also satisfied that the order has ceased to have effect.

(3) Where such an order has been made, then, for the purposes of sub-paragraph (2), the spouse or civil partner entitled to the charge affected by the order may –
    (a) if before the date of the order the charge was registered under section 31(10) or under section 2 of the Land Charges Act 1972, renew the registration of the charge, and
    (b) if before the said date the charge was not so registered, register the charge under section 31(10) or under section 2 of the Land Charges Act 1972.

(4) Renewal of the registration of a charge in pursuance of sub-paragraph (3) shall be effected in such manner as may be prescribed, and an application for such renewal or for

registration of a charge in pursuance of that sub-paragraph shall contain such particulars of any order affecting the charge made under section 33(5) as may be prescribed.

(5) The renewal in pursuance of sub-paragraph (3) of the registration of a charge shall not affect the priority of the charge.

(6) In this paragraph "prescribed" means prescribed by rules made under section 16 of the Land Charges Act 1972 or by land registration rules under the Land Registration Act 2002, as the circumstances of the case require.

Amendments—CPA 2004, s 82, Sch 9, para 15(1)–(8); Land Registration Act 2002, s 34(3).

5 Release of home rights

(1) A spouse or civil partner entitled to home rights may by a release in writing release those rights or release them as respects part only of the dwelling-house affected by them.

(2) Where a contract is made for the sale of an estate or interest in a dwelling-house, or for the grant of a lease or underlease of a dwelling-house, being (in either case) a dwelling-house affected by a charge registered under section 31(10) or under section 2 of the Land Charges Act 1972, then, without prejudice to sub-paragraph (1), the home rights constituting the charge shall be deemed to have been released on the happening of whichever of the following events first occurs –

    (a)   the delivery to the purchaser or lessee, as the case may be, or his legal representative on completion of the contract of an application by the spouse or civil partner entitled to the charge for the cancellation of the registration of the charge; or

    (b)   the lodging of such an application at Her Majesty's Land Registry.

Amendments—CPA 2004, s 82, Sch 9, para 15(1),(9)–(11); Legal Services Act 2007, s 208(1), Sch 21, para 121.

General note—Irrespective of this provision allowing voluntary release of matrimonial home rights, the court retains jurisdiction to set aside the registration of matrimonial home rights where they have been improperly registered or where the registration is causing severe prejudice to the other party (see **Removing a "Class F land charge"** under s 31).

6 Postponement of priority of charge

A spouse or civil partner entitled by virtue of section 31 to a charge on an estate or interest may agree in writing that any other charge on, or interest in, that estate or interest shall rank in priority to the charge to which that spouse or civil partner is so entitled.

Amendments—CPA 2004, s 82, Sch 9, para 15(1),(12).

SCHEDULE 5

POWERS OF HIGH COURT AND COUNTY COURT TO REMAND

1 Interpretation

In this Schedule "the court" means the High Court or a county court and includes –

    (a)   in relation to the High Court, a judge of that court, and

    (b)   in relation to a county court, a judge or district judge of that court.

2 Remand in custody or on bail

(1) Where a court has power to remand a person under section 47, the court may –

PART II

(a) remand him in custody, that is to say, commit him to custody to be brought before the court at the end of the period of remand or at such earlier time as the court may require, or

(b) remand him on bail –

    (i) by taking from him a recognizance (with or without sureties) conditioned as provided in sub-paragraph (3), or

    (ii) by fixing the amount of the recognizances with a view to their being taken subsequently in accordance with paragraph 4 and in the meantime committing the person to custody in accordance with paragraph (a).

(2) Where a person is brought before the court after remand, the court may further remand him.

(3) Where a person is remanded on bail under sub-paragraph (1), the court may direct that his recognizance be conditioned for his appearance –

(a) before that court at the end of the period of remand, or

(b) at every time and place to which during the course of the proceedings the hearing may from time to time be adjourned.

(4) Where a recognizance is conditioned for a person's appearance in accordance with sub-paragraph (1)(b), the fixing of any time for him next to appear shall be deemed to be a remand; but nothing in this sub-paragraph or sub-paragraph (3) shall deprive the court of power at any subsequent hearing to remand him afresh.

(5) Subject to paragraph 3, the court shall not remand a person under this paragraph for a period exceeding 8 clear days, except that –

(a) if the court remands him on bail, it may remand him for a longer period if he and the other party consent, and

(b) if the court adjourns a case under section 48(1), the court may remand him for the period of the adjournment.

(6) Where the court has power under this paragraph to remand a person in custody it may, if the remand for a period not exceeding 3 clear days, commit him to the custody of a constable.

Scope—Schedule 5 introduced a remand scheme for the High Court and county courts. Magistrates' courts already had power to remand in civil cases pursuant to MCA 1980, ss 128, 129.

Persons alleged to be in breach of injunctions will appear before the court in one of three ways:

(a) persons arrested pursuant to a power of arrest under s 47(6);

(b) persons arrested pursuant to a warrant of arrest issued under s 47(8);

(c) persons brought before the court under an application to show cause why they should not be committed (generally in Form N78) under CPR 1998, Sch 2, CCR Ord 29.

In all cases the court would prefer to deal with the matter at the first hearing. However, before dealing with the person for contempt of court, the court must record findings of fact and therefore the facts have to be either admitted or proved by evidence. If the facts are not admitted and the evidence is not before the court, the court will not be able to deal with the matter. This may arise, for example, where the respondent has been arrested pursuant to a power of arrest but the person who has the benefit of the injunction is not before the court to give evidence (the arresting officer is not usually required to attend). In such circumstances, as an alternative to merely adjourning, the court can remand and has to decide whether the remand should be in custody or on bail. A remand in custody cannot be for a period exceeding 8 clear days (3 clear days, if in the custody of a constable).

Although Sch 5 clearly envisages conditional bail, it is submitted that this in practice is not necessary. The injunction will still be in force and therefore imposing similar terms as a condition of bail achieves no purpose. The injunction itself could still be enforced whereas there is no procedure for enforcing breach of bail conditions. It is respectfully submitted that the Schedule has overlooked the fundamental distinction between bail in criminal matters and bail in civil matters. Bail in a criminal case is primarily to ensure that the defendant is before the court when his case comes up for trial. The criminal trial may have to be adjourned, and a bench warrant issued, if the defendant does not answer to his bail. The situation is different in a civil matter whereby, provided the court is satisfied that the respondent has notice of the hearing date, and that it is just to do so, the court can proceed in the absence of a party. Thus no practical purpose is served by conditional bail in the context of civil cases. Indeed, it is submitted that bail itself, conditional or not, serves no practical purpose in the context of injunction cases. If the court is unable to deal with the alleged breach of the injunction at the first hearing and has decided that a remand in custody is not necessary, how does a remand on bail differ from an adjournment, given that the injunction itself is still in force? An adjournment without a remand on bail is adequate, and if conditions are required to protect the applicant they could be in the form of an amended or expanded injunction, with a power of arrest. However, the term "bail" is widely understood, and perhaps a remand on bail, following arrest, could have a psychological impact, given that the court's main purpose will be to secure future compliance with its order. If the court does remand a person on bail it is obliged to take from him a recognizance (para 2(1)(b)(i)).

Re-remand—The maximum period of any remand in custody is 8 days (see Sch 5, para 2(5)). The alleged contemnor has to be brought before the court again on expiry of the remand and the order in Form FL409 should expressly provide for this. However, Sch 5, para 2(2) gives express power to further remand and does not limit the maximum number of remands nor number of days in total for a remand in custody. In practice, contempt proceedings are to be treated as urgent and dealt with as quickly as possible. A remand in custody has to be taken into consideration in any subsequent sentence. See further *Kerai v Patel* [2008] 2 FLR 2137 and commentary to CCA 1981 and to FPR 2010, Pt 10.

Contempt of court—The court's powers to commit for contempt of court are in CCA 1981. See that Act and commentary thereon.

3 Further remand

(1) If the court is satisfied that any person who has been remanded under paragraph 2 is unable by reason of illness or accident to appear or be brought before the court at the expiration of the period for which he was remanded, the court may, in his absence, remand him for a further time; and paragraph 2(5) shall not apply.

(2) Notwithstanding anything in paragraph 2(1), the power of the court under sub-paragraph (1) to remand a person on bail for a further time may be exercised by enlarging his recognizance and those of any sureties for him to a later time.

(3) Where a person remanded on bail under paragraph 2 is bound to appear before the court at any time and the court has no power to remand him under sub-paragraph (1), the court may in his absence enlarge his recognizance and those of any sureties for him to a later time; and the enlargement of his recognizance shall be deemed to be a further remand.

4 Postponement of taking of recognizance

Where under paragraph 2(1)(b)(ii) the court fixes the amount in which the principal and his sureties, if any, are to be bound, the recognizance may thereafter be taken by such person as may be prescribed by rules of court, and the same consequences shall follow as if it had been entered into before the court.

"prescribed by rules of court"—The relevant rule is FPR 2010, r 10.17. The persons prescribed in the High Court or a county court are a district judge, a police officer of at least the rank of inspector or in charge of a police station, and (where the person making the application is in his custody) the governor or keeper of a prison.

****

SCHEDULE 7

TRANSFER OF CERTAIN TENANCIES ON DIVORCE ETC OR ON SEPARATION OF COHABITANTS

Scope—Taking into account the matters set out in para 5, including the suitability of the parties as tenants (the landlord has the right to be heard by virtue of para 14), the court can transfer a range of tenancies including statutory tenancies held by one or both spouses, civil partners or former spouses or former civil partners (subject to the pronouncement of an appropriate decree and the applicant has not remarried or entered into a new civil partnership), cohabitants or former cohabitants. The transferee can be ordered to pay compensation to the transferor (para 10). If immediate payment of the compensation causes the transferee greater financial hardship than the transferor, payment can be deferred or be by instalments. The court can direct that both be liable under the obligations of the tenancy and that one indemnify the other (para 11). If jurisdiction is founded on a decree of divorce or nullity, the order cannot take effect until the decree is absolute (para 12).

Procedure—Applications for a transfer of a tenancy under s 53 and Sch 7 are governed by FPR 2010, rr 8.29–8.34. See Procedural Guide A13.

PART I
GENERAL

Interpretation

1   In this Schedule –

"civil partner", except in paragraph 2, includes (where the context requires) former civil partner;

"cohabitant", except in paragraph 3, includes (where the context requires) former cohabitant,

"the court" does not include a magistrates' court,

"landlord" includes –

(a)   any person from time to time deriving title under the original landlord; and

(b)   in relation to any dwelling-house, any person other than the tenant who is, or (but for Part VII of the Rent Act 1977 or Part II of the Rent (Agriculture) Act 1976) would be, entitled to possession of the dwelling-house;

"Part II order" means an order under Part II of this Schedule;

"a relevant tenancy" means –

(a)   a protected tenancy or statutory tenancy within the meaning of the Rent Act 1977;

(b)   a statutory tenancy within the meaning of the Rent (Agriculture) Act 1976;

(c)   a secure tenancy within the meaning of section 79 of the Housing Act 1985;

(d)   an assured tenancy or assured agricultural occupancy within the meaning of Part I of the Housing Act 1988; or

(e)   an introductory tenancy within the meaning of Chapter I of Part V of the Housing Act 1996;

"spouse", except in paragraph 2, includes (where the context requires) former spouse; and

"tenancy" includes sub-tenancy.

Amendments—SI 1997/74; CPA 2004, s 82, Sch 9, para 16(1),(2).

Costs—The costs rule in FPR 2010, r 28.3 does not apply to applications under FLA 1996, Sch 7. The court may exercise its discretion as to costs in the light of CPR 1998, r 44.2. See FPR PD28A.

Cases in which court may make order

2   (1)   This paragraph applies if one spouse or civil partner is entitled, either in his own right or jointly with the other spouse or civil partner, to occupy a dwelling-house by virtue of a relevant tenancy.

(2)   The court may make a Part II order –

(a)   on granting a decree of divorce, a decree of nullity of marriage or a decree of judicial separation or at any time thereafter (whether, in the case of a decree of divorce or nullity of marriage, before or after the decree is made absolute), or

(b)   at any time when it has power to make a property adjustment order under Part 2 of Schedule 5 to the Civil Partnership Act 2004 with respect to the civil partnership.

Amendments—SI 1997/1892; CPA 2004, s 82, Sch 9, para 16(1),(3),(4).

"dwelling-house"—In contrast to s 30, 33 et seq, this term is restricted so that it does not include a caravan or houseboat (see s 63(1),(4)). Additionally, by virtue of para 4 below, a court may only make an order in respect of a dwelling-house which is or was a matrimonial home, as opposed to one intended to be a matrimonial home.

3 (1) This paragraph applies if one cohabitant is entitled, either in his own right or jointly with the other cohabitant, to occupy a dwelling-house by virtue of a relevant tenancy.

(2) If the cohabitants cease to cohabit, the court may make a Part II order.

Amendments—By virtue of Domestic Violence, Crime and Victims Act 2004, s 58(1), Sch 10, para 42(1),(2).

Note—The court cannot transfer a tenancy to one cohabitant if that tenancy is held jointly by the other cohabitant with a third party. Nor can it do so if it is a statutory tenancy whose security has been lost by the tenant being out of occupation (*Gay v Sheeran* [1999] 2 FLR 519).

4 The court shall not make a Part II order unless the dwelling-house is or was –

(a)   in the case of spouses, a matrimonial home;
(aa) in the case of civil partners, a civil partnership home; or
(b)   in the case of cohabitants, a home in which they cohabited.

Amendments—CPA 2004, s 82, Sch 9, para 16(1),(5); by virtue of Domestic Violence, Crime and Victims Act 2004, s 58(1), Sch 10, para 42(1), (3).

Matters to which the court must have regard

5 In determining whether to exercise its powers under Part II of this Schedule and, if so, in what manner, the court shall have regard to all the circumstances of the case including –

(a)   the circumstances in which the tenancy was granted to either or both of the spouses, civil partners or cohabitants or, as the case requires, the circumstances in which either or both of them became tenant under the tenancy;
(b)   the matters mentioned in section 33(6)(a), (b) and (c) and, where the parties are cohabitants and only one of them is entitled to occupy the dwelling-house by virtue of the relevant tenancy, the further matters mentioned in section 36(6)(e), (f), (g) and (h); and
(c)   the suitability of the parties as tenants.

Amendments—By virtue of CPA 2004, s 82, Sch 9, para 16(1),(6).

Scope—The Court of Appeal have noted the absence of reference in Sch 7, para 5 to FLA 1996, s 33(6), which provides that the court in making an occupation order should have regard to "all the circumstances" including s 33(6)(d): "the conduct of the parties in relation to each other and otherwise". In *Lake v Lake* [2007] 1 FLR 427 the court had to take a balanced and fair decision as to which spouse should have the benefit of a joint tenancy following the dissolution of the marriage, having regard to all the circumstance of the case, including the conduct of the parties.

PART II

PART II
ORDERS THAT MAY BE MADE

References to entitlement to occupy

6 References in this Part of this Schedule to a spouse, a civil partner or a cohabitant being entitled to occupy a dwelling-house by virtue of a relevant tenancy apply whether that entitlement is in his own right or jointly with the other spouse, civil partner or cohabitant.

Amendments—CPA 2004, s 82, Sch 9, para 16(1),(7).

Protected, secure or assured tenancy or assured agricultural occupancy

7 (1) If a spouse, civil partner or cohabitant is entitled to occupy the dwelling-house by virtue of a protected tenancy within the meaning of the Rent Act 1977, a secure tenancy within the meaning of the Housing Act 1985, an assured tenancy or assured agricultural occupancy within the meaning of Part I of the Housing Act 1988 or an introductory tenancy within the meaning of Chapter I of Part V of the Housing Act 1996, the court may by order direct that, as from such date as may be specified in the order, there shall, by virtue of the order and without further assurance, be transferred to, and vested in, the other spouse, civil partner or cohabitant –

    (a)   the estate or interest which the spouse or cohabitant so entitled had in the dwelling-house immediately before that date by virtue of the lease or agreement creating the tenancy and any assignment of that lease or agreement, with all rights, privileges and appurtenances attaching to that estate or interest but subject to all covenants, obligations, liabilities and incumbrances to which it is subject; and

    (b)   where the spouse or cohabitant so entitled is an assignee of such lease or agreement, the liability of that spouse or cohabitant under any covenant of indemnity by the assignee express or implied in the assignment of the lease or agreement to that spouse or cohabitant.

(2) If an order is made under this paragraph, any liability or obligation to which the spouse or cohabitant so entitled is subject under any covenant having reference to the dwelling-house in the lease or agreement, being a liability or obligation falling due to be discharged or performed on or after the date so specified, shall not be enforceable against that spouse or cohabitant.

(3) If the spouse, civil partner or cohabitant so entitled is a successor within the meaning of Part 4 of the Housing Act 1985 –

    (a)   his former spouse (or, in the case of judicial separation, his spouse),

    (b)   his former civil partner (or, if a separation order is in force, his civil partner), or

    (c)   his former cohabitant,

is to be deemed also to be a successor within the meaning of that Part.

(3A) If the spouse, civil partner or cohabitant so entitled is a successor within the meaning of section 132 of the Housing Act 1996 –

    (a)   his former spouse (or, in the case of judicial separation, his spouse),

    (b)   his former civil partner (or, if a separation order is in force, his civil partner), or

    (c)   his former cohabitant,

is to be deemed also to be a successor within the meaning of that section.

(4) If the spouse, civil partner or cohabitant so entitled is for the purposes of section 17 of the Housing Act 1988 a successor in relation to the tenancy or occupancy –

(a)   his former spouse (or, in the case of judicial separation, his spouse),

(b)   his former civil partner (or, if a separation order is in force, his civil partner), or

(c)   his former cohabitant,

is to be deemed to be a successor in relation to the tenancy or occupancy for the purposes of that section.

(5) If the transfer under sub-paragraph (1) is of an assured agricultural occupancy, then, for the purposes of Chapter III of Part I of the Housing Act 1988 –

(a)   the agricultural worker condition is fulfilled with respect to the dwelling-house while the spouse, civil partner or cohabitant to whom the assured agricultural occupancy is transferred continues to be the occupier under that occupancy, and

(b)   that condition shall be treated as so fulfilled by virtue of the same paragraph of Schedule 3 to the Housing Act 1988 as was applicable before the transfer.

(6) ...

Amendments—SI 1997/74; SI 1997/1892; CPA 2004, ss 82, 261(4), Sch 9, para 16(1),(8)–(11).

Interrelation with MCA 1973, s 24 where parties are married—By virtue of MCA 1973, s 24, the court can transfer a tenancy but not a statutory tenancy, as it is not property. The advantages of applying for a transfer of a tenancy under this Schedule as opposed to MCA 1973 are:

(a)   the court order operates as the transfer "without further assurance" so that, in the case of a reluctant transferor, there is no need to apply for the district judge to execute the transfer on his behalf;

(b)   if there is a covenant against assignment, an order under MCA, s 24 is a breach of that covenant (except in the case of a secured tenancy under Housing Act 1985, s 91(3)). However, under Sch 7, para 7(1), the transfer operates to vest the interest as it existed immediately before the date of the transfer, so on the literal wording of this provision no assignment has taken place.

Statutory tenancy within the meaning of the Rent Act 1977

8 (1) This paragraph applies if the spouse, civil partner or cohabitant is entitled to occupy the dwelling-house by virtue of a statutory tenancy within the meaning of the Rent Act 1977.

(2) The court may by order direct that, as from the date specified in the order –

(a)   that spouse or cohabitant is to cease to be entitled to occupy the dwelling-house; and

(b)   the other spouse or cohabitant is to be deemed to be the tenant or, as the case may be, the sole tenant under that statutory tenancy.

(3) The question whether the provisions of paragraphs 1 to 3, or (as the case may be) paragraphs 5 to 7 of Schedule 1 to the Rent Act 1977, as to the succession by the surviving spouse or surviving civil partner of a deceased tenant, or by a member of the deceased tenant's family, to the right to retain possession are capable of having effect in the event of the death of the person deemed by an order under this paragraph to be the tenant or sole tenant under the statutory tenancy is to be determined according as those provisions have or have not already had effect in relation to the statutory tenancy.

Amendments—CPA 2004, s 82, Sch 9, para 16(1),(12),(13).

PART II

Statutory tenancy within the meaning of the Rent (Agriculture) Act 1976

9 (1) This paragraph applies if the spouse or cohabitant is entitled to occupy the dwelling-house by virtue of a statutory tenancy within the meaning of the Rent (Agriculture) Act 1976.

(2) The court may by order direct that, as from such date as may be specified in the order –

    (a)   that spouse or cohabitant is to cease to be entitled to occupy the dwelling-house; and

    (b)   the other spouse or cohabitant is to be deemed to be the tenant or, as the case may be, the sole tenant under that statutory tenancy.

(3) A spouse, civil partner or cohabitant who is deemed under this paragraph to be the tenant under a statutory tenancy is (within the meaning of that Act) a statutory tenant in his own right, or a statutory tenant by succession, according as the other spouse, civil partner or cohabitant was a statutory tenant in his own right or a statutory tenant by succession.

Amendments—CPA 2004, s 82, Sch 9, para 16(1),(14).

PART III
SUPPLEMENTARY PROVISIONS

Compensation

10 (1) If the court makes a Part II order, it may by the order direct the making of a payment by the spouse, civil partner or cohabitant to whom the tenancy is transferred ("the transferee") to the other spouse or cohabitant ("the transferor").

(2) Without prejudice to that, the court may, on making an order by virtue of sub-paragraph (1) for the payment of a sum –

    (a)   direct that payment of that sum or any part of it is to be deferred until a specified date or until the occurrence of a specified event, or

    (b)   direct that that sum or any part of it is to be paid by instalments.

(3) Where an order has been made by virtue of sub-paragraph (1), the court may, on the application of the transferee or the transferor –

    (a)   exercise its powers under sub-paragraph (2), or

    (b)   vary any direction previously given under that sub-paragraph,

at any time before the sum whose payment is required by the order is paid in full.

(4) In deciding whether to exercise its powers under this paragraph and, if so, in what manner, the court shall have regard to all the circumstances including –

    (a)   the financial loss that would otherwise be suffered by the transferor as a result of the order;

    (b)   the financial needs and financial resources of the parties; and

    (c)   the financial obligations which the parties have, or are likely to have in the foreseeable future, including financial obligations to each other and to any relevant child.

(5) The court shall not give any direction under sub-paragraph (2) unless it appears to it that immediate payment of the sum required by the order would cause the transferee financial hardship which is greater than any financial hardship that would be caused to the transferor if the direction were given.

Amendments—CPA 2004, s 82, Sch 9, para 16(1),(14).

Liabilities and obligations in respect of the dwelling-house

11 (1) If the court makes a Part II order, it may by the order direct that both spouses, civil partners or cohabitants are to be jointly and severally liable to discharge or perform any or all of the liabilities and obligations in respect of the dwelling-house (whether arising under the tenancy or otherwise) which –

    (a)   have at the date of the order fallen due to be discharged or performed by one only of them; or

    (b)   but for the direction, would before the date specified as the date on which the order is to take effect fall due to be discharged or performed by one only of them.

(2) If the court gives such a direction, it may further direct that either spouse, civil partner or cohabitant is to be liable to indemnify the other in whole or in part against any payment made or expenses incurred by the other in discharging or performing any such liability or obligation.

Amendments—CPA 2004, s 82, Sch 9, para 16(1),(15),(16).

Date when order made between spouses is to take effect

12 Date when order made between spouses or civil partners takes effect

The date specified in a Part II order as the date on which the order is to take effect must not be earlier than –

    (a)   in the case of a marriage in respect of which a decree of divorce or nullity has been granted, the date on which the decree is made absolute;

    (b)   in the case of a civil partnership in respect of which a dissolution or nullity order has been made, the date on which the order is made final.

Amendments—Substituted by CPA 2004, s 82, Sch 9, para 16(1),(17).

Remarriage of either spouse

13 Effect of remarriage or subsequent civil partnership

(1) If after the grant of a decree dissolving or annulling a marriage either spouse remarries or forms a civil partnership, that spouse is not entitled to apply, by reference to the grant of that decree, for a Part II order.

(2) If after the making of a dissolution or nullity order either civil partner forms a subsequent civil partnership or marries, that civil partner is not entitled to apply, by reference to the making of that order, for a Part II order.

(3) In sub-paragraphs (1) and (2) –

    (a)   the references to remarrying and marrying include references to cases where the marriage is by law void or voidable, and

(b)   the references to forming a civil partnership include references to cases where the civil partnership is by law void or voidable.

Amendments—Substituted by CPA 2004, s 82, Sch 9, para 16(1),(18).

Rules of court

14 (1) Rules of court shall be made requiring the court, before it makes an order under this Schedule, to give the landlord of the dwelling-house to which the order will relate an opportunity of being heard.

(2) Rules of court may provide that an application for a Part II order by reference to an order or decree may not, without the leave of the court by which that order was made or decree was granted, be made after the expiration of such period from the order or grant as may be prescribed by the rules.

Scope—FPR 2010, rr 8.29–8.34 provides for applications under FLA 1996, Pt IV. No rules have been made under para 14(2) prohibiting the application if not made within a specific time, although para 13 provides that an application must be made before remarriage. The landlord must be served, unless the court directs otherwise, and may be a party to the proceedings: FPR 2010, rr 8.31, 8.32.

Saving for other provisions of Act

15 (1) If a spouse or civil partner is entitled to occupy a dwelling-house by virtue of a tenancy, this Schedule does not affect the operation of sections 30 and 31 in relation to the other spouse's or civil partner's home rights.

(2) If a spouse, civil partner or cohabitant is entitled to occupy a dwelling-house by virtue of a tenancy, the court's powers to make orders under this Schedule are additional to those conferred by sections 33, 35 and 36.

Amendments—CPA 2004, s 82, Sch 9, para 16(1),(19),(20).

****

Family Law Reform Act 1969

ARRANGEMENT OF SECTIONS

PART I
REDUCTION OF AGE OF MAJORITY AND RELATED PROVISIONS

PART III
PROVISIONS FOR USE OF SCIENTIFIC TESTS IN DETERMINING PATERNITY

PART I
REDUCTION OF AGE OF MAJORITY AND RELATED PROVISIONS

1 Reduction of age of majority from 21 to 18

(1) As from the date on which this section comes into force a person shall attain full age on attaining the age of eighteen instead of on attaining the age of twenty-one; and a person shall attain full age on that date if he has then already attained the age of eighteen but not the age of twenty-one.

(2) The foregoing subsection applies for the purposes of any rule of law, and, in the absence of a definition or of any indication of a contrary intention, for the construction of "full age", "infant", "infancy", "minor", "minority" and similar expressions in –

    (a)   any statutory provision, whether passed or made before, on or after the date on which this section comes into force; and

    (b)   any deed, will or other instrument of whatever nature (not being a statutory provision) made on or after that date.

(3) In the statutory provisions specified in Schedule 1 to this Act for any reference to the age of twenty-one years there shall be substituted a reference to the age of eighteen years; but the amendment by this subsection of the provisions specified in Part II of that Schedule shall be without prejudice to any power of amending or revoking those provisions.

(4) This section does not affect the construction of any such expression as is referred to in subsection (2) of this section in any of the statutory provisions described in Schedule 2 to this Act, and the transitional provisions and savings contained in Schedule 3 to this Act shall have effect in relation to this section.

(5) The Lord Chancellor may by order made by statutory instrument amend any provision in any local enactment passed on or before the date on which this section comes into force (not being a provision described in paragraph 2 of Schedule 2 to this Act) by substituting a reference to the age of eighteen years for any reference therein to the age of twenty-one years; and any statutory instrument containing an order under this subsection shall be subject to annulment in pursuance of a resolution of either House of Parliament.

(6) In this section "statutory provision" means any enactment (including, except where the context otherwise requires, this Act) and any order, rule, regulation, byelaw or other instrument made in the exercise of a power conferred by any enactment.

(7) Notwithstanding any rule of law, a will or codicil executed before the date on which this section comes into force shall not be treated for the purposes of this section as made on or after that date by reason only that the will or codicil is confirmed by a codicil executed on or after that date.

****

8 Consent by persons over 16 to surgical, medical and dental treatment

(1) The consent of a minor who has attained the age of sixteen years to any surgical, medical or dental treatment which, in the absence of consent, would constitute a trespass to his person, shall be as effective as it would be if he were of full age; and where a minor has by virtue of this section given an effective consent to any treatment it shall not be necessary to obtain any consent for it from his parent or guardian.

(2) In this section "surgical, medical or dental treatment" includes any procedure undertaken for the purposes of diagnosis, and this section applies to any procedure (including, in particular, the administration of an anaesthetic) which is ancillary to any treatment as it applies to that treatment.

(3) Nothing in this section shall be construed as making ineffective any consent which would have been effective if this section had not been enacted.

Scope—This section gives to minors who have attained the age of 16 a right to consent to surgical, medical or dental treatment. The effect of consent to treatment by the minor, or someone else with authority to give it, is limited to protecting the medical or dental practitioner from claims for damages for trespass to the person. Such consent cannot be overridden by those with parental responsibility for the minor, although it can be overridden by the court. This statutory right does not extend to the donation of blood or organs (*Re W (A Minor) (Consent to Medical Treatment)* [1993] 1 FLR 1). This section is of no significance where the case concerns the effect of a *refusal* as distinct from a *consent* to treatment. The court or any person with parental responsibility can override the refusal of any minor who is under or over 16 years to consent to medical treatment, although the minor's wishes are a crucial consideration to be taken into account. In *Re W (A Minor) (Consent to Medical Treatment)* (above), a 16-year-old girl suffering from anorexia nervosa opposed the plans of the local authority to move her to a new treatment unit and to give her medical treatment without her consent. The local authority applied under CA 1989, s 100(3) for leave of the court to carry out its plans. The Court of Appeal held that the only purpose of FLRA 1969, s 8 was to enable a 16-year-old to consent to medical treatment which, in the absence of consent by the child or its parents, would constitute a trespass to the person; further, as the section was silent on the question whether a minor of 16 had an absolute right to refuse medical treatment, it could not be construed to confer such a right. There was no overriding limitation to preclude the exercise by the court of its inherent jurisdiction over minors to act in the minor's best interests. The court authorised the plans of the local authority.

Guidance where children are nearly 16 years of age—Useful guidance in this area is to be found in the conclusions set out by Lord Donaldson MR in *Re R (A Minor) (Wardship: Consent to Treatment)* [1992] 1 FLR 190, where the court considered the case of a 15-year-old girl who refused medication for her psychotic state. The court found that, due to her mental state, she was not "*Gillick* competent" within the guidelines set out in *Gillick v West Norfolk and Wisbech Area Health Authority and Another* [1986] 1 FLR 224, HL. The court authorised the proposed treatment, holding as follows:

(a) No doctor could be required to treat a child since the decision to do so was a matter for his own professional judgement, subject only to obtaining, where necessary, the consent of someone with the authority to give that consent. In forming that judgement, the wishes of the child were a factor whose importance increases with the increase in the child's intelligence and understanding.

(b) There can be concurrent powers to consent. If more than one body or person has a power to consent, only a failure to, or refusal of, consent by all having that power will create a veto.

(c) A "*Gillick*-competent" child or a child over the age of 16 will have a power to consent, but that will be concurrent with that of a parent or guardian.

(d) "*Gillick* competence" is a developmental concept and will not be lost or acquired on a day-to-day or a week-by-week basis. In the case of mental disability, that disability must also be taken into account, particularly where it is fluctuating in its effect.

(e) The court, in the exercise of its wardship or statutory jurisdiction, has power to override the decisions of a "*Gillick*-competent" child as much as those of parents or guardians.

In the case of *R (Axon) v The Secretary of State for Health and the Family Planning Association* [2006] 2 FLR 206 Silber J reaffirmed the principles set out in *Gillick* and held that a medical professional is entitled to provide advice and treatment on sexual matters, including abortion, without a parent's knowledge provided that he or she is satisfied that:

(a) the young person, although under 16, understands all aspects of the advice and that this understanding includes all relevant matters and is not limited to family and moral aspects, as well as all adverse consequences which might follow from the advice;

(b) the medical professional cannot persuade the young person to inform the parents or to allow the medical professional to inform them that their child is seeking advice and/or treatment on sexual matters;

(c) the young person is very likely to begin or to continue having sexual intercourse with or without contraceptive treatment or treatment for a sexually transmissible disease;

(d) unless the young person receives advice and treatment on the relevant sexual matters, his or her physical or mental health or both are likely to suffer; and

(e) the best interests of the young person require him or her to receive advice and treatment on sexual matters without parental consent or notification.

Silber J also stated that the parent's right to respect for family life under ECHR 1950, Art 8 dwindles as his or her child gets older and is able to understand the consequence of different choices and then to make decisions relating to them. It remains to be seen whether these principles of autonomy, when an appropriate level of maturity is reached, will be applied to the refusal of treatment or whether the guidance in *Re R* (above) will continue to apply.

9 Time at which a person attains a particular age

(1) The time at which a person attains a particular age expressed in years shall be the commencement of the relevant anniversary of the date of his birth.

(2) This section applies only where the relevant anniversary falls on a date after that on which this section comes into force, and, in relation to any enactment, deed, will or other instrument, has effect subject to any provision therein.

****

PART III
PROVISIONS FOR USE OF SCIENTIFIC TESTS IN DETERMINING PATERNITY

20 Power of court to require use of scientific tests

(1) In any civil proceedings in which the parentage of any person falls to be determined, the court may, either of its own motion or on an application by any party to the proceedings, give a direction –

(a) for the use of scientific tests to ascertain whether such tests show that a party to the proceedings is or is not the father or mother of that person; and

(b) for the taking, within a period specified in the direction, of bodily samples from all or any of the following, namely, that person, any party who is alleged to be the father or mother of that person and any other party to the proceedings;

and the court may at any time revoke or vary a direction previously given by it under this subsection.

(1A) Tests required by a direction under this section may only be carried out by a body which has been accredited for the purposes of this section by –

(a) the Lord Chancellor, or

(b) a body appointed by him for the purpose.

(2) The individual carrying out scientific tests in pursuance of a direction under subsection (1) above ("the tester") shall make to the court a report in which he shall state –

(a) the results of the tests;

(b) whether the party to whom the report relates is or is not excluded by the results from being the father or mother of the person whose parentage is to be determined; and

(c) in relation to any party who is not so excluded, the value, if any, of the results in determining whether that party is the father or mother of that person;

and the report shall be received by the court as evidence in the proceedings of the matters stated in it.

(2A) Where the proceedings in which the parentage of any person falls to be determined are proceedings on an application under section 55A or 56 of the Family Law Act 1986, any reference in subsection (1) or (2) of this section to any party to the proceedings shall include a reference to any person named in the application.

(3) A report under subsection (2) of this section shall be in the form prescribed by regulations made under section 22 of this Act.

(4) Where a report has been made to a court under subsection (2) of this section, any party may, with the leave of the court, or shall, if the court so directs, obtain from "the tester" a written statement explaining or amplifying any statement made in the report, and that statement shall be deemed for the purposes of this section (except subsection (3) thereof) to form part of the report made to the court.

(5) Where a direction is given under this section in any proceedings, a party to the proceedings, unless the court otherwise directs, shall not be entitled to call as a witness the tester, or any other person by whom any thing necessary for the purpose of enabling those tests to be carried out was done, unless within fourteen days after receiving a copy of the report he serves notice on the other parties to the proceedings, or on such of them as the court may direct, of his intention to call the tester, or that other person; and where the tester or any such person is called as a witness the party who called him shall be entitled to cross-examine him.

(6) Where a direction is given under this section the party on whose application the direction is given shall pay the cost of taking and testing bodily samples for the purpose of giving effect to the direction (including any expenses reasonably incurred by any person in taking any steps required of him for the purpose), and of making a report to the court under this section, but the amount paid shall be treated as costs incurred by him in the proceedings.

Amendments—FLRA 1987, ss 23(1), 33(1), Sch 2, para 21; CA 1989, s 89; CLSA 1990, s 116, Sch 16, para 3; CSPSSA 2000, s 82(1),(2), Sch 8, para 9.

Defined terms—"bodily samples", "scientific tests", "excluded": s 25.

"civil proceedings" (s 20(1))—This includes proceedings under FPR 2010.

"the parentage of any person falls to be determined" (s 20(1))—This section adopts terminology similar to that of FLA 1986, s 55A and enables the court to give a direction designed to show whether or not a person is the parent of the child ("the person") concerned. Section 55A enables a parent or other party "with sufficient personal interest" (FLA 1986, s 55A(3)) to make a freestanding application for parentage. However, application for a scientific tests direction can only be made in existing civil (including family) proceedings in which the issue of parentage arises (e g under FLA 1986, s 55A). The direction can be made by the court of its own initiative or on application by a party to the proceedings.

Procedure—Application for a test is by the FPR 2010, Pt 8 procedure (*Practice Direction – Practice Directions relating to family proceedings in force before 6 April 2011 which support Family Procedure Rules 2010*, para 2.1, which also applies the provisions of CPR PD23B, paras 1.1, 1.2, 1.4 and 1.5 to proceedings under FPR 2010).

Responsible adult—CPR PD23B, para 1.1(3) defines a responsible adult as (1) a person who has "care and control" of a person under 16 and (2) where a person lacks capacity under MCA 2005 to give consent to tests, a person who has power to give consent or, lacking that, a person with whom he lives or in whose care he is (and see discussion under FPR 2010, r 15.1). Where application is made in respect of a person who is under 16 or who lacks capacity, the application notice must include the name and address of the responsible adult (para 1.2).

"party to the proceedings" (s 20(1),(2A))—In proceedings under FLA 1986, ss 55A and 56, individuals may be named in an application (see FPR 2010, r 8.20). If so named in the application, the individual may be joined as a party, or may apply to be joined for the purposes of a direction under s 20(1) (FPR 2010, r 8.20(4),(5)).

Interests of justice—The interests of justice in terms of exercise of the discretion whether to make a direction was explained by Thorpe LJ in *Re H and A (Paternity: Blood Tests)* [2002] 1 FLR 1145, CA at [29] as follows:

"The points of principle to be drawn from [recent cases are]: first, that the interests of justice are best served by the ascertainment of the truth and, secondly, that the court should be furnished with the best available science and not confined to such unsatisfactory alternatives as presumptions and inferences."

Discretion to direct—The direction of a blood test is a discretionary remedy and should only be made if in the interests of the child concerned. In *Re H (Paternity: Blood Test)* [1996] 2 FLR 65, CA, Ward LJ explained fully the factors to be borne in mind when the court exercises its discretion, and concluded:

(1) A parent's refusal to comply with a direction was not determinative of the issue of whether or not a direction should be made;
(2) The welfare of the child is a relevant but not paramount factor in deciding whether or not to make a direction; the interests of other persons may also be involved (and see *S v S, W v Official Solicitor* (above));
(3) The outcome of the proceedings in which the direction is sought is not a factor in deciding whether to make a direction: the paternity question was a freestanding application entitled to its own considerations; and
(4) A child's welfare generally demands that it know the truth about his or her parentage.

The tests direction—In *Re H (Paternity: Blood Test)* [1996] 2 FLR 65, CA, Ward LJ stressed the fact that the court is required to make a direction for tests, and not an order, since the court cannot order the taking of samples against a person's consent (s 21(1)). He proposed (at [83D]) a form of words for the direction as follows:

"It is directed pursuant to s 20(1) of the Family Law Reform Act 1969:
(a) that blood tests (including DNA tests) be used to ascertain whether such tests show that [Mr A] is or is not excluded from being the father of [child B] born on [   ]; and
(b) that for that purpose blood samples be taken on or before [   ] from the following persons: [Mr A], [Mrs X (mother of child B)] and [child B]; and
(c) that the person appearing to the court to have care and control of [child B], who is under the age of 16, is [Mrs X];
(d) that such tests be carried out by [Mr CD of   ]."

"any party" (s 20(1))—An intervener would be included in this definition as would, for example, a non-parent who had obtained leave (pursuant to CA 1989, s 10) to apply for a CA 1989, s 8 order. Where a person not already a party to the proceedings is made the subject of a direction the court may at any time direct that he be made a party to the proceedings (FPR 2010, r 8.20(4)).

Two or more putative fathers—In *Re A (A Minor) (Paternity: Refusal of Blood Test)* [1994] 2 FLR 463, CA, Waite LJ left open the issue of whether or not a mother could make successive claims, leading to further applications under s 20, against two or more putative fathers where a first or subsequent claim had failed, although he felt that to deny her the ability to do this would be illogical.

"regulations made under section 22" (s 20(3))—The regulations are the Blood Tests (Evidence of Paternity) Regulations 1971, as amended by Blood Tests (Evidence of Paternity) (Amendment) Regulations 2008 (which amend the earlier regulations mostly to bring them into line with MCA 2005).

"report … in the form prescribed" (s 20(3))—The form prescribed is defined by BT(EP)R 1971, reg 10 and is prepared by the tester who has been appointed to carry out tests. When received by the court it must be sent to every party and to anyone else involved in giving a sample (CPR PD23B, para 1.5).

"treated as costs incurred by him in the proceedings" (s 20(6))—In the first instance the applicant for the direction bears liability for the cost of the tests; if ultimately his costs are ordered to be paid by another party the cost of the test will be included.

21 Consents etc required for taking of bodily samples

(1) Subject to the provisions of subsections (3) and (4) of this section, a bodily sample which is required to be taken from any person for the purpose of giving effect to a direction under section 20 of this Act shall not be taken from that person except with his consent.

(2) The consent of a minor who has attained the age of sixteen years to the taking from himself of a bodily sample shall be as effective as it would be if he were of full age; and

where a minor has by virtue of this subsection given an effective consent to the taking of a bodily sample it shall not be necessary to obtain any consent for it from any other person.

(3) A bodily sample may be taken from a person under the age of sixteen years, not being such a person as is referred to in subsection (4) of this section –

    (a)   if the person who has the care and control of him consents; or

    (b)   where that person does not consent, if the court considers that it would be in his best interests for the sample to be taken.

(4) A bodily sample may be taken from a person who lacks capacity (within the meaning of the Mental Capacity Act 2005) to give his consent, if consent is given by the court giving the direction under section 20 or by –

    (a)   a donee of an enduring power of attorney or lasting power of attorney (within the meaning of that Act), or

    (b)   a deputy appointed, or any other person authorised, by the Court of Protection,

with power in that respect.

(5) The foregoing provisions of this section are without prejudice to the provisions of section 23 of this Act.

Amendments—MHA 1983, s 148, Sch 4, para 25; FLRA 1987, s 33(1), Sch 2, para 22; CSPSSA 2000, s 82(1),(3); MCA 2005, s 67(1), Sch 6, para 15.

Defined terms—"bodily sample": s 25.

"consent" (s 21(1))—The effect of failing to comply with a direction which, by virtue of s 23(3), is implicit in refusing to consent, is dealt with in s 23.

Direction where court considers that it is in a child's best interests for sample to be taken (s 21(3))—The amendment to s 21(3), by the addition of s 21(3)(b), enables the court to direct tests where a person having care and control of the child does *not* consent. This reverses the decision in *Re O and J (Paternity: Blood Tests)* [2000] 1 FLR 418. In considering whether to make such a direction the court will, in appropriate cases, want to take account of *Gillick v West Norfolk and Wisbech Area Health Authority* [1986] 1 FLR 224 and CA 1989 (see in particular ss 38(6), 43(8), 44(7): children, if of sufficient understanding, may refuse to submit to medical examination or other assessment). Balanced against the interests of a child's mother and her husband it may, nevertheless, be in a child's interests to have a test against the wishes of the person with care and control (*Re T (Paternity: Ordering Blood Tests)* [2001] 2 FLR 1190).

Lacks capacity (s 21(4))—On a properly constituted application, the Court of Protection can give consent to bodily sample tests in respect of a person who lacks capacity, depending on the evidence in the particular case (*LG v DK* [2012] COPLR 80). In the first instance, application for a declaration of parentage (FLA 1986, s 55A) is in the family courts (see under FPR 2010, r 8.20).

22 Power to provide for manner of giving effect to direction for use of scientific tests

(1) The Lord Chancellor may by regulations make provision as to the manner of giving effect to directions under section 20 of this Act and, in particular, any such regulations may –

    (a)   provide that bodily samples shall not be taken except by registered medical practitioners or members of such professional bodies as may be prescribed by the regulations;

    (aa) prescribe the bodily samples to be taken;

    (b)   regulate the taking, identification and transport of bodily samples;

    (c)   require the production at the time when a bodily sample is to be taken of such evidence of the identity of the person from whom it is to be taken as may be prescribed by the regulations;

    (d)   require any person from whom a bodily sample is to be taken, or, in such cases as may be prescribed by the regulations, such other person as may be so prescribed, to state in writing whether he or the person from whom the sample is to be taken, as the case may be, has during such period as may be specified in the regulations suffered from any such illness or condition or undergone any such treatment as may be so specified or received a transfusion of blood;

(e)   prescribe conditions which a body must meet in order to be eligible for accreditation for the purposes of section 20 of this Act;

(f)   prescribe the scientific tests to be carried out and the manner in which they are to be carried out;

(g)   regulate the charges that may be made for the taking and testing of bodily samples and for the making of a report to a court under section 20 of this Act;

(h)   make provisions for securing that so far as practicable the bodily samples to be tested for the purpose of giving effect to a direction under section 20 of this Act are tested by the same person;

(i)   prescribe the form of the report to be made to a court under section 20 of this Act;

(j)   make different provision for different cases or for different descriptions of case.

(2) The power to make regulations under this section shall be exercisable by statutory instrument which shall be subject to annulment in pursuance of a resolution of either House of Parliament.

Amendments—FLRA 1987, s 33(1), Sch 2, para 23; SI 1992/709; CSPSSA 2000, s 82(1),(4).

Defined terms—"bodily sample", "scientific test": s 25.

Regulations—The regulations are the Blood Tests (Evidence of Paternity) Regulations 1971.

23 Failure to comply with direction for taking scientific tests

(1) Where a court gives a direction under section 20 of this Act and any person fails to take any step required of him for the purpose of giving effect to the direction, the court may draw such inferences, if any, from that fact as appear proper in the circumstances.

(2) Where in any proceedings in which the parentage of any person falls to be determined by the court hearing the proceedings there is a presumption of law that that person is legitimate, then if –

(a)   a direction is given under section 20 of this Act in those proceedings, and

(b)   any party who is claiming any relief in the proceedings and who for the purpose of obtaining that relief is entitled to rely on the presumption fails to take any step required of him for the purpose of giving effect to the direction,

the court may adjourn the hearing for such period as it thinks fit to enable that party to take that step, and if at the end of that period he has failed without reasonable cause to take it the court may, without prejudice to subsection (1) of this section, dismiss his claim for relief notwithstanding the absence of evidence to rebut the presumption.

(3) Where any person named in a direction under section 20 of this Act fails to consent to the taking of a bodily sample from himself or from any person named in the direction of whom he has the care and control, he shall be deemed for the purposes of this section to have failed to take a step required of him for the purpose of giving effect to the direction.

Amendments—FLRA 1987, s 33(1), Sch 2, para 24.

Defined terms—"scientific test": s 25.

"the court may draw such inference" (s 23(1))—Where a sample is refused, the court is entitled to infer that this corroborates the applicant's case (see e g *McV v B* [1988] 2 FLR 67). The fact that more than one man might also be the father of the child, and none of those men was being proceeded against, did not entitle a respondent father to avoid the consequences of refusing to consent to a test (*Re A (A Minor) (Paternity: Refusal of Blood Test)* [1994] 2 FLR 463, CA).

Refusal of tests—If an inference is to be drawn from the refusal of a test, such inference can be drawn, even though a direction has not been made, if a parent clearly indicates an intention not to comply with any direction made by the court (*Re H (Paternity: Blood Test)* [1996] 2 FLR 65, CA).

"presumption of law" (s 23(2))—There is a presumption that a child born in wedlock is legitimate. If, in reliance on this, application is made to the court and paternity is challenged, the applicant for the test must submit to any tests directed (*Secretary of State for Work and Pensions v Jones* [2004] 1 FLR 282). If he does not, he risks having his application dismissed even though there is no evidence to rebut the presumption which would otherwise operate in his favour. For example, a person over 18 can apply for his parent to provide financial relief (CA 1989, s 15, Sch 1, para 2). If he applies against his mother's estranged husband, who then challenges his paternity, he will have to submit to a test if one is directed; and if he does not comply with the direction, the court has a discretion to dismiss his application.

"deemed ... to have failed to take a step required" (s 23(3))—This subsection refers back to consent under s 21(3) and involves children under 16.

24 Penalty for personating another, etc, for purpose of providing bodily sample

If for the purpose of providing a bodily sample for a test required to give effect to a direction under section 20 of this Act any person personates another, or proffers a child knowing that it is not the child named in the direction, he shall be liable –

(a) on conviction on indictment, to imprisonment for a term not exceeding two years, or

(b) on summary conviction, to a fine not exceeding the prescribed sum.

Amendments—MCA 1980, s 32(2); FLRA 1987, s 33(1), Sch 2, para 25.

Defined terms—"bodily sample": s 25.

25 Interpretation of Part III

In this Part of this Act the following expressions have the meanings hereby respectively assigned to them, that is to say –

"bodily sample" means a sample of bodily fluid or bodily tissue taken for the purpose of scientific tests;

"excluded" means excluded subject to the occurrence of mutation to section 27 of the Family Law Reform Act 1987, to sections 27 to 29 of the Human Fertilisation and Embryology Act 1990 and to sections 33 to 47 of the Human Fertilisation and Embryology Act 2008;

"scientific tests" means scientific tests carried out under this Part of this Act and made with the object of ascertaining the inheritable characteristics of bodily fluids or bodily tissue.

Amendments—FLRA 1987, s 23(2); HFEA 1990, s 49(5), Sch 4, para 1; HFEA 2008, s 56, Sch 6, Pt 1, para 13(a).

PART IV
MISCELLANEOUS AND GENERAL

26 Rebuttal of presumption as to legitimacy and illegitimacy

Any presumption of law as to the legitimacy or illegitimacy of any person may in any civil proceedings be rebutted by evidence which shows that it is more probable than not that that person is illegitimate or legitimate, as the case may be, and it shall not be necessary to prove that fact beyond reasonable doubt in order to rebut the presumption.

Standard of proof—For a discussion of the subject of "standard of proof", see *Cross and Tapper on Evidence* (12th Edn; Oxford), at [154] et seq. The "civil standard" is required here, although it has been suggested that the standard should reflect the seriousness of the question in issue, namely the parentage of a child (*Serio v Serio* (1983) 4 FLR 756), summarised in *Re A (A Minor) (Paternity: Refusal of Blood Test)* [1994] 2 FLR 463, CA (at [470B]) as follows:

"(1) The question raised by an issue of paternity is a serious one – more serious in the scale of gravity than, for example, proof of debt or minor negligence.

(2) The balance of probability has to be established to a degree of sureness in the mind of the court which matches the seriousness of the issue.

(3) The weighing process involved in (2) must not however be over-elaborate. The court should not attempt, in a precise – almost mathematical – way to determine precisely what degree of probability is appropriate to the gravity of the issue. There is still ample scope for the influence of common sense and the insight gained from first impression."

A simplification of the explanation of the working of the standard of proof in family proceedings generally is provided in *Re B (Children) (Care Proceedings: Standard of Proof)* [2008] 2 FLR 141.

****

Family Law Reform Act 1987

1 General principle

(1) In this Act and enactments passed and instruments made after the coming into force of this section, references (however expressed) to any relationship between two persons shall, unless the contrary intention appears, be construed without regard to whether or not the father and mother of either of them, or the father and mother of any person through whom the relationship is deduced, have or had been married to each other at any time.

(2) In this Act and enactments passed after the coming into force of this section, unless the contrary intention appears –

    (a)   references to a person whose father and mother were married to each other at the time of his birth include; and

    (b)   references to a person whose father and mother were not married to each other at the time of his birth do not include,

references to any person to whom subsection (3) below applies, and cognate references shall be construed accordingly.

(3) This subsection applies to any person who –

    (a)   is treated as legitimate by virtue of section 1 of the Legitimacy Act 1976;

    (b)   is a legitimated person within the meaning of section 10 of that Act;

    (ba) has a parent by virtue of section 42 of the Human Fertilisation and Embryology Act 2008 (which relates to treatment provided to a woman who is at the time of treatment a party to a civil partnership or, in certain circumstances, a void civil partnership);

    (bb) has a parent by virtue of section 43 of that Act (which relates to treatment provided to woman who agrees that second woman to be parent) who –

        (i)   is the civil partner of the child's mother at the time of the child's birth, or

        (ii) was the civil partner of the child's mother at any time during the period beginning with the time mentioned in section 43(b) of that Act and ending with the child's birth;

    (c)   is an adopted person within the meaning of Chapter 4 of Part 1 of the Adoption and Children Act 2002; or

    (d)   is otherwise treated in law as legitimate.

PART II

(4) For the purpose of construing references falling within subsection (2) above, the time of a person's birth shall be taken to include any time during the period beginning with –

    (a)   the insemination resulting in his birth; or

    (b)   where there was no such insemination, his conception,

and (in either case) ending with his birth.

(5) A child whose parents are parties to a void civil partnership shall, subject to subsection (6), be treated as falling within subsection (3)(bb) if at the time when the parties registered as civil partners of each other both or either of the parties reasonably believed that the civil partnership was valid.

(6) Subsection (5) applies only where the woman who is a parent by virtue of section 43 was domiciled in England and Wales at the time of the birth or, if she died before the birth, was so domiciled immediately before her death.

(7) Subsection (5) applies even though the belief that the civil partnership was valid was due to a mistake as to law.

(8) It shall be presumed for the purposes of subsection (5), unless the contrary is shown, that one of the parties to a void civil partnership reasonably believed at the time of the formation of the civil partnership that the civil partnership was valid.

Amendments—ACA 2002, Sch 3, para 51; HFEA 2008, s 56, Sch 6, Pt 1, paras 24(1)–(3).

****

18 Succession on intestacy

(1) In Part IV of the Administration of Estates Act 1925 (which deals with the distribution of the estate of an intestate), references (however expressed) to any relationship between two persons shall be construed in accordance with section 1 above.

(2) For the purposes of subsection (1) above and that Part of that Act, a person whose father and mother were not married to each other at the time of his birth shall be presumed not to have been survived by his father, or by any person related to him only through his father, unless the contrary is shown.

(2A) In the case of a person who has a parent by virtue of section 43 of the Human Fertilisation and Embryology Act 2008 (treatment provided to woman who agrees that second woman to be parent), the second and third references in subsection (2) to the person's father are to be read as references to the woman who is a parent of the person by virtue of that section.

(3) In section 50(1) of the Administration of Estates Act 1925 (which relates to the construction of documents), the reference to Part IV of that Act, or to the foregoing provisions of that Part, shall in relation to an instrument inter vivos made, or a will or codicil coming into operation, after the coming into force of this section (but not in relation to instruments inter vivos made or wills or codicils coming into operation earlier) be construed as including references to this section.

(4) This section does not affect any rights under the intestacy of a person dying before the coming into force of this section.

Amendments—HFEA 2008, s 56, Sch 6, Pt 1, para 25(1),(3).

19 Dispositions of property

(1) In the following dispositions, namely –

    (a) dispositions inter vivos made on or after the date on which this section comes into force; and

    (b) dispositions by will or codicil where the will or codicil is made on or after that date,

references (whether express or implied) to any relationship between two persons shall be construed in accordance with section 1 above.

(2) It is hereby declared that the use, without more, of the word "heir" or "heirs" or any expression purporting to create an entailed interest in real or personal property does not show a contrary intention for the purposes of section 1 as applied by subsection (1) above.

(3) In relation to the dispositions mentioned in subsection (1) above, section 33 of the Trustee Act 1925 (which specifies the trust implied by a direction that income is to be held on protective trusts for the benefit of any person) shall have effect as if any reference (however expressed) to any relationship between two persons were construed in accordance with section 1 above.

(4) Where under any disposition of real or personal property, any interest in such property is limited (whether subject to any preceding limitation or charge or not) in such a way that it would, apart from this section, devolve (as nearly as the law permits) along with a dignity or title of honour, then –

    (a) whether or not the disposition contains an express reference to the dignity or title of honour; and

    (b) whether or not the property or some interest in the property may in some event become severed from it,

nothing in this section shall operate to sever the property or any interest in it from the dignity or title, but the property or interest shall devolve in all respects as if this section had not been enacted.

(5) This section is without prejudice to section 42 of the Adoption Act 1976 or section 69 of the Adoption and Children Act 2002 (construction of dispositions in cases of adoption).

(6) In this section "disposition" means a disposition, including an oral disposition, of real or personal property whether inter vivos or by will or codicil.

(7) Notwithstanding any rule of law, a disposition made by will or codicil executed before the date on which this section comes into force shall not be treated for the purposes of this section as made on or after that date by reason only that the will or codicil is confirmed by a codicil executed on or after that date.

Amendments—TLATA 1996, s 25(1), Sch 3, para 25; ACA 2002, Sch 3, para 52.

****

21 Entitlement to grant probate etc

(1) For the purpose of determining the person or persons who would in accordance with probate rules be entitled to a grant of probate or administration in respect of the estate of a deceased person, the deceased shall be presumed, unless the contrary is shown, not to have been survived –

    (a) by any person related to him whose father and mother were not married to each other at the time of his birth; or

(b) by any person whose relationship with him is deduced through such a person as is mentioned in paragraph (a) above.

(2) In this section "probate rules" means rules of court made under section 127 of the Senior Courts Act 1981.

(3) This section does not apply in relation to the estate of a person dying before the coming into force of this section.

Amendments—CRA 2005, Sch 11, para 1(2).

****

Gender Recognition Act 2004

ARRANGEMENT OF SECTIONS

Applications for gender recognition certificate

General note—The purpose of the Act, which came into force on 4 April 2005 (SI 2005/54, art 2), is to provide transsexual people with legal recognition in their acquired gender. It remedies breaches of the human rights of transsexuals revealed by decisions of the ECtHR and the House of Lords, e g *Goodwin v United Kingdom* [2002] 2 FLR 487, ECtHR; *Bellinger v Bellinger* [2003] 1 FLR 1043. Legal recognition in the acquired gender follows from the issue of a full gender recognition certificate. Sections 1–8 and Schs 1 and 2 establish the process for the issue of a gender recognition certificate to a transsexual person and create a Gender Recognition Panel (*www.justice.gov.uk/tribunals/gender-recognition-panel*; tel: 0845 355 5155). Sections 9–21 and Schs 3–6 set out the consequences of the issue of a full gender recognition certificate.

It is an offence under s 22 of the Act for a person who has acquired protected information, being information concerning an application under ss 1(1), 5(2), 5A(2) or 6(1) or concerning the person's gender before it becomes an acquired gender, in an official capacity to disclose the information to any other person subject to certain exceptions (s 22(4),(5),(7)).

Section 13 and Sch 5 ensure that transsexual persons are treated according to their acquired gender in respect of certain gender specific benefits, e g widowed mother's allowance, widow's pension, widowed parent's allowance, long-term incapacity benefit and state retirement pension.

Section 14 and Sch 6 provide that a person who is recognised under the Act as being of an acquired gender is to be treated as being of the acquired gender under the Sex Discrimination Act 1975. The relevant parts of FPR 2010 are r 7.11 (Nullity: Interim and full gender recognition certificate), Pt 8, Ch 2 (rr 8.2–8.5) (Application for corrected gender recognition certificate) and r 29.6 (Documents in proceedings).

Applications for gender recognition certificate

1 Applications

(1) A person of either gender who is aged at least 18 may make an application for a gender recognition certificate on the basis of –

    (a)   living in the other gender, or

    (b)   having changed gender under the law of a country or territory outside the United Kingdom.

(2) In this Act "the acquired gender", in relation to a person by whom an application under subsection (1) is or has been made, means –

    (a)   in the case of an application under paragraph (a) of that subsection, the gender in which the person is living, or

    (b)   in the case of an application under paragraph (b) of that subsection, the gender to which the person has changed under the law of the country or territory concerned.

(3) An application under subsection (1) is to be determined by a Gender Recognition Panel.

(4) Schedule 1 (Gender Recognition Panels) has effect.

Defined terms—"gender recognition certificate", "the acquired gender": s 25; "Gender Recognition Panel": s 25, Sch 1.

Scope—An application may be made for a gender recognition certificate by a person aged at least 18 living in another gender or by a person who has changed gender in another jurisdiction. The application is determined by a Gender Recognition Panel, the composition of which is prescribed in Sch 1.

"having changed gender under the law of a country or territory outside the United Kingdom" (s 1(1)(b))—See s 21.

2 Determination of applications

(1) In the case of an application under section 1(1)(a), the Panel must grant the application if satisfied that the applicant –

    (a)   has or has had gender dysphoria,

    (b)   has lived in the acquired gender throughout the period of two years ending with the date on which the application is made,

    (c)   intends to continue to live in the acquired gender until death, and

    (d)   complies with the requirements imposed by and under section 3.

(2) In the case of an application under section 1(1)(b), the Panel must grant the application if satisfied –

    (a)   that the country or territory under the law of which the applicant has changed gender is an approved country or territory, and

    (b)   that the applicant complies with the requirements imposed by and under section 3.

PART II

(3) The Panel must reject an application under section 1(1) if not required by subsection (1) or (2) to grant it.

(4) In this Act "approved country or territory" means a country or territory prescribed by order made by the Secretary of State after consulting the Scottish Ministers and the Department of Finance and Personnel in Northern Ireland.

Defined terms—"gender dysphoria": s 25; "the acquired gender": ss 1(2) and 25; "Panel": s 25, Sch 1; "approved country or territory": s 2(4) and Gender Recognition (Approved Countries and Territories) Order 2011.

Scope—This section contains the criteria to be met when determining an application for a gender recognition certificate.

"2 years" (s 2(1)(b))—See, for example, *M v Revenue and Customs Commissioners* [2010] UKFTT 356 (TC).

3 Evidence

(1) An application under section 1(1)(a) must include either –

    (a) a report made by a registered medical practitioner practising in the field of gender dysphoria and a report made by another registered medical practitioner (who may, but need not, practise in that field), or

    (b) a report made by a registered psychologist practising in that field and a report made by a registered medical practitioner (who may, but need not, practise in that field).

(2) But subsection (1) is not complied with unless a report required by that subsection and made by –

    (a) a registered medical practitioner, or

    (b) a registered psychologist,

practising in the field of gender dysphoria includes details of the diagnosis of the applicant's gender dysphoria.

(3) And subsection (1) is not complied with in a case where –

    (a) the applicant has undergone or is undergoing treatment for the purpose of modifying sexual characteristics, or

    (b) treatment for that purpose has been prescribed or planned for the applicant,

unless at least one of the reports required by that subsection includes details of it.

(4) An application under section 1(1)(a) must also include a statutory declaration by the applicant that the applicant meets the conditions in section 2(1)(b) and (c).

(5) An application under section 1(1)(b) must include evidence that the applicant has changed gender under the law of an approved country or territory.

(6) Any application under section 1(1) must include –

    (a) a statutory declaration as to whether or not the applicant is married or a civil partner,

    (b) any other information or evidence required by an order made by the Secretary of State, and

    (c) any other information or evidence which the Panel which is to determine the application may require,

and may include any other information or evidence which the applicant wishes to include.

(7) The Secretary of State may not make an order under subsection (6)(b) without consulting the Scottish Ministers and the Department of Finance and Personnel in Northern Ireland.

(8) If the Panel which is to determine the application requires information or evidence under subsection (6)(c) it must give reasons for doing so.

Amendments—CPA 2004, s 250(1),(2); SI 2009/1182.

Defined terms—"gender dysphoria", "chartered psychologist": s 25; "approved country or territory": ss 2(4), 25; "Panel": s 25, Sch 1.

Scope—This section sets out the evidential requirements to support an application under s 1(1). The evidence required for an application under s 1(1)(a) is a report from a registered medical practitioner or chartered psychologist practising in the field of gender dysphoria and a second report from any registered medical practitioner. At least one report must include details of the diagnosis of the applicant's gender dysphoria and of any treatment undergone, prescribed or planned for the purpose of modifying sexual characteristics.

4 Successful applications

(1) If a Gender Recognition Panel grants an application under section 1(1) it must issue a gender recognition certificate to the applicant.

(2) Unless the applicant is married or a civil partner, the certificate is to be a full gender recognition certificate.

(3) If the applicant is married or a civil partner, the certificate is to be an interim gender recognition certificate.

(4) Schedule 2 (annulment or dissolution of marriage after issue of interim gender recognition certificate) has effect.

(5) The Secretary of State may, after consulting the Scottish Ministers and the Department of Finance and Personnel in Northern Ireland, specify the content and form of gender recognition certificates.

Amendments—CPA 2004, s 250(1),(2).

Defined terms—"Gender Recognition Panel": s 25, Sch 1; "gender recognition certificate": s 25; "full gender recognition certificate": ss 5, 5A and 25; "interim gender recognition certificate": s 25.

Scope—This section provides that the Gender Recognition Panel must issue a gender recognition certificate to a successful applicant. Where the applicant is single, a full gender recognition certificate is issued. Where the applicant is married or a civil partner, an interim gender recognition certificate is issued. Section 4(4) and Sch 2 provide that the grant of an interim gender recognition certificate to *either* party to a marriage is in England and Wales a ground on which a marriage is voidable. The MCA 1973, s 12 (marriage celebrated *after* 31 July 1971) and Sch 1, para 11 (marriages celebrated *before* 1 August 1971) are amended accordingly. Nullity proceedings must be commenced within 6 months of the grant of the interim gender recognition certificate (MCA 1973, s 13(2A) and Sch 1, para 11(3A) as inserted by Sch 2, paras 3 and 4).

Section 11 and Sch 4, para 5 provide a further ground upon which a marriage celebrated *after* 31 July 1971 is voidable (MCA 1973, s 12(h)), namely, that the respondent is a person whose gender at the time of the marriage had become the acquired gender under the Act. The petitioner must have been ignorant of the fact that the respondent was previously of another gender.

Section 6 provides for the correction of an error in a gender recognition certificate on the application of the person to whom it has been issued or the Secretary of State by the court or the Gender Recognition Panel which issued the certificate. Section 8 permits an appeal to the High Court by an applicant to a Gender Recognition Panel under ss 1(1), 5(2), 5A(2) or 6(1) on a point of law against a decision by the Panel to reject the application. Section 8(5) provides for the Secretary of State to refer cases to the High Court where he considers an application for a gender recognition certificate has been secured by fraud. Proceedings under ss 6 and 8 are assigned to the Family Division (High Court (Distribution of Business) Order 2004).

"full gender recognition certificate" (s 4(2))—On the issue of a full gender recognition certificate, s 10 and Sch 3 establish a procedure for the creation of a new entry in the UK birth registers which supersede the original entry, thereby reversing *Rees v United Kingdom* [1987] 2 FLR 111, ECtHR and *Cossey v United Kingdom* [1991] 2 FLR 492, ECtHR.

5 Issue of full certificates where applicant has been married

(1) A court which –

    (a)   makes absolute a decree of nullity granted on the ground that an interim gender recognition certificate has been issued to a party to the marriage, or

    (b)   (in Scotland) grants a decree of divorce on that ground,

must, on doing so, issue a full gender recognition certificate to that party and send a copy to the Secretary of State.

(2) If an interim gender recognition certificate has been issued to a person and either –

    (a)   the person's marriage is dissolved or annulled (otherwise than on the ground mentioned in subsection (1)) in proceedings instituted during the period of six months beginning with the day on which it was issued, or

    (b)   the person's spouse dies within that period,

the person may make an application for a full gender recognition certificate at any time within the period specified in subsection (3) (unless the person is again married or is a civil partner).

(3) That period is the period of six months beginning with the day on which the marriage is dissolved or annulled or the death occurs.

(4) An application under subsection (2) must include evidence of the dissolution or annulment of the marriage and the date on which proceedings for it were instituted, or of the death of the spouse and the date on which it occurred.

(5) An application under subsection (2) is to be determined by a Gender Recognition Panel.

(6) The Panel –

    (a)   must grant the application if satisfied that the applicant is neither married nor a civil partner, and

    (b)   otherwise must reject it.

(7) If the Panel grants the application it must issue a full gender recognition certificate to the applicant.

Amendments—CPA 2004, s 250(1),(3).

Defined terms—"interim gender recognition certificate": ss 4(1) and 25; "Gender Recognition Panel": s 25, Sch 1; "full gender recognition certificate": ss 4(2) and 25.

Scope—This section provides for the issue of a full gender recognition certificate in two situations. First, where an interim gender recognition certificate has been issued to a party to a marriage and a decree of nullity is subsequently granted on the ground of the issue of such a certificate (s 4(3),(4)), a full gender recognition certificate must be issued. Secondly, if an interim gender recognition certificate has been issued to a person whose marriage is dissolved or annulled (otherwise than on the ground of the issue of an interim gender recognition certificate) in proceedings instituted during the 6-month period beginning with the issue of the interim gender recognition certificate, or the person's spouse dies within that period, the person may apply to the Gender Recognition Panel for a full gender recognition certificate within three months of the date of dissolution, annulment or death, unless the person is again married or is a civil partner.

5A Issue of full certificates where applicant has been a civil partner

(1) A court which –

    (a)   makes final a nullity order made on the ground that an interim gender recognition certificate has been issued to a civil partner, or

    (b)   (in Scotland) grants a decree of dissolution on that ground,

must, on doing so, issue a full gender recognition certificate to that civil partner and send a copy to the Secretary of State.

(2) If an interim gender recognition certificate has been issued to a person and either –

   (a) the person's civil partnership is dissolved or annulled (otherwise than on the ground mentioned in subsection (1)) in proceedings instituted during the period of six months beginning with the day on which it was issued, or

   (b) the person's civil partner dies within that period,

the person may make an application for a full gender recognition certificate at any time within the period specified in subsection (3) (unless the person is again a civil partner or is married).

(3) That period is the period of six months beginning with the day on which the civil partnership is dissolved or annulled or the death occurs.

(4) An application under subsection (2) must include evidence of the dissolution or annulment of the civil partnership and the date on which proceedings for it were instituted, or of the death of the civil partner and the date on which it occurred.

(5) An application under subsection (2) is to be determined by a Gender Recognition Panel.

(6) The Panel –

   (a) must grant the application if satisfied that the applicant is neither a civil partner nor married, and

   (b) otherwise must reject it.

(7) If the Panel grants the application it must issue a full gender recognition certificate to the applicant.

Amendments—Inserted by CPA 2004, s 250(1),(4).

Defined terms—"Gender Recognition Panel": s 25, Sch 1; "interim gender recognition certificate": ss 4(1) and 25; "full gender recognition certificate": ss 4(2) and 25.

Scope—This section makes provision where the applicant has been a civil partner comparable to that applicable to a married applicant found in s 5.

6 Errors in certificates

(1) Where a gender recognition certificate has been issued to a person, the person or the Secretary of State may make an application for a corrected certificate on the ground that the certificate which has been issued contains an error.

(2) If the certificate was issued by a court the application is to be determined by the court but in any other case it is to be determined by a Gender Recognition Panel.

(3) The court or Panel –

   (a) must grant the application if satisfied that the gender recognition certificate contains an error, and

   (b) otherwise must reject it.

(4) If the court or Panel grants the application it must issue a corrected gender recognition certificate to the applicant.

Defined terms—"gender recognition certificate": s 25; "Gender Recognition Panel": s 25, Sch 1.

"Determined by the court" (s 6(2))—The procedure is set out in FPR 2010, Pt 8, Ch 2 (rr 8.2–8.5).

Scope—This section enables a gender recognition certificate containing an error to be corrected on application to the court (where the certificate was issued by the court) or otherwise by a Gender Recognition Panel. Where the application is to a court, the procedure is governed by FPR 2010, Pt 8, Ch 2.

7 Applications: supplementary

(1) An application to a Gender Recognition Panel under section 1(1), 5(2), 5A(2) or 6(1) must be made in a form and manner specified by the Secretary of State after consulting the Scottish Ministers and the Department of Finance and Personnel in Northern Ireland.

(2) The applicant must pay to the Secretary of State a non-refundable fee of an amount prescribed by order made by the Secretary of State unless the application is made in circumstances in which, in accordance with provision made by the order, no fee is payable; and fees of different amounts may be prescribed for different circumstances.

Amendments—CPA 2004, s 250(1),(5).

Defined terms—"Gender Recognition Panel": s 25, Sch 1; "fee": Gender Recognition (Application Fees) Order 2006, as amended.

8 Appeals etc

(1) An applicant to a Gender Recognition Panel under section 1(1), 5(2), 5(A)2 or 6(1) may appeal to the High Court or Court of Session on a point of law against a decision by the Panel to reject the application.

(2) An appeal under subsection (1) must be heard in private if the applicant so requests.

(3) On such an appeal the court must –

    (a) allow the appeal and issue the certificate applied for,

    (b) allow the appeal and refer the matter to the same or another Panel for re-consideration, or

    (c) dismiss the appeal.

(4) If an application under section 1(1) is rejected, the applicant may not make another application before the end of the period of six months beginning with the date on which it is rejected.

(5) If an application under section 1(1), 5(2), 5A(2) or 6(1) is granted but the Secretary of State considers that its grant was secured by fraud, the Secretary of State may refer the case to the High Court or Court of Session.

(6) On a reference under subsection (5) the court –

    (a) must either quash or confirm the decision to grant the application, and

    (b) if it quashes it, must revoke the gender recognition certificate issued on the grant of the application and may make any order which it considers appropriate in consequence of, or otherwise in connection with, doing so.

Amendments—CPA 2004, s 250(1),(5).

Defined terms—"gender recognition certificate": s 25; "Gender Recognition Panel": s 25, Sch 1.

Scope—This section provides the applicant with a right of appeal against a rejection decision on a point of law to the High Court, or Court of Session in Scotland. Where such an appeal is rejected, the applicant may not lodge a further appeal until 6 months have elapsed. The Secretary of State has a right to refer a case to the High Court or Court of Session if he considers that the grant of an application was secured by fraud. An appeal will only lie where there has been a decision to reject the application and not as a result of, for example, distress arising from the delayed progress of an application or loss of state pension rights (*Carpenter v Secretary of State for Justice* [2012] All ER (D) 93 (Oct)).

Consequences of issue of gender recognition certificate etc.

9 General

(1) Where a full gender recognition certificate is issued to a person, the person's gender becomes for all purposes the acquired gender (so that, if the acquired gender is the male gender, the person's sex becomes that of a man and, if it is the female gender, the person's sex becomes that of a woman).

(2) Subsection (1) does not affect things done, or events occurring, before the certificate is issued; but it does operate for the interpretation of enactments passed, and instruments and other documents made, before the certificate is issued (as well as those passed or made afterwards).

(3) Subsection (1) is subject to provision made by this Act or any other enactment or any subordinate legislation.

Defined terms—"full gender recognition certificate": ss 4(2) and 25; "acquired gender": ss 1(2) and 25; "enactment", "subordinate legislation": s 25.

Scope—The general principle of the Act is that, where a full gender recognition certificate is issued to a transsexual person, he/she will for all purposes be regarded as being of the acquired gender without any presumption that the person has physical characteristics other than those that he/she actually possesses (e g *R (on the application of AB) v Secretary of State for Justice and another* [2010] 2 All ER 151). Recognition of the acquired gender is not retrospective (*J v C (Void Marriage: Status of Children)* [2006] 2 FLR 1098; *Timbrell v Secretary of State for Work & Pensions* [2011] 1 FLR 332). This general principle is subject to exceptions contained in the Act (e g parenthood (s 12), peerages (s 16), sport (s 19) or gender-specific offences (s 20)) or in later primary or subordinate legislation.

Much of the case-law relating to the consequences of the issue of a gender recognition certificate has related to the statutory provisions about state pensionable age. Originally, before the Act, it had been held that a male at birth who had successfully undergone gender reassignment surgery had to be treated as a male (for the purposes of the MCA 1973) (*Bellinger v Bellinger* [2003] 1 FLR 1043). In *Goodwin v UK* [2002] 2 FLR 487, it was held that the UK's failure to provide a means to obtain legal recognition of gender reassignment had been a breach of that applicant's rights under ECHR, Art 8, which decision led to the enactment of the Act. Following *Goodwin*, the ECtHR held in *Grant v United Kingdom* [2007] 44 EHRR 1 that there was no justification for failing to recognise the change of gender of post-operative transsexuals. The applicant was entitled to claim to be the victim of the denial of legal recognition of gender reassignment from the date of the decision in *Goodwin* until the Act came into force as violating her rights under ECHR, Art 8. A different approach was adopted in *Richards v Secretary of State for Work & Pensions* [2006] 2 FLR 487, where it was held on a preliminary ruling from the ECJ that the Pensions Act 1995 was discriminatory (under the directly effective right under art 4(1) of Council Directive 79/7 on the equal treatment for men and women in matters of social security) as it constituted unequal treatment for the claimant as a result of her inability to have her new gender recognised under the 1995 Act. This approach, under which it was found that UK legislation before the Act was discriminatory with regard to acquired gender and pension entitlement, was followed in *Timbrell v Secretary of State for Work & Pensions* [2011] 1 FLR 332. The decision in *Timbrell* was, however, distinguished in *M v Revenue and Customs Commissioners* [2010] SFTD 1141, where the appellant's gender reassignment surgery had been performed after the Act came into force.

Section 11 and Sch 4 amend MA 1949 so that, for example, a male is able to contract a valid marriage with a transsexual whose acquired gender under the Act is female, thereby reversing decisions such as *Corbett v Corbett* [1971] P 83 and *Bellinger v Bellinger* [2003] 1 FLR 1043, HL.

10 Registration

(1) Where there is a UK birth register entry in relation to a person to whom a full gender recognition certificate is issued, the Secretary of State must send a copy of the certificate to the appropriate Registrar General.

(2) In this Act "UK birth register entry", in relation to a person to whom a full gender recognition certificate is issued, means –

    (a)   an entry of which a certified copy is kept by a Registrar General, or

    (b)   an entry in a register so kept,

containing a record of the person's birth or adoption (or, if there would otherwise be more than one, the most recent).

(3) "The appropriate Registrar General" means whichever of –

(a) the Registrar General for England and Wales,

(b) the Registrar General for Scotland, or

(c) the Registrar General for Northern Ireland,

keeps a certified copy of the person's UK birth register entry or the register containing that entry.

(4) Schedule 3 (provisions about registration) has effect.

Defined term—"full gender recognition certificate": s 25.

Scope—Sch 3 provides for the maintenance of a Gender Recognition Register, which is not open to public inspection and which is regulated by the Gender Recognition Register Regulations 2005, as amended.

****

12 Parenthood

The fact that a person's gender has become the acquired gender under this Act does not affect the status of the person as the father or mother of a child.

Defined terms—"acquired gender": ss 1(2), 25.

Scope—This section aims to ensure continuity of parental rights and responsibilities given that, though a person is regarded as being of the acquired gender, that person will retain their original status either as father or mother of a child.

****

15 Succession etc

The fact that a person's gender has become the acquired gender under this Act does not affect the disposal or devolution of property under a will or other instrument made before the appointed day.

Defined terms—"acquired gender": ss 1(2), 25; "the appointed day": ss 25, 26 (4 April 2005; SI 2005/54, art 2).

Scope—This section contains one of the exceptions to the general rule contained in s 9 that, following the issue of a full gender recognition certificate, a person's gender becomes for all purposes the acquired gender. Under s 17, trustees and personal representatives are not placed under a duty to enquire whether a full gender recognition certificate has been issued or revoked before conveying or distributing property if that fact could affect entitlement to the property (s 17(1)). Trustees/personal representatives are not liable to any person in the circumstances envisaged by s 17(1) where no notice of the issue or revocation had been received before the conveyance or distribution (s 17(2)). A person will still be able to trace to the property or its proceeds into the hands of another person, unless that person has purchased it for value in good faith and without notice (s 17(3)). This section deals with wills made before 4 April 2005; where the will is made on or after 5 April 2005, see s 18.

****

17 Trustees and personal representatives

(1) A trustee or personal representative is not under a duty, by virtue of the law relating to trusts or the administration of estates, to enquire, before conveying or distributing any property, whether a full gender recognition certificate has been issued to any person or revoked (if that fact could affect entitlement to the property).

(2) A trustee or personal representative is not liable to any person by reason of a conveyance or distribution of the property made without regard to whether a full gender recognition certificate has been issued to any person or revoked if the trustee or personal representative has not received notice of the fact before the conveyance or distribution.

(3) This section does not prejudice the right of a person to follow the property, or any property representing it, into the hands of another person who has received it unless that person has purchased it for value in good faith and without notice.

Defined term—"full gender recognition certificate": s 25.

Scope—This section relieves a trustee or personal representative from any fiduciary duty to inquire whether a gender recognition certificate has been issued to any person or revoked, even if that fact could affect entitlement to property which he/she is responsible for distributing. The beneficiary will nevertheless retain his/her claim to the property and may enforce this claim.

18 Orders where expectations defeated

(1) This section applies where the disposition or devolution of any property under a will or other instrument (made on or after the appointed day) is different from what it would be but for the fact that a person's gender has become the acquired gender under this Act.

(2) A person may apply to the High Court or Court of Session for an order on the ground of being adversely affected by the different disposition or devolution of the property.

(3) The court may, if it is satisfied that it is just to do so, make in relation to any person benefiting from the different disposition or devolution of the property such order as it considers appropriate.

(4) An order may, in particular, make provision for –

    (a)   the payment of a lump sum to the applicant,
    (b)   the transfer of property to the applicant,
    (c)   the settlement of property for the benefit of the applicant,
    (d)   the acquisition of property and either its transfer to the applicant or its settlement for the benefit of the applicant.

(5) An order may contain consequential or supplementary provisions for giving effect to the order or for ensuring that it operates fairly as between the applicant and the other person or persons affected by it; and an order may, in particular, confer powers on trustees.

Defined terms—"the appointed day": ss 25, 26 (4 April 2005 (SI 2005/54, art 2)); "acquired gender": ss 1(2), 25.

Scope—This section applies where disposition of property under a will made on or after 5 April 2005 is different from what it would be but for the fact that a person's gender has become the acquired gender under the Act. For the position in relation to wills made before 4 April 2005, see s 15. The section gives the High Court power to make orders of the type set out in s 18(4) and (5) on the sole ground of a person being adversely affected by the different disposition (s 18(2)). In considering such an application, the court must be satisfied that it is just to make an order (s 18(3)).

****

21 Foreign gender change and marriage

(1) A person's gender is not to be regarded as having changed by reason only that it has changed under the law of a country or territory outside the United Kingdom.

(2) Accordingly, a person is not to be regarded as being married by reason of having entered into a foreign post-recognition marriage.

(3) But if a full gender recognition certificate is issued to a person who has entered into a foreign post-recognition marriage, after the issue of the certificate the marriage is no

longer to be regarded as being void on the ground that (at the time when it was entered into) the parties to it were not respectively male and female.

(4) However, subsection (3) does not apply to a foreign post-recognition marriage if a party to it has entered into a later (valid) marriage or civil partnership before the issue of the full gender recognition certificate.

(5) For the purposes of this section a person has entered into a foreign post-recognition marriage if (and only if) –

(a)   the person has entered into a marriage in accordance with the law of a country or territory outside the United Kingdom,

(b)   before the marriage was entered into the person had changed gender under the law of that or any other country or territory outside the United Kingdom,

(c)   the other party to the marriage was not of the gender to which the person had changed under the law of that country or territory, and

(d)   by virtue of subsection (1) the person's gender was not regarded as having changed under the law of any part of the United Kingdom.

(6) Nothing in this section prevents the exercise of any enforceable Community right.

Amendments—CPA 2004, s 250(1),(6).

Defined terms—"foreign post-recognition marriage": s 21(5); "full gender recognition certificate": ss 4(2), 25.

Scope—This section provides that a person's gender is not to be regarded as having changed only by reason of a foreign gender change (s 21(1)). Accordingly, a person will not be regarded as being married by reason of having entered into a foreign post-recognition marriage as defined by s 21(5) (s 21(2)). Where, however, a full gender recognition certificate is issued to a person who has entered into a foreign post-recognition marriage, the marriage will no longer be regarded as being void (subject to the exceptions in s 21(4)) after the issue of the certificate on the ground that at the time it was entered into the parties were not respectively male and female (s 21(3)).

Supplementary

22 Prohibition on disclosure of information

(1) It is an offence for a person who has acquired protected information in an official capacity to disclose the information to any other person.

(2) "Protected information" means information which relates to a person who has made an application under section 1(1) and which –

(a)   concerns that application or any application by the person under section 5(2), 5A(2) or 6(1), or

(b)   if the application under section 1(1) is granted, otherwise concerns the person's gender before it becomes the acquired gender.

(3) A person acquires protected information in an official capacity if the person acquires it –

(a)   in connection with the person's functions as a member of the civil service, a constable or the holder of any other public office or in connection with the functions of a local or public authority or of a voluntary organisation,

(b)   as an employer, or prospective employer, of the person to whom the information relates or as a person employed by such an employer or prospective employer, or

(c)   in the course of, or otherwise in connection with, the conduct of business or the supply of professional services.

(4) But it is not an offence under this section to disclose protected information relating to a person if –

(a) the information does not enable that person to be identified,
(b) that person has agreed to the disclosure of the information,
(c) the information is protected information by virtue of subsection (2)(b) and the person by whom the disclosure is made does not know or believe that a full gender recognition certificate has been issued,
(d) the disclosure is in accordance with an order of a court or tribunal,
(e) the disclosure is for the purpose of instituting, or otherwise for the purposes of, proceedings before a court or tribunal,
(f) the disclosure is for the purpose of preventing or investigating crime,
(g) the disclosure is made to the Registrar General for England and Wales, the Registrar General for Scotland or the Registrar General for Northern Ireland,
(h) the disclosure is made for the purposes of the social security system or a pension scheme,
(i) the disclosure is in accordance with provision made by an order under subsection (5), or
(j) the disclosure is in accordance with any provision of, or made by virtue of, an enactment other than this section.

(5) The Secretary of State may by order make provision prescribing circumstances in which the disclosure of protected information is not to constitute an offence under this section.

(6) The power conferred by subsection (5) is exercisable by the Scottish Ministers (rather than the Secretary of State) where the provision to be made is within the legislative competence of the Scottish Parliament.

(6A) The power conferred by subsection (5) is exercisable by the Department of Justice in Northern Ireland (rather than the Secretary of State) where the provision to be made could be made by an Act of the Northern Ireland Assembly without the consent of the Secretary of State (see sections 6 to 8 of the Northern Ireland Act 1998).

(7) An order under subsection (5) may make provision permitting –

(a) disclosure to specified persons or persons of a specified description,
(b) disclosure for specified purposes,
(c) disclosure of specified descriptions of information, or
(d) disclosure by specified persons or persons of a specified description.

(8) A person guilty of an offence under this section is liable on summary conviction to a fine not exceeding level 5 on the standard scale.

Amendments—CPA 2004, s 250(1),(5); SI 2010/976.

Defined terms—"the acquired gender": ss 1(2), 25; "enactment", "full gender recognition certificate": s 25.

Scope—This section makes it an offence for a person who has acquired protected information (s 22(2)) in an official capacity to disclose that information. Circumstances in which disclosure of protected information does not constitute an offence (s 22(5) and (7)) are contained in the Gender Recognition (Disclosure of Information) (England, Wales and Northern Ireland) (No 2) Order 2005, which concerns disclosure for the purpose of obtaining legal advice (art 3); for religious purposes (art 4); or medical purposes (art 5); by or on behalf of a credit reference agency (art 6); and in relation to insolvency (art 7).

****

25 Interpretation

In this Act –

"the acquired gender" is to be construed in accordance with section 1(2),
"approved country or territory" has the meaning given by section 2(4),
"the appointed day" means the day appointed by order under section 26,

"enactment" includes an enactment contained in an Act of the Scottish Parliament or in any Northern Ireland legislation,

"full gender recognition certificate" and "interim gender recognition certificate" mean the certificates issued as such under section 4 or 5 or 5A and "gender recognition certificate" means either of those sorts of certificate,

"gender dysphoria" means the disorder variously referred to as gender dysphoria, gender identity disorder and transsexualism,

"Gender Recognition Panel" (and "Panel") is to be construed in accordance with Schedule 1,

"registered psychologist" means a person registered in the part of the register maintained under the Health and Social Work Professions Order 2001 which relates to practitioner psychologists,

"subordinate legislation" means an Order in Council, an order, rules, regulations, a scheme, a warrant, bye-laws or any other instrument made under an enactment, and

"UK birth register entry" has the meaning given by section 10(2).

Amendments—CPA 2004, s 250(1),(7); SI 2009/1182; Health and Social Care Act 2012, s 213(8).

26 Commencement

Apart from sections 23 to 25, this section and sections 28 and 29, this Act does not come into force until such day as the Secretary of State may appoint by order made after consulting the Scottish Ministers and the Department of Finance and Personnel in Northern Ireland.

Orders under this section—The Gender Recognition Act 2004 (Commencement) Order 2005 brought the Act into force, insofar as it was not already in force, on 4 April 2005.

****

Human Fertilisation and Embryology Act 1990

ARRANGEMENT OF SECTIONS

Principal terms used

PART II

Principal terms used

1 Meaning of "embryo", "gamete" and associated expressions

(1) In this Act (except in section 4A or in the term "human admixed embryo") –

(a) embryo means a live human embryo and does not include a human admixed embryo (as defined by section 4A(6)), and

(b) references to an embryo include an egg that is in the process of fertilisation or is undergoing any other process capable of resulting in an embryo.

(2) This Act, so far as it governs bringing about the creation of an embryo, applies only to bringing about the creation of an embryo outside the human body; and in this Act –

(a) references to embryos the creation of which was brought about in vitro (in their application to those where fertilisation or any other process by which an embryo is created is complete) are to those where fertilisation or any other process by which the embryo was created began outside the human body whether or not it was completed there, and

(b) references to embryos taken from a woman do not include embryos whose creation was brought about in vitro.

(3) This Act, so far as it governs the keeping or use of an embryo, applies only to keeping or using an embryo outside the human body.

(4) In this Act (except in section 4A) –

(a) references to eggs are to live human eggs, including cells of the female germ line at any stage of maturity, but (except in subsection (1)(b)) not including eggs that are in the process of fertilisation or are undergoing any other process capable of resulting in an embryo,

(b) references to sperm are to live human sperm, including cells of the male germ line at any stage of maturity, and

(c) references to gametes are to be read accordingly.

(5) For the purposes of this Act, sperm is to be treated as partner-donated sperm if the donor of the sperm and the recipient of the sperm declare that they have an intimate physical relationship.

(6) If it appears to the Secretary of State necessary or desirable to do so in the light of developments in science or medicine, regulations may provide that in this Act (except in section 4A) "embryo", "eggs", "sperm" or "gametes" includes things specified in the regulations which would not otherwise fall within the definition.

(7) Regulations made by virtue of subsection (6) may not provide for anything containing any nuclear or mitochondrial DNA that is not human to be treated as an embryo or as eggs, sperm or gametes.

Amendments—SI 2007/1522; HFEA 2008, s 1.

Definition—The Act redefines "embryo" and "gametes", introduces and defines "human admixed embryo" and is drafted widely enough to include any possible future scientific changes that may be developed. It gives the Secretary of State new powers to make regulations in the light of any new scientific developments but excluding those set out in s 1(7).

"embryo"—Human embryos created by cell nuclear replacement fall within the definition of embryo in s 1(1) and are subject to regulation under the 1990 Act (*R (Quintavelle) v Secretary of State for Health* [2002] QB 628).

"embryo and human rights"—An embryo cannot be considered to be a person or to have a "qualified" right to life, and ECHR 1950, Art 2 does not apply to it (*Evans v Amicus Healthcare and others; Hadley v Midland Fertility Services Ltd and others* [2004] 1 FLR 67. See also *Re F (In Utero) (Wardship)* [1988] 2 FLR 307; *Re MB (Medical Treatment)* [1997] 2 FLR 426 and *Paton v United Kingdom* (1980) 3 EHHR 408.

1A Reference to Directives

In this Act –

"the first Directive" means Directive 2004/23/EC of the European Parliament and of the Council of 31 March 2004 on setting standards of quality and safety for the donation, procurement, testing, processing, preservation, storage and distribution of human tissues and cells,

"the second Directive" means Commission Directive 2006/17/EC of 8 February 2006 implementing Directive 2004/23/EC of the European Parliament and of the Council as regards certain technical requirements for the donation, procurement and testing of human tissues and cells, and

"the third Directive" means Commission Directive 2006/86/EC of 24 October 2006 implementing Directive 2004/23/EC of the European Parliament and of the Council as regards traceability requirements, notification of serious adverse reactions and events and certain technical requirements for the coding, processing, preservation, storage and distribution of human tissues and cells.

Amendments—Inserted by SI 2007/1522.

"the First Directive"—For notes generally on consent see footnote to Sch 3 below.

2 Other terms

(1) In this Act –

"the Authority" means the Human Fertilisation and Embryology Authority established under section 5 of this Act,

"basic partner treatment services" means treatment services that are provided for a woman and a man together without using –

(a) the gametes of any other person, or

(b) embryos created outside the woman's body,

"competent authority", in relation to an EEA state other than the United Kingdom or in relation to Gibraltar, means an authority designated in accordance with the law of that state or territory as responsible for implementing the requirements of the first, second and third Directives,

"directions" means directions under section 23 of this Act,

"distribution", in relation to gametes or embryos intended for human application, means transportation or delivery, and related terms are to be interpreted accordingly,

"human application" means use in a human recipient,

"licence" means a licence under Schedule 2 to this Act and, in relation to a licence, "the person responsible" has the meaning given by section 17 of this Act, and "non-medical fertility services" means any services that are provided, in the course of a business, for the purpose of assisting women to carry children, but are not medical, surgical or obstetric services,

"nuclear DNA", in relation to an embryo, includes DNA in the pronucleus of the embryo,

"processing", in relation to gametes or embryos intended for human application, means any operation involved in their preparation, manipulation or packaging, and related terms are to be interpreted accordingly,

"procurement", in relation to gametes or embryos intended for human application, means any process by which they are made available, and related terms are to be interpreted accordingly,

"serious adverse event" means –

    (a) any untoward occurrence which may be associated with the procurement, testing, processing, storage or distribution of gametes or embryos intended for human application and which, in relation to a donor of gametes or a person who receives treatment services or non-medical fertility services –

        (i) might lead to the transmission of a communicable disease, to death, or life-threatening, disabling or incapacitating conditions, or

        (ii) might result in, or prolong, hospitalisation or illness, or

    (b) any type of gametes or embryo misidentification or mix-up,

"serious adverse reaction" means an unintended response, including a communicable disease, in a donor of gametes intended for human application or a person who receives treatment services or non-medical fertility services, which may be associated with the procurement or human application of gametes or embryos and which is fatal, life-threatening, disabling, incapacitating or which results in, or prolongs, hospitalisation or illness,

"store", in relation to gametes, embryos or human admixed embryos, means preserve, whether by cryopreservation or in any other way, and "storage" and "stored" are to be interpreted accordingly,

"traceability" means the ability –

    (a) to identify and locate gametes and embryos during any step from procurement to use for human application or disposal,

    (b) to identify the donor and recipient of particular gametes or embryos,

    (c) to identify any person who has carried out any activity in relation to particular gametes or embryos, and

    (d) to identify and locate all relevant data relating to products and materials coming into contact with particular gametes or embryos and which can affect their quality or safety,

"treatment services" means medical, surgical or obstetric services provided to the public or a section of the public for the purpose of assisting women to carry children.

(2) References in this Act to keeping, in relation to embryos, gametes or human admixed embryos, include keeping while preserved in storage.

(2A) For the purposes of this Act, a person who, from any premises, controls the provision of services for transporting gametes or embryos is to be taken to distribute gametes or embryos on those premises.

(2B) In this Act, any reference to a requirement of a provision of the first, second or third Directive is a reference to a requirement which that provision requires to be imposed.

(3) For the purposes of this Act, a woman is not to be treated as carrying a child until the embryo has become implanted.

Amendments—SI 2007/1522; HFEA 2008, s 2, Sch 7, para 2.

"**treatment … for the purpose of assisting women to carry children**"—Treatment for producing a child free from genetic defects or producing a child with stem cells matching a sick or dying sibling (tissue typing) constitutes treatment for the purpose of assisting a woman to carry children (*Quintavelle v Human Fertilisation and Embryology Authority* [2005] 2 FLR 349).

2A Third party agreements

(1) For the purposes of this Act, a "third party agreement" is an agreement in writing between a person who holds a licence and another person which is made in accordance with any licence conditions imposed by the Authority for the purpose of securing compliance with the requirements of Article 24 of the first Directive (relations between tissue establishments and third parties) and under which the other person –

- (a) procures, tests or processes gametes or embryos (or both), on behalf of the holder of the licence, or
- (b) supplies to the holder of the licence any goods or services (including distribution services) which may affect the quality or safety of gametes or embryos.

(2) In this Act –

"relevant third party premises", in relation to a licence, means any premises (other than premises to which the licence relates) –

- (a) on which a third party procures, tests, processes or distributes gametes or embryos on behalf of any person in connection with activities carried out by that person under a licence, or
- (b) from which a third party provides any goods or services which may affect the quality or safety of gametes or embryos to any person in connection with activities carried out by that person under a licence;

"third party" means a person with whom a person who holds a licence has a third party agreement.

(3) References in this Act to the persons to whom a third party agreement applies are to –

- (a) the third party,
- (b) any person designated in the third party agreement as a person to whom the agreement applies, and
- (c) any person acting under the direction of a third party or of any person so designated.

Amendments—Inserted by SI 2007/1522.

Activities governed by the Act

3 Prohibitions in connection with embryos

(1) No person shall bring about the creation of an embryo except in pursuance of a licence.

(1A) No person shall keep or use an embryo except –

- (a) in pursuance of a licence, or
- (b) in the case of –
  - (i) the keeping, without storage, of an embryo intended for human application, or
  - (ii) the processing, without storage, of such an embryo,

in pursuance of a third party agreement.

(1B) No person shall procure or distribute an embryo intended for human application except in pursuance of a licence or a third party agreement.

(2) No person shall place in a woman –

    (a)   an embryo other than a permitted embryo (as defined by section 3ZA), or

    (b)   any gametes other than permitted eggs or permitted sperm (as so defined).

(3) A licence cannot authorise –

    (a)   keeping or using an embryo after the appearance of the primitive streak,

    (b)   placing an embryo in any animal, or

    (c)   keeping or using an embryo in any circumstances in which regulations prohibit its keeping or use.

    (d)   (*repealed*)

(4) For the purposes of subsection (3)(a) above, the primitive streak is to be taken to have appeared in an embryo not later than the end of the period of 14 days beginning with the day on which the process of creating the embryo began, not counting any time during which the embryo is stored.

Amendments—SI 2007/1522; HFEA 2008, s 3.

"Prohibition"—Contravention of s 3(1) is an offence (s 41(2)(a)) and see *R v HFEA ex parte Blood* [1997] 2 FLR 742.

Use of an embryo—See *Quintavelle v Human Fertilisation and Embryology Authority* [2005] 2 FLR 349; *Evans v Amicus Healthcare and others; Hadley v Midland Fertility Services Ltd and others* [2004] 1 FLR 67.

"placing in a woman a human embryo"—The Human Reproductive Cloning Act 2001 makes it an offence to place in a woman a human embryo which has been created otherwise than by fertilisation (which on conviction on indictment carries a maximum sentence of 10 years or a fine or both).

3ZA Permitted eggs, permitted sperm and permitted embryos

(1) This section has effect for the interpretation of section 3(2).

(2) A permitted egg is one –

    (a)   which has been produced by or extracted from the ovaries of a woman, and

    (b)   whose nuclear or mitochondrial DNA has not been altered.

(3) Permitted sperm are sperm –

    (a)   which have been produced by or extracted from the testes of a man, and

    (b)   whose nuclear or mitochondrial DNA has not been altered.

(4) An embryo is a permitted embryo if –

    (a)   it has been created by the fertilisation of a permitted egg by permitted sperm,

    (b)   no nuclear or mitochondrial DNA of any cell of the embryo has been altered, and

    (c)   no cell has been added to it other than by division of the embryo's own cells.

(5) Regulations may provide that –

    (a)   an egg can be a permitted egg, or

    (b)   an embryo can be a permitted embryo, even though the egg or embryo has had applied to it in prescribed circumstances a prescribed process designed to prevent the transmission of serious mitochondrial disease.

(6) In this section –

    (a)   "woman" and "man" include respectively a girl and a boy (from birth), and

    (b)   "prescribed" means prescribed by regulations.

Amendments—Inserted by HFEA 2008, s 3(5).

Scope—The amendments prohibit the placing into any woman of any embryo other than a "permitted embryo" as defined in s 3ZA to ensure that embryos created by the use of artificial or genetically modified gametes or embryos created by cloning cannot be placed into a woman.

3A Prohibition in connection with germ cells

(1) No person shall, for the purpose of providing fertility services for any woman, use female germ cells taken or derived from an embryo or a foetus or use embryos created by using such cells.

(2) In this section –

"female germ cells" means cells of the female germ line and includes such cells at any stage of maturity and accordingly includes eggs; and

"fertility services" means medical, surgical or obstetric services provided for the purpose of assisting women to carry children.

Amendments—Inserted by Criminal Justice and Public Order Act 1994, s 156(1),(2).

4 Prohibitions in connection with gametes

(1) No person shall –

    (a)   store any gametes, or

    (b)   in the course of providing treatment services for any woman, use –

        (i)   any sperm, other than partner-donated sperm which has been neither processed nor stored,

        (ii) the woman's eggs after processing or storage, or

        (iii) the eggs of any other woman,

    (c)   (*repealed*)

except in pursuance of a licence.

(1A) No person shall procure, test, process or distribute any gametes intended for human application except in pursuance of a licence or a third party agreement.

(2) A licence cannot authorise storing or using gametes in any circumstances in which regulations prohibit their storage or use.

(3) No person shall place sperm and eggs in a woman in any circumstances specified in regulations except in pursuance of a licence.

(4) Regulations made by virtue of subsection (3) above may provide that, in relation to licences only to place sperm and eggs in a woman in such circumstances, sections 12 to 22 of this Act shall have effect with such modifications as may be specified in the regulations.

(5) Activities regulated by this section or section 3 or 4A of this Act are referred to in this Act as "activities governed by this Act".

Amendments—SI 2007/1522; HFEA 2008, s 4(1).

Defined terms—"treatment services": Sch 2, para 1.

4A Prohibitions in connection with genetic material not of human origin

(1) No person shall place in a woman –

    (a)   a human admixed embryo,

    (b)   any other embryo that is not a human embryo, or

    (c)   any gametes other than human gametes.

(2) No person shall –

    (a)   mix human gametes with animal gametes,

(b) bring about the creation of a human admixed embryo, or

(c) keep or use a human admixed embryo, except in pursuance of a licence.

(3) A licence cannot authorise keeping or using a human admixed embryo after the earliest of the following –

(a) the appearance of the primitive streak, or

(b) the end of the period of 14 days beginning with the day on which the process of creating the human admixed embryo began, but not counting any time during which the human admixed embryo is stored.

(4) A licence cannot authorise placing a human admixed embryo in an animal.

(5) A licence cannot authorise keeping or using a human admixed embryo in any circumstances in which regulations prohibit its keeping or use.

(6) For the purposes of this Act a human admixed embryo is –

(a) an embryo created by replacing the nucleus of an animal egg or of an animal cell, or two animal pronuclei, with –
   (i)   two human pronuclei,
   (ii) one nucleus of a human gamete or of any other human cell, or
   (iii) one human gamete or other human cell,

(b) any other embryo created by using –
   (i)   human gametes and animal gametes, or
   (ii) one human pronucleus and one animal pronucleus,

(c) a human embryo that has been altered by the introduction of any sequence of nuclear or mitochondrial DNA of an animal into one or more cells of the embryo,

(d) a human embryo that has been altered by the introduction of one or more animal cells, or

(e) any embryo not falling within paragraphs (a) to (d) which contains both nuclear or mitochondrial DNA of a human and nuclear or mitochondrial DNA of an animal ("animal DNA") but in which the animal DNA is not predominant.

(7) In subsection (6) –

(a) references to animal cells are to cells of an animal or of an animal embryo, and

(b) references to human cells are to cells of a human or of a human embryo.

(8) For the purposes of this section an "animal" is an animal other than man.

(9) In this section "embryo" means a live embryo, including an egg that is in the process of fertilisation or is undergoing any other process capable of resulting in an embryo.

(10) In this section –

(a) references to eggs are to live eggs, including cells of the female germ line at any stage of maturity, but (except in subsection (9)) not including eggs that are in the process of fertilisation or are undergoing any other process capable of resulting in an embryo, and

(b) references to gametes are to eggs (as so defined) or to live sperm, including cells of the male germ line at any stage of maturity.

(11) If it appears to the Secretary of State necessary or desirable to do so in the light of developments in science or medicine, regulations may –

(a) amend (but not repeal) paragraphs (a) to (e) of subsection (6);

(b) provide that in this section "embryo", "eggs" or "gametes" includes things specified in the regulations which would not otherwise fall within the definition.

(12) Regulations made by virtue of subsection (11)(a) may make any amendment of subsection (7) that appears to the Secretary of State to be appropriate in consequence of any amendment of subsection (6).

Amendments—Inserted by HFEA 2008, s 4(2).

Scope—Section 4A provides for certain types of embryos to be subject to regulations. It prohibits the placing into a woman of a human admixed embryo or any other embryo or gametes that are not human. It also prohibits the placing of an admixed embryo in an animal.

The Human Fertilisation and Embryology Authority, its functions and procedure

5 The Human Fertilisation and Embryology Authority

(1) There shall be a body corporate called the Human Fertilisation and Embryology Authority.

(2) The Authority shall consist of –

    (a)   a chairman and deputy chairman, and

    (b)   such number of other members as the Secretary of State appoints.

(3) Schedule 1 to this Act (which deals with the membership of the Authority, etc.) shall have effect.

****

Scope of licences

11 Licences for treatment, storage and research

(1) The Authority may grant the following and no other licences –

    (a)   licences under paragraph 1 of Schedule 2 to this Act authorising activities in the course of providing treatment services,

    (aa) licences under paragraph 1A of that Schedule authorising activities in the course of providing non-medical fertility services,

    (b)   licences under that Schedule authorising the storage of gametes, embryos or human admixed embryos, and

    (c)   licences under paragraph 3 of that Schedule authorising activities for the purposes of a project of research.

(2) Paragraph 4 of that Schedule has effect in the case of all licences.

Amendments—SI 2007/1522; HFEA 2008, s 11(1).

"providing treatment services"—See s 2 and Sch 2, paras 1–1ZC.

Licence conditions

12 General conditions

(1) The following shall be conditions of every licence granted under this Act –

    (a)   except to the extent that the activities authorised by the licence fall within paragraph (aa), that those activities shall be carried on only on the premises to which the licence relates and under the supervision of the person responsible,

    (aa) that any activities to which section 3(1A)(b) or (1B) or 4(1A) applies shall be carried on only on the premises to which the licence relates or on relevant third party premises,

(b) that any member or employee of the Authority, on production, if so required, of a document identifying the person as such, shall at all reasonable times be permitted to enter those premises and inspect them (which includes inspecting any equipment or records and observing any activity),

(c) except in relation to the use of gametes in the course of providing basic partner treatment services, that the provisions of Schedule 3 to this Act shall be complied with,

(d) that proper records shall be maintained in such form as the Authority may specify in directions,

(e) that no money or other benefit shall be given or received in respect of any supply of gametes, embryos or human admixed embryos unless authorised by directions,

(f) that, where gametes, embryos or human admixed embryos are supplied to a person to whom another licence applies, that person shall also be provided with such information as the Authority may specify in directions, and

(g) that the Authority shall be provided, in such form and at such intervals as it may specify in directions, with such copies of or extracts from the records, or such other information, as the directions may specify.

(2) Subsection (3) applies to –

(a) every licence under paragraph 1 or 1A of Schedule 2,

(b) every licence under paragraph 2 of that Schedule, so far as authorising the storage of gametes or embryos intended for human application, and

(c) every licence under paragraph 3 of that Schedule, so far as authorising activities in connection with the derivation from embryos of stem cells that are intended for human application.

(3) It shall be a condition of every licence to which this subsection applies that –

(a) such information as is necessary to facilitate the traceability of gametes and embryos, and

(b) any information relating to the quality or safety of gametes or embryos,

shall be recorded and provided to the Authority upon request.

Amendments—SI 2007/1522; HFEA 2008, s 12.

13 Conditions of licences for treatment

(1) The following shall be conditions of every licence under paragraph 1 of Schedule 2 to this Act.

(2) Such information shall be recorded as the Authority may specify in directions about the following –

(a) the persons for whom services are provided in pursuance of the licence,

(b) the services provided for them,

(c) the persons whose gametes are kept or used for the purposes of services provided in pursuance of the licence or whose gametes have been used in bringing about the creation of embryos so kept or used,

(d) any child appearing to the person responsible to have been born as a result of treatment in pursuance of the licence,

(e) any mixing of egg and sperm and any taking of an embryo from a woman or other acquisition of an embryo, and

(f) such other matters as the Authority may specify in directions.

(3) The records maintained in pursuance of the licence shall include any information recorded in pursuance of subsection (2) above and any consent of a person whose consent is required under Schedule 3 to this Act.

(4) No information shall be removed from any records maintained in pursuance of the licence before the expiry of such period as may be specified in directions for records of the class in question.

(5) A woman shall not be provided with treatment services unless account has been taken of the welfare of any child who may be born as a result of the treatment (including the need of that child for supportive parenting), and of any other child who may be affected by the birth.

(6) A woman shall not be provided with treatment services of a kind specified in Part 1 of Schedule 3ZA unless she and any man or woman who is to be treated together with her have been given a suitable opportunity to receive proper counselling about the implications of her being provided with treatment services of that kind, and have been provided with such relevant information as is proper.

(6A) A woman shall not be provided with treatment services after the happening of any event falling within any paragraph of Part 2 of Schedule 3ZA unless (before or after the event) she and the intended second parent have been given a suitable opportunity to receive proper counselling about the implications of the woman being provided with treatment services after the happening of that event, and have been provided with such relevant information as is proper.

(6B) The reference in subsection (6A) to the intended second parent is a reference to –

(a) any man as respects whom the agreed fatherhood conditions in section 37 of the Human Fertilisation and Embryology Act 2008 ("the 2008 Act") are for the time being satisfied in relation to treatment provided to the woman mentioned in subsection (6A), and

(b) any woman as respects whom the agreed female parenthood conditions in section 44 of the 2008 Act are for the time being satisfied in relation to treatment provided to the woman mentioned in subsection (6A).

(6C) In the case of treatment services falling within paragraph 1 of Schedule 3ZA (use of gametes of a person not receiving those services) or paragraph 3 of that Schedule (use of embryo taken from a woman not receiving those services), the information provided by virtue of subsection (6) or (6A) must include such information as is proper about –

(a) the importance of informing any resulting child at an early age that the child results from the gametes of a person who is not a parent of the child, and

(b) suitable methods of informing such a child of that fact.

(6D) Where the person responsible receives from a person ("X") notice under section 37(1)(c) or 44(1)(c) of the 2008 Act of X's withdrawal of consent to X being treated as the parent of any child resulting from the provision of treatment services to a woman ("W"), the person responsible –

(a) must notify W in writing of the receipt of the notice from X, and

(b) no person to whom the licence applies may place an embryo or sperm and eggs in W, or artificially inseminate W, until W has been so notified.

(6E) Where the person responsible receives from a woman ("W") who has previously given notice under section 37(1)(b) or 44(1)(b) of the 2008 Act that she consents to another person ("X") being treated as a parent of any child resulting from the provision of treatment services to W –

(a) notice under section 37(1)(c) or 44(1)(c) of the 2008 Act of the withdrawal of W's consent, or

(b) a notice under section 37(1)(b) or 44(1)(b) of the 2008 Act in respect of a person other than X,

the person responsible must take reasonable steps to notify X in writing of the receipt of the notice mentioned in paragraph (a) or (b).

(7) Suitable procedures shall be maintained –

    (a)   for determining the persons providing gametes or from whom embryos are taken for use in pursuance of the licence, and

    (b)   for the purpose of securing that consideration is given to the use of practices not requiring the authority of a licence as well as those requiring such authority.

(8) Subsections (9) and (10) apply in determining any of the following –

    (a)   the persons who are to provide gametes for use in pursuance of the licence in a case where consent is required under paragraph 5 of Schedule 3 for the use in question;

    (b)   the woman from whom an embryo is to be taken for use in pursuance of the licence, in a case where her consent is required under paragraph 7 of Schedule 3 for the use of the embryo;

    (c)   which of two or more embryos to place in a woman.

(9) Persons or embryos that are known to have a gene, chromosome or mitochondrion abnormality involving a significant risk that a person with the abnormality will have or develop –

    (a)   a serious physical or mental disability,

    (b)   a serious illness, or

    (c)   any other serious medical condition, must not be preferred to those that are not known to have such an abnormality.

(10) Embryos that are known to be of a particular sex and to carry a particular risk, compared with embryos of that sex in general, that any resulting child will have or develop –

    (a)   a gender-related serious physical or mental disability,

    (b)   a gender-related serious illness, or

    (c)   any other gender-related serious medical condition, must not be preferred to those that are not known to carry such a risk.

(11) For the purposes of subsection (10), a physical or mental disability, illness or other medical condition is gender-related if –

    (a)   it affects only one sex, or

    (b)   it affects one sex significantly more than the other.

(12) No embryo appropriated for the purpose mentioned in paragraph 1(1)(ca) of Schedule 2 (training in embryological techniques) shall be kept or used for the provision of treatment services.

(13) The person responsible shall comply with any requirement imposed on that person by section 31ZD.

Amendments—SI 2007/1522; HFEA 2008, ss 14(2)–(4).

"unless account has been taken of the welfare of any child" (s 13(5))—Note that this includes the need of that child for supportive parenting rather than a father. See Code of Practice (8th Edn, 2009), laid down by the Human Fertilisation and Embryology Authority, which sets out every aspect of the "welfare checklist" with which the licence holders must comply (*Evans v Amicus Healthcare and others; Hadley v Midland Fertility Services Ltd and others* [2004] 1 FLR 67; *Centre for Reproductive Medicine v U* [2002] 1 FLR 927; *Leeds Teaching Hospitals NHS Trust v A* [2003] 1 FLR 412). See also DHSS Circular (LAC(85)12), which draws attention to the need to be aware of possible risks to the child in such circumstances and the duty to investigate.

13A Conditions of licences for non-medical fertility services

(1) The following shall be conditions of every licence under paragraph 1A of Schedule 2.

(2) The requirements of section 13(2) to (4) and (7) shall be complied with.

(3) A woman shall not be provided with any non-medical fertility services involving the use of sperm other than partner-donated sperm unless the woman being provided with the services has been given a suitable opportunity to receive proper counselling about the implications of taking the proposed steps, and has been provided with such relevant information as is proper.

(4) (*repealed*)

Amendments—Inserted by SI 2007/1522; amended by HFEA 2008, Sch 7, para 5.

14 Conditions of storage licences

(1) The following shall be conditions of every licence authorising the storage of gametes, embryos or human admixed embryos –

- (a)   that gametes of a person shall be placed in storage only if –
  - (i)   received from that person,
  - (ii)   acquired in circumstances in which by virtue of paragraph 9 or 10 of Schedule 3 that person's consent to the storage is not required, or
  - (iii) acquired from a person to whom a licence or third party agreement applies,
- (aa) that an embryo taken from a woman shall be placed in storage only if –
  - (i)   received from that woman, or
  - (ii)   acquired from a person to whom a licence or third party agreement applies,
- (ab) that an embryo the creation of which has been brought about in vitro otherwise than in pursuance of that licence shall be placed in storage only if acquired from a person to whom a licence or third party agreement applies,
- (ac) that a human admixed embryo the creation of which has been brought about in vitro otherwise than in pursuance of that licence shall be placed in storage only if acquired from a person to whom a licence under paragraph 2 or 3 of Schedule 2 applies,
- (b)   that gametes or embryos which are or have been stored shall not be supplied to a person otherwise than in the course of providing treatment services unless that person is a person to whom a licence applies,
- (ba) that human admixed embryos shall not be supplied to a person unless that person is a person to whom a licence applies,
- (c)   that no gametes, embryos or human admixed embryos shall be kept in storage for longer than the statutory storage period and, if stored at the end of the period, shall be allowed to perish, and
- (d)   that such information as the Authority may specify in directions as to the persons whose consent is required under Schedule 3 to this Act, the terms of their consent and the circumstances of the storage and as to such other matters as the Authority may specify in directions shall be included in the records maintained in pursuance of the licence.

(2) No information shall be removed from any records maintained in pursuance of such a licence before the expiry of such period as may be specified in directions for records of the class in question.

(3) The statutory storage period in respect of gametes is such period not exceeding ten years as the licence may specify.

(4) The statutory storage period in respect of embryos is such period not exceeding ten years as the licence may specify.

(4A) The statutory storage period in respect of human admixed embryos is such period not exceeding ten years as the licence may specify.

(5) Regulations may provide that subsection (3), (4) or (4A) above shall have effect as if for ten years there were substituted –

    (a)   such shorter period, or

    (b)   in such circumstances as may be specified in the regulations, such longer period,

as may be specified in the regulations.

Amendments—SI 2007/1522; HFEA 2008, ss 15(2)–(5).

14A Conditions of licences: human application

(1) This section applies to –

    (a)   every licence under paragraph 1 or 1A of Schedule 2,

    (b)   every licence under paragraph 2 of that Schedule, so far as authorising storage of gametes or embryos intended for human application, and

    (c)   every licence under paragraph 3 of that Schedule, so far as authorising activities in connection with the derivation from embryos of stem cells that are intended for human application.

(2) A licence to which this section applies may not authorise the storage, procurement, testing, processing or distribution of gametes or embryos unless it contains the conditions required by Schedule 3A.

(3) In relation to any gametes or embryos imported into the United Kingdom from an EEA state other than the United Kingdom or from Gibraltar, compliance with the requirements of the laws or other measures adopted in the relevant state or territory for the purpose of implementing the first, second and third Directives shall be taken to be compliance with the conditions required by Schedule 3A.

(4) Subsection (3) shall not apply to any licence conditions imposed by the Authority which amount to more stringent protective measures for the purposes of Article 4(2) of the first Directive.

Amendments—Inserted by SI 2007/1522; amended by HFEA 2008, Sch 7, para 6.

****

34 Disclosure in interests of justice

(1) Where in any proceedings before a court the question whether a person is or is not the parent of a child by virtue of sections 27 to 29 of this Act or sections 33 to 47 of the Human Fertilisation and Embryology Act 2008 falls to be determined, the court may on the application of any party to the proceedings make an order requiring the Authority –

    (a)   to disclose whether or not any information relevant to that question is contained in the register kept in pursuance of section 31 of this Act, and

    (b)   if it is, to disclose so much of it as is specified in the order,

but such an order may not require the Authority to disclose any information falling within section 31(2)(c) to (e) of this Act.

(2) The court must not make an order under subsection (1) above unless it is satisfied that the interests of justice require it to do so, taking into account –

    (a)   any representations made by any individual who may be affected by the disclosure, and

   (b)   the welfare of the child, if under 18 years old, and of any other person under that age who may be affected by the disclosure.

(3) If the proceedings before the court are civil proceedings, it –

   (a)   may direct that the whole or any part of the proceedings on the application for an order under subsection (2) above shall be heard in camera, and

   (b)   if it makes such an order, may then or later direct that the whole or any part of any later stage of the proceedings shall be heard in camera.

(4) An application for a direction under subsection (3) above shall be heard in camera unless the court otherwise directs.

Amendments—HFEA 2008, Sch 6, para 34, Sch 7, para 12.

Defined terms—"the Authority": s 2(1).

Sections 33–47—These provisions of the 2008 Act contain the "fatherhood conditions" and "female parenthood conditions" that must be satisfied when a woman carries a child as a result of placing in her an embryo or sperm and eggs, or her artificial insemination, to determine who is to be treated as the other parent of the child.

"register" (s 34(1)(a))—A register is required to be maintained by the Authority under s 31 containing information relating to the provision of treatment services for any identifiable individual or the keeping or use of any gametes of any identifiable individual or of an embryo taken from any identifiable woman or information showing that any identifiable individual was, or may have been, born as a consequence of treatment services.

"information falling within section 31(2)(b)" (s 34(1))—This is information obtained by any member or employee of the Authority on terms or in circumstances requiring it to be held in confidence.

35 Disclosure in interests of justice: congenital disabilities etc

(1) Where for the purpose of instituting proceedings under section 1 of the Congenital Disabilities (Civil Liability) Act 1976 (civil liability to child born disabled) it is necessary to identify a person who would or might be the parent of a child but for the relevant statutory provisions, the court may, on the application of the child, make an order requiring the Authority to disclose any information contained in the register kept in pursuance of section 31 of this Act identifying that person.

(2) ...

(2A) In subsections (1) and (2) "the relevant statutory provisions" means –

   (a)   sections 27 to 29 of this Act, and

   (b)   sections 33 to 47 of the Human Fertilisation and Embryology Act 2008.

(3) Subsections (2) to (4) of section 34 of this Act apply for the purposes of this section as they apply for the purposes of that.

(4) ...

Amendments—HFEA 2008, Sch 6, para 35.

35A Mitochondrial donation

(1) Regulations may provide for any of the relevant provisions to have effect subject to specified modifications in relation to cases where –

   (a)   an egg which is a permitted egg for the purposes of section 3(2) by virtue of regulations made under section 3ZA(5), or

   (b)   an embryo which is a permitted embryo for those purposes by virtue of such regulations, has been created from material provided by two women.

(2) In this section "the relevant provisions" means –

   (a)   the following provisions of this Act –

(i) section 13(6C) (information whose provision to prospective parents is required by licence condition),

(ii) section 31 (register of information),

(iii) sections 31ZA to 31ZE (provision of information), and

(iv) Schedule 3 (consents to use or storage of gametes, embryos or human admixed embryos etc.), and

(b) section 54 of the Human Fertilisation and Embryology Act 2008 (parental orders).

Amendments—Inserted by HFEA 2008, s 26.

35B Fees

(1) The Authority may charge a fee in respect of any of the following –

(a) an application for a licence,

(b) the grant or renewal of a licence,

(c) an application for the revocation or variation of a licence, or

(d) the exercise by the Authority of any other function conferred on it by or under this Act or by or under any other enactment –

(i) in relation to a licence,

(ii) in relation to premises which are or have been premises to which a licence relates,

(iii) in relation to premises which are or have been relevant third party premises in relation to a licence, or

(iv) in relation to premises which, if an application is granted, will be premises to which a licence relates or relevant third party premises.

(2) The amount of any fee charged by virtue of subsection (1) is to be fixed in accordance with a scheme made by the Authority with the approval of the Secretary of State and the Treasury.

(3) In fixing the amount of any fee to be charged by virtue of that subsection, the Authority may have regard to the costs incurred by it –

(a) in exercising the functions conferred on it by or under this Act (apart from sections 31ZA to 31ZG and 33D), and

(b) in exercising any other function conferred on it by or under any other enactment.

(4) The Authority may also charge such fee as it thinks fit in respect of any of the following –

(a) the giving of notice under section 31ZA(1) or 31ZB(1), or

(b) the provision of information under section 31ZA, 31ZB or 31ZE.

(5) In fixing the amount of any fee to be charged by virtue of subsection (4) the Authority may have regard to the costs incurred by it in exercising the function to which the fee relates.

(6) When exercising its power to charge fees under section 8(2), 31ZF(2)(d) or this section, the Authority may fix different fees for different circumstances.

Amendments—Inserted by HFEA 2008, s 27.

****

SCHEDULE 2
ACTIVITIES FOR WHICH LICENCES MAY BE GRANTED

1 Licences for treatment

(1) A licence under this paragraph may authorise any of the following in the course of providing treatment services –

- (a) bringing about the creation of embryos in vitro,
- (b) procuring, keeping, testing, processing or distributing embryos,
- (c) procuring, testing, processing, distributing or using gametes,
- (ca) using embryos for the purpose of training persons in embryo biopsy, embryo storage or other embryological techniques,
- (d) other practices designed to secure that embryos are in a suitable condition to be placed in a woman,
- (e) placing any permitted embryo in a woman,
- (f) mixing sperm with the egg of a hamster, or other animal specified in directions, for the purpose of testing the fertility or normality of the sperm, but only where anything which forms is destroyed when the test is complete and, in any event, not later than the two cell stage, and
- (g) such other practices, apart from practices falling within section 4A(2), as may be specified in, or determined in accordance with, regulations.

(2) Subject to the provisions of this Act, a licence under this paragraph may be granted subject to such conditions as may be specified in the licence and may authorise the performance of any of the activities referred to in sub-paragraph (1) above in such manner as may be so specified.

(3) A licence under this paragraph cannot authorise any activity unless it appears to the Authority to be necessary or desirable for the purpose of providing treatment services.

(4) A licence under this paragraph cannot authorise altering the nuclear or mitochondrial DNA of a cell while it forms part of an embryo, except for the purpose of creating something that will by virtue of regulations under section 3ZA(5) be a permitted embryo.

(4A) A licence under this paragraph cannot authorise the use of embryos for the purpose mentioned in sub-paragraph (1)(ca) unless the Authority is satisfied that the proposed use of embryos is necessary for that purpose.

(5) A licence under this paragraph shall be granted for such period not exceeding five years as may be specified in the licence.

(6) In this paragraph, references to a permitted embryo are to be read in accordance with section 3ZA.

Amendments—HFEA 2008, Sch 2, para 2.

"treatment services"—See annotation under s 2 above.

"designed to secure that embryos are in a suitable condition to be placed in a woman"—The meaning of "suitable" has to be determined having regard to its context. When the object of the treatment is to enable a woman to bear a child with a tissue type that will allow stem cells to be provided to a sick sibling, an embryo would only be suitable for the purpose of being placed within her if it will lead to the birth of a child with the tissue type in question. The HFEA therefore has the authority to grant a treatment licence for the purpose of tissue typing, subject to such conditions as it considers appropriate. The suitability of the embryo to be placed in a particular woman may be considered in the context of objectively established aims and perceived needs relating to the child-to-be-born's parents and to an affected sibling (*R (Quintavelle) v Human Fertilisation and Embryology Authority (Secretary of State for Health Intervening)* [2003] 2 FLR 335).

1ZA Embryo testing

(1) A licence under paragraph 1 cannot authorise the testing of an embryo, except for one or more of the following purposes –

    (a) establishing whether the embryo has a gene, chromosome or mitochondrion abnormality that may affect its capacity to result in a live birth,

    (b) in a case where there is a particular risk that the embryo may have any gene, chromosome or mitochondrion abnormality, establishing whether it has that abnormality or any other gene, chromosome or mitochondrion abnormality,

    (c) in a case where there is a particular risk that any resulting child will have or develop –

        (i) a gender-related serious physical or mental disability,

        (ii) a gender-related serious illness, or

        (iii) any other gender-related serious medical condition, establishing the sex of the embryo,

    (d) in a case where a person ("the sibling") who is the child of the persons whose gametes are used to bring about the creation of the embryo (or of either of those persons) suffers from a serious medical condition which could be treated by umbilical cord blood stem cells, bone marrow or other tissue of any resulting child, establishing whether the tissue of any resulting child would be compatible with that of the sibling, and

    (e) in a case where uncertainty has arisen as to whether the embryo is one of those whose creation was brought about by using the gametes of particular persons, establishing whether it is.

(2) A licence under paragraph 1 cannot authorise the testing of embryos for the purpose mentioned in sub-paragraph (1)(b) unless the Authority is satisfied –

    (a) in relation to the abnormality of which there is a particular risk, and

    (b) in relation to any other abnormality for which testing is to be authorised under sub-paragraph (1)(b), that there is a significant risk that a person with the abnormality will have or develop a serious physical or mental disability, a serious illness or any other serious medical condition.

(3) For the purposes of sub-paragraph (1)(c), a physical or mental disability, illness or other medical condition is gender-related if the Authority is satisfied that –

    (a) it affects only one sex, or

    (b) it affects one sex significantly more than the other.

(4) In sub-paragraph (1)(d) the reference to "other tissue" of the resulting child does not include a reference to any whole organ of the child.

Amendments—Inserted by HFEA 2008, Sch 2, para 3.

1ZB Sex selection

(1) A licence under paragraph 1 cannot authorise any practice designed to secure that any resulting child will be of one sex rather than the other.

(2) Sub-paragraph (1) does not prevent the authorisation of any testing of embryos that is capable of being authorised under paragraph 1ZA.

(3) Sub-paragraph (1) does not prevent the authorisation of any other practices designed to secure that any resulting child will be of one sex rather than the other in a case where there is a particular risk that a woman will give birth to a child who will have or develop –

    (a) a gender-related serious physical or mental disability,

    (b) a gender-related serious illness, or

(c)   any other gender-related serious medical condition.

(4) For the purposes of sub-paragraph (3), a physical or mental disability, illness or other medical condition is gender-related if the Authority is satisfied that –

(a)   it affects only one sex, or
(b)   it affects one sex significantly more than the other.

Amendments—Inserted by HFEA 2008, Sch 2, para 3.

1ZC Power to amend paragraphs 1ZA and 1ZB

(1) Regulations may make any amendment of paragraph 1ZA (embryo testing).

(2) Regulations under this paragraph which amend paragraph 1ZA may make any amendment of sub-paragraphs (2) to (4) of paragraph 1ZB (sex selection) which appears to the Secretary of State to be necessary or expedient in consequence of the amendment of paragraph 1ZA.

(3) Regulations under this paragraph may not enable the authorisation of –

(a)   the testing of embryos for the purpose of establishing their sex, or
(b)   other practices falling within paragraph 1ZB(1), except on grounds relating to the health of any resulting child.

(4) For the purposes of this paragraph, "amend" includes add to and repeal, and references to "amendment" are to be read accordingly.

Amendments—Inserted by HFEA 2008, Sch 2, para 3.

1A Licences for non-medical fertility services

(1) A licence under this paragraph may authorise any of the following in the course of providing non-medical fertility services –

(a)   procuring sperm, and
(b)   distributing sperm.

(1A) A licence under this paragraph cannot authorise the procurement or distribution of sperm to which there has been applied any process designed to secure that any resulting child will be of one sex rather than the other.

(2) Subject to the provisions of this Act, a licence under this paragraph may be granted subject to such conditions as may be specified in the licence and may authorise the performance of any of the activities referred to in sub-paragraph (1) above in such manner as may be so specified.

(3) A licence under this paragraph shall be granted for such period not exceeding five years as may be specified in the licence.

Amendments—SI 2007/1522; HFEA 2008, Sch 2, para 4.

****

SCHEDULE 3A
SUPPLEMENTARY LICENCE CONDITIONS: HUMAN APPLICATION

1 Traceability and coding system

Licence conditions shall require that all persons to whom a licence applies adopt such systems as the Authority considers appropriate to secure –

(a) in relation to traceability, compliance with the requirements of Article 8 (traceability) of the first Directive and Article 9 (traceability) of the third Directive, and

(b) in relation to the coding of information, compliance with the requirements of Article 25 (coding of information) of the first Directive and Article 10 (European coding system) of the third Directive.

2 Licence conditions imposed in accordance with paragraph 1 may specify the coding system which must be applied in relation to gametes and embryos intended for human application.

3 Serious adverse events and serious adverse reactions

Licence conditions shall require such –

(a) systems to report, investigate, register and transmit information about serious adverse events and serious adverse reactions, and

(b) accurate, rapid and verifiable procedures for recalling from distribution any product which may be related to a serious adverse event or serious adverse reaction,

to be in place as are necessary to secure compliance with the requirements of Article 11 (notification of serious adverse events and reactions) of the first Directive and Article 5 (notification of serious adverse reactions) and Article 6 (notification of serious adverse events) of the third Directive.

4 Third party agreements and termination of licensed activities

For the purpose of securing compliance with the requirements of Articles 21(5) (tissue and cell storage conditions) and 24 (relations between tissue establishments and third parties) of the first Directive, licence conditions shall specify the requirements that must be met in relation to the termination of storage activities authorised by the licence and in relation to third party agreements.

5 Requirements for procurement of gametes and embryos

Licence conditions shall require all persons to whom a licence applies who are authorised to procure gametes or embryos, or both, to comply with the requirements (including as to staff training, written agreements with staff, standard operating procedures, and appropriate facilities and equipment) laid down in Article 2 (requirements for the procurement of human tissues and cells) of the second Directive.

6 Selection criteria and laboratory tests required for donors of reproductive cells

In relation to partner-donated sperm which is not intended to be used without processing or storage, licence conditions shall require compliance with the selection criteria for donors and the requirements for laboratory tests laid down in section 2 (partner donation (not direct use)) of Annex III (selection criteria and laboratory tests required for donors of reproductive cells) to the second Directive.

7 In relation to donations of gametes or embryos other than partner-donated sperm or partner-created embryos, licence conditions shall require compliance with the selection criteria for donors and the requirements for laboratory tests laid down in section 3 (donations other than by partners) of Annex III to the second Directive.

8 Licence conditions shall require that the laboratory tests required by sections 2 and 3 of Annex III to the second Directive to be carried out for the purpose of selecting gametes or embryos for donation, meet the requirements of section 4 (general requirements to be met for determining biological markers) of Annex III to the second Directive.

9 Donation and procurement procedures and reception at the tissue establishment

In relation to –

(a)   donation and procurement procedures, and

(b)   the reception of gametes and embryos at the premises to which a licence relates or at relevant third party premises,

licence conditions shall require compliance with the requirements of Article 15(3) (selection, evaluation and procurement) and Article 19(4) to (6) (tissue and cell reception) of the first Directive and with the requirements laid down in the provisions of the second Directive listed in the right-hand column, the subject-matter of which are described in the left-hand column in respect of those provisions.

Amendments—Inserted by SI 2007/1522.

****

Human Fertilisation and Embryology Act 2008

****

PART II
PARENTHOOD IN CASES INVOLVING ASSISTED REPRODUCTION

Meaning of "mother"

33 Meaning of "mother"

(1) The woman who is carrying or has carried a child as a result of the placing in her of an embryo or of sperm and eggs, and no other woman, is to be treated as the mother of the child.

(2) Subsection (1) does not apply to any child to the extent that the child is treated by virtue of adoption as not being the woman's child.

(3) Subsection (1) applies whether the woman was in the United Kingdom or elsewhere at the time of the placing in her of the embryo or the sperm and eggs.

Application of sections 35 to 47

34 Application of sections 35 to 47

(1) Sections 35 to 47 apply, in the case of a child who is being or has been carried by a woman (referred to in those sections as "W") as a result of the placing in her of an embryo or of sperm and eggs or her artificial insemination, to determine who is to be treated as the other parent of the child.

(2) Subsection (1) has effect subject to the provisions of sections 39, 40 and 46 limiting the purposes for which a person is treated as the child's other parent by virtue of those sections.

Meaning of "father"

35 Woman married at time of treatment

(1) If –

    (a)   at the time of the placing in her of the embryo or of the sperm and eggs or of her artificial insemination, W was a party to a marriage, and

    (b)   the creation of the embryo carried by her was not brought about with the sperm of the other party to the marriage,

then, subject to section 38(2) to (4), the other party to the marriage is to be treated as the father of the child unless it is shown that he did not consent to the placing in her of the embryo or the sperm and eggs or to her artificial insemination (as the case may be).

(2) This section applies whether W was in the United Kingdom or elsewhere at the time mentioned in subsection (1)(a).

Meaning of "father"—The definition is made subject to the common law presumption that the child is the legitimate child of the married couple, so that the husband will be treated as the father of the child even where the woman becomes pregnant with a child conceived through assisted reproduction and the fatherhood conditions set out in s 37 below have been satisfied in relation to another man.

36 Treatment provided to woman where agreed fatherhood conditions apply

If no man is treated by virtue of section 35 as the father of the child and no woman is treated by virtue of section 42 as a parent of the child but –

    (a)   the embryo or the sperm and eggs were placed in W, or W was artificially inseminated, in the course of treatment services provided in the United Kingdom by a person to whom a licence applies,

    (b)   at the time when the embryo or the sperm and eggs were placed in W, or W was artificially inseminated, the agreed fatherhood conditions (as set out in section 37) were satisfied in relation to a man, in relation to treatment provided to W under the licence,

    (c)   the man remained alive at that time, and

    (d)   the creation of the embryo carried by W was not brought about with the man's sperm,

then, subject to section 38(2) to (4), the man is to be treated as the father of the child.

"Fatherhood" conditions—Section 36 must be read together with s 37 to identify all the criteria that need to be satisfied.

37 The agreed fatherhood conditions

(1) The agreed fatherhood conditions referred to in section 36(b) are met in relation to a man ("M") in relation to treatment provided to W under a licence if, but only if, –

    (a)   M has given the person responsible a notice stating that he consents to being treated as the father of any child resulting from treatment provided to W under the licence,

    (b)   W has given the person responsible a notice stating that she consents to M being so treated,

(c)   neither M nor W has, since giving notice under paragraph (a) or (b), given the person responsible notice of the withdrawal of M's or W's consent to M being so treated,

(d)   W has not, since the giving of the notice under paragraph (b), given the person responsible –

  (i)   a further notice under that paragraph stating that she consents to another man being treated as the father of any resulting child, or

  (ii) a notice under section 44(1)(b) stating that she consents to a woman being treated as a parent of any resulting child, and

(e)   W and M are not within prohibited degrees of relationship in relation to each other.

(2) A notice under subsection (1)(a), (b) or (c) must be in writing and must be signed by the person giving it.

(3) A notice under subsection (1)(a), (b) or (c) by a person ("S") who is unable to sign because of illness, injury or physical disability is to be taken to comply with the requirement of subsection (2) as to signature if it is signed at the direction of S, in the presence of S and in the presence of at least one witness who attests the signature.

Scope—The conditions set out and the requirements relating to consent are to ensure that both parties carefully consider and record in approved forms their intentions regarding fatherhood of the child and its implications, as well as their consent. Once the gametes or embryo are placed in the woman, neither party can withdraw consent in relation to that cycle of treatment.

38 Further provision relating to sections 35 and 36

(1) Where a person is to be treated as the father of the child by virtue of section 35 or 36, no other person is to be treated as the father of the child.

(2) In England and Wales and Northern Ireland, sections 35 and 36 do not affect any presumption, applying by virtue of the rules of common law, that a child is the legitimate child of the parties to a marriage.

(3) In Scotland, sections 35 and 36 do not apply in relation to any child who, by virtue of any enactment or other rule of law, is treated as the child of the parties to a marriage.

(4) Sections 35 and 36 do not apply to any child to the extent that the child is treated by virtue of adoption as not being the man's child.

39 Use of sperm, or transfer of embryo, after death of man providing sperm

(1) If –

(a)   the child has been carried by W as a result of the placing in her of an embryo or of sperm and eggs or her artificial insemination,

(b)   the creation of the embryo carried by W was brought about by using the sperm of a man after his death, or the creation of the embryo was brought about using the sperm of a man before his death but the embryo was placed in W after his death,

(c)   the man consented in writing (and did not withdraw the consent) –

  (i)   to the use of his sperm after his death which brought about the creation of the embryo carried by W or (as the case may be) to the placing in W after his death of the embryo which was brought about using his sperm before his death, and

  (ii) to being treated for the purpose mentioned in subsection (3) as the father of any resulting child,

(d)   W has elected in writing not later than the end of the period of 42 days from the day on which the child was born for the man to be treated for the purpose mentioned in subsection (3) as the father of the child, and

(e) no-one else is to be treated –

    (i) as the father of the child by virtue of section 35 or 36 or by virtue of section 38(2) or (3), or

    (ii) as a parent of the child by virtue of section 42 or 43 or by virtue of adoption, then the man is to be treated for the purpose mentioned in subsection (3) as the father of the child.

(2) Subsection (1) applies whether W was in the United Kingdom or elsewhere at the time of the placing in her of the embryo or of the sperm and eggs or of her artificial insemination.

(3) The purpose referred to in subsection (1) is the purpose of enabling the man's particulars to be entered as the particulars of the child's father in a relevant register of births.

(4) In the application of this section to Scotland, for any reference to a period of 42 days there is substituted a reference to a period of 21 days.

Scope—This section replaces the provisions inserted into HFEA 1990 by the Human Fertilisation and Embryology (Deceased Fathers) Act 2003. It sets out the conditions that must be satisfied before the man who provided the sperm may be treated as the child's father for registration of birth only.

40 Embryo transferred after death of husband etc. who did not provide sperm

(1) If –

(a) the child has been carried by W as a result of the placing in her of an embryo,

(b) the embryo was created at a time when W was a party to a marriage,

(c) the creation of the embryo was not brought about with the sperm of the other party to the marriage,

(d) the other party to the marriage died before the placing of the embryo in W,

(e) the other party to the marriage consented in writing (and did not withdraw the consent) –

    (i) to the placing of the embryo in W after his death, and

    (ii) to being treated for the purpose mentioned in subsection (4) as the father of any resulting child,

(f) W has elected in writing not later than the end of the period of 42 days from the day on which the child was born for the man to be treated for the purpose mentioned in subsection (4) as the father of the child, and

(g) no-one else is to be treated –

    (i) as the father of the child by virtue of section 35 or 36 or by virtue of section 38(2) or (3), or

    (ii) as a parent of the child by virtue of section 42 or 43 or by virtue of adoption, then the man is to be treated for the purpose mentioned in subsection (4) as the father of the child.

(2) If –

(a) the child has been carried by W as a result of the placing in her of an embryo,

(b) the embryo was not created at a time when W was a party to a marriage or a civil partnership but was created in the course of treatment services provided to W in the United Kingdom by a person to whom a licence applies,

(c) a man consented in writing (and did not withdraw the consent) –

    (i) to the placing of the embryo in W after his death, and

    (ii) to being treated for the purpose mentioned in subsection (4) as the father of any resulting child,

PART II

(d)   the creation of the embryo was not brought about with the sperm of that man,

(e)   the man died before the placing of the embryo in W,

(f)   immediately before the man's death, the agreed fatherhood conditions set out in section 37 were met in relation to the man in relation to treatment proposed to be provided to W in the United Kingdom by a person to whom a licence applies,

(g)   W has elected in writing not later than the end of the period of 42 days from the day on which the child was born for the man to be treated for the purpose mentioned in subsection (4) as the father of the child, and

(h)   no-one else is to be treated –

    (i)   as the father of the child by virtue of section 35 or 36 or by virtue of section 38(2) or (3), or

    (ii)   as a parent of the child by virtue of section 42 or 43 or by virtue of adoption,

then the man is to be treated for the purpose mentioned in subsection (4) as the father of the child.

(3) Subsections (1) and (2) apply whether W was in the United Kingdom or elsewhere at the time of the placing in her of the embryo.

(4) The purpose referred to in subsections (1) and (2) is the purpose of enabling the man's particulars to be entered as the particulars of the child's father in a relevant register of births.

(5) In the application of this section to Scotland, for any reference to a period of 42 days there is substituted a reference to a period of 21 days.

Scope—This section deals with cases where a child is born as a result of posthumous use of donated sperm. It sets out the conditions that must be satisfied before the deceased husband/partner of the woman can be treated as the father/parent of the resulting child for registration of birth only.

41 Persons not to be treated as father

(1) Where the sperm of a man who had given such consent as is required by paragraph 5 of Schedule 3 to the 1990 Act (consent to use of gametes for purposes of treatment services or non-medical fertility services) was used for a purpose for which such consent was required, he is not to be treated as the father of the child.

(2) Where the sperm of a man, or an embryo the creation of which was brought about with his sperm, was used after his death, he is not, subject to section 39, to be treated as the father of the child.

(3) Subsection (2) applies whether W was in the United Kingdom or elsewhere at the time of the placing in her of the embryo or of the sperm and eggs or of her artificial insemination.

Scope—This section provides that the donor of the sperm is not to be treated as the father of the child, nor is a person who has not consented to the use of his sperm after his death (see under s 42 for the position regarding a known male donor who has developed a relationship with the child).

Cases in which woman to be other parent

42 Woman in civil partnership at time of treatment

(1) If at the time of the placing in her of the embryo or the sperm and eggs or of her artificial insemination, W was a party to a civil partnership, then subject to section 45(2) to (4), the other party to the civil partnership is to be treated as a parent of the child unless it is shown that she did not consent to the placing in W of the embryo or the sperm and eggs or to her artificial insemination (as the case may be).

(2) This section applies whether W was in the United Kingdom or elsewhere at the time mentioned in subsection (1).

Scope—Similar provisions to those that apply to heterosexual couples are made in ss 42–47 in relation to same-sex female couples in a civil partnership and those who have not entered into a civil partnership. The female couple is regarded in law as the legal parents of the child with full parental responsibility. The biological father is denied this status but it does not prevent the female couple in whom legal parenthood is vested from encouraging or enabling the biological father to become a psychological parent. If such a relationship is encouraged and developed, this relationship is likely to fall within the scope of private family life within Art 8 of the European Convention on Human Rights. Depending on the circumstances, it is also likely to provide the biological father grounds under CA 1989, s 10(9) for seeking permission to apply for contact under s 8 of that Act: *Re G (A minor); Re Z (A minor)* [2013] EWHC 134 (Fam) (and see also the judgment of Baroness Hale in *Re G (Children)* [2006] 2 FLR 629.

43 Treatment provided to woman who agrees that second woman to be parent

If no man is treated by virtue of section 35 as the father of the child and no woman is treated by virtue of section 42 as a parent of the child but –

(a) the embryo or the sperm and eggs were placed in W, or W was artificially inseminated, in the course of treatment services provided in the United Kingdom by a person to whom a licence applies,

(b) at the time when the embryo or the sperm and eggs were placed in W, or W was artificially inseminated, the agreed female parenthood conditions (as set out in section 44) were met in relation to another woman, in relation to treatment provided to W under that licence, and

(c) the other woman remained alive at that time,

then, subject to section 45(2) to (4), the other woman is to be treated as a parent of the child.

44 The agreed female parenthood conditions

(1) The agreed female parenthood conditions referred to in section 43(b) are met in relation to another woman ("P") in relation to treatment provided to W under a licence if, but only if, –

(a) P has given the person responsible a notice stating that P consents to P being treated as a parent of any child resulting from treatment provided to W under the licence,

(b) W has given the person responsible a notice stating that W agrees to P being so treated,

(c) neither W nor P has, since giving notice under paragraph (a) or (b), given the person responsible notice of the withdrawal of P's or W's consent to P being so treated,

(d) W has not, since the giving of the notice under paragraph (b), given the person responsible –

(i) a further notice under that paragraph stating that W consents to a woman other than P being treated as a parent of any resulting child, or

(ii) a notice under section 37(1)(b) stating that W consents to a man being treated as the father of any resulting child, and

(e) W and P are not within prohibited degrees of relationship in relation to each other.

(2) A notice under subsection (1)(a), (b) or (c) must be in writing and must be signed by the person giving it.

(3) A notice under subsection (1)(a), (b) or (c) by a person ("S") who is unable to sign because of illness, injury or physical disability is to be taken to comply with the requirement of subsection (2) as to signature if it is signed at the direction of S, in the presence of S and in the presence of at least one witness who attests the signature.

45   Further provision relating to sections 42 and 43

(1) Where a woman is treated by virtue of section 42 or 43 as a parent of the child, no man is to be treated as the father of the child.

(2) In England and Wales and Northern Ireland, sections 42 and 43 do not affect any presumption, applying by virtue of the rules of common law, that a child is the legitimate child of the parties to a marriage.

(3) In Scotland, sections 42 and 43 do not apply in relation to any child who, by virtue of any enactment or other rule of law, is treated as the child of the parties to a marriage.

(4) Sections 42 and 43 do not apply to any child to the extent that the child is treated by virtue of adoption as not being the woman's child.

Status of the biological father—This provision denies the biological father the status of a legal parent but where a relationship between him and the child is encouraged and enabled to be developed in an appropriate case it will be a relevant consideration with those under CA 1989, s 10(9) to support his application for permission to apply for an order under s 8 of that Act (see above under s 42).

46   Embryo transferred after death of civil partner or intended female parent

(1) If –
- (a)   the child has been carried by W as the result of the placing in her of an embryo,
- (b)   the embryo was created at a time when W was a party to a civil partnership,
- (c)   the other party to the civil partnership died before the placing of the embryo in W,
- (d)   the other party to the civil partnership consented in writing (and did not withdraw the consent) –
  - (i)   to the placing of the embryo in W after the death of the other party, and
  - (ii)   to being treated for the purpose mentioned in subsection (4) as the parent of any resulting child,
- (e)   W has elected in writing not later than the end of the period of 42 days from the day on which the child was born for the other party to the civil partnership to be treated for the purpose mentioned in subsection (4) as the parent of the child, and
- (f)   no one else is to be treated –
  - (i)   as the father of the child by virtue of section 35 or 36 or by virtue of section 45(2) or (3), or
  - (ii)   as a parent of the child by virtue of section 42 or 43 or by virtue of adoption,

then the other party to the civil partnership is to be treated for the purpose mentioned in subsection (4) as a parent of the child.

(2) If –
- (a)   the child has been carried by W as the result of the placing in her of an embryo,
- (b)   the embryo was not created at a time when W was a party to a marriage or a civil partnership, but was created in the course of treatment services provided to W in the United Kingdom by a person to whom a licence applies,
- (c)   another woman consented in writing (and did not withdraw the consent) –
  - (i)   to the placing of the embryo in W after the death of the other woman, and

      (ii)   to being treated for the purpose mentioned in subsection (4) as the parent of any resulting child,

  (d)   the other woman died before the placing of the embryo in W,

  (e)   immediately before the other woman's death, the agreed female parenthood conditions set out in section 44 were met in relation to the other woman in relation to treatment proposed to be provided to W in the United Kingdom by a person to whom a licence applies,

  (f)   W has elected in writing not later than the end of the period of 42 days from the day on which the child was born for the other woman to be treated for the purpose mentioned in subsection (4) as the parent of the child, and

  (g)   no one else is to be treated –

      (i)   as the father of the child by virtue of section 35 or 36 or by virtue of section 45(2) or (3), or

      (ii)   as a parent of the child by virtue of section 42 or 43 or by virtue of adoption,

then the other woman is to be treated for the purpose mentioned in subsection (4) as a parent of the child.

(3) Subsections (1) and (2) apply whether W was in the United Kingdom or elsewhere at the time of the placing in her of the embryo.

(4) The purpose referred to in subsections (1) and (2) is the purpose of enabling the deceased woman's particulars to be entered as the particulars of the child's other parent in a relevant register of births.

(5) In the application of subsections (1) and (2) to Scotland, for any reference to a period of 42 days there is substituted a reference to a period of 21 days.

47 Woman not to be other parent merely because of egg donation

A woman is not to be treated as the parent of a child whom she is not carrying and has not carried, except where she is so treated –

  (a)   by virtue of section 42 or 43, or

  (b)   by virtue of section 46 (for the purpose mentioned in subsection (4) of that section), or

  (c)   by virtue of adoption.

Effect of sections 33 to 47

48 Effect of sections 33 to 47

(1) Where by virtue of section 33, 35, 36, 42 or 43 a person is to be treated as the mother, father or parent of a child, that person is to be treated in law as the mother, father or parent (as the case may be) of the child for all purposes.

(2) Where by virtue of section 33, 38, 41, 45 or 47 a person is not to be treated as a parent of the child, that person is to be treated in law as not being a parent of the child for any purpose.

(3) Where section 39(1) or 40(1) or (2) applies, the deceased man –

  (a)   is to be treated in law as the father of the child for the purpose mentioned in section 39(3) or 40(4), but

  (b)   is to be treated in law as not being the father of the child for any other purpose.

(4) Where section 46(1) or (2) applies, the deceased woman –

  (a)   is to be treated in law as a parent of the child for the purpose mentioned in section 46(4), but

(b)   is to be treated in law as not being a parent of the child for any other purpose.

(5) Where any of subsections (1) to (4) has effect, references to any relationship between two people in any enactment, deed or other instrument or document (whenever passed or made) are to be read accordingly.

(6) In relation to England and Wales and Northern Ireland, a child who –

(a)   has a parent by virtue of section 42, or

(b)   has a parent by virtue of section 43 who is at any time during the period beginning with the time mentioned in section 43(b) and ending with the time of the child's birth a party to a civil partnership with the child's mother,

is the legitimate child of the child's parents.

(7) In relation to England and Wales and Northern Ireland, nothing in the provisions of section 33(1) or sections 35 to 47, read with this section –

(a)   affects the succession to any dignity or title of honour or renders any person capable of succeeding to or transmitting a right to succeed to any such dignity or title, or

(b)   affects the devolution of any property limited (expressly or not) to devolve (as nearly as the law permits) along with any dignity or title of honour.

(8) In relation to Scotland –

(a)   those provisions do not apply to any title, coat of arms, honour or dignity transmissible on the death of its holder or affect the succession to any such title, coat of arms or dignity or its devolution, and

(b)   where the terms of any deed provide that any property or interest in property is to devolve along with a title, coat of arms, honour or dignity, nothing in those provisions is to prevent that property or interest from so devolving.

Effect of ss 33 to 47—See annotations to ss 42 and 45.

References to parties to marriage or civil partnership

49 Meaning of references to parties to a marriage

(1) The references in sections 35 to 47 to the parties to a marriage at any time there referred to –

(a)   are to the parties to a marriage subsisting at that time, unless a judicial separation was then in force, but

(b)   include the parties to a void marriage if either or both of them reasonably believed at that time that the marriage was valid; and for the purposes of those sections it is to be presumed, unless the contrary is shown, that one of them reasonably believed at that time that the marriage was valid.

(2) In subsection (1)(a) "judicial separation" includes a legal separation obtained in a country outside the British Islands and recognised in the United Kingdom.

50 Meaning of references to parties to a civil partnership

(1) The references in sections 35 to 47 to the parties to a civil partnership at any time there referred to –

(a)   are to the parties to a civil partnership subsisting at that time, unless a separation order was then in force, but

(b)   include the parties to a void civil partnership if either or both of them reasonably believed at that time that the civil partnership was valid; and for the purposes of those sections it is to be presumed, unless the contrary is shown, that one of them reasonably believed at that time that the civil partnership was valid.

(2) The reference in section 48(6)(b) to a civil partnership includes a reference to a void civil partnership if either or both of the parties reasonably believed at the time when they registered as civil partners of each other that the civil partnership was valid; and for this purpose it is to be presumed, unless the contrary is shown, that one of them reasonably believed at that time that the civil partnership was valid.

(3) In subsection (1)(a), "separation order" means –

(a)   a separation order under section 37(1)(d) or 161(1)(d) of the Civil Partnership Act 2004,

(b)   a decree of separation under section 120(2) of that Act, or

(c)   a legal separation obtained in a country outside the United Kingdom and recognised in the United Kingdom.

Further provision about registration by virtue of section 39, 40 or 46

51 Meaning of "relevant register of births"

For the purposes of this Part a "relevant register of births", in relation to a birth, is whichever of the following is relevant –

(a)   a register of live-births or still-births kept under the Births and Deaths Registration Act 1953,

(b)   a register of births or still-births kept under the Registration of Births, Deaths and Marriages (Scotland) Act 1965, or

(c)   a register of live-births or still-births kept under the Births and Deaths Registration (Northern Ireland) Order 1976 (S.I. 1976/1041 (N.I. 14)).

52 Late election by mother with consent of Registrar General

(1) The requirement under section 39(1), 40(1) or (2) or 46(1) or (2) as to the making of an election (which requires an election to be made either on or before the day on which the child was born or within the period of 42 or, as the case may be, 21 days from that day) is nevertheless to be treated as satisfied if the required election is made after the end of that period but with the consent of the Registrar General under subsection (2).

(2) The Registrar General may at any time consent to the making of an election after the end of the period mentioned in subsection (1) if, on an application made to him in accordance with such requirements as he may specify, he is satisfied that there is a compelling reason for giving his consent to the making of such an election.

(3) In this section "the Registrar General" means the Registrar General for England and Wales, the Registrar General of Births, Deaths and Marriages for Scotland or (as the case may be) the Registrar General for Northern Ireland.

Interpretation of references to father etc. where woman is other parent

53 Interpretation of references to father etc.

(1) Subsections (2) and (3) have effect, subject to subsections (4) and (6), for the interpretation of any enactment, deed or any other instrument or document (whenever passed or made).

(2) Any reference (however expressed) to the father of a child who has a parent by virtue of section 42 or 43 is to be read as a reference to the woman who is a parent of the child by virtue of that section.

(3) Any reference (however expressed) to evidence of paternity is, in relation to a woman who is a parent by virtue of section 42 or 43, to be read as a reference to evidence of parentage.

(4) This section does not affect the interpretation of the enactments specified in subsection (5) (which make express provision for the case where a child has a parent by virtue of section 42 or 43).

(5) Those enactments are –

   (a)   the Legitimacy Act (Northern Ireland) 1928,
   (b)   the Schedule to the Population (Statistics) Act 1938,
   (c)   the Births and Deaths Registration Act 1953,
   (d)   the Registration of Births, Deaths and Marriages (Special Provisions) Act 1957,
   (e)   Part 2 of the Registration of Births, Deaths and Marriages (Scotland) Act 1965,
   (f)   the Congenital Disabilities (Civil Liability) Act 1976,
   (g)   the Legitimacy Act 1976,
   (h)   the Births and Deaths Registration (Northern Ireland) Order 1976 (S.I. 1976/1041 (N.I. 14)),
   (i)   the British Nationality Act 1981,
   (j)   the Family Law Reform Act 1987,
   (k)   Parts 1 and 2 of the Children Act 1989,
   (l)   Part 1 of the Children (Scotland) Act 1995,
   (m)   section 1 of the Criminal Law (Consolidation) (Scotland) Act 1995, and
   (n)   Parts 2, 3 and 14 of the Children (Northern Ireland) Order 1995 (S.I. 1995/755 (N.I. 2)).

(6) This section does not affect the interpretation of references that fall to be read in accordance with section 1(2)(a) or (b) of the Family Law Reform Act 1987 or Article 155(2)(a) or (b) of the Children (Northern Ireland) Order 1995 (references to a person whose father and mother were, or were not, married to each other at the time of the person's birth).

Parental orders

54 Parental orders

(1) On an application made by two people ("the applicants"), the court may make an order providing for a child to be treated in law as the child of the applicants if –

   (a)   the child has been carried by a woman who is not one of the applicants, as a result of the placing in her of an embryo or sperm and eggs or her artificial insemination,
   (b)   the gametes of at least one of the applicants were used to bring about the creation of the embryo, and
   (c)   the conditions in subsections (2) to (8) are satisfied.

(2) The applicants must be –

   (a)   husband and wife,
   (b)   civil partners of each other, or
   (c)   two persons who are living as partners in an enduring family relationship and are not within prohibited degrees of relationship in relation to each other.

(3) Except in a case falling within subsection (11), the applicants must apply for the order during the period of 6 months beginning with the day on which the child is born.

(4) At the time of the application and the making of the order –

    (a)   the child's home must be with the applicants, and

    (b)   either or both of the applicants must be domiciled in the United Kingdom or in the Channel Islands or the Isle of Man.

(5) At the time of the making of the order both the applicants must have attained the age of 18.

(6) The court must be satisfied that both –

    (a)   the woman who carried the child, and

    (b)   any other person who is a parent of the child but is not one of the applicants (including any man who is the father by virtue of section 35 or 36 or any woman who is a parent by virtue of section 42 or 43),

have freely, and with full understanding of what is involved, agreed unconditionally to the making of the order.

(7) Subsection (6) does not require the agreement of a person who cannot be found or is incapable of giving agreement; and the agreement of the woman who carried the child is ineffective for the purpose of that subsection if given by her less than six weeks after the child's birth.

(8) The court must be satisfied that no money or other benefit (other than for expenses reasonably incurred) has been given or received by either of the applicants for or in consideration of –

    (a)   the making of the order,

    (b)   any agreement required by subsection (6),

    (c)   the handing over of the child to the applicants, or

    (d)   the making of arrangements with a view to the making of the order,

unless authorised by the court.

(9) For the purposes of an application under this section –

    (a)   in relation to England and Wales, section 92(7) to (10) of, and Part 1 of Schedule 11 to, the Children Act 1989 (jurisdiction of courts) apply for the purposes of this section to determine the meaning of "the court" as they apply for the purposes of that Act and proceedings on the application are to be "family proceedings" for the purposes of that Act,

    (b)   in relation to Scotland, "the court" means the Court of Session or the sheriff court of the sheriffdom within which the child is, and

    (c)   in relation to Northern Ireland, "the court" means the High Court or any county court within whose division the child is.

(10) Subsection (1)(a) applies whether the woman was in the United Kingdom or elsewhere at the time of the placing in her of the embryo or the sperm and eggs or her artificial insemination.

(11) An application which –

    (a)   relates to a child born before the coming into force of this section, and

    (b)   is made by two persons who, throughout the period applicable under subsection (2) of section 30 of the 1990 Act, were not eligible to apply for an order under that section in relation to the child as husband and wife,

may be made within the period of six months beginning with the day on which this section comes into force.

Scope—Married couples, civil partners, unmarried heterosexual couples and same-sex couples in an enduring family relationship are eligible to apply for a parental order. A single person cannot apply for a parental order. SIs 2010/985, 2010/986 and 2010/987 make provisions for the commencement of the section and other related issues, consequential, transitional and savings provisions, and with appropriate modification for many sections of the ACA 2002 to apply to applications for a parental order. For procedure, see FPR 2010, r 13. Where foreign surrogacy arrangements are made, Hedley J in *Re IJ (Foreign Surrogacy Agreement: Parental Order)* [2011] 2 FLR 646 per curiam suggested that "those who travel abroad to make these arrangements really should take advice from those skilled in our domestic law to be sure as to the problems that will confront them (not the least of which is immigration) and how they can be addressed. Reliance on advice from overseas agencies is dangerous as the provisions of our domestic and immigration law are often not fully understood".

Application made by two people (applicants)—Although s 54(1) requires the application to be made by two people, it does not require that there be two living applicants at the time when the order is made. Hence, where one of two applicants dies, since all of the relevant welfare considerations in s 54 relate to the child, as a matter of law the court retains jurisdiction to consider the application: *A v P (Surrogacy: Parental Order: Death of Applicant)* [2012] 2 FLR 145. Where an application has been made jointly by two people who are eligible under s 54(2), if the evidence at the hearing suggests that their relationship is close to a breakdown and that the mother's consent would not be available if this fact was disclosed to her, it is unlikely that an order will be made as such a situation would be outside that contemplated by the section. Whether a parental order would be set aside if the breakdown occurs immediately after the parental order is very much fact-specific. As there is no statutory provision that deals with the criteria to be applied on such an application, the court will draw guidance from adoption cases and will consider the need for certainty. *G v G (Parental Order: Revocation)* [2013] 1 FLR 286 is an illustration of the principles that are relevant to such a case and the need to ensure that the procedure set out in the FPR 2010, Pt 13 is not short-circuited.

Child's home with the applicants and jurisdiction—This home does not need to be within England and Wales (*Re X and Y (Foreign Surrogacy)* [2009] 1 FLR 733) but one or both of the applicants must be domiciled in England and Wales (*Re G (Surrogacy: Foreign Domicile)* [2008] 1 FLR 1047. In *Re K (Foreign Surrogacy)* [2011] 1 FLR 533, where the children were outside the jurisdiction when the application was made and would have required entry clearance for the children to be brought to England and Wales, it was held that the court had no jurisdiction to entertain the application because the child was not habitually resident in England and Wales. Neither FLA 1986 nor the 2008 Act refers to the basis on which jurisdiction is founded in s 54 applications. It is assumed that the court applied Brussels IIA, Art 8.

Agreement of the mother and any other person who is a parent of the child—It is essential that the consent is given freely and with full understanding of the process and its implication and must be unconditional. The parental reporter's report must, therefore, be a full inquiry into the applicants' circumstances and must ensure that the basis on which the mother has given her consent remains valid, for example if it was given on the basis of a functional family when in fact the applicants' relationship is unstable and at breaking point (*G v G (Parental Order: Revocation)* [2013] 1 FLR 286). It is also essential, particularly when the surrogacy arrangement is made overseas, that appropriate steps are taken "to ensure that clear lines of communication with the surrogate are established before the birth to facilitate the giving of consent after the expiry of the six week period" (*Re D and L (Surrogacy)* [2012] EWHC 2631 (Fam)). Consent given before the expiry of 6 weeks after the birth is not valid for the purposes of s 54 but in an exceptional case the court is entitled to take into account evidence that the woman did give consent at an earlier time to giving up the baby. The weight attached to such earlier consent is likely to be limited and the court is unlikely to allow such evidence, as to do so would undermine the legal requirement that consent is only valid when it is given after 6 weeks following the birth of the child. Where the surrogate mother genuinely changes her mind and refuses to hand over the child and proceedings are commenced under CA 1989, the court will deal with the matter applying the welfare checklist and weighing the respective factors set out in s 1(3) (*Re TT (Surrogacy)* [2011] 2 FLR 392).

No requirement of the agreement of a person who cannot be found—There is power to make a parental order without the mother's consent if she cannot be found, but the court will scrutinise the evidence as to the efforts that have been made to find her and it is only when all reasonable steps have been taken to locate her without success that a court is likely to dispense with the need for a valid consent. The court will take account of the welfare of the child as the paramount consideration when arriving at its decision: *Re D and L (Surrogacy)* [2012] EWHC 2631 (Fam).

No money or other benefit (other than for expenses reasonably incurred) has been given—The provisions of s 54(8) are mandatory. The parental reporter's report must deal comprehensively with the matters set out in this subsection, applying the statutory checklist in ACA 2002. The question of whether payments go beyond "reasonable expense" is fact-specific but it is contrary to the principles embodied in s 54(8) to sanction excessive payments. However, applying the changes brought about by the Human Fertilisation and Embryology (Parental Orders) Regulations 2010, welfare considerations are paramount and will be balanced with public policy consideration but with the scales being weighted in favour of welfare: see *G v G (Parental Order: Revocation)* [2013] 1 FLR 286) and see *Re S (Parental Order)* [2010] 1 FLR 1156 (applied in *Re L (Commercial Surrogacy)* [2011] 1 FLR 1423, *Re X and Y (s 54 HFEA 2008)* [2012] 1 FLR 1347 and *Re D and L (Surrogacy)* [2012] EWHC 2631 (Fam)) for the principles that the court will apply. "It will only be in the clearest case of the abuse of public policy that the court will be able to withhold an order if otherwise welfare considerations supports its making". It was also emphasised that in such cases the court should nevertheless continue carefully to scrutinise applications for authorisations under s 54(8) with a view to policing the public policy issues identified in *Re S* (above). As a matter of procedure, Hedley J also suggested that (a) where an application (made in the first instance to the family proceedings court) has an international element "legal advisers may wish to consider a lateral transfer to the Inner London Family Proceedings Court which has specialist expertise in this area and is able to utilise specialist expertise in Cafcass when appointing a parental order reporter" and (b) that given the extension of the categories of applicants and of new issues emerging, such "matters for the time being should still come to the High Court" (*Re L*, above). See also *Re IJ (Foreign Surrogacy Agreement: Parental Order)* [2011] 2 FLR 646, where retrospective approval of monies paid was granted. In *Re X and Y (s 54 HFEA 2008)* (above), the President confirmed the approach adopted in *Re X and Y (Foreign Surrogacy)* [2009] 1 FLR 733: (a) in such cases, the court should consider the issue of welfare on the basis of lifelong perspective of welfare as in cases of adoption and not the "minority" perspective of CA 1989; (b) as regards payments made to the surrogates and public policy issues, the President particularly endorsed the passage in para 24 that that highlights two competing and potentially irreconcilable concepts (ie welfare and public policy). The court should consider the sums involved together with the element of gain in the context of the surrogate's particular circumstances and the economic circumstances in the country where the surrogacy agreement was made to ensure that the payments made were not of such magnitude to overbear the will of the surrogate. It is also a vital part of the court's public-policy assessment to ensure that the surrogacy arrangement is not a mere purchase of a child overseas; and (c) the examination of these issues should be undertaken at an early stage in the proceedings rather than at the final hearing and preferably at the point of entry into the UK.

****

Human Rights Act 1998

ARRANGEMENT OF SECTIONS

Introduction

Introduction

1 The Convention Rights

(1) In this Act "the Convention rights" means the rights and fundamental freedoms set out in –

    (a)   Articles 2 to 12 and 14 of the Convention,

    (b)   Articles 1 to 3 of the First Protocol, and

    (c)   Article 1 of the Thirteenth Protocol,

as read with Articles 16 to 18 of the Convention.

(2) Those Articles are to have effect for the purposes of this Act subject to any designated derogation or reservation (as to which see sections 14 and 15).

(3) The Articles are set out in Schedule 1.

(4) The Secretary of State may by order make such amendments to this Act as he considers appropriate to reflect the effect, in relation to the United Kingdom, of a protocol.

(5) In subsection (4) "protocol" means a protocol to the Convention –

    (a)   which the United Kingdom has ratified; or

    (b)   which the United Kingdom has signed with a view to ratification.

(6) No amendment may be made by an order under subsection (4) so as to come into force before the protocol concerned is in force in relation to the United Kingdom.

Amendments—SI 2001/3500; SI 2003/1887; SI 2004/1574.

Scope—It is important to note that *only* those Articles of ECHR 1950 set out in Schedule 1 are to be read into domestic law. Articles not listed (e g Articles 1 and 13) are specifically excluded and are not formally incorporated into UK law.

Jurisdiction—Notwithstanding the exclusion of Article 1, dealing with jurisdiction, the House of Lords held that the principles of extraterritoriality developed by the ECtHR were applicable to claims under HRA 1998: *R (Mazim Jumaa Gatteh Al Skeina & Others) v The Secretary of State for Defence* [2008] 1 AC 153; *Ghaidan v Godin-Mendoza* [2004] 2 FLR 600 (HL). Thus, although the application of the Convention is usually limited to the jurisdiction of the contracting state, there may be an exception where a state is in "effective control" of a foreign territory through military occupation, acquiescence or invitation. In such circumstances the territory could be within the jurisdiction of the state and the Convention would then apply to acts undertaken by the state within that territory.

    The Court of Appeal appears to have limited the principle of extraterritoriality by imposing a narrower test, namely that the UK "had the legal power to fulfil substantial governmental functions as a sovereign state": *R (Al-Saadoon & Anthr) v Secretary of State for Defence* [2010] QB 486. The Supreme Court, however, has concluded that the art 1 jurisdiction is essentially territorial in nature and that other bases of jurisdiction are exceptional and require special justification in the particular circumstances of each case. So far as the exercise of executive authority is concerned as a basis for establishing article 1 jurisdiction, the Strasbourg Court has not propounded any such general principle: *R(Smith) v Secretary of State for Defence* [2011] 1 AC 1.

2 Interpretation of Convention rights

(1) A court or tribunal determining a question which has arisen in connection with a Convention right must take into account any –

    (a)   judgment, decision, declaration or advisory opinion of the European Court of Human Rights,

    (b)   opinion of the Commission given in a report adopted under Article 31 of the Convention,

    (c)   decision of the Commission in connection with Article 26 or 27(2) of the Convention, or

(d) decision of the Committee of Ministers taken under Article 46 of the Convention,

whenever made or given, so far as, in the opinion of the court or tribunal, it is relevant to the proceedings in which that question has arisen.

(2) Evidence of any judgment, decision, declaration or opinion of which account may have to be taken under this section is to be given in proceedings before any court or tribunal in such manner as may be provided by rules.

(3) In this section "rules" means rules of court or, in the case of proceedings before a tribunal, rules made for the purposes of this section –

(a) by the Lord Chancellor or Secretary of State, in relation to any proceedings outside Scotland;

(b) by the Secretary of State, in relation to proceedings in Scotland; or

(c) by a Northern Ireland department, in relation to proceedings before a tribunal in Northern Ireland –

(i)   which deals with transferred matters; and

(ii) for which no rules made under paragraph (a) are in force.

Amendments—SI 2003/1887; SI 2005/3429.

"must take into account" (s 2(1))—The court is required to take account of Strasbourg case-law but is not required to follow it. However, the circumstances in which domestic courts would not follow Strasbourg will be rare (e g the decision is based on an unambiguous misunderstanding of domestic law or procedure: *Doherty v Birmingham City Council* [2009] AC 367 at [20] and [82]). The purpose of the requirement is to ensure Convention rights are enforced under HRA 1998 as they would be enforced by the ECtHR (see *R (Al Jedda) v Secretary of State for Defence* [2008] 1 AC 332), but that should not prohibit the UK courts from developing its domestic human rights jurisprudence under the common law: HRA 1998, s 11. However, the Supreme Court appears to have signalled a broadening of the circumstances in which the domestic courts will not follow decisions of the ECtHR. Lord Phillips said, "There will, however, be rare occasions where this court has concerns as to whether a decision of the Strasbourg Court sufficiently appreciates or accommodates particular aspects of our domestic process. In such circumstances it is open to this court to decline to follow the Strasbourg decision, giving reasons for adopting this course. This is likely to give the Strasbourg Court the opportunity to reconsider the particular aspect of the decision that is in issue, so that there takes place what may prove to be a valuable dialogue between this court and the Strasbourg Court." (*R v Horncastle* [2010] 2 AC 373). Lord Neuberger, giving the judgment of the Supreme Court, said that "this Court is not bound to follow every decision of the ECtHR. Not only would it be impractical to do so: it would sometimes be inappropriate, as it would destroy the ability of the Court to engage in the constructive dialogue with the ECtHR which is of value to the development of Convention law ... Where, however, there is a clear and constant line of decisions whose effect is not inconsistent with some fundamental substantive or procedural aspect of our law, and whose reasoning does not appear to overlook or misunderstand some argument or point of principle, we consider that it would be wrong for this Court not to follow that line" *Manchester City Council v Pinnock* [2011] 2 AC 104, at [48].

"a question which has arisen" (s 2(1))—A question may arise in ongoing proceedings, in which case the issue must be determined (if possible) within those proceedings (see annotations to s 7). Alternatively, a question may arise as an issue where there are no current proceedings. In this case, an application may be made by way of freestanding proceedings under HRA 1998 or by way of judicial review to determine the question (see annotations to s 7).

"Evidence of any judgment" (s 2(2))—By FPR PD29B the President has directed that when an authority is to be cited at a hearing, the authority must be an authoritative and complete report and copies of the report, with a list of authorities, must be filed in accordance with FPR PD27A, or otherwise not less than 2 days before the hearing. The *President's Direction* states that these must be copies of the complete original text issued by the European Court and Commission (either paper-based or through HUDOC which is available on the internet at *www.echr.coe.int/hudoc*).

Precedent—The court at first instance must adhere to the English rules of precedent. If a judge feels a decision is inconsistent with Strasbourg authority he has to follow the binding precedent but could give leave to appeal as appropriate: see *Kay and Ors v London Borough of Lambeth and Ors; Leeds City Council v Price and Ors* [2006] 2 AC 465.

Competing Convention rights—Where competing Convention rights are in issue, neither has precedence over the other: *Campbell v MGN Ltd* [2004] 2 AC 457 and *R (ota L) v Commissioner of the Metropolis* [2010] 1 FLR 643.

Legislation

3 Interpretation of legislation

(1) So far as it is possible to do so, primary legislation and subordinate legislation must be read and given effect in a way which is compatible with the Convention rights.

(2) This section –

   (a)   applies to primary legislation and subordinate legislation whenever enacted;
   (b)   does not affect the validity, continuing operation or enforcement of any incompatible primary legislation; and
   (c)   does not affect the validity, continuing operation or enforcement of any incompatible subordinate legislation if (disregarding any possibility of revocation) primary legislation prevents removal of the incompatibility.

Scope—This section is the lynchpin of the Act. It imposes a strong interpretative obligation in respect both of primary and secondary legislation whenever it was enacted.

"So far as it possible to do so" (s 3(1))—This has been held to mean that primary legislation and subordinate legislation must be read and given effect in a way that is compatible with the Convention rights "unless it is plainly impossible to do so": *R v A* [2002] 1 AC 45 at [44]. The section is not available where the suggested interpretation is contrary to express statutory words or is by implication necessarily contradicted by the statute: *Re S (Minors) (Care Order: Implementation of Care Plan)* [2002] 1 FLR 815 at [40]. Lord Hope has said that "In the face of such strong statutory language, any reading down of the section to enable the court to postpone the execution of an order for possession of a dwelling-house which was not let on a secure tenancy for a longer period than the statutory maximum would go well beyond what section 3(1) of the 1998 Act permits". As Lord Nicholls of Birkenhead said in *Ghaidan v Godin-Mendoza* [2004] 2 FLR 600 at [33], for the courts to adopt a meaning inconsistent with a fundamental feature of legislation would be to cross the constitutional boundary that section 3 of the 1998 Act seeks to demarcate and preserve: *Hounslow LBC v Powell* [2011] 2 AC 186 at [62]. If it is unavailable, recourse must be had to s 4 and an application made for a declaration of incompatibility of legislation with a Convention right.

Effect of the provision—The strong interpretative obligation of s 3 is vital to the working of HRA 1998. "What is necessary, however, is to emphasise that interpretation under s 3(1) is the prime remedial remedy and that resort to s 4 must always be an exceptional course. In practical effect there is a strong rebuttable presumption in favour of an interpretation consistent with Convention rights": per *Ghaidan v Godin-Mendoza* [2004] 2 FLR 600 at [50]. In the first instance the court must decide whether the statute is consistent with a Convention right using the ordinary principles of statutory interpretation and identify the word or phrase that is or is claimed to be incompatible. A claimant should identify "precisely (a) the words used by the legislature which would otherwise be incompatible with the Convention right and (b) how these words were to be construed, according to the rule which s 3 lays down, to make them compatible": *R v A* (above) at [110]. The obligation may require the courts to:

   (a)   give legislation a Convention-compliant meaning even where there is no ambiguity in the statute;
   (b)   on occasions adopt a linguistically strained interpretation of legislation;
   (c)   modify the meaning and effect of primary and secondary legislation (which may require the court to depart from the parliamentary intention behind the legislation);
   (d)   read in additional words to the legislation to achieve Convention compliance;
   (e)   read down the legislation so as to narrow the interpretation of the provision; or
   (f)   clarify the effect of the provision without altering the words used.

See *Re S (Care Order: Implementation of a Care Plan)* (above) at [36]–[41]; *Ghaidan v Godin-Mendoza* (above) paras 28–34; *R v A* (above) at [4]–[68]; and *R v Lambert* [2002] 2 AC 545 at [79]–[81].

Limitations—Lord Hope identified the limitations on the use of s 3 when he observed, "The rule of construction which section 3 lays down is quite unlike any previous rule of statutory interpretation … But the rule is only a rule of interpretation. It does not entitle the judges to act as legislators … Section 3 does not entitle the court to legislate; its task is still one of interpretation. The compatibility is to be achieved only so far as this is possible. Plainly this will not be possible if the legislation contains provisions that expressly contradict the meaning that the enactment would have to be given to make it compatible: *R v A* (above) at [108].

Victim—The obligation imposed by the section is a general one. There is no need to satisfy the test of being a victim (cf the provisions of s 7) to be entitled to seek a declaration of the meaning of legislation: *R (Rusbridger) v Attorney General* [2004] AC 357 at [21].

4 Declaration of incompatibility

(1) Subsection (2) applies in any proceedings in which a court determines whether a provision of primary legislation is compatible with a Convention right.

(2) If the court is satisfied that the provision is incompatible with a Convention right, it may make a declaration of that incompatibility.

(3) Subsection (4) applies in any proceedings in which a court determines whether a provision of subordinate legislation, made in the exercise of a power conferred by primary legislation, is compatible with a Convention right.

(4) If the court is satisfied –

    (a)   that the provision is incompatible with a Convention right, and

    (b)   that (disregarding any possibility of revocation) the primary legislation concerned prevents removal of the incompatibility,

it may make a declaration of that incompatibility.

(5) In this section "court" means –

    (a)   the Supreme Court;

    (b)   the Judicial Committee of the Privy Council;

    (c)   the Courts-Martial Appeal Court;

    (d)   in Scotland, the High Court of Justiciary sitting otherwise than as a trial court or the Court of Session;

    (e)   in England and Wales or Northern Ireland, the High Court or the Court of Appeal

    (f)   the Court of Protection, in any matter being dealt with by the President of the Family Division, the Vice-Chancellor or a puisne judge of the High Court.

(6) A declaration under this section ("a declaration of incompatibility") –

    (a)   does not affect the validity, continuing operation or enforcement of the provision in respect of which it is given; and

    (b)   is not binding on the parties to the proceedings in which it is made.

Amendments—MCA 2005, s 67(1), Sch 6, para 43; CRA 2005, Sch 9, para 66(2).

Scope—This section provides the higher courts (as defined in s 4(4)) with power to make a "declaration of incompatibility" if satisfied that a provision of primary or subordinate legislation is incompatible with the Convention. Such a declaration is not binding upon the parties and it does not change the law, which the court is required to continue to apply (s 4(6)). This provision enables the Crown to take a different position from the court making the declaration if the matter proceeds to the ECtHR. The court therefore cannot set aside the primary legislation but can disapply subordinate legislation unless the terms of the enabling statute prevent this (s 3(2)(b),(c)). Such a declaration should have the effect of prompting the government to change the law.

Procedure—A claim for a declaration of incompatibility must be made on a claim form. The procedure for an application under s 4 is contained within FPR 2010, r 29.5 and PD29A. The court may not make a declaration of incompatibility unless 21 days' notice, or such other period as the court directs, has been given to the Crown (CPR 1998, r 19.4A and FPR 2010, r 29.5(3)). Where notice has been given to the Crown, a Minister, or other person permitted by the HRA, shall be joined as a party on giving notice to the court (CPR 1998, r 19.4A(2) and FPR 2010, r 29.5(4)).

Making a declaration—A court must use the rule of construction in s 3 to read and give effect to legislation so that it is Convention-compliant unless it is plainly impossible to do so. Where, however, the

PART II

whole scheme of the legislation is incompatible with the Convention or where there are multiple incompatibilities, it is unlikely that s 3 could be used to remedy the defects. In *R (Wright & others) v Secretary of State for Health* [2009] 1 AC 739, at [39], Baroness Hale said, when approving the first instance decision to make a declaration of incompatibility, "However, I would not make any attempt to suggest ways in which the scheme could be made compatible ... the incompatibility arises from the interaction between the three elements of the scheme – the procedure, the criterion and the consequences. It is not for us to attempt to rewrite the legislation. There is, as I have already said, a delicate balance to be struck ... It is right that that balance be struck in the first instance by the legislature."

A declaration of compatibility is a discretionary remedy. The court will consider a number of factors: that the matter has been fully argued before the court; the legislation cannot be read or given effect in a way that is compliant with Convention rights; the making of the declaration gives legitimacy to the court's order; and that the declaration will serve a legislative purpose under the 1998 Act, in that it provides a basis, under s 10(1)(a), for a Minister of the Crown to consider whether there are compelling reasons to make amendments to the legislation by remedial order (under Schedule 2 to the Act) for the purpose of removing the incompatibility that the court has identified: *Wilson v First County Trust Ltd (No.2)* [2002] QB 74 at [46], [47].

Declarations of incompatibility—The Home Secretary's scheme to control the right of any person subject to immigration control to marry in the UK was the subject of a declaration of incompatibility as being inconsistent with the Convention rights enshrined in Art 12 (*R (Baiai) v Secretary of State for the Home Department* [2008] 2 FLR 1462 (HL)) and *Aguilar v Secretary of State for the Home Department* [2011] 1 FLR 1187). The rejection of unmarried couples in Northern Ireland as prospective adopter parents was the subject of a declaration of incompatibility as being inconsistent with Convention rights of Art 14 (*Re P and Ors* [2008] 2 FLR 1084). However, a school's decision to refuse to permit a pupil to wear a "purity" ring as an expression of her Christian faith and as a sign of her belief of celibacy before marriage did not breach ECHR Art 9 (*R (Lydia Playfoot) v Millais School Governing Body* [2007] ELR 484). Further, although a school's decision to refuse to allow a pupil to wear a niqab veil at school engaged her ECHR Art 9 rights, it did not infringe that right and, even if it had, the decision was objectively justifiable under Art 9(2) (*R (X) v Governors of Y School* [2007] ELR 278).

Lacuna in legislation—A lacuna in legislation cannot be the subject of a declaration of incompatibility: *Re S (Minors) (Care Order: Implementation of Care Plan)* [2002] 1 FLR 815 (concerning the Court of Appeal's attempt to create "starred" care plans).

Effective remedy—The ECHR does not yet consider that a "declaration of incompatibility" constitutes an effective remedy within Convention terms: *Burden v UK* [2008] ECHR 357 at [35]–[40].

Hopeless applications—Where the court considers that a claim for a declaration of incompatibility has no chance of success, there is no need to transfer the case to the High Court (*Re V (Care Proceedings: Human Rights Claims)* [2004] 1 FLR 944).

Rectification—The Government may remedy incompatibility, following a final declaration of incompatibility or following a decision of the ECtHR, by later primary legislation or by making a remedial order pursuant to s 10 HRA 1998 (either by the standard procedure (Sch 2, para 2(a)) or the emergency procedure (Sch 2, para 2(b))).

5 Right of Crown to intervene

(1) Where a court is considering whether to make a declaration of incompatibility, the Crown is entitled to notice in accordance with rules of court.

(2) In any case to which subsection (1) applies –

(a) a Minister of the Crown (or a person nominated by him),
(b) a member of the Scottish Executive,
(c) a Northern Ireland Minister,
(d) a Northern Ireland department,

is entitled, on giving notice in accordance with rules of court, to be joined as a party to the proceedings.

(3) Notice under subsection (2) may be given at any time during the proceedings.

(4) A person who has been made a party to criminal proceedings (other than in Scotland) as the result of a notice under subsection (2) may, with leave, appeal to the Supreme Court against any declaration of incompatibility made in the proceedings.

(5) In subsection (4) –

"criminal proceedings" includes all proceedings before the Courts-Martial Appeal Court; and

"leave" means leave granted by the court making the declaration of incompatibility or by the Supreme Court.

Amendments—CRA 2005, Sch 9, para 66(3).

Scope—Where consideration is being given to a "declaration of incompatibility", the Crown, or in a case relating to Scotland or Northern Ireland the person mentioned in s 5(2)(b)–(d), should be notified and allowed to become a party to the proceedings. A court may not make a declaration unless 21 days' notice, or such other period as the court directs, has been given to the Crown (CPR 1998, r 19.4A and FPR 2010, r 29.5(3)). Where such notice has been given, a Minister, on giving notice to the court, will be joined as a party (CPR 1998, r 19.4A(2) and FPR 2010, r 29.5(4)).

Notice to the Crown—The notice must be served on the person named in the list published under the Crown Proceedings Act 1947, s 17. The list is annexed to CPR PD66 (see CPR PD19A, para 6.4(1)).

Criminal Proceedings—The Crown is given a right – subject to the grant of leave – to appeal against a declaration of incompatibility made in criminal proceedings direct to the Supreme Court (s 5(4)).

Public authorities

6 Acts of public authorities

(1) It is unlawful for a public authority to act in a way which is incompatible with a Convention right.

(2) Subsection (1) does not apply to an act if –

(a) as the result of one or more provisions of primary legislation, the authority could not have acted differently; or

(b) in the case of one or more provisions of, or made under, primary legislation which cannot be read or given effect in a way which is compatible with the Convention rights, the authority was acting so as to give effect to or enforce those provisions.

(3) In this section "public authority" includes –

(a) a court or tribunal, and

(b) any person certain of whose functions are functions of a public nature,

but does not include either House of Parliament or a person exercising functions in connection with proceedings in Parliament.

(4) (*repealed*)

(5) In relation to a particular act, a person is not a public authority by virtue only of subsection (3)(b) if the nature of the act is private.

(6) "An act" includes a failure to act but does not include a failure to –

(a) introduce in, or lay before, Parliament a proposal for legislation; or

(b) make any primary legislation or remedial order.

Amendments—CRA 2005, Sch 9, para 66(4).

Scope—It is unlawful for a public authority (meaning, inter alia, a court, tribunal or local authority) to act in a way which is incompatible with Convention rights unless it could not have acted differently because of primary legislation or the primary legislation could not be read in a manner compatible with Convention rights. Where the provision cannot be read as compatible, an application can be made for a declaration of incompatibility (pursuant to s 4). Accordingly, individuals have a direct cause of action against public authorities. There is no direct cause of action for acting incompatibly with Convention rights between private individuals although, of course, in all proceedings the courts are required to give effect to Convention rights and obligations: *Venables and Thompson v Newsgroup Newspapers and Associated Newspapers Ltd* [2001] 1 FLR 791 (CA); *Campbell v MGN Ltd* [2004] 2 AC 457.

Public authority—A distinction is to be drawn between "core public authorities" (e g government departments, local authorities, NHS trusts and the police) and "hybrid public authorities" (otherwise referred to as "functional public authorities") some of whose functions may be of a public nature but others of which will be of a private nature (e g a private security company would be exercising public functions in relation to the management of a contracted-out prison but would be acting privately when guarding ordinary commercial premises). There is no single test of universal application to determine whether a body is a core public authority or a hybrid public authority given the diverse nature of governmental functions and the variety of means by which these functions are discharged. "Factors to be taken into account include the extent to which in carrying out the relevant function the body is publicly funded, or is exercising statutory powers, or is taking the place of central government or local authorities, or is providing a public service": *Aston Cantlow and Wilmcote with Billesley Parochial Church Council v Wallbank* [2004] 1 AC 546 at [12]. In *Aston* the House of Lords sought to narrow the scope of core public authorities (which cannot enjoy Convention rights) and to widen the scope of hybrid public authorities (which in relation to its private acts is not disabled from having Convention rights).

Functions of a public/a private nature—In the leading case of *YL v Birmingham City Council* [2008] 1 AC 95 the House of Lords interprets the meaning of "functions of a public nature" more narrowly than that given in *Aston Cantlow* (above). The majority drew a distinction between a council's provision of services pursuant to a statutory duty and the like provision of services provided by a private company under a commercial contract paid for by public money: they emphasised the commercial nature of the operation of the private company. By contrast, the minority view was that if a private body performed functions by arrangement with a public body and at its expense, which functions if carried out by the latter would be a "public function", then the private body was undertaking "functions of a public nature" and was thus a hybrid public authority.

Primary legislation defence—The distinction between the two limbs of the statutory defence is neither obvious nor clear. In *R (Hooper) v Secretary of State for Work & Pensions* [2005] 1 WLR 1681, two law lords thought the appropriate defence was s 6(2)(a) and two thought it was s 6(2)(b). In practice the defence is rarely relied upon because most powers and duties can be read to be Convention-compliant.

Parliament (s 6(3))—Parliament, as the legislature, is not a public authority for the purposes of the section and is not bound by s 6(1).

Exclusion of failure to legislate or make a remedial order—The failure to make primary legislation or a remedial order to remedy an incompatibility or to give effect to a Convention right is not "an act" within the meaning of s 6(1) and thus may not be challenged in the UK courts (s 6(6)(b)): *Chester v Secretary of State for Justice & Anthr* [2011] 1 WLR 1436 and *Tovey & Othrs v Ministry of Justice* [2011] EWHC 271 (QB).

7 Proceedings

(1) A person who claims that a public authority has acted (or proposes to act) in a way which is made unlawful by section 6(1) may –

    (a) bring proceedings against the authority under this Act in the appropriate court or tribunal, or

    (b) rely on the Convention right or rights concerned in any legal proceedings,

but only if he is (or would be) a victim of the unlawful act.

(2) In subsection (1)(a) "appropriate court or tribunal" means such court or tribunal as may be determined in accordance with rules; and proceedings against an authority include a counterclaim or similar proceeding.

(3) If the proceedings are brought on an application for judicial review, the applicant is to be taken to have a sufficient interest in relation to the unlawful act only if he is, or would be, a victim of that act.

(4) If the proceedings are made by way of a petition for judicial review in Scotland, the applicant shall be taken to have title and interest to sue in relation to the unlawful act only if he is, or would be, a victim of that act.

(5) Proceedings under subsection (1)(a) must be brought before the end of –

    (a) the period of one year beginning with the date on which the act complained of took place; or

(b) such longer period as the court or tribunal considers equitable having regard to all the circumstances,

but that is subject to any rule imposing a stricter time limit in relation to the procedure in question.

(6) In subsection (1)(b) "legal proceedings" includes –

(a) proceedings brought by or at the instigation of a public authority; and

(b) an appeal against the decision of a court or tribunal.

(7) For the purposes of this section, a person is a victim of an unlawful act only if he would be a victim for the purposes of Article 34 of the Convention if proceedings were brought in the European Court of Human Rights in respect of that act.

(8) Nothing in this Act creates a criminal offence.

(9) In this section "rules" means –

(a) in relation to proceedings before a court or tribunal outside Scotland, rules made by the Lord Chancellor or Secretary of State for the purposes of this section or rules of court,

(b) in relation to proceedings before a court or tribunal in Scotland, rules made by the Secretary of State for those purposes,

(c) in relation to proceedings before a tribunal in Northern Ireland –

(i) which deals with transferred matters; and

(ii) for which no rules made under paragraph (a) are in force,

rules made by a Northern Ireland department for those purposes,

and includes provision made by order under section 1 of the Courts and Legal Services Act 1990.

(10) In making rules, regard must be had to section 9.

(11) The Minister who has power to make rules in relation to a particular tribunal may, to the extent he considers it necessary to ensure that the tribunal can provide an appropriate remedy in relation to an act (or proposed act) of a public authority which is (or would be) unlawful as a result of section 6(1), by order add to –

(a) the relief or remedies which the tribunal may grant; or

(b) the grounds on which it may grant any of them.

(12) An order made under subsection (11) may contain such incidental, supplemental, consequential or transitional provision as the Minister making it considers appropriate.

(13) "The Minister" includes the Northern Ireland department concerned.

Amendments—SI 2003/1887; SI 2005/3429.

Scope—This section provides the mechanism for complaints about acts which are unlawful, being incompatible with Convention rights. There are two routes: under s 7(1)(b) in legal proceedings in any court or tribunal in which the proceedings are brought by or at the instigation of a public authority, or constitute an appeal against the decision of a court or tribunal (s 7(6)). The other route is a separate claim under s 7(1)(a). Where the claim under s 7(1)(a) relates to a judicial act, the claim must be way of judicial review or by way of an appeal (HRA 1998, s 9). Otherwise, it seems that a freestanding claim should be made under CPR 1998, Pt 8.

"public authority"—A claim under s 7(1)(a) in relation to a judicial act must be brought in the High Court. Otherwise a claim in relation to an act of a public authority may be brought in any court (CPR 1998, r 7.11) in ongoing proceedings. The more usual procedure in relation to a claim concerning a judicial act will be by way of appeal from the decision made. For assistance in determining what is a "public authority" or when a body is "exercising functions of a public nature" see the notes to s 6 above.

"victim"—A claim of breach of Convention rights can only be made by a victim or prospective victim. Articles 6, 8 and 14 are generally only applicable to those within the jurisdiction of the court (*Re J (Child Returned Abroad: Human Rights)* [2004] 2 FLR 85) but there may be exceptions: see the note to s 1 above.

Procedure—Where the complaint is in relation to a local authority care plan, the application under this provision should be heard in the Family Division of the High Court, if possible by a judge with experience of sitting in the Administrative Court; see *CF v The Secretary of State for the Home Department* [2004] 2 FLR 517 and *Re S and W (Care Proceedings)* [2007] 2 FLR 275, CA. Oral evidence may be heard and this should be determined at a directions hearing (*C v Bury Metropolitan Borough Council* [2002] 2 FLR 868). Where a freestanding application is made concerning a child the matter should be referred to Cafcass Legal.

Where a parent seeks to rely on a breach of Arts 6 and 8 within public law proceedings he must act without delay and should seek interim relief as a matter of urgency (e g breach of care plan by a local authority: see *Re P (Adoption: Breach of Care Plan)* [2004] 2 FLR 1109, CA.

The provisions of the Convention may not be used to mount a collateral challenge to the decision of a court in public law proceedings (in particular where the original decision was not challenged on appeal) (*Hinds v Liverpool County Court and Ors* [2008] 2 FLR 63, QBD).

The mistaken judgments or assessments of professionals or medical experts as to the cause of child's injuries or presenting symptoms, did not of themselves establish a breach of Art 8. However, the absence of an effective remedy for any arguable violation of the child's parents' human rights constituted a breach of Art 13. (*RK and AK v UK* [2009] 1 FLR 274). Note: Article 13 is not incorporated into domestic UK law by HRA 1998. Accordingly, a failure to afford a victim an effective remedy is not, of itself, actionable in this jurisdiction. Ex turpi causa – the principle that a person may not benefit from his own wrongdoing is not recognised under Convention law and is not a legitimate basis for denying a claimant relief to which he would otherwise be entitled: *Al Hassan-Daniel v Revenue and Customs Commissioners* [2011] QB 866.

8 Judicial remedies

(1) In relation to any act (or proposed act) of a public authority which the court finds is (or would be) unlawful, it may grant such relief or remedy, or make such order, within its powers as it considers just and appropriate.

(2) But damages may be awarded only by a court which has power to award damages, or to order the payment of compensation, in civil proceedings.

(3) No award of damages is to be made unless, taking account of all the circumstances of the case, including –

    (a)   any other relief or remedy granted, or order made, in relation to the act in question (by that or any other court), and

    (b)   the consequences of any decision (of that or any other court) in respect of that act,

the court is satisfied that the award is necessary to afford just satisfaction to the person in whose favour it is made.

(4) In determining –

    (a)   whether to award damages, or

    (b)   the amount of an award,

the court must take into account the principles applied by the European Court of Human Rights in relation to the award of compensation under Article 41 of the Convention.

(5) A public authority against which damages are awarded is to be treated –

    (a)   in Scotland, for the purposes of section 3 of the Law Reform (Miscellaneous Provisions) (Scotland) Act 1940 as if the award were made in an action of damages in which the authority has been found liable in respect of loss or damage to the person to whom the award is made;

    (b)   for the purposes of the Civil Liability (Contribution) Act 1978 as liable in respect of damage suffered by the person to whom the award is made.

(6) In this section –

    "court" includes a tribunal;

    "damages" means damages for an unlawful act of a public authority; and

    "unlawful" means unlawful under section 6(1).

Scope—This section does not grant additional powers. Damages can only be awarded by a court with jurisdiction to do so.

Act or proposed act—It is plain from the wording of the section that a claim may be brought in anticipation of an act that would be unlawful if carried out and the court may grant the appropriate relief or remedy.

Grant relief or remedy (s 8(1))—The court may quash a decision made by a local authority in the care planning for a child where the parents' Convention rights have been breached by the authority in coming to that decision: *Re M (Care: Challenging Decisions made by Local Authority)* [2001] 2 FLR 1300. The court has jurisdiction in appropriate cases to make an injunction against a local authority preventing, for example, a child being removed from foster carers pending the full hearing of the matter (*Coventry CC v O (Adoption)* [2011] 2 FLR 936) or to prevent the separation of a mother and child pending a full hearing (*Re H (Care Plan: Human Rights)* [2012] 1 FLR 191).

Findings of breach of Convention rights—The Court of Appeal has given guidance on the approach that courts should adopt when invited to make findings that a local authority has breached a parent's or a child's Convention rights when, for example, it has removed a child from the parent's care. The court should focus on the issues in terms of the 1950 Convention. The court could pose the simple question "What would an impartial observer be saying if the local authority had delayed and something had gone wrong?": *Re S (Care Proceedings: Human Rights)* [2012] 2 FLR 209.

Where placement orders had been made in respect of two children but they had never been adopted, their ties with their natural family had been cut without a new family being found for them. Accordingly, the court made declarations that the local authority and the IRO had acted incompatibly with the Arts 3, 6 and 8 rights of the children: *A and S v Lancashire County Council* [2012] EWHC 1689 (Fam).

Judicial review—The courts' traditional powers of review should be expanded to permit a court to assess any relevant facts which may be in issue in a case. The expansion of the court's powers was required by the jurisprudence of the ECtHR: *Manchester City Council v Pinnock* [2011] 2 AC 104, per Lord Neuberger at [73].

Just satisfaction (s 8(3))—The court may decline to make an award of damages where the court decides that the declaratory or other relief granted is sufficient remedy for the breach of Convention rights. Wilson LJ observed in *Re C (Breach of Human Rights: Damages)* [2007] 1 FLR 1957: "In general the 'principles' applied by the European Court, which we are thus enjoined to 'take into account', are not clear or coherent … What is clear, however, is that the European Court generally favours an award of damages in cases in which local authorities have infringed the right of parents under Article 8 to respect for their family life by shortcomings in the procedures by which they have taken children into care or kept them in care, whether temporarily or permanently". In that case the infringement of the mother's human rights, as found by the court, was seen to be at the low end of the spectrum and it was unnecessary to award her damages to afford her just satisfaction.

The ECtHR assesses "just satisfaction" under three heads: pecuniary loss, non-pecuniary loss and costs.

Award of damages—The Court of Appeal laid down procedural guidelines in respect of the award of damages and the circumstances in which maladministration will constitute a breach of Art 8: the guidelines are of general application:

(a) claims for damages alone may not be brought by way of judicial review but should be started in the Administrative Court by ordinary claim;

(b) courts should examine carefully attempts to recover damages for maladministration other than by way of judicial review;

(c) claimants must first exhaust all available complaints procedures including reference to an ombudsman;

(d) if there is a claim for relief in addition to a claim for damages, only the former should be granted permission and the latter should be adjourned or stayed pending determination of the substantive application; and

(e) citation of authorities in support of arguments about the quantum of damages should be limited to three and, save for exceptional cases, the hearing should be listed for no more than half a day: *Anufrijeva v Southwark LBC* [2004] 1 FLR 8.

Quantum of damages—The court must take account of the principles applied by the ECtHR under Article 41 of the Convention when deciding whether to award damages and the quantum to be awarded: s 8(4) and see *Re C* (above). The awards of damages made by the ECtHR are generally modest. Lord Bingham said in *R (Greenfield) v Secretary of State for the Home Department* [2005] 1 WLR 673 at [19] that courts "should not aim to be significantly more or less generous that the [ECtHR] might be expected to be, in a case where it was willing to make an award at all".

PART II

9 Judicial acts

(1) Proceedings under section 7(1)(a) in respect of a judicial act may be brought only –

    (a)   by exercising a right of appeal;

    (b)   on an application (in Scotland a petition) for judicial review; or

    (c)   in such other forum as may be prescribed by rules.

(2) That does not affect any rule of law which prevents a court from being the subject of judicial review.

(3) In proceedings under this Act in respect of a judicial act done in good faith, damages may not be awarded otherwise than to compensate a person to the extent required by Article 5(5) of the Convention.

(4) An award of damages permitted by subsection (3) is to be made against the Crown; but no award may be made unless the appropriate person, if not a party to the proceedings, is joined.

(5) In this section –

    "appropriate person" means the Minister responsible for the court concerned, or a person or government department nominated by him;

    "court" includes a tribunal;

    "judge" includes a member of a tribunal, a justice of the peace (or, in Northern Ireland, a lay magistrate) and a clerk or other officer entitled to exercise the jurisdiction of a court;

    "judicial act" means a judicial act of a court and includes an act done on the instructions, or on behalf, of a judge; and

    "rules" has the same meaning as in section 7(9).

Amendments—Justice (Northern Ireland) Act 2002, Sch 4, para 39; SI 2005/109.

Scope—Where there are freestanding proceedings in which a complaint is made of a judicial act, the appropriate procedure is to appeal. The objective of the provision is to prevent collateral attacks on the decisions of courts and tribunals. Where the judicial act is not within existing proceedings or there is no right of appeal, the appropriate procedure is by way of an application for judicial review under CPR 1998, Pt 54. Otherwise, a separate freestanding application under HRA 1998 should be by proceedings commenced under CPR 1998, Pt 8; however see the case of *Hinds* (s 7 above).

Judicial act—The interpretation of the phrase is wide and includes any tribunal, any member of court or tribunal (including any legal advisor or other official entitled to exercise the powers of the court) and the act of any person acting on the instructions of or on behalf of any of the foregoing individuals.

Article 5(5)—This relates to the unlawful detention of the victim (e g continued detention after a bail application). In such circumstances damages are awarded against the Crown and not the court concerned. The government minister responsible for the court must be joined as a party to the proceedings: s 9(3),(4).

****

12 Freedom of expression

(1) This section applies if a court is considering whether to grant any relief which, if granted, might affect the exercise of the Convention right to freedom of expression.

(2) If the person against whom the application for relief is made ("the respondent") is neither present nor represented, no such relief is to be granted unless the court is satisfied –

    (a)   that the applicant has taken all practicable steps to notify the respondent; or

    (b)   that there are compelling reasons why the respondent should not be notified.

(3) No such relief is to be granted so as to restrain publication before trial unless the court is satisfied that the applicant is likely to establish that publication should not be allowed.

(4) The court must have particular regard to the importance of the Convention right to freedom of expression and, where the proceedings relate to material which the respondent claims, or which appears to the court, to be journalistic, literary or artistic material (or to conduct connected with such material), to –

    (a)   the extent to which –
          (i)   the material has, or is about to, become available to the public; or
          (ii) it is, or would be, in the public interest for the material to be published;
    (b)   any relevant privacy code.

(5) In this section –

    "court" includes a tribunal; and
    "relief" includes any remedy or order (other than in criminal proceedings).

Applications for reporting restrictions order—Applications for reporting restriction orders are to be heard in the High Court and, if required, can be dealt with speedily and out of normal court hours (out of hours number 020 7947 6000). Service of an application on the national media can be effected via the Press Association's CopyDirect service, but note the *Guardian* and the *Telegraph* do not subscribe to CopyDirect and must be served directly with the application. Similarly, if it is proposed to seek relief against a local newspaper, most do not subscribe to the CopyDirect service and must be served directly. A party who proposes to use CopyDirect to effect service on the national media should contact the service on 0870 837 6429.

Without notice orders—The court retains the power to entertain without-notice applications but such cases will be exceptional and will permit those affected by the order to apply on short notice to vary or discharge the order made: see FPR PD12I. For further guidance, see CAFCASS Practice Note of 18 March 2005: *Applications for Reporting Restriction Orders* issued by the Official Solicitor and the Deputy Director of Legal Services.

****

21 Interpretation, etc

(1) In this Act –

    "amend" includes repeal and apply (with or without modifications);
    "the appropriate Minister" means the Minister of the Crown having charge of the appropriate authorised government department (within the meaning of the Crown Proceedings Act 1947);
    "the Commission" means the European Commission of Human Rights;
    "the Convention" means the Convention for the Protection of Human Rights and Fundamental Freedoms, agreed by the Council of Europe at Rome on 4 November 1950 as it has effect for the time being in relation to the United Kingdom;
    "declaration of incompatibility" means a declaration under section 4;
    "Minister of the Crown" has the same meaning as in the Ministers of the Crown Act 1975;
    "Northern Ireland Minister" includes the First Minister and the deputy First Minister in Northern Ireland;
    "primary legislation" means any –
        (a)   public general Act;
        (b)   local and personal Act;
        (c)   private Act;
        (d)   Measure of the Church Assembly;
        (e)   Measure of the General Synod of the Church of England;
        (f)   Order in Council –
            (i)   made in exercise of Her Majesty's Royal Prerogative;

PART II

(ii)   made under section 38(1)(a) of the Northern Ireland Constitution Act 1973 or the corresponding provision of the Northern Ireland Act 1998; or

(iii)   amending an Act of a kind mentioned in paragraph (a), (b) or (c);

and includes an order or other instrument made under primary legislation (otherwise than by the Welsh Ministers, the First Minister for Wales, the Counsel General to the Welsh Assembly Government, a member of the Scottish Executive, a Northern Ireland Minister or a Northern Ireland department) to the extent to which it operates to bring one or more provisions of that legislation into force or amends any primary legislation;

"the First Protocol" means the protocol to the Convention agreed at Paris on 20th March 1952;

"the Eleventh Protocol" means the protocol to the Convention (restructuring the control machinery established by the Convention) agreed at Strasbourg on 11 May 1994;

"the Thirteenth Protocol" means the protocol to the Convention (concerning the abolition of the death penalty in all circumstances) agreed at Vilnius on 3 May 2002;

"remedial order" means an order under section 10;

"subordinate legislation" means any –

(a)   Order in Council other than one –

(i)   made in exercise of Her Majesty's Royal Prerogative;

(ii)   made under section 38(1)(a) of the Northern Ireland Constitution Act 1973 or the corresponding provision of the Northern Ireland Act 1998; or

(iii)   amending an Act of a kind mentioned in the definition of primary legislation;

(b)   Act of the Scottish Parliament;

(ba) Measure of the National Assembly for Wales;

(bb) Act of the National Assembly for Wales;

(c)   Act of the Parliament of Northern Ireland;

(d)   Measure of the Assembly established under section 1 of the Northern Ireland Assembly Act 1973;

(e)   Act of the Northern Ireland Assembly;

(f)   order, rules, regulations, scheme, warrant, byelaw or other instrument made under primary legislation (except to the extent to which it operates to bring one or more provisions of that legislation into force or amends any primary legislation);

(g)   order, rules, regulations, scheme, warrant, byelaw or other instrument made under legislation mentioned in paragraph (b), (c), (d) or (e) or made under an Order in Council applying only to Northern Ireland;

(h)   order, rules, regulations, scheme, warrant, byelaw or other instrument made by a member of the Scottish Executive, Welsh Ministers, the First Minister for Wales, the Counsel General to the Welsh Assembly Government, a Northern Ireland Minister or a Northern Ireland department in exercise of prerogative or other executive functions of Her Majesty which are exercisable by such a person on behalf of Her Majesty;

"transferred matters" has the same meaning as in the Northern Ireland Act 1998; and

"tribunal" means any tribunal in which legal proceedings may be brought.

(2) The references in paragraphs (b) and (c) of section 2(1) to Articles are to Articles of the Convention as they had effect immediately before the coming into force of the Eleventh Protocol.

(3) The reference in paragraph (d) of section 2(1) to Article 46 includes a reference to Articles 32 and 54 of the Convention as they had effect immediately before the coming into force of the Eleventh Protocol.

(4) The references in section 2(1) to a report or decision of the Commission or a decision of the Committee of Ministers include references to a report or decision made as provided by paragraphs 3, 4 and 6 of Article 5 of the Eleventh Protocol (transitional provisions).

(5) Any liability under the Army Act 1955, the Air Force Act 1955 or the Naval Discipline Act 1957 to suffer death for an offence is replaced by a liability to imprisonment for life or any less punishment authorised by those Acts; and those Acts shall accordingly have effect with the necessary modifications.

Amendments—SI 2004/1574; Government of Wales Act 2006, Sch 10, para 56.

Primary legislation—This is not limited to Acts of Parliament (public general, local and personal or private) but includes Orders made in Council (a) under the Royal Prerogative and (b) amending Acts of Parliament.

Subordinate legislation—In the interests of maintaining the sovereignty of the UK Parliament, Acts and other measures passed by the Scottish Parliament, the National Assembly for Wales or the Northern Ireland Assembly are all subordinate and not primary legislation.

Remedial order—A remedial order pursuant to s 10 is the fast-track procedure by which a minister may amend primary or secondary legislation to remove its incompatibility with the Convention either as a result of a declaration of incompatibility or in consequence of a decision of the ECtHR, if there are "compelling reasons" for so doing. The "standard procedure" requires the minister to lay a draft statutory instrument before Parliament that will not come into effect unless approved by a resolution of both Houses: Sch 2, para 2(a). The emergency procedure requires the minister to lay a draft statutory instrument before Parliament but it has immediate effect and will cease to have effect 120 days after it was made unless approved by a resolution of both Houses: Schedule 2, para 2(b). The emergency procedure must only be used where it appears to the minister that the urgency of the matter requires it.

****

SCHEDULE 1

THE ARTICLES

PART I
THE CONVENTION

Rights and Freedoms

Article 2 – Right to life

1 Everyone's right to life shall be protected by law. No one shall be deprived of his life intentionally save in the execution of a sentence of a court following his conviction of a crime for which this penalty is provided by law.

2 Deprivation of life shall not be regarded as inflicted in contravention of this Article when it results from the use of force which is no more than absolutely necessary:

(a) in defence of any person from unlawful violence;
(b) in order to effect a lawful arrest or to prevent the escape of a person lawfully detained;
(c) in action lawfully taken for the purpose of quelling a riot or insurrection.

Death penalty—The use of the death penalty was abolished by Protocol 6, save during time of war or of imminent threat of war, and in all circumstances by Protocol 13. No derogations or reservations may be made in respect of the abolition of the death penalty.

Everyone's right to life—The issue arises of whether an unborn foetus has the right to life. In *Vo v France* [2004] ECHR 326 at [75], [82], the Grand Chamber of the ECtHR held that in the absence of a European consensus on when human life begins, the issue falls within the margin of appreciation to be accorded to each State. In *Evans v United Kingdom* [2007] 1 FLR 1990 at [55], [56], the Grand Chamber referred to the English authorities that a foetus does not have a right to life and accordingly found there had been no breach of Art 2. In *A, B & C v Ireland* [2010] ECHR 2032 at [237] the Grand Chambers held that "of central importance is the finding in the above-cited *Vo* case, referred to above, that the question of when the right to life begins came within the States' margin of appreciation because there was no European consensus on the scientific and legal definition of the beginning of life, so that it was impossible to answer the question whether the unborn was a person to be protected for the purposes of Article 2. Since the rights claimed on behalf of the foetus and those of the mother are inextricably interconnected ... the margin of appreciation accorded to a State's protection of the unborn necessarily translates into a margin of appreciation for that State as to how it balances the conflicting rights of the mother".

Positive obligations—The Article imposes positive obligations on the State to protect the right to life. To be engaged the State authorities must have known or ought to have known that there was a real and immediate risk to life and yet failed to take measures within the scope of their power which, judged reasonably, might have been expected to avoid that risk: *Osman v UK* [1999] 1 FLR 193; *Van Colle v Chief Constable of Hertfordshire Police* [2009] 1 AC 225. The article imposed on the State operational obligations to protect mentally ill patients who were not detained under MHA 1983 where there was a real and immediate risk of suicide: *Rabone & Othrs v Pennine Care NHS Trust* [2012] UKSC 2.

Prohibition—The Article prohibits the taking of life intentionally or unintentionally, where the force used is more than absolutely necessary: *Osman* (above) and *McShane v UK* [2002] ECHR 469.

Right to die—The House of Lords and the ECtHR have held that the Article does not confer a right to die: *R (Pretty) v DPP* [2002] 1 FLR 268; *Pretty v UK* [2002] 2 FLR 45. However, the House of Lords and the ECtHR disagreed on whether Article 8 was engaged in "right to die" cases: the former found not, whereas the latter found it was. The House of Lords has subsequently departed from the decision in *R (Pretty)* and found that Article 8 is engaged: *R (Purdy) v DPP* [2010] 1 AC 345.

Article 3 – Prohibition of torture

No one shall be subjected to torture or to inhuman or degrading treatment or punishment.

Prohibited activities—Torture (inhuman treatment that causes very serious and cruel suffering); inhuman treatment (treatment that causes intense physical and mental suffering); and degrading treatment (treatment that arouses in the victim a feeling of fear, anguish and inferiority capable of humiliating and debasing the victim and possibly breaking his or her physical or moral resistance): *Ireland v UK* [1978] ECHR 1. The treatment must attain a "minimum level of severity" to engage the Article (i e a high level of severity): *Chalal v UK* [1996] ECHR 54.

Negative and positive obligations—The Article imposes negative and positive obligations on the State. "There must be some distinction between the scope of the state's duty not to take life or ill-treat people in a way which falls foul of Article 3 [the negative obligation] and its duty to protect people from the harm which others may do to them [the positive obligation]. In the one case, there is an absolute duty not to do it. In the other, there is a duty to do what is reasonable in all the circumstances to protect people from a real and immediate risk of harm": *Re E (A Child) (Northern Ireland)* [2009] AC 536, per Baroness Hale at [10].

Prevention—The State is under a positive duty to protect children from chronic neglect and abuse. Where children have so suffered and where the authorities knew but failed to take any action or any timeous action, the State is likely to be found in breach of the Article and liable to the children for damages: *A v UK* [1998] 2 FLR 959; *Z v UK* [2001] 2 FLR 612; *E & Others v UK* [2003] 1 FLR 348; *Mayeka v Belgium* [2007] 1 FLR 1726 (ECHR).

Article 4 – Prohibition of slavery and forced labour

1 No one shall be held in slavery or servitude.

2 No one shall be required to perform forced or compulsory labour.

3 For the purpose of this Article the term "forced or compulsory labour" shall not include:

   (a)   any work required to be done in the ordinary course of detention imposed according to the provisions of Article 5 of this Convention or during conditional release from such detention;

   (b)   any service of a military character or, in case of conscientious objectors in countries where they are recognised, service exacted instead of compulsory military service;

   (c)   any service exacted in case of an emergency or calamity threatening the life or well-being of the community;

   (d)   any work or service which forms part of normal civic obligations.

Article 5 – Right to liberty and security

1 Everyone has the right to liberty and security of person. No one shall be deprived of his liberty save in the following cases and in accordance with a procedure prescribed by law –

   (a)   the lawful detention of a person after conviction by a competent court;

   (b)   the lawful arrest or detention of a person for non-compliance with the lawful order of a court or in order to secure the fulfilment of any obligation prescribed by law;

   (c)   the lawful arrest or detention of a person effected for the purpose of bringing him before the competent legal authority on reasonable suspicion of having committed an offence or when it is reasonably considered necessary to prevent his committing an offence or fleeing after having done so;

   (d)   the detention of a minor by lawful order for the purpose of educational supervision or his lawful detention for the purpose of bringing him before the competent legal authority;

   (e)   the lawful detention of persons for the prevention of the spreading of infectious diseases, of persons of unsound mind, alcoholics or drug addicts or vagrants;

   (f)   the lawful arrest or detention of a person to prevent his effecting an unauthorised entry into the country or of a person against whom action is being taken with a view to deportation or extradition.

2 Everyone who is arrested shall be informed promptly, in a language which he understands, of the reasons for his arrest and of any charge against him.

3 Everyone arrested or detained in accordance with the provisions of paragraph 1(c) of this Article shall be brought promptly before a judge or other officer authorised by law to exercise judicial power and shall be entitled to trial within a reasonable time or to release pending trial. Release may be conditioned by guarantees to appear for trial.

4 Everyone who is deprived of his liberty by arrest or detention shall be entitled to take proceedings by which the lawfulness of his detention shall be decided speedily by a court and his release ordered if the detention is not lawful.

5 Everyone who has been the victim of arrest or detention in contravention of the provisions of this Article shall have an enforceable right to compensation.

Deprivation of liberty—Has three elements; (i) the objective element of a person's confinement to a certain limited place for a not negligible length of time; (ii) the additional subjective element that they had not validly consented to the confinement in question; and (iii) the confinement had to be imputable to the state: *Storck v Germany* (2006) 43 EHRR 6.

Assessing whether Art 5 engaged—The criteria for assessing whether there had been a deprivation of liberty such as to engage art 5 are: (i) whether objections to the arrangements had been expressed; (ii) whether drugs which might suppress the expression of objections had been used; and (iii) the normality of the living arrangements and the opportunities for leaving the place of residence for the purposes of recreation, education and social contact: *P & Q (by their Litigation Friend The Official Solicitor) v Surrey County Council & Othrs* [2011] COPLR Con Vol 931.

Article 6 – Right to a fair trial

1 In the determination of his civil rights and obligations or of any criminal charge against him, everyone is entitled to a fair and public hearing within a reasonable time by an independent and impartial tribunal established by law. Judgment shall be pronounced publicly but the press and public may be excluded from all or part of the trial in the interest of morals, public order or national security in a democratic society, where the interests of juveniles or the protection of the private life of the parties so require, or to the extent strictly necessary in the opinion of the court in special circumstances where publicity would prejudice the interests of justice.

2 Everyone charged with a criminal offence shall be presumed innocent until proved guilty according to law.

3 Everyone charged with a criminal offence has the following minimum rights –

    (a)   to be informed promptly, in a language which he understands and in detail, of the nature and cause of the accusation against him;

    (b)   to have adequate time and facilities for the preparation of his defence;

    (c)   to defend himself in person or through legal assistance of his own choosing or, if he has not sufficient means to pay for legal assistance, to be given it free when the interests of justice so require;

    (d)   to examine or have examined witnesses against him and to obtain the attendance and examination of witnesses on his behalf under the same conditions as witnesses against him;

    (e)   to have the free assistance of an interpreter if he cannot understand or speak the language used in court.

Scope—The right to a fair trial is absolute but the constituent rights are not and may be limited: the only balancing permitted is what the concept of a fair trial entails. Any limitation must satisfy the test of proportionality: *R v A* [2002] 1 AC 45 at [38].

Civil rights and obligations—Although they recognise that the meaning of the phrase is autonomous, the UK courts have tended to adopt a more restrictive interpretation than the ECtHR of what constitutes "civil rights and obligations": *R (Kehoe) v Secretary of State for Work & Pensions* [2005] 2 FLR 1249 (no right to apply to court to recover child maintenance); *R (A) v Croydon LBC; R (M) v Lambeth LBC* [2009] 1 FLR 1324 (CA) at [50]–[59] (asylum-seeker's "right" to accommodation under s 20 CA 1989); and *Ali & Others v Birmingham City Council & Others* [2010] 2 AC 39 (cases where the award of services or benefits in kind was not an individual right of which the applicant could consider himself the holder, but rather was dependent upon a series of evaluative judgments by the provider did not engage Art 6(1)).

Rights protected—The rights protected by the Article include: (i) access to a court (*Golder v UK* (1975) 1 EHRR 524); (ii) which is real and effective (*Steel & Morris v UK* [2005] ECHR 103); (iii) a hearing before an independent and impartial tribunal established by law (*McGonnell v UK* [2000] ECHR 62); (iv) in public; (v) within a reasonable time (*Adam v Germany* [2009] 1 FLR 560 (ECtHR)); (vi) with a real opportunity to present a case, including "equality of arms" or an oral hearing if required in the circumstances (*Ruiz-Mateos v Spain* (1993) 16 EHRR 505); and (vii) a reasoned decision (*English v Emery, Reimbold & Strick* [2002] 1 WLR 2409).

Public hearing—There are exceptions to the right to a public hearing and the ECtHR has accepted the general presumption of hearings concerning children being held in private (*B v UK* [2000] 1 FLR 1). The requirement for judgment to be pronounced publicly does not necessarily require the judgment to be delivered in open court but simply that the decision is made public.

Provision of legal assistance—There is no automatic right under the Convention for legal aid or legal representation (save in respect of those charged with a criminal offence under Article 6.3(c)), but where fairness or the right of a party to put forward his case in a proper and effective manner so requires, the absence of a lawyer to represent the party may render the proceedings unfair (*P, C & S v UK* [2002] 2 FLR 631 (ECHR) (contested care and freeing for adoption proceedings)).

Requirements—"The single theme which runs through the whole of Article 6 is the right of a litigant or an accused to have a fair trial ... But while there can be no doubt that the right to a fair trial is an absolute right, precisely what is comprised in the concept of fairness may be open to a varied analysis. It is not to be supposed that the content of the right is necessarily composed of rigid rules which provide an absolute protection for an accused person under every circumstance ...The jurisprudence of the ECtHR demonstrates that several of the particular rights which ... by implication fall within the scope of Article 6 are not absolute rights.": *Brown v Stott (Procurator Fiscal, Dunfermline) & Another* [2003] 1 AC 681, per Lord Clyde. For an overview of the principles for and requirements of a fair trial see *Re B (Disclosure to Other Parties)* [2001] 2 FLR 1017 at [33]–[68]; *Re L (Care: Assessment: Fair Trial)* [2002] 2 FLR 730, at [86]–[106].

Article 7 – No punishment without law

1 No one shall be held guilty of any criminal offence on account of any act or omission which did not constitute a criminal offence under national or international law at the time when it was committed. Nor shall a heavier penalty be imposed than the one that was applicable at the time the criminal offence was committed.

2 This Article shall not prejudice the trial and punishment of any person for any act or omission which, at the time when it was committed, was criminal according to the general principles of law recognised by civilised nations.

Article 8 – Right to respect for private and family life

1 Everyone has the right to respect for his private and family life, his home and his correspondence.

2 There shall be no interference by a public authority with the exercise of this right except such as is in accordance with the law and is necessary in a democratic society in the interests of national security, public safety or the economic well-being of the country, for the prevention of disorder or crime, for the protection of health or morals, or for the protection of the rights and freedoms of others.

Scope—There are four elements protected by the Article: (i) private life; (ii) family life; (iii) home; and (iv) correspondence, but the effect of the Article, as interpreted by the ECtHR and domestic courts, protects a diverse range of rights most notably a right to privacy. The protection afforded by the Article is qualified: an interference with a right protected by Article 8(1) is only permissible insofar as it is (i) in accordance with the law; (ii) necessary in a democratic society; and (iii) the degree of interference is proportionate to the objective sought to be achieved by the state.

Private life—The extent of the meaning of the phrase "private life" cannot be identified but it includes the notion of "personal autonomy", "physical & mental integrity", the protection of one's reputation" and extends to "those features which are integral to a person's identity or ability to function socially as a person": *R (Razgar) v Secretary of State for the Home Department* [2004] 2 AC 368. The House of Lords has held that the right to private life is engaged when an individual suffering from a terminal illness chooses death rather than life: *R (Purdy) v DPP* [2010] 1 AC 345.

Family life—There is no clear definition of what is meant by "family life". "The existence or non-existence of 'family life' for the purposes of Art 8 is essentially a question of fact depending upon the real existence in practice of close personal ties", which "has sufficient constancy and substance to create de facto 'family ties'": *Lebbink v The Netherlands* [2004] 2 FLR 463 at [36]. Family life is not confined to married couples or to cohabiting couples and can exist even where there is no biological relationship between parent and child: *Singh v Entry Clearance Officer, New Delhi* [2005] 1 FLR 308 at [58]–[80]. The right to start a family is not protected by the right to respect for family life: *Evans v UK* [2007] 1 FLR 1990 (ECHR Grand Chamber).

Balancing of rights—Where the rights under Art 8 of parents and those of a child are at stake, the child's rights must be the paramount consideration. If any balancing of the interests of the child, on the one hand, and of the parents, on the other, is necessary, the interests of the child must prevail: *Yousef v The Netherlands* [2003] 1 FLR 210.

Home—Whether a place is or is not a "home" is fact-specific and depends on there being sufficient and continuous links. "Home" has been held to include a long-stay hospital and second homes: *R v North &*

East Devon District Health Authority, ex p Coughlan [2001] QB 213 (CA). An order for possession of a property does infringe Article 8(1) but county courts may assume that domestic law satisfies the requirements of 8(2) and would not generally need to apply the proportionality test: *Kay v Lambeth LBC* [2006] 2 AC 465.

Right to privacy—The approach of the domestic courts to an action for breach of confidence has dramatically changed in light of Article 8. The new approach "focuses upon the protection of human autonomy and dignity – the right to control the dissemination of information about one's private life and the right to the esteem and respect of other people": *Campbell v MGN* [2004] 2 AC 457 at [51]. See the notes below to Article 10 and the balance between the protection of private life and right to freedom of expression.

Fairness—Although the Article contains no explicit procedural requirements, it is clear that the provision affords significant procedural safeguards: thus "the decision-making process leading to measures of interference must be fair and such as to afford due respect to the interests safeguard by Art 8": *McMichael v UK* (1995) 20 EHRR 205 at [87]. Accordingly, local authorities must ensure that parents are sufficiently involved in the decision-making process before and during court proceedings and must make full and proper disclosure: *Re L (Care: Assessment: Fair Trial)* (above); *Re G (Care: Challenge to Local Authority's Decision)* [2003] 2 FLR 42 at [28]–[60]. However, the mere failure to observe these precepts does not automatically or necessarily result in a finding that a parent's human rights have been breached or render the proceedings unfair: *Re V (Care: Pre-Birth Actions)* [2005] 1 FLR 627 at [4], [24], [29], [33]; *Re J (Care: Assessment: Fair Trial)* [2007] 1 FLR 77 at [25]–[30].

Care orders—A court must not sanction a care plan providing for the removal of a child from his family "unless he is satisfied that that is both necessary and proportionate and that no other less radical form of order would achieve the essential end of promoting the welfare of the child": *Re B (Care: Interference with Family Life)* [2003] 2 FLR 813 at [34].

Forced marriages—Under an amendment to the Immigration Rules, the age at which foreign spouses were banned from entering the UK for settlement was increased from 18 to 21. The Supreme Court held that the amendment pursued a legitimate aim of deterring forced marriage but was not necessary in a democratic society in that it was not a proportionate response to the problem caused by forced marriage: *R (Quila); R (Bibi) v Secretary of State for the Home Department* [2012] 1 FLR 788.

Lack of capacity—The force-feeding of a patient who lacked capacity for the purposes of MCA 2005, s 2(1) was found to be in her best interests. The resulting interference in her Arts 3 and 8 rights was proportionate and necessary to protect her right to life: *A Local Authority v E and Others* [2012] COPLR 441.

Immigration and extradition cases—*Norris v United States* [2010] UKSC 9 had not decided that the Art 8 rights of the family of a proposed extradite could never prevail unless an exceptionality test was satisfied: exceptionality was a prediction and not a test. The need to examine the way the process would interfere with the children's best interests was just as great in extradition cases as it was in cases of immigration control: *HH & PH v Italy; FK v Poland* [2013] 1 AC 338.

Article 9 – Freedom of thought, conscience and religion

1 Everyone has the right to freedom of thought, conscience and religion; this right includes freedom to change his religion or belief and freedom, either alone or in community with others and in public or private, to manifest his religion or belief, in worship, teaching, practice and observance.

2 Freedom to manifest one's religion or beliefs shall be subject only to such limitations as are prescribed by law and are necessary in a democratic society in the interests of public safety, for the protection of public order, health or morals, or for the protection of the rights and freedoms of others.

Foster carers—A local authority did not discriminate against a couple on grounds of religion when refusing to approve them as foster carers because of their views on sexuality, namely that sexual relations other than those within marriage between one man and one woman were morally wrong: *R (Eunice Johns & Owen Johns) v Derby City Council & Othrs* [2011] 1 FLR 2094).

Article 10 – Freedom of expression

1 Everyone has the right to freedom of expression. This right shall include freedom to hold opinions and to receive and impart information and ideas without interference by public authority and regardless of frontiers. This Article shall not prevent States from requiring the licensing of broadcasting, television or cinema enterprises.

2 The exercise of these freedoms, since it carries with it duties and responsibilities, may be subject to such formalities, conditions, restrictions or penalties as are prescribed by law and are necessary in a democratic society, in the interests of national security, territorial integrity or public safety, for the prevention of disorder or crime, for the protection of health or morals, for the protection of the reputation or rights of others, for preventing the disclosure of information received in confidence, or for maintaining the authority and impartiality of the judiciary.

Scope—The rights protected under Article 10 are seen to be essential to a democratic society. The protection is afforded to natural and legal persons, including commercial companies. The rights are not limited to freedom of expression but include rights to receive information but the Article does not give rise to a general right to freedom of information: the latter may arise consequentially to protect another right: *Gaskin v UK* [1990] 1 FLR 167.

Press freedom—The courts have long recognised the importance to be accorded to the freedom of the press. Lord Bingham noted that "the proper functioning of a modern participatory democracy requires that the media be free, active, professional and inquiring. For this reason, the courts, here and elsewhere, have recognised the cardinal importance of press freedom": *Turkington & Others v Times Newspapers Ltd (Northern Ireland)* [2001] 2 AC 277.

s 12 HRA—The courts are enjoined to have "particular regard" to the importance of the freedom of expression when considering the grant of injunctive relief. By ss 12(2),(3) courts should not grant without notice orders restraining freedom of expression without strong justification for so doing.

Limitations—Although the possible limitations on the rights are couched in wide terms, the ECtHR requires a strong justification for interfering with the right. To justify interference it must be (i) in accordance with law, (ii) in pursuance of a legitimate aim and (iii) necessary in a democratic society: *Sunday Times v UK (No.1)* (1979) 2 EHRR 245. The extent and duration of an obstruction of the highway and the public nuisance inherent in that obstruction may warrant an interference with protesters' rights under Arts 10 and 11 if lawful, necessary and proportionate (*City of London v Tammy Samede (Representative of those Persons Taking Part in a Protest Camp at St Paul's Churchyard, London EC4) & Othrs* [2012] EWHC 34 (QB)).

Court of Protection—Art 10 is engaged when the media first make an application to attend a hearing and not merely once a "good reason" for the application had been established: *Independent News & Media v A* [2010] COPLR Con Vol 686.

When determining issues under MCA 2005, a judge should first ascertain the best interests of the patient by applying the s 4 checklist of factors and only then consider whether the resulting conclusion amounted to a violation of the patient's rights under Art 8 and whether the violation was necessary and proportionate; Art 8 is not the starting point: *K v LBX and Others* [2012] COPLR 411.

Conflict with other Convention rights—The leading case in domestic law is *Re S (A Child) (Identification Restrictions on Publication)* [2005] 1 FLR 591. Lord Steyn said, at [17], "First, neither Article has as such precedence over the other. Secondly, where the values under the two Articles are in conflict, an intense focus on the comparative importance of the specific rights being claimed in the individual case is necessary. Thirdly, the justifications for interfering with or restricting each right must be taken into account. Finally, the proportionality test must be applied to each. For convenience I will call this the ultimate balancing test."

Injunctions preventing publication—Where a court proposed to make an injunction prohibiting the publication of information with a view to preventing an interference in the claimant's Art 8 rights, it was important that the order contained the undertakings required by CPR PD25A and the Master of the Rolls' Practice Guidance: *Interim Non-Disclosure Orders: AM v News Group Newspapers Ltd & Persons Unknown* [2012] EWHC 308.

Anonymisation of proceedings—When granting an injunction to restrain the publication of information in order to prevent an interference with a claimant's Art 8 rights, the general rule was that parties' names would be included in the court's orders and judgments; there was no general exception for cases where private matters were in issue. Anonymising the proceedings was an exceptional course to take: *Spelman (A Child by his Litigation Friends) v Express Newspapers* [2012] EWHC 239 (QB).

Article 11 – Freedom of assembly and association

1 Everyone has the right to freedom of peaceful assembly and to freedom of association with others, including the right to form and to join trade unions for the protection of his interests.

2 No restrictions shall be placed on the exercise of these rights other than such as are prescribed by law and are necessary in a democratic society in the interests of national security or public safety, for the prevention of disorder or crime, for the protection of health or morals or for the protection of the rights and freedoms of others. This Article shall not prevent the imposition of lawful restrictions on the exercise of these rights by members of the armed forces, of the police or of the administration of the State.

Article 12 – Right to marry

Men and women of marriageable age have the right to marry and to found a family, according to the national laws governing the exercise of this right.

Scope—Two rights are expressed in this Article: (i) the right to marry and (ii) the right to found a family. National States are, however, given a wide discretion to govern the exercise of these rights. The ECtHR has construed the provisions more narrowly than those under Article 8. An interference with family life that is justified under 8(2) cannot be a violation of Article 12: *Boso v Italy* [2002] ECHR 846.

National laws—There is a limit to the extent to which national laws may regulate the exercise of Article 12 rights – the rules must not be arbitrary or interfere with the essence of the right: *B v UK* (2004) 39 EHRR 30 (prohibition on father-in-law and daughter-in-law marrying save if waiver obtained by way of private Act of Parliament). The government is entitled to enact measures to prevent "sham" marriages by those subject to immigration control, but the scheme must not disproportionately infringe the rights of non-nationals: *R (Baiai & Others) v Secretary of State for the Home Department* [2008] 2 FLR 1462 (HL) and *Aguilar v Secretary of State for the Home Department* [2011] 1 FLR 1187). A ban on transsexuals, who had undergone gender reassignment, to marry was held not to be justified and in the UK led to the passing of the GRA 2004: *Goodwin v UK* [2002] 2 FLR 487; *Bellinger v Bellinger* [2003] 1 FLR 1043.

Same-sex marriages—These are not recognised or protected by the Article: *Wilkinson v Kitzinger* [2006] 2 FLR 397 and [2007] 1 FLR 295.

Right to found a family—The Article does not create a freestanding right to found a family in the absence of a marital relationship: *Marckx v Belgium* (1979) 2 EHRR 330.

****

Article 14 – Prohibition of discrimination

The enjoyment of the rights and freedoms set forth in this Convention shall be secured without discrimination on any ground such as sex, race, colour, language, religion, political or other opinion, national or social origin, association with a national minority, property, birth or other status.

Scope—The Article provides a limited degree of protection. It does not create a freestanding right of equal treatment but merely a right to equal treatment in the application of other rights afforded by the Convention. A breach of another Convention right is not a prerequisite for the finding of a breach of the Article but the facts relied on to demonstrate discrimination must come within the ambit of one or more other Convention rights: *Abdulaziz & Others v UK* (1985) 7 EHRR 471; *Ghaidan v Godin-Mendoza* [2004] 2 FLR 600.

Foreign nationals—In the absence of exceptional circumstances, aliens could not claim any entitlement under the European Convention to remain in England to escape from the discriminatory effects of the system of family law in their country of origin and could not rely on the rights protected by Article 14. It was not enough to show that a child custody regime was arbitrary and discriminatory; an applicant had to show that return to such a regime would completely deny or nullify her own and the child's right to respect for family life together: *EM (Lebanon) v Secretary of State for the Home Department* [2008] 2 FLR 2067 (HL).

European case-law—In cases where an applicant alleges a breach of a substantive Convention right and a breach of Article 14, the ECtHR invariably will not consider the claim under Article 14 if it finds a breach of the former (e g *S & Marper v UK* [2008] ECHR 1581).

****

Article 16 – Restrictions on political activity of aliens

Nothing in Articles 10, 11 and 14 shall be regarded as preventing the High Contracting Parties from imposing restrictions on the political activity of aliens.

Article 17 – Prohibition of abuse of rights

Nothing in this Convention may be interpreted as implying for any State, group or person any right to engage in any activity or perform any act aimed at the destruction of any of the rights and freedoms set forth herein or at their limitation to a greater extent than is provided for in the Convention.

Article 18 – Limitation on use of restrictions on rights

The restrictions permitted under this Convention to the said rights and freedoms shall not be applied for any purpose other than those for which they have been prescribed.

PART II
THE FIRST PROTOCOL

Article 1 – Protection of property

Every natural or legal person is entitled to the peaceful enjoyment of his possessions. No one shall be deprived of his possessions except in the public interest and subject to the conditions provided for by law and by the general principles of international law.

The preceding provisions shall not, however, in any way impair the right of a State to enforce such laws as it deems necessary to control the use of property in accordance with the general interest or to secure the payment of taxes or other contributions or penalties.

Scope—The Article comprises three distinct but not unconnected rules: the principle of the peaceful enjoyment of property; the deprivation of possessions subject to conditions; and the recognition that states are entitled to control the use of property (*Allard v Sweden* (2004) 39 EHRR 321).

Positive obligations—The ECtHR has held that a "state may be responsible under Art 1 for interferences with peaceful enjoyment of possessions resulting from transactions between private individuals" (*Gustafson v Sweden* (1996) 22 EHRR 409).The court's approach to positive and negative obligations under Art 1 are similar. In both contexts, regard must be had "to the fair balance to be struck between the competing interests of the individual and of the community as a whole" and "the state enjoys a certain margin of appreciation in determining the steps to be taken to ensure compliance with the Convention..." (*Broniowski v Poland* (2005) 40 EHRR 495).

Possessions—The term embraces a broad range of property rights. The concept, however, extends far beyond real and personal property to include all manner of things that have an economic value (e g planning permission: *Pine Valley Developments Ltd v Ireland* (1992) 14 EHRR 319).

Deprivation—Destruction of property constitutes a deprivation (*Isayeva v Russia* (2005) 41 EHRR 847. For a de facto deprivation through expropriation to arise, there must effectively be an extinction of property rights (*Papamichalopoulos v Greece* (1993) 16 EHRR 440).

Conditions for permitted deprivations—The measure must be in accordance with national law, respect the general principles of international law and be in the public interest, which requires a balancing of the public interest against individual rights. Thus, the measure must be sufficiently precise and foreseeable in its consequences and have appropriate procedural guarantees (*Hentrich v France* (1994) 18 EHRR 440; *R (on the application of Bizzy B Management Ltd) v Stockton-on-Tees Borough Council)* [2011] EWHC 2325 (Admin)).

Balancing public interest against individual rights—A compulsory purchase order for the acquisition of a derelict residential property by a local authority did not contravene the property owner's rights under the Article (*Terry Navarro Peart v Secretary of State for Transport, Local Government & Regions* [2003] EWCA Civ 295). Legislation banning the sale of tobacco from automatic vending machines pursued a legitimate public health aim and was not a disproportionate interference with the claimant's economic rights (*R (on the application of Sinclair Collis Ltd) v Secretary of State for Health* [2011] LLR 592).

Article 2 – Right to education

No person shall be denied the right to education. In the exercise of any functions which it assumes in relation to education and to teaching, the State shall respect the right of parents to ensure such education and teaching in conformity with their own religious and philosophical convictions.

Scope—The negative formulation of the first sentence means that "there is no obligation on a state to establish at its own expense, or to subsidise, education of any particular type or at any level" (*Belgian Linguistic Case* (1979–80) 1 EHRR 252). The scope of the second sentence is far wider and the rights protected are those of parents. The objectives of this provision are to safeguard the possibility of pluralism in education and to prevent the state pursuing an aim of indoctrination that might be considered as not respecting parents' religious and philosophical convictions (*Kjeldsen & Othrs v Denmark* (1979–80) 1 EHRR 711; *Campbell & Cosans v UK* (1982) 4 EHRR 293).

Limitations—The Article does not confer a right to be educated at a particular school but rather confers a right not to be denied access to the general level of educational provision available in the Member State (*Ali v Headteacher and Governors of Lord Grey School* [2006] 2 AC 363). The Article does not impose on contracting states a positive obligation to provide education that caters for the special needs of the small, if significant, portion of the population who could not profit from mainstream education (e g those with special education needs). The authorities assumed that all contracting states had an education system and limited the positive obligation imposed by the Article to regulating education in such a way as to give access without discrimination to that system (*A v Essex County Council* [2011] AC 280).

****

Inheritance (Provision for Family and Dependants) Act 1975

ARRANGEMENT OF SECTIONS

Powers of court to order financial provision from deceased's estate

Powers of court to order financial provision from deceased's estate

1 Application for financial provision from deceased's estate

(1) Where after the commencement of this Act a person dies domiciled in England and Wales and is survived by any of the following persons –

(a) the spouse or civil partner of the deceased;

(b) a former spouse or former civil partner of the deceased, but not one who has formed a subsequent marriage or civil partnership;

(ba) any person (not being a person included in paragraph (a) or (b) above) to whom subsection (1A) or (1B) below applies;

(c) a child of the deceased;

(d) any person (not being a child of the deceased) who, in the case of any marriage or civil partnership to which the deceased was at any time a party, was treated by the deceased as a child of the family in relation to that marriage or civil partnership;

(e) any person (not being a person included in the foregoing paragraphs of this subsection) who immediately before the death of the deceased was being maintained, either wholly or partly, by the deceased;

that person may apply to the court for an order under section 2 of this Act on the ground that the disposition of the deceased's estate affected by his will or the law relating to intestacy, or the combination of his will and that law, is not such as to make reasonable financial provision for the applicant.

(1A) This subsection applies to a person if the deceased died on or after 1 January 1996 and, during the whole of the period of two years ending immediately before the date when the deceased died, the person was living –

  (a)   in the same household as the deceased, and
  (b)   as the husband or wife of the deceased.

(1B) This subsection applies to a person if for the whole of the period of two years ending immediately before the date when the deceased died the person was living –

  (a)   in the same household as the deceased, and
  (b)   as the civil partner of the deceased.

(2) In this Act "reasonable financial provision" –

  (a)   in the case of an application made by virtue of subsection (1)(a) above by the husband or wife of the deceased (except where the marriage with the deceased was the subject of a decree of judicial separation and at the date of death the decree was in force and the separation was continuing), means such financial provision as it would be reasonable in all the circumstances of the case for a husband or wife to receive, whether or not that provision is required for his or her maintenance;

  (aa) in the case of an application made by virtue of subsection (1)(a) above by the civil partner of the deceased (except where, at the date of death, a separation order under Chapter 2 of Part 2 of the Civil Partnership Act 2004 was in force in relation to the civil partnership and the separation was continuing), means such financial provision as it would be reasonable in all the circumstances of the case for a civil partner to receive, whether or not that provision is required for his or her maintenance;

  (b)   in the case of any other application made by virtue of subsection (1) above, means such financial provision as it would be reasonable in all the circumstances of the case for the applicant to receive for his maintenance.

(3) For the purposes of subsection (1)(e) above, a person shall be treated as being maintained by the deceased, either wholly or partly, as the case may be, if the deceased, otherwise than for full valuable consideration, was making a substantial contribution in money or money's worth towards the reasonable needs of that person.

Amendments—Law Reform (Succession) Act 1995, s 2; CPA 2004, s 71, Sch 4, para 15(1)–(6).

Defined terms—"former wife", "former husband": s 25(1).

"person dies domiciled in England and Wales" (s 1(1))—The issue of domicile of the deceased is the first precondition that must be established when applying for relief under the Act. Domicile is a legal concept that is not easily defined. For a summary of the law and reported cases, see Andrew Francis: *Inheritance Act Claims Law Practice and Procedure* (Jordan Publishing Ltd) and Nasreen Pearce *Inheritance Act Claims* (Wildy, Simmonds & Hill Publishing) and *Wills, Probate and Administration Service* (Butterworths). The issue of the court's jurisdiction on the basis that the deceased, who was of Turkish Cypriot extraction, had not lost his domicile of origin was raised by the defendants in *Holliday v Musa* [2010] 2 FLR 702 in a claim made by the deceased's partner under the Act. The Court of Appeal, in dismissing their appeal, followed the decision in *Cyganik v Agulian* [2006] EWCA Civ 129 and the principles laid down in *Re Fuld's Estate (No 3)* [1968] P 675. In relation to jurisdiction in divorce proceedings, see in *Olafisoye v Olafisoye* [2011] 2 FLR 553. See also *Perdoni v Curati* [2011] EWHC 3442 (Ch).

"spouse of the deceased" (s 1(1)(a))—For meaning see s 25(4). The meaning of a void marriage under s 25(4) is the same as in MCA 1973, s 11. For a ceremony of marriage to create a void marriage it has to at least purport to be a marriage contemplated by the Marriage Acts and it must have been entered into in good faith (*Gandhi v Patel* [2002] 1 FLR 603). Where a presumption of marriage by cohabitation and reputation is claimed, the presumption requires extended period of cohabitation, the couple's acquisition of reputation of being husband and wife and some positive evidence from which it could be inferred that the statutory requirements for marriage had been complied (*Al-Saedy v Musawi (Presumption of Marriage)* [2011] 2 FLR 287). In relation to a religious ceremony entered into in Pakistan by a couple from the Pakistani Ahmadi community, the court regarded it as a customary marriage that was informally recognised in Pakistan as a valid marriage and was thus entitled to be recognised in England (*R v M (Validity of Foreign Marriage)* [2011] Fam Law 1074). Furthermore, having regard to the decision in *Al-Saedy* (above), it may be argued that on the facts a presumption of marriage was made out. In relation to a religious marriage generally, see *El Gamal v Al-Maktoum* [2012] 2 FLR 387 and *Dukali v Lamrani (Attorney-General Intervening)* [2012] 2 FLR 1099, where the court declared a non-marriage. Contrast with *MA v JA* [2012] EWHC 2219 (Fam), where the religious ceremony was recognised on the basis that the marriage ceremony was conducted by an authorised person, was celebrated in an authorised place and both parties genuinely believed that they had undergone a valid marriage recognised under English Law. In relation to marriages of convenience, see *Adetola v First-Tier Tribunal (Immigration and Asylum Chamber) and SSHD* [2011] 2 FLR 611 and the cases cited therein). Although it is a case concerning succession on intestacy in relation to Administration of Estates Act 1925, s 46, *Official Solicitor to the Senior Courts v Yemoh and others* [2011] 2 FLR 371 may be relevant in cases under the Act where there are surviving polygamous spouses since it was held that for the purposes so s 46(2) of the 1925 Act surviving polygamous spouses lawfully married in accordance with the law of his or her domicile to someone dying intestate was entitled to be recognised in England and Wales as a surviving spouse in relation to the property of the intestate. By virtue of the Matrimonial Proceedings (Polygamous Marriages) Act 1972, a party to a polygamous marriage is a spouse of the deceased (*Re Sehota (dec'd), Kaur v Kaur* [1978] 1 WLR 1506). Where the marriage is polygamous and the deceased has more than one wife, each of the wives would become a widow on his death. However, their entitlement to financial provision may vary (*Bibi v Chief Adjudication Officer* [1998] 1 FLR 375). Furthermore, where, within 12 months from the date on which a decree of divorce or nullity of marriage has been made absolute or a decree of judicial separation has been granted, a party to the marriage dies and either no application for a financial provision order under MCA 1973, s 23 or s 24 has been made by the surviving spouse or such an application has been made but the proceedings thereon have not been determined at the time of death of the deceased, then, if an application under s 2 is made, the court has power, notwithstanding anything in ss 1 and 3, to treat that person as if he or she were a spouse of the deceased (s 14). The common law does not recognise same-sex marriage but the GRA 2004, which came into force on 4 April 2005, allows those who have obtained a certificate from the Gender Recognition Panel to enter into a valid marriage.

Civil partner of the deceased—For meaning see s 25(4A). CPA 2004, Sch 4 amends s 14 by extending the provisions to civil partners.

Former spouse of the deceased—In *Barrass v Harding and Newman* [2001] 1 FLR 138, where the ancillary relief proceedings were concluded 32 years before the death of the deceased and in the intervening years there was no ongoing relationship between the deceased and his first wife (but as a result of an improvement in the relationship between the deceased and his son, the deceased had given him some modest financial assistance), the Court of Appeal held that there was no basis on which an order under the Act could be justified.

"child of the deceased" (s 1(1)(c))—For meaning see s 25(1). An adopted child is treated as a legitimate child (ACA 2002, s 67). However, the provisions of these Acts are not retrospective and an illegitimate child who is later adopted by his father cannot inherit under a will made before the statutory provisions coming into effect (*Timothy Everard Upton v National Westminster Bank PLC and Others* (2004) Lawtel) but see *Pla and Puncernau v Andorra* (Application No 69498/01 ECtHR) [2004] 2 FCR 690 where it was held that an adopted child was in the same legal position as a biological child in all respects. Although not a case under the Act, in *Re Erskine Trust* [2012] 2 FLR 725 the court when construing an existing trust fund applied the European Convention and followed *Pla and Puncernau v Andorra* (above) when granting a £3.2m trust fund to two adopted children of the deceased. Any interpretation of a will/testamentary disposition should be made in the light of social, economic and legal changes and the application of the ECHR 1950, and not with regard to the conditions which existed at the time when the will or trust was made. A child who is adopted after his parent's death but before he makes his application is not a child of the deceased because, by virtue of ACA 2002, an adopted child is treated in law as the child of the adopters. The Act does not confer on such an applicant an interest expectant as he merely has a right to apply to the court for relief (*Re Collins (dec'd)* [1990] 2 FLR 72). The Law Commission in a draft Bill annexed to its report of 14 December 2011 has included provisions to protect such a child from losing an inheritance from the death of a parent. The Legitimacy Act 1976 provides that a child of a void marriage whenever born is, subject to s 2 of and Sch 1 to the Act, to be treated as a legitimate child of his parents if, at the time of the insemination resulting in the birth or, where there was no such insemination, the child's conception (or at the time of the celebration of the marriage, if later), both parties to the marriage or either of them reasonably believed that the marriage was valid. See also *Re Spence (dec'd)* [1990] 2 FLR 278. See further the provisions of the Legitimacy Act 1976 FLRA 1987 and the HFEAs 1990 and 2008, to determine who can be treated as the "father", "mother" and "parent" of a child, and the decisions in *Re B (Minors) (Parentage)* [1996] 2 FLR 15; *Re Q (Parental Order)* [1996] 1 FLR

369; and *R v Human Fertilisation and Embryology Authority ex parte Blood* [1997] 2 FLR 742. Where a child is conceived by artificial insemination before the commencement of HFEA 1990 and the provisions of FLRA 1987 apply, the reference in FLRA 1987, s 27(1)(b) to "the other party to that marriage" refers to a man and not to same-sex relationship (*J v C (Void Marriage: Status of Children)* [2006] 2 FLR 1098). Where parentage is in issue, paternity should be established by scientific means, ie, DNA (*Re H & A (Paternity: Blood Tests)* [2002] 1 FLR 1145). Where the child is a minor, FLRA 1969, s 21(3) authorises the court to order that a bodily sample be taken from a person under the age of 16 who does not consent if the court considers that it would be in his interests for the sample to be taken. The court may also draw adverse inferences if a person fails to consent to such tests.

Pursuant to regulations made under HFEA 1990 and under HFEA 2008, where a parental order has been made under s 30 of the 1990 Act and s 54 of the 2008 Act, the child who is the subject of a parental order will be treated as the child of the couple in whose favour the parental order is made. These provisions will apply to enactments and instruments, such as wills and other dispositions of property or inheritance of title, effective before the parental order was made. Practitioners should note that s 30 of HFEA 1990 has been replaced by HFEA 2008, s 54 as of 6 April 2010 to enable heterosexual married and unmarried couples and civil partners whether in a civil partnership or not to apply for a parental order. The provisions of HFEA 2008 ss 33–45 will in future result in a child born as a result of assisted reproduction to heterosexual couples or same-sex female couples being considered as a child of both parents provided that the "fatherhood" and "parenthood" conditions as appropriate are met. The provisions of AA 1976, s 42 also apply to children who are the subject of a parental order.

Cohabitant of the deceased (s 1(1)(ba),(1A))—This includes a cohabitant of the deceased who has lived with him or her in the same household as the husband or wife or as a civil partner of the deceased for a period of 2 years immediately preceding the deceased's death (see the Law Commission's Report dated 14 December 2011, which recommends and proposes in a Bill attached to the report that a person who has lived with the deceased for 5 years if there are no children and 2 years if the couple have had a child together to inherit under the intestacy rules without having to bring a claim under the Act). In *Gully v Dix* [2004] 1 FLR 918, although they had been living separately, the claimant was held to be living with the deceased in the same household at the moment of his death because their relationship had not come to an end. Where these conditions are not satisfied, the applicant will have to rely on s 1(1)(e). The question whether a person falls within s 1(1A) should be determined by asking whether in the opinion of a reasonable person with normal perceptions, it could be said that the two people in question were living together as husband and wife (*Re Watson (Deceased)* [1999] 1 FLR 878). Stability, financial support, sexual relationship, children and public acknowledgement are also relevant factors in determining whether a household has existed. The claimant's continued links with his/her country of origin, the fact that he/she has property there and a child by a previous relationship are also relevant considerations in determining whether the claim should be treated as one by a cohabitant or a dependant (*Witkowska v Kaminski* [2007] 1 FLR 1547). The mere fact that the deceased had retained a separate property, of which he made occasional use, is not in itself a barrier to establishing that he was living with the claimant in the same household. It could only be regarded as a barrier, if the fact and the extent to which the deceased maintained and made use of it and treated himself as still resident there, indicated that he and the claimant had not yet established a mutual home (*Kotke v Saffarini* [2005] 2 FLR 517). In *Lindop v Agus, Bass and Hedley* [2010] 1 FLR 631, the claimant in addition to claiming that she had lived with the deceased in the same household as husband and wife also claimed in the alternative that she had been maintained by him although she retained her postal address at her father's home. It was held that she had been maintained for the purposes of the Act at least partly by the deceased before his death in that he provided a home for which he paid all the outgoings and for transport to and from work. He had also paid for her holidays and some of her wardrobe. In *Cattle v Evans* [2011] 2 FLR 843 the final property in which the parties lived as husband and wife before the deceased died was in the sole name of the deceased. The cohabitant's claim under constructive trust failed, but on the facts the court found that no provision had been made for her and applying the s 3 criteria concluded that the claimant reasonably required housing in a property worth £100,000. In *Musa v Holliday* [2013] 1 FLR 806, the Court of Appeal approved the award to the applicant from English assets to meet her reasonable needs.

"child of the family" (s 1(1)(d))—There is no definition of "child of the family" nor any guidance in the Act as to when a person is regarded as having been treated as a child of the family. The treatment need not have occurred during the marriage provided it was "in relation to the marriage" (*Re Debenham (dec'd)* [1986] 1 FLR 404). An adult child is included. The nature of the relationship between the deceased and the applicant is the relevant factor (*Re Callaghan (dec'd)* [1985] FLR 116; *Re Leach, Leach v Lindeman* [1984] FLR 590. In each case the question will be judged by an objective test on the basis of all the facts, so that where grandparents had assumed primary responsibility for their grandchild for the foreseeable future the grandchild was a "child of the family" (*Re A (Child of the Family)* [1998] 1 FLR 347). A person may apply against the estate of his parent's civil partner if he was a child of the family (CPA 2004, Sch 4, para 15(4)). See **Other persons** for the Law Commission's recommendations. Western Australia's

Inheritance (Family and Dependants Provision) Amendment Act 2011 gives a step-child in some circumstances the right to challenge the will of his deceased parent.

"court"—Pursuant to CLSA 1990, s 1, CCA 1984, s 25 and HCCCJO 1991, art 2(1), unlimited jurisdiction is conferred on the county court in respect of claims under the I(PFD)A 1975. However, under art 7 of the 1991 Order, subject to the criteria set out in art 7(5), any action where the value of the claim (the sum which the applicant has reasonable expectancy of recovering) is less than £25,000 must be tried in the county court. Where the value of the claim is £50,000 or more, the action must be tried in the High Court unless it is commenced in the county court and the court does not consider it ought to be transferred up to the High Court. Similarly, if the action has been commenced in the High Court, that court may transfer the action down to the county court.

Other persons (s 1(1)(e))—An applicant under s 1(1)(e) must establish that he or she was being maintained, either wholly or partly, by the deceased immediately before the deceased's death (s 1(1)(e)). The Law Commission in its report and a Bill annexed to the report recommends the removal of arbitrary obstacles to claims by dependants of the deceased and anyone who is treated as a child of the family outside the context of marriage or civil partnership. The applicant must establish some sort of obligation to be maintained by the deceased beyond the fact of a relationship (*Williams v Johns* [1988] 2 FLR 475). A person is treated as being so maintained if the deceased, otherwise than for valuable consideration, was making a substantial contribution in money or money's worth towards the reasonable needs of that person (s 1(3)). For the purposes of the Act, "valuable consideration" does not include marriage or a promise of marriage (s 25(1)). In determining whether the applicant had been maintained by the deceased, the court should have regard to the extent to which, the basis upon which and the length of time for which the deceased discharged that responsibility (s 3(4)). "The court will look at the problem in the round, applying a commonsense approach, avoiding fine balancing computations involving the value of normal exchanges of support in the domestic sense" (*Bishop v Plumley* [1991] 1 FLR 121; see also *Rees v Newbery and the Institute of Cancer Research* [1998] 1 FLR 1041; *Graham v Murphy and Another* [1997] 1 FLR 860 where a male applicant succeeded in his claim, made before 1 January 1996, for financial provision from the estate of his cohabitant; as did the applicant in *Re Wilkinson, Neale v Newell* [1978] Fam 22, who had left her employment at the age of 61 to look after her brother; *Re Haig, Powers v Haig* (1979) 129 NLJ 420, where a mistress's claim was upheld; *Harrington v Gill* (1983) 4 FLR 265, where 8 years' cohabitation was held sufficient evidence of dependency; *Re Viner, Kreeger v Cooper* [1978] CLY 3091, where a weekly payment of £5 for 6 months before death was considered sufficient). In *Beaumont, Martin v Midland Bank Trust Co Ltd* [1980] Ch 444, the claim failed because the applicant had regularly paid the outgoings and other expenses. In *Baynes v Hedger* [2009] 2 FLR 767, the court dismissed a goddaughter's claim on the grounds that she was not eligible to make a claim under s 1(1)(e) as she had not been able to satisfy the court that the deceased had assumed responsibility for her maintenance. In any event there had been no failure to make reasonable financial provision for her.

The settled basis or general arrangement between the parties during the lifetime of the deceased has to be looked at, not the actual, perhaps fluctuating, variations of it which exist immediately before death. The court has to consider whether the deceased was in fact making a substantial contribution in money or money's worth towards the reasonable needs of the applicant either immediately before death or to the time that the approach of death made it impossible for either party to continue to carry out the arrangement (*Jelley v Illife* [1981] Fam 128). "Whether one person makes a substantial gratuitous contribution to another person's needs is essentially a question of fact, and the benefactor's motives or intentions are irrelevant except so far as s 3(4) makes them relevant to the court's task in deciding whether to make provision for the claimant, and if so in what form and on what scale. Even when s 3(4) is taken into account this court has taken the view that actions speak louder than words" (per Robert Walker LJ in *Bouette v Rose* [2000] 1 FLR 363).

"immediately before the death" (s 1(1)(e))—See *Re Beaumont, Martin v Midland Bank Trust Ltd*; *Kourkgy v Lusher* (1983) 4 FLR 65, where the claim failed because cohabitation came to an end nine days before the deceased's death; and *Layton v Martin* [1986] 2 FLR 227, where cohabitation had ended 2 years before death.

Reasonable financial provision (s 1(2)(a),(b))—The Act does not distinguish between claims made by a surviving wife or husband of the deceased. In view of the decisions in *White v White* [2000] 2 FLR 981, HL and *Cowan v Cowan* [2001] 2 FLR 192, there is no place for discrimination based on gender. This principle was applied in *Barron v Woodhead* [2009] 1 FLR 747. The court considered his case on the basis of what he might have expected to receive had the marriage terminated by divorce. It rejected the suggestion that his claim should be decreased by reason of his conduct during the marriage, and in awarding him a life interest in the sum of £100,000 to enable him to buy a house to live in together with a lump sum of £25,000, the court took into account the factors under s 3. In defining reasonable financial provision, the Act distinguishes between a surviving spouse/civil partner and the other categories of applicants. In the case of a surviving spouse/civil partner, it need not be an amount required for maintenance (*Jessop v Jessop* [1992] 1 FLR 591, where it was held to be unreasonable for the widow not to be given some capital reserve for future contingencies, but see *Davis v Davis* [1993] 1 FLR 54, where the deceased before his death had provided his widow with a substantial capital sum together with all his chattels and a life interest in real estate. He was held to have made reasonable financial provision for her). The case of *Re Besterman (dec'd), Besterman v Grusin* [1984] FLR 503 should be viewed with a substantial element of caution (*Fielden v Cunliffe* [2006] 1 FLR 745). The test of "reasonable requirements" as a tool for assessing the needs of a spouse was disapproved of in *White v White* (above). The objective must be to achieve a fair outcome which is considered against the yardstick of equal division and the approach adopted in *White v White*. However, in cases under the 1975 Act, there is no presumption of equal division of assets, and caution needs to be exercised in using the divorce comparison in such cases (*P v G, P and P (Family Provision: Relevance of Divorce Provision)* [2006] 1 FLR 431). See also *Aston v Aston* [2007] WTLR 1349, [2008] CL 348; *Baker v Baker (Financial Provision: Divorce Comparison)* [2008] 2 FLR 1956; and *Moore v Holdsworth* [2010] 2 FLR 1501 where the application of the "divorce fiction" was considered. In *Iqbal v Ahmed* [2012] 1 FLR 31, the CA upheld the decision at first instance that had applied the observation of Lord Nicholls in *Miller v Miller; McFarlane v McFarlane* [2006] 1 FLR 1186 and in so doing had awarded the widow a life interest in the home (with the net proceeds to be held on trust for sale in equal shares for her and the deceased's son) and transferred the residuary estate to her to be available for repairs. The CA held that practical considerations were, in the circumstances, more important than abstract considerations and that the primary practical consideration in the case was to give the widow a capital cushion to cope with future eventualities. However, departure from equality based on need may be justified where the estate is insufficient to meet the needs of all the beneficiaries. The court has to strike a fair balance (*A v L* [2012] 1 FLR 985). Where the marriage has been short, the widow is entitled to a "reasonable expectation that her life again as a single woman need not revert to what it was before her marriage", but the brevity of the marriage and the limited nature of the widow's contribution are relevant factors that may affect issues of housing needs and the level of income: *Fielden v Cunliffe* (above) and *Miller v Miller* [2006] 1 FLR 151. Briggs J applied the "divorce check" in *Lilleyman v Lilleyman* [2013] 1 FLR 47, although the marriage was a short one. In *Adams v Adams* [2001] 1 WLR 493 the court considered that the provisions of MCA 1973, s 25 were the most important factor. It is submitted that there is nothing in the 1975 Act to suggest that this factor should be given more weight than the other factors referred to in s 3 of the Act: in *Re Rowlands (dec'd)* [1984] FLR 813 the widow was 90, had been separated from the deceased for 47 years and was unable to formulate what her needs were and what she would do if a substantial sum was awarded to her; she received £3000. See also *Re Bunning (dec'd), Bunning v Salmon* [1985] FLR 1 and *Re Gregory, Gregory v Goodenough* [1970] 1 WLR 1455. Where the former husband and wife settle their financial claims on divorce without a court order, the court will be slow to order further provision under the Act (*Re Fullard* [1982] Fam 42). Where a party to a consent order for financial relief dies shortly after the order is made it could be argued that the death of the other party was not a contemplated event when the order was made and was therefore a new event. In such a case the application to set aside the consent order must be made promptly. In relation to non-matrimonial property, property acquired before the marriage and post-separation or divorce, and inherited property and prenuptial agreements, see under MCA 1973, s 25.

In respect of any other applicant, including a judicially separated or divorced spouse/civil partner and a cohabitant as defined by ss 1(1A) or 1(1B), reasonable financial provision is limited to what would be reasonable in all the circumstances for the applicant to receive for his maintenance. In *Negus v Bahouse* [2008] 1 FLR 381 the court took account of the lifestyle provided by the deceased for his partner, his promises and the assurance he had given her that she would always have a roof over her head. This was balanced against the claims of the other beneficiaries and it was held that the applicant was entitled to a reasonable degree of financial security. The court ordered that the flat in which the applicant had lived be transferred to her and also awarded her a lump sum of £200,000. In *Webster v Webster* [2009] 1 FLR 1240 on the basis of the cohabitant's indirect contribution to the family budget and applying the decision in *Lloyds Bank plc v Rosset* [1990] 2 FLR 155 the court inferred that she had an interest in the family home. The court also took account of the long period of cohabitation, the claimant's age and needs and the needs of the other beneficiaries, and applied the clean break principle and a *Duxbury* capitalisation when ordering the transfer of the home to her free of mortgage. See also *Baker v Baker* [2008] 2 FLR 767, where the cohabitant's maintenance needs were adjudged to be a place to live and some financial security. See *Re Abram (Deceased)* [1996] 2 FLR 379 and *Rhodes v Dean* [1996] 7 CL 593. In *Graham v Murphy and Another* [1997] 1 FLR 860 it was held that the deceased's intestacy had resulted in a lack of reasonable provision for the applicant but on the facts it was decided that reasonable financial provision did not mean that the applicant should be provided for on a lavish scale, such as would relieve him from the need to earn a living or provide himself with a home. The application in this case pre-dated 1 January 1996 and would now be governed by Law Reform (Succession) Act 1995, s 2. An adult child, towards whom the deceased failed to discharge his responsibility, is not entitled to make a claim where he is in comfortable circumstances, in order to maintain his standard of living (*Re Jennings (deceased)*; *Harlow v National Westminster Bank plc and Others* [1994] 1 FLR 536; *Re Hancock (dec'd)* [1998] 2 FLR 346; *Re Abram (dec'd)* [1996] 2 FLR 379). In *H v J's Personal Representatives, Blue Cross, RSPB and RSPCA* [2010] 1 FLR 1613, the deceased left a substantial part of her estate to various charities and made no provision for her daughter, who lived in modest circumstances. The daughter succeeded in her claim at first instance but on the first appeal it was ruled that the test in such cases was whether on an objective basis having considered all of the factors it could be said that the provision or lack of it was unreasonable. On the facts it was not and no provision was to be made from the estate for the daughter. On further appeal (*Illot v Mitson and others* [2012] 2 FLR 170), the Court of Appeal ruled that the district judge was entitled to find the failure to make provision for the daughter unreasonable. In advising a client, consideration should be given to the s 3 criteria so that the client can make an informed choice. However, the client should nevertheless be advised that there is no guarantee that it will have the effect of preventing a claim being made and if a claim is made of its success, as much will depend on the circumstances at the date of the hearing of the claim. See also the recommendations made by the Law Commission in its report of 14 December 2011.

The court must have regard to all of the matters set out under s 3. Relevant to this issue is also the fact that the deceased's assets have been acquired from the inheritance of the applicant's mother (*Gora v Treasury Solicitor* [2003] Fam Law 93). It is not necessary in every case for the applicant to establish "a moral obligation". For a discussion of this issue see *Re Coventry, Coventry v Coventry* (1979) FLR Rep 142; *Re Jennings (deceased)* (above); *Re Pearce (deceased)* [1998] 2 FLR 705; *Re Hancock (dec'd)* (above); and *Gora v Treasury Solicitor* (above). There are no clear decisions on whether the financial resources of the claimant should include means-tested benefits. In *Re Collins* [1990] 2 FLR 72, Hollins J said "I do not consider that the fact of support from the DSS precludes consideration of whether the intestacy has or has not made reasonable financial provision for her". It is submitted that the decision in that case turned on its own facts. Furthermore, the case considered only the claim to social security benefits. It did not consider cases of funding or means-tested local authority provisions. Consideration must be given in each individual case where the applicant is on state benefit to whether an award under the Act would benefit the applicant or merely have the effect of removing entitlement to state benefit and thereby reducing the applicant's standard of living. See also *Re E, E v E* [1966] 1 WLR 709, where it was stated that if the estate is so small and the means of the applicant so exiguous that the only effect of making provision for the applicant would be to relieve the national insurance fund, there might well be no point in making provision for the applicant. See also *Re Watkins, Hayward v Chatterton* [1949] 1 All ER 695.

2 Powers of court to make orders

(1) Subject to the provisions of this Act, where an application is made for an order under this section, the court may, if it is satisfied that the disposition of the deceased's estate effected by his will or the law relating to intestacy, or the combination of his will and that law, is not such as to make reasonable financial provision for the applicant, make any one or more of the following orders –

(a) an order for the making to the applicant out of the net estate of the deceased of such periodical payments and for such term as may be specified in the order;

(b) an order for the payment to the applicant out of that estate of a lump sum of such amount as may be so specified;

(c) an order for the transfer to the applicant of such property comprised in that estate as may be so specified;

(d) an order for the settlement for the benefit of the applicant of such property comprised in that estate as may be so specified;

(e) an order for the acquisition out of property comprised in that estate of such property as may be so specified and for the transfer of the property so acquired to the applicant or for the settlement thereof for his benefit;

(f) an order varying any ante-nuptial or post-nuptial settlement (including such a settlement made by will) made on the parties to a marriage to which the deceased was one of the parties, the variation being for the benefit of the surviving party to that marriage, or any child of that marriage, or any person who was treated by the deceased as a child of the family in relation to that marriage;

(g) an order varying any settlement made –
(i)   during the subsistence of a civil partnership formed by the deceased, or
(ii) in anticipation of the formation of a civil partnership by the deceased,
on the civil partners (including such a settlement made by will), the variation being for the benefit of the surviving civil partner, or any child of both the civil partners, or any person who was treated by the deceased as a child of the family in relation to that civil partnership.

(2) An order under subsection (1)(a) above providing for the making out of the net estate of the deceased of periodical payments may provide for –

(a) payments of such amount as may be specified in the order,
(b) payments equal to the whole of the income of the net estate or of such portion thereof as may be so specified,
(c) payments equal to the whole of the income of such part of the net estate as the court may direct to be set aside or appropriated for the making out of the income thereof of payments under this section,

or may provide for the amount of the payments or any of them to be determined in any other way the court thinks fit.

(3) Where an order under subsection (1)(a) above provides for the making of payments of an amount specified in the order, the order may direct that such part of the net estate as may be so specified shall be set aside or appropriated for the making out of the income thereof of those payments; but no larger part of the net estate shall be so set aside or appropriated than is sufficient, at the date of the order, to produce by the income thereof the amount required for the making of those payments.

(4) An order under this section may contain such consequential and supplemental provisions as the court thinks necessary or expedient for the purpose of giving effect to the order or for the purpose of securing that the order operates fairly as between one beneficiary of the estate of the deceased and another and may, in particular, but without prejudice to the generality of this subsection –

(a) order any person who holds any property which forms part of the net estate of the deceased to make such payment or transfer such property as may be specified in the order;
(b) vary the disposition of the deceased's estate effected by the will or the law relating to intestacy, or by both the will and the law relating to intestacy, in such manner as the court thinks fair and reasonable having regard to the provisions of the order and all the circumstances of the case;
(c) confer on the trustees of any property which is the subject of an order under this section such powers as appear to the court to be necessary or expedient.

Amendments—CPA 2004, s 71, Sch 4, para 16.

"net estate"—Defined in s 25, and see ss 8, 9. A severable share in property in which the deceased held a joint tenancy may be treated as part of the net estate pursuant to s 9 (*Jessop v Jessop* [1992] 1 FLR 591).

Periodical payments (s 2(1)(a))—Unless an application has been made for an interim order, the order for periodical payments will normally be made from the date of the deceased's death, even where the applicant has been in receipt of state benefits (*Re Goodwin, Goodwin v Goodwin* [1969] 1 Ch 283). The matter is one for the discretion of the court. The court may specify the amount to be paid under the order, express the amount to be paid to be such sum as is equivalent to the whole or a specified portion of the income of the net estate, direct that a specified part of the net estate be appropriated or set aside for meeting periodical payments and express the amount of such periodical payments to be equivalent to the whole of the income of such part of the net estate or provide for the amount of the payment to be determined in any other way it thinks fit (s 2(2)).

Lump sum (s 2(1)(b))—In the case of a lump sum order, particularly where the capital sum is provided to produce an income, the fact that the applicant will not be able to return to the court for further orders means that in assessing the amount the court should make allowances for inflation and possible future contingencies (*Re Besterman* [1984] FLR 503); but see *A v A (Financial Provision)* [1998] 2 FLR 180, a case concerning an application for financial provision under MCA 1973, where it was held that the concept of awarding a lump sum as a cushion had not survived the introduction of *Duxbury* calculations). See also *Fielden v Cunliffe* and *P v G, P and P (Family Provision: Relevance of Divorce Provision)* (above). A lump sum may also be made on an application for a variation of periodical payments order under s 6. The court has the power to order that the lump sum payment be made by instalments and may vary the number of instalments payable, the amount of the instalments and the date on which any instalment becomes payable (s 7(2)).

Order varying any antenuptial or postnuptial settlement—See **nuptial agreements** under MCA 1973, s 25.

Settlement of property and the mentally disabled (s 2(1)(d))—It is not unusual to find that parents refrain from making provision for a mentally disabled child, particularly an adult child, in the belief that the child will be provided for adequately by the state and any benefit under a testamentary provision will have the effect of reducing the benefit. With the increasing tendency of care for such persons being provided within the community, some financial support could make a difference to the quality of life of that person. Although there are no decided cases on the subject it is submitted that under the wide powers given to the court by s 2, and in particular s 2(4), the court could make an order for the settlement of property for the benefit of a mentally handicapped claimant by setting up a discretionary trust so as to permit the whole or any part of the income of the trust fund to be applied for the maintenance, care and benefit of the claimant as the trustees in their absolute discretion deem fit. For further information on the provisions which may be included in the trust, see *Butterworths Wills, Probate and Administration Service* and Ashton and Ward, *Mental Handicap and the Law* (Sweet & Maxwell 1992).

Order for costs—Costs in claims under the Act is governed by CPR 1998, Pts 36 and 44. In considering whether to make any orders in respect of costs, the court will have regard to any Pt 36 offers but it has the discretion to disapply the normal consequences if it considers that to do so would result in injustice. In exercising its discretion, the court will have regard to the factors set out in Pt 44 and to the overriding objective (see *Lilleyman v Lilleyman* [2013] 1 FLR 47, where the court, when making an order against the claimant after a Pt 36 offer took account of the defendant's conduct. See also *Graham v Murphy and Another* [1997] 1 FLR 860).

3 Matters to which the court is to have regard in exercising powers under s 2

(1) Where an application is made for an order under section 2 of this Act, the court shall, in determining whether the disposition of the deceased's estate effected by his will or the law relating to intestacy, or the combination of his will and that law, is such as to make reasonable financial provision for the applicant and, if the court considers that reasonable financial provision has not been made, in determining whether and in what manner it shall exercise its powers under that section, have regard to the following matters, that is to say –

(a) the financial resources and financial needs which the applicant has or is likely to have in the foreseeable future;

(b) the financial resources and financial needs which any other applicant for an order under section 2 of this Act has or is likely to have in the foreseeable future;

(c) the financial resources and financial needs which any beneficiary of the estate of the deceased has or is likely to have in the foreseeable future;

(d) any obligations and responsibilities which the deceased had towards any applicant for an order under the said section 2 or towards any beneficiary of the estate of the deceased;

(e) the size and nature of the net estate of the deceased;

(f) any physical or mental disability of any applicant for an order under the said section 2 or any beneficiary of the estate of the deceased;

(g) any other matter, including the conduct of the applicant or any other person, which in the circumstances of the case the court may consider relevant.

(2) This subsection applies, without prejudice to the generality of paragraph (g) of subsection (1) above, where an application for an order under section 2 of this Act is made by virtue of section 1(1)(a) or (b) of this Act. The court shall, in addition to the matters specifically mentioned in paragraphs (a) to (f) of that subsection, have regard to –

    (a) the age of the applicant and the duration of the marriage or civil partnership;

    (b) the contribution made by the applicant to the welfare of the family of the deceased, including any contribution made by looking after the home or caring for the family.

In the case of an application by the wife or husband of the deceased, the court shall also, unless at the date of death a decree of judicial separation was in force and the separation was continuing, have regard to the provision which the applicant might reasonably have expected to receive if on the day on which the deceased died the marriage, instead of being terminated by death, had been terminated by a decree of divorce. In the case of an application by the civil partner of the deceased, the court shall also, unless at the date of the death a separation order under Chapter 2 of Part 2 of the Civil Partnership Act 2004 was in force and the separation was continuing, have regard to the provision which the applicant might reasonably have expected to receive if on the day on which the deceased died the civil partnership, instead of being terminated by death, had been terminated by a dissolution order.

(2A) Without prejudice to the generality of paragraph (g) of subsection (1) above, where an application for an order under section 2 of this Act is made by virtue of section 1(1)(ba) of this Act, the court shall, in addition to the matters specifically mentioned in paragraphs (a) to (f) of that subsection, have regard to –

    (a) the age of the applicant and the length of the period during which the applicant lived as the husband or wife or civil partner of the deceased and in the same household as the deceased;

    (b) the contribution made by the applicant to the welfare of the family of the deceased, including any contribution made by looking after the home or caring for the family.

(3) Without prejudice to the generality of paragraph (g) of subsection (1) above, where an application for an order under section 2 of this Act is made by virtue of section 1(1)(c) or 1(1)(d) of this Act, the court shall, in addition to the matters specifically mentioned in paragraphs (a) to (f) of that subsection, have regard to the manner in which the applicant was being or in which he might expect to be educated or trained, and where the application is made by virtue of section 1(1)(d) the court shall also have regard –

    (a) to whether the deceased had assumed any responsibility for the applicant's maintenance and, if so, to the extent to which and the basis upon which the deceased assumed that responsibility and to the length of time for which the deceased discharged that responsibility;

    (b) to whether in assuming and discharging that responsibility the deceased did so knowing that the applicant was not his own child;

    (c) to the liability of any other person to maintain the applicant.

(4) Without prejudice to the generality of paragraph (g) of subsection (1) above, where an application for an order under section 2 of this Act is made by virtue of section 1(1)(e) of this Act, the court shall, in addition to the matters specifically mentioned in paragraphs (a) to (f) of that subsection, have regard to the extent to which and the basis upon which the deceased assumed responsibility for the maintenance of the applicant, and to the length of time for which the deceased discharged that responsibility.

(5) In considering the matters to which the court is required to have regard under this section, the court shall take into account the facts as known to the court at the date of the hearing.

(6) In considering the financial resources of any person for the purposes of this section the court shall take into account his earning capacity and in considering the financial needs of any person for the purposes of this section the court shall take into account his financial obligations and responsibilities.

Amendments—Law Reform (Succession) Act 1995, s 2; CPA 2004, s 71, Sch 4, paras 17(1)–(5), 18.

Matters to be considered in determining reasonable financial provision (s 3(1))—See **Reasonable financial provision** under s 1. In the case of an application by a cohabitant, the further specific matters that the court is required to take into account under s 3(2A) are identical to those which apply in the case of a spouse or former spouse who has not married.

"financial resources and financial needs" (s 3(1)(b))—"Financial needs" means reasonable requirements. The standard of living enjoyed by the applicant during the lifetime of the deceased and the extent to which the deceased contributed to that standard will be relevant (*Negus v Bahouse* [2008] 1 FLR 381). The court may also restrict the distribution of the liquid assets of the estate to ensure the preservation of the capital of the estate to cover unforeseen circumstances (*Stead v Stead* [1985] FLR 16; see also *Malone v Harrison* [1979] 1 WLR 1353). In considering the applicant's claim the court may need to balance the applicant's needs and those of the beneficiaries (*Kusminow v Barclay's Bank Trust Co Ltd and Sokolow and Sitnikova* [1989] Fam Law 66).

Obligations and responsibilities—"Obligations and responsibilities" in s 3(1)(d) extends beyond legal obligation and the deceased's obligations are not to be construed too narrowly, but in a broad sense (*Gora v Treasury Solicitor* [2003] Fam Law 93; *Espinosa v Bourke* [1999] 1 FLR 747). The court is entitled to have regard to the entire estate, including foreign property, when considering whether the estate made reasonable provision for the applicant and assessing the financial resources and needs of any beneficiary of the estate (*Bheekhun v Williams* [1999] 2 FLR 229, CA). The deceased's moral obligation and the morality of the applicant's claim may be relevant. (See *Re Goodchild (Deceased) and Another* [1997] 2 FLR 644, CA and see also *Re Debenham (dec'd)* [1986] 1 FLR 404). The applicant must establish some sort of a moral claim to be maintained by the deceased beyond the mere fact of blood relationship (*Re Coventry (dec'd), Coventry v Coventry* (1979) FLR Rep 142; *Re Abram (Deceased)* [1996] 2 FLR 379; *H v J's Personal Representatives, Blue Cross, RSPB and RSPCA* [2010] 1 FLR 1613). In *Re Debenham (dec'd)* [1986] 1 FLR 404, the court found that, although the deceased did not have any legal obligation to the applicant, she owed her a moral obligation; in *Re Jennings (deceased), Harlow v National Westminster Bank plc and Others* [1994] 1 FLR 536, a claim made by an adult son of the deceased, which was based on the fact that the deceased had failed to discharge his responsibilities to the son during his minority, failed; see also *Re Wood, Wood v Wood* (1982) LS Gaz 774 and *Re Rowlands (dec'd)* [1984] FLR 813 and *Garland v Morris* [2007] 2 FLR 528 where an adult child's claim against her father's estate failed on the facts.

Size and nature of the net estate—Where the size of the estate is limited, the court will be slow to deprive the deceased of his freedom to dispose of his estate as he willed (*Re Gregory, Gregory v Goodenough* [1970] 1 WLR 1455; *Gora v Treasury Solicitor* [2003] Fam Law 93).

Physical and mental disability—See final paragraph of **Reasonable financial provision** under s 1 and **Settlement of property and the mentally disabled** under s 2.

Conduct—In *Re Snoek (dec'd)* [1983] Fam Law 18, Wood J said that he could see no reason why conduct under s 3 should be understood differently from that under MCA 1973, s 25. This decision was applied in *Barron v Woodhead* [2009] 1 FLR 747. See also *Miller v Miller; McFarlane v McFarlane* [2006] 1 FLR 1186 on the issue of conduct. Conduct that has been considered relevant includes: concealment by the applicant widow of her true financial position after her marriage had broken down and had been dissolved, resulting in her continuing to receive maintenance at a much higher level than she would have been entitled to (*Re Harker-Thomas* [1969] P 28); the deceased being secretive about his financial position (*Re W (dec'd)* (1975) 119 SJ 439); and the deceased encouraging the applicant to believe that the applicant would acquire an interest in the estate and, on that belief, allowing her to act to her detriment, which can give rise to an estoppel (*Re Basham* [1987] 2 FLR 264). Where the applicant has unlawfully killed the deceased, the forfeiture rule applies (see below).

Deceased's reason—The Act does not specifically provide for the deceased's reason for making or not making any provision to be considered, but the section is wide enough for the court to consider his reasons and can infer his intention from all the circumstances and weigh these against all other factors (see *Re Coventry (dec'd), Coventry v Coventry* (1979) FLR Rep 142; *Re Leach (dec'd), Leach v Linderman* [1984] FLR 590). See *Myers v Myers* [2004] EWHC 1944 (Fam).

Any other matter—See *Re Wood, Wood v Wood* (1982) LS Gaz 774.

Proprietary estoppel—The conduct of the deceased in encouraging the claimant to believe that he/she would acquire an interest in his/her estate and thereby, upon that belief, to act to his/her detriment, can give rise to estoppel on which a claim may be based. To establish such a claim, the claimant must prove that: (a) the claimant had a belief at all material times that he/she would receive the property that is the subject of the claim; (b) that belief was encouraged by the deceased; and (c) in reliance on that belief and assurance, the claimant acted to his/her detriment (*Re Basham* [1987] 2 FLR 264). For cases where the conditions that must be satisfied to found a claim in estoppel, see *HM Revenue and Customs v Benchdollar Ltd & others* [2010] 1 All ER 174 and *Thorner v Majors* [2009] 2 FLR 405, where the House of Lords set out the conditions that must be satisfied, namely: (a) the relevant assurances must be clear and unequivocal and must appear to have been intended to be taken seriously and might reasonably be expected to be relied upon by the person to whom it was made; and (b) the assurances given to the claimant whether expressly, impliedly or tacitly should relate to identified property owned by the defendant. This doctrine was applied in *Wayling v Jones* [1995] 2 FLR 1029, where the claimant and the deceased had been in a homosexual relationship. In *MacDonald & Anor v Frost* [2009] EWHC 2276 (Ch) a claim in estoppel made by the deceased's daughters failed on the facts. In *Evans v HSBC Trust Co (UK) Ltd* [2005] WTLR 1289, a claim brought by two brothers who were unrelated to the deceased but whom she had treated as her grandchildren was allowed as it was established that the deceased had given them assurances upon which they had acted to their detriment. In *Suggitt v Suggitt* [2011] 2 FLR 875, the deceased, who was a farmer with an agricultural estate worth £4m, left his estate to his daughter with the proviso that if his son should show himself capable of managing the farmland the daughter should transfer the farmland to him. The son, having attended agricultural college and assisted the deceased in the farming business, brought a successful claim on proprietary estoppel. It was held that once proprietary estoppel had been established, the court had to do what was necessary to avoid an unconscionable result. The court granted him the farmland and a home but no other assets. See also, *Edgerton v Edgerton and Shaikh* [2012] 2 FLR 273, in which the Master of the Rolls considered other authorities on estoppels and as to the effect of a determination of a Family Division judge on proceedings issued in the Chancery Division.

Mutual wills—The doctrine of mutual wills applies where the agreement to enter into mutual wills is reinforced by undertakings that the wills not be revoked. If the first testator dies having made a will in compliance with the agreement, the agreement is binding on the second testator and gives rise to an equitable obligation to give effect to the mutually agreed disposition. The legal principles that apply to mutual wills were summarised in *Charles & Ors v Fraser* [2010] EWHC 2154 (Ch). Where the legal formalities relating to mutual wills have not been complied with but the parties believed that they had created mutually binding wills, a constructive trust may be applied to prevent the second testator from dealing with the deceased's estate in a way that is incompatible with the agreement (*Healey v Brown* [2002] EWHC 1405 (Ch)). Practitioners should take care to supervise the execution of mutual wills to ensure that each client signs his/her own will and not that of the other spouse, as occurred in *Marley v Rawlings* [2012] 2 FLR 556.

Forfeiture rule—This rule disentitles a person from acquiring a benefit from the estate of another whom he has unlawfully killed. However, it does not preclude that person from making a claim under this Act since the Forfeiture Act 1982 gives the court a discretion to modify the application of the rule if it takes the view that the moral culpability of the applicant is such that it would be unjust to deny him any benefit (*Re K* [1985] FLR 558; *Re S (Deceased) (Forfeiture Rule)* [1996] 1 FLR 910). An application in respect of the unlawful killing must be made within 3 months of the applicant's conviction. The effect of the rule is to preclude the applicant from acquiring an interest in property (as defined in the Forfeiture Act 1982). When applying the forfeiture rule, and in exercising its discretion, the court does not draw any distinction between murder and manslaughter. In both cases the assailant remains criminally responsible for his actions (*Jones v Roberts* [1995] 2 FLR 422 and *Re Jones (Deceased), Jones v Midland Bank Trust Co Ltd and Others* [1998] 1 FLR 246). See also *Re Land (Deceased); Land v Land* [2007] 1 WLR 1009, where the claim was allowed and provision made for the deceased's son although his application was out of time under the Forfeiture Act 1982. The rule also applies to offences under the Suicide Act 1961, including aiding and abetting a suicide in pursuance of a suicide pact. Where one of the parties to a suicide pact succeeded in taking his life and the other survived, public policy would not normally require forfeiture by the survivor (*Dunbar v Plant* [1998] 1 FLR 157). It is submitted that the decision whether to exercise the discretion, and in what manner, will depend upon the facts of each case. In *Dunbar v Plant* (above) the circumstances of the suicide were extremely tragic and the events which occurred were horrific for the parties involved in the suicide pact and their families.

Provision which the deceased's spouse might have expected to receive on divorce—Any disposition by the deceased with the intention of defeating the spouse's claim would be a relevant factor (*Re Dawkins, Dawkins v Judd* [1986] 2 FLR 360), as is the length of the marriage and the contribution made by the applicant (*Kusminow v Barclay's Bank Trust Co Ltd and Sokolow and Sitnikova* [1989] Fam Law 66). However, it is not the duty of the court to alter the disposition so as to make an equitable redistribution of the available assets. The provision that the spouse might reasonably have expected to receive on divorce is only one of the matters which the court is required to consider. The major element is what is reasonable in all the circumstances of the case (*Re Krubert (Deceased)* [1997] 1 FLR 42). See further **Reasonable financial provision** under s 1 above.

Responsibility assumed for maintenance—The court is required to have regard to (a) the extent to which the deceased assumed responsibility for the applicant, (b) the basis on which the responsibility had been assumed, and (c) the length of time for which he had maintained the applicant. In *Rhodes v Dean* [1996] 7 CL 593, where the responsibility did not include the daily living expenses, the relationship was not like a marriage, and the applicant, who had cohabited with the deceased, was entitled to capital held in a joint account; the application failed. See also **Other persons** and **"immediately before the death"** under s 1.

4 Time-limit for applications

An application for an order under section 2 of this Act shall not, except with the permission of the court, be made after the end of the period of six months from the date on which representation with respect to the estate of the deceased is first taken out.

Time-limit—An application cannot be made if no grant is taken out (*Re McBroom (Deceased)* [1992] 2 FLR 49 but see *Baker v Baker* [2008] 2 FLR 1956, where although a grant of representation had not been made, because the dispute before the court related to the validity of the will and the doctrine of estoppel, both sides agreed that the court should proceed and rule on the question of any claim the cohabitant may have under the 1975 Act on the material before the court, leaving the question as to the making of any order consequential upon the court's finding). Provided the application is issued within 6 months of the grant, there is no time-limit for service (*Re Miller, Miller v De Courcey* [1969] 1 WLR 583; *Re Kay, Kay v West* [1965] 1 WLR 1463 and *Re Chittenden, Chittenden v Doe* [1970] 1 WLR 1618). The period of 6 months begins to run from the grant in common form (*Re Miller*). Where a grant of probate is replaced by letters of administration, time begins to run from the date of the grant of letters of administration and vice versa (*Re Freeman (dec'd), Weston v Freeman* [1985] FLR 543). An application is not rendered invalid if it is issued before the date on which representation is taken out (*Re Searle, Searle v Siems* [1949] Ch 73).

Standing searches—In order to gain protection against the possibility that a grant may be issued without its existence coming to the attention of an interested party, facilities are available for a standing search to be made at the Principal Registry or sub-registry (see *Practice Note of 26 September 1991* in Part V). An application for such a search is made in accordance with the Non-Contentious Probate Rules 1987, r 43 by completing the notice in Form 2 and paying the appropriate £5 fee (fee 5 of the Non-Contentious Probate Fees Order 1999). The name and date of death of the deceased, as recorded in the Register of Deaths, must be included in the notice lodged for a standing search and in any case where the name of the deceased differs from that recorded in the Register, that name shall also be included in the oath or the notice, as appropriate (see *PD of 12 January 1999* in Part V). The court will then make an entry and acknowledge it. Once an entry is made the applicant for a standing search will receive an office copy of any grant which tallies with the particulars given and which either has been issued not more than 12 months before the receipt of the application for the search or is issued within a period of 6 months thereafter. An application for the search to be extended may be made within the last month of the 6 months' period by completing a request in the following form and lodging it or sending it by post to the registry or sub-registry at which the standing search was entered:

"I Hereby request that the above standing search be extended for a further period of 6 months from the date on which it is due to expire. I enclose the further fee.
Signed . . . . Dated . . . . . "

Application out of time—The court's power to extend time is discretionary (*Fielden v Cunliffe* (above)). An application for an extension must be expressly asked for in the claim form and the grounds on which the court's leave to entertain the application is sought must be included in the supporting witness statement or affidavit. If the application is opposed, the defendant must file an affidavit in answer, setting out the grounds of opposition and the personal representative is required to file a witness statement or affidavit in answer setting out the matters required by CPR 1998, r 57.16(5) and PD57, para 16. In exercising its discretion the court will look at all the circumstances and consider whether extension of

PART II

time is required in the interests of justice (*Re Ruttie, Ruttie v Saul* [1970] 1 WLR 89). In *Re Salmon (dec'd), Coard v National Westminster Bank Ltd and Others* [1981] Ch 167, Sir Robert Megarry VC considered *Re Ruttie* and gave a full account of the matters which might be considered material on an application for permission to apply out of time.

Examples of cases where leave was granted are *Re Trott, Trott v Miles* [1958] 1 WLR 604, where the widow gave posthumous birth to a child; *Re McNare, McNare v McNare* [1964] 1 WLR 1255, where the widow, who was blind, crippled and aged 71, was unaware of the husband's death until five months after probate had been granted and had no information regarding the deceased's assets. Leave was refused in *Longley, Longley and Longley v Longley* [1981] CLY 2885 (but *cf Adams v Schofeld* [1983] CLY 594), *Escritt v Escritt* (1982) 3 FLR 280, where there was a delay of more than 3 years, and *Vodanas v Kriaris* [2012] VSC 248 (a decision of the Victorian Supreme Court in Australia), where 25 days had elapsed after the time limitation period had expired.

The crucial factor in deciding whether to grant leave to apply out of time is the balance of prejudice over and above that which is inherent in the granting or withholding of leave (*Bouette v Rose* [1999] 2 FLR 466). The court will consider all the circumstances of the case, including whether it is in the interest of justice to allow an extension of time; the reasons for the delay; what efforts have been made to mitigate any effects of the delay; whether any negotiations are being carried out; whether the estate has been distributed before notice of the claim is given; whether the applicant would have a claim against the solicitors if the application were refused; whether refusal would cause hardship and operate unfairly against the applicant and, in particular, whether it would leave the applicant without redress against anyone; and whether the applicant has an arguable case (*Re Salmon (dec'd), Coard v National Westminster Bank* (above), *Re C (Deceased) (Leave to Apply for Provision)* [1995] 2 FLR 24 (where an 8-year-old illegitimate child of the deceased was granted leave, although her mother had taken no steps to make a claim for two and a half years)). See also *Stock v Brown* [1994] 1 FLR 840 (where the time-limit had been exceeded by 6 years). See *Hashtroodi v Hancock* [2004] 1 WLR 3206 for the possible effect of a solicitor's failure to serve the claim form before the due date and *Vodanas v Kriaris* (above), where the Australian court found that there was an arguable case, the applicant had acted promptly once H became aware of the his rights and there was no prejudice to the beneficiaries. It is submitted that the court should also consider any possible infringement of ECHR 1950, Art 6 rights.

5 Interim orders

(1) Where on an application for an order under section 2 of this Act it appears to the court –

    (a)   that the applicant is in immediate need of financial assistance, but it is not yet possible to determine what order (if any) should be made under that section; and

    (b)   that property forming part of the net estate of the deceased is or can be made available to meet the need of the applicant;

the court may order that, subject to such conditions or restrictions, if any, as the court may impose and to any further order of the court, there shall be paid to the applicant out of the net estate of the deceased such sum or sums and (if more than one) at such intervals at the court thinks reasonable; and the court may order that, subject to the provisions of this Act, such payments are to be made until such date as the court may specify, not being later than the date on which the court either makes an order under the said section 2 or decides not to exercise its powers under that section.

(2) Subsections (2), (3) and (4) of section 2 of this Act shall apply in relation to an order under this section as they apply in relation to an order under that section.

(3) In determining what order, if any, should be made under this section the court shall, so far as the urgency of the case admits, have regard to the same matters as those to which the court is required to have regard under section 3 of this Act.

(4) An order made under section 2 of this Act may provide that any sum paid to the applicant by virtue of this section shall be treated to such an extent and in such manner as may be provided by that order as having been paid on account of any payment provided for by that order.

Procedure—The rules do not prescribe the procedure for such an application. Since the application is made in the main proceedings, it should be made by summons in those proceedings and supported by affidavit. The applicant must show that the conditions in s 5(1)(a) and (b) are satisfied.

"in immediate need of financial assistance" (s 5(1)(a))—Note that the court is required to have regard to the matters set out in s 3 when determining an application for an interim order (see *Smith v Smith and others* [2012] 2 FLR 230, where the requirement of "immediate need" was not established).

Sanctioning interim payments—Personal representatives may find themselves in difficulties when such an application is made, particularly when the parties are on bad terms. In such cases they should form their own view, with the assistance of their legal advisers, as to the payments that can properly be made. Alternatively, they should ask the parties who might conceivably be affected – whether applicant or residuary legatee – for their consent. If such consent is not forthcoming the executors can apply to the court for leave to make the payment in question. In the event that the court finds that consent was unreasonably withheld it may order costs against the party who acted unreasonably (*Re Ralphs, Ralphs v District Bank* [1968] 1 WLR 1522).

6 Variation, discharge, etc of orders for periodical payments

(1) Subject to the provisions of this Act, where the court has made an order under section 2(1)(a) of this Act (in this section referred to as "the original order") for the making of periodical payments to any person (in this section referred to as "the original recipient"), the court, on an application under this section, shall have power by order to vary or discharge the original order or to suspend any provision of it temporarily and to revive the operation of any provision so suspended.

(2) Without prejudice to the generality of subsection (1) above, an order made on an application for the variation of the original order may –

  (a) provide for the making out of any relevant property of such periodical payments and for such term as may be specified in the order to any person who has applied, or would but for section 4 of this Act be entitled to apply, for an order under section 2 of this Act (whether or not, in the case of any application, an order was made in favour of the applicant);

  (b) provide for the payment out of any relevant property of a lump sum of such amount as may be so specified to the original recipient or to any such person as is mentioned in paragraph (a) above;

  (c) provide for the transfer of the relevant property, or such part thereof as may be so specified, to the original recipient or to any such person as is so mentioned.

(3) Where the original order provides that any periodical payments payable thereunder to the original recipient are to cease on the occurrence of an event specified in the order (other than the formation of a subsequent marriage or civil partnership by a former spouse or former civil partner) or on the expiration of a period so specified, then, if, before the end of the period of six months from the date of the occurrence of that event or of the expiration of that period, an application is made for an order under this section, the court shall have power to make any order which it would have had power to make if the application had been made before that date (whether in favour of the original recipient or any such person as is mentioned in subsection (2)(a) above and whether having effect from that date or from such later date as the court may specify).

(4) Any reference in this section to the original order shall include a reference to an order made under this section and any reference in this section to the original recipient shall include a reference to any person to whom periodical payments are required to be made by virtue of an order under this section.

(5) An application under this section may be made by any of the following persons, that is to say –

(a)   any person who by virtue of section 1(1) of this Act has applied, or would but for section 4 of this Act be entitled to apply, for an order under section 2 of this Act,

(b)   the personal representatives of the deceased,

(c)   the trustees of any relevant property, and

(d)   any beneficiary of the estate of the deceased.

(6) An order under this section may only affect –

(a)   property the income of which is at the date of the order applicable wholly or in part for the making of periodical payments to any person who has applied for an order under this Act, or

(b)   in the case of an application under subsection (3) above in respect of payments which have ceased to be payable on the occurrence of an event or the expiration of a period, property the income of which was so applicable immediately before the occurrence of that event or the expiration of that period, as the case may be,

and any such property as is mentioned in paragraph (a) or (b) above is in subsections (2) and (5) above referred to as "relevant property".

(7) In exercising the powers conferred by this section the court shall have regard to all the circumstances of the case, including any change in any of the matters to which the court was required to have regard when making the order to which the application relates.

(8) Where the court makes an order under this section, it may give such consequential directions as it thinks necessary or expedient having regard to the provisions of the order.

(9) No such order as is mentioned in section 2(1)(d), (e) or (f), 9, 10 or 11 of this Act shall be made on an application under this section.

(10) For the avoidance of doubt it is hereby declared that, in relation to an order which provides for the making of periodical payments which are to cease on the occurrence of an event specified in the order (other than the formation of a subsequent marriage or civil partnership by a former spouse or former civil partner) or on the expiration of a period so specified, the power to vary an order includes power to provide for the making of periodical payments after the expiration of that period or the occurrence of that event.

Amendments—CPA 2004, s 71, Sch 4, para 19.

7 Payment of lump sums by instalments

(1) An order under section 2(1)(b) or 6(2)(b) of this Act for the payment of a lump sum may provide for the payment of that sum by instalments of such amount as may be specified in the order.

(2) Where an order is made by virtue of subsection (1) above, and court shall have power, on an application made by the person to whom the lump sum is payable, by the personal representatives of the deceased or by the trustees of the property out of which the lump sum is payable, to vary that order by varying the number of instalments payable, the amount of any instalment and the date on which any instalment becomes payable.

Property available for financial provision

8 Property treated as part of "net estate"

(1) Where a deceased person has in accordance with the provisions of any enactment nominated any person to receive any sum of money or other property on his death and that nomination is in force at the time of his death, that sum of money, after deducting

therefrom any capital transfer tax payable in respect thereof, or that other property, to the extent of the value thereof at the date of the death of the deceased after deducting therefrom any capital transfer tax so payable, shall be treated for the purposes of this Act as part of the net estate of the deceased; but this subsection shall not render any person liable for having paid that sum or transferred that other property to the person named in the nomination in accordance with the directions given in the nomination.

(2) Where any sum of money or other property is received by any person as a donatio mortis causa made by a deceased person, that sum of money, after deducting therefrom any capital transfer tax payable thereon, or that other property, to the extent of the value thereof at the date of the death of the deceased after deducting therefrom any capital transfer tax so payable, shall be treated for the purposes of this Act as part of the net estate of the deceased; but this subsection shall not render any person liable for having paid that sum or transferred that other property in order to give effect to that donatio mortis causa.

(3) The amount of capital transfer tax to be deducted for the purpose of this section shall not exceed the amount of that tax which has been borne by the person nominated by the deceased or, as the case may be, the person who has received a sum of money or other property as a donatio mortis causa.

Defined terms—"net estate": s 25(1) (see also under s 2).

"property"—This term includes a chose in action (s 25(1)).

"donatio mortis causa"—Land is capable of passing through a donatio mortis causa (*Sen v Headley* [1991] 2 FLR 449).

9 Property held on a joint tenancy

(1) Where a deceased person was immediately before his death beneficially entitled to a joint tenancy of any property, then, if, before the end of the period of six months from the date on which representation with respect to the estate of the deceased was first taken out, an application is made for an order under section 2 of this Act, the court for the purpose of facilitating the making of financial provision for the applicant under this Act may order that the deceased's severable share of that property, at the value thereof immediately before his death, shall, to such extent as appears to the court to be just in all the circumstances of the case, be treated for the purposes of this Act as part of the net estate of the deceased.

(2) In determining the extent to which any severable share is to be treated as part of the net estate of the deceased by virtue of any order under subsection (1) above, the court shall have regard to any capital transfer tax payable in respect of that severable share.

(3) Where an order is made under subsection (1) above, the provisions of this section shall not render any person liable for anything done by him before the order was made.

(4) For the avoidance of doubt it is hereby declared that for the purposes of this section there may be a joint tenancy of a chose in action.

Defined terms—"net estate": s 25(1).

"joint tenancy of any property" (s 9(1))—In the case of a joint life policy, in the absence of evidence to the contrary, the death benefit is taken to be intended by the parties to be payable to the survivor of the two policy-holders (*Murphy v Murphy & Others* [2004] 1 FCR 1). In *Jessop v Jessop* [1992] 1 FLR 591, the court ordered the deceased's severable share of his cohabitee's house which had been jointly owned before the deceased's death, to be treated as part of the net estate of the deceased and ordered the cohabitee to pay a lump sum to the widow. In *Re Crawford* (1983) 4 FLR 273, a lump sum received by the deceased on his retirement had been paid into an account held jointly with his second wife. The court made an order under s 9 that the deceased's share of the lump sum should be treated as part of his estate. Where the deceased's net estate consists of a beneficial half share to a joint tenancy of property which is subject to a mortgage secured by a collateral endowment insurance policy the value of the deceased's net estate is determined for the purposes of s 9(1) at the time immediately before his death (*Powell v Osbourne* [1993] 1 FLR 1001). Where a deceased person's estate is found to be insolvent, administration takes place under Insolvency Act 1986, s 421 and the matter is governed by the Administration of Insolvent Estates of Deceased Persons Order 1986. However, the making of an insolvency administration order does not relate back to sever the deceased's beneficial interest in property owned by the deceased and his wife immediately before the deceased's death, as the deceased's interest in the property passes to the widow by survivorship at the moment of death (*Re Palmer (Deceased) (Insolvent Estate)* [1994] 2 FLR 609). Where, on an application for ancillary relief following a divorce, an agreement is reached between the parties for the sale of the former matrimonial home and the division of the proceeds of sale, the joint tenancy is severed so that, if one of the parties dies before the agreement is approved by the court and an order made, the joint tenancy remains severed by the agreement. The agreement does not have to be enforceable, provided it indicates a common intention to sever (*Davis v Smith* [2012] 1 FLR 1177; *Quigley v Masterson* [2012] 1 All ER 1224).

"at the value thereof immediately before his death"—For the meaning of this term see *Dingmar v Dingmar* [2007] 1 FLR 210.

"for the purpose of facilitating the making of financial provision" (s 9(1))—This should not be understood to narrow the broad discretionary power given by s 9 (*Kourkgy v Lusher* (1983) 4 FLR 65), but the broad discretionary power is no more than a power to facilitate the making of an order under s 2 (*Jessop v Jessop* [1992] 1 FLR 591).

Powers of court in relation to transactions intended to defeat applications for financial provision

10 Dispositions intended to defeat applications for financial provision

(1) Where an application is made to the court for an order under section 2 of this Act, the applicant may, in the proceedings on that application, apply to the court for an order under subsection (2) below.

(2) Where on an application under subsection (1) above the court is satisfied –

    (a)   that, less than six years before the date of the death of the deceased, the deceased with the intention of defeating an application for financial provision under this Act made a disposition, and

    (b)   that full valuable consideration for that disposition was not given by the person to whom or for the benefit of whom the disposition was made (in this section referred to as "the donee") or by any other person, and

    (c)   that the exercise of the powers conferred by this section would facilitate the making of financial provision for the applicant under this Act,

then, subject to the provisions of this section and of sections 12 and 13 of this Act, the court may order the donee (whether or not at the date of the order he holds any interest in the property disposed of to him or for his benefit by the deceased) to provide, for the purpose of the making of that financial provision, such sum of money or other property as may be specified in the order.

(3) Where an order is made under subsection (2) above as respects any disposition made by the deceased which consisted of the payment of money to or for the benefit of the donee, the amount of any sum of money or the value of any property orders to be provided under that subsection shall not exceed the amount of the payment made by the deceased after deducting therefrom any capital transfer tax borne by the donee in respect of that payment.

(4) Where an order is made under subsection (2) above as respects any disposition made by the deceased which consisted of the transfer of property (other than a sum of money) to or for the benefit of the donee, the amount of any sum of money or the value of any property ordered to be provided under that subsection shall not exceed the value at the date of the death of the deceased of the property disposed of by him to or for the benefit of the donee (or if that property has been disposed of by the person to whom it was

transferred by the deceased, the value at the date of that disposal thereof) after deducting therefrom any capital transfer tax borne by the donee in respect of the transfer of that property by the deceased.

(5) Where an application (in this subsection referred to as "the original application") is made for an order under subsection (2) above in relation to any disposition, then, if on an application under this subsection by the donee or by any applicant for an order under section 2 of this Act the court is satisfied –

    (a)   that, less than six years before the date of the death of the deceased, the deceased with the intention of defeating an application for financial provision under this Act made a disposition other than the disposition which is the subject of the original application, and

    (b)   that full valuable consideration for that other disposition was not given by the person to whom or for the benefit of whom that other disposition was made or by any other person,

the court may exercise in relation to the person to whom or for the benefit of whom that other disposition was made the powers which the court would have had under subsection (2) above if the original application had been made in respect of that other disposition and the court had been satisfied as to the matters set out in paragraphs (a), (b) and (c) of that subsection; and where any application is made under this subsection, any reference in this section (except in subsection (2)(b)) to the donee shall include a reference to the person to whom or for the benefit of whom that other disposition was made.

(6) In determining whether and in what manner to exercise its powers under this section, the court shall have regard to the circumstances in which any disposition was made and any valuable consideration which was given therefor, the relationship, if any, of the donee to the deceased, the conduct and financial resources of the donee and all the other circumstances of the case.

(7) In this section "disposition" does not include –

    (a)   any provision in a will, any such nomination as is mentioned in section 8(1) of this Act or any donatio mortis causa, or

    (b)   any appointment of property made, otherwise than by will, in the exercise of a special power of appointment,

but, subject to these exceptions, includes any payment of money (including the payment of a premium under a policy of assurance) and any conveyance, assurance, appointment or gift of property of any description, whether made by an instrument or otherwise.

(8) The provisions of this section do not apply to any disposition made before the commencement of this Act.

Defined terms—"valuable consideration": s 25.

Avoidance of disposition intended to defeat a claim—An applicant who applies for an order under s 2 may also apply for an order that the donee of a disposition made less than 6 years before the deceased's death with the intention of defeating a claim under the Act and without full valuable consideration should provide such sum or property as may be necessary for the making of reasonable financial provision for the applicant. The court's power under this section is subject to the matters referred to in ss 12 and 13.

See *Clifford v Tanner* [1987] CLY 3881, where it was held that a deed releasing a donee from a covenant allowing the donor and his wife to occupy a house, which was the subject of a gift to the donee, is a disposition within s 10(7).

"intention of defeating an application" (s 10(2)(a),(5)(a))—It is not essential to show that the deceased had the provision of the Act in mind when the transaction in issue was made, but the evidence must show that he intended to defeat a claim against his estate made after his death (*Re Kennedy (dec'd)* [1980] CLY 2820).

11 Contracts to leave property by will

(1) Where an application is made to a court for an order under section 2 of this Act, the applicant may, in the proceedings on that application, apply to the court for an order under this section.

(2) Where on an application under subsection (1) above the court is satisfied –

(a) that the deceased made a contract by which he agreed to leave by his will a sum of money or other property to any person or by which he agreed that a sum of money or other property would be paid or transferred to any person out of his estate, and

(b) that the deceased made that contract with the intention of defeating an application for financial provision under this Act, and

(c) that when the contract was made full valuable consideration for that contract was not given or promised by the person with whom or for the benefit of whom the contract was made (in this section referred to as "the donee") or by any other person, and

(d) that the exercise of the powers conferred by this section would facilitate the making of financial provision for the applicant under this Act,

then, subject to the provisions of this section and of sections 12 and 13 of this Act, the court may make any one or more of the following orders, that is to say –

(i) if any money has been paid or any other property has been transferred to or for the benefit of the donee in accordance with the contract, an order directing the donee to provide, for the purpose of the making of that financial provision, such sum of money or other property as may be specified in the order;

(ii) if the money or all the money has not been paid or the property or all the property has not been transferred in accordance with the contract, an order directing the personal representatives not to make any payment or transfer any property, or not to make any further payment or transfer any further property, as the case may be, in accordance therewith or directing the personal representatives only to make such payment or transfer such property as may be specified in the order.

(3) Notwithstanding anything in subsection (2) above, the court may exercise its powers thereunder in relation to any contract made by the deceased only to the extent that the court considers that the amount of any sum of money paid or to be paid or the value of any property transferred or to be transferred in accordance with the contract exceeds the value of any valuable consideration given or to be given for that contract, and for this purpose the court shall have regard to the value of property at the date of the hearing.

(4) In determining whether and in what manner to exercise its powers under this section, the court shall have regard to the circumstances in which the contract was made, the relationship, if any, of the donee to the deceased, the conduct and financial resources of the donee and all the other circumstances of the case.

(5) Where an order has been made under subsection (2) above in relation to any contract, the rights of any person to enforce that contract or to recover damages or to obtain other relief for the breach thereof shall be subject to any adjustment made by the court under section 12(3) of this Act and shall survive to such extent only as is consistent with giving effect to the terms of that order.

(6) The provision of this section do not apply to a contract made before the commencement of this Act.

Avoidance of contracts to leave property by will—An applicant who applies for an order under s 2 may also apply for an order directing the donee under a contract which was made with the intention of defeating a claim under the Act and without full valuable consideration to provide such sum of money or other property as may be necessary for the making of reasonable financial provision for the applicant. Where the sum of money or the property has not been transferred, the order should direct that the personal representatives must not make the payment or transfer the property, or make any further payment or transfer any further property, or that they may make only such payment or transfer as the court may direct. Under this section the court has power to make such further consequential directions as it thinks fit for giving effect to any order it makes.

12 Provisions supplementary to ss 10 and 11

(1) Where the exercise of any of the powers conferred by section 10 or 11 of this Act is conditional on the court being satisfied that a disposition or contract was made by a deceased person with the intention of defeating an application for financial provision under this Act, that condition shall be fulfilled if the court is of the opinion that, on a balance of probabilities, the intention of the deceased (though not necessarily his sole intention) in making the disposition or contract was to prevent an order for financial provision being made under this Act or to reduce the amount of the provision which might otherwise be granted by an order thereunder.

(2) Where an application is made under section 11 of this Act with respect to any contract made by the deceased and no valuable consideration was given or promised by any person for that contract then, notwithstanding anything in subsection (1) above, it shall be presumed, unless the contrary is shown, that the deceased made that contract with the intention of defeating an application for financial provision under this Act.

(3) Where the court makes an order under section 10 or 11 of this Act it may give such consequential directions as it thinks fit (including directions requiring the making of any payment or the transfer of any property) for giving effect to the order or for securing a fair adjustment of the rights of the persons affected thereby.

(4) Any power conferred on the court by the said section 10 or 11 to order the donee, in relation to any disposition or contract, to provide any sum of money or other property shall be exercisable in like manner in relation to the personal representative of the donee, and –

(a) any reference in section 10(4) to the disposal of property by the donee shall include a reference to disposal by the personal representative of the donee, and

(b) any reference in section 10(5) to an application by the donee under that subsection shall include a reference to an application by the personal representative of the donee;

but the court shall not have power under the said section 10 or 11 to make an order in respect of any property forming part of the estate of the donee which has been distributed by the personal representative; and the personal representative shall not be liable for having distributed any such property before he has notice of the making of an application under the said section 10 or 11 on the ground that he ought to have taken into account the possibility that such an application would be made.

13 Provisions as to trustees in relation to ss 10 and 11

(1) Where an application is made for –

(a) an order under section 10 of this Act in respect of a disposition made by the deceased to any person as a trustee, or

(b) an order under section 11 of this Act in respect of any payment made or property transferred, in accordance with a contract made by the deceased, to any person as a trustee,

the powers of the court under the said section 10 or 11 to order that trustee to provide a sum of money or other property shall be subject to the following limitation (in addition, in a case of an application under section 10, to any provision regarding the deduction of capital transfer tax) namely, that the amount of any sum of money or the value of any property ordered to be provided –

(i)   in the case of an application in respect of a disposition which consisted of the payment of money or an application in respect of the payment of money in accordance with a contract, shall not exceed the aggregate of so much of that money as is at the date of the order in the hands of the trustee and the value at that date of any property which represents that money or is derived therefrom and is at that date in the hands of the trustee;

(ii) in the case of an application in respect of a disposition which consisted of the transfer of property (other than a sum of money) or an application in respect of the transfer of property (other than a sum of money) in accordance with a contract, shall not exceed the aggregate of the value at the date of the order of so much of that property as is at that date in the hands of the trustee and the value at that date of any property which represents the first mentioned property or is derived therefrom and is at that date in the hands of the trustee.

(2) Where any such application is made in respect of a disposition made to any person as a trustee or in respect of any payment made or property transferred in pursuance of a contract to any person as a trustee, the trustee shall not be liable for having distributed any money or other property on the ground that he ought to have taken into account the possibility that such an application would be made.

(3) Where any such application is made in respect of a disposition made to any person as a trustee or in respect of any payment made or property transferred in accordance with a contract to any person as a trustee, any reference in the said section 10 or 11 to the donee shall be construed as including a reference to the trustee or trustees for the time being of the trust in question and any reference in subsection (1) or (2) above to a trustee shall be construed in the same way.

Special provisions relating to cases of divorce, separation etc

14 Provision as to cases where no financial relief was granted in divorce proceedings etc

(1) Where, within twelve months from the date on which a decree of divorce or nullity of marriage has been made absolute or a decree of judicial separation has been granted, a party to the marriage dies and –

(a) an application for a financial provision order under section 23 of the Matrimonial Causes Act 1973 or a property adjustment order under section 24 of that Act has not been made by the other party to that marriage, or

(b) such an application has been made but the proceedings thereon have not been determined at the time of the death of the deceased,

then, if an application for an order under section 2 of this Act is made by that other party, the court shall, notwithstanding anything in section 1 or section 3 of this Act, have power, if it thinks it just to do so, to treat that party for the purposes of that application as if the decree of divorce or nullity of marriage had not been made absolute or the decree of judicial separation had not been granted, as the case may be.

(2) This section shall not apply in relation to a decree of judicial separation unless at the date of the death of the deceased the decree was in force and the separation was continuing.

Defined terms—"financial provision": MCA 1973, s 23; "property adjustment order": MCA 1973, s 24.

14A Provision as to cases where no financial relief was granted in proceedings for the dissolution etc. of a civil partnership

(1) Subsection (2) below applies where –

- (a) a dissolution order, nullity order, separation order or presumption of death order has been made under Chapter 2 of Part 2 of the Civil Partnership Act 2004 in relation to a civil partnership,
- (b) one of the civil partners dies within twelve months from the date on which the order is made, and
- (c) either –
  - (i) an application for a financial provision order under Part 1 of Schedule 5 to that Act or a property adjustment order under Part 2 of that Schedule has not been made by the other civil partner, or
  - (ii) such an application has been made but the proceedings on the application have not been determined at the time of the death of the deceased.

(2) If an application for an order under section 2 of this Act is made by the surviving civil partner, the court shall, notwithstanding anything in section 1 or section 3 of this Act, have power, if it thinks it just to do so, to treat the surviving civil partner as if the order mentioned in subsection (1)(a) above had not been made.

(3) This section shall not apply in relation to a separation order unless at the date of the death of the deceased the separation order was in force and the separation was continuing.

Amendments—Inserted by CPA 2004, s 71, Sch 4, para 20.

15 Restriction imposed in divorce proceedings etc on application under this Act

(1) On the grant of a decree of divorce, a decree of nullity of marriage or a decree of judicial separation or at any time thereafter the court, if it considers it just to do so, may, on the application of either party to the marriage, order that the other party to the marriage shall not on the death of the applicant be entitled to apply for an order under section 2 of this Act.

In this subsection "the court" means the High Court or, where a county court has jurisdiction by virtue of Part V of the Matrimonial and Family Proceedings Act 1984, a county court.

(2) In the case of a decree of divorce or nullity of marriage an order may be made under subsection (1) above before or after the decree is made absolute, but if it is made before the decree is made absolute it shall not take effect unless the decree is made absolute.

(3) Where an order made under subsection (1) above on the grant of a decree of divorce or nullity of marriage has come into force with respect to a party to a marriage, then, on the death of the other party to that marriage, the court shall not entertain any application for an order under section 2 of this Act made by the first-mentioned party.

(4) Where an order made under subsection (1) above on the grant of a decree of judicial separation has come into force with respect to any party to a marriage, then, if the other party to that marriage dies while the decree is in force and the separation is continuing, the court shall not entertain any application for an order under section 2 of this Act made by the first-mentioned party.

Amendments—MFPA 1984, s 8(1).

PART II

15ZA Restriction imposed in proceedings for the dissolution etc. of a civil partnership on application under this Act

(1) On making a dissolution order, nullity order, separation order or presumption of death order under Chapter 2 of Part 2 of the Civil Partnership Act 2004, or at any time after making such an order, the court, if it considers it just to do so, may, on the application of either of the civil partners, order that the other civil partner shall not on the death of the applicant be entitled to apply for an order under section 2 of this Act.

(2) In subsection (1) above "the court" means the High Court or, where a county court has jurisdiction by virtue of Part 5 of the Matrimonial and Family Proceedings Act 1984, a county court.

(3) In the case of a dissolution order, nullity order or presumption of death order ("the main order") an order may be made under subsection (1) above before (as well as after) the main order is made final, but if made before the main order is made final it shall not take effect unless the main order is made final.

(4) Where an order under subsection (1) above made in connection with a dissolution order, nullity order or presumption of death order has come into force with respect to a civil partner, then, on the death of the other civil partner, the court shall not entertain any application for an order under section 2 of this Act made by the surviving civil partner.

(5) Where an order under subsection (1) above made in connection with a separation order has come into force with respect to a civil partner, then, if the other civil partner dies while the separation order is in force and the separation is continuing, the court shall not entertain any application for an order under section 2 of this Act made by the surviving civil partner.

Amendments—Inserted by CPA 2004, s 71, Sch 4, para 21.

15A Restriction imposed in proceedings under Matrimonial and Family Proceedings Act 1984 on application under this Act

(1) On making an order under section 17 of the Matrimonial and Family Proceedings Act 1984 (orders for financial provision and property adjustment) the court, if it considers it just to do so, may, on the application of either party to the marriage, order that the other party to the marriage shall not on the death of the applicant be entitled to apply for an order under section 2 of this Act.

In this subsection "the court" means the High Court or, where a county court has jurisdiction by virtue of Part V of the Matrimonial and Family Proceedings Act 1984, a county court.

(2) Where an order under subsection (1) above has been made with respect to a party to a marriage which has been dissolved or annulled, then, on the death of the other party to that marriage, the court shall not entertain an application under section 2 of this Act made by the first-mentioned party.

(3) Where an order under subsection (1) above has been made with respect to a party to a marriage the parties to which have been legally separated, then, if the other party to the marriage dies while the legal separation is in force, the court shall not entertain an application under section 2 of this Act made by the first-mentioned party.

Amendments—Inserted by MFPA 1984, s 25.

15B Restriction imposed in proceedings under Schedule 7 to the Civil Partnership Act 2004 on application under this Act

(1) On making an order under paragraph 9 of Schedule 7 to the Civil Partnership Act 2004 (orders for financial provision, property adjustment and pension-sharing

following overseas dissolution etc. of civil partnership) the court, if it considers it just to do so, may, on the application of either of the civil partners, order that the other civil partner shall not on the death of the applicant be entitled to apply for an order under section 2 of this Act.

(2) In subsection (1) above "the court" means the High Court or, where a county court has jurisdiction by virtue of Part 5 of the Matrimonial and Family Proceedings Act 1984, a county court.

(3) Where an order under subsection (1) above has been made with respect to one of the civil partners in a case where a civil partnership has been dissolved or annulled, then, on the death of the other civil partner, the court shall not entertain an application under section 2 of this Act made by the surviving civil partner.

(4) Where an order under subsection (1) above has been made with respect to one of the civil partners in a case where civil partners have been legally separated, then, if the other civil partner dies while the legal separation is in force, the court shall not entertain an application under section 2 of this Act made by the surviving civil partner.

Amendments—Inserted by CPA 2004, s 71, Sch 4, para 22.

16 Variation and discharge of secured periodical payments orders made under Matrimonial Causes Act 1973

(1) Where an application for an order under section 2 of this Act is made to the court by any person who was at the time of the death of the deceased entitled to payments from the deceased under a secured periodical payments order made under the Matrimonial Causes Act 1973 or Schedule 5 to the Civil Partnership Act 2004, then, in the proceedings on that application, the court shall have power, if an application is made under this section by that person or by the personal representative of the deceased, to vary or discharge that periodical payments order or to revive the operation of any provision thereof which has been suspended under section 31 of that Act of 1973 or Part 11 of that Schedule.

(2) In exercising the powers conferred by this section the court shall have regard to all the circumstances of the case, including any order which the court proposes to make under section 2 or section 5 of this Act and any change (whether resulting from the death of the deceased or otherwise) in any of the matters to which the court was required to have regard when making the secured periodical payments order.

(3) The powers exercisable by the court under this section in relation to an order shall be exercisable also in relation to any instrument executed in pursuance of the order.

Amendments—CPA 2004, s 71, Sch 4, para 23.

Defined terms—"secured periodical payments": MCA 1973, s 23.

17 Variation and revocation of maintenance agreements

(1) Where an application for an order under section 2 of this Act is made to the court by any person who was at the time of the death of the deceased entitled to payments from the deceased under a maintenance agreement which provided for the continuation of payments under the agreement after the death of the deceased, then, in the proceedings on that application, the court shall have power, if an application is made under this section by that person or by the personal representative of the deceased, to vary or revoke that agreement.

(2) In exercising the powers conferred by this section the court shall have regard to all the circumstances of the case, including any order which the court proposes to make

under section 2 or section 5 of this Act and any change (whether resulting from the death of the deceased or otherwise) in any of the circumstances in the light of which the agreement was made.

(3) If a maintenance agreement is varied by the court under this section the like consequences shall ensue as if the variation had been made immediately before the death of the deceased by agreement between the parties and for valuable consideration.

(4) In this section "maintenance agreement", in relation to a deceased person, means any agreement made, whether in writing or not and whether before or after the commencement of this Act, by the deceased with any person with whom he formed a marriage or civil partnership, being an agreement which contained provisions governing the rights and liabilities towards one another when living separately of the parties to that marriage or of the civil partners (whether or not the marriage or civil partnership has been dissolved or annulled) in respect of the making or securing of payments or the disposition or use of any property, including such rights and liabilities with respect to the maintenance or education of any child, whether or not a child of the deceased or a person who was treated by the deceased as a child of the family in relation to that marriage or civil partnership.

Amendments—CPA 2004, s 71, Sch 4, para 24.

Scope—The provision is similar to that under s 16, to vary or revoke a maintenance agreement which provided for the continuation of payment under the agreement after the death of the deceased. MCA 1973, s 36 also provides for an application to be made for the alteration of a maintenance agreement after the death of one of the spouses, and FPR 2010, rr 8.6–8.11 prescribes the procedure that must be followed. When making an application under this section reference should be made to the annotation to MCA 1973, s 36 and FPR 2010, Pt 8, Ch 3.

18 Availability of court's powers under this Act in applications under ss 31 and 36 of the Matrimonial Causes Act 1973

(1) Where –

  (a)   a person against whom a secured periodical payments order was made under the Matrimonial Causes Act 1973 has died and an application is made under section 31(6) of that Act for the variation or discharge of that order or for the revival of the operation of any provision thereof which has been suspended, or

  (b)   a party to a maintenance agreement within the meaning of section 34 of that Act has died, the agreement being one which provides for the continuation of payments thereunder after the death of one of the parties, and an application is made under section 36(1) of that Act for the alteration of the agreement under section 35 thereof,

the court shall have power to direct that the application made under the said section 31(6) or 36(1) shall be deemed to have been accompanied by an application for an order under section 2 of this Act.

(2) Where the court gives a direction under subsection (1) above it shall have power, in the proceedings on the application under the said section 31(6) or 36(1), to make any order which the court would have had power to make under the provisions of this Act if the application under the said section 31(6) or 36(1), as the case may be, had been made jointly with an application for an order under the said section 2; and the court shall have power to give such consequential directions as may be necessary for enabling the court to exercise any of the powers available to the court under this Act in the case of an application for an order under section 2.

(3) Where an order made under section 15(1) of this Act is in force with respect to a party to a marriage, the court shall not give a direction under subsection (1) above with respect to any application made under the said section 31(6) or 36(1) by that party on the death of the other party.

18A Availability of court's powers under this Act in applications under paragraphs 60 and 73 of Schedule 5 to the Civil Partnership Act 2004

(1) Where –

(a) a person against whom a secured periodical payments order was made under Schedule 5 to the Civil Partnership Act 2004 has died and an application is made under paragraph 60 of that Schedule for the variation or discharge of that order or for the revival of the operation of any suspended provision of the order, or

(b) a party to a maintenance agreement within the meaning of Part 13 of that Schedule has died, the agreement being one which provides for the continuation of payments under the agreement after the death of one of the parties, and an application is made under paragraph 73 of that Schedule for the alteration of the agreement under paragraph 69 of that Schedule,

the court shall have power to direct that the application made under paragraph 60 or 73 of that Schedule shall be deemed to have been accompanied by an application for an order under section 2 of this Act.

(2) Where the court gives a direction under subsection (1) above it shall have power, in the proceedings on the application under paragraph 60 or 73 of that Schedule, to make any order which the court would have had power to make under the provisions of this Act if the application under that paragraph had been made jointly with an application for an order under section 2 of this Act; and the court shall have power to give such consequential directions as may be necessary for enabling the court to exercise any of the powers available to the court under this Act in the case of an application for an order under section 2.

(3) Where an order made under section 15ZA(1) of this Act is in force with respect to a civil partner, the court shall not give a direction under subsection (1) above with respect to any application made under paragraph 60 or 73 of that Schedule by that civil partner on the death of the other civil partner.

Amendments—Inserted by CPA 2004, s 71, Sch 4, para 25.

Miscellaneous and supplementary provisions

19 Effect, duration and form of orders

(1) Where an order is made under section 2 of this Act then for all purposes, including the purposes of the enactments relating to inheritance tax, the will or the law relating to intestacy, or both the will and the law relating to intestacy, as the case may be, shall have effect and be deemed to have had effect as from the deceased's death subject to the provisions of the order.

(2) Any order made under section 2 or 5 of this Act in favour of –

(a) an applicant who was the former spouse or former civil partner of the deceased, or

(b) an applicant who was the husband or wife of the deceased in a case where the marriage with the deceased was the subject of a decree of judicial separation and at the date of death the decree was in force and the separation was continuing, or

(c)   an applicant who was the civil partner of the deceased in a case where, at the date of death, a separation order under Chapter 2 of Part 2 of the Civil Partnership Act 2004 was in force in relation to their civil partnership and the separation was continuing,

shall, in so far as it provides for the making of periodical payments, cease to have effect on the remarriage of the applicant on the formation by the applicant of a subsequent marriage or civil partnership, except in relation to any arrears due under the order on the date of the formation of the subsequent marriage or civil partnership.

(3) A copy of every order made under this Act other than an order made under section 15(1) or 15ZA(1) of this Act shall be sent to the principal registry of the Family Division for entry and filing, and a memorandum of the order shall be endorsed on, or permanently annexed to, the probate or letters of administration under which the estate is being administered.

Amendments—AJA 1982, s 52; CPA 2004, s 71, Sch 4, para 26.

****

25 Interpretation

(1) In this Act –
"beneficiary", in relation to the estate of a deceased person, means –
(a)   a person who under the will of the deceased or under the law relating to intestacy is beneficially interested in the estate or would be so interested if an order had not been made under this Act, and
(b)   a person who has received any sum of money or other property which by virtue of section 8(1) or (2) of this Act is treated as part of the net estate of the deceased or would have received that sum or other property if an order had not been made under this Act;
"child" includes an illegitimate child and a child en ventre sa mere at the death of the deceased;
"the court" means, unless the context otherwise requires, the High Court, or where a county court has jurisdiction by virtue of section 22 of this Act, a county court;
"former civil partner" means a person whose civil partnership with the deceased was during the lifetime of the deceased either –
(a)   dissolved or annulled by an order made under the law of any part of the British Islands, or
(b)   dissolved or annulled in any country or territory outside the British Islands by a dissolution or annulment which is entitled to be recognised as valid by the law of England and Wales;
"former spouse" means a person whose marriage with the deceased was during the lifetime of the deceased either –
(a)   dissolved or annulled by a decree of divorce or a decree of nullity of marriage granted under the law of any part of the British Islands, or
(b)   dissolved or annulled in any country or territory outside the British Islands by a divorce or annulment which is entitled to be recognised as valid by the law of England and Wales;
"net estate", in relation to a deceased person, means –
(a)   all property of which the deceased had power to dispose by his will (otherwise than by virtue of a special power of appointment) less the amount of his funeral, testamentary and administration expenses, debts and liabilities, including any capital transfer tax payable out of his estate on his death;

(b)   any property in respect of which the deceased held a general power of appointment (not being a power exercisable by will) which has not been exercised;

(c)   any sum of money or other property which is treated for the purposes of this Act as part of the net estate of the deceased by virtue of section 8(1) or (2) of this Act;

(d)   any property which is treated for the purposes of this Act as part of the net estate of the deceased by virtue of an order made under section 9 of the Act;

(e)   any sum of money or other property which is, by reason of a disposition or contract made by the deceased, ordered under section 10 or 11 of this Act to be provided for the purpose of the making of financial provision under this Act;

"property" includes any chose in action;

"reasonable financial provision" has the meaning assigned to it by section 1 of this Act;

"valuable consideration" does not include marriage or a promise of marriage;

"will" includes codicil.

(2) For the purposes of paragraph (a) of the definition of "net estate" in subsection (1) above a person who is not of full age and capacity shall be treated as having power to dispose by will of all property of which he would have had power to dispose by will if he had been of full age and capacity.

(3) Any references in this Act to provision out of the net estate of a deceased person includes a reference to provision extending to the whole of that estate.

(4) For the purposes of this Act any reference to a spouse, wife or husband shall be treated as including a reference to a person who in good faith entered into a void marriage with the deceased unless either –

(a)   the marriage of the deceased and that person was dissolved or annulled during the lifetime of the deceased and the dissolution or annulment is recognised by the law of England and Wales, or

(b)   that person has during the lifetime of the deceased formed a subsequent marriage or civil partnership.

(4A) For the purposes of this Act any reference to a civil partner shall be treated as including a reference to a person who in good faith formed a void civil partnership with the deceased unless either –

(a)   the civil partnership between the deceased and that person was dissolved or annulled during the lifetime of the deceased and the dissolution or annulment is recognised by the law of England and Wales, or

(b)   that person has during the lifetime of the deceased formed a subsequent civil partnership or marriage.

(5) Any reference in this Act to the formation of, or to a person who has formed, a subsequent marriage or civil partnership includes (as the case may be) a reference to the formation of, or to a person who has formed, a marriage or civil partnership which is by law void or voidable.

(5A) The formation of a marriage or civil partnership shall be treated for the purposes of this Act as the formation of a subsequent marriage or civil partnership, in relation to either of the spouses or civil partners, notwithstanding that the previous marriage or civil partnership of that spouse or civil partner was void or voidable.

PART II

(6) Any reference in this Act to an order or decree made under the Matrimonial Causes Act 1973 or under any section of that Act shall be construed as including a reference to an order or decree which is deemed to have been made under that Act or under that section thereof, as the case may be.

(6A) Any reference in this Act to an order made under, or under any provision of, the Civil Partnership Act 2004 shall be construed as including a reference to anything which is deemed to be an order made (as the case may be) under that Act or provision.

(7) Any reference in this Act to any enactment is a reference to that enactment as amended by or under any subsequent enactment.

Amendments—CPA 2004, s 71, Sch 4, para 27.

****

Judicial Proceedings (Regulation of Reports) Act 1926

1 Restriction on publication of reports of judicial proceedings

(1) It shall not be lawful to print or publish, or cause or procure to be printed or published –

   (a) in relation to any judicial proceedings any indecent matter or indecent medical, surgical or physiological details being matter or details the publication of which would be calculated to injure public morals;

   (b) in relation to any judicial proceedings for dissolution of marriage, for nullity of marriage, or for judicial separation, or for the dissolution or annulment of a civil partnership or for the separation of civil partners, any particulars other than the following, that is to say:

      (i) the names, addresses and occupations of the parties and witnesses;

      (ii) a concise statement of the charges, defences and countercharges in support of which evidence has been given;

      (iii) submissions on any point of law arising in the course of the proceedings, and the decision of the court thereon;

      (iv) the summing-up of the judge and the finding of the jury (if any) and the judgment of the court and observations made by the judge in giving judgment.

Provided that nothing in this part of this subsection shall be held to permit the publication of anything contrary to the provisions of paragraph (a) of this subsection.

(2) If any person acts in contravention of the provisions of this Act, he shall in respect of each offence be liable, on summary conviction, to imprisonment for a term not exceeding four months, or to a fine not exceeding level 5 on the standard scale, or to both such imprisonment and fine:

Provided that no person, other than a proprietor, editor, master printer or publisher, shall be liable to be convicted under this Act.

(3) No prosecution for an offence under this Act shall be commenced in England and Wales by any person without the sanction of the Attorney-General.

(4) Nothing in this section shall apply to the printing of any pleading, transcript of evidence or other document for use in connection with any judicial proceedings or the communication thereof to persons concerned in the proceedings, or to the printing or publishing of any notice or report in pursuance of the directions of the court; or to the

printing or publishing of any matter in any separate volume or part of any bone fide series of law reports which does not form part of any other publication and consists solely of reports of proceedings in courts of law, or in any publication of a technical character bona fide intended for circulation among members of the legal or medical professions.

(5) (*repealed*)

Amendments—Criminal Justice Act 1982, s 46(1); CPA 2004, s 261(1),(4), Sch 27, para 8(1)–(3), Sch 30. See also under **Extension of s 1(1)(b)** below.

General note—The fact that a hearing takes place in chambers does not determine whether it should be regarded as subject to a ban on publication. Hearings relating to children and ancillary relief are covered by privacy and secrecy; information about such cases cannot be disclosed without leave of the court, but see *Lykiardopulo v Lykiardopulo and Lykiardopulo* [2011] 1 FLR 1427, where on appeal publication of the judgment without anonymisation but with redaction of sensitive commercial material was allowed. This may in part have been due to the false evidence and documents relied on which led the court to hold that where there has been fraud on the court the litigant who perpetrates that fraud loses the entitlement of confidentiality. Other family proceedings are not so protected. Whether or not they are protected depends on the applicability of AJA 1960, s 12 or the existence of other circumstances which make disclosure prejudicial to the administration of justice, including consideration of the requirement of CCA 1981, s 11 (*Clibbery v Allan and Another* [2002] 1 FLR 565). Section 12 does not prevent publication of the names of the parties or the children, nor does it prohibit discussion within certain bounds of the nature of the dispute, but it does prevent (unless directed by the court) the publication of what occurred before the court and of the documents filed in the proceedings and the evidence given (*Re B; X Council v B and Ors (No 2)* [2008] 1 FLR 1460). Practitioners' attention is drawn to the provisions of FPR 2010, r 27.11, which provide that save for certain exceptions accredited representatives of the media are by right entitled to access to family proceedings in all courts but reporting restriction under AJA 1960 and CA 1989, s 97(2) will continue to apply. The court may, at any stage of the proceedings on its own initiative or on application, direct that a duly accredited representative of the media should not attend the hearing where it is satisfied that this is necessary: in the interests of any child concerned in or connected with the proceedings; for the safety or protection of a party, a witness in the proceedings or a person connected with such a party or witness; for the orderly conduct of the proceedings; or if justice would otherwise be impeded FPR 2010, r 27.11(3). Persons affected by such a direction may apply to make representations (FPR 2010, r 27.11(5)). FPR PD10A also provides that where an occupation order or non-molestation order is made without notice, the terms of the order and the name of the person to whom it is addressed must be announced in open court. Similarly, where a person is brought before the court under a power of arrest the press and the public should be permitted to be present at the hearing unless security needs make this impracticable. See also FPR PD27B and PD27C and the *Guidance of 22 April 2009* (see Part V), *Re Child X (Residence and Contact: Rights of Media Attendance)* [2009] 2 FLR 1467, and the observations made by Sir Mark Potter in the terms set out in his judgment in that case. The PD under FPR 2010 that deals with old PDs confirms that the PD27B and PD27C should be read as if amended by *Re X*. In relation to the prohibition contained in AJA 1960, s 12 on the publication of information relating to proceedings held in private in children cases and the expectation of anonymity by experts and witnesses, see *A v Ward* [2010] 1 FLR 1497. See also *Coventry City Council v X, Y and Z (Identification of Local Authority)* [2011] 1 FLR 977, where the court permitted the identification of the local authority.

"in relation to any judicial proceedings for dissolution of marriage" (s 1(1)(b))—Proceedings are not concluded finally until any question arising as to the validity of any decree or order which might have been made is finally resolved; thus, proceedings concerning an application to render a decree of divorce null and void are covered by the 1926 Act and the evidence given at the hearing cannot be reported (*Moynihan v Moynihan (Nos 1 and 2)* [1997] 1 FLR 59), but "there would appear to be ample scope in the context of the subparagraphs of subpara (b) for clear and full details to be given, though not necessarily a line-by-line account of what a particular witness says at any particular time" (at [62G]).

Extension of s 1(1)(b)—Although this section has not been amended textually, it has been extended, by virtue of amendments made to Domestic and Appellate Proceedings (Restriction of Publicity) Act 1968, s 2(3) by FLA 1986 and FLRA 1987, to cover proceedings under MCA 1973, s 27 (failure to maintain), proceedings under FLA 1986, Pt III (as from 4 April 1988), and applications for a declaration under FLA 1986, s 56(1) (as from 4 April 1988). The particulars specified in s 1(1)(b) are modified in their application to allow publication of the particulars of the declaration sought instead of a concise statement of charges, defences and countercharges. See further under DAP(RP)A 1968, s 2 above.

Procedure—See *Emergency Remedies in the Family Courts* (Family Law).

Law Reform (Miscellaneous Provisions) Act 1970

1 Engagements to marry not enforceable at law

(1) An agreement between two persons to marry one another shall not under the law of England and Wales have effect as a contract giving rise to legal rights and no action shall lie in England and Wales for breach of such an agreement, whatever the law applicable to the agreement.

(2) This section shall have effect in relation to agreements entered into before it comes into force, except that it shall not affect any action commenced before it comes into force.

2 Property of engaged couples

(1) Where an agreement to marry is terminated, any rule of law relating to the rights of husbands and wives in relation to property in which either or both has or have a beneficial interest, including any such rule as explained by section 37 of the Matrimonial Proceedings and Property Act 1970, shall apply, in relation to any property in which either or both of the parties to the agreement had a beneficial interest while the agreement was in force, as it applies in relation to property in which a husband or wife has a beneficial interest.

(2) Where an agreement to marry is terminated, section 17 of the Married Women's Property Act 1882 and section 7 of the Matrimonial Causes (Property and Maintenance) Act 1958 (which sections confer power on a judge of the High Court or a county court to settle disputes between husband and wife about property) shall apply, as if the parties were married, to any dispute between, or claim by, one of them in relation to property in which either or both had a beneficial interest while the agreement was in force; but an application made by virtue of this section to the judge under the said section 17, as originally enacted or as extended by the said section 7, shall be made within three years of the termination of the agreement.

3 Gifts between engaged couples

(1) A party to an agreement to marry who makes a gift of property to the other party to the agreement on the condition (express or implied) that it shall be returned if the agreement is terminated shall not be prevented from recovering the property by reason only of his having terminated the agreement.

(2) The gift of an engagement ring shall be presumed to be an absolute gift; this presumption may be rebutted by proving that the ring was given on the condition, express or implied, that it should be returned if the marriage did not take place for any reason.

****

Legal Aid, Sentencing and Punishment of Offenders Act 2012

****

25 Charges on property in connection with civil legal services

(1) Where civil legal services are made available to an individual under this Part, the amounts described in subsection (2) are to constitute a first charge on –

(a) any property recovered or preserved by the individual in proceedings, or in any compromise or settlement of a dispute, in connection with which the services were provided (whether the property is recovered or preserved for the individual or another person), and

(b) any costs payable to the individual by another person in connection with such proceedings or such a dispute.

(2) Those amounts are –

(a) amounts expended by the Lord Chancellor in securing the provision of the services (except to the extent that they are recovered by other means), and

(b) other amounts payable by the individual in connection with the services under section 23 or 24.

(3) Regulations may make provision for exceptions from subsection (1).

(4) Regulations may make provision about the charge under subsection (1) including, in particular –

(a) provision as to whether the charge is in favour of the Lord Chancellor or a person by whom the services were made available,

(b) provision modifying the charge for the purposes of its application in prescribed cases or circumstances, and

(c) provision about the enforcement of the charge.

(5) Regulations under subsection (4)(c) may, in particular, include –

(a) provision requiring amounts recovered by the individual in proceedings or as part of a compromise or settlement of a dispute, and costs payable to the individual, to be paid to the Lord Chancellor or a person by whom the services were made available,

(b) provision about the time and manner in which the amounts must be paid,

(c) provision about what the Lord Chancellor or the person by whom the services were made available must do with the amounts,

(d) provision for the payment of interest on all or part of the amounts,

(e) provision for the payment to the individual concerned of any amount in excess of the amounts described in subsection (2), and

(f) provision for the enforcement of requirements described in paragraph (a).

(6) Regulations under this section may include provision requiring information and documents to be provided.

"a first charge on any property recovered or preserved" (s 25(1)(a))—Assessment of whether the charge arises turns on the following (as it has under successive legal aid legislation):

(i) *What are the proceedings?* This refers to the proceedings for which the certificate was issued (*Hanlon v Law Society* [1981] AC 124, HL).

(ii) *What is the property?* In most matrimonial proceedings, "property" will be all the parties' matrimonial assets – i e property owned by both parties whether jointly or individually. For guidance on CLS charge attaching to pension sharing and attachment, see note under MCA 1973, s 21A. To property in the proceedings, s 25(1)(b) has added a charge upon costs payable to the funded individual.

(iii) *Was the property in issue?*   Whether or not the charge applies to particular property turns on whether or not it was in issue in the proceedings. This is determined by looking at any court order, affidavits or pleadings, and even the correspondence between the parties (*Hanlon v Law Society* (above)).

(iv) *Was the property "recovered or preserved"?*   If property is in issue in proceedings then it will have been "recovered or preserved" and the charge applies, subject to any of the exemptions set out in the regulations. Thus property is recovered if a person takes proceedings to convert it to his own use – e g a property adjustment order or a lump sum order (*Curling v Law Society* [1985] FLR 831, CA); property is preserved if a person successfully resists a claim to his property – e g an order for sale or a property adjustment order (*Parkes v Legal Aid Board* [1997] 1 FLR 77, CA).

"whether for himself or any other person" s 25(1)(a)—The aim of drafting the section in this way was to ensure that the charge arises even though property or money is transferred to a third party, such as a child (see for example *Draskovic v Draskovic* (1981) Fam Law 87, although in that case the assisted person's solicitors were held to have evaded the charge). The charge will apply even though the payment is made to the funded client personally.

"in any compromise or settlement of any dispute" (s 25(1)(a))—The charge arises even though the liability to costs of the funded client arose as a result of "any compromise or settlement of any dispute". Thus the charge applies, even though the property recovered in the settlement was not the property directly in issue in the proceedings (*Van Hoorn v Law Society* [1984] FLR 203).

26 Costs in civil proceedings

(1) Costs ordered against an individual in relevant civil proceedings must not exceed the amount (if any) which it is reasonable for the individual to pay having regard to all the circumstances, including –

    (a)   the financial resources of all of the parties to the proceedings, and

    (b)   their conduct in connection with the dispute to which the proceedings relate.

(2) In subsection (1) "relevant civil proceedings", in relation to an individual, means –

    (a)   proceedings for the purposes of which civil legal services are made available to the individual under this Part, or

    (b)   if such services are made available to the individual under this Part for the purposes of only part of proceedings, that part of the proceedings.

(3) Regulations may make provision for exceptions from subsection (1).

(4) In assessing for the purposes of subsection (1) the financial resources of an individual to whom civil legal services are made available, the following must not be taken into account, except so far as prescribed –

    (a)   the individual's clothes and household furniture, and

    (b)   the implements of the individual's trade.

(5) Subject to subsections (1) to (4), regulations may make provision about costs in relation to proceedings for the purposes of which civil legal services are made available under this Part.

(6) Regulations under subsection (5) may, in particular, make provision –

    (a)   specifying the principles to be applied in determining the amount of any costs which may be awarded against a party to whom civil legal services are made available under this Part,

    (b)   limiting the circumstances in which, or the extent to which, an order for costs may be enforced against such a party,

    (c)   as to the cases in which, and the extent to which, such a party may be required to give security for costs and the manner in which it is to be given,

    (d)   requiring the payment by the Lord Chancellor of the whole or part of any costs incurred by a party to whom civil legal services are not made available under this Part,

(e) specifying the principles to be applied in determining the amount of costs which may be awarded to a party to whom civil legal services are made available under this Part,

(f) as to the court, tribunal or other person by whom the amount of any costs is to be determined, and

(g) as to the extent to which any determination of that amount is to be final.

(7) Regulations may provide that an individual is to be treated, for the purposes of subsection (1) or regulations under subsection (3) or (5), as having or not having financial resources of a prescribed description (but such regulations have effect subject to subsection (4)).

(8) Regulations under subsection (7) may, in particular, provide that the individual is to be treated as having prescribed financial resources of a person of a prescribed description.

(9) Regulations under this section may include provision requiring information and documents to be provided.

****

PART II

Legal Services Act 2007

ARRANGEMENT OF SECTIONS

PART 3
RESERVED LEGAL ACTIVITIES

Reserved legal activities

Rights of audience—The 2007 Act provides the regulatory framework for the provision of legal services, including the exercise of a right of audience. As of 1 January 2010, it replaced similar provisions in the Courts and Legal Services Act 1990. Whether or not a person has a right of audience must be determined solely in accordance with the provisions of the Act. A person must either be "authorised" or "exempt". A person will be "authorised" if granted a right of audience by an "authorised body" (ie authorised by the Legal Services Board). Thus, for example, the General Council of the Bar and the Law Society will authorise barristers and solicitors. A person who is not authorised may be "exempt" under Sch 3, para 1.

Schedule 3, para 1(2) enables the court, as a matter of discretion, to grant a right of audience to a particular person in relation to a specific case (not generally) and it is in this area that most of the case-law arises. Unqualified persons wishing to appear for a party have caused particular problems in family cases. In *Clarkson v Gilbert* [2000] 2 FLR 839, Lord Woolf explained that a party to litigation has two options: first, he may instruct a lawyer with the appropriate rights; second, he can act in person. If he exercises the second option but then does not wish to exercise his right he cannot delegate it (not even to a person with a power of attorney (*Gregory v Turner; R (on the application of Morris) v North Somerset Council* [2003] 1 WLR 1149)) and must invite the court (at the first inter partes hearing) to exercise its inherent jurisdiction preserved by para 1(2). However, this provision cannot be habitually relied on by unqualified persons who have set themselves up to provide advocacy services (whether for reward or not) and wishing to represent a litigant in person – that would be "monstrously inappropriate" (per Lord Woolf in *D v S* [1997] 1 FLR 724 at [19]) The court is inclined to look more favourably on a request that is clearly specific to the instant case, such as by a relative or family friend. But in all cases the court must have regard to the statutory framework, for it is essential not only to justice but to the administration of justice that the court has confidence in advocates. A "right of audience" means the right to appear before and address a court, including the right to call and to cross-examine witnesses (s 2 and Sch 2, para 3(1)).

A "McKenzie Friend" does not have a right of audience, but see further *Practice Guidance of 12 July 2010* (in Part V).

"Reserved family proceedings" are mentioned in Sch 3, para 1(10) and would be a category of proceedings to which the exemption referred to in para 1(7) would not apply. However, the Lord Chancellor has not exercised the power to prescribe any category of family proceedings as such.

****

PART 3
RESERVED LEGAL ACTIVITIES

Reserved legal activities

12 Meaning of "reserved legal activity" and "legal activity"

(1) In this Act "reserved legal activity" means –

   (a)   the exercise of a right of audience;
   (b)   the conduct of litigation;
   (c)   reserved instrument activities;
   (d)   probate activities;
   (e)   notarial activities;
   (f)   the administration of oaths.

(2) Schedule 2 makes provision about what constitutes each of those activities.

(3) In this Act "legal activity" means –

   (a)   an activity which is a reserved legal activity within the meaning of this Act as originally enacted, and
   (b)   any other activity which consists of one or both of the following –
       (i)   the provision of legal advice or assistance in connection with the application of the law or with any form of resolution of legal disputes;

    (ii)   the provision of representation in connection with any matter concerning the application of the law or any form of resolution of legal disputes.

(4) But "legal activity" does not include any activity of a judicial or quasi-judicial nature (including acting as a mediator).

(5) For the purposes of subsection (3) "legal dispute" includes a dispute as to any matter of fact the resolution of which is relevant to determining the nature of any person's legal rights or liabilities.

(6) Section 24 makes provision for adding legal activities to the reserved legal activities.

Carrying on the activities

13 Entitlement to carry on a reserved legal activity

(1) The question whether a person is entitled to carry on an activity which is a reserved legal activity is to be determined solely in accordance with the provisions of this Act.

(2) A person is entitled to carry on an activity ("the relevant activity") which is a reserved legal activity where –

    (a)   the person is an authorised person in relation to the relevant activity, or
    (b)   the person is an exempt person in relation to that activity.

(3) Subsection (2) is subject to section 23 (transitional protection for non-commercial bodies).

(4) Nothing in this section or section 23 affects section 84 of the Immigration and Asylum Act 1999 (which prohibits the provision of immigration advice and immigration services except by certain persons).

Offences

14 Offence to carry on a reserved legal activity if not entitled

(1) It is an offence for a person to carry on an activity ("the relevant activity") which is a reserved legal activity unless that person is entitled to carry on the relevant activity.

(2) In proceedings for an offence under subsection (1), it is a defence for the accused to show that the accused did not know, and could not reasonably have been expected to know, that the offence was being committed.

(3) A person who is guilty of an offence under subsection (1) is liable –

    (a)   on summary conviction, to imprisonment for a term not exceeding 12 months or a fine not exceeding the statutory maximum (or both), and
    (b)   on conviction on indictment, to imprisonment for a term not exceeding 2 years or a fine (or both).

(4) A person who is guilty of an offence under subsection (1) by reason of an act done in the purported exercise of a right of audience, or a right to conduct litigation, in relation to any proceedings or contemplated proceedings is also guilty of contempt of the court concerned and may be punished accordingly.

(5) In relation to an offence under subsection (1) committed before the commencement of section 154(1) of the Criminal Justice Act 2003, the reference in subsection (3)(a) to 12 months is to be read as a reference to 6 months.

15 Carrying on of a reserved legal activity: employers and employees etc

(1) This section applies for the interpretation of references in this Act to a person carrying on an activity which is a reserved legal activity.

(2) References to a person carrying on an activity which is a reserved legal activity include a person ("E") who –

    (a)   is an employee of a person ("P"), and

    (b)   carries on the activity in E's capacity as such an employee.

(3) For the purposes of subsection (2), it is irrelevant whether P is entitled to carry on the activity.

(4) P does not carry on an activity ("the relevant activity") which is a reserved legal activity by virtue of E carrying it on in E's capacity as an employee of P, unless the provision of relevant services to the public or a section of the public (with or without a view to profit) is part of P's business.

(5) Relevant services are services which consist of or include the carrying on of the relevant activity by employees of P in their capacity as employees of P.

(6) Where P is an independent trade union, persons provided with relevant services do not constitute the public or a section of the public where –

    (a)   the persons are provided with the relevant services by virtue of their membership or former membership of P or of another person's membership or former membership of P, and

    (b)   the services are excepted membership services.

(7) Subject to subsection (8), "excepted membership services" means relevant services which relate to or have a connection with –

    (a)   relevant activities of a member, or former member, of the independent trade union;

    (b)   any other activities carried on for the purposes of or in connection with, or arising from, such relevant activities;

    (c)   any event which has occurred (or is alleged to have occurred) in the course of or in connection with such relevant activities or activities within paragraph (b);

    (d)   activities carried on by a person for the purposes of or in connection with, or arising from, the person's membership of the independent trade union;

and such other relevant services as the Lord Chancellor may by order specify.

(8) The Lord Chancellor may by order make provision about the circumstances in which relevant services do or do not relate to, or have a connection with, the matters mentioned in paragraphs (a) to (d) of subsection (7).

(9) Subject to that, the Lord Chancellor may by order make provision about –

    (a)   what does or does not constitute a section of the public;

    (b)   the circumstances in which the provision of relevant services to the public or a section of the public does or does not form part of P's business.

(10) The Lord Chancellor may make an order under subsection (7), (8) or (9) only on the recommendation of the Board.

(11) If P is a body, references to an employee of P include references to a manager of P.

(12) In subsection (7), "relevant activities", in relation to a person who is or was a member of an independent trade union, means any employment (including self-employment), trade, occupation or other activity to which the person's membership of the trade union relates or related.

16 Offence to carry on reserved legal activity through person not entitled

(1) Where subsection (2) applies it is an offence for a person ("P") to carry on an activity ("the relevant activity") which is a reserved legal activity, despite P being entitled to carry on the relevant activity.

(2) This subsection applies if –

   (a)   P carries on the relevant activity by virtue of an employee of P ("E") carrying it on in E's capacity as such an employee, and

   (b)   in carrying on the relevant activity, E commits an offence under section 14.

(3) If P is a body, references in subsection (2) to an employee of P include references to a manager of P.

(4) In proceedings for an offence under subsection (1), it is a defence for the accused to show that the accused took all reasonable precautions and exercised all due diligence to avoid committing the offence.

(5) A person who is guilty of an offence under subsection (1) is liable –

   (a)   on summary conviction, to imprisonment for a term not exceeding 12 months or a fine not exceeding the statutory maximum (or both), and

   (b)   on conviction on indictment, to imprisonment for a term not exceeding 2 years or a fine (or both).

(6) A person who is guilty of an offence under subsection (1) by reason of an act done in the purported exercise of a right of audience, or a right to conduct litigation, in relation to any proceedings or contemplated proceedings is also guilty of contempt of the court concerned and may be punished accordingly.

(7) In relation to an offence under subsection (1) committed before the commencement of section 154(1) of the Criminal Justice Act 2003, the reference in subsection (5)(a) to 12 months is to be read as a reference to 6 months.

17 Offence to pretend to be entitled

(1) It is an offence for a person –

   (a)   wilfully to pretend to be entitled to carry on any activity which is a reserved legal activity when that person is not so entitled, or

   (b)   with the intention of implying falsely that that person is so entitled, to take or use any name, title or description.

(2) A person who is guilty of an offence under subsection (1) is liable –

   (a)   on summary conviction, to imprisonment for a term not exceeding 12 months or a fine not exceeding the statutory maximum (or both), and

   (b)   on conviction on indictment, to imprisonment for a term not exceeding 2 years or a fine (or both).

(3) In relation to an offence under subsection (1) committed before the commencement of section 154(1) of the Criminal Justice Act 2003, the reference in subsection (2)(a) to 12 months is to be read as a reference to 6 months.

Interpretation

18 Authorised persons

(1) For the purposes of this Act "authorised person", in relation to an activity ("the relevant activity") which is a reserved legal activity, means –

(a)   a person who is authorised to carry on the relevant activity by a relevant
       approved regulator in relation to the relevant activity (other than by virtue of a
       licence under Part 5), or

(b)   a licensable body which, by virtue of such a licence, is authorised to carry on
       the relevant activity by a licensing authority in relation to the reserved legal
       activity.

(2) A licensable body may not be authorised to carry on the relevant activity as
mentioned in subsection (1)(a).

(3) But where a body ("A") which is authorised as mentioned in subsection (1)(a)
becomes a licensable body, the body is deemed by virtue of this subsection to continue to
be so authorised from that time until the earliest of the following events –

(a)   the end of the period of 90 days beginning with the day on which that time falls;
(b)   the time from which the relevant approved regulator determines this subsection
       is to cease to apply to A;
(c)   the time when A ceases to be a licensable body.

(4) Subsection (2) is subject to Part 2 of Schedule 5 (by virtue of which licensable
bodies may be deemed to be authorised as mentioned in subsection (1)(a) in relation to
certain activities during a transitional period).

(5) A person other than a licensable body may not be authorised to carry on the relevant
activity as mentioned in subsection (1)(b).

(6) But where a body ("L") which is authorised as mentioned in subsection (1)(b) ceases
to be a licensable body, the body is deemed by virtue of this subsection to continue to be
so authorised from that time until the earliest of the following events –

(a)   the end of the period of 90 days beginning with the day on which that time falls;
(b)   the time from which the relevant licensing authority determines this subsection
       is to cease to apply to L;
(c)   the time when L becomes a licensable body.

19 Exempt persons

In this Act, "exempt person", in relation to an activity ("the relevant activity") which is a
reserved legal activity, means a person who, for the purposes of carrying on the relevant
activity, is an exempt person by virtue of –

(a)   Schedule 3 (exempt persons), or
(b)   paragraph 13 or 18 of Schedule 5 (additional categories of exempt persons
       during transitional period).

20 Approved regulators and relevant approved regulators

(1) In this Act, the following expressions have the meaning given by this section –
"approved regulator";
"relevant approved regulator".

(2) "Approved regulator" means –

(a)   a body which is designated as an approved regulator by Part 1 of Schedule 4 or
       under Part 2 of that Schedule (or both) and whose regulatory arrangements are
       approved for the purposes of this Act, and
(b)   if an order under section 62(1)(a) has effect, the Board.

(3) An approved regulator is a "relevant approved regulator" in relation to an activity
which is a reserved legal activity if –

(a) the approved regulator is designated by Part 1, or under Part 2, of Schedule 4 in relation to that reserved legal activity, or

(b) where the approved regulator is the Board, it is designated in relation to that reserved legal activity by an order under section 62(1)(a).

(4) An approved regulator is a "relevant approved regulator" in relation to a person if the person is authorised by the approved regulator to carry on an activity which is a reserved legal activity.

(5) Schedule 4 makes provision with respect to approved regulators other than the Board.

In that Schedule –

(a) Part 1 designates certain bodies as approved regulators in relation to certain reserved legal activities,

(b) Part 2 makes provision for bodies to be designated by order as approved regulators in relation to one or more reserved legal activities, and

(c) Part 3 makes provision relating to the approval of changes to an approved regulator's regulatory arrangements.

(6) An approved regulator may authorise persons to carry on any activity which is a reserved legal activity in respect of which it is a relevant approved regulator.

21 Regulatory arrangements

(1) In this Act references to the "regulatory arrangements" of a body are to –

(a) its arrangements for authorising persons to carry on reserved legal activities,

(b) its arrangements (if any) for authorising persons to provide immigration advice or immigration services,

(c) its practice rules,

(d) its conduct rules,

(e) its disciplinary arrangements in relation to regulated persons (including its discipline rules),

(f) its qualification regulations,

(g) its indemnification arrangements,

(h) its compensation arrangements,

(i) any of its other rules or regulations (however they may be described), and any other arrangements, which apply to or in relation to regulated persons, other than those made for the purposes of any function the body has to represent or promote the interests of persons regulated by it, and

(j) its licensing rules (if any), so far as not within paragraphs (a) to (i),

(whether or not those arrangements, rules or regulations are contained in, or made under, an enactment).

...

Continuity of existing rights and transitional protection

22 Continuity of existing rights to carry on reserved legal activities

Schedule 5 makes provision for the continuity of existing rights and for certain persons to be deemed, during a transitional period, to be authorised by approved regulators to carry on certain activities.

****

Alteration of reserved legal activities

24 Extension of the reserved legal activities

(1) The Lord Chancellor may, by order, amend section 12 or Schedule 2 (reserved legal activities) so as to add any legal activity to the activities which are reserved legal activities for the purposes of this Act.

(2) An order under subsection (1) may be made only on the recommendation of the Board.

(3) Schedule 6 makes provision about the making of recommendations for the purposes of this section.

(4) Where a recommendation is made in relation to an activity, the Lord Chancellor must –

  (a) consider the report containing the recommendation given to the Lord Chancellor under paragraph 16(3)(a) of that Schedule,
  (b) decide whether or not to make an order under this section in respect of the activity, and
  (c) publish a notice of that decision,

within the period of 90 days beginning with the day on which the report was given to the Lord Chancellor.

(5) Where the Lord Chancellor decides not to make an order under this section in respect of an activity, the notice under subsection (4)(c) must state the reasons for that decision.

25 Provisional designation as approved regulators and licensing authorities

(1) The Lord Chancellor may, by order, make provision –

  (a) enabling applications to be made, considered and determined under Part 2 of Schedule 4 or Part 1 of Schedule 10 in relation to a provisional reserved activity, as if the activity were a reserved legal activity;
  (b) enabling provisional designation orders to be made by the Lord Chancellor in respect of a provisional reserved activity, as if the activity were a reserved legal activity.

(2) An order under subsection (1) may, in particular, provide that Part 2 of Schedule 4 or Part 1 of Schedule 10 is to apply, in relation to such cases as may be specified by the order, with such modifications as may be so specified.

(3) The Lord Chancellor may also, by order, make provision –

  (a) for the purpose of enabling applications for authorisation to carry on an activity which is a provisional reserved activity to be made to and considered and determined by –
    (i)   a body in respect of which a provisional designation order is made, or
    (ii) the Board in its capacity as a licensing authority;
  (b) for the purpose of enabling persons to be deemed to be authorised to carry on an activity which is a new reserved legal activity by a relevant approved regulator in relation to the activity, or by the Board in its capacity as a licensing authority, for a period specified in the order.

(4) For this purpose –

"provisional reserved activity" means an activity in respect of which a provisional report under paragraph 10 of Schedule 6 states that the Board is minded to make a recommendation for the purposes of section 24;

"provisional designation order" means an order made by the Lord Chancellor under Part 2 of Schedule 4 or Part 1 of Schedule 10 which is conditional upon the Lord Chancellor making an order under section 24 in respect of the provisional reserved activity, pursuant to a recommendation made by the Board following the provisional report;

"new reserved legal activity" means a legal activity which has become a reserved legal activity by virtue of an order under section 24.

26 Recommendations that activities should cease to be reserved legal activities

(1) The Board may recommend that an activity should cease to be a reserved legal activity.

(2) Schedule 6 makes provision about the making of recommendations for the purposes of this section.

(3) The Lord Chancellor must consider any recommendation made by the Board for the purposes of this section (but nothing in section 208 (minor and consequential provision etc) authorises the Lord Chancellor to give effect to such a recommendation).

(4) Where the Lord Chancellor disagrees with a recommendation (or any part of it), the Lord Chancellor must publish a notice to that effect which must include the Lord Chancellor's reasons for disagreeing.

****

SCHEDULE 2

THE RESERVED LEGAL ACTIVITIES

1 Introduction

This Schedule makes provision about the reserved legal activities.

2 In this Schedule "the appointed day" means the day appointed for the coming into force of section 13 (entitlement to carry on reserved legal activities).

3 Rights of audience

(1) A "right of audience" means the right to appear before and address a court, including the right to call and examine witnesses.

(2) But a "right of audience" does not include a right to appear before or address a court, or to call or examine witnesses, in relation to any particular court or in relation to particular proceedings, if immediately before the appointed day no restriction was placed on the persons entitled to exercise that right.

4 Conduct of litigation

(1) The "conduct of litigation" means –

    (a)   the issuing of proceedings before any court in England and Wales,

    (b)   the commencement, prosecution and defence of such proceedings, and

    (c)   the performance of any ancillary functions in relation to such proceedings (such as entering appearances to actions).

(2) But the "conduct of litigation" does not include any activity within paragraphs (a) to (c) of sub-paragraph (1), in relation to any particular court or in relation to any particular proceedings, if immediately before the appointed day no restriction was placed on the persons entitled to carry on that activity.

****

SCHEDULE 3

EXEMPT PERSONS

1 Rights of audience

(1) This paragraph applies to determine whether a person is an exempt person for the purpose of exercising a right of audience before a court in relation to any proceedings (subject to paragraph 7).

(2) The person is exempt if the person –

    (a)   is not an authorised person in relation to that activity, but

    (b)   has a right of audience granted by that court in relation to those proceedings.

(3) The person is exempt if the person –

    (a)   is not an authorised person in relation to that activity, but

    (b)   has a right of audience before that court in relation to those proceedings granted by or under any enactment.

(4) The person is exempt if the person is the Attorney General or the Solicitor General and –

    (a)   the name of the person is on the roll kept by the Law Society under section 6 of the Solicitors Act 1974, or

    (b)   the person has been called to the Bar by an Inn of Court.

(5) The person is exempt if the person is the Advocate General for Scotland and is admitted –

    (a)   as a solicitor in Scotland under section 6 of the Solicitors (Scotland) Act 1980, or

    (b)   to practise as an advocate before the courts of Scotland.

(6) The person is exempt if the person –

    (a)   is a party to those proceedings, and

    (b)   would have a right of audience, in the person's capacity as such a party, if this Act had not been passed.

(7) The person is exempt if –

    (a)   the person is an individual whose work includes assisting in the conduct of litigation,

    (b)   the person is assisting in the conduct of litigation –

        (i)   under instructions given (either generally or in relation to the proceedings) by an individual to whom sub-paragraph (8) applies, and

        (ii) under the supervision of that individual, and

    (c)   the proceedings are being heard in chambers in the High Court or a county court and are not reserved family proceedings.

(8) This sub-paragraph applies to –

    (a)   any authorised person in relation to an activity which constitutes the conduct of litigation;

(b)   any person who by virtue of section 193 is not required to be entitled to carry on such an activity.

(9) The person is an exempt person in relation to the exercise of a right of audience in proceedings on an appeal from the Comptroller-General of Patents, Designs and Trade Marks to the Patents Court under the Patents Act 1977, if the person is a solicitor of the Court of Judicature of Northern Ireland.

(10) For the purposes of this paragraph –

"family proceedings" has the same meaning as in the Matrimonial and Family Proceedings Act 1984 and also includes any other proceedings which are family proceedings for the purposes of the Children Act 1989;

"reserved family proceedings" means such category of family proceedings as the Lord Chancellor may, after consulting the President of the Law Society and with the concurrence of the President of the Family Division, by order prescribe;

and any order made under section 27(9) of the Courts and Legal Services Act 1990 before the day appointed for the coming into force of this paragraph is to have effect on and after that day as if it were an order made under this sub-paragraph.

2 Conduct of litigation

(1) This paragraph applies to determine whether a person is an exempt person for the purpose of carrying on any activity which constitutes the conduct of litigation in relation to any proceedings (subject to paragraph 7).

(2) The person is exempt if the person –

(a)   is not an authorised person in relation to that activity, but
(b)   has a right to conduct litigation granted by a court in relation to those proceedings.

(3) The person is exempt if the person –

(a)   is not an authorised person in relation to that activity, but
(b)   has a right to conduct litigation in relation to those proceedings granted by or under any enactment.

(4) The person is exempt if the person –

(a)   is a party to those proceedings, and
(b)   would have a right to conduct the litigation, in the person's capacity as such a party, if this Act had not been passed.

(5) The person is an exempt person in relation to any activity which is carried on in or in connection with proceedings on an appeal from the Comptroller-General of Patents, Designs and Trade Marks to the Patents Court under the Patents Act 1977, if the person is a solicitor of the Court of Judicature of Northern Ireland.

****

7 European lawyers

A European lawyer (within the meaning of the European Communities (Services of Lawyers) Order 1978 (SI 1978/1910)) is an exempt person for the purposes of carrying on an activity which is a reserved legal activity and which the European lawyer is entitled to carry on by virtue of that order.

****

9 Further exempt persons

(1) The Lord Chancellor may, by order, amend this Schedule so as to provide –

- (a)   for persons to be exempt persons in relation to any activity which is a reserved legal activity (including any activity which is a reserved legal activity by virtue of an order under section 24 (extension of reserved legal activities)),
- (b)   for persons to cease to be such persons, or
- (c)   for the amendment of any provision made in respect of an exempt person.

(2) The Lord Chancellor may make an order under sub-paragraph (1) only on the recommendation of the Board.

****

SCHEDULE 5
AUTHORISED PERSONS

PART 1
CONTINUITY OF RIGHTS

1 Rights of audience and conduct of litigation

(1) For the purposes of section 18 (authorised persons), in the case of a person who is authorised by a listed body –

- (a)   to exercise a right of audience before a court in relation to any proceedings, or
- (b)   to conduct litigation in relation to any proceedings,

it is irrelevant whether the person's authorisation was granted before or on or after the appointed day.

(2) The "listed bodies" are –

- (a)   The Law Society,
- (b)   The General Council of the Bar,
- (c)   The Chartered Institute of Patent Attorneys,
- (d)   The Institute of Trade Mark Attorneys,
- (e)   The Association of Law Costs Draftsmen, and
- (f)   for the purposes of sub-paragraph (1)(a) only, The Institute of Legal Executives.

(3) For the purposes of sub-paragraph (1), any authority conferred by section 31 of the Courts and Legal Services Act 1990 (barristers and solicitors deemed to have rights of audience and rights to conduct litigation) is to be disregarded (see paragraphs 4 and 7 below).

****

PART 2
RIGHTS DURING TRANSITIONAL PERIOD

3 The transitional period

(1) In this Part of this Schedule references to "the transitional period" are to the period which –

- (a)   begins with the appointed day (within the meaning given by paragraph 19), and
- (b)   ends with the day appointed by the Lord Chancellor by order for the purposes of this paragraph.

(2) Different days may be appointed under sub-paragraph (1)(b) for different purposes.

(3) An order may be made under sub-paragraph (1)(b) only on the recommendation of the Board.

4 Barristers etc

(1) During the transitional period, every barrister is deemed to be authorised by the General Council of the Bar to carry on the activities in sub-paragraph (2).

(2) Those activities are –

    (a)   the exercise of a right of audience before every court in relation to all proceedings;

    (b)   reserved instrument activities;

    (c)   probate activities;

    (d)   the administration of oaths.

(3) The authority conferred on a barrister by this paragraph is exercisable in accordance with, and subject to, the regulatory arrangements of the General Council of the Bar.

(4) A person is not authorised under sub-paragraph (1) unless the person has in force a certificate issued by the General Council of the Bar authorising the person to practise as a barrister.

5 (1) During the transitional period, every registered European lawyer registered with the Inns of Court and the General Council of the Bar is deemed to be authorised by the General Council of the Bar to carry on activities which –

    (a)   are within paragraph 4(2), and

    (b)   the registered European lawyer is entitled to carry on under his home professional title by virtue of the European regulations.

(2) The authority conferred on a registered European lawyer by virtue of this paragraph is exercisable in accordance with, and subject to, the regulatory arrangements of the General Council of the Bar (as they apply to the registered European lawyer by virtue of the European regulations).

(3) In this paragraph –

    "European regulations" means the European Communities (Lawyer's Practice) Regulations 2000 (SI 2000/1119);

    "home professional title" and "registered European lawyer" have the same meaning as in the European regulations.

6 During the transitional period members of the Bar not in actual practice are to continue to have the rights conferred by section 102A(2) of the Patents Act 1977 (right of audience, etc in proceedings on appeal from the comptroller).

7 Solicitors etc

(1) During the transitional period –

    (a)   every qualified solicitor,

    (b)   every legal partnership, and

    (c)   every body recognised under section 9 of the Administration of Justice Act 1985 (incorporated practices) ("a recognised body"),

is deemed to be authorised by the Law Society to carry on the activities in sub-paragraph (2).

PART II

(2) Those activities are –

(a) the exercise of a right of audience before every court in relation to all proceedings;

(b) the conduct of litigation in relation to every court and all proceedings;

(c) reserved instrument activities;

(d) probate activities;

(e) the administration of oaths.

(3) The authority conferred on a qualified solicitor, legal partnership or recognised body by this paragraph is exercisable in accordance with, and subject to, the regulatory arrangements of the Law Society.

(4) In this paragraph –

"legal partnership" means a partnership in which a qualified solicitor, a registered European Lawyer or a body recognised under section 9 of the Administration of Justice Act 1985 is permitted to practise by virtue of rules made under that section or section 31 of the Solicitors Act 1974;

"qualified solicitor" means a person who is qualified under section 1 of the Solicitors Act 1974 to act as a solicitor;

"registered European lawyer" means a registered European lawyer within the meaning of the European Communities (Lawyer's Practice) Regulations 2000 (SI 2000/1119) who is registered with the Law Society.

8 (1) During the transitional period, every registered European lawyer registered with the Law Society is deemed to be authorised by the Law Society to carry on activities which –

(a)   are within paragraph 7(2), and

(b)   the registered European lawyer is entitled to carry on under his home professional title by virtue of the European regulations.

(2) The authority conferred on a registered European lawyer by virtue of this paragraph is exercisable in accordance with, and subject to, the regulatory arrangements of the Law Society (as they apply to the registered European lawyer by virtue of the European regulations).

(3) In this paragraph –

"European regulations" means the European Communities (Lawyer's Practice) Regulations 2000 (SI 2000/1119);

"home professional title" and "registered European lawyer" have the same meaning as in the European regulations.

9 (1) During the transitional period, solicitors are to continue to have the rights conferred on them by subsection (1) of section 102A of the Patents Act 1977 (rights of audience, etc in proceedings on appeal from the comptroller).

(2) During that period, registered European lawyers are to continue to have the rights conferred on them by that subsection by virtue of the European regulations.

(3) In this paragraph "European regulations" and "registered European lawyer" have the same meaning as in paragraph 8.

10 Legal Executives

(1) During the transitional period, a person authorised by the Institute of Legal Executives to practise as a member of the profession of legal executives is deemed to be authorised by that Institute to administer oaths.

(2) The authority conferred by sub-paragraph (1) is exercisable in accordance with and subject to the regulatory arrangements of the Institute of Legal Executives.

(3) A person is not authorised under sub-paragraph (1) unless the person has in force a certificate issued by the Institute of Legal Executives authorising the person to practise as a legal executive.

****

17 Law costs draftsmen

(1) During the transitional period, every authorised member of the Association of Law Costs Draftsmen is deemed to be authorised by that Association to administer oaths.

(2) In this paragraph, "authorised member of the Association of Law Costs Draftsmen" means a member of that Association who has been authorised by that Association to carry on one or both of the following activities –

    (a) the exercise of a right of audience;

    (b) the conduct of litigation.

(3) The authority conferred by sub-paragraph (1) is exercisable in accordance with and subject to the regulatory arrangements of the Association of Law Costs Draftsmen.

18 (1) During the transitional period, a person ("P") is an exempt person in relation to the carrying on of an activity ("the relevant activity") which is a reserved legal activity within sub-paragraph (2), if –

    (a) P carries on the relevant activity by virtue of an employee of P ("E") carrying it on in E's capacity as such an employee, and

    (b) E is an authorised member of the Association of Law Costs Draftsmen (within the meaning of paragraph 17(2) of this Schedule).

(2) The reserved legal activities mentioned in sub-paragraph (1) are –

    (a) the exercise of a right of audience;

    (b) the conduct of litigation;

    (c) the administration of oaths.

(3) If P is a body, in this paragraph references to an employee of P include references to a manager of P.

PART 3
INTERPRETATION

19 In this Schedule –

    "the appointed day" means the day appointed for the coming into force of section 13 (entitlement to carry on a reserved legal activity);

****

Legitimacy Act 1976

ARRANGEMENT OF SECTIONS

1 Legitimacy of children of certain void marriages

(1) The child of a void marriage, whenever born, shall, subject to subsection (2) below and Schedule 1 to this Act, be treated as the legitimate child of his parents if at the time of the insemination resulting in the birth or, where there was no such insemination, the child's conception (or at the time of the celebration of the marriage if later) both or either of the parties reasonably believed that the marriage was valid.

(2) This section only applies where the father of the child was domiciled in England and Wales at the time of the birth or, if he died before the birth, was so domiciled immediately before his death.

(3) It is hereby declared for the avoidance of doubt that subsection (1) above applies notwithstanding that the belief that the marriage was valid was due to a mistake as to law.

(4) In relation to a child born after the coming into force of section 28 of the Family Law Reform Act 1987, it shall be presumed for the purposes of subsection (1) above, unless the contrary is shown, that one of the parties to the void marriage reasonably believed at the time of the insemination resulting in the birth or, where there was no such insemination, the child's conception (or at the time of the celebration of the marriage if later) that the marriage was valid.

Amendments—FLRA 1987, s 28.

Defined terms—"void marriage": s 10(1).

"child of a void marriage"—The decision in *Spence, Spence v Dennis* [1990] 2 FLR 278 suggests that this definition includes only a child who would be born *in wedlock* if the marriage were valid; there is a distinction between a child of a void marriage and a child legitimated by the subsequent marriage of its parents (see s 2). In the case of a child born *after* a void marriage, the child will be treated as a legitimate child, but a child born *before* the void marriage will be treated as illegitimate (see also *F and F v AG and F* [1980] Fam Law 60).

2 Legitimation by subsequent marriage of parents

Subject to the following provisions of this Act, where the parents of an illegitimate person marry one another, the marriage shall, if the father of the illegitimate person is at the date of marriage domiciled in England and Wales, render that person, if living, legitimate from the date of the marriage.

2A Legitimation by subsequent civil partnership of parents

Subject to the following provisions of this Act, where –

    (a)   a person ("the child") has a parent ("the female parent") by virtue of section 43 of the Human Fertilisation and Embryology Act 2008 (treatment provided to woman who agrees that second woman to be parent),

    (b)   at the time of the child's birth, the female parent and the child's mother are not civil partners of each other,

    (c)   the female parent and the child's mother subsequently enter into a civil partnership, and

    (d)   the female parent is at the date of the formation of the civil partnership domiciled in England and Wales,

the civil partnership shall render the child, if living, legitimate from the date of the formation of the civil partnership.

Amendments—Inserted by HFEA 2008, s 56, Sch 6, Pt 1, para 16.

Scope—This provision extends the legitimation provision to same-sex female couples who have a child together by means of assisted reproduction (see HFEA 2008, ss 43–45) and they subsequently enter into a civil partnership so that they can legitimise the child as from the date of the civil partnership, provided the conditions set out in the section are met.

3 Legitimation by extraneous law

(1) Subject to the following provisions of this Act, where the parents of an illegitimate person marry one another and the father of the illegitimate person is not at the time of the marriage domiciled in England and Wales but is domiciled in a country by the law of which the illegitimate person became legitimated by virtue of such subsequent marriage, that person, if living, shall in England and Wales be recognised as having been so legitimated from the date of the marriage notwithstanding that, at the time of his birth, his father was domiciled in a country the law of which did not permit legitimation by subsequent marriage.

(2) Subject to the following provisions of this Act, where –

    (a)   a person ("the child") has a parent ("the female parent") by virtue of section 43 of the Human Fertilisation and Embryology Act 2008 (treatment provided to woman who agrees that second woman to be parent),

    (b)   at the time of the child's birth, the female parent and the child's mother are not civil partners of each other,

    (c)   the female parent and the child's mother subsequently enter into a civil partnership, and

    (d)   the female parent is not at the time of the formation of the civil partnership domiciled in England and Wales but is domiciled in a country by the law of which the child became legitimated by virtue of the civil partnership,

the child, if living, shall in England and Wales be recognised as having been so legitimated from the date of the formation of the civil partnership notwithstanding that, at the time of the child's birth, the female parent was domiciled in a country the law of which did not permit legitimation by subsequent civil partnership.

Amendments—HFEA 2008, s 56, Sch 6, Pt 1, para 17.

Scope—See above under s 2A.

4 Legitimation of adopted child

(1) Section 39 of the Adoption Act 1976 or section 67 of the Adoption and Children Act 2002 does not prevent an adopted child being legitimated under section 2 or 3 above if either natural parent is the sole adoptive parent.

(2) Where an adopted child (with a sole adoptive parent) is legitimated –

    (a)   subsection (2) of the said section 39 or subsection (3)(b) of the said section 67 shall not apply after the legitimation to the natural relationship with the other natural parent, and

    (b)   revocation of the adoption order in consequence of the legitimation shall not affect section 39, 41 or 42 of the Adoption Act 1976 or section 67, 68 or 69 of the Adoption and Children Act 2002 as it applies to any instrument made before the date of legitimation.

Amendments—AA 1976, s 73(2), Sch 3, para 23; ACA 2002, Sch 3, para 17.

5 Rights of legitimated persons and others to take interests in property

(1) Subject to any contrary indication, the rules of construction contained in this section apply to any instrument other than an existing instrument, so far as the instrument contains a disposition of property.

(2) For the purposes of this section, provisions of the law of intestate succession applicable to the estate of a deceased person shall be treated as if contained in an instrument executed by him (while of full capacity) immediately before his death.

(3) A legitimated person, and any other person, shall be entitled to take any interest as if the legitimated person had been born legitimate.

(4) A disposition which depends on the date of birth of a child or children of the parent or parents shall be construed as if –

    (a)   a legitimated child had been born on the date of legitimation,

    (b)   two or more legitimated children legitimated on the same date had been born on that date in the order of their actual births,

but this does not affect any reference to the age of a child.

(5) Examples of phrases in wills on which subsection (4) above can operate are –

    1   Children of A "living at my death or born afterwards".

    2   Children of A "living at my death or born afterwards before any one of such children for the time being in existence attains a vested interest, and who attain the age of 21 years".

    3   As in example 1 or 2, but referring to grandchildren of A, instead of children of A.

    4   A for life "until he has a child" and then to his child or children.

        Note. Subsection (4) above will not affect the reference to the age of 21 years in example 2.

(6) If an illegitimate person or a person adopted by one of his natural parents dies, or has died before the commencement of this Act, and –

    (a)   after his death his parents marry or have married; and

    (b)   the deceased would, if living at the time of the marriage, have become a legitimated person,

this section shall apply for the construction of the instrument so far as it relates to the taking of interests by, or in succession to, his spouse, children and remoter issue as if he had been legitimated by virtue of the marriage.

(7) In this section "instrument" includes a private Act settling property, but not any other enactment.

Defined terms—"disposition", "legitimated person": s 10(1).

6 Dispositions depending on date of birth

(1) Where a disposition depends on the date of birth of a child who was born illegitimate and who is legitimated (or, if deceased, is treated as legitimated), section 5(4) above does not affect entitlement under Part II of the Family Law Reform Act 1969 (illegitimate children).

(2) Where a disposition depends on the date of birth of an adopted child who is legitimated (or, if deceased, is treated as legitimated) section 5(4) above does not affect entitlement by virtue of section 42(2) of the Adoption Act 1976 or section 69(2) of the Adoption and Children Act 2002.

(3) This section applies for example where –

    (a) a testator dies in 1976 bequeathing a legacy to his eldest grandchild living at a specified time,

    (b) a daughter has an illegitimate child in 1977 who is the first grandchild,

    (c) his married son has a child in 1978,

    (d) subsequently the illegitimate child is legitimated,

and in all those cases the daughter's child remains the eldest grandchild of the testator throughout.

Amendments—AA 1976, s 73(2), Sch 3, para 24; ACA 2002, Sch 3, para 18.

7 Protection of trustees and personal representatives

(1) A trustee or personal representative is not under a duty, by virtue of the law relating to trusts or the administration of estates, to enquire, before conveying or distributing any property, whether any person is illegitimate or has been adopted by one of his natural parents, and could be legitimated (or if deceased be treated as legitimated), if that fact could affect entitlement to the property.

(2) A trustee or personal representative shall not be liable to any person by reason of a conveyance or distribution of the property made without regard to any such fact if he has not received notice of the fact before the conveyance or distribution.

(3) This section does not prejudice the right of a person to follow the property, or any property representing it, into the hands of another person, other than a purchaser, who has received it.

8 Personal rights and obligations

A legitimated person shall have the same rights, and shall be under the same obligations in respect of the maintenance and support of himself or of any other person as if he had been born legitimate, and, subject to the provisions of this Act, the provisions of any Act relating to claims for damages, compensation, allowance, benefit or otherwise by or in respect of a legitimate child shall apply in like manner in the case of a legitimated person.

9 Re-registration of birth of legitimated person

(1) It shall be the duty of the parents of a legitimated person or, in cases where re-registration can be effected on information furnished by one parent and one of the parents is dead, of the surviving parent to furnish to the Registrar General information

with a view to obtaining the re-registration of the birth of that person within 3 months after the date of the marriage or of the formation of the civil partnership by virtue of which he was legitimated.

(2) The failure of the parents or either of them to furnish information as required by subsection (1) above in respect of any legitimated person shall not affect the legitimation of that person.

(3) This section does not apply in relation to a person who was legitimated otherwise than by virtue of the subsequent marriage or civil partnership of his parents.

(4) Any parent who fails to give information as required by this section shall be liable on summary conviction to a fine not exceeding level 1 on the standard scale.

Amendments—Criminal Justice Act 1982, ss 38, 46; HFEA 2008, s 56, Sch 6, Pt 1, para 18(b).

Scope—The provisions of s 9 have been extended to include the re-registration of birth of a legitimated child born to same-sex female couples who enter into a subsequent civil partnership.

10 Interpretation

(1) In this Act, except where the context otherwise requires, –

"disposition" includes the conferring of a power of appointment and any other disposition of an interest in or right over property;

"existing", in relation to an instrument, means one made before 1 January 1976;

"legitimated person" means a person legitimated or recognised as legitimated –

    (a)   under section 2, 2A or 3 above; or

    (b)   under section 1 or 8 of the Legitimacy Act 1926; or

    (c)   except in section 8, by a legitimation (whether or not by virtue of the subsequent marriage of his parents) recognised by the law of England and Wales and effected under the law of any other country:

and cognate expressions shall be construed accordingly;

"power of appointment" includes any discretionary power to transfer a beneficial interest in property without the furnishing of valuable consideration;

"void marriage" means a marriage, not being voidable only, in respect of which the High Court has or had jurisdiction to grant a decree of nullity, or would have or would have had such jurisdiction if the parties were domiciled in England and Wales.

(2) For the purposes of this Act "legitimated person" includes, where the context admits, a person legitimated, or recognised as legitimated, before the passing of the Children Act 1975.

(3) For the purpose of this Act, except where the context otherwise requires, –

    (a)   the death of the testator is the date at which a will or codicil is to be regarded as made;

    (b)   an oral disposition of property shall be deemed to be contained in an instrument made when the disposition was made.

(4) (*repealed*)

(5) Except in so far as the context otherwise requires, any reference in this Act to an enactment shall be construed as a reference to that enactment as amended by or under any other enactment, including this Act.

Amendments—TLATA 1996, s 25(2),(4),(5), Sch 4; HFEA 2008, s 56, Sch 6, Pt 1, para 19.

Definition—"legitimated person" includes a child born to same-sex female couples to whom ss 2A and 3 apply.

****

Magistrates' Courts Act 1980

ARRANGEMENT OF SECTIONS

PART II

CIVIL JURISDICTION AND PROCEDURE

Jurisdiction to issue summons and deal with complaints

PART III

SATISFACTION AND ENFORCEMENT

General provisions

PART IV
WITNESSES AND EVIDENCE
Procuring attendance of witness

Evidence generally

Offences

PART VI
RECOGNIZANCES
Other provisions

PART VII
MISCELLANEOUS AND SUPPLEMENTARY
Constitution and place of sitting of magistrates' courts

Appearance by a legal representative

Process

Limitation of time

Remand

****

PART II
CIVIL JURISDICTION AND PROCEDURE

Jurisdiction to issue summons and deal with complaints

51 Issue of summons on complaint

Where a complaint relating to a person is made to a justice of the peace, the justice of the peace may issue a summons to the person requiring him to appear before a magistrates' court to answer to the complaint.

Amendments—Substituted by Courts Act 2003, s 47(1).

Scope—The power may also be exercised, by virtue of JCR 2005, Sch 1, paras 1 and 2, by a justices' clerk provided the complaint is not made on oath.

"may issue"—The decision whether to issue a summons is a judicial decision and may not be delegated (*R v Manchester Stipendiary Magistrate ex parte Hill* [1983] 1 AC 328). The justice of the peace or the justices' clerk must apply his mind to the complaint and decide whether or not the summons should be issued. See *R v Brentford Justices ex parte Catlin* [1975] QB 455.

52 Jurisdiction to deal with complaints

(1) A magistrates' court has jurisdiction to hear any complaint.

(2) But subsection (1) is subject to provision made by any enactment.

Amendments—Justices of the Peace Act 1997, s 73(2), Sch 5, para 19; AJA 1999, s 106, Sch 15; substituted by Courts Act 2003, s 47(2).

Hearing of complaint

53 Procedure on hearing

(1) On the hearing of a complaint, the court shall, if the defendant appears, state to him the substance of the complaint.

(2) The court, after hearing the evidence and the parties, shall make the order for which the complaint is made or dismiss the complaint.

(3) Where a complaint is for an order for the payment of a sum recoverable summarily as a civil debt, or for the variation of the rate of any periodical payments ordered by a magistrates' court to be made, or for such other matter as may be prescribed, the court may make the order with the consent of the defendant without hearing evidence.

(4) Subsections (1) to (3) are subject, for the purposes of family proceedings in any magistrates' court, to other provision made by Family Procedure Rules.

Amendments—SI 2011/1045.

Orders made without hearing evidence—See, for example, *R v King's Lynn Magistrates' Court ex parte M* [1988] 2 FLR 79.

54 Adjournment and stays

(1) A magistrates' court may at any time, whether before or after beginning to hear a complaint, adjourn the hearing, and may do so, notwithstanding anything in this Act, when composed of a single justice.

(2) The court may when adjourning either fix the time and place at which the hearing is to be resumed or, unless it remands the defendant under section 55 below, leave the time and place to be determined later by the court; but the hearing shall not be resumed at that time and place unless the court is satisfied that the parties have had adequate notice thereof.

(3) In family proceedings a magistrates' court may stay the whole or part of any proceedings or order either generally or until a specified date or event.

(4) Subsections (1) and (2) are subject, for the purpose of family proceedings in any magistrates' court, to other provision made by Family Procedure Rules.

Amendments—SI 2011/1045.

Defined terms—"magistrates' court": s 148(1).

Scope—Under the JCR 2005, Sch 1, para 7, a justices' clerk is permitted to adjourn the hearing with the consent of the parties. Only a full court has power to stay proceedings (FPR PD2A, para 1.1).

"adequate notice"—The service of a summons and other documents is governed by MCR 1981, r 99. The same rule applies to the service of an adjournment notice (*Unitt v Unitt* (1981) 2 FLR 89).

55 Non-appearance of defendant

(1) Where at the time and place appointed for the hearing or adjourned hearing of a complaint the complainant appears but the defendant does not, the court may, subject to subsection (3) below, proceed in his absence.

(2) Where the court, instead of proceedings in the absence of the defendant, adjourns, or further adjourns, the hearing, the court may, if the complaint has been substantiated on oath, and subject to the following provisions of this section, issue a warrant for his arrest.

(3) The court shall not begin to hear the complaint in the absence of the defendant or issue a warrant under this section unless either it is proved to the satisfaction of the court, on oath or in such other manner as may be prescribed, that the summons was served on him within what appears to the court to be a reasonable time before the hearing or adjourned hearing or the defendant has appeared on a previous occasion to answer to the complaint.

(4) Where the defendant fails to appear at an adjourned hearing, the court shall not issue a warrant under this section unless it is satisfied that he has had adequate notice of the time and place of the adjourned hearing.

(5) Where the defendant is arrested under a warrant issued under this section, the court may, on any subsequent adjournment of the hearing, but subject to the provisions of subsection (6) below, remand him.

(6) The court shall not issue a warrant or remand a defendant under this section or further remand him by virtue of section 128(3) below after he has given evidence in the proceedings.

(7) Where the court remands the defendant, the time fixed for the resumption of the hearing shall be that at which he is required to appear to be brought before the court in pursuance of the remand.

(8) A warrant under this section shall not be issued in any proceedings for the recovery or enforcement of a sum recoverable summarily as a civil debt or in proceedings in any matter of bastardy.

(9) Subsections (1) to (8) are subject, for the purpose of family proceedings in any magistrates' court, to other provision made by Family Procedure Rules.

Amendments—SI 2011/1045.

Issue of warrant for arrest (s 55(2))—The warrant may be endorsed with bail under s 117. The Bail Act 1976 does not apply to civil proceedings, and a recognizance must be set (see s 117(2)(b)).

56 Non-appearance of complainant

Subject to other provision made by Family Procedure Rules for the purposes of family proceedings in any magistrates' court, where at the time and place appointed for the hearing or adjourned hearing of a complaint the defendant appears but the complainant does not, the court may dismiss the complaint or, if evidence has been received on a previous occasion, proceed in the absence of the complainant.

Amendments—SI 2011/1045.

57 Non-appearance of both parties

Subject to other provision made by Family Procedure Rules for the purposes of family proceedings in any magistrates' court, where at the time and place appointed for the hearing or adjourned hearing of a complaint neither the complainant nor the defendant appears, the court may dismiss the complaint.

Amendments—SI 2011/1045.

Civil debt

58 Money recoverable summarily as civil debt

(1) A magistrates' court shall have power to make an order on complaint for the payment of any money recoverable summarily as a civil debt.

(2) Any sum payment of which may be ordered by a magistrates' court shall be recoverable summarily as a civil debt except –

  (a) a sum recoverable on complaint for a magistrates' court maintenance order; or
  (b) a sum that may be adjudged to be paid by a summary conviction or by an order enforceable as if it were a summary conviction.

Amendments—FLRA 1987, s 33(1), Sch 2, para 80.

Scope—This section gives magistrates the power to order the payment of a sum as a civil debt but provides that that power shall not apply to certain sums. The power of recovery is restricted by s 96 and MCR 1981, rr 53, 54, and 58, which impose procedural requirements before committal for civil debt.

Other restrictions include the protection under the Reserve and Auxiliary Forces (Protection of Civil Interests) Act 1951, Insolvency Act 1986, ss 264 (bankruptcy order) and 268 (bankruptcy notice) and CCA 1984, s 112 (administration order).

Orders for periodical payment

59 Orders for periodical payment: means of payment

(1) In any case where a magistrates' court orders money to be paid periodically by one person (in this section referred to as "the debtor") to another (in this section referred to as "the creditor"), then –

  (a) if the order is a qualifying maintenance order, the court shall at the same time exercise one of its powers under paragraphs (a) to (d) of subsection (3) below;

  (b) if the order is not a maintenance order, the court shall at the same time exercise one of its powers under paragraphs (a) and (b) of that subsection.

(2) For the purposes of this section a maintenance order is a "qualifying maintenance order" if, at the time it is made, the debtor is ordinarily resident in England and Wales.

(3) The powers of the court are –

  (a) the power to order that payments under the order be made directly by the debtor to the creditor;

  (b) the power to order that payments under the order be made to the designated officer for the court or for any other magistrates' court;

  (c) the power to order that payments under the order be made by the debtor to the creditor by such method of payment falling within subsection (6) below as may be specified;

  (cc) the power to order that payments under the order be made in accordance with arrangements made by the Secretary of State for their collection;

  (d) the power to make an attachment of earnings order under the Attachment of Earnings Act 1971 to secure payments under the order.

(3A) No order made by a magistrates' court under paragraphs (a) to (d) of subsection (3) above (other than one made under paragraph (cc)) shall have effect at any time when the Secretary of State is arranging for the collection of payments under the qualifying maintenance order concerned.

(4) In any case where –

  (a) the court proposes to exercise its power under paragraph (c) of subsection (3) above, and

  (b) having given the debtor an opportunity of opening an account from which payments under the order may be made in accordance with the method of payment proposed to be ordered under that paragraph, the court is satisfied that the debtor has failed, without reasonable excuse, to open such an account.

the court in exercising its power under that paragraph may order that the debtor open such an account.

(5) In deciding, in the case of a maintenance order, which of the powers under paragraphs (a) to (d) of subsection (3) above (other than paragraph (cc)) it is to exercise, the court having (if practicable) given them an opportunity to make representations shall have regard to any representations made –

  (a) by the debtor,

  (b) by the creditor, and

  (c) if the person who applied for the maintenance order is a person other than the creditor, by that other person.

(6) The methods of payment referred to in subsection (3)(c) above are the following, that is to say –

    (a)   payment by standing order; or

    (b)   payment by any other method which requires one person to give his authority for payments of a specific amount to be made from an account of his to an account of another's on specific dates during the period for which the authority is in force and without the need for any further authority from him.

(7) Where the maintenance order is an order –

    (a)   under the Guardianship of Minors Acts 1971 and 1973,

    (b)   under Part I of the Domestic Proceedings and Magistrates' Courts Act 1978 or Schedule 6 to the Civil Partnership Act 2004, or

    (c)   under, or having effect as if made under, Schedule 1 to the Children Act 1989,

and the court does not propose to exercise its powers under paragraph (c), (cc) or (d) of subsection (3) above, the court shall, unless upon representations expressly made in that behalf by the person who applied for the maintenance order it is satisfied that it is undesirable to do so, exercise its power under paragraph (b) of that subsection.

(8) The Lord Chancellor may by regulations confer on magistrates' courts, in addition to their powers under paragraphs (a) to (d) of subsection (3) above, the power (the "additional power") to order that payments under a qualifying maintenance order be made by the debtor to the creditor or the designated officer for a magistrates' court (as the regulations may provide) by such method of payment as may be specified in the regulations.

(9) Any reference in any enactment to paragraphs (a) to (d) of subsection (3) above (but not a reference to any specific paragraph of that subsection) shall be taken to include a reference to the additional power, and the reference in subsection (10) below to the additional power shall be construed accordingly.

(10) Regulations under subsection (8) above may make provision for any enactment concerning, or connected with, payments under maintenance orders to apply, with or without modifications, in relation to the additional power.

(11) The power of the Lord Chancellor to make regulations under subsection (8) above shall be exercisable by statutory instrument and any such statutory instrument shall be subject to annulment in pursuance of a resolution of either House of Parliament.

(12) For the purposes of this section –

    (a)   the reference in subsection (1) above to money paid periodically by one person to another includes, in the case of a maintenance order, a reference to a lump sum paid by instalments by one person to another; and

    (b)   references to arrangements made by the Secretary of State for the collection of payments are to arrangements made by him under section 30 of the Child Support Act 1991 and regulations made under that section.

Amendments—MEA 1991, s 2; SI 1992/709; SI 1994/731; AJA 1999, s 90, Sch 13, para 99; CPA 2004, s 261(1), Sch 27, para 64; Courts Act 2003, Sch 8, para 208.

Defined terms—"magistrates' court": s 148(1).

Scope—Where the order is not a maintenance order, the court is restricted to ordering direct payments or payments through any magistrates' court. For the duties of the clerk and designated officer where a means of payment order has been made, see MCR 1981, r 39.

59A Orders for periodical payment: proceedings by designated officer

(1) Where payments under a relevant UK order are required to be made periodically –

    (a)   to or through the designated officer for a magistrates' court, or

(b)   by any method of payment falling within section 59(6) above,

and any sums payable under the order are in arrear, the relevant designated officer shall, if the person for whose benefit the payments are required to be made so requests in writing, and unless it appears to that designated officer that it is unreasonable in the circumstances to do so, proceed in his own name for the recovery of those sums.

(2) Where payments under a relevant UK order are required to be made periodically to or through the designated officer for a magistrates' court, the person for whose benefit the payments are required to be made may, at any time during the period in which the payments are required to be so made, give authority in writing to the relevant designated officer for him to proceed as mentioned in subsection (3) below.

(3) Where authority under subsection (2) above is given to the relevant designated officer, he shall, unless it appears to him that it is unreasonable in the circumstances to do so, proceed in his own name for the recovery of any sums payable to or through him under the order in question which, on or after the date of the giving of the authority, fall into arrear.

(4) In any case where –

(a)   authority under subsection (2) above has been given to the relevant designated officer, and

(b)   the person for whose benefit the payments are required to be made gives notice in writing to the relevant designated officer cancelling the authority,

the authority shall cease to have effect and, accordingly, the relevant designated officer shall not continue any proceedings already commenced by virtue of the authority.

(5) The person for whose benefit the payments are required to be made shall have the same liability for all the costs properly incurred in or about proceedings taken under subsection (1) above at his request or under subsection (3) above by virtue of his authority (including any costs incurred as a result of any proceedings commenced not being continued) as if the proceedings had been taken by him.

(6) Nothing in subsection (1) or (3) above shall affect any right of a person to proceed in his own name for the recovery of sums payable on his behalf under an order of any court.

(7) In this section –

"the relevant designated officer", in relation to an order, means –

(a)   in a case where payments under the order are required to be made to or through the designated officer for a magistrates' court, the designated officer for that magistrates' court;

(b)   in a case where such payments are required to be made by any method of payment falling within section 59(6) and the order was made by a magistrates' court, the designated officer for that magistrates' court; and

(c)   in a case where such payments are required to be made by any method of payment falling within section 59(6) and the order was not made by a magistrates' court, the designated officer for the magistrates' court in which the order is registered;

"relevant UK order" means –

(a)   an order made by a magistrates' court, other than an order made by virtue of Part II of the Maintenance Orders (Reciprocal Enforcement) Act 1972;

(b)   an order made by the High Court or a county court (including an order deemed to be made by the High Court by virtue of section 1(2) of the Maintenance Orders Act 1958) and registered under Part I of that Act of 1958 in a magistrates' court; or

(c)   an order made by a court in Scotland or Northern Ireland and registered under Part II of the Maintenance Orders Act 1950 in a magistrates' court;

and any reference to payments required to be made periodically includes, in the case of a maintenance order, a reference to instalments required to be paid in respect of a lump sum payable by instalments.

Amendments—Inserted by MEA 1991, s 3; amended by AJA 1999, s 90, Sch 13, para 100; Courts Act 2003, Sch 8, para 209.

Defined terms—"maintenance order": s 150(1).

Scope—This section requires the designated officer, ie a member of Her Majesty's Court Service designated by the Lord Chancellor under Courts Act 2003, s 37, to proceed to recover any arrears under a relevant UK order where payment has been ordered through a magistrates' court or by standing order on the written authority of the person entitled to payment. Liability to costs may be incurred by the person who gives the written authority to enforce. The designated officer has a discretion not to take proceedings and, if the designated officer chooses not to do so, the person entitled to payment may proceed in his own name under s 59A(6).

"in arrear" (s 59A(1))—The designated officer is required by MCR 1981, r 40 to notify arrears to the person entitled to payment.

59B Maintenance orders: penalty for breach

(1) In any case where –

    (a)   payments under a relevant English maintenance order are required to be made periodically in the manner mentioned in paragraph (a) or (b) of section 59A(1) above, and

    (b)   the debtor fails, on or after the date of commencement of this section, to comply with the order in so far as the order relates to the manner of payment concerned,

the person for whose benefit the payments are required to be made may make a complaint to a relevant justice giving details of the failure to comply.

(2) If the relevant justice is satisfied that the nature of the alleged failure to comply may be such as to justify the relevant court in exercising its power under subsection (3) below, he shall issue a summons directed to the debtor requiring him to appear before the relevant court to answer the complaint.

(3) On the hearing of the complaint, the relevant court may order the debtor to pay a sum not exceeding £1,000.

(4) Any sum ordered to be paid under subsection (3) above shall for the purposes of this Act be treated as adjudged to be paid by a conviction of a magistrates' court.

(5) In this section –

    "debtor" has the same meaning as it has in section 59 above;
    "the relevant court", in relation to an order, means –

    (a)   in a case where payments under the order are required to be made to or through the designated officer for a magistrates' court, that magistrates' court;

    (b)   in a case where such payments are required to be made by any method of payment falling within section 59(6) and the order was made by a magistrates' court, that magistrates' court; and

    (c)   in a case where such payments are required to be made by any method of payment falling within section 59(6) and the order was not made by a magistrates' court, the magistrates' court in which the order is registered;

    "relevant English maintenance order" means –

    (a)   a maintenance order made by a magistrates' court, other than an order made by virtue of Part II of the Maintenance Orders (Reciprocal Enforcement) Act 1972; or

    (b)   an order made by the High Court or a county court (other than an order

deemed to be made by the High Court by virtue of section 1(2) of the
Maintenance Orders Act 1958) and registered under Part I of that Act of
1958 in a magistrates' court;

"relevant justice", in relation to a relevant court, means a justice of the peace acting
in the local justice area in which the relevant court is acting;

and any reference to payments required to be made periodically includes a reference to
instalments required to be paid in respect of a lump sum payable by instalments.

Amendments—Inserted by MEA 1991, s 3; amended by Courts Act 2003, Sch 8, para 210.

Defined terms—"maintenance order": s 150(1).

60 Revocation, variation etc of orders for periodical payment

(1) Where a magistrates' court has made an order for money to be paid periodically by
one person to another, the court may, by order on complaint, revoke, revive or vary the
order.

(2) The power under subsection (1) above to vary an order shall include power to
suspend the operation of any provision of the order temporarily and to revive the
operation of any provision so suspended.

(3) Where the order mentioned in subsection (1) above is a maintenance order, the
power under that subsection to vary the order shall include power, if the court is satisfied
that payment has not been made in accordance with the order, to exercise one of its
powers under paragraphs (a) to (d) of section 59(3) above.

(4) In any case where –

    (a)   a magistrates' court has made a maintenance order, and

    (b)   payments under the order are required to be made by any method of payment
falling within section 59(6) above,

an interested party may apply in writing to the court for the order to be varied as
mentioned in subsection (5) above.

(5) Subject to subsection (8) below, where an application has been made under
subsection (4) above, a justices' clerk, after giving written notice (by post or otherwise)
of the application to any other interested party and allowing that party, within the period
of 14 days beginning with the date of the giving of that notice, an opportunity to make
written representations, may vary the order to provide that payments under the order
shall be made to the designated officer for the court.

(6) The clerk may proceed with an application under subsection (4) above
notwithstanding that any such interested party as is referred to in subsection (5) above
has not received written notice of the application.

(7) In subsections (4) to (6) above "interested party", in relation to a maintenance order,
means –

    (a)   the debtor;

    (b)   the creditor; and

    (c)   if the person who applied for the maintenance order is a person other than the
creditor, that other person.

(8) Where an application has been made under subsection (4) above, the clerk may, if he
considers it inappropriate to exercise his power under subsection (5) above, refer the
matter to the court which may vary the order by exercising one of its powers under
paragraphs (a) to (d) of section 59(3) above.

(9) Subsections (4), (5) and (7) of section 59 above shall apply for the purposes of
subsections (3) and (8) above as they apply for the purposes of that section.

(10) None of the powers of the court, or of a justices' clerk, conferred by subsections (3) to (9) above shall be exercisable in relation to a maintenance order which is not a qualifying maintenance order (with the meaning of section 59 above).

(10A) The power in subsection (1) is not exercisable in relation to a maintenance order which falls to be enforced by a magistrates' court by virtue of –

    (a)   the Maintenance Regulation and the Civil Jurisdiction and Judgments (Maintenance) Regulations 2011, or

    (b)   the Council Regulation.

(10B) In subsection (10A) –

    "the Maintenance Regulation" means Council Regulation (EC) No 4/2009 including as applied in relation to Denmark by virtue of the Agreement made on 19 October 2005 between the European Community and the Kingdom of Denmark;

    "the Council Regulation" means Council Regulation (EC) No 44/2001 including as applied in relation to Denmark by virtue of the Agreement made on 19 October 2005 between the European Community and the Kingdom of Denmark.

(11) For the purposes of this section –

    (a)   "creditor" and "debtor" have the same meaning as they have in section 59 above; and

    (b)   the reference in subsection (1) above to money paid periodically by one person to another includes, in the case of a maintenance order, a reference to a lump sum paid by instalments by one person to another.

Amendments—Substituted by MEA 1991, s 4; amended by AJA 1999, s 90, Sch 13, para 101; Courts Act 2003, Sch 8, para 211; SI 2011/1484.

Defined terms—"maintenance order": s 150(1).

Scope—This section provides for the revocation, revival or variation of orders for periodical payments. For the procedure to be followed, see MCR 1981, rr 41 and 106. This section does not apply to orders made under DPMCA 1978 (see instead ss 20–24 of that Act) or orders made under CPA 2004, Sch 6 (see instead Sch 6, Pt 6 of that Act) or orders with a foreign element (see e g MO(RE)A 1972, ss 5, 32; CJJ(M)R 2011 and Council Regulation (EC) No 4/2009 ("the Maintenance Regulation")) or to registered High Court or county court orders (see MOA 1958, s 4). Special powers of variation relating to payments methods are conferred under subsections (4) to (10).

"complaint" (s 60(1))—Any person entitled to recover the sum payable under the order for his own benefit is entitled to make complaint (*Moore v Ball* [1984] FLR 555).

Fee payable—See MCFO 2008, fee 12.1.

61 Periodical payments payable by one person under more than one order

(1) Rules of court may make provision –

    (a)   for enabling a person to make one complaint for the recovery of payments required to be made to him by another person under more than one periodical payments order; and

    (b)   for apportioning between two or more periodical payments orders, in such manner as may be prescribed by the rules, any sum paid to the designated officer for a magistrate's court on any date by the person liable to make payments under the orders which is less than the total sum required to be paid on that date to that designated officer by that person in respect of those orders (being orders one of which requires payments to be made for the benefit of a child to that person with whom the child has his home and one or more of which requires payments to be made to that person either for his own benefit or for the benefit of another child who has his home with him).

(2) In this section –

"child" means a person who has not attained the age of 18;

"periodical payments order" means an order made by a magistrates' court, or registered in a magistrates' court under Part II of the Maintenance Orders Act 1950 or Part I of the Maintenance Orders Act 1958, which requires the making of periodical payments,

and any payments required under a periodical payments order to be made to a child shall for the purposes of subsection (1) above be treated as if they were required to be made to the person with whom the child has his home.

Amendments—AJA 1999, s 90, Sch 13, para 102; Courts Act 2003, Sch 8, para 212.

Scope—This section provides for rules to be made for a number of periodical payments to be enforced in one complaint and for the apportionment of payments between two or more periodical payments orders, see MCR 1981, r 60.

Payments to children

62 Provisions as to payments required to be made to a child etc

(1) Where –

(a)   periodical payments are required to be made, or a lump sum is required to be paid, to a child under an order made by a magistrates' court, or

(b)   periodical payments are required to be made to a child under an order which is registered in a magistrates' court,

any sum required under the order to be paid to the child may be paid to the person with whom the child has his home, and that person –

(i)   may proceed in his own name for the variation, revival or revocation of the order, and

(ii)   may either proceed in his own name for the recovery of any sum required to be paid under the order or request or authorise the designated officer for the magistrates' court under subsection (1) or subsection (2) respectively of section 59A above to proceed for the recovery of that sum.

(2) Where a child has a right under any enactment to apply for the revival of an order made by a magistrates' court which provided for the making of periodical payments to or for the benefit of the child, the person with whom the child has his home may proceed in his own name for the revival of that order.

(3) Where any person by whom periodical payments are required to be paid to a child under an order made by or registered in a magistrates' court makes a complaint for the variation or revocation of that order, the person with whom the child has his home may answer the complaint in his own name.

(4) Nothing in subsections (1) and (2) above shall affect any right of a child to proceed in his own name for the variation, revival or revocation of an order or for the recovery of any sum payable thereunder.

(5) In this section references to the person with whom a child has his home –

(a)   in the case of any child who is being looked after by a local authority (within the meaning of section 22 of the Children Act 1989), are references to that local authority; and

(b)   in any other case, are references to the person who, disregarding any absence of the child at a hospital or boarding school and any other temporary absence, has care of the child.

(6) In this section any reference to an order registered in a magistrates' court is a reference to an order registered in a magistrates' court under Part II of the Maintenance Orders Act 1950 or Part I of the Maintenance Orders Act 1958.

(7) In this section "child" means a person who has not attained the age of 18.

Amendments—CA 1989, s 108(5), Sch 13, para 44(2); MEA 1991, s 11(1), Sch 2, para 5; AJA 1999, s 90, Sch 13, para 103; Courts Act 2003, Sch 8, para 213.

Defined terms—"child": s 62(7); "magistrates' court": s 148(1).

Orders other than for payment of money

63 Orders other than for payment of money

(1) Where under any Act passed after 31 December 1879 a magistrates' court has power to require the doing of anything other than the payment of money, or to prohibit the doing of anything, any order of the court for the purpose of exercising that power may contain such provisions for the manner in which anything is to be done, for the time within which anything is to be done, or during which anything is not to be done, and generally for giving effect to the order, as the court thinks fit.

(2) The court may by order made on complaint suspend or rescind any such order as aforesaid.

(3) Where any person disobeys an order of a magistrates' court made under an Act passed after 31 December 1879 to do anything other than the payment of money or to abstain from doing anything the court may –

    (a)   order him to pay a sum not exceeding £50 for every day during which he is in default or a sum not exceeding £5,000; or

    (b)   commit him to custody until he has remedied his default or for a period not exceeding 2 months;

but a person who is ordered to pay a sum for every day during which he is in default or who is committed to custody until he has remedied his default shall not by virtue of this section be ordered to pay more than £1,000 or be committed for more than 2 months in all for doing or abstaining from doing the same thing contrary to the order (without prejudice to the operation of this section in relation to any subsequent default).

(4) Any sum ordered to be paid under subsection (3) above shall for the purposes of this Act be treated as adjudged to be paid by a conviction of a magistrates' court.

(5) The preceding provisions of this section shall not apply to any order for the enforcement of which provision is made by any other enactment.

Amendments—Criminal Justice Act 1991, s 17(3)(a), Sch 4, Pt I.

Defined terms—"commit him to custody": s 150(1).

Scope—This section provides for the enforcement of orders of magistrates' courts other than those for the payment of money and can be used to enforce non-molestation orders and occupation orders made under FLA 1996, Pt IV and orders for contact with a child (*P v W (Access Order: Breach)* [1984] FLR 408). The proceedings are not family proceedings unless the court treats them as family proceedings under s 65(2) or unless s 65(3) applies. Failure to obey orders may amount to contempt (see CCA 1981, s 17 and Sch 3).

Power to suspend or rescind (s 63(2))—DPMCA 1978, s 23(2) and. CPA 2004, Sch 6, Pt 6, disapply s 63(2) in respect of orders made under Pt 1 of the 1978 Act and Sch 6, Pt 6, of the 2004 Act.

"disobeys" (s 63(3))—An unintentional breach is not sufficient. The breach must be deliberate and wilful. For the approach to be adopted when enforcing a contact order, see *T v T* (1984) *The Times*, 19 July.

"the court may" (s 63(3))—For the procedure to be followed, see CCA 1981, Sch 3. Where the breach is proved, the court has a discretion to take no action, impose a financial penalty or commit to custody. Where payment of a sum is ordered, time to pay or payment by instalments may be allowed (s 75). A committal under this section may not be suspended (*B(BPM) v B(MM)* [1969] P 103). However, see FLA 1996, s 50 for power to suspend committal on breach of a non-molestation order or occupation order or breach of an exclusion requirement included in an interim care order or emergency protection order.

Appeal against order or committal (s 63(3))—Under AJA 1960, s 13, appeal lies to a Divisional Court of the High Court. For procedure on appeal, see CPR 1998, Sch 1, RSC Ord 109, r 2.

Remedying default (s 63(3))—No procedure is prescribed for notifying the prison that the default has been remedied or for ending the daily penalty. Natural justice would seem to require that the original applicant should be given an opportunity to make representations and some sort of hearing appears necessary. Following committal for breach of a non-molestation order and/or an occupation order, FPR 2010, r 10.18(17) as applied by MC(EVOFP & MP)R 2011, r 80, makes specific provision for such a hearing, with notice to the original applicant, upon the contemnor's application to purge his contempt. The difficulty arises only where committal or a daily penalty is ordered until the default is remedied. Where a period of committal is ordered for a past breach of the order, there does not appear to be any power of review.

Use of s 63—In order for contact to be enforced under this provision, it must be precisely defined as an active rather than a passive order; s 63 should be used only as a last resort, and is to be approached with the utmost caution. The question of punishment for past behaviour, or of damage to the dignity of the court if the order is disobeyed, should not enter into consideration (*Re H (Contact: Enforcement)* [1996] 1 FLR 614). Alternative provision exists in CA 1989, s 11J inserted by the CAA 2006, for breach of a contact order to be enforced on application for an enforcement order (unpaid work) or by application under CA 1989, s 11O for an order for compensation for financial loss.

Enforcement of payment (s 63(4))—The sum is treated as adjudged to be paid by a conviction; the provisions as to enforcement are contained in ss 75 to 91.

Costs

64 Power to award costs and enforcement of costs

(1) On the hearing of a complaint, a magistrates' court shall have power in its discretion to make such order as to costs –

   (a) on making the order for which the complaint is made, to be paid by the defendant to the complainant;

   (b) on dismissing the complaint, to be paid by the complainant to the defendant,

as it thinks just and reasonable; but if the complaint is for an order for the variation of an order for the periodic payment of money, or for the enforcement of such an order, the court may, whatever adjudication it makes, order either party to pay the whole or any part of the other's costs.

(1A) Subsection (1) does not apply to family proceedings.

(2) The amount of any sum ordered to be paid under subsection (1) or (4A) shall be specified in the order, or order of dismissal, as the case may be.

(3) Subject to subsection (4) below, costs ordered to be paid under this section shall be enforceable as a civil debt.

(4) Any costs awarded on a complaint for a maintenance order, or for the enforcement, variation, revocation, discharge or revival of such an order, against the person liable to make payments under the order shall be enforceable as a sum ordered to be paid by a magistrates' court maintenance order.

(4A) Subject to the provisions of any other enactment, the costs of and incidental to all family proceedings in any magistrates' court (including those required to be issued by complaint and those relating to the making of a periodic payment order) shall be in the discretion of that court and that court shall have full power to determine by whom and to what extent costs are to be paid.

(5) The preceding provisions of this section shall have effect subject to any other Act enabling a magistrates' court to order a successful party to pay the other party's costs.

Amendments—FLRA 1987, s 33(1), Sch 2, para 81; SI 2011/1045.

Defined terms—"enforceable as a civil debt": s 150(1).

Scope—The power to order costs where the complaint is not proceeded with is contained in Courts Act 1971, s 52(3).

"On the hearing of a complaint" (s 64(1))—This section does not empower the court to make orders for costs when an application is dealt with (*R v Salisbury and Tisbury and Mere Combined Juvenile Court ex parte Ball* [1986] 1 FLR 1).

"just and reasonable" (s 64(1))—The order should not be for more than the proper costs incurred. The costs order is not a penalty (*R v Highgate Justices ex parte Petrou* [1954] 1 WLR 485). However, the court has a wide discretion to order costs and, in *R v Southend Stipendiary Magistrates ex parte Rochford DC* [1994] TLR 257, a sum of £75,000 was upheld.

"the amount ... shall be specified" (s 64(2))—The amount of the costs order must be fixed by the court. It is not permissible to make a non-specific order and to delegate the task of assessment to the justices' clerk. Contrast the position in criminal cases.

"enforceable as a civil debt" (s 64(3))—See under s 58.

Family proceedings

65 Meaning of family proceedings

(1) In this Act "family proceedings" means proceedings under any of the following enactments and other instruments, that is to say –

(a) the Maintenance Orders (Facilities for Enforcement) Act 1920;
(b) (*repealed*)
(c) section 3 of the Marriage Act 1949;
(ca) Schedule 2 to the Civil Partnership Act 2004;
(d), (e) (*repealed*)
(ee) section 35 of the Matrimonial Causes Act 1973;
(ef) paragraphs 69 to 72 of Schedule 5 to the Civil Partnership Act 2004;
(f) Part I of the Maintenance Orders (Reciprocal Enforcement) Act 1972;
(g) (*repealed*)
(h) the Adoption and Children Act 2002;
(i) section 18 of the Supplementary Benefits Act 1976;
(j) Part I of the Domestic Proceedings and Magistrates' Courts Act 1978;
(ja) Schedule 6 to the Civil Partnership Act 2004;
(k) (*repealed*)
(l) section 60 of this Act;
(m) Part I of the Civil Jurisdiction and Judgments Act 1982, so far as that Part relates to the recognition or enforcement of maintenance orders;
(mm) section 55A of the Family Law Act 1986;
(n) the Children Act 1989;
(nza) section 72 or section 79 of the Childcare Act 2006;
(na) section 30 of the Human Fertilisation and Embryology Act 1990;
(nb) section 106 of the Social Security Administration Act 1992;
(o) section 20 (so far as it provides, by virtue of an order under section 45, for appeals to be made to a court) of the Child Support Act 1991;
(p) Part IV of the Family Law Act 1996;

(q) sections 11 and 12 of the Crime and Disorder Act 1998;

(r) Council Regulation (EC) No 44/2001 of 22 December 2000 on jurisdiction and the recognition and enforcement of judgments in civil and commercial matters, as amended from time to time and as applied by the Agreement made on 19 October 2005 between the European Community and the Kingdom of Denmark on jurisdiction and the recognition and enforcement of judgments in civil and commercial matters (OJ No. L 299 16.11.2005 at p 62), so far as that Regulation relates to the recognition or enforcement of maintenance orders;

(ra) Council Regulation (EC) No 4/2009 including as applied in relation to Denmark by virtue of the Agreement made on 19 October 2005 between the European Community and the Kingdom of Denmark;

(s) Council Regulation (EC) No 2201/2003 of 27 November 2003 concerning jurisdiction and the recognition and enforcement of judgments in matrimonial matters and matters of parental responsibility, so far as that Regulation relates to jurisdiction, recognition and enforcement in parental responsibility matters;

(t) the Convention on Jurisdiction, Applicable Law, Recognition, Enforcement and Co-Operation in respect of Parental Responsibility and Measures for the Protection of Children that was signed at The Hague on 19 October 1996;

(u) the Convention on the International Recovery of Child Support and other forms of Family Maintenance done at The Hague on 23 November 2007;

except that, subject to subsection (2) below, it does not include –

(i) proceedings for the enforcement of any order made, confirmed, registered or enforceable under any of those enactments or instruments;

(ii) proceedings for the variation of any provision for the periodical payment of money contained in an order made, confirmed, registered or enforceable under any of those enactments or instruments; or

(iii) proceedings on an information in respect of the commission of an offence under any of these enactments.

(2) The court before which there fall to be heard any of the following proceedings, that is to say –

(a) proceedings (whether under this Act or any other enactment) for the enforcement of any order made, confirmed, registered or enforceable under any of the enactments or instruments specified in paragraphs (a) to (k), (m), (n), (p), (r), (ra) and (u) of subsection (1) above;

(b) proceedings (whether under this Act or any other enactment) for the variation of any provision for the making of periodical payments contained in an order made, confirmed, registered or enforceable under any of those enactments or instruments;

(c) proceedings for an attachment of earnings order to secure maintenance payments within the meaning of the Attachment of Earnings Act 1971 or for the discharge or variation of such an order; or

(d) proceedings for the enforcement of a maintenance order which is registered in a magistrates' court under Part II of the Maintenance Orders Act 1950 or Part I of the Maintenance Orders Act 1958 or for the variation of the rate of payments specified by such an order,

(e) proceedings under section 20 (so far as it provides, by virtue of an order under section 45, for appeals to be made to a court) of the Child Support Act 1991,

may if it thinks fit order that those proceedings and any other proceedings being heard therewith shall, notwithstanding anything in subsection (1) above, be treated as family proceedings for the purposes of this Act.

(3) Where the same parties are parties –

   (a)   to proceedings which are family proceedings by virtue of subsection (1) above, and

   (b)   to proceedings which the court has power to treat as family proceedings by virtue of subsection (2) above,

and the proceedings are heard together by a magistrates' court, the whole of those proceedings shall be treated as family proceedings for the purposes of this Act.

(4) No appeal shall lie from the making of, or refusal to make, an order under subsection (2) above.

(5), (6) ...

Amendments—CJJA 1982, s 15(4), Sch 12, para 7; MFPA 1984, s 44; Social Security Act 1986, Sch 10; FLRA 1987, s 33(4), Sch 4; CA 1989, ss 92(11), 108(7), Sch 11, para 8, Sch 15; CLSA 1990, s 125(7), Sch 20; Social Security (Consequential Provisions) Act 1992, ss 3, 4, Schs 1, 2, para 60; FLA 1996, s 66(1), Sch 8, para 49; SI 1997/1898; Crime and Disorder Act 1998, s 119, Sch 8, para 42; CSPSSA 2000, s 83(5), Sch 8, para 2, Sch 9; SI 2001/3929; SI 2005/265; ACA 2002, s 139(1), Sch 3, paras 36, 37; CPA 2004, s 261(1), Sch 27, para 65(1)–(4); Courts Act 2003, Sch 8, para 214; Childcare Act 2006, Sch 2, para 2; SI 2007/1655; Health and Social Care Act 2008, Sch 15; SI 2010/1898; SI 2011/1215; SI 2012/1770.

Scope—Proceedings included in s 65(1) are always family proceedings, while proceedings included in s 65(2) and proceedings being heard at the same time may be treated as family proceedings by the court. FPR 2010 do not apply automatically to proceedings included in s 65(2) and reference should be made instead to MC(EVOFP & MP)R 2011, which consolidate former freestanding rules (e g MC(MOA 1958)R 1959) or apply FPR 2010 with modifications, to certain magistrates' courts proceedings. The right of appeal by way of case stated under MCA 1980, s 111 is no longer available for proceedings included in ss 65(1) and (2). Instead, provision is made for appeal to a county court on grounds of error of law or excess of jurisdiction under MCA 1980, s 111A.

65A Meaning of family procedure rules

In this Act, "Family Procedure Rules" means rules made under section 75 of the Courts Act 2003.

Amendments—Inserted by SI 2011/1045.

66 Composition of magistrates' courts for family proceedings: general

(1) A magistrates' court when hearing family proceedings shall be composed of –

   (a)   two or three lay justices; or

   (b)   a District Judge (Magistrates' Courts) as chairman and one or two lay justices;

or, if it is not practicable for such a court to be so composed, a District Judge (Magistrates' Courts) sitting alone.

(2) Except where such a court is composed of a District Judge (Magistrates' Courts) sitting alone, it shall, so far as practicable, include both a man and a woman.

(3) In this section "lay justice" has the same meaning as in the Courts Act 2003.

Amendments—Substituted by AJA 1999, s 78, Sch 11, para 27; Courts Act 2003, s 109(1), Sch 8, para 215.

Defined terms—"family proceedings": s 65.

67 Family proceedings courts

(1) Magistrates' courts –

   (a)   constituted in accordance with this section or section 66 of the Courts Act 2003 (judges having powers of District Judges (Magistrates' Courts)), and

(b) sitting for the purpose of hearing family proceedings,

are to be known as family proceedings courts.

(2) A justice of the peace is not qualified to sit as a member of a family proceedings court to hear family proceedings of any description unless he has an authorisation extending to the proceedings.

(3) He has an authorisation extending to the proceedings only if he has been authorised by the Lord Chief Justice to sit as a member of a family proceedings court to hear –

(a) proceedings of that description, or
(b) all family proceedings.

(4) The Lord Chief Justice may, after consulting the Lord Chancellor, by rules make provision about –

(a) the grant and revocation of authorisations,
(b) the appointment of chairmen of family proceedings courts, and
(c) the composition of family proceedings courts.

(5) Rules under subsection (4) may confer powers on the Lord Chief Justice with respect to any of the matters specified in the rules.

(6) Rules under subsection (4) may be made only after consultation with the Family Procedure Rule Committee.

(7) Rules under subsection (4) are to be made by statutory instrument.

(8) A statutory instrument containing rules under subsection (4) is subject to annulment in pursuance of a resolution of either House of Parliament.

(9) The Lord Chief Justice may nominate a judicial office holder (as defined in section 109(4) of the Constitutional Reform Act 2005) to exercise his functions under subsection (3) or (4) or the powers conferred on him by rules under subsection (4).

Amendments—Substituted by Courts Act 2003, s 49(1); amended by CRA 2005, s 15(1), Sch 4, Pt 1, paras 99, 101.

Defined terms—"family proceedings": s 65.

Rules (s 67(4)–(7))—The relevant rules are contained in the Family Proceedings Courts (Constitution of Committees and Right to Preside) Rules 2007.

68 (repealed)

68A Power of the magistrates' court to order disclosure of documents, inspection of property etc. in family proceedings

(1) On the application, in accordance with rules of court, of a party to any family proceedings, a magistrates' court, in such circumstances as may be prescribed, has the power to order a person who is not a party to the proceedings and who appears to the court to be likely to have in his or her possession, custody or power any documents which are relevant to any issue arising out of the proceedings –

(a) to disclose whether those documents are in that person's possession, custody or power; and
(b) to produce such of those documents as are in that person's possession, custody or power to the applicant or, on such conditions as may be specified in the order –
    (i)   to the applicant's legal advisers; or
    (ii) to the applicant's legal advisers and any medical or other professional adviser of the applicant; or

(iii) if the applicant has no legal adviser, to any medical or other professional adviser of the applicant.

(2) On the application, in accordance with rules of court, of a party to any family proceedings, a magistrates' court, in such circumstances as may be prescribed, has the power to make an order providing for any one or more of the following –

(a) the inspection, photographing, preservation, custody and detention of property which is not the property of, or in the possession of, any party to the proceedings but which is the subject matter of the proceedings or as to which any question arises in the proceedings;

(b) the taking of samples of any such property as is mentioned in paragraph (a) and the carrying out of any experiment on or with any such property.

(3) This section is without prejudice to the exercise by a magistrates' court of any power to make orders which is exercisable apart from the provisions of this section.

Amendments—Inserted by SI 2011/1045.

69 Sittings of magistrates' courts for family proceedings

(1) The business of magistrates' courts shall, so far as is consistent with the due dispatch of business, be arranged in such manner as may be requisite for separating the hearing and determination of family proceedings from other business.

(2) In the case of family proceedings in a magistrates' court other than proceedings under the Adoption Act 1976, no person shall be present during the hearing and determination by the court of the proceedings except –

(a) officers of the court;

(b) parties to the case before the court, their legal representatives, witnesses and other persons directly concerned in the case;

(c) representatives of newspapers or news agencies;

(d) any other person whom the court may in its discretion permit to be present, so, however, that permission shall not be withheld from a person who appears to the court to have adequate grounds for attendance.

(3) In relation to any family proceedings under the Adoption Act 1976, subsection (2) above shall apply with the omission of paragraphs (c) and (d).

(4) When hearing family proceedings, a magistrates' court may, if it thinks it necessary in the interest of the administration of justice or of public decency, direct that any persons, not being officers of the court or parties to the case, the parties' legal representatives, or other persons directly concerned in the case, be excluded during the taking of any indecent evidence.

(5) The powers conferred on a magistrates' court by this court by this section shall be in addition and without prejudice to any other powers of the court to hear proceedings in camera.

(6) Nothing in this section shall affect the exercise by a magistrates' court of the power to direct that witnesses shall be excluded until they are called for examination.

(7) ...

Amendments—CA 1989, s 92(11), Sch 11, para 8; CLSA 1990, s 125(3), Sch 18, para 25.

Defined terms—"family proceedings": s 65; "legal representative": s 150(1).

70 Jurisdiction of magistrates' courts in inner London for family proceedings

(1) A relevant court acting in an inner London local justice area shall, in addition to hearing proceedings which (apart from subsection (2) below) may be heard by a relevant court acting in that area, have jurisdiction to hear proceedings which could be heard before a relevant court acting in any other such area, but shall not exercise the jurisdiction conferred by this subsection except in such cases or classes of case as may be determined by the Lord Chancellor.

(2) A magistrates' court acting in an inner London local justice area shall not hear any family proceedings if the Lord Chancellor so determines.

(3) In this section –

   "relevant court" means a magistrates' court when composed for the purpose of exercising jurisdiction to hear family proceedings;

   "inner London local justice area' means any local justice area falling wholly or partly within the area consisting of the inner London boroughs and the City of London.

Amendments—CA 1989, s 92(11), Sch 11, para 8; Police and Magistrates' Courts Act 1994, s 91, Sch 8, para 30; AJA 1999, s 76(2), Sch 10, para 34; Courts Act 2003, Sch 8, para 216.

Defined terms—"family proceedings": s 65.

71 Newspaper reports of family proceedings

(1) In the case of family proceedings in a magistrates' court (other than proceedings under the Adoption Act 1976) it shall not be lawful for a person to whom this subsection applies –

   (a)   to print or publish, or cause or procure to be printed or published, in a newspaper or periodical, or

   (b)   to include, or cause or procure to be included, in a programme included in a programme service (within the meaning of the Broadcasting Act 1990) for reception in Great Britain,

any particulars of the proceedings other than such particulars as are mentioned in subsection (1A) below.

(1A) The particulars referred to in subsection (1) above are –

   (a)   the names, addresses and occupations of the parties and witnesses;

   (b)   the grounds of the application, and a concise statement of the charges, defences and counter-charges in support of which evidence has been given;

   (c)   submissions on any point of law arising in the course of the proceedings and the decision of the court on the submissions;

   (d)   the decision of the court, and any observations made by the court in giving it.

(1B) Subsection (1) above applies –

   (a)   in relation to paragraph (a) of that subsection, to the proprietor, editor or publisher of the newspaper or periodical, and

   (b)   in relation to paragraph (b) of that subsection, to any body corporate which provides the service in which the programme is included and to any person having functions in relation to the programme corresponding to those of an editor of a newspaper.

(2) In the case of family proceedings in a magistrates' court under the Adoption Act 1976, subsection (1A) above shall apply with the omission of paragraphs (a) and (b) and the reference in that subsection to the particulars of the proceedings shall, in relation to any child concerned in the proceedings, include –

   (a)   the name, address or school of the child,

(b)   any picture as being, or including, a picture of the child, and

(c)   any other particulars calculated to lead to the identification of the child.

(3) Any person acting in contravention of this section shall be liable on summary conviction to a fine not exceeding level 4 on the standard scale.

(4) No prosecution for an offence under this section shall be begun without the consent of the Attorney General.

(5) Nothing in this section shall prohibit the printing or publishing of any matter in a newspaper or periodical of a technical character bona fide intended for circulation among members of the legal or medical professions.

(6) ...

Amendments—Criminal Justice Act 1982, ss 38, 46; CA 1989, s 92(11), Sch 11, para 8; Broadcasting Act 1990, s 203, Sch 20, para 29.

Defined terms—"family proceedings": s 65.

"level 4 on the standard scale" (s 71(3))—Currently £2500 (Criminal Justice Act 1982, s 37(2), as substituted).

72 (*repealed*)

73 Examination of witnesses by court

Where in any family proceedings, or in any proceedings for the enforcement or variation of an order made in family proceedings, it appears to a magistrates' court that any party to the proceedings who is not legally represented is unable effectively to examine or cross-examine a witness, the court shall ascertain from that party what are the matters about which the witness may be able to depose or on which the witness ought to be cross-examined, as the case may be, and shall put, or cause to be put, to the witness such questions in the interests of that party as may appear to the court to be proper.

Amendments—CA 1989, s 92(11), Sch 11, para 8.

Defined terms—"family proceedings": s 65.

Scope—This section imposes a statutory duty upon the court to assist an unrepresented party, where necessary, to examine or cross-examine a witness. The cross-examination must be justified (*Brewster v Brewster* [1971] 1 WLR 1102).

"unable effectively"—The duty will also arise where a party is not present and writes a letter to the court containing his case (*Marjoram v Marjoram* [1955] 1 WLR 520).

74 Reasons for decisions in family proceedings

(1) Rules of court may make provision for the recording by a magistrates' court, in such manner as may be prescribed by the rules, of reasons for a decision made in such family proceedings or class of family proceedings as may be so prescribed, and for making available a copy of any record made in accordance with those rules of the reasons for a decision of a magistrates' court to any person who requests a copy thereof for the purposes of an appeal against that decision or for the purpose of deciding whether or not to appeal against that decision.

(2) A copy of any record made by virtue of this section of the reasons for a decision of a magistrates' court shall, if certified by such officer of the court as may be prescribed, be admissible as evidence of those reasons.

Amendments—CA 1989, s 92(11), Sch 11, para 8; Courts Act 2003, Sch 8, para 217.

Defined terms—"family proceedings": s 65.

Scope—FPR 2010, r 27.2 makes provision for written reasons to be given by the court for its decisions made in family proceedings. The provision also applies in respect of proceedings falling within MCA 1980, s 65(2), for example enforcement of orders or variation of periodical payments orders in cases heard under DPMCA 1978, CA 1989 and FLA 1996, Pt IV by virtue of MC(EVOFP & MP)R 2011, which apply FPR 2010, with modifications, to these "non-family" proceeding. Although there is no requirement to state reasons before or when making an order in proceedings concerning periodical payments orders made in the High Court or a county court and subsequently registered in the magistrates' courts, it is good practice for reasons to be recorded (*Hackshaw v Hackshaw* [1999] 2 FLR 876; see also *Stray v Stray* [1999] 2 FLR 610).

PART III
SATISFACTION AND ENFORCEMENT

General provisions

75 Power to dispense with immediate payment

(1) A magistrates' court by whose conviction or order a sum is adjudged to be paid may, instead of requiring immediate payment, allow time for payment, or order payment by instalments.

(2) Where a magistrates' court has allowed time for payment, the court may, on application by or on behalf of the person liable to make the payment, allow further time or order payment by instalments.

(2A) An order under this section that a lump sum required to be paid under a maintenance order shall be paid by instalments (a "maintenance instalments order") shall be treated for the purposes of section 59, 59B and 60 above as a maintenance order.

(2B) Subsections (5) and (7) of section 59 above (including those sub-sections as they apply for the purposes of section 60 above) shall have effect in relation to a maintenance instalments order –

    (a)   as if in subsection (5), paragraph (c) and the word "and" immediately preceding it were omitted; and

    (b)   as if in subsection (7) –

        (i)   the reference to the maintenance order were a reference to the maintenance order in respect of which the maintenance instalments order in question is made;

        (ii) for the words "the person who applied for the maintenance order" there were substituted "the debtor".

(2C) Section 60 above shall have effect in relation to a maintenance instalments order as if in subsection (7), paragraph (c) and the word "and" immediately preceding it were omitted.

(3) Where a court has ordered payment by instalments and default is made in the payment of any one instalment, proceedings may be taken as if the default had been made in the payment of all the instalments then unpaid.

Amendments—MEA 1991, s 11(1), Sch 2, para 6.

"the court" (s 75(2))—By JCR 2005, Sch, para 30, the justices clerk also has this power.

"on application" (s 75(2))—The application may be in writing (MCR 1981, r 51).

76 Enforcement of sums adjudged to be paid

(1) Subject to the following provisions of this Part of this Act, and to section 132 below, where default is made in paying a sum adjudged to be paid by a conviction or order of a

magistrates' court, the court may issue a warrant of distress for the purpose of levying the sum or issue a warrant committing the defaulter to prison.

(2) A warrant of commitment may be issued as aforesaid either –

(a)   where it appears on the return to a warrant of distress that the money and goods of the defaulter are insufficient to satisfy the sum with the costs and charges of levying the sum; or

(b)   instead of a warrant of distress.

(3) The period for which a person may be committed to prison under such a warrant as aforesaid shall not, subject to the provisions of any enactment passed after 31 December 1879, exceed the period applicable to the case under Schedule 4 to this Act.

(4) Where proceedings are brought for the enforcement of a magistrates' court maintenance order under this section, the court may vary the order by exercising one of its powers under paragraphs (a) to (d) of section 59(3) above.

(5) Subsections (4), (5) and (7) of section 59 above shall apply for the purposes of subsection (4) above as they apply for the purposes of that section.

(6) Subsections (4) and (5) above shall not have effect in relation to a maintenance order which is not a qualifying maintenance order (within the meaning of section 59 above).

Amendments—Criminal Justice Act 1982, s 78, Sch 16; MEA 1991, s 7.

Scope—The section is subject to the restrictions imposed by ss 92, 96 and Sch 4 and to the additional procedural requirements of MOA 1958, s 18. For issue and execution of distress warrants see MCR 1981, r 54.

"section 132" (s 76(1))—The minimum period of imprisonment is 5 days.

"the court may issue" (s 76(1))—A discretion arises and the justices must have regard to the means of the defaulter and to the assets which may be available for distress. For exercise of the discretion see *R v Swindon Justices* (1878) 42 JP 407 (duty to enforce order improperly made but within jurisdiction and not appealed from) and *R v Gravesend Justices ex parte Doodney* [1971] 1 WLR 818 (availability of enforcement proceedings even where the creditor lived out of the jurisdiction and could not be served with summons to vary the order).

"warrant committing" (s 76(1))—Section 92 restricts the exercise of the power to commit to prison, but excludes magistrates' court maintenance orders from this particular restriction. Section 96 makes special provision for the enforcement by committal of civil debts. Complaints for arrears of maintenance must be made under s 93.

Warrant of distress—If there is a reasonable likelihood that the debtor has sufficient goods to satisfy the debt, the court should issue a distress warrant rather than commit to prison (*R v Birmingham Justices ex parte Bennett* [1983] 1 WLR 114). Special protection against execution is given by the Reserve and Auxiliary Forces (Protection of Civil Interests) Act 1951.

Warrant of commitment (s 76(2))—See s 125 for general provisions as to warrants and s 126 for execution of warrants outside England and Wales.

77 Postponement of issue of warrant

(1) Where a magistrates' court has power to issue a warrant of distress under this Part of this Act, it may, if it thinks it expedient to do so, postpone the issue of the warrant until such time and on such conditions, if any, as the court thinks just.

(2) Where a magistrates' court has power to issue a warrant of commitment under this Part of this Act, it may, if it thinks it expedient to do so, fix a term of imprisonment or detention under section 108 of the Powers of Criminal Courts (Sentencing) Act 2000 (detention of persons aged 18 to 20 for default) and postpone the issue of the warrant until such time and on such conditions, if any, as the court thinks just.

(3) A magistrates' court shall have power at any time to do either or both of the following –

(a)   to direct that the issue of the warrant of commitment shall be postponed until a time different from that to which it was previously postponed;

(b)   to vary any of the conditions on which its issue is postponed,

but only if it thinks it just to do so having regard to a change of circumstances since the relevant time.

(4) In this section "the relevant time" means –

(a)   where neither of the powers conferred by subsection (3) above has been exercised previously, the date when the issue of the warrant was postponed under subsection (2) above; and

(b)   in any other case, the date of the exercise or latest exercise of either or both of the powers.

(5) Without prejudice to the generality of subsection (3) above, if on an application by a person in respect of whom issue of a warrant has been postponed it appears to a justice of the peace acting in the local justice area in which the warrant has been or would have been issued that since the relevant time there has been a change of circumstances which would make it just for the court to exercise one or other or both of the powers conferred by that subsection, he shall refer the application to the court.

(6) Where such an application is referred to the court –

(a)   the clerk of the court shall fix a time and place for the application to be heard; and

(b)   the designated officer for the court shall give the applicant notice of that time and place

(7) Where such a notice has been given but the applicant does not appear at the time and place specified in the notice, the court may proceed with the consideration of the application in his absence.

(8) If a warrant of commitment in respect of the sum adjudged to be paid has been issued before the hearing of the application, the court shall have power to order that the warrant shall cease to have effect and, if the applicant has been arrested in pursuance of it, to order that he shall be released, but it shall only make an order under this subsection if it is satisfied that the change of circumstances on which the applicant relies was not put before the court when it was determining whether to issue the warrant.

Amendments—Criminal Justice Act 1982, s 77, Sch 14, para 50; Criminal Justice Act 1988, s 61; Powers of Criminal Courts (Sentencing) Act 2000, s 165, Sch 9, para 66; SI 2001/618; Courts Act 2003, Sch 8, para 218 .

Scope—See MOA 1958, s 18 for the duty to review the issue of the postponed warrant.

"this Part" (s 77(1))—Pt III covers sums adjudged to be paid by conviction or order (s 76), civil debt (s 96) and maintenance orders (s 93).

Conditional postponement of warrant of commitment (s 77(2))—While it is good practice when postponing the issue of a committal warrant in relation to a maintenance order to make it a condition that the debtor pays the current order together with an amount off the arrears (*Fowler v Fowler* (1981) 2 FLR 141), the court collecting officer is obliged to apply all amounts paid first to the arrears in respect of which the committal order was made (*R v Miskin Lower Justices ex parte Young* [1953] 1 QB 533). If the debtor fails to comply with the terms of the postponement, the warrant may be issued but arrears which have accrued since the warrant was ordered may not be added to the warrant (*R v Bedford Prison (Governor) ex parte Ames* [1953] 1 WLR 607).

78 Defect in distress warrant and irregularity in its execution

(1) A warrant of distress issued for the purpose of levying a sum adjudged to be paid by the conviction or order of a magistrates' court shall not, if it states that the sum has been so adjudged to be paid, be held void by reason of any defect in the warrant.

(2) A person acting under a warrant of distress shall not be deemed to be a trespasser from the beginning by reason only of any irregularity in the execution of the warrant.

(3) Nothing in this section shall prejudice the claim of any person for special damages in respect of any loss caused by a defect in the warrant or irregularity in its execution.

(4) If any person removes any goods marked in accordance with rules of court as articles impounded in the execution of a warrant of distress, or defaces or removes any such mark, he shall be liable on summary conviction to a fine not exceeding level 1 on the standard scale.

(5) If any person charged with the execution of a warrant of distress wilfully retains from the proceeds of a sale of the goods on which distress is levied, or otherwise exacts, any greater costs and charges than those properly payable, or makes any improper charge, he shall be liable on summary conviction to a fine not exceeding level 1 on the standard scale.

Amendments—Criminal Justice Act 1982, ss 38, 46; Courts Act 2003, s 109(1), Sch 8, para 219.

Rules (s 78(4))—For the relevant rules, see MCR 1981, r 58.

"level 1 on the standard scale" (s 78(4),(5))—Currently £200 (Criminal Justice Act 1982, s 37(2), as substituted).

79 Release from custody and reduction of detention on payment

(1) Where imprisonment or other detention has been imposed on any person by the order of a magistrates' court in default of payment of any sum adjudged to be paid by the conviction or order of a magistrates' court or for want of sufficient distress to satisfy such a sum, then, on the payment of the sum, together with the costs and charges, if any, of the commitment and distress, the order shall cease to have effect; and if the person has been committed to custody he shall be released unless he is in custody for some other cause.

(2) Where, after a period of imprisonment or other detention has been imposed on any person in default of payment of any sum adjudged to be paid by the conviction or order of a magistrates' court or for want of sufficient distress to satisfy such a sum, payment is made in accordance with rules of court of part of the sum, the period of detention shall be reduced by such number of days as bears to the total number of days in that period less one day the same proportion as the amount so paid bears to so much of the said sum, and the costs and charges of any distress levied to satisfy that sum, as was due at the time the period of detention was imposed.

(3) In calculating the reduction required under subsection (2) above any fraction of a day shall be left out of account.

Amendments—Courts Act 2003, s 109(1), Sch 8, para 219.

80 Application of money found on defaulter to satisfy sum adjudged

(1) Where a magistrates' court has adjudged a person to pay a sum by a conviction or has ordered the enforcement of a sum due from a person under a magistrates' court maintenance order, the court may order him to be searched.

(2) Any money found on the arrest of a person adjudged to pay such a sum as aforesaid, or on a search as aforesaid, or on his being taken to a prison or other place of detention in default of payment of such a sum or for want of sufficient distress to satisfy such a sum, may, unless the court otherwise directs, be applied towards payment of the said sum; and the balance, if any, shall be returned to him.

(3) A magistrates' court shall not allow the application as aforesaid of any money found on a person if it is satisfied that the money does not belong to him or that the loss of the money would be more injurious to his family than would be his detention.

Amendments—FLRA 1987, s 33(1), Sch 2, para 83.

Defined terms—"magistrates' court maintenance order": s 150(1).

****

Sums adjudged to be paid by an order

92 Restriction on power to impose imprisonment for default

(1) A magistrates' court shall not exercise its power under section 76 above to issue a warrant to commit to prison a person who makes default in paying a sum adjudged to be paid by an order of such a court except where the default is under –

   (a) a magistrates' court maintenance order;

   (b) an order made by a court under regulations under section 23 of the Legal Aid, Sentencing and Punishment of Offenders Act 2012 (payment by individual in respect of legal aid); or

   (c) an order for the payment of any of the taxes, contributions, premiums or liabilities specified in Schedule 4 to the Administration of Justice Act 1970.

(2) This section does not affect the power of a magistrates' court to issue such a warrant as aforesaid in the case of default in paying a sum adjudged to be paid by a conviction, or treated (by any enactment relating to the collection or enforcement of fines, costs, compensation or forfeited recognizances) as so adjudged to be paid.

(3) (*repealed*)

Amendments—FLRA 1987, s 33(4), Sch 4; Legal Aid Act 1988, s 45, Sch 5, para 9; AJA 1999, s 24, Sch 4, paras 15, 17; LASPOA 2012, s 39, Sch 5, para 16.

"magistrates' court maintenance order" (s 92(1)(a))—This term is defined in s 150(1), and includes orders made under the following provisions: DPMCA 1978, Pt I; CPA 2004, Sch 6, Pt 6; National Assistance Act 1948, s 43; Supplementary Benefits Act 1976, s 18; Social Security Act 1986, s 24; MOA 1958; MOA 1950, Pt II; MO(FE)A 1920; MO(RE)A 1972; Matrimonial Proceedings (Magistrates' Courts) Act 1960 and CA 1989, Sch 1.

93 Complaint for arrears

(1) Where default is made in paying a sum ordered to be paid by a magistrates' court maintenance order, the court shall not enforce payment of the sum under section 76 above except by an order made on complaint.

(2) A complaint under this section shall be made not earlier than the fifteenth day after the making of the order for the enforcement of which it is made; but subject to this such a complaint may be made at any time notwithstanding anything in this or any other Act.

(3) In relation to complaints under this section, section 55 above shall not apply and section 56 above shall have effect as if the words "if evidence has been received on a previous occasion" were omitted.

(4) Where at the time and place appointed for the hearing or adjourned hearing of a complaint under this section the complainant appears but the defendant does not, the court may proceed in his absence; but the court shall not begin to hear the complaint in the absence of the defendant unless either it is proved to the satisfaction of the court, on oath or in such other manner as may be prescribed, that the summons was served on him within what appears to the court to be a reasonable time before the hearing or adjourned hearing or the defendant has appeared on a previous occasion to answer the complaint.

(5) If a complaint under this section is substantiated on oath, any justice of the peace acting in the same local justice area as a court having jurisdiction to hear the complaint may issue a warrant for the defendant's arrest, whether or not a summons has been previously issued.

(6) A magistrates' court shall not impose imprisonment in respect of a default to which a complaint under this section relates unless the court has inquired in the presence of the defendant whether the default was due to the defendant's wilful refusal or culpable neglect, and shall not impose imprisonment as aforesaid if it is of opinion that the default was not so due; and, without prejudice to the preceding provisions of this subsection, a magistrates' court shall not impose imprisonment as aforesaid –

    (a)   in the absence of the defendant; or

    (b)   in a case where the court has power to do so, if it is of the opinion that it is appropriate –

        (i)   to make an attachment of earnings order; or

        (ii) to order that payments under the order be made by any method of payment falling within section 59(6) above; or

    (c)   where the sum to which the default relates comprises only interest which the defendant has been ordered to pay by virtue of section 94A(1) below.

(7) Notwithstanding anything in section 76(3) above, the period for which a defendant may be committed to prison under a warrant of commitment issued in pursuance of a complaint under this section shall not exceed 6 weeks.

(8) The imprisonment or other detention of a defendant under a warrant of commitment issued as aforesaid shall not operate to discharge the defendant from his liability to pay the sum in respect of which the warrant was issued.

Amendments—FLRA 1987, s 33(1), Sch 2, para 84; MEA 1991, s 11(1), Sch 2, para 7; Courts Act 2003, Sch 8, para 229.

Defined terms—"magistrates' court maintenance order": s 150(1).

Scope—For enforcement of an order against members of the armed forces, see Army Act 1955, ss 150 and 151, Air Force Act 1955, ss 150 and 151 and Naval Forces (Enforcement of Maintenance Liabilities) Act 1947.

"shall not enforce" (s 93(1))—The obligation to serve a copy of the order before enforcement which applies to civil debt does not apply to enforcement of orders under this section.

"proved ... in such other manner as may be prescribed" (s 93(4))—The procedure is prescribed by MCR 1981, r 67.

Imposition of imprisonment (s 93(6))—The obligation to inform the defendant of a right to legal aid (public funding) which applies to the imposition of imprisonment in criminal proceedings does not apply to proceedings under this section (*R v Cardiff Justices ex parte Salter* [1986] 1 FLR 162).

"wilful refusal or culpable neglect" (s 93(6))—The court has to be satisfied beyond reasonable doubt as to wilful refusal or culpable neglect. Committal for non-payment is a sanction of last resort and something in the nature of a deliberate defiance or reckless disregard of the court order is required (*R v Luton Magistrates' Court ex parte Sullivan* [1992] 2 FLR 196). Clear evidence and a full means enquiry are required to justify the debtor's immediate committal to prison on a finding of culpable neglect (*R v Slough Magistrates' Court ex parte Lindsay* [1997] 1 FLR 695). The receipt of benefits from the Department for Work and Pensions is only a factor in reaching a decision as to whether conduct amounts to wilful refusal or culpable neglect and is not a conclusive factor (*R v Cardiff Justices ex parte Salter* [1986] 1 FLR 162).

Warrant of commitment (s 93(8))—For execution of the warrant outside England and Wales see s 126. Enforcement of imprisonment may be used only once in respect of the same arrears.

94 Effect of committal on arrears

Where a person is committed to custody under this Part of this Act for failure to pay a sum due under a magistrates' court maintenance order, then, unless the court that commits him otherwise directs, no arrears shall accrue under the order while he is in custody.

Amendments—FLRA 1987, s 33(1), Sch 2, para 85.

Defined terms—"magistrates' court maintenance order": s 150(1).

Scope—A direction may be inappropriate where the defendant was committed to custody on the basis of culpable neglect, but see *Starkey v Starkey* [1954] P 449 where it was indicated that a direction may be appropriate for wilful refusal to pay.

"while he is in custody"—See MCR 1981, r 63 for the duty of the prison governor to notify the clerk of the court of details of the dates of reception and discharges.

94A Interest on arrears

(1) The Lord Chancellor may by order provide that a magistrates' court, on the hearing of a complaint for the enforcement, revocation, revival, variation or discharge of an English maintenance order, may order that interest of an amount calculated at the prescribed rate shall be paid on so much of the sum due under the order as they may determine.

(2) In subsection (1) above "the prescribed rate" means such rate of interest as the Lord Chancellor may by order prescribe.

(3) An order under this section may make provision for the manner in which and the periods by reference to which interest is to be calculated.

(4) Where, by virtue of subsection (1) above, a magistrates' court orders the payment of interest on any sum due under a maintenance order –

    (a) then if it orders that the whole or any part of the interest be paid by instalments that order shall be regarded as an instalments order for the purposes of section 95 below and that section shall accordingly apply in relation to it; and

    (b) the whole of the interest shall be enforceable as a sum adjudged to be paid by the maintenance order.

(5) In this section –

"English maintenance order" means –

    (a) a qualifying maintenance order made by a magistrates' court, other than an order made by virtue of Part II of the Maintenance Orders (Reciprocal Enforcement) Act 1972; or

    (b) an order made by the High Court or a county court (other than an order deemed to be made by the High Court by virtue of section 1(2) of the Maintenance Orders Act 1958) and registered under Part I of that Act of 1958 in a magistrates' court;

"qualifying maintenance order" has the same meaning as it has in section 59 above.

(6) The power of the Lord Chancellor to make an order under this section shall be exercisable by statutory instrument made with the concurrence of the Treasury and any such statutory instrument shall be subject to annulment in pursuance of a resolution of either House of Parliament.

Amendments—Inserted by MEA 1991, s 8; amended by SI 1992/709.

"may by order prescribe"—No such order has yet been made.

95 Remission of arrears and manner in which arrears to be paid

(1) On the hearing of a complaint for the enforcement, revocation, revival, variation or discharge of a magistrates' court maintenance order, a magistrates' court may remit the whole or any part of the sum due under the order.

(1A) The power in subsection (1) is not exercisable in relation to a maintenance order which falls to be enforced by a magistrates' court by virtue of –

(a) the Maintenance Regulation and the Civil Jurisdiction and Judgments (Maintenance) Regulations 2011, or

(b) the Council Regulation.

(2) If, on the hearing of a complaint for the enforcement, revocation, revival, variation or discharge of a magistrates' court maintenance order, a magistrates' court orders that the whole or any part of the sum due under the order be paid by instalments (an "instalments order"), then –

(a) if the maintenance order is an English maintenance order, the court shall at the same time exercise one of its powers under paragraphs (a) to (d) of section 59(3) above in relation to the instalments orders;

(b) if the maintenance order is a non-English maintenance order, the court shall at the same time exercise one of its powers under subsection (3) below in relation to the instalments order.

(3) The powers of the court referred to in subsection (2)(b) above are –

(a) the power to order that payments under the order be made directly to the designated officer for the court or for any other magistrates' court;

(b) the power to order that payments under the order be made to the designated officer for the court or for any other magistrates' court, by such method of payment falling within section 59(6) above as may be specified;

(c) the power to make an attachment of earnings order under the Attachment of Earnings Act 1971 to secure payments under the order.

(4) The court may in the course of any proceedings concerning an instalments order or the magistrates' court maintenance order to which it relates vary the instalments order by exercising –

(a) in respect of an English maintenance order, one of the powers referred to in subsection (2)(a) above;

(b) in respect of a non-English maintenance order, one of its powers under subsection (3) above.

(5) In respect of an English maintenance order, subsections (4), (5) and (7) of section 59 above shall apply for the purposes of subsections (2)(a) and (4)(a) above as they apply for the purposes of that section.

(6) In respect of a non-English maintenance order –

(a) subsection (4) of section 59 above shall apply for the purposes of subsections (2)(b) and (4)(b) above as it applies for the purposes of that section but as if for paragraph (a) there were substituted –

"(a) the court proposes to exercise its power under paragraph (b) of section 95(3) below;"; and

(b) in deciding which of the powers under subsection (3) above it is to exercise the court shall have regard to any representations made by the debtor (within the meaning of section 59 above).

(7) In this section –

"the Council Regulation" means Council Regulation (EC) No 44/2001 including as applied in relation to Denmark by virtue of the Agreement made on 19 October 2005 between the European Community and the Kingdom of Denmark;

"English maintenance order" has the same meaning as it has in section 94A above;

"the Maintenance Regulation" means Council Regulation (EC) No 4/2009 including as applied in relation to Denmark by virtue of the Agreement made on 19 October 2005 between the European Community and the Kingdom of Denmark;

"non-English maintenance order" means –

  (a) a maintenance order registered in, or confirmed, by, a magistrates' court –

    (i)   under the Maintenance Orders (Facilities for Enforcement) Act 1920;

    (ii) under Part II of the Maintenance Orders Act 1950;

    (iii) under Part I of the Maintenance Orders (Reciprocal Enforcement) Act 1972;

    (iv) under Part I of the Civil Jurisdiction and Judgments Act 1982; or

    (v)   under the Council Regulation;

  (b) an order deemed to be made by the High Court by virtue of section 1(2) of the Maintenance Orders Act 1958 and registered under Part I of that Act in a magistrates' court;

  (c) a maintenance order made by a magistrates' court by virtue of Part II of the Maintenance Orders (Reciprocal Enforcement) Act 1972; or

  (d) a maintenance order which falls to be enforced by a magistrates' court by virtue of the Maintenance Regulation and the Civil Jurisdiction and Judgments (Maintenance) Regulations 2011.

Amendments—MEA 1991, s 11(1), Sch 2, para 8; AJA 1999, s 90, Sch 13, para 110; SI 2001/3929; Courts Act 2003, Sch 8, para 229; SI 2007/1655; SI 2011/1484.

Defined terms—"English maintenance order": s 94A; "magistrates' court maintenance order": s 150(1); "non-English maintenance order": s 95(7).

Remission of sum due—As a general rule, arrears which have accrued more than 12 months before the complaint for enforcement will not be enforced (see, for example, *Bernstein v O'Neill* [1989] 2 FLR 1 and *B v C (Enforcement: Arrears)* [1995] 1 FLR 467). The proper approach of the court in this situation is to decide how to exercise its discretion to enforce the arrears rather than to decide how to exercise its discretion to remit (*B v C (Enforcement: Arrears)* (above); *R (King) v Bunyon* [2008] 1 FLR 1564). The court may not, on discharge, remit monies paid before the date of complaint (*Fildes (formerly Simkin) v Simkin* [1960] P 70). Courts should act cautiously and only if the evidence justifies it, when basing decisions not to remit arrears upon anticipated changes in circumstances (*C v S (Maintenance Order: Enforcement)* [1997] 1 FLR 298). The court may not order the refund of monies paid without the knowledge that a divorced wife had remarried (*Young v Young (No 2)* [1962] P 218). The payment by a husband of his wife's debts is not a ground for remittal of arrears payable to the children (*Parry v Meugens* [1986] 1 FLR 125). Remission of arrears is not a penalty (*R v Halifax Justices ex parte Woolverton* (1981) 2 FLR 369). The magistrates' power to remit arrears does not apply to certain orders with an international element either because they fall to be enforced under EC Reg 44/2001 or EC Reg 4/2009 (MCA 1980, s 95(1A)) or following guidance from Thorpe LJ as Head of International Justice for England and Wales, in respect of orders registered for enforcement in accordance with the Hague or Lugano Conventions. In these circumstances, if it appears that the defaulter is without the means to pay the arrears, enforcement action should be suspended and the defaulter should be advised to apply to the originating country for variation of the order and/or remission of the arrears. Thorpe LJ also suggested that the 12 month rule should never be applied to such arrears where the defaulter can pay as there can often be good reason for delay in the enforcement of international orders.

For the duty to give notice and to consider representations see MCR 1981, r 44. Appeal against the order is by appeal to a county court on grounds of error of law or excess of jurisdiction under MCA 1980, s 111A.

96 Civil debt: complaint for non-payment

(1) A magistrates' court shall not commit any person to prison or other detention in default of payment of a sum enforceable as a civil debt or for want of sufficient distress to satisfy such a sum except by an order made on complaint and on proof to the satisfaction of the court that that person has, or has had since the date on which the sum was adjudged to be paid, the means to pay the sum or any instalment of it on which he has defaulted, and refuses or neglects or, as the case may be, has refused or neglected to pay it.

(2) A complaint under this section may be made at any time notwithstanding anything in this or any other Act.

(3) Where on any such complaint the defendant is committed to custody, such costs incurred by the complainant in proceedings for the enforcement of the sum as the court may direct shall be included in the sum on payment of which the defendant may be released from custody.

Defined terms—"committed to custody": s 150(1); "sum enforceable as a civil debt": s 150(1).

Scope—This section provides for the making of a complaint for the enforcement of a sum enforceable as a civil debt and, in conjunction with s 92, limits the use of committal to custody for non-payment. Some protection is afforded by the Reserve and Auxiliary Forces (Protection of Civil Interests) Act 1951.

Committal to prison (s 96(1))—The maximum period of committal is 6 weeks (Sch 4, para 3). If the court has allowed time to pay, a summons to show cause is required before committal can be ordered (*Kinnings Case* (1847) 10 QB 730). For the execution of the warrant outside England and Wales see s 126.

"order made on complaint" (s 96(1))—See MCR 1981, r 58 for the requirement to serve a judgment summons and the requirement for 3 days to elapse between service and hearing except with the debtor's consent.

Application of other sections to civil debt enforcement—Section 76 (distraint) applies to civil debt enforcement but neither s 88 (money payments supervision order) nor s 95 (remission of arrears etc) applies to civil debts enforceable under this section.

Costs (s 96(3))—Section 64 (power to award costs) applies to costs awarded under this section.

****

PART IV
WITNESSES AND EVIDENCE

Procuring attendance of witness

97 Summons to witness and warrant for his arrest

(1) Where a justice of the peace is satisfied that –

    (a)   any person in England or Wales is likely to be able to give material evidence, or produce any document or thing likely to be material evidence, at the summary trial of an information or hearing of a complaint or of an application in family proceedings by a magistrates' court, and

    (b)   it is in the interests of justice to issue a summons under this subsection to secure the attendance of that person to give evidence or produce the document or thing,

the justice shall issue a summons directed to that person requiring him to attend before the court at the time and place appointed in the summons to give evidence or to produce the document or thing

(2) If a justice of the peace is satisfied by evidence on oath of the matters mentioned in subsection (1) above, and also that it is probable that a summons under that subsection

would not procure the attendance of the person in question, the justice may instead of issuing a summons issue a warrant to arrest that person and bring him before such a court as aforesaid at a time and place specified in the warrant; but a warrant shall not be issued under this subsection where the attendance is required for the hearing of a complaint or of an application in family proceedings.

(2A) A summons may also be issued under subsection (1) above if the justice is satisfied that the person in question is outside the British Islands but no warrant shall be issued under subsection (2) above unless the justice is satisfied by evidence on oath that the person in question is in England or Wales.

(2B) A justice may refuse to issue a summons under subsection (1) above in relation to the summary trial of an information if he is not satisfied that an application for the summons was made by a party to the case as soon as reasonably practicable after the accused pleaded not guilty.

(2C) In relation to the summary trial of an information, subsection (2) above shall have effect as if the reference to the matters mentioned in subsection (1) above included a reference to the matter mentioned in subsection (2B) above.

(3) On the failure of any person to attend before a magistrates' court in answer to a summons under this section, if –

    (a) the court is satisfied by evidence on oath that he is likely to be able to give material evidence or produce any document or thing likely to be material evidence in the proceedings; and

    (b) it is proved on oath, or in such other manner as may be prescribed, that he has been duly served with the summons, and that a reasonable sum has been paid or tendered to him for costs and expenses; and

    (c) it appears to the court that there is no just excuse for the failure,

the court may issue a warrant to arrest him and bring him before the court at a time and place specified in the warrant.

(4) If any person attending or brought before a magistrates' court refuses without just excuse to be sworn or give evidence, or to produce any document or thing, the court may commit him to custody until the expiration of such period not exceeding one month as may be specified in the warrant or until he sooner gives evidence or produces the document or thing or impose on him a fine not exceeding £2,500 or both.

(5) A fine imposed under subsection (4) above shall be deemed, for the purposes of any enactment, to be a sum adjudged to be paid by a conviction.

Amendments—CCA 1981, Sch 2; SI 1984/447; Criminal Justice (International Co-operation) Act 1990, s 31(1), Sch 4, para 2; Criminal Justice Act 1991, s 17(3), Sch 4, Pt I, Pt V, para 2; Criminal Justice Act 1993, s 65(3), Sch 3, para 6(3); Criminal Procedure and Investigations Act 1996, ss 47, 51(1),(2), 80, Sch 1, Pt I, paras 1, 7, Sch 5, para 10; SI 1996/674; SI 1996/675; Courts Act 2003, Sch 8, para 230; Serious Organised Crime and Police Act 2005, s 169; SI 2005/3275; SI 2011/1045.

"justice of the peace" (s 97(1))—By virtue of JCR 2005, Sch, paras 41 and 43, this power may also be exercised by a justices' clerk or a specifically authorised court clerk.

Grounds for issuing summons (s 97(1))—The court should enquire into the nature of the evidence. The evidence should be material to the party making application for the summons (*R v Peterborough Magistrates' Court, ex parte Willis and Amos* (1987) 151 JP 785). The evidence of a hostile witness is not material to the applicant party (*R v Marylebone Magistrates' Court ex parte Gatting and Emburey* (1990) 154 JP 549). See also *R v Hove Justices ex parte Donne* [1967] 2 All ER and *R v Cheltenham Justices ex parte Secretary of State for Trade* [1977] 1 WLR 95. An application for a witness summons should not be a "fishing expedition" (*R v Tower Bridge Magistrates' Court ex parte DPP* [1988] Crim LR 693). A witness summons should not be allowed to produce a record of instructions to solicitors where the witness had not waived legal professional privilege (*R v Derby Magistrates' Court ex parte B* [1996]

1 FLR 513). See annotation **Children as witnesses in family proceedings** under CA 1989, s 96 for the principles to be applied when the court is considering whether to order a child to give evidence in family proceedings.

Production of documents (s 97(1))—If production of a number of documents is sought, the relevance of each document must be considered individually (*R v Greenwich Juvenile Court ex parte Greenwich London Borough Council* (1977) 76 LGR 99). An order for the production of a privileged document should not be made (see, for example, *R v Bournemouth Justices ex parte Grey* [1987] 1 FLR 36).

"duly served" (s 97(3)(b))—See MCR 1981, r 99(6) for method of service.

"may issue a warrant to arrest him" (s 97(3))—A warrant may be issued under s 97(3) in civil proceedings after the failure of the witness summons. A warrant should be issued only where the evidence sought is critical to the case (*R v Bradford Justices ex parte Wilkinson* [1990] 1 WLR 692; *R v Nottingham Justices ex parte Fraser* [1995] JP Rep 613).

"refuses without just excuse" (s 97(4))—Duress may amount to a defence (*R v K* (1983) 148 JP 410).

****

Evidence generally

98 Evidence on oath

Subject to the provisions of any enactment or rule of law authorising the reception of unsworn evidence, evidence given before a magistrates' court shall be given on oath.

99 Proof of non-payment of sum adjudged

Where a magistrates' court has ordered one person to pay to another any sum of money, and proceedings are taken before that or any other magistrates' court to enforce payment of that sum, then –

(a) if the person to whom the sum is ordered to be paid is the designated officer for the magistrates' court, a certificate purporting to be signed by the designated officer that the sum has not been paid to him; and

(b) in any other case a document purporting to be a statutory declaration by the person to whom the sum is ordered to be paid that the sum has not been paid to him,

shall be admissible as evidence that the sum has not been paid to him, unless the court requires the justices' chief executive or other person to be called as a witness.

Amendments—AJA 1999, s 90, Sch 13, para 112; Courts Act 2003, Sch 8, para 232.

100 Statement of wages to be evidence

A statement in writing to the effect that wages of any amount have been paid to a person during any period, purporting to be signed by or on behalf of his employer, shall be evidence of the facts therein stated in any proceedings taken before a magistrates' court –

(a) for enforcing payment by the person to whom the wages are stated to have been paid of a sum adjudged to be paid by a summary conviction or order; or

(b) on any application made by or against that person for the making of a magistrates' court maintenance order, or for the variation, revocation, discharge or revival of such an order.

Amendments—FLRA 1987, s 33(1), Sch 2, para 87.

****

Offences
****

107 False statements in declaration proving service etc

If, in any solemn declaration, certificate or other writing made or given for the purpose of its being used in pursuance of rules of court as evidence of the service of any document or the handwriting or seal of any person, a person makes a statement that he knows to be false in a material particular, or recklessly makes any statement that is false in a material particular, he shall be liable on summary conviction to imprisonment for a term not exceeding 6 months or a fine not exceeding level 3 on the standard scale or both.

Amendments—Criminal Justice Act 1982, ss 38, 46; Courts Act 2003, Sch 8, para 233.

Scope—This section makes it an offence to make a false statement in a solemn declaration or certificate as to service under MCR 1981, r 67. Proceedings under the Perjury Act 1911 remain an alternative course of action (see s 16(3) of that Act).

"level 3 on the standard scale"—Currently £1000 (Criminal Justice Act 1982, s 37(2), as substituted).

****

111A Appeals on ground of error of law etc in family proceedings

(1) This section applies in relation to family proceedings in a magistrates' court.

(2) Any person who was a party to any proceeding before the court, or is aggrieved by the order, determination or other proceeding of the court, may question the proceeding on the ground that it is wrong in law or is in excess of jurisdiction by appealing to a county court.

(3) But a person may not appeal under subsection (2) in respect of a decision if –

   (a) the person has a right of appeal to a county court against the decision otherwise than under this section, or

   (b) the decision is final by virtue of any enactment passed after 31 December 1879.

(4) A notice of appeal under subsection (2) shall be filed within 21 days after the day on which the decision of the magistrates' court was given.

(5) In this section "family proceedings" means –

   (a) proceedings which, by virtue of section 65 of this Act, are or may be treated as family proceedings for the purposes of this Act; and

   (b) proceedings under the Child Support Act 1991.

Amendments—Inserted by SI 2009/871.

Defined terms—"family proceedings"; ss 65, 111A(5).

Appeals from magistrates—The majority of appeals from magistrates' orders in family proceedings (as defined by s 111A(5)) proceed under s 111A(2). (This section has done away entirely with case-stated appeals for magistrates' family proceedings.) Once notice of appeal has been filed, the appeal proceeds under FPR 2010, Pt 30 and PD30A, in particular paras 9.2–9.12. This combination of statutory provisions creates a number of anomalies:

   (a) *Grounds for appeal: conflict between statute and rules*   An appeal under s 111A(2) is on grounds that the decision was wrong in law (or in excess of jurisdiction), whereas an appeal, once in the county court, proceeds under FPR 2010, Pt 30, where the appeal may be allowed on grounds that the decision below was wrong (FPR 2010, r 30.12(3)(a)): that is, it could be wrong in law (per s 111A(2)) but also on the facts (see for example *Assicurazioni Generali SpA v Arab Insurance Group* [2002] EWCA Civ 1642) or (in rare circumstances) on an erroneous exercise of discretion. These options for the appellate court appear to be excluded by s 111A(2), but permitted as grounds once the case is in the appellate court.

   (b) *Practice direction and conduct of appeals*   PD30A, para 9.4 states that it applies six specific rules to s 111A appeals (rr 30.1, 30.2, 30.4, 30.6, 30.8 and 30.9). It is improbable that the remaining rules within Pt 30 are intended to be excluded, given for example that r 30.11 sets out the Appeal Court's powers and r 30.12 governs the conduct of appeals.

Permission to appeal—Permission to appeal is not required for an appeal under s 111A. This remains unaffected by the provisions of FPR 2010, r 30.3 as to permission to appeal.

Time for filing notice of appeal (s 111A(4))—The 21-day time-limit is fixed and cannot be extended (*Giltinane v Child Support Agency* [2006] 2 FLR 857), although if a judge can be persuaded to transfer a meritorious out-of-time appeal to the High Court and then to deal with it as a judicial review application (as in *Giltinane*) then time could be extended under judicial review powers (CPR 1998, rr 3.9 (court's powers to give relief from sanctions, such as time limits), 54.5 (time limits for filing of a judicial review application).

****

PART VI
RECOGNIZANCES
****

Other provisions

117 Warrant endorsed for bail

(1) A justice of the peace on issuing a warrant for the arrest of any person may grant him bail by endorsing the warrant for bail, that is to say, by endorsing the warrant with a direction in accordance with subsection (2) below.

(1A) Subsection (1) is subject to section 115(1) of the Coroners and Justice Act 2009 (bail decisions in murder cases to be made by Crown Court judge).

(2) A direction for bail endorsed on a warrant under subsection (1) above shall –

(a) in the case of bail in criminal proceedings, state that the person arrested is to be released on bail subject to a duty to appear before such magistrates' court and at such time as may be specified in the endorsement;

(b) in the case of bail otherwise than in criminal proceedings, state that the person arrested is to be released on bail on his entering into such a recognizance (with or without sureties) conditioned for his appearance before a magistrates' court as may be specified in the endorsement;

and the endorsement shall fix the amounts in which any sureties and, in a case falling within paragraph (b) above, that person is or are to be bound.

(3) Where a warrant has been endorsed for bail under subsection (1) above –

(a) where the person arrested is to be released on bail on his entering into a recognizance without sureties, it shall not be necessary to take him to a police station, but if he is so taken, he shall be released from custody on his entering into the recognizance; and

(b) where he is to be released on his entering into a recognizance with sureties, he shall be taken to a police station on his arrest, and the custody officer there shall (subject to his approving any surety tendered in compliance with the endorsement) release him from custody as directed in the endorsement.

Amendments—PACE 1984, s 47(8); Coroners and Justice Act 2009, s 177, Sch 21, para 75.

"custody officer" (s 117(3)(b))—Custody officers are appointed under PACE 1984, s 36.

118 Varying or dispensing with requirement as to sureties

(1) Subject to subsection (2) below, where a magistrates' court has committed a person to custody in default of finding sureties, the court may, on application by or on behalf of the person committed, and after hearing fresh evidence, reduce the amount in which it is proposed that any surety should be bound or dispense with any of the sureties or otherwise deal with the case as it thinks just.

(2) Subsection (1) above does not apply in relation to a person granted bail in criminal proceedings.

119 Postponement of taking recognizance

(1) Where a magistrates' court has power to take any recognizance, the court may, instead of taking it, fix the amount in which the principal and his sureties, if any, are to be bound; and thereafter the recognizance may be taken by any such person as may be prescribed.

(2) Where, in pursuance of this section, a recognizance is entered into otherwise than before the court that fixed the amount of it, the same consequences shall follow as if it had been entered into before that court; and references in this or any other Act to the court before which a recognizance was entered into shall be construed accordingly.

(3) Nothing in this section shall enable a magistrates' court to alter the amount of a recognizance fixed by the High Court or the Crown Court.

Amendments—Criminal Justice Act 1982, s 77, Sch 14, para 55.

Scope—This section permits recognizances to be fixed and for them to be taken subsequently. See MCR 1981, rr 86–88 for persons prescribed for the taking of recognizances and for taking recognizances out of court.

120 Forfeiture of recognizance

(1) This section applies where –

    (a)   a recognizance to keep the peace or to be of good behaviour has been entered into before a magistrates' court; or

    (b)   any recognizance is conditioned for the appearance of a person before a magistrates' court, or for his doing any other thing connected with a proceeding before a magistrates' court.

(1A) If, in the case of a recognizance which is conditioned for the appearance of an accused before a magistrates' court, the accused fails to appear in accordance with the condition, the court shall –

    (a)   declare the recognizance to be forfeited;

    (b)   issue a summons directed to each person bound by the recognizance as surety, requiring him to appear before the court on a date specified in the summons to show cause why he should not be adjudged to pay the sum in which he is bound;

and on that date the court may proceed in the absence of any surety if it is satisfied that he has been served with the summons.

(2) If, in any other case falling within subsection (1) above, the recognizance appears to the magistrates' court to be forfeited, the court may –

    (a)   declare the recognizance to be forfeited; and

    (b)   adjudge each person bound by it, whether as principal or surety, to pay the sum in which he is bound;

but in a case falling within subsection (1)(a) above, the court shall not declare the recognizance to be forfeited except by order made on complaint.

(3) The court which declares the recognizance to be forfeited may, instead of adjudging any person to pay the whole sum in which he is bound, adjudge him to pay part only of the sum or remit the sum.

(4) Payment of any sum adjudged to be paid under this section, including any costs awarded against the defendant, may be enforced, and any such sum shall be applied, as if it were a fine and as if the adjudication were a summary conviction of an offence not punishable with imprisonment and so much of section 85(1) above as empowers a court to remit fines shall not apply to the sum but so much thereof as relates to remission after a term of imprisonment has been imposed shall so apply; but at any time before the issue of a warrant of commitment to enforce payment of the sum, or before the sale of goods under a warrant of distress to satisfy the sum, the court may remit the whole or any part of the sum either absolutely or on such conditions as the court thinks just.

(5) A recognizance such as is mentioned in this section shall not be enforced otherwise than in accordance with this section, and accordingly shall not be transmitted to the Crown Court nor shall its forfeiture be certified to that Court.

Amendments—Crime and Disorder Act 1998, s 55.

Defined terms—"fine": s 150(1).

PART VII
MISCELLANEOUS AND SUPPLEMENTARY

Constitution and place of sitting of magistrates' courts

121 Constitution and place of sitting of court

(1) A magistrates' court shall not try an information summarily or hear a complaint except when composed of at least 2 justices unless the trial or hearing is one that by virtue of any enactment may take place before a single justice.

(2) A magistrates' court shall not hold an inquiry into the means of an offender for the purposes of section 82 above or determine under that section at a hearing at which the offender is not present whether to issue a warrant of commitment except when composed of at least 2 justices.

(3) *(repealed)*

(4) Subject to the provisions of any enactment to the contrary, a magistrates' court must sit in open court if it is –

    (a)   trying summarily an information for an indictable offence,
    (b)   trying an information for a summary offence,
    (c)   imposing imprisonment,
    (d)   hearing a complaint, or
    (e)   holding an inquiry into the means of an offender for the purposes of section 82.

(5) A magistrates' court composed of a single justice, shall not impose imprisonment for a period exceeding 14 days or order a person to pay more than £1.

(6) Subject to the provisions of subsection (7) below, the justices composing the court before which any proceedings take place shall be present during the whole of the proceedings; but, if during the course of the proceedings any justice absents himself, he shall cease to act further therein and, if the remaining justices are enough to satisfy the requirements of the preceding provisions of this section, the proceedings may continue before a court composed of those justices.

(7) Where the trial of an information is adjourned after the accused has been convicted and before he is sentenced or otherwise dealt with, the court which sentences or deals with him need not be composed of the same justices as that which convicted him; but, where among the justices composing the court which sentences or deals with an offender there are any who were not sitting when he was convicted, the court which sentences or deals with the offender shall before doing so make such inquiry into the facts and circumstances of the case as will enable the justices who were not sitting when the offender was convicted to be fully acquainted with those facts and circumstances.

(8) This section shall have effect subject to the provisions of this Act relating to family proceedings.

Amendments—Criminal Justice Act 1988, s 61; CA 1989, s 92(11), Sch 11, para 8; Courts Act 2003, Sch 8, para 237.

Defined terms—"family proceedings": s 65.

Appearance by a legal representative

122 Appearance by a legal representative

(1) A party to any proceedings before a magistrates' court may be represented by a legal representative.

(2) Subject to subsection (3) below, an absent party so represented shall be deemed not to be absent.

(3) Appearance of a party by a legal representative shall not satisfy any provision of any enactment or any condition of a recognizance expressly requiring his presence.

Amendments—CLSA 1990, s 125(3), Sch 18, para 25.

Defined terms—"legal representative": s 150(1).

Scope—This section will not operate to excuse a person's presence when it is required as a matter of law, for example as under s 93(6) or in answer to bail.

Process

123 Defect in process

(1) No objection shall be allowed to any information or complaint, or to any summons or warrant to procure the presence of the defendant, for any defect in it in substance or in form, or for any variance between it and the evidence adduced on behalf of the prosecutor or complainant at the hearing of the information or complaint.

(2) If it appears to a magistrates' court that any variance between a summons or warrant and the evidence adduced on behalf of the prosecutor or complainant is such that the defendant has been misled by the variance, the court shall, on the application of the defendant, adjourn the hearing.

Scope—This section is designed to prevent the dismissal of information and complaints on the basis of minor defects where no injustice is done to the defendant.

"No objection shall be allowed" (s 123(1))—There is little case-law regarding the application of this section to complaints, whereas a considerable line of cases has examined the application of the section to alleged defects in information: see, for example *Garfield v Maddocks* [1974] QB 7 (circumstances in which the prosecution may be required to amend the information); *Lawrence v Same* [1968] 2 QB 93 (circumstances in which a fresh information must be laid). The general principles seem to be the same, and it appears that amendment is allowed, provided no injustice is caused to the defendant thereby.

"the court shall" (s 123(2))—If the court finds that the defendant has been misled by any variance between a summons (or warrant) and the evidence adduced by the complainant, there is no discretion to refuse an application for an adjournment by the defendant.

124 Process valid notwithstanding death etc of justice

A warrant or summons issued by a justice of the peace shall not cease to have effect by reason of his death or his ceasing to be a justice.

125 Warrants

(1) A warrant of arrest issued by a justice of the peace shall remain in force until it is executed or withdrawn or it ceases to have effect in accordance with rules of court.

(2) A warrant of arrest, warrant of commitment, warrant of detention, warrant of distress or search warrant issued by a justice of the peace may be executed anywhere in England and Wales by any person to whom it is directed or by any constable within his police area.

This subsection does not apply to a warrant of commitment or a warrant of distress issued under Part VI of the General Rate Act 1967.

(3), (4) (*repealed*)

Amendments—PACE 1984, s 33; Criminal Justice Act 1988, s 65(1); CLSA 1990, s 125(2), Sch 17, para 11; Reserve Forces Act 1996, s 131(1), Sch 10, para 18; SI 1997/1898; Crime and Disorder Act 1998, s 119, Sch 8, para 44; AJA 1999, s 95(1), Sch 15; Youth Justice and Criminal Evidence Act 1999, s 67, Sch 4, para 8; Powers of Criminal Courts (Sentencing) Act 2000, s 165, Sch 9, para 73; Courts Act 2003, s 109(1), Sch 8, para 238.

"A warrant ... shall remain in force" (s 125(1))—A warrant remains in force even if the document is lost or mislaid. If satisfied of such circumstances, a justice may issue a duplicate warrant (*R v Leigh Justices ex parte Kara* (1980) 72 Cr App Rep 327); it is good practice to mark all such warrants as duplicates.

"ceases to have effect in accordance with the rules" (s 125(1))—As provided in MCR 1981, r 96(5).

"any person to whom it is directed" (s 125(2))—The persons to whom a warrant may be directed are specified in MCR 1981, rr 54, 96 and 97.

****

126 Execution of certain warrants outside England and Wales

Sections 13(1) and (2) of the Indictable Offences Act 1848 (which relate, among other things, to the execution in Scotland, Northern Ireland, the Isle of Man and the Channel Islands of warrants of arrest for the offences referred to in those sections) shall, so far as applicable, apply to –

(a) warrants of arrest issued under section 1 above for offences other than indictable offences;

(b) warrants of arrest issued under section 13 above;

(c) warrants of arrest issued under section 97 above other than warrants issued in bastardy proceedings to arrest a witness;

(cc) warrants of arrest issued under section 97A above;

(d) warrants of commitment issued under this Act;

(e) warrants of arrest issued under paragraph 4 of Schedule 3 to the Crime and Disorder Act 1998; and

(f) warrants of arrest issued under paragraph 3(2) of Schedule 1 to the Powers of Criminal Courts (Sentencing) Act 2000 (offender referred to court by youth offender panel).

Amendments—Crime and Disorder Act 1998, s 119, Sch 8, para 45; Youth Justice and Criminal Evidence Act 1999, s 67, Sch 4, para 9; Powers of Criminal Courts (Sentencing) Act 2000, s 165, Sch 9, para 74; Courts Act 2003, Sch 8, para 241.

Limitation of time

127 Limitation of time

(1) Except as otherwise expressly provided by any enactment and subject to subsection (2) below, a magistrates' court shall not try an information or hear a complaint unless the information was laid, or the complaint made, within 6 months from the time when the offence was committed, or the matter of complaint arose.

(2) Nothing in –

    (a) subsection (1) above; or

    (b) subject to subsection (4) below, any other enactment (however framed or worded) which, as regards any offence to which it applies, would but for this section impose a time-limit on the power of a magistrates' court to try an information summarily or impose a limitation on the time for taking summary proceedings,

shall apply in relation to any indictable offence.

(3) Without prejudice to the generality of paragraph (b) of subsection (2) above, that paragraph includes enactments which impose a time-limit that applies only in certain circumstances (for example, where the proceedings are not instituted by or with the consent of the Director of Public Prosecutions or some other specified authority).

(4) Where, as regards any indictable offence, there is imposed by any enactment (however framed or worded, and whether falling within subsection (2)(b) above or not) a limitation on the time for taking proceedings on indictment for that offence no summary proceedings for that offence shall be taken after the latest time for taking proceedings on indictment.

Scope—This section does not apply where it is specifically excluded by statute (for example in civil contempt proceedings under s 63(3): see CCA 1981, Sch 3).

Remand

128 Remand in custody or on bail

(1) Where a magistrates' court has power to remand any person, then, subject to section 4 of the Bail Act 1976 and to any other enactment modifying that power, the court may –

    (a) remand him in custody, that is to say, commit him to custody to be brought before the court, subject to subsection (3A) below, at the end of the period of remand or at such earlier time as the court may require; or

    (b) where it is trying an offence alleged to have been committed by that person or has convicted him of an offence, remand him on bail in accordance with the Bail Act 1976, that is to say, by directing him to appear as provided in subsection (4) below; or

    (c) except in a case falling within paragraph (b) above, remand him on bail by taking from him a recognizance (with or without sureties) conditioned as provided in that subsection;

and may, in a case falling within paragraph (c) above, instead of taking recognizances in accordance with that paragraph, fix the amount of the recognizances with a view to their being taken subsequently in accordance with section 119 above.

(1A)–(1C) ...

(2) Where the court fixes the amount of a recognizance under subsection (1) above or section 8(3) of the Bail Act 1976 with a view to its being taken subsequently the court shall in the meantime commit the person so remanded to custody in accordance with paragraph (a) of the said subsection (1).

(3) Where a person is brought before the court after remand, the court may further remand him.

(3A)–(3E) ...

(4) Where a person is remanded on bail under subsection (1) above the court may, where it remands him on bail in accordance with the Bail Act 1976 direct him to appear or, in any other case, direct that his recognizance be conditioned for his appearance –

    (a) before that court at the end of the period of remand; or

    (b) at every time and place to which during the course of the proceedings the hearing may be from time to time adjourned;

and, where it remands him on bail conditionally on his providing a surety during an inquiry into an offence alleged to have been committed by him, may direct that the recognizance of the surety be conditioned to secure that the person so bailed appears –

    (c) at every time and place to which during the course of the proceedings the hearing may be from time to time adjourned and also before the Crown Court in the event of the person so bailed being committed for trial there.

(5) Where a person is directed to appear or a recognizance is conditioned for a person's appearance in accordance with paragraph (b) or (c) of subsection (4) above, the fixing at any time of the time for him next to appear shall be deemed to be a remand; but nothing in this subsection or subsection (4) above shall deprive the court of power at any subsequent hearing to remand him afresh.

(6) Subject to the provisions of section 129 below, a magistrates' court shall not remand a person for a period exceeding 8 clear days, except that –

    (a) if the court remands him on bail, it may remand him for a longer period if he and the other party consent;

    ...

Amendments—Criminal Justice Act 1982, s 59, Sch 9, paras 2–4; CJA 2003, s 332, Sch 37, Pt 4, subject to saving provisions.

Defined terms—"commit to custody": s 150(1); "magistrates' court": s 148(1).

Scope—This section defines the power of the court to remand in custody or on bail. In civil proceedings, the power to remand arises under s 55. The reception of evidence on oath is not a precondition to a remand in custody (*R v Guest ex parte Metropolitan Police Commissioner* [1961] 3 All ER 1118).

"8 clear days" (s 128(6))—The day of the remand and the day of the return to court are excluded from the period of 8 days.

****

129 Further remand

(1) If a magistrates' court is satisfied that any person who has been remanded is unable by reason of illness or accident to appear or be brought before the court at the expiration of the period for which he was remanded, the court may, in his absence, remand him for a further time; and section 128(6) above shall not apply.

(2) Notwithstanding anything in section 128(1) above, the power of a court under subsection (1) above to remand a person on bail for a further time –

PART II

(a)   where he was granted bail in criminal proceedings, includes power to enlarge the recognizance of any surety for him to a later time;

(b)   where he was granted bail otherwise than in criminal proceedings, may be exercised by enlarging his recognizance and those of any sureties for him to a later time.

(3) Where a person remanded on bail is bound to appear before a magistrates' court at any time and the court has no power to remand him under subsection (1) above, the court may in his absence –

(a)   where he was granted bail in criminal proceedings, appoint a later time as the time at which he is to appear and enlarge the recognizances of any sureties for him at that time;

(b)   where he was granted bail otherwise than in criminal proceedings, enlarge his recognizance and those of any sureties for him to a later time;

and the appointment of the time or the enlargement of his recognizance shall be deemed to be a further remand.

(4) Where a magistrates' court commits a person for trial on bail and the recognizance of any surety for him has been conditioned in accordance with paragraph (a) of subsection (4) of section 128 above the court may, in the absence of the surety, enlarge his recognizance so that he is bound to secure that the person so committed for trial appears also before the Crown Court.

****

Restrictions on imprisonment

132 Minimum term

A magistrates' court shall not impose imprisonment for less than 5 days.

****

Power to alter sums specified in certain provisions

143 Power to alter sums specified in certain provisions

(1) If it appears to the Secretary of State that there has been a change in the value of money since the relevant date, he may by order substitute for the sum or sums for the time being specified in any provision mentioned in subsection (2) below such other sum or sums as appear to him justified by the change.

(2) The said provisions are –

(a)   section 22(1) above;

(aa) section 24(3) and (4) above;

(b)   the definition of "the prescribed sum" in section 32(9) above;

(c)   paragraph (a) of section 33(1) above;

(ca) section 34(3)(b) above;

(cb) section 131(1) of the Powers of Criminal Courts (Sentencing) Act 2000 (limit on compensation order of magistrates' court);

(d)   section 135 of that Act (limit on fine imposed on young offender by magistrates' court);

(dd) section 59B(3) above;

(e)   the Table in paragraph 1 of Schedule 4 to this Act;

(f)   any provision mentioned in Schedule 6A to this Act;

(g)   paragraph 11(2) of Schedule 5A to the Army Act 1955 and to the Air Force Act 1955 (compensation orders);

(h)   paragraph 14(1) of that Schedule and paragraph 14(1) of Schedule 4A to the Naval Discipline Act 1957 (recognizance from parents and guardians);

(i)   *(repealed)*

(j)   the Table in section 139(4) of the Powers of Criminal Courts (Sentencing) Act 2000;

(k)   section 8(1)(b) of the Armed Forces Act 1976 (maximum fine awarded by Standing Civilian Courts);

(l)–(n)   *(repealed)*

(o)   section 37(2) of the Criminal Justice Act 1982;

(p)   section 150(2) and (3) of the Powers of Criminal Courts (Sentencing) Act 2000 (recognizance from parents or guardians);

(q)   column 5 or 6 of Schedule 4 to the Misuse of Drugs Act 1971 so far as the column in question relates to the offences under provisions of that Act specified in column 1 of that Schedule in respect of which the maximum fines were increased by Part II of Schedule 8 to the Criminal Justice and Public Order Act 1994.

(3) In subsection (1) above "the relevant date" means –

(a)   the date of the coming into force of section 17 of the Criminal Justice Act 1991 (increase of certain maxima); or

(b)   where the sums specified in a provision mentioned in subsection (2) above have been substituted by an order under subsection (1) above, the date of that order.

(4), (5) *(repealed)*

(6) An order under subsection (1) above –

(a)   shall be made by statutory instrument subject to annulment in pursuance of a resolution of either House of Parliament and may be revoked by a subsequent order thereunder; and

(b)   shall not affect the punishment for an offence committed before that order comes into force.

Amendments—Criminal Justice Act 1982, s 48(1); Criminal Justice Act 1988, s 170(2), Sch 16; CA 1989, s 108(7), Sch 15; Criminal Justice Act 1991, s 100, Sch 11, para 7; MEA 1991, s 11(1), Sch 2, para 9; Criminal Justice and Public Order Act 1994, s 157(6); Powers of Criminal Courts (Sentencing) Act 2000, s 165, Sch 9, para 79.

Rules

144 Rules of procedure

(A1) *(repealed)*

(1) The Lord Chief Justice may with the concurrence of the Lord Chancellor, make rules for regulating and prescribing except in relation to –

(a)   any criminal cause or matter, or

(b)   family proceedings,

the procedure and practice to be followed in magistrates' courts and by justices' clerks and designated officers for magistrates' courts.

(1A) If the Lord Chancellor does not agree rules made by the Lord Chief Justice, the Lord Chancellor must give the Lord Chief Justice written reasons for doing so.

(2)–(3A) *(repealed)*

(4) The power to make rules conferred by this section shall be exercisable by statutory instrument which shall be subject to annulment by resolution of either House of Parliament.

(4A) The Lord Chief Justice may nominate a judicial office holder (as defined in section 109(4) of the Constitutional Reform Act 2005) to exercise his functions under this section.

(5) (*repealed*)

Amendments—CLSA 1990, s 125(3), Sch 18, para 25; AJA 1999, s 78, Sch 11, para 29, Sch 13, para 116; Courts Act 2003, Sch 8, para 245; CRA 2005, s 15(1), Sch 4, Pt 1, paras 99, 102· Sch 11, para 4(1); Legal Services Act 2007, s 208(1), Sch 21, para 43, SI 2012/2398.

144A Rules to be made if required by Lord Chancellor

(1) This section applies if the Lord Chancellor gives the Lord Chief Justice written notice that he thinks it is expedient for rules made under section 144 to include provision that would achieve a purpose specified in the notice.

(2) The Lord Chief Justice must make such rules as he considers necessary to achieve the specified purpose.

(3) Those rules must be –

    (a)   made within a reasonable period after the Lord Chancellor gives notice to the Lord Chief Justice;

    (b)   made in accordance with section 144.

(4) The Lord Chief Justice may nominate a judicial office holder (as defined in section 109(4) of the Constitutional Reform Act 2005) to exercise his functions under this section.

Amendments—Inserted by CRA 2005, s 15(1), Sch 4, Pt 1, paras 99, 103.

145 Rules: supplementary provisions

(1) The power to make rules conferred by section 144 above shall, without prejudice to the generality of subsection (1) of that section, include power to make provision –

    (a)   as to the practice and procedure of justices in exercising functions preliminary or incidental to proceedings before a magistrates' court;

    (b)   as to the service and execution of process issued by or for the purposes of a magistrates' court, including the service and execution in England and Wales of process issued in other parts of the United Kingdom;

    (c)   as to the keeping of records of proceedings before magistrates' courts and the manner in which things done in the course of, or as preliminary or incidental to, any such proceedings, or any proceedings on appeal from a magistrates' court to the Crown Court, may be proved in any legal proceedings;

    (d)–(f)   (*repealed*)

    (g)   as to what magistrates' court shall have jurisdiction to hear any complaint;

    (h)   as to the matters additional to those specified in section 53 above on complaint for which a magistrates' court shall have power to make an order with the consent of the defendant without hearing evidence;

    (i)   (*repealed*)

(2) Where any Act expressly confers jurisdiction on any magistrates' court to hear a complaint, rules made under subsection (1)(g) above shall not take away that jurisdiction, but may extend it to any other magistrates' court.

(3) Any Act passed before 16 December 1949, in so far as that Act relates to matters about which rules may be made under section 144 above, shall have effect subject to any

rules so made and may be amended or repealed by the rules accordingly; but nothing in the said section shall authorise the rules to reduce the number of justices required for any purpose by any Act.

(4) (*repealed*)

(5) Any rules, directions, forms or other instrument having effect immediately before this subsection comes into force as if contained in rules made under section 15 of the Justices of the Peace Act 1949 by virtue of section 15(8) of that Act (rules etc which previously had effect under the enactments repealed by Part II of Schedule 7 to that Act) shall have effect as if contained in rules made under section 144 above.

Amendments—CLSA 1990, s 125(3), Sch 18, para 25; Police and Magistrates' Courts Act 1994, ss 91, 93, Sch 8, para 31, Sch 9; Criminal Procedure and Investigations Act 1996, ss 65(3), 80, Sch 5, para 6; Courts Act 2003, Sch 8, para 246; CJA 2003, s 332, Sch 37, Pt 4, subject to saving provisions.

145A Rules: costs order against legal representative

(1) In any civil proceedings, a magistrates' court may disallow or (as the case may be) order the legal or other representative concerned to meet the whole of any wasted costs or such part of them as may be determined in accordance with rules.

(2) In subsection (1), "wasted costs" means any costs incurred by a party –

(a) as a result of any improper, unreasonable or negligent act or omission on the part of any legal or other representative or any employee of such a representative; or

(b) which, in the light of any such act or omission occurring after they were incurred, the court considers it is unreasonable to expect that party to pay.

(3) In this section "legal or other representative", in relation to any proceedings, means any person who is exercising a right of audience, or a right to conduct litigation, on behalf of any party to the proceedings.

(4) Rules made by virtue of this section may, in particular, make provision as to the destination of any payment required to be made under the rules (including provision for the reimbursement of sums paid by the Lord Chancellor under arrangements made for the purposes of Part 1 of the Legal Aid, Sentencing and Punishment of Offenders Act 2012).

(5) Rules made by virtue of this section –

(a) shall require a magistrates' court which proposes to act under the rules against a legal or other representative to allow him a reasonable opportunity to appear before it and show cause why it should not do so,

(b) shall provide that action may be taken under the rules either on the application of any party to the proceedings or on the motion of the court;

(c) shall provide that no such action shall be taken after the end of the period of six months beginning with the date on which the proceedings are disposed of by the court; and

(d) shall provide that a legal or other representative against whom action is taken under the rules may appeal to the Crown Court.

Amendments—Inserted by CLSA 1990, s 112; amended by AJA 1999, s 24, Sch 4, para 19; LASPOA 2012, s 39, Sch 5, para 18.

****

Interpretation

148 "Magistrates' court"

(1) In this Act the expression "magistrates' court" means any justice or justices of the peace acting under any enactment or by virtue of his or their commission or under the common law.

(2) Except where the contrary is expressed, anything authorised or required by this Act to be done by, to or before the magistrates' court by, to or before which any other thing was done, or is to be done, may be done by, to or before any magistrates' court acting in the same local justice area as that court.

Amendments—Courts Act 2003, Sch 8, para 248.

149 *(repealed)*

150 Interpretation of other terms

(1) In this Act, unless the context otherwise requires, the following expressions have the meaning hereby assigned to them, that is to say –

"Act" includes local Act;

"bail in criminal proceedings" has the same meaning as in the Bail Act 1976;

"collection order" means an order made under Part 4 of Schedule 5 to the Courts Act 2003;

"commit to custody" means commit to prison or, where any enactment authorises or requires committal to some other place of detention instead of committal to prison, to that other place;

...

"Family Procedure Rules" has the meaning assigned by section 65A above;

"family proceedings" has the meaning assigned to it by section 65 above;

"enactment" includes an enactment contained in a local Act or in any order, regulation or other instrument having effect by virtue of an Act;

"fine", except for the purposes of any enactment imposing a limit on the amount of any fine, includes any pecuniary penalty or pecuniary forfeiture or pecuniary compensation payable under a conviction;

"the fines officer", in relation to a person subject to a collection order, means any fines officer working at the fines office specified in that order;

"impose imprisonment" means pass a sentence of imprisonment or fix a term of imprisonment for failure to pay any sum of money, or for want of sufficient distress to satisfy any sum of money, or for failure to do or abstain from doing anything required to be done or left undone;

"legal representative" means a person who, for the purposes of the Legal Services Act 2007, is an authorised person in relation to an activity which constitutes the exercise of a right of audience or the conduct of litigation (within the meaning of that Act);

"magistrates' court maintenance order" means a maintenance order enforceable by a magistrates' court;

"maintenance order" means any order, decision, settlement or instrument specified in Schedule 8 to the Administration of Justice Act 1970 and includes one which has been discharged or has otherwise ceased to operate, if any arrears are recoverable thereunder;

"prescribed" means prescribed by rules of court;

"sentence" does not include a committal in default of payment of any sum of money, or for want of sufficient distress to satisfy any sum of money, or for failure to do or abstain from doing anything required to be done or left undone;

"sum enforceable as a civil debt" means –

    (a)   any sum recoverable summarily as a civil debt which is adjudged to be paid by the order of a magistrates' court;

    (b)   any other sum expressed by this or any other Act to be so enforceable;

"transfer of fine order" has the meaning assigned to it by section 89 above.

(2) Except where the contrary is expressed or implied, anything required or authorised by this Act to be done by justices may, where two or more justices are present, be done by one of them on behalf of the others.

(3) Any reference in this Act to a sum adjudged to be paid by a conviction or order of a magistrates' court shall be construed as including a reference to any costs, damages or compensation adjudged to be paid by the conviction or order of which the amount is ascertained by the conviction or order; but this subsection does not prejudice the definition of "sum adjudged to be paid by a conviction" contained in subsection (8) of section 81 above for the purposes of that section.

(4) Where the age of any person at any time is material for the purposes of any provision of this Act regulating the powers of a magistrates' court, his age at the material time shall be deemed to be or to have been that which appears to the court after considering any available evidence to be or to have been his age at that time.

(5) Except where the context otherwise requires, any reference in this Act to an offence shall be construed as including a reference to an alleged offence; and any reference in this Act to an offence committed, completed or begun anywhere shall be construed as including a reference to an offence alleged to have been committed, completed or begun there.

(6) References in this Act to an offence punishable with imprisonment or punishable on summary conviction with imprisonment shall be construed without regard to any prohibition or restriction imposed by or under this or any other Act on imprisonment of young offenders.

(7) The provisions of this Act authorising a magistrates' court on conviction of an offender to pass a sentence or make an order instead of dealing with him in any other way shall not be construed as taking away any power to order him to pay costs, damages or compensation.

Amendments—Local Government Act 1985, s 12; FLRA 1987, s 33, Sch 2, para 88, Sch 4; CA 1989, s 92(11), Sch 11, para 8; CLSA 1990, s 125(3), Sch 18, para 25; SI 1996/674; SI 1996/675; Justices of the Peace Act 1997, s 73(2), Sch 5, para 19; AJA 1999, ss 76(2), 78, 106, Sch 10, para 36, Sch 11, para 30, Sch 15; Courts Act 2003, Sch 8, para 250; CJA 2003, s 332, Sch 37, Pt 4, subject to saving provisions; SI 2006/1737; Legal Services Act 2007, s 208(1), Sch 21, para 44; SI 2011/1045; SI 2011/1484.

****

SCHEDULE 4

MAXIMUM PERIODS OF IMPRISONMENT IN DEFAULT OF PAYMENT

1 Subject to the following provisions of this Schedule, the periods set out in the second column of the following Table shall be the maximum periods applicable respectively to the amounts set out opposite thereto, being amounts due at the time the imprisonment or detention is imposed.

TABLE

An amount not exceeding £200	7 days
An amount exceeding £200 but not exceeding £500	14 days
An amount exceeding £500 but not exceeding £1,000	28 days
An amount exceeding £1,000 but not exceeding £2,500	45 days
An amount exceeding £2,500 but not exceeding £5,000	3 months
An amount exceeding £5,000 but not exceeding £10,000	6 months
An amount exceeding £10,000	12 months

2 (1) Where the amount due at the time imprisonment or detention is imposed is so much of a sum adjudged to be paid by a summary conviction as remains due after part payment, then, subject to sub-paragraph (2) below, the maximum period applicable to the amount shall be the period applicable to the whole sum reduced by such number of days as bears to the total number of days therein the same proportion as the part paid bears to the whole sum.

(2) In calculating the reduction required under sub-paragraph (1) above any fraction of a day shall be left out of account and the maximum period shall not be reduced to less than 7 days.

3 The maximum period applicable to a sum of any amount enforceable as a civil debt shall be 6 weeks.

Amendments—Criminal Justice Act 1982, s 77, Sch 14, para 59: SI 1984/447; Criminal Justice Act 1988, s 60; Criminal Justice Act 1991, ss 23, 100, Sch 11, para 28.

****

Maintenance Enforcement Act 1991

1 Maintenance orders in the High Court and county courts: means of payment, attachment of earnings and revocation, variation, etc

(1) Where the High Court or a county court makes a qualifying periodical maintenance order, it may at the same time exercise either of its powers under subsection (4) below in relation to the order, whether of its own motion or on an application made under this subsection by an interested party.

(2) For the purposes of this section, a periodical maintenance order is an order –

    (a)   which requires money to be paid periodically by one person ("the debtor") to another ("the creditor"); and

    (b)   which is a maintenance order;

and such an order is a "qualifying periodical maintenance order" if, at the time it is made, the debtor is ordinarily resident in England and Wales.

(3) Where the High Court or a county court has made a qualifying periodical maintenance order, it may at any later time –

    (a)   on an application made under this subsection by an interested party, or

    (b)   of its own motion, in the course of any proceedings concerning the order,

exercise either of its powers under subsection (4) below in relation to the order.

(4) The powers mentioned in subsections (1) and (3) above are –

   (a)   the power to order that payments required to be made by the debtor to the creditor under the qualifying periodical maintenance order in question shall be so made by such a method of payment falling within subsection (5) below as the court may specify in the particular case; or

   (b)   the power, by virtue of this section, to make an attachment of earnings order under the Attachment of Earnings Act 1971 to secure payments under the qualifying periodical maintenance order in question.

(5) The methods of payment mentioned in subsection (4)(a) above are –

   (a)   payment by standing order; or

   (b)   payment by any other method which requires the debtor to give his authority for payments of a specific amount to be made from an account of his to an account of the creditor's on specific dates during the period for which the authority is in force and without the need for any further authority from the debtor.

(6) In any case where –

   (a)   the court proposes to exercise its power under paragraph (a) of subsection (4) above, and

   (b)   having given the debtor an opportunity of opening an account from which payments under the order may be made in accordance with the method of payment proposed to be ordered under that paragraph, the court is satisfied that the debtor has failed, without reasonable excuse, to open such an account,

the court in exercising its power under that paragraph may order that the debtor open such an account.

(7) Where in the exercise of its powers under subsection (1) or (3) above, the High Court or a county court has made in relation to a qualifying periodical maintenance order such an order as is mentioned in subsection (4)(a) above (a "means of payment order"), it may at any later time –

   (a)   on an application made under this subsection by an interested party, or

   (b)   of its own motion, in the course of any proceedings concerning the qualifying periodical maintenance order,

revoke, suspend, revive or vary the means of payment order.

(8) In deciding whether to exercise any of its powers under this section the court in question having (if practicable) given every interested party an opportunity to make representations shall have regard to any representations made by any such party.

(9) Nothing in this section shall be taken to prejudice –

   (a)   any power under the Attachment of Earnings Act 1971 which would, apart from this section, be exercisable by the High Court or a county court; or

   (b)   any right of any person to make any application under that Act;

and subsection (7) above is without prejudice to any other power of the High Court or a county court to revoke, suspend, revive or vary an order.

(10) For the purposes of this section –

   "debtor" and "creditor" shall be construed in accordance with subsection (2) above;

   "interested party" means any of the following, that is to say –

      (a)   the debtor;

      (b)   the creditor; and

      (c)   in a case where the person who applied for the qualifying periodical maintenance order in question is a person other than the creditor, that other person;

PART II

"maintenance order" means any order specified in Schedule 8 to the Administration of Justice Act 1970 and includes any such order which has been discharged, if any arrears are recoverable under it;

"qualifying periodical maintenance order" shall be construed in accordance with subsection (2) above, and the references to such an order in subsections (3) and (7) above are references to any such order, whether made before or after the coming into force of this section;

and the reference in subsection (2) above to an order requiring money to be paid periodically by one person to another includes a reference to an order requiring a lump sum to be paid by instalments by one person to another.

Defined terms—"creditor", "debtor": s 1(2); "interested party", "maintenance order": s 1(10); "qualifying maintenance order": s 1(2),(10).

"qualifying periodical maintenance order" (s 1(2))—The powers created or extended by this section apply only on making such an order or in relation to such an order already made.

"application ... by an interested party" (s 1(3)(a))—The expression "interested party" includes both the person who applied for the qualifying periodical maintenance order and, if different, the person entitled to receive the payments. Thus it would appear that the latter, though not a party, can apply directly and presumably would not need leave to intervene in the main proceedings or cause. The debtor is also an interested party; in the case of a qualifying periodical maintenance order s 1(3)(a) seems to enable the debtor to apply for an attachment of earnings order at any time, not only on the maintenance order being made or varied under CPR 1998, Sch 2, CCR Ord 27, r 17(4).

"of its own motion" (s 1(3)(b))—The court may exercise its powers in the course of any proceedings relating to the qualifying periodical maintenance order. This provision is general so, for example, the powers may be exercised not only on an application to vary or discharge but also on an enforcement application or an application by the debtor to suspend a warrant of execution. Since the powers include the power to make an attachment of earnings order, s 1(3) has the effect of extending to such an occasion the powers to require information given by AEA 1971, s 14.

"order that payments ... shall be made by such a method" (s 1(4)(a))—It would seem that such an order (if served endorsed with a "penal" notice) would be enforceable by committal under CPR 1998, Sch 1, RSC Ord 52, r 1 or CPR 1998, Sch 2, CCR Ord 29, r 1. However if the essence of the complaint was that the debtor had failed to maintain the payments under the underlying order it appears unlikely that the court would impose a penalty in circumstances where it would not make a committal order on a judgment summons under DA 1869, s 5.

Methods of payment (s 1(5))—It is perhaps unlikely that banks would accept a direct debit authority in favour of a personal maintenance creditor, but this power might be used where the person entitled to receive the payments had authorised an institution or Government department to collect them on his behalf.

"opportunity to make representations" (s 1(8))—This requirement will be satisfied if the debtor is present at the hearing at which the question is considered or if he has been given notice of the intention to apply for the order. Otherwise, the court must adjourn and cause notice to be given to him that it is minded to make the order.

Lump sums (s 1(10))—Although a lump sum order is a maintenance order, it is not a qualifying periodical maintenance order unless the lump sum has been ordered to be paid by instalments.

Rules and forms—If an attachment of earnings order is sought in the county court the procedure described in CPR 1998, Sch 2, CCR Ord 27 should normally be followed. Otherwise an interlocutory summons or notice of application may be used, or the court may permit the application to be made orally if proceedings concerning the maintenance order are already before it.

Maintenance Orders Act 1950

ARRANGEMENT OF SECTIONS

PART I
JURISDICTION

****

4 Contributions under the Children and Young Persons Act 1933, and National Assistance Act 1948

(1) A court of summary jurisdiction in England shall have jurisdiction in proceedings against a person residing in Scotland or Northern Ireland –

(a), (b) *(repealed)*

(c) for an order under section 18 of the Supplementary Benefits Act 1976 (which provides for the recovery of expenditure on supplementary benefits from persons liable for maintenance)

(d) for an order under section 106 of the Social Security Administration Act 1992 (which provides for the recovery of expenditure on income support or universal credit from such persons).

(2) A court in England by which an order has been made under the said section 18 or the said section 106 shall have jurisdiction in proceedings by or against a person residing in Scotland or Northern Ireland for the revocation, revival or variation of that order.

Amendments—Supplementary Benefits Act 1976, s 35(2), Sch 7, para 8; Child Care Act 1980, s 89(3), Sch 6; Social Security Act 1986, s 86(1), Sch 10, para 35; Social Security (Consequential Provisions) Act 1992, s 4, Sch 2, para 3, Health and Social Care Act 2008, Sch 15; SI 2013/630.

"**revocation, revival or variation**" (s 1(2))—MCA 1980, s 60 applies to such proceedings.

****

15 Service of process

(1) Where –

    (a) proceedings are begun in a court having jurisdiction under or by virtue of the following, namely –

        (i)   this Part of this Act; or

        (ii) sections 24(1) and 30(3) of the Domestic Proceedings and Magistrates' Courts Act 1978;

        (iii) section 92 of and Schedule 11 to the Children Act 1989; or

        (iv) section 93(2)(g) of that Act (including that provision as applied in relation to Northern Ireland by section 116(3) of the Courts and Legal Services Act 1990; or

        (v)   Article 164 of and Schedule 7 to the Children (Northern Ireland) Order 1995 or Article 165(2)(g) of that Order; or

        (vi) Council Regulation (EC) No 4/2009 including as applied in relation to Denmark by virtue of the Agreement made on 19 October 2005 between the European Community and the Kingdom of Denmark and Schedule 6 to the Civil Jurisdiction and Judgments (Maintenance) Regulations 2011; or

    (b) an action which contains a conclusion for aliment not falling within the scope of paragraph (a)(i) above is commenced in a sheriff court in Scotland,

and the person against whom the action or other proceedings is or are brought resides in another part of the United Kingdom, any summons or initial writ addressed to him in the proceedings may, if endorsed in accordance with the provisions of this section in that part of the United Kingdom, be served within that part of the United Kingdom as if it had been issued or authorised to be served, as the case may be, by the endorsing authority.

(2) A summons or writ may be endorsed under this section, in England by a justice of the peace, in Scotland by a sheriff, and in Northern Ireland by a resident magistrate; and the endorsement shall be made in the form numbered 1 in the Second Schedule to this Act, or any form to the like effect.

(3) In any proceedings in which a summons or writ is served under this section, the service may be proved by means of a declaration made in the form numbered 2 in the Second Schedule to this Act, or any form to the like effect, before a justice of the peace, sheriff, or resident magistrate, as the case may be.

(4) Nothing in this section shall be construed as authorising the service of a summons or writ otherwise than personally.

(5) Section four of the Summary Jurisdiction (Process) Act 1881 shall not apply to any process which may be served under this section; and nothing in this section or in any other enactment shall be construed as authorising the execution in one part of the United Kingdom of a warrant for the arrest of a person who fails to appear in answer to any such process issued in another part of the United Kingdom.

Amendments—Children Act 1975, s 108(1), Sch 3, para 10; AJA 1977, s 3, Sch 3, para 11; DPMCA 1978, s 89(2)(a), Sch 2, para 12; Child Care Act 1980, s 89, Sch 5, para 2; SI 1980/564; CJJA 1982, ss 16(5), 23(2), Sch 12, para 2; CLSA 1990, s 116, Sch 16, para 34; SI 1995/756; SI 2011/1484.

"**declaration**" (s 15(3))—For proof of declarations, see s 26.

PART II
ENFORCEMENT

16 Application of Part II

(1) Any order to which this section applies (in this Part of this Act referred to as a maintenance order) made by a court in any part of the United Kingdom may, if registered in accordance with the provisions of this Part of this Act in a court in another part of the United Kingdom, be enforced in accordance with those provisions in that other part of the United Kingdom.

(2) This section applies to the following orders, that is to say –

  (a) an order for alimony, maintenance or other payments made or deemed to be made by a court in England under any of the following enactments –

   (i)   sections 15 to 17, 19 to 22, 30, 34 and 35 of the Matrimonial Causes Act 1965 and sections 22, 23(1), (2) and (4) and 27 of the Matrimonial Causes Act 1973 and section 14 or 17 of the Matrimonial and Family Proceedings Act 1984;

   (ii) Part I of the Domestic Proceedings and Magistrates' Courts Act 1978;

   (iii) Schedule 1 to the Children Act 1989;

   (iv) (*repealed*)

   (v)   paragraph 23 of Schedule 2 to the Children Act 1989;

   (vi) section 18 of the Supplementary Benefits Act 1976;

   (vii) (*repealed*)

   (viii) section 106 of the Social Security Administration Act 1992;

   (ix) Part 1, 8 or 9 of Schedule 5 to the Civil Partnership Act 2004, Schedule 6 to that Act or paragraph 5 or 9 of Schedule 7 to that Act;

  (b) a decree for payment of aliment granted by a court in Scotland, including –

   (i)   an order for the payment of an annual or periodical allowance under section two of the Divorce (Scotland) Act 1938 or an order for the payment of a periodical allowance or a capital sum under section 26 of the Succession (Scotland) Act 1964 or section 5 of the Divorce (Scotland) Act 1976 or an order for financial provision in the form of a monetary payment under s 8 of the Family Law (Scotland) Act 1985;

   (ii) an order for the payment of weekly or periodical sums under subsection (2) of section 3 or subsection (4) of section 5 of the Guardianship of Infants Act 1925;

   (iii) an order for the payment of sums in respect of aliment under subsection (3) of section 1 of the Illegitimate Children (Scotland) Act 1930;

   (iv) a decree for payment of aliment under section 44 of the National Assistance Act 1948, or under section 26 of the Children Act 1948; and

   (v)   (*repealed*)

   (vi) a contribution order under section 80 of, or a decree or an order made under section 81 of, the Social Work (Scotland) Act 1968;

   (vii) an order for the payment of weekly or other periodical sums under subsection (3) of section 11 of the Guardianship Act 1973;

   (viii) an order made on an application under section 18 or section 19(8) of the Supplementary Benefits Act 1976;

   (ix) an order made on an application under section 106 of the Social Security Administration Act 1992;

   (x)   an order made on an application under Schedule 11 to the Civil Partnership Act 2004;

  (c) an order for alimony, maintenance or other payments made by a court in Northern Ireland under or by virtue of any of the following enactments: –

(i) subsection (2) of section 17, subsections (2) to (7) of section 19, subsection (2) of section 20, section 22 or subsection (1) of section 28 of the Matrimonial Causes Act (Northern Ireland) 1939;

(ii) Schedule 1 to the Children (Northern Ireland) Order 1995;

(iii) (*repealed*)

(iv) Article 41 of the Children (Northern Ireland) Order 1995 or Article 101 of the Health and Personal Social Services (Northern Ireland) Order 1972;

(v) any enactment of the Parliament of Northern Ireland containing provisions corresponding with section 22(1), 34 or 35 of the Matrimonial Causes Act 1965, with section 22, 23(1), (2) or (4) or 27 of the Matrimonial Causes Act 1973;

(vi) Article 23 or 24 of the Supplementary Benefits (Northern Ireland) Order 1977;

(vii) the Domestic Proceedings (Northern Ireland) Order 1980;

(viii) any enactment applying in Northern Ireland and corresponding to section 106 of the Social Security Administration Act 1992;

(ix) Articles 18 or 21 of the Matrimonial and Family Proceedings (Northern Ireland) Order 1989

(x) Part 1, 7 or 8 of Schedule 15 to the Civil Partnership Act 2004, Schedule 16 to that Act or paragraph 5 or 9 of Schedule 17 to that Act.

Amendments—Social Work (Scotland) Act 1968, s 95(1), Sch 8, para 34; Guardianship of Minors Act 1971, s 18(1), Sch 1; Guardianship Act 1973, ss 9(3), 14, 15(3), Sch 5, para 4; MCA 1973, s 54, Sch 2, para 3(1); Children Act 1975, s 108(1), Sch 3, para 11; Supplementary Benefits Act 1976, s 35(2), Sch 7, para 13; Divorce (Scotland) Act 1976, s 12(1), Sch 1, para 1; AJA 1977, s 3, Sch 3, para 12; SI 1977/2158; DPMCA 1978, s 89(2), Sch 2, para 13; Child Care Act 1980, s 89, Sch 5, para 3; SI 1980/564; Social Security and Housing Benefit Act 1982, s 48(5), Sch 4, para 2; CJJA 1982, s 54, Sch 14; MFPA 1984, s 46(1), Sch 1, para 1; Family Law (Scotland) Act 1985, s 28(1), Sch 1, para 3; Social Security Act 1986, Sch 10; FLRA 1987, Schs 2 and 4; SI 1989/678; CLSA 1990, Schs 16 and 20; Social Security (Consequential Provisions) Act 1992, s 4, Sch 2, para 3; SI 1995/756; CPA 2004, s 261(1), Sch 27, para 18(1)–(4); Health and Social Care Act 2008, Sch 15, Pt 5.

17 Procedure for registration of maintenance orders

(1) An application for the registration of a maintenance order under this Part of this Act shall be made in the prescribed manner to the appropriate authority, that is to say –

(a) where the maintenance order was made by a court of summary jurisdiction in England, a justice or justices acting in the same local justice area as the court which made the order;

(b) where the maintenance order was made by a court of summary jurisdiction in Northern Ireland, a resident magistrate acting for the same petty sessions district as the court which made the order;

(c) in every other case, the prescribed officer of the court which made the order.

(2) If upon application made as aforesaid by or on behalf of the person entitled to payments under a maintenance order it appears that the person liable to make those payments resides in another part of the United Kingdom, and that it is convenient that the order should be enforceable there, the appropriate authority shall cause a certified copy of the order to be sent to the prescribed officer of a court in that part of the United Kingdom in accordance with the provisions of the next following subsection.

(3) The court to whose officer the certified copy of a maintenance order is sent under this section shall be –

(a) where the maintenance order was made by a superior court, the Senior Courts, the Court of Session or the Court of Judicature, as the case may be;

(b) in any other case, a court of summary jurisdiction acting for the place in

England or Northern Ireland in which the defendant appears to be, or, as the case may be, the sheriff court in Scotland within the jurisdiction of which he appears to be.

(4) Where the prescribed officer of any court receives a certified copy of a maintenance order sent to him under this section, he shall cause the order to be registered in that court in the prescribed manner, and shall give notice of the registration in the prescribed manner to the prescribed officer of the court which made the order.

(5) The officer to whom any notice is given under the last foregoing subsection shall cause particulars of the notice to be registered in his court in the prescribed manner.

(6) Where the sums payable under a maintenance order, being an order made by a court of summary jurisdiction in England or Northern Ireland, are payable to or through an officer of any court, that officer shall, if the person entitled to the payments so requests, make an application on behalf of that person for the registration of the order under this Part of this Act; but the person at whose request the application is made shall have the same liability for costs properly incurred in or about the application as if the application had been made by him.

(7) An order which is for the time being registered under this Part of this Act in any court shall not be registered thereunder in any other court.

Amendments—Courts Act 2003, s 109(1), Sch 8, para 87; CRA 2005, Sch 11, para 19(2).

Scope—The registration in magistrates' courts of orders made by the Court of Session or High Court in Northern Ireland which were first registered in the High Court is validated by AJA 1977, Sch 3, para 10.

"maintenance order" (s 17(1))—See s 16(2).

"prescribed manner" (s 17(1))—The manner of application is prescribed, for cases in the High Court or county court, in FPR 2010, rr 32.2–32.12 and, for cases in the magistrates' court, in the Maintenance Orders Act 1950 (Summary Jurisdiction) Rules 1950.

18 Enforcement of registered orders

(1) Subject to the provisions of this section, a maintenance order registered under this Part of this Act in a court in any part of the United Kingdom may be enforced in that part of the United Kingdom in all respects as if it had been made by that court and as if that court had had jurisdiction to make it; and proceedings for or with respect to the enforcement of any such order may be taken accordingly.

(1A) A maintenance order registered under this Part of this Act in a court of summary jurisdiction in England or Northern Ireland shall not carry interest; but where a maintenance order so registered is registered in the High Court under Part I of the Maintenance Orders Act 1958 or section 36 of the Civil Jurisdiction and Judgments Act 1982, this subsection shall not prevent any sum for whose payment the order provides from carrying interest in accordance with section 2A of the said Act of 1958 or section 11A of the Maintenance and Affiliation Orders Act (Northern Ireland) 1966.

(1B) A maintenance order made in Scotland which is registered under this Part of this Act in the Senior Courts or the Court of Judicature shall, if interest is by the law of Scotland recoverable under the order, carry the like interest in accordance with subsection (1) of this section.

(2) Every maintenance order registered, under this Part of this Act in a magistrates' court in England and Wales shall, subject to the modifications of sections 76 and 93 of the Magistrates' Courts Act 1980 specified in subsections (2ZA) and (2ZB) of this section, be enforceable as a magistrates' court maintenance order within the meaning of section 150(1) of the Magistrates' Courts Act 1980.

(2ZA) Section 76 (enforcement of sums adjudged to be paid) shall have effect as if for subsections (4) to (6) there were substituted the following subsections –

"(4) Where proceedings are brought for the enforcement of a magistrates' court maintenance order under this section, the court may vary the order by exercising one of its powers under subsection (5) below.

(5) The powers of the court are –

(a) the power to order that payments under the order be made directly to the designated officer for the court or for any other magistrates' court;

(b) the power to order that payments under the order be made to the designated officer for the court or for any other magistrates' court by such method of payment falling within section 59(6) above (standing order, etc) as may be specified;

(c) the power to make an attachment of earnings order under the Attachment of Earnings Act 1971 to secure payments under the order.

(6) In deciding which of the powers under subsection (5) above it is to exercise, the court shall have regard to any representations made by the debtor (within the meaning of section 59 above).

(7) Subsection (4) of section 59 above (power of court to require debtor to open account) shall apply for the purposes of subsection (5) above as it applies for the purposes of that section but as if for paragraph (a) there were substituted –

'(a) the court proposes to exercise its power under paragraph (b) of section 76(5) below, and'."

(2ZB) In section 93 (complaint for arrears), subsection (6) (court not to impose imprisonment in certain circumstances) shall have effect as if for paragraph (b) there were substituted –

"(b) if the court is of the opinion that it is appropriate –

(i) to make an attachment of earnings order; or

(ii) to exercise its power under paragraph (b) of section 76(5) above."

(2A) Any person under an obligation to make payments under a maintenance order registered under this Part of this Act in a court of summary jurisdiction in England or Northern Ireland shall give notice of any change of address to the proper officer of the court; and any person who without reasonable excuse fails to give such a notice shall be liable on summary conviction to a fine not exceeding level 2 on the standard scale.

(2B) In subsection (2A) of this section "proper officer" means –

(a) in relation to a court of summary jurisdiction in England and Wales, the designated officer for the court; and

(b) in relation to a court of summary jurisdiction in Northern Ireland, the clerk of the court.

(3) Every maintenance order registered under this Part of this Act in a court of summary jurisdiction in Northern Ireland shall be enforceable as an order made by that court to which Article 98 of the Magistrates' Courts (Northern Ireland) Order 1981 applies, subject to the modifications of that Article specified in subsection (3ZA) of this section.

(3ZA) Article 98 (enforcement of sums adjudged to be paid) shall have effect –

(a) as if for paragraph (7)(a) there were substituted the following sub-paragraph –
"(a) if the court is of the opinion that it is appropriate –

(i) to make an attachment of earnings order; or

(ii) to exercise its power under paragraph (8C)(b)";

(b) as if for paragraphs (8B) to (8D) there were substituted the following paragraphs –

"(8B) Upon the appearance of a person or proof of service of the summons on him as mentioned in paragraph (4) for the enforcement of an order to which this Article applies, the court or resident magistrate may vary the order by exercising one of the powers under paragraph (8C).

(8C) The powers mentioned in paragraph (8B) are –

(a) the power to order that payments under the order be made directly to the collecting officer;

(b) the power to order that payments under the order be made to the collecting officer by such method of payment falling within Article 85(7) (standing order, etc) as may be specified;

(c) the power to make an attachment of earnings order under Part IX to secure payments under the order.

(8D) In deciding which of the powers under paragraph (8C) is to be exercised, the court or, as the case may be, a resident magistrate shall have regard to any representations made by the debtor (within the meaning of Article 85).

(8E) Paragraph (5) of Article 85 (power of court to require debtor to open account) shall apply for the purposes of paragraph (8C) as it applies for the purposes of that Article but as if for sub-paragraph (a) there were substituted –

'(a) the court proposes to exercise its power under sub-paragraph (b) of Article 98(8C), and'".

(3A) Notwithstanding subsection (1) above, no court in England in which a maintenance, order is registered under this Part of this Act shall enforce that order to the extent that it is for the time being registered in another court in England under Part I of the Maintenance Orders Act 1958.

(3B) Notwithstanding subsection (1) above, no court in Northern Ireland in which a maintenance order is registered under this Part of this Act shall enforce that order to the extent that it is for the time being registered in another court in Northern Ireland under section 36 of the Civil Jurisdiction and Judgments Act 1982.

(4), (5) (*repealed*)

(6) Except as provided by this section, no proceedings shall be taken for or with respect to the enforcement of a maintenance order which is for the time being registered in any court under this Part of this Act.

Amendments—Ministry of Social Security Act 1966, s 39(3), Sch 8; AJA 1977, s 3, Sch 3, para 6; SI 1981/1675; CJJA 1982, ss 36(6), 37(1), Sch 11, paras 1, 5, Sch 12, para 1; MFPA 1984, s 46(1), Sch 1, para 2; FLRA 1987, Sch 2; SI 1989/678; MEA 1991, s 10, Sch 1, para 3; Statute Law (Repeals) Act 1993; SI 1993/1577; SI 1995/756; AJA 1999, s 90, Sch 13, para 13; Courts Act 2003, Sch 8, para 88; CRA 2005, Sch 11, para 19(3).

Scope—For the duties of the justices' chief executive when a method of payments order is made under s 18(2ZA) see Maintenance Orders Act 1950 (Summary Jurisdiction) Rules 1950, r 9B in Part IV.

"proceedings ... may be taken" (s 18(1))—In magistrates' courts in England and Northern Ireland, enforcement proceedings may be taken by the court on behalf of the person entitled to payment. In Scotland, the sheriff's court will not act on behalf of the person entitled to payment, and legal representation is therefore advisable.

"standing order, etc" (s 18(2ZA),(3ZA))—The methods of payment which may be required do not include payment by direct debit.

"level 2 on the standard scale" (s 18(2A))—Currently £500 (Criminal Justice Act 1982, s 37(2)).

19 Functions of collecting officer etc

(1) Where a maintenance order made in England or Northern Ireland by a court of summary jurisdiction is registered in any court under this Part of this Act, any provision

of the court by virtue of which sums payable thereunder are required to be paid through or to any officer or person on behalf of the person entitled thereto shall be of no effect so long as the order is so registered.

(2) Where a maintenance order is registered under this Part of this Act in a court of summary jurisdiction in England or Northern Ireland, the court shall order that all payments to be made under the maintenance order (including any arrears accrued before the date of the registration) shall be made through the collecting officer of the court or the collecting officer of some other court of summary jurisdiction in England or Northern Ireland, as the case may be.

(3) An order made under subsection (2) of this section –

(a) by a court of summary jurisdiction in England may be varied or revoked by an exercise of the powers conferred by virtue of section 18(2ZA) or section 22(1A) or (1E) of this Act;

(b) by a court of summary jurisdiction in Northern Ireland may be varied or revoked by an exercise of the powers conferred by virtue of section 18(3ZA) or section 22(1F) or (1J) of this Act.

(4) Where by virtue of the provisions of this section or any order made thereunder payments under a maintenance order cease to be or become payable through or to any officer or person, the person liable to make the payments shall, until he is given the prescribed notice to that effect, be deemed to comply with the maintenance order if he makes payments in accordance with the maintenance order and any order under this section of which he had received such notice.

(5) (*repealed*)

Amendments—SI 1981/1675; MEA 1991, s 10, Sch 1, para 4; SI 1993/1577.

Scope—This section prescribes the duties of court collecting officers in relation to the enforcement of orders registered under the Act. See, however, **"proceedings ... may be taken"** under s 18.

20 Arrears under registered maintenance orders

(1) Where application is made for the registration of a maintenance order under this Part of this Act, the applicant may lodge with the appropriate authority –

(a) if the payments under the order are required to be made to or through an officer of any court, a certificate in the prescribed form, signed by that officer, as to the amount of any arrears due under the order;

(b) in any other case, a statutory declaration or affidavit as to the amount of those arrears;

and if a certified copy of the maintenance order is sent to the prescribed officer of any court in pursuance of the application, the certificate, declaration or affidavit shall also be sent to that officer.

(2) In any proceedings for or with respect to the enforcement of a maintenance order which is for the time being registered in any court under this Part of this Act, a certificate, declaration or affidavit sent under this section to the appropriate officer of that court shall be evidence, and in Scotland sufficient evidence, of the facts stated therein.

(3) Where a maintenance order made by a court in England or Northern Ireland is registered in a court in Scotland, a person shall not be entitled, except with the leave of the last-mentioned court, to enforce, whether by diligence or otherwise, the payment of any arrears accrued and due under the order before the commencement of this Act; and on any application for leave to enforce the payment of any such arrears, the court may refuse leave, or may grant leave subject to such restrictions and conditions (including

conditions as to the allowing of time for payment or the making of payment by instalments) as the court thinks proper, or may remit the payment of such arrears or of any part thereof.

"appropriate authority" (s 20(1))—See s 17(1).

"prescribed form" (s 20(1))—See Maintenance Orders Act 1950 (Summary Jurisdiction) Rules 1950, Form 3.

21 Discharge and variation of maintenance orders registered in superior courts

(1) The registration of a maintenance order in a superior court under this Part of this Act shall not confer on that court any power to vary or discharge the order, or affect any jurisdiction of the court in which the order was made to vary or discharge the order.

(2) Where a maintenance order made in Scotland is for the time being –

    (a)   registered under this Part of this Act in a superior court and not registered under Part I of the Maintenance Orders Act 1958 or under section 36 of the Civil Jurisdiction and Judgments Act 1982, or

    (b)   registered in a court in England under that Part of that Act of 1958 by virtue of section 1(2) of that Act of 1958,

    (c)   registered in a court in Northern Ireland under section 36 of the Civil Jurisdiction and Judgments Act 1982,

the person liable to make payments under the order may, upon application made to that court in the prescribed manner, adduce before that court any evidence upon which he would be entitled to rely in any proceedings brought before the court by which the order was made for the variation or discharge of the order.

(3) A court before which evidence is adduced in accordance with the foregoing subsection shall cause a transcript or summary of that evidence, signed by the deponent, to be sent to the prescribed officer of the court by which the order was made; and in any proceedings before the last-mentioned court for the variation or discharge of the order, the transcript or summary shall be evidence of the facts stated therein.

Amendments—AJA 1977, s 3, Sch 3, para 7; CJJA 1982, s 36(6), Sch 12, Pt III, para 1(3).

"prescribed manner" (s 21(2))—See FPR 2010, rr 32.2–32.12.

22 Discharge and variation of maintenance orders registered in summary or sheriff courts

(1) Subject to subsection (1ZA), where a maintenance order is for the time being registered under this Part of this Act in a court of summary jurisdiction or sheriff court, that court may, upon application made in the prescribed manner by or on behalf of the person liable to make periodical payments under the order or the person entitled to those payments, by order make such variation as the court thinks fit in the rate of the payments under the maintenance order; but no such variation shall impose on the person liable to make payments under the maintenance order a liability to make payments in excess of the maximum rate (if any) authorised by the law for the time being in force in the part of the United Kingdom in which the maintenance order was made.

(1ZA) The power under subsection (1) to vary the rate of payments may not be exercised where paragraph 9(2) of Schedule 6 to the Civil Jurisdiction and Judgments (Maintenance) Regulations 2011 applies (restriction on modifying maintenance decision where creditor remains habitually resident in the part of the United Kingdom in which the decision was made).

(1A) The power of a magistrates' court in England and Wales to vary a maintenance order under subsection (1) of this section shall include power, if the court is satisfied that payment has not been made in accordance with the order, to vary the order by exercising one of its powers under subsection (1B) of this section.

(1B) The powers of the court are –

- (a) the power to order that payments under the order be made directly to the designated officer for the court or for any other magistrates' court in England and Wales;
- (b) the power to order that payments under the order be made to a the designated officer for the court or for any other magistrates' court in England and Wales, by such method of payment falling within section 59(6) of the Magistrates' Courts Act 1980 (standing order etc) as may be specified;
- (c) the power to make an attachment of earnings order under the Attachment of Earnings Act 1971 to secure payments under the order.

(1C) In deciding which of the powers under subsection (1B) of this section it is to exercise, the court shall have regard to any representations made by the person liable to make payments under the order.

(1D) Subsection (4) of section 59 of the Magistrates' Courts Act 1980 (power of court to require debtor to open account) shall apply for the purposes of subsection (1B) of this section as it applies for the purposes of that section but as if for paragraph (a) there were substituted –

> "(a) the court proposes to exercise its power under paragraph (b) of section 22(1B) of the Maintenance Orders Act 1950, and".

(1E) Subsections (4) to (11) of section 60 of the Magistrates' Courts Act 1980 (power of clerk and court to vary maintenance order) shall apply in relation to a maintenance order for the time being registered under this Part of this Act in a magistrates' court in England and Wales as they apply in relation to a maintenance order made by a magistrates' court in England and Wales but –

- (a) as if in subsection (4) for paragraph (b) there were substituted –
  > "(b) payments under the order are required to be made to the designated officer for the court or for any other magistrates' court by any method of payment falling within section 59(6) above (standing order, etc)";
- (b) as if in subsection (5) for the words "to the designated officer for the court" there were substituted "in accordance with paragraph (a) of section 22(1B) of the Maintenance Orders Act 1950";
- (c) as if in subsection (7), paragraph (c) and the word "and" immediately preceding it were omitted;
- (d) as if in subsection (8) for the words "paragraphs (a) to (d) of section 59(3) above" there were substituted "section 22(1B) of the Maintenance Orders Act 1950";
- (e) as if for subsections (9) and (10) there were substituted the following subsections –

> "(9) In deciding which of the powers under section 22(1B) of the Maintenance Orders Act 1950 it is to exercise, the court shall have regard to any representations made by the debtor.
>
> (10) Subsection (4) of section 59 above (power of court to require debtor to open account) shall apply for the purposes of subsection (8) above as it applies for the purposes of that section but as if for paragraph (a) there were substituted –
>
> > '(a) the court proposes to exercise its power under paragraph (b) of section 22(1B) of the Maintenance Orders Act 1950, and'."

(1F) The power of a court of summary jurisdiction in Northern Ireland to vary a maintenance order under subsection (1) of this section shall include power, if the court is satisfied that payment has not been made in accordance with the order, to vary the order by exercising one of its powers under subsection (1G) of this section.

(1G) The powers of the court are –

    (a)   the power to order that payments under the order be made directly to the collecting officer;

    (b)   the power to order that payments under the order be made to the collecting officer by such method of payment falling within Article 85(7) of the Magistrates' Courts (Northern Ireland) Order 1981 (standing order, etc) as may be specified;

    (c)   the power to make an attachment of earnings order under Part IX of the Order of 1981 to secure payments under the order;

and in this subsection "collecting officer" means the officer mentioned in Article 85(4) of the Order of 1981.

(1H) In deciding which of the powers under subsection (1G) of this section it is to exercise, the court shall have regard to any representations made by the person liable to make payments under the order.

(1I) Paragraph (5) of Article 85 of the Magistrates' Courts (Northern Ireland) Order 1981 (power of court to require debtor to open account) shall apply for the purposes of subsection (1G) of this section as it applies for the purposes of that Article but as if for sub-paragraph (a) there were substituted –

    "(a)   the court proposes to exercise its power under paragraph (b) of section 22(1G) of the Maintenance Orders Act 1950, and".

(1J) Paragraphs (4) to (11) of Article 86 of the Magistrates' Courts (Northern Ireland) Order 1981 (power of clerk and court to vary maintenance order) shall apply in relation to a maintenance order for the time being registered under this Part of this Act in a court of summary jurisdiction in Northern Ireland as they apply in relation to a maintenance order made by a court of summary jurisdiction in Northern Ireland but –

    (a)   as if in paragraph (4) for sub-paragraph (b) there were substituted –

    "(b)   payments under the order are required to be made to the collecting officer by any method of payment falling within Article 85(7) (standing order, etc)";

    and as if after the words "petty sessions" there were inserted "for the petty sessions district for which the court which made the order acts";

    (b)   as if in paragraph (5) for the words "to the collecting officer" there were substituted "in accordance with paragraph (a) of section 22(1G) of the Maintenance Orders Act 1950";

    (c)   as if in paragraph (7), sub-paragraph (c) and the word "and" immediately preceding it were omitted;

    (d)   as if in paragraph (8) for the words "sub-paragraphs (a) to (d) of Article 85(3)" there were substituted "section 22(1G) of the Maintenance Orders Act 1950";

    (e)   as if for paragraphs (9) and (10) there were substituted the following paragraphs –

"(9) In deciding which of the powers under section 22(1G) of the Maintenance Orders Act 1950 it is to exercise, the court shall have regard to any representations made by the debtor.

(10) Paragraph (5) of Article 85 (power of court to require debtor to open account) shall apply for the purposes of paragraph (8) as it applies for the purposes of that Article but as if for sub-paragraph (a) there were substituted –

'(a) the court proposes to exercise its power under paragraph (b) of section 22(1G) of the Maintenance Orders Act 1950, and'."

(2) For the purposes of subsection (1) of this section, a court in any part of the United Kingdom may take notice of the law in force in any other part of the United Kingdom.

(3) Section 15 of this Act shall apply to the service of process for the purposes of this section as it applies to the service of process in proceedings begun in a court having jurisdiction by virtue of Part I of this Act.

(4) Except as provided by subsection (1) of this section, no variation shall be made in the rate of the payments under a maintenance order which is for the time being registered under this Part of this Act in a court of summary jurisdiction or sheriff court, but without prejudice to any power of the court which made the order to discharge it or vary it otherwise than in respect of the rate of the payments thereunder.

(5) Where a maintenance order is for the time being registered under this Part of this Act in a court of summary jurisdiction or sheriff court –

(a) the person entitled to payments under the order or the person liable to make payments under the order may, upon application made in the prescribed manner to the court by which the order was made, or in which the order is registered, as the case may be, adduce in the prescribed manner before the court in which the application is made any evidence on which he would be entitled to rely in proceedings for the variation or discharge of the order;

(b) the court in which the application is made shall cause a transcript or summary of that evidence, signed by the deponent, to be sent to the prescribed officer of the court in which the order is registered or of the court by which the order was made, as the case may be; and in any proceedings for the variation or discharge of the order the transcript or summary shall be evidence of the facts stated therein.

Amendments—DPMCA 1978, s 89(2), Sch 2, para 14; MEA 1991, s 10, Sch 1, para 5; SI 1993/1577; AJA 1999, s 90, Sch 13, para 14, Sch 15; Courts Act 2003, Sch 8, para 89; SI 2011/1484.

Scope—For the duties of the justices' chief executive when a method of payments order is made under s 22(1A), s 22(1E) or s 22(1F) see Maintenance Orders Act 1950 (Summary Jurisdiction) Rules 1950, r 9B in Part IV.

"prescribed manner" (s 22(1),(5))—The manner of application is prescribed in Maintenance Orders Act 1950 (Summary Jurisdiction) Rules 1950, rr 8 and 9.

"standing order etc" (s 22(1B),(1E),(1G))—This does not include the power to order payment by direct debit.

23 Notice of variation etc

(1) Where a maintenance order registered under this Part of this Act is discharged or varied by any court, the prescribed officer of that court shall give notice of the discharge or variation in the prescribed manner –

(a) to the prescribed officer of any court in which the order is registered; and

(b) if the order was made by another court, to the prescribed officer of that court.

(2) Any officer to whom a notice is given under this section shall cause particulars of the notice to be registered in his court in the prescribed manner.

Amendments—AJA 1977, s 3, Sch 3, para 8.

"prescribed manner" (s 23(1))—See FPR 2010, rr 32.5–32.7 and Maintenance Orders Act 1950 (Summary Jurisdiction) Rules 1950, rr 4 and 10.

"prescribed officer" (s 23(1)(a))—See FPR 2010, rr 32.5–32.7.

24 Cancellation of registration

(1) At any time while a maintenance order is registered under this Part of this Act in any court, an application for the cancellation of the registration may be made in the prescribed manner to the prescribed officer of that court by or on behalf of the person entitled to payments under the order; and upon any such application that officer shall (unless proceedings for the variation of the order are pending in that court), cancel the registration, and thereupon the order shall cease to be registered in that court.

(2) Where, after a maintenance order has been registered under this Part of this Act in a court of summary jurisdiction in England or Northern Ireland or a sheriff court in Scotland, it appears to the appropriate authority (as defined by section seventeen of this Act), upon application made in the prescribed manner by or on behalf of the person liable to make payments under the order, that the person has ceased to reside in England, Northern Ireland or Scotland, as the case may be, the appropriate authority may cause a notice to that effect to be sent to the prescribed officer of any court in which the order is registered; and where such a notice is sent the prescribed officer shall cancel the registration of the maintenance order, and thereupon the order shall cease to be registered in that court.

(3) Where the prescribed officer of any court cancels the registration of a maintenance order under this section, he shall give notice of the cancellation in the prescribed manner –

    (a)   to the prescribed officer of the court by which the order was made; and

    (b)   to the prescribed officer of any court in which it is registered under Part I of the Maintenance Orders Act 1958 or section 36 of the Civil Jurisdiction and Judgments Act 1982.

(3A) On receipt of a notice under subsection 3 above –

    (a)   any such officer as is mentioned in paragraph (a) of that subsection shall cause particulars of the notice to be registered in his court in the prescribed manner; and

    (b)   any such officer as is mentioned in paragraph (b) of that subsection shall cause particulars of the notice to be registered in his court in the prescribed manner and shall cancel the registration of the order.

(4) Except as provided by subsection (5) of this section, the cancellation of the registration of a maintenance order shall not affect anything done in relation to the maintenance order while it was registered.

(5) On the cancellation of the registration of a maintenance order, any order made in relation thereto under subsection (2) of section 19 of this Act shall cease to have effect; but until the person liable to make payments under the maintenance order receives the prescribed notice of the cancellation, he shall be deemed to comply with the maintenance order if he makes payments in accordance with any order under the said subsection (2) which was in force immediately before the cancellation.

(5A) On the cancellation of the registration of a maintenance order registered in a magistrates' court in England and Wales, any order –

    (a)   made in relation thereto by virtue of the powers conferred by section 18(2ZA) or section 22(1A) or (1E) of this Act, and

    (b)   requiring payment to the designated officer for a magistrates' court in England and Wales (whether or not by any method of payment falling within section 59(6) of the Magistrates' Courts Act 1980),

shall cease to have effect; but until the person liable to make payments under the maintenance order receives the prescribed notice of the cancellation, he shall be deemed to comply with the maintenance order if he makes payments in accordance with any such order which was in force immediately before the cancellation.

(5B) On the cancellation of the registration of a maintenance order registered in a court of summary jurisdiction in Northern Ireland, any order –

    (a)   made in relation thereto by virtue of the powers conferred by section 18(3ZA) or section 22(1F) or (1J) of this Act, and

    (b)   requiring payment to the collecting officer in Northern Ireland (whether or not by any method of payment falling within Article 85(7) of the Magistrates' Court (Northern Ireland) Order 1981),

shall cease to have effect; but until the person liable to make payments under the maintenance order receives the prescribed notice of the cancellation, he shall be deemed to comply with the maintenance order if he makes payments in accordance with any such order which was in force immediately before the cancellation.

(6) Where, by virtue of an order made under subsection (2) of section nineteen of this Act, sums payable under a maintenance order registered in a court of summary jurisdiction in England or Northern Ireland are payable through the collecting officer of any court, that officer shall, if the person entitled to the payments so requests, make an application on behalf of that person for the cancellation of the registration.

Amendments—AJA 1977, s 3, Sch 3, para 9; CJJA 1982, s 36(6), Sch 12, para 1; MEA 1991, s 10, Sch 1, para 6; SI 1993/1577; AJA 1999, s 90, Sch 13, para 15; Courts Act 2003, Sch 8, para 90.

"prescribed manner" (s 24(1),(3),(5))—For the High Court and county courts, see FPR 2010, r 32.3–32.6; for magistrates' courts, see Maintenance Orders Act 1950 (Summary Jurisdiction) Rules 1950 (see Part IV), rr 5, 6, 11 and 12 and Form 4.

25 Rules as to procedure of courts of summary jurisdiction

(1) (*repealed*)

(2) Rules made under section 23 of the Magistrates' Courts Act (Northern Ireland) 1964 may regulate the practice to be followed in courts of summary jurisdiction in Northern Ireland under this Part of this Act.

(2A) Without prejudice to the generality of the power to make rules under Article 13 of the Magistrates' Courts (Northern Ireland) Order 1981, for the purposes of giving effect to this Part of this Act such rules may make, in relation to any proceedings brought under or by virtue of this Part of this Act, any provision not covered by subsection (2) above which –

    (a)   falls within paragraph (2) of Article 165 of the Children (Northern Ireland) Order 1995, and

    (b)   may be made in relation to relevant proceedings under that Article.

(3) Rules of court made for the purposes of this Part of this Act may require that any order or other matter required under this Part of this Act to be registered in a court of summary jurisdiction in England shall be registered –

    (a)   in England, in accordance with the rules;

    (b)   (*repealed*)

Amendments—SI 1977/2158; Judicature (Northern Ireland) Act 1978, s 122(1), Sch 5, Pt II; MCA 1980, s 154, Sch 7, para 8; SI 1995/756; Courts Act 2003, Sch 8, para 91; CRA 2005, s 15(1), Sch 4, Pt 2, para 365(1).

Duty to keep the register—The register is kept in pursuance of a duty imposed by MCR 1981, r 66.

PART III
GENERAL

26 Proof of declarations etc

(1) Any document purporting to be a declaration made under section 15 of this Act, or to be a certified copy, statutory declaration, affidavit, certificate, transcript or summary made for the purposes of this Act or of any rules made thereunder shall, unless the contrary is shown, be deemed without further proof to be the document which it purports to be, and to have been duly certified, made or signed by or before the person or persons by or before whom it purports to have been certified, made or signed.

(2) Paragraph 7 of the Second Schedule to the Emergency Laws (Miscellaneous Provisions) Act 1947 (which relates to the proof of affiliation orders and maintenance orders and of orders for the discharge or variation of such orders), shall apply to the registration of orders under Part II of this Act, and to the cancellation of such registration, as it applies to the variation of orders; and for the purposes of that paragraph –

(a) a maintenance order registered under the said Part II in a court of summary jurisdiction; and

(b) any proceedings under the said Part II relating to a maintenance order made by or registered in such a court, being a proceeding of which a memorandum is required to be entered in the register kept by the clerk of that court pursuant to section 22 of the Summary Jurisdiction Act 1879,

shall be deemed to be an order made by that court.

****

Maintenance Orders Act 1958

ARRANGEMENT OF SECTIONS

PART I
REGISTRATION, ENFORCEMENT AND VARIATION OF CERTAIN MAINTENANCE ORDERS

PART III
MISCELLANEOUS AND SUPPLEMENTAL

Miscellaneous

PART I
REGISTRATION, ENFORCEMENT AND VARIATION OF CERTAIN MAINTENANCE ORDERS

1 Application of Part I

(1) The provisions of this Part of this Act shall have effect for the purpose of enabling maintenance orders to which this Part of this Act applies to be registered –

(a) in the case of an order made by the High Court or a county court, in a magistrates' court; and

(b) in the case of an order made by a magistrates' court, in the High Court,

and, subject to those provisions, while so registered –

(i)   to be enforced in like manner as an order made by the court of registration; and

(ii) in the case of an order registered in a magistrates' court, to be varied by a magistrates' court.

(1A) In the following provisions of this Act "maintenance order" means any order, decision, settlement or instrument specified in Schedule 8 to the Administration of Justice Act 1970.

(2) For the purposes of subsection (1) above, a maintenance order made by a court in Scotland or Northern Ireland and registered in England under Part II of the Maintenance Orders Act 1950 shall be deemed to have been made by the court in England in which it is so registered.

(2A) This Part of this Act applies –

(a) to maintenance orders made by the High Court or a county court or a magistrates' court, other than orders registered in Scotland or Northern Ireland under Part II of the Maintenance Orders Act 1950, and

(b) to maintenance orders made by a court in Scotland or Northern Ireland and registered in England under Part II of the Maintenance Orders Act 1950.

(3) Without prejudice to the provisions of section 21 of this Act, in this Part of this Act, unless the context otherwise requires, the following expressions have the following meanings –

"High court order", "county court order" and "magistrates' court order" mean an order made by the High Court, a county court or a magistrates' court, as the case may be;

"order" means a maintenance order to which this Part of this Act applies;

"original court" and "court of registration", in relation to an order mean the court by which the order was made or, as the case may be, the court in which the order is registered;

"registered" means registered in accordance with the provisions of this Part of this Act, and "registration" shall be construed accordingly;

and for the purposes of this Part of this Act an order for the payment by the defendant of any costs incurred in proceedings relating to a maintenance order, being an order for the payment of costs made while the maintenance order is not registered, shall be deemed to form part of that maintenance order.

(4) For the purposes of this section a maintenance order which is registered in a magistrates' court under Part I of the Maintenance Orders (Reciprocal Enforce-ment) Act 1972 or Part I of the Civil Jurisdiction and Judgments Act 1982 or Council Regulation (EC) No 44/2001 of 22 December 2000 on jurisdiction and the recognition and enforcement of judgments in civil and commercial matters, as amended from time to time and as applied by the Agreement made on 19 October 2005 between the European Community and the Kingdom of Denmark on jurisdiction and the recognition and enforcement of judgments in civil and commercial matters (OJ No. L 299 16.11.2005 at p 62) shall be deemed to be a maintenance order made by that court.

(5) For the purposes of this section –

    (a)   a maintenance decision which is enforceable by a magistrates' court by virtue of Section 1 of Chapter IV of the Maintenance Regulation and the Civil Jurisdiction and Judgments (Maintenance) Regulations 2011 is to be deemed to be a maintenance order made by that court;

    (b)   a maintenance decision which is registered by a magistrates' court under the Civil Jurisdiction and Judgments (Maintenance) Regulations 2011 is to be deemed to be a maintenance order made by that court;

    (c)   an authentic instrument or court settlement which is enforceable by a magistrates' court by virtue of Article 48 of the Maintenance Regulation (application of provisions relating to maintenance decisions to authentic instruments and court settlements) and the Civil Jurisdiction and Judgments (Maintenance) Regulations 2011 is to be deemed to be a maintenance order made by that court.

(6) In subsection (5) –

"the Maintenance Regulation" means Council Regulation (EC) No 4/2009 including as applied in relation to Denmark by virtue of the Agreement made on 19 October 2005 between the European Community and the Kingdom of Denmark;

"authentic instrument" and "court settlement" have the meanings given by Article 2 of the Maintenance Regulation;

"maintenance decision" has the meaning given to "decision" by Article 2 of the Maintenance Regulation.

Amendments—AJA 1970, s 27(3); MO(RE)A 1972, s 22(1), Sch, para 4; AJA 1977, s 3, Sch 3, para 1; CJJA 1982, s 15(4), Sch 12, para 3; SI 2001/3929; SI 2007/1655; SI 2011/1484.

Defined terms—"costs": s 21(4); "defendant", "England": s 21(1).

2 Registration of orders

(1) A person entitled to receive payments under a High Court or county court order may apply for the registration of the order to the original court, and the court may, if it thinks fit, grant the application.

(2) Where an application for the registration of such an order is granted –

    (a)   no proceedings shall be begun, and no writ, warrant or other process shall be issued, for the enforcement of the order before the registration of the order or the expiration of the prescribed period from the grant of the application, whichever first occurs; and

    (b)   the original court shall, on being satisfied within the period aforesaid by the person who made the application that no such proceedings or process begun or issued before the grant of the application remain pending or in force, cause a certified copy of the order to be sent to the designated officer for the magistrates' court acting in the local justice area in which the defendant appears to be;

but if at the expiration of the period aforesaid the original court has not been so satisfied, the grant of the application shall become void.

(3) A person entitled to receive payments under a magistrates' court order who considers that the order could be more effectively enforced if it were registered may apply for the registration of the order to the original court, and the court may, if it thinks fit, grant the application.

(3A) Without prejudice to subsection (3) of this section, where a magistrates' court order provides both for the payment of a lump sum and for the making of periodical payments, a person entitled to receive a lump sum under the order who considers that, so far as it relates to that sum, the order could be more effectively enforced if it were registered may apply to the original court for the registration of the order so far as it so relates, and the court may, if it thinks fit, grant the application.

(3B) Where an application under subsection (3A) of this section is granted in the case of a magistrates' court order, the provisions of this Part of this Act shall have effect in relation to that order as if so far as it relates to the payment of a lump sum it were a separate order.

(4) Where an application for the registration of a magistrates' court order is granted –

    (a)   no proceedings for the enforcement of the order shall be begun before the registration takes place and no warrant or other process for the enforcement thereof shall be issued in consequence of any such proceedings begun before the grant of the application; and

    (b)   (*repealed*)

    (c)   the original court shall, on being satisfied in the prescribed manner that no process for the enforcement of the order issued before the grant of the application remains in force, cause a certified copy of the order to be sent to the prescribed officer of the High Court.

(5) The officer of, or for, a court who receives a certified copy of an order sent to him under this section shall cause the order to be registered in that court.

(6) Where a magistrates' court order is registered under this Part of this Act in the High Court, then –

    (a)   if payments under the magistrates' court order are required to be made (otherwise than to the designated officer for a magistrates' court) by any method of payment falling within section 59(6) of the Magistrates' Courts Act 1980 (standing order, etc), any order requiring payment by that method shall continue to have effect after registration;

    (b)   any order by virtue of which sums payable under the magistrates' court order are required to be paid to the designated officer for a magistrates' court (whether or not by any method of payment falling within section 59(6) of that Act) on behalf of the person entitled thereto shall cease to have effect.

(6ZA) Where a High Court or county court order is registered under this Part of this Act in a magistrates' court, then –

    (a)   if a means of payment order (within the meaning of section 1(7) of the Maintenance Enforcement Act 1991) has effect in relation to the order in question, it shall continue to have effect after registration; and

    (b)   in any other case, the magistrates' court shall order that all payments to be made under the order in question (including any arrears accrued before registration) shall be made to the designated officer for the court or for any other magistrates' court.

(6ZB) Any such order as to payment –

    (a) as is referred to in paragraph (a) of subsection (6) of this section may be revoked, suspended, revived or varied by an exercise of the powers conferred by section 4A of this Act; and

    (b) as is referred to in paragraph (a) or (b) of subsection (6ZA) of this section may be varied or revoked by an exercise of the powers conferred by section 3(2A) or (2B) or section 4(2A), (5A) or (5B) of this Act.

(6ZC) Where by virtue of the provisions of this section or any order under subsection (6ZA)(b) of this section payments under an order cease to be or become payable to the designated officer for a magistrates' court, the person liable to make the payments shall, until he is given the prescribed notice to that effect, be deemed to comply with the order if he makes payments in accordance with the order and any order under subsection (6ZA)(b) of this section of which he has received such notice.

(6A) In this section –

    "High Court order" includes a maintenance order deemed to be made by the High Court by virtue of section 1(2) above, and

    "magistrates' court order" includes a maintenance order deemed to be made by a magistrates' court by virtue of that subsection.

(7) In this section "certified copy" in relation to an order of a court means a copy certified by the proper officer of the court to be a true copy of the order or of the official record thereof.

Amendments—AJA 1977, s 3, Sch 3, para 2; CJJA 1982, s 37(1), Sch 11, para 2; MEA 1991, s 10, Sch 1, para 7; AJA 1999, s 90, Sch 13, para 26, Sch 15; Courts Act 2003, Sch 8, para 98.

Defined terms—"certified copy": s 2(7); "county court order": s 1(3); "defendant": s 21(1); "High Court order": s 1(3); "magistrates' court": s 21(1); "magistrates' court order", "original court": s 1(3); "person entitled to receive payments": s 21(2).

Scope—For the duties of the designated officer when a means of payment order is made, see Magistrates' Courts (Maintenance Orders Act 1958) Rules 1959, r 5A in Part IV.

"the court may" (s 2(1))—The registration of nominal or interim orders is discouraged.

"The officer or clerk ... shall" (s 2(5))—If the original court has granted the application, the recipient court cannot decline to effect the registration.

"prescribed period" (s 2(2))—The prescribed period is 14 days (FPR 2010, r 32.14).

"person entitled to receive payments" (s 2(3))—Although this expression includes a court collecting officer, he or she is prevented from applying for registration except in accordance with the provisions of s 20.

"prescribed officer of the High Court" (s 2(4))—At the Principal Registry or such district registry as may be specified by the applicant (Magistrates' Courts (Maintenance Orders Act 1958) Rules 1959, rr 3, 25).

"standing order, etc" (s 2(6)(a))—This does not include payment by direct debit.

2A Interest on sums recoverable under certain orders registered in the High Court

(1) Where, in connection with an application under section 2(3) of this Act for the registration of a magistrates' court order, the applicant shows in accordance with rules of court –

    (a) that the order, though deemed for the purposes of section 1 of this Act to have been made by a magistrates' court in England, was in fact made in another part of the United Kingdom or in a country or territory outside the United Kingdom, and

(b)   that, as regards any sum for whose payment the order provides, interest on that sum at a particular rate is, by the law of that part or of that country or territory, recoverable under the order from a particular date or time,

then, if the original court grants the application and causes a certified copy of the order to be sent to the prescribed officer of the High Court under section 2(4)(c) of this Act, it shall also cause to be sent to him a certificate in the prescribed form showing, as regards that sum, the rate of interest so recoverable and the date or time from which it is so recoverable.

(2) The officer of the court who receives a certificate sent to him under the preceding subsection shall cause the certificate to be registered in that court together with the order to which it relates.

(3) Where an order is registered together with a certificate under this section, then, subject to any provision made under the next following subsection, sums payable under the order shall carry interest at the rate specified in the certificate from the date or time so specified.

(4) Provision may be made by rules of court as to the manner in which and the periods by reference to which any interest payable by virtue of subsection (3) is to be calculated and paid, including provision for such interest to cease to accrue as from a prescribed date.

(5) Except as provided by this section sums payable under registered orders shall not carry interest.

Amendments—Inserted by CJJA 1982, s 37(1), Sch 11, para 6.

Defined terms—"certified copy": s 2(7); "magistrates' court": s 21(1); "magistrates' court order", "registered": s 1(3).

"rules of court"—Magistrates' Courts (Maintenance Orders Act 1958) Rules 1959, r 2A.

3 Enforcement of registered orders

(1) Subject to the provisions of section 2A of this Act and this section, a registered order shall be enforceable in all respects as it if had been made by the court of registration and as if that court had had jurisdiction to make it; and proceedings for or with respect to the enforcement of a registered order may be taken accordingly.

(2) Subject to the provisions of subsections (2A) to (3) of this section, an order registered in a magistrates' court shall be enforceable as a magistrates' court maintenance order within the meaning of section 150(1) of the Magistrates' Courts Act 1980.

(2A) Where an order registered in a magistrates' court is an order other than one deemed to be made by the High Court by virtue of section 1(2) of this Act, section 76 of the Magistrates' Courts Act 1980 (enforcement of sums adjudged to be paid) shall have effect as if for subsections (4) to (6) there were substituted the following subsections –

"(4) Where proceedings are brought for the enforcement of a magistrates' court maintenance order under this section, the court may vary the order by exercising one of its powers under paragraphs (a) to (d) of section 59(3) above.

(5) In deciding which of the powers under paragraphs (a) to (d) of section 59(3) above it is to exercise, the court shall have regard to any representations made by the debtor and the creditor (which expressions have the same meaning as they have in section 59 above).

(6) Subsection (4) of section 59 above shall apply for the purposes of subsection (4) above as it applies for the purposes of that section."

(2B) Where an order registered in a magistrates' court is an order deemed to be made by the High Court by virtue of section 1(2) of this Act, sections 76 and 93 of the

Magistrates' Courts Act 1980 (enforcement of sums adjudged to be paid and complaint for arrears) shall have effect subject to the modifications specified in subsections (2ZA) and (2ZB) of section 18 of the Maintenance Orders Act 1950 (enforcement of registered orders).

(3) Where an order remains or becomes registered after the discharge of the order, no proceedings shall be taken by virtue of that registration except in respect of arrears which were due under the order at the time of the discharge and have not been remitted.

(3A) Any person under an obligation to make payments under an order registered in a magistrates' court shall give notice of any change of address to the designated officer for the court; and any person who without reasonable excuse fails to give such a notice shall be liable on summary conviction to a fine not exceeding level 2 on the standard scale.

(4) Except as provided by this section, no proceedings shall be taken for or with respect to the enforcement of a registered order.

Amendments—CJJA 1982, Sch 11; MFPA 1984, Sch 1; FLRA 1987, Sch 2; MEA 1991, s 10, Sch 1, para 8; Statute Law (Repeals) Act 1993; AJA 1999, s 90, Sch 13, para 27; Courts Act 2003, Sch 8, para 99.

Defined terms—"court of registration": s 1(3); "magistrates' court": s 21(1); "registered": s 1(3).

"paragraphs (a) to (d) of section 59(3)" (s 3(2A))—Section 59(3) of MCA 1980 permits orders for payments direct between the parties, through a designated officer, by standing order or by attachment of earnings.

"subsection (2ZA)" (s 3(2B))—This permits the full range of means of payments orders to be used on enforcement of an order.

"subsection (2ZB)" (s 3(2B))—This prevents the use of imprisonment for enforcement of an order if the court is of opinion that an attachment of earnings order or an order for payment by standing order is appropriate. For the duties of the designated officer when a means of payment order is made, see Magistrates' Court (Maintenance Orders Act 1958) Rules 1959, r 5A in Part IV.

"shall be enforceable" (s 3(1))—For enforcement, see MCA 1980, ss 76 and 93.

"level 2 on the standard scale" (s 3(3A))—Currently £500 (Criminal Justice Act 1982, s 37(2)).

"Except as provided by this section, no proceedings shall be taken" (s 3(4))—In particular, there is no power to remit enforcement proceedings analogous to that under s 4(4) relating to variation proceedings. See in this respect *X v Y (Maintenance Arrears – Cohabitation)* [2012] EW Misc 4 (CC) (HHJ Bellamy). Similarly, magistrates have no power to cancel the registration of an order (*X v Y*).

4 Variation of orders registered in magistrates' courts

(1) The provisions of this section shall have effect with respect to the variation of orders registered in magistrates' courts, and references in this section to registered orders shall be construed accordingly.

(2) Subject to the following provisions of this section –

    (a) the court of registration may exercise the same jurisdiction to vary any rate of payments specified by a registered order (other than jurisdiction in a case where a party to the order is not present in England when the application for variation is made) as is exercisable, apart from this subsection, by the original court; and

    (b) a rate of payments specified by a registered order shall not be varied except by the court of registration or any other magistrates' court to which the jurisdiction conferred by the foregoing paragraph is extended by rules of court.

(2A) The power of a magistrates' court to vary a registered order under subsection (2) of this section shall include power, if the court is satisfied that payment has not been made in accordance with the order, to vary the order by exercising one of its powers under paragraphs (a) to (d) of section 59(3) of the Magistrates' Courts Act 1980.

(2B) Subsection (4) of section 59 of that Act shall apply for the purposes of subsection (2A) of this section as it applies for the purposes of that section.

(2C) In deciding which of the powers under paragraphs (a) to (d) of section 59(3) of that Act it is to exercise, the court shall have regard to any representations made by the debtor and the creditor (which expressions have the same meaning as they have in section 59 of that Act).

(3) (*repealed*)

(4) If it appears to the court to which an application is made by virtue of subsection (2) of this section for the variation of a rate of payments specified by a registered order that it is for any reason appropriate to remit the application to the original court, the first-mentioned court shall so remit the application, and the original court shall thereupon deal with the application as if the order were not registered.

(5) Nothing in subsection (2) of this section shall affect the jurisdiction of the original court to vary a rate of payments specified by a registered order if an application for the variation of that rate is made to that court –

    (a)   in proceedings for a variation of provisions of the order which do not specify a rate of payments; or

    (b)   at a time when a party to the order is not present in England.

(5A) Subject to the following provisions of this section, subsections (4) to (11) of section 60 of the Magistrates' Courts Act 1980 (power of clerk and court to vary maintenance orders) shall apply in relation to a registered order (other than one deemed to be made by the High Court by virtue of section 1(2) of this Act) as they apply in relation to a maintenance order made by a magistrates' court (disregarding section 23(2) of the Domestic Proceedings and Magistrates' Courts Act 1978, section 15(2) of the Children Act 1989 and paragraph 42 of Schedule 6 to the Civil Partnership Act 2004) but –

    (a)   as if in subsection (8) after the words "the court which may" there were inserted "subject to subsection (10) below"; and

    (b)   as if for subsections (9) and (10) there were substituted the following subsections –

"(9) Subsection (4) of section 59 above shall apply for the purposes of subsection (8) above as it applies for the purposes of that section.

(10) In deciding which of the powers under paragraphs (a) to (d) of section 59(3) above it is to exercise, the court shall have regard to any representations made by the debtor and the creditor."

(5B) Subject to the following provisions of this section, subsections (4) to (11) of section 60 of the Magistrates' Courts Act 1980 (power of clerk and court to vary maintenance orders) shall apply in relation to a registered order deemed to be made by the High Court by virtue of section 1(2) of this Act as they apply in relation to a maintenance order made by a magistrates' court (disregarding section 23(2) of the Domestic Proceedings and Magistrates' Courts Act 1978, section 15(2) of the Children Act 1989 and paragraph 42 of Schedule 6 to the Civil Partnership Act 2004) but –

    (a)   as if in subsection (4) for paragraph (b) there were substituted –

       "(b) payments under the order are required to be made to the designated officer for the court or for any other magistrates' court, by any method of payment falling within section 59(6) above (standing order, etc)";

    (b)   as if in subsection (5) for the words "to the designated officer for the court" there were substituted "in accordance with paragraph (a) of subsection (9) below";

(c)   as if in subsection (7), paragraph (c) and the word "and" immediately preceding it were omitted;

(d)   as if in subsection (8) for the words "paragraphs (a) to (d) of section 59(3) above" there were substituted "subsection (9) below";

(e)   as if for subsections (9) and (10) there were substituted the following subsections –

"(9)   The powers of the court are –

(a)   the power to order that payments under the order be made directly to the designated officer for the court or for any other magistrates' court;

(b)   the power to order that payments under the order be made to the designated officer for the court or for any other magistrates' court, by such method of payment falling within section 59(6) above (standing order, etc) as may be specified;

(c)   the power to make an attachment of earnings order under the Attachment of Earnings Act 1971 to secure payments under the order.

(10)   In deciding which of the powers under subsection (9) above it is to exercise, the court shall have regard to any representations made by the debtor.

(10A)   Subsection (4) of section 59 above (power of court to require debtor to open account) shall apply for the purposes of subsection (9) above as it applies for the purposes of that section but as if for paragraph (a) there were substituted –

'(a)   the court proposes to exercise its powers under paragraph (b) of section 60(9) below'."

(6)   No application for any variation of a registered order shall be made to any court while proceedings for any variation of the order are pending in any other court.

(6A)   Except as provided by subsection (5B) of this section no application for any variation in respect of a registered order shall be made to any court in respect of an order made by the Court of Session or the High Court in Northern Ireland and registered in that court in accordance with the provisions of this Part of this Act by virtue of section 1(2) above.

(6B)   No application for any variation of a registered order shall be made to any court in respect of an order for periodical or other payments made under Part III of the Matrimonial and Family Proceedings Act 1984 or under Schedule 7 to the Civil Partnership Act 2004.

(7)   Where a magistrates' court, in exercise of the jurisdiction conferred by subsection (2) of this section, varies or refuses to vary a registered order, an appeal from the variation or refusal shall lie to a county court.

Amendments—AJA 1970, s 48, Sch 11; AJA 1977, ss 3, 32, Schs 3, 5; MFPA 1984, s 46(1), Sch 1, para 5; MEA 1991, s 10, Sch 1, para 9; AJA 1999, s 90, Sch 13, para 28, Sch 15; CPA 2004, s 261(1), Sch 27, para 22; SI 2009/871.

Defined terms—"court of registration": s 1(3); "England", "magistrates' court": s 21(1); "original court", "registered": s 1(3).

Scope—This section provides for the variation of the rate of payment under registered orders. The section does not allow the revocation or revival of registered orders, or the extension (after expiry) of a child periodical payments order where the child remains dependent. The section also allows the making of a means of payment order if satisfied that payment has not been made in accordance with the order. See FPR 2010, rr 32.19, 32.20 and Magistrates' Courts (Maintenance Orders Act 1958) Rules 1959, r 7.

Variation—In exercising the power of variation, the court must apply the same principles as the court which made the original order (*Miller v Miller* [1961] P 1). Where the application is made a short time after the original order and there is no change of circumstances, the court should refuse the application

(*Bromiley v Bromiley* [1987] 2 FLR 207). The variation of the order may be backdated to the date of complaint (*Moon v Moon* (1980) 1 FLR 115). The prohibition on variation in s 4(2) is subject to the exceptions contained in s 4(5).

"section 59(3)" (s 4(2A))—The court may exercise its power under MCA 1980, s 59(3) to make a means of payment order.

Remittal of the application (s 4(4))—In appropriate cases, the High Court encourages magistrates to consider remitting a variation application to the original court: *Goodall v Jolly* [1984] FLR 143. The matters to be taken into account include the length of the case, the consideration of a large number of documents or the need to exercise one of the special powers of the High Court (e g the power to order disclosure of documents). As noted below, however, there is no power to remit enforcement proceedings.

Appeals (s 4(7))—Similarly, an appeal now lies to the county court against a decision on the remission of arrears (MCA 1980, s 111A).

4A Variation etc of orders registered in the High Court

(1) The provisions of this section shall have effect with respect to orders registered in the High Court other than maintenance orders deemed to be made by a magistrates' court by virtue of section 1(4) or (5) of this Act, and the reference in subsection (2) of this section to a registered order shall be construed accordingly.

(2) The High Court may exercise the same powers in relation to a registered order as are exercisable by the High Court under section 1 of the Maintenance Enforcement Act 1991 in relation to a qualifying periodical maintenance order (within the meaning of that section) which has been made by the High Court, including the power under subsection (7) of that section to revoke, suspend, revive or vary –

   (a) any such order as is referred to in paragraph (a) of section 2(6) of this Act which continues to have effect by virtue of that paragraph; and

   (b) any means of payment order (within the meaning of section 1(7) of that Act of 1991) made by virtue of the provisions of this section.

Amendments—Inserted by MEA 1991, s 10, Sch 1, para 10; amended by SI 2011/1484.

Defined terms—"magistrates' court": s 21(1); "registered": s 1(3).

5 Cancellation of registration

(1) If a person entitled to receive payments under a registered order desires the registration to be cancelled, he may give notice under this section.

(2) Where the original court varies or discharges an order registered in a magistrates' court, the original court may, if it thinks fit, give notice under this section.

(3) Where the original court discharges an order registered in the High Court and it appears to the original court whether by reason of the remission of arrears by that court or otherwise, that no arrears under the order remain to be recovered, the original court shall give notice under this section.

(4) Notice under this section shall be given to the court of registration; and where such notice is given –

   (a) no proceedings for the enforcement of the registered order shall be begun before the cancellation of the registration and no writ, warrant or other process for the enforcement thereof shall be issued in consequence of any such proceedings begun before the giving of the notice; and

   (b) (*repealed*)

   (c) the court of registration shall cancel the registration on being satisfied in the prescribed manner –

      (i) that no process for the enforcement of the registered order issued before the giving of the notice remains in force; and

        (ii)   in the case of an order registered in a magistrates' court, that no proceedings for the variation of the order are pending in a magistrates' court.

(4A) For the purposes of a notice under subsection (2) or (3) above –

"court of registration" includes any court in which an order is registered under Part II of the Maintenance Orders Act 1950, and

"registration" includes registration under that Act.

(5) On the cancellation of the registration of a High Court or county court order –

    (a)   any order which requires payments under the order in question to be made (otherwise than to the designated officer for a magistrates' court) by any method of payment falling within section 59(6) of the Magistrates' Courts Act 1980 or section 1(5) of the Maintenance Enforcement Act 1991 (standing order, etc) shall continue to have effect; and

    (b)   any order made under section 2(6ZA)(b) of this Act or by virtue of the powers conferred by section 3(2A) or (2B) or section 4(2A), (5A) or (5B) of this Act and which requires payments under the order in question to be made to the designated officer for a magistrates' court (whether or not by any method of payment falling within section 59(6) of the Magistrates' Courts Act 1980) shall cease to have effect;

but, in a case falling within paragraph (b) of this subsection, until the defendant receives the prescribed notice of the cancellation he shall be deemed to comply with the High Court or county court order if he makes payment in accordance with any such order as is referred to in paragraph (b) of this subsection which was in force immediately before the cancellation and of which he has notice.

(6) On the cancellation of the registration of a magistrates' court order –

    (a)   any order which requires payments under the magistrates' court order to be made by any method of payment falling within section 59(6) of the Magistrates' Courts Act 1980 or section 1(5) of the Maintenance Enforcement Act 1991 (standing order, etc) shall continue to have effect; and

    (b)   in any other case, payments shall become payable to the designated officer for the original court;

but, in a case falling within paragraph (b) of this subsection, until the defendant receives the prescribed notice of the cancellation he shall be deemed to comply with the magistrates' court order if he makes payments in accordance with any order which was in force immediately before the cancellation and of which he has notice.

(7) In subsection (5) and (6) of this section "High Court order" and "magistrates' court order" shall be construed in accordance with section 2(6A) of this Act.

Amendments—AJA 1977, s 3, Sch 3, para 4; MEA 1991, s 10, Sch 1, para 11; AJA 1999, s 90, Sch 13, para 29, Sch 15; Courts Act 2003, Sch 8, para 101.

Defined terms—"court of registration": ss 1(3), 5(4A); "defendant", "magistrates' court", "original court": s 21(1); "person entitled to receive payments": s 21(2).

Scope—This section enables the person entitled to receive the payments or the original court to cancel the registration; and sets out the procedure for and the consequences of cancellation, see FPR 2010, rr 32.21, 32.22. For notices to be given on cancellation, see Magistrates' Courts (Maintenance Orders Act 1958) Rules 1959, r 7 in Part IV. There is no power for the magistrates' court to cancel the registration, even if further proceedings relating to the order might be more conveniently dealt with in the original court: *X v Y (Maintenance Arrears – Cohabitation)* [2012] EW Misc 4 (CC) (HHJ Bellamy) (permission to appeal on other issues refused: *Re H-J (Children)* [2012] EWCA Civ 1080).

"person entitled to receive payments" (s 5(1))—The court collecting officer is included within this description, but the officer's power to give notice is restricted by s 20(1).

"prescribed notice" (s 5(5))—See Magistrates' Courts (Maintenance Orders Act 1958) Rules 1959, r 2 in Part IV.

****

PART III
MISCELLANEOUS AND SUPPLEMENTAL

Miscellaneous

17 Prohibition of committal more than once in respect of same arrears

Where a defendant has been imprisoned or otherwise detained under an order or warrant of commitment issued in respect of his failure to pay a sum due under a maintenance order, then, notwithstanding anything in this Act, no such order or warrant (other than a warrant of which the issue has been postponed under paragraph (ii) of subsection (5) of the next following section) shall thereafter be issued in respect of that sum or any part thereof.

Defined terms—"defendant": s 21(1).

18 Power of magistrates to review committals etc

(1) Where, for the purpose of enforcing a maintenance order, a magistrates' court has exercised its power under subsection 2 of section 77 of the Magistrates' Courts Act 1980, or this section to postpone the issue of a warrant of commitment and under the terms of the postponement the warrant falls to be issued, then –

    (a) the warrant shall not be issued except in pursuance of subsection (2) or paragraph (a) of subsection (3) of this section; and

    (b) the designated officer for the court shall give notice to the defendant stating that if the defendant considers there are grounds for not issuing the warrant he may make an application to the court in the prescribed manner requesting that the warrant shall not be issued and stating those grounds.

(2) If no such application is received by the designated officer for the court within the prescribed period, any justice of the peace acting in the same local justice area as the court may issue the warrant of commitment at any time after the expiration of that period; and if such an application is so received any such justice may, after considering the statements contained in the application –

    (a) if he is of opinion that the application should be further considered, refer it to the court;

    (b) if he is not of that opinion, issue the warrant forthwith;

and when an application is referred to the court under this subsection, the designated officer for the court shall give to the defendant and the person in whose favour the maintenance order in question was made notice of the time and place appointed for the consideration of the application by the court.

(3) On considering an application referred to it under the last foregoing subsection the court shall, unless in pursuance of subsection (6) of this section it remits the whole of the sum in respect of which the warrant could otherwise be issued, either –

    (a) issue the warrant; or

    (b) further postpone the issue thereof until such time and on such conditions, if any, as the court thinks just; or

    (c) if in consequence of any change in the circumstances of the defendant the court considers it appropriate so to do, order that the warrant shall not be issued in any event.

(4) A defendant who is for the time being imprisoned or otherwise detained under a warrant of commitment issued by a magistrates' court for the purpose of enforcing a maintenance order, and who is not detained otherwise than for the enforcement of such an order, may make an application to the court in the prescribed manner requesting that the warrant shall be cancelled and stating the grounds of the application; and thereupon any justice of the peace acting in the same local justice area as the court may, after considering the statements contained in the application –

    (a)   if he is of opinion that the application should be further considered refer it to the court;

    (b)   if he is not of that opinion, refuse the application;

and when an application is referred to the court under this subsection, the designated officer for the court shall give to the person in charge of the prison or other place in which the defendant is detained and the person in whose favour the maintenance order in question was made notice of the time and place appointed for the consideration of the application by the court.

(5) On considering an application referred to it under the last foregoing subsection, the court shall, unless in pursuance of the next following subsection it remits the whole of the sum in respect of which the warrant was issued or such part thereof as remains to be paid, either –

    (a)   refuse the application; or

    (b)   if the court is satisfied that the defendant is unable to pay, or to make any payment or further payment towards, the sum aforesaid and if it is of opinion that in all the circumstances of the case the defendant ought not to continue to be detained under the warrant, order that the warrant shall cease to have effect when the person in charge of the prison or other place aforesaid is informed of the making of the order;

and where the court makes an order under paragraph (b) of this subsection, it may if it thinks fit also –

    (i)   fix a term of imprisonment in respect of the sum aforesaid or such part thereof as remains to be paid, being a term not exceeding so much of the term of the previous warrant as, after taking into account any reduction thereof by virtue of the next following subsection, remained to be served at the date of the order; and

    (ii)   postpone the issue of a warrant for the commitment of the defendant for that term until such time and on such conditions, if any, as the court thinks just.

(6) On considering an application under this section in respect of a warrant or a postponed warrant, the court may, if the maintenance order in question is an affiliation order or an order enforceable as an affiliation order, remit the whole or any part of the sum due under the order; and where the court remits the sum or part of the sum in respect of which the warrant was issued or the postponed warrant could have been issued section 79 of the Magistrates' Courts Act 1980 (which provides that on payment of the sum for which imprisonment has been ordered by a magistrates' court the order shall cease to have effect and that on payment of part of that sum the period of detention shall be reduced proportionately) shall apply as if payment of that sum or part had been made as therein mentioned.

(7) Where notice of the time and place appointed for the consideration of an application is required by this section to be given to the defendant or the person in whose favour the maintenance order in question was made and the defendant or, as the case may be, that person does not appear at that time and place, the court may proceed with the consideration of the application in his absence.

(8) A notice required by this section to be given by the designated officer for a magistrates' court to any person shall be deemed to be given to that person if it is sent by registered post addressed to him at his last known address, notwithstanding that the notice is returned as undelivered or is for any other reason not received by that person.

Amendments—MCA 1980, s 154, Sch 7, para 23; AJA 1999, s 90, Sch 13, para 30; Courts Act 2003, Sch 8, para 102.

Defined terms—"defendant": s 21(1).

"shall give notice" (s 18(1))—Notice is to be served by registered post or, under the Recorded Delivery Service Act 1962, by recorded delivery. Delivery is not required provided the notice was addressed to the defendant at his last known address (s 18(8)). Separate notice is required on each occasion that the court is considering the issue of the warrant of committal (*Slater v Calder Justices* [1984] FLR 719).

"prescribed manner" (s 18(1),(4))—See Magistrates' Courts (Maintenance Orders Act 1958) Rules 1959, r 22 in Part IV.

"prescribed period" (s 18(2))—The period prescribed by Magistrates' Courts (Maintenance Orders Act 1958) Rules 1959, r 22(3) is 8 days beginning with the day the designated officer sends notice to the defendant.

"refer" (s 18(2),(4))—The justices' discretion is limited to referring the application to the court or issuing the warrant forthwith. Where there is, prima facie, a change in circumstances, the justice should refer the application to the court (*Wood v Warley Justices* (1974) Fam Law 130).

"order enforceable as an affiliation order" (s 18(6))—This includes an order registered under s 3.

****

Supplemental

20 Special provisions as to magistrates' courts

(1) Notwithstanding anything in this Act, the designated officer for a magistrates' court who is entitled to receive payments under a maintenance order for transmission to another person shall not apply for the registration of the maintenance order under Part I of this Act or give notice in relation to the order in pursuance of subsection (1) of section five thereof unless he is requested in writing to do so by a person entitled to receive the payments through him; and where the designated officer is requested as aforesaid –

  (i)   he shall comply with the request unless it appears to him unreasonable in the circumstances to do so;
  (ii) the person by whom the request was made shall have the same liabilities for all the costs properly incurred in or about any proceedings taken in pursuance of the request as if the proceedings had been taken by that person.

(2) An application to a magistrates' court by virtue of subsection (2) of section four of this Act for the variation of a maintenance order shall be made by complaint.

(3)–(7) …

(8) For the avoidance of doubt it is hereby declared that a complaint may be made to enforce payment of a sum due and unpaid under a maintenance order notwithstanding that a previous complaint has been made in respect of that sum or a part thereof and whether or not an order was made in pursuance of the previous complaint.

Amendments—AEA 1971, Sch 5; MCA 1980, s 154, Sch 9; AJA 1999, s 90, Sch 13, para 31; Courts Act 2003, Sch 8, para 103.

Defined terms—"magistrates' court": s 21(1).

21 Interpretation etc

(1) In this Act, unless the context otherwise requires, the following expressions have the following meanings –

"magistrates' court" has the meaning assigned to it by the Magistrates' Courts Act 1980 and the reference to that Act in subsection (2) of section 148 thereof shall be construed as including a reference to this Act;

"defendant", in relation to a maintenance order or a related attachment of earnings order, means the person liable to make payments under the maintenance order;

"England" includes Wales;

"prescribed" means prescribed by rules of court.

(2) Any reference in this Act to a person entitled to receive payments under a maintenance order is a reference to a person entitled to receive such payments either directly or through another person or for transmission to another person.

(3) Any reference in this Act to proceedings relating to an order includes a reference to proceedings in which the order may be made.

(4) Any reference in this Act to costs incurred in proceedings relating to a maintenance order shall be construed, in the case of a maintenance order made by the High Court, as a reference to such costs as are included in an order for costs relating solely to that maintenance order.

(5) (*repealed*)

(6) Any reference in this Act to any enactment is a reference to that enactment as amended by or under any subsequent enactment.

Amendments—AJA 1970, s 54(3), Sch 11; MCA 1980, s 154, Sch 7, para 24; FLRA 1987, s 33(4), Sch 4; AJA 1999, s 76, Sch 10, para 22, Sch 15; Courts Act 2003, Sch 8, para 104.

****

Maintenance Orders (Facilities for Enforcement) Act 1920

ARRANGEMENT OF SECTIONS

1 Enforcement in England and Ireland of maintenance orders made in His Majesty's dominions outside the United Kingdom

(1) Where a maintenance order has, whether before or after the passing of this Act, been made against any person by any court in any part of His Majesty's dominions outside the United Kingdom to which this Act extends, and a certified copy of the order has been transmitted by the governor of that part of His Majesty's dominions to the Lord Chancellor, the Lord Chancellor shall send a copy of the order to the prescribed officer of a court in England or Ireland for registration; and on receipt thereof the order shall be registered in the prescribed manner, and shall, from the date of such registration, be of the same force and effect, and, subject to the provisions of this Act, all proceedings may be taken on such order as if it had been an order originally obtained in the court in which it is so registered, and that court shall have power to enforce the order accordingly.

(2) The Court in which an order is to be so registered as aforesaid shall, if the court by which the order was made was a court of superior jurisdiction, be the Family Division of the High Court, or in Ireland the King's Bench Division (Matrimonial) of the High Court of Justice in Ireland, and, if the court was not a court of superior jurisdiction, be a court of summary jurisdiction.

Amendments—AJA 1970, s 1(6), Sch 2, para 2; SI 1992/709.

Defined terms—"certified copy", "maintenance order": s 10.

Areas to which the Act extends—The Act remains in force only for Commonwealth countries that are not designated as reciprocating countries under MO(RE)A 1972. Although the 1972 Act provides for the repeal of the whole of this Act, that provision (s 22(2) of the 1972 Act) has been brought into force only as regards such designated countries. This Act currently applies to:

(a) *Africa*   Botswana, Lesotho, Malawi, Mauritius, Nigeria, Seychelles, Sierra Leone, Swaziland, The Gambia, Uganda, Zambia, Zanzibar.
(b) *America*   Antigua, Bahamas, Belize, Cayman Islands, Dominica, Grenada, Guyana, Jamaica, Montserrat, St Christopher and Nevis, St Lucia, St Vincent, Trinidad and Tobago, Virgin Islands, Yukon Territory and Prince Edward Island.
(c) *Asia*   Malaysia, Sri Lanka.
(d) *Australasia*   Solomon Islands, Kiribati, Tuvalu.
(e) *Europe*   Cyprus, Guernsey, Jersey.

See also s 12.

"shall be registered" (s 1(1))—For procedure in the High Court and county court, see FPR 2010, rr 34.9–34.11 and, in magistrates' courts, see FPR 2010, rr 34.1–34.8. Registration is an administrative and not a judicial act, and the payer cannot object to or appeal against registration (*Pilcher v Pilcher* [1955] P 318).

Date from which order takes effect—An order registered under this section takes effect from the date specified in the original order or from the date of the original order. Contrast the position for the confirmation of provisional orders under s 4.

"power to enforce" (s 1(1))—This does not include the power to vary or discharge the order (see *Pilcher v Pilcher* (above) and *R v Rose ex parte McGibbon* (1959) 123 JP 374).

2 Transmission of maintenance orders made in England or Ireland

Where a court in England or Ireland has, whether before or after the commencement of this Act, made a maintenance order against any person, and it is proved to that court that the person against whom the order was made is resident in some part of His Majesty's dominions outside the United Kingdom to which this Act extends, the court shall send to the Lord Chancellor for transmission to the governor of that part of His Majesty's dominions a certified copy of the order.

Amendments—SI 1992/709.

Defined terms—"certified copy", "maintenance order": s 10.

Scope—Application in the High Court or county court is made to a district judge; for procedure, see FPR 2010, r 34.10.

3 Power to make provisional orders of maintenance against persons resident in His Majesty's dominions outside the United Kingdom

(1) Where an application is made to a court of summary jurisdiction in England or Ireland for a maintenance order against any person, and it is proved that that person is resident in a part of His Majesty's dominions outside the United Kingdom to which this Act extends, the court may, in the absence of that person, if after hearing the evidence it is satisfied of the justice of the application, make any such order as it might have made if that person had been habitually resident in England and Wales, had received reasonable notice of the date of the hearing of the application and had failed to appear at the hearing, but in such case the order shall be provisional only, and shall have no effect unless and until confirmed by a competent court in such part of His Majesty's dominions as aforesaid.

(2) The evidence of any witness who is examined on any such application shall be put into writing, and such deposition shall be read over to and signed by him.

(3) Where such an order is made, the court shall send to the Lord Chancellor for transmission to the governor of the part of His Majesty's dominions in which the person against whom the order is made is alleged to reside the depositions so taken and a certified copy of the order, together with a statement of the grounds on which the making of the order might have been opposed if the person against whom the order is made had been habitually resident in England and Wales, had received reasonable notice of the date of the hearing and had appeared at the hearing, and such information as the court possesses for facilitating the identification of that person, and ascertaining his whereabouts.

(4) Where any such provisional order has come before a court in a part of His Majesty's dominions outside the United Kingdom to which this Act extends for confirmation, and the order has by that court been remitted to the court of summary jurisdiction which made the order for the purpose of taking further evidence, that court or any other court of summary jurisdiction shall, after the prescribed notice, proceed to take the evidence in like manner and subject to the like conditions as the evidence in support of the original application.

If upon the hearing of such evidence it appears to the court that the order ought not to have been made, the court may revoke the order, but in any other case the depositions shall be sent to the Lord Chancellor and dealt with in like manner as the original depositions.

(5) The confirmation of an order made under this section shall not affect any power of a court of summary jurisdiction to vary or revoke that order:

Provided that on the making of a varying or revoking order the court shall send a certified copy thereof to the Lord Chancellor for transmission to the governor of the part of His Majesty's dominions in which the original order was confirmed, and that in the case of an order varying the original order the order shall not have any effect unless and until confirmed in like manner as the original order.

(6) The applicant shall have the same right of appeal, if any, against a refusal to make a provisional order as he would have had against a refusal to make the order had the person against whom the order is sought to be made been habitually resident in England and Wales and received reasonable notice of the date of the hearing of the application.

(7) Where subsection (1) of section 60 of the Magistrates' Courts Act 1980 (revocation, variation etc of orders for periodical payment) applies in relation to an order made under

this section which has been confirmed, that subsection shall have effect as if for the words "by order on complaint", there were substituted "on an application being made, by order".

(8) In this section "revoke" includes discharge.

Amendments—DPMCA 1978, s 89(2), Sch 2, para 2; Justices of the Peace Act 1979, s 71, Sch 2, para 1; MO(RE)A 1992, s 1, Sch 1, para 1; SI 1992/709; Justices of the Peace Act 1997, s 73(2), Sch 5, para 2; AJA 1999, s 106, Sch 15; Courts Act 2003, s 109(1), Sch 8, para 68; SI 2012/2814.

"habitually resident" (s 3(1))—The Act is amended to refer to habitual residence as part of the exercise of bringing the law into line with the Convention on the International Recovery of Child Support and other forms of Family Maintenance done at The Hague on 23 November 2007 ("the Hague Convention 2007").

Application to court of summary jurisdiction (s 3(1))—Jurisdiction is based on the residence of the applicant (see DPMCA 1978, s 30 and *Collister v Collister* [1972] 1 WLR 54). For procedure, see FPR 2010, rr 2.5, 2.7, 6.23, 6.34, 22.2, 22.4, 22.5, 23.9, 27.2, 27.3, 27.4 and PD22A.

"the order shall be provisional only" (s 3(1))—Liability to make payments cannot precede the date of registration.

"deposition" (s 3(2))—See 86 JP Jo 225 for a form of deposition.

"prescribed notice" (s 3(4))—The notice should specify the further evidence required and the date, time and place fixed for taking the evidence. The notice should be sent by the clerk to the person who applied for the provisional order.

"right of appeal" (s 3(6))—As to the right of appeal, see DPMCA 1978, s 29.

4 Power of court of summary jurisdiction to confirm maintenance order made out of the United Kingdom

(1) Where a maintenance order has been made by a court in a part of His Majesty's dominions outside the United Kingdom to which this Act extends, and the order is provisional only and has no effect unless and until confirmed by a court of summary jurisdiction in England or Ireland, and a certified copy of the order, together with the depositions of witnesses and a statement of the grounds on which the order might have been opposed has been transmitted to the Lord Chancellor, and it appears to the Lord Chancellor that the person against whom the order was made is resident in England or Ireland, the Lord Chancellor may send the said documents to the prescribed officer of a court of summary jurisdiction, with a requisition that a notice be served on the person informing him that he may attend a hearing at the time and place specified in the notice to show cause why that order should not be confirmed, and upon receipt of such documents and requisition the court shall cause such a notice to be served upon such a person.

(2) A notice required to be served under this section may be served by post.

(3) At the hearing it shall be open to the person on whom the notice was served to oppose the confirmation of the order on any grounds on which he might have opposed the making of the order in the original proceedings had he been a party to them, but on no other grounds, and the certificate from the court which made the provisional order stating the grounds on which the making of the order might have been opposed if the person against whom the order was made had been a party to the proceedings shall be conclusive evidence that those grounds are grounds on which objection may be taken.

(4) If at the hearing the person served with the notice does not appear or, on appearing, fails to satisfy the court that the order ought not to be confirmed, the court may confirm the order either without modification or with such modifications as to the court after hearing the evidence may seem just.

(5) If the person served with the notice appears at the hearing and satisfies the court that for the purpose of establishing any grounds on which he opposes the confirmation of the order it is necessary to remit the case to the court which made the provisional order for the taking of any further evidence, the court may so remit the case and adjourn the proceedings for the purpose.

(5A) Where a magistrates' court confirms a provisional order under this section, it shall at the same time exercise one of its powers under subsection (5B).

(5B) The powers of the court are –

(a) the power to order that payments under the order be made directly to a designated officer for the court or for any other magistrates' court;

(b) the power to order that payments under the order be made to a designated officer for the court or for any other magistrates' court by such method of payment falling within section 59(6) of the Magistrates' Courts Act 1980 (standing order, etc) as may be specified;

(c) the power to make an attachment of earnings order under the Attachment of Earnings Act 1971 to secure payments under the order.

(5C) In deciding which of the powers under subsection (5B) it is to exercise, the court shall have regard to any representations made by the person liable to make payments under the order.

(5D) Subsection (4) of section 59 of the Magistrates' Courts Act 1980 (power of court to require debtor to open account) shall apply for the purposes of subsection (5B) as it applies for the purposes of that section but as if for paragraph (a) there were substituted –

"(a) the court proposes to exercise its power under paragraph (b) of section 4(5B) of the Maintenance Orders (Facilities for Enforcement) Act 1920, and".

(6) Subject to subsection (6A), where a provisional order has been confirmed under this section, it may be varied or revoked in like manner as if it had originally been made by the confirming court.

(6A) Where the confirming court is a magistrates' court, section 60 of the Magistrates' Courts Act 1980 (revocation, variation etc of orders for periodical payment) shall have effect in relation to a provisional order confirmed under this section –

(za) as if in subsection (1) for the words "by order on complaint" there were substituted "on an application being made, by order";

(a) as if in subsection (3) for the words "paragraphs (a) to (d) of section 59(3) above" there were substituted "section 4(5B) of the Maintenance Orders (Facilities for Enforcement) Act 1920";

(b) as if in subsection (4) for paragraph (b) there were substituted –
"(b) payments under the order are required to be made to the designated officer for the court or for any other magistrates' court by any method of payment falling within section 59(6) above (standing order, etc)";

(c) as if in subsection (5) for the words "to the designated officer for the court" there were substituted "in accordance with paragraph (a) of section 4(5B) of the Maintenance Orders (Facilities for Enforcement) Act 1920";

(d) as if in subsection (7), paragraph (c) and the word "and" immediately preceding it were omitted;

(e) as if in subsection (8) for the words "paragraphs (a) to (d) of section 59(3) above" there were substituted "section 4(5B) of the Maintenance Orders (Facilities for Enforcement) Act 1920";

(f) as if for subsections (9) and (10) there were substituted the following subsections –

"(9) In deciding, for the purposes of subsection (3) and (8) above, which of the powers under section 4(5B) of the Maintenance Orders (Facilities for Enforcement) Act 1920 it is to exercise, the court shall have regard to any representations made by the debtor.

(10) Subsection (4) of section 59 above (power of court to require debtor to open account) shall apply for the purposes of subsections (3) and (8) above as it applies for the purposes of that section but as if for paragraph (a) there were substituted –

'(a)   the court proposes to exercise its powers under paragraph (b) of section 4(5B) of the Maintenance Orders (Facilities for Enforcement) Act 1920, and'."

(6B) Where on an application for variation or revocation the confirming court is satisfied that it is necessary to remit the case to the court which made the order for the purpose of taking any further evidence, the court may so remit the case and adjourn the proceedings for the purpose.

(7) Where an order has been so confirmed the person bound thereby shall have the same right of appeal, if any, against the confirmation of the order as he would have had against the making of the order had the order been an order made by the court confirming the order.

Amendments—MEA 1991, s 10, Sch 1, para 1; MO(RE)A 1992, s 1, Sch 1, para 2; SI 1992/709; AJA 1999, s 90, Sch 13, para 7, Sch 15; Courts Act 2003, s 109(1), Sch 8, para 69.

Scope—If the relevant law of the foreign court permits the making of an order for custody and maintenance, this may also be confirmed under the Act.

"prescribed officer" (s 4(1))—See FPR 2010, rr 34.3, 34.5–34.7 for the duties of the justices' chief executive.

Defences that may be raised (s 4(3))—Although the certificate is said to be conclusive as to the grounds of objection which may be taken, other defences have been allowed; in *Harris v Harris* [1949] 2 All ER 318, a challenge on the grounds of want of jurisdiction was allowed (see also *Re Wheat* [1932] 2 KB 716).

"standing order, etc" (s 4(5B))—This does not include the power to order payment by direct debit.

"right of appeal" (s 4(7))—As to the right of appeal, see DPMCA 1978, s 29.

Conversion to sterling—The order, on confirmation, should be converted to sterling (see Home Office Circular 469, 726/4). It is suggested that the rate of exchange applicable on the date of registration should apply throughout the life of the order.

4A Variation and revocation of maintenance orders

(1) This section applies to –

(a)   any maintenance order made by virtue of section 3 of this Act which has been confirmed as mentioned in that section; and

(b)   any maintenance order which has been confirmed under section 4 of this Act.

(2) Where the respondent to an application for the variation or revocation of a maintenance order to which this section applies is residing in a part of Her Majesty's dominions outside the United Kingdom to which this Act extends, a magistrates' court in England and Wales shall have jurisdiction to hear the application (where it would not have such jurisdiction apart from this subsection) if that court would have had jurisdiction to hear it had the respondent been habitually resident in England and Wales.

(3) Where the respondent to an application for the variation or revocation of a maintenance order to which this section applies is residing in a part of Her Majesty's dominions outside the United Kingdom to which this Act extends, a court of summary jurisdiction in Northern Ireland shall have jurisdiction to hear the application (where it

would not have such jurisdiction apart from this subsection) if that court would have had jurisdiction to hear it had the respondent been habitually resident in Northern Ireland.

(4) Where –

    (a)   the respondent to an application for the variation or revocation of a maintenance order to which this section applies does not appear at the time and place appointed for the hearing of the application by a magistrates' court in England and Wales, and

    (b)   the court is satisfied that the respondent is residing in a part of Her Majesty's dominions outside the United Kingdom to which this Act extends,

the court may proceed to hear and determine the application at the time and place appointed for the hearing or for any adjourned hearing in like manner as if the respondent had appeared at that time and place.

(5) Subsection (4) shall apply to Northern Ireland with the following modifications –

    (a), (b)   (*repealed*)

    (c)   for the words "a magistrates' court in England and Wales" there shall be substituted "a court of summary jurisdiction in Northern Ireland".

(6) In this section "revocation" includes "discharge".

Amendments—Inserted by MO(RE)A 1992, s 1, Sch 1, para 3; amended by SI 1995/755; SI 2012/2814.

5 Power of Lord Chancellor to make regulations for facilitating communications between courts

The Lord Chancellor may make regulations as to the manner in which a case can be remitted by a court authorised to confirm a provisional order to the court which made the provisional order, and generally for facilitating communications between such courts.

Amendments—SI 1992/709.

Regulations—No regulations have yet been made in exercise of this power.

6 Mode of enforcing orders

(1) A court of summary jurisdiction in which an order has been registered under this Act or by which an order has been confirmed under this Act, and the officers of such court, shall take all such steps for enforcing the order as may be prescribed.

(2) Every such order shall be enforceable in like manner as if the order were for the payment of a civil debt recoverable summarily;

Provided that, if the order is of such a nature that if made by the court in which it is so registered, or by which it is so confirmed, it would be enforceable in like manner as an order of affiliation, the order shall, subject to the modifications of sections 76 and 93 of the Magistrates' Courts Act 1980 (enforcement of sums adjudged to be paid and complaint for arrears) specified in subsections (2ZA) and (2ZB) of section 18 of the Maintenance Orders Act 1950 (enforcement of registered orders), be so enforceable.

(3) A warrant of distress or commitment issued by a court of summary jurisdiction for the purpose of enforcing any order so registered or confirmed may be executed in any part of the United Kingdom in the same manner as if the warrant had been originally issued or subsequently endorsed by a court of summary jurisdiction having jurisdiction in the place where the warrant is executed.

Amendments—MEA 1991, s 10, Sch 1, para 2.

"subsections (2ZA) and (2ZB) of section 18 of the Maintenance Orders Act 1950" (s 6(2))—These sections modify the means of payments orders available on variation and restrict the use of imprisonment for enforcement where the court is of the view that it is appropriate to make an attachment of earnings order or an order for payment by standing order.

7 Application of Summary Jurisdiction Acts

(1) The Summary Jurisdiction Acts shall apply to proceedings before courts of summary jurisdiction under this Act in like manner as they apply to proceedings under those Acts.

(2) For the purpose of giving effect to this Act rules of court may make, in relation to any proceedings brought under or by virtue of this Act, any provision which –

    (a)   falls within subsection (2) of section 93 of the Children Act 1989, and

    (b)   may be made in relation to relevant proceedings under that section.

Amendments—Justices of the Peace Act 1949, s 46(2), Sch 7, Pt II; MO(RE)A 1992, s 1, Sch 1, para 4; Courts Act 2003, s 109(1), Sch 8, para 70.

8 Proof of documents signed by officers of court

Any documents purporting to be signed by a judge or officer of a court outside the United Kingdom shall, until the contrary is proved, be deemed to have been so signed without proof of the signature or judicial or official character of the person appearing to have signed it, and the officer of a court by whom a document is signed shall, until the contrary is proved, be deemed to have been the proper officer of the court to sign the document.

9 Depositions to be evidence

Depositions taken in a court in a part of His Majesty's dominions outside the United Kingdom to which this Act extends for the purposes of this Act, may be received in evidence in proceedings before courts of summary jurisdiction under this Act.

10 Interpretation

For the purposes of this Act, the expression "maintenance order" means an order other than an order of affiliation for the periodical payment of sums of money towards the maintenance of the wife or other dependants of the person against whom the order is made, and the expression "dependants" means such persons as that person is, according to the law in force in the part of His Majesty's dominions in which the maintenance order was made, liable to maintain; the expression "certified copy" in relation to an order of a court means a copy of the order certified by the proper officer of the court to be a true copy, and the expression "prescribed" means prescribed by rules of court.

"rules of court"—The rules of court for the purposes of the Act are FPR 2010, rr 34.5–34.11.

****

12 Extent of Act

(1) Where His Majesty is satisfied that reciprocal provisions have been made by the legislature of any part of His Majesty's dominions outside the United Kingdom for the enforcement within that part of maintenance orders made by courts within England and Ireland, His Majesty may by Order in Council extend this Act to that part, and thereupon that part shall become a part of His Majesty's dominions to which this Act extends.

(2) His Majesty may by Order in Council extend this Act to any British protectorate and where so extended this Act shall apply as if any such protectorate was a party of His Majesty's dominions to which this Act extends.

"dominions to which this Act extends"—See **Areas to which the Act extends** under s 1.

****

Maintenance Orders (Reciprocal Enforcement) Act 1972

PART II

ARRANGEMENT OF SECTIONS

PART I
RECIPROCAL ENFORCEMENT OF MAINTENANCE ORDERS MADE IN UNITED KINGDOM OR RECIPROCATING COUNTRY

PART II
RECIPROCAL ENFORCEMENT OF CLAIMS FOR THE RECOVERY OF MAINTENANCE

Convention countries

Application by person in the United Kingdom for recovery etc of maintenance in Convention country

Application by person in Convention country for recovery of maintenance in England, Wales or Northern Ireland

Transfer, enforcement, variation and revocation of registered orders

Supplemental

PART II

PART I
RECIPROCAL ENFORCEMENT OF MAINTENANCE ORDERS MADE IN UNITED KINGDOM OR RECIPROCATING COUNTRY

Designation of reciprocating countries

1 Orders in Council designating reciprocating countries

(1) Her Majesty, if satisfied that, in the event of the benefits conferred by this Part of this Act being applied to, or to particular classes of, maintenance orders made by the courts of any country or territory outside the United Kingdom, similar benefits will in that country or territory be applied to, or to those classes of, maintenance orders made by the courts of the United Kingdom, may by Order in Council designate that country or territory as a reciprocating country for the purposes of this Part of this Act; and, subject to subsection (2) below, in this Part of this Act "reciprocating country" means a country or territory that is for the time being so designated.

(2) A country or territory may be designated under subsection (1) above as a reciprocating country either as regards maintenance orders generally, or as regards maintenance orders other than those of any specified class, or as regards maintenance orders of one or more specified classes only; and a country or territory which is for the time being so designated otherwise than as regards maintenance orders generally shall for the purposes of this Part of this Act be taken to be a reciprocating country only as regards maintenance orders of the class to which the designation extends.

Modifications—In relation to the USA and Hague Convention countries, to which the Maintenance Regulation (EC) No 4/2009 does not apply, the provisions of this Act are excepted, adapted and modified as summarised in FPR PD34A.

Defined terms—"court", "maintenance order": s 21(1); "reciprocating country": s 1(1).

"may by Order in Council designate" (s 1(1))—The Reciprocal Enforcement of Maintenance Orders (Designation of Reciprocating Countries) Order 1974 has been made for this purpose. It is important to note that a country does not become a reciprocating country for the purposes of this Act merely by acceding to the 1956 UN Convention on the Recovery Abroad of Maintenance as, for example, the Ukraine did in 2006. It is necessary for the UK Government to make an Order under the Act designating the country in question.

Orders made by courts in the United Kingdom

2 Transmission of maintenance order made in United Kingdom for enforcement in reciprocating country

(1) Subject to subsection (2) below, where the payer under a maintenance order made, whether before or after the commencement of this Part of this Act, by a court in the United Kingdom is residing or has assets in a reciprocating country, the payee under the order may apply for the order to be sent to that country for enforcement.

(2) Subsection (1) above shall not have effect in relation to a provisional order or to an order made by virtue of a provision of Part II of this Act.

(3) Every application under this section shall be made in the prescribed manner to the prescribed officer of the court which made the maintenance order to which the application relates.

(4) If, on an application duly made under this section to the prescribed officer of a court in the United Kingdom, that officer is satisfied that the payer under the maintenance order to which the application relates is residing or has assets in a reciprocating country, the following documents, that is to say –

  (a) a certified copy of the maintenance order;
  (b) a certificate signed by that officer certifying that the order is enforceable in the United Kingdom;
  (c) a certificate of arrears so signed;
  (d) a statement giving such information as the officer possesses as to the whereabouts of the payer and the nature and location of his assets in that country;
  (e) a statement giving such information as the officer possesses for facilitating the identification of the payer; and
  (f) where available, a photograph of the payer;

shall be sent by that officer to the Lord Chancellor with a view to their being transmitted by the Lord Chancellor to the responsible authority in the reciprocating country if he is satisfied that the statement relating to the whereabouts of the payer and the nature and location of his assets in that country gives sufficient information to justify that being done.

(5) Nothing in this section shall be taken as affecting any jurisdiction of a court in the United Kingdom with respect to a maintenance order to which this section applies, and any such order may be enforced, varied or revoked accordingly.

Amendments—CJJA 1982, s 37(1), Sch 11, para 9; SI 1992/709.

Defined terms—"certificate of arrears", "certified copy", "court", "maintenance order", "payee", "payer", "provisional order": s 21(1); "reciprocating country": s 1(1).

"reciprocating country"—For Hague Convention countries, see REMO(HCC)O 1993; for the USA, see REMO(USA)O 2007, summarised in FPR PD34A.

"habitually resident" (s 3(1)(a))—The Act is amended to refer to habitual residence as part of the exercise of bringing the law into line with the Hague Convention 2007).

"prescribed manner" (s 2(3))—See FPR 2010, rr 34.14 and PD34A.

"prescribed officer" (s 2(3),(4))—See FPR 2010, r 34.2.

3 Power of magistrates' court to make provisional maintenance order against person residing in reciprocating country

(1) Where an application is made to a magistrates' court for a maintenance order against a person residing in a reciprocating country and the court would have jurisdiction to

determine the application under the Domestic Proceedings and Magistrates' Courts Act 1978 or the Children Act 1989 if that person –

   (a)   were habitually resident in England and Wales, and

   (b)   received reasonable notice of the date of the hearing of the application,

the court shall (subject to subsection (2) below) have jurisdiction to determine the application.

(2) A maintenance order made by virtue of this section shall be a provisional order.

(3) (*repealed*)

(4) No enactment (or provision made under an enactment) requiring or enabling –

   (a)   a court to transfer proceedings from a magistrates' court to a county court or the High Court, or

   (b)   a magistrates' court to refuse to make an order on an application on the ground that any matter in question is one that would be more conveniently dealt with by the High Court,

shall apply in relation to an application to which subsection (1) above applies.

(5) Where a court makes a maintenance order which is by virtue of this section a provisional order, the following documents, that is to say –

   (a)   a certified copy of the maintenance order;

   (b)   a document, authenticated in the prescribed manner, setting out or summarising the evidence given in the proceedings;

   (c)   a certificate signed by the prescribed officer of the court certifying that the grounds stated in the certificate are the grounds on which the making of the order might have been opposed by the payer under the order;

   (d)   a statement giving such information as was available to the court as to the whereabouts of the payer;

   (e)   a statement giving such information as the officer possesses for facilitating the identification of the payer, and

   (f)   where available, a photograph of the payer;

shall be sent by that officer to the Lord Chancellor with a view to their being transmitted by the Lord Chancellor to the responsible authority in the reciprocating country in which the payer is residing if he is satisfied that the statement relating to the whereabouts of the payer gives sufficient information to justify that being done.

(6) A maintenance order made by virtue of this section which has been confirmed by a competent court in a reciprocating country shall be treated for all purposes as if the magistrates' court which made the order had made it in the form in which it was confirmed and as if the order had never been a provisional order, and subject to section 5 of this Act, any such order may be enforced, varied or revoked accordingly.

(7) In the application of this section to Northern Ireland –

   (a)   for subsection (1) there shall be substituted –

"(1) Where an application is made to a magistrates' court against a person residing in a reciprocating country and the court would have jurisdiction to determine the application under the Domestic Proceedings (Northern Ireland) Order 1980 or the Children (Northern Ireland) Order 1995 if that person –

   (a)   were habitually resident in Northern Ireland, and

   (b)   received reasonable notice of the date of the hearing of the application,

the court shall (subject to subsection (2) below) have jurisdiction to determine the application.";

PART II

(b) in subsection (4), for references to the High Court there shall be substituted references to the High Court of Justice in Northern Ireland.

Amendments—FLRA 1987, s 33(4), Sch 4; MO(RE)A 1992, s 1, Sch 1, para 6; SI 1992/709; SI 1995/755; SI 2012/2814.

Defined terms—"certified copy", "court": s 21(1); "jurisdiction": s 47(3); "maintenance order", "payer", "provisional order": s 21(1); "reciprocating country": s 1(1); "responsible authority": s 21(1).

"prescribed manner" (s 3(5)(b))—See FPR 2010, r 35.15.

"prescribed officer" (s 3(5))—See FPR 2010, r 35.2.

****

5 Variation and revocation of maintenance order made in United Kingdom

(1) This section applies to a maintenance order a certified copy of which has been sent to a reciprocating country in pursuance of section 2 of this Act and to a maintenance order made by virtue of section 3 or 4 thereof which has been confirmed by a competent court in such a country.

(2) A court in the United Kingdom having power to vary a maintenance order to which this section applies shall have power to vary that order by a provisional order.

(3) Where the court hearing an application for the variation of a maintenance order to which this section applies proposes to vary it by increasing the rate of the payments under the order then, unless either –

(a) both the payer and the payee under the order appear in the proceedings, or
(b) the applicant appears and the appropriate process has been duly served on the other party,

the order varying the order shall be a provisional order.

(3A) Where subsection (1) of section 60 of the Magistrates' Courts Act 1980 (revocation, variation etc of orders for periodical payment) applies in relation to a maintenance order to which this section applies, that subsection shall have effect as if for the words "by order on complaint", there were substituted "on an application being made, by order".

(3B) Where paragraph (1) of Article 86 of the Magistrates' Courts (Northern Ireland) Order 1981 applies in relation to a maintenance order to which this section applies, that paragraph shall have effect as if for the words "by order on complaint," there were substituted "on an application being made, by order".

(4) Where a court in the United Kingdom makes a provisional order varying a maintenance order to which this section applies, the prescribed officer of the court shall send in the prescribed manner to the court in a reciprocating country having power to confirm the provisional order a certified copy of the provisional order together with a document, authenticated in the prescribed manner, setting out or summarising the evidence given in the proceedings.

(5) Where a certified copy of a provisional order made by a court in a reciprocating country, being an order varying or revoking a maintenance order, to which this section applies, together with a document, duly authenticated, setting out or summarising the evidence given in the proceedings in which the provisional order was made, is received by the court in the United Kingdom which made the maintenance order, that court may confirm or refuse to confirm the provisional order and, if that order is an order varying the maintenance order, confirm it either without alteration or with such alterations as it thinks reasonable.

(6) For the purpose of determining whether a provisional order should be confirmed under subsection (5) above, the court shall proceed as if an application for the variation or revocation, as the case may be, of the maintenance order in question, had been made to it.

(7) Where a maintenance order to which this section applies has been varied by an order (including a provisional order which has been confirmed) made by a court in the United Kingdom or by a competent court in a reciprocating country, the maintenance order shall, as, from the date on which under the provisions of the order the variation is to take effect, have effect as varied by that order and, where that order was a provisional order, as if that order had been made in the form in which it was confirmed, and as if it had never been a provisional order.

(8) Where a maintenance order to which this section applies has been revoked by an order made by a court in the United Kingdom or by a competent court in a reciprocating country, including a provisional order made by the last-mentioned court which has been confirmed by a court in the United Kingdom, the maintenance order shall, as from the date on which under the provisions of the order the revocation is to take effect, be deemed to have ceased to have effect except as respects any arrears due under the maintenance order at that date.

(9) Where before a maintenance order made by virtue of section 3 or 4 of this Act is confirmed a document, duly authenticated, setting out or summarising evidence taken in a reciprocating country for the purpose of proceedings relating to the confirmation of the order is received by the court in the United Kingdom which made the order, or that court, in compliance with a request made to it by a court in such a country, takes the evidence of a person residing in the United Kingdom for the purpose of such proceedings, the court in the United Kingdom which made the order shall consider that evidence and if, having done so, it appears to it that the order ought not to have been made –

    (a)   it shall, in such manner as may be prescribed, give to the person on whose application the maintenance order was made an opportunity to consider that evidence, to make representations with respect to it and to adduce further evidence; and

    (b)   after considering all the evidence and any representations made by that person, it may revoke the maintenance order.

(10) ...

Amendments—DPMCA 1978, s 54; MO(RE)A 1992, s 1, Sch 1, para 7; SI 1995/755.

Defined terms—"certified copy", "court", "maintenance order", "payee", "payer", "provisional order": s 21(1); "reciprocating country": s 1(1).

"prescribed officer" (s 5(4))—See FPR 2010, rr 34.2, 34.15.

"prescribed manner" (s 5(4)—See FPR 2010, rr 34.15, 34.18, 34.22.

"court may confirm or refuse to confirm" (s 5(5))—The discretion is as wide as if the application had been made to that court (*Horn v Horn* [1985] FLR 984).

"prescribed" (s 5(9)(a))—See FPR 2010, r 34.17.

Orders made by courts in reciprocating countries

6 Registration in United Kingdom court of maintenance order made in reciprocating country

(1) This section applies to a maintenance order made, whether before or after the commencement of this Part of this Act, by a court in a reciprocating country, including

PART II

such an order made by such a court which has been confirmed by a court in another reciprocating country but excluding a provisional order which has not been confirmed.

(2) Where a certified copy of an order to which this section applies is received by the Lord Chancellor from the responsible authority in a reciprocating country, and it appears to the Lord Chancellor that the payer under the order is residing or has assets in the United Kingdom, he shall send the copy of the order to the prescribed officer of the appropriate court.

(3) Where the prescribed officer of the appropriate court receives from the Lord Chancellor a certified copy of an order to which this section applies, he shall, subject to subsection (4) below, register the order in the prescribed manner in that court.

(4) Before registering an order under this section an officer of a court shall take such steps as he thinks fit for the purpose of ascertaining whether the payer under the order is residing or has assets within the jurisdiction of the court, and if after taking those steps he is satisfied that the payer is not residing and has no assets within the jurisdiction of the court he shall return the certified copy of the order to the Lord Chancellor with a statement giving such information as he possesses as to the whereabouts of the payer and the nature and location of his assets.

Amendments—CJJA 1982, s 37(1), Sch 11, para 10; SI 1992/709.

Defined terms—"appropriate court", "certified copy", "court", "maintenance order", "payer", "provisional order": s 21(1); "reciprocating country": s 1(1); "responsible authority": s 21(1).

"prescribed officer" (s 6(2))—See FPR 2010, r 34.2.

"prescribed manner" (s 6(3))—See FPR 2010, r 34.3.

7 Confirmation by United Kingdom court of provisional maintenance order made in reciprocating country

(1) This section applies to a maintenance order made, whether before or after the commencement of this Part of this Act, by a court in a reciprocating country being a provisional order.

(2) Where a certified copy of an order to which this section applies together with –

(a) a document, duly authenticated, setting out or summarising the evidence given in the proceedings in which the order was made; and

(b) a statement of the grounds on which the making of the order might have been opposed by the payer under the order,

is received by the Lord Chancellor from the responsible authority in a reciprocating country, and it appears to the Lord Chancellor that the payer under the order is residing in the United Kingdom, he shall send the copy of the order and documents which accompanied it to the prescribed officer of the appropriate court, and that court shall –

(i) if the payer under the order establishes any grounds on which he might have opposed the making of the order in the proceedings in which the order was made, refuse to confirm the order; and

(ii) in any other case, confirm the order either without alteration or with such alterations as it thinks reasonable.

(3) In any proceedings for the confirmation under this section of a provisional order the statement received from the court which made the order of the grounds on which the making of the order might have been opposed by the payer under the order shall be conclusive evidence that the payer might have opposed the making of the order on any of those grounds.

(4) For the purpose of determining whether a provisional order should be confirmed under this section a magistrates' court in Northern Ireland shall proceed as if an application for a maintenance order against the payer under the provisional order had been made to it.

(5) The prescribed officer of a court having power under this section to confirm a provisional order shall, if the court confirms the order, register the order in the prescribed manner in that court, and shall, if the court refuses to confirm the order, return the certified copy of the order and the documents which accompanied it to the Lord Chancellor.

(5A) Where a magistrates' court in England and Wales confirms a provisional order under this section, it shall at the same time exercise one of its powers under subsection (5B) below.

(5B) The powers of the court are –

    (a)   the power to order that payments under the order be made directly to the designated officer for the court or for any other magistrates' court in England and Wales;

    (b)   the power to order that payments under the order be made to the designated officer for the court or for any other magistrates' court in England and Wales by such method of payment falling within section 59(6) of the Magistrates' Courts Act 1980 (standing order, etc) as may be specified;

    (c)   the power to make an attachment of earnings order under the Attachment of Earnings Act 1971 to secure payments under the order.

(5C) In deciding which of the powers under subsection (5B) above it is to exercise, the court shall have regard to any representations made by the payer under the order.

(5D) Subsection (4) of section 59 of the Magistrates' Courts Act 1980 (power of court to require debtor to open account) shall apply for the purposes of subsection (5B) above as it applies for the purposes of that section but as if for paragraph (a) there were substituted –

       "(a)   the court proposes to exercise its power under paragraph (b) of section 7(5B) of the Maintenance Orders (Reciprocal Enforcement) Act 1972, and".

(5E) Where a court of summary jurisdiction in Northern Ireland confirms a provisional order under this section, it shall at the same time exercise one of its powers under subsection (5F) below.

(5F) The powers of the court are –

    (a)   the power to order that payments under the order be made directly to the collecting officer;

    (b)   the power to order that payments under the order be made to the collecting officer, by such method of payment falling within Article 85(7) of the Magistrates' Court (Northern Ireland) Order 1981 (standing order, etc) as may be specified;

    (c)   the power to make an attachment of earnings order under Part IX of the Order of 1981 to secure payments under the order;

and in this subsection "collecting officer" means the officer mentioned in Article 85(4) of the Order of 1981.

(5G) In deciding which of the powers under subsection (5F) above it is to exercise, the court shall have regard to any representations made by the payer under the order.

(5H) Paragraph (5) of Article 85 of the Magistrates' Courts (Northern Ireland) Order 1981 (power of court to require debtor to open account) shall apply for the purposes of subsection (5F) above as it applies for the purposes of that Article but as if for sub-paragraph (a) there were substituted –

"(a) the court proposes to exercise its powers under paragraph (b) of section 7(5F) of the Maintenance Orders (Reciprocal Enforcement) Act 1972, and".

(6) If notice of the proceedings for the confirmation of the provisional order cannot be duly served on the payer under that order the officer by whom the certified copy of the order was received shall return that copy and the documents which accompanied it to the Lord Chancellor with a statement giving such information as he possesses as to the whereabouts of the payer.

(7) …

(8) (*repealed*)

Amendments—MEA 1991, s 10, Sch 1, para 12; MO(RE)A 1992, s 1, Sch 1, para 8; SI 1992/709; SI 1993/1576; SI 1995/755; AJA 1999, s 90, Sch 13, para 72; Courts Act 2003, s 109(1), Sch 8, para 151.

Defined terms—"court", "maintenance order", "payer", "provisional order": s 21(1); "reciprocating country": s 1(1); "responsible authority": s 21(1).

"prescribed officer" (s 7(2),(5))—See FPR 2010, r 34.2.

Alteration of order (s 7(2)(ii))—The laws of the reciprocating country are to be applied to the making of the order (*Peagram v Peagram* [1926] 2 KB 165; *Harris v Harris* [1949] 2 All ER 318).

"statement … shall be conclusive evidence" (s 7(3))—The statement of possible grounds of opposition received from the reciprocating country does not prevent other defences being raised (*Re Wheat* [1932] 2 KB 716; see also *Harris v Harris* (above), where the payer was permitted to raise the issue of jurisdiction).

"prescribed manner" (s 7(5))—See FPR 2010, r 34.3.

"standing order, etc" (s 7(5B)(b),(5E)(b))—The methods of payment available do not include power to order payment by direct debit.

8 Enforcement of maintenance order registered in United Kingdom court

(1) Subject to subsection (2) below, a registered order may be enforced in the United Kingdom as if it had been made by the registering court and as if that court had had jurisdiction to make it; and proceedings for or with respect to the enforcement of any such order may be taken accordingly.

(2) Subsection (1) above does not apply to an order which is for the time being registered in the High Court under Part I of the Maintenance Orders Act 1958 or to an order which is for the time being registered in the High Court of Justice in Northern Ireland under Part II of the Maintenance and Affiliation Orders Act (Northern Ireland) 1966.

(3) Any person for the time being under an obligation to make payments in pursuance of a registered order shall give notice of any change of address to the clerk of the registering court, and any person failing without reasonable excuse to give such a notice shall be liable on summary conviction to a fine not exceeding level 2 on the standard scale.

(3A) …

(4) An order which by virtue of this section is enforceable by a magistrates' court shall subject to the modifications of sections 76 and 93 of the Magistrates' Courts Act 1980 specified in subsections (4A) and (4B) below be enforceable as if it were a magistrates' court maintenance order made by that court.

In this subsection "magistrates' court maintenance order" has the same meaning as in s 150(1) of the Magistrates' Courts Act 1980.

(4A) Section 76 (enforcement of sums adjudged to be paid) shall have effect as if for subsections (4) to (6) there were substituted the following subsections –

"(4) Where proceedings are brought for the enforcement of a magistrates' court maintenance order under this section, the court may vary the order by exercising one of its powers under subsection (5) below.

(5) The powers of the court are –

(a) the power to order that payments under the order be made directly to the designated officer for the court or for any other magistrates' court;

(b) the power to order that payments under the order be made to the designated officer for the court or for any other magistrates' court by such method of payment falling within section 59(6) above (standing order, etc) as may be specified;

(c) the power to make an attachment of earnings order under the Attachment of Earnings Act 1971 to secure payments under the order.

(6) In deciding which of the powers under subsection (5) above it is to exercise, the court shall have regard to any representations made by the debtor (within the meaning of section 59 above).

(7) Subsection (4) of section 59 above (power of court to require debtor to open account) shall apply for the purposes of subsection (5) above as it applies for the purposes of that section but as if for paragraph (a) there were substituted –

'(a) the court proposes to exercise its power under paragraph (b) of section 76(5) below, and'."

(4B) In section 93 (complaint for arrears), subsection (6) (court not to impose imprisonment in certain circumstances) shall have effect as if for paragraph (b) there were substituted –

"(b) if the court is of the opinion that it is appropriate –

(i) to make an attachment of earnings order; or

(ii) to exercise its power under paragraph (b) of section 76(5) above."

(5) The magistrates' court by which an order is enforceable by virtue of this section, and the officers thereof, shall take all such steps for enforcing the order as may be prescribed.

(6) In any proceedings for or with respect to the enforcement of an order which is for the time being registered in any court under this Part of this Act a certificate of arrears sent to the prescribed officer of the court shall be evidence of the facts stated therein.

(7) Subject to subsection (8) below, sums of money payable under a registered order shall be payable in accordance with the order as from the date on which they are required to be paid under the provisions of the order.

(8) The court having power under section 7 of this Act to confirm a provisional order may, if it decides to confirm the order, direct that the sums of money payable under it shall be deemed to have been payable in accordance with the order as from the date on which they are required to be paid under the provisions of the order or such later date as it may specify; and subject to any such direction, a maintenance order registered under the said section 7 shall be treated as if it had been made in the form in which it was confirmed and as if it had never been a provisional order.

(9) ...

(10) (*repealed*)

Amendments—DPMCA 1978, s 54; SI 1981/1675; Criminal Justice Act 1982, s 46; CJJA 1982, s 37(1), Sch 11, para 11; FLRA 1987, s 33(1), Sch 2, para 45; MEA 1991, s 10, Sch 1, para 13; AJA 1999, s 90, Sch 13, para 73; Courts Act 2003, Sch 8, para 152.

Defined terms—"certificate of arrears", "maintenance order", "provisional order", "registered order", "registering court": s 21(1).

Application to Northern Ireland—Enforcement in Northern Ireland is effected under a modified Magistrates' Court (Northern Ireland) Order 1981. The provisions are similar to the powers outlined here but reference should be made to the Family Law (Northern Ireland) Order 1993.

"standing order, etc" (s 8(4A))—The methods of payment available do not include power to order payment by direct debit.

"prescribed" (s 8(5))—See FPR 2010, r 34.24.

"prescribed officer" (s 8(6))—See FPR 2010, r 34.2.

Payment of monies collected—Monies collected are to be sent to the court that made the order, except for the following countries and territories: Gibraltar, Barbados, Bermuda, Ghana, Kenya, Fiji, Hong Kong, Singapore, Turks and Caicos Islands, Tanzania (except for Zanzibar), Anguilla, Falkland Islands and dependencies, St Helena. In the case of these territories, monies are payable through the Crown Agents for Overseas Governments and Territories.

9 Variation and revocation of maintenance order registered in United Kingdom court

(1) Subject to the provisions of this section, the registering court –

    (a)   shall have the like power, on an application made by the payer or payee under a registered order, to vary or revoke the order as if it had been made by the registering court and as if that court had had jurisdiction to make it; and

    (b)   shall have power to vary or revoke a registered order by a provisional order.

(1ZA) Where the registering court is a magistrates' court in England and Wales, section 60 of the Magistrates' Courts Act 1980 (revocation, variation etc of orders for periodical payment) shall have effect in relation to the registered order –

    (za) as if in subsection (1) for the words "by order on complaint", there were substituted "on an application being made, by order";

    (a)   as if in subsection (3) for the words "paragraphs (a) to (d) of section 59(3) above" there were substituted "subsection (3A) below" and after that subsection there were inserted –

"(3A) The powers of the court are –

    (a)   the power to order that payments under the order be made directly to the designated officer for the court or for any other magistrates' court;

    (b)   the power to order that payments under the order be made to a the designated officer for the court or for any other magistrates' court by such method of payment falling within section 59(6) above (standing order, etc) as may be specified;

    (c)   the power to make an attachment of earnings order under the Attachment of Earnings Act 1971 to secure payments under the order.";

    (b)   as if in subsection (4) for paragraph (b) there were substituted –

"(b) payments under the order are required to be made to the designated officer for the court or for any other magistrates' court by any method of payment falling within section 59(6) above (standing order, etc)";

    (c)   as if in subsection (5) for the words "to the designated officer for the court" there were substituted "in accordance with paragraph (a) of subsection (3A) above";

    (d)   as if in subsection (7), paragraph (c) and the word "and" immediately preceding it were omitted;

    (e)   as if in subsection (8) for the words "paragraphs (a) to (d) of section 59(3) above" there were substituted "subsection (3A) above";

(f) as if for subsections (9) and (10) there were substituted the following subsections –

"(9) In deciding, for the purposes of subsections (3) and (8) above, which of the powers under subsection (3A) above it is to exercise, the court shall have regard to any representations made by the debtor.

(10) Subsection (4) of section 59 above (power of court to require debtor to open account) shall apply for the purposes of subsection (3A) above as it applies for the purposes of that section but as if for paragraph (a) there were substituted –

'(a) the court proposes to exercise its power under paragraph (b) of section 60(3A) below, and'."

(1ZB) Where the registering court is a court of summary jurisdiction in Northern Ireland, Article 86 of the Magistrates' Courts (Northern Ireland) Order 1981 (revocation, variation etc, of orders for periodical payment) shall have effect in relation to the registered order –

(za) as if in paragraph (1) for the words "by order on complaint," there were substituted "on an application being made, by order";

(a) as if in paragraph (3) for the words "sub-paragraphs (a) to (d) of Article 85(3)" there were substituted "paragraph (3A)" and after that paragraph there were inserted –

"(3A) The powers of the court are –

(a) the power to order that payments under the order be made directly to the collecting officer;

(b) the power to order that payments under the order be made to the collecting officer by such method of payment falling within Article 85(7) (standing order, etc) as may be specified;

(c) the power to make an attachment of earnings order under Part IX to secure payments under the order.";

(b) as if in paragraph (4) for sub-paragraph (b) there were substituted –

"(b) payments under the order are required to be made to the collecting officer by any method of payment falling within Article 85(7) (standing order, etc)";

and as if after the words "petty sessions" there were inserted "for the petty sessions district for which the court which made the order acts";

(c) as if in paragraph (5) for the words "to the collecting officer" there were substituted "in accordance with sub-paragraph (a) of paragraph (3A)";

(d) as if in paragraph (7), sub-paragraph (c) and the word "and" immediately preceding it were omitted;

(e) as if in paragraph (8) for the words "sub-paragraphs (a) to (d) of Article 85(3)" there were substituted "paragraph (3A)";

(f) as if for paragraphs (9) and (10) there were substituted the following paragraphs –

"(9) In deciding, for the purposes of paragraphs (3) and (8), which of the powers under paragraph (3A) it is to exercise, the court shall have regard to any representations made by the debtor.

(10) Paragraph (5) of Article 85 (power of court to require debtor to open account) shall apply for the purposes of paragraph (3A) as it applies for the purposes of that Article but as if for sub-paragraph (a) there were substituted –

'(a) the court proposes to exercise its powers under sub-paragraph (b) of Article 86(3A), and'.".

(2) The registering court shall not vary a registered order otherwise than by a provisional order unless –

(a) both the payer and the payee under the registered order are for the time being residing in the United Kingdom; or

(b) the application is made by the payee under the registered order; or

(c) the variation consists of a reduction in the rate of the payments under the registered order and is made solely on the ground that there has been a change in the financial circumstances of the payer since the registered order was made or, in the case of an order registered under section 7 of this Act, since the registered order was confirmed, and the courts in the reciprocating country in which the maintenance order in question was made do not have power, according to the law in force in that country, to confirm provisional orders varying maintenance orders.

(3) The registering court shall not revoke a registered order otherwise than by a provisional order unless both the payer and the payee under the registered order are for the time being residing in the United Kingdom.

(4) On an application for the revocation of a registered order the registering court shall, unless both the payer and the payee under the registered order are for the time being residing in the United Kingdom, apply the law applied by the reciprocating country in which the registered order was made; but where by virtue of this subsection the registering court is required to apply that law, that court may make a provisional order if it has reason to believe that the ground on which the application is made is a ground on which the order could be revoked according to the law applied by the reciprocating country, notwithstanding that it has not been established that it is such a ground.

(5) Where the registering court makes a provisional order varying or revoking a registered order the prescribed officer of the court shall send in the prescribed manner to the court in the reciprocating country which made the registered order a certified copy of the provisional order together with a document, authenticated in the prescribed manner, setting out or summarising the evidence given in the proceedings.

(6) Where a certified copy of a provisional order made by a court in a reciprocating country, being an order varying a registered order, together with a document, duly authenticated, setting out or summarising the evidence given in the proceedings in which the provisional order was made, is received by the registering court, that court may confirm the order either without alteration or with such alterations as it thinks reasonable or refuse to confirm the order.

(7) For the purpose of determining whether a provisional order should be confirmed under subsection (6) above the court shall proceed as if an application for the variation of the registered order had been made to it.

(8) Where a registered order has been varied by an order (including a provisional order which has been confirmed) made by a court in the United Kingdom or by a competent court in a reciprocating country, the registered order shall, as from the date on which under the provisions of the order the variation is to take effect, have effect as varied by that order and, where that order was a provisional order, as if that order had been made in the form in which it was confirmed and as if it had never been a provisional order.

(9) Where a registered order has been revoked by an order made by a court in the United Kingdom or by a competent court in a reciprocating country, including a provisional order made by the first-mentioned court which has been confirmed by a competent court in a reciprocating country, the registered order shall, as from the date on which under the provisions of the order the revocation is to take effect, be deemed to have ceased to have effect except as respects any arrears due under the registered order at that date.

(10) The prescribed officer of the registering court shall register in the prescribed manner any order varying a registered order other than a provisional order which is not confirmed.

(11) ...

Amendments—DPMCA 1978, s 54; CJJA 1982, s 37(1), Sch 11, paras 4, 12; MEA 1991, s 10, Sch 1, para 14; MO(RE)A 1992, s 1, Sch 1, para 9; SI 1993/1576; SI 1995/755; AJA 1999, s 90, Sch 13, para 74, Sch 15; Courts Act 2003, Sch 8, para 153.

Defined terms—"payee", "payer", "provisional order": s 21(1); "reciprocating country": s 1(1); "registered order", "registering court": s 21(1).

"standing order, etc" (s 9(1ZA))—See under s 7.

"prescribed officer" (s 9(5),(10))—See FPR 2010, r 34.2.

"prescribed manner" (s 9(10))—See FPR 2010, rr 34.18, 34.19.

"the powers of the court" (s 9(1))—On an application to vary or revoke a registered maintenance order, a magistrates' court does not have the power to award costs (*MSJ v BKJ* [1999] EWHC 374 (Admin)) although it does have that power in relation to enforcement proceedings.

10 Cancellation of registration and transfer of order

(1) Where –

(a) a registered order is revoked by an order made by the registering court; or
(b) a registered order is revoked by a provisional order made by that court which has been confirmed by a court in a reciprocating country and notice of the confirmation is received by the registering court; or
(c) a registered order is revoked by an order made by a court in such a country and notice of the revocation is received by the registering court,

the prescribed officer of the registering court shall cancel the registration; but any arrears due under the registered order at the date when its registration is cancelled by virtue of this subsection shall continue to be recoverable as if the registration had not been cancelled.

(2) Where the prescribed officer of the registering court is of opinion that the payer under a registered order is not residing within the jurisdiction of that court and has no assets within that jurisdiction against which the order can be effectively enforced, he shall cancel the registration of the order and, subject to subsection (3) below, shall send the certified copy of the order to the Lord Chancellor.

(3) Where the prescribed officer of the registering court, being a magistrates' court, is of opinion that the payer is residing or has assets within the jurisdiction of another magistrates' court in that part of the United Kingdom in which the registering court is, he shall transfer the order to that other court by sending the certified copy of the order to the prescribed officer of that other court.

(4) On the transfer of the order under subsection (3) above the prescribed officer of the court to which it is transferred shall, subject to subsection (6) below, register the order in the prescribed manner in that court.

(5) Where the certified copy of an order is received by the Lord Chancellor under this section and it appears to him that the payer under the order is residing or has assets in the United Kingdom, he shall transfer the order to the appropriate court by sending the certified copy of the order together with the related documents to the prescribed officer of the appropriate court and, subject to subsection (6) below, that officer shall register the order in the prescribed manner in that court.

(6) Before registering an order in pursuance of subsection (4) or (5) above an officer of a court shall take such steps as he thinks fit for the purpose of ascertaining whether the

payer is residing or has assets within the jurisdiction of the court, and if after taking those steps he is satisfied that the payer is not residing and has no assets within the jurisdiction of the court he shall send the certified copy of the order to the Lord Chancellor.

(7) The officer of a court who is required by any of the foregoing provisions of this section to send to the Lord Chancellor or to the prescribed officer of another court the certified copy of an order shall send with that copy –

    (a)   a certificate of arrears signed by him;

    (b)   a statement giving such information as he possesses as to the whereabouts of the payer and the nature and location of his assets; and

    (c)   any relevant documents in his possession relating to the case.

(8) ...

Amendments—CJJA 1982, s 37(1), Sch 11, para 13; SI 1992/709.

Defined terms—"certified copy", "court": s 21(1); "jurisdiction": s 47(3); "provisional order": s 21(1); "reciprocating country": s 1(1); "registered order", "registering court": s 21(1).

"prescribed officer" (s 10(1)–(3))—See FPR 2010, r 34.2.

"prescribed manner" (s 10(4),(5))—See FPR 2010, r 34.3.

11 Steps to be taken by Lord Chancellor where payer under certain orders is not residing in the United Kingdom

(1) If at any time it appears to the Lord Chancellor that the payer under a maintenance order, a certified copy of which has been received by him from a reciprocating country, is not residing and has no assets in the United Kingdom, he shall send to the responsible authority in that country or, if having regard to all the circumstances he thinks it proper to do so, to the responsible authority in another reciprocating country –

    (a)   the certified copy of the order in question and a certified copy of any order varying that order;

    (b)   if the order has at any time been a registered order, a certificate of arrears signed by the prescribed officer;

    (c)   a statement giving such information as the Lord Chancellor possesses as to the whereabouts of the payer and the nature and location of his assets; and

    (d)   any other relevant documents in his possession relating to the case.

(2) Where the documents mentioned in subsection (1) above are sent to the responsible authority in a reciprocating country other than that in which the order in question was made, the Lord Chancellor shall inform the responsible authority in the reciprocating country in which that order was made of what he has done.

Amendments—CJJA 1982, s 37(1), Sch 11, para 13; SI 1992/709.

Defined terms—"certified copy", "maintenance order", "payer": s 21(1); "reciprocating country": s 1(1); "registered order", "responsible authority": s 21(1).

"prescribed officer" (s 11(1))—See FPR 2010, r 34.2.

Appeals

12 Appeals

(1) No appeal shall lie from a provisional order made in pursuance of any provision of this Part of this Act by a court in the United Kingdom.

(2) Where in pursuance of any such provision any such court confirms or refuses to confirm a provisional order made by a court in a reciprocating country, whether a

maintenance order or an order varying or revoking a maintenance order, the payer or payee under the maintenance order shall have the like right of appeal (if any) from the confirmation of, or refusal to conform, the provisional order as he would have if that order were not a provisional order and the court which confirmed or refused to confirm it had made or, as the case may be, refused to make it.

(3) Where in pursuance of any such provision any such court makes, or refuses to make, an order varying or revoking a maintenance order made by a court in a reciprocating country, then, subject to subsection (1) above, the payer or payee under the maintenance order shall have the like right of appeal (if any) from that order or from the refusal to make it as he would have if the maintenance order had been made by the first-mentioned court.

(4) Nothing in this section (except subsection (1)) shall be construed as affecting any right of appeal conferred by any other enactment.

Defined terms—"court", "payee", "payer", "provisional order": s 21(1); "reciprocating country": s 1(1).

Evidence

13 Admissibility of evidence given in reciprocating country

(1) A statement contained in –

    (a)   a document, duly authenticated, which purports to set out or summarise evidence given in proceedings in a court in a reciprocating country; or

    (b)   a document, duly authenticated, which purports to set out or summarise evidence taken in such a country for the purpose of proceedings in a court in the United Kingdom under this Part of this Act, whether in response to a request made by such a court or otherwise; or

    (c)   a document, duly authenticated, which purports to have been received in evidence in proceedings in a court in such a country or to be a copy of a document so received,

shall in any proceedings in a court in the United Kingdom relating to a maintenance order to which this Part of this Act applies be admissible as evidence of any fact stated therein to the same extent as oral evidence of that fact is admissible in those proceedings.

(2) A document purporting to set out or summarise evidence given as mentioned in subsection (1)(a) above, or taken as mentioned in subsection (1)(b) above, shall be deemed to be duly authenticated for the purposes of that subsection if the document purports to be certified by the judge, magistrate or other person before whom the evidence was given, or, as the case may be, by whom it was taken, to be the original document containing or recording, or, as the case may be, summarising, that evidence or a true copy of that document.

(3) A document purporting to have been received in evidence as mentioned in subsection (1)(c) above, or to be a copy of a document so received, shall be deemed to be duly authenticated for the purposes of that subsection if the document purports to be certified by a judge, magistrate or officer of the court in question to have been, or to be a true copy of a document which has been, so received.

(4) It shall not be necessary in any such proceedings to prove the signature or official position of the person appearing to have given such a certificate.

(5) Nothing in this section shall prejudice the admission in evidence of any document which is admissible in evidence apart from this section.

Defined terms—"court", "maintenance order": s 21(1); "reciprocating country": s 1(1).

14 Obtaining of evidence needed for purpose of certain proceedings

(1) Where for the purpose of any proceedings in a court in a reciprocating country relating to a maintenance order to which this Part of this Act applies a request is made by or on behalf of that court for the taking in the United Kingdom of the evidence of a person residing therein relating to matters specified in the request, such court in the United Kingdom as may be prescribed shall have power to take that evidence and, after giving notice of the time and place at which the evidence is to be taken to such persons and in such manner as it thinks fit, shall take the evidence in such manner as may be prescribed.

Evidence taken in compliance with such a request shall be sent in the prescribed manner by the prescribed officer of the court to the court in the reciprocating country by or on behalf of which the request was made.

(2) Where any person, not being the payer or the payee under the maintenance order to which the proceedings in question relate, is required by virtue of this section to give evidence before a court in the United Kingdom, the court may order that there shall be paid –

(a)   if the court is a court in England, Wales or Scotland, out of moneys provided by Parliament; and

(b)   if the court is a court in Northern Ireland, out of moneys provided by the Northern Ireland Assembly,

such sums as appear to the court reasonably sufficient to compensate that person for the expense, trouble or loss of time properly incurred in or incidental to his attendance.

(3) Section 97(1), (3) and (4) of the Magistrates' Courts Act 1980 (which provide for compelling the attendance of witnesses, etc) shall apply in relation to a magistrates' court having power under subsection (1) above to take the evidence of any person as if the proceedings in the court in a reciprocating country for the purpose of which a request for the taking of the evidence has been made were proceedings in the magistrates' court and had been begun by complaint.

(4) ...

(5) A court in the United Kingdom may for the purpose of any proceedings in that court under this Part of this Act relating to a maintenance order to which this Part of this Act applies request a court in a reciprocating country to take or provide evidence relating to such matters as may be specified in the request and may remit the case to that court for that purpose.

(6) In the application of this section to Northern Ireland, in subsection (3), for the reference to section 97(1), (3) and (4) of the Magistrates' Courts Act 1980 there shall be substituted a reference to Articles 118(1), (3) and (4), 119 and 120 of the Magistrates' Courts (Northern Ireland) Order 1981.

Amendments—SI 1973/2163; MCA 1980, s 154, Sch 7, para 105; SI 1981/1675; SI 2010/976.

Defined terms—"court", "maintenance order": s 21(1); "reciprocating country": s 1(1).

"such court … as may be prescribed" (s 14(1))—See FPR 2010, r 34.20.

"prescribed manner" (s 14(1))—See FPR 2010, r 34.20.

"prescribed officer" (s 14(1))—See FPR 2010, r 34.2.

15 Order etc made abroad need not be proved

For the purposes of this Part of this Act, unless the contrary is shown –

(a)   any order made by a court in a reciprocating country purporting to bear the seal of that court or to be signed by any person in his capacity as a judge, magistrate or officer of the court, shall be deemed without further proof to have been duly sealed or, as the case may be, to have been signed by that person;

(b) the person by whom the order was signed shall be deemed without further proof to have been a judge, magistrate or officer, as the case may be, of that court when he signed it and, in the case of an officer, to have been authorised to sign it; and

(c) a document purporting to be a certified copy of an order made by a court in a reciprocating country shall be deemed without further proof to be such a copy.

Defined terms—"certified copy", "court": s 21(1); "reciprocating country": s 1(1).

Supplemental

16 Payment of sums under orders made abroad: conversion of currency

(1) Payment of sums due under a registered order shall, while the order is registered in a court in England, Wales or Northern Ireland, be made in such manner and to such person as may be prescribed.

(2) Where the sums required to be paid under a registered order are expressed in a currency other than the currency of the United Kingdom, then, as from the relevant date, the order shall be treated as if it were an order requiring the payment of such sums in the currency of the United Kingdom as, on the basis of the rate of exchange prevailing at that date, are equivalent to the sums so required to be paid.

(3) Where the sum specified in any statement, being a statement of the amount of any arrears due under a maintenance order made by a court in a reciprocating country is expressed in a currency other than the currency of the United Kingdom, that sum shall be deemed to be such sum in the currency of the United Kingdom as, on the basis of the rate of exchange prevailing at the relevant date, is equivalent to the sum so specified.

(4) For the purposes of this section a written certificate purporting to be signed by an officer of any bank in the United Kingdom certifying that a specified rate of exchange prevailed between currencies at a specified date and that at such rate a specified sum in the currency of the United Kingdom is equivalent to a specified sum in another specified currency shall be evidence of the rate of exchange so prevailing on that date and of the equivalent sums in terms of the respective currencies.

(5) In this section "the relevant date" means –

(a) in relation to a registered order or to a statement of arrears due under a maintenance order made by a court in a reciprocating country, the date on which the order first becomes a registered order or (if earlier) the date on which it is confirmed by a court in the United Kingdom;

(b) in relation to a registered order which has been varied, the date on which the last order varying that order is registered in a court in the United Kingdom or (if earlier) the date on which the last order varying that order is confirmed by such a court.

(6) ...

Defined terms—"maintenance order", "registered order": s 21(1); "reciprocating country": s 1(1).

"to such person as may be prescribed" (s 16(1))—See FPR 2010, r 34.23.

17 Proceedings in magistrates' courts

(1)–(3) (*repealed*)

(4) Anything authorised or required by this Part of this Act to be done by, to or before the magistrates' court by, to or before which any other thing was done may be done by, to

or before any magistrates' court acting in the same local justice area (or, in Northern Ireland, acting for the same petty sessions district) as that court.

(5) (*repealed*)

(5A) Where the respondent to an application for the variation or revocation of –

    (a) a maintenance order made by a magistrates' court in England and Wales, being an order to which section 5 of this Act applies; or

    (b) a registered order which is registered in such a court,

is residing in a reciprocating country, a magistrates' court in England and Wales shall have jurisdiction to hear the application (where it would not have such jurisdiction apart from this subsection) if it would have had jurisdiction to hear it had the respondent been habitually resident in England and Wales.

(6) Where the respondent to an application for the variation or revocation of –

    (a) a maintenance order made by a magistrates' court in Northern Ireland, being an order to which section 5 of this Act applies; or

    (b) a registered order which is registered in such a court,

is residing in a reciprocating country, a magistrates' court in Northern Ireland shall have jurisdiction to hear the application (where it would not have jurisdiction apart from this subsection) if it would have had jurisdiction to hear it had the respondent been habitually resident in Northern Ireland.

(7) Where the respondent to an application for the variation or revocation –

    (a) of a maintenance order made by a magistrates' court, being an order to which section 5 of this Act applies; or

    (b) of a registered order registered in a magistrates' court,

does not appear at the time and place appointed for the hearing of the application, but the court is satisfied that the respondent is residing in a reciprocating country, the court may proceed to hear and determine the application at the time and place appointed for the hearing or for any adjourned hearing in like manner as if the respondent had appeared at that time and place.

(7A), (8) (*repealed*)

Amendments—DPMCA 1978, s 89(2), Sch 3; SI 1981/1675; MO(RE)A 1992, s 1, Sch 1, para 10; SI 1995/755; Courts Act 2003, Sch 8, para 154; SI 2012/2814.

Defined terms—"maintenance order": s 21(1); "reciprocating country": s 1(1); "registered order": s 21(1).

18 Magistrates' courts rules

(1) Rules of court may make provision with respect to –

    (a) Rules of court may make provision with respect to the circumstances in which anything authorised or required by this Part of this Act to be done by, to or before a magistrates' court acting in a particular local justice area or by, to or before an officer of that court may be done by, to or before a magistrates' court acting in such other local justice area as the rules may provide or by, to or before an officer of that court;

    (b) the orders made, or other things done, by a magistrates' court, or an officer of such a court, under this Part of this Act, or by a court in a reciprocating country, notice of which is to be given to such persons as the rules may provide and the manner in which such notice shall be given;

    (c) the cases and manner in which courts in reciprocating countries are to be informed of orders made, or other things done, by a magistrates' court under this Part of this Act;

(d) the cases and manner in which a justices' clerk may take evidence needed for the purpose cf proceedings in a court in a reciprocating country relating to a maintenance order to which this Part of this Act applies;

(e) the circumstances and manner in which cases may be remitted by magistrates' courts to courts in reciprocating countries;

(f) the circumstances and manner in which magistrates' courts may for the purposes of this Part of this Act communicate with courts in reciprocating countries.

(1A) For the purpose of giving effect to this Part of this Act, rules of court may make, in relation to any proceedings brought under or by virtue of this Part of this Act, any provision not covered by subsection (1) above which –

(a) falls within subsection (2) of section 93 of the Children Act 1989, and

(b) may be made in relation to relevant proceedings under that section.

(2) Rules with respect to the matter mentioned in subsection (1) above may be made in accordance with Article 13 of the Magistrates' Courts (Northern Ireland) Order 1981 in relation to proceedings or matters in magistrates' courts in Northern Ireland under this Part of this Act.

(2A) For the purpose of giving effect to this Part of this Act, rules made in accordance with Article 13 of the Magistrates' Courts (Northern Ireland) Order 1981 may make, in relation to any proceedings brought under or by virtue of this Part of this Act, any provision not covered by subsection (2) above which –

(a) falls within paragraph (2) of Article 165 of the Children (Northern Ireland) Order 1995, and

(b) may be made in relation to relevant proceedings under that Article.

Amendments—MCA 1980, s 154, Sch 7, para 106; SI 1981/1675; MO(RE)A 1992, s 1, Sch 1, para 11; SI 1995/755; Courts Act 2003, s 109(1), Sch 8, para 155.

Defined terms—"maintenance order": s 21(1); "reciprocating country": s 1(1).

****

20 Restriction on enforcement of arrears under maintenance order registered in Scotland

Where a maintenance crder is for the time being registered in the sheriff court under this Part of this Act, a person shall not be entitled, except with the leave of the sheriff, to enforce, whether by diligence or otherwise, the payment of any arrears due under the order, if either –

(a) the sheriff has made a provisional order under section 9 of this Act revoking the said maintenance order and the arrears accrued after the making of the said provisional order, or

(b) the arrears accrued before the commencement of this Part of this Act;

and on any application for leave to enforce the payment of any such arrears, the sheriff may refuse leave, or may grant leave subject to such restrictions and conditions (including conditions as to the allowing of time for payment or the making of payment by instalments) as he thinks appropriate, or may remit the payment of such arrears or of any part thereof.

Defined terms—"maintenance order", "provisional order": s 21(1).

21 Interpretation of Part I

(1) In this Part of this Act –

"affiliation order" means an order (however described) adjudging, finding or declaring a person to be the father of a child, whether or not it also provides for the maintenance of the child;

"the appropriate court" in relation to a person residing or having assets in England and Wales or in Northern Ireland means a magistrates' court, and in relation to a person residing or having assets in Scotland means a sheriff court, within the jurisdiction of which that person is residing or has assets;

"certificate of arrears", in relation to a maintenance order, means a certificate certifying that the sum specified in the certificate is to the best of the information or belief of the officer giving the certificate the amount of the arrears due under the order at the date of the certificate or, as the case may be, that to the best of his information or belief there are no arrears due thereunder at that date;

"certified copy", in relation to an order of a court, means a copy of the order certified by the proper officer of the court to be a true copy;

"court" includes any tribunal or person having power to make, confirm, enforce, vary or revoke a maintenance order;

"maintenance order" means an order (however described) of any of the following descriptions, that is to say –

(a) an order (including an affiliation order or order consequent upon an affiliation order) which provides for the payment of a lump sum or the making of periodical payments towards the maintenance of any person, being a person whom the person liable to make payments under the order is, according to the law applied in the place where the order was made, liable to maintain; and

(b) an affiliation order or order consequent upon an affiliation order, being an order which provides for the payment by a person adjudged, found or declared to be a child's father of expenses incidental to the child's birth or, where the child has died, of his funeral expenses,

and, in the case of a maintenance order which has been varied, means that order as varied;

"payee", in relation to a maintenance order, means the person entitled to the payments for which the order provides;

"payer", in relation to a maintenance order, means the person liable to make payments under the order;

"prescribed", in relation to a magistrates' court in Northern Ireland, means prescribed by rules made in accordance with Article 13 of the Magistrates' Courts (Northern Ireland) Order 1981, and in relation to any other court means prescribed by rules of court;

"provisional order" means (according to the context) –

(a) an order made by a court in the United Kingdom which is provisional only and has no effect unless and until confirmed, with or without alteration, by a competent court in a reciprocating country; or

(b) an order made by a court in a reciprocating country which is provisional only and has no effect unless and until confirmed, with or without alteration, by a court in the United Kingdom having power under this Part of this Act to confirm it;

"reciprocating country" has the meaning assigned to it by section 1 of this Act;

"registered order" means a maintenance order which is for the time being registered in a court in the United Kingdom under this Part of this Act;

"registering court", in relation to a registered order, means the court in which that order is for the time being registered under this Part of this Act;

"the responsible authority", in relation to a reciprocating country, means any person who in that country has functions similar to those of the Lord Chancellor under this Part of this Act;

"revoke" and "revocation" include discharge.

(2) For the purposes of this Part of this Act an order shall be taken to be a maintenance order so far (but only so far) as it relates to the payment of a lump sum or the making of periodic payments as mentioned in paragraph (a) of the definition of "maintenance order" in subsection (1) above or to the payment by a person adjudged, found or declared to be a child's father of any such expenses as are mentioned in paragraph (b) of that definition.

(3) Any reference in this Part of this Act to the payment of money for the maintenance of a child shall be construed as including a reference to the payment of money for the child's education.

Amendments—MCA 1980, s 154, Sch 7, para 107; SI 1981/1675; CJJA 1982, s 37(1), Sch 11, paras 4, 15; MO(RE)A 1992, s 1, Sch 1, para 12; SI 1992/709; Courts Act 2003, Sch 8, para 156.

Amendments, repeals and transitional provisions

22 Amendments and repeals

(1) The enactments mentioned in the Schedule to this Act shall have effect subject to the minor and consequential amendments specified therein.

(2) The following are hereby repealed –

    (a)   the Maintenance Orders (Facilities for Enforcement) Act 1920;

    (b)   (*repealed*)

    (c)   in the Maintenance Orders Act 1958, section 19 and, in section 23(2), the words "section nineteen";

    (d)   (*repealed*)

Amendments—MCA 1980, s 154, Sch 9; South Africa Act 1995, s 1, Sch, para 7(2).

23 Maintenance order registered in High Court under the Maintenance Orders etc Act 1920

(1) Where a country or territory, being a country or territory to which at the commencement of section 1 of this Act the Maintenance Orders (Facilities for Enforcement) Act 1920 extended becomes a reciprocating country, then, if immediately before the Order in Council made under section 12 of that Act extending that Act to that country or territory was revoked any maintenance order made by a court in that country or territory was registered in the High Court under section 1 of that Act, the High Court may, on an application by the payer or the payee under the order or of its own motion, transfer the order to such magistrates' court as having regard to the place where the payer is residing and to all the circumstances it thinks most appropriate, with a view to the order being registered in that court under this Part of this Act.

(2) Where the High Court transfers an order to a magistrates' court under this section it shall –

    (a)   cause a certified copy of the order to be sent to the appropriate officer of that court, and

    (b)   cancel the registration of the order in the High Court.

(3) The appropriate officer of the court who receives a certified copy of an order sent to him under this section shall register the order in the prescribed manner in that court.

(4) On registering a maintenance order in the magistrates' court by virtue of this section the appropriate officer of the court shall, if the order is registered in that court under Part I of the Maintenance Orders Act 1958 cancel that registration.

(5) In the application of this section to Northern Ireland, for references to the High Court there shall be substituted references to the High Court of Justice in Northern Ireland.

(6) ...

Amendments—AJA 1999, s 90, Sch 13, para 75.

Defined terms—"certified copy", "court", "maintenance order", "payee", "payer": s 21(1); "reciprocating country": s 1(1).

"prescribed manner" (s 23(3))—See FPR 2010, r 34.3.

24 Application of Part I to certain orders and proceedings under the Maintenance Orders etc Act 1920

Where Her Majesty proposes by an Order in Council under section 1 of this Act to designate as a reciprocating country a country or territory to which at the commencement of that section the Maintenance Orders (Facilities for Enforcement) Act 1920 extended, that Order in Council may contain such provisions as Her Majesty considers expedient for the purpose of securing –

  (a) that the provisions of this Part of this Act apply, subject to such modifications as may be specified in the Order, to maintenance orders, or maintenance orders of a specified class –

  (i)   made by a court in England, Wales or Northern Ireland against a person residing or having assets in that country or territory, or

  (ii) made by a court in that country or territory against a person residing or having assets in England, Wales or Northern Ireland,

  being orders to which immediately before the date of the coming into operation of the Order in Council the said Act of 1920 applied, except any order which immediately before that date is registered in the High Court or the High Court of Justice in Northern Ireland under section 1 of that Act;

  (b) that any maintenance order, or maintenance order of a specified class, made by a court in that country or territory which has been confirmed by a court in England, Wales or Northern Ireland under section 4 of the said Act of 1920 and is in force immediately before that date is registered under section 7 of this Act;

  (c) that any proceedings brought under or by virtue of a provision of the said Act of 1920 in a court in England, Wales or Northern Ireland which are pending at that date, being proceedings affecting a person resident in that country or territory, are continued as if they had been brought under or by virtue of the corresponding provision of this Part of this Act.

Amendments—CJJA 1982, s 37(1), Sch 11, para 16.

Defined terms—"court", "maintenance order": s 21(1); "reciprocating country": s 1(1).

Jersey—The Reciprocal Enforcement of Maintenance Orders (Designation of Reciprocating Countries) Order 2008, Art 4 to include the Bailiwick of Jersey, providing that: (a) a relevant maintenance order is transmitted under s 2 or s 3 of the Maintenance Orders (Facilities for Enforcement) Act 1920 Act to Jersey; and (b) immediately before the commencement date the 1920 Act applied to that order.

(1) Where this applies, sections 5, 12 to 15, 17, 18 and 21 of the 1972 Act shall apply in relation to Jersey, as they apply in relation to a maintenance order of the same description: (a) sent to Jersey pursuant to section 2 of the 1972 Act; (b) made under section 3 or 4 of the 1972 Act; and (c) confirmed by a competent court in Jersey.

(2) If: (a) a relevant maintenance order is transmitted under section 2 or 3 of the 1920 Act to Jersey; and (b) immediately before the commencement date: (i) the 1920 Act applied to that order; and (ii) the

order was not registered, then sections 8 to 21 of the 1972 Act shall apply in relation to a relevant maintenance order referred to under paragraph 1, as they apply in relation to a maintenance order of the same description made under the 1972 Act which is so registered.

(3) If (a) a relevant maintenance order has been confirmed by a court in England, Wales or Northern Ireland under section 4 of the Maintenance Orders (Facilities for Enforcement) Act 1920 and (b) is in force immediately before the commencement date, then a relevant maintenance order as referred to under paragraph (1) shall be registered under section 7(5) of the 1972 Act in the same manner as if it had been confirmed by that court in England, Wales or Northern Ireland under subsection (2) of that section.

(4) Any proceedings brought under or by virtue of any provision of the 1920 Act in a court in England, Wales or Northern Ireland which are pending immediately before the commencement date, being proceedings affecting a person resident in Jersey, shall be continued as if they had been brought under or by virtue of the corresponding provision of the 1972 Act.

PART II
RECIPROCAL ENFORCEMENT OF CLAIMS FOR THE RECOVERY OF MAINTENANCE

Convention countries

25 Convention countries

(1) Her Majesty may by Order in Council declare that any country or territory specified in the Order, being a country or territory outside the United Kingdom to which the Maintenance Convention extends, is a Convention country for the purposes of this Part of this Act.

(2) In this section "the Maintenance Convention" means the United Nations Convention on the Recovery Abroad of Maintenance done at New York on 20 June 1956.

Scope—This section provides that a country or territory may be declared a Convention country for the purposes of Pt II by Order in Council. The Recovery Abroad of Maintenance (Convention Countries) Order 1975 and the RM(USA)O 1993 have been made for this purpose. For guidance on the application of Pt II, see Home Office Circular No 54/1975. See also the MC(RAM)R 1975.

Application by person in the United Kingdom for recovery etc of maintenance in Convention country

26 Application by person in United Kingdom for recovery etc of maintenance in Convention country

(1) Where a person in the United Kingdom ("the applicant") claims to be entitled to recover in a Convention country maintenance from another person, and that other person is for the time being subject to the jurisdiction of that country, the applicant may apply to the Lord Chancellor, in accordance with the provisions of this section, to have his claim for the recovery of maintenance from that other person transmitted to that country.

(2) Where the applicant seeks to vary any provision made in a Convention country for the payment by any other person of maintenance to the applicant, and that other person is for the time being subject to the jurisdiction of that country, the applicant may apply to the Lord Chancellor, in accordance with the provisions of this section, to have his application for the variation of that provision transmitted to that country.

(3) An application to the Lord Chancellor under subsection (1) or (2) above shall be made through the appropriate officer, and that officer shall assist the applicant in completing an application which will comply with the requirements of the law applied by the Convention country and shall send the application to the Lord Chancellor, together with such other documents, if any, as are required by that law.

(4) On receiving an application from the appropriate officer the Lord Chancellor shall transmit it, together with any accompanying documents, to the appropriate authority in the Convention country, unless he is satisfied that the application is not made in good faith or that it does not comply with the requirements of the law applied by that country.

(5) The Lord Chancellor may request the appropriate officer to obtain from the court of which he is an officer such information relating to the application as may be specified in the request, and it shall be the duty of the court to furnish the Lord Chancellor with the information he requires.

(6) ...

Amendments—SI 1992/709.

Defined terms—"Convention country": s 25(1).

Application by person in Convention country for recovery of maintenance in England, Wales or Northern Ireland

27 (*repealed*)

27A Applications for recovery of maintenance in England and Wales

(1) This section applies to any application which –

  (a) is received by the Lord Chancellor from the appropriate authority in a Convention country, and

  (b) is an application by a person in that country for the recovery of maintenance from another person who is for the time being residing in England and Wales.

(2) Subject to sections 27B to 28B of this Act, an application to which this section applies shall be treated for the purposes of any enactment as if it were an application for a maintenance order under the relevant Act, made at the time when the application was received by the Lord Chancellor. This subsection does not confer jurisdiction on a court in England and Wales that it would not otherwise have.

(3) In the case of an application for maintenance for a child (or children) alone, the relevant Act is the Children Act 1989.

(4) In any other case, the relevant Act is the Domestic Proceedings and Magistrates' Courts Act 1978.

(5) In subsection (3) above, "child" means the same as in Schedule 1 to the Children Act 1989.

Amendments—Inserted by MO(RE)A 1992, s 1, Sch 1, para 13; amended by SI 2012/2814.

Defined terms—"Convention country": s 25(1).

27B Sending application to the appropriate magistrates' court

(1) On receipt of an application to which section 27A of this Act applies, the Lord Chancellor shall send it, together with any accompanying documents, to the designated officer for a magistrates' court which is acting in the local justice area in which the respondent is residing.

(2) Subject to subsection (4) below, if notice of the hearing of the application by a magistrates' court having jurisdiction to hear it cannot be duly served on the respondent, the designated officer for the court shall return the application and the accompanying documents to the Lord Chancellor with a statement giving such information as he possesses as to the whereabouts of the respondent.

(3) If the application is returned to the Lord Chancellor under subsection (2) above, then, unless he is satisfied that the respondent is not residing in the United Kingdom, he shall deal with it in accordance with subsection (1) above or section 28D(1) of this Act or send it to the Secretary of State to be dealt with in accordance with section 31 of this Act (as the circumstances of the case require).

(4) If the designated officer for a court to whom the application is sent under this section is satisfied that the respondent is residing within another local justice area, he shall send the application and accompanying documents to the designated officer for a magistrates' court acting in that other area and shall inform the Lord Chancellor that he has done so.

(5) If the application is sent to the designated officer for a court under subsection (4) above, he shall proceed as if it had been sent to him under subsection (1) above.

Amendments—Inserted by MO(RE)A 1992, s 1, Sch 1, para 13; SI 1995/756; amended by AJA 1999, s 90, Sch 13, para 77; Courts Act 2003, Sch 8, para 159.

Defined terms—"jurisdiction": s 47(3).

PART II

27C Applications to which section 27A applies: general

(1) This section applies where a magistrates' court makes an order on an application to which section 27A of this Act applies.

(2) Section 59 of the Magistrates' Courts Act 1980 (orders for periodical payment: means of payment) shall not apply.

(3) The court shall, at the same time that it makes the order, exercise one of its powers under subsection (4) below.

(4) Those powers are –

(a) the power to order that payment under the order be made directly to the designated officer for the court or for any other magistrates' court in England and Wales;

(b) the power to order that payments under the order be made to the designated officer for the court or for any other magistrates' court in England and Wales, by such method of payment falling within section 59(6) of the Magistrates' Courts Act 1980 (standing order, etc) as may be specified;

(c) the power to make an attachment of earnings order under the Attachment of Earnings Act 1971 to secure payments under the order.

(5) In deciding which of the powers under subsection (4) above it is to exercise, the court shall have regard to any representations made by the person liable to make payments under the order.

(6) Subsection (4) of section 59 of the Magistrates' Courts Act 1980 (power of court to require debtor to open account) shall apply for the purposes of subsection (4) above as it applies for the purposes of that section, but as if for paragraph (a) there were substituted –

"(a) the court proposes to exercise its power under paragraph (b) of section 27C(4) of the Maintenance Orders (Reciprocal Enforcement) Act 1972, and".

(7) The designated officer for the court shall register the order in the prescribed manner in the court.

Amendments—Inserted by MO(RE)A 1992, s 1, Sch 1, para 13; amended by AJA 1999, s 90, Sch 13, para 78; Courts Act 2003, Sch 8, para 160.

28 Applications by spouses under the Domestic Proceedings and Magistrates' Courts Act 1978

(1) The magistrates' court hearing an application which by virtue of section 27A of this Act is to be treated as if it were an application for a maintenance order under the Domestic Proceedings and Magistrates' Courts Act 1978 may make any order on the application which it has power to make under section 2 or 19(1) of that Act.

(2) Part I of that Act shall apply in relation to such an application, and to any order made on such an application, with the following modifications –

    (a)   sections 6 to 8, 16 to 18, 20ZA, 25 to 27 and 28(2) shall be omitted,

    (b)   in section 30(1), for the words "either the applicant or the respondent ordinarily resides" there shall be substituted "the respondent resides", and

    (c)   section 32(2) shall be omitted.

(3) Subsections (1) and (2) above do not apply where section 28A of this Act applies.

Amendments—MO(RE)A 1992, s 1, Sch 1, para 13.

28A Applications by former spouses under the Domestic Proceedings and Magistrates' Courts Act 1978

(1) This section applies where in the case of any application which by virtue of section 27A of this Act is to be treated as if it were an application for a maintenance order under the Domestic Proceedings and Magistrates' Courts Act 1978 ("the 1978 Act") –

    (a)   the applicant and respondent were formerly married,

    (b)   their marriage was dissolved or annulled in a country or territory outside the United Kingdom by a divorce or annulment which is recognised as valid by the law of England and Wales,

    (c)   an order for the payment of maintenance for the benefit of the applicant or a child of the family has, by reason of the divorce or annulment, been made by a court in a Convention country, and

    (d)   where the order for the payment of maintenance was made by a court of a different country from that in which the divorce or annulment was obtained, either the applicant or the respondent was resident in the Convention country whose court made that order at the time that order was applied for.

(2) Any magistrates' court that would have jurisdiction to hear the application under section 30 of the 1978 Act (as modified in accordance with subsection (6) below) if the applicant and the respondent were still married shall have jurisdiction to hear it notwithstanding the dissolution or annulment of the marriage.

(3) If the magistrates' court hearing the application is satisfied that the respondent has failed to comply with the provisions of any order such as is mentioned in subsection (1)(c) above, it may (subject to subsections (4) and (5) below) make any order which it has power to make under section 2 or 19(1) of the 1978 Act.

(4) The court shall not make an order for the making of periodical payments for the benefit of the applicant or any child of the family unless the order made in the Convention country provides for the making of periodical payments for the benefit of the applicant or, as the case may be, that child.

(5) The court shall not make an order for the payment of a lump sum for the benefit of the applicant or any child of the family unless the order made in the Convention country provides for the payment of a lump sum to the applicant or, as the case may be, to that child.

(6) Part I of the 1978 Act shall apply in relation to the application, and to any order made on the application, with the following modifications –

(a) section 1 shall be omitted,

(b) for the reference in section 2(1) to any ground mentioned in section 1 of that Act there shall be substituted a reference to non-compliance with any such order as is mentioned in subsection (1)(c) of this section,

(c) for the references in section 3(2) and (3) to the occurrence of the conduct which is alleged as the ground of the application there shall be substituted references to the breakdown of the marriage,

(d) the reference in section 4(2) to the subsequent dissolution or annulment of the marriage of the parties affected by the order shall be omitted,

(e) sections 6 to 8, 16 to 18, 20ZA and 25 to 28 shall be omitted,

(f) in section 30(1), for the words "either the applicant or the respondent ordinarily resides" there shall be substituted "the respondent resides", and

(g) section 32(2) shall be omitted.

(7) A divorce or annulment obtained in a country or territory outside the United Kingdom shall be presumed for the purposes of this section to be one the validity of which is recognised by the law of England and Wales, unless the contrary is proved by the respondent.

(8) In this section, "child of the family" has the meaning given in section 88 of the 1978 Act.

Amendments—Inserted by MO(RE)A 1992, s 1, Sch 1, para 13.

Defined terms—"Convention country": s 25(1); "jurisdiction": s 47(3).

28B Applications under the Children Act 1989

No provision of an order made under Schedule 11 to the Children Act 1989 requiring or enabling a court to transfer proceedings from a magistrates' court to a county court or the High Court shall apply in relation to an application which by virtue of section 27A of this Act is to be treated as if it were an application for a maintenance order under that Act.

Amendments—Inserted by MO(RE)A 1992, s 1, Sch 1, para 13.

28C Applications for recovery of maintenance in Northern Ireland

(1) This section applies to any application which –

(a) is received by the Lord Chancellor from the appropriate authority in a convention country, and

(b) is an application by a person in that country for the recovery of maintenance from another person who is for the time being residing in Northern Ireland.

(2) Subject to sections 28D to 29B of this Act, an application to which this section applies shall be treated for the purposes of any enactment as if it were an application for a maintenance order under the relevant Order, made at the time when the application was received by the Lord Chancellor. This subsection does not confer jurisdiction on a court in Northern Ireland that it would not otherwise have.

(3) In the case of an application for maintenance for a child (or children) alone, the relevant Order is the Children (Northern Ireland) Order 1995.

(4) In any other case, the relevant Order is the Domestic Proceedings (Northern Ireland) Order 1980.

(5) In subsection (3) above, "child" means the same as in Schedule 1 to the Children (Northern Ireland) Order 1995.

Amendments—Inserted by MO(RE)A 1992, s 1, Sch 1, para 13; substituted by SI 1995/755; amended by SI 2012/2814.

Defined terms—"Convention country": s 25(1).

28D Sending application to the appropriate magistrates' court

(1) On receipt of an application to which section 28C of this Act applies, the Lord Chancellor shall send it, together with any accompanying documents, to the clerk of a magistrates' court acting for the petty sessions district in which the respondent is residing.

(2) Subject to subsection (4) below, if notice of the hearing of the application by a magistrates' court having jurisdiction to hear it cannot be duly served on the respondent, the clerk of the court shall return the application and the accompanying documents to the Lord Chancellor with a statement giving such information as he possesses as to the whereabouts of the respondent.

(3) If the application is returned to the Lord Chancellor under subsection (2) above, then, unless he is satisfied that the respondent is not residing in the United Kingdom, he shall deal with it in accordance with subsection (1) above or section 27B of this Act or send it to the Secretary of State to be dealt with in accordance with section 31 of this Act (as the circumstances of the case require).

(4) If the clerk of a court to whom the application is sent under this section is satisfied that the respondent is residing within the petty sessions district for which another magistrates' court acts, he shall send the application and accompanying documents to the clerk of that other court and shall inform the Lord Chancellor that he has done so.

(5) If the application is sent to the clerk of a court under subsection (4) above, he shall proceed as if it had been sent to him under subsection (1) above.

Amendments—Inserted by SI 1995/755.

28E Applications to which section 28C applies: general

(1) This section applies where a magistrates' court makes an order on an application to which section 28C of this Act applies.

(2) Article 85 of the Magistrates' Courts (Northern Ireland) Order 1981 ("the 1981 Order") (orders for periodical payment: means of payment) shall not apply.

(3) The court shall, at the same time that it makes the order, exercise one of its powers under subsection (4) below.

(4) Those powers are –

    (a)   the power to order that payments under the order be made directly to the collecting officer;

    (b)   the power to order that payments under the order be made to the collecting officer, by such method of payment falling within Article 85(7) of the 1981 Order (standing order, etc.) as may be specified;

    (c)   the power to make an attachment of earnings order under Part IX of the 1981 Order to secure payments under the order;

and in this subsection "collecting officer" means the officer mentioned in Article 85(4) of the 1981 Order.

(5) In deciding which of the powers under subsection (4) above it is to exercise, the court shall have regard to any representation made by the person liable to make payments under the order.

(6) Paragraph (5) of Article 85 of the 1981 Order (power of court to require debtor to open account) shall apply for the purposes of subsection (4) above as it applies for the purposes of that Article, but as if for sub-paragraph (a) there were substituted –

> "(a) the court proposes to exercise its power under paragraph (b) of section 28E(4) of the Maintenance Orders (Reciprocal Enforcement) Act 1972, and".

(7) The clerk of the court shall register the order in the prescribed manner in the court.

Amendments—Inserted by SI 1995/755.

****

Transfer, enforcement, variation and revocation of registered orders

32 Transfer of orders

(1) Where the prescribed officer of the registering court is of opinion that the payer under a registered order has ceased to reside within the jurisdiction of that court, then, unless he is of opinion that the payer has ceased to reside in the United Kingdom, he shall, subject to subsection (2) below, send a certified copy of the order and the related documents to the Lord Chancellor, and if he is of opinion that the payer has ceased to reside in the United Kingdom he shall send a notice to that effect to the Lord Chancellor.

(2) Where the appropriate officer of the registering court, being a magistrates' court, is of opinion that the payer is residing within the jurisdiction of another magistrates' court in that part of the United Kingdom in which the registering court is, he shall transfer the order to that other court by sending a certified copy of the order and the related documents to the appropriate officer of that other court and, subject to subsection (4) below, the appropriate officer shall register the order in the prescribed manner in that court.

(2A) …

(3) Where a certified copy of an order is received by the Lord Chancellor under this section and it appears to him that the payer under the order is still residing in the United Kingdom, he shall transfer the order to the appropriate court by sending the copy of the order and the related documents to the prescribed officer of the appropriate court and subject to subsection (4) below, that officer shall register the order in the prescribed manner in that court.

(4) Before registering an order in pursuance of subsection (2) or (3) above an officer of a court shall take such steps as he thinks fit for the purpose of ascertaining whether the payer under the order is residing within the jurisdiction of the court, and if after taking those steps he is satisfied that the payer is not so residing he shall return the certified copy of the order and the related documents to the officer of the court or the Lord Chancellor, as the case may be, from whom he received them, together with a statement giving such information as he possesses as to the whereabouts of the payer.

(5) Where a certified copy of an order is received by the Lord Chancellor under this section and it appears to him that the payer under the order has ceased to reside in the United Kingdom he shall return the copy of the order and the related documents to the registering court.

(6) An officer of a court on registering an order in the court in pursuance of subsection (2) or (3) above shall give notice of the registration in the prescribed manner to the prescribed officer of the court in which immediately before its registration under this section the order was registered.

(7) The officer to whom notice is given under subsection (6) above shall on receiving the notice cancel the registration of the order in that court.

(7A), (7B) …

(8) In this section –

"the appropriate court", in relation to a person residing in England and Wales or in Northern Ireland, means a magistrates' court within the jurisdiction of which that person is residing;

"certificate of arrears" and "certified copy" have the same meanings respectively as in Part I of this Act;

"payer", in relation to a registered order, means the person liable to make payments under the order; and

"related documents" means –

    (a)   the application on which the order was made;

    (b)   a certificate of arrears signed by the prescribed officer of the registering court;

    (c)   a statement giving such information as he possesses as to the whereabouts of the payer; and

    (d)   any relevant documents in his possession relating to the case.

(9) …

Amendments—SI 1992/709; AJA 1999, s 90, Sch 13, para 79.

Defined terms—"certificate of arrears", "certified copy": s 21(1); "jurisdiction": s 47(3); "part of the United Kingdom": s 47(2); "registered order", "registering court": s 39.

33 Enforcement of orders

(1) Subject to subsection (2) below, a registered order which is registered in a court other than the court by which the order was made may be enforced as if it had been made by the registered court and as if that court had had jurisdiction to make it; and proceedings for or with respect to the enforcement of any such order may be taken in accordance with this subsection but not otherwise.

(2) Subsection (1) above does not apply to an order which is for the time being registered in the High Court under Part I of the Maintenance Orders Act 1958 or to an order which is for the time being registered in the High Court of Justice in Northern Ireland under Part II of the Maintenance and Affiliation Orders Act (Northern Ireland) 1966.

(3) An order which by virtue of subsection (1) above is enforceable by a magistrates' court shall, subject to the modifications of sections 76 and 93 of the Magistrates' Courts Act 1980 (enforcement of sums adjudged to be paid and complaint for arrears) specified in subsections (4A) and (4B) of section 8 of this Act, be enforceable as if it were a magistrates' court maintenance order made by that court.

In this subsection "magistrates' court maintenance order" has the same meaning as in section 150(1) of the Magistrates' Courts Act 1980.

(3A) Where, by virtue of being registered in the magistrates' court in which it was made, a registered order is enforceable as a magistrates' court maintenance order, sections 76 and 93 of the Magistrates' Courts Act 1980 shall have effect subject to the modifications specified in subsections (4A) and (4B) of section 8 of this Act.

(4) A magistrates' court in which an order is registered under this Part of this Act, and the officers thereof, shall take all such steps for enforcing the order as may be prescribed.

(5) In any proceedings for or with respect to the enforcement of an order which is for the time being registered in any court under this Part of this Act a certificate of arrears sent under section 32 of this Act to the prescribed officer of the court shall be evidence of the facts stated therein.

(6) Part II of the Maintenance Orders Act 1950 (enforcement of certain orders throughout the United Kingdom) shall not apply to a registered order.

(7) ...

Amendments—FLRA 1987, s 33, Sch 2, para 50; MEA 1991, s 10, Sch 1, para 18.

Defined terms—"certificate of arrears": s 21(1); "registered order", "registering court": s 39.

Application to Northern Ireland—In Northern Ireland, subsection (3) is modified and an additional subsection (3B) is added by Family Law (Northern Ireland) Order 1993 and Children (Northern Ireland) Order 1995.

34 Variation and revocation of orders

(1) Subject to subsection (3A) below and section 34A of this Act, where a registered order is registered in a court other than the court by which the order was made, the registering court shall have the like power to vary or revoke the order as if it had been made by the registering court and as if that court had had jurisdiction to make it; and no court other than the registering court shall have power to vary or revoke a registered order.

(2) Where the registering court revokes a registered order it shall cancel the registration.

(3) Where the Lord Chancellor receives from the appropriate authority in a Convention country an application by a person in that country for the variation of a registered order, he shall, if the registering court is a magistrates' court, send the application together with any documents accompanying it to –

    (a) the designated officer for the court, if the court is in England and Wales; or

    (b) the clerk of the court, if the court is in Northern Ireland.

(3A) Where subsection (1) of section 60 of the Magistrates' Courts Act 1980 (revocation, variation etc of orders for periodical payment) applies in relation to a registered order, that subsection shall have effect as if for the words "by order on complaint", there were substituted "on an application being made, by order".

(4) Where a court in a part of the United Kingdom makes, or refuses to make, an order varying or revoking a registered order made by a court in another part thereof, any person shall have the like right of appeal (if any) against the order or refusal as he would have if the registered order had been made by the first-mentioned court.

(5) ...

Amendments—MEA 1991, s 10, Sch 1, para 19(1); MO(RE)A 1992, s 1, Sch 1, para 14; SI 1992/709; AJA 1999, s 90, Sch 13, para 80; Courts Act 2003, s 109(1), Sch 8, para 162.

Defined terms—"Convention country": s 25(1); "part of the United Kingdom": s 47(2); "registered order", "registering court": s 39.

Application to Northern Ireland—See note under s 33.

34A Variation of orders by magistrates' courts in England and Wales

(1) The provisions of this section shall have effect in relation to a registered order which is registered in a magistrates' court in England and Wales (whether or not the court made the order) in place of the following enactments, that is to say –

    (a) subsections (3) to (11) of section 60 of the Magistrates' Courts Act 1980;

(b) section 20ZA of the Domestic Proceedings and Magistrates' Courts Act 1978; and

(c) paragraph 6A of Schedule 1 to the Children Act 1989.

(2) The power of a magistrates' court in England and Wales to vary a registered order shall include power, if the court is satisfied that payment has not been made in accordance with the order, to exercise one of its powers under subsection (3) below.

(3) The powers of the court are –

(a) the power to order that payments under the order be made directly to the designated officer for the court or for any other magistrates' court in England and Wales;

(b) the power to order that payments under the order be made to the designated officer for the court or for any other magistrates' court in England and Wales by such method of payment falling within section 59(6) of the Magistrates' Courts Act 1980 (standing order, etc) as may be specified;

(c) the power to make an attachment of earnings order under the Attachment of Earnings Act 1971 to secure payments under the order.

(4) In any case where –

(a) a registered order is registered in a magistrates' court in England and Wales, and

(b) payments under the order are required to be made to the designated officer for the court or for any other magistrates' court in England and Wales by any method of payment falling within section 59(6) of the Magistrates' Courts Act 1980 (standing order, etc),

an interested party may apply in writing to the court in which the order is registered for the order to be varied as mentioned in subsection (5) below.

(5) Subject to subsection (8) below, where an application has been made under subsection (4) above, a justices' clerk, after giving written notice (by post or otherwise) of the application to any other interested party and allowing that party, within the period of 14 days beginning with the date of the giving of that notice, an opportunity to make written representations, may vary the order to provide that payments under the order shall be made in accordance with paragraph (a) of subsection (3) above.

(6) The clerk may proceed with an application under subsection (4) above notwithstanding that any such interested party as is referred to in subsection (5) above has not received written notice of the application.

(7) In subsections (4) to (6) above "interested party", in relation to an order, means the debtor or the creditor.

(8) Where an application has been made under subsection (4) above, the clerk may, if he considers it inappropriate to exercise his power under subsection (5) above, refer the matter to the court which may vary the order by exercising one of its powers under subsection (3) above.

(9) In deciding, for the purposes of subsections (2) and (8) above, which of the powers under subsection (3) above it is to exercise, the court shall have regard to any representations made by the debtor.

(10) Subsection (4) of section 59 of the Magistrates' Courts Act 1980 (power of court to require debtor to open account) shall apply for the purposes of subsection (3) above as it applies for the purposes of that section but as if for paragraph (a) there were substituted –

"(a) the court proposes to exercise its power under paragraph (b) of section 34A(3) of the Maintenance Orders (Reciprocal Enforcement) Act 1972, and".

(11) In this section "creditor" and debtor" have the same meaning as they have in section 59 of the Magistrates' Courts Act 1980.

Amendments—Inserted by MEA 1991, s 10, Sch 1, para 19(2); amended by AJA 1999, s 90, Sch 13, para 81; Courts Act 2003, Sch 8, para 163.

Defined terms—"registered order": s 39.

"standing order, etc" (s 34A(3)(b))—The methods of payment available do not include power to order payment by direct debit.

34B Variation of orders by courts of summary jurisdiction in Northern Ireland

(1) The provisions of this section shall have effect in relation to a registered order which is registered in a court of summary jurisdiction in Northern Ireland (whether or not the court made the order) in place of the following enactments, that is to say –

    (a) paragraphs (3) to (11) of Article 86 of the Magistrates' Courts (Northern Ireland) Order 1981; and

    (b) Article 22A of the Domestic Proceedings (Northern Ireland) Order 1980.

(2) The power of a court of summary jurisdiction in Northern Ireland to vary a registered order shall include power, if the court is satisfied that payment has not been made in accordance with the order, to exercise one of its powers under subsection (3) below.

(3) The powers of the court are –

    (a) the power to order that payments under the order be made directly to the collecting officer;

    (b) the power to order that payments under the order be made to the collecting officer by such method of payment falling within Article 85(7) of the Magistrates' Courts (Northern Ireland) Order 1981 (standing order, etc) as may be specified;

    (c) the power to make an attachment of earnings order under Part IX of the Order of 1981 to secure payments under the order;

and in this subsection "collecting officer" means the officer mentioned in Article 85(4) of the Order of 1981.

(4) In any case where –

    (a) a registered order is registered in a court of summary jurisdiction in Northern Ireland, and

    (b) payments under the order are required to be made to the collecting officer in Northern Ireland, by any method of payment falling within Article 85(7) of the Magistrates' Courts (Northern Ireland) Order 1981 (standing order, etc),

an interested party may apply in writing to the clerk of petty sessions in which the order is registered for the order to be varied as mentioned in subsection (5) below.

(5) Subject to subsection (8) below, where an application has been made under subsection (4) above, the clerk, after giving written notice (by post or otherwise) of the application to any other interested party and allowing that party, within the period of 14 days beginning with the date of the giving of that notice, an opportunity to make written representations, may vary the order to provide that payments under the order shall be made in accordance with paragraph (a) of subsection (3) above.

(6) The clerk may proceed with an application under subsection (4) above notwithstanding that any such interested party as is referred to in subsection (5) above has not received written notice of the application.

(7) In subsections (4) to (6) above "interested party", in relation to an order, means the debtor or the creditor.

(8) Where an application has been made under subsection (4) above, the clerk may, if he considers it inappropriate to exercise his power under subsection (5) above, refer the matter to the court which may vary the order by exercising one of its powers under subsection (3) above.

(9) In deciding, for the purposes of subsections (2) and (8) above, which of the powers under subsection (3) above it is to exercise, the court shall have regard to any representations made by the debtor.

(10) Paragraph (5) of Article 85 of the Magistrates' Courts (Northern Ireland) Order 1981 (power of court to require debtor to open account) shall apply for the purposes of subsection (3) above as it applies for the purposes of that Article but as if for sub-paragraph (a) there were substituted –

> "(a)   the court proposes to exercise its power under paragraph (b) of section 34B(3) of the Maintenance Orders (Reciprocal Enforcement) Act 1972, and".

(11) In this section "creditor" and "debtor" have the same meaning as they have in Article 85 of the Magistrates' Courts (Northern Ireland) Order 1981.

Amendments—Inserted by SI 1993/1576.

35 Further provisions with respect to variation etc of orders by magistrates' courts in England and Wales

(1) Subsection (1A) applies in relation to an application for the variation or revocation of a registered order registered in a magistrates' court in England and Wales ("the registering court") made –

(a)   by the person against whom or on whose application the registered order was made, and

(b)   in circumstances where the person by or against whom the application is made is residing outside England and Wales.

(1A) The registering court has jurisdiction to hear the application even though –

(a)   a party to the application is residing outside England and Wales, and

(b)   the requirement in section 30(1) of the Domestic Proceedings and Magistrates' Courts Act 1978 as applied by section 28(2) or 28A(6) of this Act, is not satisfied.

(1B) But if the application or part of it relates to a matter where jurisdiction falls to be determined by reference to the jurisdictional requirements of the Maintenance Regulation and Schedule 6 to the Civil Jurisdiction and Judgments (Maintenance) Regulations 2011, the registering court may not entertain the application or that part of it unless it has jurisdiction to do so by virtue of that Regulation and that Schedule.

(2) None of the powers of the court, or of the clerk of the court, under section 34A of this Act shall be exercisable in relation to such an application.

(3) Where the respondent to an application for the variation or revocation of a registered order which is registered in a magistrates' court in England and Wales does not appear at the time and place appointed for the hearing of the application, but the court is satisfied –

(a)   that the respondent is residing outside England and Wales, and

(b)   that the prescribed notice of the making of the application and of the time and place appointed for the hearing has been given to the respondent in the prescribed manner,

the court may proceed to hear and determine the application at the time and place appointed for the hearing or for any adjourned hearing in like manner as if the respondent had appeared at that time and place.

(4) In subsection (1B) "the Maintenance Regulation" means Council Regulation (EC) No 4/2009 including as applied in relation to Denmark by virtue of the Agreement made on 19 October 2005 between the European Community and the Kingdom of Denmark.

Amendments—MO(RE)A 1992, s 1, Sch 1, para 16; SI 2012/2814.

Defined terms—"registered order": s 39.

35A Further provisions with respect to variation etc of orders by magistrates' courts in Northern Ireland

(1) Subsection (1A) applies in relation to an application for the variation or revocation of a registered order registered in a magistrates' court in Northern Ireland ("the registering court") made –

    (a)   by the person against whom or on whose application the registered order was made, and

    (b)   in circumstances where the person by or against whom the application is made is residing outside Northern Ireland.

(1A) The registering court has jurisdiction to hear the application even though –

    (a)   a party to the application is residing outside England and Wales, and

    (b)   the requirement in Article 32 of the Domestic Proceedings (Northern Ireland) Order 1980, as applied by section 29(2) or 29A(6) of this Act, is not satisfied.

(1B) But if the application or part of it relates to a matter where jurisdiction falls to be determined by reference to the jurisdictional requirements of the Maintenance Regulation and Schedule 6 to the Civil Jurisdiction and Judgments (Maintenance) Regulations 2011, the registering court may not entertain the application or that part of it unless it has jurisdiction to do so by virtue of that Regulation and that Schedule.

(2) None of the powers of the court, or of the clerk, under section 34B of this Act shall be exercisable in relation to such an application.

(3) Where the respondent to an application for the variation or revocation of a registered order which is registered in a magistrates' court in Northern Ireland does not appear at the time and place appointed for the hearing of the application, but the court is satisfied –

    (a)   that the respondent is residing outside Northern Ireland, and

    (b)   that the prescribed notice of the making of the application and of the time and place appointed for the hearing has been given to the respondent in the prescribed manner,

the court may proceed to hear and determine the application at the time and place appointed for the hearing or for any adjourned hearing in like manner as if the respondent had appeared at that time and place.

(4) In subsection (1B) "the Maintenance Regulation" means Council Regulation (EC) 4/2009 including as applied in relation to Denmark by virtue of the Agreement made on 19 October 2005 between the European Community and the Kingdom of Denmark.

Amendments—Inserted by MO(RE)A 1992, s 1, Sch 1, para 16; substituted by SI 1995/755; amended by SI 2012/2814.

Defined terms—"registered order": s 39.

Scope—A means of payment order may not be made under this section.

Supplemental

36 Admissibility of evidence given in Convention country

(1) A statement contained in –

   (a) a document, duly authenticated, which purports to set out or summarise evidence given in proceedings in a court in a Convention country; or

   (b) a document, duly authenticated, which purports to set out or summarise evidence taken in such a country for the purpose of proceedings in a court in the United Kingdom under this Part of this Act, whether in response to a request made on behalf of such a court or otherwise; or

   (c) a document, duly authenticated, which purports to have been received in evidence in proceedings in a court in such a country, or to be a copy of a document so received,

shall, in any proceedings in a magistrates' court or in, or remitted from, a sheriff court arising out of an application to which section 27A(1) of this Act applies, an application to which section 28C(1) of this Act applies, an application received by the Secretary of State as mentioned in section 31(1) of this Act or an application made by any person for the variation or revocation of a registered order or in proceedings on appeal from any such proceedings, be admissible as evidence of any fact stated therein to the same extent as oral evidence of that fact is admissible in those proceedings.

(2) A document purporting to set out or summarise evidence given as mentioned in subsection (1)(a) above, or taken as mentioned in subsection (1)(b) above, shall be deemed to be duly authenticated for the purposes of that subsection if the document purports to be certified by the judge, magistrate or other person before whom the evidence was given or, as the case may be, by whom it was taken, to be the original document containing or recording, or, as the case may be, summarising, that evidence or a true copy of that document.

(3) A document purporting to have been received in evidence as mentioned in subsection (1)(c) above, or to be a copy of a document so received, shall be deemed to be duly authenticated for the purposes of that subsection if the document purports to be certified by a judge, magistrate or officer of the court in question to have been, or to be a true copy of a document which has been, so received.

(4) It shall not be necessary in any such proceedings to prove the signature or official position of the person appearing to have given such a certificate.

(5) Nothing in this section shall prejudice the admission in evidence of any document which is admissible in evidence apart from this section.

Amendments—DPMCA 1978, s 60(3); MO(RE)A 1992, s 1, Sch 1, para 17; SI 1992/709; SI 1995/755.

Defined terms—"Convention country": s 25(1); "registered order": s 39.

37 Obtaining of evidence for purpose of proceedings in United Kingdom court

(1) A court in the United Kingdom may for the purpose of any proceedings in that court under this Part of this Act arising out of an application received by the Lord Chancellor from a Convention country request the Lord Chancellor to make to the appropriate authority or court in the Convention country a request for the taking in that country of the evidence of a person residing therein relating to matters connected with the application.

(2) A request made by a court under this section shall –

   (a) give details of the application in question;

   (b) state the name and address of the person whose evidence is to be taken; and

(c)   specify the matters relating to which the evidence of that person is required.

(3) If the Lord Chancellor is satisfied that a request made to him under this section contains sufficient information to enable the evidence of the person named in the request relating to the matters specified therein to be taken by a court or person in the Convention country, he shall transmit the request to the appropriate authority or court in that country.

Amendments—SI 1992/709.

Defined terms—"Convention country": s 25(1).

38 Taking of evidence at request of court in Convention country

(1) Where a request is made to the Lord Chancellor by or on behalf of a court in a Convention country to obtain the evidence of a person residing in the United Kingdom relating to matters connected with an application to which section 26 of this Act applies, the Lord Chancellor shall request such court, or such officer of a court, as he may determine to take the evidence of that person relating to such matters connected with that application as may be specified in the request.

(2) The court by which or officer by whom a request under subsection (1) above is received from the Lord Chancellor shall have power to take the evidence and, after giving notice of the time and place at which the evidence is to be taken to such persons and in such manner as it or he thinks fit, shall take the evidence of the person named in the request relating to the matters specified therein in such manner as may be prescribed; and the evidence so taken shall be sent in the prescribed manner by the prescribed officer to the court in the Convention country by or on behalf of which the request referred to in subsection (1) above was made.

(3) Where any person, not being the person by whom the application mentioned in subsection (1) above was made, is required by virtue of this section to give evidence before a court in the United Kingdom, the court may order that there shall be paid –

(a)   if the court is a court in England, Wales or Scotland, out of moneys provided by Parliament; and

(b)   if the court is a court in Northern Ireland, out of moneys provided by the Northern Ireland Assembly,

such sums as appear to the court reasonably sufficient to compensate that person for the expense, trouble or loss of time properly incurred in or incidental to his attendance.

(4) Section 97(1), (3) and (4) of the Magistrates' Courts Act 1980 (which provide for compelling the attendance of witnesses, etc) shall apply in relation to a magistrates' court to which a request under subsection (1) above is made as if the application to which the request relates were a complaint to be heard by that court.

(5) …

(6) In the application of this section to Northern Ireland, in subsection (4), for the reference to section 97(1), (3) and (4) of the Magistrates' Courts Act 1980 there shall be substituted a reference to Articles 118(1), (3) and (4), 119 and 120 of the Magistrates' Courts (Northern Ireland) Order 1981.

Amendments—SI 1973/2163; MCA 1980, s 154, Sch 7, para 109; SI 1981/1675; SI 1992/709; SI 2010/976.

Defined terms—"Convention country": s 25(1).

38A Rules of court

(1) Rules of court may make provision with respect to the orders made or other things done by a magistrates' court, or an officer of such a court, by virtue of this Part of this Act, notice of which is to be given to such persons as the rules may provide and the manner in which such notice shall be given.

(2) For the purpose of giving effect to this Part of this Act, rules of court may make, in relation to any proceedings brought under or by virtue of this Part of this Act, any provision not covered by subsection (1) above which –

  (a)   falls within subsection (2) of section 93 of the Children Act 1989, and
  (b)   may be made in relation to relevant proceedings under that section.

(3) (*repealed*)

(4) For the purpose of giving effect to this Part of this Act, rules made under Article 13 of the Magistrates' Courts (Northern Ireland) Order 1981 may make, in relation to any proceedings brought under or by virtue of this Part of this Act, any provision not covered by subsection (1) above which –

  (a)   falls within paragraph (2) of Article 165 of the Children (Northern Ireland Order) 1995, and
  (b)   may be made in relation to relevant proceedings under that Article.

Amendments—Inserted by MO(RE)A 1992, s 1, Sch 1, para 18; amended by SI 1995/755; SI 2004/2035.

39 Interpretation of Part II

In this Part of this Act –

  "maintenance order" has the same meaning as in Part I of this Act;
  "prescribed" has the same meaning as in Part I of this Act;
  "registered order" means an order which is for the time being registered in a court in
      the United Kingdom under this Part of this Act;
  "registering court", in relation to a registered order, means the court in which that
      order is for the time being registered under this Part of this Act;
  "revoke" and "revocation" include "discharge".

Amendments—MO(RE)A 1992, s 1, Sch 1, para 19.

PART III
MISCELLANEOUS AND SUPPLEMENTAL

Further provisions relating to enforcement of maintenance orders and to applications for recovery of maintenance

40 Power to apply Act to maintenance orders and applications for recovery of maintenance made in certain countries

Where Her Majesty is satisfied –

  (a)   that arrangements have been or will be made in a country or territory outside the United Kingdom to ensure that maintenance orders made by courts in the United Kingdom can be enforced in that country or territory or that applications by persons in the United Kingdom for the recovery of maintenance from persons in that country or territory can be entertained by courts in that country or territory; and
  (b)   that in the interest of reciprocity it is desirable to ensure that maintenance orders made by courts in that country or territory can be enforced in the United

Kingdom or, as the case may be, that applications by persons in that country or territory for the recovery of maintenance from persons in the United Kingdom can be entertained by courts in the United Kingdom,

Her Majesty may by Order in Council make provision for applying the provisions of this Act, with such exceptions, adaptations and modifications as may be specified in the Order, to such orders or applications as are referred to in paragraph (a) or (b) above and to maintenance and other orders made in connection with such applications by courts in the United Kingdom or in that country or territory.

Amendments—CJJA 1982, ss 37(1), 54, Sch 11, para 17, Sch 14.

Scope—This section allows the application of the Act to be extended to other countries by Order in Council, with such modifications as may be necessary. The following Orders (see Part IV) have been made under this section: Recovery of Maintenance (United States of America) Order 1993; REMO(HCC)O 1993; REMO(USA)O 2007. Reference should also be made to Procedural Guide C3.

****

Provisions with respect to certain orders of magistrates' courts

42 Provisional order for maintenance of party to marriage made by magistrates' court to cease to have effect on remarriage of party

(1) Where a magistrates' court has, by virtue of section 3 of this Act, made a provisional maintenance order consisting of, or including, a provision such as is mentioned in section 2(1)(a) of the Domestic Proceedings and Magistrates' Courts Act 1978 (making of periodical payments by husband or wife) or Article 4(1)(a) of the Domestic Proceedings (Northern Ireland) Order 1980 and the order has been confirmed by a competent court in a reciprocating country, then, if after the making of that order the marriage of the parties to the proceedings in which the order was made is dissolved or annulled but the order continues in force, that order or, as the case may be, that provision thereof shall cease to have effect on the remarriage of the party in whose favour it was made, except in relation to any arrears due under it on the date of such remarriage and shall not be capable of being revived.

(2) For the avoidance of doubt it is hereby declared that reference in this section to remarriage include references to a marriage which is by law void and voidable.

(3) ...

Amendments—DPMCA 1978, s 89(2), Sch 2, para 37; SI 1980/564.

****

Supplemental provisions

44 Exclusion of certain enactments relating to evidence

(1) Section 20 of the Family Law Reform Act 1969 (power of court hearing certain proceedings to require use of blood tests to determine paternity) and any corresponding enactment of the Parliament of Northern Ireland shall not apply to any proceedings under this Act, but the foregoing provision is without prejudice to the power of a court to allow the report of any person who has carried out such tests to be given in evidence in those proceedings.

PART II

(2) The Evidence (Proceedings in Other Jurisdictions) Act 1975 shall not apply to the taking of evidence in the United Kingdom for the taking of which section 14 or section 38 of this Act provides.

Amendments—Evidence (Proceedings in Other Jurisdictions) Act 1975, s 8(1), Sch 1.

****

47 Interpretation: general

(1) In this Act –

"enactment" includes an enactment of the Parliament of Northern Ireland;

"magistrates' court", in relation to Northern Ireland, means a court of summary jurisdiction within the meaning of Article 2(2)(a) of the Magistrates' Courts (Northern Ireland) Order 1981.

(2) References in this Act to a part of the United Kingdom are references to England and Wales, to Scotland, or to Northern Ireland.

(3) Any reference in this Act to the jurisdiction of a court, where the reference is to assets being located or to a person residing within the jurisdiction of a court, shall be construed –

(a)   in relation to a magistrates' court in England and Wales as a reference to the local justice area in which the court acts, and

(b)   in relation to a magistrates' court in Northern Ireland as a reference to the petty sessions district for which the court acts.

(4) Any reference to this Act to any other enactment is a reference thereto as amended, and includes a reference thereto as extended or applied, by or under any other enactment.

Amendments—SI 1981/1675; CJJA 1982, ss 37(1), 54, Sch 11, para 18, Sch 14; Courts Act 2003, Sch 8, para 164.

****

Married Women's Property Act 1882

****

17 Questions between husband and wife as to property to be decided in summary way

In any question between husband and wife as to the title to or possession of property, either party may apply by summons or otherwise in a summary way to the High Court or such county court as may be prescribed and the court may, on such an application (which may be heard in private), make such order with respect to the property as it thinks fit.

In this section "prescribed" means prescribed by rules of court and rules made for the purposes of this section may confer jurisdiction on county courts whatever the situation or value of the property in dispute.

Amendments—Statute Law (Repeals) Act 1969; MFPA 1984, s 43.

Scope—This section enables the court to declare and enforce the proprietary rights of each party as they are found to exist in accordance with trust and common law principles. It does not give the court power to adjust those rights to produce a fair allocation of capital and income in the way that is done on an application for financial provision and property adjustment orders under MCA 1973, s 25. Where there is or will be an application for financial relief under MCA 1973 it is, generally speaking, a waste of time and money to apply under this section (*Fielding v Fielding* [1977] 1 WLR 1146). Two situations where s 17 still has a useful purpose are:

(a) where it is believed that one party may shortly become bankrupt, a declaration as to each party's respective beneficial interests in an asset may be of some value against any claim that a trustee in bankruptcy may subsequently mount; and

(b) where it is desired to obtain a sale before the final ancillary relief hearing.

Procedure—See FPR 2010, rr 8.12–8.17, which govern applications under MWPA 1882, s 17. The application may be made to the High Court or a county court under r 8.14. Where particulars of a mortgage are provided, the mortgagee must be served and may be made a party: r 8.15(1),(2).

As explained in **Extension of court's powers** below, s 17 contains a power of sale. In *Wicks v Wicks* [1998] 1 FLR 470 the Court of Appeal suggested that an application under s 17, combined with an application under FLA 1996, Pt IV if possession was required, allowed the court to order a sale before the final ancillary relief hearing.

"property"—Property is defined by s 24 to include a thing in action. The Matrimonial Causes (Property and Maintenance) Act 1958, an Act which enables the court to make orders in respect of property which a party has had in his possession or control, defines "property" (in s 8) to mean any real or personal property, any money, any negotiable instrument, debt or other chose in action and any other right or interest whether in possession or not.

Extension of court's powers—Matrimonial Causes (Property and Maintenance) Act 1958, s 7 extends this section to enable the court to make orders where money or property has ceased to be in the possession or under the control of one of the parties. In such a case the court is able to order one party to pay to the other the value of the applicant's interest in the asset that has been disposed of or to transfer to the applicant any property which can be traced to the original asset. Section 7(7) of that Act confirms the court's power to order a sale of property but a sale may be ordered only if there is some question between the parties as to the title to or possession of the property other than the issue of whether the property should be sold (*Rawlings v Rawlings* [1964] P 398).

Engaged parties—Law Reform (Miscellaneous Provisions) Act 1970, s 2(2) provides that an application under this section may be made by parties who have been engaged but not married. Jurisdiction exists even if the agreement to marry is unenforceable at common law, e g because it was made at a time when one of the parties was already married (*Shaw v Fitzgerald* [1992] 1 FLR 357).

Civil partners—Subject to a limitation period of 3 years from dissolution or annulment, application may be made by civil partners for orders equivalent to the relief provided by this section (see CPA 2004, s 66).

Polygamous marriages—The reference to "husband and wife" includes parties to a polygamous or potentially polygamous marriage (*Chaudhry v Chaudhry* [1976] Fam 148).

Time-limit for making application—Under MPPA 1970, s 39, a husband or wife must apply within 3 years of decree absolute. Engaged parties must apply within 3 years after the termination of the engagement (Law Reform (Miscellaneous Provisions) Act 1970, s 2(2)).

Court's powers—The court's jurisdiction to declare and enforce proprietary rights includes the power to restrain by injunction one party from disposing of a matrimonial home while the other wishes to live in it (*Lee v Lee* [1952] 2 QB 489; *Halden v Halden* [1966] 1 WLR 1481), and the power to assess the monetary value of a party's interest in an asset and to order the other party to pay a lump sum in that amount (*Bothe v Amos* [1976] Fam 46).

****

Married Women's Property Act 1964

1 Money and property derived from housekeeping allowance

If any question arises as to the right of a husband or wife to money derived from any allowance made by the husband for the expenses of the matrimonial home or for similar purposes, or to any property acquired out of such money, the money or property shall, in the absence of any agreement between them to the contrary, be treated as belonging to the husband and the wife in equal shares.

****

Matrimonial and Family Proceedings Act 1984

ARRANGEMENT OF SECTIONS

PART III
FINANCIAL RELIEF IN ENGLAND AND WALES AFTER OVERSEAS DIVORCE ETC

Applications for financial relief

Orders for Financial Provision and Property Adjustment

Orders for transfer of tenancies

Avoidance of transactions intended to prevent or reduce financial relief

Interpretation

PART V
FAMILY BUSINESS: DISTRIBUTION AND TRANSFER

Preliminary

Jurisdiction of county courts in matrimonial causes and matters

****

PART III
FINANCIAL RELIEF IN ENGLAND AND WALES AFTER OVERSEAS DIVORCE ETC

Applications for financial relief

12 Applications for financial relief after overseas divorce etc

(1) Where –

    (a) a marriage has been dissolved or annulled, or the parties to a marriage have been legally separated, by means of judicial or other proceedings in an overseas country, and

    (b) the divorce, annulment or legal separation is entitled to be recognised as valid in England and Wales,

either party to the marriage may apply to the court in the manner prescribed by rules of court for an order for financial relief under this Part of this Act.

(2) If after a marriage has been dissolved or annulled in an overseas country one of the parties to the marriage forms a subsequent marriage or civil partnership, that party shall not be entitled to make an application in relation to that marriage.

(3) The reference in subsection (2) above to the forming of a subsequent marriage or civil partnership includes a reference to the forming of a marriage or civil partnership which is by law void or voidable.

(4) In this Part of this Act except sections 19, 23, and 24 "order for financial relief" means an order under section 17 or 22 below of a description referred to in that section.

Amendments—CPA 2004, s 261(1), Sch 27, para 90(1)–(3).

Scope—This section enables a party whose marriage has been ended by proceedings taken overseas (including by talaq) that are recognised as valid in accordance with FLA 1986, Pt II to apply for financial relief in this country. In making the application, there must be compliance with the formal requirements of English law, in that there must have been a marriage under s 12(a), recognised under English law as valid, or at least void. In *Sharbatly v Shagroon* [2012] EWCA Civ 1507, a ceremony in a London hotel between Saudi nationals was not a marriage for the purposes of matrimonial relief under MCA 1973, approving *Dukali v Lamrani (Attorney-General Intervening)* [2012] 2 FLR 1099 (marriage ceremony within Moroccan consulate not a marriage). The orders by way of financial relief to which a party may be entitled are practically identical to the orders that may be made under MCA 1973, ss 22–24A and Matrimonial Homes Act 1983, Sch 1 except that, where the only ground conferring jurisdiction is the existence of a matrimonial home within the jurisdiction, special rules apply. Remarriage bars an application in the same way as under MCA 1973, s 28(3).

Costs—Applications under MFPA 1984, Pt III are financial remedy proceedings under FPR 2010, rr 2.3, 28.3(4)(b)(ii). Save where conduct arises, the general rule is that in financial remedy proceedings, the court will not make a costs order against a party: FPR 2010, r 28.3(6).

13 Leave of the court required for applications for financial relief

(1) No application for an order for financial relief shall be made under this Part of this Act unless the leave of the court has been obtained in accordance with rules of court; and the court shall not grant leave unless it considers that there is substantial ground for the making of an application for such an order.

(2) The court may grant leave under this section notwithstanding that an order has been made by a court in a country outside England and Wales requiring the other party to the marriage to make any payment or transfer any property to the applicant or a child of the family.

(3) Leave under this section may be granted subject to such conditions as the court thinks fit.

Defined terms—"child of the family": s 27; "order for financial relief": s 12(4).

Scope—In *Agbaje v Agbaje* [2010] 1 FLR 1813, the Supreme Court has given guidance to the operation of MFPA 1984 in the grant of financial relief in England, following overseas divorce. The threshold for leave under s 13 is "a substantial ground for the making of an application", which meant "a solid ground"; this is specifically a higher standard than "a serious issue to be tried" or "a good arguable case". The guidance set down in *Agbaje* in the interpretation and application of s 13 should be followed. A test of a 50% probability of the claimant receiving a substantive order as in *CG v IF* [2010] 2 FLR 1790 was disapproved by the Court of Appeal in *Traversa v Freddi* [2011] 2 FLR 272, applying *Agbaje* and granting leave to apply. See also *Schofield v Schofield* [2011] 1 FLR 2129, where a wife's earnings were modest and her husband's army pension a significant resource.

   In considering a leave application under s 13, the s 16 duty of the court to consider whether England and Wales is the appropriate venue for the application should be considered.

   The procedure to obtain permission is set out in FPR 2010, rr 8.24–8.28. The application is made to the Principal Registry of the Family Division. Applications should be made without notice: r 8.25 applies. The application is heard by a judge of the division and should be given an appropriately short listing of 30 mins. If permission is granted, the substantive application may be heard by a judge of the PRFD.

   Leave, once given, should be set aside only where there is a compelling reason to do so. An application to set aside leave should be heard with the substantive application, unless the respondent could deliver a "knockout blow": *Traversa v Freddi*.

14 Interim orders for maintenance

(1) Where leave is granted under section 13 above for the making of an application for an order for financial relief and it appears to the court that the applicant or any child of the family is in immediate need of financial assistance, the court may make an interim order for maintenance, that is to say, an order requiring the other party to the marriage to make to the applicant or to the child such periodical payments, and for such term, being a term beginning not earlier than the date of the grant of leave and ending with the date of the determination of the application for an order for financial relief, as the court thinks reasonable.

(2) If it appears to the court that the court has jurisdiction to entertain the application for an order for financial relief by reason only of paragraph (c) of section 15(1) below the court shall not make an interim order under this section.

(3) An interim order under subsection (1) above may be made subject to such conditions as the court thinks fit.

Scope—Where jurisdiction arises solely through the ownership of a matrimonial home in England and Wales, the court shall not make interim orders under this section. However, this section enables the court to make an interim order for maintenance of the applicant and/or the children of the family, pending final hearing. The limitations imposed by s 14 were (i) no order for interim maintenance would be made until leave had been given to make a Pt III application; (ii) under s 14(2), the jurisdiction must be founded on domicile or habitual residence, as opposed to an interest in a former matrimonial home in the jurisdiction; (iii) the applicant must be in "immediate need" and the provision must be reasonable in the sense of "current" rather than "urgent", as with application for interim maintenance under MCA 1973: *M v M (Financial Provision)* [2011] 1 FLR 1773.

15 Jurisdiction of the court

(1) Subject to subsections (1A) and (2) below, the court shall have jurisdiction to entertain an application for an order for financial relief if any of the following jurisdictional requirements are satisfied that is to say –

    (a)   either of the parties to the marriage was domiciled in England and Wales on the date of the application for leave under section 13 above or was so domiciled on the date on which the divorce, annulment or legal separation obtained in the overseas country took effect in that country; or

    (b)   either of the parties to the marriage was habitually resident in England and Wales throughout the period of one year ending with the date of the application for leave or was so resident throughout the period of one year ending with the date on which the divorce, annulment or legal separation obtained in the overseas country took effect in that country; or

    (c)   either or both of the parties to the marriage had at the date of the application for leave a beneficial interest in possession in a dwelling-house situated in England or Wales which was at some time during the marriage a matrimonial home of the parties to the marriage.

(1A) If an application or part of an application relates to a matter where jurisdiction falls to be determined by reference to the jurisdictional requirements of the Maintenance Regulation and Schedule 6 to the Civil Jurisdiction and Judgments (Maintenance) Regulations 2011, those requirements are to determine whether the court has jurisdiction to entertain the application or that part of it.

(2) Where the jurisdiction of the court to entertain proceedings under this Part of this Act would fall to be determined by reference to the jurisdictional requirements imposed by virtue of Part I of the Civil Jurisdiction and Judgments Act 1982 (implementation of certain European conventions) then –

    (a)   satisfaction of the requirements of subsection (1) above shall not obviate the need to satisfy the requirements imposed by virtue of Part I of that Act; and

    (b)   satisfaction of the requirements imposed by virtue of Part I of that Act shall obviate the need to satisfy the requirements of subsection (1) above;

and the court shall entertain or not entertain the proceedings accordingly.

(3) In this section, "the Maintenance Regulation" means Council Regulation (EC) No 4/2009 including as applied in relation to Denmark by virtue of the Agreement made on 19 October 2005 between the European Community and the Kingdom of Denmark.

Amendments—SI 2001/3929; SI 2007/1655; SI 2011/1484.

"matrimonial home" (s 15(1)(c))—Whether a property has been a matrimonial home is a question of fact, evidenced by any period of time spent living there or any agreement to so treat it (*King v King* [1941] 2 All ER 103).

Civil Jurisdiction and Judgments Act 1982, Pt I (s 15(2))—The 1982 Act applies only where the respondent is domiciled in a contracting state. With the exception of Greece, all the contracting states are in Western Europe; they include Belgium, Germany, France, Italy, Luxembourg, The Netherlands, Denmark, Republic of Ireland and the UK. By Sch 1, Art 1, the 1982 Act does not apply to rights in property arising out of a matrimonial relationship, but subject to that exception the basic theme of the 1982 Act, Pt I is that if a proposed respondent is domiciled in a contracting state he must be sued there. There is one further exception, namely that in matters relating to maintenance even though the respondent is domiciled in a contracting state he may nevertheless be sued in the courts of the country where the maintenance creditor is either domiciled or habitually resident. In summary, if the proposed respondent is resident outside the contracting states, CJJA, Pt I is irrelevant. If the respondent is resident within a contracting state, careful attention should be paid to the provisions of Pt I.

16 Duty of the court to consider whether England and Wales is appropriate venue for application

(1) Subject to subsection (3), before making an order for financial relief the court shall consider whether in all the circumstances of the case it would be appropriate for such an order to be made by a court in England and Wales, and if the court is not satisfied that it would be appropriate, the court shall dismiss the application.

(2) The court shall in particular have regard to the following matters –

- (a) the connection which the parties to the marriage have with England and Wales;
- (b) the connection which those parties have with the country in which the marriage was dissolved or annulled or in which they were legally separated;
- (c) the connection which those parties have with any other country outside England and Wales;
- (d) any financial benefit which the applicant or a child of the family has received or is likely to receive, in consequence of the divorce, annulment or legal separation, by virtue of any agreement or the operation of the law of a country outside England and Wales,
- (e) in a case where an order has been made by a court in a country outside England and Wales requiring the other party to the marriage to make any payment or transfer any property for the benefit of the applicant or a child of the family, the financial relief given by the order and the extent to which the order has been complied with or is likely to be complied with;
- (f) any right which the applicant has, or has had, to apply for financial relief from the other party to the marriage under the law of any country outside England and Wales and if the applicant has omitted to exercise that right the reason for that omission;
- (g) the availability in England and Wales of any property in respect of which an order under this Part of this Act in favour of the applicant could be made;
- (h) the extent to which any order made under this Part of this Act is likely to be enforceable;
- (i) the length of time which has elapsed since the date of the divorce, annulment or legal separation.

(3) If the court has jurisdiction in relation to the application or part of it by virtue of the Maintenance Regulation and Schedule 6 to the Civil Jurisdiction and Judgments (Maintenance) Regulations 2011, the court may not dismiss the application or that part of it on the ground mentioned in subsection (1) if to do so would be inconsistent with the jurisdictional requirements of that Regulation and that Schedule.

(4) In this section, "the Maintenance Regulation" means Council Regulation (EC) No 4/2009 including as applied in relation to Denmark by virtue of the Agreement made on 19 October 2005 between the European Community and the Kingdom of Denmark.

Amendments—SI 2011/1484.

Scope—In seeking leave under the Act, ss 13 and 16 should be taken in conjunction. The court must consider whether under s 16(1), England and Wales is the appropriate venue for the application. Regard must be had for the principle of comity, which demands respect for overseas orders, and forum (non) conveniens: *Moore v Moore* [2007] 2 FLR 339, CA. In *Agbaje v Agbaje* [2010] 1 FLR 1813, the Supreme Court said that the doctrine of forum conveniens did not apply, as no choice between the jurisdictions was involved.

Orders for Financial Provision and Property Adjustment

17 Orders for financial provision and property adjustment

(1) Subject to section 20 below, on an application by a party to a marriage for an order for financial relief under this section, the court may –

    (a) make any one or more of the orders which it could make under Part II of the 1973 Act if a decree of divorce, a decree of nullity of marriage or a decree of judicial separation in respect of the marriage had been granted in England and Wales, that is to say –

        (i) any order mentioned in section 23(1) of the 1973 Act (financial provision orders); and

        (ii) any order mentioned in section 24(1) of that Act (property adjustment orders); and

    (b) if the marriage has been dissolved or annulled, make one or more orders each of which would, within the meaning of that Part of that Act, be a pension sharing order in relation to the marriage.

    (c) if the marriage has been dissolved or annulled, make an order which would, within the meaning of that Part of that Act, be a pension compensation sharing order in relation to the marriage.

(2) Subject to section 20 below, where the court makes a secured periodical payments order, an order for the payment of a lump sum or a property adjustment order under subsection (1) above, then, on making that order or at any time thereafter, the court may make any order mentioned in section 24A(1) of the 1973 Act (orders for sale of property) which the court would have power to make if the order under subsection (1) above had been made under Part II of the 1973 Act.

Amendments—WRPA 1999, s 84(1), Sch 12, para 3; Pensions Act 2008, Sch 6, Pt 2.

Scope—This section incorporates the principles of MCA 1973, ss 25 and 25A, including the obligation to consider whether a clean break is appropriate, where the court is considering whether and in what manner to exercise its powers under the Act. In *Agbaje v Agbaje* [2010] 1 FLR 1813, the Supreme Court said that MCA 1973, P t III contains no express reference to hardship, justice or exceptionality and these were not conditions for the making of an award. Mere disparity between a foreign award and what would be awarded on an English divorce would be insufficient to trigger the application of Pt III, but the presence of hardship or injustice might make it appropriate for an order to be made. In *Agbaje*, the case was characterised not by the disparity between what the wife would receive in Nigeria and England, but the large disparity between what the husband and wife had received in the Nigerian courts, such as to create a real hardship and a serious injustice for the wife. *Agbaje* has established that the amount of financial provision would depend on all the circumstances of the case, not the minimum amount required to overcome injustice. The Court has a broad jurisdiction, subject to three principles that (i) primary consideration must be given to the welfare of any child of the marriage, (ii) it is wrong in principle to award more than the English court would have awarded and (iii) where possible, the order should provide for the "reasonable needs" of the spouse.

Pension Sharing/Pension Attachment—For an overview of pension sharing and pension attachment see the annotations to MCA 1973, s 21.

18 Matters to which the court is to have regard in exercising its powers under s 17

(1) In deciding whether to exercise its powers under section 17 above and, if so, in what manner the court shall act in accordance with this section.

(2) The court shall have regard to all the circumstances of the case, first consideration being given to the welfare while a minor of any child of the family who has not attained the age of eighteen.

PART II

(3) As regards the exercise of those powers in relation to a party to the marriage, the court shall in particular have regard to the matters mentioned in section 25(2)(a) to (h) of the 1973 Act and shall be under duties corresponding with those imposed by section 25A(1) and (2) of the 1973 Act where it decides to exercise under section 17 above powers corresponding with the powers referred to in those subsections.

(3A) The matters to which the court is to have regard under subsection (3) above –

(a)   so far as relating to paragraph (a) of section 25(2) of the 1973 Act, include any benefits under a pension arrangement which a party to the marriage has or is likely to have and any PPF compensation to which a party to the marriage is or is likely to be entitled (whether or not in the foreseeable future), and

(b)   so far as relating to paragraph (h) of that provision, include –

(i)   any benefits under a pension arrangement which, by reason of the dissolution or annulment of the marriage, a party to the marriage will lose the chance of acquiring, and

(ii)   any PPF compensation which, by reason of the dissolution or annulment of the marriage, a party to the marriage will lose the chance of acquiring entitlement to.

(4) As regards the exercise of those powers in relation to a child of the family, the court shall in particular have regard to the matters mentioned in section 25(3)(a) to (e) of the 1973 Act.

(5) As regards the exercise of those powers against a party to the marriage in favour of a child of the family who is not the child of that party, the court shall also have regard to the matters mentioned in section 25(4)(a) to (c) of the 1973 Act.

(6) Where an order has been made by a court outside England and Wales for the making of payments or the transfer of property by a party to the marriage, the court in considering in accordance with this section the financial resources of the other party to the marriage or a child of the family shall have regard to the extent to which that order has been complied with or is likely to be complied with.

(7) In this section –

(a)   "pension arrangement" has the meaning given by section 25D(3) of the 1973 Act, and

(b)   references to benefits under a pension arrangement include any benefits by way of pension, whether under a pension arrangement or not, and

(c)   "PPF compensation" means compensation payable under –

(i)   Chapter 3 of Part 2 of the Pensions Act 2004 (pension protection) or any regulations or order made under it,

(ii)   Chapter 1 of Part 3 of the Pensions Act 2008 (pension compensation sharing) or any regulations or order made under it, or

(iii)   any provision corresponding to the provisions mentioned in sub-paragraph (i) or (ii) in force in Northern Ireland.

Amendments—WRPA 1999, s 22(2),(3); Pensions Act 2004, Sch 12, para 4; Pensions Act 2008, Sch 6, Pt 2.

Scope—This section incorporates the principles of MCA 1973, ss 25 and 25A, including the obligation to consider whether a clean break is appropriate, where the court is considering whether and in what manner to exercise its powers under the Act. In *Agbaje v Agbaje* [2010] 1 FLR 1813, the Supreme Court said that Pt III contains no express reference to hardship, justice or exceptionality and these were not conditions for the making of an award. Mere disparity between a foreign award and what would be awarded on an English divorce would be insufficient to trigger the application of Pt III, but the presence of hardship or injustice might make it appropriate for an order to be made. In *Agbaje*, the case was characterised not by the disparity between what the wife would receive in Nigeria and England, but the large disparity in what the husband and wife had received in the Nigerian courts, such as to create a real hardship and a serious injustice for the wife. *Agbaje* has established that the amount of financial provision depends on all the circumstances of the case, not the minimum amount required to overcome injustice. The court had a broad jurisdiction, subject to three principles that (i) primary consideration must be given to the welfare of any child of the marriage, (ii) it was wrong in principle to award more than the English court would have awarded and (iii) where possible, the order should provide for the "reasonable needs" of the spouse.

19 Consent orders for financial provision or property adjustment

(1) Notwithstanding anything in section 18 above, on an application for a consent order for financial relief the court may, unless it has reason to think that there are other circumstances into which it ought to inquire, make an order in the terms agreed on the basis only of the prescribed information furnished with the application.

(2) Subsection (1) above applies to an application for a consent order varying or discharging an order for financial relief as it applies to an application for an order for financial relief.

(3) In this section –

"consent order", in relation to an application for an order, means an order in the terms applied for to which the respondent agrees;
"order for financial relief" means an order under section 17 above; and
"prescribed" means prescribed by rules of court.

Scope—MFPA 1984, s 19 mirrors MCA 1973, s 33A(1). This section empowers the court to make a consent order without a full investigation and without hearing oral evidence. There is a requirement for up-to-date information of the parties' circumstances. This is provided in each party's separate or joint statement of information: if separate documents, each party must sign the other's statement. There is no requirement for the parties to attend court. See FPR 2010, r 9.26.

20 Restriction of powers of court where jurisdiction depends on matrimonial home in England or Wales

(1) Where the court has jurisdiction to entertain an application for an order for financial relief by reason only of the situation in England or Wales of a dwelling-house which was a matrimonial home of the parties, the court may make under section 17 above any one or more of the following orders (but no other) –

(a)   an order that either party to the marriage shall pay to the other such lump sum as may be specified in the order;

(b)   an order that a party to the marriage shall pay to such person as may be so specified for the benefit of a child of the family, or to such a child, such lump sum as may be so specified;

(c)   an order that a party to the marriage shall transfer to the other party, to any child of the family or to such person as may be so specified for the benefit of such a child, the interest of the first-mentioned party in the dwelling-house or such part of that interest as may be so specified;

(d)   an order that a settlement of the interest of a party to the marriage in the dwelling-house, or such part of that interest as may be so specified, be made to the satisfaction of the court for the benefit of the other party to the marriage and of the children of the family or either or any of them;

(e)   an order varying for the benefit of the parties to the marriage and of the children of the family or either or any of them any ante-nuptial or post-nuptial settlement (including such a settlement made by will or codicil) made on the parties to the marriage so far as that settlement relates to an interest in the dwelling-house;

(f)   an order extinguishing or reducing the interest of either of the parties to the marriage under any such settlement so far as that interest is an interest in the dwelling-house;

(g)   an order for the sale of the interest of a party to the marriage in the dwelling-house.

(2) Where, in the circumstances mentioned in subsection (1) above, the court makes an order for the payment of a lump sum by a party to the marriage, the amount of the lump sum shall not exceed, or where more than one such order is made the total amount of the lump sums shall not exceed in aggregate, the following amount, that is to say –

(a)   if the interest of that party in the dwelling-house is sold in pursuance of an order made under subsection (1)(g) above, the amount of the proceeds of the sale of that interest after deducting therefrom any costs incurred in the sale thereof;

(b)   if the interest of that party is not so sold, the amount which in the opinion of the court represents the value of that interest.

(3) Where the interest of a party to the marriage in the dwelling-house is held jointly or in common with any other person or persons –

(a)   the reference in subsection (1)(g) above to the interest of a party to the marriage shall be construed as including a reference to the interest of that other person, or the interest of those other persons in the dwelling-house, and

(b)   the reference in subsection (2)(a) above to the amount of the proceeds of a sale ordered under subsection (1)(g) above shall be construed as a reference to that part of those proceeds which is attributable to the interest of that party to the marriage in the dwelling-house.

Scope—Where the only fact establishing jurisdiction is the existence of a matrimonial home in this country, the court cannot make any maintenance order and it must not make a capital order which exceeds the monetary value of the matrimonial home.

21 Application to orders under ss 14 and 17 of certain provisions of Part II of Matrimonial Causes Act 1973

(1) The following provisions of Part II of the 1973 Act (financial relief for parties to marriage and children of family) shall apply in relation to an order under section 14 or 17 above as they apply in relation to a like order under that Part of that Act, that is to say –

(a)   section 23(3) (provisions as to lump sums);
(b)   section 24A(2), (4), (5) and (6) (provisions as to orders for sale);
(ba)   section 24B(3) to (5) (provisions about pension sharing orders in relation to divorce and nullity);
(bb)   section 24C (duty to stay pension sharing orders);
(bc)   section 24D (apportionment of pension sharing charges);
(bca) section 24E(3) to (10) (provisions about pension compensation orders in relation to divorce and nullity);
(bcb) section 24F (duty to stay pension compensation sharing orders);
(bcc) section 24G (apportionment of pension compensation sharing charges);
(bd)   section 25B(3) to (7B) (power, by financial provision order, to attach payments under a pension arrangement, or to require the exercise of a right of commutation under such an arrangement);
(be)   section 25C (extension of lump sum powers in relation to death benefits under a pension arrangement);
(bf)   section 25E(2) to (10) (the Pension Protection Fund);
(bg)   section 25F (power, by financial provision order, to attach pension compensation payments, or to require the exercise of a right of commutation of pension compensation);
(c)   section 28(1) and (2) (duration of continuing financial provision orders in favour of party to marriage);
(d)   section 29 (duration of continuing financial provision orders in favour of children, and age limit on making certain orders in their favour);

(e) section 30 (direction for settlement of instrument for securing payments or effecting property adjustment), except paragraph (b);

(f) section 31 variation, discharge etc of certain orders for financial relief), except subsection (2)(e) and subsection (4);

(g) section 32 (payment of certain arrears unenforceable without the leave of the court);

(h) section 33 (orders for repayment of sums paid under certain orders);

(i) section 38 (orders for repayment of sums paid after cessation of order by reason of remarriage);

(j) section 39 (settlements etc made in compliance with a property adjustment order may be avoided on bankruptcy of settlor); and

(k) section 40 (payments etc under order made in favour of person suffering from mental disorder).

(l) section 40A (appeals relating to pension sharing orders which have taken effect).

(m) section 40B (appeals relating to pension compensation sharing orders which have taken effect).

(2) Subsection (1)(bd), (be) and (bg) above shall not apply where the court has jurisdiction to entertain an application for an order for financial relief by reason only of the situation in England or Wales of a dwelling-house which was a matrimonial home of the parties.

(3) Section 25D(1) of the 1973 Act (effect of transfers on orders relating to rights under a pension arrangement) shall apply in relation to an order made under section 17 above by virtue of subsection (1)(bd) or (be) above as it applies in relation to an order made under section 23 of that Act by virtue of section 25B or 25C of the 1973 Act.

(4) The Lord Chancellor may by regulations make for the purposes of this Part of this Act provision corresponding to any provision which may be made by him under subsections (2) to (2B) of section 25D of the 1973 Act or under subsections (1) to (3) of section 25G of that Act.

(5) Power to make regulations under this section shall be exercisable by statutory instrument which shall be subject to annulment in pursuance of a resolution of either House of Parliament.

Amendments—WRPA 1999, ss 22(4),(5), 84(1), Sch 12, para 4, Sch 13, Pt II; Pensions Act 2004, Sch 12, para 4; Pensions Act 2008, Sch 6, Pt 2.

Scope—Subject to CSA 1991, which restricts the court's power to order child maintenance (see Procedural Guide B7), this section imports into the provisions for providing financial relief following an overseas divorce the vast majority of the powers of the court which apply where a financial application is brought following a divorce in this country. The three conspicuous absentees are the power to award interest on a lump sum under MCA 1973, s 23(6), the power to make a direction under s 25A(3) that there may be no further application for a periodical payments or secured periodical payments order, and the prohibition from applying to extend the term of a maintenance order under s 28(1A).

Mental disorder under s 21(1)(k)—See MCA 2005: a person who lacks capacity is defined in s 2(1) as a person who at the material time "is unable to make a decision for himself ... because of an impediment of, or a disturbance in the functioning of, the mind or brain".

Orders for transfer of tenancies

22 Powers of the court in relation to certain tenancies of dwelling-houses

(1) This section applies if –

(a) an application is made by a party to a marriage for an order for financial relief; and

(b) one of the parties is entitled, either in his own right or jointly with the other party, to occupy a dwelling-house situated in England or Wales by virtue of a tenancy which is a relevant tenancy within the meaning of Schedule 7 to the Family Law Act 1996 (certain statutory tenancies).

(2) The court may make in relation to that dwelling-house any order which it could make under Part II of that Schedule if a decree of divorce, a decree of nullity of marriage or a decree of judicial separation has been granted in England and Wales in respect of the marriage.

(3) The provisions of paragraphs 10, 11 and 14(1) in Part III of that Schedule apply in relation to any order under this section as they apply to any order under Part II of that Schedule.

Amendments—Substituted by FLA 1996, s 66(1), Sch 8, para 52; amended by SI 1997/1892.

Avoidance of transactions intended to prevent or reduce financial relief

23 Avoidance of transactions intended to defeat applications for financial relief

(1) For the purposes of this section "financial relief" means relief under section 14 or 17 above and any reference to defeating a claim by a party to a marriage for financial relief from being granted is a reference to preventing financial relief from being granted or reducing the amount of relief which might be granted, or frustrating or impeding the enforcement of any order which might be or has been made under either of those provisions at the instance of that party.

(2) Where leave is granted under section 13 above for the making by a party to a marriage of an application for an order for financial relief under section 17 above, the court may, on an application by that party –

(a) if it is satisfied that the other party to the marriage is, with the intention of defeating the claim for financial relief, about to make any disposition or to transfer out of the jurisdiction or otherwise deal with any property, make such order as it thinks fit for restraining the other party from so doing or otherwise for protecting the claim;

(b) if it is satisfied that the other party has, with that intention, made a reviewable disposition and that if the disposition were set aside financial relief or different financial relief would be granted to the applicant, make an order setting aside the disposition.

(3) Where an order for financial relief under section 14 or 17 above has been made by the court at the instance of a party to a marriage, then, on an application made by that party, the court may, if it is satisfied that the other party to the marriage has, with the intention of defeating the claim for financial relief, made a reviewable disposition, make an order setting aside the disposition.

(4) Where the court has jurisdiction to entertain the application for an order for financial relief by reason only of paragraph (c) of section 15(1) above, it shall not make any order under subsection (2) or (3) above in respect of any property other than the dwelling-house concerned.

(5) Where the court makes an order under subsection (2)(b) or (3) above setting aside a disposition it shall give such consequential directions as it thinks fit for giving effect to the order (including directions requiring the making of any payments or the disposal of any property).

(6) Any disposition made by the other party to the marriage (whether before or after the commencement of the application) is a reviewable disposition for the purposes of

subsections (2)(b) and (3) above unless it was made for valuable consideration (other than marriage) to a person who, at the time of the disposition, acted in relation to it in good faith and without notice of any intention on the part of the other party to defeat the applicant's claim for financial relief.

(7) Where an application is made under subsection (2) or (3) above with respect to a disposition which took place less than three years before the date of the application or with respect to a disposition or other dealing with property which is about to take place and the court is satisfied –

    (a)   in a case falling within subsection (2)(a) or (b) above, that the disposition or other dealing would (apart from this section) have the consequence, or

    (b)   in a case falling within subsection (3) above, that the disposition has had the consequence,

of defeating a claim by the applicant for financial relief, it shall be presumed unless the contrary is shown, that the person who disposed of or is about to dispose of or deal with the property did so or, as the case may be, is about to do so, with the intention of defeating the applicant's claim for financial relief.

(8) In this section "disposition" does not include any provision contained in a will or codicil but, with that exception, includes any conveyance, assurance or gift of property of any description, whether made by an instrument or otherwise.

(9) The preceding provisions of this section are without prejudice to any power of the High Court to grant injunctions under section 37 of the Senior Courts Act 1981.

Amendments—CRA 2005, Sch 11, para 1(2).

Scope—This section is the equivalent of MCA 1973, s 37. It enables an applicant who has been granted leave to apply for financial relief to restrain future, and set aside past, disposals made with the intention of defeating the claim.

24 Prevention of transactions intended to defeat prospective applications for financial relief

(1) Where, on an application by a party to a marriage, it appears to the court –

    (a)   that the marriage has been dissolved or annulled, or that the parties to the marriage have been legally separated, by means of judicial or other proceedings in an overseas country; and

    (b)   that the applicant intends to apply for leave to make an application for an order for financial relief under section 17 above as soon as he or she has been habitually resident in England and Wales for a period of one year; and

    (c)   that the other party to the marriage is, with the intention of defeating a claim for financial relief, about to make any disposition or to transfer out of the jurisdiction or otherwise deal with any property,

the court may make such order as it thinks fit for restraining the other party from taking such action as is mentioned in paragraph (c) above.

(2) For the purposes of an application under subsection (1) above –

    (a)   the reference to defeating a claim for financial relief shall be construed in accordance with subsection (1) of section 23 above (omitting the reference to any order which has been made); and

    (b)   subsections (7) and (8) of section 23 above shall apply as they apply for the purposes of an application under that section.

(3) The preceding provisions of this section are without prejudice to any power of the High Court to grant injunctions under section 37 of the Senior Courts Act 1981.

Amendments—CRA 2005, Sch 11, para 1(2).

Defined terms—"the court", "overseas country": s 27.

Scope—Although the major restraining provisions, equivalent to MCA 1973, s 37, are contained in s 23, this provides a remedy, equivalent to that contained in MCA 1973, s 37(2)(a), for an applicant who has not yet obtained leave but who intends to do so as soon as there has been 1 year's habitual residence. Without prejudice to the court's power under SCA 1981, s 37, this section enables an applicant to restrain anticipated dealings made with the intention of defeating the claim.

****

Interpretation

27 Interpretation of Part III

In this Part of this Act –

"the 1973 Act" means the Matrimonial Causes Act 1973;

"child of the family" has the meaning as in section 52(1) of the 1973 Act;

"the court" means the High Court or, where a county court has jurisdiction by virtue of Part V of this Act, a county court;

"dwelling-house" includes any building or part thereof which is occupied as a dwelling, and any yard, garden, garage or outhouse belonging to the dwelling-house and occupied therewith;

"order for financial relief" has the meaning given by section 12(4) above;

"overseas country" means a country or territory outside the British Islands;

"possession" includes receipt of, or the right to receive, rents and profits;

"property adjustment order" means such an order as is specified in section 24(1)(a), (b), (c) or (d) of the 1973 Act;

"rent" does not include mortgage interest;

"secured periodical payments order" means such an order as is specified in section 23(1)(b) or (e) of the 1973 Act.

"where a county court has jurisdiction by virtue of Part V of this Act"—This is a reference to a divorce county court.

****

PART V
FAMILY BUSINESS: DISTRIBUTION AND TRANSFER

Preliminary

32 What is family business

In this Part of this Act –

"family business" means business of any description which in the High Court is for the time being assigned to the Family Division and to no other Division by or under section 61 of (and Schedule 1 to) the Senior Courts Act 1981;

"family proceedings" means proceedings which are family business;

"civil partnership cause" means an action for the dissolution or annulment of a civil partnership or for the legal separation of civil partners;

"matrimonial cause" means an action for divorce, nullity of marriage or judicial separation;

and "the 1973 Act" means the Matrimonial Causes Act 1973.

Amendments—FLA 1986, s 68(1), Sch 1, para 27; CPA 2004, s 261(1), Sch 27, para 91; CRA 2005, Sch 11, para 1(2).

Jurisdiction of county courts in matrimonial causes and matters

33 Jurisdiction of county courts in matrimonial causes

(1) The Lord Chancellor may, with the concurrence of the Lord Chief Justice, by order designate any county court as a divorce county court and any court so designated shall have jurisdiction to hear and determine any matrimonial cause, except that it shall have jurisdiction to try such a cause only if it is also designated in the order as a court of trial.

In this Part of this Act "divorce county court" means a county court so designated.

(2) The jurisdiction conferred by this section on a divorce county court shall be exercisable throughout England and Wales, but rules of court may provide for a matrimonial cause pending in one such court to be heard and determined in another or partly in that and partly in another.

(3) Every matrimonial cause shall be commenced in a divorce county court and shall be heard and determined in that or another such court unless or except to the extent it is transferred to the High Court under section 39 below or section 41 of the County Courts Act 1984 (transfer to High Court by order of High Court).

(4) The Lord Chancellor, with the concurrence of the Lord Chief Justice, may by order designate a divorce county court as a court for the exercise of jurisdiction in matrimonial matters arising under Part III of this Act.

(5) The power to make an order under subsection (1) to (4) above shall be exercisable by statutory instrument.

(6) The Lord Chief Justice may nominate a judicial office holder (as defined in section 109(4) of the Constitutional Reform Act 2005) to exercise his functions under this section.

Amendments—CRA 2005, s 15(1), Sch 4, Pt 1, paras 171, 172.

34 Jurisdiction of divorce county courts as respects financial relief and protection of children

(1) Subject to subsections (2) and (3) below, a divorce county court shall have the following jurisdiction, namely –

(a) a jurisdiction to exercise any power exercisable under Part II or Part III of the 1973 Act in connection with any petition, decree or order pending in or made by such a court and to exercise any power under section 27 or 35 of that Act;

(b) if designated by an order under section 33(4) above, jurisdiction to exercise any power under Part III of this Act.

(2) Any proceedings for the exercise of a power which a divorce county court has jurisdiction to exercise by virtue of subsection (1)(a) or (b) above shall be commenced in such divorce county court as may be prescribed by rules of court.

(3) A divorce county court shall not by virtue of subsection (1)(a) above have jurisdiction to exercise any power under section 32, 33, 36 or 38 of the 1973 Act; but nothing in this section shall prejudice the exercise by a county court of any jurisdiction conferred on county courts by any of those sections.

(4) Nothing in this section shall affect the jurisdiction of a magistrates' court under section 35 of the 1973 Act.

35 Consideration of agreements or arrangements

Any provision to be made by rules of court for the purposes of section 7 of the 1973 Act with respect to any power exercisable by the court on an application made before the presentation of a petition shall confer jurisdiction to exercise the power on divorce county courts.

36 Assignment of Circuit judges to matrimonial proceedings

(1) The jurisdiction conferred by the preceding provisions of this Part of this Act on divorce county courts, so far as it is exercisable by judges of such courts, shall be exercised by such Circuit judges as the Lord Chief Justice may, after consulting the Lord Chancellor, direct.

(2) The Lord Chief Justice may nominate a judicial office holder (as defined in section 109(4) of the Constitutional Reform Act 2005) to exercise his functions under this section.

Amendments—CRA 2005, s 15(1), Sch 4, Pt 1, paras 171, 173.

36A Jurisdiction of county courts in civil partnership causes and matters

(1) The Lord Chancellor may, with the concurrence of the Lord Chief Justice, by order –

   (a)   designate any county court as a civil partnership proceedings county court, and
   (b)   designate, as a court of trial, any county court designated as a civil partnership proceedings county court.

(2) In this Part of this Act "civil partnership proceedings county court" means a county court designated under subsection (1)(a) above.

(3) A civil partnership proceedings county court shall have jurisdiction to hear and determine any civil partnership cause, subject to subsection (4) below.

(4) A civil partnership proceedings county court shall have jurisdiction to try a civil partnership cause only if it is designated under subsection (1)(b) above as a court of trial.

(5) The jurisdiction conferred by this section on a civil partnership proceedings county court shall be exercisable throughout England and Wales, but rules of court may provide for a civil partnership cause pending in one such court to be heard and determined –

   (a)   partly in that court and partly in another such court, or
   (b)   in another such court.

(6) Every civil partnership cause shall be commenced in a civil partnership proceedings county court.

(7) Every civil partnership cause shall be heard and determined in a civil partnership proceedings county court unless, or except to the extent, it is transferred to the High Court under –

   (a)   section 39 below, or
   (b)   section 41 of the County Courts Act 1984 (transfer to High Court by order of High Court).

(8) The Lord Chancellor may, with the concurrence of the Lord Chief Justice, by order designate a civil partnership proceedings county court as a court for the exercise of jurisdiction in civil partnership matters under Schedule 7 to the Civil Partnership Act 2004.

(9) The power to make an order under subsection (1) or (8) above shall be exercisable by statutory instrument.

(10) The Lord Chief Justice may nominate a judicial office holder (as defined in section 109(4) of the Constitutional Reform Act 2005) to exercise his functions under this section.

Amendments—Inserted by CPA 2004, s 261(1), Sch 27, para 92; SI 2006/1016.

36B Jurisdiction of civil partnership proceedings county courts as respects financial relief and protection of children

(1) Subject to subsection (2) below, a civil partnership proceedings county court shall have the following jurisdiction –

   (a)   a jurisdiction to exercise any power exercisable under –
      (i)   section 63 of the Civil Partnership Act 2004 (restrictions on making of orders affecting children), or
      (ii)   Schedule 5 to that Act (financial relief in the courts), other than Part 12 (arrears and repayments) and paragraph 73 (alteration of maintenance agreements by court after death of one party),
      in connection with any application or order pending in, or made by, a civil partnership proceedings county court;
   (b)   a jurisdiction to exercise any power exercisable under –
      (i)   Part 9 of that Schedule (failure to maintain: financial provision (and interim orders)), or
      (ii)   paragraphs 69 to 71 of that Schedule (alteration of maintenance agreements by court during lives of parties);
   (c)   if designated under section 36A(8) above, jurisdiction to exercise any power under Schedule 7 to that Act.

(2) Any proceedings for the exercise of a power which a civil partnership proceedings county court has jurisdiction to exercise by virtue of subsection (1) above shall be commenced in such civil partnership proceedings county court as may be prescribed by rules of court.

(3) Nothing in this section shall affect the jurisdiction of a magistrates' court under paragraphs 69 to 71 of Schedule 5 to the Civil Partnership Act 2004.

Amendments—Inserted by CPA 2004, s 261(1), Sch 27, para 92.

36C Consideration of agreements or arrangements

Where rules of court make provision for the purposes of section 43 of the Civil Partnership Act 2004 with respect to any power exercisable by the court on an application made under that section before an application is made for a dissolution or separation order, the rules shall confer jurisdiction to exercise the power on civil partnership proceedings county courts.

Amendments—Inserted by CPA 2004, s 261(1), Sch 27, para 92.

36D Assignment of circuit judges to civil partnership proceedings

(1) The jurisdiction conferred by the preceding provisions of this Part of this Act on civil partnership proceedings county courts, so far as it exercisable by judges of such courts, shall be exercised by such Circuit judges as the Lord Chief Justice may, after consulting the Lord Chancellor, direct.

(2) The Lord Chief Justice may nominate a judicial office holder (as defined in section 109(4) of the Constitutional Reform Act 2005) to exercise his functions under this section.

Amendments—Inserted by CPA 2004, s 261(1), Sch 27, para 92; amended by SI 2006/1016.

Distribution and transfer of family business and proceedings

37 Directions as to distribution and transfer of family business and proceedings

The President of the Family Division may, with the concurrence of the Lord Chancellor, give directions with respect to the distribution and transfer between the High Court and county courts of family business and family proceedings.

Scope—Allocation and transfer is governed by *PD: Allocation and Transfer of Proceedings* (3 November 2008) [2009] 1 FLR 365.

38 Transfer of family proceedings from High Court to county court

(1) At any stage in any family proceedings in the High Court the High Court may, if the proceedings are transferable under this section, either of its own motion or on the application of any party to the proceedings, order the transfer of the whole or any part of the proceedings to a county court.

(2) The following family proceedings are transferable to a county court under this section, namely –

    (a)   all family proceedings commenced in the High Court which are within the jurisdiction of a county court, divorce county court or civil partnership proceedings county court;

    (b)   wardship proceedings, except applications for an order that a minor be made, or cease to be, a ward of court or any other proceedings which relate to the exercise and the inherent jurisdiction of the High Court with respect to minors; and

    (c)   all family proceedings transferred from a county court to the High Court under section 39 below or section 41 of the County Courts Act 1984 (transfer to High Court by order of High Court); and

    (d)   all matrimonial causes and matters transferred from a county court otherwise than as mentioned in paragraph (c) above.

(3) Proceedings transferred under this section shall be transferred to such county court as the High Court directs, subject to subsections (3A) and (3B) below.

(3A) Where a matrimonial cause or matter within the jurisdiction of a divorce county court only is transferred under this section, it shall be transferred to such divorce county court as the High Court directs.

(3B) Where a civil partnership cause or matter within the jurisdiction of a civil partnership proceedings county court only is transferred under this section, it shall be transferred to such civil partnership proceedings county court as the High Court directs

(4) The transfer shall not affect any right of appeal from the order directing the transfer, or the right to enforce in the High Court any judgment signed, or order made, in that Court before the transfer.

(5) Where proceedings are transferred to a county court under this section, the county court –

    (a)   if it has no jurisdiction apart from this paragraph, shall have jurisdiction to hear and determine those proceedings;

    (b)   shall have jurisdiction to award any relief which could have been awarded by the High Court.

Amendments—Matrimonial Proceedings (Transfer) Act 1988, s 1(1); CA 1989, s 108(5), Sch 13, para 51; CPA 2004, s 261(1), Sch 27, para 93; SI 2005/3336.

39 Transfer of family proceedings to High Court from county court

(1) At any stage in any family proceedings in a county court, the county court may, if the proceedings are transferable under this section, either of its own motion or on the application of any party to the proceedings, order the transfer of the whole or any part of the proceedings to the High Court.

(2) The following family proceedings are transferable to the High Court under this section, namely –

(a) all family proceedings commenced in a county court, divorce county court or civil partnership proceedings county court; and

(b) all family proceedings transferred from the High Court to a county court, divorce county court or civil partnership proceedings county court under section 38 above.

Amendments—CPA 2004, s 261(1), Sch 27, para 94.

****

County court proceedings in principal registry

42 County court proceedings in principal registry of Family Division

(1) Sections 33 to 35 and 36A to 36C above shall not prevent the commencement of any proceedings in the principal registry except where rules of court under section 34(2) or 36B(2) above otherwise provide; and the following provisions of this section shall have effect for the purposes of enabling proceedings to be dealt with in that registry as in a divorce county court or civil partnership proceedings county court.

(1A) Subsection (2) below applies to –

(a) the jurisdiction in matrimonial causes or matters conferred by sections 33, 34 and 35 above on divorce county courts, and

(b) the jurisdiction in civil partnership causes or matters conferred by sections 36A, 36B and 36C above on civil partnership proceedings county courts.

(2) A jurisdiction to which this subsection applies shall be exercised in the principal registry –

(a) so far as it is exercisable by judges of such courts, at such sittings and in such places as the Lord Chancellor may, after consulting the Lord Chief Justice, direct; and

(b) so far as it is exercisable by registrars of such courts, by such registrars or by registrars and other officers of the principal registry according as rules of court may provide.

(2A) Rules of court may make provision –

(a) for treating, for any purposes specified in the rules, matrimonial causes and matters pending in the registry with respect to which the jurisdiction mentioned in subsection (1A)(a) above is exercisable as pending in a divorce county court,

(b) for treating, for any purposes specified in the rules, civil partnership causes and matters pending in the registry with respect to which the jurisdiction mentioned in subsection (1A)(b) above is exercisable as pending in a civil partnership proceedings county court, and

(c) for the application of section 74(3) of the Solicitors Act 1974 (costs) with respect to proceedings treated as mentioned in paragraph (a) or (b) above.

(3) Where, by virtue of rules under subsection (2A) above, a matrimonial cause is pending in the registry as in a divorce county court, any ancillary or related proceedings

which could be taken in a divorce county court and which are not of a description excluded by the rules from the operation of this subsection may be taken and dealt with in the registry as in a divorce county court.

(3A) Where, by virtue of rules under subsection (2A) above, a civil partnership cause or matter is pending in the registry as in a civil partnership proceedings county court, any ancillary or related proceedings which could be taken in a civil partnership proceedings county court and which are not of a description excluded by the rules from the operation of this subsection may be taken and dealt with in the registry as in a civil partnership proceedings county court.

(4) The principal registry shall be treated as a divorce county court –

    (a) for the purposes of any provision to be made by rules of court under section 33(2) above;

    (b) for the purpose of any provision to be made under section 34(2) above prescribing the county court in which any proceedings are to be commenced; and

    (c) for the purpose of any transfer of family proceedings under section 38 or 39 above between the High Court and a divorce county court.

(4ZA) The principal registry shall be treated as a civil partnership proceedings county court –

    (a) for the purposes of any provision to be made by rules of court under section 36A(5) above;

    (b) for the purpose of any provision to be made under section 36B(2) above prescribing the county court in which any proceedings are to be commenced; and

    (c) for the purpose of any transfer of family proceedings under section 38 or 39 above between the High Court and a civil partnership proceedings county court.

(4A) Where a district judge of the principal registry is exercising jurisdiction in any matrimonial cause or matter, or in any civil partnership cause or matter, which could be exercised by a district judge of a county court, he shall have the same powers in relation to those proceedings as if he were a district judge of a county court and the proceedings were in a county court.

(5) Rules of court shall make provision for securing, with respect to family proceedings dealt with under this section, that, as nearly as may be, the same consequences shall follow –

    (a) as regards service of process –

        (i) as if proceedings commenced in the principal registry in a matrimonial cause or matter had been commenced in a divorce county court, and

        (ii) as if proceedings commenced in that registry in a civil partnership cause or matter had been commenced in a civil partnership proceedings county court; and

    (b) as regards enforcement of orders –

        (i) as if orders made in that registry in the exercise of the family jurisdiction conferred by sections 33, 34 and 35 above on divorce county courts were orders made by such a court, and

        (ii) as if orders made in that registry in the exercise of the family jurisdiction conferred by sections 36A, 36B and 36C above on civil partnership proceedings county courts were orders made by such a court.

(5A) For the purposes of subsection (3A) above, proceedings –

    (a) are "ancillary" to a civil partnership cause if they are connected with the cause, and

(b) are "related" to a civil partnership cause if they are for protecting or otherwise relate to any rights, or the exercise of any rights, of –
  (i)   the civil partners as civil partners, or
  (ii) any children of the family

(6) In this section "the principal registry" means the principal registry of the Family Division of the High Court and, for the purposes of subsection (3) above, proceedings are "ancillary" to a matrimonial cause if they are connected with the cause and are "related" to a matrimonial cause if they are for protecting or otherwise relate to any rights, or the exercise of any rights, of the parties to the marriage as husband and wife or any children of the family.

(7) The Lord Chief Justice may nominate a judicial office holder (as defined in section 109(4) of the Constitutional Reform Act 2005) to exercise his functions under this section.

Amendments—CLSA 1990, ss 74(7), 125(3), Sch 18, para 50; CPA 2004, s 261(1), Sch 27, para 96; CRA 2005, s 15(1), Sch 4, Pt 1, paras 171, 174.

****

Matrimonial Causes Act 1973

ARRANGEMENT OF SECTIONS

PART I
DIVORCE, NULLITY AND OTHER MATRIMONIAL SUITS

Divorce

PART II

PART I
DIVORCE, NULLITY AND OTHER MATRIMONIAL SUITS

Divorce

1 Divorce on breakdown of marriage

(1) Subject to section 3 below, a petition for divorce may be presented to the court by either party to a marriage on the ground that the marriage has broken down irretrievably.

(2) The court hearing a petition for divorce shall not hold the marriage to have broken down irretrievably unless the petitioner satisfies the court of one or more of the following facts, that is to say –

(a)   that the respondent has committed adultery and the petitioner finds it intolerable to live with the respondent;
(b)   that the respondent has behaved in such a way that the petitioner cannot reasonably be expected to live with the respondent;
(c)   that the respondent has deserted the petitioner for a continuous period of at least two years immediately preceding the presentation of the petition;
(d)   that the parties of the marriage have lived apart for a continuous period of at

least two years immediately preceding the presentation of the petition (hereafter in this Act referred to as "two years' separation") and the respondent consents to a decree being granted;

(e)   that the parties to the marriage have lived apart for a continuous period of at least five years immediately preceding the presentation of the petition (hereafter in this Act referred to as "five years' separation").

(3) On a petition for divorce it shall be the duty of the court to inquire, so far as it reasonably can, into the facts alleged by the petitioner and into any facts alleged by the respondent.

(4) If the court is satisfied on the evidence of any such fact as is mentioned in subsection (2) above, then, unless it is satisfied on all the evidence that the marriage has not broken down irretrievably, it shall, subject to section 5 below, grant a decree of divorce.

(5) Every decree of divorce shall in the first instance be a decree nisi and shall not be made absolute before the expiration of six months from its grant unless the High Court by general order from time to time fixes a shorter period, or unless in any particular case the court in which the proceedings are for the time being pending from time to time by special order fixes a shorter period than the period otherwise applicable for the time being by virtue of this subsection.

Amendments—MFPA 1984, s 46(1), Sch 1, para 10.

Defined terms—"the court": s 52.

Scope—This section defines the ground for divorce (irretrievable breakdown of marriage) and sets out the facts which must be proved to establish that ground. Procedurally, it places on the court the duty to inquire into the fact alleged and to grant a decree – initially a decree nisi followed by a decree absolute – if the fact is proved; unless the court is not satisfied as to irretrievable breakdown.

Procedure—Procedure for divorce and most other matrimonial causes is covered by FPR 2010, Pt 7; see also Procedural Guides B2 and B4.

"duty of the court to inquire ... into the facts alleged" (s 1(3))—The court's duty is performed by a district judge under the procedure in FPR 2010, r 7.20, but it may be performed under the standard procedure in open court if the petition is defended or the district judge is not prepared to sign his certificate under r 7.20; and after a case-management hearing (FPR 2010, r 7.22).

"facts alleged by the petitioner [or] by the respondent" (s 1(3))—Where an answer has been filed with a cross-prayer, there will be cases where a decree is granted solely on the fact(s) in the answer. The respondent is therefore the spouse who has obtained the decree nisi.

"decree of divorce" (s 1(4),(5))—In the first instance, a decree nisi is issued (FPR 2010, r 7.20(2)(a)). This decree can be made absolute on application by the spouse who obtained the decree (FPR 2010, r 7.32(2)) or, failing that, by the other spouse.

Time for application for decree absolute (s 1(5))—The time for application for a decree absolute is as follows:

(a)   *Application by party who obtained the decree nisi*   The general rule is that a decree nisi can be made absolute on application by the party who obtained the decree nisi after 6 weeks from grant of the decree. Application for decree absolute is under FPR 2010, r 7.32.

(b)   *Expedited decree*   Application may be made to the court to "fix a shorter period" (s 1(5)) where grounds for expedition exist (e g impending death, birth of a child to one party or perhaps travel abroad). Application is made at the time of the decree nisi application or later if the urgency is not discovered until then (see **Application for expedited decree** under FPR 2010, r 7.32 and PD7A, paras 8.1–8.4).

(c)   *Application by spouse against whom decree pronounced*   The party against whom the decree was obtained can apply for a decree absolute on notice 3 months after the other spouse could have applied (MCA 1973, s 9(2)). Application is made under FPR 2010, r 7.33(2)(c). In *Re G (Decree Absolute: Prejudice)* [2003] 1 FLR 870, Bennett J allowed a respondent husband's application for decree absolute, which was opposed by the wife petitioner. Although the husband might not be prejudiced by the delay, in the absence of good grounds to refuse a decree, it should issue. Had the wife applied, a decree would have been granted. Outstanding ancillary relief proceedings were not a reason to delay grant.

2 Supplemental provisions as to facts raising presumption of breakdown

(1) One party to a marriage shall not be entitled to rely for the purposes of section 1(2)(a) above on adultery committed by the other if, after it became known to him that the other had committed that adultery, the parties have lived with each other for a period exceeding, or periods together exceeding, six months.

(2) Where the parties to a marriage have lived with each other after it became known to one party that the other had committed adultery, but subsection (1) above does not apply, in any proceedings for divorce in which the petitioner relies on that adultery the fact that the parties have lived with each other after that time shall be disregarded in determining for the purposes of section 1(2)(a) above whether the petitioner finds it intolerable to live with the respondent.

(3) Where in any proceedings for divorce the petitioner alleges that the respondent has behaved in such a way that the petitioner cannot reasonably be expected to live with him, but the parties to the marriage have lived with each other for a period or periods after the date of the occurrence of the final incident relied on by the petitioner and held by the court to support his allegation, that fact shall be disregarded in determining for the purposes of section 1(2)(b) above whether the petitioner cannot reasonably be expected to live with the respondent if the length of that period or of those periods together was six months or less.

(4) For the purposes of section 1(2)(c) above the court may treat a period of desertion as having continued at a time when the deserting party was incapable of continuing the necessary intention if the evidence before the court is such that, had that party not been so incapable, the court would have inferred that his desertion continued at that time.

(5) In considering for the purposes of section 1(2) above whether the period for which the respondent has deserted the petitioner or the period for which the parties to a marriage have lived apart has been continuous, no account shall be taken of any one period (not exceeding six months) or of any two or more periods (not exceeding six months in all) during which the parties resumed living with each other, but no period during which the parties lived with each other shall count as part of the period of desertion or of the period for which the parties to the marriage lived apart, as the case may be.

(6) For the purposes of section 1(2)(d) and (e) above and this section a husband and wife shall be treated as living apart unless they are living with each other in the same household, and references in this section to the parties to a marriage living with each other shall be construed as references to their living with each other in the same household.

(7) Provision shall be made by rules of court for the purpose of ensuring that where in pursuance of section 1(2)(d) above the petitioner alleges that the respondent consents to a decree being granted the respondent has been given such information as will enable him to understand the consequences to him of his consenting to a decree being granted and the steps which he must take to indicate that he consents to the grant of a decree.

Defined terms—"the court": s 52.

Scope—This section sets out a variety of provisions (s 2(1)–(5)) which have the effect of enabling the parties to live together for 6 months, or periods totalling 6 months, without jeopardising the evidence on which they may ultimately wish to found a divorce petition. It defines living apart as a state of not living together in the same household.

Rescission of decree nisi—The provisions of s 2(1) may apply if the court is asked to exercise any discretion it may have to rescind a decree nisi (*Kim v Morris* [2012] EWHC 1103 (Fam) at [63]), but only after 1 year from decree nisi (ie when provisions of FPR 2010, r 7.32(3) become effective) and requires rules to be made that will ensure that the respondent to a petition based on s 1(2)(d) is properly able to give informed consent. The FPR Committee is considering the subject of rescission, including in this context.

Information as to consent (s 2(7))—None has been included in FPR 2010.

3 Bar on petitions for divorce within one year of marriage

(1) No petition for divorce shall be presented to the court before the expiration of the period of one year from the date of the marriage.

(2) Nothing in this section shall prohibit the presentation of a petition based on matters which occurred before the expiration of that period.

Amendments—MFPA 1984, s 1.

Defined terms—"the court": s 52.

"matters which occurred before" (s 3(2))—Facts arising before the 1-year period can be pleaded as a basis for a divorce petition.

Judicial separation—Section 3 is no bar, for example, to a petition for judicial separation. Most other forms of relief under MCA 1973 (e g financial relief) are thus available to a petitioner, even though her marriage cannot be dissolved. If dissolution is subsequently sought, leave to present a petition is not necessary (FPR 2010, r 7.7(2)); however, leave is required to file a fresh petition even if the facts relied on pre-date the 1-year period and no decree in the judicial separation proceedings has been granted (*Butler v Butler, The Queen's Proctor Intervening* [1990] 1 FLR 114).

4 Divorce not precluded by previous judicial separation

(1) A person shall not be prevented from presenting a petition for divorce, or the court from granting a decree of divorce, by reason only that the petitioner or respondent has at any time, on the same facts or substantially the same facts as those proved in support of the petition, been granted a decree of judicial separation or an order under, or having effect as if made under, the Matrimonial Proceedings (Magistrates' Courts) Act 1960 or Part I of the Domestic Proceedings and Magistrates' Courts Act 1978 or any corresponding enactments in force in Northern Ireland, the Isle of Man or any of the Channel Islands.

(2) On a petition for divorce in such a case as is mentioned in subsection (1) above, the court may treat the decree or order as sufficient proof of any adultery, desertion or other fact by reference to which it was granted, but shall not grant a decree of divorce without receiving evidence from the petitioner.

(3) Where a petition for divorce in such a case follows a decree of judicial separation or (subject to subsection (5) below) an order containing a provision exempting one party to the marriage from the obligation to cohabit with the other, for the purposes of that petition a period of desertion immediately preceding the institution of the proceedings for the decree or order shall, if the parties have not resumed cohabitation and the decree or order has been continuously in force since it was granted, be deemed immediately to precede the presentation of the petition.

(4) For the purposes of section 1(2)(c) above the court may treat as a period during which the respondent has deserted the petitioner any of the following periods, that is to say –

   (a)   any period during which there is in force an injunction granted by the High Court or a county court which excludes the respondent from the matrimonial home;

   (b)   any period during which there is in force an order made by the High Court or a county court under section 1 or 9 of the Matrimonial Homes Act 1983 which prohibits the exercise by the respondent of the right to occupy a dwelling-house in which the applicant and the respondent have or at any time have had a matrimonial home;

(c)   any period during which there is in force an order made by a magistrates' court under section 16(3) of the Domestic Proceedings and Magistrates' Courts Act 1978 which requires the respondent to leave the matrimonial home or prohibits the respondent from entering the matrimonial home.

(5) Where –

(a)   a petition for divorce is presented after the date on which Part I of the Domestic Proceedings and Magistrates' Courts Act 1978 comes into force, and

(b)   an order made under the Matrimonial Proceedings (Magistrates' Courts) Act 1960 containing a provision exempting the petitioner from the obligation to cohabit with the respondent is in force on that date,

then, for the purpose of section 1(2)(c) above, the court may treat a period during which such a provision was included in that order (whether before or after that date) as a period during which the respondent has deserted the petitioner.

Amendments—DPMCA 1978, ss 62, 89(2)(a), Sch 2, para 38; Matrimonial Homes Act 1983, s 12, Sch 2.

Defined terms—"the court": s 52.

Scope—This section enables a spouse who has obtained a decree of judicial separation to seek a divorce on substantially the same facts and relying on findings in the previous proceedings. The section also sets out a number of factors which do not prevent the petitioner from seeking a decree under s 1(2)(c) (desertion).

Petition for divorce after decree of judicial separation (s 4(1))—If a decree of divorce is sought by a petitioner who has, or who is proceeding with, a judicial separation petition where the parties have not been married for a year, it is necessary to file a fresh petition (*Butler v Butler, The Queen's Proctor Intervening* [1990] 1 FLR 114). If the petition is presented after the 1-year period has expired, it may be amended, provided no decree has already been granted.

No decree "without receiving evidence from the petitioner" (s 4(2))—Not only is a fresh petition needed where there has already been a decree, but the petitioner will also need to prove formally that the facts have already been found by a court.

5 Refusal of decree in five year separation cases on grounds of grave hardship to respondent

(1) The respondent to a petition for divorce in which the petitioner alleges five years' separation may oppose the grant of a decree on the ground that the dissolution of the marriage will result in grave financial or other hardship to him and that it would in all the circumstances be wrong to dissolve the marriage.

(2) Where the grant of a decree is opposed by virtue of this section, then –

(a)   if the court finds that the petitioner is entitled to rely in support of his petition on the fact of five years' separation and makes no such finding as to any other fact mentioned in section 1(2) above, and

(b)   if apart from this section the court would grant a decree on the petition,

the court shall consider all the circumstances, including the conduct of the parties to the marriage and the interests of those parties and of any children or other persons concerned, and if of opinion that the dissolution of the marriage will result in grave financial or other hardship to the respondent and that it would in all the circumstances be wrong to dissolve the marriage it shall dismiss the petition.

(3) For the purposes of this section hardship shall include the loss of the chance of acquiring any benefit which the respondent might acquire if the marriage were not dissolved.

Scope—This section enables the respondent to a petition under s 1(2)(e) (5 years' living apart), if no other fact under s 1(2) is pleaded by the petitioner, to oppose the grant of a decree on the grounds that divorce will cause grave financial hardship and that it would in all the circumstances be wrong to dissolve the marriage. If, after consideration of all the circumstances including those in s 5(2)(b), the court finds the grounds established by the respondent then the petition must be dismissed. Proceedings under this section are to be distinguished from those under s 10(2)–(4), where the court's power is limited to delaying the grant of a decree absolute.

Procedure—To oppose the grant of a decree under this section the respondent must file an answer within 21 days from the date by which the acknowledgment of service is required to be filed. The answer must plead details of the financial hardship which the respondent will suffer and the circumstances which it is alleged would make it wrong to dissolve the marriage. The answer should conclude with a prayer that the petition be dismissed. The cause then proceeds as a defended cause; the court must direct that the case be listed for a case management hearing: FPR 2010, r 7.20(4). See r 7.22 for the duties of the court at case management, including deciding where the hearing should take place, setting a timetable for the filing of evidence, and giving directions in relation to disclosure and witnesses.

A defended divorce may be heard in a designated county court, the Royal Courts of Justice or a court authorised for High Court matrimonial proceedings: FPR 2010, r 7.23.

Financial provision for the respondent—While the petition subsists the respondent may seek maintenance pending suit; but upon "determination of the suit" (which includes dismissal of the petition under s 5(2)(b)) the maintenance pending suit ceases (s 22). If the respondent seeks continuing financial provision and the petitioner has failed to provide her with reasonable maintenance, application may be made under s 27. The respondent may seek to have such an application consolidated with the petition and tried immediately thereafter in the event of dismissal (CPR 1998, Sch 1, RSC Ord 4, r 9; CCR Ord 13, r 9); if the petition is dismissed many of the factors considered by the court in its dismissal will be similar to those in a consideration of the respondent's financial circumstances under ss 25(2) and 27(3) (CPR 1998, Sch 1, RSC Ord 4, r 9(1)(a); Sch 2, CCR Ord 13, r 9(1)(a)).

"grave financial or other hardship" (s 5(1))—The hardship, whether financial or otherwise, must be caused by the dissolution, as opposed to the breakdown, of the marriage. The usual case of financial hardship is where dissolution will result in one of the parties (usually the wife) losing a widow's pension (contingent upon her husband's death), the pension often being index-linked. In such a case, she must set out her case in her answer (probably referring to the Value of Lost Pension Table in *At A Glance*) and it is then for the husband in his reply to set out his proposals, if any, for compensating the wife for that financial hardship, for example by offering to fund a policy providing the wife with a lump sum should he predecease her, offering to agree a pension sharing order or, so as to cover the death in benefit lump sum, a pension attachment order – although both forms of relief may not be given against the same pension scheme. Additionally, he will point out that, while on decree absolute the wife will lose the chance of obtaining a widow's pension under the terms of his employer's scheme, the realisation of that chance depends on her outliving him and, by virtue of the divorce, she can rely on his national insurance contributions during the marriage, whereby she will receive the certainty of a State retirement pension at age 60 (for women who attain that age by 2010 and under the Government's current equalisation proposals staggered to age 65 up to 2020, and age 65 for those who attain that age after that date) whereas she would otherwise receive a much lesser amount by way of State retirement pension, i e the difference between a married couple's pension and a single person's pension. Pound for pound compensation for loss of contingent widow's pension rights is not appropriate (*Le Marchant v Le Marchant* [1977] 1 WLR 559). Hardship other than financial hardship, such as being regarded as a social outcast in one's own community (*Banik v Banik* (1973) FLR Rep 65), must also be pleaded in the answer but is very difficult to establish. If, for example, a wife petitions for divorce on the ground of the husband's behaviour and the husband then cross-petitions on the ground of 5 years' separation the wife is estopped from pleading that dissolution will result in grave financial or other hardship (*Grenfell v Grenfell* [1978] Fam 128). If the party who is losing pension rights has substantial capital, grave financial hardship is unlikely to be made out (*Archer v Archer* [1999] 1 FLR 327).

6 Attempts at reconciliation of parties to marriage

(1) Provision shall be made by rules of court for requiring the legal representative acting for a petitioner for divorce to certify whether he has discussed with the petitioner the

possibility of a reconciliation and given him the names and addresses of persons qualified to help effect a reconciliation between parties to a marriage who have become estranged.

(2) If at any stage of proceedings for divorce it appears to the court that there is a reasonable possibility of a reconciliation between the parties to the marriage, the court may adjourn the proceedings for such period as it thinks fit to enable attempts to be made to effect such a reconciliation.

The power conferred by the foregoing provision is additional to any other power of the court to adjourn proceedings.

Amendments—Legal Services Act 2007, s 208(1), Sch 21, para 29.

Defined terms—"the court": s 52.

Scope—This section provides for any solicitor acting for a petitioner to certify that reconciliation has been discussed with his client. and enables the court to adjourn proceedings if reconciliation appears to be a possibility. As worded, it applies to divorce proceedings only, although s 17(3) applies it to judicial separation proceedings as well.

"Provision shall be made by rules of court" (s 6(1))—FPR 2010, r 7.6 requires the solicitor acting for a petitioner in divorce proceedings to file with the petition a "statement of reconciliation".

7 Consideration by the court of certain agreements or arrangements

Provision may be made by rules of court for enabling the parties to a marriage, or either of them, on application made either before or after the presentation of a petition for divorce, to refer to the court any agreement or arrangement made or proposed to be made between them, being an agreement or arrangement which relates to, arises out of, or is connected with, the proceedings for divorce which are contemplated or, as the case may be, have begun, and for enabling the court to express an opinion, should it think it desirable to do so, as to the reasonableness of the agreement or arrangement and to give such directions, if any, in the matter as it thinks fit.

Defined terms—"the court": s 52.

Rules of court—No rules have been made under this section, but practices have developed which have given some effect to what is proposed here:

(a) *Pounds v Pounds [1994] 1 FLR 775*, CA   Where a consent application is lodged before decree, but after the filling of a petition, this can be made the subject of an order effective on grant of decree nisi.
(b) *Agreement between the parties*   In *Smith v McInerney* [1994] 2 FLR 1077, Thorpe J (following *Edgar v Edgar* (1981) 2 FLR 19, CA) held that parties should be required to adhere to any "contract (sic)" entered into by them at the time of separation:
"As a matter of general policy I think it is very important that what the parties themselves agree at the time of separation should be upheld by the courts unless there are overwhelmingly strong considerations for interference." (at [1081A]).
However, see also Prohibition of any restriction on right to apply under MCA 1973, s 34.
(c) *Agreement at FDR*   Where agreement is reached at FDR in terms agreed by the judge, but not incorporated immediately into a fully drafted consent order, the court will uphold that approved agreement as an order (*Rose v Rose* [2002] 1 FLR 978, CA).
(d) *Pre-proceedings approval of an agreement*   FPR PD19A, para 1.5 suggests that it may be possible to use the Pt 19 procedure to seek the court's approval of a financial agreement between spouses, civil partners or unmarried parents at a pre-proceedings stage

Agreement as a preliminary issue—In *Xydhias v Xydhias* [1999] 1 FLR 683, CA, Thorpe LJ suggested that where one party thought there was an agreement (eg in a draft consent application) but the other party denied it, then the question of whether or not an agreement had been reached should be tried as a separate and preliminary issue. Below is a procedure for dealing with this question which avoids the full ancillary relief procedure until the agreement issue is resolved:

(i) File application in Form A.
(ii) Seek immediate directions:
   – to stay requirements of FPR 2010, r 9.14 that Form E etc be filed

- to vacate first appointment
- for trial of a preliminary issue: "whether there is an agreement on the face of any documents produced which settles financial issues between the parties" subject to the subsequent consideration of the agreement in the light of MCA 1973, s 25.
- as to the filing of evidence including documents, many of which may be marked "without prejudice" (for an example of trial of a preliminary issue as to whether or not correspondence is covered by "without prejudice" see *Williams v Hull* [2009] EWHC 2844 (Ch)).

(iii) List the preliminary issue as to whether there is agreement before a district judge (who, if he finds no agreement, cannot hear any final application if he has seen "without prejudice" correspondence which is privileged from disclosure).

Antenuptial agreement—In *Radmacher (formerly Granatino) v Granatino* [2010] 2 FLR 1900, the Supreme Court considered the effects of an antenuptial agreement on the outcome of financial remedy order proceedings and held that it should be taken into consideration, subject to suitable safeguards. The alleged existence of an antenuptial agreement (a pre-nup) or its effect would be a matter for evidence at the time of negotiations for settlement or of argument in any financial remedy order proceedings as to the weight to be given to it (and see *Z v Z (No 2)* [2012] 1 FLR 1100 and *V v V* [2012] 1 FLR 1315 for further guidance on the impact of *Radmacher*). Such agreement could not be caught by s 7.

8 Intervention of Queen's Proctor

(1) In the case of a petition for divorce –

   (a) the court may, if it thinks fit, direct all necessary papers in the matter to be sent to the Queen's Proctor, who shall under the directions of the Attorney-General instruct counsel to argue before the court any question in relation to the matter which the court considers it necessary or expedient to have fully argued;

   (b) any person may at any time during the progress of the proceedings or before the decree nisi is made absolute give information to the Queen's Proctor on any matter material to the due decision of the case, and the Queen's Proctor may thereupon take such steps as the Attorney-General considers necessary or expedient.

(2) Where the Queen's Proctor intervenes or shows cause against a decree nisi in any proceedings for divorce, the court may make such order as may be just as to the payment by other parties to the proceedings of the costs incurred by him in so doing or as to the payment by him of any costs incurred by any of those parties by reason of his so doing.

(3) The Queen's Proctor shall be entitled to charge as part of the expenses of his office –

   (a) the costs of any proceedings under subsection (1)(a) above;

   (b) where his reasonable costs of intervening or showing cause as mentioned in subsection (2) above are not fully satisfied by any order under that subsection, the amount of the difference;

   (c) if the Treasury so directs, any costs which he pays to any parties under an order made under subsection (2).

Defined terms—"the court": s 52.

Divorce and nullity—As worded, this section applies to divorce proceedings only, although s 15 applies it to nullity proceedings as well.

Procedure (s 8(1))—Despite the breadth of s 8(1), the rules apply only to an application by the Queen's Proctor to show cause against a decree nisi being made absolute (FPR 2010, r 7.31).

9 Proceedings after decree nisi: general powers of court

(1) Where a decree of divorce has been granted but not made absolute, then, without prejudice to section 8 above, any person (excluding a party to the proceedings other than the Queen's Proctor) may show cause why the decree should not be made absolute by reason of material facts not having been brought before the court; and in such a case the court may –

(a) notwithstanding anything in section 1(5) above (but subject to sections 10(2) to (4) and 41 below) make the decree absolute; or

(b) rescind the decree; or

(c) require further inquiry; or

(d) otherwise deal with the case as it thinks fit.

(2) Where a decree of divorce has been granted and no application for it to be made absolute has been made by the party to whom it was granted, then, at any time after the expiration of three months from the earliest date on which that party could have made such an application, the party against whom it was granted may make an application to the court, and on that application the court may exercise any of the powers mentioned in paragraphs (a) to (d) of subsection (1) above.

Defined terms—"the court": s 52.

Divorce and nullity—As worded, this section applies to divorce proceedings only, although s 15 applies it to nullity proceedings as well.

Applications under MCA 1973, s 9—Section 9 deals with two separate forms of application:

(1) *Application to show cause (s 9(1))*   The procedure for the Queen's Proctor or "any person" to apply to the court to assert why a decree nisi should not be made absolute is set out in FPR 2010, r 7.31.

(2) *Application for decree absolute by spouse against whom the decree nisi was obtained (s 9(2))*   The procedure for the spouse who did not obtain the decree nisi to apply for a decree absolute is set out in FPR 2010, r 7.33(2)(c).

An application for a decree nisi to be made absolute that is made before the time-limit of 3 months renders void (as distinct from voidable) a decree made on that application, and the decree must be set aside (*Manchanda v Manchanda* [1995] 2 FLR 590, CA).

10 Proceedings after decree nisi: special protection for respondent in separation cases

(1) Where in any case the court has granted a decree of divorce on the basis of a finding that the petitioner was entitled to rely in support of his petition on the fact of two years' separation coupled with the respondent's consent to a decree being granted and has made no such finding as to any other fact mentioned in section 1(2) above, the court may, on an application made by the respondent at any time before the decree is made absolute, rescind the decree if it is satisfied that the petitioner misled the respondent (whether intentionally or unintentionally) about any matter which the respondent took into account in deciding to give his consent.

(2) The following provisions of this section apply where –

(a) the respondent to a petition for divorce in which the petitioner alleged two years' or five years' separation coupled, in the former case, with the respondent's consent to a decree being granted, has applied to the court for consideration under subsection (3) below of his financial position after the divorce; and

(b) the court has granted a decree on the petition on the basis of a finding that the petitioner was entitled to rely in support of his petition on the fact of two years' or five years' separation (as the case may be) and has made no such finding as to any other fact mentioned in section 1(2) above.

(3) The court hearing an application by the respondent under subsection (2) above shall consider all the circumstances, including the age, health, conduct, earning capacity, financial resources and financial obligations of each of the parties, and the financial position of the respondent as, having regard to the divorce, it is likely to be after the death of the petitioner should the petitioner die first; and, subject to subsection (4) below, the court shall not make the decree absolute unless it is satisfied –

(a)   that the petitioner should not be required to make any financial provision for the respondent, or

(b)   that the financial provision made by the petitioner for the respondent is reasonable and fair or the best that can be made in the circumstances.

(4) The court may if it thinks fit make the decree absolute notwithstanding the requirements of subsection (3) above if –

(a)   it appears that there are circumstances making it desirable that the decree should be made absolute without delay, and

(b)   the court has obtained a satisfactory undertaking from the petitioner that he will make such financial provision for the respondent as the court may approve.

Scope—This section contains two distinct provisions. First, s 10(1) enables a respondent who claims to have been misled when giving his consent to seek rescission of a decree of divorce, but not judicial separation, under MCA 1973, s 1(2)(d) (2 years' living apart with consent), provided that no other fact in MCA 1973, s 1(2) was proved by the petitioner. It makes no difference whether the petitioner misled him intentionally or unintentionally. The second aspect of the section is contained in s 10(2)–(4) which is a half-way house between the full defence to the grant of a decree nisi on the ground of financial (or other) hardship under s 5 and the range of income and capital orders available under ss 23 and 24. Where there is a loss of widow's pension rights, before issuing a s 10(2) application consideration should be given as to whether an application for a pension attachment and/or sharing order (although the two forms of relief may not be granted in respect of the same pension scheme) will meet the requirements of the applicant. In *Garcia v Garcia* [1992] Fam 83, this section was successfully used when the petitioner was in breach of a past obligation to contribute equally to the maintenance of a child.

Procedure for application for rescission under s 10(1)—See FPR 2010, r 7.28. It is probable that a decree under MCA 1973, s 1(2)(d) obtained on a respondent's answer would also be covered by this procedure.

Procedure for application under s 10(2)—Where the court makes a decree absolute following an application under s 10(2), it must make a written record of the reasons for making the decree absolute.

Effect of s 10(2) application—Making the application has the effect that the decree cannot be made absolute until the application has been heard, unless there are both circumstances making it desirable for the decree to be made absolute before hearing the application and the petitioner has given an undertaking to make suitable financial provision. The undertaking must contain concrete specific proposals and not merely be a general undertaking to carry out whatever the court may consider appropriate at some future time (see *Grigson v Grigson* [1974] 1 WLR 228).

10A Proceedings after decree nisi: religious marriage

(1) This section applies if a decree of divorce has been granted but not made absolute and the parties to the marriage concerned –

(a)   were married in accordance with –

(i)   the usages of the Jews, or

(ii)   any other prescribed religious usages; and

(b)   must co-operate if the marriage is to be dissolved in accordance with those usages.

(2) On the application of either party, the court may order that a decree of divorce is not to be made absolute until a declaration made by both parties that they have taken such steps as are required to dissolve the marriage in accordance with those usages is produced to the court.

(3) An order under subsection (2) –

(a)   may be made only if the court is satisfied that in all the circumstances of the case it is just and reasonable to do so; and

(b)   may be revoked at any time.

(4) A declaration of a kind mentioned in subsection (2) –

(a)   must be in a specified form;

(b) must, in specified cases, be accompanied by such documents as may be specified; and

(c) must, in specified cases, satisfy such other requirements as may be specified.

(5) The validity of a decree of divorce made by reference to such a declaration is not to be affected by any inaccuracy in that declaration.

(6) "Prescribed" means prescribed in an order made by the Lord Chancellor after consulting the Lord Chief Justice and such an order –

(a) must be made by statutory instrument;

(b) shall be subject to annulment in pursuance of a resolution of either House of Parliament.

(7) "Specified" means specified in rules of court.

(8) The Lord Chief Justice may nominate a judicial office holder (as defined in section 109(4) of the Constitutional Reform Act 2005) to exercise his functions under this section.

Amendments—Inserted by Divorce (Religious Marriages) Act 2002, s 1; amended by CRA 2005, s 15(1), Sch 4, Pt 1, para 76.

Procedure—Applications under s 10A(2) are governed by FPR 2010, r 7.30, which determines the form of the declaration and the necessary documentation in support.

Nullity

11 Grounds on which a marriage is void

A marriage celebrated after 31 July 1971 shall be void on the following grounds only, that is to say –

(a) that it is not a valid marriage under the provisions of the Marriage Acts 1949 to 1986 (that is to say where –
  (i) the parties are within the prohibited degrees of relationship;
  (ii) either party is under the age of sixteen; or
  (iii) the parties have intermarried in disregard of certain requirements as to the formation of marriage);

(b) that at the time of the marriage either party was already lawfully married or a civil partner;

(c) that the parties are not respectively male and female;

(d) in the case of a polygamous marriage entered into outside England and Wales, that either party was at the time of the marriage domiciled in England and Wales.

For the purposes of paragraph (d) of this subsection a marriage is not polygamous if at its inception neither party has any spouse additional to the other.

Amendments—Marriage (Prohibited Degrees of Relationship) Act 1986, s 6(4); Private International Law (Miscellaneous Provisions) Act 1995, s 8, Sch, para 2; CPA 2004, s 261(1), Sch 27, para 40.

Procedure—The procedure for petitions for nullity of marriage are, as for divorce, set out in FPR 2010, Pt 7.

12 Grounds on which a marriage is voidable

A marriage celebrated after 31 July 1971 shall be voidable on the following grounds only, that is to say –

(a) that the marriage has not been consummated owing to the incapacity of either party to consummate it;

(b)   that the marriage has not been consummated owing to the wilful refusal of the respondent to consummate it;

(c)   that either party to the marriage did not validly consent to it, whether in consequence of duress, mistake, unsoundness of mind or otherwise;

(d)   that at the time of the marriage either party, though capable of giving a valid consent, was suffering (whether continuously or intermittently) from mental disorder within the meaning of the Mental Health Act 1983 of such a kind or to such an extent as to be unfitted for marriage;

(e)   that at the time of the marriage the respondent was suffering from venereal disease in a communicable form;

(f)   that at the time of the marriage the respondent was pregnant by some person other than the petitioner;

(g)   that an interim gender recognition certificate under the Gender Recognition Act 2004 has, after the time of the marriage, been issued to either party to the marriage;

(h)   that the respondent is a person whose gender at the time of the marriage had become the acquired gender under the Gender Recognition Act 2004.

Amendments—MHA 1983, s 148, Sch 4, para 34; GRA 2004, ss 4, 11, Sch 2, para 2, Sch 4, para 5.

Procedure—The procedure for petitions for nullity of marriage is dealt with in FPR 2010, Pt 7. Rule 7.11 contains particular rules for medical evidence where the allegation is that a spouse has been incapable of consummating the marriage (s 12(a)).

"mental disorder" (s 12(d))—By virtue of MHA 1983, s 1(2), this means "mental illness, arrested or incomplete development of mind, psychopathic disorder and any other disorder or disability of mind and 'mentally disordered' shall be construed accordingly".

13 Bars to relief where marriage is voidable

(1) The court shall not, in proceedings instituted after 31 July 1971, grant a decree of nullity on the ground that a marriage is voidable if the respondent satisfies the court –

(a)   that the petitioner, with knowledge that it was open to him to have the marriage avoided, so conducted himself in relation to the respondent as to lead the respondent reasonably to believe that he would not seek to do so; and

(b)   that it would be unjust to the respondent to grant the decree.

(2) Without prejudice to subsection (1) above, the court shall not grant a decree of nullity by virtue of section 12 above on the grounds mentioned in paragraph (c), (d), (e), (f) or (h) of that section unless –

(a)   it is satisfied that proceedings were instituted within the period of three years from the date of marriage, or

(b)   leave for the institution of proceedings after the expiration of that period has been granted under subsection (4) below.

(2A) Without prejudice to subsection (1) above, the court shall not grant a decree of nullity by virtue of section 12 above on the ground mentioned in paragraph (g) of that section unless it is satisfied that proceedings were instituted within the period of six months from the date of issue of the interim gender recognition certificate.

(3) Without prejudice to subsections (1) and (2) above, the court shall not grant a decree of nullity by virtue of section 12 above on the grounds mentioned in paragraph (e), (f) or (h) of that section unless it is satisfied that the petitioner was at the time of the marriage ignorant of the facts alleged.

(4) In the case of proceedings for the grant of a decree of nullity by virtue of section 12 above on the grounds mentioned in paragraph (c), (d), (e), (f) or (h) of that section, a

judge of the court may, on an application made to him, grant leave for the institution of proceedings after the expiration of the period of three years from the date of the marriage if –

(a) he is satisfied that the petitioner has at some time during that period suffered from mental disorder within the meaning of the Mental Health Act 1983, and

(b) he considers that in all the circumstances of the case it would be just to grant leave for the institution of proceedings.

(5) An application for leave under subsection (4) above may be made after the expiration of the period of three years from the date of the marriage.

Amendments—MFPA 1984, s 2; GRA 2004, ss 4, 11, Sch 2, para 3, Sch 4, para 6.

Defined terms—"the court": s 52.

Application for leave after 3 years (s 13(4))—No procedure is prescribed for application under this provision. The application is likely to be dealt with under FPR 2010, Pt 18 procedure to start Pt 7 nullity proceedings. Application should be made without notice with an affidavit in support containing the following:

(a) a draft nullity application (petition);

(b) the medical evidence on which the petitioner relies in support of her contention that she was a patient;

(c) a statement of the background to the marriage and application; and

(d) a statement of why the petitioner believes the interests of justice require that she be granted leave.

"mental disorder" (s 13(4)(a))—By virtue of MHA 1983, s 1(2), this means "mental illness, arrested or incomplete development of mind, psychopathic disorder and any other disorder or disability of mind and 'mentally disordered' shall be construed accordingly".

"at some time during that period" (s 13(4)(a))—The disorder may have existed at the time of the marriage, or may have developed during the 3 years since the marriage.

14 Marriages governed by foreign law or celebrated abroad under English law

(1) Subject to subsection (3), where, apart from this Act, any matter affecting the validity of a marriage would fall to be determined (in accordance with the rules of private international law) by reference to the law of a country outside England and Wales, nothing in section 11, 12 or 13(1) above shall –

(a) preclude the determination of that matter as aforesaid; or

(b) require the application to the marriage of the grounds or bar there mentioned except so far as applicable in accordance with those rules.

(2) In the case of a marriage which purports to have been celebrated under the Foreign Marriage Acts 1892 to 1947 or has taken place outside England and Wales and purports to be a marriage under common law, section 11 above is without prejudice to any ground on which the marriage may be void under those Acts or, as the case may be, by virtue of the rules governing the celebration of marriages outside England and Wales under common law.

(3) No marriage is to be treated as valid by virtue of subsection (1) if, at the time when it purports to have been celebrated, either party was already a civil partner.

Amendments—CPA 2004, s 261(1), Sch 27, para 41(1)–(3).

15 Application of ss 1(5), 8 and 9 to nullity proceedings

Sections 1(5), 8 and 9 above shall apply in relation to proceedings for nullity of marriage as if for any reference in those provisions to divorce there were substituted a reference to nullity of marriage.

16 Effect of decree of nullity in case of voidable marriage

A decree of nullity granted after 31 July 1971 in respect of a voidable marriage shall operate to annul the marriage only as respects any time after the decree has been made absolute, and the marriage shall, notwithstanding the decree, be treated as if it had existed up to that time.

Scope—This section provides that a voidable marriage (ie covered by one or more of the grounds under s 12) only becomes void on decree absolute and is deemed to subsist until that time.

Other matrimonial suits

17 Judicial separation

(1) A petition for judicial separation may be presented to the court by either party to a marriage on the ground that any such fact as is mentioned in section 1(2) above exists, and the provisions of section 2 above shall apply accordingly for the purposes of a petition for judicial separation alleging any such fact, as they apply in relation to a petition for divorce alleging that fact.

(2) On a petition for judicial separation it shall be the duty of the court to inquire, so far as it reasonably can, into the facts alleged by the petitioner and into any facts alleged by the respondent, but the court shall not be concerned to consider whether the marriage has broken down irretrievably, and if it is satisfied on the evidence of any such fact as is mentioned in section 1(2) above it shall, subject to section 41 below, grant a decree of judicial separation.

(3) Sections 6 and 7 above shall apply for the purpose of encouraging the reconciliation of parties to proceedings for judicial separation and of enabling the parties to a marriage to refer to the court for its opinion an agreement or arrangement relevant to actual or contemplated proceedings for judicial separation, as they apply in relation to proceedings for divorce.

Defined terms—"the court": s 52.

Procedure—The procedure for judicial separation is covered by FPR 2010, Pt 7; see also Procedural Guides B2 and B4.

"duty of the court to inquire … into the facts alleged" (s 17(2))—The court's duty is dealt with by a district judge under the procedure in FPR 2010, r 7.20(2)(a).

"decree of judicial separation" (s 17(2))—In the case of judicial separation only a single decree is issued, but this cannot be granted until after the court has dealt with any issues which may arise under s 41 (arrangements for the children of the family).

18 Effects of judicial separation

(1) Where the court grants a decree of judicial separation it shall no longer be obligatory for the petitioner to cohabit with the respondent.

(2) If while a decree of judicial separation is in force and the separation is continuing either of the parties to the marriage dies intestate as respects all or any of his or her real or personal property, the property as respects which he or she died intestate shall devolve as if the other party to the marriage had then been dead.

(3) Notwithstanding anything in section 2(1)(a) of the Matrimonial Proceedings (Magistrates' Courts) Act 1960, a provision in force under an order made, or having effect as if made, under that section exempting one party to a marriage from the obligation to cohabit with the other shall not have effect as a decree of judicial separation for the purposes of subsection (2) above.

Defined terms—"the court": s 52.

Divorce after judicial separation—If divorce is sought where there are judicial separation proceedings not yet disposed of by dismissal or decree, leave to present a further petition is necessary (FPR 2010, r 7.7(1)); save where the petition follows a judicial separation petition filed within 1 year of the marriage and the new petition is based on the same facts as the old (FPR 2010, r 7.7(2)).

19 Presumption of death and dissolution of marriage

(1) Any married person who alleges that reasonable grounds exist for supposing that the other party to the marriage is dead may present a petition to the court to have it presumed that the other party is dead and to have the marriage dissolved, and the court may, if satisfied that such reasonable grounds exist, grant a decree of presumption of death and dissolution of the marriage.

(2) (*repealed*)

(3) In any proceedings under this section the fact that for a period of seven years or more the other party to the marriage has been continually absent from the petitioner and the petitioner has no reason to believe that the other party has been living within that time shall be evidence that the other party is dead until the contrary is proved.

(4) Sections 1(5), 8 and 9 above shall apply to a petition and a decree under this section as they apply to a petition for divorce and a decree of divorce respectively.

(5) (*repealed*)

(6) It is hereby declared that neither collusion nor any other conduct on the part of the petitioner which has at any time been a bar to relief in matrimonial proceedings constitutes a bar to the grant of a decree under this section.

Amendments—DMPA 1973, ss 6(4), 17(2), Sch 6.

Defined terms—"the court": s 52.

Scope—The fact that a spouse has been continually absent for 7 years and the petitioner has no reason to believe him to be alive during that time creates a rebuttable presumption of the death of that spouse.

Procedure—The procedure for seeking a decree of presumption of death is omitted from FPR 2010: the definition of matrimonial proceedings in r 2.3(1) does not refer to s 19 proceedings, although the effect of the definition in r 2.3(1) of civil partnership proceedings is to include the parallel civil partner provision.

"the court may, if satisfied" (s 19(1))—These words impose on the court a duty equivalent to "duty of the court to inquire ... into the facts alleged" under ss 1(3) and 17(2).

Decree of presumption of death and dissolution of marriage (s 19(4))—The reference to s 1(5) applies a procedure for decrees in the case of presumption of death similar to that for decrees of divorce. FPR 2010, r 2.3(2)(a)(ii) includes a presumption of death petition or application for a dissolution order (under MCA 1973, s 19) as enabling application to be made for the procedures under Pt 7 or for a financial order in such proceedings.

General

20 Relief for respondent in divorce proceedings

If in any proceedings for divorce the respondent alleges and proves any such fact as is mentioned in subsection (2) of section 1 above (treating the respondent as the petitioner and the petitioner as the respondent for the purposes of that subsection) the court may give to the respondent the relief to which he would have been entitled if he had presented a petition seeking that relief.

Defined terms—"the court": s 52.

"the court may give to the respondent the relief"—This situation may arise, for example, where a respondent files an answer to a petition and the suit proceeds on the prayer in his answer instead of on the prayer in the petition. In such a case, the court may grant a decree (with costs, as appropriate) to the respondent. That decree will have the effect of dissolving the marriage (although on the respondent's application or prayer) in the same way as if the decree were based on the prayer in the petition (or application).

PART II
FINANCIAL RELIEF FOR PARTIES TO MARRIAGE AND CHILDREN OF FAMILY

Financial provision and property adjustment orders

21 Financial provision and property adjustment orders

(1) The financial provision orders for the purposes of this Act are the orders for periodical or lump sum provision available (subject to the provisions of this Act) under section 23 below for the purpose of adjusting the financial position of the parties to a marriage and any children of the family in connection with proceedings for divorce, nullity of marriage or judicial separation and under section 27(6) below on proof of neglect by one party to a marriage to provide, or to make a proper contribution towards, reasonable maintenance for the other or a child of the family, that is to say –

  (a)   any order for periodical payments in favour of a party to a marriage under section 23(1)(a) or 27(6)(a) or in favour of a child of the family under section 23(1)(d), (2) or (4) or 27(6)(d);

  (b)   any order for secured periodical payments in favour of a party to a marriage under section 23(1)(b) or 27(6)(b) or in favour of a child of the family under section 23(1)(e), (2) or (4) or 27(6)(e); and

  (c)   any order for lump sum provision in favour of a party to a marriage under section 23(1)(c) or 27(6)(c) or in favour of a child of the family under section 23(1)(f), (2) or (4) or 27(6)(f);

and references in this Act (except in paragraphs 17(1) and 23 of Schedule 1 below) to periodical payments orders, secured periodical payments orders, and orders for the payment of a lump sum are references to all or some of the financial provision orders requiring the sort of financial provision in question according as the context of each reference may require.

(2) The property adjustment orders for the purposes of this Act are the orders dealing with property rights available (subject to the provisions of this Act) under section 24 below for the purpose of adjusting the financial position of the parties to a marriage and any children of the family on or after the grant of a decree of divorce, nullity of marriage or judicial separation, that is to say –

  (a)   any order under subsection (1)(a) of that section for a transfer of property;

  (b)   any order under subsection (1)(b) of that section for a settlement of property; and

  (c)   any order under subsection (1)(c) or (d) of that section for a variation of settlement.

"Any children of the family"—For the statutory definition of "child of the family" see MCA 1973, s 52. For practical purposes there must be a family in existence, and the relevant child must be treated as a child of that family by both parties. This is a question of fact and degree. In *Teeling* [1984] FLR 808, CA, a child of another man brought up within the matrimonial household for 6 months was a child of the family. In *Carron* [1984] FLR 805, CA, the wife's children by other men were still children of the family, despite being maintained by the birth fathers, because they had been treated as children of the family.

Judicial separation—This section deals with the court's global powers to adjust the financial position of the parties. The court's powers to make orders in a suit for judicial separation are more circumscribed than in divorce or nullity. A party seeking judicial separation may apply under s 23 (periodical payments) and s 24 (property adjustment). Section 25 considerations are therefore engaged. Other remedies available to the judicially separated are under s 22 (maintenance pending suit) and s 27 (neglect to maintain). There is no jurisdiction to make a clean break order under s 25A or a pension share under s 24B in judicial separation cases.

Relationship of ancillary relief with criminal compensation orders—Following the implementation of the Proceeds of Crime Act 2002, issues of confiscation and enforcement lie with the Crown Court (*Webber v Webber* [2007] 2 FLR 116). Ancillary relief and applications for confiscation orders are no longer heard together. In *Stodgell v Stodgell* [2009] 2 FLR 244 (CA), a wife's application for ancillary relief could not proceed until after a compensation order imposed on the husband following his conviction for tax evasion was discharged. Where the husband's assets are extinguished by moneys due under a confiscation order, a wife would fail in her ancillary relief claim, even where she was non-complicit in the husband's fraud.

Procedure—An application for financial orders under MCA 1973 is an application for a financial remedy. The procedure under FPR 2010, Pt 9 applies.

21A Pension sharing orders

(1) For the purposes of this Act, a pension sharing order is an order which –

    (a)   provides that one party's –

        (i)   shareable rights under a specified pension arrangement, or

        (ii)   shareable state scheme rights,

        be subject to pension sharing for the benefit of the other party, and

    (b)   specifies the percentage value to be transferred.

(1A) Where section 25E(7) applies, the reference in subsection (1) –

    (a)   to shareable rights under a specified pension arrangement shall include a reference to entitlement to PPF compensation (as defined in section 25E(9)); and

    (b)   to pension sharing shall include a reference to sharing of that compensation.

(2) In subsection (1) above –

    (a)   the reference to shareable rights under a pension arrangement is to rights in relation to which pension sharing is available under Chapter I of Part IV of the Welfare Reform and Pensions Act 1999, or under corresponding Northern Ireland legislation,

    (b)   the reference to shareable state scheme rights is to rights in relation to which pension sharing is available under Chapter II of Part IV of the Welfare Reform and Pensions Act 1999, or under corresponding Northern Ireland legislation, and

    (c)   "party" means a party to a marriage.

Amendments—Inserted by WRPA 1999, s 19, Sch 3, para 2.

Modifications—By virtue of the Divorce etc (Pension Protection Fund) Regulations 2006, reg 4, s 21A is modified so as to apply in certain circumstances as if after s 21A(1) there were inserted s 21A(1A). See SI 2006/1932 for further details.

Defined terms—"PPF compensation": s 21C.

"shareable rights under a specified pension arrangement" (s 21A(1)(a))—Widely defined in WRPA 1999, ss 19–46 to include all pension arrangements and unfunded public service pensions except for:

(i)   The Great Offices of State (the Prime Minister, the Lord Chancellor and the Speaker) (Pension Sharing (Exceptional Schemes) Order 2000 (SI 2000/3088));

(ii)   Those arising from being the widow, widower or other dependant of a deceased person and equivalent pension benefits when those rights are the only rights held by a person under a pension scheme (Pension Sharing (Valuation) Regulations 2000 (SI 2000/1052), reg 2).

"shareable state scheme rights" (s 21A(1)(a))—Defined by WRPA 1999, s 47 as the State Earnings Related Pension scheme ((SERPs) (now the State Second Pension (S2P) or (compositely) the Additional

State Pension (ASP)) and shared additional pension, i e rights derived from a pension share relating to ASP made in previous family proceedings. The basic state retirement pension cannot be shared.

"percentage value" (s 21A(1)(b))—Although a court may calculate the percentage by taking the capital sum that seems appropriate and undertaking a calculation to determine the relevant percentage, the result contained in the pension sharing order annex must be specified only in percentage terms and not "such sum as will give such percentage" (*H v H* [2010] 2 FLR 173).

Scope—Pension sharing enables the court to share a pension at the time of divorce so that (typically) the wife either becomes a member of (typically) the husband's pension scheme in her own right by provision of what has been termed "shadow membership" ("internal transfer") or, alternatively, takes a transfer of a designated amount into her own pension ("external transfer"). Central to the concept of pension sharing is the creation of pension debits and pension credits. On the making of a pension sharing order, the transferor loses the percentage required to be transferred (the pension debit) so that his pension fund is reduced in value. The transferee acquires the right to require the pension arrangement to credit her with that amount (the pension credit) so that she gains a pension fund of that value (WRPA 1999, s 29(1)). In an unfunded public service scheme, only an internal transfer is possible. Otherwise, dependent on the position of the person responsible for managing the pension arrangements, there will be either an internal transfer within the scheme or an external transfer to some other pension arrangement. However, an external transfer must be offered. In either case, the applicant receives an indefeasible pension fund in her own right which does not end on remarriage and (subject to a limited exception, mentioned below) is not capable of variation. Broadly speaking, the charges are met by the parties and not by the pension arrangement (see annotations to s 24D). The court is able to make a pension sharing order against a foreign pension. Whether or not it will exercise its jurisdiction to do so will depend upon the reaction of the pension scheme when served with the application (Pension Schemes (Application of UK Provisions to Relevant Non-UK Schemes) Regulations 2006, SI 2006/207, as amended). As to PPF compensation, see under ss 21B and 25E.

21B Pension compensation sharing orders

(1) For the purposes of this Act, a pension compensation sharing order is an order which –

    (a)   provides that one party's shareable rights to PPF compensation that derive from rights under a specified pension scheme are to be subject to pension compensation sharing for the benefit of the other party, and

    (b)   specifies the percentage value to be transferred.

(2) In subsection (1) –

    (a)   the reference to shareable rights to PPF compensation is to rights in relation to which pension compensation sharing is available under Chapter 1 of Part 3 of the Pensions Act 2008 or under corresponding Northern Ireland legislation;

    (b)   "party" means a party to a marriage;

    (c)   "specified" means specified in the order.

Amendments—Inserted by Pensions Act 2008, Sch 6, Pt 1.

Defined terms—"PPF compensation": s 21C.

Scope—Reference should be made to the annotations to s 25E for a discussion of the Pension Protection Fund (PPF). Until the provisions of the Pensions Act 2008 (PA 2008) came into force, it was not possible to make pension sharing orders or pension attachment orders against PPF compensation because such compensation was not a pension. The PA 2008 has amended MCA 1973 and CPA 2004, providing the necessary regulation-making powers to allow for PPF compensation to be treated in much the same way as pensions are treated on divorce, dissolution or annulment. The provision mirrors as closely as possible the legislation relating to pensions. The two main differences are that there is no death-in-service benefit as part of PPF compensation and that any "credit member" created as a result of a pension compensation sharing order will not in any circumstances have the option of an external transfer from the PPF.

The relevant rules are FPR 2010, Pt 9, Ch 9, the Pension Protection Fund (Pension Compensation on Divorce etc) Regulations 2011 and the Divorce and Dissolution etc (Pension Protection Fund) Regulations 2011. The Rules and Regulations again closely mirror those for pensions with two differences due to the differing nature of PPF compensation. First, the valuation of PPF compensation entitlement to be used in financial remedy applications is only produced for that express purpose. Therefore, such a valuation must always be requested for use in proceedings, whereas (in the case of a pension) the member may already be in possession of a "relevant valuation". The second difference is that it is unnecessary to allow the PPF 21 days to lodge an objection with the court where it has received notice that an attachment order is being sought (FPR 2010, r 9.42, c f r 9.33).

21C Pension compensation: interpretation

In this Part –

"PPF compensation" means compensation payable under the pension compensation provisions;

"the pension compensation provisions" means –

    (a)   Chapter 3 of Part 2 of the Pensions Act 2004 (pension protection) and any regulations or order made under it,

    (b)   Chapter 1 of Part 3 of the Pensions Act 2008 (pension compensation on divorce etc) and any regulations or order made under it, and

    (c)   any provision corresponding to the provisions mentioned in paragraph (a) or (b) in force in Northern Ireland.

Amendments—Inserted by Pensions Act 2008, Sch 6, Pt 1.

Scope—This section defines terms in relation to pension compensation used in this Part. See, further, annotations to s 21B.

Ancillary relief in connection with divorce proceedings etc

22 Maintenance pending suit

(1) On a petition for divorce, nullity of marriage or judicial separation, the court may make an order for maintenance pending suit, that is to say, an order requiring either party to the marriage to make to the other such periodical payments for his or her maintenance and for such term, being a term beginning not earlier than the date of the presentation of the petition and ending with the date of the determination of the suit, as the court thinks reasonable.

(2) An order under this section may not require a party to a marriage to pay to the other party any amount in respect of legal services for the purposes of the proceedings.

(3) In subsection (2) "legal services" has the same meaning as in section 22ZA.

Amendments—LASPOA 2012, s 49.

Procedure—The procedure on an application for maintenance pending suit is set out in FPR 2010, Pt 9; see Procedural Guide B5.

Conversion to final order—The procedure for converting a maintenance pending suit order into a periodical payments order on decree absolute is prescribed by FPR 2010, r 9.8 and is governed by Pt 18 procedure.

Scope—This section applies to periodical payments in the period following the filing of the petition (for divorce, nullity or judicial separation) but before the grant of decree. The section is intended to address the immediate needs of a spouse by making income-based orders: issues of capital or long-term expenditure are better dealt with at the final hearing.

    The principles derived from the leading cases are distilled in *TL v ML and others (Ancillary Relief: Claim against Assets of Extended Family)* [2006] 1 FLR 1263 at [124]. The sole criterion to be applied is "reasonableness", which is synonymous with "fairness", and the marital standard of living is an important factor in determining fairness. There should be a specific budget relating to immediate expenditure needs, which the court should examine critically. Where the information provided by the payer is deficient, the court may make robust assumptions on behalf of the applicant payee. Where there has historically been support from a third party, the court may assume that support will continue at least until trial. For maintenance pending suit following the dismissal of the suit, see *M v M (Maintenance Pending Suit: Enforcement on Dismissal of Suit)* [2009] 1 FLR 790. Maintenance pending suit paid before trial is not refundable to the payer and maintenance pending suit that is unpaid in breach of a court order is an enforceable debt, absent special circumstances: *Moore v Moore* [2010] 1 FLR 1413, CA.

Costs orders following maintenance pending suit hearing—The general rule in financial remedy proceedings is that, save where conduct arises, the court will not make a costs order against a party: FPR 2010, r 28.3(6). This rule does not apply to interim financial orders: r 28.3(4)(a). On an application under s 22 for maintenance pending suit or outcome, or interim periodical payments, a party may apply for a costs order. CPR 1998, r 44.2 therefore applies. The court has discretion as to whether costs are payable and in what amount, according to the guidelines in CPR 1998, r 44.2(4),(5) and may summarily assess costs under r 44.6.

22ZA Orders for payment in respect of legal services

(1) In proceedings for divorce, nullity of marriage or judicial separation, the court may make an order or orders requiring one party to the marriage to pay to the other ("the applicant") an amount for the purpose of enabling the applicant to obtain legal services for the purposes of the proceedings.

(2) The court may also make such an order or orders in proceedings under this Part for financial relief in connection with proceedings for divorce, nullity of marriage or judicial separation.

(3) The court must not make an order under this section unless it is satisfied that, without the amount, the applicant would not reasonably be able to obtain appropriate legal services for the purposes of the proceedings or any part of the proceedings.

(4) For the purposes of subsection (3), the court must be satisfied, in particular, that –

    (a)   the applicant is not reasonably able to secure a loan to pay for the services, and

    (b)   the applicant is unlikely to be able to obtain the services by granting a charge over any assets recovered in the proceedings.

(5) An order under this section may be made for the purpose of enabling the applicant to obtain legal services of a specified description, including legal services provided in a specified period or for the purposes of a specified part of the proceedings.

(6) An order under this section may –

    (a)   provide for the payment of all or part of the amount by instalments of specified amounts, and

    (b)   require the instalments to be secured to the satisfaction of the court.

(7) An order under this section may direct that payment of all or part of the amount is to be deferred.

(8) The court may at any time in the proceedings vary an order made under this section if it considers that there has been a material change of circumstances since the order was made.

(9) For the purposes of the assessment of costs in the proceedings, the applicant's costs are to be treated as reduced by any amount paid to the applicant pursuant to an order under this section for the purposes of those proceedings.

(10) In this section "legal services", in relation to proceedings, means the following types of services –

    (a)   providing advice as to how the law applies in the particular circumstances,

    (b)   providing advice and assistance in relation to the proceedings,

    (c)   providing other advice and assistance in relation to the settlement or other resolution of the dispute that is the subject of the proceedings, and

    (d)   providing advice and assistance in relation to the enforcement of decisions in the proceedings or as part of the settlement or resolution of the dispute,

and they include, in particular, advice and assistance in the form of representation and any form of dispute resolution, including mediation.

(11) In subsections (5) and (6) "specified" means specified in the order concerned.

Amendments—Inserted by LASPOA 2012, s 49.

Defined terms—"legal services": s 22ZA(10); "specified": s 22ZA(11).

Scope—Hitherto, costs allowances have been a matter of common law (referred to specifically in FPR PD28A, para 4.6). Parliament has now (via amendments introduced by LASPOA 2012) both defined and restricted judicial discretion in two critical areas (costs and financial provision), but only under MCA 1973 and the parallel provisions of CPA 2004.

"legal services ... for the proceedings" and "for financial relief" (s 22ZA(1),(2))—Legal services may be for a matrimonial cause (divorce, judicial separation etc, ie "the proceedings": s 22ZA(1)) and for financial relief (s 22ZA(2)). "Financial relief", as a term, is not defined in MCA 1973, which still uses "ancillary relief" (although the term is used (undefined) in CPA 2004, Sch 5). In this context, it can perhaps be connoted with financial remedy proceedings under MCA 1973 and CPA 2004 (but not financial remedy proceedings under, for example, CA 1989, Sch 1).

"Financial relief" and "financial remedy proceedings"—In the costs order lexicon (see notes to FPR 2010, r 28.3), there is a difference between (1) "proceedings for a financial order" and (2) "financial remedy proceedings". It remains to be seen which of these two forms of "financial relief" – or whether yet another – is judicially regarded as the preferred definition for "financial relief" under s 22ZA(2).

What is not "financial relief"—The following are examples of family proceedings covered by FPR 2010, Pt 9 that are not covered by the term "financial relief" in s 22ZA:

- Proceedings under CA 1989, Sch 1
- Proceedings under MFPA 1984, Pt III
- Proceedings under DFMCA 1978.

The question may arise as to whether in these proceedings – and perhaps under I(PFD)A 1975 – costs allowances orders (as has happened hitherto under CA 1989, Sch 1) will still be ordered under common law principles by analogy with s 22ZA (see under FPR 2010, r 28.3: **Costs allowances).**

"The court must not make an order" (s 22ZA(3))—The burden is on the applicant to show that she cannot "reasonably ... obtain appropriate legal services" for the proceedings without an order under this section. The court has to be satisfied that the applicant is not reasonably able to secure a loan or to obtain a charge over recoverable assets (*Currey v Currey (No 2)* [2007] 1 FLR 946, CA).

"charge over any assets recovered" (s 22ZA(4)(b))—The court needs to establish whether a solicitor will accept a charge over as yet inchoate property in consideration for agreeing to act for a client (*Sears Tooth (A Firm) v Payne Hicks Beach (A Firm) and others* [1997] 2 FLR 116). The solicitor must be sure that his client will recover or preserve, in the action, such capital as will attract the charge under Solicitors Act 1974, s 73.

"specified description" and "specified amounts" (s 22ZA(5) and (6))—The court may restrict the legal representation available to a party by defining, from the menu at s 22ZA(10), for what "part of the proceedings" (s 22ZA(5)) an applicant will be able to secure funding and the "amount" (s 22ZA(1),(6)(a)).

"assessment of costs" (s 22ZA(9))—If an order for costs is made in favour of the applicant, her award will be reduced by an amount paid to her under a costs allowance order.

Scope of "legal services" (s 22ZA(10))—As with the scope of a legal aid certificate, so too with a legal services order: judges and parties will need to define the scope of the services to be covered within the terms of s 22ZA(10) and, for instance, the scope of "enforcement of decisions" (s 22ZA(10)(a)) and a dispute resolution (s 22ZA(10)(d)). Caution is likely to continue to be exercised in relation to the amount and duration of an order for payment of legal services. Knowledge that the order may conclude at a financial dispute resolution (FDR) hearing may be a reasonable encouragement to settle. A judge at the FDR hearing should not hear an application to vary or extend a legal costs order under FPR 2010, r 9.17(2).

22ZB Matters to which court is to have regard in deciding how to exercise power under section 22ZA

(1) When considering whether to make or vary an order under section 22ZA, the court must have regard to –

(a)   the income, earning capacity, property and other financial resources which each of the applicant and the paying party has or is likely to have in the foreseeable future,

(b)   the financial needs, obligations and responsibilities which each of the applicant and the paying party has or is likely to have in the foreseeable future,

(c)   the subject matter of the proceedings, including the matters in issue in them,

(d)   whether the paying party is legally represented in the proceedings,

(e)   any steps taken by the applicant to avoid all or part of the proceedings, whether by proposing or considering mediation or otherwise,

(f)   the applicant's conduct in relation to the proceedings,

(g)   any amount owed by the applicant to the paying party in respect of costs in the proceedings or other proceedings to which both the applicant and the paying party are or were party, and

(h)   the effect of the order or variation on the paying party.

(2) In subsection (1)(a) "earning capacity", in relation to the applicant or the paying party, includes any increase in earning capacity which, in the opinion of the court, it would be reasonable to expect the applicant or the paying party to take steps to acquire.

(3) For the purposes of subsection (1)(h), the court must have regard, in particular, to whether the making or variation of the order is likely to –

(a)   cause undue hardship to the paying party, or

(b)   prevent the paying party from obtaining legal services for the purposes of the proceedings.

(4) The Lord Chancellor may by order amend this section by adding to, omitting or varying the matters mentioned in subsections (1) to (3).

(5) An order under subsection (4) must be made by statutory instrument.

(6) A statutory instrument containing an order under subsection (4) may not be made unless a draft of the instrument has been laid before, and approved by a resolution of, each House of Parliament.

(7) In this section "legal services" has the same meaning as in section 22ZA.

Amendments—Inserted by LASPOA 2012, s 50.

Defined terms—"legal services": MCA 1973, s 22ZA(10).

Scope—This is a new section introducing orders for payment of legal services, following changes introduced by LASPO 2012. It replaces the discretionary remedy represented by costs allowances, previously made under MCA 1973, s 22. The court is empowered to order payments between the parties to enable the receiving party to obtain legal services, as defined in s 22ZA(10), for the purpose of proceedings. The statute now reflects the previous case-law, in that the court has to be satisfied that the applicant is not reasonably able to secure a loan or to obtain a charge over recoverable assets, principles set out in *Currey v Currey (No 2)* [2007] 1 FLR 946, CA. Payment may be in a lump sum or instalments, which may be secured and may be varied subject to a material change of circumstances. Principles from previous case-law are likely still to be relevant. An application for a legal costs order should be accompanied by a detailed costs estimate, current bank statements and evidence from a party's solicitors that an instalment *Sears Tooth*-type agreement is not possible: *TL v ML (Ancillary Relief: Claim against Assets of Extended Family)* [2006] 1 FLR 1263. Lack of alternative funding is a necessary, but may not be a sufficient, precondition for a costs order. The factors listed under s 22ZB are to be considered by the court when making or varying an order.

"must have regard to" (s 22ZB(1))—The list is exclusive: only the factors set out in s 22ZB(1) can be considered by the court when it decides whether to make an order. The first two mirror MCA 1973, s 25(2).

"subject matter of the proceedings" including matters in issue (s 22ZB(1)(c))—One of the more formidable tasks of the court will be to gauge what is the cost of the case. This subsection, if the parties provide the information to comply with it, will enable the court to conduct its enquiry on that particular aspect.

"the applicant's conduct in relation to the proceedings" (s 22ZB(1)(f))—It is likely that this subsection touches on "conduct" as defined in the costs jurisdiction (see FPR 2010, r 28.3) and that the term should be construed accordingly.

"steps taken by the applicant to avoid all or part of the proceedings" (s 22ZB(1)(e))—This is a reference to alternative dispute resolution. It appears unnecessary for both parties to take steps to avoid litigation, only the applicant.

"undue hardship" (s 22ZB(3)(a))—In connection with legal aid, costs and legal services, the term "undue hardship" has a particular meaning (*Hanning v Maitland (No 2)* [1970] 1 All ER 812, CA). It does not require too serious a degree of hardship as "undue" might imply, but (per Lord Denning MR) only palpable hardship. That is to say, in this context the respondent need not show that any order would reduce him to penury (as "undue hardship" might imply) but merely cause provable hardship (*Adams v Riley* [1988] QB 372).

23 Financial provision orders in connection with divorce proceedings etc

(1) On granting a decree of divorce, a decree of nullity of marriage or a decree of judicial separation or at any time thereafter (whether, in the case of a decree of divorce or of nullity of marriage, before or after the decree is made absolute), the court may make any one or more of the following orders, that is to say –

(a) an order that either party to the marriage shall make to the other such periodical payments, for such term, as may be specified in the order;

(b) an order that either party to the marriage shall secure to the other to the satisfaction of the court such periodical payments, for such term, as may be so specified;

(c) an order that either party to the marriage shall pay to the other such lump sum or sums as may be so specified;

(d) an order that a party to the marriage shall make to such person as may be specified in the order for the benefit of a child of the family, or to such a child, such periodical payments, for such term, as may be so specified;

(e) an order that a party to the marriage shall secure to such person as may be so specified for the benefit of such a child, or to such a child, to the satisfaction of the court, such periodical payments, for such term, as may be so specified;

(f) an order that a party to the marriage shall pay to such person as may be so specified for the benefit of such a child, or to such a child, such lump sum as may be so specified;

subject, however, in the case of an order under paragraph (d), (e) or (f) above, to the restrictions imposed by section 29(1) and (3) below on the making of financial provision orders in favour of children who have attained the age of eighteen.

(2) The court may also, subject to those restrictions, make any one or more of the orders mentioned in subsection (1)(d), (e) and (f) above –

(a) in any proceedings for divorce, nullity of marriage or judicial separation, before granting a decree; and

(b) where any such proceedings are dismissed after the beginning of the trial, either forthwith or within a reasonable period after the dismissal.

(3) Without prejudice to the generality of subsection (1)(c) or (f) above –

(a) an order under this section that a party to a marriage shall pay a lump sum to the other party may be made for the purpose of enabling that other party to meet any liabilities or expenses reasonably incurred by him or her in maintaining himself or herself or any child of the family before making an application for an order under this section in his or her favour;

(b) an order under this section for the payment of a lump sum to or for the benefit of a child of the family may be made for the purpose of enabling any liabilities or expenses reasonably incurred by or for the benefit of that child before the making of an application for an order under this section in his favour to be met; and

(c)   an order under this section for the payment of a lump sum may provide for the payment of that sum by instalments of such amount as may be specified in the order and may require the payment of the instalments to be secured to the satisfaction of the court.

(4) The power of the court under subsection (1) or (2)(a) above to make an order in favour of a child of the family shall be exercisable from time to time; and where the court makes an order in favour of a child under subsection (2)(b) above, it may from time to time, subject to the restrictions mentioned in subsection (1) above, make a further order in his favour of any of the kinds mentioned in subsection (1)(d), (e) or (f) above.

(5) Without prejudice to the power to give a direction under section 30 below for the settlement of an instrument by conveyancing counsel, where an order is made under subsection (1)(a), (b) or (c) above on or after granting a decree of divorce or nullity of marriage, neither the order nor any settlement made in pursuance of the order shall take effect unless the decree has been made absolute.

(6) Where the court –

(a)   makes an order under this section for the payment of a lump sum; and
(b)   directs –
    (i)   that payment of that sum or any part of it shall be deferred; or
    (ii)   that the sum or any part of it shall be paid by instalments,

the court may order that the amount deferred or the instalments shall carry interest at such rate as may be specified by the order from such date, not earlier than the date of the order, as may be so specified, until the date when payment of it is due.

Amendments—AJA 1982, s 16.

Procedure—The procedure for an application under s 23 is set out in FPR 2010, Pt 9 and see Procedural Guide B5.

Jurisdiction—An order of the Chancery Division relating to the ownership of assets is a final determination of those issues between the parties and operates as an estoppel for the wife disputing the ownership of those assets in the Family Division: *Edgerton v Edgerton and Shaikh* [2012] 2 FLR 273. Note that the court's jurisdiction may be excluded in relation to "maintenance" (which is not necessarily limited to periodical payments) if the paying party remains resident in another EU Member State in which a decision as to maintenance, including a dismissal of a spouse's claim, has previously been made: Council Regulation (EC) No 4/2009 (Maintenance Regulation), Art 8. Jurisdiction may also be excluded if the parties have previously agreed in writing that another Member State shall have jurisdiction (Art 4).

Timing of application—If an order is made before there has been a decree, it is made without jurisdiction and cannot be validated either under the slip rule or the inherent jurisdiction of the court (*Board (Board Intervening) v Checkland* [1987] 2 FLR 257), save in the case of a pure clerical error (*Pounds v Pounds* [1994] 1 FLR 775, CA). Further, by s 23(5), the order only takes effect on the decree being made absolute.

Although there is no jurisdiction to make an order under this section (or s 24) before decree nisi, in view of the time it will take to get the application ready for a final hearing, the application should normally be made as soon after the filing of the petition as possible. There is no statute of limitation in the matrimonial jurisdiction so that, for example, the fact that an application for a lump sum order is made 17 years after a maintenance order is no bar (*Twiname v Twiname* [1992] 1 FLR 29).

Number of applications for periodical payments (s 23(1)(a))—A party to the marriage may make any number of applications for a periodical payments order (but see **Power to prevent further application** under s 25A). The earliest date on which the order can commence is the date when the claim is made; the order can continue until the death of either of the parties or the remarriage of the recipient, whichever is the earlier (see s 28(1)(a)).

Duration and form of periodical payments order—The options available to the courts are for:

(i)   No order and a clean break as to income;

(ii) A nominal order permitting the income claim to be kept alive;

(iii) A joint lives order expressed to be until the death of either party, the remarriage or cohabitation for more than a stated period of the receiving party, or further order;

(iv) A term order until a defined event, such as the children completing education; and

(v) A term order with a s 28(1A) bar preventing a party from applying for an extension of the order under s 31.

Joint lives orders—There are certain circumstances in which the court will consider that the dependant spouse is likely to require a joint lives order, notwithstanding the duty of the court to consider whether it is just and reasonable to terminate the financial obligations of each party to the other under s 25A. Joint lives maintenance may be appropriate where needs or compensation are established, but not sharing, as sharing applies to the assets already acquired within the marriage, not future earnings:

(i) where the wife is at a disadvantage in economic terms through caring for young children, age, health or impaired earning capacity through lack of an employment history. This derives from decisions made by the parties during the marriage and may have lifelong consequences for the primary carer: see *G v G (Financial Remedies: Short Marriage: Trust Assets)* [2012] 2 FLR 48. The CA in *Flavell v Flavell* [1997] 1 FLR 353 considered that it was not usually appropriate to provide for the termination of periodical payments where a woman was in her mid-50s: such orders would be only justified where the wife had her own substantial capital and a significant earning capacity.

(ii) where there is real uncertainty whether and to what extent the wife may become financially self-supporting: in such circumstances, the CA has preferred not to impose a term, as it is open to the husband to seek a variation in the future: *C v C (Financial Relief: Short Marriage)* [1997] 2 FLR 26.

(iii) where the wife requires compensation for the interruption from her career, and capital assets are not available for this purpose: *Miller v Miller; McFarlane v McFarlane* [2006] 1 FLR 1186, HL.

As the threshold needed for the extension of a term order is high, the burden should not be on the wife to make renewed applications to extend; it is better to make a joint lives order, so that it should be for the husband to apply for and justify termination or reduction, at which stage the court could consider a clean break among other options: *Miller; McFarlane* at [97].

Joint lives orders may be expressed to be until death, remarriage or cohabitation. A period of settled cohabitation may be a factor ending the liability of a spouse to continued periodical payments. For the court's approach to cohabitation, see the commentary to MCA 1973, s 31. See also the commentary on clean breaks under s 25A.

Number of applications for secured periodical payments (s 23(1)(b))—Any number of applications may be made for a secured periodical payments order in the absence of a direction under s 25A(3) (see **Power to prevent further application** under s 25A).

Duration and form of secured periodical payments order—The earliest date on which a secured periodical payments order can commence is the date when the claim is made but, by s 28(1)(b), it can be defined to continue beyond the death of the payer.

Number of applications for lump sum order (s 23(1)(c))—Only one lump sum order may be made for a party to the marriage (*Coleman v Coleman* [1973] Fam 10; *Banyard v Banyard* [1984] FLR 643). Lump sums to children are not subject to the same restriction (see s 23(4)). Difficulties in the mortgage market do not justify a delay in making lump-sum payments, especially without provision for interest (*Milton v Milton* [2009] 1 FLR 661, CA).

Rollover of statutory charge—The Legal Aid Agency (which replaced the Legal Services Commission on 1 April 2013) may postpone the enforcement of the statutory charge as set out in CLS(F)R 2000, reg 52 where, "by order of the court or agreement it relates to property to be used as a home by the client or his dependants, or, where the relevant proceedings were family proceedings, to money to pay for such a home".

Outline of new bases for child support calculation—See under CSA 1991, s 4.

Duration and form of child periodical payments order (s 23(1)(d),(e))—This section provides that unless there are special circumstances (such as physical or mental disability), or the child remains in education, an order for child periodical payments should cease when a child reached 18: (s 29(1),(3)). Payments for tertiary education are increasingly sought and are permissible under the section. The court may permit payment for a gap year before or after tertiary education: see *Re N (Payments for Benefit of Child)* [2009] 1 FLR 1442 for the application of the principle in Sch 1 Children Act cases. Care should be taken to consider the needs of a child for future provision for tertiary education or a gap year, to avoid a child having to make his or her own application against a parent. By s 29(2)(a), the order should in the first instance be expressed not to extend beyond the age of 17. It is usual to have the following words: "until the said child attains the age of 17 years or ceases full-time (secondary/tertiary) education, whichever is the later".

School fees—A suggested form of wording for a school fees order is:

"As from ... the Petitioner/Respondent do pay or cause to be paid to the Respondent/ Petitioner for the benefit of ... until he/she shall attain the age of 17 years or cease full-time secondary education if later or further order periodical payments of an amount equivalent to the school fees (but not extras/including the following extras) at the school the said child shall from time to time attend by way of three payments at the start of each term and it is further directed that the school fees shall be paid to the headmaster/bursar/school secretary as agent for the Respondent/Petitioner and the receipt of that payee shall be sufficient discharge."

There is power to order lump sums for school fees and for the property of the payer to be charged until payment in full (*T v T (Financial Provision: Private Education)* [2006] 1 FLR 903).

Assignment of pensions by service personnel—Pensions Act 1995, s 166 provides that the statutory provisions that prohibit service personnel from assigning their pensions do not prevent a divorce court from making orders in respect of those pension benefits, thus overruling the line of cases, such as *Walker v Walker* (1983) 4 FLR 779, which had previously prevented the court from exercising jurisdiction in respect of terminal grants and other pension rights. Section 166(4)–(6) provides as follows:

"(4) Nothing in the provisions mentioned in subsection (5) applies to a court exercising its powers under section 23 of MCA 1973 (financial provision orders in connection with divorce proceedings etc) in respect of any benefits under a pension scheme (within the meaning of section 25B of MCA 1973) which a party to the marriage has or is likely to have.

(5) The provisions referred to in subsection (4) are:

(a) section 203(1) and (2) of the Army Act 1955, s 203(1) and (2) of the Air Force Act 1955, s 128G(1) and (2) of the Naval Discipline Act 1957 or s 159(4) or (4A) of the Pension Schemes Act 1993 (which prevent assignment, or orders being made restraining a person from receiving anything which he is prevented from assigning),

(b) section 91 of this Act,

(c) any provision of any Act (whether passed or made before or after this Act is passed) corresponding to any of the enactments mentioned in paragraphs (a) and (b), and

(d) any provision in the scheme in question corresponding to any of those enactments.

(6) Subsections (3) to (7) of section 25B and section 25C of MCA 1973, as inserted by this section, do not affect the powers of the court under section 31 of that Act (variation, discharge etc) in relation to any order made before the commencement of this section.".

Interim orders—While the court can make a maintenance pending suit order, it does not have power to make an interim lump sum order under s 23 (*Bolsom v Bolsom* (1983) 4 FLR 21; *Barry v Barry* [1992] 2 FLR 233), except under s 23(3)(a) for meeting expenses for maintaining an applicant or child before applying for an order under s 23(1)(c); but this limited type of order cannot be applied for before decree nisi and does not take effect until decree absolute. Under s 23(4), where the court has the power to make periodical payments orders in favour of a child of the family, that power shall be exercisable "from time to time", giving the flexibility of making further orders, in line with a child's needs. In *Wicks v Wicks* [1998] 1 FLR 470 the Court of Appeal held that the court does not have an administrative power of appropriation which it may exercise before the substantive hearing by allocating a particular asset, thus overruling *Barry v Barry* [1992] 2 FLR 233. To obtain a sale before the final ancillary relief hearing, there appear to be two alternatives:

(i) an application under MWPA 1882 with, if an order for possession is required, an application under FLA 1996, Pt IV (see Procedural Guide A4); or

(ii) an application under TLATA 1996 (see Procedural Guide A5).

Interest—A lump sum cannot take affect before decree absolute. An order may provide for payment to be made on or by a specific date, or the grant of decree absolute, whichever was later. Interest at judgment debt rate could only run from the date when the judgment became effective, that is, on grant of the decree absolute: *Robson v Robson* [2011] 1 FLR 751, CA.

Relationship with bankruptcy—There is a discretion under Insolvency Act 1986, s 281(5) to release a spouse from orders to pay lump sums in financial proceedings where the payer is a discharged bankrupt. The discretion may be exercised where the debt is unlikely to be satisfied or where release is necessary to allow the debtor to re-establish himself, but not for the purpose of reviewing or varying the debt: *McRoberts v McRoberts* [2013] BPIR 77, applying *Hayes v Hayes* [2012] BPIR 739.

24 Property adjustment orders in connection with divorce proceedings etc

(1) On granting a decree of divorce, a decree of nullity of marriage or a decree of judicial separation or at any time thereafter (whether, in the case of a decree of divorce or of nullity of marriage, before or after the decree is made absolute), the court may make any one or more of the following orders, that is to say –

(a) an order that a party to the marriage shall transfer to the other party, to any child of the family or to such person as may be specified in the order for the benefit of such a child such property as may be so specified, being property to which the first-mentioned party is entitled, either in possession or reversion;

(b) an order that a settlement of such property as may be so specified, being property to which a party to the marriage is so entitled, be made to the satisfaction of the court for the benefit of the other party to the marriage and of the children of the family or either or any of them;

(c) an order varying for the benefit of the parties to the marriage and of the children of the family or either or any of them any ante-nuptial or post-nuptial settlement (including such a settlement made by will or codicil) made on the parties to the marriage, other than one in the form of a pension arrangement (within the meaning of section 25D below);

(d) an order extinguishing or reducing the interest of either of the parties to the marriage under any such settlement, other than one in the form of a pension arrangement (within the meaning of section 25D below);

subject, however, in the case of an order under paragraph (a) above, to the restrictions imposed by section 29(1) and (3) below on the making of orders for a transfer of property in favour of children who have attained the age of eighteen.

(2) The court may make an order under subsection (1)(c) above notwithstanding that there are no children of the family.

(3) Without prejudice to the power to give a direction under section 30 below for the settlement of an instrument by conveyancing counsel, where an order is made under this section on or after granting a decree of divorce or nullity of marriage, neither the order nor any settlement made in pursuance of the order shall take effect unless the decree has been made absolute.

Amendments—WRPA 1999, s 19, Sch 3, para 3.

Procedure—Applications under s 24 are governed by FPR 2010, Pt 9 and see Procedural Guide B5.

Scope—The jurisdiction to make an order under this section arises only after decree nisi. This section defines a court's power to make a property adjustment order for a party to a marriage or any children. A wife in occupation of the matrimonial home seeking a transfer of property in preference to a sale, with primary regard for the children's need for a home, should ordinarily succeed, subject to securing the release of the husband's mortgage liability: *Fisher-Aziz v Aziz* [2010] 2 FLR 1053, CA. There is no jurisdiction to make an order to a child under s 24(1)(a) where the child is over 18, unless there are special circumstances such as disability or continuing education.

"property"—Property includes a council tenancy. In *Jones v Jones* [1997] 1 FLR 27, the Court of Appeal gave guidance in the approach to the transfer of tenancies in needs cases. The court had to have regard to the effect on the parties, including what would happen to the party deprived of the right to live in the former matrimonial home, and the effect of the local authority's housing policy in relation to the timescale for rehousing. The possibility that the outgoing spouse could afford accommodation in the private sector was a consideration for the court. See also *Newlon Housing Trust v Alsulaimen* [1998] 2 FLR 690. As the court may make an order under s 37 to restrain dealing with property outside the jurisdiction (*Hamlin v Hamlin* [1986] 1 FLR 61) it has by implication power to make a property adjustment order in respect of overseas property. Where property in issue is a tenancy, an alternative way of obtaining a transfer is under FLA 1996, Sch 7. Where there is a covenant against assignment, such an application is the preferred option (see under Sch 7, para 7 of that Act).

"Property" may include company property but only where there are legitimate grounds for piercing the corporate veil. For the current view of the Court of Appeal, see *Petrodel Resources Ltd and others v Prest and others* [2012] EWCA Civ 1395, in which the Court (Thorpe LJ dissenting) held that the principles in *Salomon v Salomon and Co Ltd* [1897] AC 22 apply to all jurisdictions and the principles of legal personality have to be respected: a company's assets belong beneficially to the company itself, not to its shareholders, even where a single shareholder controls all its shares. The requisite impropriety established in *Ben Hashem v Ali Sharif* [2009] 1 FLR 115 has to be found to "pierce the corporate veil". Piercing the corporate veil requires not only the control of the company by wrongdoers, but also impropriety in the misuse of the company by wrongdoers as a device to conceal wrongdoing that exists entirely outside the company.

The Court of Appeal in *Petrodel* disapproved obiter dicta in *Nicholas v Nicholas* [1984] FLR 285 that where husband has sole control of a company, the company can be treated as his property; the line of cases accepting the *Nicholas* dicta, such as *Mubarak v Mubarak* [2001] 1 FLR 673 overruled; *Kremen v Agrest (No 2)* [2011] 2 FLR 490 and *Hope v Krejci and Others* [2013] 1 FLR 182 doubted.

In *Gowers v Gowers* [2012] 1 FLR 1040, cash sums paid into court by a company subject to a freezing order could not be diverted to a wife without notice to the company: there was a risk of prejudice to third party interests and the corporate veil had not been pierced.

Obtaining office copy entries and registration of protective charges—Land Registration Act 2002, s 66 permits inspection and copying of entries on the register. At each stage in the proceedings, before and after decree absolute, the practitioner should check that he has registered the appropriate charge against the property subject to the claim. Thus, on decree absolute, any Class F land charge should be replaced by a pending action land charge or its registered land equivalent, ie a caution or restriction against dealings.

"settlement"—Settlement means any provision (other than an absolute gift) made for the benefit of the parties to the marriage by either one or both of them or by a third party (*Ulrich v Ulrich and Felton* [1968] 1 WLR 180). It includes a pension fund, although the court will not exercise jurisdiction to vary if the interests of third parties, including the Inland Revenue, will be prejudiced (*Brooks v Brooks* [1995] 2 FLR 13, HL). A *Brooks v Brooks* variation of a pension fund settlement is permissible only if made in proceedings commenced by petition before 1 December 2000 (WRPA 1999, s 85(4) and Sch 3, para 3). Section 24(1)(c) permits a spouse to apply to vary a family settlement in ancillary relief proceedings: *K v K (Ancillary Relief: Deed of Appointment)* [2009] 2 FLR 936 (FD).

Number of applications—In general terms, the fact that an order has been made under one subsection of this section does not preclude a later application for an order under another subsection (*Carson v Carson* (1981) 2 FLR 352). However, on the subsequent application, any earlier order and any admissible material relating to it should be examined to establish whether it was intended as a final and conclusive financial settlement (either overall or in relation to a particular property). If it was intended to be a once and for all settlement of all claims any further claim under this section is precluded. It follows that if the earlier order was intended as a once and for all settlement in respect of one property only, a second application in respect of another property may be made (*Dinch v Dinch* [1987] 2 FLR 162; *Sandford v Sandford* [1986] 1 FLR 412).

No power to make interim property adjustment order—The court does not have power to make an interim property adjustment order, and the line of authority starting in *Barry v Barry* [1992] 2 FLR 233 that it may make an order to a similar effect under its administrative power of appropriation has been overruled by *Wicks v Wicks* [1998] 1 FLR 470.

Timing of application—An order under this section does not take effect until decree absolute, but there is good reason to make the application and prepare it for hearing as soon as the petition is filed. There is no time-limit for making an application. For greater detail see **Timing of application** under s 23.

Rollover of statutory charge—For a suggested form of wording for an order which is to be adopted to allow for rollover of the Legal Aid Agency's (which replaced the Legal Services Commission on 1 April 2013) statutory charge where property is to be used as a home.

Rights of third parties—Whereas s 24A (in the context of applying for an order for sale where a property is owned by a party to the marriage and a third party) expressly provides for that third party to be served with the application so that he can be heard on it, there is no similar express provision on an application under this section where the property is owned jointly with another or is subject to third party rights. Two points should be noted:

(a) The court cannot adversely affect third party rights unless those third parties have been given notice of the proceedings and the opportunity to intervene, in which case they will be bound by the court's decision (*Tebbutt v Haynes* [1981] 2 All ER 238).

(b) Where a third party does have such an interest there should be service under FPR 2010, r 9.13.

Third Party attacks on property transfers—The circumstances in which the state may claim the proceeds of crime under a confiscation order have been narrowed. In *R v Rastelli* [2008] EWCA Crim 373 a confiscation order was overturned by the Court of Appeal, where money fraudulently obtained by the husband and then paid to the former wife to pay off the mortgage on jointly owned property was held to be payment for good consideration and not a gift. In *Re B (Confiscation Order)* [2008] 2 FLR 1, a gift made by a husband to his wife on advice from financial institutions to place the family finances in order was made without consideration, and was therefore available to pay the husband's confiscation order.

Rights of trustees in bankruptcy—Transfers of property and settlements may be challenged by trustees in bankruptcy (see MCA 1973, s 39). A property transfer pursuant to s 24 gives consideration for the purpose of Insolvency Act 1986, s 339: *Hill v Haines* [2008] 1 FLR 1192), followed in *Paulin v Paulin* [2009] 2 FLR 354, CA, where the CA said that there is very little risk that an ancillary relief award to a wife would be set aside at an undervalue in any subsequent bankruptcy proceedings.

Relationship between ancillary relief and bankruptcy—A spouse may apply to set aside the bankruptcy of the other spouse, in which case the bankruptcy proceedings may be heard together with ancillary relief proceedings: see *Paulin* (above), which provides a useful review of case-law and the relevant sections of the Insolvency Act 1986.

Pension sharing—See **Inter-Relation of Pension Sharing, Pension Attachment etc** under MCA 1973, s 21A.

24A Orders for sale of property

(1) Where the court makes an order under section 22ZA or makes under section 23 or 24 of this Act a secured periodical payments order, an order for the payment of a lump sum or a property adjustment order, then, on making that order or at any time thereafter, the court may make a further order for the sale of such property as may be specified in the order, being property in which or in the proceeds of sale of which either or both of the parties to the marriage has or have a beneficial interest, either in possession or reversion.

(2) Any order made under subsection (1) above may contain such consequential or supplementary provisions as the court thinks fit and, without prejudice to the generality of the foregoing provision, may include –

(a) provision requiring the making of a payment out of the proceeds of sale of the property to which the order relates, and

(b) provision requiring any such property to be offered for sale to a person, or class of persons, specified in the order.

(3) Where an order is made under subsection (1) above on or after the grant of a decree of divorce or nullity of marriage, the order shall not take effect unless the decree has been made absolute.

(4) Where an order is made under subsection (1) above, the court may direct that the order, or such provision thereof as the court may specify, shall not take effect until the occurrence of an event specified by the court or the expiration of a period so specified.

(5) Where an order under subsection (1) above contains a provision requiring the proceeds of sale of the property to which the order relates to be used to secure periodical payments to a party to the marriage, the order shall cease to have effect on the death or re-marriage of, or formation of a civil partnership by, that person.

(6) Where a party to a marriage has a beneficial interest in any property, or in the proceeds of sale thereof, and some other person who is not a party to the marriage also has a beneficial interest in that property or in the proceeds of sale thereof, then, before deciding whether to make an order under this section in relation to that property, it shall be the duty of the court to give that other person an opportunity to make representations with respect to the order; and any representations made by that other person shall be included among the circumstances to which the court is required to have regard under section 25(1) below.

Amendments—Inserted by Matrimonial Homes and Property Act 1981, s 7; amended by MFPA 1984, s 46(1), Sch 1, para 11; CPA 2004, s 261(1), Sch 27, para 42; LASPOA 2012, s 51.

Procedure—Applications under s 24A are governed by FPR 2010, Pt 9 and see Procedural Guide B5.

Scope—This section gives the court jurisdiction to make an order for sale if there has been a lump sum or property adjustment order. Pursuant to s 24A(3), an order for sale can only take effect upon Decree Absolute. Therefore there is no jurisdiction under this section to order a sale until the final hearing of the claims for ancillary relief. Where an order for sale is contemplated, the conventional costs of sale in England and Wales should be taken to be 3%, in the absence of evidence to the contrary: *Behzadi v Behzadi* [2009] 2 FLR 649. An order for the sale of property under s 24A may be varied under s 31(2)(f).

Property jointly owned with third parties (s 24A(6))—Section 24(6) requires that a third party who has a beneficial interest in the property which it is proposed be sold must be given the opportunity to be heard on whether there should be a sale.

24B Pension sharing orders in connection with divorce proceedings etc

(1) On granting a decree of divorce or a decree of nullity of marriage or at any time thereafter (whether before or after the decree is made absolute), the court may, on an application made under this section, make one or more pension sharing orders in relation to the marriage.

(2) A pension sharing order under this section is not to take effect unless the decree on or after which it is made has been made absolute.

(3) A pension sharing order under this section may not be made in relation to a pension arrangement which –

    (a) is the subject of a pension sharing order in relation to the marriage, or
    (b) has been the subject of pension sharing between the parties to the marriage.

(4) A pension sharing order under this section may not be made in relation to shareable state scheme rights if –

    (a) such rights are the subject of a pension sharing order in relation to the marriage, or
    (b) such rights have been the subject of pension sharing between the parties to the marriage.

(5) A pension sharing order under this section may not be made in relation to the rights of a person under a pension arrangement if there is in force a requirement imposed by virtue of section 25B or 25C below which relates to benefits or future benefits to which he is entitled under the pension arrangement.

Amendments—Inserted by WRPA 1999, s 19, Sch 3, para 4.

Defined terms—"pension sharing order": ss 21A, 52(2); "the court": s 52(1).

Scope—This section empowers the court in proceedings for divorce or nullity, but not judicial separation, to make on or at any time after a decree one or more pension sharing orders. (See also the annotations to s 21A.) Provided orders at different points in time relate to different schemes, the court, having made one pension sharing order, can subsequently make another in the absence of an appropriate dismissal. The order does not take effect until the later of the date of decree absolute (s 24B(2) or 7 days after the time for appealing the order (Divorce etc (Pensions) Regulations 2000, reg 9).

It is not possible to make a deferred pension sharing order to overcome what has been termed "income gap syndrome". Where therefore the pension of the pension debit member is already in payment, the amount of his pension will be adversely affected by a pension sharing order with no corresponding immediate benefit to the pension credit member if she has not attained the age specified by the pension scheme for pension credit benefit (*Stevenson v Police Pension Scheme* [2004] (30 April), Pensions Ombudsman ref M00258; *Langley v Police Pension Scheme* [2006] (21 January), Pensions Ombudsman ref P00586; *Kerbel v Southwark Council* (2009) 26 January, ref 725771, Pensions Ombudsman). These provisions do not contravene ECHR 1950 (*R (Smith) v Secretary of State for Defence and Secretary of State for Work and Pensions* [2005] 1 FLR 97 affirmed on appeal [2004] EWCA Civ 1664; *R (Thomas) v Ministry of Defence* [2008] 2 FLR 1385). However, by virtue of Occupational, Personal and Stakeholder Pensions (Miscellaneous Amendments) Regulations 2009, reg 15, which came into force on 6 April 2009, the age at which pension credit benefit will be paid has been aligned in the case of occupational pension schemes with other pension rights (subject to amendment of the relevant scheme rules) from 6 April 2010. The position in relation to public sector schemes depends on the terms of the individual scheme.

Prohibition if other pension sharing or attachment orders made (s 24B(3)–(5))—An order for pension sharing against a particular scheme or shareable state scheme rights cannot be made if there either is or has been a pension sharing order made in relation to the marriage before the court against that scheme. However, if the pension sharing order has been made in proceedings relating to a previous marriage, a further pension sharing order *can* be made. A pension attachment order which is in force for this or any previous marriage prevents a pension sharing order being made.

Valuation—The valuation of the pension benefits is prescribed by Pensions on Divorce etc (Provision of Information) Regulations 2000, reg 3 as the Cash Equivalent (CE) of the benefits acquired to date on the assumption that the member ceased employment on the date of the valuation. As set out in the annotations to the Pensions on Divorce etc (Provision of Information) Regulations, the CE does not include the value of the death in service package nor past service reserve. Where a pension sharing order is made against a pension in payment, that payment ceases to be paid to the member at the former higher rate from the date the pension sharing order takes effect (being the later of the date of decree absolute and 7 days after the end of the period for filing notice of appeal against the pension sharing order (*Shepherd v Trustees of the Air Products plc Pension Plan* [2006] (21 September), Pensions Ombudsman ref Q00278; *Pike v Teachers Pension Scheme* (2008) 26 March, ref 26355, Pensions Ombudsman; *Davis v Windsor Life Assurance Co Ltd* (2012) 6 March, ref 80998/1, Deputy Pensions Ombudsman).

The date of the CE to be used for valuation purposes is determined for evidential purposes by the Divorce etc (Pensions) Regulations 2000, reg 3 and for implementation purposes by WRPA 1999, s 29. As to "moving target syndrome", see annotations to WRPA 1999, s 29.

24C Pension sharing orders: duty to stay

(1) No pension sharing order may be made so as to take effect before the end of such period after the making of the order as may be prescribed by regulations made by the Lord Chancellor.

(2) The power to make regulations under this section shall be exercisable by statutory instrument which shall be subject to annulment in pursuance of a resolution of either House of Parliament.

Amendments—Inserted by WRPA 1999, s 19, Sch 3, para 4.

Defined terms—"pension sharing order": ss 21A, 52(2).

Scope—A pension sharing order cannot take effect until, as provided by Divorce etc (Pensions) Regulations 2000, reg 9, 7 days have elapsed after the time for filing notice of appeal (21 days: FPR 2010, r 30.4). Subject to decree absolute, the order takes effect after 28 days, the 7-day period prescribed by the Divorce etc (Pensions) Regulations 2000, reg 9, not being subject to the computation of time provisions of FPR 2010, r 2.9(4).

24D Pension sharing orders: apportionment of charges

If a pension sharing order relates to rights under a pension arrangement, the court may include in the order provision about the apportionment between the parties of any charge under section 41 of the Welfare Reform and Pensions Act 1999 (charges in respect of pension sharing costs), or under corresponding Northern Ireland legislation.

Amendments—Inserted by WRPA 1999, s 19, Sch 3, para 4.

Defined terms—"the court": s 52(1); "pension sharing order": ss 21A, 52(2).

Scope—This section enables the court to order who should pay the charges of the person responsible for the pension arrangement. This issue is dealt with in the annex to the pension sharing order (Form P1).The core features of WRPA 1999, s 41 and the Pensions on Divorce etc (Charging) Regulations 2000 are as follows:

(i)   There is no charge for providing a CE provided that only one valuation is given in 12 months or it is not required in less than 3 months from the date of request/order.

(ii) Provided that the person responsible for the pension arrangement has stated his costs in writing in

advance and that those costs are reasonable, the parties must pay for the cost of implementing the pension sharing order and not the arrangement itself.
(iii) If the court's order is silent as to who should pay the charges, the costs fall on the transferor (WRPA 1999, s 41(3)(b)).
(iv) The resolution of a dispute as to pension-sharing charges is an issue for the Pensions Ombudsman and not for the court, eg on a detailed assessment of costs.

See, further, the annotations to Pensions on Divorce etc (Provision of Information) Regulations 2000, reg 2 in Part IV.

The National Association of Pension Funds (*www.napf.co.uk*; tel 020 7601 1700) provides a recommended scale of charges for private sector occupational pension schemes to use when providing information in relation to, and for the implementation of, pension sharing orders. The guidance also includes a flowchart showing the circumstances in which a charge may be made. The scale and flowchart may be downloaded from the website.

24E Pension compensation sharing orders in connection with divorce proceedings

(1) On granting a decree of divorce or a decree of nullity of marriage or at any time thereafter (whether before or after the decree is made absolute), the court may, on an application made under this section, make a pension compensation sharing order in relation to the marriage.

(2) A pension compensation sharing order under this section is not to take effect unless the decree on or after which it is made has been made absolute.

(3) A pension compensation sharing order under this section may not be made in relation to rights to PPF compensation that –
  (a) are the subject of pension attachment,
  (b) derive from rights under a pension scheme that were the subject of pension sharing between the parties to the marriage,
  (c) are the subject of pension compensation attachment, or
  (d) are or have been the subject of pension compensation sharing between the parties to the marriage.

(4) For the purposes of subsection (3)(a), rights to PPF compensation "are the subject of pension attachment" if any of the following three conditions is met.

(5) The first condition is that –
  (a) the rights derive from rights under a pension scheme in relation to which an order was made under section 23 imposing a requirement by virtue of section 25B(4), and
  (b) that order, as modified under section 25E(3), remains in force.

(6) The second condition is that –
  (a) the rights derive from rights under a pension scheme in relation to which an order was made under section 23 imposing a requirement by virtue of section 25B(7), and
  (b) that order –
    (i) has been complied with, or
    (ii) has not been complied with and, as modified under section 25E(5), remains in force.

(7) The third condition is that –
  (a) the rights derive from rights under a pension scheme in relation to which an order was made under section 23 imposing a requirement by virtue of section 25C, and
  (b) that order remains in force.

(8) For the purposes of subsection (3)(b), rights under a pension scheme "were the subject of pension sharing between the parties to the marriage" if the rights were at any time the subject of a pension sharing order in relation to the marriage or a previous marriage between the same parties.

(9) For the purposes of subsection (3)(c), rights to PPF compensation "are the subject of pension compensation attachment" if there is in force a requirement imposed by virtue of section 25F relating to them.

(10) For the purposes of subsection (3)(d), rights to PPF compensation "are or have been the subject of pension compensation sharing between the parties to the marriage" if they are or have ever been the subject of a pension compensation sharing order in relation to the marriage or a previous marriage between the same parties.

Amendments—Inserted by Pensions Act 2008, Sch 6, Pt 1.

Defined terms—"pension compensation sharing order": s 21B; "the court": s 52(1); "PPF compensation": s 21C.

Scope—See under s 25E for a discussion of the Pension Protection Fund (PPF) and under s 21B in relation to pension compensation sharing orders. This section is the counterpart of s 24B in relation to pension sharing orders.

Prohibition if other pension or sharing order attachment orders made (s 24E(3)–(10))—The restrictions contained in s 24B(3)–(5) are replicated so that the court may not make a pension compensation sharing order in relation to PPF compensation that is subject to pension attachment (as defined by s 24E(4)), pension compensation attachment, pension compensation sharing order or that derives from pension rights that have been subject to pension sharing. However, in the case of pension compensation sharing or PPF compensation derived from pension rights that had previously been the subject of pension sharing, the order will only preclude a pension compensation sharing order if it was between the parties to the marriage: if the prior pension sharing order or pension compensation sharing order related to a previous marriage between different parties, a further pension compensation sharing order may be made. A prior pension attachment order or pension compensation attachment order for this or any previous marriage prevents a pension compensation sharing order being made.

Valuation—The valuation of PPF compensation is prescribed by the Divorce and Dissolution etc (Pension Protection Fund) Regulations 2011, reg 3, which cross-refers to the Pension Protection Fund (Pension Compensation Sharing and Attachment on Divorce etc) Regulations 2011, regs 3 and 4, under which the value of shareable rights to PPF compensation is to be calculated in accordance with actuarial assumptions approved by the PPF Board on the date that the PPF Board receives the request for a valuation.

24F Pension compensation sharing orders: duty to stay

(1) No pension compensation sharing order may be made so as to take effect before the end of such period after the making of the order as may be prescribed by regulations made by the Lord Chancellor.

(2) The power to make regulations under this section shall be exercisable by statutory instrument which shall be subject to annulment in pursuance of a resolution of either House of Parliament.

Amendments—Inserted by Pensions Act 2008, Sch 6, Pt 1.

Defined term—"pension compensation sharing order": s 21B.

Scope—See under s 25E for a discussion of the Pension Protection Fund (PPF) and under s 21B in relation to pension compensation sharing orders. This section is the counterpart of s 24C in relation to pension sharing orders. A pension compensation sharing order cannot take effect until (as provided by the Divorce and Dissolution etc (Pension Protection Fund) Regulations 2011, reg 6) 7 days have elapsed after the time for filing notice of appeal (21 days: FPR 2010, r 30.4). Subject to decree absolute, the order takes effect after 28 days, the 7-day period prescribed by the Divorce and Dissolution etc (Pension Protection Fund) Regulations 2011, reg 6 not being subject to the computation of time provisions of FPR 2010, r 2.9(4).

24G Pension compensation sharing orders: apportionment of charges

The court may include in a pension compensation sharing order provision about the apportionment between the parties of any charge under section 117 of the Pensions Act 2008 (charges in respect of pension compensation sharing costs), or under corresponding Northern Ireland legislation.

Amendments—Inserted by Pensions Act 2008, Sch 6, Pt 1.

Defined terms—"pension compensation sharing order": s 21B; "the court": s 52(1).

Scope—See under s 25E for a discussion of the Pension Protection Fund (PPF) and under s 21B in relation to pension compensation sharing orders. This section is the counterpart of s 24D in relation to the apportionment of charges on the making of the pension sharing order. Reference should be made to the annotations to s 24D.

See also the Pension Protection Fund (Pension Compensation Sharing and Attachment on Divorce etc) Regulations 2011, regs 16 and 17.

25 Matters to which court is to have regard in deciding how to exercise its powers under ss 23, 24, 24A, 24B and 24E

(1) It shall be the duty of the court in deciding whether to exercise its powers under section 23, 24, 24A, 24B and 24E above and, if so, in what manner, to have regard to all the circumstances of the case, first consideration being given to the welfare while a minor of any child of the family who has not attained the age of eighteen.

(2) As regards the exercise of the powers of the court under section 23(1)(a), (b) or (c), 24, 24A, 24B and 24E above in relation to a party to the marriage, the court shall in particular have regard to the following matters –

    (a)   the income, earning capacity, property and other financial resources which each of the parties to the marriage has or is likely to have in the foreseeable future, including in the case of earning capacity any increase in that capacity which it would in the opinion of the court be reasonable to expect a party to the marriage to take steps to acquire;

    (b)   the financial needs, obligations and responsibilities which each of the parties to the marriage has or is likely to have in the foreseeable future;

    (c)   the standard of living enjoyed by the family before the breakdown of the marriage;

    (d)   the age of each party to the marriage and the duration of the marriage;

    (e)   any physical or mental disability of either of the parties to the marriage;

    (f)   the contributions which each of the parties has made or is likely in the foreseeable future to make to the welfare of the family, including any contribution by looking after the home or caring for the family;

    (g)   the conduct of each of the parties, if that conduct is such that it would in the opinion of the court be inequitable to disregard it;

    (h)   in the case of proceedings for divorce or nullity of marriage, the value to each of the parties to the marriage of any benefit which, by reason of the dissolution or annulment of the marriage, that party will lose the chance of acquiring.

(3) As regards the exercise of the powers of the court under section 23(1)(d), (e) or (f), (2) or (4), 24 or 24A above in relation to a child of the family, the court shall in particular have regard to the following matters –

    (a)   the financial needs of the child;

    (b)   the income, earning capacity (if any), property and other financial resources of the child;

    (c)   any physical or mental disability of the child;

    (d)   the manner in which he was being and in which the parties to the marriage expected him to be educated or trained;

(e) the considerations mentioned in relation to the parties to the marriage in paragraphs (a), (b), (c) and (e) of subsection (2) above.

(4) As regards the exercise of the powers of the court under section 23(1)(d), (e) or (f), (2) or (4), 24 or 24A above against a party to a marriage in favour of a child of the family who is not the child of that party, the court shall also have regard –

(a) to whether that party assumed any responsibility for the child's maintenance, and, if so, to the extent to which, and the basis upon which, that party assumed such responsibility and to the length of time for which that party discharged such responsibility;

(b) to whether in assuming and discharging such responsibility that party did so knowing that the child was not his or her own;

(c) to the liability of any other person to maintain the child.

Amendments—MFPA 1984, s 3; Pensions Act 1995, s 166; WRPA 1999, s 19, Sch 3, para 5; Pensions Act 2008, Sch 6, Pt 1.

Section 25 and the inquisitorial jurisdiction—This section and s 25A (clean break) contain the statutory criteria for determining how claims by a party to a marriage for income and capital should be decided. "It shall be the duty of the court" (s 25(1)) emphasises the quasi-inquisitorial duty of the court to investigate in ancillary relief litigation. The CA in *Grey v Grey* [2010] 1 FLR 1764 stated that "in ancillary relief proceedings the judge is not confined in the search for fairness by the nature of counsels' submissions nor is he bound by the evidence the parties choose to adduce". The judge must be satisfied that the court has or has sought all the information needed to discharge the duty to find the fairest solution: *Lykiardopulo v Lykiardopulo and Lykiardopulo* [2011] 1 FLR 1427. Accordingly, the parties owe the court the duty of full, frank and clear disclosure, which is absolute: *NG v SG (Appeal: Non-Disclosure)* [2012] 1 FLR 1211.

Recent case-law has shaped the approaches of the courts to the s 25 directed imperative. In considering the s 25 criteria, the House of Lords has considered three main distributive principles: needs, compensation and sharing, shaped by the overarching requirement of fairness; "each [party] is entitled to an equal share of the assets of the partnership, unless there is good reason to the contrary", but the yardstick of equality is to be used as an aid not a rule: *Miller v Miller; McFarlane v McFarlane* [2006] 1 FLR 1186, HL.

In *Charman v Charman (No 4)* [2007] 1 FLR 1246 the Court of Appeal has said that "the starting point of every enquiry in application for ancillary relief was the financial position of the parties, and was always in two stages, first computation and then distribution". Extending the approach of *Charman*, a third stage after computation and distribution is to decide whether the result produced by the sharing principle meets the needs (generously interpreted) of the parties: *L v L* [2008] 1 FLR 142. Only if the application of the sharing principle failed to meet the parties' requirements would unmet needs then dictate a greater share. This approach means that the sharing principle is, therefore, cross-checked against s 25 factors. See Wilson LJ in *Jones v Jones* [2011] 1 FLR 1723: in applying needs and sharing, the court was engaged in two separate exercises, involving different considerations: the higher of the two separate assessments should found the final award. See also *A v L* [2012] 1 FLR 985: the court must given reasons for any significant departure from equality and demonstrate how the resulting capital order will fairly meet the needs of both parties.

The court, in its duty to see if fairness is being achieved, should embark on rough calculations to the extent of compiling a balance sheet as a basis for the financial award, so that the court understands the financial consequences of the exercise of its discretion: see *MD v D* [2009] 1 FLR 810; *Behzadi v Behzadi* [2009] 2 FLR 649, CA.

Where the matrimonial assets comprise liquid and illiquid or risk-laden assets, fairness may require that consideration should be given to distributing these between each of the parties: *Wells v Wells* [2002] 2 FLR 97, CA; *P v P (Financial Relief: Illiquid Assets)* [2005] 1 FLR 548. Where the entirety of the matrimonial assets have their origins in money brought into the marriage by one of the spouses, a departure from equality may be necessary in the interests of fairness: *Smith v Smith* [2007] 2 FLR 1103, CA. The Court of Appeal has commented that "there was no rule that equal division was the starting point in all cases; on the contrary, the starting point in all cases was the financial position of the parties, and s 25 of the Act": see *B v B (Ancillary Relief: Distribution of Assets)* [2008] 2 FLR 1627, CA.

The concept of compensation raises the possibility that financial payment may be ordered, not just to meet financial needs, but as a measure of compensation to reflect that the spouse who stayed at home may have put his/her career on hold, to future economic disadvantage if the marriage ends. In *Lauder v Lauder* [2007] 2 FLR 802, a wife aged 70 with disabilities and a long marriage was entitled to an element of compensation, because of relationship-generated disadvantage that went beyond need.

However, "compensation" has been criticised as not being a statutory term under MCA 1973, s 25 and should not be applied as a separate head of claim. Parties who make lifestyle choices about careers or the domestic sphere may make a combined and equal contribution, entitling each to a full share of the fruits of the marriage, and to give an additional entitlement for "compensation" for perceived loss of economic opportunity may risk double counting: *RP v RP* [2007] 1 FLR 2105. The CA has said that "contribution, not relationship generated disadvantage, was the language of the statute": *Hvorostovsky v Hvorostovsky* [2009] 2 FLR 1574.

Nuptial agreements—The importance of the judge's discretionary powers has been emphasised by the Court of Appeal in *Crossley v Crossley* [2008] 1 FLR 1467, followed in *S v S (Ancillary Relief)* [2009] 1 FLR 254.

On nuptial agreements generally, agreements executed in a foreign jurisdiction following independent legal advice have been recognised by the English courts, to the extent that the English divorce petition has been stayed: *S v S (Divorce: Staying Proceedings)* [1997] 2 FLR 100; *C v C (Divorce: Stay of English Proceedings)* [2001] 1 FLR 624. See also *MacLeod v MacLeod* [2009] 1 FLR 641 Privy Council, where a prenuptial agreement confirmed in principle by a postnuptial agreement 8 years into the marriage was held to be a valid and enforceable agreement.

The leading case is *Radmacher v Granatino* [2010] 2 FLR 1900, the Supreme Court holding that prenuptial agreements would be given decisive weight as part of the s 25 exercise, if entered into willingly by the parties, with full information available to them and each intending that the agreement should be applied should the marriage come to an end. The agreement would be given less weight if there had been duress, fraud, misrepresentation or undue pressure, and could be set aside if circumstances meant that it would be unfair to hold a party to it, through the need to provide for the reasonable requirements of children or those of a party to the marriage. It was recognised that the longer a marriage lasted, the greater likelihood of unfairness in upholding the agreement. Pending parliamentary reform, prenuptial agreements should be taken into account to reduce the divergence between the English jurisdiction and Europe. In *Z v Z (No 2)* [2012] 1 FLR 1100, a French prenuptial agreement was upheld to the extent that it excluded sharing.

Post-*Granatino*, it is important to give weight to the autonomy of the parties who made the agreement. The fact of the agreement can alter what would otherwise be a fair award: *V v V (Pre-Nuptial Agreement)* [2012] 1 FLR 1315.

Not all prenuptial agreements carry weight, as in *F v F (Pre-nuptial Agreement)* [2010] 1 FLR 1743, where a French prenuptial agreement was perceived by the parties to be merely an administrative inconvenience imposed by the state, which they believed they had to comply with in order to marry, and placed no particular weight upon when divorcing after 15 years of marriage.

Section 25 principles—In performing the inquisitorial task, first consideration must be given to the welfare of any minor child of the family under s 25(1). Thereafter, the factors listed under s 25(2) should be considered individually: "confusion would be avoided if resort was had to the precise language of the statute": *Robson v Robson* [2011] 1 FLR 751. The CA has emphasised that there is no order of importance in the s 25(2) factors – each had to be given its due weight in the exercise of the court's discretion, with the objective of reaching a just result.

The s 25(2)(a) resources will always be balanced against the s 25(2)(b) needs of each party. The court is also concerned with the foreseeable future, as well as with the past history and present position of the parties.

Income, earning capacity, property and other financial resources (s 25(2)(a))—This was extended in 1984 to include consideration of "any increase in that capacity which it would in the in the opinion of the court be reasonable to expect a party to the marriage to take steps to acquire". This implies a rebuttable presumption of future economic self-sufficiency. A primary task of the court is to identify what is matrimonial and non-matrimonial property. Non-matrimonial property may include property brought in by one party through gift or inheritance, or may be created or acquired post-separation. Pre-acquired non-matrimonial assets should be apportioned in the light of the "sharing principle": see *Jones v Jones* [2011] 1 FLR 1723.

The cut-off date for defining matrimonial property is the date when mutual support ends, usually but not necessarily when cohabitation ends. The weight to be given to post-separation assets is a matter for the court's discretion, but future earning capacity is expressly listed in s 25(2)(a), and therefore cannot be ignored: see *P v P (Post-separation Accruals and Earning Capacity)* [2008] 2 FLR 1135; *H v H (Financial Provision)* [2009] 2 FLR 795; *CR v CR* [2008] 1 FLR 323. Income and bonuses accrued post-separation may be as a result of the husband's sole endeavours and there may be a reluctance to include them as marital property: *H v H* [2007] 2 FLR 548; *Jenifer E v Mark E* [2013] EWHC 506 (Fam).

The cut-off date for defining matrimonial property is the date when mutual support ends, usually when cohabitation ceases. There may be a reluctance to include bonuses or income accrued post-separation: *H v H* [2007] 2 FLR 548. The weight to be given to post-separation assets is a matter for the court's discretion, but future earning capacity is expressly listed in s 25(2)(a) and therefore cannot be ignored: *P v P (Post-separation Accruals and Earning Capacity)* [2008] 2 FLR 1135; *H v H (Financial Provision)* [2009] 2 FLR 795; *CR v CR* [2008] 1 FLR 323. See **Non-matrimonial resources – post-separation accruals**, below.

As a starting point, all assets should be valued at the date of trial (*Rossi v Rossi* [2007] 1 FLR 790; *S v S (Ancillary Relief after Lengthy Separation)* [2007] 1 FLR 2120). Residential property should be valued in net terms after deduction of mortgage and costs of sale, conventionally 3% in England in Wales in the absence of evidence to the contrary (*Behzadi v Behzadi* [2009] 2 FLR 649). Valuations should be at present market value, not based on future optimism: *FZ v SZ and Others (Ancillary Relief: Conduct: Valuations)* [2011] 1 FLR 64. The court must do its best on the valuation current and available at trial, even where a husband's assets have dramatically reduced in value: *Marano v Marano* [2010] 1 FLR 1903, CA.

Where disclosure is deficient, the court is required by adverse inferences to attempt "realistic and reasonable quantification, even in the broadest terms of the hidden funds" – see *NG v SG (Appeal: Non-Disclosure)* [2012] 1 FLR 1211; *Kremen v Agrest (Financial Remedy: Non-Disclosure: Post Nuptial Agreement)* [2012] 2 FLR 414.

It may be proper to "add back" a notional sum into the assets of a spouse who has recklessly depleted the matrimonial assets, thereby potentially disadvantaging the other spouse: principle developed in *Norris v Norris* [2003] 1 FLR 1142. The principle was applied to the wife in *McCartney v Mills McCartney* [2008] 1 FLR 508. In *Vaughan v Vaughan* [2008] 1 FLR 1108, CA "add backs" were considered further: the requirement was of clear evidence of dissipation with a "wanton element" and could not apply to sums expended in meeting living costs or needs. The court was not obliged to limit its orders to known resources of capital or income, but may infer the availability of other unidentified resources available to the husband.

Inherited wealth is a resource under s 25(2)(a), but it may be treated differently from wealth earned by the parties' efforts during the marriage. The nature and source of the inherited wealth may determine how it is treated by the courts and be a reason to depart from equality. Ancestral property and family heirlooms may be treated differently from inherited stocks and shares. Property inherited before the marriage may be left with that spouse, especially in a short marriage. Conversely, inherited property that has been applied within the marriage and long enjoyed by both parties may be more likely to be made available to meet a party's needs, although "judges should be cautious and not invade inherited property unnecessarily": *Robson v Robson* [2011] 1 FLR 751. In *K v L (Non-Matrimonial Property: Special Contribution)* [2011] 2 FLR 980, an award from a wife's inheritance that was based upon a generous assessment of need, not upon sharing, was upheld on appeal. See also *AR v AR (Treatment of Inherited Wealth)* [2012] 2 FLR 1.

Financial resources provided by parents to enable spouses to acquire a home may be inferred as being intended to be a gift to husband and wife jointly; a house acquired with parents' help may be held on trust for spouses in equal shares: *Abbot v Abbot* [2008] 1 FLR 1451, PC, following *Stack v Dowden* [2007] 1 FLR 1858, HL. Where the needs of the parties are the main consideration, it may be wrong to ringfence inherited assets, where all available assets are needed to meet the parties' requirements: *S v S (Ancillary Relief: Importance of FDR)* [2008] 1 FLR 944.

"other financial resources"—The potential availability of wealth owned by others could be taken into account by the court. A trust may be a financial resource, where a husband's interest has vested, and there was a likelihood that the husband would ultimately receive a significant part of the trust fund: *C v C (Ancillary Relief: Trust Fund)* [2010] 1 FLR 337; *B v B (Ancillary Relief)* [2010] 2 FLR 887; *Whaley v Whaley* [2012] 1 FLR 735. However, while the court could encourage trustees to act in the interests of a spouse, they could not be compelled, see *Thomas v Thomas* [1995] 2 FLR 668, CA; *A v A* [2007] 2 FLR 467. The court could make an award that would put pressure on the husband's parents, who had historically provided bounty, as in *TL v ML (Ancillary Relief: Claim against Assets of Extended Family)* [2006] 1 FLR 1263. Family shares held for the benefit of the husband's children were held to constitute a constructive trust and the proceeds of the shares were not matrimonial property: *De Bruyne v De Bruyne* [2010] 2 FLR 1240. A husband's entitlement under a discretionary trust was a matrimonial resource: *SR v CR (Ancillary Relief: Family Trusts)* [2009] 2 FLR 1083.

The family company is a potential resource, but valuation can present difficulties. Judges are required to consider the division of the assets using the yardstick of equality, so they should make specific findings about the value of a company, particularly where the parties disagree: *Re C (Divorce: Financial Relief)* [2008] 1 FLR 625. Valuation should be by a single joint expert: *P v P (Financial Relief: Illiquid Assets)* [2005] 1 FLR 548; *H v H* [2008] 2 FLR 2092. The purpose of the valuation is to assist the court in testing the fairness of the proposed outcome; it should not be a detailed accounting exercise and should be proportionate to the overall value of the assets. A minority shareholding held by a spouse may attract a discounted value, unless the relationship between the spouse and other shareholders is a quasi-partnership, with shareholders cooperating and likely to sell together, so that full market value may apply: see *Re Bird Precision Bellows Ltd* [1984] 1 Ch 419, CA; *G v G (Financial Provision: Equal Division)* [2002] 2 FLR 1143; *Irvine v Irvine* [2006] 4 All ER 102 Ch; *Charman v Charman (No 2)* [2007] 1 FLR 593; *NA v MA* [2007] 1 FLR 1760. The court should be cautious about ordering a sale, because it is difficult to value and the best price is rarely obtainable: *A v A* [2006] 2 FLR 115; *R v R (Financial Relief: Company Valuation)* [2005] 2 FLR 365. A wife may not merit a share in the capital value of the business where the income stream is needed to finance her maintenance, and there is a danger of double counting: *V v V (Financial Relief)* [2005] 2 FLR 697.

Personal injury awards—Damages received by one spouse may be a relevant factor to be considered in the s 25 exercise. Damages may not be sacrosanct against the needs of the other spouse. Each case turns on its facts: the application of the general sharing rule must be tempered to reflect the particular needs of the recipient of the damages and the fact that damages were acquired as compensation for pain, suffering or loss. See *Daubney v Daubney* [1976] Fam 267, *Pritchard v Cobden Ltd and Another (No 1)* [1987] 2 FLR 30, CA, *Wagstaff v Wagstaff* [1992] 1 FLR 333, CA and *Mansfield v Mansfield* [2012] 1 FLR 117.

Pensions—Pensions are increasingly an important element in future resources of the parties, where a marriage has subsisted long enough for pensions to be built up by the efforts of both parties. Pensions may be a significant element in the domestic economy of the parties, the capital value being clear and quantifiable at the end of the marriage. The CA has emphasised that the capital value of the pensions should be included on a balance sheet to assist in the computation of the available assets, and failure to do so may distort the distribution of assets: *Vaughan v Vaughan* [2008] 1 FLR 1108, CA; *Behzadi v Behzadi* [2009] 2 FLR 649.

Non-matrimonial resources – pre-acquired assets—The argument that pre-acquired assets should be excluded from distribution may be raised where parties marry later in life, or not for the first time, or where the length of the marriage is short. The existence of pre-acquired assets has previously been recognised by a percentage approach: in *C v C* [2009] 1 FLR 8, the court should not undertake a precise account of the parties' premarital wealth, especially after a long marriage, but where a husband had a successful company with a substantial asset base, a departure from equality, to be expressed in percentage terms, was justified. The approach has been further developed by the CA in *Jones v Jones* [2011] 1 FLR 1723: the non-matrimonial assets should be defined and valued where possible and may lie with the spouse who brought them into the marriage; the matrimonial assets then fall to be divided on the sharing principle. The result should then be cross-checked by a reference to a percentage division of the assets to achieve a fair result. See *N v F (Financial Orders: Pre-Acquired Wealth)* [2011] 2 FLR 533 for further refinement of the principle in *Jones*. It remains the case that non-matrimonial property belonging to one spouse may be awarded to the other where need is established: *K v L (Non-matrimonial Property: Special Contribution)* [2011] 2 FLR 980.

Non-matrimonial resources – post separation accruals—A valuable asset that comes to fruition after parties have separated may nevertheless on the facts be a matrimonial asset, where founded and developed during the marriage: 40% awarded to the wife in *SK v WL (Ancillary Relief: Post-Separation Accrual)* [2011] 1 FLR 1471. In *Gordon (formerly Stefanou) v Stefanou* [2011] 1 FLR 1582, a company created by a husband some years after separation but before divorce, to which the wife had made no contribution, was treated as a non-matrimonial asset not available for sharing. See also *S v S (Ancillary Relief after Lengthy Separation)* [2007] 1 FLR 2120. In *B v B (Ancillary Relief: Post-Separation Income)* [2010] 2 FLR 1214, the husband's assets had increased considerably through his performance-related bonuses post-separation, but before trial. The wife received 15% of additional sums if subsequently received, but an equal division of the assets at date of trial was not justified. Where a husband may expect an increase in the future value of the business and therefore in his income, such future income is not an asset that is susceptible to the sharing principle: *H v H* [2010] 1 FLR 1864.

Cohabitation as a resource—The court should be alive to the practical impact of cohabitation, including its financial consequences and duration. A cohabiting wife has no legal claim to be maintained by a third party, so the burden of maintenance may still rest with the husband. However, in the exercise of its s 25 discretion, the court must attach a significant weight to a settled relationship and should be able to conduct a full investigation of its financial consequences, to the extent of assessing what the third party is, or ought to be, contributing to the wife: *Grey v Grey* [2010] 1 FLR 1764, CA. See notes to MCA 1973, s 31 for commentary on cohabitation cases.

Needs and obligations (s 25(2)(b))—The needs of the parties are a question of fact for the court. Non-matrimonial property may be brought in if the needs of the parties dictate it *S v S (Non-matrimonial Property: Conduct)* [2007] 1 FLR 1496. The need to provide for the continuing care of children of the marriage is the responsibility of both parties and is part of the relationship-generated disadvantage of the primary carer, who may have given up work during the marriage, with lifelong consequences, which may need to be met by spousal maintenance: *G v G* [2012] EWHC 167 (Fam). The needs of the applicant may be the dominant factor in a case, but a husband was not liable for needs created by the wife's financial mismanagement and irresponsibility: *North v North* [2008] 1 FLR 158, CA. In small money cases, the focus will be on the parties' minimal future needs, rather than the strict division of the matrimonial acquest, *M-D v D* [2009] 1 FLR 810. The moral obligation to maintain an elderly parent may reduce the level of legal obligation to an applicant spouse: *Judge v Judge* [2009] 1 FLR 1287, CA.

The age of the parties and the duration of the marriage—The duration of the marriage is to be considered with the other s 25 factors. A period of cohabitation immediately before the marriage may be treated as part of the marriage for the purposes of s 25(2)(d) and is relevant to short-marriage cases: *GW v RW (Financial Provision: Departure from Equality)* [2003] 2 FLR 108; *CO v CO (Ancillary Relief: Pre-marriage cohabitation)* [2004] 1 FLR 1095.

In a short marriage, the absence of children and consequent enhanced housing needs may mean that the nature and source of property brought to the marriage will be accorded a greater significance than in a longer marriage, justifying a departure from equality where one party has contributed significantly more than the other: *Foster v Foster* [2003] 2 FLR 299, CA, where the wife received 61% of the assets. The longer the marriage, the more likely that non-matrimonial property has become merged with matrimonial or inherited property: *Robson v Robson* [2011] 1 FLR 751. In a short marriage, non-matrimonial or inherited property may be less likely to be shared, unless the needs of a spouse require it: *Rossi v Rossi* [2007] 1 FLR 790. In a short marriage, spousal maintenance may provide a transition over an appropriate period to an independent lifestyle, which may be less than that enjoyed during the marriage: *G v G* [2012] EWHC 167 (Fam). Where a child has been born in a short marriage, periodical payments may nevertheless be required without term.

In short marriages, fairness may mean that a claimant is not entitled to a share of the other spouse's non-matrimonial property, and the parties will have less of a claim against the other, even if the resulting division of capital is unequal: *Miller v Miller; McFarlane v McFarlane* [2006] 1 FLR 1186, HL, which were directed at providing for the financial need of the wife. In a short marriage of 4 years, where the husband had acquired his capital after the marriage had ended, the transfer of 30% of his assets to the wife was held to be plainly excessive: *Fallon v Fallon* [2010] 1 FLR 910. In long-marriage cases, factors of substance are required to justify departing from broad equality, such as a substantial asset base pre-dating the relationship: see **Non-matrimonial resources – pre-acquired assets**, above.

Standard of living (s 25(2)(c))—Where there is sufficient money, the continuation of the marital lifestyle choices may be sanctioned by the court. In *S v S* [2008] 2 FLR 113, the President upheld an award permitting the wife to keep horses, for so long as the husband could afford to finance it, equestrian activities having been integral to the parties' marriage. The lifestyle enjoyed in the marriage is a benchmark relevant to the consideration of the future lifestyles of the parties after separation: *G v G* [2012] EWHC 167 (Fam).

Contribution (s 25(2)(f))—The generation of wealth is to be regarded as a contribution to the welfare of the family. Special or stellar contributions may still be grounds for departing from equality. In a long marriage, the wife had done everything required of her, but the husband had the spark of genius which created the wealth, so he was nevertheless entitled to 60% of the capital: *Sorrell v Sorell* [2006] 1 FLR 497. The wife's share of the assets in Charman was held at 36.5%, partly because of the special contribution of the husband: *Charman v Charman (No 4)* [2007] 1 FLR 1246, CA. It is suggested that where a special contribution is established, the departure from equality would not be less that 55:45 or greater than 66:33 in the circumstances of a long marriage. A special contribution is not necessarily demonstrated because the assets are substantial. In *G v G (Financial Provision: Equal Division)* [2002] 2 FLR 1143 and *H v H* [2010] 1 FLR 1864, the husband (although wealthy) was not a genius and was found to have made no special contribution.

Conduct (s 25(2)(g))—This is only to be considered if it would be "inequitable to disregard it". A broader approach to conduct, involving appraisals as to why the marriage broke down, was seen in *G v G (Financial Provision: Separation Agreement)* [2004] 1 FLR 1011. This approach in now disapproved by the HL in *Miller v Miller; McFarlane v McFarlane* [2006] 1 FLR 1186: "in most cases, misconduct is not relevant to the bases upon which financial ancillary relief is ordered today" (at [1202]). Conduct may include litigation conduct, through failure to disclose. In *WF v NF* [2007] EWHC 3050 (Fam), a husband who caused costs of £4 million and thus dissipated 40% of the assets was held to have conspired to deceive the court and the wife: the court was entitled to regard this as conduct under s 25(2)(g), as the wife could not be compensated by a costs order alone. Litigation conduct through failure to disclose assets and to engage in proceedings resulted in wife being awarded 50% of assets, plus uplift in respect of husband's conduct: *A v A* [2012] All ER (D) 108 (Dec). Financial dissipation through gambling has also been held to be conduct within the section: *M v M (Third Party Subpoena: Financial Conduct)* [2006] 2 FLR 1253. Conduct will not normally extend beyond the financial: in *S v S (Non-matrimonial Property: Conduct)* [2007] 1 FLR 1496, an assault occasioning actual bodily harm upon a wife to which the husband had pleaded guilty was not considered as "conduct". However, physical assault may have financial consequences: in *H v H (Financial Relief: Attempted Murder as Conduct)* [2006] 1 FLR 990, the conduct of a husband who stabbed his wife so that she was unable to work, and refused the sale or letting of the family home, was described as conduct at the very top end of the scale, because of its financial consequences, thus entitling the wife's needs to be given a higher priority than the husband's. Cohabitation may be seen as conduct: see *Atkinson v Atkinson* [1988] 2 FLR 353. For cohabitation, see resources under **Section 25 principles**, above, and the commentary to MCA 1973, s 31. A false report by a wife to the police to obtain an occupation order has been considered to be conduct: *FZ v SZ and Others (Ancillary Relief: Conduct: Valuations)* [2011] 1 FLR 64.

25A Exercise of court's powers in favour of party to marriage on decree of divorce or nullity of marriage

(1) Where on or after the grant of a decree of divorce or nullity of marriage the court decides to exercise its powers under section 23(1)(a), (b) or (c), 24, 24A, 24B or 24E above in favour of a party to the marriage, it shall be the duty of the court to consider whether it would be appropriate so to exercise those powers that the financial obligations of each party towards the other will be terminated as soon after the grant of the decree as the court considers just and reasonable.

(2) Where the court decides in such a case to make a periodical payments or secured periodical payments order in favour of a party to the marriage, the court shall in particular consider whether it would be appropriate to require those payments to be made or secured only for such term as would in the opinion of the court be sufficient to enable the party in whose favour the order is made to adjust without undue hardship to the termination of his or her financial dependence on the other party.

(3) Where on or after the grant of a decree of divorce or nullity of marriage an application is made by a party to the marriage for a periodical payments or secured periodical payments order in his or her favour, then, if the court considers that no continuing obligation should be imposed on either party to make or secure periodical payments in favour of the other, the court may dismiss the application with a direction that the applicant shall not be entitled to make any future application in relation to that marriage for an order under section 23(1)(a) or (b) above.

Amendments—Inserted by MFPA 1984, s 3; amended by WRPA 1999, s 19, Sch 3, para 6; Pensions Act 2008, Sch 6, Pt 1.

Scope—The "clean break" section is to be read with s 25(2)(a) to provide that earning capacity includes "any increase in that capacity which it would in the opinion of the court be reasonable to expect a party to the marriage to take steps to acquire" with a view to a clean break. The court must consider:

(i)   termination: whether it is appropriate to terminate the financial obligations as soon after the decree as is "just and reasonable";

(ii) term: if periodical payments are to be made, whether they should be made or secured only for such period as to allow adjustment without undue hardship to termination;

(iii) dismissal: if there is no continuing obligation for periodical payments, the court may dismiss the application, with a direction under s 28(1A) that there be no future application for an order under s 23(1)(a) or (b).

At any stage when the court is considering orders under s 23 or s 24, the court has a duty to consider whether an immediate or future clean break is appropriate. This principle was developed in *Minton v Minton* (1978) FLR Rep 461 and had survived *White v White* [2000] 2 FLR 981 to be reiterated in *Miller; McFarlane* [2006] 1 FLR 1186. See also *Robson v Robson* [2011] 1 FLR 751, CA.

The statute is silent as to the circumstances in which it may be appropriate to make a clean break order. In *C v C (Financial Relief: Short Marriage)* [1997] 2 FLR 26, the Court of Appeal summarised the proper approach to assessing whether a clean break order should be made, which depends on all the circumstances of the case, including the welfare of any minor child and the s 25 checklist factors. A short marriage will not of itself require a term order. If a term is appropriate, there must be evidence to support that conclusion, as opposed to hope or crystal ball gazing. If there is doubt about when self-sufficiency will be attained, it is wrong to require the payee to apply to extend the term. If there is uncertainty about the appropriate length of the term, the proper course is to impose no term but leave the payer to seek variation or discharge.

Therefore, a clean break order may be appropriate where there is evidence that the applicant is financially self-sufficient, or is expected to be in the near future, or where the parties are impecunious with no prospect of future financial contribution. In *L v L (Financial Remedies: Deferred Clean Break)* [2012] 1 FLR 1283 on appeal from the PRFD, a joint lives order was set aside in favour of a non-extendable term order of just over 2 years, where a 44-year-old wife worked in an established business and retained a valuable farm that was capable of generating income, the children were subject to shared care arrangements and the wife additionally expected to benefit from a family trust.

Clean break orders may be inappropriate where the parties have a continuing responsibility for the housing and maintenance of dependent children. The situation of a dependent wife may be relevant: the Court of Appeal in *Flavell v Flavell* [1997] 1 FLR 353 considered that it is not usually appropriate to terminate periodical payments where a woman is in her mid-50s; such an order would be justified only where a woman had her own substantial capital and a significant earning capacity. In *Miller; McFarlane* [2006] 1 FLR 1186, it was held that a clean break should not be imposed at the expense of a fair result: where a party is likely to need financial support or is entitled to compensation, and capital assets are not available, periodical payments might properly be ordered.

25B Pensions

(1) The matters to which the court is to have regard under section 25(2) above include –

    (a)   in the case of paragraph (a), any benefits under a pension arrangement which a party to the marriage has or is likely to have, and

    (b)   in the case of paragraph (h), any benefits under a pension arrangement which, by reason of the dissolution or annulment of the marriage, a party to the marriage will lose the chance of acquiring,

and, accordingly, in relation to benefits under a pension arrangement, section 25(2)(a) above shall have effect as if "in the foreseeable future" were omitted.

(2) *(repealed)*

(3) The following provisions apply where, having regard to any benefits under a pension arrangement, the court determines to make an order under section 23 above.

(4) To the extent to which the order is made having regard to any benefits under a pension arrangement, the order may require the person responsible for the pension arrangement in question, if at any time any payment in respect of any benefits under the arrangement becomes due to the party with pension rights, to make a payment for the benefit of the other party.

(5) The order must express the amount of any payment required to be made by virtue of subsection (4) above as a percentage of the payment which becomes due to the party with pension rights.

(6) Any such payment by the person responsible for the arrangement –

    (a)   shall discharge so much of his liability to the party with pension rights as corresponds to the amount of the payment, and

    (b)   shall be treated for all purposes as a payment made by the party with pension rights in or towards the discharge of his liability under the order.

(7) Where the party with pension rights has a right of commutation under the arrangement, the order may require him to exercise it to any extent; and this section applies to any payment due in consequence of commutation in pursuance of the order as it applies to other payments in respect of benefits under the arrangement.

(7A) The power conferred by subsection (7) above may not be exercised for the purpose of commuting a benefit payable to the party with pension rights to a benefit payable to the other party.

(7B) The power conferred by subsection (4) or (7) above may not be exercised in relation to a pension arrangement which –

    (a)   is the subject of a pension sharing order in relation to the marriage, or

    (b)   has been the subject of pension sharing between the parties to the marriage.

(7C) In subsection (1) above, references to benefits under a pension arrangement include any benefits by way of pension, whether under a pension arrangement or not.

Amendments—Inserted by Pensions Act 1995, s 166; amended by WRPA 1999, ss 21, 88, Sch 4, para 1, Sch 13, Pt II.

Modification—See the Divorce etc (Pension Protection Fund) Regulations 2006 for modifications to s 25B.

Defined terms—"the court": s 52(1); "financial provision order": ss 21(1), 52(2); "the other party": s 25D(3); "the party with pension rights": s 25D(3); "pension arrangement": s 25D(3); "pension sharing order": ss 21A, 52(2); "person responsible for the pension arrangement": s 25D(4).

Scope—This section, taken together with the following two sections, sets out the basis for pension attachment (previously known as earmarking), which is less favoured by applicants than pension sharing:

1 Applies to all forms of relief including judicial separation.
2 Attaches a percentage (rather than a cash amount) of:
   (a) member's pension in retirement (s 25B(4));
   (b) lump sum payable on retirement (s 25B(7): court can require commutation); or
   (c) lump sum payable on death in service, after leaving service but before retirement, and after retirement (s 25C: the court can require trustees to exercise discretion as regards lump sum or can require respondent to nominate for the benefit of the applicant, e g under a personal pension).
3 No power to create spouse's pension on member's death.
4 Court cannot order member to take pension benefits on any specific date (*Field v Field* [2003] 1 FLR 376).
5 Pension attachment is a species of financial provision order. Pension attachment periodical payment orders, therefore, end on remarriage and can be varied at any time. A pension attachment lump sum order can be varied (even as to amount) before either party's death.
6 Not available if pension arrangement is or has been subject to pension sharing between parties to this marriage.
7 Periodical payments element taxable in the hands of the member.
8 For the order to be effective, the person responsible for the pension arrangement must be given notice of the proceedings, order and subsequent changes of address of the applicant after the order is made.
9 Statutory charge crystallises on lump sum element only of pension fund attached.
10 The court must have regard to the benefits of all pension schemes, not just those in the foreseeable future (s 25B(1)), thus abrogating the rule in *Milne v Milne* (1981) 2 FLR 286, CA (which restricted foreseeable future to 10 years).
11 Armed Services pensions are amenable to pension attachment orders (Pensions Act 1995, s 166(4)–(6)), the full text to which is set out in **Assignment of pensions by service personnel** under s 23.
12 As to PPF compensation, see annotations to ss 21B and 25E.

T v T (Financial Relief: Pensions) [1998] 1 FLR 1072 and *Burrow v Burrow* [1999] 1 FLR 508 comprehensively review these sections.

"matters to which the court is to have regard" (s 25B(1))—Section 25B(1) is not restricted to pension attachment, but applies also to, for example, pension sharing and off-setting.

25C Pensions: lump sums

(1) The power of the court under section 23 above to order a party to a marriage to pay a lump sum to the other party includes, where the benefits which the party with pension rights has or is likely to have under a pension arrangement include any lump sum payable in respect of his death, power to make any of the following provision by the order.

(2) The court may –
   (a) if the person responsible for the pension arrangement in question has power to determine the person to whom the sum, or any part of it, is to be paid, require him to pay the whole or part of that sum, when it becomes due, to the other party,
   (b) if the party with pension rights has power to nominate the person to whom the

sum, or any part of it, is to be paid, require the party with pension rights to nominate the other party in respect of the whole or part of that sum,

(c) in any other case, require the person responsible for the pension arrangement in question to pay the whole or part of that sum, when it becomes due, for the benefit of the other party instead of to the person to whom, apart from the order, it would be paid.

(3) Any payment by the person responsible for the pension arrangement under an order made under section 23 above by virtue of this section shall discharge so much of his liability in respect of the party with pension rights as corresponds to the amount of the payment.

(4) The powers conferred by this section may not be exercised in relation to a pension arrangement which –

(a) is the subject of a pension sharing order in relation to the marriage, or

(b) has been the subject of pension sharing between the parties to the marriage.

Amendments—Inserted by Pensions Act 1995, s 166; amended by WRPA 1999, s 21, Sch 4, para 2.

Defined terms—"the court": s 52(1); "the other party": s 25D(3); "the party with pension rights": s 25D(3); "pension arrangement": s 25D(3); "pension sharing order": ss 21A, 52(2); "person responsible for the pension arrangement": s 25D(4).

Scope—This section enables the court, except where there is or has been a pension sharing order in relation to this marriage, to attach the lump sum payable if the person with pension benefits dies before taking his benefits (e g death in service, death after leaving service but before retirement or the lump sum payable on death after retirement). This power may only be exercised for the benefit of a party to a marriage. An obligation in favour of a child of the family can only be created by a suitable undertaking in the preamble to a consent order. Lump sums defined as a multiple of pensionable salary are common in public service and occupational pension schemes. The terms of most personal pension and retirement annuity contracts allow for the return of the fund (with or without interest) in the event of the policyholder's death before taking his retirement benefits. See annotations to s 25B.

25D Pensions: supplementary

(1) Where –

(a) an order made under section 23 above by virtue of section 25B or 25C above imposes any requirement on the person responsible for a pension arrangement ("the first arrangement") and the party with pension rights acquires rights under another pension arrangement ("the new arrangement") which are derived (directly or indirectly) from the whole of his rights under the first arrangement, and

(b) the person responsible for the new arrangement has been given notice in accordance with regulations made by the Lord Chancellor,

the order shall have effect as if it had been made instead in respect of the person responsible for the new arrangement.

(2) The Lord Chancellor may by regulations –

(a) in relation to any provision of sections 25B or 25C above which authorises the court making an order under section 23 above to require the person responsible for a pension arrangement to make a payment for the benefit of the other party, make provision as to the person to whom, and the terms on which, the payment is to be made.

(ab) make, in relation to payment under a mistaken belief as to the continuation in force of a provision included by virtue of section 25B or 25C above in an order under section 23 above, provision about the rights or liabilities of the payer, the payee or the person to whom the payment was due,

(b) require notices to be given in respect of changes of circumstances relevant to such orders which include provision made by virtue of sections 25B and 25C above,

(ba) make provision for the person responsible for a pension arrangement to be discharged in prescribed circumstances from a requirement imposed by virtue of section 25B or 25C above,

(c), (d)   (*repealed*)

(e) make provision about calculation and verification in relation to the valuation of –

(i)   benefits under a pension arrangement, or

(ii)   shareable state scheme rights,

for the purposes of the court's functions in connection with the exercise of any of its powers under this Part of this Act.

(2A) Regulations under subsection (2)(e) above may include –

(a) provision for calculation or verification in accordance with guidance from time to time prepared by a prescribed person, and

(b) provision by reference to regulations under section 30 or 49(4) of the Welfare Reform and Pensions Act 1999.

(2B) Regulations under subsection (2) above may make different provision for different cases.

(2C) Power to make regulations under this section shall be exercisable by statutory instrument which shall be subject to annulment in pursuance of a resolution of either House of Parliament.

(3) In this section and sections 25B and 25C above –

"occupational pension scheme" has the same meaning as in the Pension Schemes Act 1993;

"the party with pension rights" means the party to the marriage who has or is likely to have benefits under a pension arrangement and "the other party" means the other party to the marriage;

"pension arrangement" means –

(a) an occupational pension scheme,

(b) a personal pension scheme,

(c) a retirement annuity contract,

(d) an annuity or insurance policy purchased, or transferred, for the purpose of giving effect to rights under an occupational pension scheme or a personal pension scheme, and

(e) an annuity purchased, or entered into, for the purpose of discharging liability in respect of a pension credit under section 29(1)(b) of the Welfare Reform and Pensions Act 1999 or under corresponding Northern Ireland legislation;

"personal pension scheme" has the same meaning as in the Pension Schemes Act 1993;

"prescribed" means prescribed by regulations;

"retirement annuity contract" means a contract or scheme approved under Chapter III of Part XIV of the Income and Corporation Taxes Act 1988;

"shareable state scheme rights" has the same meaning as in section 21A(1) above; and

"trustees or managers", in relation to an occupational pension scheme or a personal pension scheme, means –

(a) in the case of a scheme established under a trust, the trustees of the scheme, and

(b) in any other case, the managers of the scheme.

(4) In this section and sections 25B and 25C above, references to the person responsible for a pension arrangement are –

 (a) in the case of an occupational pension scheme or a personal pension scheme, to the trustees or managers of the scheme,

 (b) in the case of a retirement annuity contract or an annuity falling within paragraph (d) or (e) of the definition of "pension arrangement" above, the provider of the annuity, and

 (c) in the case of an insurance policy falling within paragraph (d) of the definition of that expression, the insurer.

Amendments—Inserted by Pensions Act 1995, s 166; amended by WRPA 1999, ss 21, 88, Sch 4, para 3, Sch 13, Pt II.

Defined terms—"the court": s 52(1).

Scope—This section defines various terms and provides for regulations to be made, particularly for enabling pension benefits to be valued. As outlined in the annotations to MCA 1973, s 24B the method of calculating the value of the Cash Equivalent (CE) is prescribed by Pensions on Divorce etc (Provision of Information) Regulations 2000, reg 3. The prescribed method of valuation is calculated on the basis that the member's service ends at the date of valuation. For the constituent elements of the CE and the fact that the death in service benefit is excluded, as are past service reserves, see annotations to the Pensions on Divorce etc (Provision of Information) Regulations 2000 in Part IV.

The only regulations that the reader need have a working knowledge of are the Pensions on Divorce etc (Provision of Information) Regulations 2000, the Divorce etc (Pensions) Regulations 2000 and the Sharing of State Scheme Rights (Provision of Information and Valuations) (No 2) Regulations 2000; see Part IV. As to PPF compensation, see under ss 21B and 25E.

25E The Pension Protection Fund

(1) The matters to which the court is to have regard under section 25(2) include –

 (a) in the case of paragraph (a), any PPF compensation to which a party to the marriage is or is likely to be entitled, and

 (b) in the case of paragraph (h), any PPF compensation which, by reason of the dissolution or annulment of the marriage, a party to the marriage will lose the chance of acquiring entitlement to,

and, accordingly, in relation to PPF compensation, section 25(2)(a) shall have effect as if "in the foreseeable future" were omitted.

(2) Subsection (3) applies in relation to an order under section 23 so far as it includes provision made by virtue of section 25B(4) which –

 (a) imposed requirements on the trustees or managers of an occupational pension scheme for which the Board has assumed responsibility in accordance with Chapter 3 of Part 2 of the Pensions Act 2004 (pension protection) or any provision in force in Northern Ireland corresponding to that Chapter, and

 (b) was made before the trustees or managers of the scheme received the transfer notice in relation to the scheme.

(3) The order is to have effect from the time when the trustees or managers of the scheme receive the transfer notice –

 (a) as if, except in prescribed descriptions of case –

  (i) references in the order to the trustees or managers of the scheme were references to the Board, and

  (ii) references in the order to any pension or lump sum to which the party with pension rights is or may become entitled under the scheme were references to any PPF compensation to which that person is or may become entitled in respect of the pension or lump sum, and

 (b) subject to such other modifications as may be prescribed.

(4) Subsection (5) applies to an order under section 23 if –

  (a)   it includes provision made by virtue of section 25B(7) which requires the party
        with pension rights to exercise his right of commutation under an occupational
        pension scheme to any extent, and
  (b)   before the requirement is complied with the Board has assumed responsibility
        for the scheme as mentioned in subsection (2)(a).

(5) From the time the trustees or managers of the scheme receive the transfer notice, the
order is to have effect with such modifications as may be prescribed.

(6) Regulations may modify section 25C as it applies in relation to an occupational
pension scheme at any time when there is an assessment period in relation to the scheme.

(7) Where the court makes a pension sharing order in respect of a person's shareable
rights under an occupational pension scheme, or an order which includes provision made
by virtue of section 25B(4) or (7) in relation to such a scheme, the Board subsequently
assuming responsibility for the scheme as mentioned in subsection (2)(a) does not
affect –

  (a)   the powers of the court under section 31 to vary or discharge the order or to
        suspend or revive any provision of it, or
  (b)   on an appeal, the powers of the appeal court to affirm, reinstate, set aside or
        vary the order.

(8) Regulations may make such consequential modifications of any provision of, or
made by virtue of, this Part as appear to the Lord Chancellor necessary or expedient to
give effect to the provisions of this section.

(9) In this section –

  "assessment period" means an assessment period within the meaning of Part 2 of the
      Pensions Act 2004 (pension protection) (see sections 132 and 159 of that Act) or
      an equivalent period under any provision in force in Northern Ireland
      corresponding to that Part;
  "the Board" means the Board of the Pension Protection Fund;
  "occupational pension scheme" has the same meaning as in the Pension Schemes
      Act 1993;
  "prescribed" means prescribed by regulations;
  "regulations" means regulations made by the Lord Chancellor;
  "shareable rights" are rights in relation to which pension sharing is available under
      Chapter 1 of Part 4 of the Welfare Reform and Pensions Act 1999 or any
      provision in force in Northern Ireland corresponding to that Chapter;
  "transfer notice" has the same meaning as in section 160 of the Pensions Act 2004 or
      any corresponding provision in force in Northern Ireland.

(10) Any power to make regulations under this section is exercisable by statutory
instrument, which shall be subject to annulment in pursuance of a resolution of either
House of Parliament.

Amendments—Inserted by Pensions Act 2004, Sch 12, para 3; amended by Pensions Act 2008, Sch 6,
Pt 1.

Defined terms—"the court": s 52(1).

"Regulations may make such consequential modifications" (s 25E(8))—The relevant regulations are
the Divorce etc (Pension Protection Fund) Regulations 2006, which came into force on 8 August 2006.

Scope—This section (along with the Pensions Act 2004, s 220) makes provision for where a pension
sharing or attachment order is made before the PPF assumes responsibility for a scheme (*cf* pension
compensation sharing orders (s 21B) and pension compensation attachment orders (s 25F)). The PPF acts
as a form of insurance to ensure the payment of certain defined benefit occupational scheme and hybrid
scheme benefits if the scheme is of insufficient funds to pay them and the employer is insolvent (where
there is no prospect of a corporate rescue or business rescue with pension liabilities attached) and the

scheme was not in wind-up as at 6 April 2005. Certain schemes are exempt from the PPF. However, schemes that are not in wind-up will not be covered if a "qualifying insolvency event" (voluntary administration, appointment of receiver, administration or winding up) has already taken place before 6 April 2005, unless a further insolvency event takes place after that date. Nonetheless, the Financial Assistance Scheme (FAS), established on 1 September 2005 by the Pensions Act 2004, s 286 and by the Financial Assistance Scheme Regulations 2005 may provide assistance rather than compensation for those who cannot benefit from the PPF where a wind-up occurs between 1 January 1997 and 5 April 2005 or, alternatively, where the underfunded scheme started to wind up after 5 April 2005 but before 22 December 2008 having become insolvent before 6 April 2005. On 10 July 2009, the PPF became the FAS scheme manager. No separate statutory framework has as yet been created for pension sharing or pension attachment in relation to the FAS.

The PPF covers 100% of pension benefits in payment for those who have reached normal scheme retirement age (or earlier because of incapacity) and 90% of the accrued pensions for all others with spouses, civil partners or dependants receiving a percentage of the member's PPF benefit. PPF compensation is capped at £34, 867.04 a year (PPF and Occupational Pension Schemes (Levy Ceiling and Compensation Cap) Order 2013), or less if the member retired early (such amount to be increased in line with average earnings). Pensions in payment derived from pensionable service on or after 6 April 1997 will be increased in line with RPI (or CPI from 1 January 2012) or 2.5% per annum, if less; pensions in deferment will be revalued in line with RPI (or CPI from 31 March 2011 with first payments being made on 1 January 2012) or 5% per annum for service before 6 April 2009 and 2.5% for service on or after that date, if less. Payments relating to service before 5 April 1997 will not increase. PPF compensation does not include payment of death-in-service lump sums.

If an insolvency practitioner is appointed in relation to a scheme sponsoring employer, he must inform the PPF that an insolvency event has occurred. If the insolvency practitioner concludes that a scheme rescue is not possible, he must so notify the PPF. There follows an assessment period (s 25E(9)), which will last for at least 1 year, with most assessments completed within 2 years, following which the PPF will assume responsibility for a scheme where the scheme cannot be rescued and cannot afford to pay its members at least the PPF level of benefits. The PPF assumes responsibility for a scheme under the Pensions Act 2004, s 161 when a transfer notice (s 25E(9)) is given to the trustees or managers under the Pensions Act 2004, s 160. When the PPF assumes responsibility, all of the scheme's assets transfer to the PPF along with all of the scheme's pensions obligations.

Details of schemes that have transferred into the PPF (as well as schemes that have completed assessment but will not be transferring into the PPF) may be accessed online at *www.pensionprotectionfund.org.uk/TransferredSchemes/pages/Transferred-Schemes.aspx.*

PPF compensation is included as a matter to which the court must have regard under MCA 1973, s 25(2)(a) or (h) (s 25E(1)).

Section 25E(2)–(6) address pension attachment; s 25E(7) addresses both pension sharing and attachment in the context of variations and appeals. Pension sharing is also addressed by the Pensions Act 2004, s 220 (see below). The broad regime is that pension attachment orders made before the PPF assumes responsibility for a scheme will be honoured. During the assessment period, it will be possible for pension attachment orders to be made, even if they will be implemented after the PPF assumes responsibility. Assumption of responsibility by the PPF will not affect the court's powers (limited as they are in the case of pension sharing) to vary a pension sharing or pension attachment order or the powers of an appeal court (s 25E(7)).

When a scheme is in the assessment period, it may only pay out benefits which would be payable under PPF compensation, which will not include death-in-service lump sums. If a person with pension benefits dies during an assessment period, the pension provider will not be able to pay out a death-in-service lump sum and any pension attachment order made under MCA 1973, s 25C will fail. This affects all pension attachment orders relating to death-in-service lump sums including those made before the introduction of the PPF. However, if the pension scheme is not taken over by the PPF, death-in-service benefits accrued but not paid during the assessment period will be paid out at that stage and the order made under MCA 1973, s 25C will then become operative. It should be borne in mind that it is not possible to apply to vary an order under MCA 1973, s 25C on the death of either of the parties to the marriage (MCA 1973, s 31(2B)).

When the PPF assumes responsibility for a scheme, it is required under the Pension Protection Fund (Provision of Information) Regulations 2005 to inform both members and "beneficiaries" of this fact. A "beneficiary" is defined (reg 2(1)) as "any person, other than a member of that scheme, who is entitled to compensation in accordance with the pension compensation provisions" and will therefore include the other party to a pension attachment order.

Pensions Act 2004, s 220 enables regulations to be made modifying the Pensions Act 2004 or WRPA 1999 in relation to pension sharing. The relevant regulations are the Pension Protection Fund (Pension Sharing) Regulations 2006. Broadly, the regulations make provision for the PPF to discharge liability for a pension sharing order made before the date on which the PPF assumes responsibility for the scheme, but which had either not come into effect or remained unimplemented as at that date. The PPF is substituted for the trustees or managers of the scheme and PPF compensation replaces any pension previously payable. The person entitled to the pension credit is to be treated as if he or she had been a member of the relevant scheme immediately before the assessment date in relation to the scheme and the PPF is obliged to determine the PPF compensation payable to that person from the effective date of the pension sharing order to which the credit relates. The valuation methodology remains the CE, even if the pension were in payment and would therefore be subject to the compensation cap (Pension Protection Fund (Pensions Sharing) Regulations 2006, reg 2(2)(b)).

Reference should also be made to FPR 2010, r 9.37.

25F Attachment of pension compensation

(1) This section applies where, having regard to any PPF compensation to which a party to the marriage is or is likely to be entitled, the court determines to make an order under section 23.

(2) To the extent to which the order is made having regard to such compensation, the order may require the Board of the Pension Protection Fund, if at any time any payment in respect of PPF compensation becomes due to the party with compensation rights, to make a payment for the benefit of the other party.

(3) The order must express the amount of any payment required to be made by virtue of subsection (2) as a percentage of the payment which becomes due to the party with compensation rights.

(4) Any such payment by the Board of the Pension Protection Fund –

    (a)   shall discharge so much of its liability to the party with compensation rights as corresponds to the amount of the payment, and

    (b)   shall be treated for all purposes as a payment made by the party with compensation rights in or towards the discharge of that party's liability under the order.

(5) Where the party with compensation rights has a right to commute any PPF compensation, the order may require that party to exercise it to any extent; and this section applies to any payment due in consequence of commutation in pursuance of the order as it applies to other payments in respect of PPF compensation.

(6) The power conferred by subsection (5) may not be exercised for the purpose of commuting compensation payable to the party with compensation rights to compensation payable to the other party.

(7) The power conferred by subsection (2) or (5) may not be exercised in relation to rights to PPF compensation that –

    (a)   derive from rights under a pension scheme that were at any time the subject of a pension sharing order in relation to the marriage, or a previous marriage between the same parties, or

    (b)   are or have ever been the subject of a pension compensation sharing order in relation to the marriage or a previous marriage between the same parties.

Amendments—Inserted by Pensions Act 2008, Sch 6, Pt 1.

Defined terms—"PPF compensation": s 21C; "the other party": s 25G; "the party with compensation rights": s 25G.

Scope—This section enables the court to make attachment orders in relation to pension compensation where a scheme has already entered the PPF. This section and s 25G are the counterparts of ss 25B, 25C and 25D, which permit pension attachment orders to be made against pensions. However, the court cannot attach death-in-service lump sums under this provision as PPF compensation does not include payment of such lump sums (see annotations to s 25E). It is not possible to make an order under this section in relation to PPF compensation derived from pension rights that have previously been the subject of pension sharing in relation to *any* marriage between the same parties or have previously been the subject of a pension compensation sharing order in relation to *any* marriage between the same parties (s 25F(7) *cf* s 25B(7B)).

25G Pension compensation: supplementary

(1) The Lord Chancellor may by regulations –

(a) make provision, in relation to any provision of section 25F which authorises the court making an order under section 23 to require the Board of the Pension Protection Fund to make a payment for the benefit of the other party, as to the person to whom, and the terms on which, the payment is to be made;

(b) make provision, in relation to payment under a mistaken belief as to the continuation in force of a provision included by virtue of section 25F in an order under section 23, about the rights or liabilities of the payer, the payee or the person to whom the payment was due;

(c) require notices to be given in respect of changes of circumstances relevant to orders under section 23 which include provision made by virtue of section 25F;

(d) make provision for the Board of the Pension Protection Fund to be discharged in prescribed circumstances from a requirement imposed by virtue of section 25F;

(e) make provision about calculation and verification in relation to the valuation of PPF compensation for the purposes of the court's functions in connection with the exercise of any of its powers under this Part.

(2) Regulations under subsection (1)(e) may include –

(a) provision for calculation or verification in accordance with guidance from time to time prepared by a prescribed person;

(b) provision by reference to regulations under section 112 of the Pensions Act 2008.

(3) Regulations under subsection (1) may make different provision for different cases.

(4) The power to make regulations under subsection (1) is exercisable by statutory instrument which shall be subject to annulment in pursuance of a resolution of either House of Parliament.

(5) In this section and section 25F –

"the party with compensation rights" means the party to the marriage who is or is likely to be entitled to PPF compensation, and "the other party" means the other party to the marriage;

"prescribed" means prescribed by regulations."

Amendments—Inserted by Pensions Act 2008, Sch 6, Pt 1.

Defined terms—"PPF compensation": s 21C; "the court": s 52(1).

Scope—This section defines the various terms and provides for regulations to be made. The relevant regulations are the Divorce and Dissolution etc (Pension Protection Fund) Regulations 2011.

26 Commencement of proceedings for ancillary relief etc

(1) Where a petition for divorce, nullity of marriage or judicial separation has been presented, then, subject to subsection (2) below, proceedings for maintenance pending suit under section 22 above, for a financial provision order under section 23 above, or for a property adjustment order may be begun, subject to and in accordance with rules of court, at any time after the presentation of the petition.

(2) Rules of court may provide, in such cases as may be prescribed by the rules –

(a)   that applications for any such relief as is mentioned in subsection (1) above shall be made in the petition or answer; and

(b)   that applications for any such relief which are not so made, or are not made until after the expiration of such period following the presentation of the petition or filing of the answer as may be so prescribed, shall be made only with the leave of the court.

Procedure—An application for a financial order may be made in an application for a matrimonial order (divorce, financial separation, nullity) or at any time after an application for a matrimonial order has been made, under FPR 2010, r 9.4.

Financial provision in case of neglect to maintain

27 Financial provision orders etc in case of neglect by party to marriage to maintain other party or child of the family

(1) Either party to a marriage may apply to the court for an order under this section on the ground that the other party to the marriage (in this section referred to as the respondent) –

(a)   has failed to provide reasonable maintenance for the applicant, or

(b)   has failed to provide, or to make a proper contribution towards, reasonable maintenance for any child of the family.

(2) The court may not entertain an application under this section unless it has jurisdiction to do so by virtue of the Maintenance Regulation and Schedule 6 to the Civil Jurisdiction and Judgments (Maintenance) Regulations 2011.

(3) Where an application under this section is made on the ground mentioned in subsection (1)(a) above, then, in deciding –

(a)   whether the respondent has failed to provide reasonable maintenance for the applicant, and

(b)   what order, if any, to make under this section in favour of the applicant,

the court shall have regard to all the circumstances of the case including the matters mentioned in section 25(2) above, and where an application is also made under this section in respect of a child of the family who has not attained the age of eighteen, first consideration shall be given to the welfare of the child while a minor.

(3A) Where an application under this section is made on the ground mentioned in subsection (1)(b) above then, in deciding –

(a)   whether the respondent has failed to provide, or to make a proper contribution towards, reasonable maintenance for the child of the family to whom the application relates, and

(b)   what order, if any, to make under this section in favour of the child,

the court shall have regard to all the circumstances of the case including the matters mentioned in section 25(3)(a) to (e) above, and where the child of the family to whom the application relates is not the child of the respondent, including also the matters mentioned in section 25(4) above.

(3B) In relation to an application under this section on the ground mentioned in subsection (1)(a) above, section 25(2)(c) above shall have effect as if for the reference therein to the breakdown of the marriage there were substituted a reference to the failure to provide reasonable maintenance for the applicant, and in relation to an application under this section on the ground mentioned in subsection (1)(b) above, section 25(2)(c) above (as it applies by virtue of section 25(3)(e) above) shall have effect as if for the reference therein to the breakdown of the marriage there were substituted a reference to the failure to provide, or to make a proper contribution towards, reasonable maintenance for the child of the family to whom the application relates.

(4) (*repealed*)

(5) Where on an application under this section it appears to the court that the applicant or any child of the family to whom the application relates is in immediate need of financial assistance, but it is not yet possible to determine what order, if any, should be made on the application, the court may make an interim order for maintenance, that is to say, an order requiring the respondent to make to the applicant until the determination of the application such periodical payments as the court thinks reasonable.

(6) Where on an application under this section the applicant satisfies the court of any ground mentioned in subsection (1) above, the court may make any one or more of the following orders, that is to say –

    (a)   an order that the respondent shall make to the applicant such periodical payments, for such term, as may be specified in the order;

    (b)   an order that the respondent shall secure to the applicant, to the satisfaction of the court, such periodical payments, for such term, as may be so specified;

    (c)   an order that the respondent shall pay to the applicant such lump sum as may be so specified;

    (d)   an order that the respondent shall make to such person as may be specified in the order for the benefit of the child to whom the application relates, or to that child, such periodical payments, for such term, as may be so specified;

    (e)   an order that the respondent shall secure to such person as may be so specified for the benefit of that child, or to that child, to the satisfaction of the court, such periodical payments, for such term, as may be so specified;

    (f)   an order that the respondent shall pay to such person as may be so specified for the benefit of that child, or to that child, such lump sum as may be so specified;

subject, however, in the case of an order under paragraph (d), (e) or (f) above, to the restrictions imposed by section 29(1) and (3) below on the making of financial provision orders in favour of children who have attained the age of eighteen.

(6A) An application for the variation under section 31 of this Act of a periodical payments order or secured periodical payments order made under this section in favour of a child may, if the child has attained the age of sixteen, be made by the child himself.

(6B) Where a periodical payments order made in favour of a child under this section ceases to have effect on the date on which the child attains the age of sixteen or at any time after that date but before or on the date on which he attains the age of eighteen, then, if at any time before he attains the age of twenty-one an application is made by the child for an order under this subsection, the court shall have power by order to revive the first-mentioned order from such date as the court may specify, not being earlier than the date of the making of the application, and to exercise its powers under section 31 of this Act in relation to any order so revived.

(7) Without prejudice to the generality of subsection (6)(c) or (f) above, an order under this section for the payment of a lump sum –

    (a)   may be made for the purpose of enabling any liabilities or expenses reasonably incurred in maintaining the applicant or any child of the family to whom the application relates before the making of the application to be met;

    (b)   may provide for the payment of that sum by instalments of such amount as may be specified in the order and may require the payment of the instalments to be secured to the satisfaction of the court.

(8) (*repealed*)

Amendments—DMPA 1973, s 6(1); DPMCA 1978, ss 63, 89(2)(b), Sch 3; MFPA 1984, ss 4, 46(1), Sch 1, para 12; FLRA 1987, s 33(1), Sch 2, para 52; SI 2011/1484.

Procedure—An application under s 27 is governed by FPR 2010, Pt 9 and see Procedural Guide A6.

Scope—Subject to CSA 1991, which restricts the court's power to order child maintenance (see further **Outline of new bases for child support calculation** under CSA 1991, s 4), this section enables an applicant (once he has established the domicile/residence requirement under s 27(2) and the fact that the other party has failed to provide reasonable maintenance) to obtain a financial provision order (ie periodical payments, secured periodical payments or lump sum) for herself/himself and any children of the family without petitioning. The same principles apply to an application under this section as to an application for ancillary relief where a petition has been filed. The right to pursue an application under joint lives to judgment does not endure beyond the death of the respondent (*Harb v King Fahd Bin Abdul Aziz* [2006] 1 FLR 825, CA).

Interim orders—An interim order for periodical payments or secured periodical payments may be made under this section. However, only one lump sum order may be made, so an interim lump sum order cannot be made (see **Interim orders** under s 23).

Costs—The costs rule in FPR 2010, r 28.3 does not apply to applications under s 27. The court may exercise its discretion as to costs in the light of CPR 1998, r 44.2. See FPR PD28A.

Additional provisions with respect to financial provision and property adjustment orders

28 Duration of continuing financial provision orders in favour of party to marriage, and effect of remarriage or formation of civil partnership

(1) Subject in the case of an order made on or after the grant of a decree of a divorce or nullity of marriage to the provisions of sections 25A(2) above and 31(7) below, the term to be specified in a periodical payments or secured periodical payments order in favour of a party to a marriage shall be such term as the court thinks fit, except that the term shall not begin before or extend beyond the following limits, that is to say –

    (a)   in the case of a periodical payments order, the term shall begin not earlier than the date of the making of an application for the order, and shall be so defined as not to extend beyond the death of either of the parties to the marriage or, where the order is made on or after the grant of a decree of divorce or nullity of marriage, the remarriage, or formation of a civil partnership by, of the party in whose favour the order is made; and

    (b)   in the case of a secured periodical payments order, the term shall begin not earlier than the date of the making of an application for the order, and shall be so defined as not to extend beyond the death or, where the order is made on or after the grant of such a decree, the remarriage, or formation of a civil partnership by, of the party in whose favour the order is made.

(1A) Where a periodical payments or secured periodical payments order in favour of a party to a marriage is made on or after the grant of a decree of divorce or nullity of marriage, the court may direct that that party shall not be entitled to apply under section 31 below for the extension of the term specified in the order.

(2) Where a periodical payments or secured periodical payments order in favour of a party to a marriage is made otherwise than on or after the grant of a decree of divorce or nullity of marriage, and the marriage in question is subsequently dissolved or annulled but the order continues in force, the order shall, notwithstanding anything in it, cease to have effect on the remarriage of, or formation of a civil partnership by, that party, except in relation to any arrears due under it on the date of the remarriage or formation of the civil partnership.

(3) If after the grant of a decree dissolving or annulling a marriage either party to that marriage remarries whether at any time before or after the commencement of this Act or

forms a civil partnership, that party shall not be entitled to apply, by reference to the grant of that decree, for a financial provision order in his or her favour, or for a property adjustment order, against the other party to that marriage.

Amendments—MFPA 1984, s 5; CPA 2004, s 261(1), Sch 27, para 43(1)–(5).

Maximum term of periodical payments order and secured periodical payments order (s 28(1))—This section is the source of the important difference that, while a periodical payments order must end on the death of the payer (or earlier remarriage of the payee), a secured periodical payments order can continue after the payer's death.

Power to prohibit extension of term (s 28(1A))—Section 28(1A) enables the court to prohibit a person who has the benefit of a maintenance order from applying to extend its term. See **Scope** under s 25A for the crucial importance of inserting this prohibition in an order where a complete clean break is required. A s 28(1A) direction is inappropriate where there are young children (*Mawson v Mawson* [1994] 2 FLR 985). If the applicant's right to extend the term is to be excluded, the order must expressly state that fact (*Richardson v Richardson* [1994] 1 FLR 286). Even if a court order does not contain this prohibition against applying to extend the term, any application to extend must be made before the order has expired. An order for periodical payments which ceased on a determined event cannot be varied after that event (*T v T (Financial Provision)* [1988] 1 FLR 480). The application for variation must be made in the life of the order but the fact that the order has expired at the time of the hearing of the application to vary does not prevent jurisdiction (*Jones v Jones* [2000] 2 FLR 307).

Prohibition on application after remarriage (s 28(3))—Section 28(3) imposes an almost absolute bar on the court's jurisdiction to entertain an application made after remarriage. However, s 28(3) does not apply to an application for a pension sharing order.

If the application is made before remarriage but is then proceeded with after remarriage, there is no jurisdictional problem, although the remarriage will be relevant on the merits. The prohibition is against a husband or wife making an application for their own benefit; applications for children are not affected. The fact that the other party has made an application for property adjustment does not enable the court to make an order in favour of the party who has not applied (*Robin v Robin* (1983) 4 FLR 632, considered in *Whitehouse-Piper v Stokes* [2009] 1 FLR 983, CA).

The application has to be made either in the petition or answer (if it is an answer claiming relief) or by notice in Form A (with leave if the application ought to have been made in the petition or answer) in accordance with procedure specified in FPR 2010, r 9.4. See *Nixon v Fox (formerly Nixon)* [1978] Fam 173; *Doherty v Doherty* [1976] Fam 71 and *Wilson v Wilson* [1976] Fam 142. In *Hargood (formerly Jenkins) v Jenkins* [1978] Fam 148 it was held that an answer in an acknowledgement of service did not amount to an application for ancillary relief.

It is therefore wise practice, in order to avoid the effect of this prohibition, always to include in the petition (or answer claiming relief) the full range of ancillary relief or, in the case of a respondent who has not filed an answer claiming relief, to file a Form A claiming the full range of relief as soon as possible.

29 Duration of continuing financial provision orders in favour of children, and age limit on making certain orders in their favour

(1) Subject to subsection (3) below, no financial provision order and no order for a transfer of property under section 24(1)(a) above shall be made in favour of a child who has attained the age of eighteen.

(2) The term to be specified in a periodical payments or secured periodical payments order in favour of a child may begin with the date of the making of an application for the order in question or any later date or a date ascertained in accordance with subsection (5) or (6) below but –

    (a) shall not in the first instance extend beyond the date of the birthday of the child next following his attaining the upper limit of the compulsory school age (construed in accordance with section 8 of the Education Act 1996) unless the court considers that in the circumstances of the case the welfare of the child requires that it should extend to a later date; and

    (b) shall not in any event, subject to subsection (3) below, extend beyond the date of the child's eighteenth birthday.

(3) Subsection (1) above, and paragraph (b) of subsection (2), shall not apply in the case of a child, if it appears to the court that –

    (a)   the child is, or will be, or if an order were made without complying with either or both of those provisions would be, receiving instruction at an educational establishment or undergoing training for a trade, profession or vocation, whether or not he is also, or will also be, in gainful employment; or

    (b)   there are special circumstances which justify the making of an order without complying with either or both of those provisions.

(4) Any periodical payments order in favour of a child shall, notwithstanding anything in the order, cease to have effect on the death of the person liable to make payments under the order, except in relation to any arrears due under the order on the date of the death.

(5) Where –

    (a)   a maintenance calculation ("the current calculation") is in force with respect to a child; and

    (b)   an application is made under Part II of this Act for a periodical payments or secured periodical payments order in favour of that child –

       (i)   in accordance with section 8 of the Child Support Act 1991, and

      (ii)   before the end of the period of 6 months beginning with the making of the current calculation,

the term to be specified in any such order made on that application may be expressed to begin on, or at any time after, the earliest permitted date.

(6) For the purposes of subsection (5) above, "the earliest permitted date" is whichever is the later of –

    (a)   the date 6 months before the application is made; or

    (b)   the date on which the current calculation took effect or, where successive maintenance calculations have been continuously in force with respect to a child, on which the first of those calculations took effect.

(7) Where –

    (a)   a maintenance calculation ceases to have effect by or under any provision of the Child Support Act 1991; and

    (b)   an application is made, before the end of the period of 6 months beginning with the relevant date, for a periodical payments or secured periodical payments order in favour of a child with respect to whom that maintenance calculation was in force immediately before it ceased to have effect,

the term to be specified in any such order made on that application may begin with the date on which that maintenance calculation ceased to have effect, or any later date.

(8) In subsection (7)(b) above, –

    (a)   where the maintenance calculation ceased to have effect, the relevant date is the date on which it so ceased

    (b)   (*repealed*)

Amendments—MFPA 1984, s 5; SI 1993/623; Education Act 1996, s 582(1), Sch 37, para 136; CSPSSA 2000, ss 26, 85, Sch 3, para 3, Sch 9.

Scope—This section provides that no financial provision order and no property adjustment order shall be made for children who have reached the age of 18 unless either they are continuing in education or there are special circumstances such as physical or mental disability. It also provides that in the first instance a child maintenance order should be specified to extend to the age of 17. The standard wording is "until the said child shall attain the age of 17 years or ceases full time education if later or further order".

"special circumstances" (s 29(3)(b))—Compare CA 1989, Sch 1, para 3(2)(b). Where there are special circumstances the order can continue beyond 18 years despite CSA 1991, ss 8 and 55. Special circumstances may include physical or other handicap, and the expenses attributed to the child's disability should be taken into account in the broadest sense (*C v F (Disabled Child: Maintenance Orders)* [1998] 2 FLR 1).

30 Direction for settlement of instrument for securing payments or effecting property adjustment

Where the court decides to make a financial provision order requiring any payments to be secured or a property adjustment order –

(a) it may direct that the matter be referred to one of the conveyancing counsel of the court for him to settle a proper instrument to be executed by all necessary parties; and

(b) where the order is to be made in proceedings for divorce, nullity of marriage or judicial separation it may, if it thinks fit, defer the grant of the decree in question until the instrument has been duly executed.

Scope—This section provides for the relatively rare event of instructing conveyancing counsel. For the standard wording of a secured periodical payments order see **Duration and form of secured periodical payments order** under s 23.

Variation, discharge and enforcement of certain orders etc

31 Variation, discharge etc of certain orders for financial relief

(1) Where the court has made an order to which this section applies, then, subject to the provisions of this section and of section 28(1A) above, the court shall have power to vary or discharge the order or to suspend any provision thereof temporarily and to revive the operation of any provision so suspended.

(2) This section applies to the following orders, that is to say –

(a) any order for maintenance pending suit and any interim order for maintenance;
(b) any periodical payments order;
(c) any secured periodical payments order;
(d) any order made by virtue of section 23(3)(c) or 27(7)(b) above (provision for payment of a lump sum by instalments);
(dd) any deferred order made by virtue of section 23(1)(c) (lump sums) which includes provision made by virtue of –
(i) section 25B(4),
(ii) section 25C, or
(iii) section 25F(2),
(provision in respect of pension rights or pension compensation rights);
(e) any order for a settlement of property under section 24(1)(b) or for a variation of settlement under section 24(1)(c) or (d) above, being an order made on or after the grant of a decree of judicial separation;
(f) any order made under section 24A(1) above for the sale of property.
(g) a pension sharing order under section 24B above or a pension compensation sharing order under section 24E above which is made at a time before the decree has been made absolute.

(2A) Where the court has made an order referred to in subsection (2)(a), (b) or (c) above, then, subject to the provisions of this section, the court shall have power to remit the payment of any arrears due under the order or of any part thereof.

(2B) Where the court has made an order referred to in subsection (2)(dd)(ii) above, this section shall cease to apply to the order on the death of either of the parties to the marriage.

(3) The powers exercisable by the court under this section in relation to an order shall be exercisable also in relation to any instrument executed in pursuance of the order.

(4) The court shall not exercise the powers conferred by this section in relation to an order for a settlement under section 24(1)(b) or for a variation of settlement under section 24(1)(c) or (d) above except on an application made in proceedings –

(a) for the rescission of the decree of judicial separation by reference to which the order was made, or

(b) for the dissolution of the marriage in question.

(4A) In relation to an order which falls within paragraph (g) of subsection (2) above ("the subsection (2) order") –

(a) the powers conferred by this section may be exercised –
    (i)   only on an application made before the subsection (2) order has or, but for paragraph (b) below, would have taken effect; and
    (ii) only if, at the time when the application is made, the decree has not been made absolute; and

(b) an application made in accordance with paragraph (a) above prevents the subsection (2) order from taking effect before the application has been dealt with.

(4B) No variation of a pension sharing order, or a pension compensation sharing order, shall be made so as to take effect before the decree is made absolute.

(4C) The variation of a pension sharing order, or a pension compensation sharing order, prevents the order taking effect before the end of such period after the making of the variation as may be prescribed by regulations made by the Lord Chancellor.

(5) Subject to subsections (7A) to (7G) below and without prejudice to any power exercisable by virtue of subsection (2)(d), (dd), (e) or (g) above or otherwise than by virtue of this section, no property adjustment order or pension sharing order, or pension compensation sharing order shall be made on an application for the variation of a periodical payments or secured periodical payments order made (whether in favour of a party to a marriage or in favour of a child of the family) under section 23 above, and no order for the payment of a lump sum shall be made on an application for the variation of a periodical payments or secured periodical payments order in favour of a party to a marriage (whether made under section 23 or under section 27 above).

(6) Where the person liable to make payments under a secured periodical payments order has died, an application under this section relating to that order (and to any order made under section 24A(1) above which requires the proceeds of sale of property to be used for securing those payments) may be made by the person entitled to payments under the periodical payments order or by the personal representatives of the deceased person, but no such application shall, except with the permission of the court, be made after the end of the period of six months from the date on which representation in regard to the estate of that person is first taken out.

(7) In exercising the powers conferred by this section the court shall have regard to all the circumstances of the case, first consideration being given to the welfare while a minor of any child of the family who has not attained the age of eighteen, and the circumstances of the case shall include any change in any of the matters to which the court was required to have regard when making the order to which the application relates, and –

(a) in the case of a periodical payments or secured periodical payments order made on or after the grant of a decree of divorce or nullity of marriage, the court shall consider whether in all the circumstances and after having regard to any such change it would be appropriate to vary the order so that payments under the order are required to be made or secured only for such further period as will in the opinion of the court be sufficient (in the light of any proposed exercise by the court, where the marriage has been dissolved, of its powers under subsection (7E) below) to enable the party in whose favour the order was made to adjust without undue hardship to the termination of those payments;

(b) in a case where the party against whom the order was made has died, the circumstances of the case shall also include the changed circumstances resulting from his or her death.

(7A) Subsection (7B) below applies where, after the dissolution of a marriage, the court –

(a) discharges a periodical payments order or secured periodical payments order made in favour of a party to the marriage; or

(b) varies such an order so that payments under the order are required to be made or secured only for such further period as is determined by the court.

(7B) The court has power, in addition to any power it has apart from this subsection, to make supplemental provision consisting of any of –

(a) an order for the payment of a lump sum in favour of a party to the marriage;

(b) one or more property adjustment orders in favour of a party to the marriage;

(ba) one or more pension sharing orders;

(bb) a pension compensation sharing order;

(c) a direction that the party in whose favour the original order discharged or varied was made is not entitled to make any further application for –

(i) a periodical payments or secured periodical payments order, or

(ii) an extension of the period to which the original order is limited by any variation made by the court.

(7C) An order for the payment of a lump sum made under subsection (7B) above may –

(a) provide for the payment of that sum by instalments of such amount as may be specified in the order; and

(b) require the payment of the instalments to be secured to the satisfaction of the court.

(7D) Section 23(6) above applies where the court makes an order for the payment of a lump sum under subsection (7B) above as it applies where the court makes such an order under section 23 above.

(7E) If under subsection (7B) above the court makes more than one property adjustment order in favour of the same party to the marriage, each of those orders must fall within a different paragraph of section 21(2) above.

(7F) Sections 24A and 30 above apply where the court makes a property adjustment order under subsection (7B) above as they apply where it makes such an order under section 24 above.

(7G) Subsections (3) to (5) of section 24B above apply in relation to a pension sharing order under subsection (7B) above as they apply in relation to a pension sharing order under that section.

(7H) Subsections (3) to (10) of section 24E above apply in relation to a pension compensation sharing order under subsection (7B) above as they apply in relation to a pension compensation sharing order under that section.

(8) The personal representatives of a deceased person against whom a secured periodical payments order was made shall not be liable for having distributed any part of the estate of the deceased after the expiration of the period of six months referred to in subsection (6) above on the ground that they ought to have taken into account the possibility that the court might permit an application under this section to be made after that period by the person entitled to payments under the order; but this subsection shall

not prejudice any power to recover any part of the estate so distributed arising by virtue of the making of an order in pursuance of this section.

(9) In considering for the purposes of subsection (6) above the question when representation was first taken out, a grant limited to settled land or to trust property shall be left out of account and a grant limited to real estate or to personal estate shall be left out of account unless a grant limited to the remainder of the estate has previously been made or is made at the same time.

(10) Where the court, in exercise of its powers under this section, decides to vary or discharge a periodical payments or secured periodical payments order, then, subject to section 28(1) and (2) above, the court shall have power to direct that the variation or discharge shall not take effect until the expiration of such period as may be specified in the order.

(11) Where –

    (a)   a periodical payments or secured periodical payments order in favour of more than one child ("the order") is in force;

    (b)   the order requires payments specified in it to be made to or for the benefit of more than one child without apportioning those payments between them;

    (c)   a maintenance calculation ("the calculation") is made with respect to one or more, but not all, of the children with respect to whom those payments are to be made; and

    (d)   an application is made, before the end of the period of 6 months beginning with the date on which the assessment was made, for the variation or discharge of the order,

the court may, in exercise of its powers under this section to vary or discharge the order, direct that the variation or discharge shall take effect from the date on which the calculation took effect or any later date.

(12) Where –

    (a)   an order ("the child order") of a kind prescribed for the purposes of section 10(1) of the Child Support Act 1991 is affected by a maintenance calculation;

    (b)   on the date on which the child order became so affected there was in force a periodical payments or secured periodical payments order ("the spousal order") in favour of a party to a marriage having the care of the child in whose favour the child order was made; and

    (c)   an application is made, before the end of the period of 6 months beginning with the date on which the maintenance calculation was made, for the spousal order to be varied or discharged,

the court may, in exercise of its powers under this section to vary or discharge the spousal order, direct that the variation or discharge shall take effect from the date on which the child order became so affected or any later date.

(13) For the purposes of subsection (12) above, an order is affected if it ceases to have effect or is modified by or under section 10 of the Child Support Act 1991.

(14) Subsections (11) and (12) above are without prejudice to any other power of the court to direct that the variation of discharge of an order under this section shall take effect from a date earlier than that on which the order for variation or discharge was made.

(15) The power to make regulations under subsection (4C) above shall be exercisable by statutory instrument which shall be subject to annulment in pursuance of a resolution of either House of Parliament.

Amendments—Matrimonial Homes and Property Act 1981, s 8(2); AJA 1982, s 51; MFPA 1984, s 6; SI 1993/623; Pensions Act 1995, s 166; FLA 1996, Sch 8, para 16(5)(a),(6)(b),(7) (as modified by SI 1998/2572); WRPA 1999 s 19, Sch 3, para 7; CSPSSA 2000, s 26, Sch 3, para 3; Pensions Act 2008, Sch 6, Pt 1.

Procedure—An application for variation under s 31 is governed by FPR 2010, Pt 9 and see Procedural Guide B5.

Scope—This section gives the court the power to vary its own financial orders, as listed in s 31(2)(a)–(g). It follows that property orders may not be varied, save for any order made under s 24A(1) for the sale of property. Orders may be amended under the inherent jurisdiction of the court only to give effect to the intention of the court (*Swinaale v Forder (Forder Intervening)* [2007] 1 FLR 1905). There is jurisdiction under s 31(2)(d) to vary the timing of instalments and the manner of payment (*G v G (Role of FDR Judge)* [2007] 1 FLR 237). The power to vary agreements is contained in ss 35 and 36.

Limits upon the court's power to vary—The court's power to vary applies only to orders requiring the payment of income to another, and orders for the sale of property. The court has no jurisdiction to vary capital orders, save in four limited exceptions:

(i) where the order is for a lump sum payable by instalments (*Penrose v Penrose* [1994] 2 FLR 621);
(ii) where settlement of property or variation of settlement order has been made in the course of judicial separation proceedings, and there is a subsequent application for a divorce, or the rescission of the decree of judicial separation;
(iii) where a pension attachment lump sum order under s 25B(4) or s 25C has been made;
(iv) where a pension sharing order has been made and the application to vary is made both before the order has taken effect and before decree absolute. The court has the power to extend the time to pay a lump sum under its inherent power to regulate executory orders, provided the application to extend time does not strike at the heart of the order (*Masefield v Alexander (Lump sum: Extension of time)* [1995] 1 FLR 100).

In *Richardson v Richardson* [2011] 2 FLR 244, a variation of the capital sum payable by a husband to the wife was varied where the parties became unexpectedly liable for damages and costs arising out of a personal injury claim against them: the husband's payment to the wife was reduced by one half of the personal injury claim.

Power to vary child periodical payments—The court has the power to vary a child maintenance order, even where the order is a nominal order by consent (*V v V (Child Maintenance)* [2001] 2 FLR 799). However, if the parent with care is on benefits, the court only has power to vary if there is no application for a child support assessment, and notice of the application to vary should be given to the Child Support Agency.

Power to extend the term of a periodical payments order—The application for variation must be made in the life of the order. The fact that the order has expired at the time of the hearing does not prevent the court having jurisdiction (*Jones v Jones* [2000] 2 FLR 307). Where parties agree and intend to be bound by a term order, the exercise of the power to extend the obligations is held to require "some exceptional justification": *Fleming v Fleming* [2004] 1 FLR 667; *Yates v Yates* [2012] EWCA Civ 532.

Power to vary due to death—If the application to vary a secured periodical payments order arises because of the payer's death, the application to vary requires leave, if it is made later that 6 months from the grant of probate or letters of administration. The personal representatives of the deceased will not be liable for distributing the estate before an application being made, if it is made after the 6-month period has elapsed.

Capitalization of periodical payments on the application of either party for a clean break—Section 31(5) prohibits the making of a property adjustment or lump sum order on an application for the variation of maintenance, save in defined circumstances. Where no lump sum or property adjustment order has been made, an application may be made and heard at the same time as an application for the variation of periodical payments (*Pearce v Pearce* (1980) 1 FLR 261).

The court has the power to make a pension sharing order upon a variation application. This power applies only to petitions filed after 1 December 2000 (WRPA 1999 s 85(3)(b)).

Under s 31(7A) and (7B), upon the application of either party for a clean break, the court may make a lump sum order, or a further property adjustment order. The court has no power under s 37 to reopen capital claims, but may substitute such sum as would compensate the payee and achieve the clean break. There are three questions to consider: (i) what variation if any should be ordered to periodical payments? (ii) when the variation should take effect and (iii) whether the payments should be capitalized (*Pearce v Pearce* [2003] 2 FLR 1144 (CA)). In *Vaughan v Vaughan* [2010] 2 FLR 242, CA, these questions are reinterpreted as (i) whether periodical payments should terminate or continue, and if so, at what level; (ii) if continuing, the capital equivalent, applying the Duxbury formula; and (iii) whether it is fair to both parties to capitalise periodical payments and whether it is reasonably practical for the payer to pay a capital sum, as opposed to periodical payments.

Capitalisation may be calculated from Duxbury Tables based upon interest rates of 3.75%, (see *At A Glance*, Family Law Bar Association, 2008). The court has the discretion to adopt the figure suggested in the tables, or to depart from it (*Harris v Harris* [2001] 1 FCR 68 (CA)). The issue is "what is a fair capital sum?". There is also a discretion to depart from the tables to reflect individual special factors, but it should be exercised narrowly.

Principles upon which the court will act in variation and capitalization cases (s 31(7))—The discretion has been described as "almost unfettered", but the principles governing an original consent order should not be interfered with, so that where the principle of joint lives had been accepted, the quantum to be capitalised should not extend beyond the husband's death (*Harris v Harris* [2001] 1 FCR 68, CA).

The clean break provisions apply upon an application to vary: the court has an ongoing duty to consider whether financial dependence may be terminated without undue hardship, normally to the wife (*Boylan* [1988] 1 FLR 282; *Fleming* [2004] 1 FLR 667).

Changes in s 25(2) factors since the order was made should be considered. Cohabitation with a new partner may commonly arise to be considered as a "circumstance of the case". For the court's approach to cohabitation in variation applications, see *Atkinson v Atkinson* [1988] 2 FLR 353, CA, and *Fleming v Fleming* [2004] 1 FLR 667, CA. In *K v K (Periodical Payments: Cohabitation)* [2006] 2 FLR 468, a 3-year cohabitation was a factor in varying the term of periodical payments to a shorter period. The court should be alive to the practical implications of cohabitation, including its financial consequences and duration. In *W v W (Periodical Payments: Variation)* [2010] 2 FLR 985, a wife's 6-year cohabitation was not material because the financial contribution of the cohabitee meant that the wife was not subsidising him to any significant extent. The wife received increased periodical payments that were capitalised, in part because of her ongoing contributions as a mother. The CA has stated that post-divorce cohabitation would not lead to an inevitable revaluation of a wife's claim for periodical payments: *Grey v Grey* [2010] 1 FLR 1764, CA. Where the payer has remarried, priority should not be given to the interests of the second wife, to the extent that the claims of the applicant first wife are undervalued: *Roberts v Roberts* [1968] 3 All ER 479, approved in *Vaughan v Vaughan* [2010] 2 FLR 242, CA.

The principles of both *Miller* and *McFarlane* [2006] 1 FLR 1186 have been specifically applied to variation and capitalization cases: *Lauder* [2007] 2 FLR 802; *VB v JP* [2008] 1 FLR 742.

In assessing the upward variation, the court will have regard to the original award. In *Lauder*, the fact that the original award had given the wife a high proportion of the husband's net income was not solely determinative in percentage terms, but was a relevant circumstance as one of the background factors. In *VB v JP*, the President found that the percentage of the husband's net income previously awarded was "an appropriate cross check (if not a starting point)", in an application based on the substantial increase in the husband's income. In *Hvorostovsky v Hvorostovsky* [2009] 2 FLR 1574, the Court of Appeal stressed the usefulness of a percentage comparison between the original order and the order on variation, to judge the overall proportionality of the conclusions. Consideration of the standard of living immediately before the breakdown of the marriage was not a determinative factor and it was unnecessary to assert relationship-generated disadvantage. The "reasonable requirements" argument was expressly disapproved where a rich husband who had experienced a significant increase in income had the means to pay more than the wife's needs, even where interpreted generously. See *McFarlane v McFarlane* [2009] 2 FLR 1322, where a husband's rising income in the light of the application of the principles of financial needs, compensation and sharing led to an order for payments to be paid to the wife as a percentage of his banded income.

32 Payment of certain arrears unenforceable without the leave of the court

(1) A person shall not be entitled to enforce through the High Court or any county court the payment of any arrears due under an order for maintenance pending suit, an interim order for maintenance or any financial provision order without the leave of that court if those arrears became due more than twelve months before proceedings to enforce the payment of them are begun.

(2) The court hearing an application for the grant of leave under this section may refuse leave, or may grant leave subject to such restrictions and conditions (including conditions as to the allowing of time for payment or the making of payment by instalments) as that court thinks proper, or may remit the payment of the arrears or of any part thereof.

(3) An application for the grant of leave under this section shall be made in such manner as may be prescribed by rules of court.

Procedure—An application for the issue of a judgment summons is governed by FPR 2010, rr 33.9–33.18. Where an attachment of earnings order is sought, it may be convenient to issue the summons or notice of application under this section simultaneously with and returnable on the same date as the attachment of earnings application. The same practice may be adopted on an application for the appointment of a receiver by way of equitable execution or on an application for a means of payment order under MEA 1991, s 1(4)(a). In the case of execution, and in the case of applications for garnishee or charging orders where relief is given initially on an ex parte application, leave must be sought under this section as a preliminary step.

"financial provision order" (s 32(1))—The Court has suggested that this includes a foreign judgment for financial provision and in considering enforcement under this section the English court is not reviewing the foreign judgment as to its merits contrary to the Judgments Regulation: *O'Farrell v O'Farrell* [2013] 1 FLR 77.

"may refuse leave, or may grant leave" (s 32(2))—There is no presumption that leave should be granted only in special circumstances (*Lumsden v Lumsden* 11 November 1998, CA).

"application for the grant of leave" (s 32(3))—Leave to enforce accrued arrears due during a period in excess of 12 months can be sought by making an application in general form supported by a sworn statement/affidavit by the party applying setting out the arrears sought to be enforced and giving the reasons for failure to apply to enforce earlier together with any other relevant information which may assist the court.

33 Orders for repayment in certain cases of sums paid under certain orders

(1) Where on an application made under this section in relation to an order to which this section applies it appears to the court that by reason of –

    (a)   a change in the circumstances of the person entitled to, or liable to make, payments under the order since the order was made, or

    (b)   the changed circumstances resulting from the death of the person so liable,

the amount received by the person entitled to payments under the order in respect of a period after those circumstances changed or after the death of the person liable to make payments under the order, as the case may be, exceeds the amount which the person so liable or his or her personal representatives should have been required to pay, the court may order the respondent to the application to pay to the applicant such sum, not exceeding the amount of the excess, as the court thinks just.

(2) This section applies to the following orders, that is to say –

    (a)   any order for maintenance pending suit and any interim order for maintenance;

    (b)   any periodical payments order; and

    (c)   any secured periodical payments order.

(3) An application under this section may be made by the person liable to make payments under an order to which this section applies or his or her personal representatives and may be made against the person entitled to payments under the order or her or his personal representatives.

(4) An application under this section may be made in proceedings in the High Court or a county court for –

    (a)   the variation or discharge of the order to which this section applies, or

    (b)   leave to enforce, or the enforcement of, the payment of arrears under that order;

but when not made in such proceedings shall be made to a county court, and accordingly references in this section to the court are references to the High Court or a county court, as the circumstances require.

(5) The jurisdiction conferred on a county court by this section shall be exercisable notwithstanding that by reason of the amount claimed in the application the jurisdiction would not but for this subsection be exercisable by a county court.

(6) An order under this section for the payment of any sum may provide for the payment of that sum by instalments of such amount as may be specified in the order.

Procedure—An application under s 33 is governed by FPR 2010, Pt 9.

Scope—This section empowers the court to order the party who has received maintenance to repay monies that have been received where there has been a change in circumstances of the payee or a change of circumstances which results from the payer's death. The power to order repayment relates to the period before the order is varied and is distinct from the court's powers to remit arrears and to vary the order itself. Section 38 covers the situation where payments have been made at a time when the order no longer existed because it had been determined by, for instance, the remarriage of the payee.

No repayment in respect of capital orders (s 33(2))—The power to order repayment applies only to orders for maintenance pending suit and periodical payments orders and not to capital orders. For the impeachability of a capital order where there has been a drastic change of circumstances, see the principles established by the House of Lords in *Barder v Barder* [1987] 2 FLR 480. For a discussion of *Barder*-type events, see **Power to reopen consent orders** at FPR 2010, r 9.26.

Mode of application (s 33(4),(5))—Where application is made under this section, the county court's jurisdiction is unlimited. Normally the party applying will be seeking a discharge of the order and it is likely that there will be a linked application to vary the order so that the procedure set out in FPR 2010, Pt 9 applies. If there are no variation proceedings and the application stands on its own, no form of application is specified by FPR 2010.

Consent orders

33A   Consent orders for financial provision on property adjustment

(1) Notwithstanding anything in the preceding provisions of this Part of this Act, on an application for a consent order for financial relief the court may, unless it has reason to think that there are other circumstances into which it ought to inquire, make an order in the terms agreed on the basis only of the prescribed information furnished with the application.

(2) Subsection (1) above applies to an application for a consent order varying or discharging an order for financial relief as it applies to an application for an order for financial relief.

(3) In this section –
"consent order", in relation to an application for an order, means an order in the terms applied for to which the respondent agrees;
"order for financial relief" means an order under any of sections 23, 24, 24A, 24B or 27 above; and
"prescribed" means prescribed by rules of court.

Amendments—Inserted by MFPA 1984, s 7; amended by WRPA 1999, s 19, Sch 3, para 8.

Procedure—An application for a consent order is governed by FPR 2010, Pt 9.

Scope—This section empowers the court to make a consent order without a full investigation and without hearing oral evidence. The court cannot exercise its mandatory duties under ss 25 and 25A without up-to-date information of the salient facts (*Jenkins v Livesey (formerly Jenkins)* [1985] FLR 813). This is provided in each party's separate or joint statement of information: if separate documents, each party must sign the other's statement. There is no requirement for the parties to attend court. See FPR 2010, r 9.26.

Maintenance agreements

34 Validity of maintenance agreements

(1) If a maintenance agreement includes a provision purporting to restrict any right to apply to a court for an order containing financial arrangements, then –

    (a)   that provision shall be void; but

    (b)   any other financial arrangements contained in the agreement shall not thereby be rendered void or unenforceable and shall, unless they are void or unenforceable for any other reason (and subject to sections 35 and 36 below), be binding on the parties to the agreement.

(2) In this section and in section 35 below –

"maintenance agreement" means any agreement in writing made, whether before or after the commencement of this Act, between the parties to a marriage, being –

    (a)   an agreement containing financial arrangements, whether made during the continuance or after the dissolution or annulment of the marriage; or

    (b)   a separation agreement which contains no financial arrangements in a case where no other agreement in writing between the same parties contains such arrangements;

"financial arrangements" means provisions governing the rights and liabilities towards one another when living separately of the parties to a marriage (including a marriage which has been dissolved or annulled) in respect of the making or securing of payments or the disposition or use of any property, including such rights and liabilities with respect to the maintenance or education of any child, whether or not a child of the family.

Prohibition of any restriction on right to apply (s 34(1))—Section 34(1) provides that it is not possible for an agreement to restrict either party's right to apply for income or capital relief from the court. However, while it is impossible to restrict the theoretical right to apply, the fact that parties have come to an agreement carefully arrived at with the benefit of legal advice (in the absence of a vitiating factor such as set out in *Edgar v Edgar* (1981) 2 FLR 19) will be an important factor but only one ingredient within a complex equation in determining whether the court should in fact make financial provision and property adjustment orders in identical terms to those that had been agreed (*Smith v Smith* [2000] 3 FCR 374).

"maintenance agreement" (s 34(2))—This term is defined as either an agreement containing financial arrangements made at any time or a separation agreement which contains no such financial arrangements.

35 Alteration of agreements by court during lives of parties

(1) Where a maintenance agreement is for the time being subsisting and each of the parties to the agreement is for the time being either domiciled or resident in England and Wales, then, subject to subsections (1A) and (3) below, either party may apply to the court or to a magistrates' court for an order under this section.

(1A) If an application or part of an application relates to a matter where jurisdiction falls to be determined by reference to the jurisdictional requirements of the Maintenance Regulation and Schedule 6 to the Civil Jurisdiction and Judgments (Maintenance) Regulations 2011 –

    (a)   the requirement as to domicile or residence in subsection (1) does not apply to the application or that part of it, but

    (b)   the court may not entertain the application or that part of it unless it has jurisdiction to do so by virtue of that Regulation and that Schedule.

(2) If the court to which the application is made is satisfied either –

    (a)   that by reason of a change in the circumstances in the light of which any financial arrangements contained in the agreement were made or, as the case may be, financial arrangements were omitted from it (including a change foreseen by the parties when making the agreement), the agreement should be altered so as to make different, or, as the case may be, so as to contain, financial arrangements, or

(b)   that the agreement does not contain proper financial arrangements with respect to any child of the family,

then subject to subsections (3), (4) and (5) below, that court may by order make such alterations in the agreement –

(i)   by varying or revoking any financial arrangements contained in it, or

(ii)   by inserting in it financial arrangements for the benefit of one of the parties to the agreement or of a child of the family,

as may appear to that court to be just having regard to all the circumstances, including, if relevant, the matters mentioned in section 25(4) above; and the agreement shall have effect thereafter as if any alteration made by the order had been made by agreement between the parties and for valuable consideration.

(3) A magistrates' court shall not entertain an application under subsection (1) above unless both the parties to the agreement are resident in England and Wales and the court acts in, or is authorised by the Lord Chancellor to act for, a local justice area in which at least one of the parties is resident, and shall not have power to make any order on such an application except –

(a)   in a case where the agreement includes no provision for periodical payments by either of the parties, an order inserting provision for the making by one of the parties of periodical payments for the maintenance of the other party or for the maintenance of any child of the family;

(b)   in a case where the agreement includes provision for the making by one of the parties of periodical payments, an order increasing or reducing the rate of, or terminating, any of those payments.

(4) Where a court decides to alter, by order under this section, an agreement by inserting provision for the making or securing by one of the parties to the agreement of periodical payments for the maintenance of the other party or by increasing the rate of the periodical payments which the agreement provides shall be made by one of the parties for the maintenance of the other, the term for which the payments or, as the case may be, the additional payments attributable to the increase are to be made under the agreement as altered by the order shall be such term as the court may specify, subject to the following limits, that is to say –

(a)   where the payments will not be secured, the term shall be so defined as not to extend beyond the death of either of the parties to the agreement or the remarriage of, or formation of a civil partnership by, the party to whom the payments are to be made;

(b)   where the payments will be secured, the term shall be so defined as not to extend beyond the death or remarriage of, or formation of a civil partnership by, that party.

(5) Where a court decides to alter, by order under this section, an agreement by inserting provision for the making or securing by one of the parties to the agreement of periodical payments for the maintenance of a child of the family or by increasing the rate of the periodical payments which the agreement provides shall be made or secured by one of the parties for the maintenance of such a child, then, in deciding the term for which under the agreement as altered by the order the payments, or as the case may be, the additional payments attributable to the increase are to be made or secured for the benefit of the child, the court shall apply the provisions of section 29(2) and (3) above as to age limits as if the order in question were a periodical payments or secured periodical payments order in favour of the child.

(6) For the avoidance of doubt it is hereby declared that nothing in this section or in section 34 above affects any power of a court before which any proceedings between the parties to a maintenance agreement are brought under any other enactment (including a provision of this Act) to make an order containing financial arrangements or any right of either party to apply for such an order in such proceedings.

Amendments—MFPA 1984, s 46(1), Sch 1, para 13; Justices of the Peace Act 1997, s 73(2), Sch 5, para 14; AJA 1999, s 106, Sch 15; CPA 2004, s 261(1), Sch 27, para 44; Courts Act 2003, Sch 8, para 169; SI 2011/1484.

Procedure—An application under s 25 is governed by FPR 2010, Pt 9 and see Procedural Guide B5.

Scope—Subject to CSA 1991, this section empowers the court to alter a maintenance agreement during the lives of the parties. The power arises if either there is a change in circumstances or there are no proper financial arrangements for the children. This is the only section within Pt II where jurisdiction is vested not only in the High Court and county courts but magistrates' courts as well. To overturn an agreed post-nuptial settlement, the court had to be satisfied that the applicant wife's will was overborne by her husband exercising undue pressure or influence upon her (*NA v MA* [2007] 1 FLR 1760). Post nuptial settlements clearly can be varied by the court, although the Privy Council has stated that prenuptial settlements might not be covered by the variation power in s 35 (*MacLeod v MacLeod* [2009] 1 FLR 641).

36 Alteration of agreements by court after death of one party

(1) Where a maintenance agreement within the meaning of section 34 above provides for the continuation of payments under the agreement after the death of one of the parties and that party dies domiciled in England and Wales, the surviving party or the personal representatives of the deceased party may, subject to subsections (2) and (3) below, apply to the High Court or a county court for an order under section 35 above.

(2) An application under this section shall not, except with the permission of the High Court or a county court, be made after the end of the period of six months from the date on which representation in regard to the estate of the deceased is first taken out.

(3) A county court shall not entertain an application under this section, or an application for permission to make an application under this section, unless it would have jurisdiction by virtue of section 22 of the Inheritance (Provision for Family and Dependants) Act 1975 (which confers jurisdiction on county courts in proceedings under that Act if the value of the property mentioned in that section does not exceed £5,000 or such larger sum as may be fixed by order of the Lord Chancellor) to hear and determine proceedings for an order under section 2 of that Act in relation to the deceased's estate.

(4) If a maintenance agreement is altered by a court on an application made in pursuance of subsection (1) above, the like consequences shall ensue as if the alteration had been made immediately before the death by agreement between the parties and for valuable consideration.

(5) The provisions of this section shall not render the personal representatives of the deceased liable for having distributed any part of the estate of the deceased after the expiration of the period of six months referred to in subsection (2) above on the ground that they ought to have taken into account the possibility that a court might permit an application by virtue of this section to be made by the surviving party after that period; but this subsection shall not prejudice any power to recover any part of the estate so distributed arising by virtue of the making of an order in pursuance of this section.

(6) Section 31(9) above shall apply for the purposes of subsection (2) above as it applies for the purposes of subsection (6) of section 31.

(7) Subsection (3) of section 22 of the Inheritance (Provision for Family and Dependants) Act 1975 (which enables rules of court to provide for the transfer from a county court to the High Court or from the High court to a county court of proceedings for an order under section 2 of that Act) and paragraphs (a) and (b) of subsection (4) of

that section (provisions relating to proceedings commenced in county court before coming into force of order of the Lord Chancellor under that section) shall apply in relation to proceedings consisting of any such application as is referred to in subsection (3) above as they apply in relation to proceedings for an order under section 2 of that Act.

Amendments—I(PFD)A 1975, s 26(1).

Procedure—An application under s 36 is governed by FPR 2010, rr 8.6–8.11. Application is by notice of application on Form D50D.

Six-month time-limit (s 36(2))—Leave to apply is required if the application is made later than six months from the grant of probate or letters of administration.

County court jurisdiction (s 36(3))—County courts have the same jurisdiction under this section as under the I(PFD)A 1975. By art 2 of HCCCJO 1991 county court jurisdiction under this section is unlimited.

Miscellaneous and supplemental

37 Avoidance of transactions intended to prevent or reduce financial relief

(1) For the purposes of this section "financial relief" means relief under any of the provisions of sections 22, 23, 24, 24B, 27, 31 (except subsection (6)) and 35 above, and any reference in this section to defeating a person's claim for financial relief is a reference to preventing financial relief from being granted to that person, or to that person for the benefit of a child of the family, or reducing the amount of any financial relief which might be so granted, or frustrating or impeding the enforcement of any order which might be or has been made at his instance under any of those provisions.

(2) Where proceedings for financial relief are brought by one person against another, the court may, on the application of the first-mentioned person –

(a) if it is satisfied that the other party to the proceedings is, with the intention of defeating the claim for financial relief, about to make any disposition or to transfer out of the jurisdiction or otherwise deal with any property, make such order as it thinks fit for restraining the other party from so doing or otherwise for protecting the claim;

(b) if it is satisfied that the other party has, with that intention, made a reviewable disposition and that if the disposition were set aside financial relief or different financial relief would be granted to the applicant, make an order setting aside the disposition;

(c) if it is satisfied, in a case where an order has been obtained under any of the provisions mentioned in subsection (1) above by the applicant against the other party, that the other party has, with that intention, made a reviewable disposition, make an order setting aside the disposition;

and an application for the purposes of paragraph (b) above shall be made in the proceedings for the financial relief in question.

(3) Where the court makes an order under subsection (2)(b) or (c) above setting aside a disposition it shall give such consequential directions as it thinks fit for giving effect to the order (including directions requiring the making of any payments or the disposal of any property).

(4) Any disposition made by the other party to the proceedings for financial relief in question (whether before or after the commencement of those proceedings) is a reviewable disposition for the purposes of subsection (2)(b) and (c) above unless it was made for valuable consideration (other than marriage) to a person who, at the time of the

disposition, acted in relation to it in good faith and without notice of any intention on the part of the other party to defeat the applicant's claim for financial relief.

(5) Where an application is made under this section with respect to a disposition which took place less than three years before the date of the application or with respect to a disposition or other dealing with property which is about to take place and the court is satisfied –

    (a) in a case falling within subsection (2)(a) or (b) above, that the disposition or other dealing would (apart from this section) have the consequence, or

    (b) in a case falling within subsection (2)(c) above, that the disposition has had the consequence,

of defeating the applicant's claim for financial relief, it shall be presumed, unless the contrary is shown, that the person who disposed of or is about to dispose of or deal with the property did so or, as the case may be, is about to do so, with the intention of defeating the applicant's claim for financial relief.

(6) In this section "disposition" does not include any provision contained in a will or codicil but, with that exception, includes any conveyance, assurance or gift of property of any description, whether made by an instrument or otherwise.

(7) This section does not apply to a disposition made before 1 January 1968.

Amendments—WRPA 1999, s 19, Sch 3, para 9.

Procedure—An application under s 37 preventing a disposition is governed by FPR 2010, Pt 18 (r 9.6(1)). An application may be made without notice to a respondent: r 9.6(2). See Procedural Guide B6.

Scope—This section has two separate functions. First, it empowers the court to restrain the future disposal of or future dealings with property in order to protect the applicant's pending claims (s 37(2)(a)). The court's inherent jurisdiction and its jurisdiction under SCA 1981, s 37(3) to freeze assets are in addition to the jurisdiction under this section (see Procedural Guide B6). Second, it empowers the court to set aside dispositions that have already been made where, if the disposition were set aside, different financial relief would be granted to the applicant (s 37(2)(b)) or where following an order of the court a disposition has been made that impedes the enforcement of an order (s 37(2)(c)). The section applies retrospectively to void the transaction from the beginning and has been described as "a bespoke alternative to the equitable right to seek rescission": *AC v DC and Eight Others* [2012] EWHC 2032 (Fam). In all cases, the applicant has to show the existence of an intention to defeat the claim for financial relief.

Essential preconditions (s 37(2),(5),(6))—Before an order may be made under this section, there must be proceedings for financial relief in existence. (Section 37(1) defines "financial relief" to mean an order for maintenance pending suit, financial provision, property adjustment, wilful neglect to maintain or a variation application.) Thus, there must be a valid notice of application either in the application for a matrimonial order/divorce, judicial separation, nullity or by an application for a financial order in Form A: FPR 2010, r 9.4.

    The applicant must also show that the act complained of was made with the intention of defeating the claim for financial relief. If the act complained of took place less than 3 years before the application (or is anticipated at the time of the application) then it shall be presumed until the contrary is shown that the person who disposed (will dispose) of the asset had (will have) the necessary intention if the disposition has (will have) the effect of reducing the amount of any financial relief which might be granted or frustrating or impeding the enforcement of any order. Otherwise, proving the necessary intention is a question of fact.

    The definition of "disposition" is wide but any provision in a will is excluded. The meaning of "property" is not defined but it is not restricted to property in England and Wales, and includes real and personal property situated abroad (*Hamlin v Hamlin* [1986] 1 FLR 61). It is usual to exclude a sum for the respondent's living expenses from the injunction, but this should not be used as a device to obtain periodical payments for the wife out of this allowance, who should apply under s 22 for maintenance pending suit (*Re M (Freezing Injunction)* [2006] 1 FLR 1031). The court would generally unfreeze assets to discharge a genuine commercial debt, while preserving the home of the wife and children (*Paulin v Paulin* [2009] 2 FLR 354, CA).

    To restrain an anticipated disposal under s 37(2)(a), the applicant should file a notice of application supported by a sworn statement. To obtain a s 37 order requires the applicant to demonstrate contemporaneous and factual evidence of the likelihood of the movement and dissipation of assets, with

PART II

the intention of defeating the applicant's claim. A without notice order would be made only where there was positive evidence that to give notice would lead to irretrievable prejudice to the applicant. An applicant is fixed with a high duty of candour, which if breached would lead to the discharge of the order: *ND v KP (Freezing Order: Ex Parte Application)* [2011] 2 FLR 662. The freezing order should contain conventional provisions permitting the use of funds for day-to-day living and business expenses: *Harrison v Harrison* [2008] 2 FLR 35.

Effect on third parties—There is no jurisdiction to freeze the assets of a third party who is not a party to the application. Third parties, such as banks served with an injunction after a hearing without notice, are entitled to have the documents which disclose the evidence relied upon, in separate affidavits if necessary. It is a breach of Article 6 of the ECHR to give the judge information in a without notice hearing, which is not revealed to a party affected by the application: *C v C (Without Notice Orders)* [2006] 1 FLR 936. A bank charge which continued to attach to a property sold on to defeat the wife's interest is not a reviewable disposition under s 37(1) where the husband had not been a party to the charge, and the bank was not a party to the wife's proceedings against the husband (*Ansari v Ansari* [2009] 1 FLR 1121). Where a third party has actual or constructive knowledge of the husband's intention to defeat a wife's claim, a third party charge may be set aside, as he had not acted in good faith, whether or not there had been valuable consideration: *Kremen v Agrest and Fishman* [2011] 2 FLR 478.

Restraining surrender of a tenancy—The surrender of a tenancy is not a disposition so, once made, it cannot be set aside under s 37(2)(b) or (c). If it is believed that a tenancy or joint tenancy is about to be surrendered then, in the absence of any undertaking, there should be an application under s 37(2)(a) to restrain the surrender. The undertaking/order should be served on the landlord (*Bater v Greenwich London Borough Council* [1999] 2 FLR 993).

Impounding of a passport—The power to impound a respondent's passport is addressed in *Young v Young* [2012] 2 FLR 470: see [26] for principles. Also, see SCA 1981, s 19.

Assignment of pensions by service personnel—Pensions Act 1995, s 166 enables the court to exercise jurisdiction in respect of terminal grants and other pension rights; see further under s 23 of this Act.

Breach of s 37 injunction—A husband who disposed of monies in his bank account in breach of a s 37 injunction was properly committed to prison for contempt: *Peyman-Fard v Peyman-Fard* [2011] EWCA Civ 959.

Costs—The costs rule in FPR 2010, r 28.3 does not apply to applications under s 37(2)(a) as it is not a financial order or remedy as defined in FPR 2010, r 2.3. The court may exercise its discretion as to costs in the light of CPR 1998, r 44.2. See FPR PD28A. Rule 28.3 does apply to applications under s 37(2)(b),(c) as these are for financial orders as defined in rr 2.3 and 9.3.

38 Orders for repayment in certain cases of sums paid after cessation of order by reason of remarriage or formation of civil partnership

(1) Where –

    (a) a periodical payments or secured periodical payments order in favour of a party to a marriage (hereafter in this section referred to as "a payments order") has ceased to have effect by reason of the remarriage of, or formation of a civil partnership by, that party, and

    (b) the person liable to make payments under the order or his or her personal representatives made payments in accordance with it in respect of a period after the date of the remarriage or formation of the civil partnership in the mistaken belief that the order was still subsisting,

the person so liable or his or her personal representatives shall not be entitled to bring proceedings in respect of a cause of action arising out of the circumstances mentioned in paragraphs (a) and (b) above against the person entitled to payments under the order or her or his personal representatives, but may instead make an application against that person or her or his personal representatives under this section.

(2) On an application under this section the court may order the respondent to pay to the applicant a sum equal to the amount of the payments made in respect of the period mentioned in subsection (1)(b) above or, if it appears to the court that it would be unjust

to make that order, it may either order the respondent to pay to the applicant such lesser sum as it thinks fit or dismiss the application.

(3) An application under this section may be made in proceedings in the High Court or a county court for leave to enforce, or the enforcement of, payment of arrears under the order in question, but when not made in such proceedings shall be made to a county court; and accordingly references in this section to the court are references to the High Court or a county court, as the circumstances require.

(4) The jurisdiction conferred on a county court by this section shall be exercisable notwithstanding that by reason of the amount claimed in the application the jurisdiction would not but for this subsection be exercisable by a county court.

(5) An order under this section for the payment of any sum may provide for the payment of that sum by instalments of such amount as may be specified in the order.

(6) The designated officer for a magistrates' court to whom any payments under a payments order are required to be made, and the collecting officer under an attachment of earnings order made to secure payments under a payments order, shall not be liable –

    (a)   in the case of the designated officer, for any act done by him in pursuance of the payments order after the date on which that order ceased to have effect by reason of the remarriage of, or formation of a civil partnership by, the person entitled to payments under it, and

    (b)   in the case of the collecting officer, for any act done by him after that date in accordance with any enactment or rule of court specifying how payments made to him in compliance with the attachment of earnings order are to be dealt with,

if, but only if, the act was one which he would have been under a duty to do had the payments order not so ceased to have effect and the act was done before notice in writing of the fact that the person so entitled had remarried or formed a civil partnership was given to him by or on behalf of that person, the person liable to make payments under the payments order or the personal representatives of either of those persons.

(7) In this section "collecting officer", in relation to an attachment of earnings order, means the officer of the High Court, the district judge of a county court or the designated officer for a magistrates' court to whom a person makes payments in compliance with the order.

Amendments—AJA 1999, s 90, Sch 13, para 82; CPA 2004, s 261(1), Sch 27, para 43(1)–(4); Courts Act 2003, Sch 8, para 170.

Procedure—The application under s 38 is governed by FPR 2010, Pt 9.

Scope—This section empowers the court to order repayment of a maintenance order when payments have been made under it after the order had in fact ceased (eg because the payee has married without informing the payer of that fact). Section 33 will apply if the reason for seeking repayment arises from a change of circumstances such as, for instance, steady cohabitation. The jurisdiction of county courts under this section is unlimited.

    Usually the application will be linked with an application to vary or discharge the order and should therefore be made in the same way as a variation application, ie on Form A with a supporting affidavit. If it is not combined with any other application, no procedure is prescribed except that it should be made to a county court.

39 Settlement etc made in compliance with a property adjustment order may be avoided on bankruptcy of settlor

The fact that a settlement or transfer of property had to be made in order to comply with a property adjustment order shall not prevent that settlement or transfer from being a transaction in respect of which an order may be made under section 339 or 340 of the Insolvency Act 1986 (transfers at an undervalue and preferences).

Amendments—Insolvency Act 1985, s 235(1), Sch 8, para 23; Insolvency Act 1986, s 439(2), Sch 14.

Scope—This section provides that the fact that a settlement or transfer of property is made pursuant to a property adjustment order does not prevent it from being attacked by a trustee in bankruptcy. A declaration of solvency as a recital to a property adjustment order may deter the trustee in bankruptcy from attacking the transfer. Since this section was amended in 1986, the ability of the trustee in bankruptcy to set aside an order made in matrimonial proceedings seems to be reduced. Concurrent bankruptcy proceedings may be transferred to the court hearing the ancillary relief application. The court has the power to annul the bankruptcy on the application of a party (*Paulin v Paulin* [2009] 2 FLR 354, CA).

"section 339 or 340 of the Insolvency Act 1986"—In essence, s 339 enables a transaction to be set aside on the application of a trustee in bankruptcy where an individual has been adjudged bankrupt and he has in the 5 years before the bankruptcy made a gift of property or transferred it at an undervalue. As s 339 requires a bankrupt individual to have entered into a transaction at an undervalue, it is difficult to see how this section would enable the trustee in bankruptcy to set aside a property adjustment order after genuinely contested proceedings. Insolvency Act 1986, s 340 enables a transaction to be set aside where a bankrupt individual does something or allows something to be done within 2 years of his bankruptcy which has the effect of putting one of his creditors into a better position than he otherwise would have been. After contested proceedings, it may be difficult for the trustee in bankruptcy to set aside a transfer of property which flows from the court exercising its mandatory duties under s 25. However, where there has been a consent order, a trustee in bankruptcy may set aside an order where a bankrupt husband transferred a property to a wife and had failed to disclose his interest in the property to the trustee (*R v R and S (Bankruptcy Jurisdiction Concerning Real Property Abroad: Setting Aside Consent Order)* [2008] 2 FLR 474 (Fam)). See also MCA 1973. s 24 annotation **Third Party attacks on property transfers**.

40 Payments etc under order made in favour of person suffering from mental disorder

(1) Where the court makes an order under this Part of this Act requiring payments (including a lump sum payment) to be made, or property to be transferred, to a party to a marriage and the court is satisfied that the person in whose favour the order is made ("P") lacks capacity (within the meaning of the Mental Capacity Act 2005) in relation to the provisions of the order then, subject to any order, direction or authority made or given in relation to P under that Act, the court may order the payments to be made, or as the case may be, the property to be transferred, to such person ("D") as it may direct.

(2) In carrying out any functions of his in relation to an order made under subsection (1), D must act in P's best interests (within the meaning of that Act).

Amendments—MCA 2005, s 67(1), Sch 6, para 19.

MCA 2005—A relevant extract is contained in this Part.

"lacks capacity mental disorder"—This term is expressly defined as being "within the meaning of MCA 2005" so as to incorporate the principles that apply within that legislation and the jurisprudence that develops in the new mental capacity jurisdiction. Nevertheless, many of the principles that have evolved under previous case-law are still relevant. MCA 2005, s 2(1) sets out the definition:
   "A person lacks capacity in relation to a matter if at the material time he is unable to make a decision for himself in relation to the matter because of an impairment of, or a disturbance in the functioning of, the mind or brain".
For a full explanation see the note to FPR 2010, r 15.1.

"order, direction or authority"—This is a reference to the powers of the Court of Protection pursuant to MCA 2005.

Use of this provision—This provision leaves considerable discretion to the court as to the future management of the financial provision but it will not always be appropriate to exercise the power conferred thereby (see notes below). The power will be useful where the incapacitated recipient has no capital or savings, only periodical payments are involved and there is an established carer who can receive and expend the money on his or her behalf. In that situation, any social security benefits will usually be dealt with under the appointeeship procedure and the person who is appointee may be suitable to handle additional weekly maintenance. But there will be no continuing supervision and it may be difficult to deal with a subsequent change of carer. Query whether this power might be used to direct payments to the local authority where the incapacitated recipient is in residential care funded by that authority.

Role of the Court of Protection—If the incapacitated party in whose favour an order is made already has income or assets which need to be administered, or if substantial provision is to be made, the Court of Protection should be left to administer the entire financial affairs. The jurisdiction of the county court or High Court under this provision should not be allowed to conflict with that of the Court of Protection (see generally notes to FPR 2010, Pt 15).

Enduring or lasting power of attorney—Where there is such power of attorney, it would normally be appropriate for the attorney who is managing the affairs to receive all payments or property pursuant to the financial provision order, if the terms of the power are capable of extending to this.

Implications on the proceedings—A party who lacks capacity (within the meaning of MCA 2005) to conduct the proceedings will be a "protected party" for whom a litigation friend must be appointed: see generally FPR 2010, Pt 15.

40A Appeals relating to pension sharing orders which have taken effect

(1) Subsections (2) and (3) below apply where an appeal against a pension sharing order is begun on or after the day on which the order takes effect.

(2) If the pension sharing order relates to a person's rights under a pension arrangement, the appeal court may not set aside or vary the order if the person responsible for the pension arrangement has acted to his detriment in reliance on the taking effect of the order.

(3) If the pension sharing order relates to a person's shareable state scheme rights, the appeal court may not set aside or vary the order if the Secretary of State has acted to his detriment in reliance on the taking effect of the order.

(4) In determining for the purposes of subsection (2) or (3) above whether a person has acted to his detriment in reliance on the taking effect of the order, the appeal court may disregard any detriment which in its opinion is insignificant.

(5) Where subsection (2) or (3) above applies, the appeal court may make such further orders (including one or more pension sharing orders) as it thinks fit for the purpose of putting the parties in the position it considers appropriate.

(6) Section 24C above only applies to a pension sharing order under this section if the decision of the appeal court can itself be the subject of an appeal.

(7) In subsection (2) above, the reference to the person responsible for the pension arrangement is to be read in accordance with section 25D(4) above.

Amendments—Inserted by WRPA 1999, s 19, Sch 3, para 10.

Defined terms—"the court": s 52(1); "pension sharing order": ss 21A, 52(2).

Scope—As set out in MCA 1973, s 24C, a pension sharing order does not take effect until 7 days after the time for appealing has expired (ie in total 28 days), assuming that the decree nisi has been made absolute. Where a pension sharing order has already taken effect, any appeal will be out of time and the court will need to grant permission on the usual principles. The special provisions contained in this section will then apply. The appeal court is not able to set aside or vary a pension sharing order if the pension arrangement/the Department of Work and Pensions (in relation to shareable state scheme rights) has acted to its detriment in reliance on the taking effect of the order. Instead, the appeal court may make such further orders (including one or more pension sharing orders) as it thinks fit for the purpose of putting the parties into the position it considers appropriate. This could include in effect a reverse pension sharing order made against the pension credit created by the pension sharing order under appeal.

40B Appeals relating to pension compensation sharing orders which have taken effect

(1) This section applies where an appeal against a pension compensation sharing order is begun on or after the day on which the order takes effect.

(2) If the Board of the Pension Protection Fund has acted to its detriment in reliance on the taking effect of the order the appeal court –

(a)   may not set aside or vary the order;

(b)   may make such further orders (including a pension compensation sharing order) as it thinks fit for the purpose of putting the parties in the position it considers appropriate.

(3) In determining for the purposes of subsection (2) whether the Board has acted to its detriment the appeal court may disregard any detriment which in the court's opinion is insignificant.

(4) Section 24F (duty to stay) only applies to a pension compensation sharing order under this section if the decision of the appeal court can itself be the subject of an appeal.

Amendments—Inserted by Pensions Act 2008, Sch 6, Pt 1.

Defined terms—"the court": s 52(1); "pension compensation order": s 21B(1).

Scope—This section provides a counterpart to s 40A in relation to a pension compensation sharing order, as to which see annotations to s 21B.

PART III
PROTECTION, CUSTODY ETC OF CHILDREN

41 Restrictions on decrees for dissolution, annulment or separation affecting children

(1) In any proceedings for a decree of divorce or nullity of marriage, or a decree of judicial separation, the court shall consider –

(a)   whether there are any children of the family to whom this section applies; and

(b)   where there are any such children, whether (in the light of the arrangements which have been, or are proposed to be, made for their upbringing and welfare) it should exercise any of its powers under the Children Act 1989 with respect to any of them.

(2) Where, in any case to which this section applies, it appears to the court that –

(a)   the circumstances of the case require it, or are likely to require it, to exercise any of its powers under the Act of 1989 with respect to any such child;

(b)   it is not in a position to exercise that power or (as the case may be) those powers without giving further consideration to the case; and

(c)   there are exceptional circumstances which make it desirable in the interests of the child that the court should give a direction under this section,

it may direct that the decree of divorce or nullity is not to be made absolute, or that the decree of judicial separation is not to be granted, until the court orders otherwise.

(3) This section applies to –

(a)   any child of the family who has not reached the age of sixteen at the date when the court considers the case in accordance with the requirements of this section; and

(b)   any child of the family who has reached that age at that date and in relation to whom the court directs that this section shall apply.

Amendments—CA 1989, s 108(4), Sch 12, para 31.

Scope—This section imposes on the court a duty in decree proceedings to consider whether there are any children of the family (as defined by s 52 and applied by s 41(3)); and, if so, to consider whether the court should exercise any of its powers under CA 1989. If the court considers that it may need so to exercise its powers and exceptional circumstances make such action desirable, the court can stay the grant of a decree absolute of divorce or nullity or a decree of judicial separation.

Procedure—The procedure for complying with s 41 is set out in FPR 2010, r 7.25. It is dealt with by the district judge as a solely paper exercise, save where s 41(1)(b) or (2) applies. Thus, consistent with the philosophy behind CA 1989, s 1(5) and subject to the limited powers of the court under s 41(2), to any applications under CA 1989, Pt II and to its power to order a report under CA 1989, s 37(1), the court has no power to intervene concerning a child of the family.

"powers under the Children Act 1989" (s 41(1)(b))—For practical purposes, the powers which the court may exercise are:

(a) to make an order under s 8, whether of its own motion or on application under s 10;
(b) to make a family assistance order under s 16;
(c) to make a direction for investigation by the local authority under s 37(1).

"exceptional circumstances" (s 41(2)(c))—In addition to the other factors in s 41(2), the district judge must be satisfied that "exceptional circumstances" exist before he can stay the grant of any decree. Thus, for example, the fact that an application for an order under CA 1989, s 8 is pending should not preclude the grant of a decree absolute. However, if care proceedings are pending, it is conceivable, but not inevitable, that a stay would be appropriate.

"child of the family" (s 41(3))—This limitation on the age of a child of the family is in contrast to, for example, the age for matrimonial financial relief (no order above 18, save where child is in full-time education or there are special circumstances: MCA 1973, s 29(1),(3)), orders under CA 1989, s 8 (no order above 16, save in exceptional circumstances: CA 1989, s 9(6)) and for child support maintenance (up to 16, and then up to 19 if in full-time or other prescribed education: CSA 1991, s 55).

****

PART IV
MISCELLANEOUS AND SUPPLEMENTAL

47 Matrimonial relief and declarations of validity in respect of polygamous marriages

(1) A court in England and Wales shall not be precluded from granting matrimonial relief or making a declaration concerning the validity of a marriage by reason only that either party to the marriage is, or has during the subsistence of the marriage been, married to more than one person.

(2) In this section "matrimonial relief" means –

(a) any decree under Part I of this Act;
(b) a financial provision order under section 27 above;
(c) an order under section 35 above altering a maintenance agreement;
(d) an order under any provision of this Act which confers a power exercisable in connection with, or in connection with proceedings for, such decree or order as is mentioned in paragraphs (a) to (c) above;
(dd) an order under Part III of the Matrimonial and Family Proceedings Act 1984;
(e) an order under Part I of the Domestic Proceedings and Magistrates' Courts Act 1978.

(3) In this section "a declaration concerning the validity of a marriage" means any declaration under Part II of the Family Law Act 1986 involving a determination as to the validity of a marriage.

(4) Provision may be made by rules of court –

(a) for requiring notice of proceedings brought by virtue of this section to be served on any additional spouse of a party to the marriage in question; and
(b) for conferring on any such additional spouse the right to be heard in the proceedings,

in such cases as may be specified in the rules.

Amendments—DPMCA 1978, s 89(2)(a), Sch 2, para 39; MFPA 1984, s 46(1), Sch 1, para 15; FLA 1986, s 68(1), Sch 1, para 14; Private International Law (Miscellaneous Provisions) Act 1995, s 8, Sch, para 2.

Defined terms—"the court": s 52; "matrimonial relief": s 47(2).

"provision may be made by rules of court" (s 47(4))—FPR PD7C makes provision for proceedings for matrimonial relief, as defined by s 47(2). The applicant for relief (eg petitioner) must state in their application (petition) that the marriage is polygamous (PD7C, para 2.1) and the court may then give notice to any additional spouse and to order that spouse to be made a party to the proceedings (para 2.4).

48 Evidence

(1) The evidence of a husband or wife shall be admissible in any proceedings to prove that marital intercourse did or did not take place between them during any period.

(2) In any proceedings for nullity of marriage, evidence on the question of sexual capacity shall be heard in camera unless in any case the judge is satisfied that in the interests of justice any such evidence ought to be heard in open court.

Scope—This section enables the admission of a spouse's evidence as to whether or not intercourse took place, and requires evidence of sexual capacity to be heard in camera unless otherwise directed by the judge.

"evidence of a husband or wife" (s 48(1))—A husband and wife can give evidence against one another in all circumstances (Evidence Amendment Act 1853, s 1), including in respect of adultery and marital intercourse, or lack of it.

"shall be heard in camera" (s 48(2))—Hearings should only be held in camera if the administration of justice would not be impeded (*Scott v Scott* (1913) FLR Rep 657). This section reverses the normal presumption that justice requires cases to be heard in open court and places on the judge the duty to say why the interests of justice would be served by the cause being heard in open court. See further SCA 1981, s 67 and commentary to FPR 2010, rr 7.16 and 27.10. Section 48(2) will be subject to the requirements of European Convention 1950, Art 6(1) that, in general, trials should be in open court subject to the exceptions in Art 6(1).

49 Parties to proceedings under this Act

(1) Where in a petition for divorce or judicial separation, or in any other pleading praying for either form of relief, one party to a marriage alleges that the other has committed adultery, he or she shall make the person alleged to have committed adultery with the other party to the marriage a party to the proceedings unless excused by the court on special grounds from doing so.

(2) Rules of court may, either generally or in such cases as may be prescribed by the rules, exclude the application of subsection (1) above where the person alleged to have committed adultery with the other party to the marriage is not named in the petition or other pleading.

(3) Where in pursuance of subsection (1) above a person is made a party to proceedings for divorce or judicial separation, the court may, if after the close of the evidence on the part of the person making the allegation of adultery it is of opinion that there is not sufficient evidence against the person so made a party, dismiss him or her from the suit.

(4) Rules of court may make provision, in cases not falling within subsection (1) above, with respect to the joinder as parties to proceedings under this Act of persons involved in allegations of adultery or other improper conduct made in those proceedings, and with respect to the dismissal from such proceedings of any parties so joined; and rules of court made by virtue of this subsection may make different provision for different cases.

(5) In every case in which adultery with any party to a suit is alleged against any person not made a party to the suit or in which the court considers, in the interest of any person not already a party to the suit, that that person should be made a party to the suit, the court may if it thinks fit allow that person to intervene upon such terms, if any, as the court thinks just.

Defined terms—"the court": s 52.

Scope—This section requires a person against whom adultery is alleged in any proceedings for divorce or judicial separation to be made a party to those proceedings, although rules may exempt this provision where the person is not named. If there is insufficient evidence against a party, that party may be dismissed from the suit. Others involved in allegations of adultery or other improper conduct may be joined as parties, and a person alleged to have committed adultery but not joined may be permitted by the court to intervene.

Rules and procedure—FPR 2010, r 7.10 deals with parties to a matrimonial cause (or matrimonial order application). Rule 7.10(3) directs where a person is not to be named as co-respondent (e g they are dead or under 16) and PD7A, para 7.1 requires (so far as it has power so to do) that a prospective co-respondent should not be named unless "likely to object to the making" of the matrimonial order.

****

52 Interpretation

(1) In this Act –

"child", in relation to one or both of the parties to a marriage, includes an illegitimate child of that party or, as the case may be, of both parties;

"child of the family", in relation to the parties to a marriage, means –

  (a)   a child of both of those parties; and

  (b)   any other child, not being a child who is placed with those parties as foster parents by a local authority or voluntary organisation, who has been treated by both of those parties as a child of their family;

"the court" (except where the context otherwise requires) means the High Court or, where a county court has jurisdiction by virtue of Part V of the Matrimonial and Family Proceedings Act 1984, a county court;

"education" includes training;

"maintenance calculation" has the same meaning as it has in the Child Support Act 1991 by virtue of section 54 of that Act as read with any regulations in force under that section.

"the Maintenance Regulation" means Council Regulation (EC) No 4/2009 including as applied in relation to Denmark by virtue of the Agreement made on 19 October 2005 between the European Community and the Kingdom of Denmark;

(2) In this Act –

  (a)   references to financial provision orders, periodical payments and secured periodical payments orders and orders for the payment of a lump sum, and references to property adjustment orders, shall be construed in accordance with section 21 above;

  (aa) references to pension sharing orders shall be construed in accordance with section 21A above; and

  (b)   references to orders for maintenance pending suit and to interim orders for maintenance shall be construed respectively in accordance with section 22 and section 27(5) above.

(3) For the avoidance of doubt it is hereby declared that references in this Act to remarriage include references to a marriage which is by law void or voidable.

(3A) References in this Act to the formation of a civil partnership by a person include references to a civil partnership which is by law void or voidable.

(4) Except where the contrary intention is indicated, references in this Act to any enactment include references to that enactment as amended, extended or applied by or under any subsequent enactment, including this Act.

Amendments—Children Act 1975, s 108(1)(b), Sch 4; MFPA 1984, s 46(1), Sch 1, para 16; CA 1989, s 108(4), (7), Sch 12, para 33, Sch 15; SI 1993/623; WRPA 1999, s 19, Sch 3, para 11; CSPSSA 2000, s 26, Sch 3, para 3; CPA 2004, s 261(1), Sch 27, para 46; SI 2011/1484.

****

Matrimonial Proceedings and Property Act 1970

****

30 Order for maintenance of party to marriage made by magistrates' court to cease to have effect on remarriage of that party

(1) (*repealed*)

(2) Section 4(2) of the Domestic Proceedings and Magistrates' Courts Act 1978 shall apply in relation to an order consisting of or including a provision such as is mentioned in section 2(1)(a) of that Act made by a magistrates' court and confirmed in accordance with section 3 of the Maintenance Orders (Facilities for Enforcement) Act 1920 (which enables a magistrates' court to make a maintenance order against a person resident in a part of Her Majesty's dominions outside the United Kingdom but provides that the order shall have no effect unless and until confirmed by a competent court in that part) as it applies in relation to an order made under section 2(1)(a) of the Domestic Proceedings and Magistrates' Courts Act 1978.

Amendments—MO(RE)A 1972, s 42(3); DPMCA 1978, s 89(2), Sch 2, para 28, Sch 3.

****

37 Contributions by spouse in money or money's worth to the improvement of property

It is hereby declared that where a husband or wife contributes in money or money's worth to the improvement of real or personal property in which or in the proceeds of sale of which either or both of them has or have a beneficial interest, the husband or wife so contributing shall, if the contribution is of a substantial nature and subject to any agreement between them to the contrary express or implied, be treated as having then acquired by virtue of his or her contribution a share or an enlarged share, as the case may be, in that beneficial interest of such an extent as may have been then agreed or, in default of such agreement, as may seem in all the circumstances just to any court before which the question of the existence or extent of the beneficial interest of the husband or wife arises (whether in proceedings between them or in any other proceedings).

****

39 Extension of s 17 of Married Women's Property Act 1882

An application may be made to the High Court or a county court under section 17 of the Married Women's Property Act 1882 (powers of the court in disputes between husband and wife about property) (including that section as extended by section 7 of the Matrimonial Causes (Property and Maintenance) Act 1958) by either of the parties to a marriage notwithstanding that their marriage has been dissolved or annulled so long as the application is made within the period of three years beginning with the date on which the marriage was dissolved or annulled; and references in the said section 17 and the said section 7 to a husband or a wife shall be construed accordingly.

****

Mental Capacity Act 2005

PART 1
PERSONS WHO LACK CAPACITY

The principles

1 The principles

(1) The following principles apply for the purposes of this Act.

(2) A person must be assumed to have capacity unless it is established that he lacks capacity.

(3) A person is not to be treated as unable to make a decision unless all practicable steps to help him to do so have been taken without success.

(4) A person is not to be treated as unable to make a decision merely because he makes an unwise decision.

(5) An act done, or decision made, under this Act for or on behalf of a person who lacks capacity must be done, or made, in his best interests.

(6) Before the act is done, or the decision is made, regard must be had to whether the purpose for which it is needed can be as effectively achieved in a way that is less restrictive of the person's rights and freedom of action.

Preliminary

2 People who lack capacity

(1) For the purposes of this Act, a person lacks capacity in relation to a matter if at the material time he is unable to make a decision for himself in relation to the matter because of an impairment of, or a disturbance in the functioning of, the mind or brain.

(2) It does not matter whether the impairment or disturbance is permanent or temporary.

(3) A lack of capacity cannot be established merely by reference to –

   (a)   a person's age or appearance, or

   (b)   a condition of his, or an aspect of his behaviour, which might lead others to make unjustified assumptions about his capacity.

(4) In proceedings under this Act or any other enactment, any question whether a person lacks capacity within the meaning of this Act must be decided on the balance of probabilities.

(5) No power which a person ("D") may exercise under this Act –

   (a)   in relation to a person who lacks capacity, or

   (b)   where D reasonably thinks that a person lacks capacity,

is exercisable in relation to a person under 16.

(6) Subsection (5) is subject to section 18(3).

3 Inability to make decisions

(1) For the purposes of section 2, a person is unable to make a decision for himself if he is unable –

   (a)   to understand the information relevant to the decision,

   (b)   to retain that information,

PART II

(c) to use or weigh that information as part of the process of making the decision, or

(d) to communicate his decision (whether by talking, using sign language or any other means).

(2) A person is not to be regarded as unable to understand the information relevant to a decision if he is able to understand an explanation of it given to him in a way that is appropriate to his circumstances (using simple language, visual aids or any other means).

(3) The fact that a person is able to retain the information relevant to a decision for a short period only does not prevent him from being regarded as able to make the decision.

(4) The information relevant to a decision includes information about the reasonably foreseeable consequences of –

(a) deciding one way or another, or

(b) failing to make the decision.

4 Best interests

(1) In determining for the purposes of this Act what is in a person's best interests, the person making the determination must not make it merely on the basis of –

(a) the person's age or appearance, or

(b) a condition of his, or an aspect of his behaviour, which might lead others to make unjustified assumptions about what might be in his best interests.

(2) The person making the determination must consider all the relevant circumstances and, in particular, take the following steps.

(3) He must consider –

(a) whether it is likely that the person will at some time have capacity in relation to the matter in question, and

(b) if it appears likely that he will, when that is likely to be.

(4) He must, so far as reasonably practicable, permit and encourage the person to participate, or to improve his ability to participate, as fully as possible in any act done for him and any decision affecting him.

(5) Where the determination relates to life-sustaining treatment he must not, in considering whether the treatment is in the best interests of the person concerned, be motivated by a desire to bring about his death.

(6) He must consider, so far as is reasonably ascertainable –

(a) the person's past and present wishes and feelings (and, in particular, any relevant written statement made by him when he had capacity),

(b) the beliefs and values that would be likely to influence his decision if he had capacity, and

(c) the other factors that he would be likely to consider if he were able to do so.

(7) He must take into account, if it is practicable and appropriate to consult them, the views of –

(a) anyone named by the person as someone to be consulted on the matter in question or on matters of that kind,

(b) anyone engaged in caring for the person or interested in his welfare,

(c) any donee of a lasting power of attorney granted by the person, and

(d) any deputy appointed for the person by the court,

as to what would be in the person's best interests and, in particular, as to the matters mentioned in subsection (6).

(8) The duties imposed by subsections (1) to (7) also apply in relation to the exercise of any powers which –

    (a)   are exercisable under a lasting power of attorney, or

    (b)   are exercisable by a person under this Act where he reasonably believes that another person lacks capacity.

(9) In the case of an act done, or a decision made, by a person other than the court, there is sufficient compliance with this section if (having complied with the requirements of subsections (1) to (7)) he reasonably believes that what he does or decides is in the best interests of the person concerned.

(10) "Life-sustaining treatment" means treatment which in the view of a person providing health care for the person concerned is necessary to sustain life.

(11) "Relevant circumstances" are those –

    (a)   of which the person making the determination is aware, and

    (b)   which it would be reasonable to regard as relevant.

4A Restriction on deprivation of liberty

(1) This Act does not authorise any person ("D") to deprive any other person ("P") of his liberty.

(2) But that is subject to–

    (a)   the following provisions of this section, and

    (b)   section 4B.

(3) D may deprive P of his liberty if, by doing so, D is giving effect to a relevant decision of the court.

(4) A relevant decision of the court is a decision made by an order under section 16(2)(a) in relation to a matter concerning P's personal welfare.

(5) D may deprive P of his liberty if the deprivation is authorised by Schedule A1 (hospital and care home residents: deprivation of liberty).

Amendments—Inserted by MHA 2007, s 50(2).

4B Deprivation of liberty necessary for life-sustaining treatment etc

(1) If the following conditions are met, D is authorised to deprive P of his liberty while a decision as respects any relevant issue is sought from the court.

(2) The first condition is that there is a question about whether D is authorised to deprive P of his liberty under section 4A.

(3) The second condition is that the deprivation of liberty –

    (a)   is wholly or partly for the purpose of –
        (i)   giving P life-sustaining treatment, or
        (ii)   doing any vital act, or

    (b)   consists wholly or partly of –
        (i)   giving P life-sustaining treatment, or
        (ii)   doing any vital act.

(4) The third condition is that the deprivation of liberty is necessary in order to –

    (a)   give the life-sustaining treatment, or

    (b)   do the vital act.

PART II

(5) A vital act is any act which the person doing it reasonably believes to be necessary to prevent a serious deterioration in P's condition.

Amendments—Inserted by MHA 2007, s 50(2).

5 Acts in connection with care or treatment

(1) If a person ("D") does an act in connection with the care or treatment of another person ("P"), the act is one to which this section applies if –

    (a) before doing the act, D takes reasonable steps to establish whether P lacks capacity in relation to the matter in question, and

    (b) when doing the act, D reasonably believes –

        (i)   that P lacks capacity in relation to the matter, and

        (ii) that it will be in P's best interests for the act to be done.

(2) D does not incur any liability in relation to the act that he would not have incurred if P –

    (a) had had capacity to consent in relation to the matter, and

    (b) had consented to D's doing the act.

(3) Nothing in this section excludes a person's civil liability for loss or damage, or his criminal liability, resulting from his negligence in doing the act.

(4) Nothing in this section affects the operation of sections 24 to 26 (advance decisions to refuse treatment).

6 Section 5 acts: limitations

(1) If D does an act that is intended to restrain P, it is not an act to which section 5 applies unless two further conditions are satisfied.

(2) The first condition is that D reasonably believes that it is necessary to do the act in order to prevent harm to P.

(3) The second is that the act is a proportionate response to –

    (a) the likelihood of P's suffering harm, and

    (b) the seriousness of that harm.

(4) For the purposes of this section D restrains P if he –

    (a) uses, or threatens to use, force to secure the doing of an act which P resists, or

    (b) restricts P's liberty of movement, whether or not P resists.

(5) (*repealed*)

(6) Section 5 does not authorise a person to do an act which conflicts with a decision made, within the scope of his authority and in accordance with this Part, by –

    (a) a donee of a lasting power of attorney granted by P, or

    (b) a deputy appointed for P by the court.

(7) But nothing in subsection (6) stops a person –

    (a) providing life-sustaining treatment, or

    (b) doing any act which he reasonably believes to be necessary to prevent a serious deterioration in P's condition,

while a decision as respects any relevant issue is sought from the court.

Amendments—MHA 2007, s 50(4)(a).

7 Payment for necessary goods and services

(1) If necessary goods or services are supplied to a person who lacks capacity to contract for the supply, he must pay a reasonable price for them.

(2) "Necessary" means suitable to a person's condition in life and to his actual requirements at the time when the goods or services are supplied.

8 Expenditure

(1) If an act to which section 5 applies involves expenditure, it is lawful for D –

    (a)   to pledge P's credit for the purpose of the expenditure, and
    (b)   to apply money in P's possession for meeting the expenditure.

(2) If the expenditure is borne for P by D, it is lawful for D –

    (a)   to reimburse himself out of money in P's possession, or
    (b)   to be otherwise indemnified by P.

(3) Subsections (1) and (2) do not affect any power under which (apart from those subsections) a person –

    (a)   has lawful control of P's money or other property, and
    (b)   has power to spend money for P's benefit.

General note—The Act creates an entirely new jurisdiction separate from the family jurisdiction but replacing (in part) the inherent jurisdiction. The principles are of general application but the Act establishes a new Court of Protection with a regional presence that deals with matters arising under the new jurisdiction. The scope of this legislation has been extended by MHA 2007, which introduces safeguards for the deprivation of liberty of a person who cannot consent to detention in a nursing or care home. Sections 1–8 are reproduced above because they are of general application and will on occasions need to be taken into account by family lawyers. An overview follows.

Background—For many years procedures for the delegation of decision-making powers have comprised:
* *agency* – bank mandate; ordinary power of attorney;
* *specific* – appointee for state benefits; litigation friend for court proceedings;
* *statutory* – enduring power of attorney; jurisdiction of the Court of Protection to appoint a receiver;
* *trusts* – bare trust; settlement.

Each has its own limitations and normal agency concepts do not survive a loss of capacity. These all relate to financial decisions and there have been no procedures for other types of decision (ie social welfare or healthcare) to be delegated or made on behalf of mentally incapacitated adults.

Overview of the new mental capacity jurisdiction—The MCA 2005 establishes a comprehensive statutory framework setting out how decisions should be made by and on behalf of those whose capacity to make their own decisions is in doubt. It also clarifies what actions can be taken by others involved in the care and medical treatment of people lacking capacity.

The framework provides a hierarchy of processes, extending from informal day-to-day care, to decision-making requiring formal powers and ultimately to court decisions. An individual can anticipate lack of capacity by completing a lasting power of attorney for either financial affairs or personal welfare decisions (which includes healthcare). Failing this, the new Court of Protection has jurisdiction to make declarations or decisions or to appoint a deputy to make decisions on the incapacitated person's behalf.

The common law relating to advance refusals of medical treatment is also placed on a statutory footing and there is an offence of "ill-treatment and neglect" on the part of carers, donees of lasting powers of attorney and deputies.

The Act's provisions apply in general only to people lacking capacity who are aged 16 years or over, but the property and financial affairs jurisdiction may be exercised in relation to a child who will lack capacity into adulthood.

A Code of Practice provides guidance for the courts, professionals and those concerned with the welfare of a mentally incapacitated adult and a Public Guardian is appointed to supervise and promote the new jurisdiction.

Fundamental concepts—There are two fundamental concepts that apply for the purposes of this Act, namely a definition of incapacity and clarification of best interests (the basis on which delegated decisions must be made).

1 *Incapacity*

Section 2(1) sets out the definition of a person who lacks capacity:

"A person lacks capacity in relation to a matter if at the material time he is unable to make a decision for himself in relation to the matter because of an impairment of, or a disturbance in the functioning of, the mind or brain."

This is a two-stage test, because it must be established first, that there is an impairment of, or disturbance in the functioning of, the person's mind or brain (the diagnostic threshold); and secondly, that the impairment or disturbance is sufficient to render the person incapable of making that particular decision. Capacity is thus decision-specific, but it does not matter whether the impairment or disturbance is permanent or temporary. A person is unable to make a decision if unable:

- to understand the information relevant to the decision;
- to retain that information;
- to use or weigh that information as part of the process of making the decision; or
- to communicate his decision (whether by talking, using sign language or any other means).

Explanations must be provided in ways that are appropriate to the person's circumstances.

2 *Best interests*

The Act sets out a checklist of factors which must be considered in deciding what is in a person's best interests aimed at identifying those issues most relevant to the individual who lacks capacity (as opposed to the decision-maker or any other persons). Not all the factors in the checklist will be relevant to all types of decisions or actions, but they must still be considered if only to be disregarded as irrelevant to that particular situation. They include:

- consideration of all relevant circumstances;
- whether the person will at some time have the required capacity;
- encouraging the person to participate in the decision;
- the person's past and present wishes and feelings;
- the beliefs and values that would be likely to influence the person's decision;
- the views of others who should be consulted.

Decision-making—There are three areas of decision-making (although the first and second are combined in the legislation):

1 personal welfare;
2 healthcare;
3 property and affairs.

There are four levels of decision-making:

(i) a person acting under ss 5–6 – the statutory defence (in effect a "general authority to act" with restrictions) or ss 7–8, which cover payment for "necessary" goods and services;
(ii) an attorney under a lasting power of attorney (or an earlier enduring power of attorney);
(iii) a deputy appointed by the Court;
(iv) the Court of Protection making decisions or declarations.

General principles—There are five general principles:

1 a decision-specific approach to capacity based on understanding and the ability to make and communicate a decision;
2 adults are presumed to have capacity so unjustified assumptions are outlawed and there is a "balance of probabilities" approach;
3 individuals should be helped to make their own decisions with simple explanations, and they may make unwise decisions;
4 there must be participation in decision-making and consultation with others;
5 a "least restrictive" approach is to be applied to any intervention.

The new public bodies

I *Court of Protection*

The new Court of Protection is a very different body to its predecessor of the same name. It is a Superior Court of Record with full status to deal with the entire range of decision-making on behalf of incapacitated persons (as defined). It takes over the financial jurisdiction of the former Court of Protection and extends this to personal welfare and healthcare decisions thus absorbing the existing declaratory jurisdiction of the Family Division of the High Court.

Most applications are dealt with "on paper" by district judges sitting in the Thomas More Building at the RCJ in London but hearings may be before nominated district judges based in regional courts in Bristol, Cardiff, Birmingham, Newcastle and Manchester/Preston (and now some other courts), with nominated circuit judges and High Court judges hearing more important cases and appeals.

New Court of Protection rules promote active case management drawing on CPR 1998.

II *Public Guardian*

The Public Guardian has a statutory appointment with an office and staff known as the Office of the Public Guardian (OPG). The new role of regulator is both administrative and supervisory and there are five key functions:

1   to maintain a register of lasting powers of attorney (and the former enduring powers that still remain valid);
2   to maintain a register of deputies;
3   to supervise and receive security from deputies;
4   to receive reports from and hear representations about attorneys and deputies;
5   to provide reports to the court and arrange reports from visitors;

The new jurisdiction—There is a wider range of cases under the new jurisdiction and a consequent increase in the volume of cases. The unmet need has now emerged (e g residence and contact disputes in respects of learning disabled adults) and there is a new variety of outcomes. The court is more accessible, but alternative dispute resolution may be imposed before contested hearings and the court should be seen as the last resort. There is a constant struggle to maintain the balance between protection and empowerment of these potentially vulnerable people, but the court and the Office of the Public Guardian has now attained greater prominence and wider influence.

Key points

- enduring powers of attorney previously executed are effective, but following implementation only lasting powers of attorney may be completed and registration of these does not point towards lack of capacity;
- the new Court of Protection is able to deal with the full range of decision-making on behalf of adults who lack capacity in accessible local courts;
- serious medical treatment decisions are dealt with by Family Division judges in the Court of Protection under the statutory jurisdiction rather than by the former declaratory procedure under the inherent jurisdiction;
- cases in the county courts involving a significant mental capacity element may be transferred to a suitable nominated judge as a "specialist" and a nominated judge may sit in a dual jurisdiction;
- a discrete body of law is developing in regard to the assessment of capacity with a more professional approach towards decision-making issues.

For a comprehensive explanation of the new mental capacity jurisdiction see *Mental Capacity: Law and Practice* and *Court of Protection Practice 2013*, which is a companion volume to the present work, and *Civil Court Service* (all Jordan Publishing Ltd).

****

Protection from Harassment Act 1997

England and Wales

1 Prohibition of harassment

(1) A person must not pursue a course of conduct –

  (a)   which amounts to harassment of another, and
  (b)   which he knows or ought to know amounts to harassment of the other.

(1A) A person must not pursue a course of conduct –

  (a)   which involves harassment of two or more persons, and
  (b)   which he knows or ought to know involves harassment of those persons, and
  (c)   by which he intends to persuade any person (whether or not one of those mentioned above) –
        (i)   not to do something that he is entitled or required to do, or
        (ii)   to do something that he is not under any obligation to do.

(2) For the purposes of this section, the person whose course of conduct is in question ought to know that it amounts to or involves harassment of another if a reasonable person in possession of the same information would think the course of conduct amounted to or involved harassment of the other.

(3) Subsection (1) does not apply to a course of conduct if the person who pursued it shows –

    (a)   that it was pursued for the purpose of preventing or detecting crime,

    (b)   that it was pursued under any enactment or rule of law or to comply with any condition or requirement imposed by any person under any enactment, or

    (c)   that in the particular circumstances the pursuit of the course of conduct was reasonable.

Amendments—Serious Organised Crime and Police Act 2005, s 125(2).

"harassment"—This term includes, but is not restricted to, "alarming the person" and "causing the person distress" (s 7(2)). "Harassment … includes within it an element of intent, intent to cause distress or harm" (*Johnson v Walton* [1990] 1 FLR 350 at [352H]).

"course of conduct"—Harassment is a "course of conduct" (s 1(1)) which "must involve conduct on at least two occasions" (s 7(3)). However proceedings can be brought based on an "apprehended breach of section 1" (see under s 3(1)). "'Conduct' includes speech" (s 7(4)). In *R v Hills* [2001] 1 FLR 580, CA it was held that assaults in April and October were not a "course of conduct", particularly since the parties had been reconciled. On the facts, a charge of assault might have been more appropriate. In *R v Curtis* [2010] 1 WLR 2770, six incidents over 9 months in a "volatile relationship" did not constitute a "course of conduct". The Court of Appeal has criticised prosecutions under this Act where a charge of assault is more appropriate (*R v Widdows* [2011] 2 FLR 869). In the family jurisdiction, parties should consider whether remedies under FLA 1996 may be more appropriate.

2 Offence of harassment

(1) A person who pursues a course of conduct in breach of section 1(1) or (1A) is guilty of an offence.

(2) A person guilty of an offence under this section is liable on summary conviction to imprisonment for a term not exceeding six months, or a fine not exceeding level 5 on the standard scale, or both.

(3) *(repealed)*

Amendments—Police Reform Act 2002, s 107(2), Sch 8; Serious Organised Crime and Police Act 2005, s 125(3).

3 Civil remedy

(1) An actual or apprehended breach of section 1(1) may be the subject of a claim in civil proceedings by the person who is or may be the victim of the course of conduct in question.

(2) On such a claim, damages may be awarded for (among other things) any anxiety caused by the harassment and any financial loss resulting from the harassment.

(3) Where –

    (a)   in such proceedings the High Court or a county court grants an injunction for the purpose of restraining the defendant from pursuing any conduct which amounts to harassment, and

    (b)   the plaintiff considers that the defendant has done anything which he is prohibited from doing by the injunction,

the plaintiff may apply for the issue of a warrant for the arrest of the defendant.

(4) An application under subsection (3) may be made –

    (a) where the injunction was granted by the High Court, to a judge of that court, and

    (b) where the injunction was granted by a county court, to a judge or district judge of that or any other county court.

(5) The judge or district judge to whom an application under subsection (3) is made may only issue a warrant if –

    (a) the application is substantiated on oath, and

    (b) the judge or district judge has reasonable grounds for believing that the defendant has done anything which he is prohibited from doing by the injunction.

(6) Where –

    (a) the High Court or a county court grants an injunction for the purpose mentioned in subsection (3)(a), and

    (b) without reasonable excuse the defendant does anything which he is prohibited from doing by the injunction,

he is guilty of an offence.

(7) Where a person is convicted of an offence under subsection (6) in respect of any conduct, that conduct is not punishable as a contempt of court.

(8) A person cannot be convicted of an offence under subsection (6) in respect of any conduct which has been punished as a contempt of court.

(9) A person guilty of an offence under subsection (6) is liable –

    (a) on conviction on indictment, to imprisonment for a term not exceeding five years, or a fine, or both, or

    (b) on summary conviction, to imprisonment for a term not exceeding six months, or a fine not exceeding the statutory maximum, or both.

Amendments—Serious Organised Crime and Police Act 2005, s 125(4).

Scope—This section creates the statutory tort of harassment. In *Tuppen and anor v Microsoft Corporation Ltd and anor* (2000) *The Times*, 15 November it was held, after referring to *Hansard*, that the Act was directed at the prevention of stalking, anti-social behaviour by neighbours and racial harassment and is not to be used to stifle litigation. The Act can be used to protect employees (*Huntingdon Life Sciences v Stop Huntingdon Animal Cruelty* [2003] EWHC 1139 (QB)).

"claim in civil proceedings", "damages"—A claim for damages is not necessary if all the applicant seeks is an injunction. A freestanding application for an injunction can be made in a county court in proceedings founded on any matter within the jurisdiction of a county court: CCA 1984, s 38. However, in many cases it will be appropriate to seek damages and the court is given express power to award damages for anxiety and any financial loss (see s 3(2)). In *Singh v Bhakar* [2007] 1 FLR 880, damages of £35,000 were awarded against the claimant's former mother-in-law.

Procedure—Proceedings under PHA 1997 are civil proceedings and are governed by CPR 1998, Pt 65. See further Procedural Guide A12. Enforcement of an order is governed by CPR 1998, Pt 81.

Service—Service should be effected in accordance with the Family Justice Council *Protocol for Process Servers: Non–Molestation Orders* (in Part V of this work); see the "Introduction" in the Protocol, which applies it to "harassment" cases despite the misleading title.

"apprehended breach of section 1"—Although the tort is incomplete until the course of conduct involves "conduct on at least two occasions" (s 7(3)), an application for an injunction can be brought for a threatened tort, provided the evidence justifies a finding that commission of the tort is likely (*South Carolina Insurance Co v Assurantie Maatschappij 'De Zeven Provincien' NV* [1987] AC 24; *Khorasandjian v Bush* [1993] 2 FLR 66).

Concurrent proceedings—Remedies under FLA 1996 may be more appropriate in a particular case. Damages can be awarded under PHA 1997 but not FLA 1996. Thus, exceptionally, concurrent proceedings under both statutes can be brought. They should be consolidated and tried together (*Lomas v Parle* [2004] 1 FLR 812).

Ambit of injunction—An injunction can forbid the defendant from entering a defined area around the applicant's home, where this is needed to make the injunction effective (*Burris v Azadani* [1996] 1 FLR 266) and from any other area such as a place of work (*Silverton v Gravett* [2001] All ER (D) 282).

"warrant of arrest"—A warrant of arrest can be obtained for the purpose of arresting the defendant and bringing him before the court following a breach of the injunction. See further Procedural Guide C15. Note that it is not possible for a power of arrest to be attached to the injunction itself.

"guilty of an offence"—By virtue of s 3(6)–(7), where the defendant has disobeyed an injunction forbidding harassment, he may be convicted of an offence, in which case contempt proceedings are no longer permissible. Where he has been punished for the contempt, criminal proceedings are no longer permissible (s 3(8)).

3A Injunctions to protect persons from harassment within section 1(1A)

(1) This section applies where there is an actual or apprehended breach of section 1(1A) by any person ("the relevant person").

(2) In such a case –

    (a)   any person who is or may be a victim of the course of conduct in question, or
    (b)   any person who is or may be a person falling within section 1(1A)(c),

may apply to the High Court or a county court for an injunction restraining the relevant person from pursuing any conduct which amounts to harassment in relation to any person or persons mentioned or described in the injunction.

(3) Section 3(3) to (9) apply in relation to an injunction granted under subsection (2) above as they apply in relation to an injunction granted as mentioned in section 3(3)(a).

Amendments—Inserted by Serious Organised Crime and Police Act 2005, s 125(5).

****

7 Interpretation of this group of sections

(1) This section applies for the interpretation of sections 1 to 5.

(2) References to harassing a person include alarming the person or causing the person distress.

(3) A "course of conduct" must involve –

    (a)   in the case of conduct in relation to a single person (see section 1(1)), conduct on at least two occasions in relation to that person, or
    (b)   in the case of conduct in relation to two or more persons (see section 1(1A)), conduct on at least one occasion in relation to each of those persons.

(3A) A person's conduct on any occasion shall be taken, if aided, abetted, counselled or procured by another –

    (a)   to be conduct on that occasion of the other (as well as conduct of the person whose conduct it is); and
    (b)   to be conduct in relation to which the other's knowledge and purpose, and what he ought to have known, are the same as they were in relation to what was contemplated or reasonably foreseeable at the time of the aiding, abetting, counselling or procuring.

(4) "Conduct" includes speech.

(5) References to a person, in the context of the harassment of a person, are references to a person who is an individual.

Amendments—Criminal Justice and Police Act 2001, s 44; Serious Organised Crime and Police Act 2005, s 125(7).

****

Senior Courts Act 1981

ARRANGEMENT OF SECTIONS

PART II
JURISDICTION

The Court of Appeal

****

PART II
JURISDICTION

The Court of Appeal

15 General jurisdiction of Court of Appeal

(1) The Court of Appeal shall be a superior court of record.

(2) Subject to the provisions of this Act, there shall be exercisable by the Court of Appeal –

    (a) all such jurisdiction (whether civil or criminal) as is conferred on it by this or any other Act; and

    (b) all such other jurisdiction (whether civil or criminal) as was exercisable by it immediately before the commencement of this Act.

(3) For all purposes of or incidental to –

    (a) the hearing and determination of any appeal to the civil division of the Court of Appeal; and

    (b) the amendment, execution and enforcement of any judgment or order made on such an appeal,

the Court of Appeal shall have all the authority and jurisdiction of the court or tribunal from which the appeal was brought.

(4) It is hereby declared that any provision in this or any other Act which authorises or requires the taking of any steps for the execution or enforcement of a judgment or order of the High Court applies in relation to a judgment or order of the civil division of the Court of Appeal as it applies in relation to a judgment or order of the High Court.

Amendments—CRA 2005, Sch 11, para 1.

Scope—This section establishes the general jurisdiction of the Court of Appeal. For the procedural regime governing appeals to the Court of Appeal see Procedural Guide E5.

"for all purposes of or incidental to" (s 15(3))—In relation to the hearing and determination of an appeal, this does not include maintenance pending suit where the appeal is subsequent to decree absolute (see *Cavendish-Bentinck v Cavendish-Bentinck* [1949] P 203, [1948] 2 All ER 285, CA).

"all the authority and jurisdiction" (s 15(3))—This includes a power conferred on the High Court after the order being appealed was made (see *Attorney-General v Vernazza* [1960] AC 965).

16 Appeals from High Court

(1) Subject as otherwise provided by this or any other Act (and in particular to the provision in section 13(2)(a) of the Administration of Justice Act 1969 excluding appeals to the Court of Appeal in cases where leave to appeal from the High Court directly to the Supreme Court is granted under Part II of that Act), or as provided by any order made by the Lord Chancellor under section 56(1) of the Access to Justice Act 1999 the Court of Appeal shall have jurisdiction to hear and determine appeals from any judgment or order of the High Court.

(2) An appeal from a judgment or order of the High Court when acting as a prize court shall not be to the Court of Appeal, but shall be to Her Majesty in Council in accordance with the Prize Acts 1864 to 1944.

Amendments—SI 2000/1071; CRA 2005, Sch 9, para 36(3).

Scope—Subject to certain exceptions, this section gives the Court of Appeal power to hear any appeal from a High Court judgment or order; for the procedure governing appeals to the Court of Appeal, see CPR 1998, Pt 52. This section must be read in conjunction with CPR 1998, r 52.3 which require permission (leave) to appeal for all appeals save for a few limited exceptions.

"judgment or order"—This phrase includes a decree (SCA 1981, s 151(1)), and a decree absolute of nullity (*Whitehead v Whitehead* [1963] P 117). An appeal cannot be pursued against the reasons for a decision, only against the judgment or order (*Lake v Lake* [1955] P 336), but it is possible to appeal findings of fact made after a split trial (*Re B (Split Hearings: Jurisdiction)* [2000] 1 FLR 334). Appeals against ex parte orders should not be made as they are provisional and expected to be revisited by the court (*WEA Records Ltd v Visions Channel 4 Ltd* [1983] 1 WLR 721).

17 Applications for new trial

(1) Where any cause or matter, or any issue in any cause or matter, has been tried in the High Court, any application for a new trial thereof, or to set aside a verdict, finding or judgment therein, shall be heard and determined by the Court of Appeal except where rules of court made in pursuance of subsection (2) provide otherwise.

(2) As regards cases where the trial was by a judge alone and no error of the court at the trial is alleged, or any prescribed class of such cases, rules of court may provide that any such application as is mentioned in subsection (1) shall be heard and determined by the High Court.

(3) Nothing in this section shall alter the practice in bankruptcy.

Scope—CPR 1998, r 52.10 sets out the powers of the Court of Appeal on hearing an appeal and specifically provides the power to order a new trial or hearing (r 52.10(2)). No rules have been made pursuant to s 17(2). Therefore any application for a new trial must be made to the Court of Appeal (see also *B-T v B-T (Divorce: Procedure)* [1990] 2 FLR 1). It is important to distinguish between orders which are capable of review by the original court: for example ex parte orders (see notes to SCA 1981, s 18), interim orders and orders where there has been an error on the face (which may be corrected in accordance with CPR 1998, r 40.12); and those orders which are covered by this section, where an appeal must be made to obtain a fresh hearing. For the purpose of considering the requirement of permission to appeal under AJA 1999, s 54, an application for a new trial is treated as an appeal to the Court of Appeal.

18 Restrictions on appeals to Court of Appeal

(1) No appeal shall lie to the Court of Appeal –

    (a)   except as provided by the Administration of Justice Act 1960, from any judgment of the High Court in any criminal cause or matter;

    (b)   from any order of the High Court or any other court or tribunal allowing an extension of time for appealing from a judgment or order;

    (c)   from any order, judgment or decision of the High Court or any other court or tribunal which, by virtue of any provision (however expressed) of this or any other Act, is final;

    (d)   from a decree absolute of divorce or nullity of marriage, by a party who, having had time and opportunity to appeal from the decree nisi on which that decree was founded, has not appealed from the decree nisi;

    (e), (f)   (*repealed*)

    (fa)   from a dissolution order, nullity order or presumption of death order under Chapter 2 of Part 2 of the Civil Partnership Act 2004 that has been made final, by a party who, having had time and opportunity to appeal from the conditional order on which that final order was founded, has not appealed from the conditional order;

(g) except as provided by Part I of the Arbitration Act 1996, from any decision of the High Court under that Part;

(h) *(repealed)*

(1A)–(2) *(repealed)*

Amendments—CA 1989, s 108(5), Sch 13, para 45(1); CLSA 1990, s 7(1)–(3), Sch 20; Arbitration Act 1996, s 107(1), Sch 3, para 37(2); Civil Procedure Act 1997, s 10, Sch 2, para 1(1),(2); AJA 1999, s 106, Sch 15; CPA 2004, s 261(1), Sch 27, para 68.

Scope—This section sets out the restrictions which apply to the apparently wide-ranging right of appeal provided by s 16. In most cases, an appeal may be made only with permission (see CPR 1998, r 52.3). There is no appeal against the refusal of permission to appeal by a court below (where the court below would have been exercising an appellate jurisdiction, for example a judge from a district judge, see *Bulled v Khayat and Another* [2002] EWCA Civ 804 and *Slot v Isaac* [2002] EWCA Civ 481).

"extension of time for appealing" (s 18(1)(b))—There is no appeal against an order allowing an extension of time for appealing, but the Court of Appeal does have jurisdiction to hear an appeal against the refusal of an application for an extension of time (*Rickards v Rickards* [1990] Fam 194).

"decree absolute" (s 18(1)(d))—A decree absolute should not be made if there is an appeal pending (*Lloyd-Davies v Lloyd-Davies* [1947] P 53; *Everitt v Everitt* [1948] 2 All ER 545).

Costs—The Court of Appeal may interfere on an order for costs where the judge has not acted judicially, without exercising his discretion at all or without material with which to exercise his discretion (see *Jones v McKie* [1964] 1 WLR 960; *Hellyer v Sheriff of Yorkshire* [1975] Ch 16; *Alltrans Express Ltd v CVA Holdings Ltd* [1984] 1 WLR 394; *Scherer v Counting Instruments Ltd* [1986] 1 WLR 615; *Taylor v UKF Fertilisers Ltd and Harvey Plant Ltd* (1988) *The Independent*, 14 November). There is a right of appeal where the appeal is genuinely as to other issues (*Crystall v Crystall* [1963] 1 WLR 564), even where the outcome to those other issues is unsuccessful (*Wheeler v Somerfield* [1966] 2 QB 94).

Ex parte orders—The Court of Appeal will not entertain appeals against ex parte orders; the proper course is to apply, if possible to the same judge, to vary or discharge the order (*WEA Records Ltd v Visions Channel 4 Ltd* [1983] 1 WLR 721; *Re P (A Minor) (Ex Parte Interim Residence Order)* [1993] 1 FLR 915).

Consent orders—In *Re R (Contact: Consent Order)* [1995] 1 FLR 123, the Court of Appeal held that, where a mother gave consent to an order for contact after the judge had warned of a risk of costs being ordered against this (being a criticism of the trial judge), such an order was for the Court of Appeal, and not the court of first instance, to set aside (distinguishing *Re F (A Minor) (Custody: Consent Order: Procedure)* [1992] 1 FLR 561). Bad advice is not a good basis to appeal a consent order (*Tibbs v Dick* [1998] 2 FLR 1118).

Permission to appeal—By virtue of AJA 1999, s 54, permission to appeal to the Court of Appeal is required in all cases, save for a few limited exceptions (as prescribed by CPR 1998, r 52.3). The application for permission should be made to the trial judge and, if refused, thereafter to the Court of Appeal. Full details of the procedure are contained within CPR PD52A–PD52E (see Part III).

In urgent cases where the judge had refused a stay of the order pending the application for permission to appeal, the prospective appellant may telephone the Court of Appeal to apply for a stay (during office hours the telephone number is 0207 947 6000 and out of hours contact is made to the security office at the RCJ on 0207 947 6260, who will refer the matter to the duty deputy master): see CPR PD52C, para 26). A deputy master will refer the matter to a Lord Justice who may grant the stay or list the matter urgently for consideration of the application for a stay (*Re S (Child Proceedings: Urgent Appeals)* [2007] 2 FLR 1044; *Re A (Residence Order)* [2008] 1 FCR 599).

Reopening of final appeals—It is possible, in exceptional circumstances, to reopen a final determination of an appeal to avoid injustice where there is no alternative remedy (see CPR 1998, r 52.17; *Re U (Re-opening of Appeal)* [2005] 2 FLR 444).

The High Court

General jurisdiction

19 General jurisdiction of High Court

(1) The High Court shall be a superior court of record.

(2) Subject to the provisions of this Act, there shall be exercisable by the High Court –

   (a) all such jurisdiction (whether civil or criminal) as is conferred on it by this or any other Act; and

   (b) all such other jurisdiction (whether civil or criminal) as was exercisable by it immediately before the commencement of this Act (including jurisdiction conferred on a judge of the High Court by any statutory provision).

(3) Any jurisdiction of the High Court shall be exercised only by a single judge of that court, except in so far as it is –

   (a) by or by virtue of rules of court or any other statutory provision required to be exercised by a divisional court; or

   (b) by rules of court made exercisable by a master, district judge or other officer of the court, or by any other person.

(4) The specific mention elsewhere in this Act of any jurisdiction covered by subsection (2) shall not derogate from the generality of that subsection.

Scope—Subject to the provisions of this Act, s 19(2) prescribes in general terms the jurisdiction of the High Court by defining its statutory and non-statutory jurisdiction. By virtue of s 19(2)(a), the High Court is empowered to exercise all the jurisdiction conferred by this Act or any Act passed after it. Thus, the High Court has jurisdiction as a court of first instance and as a court of appeal from decisions of district judges of the High Court. The High Court may hear and determine family proceedings commenced in the High Court or transferred to the High Court from the county court in accordance with ATPO 2008, and may hear and determine family proceedings appeals from a district judge of the High Court judge (FPR 2010, Pt 30 and PD30A). Other appeals from a district judge must be made in accordance with CPR 1998, Sch 1, RSC Ord 58.

High Court—For the constitution and divisions of the High Court, see s 4 et seq.

"all such other jurisdiction" (s 19(2)(b))—Subject to the provisions of this Act, the High Court has retained all such jurisdiction, whether statutory or otherwise, which was exercisable by it immediately before the commencement of this Act. This includes the "inherent jurisdiction" of the court, which has been exercisable by the superior court from the earliest days of the common law.

Inherent jurisdiction—The exercise of the court's powers under its inherent jurisdiction is unrestricted and unlimited, except where it has been specifically curtailed by statute. It is derived from the very nature of the court as a superior court of law and not from any statute or rule of law. It invests the court with power to maintain its authority and, as a reserve or residual source of power, to deal with and act effectively on any matter when it is just and equitable to do so. It can be exercised summarily, and may be invoked by or against any person, irrespective of whether they are party to the proceedings. Examples of situations where, in recent years, the court has assumed and exercised its inherent jurisdiction and made orders and declarations, and given directions, include cases relating to the administration or withdrawal of medical treatment, particularly in cases where the sterilisation of an adult mentally disabled person is considered necessary, and in cases of persistent vegetative state (PVS).

Writ ne exeat regno—The provisions of s 19(2)(b) subsume the High Court's jurisdiction to grant this prerogative writ, whereby a person may be prevented from leaving the jurisdiction of the court. Before the writ may be granted, the relevant conditions set out in Debtors Act 1869, s 6 must be satisfied: the applicant must show that he has a good cause of action against the defendant for a substantial award; there must be strong evidence for believing that the defendant is about to leave England unless he is arrested; and there must be evidence that the defendant's absence would materially prejudice the applicant in the prosecution of his case. It should be noted, however, that the issue of the writ is discretionary, and the standard and burden of proof imposed on the applicant is extremely high. The court will require convincing evidence, so that it can be sure that it is right to grant the writ. It will not generally be granted as an ancillary remedy to enforce a *Mareva* injunction or an *Anton Piller* order (see *Allied Arab*

Bank Ltd v Hajjar [1988] QB 787 and *Al Nahkel for Contracting and Trading v Lowe* [1986] QB 235). The relief was granted in *Thaha v Thaha* [1987] 2 FLR 142 by reason of the particular facts of the case. For a fuller consideration of the issue concerning the writ, see *Felton v Callis* [1969] 1 QB 200 and *Emergency Remedies in the Family Courts* (Jordan Publishing Ltd). After judgment, an injunction restraining movement out of the jurisdiction cannot be made as a freestanding enforcement measure but must be linked to another measure and be time limited: *B v B (Injunction: Restraint on Leaving Jurisdiction)* [1997] 2 FLR 148; *Bhura v Bhura* [2012] EWHC 3633 (Fam).

Impounding of a respondent's passport—The exercise of the power to impound a passport is discussed in *Young v Young* [2012] 2 FLR 470 where Mostyn J sets out the relevant principles at [26].

****

Other particular fields of jurisdiction
****

29 Orders of mandamus, prohibition and certiorari

(1) The orders of mandamus, prohibition and certiorari shall be known instead as mandatory, prohibiting and quashing orders respectively.

(1A) The High Court shall have jurisdiction to make mandatory, prohibiting and quashing orders in those classes of case in which, immediately before 1 May 2004, it had jurisdiction to make orders of mandamus, prohibition and certiorari respectively.

(2) Every such order shall be final, subject to any right of appeal therefrom.

(3), (3A) …

(4) The power of the High Court under any enactment to require justices of the peace or a judge or officer of a county court to do any act relating to the duties of their respective offices, or to require a magistrates' court to state a case for the opinion of the High Court, in any case where the High Court formerly had by virtue of any enactment jurisdiction to make a rule absolute, or an order, for any of those purposes, shall be exercisable by mandatory order.

(5), (6) …

Amendments—Armed Forces Act 2001, s 23; SI 2004/1033.

Scope—The procedure for an application for judicial review is contained within CPR 1998, Pt 54. In judicial review proceedings, the court can grant a mandatory order (formerly mandamus), a prohibiting order (formerly prohibition) or a quashing order (formerly certiorari) (SCA 1981, s 31(1), CPR 1998, r 54.2); it also has power to grant declarations and injunctions (SCA 1981, s 31, CPR 1998, r 54.3). Under SCA 1981, s 31 and CPR 1998, r 54.3, an application for a mandatory order, a prohibiting order or a quashing order must be by way of an application for judicial review; however, a declaration or injunction may be obtained in proceedings for judicial review or in other proceedings.

30 Injunctions to restrain persons from acting in offices in which they are not entitled to act

(1) Where a person not entitled to do so acts in an office to which this section applies, the High Court may –

    (a)   grant an injunction restraining him from so acting; and

    (b)   if the case so requires, declare the office to be vacant.

(2) This section applies to any substantive office of a public nature and permanent character which is held under the Crown or which has been created by any statutory provision or royal charter.

Scope—An application under this section must be made by way of judicial review in accordance with the provisions of CPR 1998, P. 54. The application may be made in conjunction with an application for any prerogative order, i e a mandatory, prohibiting or quashing order (CPR 1998, r 54.3).

31 Application for judicial review

(1) An application to the High Court for one or more of the following forms of relief, namely –

    (a)   a mandatory, prohibiting or quashing order;

    (b)   a declaration or injunction under subsection (2); or

    (c)   an injunction under section 30 restraining a person not entitled to do so from acting in an office to which that section applies,

shall be made in accordance with rules of court by a procedure to be known as an application for judicial review.

(2) A declaration may be made or an injunction granted under this subsection in any case where an application for judicial review, seeking that relief, has been made and the High Court considers that, having regard to –

    (a)   the nature of the matters in respect of which relief may be granted by mandatory, prohibiting or quashing orders;

    (b)   the nature of the persons and bodies against whom relief may be granted by such orders; and

    (c)   all the circumstances of the case,

it would be just and convenient for the declaration to be made or for the injunction to be granted, as the case may be.

(3) No application for judicial review shall be made unless the leave of the High Court has been obtained in accordance with rules of court; and the court shall not grant leave to make such an application unless it considers that the applicant has a sufficient interest in the matter to which the application relates.

(4) On an application for judicial review the High Court may award to the applicant damages, restitution or the recovery of a sum due if –

    (a)   the application includes a claim for such an award arising from any matter to which the application relates; and

    (b)   the court is satisfied that such an award would have been made if the claim had been made in an action begun by the applicant at the time of making the application.

(5) If, on an application for judicial review, the High Court quashes the decision to which the application relates, it may in addition –

    (a)   remit the matter to the court, tribunal or authority which made the decision, with a direction to reconsider the matter and reach a decision in accordance with the findings of the High Court; or

    (b)   substitute it's own decision for the decision in question.

(5A) But the power conferred by subsection (5)(b) is exercisable only if –

    (a)   the decision in question was made by a court or tribunal;

    (b)   the decision is quashed on the ground that there has been an error of law; and

    (c)   without the error, there would have been only one decision which the court or tribunal could have reached.

(5B) Unless the High Court otherwise directs, a decision substituted by it under subsection (5)(b) has effect as if it were a decision of the relevant court or tribunal.

(6) Where the High Court considers that there has been undue delay in making an application for judicial review, the court may refuse to grant –

(a)   leave for the making of the application; or

(b)   any relief sought on the application,

if it considers that the granting of the relief sought would be likely to cause substantial hardship to, or substantially prejudice the rights of, any person or would be detrimental to good administration.

(7) Subsection (6) is without prejudice to any enactment or rule of court which has the effect of limiting the time within which an application for judicial review may be made.

Amendments—SI 2004/1033; Tribunals, Courts and Enforcement Act 2007, s 141.

Scope—All applications for judicial review must be made in accordance with CPR 1998, Pt 54. CPR 1998, r 54.2 states that the procedure of judicial review must be used where the claimant is seeking a mandatory order (mandamus), a prohibiting order (prohibition), a quashing order (certiorari), or an injunction (under SCA 1981 restraining a person acting in an office in which he is not entitled). Further, r 54.3 provides that judicial review may also be used to claim a declaration or an injunction. The remedies, other than damages, may be claimed as alternatives or in addition to any other relief (CPR 1998, r 54.3). An application for judicial review may proceed only after permission has been granted (SCA 1981, s 31; CPR 1998, r 54.4).

There is an overlap between the supervisory jurisdiction of the High Court in judicial review proceedings and the inherent jurisdiction of the High Court to make orders in respect of children and incompetent adults. Where the court's task is to come to a decision for and on behalf of the child or incompetent adult, their welfare should be the court's paramount consideration and hence the inherent jurisdiction rather than judicial review would be the most appropriate procedure (*A (A Patient) v A Health Authority* [2002] 1 FLR 845). For the interplay between judicial review and CA 1989, Pt III see *Re T* [2004] 1 FLR 601, *CF v The Secretary of State of the Home Department* [2004] 2 FLR 517 and *Re S and W (Care Proceedings)* [2007] 2 FLR 275, CA.

Where there is a right of appeal to the Care Standards Tribunal, judicial review is not appropriate (*R (M) v London Borough of Bromley* [2002] 2 FLR 802). Judicial review is limited to a review of the local authority decision and not to a detailed examination of the evidence.

"just and convenient" (s 31(2))—The High Court has power to grant a declaration or injunction on an application for judicial review. Unlike the prerogative orders (mandatory, prohibiting or quashing orders), a declaration or injunction is available not only on an application for judicial review, but may also be obtained in other proceedings (CPR 1998, r 54.3).

"sufficient interest" (s 31(3))—The applicant for judicial review must have sufficient interest in the matter to which the application relates in order to proceed. "Mere busybodies do not have sufficient interest" (*Inland Revenue Commissioners v Federation of Self-employed and Small Businesses Ltd* [1982] AC 617 at [108B]; see also *Council of Civil Service Unions v Minister for the Civil Service* [1984] 1 WLR 1174 at [949F]).

"undue delay" (s 31(6))—If the court considers that there has been undue delay in making the application, it may refuse leave to move for judicial review. This provision must be read in conjunction with the time limitations imposed by CPR 1998, r 54.5, namely that the application must be made promptly and in any event within three months from the date when the grounds for the application first arose and the time limit cannot be extended by agreement of the parties.

31A Transfer of judicial review applications to Upper Tribunal

(1) This section applies where an application is made to the High Court –

(a)   for judicial review, or

(b)   for permission to apply for judicial review.

(2) If Conditions 1, 2, 3 and 4 are met, the High Court must by order transfer the application to the Upper Tribunal.

(2A) If Conditions 1, 2, 3 and 5 are met, but Condition 4 is not, the High Court must by order transfer the application to the Upper Tribunal.

(3) If Conditions 1, 2 and 4 are met, but Condition 3 is not, the High Court may by order transfer the application to the Upper Tribunal if it appears to the High Court to be just and convenient to do so.

(4) Condition 1 is that the application does not seek anything other than –

    (a)   relief under section 31(1)(a) and (b);

    (b)   permission to apply for relief under section 31(1)(a) and (b);

    (c)   an award under section 31(4);

    (d)   interest;

    (e)   costs.

(5) Condition 2 is that the application does not call into question anything done by the Crown Court.

(6) Condition 3 is that the application falls within a class specified under section 18(6) of the Tribunals, Courts and Enforcement Act 2007.

(7) Condition 4 is that the application does not call into question any decision made under –

    (a)   the Immigration Acts,

    (b)   the British Nationality Act 1981,

    (c)   any instrument having effect under an enactment within paragraph (a) or (b), or

    (d)   any other provision of law for the time being in force which determines British citizenship, British overseas territories citizenship, the status of a British National (Overseas) or British Overseas citizenship.

(8) Condition 5 is that the application calls into question a decision of the Secretary of State not to treat submissions as an asylum claim or a human rights claim within the meaning of Part 5 of the Nationality, Immigration and Asylum Act 2002 wholly or partly on the basis that they are not significantly different from material that has previously been considered (whether or not it calls into question any other decision).

Amendments—Inserted by Tribunals, Courts and Enforcement Act 2007, s 19(1); amended by Borders, Citizenship and Immigration Act 2009, s 53.

****

Powers

****

37 Powers of High Court with respect to injunctions and receivers

(1) The High Court may by order (whether interlocutory or final) grant an injunction or appoint a receiver in all cases in which it appears to the court to be just and convenient to do so.

(2) Any such order may be made either unconditionally or on such terms and conditions as the court thinks just.

(3) The power of the High Court under subsection (1) to grant an interlocutory injunction restraining a party to any proceedings from removing from the jurisdiction of the High Court, or otherwise dealing with, assets located within that jurisdiction shall be exercisable in cases where that party is, as well as in cases where he is not, domiciled, resident or present within that jurisdiction.

(4), (5) ...

Scope—This section restates the law governing the power of the court to grant injunctions and/or to appoint receivers. It does not fetter the court's powers (*Motorola Credit Corp v Uzan* (No 2) [2004] 1 WLR 113,). However, HRA 1998 requires a marginally higher threshold test in applications for interlocutory injunctions (*Imutran Ltd v Uncaged Campaigns* [2001] 2 All ER 385).

"whether interlocutory or final" (s 37(1))—These words confirm the practice which existed before the Act, and do not restrict the power to grant an injunction after judgment to assist in the process of enforcement. Thus, in family cases, an injunction can be obtained to prevent a respondent from disposing of assets to defeat enforcement (see *Orwell Steel (Erection and Fabrication) Ltd v Asphalt and Tarmac (UK) Ltd* [1984] 1 WLR 1097; *Roche v Roche* (1981) Fam Law 243; *Shipman v Shipman* [1991] 1 FLR 250).

Court's power to grant "Freezing injunctions" and "Search orders"—For clarification, see Civil Procedure Act 1997, s 7.

"Search order"—A search order is provided for by CPR 1998, r 25.1(1)(h) and was formerly often referred to as an *Anton Piller* order. It is an interlocutory order which achieves disclosure and protection of documentary and real evidence. It has been described by Lord Denning MR as a "search warrant" (*Anton Piller KG v Manufacturing Processes Ltd* [1976] Ch 55). It is a drastic order and will only be granted in the most exceptional circumstances where there is an extremely strong prima facie case of vital evidence being destroyed or otherwise disposed of and thus causing prejudice to the applicant's case and defeating justice. It is normally granted ex parte (see *Indicii Salus Ltd (in receivership) v Chandrasekaran* [2006] EWHC 521 (Ch) where these principles are re-stated). The search order is usually accompanied by a freezing injunction freezing the defendant's bank accounts and restraining him from making any disposition of his assets (see **Freezing injunctions** below). In matrimonial proceedings, it is very much an order of last resort, where all other methods of seeking the necessary information have failed. For example, where a wife maintained that her husband had failed to make full disclosure of his financial position and that he was a man of substantial means and had secreted his assets abroad, the court was prepared to make a search order (*Kepa v Kepa* (1983) 4 FLR 515). Where a party to matrimonial proceedings seeks documents which are not themselves the subject matter of the proceedings, the Family Division still has jurisdiction to grant a search order provided that the applicant has a strong prima facie case that the relevant documents are essential for his case and are at serious risk of being removed or destroyed (*Emanuel v Emanuel* [1982] 1 WLR 669). The order may permit a search of the defendant's premises and seizure of documents or other items found there which might form evidence in the applicant's action or proposed action against the defendant. The procedure must not be used oppressively. In *Burgess v Burgess* [1996] 2 FLR 34, the husband obtained a search order, but the search yielded no relevant evidence; he was ordered to pay the wife's costs on the indemnity basis, and the court reiterated that, in family proceedings, search orders are to be used only in extreme or exceptional circumstances; see also *A v A* [1997] Fam Law 301, in which the application was refused.

Procedure for search order—Interim remedies in family proceedings are governed by FPR 2010, Pt 20. Rule 20.2 expressly refers to a "search order" (r 20.2(1)(h)); see Pt 20 and the commentary thereon, in particular PD20A, which explains the procedure in detail.

Effect of search order—The search order is a draconian remedy and should be used with the utmost caution. An order made without notice must be given the earliest practicable return day. The court considering whether or not to make the order must strike a balance between the applicant's need for a remedy for a breach of his civil rights and the requirements of justice that a defendant should not be deprived of his property without being heard (*Columbia Picture Industries v Robinson* [1987] Ch 38). The order must contain a provision for the defendant to apply to vary or discharge the order, even though this will be of little immediate value because, when the order is served, he is under an obligation to allow entry and search of his premises and removal of the documents and items specified in the order. If he fails to comply, he risks the sanction of a committal order for contempt of court (*Wardle Fabrics Ltd v G Myristis Ltd* [1984] FSR 263). For the form of search order see the Annex to CPR PD25A in Part III.

Duty of disclosure—The applicant is under a duty to make a full and frank disclosure to the court in his affidavit in support of an application for a search order (*Lock International plc v Beswick* [1989] 1 WLR 1268), even where the material comes to his knowledge after the order was obtained (*O'Regan v Iambic Productions Ltd* (1989) 139 NLJ 1378). Failure to do so is likely to lead to the order being discharged without consideration of the merits (*Manor Electronics Ltd v Dickson* [1988] RPC 618) and refusal of a fresh order (*Arena Corp Ltd v Schroeder* [2003] EWHC 1089 (Ch)).

Safeguards for interests of defendant—See FPR PD20A. The order must be served by a "supervising solicitor" and carried out in his presence and under his supervision. The supervising solicitor should be an experienced solicitor, having some familiarity with the operation of search orders, who is not a member or employee of the firm acting for the applicant. The evidence in support of the application should include the identity and experience of the proposed supervising solicitor.

Search and seizure of documents and articles—Where a search order is executed at business premises, it should be conducted by the supervising solicitor named in the order, and it should be carried out in the presence of the defendant or a person appearing to be a responsible employee of the defendant. The order may only be served on a weekday between 9.30 am and 5.30 pm. When the supervising solicitor and the applicant's solicitor attend at the premises to execute the order, the defendant (or any other person appearing to be in control of the premises) may seek legal advice, and may apply to the court to vary or discharge the order, provided that he does so at once. See FPR PD20A.

Discharge of search order—An application for variation or discharge of a search order must be made immediately to the court that made the order. It should be made on notice (*Hallmark Cards Inc v Image Arts Ltd* [1977] FSR 150). The application should be accompanied by sworn evidence. So far as practicable, any application for the discharge or variation of the order should be dealt with effectively on the inter partes return date. If the order is discharged on the return date, the judge should always consider whether it is appropriate that he should assess damages at once and direct immediate payment by the applicant. It is not possible to appeal against the order until the application to set aside has been made and refused (*WEA Records Ltd v Visions Channel 4 Ltd* [1983] 1 WLR 721).

Jurisdiction (s 37(3))—Interlocutory applications for freezing injunctions and directions as to dealing with assets outside the jurisdiction should generally be dealt with in the High Court. However, county courts do have jurisdiction to grant freezing injunctions when exercising jurisdiction in family proceedings (CCRR 1991, reg 3(3)) and application can therefore be made to a divorce county court if the nature of the issues raised are suitable.

Freezing injunctions (s 37(3))—The term "freezing injunction" is the modern term for a "*Mareva* injunction". Section 37(3) embodies in statute the practice explained in *Mareva Compania Naviera SA v International Bulk Carriers SA* [1980] 1 All ER 213. Initially, the practice was confined to cases where there was a risk of assets being transferred abroad but the practice of granting freezing injunctions has been extended to cover any situation where there are grounds for believing that the defendant may transfer or dissipate assets, whether inside or outside the jurisdiction, with a view to defeating the applicant's claim.

Procedure for freezing injunctions—Interim remedies in family proceedings are governed by FPR 2010, Pt 20. Rule 20.2(1)(f) expressly refers to a "freezing injunction". See Pt 20 and the commentary thereon, in particular PD20A, which explains the procedure in detail.

Principles on which a freezing injunction is made—"It is an absolutely elementary tenet of English law that save in an emergency a court should hear both sides before giving a ruling. The only recognised exception to this rule ... is where there is a well-founded belief that the giving of notice would lead to irretrievable prejudice being caused to the applicant for relief" (*FZ v SZ and Others (Ancillary Relief: Conduct: Valuations)* [2011] 1 FLR 64 at [32]). The principles on which a freezing injunction is made were clearly set out by Lord Denning MR in *Third Chandris Shipping Corporation v Unimarine SA* [1979] QB 645. They include a duty on the applicant to make full and frank disclosure of all matters in his knowledge which are material for the judge to know. If material non-disclosure is established at a later stage, the court has a discretion to discharge the order. (See, for example, *ND v KP (Freezing Order: Ex Parte Application)* [2011] 2 FLR 662, where the order was discharged.) The applicant must make proper inquiries before making the application, and this duty applies to any additional facts he would have known if he had made such inquiries (*Bank Mellat v Nikpour* [1985] FSR 87). The applicant must give particulars of his claim against the respondent, stating his grounds and the amount involved, and fairly state the points made against the applicant by the respondent. The applicant must depose to some grounds for believing that there is a risk of the assets being removed or dissipated before the judgment or award is satisfied (*Z Ltd v A-Z and AA-LL* [1982] QB 558). As without notice freezing orders are granted on the basis of urgency and on the basis that notice would defeat the ends of justice it is inappropriate to warn of the possibility of such an order by a letter before action. Indeed such a warning might defeat the application (*Oaktree Financial Services Ltd v Higham* [2004] EWHC 2098 (Ch)). The applicant must give an undertaking in damages in case he fails in his claim or the injunction turns out to have been unjustified. The undertakings to be given by the applicant are set out in FPR PD20A. An applicant should be required, in an appropriate case, to support his cross-undertaking in damages by a payment into court or the provision of a bond by an insurance company. Alternatively, the judge may order a payment by way of such security to the applicant's solicitor to be held by the solicitor as an officer of the court pending further order. (If a freezing injunction is discharged on the return date, the judge should always consider whether it is appropriate for him to assess damages at once and direct immediate payment by the applicant). A legally aided person may be granted an injunction although his undertaking may be of little value (*Allen v Jambo Holdings Ltd* [1980] 1 WLR 1252). Where the injunction affects third parties, the applicant may have to give an undertaking to indemnify those third parties against all expenses reasonably incurred in complying with the order.

Matrimonial disputes—In addition to the principles set out above, in a matrimonial case an injunction should not extend to all the assets of the other party because it is unlikely that the applicant would be awarded all the assets. Thus the injunction should be limited to the size of the fund reasonably regarded as being in issue. For example in *Paulin v Paulin* [2009] 2 FLR 354 the wife obtained a specific order that the matrimonial home was not to be disposed of or charged and a freezing order against the husband's assets up to £4m. In *FZ v SZ and Others (Ancillary Relief: Conduct: Valuations)* [2011] 1 FLR 64, Mostyn J said: "I have been shocked by the volume of spurious ex parte applications that are made in the urgent applications list". In *ND v KP (Freezing Order: Ex Parte Application)* [2011] 2 FLR 662, the same judge set aside an ex parte freezing order for lack of candour in the application. But see also *Peyman-Fard v Peyman-Fard* [2011] EWCA Civ 959, where a sentence of imprisonment was upheld on a husband who had paid a sum to his sister in breach of a freezing order obtained during ancillary relief proceedings. Where an order is made requiring payment of a lump sum, the injunctive and receivership powers in s 37 can be used to make it effective. In *(1) Blight (2) Meredith (3) Lewis v Brewster* [2012] BPIR 476, the debtor was required to delegate to the judgment creditor's solicitor power to elect to receive a lump sum from a pension fund. In *O'Farrell v O'Farrell* [2013] 1 FLR 77, a freezing order was made to preserve a sum equal to the judgment made in German divorce proceedings.

Form of freezing injunction—FPR PD20A explains what the order must do (but, unlike CPR PD25A, does not contain a specimen order). The injunction may, in its widest form, include an order that the respondent disclose all his assets, which include chattels and choses in action (*CBS UK Ltd v Lambert* [1983] Ch 37; *Z Ltd v A-Z and AA-LL* [1982] QB 558), but at the inter partes hearing the court may consider whether the disclosure order against the respondent should be discharged (*Arab Monetary Fund v Hashim* [1989] 3 All ER 466). There is no general rule that a party against whom a freezing order is made is entitled to a stay or the disclosure obligations ancillary to that order until after it has been finally determined whether the freezing order should stand (*Motorola Credit Corp v Uzan* [2004] 1 WLR 113; *Raja v Van Hoogstraten* [2004] 4 All ER 793). Where appropriate, and especially where the injunction relates to the rights of third parties, the injunction should extend to the specified maximum amount claimed by the applicant. Where there is a risk of the respondent disposing of money owed to him, the court may, with the approval of the creditor, order that sum to be paid into court or into an account frozen by the injunction (*Bank Mellat v Kazmi* [1989] QB 541). The injunction takes effect, from the moment it is made, in respect of every asset of the respondent covered by the order. It is desirable to fix a return date when the continuation can be considered inter partes and third parties can have the opportunity to be heard. The order must be carefully drafted so as to make clear the date on which the order begins and ends. Where the court is concerned with injunctions imposing serious restrictions on the activities of litigants, the "slip rule" will be invoked to remedy a defect in the order only in exceptional circumstances (*Langley v Langley* [1994] 1 FLR 383).

Notice of freezing injunction—Notice of the injunction should be given to banks and other financial institutions, where it is believed that the respondent has assets, and they must do what they can to preserve such assets; otherwise, they risk being in contempt of court. The applicant must give to the bank as much detail as possible about the account number, branch number and so forth. The specimen order set out in CPR PD25A contains a clause which provides that the injunction does not prevent any bank from exercising any right of set-off it may have in respect of any facility which it gave to the respondent before it was notified of the order, and this proviso should be included where appropriate (*Oceanica Castelana Armadora SA v Mineralimportexport, The Theotokos* [1983] 1 WLR 1302). The bank is entitled to apply for a variation to enable it to exercise any right of facilities granted before it receives notice of the injunction and, in order to save court time, a proviso to that effect should be included in the injunction (*Oceanica Castelana Armadora SA v Mineralimportexport, The Theotokos* [1983] 1 WLR 1302).

Respondent's access to assets—The respondent should be allowed access to sums for his normal living expenses, and the injunction should specify these. Those sums may include sums for medical expenses and legal expenses where appropriate. In *Zakharov v White* [2003] EWHC 2463 (Ch), because of the respondent's lack of frankness at an earlier hearing, the court revisited its previous order and inserted provisions more strictly policing his ability to spend.

Assets outside the jurisdiction—By virtue of CJJA 1982, s 25(1), it is clear that a freezing injunction can cover assets worldwide, even though the respondent is outside the jurisdiction (*Babanaft International Co SA v Bassatne* [1990] Ch 13; *Republic of Haiti and Others v Duvaliers and Others* [1990] 1 QB 202), provided that the personal effect of such an order is limited to the particular respondents against whom it was granted. A worldwide injunction will only be granted in exceptional circumstances and should be subject to strict undertakings and provisos to prevent the injunction from being more oppressive to the respondent than beneficial to the applicant. The specimen order contained in CPR PD25A should be used for an injunction to prevent the disposal of assets worldwide. The specimen order contains the undertakings to be given to the court by the applicant.

Limitations—A freezing injunction should not be granted unless the applicant can show a substantial case for saying that, unless it is granted, there will be a serious risk of the assets which might otherwise be available to meet judgment being dissipated (*Behbehani v Salem (Note)* [1989] 1 WLR 723). Other pending proceedings against the respondent are relevant (*Jarvis Field Press v Chelton* [2003] EWHC 2674).

Contempt of court—Disobedience of a freezing order is a contempt of court. See further CCA 1981. The court has power to commit for up to 2 years and/or impose an unlimited fine. (See, for example, *W v W* [2011] 2 FLR 1268 – 1 year's imprisonment for Swedish banker suspended on terms including immediate payment.) In *Raja v Van Hoogstraten* [2004] 4 All ER 793, it was held to be inconsistent with ECHR 1950, Art 6 for a judge to proceed with an effective hearing of an application to commit in circumstances where he knew the alleged contemnor wished to be heard in person but was prevented from being present by matters over which he had no control.

No jurisdiction to grant freezing injunctions in support of enforcement of assessments under CSA 1991—The High Court has no jurisdiction to grant a freezing injunction in support of, and as ancillary to, the enforcement procedure for maintenance assessments provided for by CSA 1991 (*Department of Social Security v Butler* [1996] 1 FLR 65).

"or otherwise dealing with" (s 37(3))—These words include disposing of, selling or charging (see *CBS UK Ltd v Lambert* [1983] Ch 37).

Writ ne exeat regno—This writ cannot be issued for the purpose of enforcing a freezing injunction (see further under s 19 above).

Impounding of a passport—The power to impound a respondent's passport is addressed in *Young v Young* [2012] 2 FLR 470: see [26] for principles. Also, see s 19.

Section 46 Land Registration Act 2002—This section enables the court, for the purpose of protecting a right or claim in relation to a registered estate or charge, to make an order requiring a restriction to be entered in the register. The order may include a direction that the entry is to have overriding priority. It may be appropriate to obtain this order ancillary to a freezing order.

Appeals—Permission to appeal to the Court of Appeal from an order granting or refusing an interlocutory injunction is required pursuant to CPR 1998, r 52.3.

****

39 Execution of instrument by person nominated by High Court

(1) Where the High Court has given or made a judgment or order directing a person to execute any conveyance, contract or other document, or to indorse any negotiable instrument, then, if that person –

   (a)   neglects or refuses to comply with the judgment or order; or

   (b)   cannot after reasonable inquiry be found,

the High Court may, on such terms and conditions, if any, as may be just, order that the conveyance, contract or other document shall be executed, or that the negotiable instrument shall be indorsed, by such person as the court may nominate for that purpose.

(2) A conveyance, contract, document or instrument executed or indorsed in pursuance of an order under this section shall operate, and be for all purposes available, as if it had been executed or indorsed by the person originally directed to execute or indorse it.

"directing a person to execute" (s 39(1))—The person must of course be identified in the order, and he must have been ordered to execute a document, not merely (for example) to transfer a property. If an order has been made in the latter form, it is necessary first to secure an order requiring execution of the relevant document before an order can be made under this section.

"neglects or refuses" (s 39(1)(a))—In the case of neglect or refusal, this section provides a cheaper, more effective and less draconian remedy than an application to commit. If this ground is relied on it must be shown that the Respondent is aware of the order but personal service is not mandatory. It is normally required that he has been given the opportunity to execute the document, but not if it is patent that he refuses and will continue to refuse to do so (*Savage v Norton* [1908] 1 Ch 290).

"such person as the court may nominate" (s 39(1))—Any person may be nominated, but it is frequently the district judge (who may, it seems, nominate himself). The nominee signs not "on behalf of" the respondent but merely pursuant to the order.

"as if it had been executed ... by the person originally directed" (s 39(2))—The nominee assumes no personal liability under the document.

County court—The same power is exercised by the county court by virtue of CCA 1984, s 38.

Procedure—Normally the application is made by summons or on notice to the district judge (FPR 2010, r 18.1). If the respondent cannot be found (and has no solicitor on record), the application will usually be made without notice, unless (rarely) the court directs substituted service (e g by advertisement).

Alternative procedure—Where what is sought to be achieved is the transfer of a property from one party to another, it may be possible to avoid the expense and inconvenience of preparing a document for signature, obtaining an order that the transferor sign it, obtaining an order under this section and then having the document signed by the named person. The court can be asked instead to make an order under Trustee Act 1925, s 44(vii), vesting the property in the transferee. If such an order is available, it may particularly be appropriate where the whereabouts of the transferor are unknown or his co-operation otherwise seems unlikely.

40 Attachment of debts

(1) Subject to any order for the time being in force under subsection (4), this section applies to any deposit account, and any withdrawable share account, with a deposit-taker.

(2) In determining whether, for the purposes of the jurisdiction of the High Court to attach debts for the purpose of satisfying judgments or orders for the payment of money, a sum standing to the credit of a person in an account to which this section applies is a sum due or accruing to that person and, as such, attachable in accordance with rules of court, any condition mentioned in subsection (3) which applies to the account shall be disregarded.

(3) Those conditions are –

    (a)   any condition that notice is required before any money or share is withdrawn;

    (b)   any condition that a personal application must be made before any money or share is withdrawn;

    (c)   any condition that a deposit book or share-account book must be produced before any money or share is withdrawn; or

    (d)   any other prescribed condition.

(4) The Lord Chancellor may by order make such provision as he thinks fit, by way of amendment of this section or otherwise, for all or any of the following purposes, namely –

    (a)   including in, or excluding from, the accounts to which this section applies accounts of any description specified in the order;

    (b)   excluding from the accounts to which this section applies all accounts with any particular deposit-taker so specified or with any deposit-taker of a description so specified.

(5) Any order under subsection (4) shall be made by statutory instrument subject to annulment in pursuance of a resolution of either House of Parliament.

(6) "Deposit-taker" means a person who may, in the course of his business, lawfully accept deposits in the United Kingdom.

(7) Subsection (6) must be read with –

    (a)   section 22 of the Financial Services and Markets Act 2000;

    (b)   any relevant order under that section; and

    (c)   Schedule 2 to that Act.

Amendments—Banking Act 1987, s 108(1), Sch 6, para 11; SI 2001/3649.

Scope—This section extends the availability of third party debt order proceedings to bank and building society accounts which would otherwise not be vulnerable to such an order because of conditions attached to their operation (see CPR 1998, Pt 72 and particularly r 72.2(3)).

40A Administrative and clerical expenses of garnishees

(1) Where an interim third party debt order made in the exercise of the jurisdiction mentioned in subsection (2) of the preceding section is served on a deposit-taker, it may, subject to the provision of this section, deduct from the relevant debt or debts an amount not exceeding the prescribed sum towards its administrative and clerical expenses in complying with the order; and the right to make a deduction under this subsection shall be exercisable as from the time the interim third party debt order is served on it.

(1A) In subsection (1) "the relevant debt or debts", in relation to an interim third party debt order served on a deposit-taker, means the amount, as at the time the order is served on it, of the debt or debts of which the whole or a part is expressed to be attached by the order.

(1B) A deduction may be made under subsection (1) in a case where the amount referred to in subsection (1A) is insufficient to cover both the amount of the deduction and the amount of the judgment debt and costs in respect of which the attachment was made, notwithstanding that the benefit of the attachment to the creditor is reduced as a result of the deduction.

(2) An amount may not in pursuance of subsection (1) be deducted or, as the case may be, retained in a case where, by virtue of section 346 of the Insolvency Act 1986 or section 183 of the Insolvency Act 1986 or otherwise, the creditor is not entitled to retain the benefit of the attachment.

(3) In this section –

"deposit-taker" has the meaning given by section 40(6); and
"prescribed" means prescribed by an order made by the Lord Chancellor.

(4) An order under this section –

(a) may make different provision for different cases;
(b) without prejudice to the generality of paragraph (a) of this subsection, may prescribe sums differing according to the amount due under the judgment or order to be satisfied;
(c) may provide for this section not to apply to deposit-takers of any prescribed description.

(5) Any such order shall be made by statutory instrument subject to annulment in pursuance of a resolution of either House of Parliament.

Amendments—Inserted by AJA 1982, s 55, Sch 4, Pt I; amended by AJA 1985, s 52; Companies Consolidation (Consequential Provisions) Act 1985, s 30, Sch 2; Insolvency Act 1986, s 439(2), Sch 14; SI 2001/3649; SI 2002/439

"the prescribed sum" (s 40A(1))—The current sum is £55: SI 1996/3098.

41 Wards of court

(1) Subject to the provisions of this section, no minor shall be made a ward of court except by virtue of an order to that effect made by the High Court.

(2) Where an application is made for such an order in respect of a minor, the minor shall become a ward of court on the making of the application, but shall cease to be a ward of court at the end of such period as may be prescribed unless within that period an order has been made in accordance with the application.

(2A) Subsection (2) does not apply with respect to a child who is the subject of a care order (as defined by section 105 of the Children Act 1989).

(3) The High Court may, either upon an application in that behalf or without such an application, order that any minor who is for the time being a ward of court shall cease to be a ward of court.

Amendments—CA 1989, s 108(5), Sch 13, para 45(2).

Defined terms—"minor": FLRA 1969, s 1.

Applications without notice—It is on the issue of the application that a child becomes a ward. The court however, has the power to grant injunctions and emergency orders before the application is issued (*Re N (Infants) (No 2)* [1967] Ch 512). Applications without notice before the issue of proceedings should be used only as a matter of emergency (*Re O (Proposed Wardship Proceedings)* [1990] FCR 599). Where an application without notice is made before the issue of the substantive application on undertakings given to file the process, it is essential that the court is asked at that stage to confirm the wardship, particularly if the emergency that occasioned the issue of the wardship has been adequately protected by the judge's order or the emergency has passed.

42 Restriction of vexatious legal proceedings

(1) If, on an application made by the Attorney General under this section, the High Court is satisfied that any person has habitually and persistently and without any reasonable ground –

(a)   instituted vexatious civil proceedings, whether in the High Court or any inferior court, and whether against the same person or against different persons; or

(b)   made vexatious applications in any civil proceedings, whether in the High Court or any inferior court, and whether instituted by him or another, or

(c)   instituted vexatious prosecutions (whether against the same person or different persons),

the court may, after hearing that person or giving him an opportunity of being heard, make a civil proceedings order, a criminal proceedings order or an all proceedings order.

(1A) In this section –

"civil proceedings order" means an order that –

(a)   no civil proceedings shall without the leave of the High Court be instituted in any court by the person against whom the order is made;

(b)   any civil proceedings instituted by him in any court before the making of the order shall not be continued by him without the leave of the High Court; and

(c)   no application (other than one for leave under this section) shall be made by him, in any civil proceedings instituted in any court by any person, without the leave of the High Court;

"criminal proceedings order" means an order that –

(a)   no information shall be laid before a justice of the peace by the person against whom the order is made without the leave of the High Court; and

(b)   no application for leave to prefer a bill of indictment shall be made by him without the leave of the High Court; and

"all proceedings order" means an order which has the combined effect of the two other orders.

(2) An order under subsection (1) may provide that it is to cease to have effect at the end of a specified period, but shall otherwise remain in force indefinitely.

(3) Leave for the institution or continuance of, or for the making of an application in, any civil proceedings by a person who is the subject of an order for the time being in force under subsection (1) shall not be given unless the High Court is satisfied that the proceedings or application are not an abuse of the process of the court in question and that there are reasonable grounds for the proceedings or application.

(3A) Leave for the laying of an information or for an application for leave to prefer a bill of indictment by a person who is the subject of an order for the time being in force under subsection (1) shall not be given unless the High Court is satisfied that the institution of the prosecution is not an abuse of the criminal process and that there are reasonable grounds for the institution of the prosecution by the applicant.

(4) No appeal shall lie from a decision of the High Court refusing leave required by virtue of this section.

(5) A copy of any order made under subsection (1) shall be published in the London Gazette.

Amendments—Prosecution of Offences Act 1985, s 24.

"civil proceedings ... in the High Court or any inferior court" (s 42(1)(a))—The term "civil proceedings" is not defined by SCA 1981; nor is there an obvious definition elsewhere. Civil proceedings are any proceedings which are not criminal.

Inferior court—The term "inferior court" occurs in the judicial review jurisdiction and, coupled with tribunals – "inferior court or ... tribunal" – it occurs in the context of witness summonses (CPR 1998, r 34.4). It may be said to apply to county courts and the civil jurisdiction of the magistrates.

Vexatious litigant—Section 42 enables the Attorney-General to apply to the High Court where a "person has habitually and persistently and without reasonable ground instituted vexatious civil proceedings". The court has the power to make a "civil proceedings order", which prevents issue of further proceedings, stays any continuing proceedings and prevents any application by the defendant in any existing proceedings, without permission. In *Attorney-General v Barker* [2000] 1 FLR 759, Lord Bingham CJ (in the Divisional Court) suggested that the main characteristic of a vexatious litigant is that his applications have little or no basis in law; their effect is to subject the respondents to harassment, inconvenience and expense, and the effect is also to abuse the process of the court. In such circumstances, a s 42 order may be justified.

Civil restraint orders and orders under CA 1989, s 91(14)—Orders under s 42 are to be contrasted with civil restraint orders (see FPR 2010, r 4.8) and from orders under CA 1989, s 91(14).

****

General Provisions

Law and equity

49 Concurrent administration of law and equity

(1) Subject to the provisions of this or any other Act, every court exercising jurisdiction in England or Wales in any civil cause or matter shall continue to administer law and equity on the basis that, wherever there is any conflict or variance between the rules of equity and the rules of the common law with reference to the same matter, the rules of equity shall prevail.

(2) Every such court shall give the same effect as hitherto –

    (a)   to all equitable estates, titles, rights, reliefs, defences and counterclaims, and to all equitable duties and liabilities; and

    (b)   subject thereto, to all legal claims and demands and all estates, titles, rights, duties, obligations and liabilities existing by the common law or by any custom or created by any statute,

and, subject to the provisions of this or any other Act, shall so exercise its jurisdiction in every cause or matter before it as to secure that, as far as possible, all matters in dispute between the parties are completely and finally determined, and all multiplicity of legal proceedings with respect to any of those matters is avoided.

(3) Nothing in this Act shall affect the power of the Court of Appeal or the High Court to stay any proceedings before it, where it thinks fit to do so, either of its own motion or on the application of any person, whether or not a party to the proceedings.

Scope—This section provides for courts to act as courts of law and equity. The principle that equity prevails relates to substantive law and not practice (*La Grange v McAndrew* (1879) 4 QBD 210). The court has an inherent jurisdiction to stay any proceedings which are an abuse of its powers (see *Hinckley and South Leicestershire Permanent Benefit Building Society v Freeman* [1941] Ch 32).

****

Costs

51 Costs in civil division of Court of Appeal, High Court and county courts

(1) Subject to the provisions of this or any other enactment and to rules of court, the costs of and incidental to all proceedings in –

   (a)   the civil division of the Court of Appeal;
   (b)   the High Court; and
   (c)   any county court,

shall be in the discretion of the court.

(2) Without prejudice to any general power to make rules of court, such rules may make provision for regulating matters relating to the costs of those proceedings including, in particular, prescribing scales of costs to be paid to legal or other representatives or for securing that the amount awarded to a party in respect of the costs to be paid by him to such representatives is not limited to what would have been payable by him to them if he had not been awarded costs.

(3) The court shall have full power to determine by whom and to what extent the costs are to be paid.

(4) In subsections (1) and (2) "proceedings" includes the administration of estates and trusts.

(5) Nothing in subsection (1) shall alter the practice in any criminal cause, or in bankruptcy.

(6) In any proceedings mentioned in subsection (1), the court may disallow, or (as the case may be) order the legal or other representative concerned to meet, the whole of any wasted costs or such part of them as may be determined in accordance with rules of court.

(7) In subsection (6), "wasted costs" means any costs incurred by a party –

   (a)   as a result of any improper, unreasonable or negligent act or omission on the part of any legal or other representative or any employee of such a representative; or
   (b)   which, in the light of any such act or omission occurring after they were incurred, the court considers it is unreasonable to expect that party to pay.

(8) Where –

   (a)   a person has commenced proceedings in the High Court; but
   (b)   those proceedings should, in the opinion of the court, have been commenced in a county court in accordance with any provision made under section 1 of the Courts and Legal Services Act 1990 or by or under any other enactment,

the person responsible for determining the amount which is to be awarded to that person by way of costs shall have regard to those circumstances.

(9) Where, in complying with subsection (8), the responsible person reduces the amount which would otherwise be awarded to the person in question –

   (a)   the amount of that reduction shall not exceed 25 per cent; and

(b) on any taxation of the costs payable by that person to his legal representative, regard shall be had to the amount of the reduction.

(10) The Lord Chancellor may by order amend subsection (9)(a) by substituting, for the percentage for the time being mentioned there, a different percentage.

(11) Any such order shall be made by statutory instrument and may make such transitional or incidental provision as the Lord Chancellor considers expedient.

(12) No such statutory instrument shall be made unless a draft of the instrument has been approved by both Houses of Parliament.

(13) In this section "legal or other representative", in relation to a party to proceedings, means any person exercising a right of audience or right to conduct litigation on his behalf.

Amendments—CLSA 1990, s 4(1); AJA 1999, s 31.

Rules of court—The general rule, prescribed by CPR 1998, r 44.2 is that the unsuccessful party pays the costs of the successful party. This provision is specifically disapplied in relation to family appeals (by CPR 1998, r 44.2(3)). The court has a discretion as to costs and when exercising that discretion must have regard to the conduct of the parties, the success of the appeal and attempts or offers to settle the matter (r 44.2). The Supreme Court held that where it is reasonable that allegations of misconduct to a child should be investigated by a court "justice does not demand that the local authority responsible for placing the allegations before the court should ultimately be responsible for the legal costs of the person against whom the allegations are made": *Re T (Costs: Care Proceedings: Serious Allegation Not Proved)* [2013] 1 FLR 133, at [42].

Wasted costs orders—These orders are dealt with by CPR 1998, r 44.11.

****

PART III
PRACTICE AND PROCEDURE
****

The High Court
****

67 Proceedings in court and in chambers

Business in the High Court shall be heard and disposed of in court except in so far as it may, under this or any other Act, under rules of court or in accordance with the practice of the court, be dealt with in chambers.

Exercise of the court's discretion as to whether a hearing should take place in open court or in chambers—This section does not provide a statutory basis for making a direction that a particular hearing should be held in chambers. However, it was held in *Scott v Scott* (1913) FLR Rep 657 that, although business conducted in the High Court should normally be by way of public hearing to secure that justice is done, the court has jurisdiction in matrimonial proceedings to decide whether or not a particular hearing should be in chambers or in open court, where the case falls within the three exceptions identified by Viscount Haldane LC, that is to say: (i) wards; (ii) lunatics (in each of which the court is sitting primarily to safeguard the interests of the ward or lunatic); and (iii) litigation in respect of a secret process where the effect of publicity would be to destroy the subject matter. However, *Scott* (above) cannot be taken to prevent or restrict the enactment of rules for regulating the trial of family proceedings and there is no objection to hearing family cases in private and excluding the public where the rules permit it (*Clibbery v Allan and Another* [2002] 1 FLR 565, CA). In exercising its discretion in this matter, the court must conduct a balancing exercise between the genuine public interest in the case in holding the hearing in open court, and the competing interest of those people concerned in the case who seek the protection of a hearing in chambers (*Re G (Adult Patient: Publicity)* [1995] 2 FLR 528 – where an adult patient was maintained on life support machines in a persistent vegetative state, the court decided that the genuine public interest in the decision as to whether or not to allow the hospital to discontinue the life-sustaining treatment required that the hearing should be held in open court, but with safeguards to protect the positions and anonymity of the relatives, doctors and nursing staff involved). The general rule is that it is not a contempt of court to report what happened in a hearing in chambers unless AJA 1960, s 12 applies, or the case comes within the recognised categories of children or ancillary relief cases, or the administration of justice would otherwise be impeded or prejudiced by publication (*Clibbery v Allan and Another* [2002] 1 FLR 565, CA). See further under CCA 1981, s 11 and AJA 1960, s 12.

Attendance of the media—See the notes to AJA 1960, s 12.

****

151 Interpretation of this Act, and rules of construction for other Acts and documents

(1) In this Act, unless the context otherwise requires –

"action" means any civil proceedings commenced by writ or in any other manner prescribed by rules of court;

"appeal", in the context of appeals to the civil division of the Court of Appeal, includes –

(a)   an application for a new trial, and

(b)   an application to set aside a verdict, finding or judgment in any cause or matter in the High Court which has been tried, or in which any issue has been tried, by a jury;

"arbitration agreement" has the same meaning as it has in Part I of the Arbitration Act 1996;

"cause" means any action or any criminal proceedings;

"Division", where it appears with a capital letter, means a division of the High Court;

"judgment" includes a decree;

"jurisdiction" includes powers;

"matter" means any proceedings in court not in a cause;

"party", in relation to any proceedings, includes any person who pursuant to or by virtue of rules of court or any other statutory provision has been served with notice of, or has intervened in, those proceedings;

"prescribed" means –

(a)   except in relation to fees, prescribed by rules of court;

(b)   (*repealed*)

"qualifying judge advocate" means –

(a)   the Judge Advocate General; or

(b)   a person appointed under section 30(1)(a) or (b) of the Courts-Martial (Appeals) Act 1951 (assistants to the Judge Advocate General);

"senior judge", where the reference is to the senior judge of a Division, means the president of that Division;

"solicitor" means a solicitor of the Senior Courts;

"statutory provision" means any enactment, whenever passed, or any provision contained in subordinate legislation (as defined in section 21(1) of the Interpretation Act 1978), whenever made;

"this or any other Act" includes an Act passed after this Act.

(2) Section 128 contains definitions of expressions used in Part V and in the other provisions of this Act relating to probate causes and matters.

(3) Any reference in this Act to rules of court under section 84 includes a reference to rules of court in relation to the Supreme Court under any provision of this or any other Act which confers on the Civil Procedure Rule Committee or the Crown Court Rule Committee power to make rules of court.

(4) Except where the context otherwise requires, in this or any other Act –

"divisional court" (with or without capital letters) means a divisional court constituted under section 66;

"judge of the Senior Courts" means –

    (a)   a judge of the Court of Appeal other than an ex-officio judge within paragraph (b) or (c) of section 2(2), or

    (b)   a judge of the High Court,

and accordingly does not include, as such, a judge of the Crown Court;

"official referees' business" has the meaning given by section 68(6);

(5) The provisions of Schedule 4 (construction of references to superseded courts and officers) shall have effect.

Amendments—CLSA 1990, s 125(3), Sch 18, para 41; Arbitration Act 1996, s 107(1), Sch 3, para 37(1), (3); Civil Procedure Act 1997, s 10, Sch 2, para 2(1),(7); Courts Act 2003, s 109(1), (3), Sch 8, para 265, Sch 10; SI 2004/2035; CRA 2005, s 15(1), Sch 4, Pt 1, paras 114, 146, Sch 11, para 26(2); Armed Forces Act 2011, s 26, Sch 2, para 5.

SCHEDULE 1
DISTRIBUTION OF BUSINESS IN HIGH COURT

****

3 Family Division

To the Family Division are assigned –

    (a)   all matrimonial causes and matters (whether at first instance or on appeal);

    (b)   all causes and matters (whether at first instance or on appeal) relating to –

        (i)   legitimacy;

        (ii)   the exercise of the inherent jurisdiction of the High Court with respect to minors, the maintenance of minors and any proceedings under the Children Act 1989, except proceedings solely for the appointment of a guardian of a minor's estate;

        (iii) adoption;

        (iv) non-contentious or common form probate business;

    (c)   applications for consent to the marriage of a minor or for a declaration under section 27B(5) of the Marriage Act 1949;

    (d)   proceedings on appeal under section 13 of the Administration of Justice Act 1960 from an order or decision made under section 63(3) of the Magistrates' Courts Act 1980 to enforce an order of a magistrates' court made in matrimonial proceedings or proceedings under Part IV of the Family Law Act 1996 or with respect to the guardianship of a minor;

    (e)   applications under Part III of the Family Law Act 1986;

    (e)   proceedings under the Children Act 1989;

    (ea) proceedings under section 79 of the Childcare Act 2006;

    (f)   all proceedings under –

        (i)   Part IV or 4A of the Family Law Act 1996;

        (ii)   the Child Abduction and Custody Act 1985;

        (iii) the Family Law Act 1986;

        (iv) section 30 of the Human Fertilisation and Embryology Act 1990;

        (v)   Council Regulation (EC) No 2201/2003 of 27 November 2003 concerning jurisdiction and the recognition and enforcement of judgments in matrimonial matters and matters of parental responsibility, so far as that Regulation relates to jurisdiction, recognition and enforcement in parental responsibility matters;

        (vi) the Convention on Jurisdiction, Applicable Law, Recognition,

PART II

Enforcement and Co-Operation in respect of Parental Responsibility and Measures for the Protection of Children that was signed at The Hague on 19 October 1996;

(fa) all proceedings relating to a debit or credit under section 29(1) or 49(1) of the Welfare Reform and Pensions Act 1999;

(g)   all proceedings for the purpose of enforcing an order made in any proceedings of a type described in this paragraph;

(h)   all proceedings under the Child Support Act 1991.

(i)   all civil partnership causes and matters (whether at first instance or on appeal);

(j)   applications for consent to the formation of a civil partnership by a minor or for a declaration under paragraph 7 of Schedule 1 to the Civil Partnership Act 2004;

(k)   applications under section 58 of that Act (declarations relating to civil partnerships).

Amendments—Marriage (Prohibited Degrees of Relationship) Act 1986, s 5; FLA 1986, s 68(1), Sch 1, para 26; FLRA 1987, s 33(4), Sch 4; CA 1989, ss 92(11), 108(5), Sch 11, para 9, Sch 13, para 45(3); SI 1991/1210; SI 1993/622; FLA 1996, s 66(1), Sch 8, para 51; WRPA 1999, s 84(1), Sch 12, para 1; CPA 2004, s 261(1), Sch 27, para 70; SI 2005/265; Childcare Act 2006, Sch 2, para 3; Forced Marriage (Civil Protection) Act 2007, s 3(1), Sch 2, para 1; SI 2010/1898.

Two sub-paragraphs (e)—A sub-paragraph (e) was inserted by FLA 1986, but the draftsman of the insertion made by CA 1989 seems to have been unaware of it; it is submitted that the words of amendment in CA 1989, Sch 11, para 9 ("In paragraph 3 ... the following sub-paragraph shall be added at the end – (e)") mean that the second (e) has not inadvertently been substituted for the first (e), but merely added after it, so that both paragraphs (e) are fully effective, albeit that they inconveniently have the same name.

Two references to CA 1989—CA 1989 is referred to in both (b)(ii) and (the second) (e). This seems to have been simply a proverbial case of the "left hand and the right hand", as the two references were inserted by different provisions of CA 1989 (Sch 13, para 45 and Sch 11, para 9, respectively). The result is overkill but nothing more; although (b)(ii) more obviously includes appeals from proceedings under the Act, it would seem that the effect of each reference is identical.

****

Social Security Administration Act 1992

ARRANGEMENT OF SECTIONS

****

78 Recovery of social fund awards

(1)–(5) ...

(6) For the purposes of this section –

(a)   a man shall be liable to maintain his wife or civil partner and any children of whom he is the father;

(b) a woman shall be liable to maintain her husband or civil partner and any children of whom she is the mother;

(c) a person shall be liable to maintain another person throughout any period in respect of which the first-mentioned person has, on or after 23 May 1980 (the date of the passing of the Social Security Act 1980) and either alone or jointly with a further person, given an undertaking in writing in pursuance of immigration rules within the meaning of the Immigration Act 1971 to be responsible for the maintenance and accommodation of the other person; and

(d) "child" includes a person who has attained the age of 16 but not the age of 19 and in respect of whom either parent, or some person acting in the place of either parent, is receiving universal credit, income support or an income-based jobseeker's allowance.

(7) Any reference in subsection (6) above to children of whom the man or the woman is the father or the mother shall be construed in accordance with section 1 of the Family Law Reform Act 1987.

(8) Subsection (7) above does not apply in Scotland, and in the applications of subsection (6) above to Scotland any reference to children of whom the man or the woman is the father or the mother shall be construed as a reference to any such children whether or not their parents have ever been married to one another.

(9) A document bearing a certificate which –

(a) is signed by a person authorised in that behalf by the Secretary of State; and

(b) states that the document apart from the certificate is, or is a copy of, such an undertaking as is mentioned in subsection (6)(c) above,

shall be conclusive of the undertaking in question for the purposes of this section; and a certificate purporting to be so signed shall be deemed to be so signed until the contrary is proved.

Amendments—Jobseekers Act 1995, s 41, Sch 2, para 51; CPA 2004, s 254(1), Sch 24, para 61(1)–(4); WRA 2012, s 31, Sch 2, para 9.

****

106 Recovery of expenditure on benefit from person liable for maintenance

(1) Subject to the following provisions of this section, if income support is claimed by or in respect of a person whom another person is liable to maintain or paid to or in respect of such a person, the Secretary of State may make a complaint against the liable person to a magistrates' court for an order under this section.

(2) On the hearing of a complaint under this section the court shall have regard to all the circumstances and, in particular, to the income of the liable person, and may order him to pay such sum, weekly or otherwise, as it may consider appropriate, except that in a case falling within section 78(6)(c) above that sum shall not include any amount which is not attributable to income support (whether paid before or after the making of the order).

(3) In determining whether to order any payments to be made in respect of income support for any period before the complaint was made, or the amount of any such payments, the court shall disregard any amount by which the liable person's income exceeds the income which was his during that period.

(4) Any payments ordered to be made under this section shall be made –

(a) to the Secretary of State in so far as they are attributable to any income support (whether paid before or after the making of the order);

(b) to the person claiming income support or (if different) the dependant; or

    (c)   to such other person as appears to the court expedient in the interests of the dependant.

(5) As order under this section shall be enforceable as a magistrates' court maintenance order within the meaning of section 150(1) of the Magistrates' Courts Act 1980.

(6) In the application of this section to Scotland, subsection (5) above shall be omitted and for the references to a complaint and to a magistrates' court there shall be substituted respectively references to an application and to the sheriff.

(7) (*repealed*)

Amendments—CMOPA 2008, s 58, Sch 8.

Defined terms—"child", "liable to maintain": s 78(6).

107 (*repealed*)

108 Reduction of expenditure on income support: certain maintenance orders to be enforceable by the Secretary of State

(1) This section applies where –

    (a)   a person ("the claimant") who is the parent of one or more children is in receipt of income support either in respect of those children or in respect of both himself and those children; and

    (b)   there is in force a maintenance order made against the other parent ("the liable person") –

        (i)   in favour of the claimant or one or more of the children, or

        (ii)   in favour of some other person for the benefit of the claimant or one or more of the children;

and in this section "the primary recipient" means the person in whose favour that maintenance order was made.

(2) If, in a case where this section applies, the liable person fails to comply with any of the terms of the maintenance order –

    (a)   the Secretary of State may bring any proceedings or take any other steps to enforce the order that could have been brought or taken by or on behalf of the primary recipient; and

    (b)   any court before which proceedings are brought by the Secretary of State by virtue of paragraph (a) above shall have the same powers in connection with those proceedings as it would have had if they had been brought by the primary recipient.

(3) The Secretary of State's powers under this section are exercisable at his discretion and whether or not the primary recipient or any other person consents to their exercise; but any sums recovered by virtue of this section shall be payable to or for the primary recipient, as if the proceedings or steps in question had been brought or taken by him or on his behalf.

(4) The powers conferred on the Secretary of State by subsection (2)(a) above include power –

    (a)   to apply for the registration of the maintenance order under –

        (i)   section 17 of the Maintenance Orders Act 1950;

        (ii)   section 2 of the Maintenance Orders Act 1958; or

        (iii) the Civil Jurisdiction and Judgments Act 1982;

    (aa) to apply for recognition and enforcement of the maintenance order under the Maintenance Regulation, to the extent permitted by Article 64 of that Regulation; and

(b) to make an application under section 2 of the Maintenance Orders (Reciprocal Enforcement) Act 1972 (application for enforcement in reciprocating country).

(5) Where this section applies, the prescribed person shall in prescribed circumstances give the Secretary of State notice of any application –

(a) to alter, vary, suspend, discharge, revoke, revive or enforce the maintenance order in question; or

(b) to remit arrears under that maintenance order;

and the Secretary of State shall be entitled to appear and be heard on the application.

(6) Where, by virtue of this section, the Secretary of State commences any proceedings to enforce a maintenance order, he shall, in relation to those proceedings, be treated for the purposes of any enactment or instrument relating to maintenance orders as if he were a person entitled to payment under the maintenance order in question (but shall not thereby become entitled to any such payment).

(7) Where, in any proceedings under this section in England and Wales, the court makes an order for the whole or any part of the arrears due under the maintenance order in question to be paid as a lump sum, the Secretary of State shall inform the Lord Chancellor of the amount of that lump sum if he knows –

(a) that the primary recipient either –

(i) received legal aid under the Legal Aid Act 1974 in connection with the proceedings in which the maintenance order was made, or

(ii) was an assisted party, within the meaning of the Legal Aid Act 1988, in those proceedings, or

(iii) received services funded by the Legal Services Commission as part of the Community Legal Service; or

(iv) was provided with civil legal services (within the meaning of Part 1 of the Legal Aid, Sentencing and Punishment of Offenders Act 2012) under arrangements made for the purposes of that Part of that Act; and

(b) that a sum remains unpaid on account of the contribution required of the primary recipient –

(i) under section 9 of the Legal Aid Act 1974 in respect of those proceedings, or

(ii) under section 16 of the Legal Aid Act 1988 in respect of the costs of his being represented under Part IV of that Act in those proceedings, or

(iii) by virtue of section 10 of the Access to Justice Act 1999 in respect of services funded by the Legal Services Commission as part of the Community Legal Service, or

(iv) under regulations under section 23 or 24 of the Legal Aid, Sentencing and Punishment of Offenders Act 2012 in respect of civil legal services (within the meaning of Part 1 of that Act) provided under arrangements made for the purposes of that Part of that Act,

as the case may be.

(8) In this section "maintenance order" –

(a) in England and Wales, means –

(i) any order for the making of periodical payments which is, or has at any time been, a maintenance order within the meaning of the Attachment of Earnings Act 1971;

(ii) any order under Part 3 of the Matrimonial and Family Proceedings Act 1984 (overseas divorce) for the making of periodical payments;

(iii) any order under Schedule 7 to the Civil Partnership Act 2004 for the making of periodical payments;

(b) in Scotland, means any order, except an order for the payment of a lump sum, falling within the definition of "maintenance order" in section 106 of the Debtors (Scotland) Act 1987, but disregarding paragraph (h) (alimentary bond or agreement).

(9) In this section "the Maintenance Regulation" means Council Regulation (EC) No 4/2009 including as applied in relation to Denmark by virtue of the Agreement made on 19 October 2005 between the European Community and the Kingdom of Denmark.

Amendments—AJA 1999, s 24, Sch 4, para 48; SI 2001/3929, SI 2007/1655; CMOPA 2008, s 57(1), Sch 7, para 2(1); SI 2011/1484; LASPOA 2012, s 39, Sch 5, para 41.

Defined terms—"claimant": s 191.

****

116 Legal proceedings

(1) Any person authorised by the Secretary of State in that behalf may conduct any proceedings under any provision of this Act other than section 114 or under any provision of the Jobseekers Act 1995 before a magistrates' court although not a barrister or solicitor.

(2)–(7) …

Amendments—Jobseekers Act 1995, s 41, Sch 2, para 56; Social Security Contributions (Transfer of Functions, etc) Act 1999, s 1(1), Sch 1, para 21.

"authorised by the Secretary of State" (s 116(1))—An officer may prove his authority to conduct proceedings by producing a certified copy of the original authority. The Documentary Evidence Act 1868 is applied by Secretary of State for Social Services Order 1968, art 5(3).

****

191 Interpretation – general

In this Act, unless the context otherwise requires –

    …

    "claim" is to be construed in accordance with "claimant";
    "claimant" (in relation to contributions under Part I and to benefit under Parts II to IV of the Contributions and Benefits Act) means –
        (a) a person whose right to be excepted from liability to pay, or to have his liability deferred for, or to be credited with, a contribution, is in question;
        (b) a person who has claimed benefit;
    and includes, in relation to an award or decision a beneficiary under the award or affected by the decision;
    "claimant" (in relation to industrial injuries benefit) means a person who has claimed such a benefit and includes –
        (a) an applicant for a declaration under section 44 above that an accident was or was not an industrial accident; and
        (b) in relation to an award or decision, a beneficiary under the award or affected by the decision;

    …

****

Summary Jurisdiction (Process) Act 1881
****

4 Service of process of English court in Scotland and of Scotch court in England

Subject to the provisions of this Act, any process issued under the Summary Jurisdiction Acts may, if issued by a court of summary jurisdiction in England and endorsed by a court of summary jurisdiction in Scotland, or issued by a court of summary jurisdiction in Scotland and endorsed by a court of summary jurisdiction in England, be served and executed within the jurisdiction of the endorsing court in like manner as it may be served and executed in the jurisdiction of the issuing court, and that by an officer either of the issuing or of the endorsing court.

For the purposes of this Act –

(1) Any process may be issued and endorsed under the hand of any such person as is declared by this Act to be a court of summary jurisdiction, and may be endorsed upon proof alone of the handwriting of the person issuing it, and such proof may be either on oath or by such solemn declaration as is mentioned in section forty-one of the Summary Jurisdiction Act 1879, or by any like declaration taken in Scotland before a sheriff, justice of the peace, or other magistrate having the authority of a justice of the peace. Such indorsement may be in the form contained in the schedule to this Act annexed, or in a form to the like effect:

(2) Where any process requiring the appearance of a person to answer any information or complaint has been served in pursuance of this section, the court, before issuing a warrant for the apprehension of such person for failure so to appear, shall be satisfied on oath that there is sufficient prima facie evidence in support of such information or complaint:

(3) If the process is to procure the attendance of a witness, the court issuing the process shall be satisfied on oath of the probability that the evidence of such witness will be material, and that the witness will not appear voluntarily without such process, and the witness shall not be subject to any liability for not obeying the process, unless a reasonable amount for his expenses has been paid or tendered to him:

(4) This Act shall not apply to any process requiring the appearance of a person to answer a complaint if issued by an English court of summary jurisdiction for the recovery of a sum of money which is a civil debt within the meaning of the Summary Jurisdiction Act 1879, or if issued by a Scotch court in a case which falls within the definition of "civil jurisdiction" contained in the Summary Procedure Act 1864.

Scope—This section makes provision for reciprocal service of process in England and Scotland. Service of process in relation to maintenance orders is excluded (as separate provision is made by MOA 1950, s 15). The Act does, however, have application to process for non-molestation orders and occupation orders (FLA 1996, Pt IV) and enforcement of non-monetary orders (MCA 1980, s 63).

"form contained in the schedule to this Act" (s 4(1))—A revised form of the indorsement set out in the Schedule (not reproduced here) is as follows:

Proof by solemn declaration or oath having been produced before me that the name of [*name*] subscribed to this summons (or warrant or order etc) is of the handwriting of the justice of the peace (or sheriff) mentioned in it,
I authorise [   ] to effect the service or execution of it within the county of [   ].
Dated [   ]
[*Signature of Justice of the Peace*]
Justice of the Peace
for [   ]

5 Provision as to execution of process

Where a person is apprehended under any process executed in pursuance of this Act, such person shall be forthwith taken to some place within the jurisdiction of the court issuing the process, and be there dealt with as if he had been there apprehended.

A warrant of distress issued in England when endorsed in pursuance of this Act shall be executed in Scotland as if it were a Scotch warrant of poinding and sale, and a Scotch warrant of poinding and sale when endorsed in pursuance of this Act shall be executed in England as if it were an English warrant of distress, and the enactments relating to the said warrants respectively shall apply accordingly, except that any account of the costs and charges in connexion with the execution, or of the money levied thereby or otherwise relating to the execution, shall be made, and any money raised by the execution shall be dealt with in like manner as if the warrant had been executed within the jurisdiction of the court issuing the warrant.

Defined terms—"process": s 8.

****

7 Saving

This Act shall be in addition to and not in derogation of any power existing under any other Act relating to the execution of any warrant or other process in England and Scotland respectively.

8 Definitions

In this Act, unless the context otherwise requires, – The expression "process" includes any summons or warrant of citation to appear either to answer any information or complaint, or as a witness; also any warrant of commitment, any warrant of imprisonment, any warrant of distress, any warrant of poinding and sale, also any order or minute of a court of summary jurisdiction or copy of such order or minute, also an extract decree, and any other document or process, other than a warrant of arrestment, required for any purpose connected with a court of summary jurisdiction to be served or executed.

The expression "sheriff" shall include sheriff substitute.

The expression "court of summary jurisdiction" means any justice of the peace, also any officer or other magistrate having the authority in England or Scotland of a justice of the peace, also in Scotland the sheriff.

The expression "officer of a court of summary jurisdiction" means the constable, officer, or person to whom any process issued by the court is directed, or who is by law required or authorised to serve or execute any process issued by the court.

Amendments—Statute Law Revision Act 1894.

****

Surrogacy Arrangements Act 1985

1 Meaning of "surrogate mother", "surrogacy arrangement" and other terms

(1) The following provisions shall have effect for the interpretation of this Act.

(2) "Surrogate mother" means a woman who carries a child in pursuance of an arrangement –

    (a)   made before she began to carry the child, and

    (b)   made with a view to any child carried in pursuance of it being handed over to, and parental responsibility being met (so far as practicable) by, another person or other persons.

(3) An arrangement is a surrogacy arrangement if, were a woman to whom the arrangement relates to carry a child in pursuance of it, she would be a surrogate mother.

(4) In determining whether an arrangement is made with such a view as is mentioned in subsection (2) above regard may be had to the circumstances as a whole (and, in particular, where there is a promise or understanding that any payment will or may be made to the woman or for her benefit in respect of the carrying of any child in pursuance of the arrangement, to that promise or understanding).

(5) An arrangement may be regarded as made with such a view though subject to conditions relating to the handing over of any child.

(6) A woman who carries a child is to be treated for the purposes of subsection (2)(a) above as beginning to carry it at the time of the insemination or of the placing in her of an embryo, of an egg in the process of fertilisation or of sperm and eggs as the case may be, that results in her carrying the child.

(7) "Body of persons" means a body of persons corporate or unincorporate.

(7A) "Non-profit making body" means a body of persons whose activities are not carried on for profit.

(8) "Payment" means payment in money or money's worth.

(9) This Act applies to arrangements whether or not they are lawful.

Amendments—CA 1989, s 108(5), Sch 13, para 56; HFEA 1990, s 36; SI 1995/755; HFEA 2008, s 59(2).

1A Surrogacy arrangements unenforceable

No surrogacy arrangement is enforceable by or against any of the persons making it.

Amendments—Inserted by HFEA 1990, s 36.

Surrogacy arrangements unenforceable—See *Re TT (Surrogacy)* [2011] 2 FLR 392 where the surrogate mother who had agreed to hand over the child to the couple changed her mind during the pregnancy and refused to hand over the child. On the application of the father for a residence order of the child the court granted the order to the mother. See also the commentary under HFEA 2008.

2 Negotiating surrogacy arrangements on a commercial basis etc

(1) No person shall on a commercial basis do any of the following acts in the United Kingdom, that is –

    (a)   initiate any negotiations with a view to the making of a surrogacy arrangement,

    (aa) take part in any negotiations with a view to the making of a surrogacy arrangement,

    (b)   offer or agree to negotiate the making of a surrogacy arrangement, or

    (c)   compile any information with a view to its use in making, or negotiating the making of, surrogacy arrangements;

and no person shall in the United Kingdom knowingly cause another to do any of those acts on a commercial basis.

(2) A person who contravenes subsection (1) above is guilty of an offence; but it is not a contravention of that subsection –

(a) for a woman, with a view to becoming a surrogate mother herself, to do any act mentioned in that subsection or to cause such an act to be done, or

(b) for any person, with a view to a surrogate mother carrying a child for him, to do such an act or to cause such an act to be done.

(2A) A non-profit making body does not contravene subsection (1) merely because –

(a) the body does an act falling within subsection (1)(a) or (c) in respect of which any reasonable payment is at any time received by it or another, or

(b) it does an act falling within subsection (1)(a) or (c) with a view to any reasonable payment being received by it or another in respect of facilitating the making of any surrogacy arrangement.

(2B) A person who knowingly causes a non-profit making body to do an act falling within subsection (1)(a) or (c) does not contravene subsection (1) merely because –

(a) any reasonable payment is at any time received by the body or another in respect of the body doing the act, or

(b) the body does the act with a view to any reasonable payment being received by it or another person in respect of the body facilitating the making of any surrogacy arrangement.

(2C) Any reference in subsection (2A) or (2B) to a reasonable payment in respect of the doing of an act by a non-profit making body is a reference to a payment not exceeding the body's costs reasonably attributable to the doing of the act.

(3) For the purposes of this section, a person does an act on a commercial basis (subject to subsection (4) below) if –

(a) any payment is at any time received by himself or another in respect of it, or

(b) he does it with a view to any payment being received by himself or another in respect of making, or negotiating or facilitating the making of, any surrogacy arrangement.

In this subsection "payment" does not include payment to or for the benefit of a surrogate mother or prospective surrogate mother.

(4) In proceedings against a person for an offence under subsection (1) above, he is not to be treated as doing an act on a commercial basis by reason of any payment received by another in respect of the act if it is proved that –

(a) in a case where the payment was received before he did the act, he did not do the act knowing or having reasonable cause to suspect that any payment had been received in respect of the act; and

(b) in any other case, he did not do the act with a view to any payment being received in respect of it.

(5) Where –

(a) a person acting on behalf of a body of persons takes any part in negotiating or facilitating the making of a surrogacy arrangement in the United Kingdom, and

(b) negotiating or facilitating the making of surrogacy arrangements is an activity of the body,

then, if the body at any time receives any payment made by or on behalf of –

(i) a woman who carries a child in pursuance of the arrangement,

(ii) the person or persons for whom she carries it, or

(iii) any person connected with the woman or with that person or those persons, the body is guilty of an offence.

For the purposes of this subsection, a payment received by a person connected with a body is to be treated as received by the body.

(5A) A non-profit making body is not guilty of an offence under subsection (5), in respect of the receipt of any payment described in that subsection, merely because a person acting on behalf of the body takes part in facilitating the making of a surrogacy arrangement.

(6) In proceedings against a body for an offence under subsection (5) above, it is a defence to prove that the payment concerned was not made in respect of the arrangement mentioned in paragraph (a) of that subsection.

(7) A person who in the United Kingdom takes part in the management or control –

    (a)   of any body of persons, or

    (b)   of any of the activities of any body of persons,

is guilty of an offence if the activity described in subsection (8) below is an activity of the body concerned.

(8) The activity referred to in subsection (7) above is negotiating or facilitating the making of surrogacy arrangements in the United Kingdom, being –

    (a)   arrangements the making of which is negotiated or facilitated on a commercial basis, or

    (b)   arrangements in the case of which payments are received (or treated for the purposes of subsection (5) above as received) by the body concerned in contravention of subsection (5) above.

(8A) A person is not guilty of an offence under subsection (7) if –

    (a)   the body of persons referred to in that subsection is a non-profit making body, and

    (b)   the only activity of that body which falls within subsection (8) is facilitating the making of surrogacy arrangements in the United Kingdom.

(8B) In subsection (8A)(b) "facilitating the making of surrogacy arrangements" is to be construed in accordance with subsection (8).

(9) In proceedings against a person for an offence under subsection (7) above, it is a defence to prove that he neither knew nor had reasonable cause to suspect that the activity described in subsection (8) above was an activity of the body concerned; and for the purposes of such proceedings any arrangement falling within subsection (8)(b) above shall be disregarded if it is proved that the payment concerned was not made in respect of the arrangement.

Amendments—HFEA 2008, ss 59(3)–(8).

3 Advertisements about surrogacy

(1) This section applies to any advertisement containing an indication (however expressed) –

    (a)   that any person is or may be willing to enter into a surrogacy arrangement or to negotiate or facilitate the making of a surrogacy arrangement, or

    (b)   that any person is looking for a woman willing to become a surrogate mother or for persons wanting a woman to carry a child as a surrogate mother.

(1A) This section does not apply to any advertisement placed by, or on behalf of, a non-profit making body if the advertisement relates only to the doing by the body of acts that would not contravene section 2(1) even if done on a commercial basis (within the meaning of section 2).

(2) Where a newspaper or periodical containing an advertisement to which this section applies is published in the United Kingdom, any proprietor, editor or publisher of the newspaper or periodical is guilty of an offence.

(3) Where an advertisement to which this section applies is conveyed by means of an electronic communications network so as to be seen or heard (or both) in the United Kingdom, any person who in the United Kingdom causes it to be so conveyed knowing it to contain such an indication as is mentioned in subsection (1) above is guilty of an offence.

(4) A person who publishes or causes to be published in the United Kingdom an advertisement to which this section applies (not being an advertisement contained in a newspaper or periodical or conveyed by means of an electronic communications network) is guilty of an offence.

(5) A person who distributes or causes to be distributed in the United Kingdom an advertisement to which this section applies (not being an advertisement contained in a newspaper or periodical published outside the United Kingdom or an advertisement conveyed by means of an electronic communications network) knowing it to contain such an indication as is mentioned in subsection (1) above is guilty of an offence.

(6) *(repealed)*

Amendments—Communications Act 2003, s 406, Schs 17, 19; HFEA 2008, s 59(7).

4 Offences

(1) A person guilty of an offence under this Act shall be liable on summary conviction –

- (a) in the case of an offence under section 2 to a fine not exceeding level 5 on the standard scale or to imprisonment for a term not exceeding 3 months or both,
- (b) in the case of an offence under section 3 to a fine not exceeding level 5 on the standard scale.

(2) No proceedings for an offence under this Act shall be instituted –

- (a) in England and Wales, except by or with the consent of the Director of Public Prosecutions; and
- (b) in Northern Ireland, except by or with the consent of the Director of Public Prosecutions for Northern Ireland.

(3) Where an offence under this Act committed by a body corporate is proved to have been committed with the consent or connivance of, or to be attributable to any neglect on the part of, any director, manager, secretary or other similar officer of the body corporate or any person who was purporting to act in any such capacity, he as well as the body corporate is guilty of the offence and is liable to be proceeded against and punished accordingly.

(4) Where the affairs of a body corporate are managed by its members, subsection (3) above shall apply in relation to the acts and defaults of a member in connection with his functions of management as if he were a director of the body corporate.

(5) In any proceedings for an offence under section 2 of this Act, proof of things done or of words written, spoken or published (whether or not in the presence of any party to the proceedings) by any person taking part in the management or control of a body of persons or of any of the activities of the body, or by any person doing any of the acts mentioned in subsection (1)(a) to (c) of that section on behalf of the body, shall be admissible as evidence of the activities of the body.

(6) In relation to an offence under this Act, section 127(1) of the Magistrates' Courts Act 1980 (information must be laid within six months of commission of offence), section 136(1) of the Criminal Procedure (Scotland) Act 1995 (proceedings must be commenced within that time) and Article 19(1) of the Magistrates' Courts (Northern Ireland) Order 1981 (complaint must be made within that time) shall have effect as if for the reference to six months there were substituted a reference to two years.

Amendments—Statute Law (Repeals) Act 1993; Criminal Procedure (Consequential Provisions) (Scotland) Act 1995, ss 4, 5, Sch 4, para 57.

****

Trusts of Land and Appointment of Trustees Act 1996

****

Right of beneficiaries to occupy trust land

12 The right to occupy

(1) A beneficiary who is beneficially entitled to an interest in possession in land subject to a trust of land is entitled by reason of his interest to occupy the land at any time if at that time –

    (a)   the purposes of the trust include making the land available for his occupation (or for the occupation of beneficiaries of a class of which he is a member or of beneficiaries in general), or

    (b)   the land is held by the trustees so as to be so available.

(2) Subsection (1) does not confer on a beneficiary a right to occupy land if it is either unavailable or unsuitable for occupation by him.

(3) This section is subject to section 13.

Scope—This section defines entitlement to occupy land as arising when a beneficiary is entitled to an interest in possession, and the purpose of the trust is to make the land available for his occupation. The right to occupy enjoyed by a spouse is not passed to her son, who was not a beneficiary under s 12, and therefore not entitled to protection under s 13 (*Omotajo v Omotajo* [2008] All ER (D) 156 (Oct)).

13 Exclusion and restriction of right to occupy

(1) Where two or more beneficiaries are (or apart from this subsection would be) entitled under section 12 to occupy land, the trustees of land may exclude or restrict the entitlement of any one or more (but not all) of them.

(2) Trustees may not under subsection (1) –

    (a)   unreasonably exclude any beneficiary's entitlement to occupy land, or

    (b)   restrict any such entitlement to an unreasonable extent.

(3) The trustees of land may from time to time impose reasonable conditions on any beneficiary in relation to his occupation of land by reason of his entitlement under section 12.

(4) The matters to which trustees are to have regard in exercising the powers conferred by this section include –

    (a)   the intentions of the person or persons (if any) who created the trust,

    (b)   the purposes for which the land is held, and

(c)   the circumstances and wishes of each of the beneficiaries who is (or apart from any previous exercise by the trustees of those powers would be) entitled to occupy the land under section 12.

(5) The conditions which may be imposed on a beneficiary under subsection (3) include, in particular, conditions requiring him –

(a)   to pay any outgoings or expenses in respect of the land, or
(b)   to assume any other obligation in relation to the land or to any activity which is or is proposed to be conducted there.

(6) Where the entitlement of any beneficiary to occupy land under section 12 has been excluded or restricted, the conditions which may be imposed on any other beneficiary under subsection (3) include, in particular, conditions requiring him to –

(a)   make payments by way of compensation to the beneficiary whose entitlement has been excluded or restricted, or
(b)   forgo any payment or other benefit to which he would otherwise be entitled under the trust so as to benefit that beneficiary.

(7) The powers conferred on trustees by this section may not be exercised –

(a)   so as to prevent any person who is in occupation of land (whether or not by reason of an entitlement under section 12) from continuing to occupy the land, or
(b)   in a manner likely to result in any such person ceasing to occupy the land,

unless he consents or the court has given approval.

(8) The matters to which the court is to have regard in determining whether to give approval under subsection (7) include the matters mentioned in subsection (4)(a) to (c).

Scope—This section provides that, where beneficiaries are entitled under s 12 to occupy land, the trustees of land may exclude a beneficiary's entitlement to occupy, provided they act reasonably. The trustees can impose conditions (including apportioning occupation – *Rodway v Landy* [2001] Ch 703) and can compensate the beneficiary who has been excluded. A checklist of factors to be taken into account is set out; and the trustees cannot exclude without the person's consent or the court's approval.

Powers of court

14 Applications for order

(1) Any person who is a trustee of land or has an interest in property subject to a trust of land may make an application to the court for an order under this section.

(2) On an application for an order under this section the court may make any such order –

(a)   relating to the exercise by the trustees of any of their functions (including an order relieving them of any obligation to obtain the consent of, or to consult, any person in connection with the exercise of any of their functions), or
(b)   declaring the nature or extent of a person's interest in property subject to the trust,

as the court thinks fit.

(3) The court may not under this section make any order as to the appointment or removal of trustees.

(4) The powers conferred on the court by this section are exercisable on an application whether it is made before or after the commencement of this Act.

Provision—An application under TLATA 1996 is for a civil remedy and is therefore not governed by FPR 2010. CPR 1998 apply. See Procedural Guide A5.

Scope—Any trustee, or anyone who has an interest in property subject to a trust of land (which, by virtue of s 17(2), includes a beneficiary in the proceeds of sale of land), may apply for an order relating to the exercise by the trustees of any of their functions (including the power to exclude or the power of sale) or may apply for an order declaring the nature or extent of a person's interest in the trust of land. The court's powers under this section are wide, but do not encompass the appointment or removal of trustees, which is provided for in ss 19–21. Commonly, applications are made by cohabitees, family members, trustees in bankruptcy and creditors with a charge secured on the property. Applications by a married party against a spouse are disapproved of. In principle, property issues between divorcing spouses should be resolved under MCA 1973: *Miller-Smith v Miller-Smith* [2010] 1 FLR 1402, CA. This is the case even where divorce proceedings are in a foreign jurisdiction: *Prazic v Prazic* [2006] 2 FLR 1128.

15 Matters relevant in determining applications

(1) The matters to which the court is to have regard in determining an application for an order under section 14 include –

- (a) the intentions of the person or persons (if any) who created the trust,
- (b) the purposes for which the property subject to the trust is held,
- (c) the welfare of any minor who occupies or might reasonably be expected to occupy any land subject to the trust as his home, and
- (d) the interests of any secured creditor of any beneficiary.

(2) In the case of an application relating to the exercise in relation to any land of the powers conferred on the trustees by section 13, the matters to which the court is to have regard also include the circumstances and wishes of each of the beneficiaries who is (or apart from any previous exercise by the trustees of those powers would be) entitled to occupy the land under section 12.

(3) In the case of any other application, other than one relating to the exercise of the power mentioned in section 6(2), the matters to which the court is to have regard also include the circumstances and wishes of any beneficiaries of full age and entitled to an interest in possession in property subject to the trust or (in case of dispute) of the majority (according to the value of their combined interests).

(4) This section does not apply to an application if section 335A of the Insolvency Act 1986 (which is inserted by Schedule 3 and relates to applications by a trustee of a bankrupt) applies to it.

Scope—This section sets out the criteria to be applied under s 14. The four factors to which the court is to have regard include the intentions of the person who created the trust, the purposes for which the property subject to the trust is held, the welfare of any minor who occupies or may be expected to occupy the property as his home and the interests of any secured creditor of any beneficiary. The use of the word "include" demonstrates that the four factors listed in s 15(1) are not inclusive. The welfare of any children is established as a relevant criterion, but no factor is overriding. This section is expressly excluded from consideration by the court in applications by trustees in bankruptcy under Insolvency Act 1986, s 335A.

Relationship with MCA 1973—In principle, property disputes between spouses are better dealt with under MCA 1973: *Miller-Smith v Miller-Smith* [2010] 1 FLR 1402, CA, which considers the guidelines to be considered in applications under TLATA between spouses. Where a party delays a divorce by defending it, a spouse who is bearing the running costs of the former matrimonial home may use TLATA to achieve an order for vacant possession under s 13, or an order for sale under s 14. Section 15(1) and (2) will be considered and where the joint intention to provide a home for the joint occupation of the spouses is no longer being achieved, orders under s 13 and s 14 may be made. Contrast *Wicks v Wicks* [1998] 1 FLR 470 (CA): no statutory power under MCA 1973 to seek interim orders in relation to capital or property.

Application by cohabitees or family members—Former cohabitees may apply under s 14 to enforce a sale of property against the ex-partner. This jurisdiction is separate from but parallel to s 15 and Schedule 1 of CA 1989, where there is jurisdiction to transfer or settle property, but no power to order a sale.

Where a property has been acquired as an enterprise among family members or friends, an application may also be made under TLATA 1996. Typically, an application by a wife in respect of a property in the hands of the husband's family may be made alongside an application for financial ancillary relief under

MCA 1973. It is usual to join the interested family members as defendants, and for the Trusts of Land and matrimonial applications to be heard together, the decision in the Trusts application governing the size of the pot available for distribution between the spouses.

Determination of applications under s 14 involves a two-stage process: first it is necessary to determine whether the parties expressly or by inference intended to share the beneficial ownership. If so, then it is necessary to determine the nature and extent of the parties' beneficial interests.

Principles of land law apply—An express declaration of trust is conclusive, and a defendant may not go behind it, in the absence of fraud or mistake (*Clarke v Harlow* [2007] 1 FLR 1). In the absence of an express declaration, the various routes to be followed in establishing an entitlement to property are those familiar to practitioners of land law:

(i) proprietary estoppel, where a representation by the owner must relate to a specific property or part of a property, which must be objectively ascertainable, and in reliance the claimant was induced to act to their detriment (*Lissimore v Downing* [2003] 2 FLR 308; *Van Laethem v Brooker and Caradoc Estates Ltd* [2006] 2 FLR 495);

(ii) resulting trust, through direct or indirect contributions to the property; and

(iii) constructive trust at the time of purchase, or where parties formed a common intention that an incoming cohabitee would have a beneficial share in the property owned by the other.

Living together, a common business enterprise contributed to by the claimant and promises of future benefit were insufficiently specific to found an estoppel or a constructive trust (*James v Thomas* [2008] 1 FLR 1598 (CA); *Morris v Morris* [2008] EWCA Civ 257; *Abbot v Abbott* [2008] 1 FLR 1451), the Privy Council applying the principle of the constructive trust to a matrimonial case. In *Walsh v Singh* [2010] 1 FLR 1658, a claim for a beneficial interest failed where there was no financial contribution made, no representation that the claimant would have a share in the property, and no common intention giving rise to constructive trust or estoppel. For an overview of s 15 factors, see *Oxley v Hiscock* [2004] 2 FLR 669, CA. See *Q v Q* [2009] 1 FLR 935 for an explanation of the law relating to proprietary estoppel and constructive trusts, and the relationship between the doctrines. The leading case is *Stack v Dowden* [2007] 1 FLR 1858, HL, see below. Courts must apply strict legal principles and ignore "fairness". A claimant must show that it was jointly intended that she should have a share. A common intention that the man provide a home for the woman and children is not sufficient to establish the common intention that she should also have a share in the property: *Thomson v Humphrey* [2010] 2 FLR 107, Ch.

Registration in joint names—Where a property has been transferred into joint names after April 1998, the nature and extent of the beneficial interests should be determined by Form TR1, which provides for an express declaration of the beneficial interest.

Where the transfer of property into joint names was completed before 1 April 1998, in circumstances where Form TR1 does not expressly declare the beneficial interests, there is a presumption in the case of domestic property that the beneficial interests are also held equally, until the contrary is proved on trust principles. In *Stack v Dowden* [2007] 1 FLR 1858 (HL) a couple had cohabited over 27 years and raised four children together, latterly in jointly owned property. The woman had made the greater capital contribution and had the higher earnings and established the beneficial entitlement of two thirds. However, "cases in which the joint legal owners are to be taken to have intended their beneficial interest should be different from their legal interest will be very unusual" (and see *Fowler v Barron* [2008] 2 FLR 831).The starting point where there is joint legal ownership is that there is joint beneficial ownership. The burden is on the party who wishes to show other than joint beneficial ownership. Baroness Hale identified a non-exhaustive list of factors, as evidence of the parties' intentions: including the reason the home was acquired, the nature of the relationship, how the purchase was financed initially and subsequently, and how the parties arranged their finances and discharged their outgoings. The Supreme Court has given further guidance in *Jones v Kernott* [2012] 1 FLR 45. A family home was bought and registered in the joint names of the parties, paid for jointly and occupied by them and their two children for 8 years. Upon the relationship ending, they tried unsuccessfully to sell the property. An insurance policy was then divided equally and the man went on to buy his own property. He made no further contribution to the family home, which was thereafter solely funded by the woman. The Supreme Court has established the guiding principle that where a family home is in joint names of a cohabiting couple and both are responsible for the mortgage, without any express declaration as to beneficial interests (i) they are joint tenants in law and equity; (ii) the presumption may be displaced by a different common intention expressed when the home is purchased, or at a later stage; (iii) otherwise, a common intention may be deduced objectively from their conduct, as in *Gissing v Gissing* [1971] 1 AC 886 at [906] and *Stack v Dowden* at [69]; (iv) where there is no evidence as to their joint intentions at the outset, or that intention has changed but it is not possible to determine the new intention, each is entitled to such share as the court considers fair, having regard to the whole course of their dealings with the property: *Oxley v Hiscock* [2004] 2 FLR 669 at [69] followed; and (v) each case turns on its facts. In

Jones v Kernott, the Supreme Court determined that fairness involved an equal division between the parties of the value of the property at the conclusion of the relationship, the woman additionally retaining the value that had accrued since that date. This principle does not apply to commercial property, see *Laskar v Laskar* [2008] 2 FLR 589, CA, where shares of a rental property held by mother and daughter were defined as two-thirds: one-third because this was their respective financial contributions.

Registration in a sole name—Where a property is registered in the name of one party, but is occupied by both of them, each party may have made a financial contribution to purchase costs, mortgage costs and household bills, but there may be no express declaration of trust. The determining principles were set out by the HL in *Lloyds Bank plc v Rosset* [1990] 2 FLR 155, subsequently applied by the Court of Appeal in *Oxley v Hiscock* [2004] 2 FLR 669 and *Parris v Williams* [2009] BPIR 96. The principles where the family home is in the name of one party only has been considered in *Jones v Kernott* [2012] 1 FLR 45, at [52]. The starting point is different from joint names cases: (i) is it intended that the other party has any beneficial interest at all, as there is no co-ownership; (ii) a common intention may be deduced objectively from their conduct. If on the evidence there is a common intention to share, but not of what shares were intended, the court will have to proceed as in (iv) and (v) above. The imputations of particular intentions by way of a resulting trust are not appropriate to the ascertainment of beneficial interests in a family home. An intention to purchase in joint names, not acted upon because of financial advice, does not entitle the non-legal owner to a 50% beneficial interest: *Thompson v Hurst* [2012] EWCA Civ 1752.

The requirement for the court to establish a fair share, having regard to the whole course of the parties' dealings with the property, was established in *Stack v Dowden* [2007] 1 FLR 1858 (HL). For further authorities on this point, see *Holman v Howes* [2008] 1 FLR 1217, a sole name case in which the Court of Appeal said that inferences will be drawn from the whole course of dealing between the parties both before and after purchase, including the arrangements made to meet the outgoings of the property. A substantial financial contribution by a man to building works on a barn owned by his former cohabitee entitled him to a 25% interest: *Aspden v Elvy* [2012] 2 FLR 807. There may be a change of beneficial ownership after the property has been acquired, but the court will be slow to infer this from conduct alone, without evidence of an express agreement (*James v Thomas* [2008] 1 FLR 1598; *Morris v Morris* [2008] EWCA Civ 257 (CA)). The Court of Appeal has said on several occasions that fairness between the parties is not the basis for the court's decision; to argue what may be considered fair is the "impermissible question", in the absence of evidence of the parties' intentions derived from a survey of their whole course of dealings (*Holman v Howes* [2008] 1 FLR 1217); on "fairness", see also *James v Thomas* [2008] 1 FLR 1598; *Laskar v Laskar* [2008] 2 FLR 589 (CA); *Thomson v Humphrey* [2010] 2 FLR 107, Ch.

Application by trustee in bankruptcy—The Insolvency Act 1986 s 335A provides that a trustee in bankruptcy may apply for an order under s 14 for a sale of land. The application must be made to the court having jurisdiction in relation to the bankruptcy. The court will make such order as is just and reasonable, having regard to (a) the interests of the creditors; (b) where the application is made in respect of a dwelling house which is or has been the home of the bankrupt, his spouse or former spouse, the court will consider (i) the conduct of the spouse or former spouse in contributing to the bankruptcy, (ii) the needs and financial resources of the spouse, and (iii) the needs of any children. The court will also consider (c) all the circumstances of the case other than the needs of the bankrupt. Where the application is made more than a year after the vesting of the bankrupt's estate in the trustee, the court is entitled to assume that the interests of the creditors outweigh all other considerations, unless the circumstances of the case are exceptional. In *Dean v Stout (Trustee in Bankruptcy)* [2006] 1 FLR 725 a trustee in bankruptcy successfully sought the sale of the family home against a wife who had occupied with the children for 7 years, reduced debts and paid off the mortgage. The court did not find the necessary "exceptional circumstances" to displace the presumption that the interests of the creditors outweigh all other circumstances. The court's discretion under s 15 has to be compatible with the rights of those affected by an order for enforcement under the European Convention, but a balance would be drawn between the creditor's rights under Article 1 and the Article 8 rights to family life of those affected by the sale: *National Westminster Bank Plc v Rushmer* [2010] 2 FLR 362, Ch.

A matrimonial consent order giving a two thirds interest in the matrimonial home to the wife upon a trust for sale upon future contingencies did not give an absolute right to the wife, where the husband was entitled to one third interest upon sale. The husband's right to apply under s 14 passes intact to the trustee in bankruptcy, entitling him to apply for sale under the Insolvency Act s 335A (*Avis v Turner* [2008] 1 FLR 1127 (CA)). The trustee was subsequently granted possession and an order for sale: the existence of the consent order did not constitute an "exceptional circumstance" (*Turner v Avis and Avis* [2009] 1 FLR 74). A trustee in bankruptcy who secures an order for sale is entitled to compensation in the form of occupation rent (*Re Barcham (In Bankruptcy)* [2008] BPIR 857).

Costs—An application under TLATA 1996 is not for a financial order or remedy and is not governed by FPR 2010. CPR 1998, r 44.2 applies.

****

Welfare Reform and Pensions Act 1999

****

29 Creation of pension debits and credits

(1) On the application of this section –

(a) the transferor's shareable rights under the relevant arrangement become subject to a debit of the appropriate amount, and

(b) the transferee becomes entitled to a credit of that amount as against the person responsible for that arrangement.

(2) Where the relevant order or provision specifies a percentage value to be transferred, the appropriate amount for the purposes of subsection (1) is the specified percentage of the cash equivalent of the relevant benefits on the valuation day.

(3) Where the relevant order or provision specifies an amount to be transferred, the appropriate amount for the purposes of subsection (1) is the lesser of –

(a) the specified amount, and

(b) the cash equivalent of the relevant benefits on the valuation day.

(4) Where the relevant arrangement is an occupational pension scheme and the transferor is in pensionable service under the scheme on the transfer day, the relevant benefits for the purposes of subsections (2) and (3) are the benefits or future benefits to which he would be entitled under the scheme by virtue of his shareable rights under it had his pensionable service terminated immediately before that day.

(5) Otherwise, the relevant benefits for the purposes of subsections (2) and (3) are the benefits or future benefits to which, immediately before the transfer day, the transferor is entitled under the terms of the relevant arrangement by virtue of his shareable rights under it.

(6) The Secretary of State may by regulations provide for any description of benefit to be disregarded for the purposes of subsection (4) or (5).

(7) For the purposes of this section, the valuation day is such day within the implementation period for the credit under subsection (1)(b) as the person responsible for the relevant arrangement may specify by notice in writing to the transferor and transferee.

(8) In this section –

"relevant arrangement" means the arrangement to which the relevant order or provision relates;

"relevant order or provision" means the order or provision by virtue of which this section applies;

"transfer day" means the day on which the relevant order or provision takes effect;

"transferor" means the person to whose rights the relevant order or provision relates;

"transferee" means the person for whose benefit the relevant order or provision is made.

Defined terms—"implementation period": ss 34, 46(1); "occupational pension scheme": s 46(1); "pensionable service": s 46(1),(3); "person responsible for a pension arrangement": s 46(2); "shareable rights": ss 27(2), 46(1).

Scope—This section gives rise to what has become known as "moving target syndrome": see *Cowland v Capita SIPP Services* [2007] (3 April), ref Q00244, Pensions Ombudsman, *Chaundy v James Hay Pension Trustees Limited* [2007] (22 May), ref Q00060, Pensions Ombudsman and *Crabtree v BAE Executive Pension Scheme* (2008) 19 May, ref S00522, Pensions Ombudsman; *Slattery v Cabinet Office (Civil Service Pensions)* [2009] 1 FLR 1365; *Staley v Marlborough Investment Management Limited Retirement Scheme* (2012) 31 July, ref 81482/2, Pensions Ombudsman. It is critical to recognise that the valuation used evidentially will not be the same as that used by the pension provider for implementation purposes. The three relevant dates giving rise to this syndrome are best explained diagrammatically:

Date	Function	Source
1 Valuation date	Evidential valuation for the purposes of negotiation or court hearing. The "moving date syndrome" refers to the difference between this valuation and that on the valuation day.	Divorce etc (Pensions) Regulations 2000, reg 3
2 Transfer day	Establishes the relevant benefits to be valued for implementation purposes and is the date the pension sharing order takes effect.	WRPA 1999, s 29(4), (5) and (8)
3 Valuation day	Date chosen for actual implementation purposes, on which the relevant benefits are revalued to take account of market fluctuations (but not contributions and salary accruals)	WRPA 1999, s 29(7)

"Implementation period" (s 29(7))—For a pension credit, this is the period of 4 months beginning with the later of –
  "(a) the day on which the relevant order or provision takes effect, and
  (b) the first day on which the person responsible for the pension arrangement to which the relevant order or provision relates is in receipt of –
    (i) the relevant documents, and
    (ii) such information relating to the transferor and transferee as the Secretary of State may prescribe by regulations" (WRPA 1999, s 34(1)).
The relevant documents are 'copies of":
  "(a) the relevant order or provision, and
  (b) the order, decree or declarator responsible for the divorce, dissolution or annulment to which it relates […]" (WRPA 1999, s 34(2)).

The 4-month period of implementation is a maximum period: unnecessary delays *within* that period by a scheme administrator or trustees may give rise to an award of compensation by the Pensions Ombudsman (*Boughton v Punter Southall* (2009) 22 September, ref 74851/1, Pensions Ombudsman).

****

PART III

Procedure Rules

PART III: Procedure Rules

Contents

All relevant procedural provisions in the following legislation, as amended and fully annotated:

PART III

PART III

PART III

Family Procedure Rules 2010, SI 2010/2955

Note—Tables of Destination (old rules to new), Derivation (new rules from old) and FPR Practice Directions can be found on pages 13–91 of *The Family Court Practice 2011*.

PART 1
OVERRIDING OBJECTIVE

CONTENTS OF THIS PART

1.1 The overriding objective

(1) These rules are a new procedural code with the overriding objective of enabling the court to deal with cases justly, having regard to any welfare issues involved.

(2) Dealing with a case justly includes, so far as is practicable –

    (a)   ensuring that it is dealt with expeditiously and fairly;

    (b)   dealing with the case in ways which are proportionate to the nature, importance and complexity of the issues;

    (c)   ensuring that the parties are on an equal footing;

    (d)   saving expense; and

    (e)   allotting to it an appropriate share of the court's resources, while taking into account the need to allot resources to other cases.

Scope—The overriding objective is fundamental and the bedrock of the 2010 Rules and reflects a similar provision in CPR 1998, save that the wording differs to take account, in particular of "any welfare issues involved". The FPR are deliberately not designed to answer every possible procedural question that could arise and the overriding objective provides a compass to guide the courts, the parties and legal advisers.

"new procedural code" (r 1.1(1))—These words denote an intention to start afresh, procedurally speaking. Authorities on the interpretation of earlier rules may not be followed. However, it is the procedure that has changed, not the underlying law.

"an equal footing" (r 1.1(2)(c))—In *Maltez v Lewis* (2000) 16 Const LJ 65 Neuberger J, when applying the identical rule in the CPR, held that it did not mean that the court could prevent one party from employing leading counsel where the other could not afford to do so. However, the general rule that the unsuccessful party will be ordered to pay the costs of the successful party in CPR 1998, r 44.2(2) does not apply in family proceedings; see generally FPR 2010, Pt 28.

"saving expense" (r 1.1(2)(d))—The cost of taking a particular step has to be justified before the court can order it to be taken whether the cost will fall on the party or public funds. Clear examples of this are the court's duty to restrict expert evidence (see FPR 2010, r 25.1) and the power to control evidence (see FPR 2010, r 22.1) but saving expense is a general principle.

"the court's resources" (r 1.1(2)(e))—The identical words in the CPR have assumed increasing importance over the years. Parties and their advisers have a particular duty to keep the court informed of developments that may affect the use of court resources.

1.2 Application by the court of the overriding objective

The court must seek to give effect to the overriding objective when it –

    (a)   exercises any power given to it by these rules; or

(b)   interprets any rule.

Scope—This rule indicates that a purposive approach is to be adopted. The overriding objective is the crucial aid to interpretation of the rules.

1.3 Duty of the parties

The parties are required to help the court to further the overriding objective.

"help the court"—FPR 2010, rr 1.1 and 1.2 suggest that achieving the overriding objective is the duty of the court and r 1.3 confirms this by not imposing a duty on the parties to further the overriding objective but instead requiring them to "help the court" to further the overriding objective.

1.4 Court's duty to manage cases

(1) The court must further the overriding objective by actively managing cases.

(2) Active case management includes –
    (a)   setting timetables or otherwise controlling the progress of the case;
    (b)   identifying at an early stage –
       (i)   the issues; and
       (ii)   who should be a party to the proceedings;
    (c)   deciding promptly –
       (i)   which issues need full investigation and hearing and which do not; and
       (ii)   the procedure to be followed in the case;
    (d)   deciding the order in which issues are to be resolved;
    (e)   controlling the use of expert evidence;
    (f)   encouraging the parties to use an alternative dispute resolution procedure if the court considers that appropriate and facilitating the use of such procedure;
    (g)   helping the parties to settle the whole or part of the case;
    (h)   encouraging the parties to co-operate with each other in the conduct of proceedings;
    (i)   considering whether the likely benefits of taking a particular step justify the cost of taking it;
    (j)   dealing with as many aspects of the case as it can on the same occasion;
    (k)   dealing with the case without the parties needing to attend at court;
    (l)   making use of technology; and
    (m)   giving directions to ensure that the case proceeds quickly and efficiently.

Amendments—SI 2012/3061.

Scope—The concept of "case management" for civil proceedings was the single most important recommendation to emerge from Lord Woolf's "Access to Justice" report, which led to CPR 1998. It is no surprise to find that r 1.4 is very similar, although not identical, to the same rule number in the CPR. Thus, FPR 2010, r 1.4 contains a list of various case-management elements but is not exhaustive. It summarises aims that are implemented in various ways throughout the FPR. The list was amended in 2012. Former para (g) is reworded and elevated to (a). Para (e) is a new additional factor. The key point is that the court is under a duty to manage cases. Robust case management has a place in family proceedings but in *Re B* [2012] EWCA Civ 1742 a judge erred in holding an unnecessarily truncated hearing and making a finding of fact on limited evidence. See also *Re J (Residence and Contact Dispute)* [2013] 1 FLR 716, where the Recorder erred in stopping further cross-examination. But contrast *Re C* [2012] EWCA Civ 1489, where the judge did not err in stopping residence proceedings and giving judgment shortly after the father began his evidence. In family proceedings, the judge has an inquisitorial role and a duty to further the interests of the child.

PART 2
APPLICATION AND INTERPRETATION OF THE RULES

CONTENTS OF THIS PART

2.1 Application of these Rules

(1) Unless the context otherwise requires, these Rules apply to family proceedings in –

  (a) the High Court;
  (b) a county court; and
  (c) a magistrates' court.

(2) Nothing in these rules is to be construed as –

  (a) purporting to apply to proceedings in a magistrates' court which are not family proceedings within the meaning of section 65 of the Magistrates' Courts Act 1980; or
  (b) conferring upon a magistrate a function which a magistrate is not permitted by statute to perform.

"these Rules apply to family proceedings" (r 2.1(1))—Courts Act 2003, s 75(1) requires "[t]here … to be rules of court (to be called 'Family Procedure Rules') governing the practice and procedure to be followed in family proceedings" in the High Court, county courts and magistrates' courts.

Family proceedings in magistrates' courts—MC(EVOFP & MP)R 2011 ensures that new rules (with effect from 18 June 2011) provide for enforcement of certain maintenance orders, of child contact orders and of occupation and non-molestation orders. Magistrates' court rules that remained in operation following introduction of FPR 2010 are now revoked (MC(EVOFP & MP)R 2011, Sch 5).

2.2 The glossary

(1) The glossary at the end of these rules is a guide to the meaning of certain legal expressions used in the rules, but is not to be taken as giving those expressions any meaning in the rules which they do not have in the law generally.

(2) Subject to paragraph (3), words in these rules which are included in the glossary are followed by "GL".

(3) The word "service", which appears frequently in the rules, is included in the glossary but is not followed by "ᴳᴸ".

2.3 Interpretation

(1) In these rules –

"the 1958 Act" means the Maintenance Orders Act 1958;

"the 1973 Act" means the Matrimonial Causes Act 1973;

"the 1978 Act" means the Domestic Proceedings and Magistrates' Courts 1978;

"the 1980 Hague Convention" means the Convention on the Civil Aspects of International Child Abduction which was signed at The Hague on 25 October 1980;

"the 1984 Act" means the Matrimonial and Family Proceedings Act 1984;

"the 1986 Act" means the Family Law Act 1986;

"the 1989 Act" means the Children Act 1989;

"the 1990 Act" means the Human Fertilisation and Embryology Act 1990;

"the 1991 Act" means the Child Support Act 1991;

"the 1996 Act" means the Family Law Act 1996;

"the 1996 Hague Convention" means the Convention on Jurisdiction, Applicable Law, Recognition, Enforcement and Co-Operation in Respect of Parental Responsibility and Measures for the Protection of Children;

"the 2002 Act" means the Adoption and Children Act 2002;

"the 2004 Act" means the Civil Partnership Act 2004;

"the 2005 Act" means the Mental Capacity Act 2005;

"the 2007 Hague Convention" means the Convention on the International Recovery of Child Support and other forms of Family Maintenance done at The Hague on 23 November 2007;

"the 2008 Act" means the Human Fertilisation and Embryology Act 2008;

"adoption proceedings" means proceedings for an adoption order under the 2002 Act;

"Allocation Order" means any order made by the Lord Chancellor under Part 1 of Schedule 11 to the 1989 Act;

"alternative dispute resolution" means methods of resolving a dispute, including mediation, other than through the normal court process;

"application form" means a document in which the applicant states his intention to seek a court order other than in accordance with the Part 18 procedure;

"application notice" means a document in which the applicant states his intention to seek a court order in accordance with the Part 18 procedure;

"Article 11 form" means a form published by the Permanent Bureau of the Hague Conference under Article 11(4) of the 2007 Hague Convention for use in relation to an application under Article 10 of that Convention, and includes a Financial Circumstances Form as defined in rule 9.3(1) which accompanies such an application;

"Assembly" means the National Assembly for Wales;

"bank holiday" means a bank holiday under the Banking and Financial Dealings Act 1971 –

    (a)   for the purpose of service of a document within the United Kingdom, in the part of the United Kingdom where service is to take place; and

    (b)   for all other purposes, in England and Wales.

"business day" means any day other than –

    (a)   a Saturday, Sunday, Christmas Day or Good Friday; or

    (b)   a bank holiday;

"care order" has the meaning assigned to it by section 31(11) of the 1989 Act;

"CCR" means the County Court Rules 1981, as they appear in Schedule 2 to the CPR subject to paragraph (4);

"child" means a person under the age of 18 years who is the subject of the proceedings; except that –

    (a)   in adoption proceedings, it also includes a person who has attained the age of 18 years before the proceedings are concluded; and

    (b)   in proceedings brought under the Council Regulation, the 1980 Hague Convention or the European Convention, it means a person under the age of 16 years who is the subject of the proceedings;

"child of the family" has the meaning given to it by section 105(1) of the 1989 Act;

"children and family reporter" means an officer of the Service or a Welsh family proceedings officer who has been asked to prepare a welfare report under section 7(1)(a) of the 1989 Act or section 102(3)(b) of the 2002 Act;

"children's guardian" means –

    (a)   in relation to a child who is the subject of and a party to specified proceedings or proceedings to which Part 14 applies, the person appointed in accordance with rule 16.3(1); and

    (b)   in any other case, the person appointed in accordance with rule 16.4;

"civil partnership order" means one of the orders mentioned in section 37 of the 2004 Act;

"civil partnership proceedings" means proceedings for a civil partnership order;

"civil partnership proceedings county court" means a county court so designated by the Lord Chancellor under section 36A of the 1984 Act;

"civil restraint order" means an order restraining a party –

    (a)   from making any further applications in current proceedings (a limited civil restraint order);

    (b)   from making certain applications in specified courts (an extended civil restraint order); or

    (c)   from making any application in specified courts (a general civil restraint order);

...

"consent order" means an order in the terms applied for to which the respondent agrees;

"contact order" has the meaning assigned to it by section 8(1) of the 1989 Act;

"the Council Regulation" means Council Regulation (EC) No 2201/2003 of 27 November 2003 on jurisdiction and the recognition and enforcement of judgments in matrimonial matters and in matters of parental responsibility;

"court" means, subject to any rule or other enactment which provides otherwise, the High Court, a county court or a magistrates' court;

(rule 2.5 relates to the power to perform functions of the court.)

"court of trial" means –

    (a)   in proceedings under the 1973 Act, a divorce county court designated by the Lord Chancellor as a court of trial pursuant to section 33(1) of the 1984 Act; or

    (b)   in proceedings under the 2004 Act, a civil partnership proceedings county court designated by the Lord Chancellor as a court of trial pursuant to section 36A(1)(b) of the 1984 Act; and

    (c)   in proceedings under the 1973 Act pending in a divorce county court or proceedings under the 2004 Act pending in a civil partnership proceedings county court, the principal registry is treated as a court of trial having its place of sitting at the Royal Courts of Justice;

"court officer" means –

    (a)   in the High Court or in a county court, a member of court staff; and

PART III

(b)   in a magistrates' court, the designated officer;

("designated officer" is defined in section 37(1) of the Courts Act 2003.)

"CPR" means the Civil Procedure Rules 1998;

"deputy" has the meaning given in section 16(2)(b) of the 2005 Act;

"designated county court" means a court designated as –

    (a)   a divorce county court;

    (b)   a civil partnership proceedings county court; or

    (c)   both a divorce county court and a civil partnership proceedings county court;

"detailed assessment proceedings" means the procedure by which the amount of costs is decided in accordance with Part 47 of the CPR;

"directions appointment" means a hearing for directions;

"district judge" –

    (a)   in relation to proceedings in the High Court, includes a district judge of the principal registry and in relation to proceedings in a county court, includes a district judge of the principal registry when the principal registry is treated as if it were a county court;

    (b)   in relation to proceedings in a district registry or a county court, means the district judge or one of the district judges of that registry or county court, as the case may be;

"district registry" means –

    (a)   in proceedings under the 1973 Act, any district registry having a divorce county court within its district;

    (b)   in proceedings under the 2004 Act, any district registry having a civil partnership proceedings county court within its district; and

    (c)   in any other case, any district registry having a designated county court within its district;

"divorce county court" means a county court so designated by the Lord Chancellor pursuant to section 33(1) of the 1984 Act, including the principal registry when it is treated as a divorce county court;

"the European Convention" means the European Convention on Recognition and Enforcement of Decisions concerning Custody of Children and on the Restoration of Custody of Children which was signed in Luxembourg on 20 May 1980;

"filing", in relation to a document, means delivering it, by post or otherwise, to the court office;

"financial order" means –

    (a)   an avoidance of disposition order;

    (b)   an order for maintenance pending suit;

    (c)   an order for maintenance pending outcome of proceedings;

    (d)   an order for periodical payments or lump sum provision as mentioned in section 21(1) of the 1973 Act, except an order under section 27(6) of that Act;

    (e)   an order for periodical payments or lump sum provision as mentioned in paragraph 2(1) of Schedule 5 to the 2004 Act, made under Part 1 of Schedule 5 to that Act;

    (f)   a property adjustment order;

    (g)   a variation order;

    (h)   a pension sharing order; or

    (i)   a pension compensation sharing order;

("variation order", "pension compensation sharing order" and "pension sharing order" are defined in rule 9.3)

"financial remedy" means –

(a)   a financial order;

(b)   an order under Schedule 1 to the 1989 Act;

(c)   an order under Part 3 of the 1984 Act except an application under section 13 of the 1984 Act for permission to apply for a financial remedy;

(d)   an order under Schedule 7 to the 2004 Act except an application under paragraph 4 of Schedule 7 to the 2004 Act for permission to apply for an order under paragraph 9 or 13 of that Schedule;

(e)   an order under section 27 of the 1973 Act;

(f)   an order under Part 9 of Schedule 5 to the 2004 Act;

(g)   an order under section 35 of the 1973 Act;

(h)   an order under paragraph 69 of Schedule 5 to the 2004 Act;

(i)   an order under Part 1 of the 1978 Act;

(j)   an order under Schedule 6 to the 2004 Act;

(k)   an order under section 10(2) of the 1973 Act; or

(l)   an order under section 48(2) of the 2004 Act;

"hearing" includes a directions appointment;

"hearsay" means a statement made, otherwise than by a person while giving oral evidence in proceedings, which is tendered as evidence of the matters stated, and references to hearsay include hearsay of whatever degree;

"inherent jurisdiction" means the High Court's power to make any order or determine any issue in respect of a child, including in wardship proceedings, where it would be just and equitable to do so unless restricted by legislation or case law;

(Practice Direction 12D (Inherent Jurisdiction (including Wardship Proceedings)) provides examples of inherent jurisdiction proceedings.)

"judge", in the High Court or a county court, means, unless the context requires otherwise, a judge, district judge or a person authorised to act as such;

"jurisdiction" means, unless the context requires otherwise, England and Wales and any part of the territorial waters of the United Kingdom adjoining England and Wales;

"justices' clerk" has the meaning assigned to it by section 27(1) of the Courts Act 2003;

"legal representative" means a –

(a)   barrister

(b)   solicitor;

(c)   solicitor's employee;

(d)   manager of a body recognised under section 9 of the Administration of Justice Act 1985; or

(e)   person who, for the purposes of the Legal Services Act 2007, is an authorised person in relation to an activity which constitutes the conduct of litigation (within the meaning of the Act),

who has been instructed to act for a party in relation to proceedings;

"litigation friend" has the meaning given –

(a)   in relation to a protected party, by Part 15; and

(b)   in relation to a child, by Part 16;

"the Maintenance Regulation" means Council Regulation (EC) No 4/2009 of 18 December 2008 on jurisdiction, applicable law, recognition and enforcement of decisions and co-operation in matters relating to maintenance obligations, including as applied in relation to Denmark by virtue of the Agreement made on 19 October 2005 between the European Community and the Kingdom of Denmark;

"matrimonial cause" means proceedings for a matrimonial order;

"matrimonial order" means –

PART III

(a)   a decree of divorce made under section 1 of the 1973 Act;

(b)   a decree of nullity made on one of the grounds set out in sections 11 or 12 of the 1973 Act;

(c)   a decree of judicial separation made under section 17 of the 1973 Act;

"note" includes a record made by mechanical means;

"officer of the Service" has the meaning given by section 11(3) of the Criminal Justice and Court Services Act 2000;

"order" includes directions of the court;

"order for maintenance pending outcome of proceedings" means an order under paragraph 38 of Schedule 5 to the 2004 Act;

"order for maintenance pending suit" means an order under section 22 of the 1973 Act;

"parental order proceedings" has the meaning assigned to it by rule 13.1;

"parental responsibility" has the meaning assigned to it by section 3 of the 1989 Act;

"placement proceedings" means proceedings for the making, varying or revoking of a placement order under the 2002 Act;

"principal registry" means the principal registry of the Family Division of the High Court;

"proceedings" means, unless the context requires otherwise, family proceedings as defined in section 75(3) of the Courts Act 2003;

"professional acting in furtherance of the protection of children" includes –

(a)   an officer of a local authority exercising child protection functions;

(b)   a police officer who is –

   (i)   exercising powers under section 46 of the Act of 1989; or

   (ii)   serving in a child protection unit or a paedophile unit of a police force,

(c)   any professional person attending a child protection conference or review in relation to a child who is the subject of the proceedings to which the information regarding the proceedings held in private relates;

(d)   an officer of the National Society for the Prevention of Cruelty to Children; or

(e)   a member or employee of the Independent Safeguarding Authority, being the body established under section 1 of the Safeguarding Vulnerable Groups Act 2006;

"professional legal adviser" means a –

(a)   barrister;

(b)   solicitor;

(c)   solicitor's employee;

(d)   manager of a body recognised under section 9 of the Administration of Justice Act 1985; or

(e)   person who, for the purposes of the Legal Services Act 2007, is an authorised person in relation to an activity which constitutes the conduct of litigation (within the meaning of that Act),

who is providing advice to a party but is not instructed to represent that party in the proceedings;

"property adjustment order" means –

(a)   in proceedings under the 1973 Act, any of the orders mentioned in section 21(2) of that Act;

(b)   in proceedings under the 1984 Act, an order under section 17(1)(a)(ii) of that Act;

(c)   in proceedings under Schedule 5 to the 2004 Act, any of the orders mentioned in paragraph 7(1); or

(d)   in proceedings under Schedule 7 to the 2004 Act, an order for property adjustment under paragraph 9(2) or (3);

"protected party" means a party, or an intended party, who lacks capacity (within the meaning of the 2005 Act) to conduct proceedings;

"reporting officer" means an officer of the Service or a Welsh family proceedings officer appointed to witness the documents which signify a parent's or guardian's consent to the placing of the child for adoption or to the making of an adoption order or a section 84 order;

"risk assessment" has the meaning assigned to it by section 16A(3) of the 1989 Act;

"Royal Courts of Justice", in relation to matrimonial proceedings pending in a divorce county court or civil partnership proceedings pending in a civil partnership proceedings county court, means such place as may be specified in directions given by the Lord Chancellor pursuant to section 42(2)(a) of the 1984 Act;

"RSC" means the Rules of the Supreme Court 1965 as they appear in Schedule 1 to the CPR subject to paragraph (4);

"section 8 order" has the meaning assigned to it by section 8(2) of the 1989 Act;

"section 84 order" means an order made by the High Court under section 84 of the 2002 Act giving parental responsibility prior to adoption abroad;

"section 89 order" means an order made by the High Court under section 89 of the 2002 Act –

(a)   annulling a Convention adoption or Convention adoption order;

(b)   providing for an overseas adoption or determination under section 91 of the 2002 Act to cease to be valid; or

(c)   deciding the extent, if any, to which a determination under section 91 of the 2002 Act has been affected by a subsequent determination under that section;

"Service" has the meaning given by section 11 of the Criminal Justice and Court Services Act 2000;

"the Service Regulation" means Regulation (EC) No. 1393/2007 of the European Parliament and of the Council of 13 November 2007 on the service in the Member States of judicial and extrajudicial documents in civil or commercial matters (service of documents), and repealing Council Regulation (EC) No. 1348/2000, as amended from time to time and as applied by the Agreement made on 19 October 2005 between the European Community and the Kingdom of Denmark on the service of judicial and extrajudicial documents in civil and commercial matters;

"specified proceedings" has the meaning assigned to it by section 41(6) of the 1989 Act and rule 12.27;

"welfare officer" means a person who has been asked to prepare a report under section 7(1)(b) of the 1989 Act;

"Welsh family proceedings officer" has the meaning given by section 35(4) of the Children Act 2004.

(2)   In these rules a reference to –

(a)   an application for a matrimonial order or a civil partnership order is to be read as a reference to a petition for –

(i)   a matrimonial order;

(ii)   a decree of presumption of death and dissolution of marriage made under section 19 of the 1973 Act; or

(iii)   a civil partnership order,

and includes a petition by a respondent asking for such an order;

(b)   "financial order" in matrimonial proceedings is to be read as a reference to "ancillary relief";

(c)   "matrimonial proceedings" is to be read as a reference to a matrimonial cause or proceedings for an application for a decree of presumption of death and dissolution of marriage made under section 19 of the 1973 Act.

(3) Subject to paragraph (4), where these rules apply the CPR, they apply the CPR as amended from time to time.

(4) Where these Rules apply RSC Order 52 and CCR Order 29, they apply those rules as they appeared in Schedule 1 and Schedule 2 to the CPR on 30 September 2012.

Amendments—SI 2011/1328; SI 2012/679; SI 2012/2007; SI 2012/2046; SI 2012/2806.

Interpretation provisions in the rules—FPR 2010, r 2.3 deals with "Interpretation" for the rules as a whole and many individual Parts have their own internal sets of interpretation rules (e g FPR 2010, r 12.2 for children proceedings and FPR 2010, r 9.3 for financial remedy proceedings). Most of these apply only to the Part in question. There is a shortened version of the CPR 1998 Glossary at the end of FPR 2010, although no terms specific to family proceedings have been added.

Answer—Proceedings are started by application form (originating application, including by the FPR 2010, Pt 19 procedure) or application notice (i e interim to existing or in respect of proposed proceedings). There is no generic term – save possibly "answer – to describe the respondent's or another party's statement of case in reply to an application" (i e defence in other civil proceedings). FPR 2010, r 4.1(1) is probably the nearest that the rules approach to a definition of a term that describes the application and answer forms that parties exchange (when the rules provide for it) to describe their claim and opposition to that claim), and in r 4.1(1) the term "answer" is used.

"application form" and "application notice"—A party to FPR 2010 family proceedings applies for any remedy, either (1) by "application form" (see FPR 2010, Pt 5) for an originating process (generic or FPR 2010, Pt 19)); or (2) by "application notice" for an interim or pre/post-action remedy (FPR 2010, Pt 18; and see for example FPR 2010, Pt 20). In the body of the rules in Pt 5, the term "application form" does not appear: it is used only in the heading to FPR 2010, r 5.3. The rules leave parties to imply the term into the process of issue of originating applications in Pt 5. This is significant because the rules seem deliberately to make no reference in each Part to issue of a specific form of process, so applicants will need to depend on Pt 5, the accompanying FPR PD5A and the list of forms for issue, and the definition terminology in FPR 2010, r 2.3(1). This in its turn depends on understanding the meaning of what is "other than … the Part 18 procedure".

"application form… other than in accordance with the Part 18 procedure"—If the application is not made within the terms of Pt 18 (i e an interim order application), then r 2.3(1) provides that the application must be issued by "application form", that is to say in accordance with the applications provided for in FPR 2010, Pt 5.

Meaning of "child" and "child of the family"—The statutory provisions that deal with family law, including statutes that are relevant to FPR 2010, provide a variety of different definitions of "child". Only a restricted number of these is touched on by FPR 2010, r 2.3(1). A full list would include:

- CA 1989 – s 105(10);
- CA 1989 – Sch 1, paras 2 and 6 (over 18 for certain financial remedy proceedings);
- CSA 1991 – s 55;
- MCA 1973 – s 52 and CPA 2004;
- I(PFD)A 1975 – s 25(1);
- CPR 1998 – rr 2.3(1) and 21.1(2).

Child of age and understanding—Any reference to "child" in family proceedings must be seen also in the context of the child's age and understanding (CA 1989, s 1(3); see *Gillick v West Norfolk and Wisbech Area Health Authority and Another* [1986] 1 FLR 224, HL and the factors in Pt 16 (e g appointment of a litigation friend or not: e g *Re CT (A Minor) (Wardship: Representation)* [1993] 2 FLR 278)).

"detailed assessment proceedings" and "summary assessment"—Detailed assessment proceedings, but not either detailed assessment or summary assessment, are defined. These are to be found defined in CPR 1998, rr 44.1.

"financial order", "financial remedy" and "financial remedy proceedings"— FPR 2010, r 2.3(1) defines the first two of these terms, but does not emphasise the semantic difficulty created by FPR 2010, r 28.3(4) where "financial remedy proceedings" creates a third strand to the various ways in which financial proceedings are defined and dealt with in different parts of the rules (especially FPR 2010, Pt 9 and FPR 2010, r 28.3).

"Maintenance Regulation"—Council Regulation (EC) No 4/2009 came into effect on 18 June 2011.

2.4 Modification of rules in application to serial numbers etc.

If a serial number has been assigned under rule 14.2 or the name or other contact details of a party is not being revealed in accordance with rule 29.1 –

(a) any rule requiring any party to serve any document will not apply; and
(b) the court will give directions about serving any document on the other parties.

2.5 Power to perform functions conferred on the court by these rules and practice directions

(1) Where these rules or a practice direction provide for the court to perform any function then, except where any rule or practice direction, any other enactment or any directions made by the President of the Family Division under section 9 of the Courts and Legal Services Act 1990, provides otherwise, that function may be performed –

(a) in relation to proceedings in the High Court or in a district registry, by any judge or district judge of that Court including a district judge of the principal registry;
(b) in relation to proceedings in a county court, by any judge or district judge including a district judge of the principal registry when the principal registry is treated as if it were a county court; and
(c) in relation to proceedings in a magistrates' court –
   (i) by any family proceedings court constituted in accordance with sections 66 and 67 of the Magistrates' Courts Act 1980; or
   (ii) by a single justice of the peace who is a member of the family panel in accordance with Practice Direction 2A.

(The Justices' Clerks Rules 2005 make provision for a justices' clerk or assistant clerk to carry out certain functions of a single justice of the peace.)

(2) A deputy High Court judge and a district judge, including a district judge of the principal registry, may not try a claim for a declaration of incompatibility in accordance with section 4 of the Human Rights Act 1998.

Defined terms—"district judge", "district registry", "principal registry": r 2.3(1).

Courts and Legal Services Act 1990, s 9—CLSA 1990, s 9 deals with allocation of family proceedings to the county court judiciary (it does not apply to magistrates).

2.6 Powers of the single justice to perform functions under the 1989 Act, the 1996 Act, the 2002 Act and the Childcare Act 2006

(1) A single justice who is a member of the family panel may perform the functions of a magistrates' court –

(a) where an application without notice is made under sections 10, 44(1), 48(9), 50(4) and 102(1) of the 1989 Act;
(b) subject to paragraph (2), under sections 11(3) or 38(1) of the 1989 Act;
(c) under sections 4(3)(b), 4A(3)(b), 4ZA(6)(b), 7, 34(3)(b), 41, 44(9)(b) and (11)(b)(iii), 48(4), 91(15) or (17) or paragraph 11(4) of Schedule 14 of the 1989 Act;
(d) in accordance with the Allocation Order;
(e) where an application without notice is made under section 41(2) of the 2002 Act (recovery orders);
(f) where an application without notice is made for an occupation order or a non molestation order under Part 4 of the 1996 Act; or
(g) where an application is made for a warrant under section 79 of the Childcare Act 2006;

(2) A single justice of the peace may make an order under section 11(3) or 38(1) of the 1989 Act where –

(a)   a previous such order has been made in the same proceedings;

(b)   the terms of the order sought are the same as those of the last such order made; and

(c)   a written request for such an order has been made and –

(i)   the other parties and any children's guardian consent to the request and they or their legal representatives have signed the request; or

(ii)   at least one of the other parties and any children's guardian consent to the request and they or their legal representatives have signed the request, and the remaining parties have not indicated that they either consent to or oppose the making of the order.

(3) The proceedings referred to in paragraph (1)(a), (c) and (d) are proceedings which are prescribed for the purposes of section 93(2)(i) of the 1989 Act.

Scope—This rule sets out the functions that may be performed by a single justice under CA 1989, FLA 1996, ACA 2002 and the Childcare Act 2006. FPR PD2A provides that a single justice can perform any function that may be performed by the court under FPR 2010 and the PDs supplementing those Rules, except for those functions listed in Tables 1 and 2 of FPR PD2A.

"application without notice" (r 2.6(1)(a),(f))—Only certain orders may be sought without notice. Most of these are listed in FPR 2010, rr 10.2 and 12.16, which also set out the procedure to be followed, including the requirement that permission of the court to make such an application must be obtained. In practice, an application for leave is usually obtained from the justices' clerk or an assistant clerk, who can exercise many of the powers of a single justice in accordance with the provisions of the JCR 2005.

"sections 10, 44(1), 48(9), 50(4) and 102(1)" (r 2.6(1)(a))—These sections of CA 1989 deal with the following: s 10 (power of the court to make s 8 orders); s 44(1) (application for an emergency protection order); s 48(9) (application for a warrant authorising a constable to assist in the enforcement of an emergency protection order); s 50(4) (application for a recovery order in relation to a child who has been abducted, run away etc); and s 102(1) (application for a warrant authorising a constable to assist in the exercise of certain powers to search for children and inspect premises).

"sections 11(3) or 38(1)" (r 2.6(1)(b),(2))—CA 1989, s 11(3) empowers the court to make a s 8 order before it is in a position to dispose finally of the proceedings in question. For example, where the proceedings have to be adjourned for a period and the court feels it necessary to regulate where the child is going to live by making an interim residence order pending the resumed hearing. Section 38(1) empowers the court to make an interim care or supervision order where an application for a full care or supervision order is adjourned or where the court gives a direction under s 37(1) that the local authority should investigate the child's circumstances with a view to it possibly making a care or supervision order. FPR 2010, r 2.6(2) sets out the conditions that must apply for a single justice to be able to make such orders.

Provisions specified in r 2.6(1)(c)—The provisions specified in r 2.6(1)(c) require leave of the court before certain proceedings may be commenced or certain steps may be taken. The drafting is ambiguous in that, in relation to certain of the specified statutory provisions, it is not clear as to whether it is the leave application with which the single justice is empowered to deal (as was almost certainly intended) or the substantive application that will follow should leave be given. CA 1989, s 4(3)(b) authorises a child to seek an order terminating a parental responsibility order or agreement in respect of him provided that he has the leave of the court. CA 1989, s 7 empowers the court (which, by virtue of r 2.6(c), may comprise a single justice) to require a welfare report. Section 34 allows certain people to apply for orders with regard to contact with a child in care; under s 34(3)(b) certain applicants must first seek leave to apply. Section 41 provides for the appointment by the court of a children's guardian or a solicitor for a child concerned in specified proceedings such as care proceedings etc. CA 1989 s 44 enables the court to make emergency protection order and where it does so, it may under s 44(6) give directions as to medical, psychiatric or other assessment of the child or contact with him. Section 44(9)(b) makes provision for the variation of such directions on application.

Section 44(11) applies where, after the making of an emergency protection order, it is proposed to return a child or allow his removal from the place where he has been detained. It specifies the rules of precedence by reference to which the applicant is to determine to whom he must deliver the child. The first choice is the person from whom the child has been removed, but, if that is not reasonably practicable, one of the other possibilities is, in accordance with s 44(11)(b)(iii), such other person as the applicant (with the agreement of the court) considers appropriate. Rule 2.6(1)(c)) empowers a single justice to signify the requisite agreement.

Section 48 includes miscellaneous provisions to assist in finding children who may be in need of emergency protection. Under s 48(4), the court may authorise a search of premises for a child with respect to whom there is reasonable cause to believe that an emergency protection order ought to be made. Both s 91(15) and (17) prohibit the making of repeat applications within 6 months in certain cases without leave (for example, no application for the discharge of a care or supervision order may be made within 6 months of the last such application). A single justice is empowered by r 2.6(1)(c) to give such leave. Finally, CA 1989, Sch 14, para 11(4) prohibits a child from applying for the discharge of an existing order except with the leave of the court. Rule 2.6(1)(c) permits a single justice to give such leave.

"in accordance with the Allocation Order" (r 2.6(1)(d))—A single justice may exercise the powers of the court to transfer proceedings in accordance with ATPO 2008, arts 14 and 15. These powers may also be exercised by the Justices' Clerk or an assistant clerk under JCR 2005.

Power of Justices' Clerks—JCR 2005, Sch 2, para 7 prescribes that the justices' clerk may perform all of the functions of a single justice listed in FPR 2010, r 2.5 and the PDs supplementing the 2010 Rules, except for those functions listed in Tables 1 and 2 of the 2005 Rules. The power to make an order under ss 11(3) or 38(1) of the 1989 Act in accordance with the conditions set out in r 2.6(2) is to be found in JCR 2005, Sch 2, para 3.

Satisfying the conditions in r 2.6(2)—All three conditions must be satisfied before the order can be made. It follows that a single justice or justices' clerk can never grant the first interim order in a case but only a second or subsequent interim order, and then only if the order is in identical terms to the last such order, there is a written request for such an order and either signed consent of all parties or signed consent of at least one of the other parties and any children's guardian and no indication of opposition from remaining parties.

In *C v Solihull MBC* [1993] 1 FLR 290, Ward J reminded magistrates that, by virtue of such powers (formerly contained in FPC(CA 1989)R 1991, r 28) the extension of an interim arrangement can be made administratively while a programme of assessment is completed and then the matter restored for a full and final hearing once the inquiry is complete. In *Re J (Minors) (Care: Care Plan)* [1994] 1 FLR 253, however, Wall J expressed unhappiness, in view of the possible implications in terms of delay, about the uncritical use of CA 1989, s 38(4) and of this rule to extend interim orders. As to the duties of local authorities and courts in relation to the making of interim care orders, see also *Re G (Minors) (Interim Care Order)* [1993] 2 FLR 839, *Re W (A Minor) (Interim Care Order)* [1994] 2 FLR 892, and **Nature of interim orders** under CA 1989, s 38. Reference should also be made to June 1997 *CAAC Handbook of Best Practice in Children Act Cases*, "Section 2 – Renewal of interim care orders" (set out in Part V).

Written and signed request—There is no prescribed form for the making of such a request. The *Handbook of Best Practice* (see above) contains a draft application form that is tailored to this situation. It will not always be practical for all parties who wish to do so to endorse their consent on the written request itself and, in these circumstances, it ought to suffice if copies are signed and filed with the original.

"section 93(2)(i)" (r 2.6(3))—CA 1989, s 93(2)(i) empowers the making of rules authorising a single justice to discharge the functions of a magistrates' court with respect to such relevant proceedings as may be prescribed; r 2.6(3) is such a rule.

District judges (magistrates' court)—Only district judges (magistrates' court) nominated by the Lord Chancellor for family proceedings may hear CA 1989 cases.

2.7 Single justice's power to refer to a magistrates' court

Where a single justice –

    (a) is performing the function of a magistrates' court in accordance with rules 2.5(1)(c)(ii) and 2.6(1) and (2); and

    (b) considers, for whatever reason, that it is inappropriate to perform the function,

the single justice must refer the matter to a magistrates' court which may perform the function.

Scope—This rule provides for a single justice to refer the matter to a full court in an appropriate case. Identical provision is made for a justices' clerk performing the powers of a single justice to refer the matter to the court by virtue of JCR 2005, r 3A.

2.8 Court's discretion as to where it deals with cases

The court may deal with a case at any place that it considers appropriate.

Defined terms—"court", "hearing": r 2.3(1).

"hearing"—"Hearing" comprises any court appointment before any judge or court (eg hearing in a solicitors' office: in *Oral Contraceptive Group Litigation XYZ & Ors v Schering Health Care Ltd & Ors* [2004] EWHC 823 (QB) the scale of documents involved justified detailed assessment being dealt with in a solicitors' office).

Hearing "at any place [which the court] considers appropriate"—The court is final arbiter of where the hearing should take place. A venue more appropriate to a child or a protected party might be fixed, even if only for part of a hearing. Application could be made, for example, for the hearing of a case that involved a large volume of documents, to be held where the documents are most conveniently held (FPR 2010, rr 21.2 and 24.2(4)(b); and see *Khanna v Lovell White Durrant* [1995] 1 WLR 121), perhaps as a preliminary issue hearing on carefully defined document-based issues.

Application—The order could be made on the initiative of the court or on application under the FPR 2010, Pt 18 procedure (see especially FPR 2010, rr 18.9 and 18.10: hearings without attendance). The court will be concerned with the overriding objective, especially of "saving expense" to the parties, where it considers an alternative venue for a hearing. Where numerous witnesses and a child involved in the case are distant from the court, there may be an economic argument for a removed hearing. Alternatively, a hearing by video-link may assist (FPR 2010, r 22.3; eg *Black v Pastouna* [2005] EWCA Civ 1389, where the Court of Appeal discouraged Liverpool counsel from attending court personally (as distinct from by video-link) on an appeal renewal application (and see CPR PD32, Annex 3 and FPR PD22A, Annex 3 on video conferencing)).

2.9 Computation of time

(1) This rule shows how to calculate any period of time for doing any act which is specified –

    (a) by these rules;

    (b) by a practice direction; or

    (c) by a direction or order of the court.

(2) A period of time expressed as a number of days must be computed as clear days.

(3) In this rule "clear days" means that in computing the numbers of days –

    (a) the day on which the period begins; and

    (b) if the end of the period is defined by reference to an event, the day on which that event occurs,

are not included.

(4) Where the specified period is 7 days or less and includes a day which is not a business day, that day does not count.

(5) When the period specified –

    (a) by these rules or a practice direction; or

    (b) by any direction or order of the court,

for doing any act at the court office ends on a day on which the office is closed, that act will be in time if done on the next day on which the court office is open.

Defined terms—"business day": r 2.3(1); "clear days": rr 2.3(1), 2.9(3).

Use of a calendar date and time—Rule 2.9 must be read in conjunction with FPR 2010, r 2.10, which requires dates and times to be specified in orders. If r 2.10 is followed, it should avoid many of the pitfalls that r 2.9 seeks to mitigate or provide for.

"7 days or less" (r 2.9(4))—CPR 1998, r 2.8(4) retains the shorter period of "5 days or less".

Calculation of "within seven days", or the application will be struck out—For example, where a step in proceedings must be completed "within seven days" (which means "clear days": r 2.9(2)) of a Tuesday:

(1) The 7 days starts the next day (Wednesday), followed by 7 business days. This takes the period to Thursday in the following week (which "does not count": FPR 2010, r 2.9(4)); so filing and service is due on the Friday in the week following the order.

(2) If the Tuesday is in the week before Easter, the document must be filed and served as follows:

    (a) Time starts to run on the Wednesday (r 2.9(3)(b)) and the Easter weekend "does not count" (r 2.9(4)). There are 2 business days before, and 4 in the week after, Easter: total 6 days to the weekend after Easter).

    (b) The weekend "does not count" (r 2.9(4)), Monday is the final day of the 7, Tuesday is "not included" as the day on which the "event occurs" (r 2.9(3)(b)).

    (c) The period being "7 days or less" (r 2.9(4)) and "clear days" being specified by the order, time expires on the Wednesday, more than 2 weeks after it began to run.

2.10 Dates for compliance to be calendar dates and to include time of day

(1) Where the court makes an order or gives a direction which imposes a time limit for doing any act, the last date for compliance must, wherever practicable –

    (a) be expressed as a calendar date; and

    (b) include the time of day by which the act must be done.

(2) Where the date by which an act must be done is inserted in any document, the date must, wherever practicable, be expressed as a calendar date.

(3) Where "month" occurs in any order, direction or other document, it means a calendar month.

Defined terms—"month": r 2.10(3)

Practice Direction –
Practice Directions Relating to Family Proceedings In Force Before 6 April 2011 which Support the Family Procedure Rules 2010

Introduction and the Existing Practice Directions

1.1 The Family Procedure Rules 2010 ("the FPR 2010") come into force on 6 April 2011. The purpose of this practice direction is to inform court users of the practice directions relating (only) to family proceedings which date from before 6 April 2011 ("existing Practice Directions") but will continue to apply after that date.

1.2 The table in the Annex to this practice direction lists those existing Practice Directions which will continue to apply. The listed existing Practice Directions will apply to family proceedings on and after 6 April 2011 –

    (a) with the modifications outlined in the Annex (in particular that the numbering of the existing Practice Directions will be as set out in column one of the table in the Annex) and any other modifications necessary in consequence of the FPR 2010 coming into force; and

    (b) subject to the FPR 2010 and any other practice directions supporting those rules.

Application of Practice Direction 23B of the Civil Procedure Rules 1998

2.1 Paragraphs 1.1, 1.2, 1.4 and 1.5 of CPR Practice Direction 23B apply to applications under Part III of the Family Law Reform Act 1969 for the use of scientific tests to

determine parentage. These applications will be made using the procedure in Part 18 of
the FPR 2010 (Procedure for Other Applications in Proceedings).

ANNEX

Number	Title	Date	Court	Updated rule references
PD6C	Practice Direction (Disclosure of Addresses by Government Departments) (amending Practice Direction of 13 February 1989) (NB this practice direction does not apply to requests for disclosure from HMRC and related agencies which are covered by "Disclosure Orders against the Inland Revenue-Guidance from the President's Office (November 2003)"	20 July 1995	High Court, county court and magistrates' court	
PD7D	Gender Recognition Act 2004	5 April 2005	High Court and county court	
PD12A	Public Law Proceedings Guide to Case Management: April 2010	April 2010	High Court, county court and magistrates' court	
PD12B	The Revised Private Law Programme	April 2010	High Court, county court and magistrates' court	
PD12I	Applications for Reporting Restriction Orders (nb this practice direction applies to information about children and protected parties)	18 March 2005	High Court	
PD12J	Residence and Contact Orders: Domestic Violence and Harm	14 January 2009	High Court, county court and magistrates' court	In paragraph 10, for "the Family Proceedings Rules 1991, rule 4.17AA and by the Family Proceedings Courts (Children Act 1989) Rules 1991, rule 17AA", substitute, "rule 12.34 of the Family Procedure Rules 2010"

Number	Title	Date	Court	Updated rule references
PD12K	President's Direction (Children Act 1989: Exclusion Requirement)	17 December 1997	High Court, county court and magistrates' court	
PD12L	Children Act 1989:Risk Assessments under Section 16A	3 September 2007	High Court, county court and magistrates' court	
PD12M	Family Assistance Orders: Consultation	3 September 2007	High Court, county court and magistrates' court	
PD12N	Enforcement of Children Act 1989 Contact Orders: Disclosure of Information to Officers of the National Probation Service (High Court and county court)	6 November 2008	High Court and county court (The Lord Chief Justice issued a Practice Direction on this subject for the magistrates' courts mirroring the one for the High Court and county courts)	
PD12O	Practice Direction (Arrival of Child in England by Air)	18 January 1980	High Court and county court	
PD12P	Registrar's Direction (Removal from jurisdiction: issue of Passports)	15 May 1987	High Court and county court	
PD14A	Who Receives a Copy of the Application Form for Orders in Proceedings		High Court, county court and magistrates' court	In the heading, for "Part 5,rule 24(1)(b)(ii) of the Family Procedure (Adoption) Rules 2005", substitute "Part 14, rule 14.6(1)(b)(ii) of the Family Procedure Rules 2010"

PART III

Number	Title	Date	Court	Updated rule references
PD14B	The First Directions Hearing-Adoptions with a Foreign Element		High Court, county court and magistrates' court	In the heading, for "Part 5,rule 26(3) of the Family Procedure (Adoption) Rules 2005", substitute "Part 14, rule 14.8(3) of the Family Procedure Rules 2010"; and in paragraph 2, for "rule 26(1)", substitute "rule 14.8(1)"
PD14C	Reports by the Adoption Agency or Local Authority		High Court, county court and magistrates' court	In the heading for "Part 5,rule 29(3) of the Family Procedure (Adoption) Rules 2005", substitute "Part 14, rule 14.11(3) of the Family Procedure Rules 2010"
PD14D	Reports by a Registered Medical Practitioner ("Health Reports")		High Court, county court and magistrates' court	In the heading for "Part 5,rule 30(2) of the Family Procedure(Adoption) Rules 2005", substitute "Part 14, rule 14.12(2) of the Family Procedure Rules 2010"; and in paragraph 1.1, for "rule 30(1)", substitute "rule 14.12(1)"
PD14E	Communication of Information Relating to the Proceedings		High Court, county court and magistrates' court	In the heading for "Part 8,rule 78(1)(b) of the Family Procedure (Adoption) Rules 2005", substitute "Part 14, rule 14.14(b) of the Family Procedure Rules 2010"; and in paragraph 1.1, for "rule 78", substitute "rule 14.14"

Number	Title	Date	Court	Updated rule references
PD14F	Disclosing Information to an Adopted Adult		High Court, county court and magistrates' court	In the heading for "Part 8,rule 84(1)(d) of the Family Procedure (Adoption) Rules 2005", substitute "Part 14, rule 14.18(1)(d) of the Family Procedure Rules 2010"; in paragraphs 1,1 and 1.2, for "rule 84", substitute "rule 14.18"; and in paragraph 1.2, for "rule 17", substitute "rule 5"
PD27A	Family Proceedings: Court Bundles (Universal Practice to be applied in All Courts other than the Family Proceedings Court)	27 July 2006	High Court and county court	
PD27B	Attendance of Media Representatives at Hearings in Family Proceedings (High Court and county courts) (This practice direction should be read as if amended by *Re X (a child) (residence and contact: rights of media attendance)* (2009) EWHC 1728 (Fam) [87])	20 April 2009	High Court and county courts	For references to "rule 10.28 of the Family Proceedings Rules 1991", substitute "rule 27.11 of the Family Procedure Rules 2010"; in paragraph 2.2 for "paragraphs (4) to (6)", substitute "paragraphs (3) to (5)"; in paragraph 2.3, for "Part 11 of the Family Proceedings Rules 1991", substitute "Part 12, Chapter 7 of the Family Procedure Rules 2010 and Practice Direction 12G"; in paragraph 4.2, for "paragraph (8)", substitute "paragraph (7)"; in paragraph 4.3, for "paragraph (3)(f)", substitute "paragraph 2(f)" and for "paragraph 3(g)", substitute "paragraph (2)(g)";

Number	Title	Date	Court	Updated rule references
				in paragraph 5.1,for paragraph(4), substitute paragraph (3); in paragraph 5.2, for "paragraph (4)", substitute "paragraph (3)" and for "paragraph (4)(a)", substitute "paragraph 3(a)"; in paragraph 5.3, for "paragraph 4(a)(iii)", substitute "paragraph 3(a)(iii)"; in paragraph 5.4, for "paragraph 4(b)", substitute "paragraph 3(b)"; and in paragraph 6.1, for "paragraph (6)" substitute "paragraph (5)"
PD27C	Attendance of Media Representatives at Hearings in Family Proceedings (Family Proceedings Court) (This practice direction should be read as if amended by *Re X (a child) (residence and contact: rights of media attendance)* (2009) EWHC 1728 (Fam) at [87])	20 April 2009	Magistrates' courts	In paragraph 1.1, for "rule 16A of the Family Proceedings Courts (Children Act 1989) Rules 1991 ("the Rules")", substitute "rule 27.11 of the Family Procedure Rules 2010 ("the Rules")"; in paragraph 2.1, for references to "rule 16A(2)" where it occurs, substitute "rule 27.11(1)" and for "paragraphs (3) to (5) of rule 16A", substitute; "paragraphs (3) to (5) of rule 27.11"; in paragraph 2.2, for "rule 16A(2)", substitute "rule 27.11(1)";

Number	Title	Date	Court	Updated rule references
	[illegible]	[illegible]		in paragraph 2.3 for "Part 11C (rules relating to disclosure to third parties)", substitute "Part 12, Chapter 7 of the Family Procedure Rules 2010 and Practice Direction 12G"; in paragraph 2.4, for "rule 16A", substitute "rule 27.11"; and in paragraph 4.3, for "paragraph (1)(f)", substitute "paragraph 2(f)" and for "paragraph (1)(g)" substitute " paragraph 2(g)"
PD29B	Human Rights Act 1998	24 July 2000	High Court, county court and magistrates' court	
PD34B	Practice Note Tracing Payers Overseas	10 February 1976	High Court and county court	

PART III

Practice Direction 2A –
Functions of the Court in the Family Procedure Rules 2010 and Practice Directions which may be Performed by a Single Justice of the Peace

This Practice Direction supplements FPR Part 2, rule 2.5(1)(c)(ii) (Power to perform functions conferred on the court by these rules and practice directions)

1.1 Where the FPR or a practice direction provide for the court to perform any function, that function may be performed by a single justice of the peace who is a member of a family panel except that such a justice cannot perform the functions listed in:

    (a) column 2 of Table 1 in accordance with the rules listed in column 1; and

    (b) column 2 of Table 2 in accordance with the paragraph of the practice direction listed in column 1.

1.2 For the avoidance of doubt, unless a rule, practice direction or other enactment provides otherwise, a single justice cannot make the decision of a magistrates' court at the final hearing of an application for a substantive order. For example, a single justice cannot make a residence order on notice, placement order, adoption or care order. However, a single justice can discharge the functions of a family proceedings court under the statutory provisions listed in rule 2.6 of the FPR.

Table 1

Rule	Nature of function
4.1(3)(g)	Stay the whole or part of any proceedings or judgment either generally or until a specified date or event.
4.1(3)(l)	Exclude an issue from consideration.
4.1(3)(m)	Dismiss or give a decision on an application after a decision on a preliminary issue.
4.1(4)(a)	When the court makes an order, making that order subject to conditions.
4.1(6)	Varying and revoking an order (other than directions which the court has made).
4.3(1)	Ability of the court to make orders (other than directions) of its own initiative.
4.4, 4.5 and 4.6	All the powers of a magistrates' court under these rules (power to strike out statement of case, sanctions have effect unless defaulting party obtains relief from sanctions).
8.20(4)	A direction that a child should be made a respondent to the application for a declaration of parentage under section 55A of the Family Law Act 1986, except where the parties consent to the child being made a respondent.
9.11(2)	Direction that a child be separately represented on an application.
9.22	All the powers of a magistrates' court under this rule (relating to proceedings by or against a person outside England and Wales for variation or revocation of orders under section 20 of the 1978 Act or paragraphs 30 to 34 of Schedule 6 to the 2004 Act).
12.3(2)	Where the person with parental responsibility is a child, a direction for that child be made a party, except where the parties consent to that child being made a party.
12.3(3)	Direction that a child be made a party to proceedings or that a child who is a party be removed, except where the parties consent to the child being made a party or to the removal of that party.
12.3(4)	Consequential directions following the addition or removal of a party except where a single justice is able to make such a direction under rule 12.3(2) and (3).
12.61(1) and (2)	Considering the transfer of proceedings to the court of another member state, directions in relation to the manner in which parties may make representations and power to deal with question of transfer without a hearing with the consent of parties.
12.64(1)	Exercising court's powers under Article 15 of the Council Regulation or Article 8 of the 1996 Hague Convention.
12.68(1)	Staying the proceedings.
12.68(3)	Giving reasons for the court's decision, making a finding of fact and stating a finding of fact where such a finding has been made.

Rule	Nature of function
12.70(1)	Contemplating the placement of a child in another member state.
12.70(3)	Sending request directly to the central authority or other authority having jurisdiction in the other Member State.
12.70(4)	Sending request to Central Authority for England and Wales for onward transmission.
12.70(5)	Considering the documents which should accompany the request.
13.3(3)	Where the person with parental responsibility is a child, a direction for that child be made a party, except where the parties consent to that child being made a party.
13.3(4)	Direction that a child be made a party to proceedings or that a child who is a party be removed, except where the parties consent to the child being made a party or to the removal of that party.
13.3(5)	Consequential directions following the addition or removal of a party except where a single justice is able to make such a direction under rule 13.3(3) and (4).
13.9(7)	Variation or revocation of direction following transfer, except where a single justice would be able to make the direction in question under rule 13.9(1).
13.15(3)	Determination of the probable date of the child's birth.
13.20(1)	Specifying a later date by which a parental order takes effect.
14.3(2)	Direction that a child be made a respondent, except where the parties consent to the child being made a respondent.
14.3(3)(b)	Direction that a child who is a party be removed, except where the parties consent to the child being made a respondent.
14.3(4)	Consequential directions following the addition or removal of a party except where a single justice is able to make such a direction under rule 14.3(2) and (3)
14.8(3)	Any of the directions listed in PD14B in proceedings for – (a) a Convention adoption order (b) a section 84 order (c) a section 88 direction (d) a section 89 order; or (e) an adoption order where section 83(1) of the 2002 Act applies (restriction on bringing children in)
14.16(8)	Making an adoption order under section 50 of the 2002 Act after personal attendance of one only of the applicants if there are special circumstances.
14.16(9)	Not making a placement order unless the legal representative of the applicant attends the final hearing.
14.17(4)	Determination of the probable date of the child's birth.
14.25(1)	Specifying a later date by which an order takes effect.

PART III

Rule	Nature of function
15.3(1)	Permission to a person to take steps before the protected party has a litigation friend.
15.3(2)	Permission to a party to take steps (where during proceedings a person lacks capacity to continue to conduct proceedings) before the protected party has a litigation friend.
15.3(3)	Making an order that a step taken before a protected party has a litigation friend has effect.
15.6(1)	Making an order appointing a person as a litigation friend.
15.6(6)	Court may not appoint a litigation friend unless it is satisfied that the person complies with the conditions in rule 15.4(3).
15.7	Direction that a person may not act as a litigation friend, termination of an appointment, appointment of a litigation friend in substitution for an existing one.
16.2	Power of court to make a child a party to proceedings if it considers it is in the best interests of the child to do so.
16.6(3)(a)	Permission to a child to conduct proceedings without a children's guardian or litigation friend.
16.6(6)	Power of the court to grant an application under paragraph (3)(a) or (5) if the court considers that the child has sufficient understanding to conduct the proceedings.
16.6(7)	Power of the court to require the litigation friend or children's guardian to take such part in proceedings (referred to in paragraph (6)) as the court directs.
16.6(8)	Power of the court to revoke permission granted under paragraph (3) in specified circumstances.
16.6(10)	Power of the court, in specified circumstances, to appoint a person to be the child's litigation friend or children's guardian.
16.8(2)	Permission to a person to take steps before the child has a litigation friend.
16.8(3)	Making an order that a step taken before the child has a litigation friend has effect.
16.11(1)	Making an order appointing a person as a litigation friend.
16.12	Direction that a person may not act as a litigation friend, termination of an appointment, appointment of a litigation friend in substitution for an existing one.
16.23(2)	Permission to a person to take steps before the child has a children's guardian.
18.3(1)(c)	Direction that a child be a respondent to an application under Part 18.
18.9(1)(a)	Power of court to deal with a Part 18 application without a hearing.

Rule	Nature of function
18.12	Power of the court to proceed in absence of a party, except where a single justice has the power to make the relevant order applied for.
19.8(2)	The court's power to require or permit a party to give oral evidence at the hearing.
21.3	Power of court relating to withholding inspection or disclosure of a document.
22.1(2) to (4)	Power to exclude evidence that would otherwise be admissible, power to permit a party to adduce evidence, or to seek to rely on a document, in respect of which that party has failed to comply with requirements of Part 22 and power to limit cross examination.
22.6	Court's powers relating to use at final hearing of witness statements which have been served.
22.12	Power of court to require evidence by affidavit instead of or in addition to a witness statement.
22.15(4)	Permission for a party to amend or withdraw any admission made by that party on such terms as the court thinks just.
22.20(3)(a)	Permission for a witness statement in proceedings in the magistrates' court under Part 9 to be used for a purpose other than the proceedings in which it is served.
24.16(2)	Ordering the issue of a request to a designated court.
24.16(5)	Order for the submission of a request under article 17 of the Taking of Evidence Regulation.
27.10(1)(b)	Direction that proceedings to which the Rules apply will not be held in private, expect that a single justice may give such a direction in relation to a hearing which that single justice is conducting.
27.11(2)(g)	Power of the court to permit any other person to be present during any hearing, except that a single justice may give such permission in relation to a hearing which that single justice is conducting.
27.11(3)	Direction that persons within rule 27.11(2)(f) shall not attend the proceedings or any part of them.
Part 28	Powers of the court to make costs orders including wasted costs orders under section 145A of the Magistrates' Courts Act 1980.
29.8(1)	Court's opinion that it would be prevented by section 8 or 9 of the Child Support Act 1991 from making an order.
29.8(2)	Court's consideration of the matter without a hearing.
29.8(10)	Power of the court to determine that it would be prevented by sections 8 or 9 of the 1991 Act from making an order, and to dismiss the application.
29.8(11)	The court must give written reasons for its decision.

PART III

Rule	Nature of function
29.9(2)	Direction that the document will be treated as if it contained the application and directions as the court considers appropriate as to the subsequent conduct of the proceedings.
29.12(1)	Permission for inspection of a document, except where no party to the proceedings to which that document relates objects.
29.13(1)	Direction for a court officer not to serve a copy of an order (other than directions that the single justice has made) to every party affected by it.
29.15	Specifying alternative date for an order to take effect, except an order which the single justice has made.
29.16	Correcting an accidental slip or omission in an order, except where that order was made by a single justice.
Part 30	Any power of the magistrates' court (where it is the lower court) to grant or refuse permission to appeal, except where a single justice has the power to make the order which is subject to the appeal.
31.9	Power for court to stay the proceedings.

Amendments—FPR 2010, Update 2.

Table 2

Practice Direction: Family Assistance Orders dated 3 September 2007 – Paragraphs 2, 3, and 5	Under paragraph 2 the court must have obtained the opinion of the appropriate officer about whether it would be in the best interests of the child in question for a family assistance order to be made and, if so, how the family assistance order could operate and for what period. Under paragraph 3 the court decides on the category of officer required to be made available under the family assistance order. Under paragraph 5 the court must give to the person it proposes to name in the order an opportunity to comment.
Public Law Proceedings Guide to Case Management: 6 April 2010 – Paragraphs 8.1 to 8.5	Under paragraphs 8.1 to 8.5 determination by the court of issues as to whether an adult party or intended party to proceedings lacks capacity.
Practice Direction: Residence and Contact Orders: Domestic Violence and Harm: 14 January 2009 – Paragraphs 17, 18, 21 to 23, 28 and 29	Under paragraph 17 the court will consider whether a child who is the subject of an application should be made a party to proceedings. Under paragraph 18 the court will consider whether an interim order for residence or contact is in the best interests of the child.

	Under paragraphs 21–23, 27, 28 and 29 determinations of the court at fact finding hearings, in cases where a finding of domestic violence is made consideration of the conduct of the parents and where there has been a finding of domestic violence court directions or conditions on orders.
Practice Direction: Attendance of Media Representatives at Hearings in Family Proceedings dated 6 April 2009	Generally – court's discretion to exclude media representatives from attending hearings or part of hearings for "relevant proceedings" as defined in rule 1 of the Family Proceedings Courts (Children Act 1989) Rules 1991 (other than where a Single Justice or Justice's Clerk is conducting the hearing)
PD14B – The First Directions Hearing – adoptions with a Foreign Element – Paragraph 2	Under paragraph 2 the court's consideration of: (a) whether the requirements of the Adoption and Children Act 2002 and the Adoptions with a Foreign Element Regulations 2005 (S.I. 2005/392) appear to have been complied with and, if not, consider whether or not it is appropriate to transfer the case to the High Court; (b) whether all relevant documents are translated into English and, if not, fix a timetable for translating any outstanding documents; (c) whether the applicant needs to file an affidavit setting out the full details of the circumstances in which the child was brought to the United Kingdom, of the attitude of the parents to the application and confirming compliance with the requirements of The Adoptions with a Foreign Element Regulations 2005; and (d) give directions about: (i) the production of the child's passport and visa; (ii) the need for the Official Solicitor and a representative of the Home office to attend future hearings; and (iii) personal service on the parents (via the Central Authority in the case of an application for a Convention Adoption Order) including information about the role of the Official Solicitor and availability of legal aid to be represented within the proceedings; and

PART III

	(e) consider fixing a further directions no later than 6 weeks after the date of the first directions appointment and timetable a date by which the Official Solicitor should file an interim report in advance of that further appointment.
PD15A – Protected Parties – Paragraph 4.2(b)	Under paragraph 4.2(b) court directions on service on protected party.
PD16A – Representation of Children – Paragraphs 6.8 and 7.5	Under paragraph 6.8 the children's guardian must – (a) unless the court otherwise directs, file a written report advising on the interests of the child in accordance with the timetable set by the court; and (b) in proceedings to which Part 14 applies, where practicable, notify any person the joining of whom as a party to those proceedings would be likely, in the opinion of the children's guardian, to safeguard the interests of the child, of the court's power to join that person as a party under rule 14.3 and must inform the court (i) of any notification; (ii) of anyone whom the child's guardian attempted to notify under this paragraph but was unable to contact; and (iii) of anyone whom the children's guardian believes may wish to be joined to the proceedings Under paragraph 7.5 the court may, at the same time as deciding whether to join the child as a party, consider whether the proceedings should be transferred to another court taking into account the provisions of Part 3 of the Allocation and Transfer of Proceedings Order 2008.
PD18A – Other Applications in Proceedings Paragraphs 4.1 to 4.4(a)	Under paragraph 4.1 on receipt of an application notice containing a request for a hearing, unless the court considers that the application is suitable for consideration without a hearing, the court officer will, if serving a copy of the application notice, notify the applicant of the time and date fixed for the hearing of the application. Under paragraph 4.2 on receipt of an application notice containing a request that the application be dealt with without a hearing, the court will decide whether the application is suitable for consideration without a hearing.

	Under paragraph 4.3 where the court considers that the application is suitable for consideration without a hearing but is not satisfied that it has sufficient material to decide the application immediately it may give directions for the filing of evidence and will inform the applicant and the respondent(s) of its decision. Under paragraph 4.4(a) where the court does not consider that the application is suitable for consideration without a hearing it may give directions as to the filing of evidence.
PD22A – Written Evidence – Paragraphs 1.6, 14.1 and 14.2	Under paragraph 1.6 the court may give a direction under rule 22.12 that evidence shall be given by affidavit instead of or in addition to a witness statement on its own initiative; or after any party has applied to the court for such a direction. Under paragraph 14.1 where an affidavit, a witness statement or an exhibit to either an affidavit or a witness statement does not comply with Part 22 or PD22A in relation to its form, the court may refuse to admit it as evidence and may refuse to allow the costs arising from its preparation. Under paragraph 14.2 permission to file a defective affidavit or witness statement or to use a defective exhibit may be obtained from the court where the case is proceeding.
PD24A – Witnesses, Depositions and Taking of Evidence in Member States of the European Union – Paragraph 9.1 and 9.6	Under paragraph 9.1 where a person wishes to take a deposition from a person in another Regulation State, the court where proceedings are taking place may order the issue of a request to the designated court in the Regulation State (rule 24.16(2)). The form of request is prescribed as Form A in the Taking of Evidence Regulation. Under paragraph 9.6 Article 17 permits the court where proceedings are taking place to take evidence directly from a deponent in another Regulation State if the conditions of the article are satisfied. Direct taking of evidence can only take place if evidence is given voluntarily without the need for coercive measures. Rule 24.16(5) provides for the court to make an order for the submission of a request to take evidence directly.

PART III

> The form of request is Form I annexed to the Taking of Evidence Regulation and rule 24.16(6) makes provision for a draft of this form to be filed by the a party seeking the order. An application for an order under rule 24.16(5) should be by application notice in accordance with Part 18.

PART 3
ALTERNATIVE DISPUTE RESOLUTION: THE COURT'S POWERS

CONTENTS OF THIS PART

General note—This Part of the Rules represents an emphasis on alternative dispute resolution (ADR), reflecting the fact that many family cases are best disposed of by way of ADR, particularly mediation. If no welfare or safeguarding considerations arise, many private law issues under CA 1989 are better resolved by agreement between those who actually know the child and who are going to have to make any arrangement work, rather than by a solution being imposed by a court. Similarly, in a great many financial cases where assets are modest, the real question is not "What is the appropriate outcome having regard to the criteria in MCA 1973?" so much as "Is there some division of what is actually there that we can both live with?". But, as the rules make clear, mediation, and indeed ADR in general, has to involve the agreement of the parties. "It is one thing to encourage the parties to agree to mediation, even to encourage them in the strongest terms. It is another to order them to do so… It seems to us … likely that compulsion of ADR would be regarded as an unacceptable constraint on the right of access to the court and, therefore, a violation of article 6" (*Halsey v Milton Keynes General NHS Trust* [2004] EWCA Civ 576).

The court's role is limited to encouraging the parties. The court can, and frequently should, offer strong, even robust, encouragement. As FPR PD3A makes clear, before commencing private law proceedings relating to children or proceedings for a financial remedy, an applicant will, save in certain specified circumstances, be expected to attend a mediation information and assessment meeting. Attendance at a mediation assessment meeting can be ordered as a contact activity under CA 1989, ss 11A and 11C.

The Pre-application Protocol for Mediation and Assessment (introduced by FPR D3A) does not enable the court to decline to issue an application simply because a Form FM1 is not filed. As the PD makes clear, the court will enquire about compliance at the first hearing, but compliance is not compulsory nor a pre-condition of making an application.

A striking illustration of the court supporting ADR, in this case non-binding arbitration by the New York Beth Din in a case involving a devout Orthodox Jewish couple, is *AI v MT* [2013] EWHC 100 (Fam).

3.1 Scope of this Part

(1) This Part contains the court's powers to encourage the parties to use alternative dispute resolution and to facilitate its use.

(2) The powers in this Part are subject to any powers given to the court by any other rule or practice direction or by any other enactment or any powers it may otherwise have.

"encourage" (r 3.1(1))—As noted, the court cannot compel the parties to use ADR.

3.2 Court's duty to consider alternative dispute resolution

The court must consider, at every stage in proceedings, whether alternative dispute resolution is appropriate.

3.3 When the court will adjourn proceedings or a hearing in proceedings

(1) If the court considers that alternative dispute resolution is appropriate, the court may direct that the proceedings, or a hearing in the proceedings, be adjourned for such specified period as it considers appropriate –

    (a)   to enable the parties to obtain information and advice about alternative dispute resolution; and

    (b)   where the parties agree, to enable alternative dispute resolution to take place.

(2) The court may give directions under this rule on an application or of its own initiative.

(3) Where the court directs an adjournment under this rule, it will give directions about the timing and method by which the parties must tell the court if any of the issues in the proceedings have been resolved.

(4) If the parties do not tell the court if any of the issues have been resolved as directed under paragraph (3), the court will give such directions as to the management of the case as it considers appropriate.

(5) The court or court officer will –

    (a)   record the making of an order under this rule; and

    (b)   arrange for a copy of the order to be served as soon as practicable on the parties.

(6) Where the court proposes to exercise its powers of its own initiative the procedure set out in rule 4.3(2) to (6) applies.

    (By rule 4.1(7), any direction given under this rule may be varied or revoked.)

"such specified period" (r 3.3(1))—The court does not appear to have the power to adjourn generally under these provisions. This would seem to be an instance where the power to stay proceedings generally under FPR 2010, r 4.1(3)(g) is subject to "the rules providing otherwise".

"adjourned... to enable alternative dispute resolution to take place" (r 3.3(1)(b))—The court had power under FPR 1991, r 2.61D(2)(d)(iv) to adjourn financial proceedings for mediation or negotiation, but the power is given much greater prominence under the 2010 Rules and it is quite clear from the terms of FPR PD3A that this change of emphasis is deliberate.

Practice Direction 3A –
Pre-Application Protocol for Mediation Information and Assessment

This Practice Direction supplements FPR Part 3 (Pre-Application Protocol for Mediation Information and Assessment)

Introduction

1.1 This Practice Direction applies where a person is considering applying for an order in family proceedings of a type specified in Annex B (referred to in this Direction as "relevant family proceedings").

1.2 Terms used in this Practice Direction and the accompanying Pre-action Protocol have the same meaning as in the FPR.

1.3 This Practice Direction is supplemented by the following Annexes:

(i) Annex A: The Pre-application Protocol ("the Protocol"), which sets out steps which the court will normally expect an applicant to follow before an application is made to the court in relevant family proceedings;

(ii) Annex B: Proceedings which are "relevant family proceedings" for the purposes of this Practice Direction; and

(iii) Annex C: Circumstances in which attendance at a Mediation Information and Assessment Meeting is not expected.

Aims

2.1 The purpose of this Practice Direction and the accompanying Protocol is to:

(a) supplement the court's powers in Part 3 of the FPR to encourage and facilitate the use of alternative dispute resolution;

(b) set out good practice to be followed by any person who is considering making an application to court for an order in relevant family proceedings; and

(c) ensure, as far as possible, that all parties have considered mediation as an alternative means of resolving their disputes.

Rationale

3.1 There is a general acknowledgement that an adversarial court process is not always best suited to the resolution of family disputes, particularly private law disputes between parents relating to children, with such disputes often best resolved through discussion and agreement, where that can be managed safely and appropriately.

3.2 Litigants who seek public funding for certain types of family proceedings are (subject to some exceptions) already required to attend a meeting with a mediator as a pre-condition of receiving public funding.

3.3 There is growing recognition of the benefits of early information and advice about mediation and of the need for those wishing to make an application to court, whether publicly funded or otherwise, to consider alternative means of resolving their disputes, as appropriate.

3.4 In private law proceedings relating to children, the court is actively involved in helping parties to explore ways of resolving their dispute. The Private Law Programme, set out in Practice Direction 12B, provides for a first hearing dispute resolution appointment ('FHDRA'), at which the judge, legal advisor or magistrates, accompanied by an officer from Cafcass (the Children and Family Court Advisory and Support Service), will discuss with parties both the nature of their dispute and whether it could be resolved by mediation or other alternative means and can give the parties information about services which may be available to assist them. The court should also have information obtained through safeguarding checks carried out by Cafcass, to ensure that any agreement between the parties, or any dispute resolution process selected, is in the interests of the child and safe for all concerned.

3.5 Against that background, it is likely to save court time and expense if the parties take steps to resolve their dispute without pursuing court proceedings. Parties will therefore be expected to explore the scope for resolving their dispute through mediation before embarking on the court process.

The Pre-application Protocol

4.1 To encourage this approach, all potential applicants for a court order in relevant family proceedings will be expected, before making their application, to have followed the steps set out in the Protocol. This requires a potential applicant except in certain specified circumstances, to consider with a mediator whether the dispute may be capable of being resolved through mediation. The court will expect all applicants to have compiled with the Protocol before commencing proceedings and (except where any of the circumstances In Annex C applies) will expect any respondent to have attended a Mediation Information and Assessment Meeting, if invited to do so. If court proceedings are taken, the court will wish to know at the first hearing whether mediation has been considered by the parties. In considering the conduct of any relevant family proceedings, the court will take into account any failure to comply with the Protocol and may refer the parties to a meeting with a mediator before the proceedings continue further.

4.2 Nothing in the Protocol is to be read as affecting the operation of the Private Law Programme, set out in Practice Direction 12B, or the role of the court at the first hearing in any relevant family proceedings.

ANNEX A – THE PRE-APPLICATION PROTOCOL

1 This Protocol applies where a person ("the applicant") is considering making an application to the court for an order in relevant family proceedings.

2 Before an applicant makes an application to the court for an order in relevant family proceedings, the applicant (or the applicant's legal representative) should contact a family mediator to arrange for the applicant to attend an information meeting about family mediation and other forms of alternative dispute resolution (referred to in this Protocol as "a Mediation Information and Assessment Meeting").

3 An applicant is not expected to attend a Mediation Information and Assessment Meeting where any of the circumstances set out in Annex C applies.

4 Information on how to find a family mediator may be obtained from local family courts, from the Community Legal Advice Helpline – CLA Direct (0845 345 4345) or at www.direct.gov.uk.

Note—See now *www.gov.uk*.

5 The applicant (or the applicant's legal representative) should provide the mediator with contact details for the other party or parties to the dispute ("the respondent(s)"), so that the mediator can contact the respondent(s) to discuss that party's willingness and availability to attend a Mediation Information and Assessment Meeting.

6 The applicant should then attend a Mediation Information and Assessment Meeting arranged by the mediator. If the parties are willing to attend together, the meeting may be conducted jointly, but where necessary separate meetings may be held. If the applicant and respondent(s) do not attend a joint meeting, the mediator will invite the respondent(s) to a separate meeting unless any of the circumstances set out in Annex C applies.

7 A mediator who arranges a Mediation Information and Assessment Meeting with one or more parties to a dispute should consider with the party or parties concerned whether public funding may be available to meet the cost of the meeting and any subsequent mediation. Where none of the parties is eligible for, or wishes to seek, public funding, any charge made by the mediator for the Mediation Information and Assessment Meeting will be the responsibility of the party or parties attending, in accordance with any agreement made with the mediator.

PART III

8 If the applicant then makes an application to the court in respect of the dispute, the applicant should at the same time file a completed Family Mediation Information and Assessment Form (Form FM1) confirming attendance at a Mediation Information and Assessment Meeting or giving the reasons for not attending.

9 The Form FM1, must be completed and signed by the mediator, and countersigned by the applicant or the applicant's legal representative, where either:

(a) the applicant has attended a Mediation Information and Assessment Meeting; or
(b) the applicant has not attended a Mediation Information and Assessment Meeting and
    (i) the mediator is satisfied that mediation is not suitable because another party to the dispute is unwilling to attend a Mediation Information and Assessment Meeting and consider mediation;
    (ii) the mediator determines that the case is not suitable for a Mediation Information and Assessment Meeting; or
    (iii) a mediator has made a determination within the previous four months that the case is not suitable for a Mediation Information and Assessment Meeting or for mediation.

10 In all other circumstances, the Form FM1 must be completed and signed by the applicant or the applicant's legal representative.

11 The form may be obtained from magistrates' courts, county courts or the High Court or from www.direct.gov.uk.

Note—See now www.gov.uk.

ANNEX B – PROCEEDINGS WHICH ARE "RELEVANT FAMILY PROCEEDINGS" FOR THE PURPOSES OF THIS PRACTICE DIRECTION

1 Private law proceedings relating to children, except:

- proceedings for an enforcement order, a financial compensation order or an order under paragraph 9 or Part 2 of Schedule Al to the Children Act 1989;
- any other proceedings for enforcement of an order made in private law proceedings; or
- where emergency proceedings have been brought in respect of the same child(ren) and have not been determined.

("Private law proceedings" and "emergency proceedings" are defined in Rule 12.2)

2 Proceedings for a financial remedy, except:

- Proceedings for an avoidance of disposition order or an order preventing a disposition;
- Proceedings for enforcement of any order made in financial remedy proceedings.

("Financial remedy" is defined in Rule 2.3(1) and "avoidance of disposition order" and "order preventing a disposition" are defined in Rule 9.3(1))

ANNEX C – A PERSON CONSIDERING MAKING AN APPLICATION TO THE COURT IN RELEVANT FAMILY PROCEEDINGS IS NOT EXPECTED TO ATTEND A MEDIATION INFORMATION AND ASSESSMENT MEETING BEFORE DOING SO IF ANY OF THE FOLLOWING CIRCUMSTANCES APPLIES:

1 The mediator is satisfied that mediation is not suitable because another party to the dispute is unwilling to attend a Mediation Information and Assessment Meeting and consider mediation.

2 The mediator determines that the case is not suitable for a Mediation Information and Assessment Meeting.

3 A mediator has made a determination within the previous four months that the case is not suitable for a Mediation Information and Assessment Meeting or for mediation.

4 *Domestic abuse*

Any party has, to the applicant's knowledge, made an allegation of domestic violence against another party and this has resulted in a police investigation or the issuing of civil proceedings for the protection of any party within the last 12 months.

5 *Bankruptcy*

The dispute concerns financial issues and the applicant or another party is bankrupt.

6 The parties are in agreement and there is no dispute to mediate.

7 The whereabouts of the other party are unknown to the applicant.

8 The prospective application is for an order in relevant family proceedings which are already in existence and are continuing.

9 The prospective application is to be made without notice to the other party.

10 *Urgency*

The prospective application is urgent, meaning:

  (a) there is a risk to the life, liberty or physical safety of the applicant or his or her family or his or her home; or

  (b) any delay caused by attending a Mediation Information and Assessment Meeting would cause a risk of significant harm to a child, a significant risk of a miscarriage of justice, unreasonable hardship to the applicant or irretrievable problems in dealing with the dispute (such as an Irretrievable loss of significant evidence).

11 There is current social services involvement as a result of child protection concerns in respect of any child who would be the subject of the prospective application.

12 A child would be a party to the prospective application by virtue of Rule 12.3(1).

13 The applicant (or the applicant's legal representative) contacts three mediators within 15 miles of the applicant's home and none is able to conduct a Mediation Information and Assessment Meeting within 15 working days of the date of contact.

PART 4
GENERAL CASE MANAGEMENT POWERS

CONTENTS OF THIS PART

4.1 The court's general powers of management

(1) In this Part, "statement of case" means the whole or part of, an application form or answer.

(2) The list of powers in this rule is in addition to any powers given to the court by any other rule or practice direction or by any other enactment or any powers it may otherwise have.

(3) Except where these rules provide otherwise, the court may –

    (a) extend or shorten the time for compliance with any rule, practice direction or court order (even if an application for extension is made after the time for compliance has expired);

    (b) make such order for disclosure and inspection, including specific disclosure of documents, as it thinks fit;

    (c) adjourn or bring forward a hearing;

    (d) require a party or a party's legal representative to attend the court;

    (e) hold a hearing and receive evidence by telephone or by using any other method of direct oral communication;

    (f) direct that part of any proceedings be dealt with as separate proceedings;

    (g) stay$^{(GL)}$ the whole or part of any proceedings or judgment either generally or until a specified date or event;

    (h) consolidate proceedings;

    (i) hear two or more applications on the same occasion;

    (j) direct a separate hearing of any issue;

    (k) decide the order in which issues are to be heard;

    (l) exclude an issue from consideration;

    (m) dismiss or give a decision on an application after a decision on a preliminary issue;

    (n) direct any party to file and serve an estimate of costs; and

    (o) take any other step or make any other order for the purpose of managing the case and furthering the overriding objective.

    (Rule 21.1 explains what is meant by disclosure and inspection.)

(4) When the court makes an order, it may –

    (a) make it subject to conditions, including a condition to pay a sum of money into court; and

    (b) specify the consequence of failure to comply with the order or a condition.

(5) Where the court gives directions it will take into account whether or not a party has complied with any relevant pre-action protocol$^{(GL)}$.

(6) A power of the court under these rules to make an order includes a power to vary or revoke the order.

(7) Any provision in these rules –

    (a) requiring or permitting directions to be given by the court is to be taken as including provision for such directions to be varied or revoked; and

    (b) requiring or permitting a date to be set is to be taken as including provision for that date to be changed or cancelled.

(8) The court may not extend the period within which an application for a section 89 order must be made.

Amendments—SI 2012/679.

"The court's general powers of management"—The powers set out in r 4.1(3) are almost identical to the powers accorded to the civil courts under CPR 1998, r 3.1 and decisions on the interpretation of the CPR are likely to be of considerable assistance in construing them.

"adjourn ... a hearing" (r 4.1(3)(c))—The court is not required by HRA 1998, Sch 1, Pt I, Art 6 to adjourn a hopeless case to allow a party back into the fray simply because there has been some procedural unfairness along the way (*Lloyds Bank plc v Dix & anor* [2000] EWCA Civ 269). *Fitzroy Robinson v Mentmore Towers* [2009] EWHC 3070 (TCC) provides a useful checklist of factors to be taken into account when considering a contested last-minute application to adjourn a trial, although in dealing with family cases other considerations will also arise.

"telephone" (r 4.1(3)(e))—Parties are encouraged to save costs by taking advantage of telephone and video conferencing services. Care should be taken to organise these properly, c f *K v K (Financial Relief: Management of Difficult Cases)* [2005] 2 FLR 1137 at [23]–[31].

"a separate trial of any issue" (r 4.1(3)(j))—In *McLoughlin v Grovers (A firm)* [2001] EWCA Civ 1743, guidelines were suggested, which included the following:

(a) Only issues that are decisive or potentially decisive should be identified.
(b) Issues should be decided on the basis of a schedule of agreed or assumed facts.
(c) The issues should be triable without significant delay, making full allowance for the implications of a possible appeal.
(d) Any order should be made by the court following a case-management conference.

"specify the consequences of failure" (r 4.1(4)(b))—Care must be taken by the court to ensure that the consequences are in proportion to the fault – see *Asiansky Television Plc & Anor v Bayer-Rosin (A Firm)* [2001] EWCA Civ 1792.

"complied with any relevant pre-action protocol" (r 4.1(5))—In the civil courts, pre-action protocols have proved themselves to be a powerful agent of change for the better in daily practice. The family courts are here given explicit encouragement to enforce good practice. Practitioners (and litigants) who persist in viewing family litigation as a species of warfare are likely to be firmly dealt with.

"a power to vary or revoke" (r 4.1(6))—In *Lloyd's Investment (Scandinavia) Ltd v Ager-Hanssen* [2003] EWHC 1740 (Ch), Patten J considered that the power was not confined to procedural orders but should only be exercised where there was a material change of circumstances or the judge had been misled in some way. The Court of Appeal in *Roult (by his mother and litigation friend) v North West Strategic Health Authority* [2009] EWCA Civ 444 agreed that the power was not limited to case-management decisions but held that it could not be used by a judge to revisit his own final order disposing of a case in whole or in part. The rule did not permit a judge in effect to hear an appeal from himself. The power is not a substitute for an appeal (*Edwards v Golding* [2007] EWCA Civ 416).

"the period within which an application for a section 89 order must be made" (r 4.1(8))—That is, an order by the High Court under ACA 2002, s 89 annulling an overseas or Convention adoption, see FPR 2010, rr 2.3(1) and 14.22.

"exclude an issue from consideration" (r 4.1(3)(l))—The court may achieve much with orders under r 4.1(3)(l) excluding particular issues, such as conduct, from consideration; or by orders directing, for example, that unless particular steps are taken the final hearing will proceed on the assumption that, eg, the respondent has net earnings of not less than £X per annum, or free capital of £Y million.

4.2 Court officer's power to refer to the court

Where a step is to be taken by a court officer –

(a) the court officer may consult the court before taking that step;
(b) the step may be taken by the court instead of the court officer.

4.3 Court's power to make order of its own initiative

(1) Except where an enactment provides otherwise, the court may exercise its powers on an application or of its own initiative.

(Part 18 sets out the procedure for making an application.)

(2) Where the court proposes to make an order of its own initiative –

   (a)   it may give any person likely to be affected by the order an opportunity to make representations; and

   (b)   where it does so it must specify the time by and the manner in which the representations must be made.

(3) Where the court proposes –

   (a)   to make an order of its own initiative; and

   (b)   to hold a hearing to decide whether to make the order,

it must give each party likely to be affected by the order at least 5 days' notice of the hearing.

(4) The court may make an order of its own initiative without hearing the parties or giving them an opportunity to make representations.

(5) Where the court has made an order under paragraph 4 –

   (a)   a party affected by the order may apply to have it set aside(GL), varied or stayed(GL); and

   (b)   the order must contain a statement of the right to make such an application.

(6) An application under paragraph (5)(a) must be made –

   (a)   within such period as may be specified by the court; or

   (b)   if the court does not specify a period, within 7 days beginning with the date on which the order was served on the party making the application.

(7) If the High Court or a county court of its own initiative strikes out a statement of case or dismisses an application (including an application for permission to appeal) and it considers that the application is totally without merit –

   (a)   the court's order must record that fact; and

   (b)   the court must at the same time consider whether it is appropriate to make a civil restraint order.

4.4 Power to strike out a statement of case

(1) Except in proceedings to which Parts 12 to 14 apply, the court may strike out(GL) a statement of case if it appears to the court –

   (a)   that the statement of case discloses no reasonable grounds for bringing or defending the application;

   (b)   that the statement of case is an abuse of the court's process or is otherwise likely to obstruct the just disposal of the proceedings;

   (c)   that there has been a failure to comply with a rule, practice direction or court order; or

   (d)   in relation to applications for matrimonial and civil partnership orders and answers to such applications, that the parties to the proceedings consent.

(2) When the court strikes out a statement of case it may make any consequential order it considers appropriate.

(3) Where –

   (a)   the court has struck out an applicant's statement of case;

   (b)   the applicant has been ordered to pay costs to the respondent; and

   (c)   before paying those costs, the applicant starts another application against the same respondent, arising out of facts which are the same or substantially the same as those relating to the application in which the statement of case was struck out,

the court may, on the application of the respondent, stay(GL) that other application until the costs of the first application have been paid.

(4) Paragraph (1) does not limit any other power of the court to strike out^(GL) a statement of case.

(5) If the High Court or a county court strikes out an applicant's statement of case and it considers that the application is totally without merit –

    (a) the court's order must record that fact; and

    (b) the court must at the same time consider whether it is appropriate to make a civil restraint order.

"Except in proceedings to which Parts 12 to 14 apply" (r 4.4(1))—If a statement of case discloses no reasonable grounds for bringing or defending a claim, or is an abuse of process, the court is likely to deal with it summarily. The power to strike out a case under this rule does not apply to proceedings concerning children.

"Power to strike out a statement of case" (r 4.4)—PD4A is self-explanatory. Authorities on the corresponding provisions of the CPR establish that the court's approach to striking out must be firmly based on its view of the justice of the case in accordance with the overriding objective. Claims that are incoherent and unintelligible are liable to be struck out even if the applicant is a litigant in person, although normally an opportunity to amend should be given – *Spencer v Barclays Bank plc* [2009] EWHC 2832 (Ch).

    In *K v D and others* [1998] 1 FLR 700 an order striking out a claim for ancillary relief was "plainly intended to afford some protection to the respondent" and while the petitioner did not need leave as such to proceed with her application for ancillary relief, she needed an order reinstating it, and the matters relevant to the question whether she should be granted such an order included the lapse of time, the reasons for not pursuing the original application, the strength of the application and the effects on third parties.

4.5 Sanctions have effect unless defaulting party obtains relief

(1) Where a party has failed to comply with a rule, practice direction or court order, any sanction for failure to comply imposed by the rule, practice direction or court order has effect unless the party in default applies for and obtains relief from the sanction.

    (Rule 4.6 sets out the circumstances which the court may consider on an application to grant relief from a sanction.)

(2) Where the sanction is the payment of costs, the party in default may only obtain relief by appealing against the order for costs.

(3) Where a rule, practice direction or court order –

    (a) requires a party to do something within a specified time; and

    (b) specifies the consequence of failure to comply,

the time for doing the act in question may not be extended by agreement between the parties.

General note—The underlying idea is to maintain the momentum of judicial case management by making it unnecessary for the "innocent" party to have to apply for a sanction imposed against a "guilty" party to take effect; it will do so automatically, whatever the source of the sanction. The party in default must apply for relief under FPR 2010, r 4.6 (*Marcan Shipping (London) Ltd v George Kefalas & Candida Corporation* [2007] EWCA Civ 463). An agreement to extend time in such cases is of no effect and the court is unlikely to take any such agreement into account when considering an application for relief against the sanction imposed.

"payment of costs" (r 4.5(2))—Relief against all other sanctions should, in the first place, be considered at the level at which the sanction was imposed. But if the payment of costs and some other sanction are imposed by the same order, an appeal is necessary, if it is desired to seek relief against both.

4.6 Relief from sanctions

(1) On an application for relief from any sanction imposed for a failure to comply with any rule, practice direction or court order the court will consider all the circumstances including –

(a)   the interests of the administration of justice;

(b)   whether the application for relief has been made promptly;

(c)   whether the failure to comply was intentional;

(d)   whether there is a good explanation for the failure;

(e)   the extent to which the party in default has complied with other rules, practice directions, court orders and any relevant pre –action protocol[GL];

(f)   whether the failure to comply was caused by the party or the party's legal representative;

(g)   whether the hearing date or the likely hearing date can still be met if relief is granted;

(h)   the effect which the failure to comply had on each party; and

(i)   the effect which the granting of relief would have on each party or a child whose interest the court considers relevant.

(2) An application for relief must be supported by evidence.

General note—In *Bansal v Cheema* [2001] CP Rep 6 Brooke LJ emphasised the importance of judges systematically considering the analogous CPR 1998, r 3.9 checklist when considering any aspect of relief against sanctions. The principle that all factors must be considered was emphasised in *CIBC Mellon Trust Co v Stolzenberg* [2004] EWCA Civ 827. However, in *Tarn Insurance Services Limited (in Administration) v Kirby* [2009] EWCA Civ 19, the Court of Appeal explained that, when considering the provisions of this rule on an application for relief from sanctions imposed by an unless order, the true test to be applied was whether, notwithstanding that the unless order was a proper order to make for the purpose of furthering the overriding objective in the circumstances known at the time it was made, it remained appropriate at the time of hearing the application for relief to allow the sanction to take effect.

The Court of Appeal indicated in *Vernon v Spoudeas* [2010] EWCA Civ 666 that to deal on paper with an application for relief from sanctions was not normally to be recommended. The Court reiterated the importance of giving reasons when deciding such an application.

"all the circumstances" (r 4.6(1))—Consistent with FPR 2010, r 1.1(2)(b), the Court of Appeal paid particular regard to the proportionality of the strike-out sanction in *London Borough of Southwark v Onayamoke* [2007] EWCA Civ 1426.

"any sanction" (r 4.6(1))—This provision is unrestricted and applies to applications for relief from any sanction, whether payment for costs or other and however the application is made. When delay is under consideration, no distinction should be drawn between the litigant and his advisers (*Daryananii v Kumar and Gerry* (2000) (unreported) 12 December, CA).

"evidence" (r 4.6(2))—In particular, the court will need evidence as to the explanation for the failure (r 4.6(1)(d)) and as to who was responsible (r 4.6(1)(f)). In many cases, but not all, the other matters set out in the rule may be able to be established by argument based on the existing papers.

4.7 General power of the court to rectify matters where there has been an error of procedure

Where there has been an error of procedure such as a failure to comply with a rule or practice direction –

(a)   the error does not invalidate any step taken in the proceedings unless the court so orders; and

(b)   the court may make an order to remedy the error.

"error" (r 4.7)—Technical defects (e g the use of an incorrect form) should be looked at in the light of the overriding objective (*Hannigan v Hannigan & ors* [2000] 2 FCR 650, CA). The rule is not to be given a narrow meaning and the court's discretion will be used so as not to cause injustice to one party when relieving against another's error. However, the rule cannot be used to achieve something prohibited under another rule (*Steele v Mooney & ors* [2005] EWCA Civ 96).

4.8 Power of the court to make civil restraint orders

Practice Direction 4B sets out –

(a) the circumstances in which the High Court or a county court has the power to make a civil restraint order against a party to proceedings;

(b) the procedure where a party applies for a civil restraint order against another party; and

(c) the consequences of the court making a civil restraint order.

Power of the court to make a civil restraint order (r 4.8)—This provision follows the familiar provisions of CPR 1998, r 3.11. In family proceedings involving money, the authorities on CPR 1998, r 3.11 are likely to be of assistance. In proceedings involving children, it is submitted that the authorities on the interpretation of CA 1989, s 91(14) are likely to prove a more reliable guide.

Fees—A party who is subject to a restraint order is required to pay a fee if he seeks to appeal the order or seeks leave to make an application, even if he would otherwise qualify for fee remission, the fee being refunded if the application succeeds. This is not a breach of Art 6 of the European Convention on Human Rights: *Senior-Milne v Secretary of State* [2012] EWHC 3062 (Admin).

Practice Direction 4A – Striking Out a Statement of Case

This Practice Direction supplements FPR Part 4, rule 4.4 (Power to strike out a statement of case)

Introduction

1.1 Rule 4.4 enables the court to strike out the whole or part of a statement of case which discloses no reasonable grounds for bringing or defending the application (rule 4.4(1)(a)), or which is an abuse of the process of the court or otherwise likely to obstruct the just disposal of the proceedings (rule 4.4(1)(b)). These powers may be exercised on an application by a party or on the court's own initiative.

1.2 This practice direction sets out the procedure a party should follow to make an application for an order under rule 4.4.

Examples of cases within the rule

2.1 The following are examples of cases where the court may conclude that an application falls within rule 4.4(1)(a) –

(a) those which set out no facts indicating what the application is about;

(b) those which are incoherent and make no sense;

(c) those which contain a coherent set of facts but those facts, even if true, do not disclose any legally recognisable application against the respondent.

2.2 An application may fall within rule 4.4(1)(b) where it cannot be justified, for example because it is frivolous, scurrilous or obviously ill-founded.

2.3 An answer may fall within rule 4.4(1)(a) where it consists of a bare denial or otherwise sets out no coherent statement of facts.

2.4 A party may believe that it can be shown without the need for a hearing that an opponent's case has no real prospect of success on the facts, or that the case is bound to succeed or fail, as the case may be, because of a point of law (including the construction of a document). In such a case the party concerned may make an application under rule 4.4.

2.5 The examples set out above are intended only as illustrations.

2.6 Where a rule, practice direction or order states 'shall be struck out or dismissed' or 'will be struck out or dismissed' this means that the order striking out or dismissing the proceedings will itself bring the proceedings to an end and that no further order of the court is required.

Applications which appear to fall within rule 4.4(1)(a) or (b)

3.1 A court officer who is asked to issue an application form but believes the application may fall within rule 4.4(1)(a) or (b) should issue the application form, but may then consult the court (under rule 4.2) before returning the form to the applicant or taking any other step to serve the respondent. The court may of its own initiative make an immediate order designed to ensure that the application is disposed of or (as the case may be) proceeds in a way that accords with the rules.

3.2 The court may allow the applicant a hearing before deciding whether to make such an order.

3.3 Orders the court may make include –

(a) an order that the application be stayed until further order;
(b) an order that the application form be retained by the court and not served until the stay is lifted;
(c) an order that no application by the applicant to lift the stay be heard unless the applicant files such further documents (for example a witness statement or an amended application form) as may be specified in the order.

3.4 Where the court makes any such order or, subsequently, an order lifting the stay, it may give directions about the service on the respondent of the order and any other documents on the court file.

3.5 The fact that the court allows an application referred to it by a court officer to proceed does not prejudice the right of any party to apply for any order against the applicant.

Answers which appear to fall within rule 4.4(1)(a) or (b)

4.1 A court officer may similarly consult the court about any document filed which purports to be an answer and which the officer believes may fall within rule 4.4(1)(a) or (b).

4.2 If the court decides that the document falls within rule 4.4(1)(a) or (b) it may on its own initiative make an order striking it out. Where the court does so it may extend the time for the respondent to file a proper answer.

4.3 The court may allow the respondent a hearing before deciding whether to make such an order.

4.4 Alternatively the court may make an order requiring the respondent within a stated time to clarify the answer or to give additional information about it. The order may provide that the answer will be struck out if the respondent does not comply.

4.5 The fact that the court does not strike out an answer on its own initiative does not prejudice the right of the applicant to apply for any order against the respondent.

General provisions

5.1 The court may exercise its powers under rule 4.4(1)(a) or (b) on application by a party to the proceedings or on its own initiative at any time.

5.2 Where the court at a hearing strikes out all or part of a party's statement of case it may enter such judgment for the other party as that party appears entitled to.

Applications for orders under rule 4.4(1)

6.1 Attention is drawn to Part 18 (Procedure for Other Applications in Proceedings) and to the practice direction that supplements it. The practice direction requires all applications to be made as soon as possible.

6.2 While many applications under rule 4.4(1) can be made without evidence in support, the applicant should consider whether facts need to be proved and, if so, whether evidence in support should be filed and served.

Practice Direction 4B – Civil Restraint Orders

This Practice Direction supplements FPR rule 4.8

Introduction

1.1 This practice direction applies where the court is considering whether to make –

(a) a limited civil restraint order;
(b) an extended civil restraint order; or
(c) a general civil restraint order,

against a party who has made applications which are totally without merit.

Rules 4.3(7), 4.4(5) and 18.13 provide that where a statement of case or application is struck out or dismissed and is totally without merit, the court order must specify that fact and the court must consider whether to make a civil restraint order. Rule 30.11(5) makes similar provision where the appeal court refuses an application for permission to appeal, strikes out an appellant's notice or dismisses an appeal.

The powers of the court to make civil restraint orders are separate from and do not replace the powers given to the court by section 91(14) of the Children Act 1989.

Limited civil restraint orders

2.1 A limited civil restraint order may be made by a judge of the High Court or a county court where a party has made 2 or more applications which are totally without merit.

2.2 Where the court makes a limited civil restraint order, the party against whom the order is made –

(a) will be restrained from making any further applications in the proceedings in which the order is made without first obtaining the permission of a judge identified in the order;
(b) may apply for amendment or discharge of the order, but only with the permission of a judge identified in the order; and

(c)   may apply for permission to appeal the order and if permission is granted, may appeal the order.

2.3 Where a party who is subject to a limited civil restraint order –

(a)   makes a further application in the proceedings in which the order is made without first obtaining the permission of a judge identified in the order, such application will automatically be dismissed –

(i)   without the judge having to make any further order; and

(ii)   without the need for the other party to respond to it; and

(b)   repeatedly makes applications for permission pursuant to that order which are totally without merit, the court may direct that if the party makes any further application for permission which is totally without merit, the decision to dismiss the application will be final and there will be no right of appeal, unless the judge who refused permission grants permission to appeal.

2.4 A party who is subject to a limited civil restraint order may not make an application for permission under paragraphs 2.2(a) or (b) without first serving notice of the application on the other party in accordance with paragraph 2.5.

2.5 A notice under paragraph 2.4 must –

(a)   set out the nature and grounds of the application; and

(b)   provide the other party with at least 7 days within which to respond.

2.6 An application for permission under paragraphs 2.2(a) or (b) –

(a)   must be made in writing;

(b)   must include the other party's written response, if any, to the notice served under paragraph 2.4; and

(c)   will be determined without a hearing.

2.7 An order under paragraph 2.3(b) may only be made by a High Court judge but not a district judge.

2.8 Where a party makes an application for permission under paragraphs 2.2(a) or (b) and permission is refused, any application for permission to appeal –

(a)   must be made in writing; and

(b)   will be determined without a hearing.

2.9 A limited civil restraint order –

(a)   is limited to the particular proceedings in which it is made;

(b)   will remain in effect for the duration of the proceedings in which it is made, unless the court orders otherwise; and

(c)   must identify the judge or judges to whom an application for permission under paragraphs 2.2(a), 2.2(b) or 2.8 should be made.

Extended civil restraint orders

3.1 An extended civil restraint order may be made by a judge of the High Court but not a district judge where a party has persistently made applications which are totally without merit.

3.2 Unless the court orders otherwise, where the court makes an extended civil restraint order, the party against whom the order is made –

(a)   will be restrained from making applications in any court concerning any matter involving or relating to or touching upon or leading to the proceedings in which the order is made without first obtaining the permission of a judge identified in the order;

(b) may apply for amendment or discharge of the order, but only with the permission of a judge identified in the order; and

(c) may apply for permission to appeal the order and if permission is granted, may appeal the order.

3.3 Where a party who is subject to an extended civil restraint order –

(a) makes an application in a court identified in the order concerning any matter involving or relating to or touching upon or leading to the proceedings in which the order is made without first obtaining the permission of a judge identified in the order, the application will automatically be struck out or dismissed –

(i) without the judge having to make any further order; and

(ii) without the need for the other party to respond to it; and

(b) repeatedly makes applications for permission pursuant to that order which are totally without merit, the court may direct that if the party makes any further application for permission which is totally without merit, the decision to dismiss the application will be final and there will be no right of appeal, unless the judge who refused permission grants permission to appeal.

3.4 A party who is subject to an extended civil restraint order may not make an application for permission under paragraphs 3.2(a) or (b) without first serving notice of the application on the other party in accordance with paragraph 3.5.

3.5 A notice under paragraph 3.4 must –

(a) set out the nature and grounds of the application; and

(b) provide the other party with at least 7 days within which to respond.

3.6 An application for permission under paragraphs 3.2(a) or (b) –

(a) must be made in writing;

(b) must include the other party's written response, if any, to the notice served under paragraph 3.4; and

(c) will be determined without a hearing.

3.7 An order under paragraph 3.3(b) may only be made by a High Court judge but not a district judge.

3.8 Where a party makes an application for permission under paragraphs 3.2(a) or (b) and permission is refused, any application for permission to appeal –

(a) must be made in writing; and

(b) will be determined without a hearing.

3.9 An extended civil restraint order –

(a) will be made for a specified period not exceeding 2 years;

(b) must identify the courts in which the party against whom the order is made is restrained from making applications; and

(c) must identify the judge or judges to whom an application for permission under paragraphs 3.2(a), 3.2(b) or 3.8 should be made.

3.10 The court may extend the duration of an extended civil restraint order, if it considers it appropriate to do so, but the duration of the order must not be extended for a period greater than 2 years on any given occasion.

General civil restraint orders

4.1 A general civil restraint order may be made by a judge of the High Court but not a district judge where, the party against whom the order is made persists in making applications which are totally without merit, in circumstances where an extended civil restraint order would not be sufficient or appropriate.

4.2 Unless the court otherwise orders, where the court makes a general civil restraint order, the party against whom the order is made –

(a)   will be restrained from making any application in any court without first obtaining the permission of a judge identified in the order;

(b)   may apply for amendment or discharge of the order, but only with the permission of a judge identified in the order; and

(c)   may apply for permission to appeal the order and if permission is granted, may appeal the order.

4.3 Where a party who is subject to a general civil restraint order –

(a)   makes an application in any court without first obtaining the permission of a judge identified in the order, the application will automatically be struck out or dismissed –

(i)   without the judge having to make any further order; and

(ii)   without the need for the other party to respond to it; and

(b)   repeatedly makes applications for permission pursuant to that order which are totally without merit, the court may direct that if the party makes any further application for permission which is totally without merit, the decision to dismiss that application will be final and there will be no right of appeal, unless the judge who refused permission grants permission to appeal.

4.4 A party who is subject to a general civil restraint order may not make an application for permission under paragraphs 4.2(a) or (b) without first serving notice of the application on the other party in accordance with paragraph 4.5.

4.5 A notice under paragraph 4.4 must –

(a)   set out the nature and grounds of the application; and

(b)   provide the other party with at least 7 days within which to respond.

4.6 An application for permission under paragraphs 4.2(a) or (b) –

(a)   must be made in writing;

(b)   must include the other party's written response, if any, to the notice served under paragraph 4.4; and

(c)   will be determined without a hearing.

4.7 An order under paragraph 4.3(b) may only be made by a High Court judge but not a district judge.

4.8 Where a party makes an application for permission under paragraphs 4.2(a) or (b) and permission is refused, any application for permission to appeal –

(a)   must be made in writing; and

(b)   will be determined without a hearing.

4.9 A general civil restraint order–

(a)   will be made for a specified period not exceeding 2 years;

(b)   must identify the courts in which the party against whom the order is made is restrained from making applications; and

(c)   must identify the judge or judges to whom an application for permission under paragraphs 4.2(a), 4.2(b) or 4.8 should be made.

4.10 The court may extend the duration of a general civil restraint order, if it considers it appropriate to do so, but he duration of the order must not be extended for a period greater than 2 years on any given occasion.

General

5.1 The other party or parties to the proceedings may apply for any civil restraint order.

5.2 An application under paragraph 5.1 must be made using the procedure in Part 18 unless the court otherwise directs and the application must specify which type of civil restraint order is sought.

PART 5
FORMS AND START OF PROCEEDINGS

CONTENTS OF THIS PART

5.1 Forms

(1) Subject to rule 14.10(2) and (3), the forms referred to in a practice direction, shall be used in the cases to which they apply.

(2) A form may be varied by the court or a party if the variation is required by the circumstances of a particular case.

(3) A form must not be varied so as to leave out any information or guidance which the form gives to the recipient.

(4) Where these rules require a form to be sent by the court or by a party for another party to use, it must be sent without any variation except such as is required by the circumstances of the particular case.

(5) Paragraph (2) does not apply to the forms annexed to the Maintenance Regulation, or to an Article 11 form.

(6) Nothing in this rule requires a party to reveal any particulars referred to in rule 29.1(1) if notice of those particulars is given to the court in accordance with rule 29.1(2).

Amendments—SI 2011/1328; SI 2012/679; SI 2012/2806.

Practice Direction—PD5A supplements Pt 5 and sets out the forms prescribed for issue of applications in family proceedings.

"subject to rule 14.10(2) and (3)" (r 5.1(1))— FPR 2010, Pt 14 deals with adoption proceedings; r 14.10 deals with the consent of a parent or guardian in such proceedings and r 14.10(3) requires consent to a Convention adoption to be in accordance with any form required by the country of the child's habitual residence.

5.2 Documents to be attached to a form

Subject to any rule or practice direction, unless the court directs otherwise, a form must have attached to it any documents which, in the form, are –

   (a) stated to be required; or
   (b) referred to.

Disclosure and discovery of documents—A distinction may be allowed in Pt 5 between documents "discovered" (exhibited in the forms) and other relevant facts, documents and information that must be disclosed. In *Imerman v Tchenguiz and Others* [2010] 2 FLR 814 the Court of Appeal distinguished between "discovery" of documents and "disclosure" of information in financial order (then ancillary relief) proceedings (which the Court regarded as unique to family proceedings after *Livesey (formerly*

Jenkins) v Jenkins [1985] FLR 813, HL). The court explained their understanding of terms as follows: disclosure was of "relevant facts and matters" (e g the fact of a proposed remarriage), whereas discovery applied to "the discovery of relevant documents".

5.3 Proceedings are started by issue of application form

(1) Proceedings are started when a court officer issues an application at the request of the applicant.

(2) An application is issued on the date entered in the application form by the court officer.

(3) Where the application is made under Article 56 of the Maintenance Regulation, or under Article 10 of the 2007 Hague Convention, the applicant is deemed to have requested the issue of the application by virtue of making the application for establishment or modification of a maintenance decision forwarded on his or her behalf by the Lord Chancellor.

> [The Lord Chancellor is the Central Authority for England and Wales in relation to the 2007 Hague Convention and the Maintenance Regulation]

> (Rule 29.7 requires an application form to be authenticated with the stamp of the court when it is issued)

Amendments—SI 2012/2806.

Defined terms—"application form": r 2.3(1).

Start of proceedings—FPR 2010 distinguishes between the application form by which originating proceedings (either under a specific rule or under FPR 2010, Pt 19) are issued and the "application notice" (which is a different document (often Form D11) by which application is made under the FPR 2010, Pt 18 procedure); and see definition of application forms and notices in FPR 2010, r 2.3(1).

Applications and applications in proceedings—To commence any originating process under the rules, an application form must be filed and must then be issued by a court officer. Applications under the rules come in three categories:

(1) Procedures prescribed by the rules for a particular process. These are commenced by an application form (defined by FPR 2010, r 2.3(1)), generally in a form prescribed by FPR PD5A (e g matrimonial and civil partnership proceedings by Form D8; financial remedy proceedings under FPR 2010, Pt 9 by Forms A, A1 or A2 and children proceedings by Form C1).
(2) The FPR 2010, Pt 19 procedure is for certain particular simplified processes (e g application for a declaration of parentage by Form C63) or where not otherwise prescribed (as at (1), above). Applications by the FPR 2010, Pt 19 procedure are freestanding or originating applications; or prescribed to be by that procedure.
(3) Applications in proceedings, the FPR 2010, Pt 18 procedure: interim applications in existing or applications in proposed proceedings (such as where permission is required to start an application: e g application for permission to apply for a forced marriage protection order (FPR 2010, r 11.3(1)(a)(i)); or for interim remedies under FPR 2010, Pt 20 or FPR 2010, r 9.7).

The first two sets of application are originating processes. Each will attract an individual court number (and court fee), whereas the FPR 2010, Pt 18 procedure is entirely parasitic on another set of proceeding (or an anticipated application). The Ministry of Justice Explanatory Memorandum (para 7.7), which describes the FPR 2010, Pt 19 procedure as applicable where the Pt 18 procedure does not apply, is unhelpful. The equivalent procedures under CPR 1998 are:

(1) that CPR 1998, Pt 7 provides for all claims (if in doubt a CPR 1998 claimant issues under CPR 1998, Pt 7);
(2) CPR 1998, Pt 8 (like FPR 2010, Pt 19) provides a simplified originating procedure (e g where a claim "is unlikely to involve a substantial dispute of fact" or where the simplified CPR 1998, Pt 8 procedure is prescribed); and
(3) CPR 1998, Pt 23 is the equivalent of FPR 2010, Pt 18 and provides for applications in the course of proceedings ("an application … made to the court where the claim was started": CPR 1998, r 23.2(1)).

Practice Direction 5A – Forms

This Practice Direction supplements FPR Part 5, rule 5.1 (Forms)

Note—All of the forms listed in FPR PD5A are available on the Family Law Online service, which is available by subscription.

Scope and interpretation

1.1 This Practice Direction lists the forms to be used in family proceedings on or after 6 April 2011. Table 1 lists the forms against the part of the FPR to which they are relevant, and Table 2 lists the forms individually with their description.

1.2 The forms may be –

(a) modified as the circumstances require, provided that all essential information, especially information or guidance which the form gives to the recipient, is included;

(b) expanded to include additional pages where that may be necessary, provided that any additional pages are also verified by a statement of truth.

1.3 Any reference in family proceedings forms to a Part, rule or Practice Direction is to be read as a reference to the equivalent Part, rule or Practice Direction in the FPR and any reference to a Practice Direction in any CPR form used in family proceedings is to be read as a reference to the equivalent Practice Direction in the FPR.

Forms for committal applications

2.1 Rule 33.1(2) applies Part 50 of, and Schedules 1 and 2 to the CPR, in so far as they are relevant and with necessary modification (including the modification referred to in rule 33.7), to an application made in the High Court and a county court to enforce an order made in family proceedings. The CPR Practice Direction "RSC52 and CCR 29–Committal Applications" therefore applies with necessary modifications to the enforcement of such an order. The form to be used for a committal application is set out in that Practice Direction. Accordingly, where a committal application is made in existing proceedings, it must be commenced by filing an application notice under Part 18 in those proceedings. Otherwise a committal application must be commenced by the issue of a Part 19 application notice (a form FP1).

Amendments—FPR 2010, Update 2.

Application notices

2.2 Where an application under the Part 18 procedure is to be made by application notice, the forms to be used are:

(i) Form C2 where the application is made in the course of or in connection with proceedings under Part 12;

(ii) Form D11 where the application is made in the course of or in connection with proceedings under Parts 7, 8 or 9;

(iii) Form FP2 in any other case.

Other Forms

3.1 Other forms may be authorised by practice directions.

PART III

Table 1
Index to forms

FPR Part	Forms
Part 3 Alternative Dispute Resolution (Family Mediation)	FM1
Part 6 Service	C9, D5, D89, FL415, FP6
Part 7 Matrimonial and Civil Partnership Proceedings	C60, D6, D8, D8 Notes, D8A, D8B, D8D, D8D Notes, D8N, D8N Notes, D11, D13B, D20, D36, D80A, D80B, D80C, D80D, D80E, D80F, D80G, D81, D84,
Part 8 Miscellaneous Applications	D50, D50A, D50B, D50C, D50D, D50E, D50F, D50G, D50H, D50J, D50K
Part 8 Chapter 5 Applications for declarations	C63, C64, C65, D70
Part 9 Applications for a Financial Remedy	Form A, Form A1, Form A2, Form B, Form E, Form E Notes, Form E1, Form E2, Form F, Form I, Form P, Form P1, Form P2, Form PPF, Form PPF1, Form PPF2
Part 10 Applications under Part 4 of the Family Law Act 1996	FL401, FL403, FL407, FL415
Part 11 Applications under Part 4A of the Family Law Act 1996	FL401A, FL403A, FL407A, FL430, FL431
Part 12 Applications in respect of children	C1, C1A, C2, C3, C4, C5, C8, C9, C11, C12, C13A, C14, C15, C16, C17, C17A, C18, C19, C20, C61, C62, C66, C67, C68, C78, C79, C100, C110, C(PRA1), C(PRA2) C(PRA3), PLO8, PLO9, PLP10
Part 13 Applications under section 54 of Human Fertilisation and Embryology Act 2008	C51, C52, A64A, A101A
Part 14 Adoption	A4, A5, A50, A51, A52, A53, A54, A55, A56, A57, A58, A59, A60, A61, A62, A63, A50 Notes, A51 Notes, A52 Notes, A53 Notes, A54 Notes, A55 Notes, A56 Notes, A57 Notes, A58 Notes, A59 Notes, A60 Notes, A61 Notes, A 62 Notes, A63 Notes, A64, A65, A100, A101, A102, A103, A104, A105, A106, A107
Part 15 Representation of Protected Parties	FP9
Part 16 Representation of children	FP9
Part 18 Applications in proceedings	C2, D11, FP2
Part 19 Alternative Procedure for applications	FP1, FP1A, FP1B, FP3, FP5

FPR Part	Forms
Part 22 Evidence	N285
Part 24 Witnesses	FP25
Part 26 Notification of change of solicitor	FP8
Part 28 Costs	D252, D254, D258, D258A, D258B, D258C, D259, Form H, Form H1, N260
Part 30 Appeals	N161, N161A, N161B, N162, N162A, N162, N164
Part 31 Registration of Orders under the Council Regulation, The Civil Partnership (Jurisdiction and Recognition of Judgements) Regulations 2005 and under the Hague Convention 1996	C60, C61, C62, C69, D180
Part 32 Registration and Enforcement of Orders	D151
Part 33 Enforcement	D62, N56, N323, N336, N337, N349, N379, N380
Part 34 Reciprocal Enforcement of Maintenance Orders	REMO 1, REMO 2

Amendments—FPR 2010, Update 2.

Table 2

List of Forms

Number	Name
A4	Application For Revocation Of An Order Freeing A Child For Adoption
A5	Application For Substitution Of One Adoption Agency For Another
A50	Application for a placement order Section 22 Adoption and Children Act 2002
A51	Application for variation of a placement order Section 23 Adoption and Children Act 2002
A52	Application for revocation of a placement order Section 24 Adoption and Children Act 2002
A53	Application for a contact order Section 26 Adoption and Children Act 2002
A54	Application for variation or revocation of a contact order Section 27(1)(b) Adoption and Children Act 2002
A55	Application for permission to change a child's surname Section 28 Adoption and Children Act 2002

PART III

Number	Name
A56	Application for permission to remove a child from the United Kingdom Section 28 Adoption and Children Act 2002
A57	Application for a recovery order Section 41 Adoption and Children Act 2002
A58	Application for an adoption order Section 46 Adoption and Children Act 2002
A59	Application for a Convention adoption order Section 46 Adoption and Children Act 2002
A60	Application for an adoption order (excluding a Convention adoption order) where the child is habitually resident outside the British Islands and is brought into the United Kingdom for the purposes of adoption Section 46 Adoption and Children Act 2002
A61	Application for an order for parental responsibility prior to adoption abroad Section 84 Adoption and Children Act 2002
A62	Application for a direction under section 88(1) of the Adoption and Children Act 2002
A63	Application for an order to annul a Convention adoption or Convention adoption order or for an overseas adoption or determination under section 91 to cease to be valid Section 89 Adoption and Children Act 2002
A50 Notes	Application for a placement order Section 22 Adoption and Children Act 2002 – Notes on completing the form
A51 Notes	Application for variation of a placement order Section 23 Adoption and Children Act 2002 – Notes on completing the form
A52 Notes	Application for revocation of a placement order Section 24 Adoption and Children Act 2002 – Notes on completing the form
A53 Notes	Application for a contact order Section 26 Adoption and Children Act 2002 – Notes on completing the form
A54 Notes	Application for variation or revocation of a contact order Section 27(1)(b) Adoption and Children Act 2002 – Notes on completing the form
A55 Notes	Application for permission to change a child's surname Section 28 Adoption and Children Act 2002 – Notes on completing the form
A56 Notes	Application for permission to remove a child from the United Kingdom Section 28 Adoption and Children Act 2002 – Notes on completing the form
A57 Notes	Application for a recovery order Section 41 Adoption and Children Act 2002 – Notes on completing the form
A58 Notes	Application for an adoption order Section 46 Adoption and Children Act 2002 – Notes on completing the form

Number	Name
A59 Notes	Application for a Convention adoption order Section 46 Adoption and Children Act 2002 – Notes on completing the form
A60 Notes	Application for an adoption order (excluding a Convention adoption order) where the child is habitually resident outside the British Islands and is brought into the United Kingdom for the purposes of adoption Section 46 Adoption and Children Act 2002 – Notes on completing the form
A61 Notes	Application for an order for parental responsibility prior to adoption abroad Section 84 Adoption and Children Act 2002 – Notes on completing the form
A62 Notes	Application for a direction under section 88(1) of the Adoption and Children Act 2002 – Notes on completing the form
A63 Notes	Application for an order to annul a Convention adoption or Convention adoption order or for an overseas adoption or determination under section 91 to cease to be valid Section 89 Adoption and Children Act 2002 – Notes on completing the form
A64	Application to receive information from court records Section 60(4) Adoption and Children Act 2002
A64A	Application to receive information from court records about a parental order Section 60(4) Adoption and Children Act 2002
A65	Confidential information
A100	Consent to the placement of my child for adoption with any prospective adopters chosen by the Adoption Agency Section 19 of the Adoption and Children Act 2002
A101	Consent to the placement of my child for adoption with identified prospective adopters Section 19 of the Adoption and Children Act 2002
A101A	Agreement to the making of a parental order in respect of my child Section 54 of the Human Fertilisation and Embryology Act 2008
A102	Consent to the placement of my child for adoption with identified prospective adopter(s) and, if the placement breaks down, with any prospective adopter(s) chosen by the adoption agency Section 19 of the Adoption and Children Act 2002
A103	Advance Consent to Adoption Section 20 of the Adoption and Children Act 2002
A104	Consent to Adoption The Adoption and Children Act 2002
A105	Consent to the making of an Order under Section 84 of the Adoption and Children Act 2002
A106	Withdrawal of Consent Sections 19 and 20 of the Adoption and Children Act 2002
A107	Consent by the child's parent to adoption by their partner The Adoption and Children Act 2002

PART III

Number	Name
C1	Application for an Order
C1A	Allegations of harm and domestic violence (Supplemental information form)
C2	Application For permission to start proceedings For an order or directions in existing proceedings To be joined as, or cease to be, a party in existing family proceedings under the Children Act 1989
C3	Application for an order authorising search for, taking charge of and delivery of child
C4	Application for an order for disclosure of a child's whereabouts
C5	Local Authority application concerning the registration of a child-minder or a provider of day care
C8	Confidential contact details
C9	Statement of service
C11	Supplement for an application for an Emergency Protection Order
C12	Supplement for an application for a warrant to assist a person authorised by an Emergency Protection Order
C13A	Supplement for an application for a Special Guardianship Order Section 14A Children Act 1989
C14	Supplement for an application for authority to refuse contact with a child in care
C15	Supplement for an application for contact with a child in care
C16	Supplement for an application for a Child Assessment Order
C17	Supplement for an application for Education Supervision Order
C17A	Supplement for an application for an extension of an Education Supervision Order
C18	Supplement for an application for a Recovery Order
C19	Application for a warrant of assistance
C20	Supplement for an application for an order to hold a child in Secure Accommodation
C51	Application for a Parental Order Section 54 Human Fertilisation and Embryology Act 2008
C52	Acknowledgement of an application for a Parental Order
C60	Certificate referred to in Article 39 of Council Regulation (EC) No. 2201/ 2003 of 27 November 2003 concerning judgments on parental responsibility

Number	Name
C61	Certificate referred to in Article 41(1) of Council Regulation (EC) No. 2201/2003 of 27 November 2003 concerning judgments on rights of access
C62	Certificate referred to in Article 42(1) of Council Regulation (EC) No. 2201/2003 of 27 November 2003 concerning the return of the child
C63	Application for declaration of parentage under section 55A of the Family Law Act 1986
C64	Application for declaration of legitimacy or legitimation under section 56(1)(b) and (2) of the Family Law Act 1986
C65	Application for declaration as to adoption effected overseas under section 57 of the Family Law Act 1986
C66	Application for inherent jurisdiction order in relation to children
C67	Application under the Child Abduction and Custody Act 1985 or Article 11 of Council Regulation (EC) 2201/2003
C68	Application for international transfer of jurisdiction to or from England and Wales
C69	Application for registration, recognition or non recognition of a judgment under Council Regulation (EC) 2201/2003 or the 1996 Hague Convention
C78	Application for attachment of a warning notice to a contact order
C79	Application related to enforcement of a contact order
C100	Application under the Children Act 1989 for a residence, contact, prohibited steps, specific issue section 8 order or to vary or discharge a section 8 order
C110	Application under the Children Act 1989 for a care or supervision order
C(PRA1)	Parental Responsibility Agreement
C(PRA2)	Step Parent Parental Responsibility Agreement
C(PRA3)	Parental Responsibility Agreement Section 4ZA Children Act 1989 (Acquisition of parental responsibility by second female parent)
D5	Notice to be indorsed on documents served in accordance with rule 6.14
D6	Statement of Reconciliation
D8	Divorce/dissolution/(judicial) separation petition
D8 Notes	Supporting notes for guidance on completing a divorce/dissolution/(judicial) separation petition
D8A	Statement of arrangements for children
D8B	Answer to a divorce/dissolution/(judicial) separation or nullity petition

PART III

Number	Name
D8D	Petition for a presumption of death decree/order and the dissolution of a marriage/civil partnership
D8D Notes	Supporting notes for guidance on completing a petition for a presumption of death decree/order and the dissolution of a marriage/civil partnership
D8N	Nullity petition
D8N Notes	Supporting notes for guidance on completing a nullity petition
D11	Application Notice
D13B	Statement in support of a request to dispense with service of the divorce/dissolution/nullity/(judicial) separation petition on the Respondent
D20	Medical Examination: statement of parties & examiner
D36	Notice of Application for Decree Nisi to be made Absolute or Conditional Order to be made final
D50	Notice of application under section 17 of the Married Women's Property Act 1882/section 66 of the Civil Partnership Act 2004
D50A	Notice of proceedings and acknowledgement of service under section 17 of the Married Women's Property Act 1882/section 66 of the Civil Partnership Act 2004
D50B	Application under section 17 of the Married Women's Property Act 1882/section 66 of the Civil Partnership Act 2004/Application to transfer a tenancy under the Family Law Act 1996
D50C	Application on ground of failure to provide maintenance
D50D	Application for alteration of maintenance agreement after the death of one of the parties, under section 36 of the Matrimonial Causes Act 1973/paragraph 73 of Schedule 5 to the Civil Partnership Act 2004
D50E	Application for permission to apply for financial relief after overseas divorce/dissolution etc under section 13 of the Matrimonial and Family Proceedings Act 1984 / paragraph 4 of Schedule 7 to the Civil Partnership Act 2004
D50F	Application for financial relief after overseas divorce etc under section 12 of the Matrimonial and Family Proceedings Act 1984/paragraph 4 to Schedule 7 to the Civil Partnership Act 2004
D50G	Application to prevent transactions intended to defeat prospective applications for financial relief
D50H	Application for alteration of maintenance agreement during parties lifetime
D50J	Application for an order preventing avoidance under section 32L of the Child Support Act 1991
D50K	Notice of Application for Enforcement by such method of enforcement as the court may consider appropriate

Number	Name
D62	Request for issue of Judgment Summons
D70	Application for Declaration of Marital/Civil Partnership Status
D80A	Statement in support of divorce/(judicial) separation – adultery
D80B	Statement in support of divorce/dissolution/(judicial) separation – unreasonable behaviour
D80C	Statement in support of divorce/dissolution/(judicial) separation – desertion
D80D	Statement in support of divorce/dissolution/(judicial) separation – 2 years consent
D80E	Statement in support of divorce/dissolution/(judicial) separation – 5 years separation
D80F	Statement in support of annulment -void marriage/civil partnership
D80G	Statement in support of annulment – voidable marriage/civil partnership
D81	Statement of information for a Consent Order in relation to a financial remedy
D84	Application for a decree nisi/conditional order or (judicial) separation decree/order
D89	Request for personal service by a court bailiff
D151	Application for registration of maintenance order in a magistrates' court
D180	Concerning judgements in matrimonial matters
D252	Notice of commencement of assessment of bill of costs.
D254	Request for a default costs certificate
D258	Request for a detailed assessment of hearing
D258A	Request for detailed assessment (legal aid only)
D258B	Request for detailed assessment (Costs payable out of a fund other than the Community Legal Service Fund)
D258C	Request for detailed assessment hearing pursuant to an order under Part III of the Solicitors Act 1974
D259	Notice of appeal against a detailed assessment (divorce)
FL401	Application for a non molestation order/an occupation order
FL401A	Application for a Forced Marriage Protection Order
FL403	Application to vary, extend or discharge
FL403A	Application to vary, extend or discharge Forced Marriage Protection Orders

PART III

Number	Name
FL407	Applications for warrant of Arrest
FL407A	Application for warrant of arrest for a Forced Marriage Protection Order
FL415	Statement of service
FL430	Application for leave to apply for a Forced Marriage Protection Order
FL431	Application to join / cease as a party to Forced Marriage Protection Proceedings
FM1	Family Mediation Information and Assessment Form FM1
Form A	Notice of [intention to proceed with] an application for a financial order (NOTE: This form should be used whether the applicant is proceeding with an application in the petition or making a free standing application)
Form A1	Notice of [intention to proceed with] an application for a financial remedy (other than a financial order) in the county or high court
Form A2	Notice of [intention to proceed with] an application for a financial remedy in the magistrates court
Form B	Notice of an application to consider the financial position of the Respondent after the divorce/dissolution
Form E	Financial statement – For a financial order under the Matrimonial Causes Act 1973/Civil Partnership Act 2004 – For financial relief after an overseas divorce etc under Part 3 of the Matrimonial and Family Proceedings Act 1984/Schedule 7 to the Civil Partnership Act 2004
Form E Notes	Form E (Financial Statement for a financial order or for financial relief after an overseas divorce or dissolution etc) Notes for guidance
Form E1	Financial Statement for a financial remedy (other than a financial order or financial relief after an overseas divorce/dissolution etc) in the county or high court
Form E2	Financial Statement for a financial remedy in the magistrates court
Form F	Notice of allegation in proceedings for financial remedy
Form H	Estimate of costs (financial remedy)
Form H1	Statement of Costs (financial remedy)
Form I	Notice of request for periodical payments order at the same rate as order for interim maintenance pending outcome of proceeding
Form P	Pension inquiry form
Form P1	Pension sharing annex
Form P2	Pension attachment annex
Form PPF	Pension Protection Fund Inquiry Form

Number	Name
Form PPF 1	Pension Protection Fund sharing annex
Form PPF 2	Pension Protection Fund attachment annex
FP1	Application under Part 19 of the Family Procedure Rules 2010
FP1A	Application under Part 19 of the Family Procedure Rules 2010 Notes for applicant on completing the application (Form FP1)
FP1B	Application under Part 19 of the Family Procedure Rules 2010 Notes for respondent
FP2	Application notice Part 18 of the Family Procedure Rules 2010
FP3	Application for injunction (General form)
FP5	Acknowledgment of service Application under Part 19 of the Family Procedure Rules 2010
FP6	Certificate of service
FP8	Notice of change of solicitor
FP9	Certificate of suitability of litigation friend
FP25	Witness Summons
N56	Form for replying to an attachment of earnings application (statement of means)
N161	Appellant's Notice
N161A	Guidance Notes on Completing the Appellant's Notice
N161B	Important Notes for Respondents
N162	Respondent's Notice
N162A	Guidance Notes for Completing the Respondent's Notice
N163	Skeleton Argument
N164	Appellant's Notice
N260	Statement of costs (summary assessment)
N285	General Affidavit
N323	Request for Warrant of Execution
N336	Request and result of search in the attachment of earnings index
N337	Request for attachment of earnings order
N349	Application for a third party debt order
N379	Application for a charging order on land or property
N380	Application for charging order on securities

Number	Name
PLO8	Standard Directions on Issue
PLO9	Standard Directions at First Appointment
PLP10	Order Menu – Directions Revised Private Law Programme
REMO 1	Notice of Registration
REMO 2	Notice of Refusal of Registration.

Amendments—FPR 2010, Update 2.

PART 6
SERVICE

CONTENTS OF THIS PART

Scope—FPR 2010, Pt 6 provides a comprehensive code for the service of an application for a matrimonial order or civil partnership order and for other documents. Chapter 2 relates to the service of an application for a matrimonial order or civil partnership order in the *jurisdiction*. Chapter 3 provides for the service of other documents in the *UK*. Chapter 4 provides for service out of the jurisdiction. Part 6, Chs 2 and 3 are supplemented by FPR PD6A (service within the jurisdiction); Pt 6, Ch 4 is supplemented by FPR PD6B (service out of the jurisdiction).

Chapter 1
Scope of this Part and Interpretation

6.1 Part 6 rules about service apply generally

This Part applies to the service of documents, except where –

    (a) another Part, any other enactment or a practice direction makes a different provision; or

    (b) the court directs otherwise.

Scope—The court may "direct otherwise" under r 6.19: service by an alternative method or at an alternative place.

"another part" (r 6.1(a))—This includes FPR 2010, r 33.13 (judgment summons).

"any other enactment" (r 6.1(a))—These include: Companies Act 1985, ss 694A, 695 and 725; Crown Proceedings Act 1947, ss 17 and 18; and State Immunity Act 1978, s 12.

6.2 Interpretation

In this Part "solicitor" includes any person who, for the purposes of the Legal Services Act 2007, is an authorised person in relation to an activity which constitutes the conduct of litigation (within the meaning of that Act).

Defined term—"authorised person": Legal Services Act 2007, s 18.

Chapter 2
Service of the Application for a Matrimonial Order or Civil Partnership Order in the Jurisdiction

6.3 Interpretation

In this Chapter, unless the context otherwise requires, a reference to an application –

    (a) is a reference to an application for a matrimonial or civil partnership order; and

    (b) includes an application by a respondent as referred to in rule 7.4.

    (Part 7 deals with applications in matrimonial or civil partnership proceedings.)

Defined terms—"matrimonial order", "civil partnership order": FPR 2010, r 2.3.

6.4 Methods of service

An application may be served by any of the following methods –

    (a) personal service in accordance with rule 6.7;

    (b) first class post, or other service which provides for delivery on the next business day, in accordance with Practice Direction 6A or

    (c) where rule 6.11 applies, document exchange.

Scope—In the first instance, the application will normally be served by post. The option to serve personally is provided for as an alternative to postal service and is not obligatory. Service through a document exchange applies where a solicitor is acting for the respondent (FPR 2010, r 6.11 and FPR PD6A, para 2.1). It is also possible to effect service by another service which provides for delivery on the next business day by leaving the document with or delivering the document to the relevant service provider or having the document collected by the relevant service provider (FPR PD6A, para 3.1) (ie by a non-Royal Mail provider capable of next-day delivery service).

As to service on members of the Regular Forces and US Air Force, see FPR PD6A, para 5.1 and Annex.

6.5 Who is to serve the application

(1) Subject to the provisions of this rule, an application may be served by –

    (a)   the applicant; or

    (b)   a court officer, if so requested by the applicant.

(2) A court officer will not serve the application if the party to be served is a child or protected party.

(3) An application must not be served personally by the applicant himself or herself.

    (Rule 6.14 deals with service of the application on children and protected parties)

Scope—Primary responsibility for service of the application falls upon the applicant. However, unless the party to be served is a child or a protected party (FPR 2010, r 6.14), the applicant may on issuing the application request the court to serve the application by post under FPR 2010, r 6.8. Personal service by court bailiff is available under FPR 2010, r 6.9.

6.6 Every respondent to be served

The application must be served on every respondent.

6.7 Personal service

An application is served personally on a respondent by leaving it with that respondent.

"served personally"— FPR 2010, r 6.17 makes provision for proof of personal service where no acknowledgment of service has been filed.

6.8 Service of application by the court

(1) Where the application is to be served by a court officer, the applicant must give the court officer an address at which the respondent is to be served in accordance with rule 6.4.

(2) Where the court officer has sent a notification of failure of service to the applicant in accordance with rule 6.21, the applicant may request the court officer to serve the document on the respondent at an alternative address.

6.9 Service by the bailiff

(1) An applicant may request that an application be served by a bailiff delivering a copy of the application to the respondent personally.

(2) The request must be made in accordance with Practice Direction 6A.

(3) Where the bailiff is unable to serve the application, the applicant may apply to the court for an order under rule 6.19 (service by an alternative method or at an alternative place).

    (Practice Direction 6A contains provision about when a request under this rule is appropriate.)

    (Rule 6.22 provides for notice of non-service by a bailiff.)

Scope—An applicant may make a request to the court officer for personal service by the court bailiff. Such an application will only be considered where the address for service is in England and Wales and, normally, where postal service has already been attempted and failed. A request will rarely be granted where the applicant is legally represented unless it can be shown why bailiff service is required rather than service by a process server (FPR PD6A, para 11). The request is made in accordance with FPR PD6A, para 11.3. Personal service by bailiff must be proved in accordance with PD6A, para 12. Proceedings pending in the Principal Registry which are treated as pending in a divorce county court are sent to the court officer of the county court in whose district the document is to be served by bailiff (FPR PD6A, para 13).

PART III

Defined term—"bailiff": CCA 1984, s 147(1).

6.10 Where to serve the application – general provisions

(1) The application must be served within the jurisdiction except as provided for by Chapter 4 of this Part (service out of the jurisdiction).

(2) The applicant must include in the application an address at which the respondent may be served.

(3) Paragraph (2) does not apply where an order made by the court under rule 6.19 (service by an alternative method or at an alternative place) specifies the place or method of service of the application.

Scope—The general rule is that the application must state an address at which the respondent may be served, unless (having taken the steps required by FPR 2010, r 6.13) an application is made under FPR 2010, r 6.19 for service by an alternative method or at an alternative place.

Defined term—"jurisdiction": FPR 2010, r 2.3.

6.11 Service of the application on a solicitor within the jurisdiction or in any EEA state

(1) Where a solicitor acting for the respondent has notified the applicant in writing that the solicitor is instructed by the respondent to accept service of the application on behalf of the respondent at a business address within the jurisdiction, the application must be served at the business address of that solicitor.

(2) Subject to the provisions of Chapter 4 of this Part, where a solicitor acting for the respondent has notified the applicant in writing that the solicitor is instructed by the respondent to accept service of the application on behalf of the respondent at a business address within any EEA state, the application must be served at the business address of that solicitor.

> ("Solicitor" has the extended meaning set out in rule 6.2 and "EEA state" is defined in Schedule 1 to the Interpretation Act 1978.)

Scope—Where a solicitor within the jurisdiction or in any EEA state, who is acting for a respondent, has notified the applicant in writing that he/she is instructed to accept service, there is an obligation to serve the application at the business address of that solicitor. This rule makes explicit the principle established in *Nanglegan v Royal Free Hampstead NHS Trust* [2001] EWCA Civ 127 that, where solicitors have been nominated to accept service, the claim form (application) must be served on the solicitors.

6.12 Service of the application where the respondent gives an address at which the respondent may be served

Subject to 6.13, the respondent may be served with the application at an address within the jurisdiction which the respondent has given for the purpose of being served with the proceedings.

6.13 Service of the application where the respondent does not give an address at which the respondent may be served

(1) This rule applies where –

  (a) rule 6.11 (service of application on solicitor); and
  (b) rule 6.12 (respondent gives address at which respondent may be served),

do not apply and the applicant does not wish the application to be served personally under rule 6.7.

(2) Subject to paragraphs (3) to (5) the application must be served on the respondent at his usual or last known address.

(3) Where the applicant has reason to believe that the respondent no longer resides at his usual or last known address, the applicant must take reasonable steps to ascertain the current address of the respondent.

(4) Where, having taken the reasonable steps required by paragraph (3), the applicant –

    (a) ascertains the respondent's current address, the application must be served at that address; or

    (b) is unable to ascertain the respondent's current address, the applicant must consider whether there is –

        (i) an alternative place where; or

        (ii) an alternative method by which,

service may be effected.

(5) If, under paragraph (4)(b), there is such a place where or a method by which service could be effected, the applicant must make an application under rule 6.19.

"Usual or last known residence" (r 6.13(2),(3))—Service at the respondent's usual or last known address will be good service even where a respondent is no longer residing there, unless the applicant had, viewed objectively, reason to believe that the Respondent no longer resides at that address. In this event, reasonable steps must be taken to ascertain the respondent's current address.

Enquiries as to respondent's address—Enquiries should be made of at least the following people or organisations, where appropriate:

(a) *Relatives, friends, neighbours, former employers*   The district judge will want to know that, at the very least, letters have been sent to such of these as might know of the respondent's whereabouts.

(b) *Bank, accountant, former solicitors, doctor, dentist, etc*   Any of these may be willing to forward a stamped envelope containing the petition to a (former) customer/client/patient, even though they will not reveal his address.

(c) *Government departments generally*   In the case of applications concerning financial provision of tracing a child, certain government departments may be requested to provide a party's or a child's address. Requests for such information must be made officially by the district judge following FPR PD6C. An application for a matrimonial order containing an application for a financial order would satisfy the Practice Direction's requirement enabling an address to be requested. The departments concerned are the Department of Work and Pensions, the Office for National Statistics (which administers the National Health Service Central Register), the Passport Office and the Ministry of Defence (service personnel). The district judge asks the applicant to provide as much as possible of the information set out in the Practice Direction; the Passport Office require, in addition to the request, an undertaking that the information will be used only for the purposes of service of court process.

(d) *Department for Work and Pensions*   In addition to the facilities available under the Practice Direction (see (c) above), this department, if able to identify the respondent, will forward the application to him. Application may be made direct by the applicant to: Department for Work and Pensions, NICB, Special Section A, Newcastle-upon-Tyne NE98 1YU. As much information as possible about the respondent, by reference to the Practice Direction, should be given.

Disclosure orders against HMRC (Inland Revenue)—See annotations to FPR PD6C.

Service on members of the Regular Forces—See annex to FPR PD6A.

6.14 Service of the application on children and protected parties

(1) Where the respondent is a child, the application form must be served on –

    (a) one of the child's parents or guardians; or

    (b) if there is no parent or guardian, an adult with whom the child resides or in whose care the child is.

(2) Where the respondent is a protected party, the application must be served on –

    (a) one of the following persons with authority in relation to the protected party –

PART III

(i)   the attorney under a registered enduring power of attorney;

(ii)   the donee of a lasting power of attorney; or

(iii) the deputy appointed by the Court of Protection; or

(b)   if there is no such person, an adult with whom the protected party resides or in whose care the protected party is.

(3) Any reference in this Chapter to a respondent or party to be served includes the person to be served with the application form on behalf of a child or protected party under paragraph (1) or (2).

(4) The court may make an order permitting an application form to be served on a child or protected party, or on a person other than the person specified in paragraph (1) or (2).

(5) An application for an order under paragraph (4) may be made without notice.

(6) The court may order that, although an application form has been sent or given to someone other than the person specified in paragraph (1) or (2), it is to be treated as if it had been properly served.

(7) Where a document is served in accordance with this rule –

(a)   it must be endorsed with the notice set out in Practice Direction 6A; and

(b)   the person commencing the proceedings must file a witness statement by the person on whom the application form was served stating whether –

(i)   the contents of the application form; or

(ii)   the purpose and intention of the application,

were communicated to the child or protected party and, if not, why not.

(8) Paragraph (7)(b) does not apply where the Official Solicitor is, as the case may be –

(a)   the litigation friend of the protected party; or

(b)   the litigation friend or children's guardian of the child.

Scope—This rule makes special provision for service upon a child or protected party with service being effected in the normal way upon the category of persons specified.

Defined terms—"child", "protected party": FPR 2010, r 2.3.

Person to be served—Where there is no parent or guardian for a child, the claim form is to be served on "an adult with whom [he] resides or in whose care [he] is".

In the case of a protected party, there may be an attorney under a registered enduring power of attorney, a donee under a lasting power of attorney or a deputy appointed by the Court of Protection. Each of these people would be suitable to accept service of proceedings upon the protected party. In the absence of any such persons, the application is to be served on "an adult with whom [he] resides or in whose care [he] is".

In either case, the court can provide for service to be on the child or protected party or on some other person (r 6.14(4)) and an application under this provision may be made without notice (r 6.14(5)).

"an adult with whom the child or protected party resides or in whose care the child or protected party is" (r 6.14(1)(b) and (2)(b))—The purpose of this provision is to reach a responsible adult who will be concerned to ensure that the child or protected party is properly represented in the proceedings and will initiate the appointment of a litigation friend. There will seldom be a problem in the case of a child. In case of difficulty involving a protected party, in addition to attempts at formal service, it may be prudent to communicate with any person concerned as to the welfare of the protected party in the hope that a suitable representative will emerge.

A person cannot be in the care of someone who is himself a protected party. Where several such persons share a home (e g under supervision), it will be necessary to look beyond the occupants of the home (e g to the persons who provide the supervision). Occupants of a residential care or nursing home will be in the care of the registered proprietor who should bring the proceedings to the attention of any concerned person. If such care is funded by the local authority, it would be appropriate to involve the social services department which will have carried out a community care assessment of need. Service on a proper officer of the local social services authority or other guardian when the protected party is under a guardianship order, or the district health authority when the protected party has been compulsorily admitted to hospital under the Mental Health Act 1983 (as amended by Mental Health Act 2007) may be sufficient. Where no one can be identified, it is possible to resort to the provision for deemed service (see note below) thereby ensuring that the problem is brought before the court. When there is no response to due service, the need for a litigation friend will have to be addressed by the court in any event. Reference may be made to the Official Solicitor in case of continuing difficulty as he may need to be appointed.

Deemed service (r 6.14(6))—The provision for deemed service enables the court to proceed with the appointment of a litigation friend when service is not otherwise possible.

Communication to the child or protected party (r 6.14(7))—Communication to the child or protected party is generally required, unless an explanation is provided.

"notice" (r 6.14(7)(a))—Form D5 set out in FPR PD6A, para 9.1.

6.15 Deemed service – receipt of acknowledgment of service

(1) Subject to paragraph (2), an application is deemed to be served if the acknowledgment of service, signed by the party served or the solicitor acting on that party's behalf, is returned to the court office.

(2) Where the signature on the acknowledgment of service purports to be that of the other party to the marriage or civil partnership, the applicant must prove that it is the signature of that party by –

    (a)   giving oral evidence to that effect at the hearing; or

    (b)   if the application is undefended, confirming it to be so in the statement the applicant files under rule 7.19(4).

Amendments—SI 2012/679.

6.16 Deemed service by post or alternative service where no acknowledgment of service filed

(1) Subject to paragraph (2), if –

    (a)   an application has been served on a respondent by post or other service which provides for delivery on the next business day;

    (b)   no acknowledgment of service has been returned to the court office; and

    (c)   the court is satisfied that the respondent has received the application,

the district judge may direct that the application is deemed to be served.

(2) Where –

    (a)   the application alleges 2 years' separation and the respondent consents to a matrimonial or civil partnership order being granted; and

    (b)   none of the other facts mentioned in section 1(2) of the 1973 Act or section 44(5) of the 2004 Act, as the case may be, is alleged,

Paragraph (1) applies only if –

    (i)   the court is satisfied that the respondent has received notice of the proceedings; and

    (ii)   the applicant produces a written statement, signed by the respondent, containing the respondent's consent to the grant of an order.

General note—A common example of this form of deemed service is by production of a letter from the respondent's solicitors which states that the application was brought to them by the respondent. Such a letter may be exhibited to the applicant's application under FPR 2010, r 7.19 with an additional paragraph asking the district judge to deem service of the application in view of the contents of the letter.

6.17 Proof of personal service where no acknowledgment of service filed

(1) This rule applies where –

    (a)   an application has been served on a respondent personally; and

    (b)   no acknowledgment of service has been returned to the court office.

(2) The person serving the application must file a certificate of service stating the date and time of personal service.

(Practice Direction 6A makes provision for a certificate of service by a bailiff.)

(3) If the respondent served was the other party to the marriage or civil partnership, the certificate of service must show the means by which the person serving the application knows the identity of the party served.

Scope—If service is effected personally (other than by bailiff) and no acknowledgment of service is returned to the court, a certificate of service must be filed. If, as is generally the case, the respondent is not known to the server, his means of identifying the respondent must be described in one of the following ways, eg:

(a) by means of a photograph;
(b) by personal knowledge of the process server or other person identifying the respondent; or
(c) by admission of the person served.

In (b) or (c), corroborative evidence will be necessary. In the first instance, the process server should be asked to seek the respondent's signature on the acknowledgment of service obviating the need for a certificate of service. In no circumstances may the applicant effect personal service (FPR 2010, r 6.5(3)).

6.18 Proof of service by the court etc.

(1) Where a court officer serves an application by post, or other service which provides for delivery on the next business day, the court officer must note in the court records the date of –

(a)   posting; or
(b)   leaving with, delivering to or collection by the relevant service provider.

(2) A record made in accordance with paragraph (1) is evidence of the facts stated in it.

(3) This rule does not affect the operation of section 133 of the County Courts Act 1984.

(Section 133 of the County Courts Act 1984 provides that where a summons or other process issued from a county court is served by an officer of a court, service may be proved by a certificate in a prescribed form.)

Defined term—"officer": CCA 1984, s 147(1).

6.19 Service of the application by an alternative method or at an alternative place

(1) Where it appears to the court that there is a good reason to authorise service by a method or at a place not otherwise permitted by this Part, the court may direct that service is effected by an alternative method or at an alternative place.

(2) On an application under this rule, the court may direct that steps already taken to bring the application form to the attention of the respondent by an alternative method or at an alternative place is good service.

(3) A direction under this rule must specify –

(a)   the method or place of service;
(b)   the date on which the application form is deemed served; and
(c)   the period for filing an acknowledgment of service or answer.

Scope—This rule provides for what was previously known as "substituted service". The only issue to be decided on an application for service by an alternative method is whether service by the prescribed methods (FPR 2010, r 6.4) is impracticable. The court may then either direct that steps already taken to bring the application to the attention of the respondent constitute good service or give further directions specifying the method or place of service, the date the application will be deemed to be served and the period for filing an acknowledgment of service or answer. The method of service might be by advertisement or by posting to an address where the application might be expected to come to the respondent's attention. If validly obtained, such an order cannot be challenged, even if the party intended to be served did not receive the documents. However, the order cannot be said to be validly obtained if the district judge is not given all the necessary information relevant to the application (for example that, in the past, the respondent had a solicitor acting for him) (*Clifford v Clifford* [1985] FLR 732, CA).

6.20 Power of the court to dispense with service of the application

(1) The court may dispense with service of the application where it is impracticable to serve the application by any method provided for by this Part.

(2) An application for an order to dispense with service may be made at any time and must be supported by evidence.

(3) The court may require the applicant to attend when it decides the application.

Scope—The court is given power to dispense with service of an application where it is impracticable to serve by any of the other methods provided by FPR 2010, Pt 6. The district judge must be satisfied that full enquiries as to the respondent's whereabouts have been made. By dispensing with service, the district judge accepts that a party cannot be served and, in doing so, he balances the need for the court to be satisfied that a party to proceedings has had notice of them against the applicant's wish or need to proceed with an application. The needs of any children involved might be a factor in the district judge's consideration. The application must be supported by evidence from the applicant or his solicitor. The district judge may require the personal attendance of the applicant to clarify points in the evidence in support of the application.

6.21 Notification of failure of service by the court

Where –

(a)   the court serves the application by post or other service which provides for delivery on the next business day; and

(b)   the application is returned to the court,

the court will send notification to the applicant that the application has been returned.

6.22 Notice of non-service by bailiff

Where –

(a)   the bailiff is to serve an application; and

(b)   the bailiff is unable to serve it on the respondent,

the court officer will send notification to the applicant.

Defined terms—"officer" (including "bailiff"): CCA 1984, s 147(1).

Chapter 3
Service of Documents other than an Application for a Matrimonial Order or Civil Partnership Order in the United Kingdom

6.23 Method of service

A document may be served by any of the following methods –

(a)   personal service, in accordance with rule 6.25;

(b)   first class post, document exchange or other service which provides for delivery on the next business day, in accordance with Practice Direction 6A;

(c)   leaving it at a place specified in rule 6.26; or

(d)   fax or other means of electronic communication in accordance with Practice Direction 6A.

(Rule 6.35 provides for the court to permit service by an alternative method or at an alternative place.)

6.24 Who is to serve

(1) A party to proceedings will serve a document which that party has prepared, or which the court has prepared or issued on behalf of that party, except where –

(a) a rule or practice direction provides that the court will serve the document; or

(b) the court directs otherwise.

(2) Where a court officer is to serve a document, it is for the court to decide which method of service is to be used.

(3) Where the court officer is to serve a document prepared by a party, that party must provide a copy for the court and for each party to be served.

6.25 Personal service

(1) Where required by another Part, any other enactment, a practice direction or a court order, a document must be served personally.

(2) In other cases, a document may be served personally except where the party to be served has given an address for service under rule 6.26(2)(a).

(3) A document is served personally on an individual by leaving it with that individual.

6.26 Address for service

(1) A party to proceedings must give an address at which that party may be served with documents relating to those proceedings.

(2) Subject to paragraph (4), a party's address for service must be –

(a) the business address either within the United Kingdom or any other EEA state of a solicitor acting for the party to be served; or

(b) where there is no solicitor acting for the party to be served, an address within the United Kingdom at which the party resides or carries on business.

("EEA state" is defined in Schedule 1 to the Interpretation Act 1978.)

(3) Where there is no solicitor acting for the party to be served and the party does not have an address within the United Kingdom at which that party resides or carries on business, the party must, subject to paragraph (4), give an address for service within the United Kingdom.

(4) A party who –

(a) has been served with an application for a matrimonial or civil partnership order outside the United Kingdom; and

(b) apart from acknowledging service of the application, does not take part in the proceedings,

need not give an address for service within the United Kingdom.

(5) Any document to be served in proceedings must be sent, or transmitted to, or left at, the party's address for service unless it is to be served personally or the court orders otherwise.

(6) Where, in accordance with Practice Direction 6A, a party indicates or is deemed to have indicated that they will accept service by fax, the fax number given by that party must be at the address for service.

(7) Where a party indicates in accordance with Practice Direction 6A, that they will accept service by electronic means other than fax, the e-mail address or electronic identification given by that party will be deemed to be at the address for service.

(8) This rule does not apply where an order made by the court under rule 6.35 (service by an alternative method or at an alternative place) specifies where a document may be served.

6.27 Change of address for service

Where the address for service of a party changes, that party must give notice in writing of the change, as soon as it has taken place, to the court and every other party.

6.28 Service of an application form commencing proceedings on children and protected parties

(1) This rule applies to the service of an application form commencing proceedings other than an application for a matrimonial or civil partnership order.

(2) An application form commencing proceedings which would otherwise be served on a child or protected party must be served –

    (a)   where the respondent is a child, in accordance with rule 6.14(1); and

    (b)   where the respondent is a protected party, in accordance with rule 6.14(2).

Child—If a litigation friend has been or will be appointed, the service of documents other than the application form must served as set out in FPR 2010, r 6.29 below. If a children's guardian pursuant to FPR 2010, r 16.4 has been or will be appointed or a children's guardian pursuant to FPR 2010, r 16.3 has been appointed, the provisions for service on or by children are set out in FPR 2010, rr 6.30 and 6.31 below.

6.29 Service of other documents on or by children and protected parties where a litigation friend has been or will be appointed

(1) This rule applies to –

    (a)   a protected party; or

    (b)   a child to whom the provisions of rule 16.5 and Chapter 5 of Part 16 apply (litigation friends).

(2) An application for an order appointing a litigation friend where a protected party or child has no litigation friend must be served in accordance with rule 15.8 or rule 16.13 as the case may be.

(3) Any other document which would otherwise be served on or by a child or protected party must be served on or by the litigation friend conducting the proceedings on behalf of the child or protected party.

6.30 Service on or by children where a children's guardian has been or will be appointed under rule 16.4

(1) This rule applies to a child to whom the provisions of rule 16.4 and Chapter 7 apply.

(2) An application for an order appointing a children's guardian where a child has no children's guardian must be served in accordance with rule 16.26.

(3) Any other document which would otherwise be served on or by a child must be served on or by the children's guardian conducting the proceedings on behalf of the child.

Rule 16.4 children's guardian—Applies when the child is the subject of or a party to specified proceedings (as defined by CA 1989, s 41(6) and FPR 2010, r 12.27) or adoption or placement order proceedings etc.

PART III

6.31 Service on or by children where a children's guardian has been appointed under rule 16.3

(1) This rule applies where a children's guardian has been appointed for a child in accordance with rule 16.3.

(2) Any document which would otherwise be served on the child must be served on –

    (a)   the solicitor appointed by the court in accordance with section 41(3) of the 1989 Act; and

    (b)   the children's guardian.

(3) Any document which would otherwise be served by the child must be served by –

    (a)   the solicitor appointed by the court in accordance with section 41(3) of the 1989 Act or by the children's guardian; or

    (b)   if no solicitor has been appointed as mentioned in paragraph (a), the children's guardian.

Rule 16.3 children's guardian—Applies where the child is not the subject of proceedings referred in FPR 2010, r 16.3 but is an applicant in the proceedings, or the rules provide for the child to be a party or the court has made the child a party.

6.32 Supplementary provisions relating to service on children and protected parties

(1) The court may direct that a document be served on the protected party or child or on some person other than a person upon whom it would be served under rules 6.28 to 6.31 above.

(2) The court may direct that, although a document has been sent or given to someone other than a person upon whom it should be served under rules 6.28 to 6.31 above, the document is to be treated as if had been properly served.

(3) This rule and rules 6.28 to 6.31 do not apply where the court has made an order under rule 16.6 allowing a child to conduct proceedings without a children's guardian or litigation friend.

6.33 Supplementary provision relating to service on children

(1) This rule applies to proceedings to which Part 12 applies.

(2) Where a rule requires –

    (a)   a document to be served on a party;

    (b)   a party to be notified of any matter; or

    (c)   a party to be supplied with a copy of a document,

in addition to the persons to be served in accordance with rules 6.28 to 6.32, the persons or bodies mentioned in paragraph (3) must be served, notified or supplied with a copy of a document, as applicable, unless the court directs otherwise.

(3) The persons or bodies referred to in paragraph (2) are –

    (a)   such of the following who are appointed in the proceedings –

        (i)   the children's guardian (if the children's guardian is not otherwise to be served);

        (ii)   the welfare officer;

        (iii)   the children and family reporter;

        (iv)   the officer of the Service, Welsh family proceedings officer or local authority officer acting under a duty referred to in rule 16.38; and

(b)   a local authority preparing a report under section 14A(8) or (9) of the 1989 Act.

Part 12 proceedings—Proceedings relating to children except parental order proceedings and applications for adoption, placement and related proceedings.

6.34 Deemed service

A document, other than an application for a matrimonial or civil partnership order, served in accordance with these rules or a practice direction is deemed to be served on the day shown in the following table –

Method of service	Deemed day of service
First class post (or other service which provides for delivery on the next business day)	The second day after it was posted, left with, delivered to or collected by the relevant service provider, provided that day is a business day; or, if not, the next business day after that day
Document exchange	The second day after it was left with, delivered to or collected by the relevant service provider, provided that day is a business day; or, if not, the next business day after that day.
Delivering the document to or leaving it at a permitted address	If it is delivered to or left at the permitted address on a business day before 4.30p.m., on that day; or in any other case, on the next business day after that day.
Fax	If the transmission of the fax is completed on a business day before 4.30p.m., on that day; or, in any other case, the next business day after the day on which it was transmitted.
Other electronic method	If the e-mail or other electronic transmission is sent on a business day before 4.30p.m., on that day; or in any other case, on the next business day after the day on which it was sent.
Personal service	If the document is served personally before 4.30p.m. on a business day, on that day; or, in any other case, on the next business day after that day.

(Practice Direction 6A contains examples of how the date of deemed service is calculated.)

6.35 Service by an alternative method or at an alternative place

Rule 6.19 applies to any document in proceedings as it applies to an application for a matrimonial or civil partnership order and reference to the respondent in that rule is modified accordingly.

6.36 Power to dispense with service

The court may dispense with the service of any document which is to be served in proceedings.

6.37 Certificate of service

(1) Where a rule, practice direction or court order requires a certificate of service, the certificate must state the details set out in the following table –

PART III

Method of service	Details to be certified
Personal service	Date and time of personal service and method of identifying the person served.
First class post, document exchange or other service which provides for delivery on the next business day	Date of posting, leaving with, delivering to or collection by the relevant service provider.
Delivery of document to or leaving it at a permitted place	Date and time when the document was delivered to or left at the permitted place.
Fax	Date and time of completion of transmission.
Other electronic method	Date and time of sending the email or other electronic transmission.
Alternative method or place permitted by court	As required by the court.

(2) An applicant who is required to file a certificate of service of an application form must do so at or before the earlier of –

    (a) the first directions appointment in; or

    (b) the hearing of,

the proceedings unless a rule or practice direction provides otherwise.

        (Rule 17.2 requires a certificate of service to contain a statement of truth.)

6.38 Notification of outcome of service by the court

Where –

    (a) a document to be served by a court officer is served by post or other service which provides for delivery on the next working day; and

    (b) the document is returned to the court,

the court officer will send notification to the party who requested service that the document has been returned.

6.39 Notification of non-service by bailiff

Where –

    (a) the bailiff is to serve a document; and

    (b) the bailiff is unable to serve it,

the court officer must send notification to the party who requested service.

Chapter 4
Service Out of the Jurisdiction

6.40 Scope and interpretation

(1) This Chapter contains rules about –

    (a) service of application forms and other documents out of the jurisdiction; and

    (b) the procedure for service.

        ("Jurisdiction" is defined in rule 2.3.)

(2) In this Chapter –

"application form" includes an application notice;

"Commonwealth State" means a State listed in Schedule 3 to the British Nationality Act 1981; and

"the Hague Convention" means the Convention on the service abroad of judicial and extra-judicial documents in civil or commercial matters signed at the Hague on November 15, 1965.

Scope—This Chapter should be read in conjunction with PD6B, which contains provisions in relation to service out of the jurisdiction.

6.41 Permission to serve not required

Any document to be served for the purposes of these rules may be served out of the jurisdiction without the permission of the court.

"may be served out of the jurisdiction without the permission of the court"—The fact that proceedings may be served out of the jurisdiction does not necessarily mean that they should be. Choice of forum is a critical factor at the outset of any international case. The court will consider (other than where Brussels IIA or DMPA 1973, Sch 1, para 8 apply) whether England and Wales is the proper place to conduct the proceedings (*The Spiliada* [1987] AC 460). See annotations to DMPA 1973, s 5. Despite the epithet forum non conveniens, the question is not one of convenience so much as whether the proceedings are in the appropriate forum. As family proceedings can be served out of England and Wales as of right, it will be for the respondent to show that another forum is clearly more appropriate (*Ella v Ella* [2007] 2 FLR 35; *Prazic v Prazic* [2006] 2 FLR 1128).

6.42 Period for acknowledging service or responding to application where application is served out of the jurisdiction

(1) This rule applies where, under these rules, a party is required to file –

    (a)   an acknowledgment of service; or

    (b)   an answer to an application,

and sets out the time period for doing so where the application is served out of the jurisdiction.

(2) Where the applicant serves an application on a respondent in –

    (a)   Scotland or Northern Ireland; or

    (b)   a Member State or Hague Convention country within Europe,

the period for filing an acknowledgment of service or an answer to an application is 21 days after service of the application.

(3) Where the applicant serves an application on a respondent in a Hague Convention country outside Europe, the period for filing an acknowledgment of service or an answer to an application is 31 days after service of the application.

(4) Where the applicant serves an application on a respondent in a country not referred to in paragraphs (2) and (3), the period for filing an acknowledgment of service or an answer to an application is set out in Practice Direction 6B.

"Member State" (r 6.42(2))—See PD6B, para 2.

"period for filing an acknowledgment of service" (r 6.42(2))—The period for filing an acknowledgment of service or an answer to an application, where the respondent is in a country other than Scotland, Northern Ireland, a Member State or Hague Convention country, is prescribed by FPR PD6B, para 5.1 and the Table in FPR PD6B.

Application notices and orders—The provisions of FPR 2010, Pt 6, Ch 4 also apply to the service out of the jurisdiction of an application notice or order (FPR PD6B, para 6). Where an application notice or order is served out of the jurisdiction, the period for responding is 7 days less than the number of days listed in the Table (FPR PD6B, para 7.1).

6.43 Method of service – general provisions

(1) This rule contains general provisions about the method of service of an application for a matrimonial or civil partnership order, or other document, on a party out of the jurisdiction.

Where service is to be effected on a party in Scotland or Northern Ireland

(2) Where a party serves an application form or other document on a party in Scotland or Northern Ireland, it must be served by a method permitted by Chapter 2 (and references to "jurisdiction" in that Chapter are modified accordingly) or Chapter 3 of this Part and rule 6.26(5) applies.

Where service is to be effected on a respondent out of the United Kingdom

(3) Where the applicant wishes to serve an application form, or other document, on a respondent out of the United Kingdom, it may be served by any method –

> provided for by –
> rule 6.44 (service in accordance with the Service Regulation);
> rule 6.45 (service through foreign governments, judicial authorities and British Consular authorities); or
> permitted by the law of the country in which it is to be served.

(4) Nothing in paragraph (3) or in any court order authorises or requires any person to do anything which is contrary to the law of the country where the application form, or other document, is to be served.

"permitted by the law of the country in which it is to be served" (r 6.43(3)(b))—Although it has been held under CPR 1998, r 6.40 that this provision "should be applied with a reasonable degree of flexibility" (*Arros Invest Limited v Rafik Nishanov* [2004] EWHC 576 (Ch)), the onus is on the claimant to show, by expert evidence if necessary, that the local rules have been complied with. An alternative method of service may be permitted so long as it does not contravene the law of the country of service (*Habib Bank v Central Bank of Sudan* [2006] EWHC 1767 (Comm); *Bentinck v Bentinck* [2007] 2 FLR 1).

6.44 Service in accordance with the Service Regulation

(1) This rule applies where the applicant wishes to serve the application form, or other document, in accordance with the Service Regulation.

(2) The applicant must file –

    (a) the application form or other document;

    (b) any translation; and

    (c) any other documents required by the Service Regulation.

(3) When the applicant files the documents referred to in paragraph (2), the court officer will –

    (a) seal$^{(GL)}$, or otherwise authenticate with the stamp of the court, the copy of the application form; and

    (b) forward the documents to the Senior Master of the Queen's Bench Division.

(4) In addition to the documents referred to in paragraph (2), the applicant may file a photograph of the person to be served if the applicant considers that it would assist in ensuring effective service.

> (The Service Regulation is annexed to Practice Direction 6B.)

> (Article 20(1) of the Service Regulation provides that the Regulation prevails over other provisions contained in any other agreement or arrangement concluded by Member States.)

Amendments—SI 2011/1328.

"**the Service Regulation**" (r 6.44 generally)—The Service Regulation is an attempt to establish an efficient system for the service of documents within the European Union. Its use is complicated by the fact that States may opt out of a number of its provisions. The Regulation set out in Part VI and is also annexed to FPR PD6B. Reference should also be made to FPR PD6B, para 2. Up-to-date information on the implementation of the Regulation may be found on the Europa website at *http://eur-lex.europa.eu*. It will often be prudent to seek the advice of a practitioner in the state in which service is to be effected. Such practitioners may be located by visiting *www.iaml.org*. The Foreign Process Section (Room E06) at the Royal Courts of Justice, Strand, London WC2A 2LL (DX 44450 Strand) (tel: 020 7947 7786/6488/6691/1741/6682; fax: 0870 324 0025; email: foreignprocess.rcj@hmcts.gsi.gov.uk) will also offer guidance.

"**the applicant must file**" (r 6.44(2))—See FPR PD6B, para 3.

6.45 Service through foreign governments, judicial authorities and British Consular authorities

(1) Where the applicant wishes to serve an application form, or other document, on a respondent in any country which is a party to the Hague Convention, it may be served –

    (a)   through the authority designated under the Hague Convention in respect of that country; or

    (b)   if the law of that country permits –

        (i)   through the judicial authorities of that country; or

        (ii)   through a British Consular authority in that country.

(2) Where the applicant wishes to serve an application form, or other document, on a respondent in any country which is not a party to the Hague Convention, it may be served, if the law of that country so permits –

    (a)   through the government of that country, where that government is willing to serve it; or

    (b)   through a British Consular authority in that country.

(3) Where the applicant wishes to serve an application form, or other document, in –

    (a)   any Commonwealth State which is not a party to the Hague Convention;

    (b)   the Isle of Man or the Channel Islands; or

    (c)   any British Overseas Territory,

the methods of service permitted by paragraphs (1)(b) and (2) are not available and the applicant or the applicant's agent must effect service on a respondent in accordance with rule 6.43 unless Practice Direction 6B provides otherwise.

(4) This rule does not apply where service is to be effected in accordance with the Service Regulation.

    (A list of British overseas territories is reproduced in Practice Direction 6B.)

"**British Overseas Territories**" (r 6.45(3)(c))—FPR PD6B, para 4.2.

6.46 Procedure where service is to be through foreign governments, judicial authorities and British Consular authorities

(1) This rule applies where the applicant wishes to serve an application form, or other document, under rule 6.45(1) or (2).

(2) Where this rule applies, the applicant must file –

    (a)   a request for service of the application form, or other document, by specifying one or more of the methods in rule 6.45(1) or (2);

    (b)   a copy of the application form or other document;

    (c)   any other documents or copies of documents required by Practice Direction 6B; and

    (d)   any translation required under rule 6.47.

(3) When the applicant files the documents specified in paragraph (2), the court officer will –

   (a)   seal^(GL), or otherwise authenticate with the stamp of the court, the copy of the application form or other document; and

   (b)   forward the documents to the Senior Master of the Queen's Bench Division.

(4) The Senior Master will send documents forwarded under this rule –

   (a)   where the application form, or other document, is being served through the authority designated under the Hague Convention, to that authority; or

   (b)   in any other case, to the Foreign and Commonwealth Office with a request that it arranges for the application form or other document to be served.

(5) An official certificate which –

   (a)   states that the method requested under paragraph (2)(a) has been performed and the date of such performance;

   (b)   states, where more than one method is requested under paragraph (2)(a), which method was used; and

   (c)   is made by –

      (i)   a British Consular authority in the country where the method requested under paragraph (2)(a) was performed;

      (ii)   the government or judicial authorities in that country; or

      (iii)   the authority designated in respect of that country under the Hague Convention,

is evidence of the facts stated in the certificate.

(6) A document purporting to be an official certificate under paragraph (5) is to be treated as such a certificate, unless it is proved not to be.

"the applicant wishes to serve the application form, or other document" (r 6.44(1))—Where service is effected through the Foreign Office, service is not being effected by the court but by the applicant and, if there is a delay, the onus is on the applicant to show that all reasonable steps have been taken.

6.47 Translation of application form or other document

(1) Except where paragraphs (4) and (5) apply, every copy of the application form, or other document, filed under rule 6.45 (service through foreign governments, judicial authorities and British Consular authorities) must be accompanied by a translation of the application form or other document.

(2) The translation must be –

   (a)   in the official language of the country in which it is to be served; or

   (b)   if there is more than one official language of that country, in any official language which is appropriate to the place in the country where the application form or other document is to be served.

(3) Every translation filed under this rule must be accompanied by a statement by the person making it that it is a correct translation, and the statement must include that person's name, address and qualifications for making the translation.

(4) The applicant is not required to file a translation of the application form, or other document, filed under rule 6.45 where it is to be served in a country of which English is an official language.

(5) The applicant is not required to file a translation of the application form or other document filed under rule 6.45 where –

   (a)   the person on whom the document is to be served is able to read and understand English; and

   (b)   service of the document is to be effected directly on that person.

(This rule does not apply to service in accordance with the Service Regulation which contains its own provisions about the translation of documents.)

6.48 Undertaking to be responsible for expenses of the Foreign and Commonwealth Office

Every request for service filed under rule 6.46 (procedure where service is to be through foreign governments, judicial authorities etc.) must contain an undertaking by the person making the request –

(a) to be responsible for all expenses incurred by the Foreign and Commonwealth Office or foreign judicial authority; and

(b) to pay those expenses to the Foreign and Commonwealth Office or foreign judicial authority on being informed of the amount.

Practice Direction 6A – Service within the Jurisdiction

This Practice Direction supplements FPR Part 6, Chapters 2 and 3

GENERAL PROVISIONS

Scope of this Practice Direction

1.1 This Practice Direction supplements the following provisions of Part 6 –

(a) Chapter 2 (service of the application for a matrimonial order or civil partnership order in the jurisdiction);

(b) Chapter 3 (service of documents other than an application for a matrimonial order or civil partnership order in the United Kingdom); and

(c) rule 6.43(2) in relation to the method of service on a party in Scotland or Northern Ireland.

(Practice Direction B supplementing Part 6 contains provisions relevant to service on a party in Scotland or Northern Ireland, including provisions about the period for responding to an application notice.)

When service may be by document exchange

2.1 Subject to the provisions of rule 6.4 (which provides when an application for a matrimonial or civil partnership order may be served by document exchange) service by document exchange (DX) may take place only where –

(a) the address at which the party is to be served includes a numbered box at a DX; or

(b) the writing paper of the party who is to be served or of the solicitor acting for that party sets out a DX box number; and

(c) the party or the solicitor acting for that party has not indicated in writing that they are unwilling to accept service by DX.

How service is effected by post, an alternative service provider or DX

3.1 Service by post, DX or other service which provides for delivery on the next business day is effected by –

(a)   placing the document in a post box;

(b)   leaving the document with or delivering the document to the relevant service provider; or

(c)   having the document collected by the relevant service provider.

Service by fax or other electronic means

4.1 This paragraph applies to the service of a document other than an application for a matrimonial or civil partnership order and documents in adoption proceedings and parental order proceedings.

4.2 Subject to the provisions of rule 6.26(6) and (7), where a document is to be served by fax or other electronic means –

(a)   the party who is to be served or the solicitor acting for that party must previously have indicated in writing to the party serving –

(i)   that the party to be served or the solicitor is willing to accept service by fax or other electronic means; and

(ii)   the fax number, e-mail address or other electronic identification to which it must be sent; and

(b)   the following are to be taken as sufficient written indications for the purposes of paragraph 4.2(a) –

(i)   a fax number set out on the writing paper of the solicitor acting for the party to be served;

(ii)   an e-mail address set out on the writing paper of the solicitor acting for the party to be served but only where it is stated that the e-mail address may be used for service; or

(iii)   a fax number, e-mail address or electronic identification set out on a statement of case or an answer to a claim filed with the court.

4.3 Where a party intends to serve a document by electronic means (other than by fax) that party must first ask the party who is to be served whether there are any limitations to the recipient's agreement to accept service by such means (for example, the format in which documents are to be sent and the maximum size of attachments that may be received).

4.4 Where a document is served by electronic means, the party serving the document need not in addition send or deliver a hard copy.

Service on members of the Regular Forces and United States Air Force

5.1 The provisions that apply to service on members of the regular forces (within the meaning of the Armed Forces Act 2006) and members of the United States Air Force are annexed to this practice direction.

Application for an order for service by an alternative method or at an alternative place

6.1 An application in the High Court or a county court for an order under rule 6.19 may be made without notice.

6.2 Where an application for an order under rule 6.19 is made before the document is served, the application must be supported by evidence stating –

(a) the reason why an order is sought;

(b) what alternative method or place is proposed; and

(c) why the applicant believes that the document is likely to reach the person to be served by the method or at the place proposed.

6.3 Where the application for an order is made after the applicant has taken steps to bring the document to the attention of the person to be served by an alternative method or at an alternative place, the application must be supported by evidence stating –

(a) the reason why the order is sought;

(b) what alternative method or alternative place was used;

(c) when the alternative method or place was used; and

(d) why the applicant believes that the document is likely to have reached the person to be served by the alternative method or at the alternative place.

6.4 Examples –

(a) an application to serve by posting or delivering to an address of a person who knows the other party must be supported by evidence that if posted or delivered to that address, the document is likely to be brought to the attention of the other party;

(b) an application to serve by sending a SMS text message or leaving a voicemail message at a particular telephone number saying where the document is must be accompanied by evidence that the person serving the document has taken, or will take, appropriate steps to ensure that the party being served is using that telephone number and is likely to receive the message.

Applications for an order to dispense with service

7.1 An application in the High Court or a county court for an order under rule 6.36 (power to dispense with service) may be made without notice.

Deemed service of a document other than an application for a matrimonial or civil partnership order

8.1 Rule 6.34 contains provisions about deemed service of a document other than an application for a matrimonial or civil partnership order. Examples of how deemed service is calculated are set out below.

Example 1

8.2 Where the document is posted (by first class post) on a Monday (a business day), the day of deemed service is the following Wednesday (a business day).

Example 2

8.3 Where the document is left in a numbered box at the DX on a Friday (a business day), the day of deemed service is the following Monday (a business day).

Example 3

8.4 Where the document is sent by fax on a Saturday and the transmission of that fax is completed by 4.30p.m. on that day, the day of deemed service is the following Monday (a business day).

Example 4

8.5 Where the document is served personally before 4.30p.m. on a Sunday, the day of deemed service is the next day (Monday, a business day).

Example 5

8.6 Where the document is delivered to a permitted address after 4.30p.m. on the Thursday (a business day) before Good Friday, the day of deemed service is the following Tuesday (a business day) as the Monday is a bank holiday.

Example 6

8.7 Where the document is posted (by first class post) on a bank holiday Monday, the day of deemed service is the following Wednesday (a business day).

Service of application on children and protected parties

9.1 Rule 16.14(1) and (2) are applied to service of an application form (other than an application for a matrimonial or civil partnership order) commencing proceedings on children and protected parties by rule 6.28. Rule 6.14(7) makes provision as to how an application form must be served where the respondent is a child or protected party. A document served in accordance with rule 6.14(7) must be endorsed with the following notice which is set out in Form D5 –

Important Notice

The contents or purport of this document are to be communicated to the Respondent

[or as the case may be], [full name of Respondent]

if s/he is over 16 [add if the person to be served lacks capacity within the meaning of the Mental Capacity Act 2005 to conduct the proceedings] unless you are satisfied [after consultation with the responsible medical officer within the meaning of the Mental Health Act 1983 or, if s/he is not liable to be detained or subject to guardianship under that Act, his/her medical attendant]* that communication will be detrimental to his/her mental condition].

PROVISIONS RELATING TO APPLICATIONS FOR MATRIMONIAL AND CIVIL PARTNERSHIP ORDERS

Acknowledgment of service to be sent to applicant

10.1 Where the court office receives an acknowledgment of service the court officer must send a photographic copy of it to the applicant.

Personal service of application by bailiff

11.1 The court will only consider a request for personal service of the application by a bailiff if the address for service is in England and Wales.

11.2 In normal circumstances, a request should only be made if postal service has been attempted. In this case, if –

    (a)   a signed acknowledgment of service is not returned to the court within 14 days after posting; and

(b)   the applicant reasonably believes the respondent is still living at the stated address,

the applicant may make a request to the court for personal service by a bailiff.

11.3 A request for personal service by a bailiff should be made in writing to the court officer on the prescribed form and accompanied by the relevant fee. The request should also be accompanied by-

(a)   evidence that postal service has been attempted and failed; or

(b)   if postal service has not been attempted, an explanation as to why postal service is not considered appropriate in the circumstances of the case.

11.4 A request will rarely be granted where the applicant is legally represented and it will be necessary for the representative to show why service by bailiff is required rather than by a process server.

Proof of personal service by bailiff

12.1 Once service of the application has been effected or attempted by the bailiff he must file a certificate of service in the issuing court.

12.2 If the respondent fails to sign and return an acknowledgment of service to the court office and –

(a)   the certificate contains a signature of receipt of the application by the respondent; or

(b)   the identity of the respondent is to be proved by a photograph supplied by the applicant,

the applicant must prove the signature or photograph in the statement filed by the applicant under rule 7.19(4).

Amendments—FPR 2010, Update 2.

Service by bailiff in proceedings in the Principal Registry

13.1 This paragraph applies where proceedings which are pending in the Principal Registry of the Family Division are treated as pending in a divorce county court.

13.2 Where a document is to be served by a bailiff it must be sent for service to the Principal Registry for onward transmission to the court officer of the county court in whose district the document is to be served.

Service of application on children and protected parties

14.1 A document served in accordance with rule 6.14(7) must be endorsed with the notice contained in paragraph 9.1.

ANNEX

Service on Members of the Regular Forces

1 The following information is for litigants and legal representatives who wish to serve legal documents in civil proceedings in the courts of England and Wales on parties to the proceedings who are (or who, at the material time, were) members of the regular forces (as defined in the Armed Forces Act 2006).

PART III

2 The proceedings may take place in the county court or the High Court, and the documents to be served may be claim forms, interim application notices and pre-action application notices. Proceedings for divorce or maintenance and proceedings in the Family Courts generally are subject to special rules as to service which are explained in a practice direction issued by the Senior District Judge of the Principal Registry on 26 June 1979.

> (now see Practice Direction 1 Maintenance Orders: Service Personnel; 2 Disclosure of Addresses [1995] 2 FLR 813.)

3 In this Annex, the person wishing to effect service is referred to as the 'claimant' and the member of the regular forces to be served is referred to as 'the member'; the expression 'overseas' means outside the United Kingdom.

Enquiries as to address

4 As a first step, the claimant's legal representative will need to find out where the member is serving, if this is not already known. For this purpose the claimant's legal representative should write to the appropriate officer of the Ministry of Defence as specified in paragraph 10 below.

5 The letter of enquiry should in every case show that the writer is a legal representative and that the enquiry is made solely with a view to the service of legal documents in civil proceedings.

6 In all cases the letter must give the full name, service number, rank or rate, and Ship, Arm or Trade, Regiment or Corps and Unit or as much of this information as is available. Failure to quote the service number and the rank or rate may result either in failure to identify the member or in considerable delay.

7 The letter must contain an undertaking by the legal representative that, if the address is given, it will be used solely for the purpose of issuing and serving documents in the proceedings and that so far as is possible the legal representative will disclose the address only to the court and not to the claimant or to any other person or body. A legal representative in the service of a public authority or private company must undertake that the address will be used solely for the purpose of issuing and serving documents in the proceedings and that the address will not be disclosed so far as is possible to any other part of the legal representative's employing organisation or to any other person but only to the court. Normally on receipt of the required information and undertaking the appropriate office will give the service address.

8 If the legal representative does not give the undertaking, the only information that will be given is whether the member is at that time serving in England or Wales, Scotland, Northern Ireland or overseas.

9 It should be noted that a member's address which ends with a British Forces Post Office address and reference (BFPO) will nearly always indicate that the member is serving overseas.

10 The letter of enquiry should be addressed as follows –

Royal Navy and Royal Marine Officers, Ratings and Other Ranks

> Director Naval Personnel
> Fleet Headquarters
> MP 3.1
> Leach Building
> Whale Island
> Portsmouth
> Hampshire
> PO2 8BY

Army Officers and other Ranks –

> Army Personnel Centre
> Disclosures 1
> MP 520
> Kentigern House
> 65 Brown Street
> Glasgow
> G2 8EX

Royal Air Force Officers and Other Ranks –

> Manning 22E
> RAF Disclosures
> Room 221B
> Trenchard Hall
> RAF Cranwell
> Sleaford
> Lincolnshire
> NG34 8HB

Assistance in serving documents on members

11 Once the claimant's legal representative has ascertained the member's address, the legal representative may use that address as the address for service by post, in cases where this method of service is allowed by the Civil Procedure Rules. There are, however, some situations in which service of the proceedings, whether in the High Court or in the county court, must be effected personally; in these cases an appointment will have to be sought, through the Commanding Officer of the Unit, Establishment or Ship concerned, for the purpose of effecting service. The procedure for obtaining an appointment is described below, and it applies whether personal service is to be effected by the claimant's legal representative or the legal representative's agent or by a court bailiff, or, in the case of proceedings served overseas (with the leave of the court) through the British Consul or the foreign judicial authority.

12 The procedure for obtaining an appointment to effect personal service is by application to the Commanding Officer of the Unit, Establishment or Ship in which the member is serving. The Commanding Officer may grant permission for the document server to enter the Unit, Establishment or Ship but if this is not appropriate the Commanding Officer may offer arrangements for the member to attend at a place in the vicinity of the Unit, Establishment or Ship in order that the member may be served. If suitable arrangements cannot be made the legal representative will have evidence that personal service is impracticable, which may be useful in an application for service by an alternative method or at an alternative place.

General

13 Subject to the procedure outlined in paragraphs 11 and 12, there are no special arrangements to assist in the service of legal documents when a member is outside the United Kingdom. The appropriate office will, however, give an approximate date when the member is likely to return to the United Kingdom.

14 It sometimes happens that a member has left the regular forces by the time an enquiry as to address is made. If the claimant's legal representative confirms that the proceedings result from an occurrence when the member was in the regular forces and the legal representative gives the undertaking referred to in paragraph 7, the last known private address after discharge will normally be provided. In no other case, however, will the Ministry of Defence disclose the private address of a member of the regular forces.

Service on Members of United States Air Force

15 In addition to the information contained in the memorandum of 26 July 1979, and after some doubts having been expressed as to the correct procedure to be followed by persons having civil claims against members of the United States Air Force in England and Wales, the Lord Chancellor's Office (as it was then) issued the following notes for guidance with the approval of the appropriate United States authorities.

16 Instructions have been issued by the United States authorities to the commanding officers of all their units in England and Wales that every facility is to be given for the service of documents in civil proceedings on members of the United States Air Force. The proper course to be followed by a creditor or other person having a claim against a member of the United States Air Force is for that person to communicate with the commanding officer or, where the unit concerned has a legal officer, with the legal officer of the defendant's unit requesting the provision of facilities for the service of documents on the defendant. It is not possible for the United States authorities to act as arbitrators when a civil claim is made against a member of their forces. It is, therefore, essential that the claim should either be admitted by the defendant or judgment should be obtained on it, whether in the High Court or a county court. If a claim has been admitted or judgment has been obtained and the claimant has failed to obtain satisfaction within a reasonable period, the claimant's proper course is then to write to: Office of the Staff Judge Advocate, Headquarters, Third Air Force, R.A.F. Mildenhall, Suffolk, enclosing a copy of the defendant's written admission of the claim or, as the case may be, a copy of the judgment. Steps will then be taken by the Staff Judge Advocate to ensure that the matter is brought to the defendant's attention with a view to prompt satisfaction of the claim.

Practice Direction 6B – Service out of the Jurisdiction

This Practice Direction supplements FPR Part 6, Chapter 4

Scope of this Practice Direction

1.1 This Practice Direction supplements Chapter 4 (service out of the jurisdiction) of Part 6.

> (Practice Direction 6A contains relevant provisions supplementing rule 6.43(2) in relation to the method of service on a party in Scotland or Northern Ireland.)

Service in other Member States of the European Union

2.1 Where service is to be effected in another Member of State of the European Union, the Service Regulation applies.

2.2 The Service Regulation is Regulation (EC) No. 1393/2007 of the European Parliament and of the Council of 13 November 2007 on the service in the Member States of judicial and extrajudicial documents in civil or commercial matters (service of documents), and repealing Council Regulation (EC) no. 1348/2000, as amended from time to time and as applied by the Agreement made on 19 October 2005 between the European Community and the Kingdom of Denmark on the service of judicial and extrajudicial documents in civil and commercial matters.

2.3 The Service Regulation is annexed to this Practice Direction.

> (Article 20(1) of the Service Regulation provides that the Regulation prevails over other provisions contained in bilateral or multilateral agreements or arrangements concluded by the Member of States and in particular Article IV of the protocol to the Brussels Convention of 1968 and the Hague Convention of 15 November 1965)

Documents to be filed under rule 6.46(2)

3.1 A duplicate of –

   (a)   the application form or other document to be served under rule 6.45(1) or (2);
   (b)   any documents accompanying the application or other document referred to in paragraph (a); and
   (c)   any translation required by rule 6.47;

must be provided for each party to be served out of the jurisdiction, together with forms for responding to the application.

3.2 Some countries require legalisation of the document to be served and some require a formal letter of request which must be signed by the Senior Master. Any queries on this should be addressed to the Foreign Process Section (Room E02) at the Royal Courts of Justice.

Service in a Commonwealth State or British Overseas Territory

4.1 The judicial authorities of certain Commonwealth States which are not a party to the Hague Convention require service to be in accordance with rule 6.45(1)(b)(i) and not 6.45(3). A list of such countries can be obtained from the Foreign Process Section (Room E02) at the Royal Courts of Justice.

4.2 The list of British overseas territories is contained in Schedule 6 to the British Nationality Act 1981. For ease of reference these are –

   (a)   Anguilla;
   (b)   Bermuda;
   (c)   British Antarctic Territory;
   (d)   British Indian Ocean Territory;
   (e)   Cayman Islands;
   (f)   Falkland Islands;
   (g)   Gibraltar;
   (h)   Montserrat;
   (i)   Pitcairn, Henderson, Ducie and Oeno Islands;
   (j)   St. Helena, Ascension and Tristan da Cunha;
   (k)   South Georgia and the South Sandwich Islands;
   (l)   Sovereign Base Areas of Akrotiri and Dhekelia;

PART III

(m) Turks and Caicos Islands;
(n) Virgin Islands.

Period for responding to an application form

5.1 Where rule 6.42 applies, the period within which the respondent must file an acknowledgment of service or an answer to the application is the number of days listed in the Table after service of the application.

5.2 Where an application is served out of the jurisdiction any statement as to the period for responding to the claim contained in any of the forms required by the Family Procedure Rules to accompany the application must specify the period prescribed under rule 6.42.

Service of application notices and orders

6.1 The provisions of Chapter 4 of Part 6 (special provisions about service out of the jurisdiction) also apply to service out of the jurisdiction of an application notice or order.

6.2 Where an application notice is to be served out of the jurisdiction in accordance with Chapter 4 of Part 6 the court must have regard to the country in which the application notice is to be served in setting the date for the hearing of the application and giving any direction about service of the respondent's evidence.

Period for responding to an application notice

7.1 Where an application notice or order is served out of the jurisdiction, the period for responding is 7 days less than the number of days listed in the Table.

Further information

8.1 Further information concerning service out of the jurisdiction can be obtained from the Foreign Process Section, Room E02, Royal Courts of Justice, Strand, London WC2A 2LL (telephone 020 7947 6691).

Table

Place or country	Number of days
Afghanistan	23
Albania	25
Algeria	22
Andorra	21
Angola	22
Anguilla	31
Antigua and Barbuda	23
Antilles (Netherlands)	31
Argentina	22
Armenia	21

Place or country	Number of days
Ascension Island	31
Australia	25
Austria	21
Azerbaijan	22
Azores	23
Bahamas	22
Bahrain	22
Balearic Islands	21
Bangladesh	23
Barbados	23
Belarus	21
Belgium	21
Belize	23
Benin	25
Bermuda	31
Bhutan	28
Bolivia	23
Bosnia and Herzegovina	21
Botswana	23
Brazil	22
British Virgin Islands	31
Brunei	25
Bulgaria	23
Burkina Faso	23
Burma	23
Burundi	22
Cambodia	28
Cameroon	22
Canada	22
Canary Islands	22

PART III

Place or country	Number of days
Cape Verde	25
Caroline Islands	31
Cayman Islands	31
Central African Republic	25
Chad	25
Chile	22
China	24
China (Hong Kong)	31
China (Macau)	31
China (Taiwan)	23
China (Tibet)	34
Christmas Island	27
Cocos (Keeling) Islands	41
Colombia	22
Comoros	23
Congo (formerly Congo Brazzaville or French Congo)	25
Congo (Democratic Republic)	25
Corsica	21
Costa Rica	23
Croatia	21
Cuba	24
Cyprus	31
Czech Republic	21
Denmark	21
Djibouti	22
Dominica	23
Dominican Republic	23
East Timor	25
Ecuador	22
Egypt	22

Place or country	Number of days
El Salvador	25
Equatorial Guinea	23
Eritrea	22
Estonia	21
Ethiopia	22
Falkland Islands and Dependencies	31
Faroe Islands	31
Fiji	23
Finland	24
France	21
French Guyana	31
French Polynesia	31
French West Indies	31
Gabon	25
Gambia	22
Georgia	21
Germany	21
Ghana	22
Gibraltar	31
Greece	21
Greenland	31
Grenada	24
Guatemala	24
Guernsey	21
Guinea	22
Guinea-Bissau	22
Guyana	22
Haiti	23
Holland (Netherlands)	21
Honduras	24

PART III

Place or country	Number of days
Hungary	22
Iceland	22
India	23
Indonesia	22
Iran	22
Iraq	22
Ireland (Republic of)	21
Ireland (Northern)	21
Isle of Man	21
Israel	22
Italy	21
Ivory Coast	22
Jamaica	22
Japan	23
Jersey	21
Jordan	23
Kazakhstan	21
Kenya	22
Kiribati	23
Korea (North)	28
Korea (South)	24
Kosovo	21
Kuwait	22
Kyrgyzstan	21
Laos	30
Latvia	21
Lebanon	22
Lesotho	23
Liberia	22
Libya	21

Place or country	Number of days
Liechtenstein	21
Lithuania	21
Luxembourg	21
Macedonia	21
Madagascar	23
Madeira	31
Malawi	23
Malaysia	24
Maldives	26
Mali	25
Malta	21
Mariana Islands	26
Marshall Islands	32
Mauritania	23
Mauritius	22
Mexico	23
Micronesia	23
Moldova	21
Monaco	21
Mongolia	24
Montenegro	21
Montserrat	31
Morocco	22
Mozambique	23
Namibia	23
Nauru	36
Nepal	23
Netherlands	21
Nevis	24
New Caledonia	31

PART III

Place or country	Number of days
New Zealand	26
New Zealand Island Territories	50
Nicaragua	24
Niger (Republic of)	25
Nigeria	22
Norfolk Island	31
Norway	21
Oman (Sultanate of)	22
Pakistan	23
Palau	23
Panama	26
Papua New Guinea	26
Paraguay	22
Peru	22
Philippines	23
Pitcairn, Henderson, Ducie and Oeno Islands	31
Poland	21
Portugal	21
Portuguese Timor	31
Puerto Rico	23
Qatar	23
Reunion	31
Romania	22
Russia	21
Rwanda	23
Sabah	23
St. Helena	31
St. Kitts and Nevis	24
St. Lucia	24
St. Pierre and Miquelon	31

Place or country	Number of days
St. Vincent and the Grenadines	24
Samoa (U.S.A. Territory) (See also Western Samoa)	30
San Marino	21
Sao Tome and Principe	25
Sarawak	28
Saudi Arabia	24
Scotland	21
Senegal	22
Serbia	21
Seychelles	22
Sierra Leone	22
Singapore	22
Slovakia	21
Slovenia	21
Society Islands (French Polynesia)	31
Solomon Islands	29
Somalia	22
South Africa	22
South Georgia (Falkland Island Dependencies)	31
South Orkneys	21
South Shetlands	21
Spain	21
Spanish Territories of North Africa	31
Sri Lanka	23
Sudan	22
Surinam	22
Swaziland	22
Sweden	21
Switzerland	21
Syria	23

PART III

Place or country	Number of days
Tajikistan	21
Tanzania	22
Thailand	23
Togo	22
Tonga	30
Trinidad and Tobago	23
Tristan Da Cunha	31
Tunisia	22
Turkey	21
Turkmenistan	21
Turks & Caicos Islands	31
Tuvalu	23
Uganda	22
Ukraine	21
United Arab Emirates	22
United States of America	22
Uruguay	22
Uzbekistan	21
Vanuatu	29
Vatican City State	21
Venezuela	22
Vietnam	28
Virgin Islands – U.S.A	24
Wake Island	25
Western Samoa	34
Yemen (Republic of)	30
Zaire	25
Zambia	23
Zimbabwe	22

ANNEX – SERVICE REGULATION (RULE 6.44)

http://www.justice.gov.uk/courts/procedure-rules/family/practice_directions/pd_form_
imgs/pd_06b_pdf_eps/pd_06b_ecreg2007.pdf

Note—EC Regulation 1393/2007 is set out in Part VI.

Practice Direction 6C –
Disclosure of Addresses by Government
Departments 13 February 1989 [as amended by
Practice Direction 20 July 1995]

This Practice Direction supplements FPR Part 6

NB—This practice direction does not apply to requests for disclosure from HMRC and related agencies that are covered by "Disclosure Orders against the Inland Revenue-Guidance from the President's Office (November 2003)". Practice Direction of 20 July 1995 (*Disclosure of Addresses by Government Departments*), amending Practice Direction of 13 February 1989, still applies to family proceedings dating from before 6 April 2011.

The arrangements set out in the Registrar's Direction of 26 April 1988 whereby the court may request the disclosure of addresses by government departments have been further extended. These arrangements will now cover:

   (a) tracing the address of a person in proceedings against whom another person is seeking to obtain or enforce an order for financial provision either for himself or herself or for the children of the former marriage; and,

   (b) tracing the whereabouts of a child, or the person with whom the child is said to be, in proceedings under the Child Abduction and Custody Act 1985 or in which a [Part I order] is being sought or enforced.

Requests for such information will be made officially by the [district judge]. The request, in addition to giving the information mentioned below, should certify:

1 *In financial provision applications either*

   (a) that a financial provision order is in existence, but cannot be enforced because the person against whom the order has been made cannot be traced; or

   (b) that the applicant has filed or issued a notice, petition or originating summons containing an application for financial provision which cannot be served because the respondent cannot be traced.

[A "financial provision order" means any of the orders mentioned in s 21 of the Matrimonial Causes Act 1973, except an order under s 27(6) of that Act].

2 *In wardship proceedings* that the child is the subject of wardship proceedings and cannot be traced, and is believed to be with the person whose address is sought.

3 (*deleted*)

The following notes set out the information required by those departments which are likely to be of the greatest assistance to an applicant.

(1) Department of Social Security

The department most likely to be able to assist is the Department of Social Security, whose records are the most comprehensive and complete. The possibility of identifying one person amongst so many will depend on the particulars given. An address will not be supplied by the department unless it is satisfied from the particulars given that the record of the person has been reliably identified.

The applicant or his solicitor should therefore be asked to supply as much as possible of the following information about the person sought:

(i)   National Insurance number;
(ii)   surname;
(iii) forenames in full;
(iv)   date of birth (or, if not known, approximate age);
(v)   last known address, with date when living there;
(vi)   any other known address(es) with dates;
(vii) if the person sought is a war pensioner, his war pension and service particulars (if known);

and in applications for financial provision:

(viii) the exact date of the marriage and the wife's forenames.

Enquiries should be sent by the [district judge] to:

> Contribution Agency
> Special Section A, Room 101B
> Longbenton
> Newcastle upon Tyne
> NE98 1YX

The department will be prepared to search if given full particulars of the person's name and date of birth, but the chances of accurate identification are increased by the provision of more identifying information.

Second requests for records to be searched, provided that a reasonable interval has elapsed, will be met by the Department of Social Security.

Income Support [/Supplementary Benefit]

Where, in the case of applications for financial provision, the wife is or has been in receipt of [income support/supplementary benefit], it would be advisable in the first instance to make enquiries of the manager of the local Social Security office for the area in which she resides in order to avoid possible duplication of enquiries.

(2) [Office for National Statistics]

National Health Service Central Register

[The Office for National Statistics] administers the National Health Service Central Register for the Department of Health. The records held in the Central Register include individuals' names, with dates of birth and National Health Service number, against a record of the Family Practitioner Committee area where the patient is currently registered with a National Health Service doctor. The Central Register does not hold individual patients' addresses, but can advise courts of the last Family Practitioner Committee area registration. Courts can then apply for information about addresses to the appropriate Family Practitioner Committee for independent action.

When application is made for the disclosure of Family Practitioner Committee area registrations from these records the applicant or his solicitor should supply as much as possible of the following information about the person sought:

(i)   National Health Service number;
(ii)   surname;

(iii) forenames in full;
(iv) date of birth (or, if not known, approximate age);
(v) last known address;
(vi) mother's maiden name.

Enquiries should be sent by the [district judge] to:

> [The Office for National Statistics]
> National Health Service Central Register
> Smedley Hydro, Trafalgar Road
> Southport
> Merseyside PR8 2HH

(3) Passport Office

If all reasonable enquiries, including the aforesaid methods, have failed to reveal an address, or if there are strong grounds for believing that the person sought may have made a recent application for a passport, enquiries may be made to the Passport Office. The applicant or his solicitor should provide as much of the following information about the person as possible:

(i) surname;
(ii) forenames in full;
(iii) date of birth (or, if not known, approximate age);
(iv) place of birth;
(v) occupation;
(vi) whether known to have travelled abroad, and, if so, the destination and dates;
(vii) last known address, with date living there;
(viii) any other known address(es), with dates.

The applicant or his solicitor must also undertake in writing that information given in response to the enquiry will be used solely for the purpose for which it was requested, ie to assist in tracing the husband in connection with the making or enforcement of a financial provision order or in tracing a child in connection with a [Part 1 order] or wardship proceedings, as the case may be.

Enquiries should be sent to:

> The Chief Passport Officer
> [UK Passport Agency]
> Home Office
> Clive House, Petty France
> London SW1H 9HD

(4) Ministry of Defence

In cases where the person sought is known to be serving or to have recently served in any branch of HM Forces, the solicitor representing the applicant may obtain the address for service of financial provision or [Part I] and wardship proceedings direct from the appropriate service department. In the case of army servicemen, the solicitor can obtain a list of regiments and of the various manning and record offices from the Officer in Charge, Central Manning Support Office, Higher Barracks, Exeter EC4 4ND.

The solicitor's request should be accompanied by a written undertaking that the address will be used for the purpose of service of process in those proceedings and that so far as is possible the solicitor will disclose the address only to the court and not to the applicant or any other person, except in the normal course of the proceedings.

Alternatively, if the solicitor wishes to serve process on the person's commanding officer under the provisions contained in s 101 of the Naval Act 1957, s 153 of the Army Act 1955 and s 153 of the Air Force Act 1955 (all of which as amended by s 62 of the Armed Forces Act 1971) he may obtain that officer's address in the same way.

Where the applicant is acting in person the appropriate service department is prepared to disclose the address of the person sought, or that of his commanding officer, to a [district judge] on receipt of an assurance that the applicant has given an undertaking that the information will be used solely for the purpose of serving process in the proceedings.

In all cases, the request should include details of the person's full name, service number, rank or rating, and his ship, arm or trade, corps, regiment or unit or as much of this information as is available. The request should also include details of his date of birth, or, if not known, his age, his date of entry into the service and, if no longer serving, the date of discharge, and any other information, such as his last known address. Failure to quote the service number and the rank or rating may result in failure to identify the serviceman or at least in considerable delay.

Enquiries should be addressed as follows:

[(a)	Officers of Royal Navy and Women's Royal Naval Service	The Naval Secretary Room 161 Victory Building HM Naval Base Portsmouth Hants PO1 3LS
	Ratings in the Royal Navy WRNS Ratings QARNNS Ratings	Captain Naval Drafting Centurion Building Grange Road Gosport Hants PO13 9XA
	RN Medical and Dental Officers	The Medical Director General (Naval) Room 114 Victory Building HM Naval Base Portsmouth Hants PO1 3LS
	Naval Chaplains	Director General Naval Chaplaincy Service Room 201 Victory Building HM Naval Base Portsmouth Hants PO1 3LS
(b)	Royal Marine Officers	The Naval Secretary Room 161 Victory Building HM Naval Base Portsmouth Hants PO1 3LS
	Royal Marine Ranks	HQRM (DRORM) West Battery Whale Island Portsmouth Hants PO2 8DX

(c)	Army Officers (including WRAC and QARANC)	Army Officer Documentation Office Index Department Room F7 Government Buildings Stanmore Middlesex
	Other Ranks, Army	The Manning and Record Office which is appropriate to the Regiment or Corps
(d)	Royal Air Force Officers and Other Ranks Women's Royal Air Force Officers and Other Ranks (including PMRA FNS)	Ministry of Defence RAF Personnel Management 2b1(a) (RAF) Building 248 RAF Innsworth Gloucester GL3 1EZ]

General notes

Records held by other departments are less likely to be of use, either because of their limited scope or because individual records cannot readily be identified. If, however, the circumstances suggest that the address may be known to another department, application may be made to it by the [district judge], all relevant particulars available being given.

When the department is able to supply the address of the person sought to the [district judge], it will be passed on by him to the applicant's solicitor (or, in proper cases, direct to the applicant if acting in person) on an understanding to use it only for the purpose of the proceedings.

Nothing in this practice direction affects the service in matrimonial causes of petitions which do not contain any application for financial provision, etc. The existing arrangements whereby the Department of Social Security will at the request of the solicitor forward a letter by ordinary post to a party's last known address remain in force in such cases.

The Registrar's Direction of 26 April 1988 is hereby revoked.

Issued [in its original form] with the concurrence of the Lord Chancellor.

Amendments—FPR PD6C.

Note—Words in square brackets reflect text that has been amended to bring the PD up to date.

Inland Revenue—Concerns arising from the Data Protection legislation and the HRA 1998 have led the Inland Revenue to withdraw from these arrangements. They will, however, comply with a disclosure order made by the High Court exercising its inherent jurisdiction. In November 2003, an approved draft form of order was supplied to courts by the office of the President with the explanatory note set out below:
"Disclosure Orders against the Inland Revenue – Guidance from the President's Office
The Inland Revenue is bound by strict statutory confidentiality obligations which have created difficulties in complying with orders for disclosure of information made against it. The President has agreed with the Solicitor of the Inland Revenue procedures to ensure that orders for disclosure of information such as addresses are complied with and are compatible with the Inland Revenue's confidentiality obligations. The Inland Revenue has agreed to comply with all disclosure orders made against it provided they are made in the inherent jurisdiction of the High Court (and therefore no specific Act is cited on the face of the order).
The order can be made by any of the following classes of judge:
  High Court judge
  Deputy High Court judge
  A section 9 judge
  A district judge of the Principal Registry of the Family Division of the High Court
  A district judge of any District Registry of the Family Division of the High Court

If an application for an order arises in proceedings brought in a court other than a District Registry of the High Court, the application must be transferred, even if only temporarily for the purposes of the application. This will be a judicial decision, and the costs of such transfer will be costs in the proceeding.

Following recent departmental changes, one order made against the Inland Revenue will now provide the court with access to records held in relation to:

    income tax and national insurance contributions;

    the Tax Credits Office;

    the Child Benefit Office;

    provision of valuation services for rating and council tax; and

    collection of student loan repayments.

All disclosure orders against the Inland Revenue should be sent to the following addresses:

1   Where the request is for information about an adult, it should be sent to: Inland Revenue, National Insurance Contributions Office, Special Section A, Longbenton, Newcastle upon Tyne NE98 1YX;

2   Where the request is for information about a child (which may include information about the whereabouts of the relevant adult in receipt of child benefit), it should be sent to: Child Benefits Office (GB) Internal Security, Waterview Park, District 15, Mandarin Way, Paterson, Washington NE38 8QA."

Other agencies—It is not clear whether the other agencies referred to in the PD are taking the same stance. If similar resistance is encountered, the court should be asked to adopt and adapt the practice advised by the President's office.

PART 7
PROCEDURE FOR APPLICATIONS IN MATRIMONIAL AND CIVIL PARTNERSHIP PROCEEDINGS

CONTENTS OF THIS PART

Chapter 1
Application and Interpretation

Chapter 2
Rules about Starting and Responding to Proceedings

Chapter 3
How the Court Determines Matrimonial and Civil Partnership Proceedings

Chapter 4
Court Orders

PART III

INTRODUCTORY NOTE

Structure of Pt 7 and its PD—FPR PD7A prescribes use of the form for application for a matrimonial or civil partnership order (Form D8, and D8N (nullity), with supporting "notes for guidance"). It then provides relatively detailed pleading points and stresses the rule-maker's concern that where a co-respondent may be involved their naming will occur in a very limited number of cases.

Matrimonial and civil partnership proceedings—FPR 2010, Pt 7 deals with all forms of application in matrimonial proceedings or causes under MCA 1973; and with the various forms application in civil partnership proceedings under CPA 2004. In this context an application is the same as a petition. Applications in financial order proceedings ancillary to matrimonial and civil partnership proceedings will have their own separate application form (Form A) under FPR 2010, Pt 9.

Defended and undefended—FPR 2010, Pt 7 deals with all matrimonial and civil partnership proceedings whether defended or undefended, although the procedures run in parallel, often within individual rules.

Simplification, semantics and statutory provision—Courts Act 2003, s 75(5)(b) requires that the 2010 Rules be expressed in "simple and simply expressed" terms. To this end some terminology has been simplified. However, the rule-makers could not alter what was already provided for in statute, so that where procedure is provided for by statute – such as that a divorce "petition" shall start divorce proceedings – then the Rules accommodate that legislative fact.

Derivation—The derivation of these rules is from a combination of FPR 1991 and aspects of CPR 1998. Many concepts from CPR 1998 will, however, find their way into the FPR 2010, Pt 7 procedures, sometimes expressly (as when the case management hearing is introduced in FPR 2010, r 7.22 or requests for information are provided for in FPR 2010, r 7.15 and FPR PD7A, para 6.1–6.5).

Chapter 1
Application and Interpretation

7.1 Application and interpretation

(1) The rules in this Part apply to matrimonial and civil partnership proceedings.

(2) The rules in this Part do not apply to magistrates' courts.

(3) In this Part –

"defended case" means matrimonial proceedings or civil partnership proceedings in which –

(a) an answer has been filed opposing the grant of a matrimonial or civil partnership order on the application, and has not been struck out; or

(b) the respondent has filed an application for a matrimonial or civil partnership order in accordance with rule 7.14 and neither party's application has been disposed of; or

(c) rule 7.12(11) applies, notice has been given of intention to rebut and that notice has not been withdrawn,

and in which no matrimonial or civil partnership order has been made; and

"undefended case" means matrimonial proceedings or civil partnership proceedings other than a defended case.

(4) In this Part –

(a) a reference to a conditional order is a reference to a civil partnership order (other than a separation order) which has not been made final; and

(b) a reference to a final order is a reference to a conditional order which has been made final.

Defined terms—"civil partnership proceedings", "civil partnership order", "matrimonial order": FPR 2010, r 2.3(1).

Terminology—Rule 7.1(4) introduces the terminology for civil partnership proceedings, but does not give the equivalent terms for matrimonial proceedings. For example, a decree nisi is the same as a conditional order and a decree absolute the same as a final order.

"The rules … do not apply to magistrates' courts" (r 7.1(2))—The magistrates do not have the power to dissolve either a marriage or a civil partnership, nor can they annul or judicially separate parties to a marriage or civil partnership. Rule 7.1(2) confirms this by providing that FPR 2010, Pt 7 does not apply to the justices.

Matrimonial and civil partnership proceedings—The proceedings covered by FPR 2010, Pt 7 are matrimonial and civil partnership proceedings, which are defined as follows:

(1) A "matrimonial cause" means proceedings for a matrimonial order (FPR 2010, r 2.3(1)). "Matrimonial proceedings" is not defined in FPR 2010, r 2.3(1) or Pt 7, but such proceedings may be assumed to be proceedings for a matrimonial order. "Matrimonial order" (r 2.3(1)) means:
    (a) a decree of divorce made under MCA 1973, s 1;
    (b) a decree of nullity made on one of the grounds set out in MCA 1973, ss 11 or 12;
    (c) a decree of judicial separation made under MCA 1973, s 17;
    (d) a decree of presumption of death and dissolution under MCA 1973, s 19 (see FPR 2010, r 2.3(2)(a)(iii)).

(2) A "civil partnership order" is defined by reference to CPA 2004, s 37(1), which enables the court to make the civil partnership equivalent of each of those.

"Defended case"—A case becomes defended when a respondent files an answer (FPR 2010, r 7.12(8)) or, having failed to do so in time (r 7.12(8)) obtains permission from the court so to do. The consequence of that is that the court fixes a case management hearing (rr 7.20(4) and 7.22). If matrimonial or civil partnership proceedings are to be defended and if the respondent seeks to oppose the application for a matrimonial or civil partnership order (as the case may be), an answer must be filed.

Circumstances in which an answer must be filed—FPR 1991, r 2.12(1) set out in terms the circumstances in which an answer must be filed and this remains the law since the coming into operation of FPR 2010. By contrast, the 2010 Rules do not provide any procedure for certain statutory provisions (e g defence under MCA 1973, s 5 (with CPA 2004 s 47(1)): right to respond for a co-respondent). Thus, an answer should be filed by a respondent (or exceptionally a co-respondent) in the following circumstances:

(1) Defending an application or disputing facts in it:
   (a) If a respondent wishes to oppose the grant of a matrimonial and civil partnership order, or a co-respondent wishes to dispute facts in an application (the rights of a co-respondent here are not referred to in r 7.1(3)), he must file an answer.
   (b) If a respondent accepts that the marriage has irretrievably broken down but disputes certain particulars, he may wish to file an answer. However, if the purpose of doing so is to answer allegations that might be raised again in children or ancillary relief proceedings, it may be sufficient for him to write to the petitioner or her solicitors, at the time of filing his acknowledgement of service, in the following terms: "The respondent accepts that the marriage has irretrievably broken down but does not accept certain of the allegations in the petition. He reserves the right to reply to those allegations if raised in any subsequent proceedings relating to the children or for ancillary relief."
   (c) A co-respondent or party cited (FPR 2010, r 7.4) served with documents containing allegations that they refute are entitled to file a reply. The procedure for this is not clear: times for reply are not stated (c f time for an answer by a respondent: FPR 2010, r 7.12(8)).
(2) Respondent wishing to cross-apply or to make any charge against the petitioner – If a respondent wishes to make allegations against a petitioner or to cross-apply for an order on facts that he alleges, he must file an answer (FPR 2010, r 7.14). It is not necessary to file an answer if the respondent seeks relief other than a decree (see below, filing of answer not required).
(3) Respondent under MCA 1973, s 5(1) or CPA 2004, s 47(1) who wishes to oppose the grant of decree – Where the respondent to a petition under MCA 1973, s 1(2)(e) or CPA 2004, s 4 (5 years' living apart) wishes to oppose the grant of an order on grounds that it will result in grave financial or other hardship, she must file an answer containing particulars of the hardship alleged (and see under FPR 2010, r 7.12(8) below).

Circumstances where filing of answer not required—There is no need to file an answer where the respondent –

(1) seeks or opposes an order in respect of children;
(2) seeks an order or to be heard on an application for a financial order; or
(3) where a party wishes to be heard on a question of costs (FPR 2010, r 7.21).

"in which no matrimonial and civil partnership order has been made" (r 7.1(3)(d))—Rule 7.1(3)(d) recalls the fact that no proceedings are beyond defending until a final order is made. However, plainly if a respondent wishes to defend, his chances of so doing recede as the date when a final order can finally be made approaches. Such defences and other avenues that may delay the proceedings (including involvement of the Queen's Proctor) are in MCA 1973, ss 8–10(1), CPA 2004, ss 46–48(1), and are dealt with in FPR 2010, rr 7.28 and 7.31.

7.2 District registries

A reference in this Part to a registry for a place at which sittings of the High Court in matrimonial or civil partnership proceedings are authorised is a reference –

   (a) to the district registry for that place;
   (b) where the place has no district registry, such district registry as the Lord Chancellor may designate for the purpose; or
   (c) if the place is not situated within the district of any district registry, the principal registry.

Defined terms—"district registry", "principal registry": FPR 2010, r 2.3(1).

7.3 Principal registry

(1) A provision of this Part which refers to –

    (a)   proceedings being started or heard in a divorce county court or a civil partnership proceedings county court; or

    (b)   the transfer of proceedings to or from such a court,

includes a reference to the principal registry when treated as such a court.

(2) Proceedings to which this Part applies which were started in the principal registry or have been transferred to it as if it were a county court are treated as pending –

    (a)   if the proceedings are matrimonial proceedings, in a divorce county court; and

    (b)   if the proceedings are civil partnership proceedings, in a civil partnership proceedings county court.

Defined terms—"civil partnership proceedings", "civil partnership proceedings county court", "divorce county courts", "principal registry": FPR 2010, r 2.3(1).

7.4 References to respondents

(1) Where a respondent makes an application for a matrimonial order or a civil partnership order, unless the context otherwise requires, the rules in this Part shall apply with necessary modifications as if the reference to a respondent is a reference to the applicant in the other party's application for a matrimonial order or a civil partnership order.

(2) Where a respondent makes an application for a matrimonial order, unless the context otherwise requires, the rules in this Part shall apply with necessary modifications as if the reference to a co-respondent is a reference to a party cited in the respondent's application for a matrimonial order.

Defined terms—"civil partnership order"; "matrimonial order": FPR 2010, r 2.3(1).

"respondent", "co-respondent" and "party cited" (r 7.4(2))—

(1) *Respondent* (r 7.4(1))   Where a respondent files an answer with a cross-application for a matrimonial and civil partnership order (and see FPR 2010, r 7.14; and MCA 1973, s 20; CPA 2004, s 62), then if the application proceeds on that answer references to "applicant" in the rules become references to that respondent.

(2) *Party cited* (r 7.4(2))   Where a cross-application cites what would otherwise have been a co-respondent, that party in the answer becomes known as a "party cited", although this provision should be read with the caveats (especially in FPR PD7A, para 2.1 and see FPR 2010, r 7.10(2)) as to the naming of persons alleged to have committed adultery or to have been responsible for an improper association.

Chapter 2
Rules about Starting and Responding to Proceedings

7.5 Starting proceedings

(1) Matrimonial proceedings may be started in any divorce county court.

(2) Civil partnership proceedings may be started in any civil partnership proceedings county court.

Defined term—"civil partnership proceedings", "civil partnership proceedings county court", "divorce county court": r 2.3(1).

Matrimonial and civil partnership proceedings—See notes at FPR 2010, r 7.1.

Starting matrimonial and civil partnership proceedings—Proceedings are started when the court "issues an application at the request of an applicant" (r 5.3(1)). For the purposes of r 7.5, references to an "application" (MCA 1973, s 1 retains the terminology of petition and petitioners) are as follows:

(1) For a matrimonial order – The "application" for a matrimonial order is presented by "an applicant", who presents the application for a decree.

(2) For a civil partnership order – The applicant under civil partnership law (CPA 2004, r 44(1)) applies for a dissolution order.

Application for an order—The matrimonial or civil partnership proceedings application is started by Form D8, which is accompanied by detailed guidance, which must be followed. The content of the application is elaborated upon by FPR PD7A.

(1) Pleading the application

Pleading the application under the Practice Direction—FPR PD7A, para 1.2 stresses that the particulars in an application for a matrimonial or civil partnership proceedings order (formerly "particulars" in a petition) are sufficient "to show why the applicant is entitled to" the order. Yet, says the same paragraph of the PD, the particulars should be "as concise as possible consistent with providing the necessary evidence". The rule of pleading was that a petitioner must set out "brief particulars of the individual facts relied on but not the evidence by which they are to be proved" (FPR 1991, App 2, para 1(m)).

Pleading the application: court to be "satisfied on the evidence"—In any assessment of pleading the particulars, the applicant's first concern will be to ensure, within the terms of the indications in FPR PD7A that the particulars set out are sufficient to enable a district judge to be "satisfied on the evidence" presented (MCA 1973, s 1(4); equivalent wording is used in CPA 2004, s 44(4)) that the facts are as asserted sufficient for the court to grant a decree nisi or conditional order.

Concise pleading of particulars: answer filed—If particulars are pleaded concisely and an answer is filed, permission of the court can be applied for to amend with further particulars of behaviour (FPR 2010, r 7.13). At this stage all facts on which an application is based will have to be reviewed in any event; for then the proceedings cease to be declaratory and take the form of a contested civil claim, in this case for a particular order in matrimonial or civil partnership proceedings.

Pleading the case: periods together—Care will be needed in pleading dates and particulars where parties have resumed cohabitation for a period or periods of up to 6 months during the period of their living apart (for purposes of MCA 1973, s 1(2)(c),(d),(e) or CPA 2004 s 44(5)(b),(c),(d)) or, where there is no recent allegation of unreasonable behaviour pleaded, where a couple are still living together in the face of otherwise continuing unreasonable behaviour. MCA 1973, s 2 and CPA 2004, s 45 enable parties to resume cohabitation for up to 6 months during the time of their living apart or while behaviour is alleged (although in cases of living apart, periods of living together do not count towards the total living apart period). This time may, for example, give a couple an opportunity to attempt reconciliation. If care is not taken when drafting an application based on facts that involve periods that engage MCA 1973, s 2 or CPA 2004, s 45, then there is a risk that the court will find itself unable to be satisfied on the case as pleaded and a district judge may be unable to sign his certificate under FPR 2010, r 7.20(2).

(2) Prescribed content of the application

Content of the application—FPR PD7A, paras 2.1 and 3.1 define specific aspects of the content of an application. These paragraphs, where applicable, will need to be observed by the applicant in addition to "the detailed notes which accompany [Form D8]".

Co-respondents—Under the heading "respondents: restrictions" in FPR PD7A, para 2.1 the new scheme preserves the spirit of the old by adding as co-respondents anyone named as such by FPR 2010, r 7.10. The applicant should not name the prospective co-respondent unless it is thought that the respondent is likely to defend the proceedings. (In such circumstances, an applicant would be best advised to file an application based on unreasonable behaviour and not to name any prospective co-respondent.)

Civil Evidence Act 1968 notice—FPR PD7A, para 4.1 preserves the terms of FPR 1991, r 2.4 as to notice of convictions or findings in other courts, if sought to be relied upon, under ss 11 and 12 (e g a finding of parentage against one spouse, as evidence of adultery, in separate family proceedings in another magistrates' or county court).

(3) Documents to accompany the application

Documents to be filed at court—An applicant for a matrimonial or civil partnership order proceedings files the following:

(1) An application (petition: for forms see below) in accordance with FPR PD5A

(2) A marriage certificate, civil partnership certificate or certified or other appropriate foreign certificate (see further below); or an application and undertaking that it be filed later (FPR PD5A, para 3.4, see below)

(3) Where there are children of the family, a "statement of arrangements for children" (Form D8A)

(4) A statement of reconciliation where an applicant is legally represented (Form D6; and see FPR 2010, r 7.6).

(5) Appropriate filing fee or application for fees exemption. (If an answer with cross-application is filed and either party has public funding, a certificate of legal aid will be filed now or when funding is obtained.)

Application forms—The prescribed forms of application for matrimonial and civil partnership proceedings (which are accompanied by notes for guidance) are as follows:

- Form D8 – form for proceedings: divorce/dissolution; [judicial] separation petition
- Form D8D – presumption of death and dissolution
- Form D8N – nullity petition

Answer forms—A prescribed form of answer (without notes for guidance) is Form D8B, although a respondent or other replying party does not appear to be restricted to the use of this form. Indeed the rules are economical (FPR 2010, r 7.12(8),(10)) as to what a respondent is to do to file an answer.

Request for service—Under FPR 2010, rr 6.5(1)(b) and 6.8 (and see FPR 2010, r 7.8 below) the applicant will need to ask the court if it is to be requested to serve by posting the application (and documents prescribed by r 7.8(2)) on the respondent.

Acknowledgement of service—An acknowledgement of service will need to be served with the application (petition) (FPR 2010, r 7.8(2)(a)). The rules and PD do not make it clear whether the pre-existing arrangements for issue of a notice of proceedings and acknowledgement of service will be dealt with by the court.

Marriage and civil partnership certificate—In most matrimonial or civil partnership proceedings, the only documentary evidence that is relied upon will be the certificate of marriage or civil partnership. Without this there can be no proceedings (subject to what is said at **Application without marriage ... certificate**, below), and none of the rights and liabilities which flow from marriage or civil partnership (mostly financial and on death) can follow. Proof of the relationship in law is therefore fundamental to the process. In recognition of this FPR PD7A, paras 3.1 to 3.5 deal with "proof ... to accompany the application".

Marriage or civil partnership not in dispute—If the relationship is not in dispute it will be proved by the certificate of marriage or civil partnership recording obtained at the time of the marriage or civil partnership, the certificate obtained in the country where the registration occurred or a certified copy (FPR PD7A, para 3.1(a)).

Translation—If the certificate is not in English (or Welsh, in Welsh courts) a certified copy must be provided (FPR PD7A, para 3.1(b)).

Application without marriage or civil partnership certificate—FPR PD7A, paras 3.2–3.4 provide for steps to be taken where a certificate cannot be produced at the time of filing the application and "it is urgent that the application be filed" (para 3.2, but see *G v M*, below). The applicant (or his solicitor) must file a FPR 2010, Pt 18 application, with a statement that explains the urgency and why the certificate is not available (para 3.3). The court will require an undertaking as to the filing of the certificate within appropriate time limits (para 3.4). Application will normally be made without notice with an explanation as to why no certificate can be filed (FPR PD7A, paras 3.2 and 3.3). Proof of urgency (as indicated by FPR PD7A, paras 3.2 and 3.3) is not in law a prerequisite for an application (*G v M* [2011] EWHC 2651 (Fam), Hedley J, at [2]), since this procedure applies where it is alleged that there is no marriage certificate at all. Where there is no certificate at all (as in *G v M*) the existence of a marriage may require to be tested.

7.6 Statement of reconciliation

(1) Where the applicant is legally represented, the legal representative must, unless the court directs otherwise, complete and file with the application a statement in the form for this purpose referred to in Practice Direction 5A, certifying whether the legal representative has discussed with the applicant the possibility of a reconciliation and given the applicant the names and addresses of persons qualified to help effect a reconciliation.

(2) This rule applies to an application for –

(a) a decree of divorce made under section 1 of the 1973 Act;

(b) a decree of judicial separation made under section 17 of the 1973 Act;

(c) a dissolution order as mentioned in section 37(1)(a) of the 2004 Act; or

(d) a separation order as mentioned in section 37(1)(d) of the 2004 Act.

Amendments—SI 2012/679.

Defined terms—"legal representative": FPR 2010, s 2.3(1).

Certificate of discussion of reconciliation by legal representative—Rule 7.6 confirms the requirement under MCA 1973, s 6 and CPA 2004, s 42 that, where a petitioner/applicant is legally represented, then that representative must file a statement in accordance with Form D6. If an applicant has no legal representative, there is no bar to them applying for a matrimonial or civil partnership order.

7.7 Limitation on applications in respect of same marriage or civil partnership

(1) Subject to paragraph (2), a person may not make more than one application for a matrimonial or civil partnership order in respect of the same marriage or civil partnership unless –

(a) the first application has been dismissed or finally determined; or

(b) the court gives permission.

(2) Where a person –

(a) has, within one year of the date of the marriage or civil partnership, made an application for, as the case may be, a decree of judicial separation or an order for separation; and

(b) then, after that one-year period has passed, wishes to apply for a decree of divorce or a dissolution order on the same facts as those mentioned in the first application,

that person does not need the court's permission to make the application referred to in sub-paragraph (b).

Defined terms—"civil partnership order", "matrimonial order": FPR 2010, r 2.3(1).

Further applications for a matrimonial or civil partnership order—This rule, either expressly or by implication, deals with the following three issues in relation to matrimonial or civil partnership applications (petitions, as far as an existing matrimonial or civil partnership order applicants are concerned):

(a) the court giving permission for a fresh application where an application/petition has not been disposed of (r 7.7(1)(b));

(b) amendment of an existing application (see r 7.13 below);

(c) the filing, without permission, of a fresh application where there is an existing application for judicial separation or a civil partnership separation order application filed before the expiry of 1 year from the date of the marriage or civil partnership (r 7.7(2)).

Application by respondent: permission not required—Whereas it will rarely be appropriate to do so, there is no reason why a respondent to existing matrimonial or civil partnership proceedings should not file his own application (petition), provided that there has been no decree nisi or civil partnership conditional order granted. This might particularly be appropriate where an existing application has been filed and served, but has not been proceeded with by the applicant (for whatever reason), or following a couple's reconciliation.

Permission for a second application (r 7.7(1))—Application notice to the court to file a further application form will be made in the existing proceedings under the FPR 2010, Pt 18 procedure. Three options arise:

(a) If the application has not been served it can be withdrawn (r 7.9), in which case no question of permission for a fresh application arises;

(b) The parties themselves may wish to consider whether there is some way to deal with and for the court to determine the original application (r 7.7(1)(a): this is not possible, for example, if the parties have resumed cohabitation for more than 6 months) if only to save the court fee and dealing with further paperwork.

PART III

(c) If it comes to dealing with the application for permission, the court will want to consider whether the original application can be formally dismissed (r 7.7(1)(a)).

Amended applications—FPR 2010, r 7.13 deals with amendment of pleadings. The supplementary petition no longer appears as a creature of the 2010 Rules. Parker J accepted the proposition that this is a deliberate omission (*Kim v Morris* [2012] EWHC 1103 (Fam)). Concerns have been voiced that changes in circumstances that have arisen since the original petition was filed (for example, an attempted but unsuccessful reconciliation) cannot be adequately put before the court. The position remains under review within the Rules Committee.

Amendment of separation application—An application for a judicial separation or civil partnership separation order filed before the parties have been married for a year may not be amended, after that year, for an application for divorce (*Butler v Butler, The Queen's Proctor Intervening* [1990] 1 FLR 114; see also FPR 2010, r 2.6(4)) or dissolution. A fresh application can be filed (r 7.7(2)).

Applications: amended petitions, further evidence or permission under r 7.7—MCA 1973, s 2 and CPA 2004, s 45 have parallel provisions that enable parties to resume cohabitation for a period or periods up to 6 months during the time of their living apart or while behaviour is alleged (although in cases of living apart periods of living together do not count towards the total living apart period). These periods may, for example, give a couple a chance to attempt reconciliation. Once together for more than 6 months, time must run all over again or fresh unreasonable behaviour facts be pleaded. Mention has already been made of the need for care in pleading these periods (see under FPR 2010, r 7.5). Where such circumstances occur, up-to-date evidence must be filed (perhaps with the affidavit in support of an application for a certificate, but not as a "supplemental" pleading) or, if time under s 2 or s 45 has been exceeded, for seeking permission to file a second application (petition) or for dismissal of the first application (petition).

7.8 Service of application

(1) After an application for a matrimonial or civil partnership order has been issued by the court, a copy of it must be served on the respondent and on any co-respondent.

> (Rule 6.5 provides for who may serve an application for a matrimonial or civil partnership order.)

(2) When the application is served on a respondent it must be accompanied by –

(a) a form for acknowledging service;
(b) a notice of proceedings; and
(c) where applicable, a copy of the statement of arrangements for children.

Service of the application— FPR 2010, r 6.5 prescribes that service may be by an applicant (other than personal service: r 6.5(3)) or by the court (if requested: r 6.5(1)(b)). In the past, the forms of acknowledgement of service and notice of proceedings have been provided by the court and, in the first instance, the court has served documents by post.

Consent to a decree—Documents served on the respondent that require his consent to a decree under MCA 1973, s 1(2)(d) or CPA 2004, s 44(5)(b) must enable him "to understand the consequences of consenting to a decree". MCA 1973, s 2(7) and CPA 2004, s 45(4)(a) requires that provision for this be made by rules of court. It is not clear where this rule is in FPR 2010.

7.9 Withdrawal of application before service

An application for a matrimonial or civil partnership order may be withdrawn at any time before it has been served by giving notice in writing to the court where the proceedings were started.

"notice in writing"—FPR 1991, r 2.8 enabled a petitioner to "discontinue" a cause where a petition was not served. This provision echoes the earlier, save that the requirement only of "notice in writing" suggests no prescribed form: a letter would appear to suffice.

7.10 Who the parties are

(1) The parties to matrimonial proceedings or civil partnership proceedings are –

the parties to the marriage or civil partnership concerned; and
any other person who is to be a party in accordance with a provision of the rules in this Part.

(2) Subject to paragraph (3), where an application for a matrimonial order or an answer to such an application alleges that the other party to the marriage has committed adultery with a named person, that named person is to be the co-respondent.

(3) The named person referred to in paragraph (2) is not to be a co-respondent where –

(a)   the court so directs;
(b)   that person has died; or
(c)   unless the court directs otherwise –
   (i)   that person is under 16 years of age; or
   (ii)   the other party to the marriage is alleged in the application or answer to have committed rape on the named person.

(4) Where an application for a matrimonial or civil partnership order or an answer alleges that the other party to the marriage or civil partnership has had an improper association with a named person, the court may direct that the named person is to be the co-respondent to the application, unless the named person has died.

(5) An application for directions under paragraph (3)(a) or (c) may be made without notice if the acknowledgment of service indicates that no party intends to defend the case.

Amendments—SI 2012/679.

Defined terms—"Answer": r 7.1(3)(a); "civil partnership proceedings", "matrimonial proceedings": FPR 2010, r 2.3(1).

"Parties" to the proceedings—"Parties" under r 7.10 are parties to what was formerly "the main suit", namely the matrimonial and civil partnership proceedings (and see Pt 7 **Introductory note**). They are parties only to the FPR 2010, Pt 7 proceedings. In other ancillary or subsidiary proceedings (e g financial order proceedings – see, for example, FPR 2010, r 9.12: the "applicant" for the financial order applies for the order whether or not the same spouse or civil partnership is the applicant for the matrimonial or civil partnership order) the parties may have different party status names; additional parties may be joined who are not parties to the matrimonial and civil partnership proceedings at all; and in children proceedings party titles may disappear altogether from the face of the orders. The status names may change again in any appellate proceedings.

Parties: statutory provision—Statute law (namely MCA 1973, s 49 and CPA 2004, s 64) and the rules, are not in harmony with one another and with the rules over the naming of parties. MCA 1973, s 49 is prescriptive and takes a more stern line than the 2010 Rules (and the PD) on the naming of co-respondents. By contrast, CPA 2004, s 64 in an empowering provision only: it leaves questions dealt with in s 49 (i e by statute) to the rules. Dismissal, addition of parties to the proceedings and naming of parties in civil partnership proceedings (CPA 2004, s 64(1)) is left to the rule-makers. In matrimonial and civil partnership proceedings (as distinct from any proceedings alongside such proceedings), the parties will be the applicant (petitioner) and any one or more of the following:

- the respondent (the other spouse or civil partner)
- the co-respondent (if any)
- the party-cited (if any: FPR 2010, r 7.4(2)); and
- any parties formally added as parties to the proceedings (likely to be rare at this stage; and see MCA 1973, s 49(5) below).

Respondent and other parties—The respondent remains so called, even though he files an answer and the application (cause) proceeds on the prayer in that answer (see also FPR 2010, rr 7.4 and 7.14). Others may be added to the proceedings as co-respondent (MCA 1973, s 49(1) and see below). However, the mere service of proceedings does not make the person served a party to proceedings unless the person is formally added as a party by the court (*Re T (Divorce: Interim Maintenance: Discovery)* [1990] 1 FLR 1).

Practice Direction 7A— FPR PD7A, para 2.1 and r 7.10 read together confine the naming of a co-respondent in matrimonial and civil partnership proceedings and exclude certain categories of co-respondent (r 7.10(3)).

"named person is to be the co-respondent" (r 7.10(2))—Rule 7.10(3) excludes a narrow category of possible co-respondents from being named in the proceedings (MCA 1973, s 49(1)); but otherwise a named person is required to be a party to the proceedings. The approach of the rule is at odds with FPR PD7A, which discourages the naming of co-respondents. Under the heading "Respondents: restrictions" FPR PD7A, para 2.1 directs (so far as it is able so to do) that an applicant should not name the prospective co-respondent (i e they are strongly discouraged from naming a co-respondent) unless it is thought that the respondent is likely to defend the proceedings.

"improper association" (r 7.10(4))—Anyone named in an application as having had "an improper association" with the respondent may, by direction of the court, be named as a co-respondent. The rules do not dictate what, in either a hetero- or homosexual marital or civil partnership relationship, is regarded as an "improper association" in this context.

Intervener co-respondent—MCA 1973, s 49(5) enables a person against whom adultery is alleged to apply to be joined (added) as a party in matrimonial proceedings.

Dismissal of a party from the suit—A party against whom an allegation is made, can be "dismissed from the suit" (proceedings) if the court considers the evidence against them not to justify the allegation (MCA 1973, s 49(3)).

7.11 Nullity: Interim and full gender recognition certificates

(1) Where the application is for –

    (a) nullity of marriage under section 12(g) of, or paragraph 11(1)(e) of Schedule 1 to, the 1973 Act; or

    (b) an order of nullity of civil partnership under section 50(1)(d) of the 2004 Act,

the court officer must send to the Secretary of State a notice in writing that the application has been made.

(2) Where a copy of an interim gender recognition certificate has been filed with the application, that certificate must be attached to the notice.

(3) Where no copy of an interim gender recognition certificate has been filed the notice must also state –

    (a) in matrimonial proceedings –

        (i)   the names of the parties to the marriage and the date and place of the marriage, and

        (ii) the last address at which the parties to the marriage lived together as husband and wife;

    (b) in civil partnership proceedings –

        (i)   the names of the parties to the civil partnership and the date on, and the place at which, the civil partnership was formed, and

        (ii) the last address at which the parties to the civil partnership lived together as civil partners of each other; and

    (c) in either case, such further particulars as the court officer considers appropriate.

(4) Where –

    (a) the application is for a decree of nullity of marriage under section 12(h) of the 1973 Act or for an order of nullity of civil partnership under section 50(1)(e) of the 2004 Act; and

    (b) a full gender recognition certificate has been issued to the respondent,

the applicant must file a copy of that full certificate with the application unless the court, on an application made without notice, directs otherwise.

Scope—This rule is the counterpart of FPR 1991, rr 2.6A, 2.12A and 2.12B. See, generally, the annotations to the Gender Recognition Act 2004. If a married applicant's application for a gender recognition certificate is granted, the Gender Recognition Panel must issue an interim gender recognition certificate. An interim certificate permits either party to the marriage to apply for a decree of nullity under MCA 1973, s 12(g) (marriages celebrated after 31 July 1971) or Sch 1, para 11(1)(e) (marriages celebrated before 1 August 1971) on the ground that the marriage is voidable. The CPA 2004, s 50(1)(d) makes comparable provision for nullity of civil partnership. When the court makes absolute a decree of nullity granted on the ground that an interim gender recognition certificate has been issued to either party, the court must issue a full gender recognition certificate to that party. The Secretary of State must be notified of the proceedings, which could act as a trigger for proceedings for a reference under Gender Recognition Act 2004, s 8(5) (applications secured by fraud).

Defined terms—"interim gender recognition certificate" (r 7.11(2)): Gender Recognition Act 2004, ss 4(3) and 25; "full gender recognition certificate" (r 7.11(4)): Gender Recognition Act 2004, ss 4(2) and 25.

7.12 What the respondent and co-respondent should do on receiving the application

(1) The respondent, and any co-respondent, must file an acknowledgment of service within 7 days beginning with the date on which the application for a matrimonial or civil partnership order was served.

(2) This rule is subject to rule 6.42 (which specifies how the period for filing an acknowledgment of service is calculated where the application is served out of the jurisdiction).

(3) The acknowledgment of service must –

    (a) subject to paragraph (4), be signed by the respondent or the respondent's legal representative or, as the case may be, the co respondent or the co respondent's legal representative;

    (b) include the respondent's or, as the case may be, the co respondent's address for service; and

    (c) where it is filed by the respondent, indicate whether or not the respondent intends to defend the case.

(4) Where paragraph (5) or (6) applies, the respondent must sign the acknowledgment of service personally.

(5) This paragraph applies where –

    (a) the application for a matrimonial order alleges that the respondent has committed adultery; and

    (b) the respondent admits the adultery.

(6) This paragraph applies where –

    (a) the application for a matrimonial or civil partnership order alleges that the parties to the marriage or civil partnership concerned have been separated for more than 2 years; and

    (b) the respondent consents to the making of the matrimonial or civil partnership order.

(7) Where the respondent does not agree with the proposals set out in the applicant's statement of arrangements for children, the respondent may file a statement of arrangements for children under section 41(1) of the 1973 Act or section 63(1) of the 2004 Act.

(8) A respondent who wishes to defend the case must file and serve an answer within 21 days beginning with the date by which the acknowledgment of service is required to be filed.

(9) An answer is not required where the respondent does not object to the making of the matrimonial or civil partnership order but objects to paying the costs of the application or to the applicant's statement of arrangements for children.

(10) A respondent may file an answer even if the intention to do so was not indicated in the acknowledgment of service.

(11) Where the application is for nullity of marriage under section 12(d) of the 1973 Act or for nullity of civil partnership under section 50(1)(b) of the 2004 Act and the respondent files an answer containing no more than a simple denial of the facts stated in the application, the respondent must, if intending to rebut the matters stated in the application, give notice to the court of that intention when filing the answer.

(12) A respondent to an application for a matrimonial or civil partnership order alleging 2 years' separation and the respondent's consent may –

    (a)   indicate consent to the making of the matrimonial or civil partnership order in writing at any time after service of the application, whether in the acknowledgment of service or otherwise;

    (b)   indicate lack of consent to the making of that order, or withdraw any such consent already given, by giving notice to the court.

(13) Where a respondent gives a notice under paragraph (12)(b) and no other relevant fact is alleged, the proceedings must be stayed$^{(GL)}$, and notice of the stay$^{(GL)}$ given to the parties by the court officer.

(14) In this rule, a "relevant fact" is –

    (a)   in matrimonial proceedings, one of the facts mentioned in section (1)(2) of the 1973 Act; and

    (b)   in civil partnership proceedings, one of the facts mentioned in section 44(5) of the 2004 Act.

(15) In paragraphs (3)(c), (8), (9) and (10), any reference to a respondent is to be read as including a reference to a co-respondent where the context so requires.

    (The form of the answer is referred to in Practice Direction 5A.)

Amendments—SI 2012/679.

Defined terms—"civil partnership order", "matrimonial order": r 2.3(1); "defended case": FPR 2010, r 7.1(3).

Introduction—Rule 7.12 deals with requirements as to what a respondent does on service of the application and contains two separate components:

(1) The acknowledgement of service: the requirements of a respondent if he wishes to sign it; and
(2) Proceedings becoming defended by the filing of an answer (briefly referred to in r 7.12(8)).

Structure of the rules: defended and undefended proceedings—Rule 7.12 deals with the divide between defended and undefended matrimonial and civil partnership proceedings. Rules and procedure for the two forms of process are intermingled in FPR 2010, Pt 7, but the real divide between defended and undefended proceedings has the following procedural consequences.

    (i)   Once an answer is filed, rules of pleading (e g amendment of pleadings: FPR 2010, r 7.13; ordering of further information: FPR 2010, r 7.15) become relatively formal (akin to CPR 1998 proceedings).

    (ii)   Undefended cases will generally proceed without any further attendance at court required by the parties.

(1) The acknowledgement of service

Acknowledgement of service (r 7.12(1))—The term's function in matrimonial and civil partnership proceedings is developed in r 7.12, but is not defined in the rules or in the Glossary.

"The respondent ... must file an acknowledgement of service" (r 7.12(1))—Compulsion to file (a party "must file" a document, here the acknowledgement of service) is the terminology preferred by the 2010 rules. There is in fact, and in law there can be, no compulsion on anyone to file an answer, or an acknowledgement to a matrimonial or civil partnership order application.

Response to matrimonial and civil partnership order application (petition)

    (i)   *Signing the acknowledgement of service (r 7.12(3)–(6))* If a respondent chooses to sign an acknowledgement of service and if he wants it (1) to stand as an admission of adultery or (2) as his consent, the parties having lived apart for 2 years or more, then he must personally sign the acknowledgement of service (derived from FPR 1991, r 2.10(1)).

(ii) *Response to statement of arrangements (r 7.12(7))*   The respondent may file a reply to the statement of arrangements for the children.

Costs claimed in application (petition) (r 7.12(9))—If the respondent's only formal reply to the application is that he objects to paying costs, there is no need for a formal answer to be filed, although the respondent can file a short reply on costs in the acknowledgement of service when it is returned to the court (e g to admit to pay half the costs limited to a figure of (say) £350). Other opportunities will arise for objection to be taken in court to payment of costs (r 7.21).

Notice of consent (r 7.12(12)(a))—The fact of living apart for 2 years (MCA 1973, s 1(2)(d), CPA 2004, s 44(5)(b)) is the only fact that requires a respondent's consent to a decree or order. Thus the court needs to know not only that the respondent has received the application (petition) but also that he consents to a decree. The acknowledgement of service asks if the respondent consents to a decree being granted. Consent will be given if the respondent answers this affirmatively and signs the form personally (r 7.12(6)). Any other form of notice filed at court by the respondent and indicating his consent would appear to suffice.

No consent or withdrawal of consent (r 7.12(12)(b))—A respondent may indicate to the court that he does not consent or that he withdraws his consent, although no date by which this is to be done is specified in the rule. Once the district judge has signed his certificate under the special procedure, it may be difficult to set up the withdrawal (*Day v Day* (1980) 1 FLR 341, CA: certificate of registrar (district judge: certificate then is the same as a certificate under r 7.20(2)) under divorce rules held to be tantamount to a decree nisi).

Stay on proceedings (r 7.12(13),(14))—When the respondent gives an indication of no consent or withdrawal of consent (if this notice is in time (see previous note)), then if there is no other fact under MCA 1973, s 1(2) or CPA 2004, s 44(5) (r 7.12(14)), the proceedings must be stayed. The application remains on file and can be proceeded with only if permission is granted by the court. If there is no consent, the petitioner will be unable to proceed since consent is an essential component for proof of the fact under MCA 1973, s 1(2)(d). Where the respondent withdraws consent, the court may be able to resurrect the original consent when considering an application to remove the stay (*N v N (Divorce: Agreement not to Defend)* [1992] 1 FLR 266: husband who agreed not to defend was held to his original agreement). Application to remove the stay is by the FPR 2010, Pt 18 procedure; but in effect an application to remove could only be made by consent of the respondent (save in the unusual circumstances of *N v N*).

Withdrawal of consent after r 7.20 certificate signed—Once a district judge's r 7.20 certificate has been signed or decree nisi (or conditional order) has been obtained, withdrawal of consent is unlikely to be effective (and see *Day v Day* (above)), unless a respondent can appeal against the order, can successfully apply for it to be set aside (e g because notice was not given under MCA 1973, s 2(7)), or he can apply for rescission of the decree (FPR 2010, r 7.28)). A general rule of appeals is that it is rare to be able to appeal against an order made by consent (consent in the acknowledgement of service is not the same, but the principle is clear).

(2) Proceedings becoming defended by the filing of an answer

Filing of answer: rules of pleading—Once an answer is filed the case becomes defended (FPR 2010, r 7.1(3)). In effect rules of pleading apply (e g amendment of pleadings: FPR 2010, r 7.13; ordering of further information: FPR 2010, r 7.15; disclosure: FPR 2010, r 7.22(2)(c)).

Answer: defended proceedings (r 7.12(8))—Rule 7.12(8) requires that a respondent who wishes to defend matrimonial or civil partnership proceedings must file an answer to the application. The term "answer" is not defined in the Rules. It is a term that has been carried over from the former procedure and (like a defence in proceedings under CPR 1998) it indicates that a party does not agree – for whatever reason, but mostly it will be on the facts in matrimonial and civil partnership proceedings – to the application. Upon an answer being filed, the case becomes defended (see defended case under FPR 2010, r 7.1).

Time for filing an answer (r 7.12(8))—Computation of time for filing an answer remains as it was under FPR 1991, r 2.12. The time for working out the period within which an answer is to be filed is calculated from the date on which the application was served on the respondent (a date that only the respondent will know for certain), by reference to two periods:

(a) The date for filing the acknowledgement of service: by r 7.12(1) this is "7 days beginning with the date on which the application ... was served"; and

(b) 21 days from the last of the days in (a), above.

(i) *Date of service of application*   Calculation of the correct period under r 7.12(1) depends on a calculation of the exact date on which service took effect and how time runs from there. FPR 2010, Pt 6, Ch 2 creates a set of rules for service of matrimonial and civil partnership proceedings that are particular to those proceedings. No formal date for service is defined by Pt 6, Ch 2, so that where an acknowledgement of service is not returned to the court, the court may be asked to deem service and on a particular date (FPR 2010, rr 6.15, 6.16). Therefore, it must be assumed that the date for service is as for other documents: that is, 2 days after posting by first-class post avoiding non-business days (FPR 2010, r 6.34).

(ii) *Date for filing answer*   The date is calculated by a combination of two periods to which different rules apply – the time for filing an answer is the aggregate of the time limited for giving notice to defend (7 days) and the 21 days following that. Therefore, the time for giving notice to defend is 7 days after service of the application (petition). To this moving target is then added 21 days, ie 21 days regardless of what holidays, weekends etc may intervene.

Permission out of time to file an answer—Rule 7.12(8) is in mandatory terms. Permission from the court, by the FPR 2010, Pt 18 procedure (application notice in Form D11), is therefore required if an answer is to be filed once the time limits referred to above have expired. The court is likely to draw a distinction between an answer filed a few days late and one filed considerably out of time (see *Lawlor v Lawlor* [1995] 1 FLR 269, CA).

Test for permission application

(1) FPR 2010, r 4.6 – The court will bear in mind the factors in r 4.6 (relief from sanctions) when deciding whether or not to give permission relief to a respondent who has failed to comply with the time limit in r 7.12(8); this will include the prospects of success at trial of the matters raised by the proposed answer to the application.

(2) The prospect of success in the context of family proceedings (especially MFPA 1984, Pt III) has been considered by the Supreme Court in *Agbaje v Agbaje* [2010] 1 FLR 1813, at [33]: essentially that "wholly unmeritorious claims" are not pursued. Perhaps the criterion is that a respondent should show he has a "good arguable case" for permission to be granted (lower for example than for an appeal: r 30.3(7): the "threshold [need not] be high").

Procedure for a permission application: A "gap" practice direction—No procedure is prescribed for obtaining permission and the detail of FPR 2010, Pt 18 does not assist. Procedure for a permission application in MFPA 1984, Pt III proceedings was considered by Munby LJ in the Court of Appeal in *Traversa v Freddi* [2011] 2 FLR 272 at [54] and [58] in a "gap" practice direction (as explained in *Secretary of State for Communities and Local Government v Bovale Ltd and anor* [2009] EWCA Civ 171). The factors considered in *Traversa v Freddi* may be thought to assist with permission applications generally, especially on the question of whether or not such applications need to be dealt with on notice.

(1) An application for permissions "should be listed ex parte for a hearing which can be appropriately brief" (as with appeals (FPR PD30A, para 4.14) and judicial review applications (CPR 1998, r 54.12)).

(2) If the respondent attends the hearing she will not be heard or have any costs for so doing (as in the Court of Appeal etc). The respondent's case will be heard at any substantive hearing (if permission is given).

(3) An applicant can apply to set aside a grant of permission, but only if she can demonstrate some "knock-out blow" (a compelling reason: on analogy with CPR 1998, r 52.9(2)) why permission should be set aside (per *Agbaje* (at [33]).

(4) Subject to these points the applicant will be able to argue the merits of the answer at the final hearing.

Permission where r 7.20 certificate signed—If the district judge has already signed his certificate under r 7.20(2), permission to file an answer out of time is unlikely to be given (*Day v Day* (1980) 1 FLR 341, CA), unless the respondent (Pt 18 applicant for permission) is able successfully to apply for the certificate to be set aside. This area of law and the status of the certificate (as against the status of a formal order) may be appropriate for re-consideration by the courts under the current law: the requirement for family courts to deal with "cases justly" and the entitlement of respondents in Mr Day's position to a fair trial of an issue reasonably raised by him before the court. At present, the law is as stated by the Court of Appeal in *Day v Day*.

MCA 1973, s 5(1); CPA 2004, s 47(1)—If a respondent to an application under MCA 1973, s 1(2)(e) or CPA 2004, s 44(5)(c) wishes to say that she may suffer grave financial hardship if a matrimonial or civil partnership order is made, she must file an answer. The Rules are silent on this (but see commentary on FPR 2010, r 7.1). The respondent is left by statute and rules to deduce the need to file an answer from the wording of the statute (which does not mention an answer; it merely speaks of a "respondent", which is presumably intended to imply the need to file an answer to the s 1(2)(e) or 44(5)(e) application).

7.13 Amendments to the application and the answer

(1) Unless paragraph (2) applies –

    (a)   a party making an application for a matrimonial or civil partnership order may amend the application at any time before an answer to it has been filed;

    (b)   a party who has filed an answer may amend the answer.

(2) No amendment to an application for a matrimonial or civil partnership order or to an answer may be made under paragraph (1) if an application under rule 7.19(1) has been made in relation to the marriage or civil partnership concerned.

(3) Where an amendment is made under paragraph (1) –

    (a)   if the document amended is the application –
it must be served in accordance with rule 7.8 (service of application); and rule 7.12 (what the respondent and co respondent should do) applies;

    (b)   rule 7.10 (parties) applies; and

    (c)   any person who becomes a co-respondent to the proceedings in accordance with rule 7.10 as a consequence of such an amendment must be served with the documents required to be served on a co-respondent with an application for a matrimonial or civil partnership order.

(4) Paragraphs (1) and (2) do not apply if the amendment is made –

    (a)   with the written consent of all the other parties; or

    (b)   with the permission of the court.

(5) Where the court gives permission for a party to amend that party's application for a matrimonial or civil partnership order or answer it may give directions as to –

    (a)   the service of the amended application or answer and any accompanying documents;

    (b)   the joining of any additional parties in accordance with rule 7.10; and

    (c)   the extent to which rule 7.12 must be complied with in respect of any amended application.

(6) The court may direct that any person cease to be a party if, in consequence of any amendment made under this rule, that person –

    (a)   no longer falls within rule 7.10(2) or (4) or

    (b)   falls within rule 7.10(4) but it is no longer desirable for that person to be a party to the proceedings.

Application for decree nisi or conditional order: FPR 2010, r 7.19 (r 7.13(2))—No application to amend a pleading can be made (save with permission from the court) once application has been made (under r 7.19(1)) for a decree nisi or conditional order. The former rule (FPR 1991, r 2.14) made amendment of pleadings impossible after directions for trial had been given; only in defended causes did the issue of preventing further amendment arise.

Vires of r 7.13(2)—Rule 7.13(2) is unlikely to be intra vires the rules and it is of questionable logic. Once an application for decree nisi or conditional order has been filed (FPR 2010, r 7.19(1)), it may be some time before a r 7.20(2) certificate is signed and yet in that period where the proceedings are still pending it is suggested here that they are altogether aloof from amendment. A party who has been mislead on the facts or who wishes to promote a reconciliation can only (perhaps) apply to set aside her own r 7.19(1) application or apply to stay the applicant's r 7.19(1) application. The doubtful logic arises from the reference to "an answer" here. If application is made under r 7.19(1) it is unlikely an answer is on the file.

Amendment of an answer (r 7.13(1)(b))—A respondent who has filed an answer is able to amend without permission until an application is made under FPR 2010, r 7.19(1), whereas the applicant, once the answer has been filed, can only amend her application with permission of the court or the consent of the respondent (r 7.13(4)).

Application to amend; Practice Direction 7A—Application to amend, where there is no consent to amend, is by the FPR 2010, Pt 18 procedure (Form D11). For further guidance on procedure for amendment and other detailed requirements, assistance may be drawn from CPR PD17 (from which parts of FPR PD7A are drawn). The rules relating to the original pleading (statements of truth, signing etc) will apply to the amended pleading. FPR PD7A para 5.2 explains that the application and the proposed amendments incorporated into the existing pleading should be filed at court. If permission is given then the amended pleading should be filed at court (and served, perhaps) within 14 days (FPR PD7A, para 5.3).

Direction: cease to be a party (r 7.13(6))—The court may direct that a co-respondent or other party cease to be a party (r 7.10(2) or (4)) where allegations are no longer made against them (for example, because a petition/application is amended from adultery to unreasonable behaviour, or a respondent agrees finally to a decree nisi or conditional order based on 2 years living apart rather than unreasonable behaviour where an "improper association" had been alleged). The drafting of the rule suggests that such a direction would be made on the court's initiative; but in principle there is no reason why it should not be done on the application of a party (i e including the co-respondent) and save where the point was contentious it could presumably be done by letter to the court.

Prospects of success of the pleading as amended—In a consideration of an application to amend, the court will look at the likely effect of the amendment on the progress and outcome of the application. The overriding objective is to ensure that cases are dealt with justly: in general, amendments should be allowed (*Cobbold v Greenwich* LBC (1999) unreported, CA), but only where the proposed amendment shows a prospect of the outcome of the proceedings being altered by the amendment (*Mandrake Holdings Ltd v Countrywide Assured Group plc* [2005] EWCA Civ 638).

Costs of amendment—It does not follow automatically that the costs of an amendment should be borne by the amender. If a request is made to amend by consent (r 7.13(4)(a) that is refused, and the amendment is then permitted by the court, in principle there is no reason why costs should not be awarded to the party who amends (*La Chemise Lacoste SA v Sketchers USA Ltd* [2006] EWHC 3642 (Ch)).

7.14 How the respondent can make an application

(1) A respondent who wishes to make an application for a matrimonial or civil partnership order must make the application for that order within 21 days beginning with the date by which the respondent's acknowledgment of service is required to be filed, unless the court gives permission to make the application after that time has passed.

(2) Where the respondent makes an application under this rule, that application is to be treated as an application in the same proceedings for the purposes of this Part.

MCA 1973, s 20; CPA 2004, s 62—MCA 1973, s 20 (with its parallel in CPA 2004, s 62) provides that if a respondent obtains an order in matrimonial or civil partnership proceedings then he does so as if it were his application that had started the proceedings, and then the party names, as between applicant and respondent, are reversed. Rule 7.14 deals with the way that the position on which ss 20 and 62 are predicated is reached.

"must make the application ... within 21 days" (r 7.14(1))—This provision only partly sets out the steps that a respondent may take to make his own application. If a respondent wants to seek a matrimonial or civil partnership order (and thus bring himself within MCA 1973, s 20 or CPA 2004, s 62), as the law stands, there are four ways that he may do so (only two of these are expressly contemplated by r 7.14(1)):

(1) File and serve an answer, within the time limit referred to in r 7.14 (formerly known as an answer with cross-prayer). In the answer the respondent would, for example, deny that the marriage or civil partnership has irretrievably broken down on the basis of his behaviour, but allege that it had done so on the basis of facts arising from the behaviour of the applicant, and fact in support would require to be pleaded. He could then ask the court for a decree nisi or conditional order based on the application in his answer (on the prayer in his answer, in old terminology).

(2) File and serve an answer outside the time limit in FPR 2010, rr 7.14(1) and 7.12(8), but seek permission to proceed out of time under FPR 2010, r 7.13(4).

(3) File and serve an answer in which he defends the proceedings, then apply, with agreement of the applicant (FPR 2010, r 7.13(4)(a)), to amend his answer to plead facts on which the case could then proceed. This would then be on the application in the answer (cross-prayer in the answer).

(4) File a separate application (i e a separate set of matrimonial and civil partnership proceedings) in the same or another court seeking a matrimonial or civil partnership order.

Stay on application—In each of these instances, the case on the answer (or the separate application in (4)) could proceed as if on the application of the respondent (as under MCA 1973, s 20 and CPA 2004, s 62) and in the meantime the application of the applicant (petitioner) could be stayed (normally this would be by agreement) pending the grant of a decree nisi or conditional order to the respondent, whereupon the application would be dismissed. It would be a matter for the parties whether in (4) they arranged for the files in relation to the two applications be consolidated; this might depend on whether there were any live ancillary proceedings on the otherwise stayed file.

"application in the same proceedings" (r 7.14(2))—This provision restates MCA 1973, s 20 and CPA 2004, s 62 and enables the respondent to obtain any of the remedies available to an applicant. Thus, for example, an application for a financial order (the matrimonial and civil partnership proceedings equivalent of a financial remedy) is made in an application for a matrimonial or civil partnership order (FPR 2010, r 9.4(a)).

Respondent's application (r 7.14(2))—The introductory note to prescribed Form D8B (answer to divorce etc) states that a respondent who wishes to apply for a divorce etc: "… should complete your own petition. This will be issued within the existing case…". The rule appears to require a respondent to file a separate petition/final order application to cross-apply for a matrimonial or civil partnership order. This would be inconsistent with MCA 1973, s 20 and CPA 2004, s 62, which are based on the assumption that a cross-prayer in the same suit can result in a decree for the respondent (e g because the parties agree so to proceed or the petitioner fails on the dissolution prayer in her petition).

7.15 Further information about the contents of the application and the answer

(1) The court may at any time order a party –

    (a)   to clarify any matter which is in dispute in the proceedings; or

    (b)   to give additional information in relation to any such matter,

whether or not the matter is contained or referred to in the application for a matrimonial or civil partnership order or in the answer.

(2) Paragraph (1) is subject to any rule of law to the contrary.

(3) Where the court makes an order under paragraph (1), the party against whom it is made must –

    (a)   file the reply to the order made under paragraph (1); and

    (b)   serve a copy of it on each of the other parties,

within the time specified by the court.

(4) The court may direct that information provided by a party to another party (whether given voluntarily or following an order made under paragraph (1)) must not be used for any purpose except for the proceedings in which it is given.

Further information—The scheme is that in the first instance a party should be asked for the information (FPR PD7A, paras 6.1 and 6.2) and only if the information is not provided may application then be made to the court.

Application for information—Application (where information is not provided) will be by the FPR 2010, Pt 18 procedure (Form D11) and will be accompanied by the documents thus far exchanged in attempts to obtain the information. In exercising its discretion as to whether or not to grant an application, and if so to what extent, the judge will have in mind what is necessary and proportionate for a fair disposal of the case (*King v Telegraph Group Ltd* [2004] EWCA Civ 613), as against what is needed by the parties efficiently and justly to deal with the matters in dispute between them (*Harcourt v Griffin* [2007] EWHC 1500 (QB)). In particular, the court will be concerned to ensure that a party is in a position, as far as possible, to know the case he is meeting (*Butterworth v Butterworth* [1997] 2 FLR 336, CA).

Information and disclosure—Disclosure in the context of defended matrimonial and civil partnership proceedings is dealt with under FPR 2010, r 7.22 and generally under FPR 2010, Pt 21. Certain of the same principles for opposing an order for disclosure applies to an order to give information (such as rules in matrimonial proceedings relating to oppressive enquiry: *Hildebrand v Hildebrand* [1992] 1 FLR 244, refusal of permission for excessive or oppressive inquiry or interrogatories. The information request provisions in FPR PD7A, para 6.1–6.5 are similar to those in CPR 1998, r 18.1.

Chapter 3
How the Court Determines Matrimonial and Civil Partnership Proceedings

Introductory note—Ch 3 leads the parties through the undefended and the defended process for matrimonial and civil partnership proceedings; mostly it will be necessary, in respect of each of the main rules, to disentangle the defended and the undefended aspects to the procedure.

Procedural guides—The steps for each process are summarised in Procedural Guide B2 (undefended) and Procedural Guide B4 (defended). Critical stages in the procedure are:

(1) application for decree nisi or conditional order (FPR 2010, r 7.19);
(2) directions for decree nisi or conditional order hearing (FPR 2010, r 7.20(2));
(3) directions for defended hearing with prior case-management hearing (FPR 2010, r 7.20(4));
(4) the case-management hearing (FPR 2010, r 7.22).

7.16 General rule – hearing to be in public

(1) The general rule is that a hearing to which this Part applies is to be in public.

(2) The requirement for a hearing to be in public does not require the court to make special arrangements for accommodating members of the public.

(3) A hearing, or any part of it, may be in private if –

    (a) publicity would defeat the object of the hearing;
    (b) it involves matters relating to national security;
    (c) it involves confidential information (including information relating to personal financial matters) and publicity would damage that confidentiality;
    (d) a private hearing is necessary to protect the interests of any child or protected party;
    (e) it is a hearing of an application made without notice and it would be unjust to any respondent for there to be a public hearing; or
    (f) the court considers this to be necessary, in the interests of justice.

(4) A hearing of an application for rescission of an order by consent under rule 7.28 is, unless the court directs otherwise, to be in private.

(5) The court may order that the identity of any party or witness must not be disclosed if it considers non-disclosure necessary in order to protect the interests of that party or witness.

Defined terms—"child": FPR 2010, r 2.3(1) (and see MCA 1973, s 54); "hearing": FPR 2010, r 2.3(1); hearing "in private": FPR 2010, r 27.10(2); "protected party": FPR 2010, r 2.3(1).

Hearings—Rule 7.16 is addressed mostly to defended proceedings, but in principle it applies to all hearings under FPR 2010, Pt 7. A "hearing" includes a directions appointment, but whether this will include paperwork exercises by a district judge under FPR 2010, r 7.20 when directions are given for the decree nisi or conditional order hearing, (when the certificate for a decree or order is made) remains to be seen. A person "need not attend" the decree nisi or conditional order hearing consequent upon that certificate being signed (FPR 2010, r 7.18(b)).

Hearing in public: right to a transcript—A hearing in public normally carries a right to a transcript (CPR 1998, PD39A, para 1.11) and a hearing may be held in private, but judgment given in public, anonymised as need be.

"a hearing to which this Part applies is to be in public"—Rule 7.16 is taken from CPR 1998, r 39.2 and brings FPR 2010, Pt 7 into line with European Convention 1950, Art 6(1) and its requirement for public court hearings. It incorporates for matrimonial and civil partnership proceedings only (ie not for all family proceedings) the CPR 1998 checklist on when open court hearings may be heard in private. Rule 7.16 is to be contrasted with FPR 2010, r 27.10, which requires all hearings to be in private unless "these rules [as here] provide otherwise" (FPR 2010, r 27.10(1)(a)).

CPR PD39A—The PD makes the following points of practice in relation to private/public hearings (at paras 1.9 to 1.13):

"1.9 If the court or judge's room in which the proceedings are taking place has a sign on the door indicating that the proceedings are private, members of the public who are not parties to the proceedings will not be admitted unless the court permits.

1.10 Where there is no such sign on the door of the court or judge's room, members of the public will be admitted where practicable. The judge may, if he thinks it appropriate, adjourn the proceedings to a larger room or court.

1.11 When a hearing takes place in public, members of the public may obtain a transcript of any judgment given or a copy of any order made, subject to payment of the appropriate fee.

1.12 When a judgment is given or an order is made in private, if any member of the public who is not a party to the proceedings seeks a transcript of the judgment or a copy of the order, he must seek the leave of the judge who gave the judgment or made the order."

Vires of privacy provisions—It has been confirmed by the Court of Appeal that FPR 2010, r 39.2(3) (which is in similar terms to r 7.16(3)) is not ultra vires the rule-making bodies' statutory powers. It does not deny an open court hearing: it is "facultative" (ie not directive) of court process and not in breach of European Convention 1950, Arts 6 or 10 (*R (Pelling) v Bow County Court* [2000] EWHC 636 (Admin); a McKenzie friend case, but see *Practice Guidance of 12 July 2010* on McKenzie friends in Part V).

"personal financial matters" (r 7.16(3)(c))—CPR PD39A, para 1.5 lists a number of forms of financial proceedings that "shall in the first instance be listed by the court as hearings in private", which suggests that in the civil jurisdiction a relatively wide meaning is given to personal financial matters. In matrimonial and civil partnership proceedings, finance in that context may have a narrower meaning (*Clibbery v Allan* [2002] 1 FLR 565).

"necessary to protect the interests of any child or protected party" (r 7.16(3)(d))—The court is likely to see this basis for hearing a case in private in terms similar to FPR 2010, r 27.10, but as with "personal financial matters" it may be necessary for the parties to distinguish clearly what the issues are before the court and the extent to which protection of children might be affected by matrimonial and civil partnership proceedings being heard in public.

Order that a hearing be in private—Rule 7.16(3) is silent as to how an order for a hearing is made. It may be assumed that a judge can make such an order on his own initiative. Application by a party in advance of the hearing should be by the FPR 2010, Pt 18 procedure, although in practice it may often be that the application is made on the first day of a hearing or during its course. Hearing "in private" for the purposes of FPR 2010 means "proceedings at which the general public have no right to be present" (FPR 2010, r 27.10(2)).

7.17 Exercise of jurisdiction in cases heard at place other than the court in which the case is proceeding

Where a defended case is to be heard at a place other than the court in which it is proceeding, a judge of that other court may exercise all the powers that would be exercisable by a judge of the court in which the case is proceeding.

7.18 Notice of hearing

The court officer will give notice to the parties –

(a) of the date, time and place of every hearing which is to take place in a case to which they are a party; and

(b) in the case of a hearing following a direction under rule 7.20(2)(a), of the fact that, unless the person wishes or the court requires, the person need not attend.

Direction under r 7.20(2)(a)—This hearing is the list hearing of decrees nisi and conditional orders. Costs issues at this hearing will arise separately: see FPR 2010, r 7.21 below.

7.19 Applications for a decree nisi or a conditional order

(1) An application may be made to the court for it to consider the making of a decree nisi, a conditional order, a decree of judicial separation or a separation order in the proceedings –

(a)   at any time after the time for filing the acknowledgment of service has expired, provided that no party has filed an acknowledgment of service indicating an intention to defend the case; and

(b)   in any other case, at any time after the time for filing an answer to every application for a matrimonial or civil partnership order made in the proceedings has expired.

(2) An application under paragraph (1) may be made –

(a)   in a case within paragraph (1)(a), by the applicant; and

(b)   in any other case, by either party to the marriage or civil partnership in question.

(3) An application under this rule must, if the information which was required to be provided by the application form is no longer correct, be accompanied by a statement setting out particulars of the change.

(4) If no party has filed an answer opposing the making of a decree nisi, a conditional order, a decree of judicial separation or a separation order on another party's application then an application under this rule must be accompanied by a statement –

(a)   stating whether there have been any changes in the information given in the application or in any statement of arrangements for children;

(b)   confirming that, subject to any changes stated, the contents of the application and any statement of arrangements for children are true; and

(c)   where the acknowledgment of service has been signed by the other party to the marriage or civil partnership, confirming that party's signature on the acknowledgment of service.

(5) A statement under paragraph (4) must be verified by a statement of truth.

Amendments—SI 2012/679.

Defined terms—"decree nisi": r 2.3(1).

Application for consideration of making a decree nisi or conditional order (r 7.19(1),(2))—The 2010 rules do away with the former "request for directions for trial" (FPR 1991, r 2.24: defended or undefended, with undefended causes going into the "special procedure list": r 2.24(3)). Rule 7.19 replaces the "request for directions" with an application for a decree nisi or conditional order. Such application is made within time limits as fixed for filing of the acknowledgement of service and answer. It is likely that r 7.19(2)(b) intends (although it does not say so) that an application for consideration can only be made by a respondent where he seeks directions for a final hearing in the case of defended proceedings. That either party may apply in this way is new in these rules.

Application under r 7.19: consideration statement (r 7.19(4))—The application process commences with the filing of the application with a statement (prescribed by Forms D80A–D80G; Table 2 to FPR PD5A). The information required by the court is prescribed in r 7.19(4) and the question of "changes" recurs there and in r 7.19(3). The statement under r 7.19(4), which applies for consideration of the making of a decree or conditional order, is required to include confirmation of the other party's signature on the acknowledgement of service, which then provides evidence as to service of the application (and of any admitted adultery).

Application and statement (r 7.19(4) and (5))—Since the April 2012 amendments to FPR 2010, the application is to be in the form of a statement verified by a statement of truth.

7.20 What the court will do on an application for a decree nisi, a conditional order, a decree of judicial separation or a separation order

(1) This rule applies where an application is made under rule 7.19.

(2) If at the relevant time the case is an undefended case, the court must –

(a)   if satisfied that the applicant is entitled to –

(i)   in matrimonial proceedings, a decree nisi or a decree of judicial separation (as the case may be); or

> (ii) in civil partnership proceedings, a conditional order or a separation order (as the case may be),

so certify and direct that the application be listed before a district judge for the making of the decree or order at the next available date;

(b) if not so satisfied, direct –

> (i) that any party to the proceedings provide such further information, or take such other steps, as the court may specify; or
>
> (ii) that the case be listed for a case management hearing.

(3) If the applicant has applied for costs, the court may, on making a direction under paragraph (2)(a) –

(a) if satisfied that the applicant is entitled to an order for costs, so certify; or

(b) if not so satisfied, make no direction about costs.

(4) If at the relevant time the case is a defended case, the court must direct that the case be listed for a case management hearing.

(5) The court may, when giving a direction under paragraph (2)(b), direct that the further information provided be verified by an affidavit or a statement of truth.

(6) The court must not give directions under this rule unless at the relevant time it is satisfied –

(a) that a copy of each application for a matrimonial or civil partnership order or answer (including any amended application or answer) has been properly served on each party on whom it is required to be served; and

(b) that –

> (i) in matrimonial proceedings, the application for a decree nisi or a decree of judicial separation; or
>
> (ii) in civil partnership proceedings, the application for a conditional order or separation order,
>
> (iii) was made at a time permitted by rule 7.19(1).

(7) In this rule, "the relevant time" means the time at which the court is considering an application made under rule 7.19(1).

(8) Where a decree or order is made in accordance with a certificate under paragraph (2)(a), any person may, within 14 days after the making of the decree or order, inspect the certificate and the evidence filed under rule 7.19(4) (except any statement of arrangements for children) and may obtain copies.

(9) Paragraph (8) does not apply to a certificate which relates to –

(a) a decree of nullity of marriage under section 12(g) of, or paragraph 11(1)(e) of Schedule 1 to, the 1973 Act; or

(b) an order for nullity of civil partnership under section 50(1)(d) of the 2004 Act,

unless the court has given permission.

Amendments—SI 2012/679.

Defined terms—"defended case", "undefended case": FPR 2010, r 7.1(3); "hearing": FPR 2010, r 2.3(1); "relevant time": FPR 2010, r 7.20(7).

Courts duties on application for consideration under r 7.19 (r 7.20(1))—The steps to be taken by the court (a district judge) under r 7.20 on application for consideration of a decree nisi or conditional order under FPR 2010, r 7.19 fall into these categories:

(1) Certificate under 7.20(2)(a) leading directly to the hearing of the decree or order application;
(2) Direction that the court is not satisfied on the application for consideration (r 7.20(2)(b));
(3) Direction for case management hearing on a defended case (rr 7.20(4), 7.22).

Evidence for decree nisi or conditional order—The standard of evidence in the statement under r 7.19(4) that the court is entitled to expect is to enable it "to inquire, so far as it reasonably can, into the facts alleged by the petitioner and into any facts alleged by the respondent" (MCA 1973, s 1(3),(4): CPA 2004, s 44(2)–(4) is in terms that are to similar effect). On the face of the statute itself, there is therefore a duty on the court to "inquire" within reason into the facts alleged by the applicant and satisfy itself as to the evidence before it. This duty must be balanced against the need for proportionality (FPR 2010, r 1.1) and the duty of the court not to seek to be "over-meticulous" (*R v Nottinghamshire County Court ex parte Byers* [1985] FLR 695).

Respondent's application—Rule 7.20 refers throughout to the "applicant" and his "application", but it must be assumed also that the rule applies to cases proceeding undefended on the respondent's answer, since such cases can be dealt with under r 7.20 (r 7.19(2)(a)).

Determination of the proceedings—The 2010 Rules do nothing to lay the controversy in FPR 1991 as to when a decree nisi (or later a conditional order) becomes fully effective. The question is important since it affects:

(1) Whether or not an intended respondent can file an answer out of time (see e g *Day v Day* (1980) 1 FLR 341, CA);
(2) What is the date in law of any decree nisi or conditional order for appeal or set-aside purposes; and
(3) What is the status of any certificate under r 7.20(2)(a) (as distinct from a decree nisi or conditional order (e g for the purposes of an application to set it aside)).

The variety of terminology in FPR 2010, Pt 7, Ch 2 makes the issue more critical than before. In legal terms, the concepts that bear on the problem are considered more fully under FPR 2010, r 7.28 and Court Orders in FPR 2010, Pt 7 Ch 4.

(1) Certificate under r 7.20(2)(a): list for hearing

Certificate of entitlement to a decree nisi or conditional order (r 7.20(2)(a) and 7.20(6))—The court can only issue a certificate under r 7.20(2)(b) if satisfied as to the following:

(1) That the application for the order (divorce petition etc) or answer with application for a cross-decree or cross-order has been "properly served" (r 7.20(6)(a)): normally this will be done by the applicant having confirmed in the consideration statement identification of the respondent's signature on the acknowledgement of service (FPR 2010, rr 7.12 and 7.19(4)) and his admission there that he has received the application or answer.
(2) That the application for a decree nisi or conditional order was made at a time permitted by FPR 2010, r 7.19(1) (r 7.20(6)(b)).
(3) That the court's inquiry under MCA 1973, s 1(3) and (4) or CPA 2004, s 44(2)–(4) enable it to be "satisfied that the applicant is entitled to" the decree or order (r 7.20(2)(a)).

Court "satisfied that the applicant is entitled" to a decree or order (r 7.20(2)(a))—If the court is satisfied as to the entitlement of the applicant or respondent to a decree or order it "must ... so certify" and the court then directs a routine listing in open court before a district judge. The court will give notice of the resultant appointment to the parties (FPR 2010, r 7.18). At this stage no decree or final order has been made, but this intermediate phase has been characterised by the Court of Appeal as tantamount to an order (*Day v Day*, above; and see further FPR 2010, Pt 7, Ch 4).

Standard or detail of evidence—Although MCA 1973, s 1(3) and CPA 2004, s 44(2) place on the court a duty to inquire, it is likely still to be the case that the procedure under r 7.20(2) does not envisage a high standard for the detail of the evidence to be provided. The court can only expect to be "satisfied" within the terms of the procedure set up in FPR 2010, rr 7.19 and 7.20(2)(a), and there should be no room for excessive technicality of approach by district judges (*R v Nottinghamshire County Court ex parte Byers* [1985] FLR 695). That said, parties should anticipate areas of possible controversy (and see **(2) Court not satisfied**, below) such as to explain where they appear still to be living together but plead that they are not, or where a chronology might help explain issues under MCA 1973, s 2 or CPA 2004, s 46.

Hearing of decree nisi or conditional order application—Save for any pre-warned issue of costs (see FPR 2010, r 7.21) the hearing is a block hearing: a list is read out and decrees/orders made en bloc by the court. In the case of an undefended case there is no need for the parties to attend unless "the court requires" (FPR 2010, r 7.18(b)) or there is an issue as to costs (FPR 2010, r 7.21).

Costs (r 7.20(3))—See further FPR 2010, r 7.21.

(2) Court not satisfied

If the court is "not so satisfied"—Rule 7.20(2)(b) deals with the position where the district judge is not satisfied as to the applicant's entitlement to a decree or order (in undefended proceedings). The court has two options:

(1) The district judge may direct that "any party to the proceedings" should provide further information

or take such other steps as the court requires that party to do (r 7.20(2)(b)(i)). The court may direct that the information be provided by statement (r 7.20(5)); or

(2) The district judge may direct that the case is listed for a case-management hearing (r 7.20(2)(b)(ii)).

Further information required by the court: case management hearing (r 7.20(2)(b))—In cases where more clarification is needed, the court can fix a case-management appointment. FPR 2010, r 7.22(3) prescribes what the court "must" do at the r 7.20(2)(b) case-management hearing: namely to consider whether further evidence is required (FPR 2010, r 7.22(3)(a)) or further information concerning children called for (FPR 2010, r 7.22(3)(b)). It is likely that the appointment will only be attended by the applicant for the decree or order, and in principle there is no reason why the appointment should not be by telephone (FPR 2010, r 1.4(2)(k)) (and see further consideration of case management hearing under FPR 2010, r 7.22).

(3) Direction for case management hearing: defended case

Defended cases (r 7.20(4))—If at the time that the court considers an application for decree or order the case remains defended, then a case-management hearing "must ... be listed" (see under FPR 2010, r 7.22 below). If the defended case had been compromised by this time, there would appear to be no reason why the district judge should not adjourn consideration of the papers under r 7.20 to give one of the parties time to file a under FPR 2010, r 7.19(4) to enable the application then to proceed undefended.

(4) Setting aside a district judge's certificate

Setting aside the district judge's certificate—If a respondent fails to file an answer within 28 days of service of the petition (FPR 2010, r 7.12(8)) and the petitioner has obtained a certificate under the special procedure or if, after the certificate has been signed, the respondent decides that he wants to defend the proceedings, application must be made to the district judge to set aside his certificate and to seek permission to file an answer out of time (for permission to file an answer out of time, see under FPR 2010, r 7.12).

Application to set aside a certificate—The application is made by the FPR 2010, Pt 18 procedure (Form D11) and should be supported by a statement giving reasons (e g for the delay in filing or for the change of mind) and should exhibit a draft answer. If the set-aside application is made to enable the respondent to file an answer (as will generally be the case) the author of the statement will need to bear in mind the factors in FPR 2010, r 4.6 and the need to make a good arguable case (see *Agbaje v Agbaje* [2010] 1 FLR 1813, at [33] and the discussion under FPR 2010, r 7.12 above).

Grounds for setting aside a certificate—The court will be concerned that the applicant for set aside (respondent to the application) has good arguable grounds and the court must be alert to the particular problems encountered by respondents under the r 7.20(2) procedure in that they are not given notice of when the district judge will be considering his r 7.20(2)(a) certificate (*Day v Day* (1980) 1 FLR 341, CA). To that extent they have no notice of any hearing, neither do they see what is put before the district judge when he considers signing his certificate.

Setting aside for vitiating factor—Where a respondent can show that he was not served or was in some way deceived about the proceedings, the certificate should be set aside almost automatically, and where, for example, an adviser failed to act on the respondent's instructions or where through ignorance the respondent failed to take the necessary procedural steps to file an answer, the grounds for setting aside a r 7.20(2)(a) certificate may exist (*Mitchell v Mitchell* [1984] FLR 50, CA). In the latter instance, the court must also be satisfied that, if the certificate were not set aside, the respondent would be prevented from putting forward a defence with merit: the court must consider the respondent's prospects of success on his answer.

Appeal or set aside a decree nisi or conditional order—Once a decree nisi or conditional order has been granted, the respondent may apply by the FPR 2010, Pt 18 procedure to set it aside and seek a rehearing (FPR 2010, r 7.28) or appeal against the decree (FPR 2010, Pt 30); although note limitations on appeal against any later decree absolute in SCA 1981, s 18(1)(d).

Procedure for application—An application to set aside the certificate proceeds by the FPR 2010, Pt 18 procedure.

(1) The applicant to set aside should ensure that the court stays any further steps on the decree nisi or conditional order hearing and takes the hearing appointment out of the court list.

(2) FPR 2010, Pt 18 provides its own internal procedural steps that will lead to a hearing of the set-aside application. The court can deal with the application on the papers, so that if, upon first consideration of the application, the district judge could set aside or stay his certificate (FPR 2010, r 18.9(1)(a): e g if the district judge sees an obvious error that was missed on his original consideration), although that without notice order can then be sought to be set aside (FPR 2010, r 18.11).

(3)   The hearing should be before the district judge who signed the original certificate (if available).

(4)   Other matters on decree nisi or conditional order application

The *Pounds* procedure—In *Pounds v Pounds* [1994] 1 FLR 775 (at [790B]) the Court of Appeal held that a consent order could be approved by a district judge "as part of his 'directions for trial'" when approving the special procedure documents for divorce. This procedure would apply equally to the certificate under FPR 2010, r 7.22(2)(a). This pre-decree order can be made, even though the order is not drawn up and perfected until a date after decree nisi. Once the certificate was granted under the special procedure the decree nisi is all but made (*Day v Day* (1980) 1 FLR 341, CA).

7.21   Further provisions about costs

(1)   Subject to paragraph (2), any party to matrimonial or civil partnership proceedings may be heard on any question as to costs at the hearing of the proceedings.

(2)   In the case of a hearing following a direction under rule 7.20(2)(a), a party will not be heard unless that party has, not less than 2 days before the hearing, served on every other party written notice of that party's intention to attend the hearing and apply for, or oppose the making of, an order for costs.

Applications for costs—Rule 7.20(3) enables the court to deal with costs at the decree or order hearing (which otherwise is likely to be unattended by the parties). In principle costs, orders are made in accordance with SCA 1981, s 51(1) and CPR 1998, r 44.1 (as modified by FPR 2010, r 28.2). In practice, most courts are likely to follow a broad rule that fault applications (MCA 1973, s 1(2)(a)–(c); CPA 2004, s 44(5)(a),(d)) may attract an order for costs, but that living-apart applications only attract an order much more rarely.

Certificate for costs—Although neither FPR 2010, r 7.20(3) nor r 7.21 say it, it may be reasonable to assume that if a certificate is made by the district judge under r 7.20(3)(a) and there is no opposition to it at the hearing of the decree or order, then an order for costs will be made; the intended beneficiary of the order need do no more to secure her order at the decree/order hearing.

Application for costs on a direction under r 7.20(2)(a)—FPR 2010, r 7.20(3) enables the court to take a preliminary view on costs (although r 7.20(3) expresses this as a certificate or "no direction", neither of which are orders).

Application for costs at the hearing (r 7.21(1))—Either party can attend the hearing on any application for costs (subject to appropriate notice being given to the other party: r 7.21(2)). The respondent to a costs application has the opportunity to come to the block hearing of the decree or order to make representation as to why an order should not be made. An applicant who has been deprived of costs (as he sees it) by the district judge under FPR 2010, r 7.20(3)(b) can make representation as to why an order should be made. Although the rule does not require it, it would be prudent for the party who intends to attend on a costs application to inform the court (as well as the other party).

7.22   What the court must do for the case management hearing

(1)   This rule applies to a case in which the court has directed a case management hearing under rule 7.20.

(2)   Where a hearing has been directed under rule 7.20(4) the court must –

   (a)   decide where the hearing in the case should take place;
   (b)   set a timetable for the filing and service of evidence;
   (c)   make such order for the disclosure and inspection of documents as it considers appropriate; and
   (d)   give directions as to the conduct of the final hearing and the attendance of witnesses.

      (Rule 21.1 explains what is meant by disclosure and inspection.)

(3)   Where a hearing has been directed under rule 7.20(2)(b)(ii), the court must –

   (a)   consider what further evidence is required properly to dispose of the proceedings and give directions about the filing and service of such evidence;

(b)   consider whether any further information is required about the arrangements for the children of the family and give directions about the filing and service of such information;

(c)   give directions for the further conduct of the proceedings including –

(i)   giving a direction that on compliance with any directions under sub-paragraph (a) or (b) a further application may be made under rule 7.19(1) for the proceedings to be dealt with under rule 7.20(2)(a); or

(ii)   giving a direction that the case is not suitable for determination under that rule.

(4) Where the court gives a direction under paragraph (3)(c)(ii) it may also give directions under paragraph (2) or direct that the case be listed for a further hearing at which such directions will be given.

(5) Any party to proceedings which are not being dealt with under rule 7.20(2)(a) may apply to the court for further directions at any time.

(Part 3 sets out the court's powers to encourage the parties to use alternative dispute resolution and Part 4 sets out the court's general case management powers.)

Case-management under FPR 2010—FPR 2010, rr 1.4 and 4.1 contain duties of the court on case management (r 1.4) and its powers alongside (r 4.1). These case-management duties and powers are extensive and there are, in addition, parallel mandatory case-management provisions for matrimonial and civil partnership proceedings in r 7.22(2).

Case-management hearing—The listing of a case-management hearing under r 7.22 will be in relation to:

(1)   Defended matrimonial or civil partnership proceedings; or

(2)   Undefended proceedings – As directed under FPR 2010, r 7.20(2)(b)(ii) where a r 7.20(2) certificate has been refused (e g because the district judge wants further information).

(1) Defended hearing

Case management for a defended hearing (r 7.22(2))—In the giving of directions for a defended matrimonial or civil partnership hearing, r 7.22(2) will be only one of the aspects of case management that will concern the court. The court will have in mind the following provisions in FPR 2010:

(1)   the overriding objective, especially the need to dispose of the case expeditiously and fairly and in a way that is "proportionate to the nature ... of the issues" (FPR 2010, r 1.1(2));

(2)   the duty to manage the case (FPR 2010, r 1.4(2) and see below);

(3)   the duty to consider "whether alternative dispute resolution is appropriate" (FPR 2010, r 3.2);

(4)   the court's general powers of case management (FPR 2010, r 4.1(3)); and

(5)   the court's case management duties under r 7.22(2).

Alternative dispute resolution—Before taking any steps to prolong the progress of a defended matrimonial and civil partnership case, the court will be concerned to pursue any avenues that permit alternative dispute resolution (and see FPR 2010, r 1.4(2)(f): helping parties to settle a case). The 2010 Rules impose on the courts a duty "at every stage of proceedings, whether alternative dispute resolution is appropriate", notwithstanding that defended matrimonial and civil partnership proceedings are not one of the "relevant family proceedings" for the purposes of the mediation practice direction, FPR PD3A (see Annex B to PD3A).

Overriding objective—The overriding objective requires that all cases be dealt with justly, so that a respondent who insists that he wishes to defend decree proceedings must be entitled to do so. (It should always be remembered that decree nisi or conditional order proceedings have two components: that certain facts are proved and that a marriage/civil partnership has irretrievably broken down. The second may be obvious and the more so in the course of contested proceedings; but if the facts cannot be proved (e g adultery is denied, or behaviour not unreasonable (see *Butterworth v Butterworth* [1997] 2 FLR 336, CA)), then irretrievable breakdown does not come into issue before the court.

Case management duties—If the case is to go to trial, the court will want to pay close regard to its duties under FPR 2010, r 1.4(2) and to keep a tight control of the evidence (r 22.1) and disclosure and inspection (FPR 2010, Pt 21). It will want "promptly" to define the issues for trial (r 1.4(2)(c)) and to fix tight timetables (r 1.4(2)(g)).

PART III

Case-management hearing duties—The duties referred to by r 7.22(2) are likely to be a last resort for the court where all else (including alternative dispute resolution) has failed. The components of these duties are as follows:

(1) *Place of hearing (r 7.22(2)(a))*   See FPR 2010, rr 7.23 and 7.24.
(2) *Timetable for filing and service of evidence (r 7.22(2)(b))*   This rule echoes FPR 2010, r 1.4(2)(g) and in litigation such as defended matrimonial and civil partnership proceedings the court is as likely as in any jurisdiction to fix timetables and to guillotine the evidence of witnesses (and see **Evidence and a final hearing**, below).
(3) *Directions for disclosure and inspection of documents (r 7.22(2)(c))*   The subjects of (1) requests for further information and (2) disclosure and inspection of documents are separated in Pt 7: for matrimonial and civil partnership proceedings (whether defended or undefended), the first is dealt with in FPR 2010, r 7.15. Disclosure and inspection is touched upon in r 7.22(2) and the subject elaborated upon in FPR PD7A, paras 7.1-7.6, and then also in FPR 2010, Pt 21. For current purposes the subject is dealt with more fully in the commentary to Pt 21 (should a disclosure issue arise in defended proceedings). The court will wish to keep a tight rein on disclosure (bearing in mind what is meant by disclosure in family proceedings (see FPR 2010, r 21.1), and in the light of the overriding objective as to proportionality).
(4) *Directions as to conduct of the final hearing (r 7.22(2)(d))*   In setting down the final hearing the court may look to its case management powers under FPR 2010, r 4.1(3). The district judge will be aware of his powers to make orders, not only on application, but also on his own initiative (FPR 2010, r 4.3, subject to a party's right to ask for the order to be re-listed: FPR 2010, r 18.12(2)). A number of the powers in r 4.1(3) will enable the court to control the final hearing (even to excluding issues from trial: r 4.1(3)(j)).

Evidence and a final hearing—In listing the case for hearing the court will have regard to the pervasive rules on evidence including –

• FPR 2010, Pt 21: disclosure and inspection of documents;
• FPR 2010, Pt 22: general rules about evidence, especially concerning control of evidence (r 22.1), witness statements (rr 22.1 and 22.5) and notices to admit facts (r 22.15);
• FPR 2010, Pt 24: witness summonses (r 24.2) and evidence other than at a final hearing (r 24.2(4)(b));
• FPR 2010, Pt 25: expert evidence including the court's power to restrict (r 25.4);
• FPR 2010, Pt 27: the course of a final hearing.

Power to strike out a case—FPR 2010, r 4.4 enables the court to strike out a statement of case. That would include a pleading – application or answer, or part of either – in defended matrimonial and civil partnership proceedings. The court can do this on its own initiative (FPR 2010, r 4.3(1)) subject to proper notice being given to the parties (FPR 2010, r 4.3(3) and (4)); or on Pt 18 application of a party. (It can also strike out matrimonial and civil partnership proceedings by consent: FPR 2010, rr 4.4(1)(d) and 7.9, although this is an altogether different jurisdiction to the mainstream of r 4.4.)

(2) Court not satisfied on decree or order application

Directions under r 7.20(2)(b)(ii)—Under r 7.22(3), the district judge must give directions for further conduct of the application, including that on compliance with any case management hearing directions a further application under FPR 2010, r 7.19 can be made for a decree nisi or conditional order. Alternatively a direction can be made that the case "is not suitable for determination under that rule" (r 7.22(3)(c)(ii)), in which case the application can be set down for a further directions. Presumably if this fails, or if the application seems otherwise to be stalled, an applicant could ask for a hearing of the decree nisi or conditional order issue. The only opposition to a decree or order would then come from the court: there is no issue between the parties, nor any issue between the parties for the court to resolve. The hearing would enable a judge finally to resolve in the presence of the applicant (or both parties) whatever it was that was delaying the court's certificate and decree nisi or conditional order.

Application for further directions: Pt 18 procedure—Rule 7.22(5) permits any party to proceedings referred by r 7.20 for case management to seek, at any time, further directions, which application would be dealt with by the FPR 2010, Pt 18 procedure.

7.23 Where proceedings under this Part may be heard

A case, other than one dealt with under rule 7.20(2)(a), may be heard, where it is proceeding in the court set out in column 1 of the following table –

  (a)   in matrimonial proceedings, at the place referred to in column 2;

(b) in civil partnership proceedings, at the place referred to in column 3.

	Matrimonial proceedings	*Civil partnership proceedings*
A county court.	Any divorce county court designated as a court of trial.	Any civil partnership proceedings county court designated as a court of trial.
The principal registry when proceedings are treated as pending in a county court.	The Royal Courts of Justice.	The Royal Courts of Justice.
The High Court (including the principal registry other than when proceedings are treated as pending in a county court.).	a) The Royal Courts of Justice. b) Any court at which sittings of the High Court in matrimonial proceedings are authorised.	a) The Royal Courts of Justice. b) Any court at which sittings of the High Court in civil partnership proceedings are authorised.

Defined terms—"civil partnership proceedings county courts", "civil partnership proceedings county court", "court of trial", "divorce county court"' "matrimonial proceedings", "principal registry": r 2.3(1).

7.24 The circumstances in which proceedings may be transferred between courts

(1) A court may transfer the hearing of a case which is due to be heard in one court to another court of the same type at which hearings of those proceedings are permitted under rule 7.23.

(2) A court in which matrimonial or civil partnership proceedings are pending may order them, or an application made in the course of them –

   (a) if the proceedings are pending in the High Court, to be transferred from the registry in which they are pending to another district registry;

   (b) if the proceedings are matrimonial proceedings pending in a divorce county court, to be transferred from that county court to another divorce county court; and

   (c) if the proceedings are civil partnership proceedings pending in a civil partnership proceedings county court, to be transferred from that county court to another civil partnership proceedings county court.

(3) An order transferring the hearing of an application must not be made under paragraph (2) unless it would be more convenient than transferring the proceedings themselves.

(4) No transfer may be made under this rule or under section 38 or 39 of the 1984 Act (transfers between High Court and a county court) unless –

   (a) the parties consent to the transfer;

   (b) the court has held a hearing to determine whether a transfer should be ordered; or

   (c) the court has transferred a case without a hearing where neither party has, within 14 days of being notified in writing of the court's intention to make such an order, requested a hearing to determine whether a transfer should be ordered.

(5) Proceedings –

   (a) which are transferred from the High Court to a divorce county court or a civil partnership proceedings county court and are to continue after the transfer in

PART III

the principal registry are to be treated as pending in a divorce or civil partnership proceedings county court (as the case may be); and

(b) which are transferred from a divorce county court or a civil partnership proceedings county court to the High Court and are to continue after the transfer in the principal registry are no longer to be treated as pending in a divorce or civil partnership proceedings county court (as the case may be).

(6) Proceedings transferred from a divorce county court or a civil partnership proceedings county court to the High Court are to proceed in the registry nearest to the court from which they were transferred unless –

(a) the order transferring the proceedings directs otherwise; or
(b) the court subsequently orders.

Defined terms—"the 1984 Act", "civil partnership proceedings county courts", "civil partnership proceedings county court", "court of trial", "district registry", "divorce county court", "matrimonial proceedings", "principal registry": FPR 2010, r 2.3(1).

MFPA 1984, ss 38 and 39 (r 7.24(4))—Section 38 provides for the transfer of family proceedings from the High Court to county courts and s 39 provides for transfer in the other direction.

7.25 The procedure for complying with section 41 of 1973 Act or section 63 of 2004 Act

(1) Before the court –

(a) gives a direction under rule 7.20(2)(a); or
(b) makes –
   (i) in matrimonial proceedings, a decree nisi or decree of judicial separation; or
   (ii) in civil partnership proceedings, a conditional order or a separation order,

it must consider the matters set out in paragraph (2).

(2) The matters referred to in paragraph (1) are –

(a) whether there are any children of the family to whom section 41(1) of the 1973 Act or section 63(1) of the 2004 Act (as the case may be) applies; and
(b) if there are such children, and no application is pending in relation to them under Part 1 or 2 of the 1989 Act, the matters set out in section 41(1)(b) of the 1973 Act or in section 63(1)(b) of the 2004 Act (as the case may be).

(3) Where the court is satisfied that –

(a) there are no children of the family to whom –
   (i) in matrimonial proceedings, section 41 of the 1973 Act applies; and
   (ii) in civil partnership proceedings, section 63 of the 2004 Act applies; or
(b) there are such children but the court need not exercise its powers under the 1989 Act or its power to give a relevant direction with respect to any of them,

it must give a certificate to that effect.

(4) Where the court does not issue a certificate under paragraph (3) it may direct that –

(a) the parties, or any of them, must file further evidence relating to the arrangements for the children and may direct what specific matters must be dealt with in that evidence;
(b) a welfare report on the children, or any of them, be prepared;
(c) the parties, or any of them, attend a hearing for the court to consider the matter.

(5) Where the court makes a direction under paragraph (4) or a relevant direction, it must state in writing –

(a) its reasons for doing so; and

(b) in the case of a relevant direction, the exceptional circumstances which make it desirable in the interests of the child that the court should make such a direction.

(6) Nothing in this rule affects the court's power to make an order under the 1989 Act or a relevant direction.

(7) The court officer must send the parties –

(a) a copy of any certificate given under paragraph (3);

(b) a copy of any direction made under paragraph (4);

(c) a copy of any relevant direction; and

(d) a copy of any statement under paragraph (5).

(8) In this rule –

"parties" means a party to the marriage or civil partnership concerned and any person who appears to the court to have the care of any child of the family; and

"relevant direction" means –

(a) in matrimonial proceedings, a direction under section 41(2) of the 1973 Act;

(b) in civil partnership proceedings, a direction under section 63(2) of the 2004 Act.

Defined terms—"children of the family", "the 1973 Act", "the 1989 Act", "the 2004 Act": FPR 2010, r 2.3(1); MCA 1973, s 52(1); "court officer", "parties": r 7.25(8); "proper officer": r 1.2(1); "relevant direction': r 7.25(8).

"direction under r 7.20(2)(a)" (r 7.25(1))—A direction under FPR 2010, r 7.20 states that the court is satisfied that the applicant for decree nisi or conditional order has proved the contents of his application and is entitled to a decree nisi or conditional order on an undefended basis.

"section 41(1) of the 1973 Act or section 63(1) of the 2004 Act" (r 7.25(2))—Section 41(1) or 63(1) (as the case may be) requires the court to consider: (a) whether there are any children of the family to whom the section applies; and (b) where there are any such children, whether (in the light of the arrangements that have been, or are proposed to be, made for their upbringing and welfare) it should exercise any of its powers under CA 1989 (see below) with respect to any of them. MCA 1973, s 41(3) and CPA 2004, s 63(3) provide that the respective sections apply to (a) any child of the family who has not reached the age of 16 at the date when the court considers the case in accordance with the requirements of the section, and (b) any child of the family who has reached that age at that date and in relation to whom the court directs that the section will apply.

Court's powers under CA 1989 (r 7.25(6))—For most practical purposes, the powers under CA 1989 that the court may exercise of its own motion are those of making s 8 orders CA 1989, s 10(1)(b) and giving a direction under s 37(1).

Direction or certificate under MCA 1973, s 41(2) or CPA 2004, s 63(2) (r 7.25(3))—Sections 41(2) and 63(2), respectively, provide that, in any case where ss 41 or 63 (as the case may be) applies, if it appears to the court that: (a) the circumstances of the case require it, or are likely to require it, to exercise any of its powers under CA 1989 in respect of any such child; (b) it is not in a position to exercise that power or (as the case may be) those powers without giving further consideration to the case; and (c) there are exceptional circumstances that make it desirable in the interests of the child that the court should give a direction under the section, it may direct that the decree of divorce or nullity is not to be made absolute, or that the decree of judicial separation is not to be granted, until the court orders otherwise.

7.26 Medical examinations in proceedings for nullity of marriage

(1) Where the application is for a decree of nullity of marriage on the ground of incapacity to consummate or wilful refusal to do so, the court must determine whether medical examiners should be appointed to examine the parties or either of them.

(2) The court must only appoint medical examiners under paragraph (1) where it considers that it is necessary for the proper disposal of the case.

(3) The person to be examined must, in the presence of the medical examiner, sign a statement identifying that person as the party to whom the order for examination applies.

(4) The medical examiner must certify on the same statement that it was signed in his or her presence by the person who has been examined.

(5) The person who carries out the examination must prepare a report and file it with the court by the date directed by the court.

(6) Either party is entitled to see a copy of a report filed under paragraph (5).

PD7B—Rule 7.26 is accompanied by FPR PD7B.

Application for appointment—Rule 7.26(1) requires the court to "determine" the issue of whether a medical examiner should be appointed. Application is by the FPR 2010, Pt 18 procedure, with grounds to be provided in an accompanying statement and particular reasons why a report is necessary in undefended proceedings.

Medical examiner as expert—The examiner will be giving opinion evidence and his report will be subject to the requirements of a report under FPR 2010, Pt 25 (especially the information required by FPR PD25A). There, duty is to the court (FPR 2010, r 25.4) with whom they are required to file their report (FPR 2010, r 7.26(5)).

Appointment of a medical examiner—The appointment of an examiner should only be made where necessary for proper disposal of the case (FPR 2010, r 7.26(2)). For example, appointment will not normally be necessary where a nullity application is undefended (FPR PD7B, para 1.1). The party who seeks an appointment must deal with her attendance at the final hearing at the case-management hearing appointment (FPR PD7B, para 1.4).

7.27 Stay of proceedings

(1) Where –

(a) the court is considering an application in accordance with rule 7.20 or gives directions under rule 7.22;

(b) it appears to the court that there are proceedings continuing in any country outside England and Wales which are in respect of the marriage or civil partnership in question or which are capable of affecting its validity or subsistence; and

(c) the court considers that the question whether the proceedings should be stayed(GL) under paragraph 9 of Schedule 1 to the Domicile and Matrimonial Proceedings Act 1973 or, for civil partnership proceedings, under rules made under sections 75 and 76 of the Courts Act 2003 ought to be determined by the court,

the court must give directions for the hearing of that question.

(2) Where at any time after the making of an application under this Part it appears to the court in matrimonial proceedings that, under Articles 16 to 19 of the Council Regulation, the court does not have jurisdiction to hear the application and is or may be required to stay(GL) the proceedings, the court will –

(a) stay(GL) the proceedings; and

(b) fix a date for a hearing to determine the questions of jurisdiction and whether there should be a further stay(GL) or other order.

(3) The court must give reasons for its decision under Articles 16 to 19 of the Council Regulation and, where it makes a finding of fact, state such finding of fact.

(4) An order under Article 17 of the Council Regulation that the court has no jurisdiction over the proceedings will be recorded by the court or the court officer in writing.

(5) The court may, if all parties agree, deal with any question about the jurisdiction of the court without a hearing.

Amendments—SI 2012/679.

Defined terms—"the Council Regulation", "court": FPR 2010, r 2.3(1).

Stay of matrimonial or civil partnership proceedings—Rule 7.27 sets up a procedure by which a district judge, on considering his certificate under FPR 2010, r 7.20(2)(a) or under FPR 2010, r 7.22, imposes an obligatory stay on pending matrimonial or civil partnership proceedings. It also applies where the court exercises a discretion to impose a stay on any matrimonial or civil partnership proceedings, where other proceedings are pending outside the jurisdiction.

Stay under DMPA 1973—DMPA 1973, s 5(6) gives the court power to stay matrimonial proceedings (as defined in Sch 1, para 2) where there are concurrent proceedings in another jurisdiction in respect of the same marriage.

Application for a discretionary stay—An application for a discretionary stay under DMPA 1973, Sch 1, para 9 is heard by a judge. Application is made by the FPR 2010, Pt 18 procedure. The supporting statement should state as clearly as possible the grounds for seeking a stay. If a party seeks to persuade the court on the basis that another jurisdiction is the more appropriate or convenient for deciding the issue ("forum non conveniens"), it is important that the application be made at the outset of proceedings or at the first opportunity, before steps have been taken in the application and costs are incurred by either party (*Mansour v Mansour* [1989] 1 FLR 418, CA; *Krenge v Krenge* [1999] 1 FLR 969).

Referral at time of giving directions (r 7.27(1)(a),(2))—If the court considers, when looking at a case under FPR 2010, rr 7.20(2) or 7.22(2), that there is information in the statements of case of the parties that refer to other proceedings relating to the marriage or capable of affecting its validity or subsistence and that might lead to a discretionary stay, then the district judge does the following:

(1)   imposes a stay on the present proceedings (r 7.27(2)(a));
(2)   fixes an appointment before the judge and give notice of this to the parties (r 7.27(2)(b)).

Stay during the trial—If a party fails to provide particulars of other proceedings as required by the rules and the Act, the court can stay proceedings even after the start of the trial (DMPA 1973, Sch 1, para 9(4)).

Removal of stay—An application for removal of a stay can be made on grounds that the other proceedings are stayed or concluded, or that a party has delayed unreasonably in prosecuting them (DMPA 1973, Sch 1, para 10(1)). The application is made by the Pt 18 procedure (Form D11). The application should state the grounds on which removal of the stay is sought.

Chapter 4
Court Orders

Forms of court determination under Pt 7—FPR 2010, Pt 7 deals with three separate forms of determination by the court:

(1)   *Directions orders*   Directions for the conduct of proceedings or at a case-management hearing will be recorded in an "order". "Order" within the terms of FPR 2010 includes "directions of the court" (FPR 2010, r 2.3(1)).
(2)   *Certificate of satisfaction as to entitlement to a decree nisi or conditional order*   A certificate under FPR 2010, r 7.20(2)(a) (akin to the former special procedure certificate) that results in a case being listed for hearing in the block list for decree nisi or conditional order. It is possible that the decision in *Day v Day* (1980) 1 FLR 341, CA (above: based on the certificate being, in effect, the disposal of the application) would be decided differently since the coming into operation of Human Rights Act 1998 and European Convention 1950, Art 6(1). The introduction of FPR 2010, r 4.6 (relief from sanctions) might prompt a different approach to an application for permission to file and serve an answer out of time. The certificate is not an order in the sense intended by the rules generally or by FPR 2010, Ch 4 in particular.
(3)   *Orders: decree nisi or conditional order*   Orders made on application for a decree nisi or conditional order whether (a) on an undefended application or (b) following contested proceedings. It is these orders that are dealt with in FPR 2010, Ch 4.

Applications and orders—Practitioners and parties will find that under FPR 2010, Pt 7, Ch 2 the rules relate to orders, and occasionally to applications. That is to say, the rules sometimes indicate how application is to be made for the order (see for example FPR 2010, r 7.31(2)), but more often they are silent (e g under FPR 2010, r 7.28(1), 7.29 and 7.30(1)), so that the applicant must assume that the FPR 2010, Pt 18 procedure applies for the particular application.

Review or re-hearing of orders and certificates—Orders may be appealed against. A certificate, as a judicial disposal of an application, can be set aside (e g *Mitchell v Mitchell* [1984] FLR 50, where permission was given to file an answer and the registrar's certificate was set aside, albeit on appeal against the decree nisi granted following the certificate), but possibly not appealed against. Certain directions can be reviewed (e g as under FPR 2010, rr 18.9 and 18.12) or appealed against (FPR 2010, Pt 30).

Appeals, set aside or re-hearing—The former detailed provisions of FPR 1991, r 2.42 (applications for re-hearing) have gone; and will be part of the appeals procedures in Pt 30, or the facts may found an application to set aside (dealt with under the FPR 2010, Pt 18 procedure). Appeals from a district judge's grant of a decree following the special procedure are in accordance with the appeals procedures under FPR 2010, Pt 30, but note limitations on appeal against decrees absolute in SCA 1981, s 18(1)(d), where the appellant respondent had time to appeal against the decree nisi.

Rescission of decree nisi or conditional order—See FPR 2010, r 7.28.

7.28 The circumstances in which an order may be set aside (rescission)

(1) The court must not hear an application by a respondent for –

    (a)   the rescission of a decree of divorce under section 10(1) of the 1973 Act;

    (b)   the rescission of a dissolution order under section 48(1) of the 2004 Act,

less than 14 days after service of the application.

(2) Either party to the marriage concerned may apply –

    (a)   after the decree nisi has been made but before it has been made absolute; or

    (b)   after a decree of judicial separation has been made

for the rescission of the decree on the grounds that the parties are reconciled and both consent to the rescission.

(3) Either party to the civil partnership concerned may apply –

    (a)   after a conditional order has been made but before it has been made final; or

    (b)   after a separation order has been made,

for the rescission of the order on the grounds that the parties are reconciled and both consent to the rescission.

Setting aside of decree nisi or conditional order—In r 7.28, rescission of decrees nisi or conditional orders in two very different sets of circumstances is elided. There is no means prescribed by the 2010 Rules (c f FPR 1991, r 2.42) for setting aside a decree where no error of the court is alleged. If the court is alleged to be in error, a party is obliged to appeal (FPR 2010, Pt 30)).

Rescission under MCA 1973, s 10(1) or CPA 2004, s 48(1)—Under MCA 1973, s 10(1) or CPA 2004, s 48(1) the court is asked to exercise a set-aside jurisdiction (as the heading to the rule implies). The rules do not prescribe any procedure for the rescission application, although it is likely to be by the FPR 2010, Pt 18 procedure (Form D11). The application will be heard in open court.

Grounds of application for rescission under s 10(1) or s 48(1)—In the drafting of grounds for the application, the applicant will bear in mind that the application can only be made within the terms of MCA 1973, s 10(1) or CPA 2004, s 48(1): namely that the respondent was misled by the petitioner, whether intentionally or unintentionally. The factors that influenced the respondent in consenting can be elaborated on in his statement in support of the application. If intentional misleading is alleged, it must be borne in mind that this is a serious allegation and, as a result, the court is likely to require a high standard of proof from the respondent (e g fraud may only be alleged in drafting by an advocate if the client gives clear instructions). Since this is an application to set aside a consent order (a decree obtained on the basis of the respondent's consent) the respondent will need to explain clearly how his consent was obtained and why he was "misled ... (whether intentionally or unintentionally)" (MCA 1973, s 10(1)) or his consent is otherwise vitiated.

Setting aside of a decree or order in other circumstances—A decree nisi or conditional order may be able to be set aside for other reasons. The set aside jurisdiction of the county court under CCR 1981, Ord 37 has not been reproduced in FPR 2010, so the applicant is left to apply on general or common law principles (i e that no error of the court is alleged: e g *Peek v Peek* [1948] P 46). In none of these instances would it be open to a party to appeal (no judge was in error), yet the errors must by some means be put right.

Procedure—Application is by the FPR 2010, Pt 18 procedure. When the circumstances come to light, the court should be asked to list the matter urgently on notice to both parties to show good reason why the decree should not be set aside as a nullity. It may be wise for the parties to be alerted by telephone to minimise the risk of one of them taking steps to arrange remarriage. The matter should be listed in open court (because the decree nisi was pronounced in open court) before either a district judge (if the decree was pronounced by a district judge) or a circuit judge (if pronounced by a circuit judge). The designated family judge should be alerted and may wish the matter to be listed before him/her in any event.

7.29 Applications under section 10(2) of 1973 Act or section 48(2) of 2004 Act

Where the court makes –

    (a)   in the case of divorce, a decree absolute following an application under section 10(2) of the 1973 Act; or

    (b)   in the case of dissolution, a final order following an application under section 48(2) of the 2004 Act,

it must make a written record of the reasons for deciding to make that decree absolute or final order.

MCA 1973, s 10(2) or CPA 2004, s 48(2)—MCA 1973, s 10(4) and CPA 2004, s 48(5) enable the court to make a decree nisi or conditional order absolute or final (as the case may be), notwithstanding a respondent's application under ss 10(2) or 48(2) (respondent's application to the court to consider her financial position) and this rule provides that a proper record of the judge's reasons under ss 10(4) and 48(5) for allowing a final decree/order be made: any ss 10(2) or 48(2) application will be contested and heard in open court and a record of the judgment will be available by tape-recording (e g CPR PD39A, para 1.11).

7.30 Orders under section 10A(2) of the 1973 Act

(1) Where the court has made an order under section 10A(2) of the 1973 Act, the declaration referred to in that section must –

    (a)   be made and signed by both parties to the marriage concerned;

    (b)   give particulars of the proceedings in which the order was obtained;

    (c)   confirm that the steps required to dissolve the marriage in accordance with the religious usages appropriate to the parties have been taken;

    (d)   be accompanied by –

        (i)   a certificate from a relevant religious authority that all such steps have been taken; or

        (ii) such other documents showing the relevant steps have been taken as the court may direct; and

        (iii) be filed at the court either before or together with an application to make the decree nisi absolute,

under rule 7.32 or 7.33.

(2) Where the certificate referred to in paragraph (1)(d)(i) is not in English it must be accompanied by a translation of that certificate into English, certified by a notary public or authenticated by statement of truth.

(3) The court may direct that the declaration need not be accompanied by the material mentioned in paragraph (1)(d).

(4) In this rule a religious authority is "relevant" if the party who made the application for the order under section 10A(2) of the 1973 Act considers that authority competent to confirm that the steps referred to in paragraph (1)(c) have been taken.

Context of provision—MCA 1973, s 10A(1) provides that, where a couple were married in accordance with "the usages of the Jews" or other religious usages and these prescribe final dissolution, an application can be made under s 10A(2) for an order that stays the grant of a decree absolute. The stay will continue until the court is satisfied by a declaration of both parties that the marriage is also dissolved in accordance with "those [Jewish or other] usages". Rule 7.30 provides the regulatory framework for such application.

Application under s 10A(2)—No specific means of making the r 7.30 application under s 10A(2) is prescribed (as it was by FPR 1991, r 2.45A). It must be assumed that the rule-maker intends an application for the order delaying decree absolute shall be made by the Pt 18 procedure (Form D11; and see below for **Timing of application**). The application will be supported by the declaration as to Jewish dissolution required by s 10A(2),(4) and as further prescribed by r 7.30(1).

Timing of application—MCA 1973, s 10A(1) is engaged as soon as "a decree of divorce has been granted" (ie upon decree nisi, but not before). This will demand vigilance from practitioners, since the importance of s 10A(2) to a Jewish wife will be lost if the decree nisi is made absolute. An early return date will be needed (for a respondent wife, before the end of the 6-week period for decree absolute). If a husband manages to persuade the court to expedite a decree absolute, it is possible that little can be done, unless he has in some way misled the court.

7.31 Applications to prevent decrees nisi being made absolute or conditional orders being made final

(1) This rule applies to an application under section 8 or 9 of the 1973 Act or under section 39 or 40 of the 2004 Act to prevent –

    (a)   in the case of divorce or nullity of marriage, a decree nisi being made absolute; or

    (b)   in the case of dissolution or nullity of civil partnership, a conditional order being made final.

(2) An application to which this rule applies must be made using the Part 18 procedure, subject to paragraphs (3) to (6) of this rule.

(3) The person making an application to which this rule applies must within 28 days of filing the application apply to the court to give directions for the hearing of the application.

(4) Where the person making an application to which this rule applies does not apply for directions under paragraph (3), then the person in whose favour the decree nisi or conditional order (as the case may be) was made may do so.

(5) Rule 7.22(2) applies to an application to which this rule applies as it applies to an application for a matrimonial or civil partnership order.

(6) Where an application to which this rule applies is made by the Queen's Proctor –

    (a)   the Queen's Proctor may give written notice, to the court and to the party in whose favour the decree nisi or conditional order (as the case may be) was made, of the Queen's Proctor's intention to make an application to prevent the decree nisi being made absolute or the conditional order being made final; and

    (b)   where the Queen's Proctor does so the application under paragraph (1) must be made within 21 days beginning with the date on which the notice is given.

Application under MCA 1973, ss 8 and 9(1) and CPA 2004, ss 39 and 40(1)—Rule 7.31 deals with two separate sets of application:

(1) MCA 1973, s 8 and CPA 2004, s 39 enable the Queen's Proctor to show cause why a decree nisi or conditional order should not be made absolute or final (ss 8(2) and 39(4)); and

(2) MCA 1973, s 9(1) and CPA 2004, s 40(1) enable "any person" to bring "material facts" before the court to show that a decree nisi or conditional order should not be made absolute or final. (This has nothing to do with the entitlement of a respondent to apply for a decree absolute or final order under s 9(2) and 40(2): for which see r 7.33.)

Procedure for application (r 7.31(2)–(5))—Application is made by the Pt 18 procedure (r 7.31(2): application notice Form D11) as extended by r 7.31(3)–(6):

(1) The applicant will wish to ensure that his application (r 18.7) sets out clearly the basis of what will be serious allegations ("material facts": e g that a couple who claim to be living apart are living together; that there was no such claimed "improper association" and so on. The allegations will need to be set out to a high degree of credibility).

(2) The applicant, including the Queen's Proctor, should consider including application for a stay of the decree absolute or final order in the application notice (see reference to **Stay of application for decree absolute or final order** below and in r 7.32(2)).

(3) Service of the application and accompanying is in accordance with r 18.8 and Pt 6.

(4) The duty is on the applicant (the Queen's Proctor or other person who applies under s 9(1) or 40(1)) to apply within 28 days of its filing, for directions on his application (r 7.31(3)). (This provision is not consistent with the FPR 2010, Pt 18 procedure and in particular r 18.8. The provision is not as clear as it might be; but the implication at least of FPR 2010, r 18.8 (read alongside FPR 2010, r 18.9(1)) is that upon issue of the application a hearing date will be fixed before its service.)

(5) Failing application under r 7.31(3) (and if no date is fixed under FPR 2010, r 18.8 by the court) the spouse or civil partner who obtained the decree nisi or conditional order can apply (r 7.31(4)); or they may wish to apply to have the application (especially if by a private individual) struck out, e g as disclosing no grounds for the application (FPR 2010, r 4.4(1)(a)) or being an abuse of process if not pursued (FPR 2010, r 4.4(1)(b)).

(6) Upon application to the court under r 7.31(3) or (4) a case-management hearing is fixed in accordance with the procedures under FPR 2010, r 7.22(2).

Case management: "Rule 7.22(2) applies" (r 7.31(5))—This provision may be thought redundant: FPR 2010, Pt 18 has its own procedures. These are enhanced, in case-management hearing terms by FPR 2010, rr 1.4 and 4.1 (and see **Case management hearing duties** under FPR 2010, r 7.22). There should be no need for the further procedural gloss of r 7.22(2) to be added for this single issue application.

Stay of application for decree absolute or final order—The is no express provision in statute or rule to say that an application under this rule stays the grant of a decree absolute or final order, although FPR 2010, r 7.32(2) provides that a decree nisi or conditional order shall be made absolute or a final order, if no ss 8/9(1) or 39/40(1) application has been made.

7.32 Making decrees nisi absolute or conditional orders final by giving notice

(1) Unless rule 7.33 applies –

    (a) in matrimonial proceedings, a spouse in whose favour a decree nisi has been made may give notice to the court that he or she wishes the decree nisi to be made absolute; or

    (a) in civil partnership proceedings, a civil partner in whose favour a conditional order has been made may give notice to the court that he or she wishes the conditional order to be made final.

(2) Subject to paragraphs (3) and (4), where the court receives a notice under paragraph (1) it will make the decree nisi absolute or the conditional order final (as the case may be) if it is satisfied that –

    (a) no application for rescission of the decree nisi or the conditional order is pending;

    (b) no appeal against the making of the decree nisi or the conditional order is pending;

    (c) no order has been made by the court extending the time for bringing an appeal of the kind mentioned in sub-paragraph (b), or if such an order has been made, that the time so extended has expired;

    (d) no application for an order of the kind mentioned in sub-paragraph (c) is pending;

    (e) no application to prevent the decree nisi being made absolute or the conditional order being made final is pending;

PART III

(f) the court has complied with section 41(1) of the 1973 Act or section 63(1) of the 2004 Act, as the case may be, and has not given any direction under subsection (2) of either of those sections;

(g) the provisions of section 10(2) to (4) of the 1973 Act or section 48(2) to (4) of the 2004 Act do not apply or have been complied with;

(h) any order under section 10A(2) of the 1973 Act has been complied with; and

(i) where the decree nisi was made on the ground in section 12(g) of, or paragraph 11(1)(e) of Schedule 1 to, the 1973 Act, or the conditional order was made under section 50(1)(d) of the 2004 Act –

(i) there is not pending a reference under section 8(5) of the Gender Recognition Act 2004 in respect of the application on which the interim gender recognition certificate to which the application relates was granted;

(ii) that interim certificate has not been revoked under section 8(6)(b) of that Act; and

(iii) no appeal is pending against an order under section 8(6)(a) of that Act.

(3) Where the notice is received more than 12 months after the making of the decree nisi or the conditional order, it must be accompanied by an explanation in writing stating –

(a) why the application has not been made earlier;

(b) whether the applicant and respondent have lived together since the decree nisi or the conditional order was made, and, if so, between what dates;

(c) if the applicant is female, whether she has given birth to a child since the decree nisi or the conditional order was made and whether it is alleged that the child is or may be a child of the family;

(d) if the respondent is female, whether the applicant has reason to believe that she has given birth to a child since the decree nisi or the conditional order was made and whether it is alleged that the child is or may be a child of the family.

(4) Where paragraph (3) applies, the court may –

(a) require the applicant to file an affidavit verifying the explanation or to verify the explanation with a statement of truth; and

(b) make such order on the application as it thinks fit, but where it orders the decree nisi to be made absolute or the conditional order to be made final that order is not to take effect until the court is satisfied that none of the matters mentioned in paragraph (2)(a) to (i) applies.

Amendments—SI 2012/679.

Defined terms—"child of the family": r 2.3(1).

Application by spouse or civil partner in whose favour [a decree or order] has been made (r 7.32(1))—In the first instance, the application can only be by the spouse who obtained the decree nisi. After the final date for applying has passed (see **Time for notice**, below), the other spouse or civil partner can apply.

Application by "notice under paragraph (1)" (r 7.32(2))—The applicant under r 7.32 "applies" for a decree absolute or final order on prescribed Form D36. Application under r 7.32(2) is by "notice" (as distinct from an application made by "application" for decree absolute or final order made, e g under FPR 2010, r 7.33). The first is a request to the court to do something: the second a formal application to be dealt with on notice.

Time for notice—Generally for the applicant for decree nisi or conditional order the time for application for decree absolute or final order is 6 weeks from the earlier decree/order. Application may also be made to expedite the decree absolute or final order and if application is not made by the decree nisi or conditional order applicant, the other party can apply for a decree absolute or final order (MCA 1973, s 9(2); CPA 2004, s 40(2)). The procedure for each of these applications is as follows:

(1) *Application by party who obtained the decree nisi or conditional order* In accordance with this rule:
(a) The period prescribed by MCA 1973, s 1(5) for applying for a decree absolute has been shortened to 6 weeks by the Matrimonial Causes (Decree Absolute) Order 1972.

(b) The period prescribed by CPA 2004, s 38(1) is 6 weeks.

(2) *Expedited decree nisi or final order* Application may be made to the court, in appropriate circumstances, to "fix a shorter period" for grant of decree absolute or final order (MCA 1973, s 1(5); CPA 2004, s 38(4)).

(3) *Application by spouse against whom decree pronounced* The party against whom the decree nisi or conditional order was obtained can apply for a decree absolute on notice 3 months after the other spouse could have applied (MCA 1973, s 9(2); CPA 2004, s 40(2); and see r 7.33).

Application for expedited decree—Application may be made to the court to "fix a shorter period" than 6 weeks for grant of a decree absolute or final order (MCA 1973, s 1(5); CPA 2004, s 38(4)) where grounds for expedition exist (e g impending death or birth of a child, or perhaps a permanent move abroad). Procedure is governed by FPR PD7A, paras 8.1–8.4, as follows:

(1) *Prior to application for decree nisi* If the application can be made prior to application for decree nisi or conditional order then application can be made to the district judge for early directions at the time the district judge gives directions under FPR 2010, r 7.19 (FPR PD7A, para 8.1).

(2) *After decree nisi or conditional order application* Where the need for expedition emerges after decree nisi or conditional order then application can be made to the court using FPR 2010, Pt 18 procedure (Form D11; FPR PD7A, paras 8.2 and 8.4).

Search of court records (r 7.32(2))—The purpose of the search conducted under r 7.32(2) is to check that there is no outstanding application or question affecting the decree nisi or conditional order or preventing the grant of the decree absolute or final order, and in particular:

(1) *Compliance with MCA 1973, s 41 or CPA 2004, s 63(1) (r 7.32(f))* A stay on the decree being made absolute until satisfaction has been expressed by the judge is no longer available, but MCA 1973, s 41(2) (as substituted by CA 1989) and CPA 2004, s 63(2) enable the court in the instances set out in the respective subsections to stay the grant of a decree until further order of the court (i e until application is made to the court to lift the stay).

(2) *"the provisions of section 10(2) to (4) of the Act of 1973" (r 2.49(2)(g))* MCA 1973, s 10(2)–(4) concerns applications for consideration of the respondent's financial position in divorce proceedings under MCA 1973, s 1(2)(d),(e) (2 years' living apart with consent and 5 years' living apart) and enables the court to delay the decree absolute (MCA 1973, s 10(3)), subject to the provisions of MCA 1973, s 10(4).

"[the court] will make the decree nisi absolute or the conditional order final" (r 7.32(2))—The court is required to make the decree nisi absolute or the conditional order final if the court office is satisfied that none of the factors listed in the rule applies, subject to the proviso (in r 7.32(3) and (4)) where the application is made 12 months after decree nisi.

Court action if one or more factors in r 7.32(2) apply—Rule 7.32 does not state what the court shall do if one of the factors in r 7.32(2) applies: it only tells the court what to do (i e make the decree absolute or order final if none of the factors applies). For example, an appeal does not stay the order appealed against (a stay must be applied for: r 30.8). It is not clear from this that a stay in other circumstances in r 7.32(2) must be applied for, or whether the decree absolute or final order application remains in procedural limbo.

Stay on grant of decree absolute—It may be possible to stay grant of a decree absolute if its grant might prejudice financial rights of a party in another jurisdiction (in this case, the USA; *Evans v Evans* [2012] EWCA Civ 1293).

Where notice is lodged more than 12 months after decree nisi (r 7.32(3))—Where application is made more than 12 months after decree nisi, an explanation in writing must be provided to the district judge. This could be by letter from the applicant (if acting in person) or his solicitor. The court can call for an affidavit by the applicant to verify the explanation (r 7.32(4)), for example where the court has doubts as to the explanation or where an unusual state of affairs is described. Where there has been cohabitation in excess of 6 months, the court has a discretion as to whether a decree absolute is granted and as to whether the decree nisi should be rescinded (*Kim v Morris* [2012] EWHC 1103 (Fam)).

Explanation for delay (r 7.32(3))—The explanation must deal with the factors mentioned in the paragraph, including:

(1) *"whether the parties have lived with each other"* Living with each other means living together in the same household and sharing a common life (MCA 1973, s 2(6)). If the parties have lived together for less than 6 months during the previous 12 months MCA 1973, s 2(5) (or CPA 2004, s 45) apply; however, where the parties have lived together for longer than 6 months during that period, there is likely to be a presumption that the marriage has not irretrievably broken down, a decree absolute may be refused and the decree nisi rescinded (*Biggs v Biggs and Wheatley* [1977] Fam 1).

(2) *"relevant facts" concerning any child born to the wife* Such facts would include the date of birth and the child's parentage and, if the parties are themselves the parents, they will need to give a clear explanation concerning cohabitation (if any). If the child is a child of the family, the district judge will need to deal with him under MCA 1973, s 41 or CPA 2004, s 63 (see also FPR 2010, r 7.25) before he can consider the question of granting a decree absolute or final order.

"the court ... may (b) make such order ... as it thinks fit" (r 7.32(4)(b))—The court has a discretion as to the order that is made on the late application: whether to grant a decree absolute or final order; to refuse a decree (in which case the judge is likely to consider rescinding the decree nisi or conditional order and, where appropriate, dismissing the application: (*Kim v Morris* [2012] EWHC 1103 (Fam)); or to make another order, e g as to filing further affidavit evidence (r 7.32(4)(a)).

7.33 Applications to make decrees nisi absolute or conditional orders final

(1) An application must be made –

    (a)   in matrimonial proceedings, for the decree nisi to be made absolute; or

    (b)   in civil partnership proceedings, for the conditional order to be made final,

where the conditions set out in paragraph (2) apply.

(2) The conditions referred to in paragraph (1) are –

    (a)   the Queen's Proctor gives notice to the court under rule 7.31(6)(a) and has not withdrawn that notice;

    (b)   there are other circumstances which ought to be brought to the attention of the court before the application is granted; or

    (c)   the application is made –

        (i)   in matrimonial proceedings, by the spouse against whom the decree nisi was made; or

        (ii)   in civil partnership proceedings, by the civil partner against whom the conditional order was made.

(3) An application under this rule to which paragraph (2)(a) applies must be –

    (a)   made to a judge, but not a district judge; and

    (b)   served on the Queen's Proctor.

(4) Where the court orders –

    (a)   in matrimonial proceedings, a decree to be made absolute under this rule; or

    (b)   in civil partnership proceedings, a conditional order to be made final under this rule,

that order is not to take effect until the court is satisfied about the matters mentioned in rule 7.32(2)(a) to (i).

Defined terms—"civil partnership proceedings", "court", "district judge", "matrimonial proceedings": FPR 2010, r 2.3(1).

Application to make decree nisi or conditional order absolute or final—Rule 7.33 deals with two separate matters:

(1) *Delay of grant of decree absolute or final order* Application for a decree nisi or conditional order to be made absolute or final, where the Queen's Proctor has intervened or where "there are other circumstances which ought to be brought to the attention of the court" (r 7.33(2)(a),(3),(4));

(2) *Application for decree absolute or final order by the respondent spouse or civil partner* The wholly different, and generally uncontroversial question, of application for a decree absolute or final order by the non-applicant spouse or civil partner (r 7.33(2)(c))).

Application on notice—Application under r 7.33 is on notice to the other parties (including the Queen's Proctor, if it is a Queen's Proctor case) under the FPR 2010, Pt 18 procedure (by Form D11). The statement in support of the application under (1) will be extensive, but under (2) can be more or less routine (and see cases referred to below).

Hearing of the application (r 7.33(3))—An application involving the Queen's Proctor (in (1) above) – which will be essentially to warn off the Queen's Proctor – must be heard by a judge (r 7.33(3)(a)). An

application (at (2)) for a respondent's decree or order will be heard by a district judge. Any application involving "other circumstances" (see below) will be likely to be dealt with, in the first instance by a district judge.

Powers of the court—The powers of the court on dealing with an application by the Queen's Proctor are prescribed by MCA 1973, s 9(1) and CPA 2004, s 40(3). In summary these powers are:

(1) To make the decree nisi or conditional order absolute or final in any event;
(2) To rescind the decree nisi or conditional order;
(3) To require further inquiry and information; or
(4) Deal with the case in such other way as the court thinks fit.

"there are other circumstances which ought to be brought to the attention of the court" (r 7.33(2)(b))—There is no evidence on the face of the statute that indicates a power in the court to refer an issue of this nature to a judge. It is possible that what the rule anticipates is referral to a judge in circumstances such as those set out in FPR 2010, r 7.32(2), but this is unclear.

Application for decree absolute or final order by original applicant—There appears to be nothing in r 7.33(2)(c) to prevent the spouse or civil partner who obtained the decree nisi or conditional order filing a routine decree absolute application (under FPR 2010, r 7.32(2)) on receipt of the application notice under r 7.33 (unless 12 months have elapsed since the date of the decree nisi). If that happens, the spouse or civil partner applying under r 7.33(2)(c) should maintain his application if he wishes to seek an order for costs against the spouse who obtained the decree nisi.

Grant of decree or order under MCA 1973, s 9(2) or CPA 2004, s 40(2): discretion—Grant of a decree on the respondent's application is a matter for the court's discretion (MCA 1973, s 9(2); CPA 2004, s 40(2)). In *Re G (Decree Absolute: Prejudice)* [2003] 1 FLR 870, Bennett J allowed a respondent husband's application for decree absolute. Although the husband might not be prejudiced by the delay, in the absence of good grounds to refuse a decree, it should issue. Had the wife applied, a decree would have been granted. Such application gives the court a discretion to grant a decree absolute or final order to the other spouse or civil partner, although the court may refuse to exercise discretion in appropriate circumstances (*Smith v Smith* [1990] 1 FLR 438). The decree will not be made absolute (or a conditional order final) if the refusal to do so is the only way to ensure that a party complies with an ancillary relief order (*Wickler v Wickler* [1998] 2 FLR 326). See also, **Stay on grant of decree absolute** and *Evans v Evans* [2012] EWCA Civ 1293 under FPR 2010, r 7.23.

Service of the application notice—Care must be taken personally to serve the application and to ensure that proof of service is available to the court. Failure to serve the application notice on the other spouse or civil partner renders the decree absolute void and the order granted on the application would therefore have to be set aside (*Manchanda v Manchanda* [1995] 2 FLR 590, CA).

7.34 What the court officer must do when a decree nisi is made absolute

In matrimonial proceedings, where a decree nisi is made absolute the court officer must –

    (a) endorse that fact on the decree nisi together with the precise time at which the decree was made absolute; and

    (b) send a certificate that a decree nisi has been made absolute to the applicant, the respondent, any co-respondent and any other party.

Defined terms—"matrimonial proceedings": FPR 2010, r 2.3(1).

7.35 What the court officer must do when a conditional order is made final

Where a conditional order is made final the court officer must –

    (a) endorse that fact on the conditional order together with the precise time at which the order was made final; and

    (b) send the final order to the applicant, the respondent and any other party.

Defined terms—"matrimonial proceedings": FPR 2010, r 2.3(1).

PART III

7.36 Records of decrees absolute and final orders

(1) A central index of decrees absolute and final orders must be kept under the control of the principal registry.

(2) Any person may require a search to be made of that index and to be provided with a certificate showing the results of that search.

(3) Any person who requests it must be issued with a copy of the decree absolute or final order.

Amendments—SI 2012/679.

Defined terms—"principal registry": FPR 2010, r 2.3(1).

Practice Direction 7A –
Procedure for Applications in Matrimonial and Civil Partnership Proceedings

This Practice Direction supplements FPR Part 7

Applications for matrimonial and civil partnership orders: general

1.1 An application for a matrimonial or civil partnership order must be made in the form referred to in Practice Direction 5A. The application form sets out the documents which must accompany the application.

1.2 The application for a matrimonial order or a civil partnership order must be completed according to the detailed notes which accompany the form. It is especially important that the particulars provide evidence to show why the applicant is entitled to –

    (a) in matrimonial proceedings, a dissolution or annulment of the marriage or a decree of judicial separation;

    (b) in civil partnership proceedings, a dissolution or annulment of the civil partnership or a separation order.

The particulars should, however, be as concise as possible consistent with providing the necessary evidence.

Respondents: restrictions

2.1 Where the application refers to adultery or to an improper association with another person, that other person should not be named in the application unless the applicant believes the other party to the marriage or civil partnership in question is likely to object to the making of a matrimonial or civil partnership order on the application. Furthermore, such a person should not be a respondent if under the age of 16 or alleged to have been the victim of rape committed by the other party to the marriage or civil partnership, unless the court gives permission.

Proof of marriage or civil partnership to accompany the application

3.1 The application form for a matrimonial order or a civil partnership order sets out the documents which must accompany the application. Where the existence and validity of a marriage or civil partnership is not disputed, its validity will be proved by the application being accompanied by –

(a) one of the following –

    (i) a certificate of the marriage or civil partnership to which the application relates issued under the law in force in the country where the marriage or civil partnership registration took place;

    (ii) a similar document issued under the law in force in the country where the marriage or civil partnership registration took place; or

    (iii) a certified copy of such a certificate or document obtained from the appropriate register office; and

(b) where the certificate, document or certified copy is not in English (or, where the court is in Wales, in Welsh), a translation of that document certified by a notary public or authenticated by a statement of truth.

Amendments—FPR 2010. Update 2.

Filing without accompanying proof of marriage or civil partnership

3.2 If –

(a) the applicant cannot produce –

    (i) the certificate, similar document or a certified copy; and

    (ii) (where necessary) an authenticated translation;

at the time of filing the application; and

(b) it is urgent that the application be filed,

the applicant may apply to the court without notice for permission to file the application without the certificate, document, certified copy or authenticated translation.

3.3 The applicant or the applicant's solicitor must in such a case file with the application a statement explaining why –

(a) the required document is not available; and

(b) the application is urgent.

3.4 The court may give permission to file the application without the required document if the applicant gives an undertaking to file that document at the very earliest opportunity and within any time limit set by the court.

Other methods of proof of the marriage or civil partnership

3.5 The requirements of this Practice Direction do not prevent the existence and validity of a marriage, or of an overseas relationship which is not a marriage, being proved in accordance with –

(a) the Evidence (Foreign, Dominion and Colonial Documents) Act 1933; or

(b) any other method authorised in any other Practice Direction, rule or Act.

Information required where evidence of a conviction or finding is to be relied on

4.1 An applicant for a matrimonial or civil partnership order who wishes to rely on evidence –

(a) under section 11 of the Civil Evidence Act 1968 of a conviction of an offence; or

(b) under section 12 of that Act of a finding or adjudication of adultery or paternity,

must include in the application form a statement to that effect and give the following details –

    (i) the type of conviction, finding or adjudication and its date;

    (ii) the court or Court-Martial which made the conviction, finding or adjudication; and

    (iii) the issue in the proceedings to which it relates.

Amendments to applications and answers

5.1 An application for permission to amend an application for a matrimonial or civil partnership order or answer may be dealt with at a hearing.

5.2 When making an application for permission to amend an application for a matrimonial or civil partnership order or to amend an answer the applicant should file at court –

    (a) the notice of application for permission; and

    (b) a copy of the application for a matrimonial or civil partnership order or the answer showing the proposed amendments.

5.3 Where permission to amend has been given, the party applying to make the amendment should within 14 days of the date of the order, or within such other period as the court directs, file with the court the amended application for a matrimonial or civil partnership order or the amended answer.

Requests for further information under rule 7.15 (further information)

6.1 Before making an application under rule 7.15, the party seeking clarification or information ("the requesting party") should first serve a written request for it on the party from whom the clarification or information is sought, giving a date by which a reply should be served. The date should be such as to allow the requested party a reasonable time to respond.

6.2 A request should be made by letter or in a separate document, should contain no other subject matter, and should make clear that it is made under rule 7.15. It must be concise and confined to matters which are reasonably necessary and proportionate to enable the requesting party to prepare his or her own case or understand the case of the party to whom the request is directed.

6.3 The reply to the request must be in writing, dated and signed by the requested party or that party's legal representative.

6.4 The reply may be made by letter or in a separate document, should contain no other subject matter, and should make clear that it is a reply to the request concerned. It should repeat each request together with the reply to it. It must be served on every party to the proceedings.

6.5 A party who objects to replying to all or part of a request under rule 7.15, or who is unable to do so, must inform the requesting party promptly, and in any event within the time within which a reply has been requested, and give reasons for objecting or being unable to reply (as the case may be).

Disclosure and inspection

7.1 Where an application for a matrimonial or civil partnership order is not being dealt with as an undefended case the court may make an order for the disclosure of documents under rule 7.22(2)(c).

7.2 When an order for disclosure is made, the disclosing party must, in order to comply, make a reasonable search for the documents required to be disclosed. The extent of the search will depend upon the circumstances of the case and parties should bear in mind the overriding principle of proportionality.

7.3 Documents should be disclosed in a list which should normally list the documents in date order, numbering them consecutively and giving each a concise description. Where there are a large number of documents falling into a particular category they may be grouped together (e.g. 50 bank statements relating to x account from y date to z date).

7.4 The obligations imposed by a disclosure order continue until the proceedings come to an end. If, after the list of documents has been prepared and served, the existence of further documents to which the order applies comes to the attention of the disclosing party, that party must prepare and serve a supplemental list.

7.5 A list of documents must contain the following statement:

I, [insert name] state that I have carried out a reasonable and proportionate search to locate all the documents which I am required to disclose under the disclosure order made by the court on [insert date]. [I did not search for [insert here any limitations on search by reference to date, location, nature of documents etc]]. I understand the duty of disclosure and to the best of my knowledge I have carried out that duty. I certify that the list above is a complete list of all the documents which are or have been in my control and which I am obliged under the order to disclose.

7.6 If the disclosing party wishes to claim a right or duty to withhold inspection of a document or part of a document, that party must indicate in writing in the disclosure statement that such a right or duty is claimed, and the grounds on which it is claimed.

Decrees absolute and final orders: need for expedition

8.1 Where a party in an application for a matrimonial order has grounds for expediting the making of the decree absolute, that party should ordinarily seek directions with a view to an early hearing of the case. Where such an application has not been possible, an application should be made to the district judge making the decree nisi for the time between the decree nisi and the making absolute of that decree to be shortened.

8.2 Where the need for expedition only becomes obvious after the making of the decree nisi, or where (exceptionally) it arises in an undefended case to which the summary procedure applies, an application, on notice to the other parties to the proceedings, should be made using the procedure in Part 18 for an order shortening the time before which the decree nisi may be made absolute.

8.3 Where a party in an application for a civil partnership order has grounds for expediting the making of the final order, that party should ordinarily seek directions with a view to an early hearing of the case. Where such an application has not been possible, an application should be made to the district judge making the conditional order for the time between the conditional and final order to be shortened.

8.4 Where the need for expedition only becomes obvious after the making of the conditional order, or where (exceptionally) it arises in an undefended case to which the summary procedure applies, an application, on notice to the other parties to the proceedings, should be made using the procedure in Part 18 for an order shortening the time before which the final order may be made.

Practice Direction 7B –
Medical Examinations on Applications for
Annulment of a Marriage

This Practice Direction supplements FPR Part 7, rule 7.26 (Medical examinations in proceedings for nullity of marriage)

1.1 Where an application is made for the annulment of a marriage based on the incapacity of one of the parties to consummate, it will not usually be necessary to appoint a medical examiner where the application is undefended. Where the application is defended the court should not appoint a medical examiner unless it appears necessary to do so for the proper disposal of the case.

Amendments—FPR 2010, Update 2.

1.2 A medical examination ordered under rule 7.26 must, if the party to be examined so requests, be conducted by a doctor of the same gender as the person to be examined. Unless both parties are to be examined, each by a doctor of their own gender, it should not normally be necessary to appoint more than one medical examiner.

Amendments—FPR 2010, Update 2.

1.3 The costs of any medical examination ordered under rule 7.26 will be borne, in the first instance, by the party on whose application the medical examiner is appointed. Such costs form part of the costs of the proceedings.

Amendments—FPR 2010, Update 2.

1.4 It is the responsibility of the party on whose application the medical examiner is appointed to address, at the case management hearing, the question of whether any medical examiner is required to attend the final hearing of the proceedings. A medical examiner who is to give evidence at the proceedings is to be treated as an expert witness and the relevant rules in Part 25 (Experts and Assessors) will apply. The relevant rules in Part 25 will also apply to the medical examiner's report.

Amendments—FPR 2010, Update 2.

1.5 Nothing in this Practice Direction or in rule 7.26 affects the parties' right to adduce other evidence relevant to the proper disposal of the case. Such evidence must be verified by a statement of truth.

Practice Direction 7C –
Polygamous Marriages

This Practice Direction supplements FPR Part 7 (procedure for applications in matrimonial and civil partnership proceedings), Part 9 (applications for a financial remedy) and Part 18 (procedure for other applications in proceedings)

Scope of this Practice Direction

1.1 This practice direction applies where an application is made for –

   (a)   a matrimonial order;
   (b)   an order under section 27 of the 1973 Act;

(c) an order under section 35 of the 1973 Act;

(d) an order under the 1973 Act which is made in connection with, or with proceedings for any of the above orders; or

(e) an order under Part 3 of the 1984 Act,

and either party to the marriage is, or has during the course of the marriage, been married to more than one person (a polygamous marriage).

Polygamous marriages

2.1 Where this practice direction applies the application must state –

(a) that the marriage is polygamous;

(b) whether, as far as the party to the marriage is aware, any other spouse (that is, a spouse other than the spouse to whom the application relates) of that party is still living (the "additional spouse"); and

(c) if there is such an additional spouse –
   (i) the additional spouse's name and address;
   (ii) the date and place of the marriage to the additional spouse.

2.2 A respondent who believes that the marriage is polygamous must include the details referred to in paragraph 2.1 above in the acknowledgment of service if they are not included in the application.

2.3 The applicant in any proceedings to which this practice direction applies must apply to the court for directions as soon as possible after the filing of the application or the receipt of an acknowledgment of service mentioning an additional spouse.

2.4 On such an application or of its own initiative the court may –

(a) give the additional spouse notice of any of the proceedings to which this practice direction applies; and

(b) make the additional spouse a party to such proceedings.

2.5 In any case where the application or acknowledgment of service states that the marriage is polygamous (whether or not there is an additional spouse) a court officer must clearly mark the file with the words "Polygamous Marriage". The court officer must also check whether an application under paragraph 2.4 has been made in the case and, where no application has been made, refer the file to the court for consideration.

References in decrees to section 47 of the 1973 Act

3.1 Every decree nisi and decree absolute which is made in respect of a polygamous marriage must refer to the fact that the order is made with reference to section 47 of the 1973 Act.

Practice Direction 7D – Gender Recognition Act 2004

This Practice Direction supplements FPR Part 7

1 Introduction

The Gender Recognition Act 2004 ("the Act") provides transsexual people with the opportunity to obtain legal recognition in their acquired gender. Legal recognition follows from the issue of a full gender recognition certificate by a Gender Recognition Panel. Section 4 of the Act requires that where a Panel has granted an application to a married applicant, the gender recognition certificate that it must issue shall be an interim gender recognition certificate. The interim certificate may then be used by either party to the marriage as evidence in support of an application to annul the marriage under section 12(g) of, or paragraph 11(1)(e) of Schedule 1 to, the Matrimonial Causes Act 1973 ('*that an interim gender recognition certificate has, after the time of the marriage, been issued to either party to the marriage*').

2 Application

2.1 This Practice Direction applies to proceedings for divorce, judicial separation and annulment of marriage commenced on or after **4 April 2005**.

2.2 Where proceedings for divorce, judicial separation or annulment of marriage have been commenced prior to this date, paragraphs 3.2 to 3.5 below shall also apply to those proceedings if, but only if, the court acquires protected information (as defined by section 22 of the Act) in respect of a party to those proceedings.

3 Title of the cause

3.1 When a party to a matrimonial cause has changed his or her name since marriage, by deed poll or otherwise, the name currently being used by the party should appear first on any petition, answer and statement of arrangements followed by "formerly known as .... (married name)".

3.2 Subject to paragraph 3.3, when describing the parties in any Decree, Order, Notice or other document issued by the court, the parties should be described by their full current names only.

3.3 When giving details of the parties in any court list (including a special procedure cause list) they should be described by the initials and surname of their current names only. (For example, A B Jones v C D Jones).

3.4 For the sake of clarity, in any document or court list mentioned in paragraphs 3.2 and 3.3 above party titles (ie Mr, Mrs, Miss, etc.) should be omitted.

3.5 The Practice Note of 2 May 1940 (Title of Cause) shall cease to have effect.

4 Evidence at trial of cause

4.1 This part of the Practice Direction applies where the following conditions are met:

  (a) proceedings for annulment of marriage are brought under Section 12(g) of, or paragraph 11(1)(e) of Schedule 1 to, the Matrimonial Causes Act 1973 and paragraph 11 of Schedule 1 to, that Act; and

  (b) the cause is an undefended cause.

4.2 Any party requesting directions for trial may, in addition to the requirements of FPR rule 2.25(2), state in their request that they would wish to give their evidence at the trial of the cause in accordance with the provisions of this Practice Direction; and in that event, the request must be accompanied by an affidavit setting out the information required by the appendix to this Practice Direction.

4.3 Where directions for trial are given in accordance with FPR rule 2.24(5) in respect of a request to which paragraph 4.2 applies, a direction may also be given under Rule 2.28(3) that the affidavit lodged with the request for directions shall be treated as the evidence of that party at the trial of the cause (unless otherwise directed).

4.4 In the case of an undefended cause proceeding on the respondent's answer, this part of the Practice Direction and the contents of the appendix shall apply with appropriate modifications.

4.5 The appendix sets out a form of affidavit that may be used for the purposes of paragraph 4.2.

5 Issued with the approval and concurrence of the Lord Chancellor.

PART III

APPENDIX

A FORM OF AFFIDAVIT FOR THE PURPOSES OF PARAGRAPH 4.2

Affidavit by Petitioner in support of petition for
annulment under Section 12(g) of the Matrimonial Causes Act 1973

No. of matter:

^{* Delete as}
^{appropriate.}   IN THE   COUNTY COURT*
                    [PRINCIPAL REGISTRY OF THE FAMILY DIVISION*]

Between   (Petitioner)

and   (Respondent)

and   (Co-Respondent)

QUESTION	ANSWER
About the Petition	
1. Have you read the petition in this case?	
2. Do you wish to alter or to add to any statement in the petition? If so, state the alterations or additions.	
3. Subject to these alterations or additions (if any) is everything stated **in your petition** true? If any statement is not within your own knowledge, indicate this and say whether it is true to the best of your information and belief.	
About the interim gender recognition certificate	
4. State the date on which the interim gender recognition certificate was issued: State the serial number of the interim certificate: State the name of the person to whom the certificate has been issued:	

State the date on which you commenced
proceedings to annul your marriage:

**You must attach a copy of the interim
gender recognition certificate to this form.**

About other proceedings

5.   To the best of your knowledge and belief
     has there been or is there continuing any of
     the following proceedings;

     - an application to amend an error in
       the interim certificate;
     - an appeal against a decision to amend
       (or not to amend) an error in the interim
       certificate;
     - a reference under section 8(5) of the
       Gender Recognition Act 2004; or
     - an appeal against a decision made
       following a reference under section 8(5)?

     If so, please give details of those proceedings
     and any order made. (You should also attach
     copies of any orders made).

About the children of the family

6.   Has a Statement of Arrangements been filed
     in this case?

     If so, answer questions 7, 8 and 9.

7.   Have you read the Statement of
     Arrangements filed in this case?

8.   Do you wish to alter anything in the
     Statement of Arrangements or add to it?

     If so, state the alterations or additions.

9.   Subject to these alterations and additions (if
     any) is everything stated in the **Statement of
     Arrangements** true?

     If any statement is not within your own
     knowledge, indicate this and say whether it
     is true and correct to the best of your
     information and belief.

PART III

I,

                                            (full name)

of

                                  (full residential address)

                                            (occupation)

make oath and say as follows:-

1.   I am the petitioner in this cause.

2.   **The answers to Questions 1 to 9 above are true.**

3.[1]   I identify the signature .... [2]
appearing in the copy acknowledgement of service now produced to me and marked "A"
as the signature of my husband / wife, the respondent in this cause.

4.   I exhibit marked "B" a copy of the interim gender recognition certificate issued to myself /
the respondent in this cause.

5.   [3]

6.   I identify the signature.. [2]
appearing at Part IV of the Statement of Arrangements dated.................................
now produced to me and marked "C" as the signature of the respondent.

7.   I ask the court to grant a decree annulling my marriage with the respondent on the ground
stated in my petition [and to order the respondent / co-respondent to pay the costs of this
suit]. [4]

Sworn at

In the County of

this   day of   20

Before me, ...

A Commissioner for Oaths [5]
Officer of the Court appointed by the Judge to take Affidavits

PART 8
PROCEDURE FOR MISCELLANEOUS APPLICATIONS

CONTENTS OF THIS PART

Chapter 1
Procedure

8.1 Procedure

Subject to rules 8.13 and 8.24, applications to which this Part applies must be made in accordance with the Part 19 procedure.

General note—FPR 2010, Pt 19 provides an alternative procedure for applications, where the FPR 2010, Pt 18 procedure does not apply. See, generally, annotations to FPR 2010, r 19.1 and FPR PD19A. FPR 2010, r 8.13 relates to MWPA 1882, s 17/CPA 2004, s 66 and r 8.24 relates to MFPA 1984, Pt III/CPA 2004, Sch 7, where specific procedures and forms apply.

Chapter 2
Application for Corrected Gender Recognition Certificate

General note—This chapter makes provision for an application to the court under the Gender Recognition Act 2004, s 6 to correct an error in a gender recognition certificate issued by the court. The application is made to the court only where the application was determined by the court. In any other case, the application to correct is to a Gender Recognition Panel.

8.2 Scope of this Chapter

The rules in this Chapter apply to an application under section 6(1) of the Gender Recognition Act 2004 for the correction of a full gender recognition certificate issued under section 5(1) or 5A(1) of that Act.

8.3 Where to start proceedings

The application must be made to the court which issued the original certificate unless the court directs otherwise.

8.4 Who the parties are

Where the applicant is –

(a) the person to whom the original certificate was issued, the Secretary of State must be a respondent;

(b) the Secretary of State, the person to whom the original certificate was issued must be a respondent.

8.5 Delivery of copy certificate to Secretary of State

Where the court issues a corrected full gender recognition certificate, a court officer must send a copy of the corrected certificate to the Secretary of State.

Chapter 3
Application for Alteration of Maintenance Agreement after Death of One Party

8.6 Scope of this Chapter

The rules in this Chapter apply to an application under section 36 of the 1973 Act or paragraph 73 of Schedule 5 to the 2004 Act to alter a maintenance agreement after the death of one of the parties.

Defined terms—"maintenance agreement": MCA 1973, s 34(2).

8.7 Where to start proceedings

(1) The application may be made in the High Court or a county court.

(2) Where the application is made in a county court it must be made in the divorce county court or civil partnership proceedings county court for the district in which –

(a) the deceased resided at the time of death; or

(b) if the deceased did not reside in England and Wales at the time of death –
   (i) the respondent or one of the respondents resides or carries on business; or
   (ii) where the respondent is the personal representative of the deceased, the deceased's estate is situated; or

(c) if neither (a) nor (b) applies –
   (i) the applicant resides or carries on business; or
   (ii) where the applicant is the personal representative of the deceased, the deceased's estate is situated.

8.8 Who the parties are

(1) Where the applicant is –

(a) the surviving party to the agreement, the personal representative of the deceased must be a respondent;

(b) the personal representative of the deceased, the surviving party to the agreement must be a respondent.

(2) The court may at any time direct that –

(a) any person be made a party to proceedings; or

(b) a party be removed.

8.9 Representative parties

(1) The court may, before or after the application has been filed at court, make an order appointing a person to represent any other person or persons in the application where the person or persons to be represented –

    (a)   are unborn;

    (b)   cannot be found;

    (c)   cannot easily be ascertained; or

    (d)   are a class of persons who have the same interest in an application and –

        (i)   one or more members of that class are within sub-paragraphs (a), (b) or (c); or

        (ii)   to appoint a representative would further the overriding objective.

(2) An application for an order under paragraph (1) may be made by –

    (a)   any person who seeks to be appointed under the order; or

    (b)   any party to the application.

(3) An application for an order under paragraph (1) must be served on –

    (a)   all parties to the application to alter the maintenance agreement, if that application has been filed at court;

    (b)   the person sought to be appointed, if that person is not the applicant or a party to the application; and

    (c)   any other person as directed by the court.

(4) The court's approval is required to settle proceedings in which a party is acting as a representative.

(5) The court may approve a settlement where it is satisfied that the settlement is for the benefit of all the represented persons.

(6) Unless the court directs otherwise, any order made on an application in which a party is acting as a representative –

    (a)   is binding on all persons represented in the proceedings; and

    (b)   may only be enforced by or against a person who is not a party with the permission of the court.

(7) An application may be brought by or against trustees, executors or administrators without adding as parties any persons who have a beneficial interest in the trust or estate and any order made on the application is binding on the beneficiaries unless the court orders otherwise.

8.10 Acknowledgment of service

(1) A respondent who is a personal representative of the deceased must file with the acknowledgment of service a statement setting out –

    (a)   full particulars of the value of the deceased's estate for probate after providing for the discharge of the funeral, testamentary and administration expenses, debts and liabilities (including inheritance tax and interest); and

    (b)   the people (including names, addresses and details of any persons under disability) or classes of people beneficially interested in the estate and the value of their interests so far as ascertained.

(2) The respondent must file the acknowledgment of service and any statement required under this rule within 28 days beginning with the date on which the application is served.

8.11 Hearings may be in private

The court may decide to hear any application to which this Chapter applies in private.

Chapter 4
Application for Question as to Property to be Decided in Summary Way

8.12 Scope of this Chapter

The rules in this Chapter apply to an application under section 17 of the Married Women's Property Act 1882 or section 66 of the 2004 Act.

8.13 Procedure

Where an application for an order under section 17 of the Married Women's Property Act 1882 or section 66 of the 2004 Act is made in any proceedings for a financial order, the application must be made in accordance with the Part 18 procedure.

Defined terms—"financial order" is defined in FPR 2010, r 2.3, which provides a list of nine orders defined as a "financial order". This is drawn more widely than previously under FPR 1991, r 2.51B.

Procedure—The application may be made in the High Court or county court, in accordance with FPR 2010, Pt 18 procedure. Where particulars of a mortgage are provided with the application, a mortgagee must be served with a copy of the application, and must be made a party if requested by the mortgagee. Injunctions may be granted only if ancillary or incidental to the assistance sought by the applicant.

8.14 Where to start proceedings

(1) The application may be made in the High Court or a county court.

(2) Where the application is made in a county court it must be made in the court –

  (a) in which any matrimonial proceedings or civil partnership proceedings have been started or are intended to be started by the applicant or the respondent; or

  (b) in the absence of any such proceedings, for the district in which the applicant or respondent resides.

(3) The application may be made to the principal registry as if it were a county court if –

  (a) any matrimonial proceedings or civil partnership proceedings have been started there or are intended to be started there by the applicant or the respondent; and

  (b) those proceedings are or will be treated as pending in a divorce county court or civil partnership proceedings county court.

8.15 Mortgagees as parties

(1) Where particulars of a mortgage are provided with the application –

  (a) the applicant must serve a copy of the application on the mortgagee; and

  (b) the mortgagee may, within 14 days beginning with the date on which the application was received, file an acknowledgment of service and be heard on the application.

(2) The court must direct that a mortgagee be made a party to the proceedings where the mortgagee requests to be one.

8.16 Injunctions

(1) The court may grant an injunction$^{(GL)}$ only if the injunction$^{(GL)}$ is ancillary or incidental to the assistance sought by the applicant.

(2) Applications for injunctive relief must be made in accordance with the procedure in rule 20.4 (how to apply for an interim remedy) and the provisions of rule 20.5 (interim injunction$^{(GL)}$ to cease if application is stayed$^{(GL)}$) apply.

8.17 Application of other rules

Rule 9.24 applies where the court has made an order for sale under section 17 of the Married Women's Property Act 1882 or section 66 of the 2004 Act.

Chapter 5
Declarations

8.18 Scope of this Chapter

The rules in this Chapter apply to applications made in accordance with –

    (a)   section 55 of the 1986 Act (declarations as to marital status) and section 58 of the 2004 Act (declarations as to civil partnership status);

    (b)   section 55A of the 1986 Act (declarations of parentage);

    (c)   section 56(1)(b) and (2) of the 1986 Act (declarations of legitimacy or legitimation); and

    (d)   section 57 of the 1986 Act (declaration as to adoptions effected overseas).

Procedure: Part 19—The general rule is that all applications under FPR 2010, Pt 8 are by the FPR 2010, Pt 19 procedure and this includes applications under Pt 8, Ch 5 for declarations in relation to status (FLA 1986, Pt 3 and CPA 2004, s 58). Whereas each of the applications for a declaration had a separate rule in FPR 1991, the four under consideration here are incorporated together in Ch 5.

Jurisdiction to grant a declaration—There is no clear statutory jurisdiction to grant a declaration; but it is used as a recent (introduced in 1883) common law means of defining status (as in these remedies) or determining a state of affairs between parties (constructive trust, contractual terms) or between a public body and a private individual (administrative law and see SCA 1981, s 31). Its appropriateness was discussed in the context of administrative law proceedings (for example, *Gillick v West Norfolk and Wisbech Area Health Authority and Another* [1986] 1 FLR 224, HL, see the speech of Lord Scarman) and its use in recent proceedings (*Rolls-Royce plc v Unite the Union* [2009] EWCA Civ 387). The jurisdiction has statutory recognition in, though it is not defined by, the statutes which define the remedies covered in FPR 2010, Ch 5.

Application form—Application for a declaration is by application form, ie "other than under the Part 18 procedure" (FPR 2010, r 2.3(1)). FPR PD5A prescribes the following application forms:

- C63 – declaration of parentage under FLA 1986, s 55A;
- C64 – declaration of legitimacy or legitimation under FLA 1986, s 56(1)(b) and (2);
- C65 – declaration as to adoption effected overseas under FLA 1986, s 57;
- D70 – declaration of marital/civil partnership status.

Requirements of r 19.3—The requirements of FPR 2010, Pt 19 and specifically of r 19.3 must be borne in mind alongside the form's disclosure requirements, for example:

- Form C63 (Section 3) asks for "brief details about why you are making this application" and forbids the filing of a "full statement". FPR 2010, Pt 19 requires the applicant to state either the question to be decided or a draft order and its legal basis (r 19.3(b)) and also to file all "written evidence on which the applicant intends to rely" (r 19.7(1)). In a declaration as to marital status or adoption this may be copious.
- No section is left in comparable CPR 1998, Pt 8 applications for an application by the applicant for a scientific test direction, which will be the inevitable consequence of certain declaration applications (see FLRA 1969, s 20).
- If an alleged non-resident parent is asserting that he is not a parent, he should say somewhere in Form C63 why none of the cases in CSA 1991, s 26 apply to him.

Answer to the application—This must be by acknowledgment of service (FPR 2010, r 19.5). No form is prescribed for this. The acknowledgment of service must be accompanied by any evidence on which the respondent intends to rely (FPR 2010, r 19.7(3)). An answer might include an application by the respondent, for example:

- to apply the application to be struck out (FPR 2010, r 4.4), e g (1) where another court has already made a declaration or made a finding which proves parentage; or (2) the respondent denies that the applicant has sufficient personal interest (FLA 1986, s 55A(3)) to make application;
- to seek disclosure of particular documents.

Parentage and parenthood in issue—The procedure distinguishes between person whose parentage is in issue (i e the child, who may be an adult by the time of the application); and a person whose parenthood is in issue (i e the father or putative father, or fathers).

Parties to a parentage declaration application (r 8.20(1))—The parties to an application under FLA 1986, s 55A will depend on by whom the issue is raised and by whom and how it is responded to. For example:

(1) On an application by a father, the child will be "the person whose parentage is in issue" and the mother will also be a respondent.

(2) On an application by the Secretary of State for Work and Pensions, under CSA 1991, both parents and the child will be respondents.

Application for a parentage declaration—The remedy provided by FLA 1986, s 55A (which was inserted into the 1986 Act by CSPSSA 2000 and is closely interdependent on CSA 1991, s 27) is a declaration as to whether one person (it will always be a father) 'is or was the parent of another person' named in the application (FLA 1986, s 55A). Application for a declaration may be by others than members of the immediate family: e g a government department, local authority, Child Support Agency or other party with "sufficient interest".

Part 19 requirements—FPR 2010, Pt 19 applies to the declaration application (r 19.3(a)). A document filed with the FPR PD5A application form (see above) will be required to state:

– the issue the applicant wants the court to decide (r 19.3(b)(i));
– the "enactment" under which the application is being made, i e FLA 1986, s 55A (r 19.3(c));
– details of any representative capacity in which the application is made (r 19.3(d)) and of any representative capacity in which a respondent might appear (r 19.3(e));
– the "sufficient personal interest" of the applicant in the application (FLA 1986, s 55A(3) and (4)) or that CSA 1991, s 27(2) applies, that is:
  (a) that the applicant is the person with care of the child (i e looking after the child for child support purposes); or
  (b) that (where applicable) the applicant is the Secretary of State for Work and Pensions;
– the grounds on which the applicant relies for his assertion that he is entitled to seek the declaration; and if he is asserting that he is not a parent why none of the cases in CSA 1991, s 26 apply to him;
– the "legal basis of the application" made by the applicant (r 19.3(b)(ii)) or the terms of the order sought;
– details of any directions sought by the applicant (FPR 2010, Pt 18), e g as to disclosure of documents, scientific tests (see below).

Progress of the application— FPR 2010, Pt 19 deals with progress of the application (rr 19.5–19.7) and, in particular with evidence (rr 19.7 and 19.8). Rule 19.5 requires each respondent who wishes to take part at a final hearing (compare r 19.6(2)) must file an acknowledgement of service, together with any evidence on which she intends to rely (r 19.7(1)).

Scientific tests—The statutory ground for obtaining a scientific test is FLRA 1969, s 20, and the regulations governing the testing are Blood Tests (Evidence of Paternity) Regulations 1971 (as amended by Blood Tests (Evidence of Paternity) (Amendment) Regulations 2008). Procedure is governed by CPR PD23B, paras 1.1–1.3 and 1.5, as explained under FLRA 1969, s 20.

Applications in parentage declaration proceedings—In the application the applicant would be advised to draft into the document prepared a formal application for scientific tests. In principle, the application proceeds as a FPR 2010, Pt 18 application. An early, short court appointment (normally before a district judge) should be fixed for application for a direction to be dealt with (see **The direction** under FLRA 1969, s 20).

Respondent's acknowledgement of service and any applications— FPR 2010, Rule 19.5(3) deals with the respondent's opposition to the application. Any acknowledgement of service can indicate whether the respondent "contests the application" (r 19.5(3)(a); and see FPR 2010, r 8.20(3)); and the extent of and basis for that opposition. It will be necessary for the respondent to apply for any of these issues to be considered or tried by the court under the FPR 2010, Pt 18 procedure. Any witness statement in support would need to be supported by full grounds for the application. For example:

(1) A respondent may challenge whether the applicant has "sufficient interest" to bring the application (see FLA 1986, s 55A(3)).

(2) Application to strike out on grounds that the applicant (say) has no grounds for bringing the application or as an abuse of process (or res judicata: see for example *Law v Ahumuda & ors* [2011] 1 FLR 708).

PART III

If either of these preliminary applications succeeded, there would be no basis for the court to direct blood tests.

Case management and representation of any child respondent—If preliminary issues are raised the court will direct the order in which they are dealt with (and see FPR 2010, r 1.4(2)(c)). If the 'person named', ie the child whose parentage is in issue, is still a child, consideration may be needed for the child to be joined as a party and be represented by a litigation friend (FPR 2010, Pt 16, Ch 5).

Appeals to a court under CSA 1991, s 20 and Ch 5— FPR PD30A, para 12.1 directs that "the rules in Chs 1 and 5 of Pt 8 will apply as appropriate to an appeal" under CSA 1991, s 20. All appeals under s 20 go to the First-Tier Tribunal, save for appeals that raise a question of parentage, which go to the family proceedings courts (Child Support Appeals (Jurisdiction of Courts) Order 2002). The two sets of provisions (ie FPR 2010, Pt 8, Ch 5 and FPR PD30A, paras 12.1–12.3) have in common that the result of the process that they describe may be a declaration of parentage. It is difficult to see how Ch 5 can assist the parties. Procedure for a s 20 child support appeal is dealt with fully under Tribunal Procedure (First-tier Tribunal) (Social Entitlement Chamber) Rules 2008 and the magistrates only provide a venue for trial of the issues (ie all of the issues per Art 4 of the 2002 Order), whereas Ch 5 is procedural for a different set of application issues. Further, Ch 5 is governed by the FPR 2010, Pt 9 procedure, which need have nothing to do with CSA 1991, s 20 appeals. The justices will hear issues such as directing a scientific test report, but they do not need the FPR 2010, Pt 19 procedure for this. They will rely on the Pt 18 procedure for such a direction (CPR PD30A, paras 13.1 and 13.2).

8.19 Where to start proceedings

The application may be made in the High Court or a county court and applications under section 55A of the 1986 Act may also be made in a magistrates' court.

Declaration of parentage by magistrates—If magistrates have rejected an appeal before them under CSA 1991, s 20, then a subsequent application to them or to another court under FLA 1986, s 55A may be issue estopped (*Law v Ahumuda & ors* [2011] 1 FLR 708, at [12]: "the res judicata argument seems persuasive, and I would have thought it should have been first determined before any factual investigation was set in train").

Appeal from the magistrates' court—Appeal from the magistrates from a declaration (or refusal of declaration) under FLA 1986, s 55A is to the county court (FLA 1986, s 60(5), without the strict limitation to 21 days of MCA 1980, s 111A).

8.20 Who the parties are

(1) In relation to the proceedings set out in column 1 of the following table, column 2 sets out who the respondents to those proceedings will be.

Proceedings	Respondent
Applications for declarations as to marital or civil partnership status.	The other party to the marriage or civil partnership in question or, where the applicant is a third party, both parties to the marriage or civil partnership.
Applications for declarations of parentage.	(i) The person whose parentage is in issue; and (ii) any person who is or is alleged to be the parent of the person whose parentage is in issue, except where that person is the applicant.
Applications for declarations of legitimacy or legitimation.	The applicant's father and mother or the survivor of them.
Applications for declarations as to adoption effected overseas.	The person(s) whom the applicant is claiming are or are not the applicant's adoptive parents.

(2) The applicant must include in his application particulars of every person whose interest may be affected by the proceedings and his relationship to the applicant.

(3) The acknowledgment of service filed under rule 19.5 must give details of any other persons the respondent considers should be made a party to the application or be given notice of the application.

(4) Upon receipt of the acknowledgment of service, the court must give directions as to any other persons who should be made a respondent to the application or be given notice of the proceedings.

(5) A person given notice of proceedings under paragraph (4) may, within 21 days beginning with the date on which the notice was served, apply to be joined as a party.

(6) No directions may be given as to the future management of the case under rule 19.9 until the expiry of the notice period in paragraph (5).

Amendments—SI 2012/679.

Adding parties to the application—Rule 8.20(3)–(5) deals with the question of who might be required to be joined as a party to the application. The April 2012 amendment rules provide grounds at FPR 2010, r 9.26B(1)(b) on which a person may be joined in financial order proceedings: namely that there is an issue that is connected to the matters in dispute in the proceedings and it is desirable that the new party be added to resolve that issue. This provision does not specifically apply to proceedings under FPR 2010, Pt 8, but FPR 2010, r 9.26B (modelled as it is on CPR r 19.2) will be a useful criterion for the court to adopt in considering whether a person or body should be added as a party under either r 8.20(4) or r 8.20(5).

"respondent considers should be made a party" (r 8.20(3))—This rule gives the respondent no indication as to on what ground anyone else might be added as a party; but see the note above.

"directions as to who should be made a respondent" (r 8.20(4))—This rule requires a person to be made a party. For an assessment of grounds for this to be done, see the note above. A party added as a respondent will have to apply to have the order set aside on grounds analogous to setting aside a witness summons (see FPR 2010, r 24.2).

"apply to be joined as a party" (r 8.20(5))—FPR 2010, r 9.26B has been inserted (see above). This rule may be permitted as a criterion for joining as a party.

Application involving person who lacks capacity—An application under FLA 1986, s 55A involving a person who lacks capacity cannot be issued in the Court of Protection, but since the respondent to such an application must be a third party, probably the Official Solicitor, the application is likely to be transferred to the High Court and heard by a judge with Court of Protection jurisdiction (*LG v DK* [2012] COPLR 80, Sir Nicholas Wall P). This decision considers the approach to declarations as to paternity in different circumstances.

8.21 The role of the Attorney General

(1) The applicant must, except in the case of an application for a declaration of parentage, send a copy of the application and all accompanying documents to the Attorney General at least one month before making the application.

(2) The Attorney General may, when deciding whether to intervene in the proceedings, inspect any document filed at court relating to any family proceedings mentioned in the declaration proceedings.

(3) If the court is notified that the Attorney General wishes to intervene in the proceedings, a court officer must send the Attorney General a copy of any subsequent documents filed at court.

(4) The court must, when giving directions under rule 8.20(4), consider whether to ask the Attorney General to argue any question relating to the proceedings.

(5) If the court makes a request to the Attorney General under paragraph (4) and the Attorney General agrees to that request, the Attorney General must serve a summary of the argument on all parties to the proceedings.

"send a copy of the application to the Attorney General" (r 8.21(1))—This complies with the requirements of FLA 1986, s 59, but in requiring that the application be sent to the Attorney General before it is filed, r 8.21(1) goes further than s 59.

8.22 Declarations of parentage

(1) If the applicant or the person whose parentage or parenthood is in issue, is known by a name other than that which appears in that person's birth certificate, that other name must also be stated in any order and declaration of parentage.

(2) A court officer must send a copy of a declaration of parentage and the application to the Registrar General within 21 days beginning with the date on which the declaration was made.

Delay in registration—The time for registration could be delayed by order of the court but by a limited period only. FLA 1996, s 55A(7) provides that a period for registration of a declaration be prescribed and r 8.22 restricts this to 21 days. This should be the norm and any divergence should only occur in exceptional circumstances (*Re F (Children: Declaration of Parentage)* [2012] Fam Law 522: 4 months is permissible; 4 years was plainly too long).

Chapter 6
Application for Permission to Apply for a Financial Remedy after Overseas Proceedings

8.23 Scope of this Chapter

Subject to rule 9.26(6) the rules in this Chapter apply to an application for permission to apply for a financial remedy under section 13 of the 1984 Act and paragraph 4 of Schedule 7 to the 2004 Act.

> (Rule 9.26(6) enables the application for permission to apply for a financial remedy under section 13 of the 1984 Act or paragraph 4 of Schedule 7 to the 2004 Act to be heard at the same time as the application for a financial remedy under Part 3 of the 1984 Act or Schedule 7 to the 2004 Act where that application is an application for a consent order.)

8.24 Where and how to start proceedings

(1) Subject to paragraph (2), the application must be made in the principal registry.

(2) Where rule 9.26(6) applies, the application must be made in the court hearing the application for a financial remedy.

> (Rule 9.5(2) specifies the court where the application for the consent order should be filed.)

(3) The application must be made in accordance with the Part 18 procedure.

Defined terms—"Financial remedy" (r 2.3).

Application—Application is for permission under MFPA 1984, Pt III in Forms D50E and 50F. The application must be accompanied by a statement by the applicant. Form D50F sets out the matters that the court expects to see in the statement and this must be supplemented by the factors set out in the checklist in MFPA 1984, s 16(2). If permission is granted, the substantive application proceeds under FPR 2010, Pt 9, as if Form A had been issued and subject to any case-management directions given at the time of permission being granted.

The hearing of the application—The practice in London as provided for by Form D50E is for there to be an ex parte oral hearing before a judge of the division in the Royal Courts of Justice, normally with a time estimate of 30 mins. This is to operate a filter to prevent unmeritorious claims that may serve to oppress or blackmail a former spouse: *Agbaje v Agbaje* [2010] 1 FLR 1813. The practice of giving notice to respondents, resulting in inter partes hearings, has been disapproved of by the Court of Appeal in *Traversa v Freddi* [2011] 2 FLR 272. A respondent may apply for leave to set the decision aside, but unless the respondent can deliver a "knockout blow" the court should use its case-management powers to adjourn the application to be dealt with at the substantive hearing.

Draft order—It is central to the FPR 2010, Pt 18 procedure that an order accompanies the application. This should include disposal of the application and any case-management directions sought by the applicant if permission is granted.

8.25 Application to be made without notice

(1) The court may grant an application made without notice if it appears to the court that there are good reasons for not giving notice.

(2) If the applicant makes an application without giving notice, the applicant must state the reasons why notice has not been given.

Made without notice—Munby LJ in *Traversa v Freddi* [2011] 2 FLR 272 (at [57]) describes the wording of this provision as "slightly odd", but he explains what it means in the context of this rule and FPR 2010, Pt 18. He holds that the sense of the rule, in conjunction with *Agbaje v Agbaje* [2010] 1 FLR 1813, means that the application in the first instance is without notice and that the court can refuse to make an order when the application is listed on notice to the applicant ("not, it may be noted, to the respondent", at [57]).

8.26 Notification of hearing date

The court officer must –

    (a)   fix a date, time and place for the hearing of the application by a judge, but not a district judge; and

    (b)   give notice of the date of the hearing to the applicant.

Notification of hearing—This rule must be read in the light of *Traversa v Freddi* [2011] 2 FLR 272 and *Agbaje v Agbaje* [2010] 1 FLR 1813.

8.27 Hearings to be in private unless the court directs otherwise

An application under this Chapter must be heard in private unless the court directs otherwise.

8.28 Direction that application be dealt with by a district judge of the principal registry

If the application is granted, the judge may direct that the application for a financial remedy under Part 3 of the 1984 Act or Schedule 7 to the 2004 Act may be heard by a district judge of the principal registry.

Chapter 7
Application for the Transfer of a Tenancy under Section 53 of, and Schedule 7 to, the 1996 Act

Scope—This rule regulates the procedure for transfer of tenancies on divorce or the separation of cohabitants under FLA 1996, s 53 and Sch 7. See commentary to s 53 and Procedural Guide A13.

Procedure—The application may be made to the High Court or a county court, or to the court in which there are pending divorce or civil partnership proceedings, if applicable. The application will be served on the respondent and normally upon the landlord who will be made a party if he requests it. The court has the power to grant an injunction.

8.29 Scope of this Chapter

This Chapter applies to an application for the transfer of a tenancy under section 53 of, and Schedule 7 to, the 1996 Act.

8.30 Where to start proceedings

(1) Subject to paragraph (2), the application may be made in the High Court or a county court.

(2) The application must be made to the court in which any divorce, judicial separation, nullity or civil partnership proceedings are pending between the parties.

8.31 Service of the application

(1) The court will serve a copy of the application on –

    (a)   the respondent; and
    (b)   the landlord (as defined by paragraph 1 of Schedule 7 to the 1996 Act),

unless the court directs that the applicant must do so.

(2) Where service is effected by the applicant, the applicant must file a certificate of service.

8.32 Who the parties are

The court will direct that a landlord be made a party to the proceedings where the landlord requests to be one.

8.33 Orders for disclosure

Any party may apply to the court under rule 21.2 for an order that any person must attend an appointment before the court and produce any documents that are specified or described in the order.

8.34 Injunctions

(1) The court may grant an injunction(GL) only if the injunction(GL) is ancillary or incidental to the assistance sought by the applicant.

(2) Applications for injunctive relief must be made in accordance with the procedure in rule 20.4 (how to apply for an interim remedy) and the provisions of rule 20.5 (interim injunction(GL) to cease if application is stayed(GL)) apply accordingly.

Chapter 8
Applications for Orders Preventing Avoidance under Section 32l of the Child Support Act 1991

8.35 Scope of this Chapter

Subject to rule 8.40 the rules in this Chapter apply to applications made under section 32L(1) and (2) of the 1991 Act.

CSA 1991, s 32L—CSA 1991, s 32L (set out in Part II) was introduced into the 1991 Act by CMOPA 2008, s 24 along with a variety of intended enforcement provisions (many of which are not yet in force).

Terminology of s 32L—The similarity of terminology of s 32L with MCA 1973, s 37(2) and certain bankruptcy legislation will be noted. Case-law under that legislation may be applied (as appropriate).

Whereas the High Court has an inherent jurisdiction to make any form of freezing injunction or other order (*Shipman v Shipman* [1991] 1 FLR 250), it is likely that – even after the coming into operation of s 32L – it still cannot do so (*Department of Social Security v Butler* [1996] 1 FLR 65).

8.36 Interpretation

In this Chapter –

"child support maintenance" has the meaning assigned to it in section 3(6) of the 1991 Act;

"reviewable disposition" has the meaning assigned to it in section 32L(5) of the 1991 Act.

"child support maintenance"—Child support maintenance means child maintenance as calculated and payable under CSA 1991.

8.37 Where to start proceedings

(1) The application must be made to the High Court and be filed in –

    (a)   the principal registry; or

    (b)   any district registry.

(2) The application may be heard by a judge but not a district judge except –

    (a)   a district judge of the principal registry of the Family Division; or

    (b)   a district judge in a district registry who is directed by a judge to hear the application.

    (Section 32L(10)(a) of the 1991 Act defines "court" for the purposes of section 32L as being the High Court only)

8.38 Who the parties are

(1) The applicant to the proceedings is the Secretary of State and the respondent is the person who has failed to pay child support maintenance.

(2) The court may at any time direct that –

    (a)   any person be made a party to proceedings; or

    (b)   a party be removed from the proceedings.

Amendments—SI 2012/2007.

8.39 Service of the application

(1) The applicant must serve the application and a copy of the applicant's written evidence on –

    (a)   any respondent;

    (b)   the person in whose favour the reviewable disposition is alleged to have been made; and

    (c)   such other persons as the court directs.

(2) Where an application includes an application relating to land, the applicant must serve a copy of the application on any –

    (a)   mortgagee;

    (b)   trustee of a trust of land or settlement; and

    (c)   other person who has an interest in the land,

of whom particulars are given in the application.

(3) Any person served under paragraph (2) may make a request to the court in writing, within 14 days beginning with the date of service of the application, for a copy of the applicant's written evidence.

(4) Any person who –

(a) is served with copies of the application and the applicant's written evidence under paragraph (1); or

(b) receives a copy of the applicant's written evidence following a request under paragraph (3),

may, within 14 days beginning with the date of service or receipt, file a statement in answer.

(5) A statement in answer filed under paragraph (4) must be verified by a statement of truth.

Service of the application

(1) Service is by the applicant Secretary of State for Work and Pensions (r 8.39(1)).
(2) If an application relates to land, it will be seen that r 8.39(2)–(5) bears a substantial similarity to the service on mortgagees etc provisions of r 9.13.

8.40 Applications without notice

(1) This rule applies to an application under section 32L(1) of the 1991 Act.

(2) The court may grant an application made without notice if it appears to the court that there are good reasons for not giving notice.

(3) If the applicant makes an application without giving notice, the evidence in support of the application must state the reasons why notice has not been given.

(4) If the court grants an application under paragraph (2) –

(a) the order must include a provision allowing any respondent to apply to the court for an order to be reconsidered as soon as just and convenient at a full hearing; and

(b) the applicant must, as soon as reasonably practicable, serve upon each respondent a copy of the order and a copy of the written evidence in support of the application.

Application without notice— Rule 8.40(2) and (3) is closely modelled on FPR 2010, r 20.4(1) and (3). What is said of r 20.4 as to duties to other parties and the court, it is submitted, applies equally to the Secretary of State for Work and Pensions of an application under r 8.40. Many of these applications, as with those for interim remedies under FPR 2010, Pt 20, are likely to be made without notice.

Chapter 9
Application for Consent to Marriage of a Child or to Registration of Civil Partnership of a Child

8.41 Scope of this Chapter

The rules in this Chapter apply to an application under –

(a) section 3 of the Marriage Act 1949; or

(b) paragraph 3, 4 or 10 of Schedule 2 to the 2004 Act.

Scope—This rule (replacing FPR 1991, rr 3.20 and 3.20A) makes provision for the procedure for an application under either the Marriage Act 1949, s 3 (consent of the court to the marriage of a minor) or under CPA 2004, Sch 2, para 3 (where the required consent of a person to the registration of a civil partnership of a child is unobtainable due to absence, inaccessibility or disability, where the special procedure for registration does not apply), para 4 (where the required consent has been refused, where the special procedure does not apply) and para 10 (where the required consent is unobtainable or has been refused, where the special procedure does not apply).

8.42 Child acting without a children's guardian

The child may bring an application without a children's guardian, unless the court directs otherwise.

8.43 Who the respondents are

Where an application follows a refusal to give consent to –

(a)   the marriage of a child; or
(b)   a child registering as the civil partner of another person,

every person who has refused consent will be a respondent to the application.

PART 9
APPLICATIONS FOR A FINANCIAL REMEDY

CONTENTS OF THIS PART

Practice Direction 9A –
Application for a Financial Remedy   1654

Chapter 1
Application and Interpretation

9.1 Application

The rules in this Part apply to an application for a financial remedy.

("Financial remedy" and "financial order" are defined in rule 2.3)

Scope— FPR 2010, Rule 2.3 provides a list of orders defined as a "financial remedy" or "financial order". An order under MWPA 1882, TLATA 1996, I(PFD)A 1975 or for a tenancy transfer under FLA 1996, Pt IV is not a "financial remedy" or a "financial order". FPR 2010, PD9A, which supplements this Part, has only limited application to the magistrates' court.

9.2 Application of Magistrates' Courts Rules 1981

Unless the context otherwise requires, and subject to the rules in this Part, the following rules of the Magistrates' Courts Rules 1981 apply to proceedings in a magistrates' court which are family proceedings under section 65 of the Magistrates' Courts Act 1980 –

    (a)   rule 39(6) (method of making periodical payments);
    (b)   rule 41 (revocation etc. of orders for periodical payments);
    (c)   rule 43 (service of copy of order);
    (d)   rule 44 (remission of sums due under order);
    (e)   rule 45 (duty of designated officer to notify subsequent marriage or formation of civil partnership of person entitled to payments under a maintenance order);
    (f)   rule 48 (to whom payments are to be made);
    (g)   rule 49 (duty of designated officer to give receipt);
    (h)   rule 51 (application for further time);
    (i)   rule 62 (particulars relating to payment of lump sum under a magistrates' courts maintenance order etc. to be entered in register);
    (j)   rule 66 (register of convictions, etc.);
    (k)   rule 67 (proof of service, handwriting, etc.);
    (l)   rule 68 (proof of proceedings); and
    (m) rule 69 (proof that magistrates' court maintenance orders, etc, have not been revoked etc.).

Scope—For the avoidance of doubt, this rule makes it clear that the provisions of MCR 1981 listed therein apply to those financial proceedings in the magistrates' court that fall within the definition of family proceedings for the purpose of MCA 1980, s 65. For example, applications for orders under:

–   MO(FE)A 1920;
–   MCA 1973, s 35;
–   CPA 2004, Sch 5, paras 69–72, Sch 6;
–   MO(RE)A 1972, Pt I;
–   DPMCA 1978, Pt I; and
–   CA 1989.

Only originating applications for financial relief and applications for revival or revocation of orders invoke the procedures set out in FPR 2010, because proceedings for variation or enforcement of periodical payments orders do not fall within the definition of family proceedings, although the court may treat them as such. As far as these non-family proceedings are concerned, reference should be made instead to MC(EVOFP & MP)R 2011, which consolidate a number of the former freestanding provisions in rules dealing with enforcement of maintenance orders or apply FPR 2010 with modifications to the variation or enforcement of orders.

9.3 Interpretation

(1) In this Part –

"avoidance of disposition order" means –

    (a) in proceedings under the 1973 Act, an order under section 37(2)(b) or (c) of that Act;

    (b) in proceedings under the 1984 Act, an order under section 23(2)(b) or 23(3) of that Act;

    (c) in proceedings under Schedule 5 to the 2004 Act, an order under paragraph 74(3) or (4); or

    (d) in proceedings under Schedule 7 to the 2004 Act, an order under paragraph 15(3) or (4);

"the Board" means the Board of the Pension Protection Fund;

"FDR appointment" means a Financial Dispute Resolution appointment in accordance with rule 9.17;

"Financial Circumstances Form" means the Financial Circumstances Form published by the Permanent Bureau of the Hague Conference under Article 11(4) of the 2007 Hague Convention for use in relation to applications under Article 10 of that Convention;

"order preventing a disposition" means –

    (a) in proceedings under the 1973 Act, an order under section 37(2)(a) of that Act;

    (b) in proceedings under the 1984 Act, an order under section 23(2)(a) of that Act;

    (c) in proceedings under Schedule 5 to the 2004 Act, an order under paragraph 74(2); or

    (d) in proceedings under Schedule 7 to the 2004 Act, an order under paragraph 15(2);

"pension arrangement" means –

    (a) an occupational pension scheme;

    (b) a personal pension scheme;

    (c) shareable state scheme rights;

    (d) a retirement annuity contract;

    (e) an annuity or insurance policy purchased, or transferred, for the purpose of giving effect to rights under an occupational pension scheme or a personal pension scheme; and

    (f) an annuity purchased, or entered into, for the purpose of discharging liability in respect of a pension credit under section 29(1)(b) of the Welfare Reform and Pensions Act 1999 or under corresponding Northern Ireland legislation;

"pension attachment order" means –

    (a) in proceedings under the 1973 Act, an order making provision under section 25B or 25C of that Act;

    (b) in proceedings under the 1984 Act, an order under section 17(1)(a)(i) of that Act making provision equivalent to an order referred to in paragraph (a);

    (c) in proceedings under Schedule 5 to the 2004 Act, an order making provision under paragraph 25 or paragraph 26; or

    (d) in proceedings under Schedule 7 to the 2004 Act, an order under paragraph 9(2) or (3) making provision equivalent to an order referred to in paragraph (c);

"pension compensation attachment order" means –

    (a) in proceedings under the 1973 Act, an order making provision under section 25F of that Act;

(b) in proceedings under the 1984 Act, an order under section 17(1)(a)(i) of that Act making provision equivalent to an order referred in to paragraph (a);

(c) in proceedings under Schedule 5 to the 2004 Act, an order under paragraph 34A; and

(d) in proceedings under Schedule 7 to the 2004 Act, an order under paragraph 9(2) or (3) making provision equivalent to an order referred to in paragraph (c);

"pension compensation sharing order" means –

(a) in proceedings under the 1973 Act, an order under section 24E of that Act;

(b) in proceedings under the 1984 Act, an order under section 17(1)(c) of that Act;

(c) in proceedings under Schedule 5 to the 2004 Act, an order under paragraph 19A; and

(d) in proceedings under Schedule 7 to the 2004 Act, an order under paragraph 9(2) or (3) making provision equivalent to an order referred to in paragraph (c);

"pension sharing order" means –

(a) in proceedings under the 1973 Act, an order making provision under section 24B of that Act;

(b) in proceedings under the 1984 Act, an order under section 17(1)(b) of that Act;

(c) in proceedings under Schedule 5 to the 2004 Act, an order under paragraph 15; or

(d) in proceedings under Schedule 7 to the 2004 Act, an order under paragraph 9(2) or (3) making provision equivalent to an order referred to in paragraph (c);

"pension scheme" means, unless the context otherwise requires, a scheme for which the Board has assumed responsibility in accordance with Chapter 3 of Part 2 of the Pensions Act 2004 (pension protection) or any provision in force in Northern Ireland corresponding to that Chapter;

"PPF compensation" has the meaning given to it –

(a) in proceedings under the 1973 Act, by section 21C of the 1973 Act;

(b) in proceedings under the 1984 Act, by section 18(7) of the 1984 Act; and

(c) in proceedings under the 2004 Act, by paragraph 19F of Schedule 5 to the 2004 Act;

"relevant valuation" means a valuation of pension rights or benefits as at a date not more than 12 months earlier than the date fixed for the first appointment which has been furnished or requested for the purposes of any of the following provisions –

(a) the Pensions on Divorce etc (Provision of Information) Regulations 2000;

(b) regulation 5 of and Schedule 2 to the Occupational Pension Schemes (Disclosure of Information) Regulations 1996 and regulation 11 of and Schedule 1 to the Occupational Pension Schemes (Transfer Value) Regulations 1996;

(c) section 93A or 94(1)(a) or (aa) of the Pension Schemes Act 1993;

(d) section 94(1)(b) of the Pension Schemes Act 1993 or paragraph 2(a) (or, where applicable, 2(b)) of Schedule 2 to the Personal Pension Schemes (Disclosure of Information) Regulations 1987;

(e) the Dissolution etc. (Pensions) Regulations 2005;

"variation order" means –

(a) in proceedings under the 1973 Act, an order under section 31 of that Act; or

(b) in proceedings under the 2004 Act, an order under Part 11 of Schedule 5 to that Act.

(2) References in this Part to a county court are to be construed, in relation to proceedings for a financial order, as references to a divorce county court or a civil partnership proceedings county court, as the case may be.

(3)

    (a) Where an application is made under Article 56 of, and using the form in Annex VII to, the Maintenance Regulation, references in this Part to "financial statement" apply to the applicant as if for the words "financial statement" were substituted "the form in Annex VII to the Maintenance Regulation";

    (aa) where an application for establishment or modification of maintenance is made under Article 10 of the 2007 Hague Convention, references in this Part to "financial statement" apply to the applicant as if for "financial statement" there were substituted "Financial Circumstances Form;

    (b) Sub-paragraphs (a) and (aa) do not apply where the relief sought includes relief which is of a type to which the Maintenance Regulation or the 2007 Hague Convention, as the case may be, does not apply.

Amendments—SI 2011/1328; SI 2012/2806.

Chapter 2
Procedure for Applications

Defined terms—"financial order" is defined in FPR 2010, r 2.3, which provides a list of nine orders defined as a "financial order". This is drawn more widely than previously under FPR 1991, r 2.51B.

Pre-application protocol—This is annexed to FPR PD9A, which outlines the steps that must be taken to provide information before the commencement of all applications for a financial remedy. The "overriding objective" should be borne in mind: "applications should be resolved and a just outcome achieved as speedily as possible without costs being unreasonably incurred … in a manner designed to promote as good a continuing relationship between the parties and any children affected as is possible". There is an ongoing obligation to make "full and frank disclosure of all material facts, documents and other information relevant to the issues". The principle of proportionality in relation to costs must be borne in mind at all times.

Procedure—An application may be made within or following an application for a matrimonial or civil partnership order and is lodged in the county court or the registry of the High Court in which proceedings are taking place, or as provided under FPR 2010, r 9.5(2).

    Subject to the prohibition on application after remarriage under MCA 1973, s 28, there is no time limit for the application. A court may consider an application many years after the divorce: *Twiname v Twiname* [1991] Fam Law 520. It is not an abuse of process for one party to seek an order making provision for the other: *Dart v Dart* [1996] 2 FLR 286 at [296].

    Applications for an order preventing disposition and for interim orders including maintenance pending suit and interim orders may be made and are governed by FPR 2010, Pt 18 procedure.

9.4 When an application for a financial order may be made

An application for a financial order may be made –

    (a) in an application for a matrimonial or civil partnership order; or

    (b) at any time after an application for a matrimonial or civil partnership order has been made.

"An application for a financial order may be made"—Despite the wide terms of this rule, the court's jurisdiction may be excluded in relation to "maintenance" (although not child maintenance) if the parties have agreed in writing that the courts of another Member State shall have jurisdiction: Council Regulation (EC) No 4/2009 (Maintenance Regulation), Art 4. If the paying party remains resident in another Member State in which a decision as to maintenance (including child maintenance), including a dismissal of a spouse's claim, has previously been made, the court's jurisdiction will generally be excluded (Art 8), unlike the position under Brussels I. *M v V (Child Maintenance: Jurisdiction: Brussels I)* [2011] 1 FLR 109 is no longer good law.

Note that "maintenance" for the purposes of the Maintenance Regulation can extend to lump sums and transfers of property if they are for the purpose of providing maintenance or meeting needs: *Van den Boogard v Laumen* [1997] 2 FLR 399.

9.5 Where to start proceedings

(1) An application for a financial remedy must be filed –

  (a) if there are proceedings for a matrimonial order or a civil partnership order which are proceeding in a designated county court, in that court; or

  (b) if there are proceedings for a matrimonial order or a civil partnership order which are proceeding in the High Court, in the registry in which those proceedings are taking place.

(2) In any other case, in relation to the application set out in column 1 of the following table, column 2 sets out where the application must be filed.

Provision under which application is made	*Court where application must be filed*
Section 27 of the 1973 Act.	Divorce county court.
Part 9 of Schedule 5 to the 2004 Act.	Civil partnership proceedings county court.
Part 3 of the 1984 Act.	Principal Registry or, in relation to an application for a consent order, a divorce county court.
Schedule 7 to the 2004 Act.	Principal Registry or, in relation to an application for a consent order, a civil partnership proceedings county court.
Section 35 of the 1973 Act.	High Court, a divorce county court or a magistrates' court.
Paragraph 69 of Schedule 5 to the 2004 Act.	High Court, a civil partnership proceedings county court or a magistrates' court.
Schedule 1 to the 1989 Act.	High Court, designated county court or a magistrates' court.
Part 1 of the 1978 Act.	magistrates' court.
Schedule 6 to the 2004 Act.	magistrates' court.

(3) An application for a financial remedy under Part 3 of the 1984 Act or Schedule 7 to the 2004 Act which is proceeding in the High Court must be heard by a judge, but not a district judge, of that court unless a direction has been made that the application may be heard by a district judge of the principal registry.

> (Rule 8.28 enables a judge to direct that an application for a financial remedy under Part 3 of the 1984 Act or Schedule 7 to the 2004 Act may be heard by a district judge of the principal registry.)

9.6 Application for an order preventing a disposition

(1) The Part 18 procedure applies to an application for an order preventing a disposition.

PART III

(2) An application for an order preventing a disposition may be made without notice to the respondent.

("Order preventing a disposition" is defined in rule 9.3.)

9.7 Application for interim orders

(1) A party may apply at any stage of the proceedings for –

   (a)   an order for maintenance pending suit;
   (b)   an order for maintenance pending outcome of proceedings;
   (c)   an order for interim periodical payments;
   (d)   an interim variation order; or
   (e)   any other form of interim order.

(2) The Part 18 procedure applies to an application for an interim order.

(3) Where a party makes an application before filing a financial statement, the written evidence in support must –

   (a)   explain why the order is necessary; and
   (b)   give up to date information about that party's financial circumstances.

(4) Unless the respondent has filed a financial statement, the respondent must, at least 7 days before the court is to deal with the application, file a statement of his means and serve a copy on the applicant.

(5) An application for an order mentioned in paragraph (1)(e) may be made without notice.

Application for interim orders—The various types of interim orders are defined here, but the operation of r 9.7(1)(e) means that r 9.7 will also apply to other interim orders, such as legal services orders in relation to costs. Part 18 procedure applies: see FPR 2010, Pt 18 and PD18A. It is envisaged that an applicant may make their application at the beginning of proceedings before filing their Form E and a without notice application is permissible. Where there is no financial statement, the written evidence in support must state why the order is necessary and provide up-to-date information about that party's current financial circumstances; if the application is prior to the filing of the respondent's financial statement, the respondent must file and serve a statement of means.

9.8 Application for periodical payments order at same rate as an order for maintenance pending suit

(1) This rule applies where there are matrimonial proceedings and –

   (a)   a decree nisi of divorce or nullity of marriage has been made;
   (b)   at or after the date of the decree nisi an order for maintenance pending suit is in force; and
   (c)   the spouse in whose favour the decree nisi was made has made an application for an order for periodical payments.

(2) The spouse in whose favour the decree nisi was made may apply, using the Part 18 procedure, for an order providing for payments at the same rate as those provided for by the order for maintenance pending suit.

9.9 Application for periodical payments order at same rate as an order for maintenance pending outcome of proceedings

(1) This rule applies where there are civil partnership proceedings and –

   (a)   a conditional order of dissolution or nullity of civil partnership has been made;
   (b)   at or after the date of the conditional order an order for maintenance pending outcome of proceedings is in force;

(c) the civil partner in whose favour the conditional order was made has made an application for an order for periodical payments.

(2) The civil partner in whose favour the conditional order was made may apply, using the Part 18 procedure, for an order providing for payments at the same rate as those provided for by, the order for maintenance pending the outcome of proceedings.

Chapter 3
Applications for Financial Remedies for Children

9.10 Application by parent, guardian etc for financial remedy in respect of children

(1) The following people may apply for a financial remedy in respect of a child –

(a) a parent, guardian or special guardian of any child of the family;

(b) any person in whose favour a residence order has been made with respect to a child of the family, and any applicant for such an order;

(c) any other person who is entitled to apply for a residence order with respect to a child;

(d) a local authority, where an order has been made under section 31(1)(a) of the 1989 Act placing a child in its care;

(e) the Official Solicitor, if appointed the children's guardian of a child of the family under rule 16.24; and

(f) a child of the family who has been given permission to apply for a financial remedy.

(2) In this rule "residence order" has the meaning given to it by section 8(1) of the 1989 Act.

Defined terms—"financial remedy" is defined in FPR 2010, r 2.2 as a "financial order" made under MCA 1973 and the 2004 Act, together with orders under other specified statutes. The statutes are defined in FPR 2010, r 2.3.

Scope—This rule sets out the categories of people who may apply for a financial remedy in respect of a child. Where the application includes an application for a variation of settlement, the court must (unless satisfied that the child is not adversely affected) direct that the child be separately represented.

9.11 Children to be separately represented on certain applications

(1) Where an application for a financial remedy includes an application for an order for a variation of settlement, the court must, unless it is satisfied that the proposed variation does not adversely affect the rights or interests of any child concerned, direct that the child be separately represented on the application.

(2) On any other application for a financial remedy the court may direct that the child be separately represented on the application.

(3) Where a direction is made under paragraph (1) or (2), the court may if the person to be appointed so consents, appoint –

(a) a person other than the Official Solicitor; or

(b) the Official Solicitor,

to be a children's guardian and rule 16.24(5) and (6) and rules 16.25 to 16.28 apply as appropriate to such an appointment.

Chapter 4
Procedure in the High Court and County Court after Filing an Application

9.12 Duties of the court and the applicant upon issuing an application

(1) When an application under this Part is issued in the High Court or in a county court –

  (a) the court will fix a first appointment not less than 12 weeks and not more than 16 weeks after the date of the filing of the application; and

  (b) subject to paragraph (2), within 4 days beginning with the date on which the application was filed, a court officer will –

  (i) serve a copy of the application on the respondent; and

  (ii) give notice of the date of the first appointment to the applicant and the respondent.

(2) Where the applicant wishes to serve a copy of the application on the respondent and on filing the application so notifies the court –

  (a) paragraph (1)(b) does not apply;

  (b) a court officer will return to the applicant the copy of the application and the notice of the date of the first appointment; and

  (c) the applicant must, –

  (i) within 4 days beginning with the date on which the copy of the application is received from the court, serve the copy of the application and notice of the date of the first appointment on the respondent; and

  (ii) file a certificate of service at or before the first appointment.

  (Rule 6.37 sets out what must be included in a certificate of service)

(3) The date fixed under paragraph (1), or for any subsequent appointment, must not be cancelled except with the court's permission and, if cancelled, the court must immediately fix a new date.

(4) In relation to an application to which the Maintenance Regulation or the 2007 Hague Convention applies, where the applicant does not already know the address of the respondent at the time the application is issued, paragraph (2) does not apply and the court will serve the application in accordance with paragraph (1).

Amendments—SI 2011/1328; SI 2012/2806.

Scope—This rule deals with the duties of the court upon the issuing of an application. The application is in the prescribed form referred to in FPR PD5A, namely by a document entitled Form A. A first appointment shall be fixed within 12–16 weeks after the date of the filing of the application. Service upon the respondent may be by the court or the applicant and must be within 4 days beginning on the date that the application was filed. Pre-action disclosure of information and negotiations that are cost effective and issue-based are still required by the Pre-Application Protocol: see FPR PD9A.

  Hearing dates may not be cancelled save with the court's permission: the court, not the parties, is in control of the timetable.

9.13 Service of application on mortgagees, trustees etc

(1) Where an application for a financial remedy includes an application for an order for a variation of settlement, the applicant must serve copies of the application on –

  (a) the trustees of the settlement;

  (b) the settlor if living; and

  (c) such other persons as the court directs.

(2) In the case of an application for an avoidance of disposition order, the applicant must serve copies of the application on the person in whose favour the disposition is alleged to have been made.

(3) Where an application for a financial remedy includes an application relating to land, the applicant must serve a copy of the application on any mortgagee of whom particulars are given in the application.

(4) Any person served under paragraphs (1), (2) or (3) may make a request to the court in writing, within 14 days beginning with the date of service of the application, for a copy of the applicant's financial statement or any relevant part of that statement.

(5) Any person who –

    (a)   is served with copies of the application in accordance with paragraphs (1), (2) or (3); or

    (b)   receives a copy of a financial statement, or a relevant part of that statement, following an application made under paragraph (4),

may within 14 days beginning with the date of service or receipt file a statement in answer.

(6) Where a copy of an application is served under paragraphs (1), (2) or (3), the applicant must file a certificate of service at or before the first appointment.

(7) A statement in answer filed under paragraph (5) must be verified by a statement of truth.

9.14 Procedure before the first appointment

(1) Not less than 35 days before the first appointment both parties must simultaneously exchange with each other and file with the court a financial statement in the form referred to in Practice Direction 5A.

(2) The financial statement must –

    (a)   be verified by a statement of truth; and

    (b)   accompanied by the following documents only –

        (i)   any documents required by the financial statement;

        (ii)   any other documents necessary to explain or clarify any of the information contained in the financial statement; and

        (iii)   any documents provided to the party producing the financial statement by a person responsible for a pension arrangement, either following a request under rule 9.30 or as part of a relevant valuation; and

        (iv)   any notification or other document referred to in rule 9.37(2), (4) or (5) which has been received by the party producing the financial statement.

(2A) The requirement of paragraph (2)(a) relating to verification by a statement of truth does not apply to the financial statement of either party where the application has been made under –

    (a)   Article 56 of the Maintenance Regulation, using the form in Annex VII to that Regulation; or

    (b)   Article 10 of the 2007 Hague Convention, using the Financial Circumstances Form,

and the relief sought is limited to a type to which that Regulation or that Convention, as appropriate, applies, but the court may at any time direct that the financial statement of either party shall be verified by a statement of truth.

(3) Where a party was unavoidably prevented from sending any document required by the financial statement, that party must at the earliest opportunity –

    (a)   serve a copy of that document on the other party; and

    (b)   file a copy of that document with the court, together with a written explanation of the failure to send it with the financial statement.

(4) No disclosure or inspection of documents may be requested or given between the filing of the application for a financial remedy and the first appointment, except –

   (a)   copies sent with the financial statement, or in accordance with paragraph (3); or

   (b)   in accordance with paragraphs (5) and (6).

      (Rule 21.1 explains what is meant by disclosure and inspection.)

(5) Not less than 14 days before the hearing of the first appointment, each party must file with the court and serve on the other party –

   (a)   a concise statement of the issues between the parties;

   (b)   a chronology;

   (c)   a questionnaire setting out by reference to the concise statement of issues any further information and documents requested from the other party or a statement that no information and documents are required; and

   (d)   a notice stating whether that party will be in a position at the first appointment to proceed on that occasion to a FDR appointment.

(6) Not less than 14 days before the hearing of the first appointment, the applicant must file with the court and serve on the respondent confirmation –

   (a)   of the names of all persons served in accordance with rule 9.13(1) to (3); and

   (b)   that there are no other persons who must be served in accordance with those paragraphs.

Amendments—SI 2011/1328; SI 2012/679; SI 2012/2806.

Procedure before first appointment—This governs what the parties must do leading up to the first appointment. By 35 days before the first appointment, the parties must simultaneously exchange a financial statement in the prescribed form referred to in PD5A, namely Form E, verified by a statement of truth, accompanied by a limited category of documents. No disclosure or inspection of the parties' documents may be given between the filing of the application and the first appointment, save as laid down in r 9.14(4).

Documents to be exchanged and filed before first appointment—Rule 9.14(6) stipulates that by 14 days before the first directions appointment, each party must file and serve a concise statement, chronology, questionnaire and a notice stating whether that party will be in a position to use the hearing as a financial dispute resolution appointment. In addition, the parties should if possible exchange additional documents as defined in FPR PD9A. These are an agreed case summary, a schedule of assets and details of any directions sought by the parties, including, where appropriate, the name of any proposed expert.

9.15 Duties of the court at the first appointment

(1) The first appointment must be conducted with the objective of defining the issues and saving costs.

(2) At the first appointment the court must determine –

   (a)   the extent to which any questions seeking information under rule 9.14(5)(c) must be answered; and

   (b)   what documents requested under rule 9.14(5)(c) must be produced,

and give directions for the production of such further documents as may be necessary.

(3) The court must give directions where appropriate about –

   (a)   the valuation of assets (including the joint instruction of joint experts);

   (b)   obtaining and exchanging expert evidence, if required;

   (c)   the evidence to be adduced by each party; and

   (d)   further chronologies or schedules to be filed by each party.

(4) If the court decides that a referral to a FDR appointment is appropriate it must direct that the case be referred to a FDR appointment.

(5) If the court decides that a referral to a FDR appointment is not appropriate it must direct one or more of the following –

(a)   that a further directions appointment be fixed;

(b)   that an appointment be fixed for the making of an interim order;

(c)   that the case be fixed for a final hearing and, where that direction is given, the court must determine the judicial level at which the case should be heard.

(By rule 3.3 the court may also direct that the case be adjourned if it considers that alternative dispute resolution is appropriate.)

(6) In considering whether to make a costs order under rule 28.3(5), the court must have particular regard to the extent to which each party has complied with the requirement to send documents with the financial statement and the explanation given for any failure to comply.

(7) The court may –

(a)   where an application for an interim order has been listed for consideration at the first appointment, make an interim order;

(b)   having regard to the contents of the notice filed by the parties under rule 9.14(5)(d), treat the appointment (or part of it) as a FDR appointment to which rule 9.17 applies;

(c)   in a case where a pension sharing order or a pension attachment order is requested, direct any party with pension rights to file and serve a Pension Inquiry Form, completed in full or in part as the court may direct; and

(d)   in a case where a pension compensation sharing order or a pension compensation attachment order is requested, direct any party with PPF compensation rights to file and serve a Pension Protection Fund Inquiry Form, completed in full or in part as the court may direct.

(8) Both parties must personally attend the first appointment unless the court directs otherwise.

Scope—The procedure under the previous r 2.61D is unchanged. At the first appointment, the court in pursuance of the overriding objective in FPR 2010, Pt 1 will actively manage the financial application in relation to defining the issues and saving costs: disclosure, expert evidence and the extent of other evidence will be considered. The next hearing will be timetabled, normally to the financial dispute resolution (FDR) appointment. Costs will be considered. Both parties must attend in person. After the first appointment, there is no further provision for the disclosure of documents except with permission of the court.

Directions at the first appointment—Replies to questionnaires, requests for documents, expert evidence including valuation evidence will be directed by the court, in line with the overriding objective.

(i)   *Questionnaires seeking information*   The overriding objective determines that only relevant and necessary information will be ordered. The judge will go through the questionnaires, determining which questions should be answered, and in what manner. Questions that are irrelevant, oppressive or more appropriately asked in cross-examination will be disallowed. Conversely, issues that may prove fatal to an FDR hearing if not addressed in advance may be properly directed in questionnaires.

(ii) *Disclosure of documents*   The overriding objective suggests that only documents that are relevant, necessary and proportionate will be directed to be disclosed.

(iii) *Valuation of assets*   The use of experts in financial proceedings is now governed by amendments to Practice Directions (see FPR PD25D). Specific guidance is given for the use of single joint experts. In financial proceedings, there is no requirement for the court's permission to be obtained before the instruction of an expert. Permission is required for the report of a single joint expert to be placed before the court. The test for permission in r 3.1 follows current practice in financial remedy proceedings: the expert evidence must be in the opinion of the court necessary to assist the court to resolve the proceedings. See also FPR PD25A–PD25F.

(iv) *Other evidence*   At the first appointment, the court may give directions in relation to what other evidence may be called and the form that evidence should take. Directions may be given where a party wishes to assert a prenuptial agreement: *Crossley v Crossley* [2008] 1 FLR 1467.

(v)   *Joinder and other case management issues*   As part of the case-management function of the court, the position of third parties and interveners should be considered as early as possible. Provision for the joinder of parties derives from RSC 1965, Ord 15, r 6(2)(b) and CPR 1998, r 19.2(2), and is now expressly provided for under r 9.26B.

Where property is in a respondent's name but is held by a third party, there is a clear obligation to the applicant to join that party as a party at an early stage: *TL v ML (Ancillary Relief: Claims against Assets of Extended Family)* [2006] 1 FLR 1263, followed in *Fisher Meredith v JH and PH (Financial Remedy: Appeal: Wasted Costs)* [2012] 2 FLR 536. Conversely, where a respondent has legal title to property that is subject to a third-party claim, prima facie the legal and beneficial interests lie with the respondent: *Stack v Dowden* [2007] 1 FLR 1858 applying. The applicant could seek to join the non-legal owner if she wished, but is under no obligation to do so: *Fisher Meredith v JH and PH* (Rev 2), above.

Trustees need not routinely be joined as parties because a trust point is being run; however, a hostile trust dispute will require the joinder of the trustees: *A v A (No 2)* [2008] 1 FLR 1428. A company alleged to be the depository of most of a husband's wealth was held by the Court of Appeal to have been correctly joined in financial proceedings and the decision of the judge to apply the FPR not the CPR and to order a trial of the preliminary issue in relation to the company was "wise and well founded on authority": *Goldstone v Goldstone* [2011] 1 FLR 1926. There is power to depart from standard procedures: in *Crossley v Crossley* [2008] 1 FLR 1467, the CA approved directions for a preliminary trial on the issue of a prenuptial agreement: a Form E should be filed without documentation and questionnaires be dispensed with, pending a hearing in which the wife should demonstrate why the prenuptial agreement should not stand.

(vi) *Jurisdiction*   Cases of exceptional complexity should be transferred to the High Court for allocation to a High Court judge for case management. This should be done ideally at the outset or at the first appointment. Transfer to the High Court is governed by *PD of 3 November 2008: Allocation and Transfer of Proceedings* (see Part V). Where both parties seek transfer before the first appointment, a certificate must be filed stating why the application is suitable for the High Court. Assets in excess of £10 million, or where there are significant issues concerning non-disclosure, complex family or offshore holdings or the identification of non-matrimonial assets or a novel point of law may be certified by the parties as fit for transfer, before a judicial decision at the first appointment. The FDR will be listed with a time estimate normally of 1 day. Management from the outset by a High Court judge may prevent delay and limit costs: *P v P (Financial Relief: Procedure)* [2009] 1 FLR 696.

Fixing the next stage—The court will usually fix a FDR appointment, but may fix a final hearing, fix a further directions appointment, treat the hearing as FDR with the consent of the parties or adjourn for mediation or negotiation.

Attendance of media representatives at a first appointment—Provided for by FPR 2010, r 27.11. Representatives of accredited media have the right to attend the first appointment. The court may exclude the media, where this is necessary under r 27.11(3) or where justice would be impeded or prejudiced. The press must have the opportunity to make representations: *D v D (Divorce: Media Presence)* [2009] 2 FLR 324; *Spencer v Spencer* [2009] 2 FLR 1416, where the court refused to exclude the press. See commentary under r 27.11.

Ongoing duty of disclosure: first appointment—The duty to disclose and the standard to be expected has long been established by the Court of Appeal in *J v J* [1955] 2 All ER 617: disclosure was to be "full, frank and clear". PD9A (Application for a Financial Remedy) underlines the obligation of the parties to make full disclosure of all material facts, documents and information relevant to the issues. Solicitors have a duty to tell their clients in clear terms of this obligation and of the possible consequences of a breach. This duty of disclosure is an ongoing obligation, especially as the final hearing approaches, and includes the duty to disclose any material changes after initial disclosure has been given: FPR PD9A and CPR 1998, r 31.11. In *Bokor-Ingram v Bokor-Ingram* [2009] 2 FLR 922, the CA reminded practitioners that the principle of full and frank disclosure in *J v J* had never varied. Furthermore, "the duty to disclose in ancillary relief cases extends beyond what is certain ... to any fact relevant to the court's review of the foreseeable future": *I v I (Ancillary Relief: Disclosure)* [2009] 1 FLR 201 disapproved. See also *V v V (Financial Relief)* [2010] 2 FLR 516. Where an order for ancillary relief has been vitiated by non-disclosure, the court may make such additional or different provision as would have been made at the time had proper disclosure been given: *Kingdon v Kingdon* [2011] 1 FLR 1409, CA. For a recent review of the authorities in relation to the duty of disclosure see *NG v SG (Appeal: Non-Disclosure)* [2012] 1 FLR 1211. Full disclosure to the wife, including sensitive documents connected with the husband's criminal conviction for money-laundering was ordered, subject to the condition of her undertaking not to disclose the documents further, save for use in her financial applications: *P v P* [2012] EWHC 1733 (Fam).

Disclosure: the millionaire's defence— That a wealthy respondent may avoid giving full disclosure by asserting that he could meet any order that the court could reasonably make (*Dart v Dart* [1996] 2 FLR 286) has been limited in *White v White* [2000] 2 FLR 981 and *Lambert v Lambert* [2003] 1 FLR 139. The emphasis by the Supreme Court on "fairness" rather than "reasonable needs" in *Miller v Miller; McFarlane v McFarlane* [2006] 1 FLR 1186, and the overriding objective to deal with a case "justly", balancing proportionality and saving expense while ensuring that both parties are on an equal footing, is likely to override a party's objections to full disclosure.

Disclosure: self-help—The circumstances in which a party may acquire and use for the purpose of litigation documents belonging to the other party have long been subject to so-called "*Hildebrand* Rules" (*Hildebrand v Hildebrand* [1992] 1 FLR 244), requiring the prompt disclosure of such documents. The use of such material was permitted where non-disclosure was reasonably anticipated (*T v T (Interception of Documents)* [1994] 2 FLR 1083) and could include the recovery of documents deleted from a computer hard drive (*L v L* [2007] 2 FLR 171). However, in *White v Withers LLP and Dearle* [2010] 1 FLR 859 the court would not sanction the use of force to obtain documents or the interception of documents. The CA has given guidance in *Imerman v Tchenguiz* [2010] 2 FLR 814, where the wife was in possession of confidential documents downloaded by her brothers from the husband's password-protected computer. The husband's Article 8 rights to privacy had been breached by an unlawful act. *Hildebrand* Rules are "not good law and could not be justified on any basis including lawful excuse, self-help or public interest". The duty of full and frank disclosure still lies with the parties. Fear that the other side might conceal documents did not justify illegal self-help that breached confidence. Where there is concern that evidence should not be wrongly destroyed or concealed, the remedy lay in search and seize orders in the High Court, and in freezing orders. Where a party has had recourse to documents by unlawful means, the court had the power to exclude such documents and would be guided by what was necessary for disposing of the case fairly and would take into account the importance of the evidence and the conduct of the parties.

Disclosure from third parties—Disclosure of documents held by third parties will be considered, if necessary or proportionate to the case. For principles applied in determining such applications, see *M v M (Third Party Subpoena: Financial Conduct)* [2006] 2 FLR 1253. A third party who attends court under a subpoena duces tecum is entitled to the costs of compliance and conduct money. Where information may be held by a third party, the party seeking its disclosure may be ordered to use his best endeavours to obtain information: *G v G (Financial Provision: Discovery)* [1992] 1 FLR 40. In contrast to ordinary civil litigation, a request by a wife for documents held by a non-party is not limited to those whose existence is already known, as a wife would be unlikely to have that knowledge: "… the wife is entitled to go fishing in the Family Division within the limits of law and practice": *Charman v Charman* [2006] 2 FLR 422, CA, following *Parra v Parra* [2003] 1 FLR 942, CA. See FPR 2010, rr 20.2(1)(i) (orders for disclosure of documents against a non-party as an interim remedy) and 21.2 (orders for disclosure against a person not a party).

Enforcement of order to provide information or documents—If an order made for the disclosure of information or documents is not complied with by the designated date, an application may be made for an order that the defaulting party files serves the document within a specified date from service of the order, endorsed with a penal notice. The order endorsed with the penal notice should be served by a process server with an affidavit of service lodged at court. In default of compliance, application may be made to commit.

Power to make a costs order—See FPR 2010, r 28.3(5),(6). In considering whether to make a costs order, the court must have regard to the extent to which a party has complied with the requirement to send documents with the financial statement, and the explanation given for any failure to comply.

Pension sharing and attachment—If a pension order is sought, the person responsible for the pension arrangement must be served under FPR 2010, rr 9.31 and 9.33. Information as to the cash equivalent transfer value of any pension is required in the statement of financial information. Directions may be needed at the first appointment in relation to evidence from a pensions expert in relation to the appropriate pension share or attachment. A party with pension rights may be directed to file a Pension Inquiry Form, or a Pension Protection Fund Inquiry Form, as appropriate.

9.16 After the first appointment

(1) Between the first appointment and the FDR appointment, a party is not entitled to the production of any further documents except –

    (a)   in accordance with directions given under rule 9.15(2); or

    (b)   with the permission of the court.

(2) At any stage –

    (a)   a party may apply for further directions or a FDR appointment;

    (b)   the court may give further directions or direct that parties attend a FDR appointment.

No further production of documents without permission—The request for the disclosure of information and documents 14 days before the first appointment, together with the directions made in the hearing, is intended as a one-window opportunity to request disclosure. Permission is needed for further disclosure of documents after the first appointment, sought by separate application on notice for a directions appointment under r 9.16.

9.17 The FDR appointment

(1) The FDR appointment must be treated as a meeting held for the purposes of discussion and negotiation.

(2) The judge hearing the FDR appointment must have no further involvement with the application, other than to conduct any further FDR appointment or to make a consent order or a further directions order.

(3) Not less than 7 days before the FDR appointment, the applicant must file with the court details of all offers and proposals, and responses to them.

(4) Paragraph (3) includes any offers, proposals or responses made wholly or partly without prejudice[GL], but paragraph (3) does not make any material admissible as evidence if, but for that paragraph, it would not be admissible.

(5) At the conclusion of the FDR appointment, any documents filed under paragraph (3), and any filed documents referring to them, must, at the request of the party who filed them, be returned to that party and not retained on the court file.

(6) Parties attending the FDR appointment must use their best endeavours to reach agreement on matters in issue between them.

(7) The FDR appointment may be adjourned from time to time.

(8) At the conclusion of the FDR appointment, the court may make an appropriate consent order.

(9) If the court does not make an appropriate consent order as mentioned in paragraph (8), the court must give directions for the future course of the proceedings including, where appropriate –

    (a)   the filing of evidence, including up to date information; and

    (b)   fixing a final hearing date.

(10) Both parties must personally attend the FDR appointment unless the court directs otherwise.

Scope—The FDR is normally the second court hearing in a claim for a financial order. It is defined in FPR PD9A as a "meeting held for the purpose of discussion and negotiation". The rules do not provide for FDRs to take place in the magistrates' courts. See the Family Justice Council's *FDR Appointments: Best Practice Guidance* (December 2012) for valuable guidance on all aspects of FDRs, including preparation, documentation, conduct of the FDR, the role of the judge, agreements and costs. The court expects both parties to place their cards face up on the table and to make and respond to offers. All offers, whether expressed to be "open" or "without prejudice", must be disclosed to the court, so that the judge can advise the parties of the likely outcome if the matter were contested and examine how the issues between them may be resolved in the light of the costs implications and delay in waiting for a final hearing.

Admissibility—So that the parties approach the FDR openly and without reservation, anything said at the FDR appointment is not admissible in any subsequent proceedings, (except where an offence is committed at the hearing). See FPR PD9A.

Further judicial involvement—Where agreement is not reached, r 9.17(2) directs that the judge who conducts the appointment has no further involvement with the financial application and may not hear an application to extend the costs allowance beyond the FDR: *Currey v Currey (No 2)* [2007] 1 FLR 946, CA. A judge who made a consent order at the conclusion of a successful FDR could not then decide subsidiary issues that the parties had subsequently failed to agree: *Myerson v Myerson* [2009] 1 FLR 826, CA. Once the issues are determined and the order is made, a FDR judge may hear an application for variation of that order: *G v G (Role of FDR Judge)* [2007] 1 FLR 237.

Requirement to file details of offers—Seven days before the FDR appointment, the applicant must file details of all offers and proposals and responses to them. At the end of the appointment, the parties should request the return of the schedule of offers and proposals and any other privileged documents submitted during the course of the FDR.

Attendance of media representatives is not permitted at FDR—By FPR 2010, r 27.11(1)(a), the right of the media to be present at private hearings is specifically excluded from "judicially assisted conciliation or negotiation".

Active case management where failure to reach agreement—Rule 9.17(9) provides that if the FDR does not result in a consent order, the court will fix a date for the final hearing and give all the necessary case-management directions. The importance of the FDR is such that where a FDR has not been effective, the court may permit another appointment as soon as is practicable, so an experienced tribunal could engage with the matter: *S v S (Ancillary Relief: Importance of FDR)* [2008] 1 FLR 944. The duty of full and frank disclosure continues after FDR. Where a final hearing is unavoidable, the court should direct s 25 narrative statements to identify the issues upon which the court is being asked to adjudicate and for the broader presentation of the factual background relevant to the s 25 exercise. This is particularly important where there are factual disputes or allegations in relation to conduct or dishonesty, so that the basis of each party's case is clear and to reduce the extent of oral evidence: *J v J* [2009] EWHC 2654. The court may also consider the need to list further hearings upon the application of the parties, to deal with maintenance pending suit/interim maintenance and applications for legal services orders, to be listed before another judge in compliance with r 9.17(2).

Steps to be taken if agreement is reached at FDR—The judge should be told in full the terms of the agreement. If at all possible, a detailed consent order signed by both parties and their legal representatives should be handed to the judge, so that the order may be approved and sealed immediately. Where agreement is reached, the court may dispense with the filing of a statement of information: FPR 2010, r 9.26(5)(a). If the issues are complicated, written Heads of Agreement should be signed by the parties and their legal representatives and handed to the judge. The Heads of Agreement are important evidence of consensus and will carry weight if a party subsequently resiles from the agreement. Practitioners must be clear in explaining to their clients when making the Heads of Agreement that either (i) the agreement is understood and agreed to be a binding agreement but not yet expressed in the form of an order, because the parties are awaiting a point of drafting or detail: *Xydhias v Xydhias* [1999] 1 FLR 683, CA; or (ii) the agreement is approved as an unperfected order of the court: *Rose v Rose* [2002] 1 FLR 978. The FJC's *Best Practice Guidance* (December 2012) recommends that where appropriate, it should be recorded on the face of the signed and dated Agreement whether it is understood to be a binding agreement (*Xydhias*) or an approved agreement that is an order of the court (*Rose*). Where a final or perfected order is unavailable, it is the duty of the court to case manage the application to its conclusion, by listing for a 5-minute Mention in an appropriate time frame such as 2–4 weeks to be vacated upon the lodging of a typed draft order signed by the parties. The mention hearing may be adjourned as necessary, or further directions may be given.

Issues about agreements—In the event of a dispute about whether an agreement has been reached, and whether there is jurisdiction to make a subsequent order in those terms, a hearing will be necessary, but must not be before the judge who conducted the FDR hearing, to determine the point. The court will consider all of the circumstances, but formal agreements properly arrived at with competent legal advice should not be displaced unless there are "good and substantial grounds for concluding that an injustice would be done" by upholding the agreement. See also *Edgar v Edgar* (1981) 2 FLR 19, CA and *Xydhias v Xydhias* [1999] 1 FLR 683, CA: "ordinarily, heads of agreement signed by the parties or a clear exchange of solicitors' letters would establish consensus", although the agreement may still be vitiated by material non-disclosure. See also *Smith v McInerney* [1994] 2 FLR 1077; *X v X (Y and Z intervening)* [2002] 1 FLR 508. The same principles apply to agreements made through court-directed mediation: *Rothwell v Rothwell* [2009] 2 FLR 96.

See commentary to MCA 1973, s 7 for the procedure where there is an issue about whether an agreement has been made. Without prejudice documents will usually have to be seen by the court to determine the issue of whether an agreement has been made, and should be lodged in a sealed envelope: then, if no agreement is found, the hearing should be listed before another judge.

Bundles—In compliance with r 9.17(3),(4), the court must see written evidence of the parties offers, proposals and responses, which should be filed by the applicant. As the FDR hearing is conventionally listed for 1 hour, PD27A, para 2.4 applies: in hearings in the PRFD and in family proceedings in all other courts, cases listed for an hour or less do not require bundles. However, it is good practice to provide a concise bundle for the judge, to include skeleton arguments, asset schedules, written offers and responses and Forms E without their attached documentation. Rule 9.17(5) provides that documents filed under r 9.17(3) shall be returned to the parties at the conclusion of the hearing so that without prejudice material does not lie on the court file.

Costs at FDR stage—FPR 2010 r 28.3(5),(6) applies. The general rule is that one party will not be required to pay the costs of another party, but a costs order may be appropriate because of the conduct of a party in relation to the proceedings. Costs against a party may be ordered at FDR stage for a refusal to negotiate, or any failure to comply with the FPRs and any order of the court or practice direction. See FPR 2010, r 28(3) and FPR PD28A in relation to costs.

Chapter 5
Procedure in the Magistrates' Court after Filing an Application

9.18 Duties of the court and the applicant upon filing an application

(1) When an application for an order under this Part is issued in a magistrates' court –

- (a) the court will fix a first hearing date not less than 4 weeks and not more than 8 weeks after the date of the filing of the application; and
- (b) subject to paragraph (2), within 4 days beginning with the date on which the application was filed, a court officer will –
  - (i) serve a copy of the application on the respondent;
  - (ii) give notice of the date of the first hearing to the applicant and the respondent; and
  - (iii) send a blank financial statement to both the applicant and the respondent.

(2) Where the applicant wishes to serve a copy of the application on the respondent and, on filing the application, so notifies the court –

- (a) paragraph (1)(b) does not apply;
- (b) a court officer will return to the applicant the copy of the application and the notice of the date of the first hearing; and
- (c) the applicant must –
  - (i) within 4 days beginning with the date on which the copy of the application is received from the court, serve the copy of the application and notice of the date of the first hearing on the respondent;
  - (ii) send a blank financial statement to the respondent; and
  - (iii) file a certificate of service at or before the first hearing.

(3) The date fixed under paragraph (1), or for any other subsequent hearing or appointment must not be cancelled except with the court's permission and, if cancelled, the court must immediately fix a new date.

(4) The requirement in paragraph (1)(b)(iii) for the court officer to send a blank financial statement to the applicant does not apply where the application has been made under –

- (a) Article 56 of the Maintenance Regulation, using the form in Annex VII to that Regulation; or
- (b) Article 10 of the 2007 Hague Convention, using the Financial Circumstances Form.

(5) In relation to an application to which the Maintenance Regulation or the 2007 Hague Convention applies, where the applicant does not already know the address of the respondent at the time the application is issued, paragraph (2) does not apply and the court will serve the application in accordance with paragraph (1).

Amendments—SI 2011/1328; SI 2012/2806.

Maintenance Regulation and 2007 Hague Convention proceedings (r 9.18(4),(5))—An applicant for maintenance from another Member State of the EU must apply using forms annexed to the Maintenance Regulation rather than the usual domestic forms. Similarly, applicants from non-EU Contracting States under the 2007 Hague Convention will use the financial circumstances form published under Art 11(4) of the 2007 Convention. The court is required to serve the issued application and accompanying documentation where the applicant does not know the respondent's address so as to reduce the potential risk of domestic violence resulting from the applicant discovering the whereabouts of the respondent as a result of the service process.

9.19 Procedure before the first hearing

(1) Not more than 14 days after the date of the issue of the application both parties must simultaneously exchange with each other and file with the court a financial statement referred to in Practice Direction 5A.

(2) The financial statement must –

    (a)   be verified by a statement of truth; and

    (b)   contain the following documents only –

        (i)   any documents required by the financial statement; and

        (ii) any other documents necessary to explain or clarify any of the information contained in the financial statement.

(2A) The requirement of paragraph (2)(a) relating to verification by statement of truth does not apply to the financial statement of either party where the application has been made under –

    (a)   Article 56 of the Maintenance Regulation, using the form in Annex VII to that Regulation; or

    (b)   Article 10 of the 2007 Hague Convention, using the Financial Circumstances Form, but the court may at any time direct that the financial statement of either party shall be verified by a statement of truth.

(3) Where a party was unavoidably prevented from sending any document required by the financial statement, that party must at the earliest opportunity –

    (a)   serve a copy of that document on the other party; and

    (b)   file a copy of that document with the court, together with a statement explaining the failure to send it with the financial statement.

(4) No disclosure or inspection of documents may be requested or given between the filing of the application for a financial remedy and the first hearing except copies sent with the financial statement or in accordance with paragraph (3).

    (Rule 21.1 explains what is meant by disclosure and inspection.)

Amendments—SI 2011/1328, SI 2012/679; SI 2012/2806.

"verified by a statement of truth" (r 9.19(2)(a))—FPR 2010, Pt 17 and FPR PD17A prescribe the form that a statement of truth must take and who may sign it. This requirement does not apply, unless directed by the court, where the application is made by a party from another EU Member State under the Maintenance Regulation or from a non-EU Contracting State under the 2007 Hague Convention as the forms to be used are those prescribed by the relevant Regulation or Convention.

9.20 Power of the court to direct filing of evidence and set dates for further hearings

Unless the court is able to determine the application at the first hearing the court may direct that further evidence be filed and set a date for a directions hearing or appointment or final hearing.

9.21 Who the respondent is on an application under section 20 or section 20A of the 1978 Act or Part 6 of Schedule 6 to the 2004 Act

In relation to proceedings set out in column 1 of the following table, column 2 sets out who the respondents to those proceedings will be.

Proceedings	Respondent
Application under section 20 of the 1978 Act, except an application for variation of an order.	The other party to the marriage; and where the order to which the application relates requires periodical payments to be made to, or in respect of, a child who is 16 years of age or over, that child.
Application under paragraphs 30 to 34 of Schedule 6 to the 2004 Act, except an application for variation of an order.	The other party to the civil partnership; and where the order to which the application relates requires periodical payments to be made to, or in respect of, a child who is 16 years of age or over, that child.
Application for the revival of an order under section 20A of the 1978 Act or paragraph 40 of Schedule 6 to the 2004 Act.	The parties to the proceedings leading to the order which it is sought to have revived.

"except an application for variation of an order"—Applications for variation or enforcement of periodical payments orders do not fall within the definition of family proceedings for the purpose of MCA 1980, s 65. FPR 2010 do not apply automatically to such proceedings. However, see MC(EVOFP & MP)R 2011, r 69, which applies FPR 2010 generally to variation applications under s 20 of the 1978 Act and paras 30–34 of Sch 6 to the 2004 Act and FPR 2010, rr 9.10, 9.21 with modification.

9.22 Application in a magistrates' court for a maintenance order, or revocation of a maintenance order to which the 1982 Act, the Lugano Convention, the 1988 Convention or the Maintenance Regulation applies

(1) This rule applies where a person makes an application to a magistrates' court for a maintenance order, or for the revocation of a maintenance order, in relation to which the court has jurisdiction by virtue of the 1982 Act, the Lugano Convention, the 1988 Convention or the Maintenance Regulation, and the respondent is outside the United Kingdom.

(2) Where the respondent does not enter an appearance and is not represented at the Hearing –

   (a) the court will apply the provisions of Article 20 of the 1968 Convention, Article 20 of the 1988 Convention, Article 26 of the Lugano Convention, or Article 11 of the Maintenance Regulation as appropriate;

   (b) where the court proceeds to hear the application having applied the appropriate provision referred to in sub-paragraph (a), the court will take into account any written representations made and any evidence given by the respondent under these rules.

(3) This rule does not apply in relation to proceedings to vary a maintenance order.

(4) In this rule –

   (a) "the 1982 Act", "the Lugano Convention" and "the 1988 Convention" have the meanings given to them in rule 34.1(2);

(b) "the 1968 Convention" has the meaning given to it in the Civil Jurisdiction and Judgments Act 1982.

(Rules made under section 144 of the Magistrates' Courts Act 1980 make provision for applications to vary maintenance orders made in magistrates' courts.)

Amendments—Substituted by SI 2011/1328.

Scope—This rule prescribes the procedure where a respondent who is outside the UK does not attend a hearing on an application for maintenance in a cross-border case to which the 1982 Act, the Lugano Convention, the 1988 Convention or the Maintenance Regulation applies. The countries concerned are the Members States of the EU, Iceland, Norway and Switzerland. MC(EVOFP & MP)R 2011, Pt 7 applies FPR 2010 generally and r 9.22 with modification to variation proceedings.

9.23 Duty to make entries in the court's register

(1) Where the designated officer for the court receives notice of any direction made in the High Court or a county court under section 28 of the 1978 Act by virtue of which an order made by the court under that Act or the 2004 Act ceases to have effect, particulars of the direction must be entered in the court's register.

(2) Where –

(a) in proceedings under the 1978 Act, the hearing of an application under section 2 of that Act is adjourned after the court has decided that it is satisfied of any ground mentioned in section 1; or

(b) in proceedings under the 2004 Act, the hearing of an application under Part 1 of Schedule 6 to that Act is adjourned after the court has decided that it is satisfied of any ground mentioned in paragraph 1,

and the parties to the proceedings agree to the resumption of the hearing in accordance with section 31 of the 1978 Act by a court which includes justices who were not sitting when the hearing began, particulars of the agreement must be entered into the court's register.

Chapter 6
General Procedure

9.24 Power to order delivery up of possession etc.

(1) This rule applies where the court has made an order under –

(a) section 24A of the 1973 Act;

(b) section 17(2) of the 1984 Act;

(c) Part 3 of Schedule 5 to the 2004 Act; or

(d) paragraph 9(4) of Schedule 7 to the 2004 Act.

(2) When the court makes an order mentioned in paragraph (1), it may order any party to deliver up to the purchaser or any other person –

(a) possession of the land, including any interest in, or right over, land;

(b) receipt of rents or profits relating to it; or

(c) both.

Scope—When the court makes an order for the sale or transfer of property, it may order any party to deliver up to the purchaser or any other person possession of land and/or receipt of rents and profits.

9.25 Where proceedings may be heard

(1) Paragraph (2) applies to an application –

(a) for a financial order;

(b)   under Part 3 of the 1984 Act; or

(c)   under Schedule 7 to the 2004 Act.

(2) An application mentioned in paragraph (1) must be heard –

(a)   where the case is proceeding in the county court, at any court of trial; and

(b)   where the case is proceeding in the High Court –

(i)   at the Royal Courts of Justice; or

(ii)   in matrimonial or civil partnership proceedings, any court at which sittings of the High Court are authorised.

(3) An application for an order under –

(a)   section 27 of the 1973 Act; or

(b)   Part 9 of Schedule 5 to the 2004 Act,

must be heard in a court of trial or in the High Court.

(4) A court may transfer a case to another court exercising the same jurisdiction, either of its own initiative or on the application of one of the parties, if –

(a)   the parties consent to the transfer;

(b)   the court has held a hearing to determine whether a transfer should be ordered; or

(c)   paragraph (5) applies.

(5) A court may transfer a case without a hearing if –

(a)   the court has notified the parties in writing that it intends to order a transfer; and

(b)   neither party has, within 14 days of the notification being sent, requested a hearing to determine whether a transfer should be ordered.

9.26 Applications for consent orders for financial remedy

(1) Subject to paragraph (5) and to rule 35.2 in relation to an application for a consent order –

(a)   the applicant must file two copies of a draft of the order in the terms sought, one of which must be endorsed with a statement signed by the respondent to the application signifying agreement; and

(b)   each party must file with the court and serve on the other party, a statement of information in the form referred to in Practice Direction 5A.

(2) Where each party's statement of information is contained in one form, it must be signed by both the applicant and respondent to certify that they have read the contents of the other party's statement.

(3) Where each party's statement of information is in a separate form, the form of each party must be signed by the other party to certify that they have read the contents of the statement contained in that form.

(4) Unless the court directs otherwise, the applicant and the respondent need not attend the hearing of an application for a consent order.

(5) Where all or any of the parties attend the hearing of an application for a financial remedy the court may –

(a)   dispense with the filing of a statement of information; and

(b)   give directions for the information which would otherwise be required to be given in such a statement in such a manner as it thinks fit.

(6) In relation to an application for a consent order under Part 3 of the 1984 Act or Schedule 7 to the 2004 Act, the application for permission to make the application may be heard at the same time as the application for a financial remedy if evidence of the respondent's consent to the order is filed with the application.

(The following rules contain provision in relation to applications for consent orders – rule 9.32 (pension sharing order), rule 9.34 (pension attachment order), rule 9.41 (pension compensation sharing orders) and rule 9.43 (pension compensation attachment orders).

Scope—The draft order: this rule provides for the procedure to be followed for the court to be able to exercise its discretion under MCA 1973, s 25 by making an order in accordance with the terms agreed by the parties. Two copies of the proposed order are to be lodged, one of which should be endorsed by the respondent to the application signifying agreement. It is a wise precaution to insert at the end of the proposed order a statement that each party has read and understood the terms of the agreement, and for each party to sign personally.

Preambles—Where the agreed provisions contain terms beyond the jurisdiction of the statute, those terms should be set out as recitals to the order. The body of the order may state that the court approves the recitals and directs that they be made a rule of court and filed as such. This permits the terms to be enforced in the suit without the need to bring a separate action.

Statements of information—The Rules provide that the court must receive information in the prescribed form setting out the necessary personal information about the parties, their means and resources, so that the court may properly exercise its powers. There are requirements to ensure that the court can be satisfied that each party at the time of consenting to an order is aware of the details of the other's resources. Under r 9.26(2), where the statement of information is contained in one form, it must be signed by both parties to certify that they have read the contents. Under r 9.26(3), there may be separate forms, but each side must sign the form of the other party.

Clean break—Where the parties intend to be subject to a joint capital and/or income clean break, it is good practice, as followed at the Principal Registry of the Family Division, for the respondent to the financial application to have lodged on his behalf a Form A; without this, the respondent's claim does not exist and, therefore, cannot be dismissed. The Form A should be marked "For dismissal purposes only" to prevent inadvertent issue and so that the purpose of the Form A is apparent on its face. If a prayer for financial orders has been included in the petition (or cross-petition), a separate Form A from that party is not required for dismissal purposes.

Undertakings—Consent orders may commonly contain undertakings given by the parties on the face of the order for the payment of money, or doing or abstaining from any act other than the payment of money. In each case, the undertaking must be endorsed with a notice setting out the consequence of disobedience and must contain a signed statement that the person giving the undertaking understands its terms and the consequences of failing to comply: see FPR PD33A.

Powers of the court—The judge has full discretion to approve or reject a draft order lodged for approval. It is open to the court to decline to make the order and to list a hearing with the attendance of the parties. The court in its inquisitorial jurisdiction is not a rubber stamp and must always exercise a discretion, but not to the extent of acting "as a bloodhound or a ferret": *L v L* [2008] 1 FLR 26. The applicant and the respondent need not attend the hearing of an application for a consent order, unless the court otherwise directs. Where agreement had been reached as a result of arbitration by religious authorities, court proceedings having been stayed for this purpose, the High Court approved a consent order in relation to children and matrimonial finance where a non-binding agreement had been reached under the auspices of the Beth Din, the court respecting the agreement reached by the parties and finding the terms of the financial settlement "unobjectionable": *AI v MT* [2013] EWHC 100 (Fam).

Power to reopen or set aside consent order—In certain circumstances, it may be possible to set aside a consent order, which cannot in itself be appealed as it derives from the express agreement of the parties. The two main categories are:

(i) An erroneous basis of fact at the time of the order, such as misrepresentation, non-disclosure or fraud;

(ii) An unforeseen supervening event after the order, which changes the basis of the whole order.

See *S v S (Ancillary Relief: Consent Order)* [2002] 1 FLR 992 for a review of the authorities.

Erroneous basis of fact: the duty of full and frank disclosure before an agreement is axiomatic: see *Livesey v Jenkins* [1985] FLR 813, HL. The power to set aside a consent order arises where there is material non-disclosure, such as would have made a material difference to the order, as well as fraud and misrepresentation. See *Vicary v Vicary* [1992] 2 FLR 271, CA and *Rose v Rose* [2003] 2 FLR 197. Mistake as to value has been discounted as falling within the *Barder* principle: *Judge v Judge* [2009] 1 FLR 1287, CA.

Supervening event: the principles derive from *Barder v Barder* [1987] 2 FLR 480, where the husband agreed to transfer his interest in the former matrimonial home to the wife, who then killed the children and committed suicide. Leave to appeal may be given where a new event occurs, invalidating the basis upon which the consent order was made, where the event was close in time, where there was a prompt application and no third-party prejudice. *Barder* events are likely to be unforeseeable at the time of the consent order. Foreseeable events, such as dramatic fluctuations in the value of assets such as shares, which had been properly valued and taken into account, have been held not to be a *Barder* event: *Cornick v Cornick* [1994] 2 FLR 530; *Myerson v Myerson (No 2)* [2009] 2 FLR 147, CA; *Walkden v Walkden* [2010] 1 FLR 174. A change in the law must be unforeseeable to constitute a *Barder* event: *S v S (Ancillary Relief: Consent Order)* [2002] 1 FLR 992. In *Dixon v Marchant* [2008] 1 FLR 655, CA the wife's rapid remarriage was held not to be a *Barder* event. The parties had agreed the capitalisation of periodical payments to achieve a clean break. There was no fundamental assumption between the parties to be invalidated by the wife's remarriage. In *Richardson v Richardson* [2011] 2 FLR 244, justice required that both the husband and his late wife's estate bear equally the liability for an unforeseen damages claim against their company, where the insurance claim was voided. Thorpe LJ said that cases with a *Barder* factor as opposed to a vitiating factor are extremely rare. The principles of *Barder* should not be thought to be extendable by ingenuity or the lowering of the judicially created bar.

Procedure to set aside a consent order—A *Barder* event may require permission to appeal out of time to a higher court. Applications to set aside a consent order made on an erroneous basis of fact, misrepresentation or fraud may be to the judge who approved the consent order.

9.26A   Questions as to the court's jurisdiction or whether the proceedings should be stayed

(1) This rule applies to applications for maintenance where a question as to jurisdiction arises under –

   (a)   the 1968 Convention;
   (b)   the 1988 Convention;
   (c)   the Lugano Convention;
   (d)   the Maintenance Regulation; or
   (e)   Article 18 of the 2007 Hague Convention.

(2) If at any time after the issue of the application it appears to the court that it does not or may not have jurisdiction to hear an application, or that under the instruments referred to in paragraph (1) it is or may be required to stay the proceedings or to decline jurisdiction, the court must –

   (a)   stay the proceedings, and
   (b)   fix a date for a hearing to determine jurisdiction or whether there should be a stay or other order.

(3) The court officer will serve notice of the hearing referred to at paragraph (2)(b) on the parties to the proceedings.

(4) The court must, in writing –

   (a)   give reasons for its decision under paragraph (2), and
   (b)   where it makes a finding of fact, state such finding.

(5) The court may with the consent of all the parties deal with any question as to the jurisdiction of the court, or as to whether the proceedings should be stayed, without a hearing.

(6) In this rule –

   (a)   "the 1968 Convention" has the meaning given to it in the Civil Jurisdiction and Judgments Act 1982;
   (b)   "the 1988 Convention" and "the Lugano Convention" have the meanings given to them in rule 34.1(2).

Amendments—Inserted by SI 2011/1328; amended by SI 2012/2806.

9.26AA International Maintenance Obligations: Communication with the Central Authority for England and Wales

(1) Where the Lord Chancellor requests information or a document from the court officer for the relevant court for the purposes of Article 58 of the Maintenance Regulation or Articles 12 or 25(2) of the 2007 Hague Convention, the court officer shall provide the requested information or document to the Lord Chancellor forthwith.

(2) In this rule, "relevant court" means the court at which an application under Article 56 of the Maintenance Regulation or Article 10 of the 2007 Hague Convention has been filed.

> [The Lord Chancellor is the Central Authority for England and Wales in relation to the 2007 Hague Convention and the Maintenance Regulation]

Amendments—Inserted by SI 2012/2806.

9.26B Adding or removing parties

(1) The court may direct that a person or body be added as a party to proceedings for a financial remedy if –

  (a) it is desirable to add the new party so that the court can resolve all the matters in dispute in the proceedings; or

  (b) there is an issue involving the new party and an existing party which is connected to the matters in dispute in the proceedings, and it is desirable to add the new party so that the court can resolve that issue.

(2) The court may direct that any person or body be removed as a party if it is not desirable for that person or body to be a party to the proceedings.

(3) If the court makes a direction for the addition or removal of a party under this rule, it may give consequential directions about –

  (a) the service of a copy of the application form or other relevant documents on the new party; and

  (b) the management of the proceedings.

(4) The power of the court under this rule to direct that a party be added or removed may be exercised either on the court's own initiative or on the application of an existing party or a person or body who wishes to become a party.

(5) An application for an order under this rule must be made in accordance with the Part 18 procedure and, unless the court directs otherwise, must be supported by evidence setting out the proposed new party's interest in or connection with the proceedings or, in the case of removal of a party, the reasons for removal.

Amendments—Inserted by SI 2012/679.

Scope—This rule addresses the issue of joinder, not previously explicitly provided for under FPR 2010: see *Goldstone v Goldstone* [2011] 1 FLR 1926.

Chapter 7
Estimates of Costs

9.27 Estimates of Costs

(1) Subject to paragraph (2), at every hearing or appointment each party must produce to the court an estimate of the costs incurred by that party up to the date of that hearing or appointment.

(2) Not less than 14 days before the date fixed for the final hearing of an application for a financial remedy, each party ("the filing party") must (unless the court directs

otherwise) file with the court and serve on each other party a statement giving full particulars of all costs in respect of the proceedings which the filing party has incurred or expects to incur, to enable the court to take account of the parties' liabilities for costs when deciding what order (if any) to make for a financial remedy.

(3) This rule does not apply to magistrates' courts.

(Rule 28.3 makes provision for orders for costs in financial remedy proceedings.)

Scope—At every hearing a costs estimate must be produced to the judge. However, the requirement for the final hearing is for a statement giving full particulars of all costs incurred or envisaged. This is in the form of a more detailed and comprehensive document. The court is entitled to take into account the parties' liabilities for costs before deciding what order to make. The weight to be given to costs expended is for the discretion of the individual judge on s 25 principles. The court may credit back into the parties' assets any costs incurred by them, in accordance with the guidance in *Leadbetter v Leadbetter* [1985] FLR 789. But see comments in *TL v ML (Ancillary Relief: Claims against Assets of Extended Family)* [2006] 1 FLR 1263.

9.28 Duty to make open proposals

(1) Not less than 14 days before the date fixed for the final hearing of an application for a financial remedy, the applicant must (unless the court directs otherwise) file with the court and serve on the respondent an open statement which sets out concise details, including the amounts involved, of the orders which the applicant proposes to ask the court to make.

(2) Not more than 7 days after service of a statement under paragraph (1), the respondent must file with the court and serve on the applicant an open statement which sets out concise details, including the amounts involved, of the orders which the respondent proposes to ask the court to make.

Scope—This rule applies only to final hearings. There is no requirement to make open offers ahead of interim hearings.

"Open" proposals—The concept of the "open" proposal is distinct from a proposal made within negotiation that is privileged, ie it cannot be disclosed to the court. It remains public policy that parties are to be encouraged to negotiate; it is thought that they will do so more readily if they can do so privately: *Rush & Tompkins Ltd v Greater London Council* [1989] AC 1280. The rules do not alter the ability to negotiate privately. Reference should not be made in financial proceedings to correspondence between the parties that is privileged, except where both parties waive that privilege. By FPR 2010, r 28.3, no offer to settle that is not an open offer is admissible at any stage, except in FDRs under r 9.17.

Chapter 8
Pensions

Scope—Part 9, Ch 8 (rr 9.29–9.37) governs the procedure for pension sharing and pension attachment (as well as disclosure by a party with benefits under a pension arrangement (whether or not pension sharing or attachment is applied for) in relation to pension arrangements including where the Pension Protection Fund (PPF) becomes involved. However, where the PPF has already assumed responsibility for a pension arrangement so that either party is entitled to PPF compensation, FPR 2010, Pt 9, Ch 9 (rr 9.38–9.45) applies.

Outline of procedural framework for pension sharing applications—For pension sharing applications, this is:

1   The application is made in the application for a matrimonial or civil partnership order (petition) or at any time thereafter (FPR 2010, r 9.4).
2   The person with pension benefits must apply for a CE within 7 days of notice of the First Appointment, unless there is already one in existence dated not earlier than 12 months before the date of the First Appointment (a "relevant valuation": FPR 2010, r 9.30).
3   The person responsible for the pension arrangement must be served and given 21 days to provide information including details of any obstacles to a pension sharing order being made (FPR 2010, r 9.31 and Pensions on Divorce etc (Provision of Information) Regulations 2000, regs 2(7) and 4).

4   The form of the order must:
   (i) be expressed as a percentage (MCA 1973, s 21A; *H v H (Financial Relief: Pensions)* [2010] 2 FLR 173) of the CE calculated in accordance with the Pensions on Divorce etc (Provision of Information) Regulations 2000, reg 3;
   (ii) state in the body of the order that there is to be provision by way of pension sharing in accordance with the annex(es) (Form P1 (pension sharing annex)) for each pension arrangement (FPR 2010, r 9.35). The order must not take effect until 7 days after the time has expired for appealing or the date of decree absolute (whichever is the later) (MCA 1973, ss 24B(2) and 24C);
   (iii) Direct whether the court or other party is to send the pension sharing order, annex(es) and the relevant decree/order to the pension arrangement (FPR 2010, r 9.36).

5   The final stage is implementation. The court or one of the parties serves the order (FPR 2010, r 9.36). The information needed from the parties for implementation to take place is set out in the Pension on Divorce etc (Provision of Information) Regulation 2000, reg 5 et seq.

Outline of procedural framework for consent pension sharing applications—A special procedural framework for dealing with consent pension sharing applications, where there has been no prior service of a formal application (Form A) under FPR 2010, r 9.31, is provided for by FPR 2010, r 9.32. This procedure will apply where, for example, the parties have been in negotiations and have reached an agreement without any formal application having been made. Unless the information set out in Section C of the Pension Inquiry Form has already been provided in relation to the pension arrangement in question, that information must be requested and, on receipt, a copy sent to the other party. There is no formal requirement to seek the approval of the pension arrangement to a consent pension sharing order whether an application has been served under r 9.31 or is made under r 9.32. However, if there is any doubt as to the ability of the pension arrangement to implement the proposed order, it is good practice to seek such approval.

Outline of procedural framework for pension attachment applications—For pension attachment applications this is:

1   The application is made in the application for a matrimonial or civil partnership order (petition) or at any time thereafter (FPR 2010, r 9.4).
2   The person with pension benefits must apply for a CE within 7 days of notice of the First Appointment, unless there is already one in existence dated not earlier than 12 months before the date of the First Appointment (a "relevant valuation": FPR 2010, r 9.30).
3   The person responsible for the pension arrangement must be served with the application and the addresses referred to in FPR 2010, r 9.33(1). The person responsible for the pension arrangement may then within 21 days of service request the provision of the pension section of Form E from the party with pension rights which must be provided on exchange of Forms E or within 21 days of the date of the request (whichever is the later) (FPR 2010, r 9.33(2)–(4)).
4   The person responsible for the pension arrangement, who has received a copy of the requested section of Form E, may send to the court and to the parties a statement in answer within 21 days of receipt of the pensions section of Form E (FPR 2010, r 9.33(5)).
5   Where the person responsible for the pension arrangement files a statement in answer, that person is entitled to be given notice of the First Appointment and to be represented at that appointment (FPR 2010, r 9.33(6)).
6   The form of the order must:
   (i) be expressed as a percentage (MCA 1973, s 25B(5)) of the payment which becomes due to the party with pension rights;
   (ii) state in the body of the order that there is to be provision by way of pension attachment in accordance with an annex(es) (Form P2 (pension attachment annex)) for each arrangement (FPR 2010, r 9.35);
   (iii) within 21 days of service direct whether the court or one of the parties is to send the pension attachment order, annex(es) and accompany documents to the pension arrangement (FPR 2010, r 9.36).
7   The court or one of the parties serves the order (FPR 2010, r 9.36).

Outline of procedural framework for consent pension attachment applications—A special procedural framework is created for applications for consent pension attachment orders where an application has not been already served under FPR 2010, r 9.33(1). In these circumstances, the parties must serve on the pension arrangement a copy of the application for a consent order, a draft of the proposed order and pension attachment annex and particulars of the addresses referred to in r 9.33(1). The pension arrangement then has 21 days from the date of service of the consent order application in which to object (FPR 2010, r 9.34(3)).

Provision of information (r 9.30)—This rule provides that if one party has benefits under a pension arrangement (as opposed to shareable state scheme rights) then, irrespective of whether a pension sharing or attachment order is being sought, that person must within 7 days of being notified of the date of the First Appointment apply to the pension arrangement for information about the scheme. That information, as set out in the Pensions on Divorce etc (Provision of Information) Regulations 2000, reg 2(2), is simply the CE. Where further information is required because of pension sharing or an attachment order is sought, that information will be obtained in response to the Pension Inquiry Form (Form P) directed on the First Appointment (FPR 2010, r 9.15(7)(c)). As regards shareable state scheme rights (ie the Additional State Pension (SERPs/S2P)), these rules do not require similar information to be obtained. It is suggested that it is good practice to obtain the information at this stage. Sharing of State Scheme Rights (Provision of Information and Valuation) (No 2) Regulations 2000, reg 2) requires the Secretary of State to provide the person with shareable state scheme rights or the court with a valuation of that person's shareable state scheme rights and with an explanation of how a pension sharing order will affect that person and his spouse. See the annotations to these Regulations for details of the procedures involved.

Service and objection by pension provider—The pension arrangement must be given notice of an application for a pension sharing or attachment order (FPR 2010, r 9.31). However, in the case of a consent application for a pension sharing order, the application need not be served on the pension arrangement provided FPR 2010, r 9.32 is complied with. Further, no specific provision is given in relation to pension sharing (whether or not the order is made by consent) for the pension arrangement to require or be given further information about the application or to take any part in the proceedings. The facility for the pension arrangement to object applies only to pension attachment orders (FPR 2010, rr 9.33 and 9.34). The rationale for this distinction is that the pension attachment order imposes a continuing obligation on a pension arrangement in a way that a pension sharing order does not.

Form of order (r 9.35)—This rule sets out formalities for the form of the pension sharing or attachment order. This order must be accompanied by an annex(es) (Form P1 (pension sharing annex); Form P2 (pension attachment annex)). Important points are that:

(i)   the order is expressed as a percentage (MCA 1973, ss 21A and 25B(5); *H v H (Financial Relief: Pensions)* [2010] 2 FLR 173) of (pension sharing) the CE calculated in accordance with the Pensions on Divorce etc (Provision of Information) Regulations 2000, reg 3, (in respect of shareable state scheme rights) as provided by the Sharing of State Scheme Rights (Provision of Information and Valuation) (No 2) Regulations 2000, reg 2 or (pension attachment) the payment which becomes due to the party with pension rights;

(ii) the date of the valuation of the cash equivalent is, for evidential purposes, as specified by the court between 1 year before the application for a matrimonial or civil partnership order and the date of the order (Divorce etc (Pensions) Regulations 2000, reg 3). This is not, however, the valuation date used for implementation purposes, which is governed by WRPA 1999, s 29. For "moving target syndrome", see annotations to WRPA 1999, s 29;

(iii) responsibility between the parties for payment of the charges must be set out in the annex(es). If the annex(es) is silent, the transferor will pay (WRPA 1999, s 41(3)(i)). See, further, annotations to MCA 1973, s 24D and PD(PI)R 2000, reg 2;

(iv) a pension sharing order must not take effect until the expiry of 7 days after the time for appealing has elapsed or the date of decree absolute (whichever is the later) (MCA 1973, ss 24B(2) and 24C).

Service of order and implementation (r 9.36)—Within 7 days of the order or decree absolute, whichever is the later, the court or one of the parties (as directed by the court) sends to the pension arrangement the order including the annex(es) and a copy of the relevant decree/order.

Both parties must provide the pension arrangement with the formal information (date of birth, national insurance number, etc) set out in the Pensions on Divorce etc (Provision of Information) Regulations 2000, reg 5. Service of the order on the pension arrangement and provision by the parties of the above formal information triggers the start of the 4-month period which the pension arrangement has to implement the order (WRPA 1999, s 34(1)). The pension arrangement must, if it has not already done so, provide details of the charges within 3 weeks of receiving the order and must issue a notice of discharge within three weeks of its implementation (Pensions on Divorce etc (Provision of Information) Regulations 2000, regs 7 and 8).

9.29 Application and interpretation of this Chapter

(1) This Chapter applies

(a)   where an application for a financial remedy has been made; and

(b)   the applicant or respondent is the party with pension rights.

(2) In this Chapter –

    (a)   in proceedings under the 1973 Act and the 1984 Act, all words and phrases defined in sections 25D(3) and (4) of the 1973 Act have the meaning assigned by those subsections;

    (b)   in proceedings under the 2004 Act –

         all words and phrases defined in paragraphs 16(4) to (5) and 29 of Schedule 5 to that Act have the meanings assigned by those paragraphs; and

         "the party with pension rights" has the meaning given to "civil partner with pension rights" by paragraph 29 of Schedule 5 to the 2004 Act;

    (c)   all words and phrases defined in section 46 of the Welfare Reform and Pensions Act 1999 have the meanings assigned by that section.

9.30 What the party with pension rights must do when the court fixes a first appointment

(1) Where the court fixes a first appointment as required by rule 9.12(1)(a) the party with pension rights must request the person responsible for each pension arrangement under which the party has or is likely to have benefits to provide the information referred to in regulation 2(2) of the Pensions on Divorce etc (Provision of Information) Regulations 2000.

        (The information referred to in regulation 2 of the Pensions on Divorce etc (Provision of Information) Regulations 2000 relates to the valuation of pension rights or benefits.)

(2) The party with pension rights must comply with paragraph (1) within 7 days beginning with the date on which that party receives notification of the date of the first appointment.

(3) Within 7 days beginning with the date on which the party with pension rights receives the information under paragraph (1) that party must send a copy of it to the other party, together with the name and address of the person responsible for each pension arrangement.

(4) A request under paragraph (1) need not be made where the party with pension rights is in possession of, or has requested, a relevant valuation of the pension rights or benefits accrued under the pension arrangement in question.

Scope—This rule provides for the provision of information in relation to benefits under a pension arrangement. See, further the notes to FPR 2010, Pt 9, Ch 8.

9.31 Applications for pension sharing orders

Where an application for a financial remedy includes an application for a pension sharing order, or where a request for such an order is added to an existing application for a financial remedy, the applicant must serve a copy of the application on the person responsible for the pension arrangement concerned.

Scope—This rule provides for the service of an application for a pension sharing order on the pension arrangement. See further the notes to FPR 2010, Pt 9, Ch 8.

9.32 Applications for consent orders for pension sharing

(1) This rule applies where –

    (a)   the parties have agreed on the terms of an order and the agreement includes a pension sharing order;

    (b)   service has not been effected under rule 9.31; and

    (c)   the information referred to in paragraph (2) has not otherwise been provided.

(2) The party with pension rights must –

  (a) request the person responsible for the pension arrangement concerned to provide the information set out in Section C of the Pension Inquiry Form; and

  (b) on receipt, send a copy of the information referred to in sub-paragraph (a) to the other party.

Scope—This rule provides for the special procedure for consent applications for a pension sharing order where there has been no prior service of an application under FPR 2010, r 9.31 (Form A). See further the notes to FPR 2010, Pt 9, Ch 8.

9.33 Applications for pension attachment orders

(1) Where an application for a financial remedy includes an application for a pension attachment order, or where a request for such an order is added to an existing application for a financial remedy, the applicant must serve a copy of the application on the person responsible for the pension arrangement concerned and must at the same time send –

  (a) an address to which any notice which the person responsible is required to serve on the applicant is to be sent;

  (b) an address to which any payment which the person responsible is required to make to the applicant is to be sent; and

  (c) where the address in sub-paragraph (b) is that of a bank, a building society or the Department of National Savings, sufficient details to enable the payment to be made into the account of the applicant.

(2) A person responsible for a pension arrangement who receives a copy of the application under paragraph (1) may, within 21 days beginning with the date of service of the application, request the party with the pension rights to provide that person with the information disclosed in the financial statement relating to the party's pension rights or benefits under that arrangement.

(3) If the person responsible for a pension arrangement makes a request under paragraph (2), the party with the pension rights must provide that person with a copy of the section of that party's financial statement that relates to that party's pension rights or benefits under that arrangement.

(4) The party with the pension rights must comply with paragraph (3) –

  (a) within the time limited for filing the financial statement by rule 9.14(1); or

  (b) within 21 days beginning with the date on which the person responsible for the pension arrangement makes the request,

whichever is the later.

(5) A person responsible for a pension arrangement who receives a copy of the section of a financial statement as required pursuant to paragraph (4) may, within 21 days beginning with the date on which that person receives it, send to the court, the applicant and the respondent a statement in answer.

(6) A person responsible for a pension arrangement who files a statement in answer pursuant to paragraph (5) will be entitled to be represented at the first appointment, or such other hearing as the court may direct, and the court must within 4 days, beginning with the date on which that person files the statement in answer, give the person notice of the date of the first appointment or other hearing as the case may be.

Scope—This rule sets out the procedure for applying for a pension attachment order, including provision for objection by a pension arrangement. See further the notes to FPR 2010, Pt 9, Ch 8.

9.34 Applications for consent orders for pension attachment

(1) This rule applies where service has not been effected under rule 9.33(1).

(2) Where the parties have agreed on the terms of an order and the agreement includes a pension attachment order, then they must serve on the person responsible for the pension arrangement concerned –

    (a)   a copy of the application for a consent order;

    (b)   a draft of the proposed order, complying with rule 9.35; and

    (c)   the particulars set out in rule 9.33(1).

(3) No consent order that includes a pension attachment order must be made unless either –

    (a)   the person responsible for the pension arrangement has not made any objection within 21 days beginning with the date on which the application for a consent order was served on that person; or

    (b)   the court has considered any such objection, and for the purpose of considering any objection the court may make such direction as it sees fit for the person responsible to attend before it or to furnish written details of the objection.

Scope—This rule makes special provision for consent applications for pension attachment orders. See further the notes to FPR 2010, Pt 9, Ch 8.

9.35 Pension sharing orders or pension attachment orders

An order for a financial remedy, whether by consent or not, which includes a pension sharing order or a pension attachment order, must –

    (a)   in the body of the order, state that there is to be provision by way of pension sharing or pension attachment in accordance with the annex or annexes to the order; and

    (b)   be accompanied by a pension sharing annex or a pension attachment annex as the case may require, and if provision is made in relation to more than one pension arrangement there must be one annex for each pension arrangement.

Scope—This rule lays down the formal requirements for pension sharing or attachment orders. See further the notes to FPR 2010, Pt 9, Ch 8.

9.36 Duty of the court upon making a pension sharing order or a pension attachment order

(1) A court which varies or discharges a pension sharing order or a pension attachment order, must send, or direct one of the parties to send –

    (a)   to the person responsible for the pension arrangement concerned; or

    (b)   where the Board has assumed responsibility for the pension scheme or part of it, the Board;

the documents referred to in paragraph (4).

(2) A court which makes a pension sharing order or pension attachment order, must send, or direct one of the parties to send to the person responsible for the pension arrangement concerned, the documents referred to in paragraph (4).

(3) Where the Board has assumed responsibility for the pension scheme or part of it after the making of a pension sharing order or attachment order but before the documents have been sent to the person responsible for the pension arrangement in accordance with paragraph (2), the court which makes the pension sharing order or the pension attachment order, must send, or direct one of the parties to send to the Board the documents referred to in paragraph (4).

(4) The documents to be sent in accordance with paragraph (1) to (3) are –

    (a)   in the case of –

        (i)   proceedings under the 1973 Act, a copy of the decree of judicial separation;

        (ii) proceedings under Schedule 5 to the 2004 Act, a copy of the separation order;

        (iii) proceedings under Part 3 of the 1984 Act, a copy of the document of divorce, annulment or legal separation;

        (iv) proceedings under Schedule 7 to the 2004 Act, a copy of the document of dissolution, annulment or legal separation;

    (b)   in the case of divorce or nullity of marriage, a copy of the decree absolute under rule 7.31 or 7.32 or

    (c)   in the case of dissolution or nullity of civil partnership, a copy of the order making the conditional order final under rule 7.31 or 7.32; and

    (d)   a copy of the pension sharing order or the pension attachment order, or as the case may be of the order varying or discharging that order, including any annex to that order relating to that pension arrangement but no other annex to that order.

(5) The documents referred to in paragraph (4) must be sent –

    (a)   in proceedings under the 1973 Act and the 1984 Act, within 7 days beginning with the date on which –

        (i)   the relevant pension sharing or pension attachment order, or any order varying or discharging such an order, is made; or

        (ii) the decree absolute of divorce or nullity or decree of judicial separation is made,

    whichever is the later; and

    (b)   in proceedings under the 2004 Act, within 7 days beginning with the date on which –

        (i)   the relevant pension sharing or pension attachment order, or any order varying or discharging such an order, is made; or

        (ii) the final order of dissolution or nullity or separation order is made,

    whichever is the later.

Amendments—SI 2012/679.

Scope—This rule lays down duties upon the court when a pension sharing or attachment order is made, including the service of the order and accompanying documents. See further the notes to FPR 2010, Pt 9, Ch 8.

9.37 Procedure where Pension Protection Fund becomes involved with the pension scheme

(1) This rule applies where –

    (a)   rules 9.30 to 9.34 or 9.36 apply; and

    (b)   the party with the pension rights ("the member") receives or has received notification in compliance with the Pension Protection Fund (Provision of Information) Regulations 2005 ("the 2005 Regulations") –

        (i)   from the trustees or managers of a pension scheme, that there is an assessment period in relation to that scheme; or

        (ii) from the Board that it has assumed responsibility for the pension scheme or part of it.

(2) If the trustees or managers of the pension scheme notify or have notified the member that there is an assessment period in relation to that scheme, the member must send to the

other party, all the information which the Board is required from time to time to provide to the member under the 2005 Regulations including –

    (a) a copy of the notification; and

    (b) a copy of the valuation summary,

in accordance with paragraph (3).

(3) The member must send the information or any part of it referred to in paragraph (2) –

    (a) if available, when the member sends the information received under rule 9.30(1); or

    (b) otherwise, within 7 days of receipt.

(4) If the Board notifies the member that it has assumed responsibility for the pension scheme, or part of it, the member must –

    (a) send a copy of the notification to the other party within 7 days of receipt; and

    (b) comply with paragraph (5).

(5) Where paragraph (4) applies, the member must –

    (a) within 7 days of receipt of the notification, request the Board in writing to provide a forecast of the member's compensation entitlement as described in the 2005 Regulations; and

    (b) send a copy of the forecast of the member's compensation entitlement to the other party within 7 days of receipt.

(6) In this rule –

    "assessment period" means an assessment period within the meaning of Part 2 of the Pensions Act 2004; and

    "valuation summary" has the meaning assigned to it by the 2005 Regulations.

Scope—This rule governs the procedure for pension sharing and pension attachment where there is a supervening Pension Protection Fund (PPF) involvement. As to the PPF generally, reference should be made to the annotations to MCA 1973, s 25E. Where there is an application for a pension sharing or attachment order, and the party with pension rights has received notification that a PPF assessment period is in operation, he/she must provide certain information and documentation (namely, a copy of the notification and a copy of the valuation summary) to the other party at the same time as the documentation required by FPR 2010, r 9.30(1) or otherwise within 7 days of receipt. If the pension arrangement is in an assessment period and the PPF notifies the member that it has assumed responsibility for the scheme or part of it, the member must send a copy of the notification to the other party (within 7 days of receipt) and also, again within 7 days of receipt, request the PPF under the Pension Protection Fund (Provision of Information) Regulations 2005 to provide a forecast of his compensation entitlement, which must be sent to the other party within 7 days of receipt. There is no obligation to notify the other party if the PPF does not take over responsibility for the scheme (eg, where the scheme is wound up or rescued) simply because there is no obligation on the PPF to notify members in such circumstances. Furthermore, there is no notification provision in relation to winding up in non-PPF cases.

    Where the PPF has assumed responsibility for a pension arrangement before the issue of an application for a pension sharing or attachment order, reference should be made to FPR 2010, Pt 9, Ch 9.

Chapter 9
Pension Protection Fund Compensation

General note—This chapter provides the procedural framework for applications for pension compensation sharing orders and pension compensation attachment orders. Such orders may only be made where the Pension Protection Fund (PPF) has already assumed responsibility for a scheme. See, generally, annotations to MCA 1973, ss 21B, 25E and 25F. The procedure follows as closely as possible that in relation to pension sharing and attachment in relation to pensions contained in FPR 2010, Pt 9, Ch 8; reference might usefully be made to the notes to Ch 8. See, also, the Divorce and Dissolution etc (Pension Protection Fund) Regulations 2011 and the Pension Protection Fund (Pension Compensation Sharing and Attachment on Divorce etc) Regulations 2011.

9.38 Application and interpretation of this Chapter

(1) This Chapter applies –

    (a)   where an application for a financial remedy has been made; and

    (b)   the applicant or respondent is, the party with compensation rights.

(2) In this Chapter "party with compensation rights" –

    (a)   in proceedings under the 1973 Act and the 1984 Act, has the meaning given to it by section 25G(5) of the 1973 Act;

    (b)   in proceedings under the 2004 Act, has the meaning given to "civil partner with compensation rights" by paragraph 37(1) of Schedule 5 to the 2004 Act.

9.39 What the party with compensation rights must do when the court fixes a first appointment

(1) Where the court fixes a first appointment as required by rule 9.12(1)(a) the party with compensation rights must request the Board to provide the information about the valuation of entitlement to PPF compensation referred to in regulations made by the Secretary of State under section 118 of the Pensions Act 2008.

(2) The party with compensation rights must comply with paragraph (1) within 7 days beginning with the date on which that party receives notification of the date of the first appointment.

(3) Within 7 days beginning with the date on which the party with compensation rights receives the information under paragraph (1) that party must send a copy of it to the other party, together with the name and address of the trustees or managers responsible for each pension scheme.

(4) Where the rights to PPF Compensation are derived from rights under more than one pension scheme, the party with compensation rights must comply with this rule in relation to each entitlement.

9.40 Applications for pension compensation sharing orders

Where an application for a financial remedy includes an application for a pension compensation sharing order or where a request for such an order is added to an existing application for a financial remedy, the applicant must serve a copy of the application on the Board.

9.41 Applications for consent orders for pension compensation sharing

(1) This rule applies where –

    (a)   the parties have agreed on the terms of an order and the agreement includes a pension compensation sharing order;

    (b)   service has not been effected under rule 9.40; and

    (c)   the information referred to in paragraph (2) has not otherwise been provided.

(2) The party with compensation rights must –

    (a)   request the Board to provide the information set out in Section C of the Pension Protection Fund Inquiry Form; and

    (b)   on receipt, send a copy of the information referred to in sub-paragraph (a) to the other party.

9.42 Applications for pension compensation attachment orders

Where an application for a financial remedy includes an application for a pension compensation attachment order or where a request for such an order is added to an existing application for a financial remedy, the applicant must serve a copy of the application on the Board and must at the same time send –

  (a) an address to which any notice which the Board is required to serve on the applicant is to be sent;

  (b) an address to which any payment which the Board is required to make to the applicant is to be sent; and

  (c) where the address in sub-paragraph (b) is that of a bank, a building society or the Department of National Savings, sufficient details to enable the payment to be made into the account of the applicant.

9.43 Applications for consent orders for pension compensation attachment

(1) This rule applies where service has not been effected under rule 9.42.

(2) Where the parties have agreed on the terms of an order and the agreement includes a pension compensation attachment order, then they must serve on the Board –

  (a) a copy of the application for a consent order;

  (b) a draft of the proposed order, complying with rule 9.44; and

  (c) the particulars set out in rule 9.42.

9.44 Pension compensation sharing orders or pension compensation attachment orders

An order for a financial remedy, whether by consent or not, which includes a pension compensation sharing order or a pension compensation attachment order, must –

  (a) in the body of the order, state that there is to be provision by way of pension compensation sharing or pension compensation attachment in accordance with the annex or annexes to the order; and

  (b) be accompanied by a pension compensation sharing annex or a pension compensation attachment annex as the case may require, and if provision is made in relation to entitlement to PPF compensation that derives from rights under more than one pension scheme there must be one annex for each such entitlement.

9.45 Duty of the court upon making a pension compensation sharing order or a pension compensation attachment order

(1) A court which makes, varies or discharges a pension compensation sharing order or a pension compensation attachment order, must send, or direct one of the parties to send, to the Board –

  (a) in the case of –

    (i) proceedings under Part 3 of the 1984 Act, a copy of the document of divorce, annulment or legal separation;

    (ii) proceedings under Schedule 7 to the 2004 Act, a copy of the document of dissolution, annulment or legal separation;

  (b) in the case of –

    (i) divorce or nullity of marriage, a copy of the decree absolute under rule 7.32 or 7.33;

    (ii) dissolution or nullity of civil partnership, a copy of the order making the conditional order final under rule 7.32 or 7.33;

   (c) in the case of separation –
- (i) in the matrimonial proceedings, a copy of the decree of judicial separation;
- (ii) in civil partnership proceedings, a copy of the separation order; and

   (d) a copy of the pension compensation sharing order or the pension compensation attachment order, or as the case may be of the order varying or discharging that order, including any annex to that order relating to that PPF compensation but no other annex to that order.

(2) The documents referred to in paragraph (1) must be sent –

   (a) in proceedings under the 1973 Act and the 1984 Act, within 7 days beginning with the date on which –
- (i) the relevant pension compensation sharing or pension compensation attachment order is made; or
- (ii) the decree absolute of divorce or nullity or the decree of judicial separation is made,

     whichever is the later; and

   (b) in proceedings under the 2004 Act, within 7 days beginning with the date on which –
- (i) the relevant pension compensation sharing or pension compensation attachment order is made; or
- (ii) the final order of dissolution or nullity or separation order is made,

     whichever is the later.

Practice Direction 9A –
Application for a Financial Remedy

This Practice Direction supplements FPR Part 9

Introduction

1.1 Part 9 of the Family Procedure Rules sets out the procedure applicable to the financial proceedings that are included in the definition of a "financial remedy".

1.2 The procedure is applicable to a limited extent to applications for financial remedies that are heard in magistrates' courts (namely, those under section 35 of the Matrimonial Causes Act 1973, paragraph 69 of Schedule 5 to the Civil Partnership Act 2004, Part I of the Domestic Proceedings and Magistrates' Courts Act 1978, Schedule 1 to the Children Act 1989 and Schedule 6 to the Civil Partnership Act 2004). However, unless the context otherwise requires, this Practice Direction does not apply to proceedings in a magistrates' court.

1.3 Where an application for a financial remedy includes an application relating to land, details of any mortgagee must be included in the application.

Pre-application protocol

2.1 The "pre-application protocol" annexed to this Direction outlines the steps parties should take to seek and provide information from and to each other prior to the commencement of any application for a financial remedy. The court will expect the parties to comply with the terms of the protocol.

Costs

3.1 Rule 9.27 applies in the High Court and county court. The rule requires each party to produce to the court, at every hearing or appointment, an estimate of the costs incurred by the party up to the date of that hearing or appointment.

3.2 The purpose of this rule is to enable the court to take account of the impact of each party's costs liability on their financial situations. Parties should ensure that the information contained in the estimate is as full and accurate as possible and that any sums already paid in respect of a party's financial remedy costs are clearly set out. Where relevant, any liability arising from the costs of other proceedings between the parties should continue to be referred to in the appropriate section of a party's financial statement; any such costs should not be included in the estimates under rule 9.27.

3.3 Rule 28.3 provides that the general rule in financial remedy proceedings is that the court will not make an order requiring one party to pay the costs of another party. However the court may make such an order at any stage of the proceedings where it considers it appropriate to do so because of the conduct of a party in relation to the proceedings.

3.4 Any breach of this practice direction or the pre-application protocol annexed to it will be taken into account by the court when deciding whether to depart from the general rule as to costs.

Procedure before the first appointment

4.1 In addition to the matters listed at rule 9.14(5), the parties should, if possible, with a view to identifying and narrowing any issues between the parties, exchange and file with the court –

    (a)   a summary of the case agreed between the parties;
    (b)   a schedule of assets agreed between the parties; and
    (c)   details of any directions that they seek, including, where appropriate, the name of any expert they wish to be appointed.

4.2 Where a party is prevented from sending the details referred to in (c) above, the party should make that information available at the first appointment.

Financial Statements and other documents

5.1 Practice Direction 22A (Written Evidence) applies to any financial statement filed in accordance with rules 9.14 or 9.19 and to any exhibits to a financial statement. In preparing a bundle of documents to be exhibited to or attached to a financial statement, regard must be had in particular to paragraphs 11.1 to 11.3 and 13.1 to 13.4 of that Direction. Where on account of their bulk, it is impracticable for the exhibits to a financial statement to be retained on the court file after the First Appointment, the court may give directions as to their custody pending further hearings.

5.2 Where the court directs a party to provide information or documents by way of reply to a questionnaire or request by another party, the reply must be verified by a statement of truth. Unless otherwise directed, a reply to a questionnaire or request for information and documents shall not be filed with the court.

    (Part 17 and Practice Direction 17A make further provision about statements of truth)

Financial Dispute Resolution (FDR) Appointment

6.1 A key element in the procedure is the Financial Dispute Resolution (FDR) appointment. Rule 9.17 provides that the FDR appointment is to be treated as a meeting

PART III

held for the purposes of discussion and negotiation. Such meetings have been developed as a means of reducing the tension which inevitably arises in family disputes and facilitating settlement of those disputes.

6.2 In order for the FDR to be effective, parties must approach the occasion openly and without reserve. Non-disclosure of the content of such meetings is vital and is an essential prerequisite for fruitful discussion directed to the settlement of the dispute between the parties. The FDR appointment is an important part of the settlement process. As a consequence of *Re D (Minors) (Conciliation: Disclosure of Information)* [1993] Fam 231, evidence of anything said or of any admission made in the course of an FDR appointment will not be admissible in evidence, except at the trial of a person for an offence committed at the appointment or in the very exceptional circumstances indicated in *Re D*.

6.3 Courts will therefore expect –

    (a)   parties to make offers and proposals;

    (b)   recipients of offers and proposals to give them proper consideration; and

    (c)   (subject to paragraph 6.4), that parties, whether separately or together, will not seek to exclude from consideration at the appointment any such offer or proposal.

6.4 Paragraph 6.3(c) does not apply to an offer or proposal made during alternative dispute resolution.

6.5 In order to make the most effective use of the first appointment and the FDR appointment, the legal representatives attending those appointments will be expected to have full knowledge of the case.

6.6 The rules do not provide for FDR appointments to take place during proceedings in magistrates' courts.

> (Provision relating to experts in financial remedy proceedings is contained in Practice Direction 25D (Financial Remedy Proceedings and Other Family Proceedings (Except Children Proceedings) – The Use of Single Joint Experts and the Process Leading to Expert Evidence Being Put Before The Court).)

Consent orders

7.1 Rule 9.26(1)(a) requires an application for a consent order to be accompanied by two copies of the draft order in the terms sought, one of which must be endorsed with a statement signed by the respondent to the application signifying the respondent's agreement. The rule is considered to have been properly complied with if the endorsed statement is signed by solicitors on record as acting for the respondent; but where the consent order applied for contains undertakings, it should be signed by the party giving the undertakings as well as by that party's solicitor.

> (Provision relating to the enforcement of undertakings is contained in the Practice Direction 33A supplementing Part 33 of the FPR)

7.2 Rule 9.26(1)(b) requires each party to file with the court and serve on the other party a statement of information. Where this is contained in one form, both parties must sign the statement to certify that each has read the contents of the other's statement.

7.3 Rule 35.2 deals with applications for a consent order in respect of a financial remedy where the parties wish to have the content of a written mediation agreement to which the Mediation Directive applies made the subject of a consent order.

Section 10(2) of the Matrimonial Causes Act 1973 and section 48(2) of the Civil Partnership Act 2004

8.1 Where a respondent who has applied under section 10(2) of the Matrimonial Causes Act 1973, or section 48(2) of the Civil Partnership Act 2004, for the court to consider his or her financial position after a divorce or dissolution elects not to proceed with the application, a notice of withdrawal of the application signed by the respondent or by the respondent's solicitor may be filed without leave of the court. In this event a formal order dismissing or striking out the application is unnecessary. Notice of withdrawal should also be given to the applicant's solicitor.

8.2 An application under section 10(2) or section 48(2) which has been withdrawn is not a bar to making in matrimonial proceedings, the decree absolute and in civil partnership proceedings, the final order.

Maintenance Orders – registration in magistrates' courts

9.1 Where periodical payments are required to be made to a child under an order registered in a magistrates' court, section 62 of the Magistrates' Courts Act 1980 permits the payments to be made instead to the person with whom the child has his home. That person may proceed in his own name for variation, revival or revocation of the order and may enforce payment either in his own name or by requesting the designated officer of the court to do so.

9.2 The registration in a magistrates' court of an order made direct to a child entails a considerable amount of work. Accordingly, when the court is considering the form of an order where there are children, care should be taken not to make orders for payment direct where such orders would be of no benefit to the parties.

Pensions

10.1 The phrase "party with pension rights" is used in FPR Part 9, Chapter 8. For matrimonial proceedings, this phrase has the meaning given to it by section 25D(3) of the Matrimonial Causes Act 1973 and means "the party to the marriage who has or is likely to have benefits under a pension arrangement". There is a definition of "civil partner with pension rights" in paragraph 29 of Schedule 5 to the Civil Partnership Act 2004 which mirrors the definition of "party with pension rights" in section 25D(3) of the 1973 Act. The phrase "is likely to have benefits" in these definitions refers to accrued rights to pension benefits which are not yet in payment.

PPF Compensation

11.1 The phrase "party with compensation rights" is used in FPR Part 9, Chapter 9. For matrimonial proceedings, the phrase has the meaning given to it by section 25G(5) of the Matrimonial Causes Act 1973 and means the party to the marriage who is or is likely to be entitled to PPF compensation. There is a definition of "civil partner with compensation rights" in paragraph 37(1) of Schedule 5 to the Civil Partnership Act 2004 which mirrors the definition of "party with compensation rights" in section 25G(5). The phrase "is likely to be entitled to PPF Compensation" in those definitions refers to statutory entitlement to PPF Compensation which is not yet in payment.

ANNEX – PRE-APPLICATION PROTOCOL

Notes of guidance

Scope of the Protocol

1 This protocol is intended to apply to all applications for a financial remedy as defined by rule 2.3. It is designed to cover all classes of case, ranging from a simple application for periodical payments to an application for a substantial lump sum and property adjustment order. The protocol is designed to facilitate the operation of the procedure for financial remedy applications.

2 In considering the options of pre-application disclosure and negotiation, solicitors should bear in mind the advantage of having a court timetable and court managed process. There is sometimes an advantage in preparing disclosure before proceedings are commenced. However, solicitors should bear in mind the objective of controlling costs and in particular the costs of discovery and that the option of pre-application disclosure and negotiation has risks of excessive and uncontrolled expenditure and delay. This option should only be encouraged where both parties agree to follow this route and disclosure is not likely to be an issue or has been adequately dealt with in mediation or otherwise.

3 Solicitors should consider at an early stage and keep under review whether it would be appropriate to suggest mediation and/or collaborative law to the clients as an alternative to solicitor negotiation or court based litigation.

4 Making an application to the court should not be regarded as a hostile step or a last resort, rather as a way of starting the court timetable, controlling disclosure and endeavouring to avoid the costly final hearing and the preparation for it.

First letter

5 The circumstances of parties to an application for a financial remedy are so various that it would be difficult to prepare a specimen first letter. The request for information will be different in every case. However, the tone of the initial letter is important and the guidelines in paragraphs 14 and 15 should be followed. It should be approved in advance by the client. Solicitors writing to an unrepresented party should always recommend that he seeks independent legal advice and enclose a second copy of the letter to be passed to any solicitor instructed. A reasonable time limit for an answer may be 14 days.

Negotiation and settlement

6 In the event of pre-application disclosure and negotiation, as envisaged in paragraph 12 an application should not be issued when a settlement is a reasonable prospect.

Disclosure

7 The protocol underlines the obligation of parties to make full and frank disclosure of all material facts, documents and other information relevant to the issues. Solicitors owe their clients a duty to tell them in clear terms of this duty and of the possible consequences of breach of the duty, which may include criminal sanctions under the Fraud Act 2006. This duty of disclosure is an ongoing obligation and includes the duty to disclose any material changes after initial disclosure has been given. Solicitors are referred to the Good Practice Guides available to Resolution members at www.resolution.org.uk and can also contact the Law Society's Practice Advice Service on 0870 606 2522.

Amendments—FPR 2010, Update 2.

The Protocol

General principles

8 All parties must always bear in mind the overriding objective set out at rules 1.1 to 1.4 and try to ensure that applications should be resolved and a just outcome achieved as speedily as possible without costs being unreasonably incurred. The needs of any children should be addressed and safeguarded. The procedures which it is appropriate to follow should be conducted with minimum distress to the parties and in a manner designed to promote as good a continuing relationship between the parties and any children affected as is possible in the circumstances.

9 The principle of proportionality must be borne in mind at all times. It is unacceptable for the costs of any case to be disproportionate to the financial value of the subject matter of the dispute.

10 Parties should be informed that where a court is considering whether to make an order requiring one party to pay the costs of another party, it will take into account pre-application offers to settle and conduct of disclosure.

Identifying the issues

11 Parties must seek to clarify their claims and identify the issues between them as soon as possible. So that this can be achieved, they must provide full, frank and clear disclosure of facts, information and documents, which are material and sufficiently accurate to enable proper negotiations to take place to settle their differences. Openness in all dealings is essential.

Disclosure

12 If parties carry out voluntary disclosure before the issue of proceedings the parties should exchange schedules of assets, income, liabilities and other material facts, using the financial statement as a guide to the format of the disclosure. Documents should only be disclosed to the extent that they are required by the financial statement. Excessive or disproportionate costs should not be incurred.

Correspondence

13 Any first letter and subsequent correspondence must focus on the clarification of claims and identification of issues and their resolution. Protracted and unnecessary correspondence and "trial by correspondence" must be avoided.

14 The impact of any correspondence upon the reader and in particular the parties must always be considered. Any correspondence which raises irrelevant issues or which might cause the other party to adopt an entrenched, polarised or hostile position is to be discouraged.

Summary

15 The aim of all pre-application proceedings steps must be to assist the parties to resolve their differences speedily and fairly or at least narrow the issues and, should that not be possible, to assist the court to do so.

PART 10
APPLICATIONS UNDER PART 4 OF THE FAMILY LAW ACT 1996

CONTENTS OF THIS PART

10.1 Scope and interpretation of this Part

The rules in this Part apply to proceedings under Part 4 of the 1996 Act.

"Part 4 of the 1996 Act"—FLA 1996, Pt IV has the title "Family Homes and Domestic Violence". The Act is set out with detailed commentary in Part II of this work. FPR 2010, Pt 10 deals with all procedural aspects and includes provisions derived from FPR 1991, rr 3.8, 3.9, 3.9A and 3.10 and their equivalent rules in FPC(MP etc)R 1991. However, these four rules are replaced by 17 rules. The provisions are essentially the same, but clearer drafting makes the 2010 Rules much easier to follow.

10.2 Applications for an occupation order or a non-molestation order

(1) An application for an occupation order or a non-molestation order must be supported by a witness statement.

(2) Subject to paragraph (3), an application for an occupation order or a non-molestation order may be made without notice.

(3) An application for an occupation order or a non-molestation order may, in a magistrates' court, be made with the permission of the court without notice in which case the applicant must file the application at the time when the application is made or as directed by the court.

(4) Where an application is made without notice, the witness statement in support of the application must state the reasons why notice has not been given.

(Section 45 of the 1996 Act sets out the criteria for making an order without notice.)

"witness statement"—A witness statement, which must contain a statement of truth (see Pt 17), has replaced the "sworn statement" of the former rule.

"without notice"—In the rule, although not in the 1996 Act, the term "without notice" replaces "ex parte". Such an application is often necessary (see s 45 and commentary). Note that permission is required in the magistrates' court, although not in the county court or High Court.

"must state the reasons why notice has not been given"—Natural justice dictates that where an order, especially an order that might affect liberty of the subject, is made in the absence of a party without that party having even been told of the application, that party is entitled to know why. Thus reasons must be given in the witness statement for the dual purpose of persuading the court to make the order without notice and then explaining to the respondent. Written reasons used not to be required in the magistrates' court (oral evidence used to suffice) but the rule applies to all courts.

10.3 Service of the application

(1) In an application made on notice, the applicant must serve –

    (a)   a copy of the application together with any statement in support; and

    (b)   notice of any hearing or directions appointment set by the court,

on the respondent personally –

    (i)   not less than 2 days before the hearing; or

    (ii) within such period as the court may direct.

(2) Where the applicant is acting in person, the applicant may request the court officer to serve the application on the respondent.

(3) In an application for an occupation order under section 33, 35 or 36 of the 1996 Act, the applicant must serve on the mortgagee and any landlord of the dwelling-house in question –

    (a)   a copy of the application; and

    (b)   notice of the right to make representations in writing or orally at any hearing.

(4) The applicant must file a certificate of service after serving the application.

    (Rule 6.23 makes provision for the different methods of serving a document and rule 6.35 provides for the court to authorise service by an alternative method.)

"on notice"—The applicant must effect service "not less than 2 days before the hearing" or "within such period as the court may direct", which could be shorter. FPR 2010, Pt 6 deals with service of the application (cf service of the order: r 10.6). The signpost in r 10.3 points to FPR 2010, r 6.23 for the various methods of service. Personal service is not essential, although it is often the best method in FLA cases. Where an applicant in person requests the court to serve, it will generally do so by post.

"the mortgagee and any landlord"—Note the requirement to serve the application and notice on the mortgagee/landlord if an occupation order is sought.

"certificate of service"—Use Form FL415. This form, like all forms, is prescribed by FPR 2010, Pt 5.

10.4 Transfer of pending proceedings to another court

Subject to any enactment, where an application for an occupation order or a non-molestation order is pending, the court may transfer the proceedings to another court of its own initiative or on the application of either party.

"another court"—It is not unusual for a county court to make a without notice order and transfer the reconsideration of it to the magistrates' court. However, this rule refers to transfer of the application, which is not common and is likely of the court's own initiative only if the court considers that the application has not been made to the most convenient court.

10.5 Privacy

In the High Court and a county court, any hearing relating to an application for an occupation order or a non-molestation order will be in private unless the court directs otherwise.

"in private"—Statutes (eg Legal Services Act 2007) tend to refer to "chambers" and "open court", whereas rules refer to "in private" and "in public", which are more accurate and more helpful terms. The general rule is that hearings are in public and the general rule applies in the magistrates' court but not in the county court or High Court in FLA cases.

10.6 Service of an order

(1) The applicant must, as soon as reasonably practicable, serve on the respondent personally –

(a) a copy of the order; and

(b) where the order is made without notice –

(i) a copy of the application together with any statement supporting it; and

(ii) in a magistrates' court, a copy of the record of the reasons for a decision.

(Rule 27.2(8) makes provision for the court officer to supply a copy of the reasons for the court's decision to the persons referred to in rule 27.2(9).)

(2) The court must serve the documents listed in paragraph (1) if –

(a) an applicant, acting in person, so requests; or

(b) the court made the order of its own initiative.

(3) In an application for an occupation order under section 33, 35 or 36 of the 1996 Act, the applicant must serve a copy of any order made on the mortgagee and any landlord of the dwelling-house in question.

"serve on the respondent personally"—The rule requires personal service of the order and, in without notice cases, of the further documents specified in r 10.6(1)(b). No injunctive order is enforceable unless it is proved that the respondent is aware of it (see further the commentary on enforcement and CCA 1981). Service should be effected in accordance with the Family Justice Council *Protocol for Process Servers: Non-Molestation Orders*, November 2011 (see Part V).

10.7 Representations made by a mortgagee or landlord

The court may direct that a hearing be held in order to consider any representations made by a mortgagee or a landlord.

10.8 Applications to vary, extend or discharge an order

Rules 10.5 to 10.7 apply to applications to vary, extend or discharge an order.

10.9 Orders containing provisions to which a power of arrest is attached

Where the court makes an occupation order containing one or more provisions to which a power of arrest is attached ("relevant provisions") –

(a) each relevant provision must be set out in a separate paragraph in the order; and

(b) a paragraph containing a relevant provision must not include a provision of the order to which the power of arrest is not attached.

"power of arrest"—The law on powers of arrest is in FLA 1996, s 47. The power can only be attached to an occupation order (not a non-molestation order) and if it is, both the respondent who is being injuncted and the police who may have to use the power need to know precisely what it is that the respondent can be arrested for if he does it (or does not do it as the case may be). Clarity ought to be a feature of all court orders but is absolutely essential in injunctions and especially so in those that contain a power of arrest. Hence, the clear requirements of r 10.9. See the Family Justice Council *Protocol for Process Servers: Non-Molestation Orders*, November 2011 in Part V.

10.10 Service of an order on the officer for the time being in charge of a police station

(1) Where the court makes –

    (a)   an occupation order to which a power of arrest is attached; or

    (b)   a non-molestation order,

a copy of the order must be delivered to the officer for the time being in charge of –

    (i)   the police station for the applicant's address; or

    (ii)   such other police station as the court may specify.

(2) A copy of the order delivered under paragraph (1) must be accompanied by a statement showing that the respondent has been served with the order or informed of its terms (whether by being present when the order was made or by telephone or otherwise).

(3) The documentation referred to in paragraphs (1) and (2) must be delivered by –

    (a)   the applicant; or

    (b)   the court officer, where the order was served following a request under rule 10.6(2).

(4) Paragraph (5) applies where an order is made varying or discharging –

    (a)   a provision of an occupation order to which a power of arrest is attached; or

    (b)   a provision of a non-molestation order.

(5) The court officer must –

    (a)   immediately inform –

        (i)   the officer who received a copy of the order under paragraph (1); and

        (ii)   if the applicant's address has changed, the officer for the time being in charge of the police station for the new address; and

    (b)   deliver a copy of the order referred to in paragraph (4)(a) or (b) and the order referred to in paragraph (1) to any officer so informed.

Service on the police—Breach of a non-molestation order is a crime (see FLA 1996, s 42A). Thus, the police need to know of all such orders so that they can deal with any breach. The police do not need to know of occupation orders unless they contain a power of arrest so that the power can be exercised if necessary (and note FPR 2010, r 10.9, above). See the Family Justice Council *Protocol for Process Servers: Non-Molestation Orders*, November 2011 in Part V.

    Generally, orders must be delivered to the officer in charge of the police station for the applicant's address, but a different station can be specified and the court should be asked to specify a more appropriate station if there is one: for example, the police may have a domestic violence unit based at a particular police station.

    Note the requirements of r 10.10(2) and that the effect of it is to require service on the respondent before notification to the police so that there is no risk of the police effecting an unlawful arrest based on an order of which the respondent knows nothing.

"the court officer must" (r 10.10(5))—As stated above, the police need to be aware of relevant orders. The court has power to vary or discharge FLA 1996 orders (s 49) and if an order notified to the police is varied or discharged, the police must be notified of that. However, the duty to do so is on the court officer not the party who obtained the variation or discharge.

10.11 Proceedings following arrest in a county court or the High Court

(1) This rule applies where a person is arrested pursuant to –

    (a)   a power of arrest attached to a provision of an occupation order; or

    (b)   a warrant of arrest issued on an application under section 47(8) of the 1996 Act.

(2) The court before which a person is brought following arrest may –

    (a)   determine whether the facts, and the circumstances which led to the arrest, amounted to disobedience of the order; or

    (b)   adjourn the proceedings.

(3) Where the proceedings are adjourned and the arrested person is released –

    (a)   unless the court directs otherwise, the matter must be dealt with within 14 days beginning with the date of arrest; and

    (b)   the arrested person must be given not less than 2 days' notice of the hearing.

(4) An application notice seeking the committal for contempt of court of the arrested person may be issued if the arrested person is not dealt with within the period mentioned in paragraph (3)(a).

> (The powers of a county court and the High Court to remand in custody or on bail are contained in section 47 of and Schedule 5 to the Family Law Act 1996.)

> (For proceedings following arrest in a magistrates' court see rules made under section 144 of the Magistrates' Courts Act 1980.)

"where a person is arrested" (r 10.11(1))—There are three ways that a person said to be in breach of an FLA 1996 order can be brought before the court: arrest under a power of arrest; arrest under a warrant of arrest; and in answer to an application notice. This rule applies to the first two only, ie the procedure following arrest.

The rule contains provisions formerly in FPR 1991, r 3.9A but in terms much easier to follow. It even contains a signpost to the relevant statutory provisions, namely FLA 1996, s 47 and Sch 5 (see those provisions and commentary thereon).

"determine … the facts" (r 10.11(2)(a))—A trial is required to determine the facts. Where the facts are disputed, the evidence of the applicant will be required (and, if represented, submissions from the legal representative) but the applicant is unlikely to be present and may not even know of the arrest. Even if the facts are admitted, the court is unlikely to be able to proceed as it may not have the full facts. The respondent must be brought before the court within 24 hours of arrest pursuant to a power of arrest (s 47(7)) and is most unlikely to have had the opportunity to reflect or take legal advice. (The 24 hour rule does not apply to warrants but in practice is usually followed.) Further, an alleged contemnor is entitled to notice in writing, setting out clearly what he is alleged to have done (*Newman (t/a Mantella Publishing) v Modern Bookbinders Ltd* [2000] 1 WLR 2559). If it proceeded, the court could deal only with the alleged breach that led to the arrest, whereas the applicant may wish to issue an application alleging other breaches (Form N78 should be used) to be considered at the trial. For all of these reasons the court is unlikely to be able to proceed as envisaged by r 10.11(2)(a) and is much more likely to have to adjourn, as permitted by r 10.11(2)(b).

Contempt of court—Breach of an FLA 1996 order is a contempt of court. The powers of the High Court and county courts to punish are contained in the Contempt of Court Act 1981: see that Act and commentary thereon.

Relevant judicial authority—By FLA 1996, s 58 the power to punish contempt is exercisable by the "relevant judicial authority", which is defined in s 63(1).

"adjourn the proceedings" (r 10.11(2)(b))—Following the arrest the court can adjourn and, for the reasons explained above, often has to do so. If it adjourns, the court has to decide whether just to adjourn or also to remand. If the court decides to remand it has to decide whether to remand in custody or on bail. FLA 1996, s 47 and Sch 5 contain the powers of the High Court and county courts to remand (see those provisions and commentary thereon). The maximum period of a remand in custody is 8 days if remanded to prison and 3 days if remanded to police cells.

"within 14 days" (r 10.11(3)(a))—Dealing with a committal application promptly is desirable in all cases and r 10.11(3) states the basic rule that a respondent should be dealt with within 14 days of the arrest "unless the court directs otherwise". The rule only applies where "the arrested person is released", so would cover both a mere adjournment and a remand on bail but not a remand in custody, where the maximum period of remand is 8 days (although there is express power to further remand in FLA 1996, Sch 5, paras 2(2) and 3).

"not less than 2 days' notice of the hearing" (r 10.11(3)(b))—If the arrested person is released (whether on bail or not) and the hearing is adjourned, he must be given at least 2 days' notice of the new date. The better practice is for the judge to fix the date and announce it in court so that there is no doubt about it. Notice of the new date should still be served, but posting it would then be sufficient.

"application notice" (r 10.11(4))—There are three reasons why an application notice (Form N78) may be required where the respondent has been arrested: one is mentioned in r 10.11(4) and speaks for itself; the second is where the applicant wishes to put before the court for consideration other alleged breaches in addition to that which gave rise to the arrest; and the third is where the judge requires it to give effect to the requirement that a person alleged to be in breach is entitled to written notice of what he is alleged to have done (*Newman (t/a Mantella Publishing) v Modern Bookbinders Ltd* [2000] 1 WLR 2559).

MCA 1980, s 114—As the signpost at the end of r 10.11 makes clear, proceedings following arrest in the magistrates' court are governed by MCA 1980, s 114 (see the section and commentary thereon) and not by the FLA provisions.

10.12 Enforcement of an order in a county court

Rule 1 of Order 29 of the CCR (enforcement of judgment to do or abstain from doing any act) has effect as if, for paragraph (3), there were substituted the following –

"(3) At the time when the order is drawn up, the court officer will –

(a) where the order made is (or includes) a non-molestation order; or

(b) where the order made is an occupation order and the court so directs,

issue a copy of the order, indorsed with or incorporating a notice as to the consequences of disobedience, for service in accordance with paragraph (2).".

(For enforcement of an order generally in a county court or the High Court see Part 33. For enforcement of an order in a magistrates' court see rules made under section 144 of the Magistrates' Courts Act 1980.)

Scope—This rule has a misleading title as it is not really about enforcement of an order in the county court. Enforcement is governed by r 33.1, which applies CPR 1998, Schs 1 and 2. Of particular importance is Sch 1, RSC Ord 52 and Sch 2, CCR Ord 29.

The effect of r 10.12 is to require that a penal notice is endorsed on FLA orders. A penal notice, which warns the respondent of the consequences of disobedience, is an essential prerequisite to enforcement. Special wording, not the usual county court words, is used in FLA cases and these are incorporated on the standard forms. Service should be effected in accordance with the FJC Protocol of November 2011: *Process Servers: Non-Molestation Orders* (see Part V).

10.13 Enforcement of an undertaking in a county court

(1) This rule applies to applications for the enforcement of undertakings by committal order in a county court.

(2) Rule 1A of Order 29 of the CCR (undertaking given by party) applies with the necessary modifications, where an application is made in a county court to commit a person for breach of an undertaking.

(For enforcement of an undertaking in a magistrates' court see rules made under section 144 of the Magistrates' Courts Act 1980.)

Undertakings—The court can accept an undertaking instead of making an order: see FLA 1996, s 46 and commentary. Rule 10.13 applies the normal enforcement provisions of CPR 1998, Sch 2, CCR Ord 29 with the necessary modifications. As to enforcement of undertakings, see FPR PD33A. (CPR 1998, Pt 81 – committal proceedings – does not apply to family cases.)

10.14 Power to adjourn the hearing for consideration of the penalty

The High Court or a county court may adjourn the hearing for consideration of the penalty to be imposed for any contempt of court found proved and such a hearing may be restored if the respondent does not comply with any conditions specified by the court.

(Rules made under section 144 of the Magistrates' Courts Act 1980 contain an equivalent power for magistrates' courts.)

"may adjourn the hearing for consideration of the penalty"—The standard form (N79) used by sentencing judges includes provision for adjourning penalty as permitted by r 10.14. There are many reasons why this may be appropriate. For example, the judge may adjourn on terms (including strict compliance with the injunction) to give the respondent a final opportunity to comply. However, there is a trap here: it is not possible to remand in custody while the judge considers the appropriate penalty, as no statute has conferred such a power (*Delaney v Delaney* [1996] 1 FLR 458).

10.15 Hospital orders or guardianship orders under the Mental Health Act 1983

(1) Where the High Court or a county court makes a hospital order under the Mental Health Act 1983 the court officer must –

    (a)   send to the hospital any information which will be of assistance in dealing with the patient; and

    (b)   inform the applicant when the respondent is being transferred to hospital.

(2) Where the High Court or a county court makes a guardianship order under the Mental Health Act 1983, the court officer must send any information which will be of assistance in dealing with the patient to –

    (a)   the patient's guardian; and

    (b)   where the guardian is a person other than the local services authority, the local services authority.

        (Section 51 of the 1996 Act provides a magistrates' court with a power to make a hospital order or a guardianship order under the Mental Health Act 1983 and attention is drawn to rules made under section 144 of the Magistrates' Courts Act 1980.)

"hospital order"—The powers of the High Court and county courts to make a hospital order are found in CCA 1981, s 14: see that Act, the commentary thereon and the sections of MHA 1983 referred to. (There is a signpost to the equivalent magistrates' powers in the rule.) First, the court will normally have used the powers to remand for medical examination and report in FLA 1996, s 48. See further FPR PD10A.

10.16 Transfer directions under section 48 of the Mental Health Act 1983

(1) Where a transfer direction given by the Secretary of State under section 48 of the Mental Health Act 1983 is in force in respect of a person remanded in custody by the High Court or a county court, the court officer must notify –

    (a)   the governor of the prison to which that person was remanded; and

    (b)   the hospital where that person is detained,

of any committal hearing which that person is required to attend.

(2) The court officer must also give notice in writing of any further remand to the hospital where that person is detained.

        (Rules made under section 144 of the Magistrates' Courts Act 1980 make provision for magistrates' courts.)

10.17 Recognizances

(1) Where, in accordance with paragraph 2(1)(b)(ii) of Schedule 5 to the 1996 Act, the High Court or a county court fixes the amount of any recognizance with a view to it being taken subsequently, the recognizance may be taken by –

    (a)   a district judge;

    (b)   a police officer of the rank of inspector or above or in charge of a police station; or

    (c)   the governor or keeper of a prison where the arrested person is in custody.

(2) The person having custody of an applicant for bail must release that applicant if satisfied that the required recognizances have been taken.

        (A magistrates' court has a similar power to require a recognizance under Part 6 of the Magistrates' Courts Act 1980. Section 119 of that Act provides a magistrates' court with a power to postpone the taking of a recognizance and rules made under section 144 of the Magistrates' Courts Act 1980 set out the people who may subsequently take the recognizance.)

Recognizance—Recognizances by defendants in criminal proceedings were abolished by the Bail Act 1976, which created the offence of failure to answer to bail. But that offence only arises in criminal proceedings, so FLA 1996, Sch 5, para 2(1)(b) requires a recognizance to be taken where a person is remanded on bail under FLA 1996, s 47.

A recognizance is an obligation or bond acknowledged before a court. The person acknowledging it, that is the person bound by it, is the cognisor or conusor. The object of a recognizance is to secure the performance of an act by the cognisor, such as to appear at court on a particular day. If the obligation is not performed the recognizance is estreated.

Practice Direction 10A – Part 4 of the Family Law Act 1996

This Practice Direction supplements FPR Part 10

Scope of this Practice Direction

1.1 Paragraphs 4.1 to 7.1 of this Practice Direction do not apply to proceedings heard in a magistrates' court. Attention is drawn to rules made under section 144 of the Magistrates' Courts Act 1980.

Applications for an occupation order or non-molestation order made by a child under the age of sixteen

2.1 If an application for an occupation order or non-molestation order is made by a child under the age of sixteen attention is drawn to section 43 of the 1996 Act. This provides that leave of the court is required for an application made by a child under the age of sixteen. Article 6(b) of the Allocation and Transfer of Proceedings Order 2008 (S.I 2008/2836) provides that such an application must be started in a county court. The application should be made in accordance with Part 18.

Privacy

3.1 If at a hearing which has been held in private –

(a) a non-molestation order is made or an occupation order is made to which a power of arrest is attached; and

(b) the person to whom it is addressed was not given notice of the hearing and was not present at the hearing,

the terms of the order and the name of the person to whom it is addressed shall be announced in open court at the earliest opportunity.

3.2 This announcement may be either on the same day when the court proceeds to hear cases in open court or where there is no further business in open court on that day at the next listed sitting of the court.

3.3 When a person arrested under a power of arrest attached to an occupation order cannot conveniently be brought before the relevant judicial authority sitting in a place normally used as a courtroom within 24 hours after the arrest, that person may be brought before the relevant judicial authority at any convenient place. As the liberty of the subject is involved, the press and public should be permitted to be present, unless security needs make this impracticable.

Warrant of arrest on an application under section 47(8) of the 1996 Act

4.1 In accordance with section 47(9) of the 1996 Act, a warrant of arrest on an application under section 47(8) shall not be issued unless –

    (a)   the application is substantiated on oath; and

    (b)   the court has reasonable grounds for believing that the respondent has failed to comply with the order.

Attendance of arresting officer

5.1 Attention is drawn to section 47(7) of the 1996 Act. This provides that a person arrested under a power of arrest attached to an occupation order must be brought before a judge within the period of 24 hours beginning at the time of arrest.

5.2 When the arrested person is brought before the judge the attendance of the arresting officer will not be necessary, unless the arrest itself is in issue. A written statement from the arresting officer as to the circumstances of the arrest should normally be sufficient.

5.3 In those cases where the arresting officer was also a witness to the events leading to the arrest and his or her evidence regarding those events is required, arrangements should be made for the arresting officer to attend at a subsequent hearing to give evidence.

Application for Bail

6.1 An application for bail by a person arrested under –

    (a)   a power of arrest attached to an occupation order under section 47(2) or (3) of the 1996 Act; or

    (b)   a warrant of arrest issued on an application under section 47(8) or the 1996 Act,

may be made orally or in writing.

6.2 The court will require the following information, which an application in writing should therefore contain –

    (a)   the full name of the person making the application;

    (b)   the address of the place where the person making the application is detained at the time when the application is made;

    (c)   the address where the person making the application would reside if granted bail;

    (d)   the amount of the recognizance in which the person making the application would agree to be bound; and

    (e)   the grounds on which the application is made and, where a previous application has been refused, full particulars of any change in circumstances which has occurred since that refusal.

6.3 An application made in writing must be signed –

    (a)   by the person making the application or by a person duly authorised by that person in that behalf; or

    (b)   where the person making the application is a child or is for any reason incapable of acting, by a children's guardian or litigation friend acting on that person's behalf.

6.4 A copy of the application must be served on the person who obtained the injunction.

6.5 A copy of the bail notice must be given to a respondent who is remanded on bail.

Remand for Medical Examination and Report

7.1 Section 48(4) of the 1996 Act provides that the judge has power to make an order under section 35 of the Mental Health Act 1983 (remand to hospital for report on accused's mental condition) in certain circumstances. If the judge does so attention is drawn to section 35(8) of that Act, which provides that a person remanded to hospital under that section may obtain at his or her own expense an independent report on his or her mental condition from a registered medical practitioner or approved clinician of his or her choice and apply to the court on the basis of it for the remand to be terminated under section 35(7).

PART 11
APPLICATIONS UNDER PART 4A OF THE FAMILY LAW ACT 1996

CONTENTS OF THIS PART

11.1 Scope and interpretation

(1) The rules in this Part apply to proceedings in the High Court or a county court under Part 4A of the 1996 Act

(2) In this Part –

"a forced marriage protection order" means an order under section 63A of the 1996 Act; and

"the person who is the subject of the proceedings" means the person who will be protected by the forced marriage protection order applied for or being considered by the court of its own initiative, if that order is made, or who is being protected by such an order.

Rules apply to proceedings in the High Court or a county court—Although provision is made in FLA 1996, s 63N for extending the jurisdiction to the magistrates' courts, the Act has not yet been amended to provide for such extension.

11.2 Applications

(1) An application for a forced marriage protection order may be made without notice.

(2) Where an application is made without notice, it must be supported by a sworn statement explaining why notice has not been given.

(3) An application for a forced marriage protection order made by an organisation must state –

    (a)   the name and address of the person submitting the application; and

    (b)   the position which that person holds in the organisation.

Application/forms—Form FL401A is the prescribed form for an application for forced marriage protection order (FMPO). Proceedings for a FMPO are started when the court issues an application form, which means a document in which the applicant states his intention to seek a court order other than in accordance with the FPR 2010, Pt 18 procedure (see FPR 2010, rr 2.3, 5.3). The application notice must comply with the requirements set out in FPR PD18A, paras 3.1, 3.2. Where the applicant requires the permission of the court to make the application, the application for the court's permission should be made under Pt 18 in Form FL430 (PD5A). Pt 18 and PD18A procedure will apply to the application.

Without notice application—See FPR 2010, Pt 18, in particular para 5.

Statement in support—The statement in support must be a sworn statement and must set out the reasons for applying without notice. In addition, the statement should deal with the reasons for the urgency, how the overriding objective will best be furthered and refer to this rule, which permits such an application to be made (FPR PD18A, para 5.1).

Service—See FPR 2010, r 6 for service generally and for service out of jurisdiction.

11.3 Permission to apply

(1) Where the permission of the court is required to apply for a forced marriage protection order, the person seeking permission must file –

    (a)   a Part 18 application notice setting out –

        (i)   the reasons for the application, for the making of which permission is sought ("the proposed application");

        (ii)   the applicant's connection with the person to be protected;

        (iii)   the applicant's knowledge of the circumstances of the person to be protected; and

        (iv)   the applicant's knowledge of the wishes and feelings of the person to be protected;

        and

    (b)   a draft of the proposed application, together with sufficient copies for one to be served on each respondent and (if different) the person to be protected.

(2) As soon as practicable after receiving an application under paragraph (1), the court must –

    (a)   grant the application; or

    (b)   direct that a date be fixed for the hearing of the application and fix the date.

(3) The court officer must inform the following persons of the court's action under paragraph (2) –

    (a)   the applicant;

    (b)   the respondent;

    (c)   (if different) the person to be protected; and

    (d)   any other person directed by the court.

(4) Where permission is granted to apply for a forced marriage protection order, the application must proceed in accordance with rule 11.2.

Application for permission—FPR 2010, r 11.3(1)(a) specifically provides that the application should be made by a FPR 2010, Pt 18 notice and therefore the procedure set out in r 18 and FPR PD18A should be followed. The application notice in Form FL430 must set out the details set out in r 11.3(a)(i)–(iv).

Service of the order made—For service generally, see FPR 2010, r 6. Care should be taken to ensure that a penal notice is attached to the appropriate terms of the orders made and the order should be served personally on the persons to whom it is addressed.

11.4 Service of applications on notice

(1) Subject to paragraphs (3) and (5), where an application is made on notice, the applicant must serve a copy of the application, together with the notice of proceedings, personally on –

    (a)   the respondent,

    (b)   the person who is the subject of the proceedings (if that person is neither the applicant nor a respondent); and

    (c)   any other person directed by the court,

not less than 2 days before the date on which the application will be heard.

(2) The court may abridge the period specified in paragraph (1).

(3) Service of the application must be effected by the court if the applicant so requests (this does not affect the court's power to order substituted service).

(4) Where the application is served on the person who is the subject of the proceedings, it must be accompanied by a notice informing that person –

    (a)   how to apply to become a party to the proceedings; and

    (b)   of that person's right to make representations in writing or orally at any hearing.

(5) Where the person who is the subject of proceedings is not the applicant and is –

    (a)   a child;

    (b)   a person, not being a party, who lacks or may lack capacity within the meaning of the 2005 Act; or

    (c)   a protected party,

the court will give the directions about the persons who are to be served with the application.

(6) Where an application is served by the applicant, the applicant must file a certificate of service stating the date and time of personal service.

Amendments—SI 2012/679.

Person to be protected who lacks capacity is a vulnerable person or is a protected person—See the implications of the decision in *Re X (A Child)* [2012] 2 FLR 456 under FPR 2010, r 15.1. Where the Official Solicitor is invited to represent the person to be protected who lacks capacity or where the person is a vulnerable person or has learning difficulties or other mental health issues, the court should consider giving directions under its case management powers under FPR 2010, r 4.1(3)(o) that the person's independent mental health professional or social worker should be informed of the case and any orders made and that the independent mental health professional or social worker should attend with the person to provide support. Where the person has other disabilities (e g is hard of hearing or has a speech impediment) directions should be sought for the instruction of an appropriate person to assist the person during the whole court process. It is highly unlikely that any member of the family would be an appropriate person to offer such assistance as he/she is not likely to be sufficiently able or independent to offer support and assistance.

Service of application on notice—The respondent must be personally served unless the court directs otherwise. The person to be protected must also be served if he/she is neither the applicant or a respondent to the application. The court may direct that a person who is not a party to the proceedings be served. Where the person to be protected is a child or lacks capacity or is a protected person the court should be asked to give direction about service. See further under FPR 2010, Pt 15, which deals with representation of protected persons and the appointment of a litigation friend and guardian. Where the person is vulnerable, a person with limited capacity or with learning difficulties, see *Re X* (above) under r 15.1. In such cases, attempts should be made to contact the social worker allocated to the vulnerable person. Where the person to be protected has mental health issues and has an approved mental health professional or social worker, that person should be alerted and provided with a copy of the order to ensure that the person to be protected is properly supported independently of the family during the proceedings.

Evidence of service—Although the rule provides that it must be by filing a certificate of service that sets out the date and time of service, the certificate should also provide details of how the person served was identified (see FPR 2010, r 6.37). FPR PD5A provides a prescribed Form FL415 for a statement of service and this form should be used. The statement of service must be verified by a statement of truth (FPR 2010, r 17.2).

11.5 Transfer of proceedings

Subject to any enactment, where proceedings to which this Part applies are pending, the court may transfer the proceedings to another court of its own initiative or on the application of a party or (if not a party) the person who is the subject of the proceedings.

Form to be used for transfer—FPR PD5A does not specify the form that should be used. Form FL417 should be used until it is replaced.

11.6 Parties

(1) In proceedings under this Part, a person may file a Part 18 application notice for that person or another person to –

  (a) be joined as a party; or
  (b) cease to be a party.

(2) As soon as practicable after receiving an application under paragraph (1), the court must do one of the following –

  (a) in the case only of an application under paragraph (1)(a), grant the application;
  (b) order that the application be considered at a hearing, and fix a date for the hearing; or
  (c) invite written representations, as to whether the application should be granted, to be filed within a specified period, and upon expiry of that period act under sub-paragraph (a) or (b) as it sees fit.

(3) The court officer must inform the following persons of the court's action under paragraph (2) –

  (a) the applicant under paragraph (1);
  (b) (if different) the applicant for the forced marriage protection order and the respondent to that application;
  (c) (if different) the person who is the subject of the proceedings; and
  (d) any other person directed by the court.

(4) The court may at any time direct –

  (a) that a person who would not otherwise be a respondent under these rules be joined as a party to the proceedings; or
  (b) that a party to the proceedings cease to be a party,

and such a direction may be made by the court of its own initiative as well as upon an application under paragraph (1).

(5) Where the court directs the addition or removal of a party, it may give consequential directions about –

  (a) service on a new party of a copy of the application for the forced marriage protection order and other relevant documents; and
  (b) the management of the proceedings.

Note—Although rule 11.6(1) provides that an application to be joined or cease to be a party should be made by filing a FPR 2010, Pt 18 application notice, FPR PD5A prescribes Form FL431 for such an application. The application may be considered and granted without a hearing or on written representation the court may direct an oral hearing.

Consequential directions and case management—Rule 11.6(5) specifically makes provision for the court to consider giving consequential directions and any other directions for the management of the case at this stage of the proceedings. Thus, a duty is imposed on the court to apply the overriding objective principle and its case-management duties robustly.

11.7 Hearings and service of orders

(1) Any hearing relating to an application for a forced marriage protection order must be in private unless the court otherwise directs.

(2) The court may direct the withholding of any submissions made, or any evidence adduced, for or at any hearing in proceedings to which this Part applies –

    (a) in order to protect the person who is the subject of the proceedings or any other person; or

    (b) for any other good reason.

(3) The applicant must, as soon as reasonably practical, serve personally –

    (a) a copy of the order;

    (b) a copy of the record of the hearing; and

    (c) where the order is made without notice, a copy of the application together with any statement supporting it,

on the respondent, the person who is the subject of the proceedings (if neither the applicant nor a respondent), and any other person named in the order.

(4) The court must serve the documents listed in paragraph (3) if –

    (a) an applicant, acting in person, so requests; or

    (b) the court made the order of its own initiative.

Hearing must be in private unless the court otherwise directs—FPR 2010, r 27.11 provides that, save for certain exceptions, accredited representatives of the media are by right entitled to access to family proceedings in all courts. However, reporting restrictions under AJA 1960 and if appropriate under the CA 1989, s 97(2) will continue to apply (see further under r 27.11).

Disclosure against a third party and MARACs—See the commentary under FLA 1996, s 63D and *Family Law* [2012] page 331.

Withholding of any submissions etc—Rules 11.7(2) and 21.3 should be considered together when the issue of withholding of information is under consideration. In determining any application for withholding information or documents, consideration should be given not only to the grounds set out in the said two rules but the court should also balance the Arts 2, 3 and 8 Convention rights of the applicant/person to be protected and the Arts 6 and 8 rights of the respondents. See *A Chief Constable v YK and Others* [2011] 1 FLR 1493, *A County Council v SB & Others* [2011] 1 FLR 651 and *A (A Child) v Chief Constable of Dorset Police* [2011] 1 FLR 11. See *Re T (Wardship: Impact of Police Intelligence)* [2010] 1 FLR 1048 and *A Chief Constable v YK* on the issue of when the appointment of a special advocate might be appropriate. The provision relating to orders for disclosure against a person who is not a party to the proceedings previously set out in FPR 1991, r 3.31 is now set out in FPR 2010, r 21.2. Where an order is made without notice giving permission to withhold information, the court should be invited to consider including in the order the right of the person to whom it is addressed to apply to have the order varied or discharged, to make representations and where appropriate to consider listing the case for a hearing in any event so that the court can case manage the proceedings and give directions if necessary (see FPR 2010, r 11.9, below). One way of dealing with the issue of non-disclosure is to direct that the party seeking to withhold information should set out in summary the gist of the harm and the nature of the sensitive and confidential information that it is sought to withhold. Although the court cannot compel the person affected to give his legal advisers instructions permitting them to see the material that was not supplied to him, if such agreement was forthcoming the material could then be disclosed to the legal representatives on their written undertaking not to disclose it to their client. If this course was taken, the court must be satisfied that the agreement was given freely and voluntarily and that the person concerned had made an informed decision to give his consent to this procedure (*Re A (a child) v Chief Constable of Dorset & B* [2011] 1 FLR 11).

Service of the order ... on any other person named in the order—Service must be effected in accordance with the FJC Protocol of November 2011: *Process Servers: Non-Molestation Orders*. The statement of service must be a sworn statement and must contain all the information set out in the Protocol. To provide the maximum protection to the person to be protected, particularly because of the foreign element in such cases and the serious risk of the person being removed, kidnapped or abducted from the UK, as a matter of course the applicant should apply for a direction, and in any event the court should direct that the order must be served on: (i) the Forced Marriage Unit/Foreign and Commonwealth Office; (ii) the UK Border Agency (via the Foreign Marriage Unit); (iii) the Identity and Passport Service; (iv) the Children's Services/Adult Services; (v) the appropriate Police Authority; and (vi) where appropriate, the relevant embassy.

11.8 Orders made by the court of its own initiative

(1) Where the court makes a forced marriage protection order of its own initiative under section 63C of the 1996 Act, it must set out in the order –

    (a)   a summary of its reasons for making the order; and

    (b)   the names of the persons who are to be served with the order.

(2) The court may order service of the order on –

    (a)   any of the parties to the current proceedings;

    (b)   (if different) the person who is the subject of the proceedings; and

    (c)   any other person whom the court considers should be served.

(3) The court must give directions as to how the order is to be served.

Scope—Note that the specific provision for the court to direct a further hearing to consider any representation is set out in FPR 2010, r 11.9.

11.9 Representations in respect of orders

Where the court makes an order of a type referred to in rule 11.7 or 11.8, it may direct that a hearing (or further hearing) be held in order to consider any representations made by any of the persons named in, or directed to be served with, the order.

Amendments—SI 2012/679.

11.10 Applications to vary, extend or discharge an order

Rules 11.7 and 11.9 apply to applications to vary, extend or discharge a forced marriage protection order.

Scope—This rule reinforces the provisions of FLA 1996, s 63G. The application should be made on Form FL403A (PD5A).

11.11 Orders containing provisions to which a power of arrest is attached

Where the court makes a forced marriage protection order containing one or more provisions to which a power of arrest is attached ("relevant provision") –

    (a)   each relevant provision must be set out in a separate paragraph in the order; and

    (b)   a paragraph containing a relevant provision must not include a provision of the order to which the power of arrest is not attached.

Scope—This provision supports the provisions of FLA 1996, s 63H. It emphasises the need for the terms of any order that contains one or more provision to which a power of arrest is attached to be set out in separate paragraphs. These should not include any provision to which a power of arrest is not attached. Thus, orders to which a power of arrest is attached should be set out on the appropriate prescribed Form (see the Protocol of November 2011: *Process Servers: Non-Molestation Orders* in Part V). It should be noted that unlike the position under Pt IV of FLA 1996, in forced marriage cases a power of arrest may be attached to a non-molestation order and a breach of such an order is not yet a crime and cannot be dealt with in the magistrates' court. Although the Government has proposed criminalising forced marriage, a draft Bill has not yet been announced. When the order to which a power of arrest is attached is made in the absence of the respondent and without notice of the hearing, the terms of the order and the name of the person to whom it is addressed must be announced in open court at the earliest opportunity or at the next listed sitting of the court (FPR PD10A, paras 3.1, 3.2). This gives effect to para 1 of the previous *PD of 17 December 1997* [1998] 1 FLR 496, which has not always been observed. This PD must be complied with to ensure that the right of the media set out in FPR 2010, r 27.11 is preserved.

11.12 Service where order contains a power of arrest

(1) This rule applies where the court makes a forced marriage protection order consisting of or including a relevant provision (which has the meaning given in rule 11.11).

(2) The following documents must be delivered to the officer for the time being in charge of any police station for the address of the person being protected by the order or of such other police station as the court may specify –

    (a)   the power of arrest form; and

    (b)   a statement showing that the respondents and any persons directed by the court to be served with the order have been so served or informed of its terms (whether by being present when the order was made or by telephone or otherwise).

(3) The documents referred to in paragraph (2) must be delivered by –

    (a)   the applicant, if the applicant is responsible for serving the order in accordance with rule 11.7(3); or

    (b)   the court officer, if the court is responsible for serving the order in accordance with rule 11.7(4) or a direction given under rule 11.8(3).

(4) Where an order is made varying, extending or discharging any of the relevant provisions, the court officer must –

    (a)   immediately inform the officer who received a copy of the power of arrest form under paragraph (2) and, if the address of the person who is the subject of proceedings has changed, the officer for the time being in charge of the police station for the new address; and

    (b)   deliver a copy of the order, together with a copy of the order referred to in paragraph (1), to any officer so informed.

Delivery to the police—The relevant provision of the order made must be delivered to the police only after the order has been served on the respondent/s. (For mode and evidence of service, see the notes to FPR 2010, r 11.7.) It is best practice to ask the court to specify in the order that it should be delivered to the police station that has a domestic violence unit. If any relevant provision of the order is subsequently varied or discharged the police must be notified. Similarly, if the address of the person to whom the order is addressed or that of the person to be protected has changed, the police must be informed and if necessary the court should be informed so that any relevant provision of the order may be amended/varied if necessary.

11.13 Application for issue of warrant for arrest

(1) An application under section 63J(2) of the 1996 Act for the issue of a warrant for the arrest of a person must be supported by a sworn statement.

(2) An application for the issue of a warrant for arrest made by a person who is neither the person who is the subject of proceedings nor (if different) the person who applied for the order shall be treated, in the first instance, as an application for permission to apply for the warrant to be issued, and the court shall either –

    (a)   grant the application; or

(b) direct that a date be fixed for the hearing of the application and fix a date.

(3) The court officer must inform the following persons of the court's action under paragraph (2) –

    (a) the person applying for the issue of the warrant;
    (b) the person being protected by the order; and
    (c) any other person directed by the court.

Scope—This rule reinforces the provisions of FLA 1996, s 63J(2).

Application for a warrant—The rule reminds the applicant of the provision of FLA 1996, s 63J(4), that permission is required to make an application if made by a person other than the applicant or the person to be protected. The application must be made on Form FL407 using FPR 2010, Pt 18 procedure and must be supported by a sworn statement (previously an affidavit) setting out the interest or connection of the person applying for the warrant in making the application. It should exhibit a copy of the order, the terms that it is alleged have been breached and identify the breach or non-compliance with the terms or how it is alleged that the respondent is stated to be in contempt of court in relation to that order (s 63J(3); see also FPR PD10A, para 4.1).

11.14 Proceedings following arrest

(1) This rule applies where a person is arrested pursuant to –

    (a) a power of arrest attached to a provision of a forced marriage protection order; or
    (b) a warrant of arrest issued on an application under section 63J(2) of the 1996 Act.

(2) The court before whom a person is brought following his arrest may –

    (a) determine whether the facts and the circumstances which led to the arrest amounted to disobedience of the order; or
    (b) adjourn the proceedings.

(3) Where the proceedings are adjourned, the arrested person may be released and –

    (a) unless the court directs otherwise, be dealt with within 14 days of the day on which the person was arrested; and
    (b) be given not less than 2 days' notice of the adjourned hearing.

(4) An application notice seeking the committal for contempt of court of the arrested person may be issued if the arrested person is not dealt with within the period mentioned in paragraph (3)(a).

(The powers of a county court and the High Court to remand in custody or on bail are contained in section 47 of and Schedule 5 to the 1996 Act.)

Attendance of the arresting officer at court following arrest—FLA 1996, s 63I provides that the person arrested must be brought before the relevant judge within 24 hours of his arrest. The attendance of the arresting officer will not be necessary unless the arrest itself is in issue. A written statement from the arresting officer as to the circumstances of the arrest should normally be sufficient. In cases where the arresting officer is also a witness to the events leading to the arrest and his or her evidence regarding those events is required, arrangements should be made for the arresting officer to attend at a subsequent hearing (FPR PD10A, para 5.2).

Brought before a relevant judge within 24 hours—FPR PD10A, para 3.3 provides that where a person arrested under a power of arrest cannot conveniently be brought before the relevant judicial authority sitting in a place normally used as a court room within 24 hours after the arrest, that person may be brought before the relevant judicial authority at any convenient place. As the liberty of the subject is involved, the press and public should be permitted to be present unless security needs make this impracticable.

Committal for breach of order—Note that unless the court otherwise directs, if the person arrested under a power of arrest is not dealt with within 14 days of his arrest, the applicant will have to issue committal proceedings for contempt of court.

The court's power on committal for contempt—See the Contempt of Court Act 1981 (see note under that Act) and FLA 1996, s 58.

Power to grant bail—These are contained in FLA 1996, ss 47 and 63K and Sch 5. For the procedure on making an application for bail, see FPR PD10A, paras 6.1–6.5.

Power to remand in custody—The court's power to remand in custody is set out in FLA 1996, s 63K and Sch 5. The period of remand cannot exceed 8 clear days (Sch 5, para 2(5)), although the court can remand the person for a further 8 days (Sch 5, paras 2(2) and 3).

Power to remand for medical examination and report—See FLA 1996, s 63L. If the court considers it necessary to obtain a medical report it may remand the person in custody but the adjournment must not be for more than 3 weeks at a time. In the case of a remand on bail, the adjournment must not be for more than 4 weeks at a time.

11.15 Enforcement of orders

(1) The following provisions apply, with the necessary modifications, to the enforcement of orders made under this Part –

  (a) RSC Order 52, rule 7 (power to suspend execution of committal order);
  (b) in a case where an application for an order of committal is made to the High Court, RSC Order 52, rule 2 (application to Divisional Court);
  (c) CCR Order 29, rule 1 (enforcement of judgment to do or abstain from doing any act);
  (d) CCR Order 29, rule 1A (undertaking given by party);
  (e) CCR Order 29, rule 3 (discharge of person in custody).

(2) Rule 1 of Order 29 of the CCR (enforcement of judgment to do or abstain from doing any act) has effect as if, for paragraph (3), there were substituted the following –

  "(3) At the time when the order is drawn up, the court officer will, where the order made is (or includes) a forced marriage protection order, issue a copy of the order, indorsed with or incorporating a notice as to the consequences of disobedience, for service in accordance with paragraph (2)."

  (For enforcement of an order generally in a county court or the High Court see Part 33.)

Enforcement under RSC Ord 52 and CCR Ord 29—See commentary under the provisions in CPR 1998, Sch 1 and 2, respectively. Case-law before 6 April 2011 will be relevant in relation to service or orders and application to commit, the content of that application, the burden and standard of proof and penalty if breach is established. See also rr 11.16 and 11.17.

11.16 Power to adjourn the hearing for consideration of the penalty

The court may adjourn the hearing for consideration of the penalty to be imposed for any contempt of court found proved and such hearing may be restored if the contemnor does not comply with any conditions specified by the court.

Power to adjourn—Where the court finds the contempt proved, instead of sentencing the contemnor immediately, the court may adjourn the consideration of the penalty. The court may consider this as an option (where it is satisfied that the contemnor's remorse is sincere and there is evidence of change in his/her behaviour) to see whether the change is real, maintained and enduring. In addition and or in the alternative, it may extend and/or vary the terms of the injunction or make a new order.

11.17 Hospital orders or guardianship orders under the Mental Health Act 1983

(1) Where the court makes a hospital order under the Mental Health Act 1983, the court officer must –

(a)   send to the hospital any information which will be of assistance in dealing with the patient; and

(b)   inform the persons directed by the court to be informed about when the patient is being transferred to hospital.

(2) Where the court makes a guardianship order under the Mental Health Act 1983, the court officer must send any information which will be of assistance in dealing with the patient to –

(a)   the patient's guardian; and

(b)   where the guardian is a person other than the local services authority, the local services authority.

Hospital/guardianship order—For the court's power to make orders, see FLA 1996, ss 48 and 63L(4),(5). Where the court has reason to suspect that a person who is arrested is suffering from a mental illness or severe mental impairment it has power to make an order under Mental Health Act 1983, s 35 (remand for report on the accused's mental health) similar to the power of the Crown Court. FPR PD10A, para 7.1 also draws attention to s 35(8) of the Act, which provides that a person remanded to hospital under that section may obtain (at his own expense) an independent report on his mental condition from a registered medical practitioner or approved clinician of his choice and apply to the court on the basis of it for the remand to be terminated under s 35(7).

11.18 Transfer directions under section 48 of the Mental Health Act 1983

(1) Where a transfer direction given by the Secretary of State under section 48 of the Mental Health Act 1983 is in force in respect of a person remanded in custody by the court, the court officer must notify –

(a)   the governor of the prison to which that person was remanded; and

(b)   the hospital where that person is detained,

of any committal hearing which that person is required to attend.

(2) The court officer must also give notice in writing of any further remand to the hospital where that person is detained.

11.19 Recognizances

(1) Where, in accordance with paragraph 2(1)(b)(ii) of Schedule 5 to the 1996 Act, the court fixes the amount of any recognizance with a view to it being taken subsequently, the recognizance may be taken by –

(a)   a district judge;

(b)   a police officer of the rank of inspector or above or in charge of a police station; or

(c)   the governor or keeper of a prison where the arrested person is in the custody of that governor or keeper.

(2) The person having custody of an applicant for bail must release him if satisfied that the required recognizances have been taken.

Recognizance—See FLA 1996, Sch 5 and the commentary thereon.

PART 12
CHILDREN PROCEEDINGS EXCEPT PARENTAL ORDER PROCEEDINGS AND PROCEEDINGS FOR APPLICATIONS IN ADOPTION, PLACEMENT AND RELATED PROCEEDINGS

Amendments—SI 2012/3061.

CONTENTS OF THIS PART

Chapter 1
Interpretation and Application of this Part

Chapter 2
General Rules

Chapter 3
Special Provisions about Public Law Proceedings

Chapter 4
Special Provisions about Private Law Proceedings

PART III

PART III

Practice Direction 12P –
Removal from Jurisdiction: Issue of Passports   1835

Chapter 1
Interpretation and Application of this Part

12.1 Application of this Part

(1) The rules in this Part apply to –

(a)   emergency proceedings;

(b)   private law proceedings;

(c)   public law proceedings;

(d)   proceedings relating to the exercise of the court's inherent jurisdiction (other than applications for the court's permission to start such proceedings);

(e)   proceedings relating to child abduction and the recognition and enforcement of decisions relating to custody under the European Convention;

(f)   proceedings relating to the Council Regulation or the 1996 Hague Convention in respect of children; and

(g)   any other proceedings which may be referred to in a practice direction.

(Part 18 sets out the procedure for making an application for permission to bring proceedings.)

(Part 31 sets out the procedure for making applications for recognition and enforcement of judgments under the Council Regulation or the 1996 Hague Convention.)

(2) The rules in Chapter 7 of this Part also apply to family proceedings which are not within paragraph (1) but which otherwise relate wholly or mainly to the maintenance or upbringing of a minor.

Chapter 7 (r 12.1(2))—The rules in Pt 12, Ch 7, deal with the communication of information in proceedings relating to children. They set out the categories of persons to whom information relating to proceedings held in private may be communicated (FPR 2010, r 12.73) and the categories of persons to whom a party or his legal representative may communicate information relating to the proceedings where necessary for support, advice, assistance, mediation, alternative dispute resolution or to pursue a complaint (FPR 2010, r 12.75). See FPR PD12G for tables showing who may communicate information, to whom and for what purpose.

12.2 Interpretation

In this Part –

"the 2006 Act" means the Childcare Act 2006;

"advocate" means a person exercising a right of audience as a representative of, or on behalf of, a party;

"care proceedings" means proceedings for a care order under section 31(1)(a) of the 1989 Act;

"Case Management Order" means an order in the form referred to in Practice Direction 12A which may contain such of the provisions listed in that practice direction as may be appropriate to the proceedings;

"child assessment order" has the meaning assigned to it by section 43(2) of the 1989 Act;

"contact activity condition" has the meaning assigned to it by section 11C(2) of the 1989 Act;

"contact activity direction" has the meaning assigned to it by section 11A(3) of the 1989 Act;

"contribution order" has the meaning assigned to it by paragraph 23(2) of Schedule 2 to the 1989 Act;

"education supervision order" has the meaning assigned to it by section 36(2) of the 1989 Act;

"emergency proceedings" means proceedings for –

  (a) the disclosure of information as to the whereabouts of a child under section 33 of the 1986 Act;

  (b) an order authorising the taking charge of and delivery of a child under section 34 of the 1986 Act;

  (c) an emergency protection order;

  (d) an order under section 44(9)(b) of the 1989 Act varying a direction in an emergency protection order given under section 44(6) of that Act;

  (e) an order under section 45(5) of the 1989 Act extending the period during which an emergency protection order is to have effect;

  (f) an order under section 45(8) of the 1989 Act discharging an emergency protection order;

  (g) an order under section 45(8A) of the 1989 Act varying or discharging an emergency protection order in so far as it imposes an exclusion requirement on a person who is not entitled to apply for the order to be discharged;

  (h) an order under section 45(8B) of the 1989 Act varying or discharging an emergency protection order in so far as it confers a power of arrest attached to an exclusion requirement;

  (i) warrants under sections 48(9) and 102(1) of the 1989 Act and under section 79 of the 2006 Act; or

  (j) a recovery order under section 50 of the 1989 Act;

"emergency protection order" means an order under section 44 of the 1989 Act;

"enforcement order" has the meaning assigned to it by section 11J(2) of the 1989 Act;

"financial compensation order" means an order made under section 11O(2) of the 1989 Act;

"interim order" means an interim care order or an interim supervision order referred to in section 38(1) of the 1989 Act;

"private law proceedings" means proceedings for –

  (a) a section 8 order except a residence order under section 8 of the 1989 Act relating to a child who is the subject of a care order;

  (b) a parental responsibility order under sections 4(1)(c), 4ZA(1)(c) or 4A(1)(b) of the 1989 Act or an order terminating parental responsibility under sections 4(2A), 4ZA(5) or 4A(3) of that Act;

  (c) an order appointing a child's guardian under section 5(1) of the 1989 Act or an order terminating the appointment under section 6(7) of that Act;

  (d) an order giving permission to change a child's surname or remove a child from the United Kingdom under sections 13(1) or 14C(3) of the 1989 Act;

  (e) a special guardianship order except where that order relates to a child who is subject of a care order;

  (f) an order varying or discharging such an order under section 14D of the 1989 Act;

  (g) an enforcement order;

  (h) a financial compensation order;

  (i) an order under paragraph 9 of Schedule A1 to the 1989 Act following a breach of an enforcement order;

  (j) an order under Part 2 of Schedule A1 to the 1989 Act revoking or amending an enforcement order; or

  (k) an order that a warning notice be attached to a contact order;

"public law proceedings" means proceedings for –

    (a)   a residence order under section 8 of the 1989 Act relating to a child who is the subject of a care order;

    (b)   a special guardianship order relating to a child who is the subject of a care order;

    (c)   a secure accommodation order under section 25 of the 1989 Act;

    (d)   a care order, or the discharge of such an order under section 39(1) of the 1989 Act;

    (e)   an order giving permission to change a child's surname or remove a child from the United Kingdom under section 33(7) of the 1989 Act;

    (f)   a supervision order under section 31(1)(b) of the 1989 Act, the discharge or variation of such an order under section 39(2) of that Act, or the extension or further extension of such an order under paragraph 6(3) of Schedule 3 to that Act;

    (g)   an order making provision regarding contact under section 34(2) to (4) of the 1989 Act or an order varying or discharging such an order under section 34(9) of that Act;

    (h)   an education supervision order, the extension of an education supervision order under paragraph 15(2) of Schedule 3 to the 1989 Act, or the discharge of such an order under paragraph 17(1) of Schedule 3 to that Act;

    (i)   an order varying directions made with an interim care order or interim supervision order under section 38(8)(b) of the 1989 Act;

    (j)   an order under section 39(3) of the 1989 Act varying a supervision order in so far as it affects a person with whom the child is living but who is not entitled to apply for the order to be discharged;

    (k)   an order under section 39(3A) of the 1989 Act varying or discharging an interim care order in so far as it imposes an exclusion requirement on a person who is not entitled to apply for the order to be discharged;

    (l)   an order under section 39(3B) of the 1989 Act varying or discharging an interim care order in so far as it confers a power of arrest attached to an exclusion requirement;

    (m)   the substitution of a supervision order for a care order under section 39(4) of the 1989 Act;

    (n)   a child assessment order, or the variation or discharge of such an order under section 43(12) of the 1989 Act;

    (o)   an order permitting the local authority to arrange for any child in its care to live outside England and Wales under paragraph 19(1) of Schedule 2 to the 1989 Act;

    (p)   a contribution order, or revocation of such an order under paragraph 23(8) of Schedule 2 to the 1989 Act;

    (q)   an appeal under paragraph 8(1) of Schedule 8 to the 1989 Act;

"special guardianship order" has the meaning assigned to it by section 14A(1) of the 1989 Act;

"supervision order" has the meaning assigned to it by section 31(11) of the 1989 Act;

"supervision proceedings" means proceedings for a supervision order under section 31(1)(b) of the 1989 Act;

"warning notice" means a notice attached to an order pursuant to section 8(2) of the Children and Adoption Act 2006.

(The 1980 Hague Convention, the 1996 Hague Convention, the Council Regulation, and the European Convention are defined in rule 2.3.)

Chapter 2
General Rules

12.3 Who the parties are

(1) In relation to the proceedings set out in column 1 of the following table, column 2 sets out who may make the application and column 3 sets out who the respondents to those proceedings will be.

Proceedings for	Applicants	Respondents
A parental responsibility order (section 4(1)(c), 4ZA(1)(c), or section 4A(1)(b) of the 1989 Act).	The child's father; the step parent; or the child's parent (being a woman who is a parent by virtue of section 43 of the Human Fertilisation and Embryology Act 2008 and who is not a person to whom section 1(3) of the Family Law Reform Act 1987 applies) (sections 4(1)(c), 4ZA(1)(c) and 4A(1)(b) of the 1989 Act).	Every person whom the applicant believes to have parental responsibility for the child; where the child is the subject of a care order, every person whom the applicant believes to have had parental responsibility immediately prior to the making of the care order; in the case of an application to extend, vary or discharge an order, the parties to the proceedings leading to the order which it is sought to have extended, varied or discharged; in the case of specified proceedings, the child.
An order terminating a parental responsibility order or agreement (section 4(2A), 4ZA(5) or section 4A(3) of the 1989 Act).	Any person who has parental responsibility for the child; or with the court's permission, the child (section 4(3), 4ZA(6) and section 4A(3) of the 1989 Act).	As above.
An order appointing a guardian (section 5(1) of the 1989 Act).	An individual who wishes to be appointed as guardian (section 5(1) of the 1989 Act).	As above.
An order terminating the appointment of a guardian (section 6(7) of the 1989 Act).	Any person who has parental responsibility for the child; or with the court's permission, the child (section 6(7) of the 1989 Act).	As above.

PART III

Proceedings for	Applicants	Respondents
A section 8 order.	Any person who is entitled to apply for a section 8 order with respect to the child (section 10(4) to (7) of the 1989 Act); or with the court's permission, any person (section 10(2)(b) of the 1989 Act).	As above.
An enforcement order (section 11J of the 1989 Act).	A person who is, for the purposes of the contact order, a person with whom the child concerned lives or is to live; any person whose contact with the child concerned is provided for in the contact order; any individual subject to a condition under section 11(7)(b) of the 1989 Act or a contact activity condition imposed by a contact order; or with the court's permission, the child (section 11J(5) of the 1989 Act).	The person the applicant alleges has failed to comply with the contact order.
A financial compensation order (section 11O of the 1989 Act).	Any person who is, for the purposes of the contact order, a person with whom the child concerned lives or is to live; any person whose contact with the child concerned is provided for in the contact order; any individual subject to a condition under section 11(7)(b) of the 1989 Act or a contact activity condition imposed by a contact order; or with the court's permission, the child (section 11O(6) of the 1989 Act).	The person the applicant alleges has failed to comply with the contact order.

Proceedings for	Applicants	Respondents
An order permitting the child's name to be changed or the removal of the child from the United Kingdom (section 13(1), 14C(3) or 33(7) of the 1989 Act).	Any person (section 13(1), 14C(3), 33(7) of the 1989 Act).	As for a parental responsibility order.
A special guardianship order (section 14A of the 1989 Act).	Any guardian of the child; any individual in whose favour a residence order is in force with respect to the child; any individual listed in subsection (5)(b) or (c) of section 10 (as read with subsection (10) of that section) of the 1989 Act; a local authority foster parent with whom the child has lived for a period of at least one year immediately preceding the application; or any person with the court's permission (section 14A(3) of the 1989 Act) (more than one such individual can apply jointly (section 14A(3) and (5) of that Act)).	As above, and if a care order is in force with respect to the child, the child.
Variation or discharge of a special guardianship order (section 14D of the 1989 Act).	The special guardian (or any of them, if there is more than one); any individual in whose favour a residence order is in force with respect to the child; the local authority designated in a care order with respect to the child; any individual within section 14D(1)(d) of the 1989 Act who has parental responsibility for the child; the child, any parent or guardian of the child and any step-parent of the child who has acquired, and has not lost, parental responsibility by virtue of section 4A of that Act with the court's permission; or	As above.

PART III

Proceedings for	Applicants	Respondents
	any individual within section 14D(1)(d) of that Act who immediately before the making of the special guardianship order had, but no longer has, parental responsibility for the child with the court's permission.	
A secure accommodation order (section 25 of the 1989 Act).	The local authority which is looking after the child; or the Health Authority, Secretary of State, National Health Service Commissioning Board, clinical commissioning group, National Health Service Trust established under section 25 of the National Health Service Act 2006 or section 18(1) of the National Health Service (Wales) Act 2006, National Health Service Foundation Trust or any local authority providing or arranging accommodation for the child (unless the child is looked after by a local authority).	As above.
A care or supervision order (section 31 of the 1989 Act).	Any local authority; the National Society for the Prevention of Cruelty to Children and any of its officers (section 31(1) of the 1989 Act); or any authorised person.	As above.
An order varying directions made with an interim care or interim supervision order (section 38(8)(b) of the 1989 Act).	The parties to proceedings in which directions are given under section 38(6) of the 1989 Act; or any person named in such a direction.	As above.

Proceedings for	Applicants	Respondents
An order discharging a care order (section 39(1) of the 1989 Act).	Any person who has parental responsibility for the child; the child; or the local authority designated by the order (section 39(1) of the 1989 Act).	As above.
An order varying or discharging an interim care order in so far as it imposes an exclusion requirement (section 39(3A) of the 1989 Act).	A person to whom the exclusion requirement in the interim care order applies who is not entitled to apply for the order to be discharged (section 39(3A) of the 1989 Act).	As above.
An order varying or discharging an interim care order in so far as it confers a power of arrest attached to an exclusion requirement (section 39(3B) of the 1989 Act).	Any person entitled to apply for the discharge of the interim care order in so far as it imposes the exclusion requirement (section 39(3B) of the 1989 Act).	As above.
An order substituting a supervision order for a care order (section 39(4) of the 1989 Act).	Any person entitled to apply for a care order to be discharged under section 39(1) (section 39(4) of the 1989 Act).	As above.
A child assessment order (section 43(1) of the 1989 Act).	Any local authority; the National Society for the Prevention of Cruelty to Children and any of its officers; or any person authorised by order of the Secretary of State to bring the proceedings and any officer of a body who is so authorised (section 43(1) and (13) of the 1989 Act).	As above.
An order varying or discharging a child assessment order (section 43(12) of the 1989 Act).	The applicant for an order that has been made under section 43(1) of the 1989 Act; or the persons referred to in section 43(11) of the 1989 Act (section 43(12) of that Act).	As above.

PART III

Proceedings for	Applicants	Respondents
An emergency protection order (section 44(1) of the 1989 Act).	Any person (section 44(1) of the 1989 Act).	As for a parental responsibility order.
An order extending the period during which an emergency protection order is to have effect (section 45(4) of the 1989 Act).	Any person who – has parental responsibility for a child as the result of an emergency protection order; and is entitled to apply for a care order with respect to the child (section 45(4) of the 1989 Act).	As above.
An order discharging an emergency protection order (section 45(8) of the 1989 Act).	The child; a parent of the child; any person who is not a parent of the child but who has parental responsibility for the child; or any person with whom the child was living before the making of the emergency protection order (section 45(8) of the 1989 Act).	As above.
An order varying or discharging an emergency protection order in so far as it imposes the exclusion requirement (section 45(8A) of the 1989 Act).	A person to whom the exclusion requirement in the emergency protection order applies who is not entitled to apply for the emergency protection order to be discharged (section 45(8A) of the 1989 Act).	As above.
An order varying or discharging an emergency protection order in so far as it confers a power of arrest attached to an exclusion requirement (section 45(8B) of the 1989 Act).	Any person entitled to apply for the discharge of the emergency protection order in so far as it imposes the exclusion requirement (section 45(8B) of the 1989 Act).	As above.
An emergency protection order by the police (section 46(7) of the 1989 Act).	The officer designated officer for the purposes of section 46(3)(e) of the 1989 Act (section 46(7) of the 1989 Act).	As above.

Proceedings for	Applicants	Respondents
A warrant authorising a constable to assist in exercise of certain powers to search for children and inspect premises (section 48 of the 1989 Act).	Any person attempting to exercise powers under an emergency protection order who has been or is likely to be prevented from doing so by being refused entry to the premises concerned or refused access to the child concerned (section 48(9) of the 1989 Act).	As above.
A warrant authorising a constable to assist in exercise of certain powers to search for children and inspect premises (section 102 of the 1989 Act).	Any person attempting to exercise powers under the enactments mentioned in section 102(6) of the 1989 Act who has been or is likely to be prevented from doing so by being refused entry to the premises concerned or refused access to the child concerned (section 102(1) of that Act).	As above.
An order revoking an enforcement order (paragraph 4 of Schedule A1 to the 1989 Act).	The person subject to the enforcement order.	The person who was the applicant for the enforcement order; and where the child was a party to the proceedings in which the enforcement order was made, the child.
An order amending an enforcement order (paragraphs 5 to 7 of Schedule A1 to the 1989 Act).	The person subject to the enforcement order.	The person who was the applicant for the enforcement order. (Rule 12.33 makes provision about applications under paragraph 5 of Schedule A1 to the 1989 Act.)
An order following breach of an enforcement order (paragraph 9 of Schedule A1 to the 1989 Act).	Any person who is, for the purposes of the contact order, the person with whom the child lives or is to live; any person whose contact with the child concerned is provided for in the contact order; any individual subject to a condition under section 11(7)(b) of the 1989 Act or a contact activity condition imposed by a contact order; or	The person the applicant alleges has failed to comply with the unpaid work requirement imposed by an enforcement order; and where the child was a party to the proceedings in which the enforcement order was made, the child.

Proceedings for	Applicants	Respondents
	with the court's permission, the child (paragraph 9 of Schedule A1 to the 1989 Act).	
An order permitting the local authority to arrange for any child in its care to live outside England and Wales (Schedule 2, paragraph 19(1), to the 1989 Act).	The local authority (Schedule 2, paragraph 19(1), to the 1989 Act).	As for a parental responsibility order.
A contribution order (Schedule 2, paragraph 23(1), to the 1989 Act).	The local authority (Schedule 2, paragraph 23(1), to the 1989 Act).	As above and the contributor.
An order revoking a contribution order (Schedule 2, paragraph 23(8), to the 1989 Act).	The contributor; or the local authority.	As above.
An order relating to contact with the child in care and any named person (section 34(2) of the 1989 Act) or permitting the local authority to refuse contact (section 34(4) of that Act).	The local authority; or the child (section 34(2) or 34(4) of the 1989 Act).	As above; and the person whose contact with the child is the subject of the application.
An order relating to contact with the child in care (section 34(3) of the 1989 Act).	The child's parents; any guardian or special guardian of the child; any person who by virtue of section 4A of the 1989 Act has parental responsibility for the child; a person in whose favour there was a residence order in force with respect to the child immediately before the care order was made; a person who by virtue of an order made in the exercise of the High Court's inherent jurisdiction with respect to children had care of the child immediately before the care order was made (section 34(3)(a) of the 1989 Act); or	As above; and the person whose contact with the child is the subject of the application.

Proceedings for	Applicants	Respondents
	with the court's permission, any person (section 34(3)(b) of that Act).	
An order varying or discharging an order for contact with a child in care under section 34 (section 34((9) of the 1989 Act).	The local authority; the child; or any person named in the order (section 34(9) of the 1989 Act).	As above; and the person whose contact with the child is the subject of the application.
An education supervision order (section 36 of the 1989 Act).	Any local authority (section 36(1) of the 1989 Act).	As above; and the child.
An order varying or discharging a supervision order (section 39(2) of the 1989 Act).	Any person who has parental responsibility for the child; the child; or the supervisor (section 39(2) of the 1989 Act).	As above; and the supervisor.
An order varying a supervision order in so far as it affects the person with whom the child is living (section 39(3) of the 1989 Act).	The person with whom the child is living who is not entitled to apply for the order to be discharged (section 39(3) of the 1989 Act).	As above; and the supervisor.
An order varying a direction under section 44(6) of the 1989 Act in an emergency protection order (section 44(9)(b) of that Act).	The parties to the application for the emergency protection order in respect of which it is sought to vary the directions; the children's guardian; the local authority in whose area the child is ordinarily resident; or any person who is named in the directions.	As above, and the parties to the application for the order in respect of which it is sought to vary the directions; any person who was caring for the child prior to the making of the order; and any person whose contact with the child is affected by the direction which it is sought to have varied.
A recovery order (section 50 of the 1989 Act).	Any person who has parental responsibility for the child by virtue of a care order or an emergency protection order; or	As above; and the person whom the applicant alleges to have effected or to have been or to be responsible for the taking or keeping of the child.

Proceedings for	Applicants	Respondents
	where the child is in police protection the officer designated for the purposes of section 46(3)(e) of the 1989 Act (section 50(4) of the 1989 Act).	
An order discharging an education supervision order (Schedule 3, paragraph 17(1), to the 1989 Act).	The child concerned; a parent of the child; or the local authority concerned (Schedule 3, paragraph 17(1), to the 1989 Act).	As above; and the local authority concerned; and the child.
An order extending an education supervision order (Schedule 3, paragraph 15(2), to the 1989 Act).	The local authority in whose favour the education supervision order was made (Schedule 3, paragraph 15(2), to the 1989 Act).	As above; and the child.
An appeal under paragraph (8) of Schedule 8 to the 1989 Act.	A person aggrieved by the matters listed in paragraph 8(1) of Schedule 8 to the 1989 Act.	The appropriate local authority.
An order for the disclosure of information as to the whereabouts of a child under section 33 of the 1986 Act.	Any person with a legitimate interest in proceedings for an order under Part 1 of the 1986 Act; or a person who has registered an order made elsewhere in the United Kingdom or a specified dependent territory.	Any person alleged to have information as to the whereabouts of the child.
An order authorising the taking charge of and delivery of a child under section 34 of the 1986 Act.	The person to whom the child is to be given up under section 34(1) of the 1986 Act.	As above; and the person who is required to give up the child in accordance with section 34(1) of the 1986 Act.
An order relating to the exercise of the court's inherent jurisdiction (including wardship proceedings).	A local authority (with the court's permission); any person with a genuine interest in or relation to the child; or the child (wardship proceedings only).	The parent or guardian of the child; any other person who has an interest in or relationship to the child; and the child (wardship proceedings only and with the court's permission as described at rule 12.37).

Proceedings for	Applicants	Respondents
A warrant under section 79 of the 2006 Act authorising any constable to assist Her Majesty's Chief Inspector for Education, Children's Services and Skills in the exercise of powers conferred on him by section 77 of the 2006 Act.	Her Majesty's Chief Inspector for Education, Children's Services and Skills.	Any person preventing or likely to prevent Her Majesty's Chief Inspector for Education, Children's Services and Skills from exercising powers conferred on him by section 77 of the 2006 Act.
An order in respect of a child under the 1980 Hague Convention.	Any person, institution or body who claims that a child has been removed or retained in breach of rights of custody or claims that there has been a breach of rights of access in relation to the child.	The person alleged to have brought the child into the United Kingdom; the person with whom the child is alleged to be; any parent or guardian of the child who is within the United Kingdom and is not otherwise a party; any person in whose favour a decision relating to custody has been made if that person is not otherwise a party; and any other person who appears to the court to have sufficient interest in the welfare of the child.
An order concerning the recognition and enforcement of decisions relating to custody under the European Convention.	Any person who has a court order giving that person rights of custody in relation to the child.	As above.
An application for the High Court to request transfer of jurisdiction under Article 15 of the Council Regulation or Article 9 of the 1996 Hague Convention (rule 12.65).	Any person with sufficient interest in the welfare of the child and who would be entitled to make a proposed application in relation to that child, or who intends to seek the permission of the court to make such application if the transfer is agreed.	As directed by the court in accordance with rule 12.65.

PART III

Proceedings for	Applicants	Respondents
An application under rule 12.71 for a declaration as to the existence, or extent, of parental responsibility under Article 16 of the 1996 Convention.	Any interested person including a person who holds, or claims to hold, parental responsibility for the child under the law of another State which subsists in accordance with Article 16 of the 1996 Hague Convention following the child becoming habitually resident in a territorial unit of the United Kingdom.	Every person whom the applicant believes to have parental responsibility for the child; any person whom the applicant believes to hold parental responsibility for the child under the law of another State which subsists in accordance with Article 16 of the 1996 Hague Convention following the child becoming habitually resident in a territorial unit of the United Kingdom; and where the child is the subject of a care order, every person whom the applicant believes to have had parental responsibility immediately prior to the making of the care order
A warning notice.	The person who is, for the purposes of the contact order, the person with whom the child concerned lives or is to live; the person whose contact with the child concerned is provided for in the contact order; any individual subject to a condition under section 11(7)(b) of the 1989 Act or a contact activity condition imposed by the contact order; or with the court's permission, the child.	Any person who was a party to the proceedings in which the contact order was made. (Rule 12.33 makes provision about applications for warning notices).

(2) The court will direct that a person with parental responsibility be made a party to proceedings where that person requests to be one.

(3) Subject to rule 16.2, the court may at any time direct that –

    (a)   any person or body be made a party to proceedings; or

    (b)   a party be removed.

(4) If the court makes a direction for the addition or removal of a party under this rule, it may give consequential directions about –

    (a)   the service of a copy of the application form or other relevant documents on the new party;

    (b)   the management of the proceedings.

(5) In this rule –

"a local authority foster parent" has the meaning assigned to it by section 23(3) of the 1989 Act; and

"care home", "independent hospital", "local authority" and "clinical commissioning group" have the meanings assigned to them by section 105 of the 1989 Act.

(Part 16 contains the rules relating to the representation of children.)

Amendments—SI 2013/235.

Public Law Outline (FPR PD12A)—Under the PLO any decisions as to the joinder of parties and the making of directions as to party status will be considered by the court at the first appointment, which will take place by Day 6 (Stage 1 of the PLO). See further under FPR 2010, r 12.25.

Factors in decision whether to join or discharge a party—There is no guidance in the rules or CA 1989 as to the factors that the court should take into account in making decisions about parties. The court is required to apply the overriding objective in FPR 2010, r 1.1, so as to deal with cases justly and in ways that are expeditious, fair and proportionate. The court is asked to save expense and to ensure that it allots an appropriate share of the court's resources to the case. The following propositions can be extracted from the authorities, but practitioners are warned that a court considering similar cases in future might decide them differently in the light of the new overriding objective:

(a) It appears that CA 1989, s 1(1) does not apply in this context. Where the request is for joinder, see *North Yorkshire County Council v G* [1993] 2 FLR 732. As to discharge, in *Re W (Discharge of Party to Proceedings)* [1997] 1 FLR 128, Hogg J held that, in considering an application by a mother that the father cease to be a party to her proceedings for the discharge of a care order, the welfare of the children was important but not paramount. In exceptional circumstances the court has power to make a declaration that the local authority be absolved from the duty to provide information to a parent and from the duty to consult him or her in any way about the child (*Re C (Care: Consultation with Parents not in Child's Best Interests)* [2006] 2 FLR 787).

(b) Where an applicant seeks to become a party in existing proceedings in order to apply for a s 8 order, the factors in s 10(9) are applicable even though he does not expressly seek leave to apply for a s 8 order (*W v Wakefield City Council* [1995] 1 FLR 170 – an aunt sought a residence order in respect of her niece and applied to become a party to separate care proceedings relating to her nephew).

(c) Where the natural father of a child who does not have parental responsibility for him applies for leave to be joined as a party to care proceedings concerning the child, albeit at a late stage, there is a presumption that his application should be granted unless there is some justifiable reason for refusing it. There is no requirement for the court to consider the CA 1989, s 10(9) factors for granting leave to seek a s 8 order in this context (*Re B (Care Proceedings: Notification of Father Without Parental Responsibility)* [1999] 2 FLR 408; *Re F (Care: Party Status: Directions)* [1999] Fam Law 294; c f *Re P (Care Proceedings: Father's Application to be Joined as Party)* [2001] 1 FLR 781 – father's application refused as he had had every opportunity to participate in the care proceedings at an early stage and had chosen not to. This was not a breach of ECHR 1950, Art 6 (right to fair trial), because it was the father's fault that he had not applied earlier. Furthermore, there was no breach of Art 8 (right to respect for private and family life) as the father's rights had to be balanced against those of the children and the children needed a speedy conclusion to the proceedings).

(d) Where a grandparent applies to become a party to care proceedings, the Court of Appeal in *Re B (Paternal Grandmother: Joinder as Party)* [2012] 2 FLR 1358 has given guidance as to the approach to be taken. It held that it is appropriate to refer to the factors in CA 1989, s 10(9), albeit that no order under CA 1989, s 8 is being sought by the grandparent. Section 10(9) does not contain a test; by picking out some factors to which the court should have particular regard, it is acknowledged by implication that there may be other factors the court has to consider and it would be wrong to try to list or limit those. The prospects of success of the proposed application are relevant and leave will not be given for an application that is not arguable. However, the fact that a person has an arguable case might not necessarily be sufficient to entitle him to leave under s 10 or joinder as a party, since there may be other factors that outweigh this. The court has a broad discretion to conduct the case as is most appropriate given the issues involved and the evidence available. Some cases may properly be determined on submissions alone. It will not always be necessary for findings to be made in relation to disputed facts, perhaps because the result would not depend on them or because there are enough undisputed facts to form the basis of the decision that has to be taken. Furthermore, there is no absolute entitlement to an assessment with a view to caring for a child. The observation of Thorpe LJ in *Re J (Leave to Issue Application for Residence Order)* [2003] 1 FLR 114 that judges should be careful not to dismiss the possibility of a child being cared for by grandparents "without full inquiry" should be read in the context of the facts of that case. There are various levels of

PART III

investigation that may be appropriate, ranging from a full hearing with reports and oral evidence at one end of the spectrum, to a careful but limited examination of the situation by the local authority that may disclose overwhelming reasons why care by the grandparent is clearly not an option. The court must also consider the risk of delay occasioned by or associated with the application (s 10(9)(c)).

(e) The court may consider the overall merits of the applicant's case, but a good arguable case may suffice (contrasting *Re M (Care: Contact: Grandmother's Application for Leave)* [1995] 2 FLR 86, CA).

(f) If the applicant for leave does not have independent or separate views to put forward he might not be joined (*North Yorkshire County Council v G*, above, and see **Separate representation of parties**, below). The court will seek to control wasted time and costs in making its decision on joinder (*Re B and H (Minors) (Costs: Legal Aid)* [1994] 1 FLR 327).

(g) By analogy with the decision in *Re A (A Minor) (Residence Order: Leave to Apply)* [1993] 1 FLR 425 (determining an application for leave to apply for a residence order), no doubt the wishes of the child can also be part of the relevant circumstances.

(h) There may be situations in which current foster-parents are joined as respondents to care proceedings but, in ordinary circumstances, the court would not regard it as appropriate because, in most cases, it would run counter to the policy of CA 1989, ss 9(3) and 10(3) (*Re G (Minors) (Interim Care Order)* [1993] 2 FLR 839; see further **Separate representation of parties**, below).

(i) It is not correct (given the restrictions on applications by local authorities for private law orders) to join a local authority as a party to a father's s 8 application following its decision (pursuant to s 37) not to apply for a care or supervision order (*F v Cambridgeshire County Council* [1995] 1 FLR 516).

(j) It is not always necessary to add an individual to proceedings as a party simply to make a prohibited steps order against him, nor is it necessary for him even to be present in court, although the court should make it clear that if any person served with the order disagreed with any part of it and wished to seek to set aside or vary it, they should make an immediate application to the court to do so under s 11(7)(d) (*LLBC v TG, JG and KR* [2009] 1 FLR 414; *Re H (Prohibited Steps Order)* [1995] 1 FLR 638, CA).

(k) As to the appropriate parties to an application for sanction for the sterilisation of a minor, see FPR 2010, Pt 16 and PD16A, which govern the representation of children in family proceedings.

(l) It may be appropriate to give leave to intervene for a specific purpose rather than joining a person as a party (*Re S (Care: Residence: Intervener)* [1997] 1 FLR 497, CA). However, there is no right for satellite parties against whom allegations are being made in care proceedings to intervene and each case must be looked at on its own merits (*Re H (Care Proceedings: Intervener)* [2000] 1 FLR 775). In *Re H (Children) (Care Proceedings: Sexual Abuse)* [2000] 2 FCR 499 the court held that where, in the course of care proceedings, specific allegations of child sexual abuse are made against a non-party and brought for preliminary issue trial, it is vital that that person's evidence is before the court at that stage, even if he is unlikely to have party status at the substantive hearing. See also *Re L (Police Investigation: Privilege)* [1996] 1 FLR 731, HL, in which an application by the police for disclosure of medical reports was determined without the police being joined as a party to the care proceedings.

(m) Courts will not sanction the withholding of information about the existence of a child from his parent, or dispense with service on that parent of proceedings relating to the child, in anything other than exceptional circumstances (*Re A (Father: Knowledge of Child's Birth)* [2011] 2 FLR 123). The test simply requires a high degree of exceptionality and is not limited to significant physical risk; when evaluating the risk of future harm there is no minimum requirement (*Re A*). Where the mother challenges the legitimacy of the child concerned in care proceedings it is still necessary to serve notice of the proceedings on her husband (*Re AB (Care Proceedings: Service on Husband Ignorant of Child's Existence)* [2004] 1 FLR 527).

(n) In exceptional circumstances it may be appropriate to exclude a father with parental responsibility from care proceedings (*A Local Authority v M and F; The Children (by their Guardian)* [2010] 1 FLR 1355 – where the father presented a real and substantial risk to the children and the mother).

Joinder of child as respondent—Where a child seeks to make an application concerning himself, he must seek leave under CA 1989, s 10 and must start the proceedings in a county court (ATPO 2008, art 6(a)). In certain situations, the child is automatically a respondent to proceedings begun by others, notably where the proceedings are specified (see CA 1989, s 41). Where this is not the case, a child who seeks to become a respondent must apply under r 12.3 (*Re N (A Minor)* (unreported) 25 September 1997, CA). Where the application to be joined as a respondent succeeds, rr 16.4 and 16.6 will dictate whether the child can instruct his solicitor independently or whether he must do so through a children's guardian. See FPR PD16A, paras 7.1–7.19 for further information about the appointment of a children's guardian under FPR 2010, r 16.4.

Separate representation of parties—Guidance as to the representation of parties is given in *Re M (Minors) (Sexual Abuse: Evidence)* [1993] 1 FLR 822, where the Court of Appeal held that grandparents should not intervene in CA 1989 proceedings unless they have a separate point of view to put forward. In *North Yorkshire County Council v G* [1993] 2 FLR 732, magistrates were wrong to permit the brother of a child subject to care proceedings to be joined as a party in the proceedings when he had no independent point of view to present. In *Re BJ (Care: Third Party Intervention)* [1999] Fam Law 613 the court refused to join a 12-year-old boy as intervener to protect his own interests where allegations had been made that he had sexually abused one of the two children who were the subjects of the care proceedings in question. The current care proceedings did not directly involve the boy, his situation was being considered in another local authority area and his interests were being properly safeguarded by his mother. Furthermore, the court observed that intervener status brings with it onerous responsibilities which it would be inappropriate to impose on a child of his age. See also *Re G*, in **Factors in decision whether to join or discharge a party** (sub-paragraph (g)), above. Where a number of parties are putting forward essentially the same case, serious consideration should be given to the degree of separate representation of those parties that is strictly necessary (*Birmingham City Council v H (No 3)* [1994] 1 FLR 224, HL). As to the de-merits of local authorities using employed solicitors rather than specialist local counsel as representatives in contested child care cases, see *Re B (Local Authorities: Representation) (Note)* [1996] 1 FLR 56. Public funds should not be used to enable parties to be represented unless they have a positive case to put before the court (*Merton London Borough Council v K; Re K (Care: Representation: Public Funding)* [2005] 2 FLR 422) or to duplicate representation (*Oxfordshire County Council v X, Y and J* [2011] 1 FLR 272; *Re B and H Minors (Costs: Legal Aid)* [1994] 1 FLR 327). Where legal representation is unnecessarily duplicated, there may be adverse costs consequences (*Re TG (A Child)* [2013] EWCA Civ 5). As to representation on appeal, it should be borne in mind that it may be justifiable for a party to play an active role at first instance but not on appeal and, in those circumstances, costs might be ordered against him in relation to the appeal (*Re O (Costs: Liability of Legal Aid Board)* [1997] 1 FLR 465, CA).

Children as parties where separately represented—See FPR 2010, r 16.2 for the circumstances when the court may make a child a party to the proceedings. FPR PD16A, paras 7.1–7.5 set out the matters that the court will take into consideration before making a child a party. As to whether there is jurisdiction to order separate representation for children who are the subject of proceedings without adding them as parties, see *L v L (Minors) (Separate Representation)* [1994] 1 FLR 156.

Request to be joined as a party—Where a person wishes to apply for permission to be made a party in the course of existing proceedings the procedure in FPR 2010, rr 18.1–18.13 and FPR PD18A should be used. Note that PD18A, para 3.5 requires the application notice to include a draft of the application for the making of which permission is sought, together with sufficient copies for one to be served on each respondent. The request to be joined as a party should be made on Form C2. The reasons for the request to be joined as a party, or to cease to be a party, should be set out in as much detail as possible and, where the person making a request to be joined as a party has parental responsibility, this should be clearly stated because it will entitle him to have his request granted as of right (r 12.3(2)). The rule is wide enough to entitle a person to request that someone else be joined or cease to be a party. So, for example, where a respondent's interest in the proceedings has come to an end, perhaps because the child ceased to live with him some time ago, the applicant may apply for him to be removed as a party. Where the request is by one person that another be joined as a party, r 12.3(3) makes no provision for him to be consulted in advance as to his views with the result that a person might find himself a party to proceedings without knowing of the possibility in advance. Bearing in mind that participation in proceedings can have serious financial and other implications, the court should be alive to this danger and make what enquiries it can as to the willingness of the person concerned to be a party. Form C2 has been amended to include an additional question related to harm, which must be completed where an application is made under CA 1989, s 8 (for residence, contact, specific issue or prohibited steps orders) or s 4(1)(c) (for a parental responsibility order). Question 4 on Form C2 asks whether the child who is the subject of the application has suffered or is at risk of suffering any harm from (a) any form of domestic abuse; (b) violence within the household; (c) child abduction; or (d) other conduct or behaviour. If this question is answered in the affirmative, supplemental Form C1A must also be completed. It is intended that cases in which an allegation of harm is made should be identified as early as possible in the court process. See further under r 12.3.

Granting request without a hearing—The court has power under r 12.3(3) to direct at any time that a person be made a party to the proceedings. FPR PD18A, para 4.2 gives the court power to consider a request for an application to be made without a hearing if it considers it appropriate to do so. However, applications should, wherever possible, be made so that they are considered at the next hearing for which a date has been fixed (see PD18A, paras 4.7–4.9).

12.4 Notice of proceedings to person with foreign parental responsibility

(1) This rule applies where a child is subject to proceedings to which this Part applies and –

    (a) a person holds or is believed to hold parental responsibility for the child under the law of another State which subsists in accordance with Article 16 of the 1996 Hague Convention following the child becoming habitually resident in a territorial unit of the United Kingdom; and

    (b) that person is not otherwise required to be joined as a respondent under rule 12.3.

(2) The applicant shall give notice of the proceedings to any person to whom the applicant believes paragraph (1) applies in any case in which a person whom the applicant believed to have parental responsibility under the 1989 Act would be a respondent to those proceedings in accordance with rule 12.3.

(3) The applicant and every respondent to the proceedings shall provide such details as they possess as to the identity and whereabouts of any person they believe to hold parental responsibility for the child in accordance with paragraph (1) to the court officer, upon making, or responding to the application as appropriate.

(4) Where the existence of a person who is believed to have parental responsibility for the child in accordance with paragraph (1) only becomes apparent to a party at a later date during the proceedings, that party must notify the court officer of those details at the earliest opportunity.

(5) Where a person to whom paragraph (1) applies receives notice of proceedings, that person may apply to the court to be joined as a party using the Part 18 procedure.

"parental responsibility" (r 12.4(1)(a))—See definition in Hague Convention 1996, Art 1(2) and the commentary under Art 16 (see Part VI). The Hague Convention came into force in the UK on 1 November 2012.

12.5 What the court will do when the application has been issued

When the proceedings have been issued the court will consider –

    (a) setting a date for –

        (i) a directions appointment;

        (ii) in private law proceedings, a First Hearing Dispute Resolution Appointment;

        (iii) in care and supervision proceedings and in so far as practicable other public law proceedings, the First Appointment; or

        (iv) the hearing of the application or an application for an interim order,
and if the court sets a date it will do so in accordance with rule 12.13 and Practice Directions 12A and 12B;

    (b) giving any of the directions listed in rule 12.12 or, where Chapter 6, section 1 applies, rule 12.48; and

    (c) doing anything else which is set out in Practice Directions 12A or 12B or any other practice direction.

      (Practice Directions 12A and 12B supplementing this Part set out details relating to the First Hearing Dispute Resolution Appointment and the First Appointment.)

Pre-Application Protocol for Mediation Information and Assessment—FPR PD3A sets out the *Pre-Application Protocol for Mediation Information and Assessment*, which applies to all applications in "relevant family proceedings". The purpose is to encourage and facilitate the use of alternative dispute resolution (ADR) and to ensure, so far as possible, that all parties have considered mediation as an alternative way of resolving their disputes. In *Re W (Direct Contact)* [2013] 1 FLR 494, the Court of Appeal held that it is an integral aspect of parental responsibility that parents should work to put aside differences and ensure that their children have relationships with both parents.

Before making an application to the court, all applicants (unless Annex C applies) should contact a family mediator to arrange an information meeting about mediation and other forms of ADR (called a "mediation information and assessment meeting" (MIAM)). The court will also expect any respondent to have attended such a meeting if invited to do so. Annex A to the Protocol sets out the steps that the court will normally expect an applicant to follow before making an application to the court. Annex B sets out the definition of "relevant family proceedings" for the purpose of FPR PD3A. Annex C sets out the circumstances in which attendance at a mediation information and assessment meeting is not expected. If the applicant then makes an application to the court, a completed Form FM1 must also be filed. Form FM1 is completed and signed by the mediator and countersigned by the applicant or their solicitor, where the applicant has attended a meeting, or has not attended a meeting and: (1) the mediator is satisfied that mediation is not suitable because another party is not willing to attend; (2) the mediator determines that the case is not suitable; or (3) a mediator has made a determination within the previous 4 months that the case is not suitable for mediation. In all other circumstances, Form FM1 must be completed and signed by the applicant or their solicitor.

Draft Legislation on Family Justice—In September 2012, draft legislation was presented to Parliament in response to David Norgrove's Family Justice Review. Clause 1 proposes that in future every person who wishes to apply for a court order in family proceedings of a certain type (to be defined in FPR 2010), whether publicly or privately funded, must first attend a family mediation information and assessment meeting (MIAM) to find out about and consider mediation or other forms of dispute resolution, unless that person meets limited criteria exempting them from this requirement. The exemptions will include, for example, cases that are urgent, or where a MIAM cannot be arranged within a specified time, or where there is evidence of domestic violence.

Forms and start of proceedings—For the general rules about forms and the start of proceedings see FPR 2010, rr 5.1–5.3 and FPR PD5A. However, for certain proceedings the relevant forms to be used are specified in the appropriate PD governing that type of application.

12.6 Children's guardian, solicitor and reports under section 7 of the 1989 Act

As soon as practicable after the issue of proceedings or the transfer of the proceedings to the court, the court will –

   (a)   in specified proceedings, appoint a children's guardian under rule 16.3(1) unless –
      (i)   such an appointment has already been made by the court which made the transfer and is subsisting; or
      (ii)   the court considers that such an appointment is not necessary to safeguard the interests of the child;
   (b)   where section 41(3) of the 1989 Act applies, consider whether a solicitor should be appointed to represent the child, and if so, appoint a solicitor accordingly;
   (c)   consider whether to ask an officer of the service or a Welsh family proceedings officer for advice relating to the welfare of the child;
   (d)   consider whether a report relating to the welfare of the child is required, and if so, request such a report in accordance with section 7 of the 1989 Act.

   (Part 16 sets out the rules relating to representation of children.)

Defined terms—"child", "children's guardian", "court", "officer of the service", "Welsh family proceedings officer": FPR 2010, r 2.3(1): "specified proceedings": FPR 2010, r 12.27 and CA 1989, s 41(6).

Appointment—The obligation to appoint a children's guardian in specified proceedings unless the circumstances are as described in r 12.6(a)(ii) is imposed by CA 1989, s 41(1). CJCSA 2000, ss 11 and 12 established the Children and Family Court Advisory and Support Service (Cafcass), which is responsible for fulfilling the requirements of courts in respect of investigating and reporting; see further the annotations under those sections and CA 1989, ss 7 and 37. The purpose of r 12.6 is to require the appointment to be made as soon as practicable after the commencement of the proceedings, or the arrival of transferred proceedings if the transferring court has not already made an appointment. The phrase "as soon as practicable" is not restricted to matters internal to the court but includes problems relating to the identification and availability of an officer of the service for appointment as guardian. The reference in r 12.6(a)(i) to an existing appointment by the transferring court is not confined to the possibility that that court did not request Cafcass to make an officer of the service available for appointment, but includes the possibility that such a request was made and has not been complied with at the time of transfer (*R v Children and Family Court Advisory and Support Service* [2003] 1 FLR 953). See also the *Best Practice Guide of August 2009 (Preparing for Care and Supervision Proceedings* in Part V) and the PLO (FPR PD12A). The appointment is likely to be made by way of a direction under FPR 2010, r 12.12(2)(e) (which can be done quickly and without a hearing as long as the parties are given the opportunity to make written representations; this would have the advantage of enabling the guardian to be in place in time to attend the first directions appointment). Where proceedings in which a guardian has already been appointed are transferred, the appointment continues to subsist unless terminated in accordance with r 12.6.

The focus on "issue of proceedings" and "transfer" in r 12.6 seems inappropriate for some types of specified proceedings. Any non-specified family proceedings will become "specified" at any time while they are pending if a direction under CA 1989, s 37(1) (investigation of the child's circumstances) is given, or if the court begins to consider making a s 8 order in respect of a child who is in care (see CA 1989, s 41(6)(b),(e)). In those circumstances, the requirement really means as soon as practicable after the proceedings become specified.

Appointment of guardian as a result of a s 37 direction—See "direction under section 37(1)" under CA 1989, s 41.

Appointment not necessary (r 12.6(a)(ii))—See, for example, *Re J (A Minor) (Change of Name)* [1993] 1 FLR 699.

Duties of the children's guardian—See FPR 2010, Pt 16 for the rules relating to the representation of children, and FPR PD16A, paras 6.1–6.11 for details of the duties of a children's guardian appointed under FPR 2010, r 16.3. Note that these include a duty in cases involving unrepresented parties to ensure that there is procedural fairness (*Re G (Children)* [2012] EWCA Civ 1434).

Where interests of children conflict—There is usually no reason why a guardian ad litem (children's guardian) should not properly represent children whose interests conflict (*Re T and E (Proceedings: Conflicting Interests)* [1995] 1 FLR 581, FD).

12.7 What a court officer will do

(1) As soon as practicable after the issue of proceedings the court officer will return to the applicant the copies of the application together with the forms referred to in Practice Direction 5A.

(2) As soon as practicable after the issue of proceedings or the transfer of proceedings to the court or at any other stage in the proceedings the court officer will –

    (a)   give notice of any hearing set by the court to the applicant; and

    (b)   do anything else set out in Practice Directions 12A or 12B or any other practice direction.

12.8 Service of the application

The applicant will serve –

    (a)   the application together with the documents referred to in Practice Direction 12C on the persons referred to and within the time specified in that Practice Direction; and

    (b)   notice of any hearing set by the court on the persons referred to in Practice Direction 12C at the same time as serving the application.

Practice Direction 12C—FPR PD12C supplements r 12.8 and sets out tables showing those persons who are to receive a copy of the application form (para 1), the time for serving the application (para 2) and the persons who are to receive a copy of Form C6A (Notice to Non-Parties) (para 3).

12.9 Request for transfer from magistrates' court to county court or to another magistrates' court

(1) In accordance with the Allocation Order, a magistrates' court may order proceedings before the court (or any part of them) to be transferred to another magistrates' court or to a county court.

(2) Where any request to transfer proceedings to another magistrates' court or to a county court is refused, the court officer will send a copy of the written record of the reasons for refusing the transfer to the parties.

Allocation Order—The provisions of the 2008 Allocation Order (see Part IV) are intended to ensure that family cases are moved down the tiers of family courts. Thus most private law proceedings and many more contested hearings in public law and adoption cases should be heard in the family proceedings courts and cases concerning serious allegations of abuse which were routinely transferred to the High Court should remain in the county courts. A judge ought not to transfer a case to the High Court without first consulting with and obtaining the consent of the appropriate Family Division Liaison Judge.

Pursuant to art 14 of the order, a magistrates' court may only transfer to another magistrates' court if it will significantly accelerate the determination of the proceedings, it would be more convenient for the parties or the child or there is another good reason to transfer the case. Pursuant to art 15 of the order, a magistrates' court may only order a transfer to a county court if at least one of nine reasons are applicable to the proceedings, including significant acceleration of the determination of the proceedings, complexity or international law issues arise.

12.10 Procedure following refusal of magistrates' court to order transfer

(1) Where a request under rule 12.9 to transfer proceedings to a county court in accordance with the provisions of the Allocation Order is refused, a party to the proceedings may apply to a county court for an order transferring proceedings from the magistrates' court.

(2) Such an application must be made in accordance with Part 18 and the Allocation Order.

Allocation Order—Art 25 (see Part IV) provides that an application in respect of proceedings under AA 2002 must be made to an adoption centre county court, under Pts 3, 4 or 5 of CA 1989 to a care centre and in any other case to a family hearing centre.

12.11 Transfer of proceedings from one court to another court

Where proceedings are transferred from one court to another court in accordance with the provisions of the Allocation Order, the court officer from the transferring court will notify the parties of any order transferring the proceedings.

Allocation Order—The relevant provisions are set out in arts 16–19 inclusive (see Part IV). A county court must transfer a case back to a magistrates' court if satisfied that none of the art 15 criteria applies. The High Court must transfer a case back a county court or magistrates' court if satisfied that none of the art 18 criteria applies. Pursuant to art 17, a county court may only transfer to another county court if it would significantly accelerate the determination of the proceedings, it is more convenient for a party or the child, the matter requires determination of an issue relating to property which is situated in the area of the other court or there is another good reason to transfer the proceedings. Pursuant to art 18, a county court may only transfer a case to the High Court if the proceedings are exceptionally complex, the outcome is important to the public in general or there is another substantial reason to transfer.

12.12 Directions

(1) This rule does not apply to proceedings under Chapter 6 of this Part.

(2) At any stage in the proceedings, the court may give directions about the conduct of the proceedings including –

(a) the management of the case;

   (b)   the timetable for steps to be taken between the giving of directions and the final hearing;

   (c)   the joining of a child or other person as a party to the proceedings in accordance with rules 12.3(2) and (3);

   (d)   the attendance of the child;

   (e)   the appointment of a children's guardian or of a solicitor under section 41(3) of the 1989 Act;

   (f)   the appointment of a litigation friend;

   (g)   the service of documents;

   (h)   the filing of evidence including experts' reports; and

   (i)   the exercise by an officer of the Service, Welsh family proceedings officer or local authority officer of any duty referred to in rule 16.38(1).

(3) Paragraph (4) applies where –

   (a)   an officer of the Service or a Welsh family proceedings officer has filed a report or a risk assessment as a result of exercising a duty referred to in rule 16.38(1)(a); or

   (b)   a local authority officer has filed a report as a result of exercising a duty referred to in rule 16.38(1)(b).

(4) The court may –

   (a)   give directions setting a date for a hearing at which that report or risk assessment will be considered; and

   (b)   direct that the officer who prepared the report or risk assessment attend any such hearing.

(5) The court may exercise the powers in paragraphs (2) and (4) on an application or of its own initiative.

(6) Where the court proposes to exercise its powers of its own initiative the procedure set out in rule 4.3(2) to (6) applies.

(7) Directions of a court which are still in force immediately prior to the transfer of proceedings to another court will continue to apply following the transfer subject to –

   (a)   any changes of terminology which are required to apply those directions to the court to which the proceedings are transferred; and

   (b)   any variation or revocation of the direction.

(8) The court or court officer will –

   (a)   take a note of the giving, variation or revocation of a direction under this rule; and

   (b)   as soon as practicable serve a copy of the note on every party.

     (Rule 12.48 provides for directions in proceedings under the 1980 Hague Convention and the European Convention.)

Defined terms—"child", "children and family reporter", "children's guardian", "court", "directions appointment", "section 8 order": FPR 2010, r 2.3(1).

Non-application to Chapter 6—FPR 2010, Pt 12, Ch 6 deals with applications under the Hague Convention 1980, the European Convention, The Council Regulations and the Hague Convention 1996; for directions in these applications see FPR 2010, r 12.48.

Alternative dispute resolution—Pursuant to FPR 2010, r 3.2, the court has a duty, at every stage in family proceedings, to consider whether alternative dispute resolution (ADR) is appropriate. It has power to direct, at any stage of the proceedings, that the matter be adjourned for such specified period as it considers appropriate to enable the parties to obtain information and advice about ADR, and, where they agree, to enable ADR to take place (FPR 2010, r 3.3(1)). The court may give directions about this either on application or of its own initiative (FPR 2010, r 3.3(2)). See further **Pre-Application Protocol for Mediation Information and Assessment** under FPR 2010, r 12.5.

President's Guidance on Case Management Decisions and Appeals therefrom—The President of the Family Division has issued *Guidance on Case Management Decisions and Appeals therefrom: December 2010* (see Part V). It gives key messages about the way in which the court should approach the exercise of judicial discretion and guidance on how the court should approach applications for additional assessments and expert reports. Munby P gave a useful summary of the key aspects of judicial case management in *Re TG (A Child)* [2013] EWCA Civ 5 at [24]–[29]).

General case management powers—See also FPR 2010, r 4.1, which lists the general case-management powers that the court has in addition to those mentioned specifically in r 12.12 (except where the rules provide otherwise). These include: extending or shortening time; making orders for disclosure and inspection; adjourning or bringing forward hearings; requiring the attendance at court of parties or their legal representatives; holding telephone hearings; directing that there be separate proceedings or separate hearings; staying proceedings; consolidating proceedings; deciding the order in which issues are to be heard; excluding issues from consideration; dismissing or giving a decision on a preliminary issue; directing parties to file and serve an estimate of costs; taking any other step or making any other order for the purpose of managing the case and furthering the overriding objective.

Court's power to make an order of its own initiative—The court has power to make orders either on an application or of its own initiative (see r 4.3).

The Public Law Outline (PLO)—The PLO in FPR PD12A governs all applications in public law proceedings for care and supervision orders under CA 1989, Pt IV. Rules dealing specifically with public law proceedings are to be found in FPR 2010, rr 12.23–12.30

The Private Law Programme (PLP)—The PLP in FPR PD12B applies to any private law applications issued under CA 1989, Pt II. It sets out the structure for the management of such cases. Special provisions dealing with private law proceedings are to be found in FPR 2010, rr 12.31–12.35.

Case management—The *Best Practice Guidance (Handbook of Best Practice in Children Act Cases)* (June 1997) produced by the Children Act Advisory Committee (see Part V) gives great assistance in relation to the preparation for and conduct of hearings.

Judicial continuity in private law proceedings—The Private Law Programme in FPR PD12B imposes strict rules so as to ensure judicial continuity in private law cases to streamline the proceedings and cut down delay.

Judicial continuity in public law proceedings—The PLO in FPR PD12A imposes strict rules so as to ensure judicial continuity in public law cases, to streamline the proceedings and to cut down delay. Each case will be allocated to one or not more than two case-management judge(s), who will be responsible for every stage in the proceedings down to the final hearing and one of whom may be, and where possible should be, the judge who will conduct the final hearing (para 3.1). There are a number of cases reported before the implementation of the old Protocol that contain useful guidelines as to judicial continuity. However, where they conflict with the PLO, the PLO should take precedence: *Re G (Care Proceedings: Split Trials)* [2001] 1 FLR 872; *A Health Authority v X and Others* [2002] 1 FLR 1045. There is also a need for continuity of counsel and solicitors advising the various parties (*Re CB and JB (Care Proceedings: Guidelines)* [1998] 2 FLR 211).

Preparation of public law cases—There is useful guidance in relation to public law cases in *Re R (Care: Disclosure: Nature of Proceedings)* [2002] 1 FLR 755 (dealt with more fully in **Preparation of public law cases** under CA 1989, s 31). For useful guidance as to the conduct and recording of meetings and the provision of documents in care proceedings, see the judgment in *Re L (Care: Assessment: Fair Trial)* [2002] 2 FLR 730, which is referred to in more detail in **Disclosure – impact of ECHR 1950** (below).

Flexible powers of court to give directions in public law cases—Where an application is made under CA 1989, Pt IV, the PLO in FPR PD12A provides the court with flexible powers to make appropriate directions following the issue of the application, the transfer of the case or at any other stage (para 18). The court may give directions without a hearing, including setting a date for the final hearing. The court may cancel or repeat a particular hearing if appropriate.

Agreed directions in public law cases—Where an application is made under CA 1989, Pt IV, the PLO in FPR PD12A encourages the parties, their advisers and the children's guardian to try to agree directions wherever possible (para 21). To obtain the court's approval the agreed directions must set out a timetable for the child and include a date or period when it is proposed that the next hearing will take place (para 21.2).

Need to file care plan—In public law cases, CA 1989, s 31A places the local authority under a duty to file a care plan in every case in which it seeks a care order (see CA 1989, ss 31, 31A and *Manchester City Council v F (Note)* [1993] 1 FLR 419).

Split hearings—In May 2010, the President issued *Guidance in Relation to Split Hearings* (see Part V). This applies to both private and public law proceedings and warns that split hearings are taking place when they need not do so. Judges are reminded that a fact-finding hearing should only be ordered if the court takes the view that the case cannot properly be decided without one (para 7). Allegations of violence do not automatically justify a preliminary fact-finding hearing. The court must consider the nature of the allegations and the extent to which, if admitted or proved, they would be relevant in making its decision. If they are unlikely to have any impact on the court's order, there is no need for a separate fact-finding hearing. For the rationale for split hearings, see *Re S (Care Proceedings: Split Hearing)* [1996] 2 FLR 773. When a split hearing is ordered in care proceedings it is essential for the court and the parties to be absolutely clear about the purpose of the hearing, the issues to be decided and the nature of the relief sought (*Somerset County Council v D & Others* [2008] 1 FLR 399; *Re F (Care Proceedings)* [2007] EWCA Civ 810; *Re P (Care Proceedings: Split Hearing)* [2007] EWCA Civ 1265). Consideration should be given to whether questions of fact, such as an allegation of physical or sexual abuse, might need to be determined at a preliminary stage, so that the substantive hearing can proceed more speedily and focus on the child's welfare with greater clarity. Local authorities and children's guardians, in particular, should give assistance to the court in identifying cases that are suited to such a split hearing. Useful guidance as to the directions to be given in relation to split hearings can be found in *Re A (Children: Split Hearing)* [2007] 1 FLR 905. All public law applications issued by local authorities under Pt IV (care and supervision orders) are subject to the time limits contained in the PLO in FPR PD12A. See FPR 2010, r 12.25 **First appointment, Case management conference** and **Issues resolution hearing** and PD12A. The draft case management order requires the court to consider whether a fact-finding hearing is necessary and, if so, to identify the discrete issue of fact that is to be determined, by whom and when (paras 6 and 26(12)). See also, **Split hearings** under CA 1989, s 31. The importance of judicial continuity was emphasised in *Re G (Care Proceedings: Split Trials)* [2001] 1 FLR 872. Even where the parents make limited concessions that mean that the threshold criteria are proved, the court still has a discretion, as part of the proper management of the proceedings in the child's best interests, to order that there be a trial in relation to the threshold criteria where this is necessary to resolve a core factual issue without the determination of which the experts involved in the case are unable to advise on child protection (*Re D (Child: Threshold Criteria)* [2001] 1 FLR 274). Where an expert is asked to express an opinion, he must have all the relevant information, including a copy of any judgment given earlier in the case; the summary of a judgment is not sufficient (*Re G (Care Proceedings: Split Trials)* (above)). *Re T (A Minor) (Procedure: Alleged Sexual Abuse) (No 1)* [1996] 2 FCR 370, however, sounds a cautionary note about splitting the evidence on the primary facts as to sexual abuse from the evidence as to what risk there will be in the future if it is established. The Court of Appeal has jurisdiction to hear an appeal against findings of fact on preliminary issues made at the first part of a split hearing in care proceedings where those findings are of crucial importance to the final care decision to be made (*Re B (Split Hearing: Jurisdiction)* [2000] 1 FLR 334). Parents can be compelled to give evidence in any care proceedings. They have no right to refuse to do so, or to refuse to answer questions that may incriminate them (per curiam, *Re Y and K (Split Hearing: Evidence)* [2003] 2 FLR 273).

Timetable for public law cases—The PLO in FPR PD12A requires the court to set down a strict timetable for the disposal of public law cases. There must be timely crystallisation of the issues on which the case turns and a resolution of those issues without any unacceptable delay. The timetable for the case is set by the court and must be appropriate for the child who is the subject of the proceedings. It should take account of all significant steps in the child's life that are likely to take place during the proceedings, not just legal steps, and could include social, health and education steps (paras 3.2–3.9).

Timetable for the proceedings and time estimates (r 12.2(2)(b))—The court is put firmly in control of the timetable for proceedings under CA 1989 in an effort to avoid delay that CA 1989, s 1(2) stresses is likely to be prejudicial to the welfare of a child. Section 11(1) obliges the court, when dealing with proceedings in which any question of making a s 8 order arises, to draw up a timetable with a view to determining the question at issue without delay and to give such directions as it considers appropriate to ensure adherence to the timetable; s 32(1) is a similar provision relating to proceedings under CA 1989, Pt IV. Rule 12.13(1) obliges the court dealing with any proceedings to which Pt IV applies to fix a date for the next hearing upon the transfer of such proceedings, or adjourning or concluding an interlocutory hearing or appointment. In relation to the timetable for public law proceedings, see FPR 2010, rr 12.23–12.26 and FPR PD12A. In relation to the timetable for the first hearing dispute resolution appointment in private law proceedings see r 12.31. Subject to these positive duties, however, the court has a wide discretion as to how the timetable for a case is set. In reaching decisions about timetabling, the time limits set by the rules for various steps should be observed. Under the old FPR 1991 the court had specific power in r 4.14(2)(b) to abridge or extend time limits; this provision has been removed from the 2010 Rules. However, it is submitted that the court's wide powers under FPR 2010, r 12.12(2)(a),(b) to give directions about the management of the case and the timetable are ample to allow it to adjust time limits as and when necessary. The court can exercise these powers either on application or on its own initiative (r 12.12(5)). What is required is a timetable that prevents the case from drifting, without sacrificing the interests of the parties and the welfare of the child. For comments on the benefits of planned and purposeful delay, see *C v Solihull MBC* [1993] 1 FLR 290 and *Hounslow LBC v A* [1993] 1 FLR 702. See also **Interim care order or full care order?** under CA 1989, s 38.

In determining any application to adjourn a case involving children, as well as in fixing the timetable for the proceedings, the court has to consider delay and the interests of the other parties have to be assessed in the light of the principle that delay in determining a question concerning a child's upbringing is likely to prejudice his welfare (*Re SW (A Minor) (Care Proceedings)* [1993] 2 FLR 609, noted more fully in **Hearing in the absence of applicant** under FPR 2010, r 12.14). Where orders are not produced by the court and/or there are delays in compliance with these orders, directions should be sought from the court at an early stage (*Re K (Order Delay)* [2008] 1 FLR 572). An application for an adjournment can be granted without notice, but such application should only be made in exceptional circumstances and where it would be in the best interests of the children to justify such a course. Even then, those representing the parties should be in attendance, either having given undertakings or subject to a direction of the court not to pass on the information to their clients (*Re B (Minors) (Care: Procedure)* [1994] Fam Law 72).

Urgent hearings and applications without notice—See FPR 2010, r 12.16 and FPR PD12E (Urgent Business).

Electronic exchange of documents, video and telephone conferencing—The court is required to further the overriding objective in FPR 2010, r 1.1 by actively managing cases; this includes making use of technology (FPR 2010, r 1.4(2)(k)) and giving directions to ensure that the case proceeds quickly and efficiently (FPR 2010, r 1.4(2)(l)). The court may allow a witness to give evidence through a video link or by other means (FPR 2010, r 22.3). Video conferencing facilities are available in the Royal Courts of Justice and the procedure to be adopted where it is desired to use these facilities is specified in FPR PD22A, para 17.1 and Annex 3. In cases to which the PLO in FPR PD12A applies, the court will specifically consider whether any arrangements for video and telephone conferencing are required at the case management conference and at the issues resolution hearing (see **First appointment, Case management conference** and **Issues resolution hearing** under FPR 2010, r 12.25). The PLO in FPR PD12A requires that where facilities are available to the court and the parties, the court should consider making full use of technology, including electronic information exchange and video or telephone conferencing (FPR PD12A, para 24).

Care proceedings: more than one local authority involved—Where the applicant local authority will not be the authority responsible for operating the arrangements for the child once an order is made, the need for the second local authority to attend court to deal with issues arising must be borne in mind (*Re C (Care Order: Appropriate Local Authority)* [1997] 1 FLR 544, FD).

Disclosure by party—Representatives must address their minds in advance of the hearing to the need for pre-trial disclosure. For example, it is not uncommon for a party to public law proceedings to require sight of social work notes. It is not to be thought that in every case there should be carte blanche disclosure of social work notes and records. In each instance, a proper case for disclosure must be made out. But applications for discovery should precede the trial and be part of the preparatory process rather than taking place during the trial. This means that the lawyers should consider, as an essential part of the process of preparation, the issues in the case and the material that will be required for the presentation of those issues. If documents are material, the proper course is to request them from social services first and, if disclosure is resisted, to apply well before the trial for disclosure (*Re JC (Care Proceedings: Procedure)* [1995] 2 FLR 77, FD). If public interest immunity arises, the procedure to be followed is set out in **Public interest immunity** (below). For useful guidance as to the conduct and recording of meetings and the provision of documents in care proceedings, see the judgment in *Re L (Care: Assessment: Fair Trial)* [2002] 2 FLR 730 and **Disclosure – impact of ECHR 1950** (below).

Disclosure – waiver of legal professional privilege—Where a mother had waived her legal professional privilege in care proceedings by stating in a witness statement the reasons why, after a number of legal conferences, she had changed her account of how her child's injuries were sustained, fairness required full disclosure of the attendance notes of those conferences. The undesirability of breaching confidentiality between the mother and her legal representatives had to be balanced against the unfairness to the father if it was not breached (*Re D (Care Proceedings: Legal Privilege)* [2011] 2 FLR 1183). Counsel and solicitors ought to be aware that advice might have been given to prompt a change of attitude by their client and they should be on guard to protect their client from revealing that advice in either written or oral evidence. Judges must also be astute to anticipate an unintentional observation that may result in privilege being waived and must be ready to warn a witness of any such danger.

Disclosure by non-party in private law proceedings—In private law CA 1989 proceedings, as a matter of strict law, discovery of documents cannot be ordered against persons who are not parties, for example the police or a local authority (see below, **Disclosure by the police**). However, in *Re A and B (Minors)*

PART III

(No 2) [1995] 1 FLR 351, Wall J observed (obiter) that the court has the jurisdiction to compel such discovery by order, provided that suitable undertakings as to confidentiality and the use of the material are given.

Disclosure by the police—In *A London Borough Council v K and Others* [2009] EWHC 850 (Fam), Baker J found that there had been alarming deficiencies in the police disclosure in a case in which the mother had made false allegations against the father that he had sexually abused the children. During the evidence of the last police witness it became apparent that a large amount of material had not been disclosed. He held that better procedures needed to be put in place. At the start, one named officer should always be identified to deal with disclosure and there should always be a meeting between that officer and the lead solicitor, usually the local authority's solicitor, to ensure that disclosure has taken place as ordered. If a family court orders disclosure, that order must be obeyed. All such orders contain a "liberty to apply" clause and if the police have an objection on the grounds of public interest immunity or otherwise, they must apply to the judge to amend the order. He held that this was a matter that should be urgently reviewed by the Family Justice Council. See **Public interest immunity** (below). Cafcass has entered into a joint protocol with the Association of Chief Police Officers (ACPO) on disclosure of information from the police. It sets out the principles of information-sharing between Cafcass and all local police forces in England and Wales. See further under CA 1989, s 16A.

Multi-agency risk assessment conferences (MARACs) – disclosure in public law and private law proceedings—MARAC meetings collate information about high-risk cases of domestic abuse with a view to creating a coordinated safety plan for the victim and children (if any). The work is case-specific and all relevant agencies will attend or contribute to the conference. MARACs may be a valuable source of information in both public law and private law proceedings where domestic abuse towards an adult or a child may be an issue. Clearly, it important that generally the details of the safety plan devised by the MARAC are kept confidential if it is to be effective. A request for disclosure of documents or other information is most likely to come from the person whose conduct is under scrutiny at the MARAC. Therefore, there is a tension between the potential existence of relevant information and the need for confidentiality. In December 2011, the Working Party of the Family Justice Council issued guidance on *MARACs and Disclosure into Court Proceedings* (see Part V). The question of disclosure should always be considered well in advance of a contested hearing and be dealt with by an order for directions (para 7). If a request for disclosure will interfere significantly with a safety plan or may cause harm to a child, the chair of the MARAC has a duty to raise a formal objection (para 8). The chair will not normally be from a legal background and therefore it is important that his attention is drawn to the guidance and he is encouraged to take legal advice before he decides whether or not to object. If, however, there is no objection, the chair should follow the procedure in para 8(a)–(f). It will sometimes happen that the MARACs hold information that they believe would be useful to a court but that they do not want to disclose to all parties. In those circumstances, they should disclose the information to the relevant statutory body (the local authority, police, Cafcass) for them to use as appropriate in court proceedings. MARAC workers and independent domestic violence advisors (IDVAs) should not ordinarily be called as witnesses in court proceedings (para 10). See also the notes under FPR 2010, rr 21.2 and 21.3 and under FLA 1996, s 63A.

Disclosure – Impact of ECHR 1950—It is essential that a parent be placed in a position where he may obtain access to information that is relied on by the authorities in taking measures of protective care (*TP and KM v United Kingdom* [2001] 2 FLR 549). See further under **Public interest immunity** (below). Issues concerning the disclosure of confidential information involve the consideration of rights under ECHR 1950, Arts 6 and 8 and HRA 1998. The guidelines relevant to these issues are set out in *Re B (Disclosure to Other Parties)* [2001] 2 FLR 1017.

Public interest immunity—The rules on public interest immunity (PII) qualify the general principle that parties to an application for a care order must file and serve copies of any documents on which they intend to rely in the proceedings. The limits of immunity are not clear: the categories of public interest are not closed and may alter over time (see *D v National Society for the Prevention of Cruelty to Children* (1977) FLR Rep 181). Social work records are covered by PII and *Re M (A Minor) (Disclosure of Material)* [1990] 2 FLR 36, CA sets out the balancing exercise that must be done where application is made for disclosure. In exercising its discretion, the court must weigh up whether the public interest in protecting the social work records overrides the public interest that the party to proceedings should obtain the information sought in order to obtain legal redress. It is for the party seeking discovery to establish the need for the production of the documents and, while it may be necessary for the court to inspect the documents in some cases in order to decide whether production should be ordered, a court can only inspect documents where it has definite grounds for expecting to find material of real importance to the party seeking disclosure.

However, in *Re R (Care: Disclosure: Nature of Proceedings)* [2002] 1 FLR 755, Charles J held that *Re M* (above) should be treated with caution and be carefully reconsidered in the light of developments in the law and practice relating to PII, in particular since *R v Chief Constable of West Midlands Police ex parte Wiley* [1995] 1 AC 274, which resulted in the "class claim" to PII becoming a matter of history. Charles J emphasised the point made in *Re B (Disclosure to Other Parties)* [2001] 2 FLR 1017 (see **Disclosure – impact of ECHR 1950**, above), in respect of claims for non-disclosure based on ECHR 1950, Art 8, that a compelling case for non-disclosure based on PII needs to be made out and any non-disclosure must go no further than is strictly necessary, having regard to the competing public interests. Furthermore, he expressed the view that "both local authorities and guardians ad litem should be more willing than they seem to be at present to exhibit their notes of relevant conversations and incidents that are relied on as evidence for findings at the threshold or welfare stage of proceedings, rather than to embark on what is a time-consuming and difficult exercise of preparing summaries of those notes". Charles J commended the Official Solicitor's practice of exhibiting attendance records to his report and said that it would have been beneficial if this practice had been adopted by both the local authority and the guardian in this case and, indeed, it would be likely to be beneficial in many other cases. In *Re R* (above) the failure of the foster-parent, the children's guardian and further witnesses to disclose their contemporaneous notes until called for by the judge during the hearing led to the local authority having to abandon allegations of serious sexual abuse and to rely on other allegations to support its case for care orders. However, local authorities should abstain from introducing into proceedings, and sending to experts, material that would inevitably be perceived as unfair in the sense of being purely prejudicial (*Re S (Expert Evidence)* [2008] 2 FLR 1163).

Further guidance was given in *Re Chapman* (2002) Lawtel, 9 April, a case in which the local authority received information that the father was involved in serious criminal activity and likely to harm and abduct the child and so sought directions on disclosure from the police of information about the father. The police agreed to disclose information about the father's convictions and arrests but not otherwise, contending that to disclose further material about the father's possible criminal activity was likely to seriously harm the proper functioning of the police and the strong public interest in proper investigation and persecution of crime. Charles J held, inter alia, that:

(1) The parties to the care proceedings would not be prejudiced by not being given further detail from the police, while the public interest could have been harmed by it.
(2) *Nottinghamshire County Council v H* [1995] 1 FLR 115 had to be reconsidered in the light of *R v Chief Constable of West Midlands Police, ex parte Wiley* [1995] 1 AC 274.
(3) A person was entitled to disclosure of all material taken into account by a decision-maker when reaching a decision adverse to that person. Non-disclosure of relevant material to one party was exceptional.
(4) The general position was that confidentiality was not a valid reason for non-disclosure of material that passed the relevant threshold test.
(5) The stages of any issue relating to disclosure were:
    (a) whether the relevant threshold test was satisfied; and
    (b) if so, whether there were nevertheless grounds for refusing disclosure.

In *Re W (Disclosure to Police)* [1998] 2 FLR 135, the CA considered the status of local authority working papers, such as information and notes used to prepare an assessment report for court. The assessment report had been filed at court but the notes had not. Unless there is an order of the court to the contrary, such confidential information has to be dealt with by the local authority in accordance with the guide *Working Together to Safeguard Children 2010*. It is protected by PII from general publication but should be shared with the police without prior reference to the court where necessary for the protection of children. This decision is expressly confined, however, to documents held by and information known to social workers and has no application to the position of a children's guardian or children and family reporter appointed for court proceedings. It should also be noted that leave must be sought in the normal way to show documents that have been filed with the court (such as the assessment report here) to the police.

As to the immunity of adoption files, see *Re H (Criminal Proceedings: Disclosure of Adoption Records)* [1995] 1 FLR 964, FD and for a case concerning disclosure of Crown Prosecution Service documents, see *Nottinghamshire County Council v H* [1995] 1 FLR 115. In the latter case, attention was drawn to the children's guardian's power under CA 1989, s 42 to examine the local authority's social work records. The court's discretion in Children Act proceedings will be exercised in the light of this power.

Re C (Expert Evidence: Disclosure: Practice) [1995] 1 FLR 204 provides guidance as to the procedure to be followed where an issue arises, because of PII, as to whether certain material should or should not be disclosed. If documents held by the local authority are apparently relevant but appear to be protected from disclosure by PII, a letter should be written by the local authority to the parties' legal advisers and to the children's guardian drawing general attention to the existence of the documents and inviting an application to the court if disclosure of the relevant documents is required. The appropriate procedure would be to seek directions as to the service of documents pursuant to r 12.12(2)(g) or directions as to the filing of evidence pursuant to r 12.12(2)(h). The local authority should identify and flag the documents that they believe are, or may be, relevant and, if possible, a short précis of the information should be prepared to assist the court that is to make the decision. If the court orders disclosure of the documents and if the nature of the précis satisfies the party affected that the material identified and disclosed is sufficient, the directions hearing can proceed on a short basis. If the précis does not achieve agreement and the other party wishes to see more of the files, some further guide to the file should be provided so that the court can carry out the balancing exercise envisaged in *Re M (A Minor) (Disclosure of Material)* (above), taking into account the comments in *Re R* (above) and *Re B (Disclosure to Other Parties)* (above). It is for the court to make the decision as to disclosure of documents covered by PII. It is important for the local authority to draw the children's guardian's attention to any matters of concern within the documents, since his full knowledge of the material may enable him to assist the court as to its relevance. In *Re T (Wardship: Impact of Police Intelligence)* [2010] 1 FLR 1048, Special Advocates were used to "filter" evidence the disclosure of which was resisted. See further **Special Advocates** (below). The approach to be applied when deciding whether to order the disclosure of third party allegations against the father of sexual abuse in child contact proceedings was summarised by the Supreme Court in *Re A (A Child: Disclosure of Third Party Information)* [2012] UKSC 60. Here, the undisclosed information was at the core of the case and represented the entirety of the material relating to the only issue that had generated the mother's application to vary the contact regime. The judge at first instance had erred in conflating the issue of whether the complainant should give oral evidence with the question of disclosure of the substance of her allegations. On the facts of this case, the balance of rights under ECHR 1950, Arts 3, 6 and 8 came down in favour of disclosure by the local authority to the parents and the children's guardian of the complainant's identity and of the records of the substance of her allegations.

As to the difficult issue to which the local authority is free to waive PII without leave of the court, see inter alia, *D v NSPCC* (above), *Re M (A Minor) (Disclosure of Material)* (above), *R v Chief Constable of the West Midland Police ex p Wiley* [1995] 1 AC 274, HL, *Re C (Expert Evidence: Disclosure: Practice)* (above).

Submission of evidence (r 12.12(2)(h))—Rule 12.12 gives the court a broad power to deal with questions concerning the submission of evidence. For example, such directions may be given as are necessary for the purposes of FPR 2010, r 12.19, which lays down the rules about the filing and service of written and oral evidence in proceedings for a s 8 order or a special guardianship order (see *R v Nottinghamshire CC* [1993] Fam Law 625, discussed in **Non-compliance with r 12.19(2)** under FPR 2010, r 12.19). Questions of relevance/admissibility should normally be referred to the judge who will be conducting the final hearing (*Re CB and JB (Care Proceedings: Guidelines)* [1998] 2 FLR 211). All public law applications under CA 1989, Pt IV are subject to the PLO in PD12A and any issues as to disclosure will be addressed at the case management conference and the issues resolution hearing (see FPR 2010, rr 12.24 and 12.25).

Where disclosure of material to a party may be damaging to the child concerned in the proceedings, the court has power, in an appropriate case, to direct that the information should be withheld. Such a direction will only be given in exceptional circumstances. The principles have been set out in a number of cases including *Official Solicitor v K* (1963) FLR Rep 520, *Re B (A Minor) (Disclosure of Evidence)* [1993] 1 FLR 191, CA, *Re G (Minors) (Welfare Report: Disclosure)* [1993] 2 FLR 293, CA, and *Re M (Minors) (Disclosure of Evidence)* [1994] 1 FLR 760, CA. In *Re D (Adoption Reports: Confidentiality)* [1995] 2 FLR 687, the House of Lords gave full consideration to the whole question of disclosure. Although this was in the context of an adoption application, Lord Mustill's formulation of the test for non-disclosure is the test in Children Act proceedings as well, and was applied in care proceedings in *Re C (Disclosure)* [1996] 1 FLR 797, FD and endorsed in *Re M (Disclosure)* [1998] 2 FLR 1028, CA. Accordingly, the position is as follows:

(a) It is a fundamental principle of fairness that a party is entitled to disclosure of all materials that might be taken into account by a court when reaching a decision adverse to that party – non-disclosure is the exception and not the rule.

(b) When faced with a non-disclosure application, the court should first consider whether disclosure would involve a real possibility of significant harm to the child.

(c) If so, the court should next consider whether the overall interests of the child would benefit from non-disclosure, weighing the interest of the child in having the material properly tested against the magnitude of risk that harm would occur and the gravity of that harm.

(d) If the court is satisfied that the interests of the child point towards non-disclosure, it should finally weigh that consideration against the interest of the parent or other party in having an opportunity to see and respond to the material, taking into account the importance of the material to the issues in the case.

(e) The court should be rigorous in its examination of the risk and gravity of the feared harm to the child, and should order non-disclosure only where the case for it is compelling. To say that harm must be certain is to pitch the test too high, but "a powerful combination of likelihood and seriousness of harm will be required before the requirements for a fair trial can be overridden" (*Re D* at [694H]).

As *Re M* stresses, welfare of the child is not the paramount consideration. A proper balance has to be struck between the welfare consideration and the requirements of the administration of fair justice. See *Re BR and C (Care: Duty of Disclosure: Appeals)* [2003] Fam Law 305, where the Court of Appeal reinstated an order requiring disclosure of medical reports by the mother in family proceedings, emphasising that the court will only withhold evidence from disclosure to another party if such disclosure would be so detrimental to the children's welfare as to outweigh the normal requirements of a fair trial. In *Re X (Adoption: Confidential Procedure)* [2002] 2 FLR 476, Hale LJ added to these principles to provide that the ECHR 1950, Art 8 rights of adults may also justify non¬disclosure where the risk is of harm to them rather than the child. In *A Local Authority v A* [2010] 1 FLR 545 the court refused their application for non-disclosure, holding that disclosure is the norm and non-disclosure should only be permitted where the case for doing so is compelling. In the context of this case, non-disclosure would only be justified if there were a real risk of death or really serious bodily harm. In *KM v Lambeth MBC* [2012] 1 FLR 1278 the court held that it would not be right to allow only partial disclosure of the mother's psychiatric report to the father when the child's guardian and the local authority had had access to the whole report. However, the father was prohibited from disclosing it to anyone but his legal advisers, and this was backed by a penal notice.

Re C (Disclosure) (above) considered the procedure to be followed where an application for non-disclosure is made. Johnson J declined to lay down rigid rules, taking the view that the procedure in each case will be determined by the court in the light of the particular circumstances and demands of the case, so as to enable the court to carry out the appropriate balancing exercise. This approach was endorsed by the Court of Appeal in *Re M (Disclosure)* [1998] 2 FLR 1028 and should be the norm, subject to any necessary variations in individual cases. Accordingly:

(1) The application should be transferred to the High Court.
(2) Notice of the application should be given to the party from whom the material is intended to be withheld.
(3) It is essential that any party to whom the information was not to be revealed should have the opportunity of making representations to the court.
(4) In many cases it will be appropriate to follow the practice endorsed in *Official Solicitor v K* (1963) FLR Rep 520, namely disclosure in the first instance to counsel only and thereafter counsel would have the opportunity to apply for onward transmission to the client.

Where disclosure is resisted in complex family proceedings it may be possible to use Special Advocates to "filter" the evidence (*Re T (Wardship: Impact of Police Intelligence)* [2010] 1 FLR 1048). See **Special Advocates**, below.

The possibility of hearings or part of hearings being held without notice is not excluded but should arise only rarely. For example, where there is material in a document upon which the judge is asked to make a decision whether to disclose but the judge needs assistance from a party in some way to ascertain the meaning of the document, he could properly ask for such help before making his decision as to whether the document should be disclosed (*Re M* at p1033F). The procedure for without notice hearings is in FPR 2010, r 12.16.

Where certain information is to have limited distribution, special arrangements will have to be made with regard to filing it in court (in *Re C*, the children's guardian was to provide the restricted information to the judge in a confidential supplementary report dealing only with that information) and the court will have to take administrative steps to ensure that it is not disclosed inadvertently. See *Re K (Adoption: Disclosure of Information)* [1997] 2 FLR 74, FD, in which the procedure in adoption cases was distinguished from that contemplated by *Re C* for care cases and it was also pointed out that, where the party from whom it is sought to conceal information is not represented, giving notice of the application about the evidence may defeat the object of the exercise.

As *Re C* contemplates, circumstances can change, and the importance of maintaining confidentiality decline. *Re B (A Minor) (Disclosure of Evidence)* (above) stresses the importance of any order for non-disclosure being only for the shortest period possible consonant with preserving the child's welfare.

Confidentiality of statements by parties in conciliation meetings—In CA 1989 proceedings, statements by parties in conciliation meetings are not admissible, except in the very unusual case where the statement clearly indicates that the maker has in the past caused, or is likely in future to cause, serious harm to the well-being of a child. Even in such a case, there is a discretion whether or not to admit the evidence and it should be admitted only if the public interest in protecting the interests of the child outweighs the public interest in preserving the confidentiality of attempted conciliation (*Re D (Minors) (Conciliation: Privilege)* [1993] 1 FLR 932, CA).

Special Advocates—Special Advocates were used for (probably) the first time in *Re T (Wardship: Impact of Police Intelligence)* [2010] 1 FLR 1048 to "filter" evidence, the disclosure of which was resisted. The police informed the court dealing with the father's contact application in respect of the ward that there was credible intelligence to the effect that he had taken out a contract to have the mother murdered while

PART III

at court. However, the police had decided not to investigate further. The police requested that this information not be disclosed to the father, his family or any of his family's representatives. The police took the mother and child into police protection but stated that this would be withdrawn if interim contact with the father were established. McFarlane J described the procedure to be adopted in appointing Special Advocates and extracted the lessons to be learned. The lack of understanding between the police and the family justice system had delayed, and at times risked thwarting, the discharge of the family court's duty to act in accordance with the welfare needs of the ward. Any issue of public interest immunity material that raises issues of complexity should trigger a transfer to the High Court (see further under **Public interest immunity**, above). In *BCC v FZ, AZ, HZ and TVP* [2012] EWHC 1154 (Fam), Pauffley J gave judicial sanction to withholding from the parents the entire evidential basis for the making of an interim care order and decided that there was no need for a Special Advocate to assist with basic disclosure or issues of public interest immunity. However, she held that as a consequence of her judgment this became one of those exceptional cases in which it was essential, to give the parents proper protection of their rights under ECHR 1950, Arts 6 and 8, that a Special Advocate(s) be brought into the case forthwith to represent their interests both in relation to continuing and future disclosure and, in the event that there was to be no disclosure going forward, in the testing of the evidence at any subsequent trial.

Bundles and other particular matters—It is good practice to observe FPR PD27A in *all applications* concerning the preparation of court bundles. However, it applies specifically in: (i) all hearings before a High Court judge of the Family Division, wherever he or she is sitting; (ii) all hearings in family proceedings in the Royal Courts of Justice; (iii) all hearings in the Principal Registry of the Family Division at First Avenue House; and (iv) all hearings in family proceedings in all other courts except for family proceedings courts. The PD does not apply to: (a) cases listed for 1 hour or less; or (b) the hearing of any urgent application if and to the extent that it is impossible to comply with it. PD27A is to be read, where appropriate, in conjunction with the PLO (FPR PD12A) and FPR PD29B. However, the PD is subject to any directions that may be given in a particular case by the case-management judge.

In *Re X and Y (Bundles)* [2008] 2 FLR 2053, Munby J issued a stern warning in open court to all practitioners, pointing out that failure to observe the requirements of FPR PD27A is unacceptable. Orders for costs can be made against either the party in default or against the defaulting lawyers (see FPR PD27A, para 12) and in particularly flagrant cases, defaulters may be publicly identified in open court.

Citation of Authorities—Practice Direction of 24 March 2012: *Citation of Authorities* clarifies the practice and procedure governing the citation of authorities and applies throughout the Senior Courts of England and Wales, including the Crown Court), in county courts and in magistrates' courts. See Part V.

Public Law Outline (PLO) – instructing and calling experts—See under FPR 2010, Pt 25 and PD25A–PD25F.

Deciding whether case should be heard in the Administrative Court or Family Division—Where cases plainly involve only issues of public law, although they concern the welfare of either children or incompetent adults, then the proper course is to apply to the Administrative Court for judicial review (*A (A Patient) v A Health Authority; Re J; The Queen on the Application of S v Secretary of State for the Home Department* [2002] 1 FLR 845). But if cases may, in part, involve some issues of public law but are also private law cases about the best interests of a child or an incompetent adult then the proper course is to apply to the Family Division. Exactly the same principle applies in "family" cases where a freestanding application is made for relief in accordance with HRA 1998, s 7; such cases should be heard in the Family Division and, if possible, by judges with experience of sitting in the Administrative Court (*Re S (Habeas Corpus): S v Haringey London Borough Council* [2004] 1 FLR 590). Recourse to judicial review in the area of child protection will be rare (*A and S v London Borough of Enfield* [2008] 2 FLR 1945). Where the conduct of a local authority in care proceedings is fundamentally flawed and its decision-making process is a key issue, the court may direct a rehearing of the care proceedings before a High Court judge of the Family Division who is also authorised to sit in the Administrative Court. In this way, the care proceedings can run concurrently with judicial review proceedings, since the subject matter in each is essentially the same (*Re S and W (Care Proceedings)* [2007] 2 FLR 275).

"directions for the conduct of the proceedings" (r 12.12(2))—The court has a wide discretion to grant directions. The matters listed in r 12.12(2) are only examples of the types of issue that might arise. A directions hearing will almost inevitably be required in a case of any substance and a date for it is fixed by the court office in accordance with FPR 2010, r 12.5 when the application is commenced or when it is received from the transmitting court. Being an interlocutory matter, directions can be given by a district judge although a judge can, and may well have occasion to, give directions as well. Care proceedings are non-adversarial in character (see *Re L (Police Investigation: Privilege)* [1996] 1 FLR 731, HL) and, in practice, judges dealing with directions hearings in such cases adopt an interventionist style. Directions hearings should not be treated as a formality; they enable the court to come firmly to grips with the case and ensure that it is tightly timetabled and prepared for its final hearing at the earliest opportunity. Where a party feels that the case is not making satisfactory progress, he should apply for directions to ensure that progress is made (*B v B (Child Abuse: Contact)* [1994] 2 FLR 713; see also *Re A and B (Minors) (No 2)* [1995] 1 FLR 351, and the notes on the timetable for the proceedings, above. In public law proceedings, the court will give directions under FPR 2010, r 12.24 for the conduct of the case at three stages: the first appointment (by day 6); the case management conference (no later than Day 45); and at the issues resolution hearing (between weeks 16 and 25). See further under FPR 2010, rr 12.22–12.26 and FPR PD12A.

Parties who receive notice of the directions appointment are normally required to attend (see FPR 2010, r 12.14(2)). As to directions for the conduct of cases involving expert witnesses, see FPR 2010, Pt 25 and PD25A–PD25F.

Agreement between parties as to proposals for management of proceedings—If the parties or any children's guardian agree proposals for the management of the proceedings, and the court considers that the proposals are suitable, it may approve them without a hearing and give directions in the terms proposed (FPR 2010, r 12.15).

Repeated applications—As to the possibility of renewing an application previously refused by the court, see *Re F (A Minor) (Care Proceedings: Directions)* [1995] 3 FCR 601, FD.

Dismissal of proceedings at directions stage—In *Re B (Contact: Stepfather's Opposition)* [1997] 2 FLR 579, CA, the court held that, in an appropriate case, a contact application can be dismissed at a directions hearing. The CA pointed out that, in the exercise of that power, the court must bear in mind that the more Draconian the order and the more unique the situation, the greater the need for the court to be satisfied that grave harm is virtually certain to befall the child if the court follows its usual procedure and investigates the matter on its merits. In *Re A (Application for Leave)* [1998] 1 FLR 1, the CA reaffirmed the view that, in appropriate cases, an application may be determined at a directions appointment if the content of the statements and the children and family reporter's report indicate that it should go no further. This principle is clearly demonstrated in *Re W (Minors)* (unreported) 15 December 1998, CA, where the CA upheld the first instance decision, observing:

"Of course, it is normally the case that children's cases are heard on oral evidence ... which is tested under cross-examination. But it is quite clear from a number of decisions of this court and decisions at first instance that a judge does have a discretion as to whether or not there should be a full hearing permitted with oral evidence. This is particularly the case when there has already been one full investigation by the court which has produced a particular result, as here. The judge in so acting would obviously have to look carefully at the case and weigh a number of important considerations: Was the material available before the court sufficient to enable him to take that particular course? Was the outcome likely to be affected by fresh evidence or cross-examination? Would the denial of the opportunity for the mother to cross-examine witnesses or produce evidence of her own be likely to produce a skewed result and be unfair to her? Was the expert evidence available before the court sufficient? Would it be likely to be changed in the light of cross-examination or further evidence? and, above all, the welfare of the children and the likely effect on them of continuing litigation. If that was likely to be detrimental to the welfare of the children that would be a factor which would weigh very heavily in the scales. Finally, of course, the ultimate question for the judge: Would the full hearing be likely realistically to produce any different result to that which had already been reached?".

For further examples of situations in which an application may be brought to a premature end, see **Full hearing not always appropriate** under FPR 2010, r 12.21.

Attendance of the child (r 12.12(2)(d))—As to the attendance of the child at directions appointments and hearings, see FPR 2010, r 12.14(3),(4).

Appointment of a children's guardian (r 12.12(2)(e))—CA 1989, s 41 obliges the court to appoint a children's guardian for a child concerned in specified proceedings (such as care and supervision order proceedings) unless satisfied that it is not necessary to do so in order to safeguard his interest; FPR 2010, r 16.3 sets out the normal procedure for the appointment of such a guardian. There is no provision in CA 1989 for the appointment of a children's guardian for a child involved in non-specified proceedings. ACA 2002, s 122(1)(b),(2) inserts into CA 1989, s 41 subsection (6A) so as to include within the category of proceedings that may be "specified for the time being ... by rules of court" any proceedings for the making, varying or discharging of an order under CA 1989, s 8 (ie residence, contact, specific issue and prohibited steps orders). As far as the rules are concerned, a children's guardian can be appointed in non-specified proceedings under FPR 2010, r 16.4 (see for example *L v L (Minors) (Separate Representation)* [1994] 1 FLR 156). It appears that it is to such an appointment that the words "or otherwise" in r 12.12(2)(e) refer (*Essex CC v B* [1993] 1 FLR 866); see also *Re S (A Minor) (Independent Representation)* [1993] 2 FLR 437 at [445C], where Sir Thomas Bingham MR suggests that, where the court has dismissed a children's guardian earlier in the relevant proceedings in order to enable the child to participate as a party in his own right but then later decides that the child lacks the necessary understanding so as to participate, it can use its "general power to appoint under r 4.14(2)(d) [FPR 2010, r 12.12(2)] (and r 9.5) [FPR 2010, r 16.4]". Whether r 12.12(2)(e) might ever have a wider application, however, remains somewhat uncertain. A children's guardian appointed in non-specified proceedings will not receive funding from the Legal Aid Agency (which replaced the Legal Services Commission on 1 April 2013) and probably not from his own panel. Where a guardian has been appointed in the course of an investigation under CA 1989, s 37 at the conclusion of which the local authority decides not to apply for a care or supervision order, it would be possible for the High Court or a county court to direct that the guardian should continue to be involved under FPR 2010, r 16.4. However, this should only be done where the guardian consents, where funding is available and where the guardian has a continuing role to play despite the changed status of the proceedings (*Re CE (Section 37 Direction)* [1995] 1 FLR 26).

Appointment of a solicitor under s 41(3) (r 12.12(2)(e))—CA 1989, s 41(3) enables the court to appoint a solicitor to represent a child concerned in specified proceedings where he has no children's guardian, where he is of sufficient understanding to instruct a solicitor and wants to do so or where it appears that it would be in his best interests for him to be represented by a solicitor (see *Re H (A Minor) (Care Proceedings: Child's Wishes)* [1993] 1 FLR 440). In contrast to the position with regard to the appointment of a children's guardian, there is no rule dealing specifically with the procedure for the appointment of such a solicitor so this must be carried out under this rule, although r 12.12(8) imposes a duty on the court to record the appointment. Where there is a children's guardian, he generally has a duty to appoint a solicitor for the child under FPR PD16A, para 6.2(a). An appointment by the children's guardian is not made under s 41(3) and the court cannot therefore give directions with regard to it. However, it is presumed that should the court's assistance be required at a later stage (for example, if a question arises as to how the solicitor should carry out his duties under FPR 2010, r 16.29), directions under this rule could be sought on the basis that the matter arises in connection with the conduct of the proceedings. An application by the child or the children's guardian for termination of the solicitor's appointment would, however, have to be made under r 16.29(7),(8).

There is no power to appoint a solicitor for a child under s 41(3) in non-specified proceedings (*Re W (A Minor) (Contact)* [1994] 1 FLR 843).

Appointment of a litigation friend (r 12.12(2)(f))—Where a child is a party to proceedings, but not the subject of those proceedings, the child must have a litigation friend to conduct them on his behalf: see rr 16.5 and 16.7–16.15. For the circumstances in which a child does not need a children's guardian or a litigation friend, see r 16.6.

Appointment of the Official Solicitor—In recent times there has been a marked increase in the number of public law children cases in which the Official Solicitor (OS) is invited to act as guardian ad litem or litigation friend of a protected party. In December 2010 the President of the Family Division issued *Guidance in cases involving protected parties in which the Official Solicitor is being invited to act as guardian ad litem or litigation friend* (see Part V). It sets out the Official Solicitor's acceptance criteria, which remain: (1) satisfactory evidence or a finding by the court that the party lacks capacity to conduct the proceedings and is therefore a protected party; (2) confirmation that there is security for the costs of legal representation; (3) that there is no other person who is suitable and willing to act as guardian ad litem/litigation friend. When the Official Solicitor does consent to act, Standard Instructions to the solicitor whom he instructs for the protected party can be found at *www.justice.gov.uk/protecting-the-vulnerable/official-solicitor/acting-for-parents*. The telephone number for the Official Solicitor is 020 7911 7127 and the website is *www.justice.gov.uk/about/ospt*.

Litigants in person—See notes to FPR 2010, r 12.21.

McKenzie Friend—See notes to FPR 2010, r 12.21.

Service of documents (r 12.12(2)(g))—As to service generally, see FPR 2010, rr 6.23–6.39, 12.8 and FPR PD12C. The power to give directions about service under this rule is supplementary to the power of the court to give directions under FPR 2010, r 12.8.

Preparation of welfare reports (r 12.12(2)(i))—As to welfare reports generally, see CA 1989, s 7 and FPR 2010, r 16.33 and FPR PD16A. Directions may be sought under this rule where, for example, there are problems in complying with the request for a welfare report, either because of time constraints or for other reasons, or where the children and family reporter or welfare officer considers that part of his report contains sensitive material that ought not to be shown to the parties in the normal way.

Transfer of proceedings—The transfer of proceedings between courts is governed by the ATPO 2008. For a request for transfer from a magistrates' court to a county court or to another magistrates' court, see

FPR 2010, r 12.9; for the procedure following a refusal by the magistrates' court to order a transfer, see FPR 2010, r 12.10; for the procedure on transfer of proceedings from one court to another court, see r 12.11.

Any directions as to transfer that are not covered by FPR 2010, rr 12.9–12.11 may, presumably, be given under r 12.12(a) as part of the "management of the case". The provisions of FPR 2010, r 12.13, which deal with the obligation to fix a date for the receiving court next to consider the case and to notify the parties of the date, are also important in this context.

Consolidation with other proceedings—It is desirable wherever possible for directions to be given as to transfer between courts, consolidation etc, so that all linked proceedings can be heard and determined together; this will be the case, for example, where there are separate applications with regard to several children of the same family (see for example *W v Wakefield City Council* [1995] 1 FLR 170) or more than one set of proceedings concerning an individual child that ought logically to be heard together. If the family proceedings court refuses to transfer upwards, for example, an application under CA 1989, s 8 for consolidation with "linked" county court proceedings, no "appeal" to the district judge is permissible. In those circumstances, one possible solution may be to seek leave to withdraw the s 8 application so that it could be started afresh in the county court. However, the Legal Aid Agency (which replaced the Legal Services Commission on 1 April 2013) may well resist the granting of public funding for "restarting" such proceedings in the county court, when the family proceedings court was prepared to hear them originally. Another solution, in suitable circumstances, might be to seek judicial review of the magistrates' court's decision to refuse to transfer the proceedings (*R v South East Hampshire Family Proceedings Court ex parte D* [1994] 2 FLR 190).

Notice of court's intention to give directions of its own initiative (r 12.12(5),(6))—The court may exercise its powers on its own initiative, but where it proposes to do so it must follow the procedure in FPR 2010, r 4.3. This means that it may give any person likely to be affected by the order an opportunity to make representations (r 4.3(2)). Where the court proposes to hold a hearing to decide whether to make the order, it must give the parties affected at least 5 days' notice (r 4.3(3)). However, there will be situations in which the court may make an order without hearing the parties or giving them an opportunity to make representations (r 4.3(4)); in this event, the party affected by the order may apply to have it set aside, varied or stayed (r 4.3(6)).

Written directions in difficult child care cases—As a general rule, it is bad practice for directions in difficult child care cases to be sought and given in writing without the attendance of the parties (*Re A and B (Minors) (No 2)* [1995] 1 FLR 351).

Service—See FPR 2010, rr 12.8 and 16.23–16.39 and FPR PD12C.

Request of or order against Home Office—In April 2013, the President of the Family Division reissued a protocol *Communicating with the Home Office in Family Proceedings* (see Part V). It sets out the appropriate procedure for family courts to communicate with the Home Office to obtain information in relation to immigration, visa and passport information for family proceedings. It gives guidance about the timescale within which a response from the Home Office may be expected and includes a sample court order requesting information and a sample completed form EX660 (request for information). Further guidance as to the approach to be taken when family proceedings are running concurrently with other proceedings was given in *Re M and N (Parallel Family and Immigration Proceedings)* [2008] 2 FLR 2030, where Munby J held that:

(1) practitioners acting for parents in family proceedings have an ongoing duty to remain up to date with other related proceedings;
(2) parents are under a duty to instruct their advisers in other related proceedings to keep their family solicitors informed of progress. Those other advisers then have a duty to keep the family solicitors informed accordingly;
(3) family proceedings practitioners have a duty to take adequate steps before each hearing to find out what has been going on in the related proceedings and where a formal decision is anticipated, when that decision is likely to be given;
(4) it is preferable to obtain copies of correspondence and other documents of the other solicitors' files rather than attempting to find out what is going on through correspondence;
(5) if practitioners experience difficulty in obtaining the relevant information from the other advisers, prompt consideration should be given, as early as possible, to asking the court to make a peremptory order that the other advisers deliver a complete copy of their file to the family proceedings solicitors, or to make an order pursuant to the President's protocol; and
(6) where the outcome in family proceedings is dependent upon or likely to be affected by a third party's decision, early consideration should be given to whether, and if so how, that decision-maker should be brought into some appropriate form of direct engagement with the family proceedings.

Where immigration applications or proceedings are ongoing at the same time as an application for the summary return of children to the country from which they came, it is highly desirable for there to be communication and collaboration between the Secretary of State and the judge who is dealing with the latter application (*Re F (Abduction: Removal Outside Jurisdiction)* [2008] 2 FLR 1649). When considering the welfare of children who have been in the UK illegally for more than 7 years, the local authority must take into account the Secretary of State's policy in such cases and the reasons underlying it. Careful consideration should be given to joining the Home Office in an attempt to ascertain the Secretary of State's views in an individual case; this would reduce the risk of relevant central and public authority decision-makers reaching different conclusions and contain unnecessary expenditure in respect of persons in the jurisdiction unlawfully who would not be given leave to remain (*R (AC) v Birmingham City Council* [2009] 1 FLR 838).

Guidance in cases of stranded spouses—See *Re S (Wardship: Stranded Spouses)* [2011] 1 FLR 305 for guidance as to the approach to be adopted by the court in cases in which one parent has been left stranded abroad by the other parent. It aims to ensure that the relevant ECHR 1950, Arts 6 and 8 rights are upheld, that there is a fair trial of the factual allegations and that the child/children have contact with both parents pending a final welfare-based determination of the issues of residence and contact.

Attendance of the media in family proceedings—For the rules relating to the attendance of the media at hearings in family proceedings, see FPR 2010, r 27.11.

Court of Appeal standing instructions against identification of child—While it is highly desirable that appellate proceedings, wherever possible, should be in open court, in the great majority of cases involving children this could have adverse consequences for the children. It has been accepted, therefore, by the Court of Appeal that in general the identity of the child should be protected by means of an order restricting publication of information that could lead to his identity. Under standing instructions of the Court of Appeal, orders in such terms have almost invariably been made in cases involving children. Without standing instructions, there would always be a risk that the court might fail, through oversight, to give the direction that the restriction should be included. If there were unusual circumstances which made publicity desirable then the court could decide to depart from standing instructions (*Re R (Court of Appeal: Order Against Identification)* [1999] 2 FLR 145). Hearing children cases in England and Wales in private, without public pronouncement of judgment, does not breach ECHR 1950, Art 6 (*B v UK and P v UK* [2001] 2 FLR 261): if judgment were pronounced publicly that would to a large extent frustrate the aims of holding the proceedings in chambers. In *Pelling v Bruce-Williams (Secretary of State for Constitutional Affairs Intervening)* [2004] 2 FLR 823, the Court of Appeal followed *B v UK and P v UK*, but acknowledged that it was not clear that either the inherent or the statutory jurisdiction justified the imposition of an automatic restriction without the exercise of a specific discretion in the individual case. It was held to be desirable for the Master of the Rolls and the President of the Family Division to review the standard practice of the court to reflect the developments since *Re R (Court of Appeal: Order Against Identification)*, above, in which the Court of Appeal indicated that the automatic application of restrictions in all appeals involving children had been developed or confirmed by the court with the approval of the Master of the Rolls nearly 10 years before. In *Pelling v Bruce-Williams* counsel for the Secretary of State for Constitutional Affairs suggested that for the future the court should consider, both at the outset and at the conclusion of each appeal concerning children, exercising a specific discretion either to impose or to refuse prohibition on the identification of the parties to the appeal.

12.13 Setting dates for hearings and setting or confirming the timetable and date for the final hearing

(1) At the –

   (a)   transfer to a court of proceedings;

   (b)   postponement or adjournment of any hearing; or

   (c)   conclusion of any hearing at which the proceedings are not finally determined,

the court will set a date for the proceedings to come before the court again for the purposes of giving directions or for such other purposes as the court directs.

(2) At any hearing the court may –

   (a)   confirm a date for the final hearing or the week within which the final hearing is to begin (where a date or period for the final hearing has already been set);

   (b)   set a timetable for the final hearing unless a timetable has already been fixed, or the court considers that it would be inappropriate to do so; or

(c) set a date for the final hearing or a period within which the final hearing of the application is to take place.

(3) The court officer will notify the parties of –

(a) the date of a hearing fixed in accordance with paragraph (1);
(b) the timetable for the final hearing; and
(c) the date of the final hearing or the period in which it will take place.

(4) Where the date referred to in paragraph (1) is set at the transfer of proceedings, the date will be as soon as possible after the transfer.

(5) The requirement in paragraph (1) to set a date for the proceedings to come before the court again is satisfied by the court setting or confirming a date for the final hearing.

Defined terms—"children and family reporter", "children's guardian", "court", "directions appointment": r 2.3(1).

Related provisions—Other provisions affecting the timing of proceedings include CA 1989, ss 1(2) (general principle that delay is likely to be prejudicial to the welfare of a child), 11(1) (obligation of the court in s 8 proceedings to draw up a timetable) and 32(1) (obligation of the court in proceedings under Pt IV of the Act to draw up a timetable) and FPR 2010, rr 12.12 and 12.13 (power of the court to give directions as to time-limits, timetabling etc).

Computation of time—See r 2.9.

Variation of time-limits—Time-limits may not be extended except by direction of the court. However, if the parties or any children's guardian agree proposals for the management of the proceedings, and the court considers that the proposals are suitable, it may approve them without a hearing and give directions in the terms proposed (FPR 2010, r 12.15).

Failure to observe time-limits—Where a local authority failed to submit written evidence as directed by the court and to comply with a direction to serve documents, the family proceedings court was correct in giving leave for statements to be filed out of time because it was vital in the interests of the children that the court should have the best information available. The sanction for failure to comply with directions was a costs order, where appropriate (*R v Nottinghamshire CC* [1993] Fam Law 625).

Urgent hearings on Circuit before Family Division judges—See FPR PD12E and under FPR 2010, r 12.16.

Fixing a new date (r 12.13(1))—The court must keep a tight rein on the proceedings, ensuring that a new date is fixed, either at the end of the interim hearing or directions appointment while the parties are still at court or as soon as practicable thereafter. Fixing a new date is not only a question of finding an appropriate court slot for the matter to be heard. CA 1989, s 1(2) must always be kept in mind and other provisions of the Act may also impose constraints (see, for example, s 38(4), which limits the duration of interim care orders). Parties and their legal representatives must be in a position to inform the court of their availability for future hearings and that of their witnesses.

Notice—As to the giving of notice, see FPR 2010, rr 6.23–6.39, 29.3.

12.14 Attendance at hearings

(1) This rule does not apply to proceedings under Chapter 6 of this Part except for proceedings for a declaration under rule 12.71.

(2) Unless the court directs otherwise and subject to paragraph (3), the persons who must attend a hearing are –

(a) any party to the proceedings;
(b) any litigation friend for any party or legal representative instructed to act on that party's behalf; and
(c) any other person directed by the court or required by Practice Directions 12A or 12B or any other practice direction to attend.

(3) Proceedings or any part of them will take place in the absence of a child who is a party to the proceedings if –

(a)   the court considers it in the interests of the child, having regard to the matters to be discussed or the evidence likely to be given; and

(b)   the child is represented by a children's guardian or solicitor.

(4)   When considering the interests of the child under paragraph (3) the court will give –

(a)   the children's guardian;

(b)   the solicitor for the child; and

(c)   the child, if of sufficient understanding,

an opportunity to make representations.

(5)   Subject to paragraph (6), where at the time and place appointed for a hearing, the applicant appears but one or more of the respondents do not, the court may proceed with the hearing.

(6)   The court will not begin to hear an application in the absence of a respondent unless the court is satisfied that –

(a)   the respondent received reasonable notice of the date of the hearing; or

(b)   the circumstances of the case justify proceeding with the hearing.

(7)   Where, at the time and place appointed for a hearing one or more of the respondents appear but the applicant does not, the court may –

(a)   refuse the application; or

(b)   if sufficient evidence has previously been received, proceed in the absence of the applicant.

(8)   Where at the time and place appointed for a hearing neither the applicant nor any respondent appears, the court may refuse the application.

(9)   Paragraphs (5) to (8) do not apply to a hearing where the court –

(a)   is considering –

(i)   whether to make a contact activity direction or to attach a contact activity condition to a contact order; or

(ii)   an application for a financial compensation order, an enforcement order or an order under paragraph 9 of Schedule A1 to the 1989 Act following a breach of an enforcement order; and

(b)   has yet to obtain sufficient evidence from, or in relation to, the person who may be the subject of the direction, condition or order to enable it to determine the matter.

(10)   Nothing in this rule affects the provisions of Article 18 of the Council Regulation in cases to which that provision applies.

(The Council Regulation makes provision in Article 18 for the court to stay proceedings where the respondent is habitually resident in another Member State of the European Union and has not been adequately served with the proceedings as required by that provision.)

Non-application to Chapter 6—Pt 12, Ch 6 relates to proceedings under the 1980 Hague Convention, the European Convention, the Council Regulation and the 1996 Hague Convention; for directions in these applications see FPR 2010, r 12.48.

Defined terms—"child", "children's guardian", "court": FPR 2010, r 2.3(1).

Related provisions—Other provisions relating to attendance include: FPR 2010, r 16.20(2), which imposes a duty on the children's guardian to provide the court with such assistance as it may require; FPR PD16A, which sets out his other duties – including attending all directions hearings unless the court orders otherwise (para 6.5) and advising on the attendance of the child at court (para 6.6(b)); FPR 2010, r 12.12(2)(d), which is a general power enabling the court to give directions as to the attendance of the child; and CA 1989, s 95, which empowers a court hearing proceedings under Pt IV or V of the Act (or considering whether to make an order under those Parts) to require the attendance of the child and to make supplementary orders to secure that attendance.

"unless the court directs otherwise" (r 12.14(2))—The court is given a complete discretion as to the circumstances in which to dispense with the attendance of a party at a directions hearing and can do so either of its own initiative (for example when sending out notice of the hearing) or on the request of a party.

Seeking a direction dispensing with attendance at a hearing—It would seem that the appropriate procedure for seeking a direction dispensing with attendance at a hearing would be that set out in FPR 2010, rr 18.1–18.13.

Medical evidence required to justify non-attendance—Where a party wishes to demonstrate that he is unable to attend and participate in a hearing, he should provide medical evidence that: identifies the medical attendant and gives details of his familiarity with the party's medical condition, detailing all recent consultations; identifies with particularity his condition and the features of that condition preventing participation in the trial process; provides a reasoned prognosis; and gives the court confidence that the evidence expressed was an independent opinion following proper examination (*Levy (Trustee in Bankruptcy of Ellis-Carr) v Ellis-Carr and Another* [2012] BPIR 347).

Use of the power to exclude (r 12.14(2),(3))—Generally, all parties (including the child himself if he is a party) are entitled to be present throughout the proceedings. Rule 12.14(3) empowers the court to exclude any child who is a party where the criteria laid down are satisfied; it is in mandatory terms and contrasts with r 12.14(5),(6), which confers on the court a discretion as to whether to proceed with a hearing or appointment where a party fails to attend. Rule 12.14(3) will no doubt normally come into play when the child should be excluded for his own good. For the attitude of the courts towards the attendance of children at hearings, see **Child at court**, below. The court's power in r 12.14(2) to "direct otherwise" would presumably be used to exclude attendance where, for some reason, another party's presence would impede a proper hearing, for example in the very rare case where an older child is to give evidence and would find it distressing to do so in the presence of a parent who is alleged to be guilty of a serious sexual assault on him or her. However, in such a situation, the giving of the child's evidence by video link or behind a screen may be a better course. Exceptionally, an application for an adjournment can be granted without notice, but only where the best interests of the children justify such a course of action. Even then, those representing the parties should be in attendance, either having given undertakings or being subject to a direction of the court not to pass on the information to their clients (*Re B (Minors) (Care: Procedure)* [1994] Fam Law 72). As to the procedure to be followed where an application is made to withhold material from a party to proceedings, see *Re C (Disclosure)* [1996] 1 FLR 797, FD, which is considered fully in **Submission of evidence** under FPR 2010, r 12.12.

Child at court—The effect of r 12.14(2) is to require the child, if he is a party, to be present at hearings unless the court otherwise directs under r 12.14(3). Under the Private Law Programme in FPR PD12B, which applies to all applications issued under CA 1989, Pt II, any child concerned in the proceedings who is aged 9 or over may attend court for the first hearing dispute resolution appointment, where the local scheme provides for it and where resources exist. For the first hearing dispute resolution appointment, see FPR 2010, r 12.31.

However, the attitude of the court towards the attendance of children has consistently been cautious (*Re C (A Minor) (Care: Child's Wishes)* [1993] 1 FLR 832). In *Re W (Secure Accommodation Order: Attendance at Court)* [1994] 2 FLR 1092, Ewbank J said that attending court is likely to be harmful for a child and should only be permitted if the court is satisfied that it is in the child's interests. He held that r 4.16(2) (FPR 2010, r 12.14(3)) applies only to one set of circumstances. In other circumstances, the child's interests will prevail. In addition to the consideration of the interests of the child, the court has an inherent power to control its own proceedings that entitles it to decide to proceed in the child's absence. The fact that the child would need to be physically restrained during the hearing to control him (as in *Re W*) would, in itself, be sufficient ground for refusing to allow the child to be in court. Further examples given in *Re W* of situations in which the court would not allow a child to be present are where there is a prospect of disturbance or unruliness in court or the possibility of the child being educationally subnormal or where the child is much younger than the 10-year-old boy in that case. The presence of older children in court is unusual, but by no means unheard of in cases where a child has sufficient maturity to give instructions directly to a solicitor. Likewise, the Supreme Court has done away with the presumption that children should not give evidence: *Re W (Children) (Abuse: Oral Evidence)* [2010] 1 FLR 1485 (see notes to CA 1989, s 93). In *A City Council v T, J and K* [2011] 2 FLR 803, a case concerning secure accommodation, the court held that although it has the power to exclude a child who wants to attend court, on the grounds that it would be bad for him to be there, the rules do not contain any in-built presumption; it is a question of what is in the best interests of the child. It can no longer be presumed that a child's attendance in court is likely to be harmful, nor should children have to prove that their attendance at proceedings about them is in their interests. The starting point should be an open evaluation of the consequence of attendance or non-attendance. The relevant factors would generally include: (1) the age and level of understanding of the child; (2) the nature and strength of the child's

PART III

wishes; (3) the child's emotional and psychological state; (4) the effect of influence from others; (5) the matters to be discussed; (6) the evidence to be given; (7) the child's behaviour; (8) practical and logistical considerations; and (9) the integrity of the proceedings. An evaluation of these factors may well lead to the conclusion that a child of sufficient understanding who wants to attend an important hearing about his future should be allowed to do so for at least part of the time, unless there are clear reasons justifying refusal. This situation is most likely to arise in public law proceedings. In cases in which attendance at the hearing itself is not thought appropriate, a meeting with the judge is a possible alternative (see **Judge seeing child** under FPR 2010, r 12.21). The court, per curiam, added that in any case in which a child wishes to attend a hearing, or where he might wish to do so if told that was possible, the parties must ensure that the court is informed of any arrangements proposed. In the event of disagreement, the parties must, where possible, ensure that the matter is formally brought before the court as a preliminary issue for decision in good time before the relevant hearing; disagreement should not be resolved by informal communications between the parties and the court.

"the party is represented by a children's guardian or solicitor" (r 12.14(3)(b))—The rule appears to suggest that a party is represented only if the solicitor is actually in attendance at the relevant hearing. In *Re AS (Secure Accommodation Order)* [1999] 1 FLR 103, FD, considering the requirement for legal representation of the child concerned in secure accommodation proceedings (CA 1989, s 25(6)), the court held that to be effective, legal representation must involve the taking of instructions. It was not sufficient for the child to be represented at the hearing by a solicitor and counsel who had not been able to take any instructions because the child had not been informed of the hearing.

Child of sufficient understanding to make representations (r 12.14(4)(c))—There are a number of situations in which the rules or the Act oblige the court to evaluate the understanding of the child (see, for example, s 4(4) with regard to parental responsibility agreements, s 10(8) with regard to leave to apply for a s 8 order, and s 43(8) with regard to medical and other examinations). No criteria are laid down as to what constitutes sufficient understanding and what is sufficient for one purpose may not, of course, be sufficient for another; the court will have to take a decision on the particular facts of each case. The authorities on the understanding of a child are collected together under "able ... to give such instructions on his own behalf" under FPR 2010, r 16.29. Where there is a children's guardian he will advise the court as to the level of the child's understanding and the child's wishes in accordance with FPR 2010, r 16.20 and FPR PD16A, para 6.6, and where there is a children and family reporter he can be asked to assist (para 9.4). Alternatively, the assessment will have to be based on how the child appears and what he (or his legal representative on his behalf) says in court or the judge or district judge could, presumably, exercise his discretion to see him privately if appropriate (see **Judge seeing child** under r 12.21). In certain cases, it may be necessary for evidence to be heard on the question from the expert or experts already involved in the case.

"opportunity to make representations" (r 12.14(4))—The rules do not require that there should be an opportunity for oral representations so, although oral representations will be usual, presumably an opportunity to make written representations will suffice.

Hearing in the absence of a respondent (r 12.14(5),(6))—Rule 12.14(5),(6) gives the court a wide discretion to entertain proceedings in the absence of a respondent and even goes so far as to permit the court, in an appropriate case, to proceed to hear an application where the respondent is absent because he has not had reasonable notice of the hearing date. The court is not likely to go to this extreme very often but, where it is prepared to do so, it may be inclined to safeguard the position of the respondent by providing, for example, that he shall be entitled to apply within a certain number of days of service of the order upon him to have it varied or discharged (for a similar sort of order, see *Re D (A Minor) (Child: Removal from Jurisdiction)* [1992] 1 FLR 637). Where an application is made at the hearing itself for an order that is different in kind from that which previously applied for, the respondent must be given the opportunity to be present at the hearing and should be given the chance to cross-examine witnesses called by the applicant (*Re W (A Minor) (Interim Care Order)* [1994] 2 FLR 892, CA). In particular, a wholly different order should not be made without giving the parties an opportunity to make representations or to call evidence (*Re M (Judge's Discretion)* [2002] 1 FLR 730). *Re SW (A Minor) (Care Proceedings)* [1993] 2 FLR 609, a care order application, is an example of the type of situation in which the court may decide to proceed in the absence of a respondent.

Dismissal of proceedings at directions stage—See further under FPR 2010, r 12.12.

"reasonable notice of the date of the hearing" (r 12.14(6)(a))—Where it is the court's obligation to give notice to the respondents of a hearing date, proof will be found in the court file. Where it is the applicant's responsibility, he will have to prove that the respondent has had reasonable notice. FPR 2010, r 29.2 makes provision as to the appropriate method of giving notice and FPR 2010, rr 6.23–6.39 and 12.8 with regard to service and the filing of a statement as to service in Form C9. However, it is possible that the respondent may have had reasonable notice of the hearing date even if it has not been given (or cannot be proved) in accordance with these rules. Rule 12.14(6) does not specify that the notice has to be in writing to be reasonable and oral notice may suffice where, for example, the respondent was present at the last hearing when the new date was fixed. Alternatively, he may have shown in some way that he knows of the date of the hearing, for example by writing to the court about it or by telling one of the parties that he has no intention of coming to court on such and such a day. For a further example, see *Re SW (A Minor) (Care Proceedings)* [1993] 2 FLR 609. Where there has been an interim care or supervision order and no change in this is sought, a notification in the antecedent order that the renewal hearing will take place on a certain day is sufficient; there is no need to go through the formality of serving another piece of paper. However, if a change is intended in the nature of the order that is being sought on the subsequent occasion, then normally specific notice of at least 2 clear days should be given by the party who seeks the new form of order (*Re W (A Minor) (Interim Care Order)* [1994] 2 FLR 892).

For certain applications, minimum notice periods are laid down in the rules themselves or in FPR PD12C, para 2.1, and it may be difficult in such cases to satisfy the court that a lesser period of notice is "reasonable".

Hearing in the absence of applicant (r 12.14(5))—The court has a discretion whether or not to proceed with a hearing in the absence of the applicant. However, there will be many cases (for example where there is doubt as to whether the applicant has had reasonable notice of the time and place of a hearing) where the appropriate course is to adjourn the application, fixing another date for it to be heard. If the applicant fails to turn up for no good reason on more than one occasion or has indicated that he no longer wishes to proceed with his case, the court will no doubt give very serious consideration to refusing the application. However, it must be borne in mind that such a course of action would be tantamount to permitting the withdrawal of an application, and such leave is not granted as a matter of course (see under FPR 2010, r 29.4).

Where neither applicant nor respondent attends (r 12.14(8))—Although r 12.14(8) refers only to the court's discretion to refuse the application, it must also have power in an appropriate case either to adjourn it or to grant it.

12.15 Steps taken by the parties

If –

    (a) the parties or any children's guardian agree proposals for the management of the proceedings (including a proposed date for the final hearing or a period within which the final hearing is to take place); and

    (b) the court considers that the proposals are suitable,

it may approve them without a hearing and give directions in the terms proposed.

12.16 Applications without notice

(1) This rule applies to –

    (a) proceedings for a section 8 order;

    (b) emergency proceedings; and

    (c) proceedings relating to the exercise of the court's inherent jurisdiction (other than an application for the court's permission to start such proceedings and proceedings for collection, location and passport orders where Chapter 6 applies).

(2) An application in proceedings referred to in paragraph (1) may, in the High Court or a county court, be made without notice in which case the applicant must file the application –

    (a) where the application is made by telephone, the next business day after the making of the application; or

    (b) in any other case, at the time when the application is made.

(3) An application in proceedings referred to in paragraph (1)(a) or (b) may, in a magistrates' court, be made with the permission of the court, without notice, in which case the applicant must file the application at the time when the application is made or as directed by the court.

(4) Where –

    (a) a section 8 order;

    (b) an emergency protection order;

    (c) an order for the disclosure of information as to the whereabouts of a child under section 33 of the 1986 Act; or

    (d) an order authorising the taking charge of and delivery of a child under section 34 of the 1986 Act,

is made without notice, the applicant must serve a copy of the application on each respondent within 48 hours after the order is made.

(5) Within 48 hours after the making of an order without notice, the applicant must serve a copy of the order on –

    (a) the parties, unless the court directs otherwise;

    (b) any person who has actual care of the child or who had such care immediately prior to the making of the order; and

    (c) in the case of an emergency protection order and a recovery order, the local authority in whose area the child lives or is found.

(6) Where the court refuses to make an order on an application without notice it may direct that the application is made on notice in which case the application will proceed in accordance with rules 12.3 to 12.15.

(7) Where the hearing takes place outside the hours during which the court office is normally open, the court or court officer will take a note of the proceedings.

    (Practice Direction 12E (Urgent Business) provides further details of the procedure for out of hours applications. See also Practice Direction 12D (Inherent Jurisdiction (including Wardship Proceedings).)

    (Rule 12.47 provides for without-notice applications in proceedings under Chapter 6, section 1 of this Part, (proceedings under the 1980 Hague Convention and the European Convention).)

Non-application to Chapter 6 (r 12.16(1)(c))—FPR 2010, Pt 12, Ch 6 relates to proceedings under the 1980 Hague Convention, the European Convention, the Council Regulation and the 1996 Hague Convention; for directions in these applications see r 12.48

Out-of-hours hearings – President's Guidance—See FPR PD12E and FPR PD18A, which give details of how telephone hearings should be conducted (paras 8.1–8.5).

Urgent hearings before Court of Appeal for immediate relief—See *Re S (Authorising children's immediate removal)* [2010] 2 FLR 873 for the steps that can be taken to seek an urgent hearing before the Court of Appeal (CA) for immediate relief. In *Re A (A Child) (Residence Order)* [2007] EWCA Civ 899 at [27] the CA held that when a judge considers that a significant change in the arrangements for a child needs to be made forthwith and learns that there is an aspiration to appeal to the CA, he should always give serious consideration to making an order that affords the aspiring appellant a narrow opportunity to approach the CA for further, temporary relief before his order takes effect. The welfare of the child remains paramount, but, subject thereto, the judge needs to consider whether a refusal to afford this narrow opportunity unfairly erodes the facility for effective appeal. If he decides to afford it, he can do so either by directing that the change in the arrangements should occur only at the end (say) of the following working day or by directing that the change should occur forthwith but that execution of his order be stayed until the end (say) of the following working day. When, however, a judge declines to take either of these courses, there remains the opportunity for the aspiring appellant to approach the CA by telephone, and usually on notice to the other party. The approach can even be made out of court hours, first through the security officers of the CA (on 020 7947 6260) and then through a Deputy Master, to a Lord Justice. He may decide to grant a stay, for example until the end of the following working day, to enable documents, such as a note of the judgment and draft grounds of appeal, to be faxed or emailed to the court, for his consideration of the merits of a further stay.

Unlawful removal of a child from his usual place of residence—The seemingly unlawful removal of a child from his usual place of residence ordinarily calls for a peremptory order for his return. An application for such an order should be made without notice and at once to any court that has a 24-hour service, or at least a judge available every court day (*Re R (Children: Peremptory Return)* [2011] 2 FLR 863).

Power to make without notice orders (r 12.16(4))—It is clear that without notice orders will not be granted readily, see for example *Re G (Minors) (Ex Parte Interim Residence Order)* [1993] 1 FLR 910; *Re P (A Minor) (Ex Parte Interim Residence Order)* [1993] 1 FLR 915; *M v C (Children Orders: Reasons)* [1993] 2 FLR 584 (all with regard to the limited circumstances in which an interim residence order should be made without notice); *R v St Albans Magistrates' Court ex parte J* [1993] Fam Law 518 (CA 1989, s 75 application to cancel registration as childminder not normally to be dealt with without notice); *Re R (A Minor) (Blood Transfusion)* [1993] 2 FLR 757 (on application for authority to give a blood transfusion, strenuous efforts should be made to arrange a with notice hearing). In *Re B (Minors) (Care: Procedure)* [1994] Fam Law 72, Bracewell J held that a court should only allow without notice applications for adjournment of proceedings for reduction of contact in exceptional circumstances; if a hearing was to take place without the parents being present, their legal representatives should be permitted access, subject to undertakings or directions not to pass the information to their clients. Save in exceptional circumstances, it is highly undesirable that a without notice order should be allowed to stand for more than 7 days; a 12-week without notice residence order in favour of a grandmother was plainly wrong (*Re Y (A Minor) (Ex Parte Interim Orders)* [1994] Fam Law 127). In *Re J (Children: Ex Parte Orders)* [1997] 1 FLR 606, Hale J made certain observations about without notice orders following consultation with the President of the Family Division. She stressed that the courts have a special responsibility to ensure that without notice orders that could harm the interests of an adult or child are not made without a good reason. Orders requiring the handing over of a very young child to a parent with whom he has not lived for some time should only be made in exceptional circumstances. Applicants for without notice orders and their legal advisers must be scrupulously careful in relation to the application itself and to the implementation of any order that might be made. It is incumbent on the applicant's legal advisers to understand any order and to represent it accurately to others. If there is some doubt about their interpretation, urgent clarification should be sought from the court on a with notice basis. The police should always have a clear understanding of their role in relation to the order. Counsel should never advise on the effect of an order made in their absence without being satisfied of the exact terms of the order, which will generally involve reading it.

Procedure for without notice orders—Where without notice orders are sought, Munby J has set out in *Re S (Ex Parte Orders)* [2001] 1 FLR 308 guidelines that state:

(1) It is appropriate, generally, in the Family Division for the court to require the applicant (and, where appropriate, the applicant's solicitors) to give the following undertakings:
  (a) where proceedings have not yet been issued, to issue and serve on the respondent, either by some specified time or as soon as practicable, proceedings either in the form of the draft produced to the court or otherwise as may be appropriate;
  (b) where the application has been made otherwise than on sworn evidence, to cause to be sworn, filed and served on the respondent as soon as practicable an affidavit substantially in the terms of that produced to the court or, as the case may be, confirming the substance of what was said to the court by the applicant's counsel or solicitors; and
  (c) subject to (a) and (b), to serve on the respondent as soon as practicable: (i) the proceedings; (ii) a sealed copy of the order; (iii) copies of the affidavit(s) and exhibit(s) containing the evidence relied on by the applicant; and (iv) notice of the return date and details of the application to be made on that date.

(2) Whether or not express undertakings have been given, and subject to any order to the contrary, an applicant who obtains without notice injunctive relief is under an obligation to the court, and his solicitor is under an obligation both to the court and his client, to carry out the steps referred to above.

(3) A person who finds himself unable to comply timeously with his undertaking should apply for an extension of time before the time for compliance has expired, or pass the task to someone who has available the time in which to do it.

(4) Persons injuncted are entitled to be given, if they ask, proper information as to what happened at the hearing and told what documents etc were lodged with the court and what legal authorities were cited to the judge. The applicant's lawyers should respond forthwith to any reasonable request from the respondent or his lawyers, for copies of the materials read by the judge or for information about what took place at the hearing. It would, therefore, be prudent for those acting for the applicant to keep a proper note of the proceedings.

Three additional points of guidance for all without notice applications (and of particular importance if the relief involves the grant of a Tipstaff order) were given in *KY v DD* [2012] 2 FLR 200:

(1) Where information is put before the court to substantiate a without notice order, it should be the subject of the closest scrutiny and, if the applicant is not present to verify it in person, it should be substantiated by the production of a contemporaneous note of the instructions. Otherwise, a short adjournment might be necessary to verify that information.

(2) If additional information is put before the court orally, there must be a direction for the filing of sworn evidence to confirm the information within a very short period of time.

(3) It is incumbent on those giving advice in relation to the making of such an application to consider rigorously whether the application is justified and to be clear as to the evidential basis for it.

Flagrant breaches of these principles and procedures may well lead to a wasted costs order (*B v A* [2012] EWHC 3127 (Fam)).

Munby J gave guidance in *Re W (Ex Parte Orders)* [2000] 2 FLR 927 as to the procedure to be followed in seeking a without notice injunction in the Family Division.

Without notice application on notice—Although no provision is made for it in the Rules, a procedure has evolved, as a matter of practice and fairness, whereby a without notice application can be made on informal notice (see for example *Croydon LBC v A (No 3)* [1992] 2 FLR 350). This procedure must not be used, however, as a way of getting what should be a proper with notice hearing more quickly than would otherwise be the case.

Application on short notice as alternative to without notice application—Where possible, it is preferable for an application to be served and for notice to be abridged than for a without notice application to be made (see for example *Re B (A Minor) (Residence Order: Ex Parte)* [1992] 2 FLR 1, CA). As to the giving of notice, see FPR 2010, r 29.2 and as to service see FPR 2010, rr 6.23–6.39, 12.8 and FPR PD12C.

Service of the without notice orders (r 12.16(4))—Service of an order of the kind specified in r 12.16(4) within the period of 48 hours there prescribed is mandatory. Failure to serve within the period might generate argument as to enforceability of the order and therefore, to avoid problems, an applicant who knows that there is likely to be difficulty in complying with the time limit for service should seek directions at the same time as the initial without notice application is made. Rule 6.36 gives the court power to dispense with service, and FPR 2010, rr 6.19 and 6.35 give the court power to order that service shall be effected in an alternative manner. FPR 2010, r 12.12(2)(a),(b) provides a general power to give directions about the management of the case and the timetable for steps to be taken between the giving of directions and the final hearing. As to the computation of time, see FPR 2010, r 2.9; as to the extension of time limits, see FPR 2010, rr 4.1(3)(a), 12.12(2)(a),(b) and 12.13(1).

Refusal of an application for a without notice order (r 12.16(6))—Where it is directed that the application is to be heard with notice before there can be a hearing the applicant will have to file the application, if this has not already been done, serve copies in accordance with FPR 2010, r 12.8 and give notice in Form C6A in accordance with FPR 2010, r 12.3(1) and FPR PD12C.

Application to set aside without notice order—Where a without notice order has been made and the absent party wishes to challenge it, the appropriate course is to apply to the judge who made it to vary or rescind the order. There is no purpose, in anything other than a wholly exceptional case, in making such an application without notice. Notice (albeit short notice if justified by the urgency of the situation) should be given to the other parties (*Re P (A Minor) (Ex Parte Interim Residence Order)* [1993] 1 FLR 915; see also *Re H (Wardship: Ex Parte Orders)* [1994] 2 FLR 981, CA).

12.17 Investigation under section 37 of the 1989 Act

(1) This rule applies where a direction is given to an appropriate authority by the court under section 37(1) of the 1989 Act.

(2) On giving the direction the court may adjourn the proceedings.

(3) As soon as practicable after the direction is given the court will record the direction.

(4) As soon as practicable after the direction is given the court officer will –

    (a) serve the direction on –
        (i) the parties to the proceedings in which the direction is given; and
        (ii) the appropriate authority where it is not a party;

    (b) serve any documentary evidence directed by the court on the appropriate authority.

(5) Where a local authority informs the court of any of the matters set out in section 37(3)(a) to (c) of the 1989 Act it will do so in writing.

(6) Unless the court directs otherwise, the court officer will serve a copy of any report to the court under section 37 of the 1989 Act on the parties.

> (Section 37 of the 1989 Act refers to the appropriate authority and section 37(5) of that Act sets out which authority should be named in a particular case.)

Guidance on use of CA 1989, s 37—See **Best Practice Guidance on s 37(1) Directions** under CA 1989, s 37, which stresses the importance of the local authority being informed as quickly as possible of a s 37 direction and advises that an immediate telephone notification should be made, then confirmed in writing in compliance with r 12.17(5). See also *CAAC Handbook of Best Practice in Children Act Cases*, App A, item IV (set out in Part V of this work as *Best Practice Guidance of June 1997*). See also **Best Practice Guidance on s 37(1) Directions** under CA 1989, s 37, which sets out further judicial guidance on the use of s 37.

Public Law Outline (PLO)—In all public law proceedings under CA 1989, Pt IV, the PLO must be followed (see FPR PD12A and FPR 2010, rr 12.23–12.26). On the same day that the court makes such a direction (day 1), it must identify the local authority that is to prepare the s 37(1) report, fix a date for the next hearing and give directions as to filing and service of the report (steps 1–4). Within 24 hours of receiving the order (on day 3) the local authority must allocate the request to a social services team manager to oversee the referral and assessment processes, following the relevant Government guidance (see App F to the Protocol, *Social Services Assessment and Care Planning Aide-Memoire*). Any assessment undertaken by social services should be completed within 35 days of the allocation (ie by day 38). At the conclusion of their enquiries social services must consult the family, the child and all relevant agencies before making decisions about a plan for the child. The local authority must record the response of each person and agency consulted, decide whether to apply to the court for an order, file the report with the court and serve it on the parties on or before the date specified in the court's order (between days 38 and 40). Where social services decide not to apply for a care or supervision order they should set out in their report their decisions and reasons and any plan they have made for the child, including any services to be provided in accordance with Government guidance (see App F to the Protocol).

"appropriate authority" (r 12.17(1))—This phrase refers back to CA 1989, s 37; s 37(5) sets out which authority should be named in any given case.

"record the direction" (r 12.17(3))—This is to be recorded in Form C40 and constitutes a direction to a specified local authority to undertake an investigation under s 37(1) and it sets out the full name and date of birth of the child concerned.

"parties" (r 12.17(3))—As r 12.17 does not widen the normal meaning of "parties" to the proceedings so as to include the welfare officer as a party, it appears that the parties are simply the applicant and the respondents.

Documentary evidence that may accompany copy of direction (r 12.17(4)(b))—Rule 12.17(4) is important because it enables the court to ensure that the local authority carrying out the investigation receives the documentary evidence that it will need to do its job properly. However, the authority does not simply have access to the whole court file; the court has a discretion as to precisely which documents should be provided and must give a direction about this when making the s 37(1) direction.

Service—As to service, see FPR 2010, rr 6.23–6.39, 12.8 and FPR PD12C.

12.18 Disclosure of a report under section 14A(8) or (9) of the 1989 Act

(1) In proceedings for a special guardianship order, the local authority must file the report under section 14A(8) or (9) of the 1989 Act within the timetable fixed by the court.

(2) The court will consider whether to give a direction that the report under section 14A(8) or (9) of the 1989 Act be disclosed to each party to the proceedings.

(3) Before giving a direction for the report to be disclosed, the court must consider whether any information should be deleted from the report.

(4) The court may direct that the report must not be disclosed to a party.

(5) The court officer must serve a copy of the report in accordance with any direction under paragraph (2).

(6) In paragraph (3), information includes information which a party has declined to reveal under rule 29.1(1).

Definitions—"special guardianship order": r 12.2.

Rule 29.1 (r 12.18(6))—This rule states that a party is not required to reveal certain personal details such as his home address, contact details and so forth unless the court directs otherwise (FPR 2010, r 29.1(1)). If he does not wish to reveal these particulars he must give notice of them to the court and they will not be revealed to any person unless the court directs otherwise (r 29.1(2)). However, the party concerned must notify the court of any change of address (r 29.1(3)).

12.19 Additional evidence

(1) This rule applies to proceedings for a section 8 order or a special guardianship order.

(2) Unless the court directs otherwise, a party must not –

    (a) file or serve any document other than in accordance with these rules or any practice direction;

    (b) in completing a form prescribed by these rules or any practice direction, give information or make a statement which is not required or authorised by that form; or

    (c) file or serve at a hearing –

        (i) any witness statement of the substance of the oral evidence which the party intends to adduce; or

        (ii) any copy of any document (including any experts' report) which the party intends to rely on.

(3) Where a party fails to comply with the requirements of this rule in relation to any witness statement or other document, the party cannot seek to rely on that statement or other document unless the court directs otherwise.

Defined terms—"section 8 order": CA 1989, s 8(2).

Private Law Programme (PLP)—The PLP is contained in FPR PD12B and applies to all applications issued under CA 1989, Pt II and sets out the structure for the management of such cases (see FPR 2010, r 12.31).

Case management—See the CAAC *Handbook of Best Practice in Children Act Cases* (set out in Part V of this work as *Best Practice Guidance of June 1997*) and **Bundles and other particular matters** under FPR 2010, r 12.12. For the detailed rules about bundles see FPR PD27A.

Parties—Broadly speaking, the parties to proceedings are the applicant and the respondents set out in the relevant table entry in r 12.3(1). As to the power of the court to order that a person be joined as or cease to be a party, see FPR 2010, r 12.3(3).

Time for filing statements and documents (r 12.19(2))—Directions will normally be given under FPR 2010, r 12.12 for all but the very early stages of the proceedings. It is suggested that directions should be specific. Solicitors should identify the deponents of proposed statements and the relevance of their evidence, and a timetable for the filing of statements should be drawn up. This has the additional advantage that the court is in a far better position to assess the reasonableness of any estimate of the length of the final hearing.

Non-compliance with r 12.19(2) (r 12.19(3))—Rule 12.19(3) not only prevents a witness who has not filed a statement at all from giving evidence without permission, it also requires an application for permission before a witness who has filed a statement can give evidence on matters outside its scope. If the court feels that any party has been prejudiced by not receiving advance notice in accordance with r 12.19(1), it may refuse permission. However, as a matter of practice, most courts are reluctant to refuse to entertain evidence that has a bearing on the welfare of a child purely because of a breach of procedural rules (*R v Nottinghamshire CC* [1993] Fam Law 625). The alternative is to adjourn the proceedings for an appropriate period so that proper instructions can be taken etc. In such circumstances, an application for a costs order against the party who is in breach or for a wasted costs order may be appropriate. An application for permission should be made using the FPR 2010, Pt 18 procedure; FPR 2010, rr 18.1–18.13 provide a simplified process for straightforward applications made within existing proceedings, which in some cases may be determined summarily and without a hearing. The Pt 18 procedure will generally apply to applications for the court's permission unless the rules or PDs state otherwise

Forms and documentary evidence in s 8 and special guardianship cases (r 12.19(2))—The documentation to be filed and served in s 8 cases is strictly controlled to prevent matters becoming inflamed by comments and allegations in forms, statements and reports before the parties have had an opportunity to resolve matters amicably by negotiation. Broadly summarised, the position is as follows:

(a) In a normal case, certain documents are required by the rules to be filed and served and do not require leave. These include the application form (FPR 2010, r 5.1 and FPR PD5A), a statement of service in Form C9 (PD5A)) and the acknowledgement of the application. Care must be taken in each case to include only such information as is required by the form.

(b) An answer is not required or authorised by the rules and should not be filed or served without leave.

(c) Statements or copies of other documents (including experts' reports) on which a party intends to rely should not be filed or served until the court so directs. The court will normally address questions as to the filing of statements and documents at an early directions hearing to ensure that all relevant evidence is exchanged and filed with the court in advance of the hearing to which it relates, but not so early in proceedings that it jeopardises the possibility of an amicable resolution of the issues between the parties. Where advance planning of this kind is not possible, e g where a party wishes to rely on a statement for which leave has not yet been granted to support an urgent interim application, the statement should be prepared and taken to the hearing, and the court should be invited to give leave for it to be filed forthwith.

Secure editing of documents—Where the court makes an order permitting the omission of certain identifying information from documents and evidence, the legal representatives must adhere to the guidelines approved by the President of the Family Division and set out in *Re R (Secure Editing of Documents)* [2007] 2 FLR 759.

Service—See FPR 2010, rr 6.23–6.39, 12.8 and FPR PD12C.

12.20 *(revoked)*

12.21 Hearings

(1) The court may give directions about the order of speeches and the evidence at a hearing.

(2) Subject to any directions given under paragraph (1), the parties and the children's guardian must adduce their evidence at a hearing in the following order –

(a) the applicant;
(b) any party with parental responsibility for the child;
(c) other respondents;
(d) the children's guardian;
(e) the child, if the child is a party to proceedings and there is no children's guardian.

Defined terms—"child", "children's guardian", "court", "directions appointment": FPR 2010, r 2.3(1); "parental responsibility": CA 1989, s 3.

Case management—Great assistance is to be derived from the *Handbook of Best Practice in Children Act cases* produced by the Children Act Advisory Committee (set out in Part V of this work as *Best Practice Guidance of June 1997*). See also **Bundles and other particular matters** under FPR 2010, r 12.12 and for detailed guidance about bundles see FPR PD27A. See the practical guidance given as to the proper preparation of cases brought under CA 1989 in *Re R (Care: Disclosure: Nature of Proceedings)* [2002] 1 FLR 755. For further useful guidance as to the conduct and recording of meetings and the provision of documents in care proceedings see *Re L (Care: Assessment: Fair Trial)* [2002] 2 FLR 730, which is referred to in more detail in **Disclosure – impact of ECHR 1950** under FPR 2010, r 12.12.

Interim hearings—*Hampshire County Council v S* [1993] 1 FLR 559, provides valuable guidance as to the conduct of interim hearings. The justices in that case had, on submissions only and without reading the statements filed or the children's guardian's report, made an interim order reducing the contact that the parents had to a child in care. On appeal, it was held that they had made a number of serious errors and Cazalet J also gave some general guidance with the approval of the President. Guidance as to interim hearings can also be derived from *Re W (A Minor) (Interim Care Order)* [1994] 2 FLR 892, CA, which endorses the *Hampshire* case. As to the making of interim contact orders on the basis of the papers only, without hearing oral evidence and/or having the advice of a children and family reporter or other experts, see *Re D (Contact: Interim Order)* [1995] 1 FLR 495), further noted under **Full hearing not always appropriate** (below). For information as to interim orders in care proceedings, see under CA 1989, s 38.

Agreed orders—Although the court has an overriding judicial duty to investigate proposals that are put before it by consent, the depth of that investigation must reflect the consensus between the parties. Where the court intends to depart from the agreed terms, it must first tell the parties the nature of the proposed departure and allow submissions: *Devon CC v S and Others* [1992] 2 FLR 244. The practice adopted in the higher courts, whereby the parties submit a draft consent order setting out the agreed terms, was commended. Such a draft order cannot, of course, bind the court but it does serve to concentrate the minds of the parties on the terms they are agreeing, thus reducing the possibility of mistakes and misunderstandings, and makes it easier for the justices to define the points at which they might tentatively depart from the agreed package (*M v Warwickshire County Council* [1994] 2 FLR 593). *S v E (Access to Child)* [1993] 1 FCR 729 (decided under the pre-CA 1989 law but still relevant) stressed that, while magistrates are not bound to rubber stamp what the parties agree, there must be truly exceptional circumstances for justices to discard arrangements sensitively negotiated between the parties with the assistance of legal advice (here intended as provisional during a period when the natural father was being reintroduced to his child after an extensive break in contact).

As to the extent of the court's duty to investigate where either of the parties are agreed that there should be a care order or the parents are prepared to concede that there should be a care order, see **Agreed orders** under CA 1989, s 31.

Hearings in private—FPR 2010, r 27.10 states that proceedings to which FPR 2010 apply will be held in private, except where the rules or any other enactment provide otherwise, and subject to any enactment, where the court directs otherwise. The rules relating to attendance at private hearings are covered by FPR 2010, r 27.11.

Children's hearings in private do not breach ECHR 1950, Art 6—See under r 12.14.

Full hearing not always appropriate—There can be limited situations in which the application before the court has so remote a prospect of a positive outcome that it is wrong to allow it to go any further and the appropriate course is to dismiss it without hearing oral evidence or further investigation (*Cheshire County Council v M* [1993] 1 FLR 463; *W v Ealing London Borough Council* [1993] 2 FLR 788).

In cases that do not fall within the limited *Cheshire County Council v M* category, the court nonetheless has a broad discretion to conduct the case as is most appropriate for the issues involved and the evidence available (*Re C (Contact: Conduct of Hearings)* [2006] 2 FLR 289). Indeed, the overriding objective in FPR 2010, r 1.1(2)(b) requires the court to deal with cases in ways that are proportionate to the nature, importance and complexity of the issues. In family proceedings, a judge has an inquisitorial role and his duty is to further the welfare of the children, which is his paramount consideration. For that reason, he exercises a far broader discretion than in a civil jurisdiction to determine how an application should be pursued (*Re C (Children)* [2012] EWCA Civ 1489). It will not necessarily hold a full hearing with the parties permitted to call oral evidence and cross-examine any witnesses that they may choose. Applications for residence orders or care orders or for the revocation of a care order are likely to be decided on full oral evidence, although not invariably; contact applications may be and are heard sometimes with, and sometimes without, oral evidence or with a limited amount of oral evidence. In *Re N; A v G and N* [2010] 1 FLR 272, a case in which acrimonious family proceedings had been ongoing for more than 5 years, Munby J held that there was no need for a full hearing of either parent's applications because there was already more than enough evidence and other material before the court to enable it to make a fair and proper decision. The prospects of either parent succeeding at full trial were remote and the justice of the case did not require a full investigation with oral evidence. Moreover, the further prolongation of this litigation could only be seriously detrimental to the child's welfare, and to do otherwise than to dismiss both parents' applications would be an abdication of the court's responsibilities to the child. Important factors for the court to consider include: (a) whether there is sufficient evidence on which to make the decision; (b) whether the proposed evidence that the applicant for a full trial wishes to adduce and whether the opportunity to cross-examine the witnesses is likely to affect the outcome of the proceedings; (c) the welfare of the child and the effect of further litigation; (d) whether the delay will be so detrimental to the child's well-being that exceptionally there should not be a full hearing; (e) the prospects of success of the applicant for a full trial; and (f) whether the justice of the case requires a full investigation with oral evidence. In *Re H (Contact Order: Permissibility of Judge's Actions)* [2012] 2 FLR 1114, a variation of contact was sought in a case with a considerable litigation history; the parents and the child were all represented. An agreed note from all three counsel was submitted to the judge before the hearing, indicating that the parties, who had been negotiating, required more time; following a discussion with the judge, all counsel agreed that the matter would be dealt with by submissions rather than by oral evidence and further time was thus allowed for negotiation. The Court of Appeal held that everything the judge did on the day of the hearing was not only permissible but sensible and consistent with the general approach of judges in the trial courts to case management where the parties were engaged in lengthy negotiations that threatened to prevent the completion of a contested issue in the time permitted. While a judge should stop irrelevant or time-wasting cross-examination, he should always bear in mind that however carefully he has read the papers beforehand, counsel is likely to have a better grasp of the inner forensic realities of the case (*Re J (Residence and Contact Dispute)* [2013] 1 FLR 716).

For a further example of a curtailed hearing, see *Re B (Contact: Stepfather's Opposition)* [1997] 2 FLR 579, CA noted under **Dismissal of proceedings at directions stage** under FPR 2010, r 12.12 and the further comments of the CA in *Re A (Application for Leave)* [1998] 1 FLR 1, at p 4F. A judge has not only the right but the duty to bring proceedings to an end if he reaches the conclusion that the proceedings can go no further (*Re C-P (A Child)* (2006) *Lawtel* 24 January, CA). Where there is a split hearing there is nothing wrong with the court determining at the preliminary hearing, in advance of the local authority's final care plan, that a particular individual will not be in a position to care for a child safely within the timescale that the child needs, provided, of course, that the evidence substantiates this conclusion (*North Yorkshire CC v B* [2008] 1 FLR 1645).

However, the court has to be careful not to deal with the matter in too peremptory a way (*Re J (Residence and Contact Dispute)* [2013] 1 FLR 716 – where the recorder was wrong to curtail the cross-examination of the mother) and where there are disputed matters that go to the heart of the issue, the court must determine them rather than try to bypass them to progress the case (*Re S (Contact Order)* [2013] 1 FLR 825). Robust case management very much has a place in family proceedings, but it also has its limits (*Re B (A Child)* [2012] EWCA 1742 – where the judge held an unnecessarily truncated hearing and made a crucial finding of fact on the basis of limited evidence). Where a preliminary fact-finding hearing involves serious allegations of domestic violence, the judge should not terminate the case without hearing all the available evidence (Re *Re R (Family Proceedings: No Case to Answer)* [2009] 2 FLR 83). In *Re I and H (Contact: Right to Give Evidence)* [1998] 1 FLR 876, CA, it was said that an applicant under CA 1989 has a fundamental right to be heard. Similarly, in *H v West Sussex CC* [1998] 1 FLR 862, FD Johnson J said that evidence in such cases ought to be regulated by weight rather than admissibility, particularly in a case where a parent was at risk of being separated permanently from his child. He expressed a view that such a parent ought, surely, to be allowed to present his case in the way that he chose, subject to the evidence being tendered in a responsible and professional manner. In *Re W (Contact Application: Procedure)* [2000] 1 FLR 263, Wilson J roundly criticised a procedure that had been generally adopted in a family proceedings court in respect of applications for leave to apply for contact where the matter was dealt with summarily, neither party was invited to attend, no order was drawn up granting leave and no reasons were given in writing or orally.

It is clear that, where the court hears oral evidence from one side, it is wholly inappropriate not to hear from the other (*Re F (A Minor) (Care Order: Procedure)* [1994] 1 FLR 240). Reasons for a decision to refuse to hear oral evidence from a party should be given by the justices. In contrast to *Re F*, however, it was permissible for the magistrates to stop proceedings for the discharge of a care order/defined contact in *Re S and P (Discharge of Care Order)* [1995] 2 FLR 782, FD, after hearing only the mother's evidence, there being no reasonable prospect of her application succeeding. In *Re M (Contact)* [1995] 1 FLR 1029, FD, it was acknowledged that there were cases in which an application was so hopeless that the court would be entitled to dismiss it effectively out of hand, but the magistrates had been wrong to dismiss this application by a father for staying contact on the papers only and without hearing oral evidence. It is difficult to envisage circumstances in which an interim contact order could properly be made, where the principle of contact was genuinely in dispute and where there were substantial factual issues relating to the child that were unresolved without the court hearing oral evidence or having the advice of an expert such as the children and family reporter (*Re D (Contact: Interim Order)* [1995] 1 FLR 495). However, see *Re B (Contact: Stepfather's Opposition)*, above, for a case in which the judge took the exceptional course of dismissing a contact application at the directions stage without hearing evidence.

As to the possibility of estoppel, see *Re B (Children Act Proceedings: Issue Estoppel)* [1997] 1 FLR 285 and *Re W (Care Proceedings: Litigation Capacity)* [2010] 1 FLR 1176.

Organising expert evidence: private law – public law—See FPR 2010, Pt 25 and PD25A–PD25F.

Facilitated communication—It is dangerous for a court in family proceedings to rely on evidence provided by facilitated communication, a process in which a helper supports the hand or arm of the person with communication difficulties while using a keyboard or typing device, in support of allegations of abuse made by the individual (*Re D (Evidence: Facilitated Communication)* [2001] 1 FLR 148).

Wearing of veils in court—Guidance on the wearing of the niqab (the full veil worn by Muslim women) was published in 2007 by the Equal Treatment Advisory Committee (ETAC) of the Judicial Studies Board

(JSB). For victims and complainants, it may be possible for evidence to be given in court by a woman wearing a veil, or for the woman to agree to remove it while giving evidence. Other measures are available to the court, such as screens, video links and clearing the public gallery. A decision on these matters should ideally be reached after discussion at a preliminary hearing. For witnesses and defendants, a sensitive request to remove a veil may be appropriate. However, it may be possible to properly assess the evidence of a woman wearing a niqab in some cases. For advocates, the starting point is that an advocate wearing a full veil should be entitled to appear while wearing it. It will be a matter for the judge to decide whether in the particular circumstances the interests of justice are being impeded or not by the fact that the advocate's face cannot be seen, or that they cannot be heard clearly. The Judicial Studies Board's *Equal Treatment Advisory Committee's Guidance on Religious Dress (December 2007)* can be viewed in Part V of this work and future updates will be found at *www.judiciary.gov.uk*. In *Re S (Practice: Muslim Women Giving Evidence)* [2007] 2 FLR 461, a Muslim woman was granted a decree of nullity nisi on the grounds of duress. When giving evidence, the witness agreed to remove her veil before the female judge, provided that she was screened from the view of her male counsel, the only male member of the particular court. Macur J held that it was a matter of extreme importance that witnesses in sensitive cases were permitted to present their case to the satisfaction of the court while maintaining their religious observance of dress. The facility of screens and the ability, if at all possible, to list such cases before a female judge would obviate the objections of litigants or witnesses, subject to an assessment of the genuine nature of their unwillingness to appear before the court without the veil. In that case counsel had spoken to the Clerk to the Rules 2 days before the hearing to alert the court to the problem and this enabled proper thought to be given as to the best way to conduct the hearing.

Citation of authorities—See note to FPR 2010, r 12.12.

Order of speeches (r 12.21(1))—Whereas r 12.21(2) establishes a normal order in which the parties and children's guardian will adduce their evidence, this rule is silent as to the normal order for speeches. The court may give directions under r 12.21(1) if necessary, but tradition generally dictates that all the respondents have their say first, the applicant goes next and the children's guardian last. Where one legal representative has made oral representations, the others in the case should not be confined to written representations (*Re E (Minors)* [1991] TLR 300, CA).

Continuing duty of advocates—Where an advocate's submissions on the primary issue fail, it is very important that he continues to present the views of his client during the ensuing debate as to the implementation and drawing of the order (*Buckinghamshire County Council v M* [1994] 2 FLR 506).

Legal representation at hearing – the right to a fair trial under ECHR 1950, Art 6—Generally, it is important for parents in cases where the outcome could be the permanent loss of their children, to have equality of representation and to have a sense that a full and sympathetic hearing has taken place (*Re G (Adoption Proceedings: Representation of Children)* [2001] 1 FCR 353). The loss by parents of legal representation on the first day of care proceedings (leaving them to conduct their own case) will not necessarily amount to a breach of Art 6 (the right to a fair trial) (*Re B and T (Care Proceedings: Legal Representation)* [2001] 1 FLR 485 – where the parents had had skilled legal advice in the preparation of the case and had changed lawyers on four previous occasions, the judge had supported the parents at the final hearing and had a duty not only to the parents but also to the children who were entitled to an early determination of their future). However, in care proceedings the complexity of the case, the importance of what is at stake and the highly emotive nature of the subject matter mean that the principles of litigants having effective access to the court and of fairness require that they should receive the assistance of a lawyer (*P, C and S v UK* [2002] 2 FLR 631, ECtHR).

Litigants in person—On 19 April 2012, the Law Society published Practice Note: *Litigants in Person*, providing guidance to all solicitors who may need to deal with litigants in person as part of their work. This can be found in [2012] Family Law 727 and on the Law Society website: *www.lawsociety.org.uk*. The HMCS leaflet CB1 "Making an application – Children and the family courts" contains useful information for those wishing to make applications without representation.

McKenzie friend (MF)—On 12 July 2010 the President issued *Practice Guidance: McKenzie Friends (Civil and Family Courts)* (see Part V). It is intended to act as a reminder of the principles set out in the authorities. In appropriate cases, the court has a power to grant an application under CLSA 1990, ss 27 and 28 to allow a MF to have rights of audience. Whereas the court will be slow to grant such an application, it should be prepared to do so for good reason bearing in mind all of the circumstances of the case; such circumstances are likely to vary greatly (*Re N (A Child) (McKenzie Friend: Rights of Audience)* [2008] 2 FLR 1899). The assistance of a MF is available for the benefit of the litigant in person and whether or not a MF is paid or unpaid for his services he has no right to provide those services; the court is solely concerned with the interests of the litigant in person. There is a strong presumption in family proceedings in favour of permitting a MF to be present unless the judge is satisfied that fairness and the interests of justice do not require it (*In the Matter of the Children of Mr O'Connell, Mr Whelan* *and Mr Watson* [2005] 2 FLR 967). However, the court can prevent a MF from continuing to act where the assistance given is inimical to the efficient administration of justice, for example, where the friend is indirectly running the case or using the litigant as a puppet (*Noueiri v Paragon Finance plc* [2001] 1 WLR 2357).

Advocate to the court (amicus curiae)—The Attorney-General, Lord Goldsmith QC, in conjunction with Lord Woolf CJ, issued a *Memorandum of 19 December 2001 – Requests for the Appointment of an Advocate to the Court* (see Pt V), which details the provisions for the appointment of an advocate to the court (amicus curiae) in appropriate cases. In most cases, an advocate to the court is appointed by the Attorney-General following a request by the court. However, in some cases, an advocate to the court will be appointed by the Official Solicitor or Cafcass where the issue is one in which their experience of representing children and adults under a disability gives them special experience. The representation of children is governed by FPR 2010, Pt 16 and PD16A. The procedure and circumstances for requesting an advocate to the court to be appointed by the Official Solicitor or Cafcass are the same as those applying to requests to the Attorney-General. In cases of extreme urgency, telephone requests may be made (NB the *Memorandum* contains all relevant contact telephone numbers, addresses etc). In some cases, the Official Solicitor himself will be appointed as advocate to the court. He may be given directions by the court authorising him to obtain documents, conduct investigations and enquiries and to advise the court. He may appear by counsel or an in-house advocate (see para 12 of the *Memorandu*m). Where an advocate to the court has been involved in a first instance hearing, he can often make a vital contribution to any appeal, and judges giving directions for an oral hearing or an appeal should consider his role. If nothing has been said by the supervising Lord Justice then he should seek directions as to his future role (*Re A (Father: Knowledge of Child's Birth)* [2011] 2 FLR 123).

"parties" (r 12.21(2))—Broadly speaking, the parties to proceedings are the applicant and the respondents set out in the relevant entry in the table in FPR 2010, r 12.3(1). As to the power of the court to order that a person be joined as or cease to be a party, see FPR 2010, r 12.3(3). The children's guardian is not personally a party (although the child whose interests he represents may be) but, to an extent, he participates in the proceedings as if he were.

"child, if he is a party to the proceedings" (r 12.21(2)(e))—If the child is bringing the application, no doubt his status as applicant (within FPR 2010, r 20.21(2)(a)) will prevail over his status as child (within r 12.21(2)(e)) and he will adduce his evidence first. A child who is responding to an application and has a FPR 2010, r 16.4 children's guardian but no s 41 children's guardian will fall within r 12.21(2)(e), as a r 16.4 children's guardian is not the same as a children's guardian for the purposes of r 16.3 (see the definition in r 2.3(1)). The duties of the children's guardian are set out in FPR PD16A.

Role of National Youth Advocacy Service (NYAS)—The role of NYAS is becoming increasingly important in the separate representation of children, particularly in acrimonious contact cases. See note under CA 1989, s 7.

Where the child and his children's guardian part company (r 12.21(2))—Rule 12.21(2) does not expressly cover the situation where the child and the children's guardian part company because the child is instructing his solicitor direct (see FPR 2010, r 16.29(2)) or intends and is able to conduct the proceedings on his own behalf. In this case, r 16.21(2) dictates that the children's guardian takes such part in the proceedings as the court may direct and may, with the leave of the court, have his own legal representation. When it comes to the order of adducing evidence, the guardian falls within r 12.21(2)(d) but the child does not fall within r 12.21(2)(e) so the court will have to give directions.

Questioning the children's guardian (r 12.21(2)(d))—The children's guardian cannot simply put in his written report; he must submit to questioning on this and on any other oral or written advice that he tenders to the court if any party so requires (FPR PD16A); see also *Hampshire County Council v S* [1993] 1 FLR 559.

Court calling witness—As the semi-inquisitorial nature of Children Act proceedings has increasingly become accepted, the practice has developed of the court itself occasionally calling a witness where fairness dictates that an advocate should be able to cross-examine the witness and normal procedure would confine him to examination-in-chief (*Re P (Witness Summons)* [1997] 2 FLR 447, CA).

Witness anonymity—A court will give anonymity to a professional social worker witness in care proceedings only in highly exceptional cases (*Re W (Care Proceedings: Witness Anonymity)* [2003] 1 FLR 329 – where it was held that the guidance as to witness anonymity given in the criminal jurisdiction has parallels for public law cases such as care proceedings; in this case the threat of violence from adults who faced permanent separation from their children was held to be a professional hazard of social work, and not exceptional).

PART III

Judge seeing child—In April 2010 the President issued *Guidelines for Judges Meeting Children who are Subject to Family Proceedings* (see Part V). The judge's decision whether or not personally to interview a child is, above all, a question for the exercise of judicial discretion. Certainly, the judge is under no obligation to see a child in private before he decides what order to make (*Re R (A Minor) (Residence: Religion)* [1993] 2 FLR 163). It is becoming more common for judges to see children in private in the course of proceedings affecting the child's welfare. ECHR 1950, Art 12 provides that a child should be heard in any judicial proceedings affecting him, either directly or through a representative. Similarly, the United Nations Convention on the Rights of the Child 1989, Art 12 requires that a child who is capable of forming his own views has the right to express them freely in all matters affecting him. *Mabon v Mabon* [2005] 2 FLR 1011 reviewed the principles that apply when the court considers how best to ensure that the child's views are heard in such cases. Further important guidance from the Court of Appeal is contained in *Re W (Leave to Remove)* [2008] 2 FLR 1170 *B v B (Minors) (Interviews and Listing Arrangements)* [1994] 2 FLR 489 and *Re A (Fact-Finding Hearing: Judge meeting with Child)* [2012] 2 FLR 369. In *Re A*, the Court of Appeal gave cautions and guidance in a case in which the judge saw the child after hearing evidence but before giving judgment. The parents appealed against his finding that the children had been sexually abused on the basis that they had been denied the opportunity to make representations regarding the meeting with the child and that the judge had used that meeting to gather evidence, in breach of the 2010 *Guidelines*. The CA dismissed the appeal but augmented the judge's order to clarify what he had found, holding, inter alia, that: (1) It would be quite disproportionate to allow the appeal and order a retrial. The process, properly analysed, had been full and complete; (2) Much more care should be taken in defining the judicial task at a preliminary trial; this should be contained in an early directions order so that the parties know precisely what it is that the applicants are seeking to be determined, by a simple direction that at the trial the court will determine the issues contained within the schedule. Then when the process is complete and judgment given, the order drawn needs specifically to state which of the items within the schedule have been found proved; (3) There is a useful distinction between two levels of participation and involvement of children in proceedings: (a) meeting with children under the April 2010 *Guidelines* and (b) children giving evidence under the December 2011 *Guidelines in Relation to Children Giving Evidence in Family Proceedings*. If an application governed by (b) results in a direction for oral evidence, the risk of contamination of the proceedings is no greater than with the involvement of any other witness. However, if an application governed by (a) results in a decision from the meeting between judge and child, the risk of contamination is increased. So, a range of distinctions needs to be drawn and the judge must consider whether the objective of the proceedings is to establish what happened in the past or what should happen in the future, and the stage the proceedings have reached; (4) In this case, the objective was to establish what had happened and the proceedings were at a stage where the evidence was concluded but judgment reserved. This is the most dangerous situation in which a judge is likely to meet a child. Much safer is the ground when the issue is what should happen in the future and the judge is anxious to ascertain for himself the strength of the child's wishes and feelings and perhaps what has contributed to the formation of those wishes and feelings; (5) The judge would have been far wiser to have explained to the child at the outset that the process was complete and that all that remained was the formal expression of his reasons for his conclusion. To give the child the impression that his mind was still open and that he was susceptible to influence, was to give completely the wrong impression. Equally, when he came to recording the meeting in his judgment, it was unguarded of him to say that he had found the child to be truthful in his recollection and statement; (6) It was not enough for the appellants to show that an irregularity had taken place. The critical question was whether its effect was sufficiently serious to undermine the integrity of the judge's conclusions on the factual issues. If his judgment were read as a whole, it was clear that he had made all his findings of fact without reliance on his meeting with the child.

The judge will decide who should be present during an interview with children, but he cannot promise the children absolute confidentiality and he must tell the parties what the child has said to him so that they may deal with it (*H v H (Child: Judicial Interview)* [1974] 1 WLR 595; *Elder v Elder* [1986] 1 FLR 610). Any interview between the judge and the child should take place at the court (*L v L (Access: Contempt)* [1991] 2 FLR 43).

Judge seeing advocates—Thorpe LJ observed in *Re CH (Care or Interim Care Order)* [1998] 1 FLR 402, CA that it seemed to him undesirable that judges should encourage or permit significant exchanges between the advocates unrecorded in the privacy of the judge's room. If it is thought desirable by the advocates or by the judge that exchanges should take place without the clients and other persons being present, those exchanges can be in the court room in chambers where they will be fully recorded.

Judge recusing himself from a case—Applications to a judge to recuse himself from a case must be taken seriously, even if they are, in part, wild and extravagant (*Re F (Contact)* [2008] 1 FLR 1163). The test to be applied is whether all of the circumstances bearing on the suggestion that the judge could be biased would lead a fair-minded and informed observer, adopting a balanced approach, to conclude that there was a real possibility that the tribunal was biased. In *Re F* (above) neither the judge's approach nor manner had reached a level where he should recuse himself and Sumner J set out some useful principles to be considered in such applications.

Departing from an expert's opinion—The court is entitled to depart from the opinion of an expert although, if it does so, it must explain its reasons (*Re B (Care: Expert Witnesses)* [1996] 1 FLR 667). Where there is a conflict between experts, the court must address and resolve that conflict insofar as it is relevant to the issues before the court and it is entitled to give greater weight to the opinion of one expert as against that of another, provided that proper reasons are given (*Re J (Expert Evidence: Hearsay)* [1999] 2 FLR 661; *Re W and P (Children)* (2002) Lawtel, 30 April). Where there is a stark conflict of forensic medical evidence, a judge should not decline to choose between the medical opinions; instead he should invite the parties to agree a tertiary referral. To leave the evidence unresolved makes the disposal stage problematic (*Re W and P*, above). Where experts are unanimous in their opinion as to a person's core personality and emotional state, it is not open to the judge to reject that expert evidence purely on the basis of his own appraisal of the person when giving oral evidence (*Re M (Residence)* [2002] 2 FLR 1059). However, the role of the expert and the court are distinct. The court must make its findings based on the totality of the evidence. Expert evidence is but one part of the evidence available to the court at the fact-finding stage. It is open to the court on the totality of the evidence, to reach a decision that is different from those of the experts (*A County Council v K, D and L* [2005] 1 FLR 851; *A County Council v A Mother, A Father and X, Y and Z (by their Guardian)* [2005] 2 FLR 129).

Hearings in care proceedings—*Oxfordshire CC v M* [1994] 1 FLR 175 highlights the fact that care proceedings do not have an essentially adversarial character (*Re L (Police Investigation: Privilege)* [1996] 1 FLR 731; *Re S (Contact: Evidence)* [1998] 1 FLR 798, CA). In all public law proceedings under CA 1989, Pt IV the PLO must be followed (see FPR PD12A and FPR 2010, rr 12.23–12.30). Proceedings by a childminder challenging the refusal of a local authority to register her are, however, adversarial (*London Borough of Sutton v Davis (Costs) (No 2)* [1994] 2 FLR 569).

Split hearings—For guidance about split hearings in public law proceedings, see the notes to CA 1989, s 31 and under FPR 2010, r 12.12.

Judicial reasoning—It is an advocate's responsibility, whether invited or not, to draw the attention of the judge to any ambiguity or deficiency in the reasoning (*English v Emery, Reimbold & Strick* [2002] 1 WLR 2409; *Re T (Contact: Alienation: Permission to Appeal)* [2003] 1 FLR 531). Where permission to appeal is sought on the ground of lack of reasons, the trial judge should reconsider and, if necessary, provide additional reasons. If neither happens, an appeal court will normally remit the case to the trial judge, with a list of specific questions to be addressed (*Re A and L (Children)* [2012] 1 FLR 134).

Change of mind by judge prior to order being perfected—Where the judge makes a decision in civil or family proceedings, he has the power to reverse it at any time before the order is sealed. While this power must be exercised judicially rather than capriciously, it is not limited to exceptional circumstances. In family proceedings a judge is not to be bound by his earlier judgment to decide the future placement of a child upon what he has come to believe is a false basis (*Re L and B (Children)* [2013] UKSC 8).

Reasons for a decision of the magistrates' court—FPR 2010, r 27.2 requires that after a hearing in a magistrates' court the justices should make their decision as soon as is practicable, and must give their written reasons for the decision.

Chapter 3
Special Provisions about Public Law Proceedings

12.22 Application of rules 12.23 to 12.26

Rules 12.23 to 12.26 apply to care and supervision proceedings and in so far as practicable other public law proceedings.

Public Law Outline (PLO)—The PLO in FPR PD12A applies to all courts hearing applications issued by local authorities under CA 1989, Pt IV (care and supervision orders). As far as is practicable, it is to be applied to all other public law proceedings (para 1.1). The filing of the application starts the timetable rolling and will count as day 1. The issued documents must be served on the parties by day 3. Once the proceedings have been issued, the court will consider the standard directions listed in the PLO (para 12.4). In August 2009, the Ministry of Justice issued a *Best Practice Guide: Preparing for Care and Supervision Proceedings* (see Part V) that is for use by all professionals involved with children and families pre-proceedings, and in preparation for applications made under CA 1989, s 31. It complements the Statutory Guidance and the PLO, but is not intended to be prescriptive. On 15 April 2011, the President of the Family Division issued guidance in relation to the listing and hearing of care cases, reinforcing the PLO, and in July 2011 issued guidance on the allocation and continuity of case managers in the Family Proceedings Court, setting out the expectations on FPCs in relation to allocation and continuity of case managers in public law proceedings. The key points are that: (1) On the issue of a case in the family proceedings court (FPC) the court must nominate care manager(s) to be responsible for the management of the case throughout its FPC hearings; (2) As soon as a case is transferred from the FPC to a county court it must be allocated to one, but not more than two, case-management judges who will be responsible for it through to the final hearing; (3) As soon as a case is transferred from a county court to the High Court it must be allocated to a judge of the High Court; (4) Case managers and judges require the co-operation of the parties. Statements and reports must be filed on time. The case manager is key to the process and must be available to hear the case when it requires to be heard, and what she or he says goes; (5) No hearing at any stage of the case should conclude without a date for the next hearing having been fixed at the earliest possible date, and the date fixed should be one on which one of the case managers or management judges can sit to hear it; (6) Judges and legal advisers must fit their availability around the case and not the other way round. Continuity of representation is also important and lawyers will be expected to play their part in ensuring cases are heard without delay; (7) It is important that final hearings are not delayed by waiting for the allocated judge to become available. This will mean close liaison between the judge and the listing officer, and the judge's other commitments should be fitted around the need swiftly to hear care cases.

12.23 Timetable for the Child

(1) The court will set the timetable for the proceedings in accordance with the Timetable for the Child.

(2) The "Timetable for the Child" means the timetable set by the court in accordance with its duties under section 1 and 32 of the 1989 Act and will –

    (a) take into account dates of the significant steps in the life of the child who is the subject of the proceedings; and

    (b) be appropriate for that child.

Care monitoring system—The care monitoring system (CMS) is a judicially led management information programme intended to provide accurate ongoing information about case volumes, case progress and allocation. It is intended to assist judges, legal advisers and magistrates to focus on avoiding delay for children and to help identify the real causes of delay. The system has been piloted nationwide from 2 April 2012 from when all new care and supervision cases have been entered onto the system and orders have been required to contain information that will be monitored by the system, in particular the timetable for the child expressed as the expected number of weeks necessary to conclude the proceedings. In preparation for the reforms contemplated by the family modernisation programme, all cases will be given a standard 26-week timetable on issue.

12.24 Directions

The court will direct the parties to –

    (a) monitor compliance with the court's directions; and

    (b) tell the court or court officer about –

        (i) any failure to comply with a direction of the court; and

        (ii) any other delay in the proceedings.

Derivation—This rule derives from the Public Law Outline in FPR PD12A, para 5.6.

Timetable for public law cases—The PLO in PD12A sets down a strict timetable for the progress of public law cases. It is vital that all parties adhere to this, and that if there is any prospect of delay the court is informed immediately so that the case does not drift.

12.25 First Appointment, Case Management Conference and Issues Resolution Hearing

(1) The court may set the date for the First Appointment, Case Management Conference and Issues Resolution Hearing at the times and in the circumstances referred to in Practice Direction 12A.

(2) The matters which the court will consider at the hearings referred to in paragraph (1) are set out in Practice Direction 12A.

Derivation—This rule derives from the Public Law Outline in FPR PD12A.

Case management in public law proceedings—Before the implementation of the PLO, there were a number of cases that gave useful guidance as to the preparation of public law cases, although where that guidance conflicts with the PLO, the PLO must take precedence. See *Re G, S and M (Wasted Costs)* [2000] 1 FLR 52; *Re EC (Disclosure of Material)* [1996] 2 FLR 123; *Re R (Care: Disclosure: Nature of Proceedings)* [2002] 1 FLR 755. For further useful guidance see **Preparation of public law cases** under CA 1989, s 31 and **Disclosure – impact of ECHR 1950** under FPR 2010, r 12.12 and in particular the judgment in *Re L (Care: Assessment: Fair Trial)* [2002] 2 FLR 730.

First appointment—At the first appointment, which must take place by day 6, the court will take the steps set out in the revised PLO (FPR PD12A). These steps will include confirming the timetable for the child, making arrangements for any contested interim hearing, requesting the children's guardian to prepare a case analysis and recommendations, scrutinising the care plan, considering applications for the transfer of the case and giving such further directions as may be appropriate (para 13.3).

Case management conference—In accordance with Stage 2 of the PLO (FPR PD12A), the court will fix a case management conference (CMC) to take place no later than day 45, at which the court will identify the issues and give full case-management directions, including whether or not experts are to be instructed and, if so, why and how this is to be done (para 13.5). No later than 2 days before the CMC there must be an advocates' discussion/meeting, the aim of which is to facilitate agreement, narrow down the issues and prepare a draft case management order (para 14). The suggested content of this is set out in the glossary to the revised PLO (FPR PD12A) at para 26(12). It is to be used not only for drawing up orders at the end of a hearing, but also as a case-management check list and aide mémoire to everyone involved in the proceedings. There should be ongoing consideration of the draft case management order throughout the proceedings. The local authority will take the lead in preparing and adjusting the order, which must then be filed with the court by 11.00 am 1 working day before the CMC (paras 5.9 and 14.6). Note that only one order should be filed with the court (para 5.9).

Issues resolution hearing—In accordance with Stage 3 of the PLO (FPR PD12A), the court will fix an issues resolution hearing (IRH) to take place between weeks 16 and 25 (para 15.5) at which the court will try to resolve and narrow the issues and identify any remaining key issues, including any remaining issues concerning experts (para 16). There must be an advocates' discussion/meeting between 2 and 7 days before the IRH, the aim of which is to update the draft case management order (para 14). Once the updated order has been drafted, it must be filed with the court by 11.00 am 1 working day before the IRH (para 14.6). At the IRH the court will review and confirm the timetable for the child and give such other directions as are appropriate for the filing of evidence, skeleton arguments, bundles, agreements relating to satisfaction of the CA 1989, s 31 criteria and time estimates (para 16). It will then issue a case management order in preparation for the final hearing.

Final hearing—The final hearing is Stage 4 of the PLO (FPR PD12A). The timing will be fixed in accordance with the needs of the child. The object of the hearing is to determine the remaining issues. All parties will file and serve updated case-management documents and the bundle, together with the draft final order(s) in approved form. At the conclusion of the hearing the court will give its judgment and reasons for its decision and then make appropriate orders for disclosure of documents as required after the hearing. Cases that are suitable for an early final hearing are those in which all of the evidence necessary to determine issues of fact and welfare is immediately or shortly available to be filed. The court will identify such cases at the first appointment and set a date for the final hearing (PLO, para 13.4).

12.26 Discussion between advocates

(1) When setting a date for a Case Management Conference or an Issues Resolution Hearing the court will direct a discussion between the parties' advocates to –

    (a)   discuss the provisions of a draft of the Case Management Order; and

(b)   consider any other matter set out in Practice Direction 12A.

(2) Where there is a litigant in person the court will give directions about how that person may take part in the discussions between the parties' advocates.

(3) The court will direct that following a discussion between advocates they must prepare or amend a draft of the Case Management Order for the court to consider.

(4) Where it is not possible for the advocates to agree the terms of a draft of the Case Management Order, the advocates should specify on a draft of the Case Management Order or on a separate document if more practicable –

(a)   those provisions on which they agree; and

(b)   those provisions on which they disagree.

(5) Unless the court directs otherwise –

(a)   any discussion between advocates must take place no later than 2 days; and

(b)   a draft of the Case Management Order must be filed with the court no later than 1 day,

before the Case Management Conference or the Issues Resolution Hearing whichever may be appropriate.

(6) For the purposes of this rule "advocate" includes a litigant in person.

Derivation—This rule derives from the Public Law Outline (FPR PD12A), paras 3.15, 3.16, 5.8 and 5.9.

12.27 Matters prescribed for the purposes of the Act

(1) Proceedings for an order under any of the following provisions of the 1989 Act –

(a)   a secure accommodation order under section 25;

(b)   an order giving permission to change a child's surname or remove a child from the United Kingdom under section 33(7);

(c)   an order permitting the local authority to arrange for any child in its care to live outside England and Wales under paragraph 19(1) of Schedule 2;

(d)   the extension or further extension of a supervision order under paragraph 6(3) of Schedule 3;

(e)   appeals against the determination of proceedings of a kind set out in sub-paragraphs (a) to (d);

are specified for the purposes of section 41 of that Act in accordance with section 41(6)(i) of that Act.

(2) The persons listed as applicants in the table set out in rule 12.3 to proceedings for the variation of directions made with interim care or interim supervision orders under section 38(8) of the 1989 Act are the prescribed class of persons for the purposes of that section.

(3) The persons listed as applicants in the table set out in rule 12.3 to proceedings for the variation of a direction made under section 44(6) of the 1989 Act in an emergency protection order are the prescribed class of persons for the purposes of section 44(9) of that Act.

"specified" (r 12.27(1))—CA 1989, s 41 imposes a duty on the court in any "specified proceedings" to appoint a children's guardian for the child concerned, unless it is satisfied that it is not necessary to do so to safeguard his interests. Section 41(6) specifies many of the proceedings in which this duty arises and s 41(6)(i) provides for rules of court to specify further proceedings.

"section 38(8)" (r 12.27(2))—CA 1989, s 38(8) empowers the court to vary a direction made under s 38(6) on the application of a person within any class prescribed by rules of court. Section 38(6) empowers the court to make directions regarding medical or psychiatric examination or other assessment of a child where it makes an interim care or supervision order.

Section 44(6),(9) (r 12.27(5))—CA 1989, s 44 enables the court to make emergency protection orders and, where it does so, it may, under s 44(6), give directions as to the medical, psychiatric or other assessment of the child or contact with him. Section 44(9) provides that such directions can be varied at any time on the application of a person falling within any class of person prescribed by rules of court.

12.28 Exclusion requirements: interim care orders and emergency protection orders

(1) This rule applies where the court includes an exclusion requirement in an interim care order or an emergency protection order.

(2) The applicant for an interim care order or emergency protection order must –

    (a)   prepare a separate statement of the evidence in support of the application for an exclusion requirement;

    (b)   serve the statement personally on the relevant person with a copy of the order containing the exclusion requirement (and of any power of arrest which is attached to it);

    (c)   inform the relevant person of that person's right to apply to vary or discharge the exclusion requirement.

(3) Where a power of arrest is attached to an exclusion requirement in an interim care order or an emergency protection order, the applicant will deliver –

    (a)   a copy of the order; and

    (b)   a statement showing that the relevant person has been served with the order or informed of its terms (whether by being present when the order was made or by telephone or otherwise),

to the officer for the time being in charge of the police station for the area in which the dwelling-house in which the child lives is situated (or such other police station as the court may specify).

(4) Rules 10.6(2) and 10.10 to 10.17 will apply, with the necessary modifications, for the service, variation, discharge and enforcement of any exclusion requirement to which a power of arrest is attached as they apply to an order made on an application under Part 4 of the 1996 Act.

(5) The relevant person must serve the parties to the proceedings with any application which that person makes for the variation or discharge of the exclusion requirement.

(6) Where an exclusion requirement ceases to have effect whether –

    (a)   as a result of the removal of a child under section 38A(10) or 44A(10) of the 1989 Act;

    (b)   because of the discharge of the interim care order or emergency protection order; or

    (c)   otherwise,

the applicant must inform –

    (i)   the relevant person;

    (ii)   the parties to the proceedings;

    (iii) any officer to whom a copy of the order was delivered under paragraph (3); and

    (iv) (where necessary) the court.

(7) Where the court includes an exclusion requirement in an interim care order or an emergency protection order of its own motion, paragraph (2) will apply with the omission of any reference to the statement of the evidence.

(8) In this rule, "the relevant person" has the meaning assigned to it by sections 38A(2) and 44A(2) of the 1989 Act.

PART III

Defined terms—"care order": CA 1989, ss 31(11), 105(1); "child"; "court": r 2.3(1); "emergency protection order": r 12.2; "exclusion requirement": CA 1989, s 38A(3); "relevant person": CA 1989, s 38A(2)(a).

Applicant for interim care order or emergency protection order (r 12.28(2))—The applicant in the case of an interim care order will generally be the local authority (or other authorised person) who has made the original application under CA 1989, s 31(1). Section 38 gives the court power to make an interim care order where the care/supervision proceedings are adjourned and also gives the court power to make an interim care order where it gives a direction under s 37(1) for the local authority to investigate the child's circumstances. It is unclear who is the applicant for the purpose of r 12.28(2) in such a situation or, indeed, whether there is one at all. It may be that this is unlikely to cause a problem given that it is difficult to foresee the court being in a position to incorporate an exclusion requirement anyway at such an early stage. If the court did consider such a course appropriate, it could act of its own motion in including the requirement, in which case r 12.28(7) would dispense with the need for a statement of the evidence.

The applicant in the case of an emergency protection order can be any person (s 44(1)) though it is most likely to be a local authority.

Public Law Outline (PLO)—Although the PLO in FPR PD12A specifically applies to care and supervision proceedings, it also states that, insofar as practicable, it is to be applied to all other public law proceedings (para 1.1). FPR 2010, r 12.22 also states that FPR 2010, rr 12.23–12.26 apply to care and supervision proceedings and insofar as practicable other public law proceedings. It will therefore be a decision for the court in each case as to how and when it is appropriate for the PLO to apply when an application commences by way of an emergency protection order.

Separate statement of evidence (r 12.28(2))—The applicant will already have completed forms with regard to the application for an interim care order/emergency protection order. The statement of evidence in support of the exclusion requirement must be separate. There is no prescribed form. Reference must be made to the provisions of CA 1989, s 38A or 44A and in particular to the conditions for the inclusion of an exclusion requirement, which are set out in ss 38A(2) and 44A(2). The question of the ability of another person living in the home to care for the child and the consent of that person to the exclusion requirement (ss 38A(2)(b) and 44A(2)(b)) will no doubt be covered in the statement but it should be noted that it is also the subject of a separate procedural rule, FPR 2010, r 12.29. Best practice in respect of the separate statement of evidence to be served in support of an application for an exclusion requirement demands that the statement should:

(1) be separate and self-standing;
(2) set out in a concise form the factual material upon which the applicant relies;
(3) state the statutory requirements for obtaining an exclusion order, under CA 1989, s 38A(2) (for interim care orders) or s 44A(2) (for emergency protection orders), in particular the relevant subsections, with a summary of the evidence in support; and
(4) make it clear that the exclusion requirement sought is a requirement that a particular person should leave the dwelling-house in which the child is living, and/or prohibit the person from entering the dwelling house in which the child is living, and/or exclude the person from a defined area surrounding the dwelling-house in which the child is living (*Re W (Exclusion: Statement of Evidence)* [2000] 2 FLR 666).

If the court orders an exclusion requirement of its own motion, in the absence of the relevant person, it will usually be appropriate for the court to direct that a concise statement be prepared of the evidence laid at the hearing, with the other matters set out above, to be served personally on the relevant person. If the hearing was before justices then it will be desirable also to serve their findings and reasons on the relevant person. This will ensure that he receives the appropriate information to allow him to make an application to vary or discharge the order. If the person was present in court and heard the evidence laid against him, the court might, in appropriate circumstances, disapply any requirements as to service of the relevant statement. The consent of the other person living in the dwelling-house can be given either orally in court or in writing, signed by that person; written consent should provide the necessary details of the person able and willing to give the child the care that it would be reasonable to expect a parent to give, and it should state that that person understood that the giving of consent could lead to the exclusion of the relevant person from the dwelling-house in which the child was living. Once the appropriate statement has been served, it will not be necessary at subsequent renewals of the order to serve the separate statement again, unless there has been a further hearing, and the grounds have changed (*Re W* (above)).

Serve on relevant person (r 12.28(2))—The "relevant person" is the person who is excluded. Service on this person of the supporting statement is only required once an order has been made; there is no specific requirement that he be given advance notice that there is a question of such a provision being included. The "relevant person" may be a party to the proceedings in any event. Even if not, he is likely to know of the possibility of an exclusion requirement being imposed because an approach will have been made to another person living in the home to ensure that the requisite consent etc will be forthcoming for CA 1989, s 38A(2)(b) or 44A(2)(b). It remains to be seen to what extent the courts consider it appropriate to join as a party a relevant person, who is not a party, for the purpose of arguing the issue of an exclusion requirement or perhaps to allow him or her to intervene for this limited purpose without becoming a party. It may be that the relevant person will be excluded from the home almost summarily and then left to rely on his or her right to seek a variation or discharge of the order under s 39(3A)(3B) or s 45(8A),(8B).

"inform the relevant person of his right to apply to vary or discharge" (r 12.28(2)(c))—The rules do not say whether the "relevant person" should be informed orally or in writing. Given that personal service of the statement and order is required, it would seem sensible for the information to be given orally at the time of service but for the documents also to be accompanied by a written notice of the right to apply to vary or discharge. Where the exclusion requirement is included in an interim care order, the right to seek variation/discharge is contained in CA 1989, s 39(3A) (with regard to the exclusion requirement itself) and s 39(3B) (with regard to any attendant power of arrest). For an emergency protection order, the relevant provisions are s 45(8A) and (8B).

Power of arrest (r 12.28(3))—If a power of arrest is attached to an order, FPR PD12E requires that, unless the person to whom the exclusion requirement refers was given notice of the hearing and attended it, the name of that person and the fact that an order has been made including an exclusion requirement to which a power of arrest has been attached shall be announced in open court at the earliest opportunity. Note that, by virtue of r 12.28(3), a copy of an order including a power of arrest is only to be delivered to the police station once the relevant person is aware of its terms. This may be because he was present when it was made or because he has subsequently been told about it or service has been effected.

Rules 10.6(2) etc (r 12.28(4))—FPR 2010, r 10.6(2) dictates service of a copy of any order by the court where the applicant is acting in person and requests this. Rules 10.10–10.16 deal with enforcement of orders that have powers of arrest attached, including also the duty to inform the police where an order with a power of arrest is subsequently varied or discharged. FPR 2010, r 10.17 deals with bail after arrest. FLA 1996, Pt IV contains the provisions dealing with family homes and domestic violence.

Application for variation/discharge (r 12.28(5))—FPR 2010, r 5.3 would seem to apply given that the relevant person is making "an application". There does not appear to be a notice period for the variation/discharge application. The periods required for discharge applications under ss 39 and 45 do not apply because they refer specifically to certain subsections of ss 39 and 45 but do not mention s 39(3A) or 45(8A). Presumably, in the absence of any specific form, Form C2 should be used for the relevant person's application. The parties to the proceedings who must be served will be the parties to the care proceedings or to the emergency protection order application, as appropriate. This may not include the person who is caring for the child in the absence of the relevant person but common sense dictates that he or she is likely to be affected by any discharge or variation and ought to be notified of the application. Indeed, it may be that the court will consider it desirable that when an exclusion requirement is included in reliance upon care to be delivered by someone who is not presently a party to the proceedings, that person should be joined so that he or she is entitled to be kept aware of developments and to make representations. Alternatively, he or she may be eligible for notice under FPR 2010, r 12.3 as a person "who [is] caring for the child at the time when the proceedings are commenced".

Parties to the proceedings (r 12.28(6)(c)(ii))—This phrase refers to the parties to the care proceedings or emergency protection proceedings, depending on the type of order to which the exclusion requirement was attached. This may not include the person caring for the child in the absence of the excluded person but it would seem necessary to inform him or her as well.

"(where necessary) the court" (r 12.28(6)(c)(iv))—It is suggested that it would be sensible to inform the court as a matter of course.

12.29 Notification of consent

(1) Consent for the purposes of the following provisions of the 1989 Act –

    (a)   section 16(3);

    (b)   section 38A(2)(b)(ii) or 44A(2)(b)(ii); or

    (c)   paragraph 19(3)(c) or (d) of Schedule 2,

must be given either –

        (i)   orally to the court; or

        (ii)   in writing to the court signed by the person giving consent.

PART III

(2) Any written consent for the purposes of section 38A(2) or 44A(2) of the 1989 Act must include a statement that the person giving consent –

    (a)   is able and willing to give to the child the care which it would be reasonable to expect a parent to give; and

    (b)   understands that the giving of consent could lead to the exclusion of the relevant person from the dwelling-house in which the child lives.

Defined terms—"court": r 2.3.

Scope—This rule sets out the procedure for signifying consent in certain cases under CA 1989. It does not apply to all consents that are required under the Act, only to those specified.

"section 16(3)"—This provision states that the court may not make a family assistance order unless it has obtained the consent of every person to be named in the order other than the child.

"section 38A(2)(b)(ii) or 44A(2)(b)(ii)"—Section 38A(2)(b)(ii) sets out a condition for the making of an exclusion requirement in an interim care order that another person living in the house consents to the inclusion of the exclusion requirement. Section 44A(2)(b)(ii) sets out a similar condition for the making of an exclusion requirement in an emergency protection order.

"paragraph 19(3)(c) or (d) of Schedule 2"—This provision states that a local authority may only arrange for a child in care to live outside England and Wales if the child has consented to living in that country.

"orally in court" (r 12.29(1)(c)(i))—There is no requirement that the consent should be given in evidence, and so it appears that the person giving consent need not be sworn. Indeed, where the person who is consenting orally is represented by a lawyer, it is likely to be the general practice that the legal representative will tell the court of the consent rather than the person himself, who will simply confirm what has been said. There are no provisions that require a note to be made of the giving of consent, but it is quite plain that such a note will have to be taken by the court.

Written consent (r 12.29(2))—There is no prescribed form of written consent; the only guidance in the rules is that the consent should be signed by the person consenting. Clearly, as well as identifying the consenting party and including the signed (and dated) consent, the document must refer to any order or proceedings that are relevant (such as the family proceedings where the consent is given under CA 1989, r 16, or the care order where the consent is given under Sch 2, para 19), giving the number thereof. However, r 12.29(2) does stipulate certain matters that must be included in the written consent to be given under CA 1989, ss 38A(2) and 44A(2).

Where the making of a court order depends on the giving of consent—The giving of consent is a condition precedent to the making of a family assistance order under CA 1989, s 16(3) and also the inclusion of an exclusion requirement in an interim care order or emergency protection order (CA 1989, ss 38A(1) and 44A(1)). Although the prescribed form of family assistance order does not require it, it is therefore suggested that, for the avoidance of doubt, the order should recite the requisite consents and state whether they were given orally or in writing. The same should also be done where the court gives approval under Sch 2, para 19(1). Forms C23 and C33 provide for the recital of the requisite consents for the inclusion of an exclusion requirement in an emergency protection order and an interim care order.

12.30 Proceedings for secure accommodation orders: copies of reports

In proceedings under section 25 of the 1989 Act, the court will, if practicable, arrange for copies of all written reports filed in the case to be made available before the hearing to –

    (a)   the applicant;

    (b)   the parent or guardian of the child to whom the application relates;

    (c)   any legal representative of the child;

    (d)   the children's guardian; and

    (e)   the child, unless the court directs otherwise,

and copies of the reports may, if the court considers it desirable, be shown to any person who is entitled to notice of any hearing in accordance with Practice Direction 12C.

"parent"—This term is not defined in the rules or CA 1989 (see meaning of "parent" under CA 1989, s 10).

"any person who is entitled to notice of any hearing in accordance with Practice Direction 12C"—Namely the local authority providing accommodation for the child, persons caring for the child at the time when proceedings are commenced and in the case of proceedings brought in respect of a child who is alleged to be staying in a refuge which is certified under s 51(1) or (2) of the 1989 Act, the person who is providing the refuge.

Copies of reports—There appears to be a distinction between those persons listed in r 12.30(a)–(e) and persons who are simply entitled to notice in accordance with the rules. The former must have copies of reports made available to them if practicable, whereas the latter are allowed only sight of the reports, and then only if the court considers it desirable.

Form of application—Pt IV applies to secure accommodation proceedings, which must therefore be started in accordance with Pt 12. The prescribed forms are Form C1 and supplementary Form C20. Form C1 requires the applicant to give the name and date of birth of the child concerned, to identify himself and to give details of his relationship to the child. The form requires details of: any other proceedings which concern the child; the respondents to the application; other persons to whom notice is to be given; the present arrangements for the care of the child; any involvement with the child by Social Services; the arrangements for the health and education of the child; the identity of the child's parents; the family of the child, ie siblings etc; and other adults who live at the child's address. The applicant must then fill in the supplementary Form C20 in which he is required to set out the grounds for the application, the reasons for applying and the length of order applied for. Copies of reports or other documentary evidence on which the applicant relies should be enclosed with the prescribed forms, together with details as to the dates and authors of the documents. The respondents and the persons who are to receive notice of the proceedings are set out in FPR 2010, r 12.3 and FPR PD12C, respectively.

An application for remand in secure accommodation may also be made in criminal proceedings under Children and Young Persons Act 1969, s 25.

Hearsay—Proceedings under CA 1989, s 25 are "family proceedings", and hearsay evidence contained in reports and statements is admissible, although its weight will be a matter for judicial discretion (see *Oxfordshire County Council v R* [1992] 1 FLR 648).

Delay—It is essential that there should be no delay whatsoever in the hearing of a case which concerns the liberty of the subject, such as an appeal in a secure accommodation case. In any appeal from the justices in a matter of urgency, the procedure set out in *Oxfordshire County Council v R* [1992] 1 FLR 648 at [651H]–[652A] should be followed. Thus if, when the appeal is entered in the district registry of the appropriate care centre, no High Court judge is available to hear it, it is the duty of the appellant's solicitor to make the district registry aware of the need for urgency and to invite the district registry or the district judge to list the matter at the nearest court where an early hearing can take place before a High Court judge. Where any difficulty is encountered, an application for directions can always be made to a High Court judge sitting either at the appropriate care centre or in London (*Re W (A Minor) (Secure Accommodation Order)* [1993] 1 FLR 692).

Interim orders—A freestanding application for an interim secure accommodation order cannot be made. Where the court was satisfied it had all the information needed to determine the issues raised by the application and that it would be procedurally fair to proceed, it is unlikely there would be grounds upon which the court could properly adjourn the application. Prolonging secure accommodation proceedings simply to keep a children's guardian involved for the purposes of assisting the child or overseeing the performance of the local authority's statutory duties is not a proper use of the court's power (*Birmingham City Council v M* [2008] 2 FLR 542).

Other procedural matters—See CA 1989, s 25 and the notes to that section; see also C(SA)R 1991 and C(SA)(No 2)R 1991, both set out above.

Chapter 4
Special Provisions about Private Law Proceedings

12.31 The First Hearing Dispute Resolution Appointment

(1) The court may set a date for the First Hearing Dispute Resolution Appointment after the proceedings have been issued.

(2) The court officer will give notice of any of the dates so fixed to the parties.

> (Provisions relating to the timing of and issues to be considered at the First Hearing Dispute Resolution Appointment are contained in Practice Direction 12B.)

PART III

Private Law Programme (PLP)—The PLP is contained in FPR PD12B. It provides a framework for private law proceedings within which local arrangements should be made to ensure its effective operation. It is fundamental to the provisions of the PLP that the timescales be observed rigidly in all courts.

Judicial continuity—Judicial continuity is central to the PLP in FPR PD12B, which applies to every application issued under CA 1989, Pt II.

12.32 Answer

A respondent must file and serve on the parties an answer to the application for an order in private law proceedings within 14 days beginning with the date on which the application is served.

Defined terms—"section 8 order": CA 1989, s 8(2).

"within 14 days"—As to the computation of time, see FPR 2010, r 2.9; as to the extension of time, see FPR 2010, rr 12.12(2), 12.13(1).

Service—See FPR 2010, rr 6.23–6.39, 12.8 and FPR PD12C.

Parties—See FPR 2010, r 12.3.

Form C7—Each respondent to an application for a s 8 order or an order under CA 1989, Sch 1 must serve on the other parties to the proceedings an acknowledgement in Form C7. Form C7 requires the respondent to give details identifying himself and his solicitor (if he has one) and to give an address to which correspondence may be sent. The respondent must state when he received the application, whether he opposes it and whether he intends to apply to the court for an order. If the respondent indicates that he does wish to apply for an order himself, that indication is not tantamount to making the application, which must be launched using an application form in the normal way (see r 5.1 and FPR PD5A). Form C7 allows only a small space for the respondent to say whether or not he opposes the application. He is not invited to give his side of the picture at this early stage. This is deliberate, because in s 8 cases the filing of evidence and giving of information is strictly controlled (see FPR 2010, r 12.19(2),(3)). The acknowledgement should, therefore, restrict itself to the fact of opposition. However, Form C7 has been amended to include an additional question related to harm, which must be completed where the relevant application is made under CA 1989, s 8 (for residence, contact, specific issue or prohibited steps orders) or s 4(1)(c) (for a parental responsibility order). Question 7 on Form C7 asks whether the child who is the subject of the application has suffered or is at risk of suffering any harm. If this question is answered in the affirmative, supplemental Form C1A must also be completed by the respondent. If the applicant has asked the court to order the respondent to make a payment for a child under CA 1989, Sch 1, the respondent must also fill in a statement of his financial means in Form C10A.

Written answer—Where the prescribed forms are not applicable, the respondent's written answer must be drafted from scratch. It is suggested that a similar format to that used in the prescribed form is adopted and the same sort of matters covered. It is the respondent who must serve the answer.

12.33 Applications for warning notices or applications to amend enforcement orders by reason of change of residence

(1) This rule applies in relation to an application to the High Court or a county court for –

    (a)   a warning notice to be attached to a contact order; or

    (b)   an order under paragraph 5 of Schedule A1 to the 1989 Act to amend an enforcement order by reason of change of residence.

(2) The application must be made without notice.

(3) The court may deal with the application without a hearing.

(4) If the court decides to deal with the application at a hearing, rules 12.5, 12.7 and 12.8 will apply.

Warning notices—See under CA 1989, s 8, **Warning notices on contact orders** and **Care required when drafting contact orders to which warning notices are to be attached**, and see Procedural Guide D8.

12.34 Service of a risk assessment

(1) Where an officer of the Service or a Welsh family proceedings officer has filed a risk assessment with the court, subject to paragraph (2), the court officer will as soon as practicable serve copies of the risk assessment on each party.

(2) Before serving the risk assessment, the court must consider whether, in order to prevent a risk of harm to the child, it is necessary for –

    (a) information to be deleted from a copy of the risk assessment before that copy is served on a party; or

    (b) service of a copy of the risk assessment (whether with information deleted from it or not) on a party to be delayed for a specified period,

and may make directions accordingly.

Practice direction—CA 1989, s 16A requires a Cafcass officer carrying out any function in private law CA 1989 proceedings to carry out a risk assessment if he has cause to suspect that the child concerned is at risk of harm, and to provide that assessment to the court. See further under s 16A, FPR 2010, r 16.38 and Form C42. See also FPR PD16A, paras 11.1–11.7.

12.35 Service of enforcement orders or orders amending or revoking enforcement orders

(1) Paragraphs (2) and (3) apply where the High Court or a county court makes –

    (a) an enforcement order; or

    (b) an order under paragraph 9(2) of Schedule A1 to the 1989 Act (enforcement order made following a breach of an enforcement order).

(2) As soon as practicable after an order has been made, a copy of it must be served by the court officer on –

    (a) the parties, except the person against whom the order is made;

    (b) the officer of the Service or the Welsh family proceedings officer who is to comply with a request under section 11M of the 1989 Act to monitor compliance with the order; and

    (c) the responsible officer.

(3) Unless the court directs otherwise, the applicant must serve a copy of the order personally on the person against whom the order is made.

(4) The court officer must send a copy of an order made under paragraph 4, 5, 6 or 7 of Schedule A1 to the 1989 Act (revocation or amendment of an enforcement order) to –

    (a) the parties;

    (b) the officer of the Service or the Welsh family proceedings officer who is to comply with a request under section 11M of the 1989 Act to monitor compliance with the order;

    (c) the responsible officer; and

    (d) in the case of an order under paragraph 5 of Schedule A1 to the 1989 Act (amendment of enforcement order by reason of change of residence), the responsible officer in the former local justice area.

(5) In this rule, "responsible officer" has the meaning given in paragraph 8(8) of Schedule A1 to the 1989 Act.

Chapter 5
Special Provisions about Inherent Jurisdiction Proceedings

12.36 Where to start proceedings

(1) An application for proceedings under the Inherent Jurisdiction of the court must be started in the High Court.

(2) Wardship proceedings, except applications for an order that a child be made or cease to be a ward of court, may be transferred to the county court unless the issues of fact or law make them more suitable for hearing in the High Court.

> (The question of suitability for hearing in the High Court is explained in Practice Direction 12D (Inherent Jurisdiction (including Wardship Proceedings)).)

The nature of inherent jurisdiction—The inherent jurisdiction of the court relates to its general jurisdiction as a court of superior record and as a trustee of the Crown's duty to protect all of its subjects. The jurisdiction in respect of children and in particular its wardship jurisdiction is only one facet of the court's inherent jurisdiction. It is not synonymous with, but has many of the characteristics of, wardship. It is the duty of the court under its inherent jurisdiction to ensure that a child who is the subject of proceedings is protected and taken care of. See further under FPR PD12D, paras 1.1 and 1.3.

Distinguishing characteristics of wardship—These are now set out in FPR PD12D, para 1.3. Good examples of the need for obtaining permission are set out in FPR PD12D, paras 5 and 6. Removal of a ward from the jurisdiction requires the court's permission (PD12D, para 4.1).

Ward and criminal proceedings—See FPR PD12D, para 5, which sets out the procedure that must be followed to obtain permission where there is a need to interview a ward in relation to criminal investigations and proceedings. It also makes provision for the procedure to be followed in those cases where the police need to take urgent action without prior permission of the court.

Application to the Criminal Injuries Compensation Authority (CICA)—See FPR PD12D, para 6 for the procedure to be followed when an application to the CICA is proposed and disclosure of documents in the wardship proceedings is being considered.

Publicity and disclosure of evidence—AJA 1960, s 12(1) provides that the publication of information relating to wardship proceedings before any court sitting in private is a contempt of court (see also CCA 1981, s 12; CA 1989, ss 2, 97(2); and *Harris v Harris; Attorney-General v Harris* [2001] 2 FLR 895). In all other respects, the ward enjoys no greater protection against unwelcome publicity than other children. If the information relates to the ward but not to the proceedings, there is no contempt. No contempt is committed by the media in interviewing a ward or publishing or broadcasting such an interview. The issue in each case will be whether an injunction is necessary to protect the child from clear and identifiable harm and whether the injunction sought is proportionate to that aim. If a wider protection is required, application should be made for an order specifically providing for the wider protection. In such cases, the court will balance the rights of the media to publish information against the need to protect the welfare of the child to uphold the effective functioning of the court's wardship jurisdiction (*Re W (Wardship: Discharge: Publicity)* [1995] 2 FLR 466). For the principles that the court will apply, see *Re W (Wardship: Publication of Information)* [1992] 1 FLR 99. For an analysis of all other relevant cases, the competing issues of the child's rights under ECHR 1950, Art 8 and the rights of the press to freedom of expression under Art 10 see *Re S (Identification: Restrictions on Publication)* [2003] 2 FLR 1253 applied in *Re LM Reporting Restriction: Coroner's Inquest)* [2008] 1 FLR 1360, *Re Roddy (A Child) (Identification: Restriction on Publication)* [2004] 2 FLR 949 and *Re B (A Child) (Disclosure)* [2004] 2 FLR 142. For the effect of s 12 on a child who is not a ward of court see *Re B, X Council v B (No 2)* [2008] 1 FLR 1460 and Judicial Proceedings (Regulation of Reports) Act 1926. Reference should also be made to the FPR PD27B and PD27C (as amended by *Re Child X (Residence and Contact – Rights of Media Attendance – FPR 10.28(4))* [2009] 2 FLR 1467: FPR PD relating to old PDs) and *Guidance of 22 April 2009* (see Part V). For further details see [2010] Fam Law 708, [2011] Fam Law 670 and also the decision of the ECtHR in *Tarasag a Szabadsagjogokert v Hungary* (App No 37374/05) [2009] EHRR 130.

Where an injunction is sought, the effect of which would be to impose a restraint on the freedom of the press and the media generally, the application should be transferred to the High Court and the Official Solicitor should be invited to represent the child (*Re H (Minors) (Injunction: Public Interest)* [1994] 1 FLR 519). FPR PD12E, paras 3.1 and 3.2 set out the procedure that should be followed, particularly where it is intended to restrict publication in urgent or out-of-hours applications.

When considering such an application, the court will balance the right of a person and of the media to publish information and matters of public interest against the need to protect the welfare of the child and the risk of harm to the child (see *Re X, Y and Z (Expert Witness)* [2011] 2 FLR 1437 and *Clayton v Clayton* [2007] 1 FLR 11, at [77] and [145]). See also: *Norfolk County Council v Webster & ors* [2007] 2 FLR 415, where the restrictions were found to be too wide; *British Broadcasting Corporation v CAFCASS Legal & ors* [2007] 2 FLR 765, where limited publicity was permitted in the public interest; *BBC v Coventry CC and Others (Care Proceedings: Costs: Identification of Local Authority* [2011] 1 FLR 977, where permission was given for the local authority to be identified; *Re LM (Reporting Restrictions: Coroner's Inquest)* [2008] 1 FLR 1360, where reporting of an inquest into the death of a child was permitted; *Re S (Identification: Restrictions on Publication)* [2005] 1 FLR 591, where restrictions relating to the identity of a defendant in a murder trial to protect the privacy of the defendant's child were considered inappropriate on the ground that the freedom of the press to report a criminal trial without restraint outweighed the child's rights; and *Leeds County Council & ors v Channel 4 Television Corporation* [2007] 1 FLR 678. The welfare of the child is not the paramount consideration but, when public interest turns into public curiosity, public interest in the protection of the child becomes the greater public interest and the interest of the child becomes "the more important factor" (*Re Manda (Wardship: Disclosure of Evidence)* [1993] 1 FLR 205; see also *A v M (Family Proceedings: Publicity)* [2000] 1 FLR 562 and *Re G (Celebrities: Publicity)* [1999] 1 FLR 409). The court's jurisdiction, however, can only be invoked where the child concerned is the subject of the proceedings before the court and the court is concerned with the care and upbringing of the child (*R v Central Independent Television plc* [1994] 2 FLR 151). See also the commentary under AJA 1960, s 12. For standard forms on press/publicity orders see *Emergency Remedies in the Family Courts* (Jordan Publishing Ltd), App 8 and *Practice Note of 18 March 2005 (Official Solicitor: Deputy Director of Legal Services: CAFCASS: Applications for Reporting Restrictions Orders)* (see Part V). Reference should also be made to FPR PD12I in relation to applications for restricting publication of information about children or incapacitated adults.

Restrictions under CA 1989—CA 1989, ss 91 and 100 restrict the use of the wardship jurisdiction by local authorities in relation to children (see under CA 1989, s 100 for cases in which the court has warded the child where the situation has been unusual and also where the child has been accommodated voluntarily pursuant to CA 1989, s 20). Where a care order is made in respect of a child who is a ward of court, the making of the care order discharges the wardship (s 91(4)). The court may, however, grant an injunction as an ancillary to care orders under SCA 1981, s 37, as part of its general jurisdiction. The assertion in FPR PD12D, para 1.1 that issues concerning children in the first instance should be resolved under CA 1989 confirms the existing position as set out in case-law (see *Re CT (A Minor) (Wardship: Representation)* [1993] 2 FLR 278; *Re R (A Minor) (Blood Transfusion)* [1993] 2 FLR 757). Where the issue cannot be resolved under CA 1989 or the powers of the court under its inherent jurisdiction are required for the local authority to exercise its statutory functions, the local authority may apply for permission to seek relief under the inherent jurisdiction of the court (*Re S (Wardship: Peremptory Return)* [2010] 2 FLR 1960).

Commencement of application—An application to ward a child may only be made after its birth; an unborn child cannot be warded (*Re F (In Utero) (Wardship)* [1988] 2 FLR 307. However, the inherent jurisdiction of the court may be invoked to obtain an anticipatory declaratory relief in respect of an unborn child (see *Re D (Unborn Baby)* [2009] 2 FLR 313).

Where to start proceedings—All applications under the inherent jurisdiction of the court must be started in the High Court. No child shall be made a ward of court or cease to be a ward of court except by an order of the High Court.

Transfer of proceedings—The provision for transfer is dealt with in FPR PD12D, para 2. Whereas county courts do not have jurisdiction to deal with applications that a child be made or cease to be a ward of court, consideration should be given to transferring the case in whole or in part to a county court once a direction has been given confirming the wardship and directing that the child remain a ward of court during his minority or until further order (para 2.1). If a decision is required as to whether the child should remain a ward the county court must retransfer the case to the High Court (para 2.2).

Proceedings that should be dealt with in the High Court—FPR PD12D, para 2.3 identifies the proceedings in relation to a ward of court that will be dealt with in the High Court unless the nature of the issues of fact or law makes them more suitable for hearing in the county court. These include proceedings in which: (a) an officer of the Cafcass High Court Team or the Official Solicitor is or becomes the litigation friend or children's guardian of the ward or a party to the proceedings; (b) a local authority is or becomes a party; (c) an application for paternity testing is made; (d) there is a dispute about medical treatment; (e) an application is opposed on the grounds of lack of jurisdiction; (f) there is a substantial foreign element; and (g) there is an opposed application for leave to take the child permanently out of the jurisdiction or where there is an application for temporary removal of a child from the jurisdiction and it is opposed on the ground that the child may not be returned. See also *PD: Allocation and Transfer of Proceedings* in Part V and FPR PD12E, para 3.1.

Jurisdiction—In the exercise of its inherent jurisdiction the High Court has jurisdiction only if the child is habitually resident in England and Wales or is present in England and Wales and is not habitually resident in any other part of the UK and provided that jurisdiction is not excluded by FLA 1986, s 3(2) (*H v H (Jurisdiction to Grant Wardship)* [2012] 1 FLR 23). Where it is excluded by the 1986 Act, provided the child is present in England and Wales on the relevant date (for meaning see s 3(6)) and the court considers that the immediate exercise of its powers is necessary for the child's protection the court will exercise jurisdiction. (For the meaning of habitual residence see note under CACA 1985, Sch 1, art 4.) Where the child is habitually resident in a State within the European Union or a Contracting State that has ratified the Hague Convention 1996, the provisions of Brussels IIA and the Convention, respectively, will need to be considered to determine jurisdiction and applicable law. If a Member State or a Contracting State has jurisdiction, the court may (if the situation is urgent) take necessary measures for the protection of a child and in some instances take provisional measures. (See the Brussels IIA and the 1996 Convention in Part VI and the Parental Responsibility and Measures for the Protection of Children (International Obligations) (England and Wales and Northern Ireland) Regulations 2010 in Part IV.) The issue of habitual residence is usually to be determined on proper evidence and where there is a challenge on full argument. The court may proceed to hear a case and provide the necessary protection, where the evidence discloses that the child has lived in England for all of her life before removal out of the jurisdiction the court (*Re S (Wardship: Peremptory Return)* [2010] 2 FLR 1960). Before commencing proceedings, consideration should be given to the nature of the issues on which a determination is sought. If the court is required to review the decision of a public authority taken in the exercise of its statutory power, the governing principles that will apply will be those of public law and not those governed by reference to the inherent jurisdiction of the court. In such cases the application should be made in the Administrative Court for judicial review and not in the Family Division (*A (A Patient) v A Health Authority; Re J; The Queen on the Application of S v Secretary of State for the Home Department* [2002] 1 FLR 845). Note also that the court has exercised its inherent jurisdiction in relation to vulnerable adults and cases of stranded spouses.

Powers of the Court—The court under its inherent jurisdiction has power to make any order or determine any issue in respect of a child or an adult unless restricted by legislation. FPR PD12D, para 2.3 sets out some examples of the orders that the court may make. In addition to all of the orders that can be made in family proceedings the court may make a wide range of injunctions for the protection of a child, of which the most common are orders: (a) to restrain publicity, e g see *Thompson and Venables v News Group Newspapers, Associated Newspapers Ltd and MGN Ltd* [2001] 1 FLR 791 but, because of the need to balance the freedom of the press against the protection of a child any such order must be drawn in clear and precise terms (see *Re W (Wardship: Publication of Information)* [1992] 1 FLR 99 for the principles that will apply in such cases); (b) to prevent an undesirable association; (c) relating to medical treatment; (d) to protect abducted children or children where the case has another substantial foreign element; (e) for the return of children to and from another state (see *Re O (Child Abduction: Custody Rights)* [1997] 2 FLR 702); and (f) to grant an injunction pursuant to SCA 1981, s 37 restraining the local authority from removing children from placement with foster carers, who had given notice of their intention to adopt the children, pending the full hearing by the court (*Coventry CC v O (Adoption)* [2011] 2 FLR 936). (See also under HRA 1998, s 9· FPR 2010, r 29.5 and CPR 1998, r 19.4A.) Where a without notice order is sought, the information to be put before the court in support of the order should be the subject of the closest scrutiny and those advising the making of a without notice application should consider rigorously whether the application is justified and if there is clear evidence to support the application. If the applicant is not present when the application is made, a contemporaneous note of the instructions given should be available for production to the court. If material other than that disclosed in a written statement is relied on, the court should give direction for the filing of sworn evidence to confirm the information within a very short time: see *KY v DD* [2012] 2 FLR 200.

Undesirable association—Where the child has formed or is seeking to form an association considered to be undesirable with another person, that other person should not be made a party to an application within the proceedings for an injunction or committal. Such a person should not be added to the title of the proceedings or allowed to see any documents other than those relating directly to the proceedings for the injunction or committal. The person should be allowed time to obtain representation and any injunction should in the first instance extend over a few days only (FPR PD12D, para 3.1, which supersedes *PD of 16 June 1983*).

Medical treatment—It is only in cases concerning children or a vulnerable adult (i e those with capacity) that the High Court's inherent jurisdiction can be invoked. When dealing with such cases the court will apply the "patient's best interests" principle and will have to be satisfied that the proposed treatment is necessary (*R (N) v Doctor M* [2003] 1 FLR 667; *Portsmouth NHS Trust v Wyatt* [2006] 1 FLR 652; *Re Wyatt* [2006] 2 FLR 111; MCA 2005, s 4). Where there are serious medical issues such as surgery for a serious medical condition, initially it is for the parents who have parental responsibility for the child to seek to resolve the issue with the hospital. It is only when the parents are opposed to the advice offered by the medical team and when the matter cannot be resolved by agreement with the parents that it will become appropriate to invoke the inherent jurisdiction, provided that the issue is properly formulated. In such cases, the hospital should be invited to intervene. It is inappropriate to seek to resolve such issues within care proceedings or by seeking permission to apply for a specific issue order under CA 1989, s 8 (*A Local Authority v SB, AB & MB* [2010] 2 FLR 1203). In *An NHS Trust v MB (A Child Represented by CAFCASS as Guardian ad Litem)* [2006] 2 FLR 319 the court directed that a list specifically identifying the benefits/advantages and burdens/disadvantages of continuing or discontinuing treatment should be submitted by each party as part of the preparation of the case. In *Re B (Medical Treatment)* [2009] 1 FLR 1264, when making a declaration allowing for the withholding of resuscitation if the child's condition deteriorated, the court suggested that a short, joint experts' report be attached to the order so that in the event of a crisis any new doctor coming to that situation would have the information needed to make this difficult, sensitive and finely balanced clinical judgment. The court has given its consent: to medical treatment where the parents have refused to do so (*NHS Trust v A* [2008] 1 FLR 70, where applying an objective test based on the best interests of the child and discounting the religious faith of the parents, the court held that a 50% prospect of full normal life even with the risk of infertility, outweighed all other considerations); to medical treatment where the patient, whether a child or an adult, has refused to consent (*Re E (A Minor) (Wardship: Medical Treatment)* [1993] 1 FLR 386; *Re R (A Minor) (Wardship: Consent to Treatment)* [1992] 1 FLR 190; *Re J (A Minor) (Medical Treatment)* [1992] 2 FLR 165; *Re H (Mental Patient: Diagnosis,* [1993] 1 FLR 28); to the termination of a pregnancy (*Re P (A Minor)* [1986] 1 FLR 272). For cases relating to issues of withholding or withdrawing treatment, see *R (Burke) v General Medical Council* [2004] 2 FLR 1121; *Portsmouth NHS Trust v Wyatt and Wyatt* [2005] 1 FLR 21; *Re B* above; and *Re L (Medical Treatment: Benefit)* [2005] 1 FLR 491); to sterilisation (*Re P (A Minor) (Wardship: Sterilisation)* [1989] 1 FLR 182 – for the approach adopted in respect of male sterilisation, see *Re A (Male Sterilisation)* [2000] 1 FLR 549); and to making a choice between two alternative surgical interventions (*Re S (Sterilisation: Patient's Best Interests)* [2000] 2 FLR 389; *Re ZM and OS (Sterilisation: Patient's Best Interests)* [2000] 1 FLR 523).

However, where a patient is an adult and of sound mind and, in anticipation of entering into a condition such as persistent vegetative state or other life-threatening condition, permanent mental impairment or unconsciousness, has given clear instructions that in such an event he is not to be given medical care designed to keep him alive, the court will respect his wishes (*Re AK (Medical Treatment: Consent)* [2001] 1 FLR 129 and *Re B (Consent to Treatment: Capacity)* [2002] 1 FLR 1090). In such cases, the patient can now make an advanced decision, provided it complies with MCA 2005, ss 24–26. With regard to the patient's right to choose, see the President's guidelines in *Re B*, above. Where an urgent or out-of-hours application has to be made, the procedure set out in FPR PD12E should be followed.

Detention of a child or vulnerable adult—The court also has power to direct the placement/detention of a child or a vulnerable or incapacitated adult in a specified institution, subject to the principle that the jurisdiction must be exercised in compliance with ECHR 1950, Art 5 rights and, where appropriate, the minimum requirements set out in *Re PS (Incapacitated or Vulnerable Adult)* [2007] 2 FLR 1083 being satisfied. The existence of a remedy under mental health legislation does not preclude the court exercising its inherent jurisdiction in appropriate cases. As to when it is appropriate to invoke the court's inherent jurisdiction as opposed to an application for a specific issue order under CA 1989, see *A Local Authority v SB, AB & MB* [2010] 2 FLR 1203, *Devon County Council v S* [1993] 1 FLR 842 and *Re O (A Minor) (Medical Treatment)* [1993] 2 FLR 149; cf *Re R (A Minor) (Blood Transfusion)* [1993] 2 FLR 757. Such an application should be heard inter partes where possible in the High Court. It would seem that in such cases the procedure set out in Pt 19 should be followed.

Vulnerable adults and adults lacking capacity—Applications in relation to adults who lack capacity are governed by the provisions of MCA 2005 and the rules and directions issued under the Act. FPR PD12E, para 4.4 confirms this by providing that medical and welfare issues relating to an adult lacking capacity are brought in the Court of Protection. Enquires about such cases should be addressed to a Court of Protection healthcare and welfare lawyer at the offices of the Official Solicitor.

MCA 2005, s 2(1) defines those who lack capacity in relation to a matter: "… if at the material time he is unable to make a decision for himself in relation to the matter because of an impairment of, or disturbance in the functioning of, the mind or brain". Capacity is therefore subject- and issue-specific and is not limited to mental disability. MCA 2005, s 3 sets out the test to be applied for assessing whether a person is unable to make an informed decision on the relevant matter. Practitioners are advised to refer to MCA 2005 in relevant cases. (See also: Gordon Ashton et al *Mental Capacity – The New Law*; *Court of Protection Practice*; and *Urgent Applications in the Court of Protection* (all Jordan Publishing Ltd)). All applications in relation to a vulnerable adult lacking capacity should in future be made to the Court of

Protection, which will then refer the matter to the appropriate level of judiciary/court. It would appear that all cases concerning the issue of restraint and deprivation of liberty will be dealt with in the High Court. For practice and procedure refer to the Court of Protection Rules, PDs and Codes of Practice. Where an adult is considered to have capacity for the purposes of MCA 2005 but is incapacitated by external forces outside his/her control from reaching a decision and is vulnerable, the court's inherent jurisdiction may still be invoked to protect the vulnerable adult (*A Local Authority v DL, RL, and ML* [2011] 1 FLR 957, in which Local Government Act 1972, s 222 was also relied on for seeking relief) but not to impose a decision as to welfare or finance (*LBL v RYJ and VJ* [2010] COPLR Con Vol 795).

Experimental medical treatment—The court has permitted experimental and pioneering treatment to be carried out where the benefits and risks were unknown, but where there was no increased risk of suffering to the patient and some chance of benefit, and where there was a responsible body of relevant professional opinion that supported the treatment (*JS v An NHS Trust; JA v An NHS Trust* [2003] 1 FLR 879).

Exercise of the court's powers is discretionary—The court may refuse to exercise its powers if it considers it inappropriate to do so. There are numerous examples of cases where the court has declined to exercise its inherent jurisdiction. These include where the applicant sought to invoke the inherent jurisdiction to justify the retrieval and use of sperm taken from her dead husband without effective consent (*L v HFEA & Secretary of State* [2008] 2 FLR 1999); where the sole object of the application was to gain publicity (*Re Dunhill (An Infant)* (1967) 111 Sol Jo 11); where proceedings were issued to frustrate immigration laws or to prevent the exercise of statutory powers (*S v S* [2009] 1 FLR 241); to prevent a boy soldier being arrested under military law (*Re JS (A Minor) (Wardship: Boy Soldier)* [1991] 1 FLR 7); where relief is available under CA 1989 (*C v C (Access Order: Enforcement)* [1990] 1 FLR 462); and to direct a school to educate a child against his/her wishes (*Re C (A Minor) (Wardship: Jurisdiction)* [1991] 2 FLR 168).

Order for costs—Under FPR 2010, r 28.1, the court has a wide discretion to make such an order if it thinks it just. Where a party to the proceedings has advanced a case that amounts to "litigation conduct", the court may order that party to pay the costs (*R and R v A (Costs in Children Proceedings)* [2011] 2 FLR 672).

12.37 Child as respondent to wardship proceedings

(1) A child who is the subject of wardship proceedings must not be made a respondent to those proceedings unless the court gives permission following an application under paragraph (2).

(2) Where nobody other than the child would be a suitable respondent to wardship proceedings, the applicant may apply without notice for permission to make the wardship application –

    (a)   without notice; or

    (b)   with the child as the respondent.

Ward as a party to proceedings—See FPR 2010, rr 16.1–16.15 and FPR PD16A for representation of children and appointment of litigation friend. In cases relating to medical treatment and press injunction, it may be desirable for a child who is the subject of such proceedings to be made a party and represented by a children's guardian. Where an application is made out of hours, the urgent business officer will contact a representative of Cafcass. A child of sufficient understanding to instruct a solicitor should be made a party and given notice of the application (FPR PD12E, para 3.1).

12.38 Registration requirements

The court officer will send a copy of every application for a child to be made a ward of court to the principal registry for recording in the register of wards.

Defined terms—"principal registry": FPR 2010, r 2.3.

Scope—This provision is related to cases that are issued in the District Registry.

12.39 Notice of child's whereabouts

(1) Every respondent, other than a child, must file with the acknowledgment of service a notice stating –

(a) the respondent's address; and
(b) either –
   (i) the whereabouts of the child; or
   (ii) that the respondent is unaware of the child's whereabouts if that is the case.

(2) Unless the court directs otherwise, the respondent must serve a copy of that notice on the applicant.

(3) Every respondent other than a child must immediately notify the court in writing of –

(a) any subsequent changes of address; or
(b) any change in the child's whereabouts,

and, unless the court directs otherwise, serve a copy of that notice on the applicant.

(4) In this rule a reference to the whereabouts of a child is a reference to –

(a) the address at which the child is living;
(b) the person with whom the child is living; and
(c) any other information relevant to where the child may be found.

Whereabouts of the child—There is a duty on the Respondent to disclose the child's whereabouts. A solicitor is under a duty to disclose information that may assist in locating a ward even if such information has been conveyed to him in confidence by his client (*Ramsbotham v Senior* (1869) FLR Rep 591). Information about the child's whereabouts may also be obtained through government departments (but in the first instance usually through HM Customs and Excise) by applying to the High Court (or a judge authorised to sit as a judge of the High Court) for an order for disclosure (see FPR PD6C for the information required and procedure to be followed). The order will direct that the department to whom the order is addressed should disclose the information to the court. Where the information is disclosed to the applicant's solicitor, an undertaking will be required that the information given in response to the inquiry will be used solely for the purpose of assisting in tracing the person concerned or the child. A collection and/or a location order may be sought in the prescribed form directing the tipstaff to ascertain the child's whereabouts, to search for and recover the child and if necessary to arrest any person who fails to comply with the order. Where such an order is obtained, the tipstaff must be provided with all available information as to the child's possible whereabouts. See also PD12F and the court's powers under FLA 1986, ss 33 and 34.) Where an order is sought for the return of a child about to arrive by air and the applicant requires information to enable him to meet the aeroplane, the court should be asked to direct that the airline and (if he has the information) the immigration officer at the appropriate airport should supply the necessary information to the applicant. Where the applicant has an order for the return of the child, application should be made for such a direction. Where the child has been abducted, consideration should be given as to whether a press publicity order is required to trace the child (see FPR PD12F, paras 4.15, 4.16). If a child is believed to be in a State that has ratified the Hague Convention 1996, a request may be made for assistance in discovering the whereabouts of the child if it appears that the child may be present in that State and in need of protection and the Central Authority of a Contracting State, either directly or through public authorities or other bodies, is under a duty to provide the information (Hague Convention 1996, Art 31).

12.40 Enforcement of orders in wardship proceedings

The High Court may secure compliance with any direction relating to a ward of court by an order addressed to the tipstaff.

(The role of the tipstaff is explained in Practice Direction 12D (Inherent Jurisdiction (including Wardship Proceedings)).)

Tipstaff—For the purposes of FLA 1986, s 34 the tipstaff is the officer of the court to whom orders should be directed. FPR PD12D, para 7.1 sets out the extent and nature of the role of the tipstaff in family matters. All appropriate orders made in the High Court will be addressed to the tipstaff. The tipstaff has two assistants but he can call on any constable or bailiff to assist him. The tipstaff has authority to effect an arrest and inform the police. The tipstaff has the authority to make a forced entry but in practice the tipstaff will obtain the assistance of the police to ensure that there is no breach of the peace.

Committal—Where there has been a deliberate attempt to thwart the child's return to England in breach of an order made by the court, the breach may, as in all other cases of breach of an order, be punished by committal to prison (see *Re X (A Child by His Litigation Friend)* [2011] 2 FLR 793, where an 8-month prison sentence was upheld by the CA).

12.41 Child ceasing to be ward of court

(1) A child who, by virtue of section 41(2) of the Senior Courts Act 1981, automatically becomes a ward of court on the making of a wardship application will cease to be a ward on the determination of the application unless the court orders that the child be made a ward of court.

(2) Nothing in paragraph (1) affects the power of the court under section 41(3) of the Senior Courts Act 1981 to order that any child cease to be a ward of court.

Confirmation of wardship—The child will become a ward immediately on the application being issued. It is, however, essential to ensure that at the first opportunity thereafter a direction hearing is applied for and an order is sought that the child should remain a ward during his/her minority or until further order. In the absence of such an order the wardship will lapse.

12.42 Adoption of a child who is a ward of court

An application for permission –

    (a)   to start proceedings to adopt a child who is a ward of court;

    (b)   to place such a child for adoption with parental consent; or

    (c)   to start proceedings for a placement order in relation to such a child,

may be made without notice in accordance with Part 18.

Procedure—The application must be made in accordance with the procedure set out in FPR 2010, Pt 18 and FPR PD18A, which supplements the rule.

Chapter 6
Proceedings under the 1980 Hague Convention, the European Convention, the Council Regulation, and the 1996 Hague Convention

12.43 Scope

This Chapter applies to –

    (a)   children proceedings under the 1980 Hague Convention or the European Convention; and

    (b)   applications relating to the Council Regulation or the 1996 Hague Convention in respect of children.

Amendments—SI 2012/3061.

Section 1
Proceedings under the 1980 Hague Convention or the European Convention

12.44 Interpretation

In this section –

    "the 1985 Act" means the Child Abduction and Custody Act 1985;

    "Central Authority" means, in relation to England and Wales, the Lord Chancellor;

    "Contracting State" has the meaning given in –

        (a)   section 2 of the 1985 Act in relation to the 1980 Hague Convention; and

        (b)   section 13 of the 1985 Act in relation to the European Convention; and "decision relating to custody" has the same meaning as in the European Convention.

("the 1980 Hague Convention" and the "the European Convention" are defined in rule 2.3.)

The 1980 Hague Convention—This is the Convention on the Civil Aspects of International Child Abduction signed at The Hague on 25 October 1980 and is set out in Sch 1 to the 1985 Act (see the commentary thereunder). (See also FPR 2010, r 2.3.)

"the European Convention"—This is the European Convention on Recognition and Enforcement of Decisions Concerning Custody of Children and on the Restoration of Custody of Children signed in Luxembourg on 20 May 1980 and is set out in CACA 1985, Sch 2 in Part II (see also FPR 2010, r 2.3).

The 1996 Hague Convention—This is the Convention on Jurisdiction, Applicable Law, Recognition, Enforcement and Co-operation in Respect of Parental Responsibility and Measures for the Protection of Children signed at the Hague on 19 October 1996, which came into force in the UK on 1 November 2012 (see Part VI). The Parental Responsibility and Measures for the Protection of Children (International Obligations) (England and Wales and Northern Ireland) Regulations 2010 contain provisions relevant to applications under this Convention and the 1980 Hague Convention. For procedure for recognition, registration and enforcement of orders, see FPR 2010, Pt 31.

12.45 Where to start proceedings

Every application under the 1980 Hague Convention or the European Convention must be –

(a) made in the High Court and issued in the principal registry; and
(b) heard by a Judge of the High Court unless the application is;
  (i) to join a respondent; or
  (ii) to dispense with service or extend the time for acknowledging service.

Which court—This rule and FPR PD12F, para 2.10 set out two interlocutory applications that may be heard by a judge other than a High Court Judge.

12.46 Evidence in support of application

Where the party making an application under this section does not produce the documents referred to in Practice Direction 12F, the court may –

(a) fix a time within which the documents are to be produced;
(b) accept equivalent documents; or
(c) dispense with production of the documents if the court considers it has sufficient information.

Application—Must be made on Form C67 (FPR PD5A) and include the information set out in FPR PD12F para 2.11. The heading on the application form must comply with the provisions set out in PD12F, para 2.14, which confirms the guidance given in *Vigreux v Michel* [2006] 2 FLR 1180.

Documents that must be filed with the application— FPR PD12F requires the applicant to file with the application all relevant documents, including the following: (a) an authenticated copy of any relevant decision or agreement; (b) a certificate or an affidavit from a central authority, or other competent authority of the State of the child's habitual residence or from a qualified person, concerning the relevant law of that State; (c) a statement in support of the application by the applicant or by his legal representative on his behalf on the applicant's instructions. The statement must contain a statement of truth in accordance with FPR 2010, Pt 17 and FPR PD17A (FPR PD12F, para 2.13).

12.47 Without-notice applications

(1) This rule applies to applications –

(a) commencing or in proceedings under this section;
(b) for interim directions under section 5 or 19 of the 1985 Act;
(c) for the disclosure of information about the child and for safeguarding the child's welfare, under rule 12.57;

(d) for the disclosure of relevant information as to where the child is, under
    section 24A of the 1985 Act; or

(e) for a collection order, location order or passport order.

(2) Applications under this rule may be made without notice, in which case the applicant
must file the application –

(a) where the application is made by telephone, the next business day after the
    making of the application; or

(b) in any other case, at the time when the application is made.

(3) Where an order is made without notice, the applicant must serve a copy of the order
on the other parties as soon as practicable after the making of the order, unless the court
otherwise directs.

(4) Where the court refuses to make an order on an application without notice, it may
direct that the application is made on notice.

(5) Where any hearing takes place outside the hours during which the court office is
usually open –

(a) if the hearing takes place by telephone, the applicant's solicitors will, if
    practicable, arrange for the hearing to be recorded; and

(b) in all other cases, the court or court officer will take a note of the proceedings.

(Practice Direction 12E (Urgent Business) provides further details of the procedure
for out of hours applications. See also Practice Direction 12D (Inherent Jurisdiction
(including Wardship Proceedings)).)

Defined terms—"application form" and "application notice": FPR 2010, r 2.3.

Scope—This rule applies to all emergency applications made before and after proceedings have
commenced and specifically those that relate to the court's interim powers on disclosure of information
relating to a child, in applications under the European Convention, the disclosure of a child's whereabouts
and applications for a location and collection order (see commentary under FPR 2010, rr 12.36 and
12.48). Where the emergency application is made by telephone before commencement of the
proceedings, the substantive application must be issued on the next business day (for meaning of
"business day", see FPR 2010, r 2.3). In any other case, the substantive application should be filed at the
time when the without notice application is made. Provision is made for the court to give directions for an
on notice hearing. A without notice application should be made under FPR 2010, Pt 18 procedure. See
further under FPR PD18A, para 5.1.

Out of hours – urgent applications—For procedure, see FPR PD12E. If the hearing takes place by
telephone, it should (unless it is impracticable) be by tape-recorded conference call arranged and paid for
in the first instance by the applicant's solicitors. Solicitors acting for potential applicants should consider
having standing arrangements with their telephone service providers. All parties, especially the judge,
should be informed that the call is being recorded. The applicant's solicitors should order a transcript of
the hearing from the service provider, otherwise the applicant's legal representative should prepare a note
for approval by the judge (see further FPR PD18A, para 8.5). In all other cases the court officer is
required to take a note of the proceedings.

Service—Unless the court otherwise directs, service of any order made without notice must be effected as
soon as practicable after the order is made. In appropriate cases, application should be made for the court
to direct alternative methods of service, e g by email, text message or other electronic means or other form
of substituted service. For service generally, see FPR 2010, r 6.

Evidence of service—The applicant must ensure that an appropriate certificate of service is prepared and
filed as soon as practicable after service, setting out the date, time and place of service and describe how
the person served was identified (FPR 2010, r 6.37). The certificate of service must be verified by a
statement of truth (FPR 2010, r 17.2). Preferably, Form FL415 (the prescribed form for a statement of
service) should be used.

12.48 Directions

(1) As soon as practicable after an application to which this section applies has been
made, the court may give directions as to the following matters, among others –

(a)   whether service of the application may be dispensed with;

(b)   whether the proceedings should be transferred to another court under rule 12.54;

(c)   expedition of the proceedings or any part of the proceedings (and any direction for expedition may specify a date by which the court must issue its final judgment in the proceedings or a specified part of the proceedings);

(d)   the steps to be taken in the proceedings and the time by which each step is to be taken;

(e)   whether the child or any other person should be made a party to the proceedings;

(f)   if the child is not made a party to the proceedings, the manner in which the child's wishes and feelings are to be ascertained, having regard to the child's age and maturity and in particular whether an officer of the Service or a Welsh family proceedings officer should report to the court for that purpose;

(g)   where the child is made a party to the proceedings, the appointment of a children's guardian for that child unless a children's guardian has already been appointed;

(h)   the attendance of the child or any other person before the court;

(i)   the appointment of a litigation friend for a child or for any protected party, unless a litigation friend has already been appointed;

(j)   the service of documents;

(k)   the filing of evidence including expert evidence; and

(l)   whether the parties and their representatives should meet at any stage of the proceedings and the purpose of such a meeting.

(Rule 16.2 provides for when the court may make the child a party to the proceedings and rule 16.4 for the appointment of a children's guardian for the child who is made a party. Rule 16.5 (without prejudice to rule 16.6) requires a child who is a party to the proceedings but not the subject of those proceedings to have a litigation friend.)

(2) Directions of a court which are in force immediately prior to the transfer of proceedings to another court under rule 12.54 will continue to apply following the transfer subject to –

(a)   any changes of terminology which are required to apply those directions to the court to which the proceedings are transferred; and

(b)   any variation or revocation of the directions.

(3) The court or court officer will –

(a)   take a note of the giving, variation or revocation of directions under this rule; and

(b)   as soon as practicable serve a copy of the directions order on every party.

Scope—Other matters, save in relation to directions, will be covered where appropriate by the general provisions set out in FPR 2010, Pt 12 and under the court's general case management powers set out in FPR 2010, Pt 4. Note that the rule requires the court to address the issues that arise under Brussels IIA, Art 11 regarding the representation of children and the avoidance of delay. The court's attention is drawn to the provisions in FPR 2010, rr 16.2–16.6, which deal with the issues of whether a child should be made a party to the proceedings and the appointment of a guardian and litigation friend for a child who is either a party to the proceedings or the subject of the proceedings. In addition, the court is obliged to consider giving further directions under its case management powers under FPR 2010, rr 4.1–4.8 and to consider exercising its powers to encourage the parties to use alternative dispute resolution under FPR 2010, rr 3.1–3.3. As to representation of children, see further under CACA 1985, Sch 1, Art 12, FPR 2010, Pt 16 and *Emergency Remedies in the Family Courts* (Jordan Publishing Ltd), Div D paras 4.74, 4.74AA. For the court's general powers to make orders see under "inherent jurisdiction" and also FPR PD12F, which specifies some of the ways in which removal of a child may be prevented without a court order and the orders that may be made to obtain information from government departments.

Interim directions—CACA 1985, ss 5 and 19 empower the court at any time before the application is determined to give such interim directions as it thinks fit for the purpose of securing the welfare of the child concerned or preventing changes in the circumstances relevant to the determination of the application. The provision of CACA 1985, Sch 1, Arts 7 and 10 and Sch 2, Art 5 require all appropriate steps to be taken to ascertain the whereabouts of the child and to ensure his return (see further CACA 1985, s 5). The court may also grant injunctions, request a report from Cafcass (ss 6 and 21), give specific directions for trial, order publicity (see PD12F, paras 4.15, 4.16 and *Re D (A Minor) (Child Abduction)* [1989] 1 FLR 97), dispense with service (r 12.48) or abridge time under its case management powers under r 4.1 and adjourn the hearing (r 12.51). Where appropriate the court may direct a local housing authority to provide accommodation for an abductor and the abducted child and direct the local authority to accommodate the child (*Re C (Abduction: Interim Directions: Accommodation by Local Authority)* [2004] 1 FLR 653; *Re A (Abduction: Interim Directions: Accommodation by Local Authority)* [2011] 1 FLR 1 and see under CACA 1985, s 50 in Part II).

On the directions hearing, the court should consider including a provision in the order that each party should identify any undertakings that they seek and any undertakings that they are prepared to give for the purpose of paving the way for the child's return (*Re M (Child Abduction: Existence of Undertaking)* [2000] 3 FCR 693).

12.49 Answer

(1) Subject to paragraph (2) and to any directions given under rule 12.48, a respondent must file and serve on the parties an answer to the application within 7 days beginning with the date on which the application is served.

(2) The court may direct a longer period for service where the respondent has been made a party solely on one of the following grounds –

    (a)   a decision relating to custody has been made in the respondent's favour; or

    (b)   the respondent appears to the court to have sufficient interest in the welfare of the child.

Time for filing answer—The court may under its power to give/make interim directions/orders abridge time for service to deal with any issue that requires urgent directions or orders.

12.50 Filing and serving written evidence

(1) The respondent to an application to which this section applies may file and serve with the answer a statement verified by a statement of truth, together with any further evidence on which the respondent intends to rely.

(2) The applicant may, within 7 days beginning with the date on which the respondent's evidence was served under paragraph (1), file and serve a statement in reply verified by a statement of truth, together with any further evidence on which the applicant intends to rely.

Respondent's evidence—If the respondent wishes to file a statement and/or other evidence, he must file and serve it with his answer, ie within 7 days after service of the application. The statement must be verified by a statement of truth (see FPR 2010, r 17.2 and FPR PD17A for the form and verification of a witness statement generally and FPR 2010, rr 22.4–22.7 and FPR PD22A).

If the respondent wishes to defend the application, the statement must set out any defence to the application (e g that the removal or retention was not wrongful or that Art 13 applies or challenge the issue of habitual residence of the child) at the earliest opportunity and in any event within the time limit directed by the court (FPR PD12F, paras 2.21–2.24). In cases under the European Convention, the defendant's statement should show that the grounds set out in CACA 1985, Sch 2, Arts 9 and 10 apply and the relevant provisions of Brussels IIA and the 1996 Hague Convention, where appropriate. (See further, Part VI.)

Preparation—Care should be taken to ensure that statements in support are succinct and confined to the issues, which must be identified, excluding the inevitable emotions that underlie such cases to provoke "irrelevance, prejudice and prolixity" (*Re S (Abduction: Intolerable Situation: Beth Din)* [2000] 1 FLR 454). The rules and PDs relating to evidence and hearings should be followed in all hearings, irrespective of the duration of the hearing (see FPR 2010, Pt 27 and PD27A) In relation to the preparation of the court bundles, it is only in cases of urgency where it is not reasonably practicable to prepare a bundle that the court may excuse the absence of a proper court bundle.

Oral evidence—The provisions of FPR 2010, Pt 27 apply to oral hearings. Once a child has been found and surrendered, there is no power to order a person to give evidence. The desirability of introducing such a power by way of amendment was considered in *Re D (A Minor) (Child Abduction) Note* [1989] 1 FLR 97 and *Re E (A Minor) (Abduction)* [1989] 1 FLR 135. The evidence in proceedings under CACA 1985 is by way of affidavit. Oral evidence is only admitted at the discretion of the court. In *Re K (Abduction: Case Management)* [2011] 1 FLR 1268, Thorpe LJ emphasised this principle and directed that "not only should orders for oral evidence be extremely rare" but that they should "never be made in advance of the filing of written statements on the point in issue … If there were to be exceptional provision for oral evidence, it should be strongly expressed to ensure that the parties understood that this was not an opportunity to express their cases on the generality. It was strictly limited in its ambit and should be limited in its duration".

The proceedings under the Convention are summary in nature and designed to provide a speedy resolution of disputes over children and secure the prompt return of children wrongfully removed from the country of habitual residence. The admission of oral evidence runs the risk of delaying and frustrating the purpose of the Convention. The admission of oral evidence was refused in *Re K (Abduction: Child's Objections)* [1995] 1 FLR 977. The court held that it was not necessary for there to be specific findings of fact for the defence under Art 13(b) to succeed. However, in *Re G (Abduction: Psychological Harm)* [1995] 1 FLR 64 and *N v N (Abduction: Article 13 Defence)* [1995] 1 FLR 107, on the particular facts of the case, the oral evidence of experts was received.

Introduction of evidence after hearing—New and additional evidence in support of an application for the reversal or reconsideration of a judgment may be permitted if that evidence could not have been obtained with reasonable diligence before the conclusion of the case and if the court is satisfied that the additional evidence would materially affect the court's decision. If such an application is made after judgment has been given, it would have to satisfy the test in *Ladd v Marshall* (see below) but if made after the hearing was concluded but before judgment the applicant does not have to show strong reasons for so doing (*K v K (No 2) (Hague Convention Adjournment)* [2010] 1 FLR 1310; *K v K (Abduction) (No 1)* [2010] 1 FLR 1295).

As to the introduction on appeal of additional evidence (particularly evidence that was available at the trial), see *Re S (Minors) (Abduction)* [1993] 1 FCR 789; the principles laid down in *Ladd v Marshall* (1954) FLR Rep 422 were relaxed because the mother and her legal advisers had had only 3 days to prepare the evidence and the case was one that was difficult by reason of the fact that it dealt with children of dual nationality. The court held that, in appropriate cases, the *Ladd v Marshall* rules should be relaxed where the welfare of children required the court to see additional evidence.

Applicant's reply—The applicant has 7 days after service of the respondent's evidence to file and serve a statement in reply, which also must be verified by a statement of truth, together with any further evidence on which the applicant intends to rely.

12.51 Adjournment

The court will not adjourn the hearing of an application to which this section applies for more than 21 days at any one time.

Adjournment—In any application for an adjournment, the court will be mindful that it may be required to give reasons for any delay beyond 6 weeks in reaching a decision under CACA 1985, Sch 1, Art 11. Once a draft judgment has been sent out, the sealed order must be sent out with expedition (*Re M (Child Abduction: Delay)* (2007) *The Times* August 28). Brussels IIA, Art 11 requires the court, save where exceptional circumstances make this impossible, to issue its judgment within 6 weeks of the issue of the application. See further *Emergency Proceedings in the Family Courts* (Jordan Publishing Ltd).

12.52 Stay of proceedings upon notification of wrongful removal etc.

(1) In this rule and in rule 12.53 –

    (a) "relevant authority" means –

        (i) the High Court;

        (ii) a county court;

        (iii) a magistrates' court;

        (iv) the Court of Session;

        (v) a sheriff court;

        (vi) a children's hearing within the meaning of section 93 of the Children (Scotland) Act 1995;

(vii) the High Court in Northern Ireland;
(viii) a county court in Northern Ireland;
(ix) a court of summary jurisdiction in Northern Ireland;
(x) the Royal Court of Jersey;
(xi) a court of summary jurisdiction in Jersey;
(xii) the High Court of Justice of the Isle of Man;
(xiii) a court of summary jurisdiction in the Isle of Man; or
(xiv) the Secretary of State; and
(b) "rights of custody" has the same meaning as in the 1980 Hague Convention.

(2) Where a party to proceedings under the 1980 Hague Convention knows that an application relating to the merits of rights of custody is pending in or before a relevant authority, that party must file within the proceedings under the 1980 Hague Convention a concise statement of the nature of that application, including the relevant authority in or before which it is pending.

(3) On receipt of a statement filed in accordance with paragraph (2) above, a court officer will notify the relevant authority in or before which the application is pending and will subsequently notify the relevant authority of the result of the proceedings.

(4) On receipt by the relevant authority of a notification under paragraph (3) from the High Court or equivalent notification from the Court of Session, the High Court in Northern Ireland or the High Court of Justice of the Isle of Man –

(a) all further proceedings in the action will be stayed(GL) unless and until the proceedings under the 1980 Hague Convention in the High Court, Court of Session, the High Court in Northern Ireland or the High Court of Justice of the Isle of Man are dismissed; and
(b) the parties to the action will be notified by the court officer of the stay(GL) and dismissal.

Defined terms—"court officer": r 2.3.

Scope of the provision—This provision ensures that parties notify the court dealing with an application under the 1980 Convention of any other proceedings that may be pending in any other court and that such court stays the proceedings before it until the 1980 Convention proceedings have been concluded.

12.53 Stay of proceedings where application made under s 16 of the 1985 Act (registration of decisions under the European Convention)

(1) A person who –

(a) is a party to –
(i) proceedings under section 16 of the 1985 Act; or
(ii) proceedings as a result of which a decision relating to custody has been registered under section 16 of the 1985 Act; and
(b) knows that an application is pending under –
(i) section 20(2) of the 1985 Act;
(ii) Article 21(2) of the Child Abduction and Custody (Jersey) Law 2005; or
(iii) section 42(2) of the Child Custody Act 1987 (an Act of Tynwald),

must file within the proceedings under section 16 of the 1985 Act a concise statement of the nature of the pending application.

(2) On receipt of a statement filed in accordance with paragraph (1) above, a court officer will notify the relevant authority in or before which the application is pending and will subsequently notify the relevant authority of the result of the proceedings.

(3) On receipt by the relevant authority of a notification under paragraph (2) from the High Court or equivalent notification from the Court of Session, the High Court in Northern Ireland or the High Court of Justice of the Isle of Man, the court officer will notify the parties to the action.

Defined terms—"relevant authority": FPR 2010, r 12.52(1); "court officer": FPR 2010, r 2.3.

Scope—This rule makes similar provisions to those under FPR 2010, r 12.52 in relation to an application made for registration of decisions under the European Convention.

12.54 Transfer of proceedings

(1) At any stage in proceedings under the 1985 Act the court may –

    (a)   of its own initiative; or

    (b)   on the application of a party with a minimum of two days' notice;

order that the proceedings be transferred to a court listed in paragraph (4).

(2) Where the court makes an order for transfer under paragraph (1) –

    (a)   the court will state its reasons on the face of the order;

    (b)   a court officer will send a copy of the order, the application and the accompanying documents (if any) and any evidence to the court to which the proceedings are transferred; and

    (c)   the costs of the proceedings both before and after the transfer will be at the discretion of the court to which the proceedings are transferred.

(3) Where proceedings are transferred to the High Court from a court listed in paragraph (4), a court officer will notify the parties of the transfer and the proceedings will continue as if they had been commenced in the High Court.

(4) The listed courts are the Court of Session, the High Court in Northern Ireland, the Royal Court of Jersey or the High Court of Justice of the Isle of Man.

Scope—Rule 12.54(2) makes it clear that the court must state its reason for the transfer on the face of the order.

"two days' notice"—The court has power to dispense with service of an application under FPR 2010, r 12.48 or abridge time under its case management powers contained in r 4.1. As to computation of time, see FPR 2010, r 2.3.

12.55 Revocation and variation of registered decisions

(1) This rule applies to decisions which –

    (a)   have been registered under section 16 of the 1985 Act; and

    (b)   are subsequently varied or revoked by an authority in the Contracting State in which they were made.

(2) The court will, on cancelling the registration of a decision which has been revoked, notify –

    (a)   the person appearing to the court to have care of the child;

    (b)   the person on whose behalf the application for registration of the decision was made; and

    (c)   any other party to the application.

(3) The court will, on being informed of the variation of a decision, notify –

    (a)   the party appearing to the court to have care of the child; and

    (b)   any party to the application for registration of the decision;

and any such person may apply to make representations to the court before the registration is varied.

PART III

(4) Any person appearing to the court to have an interest in the proceedings may apply for the registration of a decision for the cancellation or variation of the decision referred to in paragraph (1).

Scope—This rule should be read together with CACA 1985, s 17, which places a duty on the person on whose behalf the application for registration was made to notify the court in which the decision of the variation or revocation is registered. Where the decision is revoked, the court will cancel the registration and will give notice to the parties of the cancellation. There is no provision for the parties to make representations before cancellation takes place. In a case where the decision has been varied, the court will notify the parties and they have the right to make representations before the registration is varied. In addition, under r 12.55(4) any person who has an interest in the matter is given the right to apply for the registration of a variation or the cancellation of a decision that has been registered under CACA 1985, s 16.

12.56 The central index of decisions registered under the 1985 Act

A central index of decisions registered under section 16 of the 1985 Act, together with any variation of those decisions made under section 17 of that Act, will be kept by the principal registry.

Central index—This provision was introduced to keep a record of such decisions.

12.57 Disclosure of information in proceedings under the European Convention

At any stage in proceedings under the European Convention the court may, if it has reason to believe that any person may have relevant information about the child who is the subject of those proceedings, order that person to disclose such information and may for that purpose order that the person attend before it or file affidavit$^{(GL)}$ evidence.

Defined terms—"child": CACA 1985, Sch 2, Art 1(a) and FPR 2010, r 2.3; "European Convention" CACA 1985, s 12(1) and FPR 2010, r 2.3.

Scope—This rule reinforces the provisions of CACA 1985, s 24A. A person is not excused from complying with an order under s 24A on the ground that to do so may incriminate him or his spouse of an offence (s 24A(2)). A statement or admission made in compliance with such an order will not be admissible in evidence against the person or his spouse in proceedings for any offence other than perjury. The court has power to order the attendance of a witness (see FPR 2010, r 24 and FPR PD24A, para 1) to give information about the whereabouts of a child (see *Re D (A Minor) (Child Abduction) Note* [1989] 1 FLR 97). Where an order for disclosure is made, the form of order should provide for the disclosure of "all information possessed by [the named person] as to the past movements and present whereabouts of the child or of the defendant" (see *Re D*, above, at [100]).

"in proceedings under the European Convention"—This rule applies only to proceedings under the European Convention, although CACA 1985, s 24A applies to proceedings under both Conventions.

Section 2
Applications relating to the Council Regulation and the 1996 Hague Convention

Scope—Part 12, Ch 6, s 2 makes provision for certain applications under Brussels IIA and the Hague Convention 1996:

(a) Procedure under Brussels IIA, art 11(6), where a non-return order has been made under the Hague Convention 1980, art 13 (FPR 2010, r 12.59);
(b) Procedure under Brussels IIA, art 11(7), where a non-return order made under the Hague Convention 1980, art 13 by a court in another Member State is received (FPR 2010, r 12.60);
(c) Transfer of proceedings under Brussels IIA, art 15 or the Hague Convention 1996, arts 8 and 9 (FPR 2010, rr 12.61–12.65 and 12.67 (service of order or request relating to transfer));
(d) Request from another Member/Contracting State to assume jurisdiction in relation to a child (FPR 2010, r 12.66);

(e) Questions as to the court's jurisdiction under Brussels IIA, arts 16–18 or whether proceedings should be stayed under Brussels IIA, art 19 or the Hague Convention 1996, art 13 (FPR 2010, r 12.68);

(f) Request for consultation on or consent to the contemplated placement of a child in England and Wales under Brussels IIA, art 56 or the Hague Convention 1996, art 33 (FPR 2010, r 12.69);

(g) Request made by court in England or Wales for consultation on or consent to the contemplated placement of a child in another Member/Contracting State under Brussels IIA, art 56 or the Hague Convention 1996, art 33 (FPR 2010, r 12.70); and

(h) Application for a declaration regarding parental responsibility under the Hague Convention 1996, art 16 (FPR 2010, r 12.71).

References should be made to the annotations to Brussels IIA and to the Hague Convention 1996, both in Part VI.

12.58 Interpretation

(1) In this section –

...

"Contracting State" means a State party to the 1996 Hague Convention;

"domestic Central Authority" means –

    (a) where the matter relates to the Council Regulation, the Lord Chancellor;

    (b) where the matter relates to the 1996 Hague Convention in England, the Lord Chancellor;

    (c) where the matter relates to the 1996 Hague Convention in Wales, the Welsh Ministers;

"judgment" has the meaning given in Article 2(4) of the Council Regulation;

"Member State" means a Member State bound by the Council Regulation or a country which has subsequently adopted the Council Regulation;

"parental responsibility" has the meaning given in –

    (a) Article 2(7) of the Council Regulation in relation to proceedings under that Regulation; and

    (b) Article 1(2) of the 1996 Hague Convention in relation to proceedings under that Convention; and

"seised" has the meaning given in Article 16 of the Council Regulation.

(2) In rules 12.59 to 12.70, references to the court of another member State or Contracting State include authorities within the meaning of "court" in Article 2(1) of the Council Regulation, and authorities of Contracting States which have jurisdiction to take measures directed to the protection of the person or property of the child within the meaning of the 1996 Hague Convention.

Amendments—SI 2012/2046.

12.59 Procedure under Article 11(6) of the Council Regulation where the court makes a non-return order under Article 13 of the 1980 Hague Convention

(1) Where the court makes an order for the non-return of a child under Article 13 of the 1980 Hague Convention, it must immediately transmit the documents referred to in Article 11(6) of the Council Regulation –

    (a) directly to the court with jurisdiction or the central authority in the Member State where the child was habitually resident immediately before the wrongful removal to, or wrongful retention in, England and Wales; or

    (b) to the domestic Central Authority for onward transmission to the court with jurisdiction or the central authority in the other Member State mentioned in sub-paragraph (a).

(2) The documents required by paragraph (1) must be transmitted by a method which, in the case of direct transmission to the court with jurisdiction in the other Member State, ensures and, in any other case, will not prevent, their receipt by that court within one month of the date of the non-return order.

Amendments—SI 2012/2046.

12.60 Procedure under Article 11(7) of the Council Regulation where the court receives a non-return order made under Article 13 of the 1980 Hague Convention by a court in another Member State

(1) This rule applies where the court receives an order made by a court in another Member State for the non-return of a child.

(2) In this rule, the order for non-return of the child and the papers transmitted with that order from the court in the other Member State are referred to as "the non-return order".

(3) Where, at the time of receipt of the non-return order, the court is already seised of a question of parental responsibility in relation to the child, –

   (a)   the court officer shall immediately –
      (i)   serve copies of the non-return order on each party to the proceedings in which a question of parental responsibility in relation to the child is at issue; and
      (ii) where the non-return order was received directly from the court or the central authority in the other Member State, transmit to the domestic Central Authority a copy of the non-return order.
   (b)   the court shall immediately invite the parties to the 1980 Hague Convention proceedings to file written submissions in respect of the question of custody by a specified date, or to attend a hearing to consider the future conduct of the proceedings in the light of the non-return order.

(4) Where, at the time of receipt of the non-return order, the court is not already seised of the question of parental responsibility in relation to the child, it shall immediately –

   (a)   open a court file in respect of the child and assign a court reference to the file;
   (b)   serve a copy of the non-return order on each party to the proceedings before the court in the Member State which made that order;
   (c)   invite each party to file, within 3 months of notification to that party of receipt of the non-return order, submissions in the form of –
      (i)   an application for an order under –
         (aa) the 1989 Act; or
         (bb) (in the High Court only) an application under the inherent jurisdiction in respect of the child; or
      (ii) where permission is required to make an application for the order in question, an application for that permission;
   (d)   where the non-return order was received directly from the court or central authority in the other Member State, transmit to the domestic Central Authority a copy of the non-return order.

(5) In a case to which paragraph (4) applies where no application is filed within the 3 month period provided for by paragraph (4)(c) the court must close its file in respect of the child.

      (Enforcement of a subsequent judgment requiring the return of the child, made under Article 11(8) by a court examining custody of the child under Article 11(7), is dealt with in Part 31 below.)

Amendments—SI 2012/2046.

12.61 Transfer of proceedings under Article 15 of the Council Regulation or under Article 8 of the 1996 Hague Convention

(1) Where the court is considering the transfer of proceedings to the court of another Member State or Contracting State under rules 12.62 to 12.64 it will –

(a) fix a date for a hearing for the court to consider the question of transfer; and
(b) give directions as to the manner in which the parties may make representations.

(2) The court may, with the consent of all parties, deal with the question of transfer without a hearing.

(3) Directions which are in force immediately prior to the transfer of proceedings to a court in another Member State or Contracting State under rules 12.62 to 12.64 will continue to apply until the court in that other State accepts jurisdiction in accordance with the provisions of the Council Regulation or the 1996 Hague Convention (as appropriate), subject to any variation or revocation of the directions.

(4) The court or court officer will –

(a) take a note of the giving, variation or revocation of directions under this rule; and
(b) as soon as practicable serve a copy of the directions order on every party.

(5) A register of all applications and requests for transfer of jurisdiction to or from another Member State or Contracting State will be kept by the principal registry.

12.62 Application by a party for transfer of the proceedings

(1) A party may apply to the court under Article 15(1) of the Council Regulation or under Article 8(1) of the 1996 Hague Convention –

(a) to stay^(GL) the proceedings or a specified part of the proceedings and to invite the parties to introduce a request before a court of another Member State or Contracting State; or
(b) to make a request to a court of another Member State or another Contracting State to assume jurisdiction for the proceedings, or a specified part of the proceedings.

(2) An application under paragraph (1) must be made –

(a) to the court in which the relevant parental responsibility proceedings are pending; and
(b) using the Part 18 procedure.

(3) The applicant must file the application notice and serve it on the respondents –

(a) where the application is also made under Article 11 of the Council Regulation, not less than 5 days, and
(b) in any other case, not less than 42 days,

before the hearing of the application.

12.63 Application by a court of another Member State or another Contracting State for transfer of the proceedings

(1) This rule applies where a court of another Member State or another Contracting State makes an application under Article 15(2)(c) of the Council Regulation or under Article 9 of the 1996 Hague Convention that the court having jurisdiction in relation to the proceedings transfer the proceedings or a specific part of the proceedings to the applicant court.

(2) When the court receives the application, the court officer will –

(a) as soon as practicable, notify the domestic Central Authority of the application; and

(b) serve the application, and notice of the hearing on all other parties in England and Wales not less than 5 days before the hearing of the application.

Amendments—SI 2012/2046.

12.64 Exercise by the court of its own initiative of powers to seek to transfer the proceedings

(1) The court having jurisdiction in relation to the proceedings may exercise its powers of its own initiative under Article 15 of the Council Regulation or Article 8 of the 1996 Hague Convention in relation to the proceedings or a specified part of the proceedings.

(2) Where the court proposes to exercise its powers, the court officer will give the parties not less than 5 days' notice of the hearing.

12.65 Application to High Court to make request under Article 15 of the Council Regulation or Article 9 of the 1996 Hague Convention to request transfer of jurisdiction

(1) An application for the court to request transfer of jurisdiction in a matter concerning a child from another Member State or another Contracting State under Article 15 of the Council Regulation, or Article 9 of the 1996 Hague Convention (as the case may be) must be made to the principal registry and heard in the High Court.

(2) An application must be made without notice to any other person and the court may give directions about joining any other party to the application.

(3) Where there is agreement between the court and the court or competent authority to which the request under paragraph (1) is made to transfer the matter to the courts of England and Wales, the court will consider with that other court or competent authority the specific timing and conditions for the transfer.

(4) Upon receipt of agreement to transfer jurisdiction from the court or other competent authority in the Member State, or Contracting State to which the request has been made, the court officer will serve on the applicant a notice that jurisdiction has been accepted by the courts of England and Wales.

(5) The applicant must attach the notice referred to in subparagraph (3) to any subsequent application in relation to the child.

(6) Nothing in this rule requires an application with respect to a child commenced following a transfer of jurisdiction to be made to or heard in the High Court.

(7) Upon allocation, the court to which the proceedings are allocated must immediately fix a directions hearing to consider the future conduct of the case.

12.66 Procedure where the court receives a request from the authorities of another Member State or Contracting State to assume jurisdiction in a matter concerning a child

(1) Where any court other than the High Court receives a request to assume jurisdiction in a matter concerning a child from a court or other authority which has jurisdiction in another Member State or Contracting State, that court must immediately refer the request to a Judge of the High Court for a decision regarding acceptance of jurisdiction to be made.

(2) Upon the High Court agreeing to the request under paragraph (1), the court officer will notify the parties to the proceedings before the other Member State or Contracting State of that decision, and the case must be allocated as if the application had been made in England and Wales.

(3) Upon allocation, the court to which the proceedings are allocated must immediately fix a directions hearing to consider the future conduct of the case.

(4) The court officer will serve notice of the directions hearing on all parties to the proceedings in the other Member State or Contracting State no later than 5 days before the date of that hearing.

12.67 Service of the court's order or request relating to transfer of jurisdiction under the Council Regulation or the 1996 Hague Convention

The court officer will serve an order or request relating to transfer of jurisdiction on all parties, the Central Authority of the other Member State or Contracting State, and the domestic Central Authority.

Amendments—SI 2012/2046.

12.68 Questions as to the court's jurisdiction or whether the proceedings should be stayed

(1) If at any time after issue of the application it appears to the court that under any of Articles 16 to 18 of the Council Regulation it does not or may not have jurisdiction to hear an application, or that under Article 19 of the Council Regulation or Article 13 of the 1996 Hague Convention it is or may be required to stay$^{(GL)}$ the proceedings or to decline jurisdiction, the court must –

    (a)   stay$^{(GL)}$ the proceedings; and

    (b)   fix a date for a hearing to determine jurisdiction or whether there should be a stay$^{(GL)}$ or other order.

(2) The court officer will serve notice of the hearing referred to at paragraph (1)(b) on the parties to the proceedings.

(3) The court must, in writing –

    (a)   give reasons for its decision under paragraph (1); and

    (b)   where it makes a finding of fact, state such finding.

(4) The court may with the consent of all the parties deal with any question as to the jurisdiction of the court, or as to whether the proceedings should be stayed$^{(GL)}$, without a hearing.

12.69 Request for consultation as to contemplated placement of child in England and Wales

(1) This rule applies to a request made –

    (a)   under Article 56 of the Council Regulation, by a court in another Member State; or

    (b)   under Article 33 of the 1996 Hague Convention by a court in another Contracting State

for consultation on or consent to the contemplated placement of a child in England and Wales.

PART III

(2) Where the court receives a request directly from a court in another Member State or Contracting State, the court shall, as soon as practicable after receipt of the request, notify the domestic Central Authority of the request and take the appropriate action under paragraph (4).

(3) Where it appears to the court officer that no proceedings relating to the child are pending before a court in England and Wales, the court officer must inform the domestic Central Authority of that fact and forward to the Central Authority all documents relating to the request sent by the court in the other Member State or Contracting State.

(4) Where the court receives a request forwarded by the domestic Central Authority, the court must, as soon as practicable after receipt of the request, either –

(a)   where proceedings relating to the child are pending before the court, fix a directions hearing; or

(b)   where proceedings relating to the child are pending before another court in England and Wales, send a copy of the request to that court.

Amendments—SI 2012/2046.

12.70 Request made by court in England and Wales for consultation as to contemplated placement of child in another Member State or Contracting State

(1) This rule applies where the court is contemplating the placement of a child in another Member State under Article 56 of the Council Regulation or another Contracting State under Article 33 of the 1996 Hague Convention, and proposes to send a request for consultation with or for the consent of the central authority or other authority having jurisdiction in the other State in relation to the contemplated placement.

(2) In this rule, a reference to "the request" includes a reference to a report prepared for purposes of Article 33 of the 1996 Hague Convention where the request is made under that Convention.

(3) Where the court sends the request directly to the central authority or other authority having jurisdiction in the other State, it shall at the same time send a copy of the request to the domestic Central Authority.

(4) The court may send the request to the domestic Central Authority for onward transmission to the central authority or other authority having jurisdiction in the other Member State.

(5) The court should give consideration to the documents which should accompany the request.

> (See Chapters 1 to 3 of this Part generally, for the procedure governing applications for an order under paragraph 19(1) of Schedule 2 to the 1989 Act permitting a local authority to arrange for any child in its care to live outside England and Wales.)

> (Part 14 sets out the procedure governing applications for an order under section 84 (giving parental responsibility prior to adoption abroad) of the Adoption and Children Act 2002.)

Amendments—SI 2012/2046.

12.71 Application for a declaration as to the extent, or existence, of parental responsibility in relation to a child under Article 16 of the 1996 Hague Convention

(1) Any interested person may apply for a declaration –

(a)   that a person has, or does not have, parental responsibility for a child; or

(b) as to the extent of a person's parental responsibility for a child,

where the question arises by virtue of the application of Article 16 of the 1996 Hague Convention.

(2) An application for a declaration as to the extent, or existence of a person's parental responsibility for a child by virtue of Article 16 of the 1996 Hague Convention must be made in the principal registry and heard in the High Court.

(3) An application for a declaration referred to in paragraph (1) may not be made where the question raised is otherwise capable of resolution in any other family proceedings in respect of the child.

Chapter 7
Communication of Information: Children Proceedings

Amendments—SI 2012/3061.

12.72 Interpretation

In this Chapter "independent reviewing officer" means a person appointed in respect of a child in accordance with regulation 2A of the Review of Children's Cases Regulations 1991, or regulation 3 of the Review of Children's Cases (Wales) Regulations 2007.

Amendments—SI 2012/679.

12.73 Communication of information: general

(1) For the purposes of the law relating to contempt of court, information relating to proceedings held in private (whether or not contained in a document filed with the court) may be communicated –

    (a) where the communication is to –
        (i) a party;
        (ii) the legal representative of a party;
        (iii) a professional legal adviser;
        (iv) an officer of the service or a Welsh family proceedings officer;
        (v) the welfare officer;
        (vi) the Director of Legal Aid Casework (within the meaning of section 4 of the Legal Aid, Sentencing and Punishment of Offenders Act 2012);
        (vii) an expert whose instruction by a party has been authorised by the court for the purposes of the proceedings;
        (viii) a professional acting in furtherance of the protection of children;
        (ix) an independent reviewing officer appointed in respect of a child who is, or has been, subject to proceedings to which this rule applies;
    (b) where the court gives permission; or
    (c) subject to any direction of the court, in accordance with rule 12.75 and Practice Direction 12G.

(2) Nothing in this Chapter permits the communication to the public at large, or any section of the public, of any information relating to the proceedings.

(3) Nothing in rule 12.75 and Practice Direction 12G permits the disclosure of an unapproved draft judgment handed down by any court.

Amendments—SI 2013/534, subject to savings.

General communication—There is no limitation on the communication of information to those people or bodies specified in r 12.73(1)(a).

PART III

Court prohibition or limitation—The wider communication of information relating to the proceedings as permitted by r 12.73 is subject to the direction of the court prohibiting or limiting the disclosure of information that would otherwise be permitted by the rules: r 12.73(1)(c). However, the power to prohibit or limit disclosure should be exercised with caution and only in limited circumstances because (i) the 2010 Rules represent a dramatic and radical change in the law, giving effect to a new public policy that it is not for the judges to whittle away, and (ii) the balance struck by r 12.73 plainly meets the requirements mandated by the Strasbourg court, even though it contains no requirement for prior judicial sanction: *Re N (Family Proceedings: Disclosure)* [2009] 2 FLR 1152. In undertaking the balancing exercise, it is essential that the court has regard to the various human rights to be protected, particularly Art 8 of the Convention; the welfare of the children, although important, is not paramount: *Lewisham LBC v D (Local Authority Disclosure of DNA Samples to Police)* [2011] 1 FLR 895.

Professional legal adviser—Bodey J has held that the phrase "professional legal adviser" includes a solicitor representing a party to family proceedings in related criminal proceedings: *Re B (A Child) (Disclosure of Evidence in Care Proceedings)* [2012] 1 FLR 142. For the avoidance of any doubt, this provision does not apply to disclosure sought by the police.

Routine disclosure of experts' reports—The President has observed that he would like to see a practice develop in which expert reports would be routinely disclosed: the practice would aid the need for the family justice system to be as transparent as possible and encourage informed debate about the quality and content of expert evidence: *Re X, Y and Z (Expert Witness)* [2011] 2 FLR 1437.

Release of information—In exceptional cases, the court may permit the disclosure of information into the public domain about the proceedings to correct inaccurate or false versions of events given by a party to the proceedings: *Doncaster MBC v Haigh, Tune and X (by the Children's Guardian)* [2012] 1 FLR 577.

12.74 (revoked)

12.75 Communication of information for purposes connected with the proceedings

(1) A party or the legal representative of a party, on behalf of and upon the instructions of that party, may communicate information relating to the proceedings to any person where necessary to enable that party –

    (a) by confidential discussion, to obtain support, advice or assistance in the conduct of the proceedings;

    (b) to engage in mediation or other forms of alternative dispute resolution;

    (c) to make and pursue a complaint against a person or body concerned in the proceedings; or

    (d) to make and pursue a complaint regarding the law, policy or procedure relating to a category of proceedings to which this Part applies.

(2) Where information is communicated to any person in accordance with paragraph (1)(a) of this rule, no further communication by that person is permitted.

(3) When information relating to the proceedings is communicated to any person in accordance with paragraphs (1)(b), (c) or (d) of this rule –

    (a) the recipient may communicate that information to a further recipient, provided that –

        (i) the party who initially communicated the information consents to that further communication; and

        (ii) the further communication is made only for the purpose or purposes for which the party made the initial communication; and

    (b) the information may be successively communicated to and by further recipients on as many occasions as may be necessary to fulfil the purpose for which the information was initially communicated, provided that on each such occasion the conditions in sub-paragraph (a) are met.

The safeguards—This rule introduces sweeping changes to the disclosure of information without the prior sanction of the court, especially r 12.75(1)(c),(d). Nevertheless, the rules contain safeguards against the improper dissemination of information relating to the proceedings –

(i) the communication of the information must be "necessary", which in "the Strasbourg sense, has a meaning lying somewhere between 'essential' or 'indispensable', on the one hand, and 'useful', 'reasonable' or 'desirable' on the other hand": *Spencer v Spencer* [2009] 2 FLR 1416 at [31];

(ii) r 12.75(3) imposes limitations on the use to which disclosed information may be put and to whom it may be further communicated; and

(iii) the third limitation and safeguard – and this is fundamental – is that imposed by r 12.73(2), namely that communication to the public at large, or any section of the public, is permitted.

See *Re N (A Child)* (above) at [64]–[70] and *Lewisham LBC v D (Local Authority Disclosure of DNA Samples to Police)* [2011] 1 FLR 895.

Contempt of court—It may no longer be necessary to obtain prior judicial sanction for disclosures permitted by r 12.75, but someone communicating information in circumstances that would otherwise involve a contempt of court because of the operation of the AJA 1960, s 12, will be able to rely on FPR 2010, Pt 12, Ch 7 and FPR PD12G as disapplying s 12, and thus as exonerating him from the penalties of contempt, only if s 12(4) of the 1960 Act applies, that is, if he has acted in a manner "authorised" by FPR 2010, Pt 12, Ch 7 and/or FPR PD12G.

Practice Direction 12A – Public Law Proceedings Guide to Case Management: April 2010

This Practice Direction supplements FPR Part 12

Scope

1.1 This Practice Direction applies to care and supervision proceedings. In so far as practicable, it is to be applied to all other Public Law Proceedings.

1.2 This Practice Direction replaces Practice Direction Guide to Case Management in Public Law Proceedings dated April 2008.

1.3 This Practice Direction will come into effect on 6 April 2010. The new form of application for a care or supervision order (Form C110) only applies to proceedings commenced on or after 6 April 2010. Subject to this it is intended that this Practice Direction should apply in so far as practicable to applications made and not disposed of before 6 April 2010. In relation to these applications –

(1) the Practice Direction Guide to Case Management in Public Law Proceedings dated April 2008 applies where it is not practicable to apply this Practice Direction; and

(2) the court may give directions relating to the application of this Practice Direction or the April 2008 Practice Direction. This is subject to the overriding objective below and to the proviso that such a direction will neither cause further delay nor involve repetition of steps already taken or decisions already made in the case.

1.4 This Practice Direction is to be read with the rules and is subject to them.

1.5 A Glossary of terms is at paragraph 26.

Note—For *PD Guide to Case Management in Public Law Proceedings* dated April 2008 see *The Family Court Practice 2009*.

The overriding objective

2.1 This Practice Direction has the overriding objective of enabling the court to deal with cases justly, having regard to the welfare issues involved. Dealing with a case justly includes, so far as is practicable –

(1)   ensuring that it is dealt with expeditiously and fairly;
(2)   dealing with the case in ways which are proportionate to the nature, importance and complexity of the issues;
(3)   ensuring that the parties are on an equal footing;
(4)   saving expense; and
(5)   allotting to it an appropriate share of the court's resources, while taking into account the need to allot resources to other cases.

APPLICATION BY THE COURT OF THE OVERRIDING OBJECTIVE

2.2 The court must seek to give effect to the overriding objective when it –

(1)   exercises the case management powers referred to in this Practice Direction; or
(2)   interprets any provision of this Practice Direction.

DUTY OF THE PARTIES

2.3 The parties are required to help the court further the overriding objective.

Court case management

The main principles

3.1 The main principles underlying court case management and the means of the court furthering the overriding objective in Public Law Proceedings are –

(1)   **Timetable for the Child**: each case will have a timetable for the proceedings set by the court in accordance with the Timetable for the Child;
(2)   **judicial continuity**: each case will be allocated to one or not more than two case management judges (in the case of magistrates' courts, case managers), who will be responsible for every case management stage in the proceedings through to the Final Hearing and, in relation to the High Court or county court, one of whom may be – and where possible should be – the judge who will conduct the Final Hearing;
(3)   **main case management tools**: each case will be managed by the court by using the appropriate main case management tools;
(4)   **active case management**: each case will be actively case managed by the court with a view at all times to furthering the overriding objective;
(5)   **consistency**: each case will, so far as compatible with the overriding objective, be managed in a consistent way and using the standardised steps provided for in this Direction.

The main case management tools

THE TIMETABLE FOR THE CHILD

3.2 The "Timetable for the Child" is defined by the rules as the timetable set by the court in accordance with its duties under section 1 and 32 of the 1989 Act and shall –

(1)   take into account dates of the significant steps in the life of the child who is the subject of the proceedings; and
(2)   be appropriate for that child. The court will set the timetable for the

proceedings in accordance with the Timetable for the Child and review this Timetable regularly. Where adjustments are made to the Timetable for the Child, the timetable for the proceedings will have to be reviewed. The Timetable for the Child is to be considered at every stage of the proceedings and whenever the court is asked to make directions whether at a hearing or otherwise.

3.3 The steps in the child's life which are to be taken into account by the court when setting the Timetable for the Child include not only legal steps but also social, care, health and education steps.

3.4 Examples of the dates the court will record and take into account when setting the Timetable for the Child are the dates of –

(1) any formal review by the Local Authority of the case of a looked after child (within the meaning of section 22(1) of the 1989 Act);

(2) the child taking up a place at a new school;

(3) any review by the Local Authority of any statement of the child's special educational needs;

(4) any assessment by a paediatrician or other specialist;

(5) the outcome of any review of Local Authority plans for the child, for example, any plans for permanence through adoption, Special Guardianship or placement with parents or relatives;

(6) any change or proposed change of the child's placement.

3.5 Due regard should be paid to the Timetable for the Child to ensure that the court remains child-focused throughout the progress of Public Law Proceedings and that any procedural steps proposed under the Public Law Outline are considered in the context of significant events in the child's life.

3.6 The applicant is required to provide the information needed about the significant steps in the child's life in the Application Form and to update this information regularly taking into account information received from others involved in the child's life such as other parties, members of the child's family, the person who is caring for the child, the children's guardian and the child's key social worker.

3.7 Before setting the timetable for the proceedings the factors which the court will consider will include the need to give effect to the overriding objective and the timescales in the Public Law Outline by which the steps in the Outline are to be taken. Where possible, the timetable for the proceedings should be in line with those timescales. However, there will be cases where the significant steps in the child's life demand that the steps in the proceedings be taken at times which are outside the timescales set out in the Outline. In those cases the timetable for the proceedings may not adhere to one or more of the timescales set out in the Outline.

3.8 Where more than one child is the subject of the proceedings, the court should consider and may set a Timetable for the Child for each child. The children may not all have the same Timetable, and the court will consider the appropriate progress of the proceedings in relation to each child.

3.9 Where there are parallel care proceedings and criminal proceedings against a person connected with the child for a serious offence against the child, linked directions hearings should where practicable take place as the case progresses. The timing of the proceedings in a linked care and criminal case should appear in the Timetable for the Child.

PART III

CASE MANAGEMENT DOCUMENTATION

3.10 Case Management Documentation includes the –

    (1)   Application Form and Annex Documents;
    (2)   Case Analysis and Recommendations provided by Cafcass or CAFCASS CYMRU;
    (3)   Local Authority Case Summary;
    (4)   Other Parties' Case Summaries.

3.11 The court will encourage the use of the Case Management Documentation which is not prescribed by the rules.

THE CASE MANAGEMENT RECORD

3.12 The court's filing system for the case will be known as the Case Management Record and will include the following main documents –

    (1)   the Case Management Documentation;
    (2)   Standard Directions on Issue and on First Appointment;
    (3)   Case Management Orders approved by the court.

3.13 Parties or their legal representatives will be expected to retain their own record containing copies of the documents on the court's Case Management Record.

THE FIRST APPOINTMENT

3.14 The purpose of the First Appointment is to confirm allocation of the case and give initial case management directions.

THE CASE MANAGEMENT ORDER

3.15 The Case Management Order is an order which will be made by the court at the conclusion of the Case Management Conference, the Issues Resolution Hearing and any other case management hearing. It is designed to achieve active case management as defined in paragraph 3.20 below. The parties are required to prepare and submit to the court a draft of this order in accordance with paragraphs 5.8 to 5.10 below. The order will include such of the provisions referred to in the Glossary at paragraph 26(12) as are appropriate to the proceedings.

ADVOCATES' MEETING/DISCUSSION

3.16 The court will consider directing advocates to have discussions before the Case Management Conference and the Issues Resolution Hearing. Advocates may well find that the best way to have these discussions is to meet. Such discussion is intended to facilitate agreement and to narrow the issues for the court to consider. Advocates and litigants in person may take part in the Advocates' Meeting or discussions.

THE CASE MANAGEMENT CONFERENCE

3.17 In each case there will be a Case Management Conference to enable the case management judge or case manager, with the co-operation of the parties, actively to manage the case and, at the earliest practicable opportunity to –

    (1)   identify the relevant and key issues; and
    (2)   give full case management directions including confirming the Timetable for the Child.

THE ISSUES RESOLUTION HEARING

3.18 In each case there will be an Issues Resolution Hearing before the Final Hearing
to –

(1)   identify any remaining key issues; and

(2)   as far as possible, resolve or narrow those issues.

ACTIVE CASE MANAGEMENT

3.19 The court must further the overriding objective by actively managing cases.

3.20 Active case management includes –

(1)   identifying the Timetable for the Child;

(2)   identifying the appropriate court to conduct the proceedings and transferring
the proceedings as early as possible to that court;

(3)   encouraging the parties to co-operate with each other in the conduct of the
proceedings;

(4)   retaining the Case Management Record;

(5)   identifying all facts and matters that are in issue at the earliest stage in the
proceedings and at each hearing;

(6)   deciding promptly which issues need full investigation and hearing and which
do not and whether a fact finding hearing is required;

(7)   deciding the order in which issues are to be resolved;

(8)   identifying at an early stage who should be a party to the proceedings;

(9)   considering whether the likely benefits of taking a particular step justify any
delay which will result and the cost of taking it;

(10) directing discussion between advocates and litigants in person before the Case
Management Conference and Issues Resolution Hearing;

(11) requiring the use of the Case Management Order and directing advocates and
litigants in person to prepare or adjust the draft of this Order where appropriate;

(12) standardising, simplifying and regulating –

(a)   the use of Case Management Documentation and forms;

(b)   the court's orders and directions;

(13) controlling –

(a)   the use and cost of experts;

(b)   the nature and extent of the documents which are to be disclosed to the
parties and presented to the court;

(c)   whether and, if so, in what manner the documents disclosed are to be
presented to the court;

(d)   the progress of the case;

(14) where it is demonstrated to be in the interests of the child, encouraging the
parties to use an alternative dispute resolution procedure if the court considers
such a procedure to be appropriate and facilitating the use of such procedure;

(15) helping the parties to reach agreement in relation to the whole or part of the
case;

(16) fixing the dates for all appointments and hearings;

(17) dealing with as many aspects of the case as it can on the same occasion;

(18) where possible dealing with additional issues which may arise from time to
time in the case without requiring the parties to attend at court;

(19) making use of technology; and

(20) giving directions to ensure that the case proceeds quickly and efficiently.

PART III

The Expectations

4.1 The expectations are that proceedings should be –

(1) conducted using the Case Management Tools and Case Management Documentation referred to in this Practice Direction in accordance with the Public Law Outline;

(2) finally determined within the timetable fixed by the court in accordance with the Timetable for the Child – the timescales in the Public Law Outline being adhered to and being taken as the maximum permissible time for the taking of the step referred to in the Outline unless the Timetable for the Child demands otherwise.

4.2 However, there may be cases where the court considers that the child's welfare requires a different approach from the one contained in the Public Law Outline. In those cases, the court will –

(1) determine the appropriate case management directions and timetable; and

(2) record on the face of the order the reasons for departing from the approach in the Public Law Outline.

How the parties should help court case management

Main methods of helping

GOOD CASE PREPARATION

5.1 The applicant should prepare the case before proceedings are issued. In care and supervision proceedings the Local Authority should use the Pre-proceedings checklist.

THE TIMETABLE FOR THE CHILD

5.2 The applicant must state in the Application Form all information concerning significant steps in the child's life that are likely to take place during the proceedings. The applicant is to be responsible for updating this information regularly and giving it to the court. The applicant will need to obtain information about these significant steps and any variations and additions to them from others involved in the child's life such as other parties, members of the child's family, the person who is caring for the child, the children's guardian and the child's key social worker. When the other persons involved in the child's life become aware of a significant step in the child's life or a variation of an existing one, that information should be given to the applicant as soon as possible.

5.3 The information about the significant steps in the child's life will enable the court to set the Timetable for the Child and to review that Timetable in the light of new information. The Timetable for the Child will be included or referred to in the draft of a Case Management Order, the Case Management Order, Standard Directions on Issue and on First Appointment and the directions given at the Case Management Conference and Issues Resolution Hearing.

CASE MANAGEMENT DOCUMENTATION

5.4 The parties must use the Case Management Documentation.

CO-OPERATION

5.5 The parties and their representatives should co-operate with the court in case management, including the fixing of timetables to avoid unacceptable delay, and in the crystallisation and resolution of the issues on which the case turns.

DIRECTIONS

5.6 The parties will –

  (1) monitor compliance with the court's directions; and
  (2) tell the court or court officer about any failure to comply with a direction of the court or any other delay in the proceedings.

THE CASE MANAGEMENT RECORD

5.7 The parties are expected to retain a record containing copies of the documents on the court's Case Management Record.

DRAFTING THE CASE MANAGEMENT ORDER

5.8 Parties should start to consider the content of the draft of the Case Management Order at the earliest opportunity either before or in the course of completing applications to the court or the response to the application. They should in any event consider the drafting of a Case Management Order after the First Appointment.

5.9 Only one draft of the Case Management Order should be filed with the court for each of the Case Management Conference and the Issues Resolution Hearing. It is the responsibility of the advocate for the applicant, which in care and supervision proceedings will ordinarily be the Local Authority, to prepare those drafts and be responsible for obtaining comments from the advocates and the parties.

5.10 There should be ongoing consideration of the Case Management Orders throughout the proceedings. The Case Management Orders should serve as an *aide memoire* to everyone involved in the proceedings of –

  (1) the Timetable for the Child;
  (2) the case management decisions;
  (3) the identified issues.

5.11 In paragraphs 5.4, 5.6 to 5.9 "parties" includes parties' legal representatives.

Findings of fact hearings

6 In a case where the court decides that a fact finding hearing is necessary, the starting point is that the proceedings leading to that hearing are to be managed in accordance with the case management steps in this Practice Direction.

Ethnicity, language, religion and culture

7 At each case management stage of the proceedings, particularly at the First Appointment and Case Management Conference, the court will consider giving directions regarding the obtaining of evidence about the ethnicity, language, religion and culture of the child and other significant persons involved in the proceedings. The court will subsequently consider the implications of this evidence for the child in the context of the issues in the case.

Adults who may be protected parties

8.1 The applicant must give details in the Application Form of any referral to or assessment by the local authority's Adult Learning Disability team (or its equivalent). The Local Authority should tell the court about other referrals or assessments if known such as a referral to Community Mental Health.

8.2 The court will investigate as soon as possible any issue as to whether an adult party or intended party to the proceedings lacks capacity (within the meaning of the Mental Capacity Act 2005) to conduct the proceedings. A representative (a litigation friend, next friend or guardian ad litem) is needed to conduct the proceedings on behalf of an adult who lacks capacity to do so ("a protected party"). The expectation of the Official Solicitor is that the Official Solicitor will only be invited to act for a protected party as guardian ad litem or litigation friend if there is no other person suitable and willing to act.

8.3 Any issue as to the capacity of an adult to conduct the proceedings must be determined before the court gives any directions relevant to that adult's role within the proceedings.

8.4 Where the adult is a protected party, that party's representative should be involved in any instruction of an expert, including the instruction of an expert to assess whether the adult, although a protected party, is competent to give evidence. The instruction of an expert is a significant step in the proceedings. The representative will wish to consider (and ask the expert to consider), if the protected party is competent to give evidence, their best interests in this regard. The representative may wish to seek advice about 'special measures'. The representative may put forward an argument on behalf of the protected party that the protected party should not give evidence.

8.5 If at any time during the proceedings, there is reason to believe that a party may lack capacity to conduct the proceedings, then the court must be notified and directions sought to ensure that this issue is investigated without delay.

Child likely to lack capacity to conduct the proceedings when aged 18

9 Where it appears that a child is –

(1)   a party to the proceedings and not the subject of them;
(2)   nearing age 18; and
(3)   considered likely to lack capacity to conduct the proceedings when 18, the court will consider giving directions relating to the investigation of a child's capacity in this respect.

Outline of the process and how to use the Main Case Management Tools

10.1 The Public Law Outline set out in the Table below contains an outline of –

(1)   the order of the different stages of the process;
(2)   the purposes of the main case management hearings and matters to be considered at them;
(3)   the latest timescales within which the main stages of the process should take place.

10.2 In the Public Law Outline –

(1)   "CMC" means the Case Management Conference;
(2)   "FA" means the First Appointment;
(3)   "IRH" means the Issues Resolution Hearing;
(4)   "LA" means the Local Authority which is applying for a care or supervision order;
(5)   "OS" means the Official Solicitor.

Public Law Outline

PRE-PROCEEDINGS	
PRE-PROCEEDINGS CHECKLIST	
Annex Documents (the documents specified in the Annex to the Application Form to be attached to that form where available): – Social Work Chronology – Initial Social Work Statement – Initial and Core Assessments – Letters Before Proceedings – Schedule of Proposed Findings – Care Plan	**Other Checklist Documents which already exist on LA's files which are to be disclosed in the event of proceedings normally before the day of the FA:** – Previous court orders & judgments/reasons – Any relevant assessment materials – Section 7 & 37 reports – Relatives & friends materials (e.g., a genogram) – Other relevant reports & records – Single, joint or inter-agency materials (e.g., health & education/Home Office & Immigration documents) – Records of discussions with the family – Key LA minutes & records for the child (including Strategy Discussion Record) – Pre-existing care plans (e.g., child in need plan, looked after child plan & child protection plan)

STAGE 1 – ISSUE AND THE FIRST APPOINTMENT	
ISSUE	**FIRST APPOINTMENT**
On DAY 1 and by DAY 3	**By DAY 6**
Objectives: To ensure compliance with pre-proceedings checklist; to allocate proceedings; to obtain the information necessary for initial case management at the FA	**Objectives: To confirm allocation; to give initial case management directions**

On Day 1:
– The LA files the Application Form and Annex Documents where available
– Court officer issues application
– Court nominates case manager(s)
– Court gives Standard Directions on Issue including:
 	
    – Pre-proceedings checklist compliance including preparation and service of any missing Annex Documents
    – Allocate and/or transfer
    – Appoint children's guardian
    – Appoint solicitor for the child
	– LA normally serves Other Checklist Documents on the parties
	– Parties notify LA & court of need for a contested hearing
	– Court makes arrangements for a contested hearing
	– Initial case management by court including:
	
	    – Confirm Timetable for the Child
	    – Confirm allocation or transfer
	    – Identify additional parties & representation (including allocation of children's guardian)
	    – Identify "Early Final Hearing" cases
	    – Scrutinise Care Plan

PART III

– Case Analysis for FA	– Court gives Standard Directions on FA including:
– Appoint a guardian ad litem or litigation friend for a protected party or any non subject child who is a party, including the OS where appropriate	– Case Analysis and Recommendations for Stages 2 & 3 – Preparation and service of any missing Annex Documents
– List FA by Day 6	– What Other Checklist Documents are to be filed
– Make arrangements for contested hearing (if necessary)	– LA Case Summary – Other Parties' Case Summaries
By Day 3 – Cafcass/CAFCASS CYMRU expected to allocate case to children's guardian – LA serves the Application Form and Annex Documents, on parties	– Parties' initial witness statements – For the Advocates' Meeting – List CMC or (if appropriate) an Early Final Hearing – Upon transfer

STAGE 2 – CASE MANAGEMENT CONFERENCE

ADVOCATES' MEETING	**CMC**
No later than 2 days before CMC	**No later than day 45**
Objectives: To prepare the Draft Case Management Order; to identify experts and draft questions for them	**Objectives: To identify issue(s); to give full case management directions**
– Consider information on the Application Form, all Other Parties' Case Summaries and Case Analysis and Recommendations	– Detailed case management by the court
– Identify proposed experts and draft questions in accordance with Experts Practice Direction – Draft Case Management Order – Notify court of need for a contested hearing – File draft of the Case Management Order with the case manager/case management judge by 11am one working day before the CMC	– Scrutinise compliance with directions – Review and confirm Timetable for the Child – Identify key issue(s) – Confirm allocation or transfer – Consider case management directions in the draft of the Case Management Order – Scrutinise Care Plan – Check compliance with Experts Practice Direction – Court issues Case Management Order – Court lists IRH and, where necessary, a warned period for Final Hearing

STAGE 3 – ISSUES RESOLUTION HEARING	
ADVOCATES' MEETING	**IRH**
Between 2 and 7 days before the IRH	**Between 16 & 25 weeks**
Objective: To prepare or update the draft Case Management Order	**Objectives: To resolve and narrow issue(s); to identify any remaining key issues**

– Consider all other parties' Case Summaries and Case Analysis and Recommendations
– Draft Case Management Order
– Notify court of need for a contested hearing/time for oral evidence to be given
– File Draft Case Management Order with the case manager/case management judge by 11am one working day before the IRH
	– Identification by the court of the key issue(s) (if any) to be determined
	
	– Final case management by the court:
	  – Scrutinise compliance with directions
	  – Review and confirm the Timetable for the Child
	  – Consider case management directions in the draft of the Case Management Order
	  – Scrutinise Care Plan
	  – Give directions for Hearing documents:
	    – Threshold agreement or facts/issues remaining to be determined
	    – Final Evidence & Care Plan
	    – Case Analysis and Recommendations
	    – Witness templates
	    – Skeleton arguments
	    – Judicial reading list/reading time/judgment writing time
	    – Time estimate
	    – Bundles Practice Direction compliance
	    – List or confirm Hearing
	– Court issues Case Management Order

STAGE 4	
HEARING	
Hearing set in accordance with the Timetable for the Child	
Objective: To determine remaining issues	
– All file & serve updated Case Management Documentation & bundle – Draft final order(s) in approved form	– Judgment/Reasons – Disclose documents as required after hearing

PART III

Starting the proceedings

PRE-PROCEEDINGS CHECKLIST

11.1 The Pre-proceedings Checklist is to be used by the applicant to help prepare for the start of the proceedings.

11.2 The Pre-proceedings Checklist contains the documents which are specified in the Annex to the Application Form. The rules require those documents which are known as the "Annex Documents" to be filed with the Application Form where available. The Annex Documents are –

(1)   Social Work Chronology;
(2)   Initial Social Work Statement;
(3)   Initial and Core Assessments;
(4)   Letters before Proceedings;
(5)   Schedule of Proposed Findings; and
(6)   Care Plan.

11.3 In addition, the Pre-proceedings Checklist contains examples of documents other than the Annex Documents which will normally be on the Local Authority file at the start of proceedings so that they can be served on parties in accordance with the Public Law Outline. These documents are known as the "Other Checklist Documents" and are not to be filed with the court at the start of the proceedings but are to be disclosed to the parties normally before the day of the First Appointment or in accordance with the court's directions and to be filed with the court only as directed by the court.

COMPLIANCE WITH PRE-PROCEEDINGS CHECKLIST

11.4 It is recognised that in some cases the circumstances are such that the safety and welfare of the child may be jeopardised if the start of proceedings is delayed until all of the documents appropriate to the case and referred to in the Pre-proceedings Checklist are available. The safety and welfare of the child should never be put in jeopardy because of lack of documentation. (Nothing in this Practice Direction affects an application for an emergency protection order under section 44 of the 1989 Act).

11.5 The court recognises that the preparation may need to be varied to suit the circumstances of the case. In cases where any of the Annex Documents required to be attached to the Application Form are not available at the time of issue of the application, the court will consider making directions on issue about when any missing documentation is to be filed. The expectation is that there will be a good reason why one or more of the documents are not available. Further directions relating to any missing documentation are likely to be made at the First Appointment. The court also recognises that some documents on the Pre-proceedings Checklist may not exist and may never exist, for example, the Section 37 report, and that in urgent proceedings no Letter Before Proceedings may have been sent.

What the court will do at the issue of proceedings

OBJECTIVES

12.1 The objectives at this stage are for the court –

(1)   to identify the Timetable for the Child;
(2)   in care and supervision proceedings, to ensure compliance with the Pre-proceedings Checklist;

(3)   to allocate proceedings;

(4)   to obtain the information necessary to enable initial case management at the First Appointment.

12.2 The steps which the court will take once proceedings have been issued include those set out in paragraphs 12.3 to 12.5 below.

ALLOCATION

12.3 By reference to the Allocation Order, the court will consider allocation of the case and transfer to the appropriate level of court those cases which are obviously suitable for immediate transfer.

Other steps to be taken by the court

DIRECTIONS

12.4 The court will –

(1)   consider giving directions –

    (a)   appropriate to the case including Standard Directions On Issue;

    (b)   in care and supervision proceedings, relating to the preparation, filing and service of any missing Annex Documents and what Other Checklist Documents are to be filed and by when;

    (c)   relating to the representation of any protected party or any child who is a party to, but is not the subject of, the proceedings by a guardian ad litem or litigation friend, including the Official Solicitor where appropriate;

(2)   appoint a children's guardian in specified proceedings (in relation to care and supervision proceedings the court will expect that Cafcass or CAFCASS CYMRU will have received notice from the Local Authority that proceedings were going to be started);

(3)   appoint a solicitor for the child under section 41(3) of the 1989 Act where appropriate;

(4)   request the children's guardian or if appropriate another officer of the service or Welsh family proceedings officer to prepare a Case Analysis and Recommendations for the First Appointment;

(5)   make arrangements for a contested hearing, if necessary.

    (A suggested form for the drafting of Standard Directions on Issue is Form PLO 8 which is available from HMCS)

SETTING A DATE FOR THE FIRST APPOINTMENT

12.5 The court will record the Timetable for the Child and set a date for the First Appointment normally no later than 6 days from the date of issue of the proceedings and in any event in line with the Timetable for the Child.

CASE MANAGERS IN THE MAGISTRATES' COURTS

12.6 In the magistrates' courts, the justices' clerk may nominate one but not more than two case managers.

The First Appointment objectives

13.1 The First Appointment is the first hearing in the proceedings. The main objectives of the First Appointment are to –

(1) confirm allocation; and
(2) give initial case management directions having regard to the Public Law Outline.

13.2 The steps which the court will take at the First Appointment include those set out in paragraphs 13.3 to 13.6 below.

STEPS TO BE TAKEN BY THE COURT

13.3 The court will –

(1) confirm the Timetable for the Child;
(2) make arrangements for any contested interim hearing such as an application for an interim care order;
(3) confirm in writing the allocation of the case or, if appropriate, transfer the case;
(4) request the children's guardian or if appropriate another officer of the service or Welsh family proceedings officer to prepare a Case Analysis and Recommendations for the Case Management Conference or Issues Resolution Hearing;
(5) scrutinise the Care Plan;
(6) consider giving directions relating to –
   (a) those matters in the Public Law Outline which remain to be considered including preparation, filing and service of any missing Annex Documents and what Other Checklist documents are to be filed and by when;
   (b) the joining of a person who would not otherwise be a respondent under the rules as a party to the proceedings;
   (c) where any person to be joined as a party may be a protected party, an investigation of that person's capacity to conduct the proceedings and the representation of that person by a guardian ad litem or litigation friend, including the Official Solicitor where appropriate;
   (d) the identification of family and friends as proposed carers and any overseas, immigration, jurisdiction and paternity issues;
   (e) any other documents to be filed with the court;
   (f) evidence to be obtained as to whether a parent who is a protected party is competent to make a statement.

(A suggested form for the drafting of Standard Directions on First Appointment is Form PLO 9 which is available from HMCS)

EARLY FINAL HEARING

13.4 Cases which are suitable for an early Final Hearing are those cases where all the evidence necessary to determine issues of fact and welfare is immediately or shortly available to be filed. Those cases are likely to include cases where the child has no parents, guardians, relatives who want to care for the child, or other carers. The court will –

(1) identify at the First Appointment whether the case is one which is suitable for an early Final Hearing; and
(2) set a date for that Final Hearing.

SETTING A DATE FOR THE CASE MANAGEMENT CONFERENCE.

13.5 The court will set a date for the Case Management Conference normally no later than 45 days from the date of issue of the proceedings and in any event in line with the Timetable for the Child.

ADVOCATES' MEETING/DISCUSSION AND THE DRAFTING OF THE CASE MANAGEMENT ORDER

13.6 The court will consider directing a discussion between the parties' advocates and any litigant in person and the preparation of a draft of the Case Management Order as outlined below.

EXPERTS

13.7 A party who wishes to instruct an expert should comply with the Experts Practice Direction. Where the parties are agreed on any matter relating to experts or expert evidence, the draft agreement must be submitted for the court's approval as early as possible in the proceedings.

Advocates' Meeting/discussion and the drafting of the Case Management Order

14.1 The main objective of the Advocates' Meeting or discussion is to prepare a draft of the Case Management Order for approval by the court.

14.2 Where there is a litigant in person the court will consider the most effective way in which that person can be involved in the advocates' discussions and give directions as appropriate including directions relating to the part to be played by any McKenzie Friend.

14.3 Timing of the discussions is of the utmost importance. Discussions of matters "outside the court room door", which could have taken place at an earlier time, are to be avoided. Discussions are to take place no later than 2 days before the Case Management Conference or the Issues Resolution Hearing whichever is appropriate. The discussions may take place earlier than 2 days before those hearings, for example, up to 7 days before them.

14.4 Following discussion the advocates should prepare or adjust the draft of the Case Management Order. In practice the intention is that the advocate for the applicant, which in care and supervision proceedings will ordinarily be the Local Authority, should take the lead in preparing and adjusting the draft of the Case Management Order following discussion with the other advocates. The aim is for the advocates to agree a draft of the Case Management Order which is to be submitted for the approval of the court.

14.5 Where it is not possible for the advocates to agree the terms of the draft of the Case Management Order, the advocates should specify on the draft, or on a separate document if more practicable –

  (1) those provisions on which they agree; and
  (2) those provisions on which they disagree.

14.6 Unless the court directs otherwise, the draft of the Case Management Order must be filed with the court no later than 11am on the day before the Case Management Conference or the Issues Resolution Hearing whichever may be appropriate.

14.7 At the Advocates' Meeting or discussion before the Case Management Conference, the advocates should also try to agree the questions to be put to any proposed expert (whether jointly instructed or not) if not previously agreed. Under the Experts Practice Direction the questions on which the proposed expert is to give an opinion are a crucial component of the expert directions which the court is required to consider at the Case Management Conference.

PART III

Case Management Conference objectives

15.1 The Case Management Conference is the main hearing at which the court manages the case. The main objectives of the Conference are to –

    (1)   identify key issues; and
    (2)   give full case management directions.

15.2 The steps which the court will take at the Case Management Conference include those steps set out in paragraphs 15.3 to 15.5 below.

STEPS TO BE TAKEN BY THE COURT

15.3 The court will –

    (1)   review and confirm the Timetable for the Child;
    (2)   confirm the allocation or the transfer of the case;
    (3)   scrutinise the Care Plan;
    (4)   identify the key issues;
    (5)   identify the remaining case management issues;
    (6)   resolve remaining case management issues set out in the draft of the Case Management Order;
    (7)   identify any special measures such as the need for access for the disabled or provision for vulnerable witnesses;
    (8)   scrutinise the Case Management Record to check whether directions have been complied with and if not, consider making further directions as appropriate;
    (9)   where expert evidence is required, check whether the parties have complied with the Experts Practice Direction, in particular the section on preparation for the relevant hearing and consider giving directions as appropriate.

CASE MANAGEMENT ORDER

15.4 The court will issue the approved Case Management Order. Parties or their legal representatives will be expected to submit in electronic form the final approved draft of the Case Management Order on the conclusion of, and the same day as, the Case Management Conference.

SETTING A DATE FOR THE ISSUES RESOLUTION HEARING/FINAL HEARING

15.5 The court will set –

    (1)   a date for the Issues Resolution Hearing normally at any time between 16 and 25 weeks from the date of issue of the proceedings and in any event in line with the Timetable for the Child; and
    (2)   if necessary, specify a period within which the Final Hearing of the application is to take place unless a date has already been set.

The Issues Resolution Hearing objectives

16.1 The objectives of this hearing are to –

    (1)   resolve and narrow issues;
    (2)   identify key remaining issues requiring resolution.

16.2 The Issues Resolution Hearing is likely to be the hearing before the Final Hearing. Final case management directions and other preparations for the Final Hearing will be made at this hearing.

STEPS TO BE TAKEN BY THE COURT

16.3 The court will –

(1) identify the key issues (if any) to be determined;

(2) review and confirm the Timetable for the Child;

(3) consider giving case management directions relating to –

    (a) any outstanding matter contained in the draft of the Case Management Order;

    (b) the preparation and filing of final evidence including the filing of witness templates;

    (c) skeleton arguments;

    (d) preparation and filing of bundles in accordance with the Bundles Practice Direction;

    (e) any agreement relating to the satisfaction of the threshold criteria under section 31 of the 1989 Act or facts and issues remaining to be determined in relation to it or to any welfare question which arises;

    (f) time estimates;

    (g) the judicial reading list and likely reading time and judgment writing time;

(4) issue the Case Management Order.

16.4 For the avoidance of doubt the purpose of an Issues Resolution Hearing is to –

(1) identify key issues which are not agreed;

(2) examine if those key issues can be agreed; and

(3) where those issues cannot be agreed, examine the most proportionate method of resolving those issues.

16.5 The expectation is that the method of resolving the key issues which cannot be agreed will be at a hearing (ordinarily the Final hearing) where there is an opportunity for the relevant oral evidence to be heard and challenged.

Attendance at the Case Management Conference and the Issues Resolution Hearing

17 An advocate who has conduct of the Final Hearing should ordinarily attend the Case Management Conference and the Issues Resolution Hearing. Where the attendance of this advocate is not possible, then an advocate who is familiar with the issues in the proceedings should attend.

Flexible powers of the court

18.1 Attention is drawn to the flexible powers of the court either following the issue of the application in that court, the transfer of the case to that court or at any other stage in the proceedings.

18.2 The court may give directions without a hearing including setting a date for the Final Hearing or a period within which the Final Hearing will take place. The steps, which the court will ordinarily take at the various stages of the proceedings provided for in the Public Law Outline, may be taken by the court at another stage in the proceedings if the circumstances of the case merit this approach.

18.3 The flexible powers of the court include the ability for the court to cancel or repeat a particular hearing. For example, if the issue on which the case turns can with reasonable practicability be crystallised and resolved by having an early Final Hearing, then in the fulfilment of the overriding objective, such a flexible approach must be taken to secure compliance with section 1(2) of the 1989 Act.

PART III

Alternative Dispute Resolution

19.1 The court will encourage the parties to use an alternative dispute resolution procedure and facilitate the use of such a procedure where it is –

    (1)   readily available;

    (2)   demonstrated to be in the interests of the child; and

    (3)   reasonably practicable and safe.

19.2 At any stage in the proceedings, the parties can ask the court for advice about alternative dispute resolution.

19.3 At any stage in the proceedings the court itself will consider whether alternative dispute resolution is appropriate. If so, the court may direct that a hearing or proceedings be adjourned for such specified period as it considers appropriate –

    (1)   to enable the parties to obtain information and advice about alternative dispute resolution; and

    (2)   where the parties agree, to enable alternative dispute resolution to take place.

Co-operation

20.1 Throughout the proceedings the parties and their representatives should cooperate wherever reasonably practicable to help towards securing the welfare of the child as the paramount consideration.

20.2 At each court appearance the court will ask the parties and their legal representatives –

    (1)   what steps they have taken to achieve co-operation and the extent to which they have been successful;

    (2)   if appropriate the reason why co-operation could not be achieved; and

    (3)   the steps needed to resolve any issues necessary to achieve co-operation.

Agreed directions

21.1 The parties, their advisers and the children's guardian, are encouraged to try to agree directions for the management of the proceedings.

21.2 To obtain the court's approval the agreed directions must –

    (1)   set out a Timetable for the Child by reference to calendar dates for the taking of steps for the preparation of the case;

    (2)   include a date when it is proposed that the next hearing will take place.

Variation of case management timetable

22 It is emphasised that a party or the children's guardian must apply to the court at the earliest opportunity if they wish to vary by extending the dates set by the court for –

    (1)   a directions appointment;

    (2)   a First Appointment;

    (3)   a Case Management Conference;

    (4)   an Issues Resolution Hearing;

    (5)   the Final Hearing;

    (6)   the period within which the Final Hearing of the application is to take place; or

    (7)   any Meeting/discussion between advocates or for the filing of the draft of the Case Management Orders.

Who performs the functions of the court

23.1 Where this Practice Direction provides for the court to perform case management functions, then except where any rule, practice direction, any other enactment or the Family Proceedings (Allocation to Judiciary) Directions ([2009] 2 FLR 51) provides otherwise, the functions may be performed –

(1) in relation to proceedings in the High Court or in a district registry, by any judge or district judge of that Court including a district judge of the principal registry;

(2) in relation to proceedings in the county court, by any judge or district judge including a district judge of the principal registry when the principal registry is treated as if it were a county court; and

(3) in relation to proceedings in a magistrates' court by –

(a) any family proceedings court constituted in accordance with sections 66 and 67 of the 1980 Act;

(b) a single justice; or

(c) a justices' clerk.

23.2 The case management functions to be exercised by a justices' clerk may be exercised by an assistant justices' clerk provided that person has been specifically authorised by a justices' clerk to exercise case management functions. Any reference in this Practice Direction to a justices' clerk is to be taken to include an assistant justices' clerk so authorised. The justices' clerk may in particular appoint one but not more than two assistant justices' clerks as case managers for each case.

23.3 In proceedings in a magistrates' court, where a party considers that there are likely to be issues arising at a hearing (including the First Appointment, Case Management Conference and Issues Resolution Hearing) which need to be decided by a family proceedings court, rather than a justices' clerk, then that party should give the court written notice of that need at least 2 days before the hearing.

23.4 Family proceedings courts may consider making arrangements to ensure a court constituted in accordance with s 66 of the 1980 Act is available at the same time as Issues Resolution Hearings are being heard by a justices' clerk. Any delay as a result of the justices' clerk considering for whatever reason that it is inappropriate for a justices' clerk to perform a case management function on a particular matter and the justices' clerk's referring of that matter to the court should then be minimal.

Technology

24 Where the facilities are available to the court and the parties, the court will consider making full use of technology including electronic information exchange and video or telephone conferencing.

Other Practice Directions

25.1 This Practice Direction must be read with the Bundles Practice Direction.

25.2 The Bundles Practice Direction is applied to Public Law Proceedings in the High Court and county court with the following adjustments –

(1) add "except the First Appointment; Case Management Conference, and Issues Resolution Hearing referred to in the Practice Direction Public Law Proceedings Guide to Case Management: April 2010 where there are no contested applications being heard at those hearings" to paragraph 2.2;

PART III

(2)   the reference to –
  (a)   the "Protocol for Judicial Case Management in Public law Children Act Cases [2003] 2 FLR 719" in paragraph 6.1;
  (b)   the "Practice Direction: Care Cases: Judicial Continuity and Judicial Case Management" in paragraph 15; and
  (c)   "the Public Law Protocol" in paragraph 15, shall be read as if it were a reference to this Practice Direction.

25.3 Paragraph 1.9 of the Practice Direction: Experts in Family Proceedings Relating to Children dated April 2008 should be read as if "Practice Direction: Guide to Case Management in Public law Proceedings, paragraphs 13.7, 14.3 and 25(29)" were a reference to "Practice Direction Public Law Proceedings Guide to Case Management: April 2010, paragraphs 14.7, 15.3 and 26(33)".

Glossary

26 In this Practice Direction –

  (1)   "the 1989 Act " means the Children Act 1989;
  (2)   "the 1980 Act" means the Magistrates' Courts Act 1980;
  (3)   "advocate" means a person exercising a right of audience as a representative of, or on behalf of, a party;
  (4)   "Allocation Order" means any order made by the Lord Chancellor under Part 1 of Schedule 11 to the 1989 Act;
  (5)   "alternative dispute resolution" means the methods of resolving a dispute other than through the normal court process;
  (6)   "Annex Documents" means the documents specified in the Annex to the Application Form;
  (7)   "Application Form" means Form C110 and Annex Documents;
  (8)   "assistant justices' clerk" has the meaning assigned to it by section 27(5) of the Courts Act 2003;
  (9)   "the Bundles Practice Direction" means the Practice Direction Family Proceedings: Court Bundles (Universal Practice to be Applied in all Courts other than Family Proceedings Court) of 27 July 2006;
  (10) "Case Analysis and Recommendations" means a written or oral outline of the case from the child's perspective prepared by the children's guardian or other officer of the service or Welsh family proceedings officer at different stages of the proceedings requested by the court, to provide –
      (a)   an analysis of the issues that need to be resolved in the case including-
          (i)   any harm or risk of harm;
          (ii)   the child's own views;
          (iii) the family context including advice relating to ethnicity, language, religion and culture of the child and other significant persons;
          (iv)   the Local Authority work and proposed care plan;
          (v)   advice about the court process including the Timetable for the Child; and
          (vi)   identification of work that remains to be done for the child in the short and longer term; and
      (b)   recommendations for outcomes, in order to safeguard and promote the best interests of the child in the proceedings;
  (11) "Case Management Documentation" includes the documents referred to in paragraph 3.10;
  (12) "Case Management Order" means an order made by the court which identifies the Timetable for the Child, any delay in the proceedings and the reason for

such delay and the key issues in the proceedings and includes such of the following provisions as are appropriate to the proceedings –

(a) preliminary information:
  (i) the names and dates of birth of the children who are the subject of the proceedings;
  (ii) the names and legal representatives of the parties, and whether they attended the hearing;
  (iii) any interim orders made in respect of the children and any provisions made for the renewal of those orders;

(b) any recitals that the court considers should be recorded in the order, including those relating to:
  (i) any findings made by the court or agreed between the parties;
  (ii) any other agreements or undertakings made by the parties;

(c) orders made at the hearing by way of case management relating to:
  (i) the joinder of parties;
  (ii) the determination of parentage of the children;
  (iii) the appointment of a guardian ad litem or litigation friend (including the Official Solicitor where appropriate);
  (iv) the transfer of the proceedings to a different court;
  (v) the allocation of the proceedings to a case management judge;
  (vi) the filing and service of threshold criteria documents;
  (vii) the preparation and filing of assessments, including Core Assessments and parenting assessments;
  (viii) in accordance with the Experts' Practice Direction, the preparation and filing of other expert evidence, and experts' meetings;
  (ix) care planning and directions in any application for placement for adoption;
  (x) the filing and service of evidence/further evidence on behalf of the local authority;
  (xi) the filing and service of evidence/further evidence on behalf of the other parties;
  (xii) the filing and service of the Case Analysis and Recommendations;
  (xiii) the disclosure of documents into the proceedings held by third parties, including medical records, police records and Home Office information;
  (xiv) the disclosure of documents and information relating to the proceedings to non-parties;
  (xv) the listing of further hearings, and case management documentation to be prepared for those hearings;
  (xvi) advocates' Meetings;
  (xvii) the filing of bundles and other preparatory material for future hearings;
  (xviii) technology/special measures;
  (xix) media attendance and reporting;
  (xx) linked or other proceedings;
  (xxi) non-compliance with any court orders;
  (xxii) such further or other directions as may be necessary for the purposes of case management;
  (xxiii) attendance at court (including child/children's guardian);

(13) "Case Management Record" means the court's filing system for the case which includes the documents referred to at paragraph 3.12;

(14) "Case manager" means the justices' clerk or assistant justices' clerk who manages the case in the magistrates' courts;

PART III

(15) "Care Plan" means a "section 31A plan" referred to in section 31A of the 1989 Act;

(16) "Core Assessment" means the assessment undertaken by the Local Authority in accordance with The Framework for the Assessment of Children in Need and their Families (Department of Health et al, 2000);

(17) "court" means the High Court, county court or the magistrates' court;

(18) "court officer" means –

(a) in the High Court or a county court, a member of court staff; and

(b) in a magistrates' court, the designated officer;

(19) "Experts Practice Direction" means the Practice Direction regarding Experts in Family Proceedings relating to Children;

(20) "genogram" means a family tree, setting out in diagrammatic form the family's background;

(21) "hearing" includes a directions appointment;

(22) "Initial Assessment" means the assessment undertaken by the Local Authority in accordance with The Framework for the Assessment of Children in Need and their Families (Department of Health et al, 2000);

(23) "Initial Social Work Statement" means a statement prepared by the Local Authority strictly limited to the following evidence –

(a) the precipitating incident(s) and background circumstances relevant to the grounds and reasons for making the application including a brief description of any referral and assessment processes that have already occurred;

(b) any facts and matters that are within the social worker's personal knowledge limited to the findings sought by the Local Authority;

(c) any emergency steps and previous court orders that are relevant to the application;

(d) any decisions made by the Local Authority that are relevant to the application;

(e) information relevant to the ethnicity, language, religion, culture, gender and vulnerability of the child and other significant persons in the form of a 'family profile' together with a narrative description and details of the social care and other services that are relevant to the same;

(f) where the Local Authority is applying for an interim order: the Local Authority's initial proposals for the child (which are also to be set out in the Care Plan) including placement, contact with parents and other significant persons and the social care services that are proposed;

(g) the Local Authority's initial proposals for the further assessment of the parties during the proceedings including twin track /concurrent planning (where more than one permanence option for the child is being explored by the Local Authority);

(24) "legal representative" means a –

(a) barrister,

(b) solicitor,

(c) solicitor's employee,

(d) manager of a body recognised under section 9 of the Administration of Justice Act 1985, or

(e) person who, for the purposes of the Legal Services Act 2007, is an authorised person in relation to an activity which constitutes the conduct of litigation (within the meaning of that Act), who has been instructed to act for a party in relation to the proceedings;

(25) "Letter Before Proceedings" means any letter from the Local Authority containing written notification to the parents and others with parental responsibility for the child of the Local Authority's plan to apply to court for a

care or supervision order and any related subsequent correspondence confirming the Local Authority's position;

(26) "Local Authority Case Summary" means a document prepared by the Local Authority advocate for all case management hearings including –
  (a) a recommended reading list and suggested reading time;
  (b) the key issues in the case;
  (c) any additional information relevant to the Timetable for the Child or for the conduct of the hearing or the proceedings;
  (d) a summary of updating information;
  (e) the issues and directions which the court will need to consider at the hearing in question, including any interim orders sought;
  (f) any steps which have not been taken or directions not complied with, an explanation of the reasons for non–compliance and the effect, if any, on the Timetable for the Child;
  (g) any relevant information relating to ethnicity, cultural or gender issues;

(27) "justices' clerk" has the meaning assigned to it by section 27(1) of the Courts Act 2003;

(28) "McKenzie Friend" means any person permitted by the court to sit beside an unrepresented litigant in court to assist the litigant by prompting, taking notes and giving advice to the litigant;

(29) "Other Checklist Documents" means the documents listed in the Pre-proceedings Checklist which will normally be on the local authority file prior to the start of proceedings but which are not –
  (a) to be filed with the court on issue; or
  (b) Annex Documents.

(30) "Other Parties' Case Summaries" means summaries by parties other than the Local Authority containing –
  (a) the party's proposals for the long term future of the child (to include placement and contact);
  (b) the party's reply to the Local Authority's Schedule of Proposed Findings;
  (c) any proposal for assessment / expert evidence; and
  (d) the names, addresses and contact details of any family or friends who it is suggested be approached in relation to long term care / contact or respite;

(31) "Pre-proceedings Checklist" means the Annex Documents and the Other Checklist Documents set out in the Public Law Outline;

(32) "Public Law Outline" means the Table contained in paragraph 10;

(33) "Public Law Proceedings" means proceedings for –
  (a) a residence order under section 8 of the 1989 Act with respect to a child who is subject of a care order;
  (b) a special guardianship order relating to a child who is subject of a care order;
  (c) a secure accommodation order under section 25 of the 1989 Act;
  (d) a care order under section 31(1)(a) of the 1989 Act or the discharge of such an order under section 39(1) of the 1989 Act;
  (e) an order giving permission to change a child's surname or remove a child from the United Kingdom under section 33(7) of the 1989 Act;
  (f) a supervision order under section 31(1)(b) of the 1989 Act, the discharge or variation of such an order under section 39(2) of that Act, or the extension or further extension of such an order under paragraph 6(3) of Schedule 3 to that Act;
  (g) an order making provision for contact under section 34(2) to (4) of the 1989 Act or an order varying or discharging such an order under section 34(9) of that Act;
  (h) an education supervision order, the extension of an education supervision

order under paragraph 15(2) of Schedule 3 to the 1989 Act, or the discharge of such an order under paragraph 17(1) of Schedule 3 to that Act;

(i)   an order varying directions made with an interim care order or interim supervision order under section 38(8)(b) of the 1989 Act;

(j)   an order under section 39(3) of the 1989 Act varying a supervision order in so far as it affects a person with whom the child is living but who is not entitled to apply for the order to be discharged;

(k)   an order under section 39(3A) of the 1989 Act varying or discharging an interim care order in so far as it imposes an exclusion requirement on a person who is not entitled to apply for the order to be discharged;

(l)   an order under section 39(3B) of the 1989 Act varying or discharging an interim care order in so far as it confers a power of arrest attached to an exclusion requirement;

(m)   the substitution of a supervision order for a care order under section 39(4) of the 1989 Act;

(n)   a child assessment order or the variation or discharge of such an order under section 43(12) of the 1989 Act;

(o)   an order permitting the Local Authority to arrange for any child in its care to live outside England and Wales under paragraph 19(1) of Schedule 2 to the 1989 Act;

(p)   a contribution order, or the variation or revocation of such an order under paragraph 23(8), of Schedule 2 to the 1989 Act;

(q)   an appeal under paragraph 8(1) of Schedule 8 to the 1989 Act.

(34) "rules" means rules of court governing the practice and procedure to be followed in Public Law Proceedings;

(35) "Schedule of Proposed Findings" means the schedule of findings of fact prepared by the Local Authority sufficient to satisfy the threshold criteria under section 31(2) of the 1989 Act and to inform the Care Plan;

(36) "section 7 report" means any report under section 7 of the 1989 Act;

(37) "section 37 report" means any report by the Local Authority to the court as a result of a direction under section 37 of the 1989 Act;

(38) "Social Work Chronology" means a schedule containing –

(a)   a succinct summary of the significant dates and events in the child's life in chronological order- a running record to be updated during the proceedings;

(b)   information under the following headings –

(i)   serial number;

(ii)   date;

(iii) event-detail;

(iv)   witness or document reference (where applicable);

(39) "specified proceedings" has the meaning assigned to it by section 41(6) of the 1989 Act;

(40) "Standard Directions on Issue" mean directions made by the court which will include such of the directions set out in the Public Law Outline, Stage 1, column 1 as are appropriate to the proceedings;

(41) "Standard Directions on First Appointment" means directions made by the court which will include such of the directions set out in the Public Law Outline, Stage 1, column 2 and directions relating to the following as are appropriate to the proceedings –

(a)   the Timetable for the Child;

(b)   the joining of a party to the proceedings;

(c) the appointment of a guardian ad litem or litigation friend including the Official Solicitor where appropriate for a protected party or non subject child;

(d) allocation of the case to a case manager or case management judge;

(e) experts in accordance with the Experts Practice Direction;

(f) the interim care plan setting out details as to proposed placement and contact;

(g) any other evidence (such as evidence relating to vulnerability, ethnicity, culture, language, religion or gender) and disclosure of evidence between the parties;

(h) filing and service of the draft of the Case Management Order before the Case Management Conference;

(i) listing the Issues Resolution Hearing and Final Hearing;

(j) media attendance and reporting;

(42) "Strategy Discussion Record" means a note of the strategy discussion within the meaning of "Working Together to Safeguard Children" (2006);

(43) "Timetable for the Child" has the meaning assigned to it by the rules (see paragraph 3.2 of this Practice Direction).

Practice Direction 12B – The Revised Private Law Programme

This Practice Direction supplements FPR Part 12

1 Introduction

1.1 The Private Law Programme has achieved marked success in enabling the resolution of the majority of cases by consent at the First Hearing Dispute Resolution Appointment ("FHDRA"). It has been revised to build on the successes of the initial programme and to take account of recent developments in the law and practice associated with private family law.

1.2 In particular, there have been several legislative changes affecting private family law. The Allocation and Transfer of Proceedings Order 2008 (the "Allocation Order"), requires the transfer of cases from the County Court to the Family Proceedings Court (FPC). Sections 1 to 5 and Schedule 1 of the Children and Adoption Act 2006 which came into force on 8 December 2008, amends the Children Act 1989 by introducing Contact Activity Directions, Contact Activity Conditions, Contact Monitoring Requirements, Financial Compensation Orders and Enforcement Orders.

1.3 There has been growing recognition of the impact of domestic violence and abuse, drug and alcohol misuse and mental illness, on the proper consideration of the issues in private family law; this includes the acceptance that Court orders, even those made by consent, must be scrutinised to ensure that they are safe and take account of any risk factors. Coupled with this is the need to take account of the duty on Cafcass, pursuant to s 16A Children Act 1989, to undertake risk assessments where an officer of the Service ("Cafcass Officer") suspects that a child is at risk of harm. (References to Cafcass include CAFCASS CYMRU and references to the Cafcass Officer include the Welsh family proceedings officer in Wales).

1.4 There is awareness of the importance of involving children where appropriate in the decision making process.

1.5 The Revised Programme incorporates these developments. It also retains the essential feature of the FHDRA as the forum for the parties to be helped to reach agreement as to, and understanding of, the issues that divide them. It recognises that having reached agreement parties may need assistance in putting it into effect in a co-operative way.

1.6 The Revised Programme is designed to provide a framework for the consistent national approach to the resolution of the issues in private family law whilst enabling local practices and initiatives to be operated in addition and within the framework.

1.7 The Revised Programme is designed to assist parties to reach safe agreements where possible, to provide a forum in which to find the best way to resolve issues in each individual case and to promote outcomes that are sustainable, that are in the best interests of children and that take account of their perspectives.

2 Principles

2.1 Where an application is made to a court under Part II of the Children Act 1989, the child's welfare is the court's paramount concern. The court will apply the principle of the "Overriding Objective" to enable it to deal with a case justly, having regard to the welfare principles involved. So far as practicable the Court will –

- (a)   Deal expeditiously and fairly with every case;
- (b)   Deal with a case in ways which are proportionate to the nature, importance and complexity of the issues;
- (c)   Ensure that the parties are on an equal footing;
- (d)   Save unnecessary expense;
- (e)   Allot to each case an appropriate share of the court's resources, while taking account of the need to allot resources to other cases.

2.2 The court will give effect to the overriding objective when applying this programme and when exercising its powers to manage cases.

The parties are required to help the court further the overriding objective and promote the welfare of the child by the application of the welfare principle, pursuant to s 1(1) of the Children Act 1989.

This Programme provides that consideration and discussion of all issues will not take place until the FHDRA when parties are on an equal footing and can hear what is said to and by each other. This excludes the safety checks and enquiries carried out by Cafcass before the first hearing that are required for that hearing and deal only with safety issues.

At the **FHDRA** the Court shall consider in particular –

- (a)   Whether and the extent to which the parties can safely resolve some or all of the issues with the assistance of the Cafcass Officer and any available mediator.
- (b)   Risk identification followed by active case management including risk assessment, and compliance with the Practice Direction 14 January 2009: "Residence and Contact Orders: Domestic Violence and Harm".
- (c)   Further dispute resolution.
- (d)   The avoidance of delay through the early identification of issues and timetabling, subject to the Allocation Order.
- (e)   Judicial scrutiny of the appropriateness of consent orders.
- (f)   Judicial consideration of the way to involve the child.
- (g)   Judicial continuity.

3 Practical arrangements before the FHDRA

3.1 Applications shall be issued on the day of receipt in accordance with the appropriate Rules of Procedure. It is important that the form C100 is fully completed, especially on pages 1, 2, 3 and 5 otherwise delay may be caused by requests for information.

Amendments—FPR 2010, Update 2.

3.2 If possible at the time of issue, and in any event by no later than 24 hours after issue, or in courts where applications are first considered on paper, by no later than 48 hours after issue, the court shall

(i)   send or hand to the Applicant
(ii) send to Cafcass

the following:

(a)   a copy of the Application Form C100, (together with Supplemental Information Form C1A) (if provided) (references to form C1A are to be read as form C100A following the introduction of this replacement form),
(b)   the Notice of Hearing,
(c)   the Acknowledgment Form C7,
(d)   a blank Form C1A,
(e)   the Certificate of Service Form C9,
(f)   information leaflets for the parties.

3.3 Save in urgent cases that require an earlier listing, the fully effective operation of this Practice Direction requires the FHDRA to take place within **4** weeks of the application. Where practicable, the first hearing must be listed to be heard in this period and in any event no later than within **6** weeks of the application. Where, at the time of introduction of this Programme, the Designated Family Judge/Justices' Clerk determines that it is not practicable to list the first hearing within 4 weeks, they should, in consultation with HMCS and Cafcass, formulate a timetable for revisiting the position and managing to list the FHDRA within 4 weeks.

3.4 Copies of each Application Form C100 and Notice of Hearing shall be sent by the court to Cafcass in accordance with 3.2 above.

3.5 The Respondent shall have at least 14 days notice of the hearing where practicable, but the court may abridge this time.

3.6 The Respondent should file a response on the Forms C7/C1A no later than 14 days before the hearing.

3.7 A copy of Forms C7/C1A shall be sent by the court to Cafcass on the day of receipt.

3.8 **NOTE:** This provision relates to cases that are placed in the FHDRA list for hearing other than by direct application in accordance with the procedure referred to in paragraph 3.1. Such listing may follow an application under the Family Law Act 1996, or a direction by the Court in other proceedings. In all such cases, or where the Court adjourns proceedings to a 'dispute resolution hearing' (sometimes called 'conciliation'), this will be treated as an adjournment to a FHDRA, and the documents referred to in para 3.2 must be filed and copied to parties and Cafcass for safety checks and enquiries, in the same way.

3.9 Before the FHDRA Cafcass shall identify any safety issues by the steps outlined below. Such steps shall be confined to matters of safety. Neither Cafcass nor a Cafcass Officer shall discuss with either party before the FHDRA any matter other than relates to safety. The Parties will not be invited to talk about other issues, for example relating to the substance of applications or replies or about issues concerning matters of welfare or the prospects of resolution. If such issues are raised by either party they will be advised that such matters will be deferred to the FHDRA when there is equality between the parties and full discussion can take place which will also be a time when any safety issues that have been identified also can be taken into account.

 (a) In order to inform the court of possible risks of harm to the child in accordance with its safeguarding framework Cafcass will carry out safeguarding enquiries, including checks of local authorities and police, and telephone risk identification interviews with parties.

 (b) If risks of harm are identified, Cafcass may invite parties to meet separately with the Cafcass Officer before the FHDRA to clarify any safety issue.

 (c) Cafcass shall record and outline any safety issues for the court.

 (d) The Cafcass Officer will not initiate contact with the child prior to the FHDRA. If contacted by a child, discussions relating to the issues in the case will be postponed to the day of the hearing or after when the Cafcass officer will have more knowledge of the issues.

 (e) At least 3 days before the hearing the Cafcass Officer shall report the outcome of risk identification work to the court by completing the Form at Schedule 2.

4 The First Hearing Dispute Resolution Appointment.

4.1 The parties and Cafcass Officer shall attend this hearing. A mediator may attend where available.

4.2 At the hearing, which is not privileged, the court should have the following documents:

 (a) C100 application, and C1A if any
 (b) Notice of Hearing
 (c) C7 response and C1A if any
 (d) Schedule 2 safeguarding information

4.3 The detailed arrangements for the participation of mediators will be arranged locally. These will include:

 (a) Arrangements for the mediator to ask the parties in a particular case to consent to the mediator seeing the papers in the case where it seems appropriate to do so.

 (b) Arrangements for the mediator to ask the parties to waive privilege for the purpose of the first hearing where it seems to the mediator appropriate to do so in order to assist the work of the mediator and the outcome of the first hearing.

 (c) In all cases it is important that such arrangements are put in place in a way that avoids any pressure being brought to bear in this connection on the parties that is inconsistent with general good mediation practice.

4.4 At the FHDRA the Court, in collaboration with the Cafcass Officer, and with the assistance of any mediator present, will seek to assist the parties in conciliation and in resolution of all or any of the issues between them. Any remaining issues will be identified, the Cafcass Officer will advise the court of any recommended means of resolving such issues and directions will be given for the future resolution of such issues. At all times the decisions of the Court and the work of the Cafcass Officer will take account of any risk or safeguarding issues that have been identified.

4.5 The Cafcass Officer shall, where practicable, speak separately to each party at court and before the hearing.

4.6 In the County Court, the Court shall have available a telephone contact to the Family Proceedings Court listing manager, diary dates for the appropriate Family Proceedings Court, or other means by which the County Court, at the time of the hearing, will be able to list subsequent hearings in the Family Proceedings Court.

5 Conduct of the Hearing. The following matters shall be considered

5.1 Safeguarding:

(a) The court shall inform the parties of the content of any screening report or other information which has been provided by Cafcass, unless it considers that to do so would create a risk of harm to a party or the child. The court may need to consider whether and how any information contained in the checks should be disclosed to the parties if Cafcass have not disclosed it.

(b) Whether a risk assessment is required and when.

(c) Whether a fact finding hearing is needed to determine allegations whose resolution is likely to affect the decision of the court.

5.2 Dispute Resolution:

(a) There will be at every FHDRA a period in which the Cafcass Officer, with the assistance of any Mediator and in collaboration with the Court, will seek to conciliate and explore with the parties the resolution of all or some of the issues between them. The procedure to be followed in this connection at the hearing will be determined by local arrangements between the Cafcass manager, or equivalent in Wales, and the Designated Family Judge or the Justices' Clerk where appropriate.

(b) What is the result of any such meeting at Court?

(c) What other options there are for resolution e.g. may the case be suitable for further intervention by Cafcass; mediation by an external provider; collaborative law or use of a parenting plan?

(d) Would the parties be assisted by attendance at Parenting Information Programmes or other activities, whether by formal statutory provision under section 11 Children Act 1989 as amended by Children and Adoption Act 2006 or otherwise?

5.3 Consent Orders:

Where agreement is reached at any hearing or submitted in writing to the court, no order will be made without scrutiny by the court. Where safeguarding checks or risk assessment work remain outstanding, the making of a final order may be deferred for such work. In such circumstances the court shall adjourn the case for no longer than 28 days to a fixed date. A written notification of this work is to be provided by Cafcass in accordance with the timescale specified by the court. If satisfactory information is then available, the order may be made at the adjourned hearing in the agreed terms without the need for attendance by the parties. If satisfactory information is not available, the order will not be made, and the case will be adjourned for further consideration with an opportunity for the parties to make further representations.

5.4 Reports:

(a) Are there welfare issues or other specific considerations which should be addressed in a report by Cafcass or the Local Authority? Before a report is ordered, the court should consider alternative ways of working with the parties such as are referred to in paragraph 5.2 above. If a report is ordered in accordance with Section 7 of the Children Act 1989, it should be directed specifically towards and limited to those issues. General requests should be avoided and the Court should state in the Order the specific factual and other issues that are to be addressed in a focused report. In determining whether a request for a report should be directed to the relevant local authority or to Cafcass, the court should consider such information as Cafcass has provided about the extent and nature of the local authority's current or recent involvement with the subject of the application and the parties, and any relevant protocol between Cafcass and the Association of Directors of Children's Services.

   (b)   Is there a need for an investigation under S 37 Children Act 1989?

   (c)   A copy of the Order requesting the report and any relevant court documents are to be sent to Cafcass or, in the case of the Local Authority, to the Legal Adviser to the Director of the Local Authority Children's Services and, where known, to the allocated social worker by the court forthwith.

   (d)   Is any expert evidence required in compliance with the Experts' Practice Direction?

5.5 Wishes and feelings of the child:

   (a)   Is the child aware of the proceedings?
How are the wishes and feelings of the child to be ascertained (if at all)?

   (b)   How is the child to be involved in the proceedings, if at all, and whether at or after the FHDRA?

   (c)   If consideration is given to the joining of the child as a party to the application, the court should consider the current Guidance from the President of the Family Division. Where the court is considering the appointment of a guardian ad litem, it should first seek to ensure that the appropriate Cafcass manager has been spoken to so as to consider any advice in connection with the prospective appointment and the timescale involved. In considering whether to make such an appointment the Court shall take account of the demands on the resources of Cafcass that such appointment would make.

   (d)   Who will inform the child of the outcome of the case where appropriate?

5.6 Case Management:

   (a)   What, if any, issues are agreed and what are the key issues to be determined?

   (b)   Are there any interim orders which can usefully be made (e.g. indirect, supported or supervised contact) pending final hearing?

   (c)   What directions are required to ensure the application is ready for final hearing – statements, reports etc?

   (d)   List for final hearing, consider the need for judicial continuity (especially if there has been or is to be a fact finding hearing or a contested interim hearing).

5.7 Transfer to FPC:

The case should be transferred to the FPC, pursuant to the Allocation and Transfer of Proceedings Order 2008 unless one of the specified exceptions applies. The date should be fixed at court and entered on the order.

6 The Order

6.1 The Order shall set out in particular:

   (a)   The issues about which the parties are agreed.

   (b)   The issues that remain to be resolved.

   (c)   The steps that are planned to resolve the issues.

   (d)   Any interim arrangements pending such resolution, including arrangements for the involvement of children.

   (e)   The timetable for such steps and, where this involves further hearings, the date of such hearings.

   (f)   A statement as to any facts relating to risk or safety; in so far as they are resolved the result will be stated and, in so far as not resolved, the steps to be taken to resolve them will be stated.

(g) If it be the case, the fact of the transfer of the case to the Family Proceedings Court with the date and purpose of the next hearing.

(h) If it be the case, the fact that the case cannot be transferred to the Family Proceedings Court and the reason for the decision.

(i) Whether in the event of an order, by consent or otherwise, or pending such an order, the parties are to be assisted by participation in mediation, Parenting Information Programmes, or other types of parenting intervention, and to detail any contact activity directions or conditions imposed by the court.

6.2 A suggested template order is available as set out in Schedule 1 below.

7 Commencement and Implementation

7.1 This Practice Direction will come into effect on 1 April 2010. So that procedural changes can be made by all agencies, the requirement for full implementation of the provisions is postponed, but in any event it should be effected by no later than 4 October 2010.

SCHEDULE 1

The suggested form of Order which courts may wish to use is PLP10 which is available from Her Majesty's Court Service.

SCHEDULE 2

Report Form on outcome of safeguarding enquiries. See version for Cafcass in England and for CAFCASS CYMRU in Wales.

Practice Direction 12C –
Service of Application in Certain Proceedings

This Practice Direction supplements FPR Part 12 (Children Proceedings except Parental Order Proceedings and Proceedings for Applications in Adoption, Placement and Related Proceedings), rule 12.8 (Service of the application)

Persons who receive copy of application form

1.1 In relation to the proceedings in column 1 of the following table, column 2 sets out the documentation which persons listed in column 3 are to receive –

Proceedings	Documentation	Who receives a copy of the documentation
1 Private law proceedings; public law proceedings; emergency proceedings (except those proceedings referred to in entries 2 and 3 of the Table below);	Application form (including any supplementary forms); Form C6 (Notice of proceedings); and in private law proceedings, the form of answer.	All the respondents to the application.

PART III

Proceedings	Documentation	Who receives a copy of the documentation
proceedings for a declaration under rule 12.71 as to the existence, or extent, of parental responsibility under Article 16 of the 1996 Hague Convention; an order relating to the exercise of the court's inherent jurisdiction (including wardship proceedings).		
2 An enforcement order (section 11J of the 1989 Act); a financial compensation order (section 11O of the 1989 Act).	As above	All the respondents to the application; and where the child was a party to the proceedings in which the contact order was made – (a) the person who was the children's guardian or litigation friend in those proceedings; or (b) where there was no children's guardian or litigation friend, the person who was the legal representative of the child in those proceedings.
3 A care or a supervision order (section 31 of the 1989 Act).	As above and such of the documents specified in the Annex to Form C110 as are available.	All the respondents to the application; and Cafcass or CAFCASS CYMRU.
4 Proceedings for an order for the return of a child under the 1980 Hague Convention or registration of an order under the European Convention.	As above and the documents referred to in part 2 of the Practice Direction 12F (International Child Abduction).	All the respondents to the application.

(Rule 12.3 sets out who the parties to the proceedings are.)

1.2 When filing the documents referred to in column 2 of the Table in paragraph 1.1, the applicant must also file sufficient copies for one to be served on each respondent and Cafcass or CAFCASS CYMRU.

1.3 Where the application for an order in proceedings referred to in column 1 of the Table in paragraph 1.1 is made in respect of more than one child all the children must be included in the same application form.

1.4 The applicant will serve Form C6A (notice to non parties) on the persons referred to in the Table in paragraph 3.1 at the same time as serving the documents in column 2 of the Table in paragraph 1.1.

Time for serving application

2.1 In relation to the proceedings in column 1 of the following table, column 2 sets out the time period within which the application and accompanying documents must be served on each respondent –

Proceedings	Minimum number of days prior to hearing or directions appointment for service
1 Private law proceedings; and proceedings for – an order permitting the child's name to be changed or the removal of the child from the United Kingdom (33(7) of the 1989 Act); an order permitting the local authority to arrange for any child in its care to live outside England and Wales (Schedule 2, paragraph 19(1) of the 1989 Act); a contribution order (Schedule 2, paragraph 23(1) of the 1989 Act); an order revoking a contribution order (Schedule 2, paragraph 23(8) of the 1989 Act); an appeal under paragraph 8(1) of Schedule 8 to the 1989 Act; an order relating to the exercise of the court's inherent jurisdiction (including wardship proceedings); a declaration under rule 12.71 as to the existence, or extent, of parental responsibility under Article 16 of the 1996 Hague Convention.	14 days.
2 Proceedings for – a residence order under section 8 of the 1989 Act relating to a child who is the subject of a care order; a special guardianship order relating to a child who is the subject of a care order (section 14A of the 1989 Act); an education supervision order (section 36 of the 1989 Act); an order discharging a care order (section 39(1) of the 1989 Act); an order varying or discharging a supervision order (section 39(2) of the 1989 Act) or extending or further extending a supervision order under paragraph 6(3) of Schedule 3 to the 1989 Act;	7 days.

Proceedings	Minimum number of days prior to hearing or directions appointment for service
an order varying a supervision order in so far as it affects the person with whom the child is living (section 39(3) of the 1989 Act); an application to substitute a supervision order for a care order (section 39(4) of the 1989 Act); an order extending an education supervision order (Schedule 3, paragraph 15(2) to the 1989 Act); an order discharging an education supervision order (Schedule 3, paragraph 17(1) to the 1989 Act).	
3 Proceedings for – a care or supervision order (section 31 of the 1989 Act); an order making provision for contact under section 34(2) to (4) of the 1989 Act or an order varying or discharging such an order under section 34(9) of the 1989 Act; an order varying directions made with an interim care order or interim supervision order under section 38(8)(b) of the 1989 Act; an order under section 39(3A) of the 1989 Act varying or discharging an interim care order in so far as it imposes an exclusion requirement on a person who is not entitled to apply for the order to be discharged; an order under section 39(3B) of the 1989 Act varying or discharging an interim care order in so far as it confers a power of arrest attached to an exclusion requirement; a child assessment order (section 43(1) of the 1989 Act).	3 days.
4 Proceedings for an order for the return of a child under the 1980 Hague Convention or registration of an order under the European Convention.	4 days.
5 An order varying or discharging a child assessment order (section 43(12) of the 1989 Act).	2 days.
6 Emergency proceedings; and proceedings for a secure accommodation order (section 25 of the 1989 Act).	1 day.

2.2 The court may extend or shorten the time period referred to in column 2 of the table in paragraph 2.1 (see rule 4.1(3)(a)).

2.3 Where the application is to be served on a child, rule 6.33 provides that, in addition to the persons to be served in accordance with rules 6.28 and 6.32, the application must also be served on the persons or bodies listed in rule 6.33(3) unless the court orders otherwise.

Persons who receive a copy of Form C6A (Notice to Non-Parties)

3.1 In relation to each type of proceedings in column 1 of the following table, the persons listed in column 2 are to receive a copy of Form C6A (Notice of Proceedings/Hearing/Directions Appointment to Non-Parties) –

Proceedings	Persons to whom notice is to be given
1 All applications.	Subject to separate entries below: local authority providing accommodation for the child; persons who are caring for the child at the time when the proceedings are commenced; and in the case of proceedings brought in respect of a child who is alleged to be staying in a refuge which is certified under section 51(1) or (2) of the 1989 Act, the person who is providing the refuge.
2 An order appointing a guardian (section 5(1) of the 1989 Act).	As for all applications; and the father or parent (being a woman who is a parent by virtue of section 43 of the Human Fertilisation and Embryology Act 2008) of the child if that person does not have parental responsibility.
3 A section 8 order (section 8 of the 1989 Act).	As for all applications; and, every person whom the applicant believes – (i) to be named in a court order with respect to the same child, which has not ceased to have effect; (ii) to be party to pending proceedings in respect of the same child; or (iii) to be a person with whom the child has lived for at least 3 years prior to the application, unless, in a case to which (i) or (ii) applies, the applicant believes that the court order or pending proceedings are not relevant to the application.
4 A special guardianship order (section 14A of the 1989 Act); variation or discharge of a special guardianship order (section 14D of the 1989 Act).	As for all applications; and every person whom the applicant believes – (i) to be named in a court order with respect to the same child, which has not ceased to have effect; (ii) to be party to pending proceedings in respect of the same child; or

PART III

Proceedings	Persons to whom notice is to be given
	(iii) to be a person with whom the child has lived for at least 3 years prior to the application,
	unless, in a case to which (i) or (ii) applies, the applicant believes that the court order or pending proceedings are not relevant to the application;
	if the child is not being accommodated by the local authority, the local authority in whose area the applicant is ordinarily resident; and
	in the case of an application under section 14D of the 1989 Act, the local authority that prepared the report under section 14A(8) or (9) in the proceedings leading to the order which it is sought to have varied or discharged, if different from any local authority that will otherwise be notified.
5 An order permitting the local authority to arrange for any child in its care to live outside England and Wales (Schedule 2, paragraph 19(1) of the 1989 Act).	As for all applications; and the parties to the proceedings leading to the care order.
6 A care or supervision order (section 31 of the 1989 Act).	As for all applications; and every person whom the applicant believes to be a party to pending relevant proceedings in respect of the same child; and every person whom the applicant believes to be a parent without parental responsibility for the child.
7 A child assessment order (section 43(1) of the 1989 Act).	As for all applications; and every person whom the applicant believes to be a parent of the child; every person whom the applicant believes to be caring for the child; every person in whose favour a contact order is in force with respect to the child; and every person who is allowed to have contact with the child by virtue of an order under section 34 of the 1989 Act.
8 An order varying or discharging a child assessment order (section 43(12) of the 1989 Act).	The persons referred to in section 43(11)(a) to (e) of the 1989 Act who were not party to the application for the order which it is sought to have varied or discharged.
9 An emergency protection order (section 44(1) of the 1989 Act).	As for all applications above; and every person whom the applicant believes to be a parent of the child.

Proceedings	Persons to whom notice is to be given
10 An order varying a direction under section 44(6) in an emergency protection order (section 44(9)(b) of the 1989 Act).	As for all applications; and the local authority in whose area the child is living; and any person whom the applicant believes to be affected by the direction which it is sought to have varied.
11 A warrant authorising a constable to assist in the exercise of certain powers to search for children and inspect premises (section 102 of the 1989 Act).	The person referred to in section 102(1) of the 1989 Act; and any person preventing or likely to prevent such a person from exercising powers under enactments mentioned in subsection (6) of that section.
12 An enforcement order (section 11J of the 1989 Act); a financial compensation order (section 11O of the 1989 Act).	Any officer of the Service or Welsh family proceedings officer who is monitoring compliance with a contact order (in accordance with section 11H(2) of the 1989 Act).
13 An order revoking or amending an enforcement order (Schedule A1, paragraphs 4 to 7 of the 1989 Act) (rule 12.33 makes provision regarding applications under Schedule A1, paragraph 5 of the 1989 Act); an order following a breach of an enforcement order (Schedule A1, paragraph 9 of the 1989 Act).	Any officer of the Service or Welsh family proceedings officer who is monitoring compliance with the enforcement order (in accordance with section 11M(1) of the 1989 Act); the responsible officer (as defined in section 197 of the Criminal Justice Act 2003, as modified by Schedule A1 to the 1989 Act).
14 A declaration under rule 12.71 as to the existence, or extent, of parental responsibility under Article 16 of the 1996 Hague Convention.	A person who the applicant believes is a parent of the child.

PART III

Practice Direction 12D –
Inherent Jurisdiction (including Wardship) Proceedings

This Practice Direction supplements FPR Part 12, Chapter 5

The nature of inherent jurisdiction proceedings

1.1 It is the duty of the court under its inherent jurisdiction to ensure that a child who is the subject of proceedings is protected and properly taken care of. The court may in exercising its inherent jurisdiction make any order or determine any issue in respect of a child unless limited by case law or statute. Such proceedings should not be commenced unless it is clear that the issues concerning the child cannot be resolved under the Children Act 1989.

1.2 The court may under its inherent jurisdiction, in addition to all of the orders which can be made in family proceedings, make a wide range of injunctions for the child's protection of which the following are the most common –

(a) orders to restrain publicity;
(b) orders to prevent an undesirable association;
(c) orders relating to medical treatment;
(d) orders to protect abducted children, or children where the case has another substantial foreign element; and
(e) orders for the return of children to and from another state.

1.3 The court's wardship jurisdiction is part of and not separate from the court's inherent jurisdiction. The distinguishing characteristics of wardship are that –

(a) custody of a child who is a ward is vested in the court; and
(b) although day to day care and control of the ward is given to an individual or to a local authority, no important step can be taken in the child's life without the court's consent.

Transfer of proceedings to county court

2.1 Whilst county courts do not have jurisdiction to deal with applications that a child be made or cease to be a ward of court, consideration should be given to transferring the case in whole or in part to a county court where a direction has been given confirming the wardship and directing that the child remain a ward of court during his minority or until further order.

2.2 The county court must transfer the case back to the High Court if a decision is required as to whether the child should remain a ward of court.

2.3 The following proceedings in relation to a ward of court will be dealt with in the High Court unless the nature of the issues of fact or law makes them more suitable for hearing in the county court –

(a) those in which an officer of the Cafcass High Court Team or the Official Solicitor is or becomes the litigation friend or children's guardian of the ward or a party to the proceedings;
(b) those in which a local authority is or becomes a party;
(c) those in which an application for paternity testing is made;
(d) those in which there is a dispute about medical treatment;
(e) those in which an application is opposed on the grounds of lack of jurisdiction;
(f) those in which there is a substantial foreign element;
(g) those in which there is an opposed application for leave to take the child permanently out of the jurisdiction or where there is an application for temporary removal of a child from the jurisdiction and it is opposed on the ground that the child may not be duly returned.

Parties

3.1 Where the child has formed or is seeking to form an association, considered to be undesirable, with another person, that other person should not be made a party to the application. Such a person should be made a respondent only to an application within the proceedings for an injunction or committal. Such a person should not be added to the title of the proceedings nor allowed to see any documents other than those relating directly to the proceedings for the injunction or committal. He or she should be allowed time to obtain representation and any injunction should in the first instance extend over a few days only.

Removal from jurisdiction

4.1 A child who is a ward of court may not be removed from England and Wales without the court's permission. Practice Direction 12F (International Child Abduction) deals in detail with locating and protecting children at risk of unlawful removal.

Criminal Proceedings

5.1 Where a child has been interviewed by the police in connection with contemplated criminal proceedings and the child subsequently becomes a ward of court, the permission of the court deciding the wardship proceedings ("the wardship court") is not required for the child to be called as a witness in the criminal proceedings.

5.2 Where the police need to interview a child who is already a ward of court, an application must be made for permission for the police to do so. Where permission is given the order should, unless there is some special reason to the contrary, give permission for any number of interviews which may be required by the prosecution or the police. If a need arises to conduct any interview beyond the permission contained in the order, a further application must be made.

5.3 The above applications must be made with notice to all parties.

5.4 Where a person may become the subject of a criminal investigation and it is considered necessary for the child who is a ward of court to be interviewed without that person knowing that the police are making inquiries, the application for permission to interview the child may be made without notice to that party. Notice should, however, where practicable be given to the children's guardian.

5.5 There will be other occasions where the police need to deal with complaints, or alleged offences, concerning children who are wards of court where it is appropriate, if not essential, for action to be taken straight away without the prior permission of the wardship court, for example –

    (a)   serious offences against the child such as rape, where a medical examination and the collection of forensic evidence ought to be carried out promptly;

    (b)   where the child is suspected by the police of having committed a criminal act and the police wish to interview the child in respect of that matter;

    (c)   where the police wish to interview the child as a potential witness.

5.6 In such instances, the police should notify the parent or foster parent with whom the child is living or another 'appropriate adult' (within the Police and Criminal Evidence Act 1984 – Code of Practice C for the Detention, Treatment and Questioning of Persons by Police Officers) so that that adult has the opportunity of being present when the police interview the child. Additionally, if practicable the child's guardian (if one has been appointed) should be notified and invited to attend the police interview or to nominate a third party to attend on the guardian's behalf. A record of the interview or a copy of any statement made by the child should be supplied to the children's guardian. Where the child has been interviewed without the guardian's knowledge, the guardian should be informed at the earliest opportunity of this fact and (if it be the case) that the police wish to conduct further interviews. The wardship court should be informed of the situation at the earliest possible opportunity thereafter by the children's guardian, parent, foster parent (through the local authority) or other responsible adult.

Applications to the Criminal Injuries Compensation Authority

6.1 Where a child who is a ward of court has a right to make a claim for compensation to the Criminal Injuries Compensation Authority ("CICA"), an application must be made by the child's guardian, or, if no guardian has been appointed, the person with care and control of the child, for permission to apply to CICA and disclose such documents on the wardship proceedings file as are considered necessary to establish whether or not the child is eligible for an award plus, as appropriate, the amount of the award.

6.2 Any order giving permission should state that any award made by CICA should normally be paid into court immediately upon receipt and, once that payment has been made, application should made to the court as to its management and administration. If it is proposed to invest the award in any other way, the court's prior approval must be sought

The role of the tipstaff

7.1 The tipstaff is the enforcement officer for all orders made in the High Court. The tipstaff's jurisdiction extends throughout England and Wales. Every applicable order made in the High Court is addressed to the tipstaff in children and family matters (e g "The Court hereby directs the Tipstaff of the High Court of Justice, whether acting by himself or his assistants or a police officer as follows…").

7.2 The tipstaff may effect an arrest and then inform the police. Sometimes the local bailiff or police will detain a person in custody until the tipstaff arrives to collect that person or give further directions as to the disposal of the matter. The tipstaff may also make a forced entry although there will generally be a uniformed police officer standing by to make sure there is no breach of the peace.

7.3 There is only one tipstaff (with two assistants) but the tipstaff can also call on any constable or bailiff to assist in carrying out the tipstaff's duties.

7.4 The majority of the tipstaff's work involves locating children and taking them into protective custody, including cases of child abduction abroad.

Practice Direction 12E – Urgent Business

This Practice Direction supplements FPR Part 12

Introduction

1.1 This Practice Direction describes the procedure to be followed in respect of urgent and out of hours cases in the Family Division of the High Court. For the avoidance of doubt, it does not relate to cases in respect of adults.

1.2 Urgent or out of hours applications, particularly those which have become urgent because they have not been pursued sufficiently promptly, should be avoided. A judge who has concerns that the urgent or out of hours facilities may have been abused may require a representative of the applicant to attend at a subsequent directions hearing to provide an explanation.

1.3 Urgent applications should whenever possible be made within court hours. The earliest possible liaison is required with the Clerk of the Rules who will attempt to accommodate genuinely urgent applications (at least for initial directions) in the Family Division applications court, from which the matter may be referred to another judge.

1.4 When it is not possible to apply within court hours, contact should be made with the security office at the Royal Courts of Justice (020 7947 6000 or 020 7947 6260) who will refer the matter to the urgent business officer. The urgent business officer can contact the duty judge. The judge may agree to hold a hearing, either convened at court or elsewhere, or by telephone.

1.5 When the hearing is to take place by telephone it should, unless not practicable, be by tape-recorded conference call arranged (and paid for in the first instance) by the applicant's solicitors. Solicitors acting for potential applicants should consider having standing arrangements with their telephone service providers under which such conference calls can be arranged. All parties (especially the judge) should be informed that the call is being recorded by the service provider. The applicant's solicitors should order a transcript of the hearing from the service provider. Otherwise the applicant's legal representative should prepare a note for approval by the judge.

General Issues

2.1 Parents, carers or other necessary respondents should whenever possible be given the opportunity to have independent legal advice or at least to have access to support or counselling.

2.2 In suitable cases, application may be made for directions providing for anonymity of the parties and others involved in the matter in any order or subsequent listing of the case. Exceptionally, a reporting restriction order may be sought.

2.3 Either the Official Solicitor or Cafcass, or CAFCASS CYMRU, as the case may be, may be invited by the court to be appointed as advocate to the court.

Medical treatment and press injunction cases

3.1 It may be desirable for a child who is the subject of such proceedings to be made a party and represented through a children's guardian (usually an officer of Cafcass or a Welsh Family Proceedings Officer). Cafcass and CAFCASS CYMRU stand ready to arrange for an officer to accept appointment as a children's guardian. They should be contacted at the earliest opportunity where an urgent application is envisaged. For urgent out of hours applications, the urgent business officer will contact a representative of Cafcass. CAFCASS CYMRU is not able to deal with cases that arise out of office hours and those cases should be referred to Cafcass who will deal with the matter on behalf of CAFCASS CYMRU until the next working day. A child of sufficient understanding to instruct his or her own solicitor should be made a party and given notice of any application.

3.2 Interim declarations/orders under the wardship jurisdiction or Children Act 1989 may be made on application either by an NHS trust, a local authority, an interested adult (where necessary with the leave of the court) or by the child if he or she has sufficient understanding to make the application.

Consultation with Cafcass, CAFCASS CYMRU and Official Solicitor

4.1 Cafcass, CAFCASS CYMRU and members of the Official Solicitor's legal staff are prepared to discuss cases before proceedings are issued. In all cases in which the urgent and out of hours procedures are to be used it would be helpful if the Official Solicitor, Cafcass or CAFCASS CYMRU have had some advance notice of the application and its circumstances.

4.2 Enquiries about children cases should be directed to the duty lawyer:

PART III

Cafcass National Office
6th Floor, Sanctuary Buildings
Great Smith Street
London SW1P 3BT
Tel: 0844 353 3350
Fax: 0844 353 3351.

Enquiries should be marked "FAO High Court Team or FAO HCT".

4.3 Enquiries about children cases in Wales should be directed to:

Social Care Team
Legal Services
Welsh Assembly Government
Cathays Park
Cardiff
CF10 3NQ
Tel: 02920 823913
Fax: 02920 826727.

4.4 Medical and welfare cases relating to an adult lacking capacity in relation to their medical treatment or welfare are brought in the Court of Protection. Enquiries about adult medical and welfare cases should be addressed to a Court of Protection healthcare and welfare lawyer at the office of the Official Solicitor:

81 Chancery Lane
London
WC2A 1DD
Tel: 0207 911 7127
Fax: 0207 911 7105
Email: enquiries@offsol.gsi.gov.uk

Reference should also be made to Practice Direction E, accompanying Part 9 of the Court of Protection Rules 2007, and to Practice Direction B accompanying Part 10 of those Rules. Information for parties and practitioners is available on the website of the Ministry of Justice www.justice.gov.uk and general information for members of the public is available on www.direct.gov.uk.

Note—See now www.gov.uk.

Practice Direction 12F – International Child Abduction

This Practice Direction supplements FPR Part 12, Chapters 5 and 6

Part I – Introduction

1.1 This Practice Direction explains what to do if a child has been brought to, or kept in, England and Wales without the permission of anyone who has rights of custody in respect of the child in the country where the child was habitually resident immediately before the removal or retention. It also explains what to do if a child has been taken out of, or kept out of, England and Wales[a] without the permission of a parent or someone who has rights of custody in respect of the child. These cases are called "international child abduction cases" and are dealt with in the High Court. This Practice Direction also explains what to do if you receive legal papers claiming that you have abducted a child. You can find the legal cases which are mentioned in this Practice Direction, and other legal material, on the website http://www.bailii.org (British and Irish Legal Information Institute).

(a) The child must be taken or kept out of the United Kingdom without the permission of a parent or someone who has rights of custody for it to be an international child abduction. This practice direction relates to the law as it applies in England and Wales. If the child has been taken or kept out of the United Kingdom when the child was habitually resident in Scotland, you should contact the Central Authority for Scotland, Scottish Government Justice Directorate, Civil Law Division, St Andrew's House, Regent Road, Edinburgh EH1 3DG Tel: +44 (0) 131 244 4827/4832 Fax: +44 (0)131 244 4848 Website: http://www.scotland.gov.uk/Topics/Justice/law/17867/fm-children-root/18533.

   If the child has been taken or kept out of the United Kingdom when the child was habitually resident in Northern Ireland, you should contact the Central Authority for Northern Ireland, Northern Ireland Courts and Tribunals Service, Civil Policy and Tribunal Reform Division, 3rd Floor Laganside House, 23-27 Oxford Street, Belfast BT1 3LA Tel: +44 (0)2890 328 594; fax + 44 (0)2890 728 944. Website: http://www.nics.gov.uk or http://www.courtsni.gov.uk/en-GB/Services/ChildAbduction.

1.2 If you have rights of custody in respect of a child and the child has been brought to England or Wales without your permission, or has been brought here with your permission but the person your child is staying with is refusing to return the child, then you can apply to the High Court of Justice, which covers all of England and Wales, for an order for the return of the child.

1.3 How you make an application to the High Court, what evidence you need to provide and what orders you should ask the court to make are all explained in this Practice Direction.

1.4 If your child is under 16 years of age and has been brought to England or Wales from a country which is a party (a "State party") to the 1980 Hague Convention on the Civil Aspects of International Child Abduction ("the 1980 Hague Convention") then you can make an application to the High Court for an order under that Convention for the return of your child to the State in which he or she was habitually resident immediately before being removed or being kept away. This is explained in Part 2 below.

1.5 If your child is over 16 years of age and under 18, or has been brought to England or Wales from a country which is not a State party to the 1980 Hague Convention, then you can make an application for the return of your child under the inherent jurisdiction of the High Court with respect to children. In exercising this jurisdiction over children, the High Court will make your child's welfare its paramount consideration. How to make an application under the inherent jurisdiction of the High Court with respect to children is explained in Part 3 below.

1.6 It might be necessary for you to make an urgent application to the court if you are not sure where your child is, or you think that there is a risk that the person who is keeping your child away from you might take the child out of the United Kingdom or hide them away. Part 4 below explains how to make an urgent application to the High Court for orders to protect your child until a final decision can be made about returning the child and also how to ask for help from the police and government agencies if you think your child might be taken out of the country.

Rights of Access

1.7 Rights of access to children (also called contact or visitation) may be enforced in England and Wales. Access orders made in other Member States of the European Union can be enforced under EU law, and the 1980 Hague Convention expects State parties to comply with orders and agreements concerning access as well as rights of custody. If you have an access order and you want to enforce it in England or Wales, you should read Part 5 below.

PART III

Part 2 – Hague Convention Cases

2.1 States which are party to the 1980 Hague Convention have agreed to return children who have been either wrongfully removed from, or wrongfully retained away from, the State where they were habitually resident immediately before the wrongful removal or retention. There are very limited exceptions to this obligation.

2.2 "Wrongfully removed" or "wrongfully retained" means removed or retained in breach of rights of custody in respect of the child attributed to a person or a body or an institution. "Rights of custody" are interpreted very widely (see paragraph 2.16 below).

2.3 The text of the 1980 Hague Convention and a list of Contracting States (that is, State parties) can be found on the website of the Hague Conference on Private International Law at http://www.hcch.net. All Member States of the European Union are State parties to the 1980 Hague Convention, and all but Denmark are bound by an EU Regulation which supplements the operation of the 1980 Hague Convention between the Member States of the EU (Council Regulation (EC) No 2201/2003, see paragraph 2.6).

2.4 In each State party there is a body called the Central Authority whose duty is to help people use the 1980 Hague Convention.

2.5 If you think that your child has been brought to, or kept in, England or Wales, and your State is a State party to the 1980 Hague Convention, then you should get in touch with your own Central Authority who will help you to send an application for the return of your child to the Central Authority for England and Wales. However, you are not obliged to contact your own Central Authority. You may contact the Central Authority for England and Wales directly, or you may simply instruct lawyers in England or Wales to make an application for you. The advantage of making your application through the Central Authority for England and Wales if you are applying from outside the United Kingdom is that you will get public funding ("legal aid") to make your application, regardless of your financial resources.

The Central Authority for England and Wales

2.6 The Child Abduction and Custody Act 1985 brings the 1980 Hague Convention into the law of England and Wales and identifies the Lord Chancellor as the Central Authority. His duties as the Central Authority are carried out by the International Child Abduction and Contact Unit (ICACU). ICACU also carries out the duties of the Central Authority for two other international instruments. These are the European Convention on Recognition and Enforcement of Decisions concerning Custody of Children signed at Luxembourg on 20 May 1980 (called "the European Convention" in this Practice Direction but sometimes also referred to as "the Luxembourg Convention") and the European Union Council Regulation (EC) No 2201/2003 of 27 November 2003 on jurisdiction and the recognition and enforcement of judgments in matrimonial matters and in matters of parental responsibility ("the Council Regulation[(b)]"). The Council Regulation has direct effect in the law of England and Wales.

(b) The Council Regulation (EC) No 2201/2003 of 27 November 2003 concerning jurisdiction and the recognition and enforcement of judgments in matrimonial matters and the matters of parental responsibility, repealing Regulation (EC) No 1347/2000 is also known as Brussels IIa, or Brussels II Revised, or Brussels II bis.

2.7 ICACU is open Mondays to Fridays from 9.00 a.m. to 5.00 p.m. It is located in the Office of the Official Solicitor and Public Trustee and its contact details are as follows:

International Child Abduction and Contact Unit
81 Chancery Lane
London WC2A 1DD
DX 0012 London Chancery Lane
Tel: + 44 (0)20 7911 7045 / 7047
Fax: + 44 (0)20 7911 7248
Email: enquiries@offsol.gsi.gov.uk

In an emergency (including out of normal working hours) contact should be made with the Royal Courts of Justice on one of the following telephone numbers:

+ 44 (0)20 7947 6000, or
+ 44 (0)20 7947 6260.

In addition, in an emergency or outside normal working hours advice on international child abduction can be sought from reunite International Child Abduction Centre on +44 (0)1162 556 234. Outside office hours you will be directed to the 24 hour emergency service. You can also see information on Reunite's website http://www.reunite.org.

What ICACU Will Do

2.8 When ICACU receives your application for the return of your child, unless you already have a legal representative in England and Wales whom you want to act for you, it will send your application to a solicitor whom it knows to be experienced in international child abduction cases and ask them to take the case for you. You will then be the solicitor's client and the solicitor will make an application for public funding to meet your legal costs. The solicitor will then apply to the High Court for an order for the return of your child.

2.9 You can find out more about ICACU and about the 1980 Hague Convention and the other international instruments mentioned at paragraph 2.6 on two websites: Information for parties and practitioners is available on http://www.justice.gov.uk and general information for members of the public is available on http://www.direct.gov.uk.

Note—See now www.gov.uk.

Applying to the High Court – the Form and Content of Application

2.10 An application to the High Court for an order under the 1980 Hague Convention must be made in the Principal Registry of the Family Division in Form C67. If the Council Regulation applies, then the application must be headed both "in the matter of the Child Abduction and Custody Act 1985" and "in the matter of Council Regulation (EC) 2201/2003". This is to ensure that the application is handled quickly (see paragraph 2.14 below) and to draw the court's attention to its obligations under the Council Regulation.

2.11 The application must include –

(a)   the names and dates of birth of the children;
(b)   the names of the children's parents or guardians;
(c)   the whereabouts or suspected whereabouts of the children;
(d)   the interest of the applicant in the matter (e.g. mother, father, or person with whom the child lives and details of any order placing the child with that person);
(e)   the reasons for the application;
(f)   details of any proceedings (including proceedings not in England or Wales, and including any legal proceedings which have finished) relating to the children;
(g)   where the application is for the return of a child, the identity of the person

PART III

alleged to have removed or retained the child and, if different, the identity of the person with whom the child is thought to be;

(h)   in an application to which the Council Regulation also applies, any details of measures of which you are aware that have been taken by courts or authorities to ensure the protection of the child after its return to the Member State of habitual residence.

2.12 The application should be accompanied by all relevant documents including (but not limited to) –

(a)   an authenticated copy of any relevant decision or agreement;

(b)   a certificate or an affidavit from a Central Authority, or other competent authority of the State of the child's habitual residence, or from a qualified person, concerning the relevant law of that State.

2.13 As the applicant you may also file a statement in support of the application, although usually your solicitor will make and file a statement for you on your instructions. The statement must contain and be verified by a statement of truth in the following terms:

"I make this statement knowing that it will be placed before the court, and I confirm that to the best of my knowledge and belief its contents are true."

(Further provisions about statements of truth are contained in Part 17 of these Rules and in Practice Direction 17A).

The Timetable for the Case

2.14 Proceedings to which the Council Regulation applies must be completed in 6 weeks "except where exceptional circumstances make this impossible". The following procedural steps are intended to ensure that applications under the 1980 Hague Convention and the Council Regulation are handled quickly –

(a)   the application must be headed both "in the matter of the Child Abduction and Custody Act 1985" and "in the matter of Council Regulation (EC) 2201/2003";

(b)   the court file will be marked to –
  (i)   draw attention to the nature of the application; and
  (ii)   state the date on which the 6 week period will expire (the "hear-by date");

(c)   listing priority will, where necessary, be given to such applications;

(d)   the trial judge will expedite the transcript of the judgment and its approval and ensure that it is sent to the Central Authority without delay.

(The above is taken from the judgment of the Court of Appeal, Civil Division in *Vigreux v Michel & anor* [2006] EWCA Civ 630, [2006] 2 FLR 1180).

Applications for Declarations

2.15 If a child has been taken from England and Wales to another State party, the judicial or administrative authorities of that State may ask for a declaration that the removal or retention of the child was wrongful. Or it might be thought that a declaration from the High Court that a child has been wrongfully removed or retained away from the United Kingdom would be helpful in securing his return. The High Court can make such declarations under section 8 of the Child Abduction and Custody Act 1985. An application for a declaration is made in the same way as an application for a return order, the only difference being that the details of relevant legal proceedings in respect of which the declaration is sought (if any), including a copy of any order made relating to the application, should be included in the documentation.

Rights of Custody

2.16 "Rights of custody" includes rights relating to the care of the person of the child and, in particular, the right to determine the child's place of residence. Rights of custody may arise by operation of law (that is, they are conferred on someone automatically by the legal system in which they are living) or by a judicial or administrative decision or as a result of an agreement having legal effect. The rights of a person, an institution or any other body are a matter for the law of the State of the child's habitual residence, but it is for the State which is being asked to return the child to decide: if those rights amount to rights of custody for the purposes of the 1980 Hague Convention; whether at the time of the removal or retention those rights were actually being exercised; and whether there has been a breach of those rights.

2.17 In England and Wales a father who is not married to the mother of their child does not necessarily have "rights of custody" in respect of the child. An unmarried father in England and Wales who has parental responsibility for a child has rights of custody in respect of that child. In the case of an unmarried father without parental responsibility, the concept of rights of custody may include more than strictly legal rights and where immediately before the removal or retention of the child he was exercising parental functions over a substantial period of time as the only or main carer for the child he may have rights of custody. An unmarried father can ask ICACU or his legal representative for advice on this. It is important to remember that it will be for the State which is being asked to return the child to decide if the father's circumstances meet that State's requirements for the establishment of rights of custody.

Custody rights and unmarried fathers—For case-law pre-2003, see *Practice Note of 14 October 1997* (set out in *The Family Court Practice 2011*) and post-December 2003, see under CACA 1985, Sch 1, Art 5 in Part II.

2.18 Sometimes, court orders impose restrictions on the removal of children from the country in which they are living. These can be orders under the Children Act 1989 ("section 8" orders) or orders under the inherent jurisdiction of the High Court (sometimes called "injunctions"). Any removal of a child in breach of an order imposing such a restriction would be wrongful under the 1980 Hague Convention.

2.19 The fact that court proceedings are in progress about a child does not of itself give rise to a prohibition on the removal of the child by a mother with sole parental responsibility from the country in which the proceedings are taking place unless:

(a) the proceedings are Wardship proceedings in England and Wales (in which case removal would breach the rights of custody attributed to the High Court and fathers with no custody rights could rely on that breach); or

(b) the court is actually considering the custody of the child, because then the court itself would have rights of custody.

Particular provisions for European Convention applications

2.20 The European Convention provides for the mutual recognition and enforcement of decisions relating to custody and access, so if a child has been brought here or retained here in breach of a custody order, then that order can be enforced. The European Convention has now been superseded to a very great extent by the Council Regulation. If however you want to make an application under the European Convention, then you make it in the same way as is described in paragraphs 2.10 and 2.11 above, but in addition you must include a copy of the decision relating to custody (or rights of access – see paragraph 5.1 below) which you are seeking to register or enforce, or about which you are seeking a declaration by the court.

Defending Abduction Proceedings

2.21 If you are served with an application – whether it is under the 1980 Hague or the European Convention or the inherent jurisdiction of the High Court – you must not delay. You must obey any directions given in any order with which you have been served, and you should seek legal advice at the earliest possible opportunity, although neither you nor the child concerned will automatically be entitled to legal aid.

2.22 It is particularly important that you tell the court where the child is, because the child will not be permitted to live anywhere else without the permission of the court, or to leave England and Wales, until the proceedings are finished.

2.23 It is also particularly important that you present to the court any defence to the application which you or the child might want to make at the earliest possible opportunity, although the orders with which you will have been served are likely to tell you the time by which you will have to do this.

2.24 If the child concerned objects to any order sought in relation to them, and if the child is of an age and understanding at which the court will take account of their views, the court is likely to direct that the child is seen by an officer of the Children and Family Court Advisory and Support Service (Cafcass) or in Wales CAFCASS CYMRU. You should cooperate in this process. Children are not usually made parties to abduction cases, but in certain exceptional circumstances the court can make them parties so that they have their own separate legal representation. These are all matters about which you should seek legal advice.

> (Provisions about the power of the court to join parties are contained in rule 12.3 and provisions about the joining and representation of children are contained in Part 16 of these Rules and the Practice Direction 16A (Representation of Children).

Part 3 – Non-Convention Cases

3.1 Applications for the return of children wrongfully removed or retained away from States which are not parties to the 1980 Hague Convention or in respect of children to whom that Convention does not apply, can be made to the High Court under its inherent jurisdiction with respect to children. Such proceedings are referred to as "non-Convention" cases. In proceedings under the inherent jurisdiction of the High Court with respect to children, the child's welfare is the court's paramount consideration. The extent of the court's enquiry into the child's welfare will depend on the circumstances of the case; in some cases the child's welfare will be best served by a summary hearing and, if necessary, a prompt return to the State from which the child has been removed or retained. In other cases a more detailed enquiry may be necessary (see *Re J (Child Returned Abroad: Convention Rights)* [2005] UKHL 40; [2005] 2 FLR 802).

3.2 Every application for the return of a child under the inherent jurisdiction must be made in the Principal Registry of the Family Division and heard in the High Court.

Provision about the inherent jurisdiction is made at Chapter 5 of Part 12 of the Rules and in Practice Direction 12D (Inherent Jurisdiction (including Wardship) Proceedings).

The Form and content of the application

3.3 An application for the return of a child under the inherent jurisdiction must be made in Form C66 and must include the information in paragraph 2.11 above.

3.4 You must file a statement in support of your application, which must exhibit all the relevant documents. The statement must contain and be verified by a statement of truth in the following terms:

"I make this statement knowing that it will be placed before the court, and confirm that to the best of my knowledge and belief its contents are true."

(Further provisions about statements of truth are contained in Part 17 of these Rules and Practice Direction 17A).

Timetable for Non-Convention Cases

3.5 While the 6 week deadline referred to in paragraph 2.14 is set out in the 1980 Hague Convention and in the Council Regulation, non-Convention child abduction cases must similarly be completed in 6 weeks except where exceptional circumstances make this impossible. Paragraph 2.14 applies to these cases as appropriate for a non-Convention case.

Part 4 – General Provisions

Urgent applications, or applications out of business hours

4.1 Guidance about urgent and out of hours applications is in Practice Direction 12E (Urgent Business).

Police assistance to prevent removal from England and Wales

4.2 The Child Abduction Act 1984 sets out the circumstances in which the removal of a child from this jurisdiction is a criminal offence. The police provide the following 24 hour service to prevent the unlawful removal of a child:

    (a)   they inform ports directly when there is a real and imminent threat that a child is about to be removed unlawfully from the country; and

    (b)   they liaise with Immigration Officers at the ports in an attempt to identify children at risk of removal.

4.3 Where the child is under 16, it is not necessary to obtain a court order before seeking police assistance. The police do not need an order to act to protect the child. If an order has already been obtained it should however be produced to the police. Where the child is between 16 and 18, an order must be obtained restricting or restraining removal before seeking police assistance.

4.4 Where the child is a ward of court (see Practice Direction 12D (Inherent Jurisdiction (including Wardship) Proceedings) the court's permission is needed to remove that child from the jurisdiction. When the court has not given that permission and police assistance is sought to prevent the removal of the ward, the applicant must produce evidence that the child is a ward such as:

    (a)   an order confirming wardship;

    (b)   an injunction; or

    (c)   where the matter is urgent and no order has been made, a certified copy of the wardship application.

4.5 The application for police assistance must be made by the applicant or his legal representative to the applicant's local police station except that applications may be made to any police station:

    (a)   in urgent cases;

    (b)   where the wardship application has just been issued; or

    (c)   where the court has just made the order relied on.

PART III

4.6 The police will, if they consider it appropriate, institute the "port alert" system (otherwise known as "an all ports warning") to try to prevent removal from the jurisdiction where the danger of removal is:

  (a) real (ie not being sought merely by way of insurance); and
  (b) imminent (ie within 24 to 48 hours).

4.7 The request for police assistance must be accompanied by as much of the following information as possible:

  (a) *the child:* the name, sex, date of birth, physical description, nationality and passport number; if the child has more than one nationality or passport, provide details;
  (b) *the person likely to remove:* the name, age, physical description, nationality, passport number, relationship to the child, and whether the child is likely to assist him or her; if the person has more than one nationality or passport, provide details;
  (c) *person applying for a port alert:* the name, relationship to the child, nationality, telephone number and (if appropriate) solicitor's or other legal representative's name and contact details; if the person has more than one nationality, provide details;
  (d) likely destination;
  (e) likely time of travel and port of embarkation and, if known, details of travel arrangements;
  (f) grounds for port alert (as appropriate) –
    (i)   suspected offence under section 1 or section 2 of the Child Abduction Act 1984;
    (ii) the child is subject to a court order.
  (g) details of person to whom the child should be returned if intercepted.

4.8 If the police decide that the case is one in which the port-alert system should be used, the child's name will remain on the stop list for **four weeks**. After that time it will be removed automatically unless a further application is made.

The Identity and Passport Service

4.9 Where the court makes an order prohibiting or otherwise restricting the removal of a child from the United Kingdom, or from any specified part of it, or from a specified dependent territory, the court may make an order under section 37 of the Family Law Act 1986 requiring any person to surrender any UK passport which has been issued to, or contains particulars of, the child.

4.10 The Identity and Passport Service ("IPS") will take action to prevent a United Kingdom passport or replacement passport being issued only where the IPS has been served with a court order expressly requiring a United Kingdom passport to be surrendered, or expressly prohibiting the issue of any further United Kingdom passport facilities to the child without the consent of the court, or the holder of such an order. Accordingly, in every case in which such an order has been made, the IPS must be served the same day if possible, or at the latest the following day, with a copy of the order. It is the responsibility of the applicant to do this. The specimen form of letter set out below should be used and a copy of the court order must be attached to the letter. Delay in sending the letter to the IPS must be kept to an absolute minimum.

"The Caveat Officer
Fraud and Intelligence Unit
Identity and Passport Service
Globe House
89 Eccleston Square
London SW1V 1PN

Dear Sir/Madam

........................v.....................

Case no: ....

This is to inform you that the court has today made an order

*prohibiting the issue of a passport/passports to [name(s)] [date of birth (if known)] of [address] without the consent of the holder of the order.

*requiring [name(s)] [date of birth (if known)] of [address] to surrender the passport(s) issued to him/her/them/the following child[ren] / or which contain(s) particulars of the following child[ren]:

NameDate of Birth

*and has granted an injunction/*made an order restraining the removal of the child[ren] from the jurisdiction.

(*Delete as appropriate)

Please add these names to your records to prevent the issue of further passport facilities for the child[ren]. I enclose a copy of the court order.

Yours faithfully

Applicant's name / Applicant's Solicitor's name"

4.11 Following service on the IPS of an order either expressly requiring a United Kingdom passport to be surrendered by, or expressly prohibiting the issue of any further United Kingdom passport facilities to the child, the IPS will maintain a prohibition on issuing a passport, or further passport facilities until the child's 16th birthday. The order should state that a passport must not be granted/applied for without the consent of the court or the holder of the order.

Note: These requests may also be sent to any of the regional Passport Offices.

4.12 Further information on communicating with the IPS where the court has made a request of, or an order against, the IPS, may be found in the Protocol: Communicating with the Identity and Passport Service in Family Proceedings of August 2003.

4.13 Information about other circumstances, in which the IPS will agree not to issue a passport to a child if the IPS receives an application, or an order in more general terms than set out at 4.11 above, from a person who claims to have parental responsibility for the child, is available from the IPS or at www.direct.gov.uk.

Note—See now www.gov.uk.

The Home Office

4.14 Information about communicating with the Home Office, where a question of the immigration status of a party arises in family proceedings, may be found in the Protocol: Communicating with the Home Office in Family Proceedings (revised and re-issued October 2010).

Note—The Protocol has been reissued as of April 2013 (see Part V).

PART III

Press Reporting

4.15 When a child has been abducted and a judge considers that publicity may help in tracing the child, the judge may adjourn the case for a short period to enable representatives of the Press to attend to give the case the widest possible publicity.

4.16. If a Child Rescue Alert has been used concerning a child, within the UK or abroad, it will give rise to media publicity. The court should be informed that this has happened. If there are already court proceedings concerning a child, it is advisable to obtain the agreement of the court before there is publicity to trace a missing child. If the court has not given its permission for a child who is the subject of children proceedings to be identified as the subject of proceedings, to do so would be contempt of court.

Other Assistance

4.17 The Missing Persons Bureau will be participating for the UK in the European Union wide 116 000 hotline for missing children. Parents and children can ring this number for assistance. (It is primarily intended to deal with criminal matters, for example stranger kidnapping.)

4.18 It may also be possible to trace a child by obtaining a court order under the inherent jurisdiction or the wardship jurisdiction of the High Court addressed to certain government departments, as set out in Practice Direction 6C.

Part 5 – Applications about rights of access

5.1 Access orders made in another Member State of the European Union (except Denmark) can be enforced in England or Wales under the Council Regulation.

5.2 Chapter III of the Council Regulation sets out provision for recognition and enforcement of parental responsibility orders, which include orders for custody and access (residence and contact) between Member States. Under Article 41 of the Council Regulation you can enforce an access order in your favour from another Member State directly, provided you produce the certificate given under Article 41(2) by the court which made the order. This is a quick procedure. The unsuccessful party is not allowed to oppose recognition of the order.

5.3 The rules on recognition and enforcement of parental responsibility orders are in Part 31. You should apply to the High Court using Form C69, Rule 31.8 covers applications for Article 41 of the Council Regulation. You can make the application without notice.

5.4 If the Council Regulation does not apply, and the access order was made by a State party to the European Convention, an application can be made to enforce the order under Article 11 of the European Convention. Paragraph 2.20 above gives further information about how to make the application.

5.5 Article 21 of the 1980 Hague Convention requires the States parties to respect rights of access. However, in the case of *Re G (A Minor) (Hague Convention: Access)* [1993] 1 FLR 669, the Court of Appeal took the view that Article 21 conferred no jurisdiction to determine matters relating to access, or to recognise or enforce foreign access orders (see Practice Note of 5 March 1993: Child Abduction Unit: Lord Chancellor's Department set out in the Annex to this Practice Direction). (The Child Abduction Unit is now called ICACU see paragraph 2.6.) An access order which does not fall within the Council Regulation or the (very limited) application of the European Convention may only be enforced by applying for a "contact order" under section 8 of the Children Act 1989.

5.6 This means that if, during the course of proceedings under the 1980 Hague Convention for a return order, the applicant decides to ask for access (contact) instead of the return of the child, but no agreement can be reached, a separate application for a contact order will have to be made, or the court invited to make a contact order without an application being made (Children Act 1989, s 10(1)(b)).

Part 6 – Child abduction cases between the United Kingdom and Pakistan

6.1 A consensus was reached in January 2003 between the President of the Family Division and the Hon. Chief Justice of Pakistan as to the principles to be applied in resolving child abduction cases between the UK and Pakistan.

The Protocol setting out that consensus can be accessed at:

http://www.fco.gov.uk/resources/en/pdf/2855621/3069133

ANNEX

See paragraph 5.5

Practice Note

5 March 1993

Citations: [1993] 1 FLR 804

Child Abduction Unit: Lord Chancellor's Department

Duties of the Central Authority for England and Wales under Article 21 of the Hague Convention on the Civil Aspects of International Child Abduction

CHILD ABDUCTION AND CUSTODY ACT 1985

In the case of *Re G (A Minor) (Hague Convention: Access)* [1993] 1 FLR 669 the Court of Appeal considered the duties of the Central Authority for England and Wales on receiving an application in respect of rights of access under Art 21 of the Hague Convention.

The Court of Appeal took the view that Art 21 conferred no jurisdiction to determine matters relating to access, or to recognise or enforce foreign access orders. It provides, however, for executive co-operation in the enforcement of such recognition as national law allows.

Accordingly, the duty of the Central Authority is to make appropriate arrangements for the applicant by providing solicitors to act on his behalf in applying for legal aid and instituting proceedings in the High Court under s 8 of the Children Act 1989.

If, during the course of proceedings under Art 21 of the Convention, the applicant decides to seek access instead of the return of the child, but no agreement can be reached and the provisions of the European Convention on the Recognition and Enforcement of Decisions Concerning Custody of Children and on Restoration of Custody of Children are not available, a separate application under s 8 of the Children Act 1989 will have to be made.

Central Authority for England and Wales

NOTE: The Child Abduction Unit is now called ICACU, see paragraph 2.6.

Practice Direction 12G –
Communication of Information

This Practice Direction supplements FPR Part 12, Chapter 7

1.1 Chapter 7 deals with the communication of information (whether or not contained in a document filed with the court) relating to proceedings which relate to children.

1.2 Subject to any direction of the court, information may be communicated for the purposes of the law relating to contempt in accordance with paragraphs 2.1, 3.1 or 4.1.

Communication of information by a party etc. for other purposes

2.1 A person specified in the first column of the following table may communicate to a person listed in the second column such information as is specified in the third column for the purpose or purposes specified in the fourth column –

A party	A lay adviser, a McKenzie Friend, or a person arranging or providing pro bono legal services	Any information relating to the proceedings	To enable the party to obtain advice or assistance in relation to the proceedings
A party	A health care professional or a person or body providing counselling services for children or families		To enable the party or any child of the party to obtain health care or counselling
A party	The Child Maintenance and Enforcement Commission, a McKenzie Friend, a lay adviser or the First-tier Tribunal dealing with an appeal made under section 20 of the Child Support Act 1991		For the purposes of making or responding to an appeal under section 20 of the Child Support Act 1991 or the determination of such an appeal
A party	An adoption panel		To enable the adoption panel to discharge its functions as appropriate

A party	A local authority's medical adviser appointed under the Adoption Agencies Regulations 2005 or the Adoption Agencies (Wales) Regulations 2005		To enable the medical adviser to discharge his or her functions as appropriate
A party	The European Court of Human Rights		For the purpose of making an application to the European Court of Human Rights
A party or any person lawfully in receipt of information	The Children's Commissioner or the Children's Commissioner for Wales		To refer an issue affecting the interests of children to the Children's Commissioner or the Children's Commissioner for Wales
A party, any person lawfully in receipt of information or a proper officer	A person or body conducting an approved research project		For the purpose of an approved research project
A legal representative or a professional legal adviser	A person or body responsible for investigating or determining complaints in relation to legal representatives or professional legal advisers		For the purposes of the investigation or determination of a complaint in relation to a legal representative or a professional legal adviser
A legal representative or a professional legal adviser	A person or body assessing quality assurance systems		To enable the legal representative or professional legal adviser to obtain a quality assurance assessment
A legal representative or a professional legal adviser	An accreditation body	Any information relating to the proceedings providing that it does not, or is not likely to, identify any person involved in the proceedings	To enable the legal representative or professional legal adviser to obtain accreditation

PART III

...ty	A police officer	The text or summary of the whole or part of a judgment given in the proceedings	For the purpose of a criminal investigation
A party or any person lawfully in receipt of information	A member of the Crown Prosecution Service		To enable the Crown Prosecution Service to discharge its functions under any enactment

"The Child Maintenance and Enforcement Commission"—By virtue of SI 2012/2007, art 5(3), this should be read as "The Secretary of State".

Communication for the effective functioning of Cafcass and CAFCASS CYMRU

3.1 An officer of the Service or a Welsh family proceedings officer, as appropriate, may communicate to a person listed in the second column such information as is specified in the third column for the purpose or purposes specified in the fourth column –

A Welsh family proceedings officer	A person or body exercising statutory functions relating to inspection of CAFCASS CYMRU	Any information relating to the proceedings which is required by the person or body responsible for the inspection	For the purpose of an inspection of CAFCASS CYMRU by a body or person appointed by the Welsh Ministers
An officer of the Service or a Welsh family proceedings officer	The Health and Care Professions Council	Any information relating to the proceedings providing that it does not, or is not likely to, identify any person involved in the proceedings	For the purpose of initial and continuing accreditation as a social worker of a person providing services to Cafcass or CAFCASS CYMRU in accordance with section 13(2) of the Criminal Justice and Courts Services Act 2000 or section 36 of the Children Act 2004 as the case may be
An officer of the Service or a Welsh family proceedings officer	A person or body providing services relating to professional development or training to Cafcass or CAFCASS CYMRU	Any information relating to the proceedings providing that it does not, or is not likely to, identify any person involved in the proceedings without that person's consent	To enable the person or body to provide the services, where the services cannot be effectively provided without such disclosure

An officer of the Service or a Welsh family proceedings officer	A person employed by or contracted to Cafcass or CAFCASS CYMRU for the purposes of carrying out the functions referred to in column 4 of this row	Any information relating to the proceedings	Engagement in processes internal to Cafcass or CAFCASS CYMRU which relate to the maintenance of necessary records concerning the proceedings, or to ensuring that Cafcass or CAFCASS CYMRU functions are carried out to a satisfactory standard

Communication to and by Ministers of the Crown and Welsh Ministers

4.1 A person specified in the first column of the following table may communicate to a person listed in the second column such information as is specified in the third column for the purpose or purposes specified in the fourth column –

A party or any person lawfully in receipt of information relating to the proceedings	A Minister of the Crown with responsibility for a government department engaged, or potentially engaged, in an application before the European Court of Human Rights relating to the proceedings	Any information relating to the proceedings of which he or she is in lawful possession	To provide the department with information relevant, or potentially relevant, to the proceedings before the European Court of Human Rights
A Minister of the Crown	The European Court of Human Rights		For the purpose of engagement in an application before the European Court of Human Rights relating to the proceedings
A Minister of the Crown	Lawyers advising or representing the United Kingdom in an application before the European Court of Human Rights relating to the proceedings		For the purpose of receiving advice or for effective representation in relation to the application before the European Court of Human Rights

PART III

A Minister of the crown or a Welsh Minister	Another Minister, or Ministers, of the Crown or a Welsh Minister		For the purpose of notification, discussion and the giving or receiving of advice regarding issues raised by the information in which the relevant departments have, or may have, an interest

5.1 This paragraph applies to communications made in accordance with paragraphs 2.1, 3.1 and 4.1 and the reference in this paragraph to "the table" means the table in the relevant paragraph.

5.2 A person in the second column of the table may only communicate information relating to the proceedings received from a person in the first column for the purpose or purposes –

    (a) for which he or she received that information; or

    (b) of professional development or training, providing that any communication does not, or is not likely to, identify any person involved in the proceedings without that person's consent.

6.1 In this Practice Direction –

"accreditation body" means –

    (a) The Law Society,

    (b) Resolution, or

    (c) The Legal Services Commission;

"adoption panel" means a panel established in accordance with regulation 3 of the Adoption Agencies Regulations 2005 or regulation 3 of the Adoption Agencies (Wales) Regulations 2005;

"approved research project" means a project of research –

    (a) approved in writing by a Secretary of State after consultation with the President of the Family Division,

    (b) approved in writing by the President of the Family Division, or

    (c) conducted under section 83 of the Act of 1989 or section 13 of the Criminal Justice and Court Services Act 2000;

"body assessing quality assurance systems" includes –

    (a) The Law Society,

    (b) The Legal Services Commission, or

    (c) The General Council of the Bar;

"body or person responsible for investigating or determining complaints in relation to legal representatives or professional legal advisers" means –

    (a) The Law Society,

    (b) The General Council of the Bar,

    (c) The Institute of Legal Executives,

    (d) The Legal Services Ombudsman; or

    (e) The Office of Legal Complaints.

"Cafcass" has the meaning assigned to it by section 11 of the Criminal Justice and Courts Services Act 2000;

"CAFCASS CYMRU" means the part of the Welsh Assembly Government exercising the functions of Welsh Ministers under Part 4 of the Children Act 2004;

"criminal investigation" means an investigation conducted by police officers with a view to it being ascertained –

    (a)   whether a person should be charged with an offence, or

    (b)   whether a person charged with an offence is guilty of it;

"health care professional" means –

    (a)   a registered medical practitioner,

    (b)   a registered nurse or midwife,

    (c)   a clinical psychologist, or

    (d)   a child psychotherapist;

"lay adviser" means a non-professional person who gives lay advice on behalf of an organisation in the lay advice sector;

"McKenzie Friend" means any person permitted by the court to sit beside an unrepresented litigant in court to assist that litigant by prompting, taking notes and giving him advice; and

"social worker" has the meaning assigned to it by section 55 of the Care Standards Act 2000.

Practice Direction 12H – Contribution Orders

This Practice Direction supplements FPR Part 12

1.1 Paragraph 23(6) of Schedule 2 to the 1989 Act provides that where –

    (a)   a contribution order is in force;

    (b)   the local authority serve another contribution notice; and

    (c)   the contributor and the local authority reach an agreement under paragraph 22(7) in respect of that other contribution notice,

the effect of the agreement shall be to discharge the order from the date on which it is agreed that the agreement shall take effect.

1.2 Where a local authority notifies the court of an agreement reached under paragraph 23(6) of Schedule 2 to the 1989 Act, the notification must be sent in writing to the designated officer of the court.

Practice Direction 12I – Applications for Reporting Restriction Orders

This Practice Direction supplements FPR Part 12

1 This direction applies to any application in the Family Division founded on Convention rights for an order restricting publication of information about children or incapacitated adults.

2 Applications to be heard in the High Court

Orders can only be made in the High Court and are normally dealt with by a Judge of the Family Division. If the need for an order arises in existing proceedings in the county court, judges should either transfer the application to the High Court or consult their Family Division Liaison Judge. Where the matter is urgent, it can be heard by the Urgent Applications Judge of the Family Division (out of hours contact number 020 7947 6000).

PART III

3 Service of application on the national news media

Section 12(2) of the Human Rights Act 1998 means that an injunction restricting the exercise of the right to freedom of expression must not be granted where the person against whom the application is made is neither present nor represented unless the court is satisfied (a) that the applicant has taken all practicable steps to notify the respondent, or (b) that there are compelling reasons why the respondent should not be notified.

Service of applications for reporting restriction orders on the national media can now be effected via the Press Association's CopyDirect service, to which national newspapers and broadcasters subscribe as a means of receiving notice of such applications.

The court will bear in mind that legal advisers to the media (i) are used to participating in hearings at very short notice where necessary; and (ii) are able to differentiate between information provided for legal purposes and information for editorial use. Service of applications via the CopyDirect service should henceforth be the norm.

The court retains the power to make without notice orders, but such cases will be exceptional, and an order will always give persons affected liberty to apply to vary or discharge it at short notice.

4 Further guidance

The *Practice Note Applications for Reporting Restriction Orders* dated 18 March 2005 and issued jointly by the Official Solicitor and the Deputy Director of Legal Services, provides valuable guidance and should be followed.

5 Issued with the concurrence and approval of the Lord Chancellor.

Practice Direction 12J –
Residence and Contact Orders: Domestic Violence and Harm

This Practice Direction supplements FPR Part 12

1 This Practice Direction applies to any family proceedings in the High Court, a county court or a magistrates' court in which an application is made for a residence order or a contact order in respect of a child under the Children Act 1989 ("the 1989 Act") or the Adoption and Children Act 2002 ("the 2002 Act") or in which any question arises about residence or about contact between a child and a parent or other family member.

2 The practice set out in this Direction is to be followed in any case in which it is alleged, or there is otherwise reason to suppose, that the subject child or a party has experienced domestic violence perpetrated by another party or that there is a risk of such violence. For the purpose of this Direction, the term 'domestic violence' includes physical violence, threatening or intimidating behaviour and any other form of abuse which, directly or indirectly, may have caused harm to the other party or to the child or which may give rise to the risk of harm.

> ('Harm' in relation to a child means ill-treatment or the impairment of health or development, including, for example, impairment suffered from seeing or hearing the ill-treatment of another: Children Act 1989, ss 31(9), 105(1))

General principles

3 The court must, at all stages of the proceedings, consider whether domestic violence is raised as an issue, either by the parties or otherwise, and if so must:

- identify at the earliest opportunity the factual and welfare issues involved;
- consider the nature of any allegation or admission of domestic violence and the extent to which any domestic violence which is admitted, or which may be proved, would be relevant in deciding whether to make an order about residence or contact and, if so, in what terms;
- give directions to enable the relevant factual and welfare issues to be determined expeditiously and fairly.

4 In all cases it is for the court to decide whether an order for residence or contact accords with Section 1(1) of the 1989 Act or section 1(2) of the 2002 Act, as appropriate; any proposed residence or contact order, whether to be made by agreement between the parties or otherwise must be scrutinised by the court accordingly. The court shall not make a consent order for residence or contact or give permission for an application for a residence or contact order to be withdrawn, unless the parties are present in court, except where it is satisfied that there is no risk of harm to the child in so doing.

5 In considering, on an application for a consent order for residence or contact, whether there is any risk of harm to the child, the court shall consider all the evidence and information available. The court may direct a report under Section 7 of the 1989 Act either orally or in writing before it makes its determination; in such a case, the court may ask for information about any advice given by the officer preparing the report to the parties and whether they or the child have been referred to any other agency, including local authority children's services. If the report is not in writing, the court shall make a note of its substance on the court file.

Issue

6 Immediately on receipt of an application for a residence order or a contact order, or of the acknowledgement of the application, the court shall send a copy of it, together with any accompanying documents, to Cafcass or Cafcass Cymru, as appropriate, to enable Cafcass or Cafcass Cymru to undertake initial screening in accordance with their safeguarding policies.

Liaison

7 The Designated Family Judge, or in the magistrates' court the Justices' Clerk, shall take steps to ensure that arrangements are in place for:

- the prompt delivery of documents to Cafcass or Cafcass Cymru in accordance with paragraph 6
- any information obtained by Cafcass or Cafcass Cymru as a result of initial screening or otherwise and any risk assessments prepared by Cafcass or Cafcass Cymru under section 16A of the 1989 Act to be placed before the appropriate court for consideration and directions
- a copy of any record of admissions or findings of fact made pursuant to paragraphs 12 & 21 below to be made available as soon as possible to any Officer of Cafcass or Welsh family proceedings officer or local authority officer preparing a report under section 7 of the 1989 Act.

PART III

Response of the court on receipt of information

8 Where any information provided to the court before the first hearing, whether as a result of initial screening by Cafcass or Cafcass Cymru or otherwise, indicates that there are issues of domestic violence which may be relevant to the court's determination, the court may give directions about the conduct of the hearing and for written evidence to be filed by the parties before the hearing.

9 If at any stage the court is advised by Cafcass or Cafcass Cymru or otherwise that there is a need for special arrangements to secure the safety of any party or child attending any hearing, the court shall ensure that appropriate arrangements are made for the hearing and for all subsequent hearings in the case, unless it considers that these are no longer necessary.

First hearing

10 At the first hearing, the court shall inform the parties of the content of any screening report or other information which has been provided by Cafcass or Cafcass Cymru, unless it considers that to do so would create a risk of harm to a party or the child.

> (Specific provision about service of a risk assessment under section 16A of the 1989 Act is made by rule 12.34 of the Family Procedure Rules 2010.)

11 The court must ascertain at the earliest opportunity whether domestic violence is raised as an issue and must consider the likely impact of that issue on the conduct and outcome of the proceedings. In particular, the court should consider whether the nature and effect of the domestic violence alleged is such that, if proved, the decision of the court is likely to be affected.

Admissions

12 Where at any hearing an admission of domestic violence to another person or the child is made by a party, the admission should be recorded in writing and retained on the court file.

Directions for a fact-finding hearing

13 The court should determine as soon as possible whether it is necessary to conduct a fact-finding hearing in relation to any disputed allegation of domestic violence before it can proceed to consider any final order(s) for residence or contact. Where the court determines that a finding of fact hearing is not necessary, the order shall record the reasons for that decision.

14 Where the court considers that a fact-finding hearing is necessary, it must give directions to ensure that the matters in issue are determined expeditiously and fairly and in particular it should consider:

- directing the parties to file written statements giving particulars of the allegations made and of any response in such a way as to identify clearly the issues for determination;
- whether material is required from third parties such as the police or health services and may give directions accordingly;
- whether any other evidence is required to enable the court to make findings of fact in relation to the allegations and may give directions accordingly.

15 Where the court fixes a fact-finding hearing, it must at the same time fix a further hearing for determination of the application. The hearings should be arranged in such a way that they are conducted by the same judge or, in the magistrates' court, by at least the same chairperson of the justices.

Reports under Section 7

16 In any case where domestic violence is raised as an issue, the court should consider directing that a report on the question of contact, or any other matters relating to the welfare of the child, be prepared under section 7 of the 1989 Act by an Officer of Cafcass or a Welsh family proceedings officer (or local authority officer if appropriate), unless the court is satisfied that it is not necessary to do so in order to safeguard the child's interests. If the court so directs, it should consider the extent of any enquiries which can properly be made at this stage and whether it is appropriate to seek information on the wishes and feelings of the child before findings of fact have been made.

Representation of the child

17 Subject to the seriousness of the allegations made and the difficulty of the case, the court shall consider whether it is appropriate for the child who is the subject of the application to be made a party to the proceedings and be separately represented. If the case is proceeding in the magistrates' court and the court considers that it may be appropriate for the child to be made a party to the proceedings, it may transfer the case to the relevant county court for determination of that issue and following such transfer the county court shall give such directions for the further conduct of the case as it considers appropriate.

Interim orders before determination of relevant facts

18 Where the court gives directions for a fact-finding hearing, the court should consider whether an interim order for residence or contact is in the interests of the child; and in particular whether the safety of the child and the residential parent can be secured before, during and after any contact.

19 In deciding any question of interim residence or contact pending a full hearing the court should –

    (a)   take into account the matters set out in section 1(3) of the 1989 Act or section 1(4) of the 2002 Act ('the welfare check-list'), as appropriate;

    (b)   give particular consideration to the likely effect on the child of any contact and any risk of harm, whether physical, emotional or psychological, which the child is likely to suffer as a consequence of making or declining to make an order.

20 Where the court is considering whether to make an order for interim contact, it should in addition consider

    (a)   the arrangements required to ensure, as far as possible, that any risk of harm to the child is minimised and that the safety of the child and the parties is secured; and in particular:

        (i)   whether the contact should be supervised or supported, and if so, where and by whom; and

        (ii)   the availability of appropriate facilities for that purpose

    (b)   if direct contact is not appropriate, whether it is in the best interests of the child to make an order for indirect contact.

PART III

The fact-finding hearing

21 At the fact-finding hearing, the court should, wherever practicable, make findings of fact as to the nature and degree of any domestic violence which is established and its effect on the child, the child's parents and any other relevant person. The court shall record its findings in writing, and shall serve a copy on the parties. A copy of any record of findings of fact or of admissions must be sent to any officer preparing a report under Section 7 of the 1989 Act.

22 At the conclusion of any fact-finding hearing, the court shall consider, notwithstanding any earlier direction for a section 7 report, whether it is in the best interests of the child for the court to give further directions about the preparation or scope of any report under section 7; where necessary, it may adjourn the proceedings for a brief period to enable the officer to make representations about the preparation or scope of any further enquiries. The court should also consider whether it would be assisted by any social work, psychiatric, psychological or other assessment of any party or the child and if so (subject to any necessary consent) make directions for such assessment to be undertaken and for the filing of any consequent report.

23 Where the court has made findings of fact on disputed allegations, any subsequent hearing in the proceedings should be conducted by the same judge or, in the magistrates' court, by at least the same chairperson of the justices. Exceptions may be made only where observing this requirement would result in delay to the planned timetable and the judge or chairperson is satisfied, for reasons recorded in writing, that the detriment to the welfare of the child would outweigh the detriment to the fair trial of the proceedings.

In all cases where domestic violence has occurred

24 The court should take steps to obtain (or direct the parties or an Officer of Cafcass or a Welsh family proceedings officer to obtain) information about the facilities available locally to assist any party or the child in cases where domestic violence has occurred.

25 Following any determination of the nature and extent of domestic violence, whether or not following a fact-finding hearing, the court should consider whether any party should seek advice or treatment as a precondition to an order for residence or contact being made or as a means of assisting the court in ascertaining the likely risk of harm to the child from that person, and may (with the consent of that party) give directions for such attendance and the filing of any consequent report.

Factors to be taken into account when determining whether to make residence or contact orders in all cases where domestic violence has occurred

26 When deciding the issue of residence or contact the court should, in the light of any findings of fact, apply the individual matters in the welfare checklist with reference to those findings; in particular, where relevant findings of domestic violence have been made, the court should in every case consider any harm which the child has suffered as a consequence of that violence and any harm which the child is at risk of suffering if an order for residence or contact is made and should only make an order for contact if it can be satisfied that the physical and emotional safety of the child and the parent with whom the child is living can, as far as possible, be secured before during and after contact.

27 In every case where a finding of domestic violence is made, the court should consider the conduct of both parents towards each other and towards the child; in particular, the court should consider;

   (a)   the effect of the domestic violence which has been established on the child and on the parent with whom the child is living;

   (b)   the extent to which the parent seeking residence or contact is motivated by a desire to promote the best interests of the child or may be doing so as a means of continuing a process of violence, intimidation or harassment against the other parent;

(c) the likely behaviour during contact of the parent seeking contact and its effect on the child;

(d) the capacity of the parent seeking residence or contact to appreciate the effect of past violence and the potential for future violence on the other parent and the child;

(e) the attitude of the parent seeking residence or contact to past violent conduct by that parent; and in particular whether that parent has the capacity to change and to behave appropriately.

Directions as to how contact is to proceed

28 Where the court has made findings of domestic violence but, having applied the welfare checklist, nonetheless considers that direct contact is in the best interests of the child, the court should consider what if any directions or conditions are required to enable the order to be carried into effect and in particular should consider:

(a) whether or not contact should be supervised, and if so, where and by whom;

(b) whether to impose any conditions to be complied with by the party in whose favour the order for contact has been made and if so, the nature of those conditions, for example by way of seeking advice or treatment (subject to any necessary consent);

(c) whether such contact should be for a specified period or should contain provisions which are to have effect for a specified period;

(d) whether or not the operation of the order needs to be reviewed; if so the court should set a date for the review and give directions to ensure that at the review the court has full information about the operation of the order.

29 Where the court does not consider direct contact to be appropriate, it shall consider whether it is in the best interests of the child to make an order for indirect contact.

The reasons of the court

30 In its judgment or reasons the court should always make clear how its findings on the issue of domestic violence have influenced its decision on the issue of residence or contact. In particular, where the court has found domestic violence proved but nonetheless makes an order, the court should always explain, whether by way of reference to the welfare check-list or otherwise, why it takes the view that the order which it has made is in the best interests of the child.

31 This Practice Direction is issued by the President of the Family Division, as the nominee of the Lord Chief Justice, with the agreement of the Lord Chancellor.

PART III

Practice Direction 12K –
Children Act 1989: Exclusion Requirement

This Practice Direction supplements FPR Part 12

Under s 38A(5) and s 44A(5) of the Children Act 1989 the court may attach a power of arrest to an exclusion requirement included in an interim care order or an emergency protection order. In cases where an order is made which includes an exclusion requirement, the following shall apply:

(1) If a power of arrest is attached to the order then unless the person to whom the exclusion requirement refers was given notice of the hearing and attended the hearing, the name of that person and that an order has been made including an exclusion requirement to which a power of arrest has been attached shall be announced in open court at the earliest opportunity. This may be either on the same day when the court proceeds to hear cases in open court or where there is no further business in open court on that day at the next listed sitting of the court.

(2) When a person arrested under a power of arrest cannot conveniently be brought before the relevant judicial authority sitting in a place normally used as a courtroom within 24 hours after the arrest, he may be brought before the relevant judicial authority at any convenient place but, as the liberty of the subject is involved, the press and the public should be permitted to be present, unless security needs make this impracticable.

(3) Any order of committal made otherwise than in public or in a courtroom open to the public, shall be announced in open court at the earliest opportunity. This may be either on the same day when the court proceeds to hear cases in open court or where there is no further business in open court on that day at the next listed sitting of the court. The announcement shall state –
(a) the name of the person committed,
(b) in general terms the nature of the contempt of the court in respect of which the order of committal has been made, and
(c) the length of the period of committal.

Practice Direction 12L –
Children Act 1989: Risk Assessments under
Section 16A

This Practice Direction supplements FPR Part 12

1 This Practice Direction applies to any family proceedings in the High Court, a county court or a magistrates' court in which a risk assessment is made under section 16A of the Children Act 1989 ("the 1989 Act"). It has effect from 1 October 2007.

2 Section 16A(2) of the 1989 Act provides that, if in carrying out any function to which the section applies (as set out in section 16A(1)), an officer of the Service or a Welsh family proceedings officer is given cause to suspect that the child concerned is at risk of harm, the officer must make a risk assessment in relation to the child and provide the risk assessment to the court.

3 The duty to provide the risk assessment to the court arises irrespective of the outcome of the assessment. Where an officer is given cause to suspect that the child concerned is

at risk of harm and makes a risk assessment in accordance with section 16A(2), the officer must provide the assessment to the court, even if he or she reaches the conclusion that there is no risk of harm to the child.

4 The fact that a risk assessment has been carried out is a material fact that should be placed before the court, whatever the outcome of the assessment. In reporting the outcome to the court, the officer should make clear the factor or factors that triggered the decision to carry out the assessment.

5 Issued by the President of the Family Division, as the nominee of the Lord Chief Justice, with the agreement of the Lord Chancellor.

Practice Direction 12M –
Family Assistance Orders: Consultation

This Practice Direction supplements FPR Part 12

1 This Practice Direction applies to any family proceedings in the High Court, a county court or a magistrates' court in which the court is considering whether to make a family assistance order under section 16 of the Children Act 1989, as amended ("the 1989 Act"). It has effect from 1 October 2007.

2 Before making a family assistance order the court must have obtained the opinion of the appropriate officer about whether it would be in the best interests of the child in question for a family assistance order to be made and, if so, how the family assistance order could operate and for what period.

3 The appropriate officer will be an officer of the Service, a Welsh family proceedings officer or an officer of a local authority, depending on the category of officer the court proposes to require to be made available under the family assistance order.

4 The opinion of the appropriate officer may be given orally or in writing (for example, it may form part of a report under section 7 of the 1989 Act).

5 Before making a family assistance order the court must give any person whom it proposes be named in the order an opportunity to comment upon any opinion given by the appropriate officer.

6 Issued by the President of the Family Division, as the nominee of the Lord Chief Justice, with the agreement of the Lord Chancellor.

Practice Direction 12N –
Enforcement of Children Act 1989 Contact Orders:
Disclosure of Information to Officers of the National
Probation Service (High Court and County Court)

This Practice Direction supplements FPR Part 12

Note—The Lord Chief Justice issued a Practice Direction on this subject for the magistrates' courts mirroring the one for the High Court and county courts. This is set out in *The Family Court Practice 2010*.

1 This Practice Direction applies to proceedings in the High Court or a county court where:

    (a)   the court is considering an application for an enforcement order[1] or for an order following an alleged breach of an enforcement order[2] and asks an officer of the Service or a Welsh family proceedings officer to provide information to the court in accordance with section 11L(5) of the Children Act 1989; or

1   Under section 11J of the Children Act 1989.
2   Under paragraph 9 of Schedule A1 to the Children Act 1989.

    (b)   the court makes an enforcement order or an order following an alleged breach of an enforcement order and asks an officer of the Service or a Welsh family proceedings officer to monitor compliance with that order and to report to the court in accordance with section 11M of the Children Act 1989.

2 In all cases in which paragraph 1 applies, the officer of the Service or Welsh family proceedings officer will need to discuss aspects of the court case with an officer of the National Probation Service.

3 In order to ensure that the officer of the Service or Welsh family proceedings officer will not potentially be in contempt of court by virtue of such discussions, the court should, when making a request under section 11L(5) or section 11M of the Children Act 1989, give leave to that officer to disclose to the National Probation Service such information (whether or not contained in a document filed with the court) in relation to the proceedings as is necessary.

4 This Practice Direction comes into force on 8 December 2008.

Practice Direction 12O – Arrival of Child in England by Air

This Practice Direction supplements FPR Part 12

Where a person seeks an order for the return to him of children about to arrive in England by air and desires to have information to enable him to meet the aeroplane, the judge should be asked to include in his order a direction that the airline operating the flight, and, if he has the information, the immigration officer at the appropriate airport, should supply such information to that person.

To obtain such information in such circumstances in a case where a person already has an order for the return to him of children, that person should apply to a judge ex parte for such a direction.

Practice Direction 12P –
Removal from Jurisdiction: Issue of Passports

This Practice Direction supplements FPR Part 12

1 Removal from jurisdiction

The President has directed that on application for leave to remove from the jurisdiction for holiday periods a ward of court who has been placed by a local authority with foster-parents whose identity the court considers should remain confidential, for example because they are prospective adopters, it is important that such foster-parents should not be identified in the court's order. In such cases the order should be expressed as giving leave to the local authority to arrange for the child to be removed from England and Wales for the purpose of holidays.

It is also considered permissible, where care and control has been given to a local authority, or to an individual, for the court to give general leave to make such arrangements in suitable cases, thereby obviating the need to make application for leave each time it is desired to remove the child from the jurisdiction.

2 Issue of passports

It is the practice of the Passport Department of the Home Office to issue passports for wards in accordance with the court's direction. This frequently results in passports being restricted to the holiday period specified in the order giving leave. It is the President's opinion that it is more convenient for wards' passports to be issued without such restriction.

The Passport Department has agreed to issue passports on this basis unless the court otherwise directs. It will, of course, still be necessary for the leave of the court to be obtained for the child's removal.

PART 13
PROCEEDINGS UNDER SECTION 54 OF THE HUMAN FERTILISATION AND EMBRYOLOGY ACT 2008

CONTENTS OF THIS PART

13.1 Interpretation and application

(1) A reference in this Part to the 2002 Act is a reference to that Act as applied with modifications by the Human Fertilisation and Embryology (Parental Order) Regulations 2010.

(1) In this Part –

"the other parent" means any person who is a parent of the child but is not one of the applicants or the woman who carried the child (including any man who is the father by virtue of section 35 or 36 of the 2008 Act or any woman who is a parent by virtue of section 42 or 43 of that Act);

"parental order" means an order under section 54 of the 2008 Act;

"parental order proceedings" means proceedings for the making of a parental order under the 2008 Act or an order under any provision of the 2002 Act;

"parental order reporter" means an officer of the service or a Welsh family proceedings officer appointed to act on behalf of a child who is the subject of parental order proceedings;

"provision for contact" means a contact order under section 8 or 34 of the 1989 Act.

(3) Except where the contrary intention appears, the rules in this Part apply to parental order proceedings.

Defined terms—"2002 Act", "2008 Act": r 2.3(1).

Scope—A uniform procedure applies to applications for a parental order irrespective of the court in which proceedings are commenced. Pursuant to the amendments made to ATPO 2008, subject to certain exceptions, applications for a parental order must be commenced in the family proceedings court. Rule 13.1 defines the terms used in rule 13.

13.2 Application of Part 12

Rules 12.9 to 12.11, 12.19 and 12.21 apply as appropriate, with any necessary modifications, to parental order proceedings.

Scope—This rule confirms that the provisions set out in FPR 2010, Pt 12 relating to transfer of proceedings from one court to another, the steps to be taken following refusal of the family proceedings court to transfer, the prohibition relating to the filing of any additional evidence in whatever form without the direction of the court and the conduct of the hearing will apply to applications under s 54 of the 2008 Act.

13.3 Who the parties are

(1) An application for a parental order may be made by such of the following who satisfy the conditions set out in section 54(1) of the 2008 Act –

    (a)   a husband and wife;

    (b)   civil partners of each other; or

(c) two persons who are living as partners in an enduring family relationship and are not within the prohibited degrees of relationship in relation to each other.

(2) The respondents to an application for a parental order are –

(a) the woman who carried the child;

(b) the other parent (if any);

(c) any person in whose favour there is provision for contact; and

(d) any other person or body with parental responsibility for the child at the date of the application.

(3) The court will direct that a person with parental responsibility for the child be made a party to proceedings where that person requests to be one.

(4) The court may at any time direct that –

(a) any other person or body be made a respondent to the proceedings; or

(b) a respondent be removed from the proceedings.

(5) If the court makes a direction for the addition or removal of a party, it may give consequential directions about –

(a) serving a copy of the application form on any new respondent;

(b) serving relevant documents on the new party; and

(c) the management of the proceedings.

Defined Terms—"other parent': r 13.1.

Application for a parental order—The application should be made on Form C51 (FPR PD5A).

"any other person with parental responsibility"—This category includes: (i) the birth mother; (ii) the birth father if he was married to the child's mother when the child was born, or if not married to the birth mother he registered the birth jointly with the birth mother or a person who has been granted parental responsibility for the child pursuant to a formal parental responsibility agreement with the child's birth mother or court order or he has since the child's birth married the child's birth mother; (iii) a guardian of the child; (iv) a person who has been granted a residence order in respect of the child or a local authority under an emergency protection order or a care order; (v) the adoptive parent(s) of the child; (vi) a second female who was the civil partner of the child's birth mother when the child was born or if she was not a civil partner she has been granted a parental responsibility order, a residence order in her favour or parental responsibility by the birth mother by a formal parental responsibility agreement or she has since the child's birth become a civil partner of the birth mother; or (vii) any person who has been appointed a special guardian of the child. See also, the Hague Convention 1996, Arts 16–18 (in Part VI) on the issue of attribution and extinction of parental responsibility and FPR 2010, r 13.4, below.

13.4 Notice of proceedings to person with foreign parental responsibility

(1) This rule applies where a child is subject to proceedings to which this Part applies and at the date of the application –

(a) a person holds or is believed to hold parental responsibility for the child under the law of another State which subsists in accordance with Article 16 of the 1996 Hague Convention following the child becoming habitually resident in a territorial unit of the United Kingdom; and

(b) that person is not otherwise required to be joined as a respondent under rule 13.3.

(2) The applicant shall give notice of the proceedings to any person to whom the applicant believes paragraph (1) applies.

(3) The applicant and every respondent to the proceedings shall provide such details as they possess as to the identity and whereabouts of any person they believe to hold parental responsibility for the child in accordance with paragraph (1) to the court officer, upon making, or responding to the application as appropriate.

(4) Where the existence of such a person only becomes apparent to a party at a later date during the proceedings, that party must notify the court officer of those details at the earliest opportunity.

(5) Where a person to whom paragraph (1) applies receives notice of proceedings, that person may apply to the court to be joined as a party using the Part 18 procedure.

Scope—This provision deals with situations where there is a foreign element and Brussels IIA and the 1996 Hague Convention apply. Under the law of a number of EU countries and Contracting States to the 1996 Convention, for example, unmarried fathers have parental responsibility or other legal rights without the need for an order or agreement. The rule requires the applicant to give notice to such a person and gives that person the right to apply to be joined as a party using the FPR 2010, Pt 18 procedure (see below). It is important, therefore, to ensure that the notice of proceedings itself or a letter accompanying it draws the attention of the person concerned to his/her right to make an application to be joined as a party.

Procedure for making an application to be joined—The application should be made on a FPR 2010, Pt 18 application notice, which if not supported by a statement in support must be verified by a statement of truth (FPR 2010, r 17.2). Pt 18 and FPR PD18A procedure should be followed, as such an application and any interlocutory application in the course of existing proceedings must be made under that rule (see further FPR 2010, r 18.1).

13.5 What the court or a court officer will do when the application has been issued

(1) As soon as practicable after the issue of proceedings –

    (a) the court will –
        (i) if section 48(1) of the 2002 Act applies (restrictions on making parental orders), consider whether it is proper to hear the application;
        (ii) subject to paragraph (2), set a date for the first directions hearing;
        (iii) appoint a parental order reporter; and
        (iv) set a date for the hearing of the application; and
    (b) a court officer will –
        (i) return to the applicants the copies of the application together with any other documents the applicant is required to serve; and
        (ii) send a certified copy of the entry in the register of live births to the parental order reporter.

(2) Where it considers it appropriate the court may, instead of setting a date for a first directions appointment, give the directions provided for in rule 13.9.

Defined terms—"court officer": FPR 2010, r 2.3.

First directions hearing—Although this rule is not drafted in mandatory terms, to avoid delay it is suggested that the court should list the application for a first directions hearing, appoint a parental reporter and give such other directions as may appear to be appropriate, e g consider whether a litigation friend needs to be appointed for any of the parties to the application or whether an interpreter may be required at the first hearing and consider whether video link facilities may be required at the final hearing or other special arrangements are likely to be needed. If payment has been made to the surrogate mother the court may also need to consider whether a preliminary hearing to determine the issue set out in s 54(6),(8) of the 2008 Act is required. The issue of whether the woman who carried the child or the other parent or a respondent to the application is a protected person (and thus incapable of giving consent) may not be apparent on the face of the application and documents filed in the proceedings. Therefore, the question of the appointment of a litigation friend under r 15.6(3) may only be identified and appropriately dealt with at an oral hearing. Where the surrogacy arrangements were made outside the UK, directions may be required for a preliminary hearing if payment was made to the mother and also to consider the issue of jurisdiction (see further under Pt 2).

Timing of the first direction hearing—Unless the court otherwise directs, a first directions hearing must take place within 4 weeks of the date of issue of the application (see above for the reason why the application should be listed for a first directions hearing and r 13.8).

Directions without a hearing—Rule 13.5(2) authorises the court, if it considers it appropriate to do so, to give the comprehensive directions set out in FPR 2010, r 13.9 without a hearing. However, it is suggested that if the court adopts this procedure, the order made should include a clause that the order was made without a hearing and that any party or person who is affected by the terms of the order and disagrees with it has the right to make an application to be heard and/or for the order or any of its terms to be varied, set aside or discharged within a time specified in the order (see FPR 2010, rr 4.3(2)–(7), 13.9(5)).

13.6 Service of the application and other documents

(1) The applicants must, within 14 days before the hearing or first directions hearing, serve on the respondents –

   (a)   the application;

   (b)   a form for acknowledging service; and

   (c)   a notice of proceedings.

(2) The applicants must serve a notice of proceedings on any local authority or voluntary organisation that has at any time provided accommodation for the child.

Duty for service—This rule makes it clear that it is for the applicant(s) and not the court to serve the application and other documents on the respondent(s) and that service must be effected 14 days before the first directions hearing. The documents that should be served are a copy of the application in Form FL51, any statement filed in support of the application, Form 52 – the acknowledgement of service and a notice of proceedings.

13.7 Acknowledgement

Within 7 days of the service of an application for a parental order, each respondent must file an acknowledgment of service and serve it on all the other parties.

Defined terms—"parental order": FPR 2010, r 13.1; "legal representatives": FPR 2010, r 2.3.

Time for service—The time for filing and service of the acknowledgment of service is 7 days and any statement in support should accompany the acknowledgment of service. If there is a genuine difficulty in doing so, application should be made for an extension of time (see FPR 2010, r 13.9(1)(f),(4)(b)) supported by good grounds for seeking an extension. The application should be made on a FPR 2010, Pt 18 application notice and the appropriate procedure set out in Pt 18 and FPR PD18A should be followed.

13.8 Date for first directions hearing

Unless the court directs otherwise, the first directions hearing must be within 4 weeks beginning with the date on which the application is issued.

Unless the court otherwise directs—Instead of listing the application for a first directions appointment the court may give directions without a hearing but if it elects to do so, the order must provide for any party or person who is affected by the terms of the order to make an application to be heard or to vary or discharge the order or any of its terms (see r 13.5).

13.9 The first directions hearing

(1) At the first directions hearing in the proceedings the court will –

   (a)   fix a timetable for the filing of –

      (i)   any report from a parental order reporter;

      (ii) if a statement of facts has been filed, any amended statement of facts; and

      (iii) any other evidence;

   (b)   give directions relating to the report of the parental order reporter and other evidence;

PART III

(c) consider whether any other person should be a party to the proceedings and, if so, give directions in accordance with rule 13.3(3) or (4) joining that person as a party;

(d) give directions relating to the appointment of a litigation friend for any protected party unless a litigation friend has already been appointed;

(e) consider whether the case needs to be transferred to another court and, if so, give directions to transfer the proceedings to another court in accordance with the Allocation Order;

(f) give directions about –
   (i)   tracing the other parent or the woman who carried the child;
   (ii) service of documents;
   (iii) subject to paragraph (2), disclosure as soon as possible of information and evidence to the parties; and
   (iv) the final hearing.

(2) Rule 13.12 (reports of the parental order reporter and disclosure to parties) applies to any direction given under paragraph (1)(f)(iii) as it applies to a direction given under rule 13.12(1).

(3) The parties or their legal representatives must attend the first directions hearing unless the court directs otherwise.

(4) Directions may also be given at any stage in the proceedings –

(a) of the court's own initiative; or

(b) on the application of a party or the parental order reporter.

(5) Where the court proposes to exercise its powers in paragraph (1) of its own initiative the procedure set out in rule 4.3(2) to (7) applies.

(6) For the purposes of giving directions or for such purposes as the court directs –

(a) the court may set a date for a further directions hearing or other hearing; and

(b) the court officer will give notice of any date so fixed to the parties and to the parental order reporter.

(7) Directions of a court which are still in force immediately prior to the transfer of proceedings to another court shall continue to apply following the transfer subject to –

(a) any changes of terminology which are required to apply those directions to the court to which the proceedings are transferred; and

(b) any variation or revocation of the direction.

(8) The court or court officer will –

(a) take a note of the giving, variation or revocation of a direction under this rule; and

(b) as soon as practicable serve a copy of the note on every party.

(9) After the first directions hearing the court will monitor compliance by the parties with the court's timetable and directions.

Defined terms—"parental order reporter": FPR 2010, r 13.1; "protected party": FPR 2010, r 2.3(1), MCA 2005, ss 1, 2(1) and CPR 1998, r 21.1(2)(d); " litigation friend": FPR 2010, r 2.3(1), FPR 2010, Pt 15 and in relation to a child, FPR 2010, Pt 16.

Directions—Apart from those listed in r 13.9(1) the court should consider making any other appropriate additional directions under its duty of case management under FPR 2010, Pt 4 and giving effect to the overriding objective under FPR 2010, Pt 1. See also **First directions hearing** under FPR 2010, r 13.5.

Transfer of proceedings—See FPR 2010, rr 12.11 and 12.12.

Tracing the other parent or person who carried the child—In view of the increase in surrogate mothers from overseas being used to carry a child, this issue is likely to arise more frequently (e g *Re D and L (Surrogacy)* [2012] EWHC 2631 (Fam)).

Service—See FPR 2010, r 6; consideration should also be given as to whether service needs to be effected on any party or person outside the jurisdiction, e g where the birth mother lives overseas.

13.10 Where the agreement of the other parent or the woman who carried the child is not required

(1) This rule applies where the agreement of the other parent or the woman who carried the child to the making of the parental order is not required as the person in question cannot be found or is incapable of giving agreement.

(2) The applicants must –

(a)   state that the agreement is not required in the application form, or at any later stage by filing a written note with the court;

(b)   file a statement of facts setting out a summary of the history of the case and any other facts to satisfy the court that the other parent or the woman who carried the child cannot be found or is incapable of giving agreement.

(3) On receipt of the application form or written note –

(a)   a court officer will –

(i)   unless the other parent or the woman who carried the child cannot be found, inform the other parent or the woman who carried the child that their agreement is not required;

(ii)   send a copy of the statement of facts filed in accordance with paragraph (2)(b) to –

(aa) the other parent unless the other parent cannot be found;

(bb) the woman who carried the child unless the woman cannot be found; and

(cc) the parental order reporter; and

(b)   if the applicants consider that the other parent or the woman who carried the child is incapable of giving agreement the court will consider whether to –

(i)   appoint a litigation friend for the other parent or the woman who carried the child under rule 15.6(1) or

(ii)   give directions for an application to be made under rule 15.6(3),

unless a litigation friend is already appointed for the other parent or the woman who carried the child.

Consent of the woman who carried the child is not required—The applicants and their advisors must take steps to ensure that clear lines of communication with the surrogate are established before the birth to facilitate the giving of consent: *Re D and L (Surrogacy)* [2012] EWHC 2631 (Fam) at [35].

13.11 Agreement

(1) Unless the court directs otherwise, the agreement of the other parent or the woman who carried the child to the making of the parental order may be given in the form referred to Practice Direction 5A or a form to the like effect.

(2) Any form of agreement executed in Scotland must be witnessed by a Justice of the Peace or a Sheriff.

(3) Any form of agreement executed in Northern Ireland must be witnessed by a Justice of the Peace.

(4) Any form of agreement executed outside the United Kingdom must be witnessed by –

(a)   any person for the time being authorised by law in the place where the document is executed to administer an oath for any judicial or other legal purpose;

(b)   a British Consular officer;

PART III

(c)   a notary public; or

(d)   if the person executing the document is serving in any of the regular armed forces of the Crown, an officer holding a commission in any of those forces.

Form of agreement—This provision mirrors that which applies in an application for an adoption order under FPR 2010, r 14.10. The agreement must be given on Form A101A (FPR PD5A). In the absence of a formal agreement (e g because the mother cannot be found), consent given (whether formal or informal, at an earlier stage or in an acknowledgement of service) may in exceptional circumstances be taken into account: *Re D and L (Surrogacy)* [2012] EWHC 2631 (Fam); *G v G (Parental Order: Revocation)* [2013] 1 FLR 286.

13.12 Reports of the parental order reporter and disclosure to the parties

(1) The court will consider whether to give a direction that a confidential report of the parental order reporter be disclosed to each party to the proceedings.

(2) Before giving such a direction the court will consider whether any information should be deleted including information which discloses the particulars referred to in rule 29.1(1) where a party has given notice under rule 29.1(2) (disclosure of personal details).

(3) The court may direct that the report shall not be disclosed to a party.

Scope—The report of the parental order reporter is confidential and should not be disclosed without permission of the court. Before permitting disclosure, the court must consider whether any information, including any personal details of a party, contained in the report should be redacted. In addition, the court is empowered to direct that the report be not disclosed to a party. When considering the withholding of information contained in the report or redacting it, the court will need to consider the Convention rights of the parties under Arts 6 and 8. (For case-law, see **Publicity and disclosure of evidence** under FPR 2010, r 12.36.)

Powers and duties of the parental order reporter—The parental order reporter has a duty to: (i) act on behalf of the child with the duty of safeguarding the interests of the child and must attend all directions hearings unless the court directs otherwise; (ii) investigate the issues that are set out in s 54(1)–(8) of the 2008 Act and any other matter contained in the application form or any other matter that may be relevant to the making of a parental order and in so doing must contact and seek to interview such persons as the parental reporter thinks appropriate or as the court directs and obtain such professional assistance as may be appropriate; (iii) advise the court if there is any reason to refuse the application; (iv) provide the court with such assistance as the court may require, including advice on the appropriate forum for the proceedings, the appropriate timing of the proceedings, the options available and the suitability of each option (including what order should be made in determining the application) and any other matter of which the parental order reporter considers that the court should be informed; (v) file a written report; and (vi) where practicable, identify any person who should be joined as a party. See further FPR 2010, rr 16.34, 16.35 and FPR PD16A, paras 10.1–10.5. The application for a parental order requires the same care and caution as an application for an adoption order and the requirement of a parental order should not be dispensed with: *Re D and L (Surrogacy)* [2012] EWHC 2631 (Fam); *G v G (Parental Order: Revocation)* [2013] 1 FLR 286.

Disclosure—See **Scope**, above.

13.13 Notice of final hearing

A court officer will give notice to the parties and to the parental order reporter –

(a)   of the date and place where the application will be heard; and

(b)   of the fact that, unless the person wishes or the court requires, the person need not attend.

13.14 The final hearing

(1) Any person who has been given notice in accordance with rule 13.13 may attend the final hearing and be heard on the question of whether an order should be made.

(2) The court may direct that any person must attend a final hearing.

13.15 Proof of identity of the child

(1) Unless the contrary is shown, the child referred to in the application will be deemed to be the child referred to in the form of agreement to the making of the parental order where the conditions in paragraph (2) apply.

(2) The conditions are –

(a) the application identifies the child by reference to a full certified copy of an entry in the registers of live-births;

(b) the form of agreement identifies the child by reference to a full certified copy of an entry in the registers of live-births attached to the form; and

(c) the copy of the entry in the registers of live-births referred to in sub-paragraph (a) is the same or relates to the same entry in the registers of live-births as the copy of the entry in the registers of live-births attached to the form of agreement.

(3) Where the precise date of the child's birth is not proved to the satisfaction of the court, the court will determine the probable date of birth.

(4) The probable date of the child's birth may be specified in the parental order as the date of the child's birth.

(5) Where the child's place of birth cannot be proved to the satisfaction of the court –

(a) the child may be treated as having been born in the registration district of the court where it is probable that the child may have been born in –
(i) the United Kingdom;
(ii) the Channel Islands; or
(iii) the Isle of Man; or

(b) in any other case, the particulars of the country of birth may be omitted from the parental order.

13.16 Disclosing information to an adult who was subject to a parental order

(1) Subject to paragraph (2), the person who is subject to the parental order has the right to receive from the court which made the parental order a copy of the following –

(a) the application form for a parental order (but not the documents attached to that form);

(b) the parental order and any other orders relating to the parental order proceedings;

(c) a transcript of the court's decision; and

(d) a report made to the court by the parental order reporter.

(2) The court will not provide a copy of a document or order referred to in paragraph (1) unless the person making the request has completed the certificate relating to counselling in the form for that purpose referred to in Practice Direction 5A.

(3) This rule does not apply to a person under the age of 18 years.

13.17 Application for recovery orders

(1) An application for any of the orders referred to in section 41(2) of the 2002 Act (recovery orders) may –

(a) in the High Court or a county court, be made without notice in which case the applicant must file the application –
(i) where the application is made by telephone, the next business day after the making of the application; or

(ii)   in any other case, at the time when the application is made; and

(b)   in a magistrates' court, be made, with the permission of the court, without notice in which case the applicant must file the application at the time when the application is made or as directed by the court.

(2) Where the court refuses to make an order on an application without notice it may direct that the application is made on notice in which case the application shall proceed in accordance with rules 13.1 to 13.14.

(3) The respondents to an application under this rule are –

(a)   in a case where parental order proceedings are pending, all parties to those proceedings;

(b)   any person having parental responsibility for the child;

(c)   any person in whose favour there is provision for contact;

(d)   any person who was caring for the child immediately prior to the making of the application; and

(e)   any person whom the applicant alleges to have effected, or to have been or to be responsible for, the taking or keeping the child.

Note—Reference is made to ACA 2002 and so it follows that the matters raised in s 41(2) of the 2002 Act will be relevant to such an application (see Part II).

Procedure—Note that in the case of a without notice application made in the High Court and county court, permission to make the application is not required. However, in the family proceedings court, permission to make the application without notice will have to be granted. In addition, in the High Court and county court provision is made for the application to be made by telephone. No such corresponding provision is made in relation to applications in the magistrates' court. Where the court refuses the application, direction will usually be given for the application to be made on notice and in this case the procedure set out in FPR 2010, rr 13.1–13.14 should be followed and the persons who should be made respondents to the application should be those that are listed in r 13.17(3). See also the commentary under s 41(2) of the 2002 Act and r 14.20. A without notice application should be made under FPR 2010, Pt 18 and the procedure set out in the rule and FPR PD18A (in particular para 5 should be complied with).

13.18 Keeping of registers, custody, inspection and disclosure of documents and information

(1) Such part of the register kept in a family proceedings court in pursuance of rules made under the Magistrates' Courts Act 1980 as relates to parental order proceedings, must be kept in a separate book and the book must not contain particulars of any other proceedings.

(2) All documents relating to parental order proceedings and related proceedings under the 2002 Act including, in a family proceedings court, the book kept in accordance with paragraph (1), must, while they are in the custody of the court, be kept in a place of special security.

(3) Any person who obtains any information in the course of, or relating to, parental order proceedings must treat that information as confidential and must only disclose it if –

(a)   the disclosure is necessary for the proper exercise of that person's duties; or

(b)   the information is requested by –

(i)   a court or public authority (whether in Great Britain or not) having power to determine parental order proceedings and related matters, for the purpose of that court or authority discharging its duties relating to those proceedings and matters; or

(ii)   a person who is authorised in writing by the Secretary of State to obtain the information for the purposes of research.

13.19 Documents held by the court not to be inspected or copied without the court's permission

Subject to the provisions of these rules, any practice direction or any direction given by the court –

(a) no document or order held by the court in parental order proceedings and related proceedings under the 2002 Act will be open to inspection by any person; and

(b) no copy of any such document or order, or of an extract from any such document or order, shall be taken by or given to any person.

13.20 Orders

(1) A parental order takes effect from the date when it is made, or such later date as the court may specify.

(2) In proceedings in Wales a party may request that an order be drawn up in Welsh as well as English.

13.21 Copies of orders

(1) Within 7 days beginning with the date on which the final order was made in proceedings, or such shorter time as the court may direct, a court officer will send –

(a) a copy of the order to the applicant;

(b) a copy, which is sealed$^{(GL)}$, authenticated with the stamp of the court or certified as a true copy of a parental order, to the Registrar General;

(c) a notice of the making or refusal of –
  (i) the final order; or
  (ii) an order quashing or revoking a parental order or allowing an appeal against an order in proceedings,
  to every respondent and, with the permission of the court, any other person.

(2) The court officer will also send notice of the making of a parental order to –

(a) any court in Great Britain which appears to the court officer to have made any such order as is referred to in section 46(2) of the 2002 Act (order relating to parental responsibility for, and maintenance of, the child); and

(b) the principal registry, if it appears to the court officer that a parental responsibility agreement has been recorded at the principal registry.

(3) A copy of any final order may be sent to any other person with the permission of the court.

(4) The court officer will send a copy of any order made during the course of the proceedings to all the parties to those proceedings unless the court directs otherwise.

(5) If an order has been drawn up in Welsh as well as in English in accordance with rule 13.20(2), any reference in this rule to sending an order is to be taken as a reference to sending both the Welsh and English orders.

Defined terms—"court officer", "2002 Act", "principal registry": FPR 2010, r 2.3(1); "parental responsibility agreement": r 2.3(1) and CA 1989, ss 4(1)(b),(2)· 4ZA(1)(b), 4A(1)(a),(2).

13.22 Amendment and revocation of orders

(1) This rule applies to an application under paragraph 4 of Schedule 1 to the 2002 Act (amendment of a parental order and revocation of direction).

(2) If the application is made in a family proceedings court it must be made to a family proceedings court for the same local justice area as the family proceedings court which made the parental order, by delivering it or sending it by post to the designated officer of the court.

(3) Subject to paragraph (4), an application may be made without serving a copy of the application notice.

(4) The court may direct that an application notice be served on such persons as it thinks fit.

(5) Where the court makes an order granting the application, a proper officer shall send the Registrar General a notice –

   (a)   specifying the amendments; or
   (b)   informing the Registrar General of the revocation,

giving sufficient particulars of the order to enable the Registrar General to identify the case.

Defined terms—See under FPR 2010, r 13.21, above.

PART 14
PROCEDURE FOR APPLICATIONS IN ADOPTION, PLACEMENT AND RELATED PROCEEDINGS

CONTENTS OF THIS PART

14.1 Application of this Part and interpretation

(1) The rules in this Part apply to the following proceedings –

    (a)   adoption proceedings;

    (b)   placement proceedings; and

    (c)   proceedings for –

        (i)   the making of a contact order under section 26 of the 2002 Act;

        (ii)   the variation or revocation of a contact order under section 27 of the 2002 Act;

        (iii) an order giving permission to change a child's surname or remove a child from the United Kingdom under section 28(2) and (3) of the 2002 Act;

        (iv)   a section 84 order;

        (v)   a section 88 direction;

        (vi)   a section 89 order; or

        (vii) any other order that may be referred to in a practice direction.

(2) In this Part –

"Central Authority" means –

    (a)   in relation to England, the Secretary of State; and

    (b)   in relation to Wales, the Welsh Ministers;

"Convention adoption order" means an adoption order under the 2002 Act which, by virtue of regulations under section 1 of the Adoption (Intercountry Aspects) Act 1999 (regulations giving effect to the Convention on Protection of Children and Co-operation in Respect of Intercountry Adoption, concluded at the Hague on 29 May 1993), is made as a Convention adoption order;

"guardian" means –

    (a)   a guardian (other than the guardian of the estate of a child) appointed in accordance with section 5 of the 1989 Act; and

    (b)   a special guardian within the meaning of section 14A of the 1989 Act;

"provision for contact" means a contact order under section 8 or 34 of the 1989 Act or a contact order under section 26 of the 2002 Act;

"section 88 direction" means a direction given by the High Court under section 88 of the 2002 Act that section 67(3) of that Act (status conferred by adoption) does not apply or does not apply to any extent specified in the direction.

Defined terms—"adoption proceedings", "child", "placement proceedings", "section 84 order", "section 89 order": FPR 2010, r 2.3(1).

Which court—Save for the following exceptions, an application under ACA 2002 may be commenced at any level of family court. The exceptions are:

(a) Proceedings for an adoption order must be commenced in a magistrates' court, unless a local authority will be a party or unless the application is for a Convention adoption or ACA 2002, s 83 (restrictions on bringing a child into the UK) applies (ATPO 2008, art 5(1)(e));

(b) Unless the character of the proceedings are such that they may be commenced in the High Court (ATPO 2008, art 7), proceedings for a Convention adoption or for an adoption order where ACA 2002, s 83 (restrictions on bringing a child into the UK) applies must be commenced in a county court;

(c) Only proceedings that are either exceptionally complex, or where the outcome is important to the public in general or there is another substantial reason for doing so, may be commenced in the High Court (ATPO 2008, art 7);

(d) Where proceedings for an adoption order are pending in a particular court, any of the applications listed at ATPO 2008, art 8(1) must be commenced in the same court;

(e) Where proceedings for a placement order are pending, any application to remove the child (ACA 2002, s 30(2)(b)) must be made to the same court (ATPO 2008, art 8(2));

(f) Where proceedings for leave to apply for an adoption order (ACA 2002, s 42(6)) are pending, any application to remove the child (ACA 2002, ss 38(3)(a) or 40(2)(a)) must be made to the same court (ATPO 2008, art 8(3)).

Adoption work in county courts—County courts authorised to undertake adoption work are designated as "adoption centres". The courts named as adoption centres are also care centres. Some 13 adoption centres are also designated as "intercountry adoption centres" (ATPO 2008, Sch 1).

Where an adoption case is commenced in, or transferred to, a county court it must go to an adoption centre. Where the case involves a Convention adoption order or ACA 2002, s 83 is engaged (bringing a child into the UK for adoption), the county court must be an intercountry adoption centre (ATPO 2008, arts 11 and 21).

Transfer between courts—ATPO 2008 applies to ACA 2002 proceedings.

14.2 Application for a serial number

(1) This rule applies to any application in proceedings by a person who intends to adopt the child.

(2) If, before the proceedings have started, the applicant requests a court officer to assign a serial number to identify the applicant in connection with the proceedings in order for the applicant's identity to be kept confidential in those proceedings, a serial number will be so assigned.

(3) The court may at any time direct that a serial number identifying the applicant in the proceedings referred to in paragraph (2) must be removed.

(4) If a serial number has been assigned to a person under paragraph (2) –

(a) the court officer will ensure that any application form or application notice sent in accordance with these rules does not contain information which discloses, or is likely to disclose, the identity of that person to any other party to that application who is not already aware of that person's identity; and

(b) the proceedings on the application will be conducted with a view to securing that the applicant is not seen by or made known to any party who is not already aware of the applicant's identity except with the applicant's consent.

Defined terms—"application form/notice", "child", "court", "court officer", "proceedings": FPR 2010, r 2.3(1).

14.3 Who the parties are

(1) In relation to the proceedings set out in column 1 of the following table, column 2 sets out who the application may be made by and column 3 sets out who the respondents to those proceedings will be.

Proceedings for	Applicants	Respondents
An adoption order (section 46 of the 2002 Act).	The prospective adopters (sections 50 and 51 of the 2002 Act).	Each parent who has parental responsibility for the child unless that parent has given notice under section 20(4)(a) of the 2002 Act (statement of wish not to be informed of any application for an adoption order) which has effect;
		any guardian of the child unless that guardian has given notice under section 20(4)(a) of the 2002 Act (statement of wish not to be informed of any application for an adoption order) which has effect;
		any person in whose favour there is provision for contact;
		any adoption agency having parental responsibility for the child under section 25 of the 2002 Act;
		any adoption agency which has taken part at any stage in the arrangements for adoption of the child;
		any local authority to whom notice under section 44 of the 2002 Act (notice of intention to adopt or apply for a section 84 order) has been given;
		any local authority or voluntary organisation which has parental responsibility for, is looking after or is caring for, the child; and the child where –
		– permission has been granted to a parent or guardian to oppose the making of the adoption order (section 47(3) or 47(5) of the 2002 Act);
		– the child opposes the making of an adoption order;

PART III

Proceedings for	Applicants	Respondents
		– a children and family reporter recommends that it is in the best interests of the child to be a party to the proceedings and that recommendation is accepted by the court;
		– the child is already an adopted child;
		– any party to the proceedings or the child is opposed to the arrangements for allowing any person contact with the child, or a person not being allowed contact with the child after the making of the adoption order;
		– the application is for a Convention adoption order or a section 84 order;
		– the child has been brought into the United Kingdom in the circumstances where section 83(1) of the 2002 Act applies (restriction on bringing children in);
		– the application is for an adoption order other than a Convention adoption order and the prospective adopters intend the child to live in a country or territory outside the British Islands after the making of the adoption order; or
		– the prospective adopters are relatives of the child.
A section 84 order.	The prospective adopters asking for parental responsibility prior to adoption abroad.	As for an adoption order.
A placement order (section 21 of the 2002 Act).	A local authority (section 22 of the 2002 Act).	Each parent who has parental responsibility for the child: any guardian of the child; any person in whose favour an order under the 1989 Act is in force in relation to the child;

Proceedings for	Applicants	Respondents
		any adoption agency or voluntary organisation which has parental responsibility for, is looking after, or is caring for, the child; the child; and the parties or any persons who are or have been parties to proceedings for a care order in respect of the child where those proceedings have led to the application for the placement order.
An order varying a placement order (section 23 of the 2002 Act).	The joint application of the local authority authorised by the placement order to place the child for adoption and the local authority which is to be substituted for that authority (section 23 of the 2002 Act).	The parties to the proceedings leading to the placement order which it is sought to have varied except the child who was the subject of those proceedings; and any person in whose favour there is provision for contact.
An order revoking a placement order (section 24 of the 2002 Act).	The child; the local authority authorised to place the child for adoption; or where the child is not placed for adoption by the authority, any other person who has the permission of the court to apply (section 24 of the 2002 Act).	The parties to the proceedings leading to the placement order which it is sought to have revoked; and any person in whose favour there is provision for contact.
A contact order (section 26 of the 2002 Act).	The child; the adoption agency; any parent, guardian or relative;	The adoption agency authorised to place the child for adoption or which has placed the child for adoption;

PART III

Proceedings for	Applicants	Respondents
	any person in whose favour there was provision for contact under the 1989 Act which ceased to have effect on an adoption agency being authorised to place a child for adoption, or placing a child for adoption who is less than six weeks old (section 26(1) of the 2002 Act); a person in whose favour there was a residence order in force immediately before the adoption agency was authorised to place the child for adoption or placed the child for adoption at a time when the child was less than six weeks old; a person who by virtue of an order made in the exercise of the High Court's inherent jurisdiction with respect to children had care of the child immediately before that time; or any person who has the permission of the court to make the application (section 26 of the 2002 Act).	the person with whom the child lives or is to live; each parent with parental responsibility for the child; any guardian of the child; and the child where – – the adoption agency authorised to place the child for adoption or which has placed the child for adoption or a parent with parental responsibility for the child opposes the making of the contact order under section 26 of the 2002 Act; – the child opposes the making of the contact order under section 26 of the 2002 Act; – existing provision for contact is to be revoked; – relatives of the child do not agree to the arrangements for allowing any person contact with the child, or a person not being allowed contact with the child; or – the child is suffering or is at risk of suffering harm within the meaning of the 1989 Act.
An order varying or revoking a contact order (section 27 of the 2002 Act).	The child; the adoption agency; or any person named in the contact order (section 27(1) of the 2002 Act).	The parties to the proceedings leading to the contact order which it is sought to have varied or revoked; and any person named in the contact order.
An order permitting the child's name to be changed or the removal of the child from the United Kingdom (section 28(2) and (3) of the 2002 Act).	Any person including the adoption agency or the local authority authorised to place, or which has placed, the child for adoption (section 28(2) of the 2002 Act).	The parties to proceedings leading to any placement order; the adoption agency authorised to place the child for adoption or which has placed the child for adoption;

Proceedings for	Applicants	Respondents
		any prospective adopters with whom the child is living; each parent with parental responsibility for the child; and any guardian of the child.
A section 88 direction.	The adopted child; the adopters; any parent; or any other person.	The adopters; the parents; the adoption agency; the local authority to whom notice under section 44 of the 2002 Act (notice of intention to apply for a section 84 order) has been given; and the Attorney-General.
A section 89 order.	The adopters; the adopted person; any parent; the relevant Central Authority; the adoption agency; the local authority to whom notice under section 44 of the 2002 Act (notice of intention to adopt or apply for a section 84 order) has been given; the Secretary of State for the Home Department; or any other person.	The adopters; the parents; the adoption agency; and the local authority to whom notice under section 44 of the 2002 Act (notice of intention to adopt or apply for a section 84 order) has been given.

(2) The court may at any time direct that a child, who is not already a respondent to proceedings, be made a respondent to proceedings where –

   (a)   the child –
      (i)   wishes to make an application; or
      (ii) has evidence to give to the court or a legal submission to make which has not been given or made by any other party; or
   (b)   there are other special circumstances.

(3) The court may at any time direct that –

   (a)   any other person or body be made a respondent to proceedings; or
   (b)   a party be removed.

(4) If the court makes a direction for the addition or removal of a party, it may give consequential directions about –

   (a)   serving a copy of the application form on any new respondent;
   (b)   serving relevant documents on the new party; and
   (c)   the management of the proceedings.

Defined terms—"the 1989 Act", "child", "children and family reporter", "jurisdiction", "proceedings", "section 84 order", "section 89 order": FPR 2010, r 2.3(1); "Central Authority", "provision for contact", "section 88 direction": FPR 2010, r 14.1.

Importance of giving notice to respondents—The court should ensure that each respondent is given notice of each hearing and that they are kept informed of the progress of the case (*X and Y v A Local Authority (Adoption: Procedure)* [2009] 2 FLR 984).

Father without parental responsibility—A father who does not have parental responsibility is not automatically a respondent to proceedings (unless there is a contact order in his favour). The court must consider the question at the first directions hearing and may direct that he be made a respondent (FPR 2010, rr 14.3(3)(a) and 14.8(1)(b)). For discussion of position of father without parental responsibility, see note to ACA 2002, s 47.

Former parent of child freed for adoption—There is no requirement to give the former parents of a child freed for adoption under AA 1976 notice of an adoption application under ACA 2002 (*Re F (Adoption: Natural Parents)* [2007] 1 FLR 363).

14.4 Notice of proceedings to person with foreign parental responsibility

(1) This rule applies where a child is subject to proceedings to which this Part applies and –

    (a) a parent of the child holds or is believed to hold parental responsibility for the child under the law of another State which subsists in accordance with Article 16 of the 1996 Hague Convention following the child becoming habitually resident in a territorial unit of the United Kingdom; and

    (b) that parent is not otherwise required to be joined as a respondent under rule 14.3.

(2) The applicant shall give notice of the proceedings to any parent to whom the applicant believes paragraph (1) applies in any case in which a person who was a parent with parental responsibility under the 1989 Act would be a respondent to the proceedings in accordance with rule 14.3.

(3) The applicant and every respondent to the proceedings shall provide such details as they possess as to the identity and whereabouts of any parent they believe to hold parental responsibility for the child in accordance with paragraph (1) to the court officer, upon making, or responding to the application as appropriate.

(4) Where the existence of such a parent only becomes apparent to a party at a later date during the proceedings, that party must notify the court officer of those details at the earliest opportunity.

(5) Where a parent to whom paragraph (1) applies receives notice of proceedings, that parent may apply to the court to be joined as a party using the Part 18 procedure.

Defined terms—"child", "court officer", "parental responsibility", "the 1989 Act", "the 1996 Hague Convention": FPR 2010, r 2.3(1).

14.5 Who is to serve

(1) The general rules about service in Part 6 are subject to this rule.

(2) In proceedings to which this Part applies, a document which has been issued or prepared by a court officer will be served by the court officer except where –

    (a) a practice direction provides otherwise; or

    (b) the court directs otherwise.

(3) Where a court officer is to serve a document, it is for the court to decide which of the methods of service specified in rule 6.23 is to be used.

Defined terms—"court officer": FPR 2010, r 2.3(1).

Service generally—See notes to FPR 2010, Pt 6.

Importance of service on parent—It is fundamental to the making of an adoption order that the natural parent should be informed of the application; the requirement for service is mandatory and the court will be very reluctant to dispense with service on a natural parent (*Re B (Adoption: Jurisdiction to Set Aside)* [1995] 2 FLR 1; *Re G (Foreign Adoption: Consent)* [1995] 2 FLR 534). Where a parent has given advance consent to adoption under ACA 2002, s 20 he may state that he does not wish to be informed of any application for an adoption order; such a parent is not required to be served with notice of any adoption proceedings.

14.6 What the court or a court officer will do when the application has been issued

(1) As soon as practicable after the application has been issued in proceedings –

  (a) the court will –

     (i) if section 48(1) of the 2002 Act (restrictions on making adoption orders) applies, consider whether it is proper to hear the application;

     (ii) subject to paragraph (4), set a date for the first directions hearing;

     (iii) appoint a children's guardian in accordance with rule 16.3(1);

     (iv) appoint a reporting officer in accordance with rule 16.30;

     (v) consider whether a report relating to the welfare of the child is required, and if so, request such a report in accordance with rule 16.33;

     (vi) set a date for the hearing of the application; and

     (vii) do anything else that may be set out in a practice direction; and

  (b) a court officer will –

     (i) subject to receiving confirmation in accordance with paragraph (2)(b)(ii), give notice of any directions hearing set by the court to the parties and to any children's guardian, reporting officer or children and family reporter;

     (ii) serve a copy of the application form (but, subject to sub-paragraphs (iii) and (iv), not the documents attached to it) on the persons referred to in Practice Direction 14A;

     (iii) send a copy of the certified copy of the entry in the register of live-births or Adopted Children Register and any health report attached to an application for an adoption order to –

      (aa) any children's guardian, reporting officer or children and family reporter; and

      (bb) the local authority to whom notice under section 44 of the 2002 Act (notice of intention to adopt or apply for a section 84 order) has been given;

     (iv) if notice under rule 14.9(2) has been given (request to dispense with consent of parent or guardian), in accordance with that rule inform the parent or guardian of the request and send a copy of the statement of facts to –

      (aa) the parent or guardian;

      (bb) any children's guardian, reporting officer or children and family reporter;

      (cc) any local authority to whom notice under section 44 of the 2002 Act (notice of intention to adopt or apply for a section 84 order) has been given; and

      (dd) any adoption agency which has placed the child for adoption; and

     (v) do anything else that may be set out in a practice direction.

(2) In addition to the matters referred to in paragraph (1), as soon as practicable after an application for an adoption order or a section 84 order has been issued the court or the court officer will –

  (a) where the child is not placed for adoption by an adoption agency –

     (i) ask either the Service or the Assembly to file any relevant form of consent to an adoption order or a section 84 order; and

      (ii)   ask the local authority to prepare a report on the suitability of the prospective adopters if one has not already been prepared; and

  (b)   where the child is placed for adoption by an adoption agency, ask the adoption agency to –

      (i)   file any relevant form of consent to –

         (aa) the child being placed for adoption;

         (bb) an adoption order;

         (cc) a future adoption order under section 20 of the 2002 Act; or

         (dd) a section 84 order;

      (ii)   confirm whether a statement has been made under section 20(4)(a) of the 2002 Act (statement of wish not to be informed of any application for an adoption order) and if so, to file that statement;

      (iii) file any statement made under section 20(4)(b) of the 2002 Act (withdrawal of wish not to be informed of any application for an adoption order) as soon as it is received by the adoption agency; and

      (iv) prepare a report on the suitability of the prospective adopters if one has not already been prepared.

(3) In addition to the matters referred to in paragraph (1), as soon as practicable after an application for a placement order has been issued –

  (a)   the court will consider whether a report giving the local authority's reasons for placing the child for adoption is required, and if so, will direct the local authority to prepare such a report; and

  (b)   the court or the court officer will ask either the Service or the Assembly to file any form of consent to the child being placed for adoption.

(4) Where it considers it appropriate the court may, instead of setting a date for a first directions hearing, give the directions provided for by rule 14.8.

Defined terms—"court", "court officer", "child", "children and family reporter", "children's guardian", "proceedings", "reporting officer": FPR 2010, r 2.3(1).

Who receives a copy of the application for orders in proceedings (r 14.6(1)(b)(ii))—See FPR PD14A.

Form of consent (r 14.6(2)(b))—The form of consent must be in the relevant form (A100–A106) or a form to like effect (FPR 2010, r 14.10).

Children's guardian—For children's guardian in adoption or placement proceedings generally, see FPR 2010, rr 16.3 and 16.6–16.21 and see FPR PD16A.

A children's guardian who interviews a child should be very careful not to make promises of complete confidentiality; in unusually sensitive cases affecting older children, it is not unreasonable for a children's guardian to promise a child that he would tell the judge that the child would prefer that a party was not told details of the conversation (*Re D (Minors) (Adoption Reports: Confidentiality)* [1995] 1 FLR 631).

The children's guardian must also, where practicable, notify any person the joining of whom as a party to those proceedings would be likely, in his opinion, to safeguard the interests of the child, of the court's power to join that person as a party under FPR 2010, r 14.3(3) and must inform the court:

(i)   of any notification;
(ii) of anyone whom he attempted to notify under this paragraph but was unable to contact; and
(iii) of anyone whom he believes may wish to be joined to the proceedings (see FPR PD16A, para 6.8(b)).

The children's guardian has a duty to ensure that, in relation to a decision made by the court in the proceedings, the child is notified of the decision (if the guardian considers that to do so is appropriate to the child's age and understanding) and that if the child is so notified, it is explained to him in an age-appropriate manner (FPR PD16A, para 6.11).

Inter-country adoptions—See note to FPR 2010, r 14.18.

Involvement of children's guardian in decision-making—While a case is proceeding, the local authority ought not to take any major decisions relating to the child or his adoption without informing the children's guardian and listening to his views (*R v North Yorkshire County Council ex parte M* [1989] 1 FLR 203). However, a guardian has no right to dictate how an adoption panel conducts its business or to insist on attending meetings (*R v North Yorkshire County Council ex parte M (No 2)* [1989] 2 FLR 79). The views of a children's guardian should be communicated to any adoption panel that is considering a proposal concerning the child (*Re R (Adoption: Disclosure)* [1999] 2 FLR 1123).

Inspection of records—A children's guardian has a right to inspect local authority records and adoption agency records (CA 1989, s 42; ACA 2002, s 103). Where the children's guardian inspects local authority or adoption agency records, he must bring all records and documents that may, in his opinion, assist in the proper determination of the proceedings to the attention of the court and (unless the court otherwise directs) the other parties (FPR PD16A, para 6.10).

14.7 Date for first directions hearing

Unless the court directs otherwise, the first directions hearing must be within 4 weeks beginning with the date on which the application is issued.

14.8 The first directions hearing

(1) At the first directions hearing in the proceedings the court will –
- (a) fix a timetable for the filing of –
  - (i) any report relating to the suitability of the applicants to adopt a child;
  - (ii) any report from the local authority;
  - (iii) any report from a children's guardian, reporting officer or children and family reporter;
  - (iv) if a statement of facts has been filed, any amended statement of facts;
  - (v) any other evidence, and
  - (vi) give directions relating to the reports and other evidence;
- (b) consider whether the child or any other person should be a party to the proceedings and, if so, give directions in accordance with rule 14.3(2) or (3) joining that child or person as a party;
- (c) give directions relating to the appointment of a litigation friend for any protected party or child who is a party to, but not the subject of, proceedings unless a litigation friend has already been appointed;
- (d) consider whether the case needs to be transferred to another court and, if so, give directions to transfer the proceedings to another court in accordance with any order made by the Lord Chancellor under Part 1 of Schedule 11 to the 1989 Act;
- (e) give directions about –
  - (i) tracing parents or any other person the court considers to be relevant to the proceedings;
  - (ii) service of documents;
  - (iii) subject to paragraph (2), disclosure as soon as possible of information and evidence to the parties; and
  - (iv) the final hearing.

  (By rule 3.3 the court may also direct that the case be adjourned if it considers that alternative dispute resolution is appropriate.)

(2) Rule 14.13(2) applies to any direction given under paragraph (1)(e)(iii) as it applies to a direction given under rule 14.13(1).

(3) In addition to the matters referred to in paragraph (1), the court will give any of the directions listed in Practice Direction 14B in proceedings for –
- (a) a Convention adoption order;
- (b) a section 84 order;
- (c) a section 88 direction;
- (d) a section 89 order; or

PART III

  (e) an adoption order where section 83(1) of the 2002 Act applies (restriction on bringing children in).

(4) The parties or their legal representatives must attend the first directions hearing unless the court directs otherwise.

(5) Directions may also be given at any stage in the proceedings –

  (a) of the court's own initiative; or

  (b) on the application of a party or any children's guardian or, where the direction concerns a report by a reporting officer or children and family reporter, the reporting officer or children and family reporter.

(6) For the purposes of giving directions or for such purposes as the court directs –

  (a) the court may set a date for a further directions hearing or other hearing; and

  (b) the court officer will give notice of any date so fixed to the parties and to any children's guardian, reporting officer or children and family reporter.

(7) After the first directions hearing the court will monitor compliance by the parties with the court's timetable and directions.

Defined terms—"the 1989 Act", "child", "children and family reporter", "children's guardian", "court officer", "filing", "legal representative", "litigation friend", "proceedings", "protected party", "reporting officer", "section 84 order", "section 89 order": FPR 2010, r 2.3(1); "section 88 direction": FPR 2010, r 14.1(2).

First directions hearing—The court may, if it considers it appropriate, give the directions provided for in r 14.8 at the time that the application is issued, rather than waiting for the first directions hearing (FPR 2010, r 14.6(4)).

Appointment of litigation friend (r 14.8(1)(c))—See FPR 2010, Pt 15.

First directions hearing: adoptions with a foreign element (r 14.8(3))—See FPR PD14B.

Intercountry adoptions—Guidance given in *Re R (Inter-Country Adoptions: Practice)* [1999] 1 FLR 1042 regarding intercountry adoption includes:

(a) drawing up a timetable to determine the application without delay;

(b) never accepting documents that do not have an English translation;

(c) early transfer to the High Court where there is a doubt concerning parental consent or adherence to proper pre-application procedures;

(d) before the directions hearing, the applicant should be directed to file and serve an affidavit setting out full details of the circumstances of the application;

(e) cross-examination of the applicants may take place at the directions hearing;

(f) directions should be given for personal service on the natural parents within 28 days, including the provision of information about the role of the children's guardian and the availability of public funding;

(g) further directions should be fixed before a judge within 6 weeks, with provision for filing an interim report from the children's guardian;

(h) at the next directions hearing, if it appears that the natural parents never consented and seek the return of the child, the court should consider whether to dismiss the adoption application summarily and consider proceeding in wardship.

14.9 Requesting the court to dispense with the consent of any parent or guardian

(1) This rule applies where the applicant wants to ask the court to dispense with the consent of any parent or guardian of a child to –

  (a) the child being placed for adoption;

  (b) the making of an adoption order except a Convention adoption order; or

  (c) the making of a section 84 order.

(2) The applicant requesting the court to dispense with the consent must –

(a) give notice of the request in the application form or at any later stage by filing a written request setting out the reasons for the request; and

(b) file a statement of facts setting out a summary of the history of the case and any other facts to satisfy the court that –

    (i) the parent or guardian cannot be found or is incapable of giving consent; or

    (ii) the welfare of the child requires the consent to be dispensed with.

(3) If a serial number has been assigned to the applicant under rule 14.2, the statement of facts supplied under paragraph (2)(b) must be framed so that it does not disclose the identity of the applicant.

(4) On receipt of the notice of the request –

(a) a court officer will –

    (i) inform the parent or guardian of the request unless the parent or guardian cannot be found; and

    (ii) send a copy of the statement of facts filed in accordance with paragraph (2)(b) to –

        (aa) the parent or guardian unless the parent or guardian cannot be found;

        (bb) any children's guardian, reporting officer or children and family reporter;

        (cc) any local authority to whom notice under section 44 of the 2002 Act (notice of intention to adopt or apply for a section 84 order) has been given; and

        (dd) any adoption agency which has placed the child for adoption; and

(b) if the applicant considers that the parent or guardian is incapable of giving consent, the court will consider whether to –

    (i) appoint a litigation friend for the parent or guardian under rule 15.6(1); or

    (ii) give directions for an application to be made under rule 15.6(3);

    (iii) unless a litigation friend is already appointed for that parent or guardian.

Defined terms—"child", "children and family reporter", "children's guardian", "court officer", "filing", "litigation friend", "reporting officer", "section 84 order": FPR 2010, r 2.3(1).

Statement of facts (r 14.9(2)(b))—As a matter of practice the statement of facts will be of most use if it sets out succinctly in numbered paragraphs the history that is relied upon.

14.10 Consent

(1) Consent of any parent or guardian of a child –

(a) under section 19 of the 2002 Act, to the child being placed for adoption; and

(b) under section 20 of the 2002 Act, to the making of a future adoption order,

must be given in the form referred to in Practice Direction 5A or a form to the like effect.

(2) Subject to paragraph (3), consent –

(a) to the making of an adoption order; or

(b) to the making of a section 84 order,

may be given in the form referred to in Practice Direction 5A or a form to the like effect or otherwise as the court directs.

(3) Any consent to a Convention adoption order must be in a form which complies with the internal law relating to adoption of the Convention country of which the child is habitually resident.

(4) Any form of consent executed in Scotland must be witnessed by a Justice of the Peace or a Sheriff.

(5) Any form of consent executed in Northern Ireland must be witnessed by a Justice of the Peace.

(6) Any form of consent executed outside the United Kingdom must be witnessed by –

    (a)   any person for the time being authorised by law in the place where the document is executed to administer an oath for any judicial or other legal purpose;

    (b)   a British Consular officer;

    (c)   a notary public; or

    (d)   if the person executing the document is serving in any of the regular armed forces of the Crown, an officer holding a commission in any of those forces.

Defined terms—"child", "section 84 order": FPR 2010, r 2.3(1).

Consequences of giving consent to placement or future adoption—Once consent has been given to placement for adoption (or to future adoption) and if that consent has not been withdrawn the consenting parent will be unable to oppose any subsequent adoption application unless there has been a subsequent change of circumstances and the court gives leave to oppose (see notes to ACA 2002, ss 47 and 52). As a result, for a consent to be validly given "with full understanding of what is involved" (ACA 2002, s 52(5)) the parent must understand that, while the consent may be to placement, it fundamentally alters the parents' ability to oppose any subsequent adoption.

Forms of consent—The form of consent must be in the relevant form (A100–A106) or a form to like effect (FPR 2010, r 5.1 and PD5A).

14.11 Reports by the adoption agency or local authority

(1) The adoption agency or local authority must file the report on the suitability of the applicant to adopt a child within the timetable fixed by the court.

(2) A local authority that is directed to prepare a report on the placement of the child for adoption must file that report within the timetable fixed by the court.

(3) The reports must cover the matters specified in Practice Direction 14C.

(4) The court may at any stage request a further report or ask the adoption agency or local authority to assist the court in any other manner.

(5) A court officer will send a copy of any report referred to in this rule to any children's guardian, reporting officer or children and family reporter.

(6) A report to the court under this rule is confidential.

Defined terms—"child", "children and family reporter", "children's guardian", "court officer", "reporting officer": FPR 2010, r 2.3(1).

Reports by the adoption agency or local authority (r 14.11(3))—See FPR PD14C.

14.12 Health reports

(1) Reports by a registered medical practitioner ("health reports") made not more than 3 months earlier on the health of the child and of each applicant must be attached to an application for an adoption order or a section 84 order except where –

    (a)   the child was placed for adoption with the applicant by an adoption agency;

    (b)   the applicant or one of the applicants is a parent of the child; or

    (c)   the applicant is the partner of a parent of the child.

(2) Health reports must contain the matters set out in Practice Direction 14D.

(3) A health report is confidential.

Defined terms—"child", "section 84 order": FPR 2010, r 2.3(1).

Health reports (r 14.12(2))—See FPR PD14D.

14.13 Confidential reports to the court and disclosure to the parties

(1) The court will consider whether to give a direction that a confidential report be disclosed to each party to the proceedings.

(2) Before giving such a direction the court will consider whether any information should be deleted including information which –

    (a)   discloses, or is likely to disclose, the identity of a person who has been assigned a serial number under rule 14.2(2); or

    (b)   discloses the particulars referred to in rule 29.1(1) where a party has given notice under rule 29.1(2) (disclosure of personal details).

(3) The court may direct that the report will not be disclosed to a party.

Defined terms—"proceedings": FPR 2010, r 2.3(1).

Confidentiality of reports—Any report provided to the court by a children's guardian, reporting officer or children and family reporter is confidential.

Under the earlier law there was a presumption in the rules (Adoption Rules 1984, r 53(2)) in favour of a party being entitled to inspect that part of any confidential report that related to them. That presumption has been replaced by an open discretion, but the leading authorities on the earlier provision may still be of relevance.

In *Re D (Minors) (Adoption Reports: Confidentiality)* [1995] 2 FLR 687, the House of Lords set out the principles on which issues about the disclosure of confidential adoption reports should be determined:

"It is a fundamental principle of fairness that a party is entitled to the disclosure of all materials which may be taken into account by the court when reaching a decision adverse to that party. This principle applies with particular force to proceedings designed to lead to an order for adoption, since the consequences of such an order are so lasting and far-reaching.

When deciding whether to direct that notwithstanding Adoption Rules 1984, r 53(2) a party referred to in a confidential report supplied by an adoption agency, a local authority, a reporting officer or a guardian ad litem shall not be entitled to inspect that part of the report which refers to him or her, the court should first consider whether disclosure of the material would involve a real possibility of significant harm to the child.

If it would, the court should next consider whether the overall interests of the child would benefit from non-disclosure, weighing on the one hand the interests of the child in having the material properly tested, and on the other both the magnitude of the risk that harm will occur and the gravity of the harm if it does occur.

If the court is satisfied that the interests of the child point towards non-disclosure, the next and final step is for the court to weigh that consideration, and its strength in the circumstances of the case, against the interest of the parent or other party in having an opportunity to see and respond to the material. In the latter regard the court should take into account the importance of the material to the issues in the case.

Non-disclosure should be the exception and not the rule. The court should be rigorous in its examination of the risk and gravity of the feared harm to the child, and should order non-disclosure only when the case for doing so is compelling."

Following the implementation of the HRA 1998, the Court of Appeal has held that the House of Lords decision in *Re D* must be extended to include, not solely those of the children, but also the interests of the adult parties (*Re B (Disclosure to Other Parties)* [2001] 2 FLR 1017, approved in *Re X (Adoption: Confidential Procedure)* [2002] 2 FLR 476).

It would seem sensible that the court should consider the extent of the inspection to be allowed far enough in advance of the hearing for instructions to be taken and any necessary evidence prepared for the hearing. Practitioners are advised to keep in touch with the court and apply as soon as possible after the reports are filed for facilities for inspection, to avoid delay. There is no provision in the rules to cause parties to be notified that a report has been filed.

The duty of confidentiality applies to documents in the custody and control of an adoption agency that have never been placed before the court (*Re H (Criminal Proceedings: Disclosure of Adoption Records)* [1995] 1 FLR 964).

An adoption agency must maintain the confidentiality and safekeeping of any adoption information and case records (Adoption Agencies Regulations 2005, regs 41 and 42 and Disclosure of Adoption Information (Post Commencement) Regs 2005, Pt 2).

Where information that is confidential to the adoption proceedings may be relevant in criminal proceedings, normally an application for disclosure should be made within the criminal proceedings, so that the judge may balance the high degree of confidentiality attaching to adoption proceedings against the benefits of disclosure (*Re H* above); an alternative course is to issue an originating summons in the High Court to determine whether disclosure should be made (*Re An Adoption Application* [1990] 1 FLR 412; *Re C (A Minor) (Disclosure of Adoption Reports)* [1994] 2 FLR 525). If appropriate, the Attorney-General should be represented before the court.

Communicating information relating to the proceedings—For the restrictions on a person communicating information relating to the proceedings to representatives and other persons, see FPR 2010, r 14.14.

14.14 Communication of information relating to proceedings

For the purposes of the law relating to contempt of court, information (whether or not it is recorded in any form) relating to proceedings held in private may be communicated –

   (a)   where the court gives permission;
   (b)   unless the court directs otherwise, in accordance with Practice Direction 14E; or
   (c)   where the communication is to –
         (i)   a party;
         (ii)   the legal representative of a party;
         (iii)   a professional legal adviser;
         (iv)   an officer of the service or a Welsh family proceedings officer;
         (v)   a welfare officer;
         (vi)   the Director of Legal Aid Casework (within the meaning of section 4 of the Legal Aid, Sentencing and Punishment of Offenders Act 2012);
         (vii) an expert whose instruction by a party has been authorised by the court for the purposes of the proceedings; or
         (viii) a professional acting in furtherance of the protection of children.

Amendments—SI 2013/534, subject to savings.

Defined terms—"the 1989 Act", "child", "legal representative", "officer of the Service", "proceedings", "Welsh family proceedings officer": FPR 2010, r 2.3(1).

Communication of information relating to proceedings (r 14.14(1)(b))—See FPR PD14E.

14.15 Notice of final hearing

A court officer will give notice to the parties, any children's guardian, reporting officer or children and family reporter and to any other person to whom a practice direction may require such notice to be given –

   (a)   of the date and place where the application will be heard; and
   (b)   of the fact that, unless the person wishes or the court requires, the person need not attend.

Defined terms—"children and family reporter", "children's guardian", "court officer", "reporting officer": FPR 2010, r 2.3(1).

14.16 The final hearing

(1) Any person who has been given notice in accordance with rule 14.15 may attend the final hearing and, subject to paragraph (2), be heard on the question of whether an order should be made.

(2) A person whose application for the permission of the court to oppose the making of an adoption order under section 47(3) or (5) of the 2002 Act has been refused is not entitled to be heard on the question of whether an order should be made.

(3) Any member or employee of a party which is a local authority, adoption agency or other body may address the court at the final hearing if authorised to do so.

(4) The court may direct that any person must attend a final hearing.

(5) Paragraphs (6) and (7) apply to –

    (a)   an adoption order;

    (b)   a section 84 order; or

    (c)   a section 89 order.

(6) Subject to paragraphs (7) and (8), the court cannot make an order unless the applicant and the child personally attend the final hearing.

(7) The court may direct that the applicant or the child need not attend the final hearing.

(8) In a case of adoption by a couple under section 50 of the 2002 Act, the court may make an adoption order after personal attendance of one only of the applicants if there are special circumstances.

(9) The court cannot make a placement order unless a legal representative of the applicant attends the final hearing.

Defined terms—"child", "legal representative", "section 84 order", "section 89 order": FPR 2010, r 2.3(1).

Serial number case (r 14.2(4))—The operation of this rule will inevitably mean that the applicant and those who do not know the applicant's identity may not be in the courtroom at the same time. The normal approach of courts is to conduct most of the hearing in the absence of the applicant. In some cases, particularly in the High Court, arrangements can be made for the absent applicant to listen to the proceedings without being present in the courtroom. If the applicant is called to give evidence, the roles are reversed and those who do not know the applicant's identity will leave the courtroom. The practice of splitting a final hearing so that the child and adopters may attend for a short ceremony at a time after the court has decided to make an adoption order has been expressly approved (*Re F (Adoption: Natural Parents)* [2007] 1 FLR 363).

Attendance of the child (r 14.16(6))—The default position is that the child must attend a FPR 2010, Pt 14 final hearing. In practice, in placement cases the court is likely to dispense with the child's attendance, but in adoption cases it is normal for the child to attend before the court either at the final hearing or at a later hearing. The underlying purpose of the provision is to ensure that a child in respect of whom an order is about to be made understands fully, as far as he or she can, the nature of the order (*Re P (Minors) (Adoption)* [1989] 1 FLR 1).

14.17 Proof of identity of the child

(1) Unless the contrary is shown, the child referred to in the application will be deemed to be the child referred to in the form of consent –

    (a)   to the child being placed for adoption;

    (b)   to the making of an adoption order; or

    (c)   to the making of a section 84 order,

where the conditions in paragraph (2) apply.

(2) The conditions are –

    (a)   the application identifies the child by reference to a full certified copy of an entry in the registers of live-births;

    (b)   the form of consent identifies the child by reference to a full certified copy of an entry in the registers of live-births attached to the form; and

    (c)   the copy of the entry in the registers of live-births referred to in sub-paragraph (a) is the same or relates to the same entry in the registers of live-births as the copy of the entry in the registers of live-births attached to the form of consent.

(3) Where the child is already an adopted child paragraph (2) will have effect as if for the references to the registers of live-births there were substituted references to the Adopted Children Register.

(4) Subject to paragraph (7), where the precise date of the child's birth is not proved to the satisfaction of the court, the court will determine the probable date of birth.

(5) The probable date of the child's birth may be specified in the placement order, adoption order or section 84 order as the date of the child's birth.

(6) Subject to paragraph (7), where the child's place of birth cannot be proved to the satisfaction of the court –

    (a)   the child may be treated as having been born in the registration district of the court where it is probable that the child may have been born in –
        (i)   the United Kingdom;
        (ii) the Channel Islands; or
        (iii) the Isle of Man; or
    (b)   in any other case, the particulars of the country of birth may be omitted from the placement order, adoption order or section 84 order.

(7) A placement order identifying the probable date and place of birth of the child will be sufficient proof of the date and place of birth of the child in adoption proceedings and proceedings for a section 84 order.

Defined terms—"adoption proceedings", "child", "proceedings", "section 84 order": FPR 2010, r 2.3(1).

14.18 Disclosing information to an adopted adult

(1) The adopted person has the right, on request, to receive from the court which made the adoption order a copy of the following –

    (a)   the application form for an adoption order (but not the documents attached to that form);
    (b)   the adoption order and any other orders relating to the adoption proceedings;
    (c)   orders allowing any person contact with the child after the adoption order was made; and
    (d)   any other document or order referred to in Practice Direction 14F.

(2) The court will remove any protected information from any copy of a document or order referred to in paragraph (1) before the copies are given to the adopted person.

(3) This rule does not apply to an adopted person under the age of 18 years.

(4) In this rule "protected information" means information which would be protected information under section 57(3) of the 2002 Act if the adoption agency gave the information and not the court.

Defined terms—"adoption proceedings", "child", "proceedings": FPR 2010, r 2.3(1).

Disclosing information to an adopted adult (r 14.18(1)(d))—See FPR PD14F.

14.19 Translation of documents

(1) Where a translation of any document is required for the purposes of proceedings for a Convention adoption order the translation must –

    (a)   unless the court directs otherwise, be provided by the applicant; and
    (b)   be signed by the translator to certify that the translation is accurate.

(2) This rule does not apply where the document is to be served in accordance with the Service Regulation.

Defined terms—"proceedings", "the Service Regulation": FPR 2010, r 2.3(1).

14.20 Application for recovery orders

(1) An application for any of the orders referred to in section 41(2) of the 2002 Act (recovery orders) may –

  (a) in the High Court or a county court, be made without notice in which case the applicant must file the application –
  (i)   where the application is made by telephone, the next business day after the making of the application; or
  (ii) in any other case, at the time when the application is made; and
  (b) in a magistrates' court, be made, with the permission of the court, without notice in which case the applicant must file the application at the time when the application is made or as directed by the court.

(2) Where the court refuses to make an order on an application without notice it may direct that the application is made on notice in which case the application will proceed in accordance with rules 14.1 to 14.17.

(3) The respondents to an application under this rule are –

  (a) in a case where –
  (i)   placement proceedings;
  (ii) adoption proceedings; or
  (iii) proceedings for a section 84 order,
  are pending, all parties to those proceedings;
  (b) any adoption agency authorised to place the child for adoption or which has placed the child for adoption;
  (c) any local authority to whom notice under section 44 of the 2002 Act (notice of intention to adopt or apply for a section 84 order) has been given;
  (d) any person having parental responsibility for the child;
  (e) any person in whose favour there is provision for contact;
  (f) any person who was caring for the child immediately prior to the making of the application; and
  (g) any person whom the applicant alleges to have effected, or to have been or to be responsible for, the taking or keeping of the child.

Defined terms—"adoption proceedings", "business day", "child", "court officer", "placement proceedings", "proceedings", "section 84 order": FPR 2010, r 2.3(1); "provision for contact": FPR 2010, r 14.1(2).

14.21 Inherent jurisdiction and fathers without parental responsibility

Where no proceedings have started an adoption agency or local authority may ask the High Court for directions on the need to give a father without parental responsibility notice of the intention to place a child for adoption.

Defined terms—"child", "jurisdiction", "proceedings": FPR 2010, r 2.3(1).

14.22 Timing of applications for section 89 order

An application for a section 89 order must be made within 2 years beginning with the date on which –

  (a) the Convention adoption or Convention adoption order; or
  (b) the overseas adoption or determination under section 91 of the 2002 Act,

to which it relates was made.

Defined terms—"section 89 order": FPR 2010, r 2.3(1).

14.23 Custody of documents

All documents relating to proceedings under the 2002 Act must, while they are in the custody of the court, be kept in a place of special security.

Defined terms—"the 2002 Act", "proceedings": FPR 2010, r 2.3(1).

14.24 Documents held by the court not to be inspected or copied without the court's permission

Subject to the provisions of these rules, any practice direction or any direction given by the court –

    (a) no document or order held by the court in proceedings under the 2002 Act will be open to inspection by any person; and

    (b) no copy of any such document or order, or of an extract from any such document or order, will be taken by or given to any person.

Defined terms—"the 2002 Act", "proceedings": FPR 2010, r 2.3(1).

14.25 Orders

(1) An order takes effect from the date when it is made, or such later date as the court may specify.

(2) In proceedings in Wales a party may request that an order be drawn up in Welsh as well as English.

Defined terms—"proceedings": FPR 2010, r 2.3(1).

14.26 Copies of orders

(1) Within 7 days beginning with the date on which the final order was made in proceedings, or such shorter time as the court may direct, a court officer will send –

    (a) a copy of the order to the applicant;

    (b) a copy, which is sealed$^{(GL)}$, authenticated with the stamp of the court or certified as a true copy, of –

        (i)   an adoption order;

        (ii)   a section 89 order; or

        (iii) an order quashing or revoking an adoption order or allowing an appeal against an adoption order,

        to the Registrar General;

    (c) a copy of a Convention adoption order to the relevant Central Authority;

    (d) a copy of a section 89 order relating to a Convention adoption order or a Convention adoption to the –

        (i)   relevant Central Authority;

        (ii)   adopters;

        (iii) adoption agency; and

        (iv) local authority;

    (e) unless the court directs otherwise, a copy of a contact order under section 26 of the 2002 Act or a variation or revocation of a contact order under section 27 of the 2002 Act to the –

        (i)   person with whom the child is living;

        (ii)   adoption agency; and

        (iii) local authority; and

    (f) a notice of the making or refusal of –

        (i)   the final order; or

(ii)   an order quashing or revoking an adoption order or allowing an appeal against an order in proceedings,

to every respondent and, with the permission of the court, any other person.

(2) The court officer will also send notice of the making of an adoption order or a section 84 order to –

   (a)   any court in Great Britain which appears to the court officer to have made any such order as is referred to in section 46(2) of the 2002 Act (order relating to parental responsibility for, and maintenance of, the child); and

   (b)   the principal registry, if it appears to the court officer that a parental responsibility agreement has been recorded at the principal registry.

(3) A copy of any final order may be sent to any other person with the permission of the court.

(4) The court officer will send a copy of any order made during the course of the proceedings to the following persons or bodies, unless the court directs otherwise –

   (a)   all the parties to those proceedings;

   (b)   any children and family reporter appointed in those proceedings;

   (c)   any adoption agency or local authority which has prepared a report on the suitability of an applicant to adopt a child;

   (d)   any local authority which has prepared a report on placement for adoption.

(5) If an order has been drawn up in Welsh as well as English in accordance with rule 14.25(2) any reference in this rule to sending an order is to be taken as a reference to sending both the Welsh and English orders.

Defined terms—"child", "court officer", "proceedings", "section 84 order", "section 89 order": FPR 2010, r 2.3(1). "Central Authority": FPR 2010, 14.1(2).

14.27 Amendment and revocation of orders

(1) Subject to paragraph (2), an application under –

   (a)   section 55 of the 2002 Act (revocation of adoptions on legitimation); or

   (b)   paragraph 4 of Schedule 1 to the 2002 Act (amendment of adoption order and revocation of direction),

may be made without serving a copy of the application notice.

(2) The court may direct that an application notice be served on such persons as it thinks fit.

(3) Where the court makes an order granting the application, a court officer will send the Registrar General a notice –

   (a)   specifying the amendments; or

   (b)   informing the Registrar General of the revocation,

giving sufficient particulars of the order to enable the Registrar General to identify the case.

Defined terms—"application notice", "court officer": FPR 2010, r 2.3(1).

14.28 Keeping registers in the family proceedings court

(1) A magistrates' court officer will keep a register in which there will be entered a minute or memorandum of every adjudication of the court in proceedings to which this Part applies.

(2) The register may be stored in electronic form on the court computer system and entries in the register will include, where relevant, the following particulars –

(a)   the name and address of the applicant;
(b)   the name of the child including, in adoption proceedings, the name of the child prior to, and after, adoption;
(c)   the age and sex of the child;
(d)   the nature of the application; and
(e)   the minute of adjudication.

(3) The part of the register relating to adoption proceedings will be kept separately to any other part of the register and will –

(a)   not contain particulars of any other proceedings; and
(b)   be kept by the court in a place of special security.

Defined terms—"adoption proceedings", "child", "court officer", "proceedings": FPR 2010, r 2.3(1).

Practice Direction 14A –
Who Receives a Copy of the Application Form for Orders in Proceedings

This Practice Direction supplements FPR Part 14, rule 14.6(1)(b)(ii)

Persons who receive copy of application form

1 In relation to each type of proceedings in column 1 of the following table, column 2 sets out which persons are to receive a copy of the application form:

Proceeding for	Who Receives a Copy of the Application Form
An adoption order (section 46 of the Act); or a section 84 order	Any appointed children's guardian, children and family reporter and reporting officer; the local authority to whom notice under section 44 (notice of intention to apply to adopt or apply for a section 84 order) has been given; the adoption agency which placed the child for adoption with the applicants; any other person directed by the court to receive a copy.
A placement order (section 21 of the Act); or an order varying a placement order (section 23 of the Act)	Each parent with parental responsibility for the child or guardian of the child; any appointed children's guardian, children and family reporter and reporting officer; any other person directed by the court to receive a copy.
An order revoking a placement order (section 24 of the Act)	Each parent with parental responsibility for the child or guardian of the child; any appointed children's guardian and children and family reporter; the local authority authorised by the placement order to place the child for adoption; any other person directed by the court to receive a copy.

Proceeding for	Who Receives a Copy of the Application Form
A contact order (section 26 of the Act); an order varying or revoking a contact order (section 27 of the Act); an order permitting the child's name to be changed or the removal of the child from the United Kingdom (section 28(2) of the Act); a recovery order (section 41(2) of the Act); a section 89 order; and a section 88 direction	All the parties; any appointed children's guardian and children and family reporter; any other person directed by the court to receive a copy.

PART III

Practice Direction 14B –
The First Directions Hearing – Adoptions with a Foreign Element

This Practice Direction supplements FPR Part 14, rule 14.8(3)

Application

1 This Practice Direction applies to proceedings for:

    (a) a Convention adoption order;
    (b) a section 84 order;
    (c) a section 88 direction;
    (d) a section 89 order; and
    (e) an adoption order where the child has been brought into the United Kingdom in the circumstances where section 83(1) of the Act applies.

The first directions hearing

2 At the first directions hearing the court will, in addition to any matters referred to in rule 14.8(1):

    (a) consider whether the requirements of the Act and the Adoptions with a Foreign Element Regulations 2005 (S.I. 2005/392) appear to have been complied with and, if not, consider whether or not it is appropriate to transfer the case to the High Court;
    (b) consider whether all relevant documents are translated into English and, if not, fix a timetable for translating any outstanding documents;
    (c) consider whether the applicant needs to file an affidavit setting out the full details of the circumstances in which the child was brought to the United

Kingdom, of the attitude of the parents to the application and confirming compliance with the requirements of The Adoptions with A Foreign Element Regulations 2005;

(d)   give directions about:
  (i)   the production of the child's passport and visa;
  (ii)   the need for an officer of the Service or a Welsh family proceedings officer and a representative of the Home Office to attend future hearings; and
  (iii)   personal service on the parents (via the Central Authority in the case of an application for a Convention Adoption Order) including information about the role of the officer of the Service or the Welsh family proceedings officer and availability of legal aid to be represented within the proceedings; and

(e)   consider fixing a further directions appointment no later than 6 weeks after the date of the first directions appointment and timetable a date by which the officer of the Service or the Welsh family proceedings officer should file an interim report in advance of that further appointment.

Amendments—FPR 2010, Update 2.

Practice Direction 14C –
Reports by the Adoption Agency or Local Authority

This Practice Direction supplements FPR Part 14, rule 14.11(3)

Matters to be contained in reports

1.1   The matters to be covered in the report on the suitability of the applicant to adopt a child are set out in Annex A to this Practice Direction.

1.2   The matters to be covered in a report on the placement of the child for adoption are set out in Annex B to this Practice Direction.

1.3   Where a matter to be covered in the reports set out in Annex A and Annex B does not apply to the circumstances of a particular case, the reasons for not covering the matter should be given.

ANNEX A – REPORT TO THE COURT WHERE THERE HAS BEEN AN APPLICATION FOR AN ADOPTION ORDER OR AN APPLICATION FOR A SECTION 84 ORDER

Section A: The Report and Matters for the Proceedings

Section B: The Child and the Birth Family

Section C: The Prospective Adopter of the Child

Section D: The Placement

Section E: Recommendations

Section F: Further information for proceedings relating to Convention Adoption Orders, Convention adoptions, section 84 Orders or adoptions where section 83(1) of the 2002 Act applies.

SECTION A: THE REPORT AND MATTERS FOR THE PROCEEDINGS

Part 1 – The report

For each of the principal author/s of the report:

(i)   name;

(ii)   role in relation to this case;

(iii)   sections completed in this report;

(iv)   qualifications and experience;

(v)   name and address of the adoption agency; and

(vi)   adoption agency case reference number.

Part 2 – Matters for the proceedings

(a)   Whether the adoption agency considers that any other person should be made a respondent or a party to the proceedings, including the child.

(b)   Whether any of the respondents is under the age of 18.

(c)   Whether a respondent is a person who, by reason of mental disorder within the meaning of the Mental Health Act 1983, is incapable of managing and administering his or her property and affairs. If so, medical evidence should be provided with particular regard to the effect on that person's ability to make decisions in the proceedings.

SECTION B: THE CHILD AND THE BIRTH FAMILY

Part 1

(i) Information about the child

(a)   Name, sex, date and place of birth and address including local authority area.

(b)   Photograph and physical description.

(c)   Nationality.

(d)   Racial origin and cultural and linguistic background.

(e)   Religious persuasion (including details of baptism, confirmation or equivalent ceremonies).

(f)   Details of any siblings, half-siblings and step-siblings, including dates of birth.

(g)   Whether the child is looked after by a local authority.

(h)   Whether the child has been placed for adoption with the prospective adopter by a UK adoption agency.

(i)   Whether the child was being fostered by the prospective adopter.

(j)   Whether the child was brought into the UK for adoption, including date of entry and whether an adoption order was made in the child's country of origin.

(k)   Personality and social development, including emotional and behavioural development and any related needs.

(l)   Details of interests, likes and dislikes.

(m)   A summary, written by the agency's medical adviser, of the child's health history, his current state of health and any need for health care which is anticipated, and date of the most recent medical examination.

(n)   Any known learning difficulties or known general medical or mental health factors which are likely to have, or may have, genetic implications.

(o)   Names, addresses and types of nurseries or schools attended, with dates.

(p)   Educational attainments.

(q)   Any special needs in relation to the child (whether physical, learning, behavioural or any other) and his emotional and behavioural development.

(r)   Whether the child is subject to a statement under the Education Act 1996.

PART III

(s)   Previous orders concerning the child:
  (i)   the name of the court;
  (ii)   the order made; and
  (iii)   the date of the order.
(t)   Inheritance rights and any claim to damages under the Fatal Accidents Act 1976 the child stands to retain or lose if adopted.
(u)   Any other relevant information which might assist the court.

(ii) Information about each parent of the child
(a)   Name, date and place of birth and address (date on which last address was confirmed current) including local authority area.
(b)   Photograph, if available, and physical description.
(c)   Nationality.
(d)   Racial origin and cultural and linguistic background.
(e)   Whether the mother and father were married to each other at the time of the child's birth or have subsequently married.
(f)   Where the parent has been previously married or entered into a civil partnership, dates of those marriages or civil partnerships.
(g)   Where the mother and father are not married, whether the father has parental responsibility and, if so, how it was acquired.
(h)   If the identity or whereabouts of the father are not known, the information about him that has been ascertained and from whom, and the steps that have been taken to establish paternity.
(i)   Past and present relationship with the other parent.
(j)   Other information about the parent, where available:
  (i)   health, including any known learning difficulties or known general medical or mental health factors which are likely to have, or may have, genetic implications;
  (ii)   religious persuasion;
  (iii)   educational history;
  (iv)   employment history; and
  (v)   personality and interests.
(k)   Any other relevant information which might assist the court.

Part 2

Relationships, contact arrangements and views.

THE CHILD
(a)   If the child is in the care of a local authority or voluntary organisation, or has been, details (including dates) of any placements with foster parents, or other arrangements in respect of the care of the child, including particulars of the persons with whom the child has had his home and observations on the care provided.
(b)   The child's wishes and feelings (if appropriate, having regard to the child's age and understanding) about adoption, the application and its consequences, including any wishes in respect of religious and cultural upbringing.
(c)   The child's wishes and feelings in relation to contact (if appropriate, having regard to the child's age and understanding).
(d)   The child's wishes and feelings recorded in any other proceedings.
(e)   Date when the child's views were last ascertained.

THE CHILD'S PARENTS (OR GUARDIAN) AND RELATIVES

    (a)   The parents' wishes and feelings before the placement, about the placement and about adoption, the application and its consequences, including any wishes in respect of the child's religious and cultural upbringing.

    (b)   Each parent's (or guardian's) wishes and feelings in relation to contact.

    (c)   Date/s when the views of each parent or guardian were last ascertained.

    (d)   Arrangements concerning any siblings, including half-siblings and step-siblings, and whether any are the subject of a parallel application or have been the subject of any orders. If so, for each case give:
        (i)   the name of the court;
        (ii) the order made, or (if proceedings are pending) the order applied for; and
        (iii) the date of order, or date of next hearing if proceedings are pending.

    (e)   Extent of contact with the child's mother and father and, in each case, the nature of the relationship enjoyed.

    (f)   The relationship which the child has with relatives, and with any other person considered relevant, including:
        (i)   the likelihood of any such relationship continuing and the value to the child of its doing so; and
        (ii) the ability and willingness of any of the child's relatives, or of any such person, to provide the child with a secure environment in which the child can develop, and otherwise to meet the child's needs.

    (g)   The wishes and feelings of any of the child's relatives, or of any such person, regarding the child.

    (h)   Whether the parents (or members of the child's family) have met or are likely to meet the prospective adopter and, if they have met, the effect on all involved of such meeting.

    (i)   Dates when the views of members of the child's wider family and any other relevant person were last ascertained.

PART III

Part 3

A summary of the actions of the adoption agency

    (a)   Brief account of the agency's actions in the case, with particulars and dates of all written information and notices given to the child and his parents and any person with parental responsibility.

    (b)   If consent has been given for the child to be placed for adoption, and also consent for the child to be adopted, the names of those who gave consent and the date such consents were given. If such consents were subsequently withdrawn, the dates of these withdrawals.

    (c)   If any statement has been made under section 20(4)(a) of the Adoption and Children Act 2002 (the "2002 Act") that a parent or guardian does not wish to be informed of any application for an adoption order, the names of those who have made such statements and the dates the statements were made. If such statements were subsequently withdrawn, the dates of these withdrawals.

    (d)   Whether an order has been made under section 21 of the 2002 Act, section 18 of the Adoption (Scotland) Act 1978 or Article 17(1) or 18(1) of the Northern Ireland Order 1987.

    (e)   Details of the support and advice given to the parents and any services offered or taken up.

    (f)   If the father does not have parental responsibility, details of the steps taken to inform him of the application for an adoption order.

    (g)   Brief details and dates of assessments of the child's needs, including expert opinions.

(h)   Reasons for considering that adoption would be in the child's best interests (with date of relevant decision and reasons for any delay in implementing the decision).

SECTION C: THE PROSPECTIVE ADOPTER OF THE CHILD

Part 1

Information about the prospective adopter, including suitability to adopt

(a)   Name, date and place of birth and address (date on which last address was confirmed current) including local authority area.

(b)   Photograph and physical description.

(c)   Whether the prospective adopter is domiciled or habitually resident in a part of the British Islands and, if habitually resident, for how long they have been habitually resident.

(d)   Racial origin and cultural and linguistic background.

(e)   Marital status or civil partnership status, date and place of most recent marriage (if any) or civil partnership (if any).

(f)   Details of any previous marriage, civil partnership, or relationship where the prospective adopter lived with another person as a partner in an enduring family relationship.

(g)   Relationship (if any) to the child.

(h)   Where adopters wish to adopt as a couple, the status of the relationship and an assessment of the stability and permanence of their relationship.

(i)   If a married person or a civil partner is applying alone, the reasons for this.

(j)   Description of how the prospective adopter relates to adults and children.

(k)   Previous experience of caring for children (including as a step-parent, foster parent, child-minder or prospective adopter) and assessment of ability in this respect, together where appropriate with assessment of ability in bringing up the prospective adopter's own children.

(l)   A summary, written by the agency's medical adviser, of the prospective adopter's health history, current state of health and any need for health care which is anticipated, and date of most recent medical examination.

(m)   Assessment of ability and suitability to bring up the child throughout his childhood.

(n)   Details of income and comments on the living standards of the household with particulars of the home and living conditions (and particulars of any home where the prospective adopter proposes to live with the child, if different).

(o)   Details of other members of the household, including any children of the prospective adopter even if not resident in the household.

(p)   Details of the parents and any siblings of the prospective adopter, with their ages or ages at death.

(q)   Other information about the prospective adopter:
   (i)   religious persuasion;
   (ii)   educational history;
   (iii) employment history; and
   (iv)   personality and interests.

(r)   Confirmation that the applicants have not been convicted of, or cautioned for, a specified offence within the meaning of regulation 23(3) of the Adoption Agencies Regulations 2005 (S.I. 2005/389).

(s)   Confirmation that the prospective adopter is still approved.

(t)   Confirmation that any referees have been interviewed, with a report of their views and opinion of the weight to be placed thereon and whether they are still valid.

(u)   Details of any previous family court proceedings in which the prospective adopter has been involved (which have not been referred to elsewhere in this report.)

Part 2

Wishes, views and contact arrangements

PROSPECTIVE ADOPTER

(a)   Whether the prospective adopter is willing to follow any wishes of the child or his parents or guardian in respect of the child's religious and cultural upbringing.

(b)   The views of other members of the prospective adopter's household and wider family in relation to the proposed adoption.

(c)   Reasons for the prospective adopter wishing to adopt the child and extent of understanding of the nature and effect of adoption. Whether the prospective adopter has discussed adoption with the child.

(d)   Any hope and expectations the prospective adopter has for the child's future.

(e)   The prospective adopter's wishes and feelings in relation to contact.

Part 3

Actions of the adoption agency

(a)   Brief account of the Agency's actions in the case, with particulars and dates of all written information and notices given to the prospective adopter.

(b)   The Agency's proposals for contact, including options for facilitating or achieving any indirect contact or direct contact.

(c)   The Agency's opinion on the likely effect on the prospective adopter and on the security of the placement of any proposed contact.

(d)   Where the prospective adopter has been approved by an agency as suitable to be an adoptive parent, the agency's reasons for considering that the prospective adopter is suitable to be an adoptive parent for this child (with dates of relevant decisions).

SECTION D: THE PLACEMENT

(a)   Where the child was placed for adoption by an adoption agency (section 18 of the 2002 Act), the date and circumstances of the child's placement with prospective adopter.

(b)   Where the child is living with persons who have applied for the adoption order to be made (section 44 of the 2002 Act), the date when notice of intention to adopt was given.

(c)   Where the placement is being provided with adoption support, this should be summarised and should include the plan and timescales for continuing the support beyond the making of the adoption order.

(d)   Where the placement is not being provided with adoption support, the reasons why.

(e)   A summary of the information obtained from the Agency's visits and reviews of the placement, including whether the child has been seen separately to the prospective adopter and whether there has been sufficient opportunity to see the family group and the child's interaction in the home environment.

PART III

(f)   An assessment of the child's integration within the family of the prospective adopter and the likelihood of the child's full integration into the family and community.

(g)   Any other relevant information that might assist the court.

SECTION E: RECOMMENDATIONS

(a)   The relative merits of adoption and other orders with an assessment of whether the child's long term interests would be best met by an adoption order or by other orders (such as residence and special guardianship orders).

(b)   Recommendations as to whether or not the order sought should be made (and, if not, alternative proposals).

(c)   Recommendations as to whether there should be future contact arrangements (or not).

SECTION F: FURTHER INFORMATION FOR PROCEEDINGS RELATING TO CONVENTION ADOPTION ORDERS, CONVENTION ADOPTIONS, SECTION 84 ORDERS OR AN ADOPTION WHERE SECTION 83(1) OF THE 2002 ACT APPLIES.

(a)   The child's knowledge of their racial and cultural origin.

(b)   The likelihood of the child's adaptation to living in the country he/she is to be placed.

(c)   Where the UK is the State of origin, reasons for considering that, after possibilities for placement of the child within the UK have been given due consideration, intercountry adoption is in the child's best interests.

(d)   Confirmation that the requirements of regulations made under sections 83(4), (5), (6) and (7) and 84(3) and (6) of the 2002 Act have been complied with.

(e)   For a Convention adoption or a Convention Adoption Order where the United Kingdom is either the State of origin or the receiving State, confirmation that the Central Authorities of both States have agreed that the adoption may proceed.

(f)   Where the State of origin is not the United Kingdom, the documents supplied by the Central Authority of the State of origin should be attached to the report, together with translation if necessary.

(g)   Where a Convention adoption order is proposed, details of the arrangements which were made for the transfer of the child to the UK and that they were in accordance with the Adoptions with a Foreign Element Regulations 2005 (S.I. 2005/392).

ANNEX B – REPORT TO THE COURT WHERE THERE HAS BEEN AN APPLICATION FOR A PLACEMENT ORDER

Section A: The Report and Matters for the Proceedings

Section B: The Child and the Birth Family

Section C: Recommendations

SECTION A: THE REPORT AND MATTERS FOR THE PROCEEDINGS

Part 1

The report

For each of the principal author/s of the report:

    (i)   name;
    (ii)   role in relation to this case;
    (iii)   section completed in this report;
    (iv)   qualifications and experience;
    (v)   name and address of the adoption agency; and
    (vi)   adoption agency case reference number.

Part 2

Matters for the proceedings

    (a)   Whether the adoption agency considers that any other person should be made a respondent or a party to the proceedings.
    (b)   Whether any of the respondents is under the age of 18.
    (c)   Whether a respondent is a person who, by reason of mental disorder within the meaning of the Mental Health Act 1983, is incapable of managing and administering his or her property and affairs. If so, medical evidence should be provided with particular regard to the effect on that person's ability to make decisions in the proceedings.

SECTION B: THE CHILD AND THE BIRTH FAMILY

Part 1

(i) Information about the child

    (a)   Name, sex, date and place of birth and address including local authority area.
    (b)   Photograph and physical description.
    (c)   Nationality.
    (d)   Racial origin and cultural and linguistic background.
    (e)   Religious persuasion (including details of baptism, confirmation or equivalent ceremonies).
    (f)   Details of any siblings, half-siblings and step-siblings, including dates of birth.
    (g)   Whether the child is looked after by a local authority.
    (h)   Personality and social development, including emotional and behavioural development and any related needs.
    (i)   Details of interests, likes and dislikes.
    (j)   A summary, written by the agency's medical adviser, of the child's health history, his current state of health and any need for health care which is anticipated, and date of the most recent medical examination.
    (k)   Any known learning difficulties or known general medical or mental health factors which are likely to have, or may have, genetic implications.
    (l)   Names, addresses and types of nurseries or schools attended, with dates.
    (m)   Educational attainments.
    (n)   Any special needs in relation to the child (whether physical, learning, behavioural or any other) and his emotional and behavioural development.
    (o)   Whether the child is subject to a statement under the Education Act 1996.
    (p)   Previous orders concerning the child:
        (i)   the name of the court;

      (ii) the order made; and

      (ii) the date of the order.

(q) Inheritance rights and any claim to damages under the Fatal Accidents Act 1976 the child stands to retain or lose if adopted.

(r) Any other relevant information which might assist the court.

(ii) Information about each parent of the child

(a) Name, date and place of birth and address (date on which last address was confirmed current) including local authority area.

(b) Photograph, if available, and physical description.

(c) Nationality.

(d) Racial origin and cultural and linguistic background.

(e) Whether the mother and father were married to each other at the time of the child's birth, or have subsequently married.

(f) Where the parent has been previously married or entered into a civil partnership, dates of those marriages or civil partnerships.

(g) Where the mother and father are not married, whether the father has parental responsibility and, if so, how it was acquired.

(h) If the identity or whereabouts of the father are not known, the information about him that has been ascertained and from whom, and the steps that have been taken to establish paternity.

(i) Past and present relationship with the other parent.

(j) Other information about the parent, where available:

    (i) health, including any known learning difficulties or known general medical or mental health factors which are likely to have, or may have, genetic implications;

    (ii) religious persuasion;

    (iii) educational history;

    (iv) employment history; and

    (v) personality and interests.

(k) Any other relevant information which might assist the court.

Part 2

Relationships, contact arrangements and views

THE CHILD

(a) If the child is in the care of a local authority or voluntary organisation, or has been, details (including dates) of any placements with foster parents, or other arrangements in respect of the care of the child, including particulars of the persons with whom the child has had his home and observations on the care provided.

(b) The child's wishes and feelings (if appropriate, having regard to the child's age and understanding) about the application, its consequences, and adoption, including any wishes in respect of religious and cultural upbringing.

(c) The child's wishes and feelings in relation to contact (if appropriate, having regard to the child's age and understanding).

(d) The child's wishes and feelings recorded in any other proceedings.

(e) Date when the child's views were last ascertained.

THE CHILD'S PARENTS (OR GUARDIAN) AND RELATIVES

(a) The parents' wishes and feelings about the application, its consequences, and adoption, including any wishes in respect of the child's religious and cultural upbringing.

(b) Each parent's (or guardian's) wishes and feelings in relation to contact.

(c) Date/s when the views of each parent or guardian were last ascertained.

(d) Arrangements concerning any siblings, including half-siblings and step-siblings, and whether any are the subject of a parallel application or have been the subject of any orders. If so, for each case give:

  (i)   the name of the court;

  (ii) the order made, or (if proceedings are pending) the order applied for; and

  (iii) the date of order, or date of next hearing if proceedings are pending.

(e) Extent of contact with the child's mother and father and in each case the nature of the relationship enjoyed.

(f) The relationship which the child has with relatives, and with any other person considered relevant, including:

  (i)   the likelihood of any such relationship continuing and the value to the child of its doing so; and

  (ii) the ability and willingness of any of the child's relatives, or of any such person, to provide the child with a secure environment in which the child can develop, and otherwise to meet the child's needs.

(g) The wishes and feelings of any of the child's relatives, or of any such person, regarding the child.

(h) Dates when the views of members of the child's wider family and any other relevant person were last ascertained.

Part 3

Summary of the actions of the adoption agency

(a) Brief account of the Agency's actions in the case, with particulars and dates of all written information and notices given to the child and his parents and any person with parental responsibility.

(b) If consent has been given for the child to be placed for adoption, and also consent for the child to be adopted, the names of those who gave consent and the date such consents were given. If such consents were subsequently withdrawn, the dates of these withdrawals.

(c) If any statement has been made under section 20(4)(a) of the 2002 Act that a parent or guardian does not wish to be informed of any application for an adoption order, the names of those who have made such statements and the dates the statements were made. If such statements were subsequently withdrawn, the dates of these withdrawals.

(d) Details of the support and advice given to the parents and any services offered or taken up.

(e) If the father does not have parental responsibility, details of the steps taken to inform him of the application for a placement order.

(f) Brief details and dates of assessments of the child's needs, including expert opinions.

(g) Reasons for considering that adoption would be in the child's best interests (with date of relevant decision and reasons for any delay in implementing the decision).

PART III

SECTION C: RECOMMENDATIONS

(a) The relative merits of a placement order and other orders (such as a residence or special guardianship order) with an assessment of why the child's long term interests are likely to be best met by a placement order rather than by any other order.

(b) Recommendations as to whether there should be future contact arrangements (or not), including whether a contact order under section 26 of the 2002 Act should be made.

Practice Direction 14D – Reports by a Registered Medical Practitioner ("Health Reports")

This Practice Direction supplements FPR Part 14, rule 14.12(2)

Matters to be contained in health reports

1.1 Rule 14.12(1) requires that health reports must be attached to an application for an adoption order or a section 84 order except where:

(a) the child was placed for adoption with the applicant by an adoption agency;

(b) the applicant or one of the applicants is a parent of the child; or

(c) the applicant is the partner of a parent of the child.

1.2 The matters to be contained in the health reports are set out in the Annex to this Practice Direction.

1.3 Where a matter to be contained in the health report does not apply to the circumstances of a particular case, the reasons for not covering the matter should be given.

ANNEX – CONTENTS OF HEALTH REPORTS

This information is required for reports on the health of children and their prospective adopter(s). Its purpose is to build up a full picture of each child's health history and current state of health, including strengths and weaknesses. This will enable local authorities' medical adviser to base their advice to the court on the fullest possible information when commenting on the health implications of the proposed adoption. The reports made by the examining doctor should cover, as far as practicable, the following matters.

1 The child

Name, date of birth, sex, weight and height.

A A health history of each natural parent, so far as is possible, including:

(i) name, date of birth, sex, weight and height;

(ii) a family health history, covering the parents, the brothers and sisters and the other children of the natural parent, with details of any serious physical or mental illness and inherited and congenital disease;

(iii) past health history, including details of any serious physical or mental illness, disability, accident, hospital admission or attendance at an out-patient department, and in each case any treatment given;

(iv) a full obstetric history of the mother, including any problems in the ante-natal, labour and post-natal periods, with the results of any tests carried out during or immediately after pregnancy;

(v) details of any present illness including treatment and prognosis;

(vi) any other relevant information which might assist the medical adviser; and

(vii) the name and address of any doctor(s) who might be able to provide further information about any of the above matters.

B A neo-natal report on the child, including:

(i) details of the birth, and any complications;

(ii) results of a physical examination and screening tests;

(iii) details of any treatment given;

(iv) details of any problem in management and feeding;

(v) any other relevant information which might assist the medical adviser; and

(vi) the name and address of any doctor(s) who might be able to provide further information about any of the above matters.

C A full health history and examination of the child, including:

(i) details of any serious illness, disability, accident, hospital admission or attendance at an out-patient department, and in each case any treatment given;

(ii) details and dates of immunisations;

(iii) a physical and developmental assessment according to age, including an assessment of vision and hearing and of neurological, speech and language development and any evidence of emotional or conduct disorder;

(iv) details, if relevant, of the impact of any addiction or substance use on the part of the natural mother before, during or following the pregnancy, and its impact or likely future impact on the child;

(v) the impact, if any, on the child's development and likely future development of any past exposure to physical, emotional or sexual abuse or neglectful home conditions and/or any non-organic failure to thrive;

(vi) for a child of school age, the school health history (if available);

(vii) any other relevant information which might assist the medical adviser; and

(viii) the name and address of any doctor(s) who might be able to provide further information about any of the above matters.

D The signature, name, address and qualifications of the registered medical practitioner who prepared the report, and the date of the report and of the examinations carried out.

2 The applicant

(If there is more than one applicant, a report on each applicant should be supplied covering all the matters listed below.)

A (i) name, date of birth, sex, weight and height;

(ii) a family health history, covering the parents, the brothers and sisters and the *children of the applicant*, with details of any serious physical or mental illness and inherited and congenital disease;

(iii) marital history, including (if applicable) reasons for inability to have children, and any history of domestic violence;

(iv) past health history, including details of any serious physical or mental illness, disability, accident, hospital admission or attendance at an out-patient department, and in each case any treatment given;

(v) obstetric history (if applicable);

PART III

(vi) details of any present illness, including treatment and prognosis;

(vii) a full medical examination;

(viii) details of any consumption of alcohol, tobacco and habit-forming drugs;

(ix) any other relevant information which might assist the medical adviser; and

(x) the name and address of any doctor(s) who might be able to provide further information about any of the above matters.

B The signature, name, address and qualifications of the registered medical practitioner who prepared the report, and the date of the report and of the examinations carried out.

Practice Direction 14E – Communication of Information Relating to Proceedings

This Practice Direction supplements FPR Part 14, rule 14.14(b)

Communication of information relating to proceedings

1.1 Rule 14.14 deals with the communication of information (whether or not it is recorded in any form) relating to proceedings.

1.2 Subject to any direction of the court, information may be communicated for the purposes of the law relating to contempt in accordance with paragraphs 1.3 or 1.4.

1.3 A person specified in the first column of the following table may communicate to a person listed in the second column such information as is specified in the third column for the purpose or purposes specified in the fourth column.

Communication of information without permission of the court

Communicated by	To	Information	Purpose
A party	A lay adviser or a McKenzie Friend	Any information relating to the proceedings	To enable the party to obtain advice or assistance in relation to the proceedings.
A party	The party's spouse, civil partner, cohabitant or close family member		For the purpose of confidential discussions enabling the party to receive support from his spouse, civil partner, cohabitant or close family member.

Communicated by	To	Information	Purpose
A party	A health care professional or a person or body providing counselling services for children or families		To enable the party or any child of the party to obtain health care or counselling.
A party	The Secretary of State, a McKenzie Friend, a lay adviser or an appeal tribunal dealing with an appeal made under section 20 of the Child Support Act 1991		For the purposes of making or responding to an appeal under section 20 of the Child Support Act 1991 or the determination of such an appeal.
A party	An adoption panel		To enable the adoption panel to discharge its functions as appropriate.
A party	A local authority's medical adviser appointed under the Adoption Agencies Regulations 2005 or the Adoption Agencies (Wales) Regulations 2005		To enable the medical adviser to discharge his or her functions as appropriate
A party or any person lawfully in receipt of information	The Children's Commissioner or the Children's Commissioner for Wales		To refer an issue affecting the interests of children to the Children's Commissioner or the Children's Commissioner for Wales.
A party or a legal representative	A mediator		For the purpose of mediation in relation to the proceedings.
A party, any person lawfully in receipt of information or a proper officer	A person or body conducting an approved research project		For the purpose of an approved research project.

PART III

Communicated by	To	Information	Purpose
A party, a legal representative or a professional legal adviser	A person or body responsible for investigating or determining complaints in relation to legal representatives or professional legal advisers		For the purposes of making a complaint or the investigation or determination of a complaint in relation to a legal representative or a professional legal adviser.
A legal representative or a professional legal adviser	A person or body assessing quality assurance systems		To enable the legal representative or professional legal adviser to obtain a quality assurance assessment.
A legal representative or a professional legal adviser	An accreditation body	Any information relating to the proceedings providing that it does not, or is not likely to, identify any person involved in the proceedings	To enable the legal representative or professional legal adviser to obtain accreditation.
A party	An elected representative or peer	The text or summary of the whole or part of a judgment given in the proceedings	To enable the elected representative or peer to give advice, investigate any complaint or raise any question of policy or procedure.
A party	The General Medical Council		For the purpose of making a complaint to the General Medical Council.
A party	A police officer		For the purpose of a criminal investigation.
A party or any person lawfully in receipt of information	A member of the Crown Prosecution Service		To enable the Crown Prosecution Service to discharge its functions under any enactment.

1.4 A person in the second column of the table in paragraph 1.3 may only communicate information relating to the proceedings received from a person in the first column for the purpose or purposes:

    (a)   for which he received that information, or

    (b)   of professional development or training, providing that any communication does not, or is not likely to, identify any person involved in the proceedings without that person's consent.

1.5 In this Practice Direction:

(1) "accreditation body" means:
   (a) The Law Society,
   (b) Resolution, or
   (c) The Legal Services Commission;

(1A) "adoption panel" means a panel established in accordance with regulation 3 of the Adoption Agencies Regulations 2005 or regulation 3 of the Adoption Agencies (Wales) Regulations 2005;

(2) "approved research project" means a project of research:
   (a) approved in writing by a Secretary of State after consultation with the President of the Family Division,
   (b) approved in writing by the President of the Family Division, or
   (c) conducted under section 83 of the Act of 1989 or section 13 of the Criminal Justice and Court Services Act 2000;

(3) "body assessing quality assurance systems" includes:
   (a) The Law Society,
   (b) The Legal Services Commission, or
   (c) The General Council of the Bar;

(4) "body or person responsible for investigating or determining complaints in relation to legal representatives or professional legal advisers" means:
   (a) The Law Society,
   (b) The General Council of the Bar,
   (c) The Institute of Legal Executives, or
   (d) The Legal Services Ombudsman;

(5) "cohabitant" means one of two persons who are neither married to each other nor civil partners of each other but are living together as husband and wife or as if they were civil partners;

(6) "criminal investigation" means an investigation conducted by police officers with a view to it being ascertained:
   (a) whether a person should be charged with an offence, or
   (b) whether a person charged with an offence is guilty of it;

(7) "elected representative" means:
   (a) a member of the House of Commons,
   (b) a member of the National Assembly for Wales, or
   (c) a member of the European Parliament elected in England and Wales;

(8) "health care professional" means:
   (a) a registered medical practitioner,
   (b) a registered nurse or midwife,
   (c) a clinical psychologist, or
   (d) a child psychotherapist;

(9) "lay adviser" means a non-professional person who gives lay advice on behalf of an organisation in the lay advice sector;

(10) "McKenzie Friend" means any person permitted by the court to sit beside an unrepresented litigant in court to assist that litigant by prompting, taking notes and giving him advice;

(11) "mediator" means a family mediator who is:
   (a) undertaking, or has successfully completed, a family mediation training course approved by the United Kingdom College of Family Mediators, or
   (b) a member of the Law Society's Family Mediation Panel;

(12) "peer" means a member of the House of Lords as defined by the House of Lords Act 1999.

PART III

Practice Direction 14F –
Disclosing Information to an Adopted Adult

This Practice Direction supplements FPR Part 14, rule 14.18(1)(d)

How to request for information

1.1 Rule 14.18 states that an adopted person who is over the age of 18 has the right to receive from the court which made the adoption order a copy of:

(a)   the application form for an adoption order (but not the documents attached to that form);

(b)   the adoption order and any other orders relating to the adoption proceedings; and

(c)   orders allowing any person contact with the child after the adoption order was made.

1.2 An application under rule 14.18 must be made in form A64 which is contained in the practice direction supplementing rule 5 and must have attached to it a full certified copy of the entry in the Adopted Children Register relating to the applicant.

1.3 The completed application form must be taken to the court which made the adoption order along with evidence of the applicant's identity showing a photograph and signature, such as a passport or driving licence.

Additional documents that the adopted person is also entitled to receive from the court

2 The adopted adult is also entitled to receive the following documents:

(a)   any transcript or written reasons of the court's decision; and

(b)   a report made to the court by:
(i)   a children's guardian, reporting officer or children and family reporter;
(ii)   a local authority; or
(iii)   an adoption agency.

Before the documents are sent to the adopted adult

3 The court will remove protected information from documents before they are sent to the adopted adult.

PART 15
REPRESENTATION OF PROTECTED PARTIES

CONTENTS OF THIS PART

Note—The contributor to this Part, who is also General Editor of *Court of Protection Practice* (Jordan Publishing Ltd), has submitted to the FPR Committee that the Rules in FPR 2010, Pt 15 do not conform to the principles of MCA 2005 for the following reasons:

1   There is no requirement for service of proceedings on a protected party or for those on whom the proceedings are served to inform or consult that party. When the appointment of a litigation friend is made without a court order (i e by someone filing a Certificate of Suitability) the protected party is not notified. It is thus possible for proceedings to be conducted on behalf of a party without that party being aware or a judicial finding of lack of capacity. That is inconsistent with the principles of MCA 2005.

2   The Rules should spell out the presumption of capacity and also that a "balance of probabilities" approach is to be adopted.

3   FPR PD15A, para 2.1 states that all steps and decisions that the litigation friend takes in the proceedings must be taken "for the benefit of the protected party", whereas MCA 2005 requires a "best interests" approach to be adopted for delegated decision-making, thereby introducing a checklist of factors to be taken into account. The Rules should clarify the basis on which the litigation friend is expected to act.

4   An individual treated as incapable should still be consulted at appropriate stages (when appropriate). Adopting the statutory "best interests" approach would require the litigation friend to enable the protected party to participate in any decisions about the conduct of the proceedings so far as reasonably practicable.

5   There is no express requirement for oversight by the court of the suitability or conduct of a litigation friend (although a judge would be expected to intervene where concerns arise).

6   The requirement for the litigation friend to give an undertaking as to costs (which, unlike CPR 1998, applies to a party responding to as well as bringing a claim) amounts to disability discrimination. How will the court find litigation friends for respondents when this costs indemnity is required? It is sufficient to provide that a litigation friend who unreasonably conducts a claim may, at the court's discretion, be ordered to pay some or all of the costs.

7   Unlike CPR 1998, there is no provision for judicial approval of settlements or compromises by litigation friends on behalf of protected parties (including withdrawal of proceedings).

8   The Rules (or accompanying PD) should make provision for any financial award to a protected party who is, or may be, incapable of administering financial affairs, and encourage co-operation with the Court of Protection.

At the invitation of the FPR Committee, the contributor drafted proposed new Rules and the Committee sought the approval of Mr Justice Charles as Judge in Charge of the Court of Protection before these were referred to public consultation. It is felt that because FPR 2010 are based on CPR 1998, any change should be made to both sets of Rules. It is, therefore, likely that it will be some time before new Rules are adopted.

15.1 Application of this Part

This Part contains special provisions which apply in proceedings involving protected parties.

Scope—This Part deals with protected parties (as defined) who were previously known as "patients" and together with children (minors) referred to as "persons under a disability". The terminology changed to protected parties in 2007 following the implementation of MCA 2005. The remainder of this rule regulates the conduct of proceedings by and against such persons, and ensures that they are represented by a "litigation friend". Proceedings involving a child as a party are dealt with under FPR 2010, Pt 16, Ch 5. For non-family proceedings, reference should be made to CPR 1998, Pt 21, which contains similar, although not identical, provisions.

PART III

For the first time, these provisions are available to the Family Proceedings Court, although it may be that proceedings involving a protected party will be transferred to the county court, which has more experience in this area.

Practice Direction—See FPR PD15A. See also the new FPR PD15B, which provides guidance as to litigation capacity, fluctuating capacity, ability to give evidence as a witness, the use of experts in regard to capacity issues and children who are likely to lack capacity on attaining 18.

"protected party"—This means "a party, or an intended party, who lacks capacity (within the meaning of MCA 2005) to conduct the proceedings" (FPR 2010, r 2.3(1)). It is possible for a child also to be a protected party and this may be relevant if that condition will continue following attainment of legal majority (e g in regard to the disposal of money awarded to the child). Thus, a child who has severe learning disabilities may continue to be a protected party even after attaining the age of 18.

The rules assume that it is known whether the party is a protected party but that will not always be the case and the annotations below illustrate just how difficult the assessment of capacity may be. Where there is doubt it is important to notify the party so as to provide an opportunity for representations to be made either on the issue of capacity or as to the identity of the litigation friend. It is good practice for anyone intending to become a litigation friend to serve upon or draw to the intention of the intended protected party the notice of intention to act as litigation friend and certificate of suitability, unless there is no prospect of a relevant response – see *Masterman-Lister v Brutton & Co and Jewell & Home Counties Dairies* [2003] 1 WLR 1511.

MCA 2005—This legislation established from 1 October 2007 a comprehensive statutory framework for decisions to be made by and on behalf of those whose capacity to make their own decisions is in doubt. A regional Court of Protection has jurisdiction to make declarations or decisions or to appoint a deputy to make decisions on the person's behalf. A small number of district judges and circuit judges are appointed to sit in the Court of Protection and difficult capacity issues may be referred to them.

The general principles that apply within the mental capacity jurisdiction are to be found in MCA 2005, ss 1–4. They include the test of "incapacity" and a "best interests" approach to any delegated decision-making according to a checklist of factors. (For an overview of MCA 2005, see Part II of this work.)

Persons who lack capacity—There are basically three categories of person who may come within the definition of a protected party, namely those with:

(1) a mental illness. The largest group comprises elderly people who become mentally impaired (e g by senile dementia or Alzheimer's disease);
(2) learning disabilities. The previous term was "mental handicap"; and
(3) brain damage. The courts generally encounter persons with an acquired brain injury. If the damage was caused during the developmental years (e g in childbirth) this will be classed as learning disabilities.

"lacks capacity"—This term is expressly defined as being "within the meaning of MCA 2005" so as to incorporate the principles that apply within that legislation and the jurisprudence that develops in the new mental capacity jurisdiction. Nevertheless, many of the principles that have evolved under previous case-law are still relevant. MCA 2005, s 2(1) sets out the definition:

"A person lacks capacity in relation to a matter if at the material time he is unable to make a decision for himself in relation to the matter because of an impairment of, or a disturbance in the functioning of, the mind or brain."

This is a two-stage test because it must be established first, that there is an impairment of, or disturbance in the functioning of, the person's mind or brain (the diagnostic threshold); and second, that the impairment or disturbance is sufficient to render the person incapable of making that particular decision. The impairment or disturbance may be permanent or temporary and no reference is made to the degree of impairment or disturbance. This provides a useful screening process – merely being eccentric is not a basis for being deprived of one's right to conduct litigation.

"Unable to make a decision"—MCA 2005, s 3(1) provides that a person is unable to make a decision if unable to:

• understand the information relevant to the decision;
• retain that information;
• use or weigh that information as part of the process of making the decision; or
• communicate his decision (whether by talking, using sign language or any other means).

Explanations must be provided in ways appropriate to the person's circumstances (using simple language, visual aids or any other means). This is not a significant change of approach because it was previously held (in regard to medical treatment, although the test was no doubt universal) that the individual must be able to: (a) understand and retain information, and (b) weigh that information in the balance to arrive at a choice (*Re MB* [1997] 2 FLR 426, CA).

"conduct the proceedings"—Tests of capacity are seen as being decision-specific, so it is the capacity of the party to conduct the particular proceedings that is relevant rather than capacity to manage and administer his property and affairs in general (as defined under the former test). Thus a person might be a protected party for complex personal injury proceedings, yet not for a simultaneous small claim. Even under the former rule that applied before MCA 2005, the Court of Appeal concentrated on the issue-specific nature of tests of capacity and decided that the test related to the individual and his immediate problems. Thus, Chadwick LJ in *Masterman-Lister v Brutton & Co and Jewell & anor* [2003] 1 WLR 151 stated:

> "[T]he test to be applied … is whether the party to legal proceedings is capable of understanding, with the assistance of such proper explanation from legal advisers and experts in other disciplines as the case may require, the issues on which his consent or decision is likely to be necessary in the course of those proceedings. If he has capacity to understand that which he needs to understand in order to pursue or defend a claim, I can see no reason why the law – whether substantive or procedural – should require the interposition of a next friend or guardian ad litem (or, as such a person is described in the CPR, a litigation friend)."

Presumptions as to capacity—There is a legal presumption that adults are competent until the contrary is proved. This presumption is relevant to the burden of proof. In general, the person who alleges that an individual lacks capacity must prove this, but the standard of proof is the civil standard, namely on the balance of probabilities rather than beyond reasonable doubt. Capacity must be assessed at the time that the decision is to be taken because it can vary. If an individual has previously been found to lack capacity there is no presumption of continuance, but if there is clear evidence of incapacity for a considerable period then the burden of proof may be more easily discharged even though it remains on whoever asserts incapacity.

Doubts about capacity may arise for several reasons, but these should not be confused with tests of capacity. Thus, the status of the individual (being elderly and living in a nursing home), the outcome of a decision (one that no person in his right mind would be expected to reach) or appearance, behaviour or conversation may cause capacity to be questioned, but these factors do not determine capacity. It is not unusual for outward appearances to create a false impression of lack of capacity (e g physical disabilities may obstruct the power of speech or movement) even where mental capacity is not affected. Conversely, a person may appear capable through social training and experience when in reality he/she lacks the understanding needed to make decisions. In all of these situations a proper assessment of capacity should be made.

Mental disorder—The existence of a mental disorder is no longer a criterion for a person being treated as incapable of conducting proceedings. The new diagnostic threshold of "an impairment of, or a disturbance in the functioning of, the mind or brain" was introduced because the term "mental disorder" had acquired distinct interpretations in the context of treatment under the Mental Health Acts. Being mentally disordered does not necessarily result in a person being a protected party, and an assessment of capacity must still be made. Thus:

(a) an individual may be sectioned under the provisions of the Mental Health Act 1983, yet not be a protected party as regards court proceedings because the criteria are different (consider *Re C (Refusal of Medical Treatment)* [1994] 1 FLR 31);

(b) an individual with learning disabilities may still have the capacity to conduct litigation depending on the complexity and the support available.

Communication difficulties—Physical disabilities may obstruct the power of speech or movement even where mental capacity is not affected, and other methods of communication must then be attempted. An interpreter may be provided for those with communication difficulties in the same way as for those who do not understand the language used in court.

Physical disabilities—Where the ability of an individual to conduct or participate in proceedings is impaired due to physical disabilities, steps can be taken by the court to overcome these. Thus the loop system may be provided for those who are hard of hearing, and enlarged print may be used on all documents for those whose sight is impaired. If necessary, hearings should be conducted in a courtroom or chambers with disabled access.

Tests of capacity—There is no universal test of capacity. Legal capacity depends on understanding rather than wisdom; the quality of the decision is irrelevant as long as the person understands what he is deciding. Legal tests vary according to the particular transaction or act involved but are generally issue-specific, ie they relate to the matters that the individual is required to understand. As capacity depends on time and context, a decision as to capacity in one context does not bind a court that has to consider the same issue in a different context.

A person found to be a protected party may nevertheless be capable of getting married, signing an enduring power of attorney (*Re K; Re F (Enduring Powers of Attorney)* [1988] 2 FLR 15) or consenting to medical treatment (*Re MB* above) because the matters to be taken into account are different. For a full explanation of the various tests that apply for different purposes reference should be made to the joint Law Society and BMA publication, *Assessment of Mental Capacity: Guidance for Doctors and Lawyers* (BMJ Publishing Group, 3rd edn, 2010).

Assessment of capacity—Mental capacity is a question of fact so any issue of capacity can only be determined by a judge in legal proceedings acting not as a medical expert, but as a lay person influenced by personal observation and on the basis of evidence not only from doctors, but also those who know the individual. For comprehensive guidance as to the manner in which capacity should be assessed reference should be made to *Assessment of Mental Capacity: Guidance for Doctors and Lawyers* (above). The mental abilities required to conduct litigation have been identified as comprising: the ability to recognise a problem, obtain and receive, understand and retain relevant information, including advice; the ability to weigh the information (including that derived from advice) in the balance in reaching a decision; and the ability to communicate that decision (*Masterman-Lister*, above). The approach adopted in *White v Fell* (1987) (unreported) was referred to by the Court of Appeal with approval and may still be of assistance:

"The expression 'incapable of managing her own affairs and property' must be construed in a common sense way as a whole. It does not call for proof of complete incapacity. On the other hand it is not enough to prove that the Plaintiff is now substantially less capable of managing her own affairs and property than she would have been had the accident not occurred."

But understanding is not by itself sufficient because the individual needs to be able to use or apply that understanding in making decisions. In *Mitchell v Alasia* [2005] EWHC 11 (QB) Cox J relied on qualities such as impulsiveness and volatility when deciding that the claimant was, by reason of his mental disorder, incapable of managing and administering his own affairs:

"he is at present extremely unstable and volatile. He demonstrates ... an inability to think carefully and to remember what he has said previously and a strong tendency to act impulsively. On occasions I accept that he may be able to listen to and to understand advice that he is given, but I am satisfied that he does not presently have that ability on any reliable or consistent basis. There would, in my judgment, be many occasions when this Claimant would simply be unable to absorb and process information he is given, to prioritise and plan his decision-making, to control his outbursts of emotion and temper and to learn from his mistakes."

In *Lindsay v Wood* [2006] EWHC 2895 (QB) Stanley Burnton J dealt with vulnerability as follows:

"When considering the question of capacity, psychiatrists and psychologists will normally wish to take into account all aspects of the personality and behaviour of the person in question, including vulnerability to exploitation. However, vulnerability to exploitation does not of itself lead to the conclusion that there is lack of capacity. Many people who have full capacity are vulnerability to exploitation ... The issue is ... whether the person concerned has the mental capacity to make a rational decision."

For an early decision on the test of capacity under the MCA 2005 jurisdiction in regard to a brain-injured claimant, see *Saulle v Nouvet* [2007] EWHC 2902 (QB). Guidance on the approach to capacity issues (in childcare proceedings but of more general application) is to be found in *RP v Nottingham City Council & Official Solicitor* [2008] 2 FLR 1516.

Ability to rely upon advice—The extent to which an individual with impaired capacity may rely upon the advice of others was considered in *White v Fell* (1987) (unreported, but quoted in *Masterman-Lister v Jewell & anor* [2002] EWHC 417 (QB) at first instance):

"Few people have the capacity to manage all their affairs unaided. In matters of law, particularly litigation, medicine, and given sufficient resources, financial professional advice is almost universally needed and sought ... she may not understand all the intricacies of litigation, or of a settlement, or of a wise investment policy ... But if that were the appropriate test then quite a substantial proportion of the adult population might be regarded as under disability."

Medical evidence—Legal practitioners and judges should not jump to conclusions about whether there is an impairment of, or a disturbance in the functioning of, the mind or brain without appropriate evidence, especially in the case of litigants who may merely be stubborn or eccentric. The evidence of a suitably qualified person is required as to the diagnosis, and this evidence will generally extend to the issue of capacity. In *Masterman-Lister* (Court of Appeal, above) Kennedy LJ said that "even where the issue does not seem to be contentious, a district judge who is responsible for case management will almost certainly require the assistance of a medical report before being able to be satisfied that incapacity exists". More recently, it has been stated on appeal that where medical evidence could not be obtained a court had to be cautious before concluding that a litigant was suffering from a disturbance of the mind preventing him from participating in litigation – *Baker Tilly (a firm) v Mira Makar* (2013) QBD, Sir Raymond Jack, 27 March.

Usually this expert will be a person with medical qualifications and ideally a psychiatrist. However, a psychologist, especially if of an appropriate speciality, may be better qualified in respect of a person with learning disabilities. Such opinion is merely part of the evidence and the factual evidence of a carer or social worker may also be relevant and even more persuasive. The typical general medical practitioner has little knowledge of mental capacity and the various legal tests that apply, so the appropriate test should be spelt out, and it should be explained that different tests apply to different types of decision. Any doctor or other medical witness asked to assist in relation to capacity needs to know the area of the alleged protected party's activities in relation to which his advice is sought (*Masterman-Lister*, above). All relevant information should be provided, so when the test is whether the individual is incapable of conducting civil proceedings the doctor must be given some idea of the nature and complexity of those proceedings. The doctor will need to know what decisions the individual will be called upon to make for the conduct of that litigation. Only then can he express an opinion whether the individual is capable of giving instructions.

Issues as to capacity—The rules make no express provision as to issues regarding whether a party is a protected party. Such an issue may be raised by the court or one of the parties, or by a litigation friend if there is doubt about whether a party has recovered capacity. It will then be necessary for the proceedings to be stayed until the issue is resolved and the court may order an inquiry to be made in the proceedings to determine the issue. Notice should be given to the party alleged to be a protected party in case he wishes to contest this or arrange representation. This inquiry would normally be heard before a district judge who can compel the attendance of witnesses (including medical attendants and the claimant or defendant himself) and the production of documents. Where there are practical difficulties in obtaining medical evidence the Official Solicitor may be consulted. The court can also direct the Official Solicitor to make inquiries and to report about such matters as the court thinks fit (*Harbin v Masterman* [1896] 1 Ch 351, CA).

Courts should always, as a matter of practice, at the first convenient opportunity investigate the question of capacity whenever there is any reason to suspect that it may be absent (e g significant head injury) other than in cases where the Court of Protection has already accepted jurisdiction. Although medical evidence will be required (see above), the judge may consider that he would be assisted by seeing the person alleged to lack capacity (*Masterman-Lister*, above).

Where, understandably, a claimant's legal team is unable to present a positive case as to whether their client is a protected party, consideration should be given to seeking an order of the court directing the Official Solicitor to review the evidence, to appoint his own medical expert, and to appear and make such submissions as he considers appropriate (*Lindsay v Wood* [2006] EWHC 2895 (QB)). The *Masterman-Lister* decision has been explored by the Court of Appeal in a subsequent case where a 50/50 settlement was agreed and proceedings later commenced with a litigation friend to assess quantum (*Bailey v Warren* [2006] EWCA Civ 51).

While evidence is required to support an application for the appointment of a litigation friend, it does not follow that the other party to the litigation is then entitled to put in evidence disputing the basis for the appointment. It cannot properly be contended that a defendant is at risk of suffering prejudice from the appointment of a litigation friend for the claimant (*Folks v Faizey* [2006] EWCA Civ 381).

Default orders—Where there is doubt as to the capacity of a respondent it would not be appropriate for the court to make an order that unless he submitted to an examination by a particular psychiatrist by a specified date he was to be treated as capable because such order may have been made against a protected party who needed a litigation friend (see *Carmarthenshire County Council v Lewis* [2010] EWCA Civ 1567). In the case of a petitioner or applicant the proceedings would normally be stayed until the doubt was resolved because they should not be allowed to continue without a litigation friend if capacity was lacking.

Official Solicitor—The Official Solicitor to the Senior Courts provided for by SCA 1981, s 90 may be contacted at 81 Chancery Lane, London WC2A 1DD; tel 020 7911 7127; fax 020 7911 7105. Where there are practical difficulties in obtaining medical evidence, the Official Solicitor may be consulted.

Care proceedings—In care proceedings the local authority is required to identify any concerns about the mental capacity of the mother to care for the child or to prepare for the proceedings. In *RP v Nottingham City Council and the Official Solicitor* [2008] 2 FLR 1516 the court gave guidance on the steps to be taken before and during care proceedings where there was an issue as to a parent's capacity. If a parent is considered to lack capacity the authority should refer the individual to the local adult learning disability team for help and advice. Judgments about capacity should not be made by social workers engaged in child protection.

Need for Court of Protection involvement—See the note under CPR 1998, r 21.11.

Human rights—When a person is treated as a protected party, whether or not as a result of an order of the court, he is thereby deprived of important rights, long cherished by English law and safeguarded by ECHR 1950. Although CPR 1998 do not contain any requirement for a judicial determination of the question, courts should always, as a matter of practice, at the first convenient opportunity investigate the question of capacity whenever there is any reason to suspect that it may be absent, other than in cases where the Court of Protection is already involved (*Masterman-Lister*, above).

Withdrawal of proceedings—The permission of the court is required for withdrawal of an application where any party is a protected party – see FPR 2010, r 29.4, which sets out the procedure.

Approval of settlements—Unlike FPR 1991 and the CPR, no provision appears to be made for the approval of any compromise or settlement where a party is a protected party, although the permission of the court is required for withdrawal (see above). In most cases, the approval of the court will in any event be required to an order, but approval on behalf of a protected party is a different (and possibly more onerous) concept and may mean an inquiry into the best interests of that party, including looking at counsel's advice. In the absence of an express requirement, there is a danger that this aspect may be overlooked.

Costs—Although a "solicitor must be bound at the outset to consider the question whether a client might be eligible for legal aid" (*Truex v Kitchin* [2007] 2 FLR 1203), there is no obligation on the Official Solicitor to seek public funding when acting for a protected party in matrimonial proceedings (*B v B* [2012] COPLR 480).

Witnesses—In *Re X (A Child)* [2012] 2 FLR 456 application was made in care proceedings for a 17 year old with Asperger's syndrome who had given an ABE interview to give oral evidence. Theis J held that:

Capacity   First, the court has to consider whether he is competent in accordance with CA 1989, s 96(2) (i e understands that it is his duty to speak the truth and has sufficient understanding to justify his evidence being heard).
Vulnerability   The objective is to achieve a fair trial but the court must balance the advantages that the giving of oral evidence will bring to the determination of the truth and the damage it may do to the welfare of the witness and any other child – see *Re W (Children)* [2010] 1 FLR 1485, at [23]. (Nine criteria were identified in the judgment.)
Intermediary's costs   Where support is required to enable the witness to give evidence, the LSC takes the view that is not "representation" but a mechanism analogous to translation that should be funded by the court. However, there is no provision for the use of registered intermediaries outside the scope of the Youth Justice and Criminal Evidence Act 1999, so there are obstacles to the funding of such support (unless there is a direct link to a criminal case in which the witness is involved).

15.2   Requirement for litigation friend in proceedings

A protected party must have a litigation friend to conduct proceedings on that party's behalf.

Scope—Rule 15.2 sets out the general rule that a protected party may only conduct proceedings by a litigation friend. There are no exceptions, although the court can waive the rule (see FPR 2010, r 15.3). FPR 2010, rr 15.5–15.8 set out the procedures for acquiring a litigation friend in various circumstances. The rule only refers to "a litigation friend", so a protected party may not have more than one in any particular proceedings but there is nothing to prevent such party having a different litigation friend in other proceedings of a different nature.

"litigation friend"—Under the former Rules the term was "next friend" for a petitioner or applicant and "guardian ad litem" for a respondent. It is now "litigation friend" for both.

Title of proceedings—In the proceedings, the protected party should be referred to in the title as "A.B. (by C.D. his/her litigation friend)" – PD15A. A similar approach was formerly adopted by the CPR, but the most recent PD provides that the tile shall be "A.B. (a protected party by C.D. his/her litigation friend)". This is more helpful because it draws attention to the reason why there is a litigation friend.

Status of litigation friend—The specific powers of the litigation friend are not expressly set out in the Rules, but as the appointment is to "conduct proceedings ... on behalf" of the protected party, subject to the provisions of the rules, it is assumed that any act that in the ordinary conduct of any proceedings is required or authorised to be done by a party shall or may be done by the litigation friend. (That was the position under the former CCR Ord 10, r 12).

Administration of funds—Unless the litigation friend is also a deputy appointed by the Court of Protection or an attorney under a registered lasting or enduring power of attorney, he will have no status in regard to the affairs of the protected party outside the proceedings in which he is appointed. So in that situation, if money is awarded to the protected party and this party is also incapable of handling that money (under the CPR described as a "protected beneficiary"), the Court of Protection will have to become involved unless the discretionary power referred to in the above note has been exercised. The money should not simply be paid to the litigation friend with no further guidance, thereby creating a potential for uncertainty and abuse, but the court is given an express discretion to permit small sums of money to be paid to someone (e g a relative or carer) so that a receipt may be obtained from that person rather than requiring Court of Protection involvement. This discretion may not be available in proceedings under CA 989, Sch 1 relating to a mentally disabled child.

Power to pay monies to another person—In financial remedy (ancillary relief) proceedings, the court may order transfer of property or payment (periodical payments or a lump sum) to another person where a party lacks capacity to handle that money. The other person must then act in the incapacitated party's best interests (MCA 1973, s 40).

Enduring power of attorney—An enduring power of attorney created under the Enduring Powers of Attorney Act 1985 – for the criteria and the requirement to register see MCA 2005, Sch 4.

Lasting power of attorney—A power of attorney under which the donor (P) confers on the donee (or donees) authority to make decisions about all or any of the following, namely: (a) P's personal welfare or specified matters concerning P's personal welfare; and (b) P's property and affairs or specified matters concerning P's property and affairs, and which includes authority to make such decisions in circumstances where P no longer has capacity. For the criteria and the requirement to register see MCA 2005.

Need for a solicitor—A litigation friend is not required to act by a solicitor but failure to instruct one may result in questions being raised as to the suitability of the litigation friend.

15.3 Stage of proceedings at which a litigation friend becomes necessary

(1) A person may not without the permission of the court take any step in proceedings except –

    (a)   filing an application form; or

    (b)   applying for the appointment of a litigation friend under rule 15.6,

until the protected party has a litigation friend.

(2) If during proceedings a party lacks capacity (within the meaning of the 2005 Act) to continue to conduct proceedings, no party may take any step in proceedings without the permission of the court until the protected party has a litigation friend.

(3) Any step taken before a protected party has a litigation friend has no effect unless the court orders otherwise.

Scope—This rule expands upon the general rule that a protected party may only conduct proceedings by a litigation friend. The only steps that may be taken following the issue of the proceedings and before such appointment are the filing of an application form including for appointment of a litigation friend. Any other step will be of no effect. But the court is given some discretion (see below).

Court's discretion—The court may permit proceedings involving a protected party to continue to a limited extent even though a litigation friend has not been appointed ("without the permission of the court": r 15.3(1),(2)) and may validate proceedings that have continued in breach of the requirements ("unless the court orders otherwise": r 15.3(3)).

Implications—It is possible to make urgent orders in proceedings involving a protected party before the appointment of a litigation friend, but the court should be made fully aware of all relevant circumstances. Where it is realised during the course of proceedings that a party is (and has been) a protected party, provided everyone has acted in good faith and there has been no manifest disadvantage to the party subsequently found to have been a protected party, it is likely that the court will regularise the position retrospectively (*Masterman-Lister*, above). This might be the case where the proceedings have effectively been guided throughout by the person being appointed as litigation friend. Proceedings inappropriately conducted by a protected party or an unsuitable person on his behalf will be treated as being of no effect and further proceedings may then be commenced in proper form.

PART III

Recovery of capacity—If the protected party recovers capacity, the appointment of the litigation friend may be terminated by court order under FPR 2010, r 15.9.

15.4 Who may be a litigation friend for a protected party without a court order

(1) This rule does not apply if the court has appointed a person to be a litigation friend.

(2) A person with authority as a deputy to conduct the proceedings in the name of a protected party or on that party's behalf is entitled to be the litigation friend of the protected party in any proceedings to which that person's authority extends.

(3) If there is no person with authority as a deputy to conduct the proceedings in the name of a protected party or on that party's behalf, a person may act as a litigation friend if that person –

    (a)   can fairly and competently conduct proceedings on behalf of the protected party;

    (b)   has no interest adverse to that of the protected party; and

    (c)   subject to paragraph (4), undertakes to pay any costs which the protected party may be ordered to pay in relation to the proceedings, subject to any right that person may have to be repaid from the assets of the protected party.

(4) Paragraph (3)(c) does not apply to the Official Solicitor.

    ("deputy" is defined in rule 2.3.)

Scope—This rule identifies a hierarchy for appointment as a litigation friend and the requirement of suitability for a person if not empowered under MCA 2005 as an attorney or deputy.

"Deputy"—Deputy is defined in FPR 2010, r 2.3 as having the meaning given in MCA 2005, s 16(2)(b), i e a person appointed by the Court of Protection to make decisions on the individual's behalf in relation to specified matters. In this context it means a deputy who has been authorised by the Court of Protection to conduct the proceedings in question.

Who is appointed—A duly authorised deputy takes precedence. An office copy of the order or other authorisation sealed with the official seal of the Court of Protection should be filed. Care should be taken to examine this document because simply being appointed a deputy does not by itself give authority to conduct proceedings. It is not clear if the court has power to appoint someone else (as under the former rules), but this situation is unlikely to arise and conflict between the court dealing with the litigation and the Court of Protection should be avoided.

There is no reference to an attorney under a registered lasting or enduring power but such attorney would normally be best placed to be a litigation friend because he will control the financial affairs of the protected party and there may, in consequence, be no need for a deputy. An ordinary power of attorney is of no significance because it ceases to have effect upon the incapacity of the donor, but of course the person acting may otherwise be suitable as litigation friend. If an EPA is registered this would normally indicate that the donor is a protected party, but that is not the case for an LPA because registration may take place at an earlier stage.

Suitability—There is no express restriction on who may be appointed apart from those stated in this rule, but obviously the person must not be a child or protected party. The litigation friend should not have any personal involvement in the proceedings, but see *Spurling v Broadhurst* [2012] EWHC 2883 (Ch). If the court becomes aware of the person's unsuitability, it may remove him under FPR 2010, r 15.9 and substitute another person as litigation friend, but there is no express duty to monitor the situation.

Official Solicitor—The Official Solicitor to the Senior Courts is only appointed by the court and the requirements of suitability do not apply.

Duty of litigation friend—The litigation friend must "fairly and competently conduct proceedings on behalf of the protected party" and have "no interest adverse to that of the protected party". FPR PD15A, para 2.1 also provides that all steps and decisions the litigation friend takes in the proceedings must be taken for the benefit of the protected party. It is not clear whether this direction is at variance with the duty imposed upon delegated decision-makers under MCA 2005 to act in the "best interests" of an incapacitated adult. A similar provision was initially included in CPR PD21, para 2.1 but removed following implementation of MCA 2005.

Costs undertaking—The prospective litigation friend (unless a deputy or the Official Solicitor) must undertake to pay any costs which the protected party may be ordered to pay in relation to the proceedings, subject to any right to be repaid from the assets of the protected party. This amounts to a severe disincentive especially in cases where the protected party is without funds, and may create problems in finding a suitable litigation friend, especially for a respondent.

Under the CPR (and the previous Rules) such indemnity is only required from the party bringing the proceedings and not from a defendant or respondent. It may be avoided by obtaining authority from the Court of Protection but that court may be cautious about granting authority where there are not sufficient funds to finance litigation. The court has a general discretion as to costs and will take into account the role of the litigation friend but may have power to impose a personal costs liability in case of misconduct quite apart from the undertaking.

15.5 How a person becomes a litigation friend without a court order

(1) If the court has not appointed a litigation friend, a person who wishes to act as a litigation friend must follow the procedure set out in this rule.

(2) A person with authority as a deputy to conduct the proceedings in the name of a protected party or on that party's behalf must file an official copy$^{(GL)}$ of the order, declaration or other document which confers that person's authority to act.

(3) Any other person must file a certificate of suitability stating that that person satisfies the conditions specified in rule 15.4(3).

(4) A person who is to act as a litigation friend must file –

    (a)   the document conferring that person's authority to act; or
    (b)   the certificate of suitability,

at the time when that person first takes a step in the proceedings on behalf of the protected party.

(5) A court officer will send the certificate of suitability to every person on whom, in accordance with rule 6.28, the application form should be served.

(6) This rule does not apply to the Official Solicitor.

Scope—This rule facilitates the appointment of a litigation friend by simply filing the required documents at the court office. It will be relied upon in most cases but does not apply if the court has already made such appointment.

Documents to be filed—A deputy merely needs to file the document issued by the Court of Protection authorising him to conduct the proceedings: FPR 2010, r 15.4(2). Any other person must file a certificate of suitability: r 15.5(2). The Official Solicitor does not need to file any of these documents but his consent to act is required.

Certificate of suitability—This states that the person signing can "fairly and competently conduct proceedings on behalf of the protected party" and has "no interest adverse to that of the protected party". It also contains the required undertaking as to costs. The certificate of suitability will be sent by the court to the persons to be served under FPR 2010, r 6.28.

Form N235 is used for civil proceedings and this confirms the maker's consent to act and belief that the party is a protected party (with reasons/medical evidence). Form FP9 is specified for family proceedings in FPR PD5A.

Time for filing—The required documents must be filed before any steps are taken as litigation friend: r 15.5(4).

Persons to be served (FPR 2010, r 6.14(2))—In the case of a protected party, service is to be on one of the following persons with authority in relation to that party, namely an attorney under a registered enduring or lasting power of attorney or a deputy appointed by the Court of Protection. If there is no such person, service must be on an adult with whom the protected party resides or in whose care the protected party is. The assumption is that such person will then take appropriate steps to arrange a representative (litigation friend). Service on a proper officer of the local social services authority or other guardian when the protected party is under a guardianship order, or the district health authority when the protected party has been compulsorily admitted to hospital under MHA 1983, may be sufficient. The court has a wide discretion as to service and may vary the general rule or dispense with service in a particular instance (see FPR 2010, Pt 6).

Notice to protected party—No provision is made for the certificate of suitability to be sent to the protected party, so under this procedure the proceedings may be commenced without the knowledge of the party stated to be incapable, notwithstanding that such party may dispute the lack of capacity or wish to make representations as to the identity of the litigation friend.

Official Solicitor—The Official Solicitor is not appointed under this provision.

15.6 How a person becomes a litigation friend by court order

(1) The court may, if the person to be appointed so consents, make an order appointing –

  (a) a person other than the Official Solicitor; or
  (b) the Official Solicitor,

as a litigation friend.

(2) An order appointing a litigation friend may be made by the court of its own initiative or on the application of –

  (a) a person who wishes to be a litigation friend; or
  (b) a party to the proceedings.

(3) The court may at any time direct that a party make an application for an order under paragraph (2).

(4) An application for an order appointing a litigation friend must be supported by evidence.

(5) Unless the court directs otherwise, a person appointed under this rule to be a litigation friend for a protected party will be treated as a party for the purpose of any provision in these Rules requiring a document to be served on, or sent to, or notice to be given to, a party to the proceedings.

(6) Subject to rule 15.4(4), the court may not appoint a litigation friend under this rule unless it is satisfied that the person to be appointed complies with the conditions specified in rule 15.4(3).

Scope—This rule sets out the process whereby the court appoints a litigation friend.

The person appointed—Any adult who can "fairly and competently conduct proceedings on behalf of the protected party" and has "no interest adverse to that of the protected party" may be appointed. It is not necessary to approach the Official Solicitor in all cases, and the court will not be concerned to ascertain whether he has declined to consent before appointing someone else.

Official Solicitor—Where the circumstances justify the involvement of the Official Solicitor, a completed questionnaire and a copy of the court file with any order provisionally appointing him should be sent to his office. He will usually consent to act and the case may be allocated within 28 days from invitation, subject to:

(a) satisfactory evidence in the form of an expert's opinion accepted by the party that he or she lacks capacity to conduct the proceedings, OR a finding by the court that the party is a protected party;
(b) confirmation that the Official Solicitor is litigation friend of last resort; and
(c) confirmation that there is security for the costs of legal representation.

Any order making such appointment should be expressed as being subject to the Official Solicitor's consent. Save in the most urgent of cases, it is unlikely that the Official Solicitor will be able to complete his enquiries in less than 3 months. Accordingly, a lengthy adjournment of the proceedings may be necessary and a substantive hearing should not be fixed within such period of his initial appointment without consulting him.

The Official Solicitor to the Senior Courts may be contacted at 81 Chancery Lane, London WC2A 1DD; tel 020 7911 7127; fax 020 7911 7105.

Service—Once appointed, the litigation friend is treated as a party for the purpose of service of documents.

15.7 Court's power to change litigation friend and to prevent person acting as litigation friend

(1) The court may –

(a) direct that a person may not act as a litigation friend;

(b) terminate a litigation friend's appointment; or

(c) appoint a new litigation friend in substitution for an existing one.

(2) An application for an order or direction under paragraph (1) must be supported by evidence.

(3) Subject to rule 15.4(4), the court may not appoint a litigation friend under this rule unless it is satisfied that the person to be appointed complies with the conditions specified in rule 15.4(3).

Scope—The court may prevent a person from being a litigation friend or replace a litigation friend during the course of proceedings. The court must be satisfied that the person to be appointed is suitable for appointment in accordance with the criteria set out in FPR 2010, r 15.4(3).

15.8 Appointment of litigation friend by court order – supplementary

(1) A copy of the application for an order under rule 15.6 or 15.7 must be sent by a court officer to –

(a) every person on whom, in accordance with rule 6.28, the application form should be served; and

(b) unless the court directs otherwise, the protected party.

(2) A copy of an application for an order under rule 15.7 must also be sent to –

(a) the person who is the litigation friend, or who is purporting to act as the litigation friend, when the application is made; and

(b) the person, if not the applicant, who it is proposed should be the litigation friend.

Scope—This rule makes provision for service of an application for the appointment of a litigation friend or the change of a litigation friend. In addition to being sent by the court to the persons to be served under FPR 2010, r 6.28, it must be sent to the purported protected party unless the court otherwise directs. The court has a wide discretion as to service and may vary the general rule or dispense with service in a particular instance (see FPR 2010, Pt 6).

Persons to be served (FPR 2010, r 6.28)—See note to FPR 2010, r 15.5 above.

Service of application for matrimonial order or civil partnership order—Special provisions apply to service of these proceedings on a protected party although the court has a general discretion. Neither the court nor the applicant personally must effect service: FPR 2010, r 6.5. The form must be endorsed with the notice set out in FPR PD6A and the person commencing the proceedings must file a witness statement by the person on whom the application form was served stating whether the contents of the application form or the purpose and intention of the application were communicated to the protected party and, if not, why not: FPR 2010, r 6.14(7). This does not apply when the Official Solicitor is to be the litigation friend (presumably because his enquiries will have included the circumstances of the party): FPR 2010, r 6.14(8).

Although these provisions as to service are designed to ensure that the purported protected party may participate, it is not clear how the required witness statement may be obtained, although lack of co-operation would indicate that the person served was not suitable and the court would then wish to give further directions.

15.9 Procedure where appointment of litigation friend comes to an end

(1) When a party ceases to be a protected party, the litigation friend's appointment continues until it is brought to an end by a court order.

(2) An application for an order under paragraph (1) may be made by –

    (a)   the former protected party;

    (b)   the litigation friend; or

    (c)   a party.

(3) On the making of an order under paragraph (1), the court officer will send a notice to the other parties stating that the appointment of the protected party's litigation friend to act has ended.

Scope—This rule makes provision for a party ceasing to be a protected party. The litigation friend will only be removed by court order following an application under r 15.9(3) and evidence will be required as to capacity.

Liability of litigation friend for costs—The litigation friend may have had to give an undertaking as to costs pursuant to r 15.4(3)(c). This liability continues until the court order discharging the litigation friend. It is not clear whether, when discharged, the litigation friend is released from all liability for costs or only costs incurred from that date, although it is probably the latter.

Practice Direction 15A – Protected Parties

This Practice Direction supplements FPR Part 15

General

1.1 A protected party must have a litigation friend to conduct proceedings on the protected party's behalf.

1.2 In the proceedings the protected party should be referred to in the title as "A.B. (by C.D. his/her litigation friend)".

Duties of the Litigation Friend

2.1 It is the duty of a litigation friend fairly and competently to conduct proceedings on behalf of a protected party. The litigation friend must have no interest in the proceedings adverse to that of the protected party and all steps and decisions the litigation friend takes in the proceedings must be taken for the benefit of the protected party.

Becoming a Litigation Friend without a court order

3.1 In order to become a litigation friend without a court order the person who wishes to act as litigation friend must –

    (a)   file an official copy of the order, declaration or other document which confers the litigation friend's authority as a deputy to conduct the proceedings in the name of a protected party or on his/her behalf; or

    (b)   file a certificate of suitability –

        (i)   stating that the litigation friend consents to act;

        (ii)   stating that the litigation friend knows or believes that the [applicant][respondent] lacks capacity (within the meaning of the 2005 Act) to conduct proceedings;

        (iii)   stating the grounds of that belief and if the belief is based upon medical opinion attaching any relevant document to the certificate;

    (iv)   stating that the litigation friend can fairly and competently conduct proceedings on behalf of the protected party and has no interest adverse to that of the protected party;

    (v)   undertaking to pay any costs which the protected party may be ordered to pay in relation to the proceedings, subject to any right the litigation friend may have to be repaid from the assets of the protected party; and

    (vi)   which the litigation friend has verified by a statement of truth.

3.2 Paragraph 3.1 does not apply to the Official Solicitor.

3.3 The court officer will send the certificate of suitability to the person who is the attorney of a registered enduring power of attorney, donee of a lasting power of attorney or deputy or, if there is no such person, to the person with whom the protected party resides or in whose care the protected party is.

3.4 The court officer is not required to send the documents referred to in paragraph 3.1(b)(iii) when sending the certificate of suitability to the person to be served under paragraph 3.3.

3.5 The litigation friend must file either the certificate of suitability or the authority referred to in paragraph 3.1(a) at a time when the litigation friend first takes a step in the proceedings on behalf of the protected party.

Application for a court order appointing a litigation friend

4.1 An application for a court order appointing a litigation friend should be made in accordance with Part 18 and must be supported by evidence.

4.2 The court officer must serve the application notice –

    (a)   on the persons referred to in paragraph 3.3; and

    (b)   on the protected party unless the court directs otherwise.

4.3 The evidence in support must satisfy the court that the proposed litigation friend –

    (a)   consents to act;

    (b)   can fairly and competently conduct proceedings on behalf of the protected party;

    (c)   has no interest adverse to that of the protected party; and

    (d)   undertakes to pay any costs which the protected party may be ordered to pay in relation to the proceedings, subject to any right the litigation friend may have to be repaid from the assets of the protected party.

4.4 Paragraph 4.3(d) does not apply to the Official Solicitor.

4.5 The proposed litigation friend may be one of the persons referred to in paragraph 3.3 where appropriate, or otherwise may be the Official Solicitor. Where it is sought to appoint the Official Solicitor, provision must be made for payment of his charges.

Change of litigation friend and prevention of person acting as litigation friend.

5.1 Where an application is made for an order under rule 15.7, the application must set out the reasons for seeking it and must be supported by evidence.

5.2 Subject to paragraph 4.4, if the order sought is substitution of a new litigation friend for an existing one, the evidence must satisfy the court of the matters set out in paragraph 4.3.

5.3 The court officer will serve the application notice on –

    (a)   the persons referred to in paragraph 3.3; and

    (b)   the litigation friend or person purporting to act as litigation friend.

PART III

Procedure where the need for a litigation friend has come to an end

6.1 Where a person who was a protected party regains or acquires capacity (within the meaning of the 2005 Act) to conduct the proceedings, an application under rule 15.9(2) must be made for an order under rule 15.9(1) that the litigation friend's appointment has ceased.

6.2 The application must be supported by the following evidence –

(a) a medical report or other suitably qualified expert's report indicating that the protected party has regained or acquired capacity (within the meaning of the 2005 Act) to conduct the proceedings; and

(b) a copy of any relevant order or declaration of the Court of Protection.

Practice Direction 15B –
Adults Who May Be Protected Parties and Children Who May Become Protected Parties in Family Proceedings

This Practice Direction supplements FPR Part 15

What the court will do where an adult may be a protected party

Litigation capacity

1.1 The court will investigate as soon as possible any issue as to whether an adult party or intended party to family proceedings lacks capacity (within the meaning of the Mental Capacity Act 2005) to conduct the proceedings. An adult who lacks capacity to conduct the proceedings is a protected party and must have a litigation friend to conduct the proceedings on his or her behalf. The expectation of the Official Solicitor is that the Official Solicitor will only be invited to act for the protected party as litigation friend if there is no other person suitable or willing to act.

1.2 Any issue as to the capacity of an adult to conduct the proceedings must be determined before the court gives any directions relevant to that adult's role in the proceedings. Where a party has a solicitor, it is the solicitor who is likely to first identify that the party may lack litigation capacity. Expert evidence as to whether a party lacks such capacity is likely to be necessary for the court to make a determination relating to the party's capacity to conduct proceedings. However, there are some cases where the court may consider that evidence from a treating clinician such as a treating psychiatrist is all the evidence of lack of litigation capacity which may be necessary. There may also be cases where it will be clear that a party does not have litigation capacity such as where the party is in a coma, minimally conscious or in a persistent vegetative state. In those cases the court may well consider that a letter from a treating doctor confirming the party's condition is sufficient evidence of lack of litigation capacity and not need a report from an expert.

1.3 If at any time during the proceedings there is reason to believe that a party may lack capacity to conduct the proceedings, then the court must be notified and directions sought to ensure that this issue is investigated without delay. The presumption of capacity should not be forgotten. For example, where a person has an identified difficulty such as a learning disability or a mental illness, that difficulty should not automatically lead to an investigation about that party's capacity to litigate. Where a party has a solicitor, the starting point is whether that solicitor has concerns about the party's capacity to litigate.

Ability to give evidence as a witness

1.4 Where the court determines that a party does not have capacity to conduct the proceedings, the court may well also have to determine whether that party is able to give evidence and if so whether 'special measures' are required. Expert evidence is also likely to be necessary for the court to make such determinations. However, as in relation to the question of litigation capacity, the court may consider that evidence from a treating clinician who has a good understanding of the party's difficulties may be sufficient. If the treating clinician is provided with information about the legal framework, the clinician may be able to provide that evidence more readily and more quickly than an expert instructed to give an opinion as to the party's ability to give evidence.

1.5 Where the protected party is able to give evidence, the representative will wish to consider (and ask the expert to consider) the impact on that party of giving evidence. When making a determination as to whether that protected party should give evidence, the court may need to consider whether the impact of giving evidence would be so adverse to their condition that it would not be in that party's best interests to do so. The representative may put forward an argument on behalf of the protected party that the protected party should not give evidence.

Instruction of an expert where an adult is a protected party

2.1 Where there is concern that a party or intended party may lack capacity to conduct the proceedings, that party's representative must take the lead in any instruction of an expert for the purpose of assessment of the party's capacity to conduct the proceedings. In the event that the assessment is that the party does lack capacity to conduct the proceedings, it may be appropriate to ask that the expert advise about a party's ability to give evidence as a witness. Such expert evidence would relate to the party's particular difficulties and vulnerabilities (in particular in the context of cross-examination) including the techniques or measures which could be used to assist the party to give his or her evidence to the best of his or her ability and to ensure that the party's support needs are identified and addressed in advance of any final hearing.

Factors to be considered when the court is deciding whether to give permission as mentioned in FPR 25.4(1) or (2)

3.1 FPR 25.5 lists factors to which the court is to have particular regard when deciding whether to give permission in all family proceedings for expert evidence to be put before the court, and in children proceedings also for an expert to be instructed or for a child to be medically or psychiatrically examined or assessed for the purposes of obtaining expert evidence. In relation to children proceedings, one factor to be considered by the court is whether evidence could be given by another person on matters on which the expert would give evidence. For the avoidance of doubt this factor is not intended to suggest that evidence of another party to the proceedings is a substitute for expert evidence relating to a party's capacity to conduct the proceedings, ability to give evidence or special measures as mentioned in paragraphs 1.2, 1.4 and 2.1 above.

3.2 In addition, in children proceedings, it should be noted that expert evidence or other evidence from a treating clinician about a party's litigation capacity in previous proceedings is no substitute for such evidence in current proceedings. Litigation capacity has to be considered in relation to the proceedings before the court. For example, a

PART III

parent may have been found to lack litigation capacity in care proceedings about child A three years before the current proceedings. That finding about litigation capacity in previous proceedings is not evidence that the parent lacks litigation capacity in subsequent proceedings about child B. It may be that the subsequent proceedings are simpler in terms of the issues and evidence before the court or that the parent's previous difficulty leading to lack of litigation capacity has improved.

Fluctuation in a party's capacity to conduct litigation

4.1 A party's capacity to conduct the litigation may fluctuate over the course of the proceedings. Litigation capacity may be lost or regained during the proceedings as a result of deterioration or improvement in the impairment of, or disturbance in the functioning of, the party's mind or brain. The necessity for expert evidence or evidence of a treating clinician as to a party's capacity can therefore arise at any time during the proceedings.

4.2 Fluctuation in a party's capacity to conduct litigation means that a litigation friend may not represent that party throughout the proceedings. It is expected that where the litigation friend has been appointed or reappointed, the court will be likely to make a direction in accordance with FPR 25.10(2) permitting such a litigation friend to put written questions to the expert after the 10 day period referred to in FPR 25.10(2)(c)where the 10 days referred to in that rule would be insufficient time for the litigation friend to become familiar with the case or latest developments in the case while assimilating the expert's report and formulating any questions.

Single joint experts

5.1 FPR 25.11 and 25.12 and paragraphs 2.1 to 2.7 of Practice Direction 25C and of Practice Direction 25D make provision for two or more parties to put expert evidence before the court from a single joint expert. 'Single joint expert' ('SJE') is defined by FPR 25.2(1) as a person who provides expert evidence for use in proceedings on behalf of two or more parties (including the applicant) to the proceedings. No provision of the FPR nor the Practice Directions compel the use of an SJE. Paragraph 2.1 of Practice Direction 25C and of Practice Direction 25D provide that a SJE should be used 'wherever possible'. The expectation is that expert evidence as mentioned in paragraphs 1.2, 1.4 and 2.1 above, including on whether a party lacks capacity to conduct the proceedings, would not be evidence which is likely to be appropriately given by a SJE. However, there may be circumstances where expert evidence is needed by two or more parties relating to, for example, the capacity of a party when he or she gave consent to the making of a consent order made by the court in financial remedy proceedings and such evidence may be considered by the court to be appropriately given by a SJE. But these are circumstances where the expert evidence relates to an issue in the proceedings.

Child aged 16–17 who is the subject of the proceedings likely to lack relevant decision making capacity at age 18

6.1 Where the child who is the subject of the proceedings is aged 16 to 17 consideration should be given as to whether it is necessary to obtain expert evidence on whether that child will lack capacity (within the meaning of the Mental Capacity Act 2005) to make one or more of the decisions relevant to the proceedings (for example, in relation to residence, contact with family or about care arrangements) when that child reaches 18.

6.2 Attention is drawn to the fact that the Mental Capacity Act 2005 provides for a framework for decision making in respect of persons over 16 who lack capacity to makes decisions about their own finances, health and welfare. The Mental Capacity Act 2005 (Transfer of Proceedings) Order 2007 (SI 2007/1899) includes provision for the transfer of proceedings from a court having jurisdiction under the Children Act 1989 to the Court of Protection.

Child who is not the subject of proceedings likely to lack capacity to conduct the proceedings when he or she reaches 18

7.1 Where it appears that a child is –

(a)   a party to the proceedings and not the subject of them;
(b)   nearing age 18; and
(c)   considered likely to lack capacity to conduct the proceedings when 18,

the court will consider giving directions for the child's capacity in this respect to be investigated.

Definition of 'expert' and 'children proceedings'

8.1 The definitions of 'expert' and 'children proceedings' in FPR 25.2(1) apply to this Practice Direction and the explanation of an expert team in paragraph 2.2 of Practice Direction 25B also applies.

PART 16
REPRESENTATION OF CHILDREN AND REPORTS IN PROCEEDINGS INVOLVING CHILDREN

CONTENTS OF THIS PART

Chapter 1
Application of this Part

16.1 Application of this Part

This Part –

    (a)   sets out when the court will make a child a party in family proceedings; and

    (b)   contains special provisions which apply in proceedings involving children.

Chapter 2
Child as Party in Family Proceedings

16.2 When the court may make a child a party to proceedings

(1) The court may make a child a party to proceedings if it considers it is in the best interests of the child to do so.

(2) This rule does not apply to a child who is the subject of proceedings –

    (a)   which are specified proceedings; or

    (b)   to which Part 14 applies.

       (The Practice Direction 16A sets out the matters which the court will take into consideration before making a child a party under this rule.)

PD16A—When a child should be made a party to proceedings and the circumstances which the court may consider to justify the making of an order are set out in FPR PD16A, paras 7.1–7.5.

Guidance note—In July 2011, the Justices' Clerks' Society issued guidance on making a child a party to proceedings (see Part V).

Chapter 3
When a Children's Guardian or Litigation Friend will be Appointed

16.3 Appointment of a children's guardian in specified proceedings or proceedings to which Part 14 applies

(1) Unless it is satisfied that it is not necessary to do so to safeguard the interests of the child, the court must appoint a children's guardian for a child who is –

    (a)   the subject of; and

    (b)   a party to,

proceedings –

       (i)   which are specified proceedings; or

(ii) to which Part 14 applies.

(Rules 12.6 and 14.6 set out the point in the proceedings when the court will appoint a children's guardian in specified proceedings and proceedings to which Part 14 respectively.)

(2) At any stage in the proceedings –

(a) a party may apply, without notice to the other parties unless the court directs otherwise, for the appointment of a children's guardian; or

(b) the court may of its own initiative appoint a children's guardian.

(3) Where the court refuses an application under paragraph (2)(a) it will give reasons for the refusal and the court or a court officer will –

(a) record the refusal and the reasons for it; and

(b) as soon as practicable, notify the parties and either the Service or the Assembly of a decision not to appoint a children's guardian.

(4) When appointing a children's guardian the court will consider the appointment of anyone who has previously acted as a children's guardian of the same child.

(5) Where the court appoints a children's guardian in accordance with this rule, the provisions of Chapter 6 of this Part apply.

Appointment—The obligation to appoint a children's guardian in specified proceedings unless the circumstances are as described in r 16.3(1) is imposed by CA 1989, s 41(1). CJCSA 2000, ss 11 and 12 established the Children and Family Court Advisory and Support Service which is responsible for fulfilling the requirements of courts in respect of investigating and reporting; see further the annotations under those sections and CA 1989, ss 7 and 37. Cafcass has a duty to appoint a guardian as soon as reasonably practicable, taking into account its general functions, duties and resources, but it does not owe a specific duty to an individual child: *R and Others v Cafcass* [2012] 2 FLR 1432.

Where interests of children conflict—There is usually no reason why a children's guardian should not properly represent children whose interests conflict (*Re T and E (Proceedings: Conflicting Interests)* [1995] 1 FLR 581, FD).

Refusal to make an appointment (r 16.3(3))—The concept of a refusal imports a request to act in the way refused, but it is submitted that it is appropriate for the prescribed form to be completed not only where the court refuses an application under r 16.3(2)(a) but also where the court initially decides not to make an appointment under r 16.3(1).

16.4 Appointment of a children's guardian in proceedings not being specified proceedings or proceedings to which Part 14 applies

(1) Without prejudice to rule 8.42 or 16.6, the court must appoint a children's guardian for a child who is the subject of proceedings, which are not proceedings of a type referred to in rule 16.3(1), if –

(a) the child is an applicant in the proceedings;

(b) a provision in these rules provides for the child to be a party to the proceedings; or

(c) the court has made the child a party in accordance with rule 16.2.

(2) The provisions of Chapter 7 of this Part apply where the appointment of a children's guardian is required in accordance with paragraph (1).

("children's guardian" is defined in rule 2.3.)

"rule 2.3"—A "children's guardian" means a person appointed in accordance with FPR 2010, r 16.3 or 16.4.

"rule 8.42 or 16.6" (r 16.4(1))—Rule 8.42 allows a child to apply for consent to marry or to register a civil partnership and r 16.6 allows a child to participate in proceedings without a guardian respectively. Therefore, a guardian should not be appointed under r 16.4 if the child wishes to act without one and the condition in FPR 2010, r 16.6 as to his capacity is satisfied.

PD16A—Pt 4 of FPR PD16A, para 7.1 makes plain that making a child a party to proceedings is a step that will be taken only in cases which involve an issue of significant difficulty and consequently will occur in only a minority of cases. The circumstances which the court may consider to justify the making of an order are set out in para 7.2: the guidance includes 10 circumstances which may justify the making of an order.

Hague Convention proceedings—A child should only be made party to Convention proceedings in exceptional circumstances (*Re H (Abduction)* [2007] 1 FLR 242). See also "the child's objections" under CACA 1985, Sch 1, Art 13.

Cafcass/Official Solicitor—The child should only be made a party in a minority of cases featuring issues of significant difficulty. Such decisions are made by a circuit judge, High Court judge or district judge in the Principal Registry or a district judge of the county court. Where it is felt that a child needs separate representation, consideration should first be given to appointing an officer of Cafcass as guardian. If Cafcass is unable to provide a guardian, FPR 2010, r 9.5(1) makes further provision for the appointment of a guardian. See "some other proper person" below. See *Practice Note of March 2013 (The Official Solicitor to the Senior Courts: Appointment in Family Proceedings and Proceedings under the Inherent Jurisdiction in Relation to Adults)*; and *CAFCASS and the National Assembly for Wales Practice Note of June 2006 (Appointment of Guardians in Private Law Proceedings)*.

Continuing role of children's guardian when "specified proceedings" cease to be "specified"—It is possible for the High Court or a county court to direct that a guardian ad litem continue to be involved under r 16.4 even though proceedings which had been "specified proceedings", within the meaning of CA 1989, s 41(6)(b), have ceased to be "specified" (for example, where a local authority, as a result of a s 37 direction by the court, investigates the circumstances of a child but decides to make no application for a public law order in respect of him). However, this course can only be taken if: (i) the children's guardian consents to it; (ii) there is funding available; and (iii) the children's guardian has a continuing role to play in the matter despite the changed status of the proceedings (*Re CE (Section 37 Direction)* [1995] 1 FLR 26).

Guidance note—In July 2011, the Justices' Clerks' Society issued guidance on the appointment of a guardian (see Part V).

16.5 Requirement for a litigation friend

(1) Without prejudice to rule 16.6, where a child is –

    (a)   a party to proceedings; but

    (b)   not the subject of those proceedings,

the child must have a litigation friend to conduct proceedings on the child's behalf.

(2) The provisions of Chapter 5 of this Part apply where a litigation friend is required in accordance with paragraph (1).

Scope—This rule introduces the provisions set out in FPR 2010, Pt 16, Ch 5, which relate to the appointment of a litigation friend for a child (cf FPR 2010, Pt 15 which makes similar provision for a protected party).

Chapter 4
Where a Children's Guardian or Litigation Friend is not Required

16.6 Circumstances in which a child does not need a children's guardian or litigation friend

(1) Subject to paragraph (2), a child may conduct proceedings without a children's guardian or litigation friend where the proceedings are proceedings –

    (a)   under the 1989 Act;

    (b)   to which Part 11 (applications under Part 4A of the Family Law Act 1996) or Part 14 (applications in adoption, placement and related proceedings) of these rules apply; or

    (c)   relating to the exercise of the court's inherent jurisdiction with respect to children, and one of the conditions set out in paragraph (3) is satisfied.

(2) Paragraph (1) does not apply where the child is the subject of and a party to proceedings –

  (a)   which are specified proceedings; or
  (b)   to which Part 14 applies.

(3) The conditions referred to in paragraph (1) are that either –

  (a)   the child has obtained the court's permission; or
  (b)   a solicitor –
      (i)   considers that the child is able, having regard to the child's understanding, to give instructions in relation to the proceedings; and
      (ii) has accepted instructions from that child to act for that child in the proceedings and, if the proceedings have begun, the solicitor is already acting.

(4) An application for permission under paragraph (3)(a) may be made by the child without notice.

(5) Where a child –

  (a)   has a litigation friend or children's guardian in proceedings to which this rule applies; and
  (b)   wishes to conduct the remaining stages of the proceedings without the litigation friend or children's guardian,

the child may apply to the court, on notice to the litigation friend or children's guardian, for permission for that purpose and for the removal of the litigation friend or children's guardian.

(6) The court will grant an application under paragraph (3)(a) or (5) if it considers that the child has sufficient understanding to conduct the proceedings concerned or proposed without a litigation friend or children's guardian.

(7) In exercising its powers under paragraph (6) the court may require the litigation friend or children's guardian to take such part in the proceedings as the court directs.

(8) The court may revoke any permission granted under paragraph (3)(a) where it considers that the child does not have sufficient understanding to participate as a party in the proceedings concerned without a litigation friend or children's guardian.

(9) Where a solicitor is acting for a child in proceedings without a litigation friend or children's guardian by virtue of paragraph (3)(b) and either of the conditions specified in paragraph (3)(b)(i) or (ii) cease to be fulfilled, the solicitor must inform the court immediately.

(10) Where –

  (a)   the court revokes any permission under paragraph (8); or
  (b)   either of the conditions specified in paragraph (3)(b)(i) or (ii) is no longer fulfilled,

the court may, if it considers it necessary in order to protect the interests of the child concerned, appoint a person to be that child's litigation friend or children's guardian.

"entitled to begin, prosecute or defend any proceedings"—This rule does not confer any rights to party status which a child would not otherwise enjoy but merely affects whether a litigation friend or guardian ad litem is required when a child is a party. Unlike "begin", "prosecute or defend" refers to a continuing course of action; therefore, if in the course of proceedings which a child had been prosecuting or defending without a litigation friend or guardian ad litem in reliance on one (or both) of the grounds in r 16.6(3), the ground (or both of them) ceases to apply, the child is unable to continue prosecuting or defending the remaining stages of the proceedings unless and until he acquires a litigation friend or guardian ad litem. The provisions of r 16.6(1) ceases to apply only if the permission is revoked by the court under r 16.6(8), in which case the court would be able to appoint a litigation friend or guardian ad litem under r 16.6(10). Where r 16.6(3)(b) ceases to apply, the solicitor concerned must so inform the court under r 16.6(9) and the court is similarly able to make an appointment under r 16.6(10).

Permission of the court (r 16.6(3)(a))—The criterion for granting permission is set out in r 16.6(6). Where a child wishes to act as a litigant in person, the court's permission must be obtained under r 16.6(5). Even where a child has retained a solicitor, the solicitor may still wish the court's permission to be sought if he is unsure of whether r 16.6(3)(b)(i) is satisfied, or he is unwilling to shoulder the responsibility of deciding that it is satisfied. The court, rather than the solicitor, always has the ultimate right to decide whether a child who comes before it as a party without a next friend or guardian ad litem has the necessary ability, having regard to his understanding, to instruct his solicitor (*Re CT (A Minor) (Wardship: Representation)* [1993] 2 FLR 278). The test in relation to an application to dispense with a guardian is a one-stage test, the essence of which is that the court has to consider whether or not the minor has "sufficient understanding to participate as a party in the proceedings concerned" (r 16.6(6); *Re N (Contact: Minor Seeking Leave to Defend and Removal of Guardian)* [2003] 1 FLR 652).

Solicitor's acceptance of instructions (r 16.6(3)(1)(b))—The test which applies under r 16.6(3)(b)(i) is, in substance, the same as that which governs whether a solicitor should accept instructions from a child who is the subject of specified proceedings (see FPR 2010, r 16.29(2)(b)). See also *Re CT (A Minor) (Wardship: Representation)* [1993] 2 FLR 278 (above) and "sufficient understanding" below.

Ex parte nature of request (r 16.6(5))—Whether a child should be allowed to dispense with a litigation friend or guardian ad litem is a matter between the minor and the court (and the litigation friend or guardian ad litem if one is already acting). It is implicit that the other parties to the proceedings (or proposed parties to proceedings which the minor wishes to begin) have no standing in relation to questions under this rule, even though they may have their own reasons for wishing a particular outcome. The rules do not expressly or implicitly confer any right on the parents of the child or anyone else to be heard on the child's application. However, the judge always has a discretion (not conferred by the rules), in the course of hearing such an application, to hear the representations of the child's parents or others in the interests of justice (*Re S (A Minor) (Independent Representation)* [1993] 2 FLR 437).

"sufficient understanding" (r 16.6(6))—In *Mabon v Mabon* [2005] 2 FLR 1011, the Court of Appeal reviewed the older authorities and recognised the growing acknowledgement of the autonomy and consequential rights of children, both nationally and internationally. Thorpe LJ stated that r 16.6 (then r 9.2A) was sufficiently widely framed to meet the UK's obligations under Art 12 of the United Nations Convention on the Rights of the Child 1989 and that Art 8 of ECHR 1950 provided that judges, when measuring the sufficiency of a child's understanding, reflected the extent to which in the 21st century there was a keener appreciation of the child's autonomy and consequential right to participate in decision-making processes that fundamentally affected his or her life. The courts must, in the case of articulate teenagers, accept that the right to freedom of expression and participation outweighed the paternalistic judgement of welfare. However, welfare had a place in testing the sufficiency of a child's understanding. If direct participation would lead to a risk of harm to the child and if the child was incapable of comprehending that risk then a judge could find that sufficient understanding had not been demonstrated. However, judges also had to be aware of the risk of emotional harm that might arise from denying the child knowledge of, and participation in, the continuing proceedings.

Revocation of leave (r 16.6(8))—The court may wish to revoke leave in two main types of case. First, the complexity of the proceedings may materially increase during the course of the interlocutory process by the making of new applications in the course of them, the joinder of new parties or the raising of new and complicated factual or evidential issues that were not originally foreseen. Without altering its assessment of the child's level of understanding, the court may conclude that it is insufficient in the changed circumstances (see "sufficient understanding" above). Second, through experiencing how the child conducts the interlocutory stages of the proceedings, the court may simply conclude that it was wrong to grant the leave in the first place. Where this occurs the court may appoint a litigation friend or guardian pursuant to the provisions of FPR 2010, Pt 16.

Chapter 5
Litigation Friend

16.7 Application of this Chapter

This Chapter applies where a child must have a litigation friend to conduct proceedings on the child's behalf in accordance with rule 16.5.

Scope—Rule 16.7 applies where a child is not excused from having a litigation friend by r 16.6. FPR 2010, rr 16.8–16.11 set out the procedures for acquiring a litigation friend in various circumstances.

Practice direction—See FPR PD16A.

"Litigation friend"—Under the former Rules the term was "next friend" for a petitioner or applicant and "guardian ad litem" for a respondent. It is now "litigation friend" for both.

Need for a solicitor—A litigation friend is not required to act by a solicitor but failure to instruct one may result in questions being raised as to the suitability of the litigation friend.

Withdrawal of proceedings—The permission of the court is likely to be required for withdrawal of an application where any party is a child – see FPR 2010, r 29.4, which sets out the procedure.

Approval of settlements—Unlike FPR 1991 and CPR 1998, there appears to be no provision for the approval of any compromise or settlement where a party is a child. However, in most, if not all, cases the approval of the court will in any event be required to an order.

16.8 Stage of proceedings at which a litigation friend becomes necessary

(1) This rule does not apply in relation to a child who is conducting proceedings without a litigation friend in accordance with rule 16.6.

(2) A person may not without the permission of the court take any step in proceedings except –

    (a)   filing an application form; or

    (b)   applying for the appointment of a litigation friend under rule 16.11,

until the child has a litigation friend.

(3) Any step taken before a child has a litigation friend has no effect unless the court orders otherwise.

Scope—This rule expands on the general rule that a child may only conduct proceedings by a litigation friend. The only steps that may be taken following the issue of the proceedings and before such appointment are the filing of an application form including for appointment of a litigation friend. Any other step will be of no effect. But the court is given some discretion (see below).

Title of proceedings—The child should be referred to in the title as "A.B. (a child by C.D. his/her litigation friend)" – FPR PD16A. A similar approach is adopted by the CPR.

Court's discretion—The court may permit proceedings involving a child to continue to a limited extent even though a litigation friend has not been appointed ("without the permission of the court": r 16.8(2)) and may validate proceedings that have continued in breach of the requirements ("unless the court orders otherwise": r 16.8(3)).

Implications—It is possible to make urgent orders in proceedings involving a child before the appointment of a litigation friend, but the court should be made fully aware of all relevant circumstances. Where it is realised during the course of proceedings that a party is a child, provided everyone has acted in good faith and there has been no manifest disadvantage to the child, it is likely that the court will regularise the position retrospectively (*Masterman-Lister*, above). This might be the case where the proceedings have effectively been guided throughout by the person being appointed as litigation friend. Proceedings inappropriately conducted by a child or an unsuitable person on his behalf will be treated as being of no effect and further proceedings may then be commenced in proper form.

Attainment of majority—When the child attains majority, the appointment of the litigation friend comes to an end: FPR 2010, r 16.15.

16.9 Who may be a litigation friend for a child without a court order

(1) This rule does not apply if the court has appointed a person to be a litigation friend.

(2) A person may act as a litigation friend if that person –

    (a)   can fairly and competently conduct proceedings on behalf of the child;

    (b)   has no interest adverse to that of the child; and

    (c)   subject to paragraph (3), undertakes to pay any costs which the child may be ordered to pay in relation to the proceedings, subject to any right that person may have to be repaid from the assets of the child.

(3) Paragraph (2)(c) does not apply to the Official Solicitor, an officer of the Service or a Welsh family proceedings officer.

Scope—This rule identifies the requirement of suitability for a person to be appointed as litigation friend.

Suitability—There is no other express restriction on who may be appointed, but the person must not be a child or protected party. The litigation friend should not have any personal involvement in the proceedings, but see *Spurling v Broadhurst* [2012] EWHC 2883 (Ch). If the court becomes aware of the person's unsuitability, it may remove him under r 16.12 and substitute another person as litigation friend, but there is no express duty to monitor the situation.

Official Solicitor—The Official Solicitor to the Senior Courts is only appointed by the court and the requirements of suitability do not apply.

Duty of litigation friend—The litigation friend must "fairly and competently conduct proceedings on behalf of the child" and have "no interest adverse to that of the child". FPR PD16A, para 2.1 also provides that all steps and decisions the litigation friend takes in the proceedings must be taken for the benefit of the child.

Costs undertaking—The prospective litigation friend (unless the Official Solicitor or an officer as defined) must undertake to pay any costs that the child may be ordered to pay in relation to the proceedings, subject to any right to be repaid from the assets of the child. This amounts to a severe disincentive especially in cases where the child is without funds, and may create problems in finding a suitable litigation friend.

Under the CPR (and the previous Rules) such indemnity is only required from the party bringing the proceedings and not from a defendant or respondent. The court has a general discretion as to costs and will take into account the role of the litigation friend but may have power to impose a personal costs liability in case of misconduct quite apart from the undertaking.

16.10 How a person becomes a litigation friend without a court order

(1) If the court has not appointed a litigation friend, a person who wishes to act as such must file a certificate of suitability stating that that person satisfies the conditions specified in rule 16.9(2).

(2) The certificate of suitability must be filed at the time when the person who wishes to act as litigation friend first takes a step in the proceedings on behalf of the child.

(3) A court officer will send the certificate of suitability to every person on whom, in accordance with rule 6.28, the application form should be served.

(4) This rule does not apply to the Official Solicitor, an officer of the Service or a Welsh family proceedings officer.

Scope—This rule facilitates the appointment of a litigation friend by simply filing the required documents at the court office. It will be relied upon in most cases but does not apply if the court has already made such appointment.

Documents to be filed—The intended litigation friend must file a certificate of suitability: r 16.10(1). The Official Solicitor does not need to file any of these documents but his consent to act is required.

Certificate of suitability—This states that the person signing can "fairly and competently conduct proceedings on behalf of the child" and has "no interest adverse to that of the child". It also contains the required undertaking as to costs. The certificate of suitability will be sent by the court to the persons to be served (which do not include the child).

Form N235 is used for civil proceedings and this confirms the maker's consent to act and belief that the party is a child. Form FP9 is specified for family proceedings in PD5A.

Time for filing—The required documents must be filed before any steps is taken as litigation friend: r 16.10(2).

Persons to be served (FPR 2010, r 6.28)—In the case of a child, these are a parent or guardian, or, if none, an adult with whom the child resides or in whose care he or she is: FPR 2010, r 6.14(1). The

PART III

assumption is that such person will then take appropriate steps to arrange a representative (litigation friend). Service on a proper officer of the local social services authority when the child is in care may be sufficient.

Notice to child—No provision is made for the certificate of suitability to be sent to the child.

Official Solicitor—The Official Solicitor to the Senior Courts is not appointed under this provision.

16.11 Appointment of litigation friend by the court

(1) The court may, if the person to be appointed consents, make an order appointing as a litigation friend –

    (a)   the Official Solicitor;
    (b)   an officer of the Service or a Welsh family proceedings officer; or
    (c)   some other person.

(2) An order appointing a litigation friend may be made by the court of its own initiative or on the application of –

    (a)   a person who wishes to be a litigation friend; or
    (b)   a party to the proceedings.

(3) The court may at any time direct that a party make an application for an order under paragraph (2).

(4) An application for an order appointing a litigation friend must be supported by evidence.

(5) Unless the court directs otherwise, a person appointed under this rule to be a litigation friend for a child will be treated as a party for the purpose of any provision in these rules requiring a document to be served on, or sent to, or notice to be given to, a party to the proceedings.

(6) Subject to rule 16.9(3), the court may not appoint a litigation friend under this rule unless it is satisfied that the person to be appointed complies with the conditions specified in rule 16.9(2).

(7) This rule is without prejudice to rule 16.6.

Scope—This rule sets out the process whereby the court appoints a litigation friend.

The person appointed—Any adult who can "fairly and competently conduct proceedings on behalf of the child" and has "no interest adverse to that of the child" may be appointed. It is not necessary to approach the Official Solicitor in all cases and the court will not be concerned to ascertain whether he has declined to consent before appointing someone else.

Official Solicitor—See note under FPR 2010, r 15.6. The Official Solicitor to the Senior Courts may be contacted at 81 Chancery Lane, London WC2A 1DD; tel 020 7911 7127; tax 020 7911 7105.

Service—Once appointed the litigation friend is treated as a party for the purpose of service of documents.

16.12 Court's power to change litigation friend and to prevent person acting as litigation friend

(1) The court may –

    (a)   direct that a person may not act as a litigation friend;
    (b)   terminate a litigation friend's appointment; or
    (c)   appoint a new litigation friend in substitution for an existing one.

(2) An application for an order or direction under paragraph (1) must be supported by evidence.

(3) Subject to rule 16.9(3), the court may not appoint a litigation friend under this rule unless it is satisfied that the person to be appointed complies with the conditions specified in rule 16.9(2).

Scope—The court may prevent a person from being a litigation friend or replace a litigation friend during the course of proceedings. The court must be satisfied that the person to be appointed is suitable for appointment in accordance with the criteria set out in FPR 2010, r 16.9(2).

16.13 Appointment of litigation friend by court order – supplementary

(1) A copy of the application for an order under rule 16.11 or 16.12 must be sent by a court officer to every person on whom, in accordance with rule 6.28, the application form should be served.

(2) A copy of an application for an order under rule 16.12 must also be sent to –

    (a) the person who is the litigation friend, or who is purporting to act as the litigation friend when the application is made; and

    (b) the person, if not the applicant, who it is proposed should be the litigation friend.

Scope—This rule makes provision for service of an application for the appointment of a litigation friend or the change of a litigation friend. It must be sent by the court to the persons to be served under FPR 2010, r 6.28 but need not be sent to the child. The court has a wide discretion as to service and may vary the general rule or dispense with service in a particular instance (see FPR 2010, Pt 6).

Persons to be served (FPR 2010, r 6.28)—The application must be served on one of the child's parents or guardians or, if there is no such person, an adult with whom the child resides or in whose care the child is: FPR 2010, r 6.14(1). See note to FPR 2010, r 16.10 above.

Service of application for matrimonial order or civil partnership order—Special provisions apply to service of these proceedings on a child although the court has a general discretion. Neither the court nor the applicant personally must effect service: FPR 2010, r 6.5. The form must be endorsed with the notice set out in FPR PD6A and the person commencing the proceedings must file a witness statement by the person on whom the application form was served stating whether the contents of the application form or the purpose and intention of the application were communicated to the child and, if not, why not: FPR 2010, r 6.14(7). This does not apply when the Official Solicitor is to be the litigation friend (presumably because his enquiries will have included the circumstances of the party): FPR 2010, r 6.14(8).

16.14 Powers and duties of litigation friend

(1) The litigation friend –

    (a) has the powers and duties set out in Practice Direction 16A; and

    (b) must exercise those powers and duties in accordance with Practice Direction 16A.

(2) Where the litigation friend is an officer of the Service or a Welsh family proceedings officer, rule 16.20 applies as it applies to a children's guardian appointed in accordance with Chapter 6.

Powers of litigation friend—The specific powers of the litigation friend are not expressly set out in the Rules or FPR PD16A, Pt 2, but as the appointment is to "conduct proceedings ... on behalf" of the child, it is assumed that any act that in the ordinary conduct of any proceedings is required or authorised to be done by the child shall or may be done by the litigation friend. (That was the position under the former CCR Ord 10, r 12.)

Duties of litigation friend—FPR PD16A, Pt 2, para 2.1 merely restates that the litigation friend must "fairly and competently conduct proceedings on behalf of the child", have "no interest adverse to that of the child" and that all steps and decisions the litigation friend takes in the proceedings must be taken for the benefit of the child.

Administration of funds—The litigation friend will have no status in regard to the affairs of the child outside the proceedings in which he is appointed. So in that situation, if money is awarded to the child, to whom should it be paid? There is a danger that the money will simply be paid to the litigation friend with no further guidance, thereby creating a potential for uncertainty and abuse. Should the court not be given an express discretion to permit money to be paid to someone (e g a relative or carer) so that a receipt may be obtained from that person?

16.15 Procedure where appointment of litigation friend comes to an end

(1) When a child who is not a protected party reaches the age of 18, a litigation friend's appointment comes to an end.

(2) A court officer will send a notice to the other parties stating that the appointment of the child's litigation friend to act has ended.

Scope—Unlike the position in respect of a protected party who regains capacity, the appointment of a litigation friend for a child ceases automatically when the child attains 18 years.

Liability of litigation friend for costs—An individual who was appointed litigation friend will have had to give an undertaking as to costs pursuant to FPR 2010, r 16.9(2)(c). It is not clear whether, when discharged, the litigation friend is released from all liability for costs or only costs incurred from that date, although it is probably the latter.

Chapter 6
Children's Guardian Appointed under Rule 16.3

16.16 Application of this Chapter

This Chapter applies where the court must appoint a children's guardian in accordance with rule 16.3.

16.17 Who may be a children's guardian

Where the court is appointing a children's guardian under rule 16.3 it will appoint an officer of the Service or a Welsh family proceedings officer.

Who may be appointed—The children's guardian must either be an officer of Cafcass or a Welsh family proceedings officer. FPR 2010, r 16.36 provides that in adoption proceedings certain individuals are ineligible for selection to act as children's guardian in particular proceedings if they have a close connection with the local authority concerned in the case or with any local authority if they have actually been involved with the arrangements for the child in that capacity within the previous 5 years and probation officers unless they have not been involved with the child or his family in that capacity. FPR 2010, r 16.3(4) requires the court to consider re-appointing anyone who has acted as the children's guardian in previous proceedings; the requirement is to do no more than consider re-appointing such a person, but the court will usually lean in favour of such a re-appointment as the previous knowledge of the child and the earlier proceedings will tend to enable the guardian better to safeguard the child's interests in the new proceedings.

Duration of appointment—When appointing a guardian, the court may specify the length of the appointment; otherwise the appointment will last until terminated by the court (r 16.19). The latter will be the more usual course. The rule does not specify what procedure is to be followed to terminate an appointment except to require the reasons to be given once the decision has been taken (FPR 2010, r 16.19(2)). If a guardian does act manifestly contrary to the child's best interests, the court will remove him even though neither his good faith nor his diligence is in issue. In reaching a responsible and considered decision, on which another mind might possibly take a different view, a guardian does not act manifestly contrary to the child's best interests (*Re A (Conjoined Twins: Medical Treatment) (No 2)* [2001] 1 FLR 267). Derivative applications, such as those to discharge a care order or to regulate contact with a child in care, are separate proceedings and not a continuation of the original care proceedings for this purpose (see the structure of s 41(6)); therefore the original guardian's appointment will not automatically carry over into the new proceedings. Once a care order has been made, the court has no power to add a direction that the guardian continue his involvement with the child (*Kent County Council v C* [1993] 1 FLR 308). However, see Adoption & Children Act 2002 – review of cases of looked-after children under CA 1989, s 26A for the role of a guardian where an Independent Reviewing Officer makes a referral to Cafcass. Following the repeal of CJCSA 2000, s 12(5)(b) by ACA 2002, there is no longer jurisdiction for a court to provide for a continuing role for a children's guardian following the making of a supervision order and therefore *Re MH (A Child) and Re SB and MB (Children)* [2001] 2 FLR 1334 is no longer a correct statement of the law. However, in *Oxfordshire County Council v L and F* [1997] 1 FLR 235 applications in respect of disclosure of documents in care proceedings to the police and the removal of injunctions restricting publication of material within care proceedings were made the day after care proceedings were concluded and the guardian ad litem (children's guardian) was allowed to continue to represent the child, despite the fact that her locus standi was far from clear. Where a children's guardian has been appointed for the purposes of an emergency protection order, she is no longer the guardian ad litem (children's guardian) when the emergency protection order has expired and there are no pending proceedings (*Re M (Prohibited Steps Order: Application for Leave)* [1993] 1 FLR 275).

16.18 What the court or a court officer will do once the court has made a decision about appointing a children's guardian

(1) Where the court appoints a children's guardian under rule 16.3 a court officer will record the appointment and, as soon as practicable, will –

    (a)   inform the parties and either the Service or the Assembly; and

    (b)   unless it has already been sent, send the children's guardian a copy of the application and copies of any document filed with the court in the proceedings.

(2) A court officer has a continuing duty to send the children's guardian a copy of any other document filed with the court during the course of the proceedings.

16.19 Termination of the appointment of the children's guardian

(1) The appointment of a children's guardian under rule 16.3 continues for such time as is specified in the appointment or until terminated by the court.

(2) When terminating an appointment in accordance with paragraph (1), the court will give reasons for doing so, a note of which will be taken by the court or a court officer.

16.20 Powers and duties of the children's guardian

(1) The children's guardian is to act on behalf of the child upon the hearing of any application in proceedings to which this Chapter applies with the duty of safeguarding the interests of the child.

(2) The children's guardian must also provide the court with such other assistance as it may require.

(3) The children's guardian, when carrying out duties in relation to specified proceedings, other than placement proceedings, must have regard to the principle set out in section 1(2) and the matters set out in section 1(3)(a) to (f) of the 1989 Act as if for the word "court" in that section there were substituted the words "children's guardian".

(4) The children's guardian, when carrying out duties in relation to proceedings to which Part 14 applies, must have regard to the principle set out in section 1(3) and the matters set out in section 1(4)(a) to (f) of the 2002 Act as if for the word "court" in that section there were substituted the words "children's guardian".

(5) The children's guardian's duties must be exercised in accordance with Practice Direction 16A.

(6) A report to the court by the children's guardian is confidential.

Duties of children's guardian—CA 1989, s 41(2)(b) places the children's guardian under a duty to safeguard the interests of the child in the manner prescribed by rules of court. This rule prescribes how this general duty is to be performed and lays far more specific duties on the children's guardian In *R v Cornwall County Council ex parte G* [1992] 1 FLR 270, it was emphasised that guardians are independent in the performance of their duties; and it was accordingly held that a local authority had acted unlawfully in seeking to restrict the number of hours spent by guardians on each individual case.

PD16A—The further duties of a children's guardian are set out in FPR PD16A, paras 6.1–6.11. If a care order is made, the guardian has no role in relation to the way in which the local authority performs its duties under the order, and the court has no power to direct the continuing involvement of the guardian (*Kent County Council v C* [1993] 1 FLR 308). The guardian may find himself requested to act as a collator of expert reports and to produce for the court a schedule of the areas of agreement and dispute (*Re C (Expert Evidence: Disclosure: Practice)* [1995] 1 FLR 204). In *Re L (Care Proceedings: Disclosure to Third Party)* [2000] 1 FLR 913 the guardian was asked, as an officer of the court, to disclose information concerning the psychiatric condition of a mother to the UK Central Council for Nursing, Midwifery and Health Visiting.

Duties of children's guardian where local authority documents appear to be protected by public interest immunity—See public interest immunity under CA 1989, s 42.

Guardian detached from child—Where the child's solicitor is taking instructions from the child himself, the children's guardian must inform the court and the role of the children's guardian remains wholly in the discretion of the court (FPR 2010, r 16.21). The court may feel that it would be beneficial, particularly if the detachment occurred at a late stage in the course of the proceedings, for the guardian to have full liberty to present a case as if he were a party to the proceedings (by calling evidence, cross-examining other parties' witnesses, addressing argument etc, for which purposes he would probably wish his own legal representation to be authorised under r 16.21(2)(c))) and by making a report in the usual way. This ensures that a neutral view of the best interests of the child is advanced since, where the guardian does retain a role, CA 1989, s 41(1)(b) continues to require him to perform it for the purpose of safeguarding the interests of the child. However, the court may think it right to permit only a smaller role or even to terminate the guardian's appointment altogether under FPR 2010, r 16.19.

In the ordinary case where conflict arises, the solicitor first appointed continues in the case putting the views, wishes and feelings of the child, and the guardian finds a fresh advocate to assist him in his continuing role as defined by the court; however, see *Re P (Representation)* [1996] 1 FLR 486.

"the children's guardian must advise the court" (FPR PD16A, para 6.6)—It is not part of the children's guardian function to adopt a judicial role or to seek to assess material which he does not have the expertise to assess (*B v B (Child Abuse: Contact)* [1994] 2 FLR 713). However, it is proper for the guardian to offer his opinion on child care and related matters to the court where he has the experience in his background to justify offering such an opinion (*G v A Borough Council* [2000] Fam Law 11). Presumably the guardian can rely on such admissible expert evidence in forming his conclusions and recommendations, while acknowledging that the final decision is that of the court.

In *Re K (Supervision Orders)* [1999] 2 FLR 303 Wall J held that a guardian's opinions about threshold criteria could not be ruled inadmissible, even if they were at odds with all the other parties. However, the guardian must be careful not to usurp the function of the court and would be wise to predicate any recommendations on the premise that the court will make certain findings of fact. The guardian had a duty to represent the child and put all matters relevant to the child's welfare before the court. The guardian is the child's protection against poor social work practice, procedural delay and collusive agreements. However, where the local authority and the mother had reached a sensible agreement which clearly protected the child and was in no sense collusive, the guardian should think long and hard before seeking to upset that agreement or before putting forward contentious alternative proposals.

Child's capacity to refuse to be examined etc (FPR 2010, r 4.11A(4)(a))—CA 1989, s 38(6) provides that a child of sufficient understanding may refuse to submit to an examination or assessment directed by a court making an interim care or supervision order; s 43(8) allows a child who is of sufficient understanding to make an informed decision to refuse to submit to a medical or psychiatric examination or other assessment which would otherwise have been authorised by a child assessment order. In *Re H (A Minor) (Care Proceedings: Child's Wishes)* [1993] 1 FLR 440 at [449A], Thorpe J said, in relation to the child's capacity under CA 1989, s 38(6) to make an informed decision whether to refuse to submit to a psychiatric examination, that "the level of understanding that enables a child to make an informed decision whether to refuse to submit to a psychiatric examination is in all practical senses a much higher level of understanding than is required to enable him to give instructions to a solicitor on his own behalf". It is useful to compare this with the power of the court, in exercising the inherent jurisdiction of the High Court, to override the child's wishes in respect of medical treatment (see *Re W (A Minor) (Consent to Medical Treatment)* [1993] 1 FLR 1).

Confidentiality—The guardian's report presumably comes within the ambit of "any information relating to the proceedings" within the provisions of FPR 2010, r 12.73(1) and therefore can be communicated by the parties and other specified people to other specified people for specified purposes without needing the permission of the court – see further rr 12.73, 12.75 and PD12G.

Where a children's guardian becomes aware of information that the child does not wish to be revealed to another party in the proceedings, it can never be proper for the guardian to promise the child that the information will be withheld from the court. In an unusually sensitive case involving an older child, a guardian could properly tell the child that the judge would be told that the child did not wish the information to be disclosed to a particular party, and why. In such a case, the court was required to balance the right of a properly concerned party to disclosure of information submitted to the court on which the judge's conclusion might in some measure be based, against the paramount interest of the child (*Re C (Disclosure)* [1996] 1 FLR 797). Such cases should be transferred to the High Court.

Written report by children's guardian—It is a matter for the discretion of the court whether a report of a children's guardian in public law proceedings can be made available to a court hearing related private law proceedings and to the parties thereto. If two courts are dealing with different sets of proceedings concerning siblings (an exceptional situation, as it is normally right for one court to deal with all proceedings where siblings are concerned), the report should normally be made available to both (*W v Wakefield City Council* [1995] 1 FLR 170).

Attendance of child at court—While the court can allow the child who is the subject of an application to attend court, it must always bear in mind that attendance is likely to be harmful to the child and should only permit it if satisfied that it is in the interests of the child (*Re W (Secure Accommodation Order: Attendance at Court)* [1994] 2 FLR 1092 set out under CA 1989, s 25 and see, further, **Use of the power to exclude** under FPR 2010, - 12.14). Young children should be discouraged from attending appeals from the justices in family proceedings. Where a guardian is proposing to arrange for a young child to be present, he should give the question very careful thought beforehand and be prepared to explain his reasons to the judge (*Re C (A Minor) (Care: Child's Wishes)* [1993] 1 FLR 832, which concerned a girl of 13).

"notify" and "notification" (FPR 2010, r 4.11A(6))—It is submitted that these words do not attract FPR 2010, r 10.7 (mode of giving notice) because, although it might have been argued that "notify" was cognate with "notice", the use of "notification" rather than "notice" in conjunction with it indicates the contrary.

Inspection of records (FPR 2010, r 4.11A(9))—See also CA 1989, ss 41 and 42. A children's guardian is entitled to see case records prepared by the local authority giving detailed information concerning prospective adopters and to include the relevant information derived from it in his report to the court (*Re T (A Minor) (Guardian ad Litem: Case Record)* [1994] 1 FLR 632).

Where court differs from children's guardian's advice—The court is not bound to follow the recommendation of the children's guardian but, just as with a welfare officer or children and family reporter, must give careful consideration to any argument advanced by him and, where it differs, must explain its reasons carefully (*S v Oxfordshire County Council* [1993] 1 FLR 452).

Duties of children's guardian and local authority to consult one another—Guardians should think long and hard before opposing an agreement between the local authority and the parents of a child subject to care proceedings if it appears to be sensible and appears to protect the child. However, where the guardian has considered the matter carefully and has reached the conclusion that the course proposed by the local authority does not protect the child, the guardian's duty is to safeguard the interests of the child and to put before the court her view as to how best the child's welfare is to be promoted (*Re N (Leave to Withdraw Care Proceedings)* [2000] 1 FLR 134; *Re K (Supervision Orders)* [1999] 2 FLR 303).

16.21 Where the child instructs a solicitor or conducts proceedings on the child's own behalf

(1) Where it appears to the children's guardian that the child –

    (a) is instructing a solicitor direct; or

    (b) intends to conduct and is capable of conducting the proceedings on that child's own behalf,

the children's guardian must inform the court of that fact.

(2) Where paragraph (1) applies the children's guardian –

    (a) must perform such additional duties as the court may direct;

    (b) must take such part in the proceedings as the court may direct; and

    (c) may, with the permission of the court, have legal representation in the conduct of those duties.

PART III

Chapter 7
Children's Guardian Appointed under Rule 16.4

16.22 Application of this Chapter

This Chapter applies where the court must appoint a children's guardian under rule 16.4.

PD16A—The circumstances when a child should be made a party to proceedings, the appointment of a children's guardian and the duties once appointed are set out in FPR PD16A, paras 7.1–7.19.

16.23 Stage of proceedings at which a children's guardian becomes necessary

(1) This rule does not apply in relation to a child who is conducting proceedings without a children's guardian in accordance with rule 16.6.

(2) A person may not without the permission of the court take any step in proceedings except –

    (a)   filing an application form; or

    (b)   applying for the appointment of a children's guardian under rule 16.24,

until the child has a children's guardian.

(3) Any step taken before a child has a children's guardian has no effect unless the court orders otherwise.

16.24 Appointment of a children's guardian

(1) The court may make an order appointing as a children's guardian, an officer of the Service or a Welsh family proceedings officer or, if the person to be appointed consents –

    (a)   a person other than the Official Solicitor; or

    (b)   the Official Solicitor.

(2) An order appointing a children's guardian may be made by the court of its own initiative or on the application of –

    (a)   a person who wishes to be a children's guardian; or

    (b)   a party to the proceedings.

(3) The court may at any time direct that a party make an application for an order under paragraph (2).

(4) An application for an order appointing a children's guardian must be supported by evidence.

(5) The court may not appoint a children's guardian under this rule unless it is satisfied that that person –

    (a)   can fairly and competently conduct proceedings on behalf of the child;

    (b)   has no interest adverse to that of the child; and

    (c)   subject to paragraph (6), undertakes to pay any costs which the child may be ordered to pay in relation to the proceedings, subject to any right that person may have to be repaid from the assets of the child.

(6) Paragraph (5)(c) does not apply to the Official Solicitor, an officer of the Service or a Welsh family proceedings officer.

(7) This rule is without prejudice to rule 16.6 and rule 9.11.

    (Rule 9.11 provides for a child to be separately represented in certain applications for a financial remedy.)

PD16A—The duties of the children's guardian once appointed are set out in FPR PD16A, paras 7.6, 7.7. A children's guardian who is an officer of Cafcass or a Welsh family proceedings officer has, in addition, the duties set out in paras 6.1–6.11.

Hague Convention proceedings—A child should only be made party to Convention proceedings in exceptional circumstances (*Re H (Abduction)* [2007] 1 FLR 242). See also "the child's objections" under CACA 1985, Sch 1, Art 13.

Cafcass/Official Solicitor—Where it is felt that a child needs separate representation, consideration should first be given to appointing an officer of Cafcass as guardian. If Cafcass is unable to provide a guardian, r 16.24(1) makes further provision for the appointment of a guardian. See "some other proper person" below. See *Practice Note of March 2013 (The Official Solicitor to the Senior Courts: Appointment in Family Proceedings and Proceedings under the Inherent Jurisdiction in Relation to Adults)* and *CAFCASS and the National Assembly for Wales Practice Note of June 2006 (Appointment of Guardians in Private Law Proceedings)*.

"some other proper person" (r 16.24(1)(a))—This sub-rule permits a solicitor to act as solicitor and guardian (*Re N (Residence: Appointment of Solicitor: Placement with Extended Family)* [2001] 1 FLR 1028). In *Re K (Replacement of Guardian ad Litem)* [2001] 1 FLR 663 it was held that such a course is generally undesirable. The use of the National Youth Advocacy Service (NYAS) has been endorsed in recent Court of Appeal decisions such as *Re H (National Youth Advocacy Service)* [2007] 1 FLR 1028 and *Re B (A Child)* [2006] EWCA Civ 716.

16.25 Court's power to change children's guardian and to prevent person acting as children's guardian

(1) The court may –

(a) direct that a person may not act as a children's guardian;
(b) terminate the appointment of a children's guardian; or
(c) appoint a new children's guardian in substitution for an existing one.

(2) An application for an order or direction under paragraph (1) must be supported by evidence.

(3) Subject to rule 16.24(6), the court may not appoint a children's guardian under this rule unless it is satisfied that the person to be appointed complies with the conditions specified in rule 16.24(5).

PD16A—The change of a children's guardian and to prevent a person acting as a children's guardian are set out in FPR PD16A, paras 7.17–7.19.

16.26 Appointment of children's guardian by court order – supplementary

(1) A copy of the application for an order under rule 16.24 or 16.25 must be sent by a court officer to every person on whom, in accordance with rule 6.28, the application form should be served.

(2) A copy of an application for an order under rule 16.25 must also be sent to –

(a) the person who is the children's guardian, or who is purporting to act as the children's guardian when the application is made; and
(b) the person, if not the applicant, who it is proposed should be the children's guardian.

16.27 Powers and duties of children's guardian

(1) The children's guardian –

(a) has the powers and duties set out in Practice Direction 16A; and
(b) must exercise those powers and duties in accordance with Practice Direction 16A.

(2) Where the children's guardian is an officer of the Service or a Welsh family proceedings officer, rule 16.20 applies to a children's guardian appointed in accordance with this Chapter as it applies to a children's guardian appointed in accordance with Chapter 6.

PD16A—The powers and duties of a children's guardian appointed under FPR 2010, r 16.4 are set out in FPR PD16A, paras 7.6, 7.7. A children's guardian who is an officer of Cafcass or a Welsh family proceedings officer has, in addition, the duties set out in paras 6.1–6.11: see the notes to FPR 2010, r 16.20 above.

16.28 Procedure where appointment of children's guardian comes to an end

(1) When a child reaches the age of 18, the appointment of a children's guardian comes to an end.

(2) A court officer will send a notice to the other parties stating that the appointment of the child's children's guardian to act has ended.

Chapter 8
Duties of Solicitor Acting for the Child

16.29 Solicitor for child

(1) Subject to paragraphs (2) and (4), a solicitor appointed –

    (a)   under section 41(3) of the 1989 Act; or
    (b)   by the children's guardian in accordance with the Practice Direction 16A,

must represent the child in accordance with instructions received from the children's guardian.

(2) If a solicitor appointed as mentioned in paragraph (1) considers, having taken into account the matters referred to in paragraph (3), that the child –

    (a)   wishes to give instructions which conflict with those of the children's guardian; and
    (b)   is able, having regard to the child's understanding, to give such instructions on the child's own behalf,

the solicitor must conduct the proceedings in accordance with instructions received from the child.

(3) The matters the solicitor must take into account for the purposes of paragraph (2) are –

    (a)   the views of the children's guardian; and
    (b)   any direction given by the court to the children's guardian concerning the part to be taken by the children's guardian in the proceedings.

(4) Where –

    (a)   no children's guardian has been appointed; and
    (b)   the condition in section 41(4)(b) of the 1989 Act is satisfied,

a solicitor appointed under section 41(3) of the 1989 Act must represent the child in accordance with instructions received from the child.

(5) Where a solicitor appointed as mentioned in paragraph (1) receives no instructions under paragraphs (1), (2) or (4), the solicitor must represent the child in furtherance of the best interests of the child.

(6) A solicitor appointed under section 41(3) of the 1989 Act or by the children's guardian in accordance with Practice Direction 16A must serve documents, and accept

service of documents, on behalf of the child in accordance with rule 6.31 and, where the child has not been served separately and has sufficient understanding, advise the child of the contents of any document so served.

(7) Where the child wishes an appointment of a solicitor –

   (a)   under section 41(3) of the 1989 Act; or

   (b)   by the children's guardian in accordance with the Practice Direction 16A,

to be terminated –

      (i)   the child may apply to the court for an order terminating the appointment; and

      (ii)   the solicitor and the children's guardian will be given an opportunity to make representations.

(8) Where the children's guardian wishes an appointment of a solicitor under section 41(3) of the 1989 Act to be terminated –

   (a)   the children's guardian may apply to the court for an order terminating the appointment; and

   (b)   the solicitor and, if of sufficient understanding, the child, will be given an opportunity to make representations.

(9) When terminating an appointment in accordance with paragraph (7) or (8), the court will give its reasons for so doing, a note of which will be taken by the court or a court officer.

(10) The court or a court officer will record the appointment under section 41(3) of the 1989 Act or the refusal to make the appointment.

Solicitors to whom the rule applies—This rule applies to two types of solicitor –

(a)   those appointed under CA 1989, s 41(3) which, in combination with s 41(4), enables the court to appoint a solicitor for a child who does not already have one if:

   (i)   no children's guardian has yet been appointed;

   (ii)   the child has sufficient understanding to instruct a solicitor and wishes to do so; and

   (iii)   it appears to the court that it would be in the child's best interests for him to be represented by a solicitor.

(b)   those appointed by the child's guardian in accordance with FPR 2010, r 16.21.

"able ... to give such instructions on his own behalf" (FPR 2010, r 4.12(1)(a))—Guidance on the application of the test in r 16.29(2) was given in *Re H (A Minor) (Care Proceedings: Child's Wishes)* [1993] 1 FLR 440. Assistance may also be obtained from authorities dealing with the understanding of a child in other contexts under CA 1989 and the associated rules; in particular see *Mabon v Mabon* [2005] 2 FLR 1011, CA, set out in "sufficient understanding" under r 16.6. In April 2010 the President issued *Guidelines for Judges Meeting Children who are Subject to Family Proceedings* (see Part V). The judge's decision whether or not personally to interview a child is, above all, a question for the exercise of judicial discretion. It is becoming more common for judges to see children in private in the course of proceedings affecting the child's welfare ECHR 1950, Art 12 provides that a child should be heard in any judicial proceedings affecting him, either directly or through a representative. Similarly, the United Nations Convention on the Rights of the Child 1989, Art 12 requires that a child who is capable of forming his own views has the right to express them freely in all matters affecting him. *Mabon v Mabon* reviewed the principles that apply when the court considers how best to ensure that the child's views are heard in such cases. Further important guidance from the Court of Appeal is contained in *Re W (Leave to Remove)* [2008] 2 FLR 1170 and in *B v B (Minors) (Interviews and Listing Arrangements)* [1994] 2 FLR 489.

Opportunity to make representations (r 16.29(7),(8))—The "opportunity to make representations" is a flexible concept that leaves the question of whether they should be oral or written, and the time within which they should be made, to be determined by the court according to the context in which the question arises.

Reasons for terminating appointment of solicitor or children's guardian to be given by the court (r 16.29(9))—Where the court terminates the appointment of a solicitor or children's guardian, this rule requires the court to give its reasons for doing so, and requires that a note of the reasons be taken by the court or by the proper officer. The simple fact that the court has ordered a termination of the solicitor's appointment is to be formally recorded in Form C48. No doubt the court's written reasons will therefore form an appendix to the duly completed Form C48.

Appeal hearings—The general admonition against unnecessary representation should not be taken to bar or fetter the responsibility of the children's representatives to take a firm line at the appeal hearing: *Re H (Children)* [2012] EWCA Civ 743.

Chapter 9
Reporting Officer

16.30 When the court appoints a reporting officer

In proceedings to which Part 14 applies, the court will appoint a reporting officer where –

(a) it appears that a parent or guardian of the child is willing to consent to the placing of the child for adoption, to the making of an adoption order or to a section 84 order; and

(b) that parent or guardian is in England or Wales.

16.31 Appointment of the same reporting officer in respect of two or more parents or guardians

The same person may be appointed as the reporting officer for two or more parents or guardians of the child.

16.32 The duties of the reporting officer

(1) The reporting officer must witness the signature by a parent or guardian on the document in which consent is given to –

(a) the placing of the child for adoption;

(b) the making of an adoption order; or

(c) the making of a section 84 order.

(2) The reporting officer must carry out such other duties as are set out in Practice Direction 16A.

(3) A report to the court by the reporting officer is confidential.

(4) The reporting officer's duties must be exercised in accordance with Practice Direction 16A.

Chapter 10
Children and Family Reporter and Welfare Officer

16.33 Request by court for a welfare report in respect of the child

(1) Where the court is considering an application for an order in proceedings, the court may ask –

(a) in proceedings to which Parts 12 and 14 apply, a children and family reporter; or

(b) in proceedings to which Part 12 applies, a welfare officer,

to prepare a report on matters relating to the welfare of the child, and, in this rule, the person preparing the report is called "the officer".

(2) It is the duty of the officer to –

    (a) comply with any request for a report under this rule; and

    (b) provide the court with such other assistance as it may require.

(3) A report to the court under this rule is confidential.

(4) The officer, when carrying out duties in relation to proceedings under the 1989 Act, must have regard to the principle set out in section 1(2) and the matters set out in section 1(3)(a) to (f) of that Act as if for the word "court" in that section there were substituted the words "children and family reporter" or "welfare officer" as the case may be.

(5) A party may question the officer about oral or written advice tendered by that officer to the court.

(6) The court officer will notify the officer of a direction given at a hearing at which –

    (a) the officer is not present; and

    (b) the welfare report is considered.

(7) The officer's duties must be exercised in accordance with Practice Direction 16A

    ("children and family reporter" and "welfare officer" are defined in rule 2.3)

PART III

Meaning of "welfare officer" (r 16.33(1)(b))—The CJCSA 2000 introduced the Children and Family Court Advisory and Support Service (Cafcass). The term "officer of the service" is defined in CJCSA 2000, s 11(3), and is used to denote the various categories of people appointed to undertake investigations and prepare reports for the court in children and family cases. Where a court directs, pursuant to s 7(1)(b), a local authority to report upon matters relating to the welfare of the child, the author of the report is described as a "welfare officer". The term "welfare officer" is retained only for the purpose of describing that local authority officer in those specified circumstances. Where the court appoints an officer of the service to report to it under CA 1989, s 7(1)(a) he is called a "children and family reporter".

PD16A—FPR PD16A, paras 9.1–9.4 set out the powers and duties of a children and family reporter and welfare officer.

Chapter 11
Parental Order Reporter

16.34 When the court appoints a parental order reporter

In proceedings to which Part 13 applies, the court will appoint a parental order reporter in accordance with rule 13.5.

16.35 Powers and duties of the parental order reporter

(1) The parental order reporter is to act on behalf of the child upon the hearing of any application in proceedings to which Part 13 applies with the duty of safeguarding the interests of the child.

(2) The parental order reporter must –

    (a) investigate the matters set out in sections 54(1) to (8) of the 2008 Act;

    (b) so far as the parental order reporter considers necessary, investigate any matter contained in the application form or other matter which appears relevant to the making of the parental order; and

    (c) advise the court on whether there is any reason under section 1 of the 2002 Act (as applied with modifications by the Human Fertilisation and Embryology (Parental Orders) Regulations 2010) to refuse the parental order.

(3) The parental order reporter must also provide the court with such other assistance as it may require.

(4) The parental order reporter's duties must be exercised in accordance with Practice Direction 16A.

(5) A report to the court by the parental order reporter is confidential.

Parental order report—See also, under FPR 2010, r 13.12 and HFEA 2008, s 54.

Chapter 12
Supplementary Appointment Provisions

16.36 Persons who may not be appointed as children's guardian, reporting officer or children and family reporter

(1) In specified proceedings (except where paragraph (2) applies), adoption proceedings or proceedings for a section 84 order or a section 89 order, no person may be appointed as a children's guardian, reporting officer or children and family reporter who –

(a) is a member, officer or servant of a local authority which is a party to the proceedings;

(b) is, or has been, a member, officer or servant of a local authority or voluntary organisation who has been directly concerned in that capacity in arrangements relating to the care, accommodation or welfare of the child during the 5 years prior to the start of the proceedings; or

(c) is a serving probation officer who has, in that capacity, been previously concerned with the child or the child's family.

(2) In placement proceedings, a person described in paragraph (1)(b) or (c) may not be appointed as a children's guardian, reporting officer or children and family reporter.

Amendments—SI 2012/679.

16.37 Appointment of the same person as children's guardian, reporting officer and children and family reporter

The same person may be appointed to act as one or more of the following –

(a) the children's guardian;

(b) the reporting officer; and

(c) the children and family reporter.

Chapter 13
Officers of the Service, Welsh Family Proceedings Officers and Local Authority Officers: Further Duties

16.38 Officers of the Service, Welsh family proceedings officers and local authority officers acting under certain duties

(1) This rule applies when –

(a) an officer of the Service or a Welsh family proceedings officer is acting under a duty in accordance with –

(i)   section 11E(7) of the 1989 Act (providing the court with information as to the making of a contact activity direction or a contact activity condition);

(ii) section 11G(2) of the 1989 Act (monitoring compliance with a contact activity direction or a contact activity condition);

(iii) section 11H(2) of the 1989 Act (monitoring compliance with a contact order);

(iv)   section 11L(5) of the 1989 Act (providing the court with information as to the making of an enforcement order);

(v)   section 11M(1) of the 1989 Act (monitoring compliance with an enforcement order);

(vi)   section 16(6) of the 1989 Act (providing a report to the court in accordance with a direction in a family assistance order); and

(vii)   section 16A of the 1989 Act (making a risk assessment); and

(b)   a local authority officer is acting under a duty in accordance with section 16(6) of the 1989 Act (providing a report to the court in accordance with a direction in a family assistance order).

(2)   In this rule, –

(a)   "contact activity direction", "contact activity condition" and "enforcement order" have the meanings given in rule 12.2; and

(b)   references to "the officer" are to the officer of the Service, Welsh family proceedings officer or local authority officer referred to in paragraph (1).

(3)   In exercising the duties referred to in paragraph (1), the officer must have regard to the principle set out in section 1(2) of the 1989 Act and the matters set out in section 1(3)(a) to (f) of the 1989 Act as if for the word "court" in that section there were substituted the words "officer of the Service, Welsh family proceedings officer or local authority officer".

(4)   The officer's duties referred to in paragraph (1) must be exercised in accordance with Practice Direction 16A.

Definitions—"contact activity condition", "contact activity direction", "enforcement order": FPR 2010, r 12.2. See also CA 1989, ss 11E–11M.

Family assistance order report—See **Practice Direction** under CA 1989, s 16.

Risk assessments—See **Risk assessments** under CA 1989, s 16 and see s 16A. See also FPR PD16A, paras 11.1–11.7.

"the principle set out in section 1(2)" (r 16.38(3))—"The delay principle".

"the matters set out in section 1(3)(a) to (f)" (r 16.38(3))—This rule makes it clear that officers must have regard to the welfare checklist when carrying out all aspects of their duties under this rule. See CA 1989, s 1(3)(a)–(f).

Practice Direction 16A—FPR PD16A sets out what is required of officers in the performance of their duties.

Chapter 14
Enforcement Orders and Financial Compensation Orders: Persons Notified

16.39 Application for enforcement orders and financial compensation orders: duties of the person notified

(1)   This rule applies where a person who was the child's children's guardian, litigation friend or legal representative in the proceedings in which a contact order was made has been notified of an application for an enforcement order or for a financial compensation order as required by Practice Direction 12C.

(2)   The person who has been notified of the application must –

(a)   consider whether it is in the best interests of the child for the child to be made a party to the proceedings for an enforcement order or a financial compensation order (as applicable); and

(b) before the date fixed for the first hearing in the case notify the court, orally or in writing, of the opinion reached on the question, together with the reasons for this opinion.

(3) In this rule, "enforcement order" and "financial compensation order" have the meanings given in rule 12.2.

Definitions—"child", "children's guardian", "litigation friend", "legal representative": r 2.3.

Enforcement orders—See CA 1989, s 11J–11N.

Financial compensation orders—See CA 1989, ss 11O–11P

Practice Direction 12C—FPR PD12C supplements r 12.8 and sets out the following requirements for the service of an application in certain proceedings relating to children: the persons who are to receive a copy of the application form (para 1.1); the time for serving the application (para 2.1); and the persons who are to receive a copy of Form C6A (Notice to Non-Parties).

Procedure—See Procedural Guide D8.

Practice Direction 16A – Representation of Children

This Practice Direction supplements FPR Part 16

PART 1: GENERAL

Reference in title of proceedings

1.1 Where a litigation friend represents a child in family proceedings in accordance with rule 16.5 and Chapter 5 of Part 16, the child should be referred to in the title of the proceedings as "A.B. (a child by C.D. his/her litigation friend)".

1.2 Where a children's guardian represents a child in family proceedings in accordance with rule 16.4 and Chapter 7 of Part 16, the child should be referred to in the title as "A.B. (a child by C.D. his/her children's guardian)".

1.3 A child who is conducting proceedings on that child's own behalf should be referred to in the title as "A.B. (a child)".

PART 2: LITIGATION FRIEND

Duties of the litigation friend

2.1 It is the duty of a litigation friend fairly and competently to conduct proceedings on behalf of the child. The litigation friend must have no interest in the proceedings adverse to that of the child and all steps and decisions the litigation friend takes in the proceedings must be taken for the benefit of the child.

2.2 A litigation friend who is an officer of the Service or a Welsh family proceedings officer has, in addition, the duties set out in Part 3 of this Practice Direction and must exercise those duties as set out in that Part.

Becoming a litigation friend without a court order

3.1 In order to become a litigation friend without a court order the person who wishes to act as litigation friend must file a certificate of suitability –

(a) stating that the litigation friend consents to act;

(b) stating that the litigation friend knows or believes that the [applicant][respondent] is a child to whom rule 16.5 and Chapter 5 of Part 16 apply;

(c) stating that the litigation friend can fairly and competently conduct proceedings on behalf of the child and has no interest adverse to that of the child;

(d) undertaking to pay any costs which the child may be ordered to pay in relation to the proceedings, subject to any right the litigation friend may have to be repaid from the assets of the child; and

(e) which the litigation friend has verified by a statement of truth.

3.2 Paragraph 3.1 does not apply to the Official Solicitor, an officer of the Service or a Welsh family proceedings officer.

3.3 The court officer will send the certificate of suitability to one of the child's parents or guardians or, if there is no parent or guardian, to the person with whom the child resides or in whose care the child is.

3.4 The litigation friend must file the certificate of suitability at a time when the litigation friend first takes a step in the proceedings on behalf of the child.

Application for a court order appointing a litigation friend

4.1 An application for a court order appointing a litigation friend should be made in accordance with Part 18 and must be supported by evidence.

4.2 The court officer must serve the application notice on the persons referred to in paragraph 3.3.

4.3 The evidence in support must satisfy the court that the proposed litigation friend –

(a) consents to act;

(b) can fairly and competently conduct proceedings on behalf of the child;

(c) has no interest adverse to that of the child; and

(d) undertakes to pay any costs which the child may be ordered to pay in relation to the proceedings, subject to any right the litigation friend may have to be repaid from the assets of the child.

4.4 Paragraph 4.3(d) does not apply to the Official Solicitor, an officer of the Service of a Welsh family proceedings officer.

4.5 The proposed litigation friend may be one of the persons referred to in paragraph 3.3 where appropriate, or otherwise may be the Official Solicitor, an officer of the Service or a Welsh family proceedings officer. Where it is sought to appoint the Official Solicitor, an officer of the Service or a Welsh family proceedings officer, provision should be made for payment of that person's charges.

Change of litigation friend and prevention of person acting as litigation friend.

5.1 Where an application is made for an order under rule 16.12, the application must set out the reasons for seeking it and the application must be supported by evidence.

5.2 Subject to paragraph 4.4, if the order sought is substitution of a new litigation friend for an existing one, the evidence must satisfy the court of the matters set out in paragraph 4.3.

PART III

5.3 The court officer will serve the application notice on –

    (a)   the persons referred to in paragraph 3.3; and

    (b)   the litigation friend or person purporting to act as litigation friend.

PART 3: CHILDREN'S GUARDIAN APPOINTED UNDER RULE 16.3

How the children's guardian exercises duties – investigations and appointment of solicitor

6.1 The children's guardian must make such investigations as are necessary to carry out the children's guardian's duties and must, in particular –

    (a)   contact or seek to interview such persons as the children's guardian thinks appropriate or as the court directs; and

    (b)   obtain such professional assistance as is available which the children's guardian thinks appropriate or which the court directs be obtained.

6.2 The children's guardian must –

    (a)   appoint a solicitor for the child unless a solicitor has already been appointed;

    (b)   give such advice to the child as is appropriate having regard to that child's understanding; and

    (c)   where appropriate instruct the solicitor representing the child on all matters relevant to the interests of the child arising in the course of proceedings, including possibilities for appeal.

6.3 Where the children's guardian is authorised in the terms mentioned by and in accordance with section 15(1) of the Criminal Justice and Court Services Act 2000 or section 37(1) of the Children Act 2004 (right of officer of the Service or Welsh family proceedings officer to conduct litigation or exercise a right of audience), paragraph 6.2(a) will not apply if the children's guardian intends to have conduct of the proceedings on behalf of the child unless –

    (a)   the child wishes to instruct a solicitor direct; and

    (b)   the children's guardian or the court considers that the child is of sufficient understanding to do so.

6.4 Where rule 16.21 (Where the child instructs a solicitor or conducts proceedings on the child's own behalf) applies, the duties set out in paragraph 6.2(a) and (c) do not apply.

How the children's guardian exercises duties – attendance at court, advice to the court and reports

6.5 The children's guardian or the solicitor appointed under section 41(3) of the 1989 Act or in accordance with paragraph 6.2(a) must attend all directions hearings unless the court directs otherwise.

6.6 The children's guardian must advise the court on the following matters –

    (a)   whether the child is of sufficient understanding for any purpose including the child's refusal to submit to a medical or psychiatric examination or other assessment that the court has the power to require, direct or order;

    (b)   the wishes of the child in respect of any matter relevant to the proceedings including that child's attendance at court;

    (c)   the appropriate forum for the proceedings;

    (d)   the appropriate timing of the proceedings or any part of them;

(e)   the options available to it in respect of the child and the suitability of each such option including what order should be made in determining the application; and

(f)   any other matter on which the court seeks advice or on which the children's guardian considers that the court should be informed.

6.7 The advice given under paragraph 6.6 may, subject to any direction of the court, be given orally or in writing. If the advice is given orally, a note of it must be taken by the court or the court officer.

6.8 The children's guardian must –

(a)   unless the court directs otherwise, file a written report advising on the interests of the child in accordance with the timetable set by the court; and

(b)   in proceedings to which Part 14 applies, where practicable, notify any person the joining of whom as a party to those proceedings would be likely, in the opinion of the children's guardian, to safeguard the interests of the child, of the court's power to join that person as a party under rule 14.3 and must inform the court –

(i)   of any notification;

(ii)   of anyone whom the children's guardian attempted to notify under this paragraph but was unable to contact; and

(iii)   of anyone whom the children's guardian believes may wish to be joined to the proceedings.

(Part 18 sets out the procedure for making an application to be joined as a party in proceedings.)

How the children's guardian exercises duties – service of documents and inspection of records

6.9 The children's guardian must serve and accept service of documents on behalf of the child in accordance with rule 6.31 and, where the child has not himself been served and has sufficient understanding, advise the child of the contents of any document so served.

6.10 Where the children's guardian inspects records of the kinds referred to in –

(a)   section 42 of the 1989 Act (right to have access to local authority records); or

(b)   section 103 of the 2002 Act (right to have access to adoption agency records)

the children's guardian must bring all records and documents which may, in the opinion of the children's guardian, assist in the proper determination of the proceedings to the attention of –

(i)   the court; and

(ii)   unless the court directs otherwise, the other parties to the proceedings.

How the children's guardian exercises duties – communication of a court's decision to the child

6.11 The children's guardian must ensure that, in relation to a decision made by the court in the proceedings –

(a)   if the children's guardian considers it appropriate to the age and understanding of the child, the child is notified of that decision; and

(b)   if the child is notified of the decision, it is explained to the child in a manner appropriate to that child's age and understanding.

PART III

PART 4: APPOINTMENT OF CHILDREN'S GUARDIAN UNDER RULE 16.4

Section 1 – When a child should be made a party to proceedings

7.1 Making the child a party to the proceedings is a step that will be taken only in cases which involve an issue of significant difficulty and consequently will occur in only a minority of cases. Before taking the decision to make the child a party, consideration should be given to whether an alternative route might be preferable, such as asking an officer of the Service or a Welsh family proceedings officer to carry out further work or by making a referral to social services or, possibly, by obtaining expert evidence.

7.2 The decision to make the child a party will always be exclusively that of the court, made in the light of the facts and circumstances of the particular case. The following are offered, solely by way of guidance, as circumstances which may justify the making of such an order –

(a)   where an officer of the Service or Welsh family proceedings officer has notified the court that in the opinion of that officer the child should be made a party;

(b)   where the child has a standpoint or interest which is inconsistent with or incapable of being represented by any of the adult parties;

(c)   where there is an intractable dispute over residence or contact, including where all contact has ceased, or where there is irrational but implacable hostility to contact or where the child may be suffering harm associated with the contact dispute;

(d)   where the views and wishes of the child cannot be adequately met by a report to the court;

(e)   where an older child is opposing a proposed course of action;

(f)   where there are complex medical or mental health issues to be determined or there are other unusually complex issues that necessitate separate representation of the child;

(g)   where there are international complications outside child abduction, in particular where it may be necessary for there to be discussions with overseas authorities or a foreign court;

(h)   where there are serious allegations of physical, sexual or other abuse in relation to the child or there are allegations of domestic violence not capable of being resolved with the help of an officer of the Service or Welsh family proceedings officer;

(i)   where the proceedings concern more than one child and the welfare of the children is in conflict or one child is in a particularly disadvantaged position;

(j)   where there is a contested issue about scientific testing.

7.3 It must be recognised that separate representation of the child may result in a delay in the resolution of the proceedings. When deciding whether to direct that a child be made a party, the court will take into account the risk of delay or other facts adverse to the welfare of the child. The court's primary consideration will be the best interests of the child.

7.4 When a child is made a party and a children's guardian is to be appointed –

(a)   consideration should first be given to appointing an officer of the Service or Welsh family proceedings officer. Before appointing an officer, the court will cause preliminary enquiries to be made of Cafcass or CAFCASS CYMRU. For the relevant procedure, reference should be made to the practice note issued by Cafcass in June 2006 and any modifications of that practice note.

(b)   If Cafcass or CAFCASS CYMRU is unable to provide a children's guardian without delay, or if for some other reason the appointment of an officer of the

Service of Welsh family proceedings officer is not appropriate, rule 16.24 makes further provision for the appointment of a children's guardian.

7.5 The court may, at the same time as deciding whether to join a child as a party, consider whether the proceedings should be transferred to another court taking into account the provisions of Part 3 of the Allocation and Transfer of Proceedings Order 2008.

Section 2 – Children's guardian appointed under rule 16.4

DUTIES OF THE CHILDREN'S GUARDIAN

7.6 It is the duty of a children's guardian fairly and competently to conduct proceedings on behalf of the child. The children's guardian must have no interest in the proceedings adverse to that of the child and all steps and decisions the children's guardian takes in the proceedings must be taken for the benefit of the child.

7.7 A children's guardian who is an officer of the Service or a Welsh family proceedings officer has, in addition, the duties set out in Part 3 of this Practice Direction and must exercise those duties as set out in that Part.

BECOMING A CHILDREN'S GUARDIAN WITHOUT A COURT ORDER

7.8 In order to become a children's guardian without a court order the person who wishes to act as children's guardian must file a certificate of suitability –

(a)   stating that the children's guardian consents to act;
(b)   stating that the children's guardian knows or believes that the [applicant][respondent] is a child to whom rule 16.4 and Chapter 7 of Part 16 apply;
(c)   stating that the children's guardian can fairly and competently conduct proceedings on behalf of the child and has no interest adverse to that of the child;
(d)   undertaking to pay any costs which the child may be ordered to pay in relation to the proceedings, subject to any right the children's guardian may have to be repaid from the assets of the child; and
(e)   which the children's guardian has verified by a statement of truth.

7.9 Paragraph 7.8 does not apply to the Official Solicitor, an officer of the Service or a Welsh family proceedings officer.

7.10 The court officer will send the certificate of suitability to one of the child's parents or guardians or, if there is no parent or guardian, to the person with whom the child resides or in whose care the child is.

7.11 The children's guardian must file either the certificate of suitability at a time when the children's guardian first takes a step in the proceedings on behalf of the child.

APPLICATION FOR A COURT ORDER APPOINTING A CHILDREN'S GUARDIAN

7.12 An application for a court order appointing a children's guardian should be made in accordance with Part 18 and must be supported by evidence.

7.13 The court officer must serve the application notice on the persons referred to in paragraph 7.10.

7.14 The evidence in support must satisfy the court that the proposed children's guardian –

(a)   consents to act;

PART III

(b) can fairly and competently conduct proceedings on behalf of the child;

(c) has no interest adverse to that of the child; and

(d) undertakes to pay any costs which the child may be ordered to pay in relation to the proceedings, subject to any right the children's guardian may have to be repaid from the assets of the child.

7.15 Paragraph 7.14 does not apply to the Official Solicitor, an officer of the Service of a Welsh family proceedings officer.

7.16 The proposed children's guardian may be one of the persons referred to in paragraph 7.10 where appropriate, or otherwise may be the Official Solicitor, an officer of the Service or a Welsh family proceedings officer. Where it is sought to appoint the Official Solicitor, an officer of the Service or a Welsh family proceedings officer, provision should be made for payment of that person's charges.

CHANGE OF CHILDREN'S GUARDIAN AND PREVENTION OF PERSON ACTING AS CHILDREN'S GUARDIAN

7.17 Where an application is made for an order under rule 16.25, the application must set out the reasons for seeking it and must be supported by evidence.

7.18 Subject to paragraph 7.15, if the order sought is substitution of a new children's guardian for an existing one, the evidence must satisfy the court of the matters set out in paragraph 7.14.

7.19 The court officer will serve the application notice on –

(a) the persons referred to in paragraph 7.10; and

(b) the children's guardian or person purporting to act as children's guardian.

PART 5: REPORTING OFFICER

How the reporting officer exercises duties

8.1 The reporting officer must –

(a) ensure so far as reasonably practicable that the parent or guardian is –
    (i) giving consent unconditionally to the placing of the child for adoption or to the making of an adoption order (as defined in section 46 of the Adoption and Children Act 2002) or a section 84 order; and
    (ii) with full understanding of what is involved;

(b) investigate all the circumstances relevant to a parent's or guardian's consent; and

(c) on completing the investigations the reporting officer must –
    (i) make a report in writing to the court in accordance with the timetable set by the court, drawing attention to any matters which, in the opinion of the reporting officer, may be of assistance to the court in considering the application; or
    (ii) make an interim report to the court if a parent or guardian of the child is unwilling to consent to the placing of the child for adoption or to the making of an adoption order or section 84 order.

8.2 On receipt of an interim report under paragraph 8.1(1)(c)(ii) a court officer must inform the applicant that a parent or guardian of the child is unwilling to consent to the placing of the child for adoption or to the making of an adoption order or section 84 order.

8.3 The reporting officer may at any time before the final hearing make an interim report to the court if the reporting officer considers it necessary and ask the court for directions.

8.4 The reporting officer must attend hearings as directed by the court.

PART 6: CHILDREN AND FAMILY REPORTER AND WELFARE OFFICER

How the children and family reporter or welfare officer exercises powers and duties

9.1 In this Part, the person preparing the welfare report in accordance with rule 16.33 is called "the officer".

9.2 The officer must make such investigations as may be necessary to perform the officer's powers and duties and must, in particular –

    (a)   contact or seek to interview such persons as appear appropriate or as the court directs; and

    (b)   obtain such professional assistance as is available which the children and family reporter thinks appropriate or which the court directs be obtained.

9.3 The officer must –

    (a)   notify the child of such contents of the report (if any) as the officer considers appropriate to the age and understanding of the child, including any reference to the child's own views on the application and the recommendation; and

    (b)   if the child is notified of any contents of the report, explain them to the child in a manner appropriate to the child's age and understanding.

9.4 The officer must –

    (a)   attend hearings as directed by the court;

    (b)   advise the court of the child's wishes and feelings;

    (c)   advise the court if the officer considers that the joining of a person as a party to the proceedings would be likely to safeguard the interests of the child;

    (d)   consider whether it is in the best interests of the child for the child to be made a party to the proceedings, and if so, notify the court of that opinion together with the reasons for that opinion; and

    (e)   where the court has directed that a written report be made –

        (i)   file the report; and

        (ii) serve a copy on the other parties and on any children's guardian,

in accordance with the timetable set by the court.

PART 7: PARENTAL ORDER REPORTER

How the parental order reporter exercises duties – investigations and reports

10.1 The parental order reporter must make such investigations as are necessary to carry out the parental order reporter's duties and must, in particular –

    (a)   contact or seek to interview such persons as the parental order reporter thinks appropriate or as the court directs; and

    (b)   obtain such professional assistance as is available which the parental order reporter thinks appropriate or which the court directs be obtained.

PART III

How the parental order reporter exercises duties – attendance at court, advice to the court and reports

10.2 The parental order reporter must attend all directions hearings unless the court directs otherwise.

10.3 The parental order reporter must advise the court on the following matters –

- (a)   the appropriate forum for the proceedings;
- (b)   the appropriate timing of the proceedings or any part of them;
- (c)   the options available to it in respect of the child and the suitability of each such option including what order should be made in determining the application; and
- (d)   any other matter on which the court seeks advice or on which the parental order reporter considers that the court should be informed.

10.4 The advice given under paragraph 10.3 may, subject to any direction of the court, be given orally or in writing. If the advice is given orally, a note of it must be taken by the court or the court officer.

10.5 The parental order reporter must –

- (a)   unless the court directs otherwise, file a written report advising on the interests of the child in accordance with the timetable set by the court; and
- (b)   where practicable, notify any person the joining of whom as a party to those proceedings would be likely, in the opinion of the parental order reporter, to safeguard the interests of the child, of the court's power to join that person as a party under rule 13.3 and must inform the court –
  - (i)   of any notification;
  - (ii)   of anyone whom the parental order reporter attempted to notify under this paragraph but was unable to contact; and
  - (iii) of anyone whom the parental order reporter believes may wish to be joined to the proceedings.

   (Part 18 sets out the procedure for making an application to be joined as a party in proceedings.)

PART 8: OFFICERS OF THE SERVICE, WELSH FAMILY PROCEEDINGS OFFICERS AND LOCAL AUTHORITY OFFICERS: FURTHER DUTIES

How officers of the Service, Welsh family proceedings officers and local authority officers exercise certain further duties

11.1 This Part applies when an officer of the Service, a Welsh family proceedings officer or a local authority officer is acting under a duty referred to in rule 16.38(1). In this Part, the person acting under a duty referred to in rule 16.38(1) is referred to as "the officer".

11.2 The officer must make such investigations as may be necessary to perform the officer's duties and must, in particular –

- (a)   contact or seek to interview such persons as the officer thinks appropriate or as the court directs; and
- (b)   obtain such professional assistance as the officer thinks appropriate or which the court directs.

11.3 The officer must –

- (a)   notify the child of such (if any) of the contents of any report or risk assessment as the officer considers appropriate to the age and understanding of the child;
- (b)   if the child is notified of any contents of a report or risk assessment, explain them to the child in a manner appropriate to the child's age and understanding;

(c)   consider whether to recommend in any report or risk assessment that the court lists a hearing for the purposes of considering the report or risk assessment;

(d)   consider whether it is in the best interests of the child for the child to be made a party to the proceedings, and, if so, notify the court of that opinion together with the reasons for that opinion.

11.4 When making a risk assessment, the officer must, if of the opinion that the court should exercise its discretion under rule 12.34(2), state in the risk assessment –

(a)   the way in which the officer considers the court should exercise its discretion (including the officer's view on the length of any suggested delay in service); and

(b)   the officer's reasons for that reaching that view.

11.5 The officer must file any report or risk assessment with the court –

(a)   at or by the time directed by the court;

(b)   in the absence of any direction, at least 14 days before a relevant hearing; or

(c)   where there has been no direction from the court and there is no relevant hearing listed, as soon as possible following the completion of the report or risk assessment.

11.6 In paragraph 11.5, a hearing is relevant if the court officer has given the officer notice that a report prepared by the officer is to be considered at it.

11.7 A copy of any report prepared as a result of acting under a duty referred to in rule 16.38(1)(a)(i) to (vi) or (b) (but not any risk assessment) must, as soon as practicable, be served by the officer on the parties.

(Rule 12.34 makes provision for the service of risk assessments.)

PART 17
STATEMENTS OF TRUTH

CONTENTS OF THIS PART

17.1 Interpretation

(1) In this Part "statement of case" has the meaning given to it in Part 4 except that a statement of case does not include –

(a)   an application for a matrimonial or a civil partnership order or an answer to such an application;

(b)   an application under Article 56 of the Maintenance Regulation made on the form in Annex VI or VII to that Regulation;

(c) an application under Article 10 of the 2007 Hague Convention using the Financial Circumstances Form.

(2) In this rule, "Financial Circumstances Form" has the meaning given to it in rule 9.3(1).

(Rule 4.1 defines "statement of case" for the purposes of Part 4.)

Amendments—Substituted by SI 2011/1328; amended by SI 2012/2806.

Defined terms—"statement of case": FPR 2010, rr 4.1(1), 17.1.

Statement of truth—The statement of truth is defined by FPR 2010, r 17.2(4) as a statement that the party to proceedings, witness or person who signs it "believes the facts stated in the document [to be] true". It comes in probative value between the document that is signed by the document's maker, on the one hand, and a document which is sworn to be true (an affidavit) on the other. It was introduced first in civil proceedings by CPR 1998, Pt 22 and provides some guarantee that the maker of the statement confirms an honest belief in the content of the statement. In certain circumstances a statement signed with a statement of truth may be used as evidence (eg FPR 2010, r 22.7(2)). A false statement may be the subject of contempt proceedings (FPR 2010, r 17.6). There is no penalty for including a statement of truth and signing it where it was not needed, so if in doubt as to whether a document requires a statement of truth it can be endorsed and signed without penalty.

PD—FPR PD17A accompanies FPR 2010, Pt 17 and, in particular, prescribes the forms of words to be used in statements of truth (especially at paras 2.1 to 2.3). An annex to PD17A provides a form of words for a statement of truth where a person cannot read.

Affidavit and signed documents distinguished—Affidavit is defined in the Glossary as a "written, sworn, statement of evidence". A narrow range of documents (eg certain interim remedies statements: see FPR PD20A, para 3.1; an affidavit may be called for by the court under FPR 2010, r 7.32(4)) is required to have the additional imprimatur of being sworn if any of the documents are to be filed (and perhaps to be admitted as evidence); others are required to be verified by statement of truth (ie the documents listed in FPR 2010, r 17.2(1) or otherwise referred to in a rule or PD, such as statements in divorce etc cases (r 7.19), Forms E, E1 and E2 and in most other proceedings).

"statement of case"—Defined in FPR 2010, r 4.1(1) as "the whole or part of, an application form or answer". The statements of case and answer (if the definition of "answer" in the next note is accepted) are the pleadings in a FPR 2010 application. Arrangements for signing of these documents are dealt with in FPR 2010, r 17.2.

Statement of case in family proceedings—"Statement of case" is defined in CPR 1998, r 2.3(1) in positive terms as a claim form, particulars of claim (if separate from the claim form), defence of reply to a defence; it includes any further information given to the court in respect of such documents. The effect of FPR 2010, rr 2.3(1) and 4.1(1) is that the equivalent documents, for the purposes of family proceedings, are defined in partly negative terms: that they are "an application form" (FPR 2010, r 4.1(1): "answer" is dealt with below). An application form is any document by which an applicant states an intention to seek a "court order other than in accordance with the [FPR 2010] Part 18 procedure" (ie the negative content). This is probably meant to comprise any application form that starts proceedings, including by the FPR 2010, Pt 19 procedure. Any document that starts proceedings and can be thus categorised is a statement of case and requires to be verified by a statement of truth under r 17.2(1)(a).

Answer: defence or reply to an application form—The term "answer" (above: from FPR 2010, r 4.1(1)) is not defined by the rules. It has a particular meaning in matrimonial and civil partnership proceedings (it must be filed if a respondent is to defend to such proceedings: FPR 2010, r 7.12(8)). It will be assumed for current purposes that it is the defence, reply or other answer to an application form (ie formal claim; document by which proceedings (other than under FPR 2010, Pt 18) are commenced: FPR 2010, r 2.3(1)) under FPR 2010 proceedings. (There is no penalty for including a statement of truth unnecessarily, so if anyone is in doubt as to whether a document is an "answer" it can still be endorsed with a statement of truth and signed.)

17.2 Documents to be verified by a statement of truth

(1) Subject to paragraph (9), the following documents must be verified by a statement of truth –

    (a)   a statement of case;

    (b)   a witness statement;

    (c)   an acknowledgement of service in a claim begun by the Part 19 procedure;

    (d)   a certificate of service;

    (e)   a statement of arrangements for children;

    (f)   a statement of information filed under rule 9.26(1)(b); and

    (g)   any other document where a court order, rule or practice direction requires it.

(2) Where a statement of case is amended, the amendments must be verified by a statement of truth unless the court orders otherwise.

(3) Subject to paragraph (10), if an applicant wishes to rely on matters set out in the application form or application notice as evidence, the application form or notice must be verified by a statement of truth.

(4) Subject to paragraph (5), a statement of truth is a statement that –

    (a)   the party putting forward the document;

    (b)   in the case of a witness statement, the maker of the witness statement; or

    (c)   in the case of a certificate of service, the person who signs the certificate,

believes the facts stated in the document are true.

(5) If a party is conducting proceedings with a litigation friend, the statement of truth in –

    (a)   a statement of case; or

    (b)   an application notice,

is a statement that the litigation friend believes the facts stated in the document being verified are true.

(6) The statement of truth must be signed by –

    (a)   in the case of a statement of case –

        (i)   the party or litigation friend; or

        (ii)   the legal representative on behalf of the party or litigation friend; and

    (b)   in the case of a witness statement or statement of arrangements for children, the maker of the statement.

(7) A statement of truth, which is not contained in the document which it verifies, must clearly identify that document.

(8) A statement of truth in a statement of case may be made by –

    (a)   a person who is not a party; or

    (b)   by two parties jointly,

where this is permitted by a practice direction.

(9) An application that does not contain a statement of facts need not be verified by a statement of truth.

(10) Notwithstanding paragraph (3), and subject to any direction given under rule 9.14(2A) or rule 9.19(2A), the court may permit a party to rely upon matters set out in an application form which has not been verified by a statement of truth as evidence where the application has been made under –

    (a)   Article 56 of the Maintenance Regulation on the form in Annex VI or VII to that Regulation; or

    (b)   Article 10 of the 2007 Hague Convention on an Article 11 form.

    (Practice Direction 17A sets out the form of statement of truth.)

Amendments—SI 2012/2806.

Defined terms—"statement of case": FPR 2010, r 17.1.

"verified by a statement of truth" (r 17.2(1))—Rules as to when a document should or should not be signed by a statement of truth are complex (eg an application in matrimonial and civil partnership proceedings cases or a document with no facts stated in it (r 17.2(9)) need not contain a statement of truth; only acknowledgements of service only in FPR 2010, Pt 19 proceedings (but no other) need have a statement of truth). The general rule must therefore be that, if in doubt, a statement of truth should be included in a document and it should be signed in accordance with r 17.2(3)–(6).

Documents to be verified or not:

(1) *Application or answer in matrimonial and civil partnership proceedings* Although these documents are not to be verified by a statement of truth, parties will need to have any document verified later if an interim application notice is filed.

(2) *Acknowledgement of service in Pt 19 proceedings* The acknowledgement of service in FPR 2010, Pt 19 proceedings partly performs the role of an answer or defence (FPR 2010, r 19.5(3)) and unlike other acknowledgements of service it is required to be verified by a statement of truth (r 17.2(1)(c)).

(3) *Statement of information for a financial remedy consent order* Although FPR 2010, r 9.26(1) does not say so, r 17.2(1)(f) requires that the financial information forms for a consent order be verified by a statement of truth, although there are also (new from the old rules) requirements also as to signing by the parties in FPR 2010, r 9.26(2), (3).

(4) *Enforcement documents* FPR PD17A, para 1.4 has added the following enforcement application documents as being required to be verified by a statement of truth:
  (i) a third party debt order (CPR Pt 72, as modified by FPR 2010, r 33.24);
  (ii) a hardship payment order (CPR Pt 72, as modified by FPR 2010, r 33.24); or
  (iii) a charging order (CPR Pt 73, as modified by FPR 2010, r 33.25).

"matters set out ... as evidence" (r 17.2(3))—Rule 17.2(3) refers to both an application form and application notice: if either are to be relied upon as evidence (other than at trial) they must be verified by a statement of truth (see also FPR 2010, rr 18.7 and 22.7(2)). This refers predominantly to interim hearings and has added relevance because such hearings, unless otherwise ordered or another rule says otherwise, will be based on written evidence only (FPR 2010, r 22.7(1)) and the court can only rely on the application form (or notice, if applicable) or the "answer" (r 22.7(2)(c)) if they are verified by a statement of truth (r 22.7(2)).

Statement of truth as to facts (FPR 2010, r 17.2(4),(9))—Paras (4) and (9) confirm that a statement of truth need relate only to facts. A statement of opinion or as to the law will not require (in logic as well as under the rules) to be signed. It will be rare for a party to disentangle fact from opinion or law (say) in a r 17.2(1) document. Again, if in doubt a party should endorse a statement of truth and arrange for it to be signed.

Expert's report—FPR PD17A (para 1.3) draws attention to the need for an expert's report to be verified by a statement of truth. For the form of the statement of truth verifying an expert's report (which differs from that set out below) see PD25A, para 3.3(i).

Signature—Generally the statement can be signed by a legal representative (r 17.2(6)(a) and see FPR PD17A, para 3.7) and children's representative, save in the case of a statement of arrangements where it must be signed by the applicant parent who makes the statement (r 17(6)(b)).

17.3 Failure to verify a statement of case

(1) If a party fails to verify that party's statement of case by a statement of truth –
  (a) the statement of case shall remain effective unless struck out; but
  (b) the party may not rely on the statement of case as evidence of any of the matters set out in it.

(2) The court may strike out(GL) a statement of case which is not verified by a statement of truth.

(3) Any party may apply for an order under paragraph (2).

Defined terms—"statement of case": FPR 2010, r 17.1.

Failure to verify: "effective unless struck out"—The statement of truth remains effective (ie it is not a nullity) unless court action is taken in respect of it (eg to strike it out: FPR 2010, r 4.4). The court may order that the error be remedied (FPR 2010, r 4.7(b)). Any application to strike out (r 17.3(3)) would be in the proceedings by FPR 2010, Pt 18 procedure application.

Evidence at interim hearing—In practice, the striking out of a document not properly verified is likely to be rare in family proceedings, but at an interim stage (where only evidence in writing generally is considered by the court (FPR 2010, r 22.7(1)) and the judge is not being asked to make a decision on the final issue), an application to strike out or at least suspend or ignore an imperfectly verified statement might be successful.

Verification—The effect of FPR 2010, r 17.2(7) is to enable a statement of truth to be included in a separate document provided that that separate document "clearly identifies [the] document" that it is intended to verify. Failure to verify by statement of truth can be rectified under this provision by a separate and subsequent short document being signed and filed with the original dealing with verification.

17.4 Failure to verify a witness statement

If the maker of a witness statement fails to verify the witness statement by a statement of truth, the court may direct that it shall not be admissible as evidence.

Defined terms—"statement of case": FPR 2010, r 17.1.

"the court may direct [that a statement] shall not be admissible"—Any evidence that is relevant is admissible. There are procedures that dictate how that evidence be adduced (e g in FPR 2010, Pts 17 and 23). It is difficult to imagine circumstance where, on a final hearing, otherwise admissible evidence was excluded because a document was not signed, especially if the witness or party to proceedings were there to sign at the final hearing (see also rules on hearsay evidence at FPR 2010, rr 23.2–23.5). It is conceivable that evidence at an interim hearing may be excluded (see under FPR 2010, r 7.3).

17.5 Power of the court to require a document to be verified

(1) The court may order a person who has failed to verify a document in accordance with rule 17.2 to verify the document.

(2) Any party may apply for an order under paragraph (1).

"verify a document in [r 17.2]"—The list of documents in FPR 2010, r 17.2 are specific, so the court does not have power, for example, to order a party to sign or verify an application notice.

Application for verification—The court may order a party to verify on its own initiative, or a party can make application for this. Proportionality in the making of such applications, and the need for them, will be borne in mind (and see **Verification** under FPR 2010, r 17.3).

17.6 False statements

(1) Proceedings for contempt of court may be brought against a person who makes, or causes to be made, a false statement in a document verified by a statement of truth without an honest belief in its truth.

(2) Proceedings under this rule may be brought only –

    (a)   by the Attorney General, or
    (b)   with the permission of the court.

(3) This rule does not apply to proceedings in a magistrates' court.

Practice Direction 17A – Statements of Truth

This Practice Direction supplements FPR Part 17

Documents to be verified by a statement of truth

1.1 Rule 17.2 sets out the documents which must be verified by a statement of truth.

1.2 If an applicant wishes to rely on matters set out in his application notice as evidence, the application notice must be verified by a statement of truth.

1.3 An expert's report should also be verified by a statement of truth. For the form of the statement of truth verifying an expert's report (which differs from that set out below), see paragraph 9.1(j) of Practice Direction 25B (The Duties of an Expert, The Expert's Report and Arrangements for an Expert to Attend Court).

1.4 In addition, the following documents must be verified by a statement of truth –

(a) an application notice for –
    (i)   a third party debt order (CPR Part 72 as modified by rule 33.24);
    (ii) a hardship payment order (CPR Part 72 as modified by rule 33.24); or
    (iii) a charging order (CPR Part 73 as modified by rule 33.25); and
(b) a notice of objections to an account being taken by the court, unless verified by an affidavit or witness statement.

1.5 The statement of truth may be contained in the document it verifies or it may be in a separate document served subsequently, in which case it must identify the document to which it relates.

1.6 Where the form to be used includes a jurat for the content to be verified by an affidavit, then a statement of truth is not required in addition.

1.7 In this Practice Direction, "statement of case" has the meaning given to it by rule 17.1.

Form of the statement of truth

2.1 The form of the statement of truth verifying a statement of case or an application notice should be as follows:

> "[I believe] [the (applicant or as may be) believes] that the facts stated in this [name document being verified] are true."

2.2 The form of the statement of truth verifying a witness statement should be as follows:

> "I believe that the facts stated in this witness statement are true."

2.3 Where the statement of truth is contained in a separate document, the document containing the statement of truth must be headed with the title of and court reference for the proceedings. The document being verified should be identified in the statement of truth as follows –

(a) application form: "the application form issued on [date]";
(b) statement of case: "the (application or answer as may be) served on [name of party] on [date]";
(c) application notice: "the application notice issued on [date] for [set out the remedy sought]";
(d) witness statement: "the witness statement filed on [date] or served on [party] on [date]".

Who may sign the statement of truth

3.1 In a statement of case or an application notice, the statement of truth must be signed by –

(a) the party or his litigation friend; or
(b) the legal representative of the party or litigation friend.

3.2 A statement of truth verifying a witness statement must be signed by the witness.

3.3 A statement of truth verifying a notice of objections to an account must be signed by the objecting party or his or her legal representative.

3.4 Where a document is to be verified on behalf of a company or corporation, subject to paragraph 3.7 below, the statement of truth must be signed by a person holding a senior position in the company or corporation. That person must state the office or position he or she holds.

3.5 Each of the following persons is a person holding a senior position:

  (a) in respect of a registered company or corporation, a director, the treasurer, secretary, chief executive, manager or other officer of the company or corporation; and

  (b) in respect of a corporation which is not a registered company, in addition to those persons set out in (a), the major, chairman, president, chief executive of a local authority or town clerk or other similar officer of the corporation.

3.6 Where the document is to be verified on behalf of a partnership, those who may sign the statement of truth are –

  (a) any of the partners; or

  (b) a person having the management or control of the partnership business.

3.7 Where a party is legally represented, the legal representative may sign the statement of truth on his or her behalf. The statement signed by the legal representative will refer to the client's belief, not his or her own. In signing he or she must state the capacity in which he or she signs and the name of his or her firm where appropriate.

3.8 Where a legal representative has signed a statement of truth, his or her signature will be taken by the court as his or her statement –

  (a) that the client on whose behalf he or she has signed had authorised him or her to do so;

  (b) that before signing he or she had explained to the client that in signing the statement of truth he or she would be confirming the client's belief that the facts stated in the document were true; and

  (c) that before signing he or she had informed the client of the possible consequences to the client if it should subsequently appear that the client did not have an honest belief in the truth of those facts (see rule 17.6).

3.9 A legal representative who signs a statement of truth must print his or her full name clearly beneath his or her signature.

3.10 The individual who signs a statement of truth must sign in his or her own name and not that of his or her firm or employer.

3.11 The following are examples of the possible application of this practice direction describing who may sign a statement of truth verifying statements in documents other than a witness statement. These are only examples and not an indication of how a court might apply the practice direction to a specific situation.

Managing Agent

An agent who manages property or investments for the party cannot sign a statement of truth. It must be signed by the party or by the legal representative of the party.

Trusts

Where some or all of the trustees comprise a single party one, some or all of the trustees comprising the party may sign a statement of truth. The legal representative of the trustees may sign it.

Companies

Paragraphs 3.4 and 3.5 apply. The word "manager" will be construed in the context of the phrase "a person holding a senior position" which it is used to define. The court will consider the size of the company and the importance and nature of the proceedings. It would expect the manager signing the statement of truth to have personal knowledge of the content of the document or to be responsible for those who have that knowledge of the content. A small company may not have a manager, apart from the directors, who holds a senior position. A large company will have many such managers. In a large company with specialist claims, insurance or legal departments the statement may be signed by the manager of such a department if he or she is responsible for handling the claim or managing the staff handling it.

Inability of persons to read or sign documents to be verified by a statement of truth

4.1 Where a document containing a statement of truth is to be signed by a person who is unable to read or sign the document, it must contain a certificate made by an authorised person.

4.2 An authorised person is a person able to administer oaths and take affidavits but need not be independent of the parties or their representatives.

4.3 The authorised person must certify –

    (a)   that the document has been read to the person signing it;
    (b)   that the person appeared to understand it and approved its content as accurate;
    (c)   that the declaration of truth has been read to that person;
    (d)   that that person appeared to understand the declaration and the consequences of making a false declaration; and
    (e)   that that person signed or made his mark in the presence of the authorised person.

4.4 The form of the certificate is set out at the Annex to this Practice Direction.

Consequences of failure to verify

5.1 If a statement of case is not verified by a statement of truth, the statement of case will remain effective unless it is struck out, but a party may not rely on the contents of a statement of case as evidence until it has been verified by a statement of truth.

5.2 Any party may apply to the court for an order that unless within such period as the court may specify the statement of case is verified by the service of a statement of truth, the statement of case will be struck out.

5.3 The usual order for the costs of an application referred to in paragraph 5.2 will be that the costs be paid by the party who had failed to verify, in any event and immediately.

Penalty

6.1 Rule 17.6 sets out the consequences of verifying a statement of case containing a false statement without an honest belief in its truth. Where a party alleges that a statement of truth is false, the party shall refer that allegation to the court dealing with the proceedings in which the statement of truth has been made.

6.2 On a reference under paragraph 6.1 the court may –

    (a)   exercise any of its powers under the FPR;
    (b)   initiate steps to consider if there is a contempt of court and, where there is, to punish it;

(Order 52 of the Rules of the Supreme Court and Order 29 of the County Court Rules (Schedules 1 and 2 to the CPR) make provision where committal to prison is a possibility if contempt is proved.)

(c) direct the party making the allegation to refer the matter to the Attorney General with a request to him or her to consider whether he or she wishes to bring proceedings for contempt of court.

6.3 A request to the Attorney General must be made in writing and sent to the Attorney General's Office at 20 Victoria Street, London, SW1H 0NF. The request must be accompanied by a copy of the order directing that the matter be referred to the Attorney General and must –

(a) identify the statement said to be false; and
(b) explain –
   (i) why it is false; and
   (ii) why the maker knew it to be false at the time it was made; and
(c) explain why contempt proceedings would be appropriate in the light of the overriding objective in Part 1 of the FPR.

6.4 The practice of the Attorney General is to prefer an application that comes from the court, and so has received preliminary consideration by a judge or district judge, to one made direct to him or her by a party to the proceedings in which the alleged contempt occurred without prior consideration by the court. An application to the Attorney General is not a way of appealing against, or reviewing, the decision of the judge or district judge.

6.5 Where a party makes an application to the court for permission for that party to commence proceedings for contempt of court, it must be supported by written evidence containing the information specified in paragraph 6.3 and the result of the application to the Attorney General made by the applicant.

6.6 The FPR do not change the law of contempt or introduce new categories of contempt. A person applying to commence such proceedings should consider whether the incident complained of does amount to contempt of court and whether such proceedings would further the overriding objective in Part 1 of the FPR.

ANNEX

Certificate to be used where a person is unable to read or sign a document to be verified by a statement of truth

> I certify that I [name and address of authorised person] have read the contents of this document and the declaration of truth to the person signing the document [if there are exhibits, add "and explained the nature and effect of the exhibits referred to in it"] who appeared to understand (a) the document and approved its content as accurate and (b) the declaration of truth and the consequences of making a false declaration, and made his or her mark in my presence.

PART 18
PROCEDURE FOR OTHER APPLICATIONS IN PROCEEDINGS

CONTENTS OF THIS PART

Derivation—FPR 2010, Pt 18 is derived from Pt 9 of the Family Procedure (Adoption) Rules 2005 but is wider and makes general provision for making applications to the court. Unless a rule requires otherwise (as does, for example, FPR 2010, r 30.3 dealing with permission to appeal) all applications for permission should be made under Pt 18.

Forms—FPR PD5A (Forms) prescribes all forms to be used under FPR 2010. Table 1 of PD5A states that forms C2, D11 and FP2 are for use in FPR 2010, Pt 18 applications. Table 2 describes these forms: C2 is the application for permission to start proceedings, for an order or directions in existing proceedings and to be joined as, or cease to be, a party in existing family proceedings under CA 1989; D11 is an application notice and FP2 is described as "application notice under Pt 18, FPR 2010". Thus (regrettably) there is no one form to be used in all Pt 18 applications and the relevant form will depend on the nature of the application.

Structure of Pt 18—The basic structure of FPR 2010, Pt 18 is that, unless excused from doing so by a rule, practice direction or court order, the applicant must submit an application notice which states what order is being sought with brief reasons and attaches a draft of the order being sought (FPR 2010, r 18.7). Any written evidence in support must be filed with the application notice (FPR 2010, r 18.8). The general rule is that the application notice must be served (FPR 2010, r 18.5). Pt 18 is well drafted and is clear and generally the rules speak for themselves.

Practice Direction—FPR 2010, Pt 18 is supplemented by FPR PD18A. It is essential to refer to this PD before making any application under Pt 18. Fortunately, PD18A is particularly clear and helpful and, in effect, provides all necessary commentary on Pt 18.

18.1 Types of application for which Part 18 procedure may be followed

(1) The Part 18 procedure is the procedure set out in this Part.

(2) An applicant may use the Part 18 procedure if the application is made –

   (a) in the course of existing proceedings;
   (b) to start proceedings except where some other Part of these rules prescribes the procedure to start proceedings; or
   (c) in connection with proceedings which have been concluded.

(3) Paragraph (2) does not apply –

   (a) to applications where any other rule in any other Part of these rules sets out the procedure for that type of application;
   (b) if a practice direction provides that the Part 18 procedure may not be used in relation to the type of application in question.

18.2 Applications for permission to start proceedings

An application for permission to start proceedings must be made to the court where the proceedings will be started if permission is granted.

18.3 Respondents to applications under this Part

The following persons are to be respondents to an application under this Part –

- (a) where there are existing proceedings or the proceedings have been concluded –
  - (i) the parties to those proceedings; and
  - (ii) if the proceedings are proceedings under Part 11, the person who is the subject of those proceedings;
- (b) where there are no existing proceedings –
  - (i) if notice has been given under section 44 of the 2002 Act (notice of intention to adopt or apply for an order under section 84 of that Act), the local authority to whom notice has been given; and
  - (ii) if an application is made for permission to apply for an order in proceedings, any person who will be a party to the proceedings brought if permission is granted; and
- (c) any other person as the court may direct.

18.4 Application notice to be filed

(1) Subject to paragraph (2) the applicant must file an application notice.

(2) An applicant may make an application without filing an application notice if –

- (a) this is permitted by a rule or practice direction; or
- (b) the court dispenses with the requirement for an application notice.

18.5 Notice of an application

(1) Subject to paragraph (2), a copy of the application notice must be served on –

- (a) each respondent;
- (b) in relation to proceedings under Part 11, the person who is, or, in the case of an application to start proceedings, it is intended will be, the subject of the proceedings; and
- (c) in relation to proceedings under Parts 12 and 14, the children's guardian (if any).

(2) An application may be made without serving a copy of the application notice if this is permitted by –

- (a) a rule;
- (b) a practice direction; or
- (c) the court.

    (Rule 18.8 deals with service of a copy of the application notice.)

18.6 Time when an application is made

When an application must be made within a specified time, it is so made if the court receives the application notice within that time.

18.7 What an application notice must include

(1) An application notice must state –

- (a) what order the applicant is seeking; and
- (b) briefly, why the applicant is seeking the order.

(2) A draft of the order sought must be attached to the application notice.

    (Part 17 requires an application notice to be verified by a statement of truth if the applicant wishes to rely on matters set out in his application as evidence.)

18.8 Service of a copy of an application notice

(1) Subject to rule 2.4, a copy of the application notice must be served in accordance with the provisions of Part 6 –

- (a) as soon as practicable after it is filed; and
- (b) in any event –
    - (i) where the application is for an interim order under rule 9.7 at least 14 days; and
    - (ii) in any other case, at least 7 days;

    before the court is to deal with the application.

(2) The applicant must, when filing the application notice, file a copy of any written evidence in support.

(3) If a copy of an application notice is served by a court officer it must be accompanied by –

- (a) a notice of the date and place where the application will be heard;
- (b) a copy of any witness statement in support; and
- (c) a copy of the draft order which the applicant has attached to the application.

(4) If –

- (a) an application notice is served; but
- (b) the period of notice is shorter than the period required by these rules or a practice direction,

the court may direct that, in the circumstances of the case, sufficient notice has been given and hear the application.

(5) This rule does not require written evidence –

- (a) to be filed if it has already been filed; or
- (b) to be served on a party on whom it has already been served.

18.9 Applications which may be dealt with without a hearing

(1) The court may deal with an application without a hearing if –

- (a) the court does not consider that a hearing would be appropriate; or
- (b) the parties agree as to the terms of the order sought or the parties agree that the court should dispose of the application without a hearing and the court does not consider that a hearing would be appropriate.

(2) Where –

- (a) an application is made for permission to make an application in proceedings under the 1989 Act; and
- (b) the court refuses the application without a hearing in accordance with paragraph (1)(a),

the court must, at the request of the applicant, re-list the application and fix a date for a hearing.

(3) Paragraph (2) does not apply to magistrates' courts.

18.10 Service of application notice following court order where application made without notice

(1) This rule applies where the court has disposed of an application which it permitted to be made without service of a copy of the application notice.

(2) Where the court makes an order, whether granting or dismissing the application, a copy of the application notice and any evidence in support must unless the court orders otherwise, be served with the order on –

(a) all the parties in proceedings; and

(b) in relation to proceedings under Part 11, the person who is, or, in the case of an application to start proceedings, it is intended will be, the subject of the proceedings.

(3) The order must contain a statement of the right to make an application to set aside$^{(GL)}$ or vary the order under rule 18.11.

18.11 Application to set aside or vary order made without notice

(1) A person who was not served with a copy of the application notice before an order was made under rule 18.10 may apply to have the order set aside$^{(GL)}$ or varied.

(2) An application under this rule must be made within 7 days beginning with the date on which the order was served on the person making the application.

18.12 Power of the court to proceed in the absence of a party

(1) Where the applicant or any respondent fails to attend the hearing of an application, the court may proceed in the absence of that person.

(2) Where –

(a) the applicant or any respondent fails to attend the hearing of an application; and

(b) the court makes an order at the hearing,

the court may, on application or of its own initiative, re-list the application.

(3) Paragraph (2) does not apply to magistrates' courts.

18.13 Dismissal of totally without merit applications

If the High Court or a county court dismisses an application (including an application for permission to appeal) and it considers that the application is totally without merit –

(a) the court's order must record that fact; and

(b) the court must at the same time consider whether it is appropriate to make a civil restraint order.

"totally without merit"—These are key words which trigger the procedure for a civil restraint order and thus must be included in the order itself.

Power of the court to make civil restraint orders—FPR 2010, Rule 4.8 deals with the power of the court to make a civil restraint order. There are three types: limited, extended and general.

Practice Direction 4B—FPR PD4B sets out the circumstances in which the High Court or a county court has power to make a civil restraint order and the procedure and consequences.

Practice Direction 18A –
Other Applications in Proceedings

This Practice Direction supplements FPR Part 18

Application of Part 18

1.1 Part 18 makes general provision for a procedure for making applications. All applications for the court's permission should be made under this Part, with the exception of applications for permission for which specific provision is made in other Parts of the FPR, in which case the application should be made under the specific provision. Examples of where specific provision has been made in another Part of the FPR for applications for permission are rule 11.3 (Permission to apply for a forced marriage protection order) and rule 30.3 (Permission to appeal).

Reference to a judge

2.1 In the High Court or a county court a district judge may refer to a judge any matter which the district judge thinks should properly be decided by a judge, and the judge may either dispose of the matter or refer it back to the district judge.

Additional requirements in relation to application notices

3.1 In addition to the requirements set out in rule 18.7, the following requirements apply to the applications to which the respective paragraph refers.

3.2 An application notice must be signed and include –

    (a)   the title of the case (if available);
    (b)   the reference number of the case (if available);
    (c)   the full name of the applicant;
    (d)   where the applicant is not already a party, the applicant's address for service, including a postcode. Postcode information may be obtained from www.royalmail.com or the Royal Mail Address Management Guide; and
    (e)   either a request for a hearing or a request that the application be dealt with without a hearing.

3.3 An application notice relating to an application under section 42(6) of the Adoption and Children Act 2002 (permission to apply for an adoption order) must include –

    (a)   the child's name, sex, date of birth and nationality;
    (b)   in relation to each of the child's parents or guardians, their name, address and nationality;
    (c)   the length of time that the child has had his or her home with the applicant;
    (d)   the reason why the child has had his or her home with the applicant;
    (e)   details of any local authority or adoption agency involved in placing the child in the applicant's home; and
    (f)   if there are or have been other court proceedings relating to the child, the nature of those proceedings, the name of the court in which they are being or have been dealt with, the date and type of any order made and, if the proceedings are still ongoing, the date of the next hearing.

3.4 An application notice relating to an application in the High Court by a local authority for permission under section 100(3) of the Children Act 1989 must include a draft of the application form.

3.5 Where permission is required to take any step under the Children Act 1989 (for example an application to be joined as a party to the proceedings) the application notice must include a draft of the application for the making of which permission is sought together with sufficient copies for one to be served on each respondent.

3.6 In an application for permission to bring proceedings under Schedule 1 of the Children Act 1989, the draft application for the making of which permission is sought must be accompanied by a statement setting out the financial details which the person seeking permission believes to be relevant to the request and contain a declaration that it is true to the maker's best knowledge and belief, together with sufficient copies for one to be served on each respondent.

3.7 The provisions in Schedule 1 which require an application for permission to bring proceedings are –

(a) paragraph 7(2) – permission is required to make an application for variation of a secured periodical payments order after the death of the parent liable to make the payments if a period of 6 months has passed from the date on which representation in regard to that parent's estate is first taken out; and

(b) paragraph 11(3) – permission is required to make an application to alter a maintenance agreement following the death of one of the parties if a period of 6 months has passed beginning with the day on which representation in regard to the estate of the deceased is first taken out.

Other provisions in relation to application notices

4.1 On receipt of an application notice containing a request for a hearing, unless the court considers that the application is suitable for consideration without a hearing, the court officer will, if serving a copy of the application notice, notify the applicant of the time and date fixed for the hearing of the application.

4.2 On receipt of an application notice containing a request that the application be dealt with without a hearing, the court will decide whether the application is suitable for consideration without a hearing.

4.3 Where the court –

(a) considers that the application is suitable for consideration without a hearing; but

(b) is not satisfied that it has sufficient material to decide the application immediately,

it may give directions for the filing of evidence and will inform the applicant and the respondent(s) of its decision. (Rule 18.11 enables a party to apply for an order made without notice to be set aside or varied.)

4.4 Where the court does not consider that the application is suitable for consideration without a hearing –

(a) it may give directions as to the filing of evidence; and

(b) the court officer will notify the applicant and the respondent of the time, date and place for the hearing of the application and any directions given.

4.5 In the High Court or a county court if the application is intended to be made to a judge, the application notice should so state. In that case, paragraphs 4.2, 4.3 and 4.4 will apply as though references to the court were references to a judge.

4.6 Every application should be made as soon as it becomes apparent that it is necessary or desirable to make it.

PART III

4.7 Applications should, wherever possible, be made so that they are considered at any directions hearing or other hearing for which a date has been fixed or for which a date is about to be fixed.

4.8 The parties must anticipate that at any hearing (including any directions hearing) the court may wish to review the conduct of the case as a whole and give any necessary directions. They should be ready to assist the court in doing so and to answer questions the court may ask for this purpose.

4.9 Where a date for a hearing has been fixed, a party who wishes to make an application at that hearing but does not have sufficient time to file an application notice should as soon as possible inform the court (if possible in writing) and, if possible, the other parties of the nature of the application and the reason for it. That party should then make the application orally at the hearing.

Applications without service of application notice

5.1 An application may be made without service of an application notice only –

(a)   where there is exceptional urgency;
(b)   where the overriding objective is best furthered by doing so;
(c)   by consent of all parties;
(d)   with the permission of the court;
(e)   where paragraph 4.9 applies; or
(f)   where a court order, rule or practice direction permits.

Giving notice of an application

6.1 Unless the court otherwise directs or paragraph 5.1 of this practice direction applies, the application notice must be served as soon as practicable after it has been issued and, if there is to be a hearing, at least 7 days before the hearing date.

6.2 Where an application notice should be served but there is not sufficient time to do so, informal notification of the application should be given unless the circumstances of the application require no notice of the application to be given.

Pre-action applications

7.1 All applications made before proceedings are commenced should be made under this Part.

Telephone hearings

8.1 The court may direct that an application be dealt with by a telephone hearing.

8.2 The applicant should, if seeking a direction under paragraph 8.1, indicate this on the application notice. Where the applicant has not indicated such an intention but nevertheless wishes to seek a direction the request should be made as early as possible.

8.3 A direction under paragraph 8.1 will not normally be made unless every party entitled to be given notice of the application and to be heard at the hearing has consented to the direction.

8.4 No representative of a party to an application being heard by telephone may attend the court in person while the application is being heard unless the other party to the application has agreed that the representative may do so.

8.5 If an application is to be heard by telephone the following directions will apply, subject to any direction to the contrary –

(a)   the applicant's legal representative is responsible for arranging the telephone conference for precisely the time fixed by the court. The telecommunications provider used must be one of the approved panel of service providers (see HMCS website at www.hmcourts-service.gov.uk);

(b)   the applicant's legal representative must tell the operator the telephone numbers of all those participating in the conference call and the sequence in which they are to be called;

(c)   it is the responsibility of the applicant's legal representative to ascertain from all the other parties whether they have instructed counsel and, if so the identity of counsel, and whether the legal representative and counsel will be on the same or different telephone numbers;

(d)   the sequence in which those involved are to be called will be –

   (i)   the applicant's legal representative and (if on a different number) his counsel;

   (ii)   the legal representative (and counsel) for all other parties; and

   (iii)   the judge or justices, as the case may be;

(e)   each speaker is to remain on the line after being called by the operator setting up the conference call. The call may be 2 or 3 minutes before the time fixed for the application;

(f)   when the judge has or justices have been connected the applicant's legal representative (or counsel) will introduce the parties in the usual way;

(g)   if the use of a "speakerphone" by any party causes the court or any other party any difficulty in hearing what is said the judge or justices may require that party to use a hand held telephone;

(h)   the telephone charges debited to the account of the party initiating the conference call will be treated as part of the costs of the application.

Video conferencing

9.1 Where the parties to a matter wish to use video conferencing facilities, and those facilities are available in the relevant court, the parties should apply to the court for directions.

(Practice Direction 22A provides guidance on the use of video conferencing)

Note of proceedings

10.1 The court or court officer should keep, either by way of a note or a tape recording, brief details of all proceedings before the court, including the dates of the proceedings and a short statement of the decision taken at each hearing.

Evidence

11.1 The requirement for evidence in certain types of applications is set out in some of the rules in the FPR and practice directions. Where there is no specific requirement to provide evidence it should be borne in mind that, as a practical matter, the court will often need to be satisfied by evidence of the facts that are relied on in support of or for opposing the application.

11.2 The court may give directions for the filing of evidence in support of or opposing a particular application. The court may also give directions for the filing of evidence in relation to any hearing that it fixes on its own initiative. The directions may specify the form that evidence is to take and when it is to be served.

PART III

11.3 Where it is intended to rely on evidence which is not contained in the application itself, the evidence, if it has not already been served, should be served with the application.

11.4 Where a respondent to an application wishes to rely on evidence, that evidence must be filed in accordance with any directions the court may have given and a court officer will serve the evidence on the other parties, unless the court directs otherwise.

11.5 If it is necessary for the applicant to serve any evidence in reply the court officer will serve it on the other parties unless the court directs otherwise.

11.6 Evidence must be filed with the court as well as served on the parties.

11.7 The contents of an application notice may be used as evidence provided the contents have been verified by a statement of truth.

Consent orders

12.1 The parties to an application for a consent order must ensure that they provide the court with any material it needs to be satisfied that it is appropriate to make the order. Subject to any rule in the FPR or practice direction a letter will generally be acceptable for this purpose.

12.2 Where a judgment or order has been agreed in respect of an application where a hearing date has been fixed, the parties must inform the court immediately.

Other applications considered without a hearing

13.1 Where rule 18.9(1)(b) applies the court will treat the application as if it were proposing to make an order on its own initiative.

13.2 Where the parties agree that the court should dispose of the application without a hearing they should so inform the court in writing and each should confirm that all evidence and other material on which he or she relies has been disclosed to the other parties to the application.

Miscellaneous

14.1 If the case is proceeding in the High Court and the draft order is unusually long or complex it should also be supplied in electronic form on such storage medium as shall be agreed with the judge or court staff, for use by the court office.

14.2 Where rule 18.12 applies the power to re-list the application in rule 18.12(2) is in addition to any other powers of the court with regard to the order (for example to set aside, vary, discharge or suspend the order).

Costs

15.1 Attention is drawn to the CPR costs practice direction and, in particular, to the court's power to make a summary assessment of costs.

15.2 Attention is also drawn to rule 44.13(1) of the CPR which provides that if an order makes no mention of costs, none are payable in respect of the proceedings to which it relates.

PART 19
ALTERNATIVE PROCEDURE FOR APPLICATIONS

CONTENTS OF THIS PART

PART III

19.1 Types of application for which Part 19 procedure may be followed

(1) The Part 19 procedure is the procedure set out in this Part.

(2) An applicant may use the Part 19 procedure where the Part 18 procedure does not apply and –

    (a) there is no form prescribed by a rule or referred to in Practice Direction 5A in which to make the application;

    (b) the applicant seeks the court's decision on a question which is unlikely to involve a substantial dispute of fact; or

    (c) paragraph (5) applies.

(3) The court may at any stage direct that the application is to continue as if the applicant had not used the Part 19 procedure and, if it does so, the court may give any directions it considers appropriate.

(4) Paragraph (2) does not apply if a practice direction provides that the Part 19 procedure may not be used in relation to the type of application in question.

(5) A rule or practice direction may, in relation to a specified type of proceedings –

    (a) require or permit the use of the Part 19 procedure; and

    (b) disapply or modify any of the rules set out in this Part as they apply to those proceedings.

Derivation—FPR 2010, Pt 19 is derived from Family Proceedings (Adoption) Rules 2005, Pt 10 which, in turn, was based on CPR 1998, Pt 8 but is now of general application. Pt 19 is used where the FPR 2010, Pt 18 procedure does not apply and either there is no form prescribed by rule or in PD5A or the applicant seeks the court's decision on a question which is unlikely to involve a substantial dispute of fact. An applicant may also use the Pt 19 procedure if a practice direction permits or requires its use. It must be used for applications under s 60(3) or s 79(4) of the 2002 Act and for orders under FPR 2010, r 14.21.

Forms—Table 1 of FPR PD5A (Forms) lists the forms relevant to FPR 2010, Pt 19 and Table 2 describes those forms as follows:

- FP1 Application under Part 19 FPR 2010
- FP1A Application under Part 19 FPR 2010 – notes for applicant on completing form FP1
- FP1B Application under Part 19 FPR 2010 – notes for respondent
- FP3 Application for Injunction (General Form)
- FP5 Acknowledgement of Service under Part 19 FPR 2010
- FP6 Certificate of Service

Structure of Pt 19—The procedure permits an application without naming a respondent (FPR 2010, r 19.4 and FPR PD19A, para 2.2) but where a respondent is named an acknowledgement of service is required (FPR 2010, r 19.5) and any written evidence must be filed with it. If the respondent contends that the FPR 2010, Pt 19 procedure is not appropriate he must say so and give reasons when filing the acknowledgement of service (FPR 2010, r 19.9). On receipt of the acknowledgement of service the court will give directions (r 19.9(2)). No written evidence may be relied on at a hearing unless it has been served or the court gives permission FPR 2010, (r 19.8). If the respondent does not file an acknowledgement of service he may attend the hearing but may not take part unless the court gives permission (FPR 2010, r 19.6). Pt 19 is clearly drafted and speaks for itself. Note the formal requirements as to contents of a Pt 19 application in FPR 2010, r 19.3.

Practice Direction—FPR 2010, Pt 19 is supplemented by FPR PD19A, which, in effect, provides all necessary commentary.

19.2 Applications for which the Part 19 procedure must be followed

(1) The Part 19 procedure must be used in an application made in accordance with –

    (a)   section 60(3) of the 2002 Act (order to prevent disclosure of information to an adopted person);

    (b)   section 79(4) of the 2002 Act (order for Registrar General to give any information referred to in section 79(3) of the 2002 Act); and

    (c)   rule 14.21 (directions of High Court regarding fathers without parental responsibility).

(2) The respondent to an application made in accordance with paragraph (1)(b) is the Registrar General.

19.3 Contents of the application

Where the applicant uses the Part 19 procedure, the application must state –

    (a)   that this Part applies;

    (b)   either –

         (i)   the question which the applicant wants the court to decide; or

         (ii) the order which the applicant is seeking and the legal basis of the application for that order;

    (c)   if the application is being made under an enactment, what that enactment is;

    (d)   if the applicant is applying in a representative capacity, what that capacity is; and

    (e)   if the respondent appears or is to appear in a representative capacity, what that capacity is.

    (Part 17 requires a statement of case to be verified by a statement of truth.)

19.4 Issue of application without naming respondents

(1) A practice direction may set out circumstances in which an application may be issued under this Part without naming a respondent.

(2) The practice direction may set out those cases in which an application for permission must be made by application notice before the application is issued.

(3) The application for permission –

    (a)   need not be served on any other person; and

    (b)   must be accompanied by a copy of the application which the applicant proposes to issue.

(4) Where the court gives permission, it will give directions about the future management of the application.

19.5 Acknowledgment of service

(1) Subject to paragraph (2), each respondent must –

   (a)   file an acknowledgment of service within 14 days beginning with the date on which the application is served; and

   (b)   serve the acknowledgment of service on the applicant and any other party.

(2) If the application is to be served out of the jurisdiction, the respondent must file and serve an acknowledgment of service within the period set out in Practice Direction 6B.

(3) The acknowledgment of service must –

   (a)   state whether the respondent contests the application;

   (b)   state, if the respondent seeks a different order from that set out in the application, what that order is; and

   (c)   be signed by the respondent or the respondent's legal representative.

19.6 Consequence of not filing an acknowledgment of service

(1) This rule applies where –

   (a)   the respondent has failed to file an acknowledgment of service; and

   (b)   the time period for doing so has expired.

(2) The respondent may attend the hearing of the application but may not take part in the hearing unless the court gives permission.

19.7 Filing and serving written evidence

(1) The applicant must, when filing the application, file the written evidence on which the applicant intends to rely.

(2) The applicant's evidence must be served on the respondent with the application.

(3) A respondent who wishes to rely on written evidence must file it when filing the acknowledgment of service.

(4) A respondent who files written evidence must also, at the same time, serve a copy of that evidence on the other parties.

(5) Within 14 days beginning with the date on which a respondent's evidence was served on the applicant, the applicant may file further written evidence in reply.

(6) An applicant who files further written evidence must also, within the same time limit, serve a copy of that evidence on the other parties.

19.8 Evidence – general

(1) No written evidence may be relied on at the hearing of the application unless –

   (a)   it has been served in accordance with rule 19.7; or

   (b)   the court gives permission.

(2) The court may require or permit a party to give oral evidence at the hearing.

(3) The court may give directions requiring the attendance for cross-examination(GL) of a witness who has given written evidence.

    (Rule 22.1 contains a general power for the court to control evidence.)

19.9 Procedure where respondent objects to use of the Part 19 procedure

(1) A respondent who contends that the Part 19 procedure should not be used because –

   (a)   there is a substantial dispute of fact; and

(b) the use of the Part 19 procedure is not required or permitted by a rule or practice direction,

must state the reasons for that contention when filing the acknowledgment of service.

(2) When the court receives the acknowledgment of service and any written evidence, it will give directions as to the future management of the case.

> (Rule 19.7 requires a respondent who wishes to rely on written evidence to file it when filing the acknowledgment of service.)

> (Rule 19.1(3) allows the court to make an order that the application continue as if the applicant had not used the Part 19 procedure.)

Practice Direction 19A – Alternative Procedure for Applications

This Practice Direction supplements FPR Part 19

Types of application in which Part 19 procedure must be used

1.1 An applicant must use the Part 19 procedure if the application is for an order under –

(a) section 60(3) of the 2002 Act, to prevent disclosure of information to an adopted person;

(b) section 79(4) of the 2002 Act, to require the Registrar General to provide information; or

(c) rule 14.21 (Inherent jurisdiction and fathers without parental responsibility) in Part 14, to request directions of the High Court regarding fathers without parental responsibility.

Types of application in which Part 19 procedure may be used

1.2 An applicant may use the Part 19 procedure if Part 18 does not apply and if –

(a) there is no prescribed form in which to make the application; or

(b) the applicant seeks the court's decision on a question which is unlikely to involve a substantial dispute of fact.

1.3 An applicant may also use the Part 19 procedure if a practice direction permits or requires its use for the type of proceedings concerned.

1.4 The practice directions referred to in paragraph 1.3 may in some respects modify or disapply the Part 19 procedure and, where that is so, it is those practice directions, rather than this one, which must be complied with.

1.5 The types of application for which the Part 19 procedure may be used include an application for an order or direction which is unopposed by each respondent before the commencement of the proceedings and the sole purpose of the application is to obtain the approval of the court to the agreement.

1.6 Where it appears to a court officer that an applicant is using the Part 19 procedure inappropriately, the officer may refer the application to the court for consideration of the point.

1.7 The court may at any stage order the application to continue as if the applicant had not used the Part 19 procedure and, if it does so, the court will give such directions as it considers appropriate (see rule 19.1(3)).

The application

2.1 Where an applicant uses the Part 19 procedure, the application form referred to in Practice Direction 5A should be used and must state the matters set out in rule 19.3 and, if paragraphs 1.3 and 1.4 apply, must comply with the requirements of the practice direction in question. In particular, the application form must state that Part 19 applies. A Part 19 application form means an application form which so states.

2.2 An application –

    (a)   in accordance with rule 19.4, to ask the High Court for directions on the need to give a father without parental responsibility notice of the intention to place a child for adoption; or

    (b)   under section 60(3) of the 2002 Act for an order to prevent disclosure of information to an adopted person,

may be issued without naming a respondent.

Responding to the application

3.1 Where a respondent who wishes to respond to a Part 19 application is required to file an acknowledgement of service, that acknowledgement of service should be in form FP5 which is referred to in Practice Direction 5A but can, alternatively be given in an informal document such as a letter.

3.2 Rule 19.5 sets out provisions relating to an acknowledgement of service of a Part 19 application.

3.3 Rule 19.6 sets out the consequence of failing to file an acknowledgement of service.

3.4 A respondent who believes that the Part 19 procedure should not be used because there is a substantial dispute of fact or, as the case may be, because its use is not authorised by any rule in the FPR or any practice direction, must state the reasons for that belief in writing when filing the acknowledgement of service (see rule 19.9). If the statement of reasons includes matters of evidence, it should be verified by a statement of truth.

Managing the application

4.1 The court may give directions immediately a Part 19 application is issued either on the application of a party or of its own initiative. The directions may include fixing a hearing date where –

    (a)   there is no dispute; or

    (b)   where there may be a dispute, but a hearing date could conveniently be given.

4.2 Where the court does not fix a hearing date when the application is issued, it will give directions for the disposal of the application as soon as practicable after the respondent has acknowledged service of the application or, as the case may be, after the period for acknowledging service has expired.

4.3 Certain applications may not require a hearing.

4.4 The court may convene a directions hearing before giving directions.

Evidence

5.1 An applicant wishing to rely on written evidence should file it when the Part 19 application form is issued.

5.2 Evidence will normally be in the form of a witness statement or an affidavit but an applicant may rely on the matters set out in the application form provided it has been verified by a statement of truth.

> (For information about statements of truth see Part 7 and Practice Direction 17A, and about written evidence see Part 22 and Practice Direction 22A.)

5.3 A respondent wishing to rely on written evidence should file it with the acknowledgement of service (see rule 19.7(3)).

5.4 Rule 19.7 sets out the times and provisions for filing and serving written evidence.

5.5 A party may apply to the court for an extension of time to serve and file evidence under rule 19.7 or for permission to serve and file additional evidence under rule 19.8(1).

> (For information about applications see Part 18 and Practice Direction 18A.)

5.6 The parties may, subject to paragraphs 5.7 and 5.8, agree in writing on an extension of time for serving and filing evidence under rule 19.7(3) or rule 19.7(5).

5.7 An agreement extending time for a respondent to file evidence in reply under rule 19.7(3) –

(a) must be filed by the respondent at the same time as the acknowledgement of service; and

(b) must not extend time by more than 17 days after the respondent files the acknowledgement of service.

5.8 An agreement extending time for an applicant to file evidence in reply under rule 19.7(5) must not extend time to more than 28 days after service of the respondent's evidence on the applicant.

Hearing

6.1 The court may on the hearing date –

(a) proceed to hear the case and dispose of the application;

(b) give case management directions.

PART 20
INTERIM REMEDIES AND SECURITY FOR COSTS

CONTENTS OF THIS PART

Chapter 1
Interim Remedies

Practice Direction 20A –
Interim Remedies

Interim remedies: terminology—FPR 2010 uses the terms "any other hearing" (i e other than a "final hearing": e g FPR 2010, r 22.2(1)) and "interim", interchangeably and to mean the same thing. The final hearing disposes of the issue before the court; whereas the interim hearing is preparatory for that. The injunction is interim to the extent that it does not dispose of a final issue (by definition) but it is often final in effect, since it provides the remedy sought by the applicant (e g FLA 1996, Pts IV and 4A; PFHA 1997).

Scope—FPR 2010, Pt 20 deals with two wholly separate subjects: application (supplementing the FPR 2010, Pt 18 procedure) for certain interim remedies not otherwise provided for in the rules; and security for costs. In CPR 1998, the subject matter of the equivalent FPR 2010, Pt 25 is extended by inclusion of interim damages.

Inherent jurisdiction—Injunctions originate from the equitable jurisdiction of the High Court, and declarations are a creation of the mid-19th century. The county court has no inherent jurisdiction; and the magistrates no equitable jurisdiction. Any powers to grant injunctive relief in those two jurisdictions are statutory. County courts have the same powers as the High Court (save where excluded: CCA 1984, s 38). Magistrates have no general powers: they are derived statute by statute (e g FLA 1996, Pt IV).

Pt 18 jurisdiction—Interim remedy applications (whether listed in FPR 2010, r 20.2(1) or not) are made by the FPR 2010, Pt 18 procedure: applications under Pt 20, by definition, will be parasitic on existing or proposed proceedings (see FPR 2010, r 18.1(2)). The provisions of Pt 20 add to the Pt 18 procedure particular steps which are appropriate to seeking an interim remedy and confirm, for example, that an interim remedy can be applied for "without notice if it appears to the court that there are good reasons for not giving notice" (FPR 2010, r 20.4(1)).

Remedy defines procedure—It is the remedy which defines or demands the procedure. Pts IV and 4A of FLA 1996 have created their own procedures (FPR 2010, Pts 10 and 11). Civil Procedure Act 1997, s 7 procedures exist independently of CPR 1998, Pt 25 (and FPR 2010, Pt 20) by which they are obtained. If the law provides a remedy, procedure must find a means to provide it. FPR 2010, r 20.2(3) confirms that the fact that a remedy is not listed does not 'affect any power the court may have to grant that remedy'.

Other interim remedies—FPR 2010, Pt 20 merely elaborates FPR 2010, Pt 18 and is specific to no particular aspect of family proceedings. Other interim remedies, which are likely to impact more frequently on the family lawyer's practice and which have their own procedures in the rules are to be found as follows:

– Interim financial remedy – FPR 2010, r 9.7
– FLA 1996, Pt IV – FPR 2010, Pt 10
– FLA 1996, Pt 4A – FPR 2010, Pt 11
– Interim orders for children (except those forms of proceedings referred in FPR PD20A, para 1.1)
– Interim costs provision where not available as periodical payments (e g in CA 1989, Sch 1 proceedings)
– Scientific tests direction: FLRA 1969, s 20 and CPR PD23B,

Chapter 1
Interim Remedies

20.1 Scope of this Part

The rules in this Part do not apply to proceedings in a magistrates' court.

Jurisdictional scope of Pt 20—See **Inherent jurisdiction**, above. Only the High Court has an inherent jurisdiction. Many of the FPR 2010, Pt 20 remedies derive from that inherent jurisdiction, acquired also by county courts under CCA 1984, s 37. The magistrates do not have any equivalent powers.

20.2 Orders for interim remedies

(1) The court may grant the following interim remedies –

    (a) an interim injunction$^{(GL)}$;
    (b) an interim declaration;
    (c) an order –

     (i)   for the detention, custody or preservation of relevant property;

     (ii) for the inspection of relevant property;

     (iii) for the taking of a sample of relevant property;

     (iv) for the carrying out of an experiment on or with relevant property;

     (v) for the sale of relevant property which is of a perishable nature or which for any other good reason it is desirable to sell quickly; and

     (vi) for the payment of income from relevant property until an application is decided;

(d) an order authorising a person to enter any land or building in the possession of a party to the proceedings for the purposes of carrying out an order under sub-paragraph (c);

(e) an order under section 4 of the Torts (Interference with Goods) Act 1977 to deliver up goods;

(f) an order (referred to as a 'freezing injunction$^{(GL)}$') –
restraining a party from removing from the jurisdiction assets located there; or restraining a party from dealing with any assets whether located within the jurisdiction or not;

(g) an order directing a party to provide information about the location of relevant property or assets or to provide information about relevant property or assets which are or may be the subject of an application for a freezing injunction$^{(GL)}$;

(h) an order (referred to as a "search order") under section 7 of the Civil Procedure Act 1997 (order requiring a party to admit another party to premises for the purpose of preserving evidence etc.);

(i) an order under section 34 of the Senior Courts Act 1981 or section 53 of the County Courts Act 1984 (order in certain proceedings for disclosure of documents or inspection of property against a non-party);

(j) an order for a specified fund to be paid into court or otherwise secured, where there is a dispute over a party's right to the fund;

(k) an order permitting a party seeking to recover personal property to pay money into court pending the outcome of the proceedings and directing that, if money is paid into court, the property must be given up to that party;

(l) an order directing a party to prepare and file accounts relating to the dispute;

(m) an order directing any account to be taken or inquiry to be made by the court.

(2) In paragraph (1)(c) and (g), 'relevant property' means property (including land) which is the subject of an application or as to which any question may arise on an application.

(3) The fact that a particular kind of interim remedy is not listed in paragraph (1) does not affect any power that the court may have to grant that remedy.

Interim remedies—The term "interim remedies" for the purposes of FPR 2010, Pt 20 is not defined. The remedies listed in FPR 2010, r 20.2(1) are taken from CPR 1998, r 25.1(1). Three of the civil proceedings remedies have been removed from the CPR 1998 list, but otherwise the rule-makers have not tailored the list to family proceedings.

Urgency—There is nothing to say that FPR 2010, Pt 20 is exclusive to remedies which are unusual or urgent, but they appear to have a tendency towards urgency (see for example without notice applications in FPR 2010, r 20.4).

Powers of High Court to grant injunctions—Section 37 of SCA 1981 confirms the inherent power of the High Court to make injunctions: "The High Court may by order (whether [interim] or final) grant an injunction ... receiver in all cases in which it appears to the court to be just and convenient to do so."

A discretionary remedy—The grant of an injunction is a matter for the court's discretion (SCA 1981, s 37(1) (above)). In *National Commercial Bank Jamaica Ltd v Olint Corp Ltd (Jamaica)* [2009] 1 WLR 1405, Lord Hoffmann considered this discretionary exercise, especially in the context of an urgent order. He emphasised, first, that the court must adopt a course which seemed "likely to cause the least irremediable prejudice to one party or the other"; and, second, in doing so the court should carry out an assessment in which, said Lord Hoffmann (adopting the words of Lord Diplock in *American*

Cyanamid Co v Ethicon Ltd [1975] AC 396): "It would be unwise to attempt even to list all the various matters which may need to be taken into consideration in deciding where the balance lies, let alone to suggest the relative weight to be attached to them." In terms of justice to the parties the court must "assess whether granting or withholding an injunction is more likely to produce a just result". Ultimately, can the court be satisfied, at the time of hearing the final application, that "it will [then] appear that ... the injunction was rightly granted"?

Jurisdiction of the county courts to grant injunctions—Section 38(1) of CCA 1984 empowers the county court to make orders which could be made in the High Court, if the applications were there, subject to the exceptions in County Court Remedies Regulations 1991, reg 3(3) (which prevents the county court from making search and freezing orders, save in family proceedings where freezing injunctions can be made in specified circumstances).

FORMS OF ORDER

(1) Search order – Civil Procedure Act 1997, s 7

Search order in family proceedings—CPA 1997, s 7 provides for search orders. In *Imerman v Tchenguiz and Others* [2010] 2 FLR 814, the court considered the availability of the search order in family proceedings (at [127]–[140]). They are as readily available in family, as in any other civil, proceedings, subject to issues such a proportionality: "Such applications should be seriously considered where there are substantial reasons for believing that a husband is concealing or dissipating assets, or intending to conceal or destroy documents." Removal of documents (or the freezing of electronic documents) should only be permitted by order of the High Court and under its supervision. It is not, therefore, open to the courts in any way to condone "self-help" by spouses (at [136] and [137]). A spouse (or civil partner) was under no duty to his spouse or to the court to disclose, or give discovery of, documents until such time as required to do so by the rules (now FPR 2010, r 9.14(1): filing and service of Form E). No justification for unlawful removal of documents by any (other than court-ordered) means could be permitted by the courts (at [139]).

Practice Direction 20A and search orders—FPR PD20A, paras 6.1–6.9 provides detailed directions as to the application for and working out of a search order. It creates the concept of "The Supervising Solicitor" (cf the parallel CPR PD25A for more explanation and information).

(2) Freezing injunction

Freezing orders and family proceedings—The spouse, parent (in CA 1989, Sch 1 proceedings), or civil partner involved in financial remedy proceedings where a restraint of disposal or other freezing order is sought from the court will consider precisely what order is sought alongside the powers of the particular court (if in the county court) to grant the order; and the extent of the urgency of the order if sought on an interim basis and with or without notice to the other party. There is a distinction between freezing orders in support of a proprietary claim and freezing orders where the claim is in debt. In the latter case (which will include claims for arrears of maintenance), it is not legitimate to use a freezing injunction to secure advance security for the claim or to seek to prohibit reasonable expenditure by the respondent: *O'Farrell v O'Farrell* [2013] 1 FLR 77

Freezing orders and matrimonial financial order proceedings—In financial order proceedings the court has power to make one of the following orders:

(1) *Order preventing a disposition* Restraining disposal where satisfied that a spouse (or civil partner) is about to make a disposition "with intent to defeat" the other party's claim (MCA 1973, s 37(2)(a); MFPA 1984, s 23; CPA 2004, s 74(2) and Sch 7, para 15).

(2) *Shipman order* The High Court (and county court if CCA 1984, s 38 applies) can make an inherent jurisdiction order in terms of *Shipman v Shipman* [1991] 1 FLR 250 (Anthony Lincoln J, as a High Court judge, made an order in his inherent jurisdiction where he felt unable to make an order under MCA 1973, s 37(2)(a)).

(3) *Freezing injunction* The court can make the wider freezing injunction order where the facts of the case and the seriousness of the risk of disposal of assets justifies it.

Family proceedings where prevention of disposition orders are unavailable—Under CA 1989, Sch 1, the order preventing disposition is not available under statute; so any order would need to be in the inherent jurisdiction (per *Shipman*) or as a freezing injunction (under CPA 1997, s 7(1)(b)). This position applies also to the freezing of assets, or prevention of their disposal, under TOLATA 1996, s 14 (e g where a constructive trust declaration is sought), when application would be by CPR 1998, Pt 25.

(3) Other applications under Part 20

SCA 1981, s 34, CCA 1984, s 53—Section 34 of SCA 1981 (with the parallel CCA 1984, s 53) deals with disclosure of documents by a third party. A similar question, with different underlying source, is dealt with:

(1) alongside disclosure at FPR 2010, r 21.2 (below); and

(2) in the context of witness summonses (FPR 2010, r 24.2).

Writ ne exeat regno—The writ ne exeat regno is applied for under FPR 2010, Pt 20 (r 20.2(3)) in the High Court and in the existing case or matter (which must be transferred to a District Registry). The FPR 2010, Pt 18 application (on an urgent basis, as need be: FPR 2010, rr 20.3 and 20.4) is supported by an affidavit (FPR PD20A, para 3.1), which will include reference to (iii)–(v) of the provisos set out in *Young v Young* [2012] 2 FLR 470, Mostyn J at [26] (see further **Writ ne exeat regno** and **Impounding of a respondent's passport** under SCA 1981, s 19).

20.3 Time when an order for an interim remedy may be made

(1) An order for an interim remedy may be made at any time, including –

    (a) before proceedings are started; and

    (b) after judgment has been given.

       (Rule 5.3 provides that proceedings are started when the court issues an application form.)

(2) However –

    (a) paragraph (1) is subject to any rule, practice direction or other enactment which provides otherwise; and

    (b) the court may grant an interim remedy before an application has been started only if –

       (i)   the matter is urgent; or

       (ii) it is otherwise desirable to do so in the interests of justice.

(3) Where the court grants an interim remedy before an application has been started, it will give directions requiring an application to be started.

(4) The court need not direct that an application be started where the application is made under section 33 of the Senior Courts Act 1981 or section 52 of the County Courts Act 1984 (order for disclosure, inspection etc. before starting an application).

Procedure for an interim remedy: urgent applications—Procedure for an interim remedy is governed by rules in relation to the FPR 2010, Pt 18 procedure supplemented by FPR 2010, rr 20.3 and 20.4 and FPR PD20A. An interim remedy can be applied for at any time:

– before issue of proceedings (e g to protect assets or documents or otherwise to preserve the status quo);

– during (i e interim, formerly interlocutory) to proceedings; and

– after judgment has been given (e g to protect disposal of assets as part of enforcement of an order).

"proceedings are started"—Proceedings are started where an "application" is issued by the court office (FPR 2010, r 5.3(1)).

Service of the application—Application and supporting evidence must be served "as soon as practicable after issue and in any event not less than 7 days before the application is heard" (FPR PD20A, para 2.2). Because 7 days excludes the day of hearing, the day of service and non-business days (r 2.8), it will always be 1 day under a fortnight (longer if Bank Holidays intervene).

"interim remedy ... before an application has been started, [the court] will give directions" (r 20.3(3))—If the court makes an order before the substantive application has been issued, it must give directions as to the filing of application forms and (perhaps) any other evidence. This provision enables the court (as appropriate) to give full case management directions (FPR 2010, rr 1.4 and 4.1).

Senior Courts Act 1981, s 33; County Court Act 1984, s 52 (r 20.3(4))—Section 33 of SCA 1981 (with parallel CCA 1984, s 52) deals with pre-action inspection, photographing and retention etc of property (s 33: not with 'disclosure' of anything as suggested). In this instance a freestanding application would have been made; but upon inspection etc the applicant may decide to proceed no further. The injunction will lapse, and the applicant may need to be wary about a costs order. Rule 20.3(4) countermands r 20.3(3) which, in the case of other pre-application interim orders, requires the court to give directions as to issue.

20.4 How to apply for an interim remedy

(1) The court may grant an interim remedy on an application made without notice if it appears to the court that there are good reasons for not giving notice.

(2) An application for an interim remedy must be supported by evidence, unless the court orders otherwise.

(3) If the applicant makes an application without giving notice, the evidence in support of the application must state the reasons why notice has not been given.

> (Part 4 lists general case-management powers of the court.)

> (Part 18 contains general rules about making an application.)

"without notice" applications and evidence in support (r 20.4(1) and (3))—Whereas application for an order is under FPR 2010, Pt 18 (see above), r 20.4 deals with:

(1) applications for an interim remedy "made without notice"; and
(2) the need to support any application "with evidence", a provision which is extended substantially by common law.

Without notice applications: order "desirable ... in the interests of justice" (r 20.3(2)(b))—Before issue of proceedings, the court may only grant an injunction on grounds of urgency or if "it is otherwise desirable to do so in the interests of justice", which will depend on the facts of each case, as explained in *National Commercial Bank Jamaica Ltd v Olint Corp Ltd (Jamaica)* [2009] 1 WLR 1405. Whether to permit the hearing of a without notice (ex parte) application is entirely a matter for the individual judge, but:

> "[A]*udi alterem partem* [hear the other party] is a salutary and important principle ... [A] judge should not entertain an application of which no notice has been given unless either giving notice would enable the defendant to take steps to defeat the purpose of the injunction (as in the case of a *Mareva* or *Anton Piller* order [ie freezing injunction or search order]) or there has been literally no time to give notice before the injunction is required to prevent the threatened wrongful act".

Cases in the latter category should be rare since "there will usually be no reason why the applicant should not have given shorter notice or even made a telephone call. Any notice is better than none." The High Court has expressed itself to be shocked at "the volume of spurious ex parte applications" in both the Family Division (*FZ v SZ and Others (Ancillary Relief: Conduct: Valuations)* [2011] 1 FLR 64) and the Queen's Bench Division (*O'Farrell v O'Farrell* [2013] 1 FLR 77): "a sort of lazy, laissez-faire practice or syndrome has grown up which says that provided the return date is soon and ... no material prejudice will be caused ... there is no harm in making the order ex parte. In my opinion this is absolutely wrong and turns principle on its head" (per Mostyn J in *FS v SZ*).

Applicant's duties to the court and other parties: full and fair disclosure—Any affidavit or witness statement in support of an application made without notice must provide the court with full and fair disclosure of the party's case and of the evidence to support it (see eg reference (for all interim remedy applications) in PD20A, para 3.3). The applicant is asking the court to exercise what originates in an equitable jurisdiction. The applicant therefore owes to the court (and to the party to be subject to any order) a duty to provide to the court not only evidence in support of, but any with information adverse to, his case (*R v Kensington Income Tax Commissioners, ex p Princess Edmond de Polignac* [1917] KB 486 at [514]). If material disclosure is not provided the court may discharge the injunction in any event, with adverse orders for costs.

Evidence in support of an application—Applications for search orders and freezing injunctions must be supported by affidavit evidence (FPR PD20A, para 3.1), whereas other applications should be supported by witness statement with statement of truth (FPR PD20A, para 3.2: if in doubt file affidavit evidence).

20.5 Interim injunction to cease if application is stayed

If –

    (a) the court has granted an interim injunction$^{(GL)}$ other than a freezing injunction$^{(GL)}$; and

(b) the application is stayed^(GL) other than by agreement between the parties,

the interim injunction^(GL) will be set aside^(GL) unless the court orders that it should continue to have effect even though the application is stayed^(GL).

"the court has granted an injunction" (r 20.5(a))—This wording logically refers to any injunction. Thus, where the injunction only is the intent of the proceedings, if the application is taken no further once the order is made, there is a real possibility that, unless application (at further cost) is made to continue the order, it may be set aside under this provision.

"application"—An application may be in the form of an "application form" (ie the proceedings as a whole) or "application notice" (ie the FPR Pt 18 application for the injunction).

Chapter 2
Security for Costs

20.6 Security for costs

(1) A respondent to any application may apply under this Chapter of this Part for security for costs of the proceedings.

> (Part 4 provides for the court to order payment of sums into court in other circumstances.)

(2) An application for security for costs must be supported by written evidence.

(3) Where the court makes an order for security for costs, it will –

    (a) determine the amount of security; and

    (b) direct –

        (i) the manner in which; and

        (ii) the time within which,

    the security must be given.

Defined terms—"court": r 2.3(1).

Application for security for costs—Such an order will be very rare in family proceedings (especially below the Court of Appeal: in *Charman v Charman (No 3)* [2007] 1 FLR 1237, CA the wife applied for security to be given by the appellant husband against stay obtained by him in respect of £28m of a £40m lump sum order. Sir Mark Potter P ordered security for costs pending the hearing under CPR 1998, r 25.13(2)(a) where the husband was resident out of the jurisdiction (and not in a Brussels or Lugano Contracting State). Application for an order will be by the FPR 2010, Pt 18 procedure.

20.7 Conditions to be satisfied

(1) The court may make an order for security for costs under rule 20.6 if –

    (a) it is satisfied, having regard to all the circumstances of the case, that it is just to make such an order; and

    (b) either –

        (i) one or more of the conditions in paragraph (2) applies; or

        (ii) an enactment permits the court to require security for costs.

(2) The conditions are –

    (a) the applicant is –

        (i) resident out of the jurisdiction; but

        (ii) not resident in a Brussels Contracting State, a State bound by the Lugano Convention, a State bound by the 2007 Hague Convention which is an EEA State, a Regulation State or a Maintenance Regulation State, as defined in section 1(3) of the Civil Jurisdiction and Judgments Act 1982, or a Member State bound by the Council Regulation;

(b) the applicant has changed address since the application was started with a view to evading the consequences of the litigation;

(c) the applicant failed to give an address in the application form, or gave an incorrect address in that form;

(d) the applicant has taken steps in relation to the applicant's assets that would make it difficult to enforce an order for costs against the applicant.

(3) The court may not make an order for security for costs under rule 20.6 in relation to the costs of proceedings under the 1980 Hague Convention.

(Rule 4.4 allows the court to strike out$^{(GL)}$ a statement of case.)

("EEA State" is defined in Schedule 1 to the Interpretation Act 1978.)

Amendments—SI 2011/1328; SI 2012/679; SI 2012/2806.

Security for costs in family proceedings—This rule has been taken directly from CPR 1998, Pt 25, which relates to a jurisdiction where costs orders are the rule, whereas in family proceedings costs are the exception especially in relation to proceedings which might most likely attract a r 20.7 order, namely financial remedy proceedings (ie proceedings covered by FPR 2010, r 28.3(4)–(7)). The rule makes no attempt to address these factors which are likely to provide a substantial stumbling block at the r 20.7(1)(a) stage: if it is unlikely that an order for costs will follow then it cannot be "just to make ... an order" for security for costs.

20.8 Security for costs of an appeal

The court may order security for costs of an appeal against –

(a) an appellant;

(b) a respondent who also appeals,

on the same grounds as it may order security for costs against an applicant under this Part.

Practice Direction 20A – Interim Remedies

This Practice Direction supplements FPR Part 20

Scope and jurisdiction

1.1 This Practice Direction does not apply to an order under section 48 (Powers to assist in discovery of children who may be in need of emergency protection), section 50 (Recovery of abducted children, etc.) of the Children Act 1989 or section 33(Power to order disclosure of child's whereabouts) or section 34 (Power to order recovery of child) of the Family Law Act 1986.

1.2 High Court Judges and any other judge duly authorised may grant 'search orders' and 'freezing injunctions' (see rules 20.2(1)(h) and 20.2(1)(f)).

1.3 In a case in the High Court, district judges have the power to grant injunctions –

(a) by consent;

(b) in connection with charging orders and appointments of receivers;

(c) in aid of execution of judgments.

1.4 In any other case any judge who has jurisdiction to conduct the hearing of the proceedings has the power to grant an injunction in those proceedings.

1.5 A district judge has the power to vary or discharge an injunction granted by any judge with the consent of all the parties.

Making an application

2.1 The application notice must state –

   (a)   the order sought; and
   (b)   the date, time and place of the hearing.

2.2 The application notice and evidence in support must be served as soon as practicable after issue and in any event not less than 7 days before the court is due to hear the application unless the court directs otherwise.

2.3 Where the court is to serve, sufficient copies of the application notice and evidence in support for the court and for each respondent should be filed for issue and service.

2.4 Whenever possible a draft of the order sought should be filed with the application notice and an electronic version of the draft should also be available to the court in a format compatible with the word processing software used by the court and on such storage medium as shall be agreed by the court. This will enable the court officer to arrange for any amendments to be incorporated and for the speedy preparation and sealing of the order.

Evidence

3.1 Applications for search orders and freezing injunctions must be supported by affidavit evidence.

3.2 Applications for other interim injunctions must be supported by evidence set out in either –

   (a)   a witness statement; or
   (b)   the application notice provided that it is verified by a statement of truth,

unless the court, an Act, a rule in the FPR or a practice direction requires evidence by affidavit.

3.3 The evidence must set out the facts on which the applicant relies for the application being made against the respondent, including all material facts of which the court should be made aware.

3.4 Where an application is made without notice to the respondent, the evidence must also set out why notice was not given.

> (See Part 22 and the practice direction that supplements it for information about evidence.)

Urgent applications and applications without notice

4.1 These fall into two categories –

   (a)   applications where an application in proceedings has already been issued; and
   (b)   applications where an application in proceedings has not yet been issued,

and, in both cases, where notice of the application has not been given to the respondent.

4.2 These applications are normally dealt with at a court hearing but cases of extreme urgency may be dealt with by telephone.

4.3 In relation to applications dealt with at a court hearing after issue of an application form –

(a) the application notice, evidence in support and a draft order (as in paragraph 2.4) should be filed with the court two hours before the hearing wherever possible;

(b) if an application is made before the application notice has been issued, a draft order (as in paragraph 2.4) should be provided at the hearing, and the application notice and evidence in support must be filed with the court on the same or next working day or as ordered by the court; and

(c) except in cases where it is essential that the respondent must not be aware of the application, the applicant should take steps to notify the respondent informally of the application.

4.4 In relation to applications made before the issue of an application –

(a) in addition to the provisions set out at paragraph 4.3, unless the court orders otherwise, either the applicant must undertake to the court to issue an application notice immediately or the court will give directions for the commencement of the application (see rule 20.3(3));

(b) where possible the application should be served with the order for the injunction;

(c) an order made before the issue of an application should state in the title after the names of the applicant and respondent 'the Applicant and Respondent in Intended Proceedings'.

4.5 In relation to applications made outside normal working hours –

(a) the applicant should either –

(i) telephone the Royal Courts of Justice on 020 7947 6000 to be put in contact with the clerk to the appropriate duty judge in the High Court (or the appropriate area Circuit Judge where known); or

(ii) telephone the Urgent Court Business Officer of the appropriate Circuit who will contact the local duty judge;

(b) where the facility is available it is likely that the judge will require a draft order to be faxed to him;

(c) the application notice and evidence in support must be filed with the court on the same or next working day or as ordered, together with two copies of the order for sealing;

(d) injunctions will be heard by telephone only where the applicant is acting by counsel or solicitors.

Orders for injunctions

5.1 Any order for an injunction, unless the court orders otherwise, must contain –

(a) an undertaking by the applicant to the court to pay any damages which the respondent sustains which the court considers the applicant should pay;

(b) if the order is made without notice to any other party, an undertaking by the applicant to the court to serve on the respondent the application notice, evidence in support and any order made as soon as practicable;

(c) if the order is made without notice to any other party, a return date for a further hearing at which the other party can be present;

(d) if the order is made before filing the application notice, an undertaking to file and pay the appropriate fee on the same or next working day; and

(e) if the order is made before issue of an application in proceedings –

(i) an undertaking to issue and pay the appropriate fee on the same or next working day; or

(ii) directions for the commencement of the application.

5.2 When the court makes an order for an injunction, it should consider whether to require an undertaking by the applicant to pay any damages sustained by a person other than the respondent, including another party to the proceedings or any other person who may suffer loss as a consequence of the order.

5.3 An order for an injunction made in the presence of all parties to be bound by it or made at a hearing of which they have had notice, may state that it is effective until final hearing or further order.

5.4 Any order for an injunction must set out clearly what the respondent must do or not do.

SEARCH ORDERS

Orders for the preservation of evidence and property

6.1 The following provisions apply to search orders in addition to those listed above.

The Supervising Solicitor

6.2 The Supervising Solicitor must be experienced in the operation of search orders. A Supervising Solicitor may be contacted either through the Law Society or, for the London area, through the London Solicitors Litigation Association.

Evidence

6.3
  (1) The affidavit must state the name, firm and its address, and experience of the Supervising Solicitor, also the address of the premises and whether it is a private or business address.
  (2) The affidavit must disclose very fully the reason the order is sought, including the probability that relevant material would disappear if the order were not made.

Service

6.4
  (1) The order must be served personally by the Supervising Solicitor, unless the court directs otherwise, and must be accompanied by the evidence in support and any documents capable of being copied.
  (2) Confidential exhibits need not be served but they must be made available for inspection by the respondent in the presence of the applicant's solicitors while the order is carried out and afterwards be retained by the respondent's solicitors on their undertaking not to permit the respondent –
       (a) to see them or copies of them except in their presence; and
       (b) to make or take away any note or record of them.
  (3) The Supervising Solicitor may be accompanied only by the persons mentioned in the order.
  (4) The Supervising Solicitor must explain the terms and effect of the order to the respondent in everyday language and advise the respondent –
       (a) of the respondent's right to take legal advice, and to apply to vary or discharge the order; and
       (b) that the respondent may be entitled to avail himself of –
            (i)   legal professional privilege; and

    (ii) the privilege against self-incrimination.

(5) Where the Supervising Solicitor is a man and the respondent is likely to be an unaccompanied woman, at least one other person named in the order must be a woman and must accompany the Supervising Solicitor.

(6) The order may only be served between 9.30 a.m. and 5.30 p.m. Monday to Friday unless the court directs otherwise.

Search and custody of materials

6.5

(1) No material shall be removed unless clearly covered by the terms of the order.

(2) The premises must not be searched and no items shall be removed from them except in the presence of the respondent or a person who appears to be a responsible employee of the respondent.

(3) Where copies of documents are sought, the documents should be retained for no more than 2 days before return to the owner.

(4) Where material in dispute is removed pending hearing, the applicant's solicitors should place it in the custody of the respondent's solicitors on their undertaking to retain it in safekeeping and to produce it to the court when required.

(5) In appropriate cases the applicant should insure the material retained in the respondent's solicitors' custody.

(6) The Supervising Solicitor must make a list of all material removed from the premises and supply a copy of the list to the respondent.

(7) No material shall be removed from the premises until the respondent has had reasonable time to check the list.

(8) If any of the listed items exists only in computer readable form, the respondent must immediately give the applicant's solicitors effective access to the computers, with all necessary passwords, to enable them to be searched, and cause the listed items to be printed out.

(9) The applicant must take all reasonable steps to ensure that no damage is done to any computer or data.

(10) The applicant and his representatives may not themselves search the respondent's computers unless they have sufficient expertise to do so without damaging the respondent's system;

(11) the Supervising Solicitor shall provide a report on the carrying out of the order to the applicant's solicitors.

(12) As soon as the report is received the applicant's solicitors shall –

(a) serve a copy of it on the respondent; and

(b) file a copy of it with the court.

(13) Where the Supervising Solicitor is satisfied that full compliance with paragraph 6.5(7) and (8) above is impracticable, that Solicitor may permit the search to proceed and items to be removed without compliance with the impracticable requirements.

General

6.6 The Supervising Solicitor must not be an employee or member of the applicant's firm of solicitors.

6.7 If the court orders that the order need not be served by the Supervising Solicitor, the reason for so ordering must be set out in the order.

6.8 The search order must not be carried out at the same time as a police search warrant.

6.9 There is no privilege against self incrimination in proceedings in which a court is hearing an application for an order under Part 4 or 5 of the Children Act 1989 (see section 98 of the Children Act 1989).

Delivery up orders

7.1 The following provision applies to orders, other than search orders, for delivery up or preservation of evidence or property where it is likely that such an order will be executed at the premises of the respondent or a third party.

7.2 In such cases the court will consider whether to include in the order for the benefit or protection of the parties similar provisions to those specified above in relation to injunctions and search orders.

Injunctions against third parties

8.1 The following provision applies to orders which will affect a person other than the applicant or respondent, who –

    (a)   did not attend the hearing at which the order was made; and

    (b)   is served with the order.

8.2 Where such a person served with the order requests –

    (a)   a copy of any materials read by the court, including material prepared after the hearing at the direction of the court or in compliance with the order; or

    (b)   a note of the hearing,

the applicant, or the applicant's legal representative, must comply promptly with the request, unless the court directs otherwise.

PART 21
MISCELLANEOUS RULES ABOUT DISCLOSURE AND INSPECTION OF DOCUMENTS

CONTENTS OF THIS PART

Disclosure and inspection—FPR 2010, Pt 21 deals with three distinct aspects of disclosure:

(1)   Disclosure and inspection of documents (r 21.1)
(2)   Disclosure of documents ordered against a third party (r 21.2)
(3)   Public interest immunity (r 21.3).

Discovery and disclosure—Disclosure of information and of documents (otherwise "discovery" as explained in *Imerman v Tchenguiz and Others* [2010] 2 FLR 814 at [25]) are central to many aspects of family litigation and a number of the Parts of FPR 2010 have their own rules that may or may not conflict with FPR 2010, Pt 21, according to how r 21.1(1) is read (see annotations to r 21.1, below). Despite the importance of disclosure of information in family proceedings (e g duty of full disclosure derived from the terms of MCA 1973 s 25(1)) as pointed out in *Imerman v Tchenguiz*, there is no formal procedure under FPR 2010 for seeking disclosure of information in family proceedings. FPR 2010, r 4.1(3)(b) suggests that as part of their case management powers the courts can make orders for "disclosure and inspection".

Continuing duty of disclosure—CPR 1998, r 31.11 stresses the common law rule that "disclosure continues until the proceedings are concluded" (and see *Vernon v Bosley (No 2)* [1998] 1 FLR 304). This duty applies in family proceedings (Thorpe LJ considered it might extend – in *Burns v Burns* [2004] EWCA Civ 1258 – as a "duty of candour" in financial remedy cases, to a period of time after the making of the order). Despite the absence of r 31.11 from FPR 2010, it represents the common law on disclosure (see per Stuart Smith LJ in *Vernon v Bosley*). As is well known, there is a duty of disclosure of evidence generally (documents and information) in family proceedings up to trial, and to appeal.

Subsequent use of disclosed documents—In *Clibbery v Allan* [2002] 1 FLR 565, the Court of Appeal explained when disclosed documents released in family proceedings could be released publicly. In the context of civil proceedings generally, the issue of disclosed documents (and the former implied undertaking as to non-disclosure) is dealt with in CPR 1998, r 31.22: a party to proceedings may only use a document "for the purpose of the proceedings" except where it has been read out in court, the court gives permission or the parties agree to its release (CPR 1998, r 31.22(1)). Beyond this, the court can restrict or prohibit the use of a document (CPR 1998, r 31.22(2)). See also, *HMRC v Charman and Charman* [2012] 2 FLR 1119.

21.1 Interpretation

(1) A party discloses a document by stating that the document exists or has existed.

(2) Inspection of a document occurs when a party is permitted to inspect a document disclosed by another person.

(3) For the purposes of disclosure and inspection –

    (a) "document" means anything in which information of any description is recorded; and

    (b) "copy" in relation to a document, means anything onto which information recorded in the document has been copied, by whatever means and whether directly or indirectly.

"Discovery" and disclosure—In *Imerman v Tchenguiz and Others* [2010] 2 FLR 814, the Court of Appeal explained the terms "discovery" and "disclosure" in financial remedy proceedings. The court adopted "terminology" (at [25]) as follows (emphasis provided by the court):

- the disclosure of relevant facts and matters
- the discovery of relevant documents; and
- the evidence required to establish the relevant facts.

In *Imerman* at [26] the court considered *Livesey (formerly Jenkins) v Jenkins* [1985] FLR 813 and pointed out that the failure to disclose was not failure in respect of a document: "it was the fact of her intended remarriage, not some failure to give proper discovery". This position is broadly in line with financial remedy proceedings under the 2010 Rules. It will be appreciated that disclosure in, for example, financial remedy proceedings (FPR 2010, rr 9.14(5)(c) and 9.15(2)) is altogether different from the rule in r 21.1, which is a duty only in relation to documents and information.

Disclosure, inspection and privilege—As a matter of law, disclosure only involves the informing of other parties of the existence of documents (ie not other information) that are in the possession of the discloser. That disclosure gives a right to the party to whom disclosure is given to seek inspection (r 21.1(2)) and, subject to any restrictions on inspection, the documents may ultimately be produced in evidence at a hearing. A right of inspection gives a balancing right to the discloser, in appropriate circumstances (mostly dealt with under FPR 2010, r 21.3), to withhold or restrict disclosure because of:

(1) Privilege – the right to privilege from inspection (generally called privilege from disclosure);

(2) Public interest immunity – the right to claim that a document is immune from inspection; or

(3) Confidentiality – the right to claim that a document need not be produced for inspection because it is confidential.

Confidentiality—Confidentiality gives a right to a private claim that documents, information or other evidence are immune from being produced as evidence; but this right may yield to the right of an opposing party to a fair trial where the right to confidentiality comes into conflict with the principle (which protects a fair trial) that all relevant evidence should be available to the court.

Privilege—By contrast, privilege establishes an unassailable right, so that if a request for disclosure of a document or other evidence (e g the substance of a party's legal advice) comes into conflict with the right to a fair trial, privilege cannot be overridden – unless waived or lost (e g because of fraud or dishonesty).

PART III

The main relevant forms of privilege can be categorised as follows:

(1) legal professional privilege (LPP) – considered here;
(2) self-incrimination privilege – briefly considered here;
(3) public interest immunity – considered under FPR 2010, r 21.3;
(4) without prejudice privilege: privilege only because the correspondence cannot be unilaterally disclosed (subject to various exceptions);
(5) mediation privilege: see FPR 2010, Pt 3.

Public interest immunity—Public interest immunity is a matter of public policy claimed by or on behalf of a public body (e g local authority, police or health authority). It is connoted with privilege to the extent that it involves excluding from production and disclosure otherwise admissible documents and with confidentiality because of the confidential nature of many documents and other evidence (for example, see *D v National Society for the Prevention of Cruelty to Children* (1977) FLR Rep 181) that might attract immunity.

Legal professional privilege: a relationship of confidence—LPP "arises out of a relationship of confidence between lawyer and client" (*Three Rivers District Council v Bank of England (No 6)* [2005] 1 AC 610 at [24]). It enables a client to make a "clean breast" (*Anderson v Bank of British Columbia* (1876) 2 ChD 644, at [649]) of his or her affairs to a legal adviser. What distinguishes the lawyer's advice from other advice he or she might give and what gives it the cloak of privilege is that the advice that is given in a "relevant legal context" (*Balabel v Air India* [1988] Ch 317, CA).

Legal professional privilege: an absolute right—Legal professional privilege comprises two privileges: legal advice privilege and litigation privilege. It covers communications between lawyers and their clients where advice in a "relevant legal context" is given; litigation privilege covers documents brought into being for the purpose of litigation or anticipated litigation. Legal professional privilege represents an individual's right, in a society based on the rule of law, to have advice given to them, and the information on which that advice is based, kept confidential. This is so "notwithstanding that as a result cases may sometimes have to be decided in ignorance of relevant probative material" (*Three Rivers (No 6)*, above, at [34]). Legal professional privilege, once established, is absolute (*R v Derby Magistrates' Court ex parte B* [1996] 1 FLR 513, HL). It cannot be a matter for judicial discretion, or a balancing exercise, as to whether or not privilege is overridden (see, for example, *R (Morgan Grenfell & Co Ltd) v Special Commissioner of Income Tax and anor* [2003] 1 AC 563: legal professional privilege "does not involve [any] balancing of interests. It is absolute and is based not merely upon the general right to privacy but also upon the right to access to justice" (at [7]).

Self-incrimination privilege—Any documents that might incriminate a person are exempt from disclosure, unless any specific amnesty is provided for (e g CA 1989, s 98(1) provides a form of amnesty). This is a qualified right (and see European Convention for the Protection of Human Rights, Art 8 and for example *Brown v Stott* [2003] 1 AC 681; *R v K* [2010] 1 FLR 807). It is categorised with privilege, here, since it consists of the right to withhold otherwise relevant information from the court; but the privilege will more usually apply to oral, than to documentary, evidence.

Waiver of privilege—Privilege can be waived, expressly or impliedly (see, for example, *Re D (Care Proceedings: Legal Privilege)* [2011] 2 FLR 1183, where a mother in care proceedings had, by referring to part of the documents and notes that arose from an interview with her lawyers, impliedly waived privilege in respect of the rest). Without prejudice privilege is joint and can only be waived by both parties.

Without prejudice privilege—Without prejudice privilege is the right of a party to a negotiation to withhold information from the court if the negotiation becomes the subject of litigation. The law permits privacy to certain otherwise admissible documents because the right of the private individual to withhold them is greater than it is just for the information or documents to be disclosed.

Justification for without prejudice privilege—Justification for the privilege is based on:

(1) Public policy: "that parties should be encouraged so far as possible to settle their disputes without resort to litigation and should not be discouraged by the knowledge that anything that is said … may be used to their prejudice in the course of the proceedings" (*Cutts v Head* [1984] Ch 290, at [306]).
(2) Contract: the privilege is a joint privilege whose roots are in contract: "an implied agreement of the parties themselves that communications in the course of their negotiations should not be admissible in evidence if, despite their negotiations, a contested hearing ensues" (*Oceanbulk Shipping & Trading SA v TMT Asia Ltd and ors* [2011] 1 AC 662).

In *Unilever PLC v The Procter & Gamble Company* [2000] 1 WLR 2436 (at [24]) Robert Walker LJ lists seven of the "most important instances" where the privilege may be denied.

Mediation or ADR privilege—The *Unilever* list (above) concludes with "(8) In matrimonial cases there has developed what is now a distinct privilege extending to communications received in confidence with a view to matrimonial conciliation [now mediation or dispute resolution]: see *Re D (Minors) (Conciliation: Disclosure of Information)* [1993] 1 FLR 932, where Sir Thomas Bingham MR thought it not … fruitful to debate the relationship of this privilege with the more familiar head of 'without prejudice' privilege. That its underlying rationale is similar, and that it developed by way of analogy with 'without prejudice' privilege, seems clear. But both Lord Hailsham and Lord Simon in *D v National Society for the Prevention of Cruelty to Children* (1977) FLR Rep 181 at [602], [610] regarded it as having developed into a new category of privilege based on the public interest in the stability of marriage."

Mediation and constructing the agreement—Where a case is settled following mediation and the agreement is accepted in principle, but detail is not agreed the *Oceanbulk* exception may be applicable to resolve final terms. If the agreement precedes the presentation of a matrimonial or civil partnership order application it may be possible to file a freestanding application under the FPR 2010, Pt 19 procedure as a basis for seeking the court's construction of the terms of the agreement (e g FPR PD19A).

Disclosure and inspection of electronic documents—CPR 1998, r 31.4 and FPR 2010, r 21(3)(a) define "document" as "anything in which anything of any description is recorded". CPR PD31B, in relation to proceedings that started on or after 1 October 2010, sets out what amounts to a protocol for disclosure and inspection of electronic documents (see note under CPR 1998, r 31.4). Insofar as this PD represents the common law, it applies also to proceedings under FPR 2010.

21.2 Orders for disclosure against a person not a party

(1) This rule applies where an application is made to the court under any Act for disclosure by a person who is not a party to the proceedings.

(2) The application –

  (a) may be made without notice; and
  (b) must be supported by evidence.

(3) The court may make an order under this rule only where disclosure is necessary in order to dispose fairly of the proceedings or to save costs.

(4) An order under this rule must –

  (a) specify the documents or the classes of documents which the respondent must disclose; and
  (b) require the respondent, when making disclosure, to specify any of those documents –
    (i) which are no longer in the respondent's control; or
    (ii) in respect of which the respondent claims a right or duty to withhold inspection.

(5) Such an order may –

  (a) require the respondent to indicate what has happened to any documents which are no longer in the respondent's control; and
  (b) specify the time and place for disclosure and inspection.

(6) An order under this rule must not compel a person to produce any document which that person could not be compelled to produce at the final hearing.

(7) This rule does not limit any other power which the court may have to order disclosure against a person who is not a party to proceedings.

  (Rule 35.3 contains provisions in relation to the disclosure and inspection of evidence arising out of mediation of cross-border disputes.)

Disclosure against a third party—Disclosure against a third party can occur in the following ways:

(1) *SCA 1981, s 34* Section 34 enables the court on a pre-application basis to order disclosure of documents (FPR 2010, r 20.2(1)(i)).

(2) *Disclosure against a person not a party (r 21.2)* The application is made in the proceedings (in Form D11 by the Pt 18 procedure). The basis for an application is that disclosure "is necessary in

order to dispose fairly of the proceedings or to save costs" (r 21.2(3)). This procedure partly replaces the former inspection appointment in ancillary relief proceedings under FPR 1991, r 2.62(7).

(3) *Witness summons*   A witness summons under r 24.2(1)(b) and (4).

Production of documents, production appointment—Rule 21.2 applies to all family proceedings (although rr 21.2(2) and 24.2(1) (witness summons) in effect replace the old ancillary relief production appointment procedure: the summons can require the proposed witness to produce documents and seek a prehearing inspection appointment: see r 24.3(2)(c)). The rule restricts disclosure (ie production) of documents (other evidence is dealt with under FPR 2010, Pt 24) from third parties. It is limited to production of documents (a) that are necessary to dispose fairly of the case (r 21.2(3)) and (b) that could have been required to be produced at a final hearing (r 21.2(6)).

Restrictions on disclosure—Rule 21.2(6) (c f r 24.2(5)) prevents disclosure being ordered against a third party where he or she could not be compelled to produce a document at the final hearing (e g because it is covered by confidentiality or public interest immunity). Similar principles will then arise as are considered at r 21.3 (below): the need for evidence to be before the court to ensure a fair trial balanced against the private interests of the third party or of the relevance of the evidence to the issues before the court.

Court restriction on prohibition or use of a document—CPR 1998, r 31.22(2) enables the court to restrict or prohibit the use of a document or other public disclosure of it where it has been used in public proceedings. In the light of the increased openness of family courts, it may be thought that this rule also represents the common law (see *Clibbery v Allan* [2002] 1 FLR 565) and that family courts may regard themselves as able to deal with applications to release documents on analogy with CPR 1998, r 31.22(2). Application is made to the court by the third party who must then justify the overriding of the privacy that otherwise attaches to a document (e g *HMRC v Charman and Charman* [2012] 2 FLR 1119).

MARACS and disclosure—Subject to what is said under FPR 2010, rr 12.12 and 21.3 and FLA 1996, s 63A, application may be made under this rule or by witness summons for disclosure of documents and information from multi-agency risk assessment conferences (MARACs) by their chair (see para 8 of the guidance of December 2011: *MARACs and Disclosure into Court Proceedings* in Part V). Disclosure will only be ordered against MARACs if it is necessary to dispose fairly of the case (r 21.2(3)). In deciding whether to seek public interest immunity (under FPR 2010, r 21.3) or otherwise to oppose disclosure (r 21.2), the committee will need to take a view on the substance of the information they have and the purpose of its being kept from disclosure. They may apply to seek court guidance within the terms of r 21.3(1).

Procedure—Application is by the Pt 18 procedure. The application must be supported by evidence as to why the documents are required and must specify what documents the court is being asked to order the third party to produce (r 21.2(4)).

21.3 Claim to withhold inspection or disclosure of a document

(1) A person may apply, without notice, for an order permitting that person to withhold disclosure of a document on the ground that disclosure would damage the public interest.

(2) Unless the court otherwise orders, an order of the court under paragraph (1) –

(a)   must not be served on any other person; and

(b)   must not be open to inspection by any other person.

(3) A person who wishes to claim a right or a duty to withhold inspection of a document, or part of a document, must state in writing –

(a)   the right or duty claimed; and

(b)   the grounds on which that right or duty is claimed.

(4) The statement referred to in paragraph (3) must be made to the person wishing to inspect the document.

(5) A party may apply to the court to decide whether a claim made under paragraph (3) should be upheld.

(6) Where the court is deciding an application under paragraph (1) or (5) it may –

(a)   require the person seeking to withhold disclosure or inspection of a document to produce that document to the court; and

(b)   invite any person, whether or not a party, to make representations.

(7)   An application under paragraph (1) or (5) must be supported by evidence.

(8)   This Part does not affect any rule of law which permits or requires a document to be withheld from disclosure or inspection on the ground that its disclosure or inspection would damage the public interest.

Withholding inspection or disclosure—This rule covers four separate aspects of restriction of production or disclosure:

(1)   Public interest immunity (r 21.3(1))
(2)   Privilege: "a right … to withhold inspection" (r 21.3(3)–(5))
(3)   Confidentiality: a "duty to withhold inspection" (r 21.3(3)–(5))
(4)   Public policy: the right to withhold evidence improperly obtained (e g *Imerman v Tchenguiz and Others* [2010] 2 FLR 814).

Disclosure, production of evidence and a fair trial—Rule 21.3 enables the court to restrict disclosure on one or more of the above bases. Trial of any issue before the court will be based on the requirement that all relevant evidence is adduced to ensure a fair trial. Any restriction of disclosure will have to be justified by the applicant (*Re D (Minors) (Adoption Reports: Confidentiality)* [1995] 2 FLR 687, CA), upon whom the burden to establish restriction is heavy (*Re B (Disclosure to Other Parties)* [2001] 2 FLR 1017 at [89]).

Public interest immunity—In *D v National Society for the Prevention of Cruelty to Children* (1977) FLR Rep 181 the House of Lords held that where documents were sought to be withheld from disclosure as a matter of public interest, then competing public interests must be balanced in each case: a public interest in the administration of justice as against the principle that, in general, all relevant documents should be disclosed. The presumption in favour of disclosure will predominate (*Re D (Minors) (Adoption Reports: Confidentiality)* [1995] 2 FLR 687, CA). The onus is on the party seeking it to prove that inspection of a document should be withheld and to justify any public interest immunity from production that is claimed.

Public interest immunity claim by third party—Similar principles as to suppression of evidence apply where public interest immunity is claimed by a third party against whom production is claimed and where that third party claims public interest immunity (see *P v P* [2012] EWHC 1733 (Fam) under FPR 2010, r 21.2).

Privilege—See under FPR 2010, r 21.1, above.

Confidentiality—Where confidentiality (as distinct from privilege) is claimed, private interests and a right to privacy (ECHR 1950, Art 8) may need to be balanced against the rule that disclosure should normally be ordered in the interests of a fair trial (Art 6(1)): *A Local Authority v A* [2010] 2 FLR 1757; *Re J (A Child: Disclosure)* [2012] EWCA Civ 1204.

Public policy—Public policy may enable a party to ask the court to exclude evidence because it has been wrongly obtained (e g *Lifely v Lifely* [2008] EWCA Civ 904 and *Imerman v Tchenguiz and Others* [2010] 2 FLR 814). Whether to exclude evidence may depend on weighing one party's Art 6 right to a fair trial with all the available evidence to the court, against the other party's Art 8 right to respect for privacy in respect of the illegally obtained material (see *Tchenguiz v Imerman* at [176]).

Partial disclosure—The right to a fair trial on which production of evidence is predicated is not necessarily denied where only partial disclosure is permitted by the court (*Re B (Disclosure to Other Parties)* [2001] 2 FLR 1017; *Brown v Stott* [2003] 1 AC 681).

Procedure—

(1)   *Public interest immunity*   Application can be without notice in the case of highly sensitive material; but normally would be by Pt 18 application by the public body seeking restriction of production. The court may proceed and restrict disclosure on its own initiative (*Duncan v Cammell Laird* [1942] AC 624 at [641]).
(2)   *Privilege and confidentiality*   Application is made in the proceedings in question by the Pt 18 procedure by the person who seeks disclosure, after he has been notified that a party asserts the right or the duty not to produce documents.

"supported by evidence" (r 21.3(7))—In *West London Pipeline and Storage Ltd v Total UK Ltd* [2008] EWHC 1729, Beatson J provides guidance as to the content of the affidavit in reply to an application to determine whether privilege applies.

Guidance as to grounds for restricting disclosure—In *West London Pipeline and Storage Ltd v Total UK Ltd* (above), Beatson J summarises the law on overriding privilege and on the factors to be considered by the court on an application.

Public interest immunity and special advocate—In *A Chief Constable v YK and Others* [2011] 1 FLR 1493, Sir Nicholas Wall P considered public interest immunity in the context of making a forced marriage protection order. He had no hesitation in granting immunity to the documents concerned, but refused to appoint a special advocate to be involved in the application.

Practice Direction 21A – Disclosure and Inspection

This Practice Direction supplements FPR Part 21

CHAPTER 1
ORDERS FOR DISCLOSURE AND INSPECTION OF DOCUMENTS

Interpretation

1.1 A party discloses a document by stating that the document exists or has existed. Inspection occurs when a party is permitted to inspect a document disclosed by another party.

1.2 For the purposes of disclosure and inspection in family proceedings –

"document" means anything in which information of any description is recorded and any copy of a document which contains a modification, obliteration or other marking or feature shall be treated as a separate document; and

"copy", in relation to a document, means anything on which information recorded in the document has been copied, by whatever means and whether directly or indirectly.

Types of order for disclosure in family proceedings

2.1 In family proceedings other than proceedings for a financial remedy, where the court orders disclosure, the normal order will be for disclosure by each party setting out, in a list or questionnaire, the documents material to the proceedings, of the existence of which that party is aware and which are or have been in that party's control. This process is known as "standard disclosure".

2.2 In proceedings for a financial remedy, the process of disclosure is staged. First, Form E (the financial statement referred to in rule 9.14(1)) is served together with the documents which are required to be attached to it. The second stage occurs by the parties requesting (further) disclosure of each other by a questionnaire served before the first appointment; the questionnaire can request both information and documents. With the court's permission, a further questionnaire can be served later in the proceedings.

2.3 In matrimonial and civil partnership proceedings, under rule 7.15, the court – either on its own initiative or on the application of the other party – may order a party to clarify any matter which is in dispute in the proceedings or give additional information in relation to any such matter, whether or not the matter is contained in or referred to in the application or in the answer.

2.4 In any family proceedings, the court may order "specific disclosure", which is an order that a party must –

(a) disclose documents or classes of documents specified in the order;

(b) carry out a search to the extent stated in the order; or

(c) disclose any documents located as a result of that search.

PART 22
EVIDENCE

CONTENTS OF THIS PART

Chapter 1
General Rules

Chapter 2
Rules Applying Only to Particular Proceedings

Practice Direction 22A –

Evidence and the overriding objective: identification of issues—Procedural rules that deal with evidence must be considered with the overriding objective (FPR 2010, r 1.1) in mind. Among other things, this objective stresses the need to deal with a case "in ways which are proportionate to ... the complexity of the issues", to identifying those issues at an early stage and to "deciding promptly which issues need full investigation" (FPR 2010, rr 1.1(2)(b) and 1.4(2)(b)(i),(c)(i)). Definition of issues is at the heart of economy in preparation of a case, to effective case management and to clarity as to relevance of evidence.

Examination of witnesses—The giving of evidence by witnesses and their examination in court arises in the following way in FPR 2010:

- The evidence of a witness is to be oral at a final hearing, in writing "at any other hearing" (r 22.2(1))
- Where a witness statement has been served, that witness must be available at the final hearing (22.6(1)), subject to hearsay rules (rr 23.2–23.4)
- Evidence-in-chief: a witness statement is to stand as that witness' evidence-in-chief (r 22.6(2))
- Cross-examination, which may be limited (r 22.1(4))

Evidence at hearings—Hearings are final and "other" (mostly interim hearings under the FPR 2010, Pt 18 procedure): e g FPR 2010, r 22.2(1). FPR 2010 aims to provide a consistent set of evidence rules for these hearings, which will be the culmination of the process for:

(1) Originating processes – a variety of different originating applications;
(2) Pt 19 procedure cases – for an undefined smaller group of Pt 19 "alternative" applications; and
(3) Pt 18 interim procedure cases – for "other", mostly interim, hearings under the Pt 18 procedure.

The "other" hearings are dealt with on written evidence (subject to permission to cross-examine: r 22.8).

Pervasive and particular procedures—The evidence rules in FPR 2010, Pts 21–25 are pervasive to all types of proceedings (save where excluded by rule, PD or implication). Many of the various types of originating application and FPR 2010, Pts 18 and 19 have their own particular procedures internal to each Part to deal with evidence specific to the procedure's demands (see further under FPR 2010, r 22.5 below).

Chapter 1
General Rules

22.1 Power of court to control evidence

(1) The court may control the evidence by giving directions as to –

(a)   the issues on which it requires evidence;
(b)   the nature of the evidence which it requires to decide those issues; and
(c)   the way in which the evidence is to be placed before the court.

(2) The court may use its power under this rule to exclude evidence that would otherwise be admissible.

(3) The court may permit a party to adduce evidence, or to seek to rely on a document, in respect of which that party has failed to comply with the requirements of this Part.

(4) The court may limit cross-examination[GL].

Defined terms—"court": FPR 2010, r 2.3(1).

Practice Direction—FPR 2010, Pt 22 is supported by FPR PD22A (Written Evidence). Despite its title, this PD ranges much wider than "written evidence", which concerns only the first half of Pt 22.

Format of witness statements— FPR PD22A, paras 3.1 et seq deal extensively with format and presentation of statements and affidavits, how to deal with inability of a deponent to read or sign (paras 7.1–7.4 and see Annexes 1 and 2) and exhibits (paras 9.1–13.4).

"issues on which [the court] requires evidence": relevant evidence (r 22.1(1)(a))—The main rule governing the relevance and admissibility of evidence is that "all evidence that is sufficiently relevant to an issue before the court is admissible and all that is irrelevant, or insufficiently relevant, should be excluded" (*Cross & Tapper on Evidence*, Colin Tapper (2010) at p 64). The importance of defining the issues for trial as part of case management is clear from r 1.4. Without that definition parties cannot define what evidence it is that they need to prove their case, neither can they be sure – to prove an issue that is essential to the outcome of the case – that they have the evidence that the court will need and in a form that proves the point that the party wishes to make.

Burden and standard of proof—The party who asserts a fact must prove it. The burden is on him to adduce the evidence and to prove the fact asserted. It falls once more to competent case management (FPR 2010, r 1.4 and Pt 4) to define what factual issues remain in dispute and on whom the burden lies (where there are disputed facts) to prove those facts. It is for the parties then to identify the evidence that they wish to adduce to prove those facts, subject to any power that the court may have under r 22.1(2) to "exclude evidence".

Standard of proof—The standard of proof refers to the level of probability required to prove a fact (*Bater v Bater* [1951] P 35 at [36]–[37]). In family cases this will be the civil standard, that is to say "the simple balance of probabilities" (*Re B (Children)* [2008] 2 FLR 141). The working of this principle is explained in *Re B* at [2]: "If a legal rule requires a fact to be proved (a 'fact in issue'), a judge or jury must decide whether or not it happened. There is no room for a finding that it might have happened. The law operates a binary system in which the only values are 0 and 1. The fact either happened or it did not. If the tribunal is left in doubt, the doubt is resolved by a rule that one party or the other carries the burden of proof. If the party who bears the burden of proof fails to discharge it, a value of 0 is returned and the fact is treated as not having happened. If he does discharge it, a value of 1 is returned and the fact is treated as having happened."

Power to control evidence—Courts Act 2003, s 76(3) provides that these rules "may modify the rules of evidence as they apply to family proceedings in any court within the scope of the rules". Any power must be operated by the court in a way that is in accordance with European Convention 1950, Art 6(1) (right to a fair trial) and with the overriding objective to deal with cases fairly.

"power ... to exclude evidence" (r 22.1(2))—A main plank of the overriding objective is proportionality; and part of that is to allot a fair share of the court's "resources", mostly of time, to a case and to ensure that parties "are on an equal footing". To permit evidence ad lib (even otherwise admissible evidence) and for a party to urge the court so to do, might be for that party to fail properly "to further the overriding objective" (FPR 2010, r 1.3). There may be instances where the court may feel justified in excluding evidence as a matter of procedure: for example, where a party has been culpably neglectful in failing to serve either in time or at all any appropriate notices of the intention to rely on hearsay evidence under Civil Evidence Act 1995, s 2(1) and FPR 2010, r 23.2 (but see r 22.1(3)), or evidence has been obtained illegally (*Lifely v Lifely* [2008] EWCA Civ 904; *Imerman v Tchenguiz and Others* [2010] 2 FLR 814).

"permit a party to adduce evidence" (r 22.1(3))—This suggests that family judges are expected to have – or perhaps to need – a more forgiving approach to allowing non-compliant parties to adduce evidence where rules in Pt 22 (although not other evidence procedural rules) have not been complied with. "Welfare issues" (see FPR 2010, r 1.1(1), for example) may demand such forgiveness.

Limits on cross-examination (r 22.1(4))—Limits on cross-examination might occur in two ways:

(1) The court may limit the issues to be explored: this would be consistent with r 22.1(1)(a), e g *Watson v Chief Constable of Cleveland* [2001] EWCA Civ 1547.
(2) The court may limit the time available for cross-examination of a particular witness: a "guillotine" order, which is unquestionably in line with the overriding objective, but see *Hayes v Transco plc* [2003] EWCA Civ 1261 at [58].

22.2 Evidence of witnesses – general rule

(1) The general rule is that any fact which needs to be proved by the evidence of witnesses is to be proved –

    (a) at the final hearing, by their oral evidence; and
    (b) at any other hearing, by their evidence in writing.

(2) The general rule does not apply –

    (a) to proceedings under Part 12 for secure accommodation orders, interim care orders or interim supervision orders; or
    (b) where an enactment, any of these rules, a practice direction or a court order provides to the contrary.

    (Section 45(7) of the Children Act 1989 (emergency protection orders) is an example of an enactment which makes provision relating to the evidence that a court may take into account when hearing an application.)

Derivation—CPR 1998, r 32.2.

"oral evidence" at a final hearing (r 22.2(1)(b))—The general rule for proof of an application or case is that the evidence of a witness be given orally and in public (FPR 2010, r 32.2(1) and see European Convention 1950, Art 6(1)). In family proceedings, this rule is altered, so that all hearings are in private (FPR 2010, r 27.10), subject as provided in FPR 2010, r 27.11 and unless otherwise provided (e g final defended matrimonial and civil partnership proceedings: FPR 2010, r 7.16(1), and all committal hearings, which are held in public).

Exceptions to general rule—Rules of evidence provide various exclusionary exceptions to this rule. Certain evidence need not be proved. This evidence can be treated as if it had been already formally proved before the court and includes: judicial notice, issue estoppel, formal admissions and existing judicial findings.

(1) *Judicial notice* Judicial notice establishes that a fact exists even where formal proof of it has not

been called and even though that fact is in issue before the court. Judicial notice may be the general knowledge that can be imputed to the judge, just as it can be to other people. For example, in most financial remedy cases the courts are likely to take judicial notice of the content of a number of the tables in *At a Glance* (FLBA).

(2) *Issue estoppel*   Issue estoppel prevents a party from denying that a point at issue has already been tried and established against that party. It operates where facts have been proved in a court of competent jurisdiction following a trial between the parties involved in the present litigation, where the earlier court was one of competent jurisdiction, and the trial that decided the earlier proceedings was on the merits as between the parties. It rarely applies in children proceedings (*Re B (Children Act Proceedings: Issue Estoppel)* [1997] 1 FLR 285) but it can apply in family proceedings, for example where there is a conflict as between family and other jurisdictions (*Edgerton v Edgerton and Zaffirili Shaikh* [2012] 2 FLR 273, at [36]).

(3) *Admissions*   See under FPR 2010, r 22.15.

(4) *Judicial findings*   For example, Civil Evidence Act 1968, s 11 enables a party to civil proceedings to rely on the conviction of another party as evidence that the offence was committed "unless the contrary is proved" (CEA 1968, s 11(2)(a)). A statutory presumption arises that the offence has been committed, so that a convicted party has the almost impossible task of seeking to persuade a judge that the conviction should not stand as evidence in the family proceedings (e g *Hunter v Chief Constable of West Midlands* [1982] AC 529). A finding of adultery or paternity in relevant matrimonial proceedings will be admissible as evidence in other civil proceedings, where such evidence is relevant (CEA 1968, s 12).

22.3 Evidence by video link or other means

The court may allow a witness to give evidence through a video link or by other means.

Video link—This provision is in line with r 1.4(2)(k): that in managing and (as here) in hearing a case, the court should make "use of technology". In *Polanski v Conde Nast* [2005] 1 WLR 637, the House of Lords permitted the claimant, a French resident who feared arrest by US authorities if he came to England, to give evidence from France by video link.

PD—Annex 3 to FPR PD22A provides guidance as to how video conferencing should be dealt with in court.

22.4 Witness statements

(1) A witness statement is a written statement signed by a person which contains the evidence which that person would be allowed to give orally.

(2) A witness statement must comply with the requirements set out in the Practice Direction 22A.

   (Part 17 requires a witness statement to be verified by a statement of truth.)

"evidence which that person would be allowed to give" (r 22.4(1))—A witness statement is that of the witness; it is not, for example, a pleading, a skeleton argument or a chronology (although a chronology may help it). The likelihood is that in family cases a witness will be permitted to "amplify his witness statement" or give updating evidence (FPR 2010, r 22.6(3)).

"evidence ... allowed to give" (r 22.4(1))—Every effort must be taken to ensure that a statement prepared by a legal representative complies with all relevant rules of evidence:

(1) Relevance – only evidence that is relevant to an issue before the court is admissible (i e "allowed");
(2) Privilege – no information covered by privilege should be included, save where the privilege is that of a witness and he is willing to waive his own privilege;
(3) Hearsay – see further under FPR 2010, rr 23.2–23.5;
(4) Frivolous or abusive evidence.

22.5 Service of witness statements for use at the final hearing

(1) The court may give directions as to service on the other parties of any witness statement of the oral evidence on which a party intends to rely in relation to any issues of fact to be decided at the final hearing.

(2) The court may give directions as to –

    (a)   the order in which witness statements are to be served; and

    (b)   whether or not the witness statements are to be filed.

(3) Where the court directs that a court officer is to serve a witness statement on the other parties, any reference in this Chapter to a party serving a witness statement is to be read as including a reference to a court officer serving the statement.

Defined terms—"court": r 2.3(1).

Service of statements in specific applications—Note that r 22.5(1) does not disapply the requirements of individual applications to be accompanied by their own evidences as directed. Thus:

(1) All applications –

    (a) FPR 2010, Pt 7 – for practical purposes the matrimonial and civil partnership proceedings application (petition) attested to by the certified affidavit will be the evidence in support of undefended Pt 7 proceedings

    (b) FPR 2010, Pt 8 – see under Pt 19 procedure, below

    (c) FPR 2010, Pt 9 – the Form E, E1 or E2 is the evidence in support of a Pt 9 financial remedy application (r 9.14) and care will be need to ensure that a district judge does not hold parties to the rigours of r 22.6(2): witness statement as evidence in chief.

    (d) FPR 2010, Pt 10 – an application under Pt 10 must be "supported by a witness statement" (r 10.2(1).

    (e) FPR 2010, Pt 11 – application for a forced marriage protection order must be supported by a sworn statement (r 11.2(2)).

    (f) FPR 2010, Pt 20 – applications for an interim remedy under Pt 20 must be "supported by evidence" (r 20.4(2)).

(2) FPR 2010, Pt 19 procedure applications – Pt 19 has specific procedures for filing "written evidence":

    (a) All written evidence on which the applicant intends to rely must be filed with the application (r 19.7(1)) and it must be served on the respondent with the application (r 19.7(2)).

    (b) A respondent's evidence, if he "wishes to rely on written evidence" must be filed with the acknowledgement of service (r 19.7(3)) and served on the applicant.

    (c) Rule 19.8 restricts the calling of evidence, although in cases of difficulty its rigours should be capable of being overcome given the terms of FPR 2010, r 22.1(3).

    (d) Directions are given once the acknowledgement of service and written evidence are received (r 19.9(2)).

(3) FPR 2010, Pt 18 procedure applications – FPR 2010, Pt 18 application notices will be dealt with on paper, often in the absence of the parties, so written evidence of some sort is essential (as confirmed by r 22.2(1)(b)). This may be a statement of case, a separate statement or the application notice itself (if verified by a statement of truth) (r 18.8(2),(3)).

22.6 Use at the final hearing of witness statements which have been served

(1) If a party –

    (a)   has served a witness statement; and

    (b)   wishes to rely at the final hearing on the evidence of the witness who made the statement,

that party must call the witness to give oral evidence unless the court directs otherwise or the party puts the statement in as hearsay evidence.

    (Part 23 (miscellaneous rules about evidence) contains provisions about hearsay evidence.)

(2) The witness statement of a witness called to give oral evidence under paragraph (1) is to stand as the evidence in chief[GL] of that witness unless the court directs otherwise.

(3) A witness giving oral evidence at the final hearing may with the permission of the court –

    (a)   amplify his witness statement; and

    (b)   give evidence in relation to new matters which have arisen since the witness statement was served on the other parties.

(4) The court will give permission under paragraph (3) only if it considers that there is good reason not to confine the evidence of the witness to the contents of the witness statement.

(5) If a party who has served a witness statement does not –

    (a)   call the witness to give evidence at the final hearing; or

    (b)   put the witness statement in as hearsay evidence,

any other party may put the witness statement in as hearsay evidence.

Hearsay evidence (r 22.6(5)(b))—See under FPR 2010, Pt 23.

22.7 Evidence at hearings other than the final hearing

(1) Subject to paragraph (2), the general rule is that evidence at hearings other than the final hearing is to be by witness statement unless the court, any other rule, a practice direction or any other enactment requires otherwise.

(2) At hearings other than the final hearing, a party may rely on the matters set out in that party's –

    (a)   application form;

    (b)   application notice; or

    (c)   answer,

if the application form, application notice or answer, as the case may be, is verified by a statement of truth or if the court gives that party permission to do so without such verification.

Amendments—SI 2012/2806.

Statements of case as evidence—FPR 2010, PD22A, para 1.3 confirms the availability of statements of case (see definition in FPR 2010, rr 4.1 and 17.1(1)) provided that they are verified by a statement of truth (FPR 2010, Pt 17).

"verified by a statement of truth" (r 22.7(2))—This provision does not prevent a party relying on other evidence (e g a written statement; r 22.7(2)), but it is intended to provide only that the documents referred to can be relied on if verified by a statement of truth. This provision repeats FPR 2010, r 17.2(3) but in the context only of "other hearings". As in FPR 2010, r 4.1 (which defines a "statement of case" to include an "answer"), no assistance is provided as to what is meant by "answer" (the context of its use in other parts of the rules suggests that it means not just a defence to a matrimonial and civil partnership proceedings application (divorce petition)).

22.8 Order for cross-examination

(1) Where, at a hearing other than the final hearing, evidence is given in writing, any party may apply to the court for permission to cross-examine[GL] the person giving the evidence.

(2) If the court gives permission under paragraph (1) but the person in question does not attend, that person's evidence may not be used unless the court directs otherwise.

       (Rules 35.3 and 35.4 contain rules in relation to evidence arising out of mediation of cross-border disputes.)

Pt 18 procedure—The probability is that the circumstances to which r 22.8 is mostly addressed will be FPR 2010, Pt 20 proceedings. Difficult issues may be at stake and in many cases the interim remedy will, in effect, be the final remedy – certainly on the declaration or injunction issue. The ability to test – or not – the evidence against a party may go to important questions of fairness as between the parties or as to third parties drawn into the litigation.

Part 19 procedure—The court may give directions for attendance of a witness for cross-examination (FPR 2010, r 19.8(3)). The implication and context of this provision is that it refers to a final hearing, but the sub-rule does not so state. It may also refer to an interim hearing, or hearing other than the final hearing, in FPR 2010, Pt 19 procedure proceedings (eg a hearing on a parent's FPR 2010, Pt 18 procedure application for a DNA test direction).

Hearsay evidence—This rule should be read alongside the hearsay provisions considered in FPR 2010, Pt 23, as to what becomes of a statement or affidavit if a party ordered to attend does not do so.

22.9 Witness summaries

(1) A party who –

(a) is required to serve a witness statement for use at any hearing; but
(b) is unable to obtain one,

may apply, without notice, for permission to serve a witness summary instead.

(2) A witness summary is a summary of –

(a) the evidence, if known, which would otherwise be included in a witness statement; or
(b) if the evidence is not known, the matters about which the party serving the witness summary proposes to question the witness.

(3) Unless the court directs otherwise, a witness summary must include the name and address of the intended witness.

(4) Unless the court directs otherwise, a witness summary must be served within the period in which a witness statement would have had to be served.

(5) Where a party serves a witness summary, so far as practicable rules 22.4(2) (form of witness statements), 22.5 (service of witness statements for use at the final hearing) and 22.6(3) (amplifying witness statements) apply to the summary.

Witness summaries—It is difficult to conceive of many circumstances where this rule, derived verbatim from CPR 1998 (with semantic changes only), would be of relevance in proceedings under FPR 2010.

22.10 Consequence of failure to serve witness statement

If a witness statement for use at the final hearing is not served in respect of an intended witness within the time specified by the court, then the witness may not be called to give oral evidence unless the court gives permission.

22.11 Cross-examination on a witness statement

A witness who is called to give evidence at the final hearing may be cross-examined[(GL)] on the witness statement, whether or not the statement or any part of it was referred to during the witness's evidence in chief[(GL)].

22.12 Affidavit evidence

(1) Evidence must be given by affidavit[(GL)] instead of or in addition to a witness statement if this is required by the court, a provision contained in any other rule, a practice direction or any other enactment.

(2) In relation to proceedings which are pending or treated as pending in a divorce county court or civil partnership county court, section 58(1)(c) of the County Courts Act 1984, shall have effect as if after paragraph (c) there were inserted –

"or

(d) a district judge of the principal registry; or
(e) any officer of the principal registry authorised by the President under section 2 of the Commissioner for Oaths Act 1889; or

(f)   any clerk in the Central Office of the Royal Courts of Justice authorised to take affidavits[GL] for the purposes of proceedings in the Supreme Court.".

(Rule 7.3 sets out when proceedings are treated as pending in a divorce county court or civil partnership proceedings county court.)

Affidavit evidence under court order—FPR PD22A, para 1.4 and 1.6 make supplementary provision concerning affidavits and when they must be used as evidence (e g FPR 2010, r 9.14(2): Forms E, E1 and E2; affidavits in FPR 2010, Pt 7 proceedings). Para 1.6 suggests that the court may direct the filing of affidavit evidence, on its own initiative or on application.

Affirmation—The term affidavit applies equally to affirmations (FPR PD22A, para 1.7).

22.13 Form of affidavit

An affidavit[GL] must comply with the requirements set out in the Practice Direction 22A.

22.14 Affidavit made outside the jurisdiction

A person may make an affidavit [GL] outside the jurisdiction in accordance with –

(a)   this Part; or
(b)   the law of the place where the affidavit[GL] is made.

22.15 Notice to admit facts

(1) A party may serve notice on another party requiring the other party to admit the facts, or the part of the case of the serving party, specified in the notice.

(2) A notice to admit facts must be served no later than 21 days before the final hearing.

(3) Where the other party makes any admission in answer to the notice, the admission may be used against that party only –

(a)   in the proceedings in which the notice to admit is served; and
(b)   by the party who served the notice.

(4) The court may allow a party to amend or withdraw any admission made by that party on such terms as it thinks just.

"notice … to admit the facts" (r 22.15(1))—No form is prescribed for notice to admit. It is a notice as between the parties: i e there is no requirement of filing at court, although the notice and any response may be included in the court bundle.

Admission by the serving party "only … in the proceedings" (r 22.15(3))—The consequences of the admission do not carry forward to other proceedings between the parties.

Costs on failure to admit facts—The former rule that costs incurred by a party in proving a fact of which he had given notice to admit (RSC 1965, Ord 62, r 6(7)) is no longer included in costs rules generally. However, the court is likely to take such costs into account (CPR 1998, r 44.2).

22.16 Notice to admit or produce documents

(1) A party to whom a document is disclosed is deemed to admit the authenticity of that document unless notice is served by that party that the party wishes the document to be proved at the final hearing.

(2) A notice to prove a document must be served –

(a)   by the latest date for serving witness statements; or
(b)   within 7 days beginning with the date of service of the document, whichever is later.

Notice to admit or prove documents—If a party discloses a document – that is to say, he or she "states that the document exists or has existed" (FPR 2010, r 21.1) – then the party provided with disclosure is deemed to admit "the authenticity of that document" unless notice to prove the document is given under r 22.16. The "authenticity" of a document is a separate question from the truthfulness or probative value of a document. It is not evidence of the facts it seeks to contain unless proved in some way: e g by its author preparing, filing and serving a witness statement (FPR 2010, r 22.5).

22.17 Notarial acts and instruments

A notarial act or instrument may be received in evidence without further proof as duly authenticated in accordance with the requirements of law unless the contrary is proved.

Chapter 2
Rules Applying Only to Particular Proceedings

22.18 Scope of this Chapter

This Chapter of this Part applies to affidavits$^{(GL)}$ and affirmations as it applies to witness statements.

22.19 Availability of witness statements for inspection during the final hearing

(1) This rule applies to proceedings under Part 7 (matrimonial and civil partnership proceedings).

(2) A witness statement which stands as evidence in chief$^{(GL)}$ is open to inspection during the course of the final hearing unless the court directs otherwise.

(3) Any person may ask for a direction that a witness statement is not open to inspection.

(4) The court will not make a direction under paragraph (2) unless it is satisfied that a witness statement should not be open to inspection because of –

    (a)   the interests of justice;
    (b)   the public interest;
    (c)   the nature of any expert medical evidence in the statement;
    (d)   the nature of any confidential information (including information relating to personal financial matters) in the statement; or
    (e)   the need to protect the interests of any child or protected party.

(5) The court may exclude from inspection words or passages in the witness statement.

"witness statement ... open to inspection" (r 22.19(2))—Rule 22.19 applies to public hearing in civil proceedings (CPR 1998, r 22.19) and in the same circumstances applies to FPR 2010, Pt 7 defended matrimonial and civil partnership proceedings hearings. It reflects concern for open justice, where statements are served and form a witness's evidence-in-chief. A member of the public, who is entitled to hear the case in open court, can inspect that part of the written evidence that is taken as read by FPR 2010, r 22.6(2).

22.20 Use of witness statements for other purposes

(1) This rule applies to proceedings under Part 7 (matrimonial and civil partnership proceedings) or Part 9 (financial remedies).

(2) Except as provided by this rule, a witness statement may be used only for the purpose of the proceedings in which it is served.

(3) Paragraph (2) does not apply if and to the extent that –

    (a)   the court gives permission for some other use; or
    (b)   the witness statement has been put in evidence at a hearing held in public.

Practice Direction 22A –
Written Evidence

This Practice Direction supplements FPR Part 22

Evidence in general

1.1 Rule 22.2(1) sets out the general rule as to how evidence is to be given and facts are to be proved. This is that, at the final hearing, witnesses will normally give oral evidence and, at any hearing other than the final hearing, by evidence in writing (which under rule 22.7(1) will usually be by witness statement).

1.2 Rule 22.2(2) excludes the general rule –

(a)   from proceedings under Part 12 (Children) for secure accommodation orders, interim care orders or interim supervision orders; or

(b)   where an enactment, any rule in the FPR, a practice direction or a court order provides to the contrary.

1.3 Application forms, application notices and answers except an application for a matrimonial order or a civil partnership order or an answer to such an application may also be used as evidence provided that their contents have been verified by a statement of truth (see Part 17 for information about statements of truth).

> (For information regarding evidence by deposition see Part 24 and the practice direction which supplements it.)

1.4 Affidavits must be used as evidence –

(a)   where sworn evidence is required by an enactment, rule, order or practice direction; and

(b)   in any application for an order against anyone for alleged contempt of court.

1.5 If a party believes that sworn evidence is required by a court in another jurisdiction for any purpose connected with the proceedings, he may apply to the court for a direction that evidence shall be given only by affidavit on any applications to be heard before the final hearing.

1.6 The court may give a direction under rule 22.12 that evidence shall be given by affidavit instead of or in addition to a witness statement –

(a)   on its own initiative; or

(b)   after any party has applied to the court for such a direction.

1.7 An affidavit, where referred to in the FPR or a practice direction, also means an affirmation unless the context requires otherwise.

AFFIDAVITS AND WITNESS STATEMENTS

Meaning of "deponent" and "witness"

2.1 For the purposes of the FPR –

a "deponent" is a person who gives evidence by affidavit, affirmation or deposition; and

a "witness" is a person who gives evidence by witness statement.

2.2 References in the following paragraphs to "the maker of", or "making", an affidavit, affirmation, deposition or witness statement are to be construed accordingly.

Heading and format

3.1 The affidavit/statement should be headed with the title of the proceedings where the proceedings are between several parties with the same status it is sufficient to identify the parties, subject to paragraph 4.2, as follows –

Number:

A.B. (and others)	Applicants
C.D. (and others)	Respondents

3.2 Subject to paragraph 4.2, at the top right-hand corner of the first page (and on the backsheet) there should be clearly written –

- (a) the party on whose behalf it is made;
- (b) the initials and surname of the maker;
- (c) the number of the affidavit/statement in relation to its maker;
- (d) the identifying initials and number of each exhibit referred to; and
- (e) the date made.

3.3 The affidavit/statement should –

- (a) be produced on durable quality A4 paper with a 3.5 cm margin;
- (b) be fully legible and should normally be typed on one side of the paper only;
- (c) where possible, should be bound securely in a manner which would not hamper filing or, where secure binding is not possible, each page should be endorsed with the case number and should bear the following initials –
  - (i) in the case of an affidavit, of the maker and of the person before whom it is sworn; or
  - (ii) in the case of a witness statement, of the maker and, where the maker is unable to read or sign the statement, of the authorised person (see paragraphs 7.3 and 7.4 below);
- (d) have the pages numbered consecutively as a separate document (or as one of several documents contained in a file);
- (e) be divided into numbered paragraphs;
- (f) have all numbers, including dates, expressed in figures; and
- (g) give the reference to any document or documents mentioned either in the margin or in bold text in the body of the affidavit/statement.

Body

4.1 Subject to paragraph 4.2 and rules 14.2 and 29.1, the affidavit/statement must, if practicable, be in the maker's own words, it should be expressed in the first person, and the maker should –

- (a) commence –
  - (i) in an affidavit, "I (full name) of (residential address) state on oath ....";
  - (ii) in a statement, by giving his or her full name and residential address;
- (b) if giving evidence in a professional, business or other occupational capacity, give the address at which he or she works in (a) above, the position held and the name of the firm or employer;
- (c) give his or her occupation or (if none) description; and
- (d) if it be the case that the maker is a party to the proceedings or is employed by a party to the proceedings, state that fact.

4.2 If, in proceedings to which Part 14 (Adoption, placement and related proceedings) applies, a serial number has been assigned under rule 14.2, the affidavit/statement must be framed so that it does not disclose the identity of the applicant.

PART III

(Rule 29.1 provides that, unless the court directs otherwise, a party to family proceedings is not required to reveal the address of his or her private residence or other contact details.)

4.3 An affidavit/statement must indicate –

(a)   which of the statements in it are made from the maker's own knowledge and which are matters of information and belief; and

(b)   the source for any matters of information and belief.

4.4 It is usually convenient to follow the chronological sequence of events or matters dealt with. Each paragraph should as far as possible be confined to a distinct portion of the subject.

4.5 The maker should, when referring to an exhibit or exhibits, state "there is now shown to me marked "…" the (description of exhibit)".

Alterations to affidavits and witness statements

5.1 Any alteration to an affidavit must be initialled by both the maker and the person before whom the affidavit is sworn.

5.2 Any alteration to a witness statement must be initialled by the maker or by the authorised person where appropriate (see paragraphs 7.3 and 7.4 below).

5.3 An affidavit/statement which contains an alteration that has not been initialled in accordance with paragraphs 5.1 and 5.2 may be filed or used in evidence only with the permission of the court.

Swearing an affidavit or verifying a witness statement

6.1 An affidavit is the testimony of the person who swears it. A witness statement is the equivalent of the oral evidence which the maker would, if called, give in evidence.

6.2 The jurat of an affidavit is a statement set out at the end of the document which authenticates the affidavit. It must –

(a)   be signed by all deponents;

(b)   be completed and signed by the person before whom the affidavit was sworn whose name and qualification must be printed beneath his signature;

(c)   contain the full address of the person before whom the affidavit was sworn; and

(d)   follow immediately on from the text and not be put on a separate page.

6.3 An affidavit must be sworn before a person independent of the parties or their representatives. Only the following may administer oaths and take affidavits –

(a)   a Commissioner for Oaths (Commissioners for Oaths Acts 1889 and 1891);

(b)   other persons specified by statute (sections 12 and 18 of, and Schedules 2 and 4 to, the Legal Services Act 2007);

(c)   certain officials of the Senior Courts (section 2 of the Commissioners for Oaths Act 1889);

(d)   a circuit judge or district judge (section 58 of the County Courts Act 1984);

(e)   any justice of the peace (section 58 of the County Courts Act 1984); and

(f)   certain officials of any county court appointed by the judge of that court for the purpose (section 58 of the County Courts Act 1984).

6.4 A witness statement must include a statement of truth by the intended maker as follows:

"I believe that the facts stated in this witness statement are true."

(Attention is drawn to rule 17.6 which sets out the consequences of verifying a witness statement containing a false statement without an honest belief in its truth.)

(For information regarding statements of truth, see Part 17 (Statements of truth) and Practice Direction 17A.)

(Paragraphs 7.1 to 7.4 below set out the procedures to be followed where the intended maker of an affidavit or witness statement is unable to read or sign the affidavit/statement.)

6.5 If, in proceedings under Part 14 (Adoption, placement and related proceedings), a serial number has been assigned under rule 14.2 or the name of the maker of the affidavit/statement is not being revealed in accordance with rule 29.1, the signature of the maker will be edited from the affidavit/statement before it is served on the other party.

Inability of maker to read or sign affidavit/statement

7.1 Where an affidavit is sworn by a deponent who is unable to read or sign it, the person before whom the affidavit is sworn must certify in the jurat that –

(a) that person read the affidavit to the deponent;
(b) the deponent appeared to understand it; and
(c) the deponent signed, or made his mark, in that person's presence.

7.2 If that certificate is not included in the jurat, the affidavit may not be used in evidence unless the court is satisfied that it was read to the deponent and that the deponent appeared to understand it. Annex 1 to this practice direction sets out forms of the jurat with the certificate for an affidavit and an affirmation respectively.

7.3 Where a witness statement is made by a person who is unable to read or sign the statement, it must contain a certificate made by an authorised person. An authorised person is a person able to administer oaths and take affidavits but need not be independent of the parties or their representatives.

7.4 The authorised person must certify –

(a) that the witness statement has been read to the witness;
(b) that the witness appeared to understand it and approved its content as accurate;
(c) that the statement of truth has been read to the witness;
(d) that the witness appeared to understand the statement of truth and the consequences of making a false witness statement; and
(e) that the witness signed or made his or her mark in the presence of the authorised person.

The form of the certificate is set out at Annex 2 to this practice direction.

Filing of affidavits and witness statements

8.1 If the court directs that an affidavit/statement is to be filed, it must be filed in the court or Division, or office or Registry of the court or Division, where the action in which it was or is to be used, is proceeding or will proceed.

8.2 Where the affidavit/statement is in a foreign language –

(a) the party wishing to rely on it must –
(i) have it translated; and
(ii) must file the foreign language affidavit/statement with the court; and
(b) the translator must sign the translation to certify that it is accurate.

EXHIBITS

Manner of Exhibiting Documents

9.1 A document used in conjunction with an affidavit/statement should be –

   (a) shown to and verified by the maker, and remain separate from the affidavit/statement; and

   (b) identified by a declaration of the person before whom the affidavit/statement was sworn.

9.2 The declaration should be headed with the name of the proceedings in the same way as the affidavit/statement is headed.

9.3 The first page of each exhibit should be marked –

   (a) as in paragraph 3.2 above; and

   (b) with the exhibit mark referred to in the affidavit/statement in accordance with paragraph 4.5 above.

9.4 Where the maker makes more than one affidavit/statement, to which there are exhibits, in the same proceedings, the numbering of the exhibits should run consecutively throughout and not start again with each affidavit/statement.

Letters

10.1 Copies of individual letters should be collected together and exhibited in a bundle or bundles. They should be arranged in chronological order with the earliest at the top, and firmly secured.

10.2 When a bundle of correspondence is exhibited, the exhibit should have a front page attached stating that the bundle consists of original letters and copies. They should be arranged and secured as above and numbered consecutively.

Other documents

11.1 Photocopies instead of original documents may be exhibited provided the originals are made available for inspection by the other parties before the hearing and by the court at the hearing.

11.2 Court documents must not be exhibited (official copies of such documents prove themselves).

11.3 Where an exhibit contains more than one document, a front page should be attached setting out a list of the documents contained in the exhibit. The list should contain the dates of the documents.

Exhibits other than documents

12.1 Items other than documents should be clearly marked with an exhibit number or letter in such a manner that the mark cannot become detached from the exhibit.

12.2 Small items may be placed in a container and the container appropriately marked.

General provisions

13.1 Where an exhibit contains more than one document –

   (a) the bundle should not be stapled but should be securely fastened in a way that does not hinder the reading of the documents; and

   (b) the pages should be numbered consecutively at bottom centre.

13.2 Every page of an exhibit should be clearly legible; typed copies of illegible documents should be included, paginated with "a" numbers.

13.3 Where affidavits/statements and exhibits have become numerous, they should be put into separate bundles and the pages numbered consecutively throughout.

13.4 Where on account of their bulk the service of exhibits or copies of exhibits on the other parties would be difficult or impracticable, the directions of the court should be sought as to arrangements for bringing the exhibits to the attention of the other parties and as to their custody pending trial.

MISCELLANEOUS

Defects in affidavits, witness statement and exhibits

14.1 Where –

    (a)   an affidavit;
    (b)   a witness statement; or
    (c)   an exhibit to either an affidavit or a witness statement,

does not comply with Part 22 or this practice direction in relation to its form, the court may refuse to admit it as evidence and may refuse to allow the costs arising from its preparation.

14.2 Permission to file a defective affidavit or witness statement or to use a defective exhibit may be obtained from the court where the case is proceeding.

Affirmations

15.1 All provisions in this or any other practice direction relating to affidavits apply to affirmations with the following exceptions –

    (a)   the deponent should commence "I (full name) of (residential address) do solemnly and sincerely affirm ..."; and
    (b)   in the jurat the word "sworn" is replaced by the word "affirmed".

Certificate of court officer

16.1 In proceedings under Part 7 (Matrimonial and Civil Partnership Proceedings), where the court has ordered that a witness statement, affidavit, affirmation or deposition is not be open to inspection by the public (see rule 22.19(2) and (3)) or that words or passages in the statement etc are not to be open to inspection (see rule 22.19(5)), the court officer will so certify on the statement etc and make any deletions directed by the court under rule 22.19(3).

Video Conferencing

17.1 Guidance on the use of video conferencing in the family courts is set out at Annex 3 to this practice direction.

A list of the sites which are available for video conferencing can be found on Her Majesty's Court Service's website at www.hm-courts-service.gov.uk.

Note—See now *www.justice.gov.uk/about/hmcts.*

ANNEX 1

Certificate to be used where a deponent to an affidavit is unable to read or sign it

Sworn at ... this ... day of ... Before me, I having first read over the contents of this affidavit to the deponent [if there are exhibits, add "and explained the nature and effect of the exhibits referred to in it"] who appeared to understand it and approved its content as accurate, and made his/her* mark on the affidavit in my presence. Or, (after "Before me") the witness to the mark of the deponent having been first sworn that the witness had read over etc. (as above) and that the witness saw the deponent make his/her* mark on the affidavit. (Witness must sign.)

* delete as appropriate

Certificate to be used where a deponent to an affirmation is unable to read or sign it

Affirmed at ... this ... day of ... Before me, I having first read over the contents of this affirmation to the deponent [if there are exhibits, add "and explained the nature and effect of the exhibits referred to in it"] who appeared to understand it and approved its content as accurate, and made his/her* mark on the affirmation in my presence. Or, (after "Before me") the witness to the mark of the deponent having been first sworn that the witness had read over etc. (as above) and that the witness saw the deponent make his/her* mark on the affirmation. (Witness must sign.)

* delete as appropriate

ANNEX 2

Certificate to be used where a witness is unable to read or sign a witness statement

I certify that I [name and address of authorised person] have read over the contents of this witness statement and the statement of truth to the witness [if there are exhibits, add "and explained the nature and effect of the exhibits referred to in it"] who (a) appeared to understand the witness statement and approved its content as accurate and (b) appeared to understand the statement of truth and the consequences of making a false witness statement, and [signed the statement] [made his/her mark]* in my presence.

* delete as appropriate.

ANNEX 3

Video conferencing guidance

1 This guidance is for the use of video conferencing (VCF) in proceedings to which the Family Procedure Rules apply. It is in part based, with permission, upon the protocol of the Federal Court of Australia. It is intended to provide a guide to all persons involved in the use of VCF, although it does not attempt to cover all the practical questions which might arise.

Any reference in this guide to a judge is to be taken as including a district judge or justices of the peace if the proceedings are before a magistrates' court.

Video conferencing generally

2 The guidance covers the use of VCF equipment both (a) in a courtroom, whether via equipment which is permanently placed there or via a mobile unit, and (b) in a separate

studio or conference room. In either case, the location at which the judge sits is referred to as the 'local site'. The other site or sites to and from which transmission is made are referred to as 'the remote site' and in any particular case any such site may be another courtroom. The guidance applies to cases where VCF is used for the taking of evidence and also to its use for other parts of any legal proceedings

3 VCF may be a convenient way of dealing with any part of proceedings – it can involve considerable savings in time and cost. Its use for the taking of evidence from overseas witnesses will, in particular, be likely to achieve a material saving of costs, and such savings may also be achieved by its use for taking domestic evidence. It is, however, inevitably not as ideal as having the witness physically present in court. Its convenience should not therefore be allowed to dictate its use. A judgment must be made in every case in which the use of VCF is being considered not only as to whether it will achieve an overall cost saving but as to whether its use will be likely to be beneficial to the efficient, fair and economic disposal of the litigation. In particular, it needs to be recognised that the degree of control a court can exercise over a witness at the remote site is or may be more limited than it can exercise over a witness physically before it.

4 When used for the taking of evidence, the objective should be to make the VCF session as close as possible to the usual practice in court where evidence is taken in open court. To gain the maximum benefit, several differences have to be taken into account. Some matters, which are taken for granted when evidence is taken in the conventional way, take on a different dimension when it is taken by VCF – for example, the administration of the oath, ensuring that the witness understands who is at the local site and what their various roles are, the raising of any objections to the evidence and the use of documents.

5 It should not be presumed that all foreign governments are willing to allow their nationals or others within their jurisdiction to be examined before a court in England or Wales by means of VCF. If there is any doubt about this, enquiries should be directed to the Foreign and Commonwealth Office (International Legal Matters Unit, Consular Division) with a view to ensuring that the country from which the evidence is to be taken raises no objection to it at diplomatic level. The party who is directed to be responsible for arranging the VCF (see paragraph 8) will be required to make all necessary inquiries about this well in advance of the VCF and must be able to inform the court what those inquiries were and of their outcome.

6 Time zone differences need to be considered when a witness abroad is to be examined in England or Wales by VCF. The convenience of the witness, the parties, their representatives and the court must all be taken into account. The cost of the use of a commercial studio is usually greater outside normal business hours.

7 Those involved with VCF need to be aware that, even with the most advanced systems currently available, there are the briefest of delays between the receipt of the picture and that of the accompanying sound. If due allowance is not made for this, there will be a tendency to 'speak over' the witness, whose voice will continue to be heard for a millisecond or so after he or she appears on the screen to have finished speaking.

8 With current technology, picture quality is good, but not as good as a television picture. The quality of the picture is enhanced if those appearing on VCF monitors keep their movements to a minimum.

Preliminary arrangements

9 The court's permission is required for any part of any proceedings to be dealt with by means of VCF. Before seeking a direction, the applicant should notify the listing officer, diary manager or other appropriate court officer of the intention to seek it, and should enquire as to the availability of court VCF equipment for the day or days of the proposed

PART III

VCF. If all parties consent to a direction, permission can be sought by letter, fax or e-mail, although the court may still require an oral hearing. All parties are entitled to be heard on whether or not such a direction should be given and as to its terms. If a witness at a remote site is to give evidence by an interpreter, consideration should be given at this stage as to whether the interpreter should be at the local site or the remote site. If a VCF direction is given, arrangements for the transmission will then need to be made. The court will ordinarily direct that the party seeking permission to use VCF is to be responsible for this. That party is hereafter referred to as 'the VCF arranging party'.

10 Subject to any order to the contrary, all costs of the transmission, including the costs of hiring equipment and technical personnel to operate it, will initially be the responsibility of, and must be met by, the VCF arranging party. All reasonable efforts should be made to keep the transmission to a minimum and so keep the costs down. All such costs will be considered to be part of the costs of the proceedings and the court will determine at such subsequent time as is convenient or appropriate who, as between the parties, should be responsible for them and (if appropriate) in what proportions.

11 The local site will, if practicable, be a courtroom but it may instead be an appropriate studio or conference room. The VCF arranging party must contact the listing officer, diary manager or other appropriate officer of the court which made the VCF direction and make arrangements for the VCF transmission. Details of the remote site, and of the equipment to be used both at the local site (if not being supplied by the court) and the remote site (including the number of ISDN lines and connection speed), together with all necessary contact names and telephone numbers, will have to be provided to the listing officer, diary manager or other court officer. The court will need to be satisfied that any equipment provided by the parties for use at the local site and also that at the remote site is of sufficient quality for a satisfactory transmission. The VCF arranging party must ensure that an appropriate person will be present at the local site to supervise the operation of the VCF throughout the transmission in order to deal with any technical problems. That party must also arrange for a technical assistant to be similarly present at the remote site for like purposes.

12 It is recommended that the judge, practitioners and witness should arrive at their respective VCF sites about 20 minutes prior to the scheduled commencement of the transmission.

13 If the local site is not a courtroom, but a conference room or studio, the judge will need to determine who is to sit where. The VCF arranging party must take care to ensure that the number of microphones is adequate for the speakers and that the panning of the camera for the practitioners' table encompasses all legal representatives so that the viewer can see everyone seated there.

14 If the local site is to be a studio or conference room, the VCF arranging party must ensure that it provides sufficient accommodation to enable a reasonable number of members of the public to attend if appropriate.

15 In cases where the local site is a studio or conference room, the VCF arranging party should make arrangements, if practicable, for the royal coat of arms to be placed above the judge's seat.

16 In cases in which the VCF is to be used for the taking of evidence, the VCF arranging party must arrange for recording equipment to be provided by the court which made the VCF direction so that the evidence can be recorded. An associate will normally be present to operate the recording equipment when the local site is a courtroom. The VCF arranging party should take steps to ensure that an associate is present to do likewise when it is a studio or conference room. The equipment should be set up and tested before the VCF transmission. It will often be a valuable safeguard for the VCF arranging party also to arrange for the provision of recording equipment at the remote site. This will provide a useful back-up if there is any reduction in sound quality during the

transmission. A direction from the court for the making of such a back-up recording must, however, be obtained first. This is because the proceedings are court proceedings and, save as directed by the court, no other recording of them must be made. The court will direct what is to happen to the back-up recording.

17 Some countries may require that any oath or affirmation to be taken by a witness accord with local custom rather than the usual form of oath or affirmation used in England and Wales. The VCF arranging party must make all appropriate prior inquiries and put in place all arrangements necessary to enable the oath or affirmation to be taken in accordance with any local custom. That party must be in a position to inform the court what those inquiries were, what their outcome was and what arrangements have been made. If the oath or affirmation can be administered in the manner normal in England and Wales, the VCF arranging party must arrange in advance to have the appropriate holy book at the remote site. The associate will normally administer the oath.

18 Consideration will need to be given in advance to the documents to which the witness is likely to be referred. The parties should endeavour to agree on this. It will usually be most convenient for a bundle of the copy documents to be prepared in advance, which the VCF arranging party should then send to the remote site.

19 Additional documents are sometimes quite properly introduced during the course of a witness's evidence. To cater for this, the VCF arranging party should ensure that equipment is available to enable documents to be transmitted between sites during the course of the VCF transmission. Consideration should be given to whether to use a document camera. If it is decided to use one, arrangements for its use will need to be established in advance. The panel operator will need to know the number and size of documents or objects if their images are to be sent by document camera. In many cases, a simpler and sufficient alternative will be to ensure that there are fax transmission and reception facilities at the participating sites.

The hearing

20 The procedure for conducting the transmission will be determined by the judge. He will determine who is to control the cameras. In cases where the VCF is being used for an application in the course of the proceedings, the judge will ordinarily not enter the local site until both sites are on line. Similarly, at the conclusion of the hearing, he will ordinarily leave the local site while both sites are still on line. The following paragraphs apply primarily to cases where the VCF is being used for the taking of the evidence of a witness at a remote site.

21 At the beginning of the transmission, the judge will probably wish to introduce himself or herself and the advocates to the witness. He will probably want to know who is at the remote site and will invite the witness to introduce himself or herself and anyone else who is with the witness. The judge may wish to give directions as to the seating arrangements at the remote site so that those present are visible at the local site during the taking of the evidence and to explain to the witness the method of taking the oath or of affirming, the manner in which the evidence will be taken, and who will be conducting the examination and cross-examination. The judge will probably also wish to inform the witness of the matters referred to in paragraphs 7 and 8 (co-ordination of picture with sound, and picture quality).

22 The examination of the witness at the remote site should follow as closely as possible the practice adopted when a witness is in the courtroom. During examination, cross-examination and re-examination, the witness must be able to see the legal representative asking the question and also any other person (whether another legal

PART III

representative or the judge) making any statements in regard to the witness's evidence. It will in practice be most convenient if everyone remains seated throughout the transmission.

PART 23
MISCELLANEOUS RULES ABOUT EVIDENCE

CONTENTS OF THIS PART

23.1 Scope and interpretation of this Part

Rules 23.2 to 23.6 apply to evidence to which the Children (Admissibility of Hearsay Evidence) Order 1993 does not apply.

23.2 Notice of intention to rely on hearsay evidence

(1) Where a party intends to rely on hearsay evidence at the final hearing and either –

    (a)   that evidence is to be given by a witness giving oral evidence; or

    (b)   that evidence is contained in a witness statement of a person who is not being called to give oral evidence,

that party complies with section 2(1)(a) of the Civil Evidence Act 1995 by serving a witness statement on the other parties in accordance with the court's directions.

(2) Where paragraph (1)(b) applies, the party intending to rely on the hearsay evidence must, when serving the witness statement –

    (a)   inform the other parties that the witness is not being called to give oral evidence; and

    (b)   give the reason why the witness will not be called.

(3) In all other cases where a party intends to rely on hearsay evidence at the final hearing, that party complies with section 2(1)(a) of the Civil Evidence Act 1995 by serving a notice on the other parties which –

    (a)   identifies the hearsay evidence;

    (b)   states that the party serving the notice proposes to rely on the hearsay evidence at the final hearing; and

    (c)   gives the reason why the witness will not be called.

(4) The party proposing to rely on the hearsay evidence must –

    (a)   serve the notice no later than the latest date for serving witness statements; and

    (b)   if the hearsay evidence is to be in a document, supply a copy to any party who requests it.

Definition of hearsay evidence—FPR 2010, rr 23.1–23.6 are closely modelled on CPR 1998, rr 33.1–33.6, but omit the definition of "hearsay" in CPR 1998, r 33.1. Thus, normal rules as to hearsay apply to all family proceedings, except those proceedings exempted by Children (Admissibility of Hearsay Evidence) Order 1993, Art 2. Civil Evidence Act 1995, s 1(2) defines hearsay as:

"(a) 'hearsay' means a statement made otherwise than by a person while giving oral evidence in the proceedings which is tendered as evidence of the matters stated; and

(b) references to hearsay include hearsay of whatever degree."

Civil Evidence Act 1995: weight of evidence—The 1995 Act steers a course between technical rules of hearsay evidence and the need in civil proceedings to take a proportionate view as to the forms of evidence that may be admitted. Thus hearsay evidence, merely because hearsay, will not be inadmissible. Thus, s 1(1) provides: "In civil proceedings evidence shall not be excluded on the ground that it is hearsay". Its cogency and the weight to be given to it can be considered by the court under s 4. The court will want to deal with all cases justly and ensure that all evidence is before it to make a decision, but the court retains the power to exclude otherwise admissible evidence (FPR 2010, r 22.1(2)).

"civil proceedings"—Civil proceedings are defined by Civil Evidence Act 1995, s 11 and depend on the proceedings taking place before "any tribunal in relation to which the strict rules of evidence apply". This includes all family proceedings covered by FPR 2010.

Notice of reliance on hearsay evidence—A party who wishes to rely on hearsay evidence must give notice in accordance with Civil Evidence Act 1995, s 2(1) and to do so must comply with r 23.2. Rule 23.2(1),(3) distinguishes between notice of hearsay evidence expected to be given at a "final hearing" (r 23.2(1)) and of notice "in all other cases" (r 23.2(3)).

(1) Notice is given, in the case of a final hearing, by the party intending to call hearsay evidence: first by indicating the intention to do so, or by saying that a witness whose evidence is before the court will not be called.

(2) In the case of all other cases of hearsay evidence, notice is given by the party intending to rely on hearsay evidence, by him or her saying what evidence is to be relied on and why the witness will not be called.

23.3 Circumstances in which notice of intention to rely on hearsay evidence is not required

Section 2(1) of the Civil Evidence Act 1995 (duty to give notice of intention to rely on hearsay evidence) does not apply –

(a) to evidence at hearings other than final hearings;

(b) to an affidavit(GL) or witness statement which is to be used at the final hearing but which does not contain hearsay evidence; or

(c) where the requirement is excluded by a practice direction.

Civil Evidence Act 1995, s 2(1)—Civil Evidence Act 1995, s 2(1) provides as follows:

"(1) A party proposing to adduce hearsay evidence in civil proceedings shall, subject to the following provisions of this section, give to the other party or parties to the proceedings –

(a) such notice (if any) of that fact, and

(b) on request, such particulars of or relating to the evidence,

as is reasonable and practicable in the circumstances for the purpose of enabling him or them to deal with any matters arising from its being hearsay."

The requirement for hearsay evidence notice under s 2(1) is excluded by r 23.3 in the case of interim hearings (and see FPR 2010, r 22.2(1)(b)) and for witness statements and affidavits that do not contain hearsay evidence. On a hearsay notice being given such further information concerning it shall be given (s 2(1)(b)).

23.4 Power to call witness for cross-examination on hearsay evidence

(1) Where a party –

(a) proposes to rely on hearsay evidence; and

(b) does not propose to call the person who made the original statement to give oral evidence, the court may, on the application of any other party, permit that party to call the maker of the statement to be cross-examined[GL] on the contents of the statement.

(2) An application for permission to cross-examine[GL] under this rule must be made within 14 days beginning with the date on which a notice of intention to rely on the hearsay evidence was served on the applicant.

> (Rules 35.3 and 35.4 contain rules in relation to evidence arising out of mediation of cross-border disputes.)

Application to cross-examine—A party to whom notice is given under FPR 2010, r 23.2 may apply to the court (under the FPR 2010, Pt 18 procedure) for an order that he be able to have called the witness concerned for their cross-examination on their statement. The court has a discretion as to whether to admit the evidence. Its importance of the evidence in the context of the case, the extent and relevance of the cross-examination and the proportionality of calling the witness as against the need to deal with the case fairly may all weigh in the judge's mind in the exercise of that discretion.

23.5 Credibility

(1) Where a party proposes to rely on hearsay evidence, but –

    (a)   does not propose to call the person who made the original statement to give oral evidence; and

    (b)   another party wishes to call evidence to attack the credibility of the person who made the statement,

the party who so wishes must give notice of that intention to the party who proposes to give the hearsay statement in evidence.

(2) A party must give notice under paragraph (1) within 14 days after the date on which a hearsay notice relating to the hearsay evidence was served on that party.

Weight of hearsay evidence—The counter-balance to Civil Evidence Act 1995, s 1(1) as to admissibility of hearsay evidence is to give the responsibility to the courts to assess the weight, or cogency, of the hearsay evidence. Accordingly, s 4 provides as follows:
"**4 Considerations relevant to weighing of hearsay evidence**
(1) In estimating the weight (if any) to be given to hearsay evidence in civil proceedings the court shall have regard to any circumstances from which any inference can reasonably be drawn as to the reliability or otherwise of the evidence.
(2) Regard may be had, in particular, to the following –
    (a) whether it would have been reasonable and practicable for the party by whom the evidence was adduced to have produced the maker of the original statement as a witness;
    (b) whether the original statement was made contemporaneously with the occurrence or existence of the matters stated;
    (c) whether the evidence involves multiple hearsay;
    (d) whether any person involved had any motive to conceal or misrepresent matters;
    (e) whether the original statement was an edited account, or was made in collaboration with another or for a particular purpose;
    (f) whether the circumstances in which the evidence is adduced as hearsay are such as to suggest an attempt to prevent proper evaluation of its weight."

Civil Evidence Act 1995, s 4: judicial findings on hearsay—Civil Evidence Act 1995, s 4 places on the court a positive duty to assess the weight of any hearsay evidence, to have regard to "any circumstances" in assessing the weight of that evidence and in particular to take into account the factors set out in s 4(2). If any evidence is hearsay, within the definition in s 1(2) then the judge must so state and make specific findings as to the weight to be given to that evidence in the court's decision.

23.6 Use of plans, photographs and models etc as evidence

(1) This rule applies to –

    (a)   evidence (such as a plan, photograph or model) which is not –

        (i)   contained in a witness statement, affidavit[GL] or expert's report;

        (ii) to be given orally at the final hearing; or

(iii) evidence of which prior notice must be given under rule 23.2; and

(b) documents which may be received in evidence without further proof under section 9 of the Civil Evidence Act 1995.

(2) Except as provided below, section 2(1)(a) of the Civil Evidence Act 1995 (notice of proposal to adduce hearsay evidence) does not apply to evidence falling within paragraph (1).

(3) Such evidence is not receivable at the final hearing unless the party intending to rely on it (in this rule, "the party") has –

(a) served it or, in the case of a model, a photograph of it with an invitation to inspect the original, on the other party in accordance with this rule; or

(b) complied with such directions as the court may give for serving the evidence on, or for giving notice under section 2(1)(a) of the Civil Evidence Act 1995 in respect of the evidence to, the other party.

(4) Where the party intends to use the evidence as evidence of any fact then, except where paragraph (6) applies, the party must serve the evidence not later than the latest date for serving witness statements.

(5) The party must serve the evidence at least 21 days before the hearing at which the party proposes to rely on it if –

(a) there are not to be witness statements; or

(b) the party intends to put in the evidence solely in order to disprove an allegation made in a witness statement.

(6) Where the evidence forms part of expert evidence, the party must serve the evidence when the expert's report is served on the other party.

(7) Where the evidence is being produced to the court for any reason other than as part of factual or expert evidence, the party must serve the evidence at least 21 days before the hearing at which the party proposes to rely on it.

(8) Where the court directs a party to give notice that the party intends to put in the evidence, the court may direct that every other party be given an opportunity to inspect it and to agree to its admission without further proof.

23.7 Evidence of finding on question of foreign law

(1) This rule sets out the procedure which must be followed by a party (in this rule, "the party") who intends to put in evidence a finding on a question of foreign law by virtue of section 4(2) of the Civil Evidence Act 1972.

(2) The party must give any other party notice of that intention.

(3) The party must give the notice –

(a) if there are to be witness statements, not later than the latest date for serving them; or

(b) otherwise, not less than 21 days before the hearing at which the party proposes to put the finding in evidence.

(4) The notice must –

(a) specify the question on which the finding was made; and

(b) enclose a copy of a document where it is reported or recorded.

23.8 Evidence of consent of trustee to act

In proceedings to which Part 9 (financial remedies) applies, a document purporting to contain the written consent of a person to act as trustee and to bear that person's signature verified by some other person is evidence of such consent.

23.9 Note of oral evidence in magistrates' courts

In proceedings in a magistrates' court, the justices' clerk or the court shall keep a note of the substance of the oral evidence given at a directions appointment or at a hearing of any proceedings.

PART 24
WITNESSES, DEPOSITIONS GENERALLY AND TAKING OF EVIDENCE IN MEMBER STATES OF THE EUROPEAN UNION

CONTENTS OF THIS PART

Chapter 1
Witnesses and Depositions

Note—FPR 2010, Pt 24 and FPR PD24A make provision for evidence in Member States of the EU. Chapter 1 makes provision for witnesses and dispositions; Chapter 2 makes provision for the taking of evidence in Member States of the EU.

Chapter 1
Witnesses and Depositions

Defined terms—"proceedings", "jurisdiction": FPR 2010, r 2.3(1).

Scope—FPR 2010, rr 24.2–24.6 and FPR PD24A, paras 1–3 make provision for the circumstances in which a person may be required to attend court to give evidence or to produce a document. The form of witness summons is set out in PD24A. The court's permission to issue a witness summons is required in certain circumstances (FPR 2010, r 24.3(2)). A witness summons is issued either by the court where the case is proceeding or the court where the hearing in question will be held (r 24.3(3)). Time for serving a witness summons is regulated by FPR 2010, r 24.4, the general rule being that a witness summons is binding if served at least 7 days before the hearing date. A witness summons is served by the issuing party except in proceedings to which FPR 2010, Part 14 applies, where it must be served by the court unless otherwise directed (FPR 2010, r 24.5). Provision for travelling expenses and compensation for loss of time is made by FPR 2010, rr 24.5(3) and 24.6 and FPR PD24A, para 3.

Evidence by deposition is provided for by FPR 2010, rr 24.7–24.14 and FPR PD24A, paras 4 and 5. The procedure enables a party to apply for an order that a person be examined before the hearing takes place before a judge, an examiner of the court (FPR 2010, rr 24.13, 24.14) or such other person as the court appoints. The procedure where depositions are to be taken in England and Wales for use as evidence in proceedings in courts in England and Wales is set out in FPR PD24A, para 4. The conduct of the examination is regulated by FPR 2010, r 24.8. The court has powers to enforce the attendance of a witness before an examiner (FPR 2010, r 24.9). The use of depositions is regulated by FPR 2010, rr 24.10, 24.11. Where the deposition is to be taken out of the jurisdiction for use as evidence in proceedings before a court in England and Wales and where Council Regulation (EC) No 1206/2001 of 28 May 2011 ("the Taking of Evidence Regulation") does not apply (i e in the case of all Member States except Denmark)), FPR 2010, r 24.12 and FPR PD24A, para 5 apply. The High Court may order the issue of a letter of request (FPR PD24A, Annex A) to the judicial authorities of the country in which the proposed deponent is for arrangements to be made for a deposition to be taken.

24.1 Scope of this Chapter

(1) This Chapter provides –

    (a)   for the circumstances in which a person may be required to attend court to give evidence or to produce a document; and

    (b)   for a party to obtain evidence before a hearing to be used at the hearing.

(2) This Chapter, apart from rule 24.10(2) to (4), does not apply to proceedings in a magistrates' court.

        (Rules 34.16 to 34.21 and 34.24 of the CPR apply to incoming requests for evidence.)

24.2 Witness summonses

(1) A witness summons is a document issued by the court requiring a witness to –

    (a)   attend court to give evidence; or

    (b)   produce documents to the court.

(2) A witness summons must be in the form set out in Practice Direction 24A.

(3) There must be a separate witness summons for each witness.

(4) A witness summons may require a witness to produce documents to the court either –

    (a)   on the date fixed for a hearing; or

    (b)   on such date as the court may direct.

(5) The only documents that a summons under this rule can require a person to produce before a hearing are documents which that person could be required to produce at the hearing.

        (Rules 35.3 and 35.4 contain rules in relation to evidence arising out of mediation of cross-border disputes.)

"such date as the court may direct" (r 24.2(4)(b))—For production of documents, this rule gives regulatory effect to *Khanna v Lovell White Durrant (A Firm)* [1995] 1 WLR 121 (applied in family proceedings in *Roker International Properties Inc* [2000] 2 FLR 976). Rule 24.3(2)(b) adds to the *Khanna* appointment that, with permission, the court may now require also that oral evidence (only documents could be dealt with under *Khanna*) be dealt with at a preliminary hearing. That hearing may be at a place other than the court itself (FPR 2010, r 2.8, e g at a venue where the documents are held).

Restrictions on production—Rule 24.2(5) (and c f r 21.2(5)) prevents a witness being required to produce a document where that witness could not be compelled to produce the document at any hearing (e g because it is covered by confidentiality or public interest immunity). Similar principles will then arise, as are considered at FPR 2010, r 21.3: the need for evidence to be before the court to ensure a fair trial balanced against the private interests of the third party, or of the relevance of the evidence to the issues before the court. A witness will also not be required to produce documents where they are not relevant to an issue before the court (see also **"set aside or vary a witness summons"** under r 24.3).

24.3 Issue of a witness summons

(1) A witness summons is issued on the date entered on the summons by the court.

(2) A party must obtain permission from the court where that party wishes to –

 (a) have a summons issued less than 7 days before the date of the final hearing;

 (b) have a summons issued for a witness to attend court to give evidence or to produce documents on any date except the date fixed for the final hearing; or

 (c) have a summons issued for a witness to attend court to give evidence or to produce documents at any hearing except the final hearing.

(3) A witness summons must be issued by –

 (a) the court where the case is proceeding; or

 (b) the court where the hearing in question will be held.

(4) The court may set aside(GL) or vary a witness summons issued under this rule.

"set aside or vary a witness summons" (r 24.3(4))—The court has a discretion – on application being made – to "set aside or vary a witness summons" on grounds similar to those for refusing disclosure (e g to require production of a document or attendance is oppressive; evidence not relevant to an issue before the court; not necessary to fair disposal; confidentiality; and see *South Tyneside Borough Council v Wickes Building Supplies Ltd* [2004] EWHC 2428 for what is "necessary for the fair disposal" of a case). In *Morgan v Morgan* (1976) FLR Rep 473, Watkins J put the test as: the court must balance the need to have the information necessary to get the answer as near as possible right – that is, to ensure "that the lump sum awarded is the correct figure" so far as it can be calculated; as against the "rights of the citizen ... to keep to himself ... details of his wealth and what he intends to do with it" (wife's father had been subpoenaed to produce his will).

Application for permission to set aside or to vary—Applications under r 24.3 are by FPR 2010, Pt 18 procedure (Form D11).

24.4 Time for serving a witness summons

(1) The general rule is that a witness summons is binding if it is served at least 7 days before the date on which the witness is required to attend before the court.

(2) The court may direct that a witness summons is binding although it will be served less than 7 days before the date on which the witness is required to attend before the court.

(3) A witness summons which is –

 (a) served in accordance with this rule; and

 (b) requires the witness to attend court to give evidence,

is binding until the conclusion of the hearing at which the attendance of the witness is required.

 (Rules 35.3 and 35.4 contain rules in relation to evidence arising out of mediation of cross-border disputes.)

24.5 Who is to serve a witness summons

(1) Subject to paragraph (2), a witness summons is to be served by the party on whose behalf it is issued unless that party indicates in writing, when asking the court to issue the summons, that that party wishes the court to serve it instead.

(2) In proceedings to which Part 14 (procedure for applications in adoption, placement and related proceedings) applies, a witness summons is to be served by the court unless the court directs otherwise.

(3) Where the court is to serve the witness summons, the party on whose behalf it is issued must deposit, in the court office, the money to be paid or offered to the witness under rule 24.6.

24.6 Right of witness to travelling expenses and compensation for loss of time

At the time of service of a witness summons the witness must be offered or paid –

(a) a sum reasonably sufficient to cover the expenses of the witness in travelling to and from the court; and

(b) such sum by way of compensation for loss of time as may be specified in Practice Direction 24A.

24.7 Evidence by deposition

(1) A party may apply for an order for a person to be examined before the hearing takes place.

(2) A person from whom evidence is to be obtained following an order under this rule is referred to as a 'deponent' and the evidence is referred to as a 'deposition'.

(3) An order under this rule is for a deponent to be examined on oath before –

(a) a judge;

(b) an examiner of the court; or

(c) such other person as the court appoints.

(Rule 24.14 makes provision for the appointment of examiners of the court.)

(4) The order may require the production of any document which the court considers is necessary for the purposes of the examination.

(5) The order must state the date, time and place of the examination.

(6) At the time of service of the order the deponent must be offered or paid –

(a) a sum reasonably sufficient to cover the expenses of the deponent in travelling to and from the place of examination; and

(b) such sum by way of compensation for loss of time as may be specified in Practice Direction 24A.

(7) Where the court makes an order for a deposition to be taken, it may also order the party who obtained the order to serve a witness statement or witness summary in relation to the evidence to be given by the person to be examined.

(Part 22 (evidence) contains the general rules about witness statements and witness summaries.)

(Rules 35.3 and 35.4 contain rules in relation to evidence arising out of mediation of cross-border disputes.)

24.8 Conduct of examination

(1) Subject to any directions contained in the order for examination, the examination must be conducted in the same way as if the witness were giving evidence at a final hearing.

(2) If all the parties are present, the examiner may conduct the examination of a person not named in the order for examination if all the parties and the person to be examined consent.

(3) In defended proceedings under Part 7 (matrimonial and civil partnership proceedings), the examiner may conduct the examination in private if of the view that it is appropriate to do so.

(4) Save in proceedings to which paragraph (3) applies, the examiner will conduct the examination in private unless of the view that it is not appropriate to do so.

(5) The examiner must ensure that the evidence given by the witness is recorded in full.

(6) The examiner must send a copy of the deposition –

    (a)   to the person who obtained the order for the examination of the witness; and
    (b)   to the court where the case is proceeding.

(7) The court will give directions as to service of the deposition on the other party.

24.9 Enforcing attendance of witness

(1) If a person served with an order to attend before an examiner –

    (a)   fails to attend; or
    (b)   refuses to be sworn for the purpose of the examination or to answer any lawful question or produce any document at the examination,

a certificate of that person's failure or refusal, signed by the examiner, must be filed by the party requiring the deposition.

(2) On the certificate being filed, the party requiring the deposition may apply to the court for an order requiring that person to attend or to be sworn or to answer any question or produce any document, as the case may be.

(3) An application for an order under this rule may be made without notice.

(4) The court may order the person against whom an order is made under this rule to pay any costs resulting from that person's failure or refusal.

> (Rules 35.3 and 35.4 contain rules in relation to evidence arising out of mediation of cross-border disputes. Rule 35.4(1)(d) relates specifically to this rule.)

24.10 Use of deposition at a hearing

(1) A deposition ordered under rule 24.7 may be given in evidence at a hearing unless the court orders otherwise.

(2) A party intending to put in evidence a deposition at a hearing must file notice of intention to do so on the court and the court will give directions about serving the notice on every other party.

(3) The party must file the notice at least 21 days before the day fixed for the hearing.

(4) The court may require a deponent to attend the hearing and give evidence orally.

(5) Where a deposition is given in evidence at the final hearing, it is treated as if it were a witness statement for the purposes of rule 22.19 (availability of witness statements for inspection).

> (Rules 35.3 and 35.4 contain rules in relation to evidence arising out of mediation of cross-border disputes. Rule 35.4(1)(e) relates specifically to this rule.)

24.11 Restrictions on subsequent use of deposition taken for the purpose of any hearing except the final hearing

(1) This rule applies to proceedings under Part 7 (matrimonial and civil partnership proceedings) or Part 9 (financial remedies).

(2) Where the court orders a party to be examined about that party's or any other assets for the purpose of any hearing except the final hearing, the deposition may be used only for the purpose of the proceedings in which the order was made.

(3) However it may be used for some other purpose –

    (a)   by the party who was examined;

    (b)   if the party who was examined agrees; or

    (c)   if the court gives permission.

24.12 Where a person to be examined is out of the jurisdiction – letter of request

(1) This rule applies where a party wishes to take a deposition from a person who is –

    (a)   out of the jurisdiction; and

    (b)   not in a Regulation State within the meaning of Chapter 2 of this Part.

(2) The High Court may order the issue of a letter of request to the judicial authorities of the country in which the proposed deponent is.

(3) A letter of request is a request to a judicial authority to take the evidence of that person, or arrange for it to be taken.

(4) The High Court may make an order under this rule in relation to county court proceedings.

(5) If the government of a country allows a person appointed by the High Court to examine a person in that country, the High Court may make an order appointing a special examiner for that purpose.

(6) A person may be examined under this rule on oath or affirmation or in accordance with any procedure permitted in the country in which the examination is to take place.

(7) If the High Court makes an order for the issue of a letter of request, the party who sought the order must file –

    (a)   the following documents and, except where paragraph (8) applies, a translation of them –

        (i)   a draft letter of request;

        (ii)   a statement of the issues relevant to the proceedings; and

        (iii)   a list of questions or the subject matter of questions to be put to the person to be examined; and

    (b)   an undertaking to be responsible for the Secretary of State's expenses.

(8) There is no need to file a translation if –

    (a)   English is one of the official languages of the country where the examination is to take place; or

    (b)   a practice direction has specified that country as a country where no translation is necessary.

    (Rules 35.3 and 35.4 contain rules in relation to evidence arising out of mediation of cross-border disputes. Rule 35.4(1)(f) relates specifically to this rule.)

24.13 Fees and expenses of examiner of the court

(1) An examiner of the court may charge a fee for the examination.

(2) The examiner need not send the deposition to the court unless the fee is paid.

(3) The examiner's fees and expenses must be paid by the party who obtained the order for examination.

(4) If the fees and expenses due to an examiner are not paid within a reasonable time, the examiner may report that fact to the court.

(5) The court may order the party who obtained the order for examination to deposit in the court office a specified sum in respect of the examiner's fees and, where it does so, the examiner will not be asked to act until the sum has been deposited.

(6) An order under this rule does not affect any decision as to the party who is ultimately to bear the costs of the examination.

24.14 Examiners of the court

(1) The Lord Chancellor will appoint persons to be examiners of the court.

(2) The persons appointed must be barristers or solicitor-advocates who have been practising for a period of not less than 3 years.

(3) The Lord Chancellor may revoke an appointment at any time.

Chapter 2
Taking of Evidence – Member States of the European Union

Scope—FPR 2010, Ch 2 and FPR PD24A, paras 6–9 regulate the taking of evidence between EU Member States. Where evidence is to be taken from a person in another Member State of the EU for use as evidence in proceedings before a court in England and Wales, Council Regulation (EC) No 1206/2001 of 28 May 2001 on cooperation between the courts of the Member States in the taking of evidence in civil or commercial matters ("the Taking of Evidence Regulation") applies. The Taking of Evidence Regulation is set out as Annex B in PD24A. The Taking of Evidence Regulation does not apply to Denmark in relation to which r 24.12 applies. Each Regulation State (ie all Member States except Denmark) has prepared a list of designated courts competent to take evidence in accordance with the Taking of Evidence Regulation. The designated courts for England and Wales are listed in Annex C to PD24A (PD24A, para 7). The Taking of Evidence Regulation requires each Regulation State to nominate a Central Body responsible for, for example, supplying information to courts. The Central Body for the UK is the Senior Master, Queen's Bench Division (PD24A, para 8). The procedure for taking evidence in another Regulation State for use in England and Wales is set out in FPR 2010, r 24.16 and PD24A, para 9.

24.15 Interpretation

In this Chapter –
　　"designated court" has the meaning given in Practice Direction 24A;
　　"Regulation State" has the same meaning as 'Member State' in the Taking of
　　　　Evidence Regulation, that is all Member States except Denmark;
　　"the Taking of Evidence Regulation" means Council Regulation (EC) No. 1206/2001
　　　　of 28 May 2001 on co-operation between the courts of the Member States in the
　　　　taking of evidence in civil or commercial matters.

24.16 Where a person to be examined is in another Regulation State

(1) This rule applies where a party wishes to take a deposition from a person who is –
　　(a)　outside the jurisdiction; and
　　(b)　in a Regulation State.

(2) The court may order the issue of a request to a designated court ('the requested court') in the Regulation State in which the proposed deponent is.

(3) If the court makes an order for the issue of a request, the party who sought the order must file –
　　(a)　a draft Form A as set out in the annex to the Taking of Evidence Regulation
　　　　(request for the taking of evidence);

(b)   except where paragraph (4) applies, a translation of the form;

(c)   an undertaking to be responsible for costs sought by the requested court in relation to –

fees paid to experts and interpreters; and

where requested by that party, the use of special procedures or communications technology; and

(d)   an undertaking to be responsible for the court's expenses.

(4)   There is no need to file a translation if –

(a)   English is one of the official languages of the Regulation State where the examination is to take place; or

(b)   the Regulation State has indicated, in accordance with the Taking of Evidence Regulation, that English is a language which it will accept.

(5)   Where article 17 of the Taking of Evidence Regulation (direct taking of evidence by the requested court) allows evidence to be taken directly in another Regulation State, the court may make an order for the submission of a request in accordance with that article.

(6)   If the court makes an order for the submission of a request under paragraph (5), the party who sought the order must file –

(a)   a draft Form I as set out in the annex to the Taking of Evidence Regulation (request for direct taking of evidence);

(b)   except where paragraph (4) applies, a translation of the form; and

(c)   an undertaking to be responsible for the court's expenses.

Practice Direction 24A –
Witnesses, Depositions and Taking of Evidence in Member States of the European Union

This Practice Direction supplements FPR Part 24

WITNESS SUMMONSES

Issue of witness summons

1.1   A witness summons may require a witness to –

(a)   attend court to give evidence;

(b)   produce documents to the court; or

(c)   both,

on either a date fixed for the hearing or such date as the court may direct (see rule 24.2).

(In relation to cases to which the Mediation Directive applies, rules 35.3 and 35.4 contain rules in relation to mediation evidence)

1.2   Two copies of the witness summons should be filed with the court for sealing, one of which will be retained on the court file.

1.3   A mistake in the name or address of a person named in a witness summons may be corrected if the summons has not been served.

1.4   The corrected summons must be re-sealed by the court and marked "Amended and Re-Sealed".

Magistrates' courts proceedings

2.1 An application for the issue of a summons or warrant under section 97 of the Magistrates' Courts Act 1980 may be made by the applicant in person or by his legal representative.

2.2 An application for the issue of such a summons may be made by delivering or sending the application in writing to the court officer for the magistrates' court.

Travelling expenses and compensation for loss of time

3.1 When a witness is served with a witness summons the witness must be offered a sum to cover travelling expenses to and from the court and compensation for loss of time (see rule 24.6).

3.2 If the witness summons is to be served by the court, the party issuing the summons must deposit with the court –

(a)   a sum sufficient to pay for the witness's expenses in travelling to the court and in returning to his or her home or place of work; and

(b)   a sum in respect of the period during which earnings or benefit are lost, or such lesser sum as it may be proved that the witness will lose as a result of attendance at court in answer to the witness summons.

3.3 The sum referred to in paragraph 3.2(b) is to be based on the sums payable to witnesses attending the Crown Court (fixed pursuant to the Prosecution of Offences Act 1985 and Costs in Criminal Cases (General) Regulations 1986).

Depositions to be taken in England and Wales for use as evidence in proceedings in courts in England and Wales

4.1 A party may apply for an order for a person to be examined on oath before –

(a)   a judge;

(b)   an examiner of the court; or

(c)   such other person as the court may appoint (see rule 24.7(3)).

   (This is subject to rules about mediation evidence in cases to which the Mediation Directive applies: see rules 35.3 and 35.4)

4.2 The party who obtains an order for the examination of a deponent (see rule 24.7(2)) before an examiner of the court must –

(a)   apply to the Foreign Process Section of the Masters' Secretary's Department at the Royal Courts of Justice for the allocation of an examiner;

(b)   when allocated, provide the examiner with copies of all documents in the proceedings necessary to inform the examiner of the issues; and

(c)   pay the deponent a sum to cover travelling expenses to and from the examination and compensation for loss of time (see rule 24.7(6)).

4.3 In ensuring that the deponent's evidence is recorded in full, the court or the examiner may permit it to be recorded on audiotape or videotape, but the deposition (see rule 24.7(2)) must always be recorded in writing by the examiner or by a competent shorthand writer or stenographer.

4.4 If the deposition is not recorded word for word, it must contain, as nearly as may be, the statement of the deponent. The examiner may record word for word any particular questions and answers which appear to have special importance.

4.5 If a deponent objects to answering any question or where any objection is taken to any question, the examiner must –

(a)   record in the deposition or a document attached to it –

    (i)   the question;

    (ii) the nature of and grounds for the objection;

    (iii) any answer given; and

(b)   give the examiner's opinion as to the validity of the objection and must record it in the deposition or a document attached to it.

The court will decide as to the validity of the objection and any question of costs arising from it.

4.6 Documents and exhibits must –

(a)   have an identifying number or letter marked on them by the examiner; and

(b)   be preserved by the party or legal representative (see rule 2.3) who obtained the order for the examination, or as the court or the examiner may direct.

4.7 The examiner may put any question to the deponent as to –

(a)   the meaning of any of the deponent's answers; or

(b)   any matter arising in the course of the examination.

4.8 Where a deponent –

(a)   fails to attend the examination; or

(b)   refuses to –

    (i)   be sworn; or

    (ii) answer any lawful question; or

    (iii) produce any document,

the examiner will sign a certificate (see rule 24.9) of such failure or refusal and may include in the certificate any comment as to the conduct of the deponent or of any person attending the examination.

4.9 The party who obtained the order for the examination must file the certificate with the court and may apply for an order that the deponent attend for examination or produce any document, as the case may be (see rule 24.9(2) and (3)). The application may be made without notice.

4.10 The court will make such order on the application as it thinks fit including an order for the deponent to pay any costs resulting from the failure or refusal (see rule 24.9(4)).

4.11 A deponent who wilfully refuses to obey an order of the High Court or the county court made under Part 24 may be proceeded against for contempt of court. (Where a person fails to attend before a magistrates' court in answer to a summons issued under section 97 of the Magistrates' Court Act 1980, the court may, under certain circumstances, issue a warrant for that party's arrest and to bring that party before the court at a time and place specified in the warrant: see section 97(3) of the 1980 Act.)

4.12 A deposition must –

(a)   be signed by the examiner;

(b)   have any amendments to it initialled by the examiner and the deponent;

(c)   be endorsed by the examiner with –

    (i)   a statement of the time occupied by the examination; and

    (ii) a record of any refusal by the deponent to sign the deposition and of the deponent's reasons for not doing so; and

(d)   be sent by the examiner to the court where the proceedings are taking place for filing on the court file.

4.13 Rule 24.13 deals with the fees and expenses of an examiner.

PART III

Depositions to be taken abroad for use as evidence in proceedings before courts in England and Wales (where the Taking of Evidence Regulation does not apply)

5.1 Where a party wishes to take a deposition from a person outside the jurisdiction, the High Court may order the issue of a letter of request to the judicial authorities of the country in which the proposed deponent is (see rule 24.12).

(Rule 35.4(1)(f) deals with letters of request where the Mediation Directive applies)

5.2 An application for an order referred to in paragraph 5.1 should be made by application notice in accordance with Part 18 (Procedure for other applications in proceedings).

5.3 The documents which a party applying for an order for the issue of a letter of request must file with the application notice are set out in rule 24.12(7). They are as follows –

(a)   a draft letter of request in the form set out in Annex A to this practice direction;
(b)   a statement of the issues relevant to the proceedings;
(c)   a list of questions or the subject matter of questions to be put to the proposed deponent;
(d)   a translation of the documents in (a), (b) and (c), unless the proposed deponent is in a country of which English is an official language; and
(e)   an undertaking to be responsible for the expenses of the Secretary of State.

In addition to the documents listed above the party applying for the order must file a draft order.

5.4 The above documents should be filed with the Masters' Secretary in Room E214, Royal Courts of Justice, Strand, London WC2A 2LL.

5.5 The application will be dealt with by the Senior Master of the Queen's Bench Division of the Senior Courts who will, if appropriate, sign the letter of request.

5.6 Attention is drawn to the provisions of rule 18.11 (Application to set aside or vary order made without notice).

5.7 If parties are in doubt as to whether a translation under paragraph 5.3(d) is required, they should seek guidance from the Foreign Process Section of the Masters' Secretary's Department.

5.8 A special examiner appointed under rule 24.12(5) may be the British Consul or the Consul-General or his deputy in the country where the evidence is to be taken if –

(a)   there is in respect of that country a Civil Procedure Convention providing for the taking of evidence in that country for the assistance of proceedings in the High Court or other court in this country; or
(b)   the Secretary of State has consented.

5.9 The provisions of paragraphs 4.1 to 4.12 apply to the depositions referred to in this paragraph.

TAKING OF EVIDENCE BETWEEN EU MEMBER STATES

Taking of Evidence Regulation

6.1 Where evidence is to be taken from a person in another Member State of the European Union for use as evidence in proceedings before courts in England and Wales Council Regulation (EC) No 1206/2001 of 28 May 2001 on co-operation between the courts of the Member States in the taking of evidence in civil or commercial matters ('the Taking of Evidence Regulation') applies.

6.2 The Taking of Evidence Regulation is annexed to this practice direction as Annex B.

6.3 The Taking of Evidence Regulation does not apply to Denmark. In relation to Denmark, therefore, rule 24.12 will continue to apply.

> (Article 21(1) of the Taking of Evidence Regulation provides that the Regulation prevails over other provisions contained in bilateral or multilateral agreements or arrangements concluded by the Member States.)

> Originally published in the official languages of the European Community in the Official Journal of the European Communities by the Office for Official Publications of the European Communities.

Meaning of 'designated court'

7.1 In accordance with the Taking of Evidence Regulation, each Regulation State has prepared a list of courts competent to take evidence in accordance with the Regulation indicating the territorial and, where appropriate, special jurisdiction of those courts.

7.2 Where Chapter 2 of this Part refers to a 'designated court' in relation to another Regulation State, the reference is to the court, referred to in the list of competent courts of that State, which is appropriate to the application in hand.

7.3 Where the reference is to the 'designated court' in England and Wales, the reference is to the appropriate competent court in the jurisdiction. The designated courts for England and Wales are listed in Annex C to this practice direction.

Central Body

8.1 The Taking of Evidence Regulation stipulates that each Regulation State must nominate a Central Body responsible for –

- (a) supplying information to courts;
- (b) seeking solutions to any difficulties which may arise in respect of a request; and
- (c) forwarding, in exceptional cases, at the request of a requesting court, a request to the competent court.

8.2 The United Kingdom has nominated the Senior Master of the Queen's Bench Division, to be the Central Body for England and Wales.

8.3 The Senior Master, as Central Body, has been designated responsible for taking decisions on requests pursuant to Article 17 of the Regulation. Article 17 allows a court to submit a request to the Central Body or a designated competent authority in another Regulation State to take evidence directly in that State.

Evidence to be taken in another Regulation State for use in England and Wales

9.1 Where a person wishes to take a deposition from a person in another Regulation State, the court where the proceedings are taking place may order the issue of a request to the designated court in the Regulation State (rule 24.16 (2)). The form of request is prescribed as Form A in the Taking of Evidence Regulation.

9.2 An application to the court for an order under rule 24.16(2) should be made by application notice in accordance with Part 18 (Procedure for other applications in proceedings).

9.3 Rule 24.16(3) provides that the party applying for the order must file a draft form of request in the prescribed form. Where completion of the form requires attachments or documents to accompany the form, these must also be filed.

9.4 If the court grants an order under rule 24.16(2), it will send the form of request directly to the designated court.

PART III

9.5 Where the taking of evidence requires the use of an expert, the designated court may require a deposit in advance towards the costs of that expert. The party who obtained the order is responsible for the payment of any such deposit which should be deposited with the court for onward transmission. Under the provisions of the Taking of Evidence Regulation, the designated court is not required to execute the request until such payment is received.

9.6 Article 17 permits the court where proceedings are taking place to take evidence directly from a deponent in another Regulation State if the conditions of the article are satisfied. Direct taking of evidence can only take place if evidence is given voluntarily without the need for coercive measures. Rule 24.16(5) provides for the court to make an order for the submission of a request to take evidence directly. The form of request is Form I annexed to the Taking of Evidence Regulation and rule 24.16(6) makes provision for a draft of this form to be filed by the party seeking the order. An application for an order under rule 24.16(5) should be by application notice in accordance with Part 18.

9.7 Attention is drawn to the provisions of rule 18.11 (Application to set aside or vary order made without notice).

ANNEX A – DRAFT LETTER OF REQUEST (WHERE THE TAKING OF EVIDENCE REGULATION DOES NOT APPLY) (SEE PARAGRAPH 5.3(A) ABOVE)

To the Competent Judicial Authority of in the of

[name] Senior Master of the Queen's Bench Division of the Senior Courts of England and Wales respectfully request the assistance of your court with regard to the following matters.

2 An application is now pending in the Division of the High Court of Justice in England and Wales entitled as follows [set out full title and case number] in which [name] of [address] is the applicant and [name] of [address] is the respondent.

3 The names and addresses of the representatives or agents of [set out names and addresses of representatives of the parties].

4 The application by the applicant is for –

    (a) [set out the nature of the application]
    (b) [the order sought] and
    (c) [a summary of the facts.]

5 It is necessary for the purposes of justice between the parties that you cause the following witnesses, who are resident within your jurisdiction, to be examined. The names and addresses of the witnesses are as follows:

6 The witnesses should be examined on oath or if that is not possible within your laws or is impossible of performance by reason of the internal practice and procedure of your court or by reason of practical difficulties, they should be examined in accordance with whatever procedure your laws provide for in these matters.

7 Either:

    The witnesses should be examined in accordance with the list of questions annexed hereto.
    Or:
    The witnesses should be examined regarding [set out full details of evidence sought]
    N.B. Where the witness is required to produce documents, these should be clearly identified.

8 I would ask that you cause me, or the agents of the parties (if appointed), to be informed of the date and place where the examination is to take place.

9 Finally, I request that you will cause the evidence of the said witnesses to be reduced into writing and all documents produced on such examinations to be duly marked for identification and that you will further be pleased to authenticate such examinations by the seal of your court or in such other way as is in accordance with your procedure and return the written evidence and documents produced to me addressed as follows –

> Senior Master of the Queen's Bench Division
> Royal Courts of Justice
> Strand
> London
> WC2A 2LL
> England

ANNEX B – TAKING OF EVIDENCE REGULATION

http://www.justice.gov.uk/courts/procedure-rules/family/practice_directions/pd_form_imgs/pd_24a_pdf_eps/pd_24a_cr_1206_2001.pdf

ANNEX C – DESIGNATED COURTS IN ENGLAND AND WALES UNDER THE TAKING OF EVIDENCE REGULATION (SEE PARAGRAPH 7.3 ABOVE)

Area	Designated court
London and South Eastern Circuit	Royal Courts of Justice (Queen's Bench Division)
Midland Circuit	Birmingham Civil Justice Centre
Western Circuit	Bristol County Court
Wales and Chester Circuit	Cardiff Civil Justice Centre
Northern Circuit	Manchester County Court
North Eastern Circuit	Leeds County Court

PART 25
EXPERTS AND ASSESSORS

CONTENTS OF THIS PART

Amendments—FPR 2010, Pt 25 substituted by SI 2012/3061.

Practice Direction—FPR 2010, Pt 25 is accompanied by FPR PD25A. This deals predominantly with opinion evidence in "proceedings relating to children", a term used by the PD but that is not "a legal term of art and has no statutory force" (para 1.2). Directions run together expert evidence in children with other family proceedings, where appropriate. It stresses the need to distinguish between permission to instruct an expert in proceedings relating to children (FPR 2010, r 25.4), but only to have permission to put in expert evidence in all other proceedings (para 1.5).

Opinion ("expert") evidence—The general rule is that a witness may only give evidence as to fact observed by them. This rule is overridden in the case of opinion evidence given by a person whose expertise justifies the court in receiving that opinion (and see Civil Evidence Act 1972, s 3). Such evidence can only be given with the court's permission (FPR 2010, r 25.4(1)), save in certain circumstances impliedly sanctioned by the rules.

Judge differing from expert's opinion—If a judge is to differ from the view of an expert, especially with a unanimous body of experts, he must give good reasons for so doing (e g *Re W (A Child)* [2005] EWCA Civ 649, which concerned the care of a child: three professional witnesses agreed on the shortcomings of the mother. The judge disagreed with the analysis of two psychiatric experts and the advice of the guardian. The Court allowed the local authority's appeal on the basis that the judge had not explained fully why she disagreed. A judge "is entitled not to accept expert evidence, and is entitled to depart from the views of the guardian. But self-evidently … a judge must give good reasons for taking such a course – the more so when the expert and professional evidence is so powerful" (at [92]).

Family Procedure (Amendment) (No 5) Rules 2012 have introduced amendments to FPR 2010, Pt 25, mostly by making procedure more prescriptive: grounds are stated for the grant of an order for expert evidence (FPR 2010, rr 25.4 and 25.5) and the use of the FPR 2010, Pt 18 procedure for obtaining expert evidence is specifically required (FPR 2010, r 25.7). The CPR 1998 expert's protocol does not apply in family proceedings.

Protected parties and children—FPR PD25A, paras 2.6–2.10 make specific reference to appointment of an expert to deal with issues as to capacity or a child's maturity where protected parties or children may be parties to proceedings.

Expert witness immunity—An expert does not have immunity from suit arising from his report, from discussions with other experts or from evidence given in court (*Jones v Kaney* [2011] 2 FLR 312).

25.1 Duty to restrict expert evidence

Expert evidence will be restricted to that which in the opinion of the court is necessary to assist the court to resolve the proceedings.

Defined terms—"expert": FPR 2010, r 25.2(1).

"in the opinion of the court"—This form of words replaces "reasonably required" (the wording that remains in CPR 1998, r 35.1). For practical purposes, the change of wording is likely to prove only cosmetic. This form of words is no more than a definition of admissibility by other words. As ever, parties must recognise where evidence is not reasonably required or is irrelevant, for example:

(1) where the court can reasonably be assumed already to have the expertise (e g business valuation by reference to *At a Glance*); and

(2) another witness (e g a children's guardian) has – or should have – expertise in matters of child development or family dynamics.

In assessing what is "reasonably required" the court will be required to have in mind always the overriding objective (FPR 2010, r 1.1).

25.2 Interpretation

(1) In this Part –

"authorised applicant" means –

(a) the National Society for the Prevention of Cruelty to Children; or

(b) a person authorised by an order under section 31 of the 1989 Act to bring proceedings under that section;

"children proceedings" means –

(a) proceedings referred to in rules 12.1 and 14.1 and any other proceedings which relate wholly or mainly to the maintenance or upbringing of a minor;

(b) applications for permission to start proceedings mentioned in paragraph (a); and

(c) applications made in the course of proceedings mentioned in paragraph (a);

"expert" means a person who provides expert evidence for use in proceedings;

"local authority" –

(a) in relation to England means –

(i) a county council;

(ii) a district council for an area for which there is no county council;

(iii) a London borough council;

(iv) the Common Council of the City of London; or

(v) the Council of the Isles of Scilly; and

(b) in relation to Wales means a county council or a county borough council;

"single joint expert" means a person who provides expert evidence for use in proceedings on behalf of two or more of the parties (including the applicant) to the proceedings.

(2) References to providing expert evidence, or putting expert evidence before a court, do not include references to –

(a) the provision or giving of evidence –

(i) by a person who is a member of the staff of a local authority or an authorised applicant;

PART III

(ii)   in proceedings to which the authority or authorised applicant is a party; and

(iii)   in the course of the person's work for the authority or the authorised applicant;

(b)   the provision or giving of evidence –

(i)   by a person within a description prescribed for the purposes of section 94(1) of the 2002 Act (suitability for adoption etc); and

(ii)   about the matters mentioned in that subsection;

(c)   the provision or giving of evidence by an officer of the service, or by a Welsh family proceedings officer when acting in those capacities.

(Regulation 3 of the Restriction on the Preparation of Adoption Reports Regulations 2005 (SI 2005/1711) sets out which persons are within a prescribed description for the purposes of section 94(1) of the 2002 Act.)

Expert gives expert evidence—The chief characteristic in law (and see Civil Evidence Act 1972) of expert evidence is the ability to give evidence of both fact and opinion.

"staff of a local authority" (r 25.2(2)(a))—Staff of a local authority can be called as witnesses, do not need the court's permission to be called, but (it seems) may not express an opinion.

25.3   Experts – overriding duty to the court

(1) It is the duty of experts to help the court on matters within their expertise.

(2) This duty overrides any obligation to the person from whom experts have received instructions or by whom they are paid.

(Particular duties of an expert are set out in Practice Direction 25B (The Duties of an Expert, the Expert's Report and Arrangements for an Expert to Attend Court.)

Overriding duty to the court: impartiality—Opinion evidence must be impartial as between the parties (whoever the expert may be instructed by: r 25.3(2); and see, for example, *National Justice Compania Naviera SA v Prudential Assurance Co; the Ikarian Reefer* [1993] 2 Lloyd's Rep 68). The impartiality of an expert witness is essential to their evidence and if an expert has a view that is controversial as between experts or that might be derived from partiality, he must declare the extent of the interest (e g *Re C (Welfare of Child: Immunisation)* [2003] 2 FLR 1095).

Duties of an expert—FPR PD25A sets out the duties of an expert in family proceedings.

Costs and the expert witness—See under CPR 1998, r 44.2, and see *Phillips v Symes* [2005] 1 WLR 2043, where an expert whose report lacked objectivity was ordered to be joined in wasted costs order proceedings.

25.4   Court's power to restrict expert evidence

(1) In any proceedings, a person may not without the permission of the court put expert evidence (in any form) before the court.

(2) In children proceedings –

(a)   an expert may not be instructed; and

(b)   a child may not be medically or psychiatrically examined or otherwise assessed for the purposes of the provision of expert evidence in the proceedings, without the court's permission.

(3) Where in contravention of paragraph 2(a) an expert is instructed, evidence resulting from the instructions is inadmissible in children proceedings unless the court rules that it is admissible.

(4) Where in contravention of paragraph 2(b) a child is medically or psychiatrically examined or otherwise assessed, evidence resulting from the examination or other assessment is inadmissible in children proceedings unless the court rules that it is admissible.

"**Controlling the use of expert evidence**"—This duty has been specifically added to the list of judicial case management duties in FPR 2010, r 1.4(2) by the Family Procedure (Amendment) (No 5) Rules 2012.

Court control of opinion evidence—Rule 25.4(1) deals with two aspects of expert evidence over which the court retains full control.

(1) A party's ability to "call an expert": that is to adduce their live evidence before the court at a final hearing or otherwise;
(2) A party's ability to commission and put in evidence an expert's written report, whether alone or as a jointly instructed expert.

Rule 25.4(1) repeats FPR 2010, r 25.1 in another form. The grant of permission by the court will not be automatic and any decision should be made with the overriding objective in mind and as part of the court's active management of the case.

Check-list for permission—There follows some questions that may arise before the court decides to permit, or not, the involvement of expert witnesses:

- Once issues have been defined (FPR 2010, r 1.4(2)(b)(i): court's duty of "identifying [issues] at an early stage" as part of its duty to manage cases), to what aspect of any issue or issues do the parties consider that the proposed expert is needed to give evidence?
- Is that opinion relevant to one or more issues and "reasonably required to resolve the proceedings" (FPR 2010, r 25.1)?
- Is the cost of the expert and any delay caused by an appointment proportionate "to the nature, importance and complexity of the issues" (FPR 2010, r 1.1(2)(b))?
- If evidence is to be permitted, its filing will be timetabled (r 1.4(2)(g): fixing timetables for the control of progress of the case).
- If expert evidence is to be permitted, would that evidence more appropriately be dealt with by joint instruction of an expert (r 25.7)?

Restrictions on disclosure of expert evidence—Whereas there is a strong presumption in favour of disclosing all relevant evidence, the court has powers to restrict disclosure, for example because of fears for the welfare of a child *(Re D (Adoption Reports: Confidentiality)* [1995] 2 FLR 687; *A Local Authority v A* [2010] 2 FLR 1757; and see **Submission of evidence** under FPR 2010, r 12.12 and restrictions on disclosure under FPR 2010, r 21.3).

New provision—Rule 25.4(2)–(4) is part of the amended FPR 2010, Pt 25 and concentrates on opinion evidence in children proceedings. It confirms that evidence that has been obtained without permission cannot be adduced without permission of the court. This is in line with ordinary public policy principles (e g *Lifely v Lifely* [2008] EWCA Civ 904; *Imerman v Tchenguiz and Others* [2010] 2 FLR 814).

25.5 Further provisions about the court's power to restrict expert evidence

(1) When deciding whether to give permission as mentioned in rule 25.4(1) or (2) in children proceedings, the court is to have regard in particular to –

(a) any impact which giving permission would be likely to have on the welfare of the children concerned, including in the case of permission as mentioned in rule 25.4(2)(b) any impact which any examination or other assessment would be likely to have on the welfare of the child who would be examined or otherwise assessed;
(b) the issues to which the expert evidence would relate;
(c) the questions which the court would require the expert to answer;
(d) what other expert evidence is available (whether obtained before or after the start of proceedings);
(e) whether evidence could be given by another person on the matters on which the expert would give evidence;
(f) the impact which giving permission would be likely to have on the timetable, duration and conduct of the proceedings;
(g) any failure to comply with rule 25.6 or any direction of the court about expert evidence; and
(h) the cost of the expert evidence.

(2) When deciding whether to give permission as mentioned in rule 25.4(1) in proceedings other than children proceedings, the court is to have regard in particular to –

    (a)   the issues to which the expert evidence would relate;

    (b)   the questions which the court would require the expert to answer;

    (c)   the impact which giving permission would be likely to have on the timetable, duration and conduct of the proceedings;

    (d)   any failure to comply with rule 25.6 or any direction of the court about expert evidence; and

    (e)   the cost of the expert evidence.

Checklist—This rule now provides the case management judge with an inclusive checklist. Any application for expert evidence (FPR 2010, r 25.7) would be prudent to address these and any other factors (as well as those in r 25.7) when the FPR 2010, Pt 18 application for the report is made.

25.6 When to apply for the court's permission

Unless the court directs otherwise, parties must apply for the court's permission as mentioned in rule 25.4 as soon as possible and –

    (a)   in public law proceedings referred to in rule 12.2, no later than the Case Management Conference;

    (b)   in private law proceedings referred to in rule 12.2, no later than the First Hearing Dispute Resolution Appointment;

    (c)   in adoption proceedings and placement proceedings, no later than the first directions hearing;

    (d)   in proceedings for a financial remedy, no later than the first appointment;

    (e)   in a defended case referred to in rule 7.1(3), no later than any case management hearing directed by the court under rule 7.20.

25.7 What an application notice requesting the court's permission must include

(1) Part 18 applies to an application for the court's permission as mentioned in rule 25.4.

(2) In any proceedings –

    (a)   the application notice requesting the court's permission as mentioned in rule 25.4 must state –

        (i)   the field in which the expert evidence is required;

        (ii)   where practicable, the name of the proposed expert;

        (iii)   the issues to which the expert evidence is to relate;

        (iv)   whether the expert evidence could be obtained from a single joint expert;

        (v)   the other matters set out in Practice Direction 25C or 25D, as the case may be; and

    (b)   a draft of the order sought is to be attached to the application notice requesting the court's permission and that draft order must set out the matters specified in Practice Direction 25C or 25D, as the case may be.

(3) In children proceedings, an application notice requesting the court's permission as mentioned in rule 25.4 must, in addition to the matters specified in paragraph (2)(a), state the questions which the expert is to be required to answer.

Formal court "application for the court's permission" (r 25.7(1))—The courts will now require formal application – "for the court's permission as mentioned in rule 25.4" – to be made at any case management appointment (e g the appointments referred to in FPR 2010, r 25.6). Application is by FPR 2010, Pt 18 procedure and must be accompanied by grounds and a draft order in the usual way (repeated in r 25.7(2)). The court can make the order without a hearing (FPR 2010, r 18.9) in advance of the case management conference (e g if there is any urgency or the order is not controversial and the court agrees to it).

25.8 Where permission is granted

(1) In any proceedings, where the court grants permission as mentioned in rule 25.4 –

    (a)   it will grant permission only in relation to the expert named or the field identified in the application notice requesting the court's permission; and

    (b)   the court will give directions specifying the date by which the expert is to provide a written report.

(2) In children proceedings, in addition to the directions in paragraph (1)(b), the court will give directions –

    (a)   approving the questions which the expert is required to answer;

    (b)   specifying the date by which the expert is to receive the letter of instruction.

Children proceedings—It is only in children proceedings that the court is required to be prescriptive about the questions to be answered and time limits as to instruction, although in practice case management judges may impose similar requirements in family proceedings other that children proceedings.

25.9 General requirement for expert evidence to be given in a written report

(1) Expert evidence is to be given in a written report unless the court directs otherwise.

(2) The court will not direct an expert to attend a hearing unless it is necessary to do so in the interests of justice.

Form of the report: expert's evidence—The form of the expert's report must be addressed to the court and it must comply with the requirements of FPR PD25A, para 3.3. It must be verified by a statement of truth.

Interests of justice (r 25.5(2))— FPR 2010, r 25.5(2) requires that the court should not direct the attendance of an expert witness save "in the interests of justice" so to do. An expert witness should only be called where a judge has found expressly that the evidence is required by the court (not just that the parties seek the witness's attendance). Brief reasons should, therefore, be given by the court where a direction is given that an expert's evidence is to be called. If an expert's report is not challenged, his report should be received in evidence without an attendance being required. The issue of his attendance or the narrowing of issues arising out of his report by the submission of questions (r 25.6) should be addressed in case management. The judge will apply the overriding objective of dealing with a case fairly (tempered by any "welfare" issue) but also of the proportionality of permitting the further expense of expert evidence. Evidence may be given by video link (FPR 2010, r 22.3).

25.10 Written questions to experts

(1) A party may put written questions about an expert's report to

    (a)   an expert instructed by another party; or

    (b)   a single joint expert appointed under rule 25.11.

(2) Unless the court directs otherwise or a practice direction provides otherwise, written questions under paragraph (1) –

    (a)   must be proportionate;

    (b)   may be put once only;

    (c)   must be put within 10 days beginning with the date on which the expert's report was served;

    (d)   must be for the purpose only of clarification of the report; and

    (e)   must be copied and sent to the other parties at the same time as they are sent to the expert.

(3) An expert's answers to questions put in accordance with paragraph (1) –

    (a)   must be given within the timetable specified by the court; and

    (b)   are treated as part of the expert's report.

PART III

(4) Where –

  (a)   a party has put a written question to an expert instructed by another party; and
  (b)   the expert does not answer that question,

the court may make one or both of the following orders in relation to the party who instructed the expert –

  (i)   that the party may not rely on the evidence of that expert; or
  (ii)   that the party may not recover the fees and expenses of that expert from any other party.

Practice Direction—FPR PD25A, para 3.3 specifies the content of an expert's report that must be addressed to the court (and see FPR 2010, r 25.3(1)).

Timetable for questions—FPR 2010, r 25.6 provides for written questions to be put to expert witnesses. FPR PD25A, para 6.1 states that the court will specify a timetable for answers to these questions (generally dealt with at the time of a direction as to the filing of expert evidence and when the court timetables preparation of the report).

25.11 Court's power to direct that evidence is to be given by a single joint expert

(1) Where two or more parties wish to put expert evidence before the court on a particular issue, the court may direct that the evidence on that issue is to be given by a single joint expert.

(2) Where the parties who wish to put expert evidence before the court ("the relevant parties") cannot agree who should be the single joint expert, the court may –

  (a)   select the expert from a list prepared or identified by the relevant parties; or
  (b)   direct that the expert be selected in such other manner as the court may direct.

Evidence from single joint expert— FPR 2010, r 25.7 enables the court to direct that evidence "on a particular" issue can be directed to be provided by "a single joint expert" and if parties do not agree as to the identity of the expert the court can chose the expert or direct how he is to be appointed. In *Daniels v Walker (Practice Note)* [2000] 1 WLR 1382, CA, Lord Woolf MR explained the working of CPR 1998, r 35.8.

Dissatisfaction with joint expert's report – for reasons "not fanciful"— *Daniels v Walker* (above), Lord Woolf MR explained what a party might do if dissatisfied with the report of a single joint expert. In appropriate circumstances and for reason "which are not fanciful", the court has a discretion to order another report. Lord Woolf explains the steps to be taken before objection is taken to a report:

(1) The first – and if possible last step – is the instruction jointly of an expert.
(2) If a joint letter is not agreed, then in civil cases each party sends separate instructions, but see above for the consequences of FPR 2010, r 25.8(2).
(3) If a party is dissatisfied with the report, then within 10 days of service of the report (r 25.6(2)(b)) that party can raise questions of the expert (FPR 2010, r 25.6(1); the rules permit this to be done of an expert jointly instructed: r 25.6(1)(b)).
(4) If both parties seek expert evidence and the court agrees then the experts should discuss their reports before a decision as to whether either, or both, should be called to give evidence is made.
(5) Calling both to be cross-examined should be a "last resort".

25.12 Instructions to a single joint expert

(1) Where the court gives a direction under rule 25.11(1) for a single joint expert to be used, the instructions are to be contained in a jointly agreed letter unless the court directs otherwise.

(2) Where the instructions are to be contained in a jointly agreed letter, in default of agreement the instructions may be determined by the court on the written request of any relevant party copied to the other relevant parties.

(3) Where the court permits the relevant parties to give separate instructions to a single joint expert, each instructing party must, when giving instructions to the expert, at the same time send a copy of the instructions to the other relevant parties.

(4) The court may give directions about –

    (a)   the payment of the expert's fees and expenses; and

    (b)   any inspection, examination or assessments which the expert wishes to carry out.

(5) The court may, before an expert is instructed, limit the amount that can be paid by way of fees and expenses to the expert.

(6) Unless the court directs otherwise, the relevant parties are jointly and severally liable for the payment of the expert's fees and expenses.

Cost saving and the joint expert—CPR 1998, r 35.8(1) plainly envisages that the parties can deliver separate letters of instruction to a joint expert (noted also by the Court of Appeal in *Yorke v Katra* [2003] EWCA Civ 867 at [14]). Rule 25.8 creates the potential for extra expense to the parties by requiring the court to be involved in settling joint instructions (FPR 2010, r 25.8(2)). CPR 1998 and those under FPR 2010 on this point also will proceed a little differently (and see commentary on CPR 1998, r 35.8).

25.13 Power of court to direct a party to provide information

(1) Subject to paragraph (2), where a party has access to information which is not reasonably available to another party, the court may direct the party who has access to the information to –

    (a)   prepare and file a document recording the information; and

    (b)   serve a copy of that document on the other party.

(2) In proceedings under Part 14 (procedure for applications in adoption, placement and related proceedings), a court officer will send a copy of the document recording the information to the other party.

In-house expertise—The derivation rule (CPR 1998, r 35.9) was designed to ensure that defendants with in-house access to expertise (eg a hospital or a large company), could be compelled to produce information. In family proceedings it might be preferable to obtain a report from an outside source (*Field v Leeds City Council* (2000) *The Times*, 18 January, CA).

25.14 Contents of report

(1) An expert's report must comply with the requirements set out in Practice Direction 25B.

(2) At the end of an expert's report there must be a statement that the expert understands and has complied with the expert's duty to the court.

(3) The instructions to the expert are not privileged against disclosure.

    (Rule 21.1 explains what is meant by disclosure.)

25.15 Use by one party of expert's report disclosed by another

Where a party has disclosed an expert's report, any party may use that expert's report as evidence at any hearing where an issue to which the report relates is being considered.

25.16 Discussions between experts

(1) The court may, at any stage, direct a discussion between experts for the purpose of requiring the experts to –

    (a)   identify and discuss the expert issues in the proceedings; and

    (b)   where possible, reach an agreed opinion on those issues.

PART III

(2) The court may specify the issues which the experts must discuss.

(3) The court may direct that following a discussion between the experts they must prepare a statement for the court setting out those issues on which –

    (a)   they agree; and

    (b)   they disagree, with a summary of their reasons for disagreeing.

Discussions between experts—Consistent with the overriding objective and with the court's concerns to keep costs to a minimum, the rules and the court are concerned to define any controversy that needs to be resolved. Where possible, the expert's bases for the controversy must be summarised for the court. If the court thinks it appropriate it can specify issues for the experts to discuss and it may direct that they prepare a summary identifying issues on which they agree and on which they disagree.

Experts' agreement—FPR PD25A, para 7.1 asserts a controversial proposition: (a) that experts can bind parties at their meeting; and (b) that the parties can be compelled to "inform the court … in writing why they do not agree with the agreement". This provision is likely to be outside any powers in the rule-makers. The law is correctly stated by CPR 1998, r 35.12 (two sub-rules not included in FPR 2010):

"(4) The content of the discussion between the experts shall not be referred to at the trial unless the parties agree.

(5) Where experts reach agreement on an issue during their discussions, the agreement shall not bind the parties unless the parties expressly agree to be bound by the agreement."

As a matter of law, experts have no agency from any party. Indeed, FPR 2010, r 25.3 does what it can to distance the expert from the party who instructs them, and to that extent FPR PD25A, para 7.1 is in direct conflict with FPR 2010, r 25.3. In any "agreement" that experts reach, they are not speaking for a party to the proceedings (as does a party's lawyer).

25.17 Expert's right to ask court for directions

(1) Experts may file written requests for directions for the purpose of assisting them in carrying out their functions.

(2) Experts must, unless the court directs otherwise, provide copies of the proposed requests for directions under paragraph (1) –

    (a)   to the party instructing them, at least 7 days before they file the requests; and

    (b)   to all other parties, at least 4 days before they file them.

(3) The court, when it gives directions, may also direct that a party be served with a copy of the directions.

Expert's right to ask for directions—If an expert requires assistance from the court "in carrying out [his] functions" he may file a written request for directions. The expert must give notice of the request for directions to all parties. There is no clear procedure within the rules or the court administration as to how these directions are to be requested or dealt with.

25.18 Copies of orders and other documents

Unless the court directs otherwise, a copy of any order or other document affecting an expert filed with the court after the expert has been instructed, must be served on the expert by the party who instructed the expert or, in the case of a single joint expert, the party who was responsible for instructing the expert, within 2 days of that party receiving the order or other document.

25.19 Action after final hearing

(1) Within 10 business days after the final hearing, the party who instructed the expert or, in the case of a single joint expert, the party who was responsible for instructing the expert, must inform the expert in writing about the court's determination and the use made by the court of the expert's evidence.

(2) Unless the court directs otherwise, the party who instructed the expert or, in the case of the single joint expert, the party who was responsible for instructing the expert, must send to the expert a copy of the court's final order and –

(a) where the decision was one of the High Court or a county court, any transcript of the court's decision;

(b) where the decision was one of a magistrates' court, the reasons for the court's decision, within 10 business days from the date when that party received the order and transcript or reasons.

25.20 Assessors

(1) This rule applies where the court appoints one or more persons under section 70 of the Senior Courts Act 1981 or section 63 of the County Courts Act 1984 as an assessor.

(2) An assessor will assist the court in dealing with a matter in which the assessor has skill and experience.

(3) The assessor will take such part in the proceedings as the court may direct and in particular the court may direct an assessor to –

(a) prepare a report for the court on any matter at issue in the proceedings; and

(b) attend the whole or any part of the hearing to advise the court on any such matter.

(4) If the assessor prepares a report for the court before the hearing has begun –

(a) the court will send a copy to each of the parties; and

(b) the parties may use it at the hearing.

(5) Unless the court directs otherwise, an assessor will be paid at the daily rate payable for the time being to a fee-paid deputy district judge of the principal registry and an assessor's fees will form part of the costs of the proceedings.

(6) The court may order any party to deposit in the court office a specified sum in respect of an assessor's fees and, where it does so, the assessor will not be asked to act until the sum has been deposited.

(7) Paragraphs (5) and (6) do not apply where the remuneration of the assessor is to be paid out of money provided by Parliament.

Assessors—Rule 25.20 is supplemented by FPR PD25F.

Senior Courts Act 1981, s 70—SCA 1981, s 70 provides as follows:
  "**70 Assessors and scientific advisers**
  (1) In any cause or matter before the High Court the court may, if it thinks it expedient to do so, call in the aid of one or more assessors specially qualified, and hear and dispose of the cause or matter wholly or partially with their assistance.
  (2) The remuneration, if any, to be paid to an assessor for his services under subsection (1) in connection with any proceedings shall be determined by the court, and shall form part of the costs of the proceedings.
  …"

County Courts Act 1984—CCA 1984, s 63 is in slightly different terms to SCA 1981, s 70 and goes beyond the different ages of the Parliamentary drafting. In the latter for example, it seems the assessor has a choice as to whether to act:
  "**63 Assessors**
  (1) In any proceedings the judge may, if he thinks fit, summon to his assistance, in such manner as may be prescribed, one or more persons of skill and experience in the matter to which the proceedings relate who may be willing to sit with the judge and act as assessors.
  (2) …
  (3) Subject to subsection (4), the remuneration of assessors for sitting under this section shall be determined by the judge and shall be costs in the proceedings unless otherwise ordered by the judge.
  …"

Practice Direction 25A –
Experts – Emergencies and Pre Proceedings Instructions

This Practice Direction supplements FPR Part 25

Introduction

1.1 This Practice Direction and Practice Directions 25B to E relate to expert evidence and supplement FPR Part 25. This Practice Direction applies to children proceedings and all other family proceedings.

Emergency and urgent cases

2.1 In emergency or urgent cases – for example, where, before formal issue of proceedings, a without-notice application is made to the court during or out of business hours; or where, after proceedings have been issued, a previously unforeseen need for (further) expert evidence arises at short notice – a party may wish to put expert evidence before the court without having complied with all or any part of Practice Directions 25B to E. In such circumstances, the party wishing to put the expert evidence before the court must apply forthwith to the court – where possible or appropriate, on notice to the other parties – for directions as to the future steps to be taken in respect of the expert evidence in question.

Note—On the making of an interim order "before an application has been started" the court must give directions (including, as here, opinion evidence) for issue of the application (FPR 2010, r 20.3(3)).

Pre-application instruction of experts

3.1 When experts' reports are commissioned before the commencement of proceedings, it should be made clear to the expert that he or she may in due course be reporting to the court and should therefore consider himself or herself bound by the duties of an expert set out in Practice Direction 25B (The Duties of An Expert, the Expert's Report and Arrangements for An Expert To Attend Court). In so far as possible the enquiries of the expert and subsequent letter of instruction should follow either Practice Direction 25C (Children Proceedings – the Use of Single Joint Experts and the Process Leading to an Expert Being Instructed or Expert Evidence Being Put Before The Court) or 25D (Financial Remedy Proceedings and other Family Proceedings (except Children Proceedings) – the Use of Single Joint Experts and the Process Leading to Expert Evidence Being Put Before The Court).

3.2 In particular, a prospective party to children proceedings (for example, a local authority) should always write a letter of instruction when asking a potential witness for a report or an opinion, whether that request is within proceedings or pre-proceedings (for example, when commissioning specialist assessment materials, reports from a treating expert or other evidential materials); and the letter of instruction should conform to the principles set out in Practice Direction 25C.

3.3 It should be noted that the court's permission is required to put expert evidence (in any form) before the court in all family proceedings (see FPR 25.4(1)). In children proceedings, the court's permission is also required for an expert to be instructed and for a child to be medically or psychiatrically examined or otherwise assessed for the purposes of the provision of expert evidence in the proceedings (FPR 25.4(2)). Where the court's permission has not been given in accordance with FPR 25.4(2), evidence resulting from such instructions or examination or other assessment is inadmissible unless the court rules otherwise (FPR 25.4(3) and (4)). The court's permission will be needed to put any expert evidence before the court which was obtained before proceedings have started.

3.4 Attention is drawn to Practice Direction 15B (*Adults Who May Be Protected Parties and Children Who May Become Protected Parties In Family Proceedings*) which gives guidance relating to proceedings where an adult party may not have capacity to conduct the litigation or to instruct an expert.

Practice Direction 25B –
The Duties of an Expert, the Expert's Report and Arrangements for an Expert to Attend Court

This Practice Direction supplements FPR Part 25

Scope of this Practice Direction

1.1 This Practice Direction focuses on the duties of an expert including the contents of the expert's report and, where an expert is to attend court, the arrangements for such attendance. Other Practice Directions supporting FPR Part 25 deal with different aspects of experts in family proceedings. The relevant Practice Directions are –

(a) Practice Direction 25A (Experts – Emergencies and Pre proceedings Instructions);

(b) Practice Direction 25C (Children Proceedings – The Use of Single Joint Experts and the Process Leading to an Expert Being Instructed or Expert Evidence Being Put Before the Court);

(c) Practice Direction 25D (Financial Remedy Proceedings and Other Family Proceedings (except Children Proceedings) – The Use of Single Joint Experts and the Process Leading to Expert Evidence Being Put Before The Court); and

(d) Practice Direction 25E (Discussions Between Experts in Family Proceedings).

1.2 Practice Direction 15B (Adults Who May Be Protected Parties and Children Who May Become Protected Parties In Family Proceedings) gives guidance relating to proceedings where an adult party may not have capacity to conduct the litigation or to instruct an expert.

The meaning of "expert"

2.1 In accordance with FPR 25.2(1), "expert" means a person who provides expert evidence for use in family proceedings. FPR 25.2 (2)(a) to (c) expressly refers to evidence that is not expert evidence. For example, evidence given by a children's guardian is not expert evidence.

Note—For the admissibility of expert evidence, see commentary to FPR 2010, r 25.2. A guardian's opinion in law may well be "expert evidence".

2.2 An expert includes a reference to an expert team which can include ancillary workers in addition to experts. In an expert team, an 'ancillary' worker may be, for example, a play therapist or similar who undertakes work with the child or family for the purpose of the expert assessment. It is perfectly possible that such workers will be experts in their own right and in their own field, but it would be cumbersome to name everyone in that position in an order giving permission for an expert to be instructed, a child to be medically or psychiatrically examined or otherwise assessed or expert evidence to be put before the court or in a letter of instruction to an expert. The purpose of the term 'expert team' is to enable a multi-disciplinary team to undertake the assessment without the order having to name everyone who may be involved. The final expert's report must, however, give information about those persons who have taken part in the assessment and their respective roles and who is responsible for the report.

Note—Assertions of law in this passage are controversial. See commentary to FPR 2010, r 25.2.

The expert's overriding duty

3.1 An expert in family proceedings has an overriding duty to the court that takes precedence over any obligation to the person from whom the expert has received instructions or by whom the expert is paid.

Particular duties of the expert

4.1 An expert shall have regard to the following, among other, duties:

   (a)   to assist the court in accordance with the overriding duty;

   (b)   to provide advice to the court that conforms to the best practice of the expert's profession;

   (c)   to answer the questions about which the expert is required to give an opinion (in children proceedings, those questions will be set out in the order of the court giving permission for an expert to be instructed, a child to be examined or otherwise assessed or expert evidence to be put before the court);

   (d)   to provide an opinion that is independent of the party or parties instructing the expert;

   (e)   to confine the opinion to matters material to the issues in the case and in relation only to the questions that are within the expert's expertise (skill and experience);

   (f)   where a question has been put which falls outside the expert's expertise, to state this at the earliest opportunity and to volunteer an opinion as to whether another expert is required to bring expertise not possessed by those already involved or, in the rare case, as to whether a second opinion is required on a key issue and, if possible, what questions should be asked of the second expert;

   (g)   in expressing an opinion, to take into consideration all of the material facts including any relevant factors arising from ethnic, cultural, religious or linguistic contexts at the time the opinion is expressed;

   (h)   to inform those instructing the expert without delay of any change in the opinion and of the reason for the change.

Note—None of these duties is provided for by law (see FPR 2010, rr 25.4, 25.5), which restricts duties.

The requirement for the court's permission

5.1 The general rule in family proceedings is that the court's permission is required to put expert evidence (in any form) before the court (FPR 25.4(1)). The court is under a duty to restrict expert evidence to that which in the opinion of the court is necessary to assist the court to resolve the proceedings. The overriding objective in FPR1.1 applies when the court is exercising this duty. In children proceedings, the court's permission is required to instruct an expert and for a child to be medically or psychiatrically examined or otherwise assessed for the purposes of the provision of expert evidence in the proceedings (FPR 25.4(2)).

Preliminary enquiries which the expert should expect to receive

6.1 In good time for the information requested to be available for -

    (a) **the court hearing** when the court will decide whether to give permission for the expert evidence to be put before the court (or also in children proceedings, for the expert to be instructed or the child to be examined or otherwise assessed); or

    (b) **the advocates' meeting or discussion** where one takes place before such a hearing,

the party or parties intending to instruct the expert shall approach the expert with some information about the case.

6.2 The details of the information to be given to the expert are set out in Practice Direction 25C, paragraph 3.2 and Practice Direction 25D paragraph 3.3 and include the nature of the proceedings, the questions for the expert, the time when the expert's report is likely to be required, the timing of any hearing at which the expert may have to give evidence and how the expert's fees will be funded.

6.3 Children proceedings are confidential which means in those proceedings parties raising preliminary enquiries of an expert who has not yet been instructed can only tell the expert information which he or she will need about the case to be able to answer the preliminary questions raised.

Balancing the needs of the court and those of the expert

7.1 It is essential that there should be proper co-ordination between the court and the expert when drawing up the case management timetable: the needs of the court should be balanced with the needs of the expert whose forensic work is undertaken as an adjunct to his or her main professional duties.

The expert's response to preliminary enquiries

8.1 **In good time for the court hearing when the court will decide whether or not to give permission for the expert evidence to be put before the court (or also in children proceedings, for the expert to be instructed or the child to be examined or otherwise assessed) or for the advocates' meeting or discussion where one takes place before that hearing,** the party or parties intending to instruct the expert will need confirmation from the expert –

    (a) that acceptance of the proposed instructions will not involve the expert in any conflict of interest;

    (b) that the work required is within the expert's expertise;

    (c) that the expert is available to do the relevant work within the suggested time scale;

    (d) when the expert is available to give evidence, of the dates and times to avoid and, where a hearing date has not been fixed, of the amount of notice the expert will require to make arrangements to come to court (or to give evidence by telephone conference or video link) without undue disruption to his or her normal professional routines;

    (e) of the cost, including hourly or other charging rates, and likely hours to be spent attending experts' meetings, attending court and writing the report (to include any examinations and interviews);

    (f) of any representations which the expert wishes to make to the court about being named or otherwise identified in any public judgment given by the court.

Content of the expert's report

9.1 The expert's report shall be addressed to the court and prepared and filed **in accordance with the court's timetable** and must –

- (a) give details of the expert's qualifications and experience;
- (b) include a statement identifying the document(s) containing the material instructions and the substance of any oral instructions and, as far as necessary to explain any opinions or conclusions expressed in the report, summarising the facts and instructions which are material to the conclusions and opinions expressed;
- (c) state who carried out any test, examination or interview which the expert has used for the report and whether or not the test, examination or interview has been carried out under the expert's supervision;
- (d) give details of the qualifications of any person who carried out the test, examination or interview;
- (e) answer the questions about which the expert is to give an opinion and which relate to the issues in the case;
- (f) in expressing an opinion to the court –
    - (i) take into consideration all of the material facts including any relevant factors arising from ethnic, cultural, religious or linguistic contexts at the time the opinion is expressed, identifying the facts, literature and any other material, including research material, that the expert has relied upon in forming an opinion;
    - (ii) describe the expert's own professional risk assessment process and process of differential diagnosis, highlighting factual assumptions, deductions from the factual assumptions, and any unusual, contradictory or inconsistent features of the case;
    - (iii) indicate whether any proposition in the report is an hypothesis (in particular a controversial hypothesis), or an opinion deduced in accordance with peer-reviewed and tested technique, research and experience accepted as a consensus in the scientific community;
    - (iv) indicate whether the opinion is provisional (or qualified, as the case may be), stating the qualification and the reason for it, and identifying what further information is required to give an opinion without qualification;
- (g) where there is a range of opinion on any question to be answered by the expert –
    - (i) summarise the range of opinion;
    - (ii) identify and explain, within the range of opinions, any "unknown cause", whether arising from the facts of the case (for example, because there is too little information to form a scientific opinion) or from limited experience or lack of research, peer review or support in the relevant field of expertise;
    - (iii) give reasons for any opinion expressed: the use of a balance sheet approach to the factors that support or undermine an opinion can be of great assistance to the court;
- (h) contain a summary of the expert's conclusions and opinions;
- (i) contain a statement that the expert –
    - (i) has no conflict of interest of any kind, other than any conflict disclosed in his or her report;
    - (ii) does not consider that any interest disclosed affects his or her suitability as an expert witness on any issue on which he or she has given evidence;
    - (iii) will advise the instructing party if, between the date of the expert's report and the final hearing, there is any change in circumstances which affects the expert's answers to (i) or (ii) above;

     (iv) understands their duty to the court and has complied with that duty; and

     (v)   is aware of the requirements of FPR Part 25 and this practice direction;

  (j)   be verified by a statement of truth in the following form –

"I confirm that I have made clear which facts and matters referred to in this report are within my own knowledge and which are not. Those that are within my own knowledge I confirm to be true. The opinions I have expressed represent my true and complete professional opinions on the matters to which they refer."

(FPR Part 17 deals with statements of truth. Rule 17.6 sets out the consequences of verifying a document containing a false statement without an honest belief in its truth.)

Arrangements for experts to give evidence

Preparation

10.1 Where the court has directed the attendance of an expert witness, the party who instructed the expert or party responsible for the instruction of the expert shall, **by a date specified by the court prior to the hearing at which the expert is to give oral evidence ("the specified date") or, where in care or supervision proceedings an Issues Resolution Hearing ("the IRH") is to be held, by the IRH,** ensure that –

  (a) a date and time (if possible, convenient to the expert) are fixed for the court to hear the expert's evidence, substantially in advance of the hearing at which the expert is to give oral evidence and no later than a specified date prior to that hearing or, where an IRH is to be held, than the IRH;

  (b) if the expert's oral evidence is not required, the expert is notified as soon as possible;

  (c) the witness template accurately indicates how long the expert is likely to be giving evidence, in order to avoid the inconvenience of the expert being delayed at court;

  (d) consideration is given in each case to whether some or all of the experts participate by telephone conference or video link, or submit their evidence in writing, to ensure that minimum disruption is caused to professional schedules and that costs are minimised.

Experts attending court

10.2 Where expert witnesses are to be called, all parties shall, **by the specified date or, where an IRH is to be held, by the IRH,** ensure that –

  (a) the parties' advocates have identified (whether at an advocates' meeting or by other means) the issues which the experts are to address;

  (b) wherever possible, a logical sequence to the evidence is arranged, with experts of the same discipline giving evidence on the same day;

  (c) the court is informed of any circumstance where all experts agree but a party nevertheless does not accept the agreed opinion, so that directions can be given for the proper consideration of the experts' evidence and opinion;

  (d) in the exceptional case the court is informed of the need for a witness summons.

PART III

Practice Direction 25C –
Children Proceedings – The Use of Single Joint Experts and the Process Leading to an Expert Being Instructed or Expert Evidence Being Put Before the Court

This Practice Direction supplements FPR Part 25

Scope of this Practice Direction

1.1 This Practice Direction applies to children proceedings and contains guidance on –

(a) the use of single joint experts;

(b) how to prepare for the hearing at which the court will consider whether to give permission for an expert to be instructed, a child to be medically or psychiatrically examined or otherwise assessed for the purposes of provision of expert evidence in the proceedings or for putting expert evidence (in any form) before the court including –

   (i) preliminary enquiries of experts;

   (ii) the content of an application for the court's permission in addition to matters mentioned in FPR 25.7;

   (iii) matters to be set out in the draft order to be attached to the application for permission; and

(c) the letter of instruction to the expert.

1.2 "Children proceedings" includes proceedings under Schedule 1 to the 1989 Act as those proceedings are proceedings which relate wholly or mainly to the maintenance or upbringing of a minor referred to in FPR 25.2(1).

Single joint experts

2.1 FPR 25.4 applies to a single joint expert ("SJE") in addition to an expert instructed by one party. This means that the court's permission is required to put expert evidence from an SJE (in any form) before the court (FPR 25.4(1)). The court's permission is also required to instruct an SJE and for a child to be medically or psychiatrically examined or otherwise assessed for the purposes of provision of evidence from an SJE (FPR 25.4(2)). Wherever possible, expert evidence should be obtained from an SJE instructed by both or all the parties. To that end, a party wishing to instruct an expert should as soon as possible after the start of the proceedings first give the other party or parties a list of the names of one or more experts in the relevant speciality whom they consider suitable to be instructed.

2.2 **Within 5 business days after receipt of the list of proposed experts**, the other party or parties should indicate any objection to one or more of the named experts and, if so, supply the name(s) of one or more experts whom they consider suitable.

2.3 Each party should disclose whether they have already consulted any of the proposed experts about the issue(s) in question.

2.4 Where the parties cannot agree on the identity of the expert, each party should think carefully before seeking the permission of the court to instruct their own expert because of the costs implications. Disagreements about the use and identity of an expert may be better managed by the court in the context of the application for the court's permission to instruct the expert and for directions for the use of an SJE (see paragraph 2.6 below).

Instructing separate experts

2.5 If the parties seek the permission of the court to instruct separate experts –

(a)   they should agree in advance that the reports will be disclosed; and

(b)   the instructions to each expert should comply, so far as appropriate, with paragraphs 4.1 and 6.1 below (Letter of instruction).

Where two or more parties wish to instruct an SJE

2.6 If two or more parties wish to instruct an SJE, before applying to the court for permission and directions for the use of an SJE, the parties should –

(a)   so far as appropriate, comply with the guidance in paragraphs 3.2 (Preliminary enquires of the expert) and paragraphs 3.10 and 3.11 below;

(b)   receive the expert's confirmation in response to preliminary enquires referred to in paragraph 8.1 of Practice Direction 25B;

(c)   have agreed in what proportion the SJE's fee is to be shared between them (at least in the first instance) and when it is to be paid; and

(d)   if applicable, have obtained agreement for public funding.

2.7 The instructions to the SJE should comply, so far as appropriate, with paragraphs 4.1 and 6.1 below (Letter of instruction).

Preparation for the permission hearing

3.1 Paragraphs 3.2 to 3.11 give guidance on how to prepare for the hearing at which the court will consider whether to give permission for an expert to be instructed, a child to be examined or otherwise assessed or expert evidence to be put before the court. The purpose of the preparation is to ensure that the court has the information required to enable it to exercise its powers under FPR 25.4 and 25.5.

Preliminary enquiries of the expert

3.2 In good time for the information requested to be available for the hearing at which the court will consider whether to give permission for an expert to be instructed, a child to be examined or otherwise assessed or expert evidence to be put before the court or for the advocates' meeting or discussion where one takes place before that hearing, the party or parties intending to instruct the expert shall approach the expert with the following information –

(a)   the nature of the proceedings and the issues likely to require determination by the court;

(b)   the issues in the proceedings to which the expert evidence is to relate;

(c)   the questions about which the expert is to be asked to give an opinion (including any ethnic, cultural, religious or linguistic contexts) and which relate to the issues in the case;

(d)   the date when the court is to be asked to give permission for the instruction (or if – unusually – permission has already been given, the date and details of that permission);

(e)   whether permission is to be asked of the court for the instruction of another expert in the same or any related field (that is, to give an opinion on the same or related questions);

(f)   the volume of reading which the expert will need to undertake;

(g)   whether or not permission has been applied for or given for the expert to examine the child;

PART III

(h)   whether or not it will be necessary for the expert to conduct interviews – and, if so, with whom;

(i)   the likely timetable of legal and social work steps;

(j)   in care and supervision proceedings, any dates in the Timetable for the Child which would be relevant to the proposed timetable for the assessment;

(k)   when the expert's report is likely to be required;

(l)   whether and, if so, what date has been fixed by the court for any hearing at which the expert may be required to give evidence (in particular the Final Hearing); and whether it may be possible for the expert to give evidence by telephone conference or video link: see paragraphs 10.1 and 10.2 (Arrangements for experts to give evidence) of Practice Direction 25B;

(m)   the possibility of making, through their instructing solicitors, representations to the court about being named or otherwise identified in any public judgment given by the court;

(n)   whether the instructing party has public funding and the legal aid rates of payment which are applicable.

Confidentiality of children proceedings and making preliminary enquiries of an expert

3.3 For the purposes of the law of contempt of court, information relating to children proceedings (whether or not contained in a document filed with the court or recorded in any form) may be communicated only to an expert whose instruction by a party has been permitted by the court (see FPR 12.73(1)(a)(vii) and 14.14(c)(vii)) as children proceedings are confidential.

3.4 Before permission is obtained from the court to instruct an expert in children proceedings, the party seeking permission needs to make the enquiries of the expert referred to above in order to provide the court with information to enable it to decide whether to give permission. In practice, enquiries may need to be made of more than one expert for this purpose. This will in turn require each expert to be given sufficient information about the case to decide whether or not he or she is in a position to accept instructions. Such preliminary enquiries, and the disclosure of information about the case which is a necessary part of such enquiries, will not require the court's permission and will not amount to a contempt of court.

Expert's response to preliminary enquiries

3.5 In good time for the hearing at which the court will consider whether to give permission for an expert to be instructed, a child to be examined or otherwise assessed or expert evidence to be put before the court, **the party or parties** intending to instruct the expert must obtain the confirmations from the expert referred to in paragraph 8.1 of Practice Direction 25B. These confirmations include that the work is within the expert's expertise, the expert is available to do the work within the relevant timescale and the expert's costs.

3.6 Where the parties **cannot agree who should be the single joint expert** before the hearing at which the court will consider whether to give permission for an expert to be instructed, a child to be examined or otherwise assessed or expert evidence to be put before the court, they should obtain the above confirmations in respect of all experts whom they intend to put to the court for the purposes of FPR 25.11(2)(a) as candidates for the appointment.

The application for the court's permission mentioned in FPR 25.4

TIMING AND ORAL APPLICATIONS FOR THE COURT'S PERMISSION MENTIONED IN FPR 25.4

3.7 An application for the court's permission for an expert to be instructed, a child to be examined or otherwise assessed or expert evidence to be put before the court should be made as soon as it becomes apparent that it is necessary to make it. FPR 25.6 makes provision about the time by which applications for the court's permission should be made.

3.8 Applications should, wherever possible, be made so that they are considered at any directions hearing or other hearing for which a date has been fixed or for which a date is about to be fixed. It should be noted that one application notice can be used by a party to make more than one application for an order or direction at a hearing held during the course of proceedings. An application for the court's permission for an expert to be instructed, a child to be examined or otherwise assessed or expert evidence to be put before the court may therefore be included in an application notice requesting other orders to be made at such a hearing.

3.9 Where a date for a hearing has been fixed, a party who wishes to make an application at that hearing but does not have sufficient time to file an application notice should as soon as possible inform the court (if possible in writing) and, if possible, the other parties of the nature of the application and the reason for it. The party should provide the court and the other party with as much as possible of the information referred to in FPR 25.7 and paragraph 3.10 below. That party should then make the application orally at the hearing. An oral application of this kind should be the exception and reserved for genuine cases where circumstances are such that it has only become apparent shortly before the hearing that an expert opinion is necessary.

THE APPLICATION

3.10 In addition to the matters specified in FPR 25.7(2)(a) and (3), an application for the court's permission for an expert to be instructed, a child to be examined or otherwise assessed or expert evidence to be put before the court, must state-

    (a) the discipline, qualifications and expertise of the expert (by way of C.V. where possible);

    (b) the expert's availability to undertake the work;

    (c) the timetable for the report;

    (d) the responsibility for instruction;

    (e) whether the expert evidence can properly be obtained by only one party (for example, on behalf of the child);

    (f) why the expert evidence proposed cannot properly be given by an officer of the service, Welsh family proceedings officer or the local authority (social services undertaking a core assessment) in accordance with their respective statutory duties or any other party to the proceedings or an expert already instructed in the proceedings;

    (g) the likely cost of the report on an hourly or other charging basis;

    (h) the proposed apportionment (at least in the first instance) of any jointly instructed expert's fee; when it is to be paid; and, if applicable, whether public funding has been approved.

THE TERMS OF THE DRAFT ORDER TO BE ATTACHED TO THE APPLICATION FOR THE COURT'S PERMISSION

3.11 FPR 25.7(2)(b) provides that a draft of the order giving the court's permission as mentioned in FPR 25.4 is to be attached to the application for the court's permission. That draft order must set out the following matters –

(a)   the issues in the proceedings to which the expert evidence is to relate and which the court is to identify;

(b)   the questions relating to the issues in the case which the expert is to answer and which the court is to approve ensuring that they
    (i)   are within the ambit of the expert's area of expertise;
    (ii) do not contain unnecessary or irrelevant detail;
    (iii) are kept to a manageable number and are clear, focused and direct;

(c)   the party who is responsible for drafting the letter of instruction and providing the documents to the expert;

(d)   the timetable within which the report is to be prepared, filed and served;

(e)   the disclosure of the report to the parties and to any other expert;

(f)   the organisation of, preparation for and conduct of any experts' discussion (see Practice Direction 25E – *Discussions between Experts in Family Proceedings*);

(g)   the preparation of a statement of agreement and disagreement by the experts following an experts' discussion;

(h)   making available to the court at an early opportunity the expert reports in electronic form;

(i)   the attendance of the expert at court to give oral evidence (alternatively, the expert giving his or her evidence in writing or remotely by video link), whether at or for the Final Hearing or another hearing; unless agreement about the opinions given by the expert is reached at or before the Issues Resolution Hearing ("IRH") or, if no IRH is to be held, by a date specified by the court prior to the hearing at which the expert is to give oral evidence.

Letter of instruction

4.1 The party responsible for instructing the expert shall prepare (in agreement with the other parties where appropriate), a letter of instruction to the expert and shall –

(a)   set out the context in which the expert's opinion is sought (including any ethnic, cultural, religious or linguistic contexts);

(b)   set out the questions approved by the court and which the expert is required to answer and any other linked questions ensuring that they –
    (i)   are within the ambit of the expert's area of expertise;
    (ii) do not contain unnecessary or irrelevant detail;
    (iii) are kept to a manageable number and are clear, focused and direct; and
    (iv) reflect what the expert has been requested to do by the court

(Annex A to this Practice Direction sets out suggested questions in letters of instruction to (1) child mental health professionals or paediatricians, and (2) adult psychiatrists and applied psychologists, in Children Act 1989 proceedings);

(c)   list the documentation provided, or provide for the expert an indexed and paginated bundle which shall include –
    (i)   an agreed list of essential reading; and
    (ii) a copy of this Practice Direction and Practice Directions 25B and E and where appropriate Practice Direction 15B;

(d)   identify any materials provided to the expert which have not been produced either as original medical (or other professional) records or in response to an instruction from a party, and state the source of that material (such materials may contain an assumption as to the standard of proof, the admissibility or otherwise of hearsay evidence, and other important procedural and substantive questions relating to the different purposes of other enquiries, for example, criminal or disciplinary proceedings);

(e) identify all requests to third parties for disclosure and their responses in order to avoid partial disclosure, which tends only to prove a case rather than give full and frank information;

(f) identify the relevant people concerned with the proceedings (for example, the treating clinicians) and inform the expert of his or her right to talk to them provided that an accurate record is made of the discussions;

(g) identify any other expert instructed in the proceedings and advise the expert of their right to talk to the other experts provided that an accurate record is made of the discussions;

(h) subject to any public funding requirement for prior authority, define the contractual basis upon which the expert is retained and in particular the funding mechanism including how much the expert will be paid (an hourly rate and overall estimate should already have been obtained), when the expert will be paid, and what limitation there might be on the amount the expert can charge for the work which they will have to do. In cases where the parties are publicly funded, there may also be a brief explanation of the costs and expenses excluded from public funding by Funding Code criterion 1.3 and the detailed assessment process.

Adult who is a protected party

5.1 Where the adult is a protected party, that party's representative shall be involved in any instruction of an expert, including the instruction of an expert to assess whether the adult, although a protected party, is competent to give evidence (see Practice Direction 15B – *Adults Who May Be Protected Parties and Children Who May Become Protected Parties in Family Proceedings*).

Asking the court to settle the letter of instruction to a single joint expert

6.1 Where possible, the written request for the court to consider the letter of instruction referred to in rule 25.12(2) should be set out in an e-mail to the court and copied by e-mail to the other instructing parties. The request should be sent to the relevant court or (by prior arrangement only) directly to the judge dealing with the proceedings. In the magistrates' court, the request should be sent to the relevant court or (by prior arrangement only) to any district judge (magistrates' courts) hearing the proceedings (and copied to the legal adviser) or to the legal adviser. The court will settle the letter of instruction, usually without a hearing to avoid delay; and will send (where practicable, by e-mail) the settled letter to the lead solicitor for transmission forthwith to the expert, and copy it to the other instructing parties for information.

ANNEX A

(drafted by the Family Justice Council)

Suggested questions in letters of instruction to child mental health professional or paediatrician in Children Act 1989 proceedings

A. *The Child(ren)*

1. Please describe the child(ren)'s current health, development and functioning (according to your area of expertise), and identify the nature of any significant changes which have occurred

- Behavioural
- Emotional
- Attachment organisation
- Social/peer/sibling relationships
- Cognitive/educational
- Physical
  – Growth, eating, sleep
  – Non-organic physical problems (including wetting and soiling)
  – Injuries
  – Paediatric conditions

2. Please comment on the likely explanation for/aetiology of the child(ren)'s problems/difficulties/injuries

- History/experiences (including intrauterine influences, and abuse and neglect)
- Genetic/innate/developmental difficulties
- Paediatric/psychiatric disorders

3. Please provide a prognosis and risk if difficulties not addressed above.

4. Please describe the child(ren)'s needs in the light of the above

- Nature of care-giving
- Education
- Treatment

in the short and long term (subject, where appropriate, to further assessment later).

B. *The parents/primary carers*

5. Please describe the factors and mechanisms which would explain the parents' (or primary carers) harmful or neglectful interactions with the child(ren) (if relevant).

6. What interventions have been tried and what has been the result?

7. Please assess the ability of the parents or primary carers to fulfil the child(ren)'s identified needs now.

8. What other assessments of the parents or primary carers are indicated?

- Adult mental health assessment
- Forensic risk assessment
- Physical assessment
- Cognitive assessment

9. What, if anything, is needed to assist the parents or primary carers now, within the child(ren)'s time scales and what is the prognosis for change?

- Parenting work
- Support
- Treatment/therapy

C. *Alternatives*

10. Please consider the alternative possibilities for the fulfilment of the child(ren)'s needs

- What sort of placement
- Contact arrangements

Please consider the advantages, disadvantages and implications of each for the child(ren).

Suggested questions in letters of instruction to adult psychiatrists and applied psychologists in Children Act 1989 proceedings

1. Does the parent/adult have – whether in his/her history or presentation – a mental illness/disorder (including substance abuse) or other psychological/emotional difficulty and, if so, what is the diagnosis?

2. How do any/all of the above (and their current treatment if applicable) affect his/her functioning, including interpersonal relationships?

3. If the answer to Q1 is yes, are there any features of either the mental illness or psychological/emotional difficulty or personality disorder which could be associated with risk to others, based on the available evidence base (whether published studies or evidence from clinical experience)?

4. What are the experiences/antecedents/aetiology which would explain his/her difficulties, if any, (taking into account any available evidence base or other clinical experience)?

5. What treatment is indicated, what is its nature and the likely duration?

6. What is his/her capacity to engage in/partake of the treatment/therapy?

7. Are you able to indicate the prognosis for, time scales for achieving, and likely durability of, change?

8. What other factors might indicate positive change?

> (It is assumed that this opinion will be based on collateral information as well as interviewing the adult).

Practice Direction 25D –
Financial Remedy Proceedings and Other Family Proceedings (Except Children Proceedings) – The Use of Single Joint Experts and the Process Leading to Expert Evidence Being Put Before the Court

This Practice Direction supplements FPR Part 25

Scope of this Practice Direction

1.1 This Practice Direction applies to financial remedy proceedings and other family proceedings except children proceedings and contains guidance on –

(a) the use of single joint experts;
(b) how to prepare for the hearing at which the court will consider whether to give permission for putting expert evidence (in any form) before the court including –
  (i) preliminary enquiries of experts;
  (ii) information to be given to the court before the hearing;
(c) the letter of instruction to the expert.

Single joint experts

2.1 FPR 25.4 applies to a single joint expert ("SJE") in addition to an expert instructed by one party. This means that the court's permission is required to put expert evidence from an SJE (in any form) before the court. However, in family proceedings (except children proceedings) there is no requirement for the court's permission to be obtained before instructing an expert. Wherever possible, expert evidence should be obtained from a single joint expert instructed by both or all the parties ("SJE"). To that end, a party wishing to instruct an expert should first give the other party or parties a list of the names of one or more experts in the relevant speciality whom they consider suitable to be instructed.

2.2 **Within 10 business days after receipt of the list of proposed experts**, the other party or parties should indicate any objection to one or more of the named experts and, if so, supply the name(s) of one or more experts whom they consider suitable.

2.3 Each party should disclose whether they have already consulted any of the proposed experts about the issue(s) in question.

2.4 Where the parties cannot agree on the identity of the expert, each party should think carefully before instructing their own expert and seeking the permission of the court to put that expert evidence before it because of the costs implications. Disagreements about the use and identity of an expert may be better managed by the court in the context of an application for the court's permission to put the expert evidence before the court and for directions for the use of an SJE (see paragraph 2.6 below).

Agreement to instruct separate experts

2.5 If the parties agree to instruct separate experts and to seek the permission of the court to put the separate expert evidence before it –

    (a)   they should agree in advance that the reports will be disclosed; and

    (b)   the instructions to each expert should comply, so far as appropriate, with paragraphs 4.1 and 6.1 below (Letter of instruction).

Agreement to instruct an SJE

2.6 If there is agreement to instruct an SJE, **before applying to the court for permission to put the expert evidence before it and directions for the use of an SJE**, the parties should –

    (a)   so far as appropriate, comply with the guidance in paragraphs 3.3 (Preliminary enquiries of the expert) and paragraphs 3.11 and 3.12 below;

    (b)   receive the expert's confirmation in response to preliminary enquires referred to in paragraph 8.1 of Practice Direction 25B;

    (c)   have agreed in what proportion the SJE's fee is to be shared between them (at least in the first instance) and when it is to be paid; and

    (d)   if applicable, have obtained agreement for public funding.

2.7 The instructions to the SJE should comply, so far as appropriate, with paragraphs 4.1 and 6.1 below (Letter of instruction).

The test for permission and preparation for the permission hearing

3.1 The test in FPR 25.1 which the court is to apply to determine whether permission should be given for expert evidence to be put before the court has been altered from one which refers to expert evidence being restricted by the court to that which is reasonably required to resolve the proceedings to one which refers to the expert evidence being in the opinion of the court necessary to assist the court to resolve the proceedings. The overriding objective of the FPR, which is to enable the court to deal with cases justly, having regard to any welfare issues involved, continues to apply when the court is making the decision whether to give permission. In addition, the rules (FPR 25.5(2)) now tell the court what factors it is to have particular regard to when deciding whether to give permission. In financial remedy proceedings the expectation is that the new test and factors are a reflection of current practice and so are unlikely in practice to alter the use of expert evidence in these proceedings.

3.2 Paragraphs 3.3 to 3.12 below give guidance on how to prepare for the hearing at which the court will apply the test in FPR 25.1 and the factors in FPR 25.5(2) and decide whether to give permission for expert evidence to be put before the court. The purpose of the preparation is to ensure that the court has the information required to enable it to exercise its powers under FPR 25.4 and 25.5 in line with FPR 25.1.

Preliminary enquiries of the expert

3.3 **In good time for the information requested to be available for the hearing** at which the court will consider whether to give permission for expert evidence to be put before the court, the party or parties intending to instruct the expert shall approach the expert with the following information –

(a) the nature of the proceedings and the issues likely to require determination by the court;

(b) the issues in the proceedings to which the expert evidence is to relate;

(c) the questions about which the expert is to be asked to give an opinion and which relate to the issues in the case;

(d) whether permission is to be asked of the court for the use of another expert in the same or any related field (that is, to give an opinion on the same or related questions);

(e) the volume of reading which the expert will need to undertake;

(f) whether or not it will be necessary for the expert to conduct interviews and, if so, with whom;

(g) the likely timetable of legal steps;

(h) when the expert's report is likely to be required;

(i) whether and, if so, what date has been fixed by the court for any hearing at which the expert may be required to give evidence (in particular the Final Hearing); and whether it may be possible for the expert to give evidence by telephone conference or video link: see paragraphs 10.1 and 10.2 (Arrangements for experts to give evidence) of Practice Direction 25B;

(j) the possibility of making, through their instructing solicitors, representations to the court about being named or otherwise identified in any public judgment given by the court;

(k) whether the instructing party has public funding and the legal aid rates of payment which are applicable.

Expert's response to preliminary enquiries

3.4 In good time for the hearing at which the court will consider whether to give permission for expert evidence to be put before the court, the solicitors or party intending to instruct the expert must obtain the confirmations from the expert referred to in paragraph 8.1 of Practice Direction 25B. These confirmations include that the work is within the expert's expertise, the expert is available to do the work within the relevant timescale and the expert's costs.

3.5 Where parties **cannot agree who should be the single joint expert** before the hearing at which the court will consider whether to give permission for expert evidence to be put before the court, they should obtain the above confirmations in respect of all experts whom they intend to put to the court for the purposes of rule 25.11(2)(a) as candidates for the appointment.

The application for the court's permission to put expert evidence before the court

TIMING AND ORAL APPLICATIONS FOR THE COURT'S PERMISSION

3.6 An application for the court's permission to put expert evidence before the court should be made as soon as it becomes apparent that it is necessary to make it. FPR 25.6 makes provision about the time by which applications for the court's permission should be made.

3.7 Applications should, wherever possible, be made so that they are considered at any directions hearing or other hearing for which a date has been fixed or for which a date is about to be fixed. It should be noted that one application notice can be used by a party to make more than one application for an order or direction at a hearing held during the course of proceedings. An application for the court's permission to put expert evidence before the court may therefore be included in an application notice requesting other orders to be made at such a hearing.

3.8 Where a date for a hearing has been fixed, a party who wishes to make an application at that hearing but does not have sufficient time to file an application notice should as soon as possible inform the court (if possible in writing) and, if possible, the other parties of the nature of the application and the reason for it. The party should provide the court and the other party with as much as possible of the information referred to in FPR 25.7 and paragraph 3.11 below. That party should then make the application orally at the hearing. An oral application of this kind should be the exception and reserved for genuine cases where circumstances are such that it has only become apparent shortly before the hearing that an expert opinion is necessary.

3.9 In financial remedy proceedings, unless the court directs otherwise, parties must apply for permission to put expert evidence before the court as soon as possible and no later than the first appointment. The expectation is that the court will give directions extending the time by which permission should be obtained where there is good reason for parties to delay the decision whether to use expert evidence and make an application for the court's permission.

3.10 Examples of situations where the time for requesting permission to put expert evidence before the court is likely to be extended are where –

   (a)   a decision about the need for expert evidence cannot be made until replies to questionnaires in relation to Forms E have been fully considered; or

   (b)   valuations of property are agreed for the purposes of the Financial Dispute Resolution appointment but no agreement is reached to resolve the proceedings at that appointment and the court cannot make a consent order as mentioned in FPR 9.17(8). In these circumstances, it may become clear to a party that he or she will want to use expert valuations of property and an application for the court's permission for such valuation to be put before it may be made orally at the end of the appointment to avoid the need for a separate hearing about this issue. As with other oral applications, the party should provide the court and the other party with as much as possible of the information referred to in FPR 25.7 and paragraph 3.11 below. FPR 9.17(9) requires the court to give directions for the future course of the proceedings where it has not made a consent order including, where appropriate, the filing of evidence.

THE APPLICATION

3.11 In addition to the matters specified in FPR 25.7(2)(a), an application for the court's permission to put expert evidence before the court must state –

(a) the discipline, qualifications and expertise of the expert (by way of C.V. where possible);

(b) the expert's availability to undertake the work;

(c) the timetable for the report;

(d) the responsibility for instruction;

(e) whether the expert evidence can properly be obtained by only one party;

(f) why the expert evidence proposed cannot properly be given by an expert already instructed in the proceedings;

(g) the likely cost of the report on an hourly or other charging basis;

(h) the proposed apportionment (at least in the first instance) of any jointly instructed expert's fee; when it is to be paid; and, if applicable, whether public funding has been approved.

THE DRAFT ORDER TO BE ATTACHED TO THE APPLICATION FOR THE COURT'S PERMISSION

3.12 FPR 25.7(2)(b) provides that a draft of the order giving the court's permission to put expert evidence before the court is to be attached to the application for the court's permission. That draft order must set out the following matters –

(a) the issues in the proceedings to which the expert evidence is to relate;

(b) the party who is to be responsible for drafting the letter of instruction and providing the documents to the expert;

(c) the timetable within which the report is to be prepared, filed and served;

(d) the disclosure of the report to the parties and to any other expert;

(e) the organisation of, preparation for and conduct of any experts' discussion (see Practice Direction 25E – *Discussions between Experts in Family Proceedings*);

(f) the preparation of a statement of agreement and disagreement by the experts following an experts' discussion;

(g) making available to the court at an early opportunity the expert reports in electronic form;

(h) the attendance of the expert at court to give oral evidence (alternatively, the expert giving his or her evidence in writing or remotely by video link), whether at or for the Final Hearing or another hearing; unless agreement about the opinions given by the expert is reached by a date specified by the court prior to the hearing at which the expert is to give oral evidence.

Letter of instruction

4.1 The party responsible for instructing the expert shall, **within 5 business days after the permission hearing**, prepare (in agreement with the other parties where appropriate), file and serve a letter of instruction to the expert which shall –

(a) set out the context in which the expert's opinion is sought (including any ethnic, cultural, religious or linguistic contexts);

(b) set out the questions which the expert is required to answer and ensuring that they –

(i) are within the ambit of the expert's area of expertise;

(ii) do not contain unnecessary or irrelevant detail;

(iii) are kept to a manageable number and are clear, focused and direct; and

(iv) reflect what the expert has been requested to do by the court;

PART III

(c)   list the documentation provided, or provide for the expert an indexed and paginated bundle which shall include –
    (i)   an agreed list of essential reading; and
    (ii)   a copy of this Practice Direction and Practice Directions 25B, 25E and where appropriate Practice Direction 15B;

(d)   identify any materials provided to the expert which have not been produced either as original medical (or other professional) records or in response to an instruction from a party, and state the source of that material (such materials may contain an assumption as to the standard of proof, the admissibility or otherwise of hearsay evidence, and other important procedural and substantive questions relating to the different purposes of other enquiries);

(e)   identify all requests to third parties for disclosure and their responses in order to avoid partial disclosure, which tends only to prove a case rather than give full and frank information;

(f)   identify the relevant people concerned with the proceedings and inform the expert of his or her right to talk to them provided that an accurate record is made of the discussions;

(g)   identify any other expert instructed in the proceedings and advise the expert of their right to talk to the other experts provided that an accurate record is made of the discussions;

(h)   subject to any public funding requirement for prior authority, define the contractual basis upon which the expert is retained and in particular the funding mechanism including how much the expert will be paid (an hourly rate and overall estimate should already have been obtained), when the expert will be paid, and what limitation there might be on the amount the expert can charge for the work which they will have to do. In cases where the parties are publicly funded, there may also be a brief explanation of the costs and expenses excluded from public funding by Funding Code criterion 1.3 and the detailed assessment process.

Adult who is a protected party

5.1 Where the adult is a protected party, that party's representative shall be involved in any instruction of an expert, including the instruction of an expert to assess whether the adult, although a protected party, is competent to give evidence (see Practice Direction 15B – *Adults Who May Be Protected Parties and Children Who May Become Protected Parties in Family Proceedings*).

Asking the court to settle the letter of instruction to a single joint expert

6.1 Where possible, the written request for the court to consider the letter of instruction referred to in rule 25.12(2) should be set out in an e-mail to the court and copied by e-mail to the other instructing parties. The request should be sent to the relevant court or (by prior arrangement only) directly to the judge dealing with the proceedings. In the magistrates' court, the request should be sent to the relevant court or (by prior arrangement only) to any district judge (magistrates' courts) hearing the proceedings (and copied to the legal adviser) or to the legal adviser. The court will settle the letter of instruction, usually without a hearing to avoid delay; and will send (where practicable, by e-mail) the settled letter to the party responsible for instructing the expert for transmission forthwith to the expert, and copy it to the other instructing parties for information.

Practice Direction 25E –
Discussions Between Experts in Family Proceedings

This Practice Direction supplements FPR Part 25

Scope

1.1 This Practice Direction supports FPR 25.16 by providing details about how and when experts discussions are to be arranged, their purpose and content. This Practice Direction applies to children proceedings and all other family proceedings.

Experts' discussion or meeting: purpose

2.1 In accordance with FPR 25.16, the court may, at any stage, direct a discussion between experts for the purpose outlined in paragraph (1) of that rule. FPR 25.16(2) provides that the court may specify the issues which the experts must discuss. The expectation is that those issues will include –

    (a)   the reasons for disagreement on any expert question and what, if any, action needs to be taken to resolve any outstanding disagreement or question;

    (b)   an explanation of existing evidence or additional evidence in order to assist the court to determine the issues.

One of the aims of specifying the issues for discussion is to limit, wherever possible, the need for the experts to attend court to give oral evidence.

Experts' discussion or meeting: arrangements

3.1 Subject to the directions given by the court under FPR 25.16, the solicitor or other professional who is given the responsibility by the court ("the nominated professional") shall **within 15 business days after the experts' reports have been filed and copied to the other parties**, make arrangements for the experts to have discussions. Subject to any specification by the court of the issues which experts must discuss under FPR 25.16(2), the following matters should be considered as appropriate –

    (a)   where permission has been given for the instruction of experts from different disciplines, a global discussion may be held relating to those questions that concern all or most of them;

    (b)   separate discussions may have to be held among experts from the same or related disciplines, but care should be taken to ensure that the discussions complement each other so that related questions are discussed by all relevant experts;

    (c)   5 business days prior to a discussion or meeting, the nominated professional should formulate an agenda including a list of questions for consideration. The agenda should, subject always to the provisions of FPR 25.16(1), focus on those questions which are intended to clarify areas of agreement or disagreement. Questions which repeat questions asked in the court order giving permission for an expert to be instructed or expert evidence to be put before the court or the letter of instruction or which seek to rehearse cross-examination in advance of the hearing should be rejected as likely to defeat the purpose of the meeting. The agenda may usefully take the form of a list of questions to be circulated among the other parties in advance and should comprise all questions that each party wishes the experts to consider.

The agenda and list of questions should be sent to each of the experts **not later than 2 business days before the discussion**;

(d)   the nominated professional may exercise his or her discretion to accept further questions after the agenda with the list of questions has been circulated to the parties. **Only in exceptional circumstances should questions be added to the agenda within the 2-day period before the meeting. Under no circumstances should any question received on the day of or during the meeting be accepted**. This does not preclude questions arising during the meeting for the purposes of clarification. Strictness in this regard is vital, for adequate notice of the questions enables the parties to identify and isolate the expert issues in the case before the meeting so that the experts' discussion at the meeting can concentrate on those issues;

(e)   the discussion should be chaired by the nominated professional. A minute must be taken of the questions answered by the experts. Where the court has given a direction under FPR 25.16(3) and subject to that direction, a Statement of Agreement and Disagreement must be prepared which should be agreed and signed by each of the experts who participated in the discussion. In accordance with FPR 25.16(3) the statement must contain a summary of the experts' reasons for disagreeing. The statement should be served and filed **not later than 5 business days after the discussion has taken place**;

(f)   in each case, whether some or all of the experts participate by telephone conference or video link to ensure that minimum disruption is caused to professional schedules and that costs are minimised.

Meetings or conferences attended by a jointly instructed expert

4.1 Jointly instructed experts should not attend any meeting or conference which is not a joint one, unless all the parties have agreed in writing or the court has directed that such a meeting may be held, and it is agreed or directed who is to pay the expert's fees for the meeting or conference. Any meeting or conference attended by a jointly instructed expert should be proportionate to the case.

(Practice Direction 25C, paragraphs 2.1 to 2.7 deals generally with single joint experts in children proceedings and Practice Direction 25D paragraphs 2.1 to 2.7 deals with single joint experts in relation to other family proceedings).

Court-directed meetings involving experts in public law Children Act cases

5.1 In public law Children Act proceedings, where the court gives a direction that a meeting shall take place between the local authority and any relevant named experts for the purpose of providing assistance to the local authority in the formulation of plans and proposals for the child, the meeting shall be arranged, chaired and minuted in accordance with the directions given by the court.

Practice Direction 25F –
Assessors in Family Proceedings

This Practice Direction supplements FPR Part 25

Scope of this Practice Direction

1.1 This Practice Direction applies to the appointment of assessors in family proceedings in England and Wales.

Appointment of assessors in family proceedings

2.1 The power to appoint one or more assessors to assist the court is conferred on the High Court by section 70(1) of the Senior Courts Act 1981, and on a county court by section 63(1) of the County Courts Act 1984. In practice, these powers have been used in appeals from a district judge or costs judge in costs assessment proceedings – although, in principle, the statutory powers permit one or more assessors to be appointed in any family proceedings where the High Court or a county court sees fit.

2.2 Not less than 21 days before making any such appointment, the court will notify each party in writing of the name of the proposed assessor, of the matter in respect of which the assistance of the assessor will be sought and of the qualifications of the assessor to give that assistance.

2.3 Any party may object to the proposed appointment, either personally or in respect of the proposed assessor's qualifications.

2.4 Any such objection must be made in writing and filed and served within 7 business days of receipt of the notification from the court of the proposed appointment, and will be taken into account by the court in deciding whether or not to make the appointment.

Scope—FPR 2010, r 25.20 makes provision for the appointment, duties and remuneration of one or more assessors. As indicated by para 2.1, the appointment of assessors normally takes place in appeals from a district judge or costs judge in costs assessment proceedings when, typically, a district judge and senior practising solicitor will be appointed as assessors to sit on the appeal alongside a High Court or circuit judge. FPR PD25F makes provision for an objection to be taken to any such appointment in appropriate circumstances. These provisions are derived from CPR 1998, r 35.15 and CPR PD35, para 10.

PART 26
CHANGE OF SOLICITOR

CONTENTS OF THIS PART

26.1 Solicitor acting for a party

Where the address for service of a party is the business address of that party's solicitor, the solicitor will be considered to be acting for that party until the provisions of this Part have been complied with.

> (Part 6 contains provisions about the address for service.)

Practice Direction—See generally FPR PD26A.

Scope—Formerly, in family proceedings, RSC Ord 67, r 6 and CCR Ord 50, r 5 applied by FPR 1991, r 1.3(1). In other proceedings CPR 1998, Pt 42 applied and still applies. The FP(A)R 2005, Pt 18 and PD applied in adoption and related proceedings. Pt 26 reproduces CPR 1998, Pt 42 with minor amendments.

Where a party employs a solicitor, the solicitor's business address will be the address for service (FPR 2010, r 6.11). All documents served by the court or another party are properly served at that address. The solicitor will be considered to be acting for that party until a notice of change has been filed with the court by the party concerned or his new solicitor and served on the other party (FPR PD26A, para 1.1).

26.2 Change of solicitor – duty to give notice

(1) This rule applies where –

    (a) a party for whom a solicitor is acting wants to change solicitor;

    (b) a party, after having conducted the application in person, appoints a solicitor to act for that party (except where the solicitor is appointed only to act as an advocate for a hearing); or

    (c) a party, after having conducted the application by a solicitor, intends to act in person.

(2) Where this rule applies, the party or the party's solicitor (where one is acting) must –

    (a) serve notice of the change on –
        every other party; and
        where paragraph (1)(a)or (c) applies, the former solicitor; and

    (b) file notice of the change.

(3) Except where a serial number has been assigned under rule 14.2 or the name or address of a party is not being revealed in accordance with rule 29.1, the notice must state the party's new address for service.

(4) The notice filed at court must state that notice has been served as required by paragraph (2)(a) or, where rule 2.4 applies, in accordance with the court's directions given under that rule.

(5) Subject to paragraph (6), where a party has changed solicitor or intends to act in person, the former solicitor will be considered to be the party's solicitor unless and until –

    (a) notice is filed and served in accordance with paragraph (2)(a) or, where rule 2.4 applies, in accordance with the court's directions given under that rule; or

    (b) the court makes an order under rule 26.3 and the order is served as required by paragraph (3) of that rule.

(6) Where the certificate of a legally aided person (in this rule "C") is revoked or withdrawn –

    (a) the solicitor who acted for C will cease to be the solicitor acting in the case as soon as the retainer is determined under regulation 24 or 41 of the Civil Legal Aid (Procedure) Regulations 2012; and

    (b) if C wishes to continue –

        (i) where C appoints a solicitor to act on C's behalf, paragraph (2) will apply as if C had previously conducted the application in person; and

  (ii) where C wants to act in person, C must give an address for service, in accordance with rule 6.26, unless the court directs otherwise.

(7) In this rule –

 …

"certificate" means a certificate issued under the Civil Legal Aid (Procedure) Regulations 2012"; and

 …

"legally aided person" means a person to whom civil legal services (within the meaning of Part 1 of the Legal Aid, Sentencing and Punishment of Offenders Act 2012) have been made available under arrangements made for the purposes of that Part of that Act).

Amendments—SI 2013/534, subject to savings.

Practice Direction—See generally FPR PD26A, in particular para 2 (notice of change of solicitor).

Scope—In the three situations referred to in r 26.2(1), it is mandatory for the party or his solicitor:

(a) to file notice of change; and
(b) to serve notice of change on every other party and (where appropriate) the former solicitor.

 No order of the court is required in the circumstances set out in r 26.2(1). Rule 26.2(5) makes it clear that, once a solicitor is appointed to act, he is considered to be the party's solicitor unless or until the requirements of Pt 26 are complied with. The notice of change of solicitor must state the party's new address for service, subject to the exceptions in r 26.2(3). The notice filed with the court must also state that the notice has been served on every other party and (where appropriate) the former solicitor.

 The court cannot order a party to appoint a new solicitor; the court may only forbid solicitors from acting and grant a stay for new solicitors to be appointed (*SMC Engineering (Bristol) Limited v Fraser* (2001) *The Times*, 26 January, CA).

"Notice of change"—PD26A, para 2.6: Form FP8.

Revocation or discharge of certificate (r 26.2(6))—A solicitor's retainer under a public funding certificate ends upon receipt by the solicitor of a notice of revocation or discharge of the certificate. The solicitor must serve notice of the revocation or discharge on all other parties and to the court. No further notice or order is required by the solicitor to come off the court record. If the LSC funded client or assisted person wishes to continue with the proceedings and appoints either the solicitor who was acting for him under the certificate or another solicitor, he must file notice of change and serve the notice on every other party. Alternatively, if the party who formerly had the benefit of a certificate wishes to act in person, then he must give an address for service within the jurisdiction.

 Where a public funding certificate is revoked, the court has a discretion to revoke the limitation in an order for costs against a previously assisted party provided that no costs attributable to the period after the grant of legal aid are recoverable until a determination in accordance with the Legal Aid Act 1988, s 17 has been carried out (*DEG – Deutsche Investitions und Entwicklungsgesellschaft mbH v Koshy & ors* [2001] EWCA Civ 79).

26.3 Order that a solicitor has ceased to act

(1) A solicitor may apply for an order declaring that that solicitor has ceased to be the solicitor acting for –

 (a) a party; or
 (b) a children's guardian.

(2) Where an application is made under this rule –

 (a) notice of the application must be given to the party, or children's guardian, for whom the solicitor is acting, unless the court directs otherwise; and
 (b) the application must be supported by evidence.

(3) Where the court makes an order declaring that a solicitor has ceased to act, a court officer will serve a copy of the order on –

 (a) every party to the proceedings; and
 (b) where applicable, a children's guardian.

Practice Direction—See generally FPR PD26A and, in particular, para 3. It should be noted that an order made under r 26.3 must be served on every party and takes effect only when it is served. If the order is not served by the court, the solicitor or person serving the order must file proof of service.

Scope—A solicitor's retainer is usually an entire contract to conduct or defend the action to the end. See, however, *Cawdrey Kaye Fireman & Taylor v Minkin* [2012] EWCA Civ 546. Whether it has determined is a matter of fact. It will usually continue until one of the following occurs: the client discharges the solicitor; the solicitor discharges himself; death (but not necessarily) (*Donsland Limited v Van Hoogstraten* [2002] EWCA Civ 253); incapacity of the party; a change in the solicitor's firm; the final conclusion of the cause or matter. The retainer is subject to implied terms allowing the solicitor to withdraw for good cause, e g where the client fails to provide a reasonable sum of money for disbursements (Solicitors Act 1974, s 65(2)) and upon reasonable notice (*Cawdrey Kaye Fireman & Taylor v Minkin*, above). As to the scope of the retainer in relation to fixed-fee legal advice, see *Inventors Friend Limited v Leathes Prior* [2011] EWHC 711 (QB). The client may end the retainer at any time. If the former client or his new solicitor has not given notice of change under FPR 2010, r 26.2, the solicitor whose retainer has determined should apply promptly for an order under this rule. Where solicitors are plainly unwilling to continue to act due to a serious breakdown in the relationship between themselves and their client, they cannot be forced to continue to act and an order removing them from the record should be made (*UCB Bank plc v Hedworth* [2003] EWCA Civ 705).

An application under this rule is made in accordance with FPR 2010, Pt 18 and must state why the applicant is seeking the order and be supported by evidence (FPR 2010, r 18.7 and FPR PD26A, para 3.2). It is the party who is the respondent to the application. The court may direct other persons to be added as respondents but, unless this occurs, the other parties to the claim must not be served. It is appropriate in a simple case to allow a solicitor to make an application pursuant to r 26.3 in writing. To require attendance would take up court time and lead to an increase in costs (*Miller v Allied Sainif* (UK) (2000) *The Times*, 31 October). Solicitors wishing to come off the record in a more complex case would be well advised to attend court. If applying in writing, they will still normally have to file evidence that the application notice has been served on the former client (r 26.3(2)(a)).

The court may direct that notice of the application need not be given to the party for whom the solicitor is or was acting e g where that party has changed address without giving the solicitor details. It is useful practice for the order declaring that the solicitor has ceased to act to set out the address for service of the party concerned. A copy of the order must be served on every party to the claim.

An order for costs on the granting of an application that a solicitor cease to act should be unnecessary, as the costs form part of the solicitor's retainer and the order made does not affect the rights of either the solicitor or the client.

26.4 Removal of solicitor who has ceased to act on application of another party

(1) Where –

    (a)   a solicitor who has acted for a party –

        (i)   has died;

        (ii) has become bankrupt;

        (iii) has ceased to practise; or

        (iv) cannot be found; and

    (b)   the party has not given notice of a change of solicitor or notice of intention to act in person as required by rule 26.2(2),

any other party may apply for an order declaring that the solicitor has ceased to be the solicitor acting for the other party in the case.

(2) Where an application is made under this rule, notice of the application must be given to the party to whose solicitor the application relates unless the court directs otherwise.

(3) Where the court makes an order made under this rule, a court officer will serve a copy of the order on every other party to the proceedings.

Practice Direction—See generally FPR PD26A, in particular para 4.

Practice Direction 26A – Change of Solicitor

This Practice Direction supplements FPR Part 26

Solicitor acting for a party

1.1 Rule 26.1 states that where the address for service of a party is the business address of his solicitor, the solicitor will be considered to be acting for that party until the provisions of Part 26 have been complied with.

1.2 Subject to rule 26.2(6) (where the certificate of a LSC funded client or assisted person is revoked or discharged), where a party has changed his solicitor or intends to act in person, the former solicitor will be considered to be the party's solicitor unless or until –

    (a) a notice of the change is –
        (i)   served on every other party (see rule 26.2(2)(a)); and
        (ii) filed with the court (see rule 26.2(2)(b)); or
    (b) the court makes an order under rule 26.3 and the order is served on the former solicitor and every other party in accordance with directions of the court (see rule 26.2(5)).

1.3 A solicitor appointed to represent a party only as an advocate at a hearing will not be considered to be acting for that party within the meaning of Part 26.

Notice of change of solicitor

2.1 Rule 26.2(1) sets out the circumstances following which a notice of the change must be filed and served.

2.2 A notice of the change giving the last known address of the former assisted person must also be filed and served on every party where, under rule 26.2(6) –

    (a) the certificate of a LSC funded client or assisted person is revoked or discharged; and
    (b) the LSC funded client or the assisted person wishes either to act in person or appoint another solicitor to act on his behalf.

2.3 Where a solicitor has given notice that he or she acts for a child directly, and an officer of the Service, a Welsh family proceedings officer or the Official Solicitor continues with the permission of the court to have legal representation, notice of that legal representation must be given to the court.

2.4 In addition, where a party or solicitor changes his address for service, a notice of that change should be filed and served on every party.

2.5 A party who, having conducted an application by a solicitor, intends to act in person must give in his notice an address for service that is within the United Kingdom (see rule 6.26).

2.6 The form giving notice of any change is referred to in Practice Direction 5A. The notice should be filed in the court office in which the application is proceeding.

Application for an order that a solicitor has ceased to act

3.1 A solicitor may apply under rule 26.3 for an order declaring that he has ceased to be the solicitor acting for a party.

PART III

3.2 The application should be made in accordance with Part 18 and must be supported by evidence (see Part 18 and the Practice Direction 18A). Unless the court directs otherwise the application notice must be served on the party (see rule 26.3(2)).

3.3 An order made under rule 26.3 will be served on every party by the court officer and takes effect when it is served.

Application by another party to remove a solicitor

4.1 Rule 26.4 sets out circumstances in which any other party may apply for an order declaring that a solicitor has ceased to be the solicitor acting for another party in the proceedings.

4.2 The application should be made in accordance with Part 18 and must be supported by evidence. Unless the court directs otherwise the application notice must be served on the party to whose solicitor the application relates.

4.3 An order made under rule 26.4 will be served on every party by the court officer.

New address for service where order made under rules 26.3 or 26.4

5.1 Where the court has made an order under rule 26.3 that a solicitor has ceased to act or under rule 26.4 declaring that a solicitor has ceased to be the solicitor for a party, the party for whom the solicitor was acting must give a new address for service to comply with rule 6.26.

> (Rule 6.26 provides that a party must give an address for service within the United Kingdom, or where a solicitor is acting for a party, an address for service either in the United Kingdom or any other EEA state, at which that party resides or carries on business. Where that party does not have such an address, an address within the United Kingdom must generally be given (see rule 6.26(3) and (4)).

> (Until such time as a new address for service is given directions may be needed under rule 6.19.)

PART 27
HEARINGS AND DIRECTIONS APPOINTMENTS

CONTENTS OF THIS PART

27.1 Application of this Part

This Part is subject to any enactment, any provision in these rules or a practice direction.

> (Rule 27.4(7) makes additional provision in relation to requirements to stay proceedings where the respondent does not appear and a relevant European regulation or international convention applies)

27.2 Reasons for a decision of the magistrates' courts

(1) This rule applies to proceedings in a magistrates' court.

(2) After a hearing, the court will make its decision as soon as is practicable.

(3) The court must give written reasons for its decision.

(4) Paragraphs (5) and (6) apply where the functions of the court are being performed by –

    (a)   two or three lay justices; or

    (b)   by a single lay justice in accordance with these rules and Practice Direction 2A.

(5) The justices' clerk must, before the court makes an order or refuses an application or request, make notes of –

    (a)   the names of the justice or justices constituting the court by which the decision is made; and

    (b)   in consultation with the justice or justices, the reasons for the court's decision.

(6) The justices' clerk must make a written record of the reasons for the court's decision.

(7) When making an order or refusing an application, the court, or one of the justices constituting the court by which the decision is made, will announce its decision and –

    (a)   the reasons for that decision; or

    (b)   a short explanation of that decision.

(8) Subject to any other rule or practice direction, the court officer will supply a copy of the order and the reasons for the court's decision to the persons referred to in paragraph (9) –

    (a)   by close of business on the day when the court announces its decision; or

    (b)   where that time is not practicable and the proceedings are on notice, no later than 72 hours from the time when the court announced its decision.

(9) The persons referred to in paragraph (8) are –

    (a)   the parties (unless the court directs otherwise);

    (b)   any person who has actual care of a child who is the subject of proceedings, or who had such care immediately prior to the making of the order;

    (c)   in the case of an emergency protection order and a recovery order, the local authority in whose area the child lives or is found;

    (d)   in proceedings to which Part 14 applies –

        (i)   an adoption agency or local authority which has prepared a report on the suitability of the applicant to adopt a child;

        (ii)   a local authority which has prepared a report on the placement of the child for adoption;

(e) any other person who has requested a copy if the court is satisfied that it is required in connection with an appeal or possible appeal.

(10) In this rule, "lay justice" means a justice of the peace who is not a District Judge (Magistrates' Courts).

(Rule 12.16(5) provides for the applicant to serve a section 8 order and an order in emergency proceedings made without notice within 48 hours after the making of the order. Rule 10.6(1) provides for the applicant to serve the order in proceedings under Part 4 of the 1996 Act. Rule 4.1(3)(a) permits the court to extend or shorten the time limit for compliance with any rule. Rule 6.33 provides for other persons to be supplied with copy documents under paragraph (8).)

The decision and the reasons for it—The Justices' Clerks' Society and the Magistrates' Association have published joint guidance on the giving of justices' reasons in family proceeding courts in CA 1989 cases; see *www.familieslink.co.uk/download/sept07/guidance_on_family_justices'_reasons.pdf*. In public law cases to which the PLO (FPR PD12A) applies, the drawing up of orders and reasons is covered by Stage 4 of the PLO. Reasons must be given whenever an order is made or an application refused including, for example, interim orders ((*Hampshire County Council v S* [1993] 1 FLR 559), a refusal to shorten a prescribed notice period or to make a without notice order (*Essex CC v F* [1993] 1 FLR 847), the determination of the length of a secure accommodation order (*Re W (A Minor) (Secure Accommodation Order)* [1993] 1 FLR 692), a decision to proceed to determine an application for leave under CA 1989, s 10 without notice and the decision whether to grant such leave (*Re M (Prohibited Steps Order: Application for Leave)* [1993] 1 FLR 275), a refusal to give leave for a child psychiatrist to become involved in the case and to transfer the matter to the High Court (*London Borough of Croydon v R* [1997] 2 FLR 675, where there was particular need to give reasons as the application for directions had been referred to the court by the justices' clerk). For consideration of whether there may be a class of quite exceptional cases in which reasons need not be given, see *T v W (Contact: Reasons for Refusing Leave)* [1996] 2 FLR 473 and see *London Borough of Croydon v R* (above) in which Wall J, not wishing to place an intolerable burden on justices, expressed his view that not every order for directions requires reasons to be given but that where the issue is contentious and requires a ruling from the court after full argument, it is good practice for succinct reasons to be given.

Although the rules require the decision to be made as soon as practicable (r 27.2(2), and see *Devon CC v S and Others* [1992] 2 FLR 244), it can be better in certain circumstances (e g where the hearing lasts beyond normal hours) to adjourn the making of the order or the giving of the decision until the following court day or the earliest possible other date, on which subsequent occasion only one justice need return to court to state the decision, findings of fact and reasons (see *Oxfordshire County Council v R* [1992] 1 FLR 648; *Hampshire CC v S* [1993] 1 FLR 559). What is not permissible, however, is for the justices to announce their order before they have finished writing down their reasons and then to give reasons and announce their findings on the following day (*Re W (A Minor) (Contact)* [1994] 1 FLR 843). The findings of fact and reasons stated in court must tally with those recorded in writing (*S v S (Children: Periodical Payments)* [1993] 1 FLR 606).

Failure to observe the requirements of r 27.2(5)–(7) can vitiate the decision of the justices and lead to their orders being set aside on appeal (*Re W (A Minor) (Contact)*, above). There are a number of cases in which the higher courts have given guidance as to how it should be done. The Court of Appeal in *Re B (Procedure: Family Proceedings Court)* [1993] Fam Law 209 stated that it was helpful if the justices first set out the relevant facts in chronological order or under convenient headings, making it clear what was in dispute and what was not, and then make findings on any disputed matters. It was also said to be helpful if, in giving reasons for their decision, the justices mentioned the factors that they had brought into the balancing exercise, even if obvious. This was not to say that every point, however trivial, had to be dealt with, but an appellate court would need to know the basis for the decision. On the format of reasons, see *Re D (Contact: Interim Order)* [1995] 1 FLR 495 as to the need to deal with matters set out in CA 1989. If, in the case of an interim application, the justices decide that they cannot make findings of fact and deliberately refrain from detailed investigation as part of the overall strategy of reaching a final conclusion only on the final hearing, this is a reasoning process that should be explained in their reasons (*F v R (Contact: Justices' Reasons)* [1995] 1 FLR 227). Where the justices give inadequate reasons for their decision, they cannot retrieve the situation by sending extended reasons to the appeal court on receiving notice of appeal (see *Hillingdon LBC v H* [1992] 2 FLR 372) or by corresponding with the appellate court (*Re F (A Minor) (Care Order: Withdrawal of Application)* [1993] 2 FLR 9). It is also inappropriate for the justices to solicit general guidance from, or to communicate with, the appellate court, particularly in the submission of considerations that they believed justified their determination; anything that supported the justices' order must be contained within their stated reasons and it was not open to them further to reason their conclusion in response to the knowledge that there was an appeal

(Re WB (Residence Orders) [1995] 2 FLR 1023). The Court of Appeal commented in *Re M (Section 94 Appeals)* [1995] 1 FLR 546 that an appellate court might be less ready to assume that magistrates have taken relevant factors into account if they have not referred to them in their reasons than it might in the case of an experienced judge, but that the justices' reasons are not intended to be a judgment and that an appellate court should be slow to interfere with magistrates' decisions as it would be to interfere with any other tribunal charged with the duty to make decisions in the exercise of discretion. See also *Re C (Care or Supervision Order)* [1999] 2 FLR 621, where Sir Stephen Brown P upheld the decision of the magistrates to follow the recommendation of the children's guardian to make a care order instead of the supervision order sought by the local authority, saying that the case revolved around the exercise of discretion by the magistrates. In *Re P (Contact: Discretion)* [1998] 2 FLR 696, FD it was recognised that the requirement that a decision to make or refuse an order could only be announced in court after the findings and reasons in support had been recorded in writing was an onerous one and it was said to be important that the appellate court did not take too pedantic an approach to a document produced in such circumstances. The key issues for the appellate court were whether the legal principles had been correctly identified, whether the material factors, particularly any under s 1(3), had been afforded sufficient weight in the balancing exercise and whether the decision was plainly wrong. For a case in which the court, dealing with an appeal in which the magistrates had failed to give adequate reasons, filled in the gaps and upheld the magistrates' decision, see *Oxfordshire CC v R* [1997] Fam Law 828.

The June 1997 *CAAC Handbook of Best Practice in Children Act Cases*, App A, item X contains detailed guidance compiled by Mr Justice Cazalet as to the preparation of justices' written findings and reasons (see Part V).

Announcing the decision (r 27.2(7))—In *Oxfordshire CC v S* [2004] 1 FLR 426, it was not clear from the justices' reasons that they had correctly applied the CA 1989, s 38 test relevant to the making of an interim care order. Munby J held that there is no legal obligation on justices to read out verbatim the whole of the document in which their reasons and findings of fact have been recorded. Rule 27.2(7)(b) provides that magistrates can choose to announce the decision and to summarise their written reasons by reading out a short explanation only. Consequently, Munby J's guidance remains valid and of particular relevance in such circumstances. Although the decision is not likely to be invalidated by a mere slip of the tongue, care should be taken that any summary does not involve a material or significant departure or deviation from the written document. Any such departure or deviation of substance rather than mere form is almost bound to lead to the decision being quashed. However, any litigant seeking to demonstrate that any such material or significant departure or deviation from the written reasons had taken place bears a heavy evidential burden and, absent admission or clear evidence, the court will be slow to find that justices have erred in this way.

Departing from an expert's opinion—The court is entitled to depart from the opinion of an expert although, if it does so, it must explain its reasons (*Re B (Care: Expert Witnesses)* [1996] 1 FLR 667). Where there is a conflict between experts, the court must address and resolve that conflict insofar as it is relevant to the issues before the court and it is entitled to give greater weight to the opinion of one expert as against that of another, provided that proper reasons are given (*Re J (Expert Evidence: Hearsay)* [1999] 2 FLR 661). It is unusual for a magistrates' court to hear a case involving a conflict of expert evidence (see ATPO 2008, art 15).

"a copy of the order" (r 27.2(8))—The order has to be made on whichever of the prescribed forms is appropriate to the case (see PD5A) or, in default of an appropriate form, in writing. Where the order is by consent, it should say so (see *Chandless-Chandless v Nicholson* [1942] 2 KB 321). Where the justices make no order, there should still be a written order to that effect (*S v R (Parental Responsibility)* [1993] 1 FCR 331). If appropriate, it is possible for the order to recite the intention of the parties at the time of the order, as a preliminary to stating that the court considered an order unnecessary (*M v M (Defined Contact Application)* [1998] 2 FLR 244, in which there was an order of "no order as to defined contact" but with the parents' joint wishes and expectations set out in the preamble). The justices should give careful consideration to the practical effect of making no order (*D v D (Application for Contact)* [1994] 1 FCR 694). As to the possibility of recording the agreement of a parent to seek treatment as a preamble to a supervision order, see *Re B (Supervision Order: Parental Undertaking)* [1996] 1 FLR 676.

27.3 Attendance at hearing or directions appointment

Unless the court directs otherwise, a party shall attend a hearing or directions appointment of which that party has been given notice.

"a party shall attend"—It is a fundamental aspect of family procedure that, whatever aspect is before the court, the parties should be present as well as their legal advisers. This is an instance of the parties' duty under FPR 2010, r 1.3 to help the court further the overriding objective. If a party fails to attend, see FPR 2010, r 27.4.

"has been given notice"—Service is dealt with in FPR 2010, Pt 6. Service on a party's solicitor is, of course, good service on the party. But whereas "service" has a technical meaning, "notice" does not.

"unless the court directs otherwise"—The court has a complete discretion as to the circumstances in which to dispense with the attendance of a party and can do so either on request of a party or of its own initiative. For example, where a court is fixing the next appointment at the conclusion of a directions hearing it could, in special circumstances, excuse a party from attending that appointment.

27.4 Proceedings in the absence of a party

(1) Proceedings or any part of them shall take place in the absence of any party, including a party who is a child, if –

    (a)   the court considers it in the interests of the party, having regard to the matters to be discussed or the evidence likely to be given; and

    (b)   the party is represented by a children's guardian or solicitor,

and when considering the interests of a child under sub-paragraph (a) the court shall give the children's guardian, the solicitor for the child and, if of sufficient understanding and the court thinks it appropriate, the child, an opportunity to make representations.

(2) Subject to paragraph (3), where at the time and place appointed for a hearing or directions appointment the applicant appears but one or more of the respondents do not, the court may proceed with the hearing or appointment.

(3) The court shall not begin to hear an application in the absence of a respondent unless –

    (a)   it is proved to the satisfaction of the court that the respondent received reasonable notice of the date of the hearing; or

    (b)   the court is satisfied that the circumstances of the case justify proceeding with the hearing.

(4) Where, at the time and place appointed for a hearing or directions appointment, one or more of the respondents appear but the applicant does not, the court may refuse the application or, if sufficient evidence has previously been received, proceed in the absence of the applicant.

(5) Where, at the time and place appointed for a hearing or directions appointment, neither the applicant nor any respondent appears, the court may refuse the application.

(6) Paragraphs (2) to (5) do not apply to a hearing to which paragraphs (5) to (8) of rule 12.14 do not apply by virtue of paragraph (9) of that rule.

(7) Nothing in this rule affects any provision of a European regulation or international convention by which the United Kingdom is bound which requires a court to stay proceedings where a respondent in another State has not been adequately served with proceedings in accordance with the requirements of that regulation or convention.

"proceedings ... shall take place in the absence of a party ... if"—Parties are under a duty to attend all hearings unless the court directs otherwise (see FPR 2010, r 27.3). But this raises the question "what if a party does not attend?" and that question is answered by r 27.4. If a child is also a party then the basic rule in r 27.3 applies to that child too but note the specific provisions in r 27.4(1), especially r 27.4(1)(b).

"the party is represented by a children's guardian or solicitor"—This rule (which merely reproduces the former r 4.16(2)(b)) is worded oddly. The words "is represented" must surely mean "is represented at the hearing". But the rule makes no mention of representation by counsel. It is submitted that if a child who is a party is not present but is represented by fully instructed counsel that is sufficient to enable the court to proceed as the court must give effect to the overriding objective when it interprets any rule (FPR 2010, r 1.2). In *Re AS (Secure Accommodation Order)* [1999] 1 FLR 103, when considering the requirement for legal representation of a child in secure accommodation proceedings, the court held that this involves the taking of instructions. Thus it was not sufficient for a child to be "represented" by solicitor and counsel who had not been able to take instructions as the child had not been informed of the hearing.

Child of sufficient understanding to make representations—Rule 27.4 is one of many situations when the court is required to assess whether a child has "sufficient understanding" to make representations in person rather than just through the guardian or legal representative. No criteria are laid down as much turns on not only the nature of the proceedings but also of the particular application before the court. Both the guardian and legal representative will be expected to assist the court in making the assessment.

Proceeding in the absence of the respondent—Paras (2) and (3) of r 27.4 must be read together. The rule refers to "reasonable notice" rather than "service" and this can take many forms. Where it is the court's obligation to give notice, proof will be on the court file. Otherwise the applicant will have to prove that the respondent has had reasonable notice. Clearly formal proof of service suffices but it would be sufficient also if the respondent was present at the previous hearing when the new date was fixed. Alternatively, for example, the respondent may have written to the court about the hearing or told the applicant that he will not be attending. Note that for certain applications (see for example FPR 2010, Pt 10 dealing with non-molestation orders etc) a particular rule requires a minimum period of notice and that, unless the court abridges time for service, anything less than the prescribed minimum would not be "reasonable notice".

Proceeding in the absence of the applicant—If the applicant does not attend, r 27.4(4) refers only to the court being able to "refuse the application" or, alternatively, proceeding with it in the absence of the applicant if "sufficient evidence has previously been received". However, the use of the word "may" clearly indicates that the court could instead adjourn to another day if it considered that to be more appropriate. The court will be reluctant to waste the time set aside to hear the application and would try to proceed if possible although the circumstances in which it could do so are prescribed by the rule: but to refuse an application which on the face of it has merit (aliter if it does not) may be draconian and lead to yet more court time being taken up by an application under r 27.5. Therefore, there will inevitably be occasions when the better course is to adjourn. However, if the applicant fails to attend on a second occasion the court would no doubt refuse the application.

"sufficient evidence has previously been received"—The best example of the court being able to proceed under r 27.4(4) is the part-heard case where the applicant's case has been closed or, at least, the applicant's own evidence has been concluded. The rule refers to "evidence" and a witness statement is not evidence until the maker swears or affirms to it (before that it is merely an advance indication of the evidence which the maker intends to give).

Where neither applicant nor respondent attends—Rule 27.4(5) gives the court a discretion to refuse the application. The use of "may" indicates that the court could adjourn and the court may prefer to do so if, for example, there is a suspicion that inappropriate pressure has been applied to keep a party away. However, where neither attends generally the application would be refused leaving either party to apply under FPR 2010, r 27.5.

Proceedings relating to children (except parental order proceedings and proceedings for applications in adoption, placement and related proceedings)—This sub-heading is the title to FPR 2010, Pt 12. FPR 2010, Rule 12.14 is titled "Attendance at hearings" and thus needs to be read in conjunction with Pt 27 in proceedings relating to children. Rule 12.14 is expressly referred to in r 27.4(6). Paragraph (9) of r 12.14 is concerned with the enforcement of contact orders.

27.5 Application to set aside judgment or order following failure to attend

(1) Where a party does not attend a hearing or directions appointment and the court gives judgment or makes an order against him, the party who failed to attend may apply for the judgment or order to be set aside[(GL)].

(2) An application under paragraph (1) must be supported by evidence.

(3) Where an application is made under paragraph (1), the court may grant the application only if the applicant –

    (a) acted promptly on finding out that the court had exercised its power to enter judgment or make an order against the applicant;

    (b) had a good reason for not attending the hearing or directions appointment; and

    (c) has a reasonable prospect of success at the hearing or directions appointment.

(4) This rule does not apply to magistrates' courts.

"set aside judgment or order"—Rule 27.5 enables a party who failed to attend a hearing or directions appointment to apply to have the judgment or order to be set aside. This provision had no equivalent in the former rules. It is clearly based on CPR 1998, r 39.3 and thus cases on that rule will aid interpretation. All cases cited in commentary on r 27.5 are cases on CPR 1998, r 39.3. It remains to be seen whether the different nature of family proceedings requires a more generous approach.

"must be supported by evidence"—At the very least a witness statement giving a full explanation and satisfying the strict requirements of r 27.5(3) will be necessary.

"the court may grant the application only …"—The three criteria in r 27.5(3) have to be met. The court has no residual discretion (*Regency Rolls Ltd v Carnall* [2000] EWCA Civ 379).

"acted promptly"—"I would construe 'promptly' here to require, not that an applicant has been guilty of no needless delay whatever, but rather that he has acted with all reasonable celerity in the circumstances" per Simon Brown LJ in *Regency Rolls Ltd v Carnall* [2000] EWCA Civ 379 where an application made over four weeks after the hearing was dismissed because the applicant had not acted promptly.

"had a good reason for not attending"—The court has to consider each application in the light of all relevant factors for non-attendance and, looking at the matter in the round, decide whether the reasons are sufficient to exercise the discretion to set aside (*Brazil v Brazil* [2002] EWCA Civ 1135). The court must be satisfied that the reason is genuine and honest but that, of itself, does not mean that the reason is "good". There are no fixed reasons that are "good" or "bad" and an over analytical approach is inconsistent with the overriding objective. The mere assertion that a party was unaware of the hearing is unlikely to be sufficient of itself. The court will enquire why this was so. Once a party is aware that proceedings are underway communications from the court and the other party are to be expected. A party who knows of proceedings is not entitled as of right to have an order set aside simply because he was not aware of a new hearing date (*Hackney London Borough Council v Driscoll* [2003] 1 WLR 2602).

"has a reasonable prospect of success"—The reasonable prospect of success condition of r 27.5(3)(c) is just as important as the other two conditions and does not offend any fundamental principle of justice or any principle of the ECHR (see both *Hackney London Borough Council v Driscoll* and *Regency Rolls Ltd v Carnall* above).

27.6 Court bundles and place of filing of documents and bundles

(1) The provisions of Practice Direction 27A must be followed for the preparation of court bundles and for other related matters in respect of hearings and directions appointments.

(2) Paragraph (3) applies where the file of any family proceedings has been sent from one designated county court or registry to another for the purpose of a hearing or for some other purpose.

(3) A document needed for the purpose for which the proceedings have been sent to the other court or registry must be filed in that court or registry.

> (Practice Direction 27A (Family Proceedings: Court Bundles (Universal Practice to be applied in All Courts other than the Family Proceedings Courts)) does not apply to magistrates' courts.)

27.7 Representation of companies or other corporations

A company or other corporation may be represented at a hearing or directions appointment by an employee if –

(a) the employee has been authorised by the company or corporation to appear at the hearing or directions appointment on its behalf; and
(b) the court gives permission.

27.8 Impounded documents

(1) Documents impounded by order of the court must not be released from the custody of the court except in compliance with –

    (a) a court order; or

    (b) a written request made by a Law Officer or the Director of Public Prosecutions.

(2) A document released from the custody of the court under paragraph (1)(b) must be released into the custody of the person who requested it.

(3) Documents impounded by order of the court, while in the custody of the court, may not be inspected except by a person authorised to do so by a court order.

"impounded by order" (r 27.8(1))—The intent of this rule is to ensure only that while documents in a case are in the custody of the court they should not leave its custody, save by court order or formal request under this rule.

27.9 Official shorthand note etc of proceedings

(1) Unless the judge directs otherwise, an official shorthand note will be taken at the hearing in open court of proceedings pending in the High Court.

(2) An official shorthand note may be taken of any other proceedings before a judge if directions for the taking of such a note are given by the Lord Chancellor.

(3) The shorthand writer will sign the note and certify it to be a correct shorthand note of the proceedings and will retain the note unless directed by the district judge to forward it to the court.

(4) On being so directed, the shorthand writer will furnish the court with a transcript of the whole or such part of the shorthand note as may be directed.

(5) Any party, any person who has intervened in the proceedings, the Queen's Proctor or, where a declaration of parentage has been made under section 55A of the 1986 Act, the Registrar General is entitled to require from the shorthand writer a transcript of the shorthand note, and the shorthand writer will, at the request of any person so entitled, supply that person with a transcript of the whole or any part of the note on payment of the shorthand writer's charges authorised by any scheme in force providing for the taking of official shorthand notes of legal proceedings.

(6) Save as permitted by this rule, the shorthand writer will not, without the permission of the court, furnish the shorthand note or a transcript of the whole or any part of it to anyone.

(7) In these rules, references to a shorthand note include references to a record of the proceedings made by mechanical means and in relation to such a record references to the shorthand writer include the person responsible for transcribing the record.

27.10 Hearings in private

(1) Proceedings to which these rules apply will be held in private, except –

    (a) where these rules or any other enactment provide otherwise;

    (b) subject to any enactment, where the court directs otherwise.

(2) For the purposes of these rules, a reference to proceedings held "in private" means proceedings at which the general public have no right to be present.

27.11 Attendance at private hearings

(1) This rule applies when proceedings are held in private, except in relation to –

(a) hearings conducted for the purpose of judicially assisted conciliation or negotiation;

(b) proceedings to which the following provisions apply –

    (i) Part 13 (proceedings under section 54 of the Human Fertilisation and Embryology Act 2008);

    (ii) Part 14 (procedure for applications in adoption, placement and related proceedings); and

    (iii) any proceedings identified in a practice direction as being excepted from this rule.

(2) When this rule applies, no person shall be present during any hearing other than –

    (a) an officer of the court;

    (b) a party to the proceedings;

    (c) a litigation friend for any party, or legal representative instructed to act on that party's behalf;

    (d) an officer of the service or Welsh family proceedings officer;

    (e) a witness;

    (f) duly accredited representatives of news gathering and reporting organisations; and

    (g) any other person whom the court permits to be present.

(3) At any stage of the proceedings the court may direct that persons within paragraph (2)(f) shall not attend the proceedings or any part of them, where satisfied that –

    (a) this is necessary –

        (i) in the interests of any child concerned in, or connected with, the proceedings;

        (ii) for the safety or protection of a party, a witness in the proceedings, or a person connected with such a party or witness; or

        (iii) for the orderly conduct of the proceedings; or

    (b) justice will otherwise be impeded or prejudiced.

(4) The court may exercise the power in paragraph (3) of its own initiative or pursuant to representations made by any of the persons listed in paragraph (5), and in either case having given to any person within paragraph (2)(f) who is in attendance an opportunity to make representations.

(5) At any stage of the proceedings, the following persons may make representations to the court regarding restricting the attendance of persons within paragraph (2)(f) in accordance with paragraph (3) –

    (a) a party to the proceedings;

    (b) any witness in the proceedings;

    (c) where appointed, any children's guardian;

    (d) where appointed, an officer of the service or Welsh family proceedings officer, on behalf of the child the subject of the proceedings;

    (e) the child, if of sufficient age and understanding.

(6) This rule does not affect any power of the court to direct that witnesses shall be excluded until they are called for examination.

(7) In this rule "duly accredited" refers to accreditation in accordance with any administrative scheme for the time being approved for the purposes of this rule by the Lord Chancellor.

General note—Reference should be made to the *President's Guidance in Relation to Applications Consequent Upon the Attendance of the Media in Family Proceedings* (issued 22 April 2009; see Part V) and the FPR PD27B and PD27C. This rule provides for the attendance of persons, especially particular members of the press, at family proceedings heard "in private" (r 27.11(2)). It gives effect, for family proceedings in the High Court and county courts, to policy changes arising out Confidence and confidentiality: openness in family courts – a new approach (Ministry of Justice, Cm 7131) and outlined in the response to Family Justice in View (Cm 7502). The court may direct the exclusion of the media from all or a part of the proceedings for one of the reasons in r 27.11(3).

"Duly accredited" media representatives—Only "duly accredited" representatives of the media are entitled to attend family proceedings. The production of a card issued by the UK Press Card Authority provides sufficient evidence of accreditation. An unaccredited representative of the media may nevertheless be permitted to attend the hearing at the court's discretion: r 27.11(2)(g).

There are limited grounds on which the court may direct that representatives of the media shall not attend the proceedings: r 27.11(3). Before exercising its power to exclude the media the court should give a party and any representatives of the media in attendance the opportunity to make representations: r 27.11(4). The *President's Guidance* (see above) sets out the principled approach courts should adopt in relation to applications under this rule: paras 20–22.

Confidentiality—The provisions permitting the attendance of the media at family proceedings do not affect or alter the statutory provisions and the rules prohibiting the publication of information relating to family proceedings: in particular AJA 1960, s 12.

"proceedings held 'in private'" (r 27.11(1))—This means proceedings at which the general public have no right to be present.

"general public … no right to be present" (r 27.11(1))—While the general public may not attend "in private" hearings, certain individuals, as listed in r 27.11(2), are entitled to be in court, including "(f) duly accredited" members of the press and "(g) any other person whom the court permits to be present". The court appears to have an unfettered discretion as to those other persons whom it may permit to be present at a hearing held in private (which may include unaccredited members of the media: para 4.3 of FPR PD27B and PD27C).

However, the power to direct that members of the media may not attend all or any part of the proceedings is not the exercise of a discretion (references to the exercise of a discretion in FPR PD27B and 27C, paras 3.1 and 5 and in the President's Guidance of 22 April 2009, para 10, are a misnomer). The court may only make a direction to exclude the media if one or more of the criteria set out in r 27.11(3) is satisfied. The burden of satisfying the court that one of the relevant criteria is satisfied rests on the party who seeks the direction to exclude the media.

The grounds for exclusion are –

(a) it is necessary (i) in the interests of any child concerned with or connected with the proceedings; (ii) for the safety or protection of a party, a witness or a person connected with a party or a witness; or (iii) for the orderly conduct of the proceedings; or
(b) justice will otherwise be impeded or prejudiced.

The President observed that where the Court has a duty to apply a test of necessity in relation to a series of questions as to legitimacy and proportionality, the duty of the Court is to proceed though the balancing exercise making a value judgment as to the conflicts that arise rather than to regard the matter simply as an exercise of discretion as between two equally legitimate courses. The court must balance the Art 8 rights of the children, the parties and of any witnesses (which may be competing) against the Art 10 rights of the media: *Re Child X (Residence and Contact – Rights of Media Attendance – FPR 10.28(4))* [2009] 2 FLR 1467 paras 51–58.

Reasons for exclusion—Reasons for exclusion should be given. No provision is made in the rules for the media to seek a review or to appeal a decision to exclude them from proceedings and there is as yet no authoritative guidance on the matter. It is suggested that the media will be entitled to seek permission to appeal against direction made to exclude them: it is unlikely that the media would be limited to seeking a judicial review or that that would be an appropriate route of challenge.

"may make representations to the court" (r 27.11(4))—That is to say, there is no need for formal application (and see FPR PD27A and FPR PD27B, para 6, especially 6.2). An application to exclude can be made at "any stage" of proceedings: r 27.11(3).

Accredited representative—See r 27.11(7).

Statutory restrictions on publication—The provisions restricting the publication of information relating to proceedings, principally AJA 1960, s 12, and CA 1989, s 97(2), are unaffected by this rule.

Court documents—The provisions of this rule do not entitle media representatives to receive or peruse court documents referred to in the course of evidence, submissions or judgment without the permission of the court or otherwise in accordance with FPR 2010, rr 12.73–12.75 and FPR PD12G (rules relating to disclosure to third parties).

Practice Direction 27A –
Family Proceedings: Court Bundles (Universal Practice to be applied in All Courts other than the Family Proceedings Court)

This Practice Direction supplements FPR Part 27

Note 1—PD27A is applied in public law proceedings in the High Court with certain adjustments as made by FPR PD12A, para 25.2.

Note 2—In *Re X and Y (Bundles)* [2008] 2 FLR 2053, Munby J issued a stern warning in open court to all practitioners, pointing out that far too often the requirements of PD27A are not observed and that this is unacceptable. Orders for costs can be made against either the party in default or against the defaulting lawyers (see para 12 of the PD). Furthermore, he warned that in particularly flagrant cases, defaulters may be publicly identified in open court. See **Bundles and other particular matters** under r 12.12.

1.1 The President of the Family Division has issued this practice direction to achieve consistency across the country in all family courts (other than the Family Proceedings Court) in the preparation of court bundles and in respect of other related matters.

Application of the practice direction

2.1 Except as specified in para 2.4, and subject to specific directions given in any particular case, the following practice applies to:

    (a) all hearings of whatever nature (including but not limited to hearings in family proceedings, Civil Procedure Rules 1998 Part 7 and Part 8 claims and appeals) before a judge of the Family Division of the High Court wherever the court may be sitting;

    (b) all hearings in family proceedings in the Royal Courts of Justice (RCJ);

    (c) all hearings in the Principal Registry of the Family Division (PRFD) at First Avenue House; and

    (d) all hearings in family proceedings in all other courts except for Family Proceedings Courts.

2.2 'Hearings' includes all appearances before a judge or district judge, whether with or without notice to other parties and whether for directions or for substantive relief.

2.3 This practice direction applies whether a bundle is being lodged for the first time or is being re-lodged for a further hearing (see para 9.2).

2.4 This practice direction does not apply to:

    (a) cases listed for one hour or less at a court referred to in para 2.1(c) or 2.1(d); or

    (b) the hearing of any urgent application if and to the extent that it is impossible to comply with it.

2.5 The designated family judge responsible for any court referred to in para 2.1(c) or 2.1(d) may, after such consultation as is appropriate (but in the case of hearings in the PRFD at First Avenue House only with the agreement of the Senior District Judge), direct that in that court this practice direction shall apply to all family proceedings irrespective of the length of hearing.

Responsibility for the preparation of the bundle

3.1 A bundle for the use of the court at the hearing shall be provided by the party in the position of applicant at the hearing (or, if there are cross-applications, by the party whose application was first in time) or, if that person is a litigant in person, by the first listed respondent who is not a litigant in person.

3.2 The party preparing the bundle shall paginate it. If possible the contents of the bundle shall be agreed by all parties.

Contents of the bundle

4.1 The bundle shall contain copies of all documents relevant to the hearing, in chronological order from the front of the bundle, paginated and indexed, and divided into separate sections (each section being separately paginated) as follows:

    (a)   preliminary documents (see para 4.2) and any other case management documents required by any other practice direction;

    (b)   applications and orders;

    (c)   statements and affidavits (which must be dated in the top right corner of the front page);

    (d)   care plans (where appropriate);

    (e)   experts' reports and other reports (including those of a guardian, children's guardian or litigation friend); and

    (f)   other documents, divided into further sections as may be appropriate.

Copies of notes of contact visits should normally not be included in the bundle unless directed by a judge.

4.2 At the commencement of the bundle there shall be inserted the following documents (the preliminary documents):

    (i)   an up to date summary of the background to the hearing confined to those matters which are relevant to the hearing and the management of the case and limited, if practicable, to one A4 page;

    (ii)   a statement of the issue or issues to be determined (1) at that hearing and (2) at the final hearing;

    (iii)   a position statement by each party including a summary of the order or directions sought by that party (1) at that hearing and (2) at the final hearing;

    (iv)   an up to date chronology, if it is a final hearing or if the summary under (i) is insufficient;

    (v)   skeleton arguments, if appropriate, with copies of all authorities relied on; and

    (vi)   a list of essential reading for that hearing.

4.3 Each of the preliminary documents shall state on the front page immediately below the heading the date when it was prepared and the date of the hearing for which it was prepared.

4.4 The summary of the background, statement of issues, chronology, position statement and any skeleton arguments shall be cross-referenced to the relevant pages of the bundle.

4.5 The summary of the background, statement of issues, chronology and reading list shall in the case of a final hearing, and shall so far as practicable in the case of any other hearing, each consist of a single document in a form agreed by all parties. Where the parties disagree as to the content the fact of their disagreement and their differing contentions shall be set out at the appropriate places in the document.

4.6 Where the nature of the hearing is such that a complete bundle of all documents is unnecessary, the bundle (which need not be repaginated) may comprise only those documents necessary for the hearing, but

(i)   the summary (para 4.2(i)) must commence with a statement that the bundle is limited or incomplete; and

(ii) the bundle shall if reasonably practicable be in a form agreed by all parties.

4.7 Where the bundle is re-lodged in accordance with para 9.2, before it is re-lodged:

(a)   the bundle shall be updated as appropriate; and

(b)   all superseded documents (and in particular all outdated summaries, statements of issues, chronologies, skeleton arguments and similar documents) shall be removed from the bundle.

Format of the bundle

5.1 The bundle shall be contained in one or more A4 size ring binders or lever arch files (each lever arch file being limited to 350 pages).

5.2 All ring binders and lever arch files shall have clearly marked on the front and the spine:

(a)   the title and number of the case;

(b)   the court where the case has been listed;

(c)   the hearing date and time;

(d)   if known, the name of the judge hearing the case; and

(e)   where there is more than one ring binder or lever arch file, a distinguishing letter (A, B, C etc).

Timetable for preparing and lodging the bundle

6.1 The party preparing the bundle shall, whether or not the bundle has been agreed, provide a paginated index to all other parties not less than 4 working days before the hearing (in relation to a case management conference to which the provisions of the *Protocol for Judicial Case Management in Public Law Children Act Cases* [2003] 2 FLR 719 apply, not less than 5 working days before the case management conference).

6.2 Where counsel is to be instructed at any hearing, a paginated bundle shall (if not already in counsel's possession) be delivered to counsel by the person instructing that counsel not less than 3 working days before the hearing.

6.3 The bundle (with the exception of the preliminary documents if and insofar as they are not then available) shall be lodged with the court not less than 2 working days before the hearing, or at such other time as may be specified by the judge.

6.4 The preliminary documents shall be lodged with the court no later than 11 am on the day before the hearing and, where the hearing is before a judge of the High Court and the name of the judge is known, shall at the same time be sent by email to the judge's clerk.

Lodging the bundle

7.1 The bundle shall be lodged at the appropriate office. If the bundle is lodged in the wrong place the judge may:

(a)   treat the bundle as having not been lodged; and

(b)   take the steps referred to in para 12.

7.2 Unless the judge has given some other direction as to where the bundle in any particular case is to be lodged (for example a direction that the bundle is to be lodged with the judge's clerk) the bundle shall be lodged:

(a) for hearings in the RCJ, in the office of the Clerk of the Rules, 1st Mezzanine (Rm 1M), Queen's Building, Royal Courts of Justice, Strand, London WC2A 2LL (DX 44450 Strand);

(b) for hearings in the PRFD at First Avenue House, at the List Office counter, 3rd floor, First Avenue House, 42/49 High Holborn, London, WC1V 6NP (DX 396 Chancery Lane); and

(c) for hearings at any other court, at such place as may be designated by the designated family judge or other judge at that court and in default of any such designation at the court office of the court where the hearing is to take place.

Amendments—FPR 2010, Update 2.

7.3 Any bundle sent to the court by post, DX or courier shall be clearly addressed to the appropriate office and shall show the date and place of the hearing on the outside of any packaging as well as on the bundle itself.

Lodging the bundle – additional requirements for cases being heard at First Avenue House or at the RCJ

8.1 In the case of hearings at the RCJ or First Avenue House, parties shall:

(a) if the bundle or preliminary documents are delivered personally, ensure that they obtain a receipt from the clerk accepting it or them; and

(b) if the bundle or preliminary documents are sent by post or DX, ensure that they obtain proof of posting or despatch.

The receipt (or proof of posting or despatch, as the case may be) shall be brought to court on the day of the hearing and must be produced to the court if requested. If the receipt (or proof of posting or despatch) cannot be produced to the court the judge may: (i) treat the bundle as having not been lodged; and (ii) take the steps referred to in para 12.

8.2 For hearings at the RCJ:

(a) bundles or preliminary documents delivered after 11 am on the day before the hearing will not be accepted by the Clerk of the Rules and shall be delivered:

(i) in a case where the hearing is before a judge of the High Court, directly to the clerk of the judge hearing the case;

(ii) in a case where the hearing is before a Circuit Judge, Deputy High Court Judge or Recorder, directly to the messenger at the Judge's entrance to the Queen's Building (with telephone notification to the personal assistant to the Designated Family Judge, 020 7947 7155, that this has been done).

(b) upon learning before which judge a hearing is to take place, the clerk to counsel, or other advocate, representing the party in the position of applicant shall no later than 3 pm the day before the hearing:

(i) in a case where the hearing is before a judge of the High Court, telephone the clerk of the judge hearing the case;

(ii) in a case where the hearing is before a circuit judge, deputy high court judge or recorder, telephone the personal assistant to the designated family judge;

to ascertain whether the judge has received the bundle (including the preliminary documents) and, if not, shall organise prompt delivery by the applicant's solicitor.

Removing and re-lodging the bundle

9.1 Following completion of the hearing the party responsible for the bundle shall retrieve it from the court immediately or, if that is not practicable, shall collect it from the court within 5 working days. Bundles which are not collected in due time may be destroyed.

9.2 The bundle shall be re-lodged for the next and any further hearings in accordance with the provisions of this practice direction and in a form which complies with para 4.7.

Time estimates

10.1 In every case a time estimate (which shall be inserted at the front of the bundle) shall be prepared which shall so far as practicable be agreed by all parties and shall:

    (a)   specify separately: (i) the time estimated to be required for judicial pre-reading; and (ii) the time required for hearing all evidence and submissions; and (iii) the time estimated to be required for preparing and delivering judgment; and

    (b)   be prepared on the basis that before they give evidence all witnesses will have read all relevant filed statements and reports.

10.2 Once a case has been listed, any change in time estimates shall be notified immediately by telephone (and then immediately confirmed in writing):

    (a)   in the case of hearings in the RCJ, to the Clerk of the Rules;

    (b)   in the case of hearings in the PRFD at First Avenue House, to the List Officer at First Avenue House; and

    (c)   in the case of hearings elsewhere, to the relevant listing officer.

Taking cases out of the list

11.1 As soon as it becomes known that a hearing will no longer be effective, whether as a result of the parties reaching agreement or for any other reason, the parties and their representatives shall immediately notify the court by telephone and by letter. The letter, which shall wherever possible be a joint letter sent on behalf of all parties with their signatures applied or appended, shall include:

    (a)   a short background summary of the case;

    (b)   the written consent of each party who consents and, where a party does not consent, details of the steps which have been taken to obtain that party's consent and, where known, an explanation of why that consent has not been given;

    (c)   a draft of the order being sought; and

    (d)   enough information to enable the court to decide (i) whether to take the case out of the list and (ii) whether to make the proposed order.

Penalties for failure to comply with the practice direction

12.1 Failure to comply with any part of this practice direction may result in the judge removing the case from the list or putting the case further back in the list and may also result in a "wasted costs" order in accordance with CPR, Part 48.7 or some other adverse costs order.

Commencement of the practice direction and application of other practice directions

13.1 This practice direction replaces *Practice Direction (Family Proceedings: Court Bundles) (10 March 2000)* [2000] 1 FLR 536 and shall have effect from 2 October 2006.

14.1 Any reference in any other practice direction to *Practice Direction (Family Proceedings: Court Bundles) (10 March 2000)* [2000] 1 FLR 536 shall be read as if substituted by a reference to this practice direction.

15.1 This practice direction should where appropriate be read in conjunction with *Practice Direction (Family Proceedings: Human Rights)* [2000] 2 FLR 429 and with *Practice Direction (Care Cases: Judicial Continuity and Judicial Case Management)* appended to the *Protocol for Judicial Case Management in Public Law Children Act Cases*. In particular, nothing in this practice direction is to be read as removing or altering any obligation to comply with the requirements of the *Public Law Protocol*.

This Practice Direction is issued:

    (i)   in relation to family proceedings, by the President of the Family Division, as the nominee of the Lord Chief Justice, with the agreement of the Lord Chancellor; and

    (ii)   to the extent that it applies to proceedings to which s 5 of the Civil Procedure Act 1997 applies, by the Master of the Rolls as the nominee of the Lord Chief Justice, with the agreement of the Lord Chancellor.

Practice Direction 27B – Attendance of Media Representatives at Hearings in Family Proceedings (High Court and County Courts)

This Practice Direction supplements FPR Part 27

1 Introduction

1.1 This Practice Direction supplements rule 27.11 of the Family Procedure Rules 2010 ("FPR 2010") and deals with the right of representatives of news gathering and reporting organisations ("media representatives") to attend at hearings of family proceedings which take place in private subject to the discretion of the court to exclude such representatives from the whole or part of any hearing on specified grounds[1] It takes effect on 27 April 2009.

1   It does not, accordingly, apply where hearings are held in open court where the general public including media representatives may attend as of right, such as committal hearings or the hearing of matrimonial or civil partnership causes.

2 Matters unchanged by the rule

2.1 Rule 27.11(1) contains an express exception in respect of hearings which are conducted for the purpose of judicially assisted conciliation or negotiation and media representatives do not have a right to attend these hearings. Financial Dispute Resolution hearings will come within this exception. First Hearing Dispute Resolution appointments in private law Children Act cases will also come within this exception to the extent that the judge plays an active part in the conciliation process. Where the judge plays no part in the conciliation process or where the conciliation element of a hearing is complete and the judge is adjudicating upon the issues between the parties, media representatives should be permitted to attend, subject to the discretion of the court to exclude them on the specified grounds. Conciliation meetings or negotiation conducted between the parties with the assistance of an officer of the service or a Welsh Family Proceedings officer, and without the presence of the judge, are not "hearings" within the meaning of this rule and media representatives have no right to attend such appointments.

The exception in rule 27.11(1) does not operate to exclude media representatives from:

- Hearings to consider applications brought under Parts IV and V of the Children Act 1989, including Case Management Conferences and Issues Resolution Hearings
- Hearings relating to findings of fact
- Interim hearings
- Final hearings.

The rights of media representatives to attend such hearings are limited only by the powers of the court to exclude such attendance on the limited grounds and subject to the procedures set out in paragraphs (3)–(5) of rule 27.11.

2.2 During any hearing, courts should consider whether the exception in rule 27.11(1) becomes applicable so that media representatives should be directed to withdraw.

2.3 The provisions of the rules permitting the attendance of media representatives and the disclosure to third parties of information relating to the proceedings do not entitle a media representative to receive or peruse court documents referred to in the course of evidence, submissions or judgment without the permission of the court or otherwise in accordance with Part 12, Chapter 7 of the Family Procedure Rules 2010 and Practice Direction 12G (rules relating to disclosure to third parties). (This is in contrast to the position in civil proceedings, where the court sits in public and where members of the public are entitled to seek copies of certain documents[1]).

1   See *GIO Services Ltd v Liverpool and London Ltd* [1999] 1 WLR 984.

2.4 The question of attendance of media representatives at hearings in family proceedings to which rule 27.11 and this guidance apply must be distinguished from statutory restrictions on publication and disclosure of information relating to proceedings, which continue to apply and are unaffected by the rule and this guidance.

2.5 The prohibition in section 97(2) of the Children Act 1989, on publishing material intended to or likely to identify a child as being involved in proceedings or the address or school of any such child, is limited to the duration of the proceedings[1]. However, the limitations imposed by section 12 of the Administration of Justice Act 1960 on publication of information relating to certain proceedings in private[2] apply during and after the proceedings. In addition, in proceedings to which s 97(2) of the Children Act 1989 applies the court should continue to consider at the conclusion of the proceedings whether there are any outstanding welfare issues which require a continuation of the protection afforded during the course of the proceedings by that provision.

1   See *Clayton v Clayton* [2006] EWCA Civ 878.
2   In particular proceedings which
    (a)   relate to the exercise of the inherent jurisdiction of the High Court with respect to minors;
    (b)   are brought under the Children Act 1989; or
    (c)   otherwise relate wholly or mainly to the maintenance or upbringing of a minor.

3 Aims of the guidance

3.1 This Practice Direction is intended to provide guidance regarding:

- the handling of applications to exclude media representatives from the whole or part of a hearing; and
- the exercise of the court's discretion to exclude media representatives whether upon the court's own motion or any such application.

3.2 While the guidance does not aim to cover all possible eventualities, it should be complied with so far as consistent in all the circumstances with the just determination of the proceedings.

"discretion to exclude"—The reference in para 3.1 to a "discretion" to exclude the media is a misnomer. The President observed that where the Court has a duty to apply a test of necessity in relation to a series of questions as to legitimacy and proportionality, the duty of the Court is to proceed though the balancing exercise making a value judgment as to the conflicts that arise rather than to regard the matter simply as an exercise of discretion as between two equally legitimate courses: *Re Child X (Residence and Contact: Rights of Media Attendance – FPR r 10.28(4))* [2009] 2 FLR 1467 at [51]–[58].

4 Identification of media representatives as "accredited"

4.1 Media representatives will be expected to carry with them identification sufficient to enable court staff, or if necessary the court itself, to verify that they are "accredited" representatives of news gathering or reporting organisations within the meaning of the rule.

4.2 By virtue of paragraph (7) of the rule, it is for the Lord Chancellor to approve a scheme which will provide for accreditation. The Lord Chancellor has decided that the scheme operated by the UK Press Card Authority provides sufficient accreditation; a card issued under that scheme will be the expected form of identification, and production of the Card will be both necessary and sufficient to demonstrate accreditation.

4.3 A media representative unable to demonstrate accreditation in accordance with the UK Press Card Authority scheme, so as to be able to attend by virtue of paragraph (2)(f) of the rule, may nevertheless be permitted to attend at the court's discretion under paragraph (2)(g).

5 Exercise of the discretion to exclude media representatives from all or part of the proceedings

5.1 The rule anticipates and should be applied on the basis that media representatives have a right to attend family proceedings throughout save and to the extent that the court exercises its discretion to exclude them from the whole or part of any proceedings on one or more of the grounds set out in paragraph (3) of the rule.

5.2 When considering the question of exclusion on any of the grounds set out in paragraph (3) of the rule the court should –

- specifically identify whether the risk to which such ground is directed arises from the mere fact of media presence at the particular hearing or hearings the subject of the application or whether the risk identified can be adequately addressed by exclusion of media representatives from a part only of such hearing or hearings;
- consider whether the reporting or disclosure restrictions which apply by operation of law, or which the court otherwise has power to order will provide sufficient protection to the party on whose behalf the application is made or any of the persons referred to in paragraph (3)(a) of the rule;
- consider the safety of the parties in cases in which the court considers there are particular physical or health risks against which reporting restrictions may be inadequate to afford protection;
- in the case of any vulnerable adult or child who is unrepresented before the court, consider the extent to which the court should of its own motion take steps to protect the welfare of that adult or child.

5.3 Paragraph (3)(a)(iii) of the rule permits exclusion where necessary "for the orderly conduct of proceedings". This enables the court to address practical problems presented

PART III

by media attendance. In particular, it may be difficult or even impossible physically to accommodate all (or indeed any) media representatives who wish to attend a particular hearing on the grounds of the restricted size or layout of the court room in which it is being heard. Court staff will use their best efforts to identify more suitable accommodation in advance of any hearing which appears likely to attract particular media attention, and to move hearings to larger court rooms where possible. However, the court should not be required to adjourn a hearing in order for larger accommodation to be sought where this will involve significant disruption or delay in the proceedings.

5.4 Paragraph (3)(b) of the rule permits exclusion where, unless the media are excluded, justice will be impeded or prejudiced for some reason other than those set out in sub-paragraph (a). Reasons of administrative inconvenience are not sufficient. Examples of circumstances where the impact on justice of continued attendance might be sufficient to necessitate exclusion may include:

- a hearing relating to the parties' finances where the information being considered includes price sensitive information (such as confidential information which could affect the share price of a publicly quoted company); or
- any hearing at which a witness (other than a party) states for credible reasons that he or she will not give evidence in front of media representatives, or where there appears to the court to be a significant risk that a witness will not give full or frank evidence in the presence of media representatives.

5.5 In the event of a decision to exclude media representatives, the court should state brief reasons for the decision.

Note—The reference in the title of this paragraph to a "discretion" to exclude the media is a misnomer: see *Re Child X* (above).

6 Applications to exclude media representatives from all or part of proceedings

6.1 The court may exclude media representatives on the permitted grounds of its own motion or after hearing representations from the interested persons listed at paragraph (5) of the rule. Where exclusion is proposed, any media representatives who are present are entitled to make representations about that proposal. There is, however, no requirement to adjourn proceedings to enable media representatives who are not present to attend in order to make such representations, and in such a case the court should not adjourn unless satisfied of the necessity to do so having regard to the additional cost and delay which would thereby be caused.

6.2 Applications to exclude media representatives should normally be dealt with as they arise and by way of oral representations, unless the court directs otherwise.

6.3 When media representatives are expected to attend a particular hearing (for example, where a party is encouraging media interest and attendance) and a party intends to apply to the court for the exclusion of the media, that party should, if practicable, give advance notice to the court, to the other parties and (where appointed) any children's guardian, officer of the service or Welsh Family Proceedings officer, NYAS or other representative of the child of any intention to seek the exclusion of media representatives from all or part of the proceedings. Equally, legal representatives and parties should ensure that witnesses are aware of the right of media representatives to attend and should notify the court at an early stage of the intention of any witness to request the exclusion of media representatives

6.4 Prior notification by the court of a pending application for exclusion will not be given to media interests unless the court so directs. However, where such an application has been made, the applicant must where possible, notify the relevant media organisations [and should do so by means of the Press Association CopyDirect service, following the procedure set out in the Official Solicitor/CAFCASS *Practice Note* dated 18 March 2005][1].

1   The additional words in square brackets were added by the President in *Re Child X (Residence and Contact: Rights of Media Attendance* – FPR r 10.28(4)) [2009] 2 FLR 1467, at [87].

Practice Direction 27C – Attendance of Media Representatives at Hearings in Family Proceedings (Family Proceedings Court)

This Practice Direction supplements FPR Part 27

1 Introduction

1.1 This Practice Direction supplements rule 27.11 of the Family Procedure Rules 2010 ("the Rules") and deals with the right of representatives of news gathering and reporting organisations ("media representatives") to attend at hearings of relevant proceedings[1] subject to the discretion of the court to exclude such representatives from the whole or part of any hearing on specified grounds.[2] It takes effect on 27 April 2009. References to a "hearing" within this Practice Direction include reference to a directions appointment, whether conducted by the justices, a district judge or a justices' clerk.

1   "relevant proceedings" are defined in rule 1 of the Rules by reference to section 93(3) of the Children Act 1989.
2   It does not, accordingly, apply where hearings are held in open court where the general public including media representatives attend as of right.

2 Matters unchanged by the rule

2.1 Rule 27.11(1) contains an express exception in respect of hearings which are conducted for the purpose of judicially assisted conciliation or negotiation and media representatives do not have a right to attend these hearings. First Hearing Dispute Resolution appointments in private law Children Act cases will come within this exception to the extent that the justices, a district judge or a justices' clerk play an active part in the conciliation process. Where the justices, a district judge or a justices' clerk play no part in the conciliation process or where the conciliation element of a hearing is complete and the court is adjudicating upon the issues between the parties, media representatives should be permitted to attend subject to the discretion of the court to exclude them on the specified grounds. Conciliation meetings or negotiation conducted between the parties with the assistance of an officer of the service or a Welsh Family Proceedings officer, and without the presence of the justices, a district judge or a justices' clerk, are not "hearings" within the meaning of this rule and media representatives have no right to attend such appointments.

The exception in rule 27.11(1) does not operate to exclude media representatives from:

- Hearings to consider applications brought under Parts IV and V of the Children Act 1989, including Case Management Conferences and Issues Resolution Hearings

- Hearings relating to findings of fact
- Interim hearings
- Final hearings.

The rights of media representatives to attend such hearings are limited only by the powers of the court to exclude such attendance on the limited grounds and subject to the procedures set out in paragraphs (3) to (5) of rule 27.11.

2.2 During any hearing, the court should consider whether the exception in rule 27.11(1) becomes applicable so that media representatives should be directed to withdraw.

2.3 The provisions of the rules permitting the attendance of media representatives and the disclosure to third parties of information relating to the proceedings do not entitle a media representative to receive or peruse court documents referred to in the course of evidence, submissions or decisions of the court (in particular, written reasons) without the permission of the court or otherwise in accordance with Part 12, Chapter 7 of the Family Procedure Rules 2010 and Practice Direction 12G.

2.4 The question of attendance of media representatives at hearings in family proceedings to which rule 27.11 and this guidance apply must be distinguished from statutory restrictions on publication and disclosure of information relating to proceedings, which continue to apply and are unaffected by the rule and this guidance.

2.5 The prohibition in section 97(2) of the Children Act 1989, on publishing material intended to or likely to identify a child as being involved in proceedings or the address or school of any such child, is limited to the duration of the proceedings[1]. However, the limitations imposed by section 12 of the Administration of Justice Act 1960 on publication of information relating to certain proceedings in private[2] apply during and after the proceedings. In addition, in the course of proceedings to which s 97(2) of the Children Act 1989 applies the court should consider whether at the conclusion of the proceedings there may be outstanding welfare issues which may require a continuation of the protection afforded during the course of the proceedings by s 97 (2) of the Children Act 1989 and which are not fully met by a direction under section 39 Children and Young Persons Act 1933,[3] so that any party seeking such protection has an opportunity to apply to the county court or High Court for the appropriate order before the proceedings are finally concluded.

1   See *Clayton v Clayton* [2006] EWCA Civ 878
2   In particular proceedings which
   (a) relate to the exercise of the inherent jurisdiction of the High Court with respect to minors;
   (b) are brought under the Children Act 1989; or
   (c) otherwise relate wholly or mainly to the maintenance or upbringing of a minor

3   Power of court to prohibit publication of certain matters in newspapers

3 Aims of the guidance

3.1 This Practice Direction is intended to provide guidance regarding:

- the handling of applications to exclude media representatives from the whole or part of a hearing: and
- the exercise of the court's discretion to exclude media representatives whether upon the court's own motion or any such application.

3.2 While the guidance does not aim to cover all possible eventualities, it should be complied with so far as consistent in all the circumstances with the just determination of the proceedings.

"discretion to exclude"—See note under FPR PD27B, para 3.1.

4 Identification of media representatives as "accredited"

4.1 Media representatives will be expected to carry with them identification sufficient to enable court staff, or if necessary the court itself, to verify that they are "accredited" representatives of news gathering or reporting organisations within the meaning of the rule.

4.2 By virtue of paragraph (7) of the rule, it is for the Lord Chancellor to approve a scheme which will provide for accreditation. The Lord Chancellor has decided that the scheme operated by the UK Press Card Authority provides sufficient accreditation: a card issued under that scheme will be the expected form of identification, and production of the Card will be both necessary and sufficient to demonstrate accreditation.

4.3 A media representative unable to demonstrate accreditation in accordance with the UK Press Card Authority scheme so as to be able to attend by virtue of paragraph (2)(f) of the rule may nevertheless be permitted to attend at the court's discretion under paragraph (2)(g).

5 Exercise of the discretion to exclude media representatives from all or part of the proceedings.

5.1 The rule anticipates and should be applied on the basis that media representatives have a right to attend family proceedings throughout save and to the extent that the court exercises its discretion to exclude them from the whole or part of any proceedings on one or more of the grounds set out in paragraph (3) of the rule.

5.2 When considering the question of exclusion on any of the grounds set out in paragraph (3) of the rule the court should –

- specifically identify whether the risk to which such ground is directed arises from the mere fact of media presence at the particular hearing or hearings the subject of the application or whether the risk identified can be adequately addressed by exclusion of media representatives from a part only of such hearing or hearings;
- consider whether the reporting or disclosure restrictions which apply by operation of law, or which the court otherwise has power to order will provide sufficient protection to the party on whose behalf the application is made or any of the persons referred to in paragraph (3)(a) of the rule;
- consider the safety of the parties in cases in which the court considers there are particular physical or health risks against which reporting restrictions may be inadequate to afford protection;
- in the case of any vulnerable adult or child who is unrepresented before the court, consider the extent to which the court should of its own motion take steps to protect the welfare of that adult or child.

5.3 Paragraph (3)(a)(iii) of the rule permits exclusion where necessary "for the orderly conduct of proceedings". This enables the court to address practical problems presented by media attendance. In particular, it may be difficult or even impossible physically to accommodate all (or indeed any) media representatives who wish to attend a particular hearing on the grounds of the restricted size or layout of the court room in which it is being heard. Court staff will use their best efforts to identify more suitable accommodation in advance of any hearing which appears likely to attract particular media attention, and to move hearings to larger court rooms where possible. However, the court should not be required to adjourn a hearing in order for larger accommodation to be sought where this will involve significant disruption or delay in the proceedings.

5.4 Paragraph (3)(b) of the rule permits exclusion where, unless the media are excluded, justice will be impeded or prejudiced for some reason other than those set out in sub-paragraph (a). Reasons of administrative inconvenience are not sufficient. An example of circumstances where the impact on justice of continued attendance might be sufficient to necessitate exclusion would be any hearing at which a witness (other than a party) states for credible reasons that he or she will not give evidence in front of media representatives, or where there appears to the court to be a significant risk that a witness will not give full or frank evidence in the presence of media representatives.

5.5 In the event of a decision to exclude media representatives, the court should state brief reasons for the decision.

Note—The reference in the title of this paragraph to a "discretion" to exclude the media is a misnomer: see *Re Child X* (above).

6 *Applications to exclude media representatives from all or part of proceedings.*

6.1 The court may exclude media representatives on the permitted grounds of its own motion or after hearing representations from the interested persons listed at paragraph (5) of the rule. Where exclusion is proposed, any media representatives who are present are entitled to make representations about that proposal. There is, however, no requirement to adjourn proceedings to enable media representatives who are not present to attend in order to make such representations, and in such a case the court should not adjourn unless satisfied of the necessity to do so having regard to the additional cost and delay which would thereby be caused.

6.2 Applications to exclude media representatives should normally be dealt with as they arise and by way of oral representations, unless the court directs otherwise.

6.3 When media representatives are expected to attend a particular hearing (for example, where a party is encouraging media interest and attendance) and a party intends to apply to the court for the exclusion of the media, such party should, if practicable, give advance notice to the court, to the other parties and (where appointed) any children's guardian, officer of the service or Welsh Family Proceedings officer, NYAS or other representative of the child of any intention to seek the exclusion of media representatives from all or part of the proceedings. Equally, legal representatives and parties should ensure that witnesses are aware of the right of media representatives to attend and should notify the court at an early stage of the intention of any witness to request the exclusion of media representatives.

6.4 Prior notification by the court of a pending application for exclusion will not be given to media interests unless the court so directs. However, where such an application has been made, the applicant must where possible, notify the relevant media organisations [and should do so by means of the Press Association CopyDirect service, following the procedure set out in the Official Solicitor/CAFCASS Practice Note dated 18 March 2005][1].

1   The additional words in square brackets were added by the President in *Re Child X (Residence and Contact: Rights of Media Attendance – FPR r 10.28(4))* [2009] 2 FLR 1467, at [87].

PART 28
COSTS

CONTENTS OF THIS PART

28.1 Costs

The court may at any time make such order as to costs as it thinks just.

SCA 1981, s 51—Section 51(1) of SCA 1981 provides that "subject to rules of court, costs ... shall be in the discretion of the court". Rule 28.1 is such a rule.

28.2 Application of other rules

(1) Subject to rule 28.3 and to paragraph (2), Parts 44 (except rules 44.2(2) and (3) and 44.10(2) and (3)), 46 and 47 and rule 45.8 of the CPR apply to costs in proceedings, with the following modifications –

    (a)   in rule 44.1(1)(f)(ii), "district judge" includes a district judge of the principal registry;

    (b)   in rule 46.8(1) after "section 51(6) of the Senior Courts Act 1981" insert "or section 145A of the Magistrates' Courts Act 1980";

    (c)   in accordance with any provisions in Practice Direction 28A; and

    (d)   any other necessary modifications.

(2) Part 47 and rules 45.8 and 46.7 of the CPR do not apply to proceedings in a magistrates' court.

Amendments—SI 2013/530.

Defined terms—"the CPR": r 2.3(1).

"the CPR apply to costs in proceedings" (r 28.2(1))—The effect of incorporation of CPR 1998, Pts 44 (except rr 44.2(2),(3) and 44.10(2),(3)), 46 and 47 and r 45.8 is that costs provisions relevant to family proceedings from CPR 1998 remain applicable, and that, as before, the exclusion of CPR 1998, r 44.2(2) (formerly r 44.3(2)) exempts all family proceedings covered by FPR 2010 from the general rule "that the unsuccessful party [should pay] the costs of the successful party" (subject to what was said in the Court of Appeal in *Gojkovic v Gojkovic (No 2)* [1991] 2 FLR 233, CA: the court needs to start somewhere and that should be that "costs follow the event").

Costs in family proceedings—The costs rules under FPR 2010 and CPR 1998 apply as follows:

(1) *Financial remedy proceedings ("no order")*   For "financial remedy proceedings" as defined by FPR 2010, r 28.3(4)(b) the no order for costs rule at FPR 2010, r 28.3(5) applies, subject to the court being required to "have regard" to conduct issues in FPR 2010, r 28.3(7).

(2) *Proceedings for a financial remedy ("clean sheet")*   Financial remedy proceedings that are outside FPR 2010, r 28.3(4)(b) are not covered by the exemptions from orders for costs in FPR 2010, r 28.3(5). The court has "a clean sheet" as to what order to make. The applicant for costs and the court must be clear under which heading – "no order" or "clean sheet" – the application proceeds and whether the proceedings are "in", "in connection with" or "for" (each preposition makes a difference) financial remedy proceedings, as explained in *Judge v Judge* [2009] 1 FLR 1287 at [51] and in *Baker v Rowe* [2010] 1 FLR 761 at [35]; and see the commentary to r 28.3). Unless the financial remedy application is for a final, first instance, inter partes financial order (as defined by

FPR 2010, rr 2.3(1) and 28.3(4)(b)), and most applications will be, then either (or any) party may apply for, or may be subject to, an order for costs.

(3) *Public law children proceedings* In *Re T (Costs: Care Proceedings: Serious Allegation Not Proved)* [2013] 1 FLR 133, the Supreme Court drew attention to the rarity of orders for costs being made in children cases if a party's conduct had not been reprehensible or that party's stance had not been beyond the band of what was reasonable. Further, it was wrong for the court to regard care proceedings as automatically involving a two-stage process (as explained in *Re B (Children)* [2008] 2 FLR 141) and to divide costs orders accordingly. "The general practice of not awarding costs against a party, including a local authority, in the absence of reprehensible behaviour or an unreasonable stance, is one that accords with the ends of justice" (*Re T* (above) at [44]) and there should be no exception to this principle in the case of split hearings.

(4) *Other children proceedings* Orders for costs in children proceedings generally will be rare (subject to the position of the Official Solicitor referred to below), but the starting point is likely to be *R v R (Costs: Child Case)* [1997] 2 FLR 95, CA (approved by the Supreme Court in passing in *Re T*, above), explained by Staughton LJ as that the judge "found that the father had behaved unreasonably in the litigation. I do not doubt that Mr R genuinely believes that his arguments are perfectly reasonable. I do not question his good faith, but I am afraid I do agree with the judge that they did not, in reality, represent a reasonable attitude for the father to take".

(5) *Other family proceedings under FPR 2010* The remainder of family proceedings under FPR 2010 – mostly divorce, civil partnership and other matrimonial causes, declaration applications etc – are covered by the general family proceedings costs principles at (2), above ("clean sheet"). Where the proceedings are parasitic on other proceedings (e g interim applications, appeals and enforcement), those parasitic proceedings will be covered by the "clean sheet rule", even if other rules (e g FPR 2010, r 28.3(5)) apply to the original decision or main proceedings.

Costs where the Official Solicitor acts for a party—The costs of the Official Solicitor are entirely a matter for the discretion of the court, but a general rule has developed, which is that the Official Solicitor should have half his costs in the absence of special features that override this "rule" (see *Re D (Costs)* [2012] COPLR 499).

28.3 Costs in financial remedy proceedings

(1) This rule applies in relation to financial remedy proceedings.

(2) Rule 44.2(1), (4) and (5) of the CPR do not apply to financial remedy proceedings.

(3) Rules 44.2(6) to (8) and 44.12 of the CPR apply to an order made under this rule as they apply to an order made under rule 44.3 of the CPR.

(4) In this rule –

    (a) "costs" has the same meaning as in rule 44.1(1)(c) of the CPR; and

    (b) "financial remedy proceedings" means proceedings for –

        (i) a financial order except an order for maintenance pending suit, an order for maintenance pending outcome of proceedings, an interim periodical payments order or any other form of interim order for the purposes of rule 9.7(1)(a), (b), (c) and (e);

        (ii) an order under Part 3 of the 1984 Act;

        (iii) an order under Schedule 7 to the 2004 Act;

        (iv) an order under section 10(2) of the 1973 Act;

        (v) an order under section 48(2) of the 2004 Act.

(5) Subject to paragraph (6), the general rule in financial remedy proceedings is that the court will not make an order requiring one party to pay the costs of another party.

(6) The court may make an order requiring one party to pay the costs of another party at any stage of the proceedings where it considers it appropriate to do so because of the conduct of a party in relation to the proceedings (whether before or during them).

(7) In deciding what order (if any) to make under paragraph (6), the court must have regard to –

    (a) any failure by a party to comply with these rules, any order of the court or any practice direction which the court considers relevant;

(b)   any open offer to settle made by a party;

(c)   whether it was reasonable for a party to raise, pursue or contest a particular allegation or issue;

(d)   the manner in which a party has pursued or responded to the application or a particular allegation or issue;

(e)   any other aspect of a party's conduct in relation to proceedings which the court considers relevant; and

(f)   the financial effect on the parties of any costs order.

(8) No offer to settle which is not an open offer to settle is admissible at any stage of the proceedings, except as provided by rule 9.17.

Amendments—SI 2013/530.

Defined terms—"costs": CPR 1998, r 44.1; "financial remedy": FPR 2010, r 2.3(1); "financial remedy proceedings": FPR 2010, r 28.3(4).

"applies in financial remedy proceedings" (r 28.3(1))—With effect from April 2006, FPR 1991, r 2.71 was introduced for MCA 1973 and CPA 2004 ancillary relief proceedings. FPR 2010, r 28.3 derives from FPR 1991, r 2.71 and seeks to replicate it. Save in the case of "conduct" (FPR 2010, r 28.3(6)), it excludes costs orders in the case of a prescribed list of matrimonial and civil partnership financial proceedings (FPR 2010, r 28.3(4)) and disallows *Calderbank* correspondence as a basis for seeking costs (FPR 2010, r 28.3(8)). In order to be effective to justify costs, all negotiations must be open.

"Financial remedy proceedings" defined—For costs rules purposes "financial remedy proceedings" is defined differently from proceedings for a "financial remedy". The list in FPR 2010, r 28.3(4) specifically excludes orders for interim financial provision, maintenance pending suit, maintenance pending outcome of proceedings and any other form of interim financial provision. In summary, costs applications are subject to FPR 2010, r 28.3 in summary as follows:

Costs and financial remedy proceedings			
Type of financial application	(1) Financial remedy[1]	(2) Financial order[2]	(3) Financial remedy proceedings[3]
Avoidance of disposition order	*	*	*
Maintenance pending suit	*	*	+
Maintenance pending outcome of proceedings	*	*	+
Order for periodical payments or lump sum under MCA 1973 (save for under s 27(6))	*	*	*
The same: under CPA 2004, Sch 5, Pt 1	*	*	*
Property adjustment order (FPR 2010, r 2.3(1))	*	*	*
A variation order (FPR 2010, r 9.3(1))	*	*	*
A pension sharing order (r 9.3(1))	*	*	*
Order under MCA 1973, s 27 (and under CPA 2004, Sch 5, Pt 9)	*		
MFPA 1984, Pt 3 (and under CPA 2004, Sch 7)	*		*
MCA 1973, s 35 (and CPA 2004)	*		
DPMCA 1978 (and CPA 2004, Sch 6)	*		
MCA 1973, s 10(2) (and CPA 2004, s 48(2))			*

Costs and financial remedy proceedings			
Type of financial application	(1) Financial remedy[1]	(2) Financial order[2]	(3) Financial remedy proceedings[3]
CA 1989, Sch 1	*		
Order preventing disposition (including MCA 1973, s 37(2)(a), CPA 2004 and MFPA 1984)	*		
Interim financial order (FPR 2010, r 9.17)			+
Other Pt 18 applications Trial of prelim issue (e g *Baker v Rowe* [2010] 1 FLR 761) Set aside application *Barder* appeal			+
Appeal; FPR 2010, Pt 30			
Appeal to Court of Appeal: CPR 1998, Pt 52			

1   FPR 2010, Pt 9
2   FPR 2010, rr 2.3(1) and 9.4
3   FPR 2010, r 28.3(4)

In column (3) above:

–   orders marked + are financial remedy proceedings, but are not covered by FPR 2010, r 28.3 costs orders; and are therefore 'clean sheet' cases;
–   those marked * are covered by FPR 2010, r 28.3; and
–   those left blank are in the "clean sheet"/*Gojkovic* category

Financial remedy proceedings subject to orders for costs—Examples of proceedings which are not financial remedy proceedings for the purposes of FPR 2010, r 28.3:

(1)   Applications under CA 1989, Sch 1
(2)   Appeals – Probably, as considered above; including appeals under FPR 2010, Pt 30
(3)   Interim applications – Interim applications, including for periodical payments, are specifically excluded by FPR 2010, r 28.3(4) from its application
(4)   Applications to set aside financial remedy orders – In *Judge v Judge* [2009] 1 FLR 1287 (and see below) Wilson LJ held that an application to set aside, though not ancillary relief proceedings and therefore outside FPR 1991, r 2.71(1), were "family proceedings", so that costs did not automatically follow the event (FPR 1991, r 2.71(1)(b)). The position is likely to be the same under FPR 2010, Pt 28, subject to any *Gojkovic* question.
(5)   Preliminary issue application – In *KSO v MJO, JMO and PSO* [2009] 1 FLR 1036, especially at [65], Munby J took the view that in the case of preliminary issue applications in the ancillary relief jurisdiction it was appropriate to make an order for costs.
(6)   Intervener proceedings – Where a person intervenes in financial remedy proceedings, they will be "family proceedings" so that FPR 2010, r 28.2(1) applies and CPR 1998, r 44.2 (costs follow the event) cannot formally apply. In any consideration of costs, the success of a party must be an important factor in consideration of an order for costs (*Baker v Rowe* (above)).
(7)   Other applications – Further, the term "financial remedy proceedings" for the purpose of FPR 2010, r 28.3 does not include the following (and, so far as these are family proceedings covered by FPR 2010, CPR 1998, r 44.2 does not formally apply either), so the "clean sheet" principle applies:
–   all appeals in family proceedings (including to the Court of Appeal);
–   applications for restraint of disposal (MCA 1973, s 37(2)(a)) or *Shipman* orders (*Shipman v Shipman* [1991] 1 FLR 250; and see Pt 20 interim remedies));
–   enforcement in family proceedings (FPR 2010, Pt 33; *X v Y (Repayment of Overpaid Maintenance)* [2012] EWCC 2 (Fam));
–   applications under CA 1989, s 15 and Sch 1.

"For" or "about" a financial remedy—In *Judge v Judge* [2009] 1 FLR 1287 and *Baker v Rowe* [2010] 1 FLR 761 the Court of Appeal had to decide the question: are proceedings "for a financial remedy" or "about a financial remedy". *Judge* concerned an unsuccessful application and appeal by a wife to set aside an order in which she asserted that the order had been vitiated by non-disclosure on the part of the husband. The court considered whether the judge, in dealing with costs, had correctly concluded that the application before him (FPR 2010 terminology is here adopted) was not financial remedy proceedings (as distinct from proceedings for a financial remedy within the meaning of FPR 2010, r 28.3(5)) and that, therefore, the general rule in CPR 1998, r 44.2 applied; also that the unsuccessful party should pay the costs of the successful party. It was held:

– These were not ancillary relief proceedings (per Wilson LJ at [51]), they were merely in connection with such proceedings. Therefore, FPR 2010, r 28.3(5) (as now is) does not apply.
– Instead, the judge has a clean sheet (per Wilson LJ at [52] and [53]), because FPR 2010, r 28.2(1) disapplies CPR 1998, r 44.2 in family proceedings.

Search for a starting point: *Gojkovic (No 2)*—When a much earlier Court of Appeal considered the same – or a very similar – point (the disapplication for family proceedings of the rule that costs follow the event) under RSC 1965, Ord 62, which applied to the costs appeal then before the court in *Gojkovic v Gojkovic (No 2)* [1991] 2 FLR 233, CA and which in effect was in very similar terms to the present 'clean sheet' rules, Butler-Sloss LJ said:

"… in the Family Division there still remains the necessity for some starting point. That starting point, in my judgment, is that costs prima facie follow the event (see Cumming-Bruce LJ in *Singer (formerly Sharegin) v Sharegin* [1984] FLR 114 at [119]) but may be displaced much more easily than, and in circumstances which would not apply, in other divisions of the High Court."

A question may arise that *Judge* and *Baker v Rowe* [2010] 1 FLR 761 were decided per curiam (the judgments in neither case make obvious reference to *Gojkovic (No 2)*).

"conduct … in relation to the proceedings" (r 28.3(6))—FPR 2010, r 28.3(7)(d),(e) are taken directly from CPR 1998, r 44.2. Examples of "conduct" might include (in addition to the list in FPR 2010, r 28.3(7)):

– oppressive enquiry (if not fully controlled by the court);
– disproportionate pursuit of a particular issue which turns out to of peripheral or of no relevance (and see FPR 1991, r 2.71(5)(c),(d)); and see for example *KSO v MJO, JMO and PSO* [2009] 1 FLR 1036; and, for examples, see costs cases referred to at [76]–[81]; *A v A (No 2) (Ancillary Relief: Costs)* [2008] 1 FLR 1428);
– persistent or unnecessary pursuit of interim applications such as for restraint of disposal (costs can be awarded in any event: see above) or for interim financial provision;
– tardy or non-disclosure of documents or information.

28.4 Wasted costs orders in the magistrates' court: appeals

A legal or other representative against whom a wasted costs order is made in the magistrates' court may appeal to the Crown Court.

"appeal to Crown Court" (r 28.4)—In the absence of any further provision relating to the time limit for giving notice of appeal and procedure to be adopted, it is suggested that reference should be made to Magistrates' Courts (Costs against Legal Representatives in Civil Proceedings) Rules 1991, r 3.

Practice Direction 28A –
Costs

This Practice Direction supplements FPR Part 28

Application and modification of the CPR

1.1 Rule 28.2 provides that subject to rule 28.3 of the FPR and to paragraph (2) of rule 28.2, Parts 43, 44 (except rules 44.3(2) and (3), 44.9 to 44.12C, 44.13(1A) and (1B) and 44.18 to 20), 47 and 48 and rule 45.6 of the CPR apply to costs in family proceedings with the modifications listed in rule 28.2(1)(a) to (d). Rule 28.2(1)(c) refers to modifications in accordance with this Practice Direction.

1.2 In addition to the modifications to the CPR listed in rule 28.2(1), in rule 48.1(1)(b) after paragraph (ii) insert "(iii) section 68A of the Magistrates' Courts Act 1980.".

1.3 Rule 28.2(2) provides that Part 47 and rules 44.3C and 45.6 of the CPR do not apply to proceedings in a magistrates' court.

Application and modification of the Practice Direction supplementing CPR Parts 43 to 48

2.1 For the purpose of proceedings to which these Rules apply, the Practice Direction about costs which supplements Parts 43 to 48 of the CPR ("the costs practice direction") will apply, but with the exclusions and modifications explained below to reflect the exclusions and modifications to those Parts of the CPR as they are applied by Part 28 of these Rules.

2.2 Rule 28.2(1) applies, with modifications and certain exceptions, Parts 43 to 48 of the CPR to costs in family proceedings. Paragraph 1.2 of this Practice Direction modifies rule 48.1(1)(b) when it applies to family proceedings. Rule 28.2(2), by way of exception, disapplies Part 47, rules 44.3C and 45.6 of the CPR in the case of family proceedings in a magistrates' court. Rule 28.3, again by way of exception, additionally disapplies CPR rule 44.3(1), (4) and (5) in the case of financial remedy proceedings, regardless of court.

2.3 The costs practice direction does not, therefore, apply in its entirety but with the exclusion of certain sections reflecting the non-application of certain rules of the CPR which those sections supplement.

2.4 The costs practice direction applies as follows –

- to family proceedings generally, other than in magistrates' courts, with the exception of sections 6, 15, 16, 17 and 23A;
- to family proceedings generally, in magistrates' courts only, with the exception of sections 6, 15, 16, 17, 23A and sections 28–49A;
- to financial remedy proceedings, other than in magistrates' courts, with the exception of section 6, paragraphs 8.1 to 8.4 of section 8 and sections 15, 16, 17 and 23A;
- to a financial remedy proceedings, in magistrates' courts only, with the exception of section 6, paragraphs 8.1 to 8.4 of section 8, sections 15, 16, 17, 23A and sections 28–49A.

2.5 All subsequent editions of the costs practice direction as and when they are published and come into effect shall in the same way extend to all family proceedings.

2.6 The costs practice direction includes provisions applicable to proceedings following changes in the manner in which legal services are funded pursuant to the Access to Justice Act 1999. It should be noted that although the cost of the premium in respect of legal costs insurance (section 29) or the cost of funding by a prescribed membership organisation (section 30) may be recoverable, family proceedings (within section 58A(2) of the Courts and Legal Services Act 1990) cannot be the subject of an enforceable conditional fee agreement.

2.7 Paragraph 1.4 of section 1 of the costs practice direction shall be modified as follows –

in the definition of "counsel" for "High court or in the county courts" substitute "High Court, county courts or in a magistrates' court".

General interpretation of references in CPR

3.1 References in the costs practice direction to "claimant" and "defendant" are to be read as references to equivalent terms used in proceedings to which these Rules apply and other terms and expressions used in the costs practice direction shall be similarly treated.

3.2 References in CPR Parts 43 to 48 to other rules or Parts of the CPR shall be read, where there is an equivalent rule or Part in these Rules, to that equivalent rule or Part.

Costs in financial remedy proceedings

4.1 Rule 28.3 relates to the court's power to make costs orders in financial remedy proceedings. For the purposes of rule 28.3, "financial remedy proceedings" are defined in accordance with rule 28.3(4)(b). That definition, which is more limited than the principal definition in rule 2.3(1), includes:

    (a)   an application for a financial order, except:
        (i)   an order for maintenance pending suit or an order for maintenance pending outcome of proceedings;
        (ii)   an interim periodical payments order or any other form of interim order for the purposes of rule 9.7(1)(a), (b), (c) and (e);
    (b)   an application for an order under Part 3 of the Matrimonial and Family Proceedings Act 1984 or Schedule 7 to the Civil Partnership Act 2004; and
    (c)   an application under section 10(2) of the Matrimonial Causes Act 1973 or section 48(2) of the Civil Partnership Act 2004.

4.2 Accordingly, it should be noted that:

    (a)   while most interim financial applications are excluded from rule 28.3, the rule does apply to an application for an interim variation order within rule 9.7(1)(d),
    (b)   rule 28.3 does not apply to an application for any of the following financial remedies:
        (i)   an order under Schedule 1 to the Children Act 1989;
        (ii)   an order under section 27 of the Matrimonial Causes Act 1973 or Part 9 of Schedule 5 to the Civil Partnership Act 2004;
        (iii)   an order under section 35 of the Matrimonial Causes Act 1973 or paragraph 69 of Schedule 5 to the Civil Partnership Act 2004; or
        (iv)   an order under Part 1 of the Domestic Proceedings and Magistrates' Courts Act 1978 or Schedule 6 to the Civil Partnership Act 2004.

4.3 Under rule 28.3 the court only has the power to make a costs order in financial remedy proceedings when this is justified by the litigation conduct of one of the parties. When determining whether and how to exercise this power the court will be required to take into account the list of factors set out in that rule. The court will not be able to take into account any offers to settle expressed to be "without prejudice" or "without prejudice save as to costs" in deciding what, if any, costs orders to make.

4.4 In considering the conduct of the parties for the purposes of rule 28.3(6) and (7) (including any open offers to settle), the court will have regard to the obligation of the parties to help the court to further the overriding objective (see rules 1.1 and 1.3) and will take into account the nature, importance and complexity of the issues in the case. This may be of particular significance in applications for variation orders and interim variation orders or other cases where there is a risk of the costs becoming disproportionate to the amounts in dispute.

4.5 Parties who intend to seek a costs order against another party in proceedings to which rule 28.3 applies should ordinarily make this plain in open correspondence or in skeleton arguments before the date of the hearing. In any case where summary assessment of costs awarded under rule 28.3 would be appropriate parties are under an obligation to file a statement of costs in CPR Form N260.

4.6 An interim financial order which includes an element to allow a party to deal with legal fees (see *A v A (maintenance pending suit: provision for legal fees)* [2001] 1 WLR 605; *G v G (maintenance pending suit; costs)* [2002] EWHC 306 (Fam); *McFarlane v McFarlane, Parlour v Parlour* [2004] EWCA Civ 872; *Moses-Taiga v Taiga* [2005] EWCA Civ 1013; *C v C (Maintenance Pending Suit: Legal Costs)* [2006] Fam Law 739; *Currey v Currey (No 2)* [2006] EWCA Civ 1338) is an order made pursuant to section 22 of the Matrimonial Causes Act 1973 or an order under paragraph 38 of Schedule 5 of the 2004 Act, and is not a "costs order" within the meaning of rule 28.3.

4.7 By virtue of rule 28.2(1), where rule 28.3 does not apply, the exercise of the court's discretion as to costs is governed by the relevant provisions of the CPR and in particular rule 44.3 (excluding r 44.3(2) and (3)).

PART 29
MISCELLANEOUS

CONTENTS OF THIS PART

29.1 Personal details

(1) Unless the court directs otherwise, a party is not required to reveal –

    (a)   the party's home address or other contact details;

    (b)   the address or other contact details of any child;

    (c)   the name of a person with whom the child is living, if that person is not the applicant; or

    (d)   in relation to an application under section 28(2) of the 2002 Act (application for permission to change the child's surname), the proposed new surname of the child.

(2) Where a party does not wish to reveal any of the particulars in paragraph (1), that party must give notice of those particulars to the court and the particulars will not be revealed to any person unless the court directs otherwise.

(3) Where a party changes home address during the course of proceedings, that party must give notice of the change to the court.

29.2 Disclosure of information under the 1991 Act

Where the Secretary of State requires a person mentioned in regulation 3(1), 4(2) or 6(2)(a) of the Child Support Information Regulations 2008 to furnish information or evidence for a purpose mentioned in regulation 4(1) of those Regulations, nothing in these rules will –

(a) prevent that person from furnishing the information or evidence sought; or
(b) require that person to seek permission of the court before doing so.

Amendments—SI 2012/2007.

Defined terms—"the 1991 Act": r 2.3(1).

Child Support Information Regulations 2008—The Child Support Information Regulations 2008, reg 4(1) provides for the disclosure to the Secretary of State for Work and Pensions of certain information or evidence required by it to perform its duties under CSA 1991 (especially calculation of child support maintenance or enforcement of arrears). This rule prevents any prohibitive measures being applied to a parent with care (reg 3(1)) or non-resident parent (reg 4(2)(a)) if they are required to produce, and do produce to the Secretary of State, documents arising in court proceedings. It enables the court to produce such documents directly to the Secretary of State (reg 6(2)(a)).

No contempt by parent who releases "required" information or evidence—The release of the parent with care to disclose information and evidence ends any possibility of contempt proceedings for a parent with care who, when requested so to do under Child Support Information Regulations 2008, reg 3(1) ("must furnish such information as the Secretary of State requires"), passes court documents (eg Form E or other financial information) to the Secretary of State. It reverses *Gelber v Griffin* [2006] EWHC 3666 (Fam) (parent with care in contempt of court where she gave Form E to the Secretary of State). It remains the case that where information is volunteered by the parent with care (as was the case in *Gelber v Griffin*), then that parent may yet be in contempt, unless she first obtains permission from the court.

Legal representatives—There is no mention of a party's legal representative in the list in Child Support Information Regulations 2008, reg 4(2) of those required to disclose documents to the Secretary of State. Documents held by a lawyer remain confidential and many will be covered by privilege. A client's file, or any part of it, should only be released to the Secretary of State with the written authority of the client.

Child Support Act 1991, s 50—CSA 1991, s 50 prevents disclosure of information by the Secretary of State to third parties; save that they are entitled to release documents for use in court proceedings (s 50(6)).

29.3 Method of giving notice

(1) Unless directed otherwise, a notice which is required by these rules to be given to a person must be given –

(a) in writing; and
(b) in a manner in which service may be effected in accordance with Part 6.

(2) Rule 6.33 applies to a notice which is required by these rules to be given to a child as it applies to a document which is to be served on a child.

Rule 6.33—In FPR 2010, Pt 12 proceedings where a rule requires a document to be served on a party who is a child, then unless the court directs otherwise, the following additional persons or bodies must be served, notified or supplied with a copy of the document (in addition to those specified in FPR 2010, rr 6.28–6.32) namely the children's guardian, the welfare officer, the children and family reporter or the person acting under a duty referred to in r 16.38 and the local authority preparing a report under CA 1989, s 14A(8),(9).

29.4 Withdrawal of applications in proceedings

(1) This rule applies to applications in proceedings –

    (a)   under Part 7;

    (b)   under Parts 10 to 14 or under any other Part where the application relates to the welfare or upbringing of a child or;

    (c)   where either of the parties is a protected party.

(2) Where this rule applies, an application may only be withdrawn with the permission of the court.

(3) Subject to paragraph (4), a person seeking permission to withdraw an application must file a written request for permission setting out the reasons for the request.

(4) The request under paragraph (3) may be made orally to the court if the parties are present.

(5) A court officer will notify the other parties of a written request.

(6) The court may deal with a written request under paragraph (3) without a hearing if the other parties, and any other persons directed by the court, have had an opportunity to make written representations to the court about the request.

Court's approach to application—An application under r 29.4(2) involves the determination of a "question with respect to the upbringing of a child", and so the paramountcy principle in CA 1989, s 1(1) applies. The paramount consideration for the court is whether the withdrawal of the proceedings would promote or conflict with the welfare of the child concerned. The court must look at each case on its facts to see if there is some "solid advantage to the child to be derived from continuing the proceedings". For an example of the application of the test see *Re N (Leave to Withdraw Care Proceedings)* [2000] 1 FLR 134 where the court refused the application of the local authority for leave to withdraw care proceedings.

Withdrawal of proceedings – ECHR 1950—Where an application is made to withdraw public law child care proceedings on the basis that to continue them would amount to an interference with the right of the parents of the child concerned under Art 8(1) of the ECHR to respect for their private and family life, the court must assess whether such interference is necessary to protect one of the interests set out in Art 8(2) (*Re N (Leave to Withdraw Care Proceedings)* [2000] 1 FLR 134). Where there is a serious conflict between the interests of the child and one of its parents which can only be resolved to the disadvantage of one of them, the interests of the child must prevail under Art 8(2) (*Hendriks v The Netherlands* (1982) 5 EHRR 223).

"written request for permission"—The written request for permission to withdraw proceedings should be made in Form C2. The form requires the names and date of birth of the child concerned, and details as to the identity of the person making the request and as to his relationship with the child. The reasons for seeking permission to withdraw the proceedings must be clearly set out, and particular attention should be paid to the effect that withdrawal will have on the child.

Service—See FPR 2010, Pt 6, Ch 3.

Oral application in the presence of the parties—The court must not entertain an oral request for leave to withdraw proceedings in the absence of the children's guardian either, even if his legal representative is present (*Re F (A Minor) (Care Order: Withdrawal of Application)* [1993] 2 FLR 9). It is possible that the applicant may change his mind almost immediately after filing the application and wish to raise the question of withdrawing the proceedings orally at the first directions hearing. At this stage, it may be that neither the children's guardian nor the children and family reporter will have been appointed, so neither could be present. This ought not to debar the making of an oral request. FPC(CA 989)R 1991, r 5(3), the equivalent provision for magistrates' courts, is much clearer on this point. It is not impossible (although it is very unusual) to have both a children's guardian and a children and family reporter in the same case. Where this occurs, the wording of the rule suggests that it will suffice if the oral application is made in the presence of one or the other though it is doubted whether, in practice, it would normally be prudent to proceed to determine the application without notification to both.

29.5 The Human Rights Act 1998

(1) In this rule –

"the 1998 Act" means the Human Rights Act 1998;

"Convention right" has the same meaning as in the 1998 Act; and

"declaration of incompatibility" means a declaration of incompatibility under section 4 of the 1998 Act.

(2) A party who seeks to rely on any provision of or right arising under the 1998 Act or seeks a remedy available under that Act must inform the court in that party's application or otherwise in writing specifying –

(a) the Convention right which it is alleged has been infringed and details of the alleged infringement; and

(b) the relief sought and whether this includes a declaration of incompatibility.

(3) The High Court may not make a declaration of incompatibility unless 21 days' notice, or such other period of notice as the court directs, has been given to the Crown.

(4) Where notice has been given to the Crown, a Minister, or other person permitted by the 1998 Act, will be joined as a party on giving notice to the court.

(5) Where a claim is made under section 7(1) of the 1998 Act (claim that public authority acted unlawfully) in respect of a judicial act –

(a) that claim must be set out in the application form or the appeal notice; and

(b) notice must be given to the Crown.

(6) Where paragraph (4) applies and the appropriate person (as defined in section 9(5) of the 1998 Act) has not applied within 21 days, or such other period as the court directs, beginning with the date on which the notice to be joined as a party was served, the court may join the appropriate person as a party.

(7) On any application concerning a committal order, if the court ordering the release of the person concludes that that person's Convention rights have been infringed by the making of the order to which the application or appeal relates, the judgment or order should so state, but if the court does not do so, that failure will not prevent another court from deciding the matter.

(8) Where by reason of a rule, practice direction or court order the Crown is permitted or required –

(a) to make a witness statement;

(b) to swear an affidavit(GL);

(c) to verify a document by a statement of truth; or

(d) to discharge any other procedural obligation,

that function will be performed by an appropriate officer acting on behalf of the Crown, and the court may if necessary nominate an appropriate officer.

(Practice Direction 29A (Human Rights – Joining the Crown) makes provision for the notices mentioned in this rule.)

Scope—An application in relation to a human rights point may be before the court as a freestanding issue, which will be by way of judicial review proceedings to the Administrative Court (see CPR 1998, Pt 54) or in existing proceedings. This rule applies to the latter. Where a human rights issue is to be raised, it should be included within the application or originating documentation. If the issue arises after the commencement of the proceedings, the application or originating documentation should be amended to include the human rights point.

Declaration of incompatibility—An application may be made under HRA 1998, s 4 to declare primary or secondary legislation incompatible with the provisions of ECHR 1950 (as defined under HRA 1998, s 1). If such an issue is raised the application must be dealt with in the High Court (HRA 1998, s 4(5)).

This means the application must be made to the High Court or transferred there. Where such an application is made, notice must also be given to the Crown to consider joinder as a party to the application (FPR 2010, r 29.5(3),(4),(6)).

Judicial acts—An application may be made claiming that there has been a failure to act in a way which is compatible with the provisions of ECHR 1950 (as defined under HRA 1998, s 1). Such a claim may only be made by way of appeal, or judicial review where an appeal may not be made (HRA 1998, s 9). On such an application, where damages are sought, notice must be given to the Crown with a view to joinder (FPR 2010, r 29.5(5)). The notice given under r 29.5(5) must be served on the person named in the list published under Crown Proceedings Act 1947, s 17, namely the Lord Chancellor and should be served on the Treasury Solicitor (FPR PD29A, paras 1.1–1.6, 2.1–2.3). The full list published under Crown Proceedings Act 1947, s 17 is annexed to CPR PD66 (set out in *Civil Court Service*, Jordan Publishing Ltd).

Injunctions—The court has jurisdiction in appropriate cases to grant an injunction restraining a local authority from, for example, seeking to remove a child from a placement pending a full hearing by the court: *Coventry CC v O (Adoption)* [2011] 2 FLR 936.

29.6 Documents in proceedings concerning gender recognition

(1) This rule applies to all documents in proceedings brought under –

    (a)   section 12(g) or (h) of, or paragraph 11(1)(e) of Schedule 1 to, the 1973 Act; or

    (b)   the Gender Recognition Act 2004.

(2) Documents to which this rule applies must, while they are in the custody of the court, be kept in a place of special security.

Scope—This rule provides for the security of documents in the custody of the court in proceedings concerning gender recognition.

29.7 Stamping or sealing court documents

(1) A court officer must, when issuing the following documents, seal$^{(GL)}$, or otherwise authenticate them with the stamp of the court –

    (a)   the application form;

    (b)   an order; and

    (c)   any other document which a rule or practice direction requires the court officer to seal$^{(GL)}$ or stamp.

(2) The court officer may place the seal$^{(GL)}$ or the stamp on the document –

    (a)   by hand; or

    (b)   by printing a facsimile of the seal$^{(GL)}$ on the document whether electronically or otherwise.

(3) A document purporting to bear the court's seal$^{(GL)}$ or stamp will be admissible in evidence without further proof.

29.8 Applications for relief which is precluded by the 1991 Act

(1) This rule applies where an application is made for an order which, in the opinion of the court, it would be prevented from making under section 8 or 9 of the 1991 Act and in this rule, "the matter" means the question of whether or not the court would be so prevented.

(2) The court will consider the matter without holding a hearing.

(3) Where the court officer receives the opinion of the court, as mentioned in paragraph (1), the court officer must send a notice to the applicant of that opinion.

(4) Paragraphs (5) to (11) apply where the court officer sends a notice under paragraph (3).

(5) Subject to paragraph (6), no requirement of these rules apply except the requirements –

    (a)   of this rule;

    (b)   as to service of the application by the court officer; and

    (c)   as to any procedural step to be taken following the making of an application of the type in question.

(6) The court may direct that the requirements of these rules apply, or apply to such extent or with such modifications as are set out in the direction.

(7) If the applicant informs the court officer, within 14 days of the date of the notice, that the applicant wishes to persist with the application, the court will give appropriate directions for the matter to be heard and determined and may provide for the hearing to be without notice.

(8) Where directions are given in accordance with paragraph (7), the court officer must –

    (a)   inform the applicant of the directions;

    (b)   send a copy of the application to the other parties;

    (c)   if the hearing is to be without notice, inform the other parties briefly –

        (i)   of the nature and effect of the notice given to the applicant under paragraph (3);

        (ii)   that the matter is being resolved without a hearing on notice; and

        (iii)   that they will be notified of the result; and

    (d)   if the hearing is to be on notice, inform the other parties of –

        (i)   the circumstances which led to the directions being given; and

        (ii)   the directions.

(9) If the applicant does not inform the court officer as mentioned in paragraph (7), the application shall be treated as having been withdrawn.

(10) Where –

    (a)   the matter is heard in accordance with directions given under paragraph (7); and

    (b)   the court determines that it would be prevented, under section 8 or 9 of the 1991 Act, from making the order sought by the applicant,

the court will dismiss the application.

(11) Where the court dismisses the application –

    (a)   the court must give its reasons in writing; and

    (b)   the court officer must send a copy of the reasons to the parties.

Defined terms—"the 1991 Act", "court officer": FPR 2010, r 2.3(1); "matter": FPR 2010, r 29.8(1).

"section 8 or 9 of the 1991 Act" (r 29.8(1))—Sections 8(3) and 9(5) of CSA 1991 prevent any court from making, varying or reviving any orders for periodical payments for children and from varying any agreement for child maintenance. These applications are financial remedy proceedings under FPR 2010, Pt 9, either with periodical payments as the sole object (r 29.8); or with periodical payments as part of a wider application for financial remedies (r 29.9). Where a party appears to have made an application precluded by CSA 1991, r 29.8 enables the court to give that party an opportunity to justify why he considers that the application should proceed.

"applicant wishes to persist" (r 29.8(7))—It is possible that the draftsman of r 29.8 has overlooked the crucial fact (to FPR 2010, rr 28.9 and 29.8) that all applications to which the rule applies will be financial remedy proceedings (not, for example, as before also under CA 1989, Sch 1 or MFPA 1984, with their bespoke procedures) and will, therefore, be covered by the first directions appointment procedure under FPR 2010, Pt 9 (r 9.15). Once a party has indicated a 'wish to persist', there seems to be no reason why this intent cannot be picked up on directions at the r 9.15 appointment. That would also obviate any separate court appointment under r 29.8(10).

29.9 Modification of rule 29.8 where the application is not freestanding

(1) Where the court officer sends a notice under rule 29.8(3) in relation to an application which is contained in another document ("the document") which contains material extrinsic to the application –

    (a)   subject to paragraph (2), the document will be treated as if it did not contain the application in respect of which the notice was served; and

    (b)   the court officer, when sending copies of the documents to the respondents under any provision of these rules, must attach –

        (i)   a copy of the notice under rule 29.8(3); and

        (ii)   a notice informing the respondents of the effect of paragraph (1)(a).

(2) If the court determines that it is not prevented by section 8 or 9 of the 1991 Act from making the order sought by the application, the court –

    (a)   must direct that the document shall be treated as if it contained the application; and

    (b)   may give such directions as it considers appropriate for the subsequent conduct of the proceedings.

Application for periodical payments included in a composite financial remedy application—This provision, like FPR 2010, r 29.8, may have been drafted without account of the points made in the note to r 29.8(7) above. So far as it is of continuing real effect, the rule deals with 'material extrinsic to the application' for child periodical payments. It enables the financial remedy application to proceed without the periodical payments application; and, if it is restored, to proceed with it.

29.10 Standard requirements

(1) Every judgment or order must state the name and judicial title of the person who made it.

(2) Every judgment or order must –

    (a)   bear the date on which it is given or made; and

    (b)   be sealed$^{(GL)}$ by the court.

Standard requirements (r 29.10)—This and the following rules, and the corresponding PD, follow CPR 1998, Pt 40 in seeking to standardise the practice of the High Court and county courts in drawing up and serving judgments and orders.

"the name and judicial title of the person who made it" (r 29.10(1))—It is necessary in dealing with appeals and applications to review or set aside orders to identify the judge of first instance. Judges frequently deal with lists back to back and it is advisable to check who the adjudicator was before drawing up an order or judgment. Draft judgments should leave space for the judge's name and title to be inserted (compare CPR PD40B, para 3.3(2)).

29.11 Drawing up and filing of judgments and orders

(1) Except as provided by a rule or a practice direction, every judgment or order will be drawn up by the court unless –

    (a)   the court orders a party to draw it up;

    (b)   a party, with the permission of the court, agrees to draw it up; or

    (c)   the court dispenses with the need to draw it up.

(2) The court may direct that –

    (a)   a judgment or an order drawn up by a party must be checked by the court before it is sealed$^{(GL)}$; or

    (b)   before a judgment or an order is drawn up by the court, the parties must file an agreed statement of its terms.

(3) Where a judgment or an order is to be drawn up by a party –

(a) that party must file it no later than 7 days after the date on which the court ordered or gave permission for the order to be drawn up so that it can be sealed by the court; and

(b) if that party fails to file it within that period, any other party may draw it up and file it.

"drawn up" (r 29.11)—A judge has jurisdiction to re-consider his decision before an order is drawn up (*Re Barrell Enterprises* [1973] 1 WLR 19; *Stewart v Engel & Anor* [2000] 1 WLR 2268), although this power must be exercised sparingly, for, as observed in *Barrell*: "When oral judgments have been given, either in a court of first instance or on appeal, the successful party ought, save in the most exceptional circumstances, to be able to assume that the judgment is a valid and effective one." The law is conveniently summarised in *Paulin v Paulin* [2009] 2 FLR 354 at [30].

In *Earl of Malmesbury v Strutt & Parker* [2007] EWHC 2199 (QB) Jack J reiterated the rule that a judicial decision will only be reconsidered in exceptional circumstances before it is sealed and that sealing is an absolute bar to reconsideration. See also **"a power to vary or revoke"** under FPR 2010, r 4.1.

"must file it no later than 7 days" (r 29.11(3)(a))—As this time limit exceeds 5 days, it includes weekends and public holidays (FPR 2010, r 2.9). It is particularly important to ensure that urgent orders are drawn up and served immediately to ensure that the time limit imposed in the order does not elapse.

29.12 Access to and inspection of documents retained in court

(1) Except as provided by this rule or by any other rule or Practice Direction, no document filed or lodged in the court office shall be open to inspection by any person without the permission of the court, and no copy of any such document shall be taken by, or issued to, any person without such permission.

(2) A copy of an order made in open court will be issued to any person who requests it.

(3) Subject to rules 14.24 and 29.1(2) and to any direction given by the court, a party to any family proceedings, or the legal representative, children's guardian or litigation friend for a party in any family proceedings, may have a search made for, and may inspect, and obtain a copy of, any document filed or lodged in the court office in those proceedings.

(4) Any person who intends to make an application in relation to a child under the 1980 Hague Convention in a Contracting State (as defined in rule 12.44) other than the United Kingdom shall, if the court is satisfied that that person intends to make such an application, be entitled to obtain a copy bearing the seal(GL) of the court of any order made in relation to the child under the 1989 Act or under the inherent jurisdiction, whether or not that person was a party to the proceedings in which the order was made.

Amendments—Substituted by SI 2012/679.

29.13 Service of judgments and orders

(1) The court officer must, unless the court directs otherwise, serve a copy of a judgment or an order made in family proceedings to every party affected by it.

(2) Where a judgment or an order has been drawn up by a party and is to be served by the court officer the party who drew it up must file a copy to be retained at court and sufficient copies for service on all the parties.

(3) A party in whose favour an order is made need not prove that a copy of the order has reached a party to whom it is required to be sent under this rule.

(4) This rule does not affect the operation of any rule or enactment which requires an order to be served in a particular way

29.14 Power to require judgment or order to be served on a party as well as the party's solicitor

Where the party on whom a judgment or order is served is acting by a solicitor, the court may order the judgment or order to be served on the party as well as on the party's solicitor.

"served on the party as well as on his solicitor" (r 29.14)—There is no guidance as to the circumstances in which such an order will be made. It is likely to be made only in exceptional circumstances, e g to ensure that it is brought to the lay party's attention that an adverse costs order has been made or that an order is penal.

29.15 When judgment or order takes effect

A judgment or order takes effect from the day when it is given or made, or such later date as the court may specify.

"takes effect" (r 29.15)—An order to do an act cannot be enforced unless and until a date for the act to be done is fixed. If a period of time is incorporated, the order should state the date from which the period of time is to run, but FPR 2010, r 2.10 (mirroring CPR 1998, r 2.9) requires that wherever practicable, the order should state a day and time by which an act is to be done. (Time and again, parties go to the trouble of obtaining "unless orders", which are then drafted to require compliance "within 7 days", say, but unless the order makes it clear *from when the 7 days runs*, getting the order is a wasted effort.)

If a party is not present when the order is made, sufficient time should, of course, be allowed for the order to be sealed and served, and, thereafter, for compliance.

29.16 Correction of errors in judgments and orders

(1) The court may at any time correct an accidental slip or omission in a judgment or order.

(2) A party may apply for a correction without notice.

"The court may at any time correct an accidental slip or omission" (r 29.16)(1))—This, the well-known "slip rule", is not limited to errors of the court or its officials but it *is* limited to genuine slips and cannot be used to correct an error of substance. It cannot enable a court to have second or additional thoughts. Once the order is drawn up, any mistakes must be corrected by an appellate court. It is sometimes possible under the slip rule to amend an order to give effect to the intention of the court (*Bristol-Myers Squibb Co v (1) Baker Norton Pharmaceuticals Inc (2) Napro Biotherapeutics Inc* [2001] EWCA Civ 414, but c f *R v Cripps ex parte Muldoon* [1984] 1 QB 686 (where an order for costs had a clear meaning in law, although a different one from that which the judge intended, and could not be "corrected" under the Slip Rule)).

Practice Direction 29A –
Human Rights, Joining the Crown

This Practice Direction supplements FPR Part 29, rule 29.5 (The Human Rights Act 1998)

Section 4 of the Human Rights Act 1998

1.1 Where a party has informed the court about –

    (a) a claim for a declaration of incompatibility in accordance with section 4 of the Human Rights Act 1998; or

    (b) an issue for the court to decide which may lead to the court considering making a declaration, then the court may at any time consider whether notice should be given to the Crown as required by that Act and give directions for the content and service of the notice. The rule allows a period of 21 days before the court will make the declaration but the court may vary this period of time.

1.2 The court will normally consider the issues and give the directions referred to in paragraph 1.1 at a directions hearing.

1.3 The notice must be served on the person named in the list published under section 17 of the Crown Proceedings Act 1947.

1.4 The notice will be in the form directed by the court and will normally include the directions given by the court. The notice will also be served on all the parties.

1.5 The court may require the parties to assist in the preparation of the notice.

1.6 Unless the court orders otherwise, the Minister or other person permitted by the Human Rights Act 1998 to be joined as a party must, if he or she wishes to be joined, give notice of his or her intention to be joined as a party to the court and every other party. Where the Minister has nominated a person to be joined as a party the notice must be accompanied by the written nomination.

(Section 5(2)(a) of the Human Rights Act 1998 permits a person nominated by a Minister of the Crown to be joined as a party. The nomination may be signed on behalf of the Minister.)

Section 9 of the Human Rights Act 1998

2.1 The procedure in paragraphs 1.1 to 1.6 also applies where a claim is made under sections 7(1)(a) and 9(3) of the Human Rights Act 1998 for damages in respect of a judicial act.

2.2 Notice must be given to the Lord Chancellor and should be served on the Treasury Solicitor on his behalf.

2.3 The notice will also give details of the judicial act, which is the subject of the claim for damages, and of the court that made it.

(Section 9(4) of the Human Rights Act 1998 provides that no award of damages may be made against the Crown as provided for in section 9(3) unless the appropriate person is joined in the proceedings. The appropriate person is the Minister responsible for the court concerned or a person or department nominated by him or her (section 9(5) of the Act).)

Practice Direction 29B – Human Rights Act 1998

This Practice Direction supplements FPR Part 29

1 It is directed that the following practice shall apply as from 2 October 2000 in all family proceedings:

Citation of authorities

2 When an authority referred to in s 2 of the Human Rights Act 1998 ("the Act") is to be cited at a hearing:

(a) the authority to be cited shall be an authoritative and complete report;

(b)   the court must be provided with a list of authorities it is intended to cite and copies of the reports:

    (i)   in cases to which *Practice Direction (Family Proceedings: Court Bundles)* (10 March 2000) [2000] 1 FLR 536 applies, as part of the bundle;

    (ii)   otherwise, not less than 2 clear days before the hearing; and

(c)   copies of the complete original texts issued by the European Court and Commission, either paper based or from the Court's judgment database (HUDOC) which is available on the internet, may be used.

Note—*PD Family Proceedings: Court Bundles* of 10 March 2000, [2000] 1 FLR 536 has been replaced by FPR PD27A (formerly *PD Family Proceedings: Court Bundles (Universal Practice to be Applied in all Courts other than the Family Proceedings Court)* of 27 July 2006, [2006] 2 FLR 199, and any reference in any other PD to *PD Family Proceedings: Court Bundles* shall be read as if substituted by a reference to PD27A.

Allocation to judges

3

(1)   The hearing and determination of the following will be confined to a High Court judge:

    (a)   a claim for a declaration of incompatibility under s 4 of the Act; or

    (b)   an issue which may lead to the court considering making such a declaration.

(2)   The hearing and determination of a claim made under the Act in respect of a judicial act shall be confined in the High Court to a High Court judge and in county courts to a circuit judge.

PART 30
APPEALS

CONTENTS OF THIS PART

30.1 Scope and interpretation

(1) The rules in this Part apply to appeals to –

    (a)   the High Court; and

    (b)   a county court.

(2) This Part does not apply to an appeal in detailed assessment proceedings against a decision of an authorised court officer.

> (Rules 47.20 to 47.23 of the CPR deal with appeals against a decision of an authorised court officer in detailed assessment proceedings.)

(3) In this Part –

"appeal court" means the court to which an appeal is made;

"appeal notice" means an appellant's or respondent's notice;

"appellant" means a person who brings or seeks to bring an appeal;

"lower court" means the court from which, or the person from whom, the appeal lies; and

"respondent" means –

    (a)   a person other than the appellant who was a party to the proceedings in the lower court and who is affected by the appeal; and

    (b)   a person who is permitted by the appeal court to be a party to the appeal.

(4) This Part is subject to any rule, enactment or practice direction which sets out special provisions with regard to any particular category of appeal.

Appeals (FPR 2010, Pt 30)—See FPR PD30A.

Scope—The rules in this Part apply to all appeals in family proceedings from:

(i)   the magistrates' courts to a county court;

(ii) district judges of a county court to a circuit judge; and

(iii) district judges of the High Court and district judges of the Principal Registry of the Family Division to the High Court.

See ACA 2002, s 100; CA 1989, s 94; Access to Justice Act 1999 (Destination of Appeals) (Family Proceedings) Order 2011; and AJA 1999(DA)(FP)O 2009.

    Part 30 replicates the provisions of CPR 1998, Pt 52 with necessary and minor modifications: reference should be made to the notes to Pt 52 for guidance.

Procedure—All appeals must comply with the provisions of Pt 30 and PD30A.

Applications—Where a party makes an application in an appeal, the provisions of FPR 2010, Pt 18 will apply (FPR PD30A, rr 13.1 and 13.2)

Interim orders—Where events changed or developed after the making of an interim order, the appropriate course was to seek a variation of the order from the judge, rather than seek to appeal against the order: *Re H (A Child)* [2011] EWCA Civ 762.

Special provisions—Special provisions are made for appeals (i) under MCA 1980, s 111A (FPR 2010, rr 9.2–9.12, FPR PD30A), (ii) Child Maintenance and Enforcement Commission (CMEC) deduction order appeals (FPR 2010, rr 9.13–9.34, FPR PD30A; note that CMEC was abolished on 30 July 2012), (iii) appeals against decisions under rr 31.10, 31.11 or 31.14 (FPR 2010, rr 10.1–10.5, FPR PD30A,), (iv) appeals against pension orders and pension sharing orders (FPR 2010, rr 11.1–11.3, FPR PD30A) and (v) appeals in respect of parentage determinations pursuant to CSA 1991, s 20 (FPR 2010, rr 12.1–12.3, PD30A)

Magistrates' courts—Magistrates may not order an appeal to be transferred to the Court of Appeal (FPR 2010, r 30.13).

Appeal to Court of Appeal—Appeals from the county court and the High Court to the Court of Appeal are still governed by CPR 1998, Pt 52 and, as from 1 October 2012, CPR PD52A–PD52E.

30.2 Parties to comply with the practice direction

All parties to an appeal must comply with Practice Direction 30A.

30.3 Permission

(1) An appellant or respondent requires permission to appeal –

    (a)   against a decision in proceedings where the decision appealed against was made by a district judge or a costs judge, unless paragraph (2) applies; or

    (b)   as provided by Practice Direction 30A.

(2) Permission to appeal is not required where the appeal is against –

    (a)   a committal order; or

    (b)   a secure accommodation order under section 25 of the 1989 Act.

(3) An application for permission to appeal may be made –

    (a)   to the lower court at the hearing at which the decision to be appealed was made; or

    (b)   to the appeal court in an appeal notice.

        (Rule 30.4 sets out the time limits for filing an appellant's notice at the appeal court. Rule 30.5 sets out the time limits for filing a respondent's notice at the appeal court. Any application for permission to appeal to the appeal court must be made in the appeal notice (see rules 30.4(1) and 30.5(3).)

(4) Where the lower court refuses an application for permission to appeal, a further application for permission to appeal may be made to the appeal court.

(5) Subject to paragraph (5A), where the appeal court, without a hearing, refuses permission to appeal, the person seeking permission may request the decision to be reconsidered at a hearing.

(5A) Where a judge of the High Court or a Designated Family Judge refuses permission to appeal without a hearing and considers that the application is totally without merit, the judge may make an order that the person seeking permission may not request the decision to be reconsidered at a hearing.

(5B) Rule 4.3(5) will not apply to an order that the person seeking permission may not request the decision to be reconsidered at a hearing made under paragraph (5A).

(6) A request under paragraph (5) must be filed within 7 days beginning with the date on which the notice that permission has been refused was served.

(7) Permission to appeal may be given only where –

    (a)   the court considers that the appeal would have a real prospect of success; or

    (b)   there is some other compelling reason why the appeal should be heard.

(8) An order giving permission may –

    (a)   limit the issues to be heard; and

    (b)   be made subject to conditions.

(9) In this rule "costs judge" means a taxing master of the Senior Courts.

Amendments—SI 2013/530.

Permission to appeal—FPR PD30A does not set out any other circumstances in which permission to appeal is required. Permission to appeal is required from a decision made by a district judge or a costs judge (save where FPR 2010, r 30.3(2) applies).

Permission not required—Permission to appeal is not required (i) a committal order (ii) a secure accommodation order under CA 1989, s 25 or (iii) against a decision made by a magistrates' court.

Material omission—Where a party's advocate considers there is a material omission from a judgment or written reasons, the advocate should before drawing the order give the lower court the opportunity to consider whether there is an omission (FPR PD30A, para 4.6).

    Where the application for permission to appeal is made to the lower court, that court must consider whether there is a material omission from the judgment and if it concludes there is, to provide additions to the judgment. Where the application is made to the appeal court, it must consider whether there is a material omission from the judgment and if it concludes there is, it may remit the matter to the lower court with an invitation to provide additions to the judgment (FPR PD30A, paras 4.7-4.9). Where an alleged lack of reasons in the judgment had not been drawn to the attention of the trial judge or the judge had subsequently failed to elaborate on his reasons, the normal procedure was remittal to the judge at first instance with a list of specific questions: *Re A and L (Children)* [2012] 1 FLR 134.

Power to change judgment after handing down—A judge has the power to change his mind after delivering a judgment at the conclusion of a fact-finding hearing: *Re L and B (Children)* [2013] UKSC 8 and the notes to CPR 1998, r 52.3.

Permission without a hearing (r 30.3(4))—The general rule is that permission to appeal will be considered without a hearing (i e on paper: FPR PD30A, para 4.10; and see **Determination by the appeal court of an application for permission to appear** under CPR 1998, r 52.3 in *Civil Court Service* (Jordan Publishing Ltd)). This procedure will be applicable also to applications for permission to appeal out of time under *Barder v Barder* [1987] 2 FLR 480 (see Baron J in *O v O (Procedure for Listing Applications for Permission to Appeal to the High Court)* [2011] EWHC 14 July 2011 (unreported)). In *Black v Pastouna* [2005] EWCA Civ 1389, the Court of Appeal referred to CPR PD32, Annex 3 (video conferencing; reproduced in FPR PD22A, Annex 3): it would expect applications under 30 mins to be disposed of with Annex 3 in mind (but see *NLW v ARC* [2012] 2 FLR 129, where Mostyn J said that applications for permission in the Family Division – and in county courts, perhaps – must be in court). It is submitted that, generally, in the first instance and in light of FPR PD30A, para 4.10, the judge will consider permission on the papers. If a court hearing is requested where permission is refused, then *Pastouna* suggests that consideration be given to a video hearing.

Request for an oral hearing—Where an appeal court refuses permission to appeal, the appellant may request the decision to refuse permission to appeal be reconsidered at an oral hearing within 7 days of service of the notice of refusal. The request must at the same time be served on the respondents (FPR PD30A, para 4.13). The appellant's advocate must, at least 4 days before the oral hearing, set out in a brief written statement (i) the points the appellant proposes to raise at the hearing (ii) the reasons why permission to appeal should be granted and (iii) in the case of a publicly funded litigant confirm that a copy of the reasons given by the appeal court for refusing permission to appeal was sent to the relevant office of the Legal Aid Agency (which replaced the Legal Services Commission on 1 April 2013) (FPR PD30A, paras 4.14 and 4.17). The respondent should not attend the oral hearing unless requested to do so by the appeal court (FPR PD30A, para 4.15).

Transcripts of the hearing or of the evidence—See notes to CPR 1998, r 52.3.

Limited permission—Where a court gives permission to appeal on some issues only it will either (i) refuse permission on remaining issues or (ii) reserve the question of permission on those remaining issues to the court hearing the appeal. If the court reserves the question of permission on the remaining issues, the appellant must within 14 days after service of the court's order notify the court and the respondent in writing whether the appellant intends to pursue the reserved issues. If the appellant intends to pursue the same, the parties must include in the time estimate for the appeal hearing their time estimate for the reserved issues (FPR PD30A, paras 4.18 and 4.19).

Once permission is granted—The appeal bundle must be served on each respondent within 7 days of receiving the order giving permission to appeal (FPR PD30A, para 6.2). Where the appeal court grants permission the appellant must add specified documents to the appeal bundle, namely (i) the respondent's notice and skeleton argument (if any), (ii) those parts of transcripts of evidence which are directly relevant to the appeal, (iii) the order granting permission to appeal and (iv) any other document which the parties have agreed should be added to the appeal bundle (FPR PD30A, para 6.4) The advocate for an appellant must give a time estimate for the hearing of the appeal: a respondent must notify the court within 7 days whether he disagrees with the appellant's time estimate (FPR PD30A, paras 6.6–6.8).

Case management appeals and appeals against discretionary decisions—See *President's Bulletin No 2* (December 2010) in Part V and *Re W (Relocation: Removal Outside Jurisdiction)* [2011] 2 FLR 409 at [7]–[12].

Procedure for listing applications for permission to appeal—Practice guidance was given on the proper procedure for listing applications for permission to appeal to the High Court. It is akin to the procedure followed in the Court of Appeal: *O v O (Procedure for Listing Applications for Permission to Appeal to the High Court)* [2011] EWHC 14 July 2011 (unreported).

Real prospect of success—There are two conflicting authorities on the meaning of a "real prospect of success". In *NLW v ARC* [2012] 2 FLR 129, Mostyn J held that "real prospect of success" meant it was more likely than not that the appeal would be allowed at the substantive hearing "anything less than a 50/50 threshold could only mean there was a real prospect of failure". Moor J, however, has held that a

PART III

"real prospect of success" is one that is realistic rather than fanciful and does not mean a greater than 50/50 chance of success. He commented that a practice direction was required to clarify the procedure for applications for permission to appeal: *AV v RM (Appeal)* [2012] 2 FLR 709.

Respondent's attendance at permission hearing (r 30.3(5))—Rule 30.3(5) permits reconsideration of a paper refusal of permission by the court. The respondent is permitted to attend, but FPR PD30A, paras 4.15, 4.22 and 4.23 in effect discourage such attendance. In *Livock v Livock* [2012] 1 FLR 776, Coleridge J was critical of the lack of notice given to the wife respondent of the permission application and that she had not been able to respond to any fresh evidence application (per *Ladd v Marshall* (1954) FLR Rep 422).

Appeals against decisions under rr 31.10, 31.11 and 31.14—Note that special provisions apply to appeals against certain FPR 2010, Pt 31 decisions. The provisions set out in FPR 2010, rr 30.3, 30.7, 30.8, 30.10 and 30.12 do not apply to these appeals. The time for filing an appellant's notice of appeal and provisions for extending or shortening time for compliance are set out in FPR 2010, r 31.15 (FPR PD30A, paras 10.1–10.5).

Appeals from district judge—The Court of Appeal determined in *Cordle v Cordle* [2002] 1 FLR 207 that in the light of AJA 1999, s 55 appeals from district judges should henceforth only be allowed if it were demonstrated that there was procedural irregularity, or that in conducting the necessary balancing exercise, the district judge took into account matters that were irrelevant, or ignored matters that were relevant, or had otherwise arrived at a decision that was plainly wrong. These factors are reflected in r 30.3(7) "real prospect of success or … some other compelling reason why the appeal should be heard", which is the necessary filter for permission to appeal. See *DE v AB (Financial Provision for Child)* [2012] 2 FLR 1396.

30.4 Appellant's notice

(1) Where the appellant seeks permission from the appeal court it must be requested in the appellant's notice.

(2) Subject to paragraph (3), the appellant must file the appellant's notice at the appeal court within –

(a)   such period as may be directed by the lower court (which may be longer or shorter than the period referred to in sub-paragraph (b)); or

(b)   where the court makes no such direction, 21 days after the date of the decision of the lower court against which the appellant wishes to appeal.

(3) Where the appeal is against an order under section 38(1) of the 1989 Act, the appellant must file the appellant's notice within 7 days beginning with the date of the decision of the lower court.

(4) Unless the appeal court orders otherwise, an appellant's notice must be served on each respondent and the persons referred to in paragraph (5) –

(a)   as soon as practicable; and

(b)   in any event not later than 7 days,

after it is filed.

(5) The persons referred to in paragraph (4) are –

(a)   any children's guardian, welfare officer, or children and family reporter;

(b)   a local authority who has prepared a report under section 14A(8) or (9) of the 1989 Act;

(c)   an adoption agency or local authority which has prepared a report on the suitability of the applicant to adopt a child;

(d)   a local authority which has prepared a report on the placement of the child for adoption; and

(e)   where the appeal is from a magistrates' court, the court officer.

MCA 1980, s 111A appeal—The time for filing and service of the notice of appeal pursuant to s 111A is fixed at 21 days and may not be extended under FPR 2010, r 4.1(3)(a) or varied under r 30.4(2).

HRA 1998—Where an appellant seeks for the first time to rely on an issue under HRA 1998 or a remedy available under that Act he must include in the appeal notice the information required by FPR 2010, r 29.5(2) and FPR PD29A (Human Rights, Joining the Crown) will apply as if references to the directions hearing were to the application for permission to appeal (FPR PD30A, paras 5.2 and 5.3).

Incidental applications—Notice to the appeal court of an incidental application may be included in the notice of appeal or in a Pt 18 (Procedure for Other Applications in Proceedings) application notice (FPR PD30A, para 5.7).

Documents—FPR PD30A, para 5.8 sets out the documents which must be filed with the appellant's notice and para 5.9 sets out the documents which must be included in the appeal bundle (see Procedural Guide E2). All extraneous documents must be excluded and only material which is directly relevant to the subject matter of the appeal should be included in the bundle (FPR PD30A, para 5.10). The appeal bundle must contain a certificate signed by the party's counsel, solicitor or representative that the appellant has read and understood para 5.10 and the appeal bundle filed complies with it. Where it is not possible to file any of the required documents, the appellant must indicate the same, provide an estimate of when the same can be filed and then file as soon as practicable (FPR PD30A, paras 5.11 and 5.12).

Skeleton arguments—The skeleton argument may be included in the appellant's notice or filed and served with the notice. Where it is impracticable to do so, the skeleton argument must be filed and served within 14 days of the filing of the notice. A skeleton argument must contain "a numbered list of the points which the party wishes to make. These should both define and confine the areas of controversy. Each point should be stated as concisely as the nature of the case allows". The skeleton argument must set out, in respect of each authority cited, the proposition of law that it demonstrates and identify the relevant page or paragraph. Where more than one authority is cited in support of a proposition, brief reasons must be given for doing so (FPR PD30A, paras 5.13–5.22, 7.7–7.12 and 7.14–7.15).

Citation of authorities—On 24 March 2012, the Lord Chief Justice issued a new practice direction: *Citation of Authorities* (see Part V). For a summary of the new requirements, see the notes to Procedural Guide E5.

Transcripts—If an approved transcript of the judgment is not available, the following documents are acceptable: (i) a written copy of the judgment endorsed with the judge's signature; (ii) in the magistrates' court, a copy of the written reasons; (iii) an agreed note of the judgment submitted to the judge for approval or, if no agreement, copies of the rival versions should be submitted to the judge with an explanatory letter; and (iv) an advocates' note of the judgment where the appellant is unrepresented (FPR PD30A, paras 5.23 and 5.24).

30.5 Respondent's notice

(1) A respondent may file and serve a respondent's notice.

(2) A respondent who –

    (a)   is seeking permission to appeal from the appeal court; or

    (b)   wishes to ask the appeal court to uphold the order of the lower court for reasons different from or additional to those given by the lower court,

must file a respondent's notice.

(3) Where the respondent seeks permission from the appeal court it must be requested in the respondent's notice.

(4) A respondent's notice must be filed within –

    (a)   such period as may be directed by the lower court; or

    (b)   where the court makes no such direction, 14 days beginning with the date referred to in paragraph (5).

(5) The date referred to in paragraph (4) is –

    (a)   the date on which the respondent is served with the appellant's notice where –
        permission to appeal was given by the lower court; or
        permission to appeal is not required;

    (b)   the date on which the respondent is served with notification that the appeal court has given the appellant permission to appeal; or

(c) the date on which the respondent is served with notification that the application for permission to appeal and the appeal itself are to be heard together.

(6) Unless the appeal court orders otherwise, a respondent's notice must be served on the appellant, any other respondent and the persons referred to in rule 30.4(5) –

(a) as soon as practicable; and

(b) in any event not later than 7 days,

after it is filed.

(7) Where there is an appeal against an order under section 38(1) of the 1989 Act –

(a) a respondent may not, in that appeal, bring an appeal from the order or ask the appeal court to uphold the order of the lower court for reasons different from or additional to those given by the lower court; and

(b) paragraphs (2) and (3) do not apply.

Respondent's notice—A respondent who wishes to ask the appeal court to vary in any way the order of the lower court must appeal and obtain permission to appeal (if required, see FPR 2010, r 30.3(1),(2) above) on the same basis as for an appellant. A respondent who wishes to appeal or to invite the appeal court to uphold the order of the lower court but for different or additional reasons, must file a respondent's notice: in the absence of which a respondent will not be entitled, without permission of the appeal court, to rely on any reason not relied on by the lower court (FPR PD30A, paras 7.1–7.3).

Skeleton arguments—For the content and form of skeleton arguments see the notes to FPR 2010, r 30.4, above. A party who files a respondent's notice but does not include a skeleton argument must file one within 14 days of filing the notice. A party who does not file a respondent's notice but who proposes to file a skeleton argument must do so at least 7 days before the appeal hearing. The respondent's skeleton argument should, where appropriate, answer the arguments set out in the appellant's skeleton argument (FPR PD30A, para 7.7–7.12).

Documents—Where a respondent considers additional documents should be included in the appeal bundle, the parties should agree amendments to the appeal bundle it possible. If unable to reach agreement, the respondent may prepare a supplemental bundle which bundle, with the requisite number of copies, must be filed at the appeal court: (i) with the respondent's notice; or (ii) within 21 days after being served with the appeal bundle (FPR PD30A, paras 7.16–7.18).

30.6 Grounds of appeal

The appeal notice must state the grounds of appeal.

30.7 Variation of time

(1) An application to vary the time limit for filing an appeal notice must be made to the appeal court.

(2) The parties may not agree to extend any date or time limit set by –

(a) these rules;

(b) Practice Direction 30A; or

(c) an order of the appeal court or the lower court.

(Rule 4.1(3)(a) provides that the court may extend or shorten the time for compliance with a rule, practice direction or court order (even if an application for extension is made after the time for compliance has expired).)

(Rule 4.1(3)(c) provides that the court may adjourn or bring forward a hearing.)

Extension of time—The application for an extension of time for filing the appellant's notice must be made in that notice with reasons for the delay. A respondent has the right to be heard on an application for an extension of time but a party who unreasonably opposes an extension of time is at risk of being ordered to pay the appellant's costs of the application (FPR PD30A, paras 5.4–5.6). An application to extend the time for filing a respondent's notice must be requested in that notice with reasons (FPR PD30A, para 7.6).

30.8 Stay

Unless the appeal court or the lower court orders otherwise, an appeal does not operate as a stay$^{(GL)}$ of any order or decision of the lower court.

Scope—An appeal (meaning an application for permission or following the grant of permission) does not automatically operate to stop the order which is the subject of the appeal taking effect. An application must be made for a stay of the order. A stay should normally be sought at the time of the application for permission to appeal, if not immediately following the decision which is to be appealed.

Imposition of conditions to grant of stay—The Supreme Court has criticised the imposition by the Court of Appeal of conditions to the grant of a stay pending determination of an application for permission to appeal by the Supreme Court. Lord Kerr said: "as a general rule, conditions such as were imposed by the Court of Appeal in this case should not be made where a party seeks permission to appeal, not least because these might be seen as an unwarranted disincentive to the pursuit of what proved in this case to be a fully merited application": *Re B (A Child)* [2010] 1 FLR 551.

30.9 Amendment of appeal notice

An appeal notice may not be amended without the permission of the appeal court.

Amendment—An application to amend should normally be made at the appeal hearing unless that would cause unnecessary expense or delay in which case a request should be made for it to be head in advance (FPR PD30A, para 5.44).

30.10 Striking out appeal notices and setting aside or imposing conditions on permission to appeal

(1) The appeal court may –

   (a) strike out$^{(GL)}$ the whole or part of an appeal notice;

   (b) set aside$^{(GL)}$ permission to appeal in whole or in part;

   (c) impose or vary conditions upon which an appeal may be brought.

(2) The court will only exercise its powers under paragraph (1) where there is a compelling reason for doing so.

(3) Where a party was present at the hearing at which permission was given that party may not subsequently apply for an order that the court exercise its powers under paragraphs (1)(b) or (1)(c).

Compelling reasons—These are required to impose conditions under this rule and under FPR 2010, r 30.3(8). This rule applies where permission to appeal has already been granted on some previous occasion: *Radmacher v Granatino* [2009] 1 FLR 1566.

30.11 Appeal court's powers

(1) In relation to an appeal the appeal court has all the powers of the lower court.

   (Rule 30.1(4) provides that this Part is subject to any enactment that sets out special provisions with regard to any particular category of appeal.)

(2) The appeal court has power to –

   (a) affirm, set aside$^{(GL)}$ or vary any order or judgment made or given by the lower court;

   (b) refer any application or issue for determination by the lower court;

   (c) order a new hearing;

   (d) make orders for the payment of interest;

   (e) make a costs order.

(3) The appeal court may exercise its powers in relation to the whole or part of an order of the lower court.

   (Rule 4.1 contains general rules about the court's case management powers.)

(4) If the appeal court –

   (a) refuses an application for permission to appeal;
   (b) strikes out an appellant's notice; or
   (c) dismisses an appeal,

and it considers that the application, the appellant's notice or the appeal is totally without merit, the provisions of paragraph (5) must be complied with.

(5) Where paragraph (4) applies –

   (a) the court's order must record the fact that it considers the application, the appellant's notice or the appeal to be totally without merit; and
   (b) the court must at the same time consider whether it is appropriate to make a civil restraint order.

"all the powers of the lower court" (r 30.11(1))—This includes the power to re-hear the matter. This is a power seldom used. The appeal is determined in accordance with the principles of *G v G (Minors: Custody Appeal)* [1985] FLR 894. The appeal court does not hear the evidence and does not exercise a discretion afresh but must consider whether the court that heard the evidence erred in principle or was otherwise plainly wrong (see *Re W, Re A, Re B* [1999] 2 FLR 930 and *Re C (Leave to remove from jurisdiction)* [2000] 2 FLR 457). However, where the court allows an appeal it may exercise the judicial discretion afresh rather than remitting the matter to the court below (*Fallon v Fallon* [2010] 1 FLR 910 (20 November)). The Court of Appeal has given guidance on the limited grounds on which the court may grant an application for permission to appeal and to allow an appeal (particularly for the benefit of litigants in person) (*Re W (Permission to Appeal)* [2008] 1 FLR 406).

Chronology—The Court of Appeal has observed that it would be "enormously helpful" if a chronology was provided in all family appeals as they are for most first instance hearings: *Re H (A Child)* [2013] EWCA Civ 72.

Fresh evidence—There is a presumption that the appeal court will determine the appeal on the basis of the evidence that was before the lower court. Fresh evidence will not be admitted without an order to that effect. Fresh evidence may be evidence of events since the decision which was the subject of the appeal or evidence relating to matters before the hearing that is the subject of the appeal but was not available at the hearing in the lower court. There is no specific requirement to be satisfied in respect of an application to admit fresh evidence. The former requirements laid down in *Ladd v Marshall* (1954) FLR Rep 422 are relevant as matters which should be considered in an exercise of the discretion whether to allow an appellant to rely on evidence not before the court below. These factors are:

(a) the evidence could not have been obtained with reasonable diligence at the trial;
(b) the evidence must be such that, if given, it would probably have had an important influence on the result of the case, though it need not be decisive; and
(c) the evidence must be such as would presumably be believed, or in other words, it must be apparently credible though it need not be incontrovertible (see *Hickey v Marks* (2000) 6 July, (unreported), CA and *Gillingham v Gillingham* [2001] EWCA Civ 906). There are dicta to suggest that in any case involving the welfare of a child fresh evidence would be admitted (*M v M (Transfer of Custody: Appeal)* [1987] 2 FLR 146 at [150B]; *Re B (Minors) (Custody)* [1991] 1 FLR 137 at [149B]; but see also *B v P (Access)* [1992] 2 FCR 576).

These conditions do not apply to evidence in relation to matters that have occurred after the trial or where there was no trial on the facts. In such a situation the question of receiving the new evidence is a matter for the discretion of the appeal court. In deciding whether to admit fresh evidence as to events since the date of the trial, the appeal court will consider the matter without the benefit of the fresh evidence and, if the decision was wrong in accordance with the principles of *G v G (Minors: Custody Appeal)* [1985] FLR 894, the court will consider the evidence and consider what weight to attach to it (*M v M (Transfer of Custody: Appeal)* [1987] 2 FLR 146 and *Re G (A Minor) (Wardship: Access)* [1988] 1 FLR 305).

Proportionality—In exceptional but appropriate cases the appeal court may decline to hear an appeal on the basis that further litigation is disproportionate to the costs and/or issues in the case (*Cook v Plummer* [2008] 2 FLR 989 and *HH v BLW (Appeal: Costs: Proportionality)* [2013] 1 FLR 420).

Second appeals—The unlawful removal of a child from his usual place of residence called for a peremptory order to be sought for his return, rather than to seek to challenge the dismissal of an appeal for an interim residence order by way of a second appeal to the Court of Appeal: *Re R (Children)* [2011] 2 FLR 863 and AJA 1999, s 55.

Reopening an appeal—In exceptional circumstances, the High Court may reopen the final determination of an appeal if there is no alternative effective remedy and it would avoid real injustice (FPR 2010, r 30.14) The jurisdiction to reopen an appeal should only be permitted where the process of justice has been corrupted. It is insufficient for these purposes to establish that there is fresh evidence available which might have had a significant impact on the result (*Re U* (*Re-opening of Appeal*) [2005] 2 FLR 444).

Hopeless appeals—Where the appeal court considers the application or appeal is totally without merit, it must record that fact in the court order and consider making a civil restraint order: see CPR 1998, Pt 3.

30.12 Hearing of appeals

(1) Every appeal will be limited to a review of the decision of the lower court unless –

    (a)   an enactment or practice direction makes different provision for a particular category of appeal; or

    (b)   the court considers that in the circumstances of an individual appeal it would be in the interests of justice to hold a re-hearing.

(2) Unless it orders otherwise, the appeal court will not receive –

    (a)   oral evidence; or

    (b)   evidence which was not before the lower court.

(3) The appeal court will allow an appeal where the decision of the lower court was –

    (a)   wrong; or

    (b)   unjust because of a serious procedural or other irregularity in the proceedings in the lower court.

(4) The appeal court may draw any inference of fact which it considers justified on the evidence.

(5) At the hearing of the appeal a party may not rely on a matter not contained in that party's appeal notice unless the appeal court gives permission.

Modifications—Modified for certain proceedings by FPR PD30A, para 9.30.

Separate representation—The Master of the Rolls has emphasised "in the strongest possible terms that it is only where it is clear that there is an unavoidable conflict of interest, as a matter of law, between two parties in the same interest that they should have separate legal representation, especially where public money is involved. The fact that the parties may have different factual points, or that one party's case may be seen as stronger than the other's, or that the parties' legal advisers may see the legal arguments or the prospects somewhat differently, are not good reasons for their incurring the expense and the court time of separate representation": *Oxfordshire County Council v X, Y and J* [2011] 1 FLR 272.

Fresh experts on appeal—The Court of Appeal emphasised that there was an obligation on an applicant seeking permission to appeal, or on an appellant who had obtained permission, to seek the appeal court's leave before instructing a fresh expert and releasing court papers to him: see notes to CPR 1998, r 52.11 (*Re M (A Child)* [2012] 2 FLR 121 and the Family Justice Council Guidelines of December 2011, *Instruction of Medical Experts from Overseas in Family Cases* (see Part V)).

Appeal against findings of fact—For Mostyn J's observations in *NG v SG (Appeal: Non-Disclosure)* [2012] 1 FLR 1211, see the introduction to Guide E5.

Role of appellate court—For further guidance on the approach that an appellate court should adopt to (a) appeals where the adequacy of a trial judge's reasoning is in issue and (b) appeals against the exercise of a discretion by a trial judge, see the notes to CPR 1998, Pt 52.

30.13 Assignment of appeals to the Court of Appeal

(1) Where the court from or to which an appeal is made or from which permission to appeal is sought ("the relevant court") considers that –

    (a)   an appeal which is to be heard by a county court or the High Court would raise an important point of principle or practice; or

    (b)   there is some other compelling reason for the Court of Appeal to hear it,

PART III

the relevant court may order the appeal to be transferred to the Court of Appeal.

(2) This rule does not apply to proceedings in a magistrates' court.

Scope—Where an appeal is to be heard in the county court or the High Court, that court may transfer the appeal to be heard by the Court of Appeal. If that court (the county court or High Court) hears and determines the appeal, there can be an appeal to the Court of Appeal from that decision only if there is some important point of principle or other compelling reason.

30.14 Reopening of final appeals

(1) The High Court will not reopen a final determination of any appeal unless –

- (a) it is necessary to do so in order to avoid real injustice;
- (b) the circumstances are exceptional and make it appropriate to reopen the appeal; and
- (c) there is no alternative effective remedy.

(2) In paragraphs (1), (3), (4) and (6), "appeal" includes an application for permission to appeal.

(3) This rule does not apply to appeals to a county court.

(4) Permission is needed to make an application under this rule to reopen a final determination of an appeal.

(5) There is no right to an oral hearing of an application for permission unless, exceptionally, the judge so directs.

(6) The judge will not grant permission without directing the application to be served on the other party to the original appeal and giving that party an opportunity to make representations.

(7) There is no right of appeal or review from the decision of the judge on the application for permission, which is final.

(8) The procedure for making an application for permission is set out in Practice Direction 30A.

Limitations—The jurisdiction to reopen an appeal should only be permitted where the process of justice has been corrupted. It is insufficient for these purposes to establish that there is fresh evidence available which might have had a significant impact on the result (*Re U (Re-opening of Appeal)* [2005] 2 FLR 444).

County courts—A county court does not have jurisdiction to reopen a final appeal (r 30.14(3)).

Procedure—The term "appeal" includes an application for permission to appeal. The application for permission must be sought from the court whose decision the applicant wishes to re-open and must be made by application notice and supported by written evidence verified by a statement of truth. The application must not be served on any other party to the original appeal unless the courts so directs. Where such a direction is given that party may file within 14 days a written statement supporting or opposing the application. The application for permission will be considered by a single judge on paper and will only be allowed to proceed if the judge so directs (FPR PD30A, paras 18.1–18.7).

Practice Direction 30A – Appeals

This Practice Direction supplements FPR Part 30

"Child Maintenance and Enforcement Commission" and "Commission"—By virtue of SI 2012/2007, art 5(3), these should be read as "Secretary of State" throughout FPR PD30A (except where explicitly referring to the Legal Aid Agency, which replaced the Legal Services Commission on 1 April 2013).

1.1 This practice direction applies to all appeals to which Part 30 applies.

Routes of appeal

2.1 The following table sets out to which court or judge an appeal is to be made (subject to obtaining any necessary permission) –

Decision of:	Appeal made to:
Magistrates' Court	Circuit judge
District judge of a county court	Circuit judge
District judge of the High Court	High Court judge
District judge of the principal registry of the Family Division	High Court judge
Costs judge	High Court Judge
Circuit judge or recorder	Court of Appeal
High Court judge	Court of Appeal

(Provisions setting out routes of appeal include section 16(1) of the Senior Courts Act 1981 (as amended); section 77(1) of the County Courts Act 1984 (as amended) and the Access to Justice Act 1999 (Destination of Appeals) (Family Proceedings) Order 2009 (see paragraphs 9.1 to 9.12 below. The Family Proceedings (Allocation to Judiciary) (Appeals) Directions 2009 provide for an appeal from a magistrates' court to be heard by a Circuit judge.

The routes of appeal from an order or decision relating to contempt of court of a magistrates' court under section 63(3) of the Magistrates' Courts Act 1980 and of a county court and the High Court are set out in section 13(2) of the Administration of Justice Act 1960. Appeals under section 8(1) of the Gender Recognition Act 2004 lie to the High Court (see section 8 of the 2004 Act). The procedure for appeals to the Court of Appeal is governed by the Civil Procedure Rules 1998, in particular CPR Part 52.).

2.2 Where the decision to be appealed is a decision in a Part 19 (Alternative Procedure For Applications) application on a point of law in a case which did not involve any substantial dispute of fact, the court to which the appeal lies, where that court is the High Court or a county court and unless the appeal would lie to the Court of Appeal in any event, must consider whether to order the appeal to be transferred to the Court of Appeal under rule 30.13 (Assignment of Appeals to the Court of Appeal).

Grounds for appeal

3.1 Rule 30.12 (hearing of appeals) sets out the circumstances in which the appeal court will allow an appeal.

3.2 The grounds of appeal should –

(a) set out clearly the reasons why rule 30.12(3)(a) or (b) is said to apply; and
(b) specify in respect of each ground, whether the ground raises an appeal on a point of law or is an appeal against a finding of fact.

Permission to appeal

4.1 Rule 30.3 (Permission) sets out the circumstances when permission to appeal is required. At present permission to appeal is required where the decision appealed against was made by a district judge or a costs judge. However, no permission is required where rule 30.3(2) (appeals against a committal order or a secure accommodation order under section 25 of the Children Act 1989) applies.

> (The requirement of permission to appeal may be imposed by a practice direction – see rule 30.3(1)(b) (Permission).)

Court to which permission to appeal application should be made

4.2 An application for permission should be made orally at the hearing at which the decision to be appealed against is made.

4.3 Where –

(a)   no application for permission to appeal is made at the hearing; or
(b)   the lower court refuses permission to appeal,

an application for permission to appeal may be made to the appeal court in accordance with rules 30.3(3) and (4) (Permission).

> (Rule 30.1(3) defines 'lower court'.)

4.4 Where no application for permission to appeal has been made in accordance with rule 30.3(3)(a) (Permission) but a party requests further time to make such an application the court may adjourn the hearing to give that party an opportunity to do so.

4.5 There is no appeal from a decision of the appeal court to allow or refuse permission to appeal to that court (although where the appeal court, without a hearing, refuses permission to appeal, the person seeking permission may request that decision to be reconsidered at a hearing- see section 54(4) of the Access to Justice Act 1999 and rule 30.3(5) (Permission)).

Material omission from a judgment of the lower court

4.6 Where a party's advocate considers that there is a material omission from a judgment of the lower court or, in a magistrates' court, the written reasons for the decision of the lower court (including inadequate reasons for the lower court's decision), the advocate should before the drawing of the order give the lower court which made the decision the opportunity of considering whether there is an omission and should not immediately use the omission as grounds for an application to appeal.

4.7 Paragraph 4.8 below applies where there is an application to the lower court for permission to appeal on the grounds of a material omission from a judgment of the lower court. Paragraph 4.9 below applies where there is an application for permission to appeal to the appeal court on the grounds of a material omission from a judgment of the lower court. Paragraphs 4.8 and 4.9 do not apply where the lower court is a magistrates' court.

4.8 Where the application for permission to appeal is made to the lower court, the court which made the decision must –

(a)   consider whether there is a material omission and adjourn for that purpose if necessary; and
(b)   where the conclusion is that there has been such an omission, provide additions to the judgment.

4.9 Where the application for permission to appeal is made to the appeal court, the appeal court –

(a)   must consider whether there is a material omission; and

(b)   where the conclusion is that there has been such an omission, may adjourn the application and remit the case to the lower court with an invitation to provide additions to the judgment.

Consideration of Permission without a hearing

4.10 An application for permission to appeal may be considered by the appeal court without a hearing.

4.11 If permission is granted without a hearing the parties will be notified of that decision and the procedure in paragraphs 6.1 to 6.8 will then apply.

4.12 If permission is refused without a hearing the parties will be notified of that decision with the reasons for it. The decision is subject to the appellant's right to have it reconsidered at an oral hearing. This may be before the same judge.

4.13 A request for the decision to be reconsidered at an oral hearing must be filed at the appeal court within 7 days after service of the notice that permission has been refused. A copy of the request must be served by the appellant on the respondent at the same time.

Video conferencing—In *Black v Pastouna* [2005] EWCA Civ 1389 at [13]–[15], Brooke LJ issued guidance on the use of video conferencing under Annex 3, which urges parties always to consider when video arrangements might save cost (and see CPR 1998, rr 1.1 and 1.3, and the same rules in FPR 2010). Where cases in the Court of Appeal are likely to last 30 mins or less, the Court will expect the parties or their advisers to consider the use of video conferencing. At [15] Brooke LJ concluded: "If the Court is not satisfied that there are any features of the application which warrant an oral hearing … it may direct that any recoverable costs may be limited to the cost of conducting the hearing by video conference [where] less than the cost of attending court and any associated travel expenses."

Permission hearing

4.14 Where an appellant, who is represented, makes a request for a decision to be reconsidered at an oral hearing, the appellant's advocate must, at least 4 days before the hearing, in a brief written statement –

(a)   inform the court and the respondent of the points which the appellant proposes to raise at the hearing;

(b)   set out the reasons why permission should be granted notwithstanding the reasons given for the refusal of permission; and

(c)   confirm, where applicable, that the requirements of paragraph 4.17 have been complied with (appellant in receipt of services funded by the Legal Services Commission).

4.15 The respondent will be given notice of a permission hearing, but is not required to attend unless requested by the court to do so.

4.16 If the court requests the respondent's attendance at the permission hearing, the appellant must supply the respondent with a copy of the appeal bundle (see paragraph 5.9) within 7 days of being notified of the request, or such other period as the court may direct. The costs of providing that bundle shall be borne by the appellant initially, but will form part of the costs of the permission application.

Appellants in receipt of services funded by the Legal Services Commission applying for permission to appeal

4.17 Where the appellant is in receipt of services funded by the Legal Services Commission (or legally aided) and permission to appeal has been refused by the appeal court without a hearing, the appellant must send a copy of the reasons the appeal court gave for refusing permission to the relevant office of the Legal Services Commission as soon as it has been received from the court. The court will require confirmation that this has been done if a hearing is requested to re-consider the question of permission.

Limited permission

4.18 Where a court under rule 30.3 (Permission) gives permission to appeal on some issues only, it will –

(a) refuse permission on any remaining issues; or

(b) reserve the question of permission to appeal on any remaining issues to the court hearing the appeal.

4.19 If the court reserves the question of permission under paragraph 4.18(b), the appellant must, within 14 days after service of the court's order, inform the appeal court and the respondent in writing whether the appellant intends to pursue the reserved issues. If the appellant does intend to pursue the reserved issues, the parties must include in any time estimate for the appeal hearing, their time estimate for the reserved issues.

4.20 If the appeal court refuses permission to appeal on the remaining issues without a hearing and the applicant wishes to have that decision reconsidered at an oral hearing, the time limit in rule 30.3(6) (Permission) shall apply. Any application for an extension of this time limit should be made promptly. The court hearing the appeal on the issues for which permission has been granted will not normally grant, at the appeal hearing, an application to extend the time limit in rule 30.3(6) for the remaining issues.

4.21 If the appeal court refuses permission to appeal on remaining issues at or after an oral hearing, the application for permission to appeal on those issues cannot be renewed at the appeal hearing (see section 54(4) of the Access to Justice Act 1999).

Respondents' costs of permission applications

4.22 In most cases, applications for permission to appeal will be determined without the court requesting –

(a) submissions from; or

(b) if there is an oral hearing, attendance by,

the respondent.

4.23 Where the court does not request submissions from or attendance by the respondent, costs will not normally be allowed to a respondent who volunteers submissions or attendance.

4.24 Where the court does request –

(a) submissions from; or

(b) attendance by the respondent,

the court will normally allow the costs of the respondent if permission is refused.

Appellant's notice

5.1 An appellant's notice must be filed and served in all cases. Where an application for permission to appeal is made to the appeal court it must be applied for in the appellant's notice.

Human Rights

5.2 Where the appellant seeks –

(a) to rely on any issue under the Human Rights Act 1998; or

(b)   a remedy available under that Act,

for the first time in an appeal the appellant must include in the appeal notice the information required by rule 29.5(2).

5.3 Practice Direction 29A (Human Rights, Joining the Crown) will apply as if references to the directions hearing were to the application for permission to appeal.

Extension of time for filing appellant's notice

5.4 If an extension of time is required for filing the appellant's notice the application must be made in that notice. The notice should state the reason for the delay and the steps taken prior to the application being made.

5.5 Where the appellant's notice includes an application for an extension of time and permission to appeal has been given or is not required the respondent has the right to be heard on that application and must be served with a copy of the appeal bundle (see paragraph 5.9). However, a respondent who unreasonably opposes an extension of time runs the risk of being ordered to pay the appellant's costs of that application.

5.6 If an extension of time is given following such an application the procedure at paragraphs 6.1 to 6.8 applies.

Applications

5.7 Notice of an application to be made to the appeal court for a remedy incidental to the appeal (e.g. an interim injunction under rule 20.2 (Orders for interim remedies)) may be included in the appeal notice or in a Part 18 (Procedure For Other Applications in Proceedings) application notice.

> (Paragraph 13 of this practice direction contains other provisions relating to applications.).

Documents

5.8 The appellant must file the following documents together with an appeal bundle (see paragraph 5.9) with his or her appellant's notice –

(a)   two additional copies of the appellant's notice for the appeal court;
(b)   one copy of the appellant's notice for each of the respondents;
(c)   one copy of the appellant's skeleton argument for each copy of the appellant's notice that is filed;
(d)   a sealed or stamped copy of the order being appealed or a copy of the notice of the making of an order;
(e)   a copy of any order giving or refusing permission to appeal, together with a copy of the court's reasons for allowing or refusing permission to appeal;
(f)   any witness statements or affidavits in support of any application included in the appellant's notice.

5.9 An appellant must include the following documents in his or her appeal bundle –

(a)   a sealed or stamped copy of the appellant's notice;
(b)   a sealed or stamped copy of the order being appealed, or a copy of the notice of the making of an order;
(c)   a copy of any order giving or refusing permission to appeal, together with a copy of the court's reasons for allowing or refusing permission to appeal;
(d)   any affidavit or witness statement filed in support of any application included in the appellant's notice;

PART III

(e) where the appeal is against a consent order, a statement setting out the change in circumstances since the order was agreed or other circumstances justifying a review or re-hearing;

(f) a copy of the appellant's skeleton argument;

(g) a transcript or note of judgment or, in a magistrates' court, written reasons for the court's decision (see paragraph 5.23), and in cases where permission to appeal was given by the lower court or is not required those parts of any transcript of evidence which are directly relevant to any question at issue on the appeal;

(h) the application form;

(i) any application notice (or case management documentation) relevant to the subject of the appeal;

(j) any other documents which the appellant reasonably considers necessary to enable the appeal court to reach its decision on the hearing of the application or appeal; and

(k) such other documents as the court may direct.

5.10 All documents that are extraneous to the issues to be considered on the application or the appeal must be excluded. The appeal bundle may include affidavits, witness statements, summaries, experts' reports and exhibits but only where these are directly relevant to the subject matter of the appeal.

5.11 Where the appellant is represented, the appeal bundle must contain a certificate signed by the appellant's solicitor, counsel or other representative to the effect that the appellant has read and understood paragraph 5.10 and that the composition of the appeal bundle complies with it.

5.12 Where it is not possible to file all the above documents, the appellant must indicate which documents have not yet been filed and the reasons why they are not currently available. The appellant must then provide a reasonable estimate of when the missing document or documents can be filed and file them as soon as reasonably practicable.

Skeleton arguments

5.13 The appellant's notice must, subject to paragraphs 5.14 and 5.15, be accompanied by a skeleton argument. Alternatively the skeleton argument may be included in the appellant's notice. Where the skeleton argument is so included it will not form part of the notice for the purposes of rule 30.9 (Amendment of appeal notice).

5.14 Where it is impracticable for the appellant's skeleton argument to accompany the appellant's notice it must be filed and served on all respondents within 14 days of filing the notice.

5.15 An appellant who is not represented need not file a skeleton argument but is encouraged to do so since this will be helpful to the court.

5.16 A skeleton argument must contain a numbered list of the points which the party wishes to make. These should both define and confine the areas of controversy. Each point should be stated as concisely as the nature of the case allows.

5.17 A numbered point must be followed by a reference to any document on which the party wishes to rely.

5.18 A skeleton argument must state, in respect of each authority cited –

(a) the proposition of law that the authority demonstrates; and

(b) the parts of the authority (identified by page or paragraph references) that support the proposition.

5.19 If more than one authority is cited in support of a given proposition, the skeleton argument must briefly state the reason for taking that course.

5.20 The statement referred to in paragraph 5.19 should not materially add to the length of the skeleton argument but should be sufficient to demonstrate, in the context of the argument –

(a)   the relevance of the authority or authorities to that argument; and

(b)   that the citation is necessary for a proper presentation of that argument.

5.21 The cost of preparing a skeleton argument which –

(a)   does not comply with the requirements set out in this paragraph; or

(b)   was not filed within the time limits provided by this Practice Direction (or any further time granted by the court),

will not be allowed on assessment except to the extent that the court otherwise directs.

5.22 The appellant should consider what other information the appeal court will need. This may include a list of persons who feature in the case or glossaries of technical terms. A chronology of relevant events will be necessary in most appeals.

Suitable record of the judgment

5.23 Where the judgment to be appealed has been officially recorded by the court, an approved transcript of that record should accompany the appellant's notice. Photocopies will not be accepted for this purpose. However, where there is no officially recorded judgment, the following documents will be acceptable –

Written judgments – Where the judgment was made in writing a copy of that judgment endorsed with the judge's signature.

Written reasons – in a magistrates' court, a copy of the written reasons for the court's decision.

Note of judgment – When judgment was not officially recorded or made in writing a note of the judgment (agreed between the appellant's and respondent's advocates) should be submitted for approval to the judge whose decision is being appealed. If the parties cannot agree on a single note of the judgment, both versions should be provided to that judge with an explanatory letter. For the purpose of an application for permission to appeal the note need not be approved by the respondent or the lower court judge.

Advocates' notes of judgments where the appellant is unrepresented – When the appellant was unrepresented in the lower court it is the duty of any advocate for the respondent to make the advocate's note of judgment promptly available, free of charge to the appellant where there is no officially recorded judgment or if the court so directs. Where the appellant was represented in the lower court it is the duty of the appellant's own former advocate to make that advocate's note available in these circumstances. The appellant should submit the note of judgment to the appeal court.

5.24 An appellant may not be able to obtain an official transcript or other suitable record of the lower court's decision within the time within which the appellant's notice must be filed. In such cases the appellant's notice must still be completed to the best of the appellant's ability on the basis of the documentation available. However it may be amended subsequently with the permission of the appeal court in accordance with rule 30.9 (Amendment of appeal notice).

Advocates' notes of judgments

5.25 Advocates' brief (or, where appropriate, refresher) fee includes –

(a)   remuneration for taking a note of the judgment of the court;

(b)   having the note transcribed accurately;

(c)   attempting to agree the note with the other side if represented;

(d)   submitting the note to the judge for approval where appropriate;

(e)   revising it if so requested by the judge,

(f)   providing any copies required for the appeal court, instructing solicitors and lay client; and

(g)   providing a copy of the note to an unrepresented appellant.

Appeals from decision made by a family proceedings court under Parts 4 and 4A of the Family Law Act 1996

5.26 Where the appeal is brought against the making of a hospital order or a guardianship order under the Mental Health Act 1983, the court officer for the court from which the appeal is brought must send a copy of any written evidence considered by the magistrates under section 37(1)(a) of that Act to the appeal court.

Appeals under section 8(1) of the Gender Recognition Act 2004

5.27 Paragraph 5.28 to 5.30 apply where the appeal is brought under section 8(1) of the Gender Recognition Act 2004 to the High Court on a point of law against a decision by the Gender Recognition Panel to reject the application under sections 1(1), 5(2), 5(A)(2) or 6(1) of the 2004 Act.

5.28 The appeal notice must be –

(a)   filed in the principal registry of the Family Division; and

(b)   served on the Secretary of State and the President of the Gender Recognition Panels.

5.29 The Secretary of State may appear and be heard in the proceedings on the appeal.

5.30 Where the High Court issues a gender recognition certificate under section 8(3)(a) of the Gender Recognition Act 2004, the court officer must send a copy of that certificate to the Secretary of State.

Transcripts or Notes of Evidence

5.31 When the evidence is relevant to the appeal an official transcript of the relevant evidence must be obtained. Transcripts or notes of evidence are generally not needed for the purpose of determining an application for permission to appeal.

Notes of evidence

5.32 If evidence relevant to the appeal was not officially recorded, a typed version of the judge's (including a district judge (magistrates' courts) or justices' clerk's /assistant clerk's notes of evidence must be obtained.

Transcripts at public expense

5.33 Where the lower court or the appeal court is satisfied that –

(a)   an unrepresented appellant; or

(b)   an appellant whose legal representation is provided free of charge to the appellant and not funded by the Community Legal Service, is in such poor financial circumstances that the cost of a transcript would be an excessive burden the court may certify that the cost of obtaining one official transcript should be borne at public expense.

5.34 In the case of a request for an official transcript of evidence or proceedings to be paid for at public expense, the court must also be satisfied that there are reasonable grounds for appeal. Whenever possible a request for a transcript at public expense should be made to the lower court when asking for permission to appeal.

Filing and service of appellant's notice

5.35 Rule 30.4 (Appellant's notice) sets out the procedure and time limits for filing and serving an appellant's notice. Subject to paragraph 5.36, the appellant must file the appellant's notice at the appeal court within such period as may be directed by the lower court, which should not normally exceed 14 days or, where the lower court directs no such period within 21 days of the date of the decision that the appellant wishes to appeal.

5.36 Rule 30.4(3) (Appellant's notice) provides that unless the appeal court orders otherwise, where the appeal is against an order under section 38(1) of the 1989 Act, the appellant must file the appellant's notice within 7 days beginning with the date of the decision of the lower court.

5.37 Where the lower court announces its decision and reserves the reasons for its judgment or order until a later date, it should, in the exercise of powers under rule 30.4(2)(a))(Appellant's notice), fix a period for filing the appellant's notice at the appeal court that takes this into account.

5.38 Except where the appeal court orders otherwise a sealed or stamped copy of the appellant's notice, including any skeleton arguments must be served on all respondents and other persons referred to in rule 30.4(5) (Appellant's notice) in accordance with the timetable prescribed by rule 30.4(4)) (Appellant's notice) except where this requirement is modified by paragraph 5.14 in which case the skeleton argument should be served as soon as it is filed.

5.39 Where the appellant's notice is to be served on a child, then rule 6.33 (supplementary provision relating to service on children) applies and unless the appeal court orders otherwise a sealed or stamped copy of the appellant's notice, including any skeleton arguments must be served on the persons or bodies mentioned in rule 6.33(2). For example, the appeal notice must be served on any children's guardian, welfare officer or children and family reporter who is appointed in the proceedings.

5.40 Unless the court otherwise directs, a respondent need not take any action when served with an appellant's notice until such time as notification is given to the respondent that permission to appeal has been given.

5.41 The court may dispense with the requirement for service of the notice on a respondent.

5.42 Unless the appeal court directs otherwise, the appellant must serve on the respondent the appellant's notice and skeleton argument (but not the appeal bundle),where the appellant is applying for permission to appeal in the appellant's notice.

5.43 Where permission to appeal –

    (a)   has been given by the lower court; or
    (b)   is not required,

the appellant must serve the appeal bundle on the respondent and the persons mentioned in paragraph 5.39 with the appellant's notice.

PART III

Amendment of Appeal Notice

5.44 An appeal notice may be amended with permission. Such an application to amend and any application in opposition will normally be dealt with at the hearing unless that course would cause unnecessary expense or delay in which case a request should be made for the application to amend to be heard in advance.

Procedure after permission is obtained

6.1 This paragraph sets out the procedure where –

(a) permission to appeal is given by the appeal court; or
(b) the appellant's notice is filed in the appeal court and –
  (i) permission was given by the lower court; or
  (ii) permission is not required.

6.2 If the appeal court gives permission to appeal, the appeal bundle must be served on each of the respondents within 7 days of receiving the order giving permission to appeal.

6.3 The appeal court will send the parties –

(a) notification of the date of the hearing or the period of time (the 'listing window') during which the appeal is likely to be heard;
(b) where permission is granted by the appeal court a copy of the order giving permission to appeal; and
(c) any other directions given by the court.

6.4 Where the appeal court grants permission to appeal, the appellant must add the following documents to the appeal bundle –

(a) the respondent's notice and skeleton argument (if any);
(b) those parts of the transcripts of evidence which are directly relevant to any question at issue on the appeal;
(c) the order granting permission to appeal and, where permission to appeal was granted at an oral hearing, the transcript (or note) of any judgment which was given; and
(d) any document which the appellant and respondent have agreed to add to the appeal bundle in accordance with paragraph 7.16.

6.5 Where permission to appeal has been refused on a particular issue, the appellant must remove from the appeal bundle all documents that are relevant only to that issue.

Time estimates

6.6 If the appellant is legally represented, the appeal court must be notified, in writing, of the advocate's time estimate for the hearing of the appeal.

6.7 The time estimate must be that of the advocate who will argue the appeal. It should exclude the time required by the court to give judgment.

6.8 A court officer will notify the respondent of the appellant's time estimate and if the respondent disagrees with the time estimate the respondent must inform the court within 7 days of the notification. In the absence of such notification the respondent will be deemed to have accepted the estimate proposed on behalf of the appellant.

Respondent

7.1 A respondent who wishes to ask the appeal court to vary the order of the lower court in any way must appeal and permission will be required on the same basis as for an appellant.

(Paragraph 3.2 applies to grounds of appeal by a respondent.)

7.2 A respondent who wishes to appeal or who wishes to ask the appeal court to uphold the order of the lower court for reasons different from or additional to those given by the lower court must file a respondent's notice.

7.3 A respondent who does not file a respondent's notice will not be entitled, except with the permission of the court, to rely on any reason not relied on in the lower court. This paragraph and paragraph 7.2 do not apply where the appeal is against an order under section 38(1) of the 1989 Act (see rule 30.5(7) (Respondent's notice)).

7.4 Paragraphs 5.3 (Human Rights and extension for time for filing appellant's notice) and 5.4 to 5.6 (extension of time for filing appellant's notice) of this practice direction also apply to a respondent and a respondent's notice.

Time limits

7.5 The time limits for filing a respondent's notice are set out in rule 30.5(4) and (5) (Respondent's notice).

7.6 Where an extension of time is required the extension must be requested in the respondent's notice and the reasons why the respondent failed to act within the specified time must be included.

7.7 Except where paragraphs 7.8 and 7.10 apply, the respondent must file a skeleton argument for the court in all cases where the respondent proposes to address arguments to the court. The respondent's skeleton argument may be included within a respondent's notice. Where a skeleton argument is included within a respondent's notice it will not form part of the notice for the purposes of rule 30.9 (Amendment of appeal notice).

7.8 A respondent who –

    (a)   files a respondent's notice; but
    (b)   does not include a skeleton argument with that notice,

must file the skeleton argument within 14 days of filing the notice.

7.9 A respondent who does not file a respondent's notice but who files a skeleton argument must file that skeleton argument at least 7 days before the appeal hearing.

    (Rule 30.5(4) (Respondent's notice) sets out the period for filing a respondent's notice.)

7.10 A respondent who is not represented need not file a skeleton argument but is encouraged to do so in order to assist the court.

7.11 The respondent must serve the skeleton argument on –

    (a)   the appellant; and
    (b)   any other respondent;

at the same time as the skeleton argument is filed at court. Where a child is an appellant or respondent the skeleton argument must also be served on the persons listed in rule 6.33(2) unless the court directs otherwise.

7.12 A respondent's skeleton argument must conform to the directions at paragraphs 5.16 to 5.22 with any necessary modifications. It should, where appropriate, answer the arguments set out in the appellant's skeleton argument.

Applications within respondent's notices

7.13 A respondent may include an application within a respondent's notice in accordance with paragraph 5.7.

Filing respondent's notices and skeleton arguments

7.14 The respondent must file the following documents with the respondent's notice in every case –

    (a)   two additional copies of the respondent's notice for the appeal court; and

    (b)   one copy each for the appellant, any other respondents and any persons referred to in paragraph 5.39.

7.15 The respondent may file a skeleton argument with the respondent's notice and –

    (a)   where doing so must file two copies; and

    (b)   where not doing so must comply with paragraph 7.8.

7.16 If the respondent considers documents in addition to those filed by the appellant to be necessary to enable the appeal court to reach its decision on the appeal and wishes to rely on those documents, any amendments to the appeal bundle should be agreed with the appellant if possible.

7.17 If the representatives for the parties are unable to reach agreement, the respondent may prepare a supplemental bundle.

7.18 The respondent must file any supplemental bundle so prepared, together with the requisite number of copies for the appeal court, at the appeal court –

    (a)   with the respondent's notice; or

    (b)   if a respondent's notice is not filed, within 21 days after the respondent is served with the appeal bundle.

7.19 The respondent must serve –

    (a)   the respondent's notice;

    (b)   the skeleton argument (if any); and

    (c)   the supplemental bundle (if any),

      on

      (i)   the appellant; and

      (ii)   any other respondent;

at the same time as those documents are filed at the court. Where a child is an appellant or respondent the documents referred to in paragraphs (a) to (c) above must also be served on the persons listed in rule 6.33(2) unless the court directs otherwise.

Appeals to the High Court

Application

8.1 The appellant's notice must be filed in –

    (a)   the principal registry of the Family Division; or

    (b)   the district registry which is nearest to the court from which the appeal lies.

8.2 A respondent's notice must be filed at the court where the appellant's notice was filed.

8.3 In the case of appeals from district judges of the High Court, applications for permission and any other applications in the appeal, appeals may be heard and directions in the appeal may be given by a High Court Judge or by any person authorised under section 9 of the Senior Courts Act 1981 to act as a judge of the High Court.

Appeals to a county court

Appeals to a judge of a county court from a district judge

9.1 The Designated Family Judge in consultation with the Family Division Liaison Judges has responsibility for the allocation of appeals from decisions of district judges to circuit judges.

Appeals to a county court from a magistrates' court

Appeals under section 111A of the Magistrates' Courts Act 1980 ("the 1980 Act") from a magistrates' court to a county court on the ground that the decision is wrong in law or in excess of jurisdiction

9.2 As a result of an amendment to section 111 of the 1980 Act by the Access to Justice Act 1999 (Destination of Appeals) (Family Proceedings) Order 2009 ("the Destination Order") an application to have a case stated for the opinion of the High Court under section 111 of that Act may not be made in relation to family proceedings. Family proceedings for those purposes are defined as –

    (a)   proceedings which, by virtue of section 65 of the 1980 Act, are or may be treated as family proceedings for the purposes of that Act; and

    (b)   proceedings under the Child Support Act 1991.

9.3 Section 111A of the 1980 Act, which is inserted by article 4(3) of the Destination Order, provides that in family proceedings as defined in paragraph 9.2 above a person may appeal to a county court on the ground that a decision is wrong in law or is in excess of jurisdiction; this appeal to a county court replaces the procedure for making an application to have a case stated. Section 111A(3)(a) provides that no appeal may be brought under section 111A if there is a right of appeal to a county court against the decision otherwise than under that section.

9.4 Subject to section 111A of the 1980 Act and any other enactment, the following rules in Part 30 apply to appeals under section 111A of the 1980 Act –

    (a)   30.1 (scope and interpretation);

    (b)   30.2 (parties to comply with the practice direction);

    (c)   30.4 (appellant's notice);

    (d)   30.6 (grounds of appeal);

    (e)   30.8 (stay); and

    (f)   30.9 (amendment of appeal notice).

9.5 Section 111A(4) of the 1980 Act provides that the notice of appeal must be filed within 21 days after the day on which the decision of the magistrates' court was given. The notice of appeal should also be served within this period of time. The time period for filing the appellant's notice in rule 30.4(2) does not apply. There can be no extension of this 21 day time limit under rule 4.1(3)(a).

Other statutory rights of appeal from a magistrates' court and the court at which the appellant's notice is to be filed-provisions applying to those appeals and appeals under section 111A of the 1980 Act

9.6 The effect of the Destination Order is that appeals against decisions of magistrates' courts in family proceedings shall lie to a county court instead of to the High Court. In addition to replacing appeals by way of case stated by amending the 1980 Act as outlined above, the Destination Order amends the statutory provisions listed in paragraph 9.7 below to provide for the appeals under those provisions to lie to a county court instead of to the High Court Paragraph 9.7 also refers to the amendment to the 1980 Act for completeness.

9.7 Paragraph 9.8 and 9.9 below apply to appeals under –

(a)   section 4(7) of the Maintenance Orders Act 1958;
(b)   section 29 of the Domestic Proceedings and Magistrates' Courts Act 1978;
(c)   section 60(5) of the Family Law 1986;
(d)   section 94(1) to (9) of the Children Act 1989;
(e)   section 61 of the Family Law Act 1996;
(f)   sections 10(1)(a) to (3) and 13 (1) and (2) of the Crime and Disorder Act 1998; or
(g)   section 111A of the 1980 Act.

9.8 Subject to any enactment or to any directions made by the President of the Family Division in exercise of the powers conferred on him under section 9 of the Courts and Legal Services Act 1990, a district judge may –

(a)   dismiss an appeal;
    (i)   for want of prosecution; or
    (ii)   with the consent of the parties; or
(b)   give leave for the appeal to be withdrawn,
and may deal with any question of costs arising out of the dismissal or withdrawal.
Unless the court directs otherwise, any interlocutory application in an appeal under the statutory provisions listed in paragraph 9.7 may be made to a district judge.

9.9 Subject to paragraph 9.10 below, the appellant's notice and other documents required to be filed by rule 30.4 and this practice direction shall where the appeal is against the making by a magistrates' court of any order or any refusal by a magistrates' court to make such an order –

(a)   in proceedings listed in Schedule 1 to this Practice Direction, be filed in a care centre within the meaning of article 2(b) of the Allocation and Transfer of Proceedings Order 2008;
(b)   in proceedings under the Adoption and Children Act 2002, be filed in an adoption centre or an intercountry adoption centre within the meaning of article 2(c) and (d) of the Allocation and Transfer of Proceedings Order 2008; and
(c)   in any other case, be filed in a family hearing centre within the meaning of article 2(a) of that Order.

9.10 Where the appeal is an appeal from a decision of a magistrates' court under section 94 of the 1989 Act or section 61 of the Family Law Act 1996, the documents required to be filed by rule 30.4 and this practice direction may be filed in the principal registry of the Family Division of the High Court.

9.11 Article 11 of the Destination Order amends article 3 of the Allocation and Transfer of Proceedings Order 2008 to provide that the principal registry of the Family Division of the High Court is treated as a county court for the purposes of appeals from decisions of a magistrates' court under section 94 of the Children Act 1989 and section 61 of the Family Law Act 1996.

9.12 This practice direction applies to appeals under the statutory provisions listed in paragraph 9.7 with the following modifications and any other necessary modifications –

(a)   after paragraph 5.6 insert –
"5.6A Paragraphs 5.4 to 5.6 do not apply to an appeal to a county court under section 111A of the Magistrates' Courts Act 1980."
(b)   in paragraph 5.35, insert "and 5.36A" after " subject to paragraph 5.36";

(c) after paragraph 5.36 insert –

"5.36A Where the appeal is to a judge of a county court under section 111A of the Magistrates' Courts Act 1980, the appellant's notice must be filed and served within 21 days after the day on which the decision of the lower court was given.".

Appeals to a county court from the Child Maintenance and Enforcement Commission ("the Commission"): Deduction order appeals

9.13 A "deduction order appeal" is an appeal under regulation 25AB(1)(a) to (d) of the Child Support (Collection and Enforcement) Regulations 1992 (S.I. 1992/1989)("the Collection and Enforcement Regulations"). A deduction order appeal is an appeal against –

(a) the making of a regular deduction order under section 32A of the Child Support Act 1991 ("the 1991 Act");

(b) a decision on an application to review a regular deduction order;

(c) a decision to withhold consent to the disapplication of sections 32G(1) and 32H(2)(b) of the 1991 Act which has the effect of unfreezing funds in the liable person's account; or

(d) the making of a final lump sum deduction order under section 32F of the 1991 Act.

A deduction order appeal lies to a county court from the Commission as a result of regulation 25AB(1) of the Collection and Enforcement Regulations.

9.14 The rules in Part 30 apply to deduction order appeals with the amendments set out in paragraphs 9.15 to 9.27 and 9.29 and 9.30 below. The rules in Part 30 also apply to appeals against the decision of a district judge in proceedings relating to a deduction order appeal with the amendments set out in paragraph 9.28 below.

9.15 "The respondent" means –

(a) the Commission and any person other than the appellant who was served with an order under section 32A(1), 32E(1) or 32F(1) of the 1991 Act; and

(b) a person who is permitted by the appeal court to be a party to the appeal.

9.16 The appellant will serve the appellant's notice on the Commission and any other respondent.

9.17 The appellant shall file and serve the appellant's notice, within 21 days of –

(a) where the appellant is a deposit-taker, service of the order;

(b) where the appellant is a liable person, receipt of the order; or

(c) where the appellant is either a deposit-taker or a liable person, the date of receipt of notification of the decision.

9.18 For the purposes of paragraph 9.17 –

(a) references to "liable person" and "deposit-taker" are to be interpreted in accordance with section 32E of the 1991 Act and regulation 25A(2) of the Collection and Enforcement Regulations and section 54 of the 1991 Act, respectively; and

(b) the liable person is to be treated as having received the order or notification of the decision 2 days after it was posted by the Commission.

9.19 Rule 4.1(3)(a) (court's power to extend or shorten the time for compliance with a rule, practice direction or court order) does not apply to an appeal against the making of a lump sum deduction order under section 32F of the 1991 Act in so far as that rule gives the court power to extend the time set out in paragraph 9.17 for filing and serving an appellant's notice after the time for filing and serving the that notice set out in paragraph 9.17 has expired.

9.20 The Commission shall provide to the court and serve on all other parties to the appeal any information and evidence relevant to the making of the decision or order being appealed, within 14 days of receipt of the appellant's notice.

9.21 Subject to paragraph 9.23, a respondent who wishes to ask the appeal court to uphold the order or decision of the Commission for reasons different from or in additional to those given by the Commission must file a respondent's notice.

9.22 A respondent's notice must be filed within 14 days of receipt of the appellant's notice.

9.23 Where the Commission as a respondent, wishes to contend that its order or decision should be –

- (a) varied, either in any event or in the event of the appeal being allowed in whole or in part; or
- (b) affirmed on different grounds from those on which it relied when making the order or decision,

it shall, within 14 days of receipt of the appellant's notice, file and serve on all other parties to the appeal a respondent's notice.

9.24 In so far as rule 30.7 (Variation of time) may permit any application for variation of the time limit for filing an appellant's notice after the time for filing the appellant's notice has expired, that rule shall not apply to an appeal made against an order under section 32F(1) of the Act of 1991.

9.25 Rule 30.8 (stay) shall not apply to an appeal made against an order under section 32F(1) of the Act of 1991.

9.26 A district judge may hear a deduction order appeal.

9.27 Rule 30.11 (appeal court's powers) does not apply to deduction order appeals.

9.28 Rule 30.11(2)(d) (making orders for payment of interest) does not apply in the case of an appeal against a decision of a district judge in proceedings relating to a deduction order appeal.

9.29 In the case of a deduction order appeal –

- (a) the appeal court has power to –
  - (i) affirm or set aside the order or decision;
  - (ii) remit the matter to the Commission for the order or decision to be reconsidered, with appropriate directions;
  - (iii) refer any application or issue for determination by the Commission;
  - (iv) make a costs order; and
- (b) the appeal court may exercise its powers in relation to the whole or part of an order or decision of the Commission.

9.30 In rule 30.12 (Hearing of appeals) –

- (a) at the beginning of paragraph (1), for "Every" substitute "Subject to paragraph (2A), every";
- (b) at the beginning of paragraph (2), for "Unless" substitute "Subject to paragraph (2A), unless";
- (c) after paragraph (2), insert –
  "(2A) In the case of a deduction order appeal, the appeal will be a re-hearing, unless the appeal court orders otherwise.";
- (d) in paragraph (3), after "lower court" insert "or, in a deduction order appeal, the order or decision of the Commission"; and

   (e)   for sub-paragraph (b) of paragraph (3), substitute –
       "(b) unjust because of a serious procedural or other irregularity in –
       (i)   the proceedings in the lower court; or
       (ii)   the making of an order or decision by the Commission."

Information about the Commission's decision

9.31 In relation to the deduction order appeals listed in column 1 of the table in Schedule 2 to this Practice Direction –

   (a)   the documents to be filed and served by the appellant include the documents set out in Column 3; and

   (b)   the relevant information to be provided by the Commission in accordance with paragraph 9.20 above includes the information set out in Column 4.

The court at which the appeal notice is to be filed

9.32 In relation to a deduction order appeal, the appellant's notice and other documents required to be filed with that notice shall be filed in a county court (the Collection and Enforcement Regulations 25AB(1)).

The Commission's address for service

9.33 For the purposes of a deduction order appeal the Commission's address for service is –

       Commission Legal Adviser
       Deduction Order Team
       Legal Enforcement (Civil)
       Antonine House
       Callendar Road
       Falkirk
       FK1 1XT

All notices or other documents for CMEC relating to a deduction order appeal should be sent to the above address.

9.34 This practice direction applies to deduction order appeals and appeals against the decision of a district judge in proceedings relating to a deduction order appeal with the following modifications and any other necessary modifications-

   (a)   in paragraph 5.35, insert "and 5.36B" after " subject to paragraph 5.36A";
   (b)   after paragraph 5.36A insert –

"5.36A Where the appeal is a deduction order appeal, the appellant's notice must be filed and served within 21 days of –

   (a)   where the appellant is a deposit-taker, service of the order;
   (b)   where the appellant is a liable person, receipt of the order; or
   (c)   where the appellant is either a deposit-taker or a liable person, the date of receipt of notification of the decision the lower court was given.".

Appeal against the court's decision under rules 31.10, 31.11 or 31.14

10.1 The rules in Part 30 apply to appeals against the court's decision under rules 31.10, 31.11 or 31.14 with the amendments set out in paragraphs 10.2 to 10.5 below. Rules 31.15 and 31.16 apply to these appeals. These modifications do not apply to appeals against the decision made on appeal under rule 31.15.

PART III

10.2 Rule 30.3 (permission to appeal) does not apply.

10.3 The time for filing an appellant's notice at the appeal court in rule 30.4(2) does not apply. Rule 31.15 sets out the time within which an appeal against the court's decision under rules 31.10, 31.11 or 31.14 must be made to a judge of the High Court.

10.4 Rule 4.1(3)(a) (court's power to extend or shorten the time for compliance with a rule, practice direction or court order) does not apply to an appeal against the court's decision under rules 31.10, 31.11 or 31.14 in so far as that rule gives the court power to extend the time set out in rules 31.15 for filing an appellant's notice.

10.5 Rules 30.7 (variation), 30.8 (stay of proceedings), 30.10 (striking out appeal notices, setting aside or imposing conditions on permission to appeal) and 30.12 (hearing of appeals) do not apply.

Appeals against pension orders and pension compensation sharing orders

11.1 Paragraph 11.2 below applies to appeals against –

(a) a pension sharing order under section 24B of the Matrimonial Causes Act 1973 or the variation of such an order under section 31 of that Act;

(b) a pension sharing order under Part 4 of Schedule 5 to the Civil Partnership Act 2004 or the variation of such an order under Part 11 of Schedule 5 to that Act;

(c) a pension compensation sharing order under section 24E of the Matrimonial Causes Act 1973 or a variation of such an order under section 31 of that Act; and

(d) a pension compensation sharing order under Part 4 of Schedule 5 to the Civil Partnership Act 2004 or a variation of such an order under Part 11 of Schedule 5 to that Act.

11.2 Rule 4.1(3)(a) (court's power to extend or shorten the time for compliance with a rule, practice direction or court order) does not apply to an appeal against the making of the orders referred to in paragraph 11.1 above in so far as that rule gives the court power to extend the time set out in rule 30.4 for filing and serving an appellant's notice after the time for filing and serving that notice has expired.

11.3 In so far as rule 30.7 (Variation of time) may permit any application for variation of the time limit for filing an appellant's notice after the time for filing the appellant's notice has expired, that rule shall not apply to an appeal made against the orders referred to in paragraph 11.1 above.

Appeals to a court under section 20 of the 1991 Act (appeals in respect of parentage determinations)

12.1 The rules in Chapters 1 and 5 of Part 8 will apply as appropriate to an appeal under section 20(1) of the 1991 Act where that appeal must be made to a court in accordance with the Child Support Appeals (Jurisdiction of Courts) Order 2002.

12.2 The respondent to such an appeal will be the Child Maintenance and Enforcement Commission.

12.3 Where the justices' clerk or the court is considering whether or not to transfer appeal proceedings under section 20(1) of the 1991 Act, rules 12.9 to 12.11 will apply as appropriate.

Applications

13.1 Where a party to an appeal makes an application whether in an appeal notice or by Part 18 (Procedure For Other Applications in Proceedings) application notice, the provisions of Part 18 will apply.

13.2 The applicant must file the following documents with the notice –

(a) one additional copy of the application notice for the appeal court, one copy for each of the respondents and the persons referred to in paragraph 5.39;

(b) where applicable a sealed or stamped copy of the order which is the subject of the main appeal or a copy of the notice of the making of an order;

(c) a bundle of documents in support which should include –

(i) the Part 18 application notice; and

(ii) any witness statements and affidavits filed in support of the application notice.

Appeals against consent orders

14.1 The rules in Part 30 and the provisions of this Practice Direction apply to appeals relating to orders made by consent in addition to orders which are not made by consent. An appeal is the only way in which a consent order can be challenged.

Disposing of applications or appeals by consent

15.1 An appellant who does not wish to pursue an application or an appeal may request the appeal court for an order that the application or appeal be dismissed. Such a request must state whether the appellant is a child, or a protected person.

15.2 The request must be accompanied by a consent signed by the other parties stating whether the respondent is a child, or a protected person and consents to the dismissal of the application or appeal.

Allowing unopposed appeals or applications on paper

16.1 The appeal court will not normally make an order allowing an appeal unless satisfied that the decision of the lower court was wrong, but the appeal court may set aside or vary the order of the lower court with consent and without determining the merits of the appeal, if it is satisfied that there are good and sufficient reasons for doing so. Where the appeal court is requested by all parties to allow an application or an appeal the court may consider the request on the papers. The request should state whether any of the parties is a child, or protected person and set out the relevant history of the proceedings and the matters relied on as justifying the proposed order and be accompanied by a copy of the proposed order.

Summary assessment of costs

17.1 Costs are likely to be assessed by way of summary assessment at the following hearings –

(a) contested directions hearings;

(b) applications for permission to appeal at which the respondent is present;

(c) appeals from case management decisions or decisions made at directions hearings; and

(d) appeals listed for one day or less.

(Provision for summary assessment of costs is made by section 13 of the Practice Direction supplementing CPR Part 44)

17.2 Parties attending any of the hearings referred to in paragraph 17.1 should be prepared to deal with the summary assessment.

Reopening of final appeals

18.1 This paragraph applies to applications under rule 30.14 (Reopening of final appeals) for permission to reopen a final determination of an appeal.

18.2 In this paragraph, "appeal" includes an application for permission to appeal.

18.3 Permission must be sought from the court whose decision the applicant wishes to reopen.

18.4 The application for permission must be made by application notice and supported by written evidence, verified by a statement of truth.

18.5 A copy of the application for permission must not be served on any other party to the original appeal unless the court so directs.

18.6 Where the court directs that the application for permission is to be served on another party, that party may within 14 days of the service on him or her of the copy of the application file a written statement either supporting or opposing the application.

18.7 The application for permission, and any written statements supporting or opposing it, will be considered on paper by a single judge, and will be allowed to proceed only if the judge so directs.

SCHEDULE 1

Description of proceedings

(1) Proceedings under section 25 of the Children Act 1989;

(2) Proceedings under Parts IV and V of the Children Act 1989;

(3) Proceedings under Schedules 2 and 3 to the Children Act 1989;

(4) Applications for leave under section 91(14), (15) or (17) of the Children Act 1989;

(5) Proceedings under section 102 of the Children Act 1989 or section 79 of the Childcare Act 2006;

(6) Proceedings for a residence order under section 8 of the Children Act 1989 or for a special guardianship order under section 14A of the Children Act 1989 with respect to a child who is the subject of a care order.

(7) Proceedings for a residence order under section 8 of the Children Act 1989 where either section 28(1) (child placed for adoption) or 29(4) (placement order in force) of the Adoption and Children Act 2002 applies;

(8) Proceedings for a special guardianship order under section 14A of the Children Act 1989 where either section 28(1)(child placed for adoption) or section 29(5) (placement order in force) of the Adoption and Children Act 2002 applies.

SCHEDULE 2

Appeal	Relevant legislation	Appellant information	Commission information
Appeal against the making of a regular deduction order (under section 32A of the 1991 Act)	Section 32C(4)(a) of the 1991 Act The Collection and Enforcement Regulations 25AB(1)(a) (appeals)	A copy of the order; A covering letter explaining that the order has been made and the reasons for the order namely that there are arrears of child maintenance and/or no other arrangements have been made for the payment of child maintenance, including arrears	The amount of the current maintenance calculation, the period of debt and the total amount of arrears (including account breakdown if appropriate) and the reasons for the Commission's decision, details of all previous attempts to negotiate payment i.e. phone calls and letters to the non resident parent, details of any previous enforcement action taken
Appeal against a decision on an application for a review of a regular deduction order	Sections 32C(4)(b) 32C(2)(k) of the 1991 Act The Collection and Enforcement Regulations 25G (review of a regular deduction order) and 25AB(1)(b) (appeals)	A decision notification setting out whether or not the review has been agreed by the Commission and the resulting action to be taken if agreed; with an enclosure setting out the specific reasons for the Commission's decision	The reasons for the Commission's decision in respect of the application for review and any evidence supporting that decision

Appeal	Relevant legislation	Appellant information	Commission information
Appeal against the withholding of consent to the disapplication of sections 32G(1) and 32H(2)(b) of the 1991 Act	Section 32I(4) of the 1991 Act The Collection and Enforcement Regulations 25N (disapplication of sections 32G(1) and 32H(2)(b) of the 1991 Act) and 25AB(1)(c) (appeals)	A decision notification setting out that either: a) consent has been refused; or b) consent has been given in relation to part of the application i.e. that only some of the funds which were requested to be released have been agreed to be released (the right of appeal will lie in respect of the part of the application which has been refused). There will be an enclosure with the notification setting out the reasons for the decision on the application.	The reasons for the Commission's decision in respect of the application for consent and any evidence supporting that decision
Appeal against the making of a final lump sum deduction order (under section 32F of the 1991 Act)	Section 32J(5) of the 1991 Act Collection and Enforcement Regulations 25AB(1)(d) (appeals)	A copy of the order; A covering letter explaining that the order has been made and the reasons for the order namely that there are arrears of child maintenance and/or no other arrangements have been made for the payment of child maintenance, including arrears	The amount of the current maintenance calculation (if applicable), the period of debt and the total amount of arrears (including account breakdown if appropriate) and the reasons for the Commission's decision, details of all previous attempts to negotiate payment i.e. phone calls and letters to the non resident parent, details of any previous enforcement action taken.

PART 31

REGISTRATION OF ORDERS UNDER THE COUNCIL REGULATION, THE
CIVIL PARTNERSHIP (JURISDICTION AND RECOGNITION OF
JUDGMENTS) REGULATIONS 2005 AND UNDER THE HAGUE
CONVENTION 1996

CONTENTS OF THIS PART

Scope—FPR 2010, Pt 31 makes provision for proceedings for the recognition, non-recognition and registration of the following incoming orders:

(a) Judgments as defined by Brussels IIA, art 2(4) (divorce, legal separation, marriage annulment or a judgment relating to parental responsibility pronounced by a court of a Member State);
(b) Measures taken by an authority with jurisdiction under the Hague Convention 1996, Chapter II (measures directed to the protection of a child's person or property); and
(c) Judgments to which the Civil Partnership (Jurisdiction and Recognition of Judgments) Regulations 2005 apply (dissolution or annulment of overseas relationships entitled to be treated as a civil partnership or legal separation of such a relationship, making corresponding provision to the relevant parts of Brussels IIA).

In relation to judgments to which Brussels IIA applies, reference should be made to the annotations to Brussels IIA, arts 11, 21, 28, 41 and 42.

31.1 Scope

This Part applies to proceedings for the recognition, non-recognition and registration of –

    (a)   judgments to which the Council Regulation applies;

    (b)   measures to which the 1996 Hague Convention applies; and

    (c)   judgments to which the Jurisdiction and Recognition of Judgments Regulations apply, and which relate to dissolution or annulment of overseas relationships entitled to be treated as a civil partnership, or legal separation of the same.

31.2 Interpretation

(1) In this Part –

    (a)   "judgment" is to be construed –

        (i)   in accordance with the definition in Article 2(4) of the Council Regulation where it applies;

        (ii) in accordance with regulation 6 of the Jurisdiction and Recognition of Judgments Regulations where those Regulations apply; or

        (iii) as meaning any measure taken by an authority with jurisdiction under Chapter II of the 1996 Hague Convention where that Convention applies;

    (b)   "the Jurisdiction and Recognition of Judgments Regulations" means the Civil Partnership (Jurisdiction and Recognition of Judgments) Regulations 2005;

    (c)   "Member State" means –

        (i)   where registration, recognition or non-recognition is sought of a judgment under the Council Regulation, a Member State of the European Union which is bound by that Regulation or a country which has subsequently adopted it;

        (ii) where recognition is sought of a judgment to which the Jurisdiction and Recognition of Judgments Regulations apply, a Member State of the European Union to which Part II of those Regulations applies;

    (d)   "Contracting State" means a State, other than a Member State within the meaning of (c) above, in relation to which the 1996 Hague Convention is in force as between that State and the United Kingdom; and

    (e)   "parental responsibility" –

        (i)   where the Council Regulation applies, has the meaning given in Article 2(7) of that Regulation; and

        (ii) where the 1996 Hague Convention applies, has the meaning given in Article 1(2) of that Convention.

(2) References in this Part to registration are to the registration of a judgment in accordance with the provisions of this Part.

    Articles of the Council Regulation and the 1996 Hague Convention—See Part VI.

31.3 Where to start proceedings

(1) Every application under this Part, except for an application under rule 31.18 for a certified copy of a judgment, or under rule 31.20 for rectification of a certificate issued under Articles 41 or 42, must be made to the principal registry.

(2) Nothing in this rule prevents the determination of an issue of recognition as an incidental question by any court in proceedings, in accordance with Article 21(4) of the Council Regulation.

(3) Notwithstanding paragraph (1), where recognition of a judgment is raised as an incidental question in proceedings under the 1996 Hague Convention or the Jurisdiction and Recognition of Judgments Regulations the court hearing those proceedings may determine the question of recognition.

Jurisdiction to hear proceedings—The High Court in England and Wales, the Court of Session in Scotland and the High Court of Northern Ireland have jurisdiction to hear applications for recognition and non-recognition under Arts 24 and 26 of the 1966 Convention (Parental Responsibility and Measures for the Protection of Children (International Obligations) (England and Wales and Northern Ireland) Regulations 2010, reg 7, set out in Part IV) but if such an issue is raised as an incidental question in another court, that court may determine the issue of recognition. See Part VI for the Council Regulations and 1996 Convention.

31.4 Application for registration, recognition or non-recognition of a judgment

(1) Any interested person may apply to the court for an order that the judgment be registered, recognised or not recognised.

(2) Except for an application under rule 31.7, an application for registration, recognition or non-recognition must be –

    (a)   made to a district judge of the principal registry; and

    (b)   in the form, and supported by the documents and the information required by a practice direction.

Any interested person may apply—Contrast with the provisions of the Hague Convention 1980 and applications under Art 26 (which deals with enforcements provisions) and Brussels IIA, both of which refer to "any interested party" rather than "person". This seems to restrict those entitled to apply to a person rather than a public body or institution.

Form of application—Must be made using the FPR 2010, Pt 19 procedure and Form C69. Where the application is for recognition only of an order, it should be made clear that the application does not extend to registration for enforcement. See FPR PD31A, para 1.

31.5 Documents – supplementary

(1) Except as regards a copy of a judgment required by Article 37(1)(a) of the Council Regulation, where the person making an application under this Part does not produce the documents required by rule 31.4(2)(b) the court may –

    (a)   fix a time within which the documents are to be produced;

    (b)   accept equivalent documents; or

    (c)   dispense with production of the documents if the court considers it has sufficient information.

(2) This rule does not apply to applications under rule 31.7.

Documents required by r 31.4(2)(b)—These are identified in FPR PD31A.

31.6 Directions

(1) As soon as practicable after an application under this Part has been made, the court may (subject to the requirements of the Council Regulation) give such directions as it considers appropriate, including as regards the following matters –

    (a)   whether service of the application may be dispensed with;

    (b)   expedition of the proceedings or any part of the proceedings (and any direction for expedition may specify a date by which the court must give its decision);

    (c)   the steps to be taken in the proceedings and the time by which each step is to be taken;

    (d)   the service of documents; and

    (e)   the filing of evidence.

(2) The court or court officer will –

    (a)   record the giving, variation or revocation of directions under this rule; and

    (b)   as soon as practicable serve a copy of the directions order on every party.

PART III

Every party—In the case of an application for registration, recognition or order for non-recognition, service of the directions order will be on the person against whom registration is sought or in the case of non-recognition in whose favour the judgment was given (FPR 2010, rr 31.8 and 31.14).

31.7 Recognition and enforcement under the Council Regulation of a judgment given in another Member State relating to rights of access or under Article 11(8) for the return of the child to that State

(1) This rule applies where a judgment has been given in another Member State –

   (a)   relating to rights of access: or
   (b)   under Article 11(8) of the Council Regulation for the return of a child to that State,

which has been certified, in accordance with Article 41(2) or 42(2) as the case may be, by the judge in the court of origin.

(2) An application for recognition or enforcement of the judgment must be –

   (a)   made in writing to a district judge of the principal registry; and
   (b)   accompanied by a copy of the certificate issued by the judge in the court of origin.

(3) The application may be made without notice.

(4) Rules 31.5 and 31.8 to 31.17 do not apply to an application made under this rule.

(5) Nothing in this rule shall prevent a holder of parental responsibility from seeking recognition and enforcement of a judgment in accordance with the provisions of rules 31.8 to 31.17.

31.8 Registration for enforcement or order for non-recognition of a judgment

(1) This rule applies where an application is made for an order that a judgment given in another Member State, or a Contracting State, should be registered, or should not be recognised, except where rule 31.7 applies.

(2) Where the application is made for an order that the judgment should be registered –

   (a)   upon receipt of the application, and subject to any direction given by the court under rule 31.6 the court officer will serve the application on the person against whom registration is sought;
   (b)   the court will not accept submissions from either the person against whom registration is sought or any child in relation to whom the judgment was given.

(3) Where the application is for an order that the judgment should not be recognised –

   (a)   upon receipt of the application, and subject to any direction given by the court under rule 31.6, the court officer will serve the application on the person in whose favour judgment was given;
   (b)   the person in whose favour the judgment was given must file an answer to the application and serve it on the applicant –
       (i)   within 1 month of service of the application; or
       (ii)   if the applicant is habitually resident in another Member State, within two months of service of the application.

(4) In cases to which the 1996 Hague Convention applies and the Council Regulation does not apply, the court may extend the time set out in subparagraph (3)(b)(ii) on account of distance.

(5) The person in whose favour the judgment was given may request recognition or registration of the judgment in their answer, and in that event must comply with

31.4(2)(b) to the extent that such documents, information and evidence are not already contained in the application for non-recognition.

(6) If, in a case to which the Council Regulation applies, the person in whose favour the judgment was given fails to file an answer as required by paragraph (3), the court will act in accordance with the provisions of Article 18 of the Council Regulation.

(7) If, in a case to which the 1996 Hague Convention applies and the Service Regulation does not, the person in whose favour the judgment was given fails to file an answer as required by paragraph (3) –

(a) where the Hague Convention of 15 November 1965 on the service abroad of judicial and extrajudicial documents in civil or commercial matters applies, the court shall apply Article 15 of that Convention; and

(b) in all other cases, the court will not consider the application unless –

(i) it is proved to the satisfaction of the court that the person in whose favour judgment was given was served with the application within a reasonable period of time to arrange his or her response; or

(ii) the court is satisfied that the circumstances of the case justify proceeding with consideration of the application.

(8) In a case to which the Jurisdiction and Recognition of Judgments Regulations apply, if the person in whose favour judgment was given fails to file an answer as required by paragraph (3), the court will apply the Service Regulation where that regulation applies, and if it does not –

(a) where the Hague Convention of 15 November 1965 on the service abroad of judicial and extrajudicial documents in civil or commercial matters applies, the court shall apply Article 15 of that Convention; and

(b) in all other cases, the court will apply the provisions of paragraph (7)(b).

Scope—This rule applies to both the Council Regulation and the 1996 Convention. It (i) identifies the person on whom service should be effected where application is made for registration or non-recognition, (ii) provides for an answer to contain a cross-request for registration and recognition and sets out the evidence documents and information that should be filed to support such a cross-application, (iii) sets out the time limits for filing the answer and (iv) sets out the circumstances in which the court may consider the application where an answer is not filed.

31.9 Stay of recognition proceedings by reason of an appeal

Where recognition or non-recognition of a judgment given in another Member State or Contracting State is sought, or is raised as an incidental question in other proceedings, the court may stay the proceedings –

(a) if an ordinary appeal against the judgment has been lodged; or

(b) if the judgment was given in the Republic of Ireland, if enforcement of the judgment is suspended there by reason of an appeal.

Scope—Where an appeal is pending in the court of origin, the court is authorised to stay the proceedings, but in any event see FPR 2010, r 31.17, which provides that the court will not enforce a registered judgment until after the expiration of the time for lodging an appeal or any extension of time granted by the court unless an urgent enforcement of the judgment is necessary to secure the welfare of the child who is the subject to the proceedings. The rule applies to both the Council Regulations and the 1996 Convention. This rule should be read with FPR 2010, r 31.20, which provides for protective measures to be taken in an urgent situation notwithstanding that the time for appeal has not expired or where the appeal is pending.

31.10 Effect of refusal of application for a decision that a judgment should not be recognised

Where the court refuses an application for a decision that a judgment should not be recognised, the court may –

(a) direct that the decision to refuse the application is to be treated as a decision that the judgment be recognised; or

(b) treat the answer under paragraph (3)(b) of rule 31.8 as an application that the judgment be registered for enforcement if paragraph (5) of that rule is complied with and order that the judgment be registered for enforcement in accordance with rule 31.11.

31.11 Notification of the court's decision on an application for registration or non-recognition

(1) Where the court has –

(a) made an order on an application for an order that a judgment should be registered for enforcement; or

(b) refused an application that a judgment should not be recognised and ordered under rule 31.10 that the judgment be registered for enforcement,

the court officer will as soon as practicable take the appropriate action under paragraph (2) or (3).

(2) If the court refuses the application for the judgment to be registered for enforcement, the court officer will serve the order on the applicant and the person against whom judgment was given in the state of origin.

(3) If the court orders that the judgment should be registered for enforcement, the court officer will –

(a) register the judgment in the central index of judgments kept by the principal registry;

(b) confirm on the order that the judgment has been registered; and

(c) serve on the parties the court's order endorsed with the court officer's confirmation that the judgment has been registered.

(4) A sealed order of the court endorsed in accordance with paragraph (3)(b) will constitute notification that the judgment has been registered under Article 28(2) of the Council Regulation or under Article 26 of the 1996 Hague Convention, as the case may be, and in this Part "notice of registration" means a sealed order so endorsed.

(5) The notice of registration must state –

(a) full particulars of the judgment registered and the order for registration;

(b) the name of the party making the application and his address for service within the jurisdiction;

(c) the right of the person against whom judgment was given to appeal against the order for registration; and

(d) the period within which an appeal against the order for registration may be made.

Scope—This rule sets out the procedure that must be followed to record, seal and serve the order made on an application for registration or non-recognition.

Effect of a sealed copy of the court order—A sealed copy of the court order endorsed in accordance with FPR 2010, r 31.11(3)(b) will constitute notification that the judgment has been registered under Art 26 of the 1996 Convention or recognised under Art 24, as the case may be. Registration of a judgment under FPR 2010, r 31.11 will serve for the purposes of Art 24 of the 1996 Convention as a decision that the judgment is recognised.

31.12 Effect of registration under rule 31.11

Registration of a judgment under rule 31.11 will serve for the purpose of Article 21(3) of the Council Regulation, Article 24 of the 1996 Hague Convention, or regulation 7 of the Jurisdiction and Recognition of Judgments Regulations (as the case may be) as a decision that the judgment is recognised.

31.13 The central index of judgments registered under rule 31.11

The central index of judgments registered under rule 31.11 will be kept by the principal registry.

31.14 Decision on recognition of a judgment only

(1) Where an application is made seeking recognition of a judgment only, the provisions of rules 31.8 and 31.9 apply to that application as they do to an application for registration for enforcement.

(2) Where the court orders that the judgment should be recognised, the court officer will serve a copy of the order on each party as soon as practicable.

(3) A sealed order of the court will constitute notification that the judgment has been recognised under Article 21(3) of the Council Regulation, Article 24 of the 1996 Hague convention or regulation 7 of the Jurisdiction and Recognition of Judgments Regulations, as the case may be.

(4) The sealed order shall indicate –

    (a)   full particulars of the judgment recognised;

    (b)   the name of the party making the application and his address for service within the jurisdiction;

    (c)   the right of the person against whom judgment was given to appeal against the order for recognition; and

    (d)   the period within which an appeal against the order for recognition may be made.

31.15 Appeal against the court's decision under rules 31.10, 31.11 or 31.14

(1) An appeal against the court's decision under rules 31.10, 31.11 or 31.14 must be made to a judge of the High Court –

    (a)   within one month of the date of service of the notice of registration; or

    (b)   if the party bringing the appeal is habitually resident in another Member State, or a Contracting State, within two months of the date of service.

(2) The court may not extend time for an appeal on account of distance unless the matter is one to which the 1996 Hague Convention applies and the Council Regulation does not apply.

(3) If, in a case to which the 1996 Hague Convention applies and the Service Regulation does not, the appeal is brought by the applicant for a declaration of enforceability or registration and the respondent fails to appear –

    (a)   where the Hague Convention of 15 November 1965 on the service abroad of judicial and extrajudicial documents in civil or commercial matters applies, the court shall apply Article 15 of that Convention; and

    (b)   in all other cases, the court will not consider the appeal unless –

        (i)   it is proved to the satisfaction of the court that the respondent was served with notice of the appeal within a reasonable period of time to arrange his or her response; or

(ii)   the court is satisfied that the circumstances of the case justify proceeding with consideration of the appeal.

(4) This rule is subject to rule 31.16.

(The procedure for applications under rule 31.15 is set out in Practice Direction 30A (Appeals).)

31.16 Stay of enforcement where appeal pending in state of origin

(1) A party against whom enforcement is sought of a judgment which has been registered under rule 31.11 may apply to the court with which an appeal is lodged under rule 31.15 for the proceedings to be stayed where –

(a)   that party has lodged an ordinary appeal in the Member State or Contracting State of origin; or

(b)   the time for such an appeal has not yet expired.

(2) Where an application for a stay is filed in the circumstances described in paragraph (1)(b), the court may specify the time within which an appeal must be lodged.

31.17 Enforcement of judgments registered under rule 31.11

(1) Subject to paragraph (1A), the court will not enforce a judgment registered under rule 31.11 until after –

(a)   the expiration of any applicable period under rules 31.15 or 31.16; or

(b)   if that period has been extended by the court, the expiration of the period so extended.

(1A) The court may enforce a judgment registered under rule 31.11 before the expiration of a period referred to in paragraph (1) where urgent enforcement of the judgment is necessary to secure the welfare of the child to whom the judgment relates.

(2) A party applying to the court for the enforcement of a registered judgment must produce to the court a certificate of service of –

(a)   the notice of registration of the judgment; and

(b)   any order made by the court in relation to the judgment.

(Service out of the jurisdiction, including service in accordance with the Service Regulation, is dealt with in chapter 4 of Part 6 and in Practice Direction 6B.)

Amendments—SI 2012/1462.

31.18 Request for a certificate or a certified copy of a judgment

(1) An application for a certified copy of a judgment, or for a certificate under Articles 39, 41 or 42 of the Council Regulation, must be made to the court which made the order and without giving notice to any other party.

(2) The application must be made in the form, and supported by the documents and information required by a practice direction.

(3) The certified copy of the judgment will be an office copy sealed with the seal of the court and signed by the district judge, or by the court where the application is made to the Magistrates' Court. It will be issued with a certified copy of any order which has varied any of the terms of the original order.

(4) Where the application is made for the purposes of applying for recognition or recognition and enforcement of the order in another Contracting State, the court must

indicate on the certified copy of the judgment the grounds on which it based its jurisdiction to make the order, for the purposes of Article 23(2)(a) of the 1996 Hague Convention.

31.19 Certificates issued in England and Wales under Articles 41 and 42 of the Council Regulation

The court officer will serve –

    (a)   a certificate issued under Article 41 or 42; or

    (b)   a certificate rectified under rule 31.20,

on all parties and will transmit a copy to the Central Authority for England and Wales.

Central Authority—The Central Authority for England and Wales is the Lord Chancellor but the function will be discharged by the International Child Abduction and Contact Unit, in Wales by the Welsh Ministers, in Scotland by the Scottish Ministers and in Northern Ireland by the Department of Justice.

31.20 Rectification of certificate issued under Article 41 or 42 of the Council Regulation

(1) Where there is an error in a certificate issued under Article 41 or 42, an application to rectify that error must be made to the court which issued the certificate.

(2) A rectification under paragraph (1) may be made –

    (a)   by the court of its own initiative; or

    (b)   on application by –

        (i)   any party to the proceedings; or

        (ii)   the court or Central Authority of another Member State.

(3) An application under paragraph (2)(b) may be made without notice being served on any other party.

31.21 Authentic instruments and agreements under Article 46 of the Council Regulation

This Chapter applies to an authentic instrument and an agreement to which Article 46 of the Council Regulation applies as it applies to a judgment.

31.22 Application for provisional, including protective measures

An application for provisional, including protective, measures under Article 20 of the Council Regulation or Articles 11 or 12 of the 1996 Hague Convention may be made notwithstanding that the time for appealing against an order for registration of a judgment has not expired or that a final determination of any issue relating to enforcement of the judgment is pending.

Scope—This rule authorises the court to take such measures as may be necessary to protect the welfare of a child who is the subject of the proceedings as a matter of urgency. The Convention does not define what may be deemed to be an urgent situation but the *Handbook* suggests that the test should be: were a State not to take the necessary measures, it would result in irreparable harm being caused to the child or the protection of the child or where the interests of the child might be compromised. See further under Art 20 of the Council Regulations or Arts 11 and 12 of the 1996 Convention (both in Part VI).

Practice Direction 31A –
Registration of Orders under the Council Regulation, the Civil Partnership (Jurisdiction and Recognition of Judgments) Regulations 2005 and under the 1996 Hague Convention

This Practice Direction supplements FPR Part 31

Form of application

1.1 An application under rule 31.4 must be made using the Part 19 procedure, except that the provisions of rules 31.8 to 31.14 and of this Practice Direction shall apply in place of rules 19.4 to 19.9.

1.2 Where the application is for recognition only of an order, it should be made clear that the application does not extend to registration for enforcement.

Evidence in support of all applications for registration, recognition or non-recognition

2.1 The requirements for information and evidence for applications differ according to whether the application is made under the Council Regulation, the Jurisdiction and Recognition of Judgments Regulations, or the 1996 Hague Convention.

2.2 All applications to which rule 31.4(2) applies must be supported by a statement that is sworn to be true or an affidavit, exhibiting the judgment, or a verified, certified or otherwise duly authenticated copy of the judgment. In the case of an application under the Jurisdiction and Recognition of Judgments Regulations or under the 1996 Hague Convention, a translation of the judgment should be supplied.

2.3 Where any other document required by this Practice Direction or by direction of the court under rule 31.5 is not in English, the applicant must supply a translation of that document into English certified by a notary public or a person qualified for the purpose, or accompanied by witness statement or affidavit confirming that the translation is accurate.

Evidence required in support of application for registration, recognition or non-recognition of a judgment under the Council Regulation

3.1 An application for a judgment to be registered, recognised or not recognised under the Council Regulation must be accompanied by a witness statement or an affidavit exhibiting the following documents and giving the information required by 3.2 or 3.3 below, as appropriate.

3.2 In the case of an application for recognition or registration –

    (a)   the certificate in the form set out in Annex I or Annex II of the Council Regulation, issued by the Member State in which judgment was given;

    (b)   in the case of a judgment given in default, the documents referred to in Article 37(2);

    (c)   whether the judgment provides for the payment of a sum or sums of money;

    (d)   whether interest is recoverable on the judgment or part of the judgment in accordance with the law of the State in which the judgment was given, and if that is the case, the rate of interest, the date from which interest is recoverable, and the date on which interest ceases to accrue;

(e) an address within the jurisdiction of the court for service of process on the party making the application and stating, in so far as is known to the applicant, the name and usual or last known address or place of business of the person against whom judgment was given; and

(f) where appropriate, whether Article 56 has been complied with, and the identity and address of the authority or authorities from whom consent has been obtained, together with evidence of that consent.

3.3 In the case of an application for an order that a judgment should not be recognised under Article 21(3) –

(a) the certificate referred to at paragraph 3.2(a);

(b) in relation to the documents identified at paragraph 3.2(b), those documents or a statement that no such service or acceptance occurred if that is the case;

(c) an address within the jurisdiction of the court for service of process on the applicant and stating, in so far as is known to the applicant, the name and usual or last known address or place of business of the person in whose favour judgment was given; and

(d) a statement of the ground or grounds under Articles 22 or 23 (as the case may be) on which it is requested that the judgment should not be recognised, the reasons why the applicant asserts that such ground or grounds is, or are, made out, and any documentary evidence on which the applicant relies.

Evidence required in support of an application for registration, recognition or non-recognition of a judgment under the 1996 Hague Convention.

4.1 An application for an order for a judgment to be registered under Article 26 or not recognised under Article 24 of the 1996 Hague Convention must be accompanied by a witness statement or affidavit exhibiting the following documents and giving the information required by 4.2, 4.3 or 4.4 below as appropriate.

4.2 In the case of an application for registration –

(a) those documents necessary to show that the judgment is enforceable according to the law of the Contracting State in which it was given;

(b) a description of the opportunities provided by the authority which gave the judgment in question for the child to be heard, except where that judgment was given in a case of urgency;

(c) where the judgment was given in a case of urgency, a statement as to the circumstances of the urgency that led to the child not having the opportunity to be heard;

(d) details of any measures taken in the non-Contracting State of the habitual residence of the child, if applicable, specifying the nature and effect of the measure, and the date on which it was taken;

(e) in as far as not apparent from the copy of the judgment provided, a statement of the grounds on which the authority which gave the judgment based its jurisdiction, together with any documentary evidence in support of that statement;

(f) where appropriate, a statement regarding whether Article 33 of the 1996 Hague Convention has been complied with, and the identity and address of the authority or authorities from which consent has been obtained, together with evidence of that consent; and

(g) the information referred to at 3.2(c) to (e) above.

4.3 In the case of an application for an order that a judgment should not be recognised –

(a) a statement of the ground or grounds under Article 23 of the 1996 Hague Convention on which it is requested that the judgment be not recognised, the reasons why the applicant asserts that such ground or grounds is or are made out, and any documentary evidence on which the Applicant relies; and

(b) an address within the jurisdiction of the court for service of process on the applicant and stating, in so far as is known to the applicant, the name and usual or last known address or place of business of the person in whose favour judgment was given.

4.4 Where is it sought to apply for recognition only of a judgment under the 1996 Hague Convention, the provisions of paragraph 4.2 apply with the exception that the applicant is not required to produce the document referred to in subparagraph 4.2(a).

Evidence required in support of an application for recognition or non-recognition of a judgment under the Jurisdiction and Recognition of Judgments Regulations

5.1 An application for recognition of a judgment under regulation 7 of the Jurisdiction and Recognition of Judgments Regulations or for non-recognition of a judgment under regulation 8 must be accompanied by a witness statement or affidavit exhibiting the following documents and giving the information at 5.2 or 5.3 below, as appropriate.

5.2 In the case of an application for recognition of a judgment –

(a) where applicable, details of any decision determining the question of the substance or validity of the civil partnership previously given by a court of civil jurisdiction in England and Wales, or by a court elsewhere;

(b) where the judgment was obtained otherwise than by means of proceedings –
   (i)   an official document certifying that the judgment is effective under the law of the country in which it was obtained;
   (ii) where either civil partner was domiciled in another country from that in which the judgment was obtained at the relevant date, an official document certifying that the judgment is recognised as valid under the law of that country; or
   (iii) a verified, certified or otherwise duly authenticated copy of the document at (i) or (ii) above, as appropriate;

(c) in relation to a judgment obtained by means of proceedings and given in default, the original or a certified true copy of the document which establishes that the party who did not respond was served with the document instituting the proceedings or with an equivalent document, or any document indicating that the respondent has accepted the judgment unequivocally; and

(d) the information referred to at paragraph 3.2(c) to (e) above.

5.3 In the case of an application for non-recognition of a judgment –

(a) an address within the jurisdiction of the court for service of process on the applicant and stating, in so far as is known to the applicant, the name and usual or last known address or place of business of the person in whose favour judgment was given;

(b) a statement of the ground or grounds under regulation 8 of the Jurisdiction and Recognition of Judgments Regulations on which it is requested that the judgment should not be recognised together with any documentary evidence on which the applicant relies; and

(c) where the judgment was obtained by means of proceedings, the document referred to at paragraph 5.2(c) or a statement that no such service or acceptance occurred if that is the case.

Evidence in support of application for a certificate under Articles 39, 41 or 42 of the Council Regulation, or for a certified copy of a judgment

6.1 The procedure described in the following paragraphs should be used where the application for the certified copy of the judgment or relevant certificate under the Council Regulation has not been made at the conclusion of the proceedings to which it relates.

6.2 An application for a certified copy of a judgment, or for a certificate under Articles 39, 41 or 42 of the Council Regulation must be made by witness statement or affidavit, containing the information and attaching the documents required under paragraph 6.3, and paragraphs 6.4, 6.5 or 6.6 below, as appropriate.

6.3 All applications must –

    (a)   provide details of the proceedings in which the judgment was obtained;

    (b)   attach a copy of the application by which the proceedings were begun;

    (c)   attach a copy of all statements of case filed in the proceedings; and

    (d)   state –

        (i)   whether the judgment provides for the payment of a sum of money; and

        (ii)   whether interest is recoverable on the judgment or part of it and if so, the rate of interest, the date from which interest is recoverable, and the date on which interest ceases to accrue.

Further, where the application relates to the Council Regulation, the applicant must attach a document showing that he or she benefitted from legal aid in the proceedings to which the judgment relates, if that is the case.

6.4 An application for a certified copy of the judgment and a certificate under Article 41 or 42 of the Council Regulation must –

    (a)   contain a statement of whether the certificate is sought under Article 41 or Article 42;

    (b)   attach a document evidencing the service of the application by which the proceedings were begun on all respondents, and if no such service occurred, details of all opportunities provided to each respondent to put their case before the court;

    (c)   provide information regarding the age of the child at the time of the judgment and the opportunities given during the proceedings, if any, for the child's wishes and feelings to be ascertained;

    (d)   state the full names, addresses and dates and places of birth (where available) of all persons holding parental responsibility in relation to the child or children to whom the judgment relates; and

    (e)   state the full names and dates of birth of each child to whom the judgment relates.

6.5 An application for a certified copy of the judgment and a certificate under Article 39 of the Council Regulation must –

    (a)   state whether the certificate sought relates to a parental responsibility matter or a matrimonial matter;

    (b)   in relation to a parental responsibility matter, attach evidence that the judgment has been served on the respondent;

    (c)   in the case of a judgment given in default, attach a document which establishes that the respondent was served with the petition or application by which the proceedings were commenced, or a document indicating that the respondent accepted the judgment unequivocally;

    (d)   state that the time for appealing has expired, or give the date on which it will expire, as appropriate, and state whether a notice of appeal against the judgment has been given;

PART III

(e)   in relation to a matrimonial matter, give the full name, address, country and place of birth, and date of birth of each party, and the country, place and date of the marriage;

(f)   in relation to a parental responsibility matter, give the full name, address, place and date of birth of each person who holds parental responsibility;

(g)   as appropriate, give the name, address, and date and place of birth of the person with access rights, or to whom the child is to be returned.

6.6   An application for a certified copy of a judgment for the purposes of recognition and enforcement of the judgment under the 1996 Hague Convention must –

(a)   provide a statement of the grounds on which the court based its jurisdiction to make the orders in question;

(b)   indicate the age of the child at the time of the judgment and the measures taken, if any, for the child's wishes and feelings to be ascertained; and

(c)   indicate which persons were provided with notice of the proceedings and, where such persons were served with the proceedings, attach evidence of such service.

PART 32
REGISTRATION AND ENFORCEMENT OF ORDERS

CONTENTS OF THIS PART

Chapter 1
Scope and Interpretation of this Part

Chapter 4
Registration and Enforcement of Custody Orders under the 1986 Act

Chapter 1
Scope and Interpretation of this Part

32.1 Scope and interpretation

(1) This Part contains rules about the registration and enforcement of maintenance orders and custody orders.

(2) In this Part, "the 1950 Act" means the Maintenance Orders Act 1950.

(3) Chapter 2 of this Part relates to –

(a) the registration of a maintenance order, made in the High Court or a county court, in a court in Scotland or Northern Ireland in accordance with the 1950 Act; and

(b) the registration of a maintenance order, made in Scotland or Northern Ireland, in the High Court in accordance with the 1950 Act.

(Provision in respect of proceedings in the magistrates' court under the 1950 Act is in rules made under section 144 of the Magistrates' Courts Act 1980).

(4) Chapter 3 of this Part contains rules to be applied in the High Court or a county court in relation –

(a) The registration of a maintenance order, made in the High Court or a county court, in the magistrates' court in accordance with the 1958 Act; and

(b) The registration of a maintenance order, made in a magistrates' court, in the High Court, in accordance with the 1958 Act.

(Provision in respect of proceedings in the magistrates' court under the 1958 Act is in rules made under section 144 of the Magistrates' Courts Act 1980).

(5) Chapter 4 of this Part relates to the registration and enforcement of custody orders in accordance with the 1986 Act.

Amendments—SI 2011/1328; SI 2012/679.

Chapter 2
Registration etc. of Orders under the 1950 Act

Section 1
Interpretation of this Chapter

32.2 Interpretation

In this Chapter –

"the clerk of the Court of Session" means the deputy principal clerk in charge of the petition department of the Court of Session;

"county court order" means a maintenance order made in a county court;

"High Court order" means a maintenance order made in the High Court;

"maintenance order" means a maintenance order to which section 16 of the 1950 Act applies;

"Northern Irish order" means a maintenance order made by the Court of Judicature of Northern Ireland;

"the register" means the register kept for the purposes of the 1950 Act;

"the registrar in Northern Ireland" means the chief registrar of the Queen's Bench Division (Matrimonial) of the High Court of Justice in Northern Ireland;

"registration" means registration under Part 2 of the 1950 Act and "registered" is to be construed accordingly; and

"Scottish Order" means a maintenance order made by the Court of Session.

Section 2
Registration etc of High Court and county court orders

32.3 Registration of a High Court order

(1) An application for the registration of a High Court order may be made by sending to a court officer at the court which made the order –

 (a)   a certified copy of the order; and
 (b)   a statement which –
  (i)   contains the address in the United Kingdom, and the occupation, of the person liable to make payments under the order;
  (ii) contains the date on which the order was served on the person liable to make payments, or, if the order has not been served, the reason why service has not been effected;
  (iii) contains the reason why it is convenient for the order to be enforced in Scotland or Northern Ireland, as the case may be;
  (iv) contains the amount of any arrears due to the applicant under the order;
  (v)   confirms that the order is not already registered; and
  (vi) is verified by a statement of truth.

(2) If it appears to the court that –

 (a)   the person liable to make payments under the order resides in Scotland or Northern Ireland; and
 (b)   it is convenient for the order to be enforced there,

the court officer will send the documents filed under paragraph (1) to the clerk of the Court of Session or to the registrar in Northern Ireland, as the case may be.

(3) On receipt of a notice of the registration of a High Court order in the Court of Session or the Court of Judicature of Northern Ireland, the court officer (who is the prescribed officer for the purposes of section 17(4) of the 1950 Act) will –

    (a)   enter particulars of the notice of registration in the register;

    (b)   note the fact of registration in the court records; and

    (c)   send particulars of the notice to the principal registry.

32.4 Notice of Variation etc. of a High Court order

(1) This rule applies where a High Court order, which is registered in the Court of Session or the Court of Judicature of Northern Ireland, is discharged or varied.

(2) A court officer in the court where the order was discharged or varied will send a certified copy of that order to the clerk of the Court of Session or the registrar in Northern Ireland, as the case may be.

32.5 Cancellation of registration of a High Court order

(1) This rule applies where –

    (a)   the registration of a High Court order registered in the Court of Session or the Court of Judicature of Northern Ireland is cancelled under section 24(1) of the 1950 Act; and

    (b)   notice of the cancellation is given to a court officer in the court in which the order was made (who is the prescribed officer for the purposes of section 24(3)(a) of the 1950 Act).

(2) On receipt of a notice of cancellation of registration, the court officer will enter particulars of the notice in Part 1 of the register.

32.6 Application of this Chapter to a county court order

Rules 32.3 to 32.5 apply to an application to register a county court order as if –

    (a)   references to a High Court order were references to a county court order;

    (b)   where the order is to be registered in Scotland, references to the Court of Session and the clerk of the Court of Session were references to the sheriff court and the sheriff-clerk of the sheriff court respectively; and

    (c)   where the order is to be registered in Northern Ireland, references to the Court of Judicature of Northern Ireland and the registrar of Northern Ireland were references to the court of summary jurisdiction and the clerk of the court of summary jurisdiction respectively.

Section 3
Registration etc. of Scottish and Northern Irish orders

32.7 Registration of Scottish and Northern Irish orders

On receipt of a certified copy of a Scottish order or a Northern Irish order for registration, a court officer in the principal registry (who is the prescribed officer for the purposes of section 17(2) of the 1950 Act) will –

    (a)   enter particulars of the order in Part 2 of the register;

    (b)   notify the clerk of the Court of Session or the registrar in Northern Ireland, as the case may be, that the order has been registered; and

(c) file the certified copy of the order and any statutory declaration, affidavit(GL) or statement as to the amount of any arrears due under the order.

32.8 Application to adduce evidence before High Court

The Part 18 procedure applies to an application by a person liable to make payments under a Scottish order registered in the High Court to adduce before that court any evidence on which that person would be entitled to rely in any proceedings brought before the court by which the order was made for the variation or discharge of the order.

32.9 Notice of variation etc. of Scottish and Northern Irish orders

(1) This rule applies where –

(a) a Scottish order or a Northern Irish order, which is registered in the High Court, is discharged or varied; and

(b) notice of the discharge or variation is given to a court officer in the High Court (who is the prescribed officer for the purposes of section 23(1)(a) of the 1950 Act).

(2) On receipt of a notice of discharge or variation, the court officer will enter particulars of the notice in Part 2 of the register.

32.10 Cancellation of registration of Scottish and Northern Irish orders

(1) The Part 18 procedure applies to an application for the cancellation of the registration of a Scottish order or a Northern Irish order in the High Court.

(2) The application must be made without notice to the person liable to make payments under the order.

(3) If the registration of the order is cancelled, the court officer will –

(a) note the cancellation in Part II of the register; and

(b) send written notice of the cancellation to –

(i)   the clerk of the Court of Session or the registrar in Northern Ireland, as the case may be; and

(ii) the court officer in any magistrates' court in which the order has been registered in accordance with section 2(5) of the 1958 Act.

32.11 Enforcement

(1) The Part 18 procedure applies to an application for or with respect to the enforcement of a Scottish order or a Northern Irish order registered in the High Court.

(2) The application may be made without notice to the person liable to make payments under the order.

32.12 Inspection of register and copies of order

Any person –

(a) who is entitled to receive, or liable to make, payments under a maintenance order made by the High Court, the Court of Session or the Court of Judicature of Northern Ireland; or

(b) with the permission of the court,

may –

(i)   inspect the register; or

    (ii)   request a copy of any order registered in the High Court under Part 2 of the 1950 Act and any statutory declaration, affidavit(GL) or statement filed with the order.

Chapter 3
Registration of Maintenance Orders under the 1958 Act

32.13 Interpretation

In this Chapter "the register" means the register kept for the purposes of the 1958 Act.

32.14 Registration of orders – prescribed period

The prescribed period for the purpose of section 2(2) of the 1958 Act is 14 days.

    (Section 2(2) sets out the period during which an order, which is to be registered in a magistrates' court, may not be enforced)

32.15 Application for registration of a maintenance order in a magistrates' court

(1) An application under section 2(1) of the 1958 Act may be made by sending to the court officer at the court which made the order –

    (a)   a certified copy of the maintenance order; and

    (b)   two copies of the application.

(2) When, on the grant of an application, the court officer sends the certified copy of the maintenance order to the magistrates' court in accordance with section 2(2), the court officer must –

    (a)   note on the order that the application for registration has been granted; and

    (b)   send to the magistrates' court a copy of the application for registration of the order.

(3) On receiving notice that the magistrates' court has registered the order, the court officer must enter particulars of the registration in the court records.

"maintenance order" (r 32.15(1))—A nominal order for a spouse only will not be registered, and a maintenance pending suit or interim order will only be registered in special circumstances, e g where a final order at the same rate is expected to follow shortly.

Method of and grounds supporting application (r 32.15(1))—The court may grant the application if it thinks fit (MOA 1958, s 2(1)); there is no absolute right to registration. The application is made simply by lodging the prescribed documents including Form D151 but the district judge may give the respondent the opportunity to make representations, and if the order granting the application is made without notice, the respondent may apply under r 18.11 for it to be reconsidered.

Effect of registration (r 32.15)—Any existing attachment of earnings order ceases to have effect on registration (AEA 1971, s 11(1)(a)). Any existing means of payment order under MEA 1991, s 1(7) continues to have effect (MOA 1958, s 2(6ZA)(a)). However, if there is no such order in force, the magistrates' court must order the payments to be made to the justices' chief executive for that or another magistrates' court (s 2(6ZA)(b)); in either case, the order may subsequently be varied or revoked (s 2(6ZB)(b)). The order is enforceable by the same procedures as if it had been made in the magistrates' court (MOA 1958, s 3(1),(2)), subject to minor modifications. No other proceedings (e g in the original court) may be taken for its enforcement (s 3(4)).

32.16 Registration in a magistrates' court of an order registered in the High Court

(1) This rule applies where –

  (a) a maintenance order is registered in the High Court in accordance with section 17(4) of the 1950 Act; and

  (b) the court officer receives notice that the magistrates' court has registered the order in accordance with section 2(5) of the 1958 Act.

(2) The court officer must enter particulars of the registration in Part II of the register.

32.17 Registration in the High Court of a magistrates' court order

(1) This rule applies where a court officer receives a certified copy of a magistrates' court order for registration in accordance with section 2(4)(c) of the 1958 Act.

(2) The court officer must register the order in the High Court by –

  (a) filing the copy of the order; and

  (b) entering particulars in –

    (i)   the register; or

    (ii) if the order is received in a district registry, the cause book or cause card.

(3) The court officer must notify the magistrates' court that the order has been registered.

32.18 Registration in the High Court of an order registered in a magistrates' court

(1) This rule applies where –

  (a) an order has been registered in the magistrates' court in accordance with section 17(4) of the 1950 Act; and

  (b) a sheriff court in Scotland or a magistrates' court in Northern Ireland has –

    (i)   made an order for the registration of that order in the High Court; and

    (ii) sent a certified copy of the maintenance order to the court officer of the High Court in accordance with section 2(4)(c) of the 1958 Act.

(2) The court officer must register the order in the High Court by –

  (a) filing the copy of the order; and

  (b) entering particulars in the register.

(3) The court officer must notify –

  (a) the court which made the order; and

  (b) the magistrates' court in which the order was registered in accordance with section 17(4) of the 1950 Act,

that the order has been registered in the High Court.

Effect of registration (r 32.18)—Any existing attachment of earnings order ceases to have effect (AEA 1971, s 11(1)(a)). Any order as to the method of payment within MCA 1980, s 59(6) (payment otherwise than to the clerk) continues to have effect but any order to pay to the clerk ceases to have effect (MOA 1958, s 2(6)). The court may vary the order as to method of payment or make a means of payment order under MEA 1991, s 1(7) (MOA 1958, s 4A). The order is enforceable as a High Court order and not otherwise (MOA 1958, s 3(1),(4)).

32.19 Variation or discharge of an order registered in a magistrates' court

(1) This rule applies where a maintenance order is registered in a magistrates' court under Part 1 of the 1958 Act.

(2) If the court which made the order makes an order varying or discharging that order the court officer must send a certified copy of the order of variation or discharge to the magistrates' court.

(3) If the court officer receives from the magistrates' court a certified copy of an order varying the maintenance order the court officer must –

    (a)   file the copy of the order; and

    (b)   enter the particulars of the variation in the place where the details required by rule 32.15(3) were entered.

Variation of order (r 2.19)—Applications to vary the rate of payment must be made to the magistrates' court (MOA 1958, s 4(2)), unless made in proceedings to vary some other provision in the order (s 4(5)(a)) or unless either party is not present in England or Wales (s 4(5)(b)). If variation proceedings are pending in one court, no variation application may be made to the other (s 4(6)). The magistrates' court may remit a variation application to be heard by the original court (s 4(4)).

Discharge of order (r 32.19)—The MOA 1958 does not give magistrates' courts power to discharge a registered order made by the High Court or county court. An application for discharge must be made to the original court. It is suggested, however, that the magistrates' court could in an appropriate case vary an order to a nominal figure.

32.20 Variation or discharge of an order registered in the High Court

(1) This rule applies where a maintenance order is registered in the High Court under Part 1 of the 1958 Act.

(2) If the court officer receives from the magistrates' court a certified copy of an order varying or discharging the maintenance order the court officer must –

    (a)   file the copy of the order;

    (b)   enter the particulars of the variation or discharge in –

        (i)   the register; or

        (ii) if the order is received in a district registry, the cause book or cause card; and

    (c)   send notice of the variation or discharge to the court officer of a county court –

        (i)   who has notified the court officer of enforcement proceedings in that court relating to the maintenance order; or

        (ii) to whom a payment is to be made under an attachment of earnings order made by the High Court for the enforcement of the registered order.

32.21 Cancellation of registration – orders registered in the High Court

(1) This rule applies where an order is registered in the High Court.

(2) A person giving notice under section 5(1) of the 1958 Act must give the notice to the court officer.

(3) The court officer must take the steps mentioned in paragraph (4) if –

    (a)   notice is given under section 5 of the 1958 Act; and

    (b)   the court officer is satisfied, by a witness statement by the person entitled to receive payments under the order that no enforcement proceedings in relation to the order, that were started before the giving of the notice, remain in force.

(4) The court officer must, if satisfied as mentioned in paragraph (3) –

    (a)   cancel the registration by entering particulars of the notice in the register or cause book (or cause card) as the case may be; and

    (b)   send notice of the cancellation to –

        (i)   the court which made the order; and

        (ii) where applicable, to the magistrates' court in which the order was registered in accordance with section 17(4) of the 1950 Act.

PART III

(5) Where the cancellation results from a notice given under section 5(1) of the 1958 Act, the court officer must state that fact in the notice of cancellation sent in accordance with paragraph (4)(b).

(6) If notice is received from a magistrates' court that the registration in that court under the 1958 Act of an order registered in the High Court in accordance with section 17(4) of the 1950 Act has been cancelled, the court officer must note the cancellation in Part II of the register.

32.22 Cancellation of registration – orders registered in a magistrates' court

(1) Where the court gives notice under section 5(2) of the 1958 Act, the court officer must endorse the notice on the certified copy of the order of variation or discharge sent to the magistrates' court in accordance with rule 32.19(2).

(2) Where notice is received from a magistrates' court that registration of an order made by the High Court or a county court under Part 1 of the 1958 Act has been cancelled, the court officer must enter particulars of the cancellation in the place where the details required by rule 32.15(3) were entered.

Chapter 4
Registration and Enforcement of Custody Orders under the 1986 Act

32.23 Interpretation

In this Chapter –
   "appropriate court" means, in relation to –
      (a)   Scotland, the Court of Session;
      (b)   Northern Ireland, the High Court in Northern Ireland; and
      (c)   a specified dependent territory, the corresponding court in that territory;
   "appropriate officer" means, in relation to –
      (a)   the Court of Session, the Deputy Principal Clerk of Session;
      (b)   the High Court in Northern Ireland, the Master (Care and Protection) of that court; and
      (c)   the appropriate court in a specified dependent territory, the corresponding officer of that court;
   "Part 1 order" means an order under Part 1 of the 1986 Act;
   "the register" means the register kept for the purposes of Part 1 of the 1986 Act; and
   "specified dependent territory" means a dependent territory specified in column 1 of
         Schedule 1 to the Family Law Act 1986 (Specified Dependent Territories) Order 1991.

Scope—The interpretation clause of this rule is in addition to FPR 2010, r 2.3(1). It deals with the terminology found in FLA 1986, ss 25–31 and in FPR 2010, rr 32.24–32.32 relating to the registration of "custody orders" within the UK. References to the Isle of Man are included within the term "specified dependant territory" pursuant to the Family Law Act 1986 (Dependent Territories) Order 1991, which brought orders made in the Isle of Man in relation to children within the reciprocal recognition and enforcement provision of FLA 1986. It also includes the Channel Island of Jersey and hence the Royal Court of Jersey (see FPR 2010, r 12.52).

32.24 Prescribed officer and functions of the court

(1) The prescribed officer for the purposes of sections 27(4) and 28(1) of the 1986 Act is the family proceedings department manager of the principal registry.

(2) The function of the court under sections 27(3) and 28(1) of the 1986 Act shall be performed by a court officer.

Defined terms—"court officer", "appropriate officer": FPR 2010, r 2.3(1).

32.25 Application for the registration of an order made by the High Court or a county court

(1) An application under section 27 of the 1986 Act for the registration of an order made in the High Court or a county court may be made by sending to a court officer at the court which made the order –

    (a)   a certified copy of the order;

    (b)   a copy of any order which has varied the terms of the original order;

    (c)   a statement which –

        (i)   contains the name and address of the applicant and the applicant's interest under the order;

        (ii)   contains –

            (aa)   the name and date of birth of the child in respect of whom the order was made;

            (bb)   the whereabouts or suspected whereabouts of the child; and

            (cc)   the name of any person with whom the child is alleged to be;

        (iii)   contains the name and address of any other person who has an interest under the order and states whether the order has been served on that person;

        (iv)   states in which of the jurisdictions of Scotland, Northern Ireland or a specified dependent territory the order is to be registered;

        (v)   states that to the best of the applicant's information and belief, the order is in force;

        (vi)   states whether, and if so where, the order is already registered;

        (vii)   gives details of any order known to the applicant which affects the child and is in force in the jurisdiction in which the order is to be registered;

        (viii)   annexes any document relevant to the application; and

        (ix)   is verified by a statement of truth; and

    (d)   a copy of the statement referred to in paragraph (c).

(2) On receipt of the documents referred to in paragraph (1), the court officer will, subject to paragraph (4) –

    (a)   keep the original statement and send the other documents to the appropriate officer;

    (b)   record in the court records the fact that the documents have been sent to the appropriate officer; and

    (c)   file a copy of the documents.

(3) On receipt of a notice that the document has been registered in the appropriate court the court officer will record that fact in the court records.

(4) The court officer will not send the documents to the appropriate officer if it appears to the court officer that –

    (a)   the order is no longer in force; or

    (b)   the child has reached the age of 16.

(5) Where paragraph (4) applies –

    (a)   the court officer must, within 14 days of the decision, notify the applicant of the decision of the court officer in paragraph (4) and the reasons for it; and

    (b)   the applicant may apply to a judge, but not a district judge, in private for an order that the documents be sent to the appropriate court.

Defined terms—"specified territory": FPR 2010, r 32.23, but also includes Jersey.

Verified by statement of truth—For documents to be verified by statement of truth, see FPR 2010, r 17 and FPR PD17A, para 1.

Form of statement of truth—See FPR 2010, r 17.2 and FPR PD17A, paras 2–4.4.

32.26   Registration of orders made in Scotland, Northern Ireland or a specified dependent territory

(1) This rule applies where the prescribed officer receives, for registration, a certified copy of an order made in Scotland, Northern Ireland or a specified dependent territory.

(2) The prescribed officer will –

    (a)   enter in the register –

        (i)   the name and address of the applicant and the applicant's interest under the order;

        (ii)   the name and date of birth of the child and the date the child will attain the age of 16;

        (iii)   the whereabouts or suspected whereabouts of the child; and

        (iv)   the terms of the order, its date and the court which made it;

    (b)   file the certified copy and accompanying documents; and

    (c)   notify –

        (i)   the court which sent the order; and

        (ii)   the applicant,

    that the order has been registered.

Defined terms—"specified territory", "the register": r 32.23; "prescribed officer": r 32.24.

Scope—This rule sets out what the prescribed officer has to do to register the order.

32.27   Revocation and variation of an order made in the High Court or a county court

(1) Where a Part 1 order, registered in an appropriate court, is varied or revoked, the court officer of the court making the order of variation or revocation will –

    (a)   send a certified copy of the order of variation or revocation to –

        (i)   the appropriate officer; and

        (ii)   if a different court, the court which made the Part 1 order;

    (b)   record in the court records the fact that a copy of the order has been sent; and

    (c)   file a copy of the order.

(2) On receipt of notice from the appropriate court that its register has been amended, this fact will be recorded by the court officer of –

    (a)   the court which made the order of variation or revocation; and

    (b)   if different, the court which made the Part 1 order.

Defined terms—"appropriate court", "appropriate officer": r 32.23; "Part 1 order": FLA 1986, s 32 and FPR 2010, r 32.23.

Scope—This rule should be read together with FLA 1986, s 28, which makes provision for the cancellation and variation of registered orders. Similar provision is made for registration of Scottish and Northern Ireland orders and orders made in the Isle of Man in FPR 2010, r 32.28. Unlike r 32.28, there is no provision for the court of its own motion to cancel an order that ceased to have effect, other than by revocation or variation.

32.28 Registration of varied, revoked or recalled orders made in Scotland, Northern Ireland or a specified dependent territory

(1) This rule applies where the prescribed officer receives a certified copy of an order made in Scotland, Northern Ireland or a specified dependent territory which varies, revokes or recalls a registered Part 1 order.

(2) The prescribed officer shall enter particulars of the variation, revocation or recall in the register and give notice of the entry to –

    (a)   the court which sent the certified copy;

    (b)   if different, the court which made the Part 1 order;

    (c)   the applicant for registration; and

    (d)   if different, the applicant for the variation, revocation of recall of the order.

(3) An application under section 28(2) of the 1986 Act must be made in accordance with the Part 19 procedure.

(4) The applicant for the Part 1 order, if not the applicant under section 28(2) of the 1986 Act, must be made a defendant to the application.

(5) Where the court cancels a registration under section 28(2) of the 1986 Act, the court officer will amend the register and give notice of the amendment to the court which made the Part 1 order.

Defined terms—"specified territory", "the register": FPR 2010, r 32.23; "prescribed officer": FPR 2010, r 32.24; "Part 1 Order": FLA 1986, s 32 and FPR 2010, r 32.23.

Scope—This rule sets out: what the prescribed officer must do when registration of a varied etc order is received; the procedure that must be followed by the applicant; and the persons who must be made respondents to the application.

Procedure—FPR 2010, Pt 19 procedure must be followed.

Cancellation—Cancellation may take place only where the court acts of its own initiative or on an application of any person who has an interest in the matter (FLA 1986, s 28(2)).

32.29 Interim directions

The following persons will be made parties to an application for interim directions under section 29 of the 1986 Act –

    (a)   the parties to the proceedings for enforcement; and

    (b)   if not a party to those proceedings, the applicant for the Part 1 order.

Section 29 of the 1986 Act—The section relates to enforcement of a registered order. See further the commentary under the provisions of that section.

32.30 Staying and dismissal of enforcement proceedings

(1) The following persons will be made parties to an application under section 30(1) or 31(1) of the 1986 Act –

    (a)   the parties to the proceedings for enforcement which are sought to be stayed[(GL)]; and

    (b)   if not a party to those proceedings, the applicant for the Part 1 order.

(2) Where the court makes an order under section 30(2) or (3) or section 31(3) of the 1986 Act, the court officer will amend the register and give notice of the amendment to –

    (a)   the court which made the Part 1 order; and

    (b)   the applicants for –

        (i)   registration;

        (ii)   enforcement; and

PART III

      (iii) stay$^{(GL)}$or dismissal of the enforcement proceedings.

Defined terms—"court officer", "Part 1 order": FLA 1986, s 32 and FPR 2010, r 32.23.

32.31 Particulars of other proceedings

A party to proceedings for or relating to a Part 1 order who knows of other proceedings which relate to the child concerned (including proceedings out of the jurisdiction and concluded proceedings) must file a witness statement which –

    (a) states in which jurisdiction and court the other proceedings were begun;

    (b) states the nature and current state of the proceedings and the relief claimed or granted;

    (c) sets out the names of the parties to the proceedings and their relationship to the child;

    (d) if applicable and if known, states the reasons why relief claimed in the proceedings for or relating to the Part 1 order was not claimed in the other proceedings; and

    (e) is verified by a statement of truth.

Defined terms—"Part 1 order": FLA 1986, s 32 and r 32.23; "witness statement": r 22.4.

Witness statement—See FPR 2010, r 17, FPR PD17A, FPR 2010, r 22.4 and FPR PD22A.

32.32 Inspection of register

The following persons may inspect any entry in the register relating to a Part 1 order and may request copies of the order any document relating to it –

    (a) the applicant for registration of the Part 1 order;

    (b) a person who, to the satisfaction of a district judge, has an interest under the Part 1 order; and

    (c) a person who obtains the permission of a district judge.

Defined terms—"the register": FPR 2010, r 32.23; "Part 1 order": FLA 1986, s 32 and FPR 2010, r 32.23; "district judge": FPR 2010, r 2.3(1).

PART 33
ENFORCEMENT

CONTENTS OF THIS PART

Chapter 1
General Rules

Chapter 1
General Rules

33.1 Application

(1) The rules in this Part apply to an application made in the High Court and a county court to enforce an order made in family proceedings.

(2) Part 50 of, and Schedules 1 and 2 to, the CPR apply, as far as they are relevant and with necessary modification (including the modifications referred to in rule 33.7), to an application made in the High Court and a county court to enforce an order made in family proceedings.

"Schedules 1 and 2 to the CPR" (r 33.1(2))—Some parts of the former RSC and CCR survive as part of the CPR 1998, as Schs 1 and 2, respectively. The rules in question, not all of which are relevant to family proceedings, are parts of RSC Ords 17 (Interpleader), 45 (Enforcement), 46 and 47 (Writs of Execution/Fieri Facias), 52 (Committal), 54 (Habeas Corpus), 64 (Sittings), 79, 115 and 116 (Criminal Proceedings), 109 (AJA 1960) and 113 (Summary Proceedings for Possession), and CCR Ords 1 (Interpretation), 16 (Transfer), 22 (Judgments and Orders), 24 (Summary Proceedings for Recovery of Land), 25 (Enforcement), 26 (Warrants), 27 (Attachment of Earnings), 28 (Judgment Summonses), 29 (Committal), 33 (Interpleader), 34 (Penal and Disciplinary), 39 (Administration Orders), 44 (Agricultural Holdings) and 49 (Miscellaneous Statutes). See generally *Civil Court Service* (Jordan Publishing Ltd).

Note that it is no longer necessary to engage in archaeology to find what the RSC and CCR were on 25 April 1999, but note the modifications to the surviving CCR set out in FPR 2010, r 33.7. However, while RSC Ord 52 and CCR Ord 29 have been revoked in relation to civil proceedings, they continue to apply as they were at 30 September 2012 in relation to family proceedings. It is understood that this is to give the Rules Committee an opportunity to consider the application of CPR 1998, Pt 81 and that this unfortunate anomaly is not intended to be permanent.

Section 1
Enforcement of orders for the payment of money

33.2 Application of the Civil Procedure Rules

Part 70 of the CPR applies to proceedings under this Section as if –

    (a)   in rule 70.1, in paragraph (2)(d), "but does not include a judgment or order for the payment of money into court" is omitted; and

    (b)   rule 70.5 is omitted.

Note—Part 70 of the CPR is reproduced as modified.

33.3 How to apply

(1) Except where a rule or practice direction otherwise requires, an application for an order to enforce an order for the payment of money must be made in a notice of application accompanied by a statement which must –

    (a)   state the amount due under the order, showing how that amount is arrived at; and

    (b)   be verified by a statement of truth.

(2) The notice of application may either –

    (a)   apply for an order specifying the method of enforcement; or

    (b)   apply for an order for such method of enforcement as the court may consider appropriate.

(3) If an application is made under paragraph (2)(b), an order to attend court will be issued and rule 71.2 (6) and (7) of the CPR will apply as if the application had been made under that rule.

"such means of enforcement as the court may consider appropriate" (r 33.3(2)(b))—This provision, which is novel, represents the partial implementation of the "long awaited reforms", the "swift implementation" of which was urged as long ago as 2003 – see *Corbett v Corbett* [2003] 2 FLR 385 at [32]. It will result in an order to attend court for questioning to which certain provisions of CPR 1998, Pt 71 will apply (see r 33.23). As it is directed to the court considering what means of enforcement are appropriate, the questioning should take place before a judge.

"an order to attend court will be issued" (r 33.3(3))—As CPR 1998, Pt 71 is incorporated (see FPR 2010, r 33.23) the appropriate form of order would appear to be County Court Form N39.

"Except where a rule or practice direction otherwise requires" (r 33.3(1))—Applications for third party debt orders (CPR 1998, Pt 72, as applied to family proceedings by FPR 2010, r 33.24) and charging orders (CPR 1998, Pt 73, as applied by FPR 2010, r 33.25) do "otherwise require". An application for a third party debt order "must be in the form, and contain the information, required by PD72" (CPR 1998, r 72.3(2)(a)); an application for a charging order "must be in the form, and contain the information, required by PD73" (CPR 1998, r 73.4(2)(a)).

33.4 Transfer of orders

(1) This rule applies to an application for the transfer –

(a) to the High Court of an order made in a designated county court; and

(b) to a designated county court of an order made in the High Court.

(2) The application must be –

(a) made without notice; and

(b) accompanied by a statement which complies with rule 33.3(1).

(3) The transfer will have effect upon the filing of the application.

(4) Where an order is transferred from a designated county court to the High Court –

(a) it will have the same force and effect; and

(b) the same proceedings may be taken on it,

as if it were an order of the High Court.

(5) This rule does not apply to the transfer of orders for periodical payments or for the recovery of arrears of periodical payments.

"as if it were an order of the High Court" (r 33.4)—Note that if it is sought to enforce an English judgment abroad under AJA 1920 or FJ(RE)A 1933, it should be borne in mind that foreign courts may well not regard a county court order transferred to the High Court as being "an order of the High Court". See for example *Re Hardwick* [1995] Jersey LR 245 (*www.jerseylaw.je*).

Section 2
Committal and injunction

33.5 General rule – committal hearings to be in public

(1) The general rule is that proceedings in the High Court for an order of committal will be heard in public.

(2) An order of committal may be heard in private where this is permitted by rule 6 of Order 52 of the RSC (cases in which a court may sit in private).

"proceedings in the High Court … will be heard in public"—Committal in the High Court is still governed by CPR 1998, Sch 1, RSC Ord 52 in family cases. The RSC were made in 1965 based on a revision of 1962. There was some tinkering with the wording when the CPR were made in 1998 but the essentials of the rule were unchanged. Evidently the rule was felt to be so opaque that FPR 2010, r 33.5 requires committal hearings in family cases to be in public (which is surely what everyone expects) save in the limited circumstances prescribed by RSC Ord 52, r 6. RSC Ord 52 has been repealed in civil cases where CPR 1998, Pt 81 applies.

"may sit in private" (r 33.5)—The most common such situation likely to be encountered in family proceedings will be that the order breached was made in proceedings concerning children.

33.6 Proceedings in the principal registry treated as pending in a designated county court

(1) This rule applies where an order for the warrant of committal of any person to prison has been made or issued in proceedings which are –

(a) in the principal registry; and

(b) treated as pending in a designated county court or a county court.

(2) The person subject to the order will, wherever located, be treated for the purposes of section 122 of the County Courts Act 1984 as being out of the jurisdiction of the principal registry.

(3) Where –

    (a)   a committal is for failure to comply with the terms of an injunction[GL]; or

    (b)   an order or warrant for the arrest or committal of any person is made or issued in proceedings under Part 4 of the 1996 Act in the principal registry which are treated as pending in a county court,

the order or warrant may, if the court so directs, be executed by the tipstaff within any county court.

"the principal registry"—It is the Principal Registry of the High Court of Justice. But for many purposes (e g the issuing of divorce petitions) it is deemed to be a county court. Thus there always has to be a special rule just to ensure that the PR has jurisdiction and to have in place workable arrangements such as the provision here to allow the tipstaff to execute warrants.

33.7 Specific modifications of the CCR

(1) CCR Order 29, rule 1 (committal for breach of an order or undertaking) applies to –

    (a)   section 8 orders, except those referred to in paragraph (2)(a); and

    (b)   orders under the following sections of the 1989 Act –

        (i)   section 14A (special guardianship orders);

        (ii)   14B(2)(b) (granting of permission on making a special guardianship order to remove a child from the United Kingdom);

        (iii)   section 14C(3)(b) (granting of permission to remove from the United Kingdom a child who is subject to a special guardianship order); and

        (iv)   section 14D (variation or discharge of a special guardianship order),

as if paragraph (3) of that rule were substituted by the following paragraph –

"(3) In the case of a section 8 order (within the meaning of section 8(2) of the Children Act 1989) or an order under section 14A, 14B(2)(b), 14C(3)(b) or 14D of the Children Act 1989 enforceable by committal order under paragraph (1), the judge or the district judge may, on the application of the person entitled to enforce the order, direct that the proper officer issue a copy of the order, endorsed with or incorporating a notice as to the consequences of disobedience, for service in accordance with paragraph (2), and no copy of the order shall be issued with any such notice endorsed or incorporated save in accordance with such a direction.".

(2) CCR Order 29, rule 1 applies to –

    (a)   contact orders to which a notice has been attached under section 11I of the 1989 Act or under section 8(2) of the Children and Adoption Act 2006;

    (b)   orders under section 11J of the 1989 Act (enforcement orders); and

    (c)   orders under paragraph 9 of Schedule A1 to the 1989 Act (orders following breach of enforcement orders),

as if paragraph (3) were omitted.

CCR Order 29—Committal in the county courts is still governed by CPR 1998, Sch 2, CCR Ord 29 in family cases. The CCR were made in 1981 but the wording of CCR Ord 29, in particular r 1(3), is not suited to all family cases and is thus varied by FPR 2010, r 33.7, as clearly set out in the rule. CCR Ord 29 has been repealed for civil cases and replaced by CPR 1998, Pt 81.

33.8 Section 118 County Courts Act 1984 and the tipstaff

For the purposes of section 118 of the County Courts Act 1984 in its application to the hearing of family proceedings at the Royal Courts of Justice or the principal registry, the tipstaff is deemed to be an officer of the court.

Chapter 2
Committal by way of Judgment Summons

33.9 Interpretation

In this Chapter, unless the context requires otherwise –

"order" means an order made in family proceedings for the payment of money;
"judgment creditor" means a person entitled to enforce an order under section 5 of the Debtors Act 1869;
"debtor" means a person liable under an order; and
"judgment summons" means a summons under section 5 of the Debtor's Act 1869 requiring a debtor to attend court.

"section 5 of the Debtors Act 1869" (r 33.9)—The section provides:

"Subject to the provisions hereinafter mentioned, and to the prescribed rules, any court may commit to prison for a term not exceeding 6 weeks, or until payment of the sum due, any person who makes default in payment of any debt or instalment of any debt due from him in pursuance of any order or judgment of that or any other competent court. Provided –

(1) That the jurisdiction by this section given of committing a person to prison shall, in the case of any court other than the superior courts of law and equity, be exercised only subject to the following restrictions; that is to say

   (a) be exercised only by a judge or his deputy, and by an order made in open court and showing on its face the ground on which it is issued;

   (b) *(repealed)*

   (c) be exercised only as respects a judgment of a county court by a county court judge or his deputy.

(2) That such jurisdiction shall only be exercised where it is proved to the satisfaction of the court that the person making default either has or has had since the date of the order or judgment the means to pay the sum in respect of which he has made default, and has refused or neglected, or refuses or neglects, to pay the same.

Proof of the means of the person making default may be given in such manner as the court thinks just. For the purpose of considering whether to commit a debtor to prison under this section, the debtor may be summoned in accordance with the prescribed rules.

For the purposes of this section any court may direct any debt due from any person in pursuance of any order or judgment of that or any other competent court to be paid by instalments, and may from time to time rescind or vary such order.

No imprisonment under this section shall operate as a satisfaction or extinguishment of any debt or demand or cause of action, or deprive any person of any right to take out execution against the lands, goods or chattels of the person imprisoned, in the same manner as if such imprisonment had not taken place.

Any person imprisoned under this section shall be discharged out of custody upon a certificate signed in the prescribed manner to the effect that he has satisfied a debt or instalment of a debt in respect of which he was imprisoned, together with the prescribed costs (if any)."

The provision that proof of the debtor's means may be given by summoning him to be examined on oath has been removed by the amendment made to the section by the Civil Procedure (Modification of Enactments) Order 2002. The amendment is a consequence of the finding in *Mubarak v Mubarak and others* [2001] 1 FLR 698, CA that the provision was incompatible with the HRA 1998, the proceedings being of a penal character and the requirement amounting to compulsory self-incrimination. It is for the creditor to prove the necessary facts (see **"the judgment creditor proves"**, under FPR 2010, r 33.14) by such other evidence as he can muster. Amendments have also been made to the CPR and, latterly, these rules in consequence of the same decision.

The jurisdiction, which the section confers may be exercised by the High Court only in respect of a High Court maintenance order (ie a maintenance order enforceable by the High Court (AJA 1970, s 28(1)), which includes an order registered in or transferred to the High Court) and by the county court in respect of a High Court or a county court maintenance order, as well as in respect of certain orders for payment of taxes etc (AJA 1970, s 11). The term "maintenance order" is defined by AJA 1970, s 28 and Sch 8; in addition to periodical payments the definitions in Sch 8 include "other payments made or having effect as if made under" the provisions there referred to, including, for example, MCA 1973, Pt II, which provides for lump sum and other orders for payment of money that would not normally be thought of as maintenance orders.

An obligation to pay pursuant to an undertaking may be enforced by this procedure if it is equivalent to a maintenance order (*Symmons v Symmons* [1993] 1 FLR 317) but not otherwise – *Farrant v Farrant* [1957] P 188 (school fees); *Nwogbe v Nwogbe* [2000] 2 FLR 744 (rent ordered to be paid under an occupation order)). An undertaking to pay money may not be enforced by committal except as permitted under DA 1869, s 5 (*Buckley v Crawford* [1893] 1 QB 105).

As to the formalities that are required if an undertaking, and in particular an undertaking to pay money, is to be enforceable by committal, see FPR PD33A.

33.10 Application

(1) An application for the issue of a judgment summons may be made –

    (a) in the case of an order of the High Court –

        (i) where the order was made in matrimonial proceedings, to the principal registry, a district registry or a divorce county court, whichever in the opinion of the judgment creditor is most convenient;

        (ii) where the order was made in civil partnership proceedings, to the principal registry, a district registry or a civil partnership proceedings county court, whichever in the opinion of the judgment creditor is the most convenient; and

        (iii) in any other case, to the principal registry, a district registry or a designated county court, whichever in the opinion of the judgment creditor is most convenient;

    (b) in the case of an order of a divorce county court, to whichever divorce county court is in the opinion of the judgment creditor most convenient; and

    (c) in the case of an order of a civil partnership proceedings county court, to whichever civil partnership proceedings county court is in the opinion of the judgment creditor most convenient,

having regard (in any case) to the place where the debtor resides or carries on business and irrespective of the court or registry in which the order was made.

(2) An application must be accompanied by a statement which –

    (a) complies with rule 33.3(1);

    (b) contains all the evidence on which the judgment creditor intends to rely; and

    (c) has exhibited to it a copy of the order.

Venue—Which venue is "convenient" depends inter alia on the debtor's residence or place of business. The summons cannot be issued in a county court that is not a divorce county court or civil partnership proceedings county court as the case may be.

Evidence (r 33.10(2)(b))—The requirement is to file all of the written evidence on which the creditor intends to rely. Copies will be served on the debtor (FPR 2010, r 33.13(2)). The object is to secure compliance with HRA 1998 as applied in *Mubarak v Mubarak* [2001] 1 FLR 698, CA. Thus, the written statements of witnesses on whose oral evidence it is intended to rely should be included. No doubt, if additional evidence came to light before the hearing, it would be admitted provided that it had been copied to the debtor promptly and in sufficient time before the hearing to enable him to deal with it.

33.11 Judgment summons

(1) If the debtor is in default under an order of committal made on a previous judgment summons in respect of the same order, a judgment summons must not be issued without the court's permission.

(2) A judgment summons must –

    (a)   be accompanied by the statement referred to in rule 33.10(2) and

    (b)   be served on the debtor personally not less than 14 days before the hearing.

(3) A debtor served with the judgment summons under paragraph (2)(b) must be paid or offered a sum reasonably sufficient to cover the expenses of travelling to and from the court at which the debtor is summoned to appear.

33.12 Successive judgment summonses

Subject to rule 33.11(1), successive judgment summonses may be issued even if the debtor has ceased to reside or carry on business at the address stated in the application for the issue of a judgment summons since the issue of the original judgment summons.

33.13 Requirement for personal service

In proceedings for committal by way of judgment summons, the following documents must be served personally on the debtor –

    (a)   where the court has summonsed the debtor to attend and the debtor has failed to do so, the notice of the date and time fixed for the adjourned hearing; and

    (b)   copies of the judgment summons and the documents mentioned in rule 33.10(2).

33.14 Committal on application for judgment summons

(1) No person may be committed on an application for a judgment summons unless –

    (a)   where the proceedings are in the High Court, the debtor has failed to attend both the hearing that the debtor was summonsed to attend and the adjourned hearing;

    (b)   where the proceedings are in a county court, an order is made under section 110(2) of the County Courts Act 1984; or

    (c)   the judgment creditor proves that the debtor –

        (i)   has, or has had, since the date of the order the means to pay the sum in respect of which the debtor has made default; and

        (ii)   has refused or neglected, or refuses or neglects, to pay that sum.

(2) The debtor may not be compelled to give evidence.

"the judgment creditor proves" (r 33.14(c))—It is not a requirement that the debtor be in attendance. Where the judge is satisfied that the judgment summons has been duly served, with evidence that proves that the debtor has or has had the means to pay and neglects or refuses (or has neglected or refused) to pay, he is not obliged to exercise his power to order the debtor to attend an adjourned hearing. See further **Order for attendance** under CPR 1998, Sch 2, CCR Ord 28, r 4. Particularly in a case where the evidence demonstrates that the debtor is aware of the hearing, chooses to absent himself, is able to pay and is defying the court's order, the judge may find that an adjournment and order to attend, with consequent costs, would serve no purpose; and exercise his power to commit under s 5 without first making such an order. (The debtor would, of course, still be able to apply to set aside the order made in his absence.) An order made in these circumstances might well be suspended for a short period to enable the debtor to pay.

The evidence must show that the debtor has or had the means to pay (*Buckley v Crawford* [1893] 1 QB 105; *R v Birmingham County Court Judge* [1902] 2 KB 283). The fact that the original order was made by consent was described as an "obvious starting point" in *Topping v Topping* [2008] EWCA Civ 1142. His conduct must be in the nature of a contempt (*Re Edgcome, ex parte Edgcome* [1902] 2 KB 403), although it is his means and not his general conduct that are the relevant consideration (*Abecasis v Brandon* [1947] LJR 325). The standard of proof of the debtor's means is the criminal standard, i e beyond reasonable doubt (*Woodley v Woodley* [1992] 2 FLR 417, CA). After the making of a bankruptcy order, the debtor will usually no longer have the means to pay and, in those circumstances, a committal order will not be made unless his failure to pay before the bankruptcy was such as to merit punishment (*Woodley v Woodley*

(No 2) [1993] 2 FLR 477, CA). The debtor's means include gifts received (*Re Park, ex parte Koster* (1885) 14 QBD 597), but not future sums that may be received such as a husband's allowance to his wife (*Barefoot v Clarke* [1949] 2 KB 97). Child benefit and certain social security benefits paid in respect of children must be ignored.

Gaps in the evidence as to the debtor's means can no longer be made good by requiring him to submit to questioning (r 33.14(2)). It seems unlikely that any evidence he gave, under compulsion, on examination under CPR 1998, Sch 2, CCR Ord 26, r 3 will be admitted.

As an alternative to a committal order the court may make an attachment of earnings order (AEA 1971, s 3(4)). For this purpose, proof of the debtor's means to the civil standard only would be needed. A further alternative is to make a new order under FPR 2010, r 33.16(1). If the proceedings concern a "qualifying periodical maintenance order" within the meaning of MEA 1991, s 1 then, under s 1(4)(a), the court may of its own motion make a "means of payment order", whether as an alternative to or in aid of a suspended committal order or a new order.

"the debtor may not be compelled to give evidence" (r 33.14(2))—While this remains correct, a debtor who fails to adduce convincing evidence does so at his peril – "there is no proper affidavit of means from him which demonstrates the truth of what he says" (*Topping*, above).

33.15 Orders for the benefit of different persons

Where an applicant has obtained one or more orders in the same application but for the benefit of different persons –

    (a)   where the judgment creditor is a child, the applicant may apply for the issue of a judgment summons in respect of those orders on behalf of the judgment creditor without seeking permission to act as the child's litigation friend; and

    (b)   only one judgment summons need be issued in respect of those orders.

33.16 Hearing of judgment summons

(1) On the hearing of the judgment summons the court may –

    (a)   where the order is for lump sum provision or costs; or

    (b)   where the order is an order for maintenance pending suit, an order for maintenance pending outcome of proceedings or an order for other periodical payments and it appears to the court that the order would have been varied or suspended if the debtor had made an application for that purpose,

make a new order for payment of the amount due under the original order, together with the costs of the judgment summons, either at a specified time or by instalments.

(2) If the court makes an order of committal, it may direct its execution to be suspended on terms that the debtor pays to the judgment creditor –

    (a)   the amount due;

    (b)   the costs of the judgment summons; and

    (c)   any sums accruing due under the original order,

either at a specified time or by instalments.

(3) All payments under a new order or an order of committal must be made to the judgment creditor unless the court directs otherwise.

(4) Where an order of committal is suspended on such terms as are mentioned in paragraph (2) –

    (a)   all payments made under the suspended order will be deemed to be made –

        (i)   first, in or towards the discharge of any sums from time to time accruing due under the original order; and

        (ii) secondly, in or towards the discharge of a debt in respect of which the judgment summons was issued and the costs of the summons; and

    (b)   the suspended order must not be executed until the judgment creditor has filed a statement of default on the part of the debtor.

New order (r 33.16(1))—This alternative to a committal order effectively gives the periodical payments debtor further time to pay the arrears. It is available only if the judge believes that an application to vary or suspend would have succeeded. It allows time for such an application to be made and for the question then to be considered whether some or all of the arrears should be remitted. Preferably, the debtor should issue an application to vary the periodical payments order and (if appropriate) remit arrears so that this can be heard with, or before an adjourned hearing of, the judgment summons (*Corbett v Corbett* [2003] 2 FLR 385). The new order (or, indeed, any committal order) will then relate only to such of the arrears as remain after the application has been determined. A new order may of course also be made in respect of a lump sum order.

An order of committal (r 33.16(2))—It is important to note that the limit of the court's jurisdiction is to commit for up to 6 weeks in accordance with DA 1869, s 5: *Zuk v Zuk* [2012] EWCA Civ 1871, where "the proceedings were peppered with errors". Also, now see *Bhura v Bhura* [2012] EWHC 3633 (Fam), where wilful refusal to pay, accompanied by the giving of "completely false evidence" (dishonesty in proceedings), attracted a suspended sentence. Semble, an approach to the Attorney-General under FPR 2010, r 17.6 may be appropriate in such a case; cf recent decisions under CPR 1998, r 32.14 discussed in *Civil Court Service* (Jordan Publishing Ltd).

Continued default after committal—Only one term of imprisonment can be imposed in respect of an unpaid amount (*Evans v Wills* (1876) 1 CPD 229). This would not prevent a second judgment summons in respect of fresh arrears under the same periodical payments order.

33.17 Special provisions as to judgment summonses in the High Court

(1) The court may summons witnesses to give evidence to prove the means of the debtor and may issue a witness summons for that purpose.

(2) Where the debtor appears at the hearing, the court may direct that the travelling expenses paid to the debtor be allowed as expenses of a witness.

(3) Where the debtor appears at the hearing and no order of committal is made, the court may allow the debtor's proper costs including compensation for any loss of earnings.

(4) When the court makes –

    (a) a new order; or

    (b) an order of committal,

a court officer must send notice of the order to the debtor and, if the original order was made in another court, to that court.

(5) An order of committal must be directed –

    (a) where the order is to be executed by the tipstaff, to the tipstaff; or

    (b) where the order is to be executed by a deputy tipstaff, to the county court within the district of which the debtor is to be found.

33.18 Special provisions as to judgment summonses in designated county courts

(1) Rules 1, 2, 3(2), 5, 7(3) and 9(2) of Order 28 of the CCR (which deal with the issue of a judgment summons in a county court and the subsequent procedure) do not apply to judgment summons issued in a designated county court.

(2) Rule 9(1) of Order 28 of the CCR (notification of order on judgment of High Court) applies to such a summons as if for the words "the High Court" there were substituted the words –

    (a) "any other court" where they first appear; and

    (b) "that other court" where they next appear.

(3) Rule 7(1) and (2) of Order 28 of the CCR (suspension of a committal order) apply to such a summons subject to rule 33.16(2) and (3).

Chapter 3
Attachment of Earnings

33.19 Proceedings in the Principal Registry

The Attachment of Earnings Act 1971 and Order 27 of the CCR (attachment of earnings) apply to the enforcement of an order made in family proceedings in the principal registry which are treated as pending in a designated county court as if they were an order made by such a court.

Chapter 4
Warrant of Execution

33.20 Applications to vary existing orders

Where an application is pending for a variation of –

    (a)   a financial order;
    (b)   an order under section 27 of the 1973 Act; or
    (c)   an order under Part 9 of Schedule 5 to the 2004 Act,

no warrant of execution may be issued to enforce payment of any sum due under those orders, except with the permission of the district judge.

33.21 Section 103 County Courts Act 1984

Where a warrant of execution has been issued to enforce an order made in family proceedings pending in the principal registry which are treated as pending in a designated county court, the goods and chattels against which the warrant has been issued must, wherever they are located, be treated for the purposes of section 103 of the County Courts Act 1984 as being out of the jurisdiction of the principal registry.

Chapter 5
Court's Power to Appoint a Receiver

33.22 Application of the CPR

Part 69 of the CPR applies to proceedings under this Part.

Chapter 6
Orders to Obtain Information from Judgment Debtors

33.23 Application of the CPR

Part 71 of the CPR applies to proceedings under this Part.

Chapter 7
Third Party Debt Orders

33.24 Application of the CPR

(1) Part 72 of the CPR applies to proceedings under this Part with the following modifications.

(2) In rule 72.4 –

    (a)   in paragraph (1), for "a judge" there is substituted "the court"; and

(b)   in paragraph (2), for "judge" there is substituted "court".

(3) In rule 72.7, in paragraph (2)(a), after "the Royal Courts of Justice" insert ", or the principal registry".

(4) Rule 72.10 is omitted.

Chapter 8
Charging Order, Stop Order, Stop Notice

33.25 Application of the CPR

(1) Part 73 of the CPR applies to proceedings under this Part with the following modifications.

(2) In rule 73.1, paragraph (2), sub-paragraphs (b) and (c) are omitted.

(3) For rule 73.2, there is substituted "This Section applies to an application by a judgment creditor for a charging order under section 1 of the 1979 Act.".

(4) In rule 73.3, paragraph (2), sub-paragraphs (b) and (c) are omitted.

(5) In rule 73.4 –
> (a)   in paragraph (1), for "a judge" there is substituted "the court,"; and
> (b)   in paragraph (2), for "judge" there is substituted "court".

(6) In rule 73.9, in the parenthesis after paragraph (1) –
> (a)   "and regulation 51.4 of the 1992 Regulations" is omitted;
> (b)   for "provides" there is substituted "provide", and
> (c)   ", or (where the 1992 Regulations apply) of the authority," is omitted.

(7) In rule 73.10 –
> (a)   in paragraph (1), for "a claim" there is substituted "an application";
> (b)   in paragraph (2) and the parenthesis following it, for "A claim" each time it appears there is substituted "An application";
> (c)   in paragraph (3), for "claimant" there is substituted "applicant";
> (d)   in paragraph (4), for "claim form" there is substituted "application"; and
> (e)   in paragraph (5), for "claimant's" there is substituted "applicant's".

(8) In rule 73.11, "funds in court or" is omitted.

(9) In rule 73.12 –
> (a)   paragraph (1)(a) is omitted;
> (b)   in paragraph (1)(b) "other than securities held in court" is omitted;
> (c)   in paragraph (2), in sub-paragraph (b), for "claim form" there is substituted "application notice"; and
> (d)   in paragraph (3) –
>> (i)   "or claim form" is omitted; and
>> (ii) for sub-paragraph (b) there is substituted "the person specified in rule 73.5(1)(d)".

(10) Rule 73.13 is omitted.

(11) In rule 73.14, in paragraph (1), "other than securities held in court" is omitted.

(12) In rule 73.16 –
> (a)   in paragraph (a) for "; and" there is substituted "."; and
> (b)   paragraph (b) is omitted.

Practice Direction 33A – Enforcement of Undertakings

This Practice Direction supplements FPR Part 33

Enforcement of undertaking to do or abstain from doing any act other than the payment of money

1.1 Rule 33.1(2) provides that Part 50 of, and Schedules 1 and 2 to, the CPR (which contain the Rules of the Supreme Court (RSC) and County Court Rules (CCR) respectively) apply, as far as they are relevant and with necessary modification, to an application made in the High Court and a county court to enforce an order made in family proceedings.

1.2 Subject to the Debtors Act 1869 (which makes provision in relation to orders for the payment of money), RSC Order 45.5 and CCR Order 29.1 enable a judgment or order to be enforced by committal for contempt of court where –

    (a)   a person who is required by a judgment or order to do an act has refused or neglected to do that act within the specified time; or

    (b)   a person disobeys a judgment or order requiring him to abstain from doing an act.

1.3 These Rules apply to undertakings as they apply to orders, with necessary modifications.

1.4 The form of an undertaking to do or abstain from doing any act must be endorsed with a notice setting out the consequences of disobedience, as follows:

    "You may be sent to prison for contempt of court if you break the promises that you have given to the court".

1.5 The person giving the undertaking must make a signed statement to the effect that he or she understands the terms of the undertaking being given and the consequences of failure to comply with it, as follows:

    "I understand the undertaking that I have given, and that if I break any of my promises to the court I may be sent to prison for contempt of court".

1.6 The statement need not be given before the court in person. It may be endorsed on the court copy of the undertaking or may be filed in a separate document such as a letter.

Enforcement of undertaking for the payment of money

2.1 Any undertaking for the payment of money that has effect as if it was an order made under Part 2 of the Matrimonial Causes Act 1973 may be enforced as if it was an order and Part 33 applies accordingly.

2.2 The form of an undertaking for the payment of money that has effect as if it were an order under Part 2 of the Matrimonial Causes Act 1973 must be endorsed with a notice setting out the consequences of disobedience, as follows:

    "If you fail to pay any sum of money which you have promised the court that you will pay, a person entitled to enforce the undertaking may apply to the court for an order. You may be sent to prison if it is proved that you –

    (a)   have, or have had since the date of your undertaking, the means to pay the sum; and

    (b)   have refused or neglected, or are refusing or neglecting, to pay that sum".

Amendments—FPR 2010, Update 2.

2.3 The person giving the undertaking must make a signed statement to the effect that he or she understands the terms of the undertaking being given and the consequences of failure to comply with it, as follows:

"I understand the undertaking that I have given, and that if I break my promise to the court to pay any sum of money, I may be sent to prison".

2.4 The statement need not be given before the court in person. It may be endorsed on the court copy of the undertaking or may be filed in a separate document such as a letter.

PART 34
RECIPROCAL ENFORCEMENT OF MAINTENANCE ORDERS

CONTENTS OF THIS PART

34.1 Scope and interpretation of this Part

(1) This Part contains rules about the reciprocal enforcement of maintenance orders.

(2) In this Part –

"the 1920 Act" means the Maintenance Orders (Facilities for Enforcement) Act 1920;

"the 1972 Act" means the Maintenance Orders (Reciprocal Enforcement) Act 1972;

"the 1982 Act" means the Civil Jurisdiction and Judgments Act 1982;

"the 1988 Convention" means the Convention on jurisdiction and the enforcement of judgments in civil and commercial matters done at Lugano on 16 September 1988;

"the Judgments Regulation" means Council Regulation (EC) No. 44/2001 of 22 December 2000 on jurisdiction and the recognition and enforcement of judgments in civil and commercial matters; and

"the Lugano Convention" means the Convention on jurisdiction and the recognition and enforcement of judgments in civil and commercial matters, between the European Community and the Republic of Iceland, the Kingdom of Norway, the Swiss Confederation and the Kingdom of Denmark signed on behalf of the European Community on 30 October 2007.

(3) Chapter 1 of this Part relates to the enforcement of maintenance orders in accordance with the 1920 Act.

(4) Chapter 2 of this Part relates to the enforcement of maintenance orders in accordance with Part 1 of the 1972 Act.

(5) Chapter 3 of this Part relates to the enforcement of maintenance orders in accordance with –

    (a)   the 1982 Act;

    (b)   the Judgments Regulation;

    (c)   the Lugano Convention;

    (d)   the Maintenance Regulation; and

    (e)   the 2007 Hague Convention.

Amendments—SI 2011/1328; SI 2012/2806.

34.2 Meaning of prescribed officer in a magistrates' court

(1) For the purposes of the 1920 Act, the prescribed officer in relation to a magistrates' court is the designated officer for that court.

(2) For the purposes of Part 1 of the 1972 Act and section 5(2) of the 1982 Act, the prescribed officer in relation to a magistrates' court is the justices' clerk for the local justice area in which the court is situated.

34.3 Registration of maintenance orders in magistrates' courts in England and Wales

Where a magistrates' court is required by any of the enactments referred to in rule 34.1(2) or by virtue of the Maintenance Regulation or the 2007 Hague Convention to register a foreign order the court officer must –

    (a)   enter a memorandum of the order in the register kept in accordance with rules made under section 144 of the Magistrates' Courts Act 1980; and

    (b)   state on the memorandum the statutory provision or international instrument under which the order is registered.

Amendments—SI 2011/1328; SI 2012/679; SI 2012/2806.

Chapter 1
Enforcement of Maintenance Orders under the Maintenance Orders (Facilities for Enforcement) Act 1920

34.4 Interpretation

(1) In this Chapter –
  "payer", in relation to a maintenance order, means the person liable to make the payments for which the order provides; and
  "reciprocating country" means a country or territory to which the 1920 Act extends.

(2) In this Chapter, an expression defined in the 1920 Act has the meaning given to it in that Act.

34.5 Confirmation of provisional orders made in a reciprocating country

(1) This rule applies where, in accordance with section 4(1) of the 1920 Act, the court officer receives a provisional maintenance order.

(2) The court must fix the date, time and place for a hearing.

(3) The court officer must register the order in accordance with rule 34.3.

(4) The court officer must serve on the payer –
  (a) certified copies of the provisional order and accompanying documents; and
  (b) a notice –
    (i) specifying the time and date fixed for the hearing; and
    (ii) stating that the payer may attend to show cause why the order should not be confirmed.

(5) The court officer must inform –
  (a) the court which made the provisional order; and
  (b) the Lord Chancellor,

whether the court confirms, with or without modification, or decides not to confirm, the order.

34.6 Payment of sums due under registered orders

Where an order made by a reciprocating country is registered in a magistrates' court, the court must order payments due to be made to the court officer.

  (Practice Direction 34A contains further provisions relating to the payment of sums due under registered orders.)

34.7 Enforcement of sums due under registered orders

(1) This rule applies to –
  (a) an order made in a reciprocating country which is registered in a magistrates' court; and
  (b) a provisional order made in a reciprocating country which has been confirmed by a magistrates' court.

(2) The court officer must –
  (a) collect the monies due under the order in the same way as for a magistrates' court maintenance order; and
  (b) send the monies collected to –
    (i) the court in the reciprocating country which made the order; or

>   (ii) such other person or authority as that court or the Lord Chancellor may from time to time direct.

(3) The court officer may take proceedings in that officer's own name for enforcing payment of monies due under the order.

"the Lord Chancellor may from time to time direct" (r 34.7(2)(b))—In Home Office Circular 139/1970 it is directed that payments under a New Zealand court order are to be made to the New Zealand Department of Social Security. The relevant addresses are listed in the appendix to the Circular.

34.8 Prescribed notice for the taking of further evidence

(1) This rule applies where a court in a reciprocating country has sent a provisional order to a magistrates' court for the purpose of taking further evidence.

(2) The court officer must send a notice to the person who applied for the provisional order specifying –

>   (a) the further evidence required; and
>   (b) the time and place fixed for taking the evidence.

34.9 Transmission of maintenance orders made in a reciprocating country to the High Court

A maintenance order to be sent by the Lord Chancellor to the High Court in accordance with section 1(1) of the 1920 Act will be –

>   (a) sent to the senior district judge who will register it in the register kept for the purpose of the 1920 Act; and
>   (b) filed in the principal registry.

34.10 Transmission of maintenance orders made in the High Court to a reciprocating country

(1) This rule applies to maintenance orders made in the High Court.

(2) An application for a maintenance order to be sent to a reciprocating country under section 2 of the 1920 Act must be made in accordance with this rule.

(3) The application must be made to a district judge in the principal registry unless paragraph (4) applies.

(4) If the order was made in the course of proceedings in a district registry, the application may be made to a district judge in that district registry.

(5) The application must be –

>   (a) accompanied by a certified copy of the order; and
>   (b) supported by a record of the sworn written evidence.

(6) The written evidence must give –

>   (a) the applicant's reason for believing that the payer resides in the reciprocating country;
>   (b) such information as the applicant has as to the whereabouts of the payer; and
>   (c) such other information as may be set out in Practice Direction 34A.

34.11 Inspection of the register in the High Court

(1) A person may inspect the register and request copies of a registered order and any document filed with it if the district judge is satisfied that that person is entitled to, or liable to make, payments under a maintenance order made in –

    (a)   the High Court; or

    (b)   a court in a reciprocating country.

(2) The right to inspect the register referred to in paragraph (1) may be exercised by –

    (a)   a solicitor acting on behalf of the person entitled to, or liable to make, the payments referred to in that paragraph; or

    (b)   with the permission of the district judge, any other person.

Chapter 2
Enforcement of Maintenance Orders under Part 1 of the 1972 Act

34.12 Interpretation

(1) In this Chapter –

    (a)   "reciprocating country" means a country to which Part 1 of the 1972 Act extends; and

    (b)   "relevant court in the reciprocating country" means, as the case may be –

        (i)   the court which made the order which has been sent to England and Wales for confirmation;

        (ii) the court which made the order which has been registered in a court in England and Wales;

        (iii) the court to which an order made in England and Wales has been sent for registration; or

        (iv) the court to which a provisional order made in England and Wales has been sent for confirmation.

(2) In this Chapter, an expression defined in the 1972 Act has the meaning given to it in that Act.

(3) In this Chapter, "Hague Convention Countries" means the countries listed in Schedule 1 to the Reciprocal Enforcement of Maintenance Orders (Hague Convention Countries) Order 1993.

Amendments—SI 2011/1328.

34.13 Scope

(1) Section 1 of this Chapter contains rules relating to the reciprocal enforcement of maintenance orders under Part 1 of the 1972 Act.

(2) Section 2 of this Chapter modifies the rules contained in Section 1 of this Chapter in their application to –

    (a)   *(revoked)*

    (b)   the Hague Convention Countries; and

    (c)   the United States of America.

       (Practice Direction 34A sets out in full the rules for the Hague Convention Countries and the United States of America as modified by Section 2 of this Chapter.)

Amendments—SI 2011/1328.

Section 1
Reciprocal enforcement of maintenance orders under Part 1 of the 1972 Act

34.14 Application for transmission of maintenance order to reciprocating country

An application for a maintenance order to be sent to a reciprocating country under section 2 of the 1972 Act must be made in accordance with Practice Direction 34A.

34.15 Certification of evidence given on provisional orders

A document setting out or summarising evidence is authenticated by a court in England and Wales by a certificate signed, as the case may be, by –

(a)   one of the justices; or

(b)   the District Judge (Magistrates' Courts),

before whom that evidence was given.

> (Section 3(5)(b), 5(4) and 9(5) of the 1972 Act require a document to be authenticated by the court.)

34.16 Confirmation of a provisional order made in a reciprocating country

(1) This rule applies to proceedings for the confirmation of a provisional order made in a reciprocating country.

(2) Paragraph (3) applies on receipt by the court of –

(a)   a certified copy of the order; and

(b)   the documents required by the 1972 Act to accompany the order.

(3) On receipt of the documents referred to in paragraph (2) –

(a)   the court must fix the date, time and place for a hearing or a directions appointment; and

(b)   the court officer must send to the payer notice of the date, time and place fixed together with a copy of the order and accompanying documents.

(4) The date fixed for the hearing must be not less than 21 days beginning with the date on which the court officer sent the documents to the payer in accordance with paragraph (2).

(5) The court officer will send to the relevant court in the reciprocating country a certified copy of any order confirming or refusing to confirm the provisional order.

(6) This rule does not apply to the confirmation of a provisional order made in a reciprocating country varying a maintenance order to which sections 5(5) or 9(6) of the 1972 Act applies.

> (Section 5(5) and 7 of the 1972 Act provide for proceedings for the confirmation of a provisional order.)

> (Provision in respect of confirmation of a provisional order varying a maintenance order under the 1972 Act is in rules made under section 144 of the Magistrates' Courts Act 1980).

> (Rule 34.22 provides for the transmission of documents to a court in a reciprocating country.)

Varying a maintenance order—Proceedings involving variation by the court of maintenance orders, whether made, confirmed or registered in the UK, do not fall within the definition of family proceedings for the purpose of MCA 1980, s 65. The provisions of FPR 2010 do not apply automatically to such proceedings, but see MC(EVOFP & MP)R 2011, Pt 5, which applies this rule with modification.

PART III

34.17 Consideration of revocation of a provisional order made by a magistrates' court

(1) This rule applies where –

  (a) a magistrates' court has made a provisional order by virtue of section 3 of the 1972 Act;

  (b) before the order is confirmed, evidence is taken by the court or received by it as set out in section 5(9) of the 1972 Act; and

  (c) on consideration of the evidence the court considers that the order ought not to have been made.

  (Section 5(9) of the 1972 Act provides that a magistrates' court may revoke a provisional order made by it, before the order has been confirmed in a reciprocating country, if it receives new evidence.)

(2) The court officer must serve on the person who applied for the provisional order ("the applicant") a notice which must –

  (a) set out the evidence taken or received by the court;

  (b) inform the applicant that the court considers that the order ought not to have been made; and

  (c) inform the applicant that the applicant may –

    make representations in relation to that evidence either orally or in writing; and adduce further evidence.

(3) If an applicant wishes to adduce further evidence –

  (a) the applicant must notify the court officer at the court which made the order;

  (b) the court will fix a date for the hearing of the evidence; and

  (c) the court officer will notify the applicant in writing of the date fixed.

34.18 Notification of variation or revocation of a maintenance order by the High Court or a county court

(1) This rule applies where –

  (a) a maintenance order has been sent to a reciprocating country in pursuance of section 2 of the 1972 Act; and

  (b) the court makes an order, not being a provisional order, varying or revoking that order.

(2) The court officer must send a certified copy of the order of variation or revocation to the relevant court in the reciprocating country.

  (Rule 34.22 provides for the transmission of documents to a court in a reciprocating country.)

34.19 Notification of confirmation or revocation of a maintenance order by a magistrates' court

(1) This rule applies where a magistrates' court makes an order –

  (a) not being a provisional order, revoking a maintenance order to which section 5 of the 1972 Act applies;

  (b) under section 9 of the 1972 Act, revoking a registered order; or

  (c) under section 7(2) of the 1972 Act, confirming an order to which section 7 of that Act applies.

(2) The court officer must send written notice of the making, revocation or confirmation of the order, as appropriate, to the relevant court in the reciprocating country.

(3) This rule does not apply to a provisional order varying a maintenance order to which sections 5 or 9 of the 1972 Act apply.

> (Section 5 of the 1972 Act applies to a provisional order made by a magistrates' court in accordance with section 3 of that Act which has been confirmed by a court in a reciprocating country.)

> (Provision in respect of notification of variation of a maintenance order by a magistrates' court under the 1972 Act is made in rules made under section 144 of the Magistrates' Courts Act 1980.)

> (Rule 34.22 provides for the transmission of documents to a court in a reciprocating country.)

Varying a maintenance order—See under FPR 2010, r 34.16.

34.20 Taking of evidence for court in reciprocating country

(1) This rule applies where a request is made by or on behalf of a court in a reciprocating country for the taking of evidence for the purpose of proceedings relating to a maintenance order to which Part 1 of the 1972 Act applies.

> (Section 14 of the 1972 Act makes provision for the taking of evidence needed for the purpose of certain proceedings.)

(2) The High Court has power to take the evidence where –

    (a)   the request for evidence relates to a maintenance order made by a superior court in the United Kingdom; and

    (b)   the witness resides in England and Wales.

(3) The county court has power to take the evidence where –

    (a)   the request for evidence relates to a maintenance order made by a county court; and

    (b)   the maintenance order has not been registered in a magistrates' court under the 1958 Act.

(4) The following magistrates' courts have power to take the evidence, that is –

    (a)   where the proceedings in the reciprocating country relate to a maintenance order made by a magistrates' court, the court which made the order;

    (b)   where the proceedings relate to an order which is registered in a magistrates' court, the court in which the order is registered; and

    (c)   a magistrates' court to which the Lord Chancellor sends the request to take evidence.

(5) A magistrates' court not mentioned in paragraph (4) has power to take the evidence if the magistrates' court which would otherwise have that power consents because the evidence could be taken more conveniently.

(6) The evidence is to be taken in accordance with Part 22.

Amendments—SI 2011/1328.

34.21 Request for the taking of evidence by a court in a reciprocating country

(1) This rule applies where a request is made by a magistrates' court for the taking of evidence in a reciprocating country in accordance with section 14(5) of the 1972 Act.

(2) The request must be made in writing to the court in the reciprocating country.

> (Rule 34.22 provides for the transmission of documents to a court in a reciprocating country.)

34.22 Transmission of documents

(1) This rule applies to any document, including a notice or request, which is required to be sent to a court in a reciprocating country by –

(a)   Part 1 of the 1972 Act; or

(b)   Section 1 of Chapter 2 of this Part of these rules.

(2) The document must be sent to the Lord Chancellor for transmission to the court in the reciprocating country.

34.23 Method of payment under registered orders

(1) Where an order is registered in a magistrates' court in accordance with section 6(3) of the 1972 Act, the court must order that the payment of sums due under the order be made –

(a)   to the court officer for the registering court; and

(b)   at such time and place as the court officer directs.

> (Section 6(3) of the 1972 Act makes provision for the registration of maintenance orders made in a reciprocating country.)

(2) Where the court orders payments to be made to the court officer, whether in accordance with paragraph (1) or otherwise, the court officer must send the payments –

(a)   by post to either –

    (i)   the court which made the order; or

    (ii)   such other person or authority as that court, or the Lord Chancellor, directs; or

(b)   if the court which made the order is a country or territory specified in the Practice Direction 34A –

    (i)   to the Crown Agents for Overseas Governments and Administrations for transmission to the person to whom they are due; or

    (ii)   as the Lord Chancellor directs.

> (Practice Direction 34A contains further provisions relating to the payment of sums due under registered orders.)

"Crown Agents for Overseas Governments and Administrations" (r 34.23(2)(b)(i))—The address of the Crown Agents is St Nicholas House, St Nicholas Road, Sutton, Surrey, SM1 1EL.

34.24 Enforcement of payments under registered orders

(1) This rule applies where a court has ordered periodical payments under a registered maintenance order to be made to the court officer.

(2) The court officer must take reasonable steps to notify the payee of the means of enforcement available.

(3) Paragraph (4) applies where periodical payments due under a registered order are in arrears.

(4) The court officer, on that officer's own initiative –

(a)   may; or

(b)   if the sums due are more than 4 weeks in arrears, must,

proceed in that officer's own name for the recovery of the sums due unless of the view that it is unreasonable to do so.

"where periodical payments ... are in arrears" (r 34.24(3))—Applying the principle established in *Vogel v Lothschütz* [2012] EWHC 3411 (QB) in respect of registration of a European Enforcement Order, registration will not be invalidated by any miscalculation of arrears if registration has been effected in accordance with the proper procedure, as any miscalculation can be corrected.

34.25 Notification of registration and cancellation

(1) The court officer must send written notice to the Lord Chancellor of the due registration of orders registered in accordance with section 6(3), 7(5), or 10(4) of the 1972 Act.

(2) The court officer must, when registering an order in accordance with section 6(3), 7(5), 9(10), 10(4) or (5) or 23(3) of the 1972 Act, send written notice to the payer stating –

 (a) that the order has been registered;
 (b) that payments under the order should be made to the court officer; and
 (c) the hours during which and the place at which the payments should be made.

(3) The court officer must, when cancelling the registration of an order in accordance with section 10(1) of the 1972 Act, send written notice of the cancellation to the payer.

Section 2
Modification of rules in Section 1 of this Chapter

Sub-section 1
(revoked)

Sub-section 2
Hague Convention Countries

34.27 Application of Section 1 of this Chapter to the Hague Convention Countries

Note—This subsection contains detailed provision for the application of the Maintenance Orders (Reciprocal Enforcement) Act 1972 to the countries listed in the Reciprocal Enforcement of Maintenance Orders (Hague Convention Countries) Order 1993, Sch 1 (ie "the Hague Convention Countries"). However, where the country concerned is also a country to which the Maintenance Regulation (EC) No 4/2009 applies (EU member states), that regulation takes precedence over other reciprocal arrangements in Conventions and agreements and reference should be made instead to the provisions at Ch 3 of FPR 2010, Pt 34. The Maintenance Regulation, therefore, replaces the separate reciprocal regime between the UK and the Republic of Ireland.

(1) In relation to the Hague Convention Countries, Section 1 of this Chapter has effect as modified by this rule.

(2) A reference in this rule, and in any rule which has effect in relation to the Hague Convention Countries by virtue of this rule to –

 (a) the 1972 Act is a reference to the 1972 Act as modified by Schedule 2 to the Reciprocal Enforcement of Maintenance Orders (Hague Convention Countries) Order 1993; and
 (b) a section under the 1972 Act is a reference to the section so numbered in the 1972 Act as so modified.

(3) A reference to a reciprocating country in rule 34.12(1) and Section 1 of this Chapter is a reference to a Hague Convention Country.

(4) Rules 34.15 (certification of evidence given on provisional orders), 34.16 (confirmation of provisional orders), 34.19 (notification of confirmation or revocation of a maintenance order by a magistrates' court) and 34.21 (request for the taking of evidence by a court in a reciprocating country) do not apply.

(5) For rule 34.17 (consideration of revocation of a provisional order made by a magistrates' court) substitute –

"34.17   Consideration of revocation of a maintenance order made by a magistrates' court

(1) This rule applies where –

    (a)   an application has been made to a magistrates' court by a payee for the revocation of an order to which section 5 of the 1972 Act applies; and

    (b)   the payer resides in a Hague Convention Country.

(2) The court officer must serve on the payee, by post, a copy of any representations or evidence adduced by or on behalf of the payer.

    (Provision relating to consideration of variation of a maintenance order made by a magistrates' court to which section 5 of the 1972 Act applies is made in rules made under section 144 of the Magistrates' Courts Act 1980.)".

(6) For rule 34.18 (notification of variation or revocation of a maintenance order by the High Court or county court) substitute –

"34.18   Notification of variation or revocation of a maintenance order by the High Court or a county court

(1) This rule applies if the High Court or a county court makes an order varying or revoking a maintenance order to which section 5 of the 1972 Act applies.

(2) If the time for appealing has expired without an appeal having been entered, the court officer will send to the Lord Chancellor –

    (a)   the documents required by section 5(8) of the 1972 Act; and

    (b)   a certificate signed by the district judge stating that the order of variation or revocation is enforceable and no longer subject to the ordinary forms of review.

(3) A party who enters an appeal against the order of variation or revocation must, at the same time, give written notice to the court officer.".

(7) For rule 34.23(2) (method of payment under registered orders) substitute –

"(2) Where the court orders payment to be made to the court officer, the court officer must send the payments by post to the payee under the order.".

(8) For rule 34.25 (notification of registration and cancellation) substitute –

"34.25   Notification of registration and cancellation

The court officer must send written notice to –

    (a)   the Lord Chancellor, on the due registration of an order under section 10(4) of the 1972 Act; and

    (b)   the payer under the order,

on –

    (i)   the registration of an order under section 10(4) of the 1972 Act; or

    (ii)   the cancellation of the registration of an order under section 10(1) of the 1972 Act.".

(9) After rule 34.25 insert –

"34.25A General provisions as to notices

(1) A notice to a payer of the registration of an order in a magistrates' court in accordance with section 6(3) of the 1972 Act must be in the form referred to in a practice direction.

(Section 6(8) of the 1972 Act requires notice of registration to be given to the payer.)

(2) If the court sets aside the registration of a maintenance order following an appeal under section 6(9) of the 1972 Act, the court officer must send written notice of the decision to the Lord Chancellor.

(3) A notice to a payee that the court officer has refused to register an order must be in the form referred to in a practice direction.

(Section 6(11) of the 1972 Act requires notice of refusal of registration to be given to the payee.)

(4) Where, under any provision of Part 1 of the 1972 Act, a court officer serves a notice on a payer who resides in a Hague Convention Country, the court officer must send to the Lord Chancellor a certificate of service.".

"variation of a maintenance order made by a magistrates' court" (r 34.17)—Proceedings involving variation by the court of maintenance orders, whether made, confirmed or registered in the UK, do not fall within the definition of family proceedings for the purpose of MCA 1980, s 65. The provisions of FPR 2010 do not apply automatically to such proceedings, but see MC(EVOFP & MP)R 2011, Pt 5, which applies this rule with modification.

Modifications—See FPR PD34A, Annex 2.

Sub-section 3
United States of America

34.28 Application of Section 1 of this Chapter to the United States of America

(1) In relation to the United States of America, Section 1 of this Chapter has effect as modified by this rule.

(2) A reference in this rule and in any rule which has effect in relation to the United States of America by virtue of this rule to –

    (a)   the 1972 Act is a reference to the 1972 Act as modified by Schedule 1 to the Reciprocal Enforcement of Maintenance Orders (United States of America) Order 2007; and

    (b)   a section under the 1972 Act is a reference to the section so numbered in the 1972 Act as so modified.

(3) A reference to a reciprocating country in rule 34.12(1) and Section 1 of this Chapter is a reference to the United States of America.

(4) Rules 34.15 (certification of evidence given on provisional orders), 34.16 (confirmation of provisional orders), 34.19 (notification of confirmation or revocation of a maintenance order made by a magistrates' court) and 34.21 (request for the taking of evidence in a reciprocating country) do not apply.

(5) For rule 34.17 (consideration of revocation of a provisional order made by a magistrates' court) substitute –

"34.17 Consideration of revocation of a maintenance order made by a magistrates' court

(1) This rule applies where –

    (a) an application has been made to a magistrates' court by a payee for the revocation of an order to which section 5 of the 1972 Act applies; and

    (b) the payer resides in the United States of America.

(2) The court officer must serve on the payee by post a copy of any representations or evidence adduced by or on behalf of the payer.

    (Provision relating to consideration of variation of a maintenance order made by a magistrates' court to which section 5 of the 1972 Act applies is made in rules made under section 144 of the Magistrates' Courts Act 1980.)".

(6) For rule 34.18 (notification of variation or revocation), substitute –

"34.18 Notification of variation or revocation

If the High Court or a county court makes an order varying or revoking a maintenance order to which section 5 of the 1972 Act applies, the court officer will send to the Lord Chancellor the documents required by section 5(7) of that Act.".

(7) For rule 34.23(2) (method of payment under registered orders) substitute –

"(2) Where the court orders payment to be made to the court officer, the court officer must send the payments by post to the payee under the order.".

(8) For rule 34.25 (notification of registration and cancellation) substitute –

"34.25 Notification of registration and cancellation

The court officer must send written notice to –

    (a) the Lord Chancellor, on the due registration of an order under section 10(4) of the 1972 Act; or

    (b) the payer under the order, on –

        (i) the registration of an order under section 10(4) of the 1972 Act; or

        (ii) the cancellation of the registration of an order under section 10(1) of that Act."

Modifications—See FPR PD34A, Annex 3.

Application to the USA—With effect from 1 October 2007 (SI 2007/2005 and SI 2007/2006) the provisions of the 1972 Act apply, with modifications, to the whole of the USA. The principal modification is that a maintenance order made in the USA may not be varied or revoked in the UK and a maintenance order made in the UK may not be varied or revoked in the USA.

"variation of a maintenance order made by a magistrates' court" (r 34.17)—Proceedings involving variation by the court of maintenance orders, whether made, confirmed or registered in the UK, do not fall within the definition of family proceedings for the purpose of MCA 1980, s 65. The provisions of FPR 2010 do not apply automatically to such proceedings, but see MC(EVOFP & MP)R 2011, Pt 5, which applies this rule with modification.

Chapter 3
Enforcement of Maintenance Orders under the Civil Jurisdiction and Judgments Act 1982, the Judgments Regulation, the Maintenance Regulation, the 2007 Hague Convention and the Lugano Convention

Amendments—SI 2011/1328; SI 2012/2806.

Note—The relevant orders to which this Chapter applies are orders made in one of the other Member States of the EU, one of the non-EU signatories to the 2007 Hague Convention being Albania, Bosnia-Herzegovina, Norway, the USA and Ukraine, or orders made in Iceland or Switzerland sent for enforcement in England and Wales or vice versa.

34.28A Application of this Chapter

(1) In this Chapter –

- (a) references to a maintenance order include –
    - (i) a decision, a court settlement or an authentic instrument within the meaning of Article 2 of the Maintenance Regulation where that Regulation applies;
    - (ii) a maintenance decision to which Chapter V of the 2007 Hague Convention applies by virtue of Article 19(1) of that Convention;
    - (iii) a maintenance arrangement (as defined in Article 3(e) of the 2007 Hague Convention) which is to be recognised and enforceable in the same way as a maintenance decision by virtue of Article 30 of that Convention;
- (b) references to the Hague Protocol are to the Protocol on the Law Applicable to Maintenance Obligations done at The Hague on 23 November 2007;
- (c) "the 1968 Convention" has the meaning given in the 1982 Act.

(2) In relation to the Maintenance Regulation –

- (a) Section 1 applies to maintenance orders to which Sections 2 and 3 of Chapter IV of the Maintenance Regulation apply (decisions given in a Member State which does not apply the rules of the Hague Protocol, that is, Denmark, and decisions to which Sections 2 and 3 of Chapter IV of that Regulation apply by virtue of Article 75(2)(a) or (b));
- (b) Section 2 applies to all maintenance orders made in a magistrates' court in England and Wales for which reciprocal enforcement is sought in any Member State of the European Union, including Denmark.

    (Provision in respect of enforcement of maintenance orders to which Section 1 of Chapter IV of the Maintenance Regulation applies (maintenance decisions given in Member States other than Denmark) is made in the Magistrates' Courts Rules 1981)

Amendments—Inserted by SI 2011/1328; amended by SI 2012/679; SI 2012/2806.

Section 1
Registration and Enforcement in a Magistrates' Court of Maintenance Orders made in a Contracting State to the 1968 Convention, a Contracting State to the 1988 Convention, a Regulation State, a State bound by the 2007 Hague Convention other than a Member State of the European Union or a State bound by the Lugano Convention

Amendments—SI 2012/2806.

Note—EU Member States will use the 2007 Hague Convention with non-EU Contracting States only; the Maintenance Regulation will be used as between Member States.

34.29 Interpretation

In this Section –

- (a) an expression defined in the 1982 Act has the meaning given to it in that Act, subject to paragraph (b); and

(b) "Regulation State" means a Member State of the European Union which does not apply the rules of the Hague Protocol, or, where registration is sought for a maintenance order to which Article 75(2)(a) or (b) of the Maintenance Regulation applies, the Member State of the European Union from which the order originated.

Amendments—SI 2011/1328.

34.29A Application under Article 30 of the Maintenance Regulation or under Article 23 of the 2007 Hague Convention for a declaration of enforceability

An application under Article 30 of the Maintenance Regulation for a declaration of enforceability of a maintenance order, or under Article 23(2) or (3) of the 2007 Hague Convention for registration of a maintenance order, will be determined by the justices' clerk for the local justice area in which the court is situated.

Amendments—Inserted by SI 2011/1328; amended by SI 2012/2806.

34.30 Registration of maintenance orders

(1) In this rule, "assets to which the 1958 Act applies" means assets against which, after registration in the High Court, the maintenance order could be enforced under Part 1 of the 1958 Act.

(2) This rule applies where the court officer for a magistrates' court receives –

(a) an application under Article 31 of the 1968 Convention for the enforcement of a maintenance order made in a Contracting State other than the United Kingdom;

(b) an application under Article 31 of the 1988 Convention for the enforcement of a maintenance order made in a State bound by the 1988 Convention other than a Member State of the European Union;

(c) an application under Article 26 of the Maintenance Regulation for a declaration of enforceability of a maintenance order made in a Regulation State other than the United Kingdom;

(d) an application under Article 38 of the Lugano Convention for the enforcement of a maintenance order made in a State bound by the Lugano Convention other than a Member State of the European Union; or

(e) an application under Article 23 of the 2007 Hague Convention for registration of a maintenance order made in a State bound by that Convention other than a Member State of the European Union.

(3) The court officer must –

(a) take such steps as appear appropriate for ascertaining whether the payer resides within the local justice area for which the court acts; and

(b) consider any available information as to the nature and location of the payer's assets.

(4) If the court officer is satisfied that the payer –

(a) does not reside within the local justice area for which the court acts; and

(b) does not have assets to which the 1958 Act applies,

the court officer must refuse the application and return the application to the Lord Chancellor stating the information the court officer has as to the whereabouts of the payer and the nature and location of the payer's assets.

(5) If the court officer is satisfied that the payer –

(a) does not reside within the local justice area for which the court acts; but

(b)   has assets to which the 1958 Act applies,

then either –

      (i)   the court officer must register the order; or

      (ii) if the court officer believes that the payer is residing within the local justice area in which another magistrates' court acts, the court officer may refuse the application and return the documents to the Lord Chancellor with the information referred to in paragraph (4) above.

(6) Except where paragraphs (4) or (5) apply, the court officer must register the order unless –

(a)   in the case of an application under Article 31 of the 1968 Convention, Articles 27 or 28 of that Convention apply;

(b)   in the case of an application under Article 31 of the 1988 Convention, Articles 27 or 28 of that Convention apply; and

(c)   in the case of an application under Article 23(2) or (3) of the 2007 Hague Convention, Article 22(a) of that Convention applies.

(7) If the court officer refuses to register an order to which this rule relates the court officer must notify the applicant.

(8) If the court officer registers an order the court officer must send written notice of that fact to –

(a)   the Lord Chancellor;

(b)   the payer; and

(c)   the applicant.

(9) If the court officer considers that it would be appropriate for all or part of a registered order to be enforced in the High Court the court officer must notify the applicant –

(a)   that the court officer so considers it appropriate; and

(b)   that the applicant may apply, or may request the court officer to apply, under the 1958 Act for the order to be registered in the High Court.

Amendments—SI 2011/1328, with savings and transitional provisions; SI 2012/2806.

34.31 Appeal from a decision relating to registration

(1) This rule applies to an appeal under –

(a)   Article 36 or Article 40 of the 1968 Convention;

(b)   Article 36 or Article 40 of the 1988 Convention;

(c)   Article 32 of the Maintenance Regulation;

(d)   Article 43 of the Lugano Convention; or

(e)   Article 23(5) of the 2007 Hague Convention.

(2) The appeal must be to the magistrates' court –

(a)   in which the order is registered; or

(b)   in which the application for registration has been refused,

as the case may be.

Amendments—SI 2011/1328, with savings and transitional provisions; SI 2012/2806.

34.32 Payment of sums due under a registered order

(1) Where an order is registered in accordance with section 5(3) of the 1982 Act, Article 38 of the Judgments Regulation, Article 38 of the Lugano Convention or

Article 23 of the 2007 Hague Convention, or declared enforceable under Article 26 of the Maintenance Regulation by virtue of registration, the court must order that payment of sums due under the order be made –

(a)   to the court officer for the registering court; and

(b)   at such time and place as the court officer directs.

(2) Where the court orders payments to be made to the court officer, whether in accordance with paragraph (1) or otherwise, the court officer must send the payments by post either –

(a)   to the court which made the order; or

(b)   to such other person or authority as that court, or the Lord Chancellor, directs.

(Practice Direction 34A contains further provisions relating to the payment of sums due under registered orders.)

Amendments—SI 2011/1328; SI 2012/2806.

34.33 Enforcement of payments under registered orders

(1) This rule applies where a court has ordered periodical payments under a registered maintenance order to be made to the court officer for a magistrates' court.

(2) The court officer must take reasonable steps to notify the payee of the means of enforcement available.

(3) Paragraph (4) applies where periodical payments due under a registered order are in arrears.

(4) The court officer, on that officer's own initiative –

(a)   may; or

(b)   if the sums due are more than 4 weeks in arrears, must,

proceed in that officer's own name for the recovery of the sums due unless of the view that it is unreasonable to do so.

"where periodical payments ... are in arrears" (r 34.33(3))—Applying the principle established in *Vogel v Lothschütz* [2012] EWHC 3411 (QB) in respect of registration of a European Enforcement Order, registration will not be invalidated by any miscalculation of arrears if registration has been effected in accordance with the proper procedure, as any miscalculation can be corrected.

34.34 Variation and revocation of registered orders

(1) This rule applies where the court officer for a registering court receives notice that a registered maintenance order has been varied or revoked by a competent court in a Contracting State to the 1968 Convention, a Contracting State to the 1988 Convention (other than a Member State of the European Union), a Regulation State or a State bound by the Lugano Convention or by the 2007 Hague Convention, other than a Member State of the European Union.

(2) The court officer for the registering court must –

(a)   register the order of variation or revocation; and

(b)   send notice of the registration by post to the payer and payee under the order.

(3) Where the court officer for a registering court receives notice that a maintenance order registered in that court by virtue of the provisions of the Judgments Regulation has been varied or revoked by a competent court in another Member State of the European Union, the court officer must –

(a)   note against the entry in the register that the original order so registered has been varied or revoked, as the case may be; and

(b) send notice of the noting of the variation or revocation, as the case may be, by post to the payer and payee under the order.

Amendments—SI 2011/1328; SI 2012/2806.

34.35 Transfer of registered order

(1) This rule applies where the court officer for the court where an order is registered considers that the payer is residing within the local justice area in England and Wales for which another magistrates' court acts.

(2) Subject to paragraph (4), the court officer must transfer the order to the other court by sending to that court –

(a) the information and documents relating to the registration;

(b) a certificate of arrears, if applicable, signed by the court officer;

(c) a statement giving such information as the court officer possesses as to the whereabouts of the payer and the nature and location of the payer's assets; and

(d) any other relevant documents which the court officer has relating to the case.

(3) The information and documents referred to in paragraph (2)(a) are those required, as appropriate, under –

(a) Articles 46 and 47 of the 1968 Convention;

(b) Articles 46 and 47 of the 1988 Convention;

(c) Article 53 of the Judgments Regulation;

(d) Article 53 of the Lugano Convention;

(e) Article 28 or 29 of the Maintenance Regulation; or

(f) Article 25 or 30 of the 2007 Hague Convention.

(4) If an application is pending in the registering court for the registration of the whole or part of the order in the High Court under Part 1 of the 1958 Act, the court officer must not transfer the order, or the part to which the application relates, under paragraph (2).

(5) The court officer must give notice of the transfer of an order to –

(a) the payee; and

(b) the Lord Chancellor.

(6) If an order is transferred, the court officer for the court to which it is transferred must register the order.

Amendments—SI 2011/1328; SI 2012/2806.

34.36 Cancellation of registered orders

(1) Where the court officer for the registering court –

(a) has no reason to transfer a registered order under rule 34.35; and

(b) considers that the payer under the registered order is not residing within the local justice area for which the court acts and has no assets to which the 1958 Act applies,

the court officer must cancel the registration of the order.

(2) The court officer must –

(a) give notice of cancellation to the payee; and

(b) send the information and documents relating to the registration and the other documents referred to in rule 34.35(2) to the Lord Chancellor.

34.36A Directions as to stays, documents and translations

At any stage in proceedings for registration of a maintenance order under this Section of this Chapter, the court may give directions about the conduct of the proceedings, including –

(a) staying of proceedings in accordance with –
  (i)   Article 30 or 38 of the 1968 Convention,
  (ii) Article 30 or 38 of the 1988 Convention,
  (iii) Article 37 or 46 of the Lugano Convention,
  (iv) Article 25 or 35 of the Maintenance Regulation, or
  (v)   Article 30(6) of the 2007 Hague Convention;
(b) the provision of documents in accordance with –
  (i)   Article 48 of the 1968 Convention,
  (ii) Article 48 of the 1988 Convention,
  (iii) Article 55 of the Lugano Convention,
  (iv) Article 29 of the Maintenance Regulation, or
  (v)   Article 25 or 30 of the 2007 Hague Convention;
(c) the provision of translations in accordance with –
  (i)   Article 48 of the 1968 Convention,
  (ii) Article 48 of the 1988 Convention,
  (iii) Article 55 of the Lugano Convention,
  (iv) Article 28 of the Maintenance Regulation, or
  (v)   in relation to an application under this Section relating to the 2007 Hague Convention, without prejudice to Article 44 of that Convention.

Amendments—Inserted by SI 2011/1328; amended by SI 2012/2806.

34.36B International Maintenance Obligations; Communication with the Central Authority for England and Wales

(1) Where the Lord Chancellor requests information or a document from the court officer for the relevant court for the purposes of Article 58 of the Maintenance Regulation, or Article 12 or 25(2) of the 2007 Hague Convention, the court officer shall provide the requested information or document to the Lord Chancellor forthwith.

(2) In this rule, "relevant court" means the court at which an application under Article 56 of the Maintenance Regulation or Article 10 of the 2007 Hague Convention has been filed.

[The Lord Chancellor is the Central Authority for the 2007 Hague Convention and the Maintenance Regulation]

Amendments—Inserted by SI 2012/2806.

Section 2
Reciprocal enforcement in a Contracting State or a Member State of the European Union of Orders of a court in England and Wales

34.37 *(revoked)*

34.38 Admissibility of documents

(1) This rule applies to a document, referred to in paragraph (2) and authenticated in accordance with paragraph (3), which comprises, records or summarises evidence given in, or information relating to, proceedings in a court in another part of the UK, another Contracting State to the 1968 Convention or the 1988 Convention, Member State of the

European Union or State bound by the Lugano Convention, or by the 2007 Hague Convention, and any reference in this rule to "the court", without more, is a reference to that court.

(2) The documents referred to at paragraph (1) are documents which purport to –

    (a)   set out or summarise evidence given to the court;

    (b)   have been received in evidence to the court;

    (c)   set out or summarise evidence taken in the court for the purpose of proceedings in a court in England and Wales to which the 1982 Act, the Judgments Regulation, the Maintenance Regulation or the 2007 Hague Convention applies; or

    (d)   record information relating to payments made under an order of the court.

(3) A document to which paragraph (1) applies shall, in any proceedings in a magistrates' court in England and Wales relating to a maintenance order to which the 1982 Act, the Judgments Regulation, the Maintenance Regulation or the 2007 Hague Convention applies, be admissible as evidence of any fact stated in it to the same extent as oral evidence of that fact is admissible in those proceedings.

(4) A document to which paragraph (1) applies shall be deemed to be authenticated –

    (a)   in relation to the documents listed at paragraph 2(a) or (c), if the document purports to be –

        (i)   certified by the judge or official before whom the evidence was given or taken; or

        (ii) the original document recording or summarising the evidence, or a true copy of that document;

    (b)   in relation to a document listed at paragraph (2)(b), if the document purports to be certified by a judge or official of the court to be, or to be a true copy of, the document received in evidence; and

    (c)   in relation to the document listed at paragraph (2)(d), if the document purports to be certified by a judge or official of the court as a true record of the payments made under the order.

(5) It shall not be necessary in any proceedings in which evidence is to be received under this rule to prove the signature or official position of the person appearing to have given the certificate referred to in paragraph (4).

(6) Nothing in this rule shall prejudice the admission in evidence of any document which is admissible in evidence apart from this rule.

(7) Any request by a magistrates' court in England and Wales for the taking or providing of evidence by a court in a State listed in paragraph (8) for the purposes of proceedings to which an instrument listed in that paragraph applies, or by a court in another part of the United Kingdom, shall be communicated in writing to the court in question.

(8) The States and instruments referred to in paragraph (7) are –

    (a)   a Contracting State to the 1968 Convention;

    (b)   a Contracting State to the 1988 Convention;

    (c)   a State bound by the Lugano Convention;

    (d)   Denmark, in relation to proceedings to which the Maintenance Regulation applies;

    (e)   a State bound by the 2007 Hague Convention,

but this paragraph and paragraph (7) do not apply where the State in question is a Member State of the European Union to which the Taking of Evidence Regulation (as defined in rule 24.15) applies.

    (Chapter 2 of Part 24 makes provision for taking of evidence by a court in another Member State of the European Union).

PART III

Amendments—SI 2011/1328; SI 2012/2806.

34.39 Enforcement of orders of a magistrates' court

(1) A person who wishes to enforce a maintenance order obtained in a magistrates' court in a State to which paragraph (2) applies must apply for a certified copy of the order and, where required by Practice Direction 34A, a certificate giving particulars relating to the judgment and proceedings in which it was given.

(2) The States referred to in paragraph (1) are –

    (a)   a Contracting State to the 1968 Convention;

    (b)   a Contracting State to the 1988 Convention (other than a Member State of the European Union);

    (c)   a Member State of the European Union;

    (d)   a State bound by the Lugano Convention (other than a Member State of the European Union); or

    (e)   a State bound by the 2007 Hague Convention (other than a Member State of the European Union).

(3) An application under this rule must be made in writing to the court officer and must specify –

    (a)   the names of the parties to the proceedings;

    (b)   the date, or approximate date, of the proceedings in which the maintenance order was made and the nature of those proceedings;

    (c)   the State in which the application for recognition or enforcement has been made or is to be made; and

    (d)   the postal address of the applicant.

(4) The court officer must, on receipt of the application, send a copy of the order to the applicant certified in accordance with practice direction 34A, together with a copy of any certificate required by that practice direction.

(5) Paragraph (6) applies where –

    (a)   a maintenance order is registered in a magistrates' court in England and Wales; and

    (b)   a person wishes to obtain a certificate giving details of any payments made or arrears accrued under the order while it has been registered, for the purposes of an application made or to be made in connection with that order in –

        (i)   another Contracting State to the 1968 Convention;

        (ii)   another Contracting State to the 1988 Convention (other than a Member State of the European Union);

        (iii)   another Member State of the European Union;

        (iv)   another State bound by the Lugano Convention (other than a Member State of the European Union);

        (v)   another part of the United Kingdom; or

        (vi)   another State bound by the 2007 Hague Convention (other than a Member State of the European Union).

(6) The person wishing to obtain the certificate referred to in paragraph (5) may make a written application to the court officer for the registering court.

(7) On receipt of an application under paragraph (6) the court officer must send to the applicant a certificate giving the information requested.

> (Rule 74.12 (application for certified copy of a judgment) and 74.13 (evidence in support) of the CPR apply in relation to the application for a certified copy of a judgment obtained in the High Court or a county court.)

Amendments—SI 2011/1328; SI 2012/679; SI 2012/2806.

34.40 Enforcement of orders of the High Court or a county court

(1) This rule applies where a person wishes to enforce a maintenance order obtained in the High Court or a county court (including the principal registry when treated as a divorce county court or, where the enforcement application relates to a civil partnership matter and the Maintenance Regulation, a civil partnership proceedings county court) in a Member State of the European Union or a State bound by the 2007 Hague Convention (other than a Member State of the European Union).

(2) Subject to the requirements of Practice Direction 34A, rules 74.12 (application for a certified copy of a judgment) and 74.13 (evidence in support) of the CPR apply in relation to –

    (a) an application under Article 40(2) of the Maintenance Regulation for a certified copy of a judgment and an extract relating to that judgment in the form of Annex II to that Regulation;

    (b) an application for a certified copy of a judgment and a certificate giving particulars relating to the judgment and the proceedings in which it was given.

Amendments—Inserted by SI 2011/1328; substituted by SI 2012/2806.

PART III

Practice Direction 34A –
Reciprocal Enforcement of Maintenance Orders

This Practice Direction supplements FPR Part 34

Note—FPR PD34A remains in force unamended, notwithstanding the application of the EU Maintenance Regulation (Council Regulation (EC) No 4/2009) from 18 June 2011. For cases concerning the Republic of Ireland, or those European Union Member States that are Contracting Parties to the 1973 Hague Convention on the Recognition and Enforcement of Decisions Relating to Maintenance Obligations, reference should be had to FPR PD34C, which identifies the transitional arrangements for these cases.

Noting Record of Means of Payment

1.1 Where a magistrates' court orders payments under a maintenance order to which Part 34 applies to be made in a particular way, the court must record that on a copy of the order.

1.2 If the court orders payment to be made to the court officer of a magistrates' court by a method referred to in section 59(6) of the Magistrates' Courts Act 1980, the court may vary the method of payment on the application of an interested party and where it does so the court must record the variation on a copy of the order.

    (Section 59(6) refers to payment by standing order or other methods which require transfer between accounts of a specific amount on a specific date during the period for which the authority to make the payment is in force.)

Notification by court officer

2.1 The court officer must, as soon as practicable, notify in writing the person liable to make the payments of the method by which they must be made.

2.2 If the court orders payment to be made to the court officer of a magistrates' court by a method referred to in section 59(6) of the Magistrates' Courts Act 1980 the court officer must inform the person liable to make the payments of the number and location of the account to which the payments must be made.

2.3 If the court varies the method of payment on the application of an interested party the court officer must, as soon as practicable, notify all interested parties in writing of the result of an application (including a decision to refer it to the court).

Applications under section 2 of the 1920 Act

3.1 This paragraph refers to an application for the transmission of a maintenance order to a reciprocating country under section 2 of the 1920 Act in accordance with rule 34.10.

3.2 The applicant's written evidence must include such information as may be required by the law of the reciprocating country for the purpose of enforcement of the order.

3.3 If, in accordance with section 2 of the 1920 Act, the court sends a maintenance order to the Lord Chancellor for transmission to a reciprocating country, it shall record the fact in the court records.

Applications under section 2 of the 1972 Act (rule 34.14)

Introduction

4.1 An application for a maintenance order to be sent to a reciprocating country under section 2 of the 1972 Act is made by lodging specified documents with the court. The documents to be lodged vary according to which country it is intended that the maintenance order is be sent and the requirements are set out in this paragraph.

General provision

4.2 The general requirement is that the following documents should be lodged with the court –

- (a) an affidavit by the applicant stating –
  - (i)   the reason that the applicant has for believing that the payer under the maintenance order is residing in the reciprocating country; and
  - (ii) the amount of any arrears due to the applicant under the order, the date to which those arrears have been calculated and the date on which the next payment under the order falls due;
- (b) a certified copy of the maintenance order;
- (c) a statement giving such information as the applicant has as to the whereabouts of the payer;
- (d) a statement giving such information as the applicant has for facilitating the identification of the payer, (including, if known to the applicant, the name and address of any employer of the payer, his occupation and the date and place of issue of any passport of the payer); and
- (e) if available to the applicant, a photograph of the payer.
  ...

Hague Convention Country

4.5 If the country to which it is intended to send the maintenance order is a Hague Convention country (as defined in rule 34.12), then the following changes to the general requirements apply.

4.6 In addition to the matters stated in that paragraph, the affidavit referred to in paragraph 4.2(a) must also state whether the time for appealing against the maintenance order has expired and whether an appeal is pending.

4.7 The applicant must lodge the following documents with the court in addition to those set out in paragraph 4.2 –

    (a)   a statement as to whether or not the payer appeared in the proceedings in which the maintenance order was made;

    (b)   if the payer did not so appear –

        (i)   the original of a document which establishes that notice of the institution of proceedings, including notice of the substance of the claim, was served on the payer; or

        (ii)   a copy of such a document certified by the applicant or the applicant's solicitor to be a true copy;

    (c)   a document which establishes that notice of the order was sent to the payer;

    (d)   a written statement as to whether or not the payee received legal aid in the proceedings in which the order was made, or in connection with the application under section 2 of the 1972 Act; and

    (e)   if the payee did receive legal aid, a copy certified by the applicant or the applicant's solicitor to be a true copy of the legal aid certificate.

United States of America

4.8 If the country to which it is intended to send the maintenance order is the United States of America, then the following changes to the general requirements apply.

4.9 There is no requirement to lodge a statement giving information as to the whereabouts of the payer since this information must be contained in the affidavit as mentioned in paragraph 4.10.

4.10 In addition to the matters stated in that paragraph, the affidavit referred to in paragraph 4.2(*a*) must also state –

    (a)   the address of the payee;

    (b)   such information as is known as to the whereabouts of the payer; and

    (c)   a description, so far as is known, of the nature and location of any assets of the payer available for execution.

4.11 The applicant must lodge three certified copies of the maintenance order.

Notification to the Lord Chancellor

5.1 Where, in accordance with Part 1 of the 1972 Act, a magistrates' court registers a maintenance order sent to it from a Hague Convention Country, the court officer must send written notice of the registration to the Lord Chancellor.

Notification of means of enforcement

6.1 The court officer of a magistrates' court must take reasonable steps to notify the person to whom payments are due under a registered order of the means of enforcement available in respect of it.

6.2 Notification of the means of enforcement includes, where appropriate, notification of the possibility of registration of the order in the High Court under Part I of the Maintenance Orders Act 1958.

PART III

Certified copies of orders issued under rule 34.39 or 34.40

7.1 In an application under rule 34.39 or 34.40 by a person wishing to enforce abroad a maintenance order, the certified copy of the order will be a sealed copy and will be accompanied by a certificate signed by the court officer.

7.2 In an application under the 1982 Act, the certificate signed by the court officer must state that it is a true copy of the order concerned and must give particulars of the proceedings in which it was made.

7.3 In an application under the Judgments Regulation, the certificate will be in the form of Annex V to the Regulation.

7.4 In an application under the Lugano Convention, the certificate will be in the form of Annex V to the Convention.

7.5 In an application under the Maintenance Regulation, the certificate will be in the form of Annex II to that Regulation.

7.6 In an application under the 2007 Hague Convention, the certificate will be comprised of the following Article 11 forms duly completed by the court officer –

   (a)   the Abstract of a Decision;
   (b)   the Statement of Enforceability; and
   (c)   the Statement of Proper Notice.

7.7 In an application under the 2007 Hague Convention, the certificate will additionally state the jurisdictional basis upon which the order was made, with reference to the jurisdictional criteria in Article 20(1) of that Convention to be applied by the State in which recognition and/or enforcement is to be sought.

Countries and Territories in which Sums are Payable through Crown Agents for Overseas Governments and Territories (rule 34.23)

8.1 Gibraltar, Barbados, Bermuda, Ghana, Kenya, Fiji, Hong Kong, Singapore, Turks and Caicos Islands, United Republic of Tanzania (except Zanzibar), Anguilla, Falkland Islands and Dependencies, St Helena.

Part 1 of the 1972 Act – Modified Rules

9.1 The annexes to this Practice Direction set out rules 34.14 to 34.25 as they are modified –

   (a)   in relation to the Republic of Ireland, by rule 34.26 (Annex 1) (but see the note in that Annex regarding the ongoing relevance of those rules following revocation of rule 34.26);
   (b)   in relation to the Hague Convention Countries, by rule 34.27 (Annex 2); and
   (c)   in relation to the United States of America, by rule 34.28 (Annex 3).

9.2 The statutory references in the annexes are construed in accordance with rule 34.26(2), 34.27(2) or 34.28(2) as the case may be.

ANNEX 1 – APPLICATION OF SECTION 1 OF CHAPTER 2 OF PART 34 TO THE REPUBLIC OF IRELAND

NOTE—Rule 34.26 was revoked by SI 2011/1328. Reciprocal enforcement of maintenance as between the UK and the Irish Republic has been governed by the Maintenance Regulation (Council Regulation (EC) no 4/2009) since 18 June 2011 and the relevant rules for that Regulation are contained in Chapter 3 of Part 34 of the Rules. The provisions of this Annex are therefore of relevance only where either –

(a) the application for registration of an order relating to an Irish maintenance order was made on or before 18 June 2011 and was still pending on that date; or

(b) the order was registered prior to 18 June 2011.

All other applications are governed by the Maintenance Regulation. Practice Direction 34C provides further information regarding which rules apply to applications relating to other European Union Member States.

34.14 Application for transmission of maintenance order to the Republic of Ireland

An application for a maintenance order to be sent to the Republic of Ireland under section 2 of the 1972 Act must be made in accordance with Practice Direction 34A.

34.15 Certification of evidence given on provisional orders

A document setting out or summarising evidence is authenticated by a court in England and Wales by a certificate signed, as appropriate, by –

(a) one of the justices; or

(b) the District Judge (Magistrates' Courts),

before whom that evidence was given.

(Section 3(5)(b) or 5(3) of the 1972 Act require a document to be authenticated by the court.)

34.16 Confirmation of a provisional order...

[This rule does not apply to the Republic of Ireland]

34.17 Consideration of confirmation of a provisional order made by a magistrates' court

(1) This rule applies where–

(a) a magistrates' court has made a provisional order by virtue of section 3 of the 1972 Act;

(b) the payer has made representations or adduced evidence to the court; and

(c) the court has fixed a date for the hearing at which it will consider confirmation of the order.

(2) The court officer must serve on the applicant for the provisional order –

(a) a copy of the representations or evidence; and

(b) written notice of the date fixed for the hearing.

34.18 Notification of variation or revocation of a maintenance order by the High Court

Where the High Court makes an order varying or revoking an order to which section 5 of the 1972 Act applies the court officer must send –

(a) a certified copy of the order of variation or revocation; and

(b) a statement as to the service on the payer of the documents mentioned in section 5(3) of the 1972 Act;

to the court in the Republic of Ireland.

(Rule 34.22 provides for the transmission of documents to a court in a reciprocating country.)

34.19 Notification of revocation of a maintenance order by a magistrates' court

Where a magistrates' court makes an order revoking an order to which section 5 of the 1972 Act applies, the court officer must send written notice of the making of the order to the Lord Chancellor.

> (Section 5 of the 1972 Act applies to a maintenance order sent to the Republic of Ireland in accordance with section 2 of that Act and a provisional order made by a magistrates' court in accordance with section 3 of that Act which has been confirmed by such a court.)

> (Provision in respect of notification of variation of a maintenance order by a magistrates' court under the 1972 Act is made in Rules made under section 144 of the Magistrates' Courts Act 1980.)

34.20 Taking of evidence for court in the Republic of Ireland

(1) This rule applies where a request is made by or on behalf of a court in the Republic of Ireland for the taking of evidence for the purpose of proceedings relating to a maintenance order to which Part 1 of the 1972 Act applies.

> (Section 14 of the 1972 Act makes provision for the taking of evidence needed for the purpose of certain proceedings.)

(2) The High Court has power to take the evidence where –

  (a) the request for evidence relates to a maintenance order made by a superior court in the United Kingdom; and

  (b) the witness resides in England and Wales.

(3) The county court has power to take the evidence where –

  (a) the request for evidence relates to a maintenance order made by a county court; and

  (b) the maintenance order has not been registered in a magistrates' court under the 1958 Act.

(4) The following magistrates' courts have power to take the evidence, that is –

  (a) where the proceedings in the Republic of Ireland relate to a maintenance order made by a magistrates' court, the court which made the order;

  (b) where the proceedings relate to an order which is registered in a magistrates' court, the court in which the order is registered; and

  (c) a magistrates' court to which the Secretary of State sends the request to take evidence.

(5) A magistrates' court not mentioned in paragraph (4) has power to take the evidence if the magistrates' court which would otherwise have that power consents because the evidence could be taken more conveniently.

(6) The evidence is to be taken in accordance with Part 22.

34.21 Request for the taking of evidence by a court

[This rule does not apply to the Republic of Ireland]

34.22 Transmission of documents

(1) This rule applies to any document, including a notice or request, which is required to be sent to a court in the Republic of Ireland by –

  (a) Part 1 of the 1972 Act; or

  (b) Section 1 of Chapter 2 of this Part of these Rules.

(2) The document must be sent to the Lord Chancellor for transmission to the court in the Republic of Ireland.

34.23 Method of payment under registered orders

(1) Where an order is registered in a magistrates' court in accordance with section 6(3) of the 1972 Act, the court must order that the payment of sums due under the order be made –

    (a) to the court officer for the registering court; and

    (b) at such time and place as the court officer directs.

        (Section 6(3) of the 1972 Act makes provision for the registration of maintenance orders made in the Republic of Ireland.)

(2) Where the court orders payment to be made to the court officer, the court officer must send the payments by post –

    (a) to the payee under the order; or

    (b) where a public authority has been authorised by the payee to receive the payments, to that public authority.

        (Practice Direction 34A contains further provisions relating to the payment of sums due under registered orders.)

34.24 Enforcement of payments under registered orders

(1) This rule applies where periodical payments under a registered order are in arrears.

(2) The court officer must, on the written request of the payee, proceed in that officer's own name for the recovery of the sums due unless of the view that it is unreasonable to do so.

(3) If the sums due are more than 4 weeks in arrears the court officer must give the payee notice in writing of that fact stating the particulars of the arrears.

34.25 Notification of registration and cancellation

The court officer must send written notice to –

    (a) the Lord Chancellor, on the due registration of an order under section 6(3) or 10(4) of the 1972 Act; and

    (b) to the payer under the order, on –

        (i) the registration of an order under section 10(4) of the 1972 Act; or

        (ii) the cancellation of the registration of an order under section 10(1) of that Act.

34.25A Other notices under section 6 of the 1972 Act

(1) A notice required under section 6(6) or (10) of the 1972 Act must be in the form referred to in a practice direction.

(2) Where a magistrates' court sets aside the registration of an order following an appeal under section 6(7) of the 1972 Act, the court officer must send written notice of the court's decision to the payee.

        (Section 6(6) of the 1972 Act provides for notice of registration in a United Kingdom court of a maintenance order made in the Republic of Ireland, and section 6(10) of that Act for notice that a maintenance order made in the Republic of Ireland has not been registered in a United Kingdom court.)

PART III

ANNEX 2 – APPLICATION OF SECTION 1 OF CHAPTER 2 OF PART 34 TO THE HAGUE CONVENTION COUNTRIES

34.14 Application for transmission of maintenance order to a Hague Convention Country

An application for a maintenance order to be sent to a Hague Convention Country under section 2 of the 1972 Act must be made in accordance with Practice Direction 34A.

34.15 Certification of evidence given on provisional orders

[This rule does not apply to the Hague Convention Countries]

34.16 Confirmation of a provisional order made in a reciprocating country

[This rule does not apply to the Hague Convention Countries]

34.17 Consideration of revocation of a maintenance order made by a magistrates' court

(1) This rule applies where –

    (a) an application has been made to a magistrates' court by a payee for the revocation of an order to which section 5 of the 1972 Act applies; and

    (b) the payer resides in a Hague Convention Country.

(2) The court officer must serve on the payee, by post, a copy of any representations or evidence adduced by or on behalf of the payer.

> (Provision relating to consideration of variation of a maintenance order made by a magistrates' court to which section 5 of the 1972 Act applies is made in Rules made under section 144 of the Magistrates' Courts Act 1980.)

34.18 Notification of variation or revocation of a maintenance order by the High Court or a county court

(1) This rule applies if the High Court or a county court makes an order varying or revoking a maintenance order to which section 5 of the 1972 Act applies.

(2) If the time for appealing has expired without an appeal having been entered, the court officer will send to the Lord Chancellor –

    (a) the documents required by section 5(8) of the 1972 Act; and

    (b) a certificate signed by the district judge stating that the order of variation or revocation is enforceable and no longer subject to the ordinary forms of review.

(3) A party who enters an appeal against the order of variation or revocation must, at the same time, give written notice to the court officer.

34.19 Notification of confirmation or revocation of a maintenance order by a magistrates' court

[This rule does not apply to the Hague Convention Countries]

34.20 Taking of evidence for court in a Hague Convention Country

(1) This rule applies where a request is made by or on behalf of a court in a Hague Convention Country for the taking of evidence for the purpose of proceedings relating to a maintenance order to which Part 1 of the 1972 Act applies.

> (Section 14 of the 1972 Act makes provision for the taking of evidence needed for the purpose of certain proceedings.)

(2) The High court has power to take the evidence where –

    (a)   the request for evidence relates to a maintenance order made by a superior court in the United Kingdom: and

    (b)   the witness resides in England and Wales.

(3) The county court has power to take the evidence where –

    (a)   the request for evidence relates to a maintenance order made by a county court; and

    (b)   the maintenance order has not been registered in a magistrates' court under the 1958 Act.

(4) The following magistrates' courts have power to take the evidence, that is –

    (a)   where the proceedings in the Hague Convention Country relate to a maintenance order made by a magistrates' court, the court which made the order;

    (b)   where the proceedings relate to an order which is registered in a magistrates' court, the court in which the order is registered; and

    (c)   a magistrates' court to which the Secretary of State sends the request to take evidence.

(5) A magistrates' court not mentioned in paragraph (4) has power to take the evidence if the magistrates' court which would otherwise have that power consents because the evidence could be taken more conveniently.

(6) The evidence is to be taken in accordance with Part 22.

34.21 Request for the taking of evidence by a court in a Hague Convention country

[This rule does not apply to the Hague Convention countries.]

34.22 Transmission of documents

(1) This rule applies to any document, including a notice or request, which is required to be sent to a court in a Hague Convention country by –

    (a)   Part 1 of the 1972 Act; or

    (b)   Section 1 of Chapter 2 of this Part of these Rules.

(2) The document must be sent to the Lord Chancellor for transmission to the court in the Hague Convention country.

34.23 Method of payment under registered orders

(1) Where an order is registered in a magistrates' court in accordance with section 6(3) of the 1972 Act, the court must order that the payment of sums due under the order be made –

    (a)   to the court officer for the registering court; and

    (b)   at such time and place as the court officer directs.

(Section 6(3) of the 1972 Act makes provision for the registration of maintenance orders made in a Hague Convention country.)

(2) Where the court orders payment to be made to the court officer, the court officer must send the payments by post to the payee under the order.

(Practice Direction 34A contains further provision relating to the payment of sums due under registered orders.)

34.24 *Enforcement of payments under registered orders*

(1) This rule applies where a court has ordered periodical payments under a registered maintenance order to be made to the court officer.

(2) The court officer must take reasonable steps to notify the payee of the means of enforcement available.

(3) Paragraph (4) applies where periodical payments due under a registered order are in arrears.

(4) The court officer, on that officer's own initiative –

(a)   may; or
(b)   if the sums due are more than 4 weeks in arrears, must,

proceed in that officer's own name for the recovery of the sums due unless of the view that it is unreasonable to do so.

34.25 *Notification of registration and cancellation*

The court officer must send written notice to –

(a)   the Lord Chancellor, on the due registration of an order under section 10(4) of the 1972 Act; and
(b)   the payer under the order, on –
  (i)   the registration of an order under section 10(4) of the 1972 Act; or
  (ii) the cancellation of the registration of an order under section 10(1) of the 1972 Act.

34.25A *General provisions as to notices*

(1) A notice to a payer of the registration of an order in a magistrates' court in accordance with section 6(3) of the 1972 Act must be in the form referred to in a practice direction.

(Section 6(8) of the 1972 Act requires notice of registration to be given to the payer.)

(2) If the court sets aside the registration of a maintenance order following an appeal under section 6(9) of the 1972 Act, the court officer must send written notice of the decision to the Lord Chancellor.

(3) A notice to a payee that the court officer has refused to register an order must be in the form referred to in a practice direction.

(Section 6(11) of the 1972 Act requires notice of refusal of registration to be given to the payee.)

(4) Where, under any provision of Part 1 of the 1972 Act, a court officer serves a notice on a payer who resides in a Hague Convention Country, the court officer must send to the Lord Chancellor a certificate of service.

ANNEX 3 – APPLICATION OF SECTION 1 OF CHAPTER 2 OF PART 34 TO THE UNITED STATES OF AMERICA

34.14 Application for transmission of maintenance order to the United States of America

An application for a maintenance order to be sent to the United States of America under section 2 of the 1972 Act must be made in accordance with Practice Direction 34A.

34.15 Certification of evidence given on provisional orders

[This rule does not apply to the United States of America]

34.16 Confirmation of a provisional order made in a reciprocating country

[This rule does not apply to the United States of America]

34.17 Consideration of revocation of a maintenance order made by a magistrates' court

(1) This rule applies where –

    (a) an application has been made to a magistrates' court by a payee for the revocation of an order to which section 5 of the 1972 Act applies; and

    (b) the payer resides in the United States of America.

(2) The court officer must serve on the payee by post a copy of any representations or evidence adduced by or on behalf of the payer.

> (Provision relating to consideration of variation of a maintenance order made by a magistrates' court to which section 5 of the 1972 Act applies is made in rules made under section 144 of the Magistrates' Courts Act 1980.)

34.18 Notification of variation or revocation

If the High Court or a county court makes an order varying or revoking a maintenance order to which section 5 of the 1972 Act applies, the court officer will send to the Lord Chancellor the documents required by section 5(7) of that Act.

34.19 Notification of confirmation or revocation of a maintenance order by a magistrates' court

[This rule does not apply to the United States of America]

34.20 Taking of evidence for court in United States of America

(1) This rule applies where a request is made by or on behalf of a court in the United States of America for the taking of evidence for the purpose of proceedings relating to a maintenance order to which Part 1 of the 1972 Act applies.

> (Section 14 of the 1972 Act makes provision for the taking of evidence needed for the purpose of certain proceedings.)

(2) The High Court has power to take the evidence where –

    (a) the request for evidence relates to a maintenance order made by a superior court in the United Kingdom; and

PART III

(b) the witness resides in England and Wales.

(3) The county court has power to take the evidence where –

(a) the request for evidence relates to a maintenance order made by a county court; and

(b) the maintenance order has not been registered in a magistrates' court under the 1958 Act.

(4) The following magistrates' courts have power to take the evidence, that is –

(a) where the proceedings in the United States of America relate to a maintenance order made by a magistrates' court, the court which made the order;

(b) where the proceedings relate to an order which is registered in a magistrates' court, the court in which the order is registered; and

(c) a magistrates' court to which the Secretary of State sends the request to take evidence.

(5) A magistrates' court not mentioned in paragraph (4) has power to take the evidence if the magistrates' court which would otherwise have that power consents because the evidence could be taken more conveniently.

(6) The evidence is to be taken in accordance with Part 22.

34.21 Request for the taking of evidence by a court in a reciprocating country

[This rule does not apply to the United States of America]

34.22 Transmission of documents

(1) This rule applies to any document, including a notice or request, which is required to be sent to a court in the United States of America by –

(a) Part 1 of the 1972 Act; or

(b) Section 1 of Chapter 2 of this Part of these Rules.

(2) The document must be sent to the Lord Chancellor for transmission to the court in the United States of America.

34.23 Method of payment under registered orders

(1) Where an order is registered in a magistrates' court in accordance with section 6(3) of the 1972 Act, the court must order that the payment of sums due under the order be made –

(a) to the court officer for the registering court; and

(b) at such time and place as the court officer directs.

(Section 6(3) of the 1972 Act makes provision for the registration of maintenance orders made in the United States of America.)

(2) Where the court orders payment to be made to the court officer, the court officer must send the payments by post to the payee under the order.

(Practice Direction 34A contains further provisions relating to the payment of sums due under registered orders.)

34.24 Enforcement of payments under registered orders

(1) This rule applies where a court has ordered periodical payments under a registered maintenance order to be made to the court officer.

(2) The court officer must take reasonable steps to notify the payee of the means of enforcement available.

(3) Paragraph (4) applies where periodic payments due under a registered order are in arrears.

(4) The court officer, on that officer's own initiative –

    (a) may; or
    (b) if the sums due are more than 4 weeks in arrears, must,

proceed in that officer's own name for the recovery of the sums due unless of the view that it is unreasonable to do so.

34.25 *Notification of registration and cancellation*

The court officer must send written notice to –

    (a) the Lord Chancellor, on the due registration of an order under section 10(4) of the 1972 Act; or
    (b) the payer under the order, on –
        (i) the registration of an order under section 10(4) of the 1972 Act; or
        (ii) the cancellation of the registration of an order under section 10(1) of that Act.

Practice Direction 34B –
Practice Note (Tracing Payers Overseas)

This Practice Direction supplements FPR Part 34

Difficulties can arise where a person in this country wishes to take proceedings under the Maintenance Orders (Facilities for Enforcement) Act 1920 or Part I of the Maintenance Orders (Reciprocal Enforcement) Act 1972 to obtain or enforce a maintenance order against a payer living overseas whose address is unknown to the applicant.

To mitigate these difficulties, arrangements have now been made with the appropriate authorities in Australia, Canada, New Zealand and South Africa, whereby the court may on request ask the authorities in those countries to make enquiries with a view to tracing the whereabouts of the payer. The following procedure should be followed.

On or before an application is made for a provisional maintenance order, or for transmission of an absolute maintenance order under the above Acts by an applicant who does not know the payer's actual address in either Australia, Canada, New Zealand or South Africa, there should be completed and lodged with the [district judge] a questionnaire, in duplicate, ([Principal] Registry Form D312 or county court Form D85 as appropriate) obtainable from the registry or court office, together with a written undertaking from the solicitor (or from the applicant if acting in person) that any address of the payer received in response to the enquiries will not be disclosed or used except for the purpose of the proceedings.

This Note is issued [in its original form] with the concurrence of the Lord Chancellor.

Practice Direction 34C –
Applications for Recognition and Enforcement To or From European Union Member States

This Practice Direction supplements FPR Part 34

This Practice Direction supplementing the Family Procedure Rules 2010 is made by the President of the Family Division under the powers delegated to him by the Lord Chief Justice under Schedule 2, Part 1, paragraph 2(2) of the Constitutional Reform Act 2005, and is agreed by Lord McNally, Minister of State, by the authority of the Lord Chancellor.

This Practice Direction comes into force on 31 October 2011.

1 Introduction

1.1 The Maintenance Regulation (Council Regulation (EC) No 4/2009 of 18 December 2008 on jurisdiction, applicable law, recognition and enforcement of decisions and cooperation in matters relating to maintenance obligations) ("the Maintenance Regulation") applies across the European Union from 18 June 2011. It applies to all cases for recognition and enforcement in or from a European Union Member State from that date. The domestic legislation facilitating the application of the Maintenance Regulation is the Civil Jurisdiction and Judgments (Maintenance) Regulations 2011[1] ("the CJJMR").

1   SI 2011/1484.

2 The Member States of the European Union are: Austria, Belgium, Bulgaria, Cyprus, Czech Republic, Denmark, Estonia, Finland, France, Germany, Greece, Hungary, Ireland, Italy, Latvia, Lithuania, Luxembourg, Malta, The Netherlands, Poland, Portugal, Romania, Slovakia, Slovenia, Spain, Sweden, and the United Kingdom.

2 Relationship between the Maintenance Regulation and other international instruments

2.1 The Maintenance Regulation replaces the relevant provisions of Regulation (EC) No 44/2001 of 22 December 2000 on jurisdiction and the recognition and enforcement of judgments in civil and commercial matters (known as "Brussels I"), subject to the transitional provisions of Article 75. It will also take precedence over any other international conventions and agreements concerning matters which the Maintenance Regulation governs as regards relations between Member States. In particular (and subject to the relevant transitional provisions (discussed below)), the Maintenance Regulation must be applied between Member States instead of the following:

(a)   The Convention on the Recognition and Enforcement of Decisions Relating to Maintenance Obligations done at The Hague on 2 October 1973 ("the 1973 Convention");[2]

(b)   the arrangements for reciprocal enforcement of maintenance between the United Kingdom and the Republic of Ireland reflected in the Reciprocal Enforcement of Maintenance Orders (Republic of Ireland) Order 1993[3] ("the Republic of Ireland Order");

(c)   as regards Malta, the provisions of the Maintenance Orders (Reciprocal Enforcement) Act 1972 Part 1 ("the 1972 Act");

(d)   the United Nations Convention on the Recovery Abroad of Maintenance done at New York on 20 June 1956 ("the 1956 New York Convention") (applied in

England and Wales by Part II of the Maintenance Orders (Reciprocal Enforcement) Act 1972) (this Convention is concerned with the reciprocal treatment of applications for maintenance rather than reciprocal enforcement of orders, but is included here for clarity).

2   This Convention previously governed relations between the UK and other European Union Member States which were Contracting Parties to it, rather than Brussels I. Those Member States were – the Czech Republic, Denmark, Germany, Finland, France, Italy, Luxembourg, the Netherlands, Portugal, Estonia, Poland, Slovakia, Spain, and Sweden. The arrangements in the Reciprocal Enforcement of Maintenance Orders (Hague Convention Countries) Order 1993 (SI 1993/593) ("the Hague Convention Countries Order") no longer apply in relations with these countries.

3   SI 1993/594.

3 Application of the Maintenance Regulation rules to recognition, registration and enforcement in England and Wales of an order from another Member State

3.1 For an application for enforcement of a maintenance order from another European Union Member State which applies the 2007 Hague Protocol on the Law Applicable to Maintenance Orders (all other Member States except Denmark), the court will apply the rules in Sections 1 and 3 of Chapter IV of the Maintenance Regulation. Orders from such Member States are not subject to registration and benefit from direct enforceability in magistrates' courts in the same manner as an order for maintenance which had been made in proceedings in England and Wales. Rules 59A and 59B of the Magistrates' Courts Rules 1981 (as amended[4]) make provision for such cases.

4   Amended by the Magistrates' Courts (Enforcement or Variation of Orders Made in Family Proceedings and Miscellaneous Provisions) Rules 2011, SI 2011/1329.

3.2 For an application from another European Union Member State which does not apply the 2007 Hague Protocol on the Law Applicable to Maintenance Orders (namely Denmark), the court will apply the rules in Sections 2 and 3 of Chapter IV of the Maintenance Regulation. These orders do require registration before they can be enforced and Section 1 of Chapter 3 of Part 34 of the Family Procedure Rules 2010 applies to these cases.

4 Application of the Maintenance Regulation to recognition and enforcement of a maintenance order from England and Wales in another Member State

4.1 Where recognition and enforcement of an England and Wales maintenance order is sought in another European Union Member State, the courts and authorities of that Member State will apply Sections 2 and 3 of Chapter IV of the Maintenance Regulation, because the United Kingdom is not a State Party to the 2007 Hague Protocol (and consequently courts and authorities of the United Kingdom are not bound to apply "applicable law" rules to the initial decision). Section 2 of Chapter 3 of Part 34 of the Family Procedure Rules 2010 applies to those decisions.

5 Transitional cases

5.1 The Maintenance Regulation makes specific provision for transitional cases in Article 75. The general rule is provided by Article 75(1), whereby the Regulation applies only to proceedings instituted after its date of application (18 June 2011). However, special rules apply in relation to applications from another European Union Member State for recognition or recognition and enforcement:

(a)   Where the maintenance decision was given in any Member State prior to 18 June 2011, but recognition and enforcement are sought after that date, the court will apply the rules of Sections 2 and 3 of Chapter IV.

(b)   Where the maintenance decision was given in any Member State after 18 June

2011 but the proceedings for that decision were commenced prior to that date, the court will also apply the rules of Sections 2 and 3 of Chapter IV.

(c)   Where there is an application in progress on 18 June 2011 for recognition and enforcement under Council Regulation (EC) No 44/2001 (Brussels I) relating to a maintenance decision from a Member State, the court will apply the rules of Chapter III of Brussels I.

5.2 It will therefore be seen that, for transitional cases (a) and (b) above, Section 1 of Chapter IV will not be used, regardless of whether the Member State in question applies the 2007 Hague Protocol – the arrangements are the same for all Member States.

5.3 As stated in paragraph 2.1 above, the Maintenance Regulation will apply as between Member States instead of other existing international agreements dealing with the same matters. The provisions of 5.1(a) and (b) above apply in all cases. Where relations in maintenance matters between the United Kingdom and another Member State were governed by Brussels I prior to the application of the Maintenance Regulation, the transitional arrangements in paragraph 5.1(c) above will apply, and transitional arrangements regarding rules of court for such cases are made in rule 38 of the Family Procedure (Amendment) Rules 2011[5].

5   SI 2011/1328.

5.4 Where maintenance matters between the United Kingdom and another Member State were governed by the 1973 Convention or the Republic of Ireland Order prior to 18 June 2011, the following provision is made for transitional cases:

(a)   As regards cases governed by the 1973 Convention, the references in the Hague Convention Countries Order to those Member States which are party to that Convention have been revoked[6]. However, those Member States continue to be treated under that Order as Hague Convention Countries for transitional purposes[7] under the CJJMR, including those proceedings for establishment, variation, or revocation of a maintenance order, or for registration of a maintenance order, which are continuing on 18 June 2011. In those circumstances, the rules at Part 34, Chapter 2, Section 2 sub-section 2 of the Family Procedure Rules 2010 will continue to apply to those proceedings.

(b)   In relation to cases concerning the Republic of Ireland, the Republic of Ireland Order has been revoked[8]. Transitional provision is made by paragraph 28 of Schedule 7 to the CJJMR. Again, this includes provision for proceedings for establishment of maintenance, variation or revocation of an order, or for registration of an order, which are continuing on 18 June 2011. The Family Procedure Rules 2010 have been amended so that Part 34, Chapter 2, Section 2 sub-section 1 has been revoked. Provision is made for the application of those rules in transitional cases in the Family Procedure (Amendment) Rules 2011 at rule 38. Annex 1 to Practice Direction 34A (which sets out rules 34.14 to 34.25 as modified by Part 34, Chapter 2, section 2 sub- section 1 prior to its revocation) should therefore be applied in accordance with the provision in rule 38 of those Amendment Rules.

6   The Civil Jurisdiction and Judgments (Maintenance) Regulations 2011 Schedule 7 paragraph 25(2) (SI 2011/1484).
7   Schedule 7 paragraph 26 ibid.
8   Schedule 7 paragraph 27 ibid.

5.5 No specific provision is currently made in domestic law for transitional provision relating to Malta or in relation to the 1956 New York Convention as it relates to applications from European Union Member States. The position is directly governed by Article 75(1) of the Maintenance Regulation. Where proceedings have been instituted by virtue of the 1956 New York Convention or the operation of Part I of the 1972 Act on or prior to 18 June 2011 and are continuing on that date, those proceedings are not affected by Maintenance Regulation rules. Such proceedings would include applications for variation and revocation of orders as well as for establishment of a maintenance order. However, recognition and enforcement in another Member State of any resulting order would occur in accordance with the Maintenance Regulation (and the transitional provisions of Article 75(2) should be considered). Enforcement in England and Wales of orders registered under either part of the 1972 Act on or prior to 18 June 2011 will not be affected by the Maintenance Regulation.

PART 35
MEDIATION DIRECTIVE

CONTENTS OF THIS PART

35.1 Scope and interpretation

(1) This Part applies to mediated cross-border disputes that are subject to Directive 2008/52/EC of the European Parliament and of the Council of 21 May 2008 on certain aspects of mediation in civil and commercial matters ("the Mediation Directive").

(2) In this Part –

"cross-border dispute" has the meaning given by article 2 of the Mediation Directive;
"mediation" has the meaning given by article 3(a) of the Mediation Directive;
"mediation administrator" means a person involved in the administration of the mediation process;
"mediation evidence" means evidence regarding information arising out of or in connection with a mediation process;
"mediator" has the meaning given by article 3(b) of the Mediation Directive; and
"relevant dispute" means a cross-border dispute that is subject to the Mediation Directive.

Scope—This Part applies only to mediated cross-border disputes subject to Directive 2008/52/EC of 21 May 2008 on certain aspects of mediation in civil and commercial matters ("the Mediation Directive"). The purpose of the Mediation Directive is to facilitate access to ADR and to promote the amicable settlement of cross-border disputes by encouraging the use of mediation and by ensuring a balanced relationship between mediation and judicial proceedings (Mediation Directive, Art 1.1). The Mediation Directive does not apply to Denmark (Mediation Directive, Art 1.3). FPR 2010, Pt 35 implements the Mediation Directive by ensuring that it is possible for the parties, or for one of them with the explicit consent of the others, to request that the content of a written agreement resulting from mediation is made enforceable. The relevant parts of the Mediation Directive are set out below:

Article 2: Cross-border disputes
1   For the purposes of this Directive a cross-border dispute shall be one in which at least one of the parties is domiciled or habitually resident in a Member State other than that of any other party on the date on which:
   (a) the parties agree to use mediation after the dispute has arisen;
   (b) mediation is ordered by a court;
   (c) an obligation to use mediation arises under national law; or
   (d) for the purposes of Article 5 an invitation is made to the parties.

2   Notwithstanding paragraph 1, for the purposes of Articles 7 and 8 a cross-border dispute shall also be one in which judicial proceedings or arbitration following mediation between the parties are initiated in a Member State other than that in which the parties were domiciled or habitually resident on the date referred to in paragraph 1(a),(b) or (c).

3   For the purposes of paragraphs 1 and 2, domicile shall be determined in accordance with Articles 59 and 60 of Regulation (EC) No 44/2001 (see, now, the Maintenance Regulation (Council Regulation (EC) No 4/2009), art 2.3 and annotations to Ch III (Applicable Law)).

Article 3: Definitions

For the purposes of this Directive the following definitions shall apply:

(a) "Mediation" means a structured process, however named or referred to, whereby two or more parties to a dispute attempt by themselves, on a voluntary basis, to reach an agreement on the settlement of their dispute with the assistance of a mediator. This process may be initiated by the parties or suggested or ordered by a court or prescribed by the law of a Member State.

It includes mediation conducted by a judge who is not responsible for any judicial proceedings concerning the dispute in question. It excludes attempts made by the court or the judge seised to settle a dispute in the course of judicial proceedings concerning the dispute in question.

(b) "Mediator" means any third person who is asked to conduct a mediation in an effective, impartial and competent way, regardless of the denomination or profession of that third person in the Member State concerned and of the way in which the third person has been appointed or requested to conduct the mediation.

Article 6: Enforceability of agreements resulting from mediation

1   Member States shall ensure that it is possible for the parties, or for one of them with the explicit consent of the others, to request that the content of a written agreement resulting from mediation be made enforceable. The content of such an agreement shall be made enforceable unless, in the case in question, either the content of that agreement is contrary to the law of the Member State where the request is made or the law of that Member State does not provide for its enforceability.

2   The content of the agreement may be made enforceable by a court or other competent authority in a judgment or decision or in an authentic instrument in accordance with the law of the Member State where the request is made.

3   Member States shall inform the Commission of the courts or other authorities competent to receive requests in accordance with paragraphs 1 and 2.

4   Nothing in this Article shall affect the rules applicable to the recognition and enforcement in another Member State of an agreement made enforceable in accordance with paragraph 1.

Article 7: Confidentiality of mediation

1   Given that mediation is intended to take place in a manner which respects confidentiality, Member States shall ensure that, unless the parties agree otherwise, neither mediators nor those involved in the administration of the mediation process shall be compelled to give evidence in civil and commercial judicial proceedings or arbitration regarding information arising out of or in connection with a mediation process, except:

(a) where this is necessary for overriding considerations of public policy of the Member State concerned, in particular when required to ensure the protection of the best interests of children or to prevent harm to the physical or psychological integrity of a person; or

(b) where disclosure of the content of the agreement resulting from mediation is necessary in order to implement or enforce that agreement.

2   Nothing in paragraph 1 shall preclude Member States from enacting stricter measures to protect the confidentiality of mediation.

35.2 Relevant disputes: applications for consent orders in respect of financial remedies

(1) This rule applies in relation to proceedings for a financial remedy where the applicant, with the explicit consent of the respondent, wishes to make an application that the content of a written agreement resulting from mediation of a relevant dispute be made enforceable by being made the subject of a consent order.

(2) The court will not include in a consent order any matter which is contrary to the law of England and Wales or which is not enforceable under that law.

(3) The applicant must file two copies of a draft of the order in the terms sought.

(4) Subject to paragraph (5), the application must be supported by evidence of the explicit consent of the respondent.

(5) Where the respondent has written to the court consenting to the making of the order sought, the respondent is deemed to have given explicit consent to the order and paragraph (4) does not apply.

(6) Paragraphs (1)(b) and (2) to (6) of rule 9.26 apply to an application to which this rule applies.

Scope—This rule gives effect to the Mediation Directive, art 6. The rule does not make specific provision that the court must make the content of a cross-border mediated agreement enforceable, but rather relies upon the courts' existing powers to make consent orders (for example, FPR 2010, r 9.26 (applications for consent orders for a financial remedy)) and to enforce the content of a consent order (for example, in relation to contact orders made by consent under CA1989, s 8). This rule addresses the requirement of the Mediation Directive, art 6 that a respondent should give "explicit consent". Without this provision, FPR 2010, r 9.25(1)(a) would apply in default. FPR 2010, r 9.25(1)(a) requires that one copy of any draft consent order must be endorsed with a statement signed by the respondent signifying agreement. FPR PD9A, para 6.1 states that this requirement is properly complied with if the endorsed statement is signed by solicitors on record as acting for the respondent. r 35.2 addresses any potential limitation on the opportunities for providing explicit consent contained in FPR 2010, r 9.25(1)(a) and FPR PD9A, para 6.1. An application under r 35.2 must be completed in English or accompanied by a translation into English. The respondent's explicit consent must similarly be in English or accompanied by a translation into English (FPR PD35A).

Defined terms—"consent order" (FPR 2010, r 2.3); "relevant dispute" (FPR 2010, r 35.1(2)).

35.3 Mediation evidence: disclosure and inspection

(1) Where a party to proceedings seeks disclosure or inspection of mediation evidence that is in the control of a mediator or mediation administrator, that party must first obtain the court's permission to seek the disclosure or inspection, by an application made in accordance with Part 18.

(2) The mediator or mediation administrator who has control of the mediation evidence must be named as a respondent to the application and must be served with a copy of the application notice.

(3) Evidence in support of the application must include evidence that –

    (a)   all parties to the mediation agree to the disclosure or inspection of the mediation evidence;

    (b)   disclosure or inspection of the mediation evidence is necessary for overriding considerations of public policy, in accordance with article 7(1)(a) of the Mediation Directive; or

    (c)   the disclosure of the content of an agreement resulting from mediation is necessary to implement or enforce that agreement.

(4) Where this rule applies, Parts 21 to 24 apply to the extent they are consistent with this rule.

Defined terms—"mediation", "mediation administrator", "mediation evidence": FPR 2010, r 35.1(2); "public policy": Mediation Directive, art 7.1(a) (a distinction is to be drawn between the narrow interpretation of "public policy" used in European law and the wider meaning in domestic law of "public interest").

Scope—FPR 2010, rr 35.3 and 35.4 relate to the implementation of the Mediation Directive, art 7 concerning the confidentiality of mediation other than in excepted cases. Where an application for disclosure and inspection is made in an excepted case, r 35.3 requires an application in accordance with FPR 2010, Pt 18 to be made.

35.4 Mediation evidence: witnesses and depositions

(1) This rule applies where a party wishes to obtain mediation evidence from a mediator or mediation administrator by –

    (a)   a witness summons;
    (b)   cross-examination with permission of the court under rule 22.8 or 23.4;
    (c)   an order under rule 24.7 (evidence by deposition);
    (d)   an order under rule 24.9 (enforcing attendance of witness);
    (e)   an order under rule 24.10(4) deponent's evidence to be given orally); or
    (f)   an order under rule 24.12 (order for the issue of a letter of request).

(2) When applying for a witness summons, permission under rule 22.8 or 23.4 or order under rule 24.7, 24.9, 24.10(4) or 24.12, the party must provide the court with evidence that –

    (a)   all parties to the mediation agree to the obtaining of the mediation evidence;
    (b)   obtaining the mediation evidence is necessary for overriding considerations of public policy in accordance with article 7(1)(a) of the Mediation Directive; or
    (c)   the disclosure of the content of an agreement resulting from mediation is necessary to implement or enforce that agreement.

(3) When considering a request for a witness summons, permission under rule 22.8 or 23.4 or order under rule 24.7, 24.9, 24.10(4) or 24.12, the court may invite any person, whether or not a party, to make representations.

(4) Where this rule applies, Parts 21 to 24 apply to the extent they are consistent with this rule.

Scope—See the notes to FPR 2010, r 35.3.

Practice Direction 35A – Mediation Directive

This Practice Direction supplements FPR rule 35.2 (Relevant disputes: applications for consent orders in respect of financial remedies)

1.1 An application for an order to which rule 35.2 applies must be completed in English or accompanied by a translation into English.

1.2 Where the application is supported by evidence of explicit consent to the application by a party, the evidence must also be in English or accompanied by a translation into English.

1.3 Where a party chooses to write to the court consenting to the making of the order the correspondence must be in English or accompanied by a translation into English.

PART 36
TRANSITIONAL ARRANGEMENTS AND PILOT SCHEMES

CONTENTS OF THIS PART

Scope—As well as making provision for pilot schemes (FPR 2010, r 36.2), FPR 2010, Pt 36 and FPR PD36A make provision for transitional arrangements dealing with the application of the FPR to proceedings started before 6 April 2011 ("existing proceedings"). The general scheme (FPR PD36A, para 2.1) is to apply the FPR to existing proceedings so far as is practicable but, where this is not practicable, to apply the previous rules (as set out in FPR PD36A, para 1.2) to such proceedings. Where proceedings have been commenced before 6 April 2011, the case will proceed in the first instance under the previous rules with subsequent pleadings being filed and served in accordance with the previous rules. However, when proceedings come before a court (whether at a hearing, including a hearing of a substantive issue, or on paper) for the first time on or after 6 April 2011 (whether or not the application was issued before 6 April 2011), the court may direct how FPR 2010 are to apply to the proceedings on the general presumption that the FPR will apply to the proceedings from then on (FPR PD36A, para 4.4). Where a new step is to be taken in any existing proceedings on or after 6 April 2011, it is to be taken under the FPR (FPR PD36A, para 4.1). The overriding objective (FPR 2010, Pt 1) applies to all existing proceedings from 6 April 2011 (FPR PD36A, para 4.2). Any assessment of costs taking place on or after 6 April 2011 is in accordance with FPR 2010, Pt 28 (and the CPR as applied by FPR 2010, Pt 28). However, the general presumption that no costs for work undertaken before 6 April 2011 will be disallowed if those costs would have been allowed on detailed assessment before that date (FPR PD36A, para 4.5).

36.1 Transitional provisions

Practice Direction 36A shall make provision for the extent to which these rules shall apply to proceedings started before the day on which they come into force.

36.2 Pilot schemes

Practice directions may modify or disapply any provision of these rules –

(a) for specified periods; and
(b) in relation to proceedings in specified courts,

during the operation of pilot schemes for assessing the use of new practices and procedures in connection with proceedings.

Practice Direction 36A – Transitional Arrangements

This Practice Direction supplements FPR Part 36

Content of this Practice Direction

1.1 This Practice Direction deals with the application of the FPR to proceedings started before 6 April 2011 ("existing proceedings").

1.2 In this Practice Direction "the previous rules" means, as appropriate, the Rules of the Supreme Court 1965 and County Court Rules 1981 as in force immediately before 26 April 1999, and –

–   the Maintenance Orders (Facilities for Enforcement) Rules 1922;
–   the Magistrates' Courts (Guardianship of Minors) Rules 1974;
–   the Magistrates' Courts (Reciprocal Enforcement of Maintenance Orders) Rules 1974;
–   the Magistrates' Courts (Reciprocal Enforcement of Maintenance Orders) (Republic of Ireland) Rules 1975;
–   the Magistrates' Courts (Reciprocal Enforcement of Maintenance Orders) (Hague Convention Countries) Rules 1980;
–   the Magistrates' Courts (Child Abduction and Custody) Rules 1986;
–   the Magistrates' Courts (Civil Jurisdiction and Judgments Act 1982) Rules 1986;
–   the Family Proceedings Rules 1991;
–   the Family Proceedings Courts (Children Act 1989) Rules 1991;
–   the Family Proceedings Courts (Matrimonial Proceedings etc.) Rules 1991 (in so far as those rules do not relate to enforcement or variation of orders);
–   the Magistrates' Courts (Costs Against Legal Representatives in Civil Proceedings) Rules 1991 (in so far as those rules relate to family proceedings);
–   the Family Proceedings Courts (Child Support Act 1991) Rules 1993;
–   the Magistrates' Courts (Reciprocal Enforcement of Maintenance Orders) (United States of America) Rules 1995 (subject to the saving in paragraph 3.6 of this Practice Direction);
–   the Magistrates' Courts (Hearsay Evidence in Civil Proceedings) Rules 1999 (in so far as those rules relate to family proceedings); and
–   the Family Procedure (Adoption) Rules 2005,

as in force immediately before 6 April 2011.

Amendments—FPR 2010, Update 2.

1.3 Insofar as they relate to family proceedings, the previous rules are revoked with effect from 6 April 2011 by operation of law and necessary implication. This is the case except where the previous rules continue to apply to existing family proceedings in accordance with this Practice Direction. The revocation of the previous rules arises from:

–   the repeal of the powers under which the previous rules were made (by section 109(1) and (3) of, and paragraph 245(2) of Schedule 8 and Schedule 10 to, the Courts Act 2003) or in the case of the Family Procedure (Adoption) Rules 2005 by remaking the rules in the FPR, and
–   the fact that the FPR are stated in terms to be a new procedural code and to apply to family proceedings in the High Court, a county court and a magistrates' court (FPR rules 1.1 and 2.1).

General scheme of transitional arrangements

2.1 The general scheme is –

(a)   to apply the FPR to existing proceedings so far as is practicable; but
(b)   where this is not practicable, to apply the previous rules to such proceedings.

Where the previous rules will normally apply

General principle

3.1 Where an initiating step has been taken in a case before 6 April 2011, in particular a step using forms or other documentation required by the previous rules, the case will proceed in the first instance under the previous rules. Where a party must take a step in response to something done by another party in accordance with the previous rules, that step must also be in accordance with those rules.

Responding to old process

3.2 A party who is served with an old type of originating process (for example, an originating summons) on or after 6 April 2011 must respond in accordance with the previous rules and the instructions on any forms received.

Filing and service of pleadings where old process served

3.3 Where a case has been begun by an old type of originating process (whether served before or after 6 April 2011), filing and service of pleadings will continue according to the previous rules.

Pre-commencement order inconsistent with FPR

3.4 Where a court order has been made before 6 April 2011, that order must still be complied with on or after that date.

Steps taken before commencement

3.5 Where a party has, before 6 April 2011, taken any step in the proceedings in accordance with the previous rules, that step will remain valid on or after that date, and a party will not normally be required to take any action that would amount to taking such a step again under the FPR.

Saving – Reciprocal enforcement of maintenance orders (United States of America)

3.6 Where, by virtue of article 6(2) of the Reciprocal Enforcement of Maintenance Orders (United States of America) Order 2007, the Reciprocal Enforcement of Maintenance (United States of America) Order 1995 continues in full force and effect, the Magistrates' Courts (Reciprocal Enforcement of Maintenance Orders) (United States of America) Rules 1995 shall, notwithstanding any provision in the FPR, continue to apply as if they had not been amended by the Magistrates' Courts (Reciprocal Enforcement of Maintenance Orders) (Miscellaneous Amendment) Rules 2007.

Where the FPR will normally apply

General principle

4.1 Where a new step is to be taken in any existing proceedings on or after 6 April 2011, it is to be taken under the FPR.

Part 1 (Overriding objective) to apply

4.2 Part 1 of the FPR (Overriding objective) will apply to all existing proceedings from 6 April 2011 onwards.

Issuing of application forms after the FPR come into force

4.3 (1) The general rule is that –
  - (a) only application forms under the FPR will be issued by the court on or after 6 April 2011; and
  - (b) if a request to issue an old type of form or originating process (summons, etc.) is received at the court on or after 6 April 2011, it will be returned unissued.

  (2) By way of exception to the general rule, the court may in cases of urgency direct that the form or process is to be issued as if the request to issue it had been a request to issue an application form under the FPR and, if it does so, the court may make such supplementary directions as it considers appropriate.

First time before a court on or after 6 April 2011

4.4

  (1) When proceedings come before a court (whether at a hearing or on paper) for the first time on or after 6 April 2011, the court may direct how the FPR are to apply to the proceedings and may disapply certain provisions of the FPR. The court may also give case management directions.

  (2) The general presumption will be that the FPR will apply to the proceedings from then on unless the court directs or this practice direction provides otherwise.

  (3) If an application has been issued before 6 April 2011 and the hearing of the application has been set on or after that date, the general presumption is that the application will be decided having regard to the FPR.

  (4) When the first occasion on which existing proceedings are before a court on or after 6 April 2011 is a hearing of a substantive issue, the general presumption is that the hearing will be conducted according to the FPR.

Costs

4.5

  (1) Any assessment of costs that takes place on or after 6 April 2011 will be in accordance with FPR Part 28 and the provisions of the Civil Procedure Rules as applied by that Part.

  (2) However, the general presumption is that no costs for work undertaken before 6 April 2011 will be disallowed if those costs would have been allowed on detailed assessment before that date.

  (3) The decision as to whether to allow costs for work undertaken on or after 6 April 2011 will generally be taken in accordance with FPR Part 28 and the provisions of the Civil Procedure Rules as applied by that Part.

GLOSSARY

Scope

This glossary is a guide to the meaning of certain legal expressions as used in these rules, but it does not give the expressions any meaning in the rules which they do not otherwise have in the law.

Expression	Meaning
Affidavit	A written, sworn, statement of evidence.
Cross-examination	Questioning of a witness by a party other than the party who called the witness.
Evidence in chief	The evidence given by a witness for the party who called him.
Injunction	A court order prohibiting a person from doing something or requiring a person to do something.
Official copy	A copy of an official document, supplied and marked as such by the office which issued the original.
Pre-action protocol	Statements of best practice about pre-action conduct which have been approved by the President of the Family Division and which are annexed to a Practice Direction.
Privilege	The right of a party to refuse to disclose a document or produce a document or to refuse to answer questions on the ground of some special interest recognised by law.
Seal	A seal is a mark which the court puts on document to indicate that the document has been issued by the court.
Service	Steps required by rules of court to bring documents used in court proceedings to a person's attention.
Set aside	Cancelling a judgment or order or a step taken by a party in the proceedings.
Stay	A stay imposes a halt on proceedings, apart from the taking of any steps allowed by the rules or the terms of the stay. Proceedings can be continued if a stay is lifted.
Strike out	Striking out means the court ordering written material to be deleted so that it may no longer be relied upon.
Without prejudice	Negotiations with a view to settlement are usually conducted "without prejudice" which means that the circumstances in which the content of those negotiations may be revealed to the court are very restricted.

PART III

Civil Procedure Rules 1998, SI 1998/3132

Amended Civil Procedure Rules Costs Provisions: Derivation and Destination Tables

Much of the existing text of the Civil Procedure Rules dealing with costs and the Costs Practice Direction is carried over to the new Rules, but almost all the rule and paragraph numbers have changed. The purpose of the following tables is to assist in cross-referring between the new material and the old; the precise text of the new Rules and Practice Directions should always be carefully examined because a number of Rules and Practice Directions have been preserved subject to small but usually significant amendment.

Where existing Rules and Practice Directions have been carried over subject to amendment, this is noted by italics, thus: *44.3*.

The following table deals only with the sections of the costs rules that are directly relevant to family proceedings; a fuller version can be found on page xix of *Civil Court Service 2013* (Jordan Publishing Ltd).

List of Tables

1   Derivation Table – Rules
2   Destination Table – Rules
3   Derivation Table – Practice Directions
4   Destination Table – The Costs Practice Direction

1 Derivation Table – Rules

CPR as amended		Existing CPR
	PART 44 – GENERAL RULES ABOUT COSTS	
	SECTION I: GENERAL	
44.1	Interpretation and application	*43.2, 43.3, 43.4, etc*
44.2	Court's discretion as to costs	*44.3*
44.3	Basis of assessment	*44.4*
44.4	Factors to be taken into account in deciding the amount of costs	44.5
44.5	Amount of costs where costs are payable under a contract	48.3
44.6	Procedure for assessing costs	44.7, 44.6
44.7	Time for complying with an order for costs	44.8
44.8	Legal representative's duty to notify the party	44.2
44.10	Where the court makes no order for costs	44.13
44.11	Court's powers in relation to misconduct	44.14
44.12	Set off	44.3(9)
	PART 46 – COSTS –SPECIAL CASES	
	SECTION I: COSTS PAYABLE BY OR TO PARTICULAR PERSONS	
46.1	Pre-commencement disclosure and orders for disclosure against a person who is not a party	48.1
46.2	Costs orders in favour of or against non-parties	48.2

CPR as amended		Existing CPR
46.3	Limitations on court's power to award costs in favour of trustee or personal representative	48.4
46.5	Litigants in person	48.6
46.7	Orders in respect of pro bono representation	44.3C
	SECTION II: COSTS RELATING TO LEGAL REPRESENTATIVES	
46.8	Personal liability of legal representative for costs – wasted costs orders	48.7
46.9	Basis of detailed assessment of solicitor and client costs	48.8
46.10	Assessment procedure	48.10
	PART 47 – PROCEDURE FOR DETAILED ASSESSMENT OF COSTS AND DEFAULT PROVISIONS	
	SECTION I: GENERAL RULES ABOUT DETAILED ASSESSMENT	
47.1	Time when detailed assessment may be carried out	47.1
47.2	No stay of detailed assessment where there is an appeal	47.2
47.3	Powers of an authorised court officer	47.3
47.4	Venue for detailed assessment proceedings	47.4
	SECTION II: COSTS PAYABLE BY ONE PARTY TO ANOTHER – COMMENCEMENT OF DETAILED ASSESSMENT PROCEEDINGS	
47.5	Application of this Section	47.5
47.6	Commencement of detailed assessment proceedings	47.6
47.7	Period for commencing detailed assessment proceedings	47.7
47.8	Sanction for delay in commencing detailed assessment proceedings	47.8
47.9	Points of dispute and consequence of not serving	47.9
47.10	Procedure where costs are agreed	47.10
	SECTION III: COSTS PAYABLE BY ONE PARTY TO ANOTHER – DEFAULT PROVISIONS	
47.11	Default costs certificate	47.11
47.12	Setting aside a default costs certificate	47.12
	SECTION IV: COSTS PAYABLE BY ONE PARTY TO ANOTHER – PROCEDURE WHERE POINTS OF DISPUTE ARE SERVED	
47.13	Optional Reply	47.13
47.14	Detailed assessment hearing	47.14

PART III

CPR as amended		Existing CPR
47.15	Provisional Assessment	*New*
	SECTION V: INTERIM COSTS CERTIFICATE AND FINAL COSTS CERTIFICATE	
47.16	Power to issue an interim certificate	47.15
47.17	Final costs certificate	47.16
	SECTION VI: DETAILED ASSESSMENT PROCEDURE FOR COSTS OF A LSC FUNDED CLIENT OR AN ASSISTED PERSON WHERE COSTS ARE PAYABLE OUT OF THE COMMUNITY LEGAL SERVICE FUND	
47.18	Detailed assessment procedure where costs are payable out of the community legal service fund	47.17
47.19	Detailed assessment procedure where costs are payable out of a fund other than the community legal service fund	47.17A
	SECTION VII: COSTS OF DETAILED ASSESSMENT PROCEEDINGS	
47.20	Liability for costs of detailed assessment proceedings	*47.18*
	SECTION VIII: APPEALS FROM AUTHORISED COURT OFFICERS IN DETAILED ASSESSMENT PROCEEDINGS	
47.21	Right to appeal	47.20
47.22	Court to hear appeal	47.21
47.23	Appeal procedure	47.22
47.24	Powers of the court on appeal	47.23

2 Destination Table – Rules

Existing CPR		CPR as amended
	PART 43 – SCOPE OF COST RULES AND DEFINITIONS	
43.2	Definitions and application	44.1
43.3	Meaning of summary assessment	44.1
43.4	Meaning of detailed assessment	44.1
	PART 44 – GENERAL RULES ABOUT COSTS	
44.2	Solicitor's duty to notify client	44.8
44.3	Court's discretion and circumstances to be taken into account when exercising its discretion as to costs	*44.2*
44.4	Basis of assessment	*44.3*
44.5	Factors to be taken into account in deciding the amount of costs	44.4

Existing CPR		CPR as amended
44.6	Fixed costs	44.6
44.7	Procedure for assessing costs	44.6
44.8	Time for complying with an order for costs	44.7
44.13	Special situations	44.10
44.14	Court's powers in relation to misconduct	44.11
	PART 47 – PROCEDURE FOR DETAILED ASSESSMENT OF COSTS AND DEFAULT PROVISIONS	
	SECTION I: GENERAL RULES ABOUT DETAILED ASSESSMENT	
47.1	Time when detailed assessment may be carried out	47.1
47.2	No stay of detailed assessment where there is an appeal	47.2
47.3	Powers of an authorised court officer	47.3
47.4	Venue for detailed assessment proceedings	47.4
	SECTION II: COSTS PAYABLE BY ONE PARTY TO ANOTHER – COMMENCEMENT OF DETAILED ASSESSMENT PROCEEDINGS	
47.5	Application of this Section	47.5
47.6	Commencement of detailed assessment procedure	47.6
47.7	Period for commencing detailed assessment procedure	47.7
47.8	Sanction for delay in commencing detailed assessment procedure	*47.8*
47.9	Points of dispute and consequences of not serving	47.9
47.10	Procedure where costs are agreed	47.10
	SECTION III: COSTS PAYABLE BY ONE PARTY TO ANOTHER – DEFAULT PROVISIONS	
47.11	Default costs certificate	47.11
47.12	Setting aside default costs certificate	*47.12*
	SECTION IV: COSTS PAYABLE BY ONE PARTY TO ANOTHER – PROCEDURE WHERE POINTS OF DISPUTE ARE SERVED	
47.13	Optional reply	47.13
47.14	Detailed assessment hearing	47.14
	SECTION V: INTERIM COSTS CERTIFICATE AND FINAL COSTS CERTIFICATE	
47.15	Power to issue an interim certificate	47.16
47.16	Final costs certificate	47.17

PART III

Existing CPR		CPR as amended
	SECTION VI: DETAILED ASSESSMENT PROCEDURE FIR COSTS OF A LSC FUNDED CLIENT OR AN AASSISTED PERSON WHERE COSTS ARE PAYABLE OUT OF THE COMMUNITY LEGAL SERVICE FUND	
47.17	Detailed assessment procedure for costs of a LSC funded client or an assisted person where costs are payable out of the Community Legal Service Fund	47.18
47.17A	Detailed assessment procedure where costs are payable out of a fund other than the Community Legal Service Fund	47.19
	SECTION VII: COSTS OF DETAILED ASSESSMENT PROCEEDINGS	
47.18	Liability for costs of detailed assessment proceedings	47.20
47.19	Offers to settle without prejudice save as to costs of the detailed assessment proceedings	Revoked
	SECTION VIII: APPEALS FROM AUTHORISED COURT OFFICERS IN DETAILED ASSESSMENT PROCEEDINGS	
47.20	Right to appeal	47.21
47.21	Court to hear appeal	47.22
47.22	Appeal procedure	47.23
47.23	Powers of the court on appeal	47.24
	PART 48 – COSTS – SPECIAL CASES	
	SECTION I: COSTS PAYABLE BY OR TO PARTICULAR PERSONS	
48.1	Pre-commencement disclosure and orders for disclosure against a person who is not a party	46.1
48.2	Costs orders in favour of or against non-parties	46.2
48.4	Limitations on court's power to award costs in favour of trustee or personal representative	46.3
48.6	Litigants in person	46.5
	SECTION II: COSTS RELATING TO SOLICITORS AND OTHER LEGAL REPRESENTATIVES	
48.7	Personal liability of legal representative for costs – wasted costs orders	46.8
48.8	Basis of detailed assessment of solicitor and client costs	46.9
48.10	Assessment procedure	46.10

3 Derivation Table – Practice Directions

New PDs		Existing Costs PD
	PRACTICE DIRECTION 44 – GENERAL RULES ABOUT COSTS	
	SECTION I: GENERAL	
	Subsection 1 – Documents and forms	
1.1		*1.5*
1.2		*3.2, 3.3, 3.5, 3.6, 3.7*
	Subsection 2 – Special provisions relating to VAT:	
2.1	Scope of this subsection	5.1
2.2	VAT Registration Number	5.2
2.3	Entitlement to VAT on Costs	5.3
2.4		5.4
2.5		*5.5*
2.6		5.6
2.7	Form of bill of costs when VAT rate changes	5.7
2.8		5.8
2.9	Apportionment	*5.9*
2.10	Change of a VAT rate between the conclusion of a detailed assessment and the issue of a final certificate	5.10
2.11	Disbursements not classified as such for VAT purposes	5.11
2.12	Litigants in person	*5.18, 5.19*
2.13	Government Departments	5.20
2.14	Payment pursuant to an order under section 194(3) of the 2007 Act	5.21
	Subsection 4 – Court's discretion as to costs: rule 44.2	
4.1		8.3(1)
4.2		8.5
	Subsection 5 – Fees of Counsel	
5.1		*8.7(2), 8.7(3)*
5.2		*8.8*
	Subsection 6 – Basis of assessment: rule 44.3	
6.1	Costs on the indemnity basis	*New*
6.2	Costs on the standard basis	*New*

PART III

	Subsection 8 – Procedure for assessing costs: rule 44.6	
8.1		*12.1*
8.2		12.2
8.3		*New*
	Subsection 9 – Summary assessment: general provisions	
9.1	When the court should consider whether to make a summary assessment	13.1
9.2	Timing of summary assessment	13.2
9.4	Consent orders	*13.4*
9.5	Duty of parties and legal representatives	13.5
9.6		13.6
9.7	No summary assessment by a costs officer	13.8
9.8	Assisted persons or LSC funded clients	*13.9*
9.9	Children or protected parties	13.11
9.10	Disproportionate or unreasonable costs	*13.13(a)*
	Subsection 10 – Legal representative's duty to notify party: rule 44.8	
10.1		*7.1*
10.2		*7.2*
10.3		*7.3*
	Subsection 11 – Court's powers in relation to misconduct: rule 44.11	
11.1		18.1
11.2		18.2
11.3		18.3
	PRACTICE DIRECTION 46 – COSTS SPECIAL CASES	
1.1	Awards of costs in favour of a trustee or personal representative: rule 46.3	50A.1, 50A.2
1.2		50A.3
2.1	Costs where money is payable by or to a child or protected party: rule 46.4	51.1
3.1	Litigants in person: rule 46.5	*52.1*
3.2		52.2
3.3		52.3
3.4		52.4
4.1	Orders in respect of pro bono representation: rule 46.7	*10A.2*

5.1	Personal liability of legal representative for costs – wasted costs orders: rule 46.8	*New*
5.2		53.1
5.3		53.2
5.4		53.3
5.5		53.4
5.6		53.5
5.7		53.6
5.8		*53.7*
5.9		53.8
6.1	Assessment of solicitor and client costs: rules 46.9 and 46.10	54.1
6.2		*54.2*
6.3		54.4
6.4		56.2
6.5		56.3
6.6		56.5
6.7		56.6
6.8		56.7
6.9		56.9
6.10		*56.10*
6.11		*56.11*
6.12		*56.12*
6.13		*56.13(1)*
6.14		*56.13(3)*
6.15		56.14
6.16		56.15
6.17		56.16
6.18		*56.17(2)*
6.19		*56.18(2)*
	PRACTICE DIRECTION 47 – PROCEDURE FOR DETAILED ASSESSMENT OF COSTS AND DEFAULT PROVISIONS	
1.1	Time when assessment may be carried out: rule 47.1	*28.1(1), 28.1(2)*
1.2		28.1(3)

PART III

1.3		28.1(4)
1.4		28.1(5)
2	No stay of detailed assessment where there is an appeal: rule 47.2	29.1(2)
3.1	Powers of an authorised court officer: rule 47.3	*30.1(1)*
3.2		30.1(3)
3.3		*30.1(4)*
4.1	Venue for detailed assessment proceedings: rule 47.4	31.1
4.2		31.1A
4.3		31.2(1), 31.2(3)
5.1	Commencement of detailed assessment proceedings: rule 47.6	*32.1*
5.2		32.3
5.3		32.8(2)
5.4		*32.9*
5.5		32.10
5.6		*32.11*
	FORM AND CONTENT OF BILLS OF COSTS	
5.7	General	4.1
5.8		4.2
5.9		*4.3*
5.10	Title page	4.4
5.11	Background information	*4.5*
5.12	Heads of costs	4.6
5.13		4.7
5.14		4.8
5.15		4.9
5.16		4.10
5.17		4.11
5.18		4.12
5.19		4.13
5.20		4.14
5.21		4.15
5.22		4.16

6.1	Period for commencing detailed assessment proceedings: rule 47.7	*33.1, 33.2*
6.2		33.3, 33.4
7	Sanction for delay in commencing detailed assessment proceedings: rule 47.8	34.1
8.1	Points of dispute and consequences of not serving: rule 47.9	*35.1*
8.2		35.2, *35.3*
8.3		*New*
9.1	Procedure where costs are agreed and on discontinuance: rule 47.10	36.1
9.2		36.2
9.3		36.4
9.4		36.5
10.1	Default costs certificate: rule 47.11	37.1, 37.2
10.2		37.3
10.3		37.4
10.4		*37.5*
10.5		37.6
10.6		37.7
10.7	Fixed costs on the issue of a default costs certificate	25.1
10.8		25.2
11.1	Setting aside default costs certificate: rule 47.12	38.1
11.2		38.2
11.3		38.3
12.1	Optional reply: rule 47.13	*New*
12.2		*New*
13.1	Detailed assessment hearing: rule 47.14	40.1
13.2		40.2
13.3		*40.4*
13.4		40.5
13.5		*New*
13.6		40.6(1)
13.7		40.8
13.8		40.9
13.10		40.10

13.11		40.11
13.12		*40.12*
13.13		40.14
13.14		*40.16*
14.1	Provisional assessment: rule 47.15	*New*
14.2		*New*
14.3		*New*
14.4		*New*
14.5		*New*
14.6		*New*
15	Power to issue an interim certificate: rule 47.16	41.1(1)
16.1	Final costs certificate: rule 47.17	42.1
16.2		42.2
16.3		42.3
16.4		42.4
16.5		42.5
16.6		42.6
16.7		*42.7*
16.8		42.8
16.9		42.9
16.10		42.10
16.11		42.11
16.12		*42.12*
17.1	Detailed assessment procedure where costs are payable out of the Community Legal Service Fund or by the Lord Chancellor under Part 1 of the Legal Aid, Sentencing and Punishment of Offenders Act 2012: rule 47.18	43.2
17.2		43.3
17.3		43.5
17.4		43.8
17.5		43.9
17.6	Costs payable by the Legal Services Commission or Lord Chancellor at Prescribed Rates	*49.1, 49.2*
17.7		49.3
17.8		49.4

17.9		49.5
17.10		49.6, 49.7
17.11		49.8
18.1	Detailed assessment procedure where costs are payable out of a fund other than the Community Legal Service Fund or by the Lord Chancellor under Part 1 of the Legal Aid, Sentencing and Punishment of Offenders Act 2012: rule 47.19	*44.1*
18.2		44.2
18.3		*44.3*
18.4		44.4
18.5		44.5
18.6		*44.6*
18.7		44.8
18.8		*44.9*
18.9		44.10
19	Costs of detailed assessment proceedings – rule 47.20: offers to settle under Part 36 or otherwise	*46.2*
20.1	Appeals from authorised court officers in detailed assessment proceedings: rules 47.22 to 47.25	*47.1*
20.2		47.2
20.3		48.1
20.4		48.2
20.5		48.3
20.6		48.4

PART III

4 Destination Table – The Costs Practice Direction

Existing Costs PD		New PDs
	SECTION 1 – INTRODUCTION	
1.5		PD44 1.1
	SECTION 3 – MODEL FORMS FOR CLAIMS FOR COSTS	
3.1	Rule 43.3 Meaning of Summary Assessment	
3.2		PD44 1.2
3.3		PD44 1.2
3.5		PD44 1.2
3.6		PD44 1.2

3.7		
	SECTION 4 – FORM AND CONTENTS OF BILLS OF COSTS	
4.1		PD47 5.7
4.2		PD47 5.8
4.3		PD47 5.9
4.4		PD47 5.10
4.5		PD47 5.11
4.6		PD47 5.12
4.7		PD47 5.13
4.8		PD47 5.14
4.9		PD47 5.15
4.10		PD47 5.16
4.11		PD47 5.17
4.12		PD47 5.18
4.13		PD47 5.19
4.14		PD47 5.20
4.15		PD47 5.21
4.16		PD47 5.22
4.17		*Revoked*
	SECTION 5 – SPECIAL PROVISIONS RELATING TO VAT	
5.1		PD44 2.1
5.2	VAT registration number	PD44 2.2
5.3	Entitlement to VAT on costs	PD44 2.3
5.4		PD44 2.4
5.5		PD44 2.5
5.6		PD44 2.6
5.7	Form of bill of costs where VAT rate changes	PD44 2.7
5.8		PD44 2.8
5.9	Apportionment	PD44 2.9
5.10		PD44 2.10
5.11	Disbursements not classified as such for VAT purposes	PD44 2.11
5.12		
5.13	Legal Aid/LSC funding	

5.14		
5.15	Tax invoice	
5.16	Vouchers	
5.17	Certificates	
5.18	Litigants acting in person	PD44 2.12
5.19		PD44 2.12
5.20	Government Departments	PD44 2.13
5.21	Payment pursuant to an order under section 194(3) of the Legal Services Act 2007	PD44 2.14
	DIRECTIONS RELATING TO PART 44 – GENERAL RULES ABOUT COSTS	
	SECTION 7 – SOLICITOR'S DUTY TO NOTIFY CLIENT: RULE 44.2	
7.1		PD44 10.1
7.2		PD44 10.2
7.3		PD44 10.3
	SECTION 8 – COURT'S DISCRETION AND CIRCUMSTANCES TO BE TAKEN INTO ACCOUNT WHEN EXERCISING ITS DISCRETION AS TO COSTS: RULE 44.3	
8.3		PD44 4.1
8.5		PD44 4.2
8.7	Fees of counsel	PD44 5.1
8.8	Fees payable to conveyancing counsel appointed by the court to assist it	PD44 5.2
	SECTION 10A – ORDERS IN RESPECT OF PRO BONO REPRESENTATION: RULE 44.3C	
10A.1		
10A.2		PD46 4.1
	SECTION 12 – PROCEDURE FOR ASSESSING COSTS: RULE 44.7	
12.1		PD44 8.1
12.2		PD44 8.2
12.3		*Revoked*
	SECTION 13 – SUMMARY ASSESSMENT: GENERAL PROVISIONS	
13.1		PD44 9.1
13.2		PD44 9.2
13.3		PD44 9.3

PART III

32.6		*Revoked*
32.7		*Revoked*
32.8		PD47 5.3
32.9		PD47 5.4
32.10		PD47 5.5
32.11		PD47 5.6
	SECTION 33 – PERIOD FOR COMMENCING DETAILED ASSESSMENT PROCEEDINGS: RULE 47.7	
33.1		PD47 6.1
33.2		PD47 6.1
33.3		PD47 6.2
33.4		PD47 6.2
	SECTION 34 – SANCTION FOR DELAY IN COMMENCING DETAILED ASSESSMENT PROCEEDINGS: RULE 47.8	
34.1		PD47 7
	SECTION 35 – POINTS OF DISPUTE AND CONSEQUENCES OF NOT SERVING: RULE 47.9	
35.1		PD47 8.1
35.2		PD47 8.2
35.3		PD47 8.2
	SECTION 36 – PROCEDURE WHERE COSTS ARE AGREED: RULE 47.10	
36.1		PD47 9.1
36.2		PD47 9.2
36.3		
36.4		PD47 9.3
36.5		PD47 9.4
	SECTION 37 – DEFAULT COSTS CERTIFICATE: RULE 47.11	
37.1		PD47 10.1
37.2		PD47 10.1
37.3		PD47 10.2
37.4		PD47 10.3
37.5		PD47 10.4
37.6		PD47 10.5
37.7		PD47 10.6

PART III

42.4		PD47 16.4
42.5		PD47 16.5
42.6		PD47 16.6
42.7		PD47 16.7
42.8		PD47 16.8
42.9		PD47 16.9
42.10		PD47 16.10
42.11		PD47 16.11
42.12		PD47 16.12
	SECTION 43 – DETAILED ASSESSMENT PROCEDURE WHERE COSTS ARE PAYABLE OUT OF THE COMMUNITY LEGAL SERVICE FUND: RULE 47.17	
43.1		
43.2		PD47 17.1
43.3		PD47 17.2
43.4		
43.5		PD47 17.3
43.6		
43.7		
43.8		PD47 17.4
43.9		PD47 17.5
	SECTION 44 – COSTS OF DETAILED ASSESSMENT PROCEEDINGS	
	Where costs are payable out of a fund other than the Community Legal Service Fund: rule 47.17A	
44.1		PD47 18.1
44.2		PD47 18.2
44.3		PD47 18.3
44.4		PD47 18.4
44.5		PD47 18.5
44.6		PD47 18.6
44.7		
44.8		PD47 18.7
44.9		PD47 18.8
44.10		PD47 18.9

PART III

	SECTION 47 – APPEALS FROM AUTHORISED COURT OFFICERS IN DETAILED ASSESSMENT PROCEEDINGS: RIGHT TO APPEAL: RULE 47.20	
47.1		PD47 20.1
47.2		PD47 20.2
	SECTION 48 – PROCEDURE ON APPEAL FROM AUTHORISED COURT OFFICERS: RULE 47. 22	
48.1		PD47 20.3
48.2		PD47 20.4
48.3		PD47 20.5
48.4		PD47 20.6
	SECTION 49 – COSTS PAYABLE BY THE LSC AT PRESCRIBED RATES	
49.1		PD47 17.6
49.2		PD47 17.6
49.3		PD47 17.7
49.4		PD47 17.8
49.5		PD47 17.9
49.6		PD47 17.10
49.7		PD47 17.10
49.8		PD47 17.11
	SECTION 50A – LIMITATION ON COURT'S POWER TO AWARD COSTS IN FAVOUR OF TRUSTEE OR PERSONAL REPRESENTATIVE: RULE 48.4	
50A.1		PD46 1.1
50A.2		PD46 1.1
50A.3		PD46 1.2
	SECTION 51 – COSTS WHERE MONEY IS PAYABLE BY OR TO A CHILD OR PROTECTED PARTY: RULE 48.5	
51.1		PD46 2.1
	SECTION 52 – LITIGANTS IN PERSON: RULE 48.6	
52.1		PD46 3.1
52.2		PD46 3.2
52.3		PD46 3.3
52.4		PD46 3.4
52.5		

	SECTION 53 – PERSONAL LIABILITY OF LEGAL REPRESENTATIVE FOR COSTS – WASTED COSTS ORDERS: RULE 48.7	
53.1		PD46 5.2
53.2		PD46 5.3
53.3		PD46 5.4
53.4		PD46 5.5
53.5		PD46 5.6
53.6		PD46 5.7
53.7		PD46 5.8
53.8		PD46 5.9
53.9		
	SECTION 54 – BASIS OF DETAILED ASSESSMENT OF SOLICITOR AND CLIENT COSTS: RULE 44.8	
54.1		PD46 6.1
54.2		PD46 6.2
54.3		
54.4		PD46 6.3
54.5		
54.6		
54.7		
54.8		
	SECTION 56 – PROCEDURE ON ASSESSMENT OF SOLICITOR AND CLIENT COSTS: RULE 48.10	
56.1		
56.2		PD46 6.4
56.3		PD46 6.5
56.4		
56.5		PD46 6.6
56.6		PD46 6.7
56.7		PD46 6.8
56.8		
56.9		PD46 6.9
56.10		PD46 6.10
56.11		PD46 6.11

PART III

56.12		PD46 6.12
56.13		PD46 6.13, 6.14
56.14		PD46 6.15
56.15		PD46 6.16
56.16		PD46 6.17
56.17		PD46 6.18
56.18		PD46 6.19
56.19		
	SECTION 57 – TRANSITIONAL ARRANGEMENTS	*Revoked*

PART 1
OVERRIDING OBJECTIVE

CONTENTS OF THIS PART

1.1 The overriding objective

(1) These Rules are a new procedural code with the overriding objective of enabling the court to deal with cases justly and at proportionate cost.

(2) Dealing with a case justly and at proportionate cost includes, so far as is practicable –

    (a)   ensuring that the parties are on an equal footing;

    (b)   saving expense;

    (c)   dealing with the case in ways which are proportionate –

        (i)   to the amount of money involved;

        (ii) to the importance of the case;

        (iii) to the complexity of the issues; and

        (iv) to the financial position of each party;

    (d)   ensuring that it is dealt with expeditiously and fairly;

    (e)   allotting to it an appropriate share of the court's resources, while taking into account the need to allot resources to other cases; and

    (f)   enforcing compliance with rules, practice directions and orders.

Amendments—SI 2013/262.

Scope of CPR 1998—The CPR 1998 are a procedural code that replaced both the former RSC 1965 and CCR 1981.

FPR 2010—FPR 2010 are the procedural code for family proceedings and came into force on 6 April 2011. The FPR have their own "overriding objective", which is not exactly the same as that in the CPR.

1.2 Application by the court of the overriding objective

The court must seek to give effect to the overriding objective when it –

    (a)   exercises any power given to it by the Rules; or

    (b)   interprets any rule, subject to rules 76.2, 79.2 and 80.2.

"interprets any rule"—The overriding objective applies to every rule. FPR 2010 have a similar, but not identical provision.

Amendments—SI 2005/656; SI 2008/3085; SI 2011/2970.

1.3 Duty of the parties

The parties are required to help the court to further the overriding objective.

1.4 Court's duty to manage cases

(1) The court must further the overriding objective by actively managing cases.

(2) Active case management includes –

    (a)   encouraging the parties to co-operate with each other in the conduct of the proceedings;

    (b)   identifying the issues at an early stage;

    (c)   deciding promptly which issues need full investigation and trial and accordingly disposing summarily of the others;

    (d)   deciding the order in which issues are to be resolved;

    (e)   encouraging the parties to use an alternative dispute resolution(GL) procedure if the court considers that appropriate and facilitating the use of such procedure;

    (f)   helping the parties to settle the whole or part of the case;

    (g)   fixing timetables or otherwise controlling the progress of the case;

    (h)   considering whether the likely benefits of taking a particular step justify the cost of taking it;

    (i)   dealing with as many aspects of the case as it can on the same occasion;

    (j)   dealing with the case without the parties needing to attend at court;

    (k)   making use of technology; and

    (l)   giving directions to ensure that the trial of a case proceeds quickly and efficiently.

PART 2
APPLICATION AND INTERPRETATION OF THE RULES

CONTENTS OF THIS PART

Practice Direction—See PD2A and PD2B, which supplement this Part generally; both are set out in Section 2 of the *Civil Court Service* (Jordan Publishing Ltd).

2.1 Application of the Rules

(1) Subject to paragraph (2), these Rules apply to all proceedings in –

    (a)   county courts;

(b)   the High Court; and
(c)   the Civil Division of the Court of Appeal.

(2) These Rules do not apply to proceedings of the kinds specified in the first column of the following Table (proceedings for which rules may be made under the enactments specified in the second column) except to the extent that they are applied to those proceedings by another enactment –

Proceedings	Enactments
1. Insolvency proceedings	Insolvency Act 1986, ss 411 and 412
2. Non-contentious or common form probate proceedings	Senior Courts Act 1981, s 127
3. Proceedings in the High Court when acting as a Prize Court	Prize Courts Act 1894, s 3
4. Proceedings before the Court of Protection	Mental Capacity Act 2005, s 51
5. Family proceedings	Courts Act 2003, s 75
6. Adoption proceedings	Adoption and Children Act 2002, s 141 or Courts Act 2003, s 75
7. Election petitions in the High Court	Representation of the People Act 1983, s 182

Amendments—SI 1999/1008; SI 2003/1242; CRA 2005, Sch 11, para 1(2); SI 2005/3515; SI 2007/2204; SI 2011/1045.

Effect of CPR 1998 on family proceedings—Rule 2.1(2) provides that the CPR do not apply to "family proceedings". In family proceedings, see FPR 2010, which expressly incorporate certain provisions in the CPR.

2.2 The glossary

(1) The glossary at the end of these Rules is a guide to the meaning of certain legal expressions used in the Rules, but is not to be taken as giving those expressions any meaning in the Rules which they do not have in the law generally.

(2) Subject to paragraph (3), words in these Rules which are included in the glossary are followed by "(GL)".

(3) The words "counterclaim", "damages", "practice form" and "service", which appear frequently in the Rules, are included in the glossary but are not followed by "(GL)".

2.3 Interpretation

(1) In these Rules –

"child" has the meaning given by rule 21.1(2);
"civil restraint order" means an order restraining a party –
    (a)   from making any further applications in current proceedings (a limited civil restraint order);
    (b)   from issuing certain claims or making certain applications in specified courts (an extended civil restraint order); or
    (c)   from issuing any claim or making any application in specified courts (a general civil restraint order).

"claim for personal injuries" means proceedings in which there is a claim for damages in respect of personal injuries to the claimant or any other person or in respect of a person's death, and "personal injuries" includes any disease and any impairment of a person's physical or mental condition;

"claimant" means a person who makes a claim;

"CCR" is to be interpreted in accordance with Part 50;

"court officer" means a member of the court staff;

"defendant" means a person against whom a claim is made;

"defendant's home court" means –

    (a)   if the claim is proceeding in a county court, the county court for the district in which the defendant resides or carries on business; and

    (b)   if the claim is proceeding in the High Court, the district registry for the district in which the defendant resides or carries on business or, where there is no such district registry, the Royal Courts of Justice;

(Rule 6.23 provides for a party to give an address for service)

"designated money claim" means any claim which –

    (a)   is started in a county court under Part 7;

    (b)   is only a claim for either or both a specified amount of money or an unspecified amount of money; and

    (c)   is not a claim for which special procedures are provided in these rules;

"filing", in relation to a document, means delivering it, by post or otherwise, to the court office;

"judge" means, unless the context otherwise requires, a judge, Master or district judge or a person authorised to act as such;

"jurisdiction" means, unless the context requires otherwise, England and Wales and any part of the territorial waters of the United Kingdom adjoining England and Wales;

"legal representative" means a –

    (a)   barrister;

    (b)   solicitor;

    (c)   solicitor's employee;

    (d)   manager of a body recognised under section 9 of the Administration of Justice Act 1985; or

    (e)   person who, for the purposes of the Legal Services Act 2007, is an authorised person in relation to an activity which constitutes the conduct of litigation (within the meaning of that Act),

who has been instructed to act for a party in relation to proceedings;

"litigation friend" has the meaning given by Part 21;

"preferred court" means, if the claim is proceeding in a county court, the county court the claimant has specified in practice form N1 as the court to which the proceedings should be transferred if necessary;

"protected party" has the meaning given by rule 21.1(2);

"RSC" is to be interpreted in accordance with Part 50;

"statement of case" –

    (a)   means a claim form, particulars of claim where these are not included in a claim form, defence, Part 20 claim, or reply to defence; and

    (b)   includes any further information given in relation to them voluntarily or by court order under rule 18.1;

"statement of value" is to be interpreted in accordance with rule 16.3;

"summary judgment" is to be interpreted in accordance with Part 24.

(2) A reference to a "specialist list" is a reference to a list$^{(GL)}$ that has been designated as such by a rule or practice direction.

(3) Where the context requires, a reference to "the court" means a reference to a particular county court, a district registry, or the Royal Courts of Justice.

Amendments—SI 2000/2092; SI 2001/4015; SI 2004/2072; SI 2007/2204; SI 2008/2178; SI 2009/3390; SI 2011/3103.

****

2.8 Time

(1) This rule shows how to calculate any period of time for doing any act which is specified –

    (a) by these Rules;
    (b) by a practice direction; or
    (c) by a judgment or order of the court.

(2) A period of time expressed as a number of days shall be computed as clear days.

(3) In this rule "clear days" means that in computing the number of days –

    (a) the day on which the period begins; and
    (b) if the end of the period is defined by reference to an event, the day on which that event occurs

are not included.

Examples
(i)   Notice of an application must be served at least 3 days before the hearing.
An application is to be heard on Friday 20 October.
The last date for service is Monday 16 October.
(ii) The court is to fix a date for a hearing.
The hearing must be at least 28 days after the date of notice.
If the court gives notice of the date of the hearing on 1 October, the earliest date for the hearing is 30 October.
(iii) Particulars of claim must be served within 14 days of service of the claim form.
The claim form is served on 2 October.
The last day for service of the particulars of claim is 16 October.

(4) Where the specified period –

    (a) is 5 days or less; and
    (b) includes –
        (i)   a Saturday or Sunday; or
        (ii) a Bank Holiday, Christmas Day or Good Friday,

that day does not count.

Example
Notice of an application must be served at least 3 days before the hearing.
An application is to be heard on Monday 20 October.
The last date for service is Tuesday 14 October.

(5) Subject to the provisions of Practice Direction 5C, when the period specified –

    (a) by these Rules or a practice direction; or
    (b) by any judgment or court order,

for doing any act at the court office ends on a day on which the office is closed, that act shall be in time if done on the next day on which the court office is open.

Amendments—SI 2009/3390.

****

PART 3
THE COURT'S CASE AND COSTS MANAGEMENT POWERS

CONTENTS OF THIS PART

Section I
Case Management

Practice Direction—See *PD (Striking out a Statement of Case)*, *PD (Sanctions for Non-Payment of Fees)* and *PD (Civil Restraint Orders)*, which supplement this Part generally; all three are set out in Section 2 of the *Civil Court Service* (Jordan Publishing Ltd).

Section I
Case Management

3.1 The court's general powers of management

(1) The list of powers in this rule is in addition to any powers given to the court by any other rule or practice direction or by any other enactment or any powers it may otherwise have.

(2) Except where these Rules provide otherwise, the court may –

   (a) extend or shorten the time for compliance with any rule, practice direction or court order (even if an application for extension is made after the time for compliance has expired);

   (b) adjourn or bring forward a hearing;

   (c) require a party or a party's legal representative to attend the court;

   (d) hold a hearing and receive evidence by telephone or by using any other method of direct oral communication;

   (e) direct that part of any proceedings (such as a counterclaim) be dealt with as separate proceedings;

   (f) stay[GL] the whole or part of any proceedings or judgment either generally or until a specified date or event;

   (g) consolidate proceedings;

   (h) try two or more claims on the same occasion;

   (i) direct a separate trial of any issue;

   (j) decide the order in which issues are to be tried;

   (k) exclude an issue from consideration;

   (l) dismiss or give judgment on a claim after a decision on a preliminary issue;

   (ll) order any party to file and serve an estimate of costs;

   (m) take any other step or make any other order for the purpose of managing the case and furthering the overriding objective.

(3) When the court makes an order, it may –

   (a) make it subject to conditions, including a condition to pay a sum of money into court; and

   (b) specify the consequence of failure to comply with the order or a condition.

(4) Where the court gives directions it will take into account whether or not a party has complied with the Practice Direction (Pre-Action Conduct) and any relevant pre-action protocol[GL].

(5) The court may order a party to pay a sum of money into court if that party has, without good reason, failed to comply with a rule, practice direction or a relevant pre-action protocol.

(6) When exercising its power under paragraph (5) the court must have regard to –

(a)   the amount in dispute; and

(b)   the costs which the parties have incurred or which they may incur.

(6A) Where a party pays money into court following an order under paragraph (3) or (5), the money shall be security for any sum payable by that party to any other party in the proceedings.

(7) A power of the court under these Rules to make an order includes a power to vary or revoke the order.

(8) The court may contact the parties from time to time in order to monitor compliance with directions. The parties must respond promptly to any such enquiries from the court.

Amendments—SI 1999/1008; SI 2005/2292; SI 2006/3435; SI 2008/3327; SI 2013/262.

General powers of management—The list of case management powers supplement those in r 1.4. FPR 2010, r 4.1 will provide for case management in family proceedings in similar terms to CPR 1998, r 3.1, although case-law under this rule will be helpful in an understanding of r 4.1.

Case management of parallel family and civil proceedings—Where an application under, for example, CA 1989, s 15 and Sch 1, and a claim under TLATA 1996, s 14, are proceedings in parallel, care is needed to ensure that the CPR 1998, Pt 8 procedure (for s 14 proceedings) and FPR 2010, Pt 9 run in parallel. Typically this occurs where there are proceedings relating to a home owned by an unmarried couple with children (see W v W (*Joinder of Trusts of Land Act and Children Act 1989 Applications*) [2004] 2 FLR 321, CA). The judge had been wrong to try the TLATA application first and separately from the CA 1989 application. The Court of Appeal did not address the question of whether FPR 2010 or CPR 1998 apply. The same question of parallel proceedings under different rules arises: where an issue as to equitable interests arises in respect of specific matrimonial property or where one spouse of civil partner is bankrupt and their interest in the former matrimonial home vests in their trustee in bankruptcy (see case management under FPR 2010, rr 1.4 and 4.1).

Directions—Given the terms of the overriding objective here and in FPR 2010, r 1.4, parties owe a duty to the court and to each other to consider whether preliminary directions, and if so which, should be applied for in any court proceedings, especially where a preliminary issue is identified by one party (see, for example, *TL v ML* above).

Application for order—Where application is made for an order in respect of any of the provisions under r 3.1(2), it is made in accordance with Pt 23 on Form N246 (and see r 3.3 below).

****

3.3 Court's power to make order of its own initiative

(1) Except where a rule or some other enactment provides otherwise, the court may exercise its powers on an application or of its own initiative.

(Part 23 sets out the procedure for making an application)

(2) Where the court proposes to make an order of its own initiative –

(a)   it may give any person likely to be affected by the order an opportunity to make representations; and

(b)   where it does so it must specify the time by and the manner in which the representations must be made.

(3) Where the court proposes –

(a)   to make an order of its own initiative; and

(b)   to hold a hearing to decide whether to make the order,

it must give each party likely to be affected by the order at least 3 days' notice of the hearing.

(4) The court may make an order of its own initiative, without hearing the parties or giving them an opportunity to make representations.

(5) Where the court has made an order under paragraph (4) –

    (a)   a party affected by the order may apply to have it set aside$^{(GL)}$, varied or stayed$^{(GL)}$; and

    (b)   the order must contain a statement of the right to make such an application.

(6) An application under paragraph (5)(a) must be made –

    (a)   within such period as may be specified by the court; or

    (b)   if the court does not specify a period, not more than 7 days after the date on which the order was served on the party making the application.

(7) If the court of its own initiative strikes out a statement of case or dismisses an application, including an application for permission to appeal or for permission to apply for judicial review) and it considers that the claim or application is totally without merit –

    (a)   the court's order must record that fact; and

    (b)   the court must at the same time consider whether it is appropriate to make a civil restraint order.

       (CCR Ord 42, in Schedule 2, sets out the circumstances when the court may not make an order of its own initiative against the Crown)

Amendments—SI 2004/2072; SI 2005/2292.

****

3.9 Relief from sanctions

(1) On an application for relief from any sanction imposed for a failure to comply with any rule, practice direction or court order the court will consider all the circumstances including –

    (a)   the interests of the administration of justice;

    (b)   whether the application for relief has been made promptly;

    (c)   whether the failure to comply was intentional;

    (d)   whether there is a good explanation for the failure;

    (e)   the extent to which the party in default has complied with other rules, practice directions, court orders and any relevant pre-action protocol$^{(GL)}$;

    (f)   whether the failure to comply was caused by the party or his legal representative;

    (g)   whether the trial date or the likely trial date can still be met if relief is granted;

    (h)   the effect which the failure to comply had on each party; and

    (i)   the effect which the granting of relief would have on each party.

(2) An application for relief must be supported by evidence.

"relief from any sanction imposed" (r 3.9(1))—In proceedings covered by CPR 1998 this rule provides an inclusive list of factors for the court to consider where failure by a party to comply with a rule, order or PD arises. In *Sayers v Clarke Walker (a firm): Practice Note* [2002] 1 WLR 3095, the Court of Appeal discouraged individual judge made check-lists where consideration of failure to comply with a rule came before the court. Rules are there to be obeyed, said Brooke LJ; but where a question arises as to whether relief should be given to a defaulting party the court should take into account "all the circumstances" of the case, and in particular the factors listed in r 3.9(1).

****

PART III

PART 7
HOW TO START PROCEEDINGS – THE CLAIM FORM

CONTENTS OF THIS PART

Application of this Part—The provisions of this Part are modified as regards particular kinds of proceedings and care needs to be paid to particular rules or practice directions:

Type of Claim	CPR Part/Practice Direction
Consumer Credit Act 1974	Rule 7.9/PD7B
Money Claims Online	PD7E
No substantial dispute of fact	Part 8
Parties and group litigation	Part 19/PD19B
Children or patients	Part 21
Pre-action disclosure of documents	Rule 31.16
Costs-only proceedings	Rule 44.12A
Injunctions and other interim remedies	Part 25
Applications under the Companies Acts 1985–89, the Insurance Companies Act 1982 and Part VII of the Financial Services and Markets Act 2000	PD49B
Appeals	Part 52
Defamation claims	Part 53
Judicial review	Part 54
Claim for possession of land	Part 55
Applications relating to business tenancies	Part 56
Probate claims	Part 57

Type of Claim	CPR Part/Practice Direction
Claims under the Inheritance (Provision for Family and Dependants) Act 1975	Part 57, Section IV
Commercial Court claims	Part 58
Mercantile court claims	Part 59
Technology and Construction Court claims	Part 60
Admiralty Court claims	Part 61
Claims or applications under the Arbitration Act 1996	Part 62
Patent claims	Part 63
Claims relating to estates, trusts and charities	Part 64
Proceedings relating to anti-social behaviour and harassment	Part 65
Proceedings relating to solicitors	Part 67
Applications for Writ of Habeas Corpus	Sch 1, RSC Ord 54

7.1 Where to start proceedings

Restrictions on where proceedings may be started are set out in the relevant practice directions supplementing this Part.

Amendments—SI 2009/3390.

7.2 How to start proceedings

(1) Proceedings are started when the court issues a claim form at the request of the claimant.

(2) A claim form is issued on the date entered on the form by the court.

> (A person who seeks a remedy from the court before proceedings are started or in relation to proceedings which are taking place, or will take place, in another jurisdiction must make an application under Part 23)

> (Part 16 sets out what the claim form must include)

> (The Costs Practice Direction sets out the information about a funding arrangement to be provided with the claim form where the claimant intends to seek to recover an additional liability)

> ("Funding arrangement" and "additional liability" are defined in rule 43.2)

Amendments—SI 2000/1317; SI 2008/2178; SI 2009/3390; SI 2011/88.

Type of Claim	Claim Form
Money (which includes a claim for damages)	N1
Consumer Credit Act or similar return of goods claim under r 7.9	N1 (FD)
Claim Production Centre claim form	N1 CPC
Probate claim	N2

Type of Claim	Claim Form
Claim for possession by landlord or mortgagor	N5 and N119/N120
Claim for relief from forfeiture	N5A
Applications for accelerated possession of assured tenancies	N5B
Claim for demotion of tenancy	N6
Injunction under Housing Act 1996, s 152	N16A
Claim for possession against trespasser	N5 and N121
Application for possession including application for interim possession order	N5 and N130
Claim where there is no substantial dispute of fact or PD8 has applied the Pt 8 procedure	N208
An additional claim	N211
Time order under Consumer Credit Act 1974	N440
Claims for judicial review	N461

7.2A Practice Direction 7A makes provision for procedures to be followed when claims are brought by or against a partnership within the jurisdiction.

Amendments—Inserted by SI 2006/1689; amended by SI 2009/3390.

7.3 Right to use one claim form to start two or more claims

A claimant may use a single claim form to start all claims which can be conveniently disposed of in the same proceedings.

7.4 Particulars of claim

(1) Particulars of claim must –

   (a)   be contained in or served with the claim form; or
   (b)   subject to paragraph (2) be served on the defendant by the claimant within 14 days after service of the claim form.

(2) Particulars of claim must be served on the defendant no later than the latest time for serving a claim form.

   (Rule 7.5 sets out the latest time for serving a claim form)

(3) Where the claimant serves particulars of claim separately from the claim form in accordance with paragraph (1)(b), the claimant must, within 7 days of service on the defendant, file a copy of the particulars except where –

   (a)   paragraph 5.2(4) of Practice Direction 7C applies; or
   (b)   paragraph 6.4 of Practice Direction 7E applies.

   (Part 16 sets out what the particulars of claim must include)

   (Part 22 requires particulars of claim to be verified by a statement of truth)

Amendments—SI 2008/2178; SI 2008/3327; SI 2009/3390.

7.5 Service of a claim form

(1) Where the claim form is served within the jurisdiction, the claimant must complete the step required by the following table in relation to the particular method of service chosen, before 12.00 midnight on the calendar day four months after the date of issue of the claim form.

Method of service	Step required
First class post, document exchange or other service which provides for delivery on the next business day	Posting, leaving with, delivering to or collection by the relevant service provider
Delivery of the document to or leaving it at the relevant place	Delivery of the document to or leaving it at the relevant place
Personal service under rule 6.5	Completing the relevant step required by rule 6.5(3)
Fax	Completing the transmission of the fax
Other electronic method	Sending the e-mail or other electronic transmission

(2) Where the claim form is to be served out of the jurisdiction, the claim form must be served in accordance with Section IV of Part 6 within 6 months of the date of issue.

Amendments—Substituted by SI 2008/2178.

7.6 Extension of time for serving a claim form

(1) The claimant may apply for an order extending the period for compliance with rule 7.5.

(2) The general rule is that an application to extend the time for compliance with rule 7.5 must be made –

  (a) within the period specified by rule 7.5; or
  (b) where an order has been made under this rule, within the period for service specified by that order.

(3) If the claimant applies for an order to extend the time for compliance after the end of the period specified by rule 7.5 or by an order made under this rule, the court may make such an order only if –

  (a) the court has failed to serve the claim form; or
  (b) the claimant has taken all reasonable steps to comply with rule 7.5 but has been unable to do so; and
  (c) in either case, the claimant has acted promptly in making the application.

(4) An application for an order extending the time for compliance with rule 7.5 –

  (a) must be supported by evidence; and
  (b) may be made without notice.

Amendments—Substituted by SI 2008/2178.

7.7 Application by defendant for service of claim form

(1) Where a claim form has been issued against a defendant, but has not yet been served on him, the defendant may serve a notice on the claimant requiring him to serve the claim form or discontinue the claim within a period specified in the notice.

PART III

(2) The period specified in a notice served under paragraph (1) must be at least 14 days after service of the notice.

(3) If the claimant fails to comply with the notice, the court may, on the application of the defendant –

    (a)   dismiss the claim; or

    (b)   make any other order it thinks just.

7.8 Form for defence etc must be served with particulars of claim

(1) When particulars of claim are served on a defendant, whether they are contained in the claim form, served with it or served subsequently, they must be accompanied by –

    (a)   a form for defending the claim;

    (b)   a form for admitting the claim; and

    (c)   a form for acknowledging service.

(2) Where the claimant is using the procedure set out in Part 8 (alternative procedure for claims) –

    (a)   paragraph (1) does not apply; and

    (b)   a form for acknowledging service must accompany the claim form.

7.9 Fixed date and other claims

A practice direction –

    (a)   may set out the circumstances in which the court may give a fixed date for a hearing when it issues a claim;

    (b)   may list claims in respect of which there is a specific claim form for use and set out the claim form in question; and

    (c)   may disapply or modify these Rules as appropriate in relation to the claims referred to in paragraphs (a) and (b).

7.10 Production Centre for claims

(1) There shall be a Production Centre for the issue of claim forms and other related matters.

(2) Practice Direction 7C makes provision for –

    (a)   which claimants may use the Production Centre;

    (b)   the type of claims which the Production Centre may issue;

    (c)   the functions which are to be discharged by the Production Centre;

    (d)   the place where the Production Centre is to be located; and

    (e)   other related matters.

(3) Practice Direction 7C may disapply or modify these Rules as appropriate in relation to claims issued by the Production Centre.

Amendments—SI 2009/3390.

7.11 Human Rights

(1) A claim under section 7(1)(a) of the Human Rights Act 1998 in respect of a judicial act may be brought only in the High Court.

(2) Any other claim under section 7(1)(a) of that Act may be brought in any court.

Amendments—Inserted by SI 2000/2092.

7.12 Electronic issue of claims

(1) A practice direction may make provision for a claimant to start a claim by requesting the issue of a claim form electronically.

(2) The practice direction may, in particular –

    (a)   specify –
        (i)   the types of claim which may be issued electronically; and
        (ii) the conditions which a claim must meet before it may be issued electronically;

    (b)   specify –
        (i)   the court where the claim will be issued; and
        (ii) the circumstances in which the claim will be transferred to another court;

    (c)   provide for the filing of other documents electronically where a claim has been started electronically;

    (d)   specify the requirements that must be fulfilled for any document filed electronically; and

    (e)   provide how a fee payable on the filing of any document is to be paid where that document is filed electronically.

(3) The practice direction may disapply or modify these Rules as appropriate in relation to claims started electronically.

> (Practice Direction 5C deals with electronic issue of claims started or continued under the Electronic Working scheme.)

Amendments—Inserted by SI 2003/3361; amended by SI 2009/3390.

Practice Direction 7A –
How to Start Proceedings

This Practice Direction supplements CPR Part 7

General

1 Subject to the following provisions of this practice direction, proceedings which both the High Court and the county courts have jurisdiction to deal with may be started in the High Court or in a county court.

Where to start proceedings

2.1 Proceedings (whether for damages or for a specified sum) may not be started in the High Court unless the value of the claim is more than £25,000.

2.2 Proceedings which include a claim for damages in respect of personal injuries must not be started in the High Court unless the value of the claim is £50,000 or more (paragraph 9 of the High Court and County Courts Jurisdiction Order 1991 (SI 1991/724 as amended) describes how the value of a claim is to be determined).

2.3 A claim must be issued in the High Court or a county court if an enactment so requires.

2.4 Subject to paragraphs 2.1 and 2.2 above, a claim should be started in the High Court if by reason of:

    (1)   the financial value of the claim and the amount in dispute, and/or

(2)   the complexity of the facts, legal issues, remedies or procedures involved, and/or

(3)   the importance of the outcome of the claim to the public in general,

the claimant believes that the claim ought to be dealt with by a High Court judge.

> (CPR Part 30 and Practice Direction 30 contain provisions relating to the transfer to the county court of proceedings started in the High Court and vice-versa.)

2.5 A claim relating to Chancery business (which includes any of the matters specified in paragraph 1 of Schedule 1 to the Senior Courts Act 1981) may, subject to any enactment, rule or practice direction, be dealt with in the High Court or in a county court. The claim form should, if issued in the High Court, be marked in the top right hand corner 'Chancery Division' and, if issued in the county court, be marked 'Chancery Business'.

> (For the equity jurisdiction of county courts, see section 23 of the County Courts Act 1984.)

2.6 A claim relating to any of the matters specified in sub-paragraphs (a) and (b) of paragraph 2 of Schedule 1 to the Senior Courts Act 1981 must be dealt with in the High Court and will be assigned to the Queen's Bench Division.

2.7 Practice directions applying to particular types of proceedings, or to proceedings in particular courts, will contain provisions relating to the commencement and conduct of those proceedings.

2.8 A claim in the High Court for which a jury trial is directed will, if not already being dealt with in the Queen's Bench Division, be transferred to that Division.

2.9 The following proceedings may not be started in ...a county court unless the parties have agreed otherwise in writing:

(1)   a claim for damages or other remedy for libel or slander, and

(2)   a claim in which the title to any toll, fair, market or franchise is in question.

2.10

(1)   The normal rules apply in deciding in which court and specialist list a claim that includes issues under the Human Rights Act 1998 should be started. They also apply in deciding which procedure to use to start the claim; this Part or CPR Part 8 or CPR Part 54 (judicial review).

(2)   The exception is a claim for damages in respect of a judicial act, which should be commenced in the High Court. If the claim is made in a notice of appeal then it will be dealt with according to the normal rules governing where the appeal is heard.

> (A county court cannot make a declaration of incompatibility in accordance with section 4 of the Human Rights Act 1998. Legislation may direct that such a claim is to be brought before a specified tribunal.)

The claim form

3.1 A claimant must use practice form N1 or practice form N208 (the Part 8 claim form) to start a claim (but see paragraphs 3.2 and 3.4 below).

3.2 Rule 7.9 deals with fixed date claims and rule 7.10 deals with the Production Centre for the issue of claims; there are separate practice directions supplementing rules 7.9 and 7.10.

3.3 If a claimant wishes the claim to proceed under Part 8, or if the claim is required to proceed under Part 8, the claim form should so state. Otherwise the claim will proceed under Part 7. But note that in respect of claims in specialist proceedings (listed in CPR Part 49) and claims brought under the RSC or CCR set out in the Schedule to the

CPR (see CPR Part 50) the CPR will apply only to the extent that they are not inconsistent with the rules and practice directions that expressly apply to those claims.

3.4 Other practice directions may require special practice forms to be used to commence particular types of proceedings, or proceedings in particular courts.

3.5 Where a claim form to be served out of the jurisdiction is one which the court has power to deal with –

(a) under the Civil Jurisdiction and Judgments Act 1982; and

(b) the Judgments Regulation (which has the same meaning as in rule 6.31(d)),

the claim form must, pursuant to rule 6.34, be filed and served with the notice referred to in that rule and paragraph 2.1 of Practice Direction 6B.

3.6 If a claim for damages or for an unspecified sum is started in the High Court, the claim form must:

(1) state that the claimant expects to recover more than £25,000 (or £50,000 or more if the claim is for personal injuries), or

(2) state that some enactment provides that the claim may only be commenced in the High Court and specify that enactment, or

(3) state that the claim is to be in one of the specialist High Court lists (see CPR Parts 49 and 58–62) and specify that list.

3.7 If the contents of a claim form commencing specialist proceedings comply with the requirements of the specialist list in question the claim form will also satisfy paragraph 3.6 above.

3.8 If a claim for damages for personal injuries is started in the county court, the claim form must state whether or not the claimant expects to recover more than £1000 in respect of pain, suffering and loss of amenity.

3.9 If a claim for housing disrepair which includes a claim for an order requiring repairs or other work to be carried out by the landlord is started in the county court, the claim form must state:

(1) whether or not the cost of the repairs or other work is estimated to be more than £1000, and

(2) whether or not the claimant expects to recover more than £1000 in respect of any claim for damages[1].

If either of the amounts mentioned in (1) and (2) is more than £1000, the small claims track will not be the normal track for that claim.

> (Section 19 of the Costs Practice Direction supplementing Parts 43 to 48 contains details of the information required to be filed with a claim form to comply with rule 44.15 (providing information about funding arrangements).)

1 See rules 16.3(4) and 26.6.

Title of proceedings

4.1 The claim form and every other statement of case, must be headed with the title of the proceedings. The title should state:

(1) the number of proceedings,

(2) the court or Division in which they are proceeding,

(3) the full name of each party,

(4) each party's status in the proceedings (i e claimant/defendant).

> (Paragraph 2.6 of Practice Direction 16 sets out what is meant by a full name in respect of each type of claimant.)

PART III

4.2 Where there is more than one claimant and/or more than one defendant, the parties should be described in the title as follows:

    (1)   AB
    (2)   CD
    (3)   EF   Claimants
         and
    (1)   GH
    (2)   IJ
    (3)   KL   Defendants

Starting a designated money claim

4A.1 In all designated money claims, practice form N1 must be sent to: County Court Money Claims Centre, PO Box 527. M5 0BY. The claims will then be issued in Northampton County Court.

4A.2 In proceedings referred to in paragraph 4A.1, the claimant must specify the preferred court on practice form N1.

Start of proceedings

5.1 Proceedings are started when the court issues a claim form at the request of the claimant (see rule 7.2) but where the claim form as issued was received in the court office on a date earlier than the date on which it was issued by the court, the claim is 'brought' for the purposes of the Limitation Act 1980 and any other relevant statute on that earlier date.

5.2 The date on which the claim form was received by the court will be recorded by a date stamp either on the claim form held on the court file or on the letter that accompanied the claim form when it was received by the court.

5.3 An enquiry as to the date on which the claim form was received by the court should be directed to a court officer.

5.4 Parties proposing to start a claim which is approaching the expiry of the limitation period should recognise the potential importance of establishing the date the claim form was received by the court and should themselves make arrangements to record the date.

5.5 Where it is sought to start proceedings against the estate of a deceased defendant where probate or letters of administration have not been granted, the claimant should issue the claim against 'the personal representatives of A.B. deceased'. The claimant should then, before the expiry of the period for service of the claim form, apply to the court for the appointment of a person to represent the estate of the deceased.

Claims by and against partnerships within the jurisdiction

5A.1 Paragraphs 5A and 5B apply to claims that are brought by or against two or more persons who –

    (1)   were partners; and
    (2)   carried on that partnership business within the jurisdiction,

at the time when the cause of action accrued.

5A.2 For the purposes of this paragraph, 'partners' includes persons claiming to be entitled as partners and persons alleged to be partners.

5A.3 Where that partnership has a name, unless it is inappropriate to do so, claims must be brought in or against the name under which that partnership carried on business at the time the cause of action accrued.

Partnership membership statements

5B.1 In this paragraph a 'partnership membership statement' is a written statement of the names and last known places of residence of all the persons who were partners in the partnership at the time when the cause of action accrued, being the date specified for this purpose in accordance with paragraph 5B.3.

5B.2 If the partners are requested to provide a copy of a partnership membership statement by any party to a claim, the partners must do so within 14 days of receipt of the request.

5B.3 In that request the party seeking a copy of a partnership membership statement must specify the date when the relevant cause of action accrued.

> (Signing of the acknowledgment of service in the case of a partnership is dealt with in paragraph 4.4 of Practice Direction 10.)

Persons carrying on business in another name

5C.1 This paragraph applies where –

(1) a claim is brought against an individual;
(2) that individual carries on a business within the jurisdiction (even if not personally within the jurisdiction); and
(3) that business is carried on in a name other than that individual's own name ('the business name').

5C.2 The claim may be brought against the business name as if it were the name of a partnership.

Particulars of claim

6.1 Where the claimant does not include the particulars of claim in the claim form, they may be served separately:

(1) either at the same time as the claim form, or
(2) within 14 days after service of the claim form provided that the service of the particulars of claim is within 4 months after the date of issue of the claim form[1] (or 6 months where the claim form is to be served out of the jurisdiction[2]).

1 See rules 7.4(2) and 7.5(1).
2 See rule 7.5(2).

6.2 If the particulars of claim are not included in or have not been served with the claim form, the claim form must contain a statement that particulars of claim will follow[1].

> (These paragraphs do not apply where the Part 8 procedure is being used. For information on matters to be included in the claim form or the particulars of claim, see Part 16 (statements of case) and Practice Direction 16.)

1 See rule 16.2(2).

Statement of truth

7.1 Part 22 requires the claim form and, where they are not included in the claim form, the particulars of claim, to be verified by a statement of truth.

7.2 The form of the statement of truth is as follows:

PART III

'[I believe][the claimant believes] that the facts stated in [this claim form] [these particulars of claim] are true.'

7.3 Attention is drawn to rule 32.14 which sets out the consequences of verifying a statement of case containing a false statement without an honest belief in its truth.

Extension of time

8.1 An application under rule 7.6 (for an extension of time for serving a claim form under rule 7.6(1)) must be made in accordance with Part 23 and supported by evidence.

8.2 The evidence should state:

    (1)   all the circumstances relied on,

    (2)   the date of issue of the claim,

    (3)   the expiry date of any rule 7.6 extension, and

    (4)   a full explanation as to why the claim has not been served.

        (For information regarding (1) written evidence see Part 32 and Practice Direction 32 and (2) service of the claim form see Part 6 and Practice Directions 6A and 6B.)

****

PART 8
ALTERNATIVE PROCEDURE FOR CLAIMS

CONTENTS OF THIS PART

8.1 Types of claim in which Part 8 procedure may be followed

(1) The Part 8 procedure is the procedure set out in this Part.

(2) A claimant may use the Part 8 procedure where –

    (a) he seeks the court's decision on a question which is unlikely to involve a substantial dispute of fact; or

    (b) paragraph (6) applies.

(3) The court may at any stage order the claim to continue as if the claimant had not used the Part 8 procedure and, if it does so, the court may give any directions it considers appropriate.

(4) Paragraph (2) does not apply if a practice direction provides that the Part 8 procedure may not be used in relation to the type of claim in question.

(5) Where the claimant uses the Part 8 procedure he may not obtain default judgment under Part 12.

(6) A rule or practice direction may, in relation to a specified type of proceedings –

    (a) require or permit the use of the Part 8 procedure; and

    (b) disapply or modify any of the rules set out in this Part as they apply to those proceedings.

> (Rule 8.9 provides for other modifications to the general rules where the Part 8 procedure is being used)

> (Part 78 provides procedures for European orders for payment and for the European small claims procedure. It also provides procedures for applications for mediation settlement enforcement orders in relation to certain cross-border disputes.)

Amendments—SI 2000/1317; SI 2008/2178; SI 2011/88.

"unlikely to involve a substantial dispute of fact" (r 8.1(2)(a))—This provision encapsulates whether a claim proceeds under Pt 8, or under the more generally used Pt 7. PD to Pt 8, para 3 sets out those claims which may proceed under Pt 8, such as approval of infant settlements (PD8, para 3.1(1)) and (2)); those which must use the Pt 8 procedure: namely a recondite list of forms of proceeding, none of them family proceedings (PD8, para 3.2); and proceedings where the originating summons procedure is prescribed by statute, rule or PD (PD8, para 3.3, e g I(PFD)A 1975, see below). Traditionally, land claims e g under TLATA 1996 and its predecessor, proceeded under Pt 8 because they were issued under the old originating summons procedure. In practice it is likely to be rare that a claim under, e g TLATA 1996, s 14, does not involve a "substantial dispute of fact", so almost invariably such claims are likely to be issued under Pt 7.

Particular uses of the Pt 8 procedure

(a) *The "judicial review procedure"* (CPR 1998, r 54.1(2)(e)) prescribes that the procedure for judicial review is the Pt 8 procedure "as modified" by the detailed provisions of Pt 54 – not always an easy fit, in practice.

(b) *Claims under I(PFD)A 1975, s 1* must be made in accordance with Pt 8.

(c) *Application for a declaration* should in the first instance be issued under Pt 8 (save where other provision is made under statute or rules.

"the claim to continue as if the claimant had not used the Part 8 procedure" (r 8.1(3))—Failure to use the procedure correctly, or where it becomes obvious, for example, that disputed issues of fact will arise, enables the court to switch the claim to the appropriate procedure and give directions accordingly.

Objection to Pt 8 procedure—A defendant who objects to the Pt 8 procedure must so state in his/her acknowledgement of service (rr 8.3 and 8.8(1)).

8.2 Contents of the claim form

Where the claimant uses the Part 8 procedure the claim form must state –

    (a) that this Part applies;

    (b) (i) the question which the claimant wants the court to decide; or

        (ii) the remedy which the claimant is seeking and the legal basis for the claim to that remedy;

    (c) if the claim is being made under an enactment, what that enactment is;

    (d) if the claimant is claiming in a representative capacity, what that capacity is; and

    (e) if the defendant is sued in a representative capacity, what that capacity is.

> (Part 22 provides for the claim form to be verified by a statement of truth)

> (Rule 7.5 provides for service of the claim form)

> (The Costs Practice Direction sets out the information about a funding arrangement to be provided with the claim form where the claimant intends to seek to recover an additional liability)

> ('Funding arrangement' and 'additional liability' are defined in rule 43.2)

Amendments—SI 2000/1317; SI 2009/3390.

Pleading the claim—The claim is in Form N208 (PD8, para 4.2). The essence of Pt 8 is simplicity and r 8.2 sets out what a Pt 8 claim must include.

Written evidence—Evidence on which the claimant intends to rely must be contained in his/her claim form or served with it (r 8.5(1)). The defendant must file his/her written evidence with his acknowledgement of service (rr 8.3 and 8.5(3)). No evidence can be relied upon unless filed in accordance with r 8.5 (r 8.6), save with permission of the court. A party may apply for time to be extended to file and serve evidence (PD8, para 7.4).

Form of evidence—Evidence will be by affidavit or statement; if a claimant relies on his/her claim form it must be verified by a statement of truth (PD8, para 7.2).

Disposal of the claim—The intention of the Pt 8 procedure is that, where possible, claims should be capable of being disposed of on the documents or with the hearing of only minimal oral evidence.

8.2A Issue of claim form without naming defendants

(1) A practice direction may set out the circumstances in which a claim form may be issued under this Part without naming a defendant.

(2) The practice direction may set out those cases in which an application for permission must be made by application notice before the claim form is issued.

(3) The application notice for permission –

    (a)   need not be served on any other person; and

    (b)   must be accompanied by a copy of the claim form that the applicant proposes to issue.

(4) Where the court gives permission it will give directions about the future management of the claim.

Amendments—Inserted by SI 2000/221; amended by SI 2001/256.

8.3 Acknowledgment of service

(1) The defendant must –

    (a)   file an acknowledgment of service in the relevant practice form not more than 14 days after service of the claim form; and

    (b)   serve the acknowledgment of service on the claimant and any other party.

(2) The acknowledgment of service must state –

    (a)   whether the defendant contests the claim; and

    (b)   if the defendant seeks a different remedy from that set out in the claim form, what that remedy is.

(3) The following rules of Part 10 (acknowledgment of service) apply –

    (a)   rule 10.3(2) (exceptions to the period for filing an acknowledgment of service); and

    (b)   rule 10.5 (contents of acknowledgment of service).

(4) (*revoked*)

        (The Costs Practice Direction sets out the information about a funding arrangement to be provided with the acknowledgment of service where the defendant intends to seek to recover an additional liability)

        ('Funding arrangement' and 'additional liability' are defined in rule 43.2)

Amendments—SI 2000/1317; SI 2001/4015; SI 2009/3390.

8.4 Consequence of not filing an acknowledgment of service

(1) This rule applies where –

(a) the defendant has failed to file an acknowledgment of service; and

(b) the time period for doing so has expired.

(2) The defendant may attend the hearing of the claim but may not take part in the hearing unless the court gives permission.

8.5 Filing and serving written evidence

(1) The claimant must file any written evidence on which he intends to rely when he files his claim form.

(2) The claimant's evidence must be served on the defendant with the claim form.

(3) A defendant who wishes to rely on written evidence must file it when he files his acknowledgment of service.

(4) If he does so, he must also, at the same time, serve a copy of his evidence on the other parties.

(5) The claimant may, within 14 days of service of the defendant's evidence on him, file further written evidence in reply.

(6) If he does so, he must also, within the same time limit, serve a copy of his evidence on the other parties.

(7) The claimant may rely on the matters set out in his claim form as evidence under this rule if the claim form is verified by a statement of truth.

8.6 Evidence – general

(1) No written evidence may be relied on at the hearing of the claim unless –

(a) it has been served in accordance with rule 8.5; or

(b) the court gives permission.

(2) The court may require or permit a party to give oral evidence at the hearing.

(3) The court may give directions requiring the attendance for cross-examination(GL) of a witness who has given written evidence.

(Rule 32.1 contains a general power for the court to control evidence)

8.7 Part 20 claims

Where the Part 8 procedure is used, Part 20 (counterclaims and other additional claims) applies except that a party may not make a Part 20 claim (as defined by rule 20.2) without the court's permission.

8.8 Procedure where defendant objects to use of the Part 8 procedure

(1) Where the defendant contends that the Part 8 procedure should not be used because –

(a) there is a substantial dispute of fact; and

(b) the use of the Part 8 procedure is not required or permitted by a rule or practice direction,

he must state his reasons when he files his acknowledgment of service.

(Rule 8.5 requires a defendant who wishes to rely on written evidence to file it when he files his acknowledgment of service)

(2) When the court receives the acknowledgment of service and any written evidence it will give directions as to the future management of the case.

> (Rule 8.1(3) allows the court to make an order that the claim continue as if the claimant had not used the Part 8 procedure)

8.9 Modifications to the general rules

Where the Part 8 procedure is followed –

    (a) provision is made in this Part for the matters which must be stated in the claim form and the defendant is not required to file a defence and therefore –
- (i) Part 16 (statements of case) does not apply;
- (ii) Part 15 (defence and reply) does not apply;
- (iii) any time limit in these Rules which prevents the parties from taking a step before a defence is filed does not apply;
- (iv) the requirement under rule 7.8 to serve on the defendant a form for defending the claim does not apply;

    (b) the claimant may not obtain judgment by request on an admission and therefore –
- (i) rules 14.4 to 14.7 do not apply; and
- (ii) the requirement under rule 7.8 to serve on the defendant a form for admitting the claim does not apply; and

    (c) the claim shall be treated as allocated to the multi-track and therefore Part 26 does not apply.

Practice Direction 8A –
Alternative Procedure for Claims

This Practice Direction supplements CPR Part 8 and Schedule 1 & Schedule 2 to the CPR

Terminology

1.1 In this Practice Direction, 'Schedule rules' means provisions contained in the Schedules to the CPR, which were previously contained in the Rules of the Supreme Court (1965) or the County Court Rules (1981).

Application of this Practice Direction

2.1 Section A contains general provisions about claims and applications to which Part 8 applies. Section B comprises a table listing claims, petitions and applications under various enactments which must be made under Part 8. Section C contains certain additions and modifications to the Part 8 procedure that apply to the particular claims and applications identified.

2.2 Some of the claims and applications listed in the table in Section B are dealt with in the Schedule Rules in the CPR. The table in Section B contains cross-reference to the relevant Schedule Rules.

SECTION A: GENERAL PROVISIONS APPLICABLE TO PART 8 CLAIMS

Types of claim in which the Part 8 procedure may be used

3.1 The types of claim for which the Part 8 procedure may be used include –

   (1)   a claim by or against a child or protected party, as defined in rule 21.1(2), which has been settled before the commencement of proceedings and the sole purpose of the claim is to obtain the approval of the court to the settlement; or

   (2)   a claim for provisional damages which has been settled before the commencement of proceedings and the sole purpose of the claim is to obtain a consent judgment.

3.2

   (1)   The Part 8 procedure must be used for those claims, petitions and applications listed in the table in Section B.

   (2)   Where a claim is listed in the table in Section B and is identified as a claim to which particular provisions of Section C apply, the Part 8 procedure shall apply subject to the additions and modifications set out in the relevant paragraphs in Section C.

3.3 The Part 8 procedure must also be used for any claim or application in relation to which an Act, rule or practice direction provides that the claim or application is brought by originating summons, originating motion or originating application.

3.4 Where it appears to a court officer that a claimant is using the Part 8 procedure inappropriately, he may refer the claim to a judge for the judge to consider the point.

3.5 The court may at any stage order the claim to continue as if the claimant had not used the Part 8 procedure and, if it does so, the court will allocate the claim to a track and give such directions as it considers appropriate.

Issuing the claim

4.1 Part 7 and Practice Direction 7A contain a number of rules and directions applicable to all claims, including those to which Part 8 applies. Those rules and directions should be applied where appropriate.

4.2 Where a claimant uses the Part 8 procedure, the claim form (practice form N208) should be used and must state the matters set out in rule 8.2 and, if rule 8.1(6) applies, must comply with the requirements of the rule or practice direction in question. In particular, the claim form must state that Part 8 applies; a Part 8 claim form means a claim form which so states.

     (The Costs Practice Direction supplementing Parts 43 to 48 contains details of the information required to be filed with a claim form to comply with rule 44.15 (providing information about funding arrangements).)

Responding to the claim

5.1 The provisions of Part 15 (defence and reply) do not apply where the claim form is a Part 8 claim form.

5.2 Where a defendant who wishes to respond to a Part 8 claim form is required to file an acknowledgment of service, that acknowledgment of service should be in practice form N210.

5.3 Where a defendant objects to the use of the Part 8 procedure, and his statement of reasons includes matters of evidence, the acknowledgment of service must be verified by a statement of truth.

PART III

Managing the claim

6.1 The court may give directions immediately a Part 8 claim form is issued either on the application of a party or on its own initiative. The directions may include fixing a hearing date where –

(1) there is no dispute, such as in child and protected party settlements; or
(2) where there may be a dispute, but a hearing date could conveniently be given.

6.2 Where the court does not fix a hearing date when the claim form is issued, it will give directions for the disposal of the claim as soon as practicable after the defendant has acknowledged service of the claim form or, as the case may be, after the period for acknowledging service has expired.

6.3 Certain applications may not require a hearing.

6.4 The court may convene a directions hearing before giving directions.

Evidence

7.1 A claimant must file the written evidence on which he relies when his Part 8 claim form is issued (unless the evidence is contained in the claim form itself).

7.2 Evidence will normally be in the form of a witness statement or an affidavit but a claimant may rely on the matters set out in his claim form provided that it has been verified by a statement of truth.

> (For information about (1) statements of truth see Part 22 and Practice Direction 22, and (2) written evidence see Part 32 and Practice Direction 32.)

7.3 A defendant wishing to rely on written evidence, must file it with his acknowledgment of service.

7.4 A party may apply to the court for an extension of time to serve and file evidence under rule 8.5 or for permission to serve and file additional evidence under rule 8.6(1).

> (For information about applications see Part 23 and Practice Direction 23A.)

7.5

(1) The parties may, subject to the following provisions, agree in writing on an extension of time for serving and filing evidence under rule 8.5(3) or rule 8.5(5).
(2) An agreement extending time for a defendant to file evidence under rule 8.5(3) –
    (a) must be filed by the defendant at the same time as he files his acknowledgement of service; and
    (b) must not extend time by more than 14 days after the defendant files his acknowledgement of service.
(3) An agreement extending time for a claimant to file evidence in reply under rule 8.5(5) must not extend time to more than 28 days after service of the defendant's evidence on the claimant.

Hearing

8.1 The court may on the hearing date –

(1) proceed to hear the case and dispose of the claim;
(2) give case management directions.

8.2 Case management directions may include the specific allocation of a case to a track.

8.3 CPR rules 26.5(3) to (5) and rules 26.6 to 26.10 apply to the allocation of a claim under paragraph 8.2.

SECTION B: CLAIMS AND APPLICATIONS THAT MUST BE MADE UNDER PART 8

9.1 The claimant must use the Part 8 procedure if the claim is listed in the table below.

9.2 Section C of this Practice Direction contains special provisions modifying the Part 8 procedure, and where it does so, those provisions should be followed. The table below refers to the relevant paragraph of Section C where it applies.

9.3 Some of the claims and applications listed in the table below are dealt with in the Schedule Rules, and those rules modify the Part 8 procedure. A cross-reference to the relevant Schedule Rule is contained in the table below.

9.4 For applications that may or must be brought in the High Court, where no other rule or practice direction assigns the application to a Division of the court, the table specifies the Division to which the application is assigned.

Type of Claim or Application	Paragraph of Section C	Division	Schedule Rule
Application under section 14 of the Bills of Sale Act 1878 (Rectification of register)	Paragraph 10A	Queen's Bench Central Office	
Application under section 15 of the Bills of Sale Act 1878 (Entry of satisfaction)	Paragraph 11	Queen's Bench Central Office	
Application under section 16 of the Bills of Sale Act 1878 (Search of the bills of sale register)	Paragraph 11A	Queen's Bench Central Office	
Application under the proviso to section 7 of the Bills of Sale Act (1878) Amendment Act 1882 (Restraining removal or sale of goods seized)		Queen's Bench Central Office	
Application under the Public Trustee Act 1906 (free-standing proceedings)	Paragraph 12	Chancery	
Application under section 7 of the Deeds of Arrangement Act 1914 (Rectification of register)	Paragraph 12A	Queen's Bench Central Office	
Proceedings under the Trustee Act 1925		Chancery	
Applications under section 2(3) of the Public Order Act 1936	Paragraph 13	Chancery	
Proceedings under jurisdiction conferred by section 1 of the Railway and Canal Commission (Abolition) Act 1949	Paragraph 14	Chancery	

Type of Claim or Application	Paragraph of Section C	Division	Schedule Rule
Administration of Justice Act 1960 (Applications under the Act)		Divisional Court	RSC O.109, r.1(3)
Administration of Justice Act 1960 (Appeals under section 13 of the Act)		Divisional Court	RSC O.109, r.2(4)
Proceedings under section 14 of the Commons Registration Act 1965		Chancery	
Application under the Mines (Working Facilities and Support) Act 1966	Paragraph 15	Chancery	
Proceedings under section 21 or 25 of the Law of Property Act 1969		Chancery	
Local Government Act 1972 (claims under section 92 – proceedings for disqualification)		Queen's Bench Central Office	
Application under article 10 of the Mortgaging of Aircraft Order 1972 (Rectification of register)	Paragraph 15A	Chancery	
Application to register an assignment of book debts (section 344 of the Insolvency Act 1986)	Paragraph 15B	Queen's Bench Central Office	
Proceedings under the Control of Misleading Advertisements Regulations 1988		Chancery	
Application under section 42 of the Senior Courts Act 1981	Paragraph 16	Administrative Court	
Proceedings in the High Court under the Representation of the People Acts	Paragraph 17A	Queen's Bench Central Office	
Applications under Part II of the Mental Health Act 1983	Paragraph 18	Administrative Court	
Applications under section 13 of the Coroners Act 1988	Paragraph 19	Administrative Court	

Type of Claim or Application	Paragraph of Section C	Division	Schedule Rule
Application for an injunction to prevent environmental harm under section 187B or 214A of the Town and Country Planning Act 1990; section 44A of the Planning (Listed Buildings and Conservation Areas) Act 1990; or section 26AA of the Planning (Hazardous Substances) Act 1990	Paragraph 20	Queen's Bench	
Confiscation and forfeiture in connection with criminal proceedings (I. Drug Trafficking Act 1994 and Criminal Justice (International Co-operation) Act 1990 – Application for a confiscation order)		Queen's Bench	RSC O.115, r.2B(1)
Confiscation and forfeiture in connection with criminal proceedings (I. Drug Trafficking Act 1994 and Criminal Justice (International Co-operation) Act 1990 – Application for a restraint order or charging order)		Queen's Bench	RSC O.115, r.3(1)
Confiscation and forfeiture in connection with criminal proceedings (I. Drug Trafficking Act 1994 and Criminal Justice (International Co-operation) Act 1990 – Realisation of property)		Queen's Bench	RSC O.115, r.7(1)
Criminal Procedure and Investigations Act 1996 (Application under section 54(3))		Administrative Court	
Confiscation and forfeiture in connection with criminal proceedings (III. Terrorism Act 2000 – Application for a restraint order)		Queen's Bench	RSC O.115, r.26(1)
Proceedings under the Financial Services and Markets Act 2000	Paragraph 21	Chancery	

PART III

Type of Claim or Application	Paragraph of Section C	Division	Schedule Rule
Application for an injunction under section 12 or 26 of the Energy Act 2008	Paragraph 20	Queen's Bench	
Interpleader (Mode of application)		Chancery or Queen's Bench	RSC O.17, r.3(1)
Criminal proceedings (estreat of recognizances)		Queen's Bench	RSC O.79, r.8(2)
Criminal proceedings (bail)		Queen's Bench	RSC O.79, r.9(2)
Application under an enactment giving the High Court jurisdiction to quash or prohibit any order, scheme, certificate or plan, any amendment or approval of a plan, any decision of a Minister or government department or any action on the part of a Minister or government department	Paragraph 22	Administrative Court	

****

PART 18
FURTHER INFORMATION

CONTENTS OF THIS PART

18.1 Obtaining further information

(1) The court may at any time order a party to –

    (a)   clarify any matter which is in dispute in the proceedings; or
    (b)   give additional information in relation to any such matter,

whether or not the matter is contained or referred to in a statement of case.

(2) Paragraph (1) is subject to any rule of law to the contrary.

(3) Where the court makes an order under paragraph (1), the party against whom it is made must –

    (a)   file his response; and
    (b)   serve it on the other parties,

within the time specified by the court.

(Part 22 requires a response to be verified by a statement of truth)

(Part 53 (defamation) restricts requirements for providing further information about sources of information in defamation claims)

Amendments—SI 2000/221.

18.2 Restriction on the use of further information

The court may direct that information provided by a party to another party (whether given voluntarily or following an order made under rule 18.1) must not be used for any purpose except for that of the proceedings in which it is given.

(RSC Order 82, in Schedule 1, provides for circumstances in which further information is not allowed in defamation claims)

Practice Direction 18 – Further Information

This Practice Direction supplements CPR Part 18

Attention is also drawn to Part 22 (Statements of Truth).

Preliminary request for further information or clarification

1.1 Before making an application to the court for an order under Part 18, the party seeking clarification or information (the first party) should first serve on the party from whom it is sought (the second party) a written request for that clarification or information (a Request) stating a date by which the response to the Request should be served. The date must allow the second party a reasonable time to respond.

1.2 A Request should be concise and strictly confined to matters which are reasonably necessary and proportionate to enable the first party to prepare his own case or to understand the case he has to meet.

1.3 Requests must be made as far as possible in a single comprehensive document and not piecemeal.

1.4 A Request may be made by letter if the text of the request is brief and the reply is likely to be brief; otherwise the Request should be made in a separate document.

1.5 If a Request is made in a letter, the letter should, in order to distinguish it from any other that might routinely be written in the course of a case,

(1) state that it contains a Request made under Part 18, and
(2) deal with no matters other than the Request.

1.6 (1) A Request (whether made by letter or in a separate document) must –

    (a) be headed with the name of the court and the title and number of the claim,

    (b) in its heading state that it is a Request made under Part 18, identify the first party and the second party and state the date on which it is made,

    (c) set out in a separate numbered paragraph each request for information or clarification,

    (d) where a Request relates to a document, identify that document and (if relevant) the paragraph or words to which it relates,

    (e) state the date by which the first party expects a response to the Request,

(2) (a) A Request which is not in the form of a letter may, if convenient, be prepared in such a way that the response may be given on the same document.

(b) To do this the numbered paragraphs of the Request should appear on the left hand half of each sheet so that the paragraphs of the response may then appear on the right.

(c) Where a Request is prepared in this form an extra copy should be served for the use of the second party.

1.7 Subject to the provisions of rule 6.23(5) and (6) and paragraphs 4.1 to 4.3 of Practice Direction 6A, a request should be served by email if reasonably practicable.

Responding to a request

2.1 A response to a Request must be in writing, dated and signed by the second party or his legal representative.

2.2

(1) Where the Request is made in a letter the second party may give his response in a letter or in a formal reply.

(2) Such a letter should identify itself as a response to the Request and deal with no other matters than the response.

2.3

(1) Unless the Request is in the format described in paragraph 1.6(2) and the second party uses the document supplied for the purpose, a response must:

(a) be headed with the name of the court and the title and number of the claim,

(b) in its heading identify itself as a response to that Request,

(c) repeat the text of each separate paragraph of the Request and set out under each paragraph the response to it,

(d) refer to and have attached to it a copy of any document not already in the possession of the first party which forms part of the response.

(2) A second or supplementary response to a Request must identify itself as such in its heading.

2.4 The second party must when he serves his response on the first party serve on every other party and file with the court a copy of the Request and of his response.

Statements of truth

3 Attention is drawn to Part 22 and to the definition of a statement of case in Part 2 of the rules; a response should be verified by a statement of truth.

General matters

4.1 (1) If the second party objects to complying with the Request or part of it or is unable to do so at all or within the time stated in the Request he must inform the first party promptly and in any event within that time.

(2) He may do so in a letter or in a separate document (a formal response), but in either case he must give reasons and, where relevant, give a date by which he expects to be able to comply.

4.2

(1) There is no need for a second party to apply to the court if he objects to a

Request or is unable to comply with it at all or within the stated time. He need only comply with paragraph 4.1(1) above.

(2) Where a second party considers that a Request can only be complied with at disproportionate expense and objects to comply for that reason he should say so in his reply and explain briefly why he has taken that view.

Applications for orders under Part 18

5.1 Attention is drawn to Part 23 (Applications) and to Practice Direction 23A.

5.2 An application notice for an order under Part 18 should set out or have attached to it the text of the order sought and in particular should specify the matter or matters in respect of which the clarification or information is sought.

5.3

(1) If a Request under paragraph 1 for the information or clarification has not been made, the application notice should, in addition, explain why not.

(2) If a Request for clarification or information has been made, the application notice or the evidence in support should describe the response, if any.

5.4 Both the first party and the second party should consider whether evidence in support of or in opposition to the application is required.

5.5

(1) Where the second party has made no response to a Request served on him, the first party need not serve the application notice on the second party, and the court may deal with the application without a hearing.

(2) Subparagraph (1) above only applies if at least 14 days have passed since the Request was served and the time stated in it for a response has expired.

5.6 Unless paragraph 5.5 applies the application notice must be served on the second party and on all other parties to the claim.

5.7 An order made under Part 18 must be served on all parties to the claim.

5.8 Costs:

(1) Attention is drawn to the Costs Practice Direction and in particular the court's power to make a summary assessment of costs.

(2) Attention is also drawn to rule 44.13(1) which provides that if an order does not mention costs no party is entitled to costs relating to that order.

PART 19
PARTIES AND GROUP LITIGATION

CONTENTS OF THIS PART

PD—See *PD (Addition and Substitution of Parties)* and *PD (Group Litigation)*, which supplement this Part generally; both are set out in Section 2 of the *Civil Court Service* (Jordan Publishing Ltd).

****

19.4A Human Rights

Section 4 of the Human Rights Act 1998

(1) The court may not make a declaration of incompatibility in accordance with section 4 of the Human Rights Act 1998 unless 21 days' notice, or such other period of notice as the court directs, has been given to the Crown.

(2) Where notice has been given to the Crown a Minister, or other person permitted by that Act, shall be joined as a party on giving notice to the court.

> (Only courts specified in section 4 of the Human Rights Act 1998 can make a declaration of incompatibility)

Section 9 of the Human Rights Act 1998

(3) Where a claim is made under that Act for damages in respect of a judicial act –

  (a) that claim must be set out in the statement of case or the appeal notice; and
  (b) notice must be given to the Crown.

(4) Where paragraph (3) applies and the appropriate person has not applied to be joined as a party within 21 days, or such other period as the court directs, after the notice is served, the court may join the appropriate person as a party.

> (Practice Direction 19A makes provision for these notices)

Amendments—Inserted by SI 2000/2092; SI 2009/3390.

Scope—In any proceedings where a human rights point is raised and there is either an issue as to whether a declaration of incompatibility of domestic legislation to ECHR 1950 should be made (as detailed in HRA 1998, s 1) or there has been a potential breach of a provision of ECHR 1950 by virtue of a judicial act, it is necessary to give notice to the Crown with a view to joinder (see also CPR 1998, r 7.11 and FPR 2010, rr 29.5(3)–(5)). The notice given under r 19.4A must be served on the person named in the list published under Crown Proceedings Act 1947, s 17. The list is annexed to CPR PD66 (see PD19, para 6.4(1)).

Declarations of incompatibility—The Home Secretary's scheme to control the right of any person subject to immigration control to marry in the UK was declared unlawful as being inconsistent with ECHR 1950, Art 12 (*R (Baiai) v Secretary of State for the Home Department* [2008] 2 FLR 1462, HL). However, a school's decision to refuse to permit a pupil to wear a "purity" ring as an expression of her Christian faith and as a sign of her belief of celibacy before marriage did not breach ECHR 1950, Art 9 (*R (Lydia Playfoot) v Millais School Governing Body* [2007] ELR 484). Further, although a school's decision to refuse to allow a pupil to wear a niqab veil at school engaged her ECHR 1950, Art 9 rights, it did not infringe that right and, even if it had, the decision was objectively justifiable under Art 9(2) (*R (X) v Governors of Y School* [2007] ELR 278).

Injunctions—The court has jurisdiction in appropriate cases to grant an injunction restraining a local authority from, for example, seeking to remove a child from a placement pending a full hearing by the court (*Coventry CC v O (Adoption)* [2011] 2 FLR 936) or to prevent the separation of a mother and child pending a full hearing (*Re H (Care Plan: Human Rights)* [2012] 1 FLR 191).

****

19.7 Representation of interested persons who cannot be ascertained etc

(1) This rule applies to claims about –

  (a) the estate of a deceased person;
  (b) property subject to a trust; or
  (c) the meaning of a document, including a statute.

(2) The court may make an order appointing a person to represent any other person or persons in the claim where the person or persons to be represented –

  (a) are unborn;
  (b) cannot be found;
  (c) cannot easily be ascertained; or

(d) are a class of persons who have the same interest in a claim and –
  (i) one or more members of that class are within sub-paragraphs (a), (b) or (c); or
  (ii) to appoint a representative would further the overriding objective.

(3) An application for an order under paragraph (2) –
  (a) may be made by –
    (i) any person who seeks to be appointed under the order; or
    (ii) any party to the claim; and
  (b) may be made at any time before or after the claim has started.

(4) An application notice for an order under paragraph (2) must be served on –
  (a) all parties to the claim, if the claim has started;
  (b) the person sought to be appointed, if that person is not the applicant or a party to the claim; and
  (c) any other person as directed by the court.

(5) The court's approval is required to settle a claim in which a party is acting as a representative under this rule.

(6) The court may approve a settlement where it is satisfied that the settlement is for the benefit of all the represented persons.

(7) Unless the court otherwise directs, any judgment or order given in a claim in which a party is acting as a representative under this rule –
  (a) is binding on all persons represented in the claim; but
  (b) may only be enforced by or against a person who is not a party to the claim with the permission of the court.

Amendments—Inserted by SI 2000/221.

Procedure for making an application—See CPR 1998, Pt 23. The application may be heard in chambers or in open court. The court may direct that it take place by telephone conference. In appropriate cases or where there is agreement the application may be handled without a hearing. The court may also use the hearing to case-manage the proceedings and give directions. A draft of the order sought should be provided to the court. The application notice and any order made must be served unless the court otherwise directs. If the application is made without notice the order should provide for the respondent to the application to apply to have the order set aside or varied within 7 days after the order is served. The court will generally serve such an application but it would be prudent to check with the court that it will effect service. When determining the application the court will have regard to the overriding objective.

19.7A Representation of beneficiaries by trustees etc

(1) A claim may be brought by or against trustees, executors or administrators in that capacity without adding as parties any persons who have a beneficial interest in the trust or estate ("the beneficiaries").

(2) Any judgment or order given or made in the claim is binding on the beneficiaries unless the court orders otherwise in the same or other proceedings.

Amendments—Inserted by SI 2002/2058.

19.7B Postal Services Act 2000

(1) An application under section 92 of the Postal Services Act 2000 for permission to bring proceedings in the name of the sender or addressee of a postal packet or his personal representative is made in accordance with Part 8.

PART III

(2) A copy of the application notice must be served on the universal service provider and on the person in whose name the applicant seeks to bring the proceedings.

Amendments—Inserted by SI 2005/2092.

****

PART 21
CHILDREN AND PROTECTED PARTIES

CONTENTS OF THIS PART

Amendments—Substituted by SI 2007/2204.

Procedural Guide—See Procedural Guide F1(2).

21.1 Scope of this Part

(1) This Part –

    (a)   contains special provisions which apply in proceedings involving children and protected parties; and

    (b)   sets out how a person becomes a litigation friend; and

    (c)   does not apply to proceedings under Part 75 where one of the parties to the proceedings is a child.

(2) In this Part –

    (a)   "the 2005 Act" means the Mental Capacity Act 2005;

    (b)   "child" means a person under 18;

    (c)   "lacks capacity" means lacks capacity within the meaning of the 2005 Act;

    (d)   "protected party" means a party, or an intended party, who lacks capacity to conduct the proceedings;

    (e)   "protected beneficiary" means a protected party who lacks capacity to manage and control any money recovered by him or on his behalf or for his benefit in the proceedings.

    (Rules 6.13 and 6.25 contain provisions about the service of documents on children and protected parties.)

(Rule 48.5 deals with costs where money is payable by or to a child or protected party.)

Amendments—SI 2003/3361; SI 2007/2204; SI 2008/2178.

Scope—This Part, which has no application to family proceedings, makes special provision in civil proceedings for those litigants who were previously described as being "persons under disability". There are two distinct categories: "child" and "protected party" (formerly "patient") as defined. FPR 2010 will apply instead to family proceedings but there are situations in the family context in which reliance may have to be placed on the CPR (e g an application under the PHA 1997). A representative known as a "litigation friend" must generally be appointed to conduct the proceedings in the name and on behalf of a child or protected party, and any settlement or compromise must be approved by the court.

"protected party" (r 21.1(2)(d))—Means "a party, or an intended party, who lacks capacity [within the meaning of MCA 2005] to conduct the proceedings". Lack of capacity is also defined (see below).

"protected beneficiary" (r 21.1(2)(e))—A separate definition is needed because a party may lack capacity to conduct the proceedings but nevertheless have the capacity to manage and control any money recovered by him or on his behalf or for his benefit in the proceedings. This definition is restricted to money recovered in the proceedings, but in practice all income and capital assets of the protected party will have to be taken into account because that is how the Court of Protection approaches its jurisdiction.

"child" or "protected party" (r 21.1(2))—It is possible for a child also to be a protected party and this may be relevant if that condition will continue to subsist on ceasing to be a child (e g in regard to the disposal of money awarded to the child). Thus a child who has severe learning disabilities will continue to be a protected party even after attaining the age of 18.

"litigation friend" (r 21.1(1)(b))—This expression replaces both next friend and guardian ad litem used in previous rules.

Mental Capacity Act 2005—This legislation established from 1 October 2007 a comprehensive new mental capacity jurisdiction. The general principles are to be found in MCA 2005, ss 1-4. They include a new test of "incapacity" and a "best interests" approach to any delegated decision-making according to a check list of factors, thus incorporated into CPR 1998, Pt 21. (For an overview of the Act see Part II).

"lacks capacity"—This term is expressly defined as being "within the meaning of MCA 2005" so as to incorporate the principles that apply within the new mental capacity jurisdiction. Nevertheless, many of the principles that have evolved under previous case-law are still relevant. MCA 2005, s 2(1) sets out the definition:

"a person lacks capacity in relation to a matter if at the material time he is unable to make a decision for himself in relation to the matter because of an impairment of, or a disturbance in the functioning of, the mind or brain."

A more comprehensive explanation is provided in the annotations to FPR 2010, Pt 15. For an early decision on the test of capacity under the new MCA 2005 jurisdiction in regard to a brain injured claimant, see *Saulle v Nouvet* [2007] EWHC 2902 (QB).

Default orders—Where there is doubt as to the capacity of a defendant it would not be appropriate for the court to make an order that unless the defendant submitted to an examination by a particular psychiatrist by a specified date he was to be debarred from defending the claim because such order may have been made against a protected party who needed a litigation friend (*Carmarthenshire County Council v Lewis* [2010] EWCA Civ 1567). Should such an order be appropriate in respect of a claimant, since the proceedings should not be allowed to continue without a litigation friend if capacity was lacking?

21.2 Requirement for litigation friend in proceedings by or against children and protected parties

(1) A protected party must have a litigation friend to conduct proceedings on his behalf.

(2) A child must have a litigation friend to conduct proceedings on his behalf unless the court makes an order under paragraph (3).

(3) The court may make an order permitting a child to conduct proceedings without a litigation friend.

(4) An application for an order under paragraph (3) –

    (a)   may be made by the child;

    (b)   if the child already has a litigation friend, must be made on notice to the litigation friend; and

    (c)   if the child has no litigation friend, may be made without notice.

(5) Where –

    (a)   the court has made an order under paragraph (3); and

    (b)   it subsequently appears to the court that it is desirable for a litigation friend to conduct the proceedings on behalf of the child,

the court may appoint a person to be the child's litigation friend.

Amendments—SI 2007/2204.

Scope—The general rule is that a child or protected party may only conduct proceedings, whether as claimant or defendant, by a litigation friend. The rule only refers to "a litigation friend" so this party may not have more than one in any particular proceedings. There is nothing to prevent that party having a different litigation friend in other proceedings of a different nature, except when a deputy (formerly a receiver) has been appointed in which event this person should generally be the only litigation friend for the protected party unless the Court of Protection otherwise orders.

Verification that a party is a child or protected party—Paragraph 2.3 of PD21 requires the litigation friend to state in the "certificate of suitability" that he consents to act and knows or believes the party to be a child or protected party. The grounds for this belief must be stated and if based upon medical opinion, this document must be attached. It is unlikely to be difficult to ascertain the age of a party, but there may be doubt as to whether a party is a protected party and in that event a preliminary issue as to capacity should be tried with notice being given to that party who may wish to make representations.

Even where the issue does not seem to be contentious, a district judge who is responsible for case management will generally require the assistance of a medical report before being able to be satisfied that incapacity exists. An admission by a person alleged to lack capacity will carry little weight. It may assist for the judge to see the person alleged to lack capacity (*Masterman-Lister v Brutton & Co and Jewell & Home Counties Dairies* [2003] 1 WLR 1511).

Notification to the child or protected party—Neither CPR 1998 nor PDs actually provide that a child or protected party must be given notice of the proceedings, unless (in the case of a protected party) the court is involved in the appointment of the litigation friend, so it is possible for proceedings in the name of a child or protected party to be commenced or defended without the personal knowledge of that party. Reliance is placed on the certificate of suitability (see above) and upon service on the parent or guardian of the child, or the person with whom the protected party resides or in whose care he is (see also PD21, para 2.4). It cannot be assumed that this person will inform the protected party in every situation where this would be prudent.

Child as a party (r 21.2(3))—An all or nothing approach to age is no longer adopted (*Gillick v West Norfolk & Wisbech Area Health Authority* [1986] 1 FLR 224, HL). The court may authorise a child to conduct proceedings, but will only do so when satisfied that the child has the required capacity (ie, is of sufficient maturity and understanding). It is both prudent and good practice for the litigation friend to consult the child once able to make a meaningful contribution and particularly as the child approaches 18, since on attaining that age the appointment of the litigation friend ceases and the child (now an adult) may take over conduct of the proceedings (r 21.9(1)).

Statement of truth—Pt 22 makes provision for certain documents to be verified by a "statement of truth". If a party is a child or a protected party it will be the litigation friend (or legal representative on his behalf) who makes and signs this statement (see r 22.1(5),(6)).

Need for a solicitor—There is no requirement in CPR 1998 for a solicitor to act on behalf of a child or protected party whose proceedings are being conducted by a litigation friend. Nevertheless, in a complex or high-value case the court may consider that the litigation friend who acts without a solicitor is not "suitable" within r 21.4(3) and appoint someone else under r 21.7(1)(c).

21.3 Stage of proceedings at which a litigation friend becomes necessary

(1) This rule does not apply where the court has made an order under rule 21.2(3).

(2) A person may not, without the permission of the court –

    (a)   make an application against a child or protected party before proceedings have started; or

    (b)   take any step in proceedings except –

        (i)   issuing and serving a claim form; or

        (ii)   applying for the appointment of a litigation friend under rule 21.6,

until the child or protected party has a litigation friend.

(3) If during proceedings a party lacks capacity to continue to conduct proceedings, no party may take any further step in the proceedings without the permission of the court until the protected party has a litigation friend.

(4) Any step taken before a child or protected party has a litigation friend, shall be of no effect unless the court orders otherwise.

Amendments—SI 2007/2204.

Scope—The general principle is that a litigation friend must be appointed before any step is taken in proceedings involving a child or protected party (unless the child has been permitted to conduct those proceedings under r 21.2(3)).

Exceptions—The court has a discretion to permit specified steps to be taken before a litigation friend is appointed ("without the permission of the court" r 21.3(2),(3)) or retrospectively to approve any steps that have been taken without such appointment ("unless the court otherwise orders" (r 21.3(4)). This alleviates the problem under former rules that, where the disability was not identified by the parties or their solicitors or arose during the proceedings without their knowledge, steps taken had no effect and liabilities could arise in respect of abortive costs.

Implications—It is possible to make urgent orders in proceedings involving a child or protected party before the appointment of a litigation friend, but the court should be made fully aware of all relevant circumstances. Where it is realised during the course of proceedings that a party is (and has been) a child or a protected party, then, provided everyone has acted in good faith and there has been no manifest disadvantage to the party subsequently found to have been a protected party, it is likely that the court will regularise the position retrospectively (*Masterman-Lister*, above). This might be the case where the proceedings have effectively been guided throughout by the person being appointed as litigation friend. Proceedings inappropriately conducted by the child or protected party or an unsuitable person on his behalf will be treated as being of no effect and further proceedings may then be commenced in proper form (the Limitation Acts are unlikely to apply).

21.4 Who may be a litigation friend without a court order

(1) This rule does not apply if the court has appointed a person to be a litigation friend.

(2) A deputy appointed by the Court of Protection under the 2005 Act with power to conduct proceedings on the protected party's behalf, is entitled to be the litigation friend of the protected party in any proceedings to which his power extends.

(3) If nobody has been appointed by the court or, in the case of a protected party, has been appointed as a deputy as set out in paragraph (2), a person may act as a litigation friend if he –

    (a)   can fairly and competently conduct proceedings on behalf of the child or protected party;

    (b)   has no interest adverse to that of the child or protected party; and

    (c)   where the child or protected party is a claimant, undertakes to pay any costs which the child or patient may be ordered to pay in relation to the proceedings, subject to any right he may have to be repaid from the assets of the child or protected party.

Amendments—SI 2007/2204.

Scope—This rule identifies who may act as a litigation friend without an order appointing him.

Authorised person—Any person authorised under MCA 2005 (ie, as a deputy appointed by the Court of Protection) to conduct legal proceedings in the name or on behalf of a protected party is entitled to become the litigation friend in accordance with such authority. An office copy of the order or other authorisation sealed with the official seal of the Court of Protection should be filed. Care should be taken to examine this document because simply being appointed a deputy does not by itself give authority to conduct proceedings. It is not clear if the court has power to appoint someone else (as under the former rules), but this situation is unlikely to arise and conflict between the court dealing with the litigation and the Court of Protection should be avoided.

Attorneys—An attorney under a registered enduring power of attorney (EPA), or donee under a lasting power of attorney for financial affairs (LPA), is not specifically mentioned but would be an obvious person to act as litigation friend because he will control the financial affairs of the protected party (see MCA 2005) and there will, in consequence, be no need for a deputy. An ordinary power of attorney is of no significance because it ceases to have effect upon the incapacity of the donor, but of course the person acting may otherwise be suitable as litigation friend. If an EPA is registered this would normally indicate that the donor is a protected party, but that is not the case for an LPA because registration may take place at an earlier stage.

The court controls its own procedures and principles of agency do not apply. So a power of attorney cannot confer a right to conduct litigation or of audience (*Gregory v Turner; R (on the application of Morris) v North Somerset Council* [2003] 1 WLR 1149). Doubt was cast as to whether a litigation friend has the right of audience of the party, although the court retains a discretion to allow this.

Suitability—There can be no doubt as to the suitability of a person authorised by the Court of Protection (if doubt arises the matter should be referred back to that Court). The rule helpfully sets out the criteria whereby other persons may be regarded as suitable to act as litigation friend (r 21.4(3)), but the court may not waive any of these criteria which the proposed person is unable to satisfy. These criteria feature throughout Pt 21, as amplified by PD21, para 2.1, and the court must be satisfied that they are complied with before appointing a litigation friend. They may be relied upon where there is a dispute as to who should be appointed. Apart from this there is no restriction on who may be a litigation friend, save that the person appointed must not be a child or a protected party and (in practice) should normally be within the jurisdiction. The litigation friend should not have any personal involvement in the proceedings, but see *Spurling v Broadhurst* [2012] EWHC 2883 (Ch). If the court becomes aware of the person's unsuitability, it may remove him under r 21.7 and substitute another person as litigation friend, but there is no express duty to monitor the situation.

Undertaking as to costs (r 21.4(3)(c))—This undertaking is required from the litigation friend of a claimant (unless appointed by the Court of Protection) but not a defendant (see PD21, para 2.2(e) and 2.3(4)). It is contained in Form N235 *Certificate of Suitability of Litigation Friend*. A mother's undertaking to meet any liability in costs "if her financial circumstances were to change, enabling her to afford them" did not satisfy the requirement of r 21.4(3)(c) and she was, accordingly, ineligible for appointment as a litigation friend (*R (Hussain) v Birmingham City Council* (above)).

The requirement imposes a severe limitation upon the ability of a child or protected party to bring a claim. Query whether it amounts to discrimination against a person with a mental disability contrary to DDA 1995 or will otherwise be in breach of HRA 1998. The Court of Protection Rules 2007 (the latest court rules to be produced) do not require this undertaking. The litigation friend is, in effect, expected to provide an indemnity so may wish to be protected by a Public Funding certificate or otherwise in control of adequate funds held by the child or protected party. One way of circumventing the undertaking in the case of a protected party is to obtain the authority of the Court of Protection to bring the proceedings. The court has a general discretion as to costs and will take into account the role of the litigation friend but may have power to impose a personal costs liability in case of misconduct quite apart from the undertaking.

21.5 How a person becomes a litigation friend without a court order

(1) If the court has not appointed a litigation friend, a person who wishes to act as a litigation friend must follow the procedure set out in this rule.

(2) A deputy appointed by the Court of Protection under the 2005 Act with power to conduct proceedings on the protected party's behalf must file an official copy^(GL) of the order of the Court of Protection which confers his power to act either –

    (a) where the deputy is to act as a litigation friend for a claimant, at the time the claim is made; or

    (b) where the deputy is to act as a litigation friend for a defendant, at the time when he first takes a step in the proceedings on behalf of the defendant.

(3) Any other person must file a certificate of suitability stating that he satisfies the conditions specified in rule 21.4(3) either –

    (a)   where the person is to act as a litigation friend for a claimant, at the time when the claim is made; or

    (b)   where the person is to act as a litigation friend for a defendant, at the time when he first takes a step in the proceedings on behalf of the defendant.

(4) The litigation friend must –

    (a)   serve the certificate of suitability on every person on whom, in accordance with rule 6.13 (service on parent, guardian etc), the claim form should be served; and

    (b)   file a certificate of service when filing the certificate of suitability.

    (Rules 6.17 and 6.29 set out the details to be contained in a certificate of service.)

Amendments—SI 2007/2204; SI 2008/2178.

Scope—This rule sets out the procedural steps for the appointment of a litigation friend otherwise than by a court order. It will be relied upon in most cases.

No need for court appointment of litigation friend—A litigation friend may be appointed simply by filing the relevant documents. The certificate is a pre-requisite for appointment without a court order, but will not be conclusive in the event of a dispute as to suitability. It is strange that there is no requirement for the child or protected party to be personally notified that proceedings are being brought or defended in his name because he may wish to make representations as to who the litigation friend should be or dispute that he is a protected party (see generally the provisions as to service in CPR 1998, Pt 6). It is good practice for anyone intending to become a litigation friend to serve upon or draw to the attention of the intended protected party the notice of his intention to act as litigation friend and certificate of suitability, unless there is no prospect of a relevant response and the court may require confirmation of this. The Court of Appeal has recommended a change in the rules so that a person cannot become a protected party without knowing what is going on (see *Masterman-Lister*, above).

"certificate of suitability" (r 21.5(3))—This document confirms that the person to be appointed meets the criteria whereby a person may be regarded as suitable for appointment as litigation friend (r 21.4(3)). As to suitability see note to r 21.4. The certificate is not required where the person is a deputy authorised by the Court of Protection to conduct the proceedings (see note to r 21.4).

    Form N235 also confirms the maker's consents to act and belief that the party is a protected party (with reasons/medical evidence). There is no specific requirement in the Rules for evidence to be provided notwithstanding that it is fundamental to the appointment.

Deputy appointed by the Court of Protection—An official copy of the order of the Court of Protection, which confers his power to act, must be filed. The rules do not contemplate the Court of Protection authorising a person to conduct proceedings without appointing him to be a deputy, but this could happen. Presumably the court would ensure that this person was appointed and exclude any competing application.

"certificate of service" (r 21.5(6)(b))—Paragraph 2.4 of PD21 clarifies the persons on whom the certificate of suitability (when required) must be served in accordance with this rule. The alleged protected party is not included (but see note **No need for court appointment of litigation friend** above).

Forms—Form N235 (Certificate of Suitability of Litigation Friend).

21.6 How a person becomes a litigation friend by court order

(1) The court may make an order appointing a litigation friend.

(2) An application for an order appointing a litigation friend may be made by –

    (a)   a person who wishes to be the litigation friend; or

    (b)   a party.

(3) Where –

    (a)   a person makes a claim against a child or protected party;

    (b)   the child or protected party has no litigation friend;

PART III

(c)   the court has not made an order under rule 21.2(3) (order that a child can conduct proceedings without a litigation friend); and

(d)   either –

(i)   someone who is not entitled to be a litigation friend files a defence; or

(ii)   the claimant wishes to take some step in the proceedings,

the claimant must apply to the court for an order appointing a litigation friend for the child or protected party.

(4) An application for an order appointing a litigation friend must be supported by evidence.

(5) The court may not appoint a litigation friend under this rule unless it is satisfied that the person to be appointed satisfies the conditions specified in rule 21.4(3).

Amendments—SI 2007/2204.

Scope—This rule sets out the procedural steps for the appointment of a litigation friend by a court order, that is, where it has not been possible to appoint a litigation friend under r 21.5. The court must be satisfied that the person to be appointed is suitable for appointment in accordance with the criteria set out in r 21.4(3). Although the rules do not so provide, the application should be served upon or at least brought to the notice of the party unless there is no prospect of a relevant response (see note **No need for court appointment of litigation friend** under r 21.5).

Official Solicitor—Where the circumstances justify the involvement of the Official Solicitor, a completed questionnaire and a copy of the court file with any order provisionally appointing him should be sent to his office. He will usually consent to act and the case may be allocated within 28 days from invitation, subject to:

(a)   satisfactory evidence in the form of an expert's opinion accepted by the party that he or she lacks capacity to conduct the proceedings, OR a finding by the court that the party is a protected party;

(b)   confirmation that the Official Solicitor is litigation friend of last resort; and

(c)   confirmation that there is security for the costs of legal representation.

Any order making such appointment should be expressed as being subject to the Official Solicitor's consent. Save in the most urgent of cases, it is unlikely that the Official Solicitor will be able to complete his enquiries in less than 3 months. Accordingly, a lengthy adjournment of the proceedings may be necessary and a substantive hearing should not be fixed within such period of his initial appointment without consulting him.

The Official Solicitor to the Senior Courts may be contacted at 81 Chancery Lane, London WC2A 1DD; tel 020 7911 7127; fax 020 7911 7105.

Service—See r 21.8(1) and (2) for the special rules that apply to an application for appointment by the court of a litigation friend. The (alleged) protected party must be served on a first application to appoint a litigation friend unless the court orders otherwise, but there is still no requirement for a child to be notified of proceedings to be conducted in his name and on his behalf even though he may be approaching 18 (see note to r 21.2).

Evidence—Paragraph 3.4 of PD21 clarifies the evidence required. This presumably includes evidence that the party is a child or protected party although this is not expressly stated.

Suitability—See note to r 21.4. The court may appoint the person proposed or any other person who complies with the conditions specified in r 21.4(3) (r 21.8(4)). Thus, the criteria of suitability in r 21.4(3) must be satisfied even though r 21.4(1) expressly states that the rule does not apply if the court has appointed a person to be a litigation friend.

21.7 Court's power to change litigation friend and to prevent person acting as litigation friend

(1) The court may –

(a)   direct that a person may not act as a litigation friend;

(b)   terminate a litigation friend's appointment; or

(c)   appoint a new litigation friend in substitution for an existing one.

(2) An application for an order under paragraph (1) must be supported by evidence.

(3) The court may not appoint a litigation friend under this rule unless it is satisfied that the person to be appointed satisfies the conditions in rule 21.4(3).

Amendments—SI 2007/2204.

Scope—The court may prevent a person from being a litigation friend or replace a litigation friend during the course of proceedings. The court must be satisfied that the person to be appointed is suitable for appointment in accordance with the criteria set out in r 21.4(3).

Service—See r 21.8(1) and (3). See generally note to r 21.6 as to service. Although this does not include the protected party, it is good practice to consult this person as capacity is not an "all or nothing" concept.

Suitability—See note to r 21.4 above. The court may appoint the person proposed or any other person who complies with the conditions specified in r 21.4(3) (r 21.8(4)). Thus the criteria of suitability in r 21.4(3) must be satisfied even though r 21.4(1) expressly states that the rule does not apply if the court has appointed a person to be a litigation friend.

Applications—This rule contemplates an application by a party or presumably a non-party, such as an alternative representative for the child or protected party. The court may, as part of its case management powers, initiate the process (r 3.3); concern as to an actual or potential litigation friend does not necessarily mean that there is someone with an interest in making the application.

Termination—The rules express no limit on the power to terminate the appointment and if the litigation friend acts manifestly contrary to the child's or protected party's best interests the court will remove him, even though neither his good faith nor his diligence is in issue (*Re A (Conjoined Twins: Medical Treatment) (No 2)* [2001] 1 FLR 267, CA). In respect of mentally incapable adults, what are this person's best interests has been clarified by MCA 2005, s 4. For an overview of MCA 2005, see Part II.

21.8 Appointment of litigation friend by court order – supplementary

(1) An application for an order under rule 21.6 or 21.7 must be served on every person on whom, in accordance with rule 6.13 (service on parent, guardian etc), the claim form must be served.

(2) Where an application for an order under rule 21.6 is in respect of a protected party, the application must also be served on the protected party unless the court orders otherwise.

(3) An application for an order under rule 21.7 must also be served on –

    (a) the person who is the litigation friend, or who is purporting to act as the litigation friend, when the application is made; and

    (b) the person who it is proposed should be the litigation friend, if he is not the applicant.

(4) On an application for an order under rule 21.6 or 21.7, the court may appoint the person proposed or any other person who satisfies the conditions specified in rule 21.4(3).

Amendments—SI 2007/2204; SI 2008/2178.

Scope—This rule makes provision for service where a party is a child or protected party and supplements r 6.13. It also provides that when an application is made to appoint or change a litigation friend the court is not obliged to appoint the person proposed.

Service—Service on the parent or guardian of the child, or the person with whom the protected party resides or in whose care he is, is required in all cases (see notes to CPR 1998, Sch 2, CCR Ord 10, r 4 for detailed consideration). Note that the application under r 21.6 must be served on the protected party but this is not a universal provision. Where it is proposed to change the litigation friend both the existing and intended litigation friend must be served. Although the rules do not so provide, the application should be served upon or at least brought to the notice of the protected party unless there is no prospect of a relevant response (see note **No need for court appointment of litigation friend** under r 21.5). There is no requirement to serve a child in any of these situations but see the note to r 21.2.

Who is appointed—The court may decide to appoint any other person who meets the criteria set out in r 21.4(3) and is willing to act.

21.9 Procedure where appointment of litigation friend ceases

(1) When a child who is not a protected party reaches the age of 18, the litigation friend's appointment ceases.

(2) Where a protected party regains or acquires capacity to conduct the proceedings, the litigation friend's appointment continues until it is ended by court order.

(3) An application for an order under paragraph (2) may be made by –

    (a)   the former protected party;

    (b)   the litigation friend; or

    (c)   a party.

(4) The child or protected party in respect of whom the appointment to act has ceased must serve notice on the other parties –

    (a)   stating that the appointment of his litigation friend to act has ceased;

    (b)   giving his address for service; and

    (c)   stating whether or not he intends to carry on the proceedings.

(5) If the child or protected party does not serve the notice required by paragraph (4) within 28 days after the day on which the appointment of the litigation friend ceases the court may, on application, strike out[(GL)] any claim brought by or defence raised by the child or protected party.

(6) The liability of a litigation friend for costs continues until –

    (a)   the person in respect of whom his appointment to act has ceased serves the notice referred to in paragraph (4); or

    (b)   the litigation friend serves notice on the parties that his appointment to act has ceased.

Amendments—SI 2007/2204.

Scope—This rule makes provision for a party ceasing to be a child or protected party.

Child—There will be no need for a litigation friend when the child attains 18 (unless the child is also a protected party) and the appointment then ceases automatically. If this party does not then continue the proceedings they may be struck out. There is no express requirement for the child to be notified of the existence of the proceedings up to that point, but notice of an application to strike out under r 21.9(5) must presumably be given to the party formerly a child. The litigation friend will remain liable for costs unless the child gives notice as aforesaid or the litigation friend gives notice under r 21.9(6)(b), which must also be given to the party formerly a child.

Protected party—The position is different in respect of a protected party who recovers capacity. The litigation friend will only be removed by court order following an application under r 21.9(3) and evidence will be required as to capacity. Notice must still be served by the former protected party under r 21.9(4) or the proceedings may be struck out, and the litigation friend will remain liable for costs until that notice is served or he serves his own notice under r 21.9(6)(b).

Liability of litigation friend for costs—The litigation friend of a claimant may have had to give an undertaking as to costs pursuant to r 21.4(3)(c). This liability continues until notice is served on the other parties either by the claimant or the former litigation friend as mentioned above. Presumably the reference in r 21.9(6) to "The liability of a litigation friend for costs" refers to such undertaking and is not sufficient to create any additional liability. It is not clear whether, when discharged, the litigation friend is released from all liability for costs or only costs incurred from that date, although it is probably the latter.

21.10 Compromise etc by or on behalf of child or protected party

(1) Where a claim is made –

    (a)   by or on behalf of a child or protected party; or

    (b)   against a child or protected party,

no settlement, compromise or payment (including any voluntary interim payment) and no acceptance of money paid into court shall be valid, so far as it relates to the claim by, on behalf of or against the child or protected party, without the approval of the court.

(2) Where –

   (a) before proceedings in which a claim is made by or on behalf of, or against a child or protected party (whether alone or with any other person) are begun, an agreement is reached for the settlement of the claim; and

   (b) the sole purpose of proceedings is to obtain the approval of the court to a settlement or compromise of the claim,

the claim must –

   (i) be made using the procedure set out in Part 8 (alternative procedure for claims); and

   (ii) include a request to the court for approval of the settlement or compromise.

(3) In proceedings to which Section II or Section III of Part 45 applies, the court shall not make an order for detailed assessment of the costs payable to the child or protected party but will assess the costs in the manner set out in that Section.

   (Rule 46.4 contains provisions about costs where money is payable to a child or protected party.)

Amendments—SI 2004/3419; SI 2007/2204; SI 2010/621; SI 2013/262.

Scope—This provision ensures that the approval of the court is obtained to any settlement or compromise on behalf of a child or protected party, and extends to accepting any Pt 36 offer. It applies to claims other than for money and where the claim is made against the child or protected party. Without this approval the settlement, compromise or payment of any claim is wholly invalid and unenforceable, and is made entirely at the risk of the parties and their solicitors. The acceptance by a defendant of a Pt 36 offer to settle made by a litigation friend (including a partial settlement relating to liability) may be withdrawn before court approval is obtained (*Drinkall v Whitwood* [2004] 1 WLR 462).

Setting aside a settlement—Although there is a public interest in the finality of litigation, there is also a public interest in the protection of vulnerable people who lack the mental state to conduct litigation, so a compromise may be set aside many years later where, unknown to the parties, the claimant was a protected party at the time. The test is whether the claimant has capacity to conduct the proceedings, not whether the claimant agrees to the compromise (*Dunhill v Burgin* [2012] COPLR 679).

Varying the settlement—Once the settlement has been approved, it is final and cannot be varied or revoked on the grounds that an unforeseen event has destroyed the assumption on which it was made pursuant to the case-management power of the court under r 3.1(7) (*Roult (by his mother and litigation friend) v North West Strategic Health Authority* [2010] 1 WLR 487).

Need for a public hearing—Although any hearing should normally be held in public to comply with ECHR 1950, Art 6(1), there are exceptions and hearings involving the interests of a child or patient may be in private (CPR 1998, r 39.2(3)(d) and PD39, para 1.4A).

Appeals—A decision not to appeal, where permission has been obtained on the express understanding that the possible appellant needs time to consider the matter, and with no consideration moving from the possible respondents, is not a "compromise" and does not require the approval of the court (*Re A (Conjoined Twins: Medical Treatment) (No 2)* [2001] 1 FLR 267, CA).

21.11 Control of money recovered by or on behalf of child or protected party

(1) Where in any proceedings –

   (a) money is recovered by or on behalf of or for the benefit of a child or protected party; or

   (b) money paid into court is accepted by or on behalf of a child or protected party, the money shall be dealt with in accordance with directions given by the court under this rule and not otherwise.

(2) Directions given under this rule may provide that the money shall be wholly or partly paid into court and invested or otherwise dealt with.

(3) Where money is recovered by or on behalf of a protected party or money paid into court is accepted by or on behalf of a protected party, before giving directions in accordance with this rule, the court will first consider whether the protected party is a protected beneficiary.

Amendments—SI 2007/2204.

Scope—This rule ensures that there is supervision of money awarded to or recovered by a child or protected party who is also a protected beneficiary. Further guidance is to be found in PD21 generally.

Control of money—This subject generally is beyond the scope of this volume. The court will control funds held on behalf of a child, but in the case of a protected beneficiary reference must usually be made to the Court of Protection. If there is a registered attorney under an enduring power or a donee under a lasting power for financial affairs it may be appropriate to release the fund to such attorney or donee. The powers of the litigation friend are restricted to the conduct of the proceedings and do not extend to dealing with the financial affairs of the infant or protected beneficiary.

Additional powers: infant—The court will control funds held on behalf of an infant, but under r 21.12 (see below) may appoint the Official Solicitor as guardian of that child's estate.

Protected beneficiary—Having approved an award of damages on behalf of a protected party, the court must then consider whether this party is also a protected beneficiary. In that event the fund will either be transferred to the Court of Protection or retained in court and dealt with in like manner to a child's fund, if under £30,000 and there are no further financial resources justifying Court of Protection involvement.

21.12 Expenses incurred by a litigation friend

(1) In proceedings to which rule 21.11 applies, a litigation friend who incurs expenses on behalf of a child or protected party in any proceedings is entitled on application to recover the amount paid or payable out of any money recovered or paid into court to the extent that it –

    (a)   has been reasonably incurred; and

    (b)   is reasonable in amount.

(2) Expenses may include all or part of –

    (a)   a premium in respect of a costs insurance policy (as defined by section 58C(5) of the Courts and Legal Services Act 1990); or

    (b)   interest on a loan taken out to pay a premium in respect of a costs insurance policy or other recoverable disbursement.

(3) No application may be made under this rule for expenses that –

    (a)   are of a type that may be recoverable on an assessment of costs payable by or out of money belonging to a child or protected party; but

    (b)   are disallowed in whole or in part on such an assessment.

(Expenses which are also 'costs' as defined in rule 44.1(1)(a) are dealt with under rule 46.4(2)).

(4) In deciding whether the expenses were reasonably incurred and reasonable in amount, the court will have regard to all the circumstances of the case including the factors set out in rule 44.4(3).

(5) When the court is considering the factors to be taken into account in assessing the reasonableness of expenses, it will have regard to the facts and circumstances as they reasonably appeared to the litigation friend or to the child's or protected party's legal representative when the expense was incurred.

(6) Where the claim is settled or compromised, or judgment is given, on terms that an amount not exceeding £5,000 is paid to the child or protected party, the total amount the litigation friend may recover under paragraph (1) must not exceed 25% of the sum so agreed or awarded, unless the court directs otherwise. Such total amount must not exceed 50% of the sum so agreed or awarded.

Amendments—SI 2005/2292; SI 2007/2204; SI 2013/262.

Scope—This rule clarifies the approach to be adopted by the court when a litigation friend seeks approval to deduct from the damages any expenses that are not recoverable from the defendant.

21.13 Appointment of guardian of child's estate

(1) The court may appoint the Official Solicitor to be a guardian of a child's estate where –

    (a)   money is paid into court on behalf of the child in accordance with directions given under rule 21.11 (control of money received by a child or protected party);

    (b)   the Criminal Injuries Compensation Authority notifies the court that it has made or intends to make an award to the child;

    (c)   a court or tribunal outside England and Wales notifies the court that it has ordered or intends to order that money be paid to the child;

    (d)   the child is absolutely entitled to the proceeds of a pension fund; or

    (e)   in any other case, such an appointment seems desirable to the court.

(2) The court may not appoint the Official Solicitor under this rule unless –

    (a)   the persons with parental responsibility (within the meaning of section 3 of the Children Act 1989) agree; or

    (b)   the court considers that their agreement can be dispensed with.

(3) The Official Solicitor's appointment may continue only until the child reaches 18.

Amendments—SI 2007/2204.

Scope—This rule enables the court to appoint the Official Solicitor to be responsible for the estate of a child in certain defined circumstances.

Official Solicitor—The expression means the Official Solicitor to the Senior Courts provided for by SCA 1981, s 90. The Official Solicitor may be contacted at 81 Chancery Lane, London WC2A 1DD; tel 020 7911 7127; fax 020 7911 7105.

Practice Direction 21 – Children and Protected Parties

This Practice Direction supplements CPR Part 21

General

1.1 In proceedings where one of the parties is a protected party, the protected party should be referred to in the title to the proceedings as 'A.B. (a protected party by C.D. his litigation friend)'.

1.2 In proceedings where one of the parties is a child, where –

    (1)   the child has a litigation friend, the child should be referred to in the title to the proceedings as 'A.B. (a child by C.D. his litigation friend)'; or

    (2)   the child is conducting the proceedings on his own behalf, the child should be referred to in the title as 'A.B. (a child)'.

1.3 A settlement of a claim by a child includes an agreement on a sum to be apportioned to a dependent child under the Fatal Accidents Act 1976.

The litigation friend

2.1 A person may become a litigation friend –

    (a)   without a court order under rule 21.5, or

    (b)   by a court order under rule 21.6.

2.2 A person who wishes to become a litigation friend without a court order pursuant to rule 21.5(3) must file a certificate of suitability in Practice Form N235 –

    (a)   stating that he consents to act,

    (b)   stating that he knows or believes that the [claimant] [defendant] [is a child][lacks capacity to conduct the proceedings],

    (c)   in the case of a protected party, stating the grounds of his belief and, if his belief is based upon medical opinion or the opinion of another suitably qualified expert, attaching any relevant document to the certificate,

    (d)   stating that he can fairly and competently conduct proceedings on behalf of the child or protected party and has no interest adverse to that of the child or protected party, and

    (e)   where the child or protected party is a claimant, undertaking to pay any costs which the child or protected party may be ordered to pay in relation to the proceedings, subject to any right he may have to be repaid from the assets of the child or protected party.

2.3 The certificate of suitability must be verified by a statement of truth.

    (Part 22 contains provisions about statements of truth.)

2.4 The litigation friend is not required to serve the document referred to in paragraph 2.2(c) when he serves a certificate of suitability on the person to be served under rule 21.5(4)(a).

Application for a court order appointing a litigation friend

3.1 Rule 21.6 sets out who may apply for an order appointing a litigation friend.

3.2 An application must be made in accordance with Part 23 and must be supported by evidence.

3.3 The evidence in support must satisfy the court that the proposed litigation friend –

    (1)   consents to act,

    (2)   can fairly and competently conduct proceedings on behalf of the child or protected party,

    (3)   has no interest adverse to that of the child or protected party, and

    (4)   where the child or protected party is a claimant, undertakes to pay any costs which the child or protected party may be ordered to pay in relation to the proceedings, subject to any right he may have to be repaid from the assets of the child or protected party.

3.4 Where it is sought to appoint the Official Solicitor as the litigation friend, provision must be made for payment of his charges.

Procedure where the need for a litigation friend has come to an end

4.1 Rule 21.9 deals with the situation where the need for a litigation friend comes to an end during the proceedings because either –

(1) a child who is not also a protected party reaches the age of 18 (full age) during the proceedings, or

(2) a protected party regains or acquires capacity to conduct the proceedings.

4.2 A child on reaching full age must serve on the other parties to the proceedings and file with the court a notice –

(1) stating that he has reached full age,

(2) stating that his litigation friend's appointment has ceased,

(3) giving an address for service, and

(4) stating whether or not he intends to carry on with or continue to defend the proceedings.

4.3 If the notice states that the child intends to carry on with or continue to defend the proceedings he must subsequently be described in the proceedings as 'A.B. (formerly a child but now of full age)'.

4.4 Whether or not a child having reached full age serves a notice in accordance with rule 21.9(4) and paragraph 4.2 above, a litigation friend may, at any time after the child has reached full age, serve a notice on the other parties that his appointment has ceased.

4.5 Where a protected party regains or acquires capacity to conduct the proceedings, an application under rule 21.9(3) must be made for an order under rule 21.9(2) that the litigation friend's appointment has ceased.

4.6 The application must be supported by the following evidence –

(1) a medical report or other suitably qualified expert's report indicating that the protected party has regained or acquired capacity to conduct the proceedings,

(2) a copy of any relevant order or declaration of the Court of Protection, and

(3) if the application is made by the protected party, a statement whether or not he intends to carry on with or continue to defend the proceedings.

4.7 An order under rule 21.9(2) must be served on the other parties to the proceedings. The former protected party must file with the court a notice –

(1) stating that his litigation friend's appointment has ceased,

(2) giving an address for service, and

(3) stating whether or not he intends to carry on with or continue to defend the proceedings.

Settlement or compromise by or on behalf of a child or protected party before the issue of proceedings

5.1 Where a claim by or on behalf of a child or protected party has been dealt with by agreement before the issue of proceedings and only the approval of the court to the agreement is sought, the claim must, in addition to containing the details of the claim and satisfying the requirements of rule 21.10(2), include the following –

(1) subject to paragraph 5.3, the terms of the settlement or compromise or have attached to it a draft consent order in Practice Form N292;

(2) details of whether and to what extent the defendant admits liability;

(3) the age and occupation (if any) of the child or protected party;

(4) the litigation friend's approval of the proposed settlement or compromise,

(5) a copy of any financial advice relating to the proposed settlement; and

(6) in a personal injury case arising from an accident –

(a) details of the circumstances of the accident,

(b)   any medical reports,

(c)   where appropriate, a schedule of any past and future expenses and losses claimed and any other relevant information relating to the personal injury as set out in Practice Direction 16, and

(d)   where considerations of liability are raised –

  (i)   any evidence or reports in any criminal proceedings or in an inquest, and

  (ii)   details of any prosecution brought.

5.2

(1)   An opinion on the merits of the settlement or compromise given by counsel or solicitor acting for the child or protected party must, except in very clear cases, be obtained.

(2)   A copy of the opinion and, unless the instructions on which it was given are sufficiently set out in it, a copy of the instructions, must be supplied to the court.

5.3   Where in any personal injury case a claim for damages for future pecuniary loss is settled, the provisions in paragraphs 5.4 and 5.5 must in addition be complied with.

5.4   The court must be satisfied that the parties have considered whether the damages should wholly or partly take the form of periodical payments.

5.5   Where the settlement includes provision for periodical payments, the claim must –

(1)   set out the terms of the settlement or compromise; or

(2)   have attached to it a draft consent order,

which must satisfy the requirements of rules 41.8 and 41.9 as appropriate.

5.6   Applications for the approval of a settlement or compromise will normally be heard by –

(1)   a Master or a district judge in proceedings involving a child; and

(2)   a Master, designated civil judge or his nominee in proceedings involving a protected party.

(For information about provisional damages claims see Part 41 and Practice Direction 41A.)

Settlement or compromise by or on behalf of a child or protected party after proceedings have been issued

6.1   Where in any personal injury case a claim for damages for future pecuniary loss, by or on behalf of a child or protected party, is dealt with by agreement after proceedings have been issued, an application must be made for the court's approval of the agreement.

6.2   The court must be satisfied that the parties have considered whether the damages should wholly or partly take the form of periodical payments.

6.3   Where the settlement includes provision for periodical payments, an application under paragraph 6.1 must –

(1)   set out the terms of the settlement or compromise; or

(2)   have attached to it a draft consent order,

which must satisfy the requirements of rules 41.8 and 41.9 as appropriate.

6.4   The court must be supplied with –

(1)   an opinion on the merits of the settlement or compromise given by counsel or solicitor acting for the child or protected party, except in very clear cases; and

(2)   a copy of any financial advice.

6.5 Applications for the approval of a settlement or compromise, except at the trial, will normally be heard by –

(1) a Master or a district judge in proceedings involving a child; and

(2) a Master, designated civil judge or his nominee in proceedings involving a protected party.

Apportionment under the Fatal Accidents Act 1976

7.1 A judgment on or settlement in respect of a claim under the Fatal Accidents Act 1976 must be apportioned between the persons by or on whose behalf the claim has been brought.

7.2 Where a claim is brought on behalf of a dependent child or children, any settlement (including an agreement on a sum to be apportioned to a dependent child under the Fatal Accidents Act 1976) must be approved by the court.

7.3 The money apportioned to any dependent child must be invested on the child's behalf in accordance with rules 21.10 and 21.11 and paragraphs 8 and 9 below.

7.4 In order to approve an apportionment of money to a dependent child, the court will require the following information:

(1) the matters set out in paragraphs 5.1(2) and (3), and

(2) in respect of the deceased –

    (a) where death was caused by an accident, the matters set out in paragraphs 5.1(6)(a), (b) and (c), and

    (b) his future loss of earnings, and

(3) the extent and nature of the dependency.

Control of money recovered by or on behalf of a child or protected party

8.1 When giving directions under rule 21.11, the court –

(1) may direct the money to be paid into court for investment,

(2) may direct that certain sums be paid direct to the child or protected beneficiary, his litigation friend or his legal representative for the immediate benefit of the child or protected beneficiary or for expenses incurred on his behalf, and

(3) may direct that the application in respect of the investment of the money be transferred to a local district registry.

8.2 The court will consider the general aims to be achieved for the money in court (the fund) by investment and will give directions as to the type of investment.

8.3 Where a child also lacks capacity to manage and control any money recovered by him or on his behalf in the proceedings, and is likely to remain so on reaching full age, his fund should be administered as a protected beneficiary's fund.

8.4 Where a child or protected beneficiary is in receipt of publicly funded legal services the fund will be subject to a first charge under section 10 of the Access to Justice Act 1999 (statutory charge) and an order for the investment of money on the child's or protected beneficiary's behalf must contain a direction to that effect.

Investment on behalf of a child

9.1 At the hearing of an application for the approval of a settlement or compromise the litigation friend or his legal representative must provide, in addition to the information required by paragraphs 5 and 6 –

(1) a CFO form 320 (initial application for investment of damages) for completion by the judge hearing the application; and

(2) any evidence or information which the litigation friend wishes the court to consider in relation to the investment of the award for damages.

9.2 Following the hearing in paragraph 9.1, the court will forward to the Court Funds Office a request for investment decision (form 212) and the Public Trustee's investment managers will make the appropriate investment.

9.3 Where an award for damages for a child is made at trial, unless paragraph 9.7 applies, the trial judge will –

(1) direct the money to be paid into court and placed into the special investment account until further investment directions have been given by the court;

(2) direct the litigation friend to make an application to a Master or district judge for further investment directions; and

(3) give such other directions as the trial judge thinks fit, including a direction that the hearing of the application for further investment directions will be fixed for a date within 28 days from the date of the trial.

9.4 The application under paragraph 9.3(2) must be made by filing with the court –

(1) a completed CFO form 320; and

(2) any evidence or information which the litigation friend wishes the court to consider in relation to the investment of the award for damages.

9.5 The application must be sent in proceedings in the Royal Courts of Justice to the Masters' Support Unit (Room E16) at the Royal Courts of Justice.

9.6 If the application required by paragraph 9.3(2) is not made to the court, the money paid into court in accordance with paragraph 9.3(1) will remain in the special investment account subject to any further order of the court or paragraph 9.8.

9.7 If the money to be invested is very small the court may order it to be paid direct to the litigation friend to be put into a building society account (or similar) for the child's use.

9.8 If the money is invested in court, it must be paid out to the child on application when he reaches full age.

Investment on behalf of a protected beneficiary

10.1 The Court of Protection has jurisdiction to make decisions in the best interests of a protected beneficiary. Fees may be charged for the administration of funds and these must be provided for in any settlement.

10.2 Where the sum to be administered for the benefit of the protected beneficiary is –

(1) £30,000 or more, unless a person with authority as –
    (a) the attorney under a registered enduring power of attorney;
    (b) the donee of a lasting power of attorney; or
    (c) the deputy appointed by the Court of Protection,
to administer or manage the protected beneficiary's financial affairs has been appointed, the order approving the settlement will contain a direction to the litigation friend to apply to the Court of Protection for the appointment of a deputy, after which the fund will be dealt with as directed by the Court of Protection; or

(2) under £30,000, it may be retained in court and invested in the same way as the fund of a child.

10.3 A form of order transferring the fund to the Court of Protection is set out in practice form N292.

10.4 In order for the Court Funds Office to release a fund which is subject to the statutory charge, the litigation friend or his legal representative or the person with authority referred to in paragraph 10.2(1) must provide the appropriate regional office of the Legal Services Commission with an undertaking in respect of a sum to cover their costs, following which the regional office will advise the Court Funds Office in writing of that sum, enabling them to transfer the balance to the Court of Protection on receipt of a CFO form 200 payment schedule authorised by the court.

10.5 The CFO form 200 should be completed and presented to the court where the settlement or trial took place for authorisation, subject to paragraphs 10.6 and 10.7.

10.6 Where the settlement took place in the Royal Courts of Justice the CFO form 200 must be completed and presented for authorisation –

    (1)   on behalf of a child, in the Masters' Support Unit, Room E105, and

    (2)   on behalf of a protected beneficiary, in the Judgment and Orders Section in the Action Department, Room E17.

10.7 Where the trial took place in the Royal Courts of Justice, the CFO form 200 is completed and authorised by the court officer.

Expenses incurred by a litigation friend

11.1 A litigation friend may make a claim for expenses under rule 21.12(1) –

    (1)   where the court has ordered an assessment of costs under rule 46.4(2), at the detailed assessment hearing;

    (2)   where the litigation friend's expenses are not of a type which would be recoverable as costs on an assessment of costs between the parties, to the Master or district judge at the hearing to approve the settlement or compromise under Part 21 (the Master or district judge may adjourn the matter to the costs judge); or

    (3)   where an assessment of costs under Part 46.4(2) is not required, and no approval under Part 21 is necessary, by a Part 23 application supported by a witness statement to a costs judge or district judge as appropriate.

11.2 In all circumstances, the litigation friend must support a claim for expenses by filing a witness statement setting out –

    (1)   the nature and amount of the expense; and

    (2)   the reason the expense was incurred.

Guardian's accounts

12 Paragraph 8 of Practice Direction 40A deals with the approval of the accounts of a guardian of assets of a child.

Payment out of funds in court

13.1 Applications to a Master or district judge –

    (1)   for payment out of money from the fund for the benefit of the child, or

    (2)   to vary an investment strategy,

may be dealt with without a hearing unless the court directs otherwise.

13.2 When the child reaches full age –

    (1)   where his fund in court is a sum of money, it will be paid out to him on application; or

(2) where his fund is in the form of investments other than money (for example shares or unit trusts), the investments will on application be –

  (a)   sold and the proceeds of sale paid out to him; or

  (b)   transferred into his name.

13.3 Where the fund is administered by the Court of Protection, any payment out of money from that fund must be in accordance with any decision or order of the Court of Protection.

13.4 If an application is required for the payment out of money from a fund administered by the Court of Protection, that application must be made to the Court of Protection.

(For further information on payments out of court, see Practice Direction 37.)

****

PART 23
GENERAL RULES ABOUT APPLICATIONS FOR COURT ORDERS

CONTENTS OF THIS PART

23.1 Meaning of "application notice" and "respondent"

In this Part –

  "application notice" means a document in which the applicant states his intention to seek a court order; and

  "respondent" means –

  (a)   the person against whom the order is sought; and

  (b)   such other person as the court may direct.

23.2 Where to make an application

(1) The general rule is that an application must be made to the court where the claim was started.

(2) If a claim has been transferred to another court since it was started, an application must be made to the court to which the claim has been transferred.

(3) If the parties have been notified of a fixed date for the trial, an application must be made to the court where the trial is to take place.

(4) Subject to paragraph (4A), if an application is made before a claim has been started, it must be made to the court where it is likely that the claim to which the application relates will be started unless there is good reason to make the application to a different court.

(4A) If –

    (a) an application is made before a claim has been started; and
    (b) the claim is a designated money claim,

the application may be made in any county court.

(5) If an application is made after proceedings to enforce judgment have begun, it must be made to any court which is dealing with the enforcement of the judgment unless any rule or practice direction provides otherwise.

Amendments—SI 2011/3103.

23.3 Application notice to be filed

(1) The general rule is that an applicant must file an application notice.

(2) An applicant may make an application without filing an application notice if –

    (a) this is permitted by a rule or practice direction; or
    (b) the court dispenses with the requirement for an application notice.

Filing of an application notice—The applicant should provide certain information (and see r 23.6 below) including in particular:

(a) a summary of the application;
(b) the grounds for the application;
(c) evidence or documents in support of the application; and
(d) a draft of the order applied for.

Interim remedies—Certain defined interim remedies may be claimed under Pt 25 (see remedies listed at r 25.1). Application for such remedies is in accordance with the procedure under Pt 23 (r 25.3).

23.4 Notice of an application

(1) The general rule is that a copy of the application notice must be served on each respondent.

(2) An application may be made without serving a copy of the application notice if this is permitted by –

    (a) a rule;
    (b) a practice direction; or
    (c) a court order.

    (Rule 23.7 deals with service of a copy of the application notice)

Not on notice applications—The court has power to make applications "not on notice" (ex parte) in certain circumstances (and see Pt 25, which deals with interim remedies). If application is made without giving notice the reason for so doing must be stated in the evidence with the application (r 25.3(3)). Rule 23.9 deals with service of a without notice application.

23.5 Time when an application is made

Where an application must be made within a specified time, it is so made if the application notice is received by the court within that time.

23.6 What an application notice must include

An application notice must state –

    (a)   what order the applicant is seeking; and

    (b)   briefly, why the applicant is seeking the order.

        (Part 22 requires an application notice to be verified by a statement of truth if the applicant wishes to rely on matters set out in his application notice as evidence)

23.7 Service of a copy of an application notice

(1) A copy of the application notice –

    (a)   must be served as soon as practicable after it is filed; and

    (b)   except where another time limit is specified in these Rules or a practice direction, must in any event be served at least 3 days before the court is to deal with the application.

(2) If a copy of the application notice is to be served by the court, the applicant must, when he files the application notice, file a copy of any written evidence in support.

(3) When a copy of an application notice is served it must be accompanied by –

    (a)   a copy of any written evidence in support; and

    (b)   a copy of any draft order which the applicant has attached to his application.

(4) If –

    (a)   an application notice is served; but

    (b)   the period of notice is shorter than the period required by these Rules or a practice direction,

the court may direct that, in the circumstances of the case, sufficient notice has been given and hear the application.

(5) This rule does not require written evidence –

    (a)   to be filed if it has already been filed; or

    (b)   to be served on a party on whom it has already been served.

        (Part 6 contains the general rules about service of documents including who must serve a copy of the application notice)

23.8 Applications which may be dealt with without a hearing

The court may deal with an application without a hearing if –

    (a)   the parties agree as to the terms of the order sought;

    (b)   the parties agree that the court should dispose of the application without a hearing, or

    (c)   the court does not consider that a hearing would be appropriate.

23.9 Service of application where application made without notice

(1) This rule applies where the court has disposed of an application which it permitted to be made without service of a copy of the application notice.

(2) Where the court makes an order, whether granting or dismissing the application, a copy of the application notice and any evidence in support must, unless the court orders otherwise, be served with the order on any party or other person –

    (a)   against whom the order was made; and

    (b)   against whom the order was sought.

(3) The order must contain a statement of the right to make an application to set aside or vary the order under rule 23.10.

23.10 Application to set aside or vary order made without notice

(1) A person who was not served with a copy of the application notice before an order was made under rule 23.9, may apply to have the order set aside(GL) or varied.

(2) An application under this rule must be made within 7 days after the date on which the order was served on the person making the application.

Amendments—SI 2000/221.

23.11 Power of the court to proceed in the absence of a party

(1) Where the applicant or any respondent fails to attend the hearing of an application, the court may proceed in his absence.

(2) Where –

    (a)   the applicant or any respondent fails to attend the hearing of an application; and

    (b)   the court makes an order at the hearing,

the court may, on application or of its own initiative, re-list the application.

    (Part 40 deals with service of orders)

23.12 Dismissal of totally without merit applications

If the court dismisses an application (including an application for permission to appeal or for permission to apply for judicial review) and it considers that the application is totally without merit –

    (a)   the court's order must record that fact; and

    (b)   the court must at the same time consider whether it is appropriate to make a civil restraint order.

Amendments—Inserted by SI 2004/2072; amended by SI 2005/2292.

Civil restraint orders—Civil restraint orders are dealt with in r 3.11 (from which FPR 2010, r 4.8 is derived) and PD3C.

PART III

Practice Direction 23A –
Applications

This Practice Direction supplements CPR Part 23

Reference to a judge

1 A master or district judge may refer to a judge any matter which he thinks should properly be decided by a judge, and the judge may either dispose of the matter or refer it back to the master or district judge.

Application notices

2.1 An application notice must, in addition to the matters set out in rule 23.6, be signed and include:

    (1) the title of the claim,

    (2) the reference number of the claim,

    (3) the full name of the applicant,

    (4) where the applicant is not already a party, his address for service, including a postcode. Postcode information may be obtained from *www.royalmail.com* or the Royal Mail Address Management Guide, and

    (5) either a request for a hearing or a request that the application be dealt with without a hearing.

      (Practice Form N244 may be used.)

2.2 On receipt of an application notice containing a request for a hearing the court will notify the applicant of the time and date for the hearing of the application.

2.3 On receipt of an application notice containing a request that the application be dealt with without a hearing, the application notice will be sent to a master or district judge so that he may decide whether the application is suitable for consideration without a hearing.

2.4 Where the master or district judge agrees that the application is suitable for consideration without a hearing, the court will so inform the applicant and the respondent and may give directions for the filing of evidence. (Rules 23.9 and 23.10 enable a party to apply for an order made without a hearing to be set aside or varied.)

2.5 Where the master or district judge does not agree that the application is suitable for consideration without a hearing, the court will notify the applicant and the respondent of the time, date and place for the hearing of the application and may at the same time give directions as to the filing of evidence.

2.6 If the application is intended to be made to a judge, the application notice should so state. In that case, paragraphs 2.3, 2.4 and 2.5 will apply as though references to the master or district judge were references to a judge.

2.7 Every application should be made as soon as it becomes apparent that it is necessary or desirable to make it.

2.8 Applications should wherever possible be made so that they can be considered at any other hearing for which a date has already been fixed or for which a date is about to be fixed. This is particularly so in relation to case management conferences, allocation and listing hearings and pre-trial reviews fixed by the court.

2.9 The parties must anticipate that at any hearing the court may wish to review the conduct of the case as a whole and give any necessary case management directions. They should be ready to assist the court in doing so and to answer questions the court may ask for this purpose.

2.10 Where a date for a hearing has been fixed and a party wishes to make an application at that hearing but he does not have sufficient time to serve an application notice he should inform the other party and the court (if possible in writing) as soon as he can of the nature of the application and the reason for it. He should then make the application orally at the hearing.

Applications without service of application notice

3 An application may be made without serving an application notice only:

(1)   where there is exceptional urgency,
(2)   where the overriding objective is best furthered by doing so,
(3)   by consent of all parties,
(4)   with the permission of the court,
(5)   where paragraph 2.10 above applies, or
(6)   where a court order, rule or practice direction permits.

Giving notice of an application

4.1 Unless the court otherwise directs or paragraph 3 or paragraph 4.1A of this practice direction applies the application notice must be served as soon as practicable after it has been issued and, if there is to be a hearing, at least 3 days before the hearing date (rule 23.7(1)(b)).

4.1A Where there is to be a telephone hearing the application notice must be served as soon as practicable after it has been issued and in any event at least 5 days before the date of the hearing.

4.2 Where an application notice should be served but there is not sufficient time to do so, informal notification of the application should be given unless the circumstances of the application require secrecy.

(Rule 2.8 explains how to calculate periods of time expressed in terms of days.)

Pre-action applications

5 All applications made before a claim is commenced should be made under Part 23 of the Civil Procedure Rules. Attention is drawn in particular to rule 23.2(4).

Telephone hearings

Interpretation

6.1 In this paragraph –

(a)   'designated legal representative' means the applicant's legal representative (if any), or the legal representative of such other party as the court directs to arrange the telephone hearing; and
(b)   'telephone conference enabled court' means-
(i)   a district registry of the High Court; or
(ii)   a county court,
in which telephone conferencing facilities are available.

PART III

When a hearing is to be conducted by telephone

6.2 Subject to paragraph 6.3, at a telephone conference enabled court the following hearings will be conducted by telephone unless the court otherwise orders –

(a)   allocation hearings;
(b)   listing hearings; and
(c)   interim applications, case management conferences and pre-trial reviews with a time estimate of no more than one hour.

6.3 Paragraph 6.2 does not apply where –

(a)   the hearing is of an application made without notice to the other party;
(b)   all the parties are unrepresented; or
(c)   more than four parties wish to make representations at the hearing (for this purpose where two or more parties are represented by the same person, they are to be treated as one party).

6.4 A request for a direction that a hearing under paragraph 6.2 should not be conducted by telephone –

(a)   must be made at least 7 days before the hearing or such shorter time as the court may permit; and
(b)   may be made by letter,

and the court shall determine such request without requiring the attendance of the parties.

6.5 The court may order that an application, or part of an application, to which paragraph 6.2 does not apply be dealt with by a telephone hearing. The court may make such order –

(a)   of its own initiative; or
(b)   at the request of the parties.

6.6 The applicant should indicate on his application notice if he seeks a court order under paragraph 6.5. Where he has not done so but nevertheless wishes to seek an order, the request should be made as early as possible.

6.7 An order under paragraph 6.5 will not normally be made unless every party entitled to be given notice of the application and to be heard at the hearing has consented to the order.

6.8 If the court makes an order under paragraph 6.5 it will give any directions necessary for the telephone hearing.

Conduct of the telephone hearing

6.9 No party, or representative of a party, to an application being heard by telephone may attend the judge in person while the application is being heard unless every other party to the application has agreed that he may do so.

6.10 If an application is to be heard by telephone the following directions will apply, subject to any direction to the contrary –

(1)   The designated legal representative is responsible for arranging the telephone conference for precisely the time fixed by the court. The telecommunications provider used must be one on the approved panel of service providers (see Her Majesty's Courts and Tribunals Service website).
(2)   The designated legal representative must tell the operator the telephone numbers of all those participating in the conference call and the sequence in which they are to be called.
(3)   It is the responsibility of the designated legal representative to ascertain from all

the other parties whether they have instructed counsel and, if so, the identity of counsel, and whether the legal representative and counsel will be on the same or different telephone numbers.

(4) The sequence in which they are to be called will be –

    (a) the designated legal representative and (if on a different number) his counsel;

    (b) the legal representative (and counsel) for all other parties; and

    (c) the judge.

(5) Each speaker is to remain on the line after being called by the operator setting up the conference call. The call shall be connected at least ten minutes before the time fixed for the hearing.

(6) When the judge has been connected the designated legal representative (or his counsel) will introduce the parties in the usual way.

(7) If the use of a 'speakerphone' by any party causes the judge or any other party any difficulty in hearing what is said the judge may require that party to use a hand held telephone.

(8) The telephone charges debited to the account of the party initiating the conference call will be treated as part of the costs of the application.

Documents

6.11 Where a document is required to be filed and served the party or the designated legal representative must do so no later than 4pm at least 2 days before the hearing.

6.12 A case summary and draft order must be filed and served in –

    (a) multi-track cases; and

    (b) small and fast track cases if the court so directs.

6.13 Any other document upon which a party seeks to rely must be filed and served in accordance with the period specified in paragraph 6.11.

    (Rule 2.8 explains how to calculate period of time expressed in terms of days.)

Video conferencing

7 Where the parties to a matter wish to use video conferencing facilities, and those facilities are available in the relevant court, they should apply to the master or district judge for directions.

Note of proceedings

8 The procedural judge should keep, either by way of a note or a tape recording, brief details of all proceedings before him, including the dates of the proceedings and a short statement of the decision taken at each hearing.

Evidence

9.1 The requirement for evidence in certain types of applications is set out in some of the rules and practice directions. Where there is no specific requirement to provide evidence it should be borne in mind that, as a practical matter, the court will often need to be satisfied by evidence of the facts that are relied on in support of or for opposing the application.

9.2 The court may give directions for the filing of evidence in support of or opposing a particular application. The court may also give directions for the filing of evidence in relation to any hearing that it fixes on its own initiative. The directions may specify the form that evidence is to take and when it is to be served.

9.3 Where it is intended to rely on evidence which is not contained in the application itself, the evidence, if it has not already been served, should be served with the application.

9.4 Where a respondent to an application wishes to rely on evidence which has not yet been served he should serve it as soon as possible and in any event in accordance with any directions the court may have given.

9.5 If it is necessary for the applicant to serve any evidence in reply it should be served as soon as possible and in any event in accordance with any directions the court may have given.

9.6 Evidence must be filed with the court as well as served on the parties. Exhibits should not be filed unless the court otherwise directs.

9.7 The contents of an application notice may be used as evidence (otherwise than at trial) provided the contents have been verified by a statement of truth[1].

1   See Part 22.

Consent orders

10.1 Rule 40.6 sets out the circumstances where an agreed judgment or order may be entered and sealed.

10.2 Where all parties affected by an order have written to the court consenting to the making of the order a draft of which has been filed with the court, the court will treat the draft as having been signed in accordance with rule 40.6(7).

10.3 Where a consent order must be made by a judge (ie rule 40.6(2) does not apply) the order must be drawn so that the judge's name and judicial title can be inserted.

10.4 The parties to an application for a consent order must ensure that they provide the court with any material it needs to be satisfied that it is appropriate to make the order. Subject to any rule or practice direction a letter will generally be acceptable for this purpose.

10.5 Where a judgment or order has been agreed in respect of an application or claim where a hearing date has been fixed, the parties must inform the court immediately. (note that parties are reminded that under rules 28.4 and 29.5 the case management timetable cannot be varied by written agreement of the parties.)

Other applications considered without a hearing

11.1 Where rule 23.8(b) applies the parties should so inform the court in writing and each should confirm that all evidence and other material on which he relies has been disclosed to the other parties to the application.

11.2 Where rule 23.8(c) applies the court will treat the application as if it were proposing to make an order on its own initiative.

Applications to stay claim where related criminal proceedings

11A.1 An application for the stay of civil proceedings pending the determination of related criminal proceedings may be made by any party to the civil proceedings or by the prosecutor or any defendant in the criminal proceedings.

11A.2 Every party to the civil proceedings must, unless he is the applicant, be made a respondent to the application.

11A.3 The evidence in support of the application must contain an estimate of the expected duration of the stay and must identify the respects in which the continuance of the civil proceedings may prejudice the criminal trial.

11A.4 In order to make an application under paragraph 11A.1, it is not necessary for the prosecutor or defendant in the criminal proceedings to be joined as a party to the civil proceedings.

Miscellaneous

12.1 Except in the most simple application the applicant should bring to any hearing a draft of the order sought. If the case is proceeding in the Royal Courts of Justice and the order is unusually long or complex it should also be supplied on disk for use by the court office.

12.2 Where rule 23.11 applies, the power to re-list the application in rule 23.11(2) is in addition to any other powers of the court with regard to the order (for example to set aside, vary, discharge or suspend the order).

Costs

13.1 Attention is drawn to the Costs Practice Direction and, in particular, to the court's power to make a summary assessment of costs.

13.2 Attention is also drawn to rule 44.13(i) which provides that if an order makes no mention of costs, none are payable in respect of the proceedings to which it relates.

Practice Direction 23B –
Applications under Particular Statutes

This Practice Direction supplements CPR Part 23

Applications under Part III of the Family Law Reform Act 1969 for use of scientific tests to determine parentage

1.1 In this section –

(1) 'the Act' means the Family Law Reform Act 1969;
(2) 'direction' means a direction under section 20(1) of the Act made in any proceedings in which a person's parentage falls to be determined;
(3) 'responsible adult' means –
   (a) in relation to a person under 16 to whom sub-paragraph (b) does not apply, the person having care and control of him;
   (b) in relation to a person who lacks capacity (within the meaning of the Mental Capacity Act 2005) to give his consent to tests –
      (i) a person having power under that Act to give consent on his behalf; or
      (ii) if there is no such person, the person with whom he resides or in whose care he is.
(4) 'samples' means bodily samples within the meaning of section 25 of the Act; and
(5) 'tests' means scientific tests within the meaning of section 25 of the Act.

1.2 Where an application is made for a direction in respect of a person who either –

(a) is under 16; or

(b) lacks capacity (within the meaning of the Mental Capacity Act 2005) to give his consent to the tests,

the application notice must state the name and address of the responsible adult.

1.3 Unless the court orders otherwise –

(1) the court will serve a copy of the application notice on every party to the proceedings other than the applicant; and

(2) the applicant must serve a copy of the application notice personally on any other person who would be directed to give samples and, where paragraph 1.2 applies, on the responsible adult.

1.4 Unless the court orders otherwise, where the court gives a direction –

(1) the court will serve a copy of the direction on every party to the proceedings;

(2) the applicant must serve a copy of the direction personally on any other person directed to give samples and, where paragraph 1.2 applies, on the responsible adult; and

(3) further consideration of the proceedings shall be adjourned until the court receives a report of the tests carried out or samples taken.

1.5 When the court receives the report of the tests carried out or samples taken, the court officer shall send a copy of the report to –

(1) every party to the proceedings;

(2) the responsible adult where paragraph 1.2 applies; and

(3) every other person directed to give samples.

****

PART 25
INTERIM REMEDIES AND SECURITY FOR COSTS

CONTENTS OF THIS PART

25.1 Orders for interim remedies

(1) The court may grant the following interim remedies –

(a) an interim injunction(GL);

(b) an interim declaration;

(c) an order –

(i) for the detention, custody or preservation of relevant property;

(ii) for the inspection of relevant property;

(iii) for the taking of a sample of relevant property;

(iv) for the carrying out of an experiment on or with relevant property;

(v) for the sale of relevant property which is of a perishable nature or which for any other good reason it is desirable to sell quickly; and

(vi) for the payment of income from relevant property until a claim is decided;
(d) an order authorising a person to enter any land or building in the possession of a party to the proceedings for the purposes of carrying out an order under sub-paragraph (c);
(e) an order under section 4 of the Torts (Interference with Goods) Act 1977 to deliver up goods;
(f) an order (referred to as a "freezing injunction") –
  (i) restraining a party from removing from the jurisdiction assets located there; or
  (ii) restraining a party from dealing with any assets whether located within the jurisdiction or not;
(g) an order directing a party to provide information about the location of relevant property or assets or to provide information about relevant property or assets which are or may be the subject of an application for a freezing injunction;
(h) an order (referred to as a "search order") under section 7 of the Civil Procedure Act 1997 (order requiring a party to admit another party to premises for the purpose of preserving evidence etc);
(i) an order under section 33 of the Senior Courts Act 1981 or section 52 of the County Courts Act 1984 (order for disclosure of documents or inspection of property before a claim has been made);
(j) an order under section 34 of the Senior Courts Act 1981 or section 53 of the County Courts Act 1984 (order in certain proceedings for disclosure of documents or inspection of property against a non-party);
(k) an order (referred to as an order for interim payment) under rule 25.6 for payment by a defendant on account of any damages, debt or other sum (except costs) which the court may hold the defendant liable to pay;
(l) an order for a specified fund to be paid into court or otherwise secured, where there is a dispute over a party's right to the fund;
(m) an order permitting a party seeking to recover personal property to pay money into court pending the outcome of the proceedings and directing that, if he does so, the property shall be given up to him;
(n) an order directing a party to prepare and file accounts relating to the dispute;
(o) an order directing any account to be taken or inquiry to be made by the court; and
(p) an order under Article 9 of Council Directive (EC) 2004/48 on the enforcement of intellectual property rights (order in intellectual property proceedings making the continuation of an alleged infringement subject to the lodging of guarantees).

(Rule 34.2 provides for the court to issue a witness summons requiring a witness to produce documents to the court at the hearing or on such date as the court may direct)

(2) In paragraph (1)(c) and (g), "relevant property" means property (including land) which is the subject of a claim or as to which any question may arise on a claim.

(3) The fact that a particular kind of interim remedy is not listed in paragraph (1) does not affect any power that the court may have to grant that remedy.

(4) The court may grant an interim remedy whether or not there has been a claim for a final remedy of that kind.

Amendments—SI 2002/2058; SI 2005/3515; CRA 2005, Sch 11, para 1(2).

Inherent jurisdiction—The court retains an inherent jurisdiction to grant an injunction (see SCA 1981 and, for example, *Shipman v Shipman* [1991] 1 FLR 250, where the court granted an injunction in the inherent jurisdiction of the High Court. (In family proceedings such an application would be under FPR 2010, r 9.7 or Pt 20 (by the Pt 18 procedure).)

"interim declaration" (r 25.1(1)(b))—Crown Proceedings Act 1947 provides that an injunction does not lie against the Crown. The remedy is by seeking a declaration in the form of order in many judicial review proceedings, or where a government department is the defendant (see discussion of the declaration remedy in *Gillick v West Norfolk and Wisbech AHA* [1986] 1 FLR 224, HL).

"freezing injunction" (r 25.1(1)(f))—The term "freezing injunction" refers to the *Mareva* order or injunction. This remains an inherent jurisdiction remedy. For further commentary see notes to SCA 1981, s 37.

Issue in High Court—All applications for freezing (*Mareva*) injunctions and search orders must be made in the High Court (CCRR 1991, reg 3). Freezing injunctions can be made in the county court in family proceedings (CCRR 1991, reg 3(3)(a)). A *Shipman* order (see above) derives from the inherent jurisdiction of the High Court and can be made in the county court (CCA 1984 s 38(1), e g where the court finds it cannot make an order under MCA 1973, s 37(2)(a)).

"search order" (r 25.1(1)(h))—The terminology for the former *Anton Piller* order has been statutorily defined (CPA 1997, s 7(1), set out in the notes under SCA 1981, s 37). This order was considered fully in *Imerman v Tchenguiz and Others* [2010] 2 FLR 814 (see further under FPR 2010, r 20.2). Alternatively, it may be appropriate to apply in a breach of confidence damages claim alongside family proceedings for an order to restrain removal of documents. In *L v L* [2007] 2 FLR 171 the documents comprised the hard drive from the husband's computer.

Impounding a party's passport—To impound a party's passport, application is under Pt 25. The Pt 23 application (on an urgent basis, as need be) is supported by an affidavit (PD25A, para 3.1) (and see further note under SCA 1981, s 19 and FPR 2010, Pt 20).

25.2 Time when an order for an interim remedy may be made

(1) An order for an interim remedy may be made at any time, including –

    (a)   before proceedings are started; and

    (b)   after judgment has been given.

       (Rule 7.2 provides that proceedings are started when the court issues a claim form)

(2) However –

    (a)   paragraph (1) is subject to any rule, practice direction or other enactment which provides otherwise;

    (b)   the court may grant an interim remedy before a claim has been made only if –

       (i)   the matter is urgent; or

       (ii) it is otherwise desirable to do so in the interests of justice; and

    (c)   unless the court otherwise orders, a defendant may not apply for any of the orders listed in rule 25.1(1) before he has filed either an acknowledgment of service or a defence.

       (Part 10 provides for filing an acknowledgment of service and Part 15 for filing a defence)

(3) Where it grants an interim remedy before a claim has been commenced, the court should give directions requiring a claim to be commenced.

(4) In particular, the court need not direct that a claim be commenced where the application is made under section 33 of the Senior Courts Act 1981 or section 52 of the County Courts Act 1984 (order for disclosure, inspection etc before commencement of a claim).

Amendments—SI 2005/3515; CRA 2005, Sch 11, para 1(2).

25.3 How to apply for an interim remedy

(1) The court may grant an interim remedy on an application made without notice if it appears to the court that there are good reasons for not giving notice.

(2) An application for an interim remedy must be supported by evidence, unless the court orders otherwise.

(3) If the applicant makes an application without giving notice, the evidence in support of the application must state the reasons why notice has not been given.

(Part 3 lists general powers of the court)

(Part 23 contains general rules about making an application)

****

Practice Direction 25A – Interim Injunctions

This Practice Direction supplements CPR Part 25

Jurisdiction

1.1 High Court judges and any other judge duly authorised may grant 'search orders'[1] and 'freezing injunctions'[2].

1   Rule 25.1(1)(h).
2   Rule 25.1(1)(f).

1.2 In a case in the High Court, masters and district judges have the power to grant injunctions:

(1)   by consent,
(2)   in connection with charging orders and appointments of receivers,
(3)   in aid of execution of judgments.

1.3 In any other case any judge who has jurisdiction to conduct the trial of the action has the power to grant an injunction in that action.

1.4 A master or district judge has the power to vary or discharge an injunction granted by any judge with the consent of all the parties.

Making an application

2.1 The application notice must state:

(1)   the order sought, and
(2)   the date, time and place of the hearing.

2.2 The application notice and evidence in support must be served as soon as practicable after issue and in any event not less than 3 days before the court is due to hear the application[1].

1   Rule 23.7(1) and (2) and see rule 23.7(4) (short service).

2.3 Where the court is to serve, sufficient copies of the application notice and evidence in support for the court and for each respondent should be filed for issue and service.

2.4 Whenever possible a draft of the order sought should be filed with the application notice and a disk containing the draft should also be available to the court in a format compatible with the word processing software used by the court. This will enable the court officer to arrange for any amendments to be incorporated and for the speedy preparation and sealing of the order.

Evidence

3.1 Applications for search orders and freezing injunctions must be supported by affidavit evidence.

3.2 Applications for other interim injunctions must be supported by evidence set out in either:

    (1) a witness statement, or

    (2) a statement of case provided that it is verified by a statement of truth[1], or

    (3) the application provided that it is verified by a statement of truth,

unless the court, an Act, a rule or a practice direction requires evidence by affidavit.

1   See Part 22.

3.3 The evidence must set out the facts on which the applicant relies for the claim being made against the respondent, including all material facts of which the court should be made aware.

3.4 Where an application is made without notice to the respondent, the evidence must also set out why notice was not given.

    (See Part 32 and Practice Direction 32 for information about evidence.)

Urgent applications and applications without notice

4.1 These fall into two categories:

    (1) applications where a claim form has already been issued, and

    (2) applications where a claim form has not yet been issued,

and, in both cases, where notice of the application has not been given to the respondent.

4.2 These applications are normally dealt with at a court hearing but cases of extreme urgency may be dealt with by telephone.

4.3 Applications dealt with at a court hearing after issue of a claim form:

    (1) the application notice, evidence in support and a draft order (as in 2.4 above) should be filed with the court 2 hours before the hearing wherever possible,

    (2) if an application is made before the application notice has been issued, a draft order (as in 2.4 above) should be provided at the hearing, and the application notice and evidence in support must be filed with the court on the same or next working day or as ordered by the court, and

    (3) except in cases where secrecy is essential, the applicant should take steps to notify the respondent informally of the application.

4.4 Applications made before the issue of a claim form:

    (1) in addition to the provisions set out at 4.3 above, unless the court orders otherwise, either the applicant must undertake to the court to issue a claim form immediately or the court will give directions for the commencement of the claim[1],

    (2) where possible the claim form should be served with the order for the injunction,

    (3) an order made before the issue of a claim form should state in the title after the names of the applicant and respondent 'the Claimant and Defendant in an Intended Action'.

1   Rule 25.2(3).

4.5 Applications made by telephone:

    (1) where it is not possible to arrange a hearing, application can be made between 10.00 am and 5.00 pm weekdays by telephoning the Royal Courts of Justice on

020 7947 6000 and asking to be put in contact with a High Court judge of the appropriate Division available to deal with an emergency application in a High Court matter. The appropriate district registry may also be contacted by telephone. In county court proceedings, the appropriate county court should be contacted,

(2) where an application is made outside those hours the applicant should either –

    (a) telephone the Royal Courts of Justice on 020 7947 6000 where he will be put in contact with the clerk to the appropriate Duty judge in the High Court (or the appropriate area circuit judge where known), or

    (b) the Urgent Court Business Officer of the appropriate Circuit who will contact the local Duty judge,

(3) where the facility is available it is likely that the judge will require a draft order to be faxed to him,

(4) the application notice and evidence in support must be filed with the court on the same or next working day or as ordered, together with two copies of the order for sealing,

(5) injunctions will be heard by telephone only where the applicant is acting by counsel or solicitors.

Orders for injunctions

5.1 Any order for an injunction, unless the court orders otherwise, must contain:

(1) subject to paragraph 5.1B, an undertaking by the applicant to the court to pay any damages which the respondent(s) (or any other party served with or notified of the order) sustain which the court considers the applicant should pay,

(2) if made without notice to any other party, an undertaking by the applicant to the court to serve on the respondent the application notice, evidence in support and any order made as soon as practicable,

(3) if made without notice to any other party, a return date for a further hearing at which the other party can be present,

(4) if made before filing the application notice, an undertaking to file and pay the appropriate fee on the same or next working day, and

(5) if made before issue of a claim form –

    (a) an undertaking to issue and pay the appropriate fee on the same or next working day, or

    (b) directions for the commencement of the claim.

5.1A Subject to paragraph 5.1B, when the court makes an order for an injunction, it should consider whether to require an undertaking by the applicant to pay any damages sustained by a person other than the respondent, including another party to the proceedings or any other person who may suffer loss as a consequence of the order.

5.1B (1) If in an Aarhus Convention claim the court is satisfied that an injunction is necessary to prevent significant environmental damage and to preserve the factual basis of the proceedings, the court will, in considering whether to require an undertaking by the applicant to pay any damages which the respondent or any other person may sustain as a result and the terms of any such undertaking –

    (a) have particular regard to the need for the terms of the order overall not to be such as would make continuing with the claim prohibitively expensive for the applicant; and

    (b) make such directions as are necessary to ensure that the case is heard promptly.

(2) "Aarhus Convention claim" has the same meaning as in rule 45.41(2).

5.2 An order for an injunction made in the presence of all parties to be bound by it or made at a hearing of which they have had notice, may state that it is effective until trial or further order.

5.3 Any order for an injunction must set out clearly what the respondent must do or not do.

Freezing injunctions

Orders to restrain disposal of assets worldwide and within England and Wales

6.1 An example of a Freezing Injunction is annexed to this practice direction.

6.2 This example may be modified as appropriate in any particular case. In particular, the court may, if it considers it appropriate, require the applicant's solicitors, as well as the applicant, to give undertakings.

Search orders

7.1 The following provisions apply to search orders in addition to those listed above.

7.2 **The Supervising Solicitor**

The supervising solicitor must be experienced in the operation of search orders. A supervising solicitor may be contacted either through the Law Society or, for the London area, through the London Solicitors Litigation Association.

7.3 **Evidence:**

(1)   the affidavit must state the name, firm and its address, and experience of the supervising solicitor, also the address of the premises and whether it is a private or business address, and

(2)   the affidavit must disclose very fully the reason the order is sought, including the probability that relevant material would disappear if the order were not made.

7.4 **Service:**

(1)   the order must be served personally by the supervising solicitor, unless the court otherwise orders, and must be accompanied by the evidence in support and any documents capable of being copied,

(2)   confidential exhibits need not be served but they must be made available for inspection by the respondent in the presence of the applicant's solicitors while the order is carried out and afterwards be retained by the respondent's solicitors on their undertaking not to permit the respondent –

    (a)   to see them or copies of them except in their presence, and

    (b)   to make or take away any note or record of them,

(3)   the supervising solicitor may be accompanied only by the persons mentioned in the order,

(4)   the Supervising Solicitor must explain the terms and effect of the order to the respondent in everyday language and advise him –

    (a)   of his right to take legal advice and to apply to vary or discharge the order; and

    (b)   that he may be entitled to avail himself of –

        (i)   legal professional privilege; and

        (ii)   the privilege against self-incrimination.

(5)   where the supervising solicitor is a man and the respondent is likely to be an unaccompanied woman, at least one other person named in the order must be a woman and must accompany the supervising solicitor, and

(6)   the order may only be served between 9.30 am and 5.30 pm Monday to Friday unless the court otherwise orders.

7.5 Search and custody of materials:

(1)   no material shall be removed unless clearly covered by the terms of the order,

(2)   the premises must not be searched and no items shall be removed from them except in the presence of the respondent or a person who appears to be a responsible employee of the respondent,

(3)   where copies of documents are sought, the documents should be retained for no more than 2 days before return to the owner,

(4)   where material in dispute is removed pending trial, the applicant's solicitors should place it in the custody of the respondent's solicitors on their undertaking to retain it in safekeeping and to produce it to the court when required,

(5)   in appropriate cases the applicant should insure the material retained in the respondent's solicitors' custody,

(6)   the supervising solicitor must make a list of all material removed from the premises and supply a copy of the list to the respondent,

(7)   no material shall be removed from the premises until the respondent has had reasonable time to check the list,

(8)   if any of the listed items exists only in computer readable form, the respondent must immediately give the applicant's solicitors effective access to the computers, with all necessary passwords, to enable them to be searched, and cause the listed items to be printed out,

(9)   the applicant must take all reasonable steps to ensure that no damage is done to any computer or data,

(10) the applicant and his representatives may not themselves search the respondent's computers unless they have sufficient expertise to do so without damaging the respondent's system,

(11) the supervising solicitor shall provide a report on the carrying out of the order to the applicant's solicitors,

(12) as soon as the report is received the applicant's solicitors shall –

    (a)   serve a copy of it on the respondent, and

    (b)   file a copy of it with the court, and

(13) where the supervising solicitor is satisfied that full compliance with paragraph 7.5(7) and (8) above is impracticable, he may permit the search to proceed and items to be removed without compliance with the impracticable requirements.

7.6 The Supervising Solicitor must not be an employee or member of the applicant's firm of solicitors.

7.7 If the court orders that the order need not be served by the Supervising Solicitor, the reason for so ordering must be set out in the order.

7.8 The search order must not be carried out at the same time as a police search warrant.

7.9 There is no privilege against self incrimination in –

(1)   Intellectual Property cases in respect of a 'related offence' or for the recovery of a 'related penalty' as defined in section 72 Senior Courts Act 1981;

(2)   proceedings for the recovery or administration of any property, for the execution of a trust or for an account of any property or dealings with property, in relation to –

    (a)   an offence under the Theft Act 1968 (see section 31 of the Theft Act 1968); or

    (b)   an offence under the Fraud Act 2006 (see section 13 of the Fraud Act 2006) or a related offence within the meaning given by section 13(4)

PART III

of that Act – that is, conspiracy to defraud or any other offence involving any form of fraudulent conduct or purpose; or

(3) proceedings in which a court is hearing an application for an order under Part IV or Part V of the Children Act 1989 (see section 98 Children Act 1989).

However, the privilege may still be claimed in relation to material or information required to be disclosed by an order, as regards potential criminal proceedings outside those statutory provisions.

7.10 Applications in Intellectual Property cases should be made in the Chancery Division.

7.11 An example of a Search Order is annexed to this practice direction. This example may be modified as appropriate in any particular case.

Delivery-up orders

8.1 The following provisions apply to orders, other than search orders, for delivery up or preservation of evidence or property where it is likely that such an order will be executed at the premises of the respondent or a third party.

8.2 In such cases the court shall consider whether to include in the order for the benefit or protection of the parties similar provisions to those specified above in relation to injunctions and search orders.

Injunctions against third parties

9.1 The following provisions apply to orders which will affect a person other than the applicant or respondent, who:

(1) did not attend the hearing at which the order was made; and
(2) is served with the order.

9.2 Where such a person served with the order requests –

(1) a copy of any materials read by the judge, including material prepared after the hearing at the direction of the judge or in compliance with the order; or
(2) a note of the hearing,

the applicant, or his legal representative, must comply promptly with the request, unless the court orders otherwise.

ANNEX

FREEZING INJUNCTION   **IN THE HIGH COURT OF JUSTICE**
                                               [   ] **DIVISION**

Before The Honourable Mr Justice   [   ]

                                          Claim No
                                          Dated

Applicant

                                           Seal

Respondent

Name, address and reference of respondent

IF YOU [ ]¹ DISOBEY THIS ORDER YOU MAY BE HELD TO BE IN CONTEMPT OF COURT AND MAY BE IMPRISONED, FINED OR HAVE YOUR ASSETS SEIZED.

ANY OTHER PERSON WHO KNOWS OF THIS ORDER AND DOES ANYTHING WHICH HELPS OR PERMITS THE RESPONDENT TO BREACH THE TERMS OF THIS ORDER MAY ALSO BE HELD TO BE IN CONTEMPT OF COURT AND MAY BE IMPRISONED, FINED OR HAVE THEIR ASSETS SEIZED.

1   Insert name of Respondent.

This order

1 This is a Freezing Injunction made against [ ] ('the Respondent') on [ ] by Mr Justice [ ] on the application of [ ] ('the Applicant'). The Judge read the Affidavits listed in Schedule A and accepted the undertakings set out in Schedule B at the end of this Order.

2 This order was made at a hearing without notice to the Respondent. The Respondent has a right to apply to the court to vary or discharge the order – see paragraph 13 below.

3 There will be a further hearing in respect of this order on [ ] ('the return date').

4 If there is more than one Respondent –

    (a) unless otherwise stated, references in this order to 'the Respondent' mean both or all of them; and

    (b) this order is effective against any Respondent on whom it is served or who is given notice of it.

Freezing injunction

[*For injunction limited to assets in England and Wales*]

5 Until the return date or further order of the court, the Respondent must not remove from England and Wales or in any way dispose of, deal with or diminish the value of any of his assets which are in England and Wales up to the value of £ .

[*For worldwide injunction*]

5 Until the return date or further order of the court, the Respondent must not –

    (1) remove from England and Wales any of his assets which are in England and Wales up to the value of £ ; or

    (2) in any way dispose of, deal with or diminish the value of any of his assets whether they are in or outside England and Wales up to the same value.

[*For either form of injunction*]

6 Paragraph 5 applies to all the Respondent's assets whether or not they are in his own name and whether they are solely or jointly owned. For the purpose of this order the Respondent's assets include any asset which he has the power, directly or indirectly, to

PART III

dispose of or deal with as if it were his own. The Respondent is to be regarded as having such power if a third party holds or controls the asset in accordance with his direct or indirect instructions.

7 This prohibition includes the following assets in particular –

    (a)   the property known as [*title/address*] or the net sale money after payment of any mortgages if it has been sold;

    (b)   the property and assets of the Respondent's business [known as [*name*]] [carried on at [*address*]] or the sale money if any of them have been sold; and

    (c)   any money standing to the credit of any bank account including the amount of any cheque drawn on such account which has not been cleared.

[*For injunction limited to assets in England and Wales*]

8 If the total value free of charges or other securities ('unencumbered value') of the Respondent's assets in England and Wales exceeds £ , the Respondent may remove any of those assets from England and Wales or may dispose of or deal with them so long as the total unencumbered value of his assets still in England and Wales remains above £ .

[*For worldwide injunction*]

8

    (1)   If the total value free of charges or other securities ('unencumbered value') of the Respondent's assets in England and Wales exceeds £ , the Respondent may remove any of those assets from England and Wales or may dispose of or deal with them so long as the total unencumbered value of the Respondent's assets still in England and Wales remains above £ .

    (2)   If the total unencumbered value of the Respondent's assets in England and Wales does not exceed £ , the Respondent must not remove any of those assets from England and Wales and must not dispose of or deal with any of them. If the Respondent has other assets outside England and Wales, he may dispose of or deal with those assets outside England and Wales so long as the total unencumbered value of all his assets whether in or outside England and Wales remains above £ .

Provision of information

9

    (1)   Unless paragraph (2) applies, the Respondent must [immediately] [within hours of service of this order] and to the best of his ability inform the Applicant's solicitors of all his assets [in England and Wales] [worldwide] [exceeding £ in value] whether in his own name or not and whether solely or jointly owned, giving the value, location and details of all such assets.

    (2)   If the provision of any of this information is likely to incriminate the Respondent, he may be entitled to refuse to provide it, but is recommended to take legal advice before refusing to provide the information. Wrongful refusal to provide the information is contempt of court and may render the Respondent liable to be imprisoned, fined or have his assets seized.

10 Within [ ] working days after being served with this order, the Respondent must swear and serve on the Applicant's solicitors an affidavit setting out the above information.

Exceptions to this order

11

(1) This order does not prohibit the Respondent from spending £ a week towards his ordinary living expenses and also £ [or a reasonable sum] on legal advice and representation. [But before spending any money the Respondent must tell the Applicant's legal representatives where the money is to come from.]

[(2) This order does not prohibit the Respondent from dealing with or disposing of any of his assets in the ordinary and proper course of business.]

(3) The Respondent may agree with the Applicant's legal representatives that the above spending limits should be increased or that this order should be varied in any other respect, but any agreement must be in writing.

(4) The order will cease to have effect if the Respondent –
   (a) provides security by paying the sum of £ into court, to be held to the order of the court; or
   (b) makes provision for security in that sum by another method agreed with the Applicant's legal representatives.

Costs

12 The costs of this application are reserved to the judge hearing the application on the return date.

Variation or discharge of this order

13 Anyone served with or notified of this order may apply to the court at any time to vary or discharge this order (or so much of it as affects that person), but they must first inform the Applicant's solicitors. If any evidence is to be relied upon in support of the application, the substance of it must be communicated in writing to the Applicant's solicitors in advance.

Interpretation of this order

14 A Respondent who is an individual who is ordered not to do something must not do it himself or in any other way. He must not do it through others acting on his behalf or on his instructions or with his encouragement.

15 A Respondent which is not an individual which is ordered not to do something must not do it itself or by its directors, officers, partners, employees or agents or in any other way.

Parties other than the applicant and respondent

16 Effect of this order

It is a contempt of court for any person notified of this order knowingly to assist in or permit a breach of this order. Any person doing so may be imprisoned, fined or have their assets seized.

17 Set off by banks

This injunction does not prevent any bank from exercising any right of set off it may have in respect of any facility which it gave to the respondent before it was notified of this order.

PART III

18 Withdrawals by the Respondent

No bank need enquire as to the application or proposed application of any money withdrawn by the Respondent if the withdrawal appears to be permitted by this order.

[For worldwide injunction]

19 Persons outside England and Wales

(1) Except as provided in paragraph (2) below, the terms of this order do not affect or concern anyone outside the jurisdiction of this court.

(2) The terms of this order will affect the following persons in a country or state outside the jurisdiction of this court –

    (a) the Respondent or his officer or agent appointed by power of attorney;

    (b) any person who –

        (i) is subject to the jurisdiction of this court;

        (ii) has been given written notice of this order at his residence or place of business within the jurisdiction of this court; and

        (iii) is able to prevent acts or omissions outside the jurisdiction of this court which constitute or assist in a breach of the terms of this order; and

    (c) any other person, only to the extent that this order is declared enforceable by or is enforced by a court in that country or state.

[For worldwide injunction]

20 Assets located outside England and Wales

Nothing in this order shall, in respect of assets located outside England and Wales, prevent any third party from complying with –

(1) what it reasonably believes to be its obligations, contractual or otherwise, under the laws and obligations of the country or state in which those assets are situated or under the proper law of any contract between itself and the Respondent; and

(2) any orders of the courts of that country or state, provided that reasonable notice of any application for such an order is given to the Applicant's solicitors.

Communications with the court

All communications to the court about this order should be sent to –

[Insert the address and telephone number of the appropriate Court Office]

If the order is made at the Royal Courts of Justice, communications should be addressed as follows –

Where the order is made in the Chancery Division

Room TM 5.07, Royal Courts of Justice, Strand, London WC2A 2LL quoting the case number. The telephone number is 020 7947 6322.

Where the order is made in the Queen's Bench Division

Room WG034, Royal Courts of Justice, Strand, London WC2A 2LL quoting the case number. The telephone number is 0207 947 6009.

Where the order is made in the Commercial Court

Room E201, Royal Courts of Justice, Strand, London WC2A 2LL quoting the case number. The telephone number is 0207 947 6826.

The offices are open between 10 am and 4.30 pm Monday to Friday.

SCHEDULE A

Affidavits

The Applicant relied on the following affidavits –

[name]	[number of affidavit]	[date sworn]	[filed on behalf of]
(1)			
(2)			

SCHEDULE B

Undertakings given to the court by the applicant

(1) If the court later finds that this order has caused loss to the Respondent, and decides that the Respondent should be compensated for that loss, the Applicant will comply with any order the court may make.

[(2) The Applicant will –

    (a) on or before [date] cause a written guarantee in the sum of £ to be issued from a bank with a place of business within England or Wales, in respect of any order the court may make pursuant to paragraph (1) above; and

    (b) immediately upon issue of the guarantee, cause a copy of it to be served on the Respondent.]

(3) As soon as practicable the Applicant will issue and serve a claim form [in the form of the draft produced to the court] [claiming the appropriate relief].

(4) The Applicant will [swear and file an affidavit] [cause an affidavit to be sworn and filed] [substantially in the terms of the draft affidavit produced to the court] [confirming the substance of what was said to the court by the Applicant's counsel/solicitors].

(5) The Applicant will serve upon the Respondent [together with this order] [as soon as practicable] –

    (i) copies of the affidavits and exhibits containing the evidence relied upon by the Applicant, and any other documents provided to the court on the making of the application;

    (ii) the claim form; and

    (iii) an application notice for continuation of the order.

[(6) Anyone notified of this order will be given a copy of it by the Applicant's legal representatives.]

(7) The Applicant will pay the reasonable costs of anyone other than the Respondent which have been incurred as a result of this order including the costs of finding out whether that person holds any of the Respondent's assets and if the court later finds that this order has caused such person loss, and decides that such person should be compensated for that loss, the Applicant will comply with any order the court may make.

(8) If this order ceases to have effect (for example, if the Respondent provides security or the Applicant does not provide a bank guarantee as provided for above) the Applicant will immediately take all reasonable steps to inform in writing anyone to whom he has given notice of this order, or who he has reasonable grounds for supposing may act upon this order, that it has ceased to have effect.

[(9) The Applicant will not without the permission of the court use any information obtained as a result of this order for the purpose of any civil or criminal proceedings, either in England and Wales or in any other jurisdiction, other than this claim.]

[(10) The Applicant will not without the permission of the court seek to enforce this order in any country outside England and Wales [or seek an order of a similar nature including orders conferring a charge or other security against the Respondent or the Respondent's assets].]

Name and address of applicant's legal representatives

The Applicant's legal representatives are –

[*Name, address, reference, fax and telephone numbers both in and out of office hours and e-mail*]

SEARCH ORDER	**IN THE HIGH COURT OF JUSTICE**
	[ ] **DIVISION**
Before The Honourable Mr Justice [	]
	Claim No
	Dated
Applicant	
	Seal
Respondent	

Name, address and reference of respondent

IF YOU [ ]¹ DISOBEY THIS ORDER YOU MAY BE HELD TO BE IN CONTEMPT OF COURT AND MAY BE IMPRISONED, FINED OR HAVE YOUR ASSETS SEIZED.

ANY OTHER PERSON WHO KNOWS OF THIS ORDER AND DOES ANYTHING WHICH HELPS OR PERMITS THE RESPONDENT TO BREACH THE TERMS OF THIS ORDER MAY ALSO BE HELD TO BE IN CONTEMPT OF COURT AND MAY BE IMPRISONED, FINED OR HAVE THEIR ASSETS SEIZED.

1   Insert name of Respondent.

This order

1 This is a Search Order made against [ ] ('the Respondent') on [ ] by Mr Justice [ ] on the application of [ ] ('the Applicant'). The Judge read the Affidavits listed in Schedule F and accepted the undertakings set out in Schedules C, D and E at the end of this order.

2 This order was made at a hearing without notice to the Respondent. The Respondent has a right to apply to the court to vary or discharge the order – see paragraph 27 below.

3 There will be a further hearing in respect of this order on [ ] ('the return date').

4 If there is more than one Respondent –

    (a) unless otherwise stated, references in this order to 'the Respondent' mean both or all of them; and

(b) this order is effective against any Respondent on whom it is served or who is given notice of it.

5 This order must be complied with by –

(a) the Respondent;

(b) any director, officer, partner or responsible employee of the Respondent; and

(c) if the Respondent is an individual, any other person having responsible control of the premises to be searched.

The search

6 The Respondent must permit the following persons[1] –

(a) [ ] ('the Supervising Solicitor');

(b) [ ], a solicitor in the firm of [ ], the Applicant's solicitors; and

(c) up to [ ] other persons[2] being [*their identity or capacity*] accompanying them,

(together 'the search party'), to enter the premises mentioned in Schedule A to this order and any other premises of the Respondent disclosed under paragraph 18 below and any vehicles under the Respondent's control on or around the premises ('the premises') so that they can search for, inspect, photograph or photocopy, and deliver into the safekeeping of the Applicant's solicitors all the documents and articles which are listed in Schedule B to this order ('the listed items').

7 Having permitted the search party to enter the premises, the Respondent must allow the search party to remain on the premises until the search is complete. In the event that it becomes necessary for any of those persons to leave the premises before the search is complete, the Respondent must allow them to re-enter the premises immediately upon their seeking re-entry on the same or the following day in order to complete the search.

1 Where the premises are likely to be occupied by an unaccompanied woman and the Supervising Solicitor is a man, at least one of the persons accompanying him should be a woman.
2 None of these persons should be people who could gain personally or commercially from anything they might read or see on the premises, unless their presence is essential.

Restrictions on search

8 This order may not be carried out at the same time as a police search warrant.

9 Before the Respondent allows anybody onto the premises to carry out this order, he is entitled to have the Supervising Solicitor explain to him what it means in everyday language.

10 The Respondent is entitled to seek legal advice and to ask the court to vary or discharge this order. Whilst doing so, he may ask the Supervising Solicitor to delay starting the search for up to 2 hours or such other longer period as the Supervising Solicitor may permit. However, the Respondent must –

(a) comply with the terms of paragraph 27 below;

(b) not disturb or remove any listed items; and

(c) permit the Supervising Solicitor to enter, but not start to search.

11

(1) Before permitting entry to the premises by any person other than the Supervising Solicitor, the Respondent may, for a short time (not to exceed two hours, unless the Supervising Solicitor agrees to a longer period) –

(a) gather together any documents he believes may be incriminating or privileged; and

(b) hand them to the Supervising Solicitor for him to assess whether they are incriminating or privileged as claimed.

(2)   If the Supervising Solicitor decides that the Respondent is entitled to withhold production of any of the documents on the ground that they are privileged or incriminating, he will exclude them from the search, record them in a list for inclusion in his report and return them to the Respondent.

(3)   If the Supervising Solicitor believes that the Respondent may be entitled to withhold production of the whole or any part of a document on the ground that it or part of it may be privileged or incriminating, or if the Respondent claims to be entitled to withhold production on those grounds, the Supervising Solicitor will exclude it from the search and retain it in his possession pending further order of the court.

12 If the Respondent wishes to take legal advice and gather documents as permitted, he must first inform the Supervising Solicitor and keep him informed of the steps being taken.

13 No item may be removed from the premises until a list of the items to be removed has been prepared, and a copy of the list has been supplied to the Respondent, and he has been given a reasonable opportunity to check the list.

14 The premises must not be searched, and items must not be removed from them, except in the presence of the Respondent.

15 If the Supervising Solicitor is satisfied that full compliance with paragraphs 13 or 14 is not practicable, he may permit the search to proceed and items to be removed without fully complying with them.

Delivery up of articles/documents

16 The Respondent must immediately hand over to the Applicant's solicitors any of the listed items, which are in his possession or under his control, save for any computer or hard disk integral to any computer. Any items the subject of a dispute as to whether they are listed items must immediately be handed over to the Supervising Solicitor for safe keeping pending resolution of the dispute or further order of the court.

17 The Respondent must immediately give the search party effective access to the computers on the premises, with all necessary passwords, to enable the computers to be searched. If they contain any listed items the Respondent must cause the listed items to be displayed so that they can be read and copied.[1] The Respondent must provide the Applicant's Solicitors with copies of all listed items contained in the computers. All reasonable steps shall be taken by the Applicant and the Applicant's solicitors to ensure that no damage is done to any computer or data. The Applicant and his representatives may not themselves search the Respondent's computers unless they have sufficient expertise to do so without damaging the Respondent's system.

1   If it is envisaged that the Respondent's computers are to be imaged (ie the hard drives are to be copied wholesale, thereby reproducing listed items and other items indiscriminately), special provision needs to be made and independent computer specialists need to be appointed, who should be required to give undertakings to the court.

Provision of information

18 The Respondent must immediately inform the Applicant's Solicitors (in the presence of the Supervising Solicitor) so far as he is aware –

(a)   where all the listed items are;

(b)   the name and address of everyone who has supplied him, or offered to supply him, with listed items;

(c)   the name and address of everyone to whom he has supplied, or offered to supply, listed items; and

(d) full details of the dates and quantities of every such supply and offer.

19 Within [ ] working days after being served with this order the Respondent must swear and serve an affidavit setting out the above information[1].

1 The period should ordinarily be longer than the period in paragraph (2) of Schedule D, if any of the information is likely to be included in listed items taken away of which the Respondent does not have copies.

Prohibited acts

20 Except for the purpose of obtaining legal advice, the Respondent must not directly or indirectly inform anyone of these proceedings or of the contents of this order, or warn anyone that proceedings have been or may be brought against him by the Applicant until 4.30 p.m. on the return date or further order of the court.

21 Until 4.30 p.m. on the return date the Respondent must not destroy, tamper with, cancel or part with possession, power, custody or control of the listed items otherwise than in accordance with the terms of this order.

22 [Insert any negative injunctions]

23 [Insert any further order]

Costs

24 The costs of this application are reserved to the judge hearing the application on the return date.

Restrictions on service

25 This order may only be served between [ ] am/pm and [ ] am/pm [and on a weekday][1].

26 This order must be served by the Supervising Solicitor, and paragraph 6 of the order must be carried out in his presence and under his supervision.

1 Normally, the order should be served in the morning (not before 9.30 am) and on a weekday to enable the Respondent more readily to obtain legal advice.

Variation and discharge of this order

27 Anyone served with or notified of this order may apply to the court at any time to vary or discharge this order (or so much of it as affects that person), but they must first inform the Applicant's solicitors. If any evidence is to be relied upon in support of the application, the substance of it must be communicated in writing to the Applicant's solicitors in advance.

Interpretation of this order

28 Any requirement that something shall be done to or in the presence of the Respondent means –

(a) if there is more than one Respondent, to or in the presence of any one of them; and

(b) if a Respondent is not an individual, to or in the presence of a director, officer, partner or responsible employee.

29 A Respondent who is an individual who is ordered not to do something must not do it himself or in any other way. He must not do it through others acting on his behalf or on his instructions or with his encouragement.

30 A Respondent which is not an individual which is ordered not to do something must not do it itself or by its directors, officers, partners, employees or agents or in any other way.

Communications with the court

All communications to the court about this order should be sent to –

[Insert the address and telephone number of the appropriate Court Office]

If the order is made at the Royal Courts of Justice, communications should be addressed as follows –

Where the order is made in the Chancery Division

Room TM 5.07, Royal Courts of Justice, Strand, London WC2A 2LL quoting the case number. The telephone number is 020 7947 6322.

Where the order is made in the Queen's Bench Division

Room WG034, Royal Courts of Justice, Strand, London WC2A 2LL quoting the case number. The telephone number is 0207 947 6009.

Where the order is made in the Commercial Court

Room E201, Royal Courts of Justice, Strand, London WC2A 2LL quoting the case number. The telephone number is 0207 947 6826.

The offices are open between 10 am and 4.30 pm Monday to Friday.

SCHEDULE A

THE PREMISES

SCHEDULE B

THE LISTED ITEMS

SCHEDULE C

Undertakings given to the court by the applicant

(1) If the court later finds that this order or carrying it out has caused loss to the Respondent, and decides that the Respondent should be compensated for that loss, the Applicant will comply with any order the court may make. Further if the carrying out of this order has been in breach of the terms of this order or otherwise in a manner inconsistent with the Applicant's solicitors' duties as officers of the court, the Applicant will comply with any order for damages the court may make.

[(2) As soon as practicable the Applicant will issue a claim form [in the form of the draft produced to the court] [claiming the appropriate relief].]

(3) The Applicant will [swear and file an affidavit] [cause an affidavit to be sworn and filed] [substantially in the terms of the draft affidavit produced to the court] [confirming the substance of what was said to the court by the Applicant's counsel/solicitors].

(4) The Applicant will not, without the permission of the court, use any information or documents obtained as a result of carrying out this order nor inform anyone else of these proceedings except for the purposes of these proceedings (including adding further Respondents) or commencing civil proceedings in relation to the same or related subject matter to these proceedings until after the return date.

[(5) The Applicant will maintain pending further order the sum of £ [ ] in an account controlled by the Applicant's solicitors.]

[(6) The Applicant will insure the items removed from the premises.]

SCHEDULE D

Undertakings given by the applicant's solicitors

(1) The Applicant's solicitors will provide to the Supervising Solicitor for service on the Respondent –

- (i) a service copy of this order;
- (ii) the claim form (with defendant's response pack) or, if not issued, the draft produced to the court;
- (iii) an application for hearing on the return date;
- (iv) copies of the affidavits [*or draft affidavits*] and exhibits capable of being copied containing the evidence relied upon by the applicant;
- (v) a note of any allegation of fact made orally to the court where such allegation is not contained in the affidavits or draft affidavits read by the judge; and
- (vi) a copy of the skeleton argument produced to the court by the Applicant's [counsel/solicitors].

(2) The Applicants' solicitors will answer at once to the best of their ability any question whether a particular item is a listed item.

(3) Subject as provided below the Applicant's solicitors will retain in their own safe keeping all items obtained as a result of this order until the court directs otherwise.

(4) The Applicant's solicitors will return the originals of all documents obtained as a result of this order (except original documents which belong to the Applicant) as soon as possible and in any event within [two] working days of their removal.

SCHEDULE E

Undertakings given by the supervising solicitor

(1) The Supervising Solicitor will use his best endeavours to serve this order upon the Respondent and at the same time to serve upon the Respondent the other documents required to be served and referred to in paragraph (1) of Schedule D.

(2) The Supervising Solicitor will offer to explain to the person served with the order its meaning and effect fairly and in everyday language, and to inform him of his right to take legal advice (including an explanation that the Respondent may be entitled to avail himself of the privilege against self-incrimination and legal professional privilege) and to apply to vary or discharge this order as mentioned in paragraph 27 above.

(3) The Supervising Solicitor will retain in the safe keeping of his firm all items retained by him as a result of this order until the court directs otherwise.

PART III

(4) Unless and until the court otherwise orders, or unless otherwise necessary to comply with any duty to the court pursuant to this order, the Supervising Solicitor shall not disclose to any person any information relating to those items, and shall keep the existence of such items confidential.

(5) Within [48] hours of completion of the search the Supervising Solicitor will make and provide to the Applicant's solicitors, the Respondent or his solicitors and to the judge who made this order (for the purposes of the court file) a written report on the carrying out of the order.

SCHEDULE F

Affidavits

The Applicant relied on the following affidavits –

[*name*]   [*number of affidavit*]   [*date sworn*]   [*filed on behalf of*]

    (1)

    (2)

Name and address of applicant's solicitors

The Applicant's solicitors are –

[Name, address, reference, fax and telephone numbers both in and out of office hours.]
****

PART 31
DISCLOSURE AND INSPECTION OF DOCUMENTS

CONTENTS OF THIS PART

31.1 Scope of this Part

(1) This Part sets out rules about the disclosure and inspection of documents.

(2) This Part applies to all claims except a claim on the small claims track.

Procedure for disclosure under Pt 31—PD31A supplements the rules and explains the steps to be taken on disclosure:

(a) Disclosure is limited to standard disclosure (r 31.5) of certain prescribed documents (r 31.6). Disclosure is predicated upon a duty of "reasonable search" for documents (r 31.7).
(b) Disclosure should be by list (r 31.10) in Form N265 with documents set out in accordance with PD31A, para 3.2. The list contains a disclosure statement (r 31.10(5) and PD31A, paras 4.1–4.4).
(c) The other party has a right to inspect the documents (r 31.3), normally in practice by receiving copies.
(d) If a party believes that documents have not been disclosed then application can be made for "specific disclosure" (r 31.12 and PD31A, para 5).

31.2 Meaning of disclosure

A party discloses a document by stating that the document exists or has existed.

Disclosure defined—Disclosure involves only the act of informing a party that a document exists, not the physical act of producing it for inspection. That is a separate concept provided for by r 31.3.

Disclosure and family proceedings—The term disclosure in CPR 1998 is comparable to the equitable remedy of "discovery". It applies only to documents (defined by CPR 1998, r 31.4, below). In family proceedings there is a wider duty of relevant (or "full and frank") disclosure of information and documents (*Livesey (formerly Jenkins) v Jenkins* [1985] FLR 813, HL). It is a duty owed between the parties and to the court (MCA 1973, s 25). See also discussion under FPR 2010, r 21.1 and *Imerman v Tchenguiz and Others* [2010] 2 FLR 814, especially at [27].

31.3 Right of inspection of a disclosed document

(1) A party to whom a document has been disclosed has a right to inspect that document except where –

(a) the document is no longer in the control of the party who disclosed it;
(b) the party disclosing the document has a right or a duty to withhold inspection of it;
(c) paragraph (2) applies; or
(d) rule 78.26 applies.

(Rule 31.8 sets out when a document is in the control of a party)

(Rule 31.19 sets out the procedure for claiming a right or duty to withhold inspection)

(Rule 78.26 contains rules in relation to the disclosure and inspection of evidence arising out of mediation of certain cross-border disputes.)

(2) Where a party considers that it would be disproportionate to the issues in the case to permit inspection of documents within a category or class of document disclosed under rule 31.6(b) –

(a) he is not required to permit inspection of documents within that category or class; but
(b) he must state in his disclosure statement that inspection of those documents will not be permitted on the grounds that to do so would be disproportionate.

(Rule 31.6 provides for standard disclosure)

(Rule 31.10 makes provision for a disclosure statement)

(Rule 31.12 provides for a party to apply for an order for specific inspection of documents)

Amendments—SI 2011/88.

Duty of disclosure—The duty to disclose only arises where the court orders disclosure (r 31.5), although the parties may themselves arrange disclosure and inspection in accordance with their duty to further the overriding objective (e g see rr 1.1(2)(d) and 1.4(2)(a)). Such disclosure will always be subject to further review by the court. Where a party seeks specific disclosure or inspection of documents, application is made under r 31.12, and when he seeks to rely on public interest immunity, application is made under r 31.19.

"duty to withhold inspection" (r 31.3(1)(b))—This expression refers to public interest immunity, for which see **Application to withhold disclosure or inspection (public interest immunity)** under r 31.19 below.

"a right or a duty to withhold inspection" (r 31.3(1)(b))—This refers to the doctrine of privilege, defined by the glossary as: "the right of a party ... recognised by law"; and (the duty to withhold) to public interest immunity. Privilege therefore consists of the right of a party to proceedings to withhold evidence otherwise relevant to an issue before the court, and can be categorised, for present purposes, as falling into three main categories: (1) legal professional privilege; (2) privilege against self-incrimination; (3) "without prejudice" privilege with its related (a) privilege arising from statements to a conciliator and (b) privilege arising from FDR appointments.

Public interest immunity—See r 31.19 below.

"a party considers that it would be disproportionate to the issues ..." (r 31.3(2))—First, the disclosing party must take a view on whether inspection of particular documents is disproportionate. Rule 31.12(3) enables the party who seeks inspection of the documents to apply for an order for "specific inspection". The court will generally refuse disclosure if to order it would be disproportionate, oppressive for a party required to disclose (see *Hildebrand* below) or it is regarded as irrelevant to the issues before the court.

(1) *Relevance*   The question of whether disclosure should be ordered on grounds of relevance is a broader ground than "proportionality". It has been applied to family proceedings, for example, to refuse disclosure that was regarded by the court as oppressive (*Hildebrand v Hildebrand* [1992] 1 FLR 244) or to refuse inspection of a third party's documents (formerly a production appointment) against a spouse's cohabitant.

(2) *Standard disclosure*   Standard disclosure is defined in rr 31.5 and 31.6. Use of the term "standard" and the setting out of the specific documents referred to in r 31.6 provide for a more restrictive approach to disclosure than the old rules of discovery. If more than standard disclosure is sought, the court will expect a party to go beyond merely establishing the relevance of the documents required. It is likely that the court will need to be satisfied to a higher standard, namely is the request, and compliance with it, proportionate to the issues before the court?

(3) *Proportionality*   At this stage, the party disclosing documents will have in mind the principle of "proportionality" within the terms of r 1.1(2)(c); in particular "the importance of the case", "the complexity of the issues" involved and the cost to the parties (in the context of the case) of disclosure and inspection of the documents concerned.

31.4 Meaning of document

In this Part –

"document" means anything in which information of any description is recorded; and

"copy", in relation to a document, means anything onto which information recorded in the document has been copied, by whatever means and whether directly or indirectly.

Electronic documents: Practice Direction 31B—PD31B (see *Civil Court Service*; Jordan Publishing Ltd) proposes that the term "documents" extends to "Electronic Documents" (para 1). These are defined (para 5(3)) as "any document held in electronic form" including text messages, email and documents stored on any form of memory device – computer drives, memory sticks and mobile telephones. PD31B, para 2 suggests that the purpose of the practice direction is to help the parties to reach agreement on disclosure of electronic documents "in a proportionate and cost-effective manner".

General principles—PD31B, para 6 sets out five general principles where parties "are considering disclosure": these comprise efficient management of data and communication of the data on inspection by which the discloser provides the same facility of access as he enjoys to the party seeking inspection. Disclosure and inspection must be in accordance with the overriding objective (especially as to what is proportionate to the issues involved) and with a firm eye on what is relevant to the issues for trial.

Discussions between the parties and court directions—The parties (and their legal representatives, if any), before the first case-management conference (for which can be read first directions or other appointments in family cases) must discuss: (1) use of technology as an aid to disclosure (PD31B, para 8); and (2) how to arrange disclosure most effectively to illuminate the case and to present electronic documents to the court (para 9). In some cases an electronic documents questionnaire may help (PD31B, para 10 and Sch). If parties cannot reach agreement as to disclosure of electronic documents they can seek directions from the court (para 17) or the court "will give written directions in relation to disclosure or order a separate hearing in relation to disclosure" (para 15). Para 20 et seq reminds parties of the requirement of reasonable search and concludes by embedding disclosure of electronic documents into the framework of standard disclosure within the terms of CPR 1998, Pt 31.

31.5 Disclosure limited to standard disclosure

(1) In all claims to which rule 31.5(2) does not apply –

    (a)   an order to give disclosure is an order to give standard disclosure unless the court directs otherwise;

    (b)   the court may dispense with or limit standard disclosure; and

    (c)   the parties may agree in writing to dispense with or to limit standard disclosure.

(2) Unless the court otherwise orders, paragraphs (3) to (8) apply to all multi-track claims, other than those which include a claim for personal injuries.

(3) Not less than 14 days before the first case management conference each party must file and serve a report verified by a statement of truth, which –

    (a)   describes briefly what documents exist or may exist that are or may be relevant to the matters in issue in the case;

    (b)   describes where and with whom those documents are or may be located;

    (c)   in the case of electronic documents, describes how those documents are stored;

    (d)   estimates the broad range of costs that could be involved in giving standard disclosure in the case, including the costs of searching for and disclosing any electronically stored documents; and

    (e)   states which of the directions under paragraphs (7) or (8) are to be sought.

(4) In cases where the Electronic Documents Questionnaire has been exchanged, the Questionnaire should be filed with the report required by paragraph (3).

(5) Not less than seven days before the first case management conference, and on any other occasion as the court may direct, the parties must, at a meeting or by telephone, discuss and seek to agree a proposal in relation to disclosure that meets the overriding objective.

(6) If –

    (a)   the parties agree proposals for the scope of disclosure; and

    (b)   the court considers that the proposals are appropriate in all the circumstances, the court may approve them without a hearing and give directions in the terms proposed.

(7) At the first or any subsequent case management conference, the court will decide, having regard to the overriding objective and the need to limit disclosure to that which is necessary to deal with the case justly, which of the following orders to make in relation to disclosure –

(a)   an order dispensing with disclosure;
(b)   an order that a party disclose the documents on which it relies, and at the same time request any specific disclosure it requires from any other party;
(c)   an order that directs, where practicable, the disclosure to be given by each party on an issue by issue basis;
(d)   an order that each party disclose any documents which it is reasonable to suppose may contain information which enables that party to advance its own case or to damage that of any other party, or which leads to an enquiry which has either of those consequences;
(e)   an order that a party give standard disclosure;
(f)   any other order in relation to disclosure that the court considers appropriate.

(8) The court may at any point give directions as to how disclosure is to be given, and in particular –
(a)   what searches are to be undertaken, of where, for what, in respect of which time periods and by whom and the extent of any search for electronically stored documents;
(b)   whether lists of documents are required;
(c)   how and when the disclosure statement is to be given;
(d)   in what format documents are to be disclosed (and whether any identification is required);
(e)   what is required in relation to documents that once existed but no longer exist; and
(f)   whether disclosure shall take place in stages.

(9) To the extent that the documents to be disclosed are electronic, the provisions of Practice Direction 31B – Disclosure of Electronic Documents will apply in addition to paragraphs (3) to (8).

Amendments—Substituted by SI 2013/262.

31.6 Standard disclosure – what documents are to be disclosed

Standard disclosure requires a party to disclose only –
(a)   the documents on which he relies; and
(b)   the documents which –
(i)   adversely affect his own case;
(ii)   adversely affect another party's case; or
(iii) support another party's case; and
(c)   the documents which he is required to disclose by a relevant practice direction.

31.7 Duty of search

(1) When giving standard disclosure, a party is required to make a reasonable search for documents falling within rule 31.6(b) or (c).

(2) The factors relevant in deciding the reasonableness of a search include the following –
(a)   the number of documents involved;
(b)   the nature and complexity of the proceedings;
(c)   the ease and expense of retrieval of any particular document; and
(d)   the significance of any document which is likely to be located during the search.

(3) Where a party has not searched for a category or class of document on the grounds that to do so would be unreasonable, he must state this in his disclosure statement and identify the category or class of document.

(Rule 31.10 makes provision for a disclosure statement)

31.8 Duty of disclosure limited to documents which are or have been in party's control

(1) A party's duty to disclose documents is limited to documents which are or have been in his control.

(2) For this purpose a party has or has had a document in his control if –

    (a)   it is or was in his physical possession;

    (b)   he has or has had a right to possession of it; or

    (c)   he has or has had a right to inspect or take copies of it.

"documents ... in his control" (r 31(1) and (2))—This rule restricts disclosure to those documents that are or have been in a party's control and should be read alongside r 31.6, which defines those documents that should be produced.

31.9 Disclosure of copies

(1) A party need not disclose more than one copy of a document.

(2) A copy of a document that contains a modification, obliteration or other marking or feature –

    (a)   on which a party intends to rely; or

    (b)   which adversely affects his own case or another party's case or supports another party's case;

shall be treated as a separate document.

(Rule 31.4 sets out the meaning of a copy of a document)

31.10 Procedure for standard disclosure

(1) The procedure for standard disclosure is as follows.

(2) Each party must make, and serve on every other party, a list of documents in the relevant practice form.

(3) The list must identify the documents in a convenient order and manner and as concisely as possible.

(4) The list must indicate –

    (a)   those documents in respect of which the party claims a right or duty to withhold inspection; and

    (b)   (i)   those documents which are no longer in the party's control; and

          (ii)   what has happened to those documents.

    (Rule 31.19(3) and (4) require a statement in the list of documents relating to any documents inspection of which a person claims he has a right or duty to withhold)

(5) The list must include a disclosure statement.

(6) A disclosure statement is a statement made by the party disclosing the documents –

    (a)   setting out the extent of the search that has been made to locate documents which he is required to disclose;

    (b)   certifying that he understands the duty to disclose documents; and

    (c)   certifying that to the best of his knowledge he has carried out that duty.

PART III

(7) Where the party making the disclosure statement is a company, firm, association or other organisation, the statement must also –

    (a)   identify the person making the statement; and

    (b)   explain why he is considered an appropriate person to make the statement.

(8) The parties may agree in writing –

    (a)   to disclose documents without making a list; and

    (b)   to disclose documents without the disclosing party making a disclosure statement.

(9) A disclosure statement may be made by a person who is not a party where this is permitted by a relevant practice direction.

Scope—Each party must prepare and serve on other parties (but not file at court) a list in the prescribed form, indicating which documents he has and which he claims the right or duty not to disclose. If necessary, the reasons why documents are no longer in a party's control must be explained. The list must have a signed disclosure statement. Parties may agree to disclose without making a list.

"a list of documents in the relevant practice form" (r 31.10(2))—The relevant form is PF N265.

"right or duty to withhold inspection" (r 31.10(4)(a))—See commentary on this subject under rr 31.3 and 31.19. If a party wishes to claim the right to withhold he must set out the grounds for so doing (*PD (Disclosure and Inspection)*, para 4.5).

"disclosure statement" (r 31.10(5)–(7))—A disclosure statement which complies with r 31.10(6) and (7) is set out in the Annex to PD31) and certain other requirements are set out in paras 4.2–4.6 of the PD.

31.11 Duty of disclosure continues during proceedings

(1) Any duty of disclosure continues until the proceedings are concluded.

(2) If documents to which that duty extends come to a party's notice at any time during the proceedings, he must immediately notify every other party.

"until the proceedings are concluded" (r 31.11(1))—The reference to the conclusion of proceedings includes until the final hearing of any appeal (*Vernon v Bosley (No 2)* [1998] 1 FLR 304). Where documents within the terms of this rule come to light a supplemental list must be prepared (PD31, para 3.3) unless such a list can be dispensed with under r 31.10(8).

31.12 Specific disclosure or inspection

(1) The court may make an order for specific disclosure or specific inspection.

(2) An order for specific disclosure is an order that a party must do one or more of the following things –

    (a)   disclose documents or classes of documents specified in the order;

    (b)   carry out a search to the extent stated in the order;

    (c)   disclose any documents located as a result of that search.

(3) An order for specific inspection is an order that a party permit inspection of a document referred to in rule 31.3(2).

        (Rule 31.3(2) allows a party to state in his disclosure statement that he will not permit inspection of a document on the grounds that it would be disproportionate to do so)

        (Rule 78.26 contains rules in relation to the disclosure and inspection of evidence arising out of mediation of certain cross-border disputes.)

Amendments—SI 2011/88.

Application for specific disclosure or inspection—An application for an order for specific disclosure/inspection is made in accordance with Pt 23. The application should state the order applied for (r 23.6(a) – ie one or more of the orders set out in r 31.12(2) and (3)) and must be supported by a statement of evidence (and see *PD (Applications)*, para 9.1, which reminds parties that "the court will often need to be satisfied by evidence of the facts that are relied on in support of or for opposing the application"). Grounds for the application may be in the application notice but a statement of evidence should also be filed setting out which documents are sought and why (PD31, para 5.3). In particular, an application for specific inspection will need to deal with the respondent's assertion that inspection is "disproportionate to the issues" (r 31.3(2)).

Proportionality and relevance—All orders for disclosure are governed by the overriding objective in Pt 1 (PD31, para 5.4). The court should bear in mind the need for "saving expense" (r 1.1(2)(b)) and that orders for disclosure or inspection should be proportionate "to the complexity of the issues" in the case (r 1.1(2)(c)(iii)). The court has a discretion as to whether to order disclosure and it retains its equitable jurisdiction to refuse disclosure, akin to its jurisdiction to refuse discovery or inspection on the ground that to order it would be oppressive (*Imerman v Tchenguiz and Others* [2010] 2 FLR 814).

31.13 Disclosure in stages

The parties may agree in writing, or the court may direct, that disclosure or inspection or both shall take place in stages.

31.14 Documents referred to in statements of case etc

(1) A party may inspect a document mentioned in –

- (a)   a statement of case;
- (b)   a witness statement;
- (c)   a witness summary; or
- (d)   an affidavit$^{(GL)}$.
- (e)   (*revoked*)

(2) Subject to rule 35.10(4), a party may apply for an order for inspection of any document mentioned in an expert's report which has not already been disclosed in the proceedings.

> (Rule 35.10(4) makes provision in relation to instructions referred to in an expert's report)

Amendments—SI 2001/4015.

31.15 Inspection and copying of documents

Where a party has a right to inspect a document –

- (a)   that party must give the party who disclosed the document written notice of his wish to inspect it;
- (b)   the party who disclosed the document must permit inspection not more than 7 days after the date on which he received the notice; and
- (c)   that party may request a copy of the document and, if he also undertakes to pay reasonable copying costs, the party who disclosed the document must supply him with a copy not more than 7 days after the date on which he received the request.

> (Rule 31.3 and 31.14 deal with the right of a party to inspect a document)

****

31.19 Claim to withhold inspection or disclosure of a document

(1) A person may apply, without notice, for an order permitting him to withhold disclosure of a document on the ground that disclosure would damage the public interest.

(2) Unless the court orders otherwise, an order of the court under paragraph (1) –

- (a)   must not be served on any other person; and
- (b)   must not be open to inspection by any person.

(3) A person who wishes to claim that he has a right or a duty to withhold inspection of a document, or part of a document must state in writing –

    (a)   that he has such a right or duty; and

    (b)   the grounds on which he claims that right or duty.

(4) The statement referred to in paragraph (3) must be made –

    (a)   in the list in which the document is disclosed; or

    (b)   if there is no list, to the person wishing to inspect the document.

(5) A party may apply to the court to decide whether a claim made under paragraph (3) should be upheld.

(6) For the purpose of deciding an application under paragraph (1) (application to withhold disclosure) or paragraph (3) (claim to withhold inspection) the court may –

    (a)   require the person seeking to withhold disclosure or inspection of a document to produce that document to the court; and

    (b)   invite any person, whether or not a party, to make representations.

(7) An application under paragraph (1) or paragraph (5) must be supported by evidence.

(8) This Part does not affect any rule of law which permits or requires a document to be withheld from disclosure or inspection on the ground that its disclosure or inspection would damage the public interest.

31.20 Restriction on use of a privileged document inspection of which has been inadvertently allowed

Where a party inadvertently allows a privileged(GL) document to be inspected, the party who has inspected the document may use it or its contents only with the permission of the court.

31.21 Consequence of failure to disclose documents or permit inspection

A party may not rely on any document which he fails to disclose or in respect of which he fails to permit inspection unless the court gives permission.

31.22 Subsequent use of disclosed documents and completed Electronic Documents Questionnaires

(1) A party to whom a document has been disclosed may use the document only for the purpose of the proceedings in which it is disclosed, except where –

    (a)   the document has been read to or by the court, or referred to, at a hearing which has been held in public;

    (b)   the court gives permission; or

    (c)   the party who disclosed the document and the person to whom the document belongs agree.

(2) The court may make an order restricting or prohibiting the use of a document which has been disclosed, even where the document has been read to or by the court, or referred to, at a hearing which has been held in public.

(3) An application for such an order may be made –

    (a)   by a party; or

    (b)   by any person to whom the document belongs.

(4) For the purpose of this rule, an Electronic Documents Questionnaire which has been completed and served by another party pursuant to Practice Direction 31B is to be treated as if it is a document which has been disclosed.

Amendments—SI 2010/1953.

Restriction on use of disclosed documents—Rule 31.22 is the CPR 1998 replacement of the former "implied undertaking" as to the further production of documents that had been disclosed (discovered) in civil proceedings, as applied in family proceedings by *Clibbery v Allan* [2002] 1 FLR 565. It has no equivalent in family proceedings, although its effect (r 31.22(1)(b)) has been applied in the case of release of disclosed documents to HMRC in *HMRC v Charman and Charman* [2012] 2 FLR 1119.

31.23 False disclosure statements

(1) Proceedings for contempt of court may be brought against a person if he makes, or causes to be made, a false disclosure statement, without an honest belief in its truth.

...

(Section 6 of Part 81 contains provisions in relation to committal for making a false disclosure statement.)

Amendments—Inserted by SI 2000/221; amended by SI 2012/2208.

Practice Direction 31A –
Disclosure and Inspection

This Practice Direction supplements CPR Part 31

General

1.1 The normal order for disclosure will be an order that the parties give standard disclosure.

1.2 In order to give standard disclosure the disclosing party must make a reasonable search for documents falling within the paragraphs of rule 31.6.

1.3 Having made the search the disclosing party must (unless rule 31.10(8) applies) make a list of the documents of whose existence the party is aware that fall within those paragraphs and which are or have been in the party's control (see rule 31.8).

1.4 The obligations imposed by an order for standard disclosure may be dispensed with or limited either by the court or by written agreement between the parties. Any such written agreement should be lodged with the court.

The search

2 The extent of the search which must be made will depend upon the circumstances of the case including, in particular, the factors referred to in rule 31.7(2). The parties should bear in mind the overriding principle of proportionality (see rule 1.1(2)(c)). It may, for example, be reasonable to decide not to search for documents coming into existence before some particular date, or to limit the search to documents in some particular place or places, or to documents falling into particular categories.

Electronic disclosure

2A.1 Rule 31.4 contains a broad definition of a document. This extends to electronic documents, including e-mail and other electronic communications, word processed documents and databases. In addition to documents that are readily accessible from computer systems and other electronic devices and media, the definition covers those documents that are stored on servers and back-up systems and electronic documents that have been 'deleted'. It also extends to additional information stored and associated with electronic documents known as metadata.

2A.2 Practice Direction 31B contains additional provisions in relation to the disclosure of electronic documents in cases that are likely to be allocated to the multi-track.

The list

3.1 The list should be in Form N265.

3.2 In order to comply with rule 31.10(3) it will normally be necessary to list the documents in date order, to number them consecutively and to give each a concise description (eg letter, claimant to defendant). Where there is a large number of documents all falling into a particular category the disclosing party may list those documents as a category rather than individually eg 50 bank statements relating to account number   at   Bank,   20 to   20 ; or, 35 letters passing between   and   between   20 and   20 .

3.3 The obligations imposed by an order for disclosure will continue until the proceedings come to an end. If, after a list of documents has been prepared and served, the existence of further documents to which the order applies comes to the attention of the disclosing party, the party must prepare and serve a supplemental list.

Disclosure statement

4.1 A list of documents must (unless rule 31.10(8)(b) applies) contain a disclosure statement complying with rule 31.10. The form of disclosure statement is set out in Annex A to this practice direction.

4.2 The disclosure statement should:

    (1)   expressly state that the disclosing party believes the extent of the search to have been reasonable in all the circumstances, and

    (2)   in setting out the extent of the search (see rule 31.10(6)) draw attention to any particular limitations on the extent of the search which were adopted for proportionality reasons and give the reasons why the limitations were adopted, eg the difficulty or expense that a search not subject to those limitations would have entailed or the marginal relevance of categories of documents omitted from the search.

4.3 Where rule 31.10(7) applies, the details given in the disclosure statement about the person making the statement must include his name and address and the office or position he holds in the disclosing party or the basis upon which he makes the statement on behalf of the party.

4.4 If the disclosing party has a legal representative acting for him, the legal representative must endeavour to ensure that the person making the disclosure statement (whether the disclosing party or, in a case to which rule 31.10(7) applies, some other person) understands the duty of disclosure under Part 31.

4.5 If the disclosing party wishes to claim that he has a right or duty to withhold a document, or part of a document, in his list of documents from inspection (see rule 31.19(3)), he must state in writing:

(1) that he has such a right or duty, and

(2) the grounds on which he claims that right or duty.

4.6 The statement referred to in paragraph 4.5 above should normally be included in the disclosure statement and must identify the document, or part of a document, to which the claim relates.

4.7 An insurer or the Motor Insurers' Bureau may sign a disclosure statement on behalf of party where the insurer or the Motor Insurers' Bureau has a financial interest in the result of proceedings brought wholly or partially by or against that party. Rule 31.10(7) and paragraph 4.3 above shall apply to the insurer or the Motor Insurers' Bureau making such a statement.

Specific disclosure

5.1 If a party believes that the disclosure of documents given by a disclosing party is inadequate he may make an application for an order for specific disclosure (see rule 31.12).

5.2 The application notice must specify the order that the applicant intends to ask the court to make and must be supported by evidence (see rule 31.12(2) which describes the orders the court may make).

5.3 The grounds on which the order is sought may be set out in the application notice itself but if not there set out must be set out in evidence filed in support of the application.

5.4 In deciding whether or not to make an order for specific disclosure the court will take into account all the circumstances of the case and, in particular, the overriding objective described in Part 1. But if the court concludes that the party from whom specific disclosure is sought has failed adequately to comply with the obligations imposed by an order for disclosure (whether by failing to make a sufficient search for documents or otherwise) the court will usually make such order as is necessary to ensure that those obligations are properly complied with.

5.5 An order for specific disclosure may in an appropriate case direct a party to –

(1) carry out a search for any documents which it is reasonable to suppose may contain information which may –

(a) enable the party applying for disclosure either to advance his own case or to damage that of the party giving disclosure; or

(b) lead to a train of enquiry which has either of those consequences; and

(2) disclose any documents found as a result of that search.

Claims to withhold disclosure or inspection of a document

6.1 A claim to withhold inspection of a document, or part of a document, disclosed in a list of documents does not require an application to the court. Where such a claim has been made, a party who wishes to challenge it must apply to the court (see rule 31.19(5)).

6.2 Rule 31.19(1) and (6) provide a procedure enabling a party to apply for an order permitting disclosure of the existence of a document to be withheld.

Inspection of documents mentioned in expert's report (Rule 31.14(2))

7.1 If a party wishes to inspect documents referred to in the expert report of another party, before issuing an application he should request inspection of the document informally, and inspection should be provided by agreement unless the request is unreasonable.

7.2 Where an expert report refers to a large number or volume of documents and it would be burdensome to copy or collate them, the court will only order inspection of such documents if it is satisfied that it is necessary for the just disposal of the proceedings and the party cannot reasonably obtain the documents from another source.

False disclosure statement

8 Attention is drawn to rule 31.23 which sets out the consequences of making a false disclosure statement without an honest belief in its truth, and to the procedures set out in rule 81.18 and paragraphs 5.1 to 5.7 of Practice Direction 81 – Applications and proceedings in relation to contempt of court.

ANNEX A

Disclosure statement

I, the above named claimant [or defendant] [if party making disclosure is a company, firm or other organisation identify here who the person making the disclosure statement is and why he is the appropriate person to make it] state that I have carried out a reasonable and proportionate search to locate all the documents which I am required to disclose under the order made by the court on   day of   . I did not search:

    (1)   for documents predating ....,

    (2)   for documents located elsewhere than ....,

    (3)   for documents in categories other than ....,

    (4)   for electronic documents

I carried out a search for electronic documents contained on or created by the following:

[list what was searched and extent of search]

I did not search for the following:

    (1)   documents created before ... ...,

    (2)   documents contained on or created by the Claimant's/Defendant's PCs/portable data storage media/databases/servers/back-up tapes/off-site storage/mobile phones/laptops/notebooks/handheld devices/PDA devices (delete as appropriate),

    (3)   documents contained on or created by the Claimant's/Defendant's mail files/document files/calendar files/spreadsheet files/graphic and presentation files/web-based applications (delete as appropriate),

    (4)   documents other than by reference to the following keyword(s)/concepts ... ... (delete if your search was not confined to specific keywords or concepts).

I certify that I understand the duty of disclosure and to the best of my knowledge I have carried out that duty. I certify that the list above is a complete list of all documents which are or have been in my control and which I am obliged under the said order to disclose.

Practice Direction 31B –
Disclosure of Electronic Documents

This Practice Direction supplements CPR Part 31

Note—CPR PD31B is set out in *Civil Court Service* (Jordan Publishing Ltd).

PART 32
EVIDENCE

CONTENTS OF THIS PART

Note—Only CPR 1998, rr 32.1–32.4, 32.18 and 32.19 have been reproduced here. Almost all of the remaining rules are replicated in FPR 2010, Pt 22. For detailed commentary specifically on civil proceedings, see *Civil Court Service* (Jordan Publishing Ltd).

32.1 Power of court to control evidence

(1) The court may control the evidence by giving directions as to –

    (a)   the issues on which it requires evidence;

    (b)   the nature of the evidence which it requires to decide those issues; and

    (c)   the way in which the evidence is to be placed before the court.

(2) The court may use its power under this rule to exclude evidence that would otherwise be admissible.

(3) The court may limit cross-examination$^{(GL)}$.

"The court may control the evidence" (r 32.1(1))—This is a helpful description of the powers derived from the overriding objective.

Evidence from third parties—It remains to be seen whether the courts will use powers akin to those assumed by the High Court in *Khanna v Lovell White Durrant (A Firm)* [1995] 1 WLR 121 to require a third party to produce documents in advance of a final hearing.

Bankers' Book Evidence Act 1879—This (or the *Khanna* hearing) is the appropriate procedure to adopt for production of entries in bankers' books. Privilege may be claimed by a third party (*Waterhouse v Barker* [1924] 2 KB 759), but a bank does not breach confidentiality to its customer if it produces his bank statements when ordered so to do (*Robertson v Canadian Imperial Bank of Commerce* [1994] 1 WLR 1493, PC).

32.2 Evidence of witnesses – general rule

(1) The general rule is that any fact which needs to be proved by the evidence of witnesses is to be proved –

    (a)   at trial, by their oral evidence given in public; and

    (b)   at any other hearing, by their evidence in writing.

(2) This is subject –

    (a)   to any provision to the contrary contained in these Rules or elsewhere; or

    (b)   to any order of the court.

(3) The court may give directions –

    (a)   identifying or limiting the issues to which factual evidence may be directed;

    (b)   identifying the witnesses who may be called or whose evidence may be read; or

    (c)   limiting the length or format of witness statements.

Amendments—SI 2013/262.

Scope—This rule stresses the importance of proving the case by oral evidence in open court at trial and see ECHR 1950, Art 6(1) entitlement to a "fair and public hearing". This "general rule" may be displaced by court order. At other hearings (e g under Pt 23), the general rule is that evidence should be in writing (and see r 32.6 below).

32.3 Evidence by video link or other means

The court may allow a witness to give evidence through a video link or by other means.

Video link and the overriding objective—This rule is consistent with the overriding objective; see r 1.4(2)(k), which provides that case management includes "making use of technology" and r 3.1(2)(d) which enables the court to "receive evidence by telephone or by using any other method of direct oral communication".

32.4 Requirement to serve witness statements for use at trial

(1) A witness statement is a written statement signed by a person which contains the evidence which that person would be allowed to give orally.

(2) The court will order a party to serve on the other parties any witness statement of the oral evidence which the party serving the statement intends to rely on in relation to any issues of fact to be decided at the trial.

(3) The court may give directions as to –

    (a)   the order in which witness statements are to be served; and

    (b)   whether or not the witness statements are to be filed.

Witness statements—Witness statements, as stipulated by r 32.8, must comply with the requirements of *PD (Written Evidence)*, paras 17.1–22.2. Hearsay evidence in witness statements is dealt with in r 33.2.

****

32.18 Notice to admit facts

(1) A party may serve notice on another party requiring him to admit the facts, or the part of the case of the serving party, specified in the notice.

(2) A notice to admit facts must be served no later than 21 days before the trial.

(3) Where the other party makes any admission in response to the notice the admission may be used against him only –

    (a)   in the proceedings in which the notice to admit is served; and

    (b)   by the party who served the notice.

(4) The court may allow a party to amend or withdraw any admission made by him on such terms as it thinks just.

"notice ... to admit the facts ... specified" (r 32.18))—Rule 32.18 enables a party to give notice to another to admit facts. Any admission can only be used in the proceedings to which it relates and it can only cause an estoppel if findings are made on the admission to question.

32.19 Notice to admit or produce documents

(1) A party shall be deemed to admit the authenticity of a document disclosed to him under Part 31 (disclosure and inspection of documents) unless he serves notice that he wishes the document to be proved at trial.

(2) A notice to prove a document must be served –

    (a) by the latest date for serving witness statements; or

    (b) within 7 days of disclosure of the document,

whichever is later.

Notice to prove a document (r 32.19(2))—The heading to this rule is misleading, since the rule provides for a presumption that a party admits that any disclosed document is authentic unless notice is given for the document to be produced at trial within the time limits set out in r 32.19(2).

****

Practice Direction 32 – Evidence

This Practice Direction supplements CPR Part 32

Evidence in general

1.1 Rule 32.2 sets out how evidence is to be given and facts are to be proved.

1.2 Evidence at a hearing other than the trial should normally be given by witness statement[1] (see paragraph 17 onwards). However a witness may give evidence by affidavit if he wishes to do so[2] (and see paragraph 1.4 below).

1   See rule 32.6(1).
2   See rule 32.15(2).

1.3 Statements of case (see paragraph 26 onwards) and application notices[1] may also be used as evidence provided that their contents have been verified by a statement of truth[2].

    (For information regarding evidence by deposition see Part 34 and Practice Direction 34A.)

1   See Part 23 for information about making an application.
2   Rule 32.6(2) and see Part 22 for information about the statement of truth.

1.4 Affidavits must be used as evidence in the following instances:

    (1) where sworn evidence is required by an enactment[1], rule, order or practice direction, and

    (2) in any application for a search order, a freezing injunction, or an order requiring an occupier to permit another to enter his land.

    (Part 81 – Applications and proceedings in relation to contempt of court, and the Practice Direction accompanying that Part, contain provisions about evidence in relation to contempt of court. Particular attention is drawn to rules 81.10, 81.11, 81.14, 81.15, 81.26 and Practice Direction 81 paragraphs 4.5 and 14.1.).

1   See, eg, s 3(5)(a) of the Protection from Harassment Act 1997.

1.5 If a party believes that sworn evidence is required by a court in another jurisdiction for any purpose connected with the proceedings, he may apply to the court for a direction that evidence shall be given only by affidavit on any pre-trial applications.

1.6 The court may give a direction under rule 32.15 that evidence shall be given by affidavit instead of or in addition to a witness statement or statement of case:

    (1) on its own initiative, or

    (2) after any party has applied to the court for such a direction.

1.7 An affidavit, where referred to in the Civil Procedure Rules or a practice direction, also means an affirmation unless the context requires otherwise.

AFFIDAVITS

Deponent

2 A deponent is a person who gives evidence by affidavit or affirmation.

Heading

3.1 The affidavit should be headed with the title of the proceedings (see paragraph 4 of Practice Direction 7A and paragraph 7 of Practice Direction 20); where the proceedings are between several parties with the same status it is sufficient to identify the parties as follows:

	Number:
AB (and others)	Claimants/Applicants
CD (and others)	Defendants/Respondents
	(as appropriate)

3.2 At the top right hand corner of the first page (and on the backsheet) there should be clearly written:

    (1) the party on whose behalf it is made,

    (2) the initials and surname of the deponent,

    (3) the number of the affidavit in relation to that deponent,

    (4) the identifying initials and number of each exhibit referred to, and

    (5) the date sworn.

Body of affidavit

4.1 The affidavit must, if practicable, be in the deponent's own words, the affidavit should be expressed in the first person and the deponent should:

    (1) commence 'I (*full name*) of (*address*) state on oath   ',

    (2) if giving evidence in his professional, business or other occupational capacity, give the address at which he works in (1) above, the position he holds and the name of his firm or employer,

    (3) give his occupation or, if he has none, his description, and

    (4) state if he is a party to the proceedings or employed by a party to the proceedings, if it be the case.

4.2 An affidavit must indicate:

    (1) which of the statements in it are made from the deponent's own knowledge and which are matters of information or belief, and

    (2) the source for any matters of information or belief.

4.3 Where a deponent:

    (1) refers to an exhibit or exhibits, he should state 'there is now shown to me marked "   " the (*description of exhibit*),' and

(2) makes more than one affidavit (to which there are exhibits) in the same proceedings, the numbering of the exhibits should run consecutively throughout and not start again with each affidavit.

Jurat

5.1 The jurat of an affidavit is a statement set out at the end of the document which authenticates the affidavit.

5.2 It must:

(1) be signed by all deponents,

(2) be completed and signed by the person before whom the affidavit was sworn whose name and qualification must be printed beneath his signature,

(3) contain the full address of the person before whom the affidavit was sworn, and

(4) follow immediately on from the text and not be put on a separate page.

Format of affidavits

6.1 An affidavit should:

(1) be produced on durable quality A4 paper with a 3.5 cm margin,

(2) be fully legible and should normally be typed on one side of the paper only,

(3) where possible, be bound securely in a manner which would not hamper filing, or otherwise each page should be endorsed with the case number and should bear the initials of the deponent and of the person before whom it was sworn,

(4) have the pages numbered consecutively as a separate document (or as one of several documents contained in a file),

(5) be divided into numbered paragraphs,

(6) have all numbers, including dates, expressed in figures, and

(7) give the reference to any document or documents mentioned either in the margin or in bold text in the body of the affidavit.

6.2 It is usually convenient for an affidavit to follow the chronological sequence of events or matters dealt with; each paragraph of an affidavit should as far as possible be confined to a distinct portion of the subject.

Inability of deponent to read or sign affidavit

7.1 Where an affidavit is sworn by a person who is unable to read or sign it, the person before whom the affidavit is sworn must certify in the jurat that:

(1) he read the affidavit to the deponent,

(2) the deponent appeared to understand it, and

(3) the deponent signed or made his mark, in his presence.

7.2 If that certificate is not included in the jurat, the affidavit may not be used in evidence unless the court is satisfied that it was read to the deponent and that he appeared to understand it. Two versions of the form of jurat with the certificate are set out at Annex 1 to this practice direction.

Alterations to affidavits

8.1 Any alteration to an affidavit must be initialled by both the deponent and the person before whom the affidavit was sworn.

8.2 An affidavit which contains an alteration that has not been initialled may be filed or used in evidence only with the permission of the court.

Who may administer oaths and take affidavits

9.1 Only the following may administer oaths and take affidavits –

    (1)   a commissioner for oaths[1];

    (2)   *(revoked)*

    (3)   other persons specified by Statute[2];

    (4)   certain officials of the Senior Courts[3];

    (5)   a circuit judge or district judge[4];

    (6)   any justice of the peace[5]; and

    (7)   certain officials of any county court appointed by the judge of that court for the purpose[6].

1   Commissioners for Oaths Acts 1889 and 1891.
2   Sections 12 and 18 of, and Schedules 2 and 4 to, the Legal Services Act 2007.
3   Section 2 of the Commissioners for Oaths Act 1889.
4   Section 58 of the County Courts Act 1984.
5   Section 58 as above.
6   Section 58 as above.

9.2 An affidavit must be sworn before a person independent of the parties or their representatives.

Filing of affidavits

10.1 If the court directs that an affidavit is to be filed[1], it must be filed in the court or Division, or Office or Registry of the court or Division where the action in which it was or is to be used, is proceeding or will proceed.

1   Rules 32.1(3) and 32.4(3)(b).

10.2 Where an affidavit is in a foreign language:

    (1)   the party wishing to rely on it –
        (a)   must have it translated, and
        (b)   must file the foreign language affidavit with the court, and

    (2)   the translator must make and file with the court an affidavit verifying the translation and exhibiting both the translation and a copy of the foreign language affidavit.

EXHIBITS

Manner of exhibiting documents

11.1 A document used in conjunction with an affidavit should be:

    (1)   produced to and verified by the deponent, and remain separate from the affidavit, and

    (2)   identified by a declaration of the person before whom the affidavit was sworn.

11.2 The declaration should be headed with the name of the proceedings in the same way as the affidavit.

11.3 The first page of each exhibit should be marked:

    (1)   as in paragraph 3.2 above, and

    (2)   with the exhibit mark referred to in the affidavit.

Letters

12.1 Copies of individual letters should be collected together and exhibited in a bundle or bundles. They should be arranged in chronological order with the earliest at the top, and firmly secured.

12.2 When a bundle of correspondence is exhibited, the exhibit should have a front page attached stating that the bundle consists of original letters and copies. They should be arranged and secured as above and numbered consecutively.

Other documents

13.1 Photocopies instead of original documents may be exhibited provided the originals are made available for inspection by the other parties before the hearing and by the judge at the hearing.

13.2 Court documents must not be exhibited (official copies of such documents prove themselves).

13.3 Where an exhibit contains more than one document, a front page should be attached setting out a list of the documents contained in the exhibit; the list should contain the dates of the documents.

Exhibits other than documents

14.1 Items other than documents should be clearly marked with an exhibit number or letter in such a manner that the mark cannot become detached from the exhibit.

14.2 Small items may be placed in a container and the container appropriately marked.

General provisions

15.1 Where an exhibit contains more than one document:

   (1)   the bundle should not be stapled but should be securely fastened in a way that does not hinder the reading of the documents, and

   (2)   the pages should be numbered consecutively at bottom centre.

15.2 Every page of an exhibit should be clearly legible; typed copies of illegible documents should be included, paginated with 'a' numbers.

15.3 Where affidavits and exhibits have become numerous, they should be put into separate bundles and the pages numbered consecutively throughout.

15.4 Where on account of their bulk the service of exhibits or copies of exhibits on the other parties would be difficult or impracticable, the directions of the court should be sought as to arrangements for bringing the exhibits to the attention of the other parties and as to their custody pending trial.

Affirmations

16 All provisions in this or any other practice direction relating to affidavits apply to affirmations with the following exceptions:

   (1)   the deponent should commence 'I (*name*) of (*address*) do solemnly and sincerely affirm   ', and

   (2)   in the jurat the word 'sworn' is replaced by the word 'affirmed'.

WITNESS STATEMENTS

Heading

17.1 The witness statement should be headed with the title of the proceedings (see paragraph 4 of Practice Direction 7A and paragraph 7 of Practice Direction 20); where the proceedings are between several parties with the same status it is sufficient to identify the parties as follows:

	Number:
AB (and others)	Claimants/Applicants
CD (and others)	Defendants/Respondents
	(as appropriate)

17.2 At the top right hand corner of the first page there should be clearly written:

(1)   the party on whose behalf it is made,
(2)   the initials and surname of the witness,
(3)   the number of the statement in relation to that witness,
(4)   the identifying initials and number of each exhibit referred to, and
(5)   the date the statement was made.

Body of witness statement

18.1 The witness statement must, if practicable, be in the intended witness's own words, the statement should be expressed in the first person and should also state:

(1)   the full name of the witness,
(2)   his place of residence or, if he is making the statement in his professional, business or other occupational capacity, the address at which he works, the position he holds and the name of his firm or employer,
(3)   his occupation, or if he has none, his description, and
(4)   the fact that he is a party to the proceedings or is the employee of such a party if it be the case.

18.2 A witness statement must indicate:

(1)   which of the statements in it are made from the witness's own knowledge and which are matters of information or belief, and
(2)   the source for any matters of information or belief.

18.3 An exhibit used in conjunction with a witness statement should be verified and identified by the witness and remain separate from the witness statement.

18.4 Where a witness refers to an exhibit or exhibits, he should state 'I refer to the (*description of exhibit*) marked "   "'.

18.5 The provisions of paragraphs 11.3 to 15.4 (exhibits) apply similarly to witness statements as they do to affidavits.

18.6 Where a witness makes more than one witness statement to which there are exhibits, in the same proceedings, the numbering of the exhibits should run consecutively throughout and not start again with each witness statement.

Format of witness statement

19.1 A witness statement should:

(1)   be produced on durable quality A4 paper with a 3.5 cm margin,
(2)   be fully legible and should normally be typed on one side of the paper only,

(3) where possible, be bound securely in a manner which would not hamper filing, or otherwise each page should be endorsed with the case number and should bear the initials of the witness,

(4) have the pages numbered consecutively as a separate statement (or as one of several statements contained in a file),

(5) be divided into numbered paragraphs,

(6) have all numbers, including dates, expressed in figures, and

(7) give the reference to any document or documents mentioned either in the margin or in bold text in the body of the statement.

19.2 It is usually convenient for a witness statement to follow the chronological sequence of the events or matters dealt with, each paragraph of a witness statement should as far as possible be confined to a distinct portion of the subject.

Statement of truth

20.1 A witness statement is the equivalent of the oral evidence which that witness would, if called, give in evidence; it must include a statement by the intended witness that he believes the facts in it are true[1].

1   See Part 22 for information about the statement of truth.

20.2 To verify a witness statement the statement of truth is as follows:

'I believe that the facts stated in this witness statement are true'

20.3 Attention is drawn to rule 32.14 which sets out the consequences of verifying a witness statement containing a false statement without an honest belief in its truth.

(Paragraph 3A of Practice Direction 22 sets out the procedure to be followed where the person who should sign a document which is verified by a statement of truth is unable to read or sign the document.)

Alterations to witness statements

22.1 Any alteration to a witness statement must be initialled by the person making the statement or by the authorised person where appropriate (see paragraph 21).

22.2 A witness statement which contains an alteration that has not been initialled may be used in evidence only with the permission of the court.

Filing of witness statements

23.1 If the court directs that a witness statement is to be filed[1], it must be filed in the court or Division, or Office or Registry of the court or Division where the action in which it was or is to be used, is proceeding or will proceed.

1   Rule 32.4(3)(b).

23.2 Where the court has directed that a witness statement in a foreign language is to be filed:

(1) the party wishing to rely on it must –
  (a) have it translated, and
  (b) file the foreign language witness statement with the court, and

(2) the translator must make and file with the court an affidavit verifying the translation and exhibiting both the translation and a copy of the foreign language witness statement.

Certificate of court officer

24.1 Where the court has ordered that a witness statement is not to be open to inspection by the public[1] or that words or passages in the statement are not to be open to inspection[2] the court officer will so certify on the statement and make any deletions directed by the court under rule 32.13(4).

1   Rule 32.13(2).
2   Rule 32.13(4).

Defects in affidavits, witness statements and exhibits

25.1 Where:

  (1)   an affidavit,
  (2)   a witness statement, or
  (3)   an exhibit to either an affidavit or a witness statement,

does not comply with Part 32 or this practice direction in relation to its form, the court may refuse to admit it as evidence and may refuse to allow the costs arising from its preparation.

25.2 Permission to file a defective affidavit or witness statement or to use a defective exhibit may be obtained from a judge[1] in the court where the case is proceeding.

1   Rule 2.3(1); definition of judge.

Statements of case

26.1 A statement of case may be used as evidence in an interim application provided it is verified by a statement of truth[1].

1   See rule 32.6(2)(a).

26.2 To verify a statement of case the statement of truth should be set out as follows:

  '[I believe] [the (*party on whose behalf the statement of case is being signed*) believes] that the facts stated in the statement of case are true'.

26.3 Attention is drawn to rule 32.14 which sets out the consequences of verifying a witness statement containing a false statement without an honest belief in its truth.

  (For information regarding statements of truth see Part 22 and Practice Direction 22.)

  (Practice Directions 7A and 17 provide further information concerning statements of case.)

Agreed bundles for hearings

27.1 The court may give directions requiring the parties to use their best endeavours to agree a bundle or bundles of documents for use at any hearing.

27.2 All documents contained in bundles which have been agreed for use at a hearing shall be admissible at that hearing as evidence of their contents, unless –

  (1)   the court orders otherwise; or
  (2)   a party gives written notice of objection to the admissibility of particular documents.

...

Video conferencing

29.1 Guidance on the use of video conferencing in the civil courts is set out at Annex 3 to this practice direction.

A list of the sites which are available for video conferencing can be found on Her Majesty's Courts and Tribunals Service website.

ANNEX 1

Certificate to be used where a deponent to an affidavit is unable to read or sign it

Sworn at   this   day of   Before me, I having first read over the contents of this affidavit to the deponent [*if there are exhibits, add* 'and explained the nature and effect of the exhibits referred to in it'] who appeared to understand it and approved its content as accurate, and made his mark on the affidavit in my presence.

Or, (after, *Before me*) the witness to the mark of the deponent having been first sworn that he had read over etc (*as above*) and that he saw him make his mark on the affidavit. (*Witness must sign*).

Certificate to be used where a deponent to an affirmation is unable to read or sign it

Affirmed at   this   day of   Before me, I having first read over the contents of this affirmation to the deponent [*if there are exhibits, add* 'and explained the nature and effect of the exhibits referred to in it'] who appeared to understand it and approved its content as accurate, and made his mark on the affirmation in my presence.

Or, (after, *Before me*) the witness to the mark of the deponent having been first sworn that he had read over etc (*as above*) and that he saw him make his mark on the affirmation. (*Witness must sign*).

ANNEX 2

(*revoked*)

ANNEX 3

Video conferencing guidance

This guidance is for the use of video conferencing (VCF) in civil proceedings. It is in part based, with permission, upon the protocol of the Federal Court of Australia. It is intended to provide a guide to all persons involved in the use of VCF, although it does not attempt to cover all the practical questions which might arise.

Video conferencing generally

1 The guidance covers the use of VCF equipment both (a) in a courtroom, whether via equipment which is permanently placed there or via a mobile unit, and (b) in a separate studio or conference room. In either case, the location at which the judge sits is referred to as the 'local site'. The other site or sites to and from which transmission is made are referred to as 'the remote site' and in any particular case any such site may be another courtroom. The guidance applies to cases where VCF is used for the taking of evidence and also to its use for other parts of any legal proceedings (for example, interim applications, case management conferences, pre-trial reviews).

2 VCF may be a convenient way of dealing with any part of proceedings: it can involve considerable savings in time and cost. Its use for the taking of evidence from overseas witnesses will, in particular, be likely to achieve a material saving of costs, and such savings may also be achieved by its use for taking domestic evidence. It is, however, inevitably not as ideal as having the witness physically present in court. Its convenience should not therefore be allowed to dictate its use. A judgment must be made in every case in which the use of VCF is being considered not only as to whether it will achieve an overall cost saving but as to whether its use will be likely to be beneficial to the efficient, fair and economic disposal of the litigation. In particular, it needs to be recognised that the degree of control a court can exercise over a witness at the remote site is or may be more limited than it can exercise over a witness physically before it.

3 When used for the taking of evidence, the objective should be to make the VCF session as close as possible to the usual practice in a trial court where evidence is taken in open court. To gain the maximum benefit, several differences have to be taken into account. Some matters, which are taken for granted when evidence is taken in the conventional way, take on a different dimension when it is taken by VCF: for example, the administration of the oath, ensuring that the witness understands who is at the local site and what their various roles are, the raising of any objections to the evidence and the use of documents.

4 It should not be presumed that all foreign governments are willing to allow their nationals or others within their jurisdiction to be examined before a court in England or Wales by means of VCF. If there is any doubt about this, enquiries should be directed to the Foreign and Commonwealth Office (International Legal Matters Unit, Consular Division) with a view to ensuring that the country from which the evidence is to be taken raises no objection to it at diplomatic level. The party who is directed to be responsible for arranging the VCF (see paragraph 8 below) will be required to make all necessary inquiries about this well in advance of the VCF and must be able to inform the court what those inquiries were and of their outcome.

5 Time zone differences need to be considered when a witness abroad is to be examined in England or Wales by VCF. The convenience of the witness, the parties, their representatives and the court must all be taken into account. The cost of the use of a commercial studio is usually greater outside normal business hours.

6 Those involved with VCF need to be aware that, even with the most advanced systems currently available, there are the briefest of delays between the receipt of the picture and that of the accompanying sound. If due allowance is not made for this, there will be a tendency to 'speak over' the witness, whose voice will continue to be heard for a millisecond or so after he or she appears on the screen to have finished speaking.

7 With current technology, picture quality is good, but not as good as a television picture. The quality of the picture is enhanced if those appearing on VCF monitors keep their movements to a minimum.

Preliminary arrangements

8 The court's permission is required for any part of any proceedings to be dealt with by means of VCF. Before seeking a direction, the applicant should notify the listing officer, diary manager or other appropriate court officer of the intention to seek it, and should enquire as to the availability of court VCF equipment for the day or days of the proposed VCF. The application for a direction should be made to the master, district judge or judge, as may be appropriate. If all parties consent to a direction, permission can be sought by letter, fax or e-mail, although the court may still require an oral hearing. All parties are entitled to be heard on whether or not such a direction should be given and as to its terms. If a witness at a remote site is to give evidence by an interpreter,

consideration should be given at this stage as to whether the interpreter should be at the local site or the remote site. If a VCF direction is given, arrangements for the transmission will then need to be made. The court will ordinarily direct that the party seeking permission to use VCF is to be responsible for this. That party is hereafter referred to as 'the VCF arranging party'.

9 Subject to any order to the contrary, all costs of the transmission, including the costs of hiring equipment and technical personnel to operate it, will initially be the responsibility of, and must be met by, the VCF arranging party. All reasonable efforts should be made to keep the transmission to a minimum and so keep the costs down. All such costs will be considered to be part of the costs of the proceedings and the court will determine at such subsequent time as is convenient or appropriate who, as between the parties, should be responsible for them and (if appropriate) in what proportions.

10 The local site will, if practicable, be a courtroom but it may instead be an appropriate studio or conference room. The VCF arranging party must contact the listing officer, diary manager or other appropriate officer of the court which made the VCF direction and make arrangements for the VCF transmission. Details of the remote site, and of the equipment to be used both at the local site (if not being supplied by the court) and the remote site (including the number of ISDN lines and connection speed), together with all necessary contact names and telephone numbers, will have to be provided to the listing officer, diary manager or other court officer. The court will need to be satisfied that any equipment provided by the parties for use at the local site and also that at the remote site is of sufficient quality for a satisfactory transmission. The VCF arranging party must ensure that an appropriate person will be present at the local site to supervise the operation of the VCF throughout the transmission in order to deal with any technical problems. That party must also arrange for a technical assistant to be similarly present at the remote site for like purposes.

11 It is recommended that the judge, practitioners and witness should arrive at their respective VCF sites about 20 minutes prior to the scheduled commencement of the transmission.

12 If the local site is not a courtroom, but a conference room or studio, the judge will need to determine who is to sit where. The VCF arranging party must take care to ensure that the number of microphones is adequate for the speakers and that the panning of the camera for the practitioners' table encompasses all legal representatives so that the viewer can see everyone seated there.

13 The proceedings, wherever they may take place, form part of a trial to which the public is entitled to have access (unless the court has determined that they should be heard in private). If the local site is to be a studio or conference room, the VCF arranging party must ensure that it provides sufficient accommodation to enable a reasonable number of members of the public to attend.

14 In cases where the local site is a studio or conference room, the VCF arranging party should make arrangements, if practicable, for the royal coat of arms to be placed above the judge's seat.

15 In cases in which the VCF is to be used for the taking of evidence, the VCF arranging party must arrange for recording equipment to be provided by the court which made the VCF direction so that the evidence can be recorded. An associate will normally be present to operate the recording equipment when the local site is a courtroom. The VCF arranging party should take steps to ensure that an associate is present to do likewise when it is a studio or conference room. The equipment should be set up and tested before the VCF transmission. It will often be a valuable safeguard for the VCF arranging party also to arrange for the provision of recording equipment at the remote site. This will provide a useful back-up if there is any reduction in sound quality during the transmission. A direction from the court for the making of such a back-up recording

PART III

must, however, be obtained first. This is because the proceedings are court proceedings and, save as directed by the court, no other recording of them must be made. The court will direct what is to happen to the back-up recording.

16 Some countries may require that any oath or affirmation to be taken by a witness accord with local custom rather than the usual form of oath or affirmation used in England and Wales. The VCF arranging party must make all appropriate prior inquiries and put in place all arrangements necessary to enable the oath or affirmation to be taken in accordance with any local custom. That party must be in a position to inform the court what those inquiries were, what their outcome was and what arrangements have been made. If the oath or affirmation can be administered in the manner normal in England and Wales, the VCF arranging party must arrange in advance to have the appropriate holy book at the remote site. The associate will normally administer the oath.

17 Consideration will need to be given in advance to the documents to which the witness is likely to be referred. The parties should endeavour to agree on this. It will usually be most convenient for a bundle of the copy documents to be prepared in advance, which the VCF arranging party should then send to the remote site.

18 Additional documents are sometimes quite properly introduced during the course of a witness's evidence. To cater for this, the VCF arranging party should ensure that equipment is available to enable documents to be transmitted between sites during the course of the VCF transmission. Consideration should be given to whether to use a document camera. If it is decided to use one, arrangements for its use will need to be established in advance. The panel operator will need to know the number and size of documents or objects if their images are to be sent by document camera. In many cases, a simpler and sufficient alternative will be to ensure that there are fax transmission and reception facilities at the participating sites.

The hearing

19 The procedure for conducting the transmission will be determined by the judge. He will determine who is to control the cameras. In cases where the VCF is being used for an application in the course of the proceedings, the judge will ordinarily not enter the local site until both sites are on line. Similarly, at the conclusion of the hearing, he will ordinarily leave the local site while both sites are still on line. The following paragraphs apply primarily to cases where the VCF is being used for the taking of the evidence of a witness at a remote site. In all cases, the judge will need to decide whether court dress is appropriate when using VCF facilities. It might be appropriate when transmitting from courtroom to courtroom. It might not be when a commercial facility is being used.

20 At the beginning of the transmission, the judge will probably wish to introduce himself and the advocates to the witness. He will probably want to know who is at the remote site and will invite the witness to introduce himself and anyone else who is with him. He may wish to give directions as to the seating arrangements at the remote site so that those present are visible at the local site during the taking of the evidence. He will probably wish to explain to the witness the method of taking the oath or of affirming, the manner in which the evidence will be taken, and who will be conducting the examination and cross-examination. He will probably also wish to inform the witness of the matters referred to in paragraphs 6 and 7 above (co-ordination of picture with sound, and picture quality).

21 The examination of the witness at the remote site should follow as closely as possible the practice adopted when a witness is in the courtroom. During examination, cross-examination and re-examination, the witness must be able to see the legal representative asking the question and also any other person (whether another legal

representative or the judge) making any statements in regard to the witness's evidence. It will in practice be most convenient if everyone remains seated throughout the transmission.

****

PART 35
EXPERTS AND ASSESSORS

CONTENTS OF THIS PART

35.1 Duty to restrict expert evidence

Expert evidence shall be restricted to that which is reasonably required to resolve the proceedings.

"reasonably required"—FPR 2010, r 25.1 uses the phrase "evidence ... which in the opinion of the court is necessary to assist".

35.2 Interpretation and definitions

(1) A reference to an "expert" in this Part is a reference to an expert who has been instructed to give or prepare evidence for the purpose of proceedings.

(2) "Single joint expert" means an expert instructed to prepare a report for the court on behalf of two or more of the parties (including the claimant) to the proceedings.

Amendments—Substituted by SI 2009/2092.

Admissibility of "expert evidence" (r 35.2)—The admissibility of expert evidence depends upon the expert being permitted to be called as a witness so that "his opinion on any relevant matter on which he is qualified to give expert evidence shall be admissible in evidence" (Civil Evidence Act 1972, s 3(1)) and that other opinion evidence if given as facts "personally perceived by him, is admissible as evidence of what he perceived" (Civil Evidence Act 1972, s 3(2)).

35.3 Experts – overriding duty to the court

(1) It is the duty of experts to help the court on matters within their expertise.

(2) This duty overrides any obligation to the person from whom experts have received instructions or by whom they are paid.

Amendments—SI 2009/2092.

35.4 Court's power to restrict expert evidence

(1) No party may call an expert or put in evidence an expert's report without the court's permission.

(2) When parties apply for permission they must provide an estimate of the costs of the proposed expert evidence and identify –

    (a) the field in which expert evidence is required and the issues which the expert evidence will address; and

    (b) where practicable, the name of the proposed expert.

(3) If permission is granted it shall be in relation only to the expert named or the field identified under paragraph (2). The order granting permission may specify the issues which the expert evidence should address.

(3A) ...

        (Paragraph 7 of Practice Direction 35 sets out some of the circumstances the court will consider when deciding whether expert evidence should be given by a single joint expert).

(4) The court may limit the amount of a party's expert's fees and expenses that may be recovered from any other party.

Amendments—SI 2009/2092; SI 2009/3390; SI 2013/262.

35.5 General requirement for expert evidence to be given in a written report

(1) Expert evidence is to be given in a written report unless the court directs otherwise.

(2) ...

Amendments—SI 2009/2092.

35.6 Written questions to experts

(1) A party may put written questions about an expert's report (which must be proportionate) to –

    (a) an expert instructed by another party; or

    (b) a single joint expert appointed under rule 35.7.

(2) Written questions under paragraph (1) –

    (a) may be put once only;

    (b) must be put within 28 days of service of the expert's report; and

    (c) must be for the purpose only of clarification of the report;

unless in any case,

        (i) the court gives permission; or

        (ii) the other party agrees.

(3) An expert's answers to questions put in accordance with paragraph (1) shall be treated as part of the expert's report.

(4) Where –

    (a) a party has put a written question to an expert instructed by another party; and

    (b) the expert does not answer that question,

the court may make one or both of the following orders in relation to the party who instructed the expert –

    (i)   that the party may not rely on the evidence of that expert; or

    (ii) that the party may not recover the fees and expenses of that expert from any other party.

Amendments—SI 2009/2092.

35.7 Court's power to direct that evidence is to be given by a single joint expert

(1) Where two or more parties wish to submit expert evidence on a particular issue, the court may direct that the evidence on that issue is to given by a single joint expert.

(2) Where the parties who wish to submit the evidence ("the relevant parties") cannot agree who should be the single joint expert, the court may –

    (a) select the expert from a list prepared or identified by the relevant parties; or

    (b) direct that the expert be selected in such other manner as the court may direct.

(3) Where the instructing parties cannot agree who should be the expert, the court may –

    (a) select the expert from a list prepared or identified by the instructing parties; or

    (b) direct that the expert be selected in such other manner as the court may direct.

Amendments—SI 2009/2092.

Dissatisfaction with joint expert's report for reasons "not fanciful"—Where a party is dissatisfied with the joint expert's report for reasons "which are not fanciful", the court has a discretion to order another report (*Daniels v Walker (Practice Note)* [2000] 1 WLR 1382, CA):

(1) Instruction of an expert on jointly agreed instructions.
(2) Failing that, each party can send separate instructions (r 35.8(1)).
(3) If a party is dissatisfied with the report, then within 28 days of service of the report (r 35.6(2)(b)) that party can raise questions of the expert (r 35.6(1); the rules permit this to be done of an expert jointly instructed: r 35.6(1)(b)).
(4) If both parties seek expert evidence and the court agrees, then the experts should discuss their reports before a decision as to whether either, or both, should be called to give evidence is made.
(5) Calling both to be cross-examined should be a "last resort".

35.8 Instructions to a single joint expert

(1) Where the court gives a direction under rule 35.7 for a single joint expert to be used, any relevant party may give instructions to the expert.

(2) When a party gives instructions to the expert that party must, at the same time, send a copy to the other relevant parties.

(3) The court may give directions about –

    (a) the payment of the expert's fees and expenses; and

    (b) any inspection, examination or experiments which the expert wishes to carry out.

(4) The court may, before an expert is instructed –

    (a) limit the amount that can be paid by way of fees and expenses to the expert; and

    (b) direct that some or all of the relevant parties pay that amount into court.

(5) Unless the court otherwise directs, the relevant parties are jointly and severally liable[(GL)] for the payment of the expert's fees and expenses.

Amendments—SI 2009/2092.

"any relevant party may give instructions to the expert" (r 35.8(1))—Separate instructions may be given to the single joint expert by individual parties (ie there is no need for both or all parties jointly to agree a letter of instruction: cf FPR 2010, r 25.12).

35.9 Power of court to direct a party to provide information

Where a party has access to information which is not reasonably available to another party, the court may direct the party who has access to the information to –

    (a)   prepare and file a document recording the information; and

    (b)   serve a copy of that document on the other party.

Amendments—SI 2009/2092.

35.10 Contents of report

(1) An expert's report must comply with the requirements set out in Practice Direction 35.

(2) At the end of an expert's report there must be a statement that the expert understands and has complied with their duty to the court.

(3) The expert's report must state the substance of all material instructions, whether written or oral, on the basis of which the report was written.

(4) The instructions referred to in paragraph (3) shall not be privileged$^{(GL)}$ against disclosure but the court will not, in relation to those instructions –

    (a)   order disclosure of any specific document; or

    (b)   permit any questioning in court, other than by the party who instructed the expert,

unless it is satisfied that there are reasonable grounds to consider the statement of instructions given under paragraph (3) to be inaccurate or incomplete.

Amendments—SI 2009/2092; SI 2009/3390.

35.11 Use by one party of expert's report disclosed by another

Where a party has disclosed an expert's report, any party may use that expert's report as evidence at the trial.

35.12 Discussions between experts

(1) The court may, at any stage, direct a discussion between experts for the purpose of requiring the experts to –

    (a)   identify and discuss the expert issues in the proceedings; and

    (b)   where possible, reach an agreed opinion on those issues.

(2) The court may specify the issues which the experts must discuss.

(3) The court may direct that following a discussion between the experts they must prepare a statement for the court setting out those issues on which –

    (a)   they agree; and

    (b)   they disagree, with a summary of their reasons for disagreeing.

(4) The content of the discussion between the experts shall not be referred to at the trial unless the parties agree.

(5) Where experts reach agreement on an issue during their discussions, the agreement shall not bind the parties unless the parties expressly agree to be bound by the agreement.

Amendments—SI 2001/4015; SI 2009/2092.

35.13 Consequence of failure to disclose expert's report

A party who fails to disclose an expert's report may not use the report at the trial or call the expert to give evidence orally unless the court gives permission.

35.14 Expert's right to ask court for directions

(1) Experts may file written requests for directions for the purpose of assisting them in carrying out their functions.

(2) An expert must, unless the court orders otherwise, provide a copies of the proposed requests for directions under paragraph (1) –

    (a)   to the party instructing them at least 7 days before they file the requests; and
    (b)   to all other parties, at least 4 days before they file them.

(3) The court, when it gives directions, may also direct that a party be served with a copy of the directions.

    (a), (b)   ...

Amendments—SI 2001/4015; SI 2009/2092.

35.15 Assessors

This rule applies where the court appoints one or more persons under section 70 of the Senior Courts Act 1981 or section 63 of the County Courts Act 1984 as an assessor.

(2) An assessor will assist the court in dealing with a matter in which the assessor has skill and experience.

(3) An assessor will take such part in the proceedings as the court may direct and in particular the court may direct an assessor to –

    (a) prepare a report for the court on any matter at issue in the proceedings; and
    (b) attend the whole or any part of the trial to advise the court on any such matter.

(4) If an assessor prepares a report for the court before the trial has begun –

    (a)   the court will send a copy to each of the parties; and
    (b)   the parties may use it at trial.

(5) The remuneration to be paid to an assessor is to be determined by the court and will form part of the costs of the proceedings.

(6) The court may order any party to deposit in the court office a specified sum in respect of an assessor's fees and, where it does so, the assessor will not be asked to act until the sum has been deposited.

(7) Paragraphs (5) and (6) do not apply where the remuneration of the assessor is to be paid out of money provided by Parliament.

Amendments—SI 2009/2092.

PART III

Practice Direction 35 – Experts and Assessors

This Practice Direction supplements CPR Part 35

Introduction

1 Part 35 is intended to limit the use of oral expert evidence to that which is reasonably required. In addition, where possible, matters requiring expert evidence should be dealt with by only one expert. Experts and those instructing them are expected to have regard to the guidance contained in the Protocol for the Instruction of Experts to give Evidence in Civil Claims annexed to this practice direction.

(Further guidance on experts is contained in Annex C to the Practice Direction (Pre-Action Conduct)).

Expert Evidence – General Requirements

2.1 Expert evidence should be the independent product of the expert uninfluenced by the pressures of litigation.

2.2 Experts should assist the court by providing objective, unbiased opinions on matters within their expertise, and should not assume the role of an advocate.

2.3 Experts should consider all material facts, including those which might detract from their opinions.

2.4 Experts should make it clear –

   (a)   when a question or issue falls outside their expertise; and
   (b)   when they are not able to reach a definite opinion, for example because they have insufficient information.

2.5 If, after producing a report, an expert's view changes on any material matter, such change of view should be communicated to all the parties without delay, and when appropriate to the court.

Form and Content of an Expert's Report

3.1 An expert's report should be addressed to the court and not to the party from whom the expert has received instructions.

3.2 An expert's report must:

   (1)   give details of the expert's qualifications;
   (2)   give details of any literature or other material which has been relied on in making the report;
   (3)   contain a statement setting out the substance of all facts and instructions which are material to the opinions expressed in the report or upon which those opinions are based;
   (4)   make clear which of the facts stated in the report are within the expert's own knowledge;
   (5)   say who carried out any examination, measurement, test or experiment which the expert has used for the report, give the qualifications of that person, and say whether or not the test or experiment has been carried out under the expert's supervision;
   (6)   where there is a range of opinion on the matters dealt with in the report –
         (a)   summarise the range of opinions; and

(b)   give reasons for the expert's own opinion;

(7)   contain a summary of the conclusions reached;

(8)   if the expert is not able to give an opinion without qualification, state the qualification; and

(9)   contain a statement that the expert –

(a)   understands their duty to the court, and has complied with that duty; and

(b)   is aware of the requirements of Part 35, this practice direction and the Protocol for Instruction of Experts to give Evidence in Civil Claims.

3.3 An expert's report must be verified by a statement of truth in the following form –

'I confirm that I have made clear which facts and matters referred to in this report are within my own knowledge and which are not. Those that are within my own knowledge I confirm to be true. The opinions I have expressed represent my true and complete professional opinions on the matters to which they refer.

(Part 22 deals with statements of truth. Rule 32.14 sets out the consequences of verifying a document containing a false statement without an honest belief in its truth.)

Information

4 Under rule 35.9 the court may direct a party with access to information, which is not reasonably available to another party to serve on that other party a document, which records the information. The document served must include sufficient details of all the facts, tests, experiments and assumptions which underlie any part of the information to enable the party on whom it is served to make, or to obtain, a proper interpretation of the information and an assessment of its significance.

Instructions

5 Cross-examination of experts on the contents of their instructions will not be allowed unless the court permits it (or unless the party who gave the instructions consents). Before it gives permission the court must be satisfied that there are reasonable grounds to consider that the statement in the report of the substance of the instructions is inaccurate or incomplete. If the court is so satisfied, it will allow the cross-examination where it appears to be in the interests of justice.

Questions to Experts

6.1 Where a party sends a written question or questions under rule 35.6 direct to an expert, a copy of the questions must, at the same time, be sent to the other party or parties.

6.2 The party or parties instructing the expert must pay any fees charged by that expert for answering questions put under rule 35.6. This does not affect any decision of the court as to the party who is ultimately to bear the expert's fees.

Single joint expert

7 When considering whether to give permission for the parties to rely on expert evidence and whether that evidence should be from a single joint expert the court will take into account all the circumstances in particular, whether:

(a)   it is proportionate to have separate experts for each party on a particular issue with reference to –

(i)   the amount in dispute;

      (ii)   the importance to the parties; and

      (iii) the complexity of the issue;

(b)   the instruction of a single joint expert is likely to assist the parties and the court to resolve the issue more speedily and in a more cost-effective way than separately instructed experts;

(c)   expert evidence is to be given on the issue of liability, causation or quantum;

(d)   the expert evidence falls within a substantially established area of knowledge which is unlikely to be in dispute or there is likely to be a range of expert opinion;

(e)   a party has already instructed an expert on the issue in question and whether or not that was done in compliance with any practice direction or relevant pre-action protocol;

(f)   questions put in accordance with rule 35.6 are likely to remove the need for the other party to instruct an expert if one party has already instructed an expert;

(g)   questions put to a single joint expert may not conclusively deal with all issues that may require testing prior to trial;

(h)   a conference may be required with the legal representatives, experts and other witnesses which may make instruction of a single joint expert impractical; and

(i)   a claim to privilege[GL] makes the instruction of any expert as a single joint expert inappropriate.

Orders

8   Where an order requires an act to be done by an expert, or otherwise affects an expert, the party instructing that expert must serve a copy of the order on the expert. The claimant must serve the order on a single joint expert.

Discussions between experts

9.1 Unless directed by the court discussions between experts are not mandatory. Parties must consider, with their experts, at an early stage, whether there is likely to be any useful purpose in holding an expert's discussion and if so when.

9.2 The purpose of discussions between experts is not for experts to settle cases but to agree and narrow issues and in particular to identify:

      (i)   the extent of the agreement between them;

      (ii) the points of and short reasons for any disagreement;

      (iii) action, if any, which may be taken to resolve any outstanding points of disagreement; and

      (iv) any further material issues not raised and the extent to which these issues are agreed.

9.3 Where the experts are to meet, the parties must discuss and if possible agree whether an agenda is necessary, and if so attempt to agree one that helps the experts to focus on the issues which need to be discussed. The agenda must not be in the form of leading questions or hostile in tone.

9.4 Unless ordered by the court, or agreed by all parties, and the experts, neither the parties nor their legal representatives may attend experts discussions.

9.5 If the legal representatives do attend –

      (i)   they should not normally intervene in the discussion, except to answer questions put to them by the experts or to advise on the law; and

      (ii) he experts may if they so wish hold part of their discussions in the absence of the legal representatives.

9.6 A statement must be prepared by the experts dealing with paragraphs 9.2(i)–(iv) above. Individual copies of the statements must be signed by the experts at the conclusion of the discussion, or as soon thereafter as practicable, and in any event within 7 days. Copies of the statements must be provided to the parties no later than 14 days after signing.

9.7 Experts must give their own opinions to assist the court and do not require the authority of the parties to sign a joint statement.

9.8 If an expert significantly alters an opinion, the joint statement must include a note or addendum by that expert explaining the change of opinion.

Assessors

10.1 An assessor may be appointed to assist the court under rule 35.15. Not less than 21 days before making any such appointment, the court will notify each party in writing of the name of the proposed assessor, of the matter in respect of which the assistance of the assessor will be sought and of the qualifications of the assessor to give that assistance.

10.2 Where any person has been proposed for appointment as an assessor, any party may object to that person either personally or in respect of that person's qualification.

10.3 Any such objection must be made in writing and filed with the court within 7 days of receipt of the notification referred to in paragraph 10.1 and will be taken into account by the court in deciding whether or not to make the appointment.

10.4 Copies of any report prepared by the assessor will be sent to each of the parties but the assessor will not give oral evidence or be open to cross-examination or questioning.
****

PART 44
GENERAL RULES ABOUT COSTS

CONTENTS OF THIS PART

Section I
General

CPR 1998 costs rules applied to FPR 2010—FPR 2010, Pt 28 incorporates substantial parts of the costs rules in CPR 1998 (as amended by SI 2013/262) into family proceedings. These rules apply to costs orders in all family proceedings, save that certain provisions in CPR 1998, Pt 44 are disapplied and costs orders do not apply in certain financial order proceedings (see FPR 2010, r 28.3).

Section I
General

44.1 Interpretation and application

(1) In Parts 44 to 47, unless the context otherwise requires –

"authorised court officer" means any officer or –

    (i)   a county court;

    (ii) a district registry;

    (iii) the Principal Registry of the Family Division; or

    (iv) the Costs Office,

whom the Lord Chancellor has authorised to assess costs;

"costs" includes fees, charges, disbursements, expenses, remuneration, reimbursement allowed to a litigant in person under rule 46.5 and any fee or reward charged by a lay representative for acting on behalf of a party in proceedings allocated to the small claims track;

"costs judge" means a taxing master of the Senior Courts;

"Costs Office" means the Senior Courts Costs Office;

"costs officer" means –

    (i)   a costs judge;

    (ii) a district judge; or

    (iii) an authorised court officer;

"detailed assessment" means the procedure by which the amount of costs is decided by a costs officer in accordance with Part 47;

"the Director (legal aid)" means the person designated as the Director of Legal Aid Casework pursuant to section 4 of the Legal Aid, Sentencing and Punishment of Offenders Act 2012, or a person entitled to exercise the functions of the Director;

…

"free of charge" has the same meaning as in section 194(10) of the 2007 Act;

"fund" includes any estate or property held for the benefit of any person or class of person and any fund to which a trustee or personal representative is entitled in that capacity;

"HMRC" means HM Revenue and Customs;

"legal aid" means civil legal services made available under arrangements made for the purposes of Part 1 of the Legal Aid, Sentencing and Punishment of Offenders Act 2012;

"paying party" means a party liable to pay costs;

"the prescribed charity" has the same meaning as in section 194(8) of the 2007 Act;

"pro bono representation" means legal representation provided free of charge;

"receiving party" means a party entitled to be paid costs;

"summary assessment" means the procedure whereby costs are assessed by the judge who has heard the case or application;

"VAT" means Value Added Tax;

"the 2007 Act" means the Legal Services Act 2007.

("Legal representative" has the meaning given in rule 2.3).

(2) The costs to which Parts 44 to 47 apply include –

    (a) the following costs where those costs may be assessed by the court –

        (i)   costs of proceedings before an arbitrator or umpire;

        (ii) costs of proceedings before a tribunal or other statutory body; and

        (iii) costs payable by a client to their legal representative; and

(b)   costs which are payable by one party to another party under the terms of a contract, where the court makes an order for an assessment of those costs.

(3)   Where advocacy or litigation services are provided to a client under a conditional fee agreement, costs are recoverable under Parts 44 to 47 notwithstanding that the client is liable to pay the legal representative's fees and expenses only to the extent that sums are recovered in respect of the proceedings, whether by way of costs or otherwise.

Amendments—Inserted by SI 2013/262.

44.2   Court's discretion as to costs

(1)   The court has discretion as to –

(a)   whether costs are payable by one party to another;
(b)   the amount of those costs; and
(c)   when they are to be paid.

(2)   If the court decides to make an order about costs –

(a)   the general rule is that the unsuccessful party will be ordered to pay the costs of the successful party; but
(b)   the court may make a different order.

(3)   The general rule does not apply to the following proceedings –

(a)   proceedings in the Court of Appeal on an application or appeal made in connection with proceedings in the Family Division; or
(b)   proceedings in the Court of Appeal from a judgment, direction, decision or order given or made in probate proceedings or family proceedings.

(4)   In deciding what order (if any) to make about costs, the court will have regard to all the circumstances, including –

(a)   the conduct of all the parties;
(b)   whether a party has succeeded on part of its case, even if that party has not been wholly successful; and
(c)   any admissible offer to settle made by a party which is drawn to the court's attention, and which is not an offer to which costs consequences under Part 36 apply.

(5)   The conduct of the parties includes –

(a)   conduct before, as well as during, the proceedings and in particular the extent to which the parties followed the Practice Direction – Pre-Action Conduct or any relevant pre-action protocol;
(b)   whether it was reasonable for a party to raise, pursue or contest a particular allegation or issue;
(c)   the manner in which a party has pursued or defended the case or a particular allegation or issue; and
(d)   whether a claimant who has succeeded in the claim, in whole or in part, exaggerated its claim.

(6)   The orders which the court may make under this rule include an order that a party must pay –

(a)   a proportion of another party's costs;
(b)   a stated amount in respect of another party's costs;
(c)   costs from or until a certain date only;
(d)   costs incurred before proceedings have begun;
(e)   costs relating to particular steps taken in the proceedings;
(f)   costs relating only to a distinct part of the proceedings; and
(g)   interest on costs from or until a certain date, including a date before judgment.

PART III

(7) Before the court considers making an order under paragraph (6)(f), it will consider whether it is practicable to make an order under paragraph (6)(a) or (c) instead.

(8) Where the court orders a party to pay costs subject to detailed assessment, it will order that party to pay a reasonable sum on account of costs, unless there is good reason not to do so.

Amendments—Inserted by SI 2013/262.

Defined terms—"assessment of costs": Pt 47; "costs": r 44.1(1)); "Part 36 offer": r 36.5.

Disapplication costs order rules in family proceedings—FPR 2010, r 28.1(1) disapplies r 44.2(2),(3) for proceedings covered by FPR 2010. This means:

(1) That there is no rule in family proceedings that costs follow the event, or that a successful party should have his costs (see **"the general rule"** below and r 44.2(2)). In *Gojkovic v Gojkovic (No 2)* [1991] 2 FLR 233, the Court of Appeal suggested that although the rule that "costs follow the event" did not apply to family proceedings, "there still remains the necessity for some starting point. That starting point, in my judgment, is that costs prima facie follow the event (see Cumming-Bruce LJ in *Singer (formerly Sharegin) v Sharegin* [1984] FLR 114 at 119)", per Butler-Sloss LJ.

(2) That the rule that the successful party should generally have his costs does apply in the Court of Appeal. The rule is disapplied by r 44.2(3) and in that disapplication being disapplied the question may arise as to whether the general rule does apply for family cases in the Court of Appeal.

Court's discretion on costs (r 44.2(1))—Rule 44.2(1) gives regulatory effect to SCA 1981, s 51(3); namely that costs can only be recovered by order of the court and that orders for costs are in the court's discretion (SCA 1981, s 51(1)). The rule prescribes bases upon which the court is to exercise its discretion.

"In deciding what order ... the court must have regard" (r 44.2(4))—It is not a matter of discretion for the court as to whether it considers the factors in r 44.2(4); though having done so it has a discretion as to whether to make an order.

"the amount of those costs" (r 44.2(1)(b))—The court's discretion as to the amount of costs "includes its discretion to decide whether some or all of the costs awarded should be on a standard or indemnity basis"; and see note under r 44.4 on standard and indemnity costs.

Practice Direction—Costs Practice Direction (CPR 1998, Pt 44), para 8.5 draws attention to a "non-exhaustive list" of "certain costs orders which the court will commonly make". The following should be particularly noted:

(a) *Respondent's costs*   A wholly successful respondent should normally be awarded his costs unless he has brought about the proceedings or has done something in connection with the institution or conduct of the proceedings intended to prolong them or cause unnecessary expense (r 44.2(5)).

(b) *"Costs in the cause" or "Costs in the application"*   Where proceedings are discontinued or withdrawn (eg domestic violence injunction proceedings where applicant does not pursue application beyond initial order) the defendant or respondent does not automatically have an order for costs in his favour where there is an order for "costs in the cause [or] application": the court retains its discretion as to costs, since no judgment on the issues has yet been given.

(c) *"Costs reserved"*   A party in whose favour an order for costs is made will be awarded costs in respect of any "costs reserved" order, unless some other order is made. Thus, where costs are reserved at an interlocutory hearing and, at the final hearing, costs either (i) are not awarded at all or (ii) are awarded to one or other party, it will be necessary to seek a specific order for the prior hearing, in respect of which costs were reserved, at that final hearing. A party who fails to seek, at the final hearing, an order for the costs which were reserved at an earlier hearing, can cure the omission by making a separate application (*S v S (Reserved Costs Order)* [1995] 1 FLR 739).

(d) *Applicant's costs in the case*   (1) If the applicant ("A") is awarded costs at the conclusion of the case, he is entitled to the costs of the application to which the order for costs in the case relates. (2) If another party is awarded costs, he cannot be required to pay A's costs on the part of the proceedings for which costs in the case were awarded.

"the general rule" (r 44.2(2)(a))—This rule replaces the former rule that "costs should follow the event", unless some other order seems appropriate. The effect of this rule in family proceeding is as follows:

(1) The general rule applies to all family proceedings covered by CPR 1998 (ie 1(PFD)A 1975 TLATA 1996, etc).

(2) The general rule does not apply to proceedings covered by FPR 2010 (r 28.1(1)), including appeals

to the Court of Appeal and all family proceedings appeals under FPR 2010, Pt 30; but see *Gojkovic v Gojkovic (No 2)* [1991] 2 FLR 233 (above).

(3) Financial remedy proceedings (as defined by r 28.3(4) and see the introductory note, above) have their own rules arising from r 28.3(5).

Wide discretion as to by whom costs paid—The court has a wide discretion as to by whom costs should be paid. For example, in *Ben Hashem v Ali Shayif and Radfan Ltd* [2009] 2 FLR 896 in ancillary relief proceedings (1) H was ordered to pay W's costs on an indemnity basis, whereas (2) in parallel Chancery proceedings involving children and a family company W was almost entirely unsuccessful and was required to pay most of their costs. In *Baker v Rowe* [2010] 1 FLR 761 (see especially at [24] and [35]), in financial remedy proceedings the real issue on costs was between the interveners: the rule in 28.3(6) that there be no order save by reason of a party's conduct did not apply. The district judge had a "clean sheet" in relation to the court's costs order but in considering an award of costs the judge could not avoid the fact that one side had succeeded as against the other.

The Act, the Rules, Practice Directions and a Protocol—In *R (on the application of Mount Cook Land Limited) v Westminster City Council* [2003] EWCA Civ 1346, CA at [67] Auld LJ examined the interrelationship between statute, CPR 1998 rules and PDs and a protocol (in this instance, judicial review). The costs award hierarchy and the extent to which each can influence the court are as follows:

(1) The court starts from SCA 1981, s 51(1): subject to any contrary enactment or "rule of court", costs are in the court's discretion;
(2) "Intrusion" on s 51 can come from r 44.3(2): costs should normally follow the event;
(3) PDs are "recognised" by CPA 1997, no more. They are guidance as to "normal practice" of the courts (no more). They are not determinative nor can they be regarded as comprised in an exception to s 51(1);
(4) Any relevant protocol.

"In deciding what order (if any) to make about costs" (r 44.2(4))—The exercise of the court's discretion was considered by Nourse LJ in the Court of Appeal in *Re Elgindata Ltd (No 2)* [1992] 1 WLR 1207 (cited with approval as applicable to a financial relief application by Thorpe LJ in *Dart v Dart* [1996] 2 FLR 286, CA). Nourse LJ set out the main principles on which he considered that an order for costs should be awarded:

(a) costs are in the discretion of the court (SCA 1981, s 51(1));
(b) orders for costs should "follow the event" (ie should be paid to the "successful party": see r 44.2(2)(a)), unless the court considers that in the circumstances of the case some other order should be made (r 44.2(2)(b));
(c) these general rules do not cease to apply because a party raises issues on which he is not successful, although if, in raising those issues, he substantially lengthens the trial he may lose part or all of his costs;
(d) where a successful party raises issues or makes allegations improperly or unreasonably, the court may deprive him of his costs (and see r 44.2(4)(a) and (5)) and order him to pay the unsuccessful party's costs (SCA 1981, s 51(6)).

"the conduct of all the parties" (r 44.2(4)(a),(5))—In the exercise of its discretion, the court will be required to pay particular attention to the conduct of the parties and r 44.3(5) provides an inclusive check-list of the factors for consideration when assessing conduct. For an example of the balancing exercise required between 'conduct" and success on the event see *McMinn v McMinn (Ancillary Relief: Death of Party to Proceedings: Costs)* [2003] 2 FLR 839 (no order for costs in that instance).

"whether a party has succeeded" (r 44.2(4)(b))—This is the terminology used to replace costs following "the event" as considered by the Court of Appeal in *Gojkovic v Gojkovic (No 2)* [1991] 2 FLR 233, CA; and see *Baker v Rowe* (above), which adopts a similar approach to *Gojkovic* in regarding success in the proceedings as an important factor in determining an order for costs.

Calderbank letters—*Calderbank* letters may be of limited application in financial remedy proceedings but they apply in all other forms of family proceedings. A *Calderbank* letter sets out proposals for settlement of any issue in proceedings (*Calderbank v Calderbank* (1975) FLR Rep 113, CA; and see CPR 1998, r 36.5(2)) "without prejudice" – ie with privilege attached as with all negotiations; but on terms that, although the privilege is joint, the correspondence can be opened when the question of costs fails to be decided. In *Gojkovic v Gojkovic (No 2)* [1991] 2 FLR 233, at [238F], Butler-Sloss LJ expressed the view that "*Calderbank* offers are required to have teeth in order for them to be effective" and this will remain the position, save in ancillary relief proceedings.

"whether a claimant ... exaggerated his claim" (r 44.2(5)(d))—A party who, though successful on the main issue before the court, has exaggerated a claim and pursued a particular allegation or issue which proves to be of no or only tangential relevance (r 44.3(5)(b) and (c)) may find their costs disallowed or substantially reduced (for an example of exaggeration of claim and cost consequences see e g *A v A (No 2) (Ancillary Relief: Costs)* [2008] 1 FLR 1428).

"an amount to be paid on account" (r 44.2(8))—It is now required positively of the court, where costs are awarded, that an amount on account be paid, unless there is some reason not to (similar in principle to *Hadjimilitis (Tsavliris) v Tsavliris* [2003] 1 FLR 81, where the court held that it was appropriate to order a payment on account "unless there are clear reasons why it would be unfair" (Costs Judgment [4](j)). In the event of an order for costs in ancillary relief proceedings, a payment on account can be requested of the court.

Official Solicitor's costs—The costs of the Official Solicitor are entirely a matter for the discretion of the judge (*B v Croydon Health Authority (No 2)* [1996] 1 FLR 253, CA). It may be appropriate to order a party to pay one half of the Official Solicitor's costs (*Re G (Minors) (Wardship: Costs)* [1982] 1 WLR 438 CA) or, where the Official Solicitor has become involved because of the position the parties find themselves in, he might be expected to bear his own costs (see *Northampton Health Authority v The Official Solicitor and the Governors of St Andrews Hospital* [1994] 1 FLR 162, CA).

Security for costs—In *Charman v Charman (No 3)* [2007] 1 FLR 1237, CA the wife applied for security to be given by the appellant husband against stay obtained by him in respect of £28m of a £40m lump sum order. This was refused. However, Sir Mark Potter P had no hesitation in ordering security for costs pending the hearing under CPR 1998, r 25.13(2)(a), namely, that the husband is resident out of the jurisdiction and not in a Brussels or Lugano Contracting State. An order under r 25.13 can only be made where CPR 1998 applies to the proceedings. It can only be applied for by a defendant or respondent to an appeal (r 25.12), and will only be ordered where justice demands it and one of the conditions in r 25.13(2) apply, including (a) residence (as above), (d) changes of address to evade the consequences of the litigation and (g) the taking of steps by the claimant/appellant to move assets to make it difficult to enforce any order for costs.

44.3 Basis of assessment

(1) Where the court is to assess the amount of costs (whether by summary or detailed assessment) it will assess those costs –

  (a)   on the standard basis; or
  (b)   on the indemnity basis,

but the court will not in either case allow costs which have been unreasonably incurred or are unreasonable in amount.

>   (Rule 44.5 sets out how the court decides the amount of costs payable under a
>   contract.)

(2) Where the amount of costs is to be assessed on the standard basis, the court will –

  (a)   only allow costs which are proportionate to the matters in issue. Costs which
        are disproportionate in amount may be disallowed or reduced even if they were
        reasonably or necessarily incurred; and
  (b)   resolve any doubt which it may have as to whether costs were reasonably and
        proportionately incurred or were reasonable and proportionate in amount in
        favour of the paying party.

  (Factors which the court may take into account are set out in rule 44.4.)

(3) Where the amount of costs is to be assessed on the indemnity basis, the court will resolve any doubt which it may have as to whether costs were reasonably incurred or were reasonable in amount in favour of the receiving party.

(4) Where –

  (a)   the court makes an order about costs without indicating the basis on which the
        costs are to be assessed; or
  (b)   the court makes an order for costs to be assessed on a basis other than the
        standard basis or the indemnity basis,

the costs will be assessed on the standard basis.

(5) Costs incurred are proportionate if they bear a reasonable relationship to –

    (a)   the sums in issue in the proceedings;

    (b)   the value of any non-monetary relief in issue in the proceedings;

    (c)   the complexity of the litigation;

    (d)   any additional work generated by the conduct of the paying party; and

    (e)   any wider factors involved in the proceedings, such as reputation or public importance.

(6) Where the amount of a solicitor's remuneration in respect of non-contentious business is regulated by any general orders made under the Solicitors Act 1974, the amount of the costs to be allowed in respect of any such business which falls to be assessed by the court will be decided in accordance with those general orders rather than this rule and rule 44.4.

(7) Paragraphs (2)(a) and (5) do not apply in relation to –

    (a)   cases commenced before 1 April 2013; or

    (b)   costs incurred in respect of work done before 1 April 2013,

and in relation to such cases or costs, rule 44.4.(2)(a) as it was in force immediately before 1 April 2013 will apply instead.

Amendments—Inserted by SI 2013/262; amended by SI 2013/515.

Defined terms—"costs": r 44.1(1); "costs officer": r 44.1(1); "detailed assessment": r 44.1(1); "summary assessment": r 44.1(1).

Assessment of costs—Rule 44.3 deals with the basis of the assessment of costs (standard or indemnity) which the court awards; r 44.4 deals with the factors to be taken into account when undertaking that assessment; and r 44.5 deals with the procedure (detailed or summary) by which the assessment is to take place.

Indemnity or standard basis (r 44.3(1))—An award of costs on the indemnity basis is only justified where a paying party has been responsible for conduct which is unreasonable to a high degree: not "merely wrong or misguided in hindsight" (*Kiam v MGN Ltd (No 2)* [2002] 1 WLR 2810, CA). Where one party makes a sensible attempt at settlement and the other party resists, the latter party puts himself at risk of an indemnity order (*Reid Minty (a firm) v Taylor* [2002] 1 WLR 2800). Implicit disapproval of the way the litigation was conducted may be reflected by such an order.

44.4 Factors to be taken into account in deciding the amount of costs

(1) The court will have regard to all the circumstances in deciding whether costs were –

    (a)   if it is assessing costs on the standard basis –

        (i)   proportionately and reasonably incurred; or

        (ii)   proportionate and reasonable in amount, or

    (b)   if it is assessing costs on the indemnity basis –

        (i)   unreasonably incurred; or

        (ii)   unreasonable in amount.

(2) In particular, the court will give effect to any orders which have already been made.

(3) The court will also have regard to –

    (a)   the conduct of all the parties, including in particular –

        (i)   conduct before, as well as during, the proceedings; and

        (ii)   the efforts made, if any, before and during the proceedings in order to try to resolve the dispute;

    (b)   the amount or value of any money or property involved;

    (c)   the importance of the matter to all the parties;

    (d)   the particular complexity of the matter or the difficulty or novelty of the questions raised;

    (e)   the skill, effort, specialised knowledge and responsibility involved;

PART III

(f)   the time spent on the case;

(g)   the place where and the circumstances in which work or any part of it was done; and

(h)   the receiving party's last approved or agreed budget.

(Rule 35.4(4) gives the court power to limit the amount that a party may recover with regard to the fees and expenses of an expert.)

Amendments—Inserted by SI 2013/262.

Defined terms—"costs": r 44.1(1); "indemnity basis": r 44.3(1)(b); "standard basis": r 44.3(1)(a).

"proportionate and reasonable in amount" (r 44.4(1)(a)(ii))—In assessing what is "proportionate and reasonable" the court considers, in its assessment on a standard basis, what costs should be awarded if "the litigation had been appropriately conducted". A reasonable sum should be awarded for the work which was carried out and was necessary (*Lownds v Home Office (Practice Note)* [2002] 1 WLR 2450, CA).

"conduct of all the parties" (r 44.4(3)(a))—In assessing one party's costs and their conduct of the dispute, the conduct of the other party is highly relevant. A co-operative opponent can contain costs: by being unco-operative he can increase costs and make work necessary which would otherwise be unnecessary (*Lownds v Home Office* (above)).

"efforts made ... in order to try to resolve the dispute" (r 44.4(3)(a)(ii))—Orders for costs can relate to work done before the issue of proceedings and to proposals for settlement made before issue (*Butcher v Wolfe and Wolfe* [1999] 1 FLR 334, CA).

"the circumstances in which work or any part of it was done" (r 44.4(3)(g))—The court may allow variable rates of remuneration according to the nature of the work done at each stage (*Re Children Act 1989 (Taxation of Costs)* [1994] 2 FLR 934).

44.5 Amount of costs where costs are payable under a contract

(1) Subject to Paragraphs (2) to (4), where the court assesses (whether by summary or detailed assessment) costs which are payable by the paying party to the receiving party under the terms of a contract, the costs payable under those terms are, unless the contract expressly provides otherwise, to be presumed to be costs which –

(a)   have been reasonably incurred; and

(b)   are reasonable in amount,

and the court will assess them accordingly.

(2) The presumptions in paragraph (1) are rebuttable.

Practice Direction 44 – General rules about costs sets out circumstances where the court may order otherwise.

(3) Paragraph (1) does not apply where the contract is between a solicitor and client.

Amendments—Inserted by SI 2013/262.

44.6 Procedure for assessing costs

(1) Where the court orders a party to pay costs to another party (other than fixed costs) it may either –

(a)   make a summary assessment of the costs; or

(b)   order detailed assessment of the costs by a costs officer,

unless any rule, practice direction or other enactment provides otherwise.

(Practice Direction 44 – General rules about costs sets out the factors which will affect the court's decision under paragraph (1).)

(2) A party may recover the fixed costs specified in Part 45 in accordance with that Part.

Amendments—Inserted by SI 2013/262.

Defined terms—"costs": r 43.2(1)(a); "costs officer": r 43.2(1)(c); "detailed assessment": r 43.4; "summary assessment": r 43.3.

Summary assessment—PD44, subsection 9 explains the operation of the rules on summary assessment.

44.7 Time for complying with an order for costs

A party must comply with an order for the payment of costs within 14 days of –

- (a) the date of the judgment or order if it states the amount of those costs;
- (b) if the amount of those costs (or part of them) is decided later in accordance with Part 47, the date of the certificate which states the amount; or
- (c) in either case, such other date as the court may specify.

(Part 47 sets out the procedure for detailed assessment of costs.)

Amendments—Inserted by SI 2013/262.

44.8 Legal representative's duty to notify the party

Where –

- (a) the court makes a costs order against a legally represented party; and
- (b) the party is not present when the order is made,

the party's legal representative must notify that party in writing of the costs order no later than 7 days after the legal representative receives notice of the order.

(Paragraph 10.1 of Practice Direction 44 defines "party" for the purposes of this rule.)

Amendments—Inserted by SI 2013/262.

****

44.10 Where the court makes no order for costs

(1) Where the court makes an order which does not mention costs –

- (a) subject to Paragraphs (2) and (3), the general rule is that no party is entitled –
  - (i) to costs; or
  - (ii) to seek an order under section 194(3) of the 2007 Act,

in relation to that order; but

- (b) this does not affect any entitlement of a party to recover costs out of a fund held by that party as trustee or personal representative, or under any lease, mortgage or other security.

(2) Where the court makes –

- (a) an order granting permission to appeal;
- (b) an order granting permission to apply for judicial review; or
- (c) any other order or direction sought by a party on an application without notice,

and its order does not mention costs, it will be deemed to include an order for applicant's costs in the case.

(3) Any party affected by a deemed order for costs under paragraph (2) may apply at any time to vary the order.

(4) The court hearing an appeal may, unless it dismisses the appeal, make orders about the costs of the proceedings giving rise to the appeal as well as the costs of the appeal.

(5) Subject to any order made by the transferring court, where proceedings are transferred from one court to another, the court to which they are transferred may deal with all the costs, including the costs before the transfer.

Amendments—Inserted by SI 2013/262.

Deemed orders for costs (r 44.10(2))—Most of the orders referred to are made in the absence of the
parties although applications for permission to appeal and to apply for judicial review may be made at
contested hearings (rr 52.3(3) and 54.12(3)). In respect of a judicial review permission hearing: if given,
costs will not normally awarded against a claimant (PD54A, para 8.6); if refused, then the application for
permission is within the terms of "proceedings" under SCA 1981, s 51(1) and therefore susceptible to an
order for costs (see e g *R (Gunn) v Secretary of State for the Home Department* [2001] 1 WLR 1634, CA).

"order for applicant's costs in the case" (r 44.10(2))—See note to r 44.2 above. As an order for costs
for a successful defendant or respondent will not include any costs relating to the application covered by
r 44.10(2), he will need to apply specifically to vary under r 44.10(3) that an order be deemed under
r 44.10(2).

"apply at any time to vary the order" (r 44.10(3)—In principle there would appear to be no reason why
such application to vary the order deemed by r 44.10(2) should not be made at the final hearing of the
particular claim or application; nor does there seem to be any reason to make formal application under
Pt 23 or otherwise to give notice to the receiving party.

The court hearing an appeal (r 44.10(4))—It will be important, in preparation for an appeal, that the
appellate court has information necessary to deal with this provision. Two distinct situations must be
borne in mind:

(i)   An appeal where costs is one of the issues under appeal. It would be advisable still to appeal against
      the order for costs, since if the court dismisses the appeal on its merits, it may find that an order for
      costs below should have been made.
(ii) An appeal where costs is the only issue under appeal.

    In the first instance a separate bundle of Pt 36/*Calderbank* correspondence will be necessary (this will
remain privileged until the appeal has been heard), with separate submissions and skeleton arguments on
the subject. The court will need to have details of the documents considered by the first instance judge
and a note of his judgment on costs.

44.11 Court's powers in relation to misconduct

(1) The court may make an order under this rule where –

  (a) a party or that party's legal representative, in connection with a summary or
       detailed assessment, fails to comply with a rule, practice direction or court
       order; or
  (b) it appears to the court that the conduct of a party or that party's legal
       representative, before or during the proceedings or in the assessment
       proceedings, was unreasonable or improper.

(2) Where paragraph (1) applies, the court may –

  (a) disallow all or part of the costs which are being assessed; or
  (b) order the party at fault or that party's legal representative to pay costs which
       that party or legal representative has caused any other party to incur.

(3) Where –

  (a) the court makes an order under paragraph (2) against a legally represented
       party; and
  (b) the party is not present when the order is made,

the party's legal representative must notify that party in writing of the order no later than
7 days after the legal representative receives notice of the order.

Amendments—Inserted by SI 2013/262.

Defined terms—"costs": r 44.1(1); "costs officer": r 44.1(1); "detailed assessment": r 42.4.

"unreasonable or improper" (r 44.11(1)(b))—These bases for judging conduct of a party or his
representative must be distinguished from the more serious "wasted costs" criteria set out in SCA 1981,
s 51(7) (see further under r 48.7). The purpose of r 44.14 is to enable the court to exercise its discretion to
disallow a party's costs and to order him to pay another party's costs (see, for example, *Langley v North
West Water Authority* [1991] 1 WLR 697 – solicitors ordered to pay costs on their failure to comply with

directions; and *R v Nottinghamshire County Council* [1993] Fam Law 625 – local authority ordered to pay costs where adjournment was necessary because of their delay).

44.12 Set Off

Where a party entitled to costs is also liable to pay costs, the court may assess the costs which that party is liable to pay and either –

(a) set off the amount assessed against the amount the party is entitled to be paid and direct that party to pay any balance; or

(b) delay the issue of a certificate for the costs to which the party is entitled until the party has paid the amount which that party is liable to pay.

Amendments—Inserted by SI 2013/262.

****

Practice Direction 44 – General Rules About Costs

PART III

This Practice Direction supplements CPR Part 44

SECTION 1: GENERAL

Subsection 1 of this Practice Direction – Documents and Forms

Documents and Forms

1.1 In respect of any document which is required by Practice Directions 44 to 47 to be signed by a party or that party's legal representative, the provisions of Practice Direction 22 relating to who may sign apply as if the document in question was a statement of truth. Statements of truth are not required in assessment proceedings unless a rule of Practice Direction so requires or the court so orders.

> (Practice Direction 22 makes provision for cases in which a party is a child, a protected party or a company or other corporation and cases in which a document is signed on behalf of a partnership.)

1.2 Form N260 is a model form of Statement of Costs to be used for summary assessments.

> (Further details about Statements of Costs are given in paragraph 9.5 below.)

Precedents A, B and C in the Schedule of Costs Precedents annexed to this Practice Direction are model forms of bills of costs to be used for detailed assessments. A party wishing to rely upon a bill which departs from the model forms should include in the background information of the bill an explanation for that departure.

> (Further details about bills of costs are given in Practice Direction 47.)

Subsection 2 of this Practice Direction – Special Provisions Relating to VAT

Scope of this subsection

2.1 This subsection deals with claims for VAT) which are made in respect of costs being dealt with by way of summary assessment or detailed assessment.

Subsection on VAT—This subsection can be found in full online at www.justice.gov.uk.

****

Subsection 4 of this Practice Direction – Court's Discretion as to Costs: Rule 44.2

Court's Discretion as to Costs

4.1 The court may make an order about costs at any stage in a case.

4.2 There are certain costs orders which the court will commonly make in proceedings before trial. The following table sets out the general effect of these orders. The table is not an exhaustive list of the orders which the court may make.

Term	Effect
Costs Costs in any event	The party in whose favour the order is made is entitled to the costs in respect of the part of the proceedings to which the order relates, whatever other costs orders are made in the proceedings.
Costs in the case Costs in the application	The party in whose favour the court makes an order for costs at the end of the proceedings is entitled to his costs of the part of the proceedings to which the order relates.
Costs reserved	The decision about costs is deferred to a later occasion, but if no later order is made the costs will be costs in the case.
Claimant's/defendant's costs in the case/application	If the party in whose favour the costs order is made is awarded costs at the end of the proceedings, that party is entitled to his costs of the part of the proceedings to which the order relates. If any other party is awarded costs at the end of the proceedings, the party in whose favour the final costs order is made is not liable to pay the costs of any other party in respect of the part of the proceedings to which the order relates.
Costs thrown away	Where, for example, a judgment or order is set aside, the party in whose favour the costs order is made is entitled to the costs which have been incurred as a consequence. This includes the costs of – (a) preparing for and attending any hearing at which the judgment or order which has been set aside was made; (b) preparing for and attending any hearing to set aside the judgment or order in question;

Term	Effect
	(c) preparing for and attending any hearing at which the court orders the proceedings or the Part In question to be adjourned;
	(d) any steps taken to enforce a judgment or order which has subsequently been set aside.
Costs of and caused by	Where, for example, the court makes this order on an application to amend a statement of case, the party in whose favour the costs order is made is entitled to the costs of preparing for and attending the application and the costs of any consequential Amendment to his own statement of case.
Costs here and below	The party in whose favour the costs order is made is entitled not only to his costs in respect of the proceedings in which the court makes the order but also to his costs of the proceedings in any lower court. In the case of an appeal from a Divisional Court the party is not entitled to any costs incurred in any court below the Divisional Court.
No order as to costs Each party to pay his own costs	Each party is to bear his own costs of the part of the proceedings to which the order relates whatever costs order the court makes at the end of the proceedings.

Subsection 5 of this Practice Direction – Fees of Counsel

Fees of Counsel

5.1

(1) When making an order for costs the court may state an opinion as to whether or not the hearing was fit for the attendance of one or more counsel, and, if it does so, the court conducting a detailed assessment of those costs will have regard to the opinion stated.

(2) The court will generally express an opinion only where –
(a) the paying party asks it to do so;
(b) more than one counsel appeared for a party; or
(c) the court wishes to record its opinion that the case was not fit for the attendance of counsel.

5.2

(1) Where the court refers any matter to the conveyancing counsel of the court the fees payable to counsel in respect of the work done or to be done will be assessed by the court in accordance with rule 44.2.

(2) An appeal from a decision of the court in respect of the fees of such counsel will be dealt with under the general rules as to appeals set out in Part 52. If the appeal is against the decision of an authorised court officer, it will be dealt with in accordance with rules 47.22 to 47.24.

Subsection 6 of This Practice Direction – Basis of Assessment: Rule 44.3

Costs on the indemnity basis

6.1 If costs are awarded on the indemnity basis, the court assessing costs will disallow any costs –

    (a)   which it finds to have been unreasonably incurred; or

    (b)   which it considers to be unreasonable in amount.

Costs on the standard basis

6.2 If costs are awarded on the standard basis, the court assessing costs will disallow any costs –

    (a)   which it finds to have been unreasonably incurred;

    (b)   which it considers to be unreasonable in amount;

    (c)   which it considers to have been disproportionately incurred or to be disproportionate in amount; or

    (d)   about which it has doubts as to whether they were reasonably or proportionately incurred, or whether they are reasonable and proportionate in amount.

****

Subsection 8 of This Practice Direction -Procedure for Assessing Costs: Rule 44.6

Procedure for Assessing Costs

8.1 Subject to paragraph 8.3, where the court does not order fixed costs (or no fixed costs are provided for) the amount of costs payable will be assessed by the court. Rule 44.6 allows the court making an order about costs either –

    (a)   to make a summary assessment of the amount of the costs; or

    (b)   to order the amount to be decided in accordance with Part 47 (a detailed assessment).

8.2 An order for costs will be treated as an order for the amount of costs to be decided by a detailed assessment unless the order otherwise provides.

8.3 Where a party is entitled to costs some of which are fixed costs and some of which are not, the court will assess those costs which are not fixed. For example, the court will assess the disbursements payable in accordance with rules 45.12 or 45.19. The decision whether such assessment should be summary or detailed will be made in accordance with paragraphs 9.1 to 9.10 of this Practice Direction.

Subsection 9 of This Practice Direction – Summary Assessment: General Provisions

When the court should consider whether to make a summary assessment

9.1 Whenever a court makes an order about costs which does not provide only for fixed costs to be paid the court should consider whether to make a summary assessment of costs.

Timing of summary assessment

9.2 The general rule is that the court should make a summary assessment of the costs –

    (a)   ...

    (b)   at the conclusion of any other hearing, which has lasted not more than one day, in which case the order will deal with the costs of the application or matter to which the hearing related. If this hearing disposes of the claim, the order may deal with the costs of the whole claim,

unless there is good reason not to do so, for example where the paying party shows substantial grounds for disputing the sum claimed for costs that cannot be dealt with summarily.

****

Consent orders

9.4 Where an application has been made and the parties to the application agree an order by consent without any party attending, the parties should seek to agree a figure for costs to be inserted in the consent order or agree that there should be no order for costs.

Duty of parties and legal representatives

9.5

(1) sment of costs in any case to which paragraph 9.2 above applies, in accordance with the following subparagraphs.

(2) Each party who intends to claim costs must prepare a written statement of those costs showing separately in the form of a schedule –
    (a) the number of hours to be claimed;
    (b) the hourly rate to be claimed;
    (c) the grade of fee earner;
    (d) the amount and nature of any disbursement to be claimed, other than counsel's fee for appearing at the hearing;
    (e) the amount of legal representative's costs to be claimed for attending or appearing at the hearing;
    (f) counsel's fees; and
    (g) any VAT to be claimed on these amounts.

(3) The statement of costs should follow as closely as possible Form N260 and must be signed by the party or the party's legal representative. Where a party is –
    (a) an assisted person;
    (b) a LSC funded client;
    (c) a person for who civil legal services (within the meaning of Part 1 of the Legal Aid, Sentencing and Punishment of Offenders Act 2012) are provided under arrangements made for the purposes of that Part of that Act; or
    (d) represented by a person in the party's employment,
    the statement of costs need not include the certificate appended at the end of Form N260.

(4) The statement of costs must be filed at court and copies of it must be served on any party against whom an order for payment of those costs is intended to be sought as soon as possible and in any event –
    (a) for a fast track trial, not less than 2 days before the trial; and
    (b) for all other hearings, not less than 24 hours before the time fixed for the hearing.

9.6 The failure by a party, without reasonable excuse, to comply with paragraph 9.5 will be taken into account by the court in deciding what order to make about the costs of the claim, hearing or application, and about the costs of any further hearing or detailed assessment hearing that may be necessary as a result of that failure.

PART III

No summary assessment by a costs officer

9.7 The court awarding costs cannot make an order for a summary assessment of costs by a costs officer. If a summary assessment of costs is appropriate but the court awarding costs is unable to do so on the day, the court may give directions as to a further hearing before the same judge.

Assisted persons

9.8 The court will not make a summary assessment of the costs of a receiving party who is an assisted person or LSC funded client or who is a person for whom civil legal services (within the meaning of Part 1 of the Legal Aid, Sentencing and Punishment of Offenders Act 2012) are provided under arrangements made for the purposes of that Part of that Act.

Children or protected parties

9.9

    (1)   The court will not make a summary assessment of the costs of a receiving party who is a child or protected party within the meaning of Part 21 unless the legal representative acting for the child or protected party has waived the right to further costs (see Practice Direction 46 paragraph 2.1).

    (2)   The court may make a summary assessment of costs payable by a child or protected party.

Disproportionate or unreasonable costs

9.10 The court will not give its approval to disproportionate or unreasonable costs. When the amount of the costs to be paid has been agreed between the parties the order for costs must state that the order is by consent.

Subsection 10 of this Practice Direction – Legal Representative's Duty to Notify Party: Rule 44.8

Legal Representative's Duty to Notify Party: Rule 44.8

10.1 For the purposes of rule 44.8 and paragraph 10.2, "party" includes any person (for example, an insurer, a trade union or the LSC or Lord Chancellor) who has instructed the legal representative to act for the party or who is liable to pay the legal representative's fees.

10.2 A legal representative who notifies a party of an order under rule 44.8 must also explain why the order came to be made.

10.3 Although rule 44.8 does not specify any sanction for breach of the rule the court may, either in the order for costs itself or in a subsequent order, require the legal representative to produce to the court evidence showing that the legal representative took reasonable steps to comply with the rule.

Subsection 11 of this Practice Direction – *Court's Powers In Relation To Misconduct: Rule 44.11*

Court's Powers In Relation To Misconduct: Rule 44.11

11.1 Before making an order under rule 44.11, the court must give the party or legal representative in question a reasonable opportunity to make written submissions or, if the legal representative so desires, to attend a hearing.

11.2 Conduct which is unreasonable or improper includes steps which are calculated to prevent or inhibit the court from furthering the overriding objective.

11.3 Although rule 44.11(3) does not specify any sanction for breach of the obligation imposed by the rule the court may, either in the order under rule 44.11(2) or in a subsequent order, require the legal representative to produce to the court evidence that the legal representative took reasonable steps to comply with the obligation.

****

PART 46
COSTS – SPECIAL CASES

CONTENTS OF THIS PART

Section I – Costs Payable by or to Particular Persons

Section I – Costs Payable by or to Particular Persons

46.1 Pre-commencement disclosure and orders for disclosure against a person who is not a party

(1) This paragraph applies where a person applies –

    (a) for an order under –
        (i)   section 33 of the Senior Courts Act 19811; or
        (ii)   section 52 of the County Courts Act 19842,

(which give the court powers exercisable before commencement of proceedings); or

    (b) for an order under –
        (i)   section 34 of the Senior Courts Act 19813; or
        (ii)   section 53 of the County Courts Act 19844,

(which give the court power to make an order against a non-party for disclosure of documents, inspection of property etc.).

(2) The general rule is that the court will award the person against whom the order is sought that person's costs –

(a)   of the application; and

(b)   of complying with any order made on the application.

(3) The court may however make a different order, having regard to all the circumstances, including –

(a)   the extent to which it was reasonable for the person against whom the order was sought to oppose the application; and

(b)   whether the parties to the application have complied with any relevant pre-action protocol.

Amendments—Inserted by SI 2013/262.

46.2 Costs orders in favour of or against non-parties

(1) Where the court is considering whether to exercise its power under section 51 of the Senior Courts Act 19815 (costs are in the discretion of the court) to make a costs order in favour of or against a person who is not a party to proceedings, that person must –

(a)   be added as a party to the proceedings for the purposes of costs only; and

(b)   be given a reasonable opportunity to attend a hearing at which the court will consider the matter further.

(2) This rule does not apply –

(a)   where the court is considering whether to –

(i)   make an order against the Lord Chancellor in proceedings in which the Lord Chancellor has provided legal aid to a party to the proceedings;

(ii)   make a wasted costs order (as defined in rule 46.8); and

(b)   in proceedings to which rule 46.1 applies (pre-commencement disclosure and orders for disclosure against a person who is not a party).

Amendments—Inserted by SI 2013/262.

Costs orders against non-parties—SCA 1981, s 51(3) gives the court discretion "to determine by whom and to what extent costs are to be paid". This includes costs against a third party who must be must be joined as a party (r 46.2(1)(a), to deal with costs only (r 46.2(1)(b)).

"costs order in favour of or against a person who is not a party to proceedings" (r 48.2(1))—Guidelines for the ordering of costs against a third party were laid down by the Court of Appeal in *Symphony Group plc v Hodgson* [1994] QB 179; and see *Sarra v Sarra* [1994] 2 FLR 880 (costs sought against accountant called as expert witness by one party) for an example of a case in the ancillary relief jurisdiction.

46.3 Limitations on court's power to award costs in favour of trustee or personal representative

(1) This rule applies where –

(a)   a person is or has been a party to any proceedings in the capacity of trustee or personal representative; and

(b)   rule 44.5 does not apply.

(2) The general rule is that that person is entitled to be paid the costs of those proceedings, insofar as they are not recovered from or paid by any other person, out of the relevant trust fund or estate.

(3) Where that person is entitled to be paid any of those costs out of the fund or estate, those costs will be assessed on the indemnity basis.

Amendments—Inserted by SI 2013/262.

Defined terms—"costs": r 44.1(1); "indemnity basis": r 44.3.

Indemnity basis—This rule re-states the general principle that a person acting in a representative capacity should have his costs paid on an indemnity basis and, as seems likely, on the basis that those costs are paid in any event (see r 44.3).

***Beddoe* orders**—Those acting in a fiduciary capacity should be aware of the need, where necessary, to seek a *Beddoe* order (*Re Beddoe* [1893] 1 Ch 547); e g personal representatives in proceedings under I(PFD)A 1975, trustees joined in ancillary relief proceedings, pension fund trustees, trustees in bankruptcy (c f *Albert v Albert* [1996] BPIR 232) and building society (not bank) mortgagees who respond when served in financial remedy proceedings. In many instances, such an application may not be strictly necessary, but in cases of doubt, where a trustee thinks there is any risk of his being criticised by the court for expending the trust, or other (e g pension) fund, application should be made for an order (and see PD46, para 1.1(a)).

Procedure on application for a *Beddoe* order—Application (other than under CPR 1998 proceedings, e g I(PFD)A 1975) will be in the proceedings by FPR 2010, Pt 18 application.

****

46.5 Litigants in person

(1) This rule applies where the court orders (whether by summary assessment or detailed assessment) that the costs of a litigant in person are to be paid by any other person.

(2) The costs allowed under this rule will not exceed, except in the case of a disbursement, two-thirds of the amount which would have been allowed if the litigant in person had been represented by a legal representative.

(3) The litigant in person shall be allowed –

- (a) costs for the same categories of –
    - (i) work; and
    - (ii) disbursements,

which would have been allowed if the work had been done or the disbursements had been made by a legal representative on the litigant in person's behalf;

- (b) the payments reasonably made by the litigant in person for legal services relating to the conduct of the proceedings; and
- (c) the costs of obtaining expert assistance in assessing the costs claim.

(4) The amount of costs to be allowed to the litigant in person for any item of work claimed will be –

- (a) where the litigant can prove financial loss, the amount that the litigant can prove to have been lost for time reasonably spent on doing the work; or
- (b) where the litigant cannot prove financial loss, an amount for the time reasonably spent on doing the work at the rate set out in Practice Direction 46.

(5) A litigant who is allowed costs for attending at court to conduct the case is not entitled to a witness allowance in respect of such attendance in addition to those costs.

(6) For the purposes of this rule, a litigant in person includes –

- (a) a company or other corporation which is acting without a legal representative; and
- (b) any of the following who acts in person (except where any such person is represented by a firm in which that person is a partner) –
    - (i) a barrister,

  (ii)   a solicitor,
  (iii) a solicitor's employee,
  (iv)   a manager of a body recognised under section 9 of the Administration of
         Justice Act 1985; or
  (v)   a person who, for the purposes of the 2007 Act, is an authorised person in
         relation to an activity which constitutes the conduct of litigation (within
         the meaning of that Act).

Amendments—Inserted by SI 2013/262.

****

46.7 Orders in respect of pro bono representation

(1) Where the court makes an order under section 194(3) of the 2007 Act –

  (a)   the court may order the payment to the prescribed charity of a sum no greater
        than the costs specified in Part 45 to which the party with pro bono
        representation would have been entitled in accordance with that Part and in
        respect of that representation had it not been provided free of charge; or

  (b)   where Part 45 does not apply, the court may determine the amount of the
        payment (other than a sum equivalent to fixed costs) to be made by the paying
        party to the prescribed charity by –
        (i)   making a summary assessment; or
        (ii) making an order for detailed assessment,

of a sum equivalent to all or part of the costs the paying party would have been ordered
to pay to the party with pro bono representation in respect of that representation had it
not been provided free of charge.

(2) Where the court makes an order under section 194(3) of the 2007 Act, the order must
direct that the payment by the paying party be made to the prescribed charity.

(3) The receiving party must send a copy of the order to the prescribed charity within
7 days of receipt of the order.

(4) Where the court considers making or makes an order under section 194(3) of the
2007 Act, Parts 44 to 47 apply, where appropriate, with the following modifications –

  (a)   references to "costs orders", "orders about costs" or "orders for the payment of
        costs" are to be read, unless otherwise stated, as if they refer to an order under
        section 194(3);

  (b)   references to "costs" are to be read, as if they referred to a sum equivalent to the
        costs that would have been claimed by, incurred by or awarded to the party with
        pro bono representation in respect of that representation had it not been
        provided free of charge; and

  (c)   references to "receiving party" are to be read, as meaning a party who has pro
        bono representation and who would have been entitled to be paid costs in
        respect of that representation had it not been provided free of charge.

Amendments—Inserted by SI 2013/262.

Section II – Costs Relating to Legal representatives

46.8 Personal liability of legal representative for costs – wasted costs orders

(1) This rule applies where the court is considering whether to make an order under
section 51(6) of the Senior Courts Act 19817 (court's power to disallow or (as the case
may be) order a legal representative to meet, "wasted costs").

(2) The court will give the legal representative a reasonable opportunity to make written submissions or, if the legal representative prefers, to attend a hearing before it makes such an order.

(3) When the court makes a wasted costs order, it will –

    (a) specify the amount to be disallowed or paid; or

    (b) direct a costs judge or a district judge to decide the amount of costs to be disallowed or paid.

(4) The court may direct that notice must be given to the legal representative's client, in such manner as the court may direct –

    (a) of any proceedings under this rule; or

    (b) of any order made under it against his legal representative.

Amendments—Inserted by SI 2013/262.

Defined terms—"costs": r 43.2(1)(a); "costs judge": r 43.2(1)(c); "legal representative": SCA 1981, s 51(13); "privileged": Glossary; "wasted costs": SCA 1981, s 51(7).

Jurisdiction—This rule derives from SCA 1981, s 51(6). Where there has been an improper, negligent or unreasonable act by a legal representative, the rule gives the court a discretion to make a wasted costs order against that legal representative personally. The court must give the representative notice of any such application.

Guidance on the court's jurisdiction—In *Ridehalgh v Horsefield, and Watson v Watson (Wasted Costs Order)* [1994] 2 FLR 194, the Court of Appeal fully considered the wasted costs jurisdiction and proposed guidelines as to its exercise. Accordingly, the court must balance two, often conflicting, questions of public interest. On the one hand, lawyers should not be deterred from pursuing their clients' interests for fear of incurring personal liability for costs; on the other hand, other parties to proceedings need to be protected from financial prejudice caused by the unjustifiable conduct of lawyers. The jurisdiction is one which is entirely discretionary.

Meaning of "improper, unreasonable or negligent"—These words from SCA 1981, s 51(7), were considered fully in *Ridehalgh v Horsefield* (above):

(a) *"Improper"* This word covers conduct which might lead to disbarment, striking off or other serious professional penalty; however, it is not restricted to this and might include other conduct stigmatised by the court in appropriate circumstances.

(b) *"Unreasonable"* This term includes conduct which is vexatious or harasses other parties, but it does not include an approach which merely leads to an unsuccessful result or which a more cautious representative might not have adopted.

(c) *"Negligent"* This term is to be approached in a non-technical way. A legal representative may come within the definition by failing to act with the competence reasonably to be expected of a member of the legal profession (as further explained in *Fisher Meredith v JH and PH (Financial Remedy: Appeal: Wasted Costs)* [2012] 2 FLR 536 at [34]–[37]).

A legal representative is not to be regarded as acting improperly, unreasonably or negligently where pursuing a hopeless case for the client, providing this does not represent an abuse of the court's process. It is the responsibility of a lawyer to present the case and of the court to judge it.

Warnings on unarguable appeals—In *Re G (A Minor) (Role of the Appellate Court)* [1987] 1 FLR 164 at [168], May LJ, firmly echoed by Nourse LJ, issued a warning to legal representatives that the court would not shrink from "investigating how public money has come to be spent in [unarguable appeals] and to make all appropriate orders to ensure that it has not been wasted".

Procedure on wasted costs orders—In *Ridehalgh v Horsefield* (above) the Court of Appeal made comments on the procedure for seeking an order.

Procedure after *Ridehalgh*—Any procedure should be as simple and summary as possible, while remaining consistent with fairness to the respondent legal representative. In *Ridehalgh v Horsefield*, Sir Thomas Bingham MR (as he then was) approved the procedure in *Re A Barrister (Wasted Costs Order) (No 1 of 1991)* [1993] QB 293; namely:

(a) Where the court intends to exercise the wasted costs jurisdiction it must set out clearly and concisely the complaint and grounds upon which the order is to be made. These measures are draconian and, as with contempt proceedings, the grounds must be clear and particularised.

(b) A three-stage test would apply: (i) Had there been an improper, unreasonable or negligent act or omission? (ii) As a result had any costs been incurred by a party? (iii) If the answers to both questions was "yes", should the court make an order; and if so what specific sum should be considered?

(c) The court should formally state its complaint, in chambers, and invite comments from the representative. After comments have been heard from any other party, the court should give a formal ruling.

(d) The court must specify the sum to be disallowed.

Procedure—There are two routes to an order (PD46, paras 5.7 and 5.8): (i) the application by a party and (ii) the order by the court of its own initiative. *Re A Barrister (Wasted Costs Order) (No 1 of 1991)* explains a procedure where the court acts or application can be by a party in the proceedings. Now the party seeking a wasted costs order must state a complaint. In either case, it is important for the legal representative to know the case to be met and to have an opportunity (often with assistance from insurers) to answer it.

Application for an order—PD46, para 5.9 requires that the party who wishes to apply for a wasted costs order must give notice of such application in accordance with Pt 23 (or FPR 2010, Pt 18 in family proceedings) or by making an oral application in the course of any hearing. Under CPR 1998, Pt 23 or FPR 2010, Pt 18, the application notice must set out "what the legal representative is alleged to have done or failed to do", accompanied by details of precisely what costs are sought against him.

"legal representative" (r 46.8(1))—SCA 1981, s 51(13) defines "legal or other representative" as "in relation to a party to proceedings, any person exercising a right of audience or right to conduct litigation on his behalf". Rule 46.8 uses "legal representative" as synonymous with that definition. CLSA 1990, s 119(1) defines "right of audience" as "the right to exercise any of the functions of appearing before and addressing a court including the calling and examining of witnesses"; it defines "right to conduct litigation" as being the right to issue process and to perform ancillary functions in relation to proceedings.

Wasted costs, proportionality and disclosure of documents—Where a party's solicitors press another party, especially a local authority, for wide-ranging disclosure which may be of dubious relevance to the case, their attention may be drawn to the case of *R v Reading Justices ex parte Berkshire County Council* [1996] 1 FLR 149, in which disclosure of documents from criminal proceedings was limited to "material evidence" (MCA 1980, s 97(1)). If the solicitors persist in seeking extensive disclosure, they risk a wasted costs order (*R v M (Wasted Costs Order)* [1996] 1 FLR 750).

Privilege and wasted costs—Where a paying party has refused to waive privilege in respect of documents relevant to assessment of wasted costs, the court will be wary of making an order against a legal representative who is unable to explain his/her actions by reference to a client's withheld documents (*Medcalf v Weatherhill* [2003] 1 AC 120).

CLS funding (Legal aid)—The court retains its inherent jurisdiction to order solicitors to repay costs to the legal aid fund where there has been a serious dereliction of duty, and presumably now where costs have been wasted, but this applies only where the Legal Aid Agency (which replaced the Legal Services Commission on 1 April 2013) pursues its remedy promptly (*Clark v Clark (No 2)* [1991] 1 FLR 179).

46.9 Basis of detailed assessment of solicitor and client costs

(1) This rule applies to every assessment of a solicitor's bill to a client except a bill which is to be paid out of the Community Legal Service Fund under the Legal Aid Act 1988 or the Access to Justice Act 1999 or by the Lord Chancellor under Part 1 of the Legal Aid, Sentencing and Punishment of Offenders Act 2012.

(2) Section 74(3) of the Solicitors Act 1974 applies unless the solicitor and client have entered into a written agreement which expressly permits payment to the solicitor of an amount of costs greater than that which the client could have recovered from another party to the proceedings.

(3) Subject to paragraph (2), costs are to be assessed on the indemnity basis but are to be presumed –

(a) to have been reasonably incurred if they were incurred with the express or implied approval of the client;

(b) to be reasonable in amount if their amount was expressly or impliedly approved by the client;

(c) to have been unreasonably incurred if –

    (i)   they are of an unusual nature or amount; and

    (ii)   the solicitor did not tell the client that as a result the costs might not be recovered from the other party.

(4) Where the court is considering a percentage increase on the application of the client, the court will have regard to all the relevant factors as they reasonably appeared to the solicitor or counsel when the conditional fee agreement was entered into or varied.

Amendments—Inserted by SI 2013/262; amended by SI 2013/534.

46.10 Assessment procedure

(1) This rule sets out the procedure to be followed where the court has made an order under Part III of the Solicitors Act 1974 for the assessment of costs payable to solicitor by the solicitor's client.

(2) The solicitor must serve a breakdown of costs within 28 days of the order for costs to be assessed.

(3) The client must serve points of dispute within 14 days after service on him of the breakdown of costs.

(4) The solicitor must serve any reply within 14 days of service on the solicitor of the points of dispute.

(5) Either party may file a request for a hearing date –

    (a)   after points of dispute have been served; but

    (b)   no later than 3 months after the date of the order for the costs to be assessed.

(6) This procedure applies subject to any contrary order made by the court.

Amendments—Inserted by SI 2013/262.

****

Practice Direction 46 – Costs Special Cases

This Practice Direction supplements CPR Part 46

Awards of Costs in Favour of a Trustee or Personal Representative: Rule 46.3

1.1 A trustee or personal representative is entitled to an indemnity out of the relevant trust fund or estate for costs properly incurred. Whether costs were properly incurred depends on all the circumstances of the case including whether the trustee or personal representative ("the trustee") –

    (a)   obtained directions from the court before bringing or defending the proceedings;

    (b)   acted in the interests of the fund or estate or in substance for a benefit other than that of the estate, including the trustee's own; and

    (c)   acted in some way unreasonably in bringing or defending, or in the conduct of, the proceedings.

1.2 The trustee is not to be taken to have acted for a benefit other than that of the fund by reason only that the trustee has defended a claim in which relief is sought against the trustee personally.

PART III

Costs Where Money Is Payable By Or To A Child Or Protected Party: Rule 46.4

2.1 The circumstances in which the court need not order the assessment of costs under rule 46.4(3) are as follows –

(a)   where there is no need to do so to protect the interests of the child or protected party or their estate;

(b)   where another party has agreed to pay a specified sum in respect of the costs of the child or protected party and the legal representative acting for the child or protected party has waived the right to claim further costs;

(c)   where the court has decided the costs payable to the child or protected party by way of summary assessment and the legal representative acting for the child or protected party has waived the right to claim further costs; and

(d)   where an insurer or other person is liable to discharge the costs which the child or protected party would otherwise be liable to pay to the legal representative and the court is satisfied that the insurer or other person is financially able to discharge those costs.

Litigants In Person: Rule 46.5

3.1 In order to qualify as an expert for the purpose of rule 46.5(3)(c) (expert assistance in connection with assessing the claim for costs), the person in question must be a –

(a)   barrister;

(b)   solicitor;

(c)   Fellow of the Institute of Legal Executives;

(d)   Fellow of the Association of Costs Lawyers;

(e)   law costs draftsman who is a member of the Academy of Experts;

(f)   law costs draftsman who is a member of the Expert Witness Institute.

3.2 Where a self represented litigant wishes to prove that the litigant has suffered financial loss, the litigant should produce to the court any written evidence relied on to support that claim, and serve a copy of that evidence on any party against whom the litigant seeks costs at least 24 hours before the hearing at which the question may be decided.

3.3 A self represented litigant who commences detailed assessment proceedings under rule 47.5 should serve copies of that written evidence with the notice of commencement.

3.4 The amount, which may be allowed to a self represented litigant under rule 45.39(5)(b) and rule 46.5(4)(b), is £18 per hour.

Orders in Respect of Pro Bono Representation: Rule 46.7

4.1 Where an order is sought under section 194(3) of the Legal Services Act 2007 the party who has pro bono representation must prepare, file and serve a written statement of the sum equivalent to the costs that party would have claimed for that legal representation had it not been provided free of charge.

Personal Liability of Legal Representative for Costs – Wasted Costs Orders: Rule 46.8

5.1 A wasted costs order is an order –

(a)   that the legal representative pay a sum (either specified or to be assessed) in respect of costs to a party; or

(b)   for costs relating to a specified sum or items of work to be disallowed.

5.2 Rule 46.8 deals with wasted costs orders against legal representatives. Such orders can be made at any stage in the proceedings up to and including the detailed assessment proceedings. In general, applications for wasted costs are best left until after the end of the trial.

5.3 The court may make a wasted costs order against a legal representative on its own initiative.

5.4 A party may apply for a wasted costs order –

    (a) by filing an application notice in accordance with Part 23; or

    (b) by making an application orally in the course of any hearing.

5.5 It is appropriate for the court to make a wasted costs order against a legal representative, only if –

    (a) the legal representative has acted improperly, unreasonably or negligently;

    (b) the legal representative's conduct has caused a party to incur unnecessary costs, or has meant that costs incurred by a party prior to the improper, unreasonable or negligent act or omission have been wasted;

    (c) it is just in all the circumstances to order the legal representative to compensate that party for the whole or part of those costs.

5.6 The court will give directions about the procedure to be followed in each case in order to ensure that the issues are dealt with in a way which is fair and as simple and summary as the circumstances permit.

5.7 As a general rule the court will consider whether to make a wasted costs order in two stages –

    (a) at the first stage the court must be satisfied –

        (i) that it has before it evidence or other material which, if unanswered, would be likely to lead to a wasted costs order being made; and

        (ii) the wasted costs proceedings are justified notwithstanding the likely costs involved;

    (b) at the second stage, the court will consider, after giving the legal representative an opportunity to make representations in writing or at a hearing, whether it is appropriate to make a wasted costs order in accordance with paragraph 5.5 above.

5.8 The court may proceed to the second stage described in paragraph 5.7 without first adjourning the hearing if it is satisfied that the legal representative has already had a reasonable opportunity to make representations.

5.9 On an application for a wasted costs order under Part 23 the application notice and any evidence in support must identify –

    (a) what the legal representative is alleged to have done or failed to do; and

    (b) the costs that the legal representative may be ordered to pay or which are sought against the legal representative.

Assessment of Solicitor and Client Costs: Rules 46.9 and 46.10

6.1 A client and solicitor may agree whatever terms they consider appropriate about the payment of the solicitor's charges. If however, the costs are of an unusual nature, either in amount or the type of costs incurred, those costs will be presumed to have been unreasonably incurred unless the solicitor satisfies the court that the client was informed that they were unusual and that they might not be allowed on an assessment of costs between the parties. That information must have been given to the client before the costs were incurred.

6.2 Costs as between a solicitor and client are assessed on the indemnity basis. The presumptions in rule 46.9(3) are rebuttable.

6.3 If a party fails to comply with the requirements of rule 46.10 concerning the service of a breakdown of costs or points of dispute, any other party may apply to the court in which the detailed assessment hearing should take place for an order requiring compliance. If the court makes such an order, it may –

(a) make it subject to conditions including a condition to pay a sum of money into court; and

(b) specify the consequence of failure to comply with the order or a condition.

6.4 The procedure for obtaining an order under Part III of the Solicitors Act 1974 is by a Part 8 claim, as modified by rule 67.3 and Practice Direction 67. Precedent J of the Schedule of Costs Precedents is a model form of claim form. The application must be accompanied by the bill or bills in respect of which assessment is sought, and, if the claim concerns a conditional fee agreement, a copy of that agreement. If the original bill is not available a copy will suffice.

6.5 Model forms of order, which the court may make, are set out in Precedents K, L and M of the Schedule of Costs Precedents.

6.6 The breakdown of costs referred to in rule 46.10 is a document which contains the following information –

(a) details of the work done under each of the bills sent for assessment; and

(b) in applications under Section 70 of the Solicitors Act 1974, a cash account showing money received by the solicitor to the credit of the client and sums paid out of that money on behalf of the client but not payments out which were made in satisfaction of the bill or of any items which are claimed in the bill.

6.7 Precedent P of the Schedule of Costs Precedents is a model form of breakdown of costs. A party who is required to serve a breakdown of costs must also serve –

(a) copies of the fee notes of counsel and of any expert in respect of fees claimed in the breakdown, and

(b) written evidence as to any other disbursement which is claimed in the breakdown and which exceeds £250.

6.8 The provisions relating to default costs certificates (rule 47.11) do not apply to cases to which rule 46.10 applies.

6.9 The time for requesting a detailed assessment hearing is within 3 months after the date of the order for the costs to be assessed.

6.10 The form of request for a hearing date must be in Form N258C. The request must be accompanied by copies of –

(a) the order sending the bill or bills for assessment;

(b) the bill or bills sent for assessment;

(c) the solicitor's breakdown of costs and any invoices or accounts served with that breakdown;

(d) a copy of the points of dispute;

(e) a copy of any replies served;

(f) a statement signed by the party filing the request or that party's legal representative giving the names and addresses for service of all parties to the proceedings.

6.11 The request must include the estimated length of hearing.

6.12 On receipt of the request the court will fix a date for the hearing, or will give directions.

6.13 The court will give at least 14 days notice of the time and place of the detailed assessment hearing.

6.14 Unless the court gives permission, only the solicitor whose bill it is and parties who have served points of dispute may be heard and only items specified in the points of dispute may be raised.

6.15 If a party wishes to vary that party's breakdown of costs, points of dispute or reply, an amended or supplementary document must be filed with the court and copies of it must be served on all other relevant parties. Permission is not required to vary a breakdown of costs, points of dispute or a reply but the court may disallow the variation or permit it only upon conditions, including conditions as to the payment of any costs caused or wasted by the variation.

6.16 Unless the court directs otherwise the solicitor must file with the court the papers in support of the bill not less than 7 days before the date for the detailed assessment hearing and not more than 14 days before that date.

6.17 Once the detailed assessment hearing has ended it is the responsibility of the legal representative appearing for the solicitor or, as the case may be, the solicitor in person to remove the papers filed in support of the bill.

6.18 If, in the course of a detailed assessment hearing of a solicitor's bill to that solicitor's client, it appears to the court that in any event the solicitor will be liable in connection with that bill to pay money to the client, it may issue an interim certificate specifying an amount which in its opinion is payable by the solicitor to the client.

6.19 After the detailed assessment hearing is concluded the court will –

   (a) complete the court copy of the bill so as to show the amount allowed;
   (b) determine the result of the cash account;
   (c) award the costs of the detailed assessment hearing in accordance with Section 70(8) of the Solicitors Act 1974; and
   (d) issue a final costs certificate.

****

PART 47
PROCEDURE FOR DETAILED ASSESSMENT OF COSTS AND DEFAULT PROVISIONS

CONTENTS OF THIS PART

Section I
General Rules about Detailed Assessment

47.1 Time when detailed assessment may be carried out

The general rule is that the costs of any proceedings or any part of the proceedings are not to be assessed by the detailed procedure until the conclusion of the proceedings but the court may order them to be assessed immediately.

> (Practice Direction 47 gives further guidance about when proceedings are concluded for the purpose of this rule.)

Amendments—Inserted by SI 2013/262.

Defined terms—"costs": r 44.1(1)).

Scope—"Detailed assessment", as distinct from "summary assessment", is the terminology preferred under CPR 1998 for what was formerly known as taxation of costs under both the old rules governing civil procedure and in legal aid legislation.

Further guidance in the practice direction—PD47, paras 1.2–1.4 provide further guidance as to when detailed assessment may be commenced or when proceedings are concluded, or treated as concluded:

(1) Treated as concluded: The parties may agree or the court order that proceedings be treated as concluded (para 1.2), for example, in long-running children proceedings with successive reviews and an order for costs has been made at some point.
(2) If a notice of commencement is served, a party may question whether the receiving party is entitled to claim at that stage of proceedings (para 1.3).
(3) Where there is no realistic prospect of a claim, continuing detailed assessment may be ordered (para 1.4).

47.2 No stay of detailed assessment where there is an appeal

Detailed assessment is not stayed pending an appeal unless the court so orders.

Amendments—Inserted by SI 2013/262.

No stay pending appeal—This is as with an appeal order. A stay on detailed assessment can be made to the court below or to that court appealed to (PD47, para 2). Application can be included in the appeal notice (which will generally be the most economic way) or must be by FPR 2010, Pt 18 or CPR 1998, Pt 23.

47.3 Powers of an authorised court officer

(1) An authorised court officer has all the powers of the court when making a detailed assessment, except –

(a) power to make a wasted costs order as defined in rule 46.8;
(b) power to make an order under –
(i) rule 44.11 (powers in relation to misconduct);
(ii) rule 47.8 (sanction for delay in commencing detailed assessment proceedings);
(iii) paragraph (2) (objection to detailed assessment by authorised court officer); and
(c) power to make a detailed assessment of costs payable to a solicitor by that solicitor's client, unless the costs are being assessed under rule 46.5 (costs where money is payable to a child or protected party).

(2) Where a party objects to the detailed assessment of costs being made by an authorised court officer, the court may order it to be made by a costs judge or a district judge.

(Practice Direction 47 sets out the relevant procedure.)

Amendments—Inserted by SI 2013/262.

The relevant procedure—The relevant procedure is set out in PD47, para 3.3.

47.4 Venue for detailed assessment proceedings

(1) All applications and requests in detailed assessment proceedings must be made to or filed at the appropriate office.

(Practice Direction 47 sets out the meaning of "appropriate office" in any particular case)

(2) The court may direct that the appropriate office is to be the Costs Office.

(3) A county court may direct that another county court is to be the appropriate office.

(4) A direction under paragraph (3) may be made without proceedings being transferred to that court.

> (Rule 30.2 makes provision for any county court to transfer the proceedings to another county court for detailed assessment of costs.)

Amendments—Inserted by SI 2013/262.

"appropriate office"—See PD47, para 4.1.

Section II
Costs Payable by one Party to Another – Commencement of Detailed Assessment Proceedings

47.5 Application of this Section

This Section of Part 47 applies where a cost officer is to make a detailed assessment of –

(a)   costs which are payable by one party to another; or

(b)   the sum which is payable by one party to the prescribed charity pursuant to an order under section 194(3) of the 2007 Act.

Amendments—Inserted by SI 2013/262.

47.6 Commencement of detailed assessment proceedings

(1) Detailed assessment proceedings are commenced by the receiving party serving on the paying party –

(a)   notice of commencement in the relevant practice form; and

(b)   a copy of the bill of costs.

> (Rule 47.7 sets out the period for commencing detailed assessment proceedings)

(2) The receiving party must also serve a copy of the notice of commencement and the bill on any other relevant persons specified in Practice Direction 47.

(3) A person on whom a copy of the notice of commencement is served under paragraph (2) is a party to the detailed assessment proceedings (in addition to the paying party and the receiving party).

> (Practice Direction 47 deals with –
>
> other documents which the party must file when requesting detailed assessment;
>
> the court's powers where it considers that a hearing may be necessary;
>
> the form of a bill; and
>
> the length of notice which will be given if a hearing date is fixed.)

Amendments—Inserted by SI 2013/262.

Defined terms—"costs": r 44.1(1); "detailed assessment": r 44.3; "paying party": r 44.1(1)); "receiving party": r 44.1(1)).

Documents for service—The receiving party must serve a combination of the documents listed in r 47.6(1) and PD47, para 5.2. These include notice of commencement, which is in Form N252.

"any other relevant persons" (r 47.6(2))—PD47, para 5.5 defines a "relevant person" for the purposes of Pt 47. This definition includes a non-party who may be required to pay costs, a trustee out of whose trust fund costs might, unusually, be paid, but not a legally assisted person (see r 47.17) and probably not a legal representative under a wasted costs order (since costs should be defined by the court at the time of the order: r 48.7(4)).

The client as "relevant person"—The party in respect of whom the costs are to be paid is not a relevant person, save where application is made by him to be joined as a party to assessment proceedings. A person can apply to be made a party under Pt 19. This will give a legally aided assisted person the right to apply to be heard on assessment of their bill, whereas, in the past, such a person's standing as a party to the taxation process was unclear. These provisions will be of greater significance where costs orders are made for differing amounts, for proportions etc. Practitioners will need to be aware that their interests may be in conflict with those of their client.

47.7 Period for commencing detailed assessment proceedings

The following table shows the period for commencing detailed assessment proceedings.

Source of right to detailed assessment	Time by which detailed assessment proceedings must be commenced
Judgment, direction, order, award or other determination	3 months after the date of the judgment etc. Where detailed assessment is stayed pending an appeal, 3 months after the date of the order lifting the stay
Discontinuance under Part 38	3 months after the date of service of notice of discontinuance under rule 38.3; or 3 months after the date of the dismissal of application to set the notice of discontinuance aside under rule 38.4
Acceptance of an offer to settle under Part 36	3 months after the date when the right to costs arose

Amendments—Inserted by SI 2013/262.

47.8 Sanction for delay in commencing detailed assessment proceedings

(1) Where the receiving party fails to commence detailed assessment proceedings within the period specified –

    (a) in rule 47.7; or

    (b) by any direction of the court,

the paying party may apply for an order requiring the receiving party to commence detailed assessment proceedings within such time as the court may specify.

(2) On an application under paragraph (1), the court may direct that, unless the receiving party commences detailed assessment proceedings within the time specified by the court, all or part of the costs to which the receiving party would otherwise be entitled will be disallowed.

(3) If –

    (a) the paying party has not made an application in accordance with paragraph (1); and

    (b) the receiving party commences the proceedings later than the period specified in rule 47.7,

the court may disallow all or part of the interest otherwise payable to the receiving party under –

    (i) section 17 of the Judgments Act 1838; or

    (ii) section 74 of the County Courts Act 1984,

but will not impose any other sanction except in accordance with rule 44.11 (powers in relation to misconduct).

(4) Where the costs to be assessed in a detailed assessment are payable out of the Community Legal Service Fund, this rule applies as if the receiving party were the solicitor to whom the costs are payable and the paying party were the Legal Services Commission.

(5) Where the costs to be assessed in a detailed assessment are payable by the Lord Chancellor under Part 1 of the Legal Aid, Sentencing and Punishment of Offenders Act 2012, this rule applies as if the receiving party were the solicitor to whom the costs are payable and the paying party were the Lord Chancellor.

Amendments—Inserted by SI 2013/262; amended by SI 2013/534.

Defined terms—"costs": r 44.1(1); "detailed assessment": r 44.3; "paying party": r 44.1(1)); "receiving party": r 44.1(1).

Delay in commencement of detailed assessment—It is not necessary to obtain court permission to start detailed assessment proceedings out of time but, where proceedings are not commenced, a paying party, including for this purpose the Legal Aid Agency (which replaced the Legal Services Commission on 1 April 2013), can seek an order to require the receiving party to do so. Thereafter, failure to commence proceedings within the requisite period of time may attract an order that all or part of the costs be disallowed. By contrast, failure to commence in accordance with the r 44.7 time-limits may only be penalised by (i) an order that interest be awarded for a shorter period and (ii) an award of costs against the legal representative on the basis of misconduct under r 44.11.

"period specified" (r 47.8(1))—See r 47.7.

"interest otherwise payable to the receiving party" (r 47.8(3))—Rule 44.2(6)(g) provides that an order for payment of interest on costs due can be made by the court at the same time as any order for costs is made.

47.9 Points of dispute and consequence of not serving

(1) The paying party and any other party to the detailed assessment proceedings may dispute any item in the bill of costs by serving points of dispute on –

(a)   the receiving party; and

(b)   every other party to the detailed assessment proceedings.

(2) The period for serving points of dispute is 21 days after the date of service of the notice of commencement.

(3) If a party serves points of dispute after the period set out in paragraph (2), that party may not be heard further in the detailed assessment proceedings unless the court gives permission.

(Practice Direction 47 sets out requirements about the form of points of dispute)

(4) The receiving party may file a request for a default costs certificate if –

(a)   the period set out in paragraph (2) for serving points of dispute has expired; and

(b)   the receiving party has not been served with any points of dispute.

(5) If any party (including the paying party) serves points of dispute before the issue of a default costs certificate the court may not issue the default costs certificate.

(Section IV of this Part sets out the procedure to be followed after points of dispute have been served).

Amendments—Inserted by SI 2013/262.

Defined terms—"costs": r 44.1(1); "detailed assessment": r 44.3; "paying party": r 44.1(1)); "receiving party": r 44.1(1).

Form of points of dispute—PD47, para 8.2 provides that Precedent G from the costs precedents must be used.

Dispute as to items—At this stage in the detailed assessment process the court is still not involved (subject to any order under r 47.8). The paying party who wishes to dispute any item on the detailed assessment bill does so by sending points of dispute, 21 days after service of the bill, to the receiving party and to anyone else interested in the assessment. Failure to send points of dispute within that time (i) prevents the paying party being heard on the detailed assessment except with the court's permission and (ii) enables the receiving party to apply to the court for a default costs certificate.

"**points of dispute**" (r 47.9(1))—Points of dispute should be briefly set out in accordance with PD47, para 8.2.

"**21 days after the date of service of the notice**" (r 47.9(2))—See r 6.7 for details of deemed service periods.

47.10 Procedure where costs are agreed

(1) If the paying party and the receiving party agree the amount of costs, either party may apply for a costs certificate (either interim or final) in the amount agreed.

> (Rule 47.16 and rule 47.17 contain further provisions about interim and final costs certificates respectively)

(2) An application for a certificate under paragraph (1) must be made to the court which would be the venue for detailed assessment proceedings under rule 47.4.

Amendments—Inserted by SI 2013/262.

Section III
Costs Payable by One Party to Another – Default Provisions

47.11 Default costs certificate

(1) Where the receiving party is permitted by rule 47.9 to obtain a default costs certificate, that party does so by filing a request in the relevant practice form.

> (Practice Direction 47 deals with the procedure by which the receiving party may obtain a default costs certificate.)

(2) A default costs certificate will include an order to pay the costs to which it relates.

(3) Where a receiving party obtains a default costs certificate, the costs payable to that party for the commencement of detailed assessment proceedings will be the sum set out in Practice Direction 47.

(4) A receiving party who obtains a default costs certificate in detailed assessment proceedings pursuant to an order under section 194(3) of the 2007 Act must send a copy of the default costs certificate to the prescribed charity.

Amendments—Inserted by SI 2013/262.

Procedure—Practice and procedure governing the application are dealt with in PD47, paras 10.1–10.6.

47.12 Setting aside a default costs certificate

(1) The court will set aside a default costs certificate if the receiving party was not entitled to it.

(2) In any other case, the court may set aside or vary a default costs certificate if it appears to the court that there is some good reason why the detailed assessment proceedings should continue.

> (Practice Direction 47 contains further details about the procedure for setting aside a default costs certificate and the matters which the court must take into account)

(3) Where the court sets aside or varies a default costs certificate in detailed assessment proceedings pursuant to an order under section 194(3) of the Legal Services Act 2007, the receiving party must send a copy of the order setting aside or varying the default costs certificate to the prescribed charity.

Amendments—Inserted by SI 2013/262.

Procedure—Practice and procedure for setting aside the certificate are dealt with in PD47, paras 11.1–11.3.

Section IV
*Costs Payable by One Party to Another – Procedure where Points of Dispute
are Served*

47.13 Optional Reply

(1) Where any party to the detailed assessment proceedings serves points of dispute, the
receiving party may serve a reply on the other parties to the assessment proceedings.

(2) The receiving party may do so within 21 days after being served with the points of
dispute to which the reply relates.

(Practice Direction 47 sets out the meaning of "reply".)

Amendments—Inserted by SI 2013/262.

Defined terms—"detailed assessment": r 44.3; "paying party": r 44.1(1)); "receiving party": r 44.1(1).

Scope—A receiving party who is served with points of dispute may serve a reply. This is entirely
voluntary but if no reply is filed it may be reflected in a later order for costs on the detailed assessment.
If a receiving party accepts a point raised in dispute, it might be prudent to indicate this in a reply under
r 47.13. However, merely to re-argue points already raised in the bill would seem to be sterile and might
risk the receiving party losing the costs so incurred.

"reply"—See PD47, para 12.1.

47.14 Detailed assessment hearing

(1) Where points of dispute are served in accordance with this Part, the receiving party
must file a request for a detailed assessment hearing within 3 months of the expiry of the
period for commencing detailed assessment proceedings as specified –

    (a)   in rule 47.7; or
    (b)   by any direction of the court.

(2) Where the receiving party fails to file a request in accordance with paragraph (1), the
paying party may apply for an order requiring the receiving party to file the request
within such time as the court may specify.

(3) On an application under paragraph (2), the court may direct that, unless the receiving
party requests a detailed assessment hearing within the time specified by the court, all or
part of the costs to which the receiving party would otherwise be entitled will be
disallowed.

(4) If –

    (a)   the paying party has not made an application in accordance with paragraph (2);
       and
    (b)   the receiving party files a request for a detailed assessment hearing later than
       the period specified in paragraph (1),

the court may disallow all or part of the interest otherwise payable to the receiving party
under –

    (i)   section 17 of the Judgments Act 1838; or
    (ii)   section 74 of the County Courts Act 1984,

but will not impose any other sanction except in accordance with rule 44.11 (powers in
relation to misconduct).

(5) No party other than –

    (a)   the receiving party;
    (b)   the paying party; and
    (c)   any party who has served points of dispute under rule 47.9,

may be heard at the detailed assessment hearing unless the court gives permission.

(6) Only items specified in the points of dispute may be raised at the hearing, unless the court gives permission.

(7) If an assessment is carried out at more than one hearing, then for the purposes of rule 52.4 time for appealing shall not start to run until the conclusion of the final hearing, unless the court orders otherwise.

> (Practice Direction 47 specifies other documents which must be filed with the request for hearing and the length of notice which the court will give when it fixes a hearing date.)

Amendments—Inserted by SI 2013/262.

Defined terms—"costs": r 44.1(1); "default costs certificate": "detailed assessment": r 44.3; "paying party": r 44.1(1)); "points of dispute": r 47.9 "receiving party": r 44.1(1)).

Request for detailed assessment—Once points of dispute are served, the receiving party must file a request for a detailed assessment within 3 months. If the receiving party is out of time for filing the request, the paying party can ask the court to specify a date for filing. In default of this requirement, all or part of the costs may be allowed and if both paying and receiving parties delay in applying under this rule, interest on costs due may be disallowed. Only the paying party, the receiving party and any other party who has filed points of dispute may be heard at the detailed assessment hearing(s). Where matters have not been raised in the points of dispute, a party will be estopped from raising them unless the court gives permission.

Practice and procedure—PD47, para 13.2 sets out specific requirements which need to be complied with in the request for a detailed assessment hearing. Applications in the assessment proceedings are made under FPR 2010, Pt 18 or CPR 1998, Pt 23.

Document giving the right to detailed assessment—This document is defined in the practice direction and is crucial to the process of detailed assessment since it underlines the fact that there is a right to proceed with such an assessment.

"request for a detailed assessment hearing" (r 47.14(1))—The request must be in Form N258.

"any party who has served points of dispute under rule 47.9" (r 47.14(6)(c))—Points of dispute may also be served by every other party to the detailed assessment proceedings (r 47.9(1)(b)); only those "other parties" who have served points of dispute can be heard.

47.15 Provisional Assessment

(1) This rule applies to any detailed assessment proceedings commenced in the High Court or a county court on or after 1 April 2013 in which the costs claimed are the amount set out in paragraph 14.1 of the practice direction supplementing this Part, or less.

(2) In proceedings to which this rule applies, the parties must comply with the procedure set out in Part 47 as modified by paragraph 14 Practice Direction 47.

(3) The court will undertake a provisional assessment of the receiving party's costs on receipt of Form N258 and the relevant supporting documents specified in Practice Direction 47.

(4) The provisional assessment will be based on the information contained in the bill and supporting papers and the contentions set out in Precedent G (the points of dispute and any reply).

(5) The court will not award more than £1,500 to any party in respect of the costs of the provisional assessment.

(6) The court may at any time decide that the matter is unsuitable for a provisional assessment and may give directions for the matter to be listed for hearing. The matter will then proceed under rule 47.14 without modification.

(7) When a provisional assessment has been carried out, the court will send a copy of the bill, as provisionally assessed, to each party with a notice stating that any party who

wishes to challenge any aspect of the provisional assessment must, within 21 days of the receipt of the notice, file and serve on all other parties a written request for an oral hearing. If no such request is filed and served within that period, the provisional assessment shall be binding upon the parties, save in exceptional circumstances.

(8) The written request referred to in paragraph (7) must –

    (a)   identify the item or items in the court's provisional assessment which are sought to be reviewed at the hearing; and

    (b)   provide a time estimate for the hearing.

(9) The court then will fix a date for the hearing and give at least 14 days' notice of the time and place of the hearing to all parties.

(10) Any party which has requested an oral hearing, will pay the costs of and incidental to that hearing unless –

    (a)   it achieves an adjustment in its own favour by 20% or more of the sum provisionally assessed; or

    (b)   the court otherwise orders.

Amendments—Inserted by SI 2013/262.

Documents in PD47 (r 47.15(2))—See para 14.3.

Section V
Interim Costs Certificate and Final Costs Certificate.

47.16   Power to issue an interim certificate

(1) The court may at any time after the receiving party has filed a request for a detailed assessment hearing –

    (a)   issue an interim costs certificate for such sum as it considers appropriate or

    (b)   amend or cancel an interim certificate.

(2) An interim certificate will include an order to pay the costs to which it relates, unless the court orders otherwise.

(3) The court may order the costs certified in an interim certificate to be paid into court.

(4) Where the court –

    (a)   issues an interim costs certificate; or

    (b)   amends or cancels an interim certificate,

in detailed assessment proceedings pursuant to an order under section 194(3) of the 2007 Act, the receiving party must send a copy of the interim costs certificate or the order amending or cancelling the interim costs certificate to the prescribed charity.

Amendments—Inserted by SI 2013/262.

Defined terms—"costs": r 44.1(1); "detailed assessment": r 44.3; "receiving party": r 44.1(1).

Costs certificates—Once the receiving party has applied under r 47.14 for a detailed assessment hearing, the court may issue an interim certificate or may cancel or amend such a certificate. Costs of the application will normally be included in the certificate and an order may be made that such costs be paid into court.

Procedure for application—In accordance with PD47, para 15 application for a certificate is in accordance with Pt 23 (FPR 2010, Pt 18 in family proceedings).

"issue an interim costs certificate" (r 47.15(1)(a))—This power appears to be additional to the power under r 44.3(8) to order costs to be paid on account before they are assessed, although any payment made under the latter rule will doubtless be taken into account when the amount to be paid under the interim costs certificate is quantified.

47.17 Final costs certificate

(1) In this rule a "completed bill" means a bill calculated to show the amount due following the detailed assessment of the costs.

(2) The period for filing the completed bill is 14 days after the end of the detailed assessment hearing.

(3) When a completed bill is filed the court will issue a final costs certificate and serve it on the parties to the detailed assessment proceedings.

(4) Paragraph (3) is subject to any order made by the court that a certificate is not to be issued until other costs have been paid.

(5) A final costs certificate will include an order to pay the costs to which it relates, unless the court orders otherwise.

(Practice Direction 47 deals with the form of a final costs certificate)

(6) Where the court issues a final costs certificate in detailed assessment proceedings pursuant to an order under section 194(3) of the 2007 Act, the receiving party must send a copy of the final costs certificate to the prescribed charity.

Amendments—Inserted by SI 2013/262.

Defined terms—"costs": r 44.1(1); "detailed assessment": r 44.3; "receiving party": r 44.1(1).

Final costs certificate—Not more than 2 weeks after completion of all detailed assessment hearings, the receiving party should lodge a final bill showing the amount due following such assessment. The court then issues a final costs certificate which includes an order to the paying party to discharge the liability for costs, unless otherwise ordered (e g because the receiving party has an outstanding liability to make payment of a lump sum or costs to the paying party). PD47, paras 16.1–16.8 deal with practice and procedure in relation to obtaining a final costs certificate.

Section VI
Detailed Assessment Procedure for Costs of a LSC Funded Client, an Assisted Person or Person to Whom Legal Aid is Made Available where Costs are Payable out of the Community Legal Service Fund or by the Lord Chancellor under Part 1 of the Legal Aid, Sentencing and Punishment of Offenders Act 2012

Amendments—SI 2013/534.

47.18 Detailed assessment procedure where costs are payable out of the Community Legal Services Fund or by the Lord Chancellor under Part 1 of the Legal Aid, Sentencing and Punishment of Offenders Act 2012

(1) Where the court is to assess costs of a LSC funded client, an assisted person or a person to whom legal aid is provided which are payable out of the Community Legal Services Fund or by the Lord Chancellor under Part 1 of the Legal Aid, Sentencing and Punishment of Offenders Act 2012, that person's solicitor may commence detailed assessment proceedings by filing a request in the relevant practice form.

(2) A request under paragraph (1) must be filed within 3 months after the date when the right to detailed assessment arose.

(3) The solicitor must also serve a copy of the request for detailed assessment on the LSC funded client, the assisted person or the person to whom legal aid is provided, if notice of that person's interest has been given to the court in accordance with community legal service or legal aid regulations.

(4) Where the solicitor has certified that the LSC funded client or that person wishes to attend an assessment hearing, the court will, on receipt of the request for assessment, fix a date for the assessment hearing.

(5) Where paragraph (3) does not apply, the court will, on receipt of the request for assessment provisionally assess the costs without the attendance of the solicitor, unless it considers that a hearing is necessary.

(6) After the court has provisionally assessed the bill, it will return the bill to the solicitor.

(7) The court will fix a date for an assessment hearing if the solicitor informs the court, within 14 days after receiving the provisionally assessed bill, that the solicitor wants the court to hold such a hearing.

Amendments—Inserted by SI 2013/262; amended by SI 2013/534.

Defined terms—"costs": r 44.1(1); "detailed assessment": r 43.4; "request for detailed assessment": r 47.14(1).

47.19 Detailed assessment procedure where costs are payable out of a fund other than the community legal service fund

(1) Where the court is to assess costs which are payable out of a fund other than the Community Legal Service Fund, the receiving party may commence detailed assessment proceedings by filing a request in the relevant practice form.

(2) A request under paragraph (1) must be filed within 3 months after the date when the right to detailed assessment arose.

(3) The court may direct that the party seeking assessment serve a copy of the request on any person who has a financial interest in the outcome of the assessment.

(4) The court will, on receipt of the request for assessment, provisionally assess the costs without the attendance of the receiving party, unless the court considers that a hearing is necessary.

(5) After the court has provisionally assessed the bill, it will return the bill to the receiving party.

(6) The court will fix a date for an assessment hearing if the receiving party informs the court, within 14 days after receiving the provisionally assessed bill, that the receiving party wants the court to hold such a hearing.

Amendments—Inserted by SI 2013/262.

Section VII
Costs of Detailed Assessment Proceedings

47.20 Liability for costs of detailed assessment proceedings

(1) The receiving party is entitled to the costs of the detailed assessment proceedings except where –

    (a) the provisions of any Act, any of these Rules or any relevant practice direction provide otherwise; or

    (b) the court makes some other order in relation to all or part of the costs of the detailed assessment proceedings.

(2) Paragraph (1) does not apply where the receiving party has pro bono representation in the detailed assessment proceedings but that party may apply for an order in respect of that representation under section 194(3) of the 2007 Act.

(3) In deciding whether to make some other order, the court must have regard to all the circumstances, including –

    (a)   the conduct of all the parties;

    (b)   the amount, if any, by which the bill of costs has been reduced; and

    (c)   whether it was reasonable for a party to claim the costs of a particular item or to dispute that item.

(4) The provisions of Part 36 apply to the costs of detailed assessment proceedings with the following modifications –

    (a)   "claimant" refers to "receiving party" and "defendant" refers to "paying party";

    (b)   "trial" refers to "detailed assessment hearing";

    (c)   in rule 36.9(5), at the end insert "or, where the Part 36 offer is made in respect of the detailed assessment proceedings, after the commencement of the detailed assessment hearing.";

    (d)   for rule 36.11(7) substitute "If the accepted sum is not paid within 14 days or such other period as has been agreed the offeree may apply for a final costs certificate for the unpaid sum.";

    (e)   a reference to "judgment being entered" is to the completion of the detailed assessment, and references to a "judgment" being advantageous or otherwise are to the outcome of the detailed assessment.

(5) The court will usually summarily assess the costs of detailed assessment proceedings at the conclusion of those proceedings.

(6) Unless the court otherwise orders, interest on the costs of detailed assessment proceedings will run from the date of default, interim or final costs certificate, as the case may be.

(7) For the purposes of rule 36.14, detailed assessment proceedings are to be regarded as an independent claim.

Amendments—Inserted by SI 2013/262. Under the transitional provisions, r 47.20(1)–(5),(7) do not apply to detailed assessments commenced before 1 April 2013. In respect of such assessments, rr 47.18 and 47.19, which were in force before then, apply instead.

Section VIII
Appeals from Authorised Court Officers in Detailed Assessment Proceedings

47.21 Right to appeal

(1) Any party to detailed assessment proceedings may appeal against a decision of an authorised court officer in those proceedings.

Amendments—Inserted by SI 2013/262.

47.22 Court to hear appeal

An appeal against a decision of an authorised court officer lies to a costs judge or a district judge of the High Court.

Amendments—Inserted by SI 2013/262.

47.23 Appeal procedure

(1) The appellant must file an appeal notice within 21 days after the date of the decision against which it is sought to appeal.

(2) On receipt of the appeal notice, the court will –

(a) serve a copy of the notice on the parties to the detailed assessment proceedings; and

(b) give notice of the appeal hearing to those parties.

Amendments—Inserted by SI 2013/262.

47.24 Powers of the court on appeal

On an appeal from an authorised court officer the court will –

(a) re-hear the proceedings which gave rise to the decision appealed against; and

(b) make any order and give any directions as it considers appropriate.

Amendments—Inserted by SI 2013/262.

Practice Direction 47 –
Procedure for Detailed Assessment of Costs and Default Provisions

This Practice Direction supplements CPR Part 47

Time When Assessment May Be Carried Out: Rule 47.1

1.1 For the purposes of rule 47.1, proceedings are concluded when the court has finally determined the matters in issue in the claim, whether or not there is an appeal, or made an award of provisional damages under Part 41.

1.2 The court may order or the parties may agree in writing that, although the proceedings are continuing, they will nevertheless be treated as concluded.

1.3 A party who is served with a notice of commencement (see paragraph 5.2 below) may apply to a costs judge or a district judge to determine whether the party who served it is entitled to commence detailed assessment proceedings. On hearing such an application the orders which the court may make include: an order allowing the detailed assessment proceedings to continue, or an order setting aside the notice of commencement.

1.4 A costs judge or a district judge may make an order allowing detailed assessment proceedings to be commenced where there is no realistic prospect of the claim continuing.

No Stay of Detailed Assessment Where There is an Appeal: Rule 47.2

2 An application to stay the detailed assessment of costs pending an appeal may be made to the court whose order is being appealed or to the court which will hear the appeal.

Powers of an Authorised Court Officer: Rule 47.3

3.1 The court officers authorised by the Lord Chancellor to assess costs in the Costs Office and the Principal Registry of the Family Division are authorised to deal with claims where the base costs excluding VAT do not exceed £35,000 in the case of senior executive officers, or their equivalent, and £110,000 in the case of principal officers.

3.2 Where the receiving party, paying party and any other party to the detailed assessment proceedings who has served points of dispute are agreed that the assessment should not be made by an authorised court officer, the receiving party should so inform the court when requesting a hearing date. The court will then list the hearing before a costs judge or a district judge.

3.3 In any other case a party who objects to the assessment being made by an authorised court officer must make an application to the costs judge or district judge under Part 23 setting out the reasons for the objection.

Venue for Detailed Assessment Proceedings: Rule 47.4

4.1 For the purposes of rule 47.4(1) the "appropriate office" means –

  (a) the district registry or county court in which the case was being dealt with when the judgment or order was made or the event occurred which gave rise to the right to assessment, or to which it has subsequently been transferred;
  (b) where a tribunal, person or other body makes an order for the detailed assessment of costs, a county court (subject to paragraph 4.2); or
  (c) in all other cases, including Court of Appeal cases, the Costs Office.

4.2

  (1) This paragraph applies where the appropriate office is any of the following county courts: Barnet, Bow, Brentford, Bromley, Central London, Clerkenwell and Shoreditch, Croydon, Edmonton, Ilford, Kingston, Lambeth, Mayors and City of London, Romford, Uxbridge, Wandsworth, West London, Willesden and Woolwich

  (2) Where this paragraph applies –
  (a) the receiving party must file any request for a detailed assessment hearing in the Costs Office and, for all purposes relating to that detailed assessment (other than the issue of default costs certificates and applications to set aside default costs certificates), the Costs Office will be treated as the appropriate office in that case;
  (b) default costs certificates should be issued and applications to set aside default costs certificates should be issued and heard in the relevant county court; and
  (c) unless an order is made under rule 47.4(2) directing that the Costs Office as part of the High Court shall be the appropriate office, an appeal from any decision made by a costs judge shall lie to the Designated Civil Judge for the London Group of County Courts or such judge as the Designated Civil Judge shall nominate. The appeal notice and any other relevant papers should be lodged at the Central London Civil Justice Centre.

4.3

  (1) A direction under rule 47.4(2) or (3) specifying a particular court, registry or office as the appropriate office may be given on application or on the court's own initiative.
  (2) Unless the Costs Office is the appropriate office for the purposes of rule 47.4(1) an order directing that an assessment is to take place at the Costs Office will be made only if it is appropriate to do so having regard to the size of the bill of costs, the difficulty of the issues involved, the likely length of the hearing, the cost to the parties and any other relevant matter.

PART III

Commencement of Detailed Assessment Proceedings: Rule 47.6

5.1 Precedents A, B, C and D in the Schedule of Costs Precedents annexed to this Practice Direction are model forms of bills of costs for detailed assessment.

5.2 The receiving party must serve on the paying party and all the other relevant persons the following documents –

(a)   a notice of commencement in Form N252;

(b)   a copy of the bill of costs;

(c)   copies of the fee notes of counsel and of any expert in respect of fees claimed in the bill;

(d)   written evidence as to any other disbursement which is claimed and which exceeds £500;

(e)   a statement giving the name and address for service of any person upon whom the receiving party intends to serve the notice of commencement.

5.3 The notice of commencement must be completed to show as separate items –

(a)   the total amount of the costs claimed in the bill;

(b)   the extra sum which will be payable by way of fixed costs and court fees if a default costs certificate is obtained.

5.4 Where the notice of commencement is to be served outside England and Wales the date to be inserted in the notice of commencement for the paying party to send points of dispute is a date (not less than 21 days from the date of service of the notice) which must be calculated by reference to Section IV of Part 6 as if the notice were a claim form and as if the date to be inserted was the date for the filing of a defence.

5.5

(1)   For the purposes of rule 47.6(2) a "relevant person" means –

(a)   any person who has taken Part In the proceedings which gave rise to the assessment and who is directly liable under an order for costs made against that person;

(b)   any person who has given to the receiving party notice in writing that that person has a financial interest in the outcome of the assessment and wishes to be a party accordingly;

(c)   any other person whom the court orders to be treated as such.

(2)   Where a party is unsure whether a person is or is not a relevant person, that party may apply to the appropriate office for directions.

(3)   The court will generally not make an order that the person in respect of whom the application is made will be treated as a relevant person, unless within a specified time that person applies to the court to be joined as a party to the assessment proceedings in accordance with Part 19 (Parties and Group Litigation).

5.6 Where –

(a)   the bill of costs is capable of being copied electronically; and

(b)   before the detailed assessment hearing,

a paying party requests an electronic copy of the bill, the receiving party must supply the paying party with a copy in its native format (for example, in Excel or an equivalent) free of charge not more than 7 days after receipt of the request.

Form and Contents of Bills of Costs – General

5.7 A bill of costs may consist of such of the following sections as may be appropriate –

(1)   title page;

(2)   background information;

(3)   items of costs claimed under the headings specified in paragraph 5.12;

(4)   summary showing the total costs claimed on each page of the bill;

(5)   schedules of time spent on non-routine attendances; and

(6)   the certificates referred to in paragraph 5.21.

If the only dispute between the parties concerns disbursements, the bill of costs shall be limited to items (1) and (2) above, a list of the disbursements in issue and brief written submissions in respect of those disbursements.

5.8 Where it is necessary or convenient to do so, a bill of costs may be divided into two or more parts, each part containing sections (2), (3) and (4) above. Circumstances in which it will be necessary or convenient to divide a bill into parts include the following –

(1)   Where the receiving party acted in person during the course of the proceedings (whether or not that party also had a legal representative at that time) the bill must be divided into different parts so as to distinguish between;

(a)   the costs claimed for work done by the legal representative; and

(b)   the costs claimed for work done by the receiving party in person.

(2)   Where the receiving party had pro bono representation for part of the proceedings and an order under section 194(3) of the Legal Services Act 2007 has been made, the bill must be divided into different parts so as to distinguish between –

(a)   the sum equivalent to the costs claimed for work done by the legal representative acting free of charge; and

(b)   the costs claimed for work not done by the legal representative acting free of charge.

(3)   Where the receiving party was represented by different legal representatives during the course of the proceedings, the bill must be divided into different parts so as to distinguish between the costs payable in respect of each legal representative.

(4)   Where the receiving party obtained legal aid or LSC funding or is a person for whom civil legal services (within the meaning of Part 1 of the Legal Aid, Sentencing and Punishment of Offenders Act 2012) were provided under arrangements made for the purposes of that Part of that Act in respect of all or part of the proceedings the bill must be divided into separate parts so as to distinguish between –

(a)   costs claimed before legal aid or LSC funding was granted or after civil legal services were provided;

(b)   costs claimed after legal aid or LSC funding was granted or after civil legal services were provided; and

(c)   any costs claimed after legal aid or LSC funding ceased or after civil legal services ceased to be provided.

(5)   Where the bill covers costs payable under an order or orders under which there are different paying parties the bill must be divided into parts so as to deal separately with the costs payable by each paying party.

(6)   Where the bill covers costs payable under an order or orders, in respect of which the receiving party wishes to claim interest from different dates, the bill must be divided to enable such interest to be calculated.

5.9 Where a party claims costs against another party and also claims costs against the LSC or Lord Chancellor only for work done in the same period, the costs claimed against the LSC or Lord Chancellor only can be claimed either in a separate part of the bill or in additional columns in the same part of the bill. Precedents B and C in the Schedule of Costs Precedents annexed to this Practice Direction show how bills should be drafted when costs are claimed against the LSC only.

PART III

Form and Content of Bills of Costs – Title page

5.10 The title page of the bill of costs must set out –

(1) the full title of the proceedings;

(2) the name of the party whose bill it is and a description of the document showing the right to assessment (as to which see paragraph 13.3 of this Practice Direction);

(3) if VAT is included as part of the claim for costs, the VAT number of the legal representative or other person in respect of whom VAT is claimed;

(4) details of all legal aid certificates, LSC certificates, certificates recording the determinations of the Directions of Legal Aid Casework and relevant amendment certificates in respect of which claims for costs are included in the bill.

Form and Content of Bills of Costs – Background information

5.11 The background information included in the bill of costs should set out –

(1) a brief description of the proceedings up to the date of the notice of commencement;

(2) a statement of the status of the legal representatives' employee in respect of whom costs are claimed and (if those costs are calculated on the basis of hourly rates) the hourly rates claimed for each such person.

(3) a brief explanation of any agreement or arrangement between the receiving party and his legal representatives, which affects the costs claimed in the bill.

Form and Content of Bills of Costs – Heads of costs

5.12 The bill of costs may consist of items under such of the following heads as may be appropriate –

(1) attendances at court and upon counsel up to the date of the notice of commencement;

(2) attendances on and communications with the receiving party;

(3) attendances on and communications with witnesses including any expert witness;

(4) attendances to inspect any property or place for the purposes of the proceedings;

(5) attendances on and communications with other persons, including offices of public records;

(6) communications with the court and with counsel;

(7) work done on documents:

(8) work done in connection with negotiations with a view to settlement if not already covered in the heads listed above;

(9) attendances on and communications with London and other agents and work done by them;

(10) other work done which was of or incidental to the proceedings and which is not already covered in the heads listed above.

5.13 In respect of each of the heads of costs –

(1) "communications" means letters out e-mails out and telephone calls;

(2) communications, which are not routine communications, must be set out in chronological order;

(3) routine communications must be set out as a single item at the end of each head;

5.14 Routine communications are letters out, e-mails out and telephone calls which because of their simplicity should not be regarded as letters or e-mails of substance or telephone calls which properly amount to an attendance.

5.15 Each item claimed in the bill of costs must be consecutively numbered.

5.16 In each part of the bill of costs which claims items under head (1) in paragraph 5.12 (attendances at court and upon counsel) a note should be made of –

(1) all relevant events, including events which do not constitute chargeable items;
(2) any orders for costs which the court made (whether or not a claim is made in respect of those costs in this bill of costs).

5.17 The numbered items of costs may be set out on paper divided into columns. Precedents A, B and C in the Schedule of Costs Precedents annexed to this Practice Direction illustrate various model forms of bills of costs.

5.18 In respect of heads (2) to (10) in paragraph 5.12 above, if the number of attendances and communications other than routine communications is twenty or more, the claim for the costs of those items in that section of the bill of costs should be for the total only and should refer to a schedule in which the full record of dates and details is set out. If the bill of costs contains more than one schedule each schedule should be numbered consecutively.

5.19 The bill of costs must not contain any claims in respect of costs or court fees which relate solely to the detailed assessment proceedings other than costs claimed for preparing and checking the bill.

5.20 The summary must show the total profit costs and disbursements claimed separately from the total VAT claimed. Where the bill of costs is divided into parts the summary must also give totals for each part. If each page of the bill gives a page total the summary must also set out the page totals for each page.

5.21 The bill of costs must contain such of the certificates, the texts of which are set out in Precedent F of the Schedule of Costs Precedents annexed to this Practice Direction, as are appropriate.

5.22 The following provisions relate to work done by legal representatives –

(1) Routine letters out, routine e-mails out and routine telephone calls will in general be allowed on a unit basis of 6 minutes each, the charge being calculated by reference to the appropriate hourly rate. The unit charge for letters out and e-mails out will include perusing and considering the routine letters in or e-mails in.
(2) The court may, in its discretion, allow an actual time charge for preparation of electronic communications sent by legal representatives, which properly amount to attendances provided that the time taken has been recorded.
(3) Local travelling expenses incurred by legal representatives will not be allowed. The definition of "local" is a matter for the discretion of the court. As a matter of guidance, "local" will, in general, be taken to mean within a radius of 10 miles from the court dealing with the case at the relevant time. Where travelling and waiting time is claimed, this should be allowed at the rate agreed with the client unless this is more than the hourly rate on the assessment.
(4) The cost of postage, couriers, out-going telephone calls, fax and telex messages will in general not be allowed but the court may exceptionally in its discretion allow such expenses in unusual circumstances or where the cost is unusually heavy.
(5) The cost of making copies of documents will not in general be allowed but the court may exceptionally in its discretion make an allowance for copying in unusual circumstances or where the documents copied are unusually numerous

PART III

in relation to the nature of the case. Where this discretion is invoked the number of copies made, their purpose and the costs claimed for them must be set out in the bill.

(6)   Agency charges as between principal legal representatives and their agents will be dealt with on the principle that such charges, where appropriate, form part of the principal legal representative's charges. Where these charges relate to head (1) in paragraph 5.12 (attendances at court and on counsel) they must be included in their chronological order in that head. In other cases they must be included in head (9) (attendances on London and other agents).

Period for Commencing Detailed Assessment Proceedings: Rule 47.7

6.1 time for commencing the detailed assessment proceedings may be extended or shortened either by agreement (rule 2.11) or by the court (rule 3.1(2)(a)). Any application is to the appropriate office.

6.2 The detailed assessment proceedings are commenced by service of the documents referred to. Permission to commence assessment proceedings out of time is not required.

Sanction for Delay in Commencing Detailed Assessment Proceedings: Rule 47.8

7 An application for an order under rule 47.8 must be made in writing and be issued in the appropriate office. The application notice must be served at least 7 days before the hearing.

Points of Dispute and Consequences of Not Serving: Rule 47.9

8.1 Time for service of points of dispute may be extended or shortened either by agreement (rule 2.11) or by the court (rule 3.1(2)(a)). Any application is to the appropriate office.

8.2 Points of dispute must be short and to the point. They must follow Precedent G in the Schedule of Costs Precedents annexed to this Practice Direction, so far as practicable. They must:

(a)   identify any general points or matters of principle which require decision before the individual items in the bill are addressed; and

(b)   identify specific points, stating concisely the nature and grounds of dispute.

Once a point has been made it should not be repeated but the item numbers where the point arises should be inserted in the left hand box as shown in Precedent G.

8.3 The paying party must state in an open letter accompanying the points of dispute what sum, if any, that party offers to pay in settlement of the total costs claimed. The paying party may also make an offer under Part 36.

PROCEDURE WHERE COSTS ARE AGREED AND ON DISCONTINUANCE: RULE 47.10

9.1 Where the parties have agreed terms as to the issue of a costs certificate (either interim or final) they should apply under rule 40.6 (Consent judgments and orders) for an order that a certificate be issued in the terms set out in the application. Such an application may be dealt with by a court officer, who may issue the certificate.

9.2 Where in the course of proceedings the receiving party claims that the paying party has agreed to pay costs but that the paying party will neither pay those costs nor join in a consent application under paragraph 9.1, the receiving party may apply under Part 23 for a certificate either interim or final to be issued.

9.3 Nothing in rule 47.10 prevents parties who seek a judgment or order by consent from including in the draft a term that a party shall pay to another party a specified sum in respect of costs.

9.4

(1) The receiving party may discontinue the detailed assessment proceedings in accordance with Part 38 (Discontinuance).

(2) Where the receiving party discontinues the detailed assessment proceedings before a detailed assessment hearing has been requested, the paying party may apply to the appropriate office for an order about the costs of the detailed assessment proceedings.

(3) Where a detailed assessment hearing has been requested the receiving party may not discontinue unless the court gives permission.

(4) A bill of costs may be withdrawn by consent whether or not a detailed assessment hearing has been requested.

Default Costs Certificate: Rule 47.11

10.1

(1) A request for the issue of a default costs certificate must be made in Form N254 and must be signed by the receiving party or his legal representative.

(2) The request must be accompanied by a copy of the document giving the right to detailed assessment and must be filed at the appropriate office. (Paragraph 13.3 below identifies the appropriate documents).

10.2 A default costs certificate will be in Form N255.

10.3 Attention is drawn to Rules 40.3 (Drawing up and Filing of Judgments and Orders) and 40.4 (Service of Judgments and Orders) which apply to the preparation and service of a default costs certificate. The receiving party will be treated as having permission to draw up a default costs certificate by virtue of this Practice Direction.

10.4 The issue of a default costs certificate does not prohibit, govern or affect any detailed assessment of the same costs which are payable out of the Community Legal Service Fund of by the Lord Chancellor under Part 1 of the Legal Aid, Sentencing and Punishment of Offenders Act 2012.

10.5 An application for an order staying enforcement of a default costs certificate may be made either –

(a) to a costs judge or district judge of the court office which issued the certificate; or

(b) to the court (if different) which has general jurisdiction to enforce the certificate.

10.6 Proceedings for enforcement of default costs certificates may not be issued in the Costs Office.

Default Costs Certificate: Fixed Costs on the Issue of a Default Costs Certificate

10.7 Unless paragraph 1.2 of Practice Direction 45 (Fixed Costs in Small Claims) applies or unless the court orders otherwise, the fixed costs to be included in a default costs certificate are £80 plus a sum equal to any appropriate court fee payable on the issue of the certificate.

10.8 The fixed costs included in a certificate must not exceed the maximum sum specified for costs and court fee in the notice of commencement.

Setting Aside Default Costs Certificate: Rule 47.12

11.1 A court officer may set aside a default costs certificate at the request of the receiving party under rule 47.12. A costs judge or a district judge will make any other order or give any directions under this rule.

11.2

    (1)   An application for an order under rule 47.12(2) to set aside or vary a default costs certificate must be supported by evidence.

    (2)   In deciding whether to set aside or vary a certificate under rule 47.12(2) the matters to which the court must have regard include whether the party seeking the order made the application promptly.

    (3)   As a general rule a default costs certificate will be set aside under rule 47.12 only if the applicant shows a good reason for the court to do so and if the applicant files with the application a copy of the bill, a copy of the default costs certificate and a draft of the points of dispute the applicant proposes to serve if the application is granted.

11.3 Attention is drawn to rule 3.1(3) (which enables the court when making an order to make it subject to conditions) and to rule 44.2(8) (which enables the court to order a party whom it has ordered to pay costs to pay an amount on account before the costs are assessed). A costs judge or a district judge may exercise the power of the court to make an order under rule 44.2(8) although he did not make the order about costs which led to the issue of the default costs certificate.

Optional Reply: Rule 47.13

12.1 A reply served by the receiving party under Rule 47.13 must be limited to points of principle and concessions only. It must not contain general denials, specific denials or standard form responses.

12.2 Whenever practicable, the reply must be set out in the form of Precedent G.

Detailed Assessment Hearing: Rule 47.14

13.1 The time for requesting a detailed assessment hearing is within 3 months of the expiry of the period for commencing detailed assessment proceedings.

13.2 The request for a detailed assessment hearing must be in Form N258. The request must be accompanied by –

    (a)   a copy of the notice of commencement of detailed assessment proceedings;

    (b)   a copy of the bill of costs,

    (c)   the document giving the right to detailed assessment (see paragraph 13.3 below);

    (d)   a copy of the points of dispute, annotated as necessary in order to show which items have been agreed and their value and to show which items remain in dispute and their value;

    (e)   as many copies of the points of dispute so annotated as there are persons who have served points of dispute;

    (f)   a copy of any replies served;

    (g)   copies of all orders made by the court relating to the costs which are to be assessed;

(h) copies of the fee notes and other written evidence as served on the paying party in accordance with paragraph 5.2 above;

(i) where there is a dispute as to the receiving party's liability to pay costs to the legal representatives who acted for the receiving party, any agreement, letter or other written information provided by the legal representative to the client explaining how the legal representative's charges are to be calculated;

(j) a statement signed by the receiving party or the legal representative giving the name, address for service, reference and telephone number and fax number, if any, of –

    (i) the receiving party;

    (ii) the paying party;

    (iii) any other person who has served points of dispute or who has given notice to the receiving party under paragraph 5.5(1)(b) above;

    and giving an estimate of the length of time the detailed assessment hearing will take;

(k) where the application for a detailed assessment hearing is made by a party other than the receiving party, such of the documents set out in this paragraph as are in the possession of that party;

(l) where the court is to assess the costs of an assisted person or LSC funded client or person to whom civil legal aid services (within the meaning of Part 1 of the Legal Aid, Sentencing and Punishment of Offenders Act 2012) are provided under arrangement made for the purposes of that Part of that Act –

    (i) the legal aid certificate, LSC certificate, the certificate recording the determination of the Direction of Legal Aid Casework and relevant amendment certificates, any authorities and any certificates of discharge or revocation or withdrawal;

    (ii) a certificate, in Precedent F(3) of the Schedule of Costs Precedents;

    (iii) if that person has a financial interest in the detailed assessment hearing and wishes to attend, the postal address of that person to which the court will send notice of any hearing;

    (iv) if the rates payable out of the LSC fund or by the Lord Chancellor under Part 1 of the Legal Aid, Sentencing and Punishment of Offenders Act 2012 are prescribed rates, a schedule to the bill of costs setting out all the items in the bill which are claimed against other parties calculated at the legal aid prescribed rates with or without any claim for enhancement: (further information as to this schedule is set out in paragraph 17 of this Practice Direction);

    (v) a copy of any default costs certificate in respect of costs claimed in the bill of costs.

13.3 "The document giving the right to detailed assessment" means such one or more of the following documents as are appropriate to the detailed assessment proceedings –

(a) a copy of the judgment or order of the court or tribunal giving the right to detailed assessment;

(b) a copy of the notice served under rule 3.7 (sanctions for non-payment of certain fees) where a claim is struck out under that rule;

(c) a copy of the notice of acceptance where an offer to settle is accepted under Part 36 (Offers to settle);

(d) a copy of the notice of discontinuance in a case which is discontinued under Part 38 (Discontinuance);

(e) a copy of the award made on an arbitration under any Act or pursuant to an agreement, where no court has made an order for the enforcement of the award;

(f) a copy of the order, award or determination of a statutorily constituted tribunal or body.

13.4 On receipt of the request for a detailed assessment hearing the court will fix a date for the hearing, or, if the costs officer so decides, will give directions or fix a date for a preliminary appointment.

13.5 Unless the court otherwise orders, if the only dispute between the parties concerns disbursements, the hearing shall take place in the absence of the parties on the basis of the documents and the court will issue its decision in writing.

13.6 The court will give at least 14 days' notice of the time and place of the detailed assessment hearing to every person named in the statement referred to in paragraph 13.2(j) above.

13.7 If either party wishes to make an application in the detailed assessment proceedings the provisions of Part 23 apply.

13.8

    (1)   This paragraph deals with the procedure to be adopted where a date has been given by the court for a detailed assessment hearing and –
        (a)   the detailed assessment proceedings are settled; or
        (b)   a party to the detailed assessment proceedings wishes to apply to vary the date which the court has fixed; or
        (c)   the parties to the detailed assessment proceedings agree about changes they wish to make to any direction given for the management of the detailed assessment proceedings.

    (2)   If detailed assessment proceedings are settled, the receiving party must give notice of that fact to the court immediately, preferably by fax.

    (3)   A party who wishes to apply to vary a direction must do so in accordance with Part 23.

    (4)   If the parties agree about changes they wish to make to any direction given for the management of the detailed assessment proceedings –
        (a)   they must apply to the court for an order by consent; and
        (b)   they must file a draft of the directions sought and an agreed statement of the reasons why the variation is sought; and
        (c)   the court may make an order in the agreed terms or in other terms without a hearing, but it may direct that a hearing is to be listed.

13.10

    (1)   If a party wishes to vary that party's bill of costs, points of dispute or a reply, an amended or supplementary document must be filed with the court and copies of it must be served on all other relevant parties.

    (2)   Permission is not required to vary a bill of costs, points of dispute or a reply but the court may disallow the variation or permit it only upon conditions, including conditions as to the payment of any costs caused or wasted by the variation.

13.11 Unless the court directs otherwise the receiving party must file with the court the papers in support of the bill not less than 7 days before the date for the detailed assessment hearing and not more than 14 days before that date.

13.12 The papers to be filed in support of the bill and the order in which they are to be arranged are as follows –

    (i)   instructions and briefs to counsel arranged in chronological order together with all advices, opinions and drafts received and response to such instructions;
    (ii)   reports and opinions of medical and other experts;
    (iii) any other relevant papers;
    (iv) a full set of any relevant statements of case
    (v)   correspondence, file notes and attendance notes;

13.13 The court may direct the receiving party to produce any document which in the opinion of the court is necessary to enable it to reach its decision. These documents will in the first instance be produced to the court, but the court may ask the receiving party to elect whether to disclose the particular document to the paying party in order to rely on the contents of the document, or whether to decline disclosure and instead rely on other evidence.

13.14 Once the detailed assessment hearing has ended it is the responsibility of the receiving party to remove the papers filed in support of the bill.

Provisional Assessment: Rule 47.15

14.1 The amount of costs referred to in rule 47.15(1) is £75,000.

14.2 The following provisions of Part 47 and this Practice Direction will apply to cases falling within rule 47.15 –

    (1)   rules 47.1, 47.2, 47.4 to 47.13, 47.14 (except Paragraphs (6) and (7)), 47.16, 47.17, 47.20 and 47.21; and

    (2)   paragraphs 1, 2, 4 to 12, 13 (with the exception of paragraphs 13.4 to 13.7, 13.9, 13.11 and 13.14), 15, and 16, of this Practice Direction.

14.3 In cases falling within rule 47.15, when the receiving party files a request for a detailed assessment hearing, that party must file –

    (a)   the request in Form N258;

    (b)   the documents set out at paragraphs 8.3 and 13.2 of this Practice Direction;

    (c)   an additional copy of the bill, including a statement of the costs claimed in respect of the detailed assessment drawn on the assumption that there will not be an oral hearing following the provisional assessment;

    (d)   the offers made (those marked "without prejudice save as to costs" or made under Part 36 must be contained in a sealed envelope, marked "Part 36 or similar offers", but not indicating which party or parties have made them);

    (e)   completed Precedent G (points of dispute and any reply).

14.4

    (1)   On receipt of the request for detailed assessment and the supporting papers, the court will use its best endeavours to undertake a provisional assessment within 6 weeks. No party will be permitted to attend the provisional assessment.

    (2)   Once the provisional assessment has been carried out the court will return Precedent G (the points of dispute and any reply) with the court's decisions noted upon it. Within 14 days of receipt of Precedent G the parties must agree the total sum due to the receiving party on the basis of the court's decisions. If the parties are unable to agree the arithmetic, they must refer the dispute back to the court for a decision on the basis of written submissions.

14.5 When considering whether to depart from the order indicated by rule 47.15(10) the court will take into account the conduct of the parties and any offers made.

14.6 If a party wishes to be heard only as to the order made in respect of the costs of the initial provisional assessment, the court will invite each side to make written submissions and the matter will be finally determined without a hearing. The court will decide what if any order for costs to make in respect of this procedure.

Power to Issue An Interim Certificate: Rule 47.16

15 A party wishing to apply for an interim certificate may do so by making an application in accordance with Part 23.

Final Costs Certificate: Rule 47.17

16.1 At the detailed assessment hearing the court will indicate any disallowance or reduction in the sums claimed in the bill of costs by making an appropriate note on the bill.

16.2 The receiving party must, in order to complete the bill after the detailed assessment hearing make clear the correct figures agreed or allowed in respect of each item and must re-calculate the summary of the bill appropriately.

16.3 The completed bill of costs must be filed with the court no later than 14 days after the detailed assessment hearing.

16.4 At the same time as filing the completed bill of costs, the party whose bill it is must also produce receipted fee notes and receipted accounts in respect of all disbursements except those covered by a certificate in Precedent F(5) in the Schedule of Costs Precedents annexed to this Practice Direction.

16.5 No final costs certificate will be issued until all relevant court fees payable on the assessment of costs have been paid.

16.6 If the receiving party fails to file a completed bill in accordance with rule 47.17 the paying party may make an application under Part 23 seeking an appropriate order under rule 3.1.

16.7 A final costs certificate will show –

    (a)   the amount of any costs which have been agreed between the parties or which have been allowed on detailed assessment;

    (b)   where applicable the amount agreed or allowed in respect of VAT on such costs.

This provision is subject to any contrary statutory provision relating to costs payable out of the Community Legal Service Fund or by the Lord Chancellor under Part 1 of the Legal Aid, Sentencing and Punishment of Offenders Act 2012.

16.8 A final costs certificate will include disbursements in respect of the fees of counsel only if receipted fee notes or accounts in respect of those disbursements have been produced to the court and only to the extent indicated by those receipts.

16.9 Where the certificate relates to costs payable between parties a separate certificate will be issued for each party entitled to costs.

16.10 Form N257 is a model form of interim costs certificate and Form N256 is a model form of final costs certificate.

16.11 An application for an order staying enforcement of an interim costs certificate or final costs certificate may be made either –

    (a)   to a costs judge or district judge of the court office which issued the certificate; or

    (b)   to the court (if different) which has general jurisdiction to enforce the certificate.

16.12 An interim or final costs certificate may be enforced as if it were a judgment for the payment of an amount of money. However, proceedings for the enforcement of interim costs certificates or final costs certificates may not be issued in the Costs Office.

Detailed Assessment Procedure Where Costs are Payable Out of The Community Legal Service Fund or by the Lord Chancellor under Part 1 of the Legal Aid, Sentencing and Punishment of Offenders Act 2012: Rule 47.18

17.1 The time for requesting a detailed assessment under rule 47.18 is within 3 months after the date when the right to detailed assessment arose.

17.2

(1) The request for a detailed assessment of costs must be in Form N258A. The request must be accompanied by –

    (a) a copy of the bill of costs;

    (b) the document giving the right to detailed assessment (see paragraph 13.3 above);

    (c) copies of all orders made by the court relating to the costs which are to be assessed;

    (d) copies of any fee notes of counsel and any expert in respect of fees claimed in the bill;

    (e) written evidence as to any other disbursement which is claimed and which exceeds £500;

    (f) the legal aid certificates, LSC certificates, certificates recording the determinations of the Direction of Legal Aid Casework, any relevant amendment certificates, any authorities and any certificates of discharge, revocation or withdrawal and;

    (g) a statement signed by the legal representative giving the representative's name, address for service, reference, telephone number, fax number, e-mail address where available and, if the assisted person has a financial interest in the detailed assessment and wishes to attend, giving the postal address of that person, to which the court will send notice of any hearing.

(2) The relevant papers in support of the bill as described in paragraph 13.12 must only be lodged if requested by the costs officer.

17.3 Where the court has provisionally assessed a bill of costs it will send to the legal representative a notice, in Form N253 annexed to this practice direction, of the amount of costs which the court proposes to allow together with the bill itself. The legal representative should, if the provisional assessment is to be accepted, then complete the bill.

17.4 If the solicitor whose bill it is, or any other party wishes to make an application in the detailed assessment proceedings, the provisions of Part 23 applies.

17.5 It is the responsibility of the legal representative to complete the bill by entering in the bill the correct figures allowed in respect of each item, recalculating the summary of the bill appropriately and completing the Community Legal Service assessment certificate (Form EX80A).

Costs Payable by the Legal Services Commission or Lord Chancellor at Prescribed Rates

17.6 Where the costs of an assisted person or LSC funded client or person to whom civil legal services (within the meaning of Part 1 of the Legal Aid, Sentencing and Punishment of Offenders Act 2012) are provided under arrangements made for the purposes of that Part of that Act are payable by another person but costs can be claimed against the LSC or Lord Chancellor at prescribed rates (with or without enhancement), the solicitor of the assisted person or LSC funded client or person to whom civil legal services are provided must file a legal aid/ LSC schedule in accordance with paragraph 13.2(1) above. The schedule should follow as closely as possible Precedent E of the Schedule of Costs Precedents annexed to this Practice Direction.

17.7 The schedule must set out by reference to the item numbers in the bill of costs, all the costs claimed as payable by another person, but the arithmetic in the schedule should claim those items at prescribed rates only (with or without any claim for enhancement).

17.8 Where there has been a change in the prescribed rates during the period covered by the bill of costs, the schedule (as opposed to the bill) should be divided into separate parts, so as to deal separately with each change of rate. The schedule must also be divided so as to correspond with any divisions in the bill of costs.

17.9 If the bill of costs contains additional columns setting out costs claimed against the LSC or Lord Chancellor only, the schedule may be set out in a separate document or, alternatively, may be included in the additional columns of the bill.

17.10 The detailed assessment of the legal aid/ LSC schedule will take place immediately after the detailed assessment of the bill of costs but on occasions, the court may decide to conduct the detailed assessment of the legal aid/ LSC schedule separately from any detailed assessment of the bill of costs. This will occur, for example, where a default costs certificate is obtained as between the parties but that certificate is not set aside at the time of the detailed assessment of the legal aid costs.

17.11 Where costs have been assessed at prescribed rates it is the responsibility of the legal representative to enter the correct figures allowed in respect of each item and to recalculate the summary of the legal aid/ LSC schedule.

Detailed Assessment Procedure Where Costs are Payable Out of a Fund or by the Lord Chancellor under Part 1 of the Legal Aid, Sentencing and Punishment of Offenders Act 2012: Rule 47.19

18.1 Rule 47.19 enables the court to direct under rule 47.19(3) that the receiving party must serve a copy of the request for assessment and copies of the documents which accompany it, on any person who has a financial interest in the outcome of the assessment.

18.2 A person has a financial interest in the outcome of the assessment if the assessment will or may affect the amount of money or property to which that person is or may become entitled out of the fund. Where an interest in the fund is itself held by a trustee for the benefit of some other person, that trustee will be treated as the person having such a financial interest unless it is not appropriate to do so. "Trustee" includes a personal representative, receiver or any other person acting in a fiduciary capacity.

18.3 The request for a detailed assessment of costs out of the fund should be in Form N258B, be accompanied by the documents set out at paragraph 17.2(1) (a) to (e) and the following –

(a) a statement signed by the receiving party giving his name, address for service, reference, telephone number,

(b) a statement of the postal address of any person who has a financial interest in the outcome of the assessment; and

(c) if a person having a financial interest is a child or protected party, a statement to that effect.

18.4 The court will decide, having regard to the amount of the bill, the size of the fund and the number of persons who have a financial interest, which of those persons should be served and may give directions about service and about the hearing. The court may dispense with service on all or some of those persons.

18.5 Where the court makes an order dispensing with service on all such persons it may proceed at once to make a provisional assessment, or, if it decides that a hearing is necessary, give appropriate directions. Before deciding whether a hearing is necessary, the court may require the receiving party to provide further information relating to the bill.

18.6

(1) The court will send the provisionally assessed bill to the receiving party with a

notice in Form N253. If the receiving party is legally represented the legal representative should, if the provisional assessment is to be accepted, then complete the bill.

(2) The court will fix a date for a detailed assessment hearing, if the receiving party informs the court within 14 days after receiving the notice in Form N253, that the receiving party wants the court to hold such a hearing.

18.7 The court will give at least 14 days notice of the time and place of the hearing to the receiving party and to any person who has a financial and who has been served with a copy of the request for assessment.

18.8 If any party or any person who has a financial interest wishes to make an application in the detailed assessment proceedings, the provisions of Part 23 (General Rules about Applications for Court Orders) apply.

18.9 If the receiving party is legally represented the legal representative must complete the bill by inserting the correct figures in respect of each item and must recalculate the summary of the bill.

Costs of Detailed Assessment Proceedings – Rule 47.20: Offers to Settle Under Part 36 or Otherwise

19 Where an offer to settle is made, whether under Part 36 or otherwise, it should specify whether or not it is intended to be inclusive of the cost of preparation of the bill, interest and VAT. Unless the offer states otherwise it will be treated as being inclusive of these.

Appeals from Authorised Court Officers in Detailed Assessment Proceedings: Rules 47.22 To 47.25

20.1 This Section relates only to appeals from authorised court officers in detailed assessment proceedings. All other appeals arising out of detailed assessment proceedings (and arising out of summary assessments) are dealt with in accordance with Part 52 and Practice Directions 52A to 52E. The destination of appeals is dealt with in accordance with the Access to Justice Act 1999 (Destination of Appeals) Order 2000.

20.2 In respect of appeals from authorised court officers, there is no requirement to obtain permission, or to seek written reasons.

20.3 The appellant must file a notice which should be in Form N161 (an appellant's notice).

20.4 The appeal will be heard by a costs judge or a district judge of the High Court, and is a re-hearing.

20.5 The appellant's notice should, if possible, be accompanied by a suitable record of the judgment appealed against. Where reasons given for the decision have been officially recorded by the court an approved transcript of that record should accompany the notice. Where there is no official record the following documents will be acceptable –

(a) the officer's comments written on the bill;
(b) advocates' notes of the reasons agreed by the respondent if possible and approved by the authorised court officer.

When the appellant was unrepresented before the authorised court officer, it is the duty of any advocate for the respondent to make a note of the reasons promptly available, free of charge to the appellant where there is no official record or if the court so directs. Where the appellant was represented before the authorised court officer, it is the duty of the appellant's own former advocate to make a note available. The appellant should submit the note of the reasons to the costs judge or district judge hearing the appeal.

PART III

20.6 Where the appellant is not able to obtain a suitable record of the authorised court officer's decision within the time in which the appellant's notice must be filed, the appellant's notice must still be completed to the best of the appellant's ability. It may however be amended subsequently with the permission of the costs judge or district.

****

PART 50
APPLICATION OF THE SCHEDULES

50 (1) The Schedules to these Rules set out, with modifications, certain provisions previously contained in the Rules of the Supreme Court 1965 and the County Court Rules 1981.

(2) These Rules apply in relation to the proceedings to which the Schedules apply subject to the provisions in the Schedules and the relevant practice directions.

(3) A provision previously contained in the Rules of the Supreme Court 1965 –

    (a) is headed "RSC";

    (b) is numbered with the Order and rule numbers it bore as part of the RSC; and

    (c) unless otherwise stated in the Schedules or the relevant practice direction, applies only to proceedings in the High Court.

(4) A provision previously contained in the County Court Rules 1981 –

    (a) is headed "CCR";

    (b) is numbered with the Order and rule numbers it bore as part of the CCR; and

    (c) unless otherwise stated in the Schedules or the relevant practice direction, applies only to proceedings in the county court.

(5) A reference in a Schedule to a rule by number alone is a reference to the rule so numbered in the Order in which the reference occurs.

(6) A reference in a Schedule to a rule by number prefixed by "CPR" is a reference to the rule with that number in these Rules.

(7) In the Schedules, unless otherwise stated, "the Act" means –

    (a) in a provision headed "RSC", the Senior Courts Act 1981; and

    (b) in a provision headed "CCR", the County Courts Act 1984.

Amendments—CRA 2005, Sch 11, para 1(2).

****

PART 52
APPEALS

CONTENTS OF THIS PART

Section I
General Rules about Appeals

Section II
Special Provisions applying to the Court of Appeal

Section III
Provisions about Reopening Appeals

Section I
General Rules about Appeals

Note—From 1 October 2012, CPR PD52 is replaced by five new practice directions, PD52A–PD52E, which shall apply to all appeals where the notice of appeal was filed or permission to appeal was given after that date. The appeal court may direct that the new provisions apply to any appeal, irrespective of the date on which the notice was filed or permission to appeal was given (CPR PD52A, paras 8.1 and 8.2). The practice directions deal with the following:
  CPR PD52A: Appeals: General Provisions
  CPR PD52B: Appeals in the County Courts and the High Court
  CPR PD52C: Appeals to the Court of Appeal
  CPR PD52D: Statutory Appeals and Appeals Subject to Special Provision
  CPR PD52E: Appeals by way of Case Stated.

52.1 Scope and interpretation

(1) The rules in this Part apply to appeals to –

   (a)   the civil division of the Court of Appeal;
   (b)   the High Court; and
   (c)   a county court.

(2) This Part does not apply to an appeal in detailed assessment proceedings against a decision of an authorised court officer.

(Rules 47.20 to 47.23 deal with appeals against a decision of an authorised court officer in detailed assessment proceedings)

(3) In this Part –

    (a)   "appeal" includes an appeal by way of case stated;

    (b)   "appeal court" means the court to which an appeal is made;

    (c)   "lower court" means the court, tribunal or other person or body from whose decision an appeal is brought;

    (d)   "appellant" means a person who brings or seeks to bring an appeal;

    (e)   "respondent" means –

        (i)   a person other than the appellant who was a party to the proceedings in the lower court and who is affected by the appeal; and

        (ii)   a person who is permitted by the appeal court to be a party to the appeal; and

    (f)   "appeal notice" means an appellant's or respondent's notice.

(4) This Part is subject to any rule, enactment or practice direction which sets out special provisions with regard to any particular category of appeal.

Amendments—Inserted by SI 2000/221; amended by SI 2000/2092; SI 2005/3515.

Scope of Pt 52—This Part applies to all appeals to the Court of Appeal and to appeals to the High Court which are not defined as family proceedings under MFPA 1984, s 40. It applies to non-family appeals to the High Court that were previously covered by RSC Ords 55 and 58. This Part also provides, in addition to appeals to the Court of Appeal, the power of the High Court or the county court on appeal to transfer a case for determination by the Court of Appeal where it is thought that that appeal raises an important point of practice, or there is some other compelling reason (r 52.14).

For the general jurisdiction of the Court of Appeal, see SCA 1981, ss 15–18. For restriction of appeals to the Court of Appeal, see SCA 1981, ss 16, 18.

Appeal—An appeal is an application to set aside or vary a decision of the court below on the ground that it was wrongly made. Baroness Hale has criticised the Court of Appeal's apparent readiness to interfere with the first instance judge's exercise of his discretion: see *Re J (Child Returned Abroad: Convention Rights)* [2005] 2 FLR 802, HL at [12]. An appeal is against the order and not the judgment (*Vaughan v Vaughan* [2008] 1 FLR 1108). Appeals against ex parte orders are discouraged (see **Ex parte orders** under SCA 1981, s 18), as are appeals against interim orders (see *G v G (Interim Custody: Appeal)* (1983) 4 FLR 327; *Edwards v Edwards* [1986] 1 FLR 205). To challenge an order that has been made by consent where the basis of the order has been frustrated by one party, the aggrieved party may appeal or should preferably return to the court which made the order (*Middleton v Middleton* [1998] 2 FLR 821). Where the court has made an order in favour of a party subject to conditions and that party fails to comply, the (most usual) appropriate course is to apply to the first instance judge to set aside the order and not to appeal: see *Walley v Walley* [2005] EWCA Civ 910.

Interim orders—Where events changed or developed after the making of an interim order, the appropriate course was to seek a variation of the order from the judge, rather than seek to appeal against the order: *Re H (A Child)* [2011] EWCA Civ 762.

Mediation—The Court of Appeal has observed that no family case, even at appellate level, is not potentially open to successful mediation; even if mediation was not attempted or failed at first instance, it was vital there be judicial supervision of the process of mediation: see *Al-Khatib v Masry* [2005] 1 FLR 381, CA. The Court of Appeal has observed that the Court's ADR scheme has a relatively low take up from family appeals but an encouragingly high success rate and "as a matter of policy it is important that this court should signify that if the parties arrive at a compromise, a clear compromise, within the mediation process, then that compromise will be robustly upheld by this court": *Rothwell v Rothwell* [2009] 2 FLR 96.

Trial judge—The Court of Appeal has emphasised that the appeal court must give great weight to those aspects of the case exclusively within the domain of the trial judge: in particular the judicial assessment of witness credibility and findings of fact (*Re M (Children) (Sexual Abuse)* [2008] EWCA Civ 3).

Reasons—Where a party alleges a judge has failed to deal with an important part of the evidence or has failed to give sufficient or adequate reasons for his decision, the aggrieved party must apply to the trial judge for further reasons: the Court of Appeal will not "fill that hole" (*Re T (Contact: Alienation: Permission to Appeal)* [2003] 1 FLR 531; *Re M (Children)* [2007] EWCA Civ 177). It is not sufficient for a party to draw attention to an alleged deficiency in a judgment by way of an application for permission to appeal. It is incumbent on the party to point out the deficiency and to request clarification or a supplemental judgment on the issue (*Re A (Child Abuse)* [2008] 1 FLR 1423 (CA). The Court of Appeal is losing patience with the failure of practitioners to follow this procedure before seeking permission to appeal: it has recently observed that it is about time the family bar woke up to the fact that the procedure set out in *English v Emery, Reimbold & Strick* [2002] 1 WLR 2409 applies to family cases and must be followed (*Re M (Fact-finding Hearing: Burden of Proof)* [2009] 1 FLR 1177)). The Court of Appeal has reiterated the proper course to be taken. Where an alleged lack of reasons in the judgment had not been drawn to the attention of the trial judge or the judge had subsequently failed to elaborate his reasons, the normal procedure was remittal to the judge at first instance with a list of specific questions: *Re A and L (Children)* [2012] 1 FLR 134.

Public funding—The Supreme Court has decided that there must be compelling reasons for withdrawing public funding from a party who had been publicly funded in the court below, had been successful in that court and wished to resist an appeal to a higher court by the unsuccessful party: *R (E) v Governing Body of JFS and the Admissions Appeal Panel of JFS and others* [2009] 1 WLR 2353.

Appeals against decree nisi—CPR PD52D, para 6.1 makes special provision for such appeals.

Contempt appeals—CPR PD52D, para 9.1 makes special provision for such appeals.

52.2 Parties to comply with Practice Directions 52A to 52E

All parties to an appeal must comply with Practice Directions 52A to 52E.

Amendments—Inserted by SI 2000/221; amended by SI 2009/3390; SI 2012/2208.

"the relevant practice direction"—See CPR PD52A-PD52E.

52.3 Permission

(1) An appellant or respondent requires permission to appeal –

    (a) where the appeal is from a decision of a judge in a county court or the High Court, except where the appeal is against –

        (i)   a committal order;

        (ii) a refusal to grant habeas corpus; or

        (iii) a secure accommodation order made under section 25 of the Children Act 1989; or

    (b) as provided by Practice Direction 52.

    (Other enactments may provide that permission is required for particular appeals)

(2) An application for permission to appeal may be made –

    (a) to the lower court at the hearing at which the decision to be appealed was made; or

    (b) to the appeal court in an appeal notice.

    (Rule 52.4 sets out the time limits for filing an appellant's notice at the appeal court. Rule 52.5 sets out the time limits for filing a respondent's notice at the appeal court. Any application for permission to appeal to the appeal court must be made in the appeal notice (see rules 52.4(1) and 52.5(3)))

    (Rule 52.13(1) provides that permission is required from the Court of Appeal for all appeals to that court from a decision of a county court or the High Court which was itself made on appeal)

(3) Where the lower court refuses an application for permission to appeal, a further application for permission to appeal may be made to the appeal court.

(4) Subject to paragraph (4A), where the appeal court, without a hearing, refuses permission to appeal, the person seeking permission may request the decision to be reconsidered at a hearing.

(4A)

    (a)   Where a judge of the Court of Appeal or of the High Court, a Designated Civil Judge or a Specialist Circuit Judge refuses permission to appeal without a hearing and considers that the application is totally without merit, the judge may make an order that the person seeking permission may not request the decision to be reconsidered at a hearing.

    (b)   For the purposes of subparagraph (a) "Specialist Circuit Judge" means a Patents County Court judge and any circuit judge in any county court nominated to hear cases in the Mercantile, Chancery or Technology and Construction Court lists.

(4B) Rule 3.3(5) will not apply to an order that the person seeking permission may not request the decision to be reconsidered at a hearing made under paragraph (4A).

(5) A request under paragraph (4) must be filed within seven days after service of the notice that permission has been refused.

(6) Permission to appeal may be given only where –

    (a)   the court considers that the appeal would have a real prospect of success; or

    (b)   there is some other compelling reason why the appeal should be heard.

(7) An order giving permission may –

    (a)   limit the issues to be heard; and

    (b)   be made subject to conditions.

       (Rule 3.1(3) also provides that the court may make an order subject to conditions)

       (Rule 25.15 provides for the court to order security for costs of an appeal)

Amendments—Inserted by SI 2000/221; amended by SI 2005/3515; SI 2006/1689; SI 2008/2178; SI 2009/3390; SI 2012/2208.

General note—The amendment made by SI 2008/2178 does not apply to proceedings where the Notice of Appeal was filed before 1 October 2008.

Scope—Save for the limited exceptions contained within r 52.3(1)(a), namely in respect of a committal order, habeas corpus and secure accommodation, permission to appeal is required in all cases (here committal order includes a suspended order – see *Wilkinson v S* [2003] 1 WLR 1254 and *Re G (Contempt: Committal)* [2003] 2 FLR 58). The application should usually be made to the judge whose decision is to be appealed, at the time the decision is made (see CPR PD52A, para 4.1(a)) and, if refused, thereafter to the Court of Appeal. An application directly to the Court of Appeal, while permissible within the terms of the rule (see CPR PD52A, para 4.1(b)), is unusual. If there has been a "paper" refusal by the Court of Appeal (see CPR PD52C, para 15.1), there may be a renewal of the application before a Lord Justice (see CPR PD52C, para 15.2). It is necessary to show a "real prospect" of success or "some other compelling reason" (r 52.3(6)). The Court of Appeal has given guidance on the limited grounds on which the court may grant permission for appeal and to allow an appeal (particularly for the benefit of litigants in person) *(Re W (Permission to Appeal)* [2008] 1 FLR 406). There is no appeal from the decision at the oral hearing. Note, however, the new power of a single judge when refusing permission to appeal on paper; if he considers the application to be wholly without merit he may direct that the application cannot be reconsidered at an oral hearing, a power which remains unavailable in family proceedings (r 52.3(4A)). Where the appeal to the Court of Appeal is a second appeal (i e an appeal from a decision of the High Court on appeal from the family proceedings court) there is an additional hurdle to overcome (see r 52.13), namely the requirement to establish an important point of principle or practice or some other compelling reason to grant permission. On a second appeal, the application for permission to appeal must be made to the Court of Appeal (see CPR PD52A, para 4.7). Where the appeal is based in whole or in part on lack of reasons given in the judgment, the first instance judge must be invited to give further reasons for his decision: see *Re T (Contact: Alienation: Permission to Appeal)* [2003] 1 FLR 531. It is not sufficient for a party to draw attention to an alleged deficiency in a judgment by way of an application for permission to appeal and see further **Reasons** under r 52.1.

Power to change judgment after handing down—In care proceedings a judge is entitled to change his mind – and thus his findings of fact – after delivering judgment, written or oral, at a fact finding hearing even in the absence of an intervening change of circumstances. The Supreme Court held that a court should not be required to make welfare decisions concerning a child on a false factual basis. It declined to offer even a provisional view on whether the power was available after the order made at the conclusion of the fact finding hearing had been perfected (i e sealed by the court): it was said the arguments either way were finely balanced. The power must be exercised "judicially and not capriciously". "The best safeguard against having to do so is a fully and properly reasoned judgment in the first place": *Re L and B (Children)* [2013] UKSC 8.

Abduction appeals—If the obligation to complete proceedings under the Hague Convention and Brussels IIA within 6 weeks was to be met, it was imperative that the Bar ensured draft judgments were returned to the judge within a brief period, the consequential order was then drafted promptly and the approved order sealed immediately thereafter (*Re M (Abduction: Appeals)* [2008] 1 FLR 699).

Case management appeals—Where an appeal is against a case management decision, the court dealing with the application may take into account whether:

(a) the issue is of sufficient significance to justify the costs of the appeal;
(b) the procedural consequences of an appeal (e g loss of a trial date) outweigh the significance of the case management decision; or
(c) it would be more convenient to determine the issue at or after the trial (CPR PD52A, para 4.6).

See also the President's observations on five basic principles relevant to the approach of the Court of Appeal to appeals against case management decisions in *Re TG (A Child)* [2013] EWCA Civ 5 at [24]–[38].

Committal appeals—CPR 1998, r 52.3(1)(a)(i) could not be construed as restricting the right to appeal as of right to a contemnor and not to an applicant who sought to have a sentence increased and, accordingly, the applicant did not require permission to appeal (*Wood v Collins* [2006] EWCA Civ 743). Any appeal against either a finding of breach or the sentence for a breach must be expedited into court and as a matter of safeguard, should be immediately referred to one of the supervising Lord Justices, so that appropriate directions could be given for an expedited hearing and for whatever else might be needed, as every day that the appeal was delayed might be a day in which the appellant was unjustifiably detained in custody (*G v G* [2007] 2 FLR 1127).

Transcripts of the hearing or of the evidence—When considering ordering a transcript of the whole, or a part, of the evidence or hearing in the court below, practitioners should bear in mind the following:

(a) The preparation of and authorisation of the payment for a transcript might take time, therefore practitioners should consider whether a transcript was an essential prerequisite before filing of a notice of appeal or before an application for permission to appeal was sought.
(b) Practitioners should consider filing a notice of appeal even though a transcript might not be available.
(c) The judge of the lower court could be contacted if necessary to speed up the process.
(d) Pursuit of a transcript, which might be peripheral, should not affect the consideration of an application for permission to appeal: *Re GB (Children)* [2013] EWCA Civ 164).

Limited permission—It is possible for there to be a grant of permission to appeal in relation to a limited issue (r 52.3(7)). The court should normally refuse permission on the other grounds (see CPR PD52C, para 18) and those issues may then not be raised at the appeal hearing without the court's permission (CPR PD52C, para 18(3)). Where a party has been present at the hearing to determine permission to appeal, he cannot apply to limit the scope of the appeal (see r 52.9).

Respondent's attendance at permission hearing (r 52.3(4))—Rule 52.3(4) permits reconsideration of a paper refusal of permission by the court. The respondent is permitted to attend, but CPR PD52C, para 20 in effect discourages such attendance. In *Livock v Livock* [2012] 1 FLR 776, Coleridge J expressed concern at the lack of notice to a respondent in these circumstances and at his order having been sent back to him for "review" without it being set aside (see FPR 2010, r 30.3(5)).

Observations by Court—Where a single Lord Justice makes observations on Form 269C1, when granting permission to appeal or directing an oral hearing on notice with the appeal to follow immediately if permission was granted, they were to be obeyed. Primary responsibility for a failure to comply will usually lie with the party who brings the appeal/application: *Re M-W (Care Proceedings: Expert Evidence)* [2010] 2 FLR 46 (CA).

Consent orders—In relation to a consent order, consideration must be given to whether the matter should be returned to the judge who heard the matter for a rehearing rather than to appeal. This seems to be the preferred course in relation to orders made as a result of fraud, mistake or material non-disclosure, or where there has been a new event to invalidate the basis of the order (see *Re C (Financial Provision: Leave to Appeal)* [1993] 2 FLR 799 and *Benson v Benson (Deceased)* [1996] 1 FLR 692). This route is the more appropriate where there are issues of fact to be determined or a substitute order is sought. Bad advice cannot found the basis for an appeal against the making of a consent order (*Tibbs v Dick* [1998] 2 FLR 1118).

PART III

Conditions—The Court of Appeal may impose conditions on the grant of permission if compelling reasons are found to exist (unlike r 52.9, r 52.3(7) does not specify the need for compelling reasons, but the court has held that the latter should be read as if those words were included in the rule). Where a party had attempted to evade enforcement and was in gross breach of court orders, it was appropriate that conditions were attached to the grant of permission to appeal including the transfer of a lump sum into this jurisdiction in a secure environment and a requirement to comply with existing court orders: *Radmacher v Granatino* [2009] 1 FLR 1566.

General observations—Recent decisions of the Court of Appeal highlight the following:

(a) the essential test is: does the judgment sufficiently explain what the judge has found and what he has concluded, as well as the process of reasoning by which he arrived at his findings and then his conclusions? (*Re B (Appeal: Lack of Reasons)* [2003] 2 FLR 1035; *Re A and L (Fact-Finding Hearing: Extempore Judgment)* [2012] 1 FLR 1243);

(b) albeit the course taken by the judge had potential adverse consequences for the child in terms of risk of harm and the delay that could result, he was aware of those consequences and had been entitled to take the approach he did in advancement of the child's welfare: *Re H (A Child)* [2012] EWCA Civ 1700;

(c) whatever the allegations, however serious, the balance of probabilities remained the standard of proof. Findings should be made without regard to the gravity of the consequences of the same: *Re D (Children)* [2012] EWCA Civ 1584;

(d) the Court of Appeal is always reluctant to interfere with a judge's assessment of the witnesses who has given evidence before him : *Re A (Removal from Jurisdiction)* [2012] EWCA Civ 1041;

(e) a trial judge has a wide discretion to accept and deal with the evidence and, fairly, to terminate or permit continuation of a case but there are limits to what is permissible: *Re C (Children)* [2012] EWCA Civ 1489, cf *Re J (Children)* [2012] EWCA Civ 1457;

(f) a trial judge is not entitled to depart from findings made in an extempore judgment delivered at the conclusion of a fact-finding hearing absent further evidence or a significant change in circumstances: *Re L-B (Reversal of Judgment)* [2013] 1 FLR 209;

(g) a trial judge was entitled, however, after reserving judgment, to change his mind about a provisional view he had expressed during the trial about the value of some of the evidence: this was a wholly legitimate aspect of the trial process and could not be characterised as procedurally unfair. The serious procedural irregularity required for an appeal to be allowed is a high hurdle: *Re R (Care Proceedings: Appeal)* [2013] 1 FLR 467;

(h) it was only appropriate to consider inviting a trial judge to provide further reasons for his decision where it might have a bearing on whether to allow the appeal. It was not appropriate to invite a judge to give reasons for his decision on the basis that it would benefit the children: *Re F (Supervised Contact: Disputed Evidence)* [2013] 1 FLR 665;

(i) following a fact-finding hearing before one judge, another judge at the welfare hearing was not entitled to make further findings of fact without giving notice of the possibility of the same to the parties: *Re C (A Child)* [2012] EWCA Civ 535; and

(j) a judge in a fact-finding hearing who is not satisfied that specific allegations in the schedule of findings are not made out is not entitled to make alternative findings that are not set out in the schedule: *Re J-L* [2012] EWCA Civ 1832.

52.4 Appellant's notice

(1) Where the appellant seeks permission from the appeal court it must be requested in the appellant's notice.

(2) The appellant must file the appellant's notice at the appeal court within –

    (a) such period as may be directed by the lower court (which may be longer or shorter than the period referred to in sub-paragraph (b); or

    (b) where the court makes no such direction, 21 days after the date of the decision of the lower court that the appellant wishes to appeal.

(3) Subject to paragraph (4) and unless the appeal court orders otherwise, an appellant's notice must be served on each respondent –

    (a) as soon as practicable; and

    (b) in any event not later than 7 days,

after it is filed.

(4) Where an appellant seeks permission to appeal against a decision to refuse to grant an interim injunction under section 41 of the Policing and Crime Act 2009 the appellant is not required to serve the appellant's notice on the respondent.

Amendments—Inserted by SI 2000/221; amended by SI 2005/3515; SI 2010/1953.

Scope—In children's cases, the Court of Appeal has observed that the period ought generally to be less than 21 days (*Re M-H (Children)* [2006] EWCA Civ 499). Applications for permission to appeal in children's cases, especially those with an international element, have to be brought on for hearing swiftly. First instance judges should, as a matter of routine, establish whether a party wishes to appeal and, whether granting or refusing permission to appeal, give directions to ensure that the inception of the appeal is achieved within the shortest possible period. The period allowed of 21 days is "over generous" (*Klentzeris v Klentzeris* [2007] 2 FLR 996; *Re EC (Child Abduction: Stayed Proceedings)* [2007] 1 FLR 57). The filing of the notice of appeal should not be delayed until the applicant has received a copy of the approved judgment under appeal (*Re A (Children: Split Hearing)* [2007] 1 FLR 905 (CA)). The respondent need do nothing until notification of the grant of permission to appeal (CPR PD52C, para 19).

Skeleton arguments—The Notice and a copy of the skeleton argument must be filed at the same time and served as soon as practicable thereafter and in any event not later than 7 days thereafter (CPR PD52C, paras 3, 21, 27 and 31). Practitioners should pay attention to the compulsory directions on the contents of skeleton arguments and the requirements in respect of the citation of authorities (see CPR PD52A, paras 5.1–5.3, CPR PD52C, paras 29 and 31 and the Practice Direction of 24 March 2012: *Citation of Authorities*). The appellant and the respondent(s) may file and serve "replacement" skeleton arguments to include cross-references to the appeal bundle but must do so no later than 14 days and 7 days, respectively, before the date of the appeal hearing (CPR PD52C, paras 1 and 21). Supplementary skeleton arguments may only be filed where strictly necessary and only with the permission of the Court of Appeal. They must be lodged and served as soon as practicable and be accompanied by a request for permission setting out the reasons why it is necessary and why they could not reasonably have been lodged earlier. Only in exceptional cases will the court allow the use of a supplementary skeleton argument if it is lodged later than 7 days before the hearing (CPR PD52C, para 32(1)–(3)).

Where the appeal is out of time, it seems that a composite application for permission to appeal must be made in order to comply with the general requirement of permission and because the time for appealing has expired. In those circumstances, the Notice of Appeal should seek permission to appeal and an extension of time for filing the Notice of Appeal (see CPR PD52C, para 4). The appellant must file the prescribed documents and an appeal bundle with his Notice of Appeal (see CPR PD52C, para 3).

Procedure following the grant of permission—CPR PD52C, para 3 sets out the documents that the appellant is required to file with the Notice of Appeal. Once permission to appeal has been granted, or the permission application is to be listed with, if granted, the appeal to follow, the appellant must serve a proposed index bundle on each respondent 7 days after the listing window notification and no later than 42 days before the hearing of the appeal must file the appropriate number of appeal bundles at the court and serve a copy of the appeal bundle on each of the respondents (CPR PD52C, para 21). The Court of Appeal shall send the parties notification of the period of time in which the appeal is likely to be heard (the "listing window notification"), together with a questionnaire (CPR PD52C, paras 1, 21 and 23). This requires the appellant to give a time estimate for the hearing of the appeal.

Policing and Crime Act 2009—Section 34 of the Act empowers the court to grant injunctions to prevent gang-related violence. Where the court adjourns a without notice application for an injunction it may grant an interim injunction if it thinks it necessary (s 41). Where the court adjourns a without notice application for an injunction but refuses to grant an interim injunction the applicant may appeal that decision without giving notice of the appeal to the respondent.

The appeal bundle—CPR PD52C, para 27 sets out the detailed provisions for the preparation of the bundle of documents.

Electronic filing—A party may file a notice by email to the email account specified in the "Guidelines for filing Appellants' Notices, Respondents' Notices and Application Notices by e-mail", which appear on the court's website at *www.civilappeals.gov.uk*, but only where permitted to do so by the guidelines. A party may file notices electronically using the online forms service on the Court of Appeal, Civil Division website where permitted to do so by the "Guidelines for filing by e-mail".

52.5 Respondent's notice

(1) A respondent may file and serve a respondent's notice.

(2) A respondent who –

(a)   is seeking permission to appeal from the appeal court; or

(b)   wishes to ask the appeal court to uphold the order of the lower court for reasons different from or additional to those given by the lower court,

must file a respondent's notice.

(3) Where the respondent seeks permission from the appeal court it must be requested in the respondent's notice.

(4) A respondent's notice must be filed within –

(a)   such period as may be directed by the lower court; or

(b)   where the court makes no such direction, 14 days, after the date in paragraph (5).

(5) The date referred to in paragraph (4) is –

(a)   the date the respondent is served with the appellant's notice where –

(i)   permission to appeal was given by the lower court; or

(ii)   permission to appeal is not required;

(b)   the date the respondent is served with notification that the appeal court has given the appellant permission to appeal; or

(c)   the date the respondent is served with notification that the application for permission to appeal and the appeal itself are to be heard together.

(6) Unless the appeal court orders otherwise a respondent's notice must be served on the appellant and any other respondent –

(a)   as soon as practicable; and

(b)   in any event not later than 7 days,

after it is filed.

(7) This rule does not apply where rule 52.4(4) applies.

Amendments—Inserted by SI 2000/221; amended by SI 2010/1953.

Scope—Unless the respondent wishes to cross-appeal or justify the order for different reasons, there is no need to provide a Notice. If the respondent wishes to file a Notice, he must do so within 14 days unless otherwise directed (r 52.5(4)) and serve it as soon as practicable and in any event within 7 days thereafter (r 52.5(6)). An appeal by a respondent will also require permission (CPR PD52C, para 8). A respondent must file and serve a skeleton argument. It must be lodged with the Respondent's Notice and served on each party (CPR PD52C, para 9). If there is no Respondent's Notice, the skeleton argument must be lodged and served 42 days after the date of the listing window notification (CPR PD52C, para 21).

r 52.4(4)—Section 34 of the Policing and Crime Act 2009 empowers the court to grant injunctions to prevent gang-related violence. Where the court adjourns a without notice application for an injunction it may grant an interim injunction if it thinks it necessary (s 41). Where the court adjourns a without notice application for an injunction but refuses to grant an interim injunction the applicant may appeal that decision without giving notice of the appeal to the respondent.

Respondent's Notices—Respondent's Notices that simply assert their support for the conclusion arrived at by the judge for the reasons he has given are entirely superfluous: *Re S (Care and Placement Orders)* [2013] 1 FLR 354.

52.6 Variation of time

(1) An application to vary the time limit for filing an appeal notice must be made to the appeal court.

(2) The parties may not agree to extend any date or time limit set by –

(a)   these Rules;

(b)   Practice Direction 52; or

(c)   an order of the appeal court or the lower court.

(Rule 3.1(2)(a) provides that the court may extend or shorten the time for compliance with any rule, practice direction or court order (even if an application for extension is made after the time for compliance has expired))

(Rule 3.1(2)(b) provides that the court may adjourn or bring forward a hearing)

Amendments—Inserted by SI 2000/221; amended by SI 2009/3390.

52.7 Stay(GL)

Unless –

(a) the appeal court or the lower court orders otherwise; or

(b) the appeal is from the Immigration and Asylum Chamber of the Upper Tribunal,

an appeal shall not operate as a stay of any order or decision of the lower court.

Amendments—Inserted by SI 2000/221; amended by SI 2006/1689; SI 2009/3390.

Scope—An appeal (meaning an application for permission or following the grant of permission) does not automatically operate to stop the order which is the subject of the appeal taking effect. An application must be made for a stay of the order. A stay should normally be sought at the time of the application for permission to appeal, if not immediately following the decision which is to be appealed. An application for a stay must be determined by a judge and is usually heard by a single Lord Justice (see r 52.16).

Imposition of conditions to grant of stay—The Supreme Court has criticised the imposition by the Court of Appeal of conditions to the grant of a stay pending determination of an application for permission to appeal by the Supreme Court. Lord Kerr said: "as a general rule, conditions such as were imposed by the Court of Appeal in this case should not be made where a party seeks permission to appeal, not least because these might be seen as an unwarranted disincentive to the pursuit of what proved in this case to be a fully merited application": *Re B (A Child)* [2010] 1 FLR 551. The Court of Appeal had approved the decision of the court below to transfer residence from the maternal grandmother to the father: in granting a stay of the transfer of residence the court imposed a provision for extensive overnight staying contact to the father.

Urgent cases—In urgent cases where the judge has refused a stay of the order pending the application for permission to appeal, the prospective appellant may telephone the Court of Appeal to apply for a stay (during office hours the telephone number is 0207 947 6000 and out of hours contact is made to the security office at the RCJ on 0207 947 6260, who will refer the matter to the duty deputy master; CPR PD52C, para 26). A deputy master will refer the matter to a Lord Justice who may grant the stay or list the matter urgently for consideration of the application for a stay (*Re S (Child Proceedings: Urgent Appeals)* [2007] 2 FLR 1044).

52.8 Amendment of appeal notice

An appeal notice may not be amended without the permission of the appeal court.

Amendments—Inserted by SI 2000/221.

52.9 Striking out(GL) appeal notices and setting aside or imposing conditions on permission to appeal

(1) The appeal court may –

(a) strike out the whole or part of an appeal notice;

(b) set aside(GL) permission to appeal in whole or in part;

(c) impose or vary conditions upon which an appeal may be brought.

(2) The court will only exercise its powers under paragraph (1) where there is a compelling reason for doing so.

(3) Where a party was present at the hearing at which permission was given he may not subsequently apply for an order that the court exercise its powers under sub-paragraphs (1)(b) or (1)(c).

PART III

Amendments—Inserted by SI 2000/221.

Scope—See notes to r 52.3 (above).

Compelling reasons—These are required to impose conditions under this rule and under r 52.3(7). This rule applies where permission to appeal has already been granted on some previous occasion: *Radmacher v Granatino* [2009] 1 FLR 1566.

52.9A Orders to limit the recoverable costs of an appeal

(1) In any proceedings in which costs recovery is normally limited or excluded at first instance, an appeal court may make an order that the recoverable costs of an appeal will be limited to the extent which the court specifies.

(2) In making such an order the court will have regard to –

    (a)   the means of both parties;

    (b)   all the circumstances of the case; and

    (c)   the need to facilitate access to justice.

(3) If the appeal raises an issue of principle or practice upon which substantial sums may turn, it may not be appropriate to make an order under paragraph (1).

(4) An application for such an order must be made as soon as practicable and will be determined without a hearing unless the court orders otherwise.

Amendments—Inserted by SI 2013/262.

52.10 Appeal court's powers

(1) In relation to an appeal the appeal court has all the powers of the lower court.

    (Rule 52.1(4) provides that this Part is subject to any enactment that sets out special provisions with regard to any particular category of appeal – where such an enactment gives a statutory power to a tribunal, person or other body it may be the case that the appeal court may not exercise that power on an appeal)

(2) The appeal court has power to –

    (a)   affirm, set aside or vary any order or judgment made or given by the lower court;

    (b)   refer any claim or issue for determination by the lower court;

    (c)   order a new trial or hearing;

    (d)   make orders for the payment of interest;

    (e)   make a costs order.

(3) In an appeal from a claim tried with a jury the Court of Appeal may, instead of ordering a new trial –

    (a)   make an order for damages; or

    (b)   vary an award of damages made by the jury.

(4) The appeal court may exercise its powers in relation to the whole or part of an order of the lower court.

(5) If the appeal court –

    (a)   refuses an application for permission to appeal;

    (b)   strikes out an appellant's notice; or

    (c)   dismisses an appeal,

and it considers that the application, the appellant's notice or the appeal is totally without merit, the provisions of paragraph (6) must be complied with.

(6) Where paragraph (5) applies –

    (a)   the court's order must record the fact that it considers the application, the appellant's notice or the appeal to be totally without merit; and

    (b)   the court must at the same time consider whether it is appropriate to make a civil restraint order.

    (Part 3 contains general rules about the court's case management powers)

Amendments—Inserted by SI 2000/221; amended by SI 2004/2072.

Scope—Like the High Court, the Court of Appeal is a Superior Court of Record (SCA 1981, s 15) and has all the authority and jurisdiction of the court from which the appeal is brought. Having decided that the decision of the lower court was wrong, the Court of Appeal may set aside the order and order a new trial, substitute an order and make such order as the case may require. This includes a power to make interim orders pending a re-hearing (*Re R (Minors) (Custody)* [1986] 1 FLR 6). SCA 1981, s 17 provides that any application for a new trial in the High Court must be made to the Court of Appeal.

"all the powers of the lower court" (r 52.10(1))—See the notes to FPR 2010, r 30.11.

Fresh evidence—See the notes to FPR 2010, r 30.11.

Reopening an appeal—See the notes to FPR 2010, r 30.11.

Hopeless appeals—Where the Court of Appeal considers the application or appeal is totally without merit, it must record that fact in the court order and consider making a civil restraint order: see CPR 1998, Pt 3.

Civil restraint order—For the power to make a civil restraint order and the procedure to be followed, see CPR 1998, r 3.11 and PD3C.

Wasted costs order—For the appropriate court to determine an appeal against a wasted costs order see *Gray v Going Places Leisure Travel Ltd* [2005] EWCA Civ 189.

52.11 Hearing of appeals

(1) Every appeal will be limited to a review of the decision of the lower court unless –

    (a)   a practice direction makes different provision for a particular category of appeal; or

    (b)   the court considers that in the circumstances of an individual appeal it would be in the interests of justice to hold a re-hearing.

(2) Unless it orders otherwise, the appeal court will not receive –

    (a)   oral evidence; or

    (b)   evidence which was not before the lower court.

(3) The appeal court will allow an appeal where the decision of the lower court was –

    (a)   wrong; or

    (b)   unjust because of a serious procedural or other irregularity in the proceedings in the lower court.

(4) The appeal court may draw any inference of fact which it considers justified on the evidence.

(5) At the hearing of the appeal a party may not rely on a matter not contained in his appeal notice unless the appeal court gives permission.

Amendments—Inserted by SI 2000/221.

Listing—Following the grant of permission to appeal, the Court of Appeal will send a questionnaire to the appellant requesting a time estimate and giving the period of time in which the appeal is likely to be heard (CPR PD52C, para 23). An application to expedite or delay a hearing must be made to a Master or single Lord Justice. Applications relating to children must be listed swiftly (*Re A (Children: Split Hearing)* [2007] 1 FLR 905). For the listing of urgent appeals, see CPR PD52C, para 26.

Counsel's convenience—It was a well-recognised principle in the Court of Appeal that a permissions application would not be adjourned for the convenience of counsel. An application should have been made by leading counsel for the Court of Appeal to sit early and the indulgence sought of the trial judge, sitting in the RCJ, for the other case to start late (*Bracknell Forest Borough Council v N* [2006] *The Times* November 6).

Separate representation—The Master of the Rolls has emphasised "in the strongest possible terms that it is only where it is clear that there is an unavoidable conflict of interest, as a matter of law, between two parties in the same interest that they should have separate legal representation, especially where public money is involved. The fact that the parties may have different factual points, or that one party's case may be seen as stronger than the other's, or that the parties' legal advisers may see the legal arguments or the prospects somewhat differently, are not good reasons for their incurring the expense and the court time of separate representation": *Oxfordshire County Council v X, Y and J* [2011] 1 FLR 272.

Case management appeals and appeals against discretionary decisions—See *President's Bulletin No 2* (December 2010) in Part V and *Re W (Relocation: Removal Outside Jurisdiction)* [2011] 2 FLR 409. The President has reiterated that appellate courts should respect brave discretionary decisions made at first instance and must be on "secure ground" if they are to reverse the exercise of a discretion: *Re W* (above) at [7]–[12].

Chronology—The Court of Appeal has observed that it would be "enormously helpful" if a chronology was provided in all family appeals as they are for most first instance hearings: *Re H (A Child)* [2013] EWCA Civ 72.

Fresh experts on appeal—The Court of Appeal emphasised that there was an obligation on an applicant seeking permission to appeal, or on an appellant who had obtained permission, to seek the Court of Appeal's leave before instructing a fresh expert and releasing court papers to him. Although the guidelines for instructing medical experts from overseas in family cases had some application to appellate proceedings, they were written for first instance hearings in the course of a trial. However, where an applicant seeking permission to appeal or an appellant sought to instruct a fresh expert from some other jurisdiction, regard had to be had to those guidelines. In particular, the matters requiring explanation included (a) why a UK expert had not been used; (b) what efforts had been made to identify UK experts; and (c) the financial implications of instructing an overseas expert (*Re M (A Child)* [2012] 2 FLR 121 and the Family Justice Council Guidelines of December 2011, *Instruction of Medical Experts from Overseas in Family Cases* (see Part V)).

Appeal against findings of fact—See notes to FPR 2010, r 30.12 and *NG v SG (Appeal: Non-Disclosure)* [2012] 1 FLR 1211.

Expediting an appeal—In *Unilever plc v Chefaro Proprietaries Ltd* [1995] 1 FLR 1102, the Court of Appeal set out the approach to applications for expedition of the hearing of an appeal (to be included in the "expedited list"). It was stated that, in the following cases, justice could be done only if the appeal was heard immediately or within a matter of days:

(a) committal appeals, particularly if there were adverse findings or the sentence was short;
(b) where children were likely to suffer extraordinary prejudice beyond that inevitably involved in the proceedings;
(c) Hague Convention cases;
(d) asylum appeals;
(e) execution of a possession order;
(f) where an irrevocable decision is to be implemented;
(g) publication of allegedly unlawful material;
(h) judicial decisions in the course of proceedings.

Further, the court recognised the need to try and arrange an expedited hearing where otherwise:

(a) a party might lose its livelihood;
(b) the appeal would become futile;
(c) the resolution of other similar cases awaiting the outcome of the appeal would be delayed;
(d) a widespread divergence of practice would continue;
(e) there would be serious detriment to public administration.

Citation of authorities—The Lord Chief Justice has issued a new practice direction in respect of the citation of authorities – see Practice Direction of 24 March 2012: *Citation of Authorities* (see Part V) and see the notes to Procedural Guide E5.

For appeals against case management decisions, see *President's Bulletin No 2, December 2010* in Part V.

52.12 Non-disclosure of Part 36 offers and payments

(1) The fact that a Part 36 offer or payment into court has been made must not be disclosed to any judge of the appeal court who is to hear or determine –

    (a)   an application for permission to appeal; or

    (b)   an appeal,

until all questions (other than costs) have been determined.

(2) Paragraph (1) does not apply if the Part 36 offer or payment into court is relevant to the substance of the appeal.

(3) Paragraph (1) does not prevent disclosure in any application in the appeal proceedings if disclosure of the fact that a Part 36 offer or payment into court has been made is properly relevant to the matter to be decided.

> (Rule 36.3 has the effect that a Part 36 offer made in proceedings at first instance will not have consequences in any appeal proceedings. Therefore, a fresh Part 36 offer needs to be made in appeal proceedings. However, rule 52.12 applies to a Part 36 offer whether made in the original proceedings or in the appeal.)

Amendments—Inserted by SI 2000/221; amended by SI 2003/3361; SI 2006/3435.

52.12A Statutory appeals – court's power to hear any person

(1) In a statutory appeal, any person may apply for permission –

    (a)   to file evidence; or

    (b)   to make representations at the appeal hearing.

(2) An application under paragraph (1) must be made promptly.

Amendments—Inserted by SI 2007/2204.

Scope—This rule is part of a package of amendments made in consequence of the reformed Court of Protection, as a Superior Court of Record, pursuant to the provisions of MCA 2005. In respect of statutory appeals and appeals subject to special provisions, including appeals from an order of the Court of Protection, see CPR PD52D.

Section II
Special Provisions applying to the Court of Appeal

52.13 Second appeals to the court

(1) Permission is required from the Court of Appeal for any appeal to that court from a decision of a county court or the High Court which was itself made on appeal.

(2) The Court of Appeal will not give permission unless it considers that –

    (a)   the appeal would raise an important point of principle or practice; or

    (b)   there is some other compelling reason for the Court of Appeal to hear it.

Amendments—Inserted by SI 2000/221.

Scope—Where it is proposed to appeal the decision of the county court or the High Court which itself was a determination of an appeal, there is an additional hurdle to overcome in obtaining permission to appeal. The proposed appellant must show that there is some compelling reason or some important point of principle. It is possible that rather than determining the appeal itself, the lower court, having considered that there is some important point of principle or there is some other compelling reason may transfer the appeal to be heard by the Court of Appeal (see r 52.14 and CPR PD52A, para 4.7). Permission to appeal may be sought in relation to the substantive order but there can be no appeal in relation to the refusal (of the lower court) to grant permission to appeal (see AJA 1999, s 54; *Bulled v Khayat and Another* [2002] EWCA Civ 804 and *Slot v Isaac* [2002] EWCA Civ 481).

Peremptory orders—The unlawful removal of a child from his usual place of residence called for a peremptory order to be sought for his return, rather than to seek to challenge the dismissal of an appeal for an interim residence order by way of a second appeal to the Court of Appeal: *Re R (Children: Peremptory Return)* [2011] 2 FLR 863.

52.14 Assignment of appeals to the Court of Appeal

(1) Where the court from or to which an appeal is made or from which permission to appeal is sought ("the relevant court") considers that –

   (a)   an appeal which is to be heard by a county court or the High Court would raise an important point of principle or practice; or

   (b)   there is some other compelling reason for the Court of Appeal to hear it,

the relevant court may order the appeal to be transferred to the Court of Appeal.

> (The Master of the Rolls has the power to direct that an appeal which would be heard by a county court or the High Court should be heard instead by the Court of Appeal – see section 57 of the Access to Justice Act 1999)

(2) The Master of the Rolls or the Court of Appeal may remit an appeal to the court in which the original appeal was or would have been brought.

Amendments—Inserted by SI 2000/221.

Scope—Where an appeal is to be heard in the county court or the High Court, that court may transfer the appeal to be heard by the Court of Appeal. If that court (the county court or High Court) hears and determines the appeal, there can be an appeal to the Court of Appeal from that decision only if there is some important point of principle or other compelling reason (see r 52.13).

52.15 Judicial review appeals

(1) Where permission to apply for judicial review has been refused at a hearing in the High Court, the person seeking that permission may apply to the Court of Appeal for permission to appeal.

(1A) Where permission to apply for judicial review of a decision of the Upper Tribunal has been refused by the High Court –

   (a)   the applicant may apply to the Court of Appeal for permission to appeal;

   (b)   the application will be determined on paper without an oral hearing.

(2) An application in accordance with paragraphs (1) or (1A) must be made within 7 days of the decision of the High Court to refuse to give permission to apply for judicial review.

(3) On an application under paragraph (1), the Court of Appeal may, instead of giving permission to appeal, give permission to apply for judicial review.

(4) Where the Court of Appeal gives permission to apply for judicial review in accordance with paragraph (3), the case will proceed in the High Court unless the Court of Appeal orders otherwise.

Amendments—Inserted by SI 2000/221; amended by SI 2012/2208.

Appeals—For the ingenuity of the Court of Appeal to rectify a want of jurisdiction to hear an appeal which had been concluded by the court and reported: see *Farley v Secretary of State for Work & Pensions (No 2)* [2005] 2 FLR 1075, CA.

52.16 Who may exercise the powers of the Court of Appeal

(1) A court officer assigned to the Civil Appeals Office who is –

   (a)   a barrister; or

   (b)   a solicitor

may exercise the jurisdiction of the Court of Appeal with regard to the matters set out in paragraph (2) with the consent of the Master of the Rolls.

(2) The matters referred to in paragraph (1) are –

    (a) any matter incidental to any proceedings in the Court of Appeal;

    (b) any other matter where there is no substantial dispute between the parties; and

    (c) the dismissal of an appeal or application where a party has failed to comply with any order, rule or practice direction.

(3) A court officer may not decide an application for –

    (a) permission to appeal;

    (b) bail pending an appeal;

    (c) an injunction(GL);

    (d) a stay(GL) of any proceedings, other than a temporary stay of any order or decision of the lower court over a period when the Court of Appeal is not sitting or cannot conveniently be convened.

(4) Decisions of a court officer may be made without a hearing.

(5) A party may request any decision of a court officer to be reviewed by the Court of Appeal.

(6) At the request of a party, a hearing will be held to reconsider a decision of –

    (a) a single judge; or

    (b) a court officer,

made without a hearing.

(6A) A request under paragraph (5) or (6) must be filed within 7 days after the party is served with notice of the decision.

(7) A single judge may refer any matter for a decision by a court consisting of two or more judges.

> (Section 54(6) of the Senior Courts Act 1981 provides that there is no appeal from the decision of a single judge on an application for permission to appeal)

> (Section 58(2) of the Senior Courts Act 1981 provides that there is no appeal to the Supreme Court from decisions of the Court of Appeal that –

>   (a) are taken by a single judge or any officer or member of staff of that court in proceedings incidental to any cause or matter pending before the civil division of that court; and

>   (b) do not involve the determination of an appeal or of an application for permission to appeal,

> and which may be called into question by rules of court. Rules 52.16(5) and (6) provide the procedure for the calling into question of such decisions)

Amendments—Inserted by SI 2000/221; amended by SI 2003/3361; CRA 2005, Sch 11, para 1(2); SI 2009/2092.

Section III
Provisions about Reopening Appeals

52.17 Reopening of final appeals

(1) The Court of Appeal or the High Court will not reopen a final determination of any appeal unless –

    (a) it is necessary to do so in order to avoid real injustice;

    (b) the circumstances are exceptional and make it appropriate to reopen the appeal; and

(c)   there is no alternative effective remedy.

(2) In paragraphs (1), (3), (4) and (6), "appeal" includes an application for permission to appeal.

(3) This rule does not apply to appeals to a county court.

(4) Permission is needed to make an application under this rule to reopen a final determination of an appeal even in cases where under rule 52.3(1) permission was not needed for the original appeal.

(5) There is no right to an oral hearing of an application for permission unless, exceptionally, the judge so directs.

(6) The judge will not grant permission without directing the application to be served on the other party to the original appeal and giving him an opportunity to make representations.

(7) There is no right of appeal or review from the decision of the judge on the application for permission, which is final.

(8) The procedure for making an application for permission is set out in Practice Direction 52.

Amendments—Inserted by SI 2003/2113; SI 2009/3390.

Limitations—The jurisdiction to re-open an appeal should only be permitted where the process of justice has been corrupted. It is insufficient for these purposes to establish that there is fresh evidence available which might have had a significant impact on the result: see *Re U (Re-Opening Of Appeal)* [2005] 2 FLR 444. See CPR PD52A, paras 7.1–7.4.

Practice Direction 52A – Appeals: General Provisions

This Practice Direction supplements CPR Part 52

Contents of this Practice Direction

This Practice Direction is divided into the following sections –

1   Practice Directions supplementing Part 52
2   Introduction
3   Destinations of Appeal
4   Obtaining permission to appeal
5   Skeleton arguments
6   Disposing of applications and appeals by consent
7   Reopening appeals
8   Transitional provisions

SECTION 1: PRACTICE DIRECTIONS SUPPLEMENTING PART 52

1.1 There are five Practice Directions supplementing Part 52 –

- PD52A – Appeals: general provisions
- PD52B – Appeals in the county courts and the High Court
- PD52C – Appeals to the Court of Appeal
- PD52D – Statutory appeals and appeals subject to special provision
- PD52E – Appeals by way of case stated

SECTION 2: INTRODUCTION

2.1 These Practice Directions apply to all appeals to which Part 52 applies.

2.2 Part 52 complements the provisions of sections 54 to 57 of the Access to Justice Act 1999 and provides a uniform procedure for appeals in the county courts and the High Court and a modified procedure for the Civil Division of the Court of Appeal. Part 52 does not apply to –

    (a)   family proceedings in the High Court or county courts but does apply to appeals to the Court of Appeal from decisions made in family proceedings with such modifications as may be required;

    (b)   appeals in detailed assessment proceedings against the decision of an authorised court officer.

SECTION 3: DESTINATIONS OF APPEAL

3.1 Section 56 of the Access to Justice Act 1999 enables the Lord Chancellor by Order to specify the destinations of appeal in different cases. The Access to Justice Act 1999 (Destination of Appeals) Order 2000, SI 2000/1071 made under section 56, specifies the general destinations of appeal which apply subject to any statutory provision to the contrary. The destinations of appeal provided by that Order are explained in the following paragraphs of this section of this Practice Direction.

3.2 "Statutory appeals" and "Appeals by way of case stated" are dealt with in PD52D – refer to those provisions for the appropriate court to which such an appeal may lie.

3.3 The court or judge to which an appeal is to be made (subject to obtaining any necessary permission) is set out in the tables below –

- Table 1 deals with appeals in proceedings other than family and insolvency proceedings;
- Table 2 deals with appeals in insolvency proceedings; and
- Table 3 deals with appeals in family proceedings which may be heard in the Family Division and to which the CPR may apply.

3.4 Definitions of terms and abbreviations used in Tables 1, 2 and 3:

"Destination": the court to which the appeal lies.

"Pt 7 Claim (not MT)": Part 7 Claim, other than a claim allocated to the multitrack.

"Pt 7 Claim (MT)": Part 7 Claim, allocated to the multi-track.

"Pt 8 Claim (not MT)": Part 8 Claim, other than a claim allocated to the multitrack.

"Pt 8 Claim (MT)": Part 8 Claim, allocated to the multi-track.

"DJ": District judge.

"CJ": Circuit judge including a recorder or a district judge who is exercising the jurisdiction of a Circuit judge with the permission of the Designated Civil Judge in respect of the case.

"CJ (CC)": Circuit judge in the county court.

"Master": Master, district judge sitting in a district registry or any other judge referred to in article 2 of the Destination of Appeals Order.

"Final": A final decision within the meaning of paragraphs 3.6 to 3.8 of this Practice Direction.

"Interim": A decision that is not a final decision within the meaning of paragraphs 3.6 to 3.8 of this Practice Direction.

"HCJ": single judge of the High Court.

"HCJ(FD): single judge of the family Division of the High Court.

"CA": Court of Appeal.

"Other": Claims or originating or pre-action applications started otherwise than by a Part 7 or Part 8 claim (for example an application under Part 23).

"Specialist": Specialist proceedings (under the Companies Act 1985 or the Companies Act 1989 or to which Sections I, II or III of Part 57 or any of Parts 58,59,60, 62 or 63 apply).

(Note: Tables 1, 2 and 3 do not include so-called "leap frog" appeals either to the Court of Appeal pursuant to section 57 of the Access to Justice Act 1999 or to the Supreme Court pursuant to section 13 of the Administration of Justice Act 1969.)

3.5 The destinations in the tables set out below apply whether the decision is interim or final. For the meaning of "final decision" for the purposes of this table see paragraphs 3.6 to 3.8 below.

Table 1: Proceedings other than family or insolvency proceedings

Court	Deciding judge	Nature of claim	Interim/final	Destination
County	DJ	Pt 7 Claim	Interim	CJ (CC)
		Pt 7 Claim (not MT)	Final	
		Pt 7 Claim (MT)	Final	CA
		Pt 8 Claim	Interim/final	CJ (CC)
		Other	Interim/final	
		Specialist	Interim	
			Final	CA
	CJ	Pt 7 Claim	Interim	HCJ
		Pt 7 Claim (not MT)	Final	
		Pt 7 Claim (MT)	Final	CA
		Pt 8 Claim	Interim/final	HCJ
		Other	Interim/final	
		Specialist	Interim	
			Final	CA
High	Master	Pt 7 Claim	Interim	HCJ
		Pt 7 Claim (not MT)	Final	
		Pt 7 Claim (MT)	Final	CA
		Pt 8 Claim	Interim/final	HCJ
		Other	Interim/final	
		Specialist	Interim	
			Final	CA
	HCJ	Any	Interim/final	CA

Table 2: Insolvency proceedings

Court	Deciding judge	Destination
County	DJ or CJ	HCJ
High	Registrar	
	HCJ	CA

Table 3: Family proceedings in the Principal Registry of the Family Division and to which the CPR will apply

The proceedings to which this table applies include proceedings under the Inheritance (Provision for Family and Dependants) Act 1975 and proceedings under the Trusts of Land and Appointment of Trustees Act 1996.

Deciding judge	Nature of claim	Decision under appeal	Destination
DJ	Part 7 Claim (not MT)	Any decision other than a final decision	HCJ (FD)
	Part 7 Claim (MT)	Final decision	CA
	Part 8 Claim (not MT)	Any decision	HCJ (FD)
	Part 8 Claim (MT)		
HCJ (FD)	Any	Any decision	CA

3.6 A "final decision" is a decision of a court that would finally determine (subject to any possible appeal or detailed assessment of costs) the entire proceedings whichever way the court decided the issues before it.

3.7 A decision is to be treated as a final decision for destination of appeal purposes where it –

(a) is made at the conclusion of part of a hearing or trial which has been split into parts; and
(b) would, if it had been made at the conclusion of that hearing or trial, have been a final decision.

3.8 (1) The following are examples of final decisions –

- a judgment on liability at the end of a split trial;
- a judgment at the conclusion of an assessment of damages following a judgment on liability.

(2) The following are examples of decisions that are not final –

- a case management decision (within the meaning of paragraph 4.6);
- a grant or refusal of interim relief;
- summary judgment;
- striking out a claim or statement of case;
- a summary or detailed assessment of costs;
- an order for the enforcement of a final decision.

Filing appellant's notice in wrong court

3.9 (1) Where a party attempts to file an appellant's notice in a court which does not have jurisdiction to issue the notice, a court officer may notify that party in writing that the appeal court does not have jurisdiction in respect of the notice.

(2) Before notifying a person under paragraph (1) the court officer must confer –

(a)   with a judge of the appeal court; or

(b)   where the Court of Appeal is the appeal court, with a court officer who exercises the jurisdiction of that Court under rule 52.16.

(3) Where a court officer, in the Court of Appeal, notifies a person under paragraph (1), rule 52.16(5) and (6) shall not apply.

SECTION 4: OBTAINING PERMISSION TO APPEAL

Where to apply for permission

4.1 An application for permission to appeal may be made –

(a)   to the lower court at the hearing at which the decision to be appealed against is given (in which case the lower court may adjourn the hearing to give a party an opportunity to apply for permission to appeal); or

(b)   where the lower court refuses permission to appeal or where no application is made to the lower court, to the appeal court in accordance with rule 52.4.

Form

4.2 An application for permission to appeal to the appeal court must be made using an appellant's notice (form N161 or N164 (small claims track)).

Appeals from Masters and district judges of High Court

4.3 In relation to appeals from Masters or district judges of the High Court: appeals, applications for permission and any other applications in the appeal may be heard and directions in the appeal may be given by a High Court Judge or by any person authorised under section 9 of the Senior Courts Act 1981 to act as a judge of the High Court.

Where the lower court is a county court

4.4 Where the lower court is a county court –

(a)   subject to sub-paragraph (b), appeals and applications for permission to appeal will be heard by a High Court Judge or by a person authorised under paragraphs (1), (2) or (4) of the Table in section 9(1) of the Senior Courts Act 1981 to act as a judge of the High Court;

(b)   an appeal or application for permission to appeal from the decision of a recorder may be heard by a Designated Civil Judge who is authorised under paragraph (5) of the Table in section 9(1) of the Senior Courts Act 1981 to act as a judge of the High Court; and

(c)   other applications in the appeal may be heard and directions in the appeal may be given either by a High Court Judge or by any person authorised under section 9 of the Senior Courts Act 1981 to act as a judge of the High Court.

4.5 The Designated Civil Judge in consultation with the Presiding Judge has responsibility for allocating appeals from decisions of district judges to circuit judges.

Appeal in relation to case management decision

4.6 Where the application is for permission to appeal from a case management decision, the court dealing with the application may take into account whether –

(a)   the issue is of sufficient significance to justify the costs of an appeal;

(b)   the procedural consequences of an appeal (e.g. loss of trial date) outweigh the significance of the case management decision;

(c)   it would be more convenient to determine the issue at or after trial.

Case management decisions include decisions made under rule 3.1(2) and decisions about disclosure, filing of witness statements or experts' reports, directions about the timetable of the claim, adding a party to a claim and security for costs.

Second appeal

4.7 An application for permission to appeal from a decision of the High Court or a county court which was itself made on appeal is a second appeal and must be made to the Court of Appeal. If permission to appeal is granted the appeal will be heard by the Court of Appeal.

SECTION 5: SKELETON ARGUMENTS

5.1 (1) The purpose of a skeleton argument is to assist the court by setting out as concisely as practicable the arguments upon which a party intends to rely.

(2) A skeleton argument must –

- be concise;
- both define and confine the areas of controversy;
- be set out in numbered paragraphs;
- be cross-referenced to any relevant document in the bundle;
- be self-contained and not incorporate by reference material from previous skeleton arguments;
- not include extensive quotations from documents or authorities.

(3) Documents to be relied on must be identified.

(4) Where it is necessary to refer to an authority, a skeleton argument must –

(a)   state the proposition of law the authority demonstrates; and

(b)   identify the parts of the authority that support the proposition.

If more than one authority is cited in support of a given proposition, the skeleton argument must briefly state why.

(5) The cost of preparing a skeleton argument which –

(a)   does not comply with the requirements set out in this paragraph; or

(b)   was not filed within the time limits provided by this Practice Direction (or any further time granted by the court),

will not be allowed on assessment except as directed by the court.

5.2 The appellant should consider what other information the appeal court will need. This may include a list of persons who feature in the case or glossaries of technical terms. A chronology of relevant events will be necessary in most appeals.

5.3 Any statement of costs must show the amount claimed for the skeleton argument separately.

PART III

SECTION 6: DISPOSING OF APPLICATIONS AND APPEALS BY CONSENT

Dismissal of applications or appeals by consent

6.1 An appellant who does not wish to pursue an application or appeal may request the appeal court to dismiss the application or the appeal. If such a request is granted it will usually be subject to an order that the appellant pays the costs of the application or appeal.

6.2 If the appellant wishes to have the application or appeal dismissed without costs, his request must be accompanied by a letter signed by the respondent stating that the respondent so consents.

6.3 Where a settlement has been reached disposing of the application or appeal, the parties may make a joint request to the court for the application or appeal to be dismissed by consent. If the request is granted the application or appeal will be dismissed.

Allowing unopposed appeals or applications on paper

6.4 The appeal court will not normally make an order allowing an appeal unless satisfied that the decision of the lower court was wrong or unjust because of a serious procedural or other irregularity. The appeal court may, however, set aside or vary the order of the lower court by consent and without determining the merits of the appeal if it is satisfied that there are good and sufficient reasons for so doing. Where the appeal court is requested by all parties to allow an application or an appeal the court may consider the request on the papers. The request should set out the relevant history of the proceedings and the matters relied on as justifying the order and be accompanied by a draft order.

Disposal of applications and appeals involving children or protected parties

6.5 Where one of the parties is a child or protected party, any disposal of an application or the appeal requires the court's approval. A draft order signed by the parties' solicitors should be sent to the appeal court, together with an opinion from the advocate acting on behalf of the child or protected party and, in the case of a protected party, any relevant documents prepared for the Court of Protection.

SECTION 7: REOPENING APPEALS (RULE 52.17)

7.1 A party applying for permission to reopen an appeal or an application for permission to appeal must apply for such permission from the court whose decision the party wishes to reopen.

7.2 The application for permission must be made by application notice and be supported by written evidence, verified by a statement of truth. A copy of the application for permission must not be served on any other party to the original appeal unless the court so directs.

7.3 Where the court directs that the application for permission is to be served on another party, that party may, within 14 days of the service on him of the copy of the application, file and serve a written statement either supporting or opposing the application.

7.4 The application for permission will be considered on paper by a single judge.

SECTION 8: TRANSITIONAL PROVISIONS

8.1 This Practice Direction and Practice Directions 52B, 52C, 52D and 52E shall come into force on 1 October 2012 and shall apply to all appeals where –

   (a) the appeal notice was filed; or

   (b) permission to appeal was given

on or after that date.

8.2 The appeal court may at any time direct that, in relation to any appeal, one or more of Practice Directions 52A, 52B, 52C, 52D or 52E shall apply irrespective of the date on which the appeal notice was filed or permission to appeal was given.

Practice Direction 52B –
Appeals in the County Courts and High Court

This Practice Direction supplements CPR Part 52

Contents of this Practice Direction

This Practice Direction is divided into the following sections –

SECTION 1: APPLICATION

This Practice Direction applies to –

   (a) appeals within a county court (from a District Judge to a Circuit Judge);

   (b) appeals from a county court to the High Court; and

   (c) appeals within the High Court (from a Master, a District Judge sitting in a District Registry, a Registrar in Bankruptcy, a Registrar of the Companies Court, a Costs Judge or an officer of the High Court to a judge of the High Court).

SECTION 2: VENUE FOR APPEALS AND FILING OF NOTICES AND APPLICATIONS

2.1 Appeals within a county court, appeals from a county court and appeals within the High Court to a judge of the High Court must be brought in the appropriate appeal centre and all other notices (including any respondent's notice) and applications must be filed at that appeal centre. The venue for an appeal within a county court will be determined by the Designated Civil Judge and may be different from the appeal centre.

2.2 The tables at the end of this Practice Direction set out the Appeal Centres for each circuit.

SECTION 3: EXTENDING TIME IN WHICH TO APPEAL

3.1 A party may apply to the lower court for an extension of time in which to file an appellant's notice. The application must be made at the same time as the appellant applies to the lower court for permission to appeal.

3.2 Where the time for filing an appellant's notice has expired, the appellant must include an application for an extension of time within the appellant's notice (form N161 or, in respect of a small claim, form N164) stating the reason for the delay and the steps taken prior to making the application.

3.3 The court may make an order granting or refusing an extension of time and may do so with or without a hearing. If an order is made without a hearing, any party seeking to set aside or vary the order may apply, within 14 days of service of the order, for a hearing.

SECTION 4: INITIATING AN APPEAL

4.1 An appellant's notice (Form N161 or, in respect of a small claim, Form N164) must be filed and served in all cases. The appellant's notice must be accompanied by the appropriate fee or, if appropriate, a fee remission application or certificate.

4.2 Documents to be filed with the appellant's notice: The appellant must file with the appellant's notice –

- (a)   three copies of the appellant's notice and one additional copy for each respondent;
- (b)   a copy of the sealed order under appeal;
- (c)   where an application was made to the lower court for permission to appeal, a copy of any order granting or refusing permission to appeal together with a copy of the reasons, if any, for allowing or refusing permission to appeal; and
- (d)   grounds of appeal, which must be set out on a separate sheet attached to the appellant's notice and must set out, in simple language, clearly and concisely, why the order of the lower court was wrong or unjust because of a serious procedural or other irregularity (Rule 52.11(3)).

4.3 Applications in the appeal: Any application to be made in the appeal (for example, for a stay of the order of the lower court, or for an extension of time) should be included within the appellant's notice. Where the applicant qualifies for fee remission, any application for a transcript of the judgment of the lower court at public expense should be made within the appellant's notice.

SECTION 5: CASE MANAGING THE APPEAL; ORDERS OF THE COURT

5.1 The appeal court may make orders for the case management of an appeal.

5.2 When making a case management order, the court may dispense with any requirements of or directions made in this Practice Direction.

SECTION 6: CONDUCT OF THE APPEAL

6.1 Service of appellant's notice on the respondent: The appellant must file a certificate of service of the appellant's notice with the court as soon as practicable after service.

6.2 Transcript of the judgment of the lower court or other record of reasons: Except where the claim has been allocated to the small claims track, the appellant must obtain a transcript or other record of reasons of the lower court as follows –

(a) where the judgment has been officially recorded, the appellant must apply for an approved transcript as soon as possible and, in any event, within 7 days of the filing of the appellant's notice;

(b) where the judgment under appeal has been handed down in writing, the appellant must obtain and retain a copy of the written judgment;.

(c) in any other case, the appellant must cause a note of the judgment under appeal to be made and typed. The parties to the appeal should agree the note, which should then be sent to the judge of the lower court for approval. The parties and their advocates have a duty to make, and to co-operate in agreeing, a note of the judgment.

6.3 Appeal bundle: As soon as practicable, but in any event within 35 days of the filing of the appellant's notice, the appellant must file an appeal bundle which must contain only those documents relevant to the appeal. The appeal bundle must be paginated and indexed.

6.4 Documents relevant to the appeal:

(1) Subject to any order made by the court, the following documents must be included in the appeal bundle –

(a) a copy of the appellant's notice;

(b) a copy of any respondent's notice;

(c) a copy of any appellant's or respondent's skeleton argument;

(d) a copy of the order under appeal;

(e) a copy of the order of the lower court granting or refusing permission to appeal together with a copy of the judge's reasons, if any, for granting or refusing permission;

(f) a copy of any order allocating the case to a track;

(g) a transcript of the judgment of the lower court or other record of reasons (except in appeals in cases which were allocated to the small claims track and subject to any order of the court).

(2) The following documents should also be considered for inclusion in the appeal bundle but should be included only where relevant to the appeal –

(a) statements of case;

(b) application notices;

(c) other orders made in the case;

(d) a chronology of relevant events;

(e) witness statements made in support of any application made in the appellant's notice;

(f) other witness statements;

(g) any other documents which any party considers would assist the appeal court.

6.5 Service of the appeal bundle: A copy of the appeal bundle must be served on each respondent –

(a) where permission to appeal was granted by the lower court, at the same time as filing the appeal bundle;

(b) where the appeal court has granted permission to appeal, as soon as practicable after notification and in any event within 14 days of the grant of permission;

(c) where the appeal court directs that the application for permission to appeal is to be heard on the same occasion as the appeal, as soon as practicable and in any event within 14 days after notification of the hearing date.

6.6 Late documents: Any relevant document which is obtained or created after the appeal bundle has been filed (for example a respondent's notice or a skeleton argument) should be added to the appeal bundle as soon as practicable and, in any event, no less than 7 days before the hearing of the appeal or any application.

PART III

SECTION 7: DETERMINATION OF APPLICATIONS

7.1 Applications made in the appeal, including applications for permission to appeal under rule 52.3(2)(a) or rule 52.5(3), may be determined with or without a hearing.

7.2 Where the court refuses an application for permission to appeal without a hearing, the appellant (or, where appropriate, the respondent) may request the application to be reconsidered at a hearing.

7.3 Where the court determines any other application without hearing the respondent (including an application for permission to bring the appeal out of time) any party affected by the determination may apply to have the order set aside or varied.

7.4 Any request or application made under this section must be made within 7 days of service of notification of the determination upon the person making the application. Where any such request or application is made –

    (a)   a copy of the request or application must be served on all other parties at the same time; and

    (b)   the court will give directions for the determination of the application.

SECTION 8: HEARINGS

8.1 Attendance at permission hearings: Where a respondent to an appeal or cross-appeal attends the hearing of an application for permission to appeal, costs will not be awarded to the respondent unless –

    (a)   the court has ordered or requested attendance by the respondent;

    (b)   the court has ordered that the appeal be listed at the same time as the determination of other applications;

    (c)   the court has ordered that the hearing of the appeal will follow the hearing of the application if permission is granted; or

    (d)   the court considers it just, in all the circumstances, to award costs to the respondent.

8.2 Respondent's documents: A respondent who has been served with an appeal bundle and who considers that relevant documents have been omitted may file and serve on all parties a respondent's supplemental appeal bundle containing copies of other relevant documents. The supplemental appeal bundle must be filed and served as soon as practicable after service of the appeal bundle, but in any event not less than 7 days before the hearing.

8.3 Skeleton arguments: Subject to any order of the court, the parties to the appeal should file and serve skeleton arguments only where –

    (a)   the complexity of the issues of fact or law in the appeal justify them; or

    (b)   skeleton arguments would assist the court in respects not readily apparent from the papers in the appeal.

Table A: Table of appeal centres for each circuit

Circuit	Court	Appeal Centre
Midland	Birmingham CJC	Birmingham CJC
	Boston	Lincoln
	Burton-upon-Trent	Nottingham
	Buxton	Nottingham
	Chesterfield	Nottingham

Circuit	Court	Appeal Centre
	Coventry	Coventry
	Derby	Nottingham
	Dudley	Walsall
	Hereford	Worcester
	Kettering	Northampton
	Kidderminster	Worcester
	Leicester	Leicester
	Lincoln	Lincoln
	Mansfield	Nottingham
	Northampton	Northampton
	Nottingham	Nottingham
	Nuneaton	Coventry
	Redditch	Worcester
	Stafford	Stoke-on-Trent
	Stoke-on-Trent	Stoke-on-Trent
	Telford	Telford
	Walsall	Walsall
	Warwick	Coventry
	Wolverhampton	Walsall
	Worcester	Worcester
North East	Barnsley	Sheffield
	Bradford	Bradford
	Darlington	Teesside
	Doncaster	Sheffield
	Durham	Newcastle-upon-Tyne
	Gateshead	Newcastle-upon-Tyne
	Grimsby	Kingston-upon-Hull
	Halifax	Halifax
	Harrogate	Leeds
	Hartlepool	Teesside
	Huddersfield	Huddersfield
	Kingston-upon-Hull	Kingston-upon-Hull
	Leeds	Leeds
	Morpeth	Newcastle-upon-Tyne
	Newcastle-upon-Tyne	Newcastle-upon-Tyne
	North Shields	Newcastle-upon-Tyne
	Rotherham	Sheffield
	Scarborough	Leeds
	Scunthorpe	Kingston-upon-Hull
	Sheffield	Sheffield
	Skipton	Skipton
	South Shields	Newcastle-upon-Tyne
	Sunderland	Newcastle-upon-Tyne

PART III

Circuit	Court	Appeal Centre
	Teesside	Teesside
	Wakefield	Leeds
	York	Leeds
Northern	Accrington	Preston
	Altrincham	Manchester CJC
	Barrow-in-Furness	Carlisle
	Birkenhead	Liverpool
	Blackburn	Preston
	Blackpool	Preston
	Bolton	Manchester CJC
	Burnley	Preston
	Bury	Manchester CJC
	Carlisle	Carlisle
	Chester CJC	Chester CJC
	Crewe	Chester CJC
	Kendal	Carlisle
	Lancaster	Preston
	Liverpool	Liverpool
	Macclesfield	Chester CJC
	Manchester CJC	Manchester CJC
	Oldham	Manchester CJC
	Preston	Preston
	St Helens	Liverpool
	Stockport	Manchester CJC
	Tameside	Manchester CJC
	Warrington	Chester CJC
	West Cumbria	Carlisle
	Wigan	Liverpool
Wales	Aberystwyth	Swansea
	Blackwood	Cardiff CJC
	Brecknock	Swansea
	Bridgend	Cardiff CJC
	Caernarfon	Wrexham
	Cardiff	Cardiff CJC
	Carmarthen	Swansea
	Conwy & Colwyn	Wrexham
	Haverfordwest	Swansea
	Llanelli	Swansea
	Llangefni	Wrexham
	Merthyr Tydfil	Cardiff CJC
	Mold	Wrexham
	Neath & Port Talbot	Swansea
	Newport (Gwent)	Cardiff CJC

Circuit	Court	Appeal Centre
	Pontypridd	Cardiff CJC
	Rhyl	Wrexham
	Swansea	Swansea
	Welshpool & Newtown	Wrexham
	Wrexham	Wrexham
Western	Aldershot & Farnham	Aldershot & Farnham
	Barnstaple	Barnstaple
	Basingstoke	Basingstoke
	Bath	Bristol CJC
	Bodmin	Bodmin
	Bournemouth	Bournemouth
	Bristol	Bristol CJC
	Cheltenham	Bristol CJC
	Exeter	Exeter
	Gloucester	Bristol CJC
	Newport (Isle of Wight)	Newport (Isle of Wight)
	Plymouth	Plymouth
	Portsmouth	Portsmouth
	Salisbury	Salisbury
	Southampton	Southampton
	Swindon	Swindon
	Taunton	Bristol CJC
	Torquay & Newton Abbot	Torquay & Newton Abbot
	Trowbridge	Trowbridge
	Truro	Truro
	Weston-Super-Mare	Bristol CJC
	Weymouth & Dorchester	Weymouth & Dorchester
	Winchester	Winchester
	Yeovil	Bristol
South East	Aylesbury	Oxford
	Banbury	Oxford
	Barnet	Barnet
	Basildon	Southend
	Bedford	Luton
	Bow	Bow
	Brentford	Brendford
	Brighton	Brighton
	Bromley	Bromley
	Bury St Edmunds	Cambridge
	Cambridge	Cambridge
	Canterbury	Canterbury
	Central London CJC	Central London CJC
	Chelmsford	Southend

PART III

Circuit	Court	Appeal Centre
	Chichester	Chichester
	Clerkenwell & Shoreditch	Clerkenwell & Shoreditch
	Colchester	Southend
	Croydon	Croydon
	Dartford	Dartford
	Eastbourne	Eastbourne
	Edmonton	Edmonton
	Guildford	Guildford
	Hastings	Hastings
	Hertford	Luton
	High Wycombe	Oxford
	Horsham	Horsham
	Hove	Hove
	Ipswich	Norwich
	Kingston-upon-Thames	Kingston-upon-Thames
	King's Lynn	Norwich
	Lambeth	Lambeth
	Lewes	Lewes
	Luton	Luton
	Maidstone	Maidstone
	Mayor's and City	Mayor's and City
	Medway	Medway
	Milton Keynes	Oxford
	Norwich	Norwich
	Oxford	Oxford
	Peterborough	Cambridge
	Reading	Oxford
	Reigate	Reigate
	Romford	Romford
	Slough	Oxford
	Southend	Southend
	St Albans	Luton
	Staines	Staines
	Thanet	Thanet
	Tunbridge Wells	Tunbridge Wells
	Uxbridge	Uxbridge
	Wandsworth	Wandsworth
	Watford	Watford
	Willesden	Willesden
	West London	West London
	Woolwich	Woolwich
	Worthing	Worthing

Table B: Appeals from a county court or within the High Court: appeal centres for each circuit

Circuit	Appeal Centre
Midland Circuit	Birmingham Nottingham
North Eastern Circuit	Leeds Newcastle Sheffield
Northern Circuit	Manchester Liverpool Preston Chester
Wales Circuit	Cardiff Swansea Mold
Western Circuit	Bristol Exeter Winchester
South Eastern Circuit	Royal Courts of Justice Lewes Luton Norwich Reading Chelmsford St Albans Maidstone Oxford

PART III

Practice Direction 52C – Appeals to the Court of Appeal

This Practice Direction supplements CPR Part 52

Contents of this Practice Direction

This Practice Direction is divided into the following sections:

1 Introduction and interpretation
2 Starting an appeal to the Court of Appeal, Grounds of Appeal and Skeleton Arguments
3 Respondent's notice and respondent's skeleton argument
4 Procedure where permission to appeal is sought from the Court of Appeal
5 Timetable

6   Management of the appeal
7   Bundles, amendment and supplementary skeleton arguments

SECTION 1: INTRODUCTION AND INTERPRETATION

1 In this Practice Direction –

"appeal notice" means either an appellant's notice in form N161 or a respondent's notice in form N162 ;

"appellant's notice" means an appeal notice filed by an appellant and a "respondent's notice" means an appeal notice filed by a respondent;

"hearing date" means the date on which the appeal is listed to be heard, including a "floating" date over two or more days;

"listing window notification" means the letter sent by the Civil Appeals Office in accordance with Section 5: Timetable Part 1 notifying the parties of the window within which the appeal is likely to be heard; and "date of the listing window notification" means the date of such letter;

"replacement skeleton argument" means a skeleton argument which has been amended in order to include cross references to the appeal bundle and is lodged and served in accordance with the timetable at Section 5 Part 2.

2 The court may make such directions as the case may require and such directions will prevail over any provision of this practice direction.

SECTION 2: STARTING AN APPEAL TO THE COURT OF APPEAL

Filing the Appellant's Notice and accompanying documents

3 (1) An appellant's notice (Form N161) must be filed and served in all cases. The appellant's notice must be accompanied by the appropriate fee or, if appropriate, a fee remission certificate.

(2) The appellant's notice and accompanying documents must be filed in the Civil Appeals Office Registry, Room E307, Royal Courts of Justice, Strand, London, WC2A 2LL.

(3) At the same time as filing an appellant's notice, the appellant must provide for the use of the court three copies of the appellant's notice and one copy of each of the following –

(a)   the sealed order or tribunal determination being appealed;
(b)   any order granting or refusing permission to appeal, together with a copy of the judge's or tribunal's reasons for granting or refusing permission to appeal;
(c)   any witness statements or affidavits relied on in support of any application included in the appellant's notice;
(d)   in cases where the decision of the lower court was itself made on appeal, the first order, the reasons given by the judge who made it, and the appellant's notice of appeal against that order;
(e)   in a claim for judicial review or a statutory appeal, the original decision which was the subject of the application to the lower court;
(f)   the order allocating the case to a track (if any);
(g)   the appellant's skeleton argument in support of the appeal;
(h)   the approved transcript of the judgment.

(4) The appellant must also provide to the court one copy of the appellant's notice for each respondent for sealing by the court and return to the appellant for service.

(5) Where the appellant applies for permission to appeal, additional documents are required: see Section 4 of this Practice Direction.

(6) Provisions in relation to the skeleton argument are set out in paragraph 31.

Extension of time for filing appellant's notice

4 (1) Where the time for filing an appellant's notice has expired, the appellant must –

    (a)   file the appellant's notice; and

    (b)   include in that appellant's notice an application for an extension of time.

(2) The appellant's notice must state the reason for the delay and the steps taken prior to the application being made.

(3) Where the appellant's notice includes an application for an extension of time and permission to appeal has been given or is not required, the respondent has the right to oppose that application and to be heard at any hearing of that application. In respect of any application to extend time –

    (a)   The respondent must –

        (i)   be served with a copy of any evidence filed in support of the application; and

        (ii)   inform the court in writing of any objections to the grant of the extension of time within 7 days of being served with the appellant's notice.

    (b)   A respondent who unreasonably opposes an application for an extension of time may be ordered to pay the costs of the application.

    (c)   An application for an extension of time will normally be determined without a hearing unless the court directs otherwise.

Grounds of Appeal

5 (1) The grounds of appeal must identify as concisely as possible the respects in which the judgment of the court below is –

    (a)   wrong; or

    (b)   unjust because of a serious procedural or other irregularity, as required by rule 52.11(3).

(2) The reasons why the decision under appeal is wrong or unjust must not be included in the grounds of appeal and must be confined to the skeleton argument.

Second appeals

5A An application to make a second appeal must identify in the grounds of appeal –

    (a)   the important point of principle or practice, or

    (b)   the compelling reason

which is said to justify the grant of permission to appeal.

Non-availability of documents

6 If the appellant is unable to provide any of the necessary documents in time, the appellant must complete the appeal notice on the basis of the available documents. The notice may be amended subsequently with the permission of the court (see paragraph 30).

Service of appellant's notice on the respondent

7.1 The Civil Appeals Office will not serve documents. Where service is required by the Rules or this Practice Direction, it must be effected by the parties.

7.2 The evidence in support of any application made in an appellant's notice must be filed and served with the appellant's notice.

7.3 An application for an order to dispense with service of the appellant's notice under rule 6.28 must be made in the appeal notice or, thereafter, by application notice under Part 23.

Section 3: Respondent's notice (Rule 52.5) and respondent's skeleton argument

Respondent's notice

8 (1) A respondent who seeks to appeal against any part of the order made by the court below must file an appeal notice.

(2) A respondent who seeks a variation of the order of the lower court must file an appeal notice and must obtain permission to appeal.

(3) A respondent who seeks to contend that the order of the court below should be upheld for reasons other than those given by that court must file a respondent's notice.

(4) The notice may be amended subsequently with the permission of the court (see paragraph 30).

Skeleton argument to be lodged with the respondent's notice

9 A respondent who files a respondent's notice must, within 14 days of filing the notice, lodge a skeleton argument with the court and serve a copy of the skeleton argument on every other party to the appeal.

(Provisions in relation to the skeleton argument are set out in paragraph 31.)

Documents to be filed with respondent's notice

10 The respondent must file the following documents with the respondent's notice –

(a)   two additional copies of the respondent's notice for the court; and

(b)   one copy each for the appellant and any other respondents.

Applications within respondent's notice

11 (1) A respondent may include an application within a respondent's notice.

(2) The parties must consider whether it would be more convenient for any application to be listed with the appeal or whether the application needs to be considered in advance.

(3) Where parties consider that the time estimate for the appeal will be affected by listing the application with the appeal, they must inform the court without delay.

Time limits: rule 52.5(4) and (5)

12 Where an extension of time is required, the respondent must apply in the respondent's notice and explain the delay.

Respondent's skeleton argument (where no respondent's notice filed)

13 (1) In all cases where the respondent is legally represented and proposes to address the court, the respondent must lodge and serve a skeleton argument.

(2) A respondent's skeleton argument must be lodged and served in accordance with Part 1 of the Timetable in Section 5.

(Provisions in relation to the skeleton argument are set out in paragraph 31.)

SECTION 4: PROCEDURE WHERE PERMISSION TO APPEAL IS SOUGHT FROM THE COURT OF APPEAL

Documents for use on an application for permission

14 (1) Within 14 days of filing the appeal notice the appellant must lodge a bundle containing only those documents which are necessary for the court to determine that application.

(2) The bundle of documents must –

    (a)   be paginated and in chronological order;

    (b)   contain an index at the front.

Determination of applications for permission to appeal

15 (1) Applications for permission to appeal will generally be considered by the court without a hearing in the first instance. The court will notify the parties of the decision and the reasons for it.

(2) If permission is refused the appellant is entitled to have the decision reconsidered at an oral hearing, except where rule 52.3(4A) (applications totally without merit) applies. The hearing may be before the same judge.

(3) A request for the decision to be reconsidered at an oral hearing must be filed within 7 days after service of the letter giving notice that permission has been refused.

A copy of the request must be served by the appellant on the respondent at the same time.

Permission hearing

16 (1) Where an appellant who is represented makes a request for a decision to be reconsidered at an oral hearing, the appellant's advocate must at least 4 days before the hearing file a brief written statement –

    (a)   informing the court and the respondent of the points which are to be raised at the hearing; and

    (b)   setting out the reasons why permission should be granted notwithstanding the reasons given for the refusal of permission.

(2) The court will notify the respondent of the hearing but the respondent is not expected to attend unless the court so directs.

(3) If the court directs the respondent to attend the permission hearing, the appellant must supply the respondent with a copy of the skeleton argument and any documents to which the appellant intends to refer.

PART III

Appellant in receipt of services funded by the Legal Services Commission applying for permission to appeal

17 Where the appellant is in receipt of services funded by the Legal Services Commission and permission to appeal has been refused by the court without a hearing, the appellant must send a copy of the court's reasons for refusing permission to the Legal Services Commission as soon as it has been received. The court will require confirmation that this has been done if a hearing is requested to re-consider the application.

Limited permission: rule 52.3

18 (1) If, under rule 52.3(7), the court grants permission to appeal on some issues only, it will –

    (a)   refuse permission on any remaining issues; or

    (b)   adjourn the application in respect of those issues to the hearing of the appeal.

(2) If the court adjourns the application under sub-paragraph (1)(b), the appellant must inform the court and the respondent in writing, within 14 days after the date of the court's order, whether the appellant intends to pursue the application. If the appellant intends to pursue the application, the parties must include in any time estimate for the appeal hearing an allowance for the adjourned application.

(3) If the court refuses permission to appeal on the remaining issues without a hearing and the applicant wishes to have that decision reconsidered at an oral hearing, the time limit in rule 52.3(5) applies. Any application for an extension of this time should be made promptly. When hearing the appeal on the issues for which permission has been given the court will not normally grant an application to extend time in relation to the remaining issues.

Respondent need not take any action when served with an appellant's notice

19 Unless the court directs otherwise, a respondent need not take any action when served with an appellant's notice until notified that permission to appeal has been granted.

Respondent's costs of permission applications

20 (1) In most cases an application for permission to appeal will be determined without the need for the respondent to file submissions or attend a hearing. In such circumstances an order for costs will not normally be made in favour of a respondent who voluntarily makes submissions or attends a hearing.

(2) If the court directs the respondent to file submissions or attend a hearing, it will normally award costs to the respondent if permission is refused.

SECTION 5: TIMETABLE

21 The timetable for the conduct of an appeal after the date of the listing window notification is set out below:

Timetable Part 1: Listing window notification to lodging bundle

Period within which step is to be taken	Action	Cross reference to relevant provisions in this Practice Direction
Within 14 days of service of: (i) the appellant's notice if permission has been given by the lower court or is not needed; (ii) notification that permission has been granted by the Court of Appeal; or (iii) notification that the permission application will be listed with the appeal to follow	**Respondent's notice** (if any) must be filed and served	Paragraph 8 (respondent's notice)
Within 14 days of filing a respondent's notice	**If respondent has filed a respondent's notice,** respondent must lodge and serve a skeleton argument on every other party	Paragraph 9 (skeleton argument to be lodged with the respondent's notice or within 14 days of filing respondent's notice)
7 days after date of listing window notification	Appellant must serve **proposed bundle index** on every respondent	Paragraph 27 (bundle of documents)
14 days after date of listing window notification	**Appeal questionnaire** must be filed and served on every respondent	Paragraph 1 (listing window notification defined) Paragraph 23 (Appeal questionnaire)
7 days after service of Appellant's Appeal Questionnaire	**If a respondent disagrees with appellant's time estimate,** that respondent must file and serve on every other party its own time estimate	Paragraph 24 (time estimate)
21 days after listing window notification	**Appeal skeleton**: appellant must serve on every respondent an appeal skeleton (without bundle cross references)	Paragraph 31 (skeleton argument)

Period within which step is to be taken	Action	Cross reference to relevant provisions in this Practice Direction
21 days after date of the listing window notification	**Agree bundle**: the respondent must either agree the contents of the appeal bundle or notify the appellant of the documents that the respondent considers should be included in, or removed from, the appeal bundle by sending a revised index. If there is no agreement in relation to inclusion of a particular document, it must be placed in a supplemental bundle prepared by the party who has proposed its inclusion.	Paragraph 27 (bundle of documents) Paragraph 28 (bundle: Appeals from Upper Tribunal Immigration and Asylum Chamber)
42 days after date of listing window notification	**Where Respondent has not filed a respondent's notice**, respondent must lodge skeleton argument and serve on every other party	Paragraph 13 (respondent's skeleton argument (where no Respondent's Notice filed)) Paragraph 31 (skeleton argument)

Timetable Part 2: Steps to be taken once hearing date fixed: lodging bundles, supplemental skeletons and bundles of authorities

Time before hearing date when step is to be taken	Action	Cross reference to relevant provisions in this Practice Direction
No later than 42 days before the appeal hearing	Lodge, as directed by the court, the appropriate number of appeal bundles and serve a copy on all other parties to the appeal	Paragraph 27 (bundle of documents) Paragraph 28 (bundle: Appeals from Upper Tribunal Immigration and Asylum Chamber)
No later than 14 days before date of appeal hearing	Appellant must lodge and serve replacement skeleton argument	Paragraph 1 (replacement skeleton argument defined) Paragraph 31 (skeleton argument content, length and format) Paragraph 32 (supplementary skeleton argument)
No later than 7 days before the date of the hearing	Respondent must lodge and serve replacement skeleton argument	Paragraph 1 (replacement skeleton argument defined) Paragraph 32 (supplementary skeleton argument)

Time before hearing date when step is to be taken	Action	Cross reference to relevant provisions in this Practice Direction
No later than 7 days before date of appeal hearing	Bundles of authorities must be lodged	Paragraph 29 (bundle of authorities)
No later than 7 days before the date of the hearing	Every document needed for the appeal hearing (if not already lodged or filed) must be lodged or filed	

SECTION 6: MANAGEMENT OF THE APPEAL

Listing and hear-by dates

22 The hear-by date is the last day of the listing window.

Appeal Questionnaire

23 The appellant must complete and file the Appeal Questionnaire and serve it on the respondent within 14 days after the date of the listing window notification.

Time estimates

24 If the respondent disagrees with the appellant's time estimate, the respondent must inform the court within 7 days of service of the Appeal Questionnaire. In the absence of such notification the respondent will be deemed to have accepted the appellant's time estimate.

Multiple Appeals

25 (1) If two or more appeals are pending in the same or related proceedings, the parties must seek directions as to whether they should be heard together or consecutively by the same judges.

(2) Whether appeals are heard together or consecutively, the parties must attempt to agree a single appeal bundle or set of bundles for all the appeals and seek directions if they are unable to do so.

Expedition

26 (1) The court may direct that the hearing of an appeal be expedited.

(2) The court will deal with requests for expedition without a hearing. Requests for expedition must be made by letter setting out succinctly the grounds on which expedition is sought. The letter (or, if time is particularly short, email) must be marked for the immediate attention of the court and copied to the other parties to the appeal.

(3) If an expedited appeal hearing is required as a matter of extreme urgency, the Civil Appeals Office must be informed as soon as possible. If necessary, parties or their legal representatives should call the Royal Courts of Justice switchboard on 020 7947 6000 and ask a member of the security staff to contact the Duty Judge.

PART III

(4) An expedited hearing will be listed at the convenience of the court and not according to the availability of counsel.

SECTION 7: BUNDLES, AMENDMENT AND SKELETON ARGUMENTS

Bundle of documents

27 (1) The appellant must lodge an appeal bundle which must contain only those documents relevant to the appeal. The bundle must –

    (a) be paginated and in chronological order;

    (b) contain an index at the front.

(2) Documents relevant to the appeal: Subject to any order made by the court, the following documents must be included in the appeal bundle –

    (a) a copy of the appellant's notice;

    (b) a copy of any respondent's notice;

    (c) a copy of any appellant's or respondent's skeleton argument;

    (d) a copy of the order under appeal;

    (e) a copy of the order of the lower court granting or refusing permission to appeal together with a copy of the judge's reasons, if any, for granting or refusing permission;

    (f) a copy of any order allocating the case to a track;

    (g) the approved transcript of the judgment of the lower court (except in appeals in cases which were allocated to the small claims track but subject to any order of the court).

(3) Documents which may be included: The following documents should also be considered for inclusion in the appeal bundle but should be included only where relevant to the appeal –

    (a) statements of case;

    (b) application notices;

    (c) other orders made in the case;

    (d) a chronology of relevant events;

    (e) witness statements made in support of any application made in the appellant's notice;

    (f) other witness statements;

    (g) other documents which the appellant or respondent consider relevant to the appeal.

(4) Bundles not to include originals: Unless otherwise directed, the appeal bundle should not include original material such as original documents, photographs and recorded media. Such material should be provided to the court, if necessary, at the hearing.

(5) Destruction of bundles: Bundles lodged with the court will not be returned to the parties but will be destroyed in the confidential waste system at the conclusion of the proceedings and without further notification.

Appeals from the Upper Tribunal Immigration and Asylum Chamber

28 (1) In an appeal from the Immigration and Asylum Chamber of the Upper Tribunal (other than an appeal relating to a claim for judicial review):

    (a) the Immigration and Asylum Chamber of the Upper Tribunal, upon request, shall send to the Civil Appeals Office copies of the documents which were before the relevant Tribunal when it considered the appeal;

(b) the appellant is not required to file an appeal bundle;

(c) the appellant must file with the appellant's notice the documents specified in paragraph 4(3)(a) to (e) and (g) of this Practice Direction.

Bundle of authorities

29 (1) After consultation with any opposing advocate, the appellant's advocate must file a bundle containing photocopies of the authorities upon which each party will rely at the hearing.

(2) The most authoritative report of each authority must be used in accordance with the Practice Direction on Citation of Authorities (2012) and must have the relevant passages marked by a vertical line in the margin.

(3) Photocopies of authorities should not be in landscape format and the type should not be reduced in size.

(4) The bundle should not –

(a) include authorities for propositions not in dispute; or

(b) contain more than 10 authorities unless the issues in the appeal justify more extensive citation.

(5) A bundle of authorities must bear a certificate by the advocates responsible for arguing the case that the requirements of sub-paragraphs (2) to (4) of this paragraph have been complied with in respect of each authority included.

Amendment of appeal notice: rule 52.8

30 (1) An appeal notice may not be amended without the permission of the court.

(2) An application for permission to amend made before permission to appeal has been considered will normally be determined without a hearing.

(3) An application for permission to amend (after permission to appeal has been granted) and any submissions in opposition will normally be dealt with at the hearing unless that would cause unnecessary expense or delay, in which case a request should be made for the application to amend to be heard in advance.

(4) Legal representatives must –

(a) inform the court at the time they make the application if the existing time estimate is affected by the proposed amendment; and

(b) attempt to agree any revised time estimate no later than 7 days after service of the application.

Skeleton argument

31 (1) Any skeleton argument must comply with the provisions of Section 5 of Practice Direction 52A and must:

(a) not normally exceed 25 pages (excluding front sheets and back sheets);

(b) be printed on A4 paper in not less than 12 point font and 1.5 line spacing.

(2) Where an appellant has filed a skeleton argument in support of an application for permission to appeal, the same skeleton argument may be relied upon in the appeal or the appellant may file an appeal skeleton argument (Timetable Section 5, Part 1).

PART III

(3) At the hearing the court may refuse to hear argument on a point not included in a skeleton argument filed within the prescribed time.

(4) The court may disallow the cost of preparing an appeal skeleton argument which does not comply with these requirements or was not filed within the prescribed time.

Supplementary skeleton arguments

32 (1) A party may file a supplementary skeleton argument only where strictly necessary and only with the permission of the court

(2) If a party wishes to rely on a supplementary skeleton argument, it must be lodged and served as soon as practicable. It must be accompanied by a request for permission setting out the reasons why a supplementary skeleton argument is necessary and why it could not reasonably have been lodged earlier.

(3) Only exceptionally will the court allow the use of a supplementary skeleton argument if lodged later than 7 days before the hearing.

Practice Direction 52D – Statutory Appeals and Appeals Subject to Special Provision

This Practice Direction supplements CPR Part 52

Contents of this Practice Direction

This Practice Direction is divided into the following sections:

    1   Introduction
    2   Routes of appeal
    3   General provisions about statutory appeals
    4   Specific appeals

SECTION 1: INTRODUCTION

1.1 This Practice Direction applies to all statutory appeals, and to other appeals which are subject to special provision, but not to appeals by way of case stated (to which Practice Direction 52E applies).

SECTION 2: ROUTES OF APPEAL

2.1 In this Practice Direction, the court to which an appeal lies is prescribed by statute.

SECTION 3: GENERAL PROVISIONS ABOUT STATUTORY APPEALS

3.1 This Section contains general provisions about statutory appeals (paragraphs 3.2–3.8). For where this Practice Direction or a statute makes additional special provision see also Section 4.

3.2 Where any of the provisions in this Section provide for documents to be filed at the appeal court, those documents are in addition to any documents required under Part 52 or Practice Direction 52B or 52C.

3.3 (1) Where the appellant wishes to appeal against a decision of the Administrative Appeals Chamber of the Upper Tribunal, the appellant's notice must be filed within 21 days of the date on which the Upper Tribunal's decision on permission to appeal to the Court of Appeal is given.

(2) Where the appellant wishes to appeal against a decision of any other Chamber of the Upper Tribunal, the appellant's notice must be filed within 28 days of the date on which the Upper Tribunal's decision on permission to appeal to the Court of Appeal is given.

Service of appellant's notice: rule 52.4(3)

3.4 (1) The appellant must serve the appellant's notice on the respondent and on the chairman of the tribunal, Minister of State, government department or other person from whose decision the appeal is brought.

(2) In the case of an appeal from the decision of a tribunal that has no chairman or member who acts as a chairman, the appellant's notice must be served on the member (or members if more than one) of the tribunal.

Variation of time: rule 52.6

3.5 Where any statute prescribes a period within which an appeal must be filed then, unless the statute otherwise provides, the appeal court may not extend that period.

Applications by third parties (rule 52.12A)

3.6 Where all the parties consent, the court may deal with an application under rule 52.12A without a hearing.

3.7 An application for permission must be made by letter to the relevant court office, identifying the appeal, explaining who the applicant is and indicating why and in what form the applicant wants to participate in the hearing.

3.8 If the applicant is seeking a prospective order as to costs, the letter must say what kind of order and on what grounds.

SECTION 4: SPECIFIC APPEALS

Provisions about specific appeals

4.1 This Section sets out special provisions about the appeals listed in the Table below. This Section is not exhaustive and does not create, amend or remove any right of appeal.

4.2 Part 52 applies to all appeals to which this Section applies subject to any special provisions set out in this Section.

4.3 Where any of the provisions in this Section provide for documents to be filed at the appeal court, these documents are in addition to any documents required under Part 52 or Practice Direction 52B or 52C.

PART III

Certain appeals to the High Court to be heard in Chancery Division

5.1 Any appeal to the High Court, and any case stated or question referred for the opinion of that court under any of the following enactments shall be heard in the Chancery Division –

(1) section 38(3) of the Clergy Pensions Measure 1961;
(2) regulation 74 of the European Public Limited-Liability Company Regulations 2004.
(3) the Industrial and Provident Societies Act 1965;
(4) section 222(3) of the Inheritance Tax Act 1984;
(5) the Land Registration Act 2002;
(6) paragraph 16 of Schedule 15 to the Law of Property Act 1922;
(7) section 215 or 217 of the Pensions Act 2003;
(8) section 151 of the Pension Schemes Act 1993;
(9) section 13 and 13B of the Stamp Act 1891;
(10) regulation 8(3) of the Stamp Duty Reserve Tax Regulations 1986.

Table

Statute (or description of appeal)	Appropriate Court	Relevant paragraph in this Practice Direction
Agricultural Land Tribunal	High Court	18.1
Architects Act 1997, s 22	High Court	19.1
Chiropractors Act 1994, s 31	High Court	19.1
Civil Partnership – conditional order for dissolution or nullity	CA	6.1
Clergy Pensions Measure 1961, s 38(3)	High Court	5.1
Competition: Articles 101 and 102 of the Treaty on the Functioning of the European Union and Chapters I and II of Part I of the Competition Act 1998	CA	7.1
Competition Appeal Tribunal	CA	8.1
Contempt of Court	CA	9.1
Court of Protection	CA	10.1
Decree nisi of divorce or nullity of marriage	CA	6.1
Dentists Act 1984, ss 29 and 44	High Court	19.1
Employment Appeal Tribunal	CA	11.1
European Public Limited-Liability Company Regulations 2004, reg 74	High Court	20.1
Extradition Act 2003	High Court	21.1
Friendly Societies Act 1974	High Court	5.1 and 22.1

Statute (or description of appeal)	Appropriate Court	Relevant paragraph in this Practice Direction
Friendly Societies Act 1992	High Court	5.1 and 22.1
Health Professions Order 2001, art 38	High Court	19.1
Housing Act 1996, ss 204 and 204A	County Court	28.1
Immigration and Asylum Act 1999, Part II	County Court	29.1
Immigration and Asylum Appeals	CA	12.1
Inheritance Tax Act 1984, s 222	High Court	5.1 and 23.1
Land Registration Act 2002	High Court	5.1 and 24.1
Law of Property Act 1922, para 16 of Sch 15	High Court	5.1
Local Government (Miscellaneous Provisions) Act 1976	County Court	30.1
Medical Act 1983, s 40	High Court	19.1
Medicines Act 1968, ss 82(3) and 83	High Court	19.1
Merchant Shipping Act 1995	High Court	25.1
Nurses, Midwives and Health Visitors Act 1997, s 12	High Court	19.1
Nursing and Midwifery Order 2001 art 38	High Court	19.1
Opticians Act 1989, s 23	High Court	19.1
Osteopaths Act 1993, s 31	High Court	19.1
Patents Court: on appeal from Comptroller	CA	13.1
Patents: Revocation of patent	CA	14.1
Pensions Act 2004, ss 215 and 217	High Court	5.1
Pension Schemes Act 1993, s 151	High Court	5.1
Pharmacy Act 1954	High Court	19.1
Pharmacy Order 2010, art 58	High Court	19.1
Planning (Listed Buildings and Conservation Areas) Act 1990, s 65	High Court	26.1
Proscribed Organisations Appeal Commission	CA	15.1
Representation of the People Act 1983, s 56	County Court	31.1-31.3
Serious Crime Prevention Orders	CA	16.1
Solicitors Disciplinary Tribunal	High Court	27.1
Special Immigration Appeals Commission	CA	17.1

PART III

Statute (or description of appeal)	Appropriate Court	Relevant paragraph in this Practice Direction
Stamp Duty Reserve Tax Regulations 1986, reg 8	High Court	5.1 and 23.1
Town and Country Planning Act 1990, s 289	High Court	26.1
UK Borders Act 2007, s 11	County Court	32.1

Appeals to the Court Of Appeal

Appeal against decree nisi of divorce or nullity of marriage or conditional dissolution or nullity order in relation to civil partnership

6.1 (1) The appellant must file the appellant's notice at the Court of Appeal within 28 days after the date on which the decree was pronounced or conditional order made.

(2) The appellant must file the following documents with the appellant's notice –

    (a)   the decree or conditional order; and

    (b)   a certificate of service of the appellant's notice.

(3) The appellant's notice must be served on the appropriate district judge (see subparagraph (6)) in addition to the persons to be served under rule 52.4(3) and in accordance with that rule.

(4) The lower court may not alter the time limits for filing of the appeal notices.

(5) Where an appellant intends to apply to the Court of Appeal for an extension of time for serving or filing the appellant's notice the appellant must give notice of that intention to the appropriate district judge (see sub-paragraph 6) before the application is made.

(6) In this paragraph "the appropriate district judge" means, where the lower court is –

    (a)   a county court, the district judge of that court;

    (b)   a district registry, the district judge of that registry;

    (c)   the Principal Registry of the Family Division, the senior district judge of that division.

Appeals relating to the application of Articles 101 and 102 of the Treaty on the Functioning of the European Union and Chapters I and II of Part I of the Competition Act 1998

7.1 (1) This paragraph applies to any appeal to the Court of Appeal relating to the application of –

    (a)   Article 101 or Article 102 of the Treaty on the Functioning of the European Union; or

    (b)   Chapter I or Chapter II of Part I of the Competition Act 1998.

(2) In this paragraph –

    (a)   "the Act" means the Competition Act 1998;

    (b)   "the Commission" means the European Commission;

    (c)   "the Competition Regulation" means Council Regulation (EC) No 1/2003 of 16 December 2002 on the implementation of the rules on competition laid down in Articles 81 and 82 of the Treaty establishing the European Community (as amended in consequence of the Treaty on the Functioning of the European Union);

(d) "national competition authority" means –
   (i) the Office of Fair Trading; and
   (ii) any other person or body designated pursuant to Article 5 of the Competition Regulation as a national competition authority of the United Kingdom;

(e) "the Treaty" means the Treaty on the Functioning of the European Union.

(3) Any party whose appeal notice raises an issue relating to the application of Article 101 or 102 of the Treaty, or Chapter I or II of Part I of the Act, must –

(a) state that fact in the appeal notice; and
(b) serve a copy of the appeal notice on the Office of Fair Trading at the same time as it is served on the other party to the appeal (addressed to the Director of Competition Policy Co-ordination, Office of Fair Trading, Fleetbank House, 2–6 Salisbury Square, London EC4Y 8JX).

(4) Attention is drawn to the provisions of article 15.3 of the Competition Regulation, which entitles competition authorities and the Commission to submit written observations to national courts on issues relating to the application of Article 101 or 102 and, with the permission of the court in question, to submit oral observations to the court.

(5) A national competition authority may also make written observations to the Court of Appeal, or apply for permission to make oral observations, on issues relating to the application of Chapter I or II.

(6) If a national competition authority or the Commission intends to make written observations to the Court of Appeal, it must give notice of its intention to do so by letter to the Civil Appeals Office at the earliest opportunity.

(7) An application by a national competition authority or the Commission for permission to make oral representations at the hearing of an appeal must be made by letter to the Civil Appeals Office at the earliest opportunity, identifying the appeal and indicating why the applicant wishes to make oral representations.

(8) If a national competition authority or the Commission files a notice under subparagraph (6) or an application under sub-paragraph (7), it must at the same time serve a copy of the notice or application on every party to the appeal.

(9) Any request by a national competition authority or the Commission for the court to send it any documents relating to an appeal should be made at the same time as filing a notice under sub-paragraph (6) or an application under sub-paragraph (7).

(10) When the Court of Appeal receives a notice under sub-paragraph (6) it may give case management directions to the national competition authority or the Commission, including directions about the date by which any written observations are to be filed.

(11) The Court of Appeal will serve on every party to the appeal a copy of any directions given or order made –

(a) on an application under sub-paragraph (7); or
(b) under sub-paragraph (10).

(12) Every party to an appeal which raises an issue relating to the application of Article 101 or 102, and any national competition authority which has been served with a copy of a party's appeal notice, is under a duty to notify the Court of Appeal at any stage of the appeal if they are aware that –

(a) the Commission has adopted, or is contemplating adopting, a decision in relation to proceedings which it has initiated; and

(b)   the decision referred to in (a) above has or would have legal effects in relation to the particular agreement, decision or practice in issue before the court.

(13) Where the Court of Appeal is aware that the Commission is contemplating adopting a decision as mentioned in sub-paragraph (12)(a), it shall consider whether to stay the appeal pending the Commission's decision.

(14) Where any judgment is given which decides on the application of Article 101 or 102, the court shall direct that a copy of the transcript of the judgment shall be sent to the Commission. Judgments may be sent to the Commission electronically to compamicus@cec.eu.int or by post to the European Commission – DG Competition, B–1049, Brussels.

Appeal from Competition Appeal Tribunal

8.1 (1) Where the appellant applies for permission to appeal at the hearing at which the decision is delivered by the tribunal and –

(a)   permission is given; or
(b)   permission is refused and the appellant wishes to make an application to the Court of Appeal for permission to appeal,

the appellant's notice must be filed at the Court of Appeal within 14 days after the date of that hearing.

(2) Where the appellant applies in writing to the Registrar of the tribunal for permission to appeal and –

(a)   permission is given; or
(b)   permission is refused and the appellant wishes to make an application to the Court of Appeal for permission to appeal,

the appellant's notice must be filed at the Court of Appeal within 14 days after the date of receipt of the tribunal's decision on permission.

(3) Where the appellant does not make an application to the tribunal for permission to appeal, but wishes to make an application to the Court of Appeal for permission, the appellant's notice must be filed at the Court of Appeal within 14 days after the end of the period within which the appellant may make a written application to the Registrar of the tribunal.

Appeals in cases of contempt of court (section 13 Administration of Justice Act 1960)

9.1 In an appeal under section 13 of the Administration of Justice Act 1960 (appeals in cases of contempt of court), the appellant must serve the appellant's notice on the court or the Upper Tribunal from whose order or decision the appeal is brought in addition to the persons to be served under rule 52.4(3) and in accordance with that rule.

Appeal from the Court of Protection

10.1 (1) In this paragraph –

(a)   'P' means a person who lacks, or who is alleged to lack, capacity within the meaning of the Mental Capacity Act 2005 to make a decision or decisions in relation to any matter that is subject to an order of the Court of Protection;
(b)   "the person effecting notification" means –
   (i)   the appellant;
   (ii)   an agent duly appointed by the appellant; or

      (iii) such other person as the Court of Protection may direct, who is required to notify P in accordance with this paragraph; and

  (c) "final order" means a decision of the Court of Appeal that finally determines the appeal proceedings before it.

(2) Where P is not a party to the proceedings, unless the Court of Appeal directs otherwise, the person effecting notification must notify P –

  (a) that an appellant's notice has been filed with the Court of Appeal and –
      (i) who the appellant is;
      (ii) what final order the appellant is seeking;
      (iii) what will happen if the Court of Appeal makes the final order sought by the appellant; and
      (iv) that P may apply under rule 52.12A (Statutory appeals: court's power to hear any person) by letter for permission to file evidence or make representations at the appeal hearing;

  (b) of the final order, the effect of the final order and what steps P can take in relation to it; and

  (c) of such other events and documents as the Court of Appeal may direct. (Paragraphs 3.6 to 3.8 of this Practice Direction 52D contain provisions on how a third party can apply for permission to file evidence or make representations at an appeal hearing.)

(3) The person effecting notification must provide P with the information specified in sub-paragraph (2) –

  (a) within 14 days of the date on which the appellant's notice was filed with the Court of Appeal;

  (b) within 14 days of the date on which the final order was made; or

  (c) within such time as the Court of Appeal may direct, as the case may be.

(4) The person effecting notification must provide P in person with the information specified in sub-paragraph (2) in a way that is appropriate to P's circumstances (for example, using simple language, visual aids or any other appropriate means).

(5) Where P is to be notified as to –

  (a) the existence or effect of a document other than the appellant's notice or final order; or

  (b) the taking place of an event,
    the person effecting notification must explain to P –
      (i) in the case of a document, what the document is and what effect, if any, it has; or
      (ii) in the case of an event, what the event is and its relevance to P.

(6) The person effecting notification must, within 7 days of notifying P, file a certificate of notification (form N165) which certifies –

  (a) the date on which P was notified; and

  (b) that P was notified in accordance with this paragraph.

(7) Where the person effecting notification has not notified P in accordance with this paragraph, a certificate of non-notification (form N165) must be filed with the Court of Appeal stating the reason why notification has not been effected.

(8) Where the person effecting notification must file a certificate of non-notification with the Court of Appeal, the certificate must be filed within the following time limits –

  (a) where P is to be notified in accordance with sub-paragraph (2)(a) (appellant's notice), within 21 days of the appellant's notice being filed with the Court of Appeal;

PART III

    (b)   where P is to be notified in accordance with sub-paragraph (2)(b) (final order), within 21 days of the final order being made by the Court of Appeal; or

    (c)   where P is to be notified of such other events and documents as may be directed by the Court of Appeal, within such time as the Court of Appeal directs.

(9) The appellant or such other person as the Court of Appeal may direct may apply to the Court of Appeal seeking an order –

    (a)   dispensing with the requirement to comply with the provisions of this paragraph; or

    (b)   requiring some other person to comply with the provisions of this paragraph.

(10) An application made under sub-paragraph (9) may be made in the appellant's notice or by Part 23 application notice.

        (Paragraphs 6.1 to 6.3 of Practice Direction 52A contain provisions about the dismissal of applications or appeals by consent. Paragraph 6.5 of Practice Direction 52A contains provisions about allowing unopposed appeals or applications involving a child or protected party.)

Appeal from Employment Appeal Tribunal

11.1 (1) This paragraph applies to an appeal to the Court of Appeal from the Employment Appeal Tribunal (EAT) under section 37 of the Employment Tribunals Act 1996.

(2) If an application for permission to appeal to the Court of Appeal is refused by the EAT or is not made, then such an application must be made to the Court of Appeal within 21 days of the date of the sealed order of the EAT.

(3) An application for extension of time for filing an appellant's notice may be entertained by the EAT but such applications should normally be made to the Court of Appeal.

Immigration and Asylum Appeals

12.1 The provisions of paragraph 28 of Practice Direction 52C (bundle of documents in immigration appeals and asylum appeals) apply to appeals from the Upper Tribunal Immigration and Asylum Chamber.

Appeal from Patents Court on appeal from Comptroller

13.1 Where the appeal is from a decision of the Patents Court which was itself made on an appeal from a decision of the Comptroller-General of Patents, Designs and Trade Marks, the appellant must serve the appellant's notice on the Comptroller in addition to the persons to be served under rule 52.4(3) and in accordance with that rule.

Appeal against order for revocation of patent

14.1 (1) This paragraph applies where an appeal lies to the Court of Appeal from an order for the revocation of a patent.

(2) The appellant must serve the appellant's notice on the Comptroller-General of Patents, Designs and Trade Marks (the "Comptroller") in addition to the persons to be served under rule 52.4(3) and in accordance with that rule.

(3) Where, before the appeal hearing, the respondent decides not to oppose the appeal or not to attend the appeal hearing, the respondent must immediately serve notice of that decision on –

(a) the Comptroller; and
(b) the appellant.

(4) Where the respondent serves a notice in accordance with sub-paragraph (3), copies of the following documents must also be served on the Comptroller with that notice –

(a) the petition;
(b) any statements of claim;
(c) any written evidence filed in the claim.

(5) Within 14 days after receiving the notice in accordance with sub-paragraph (3), the Comptroller must serve on the appellant a notice stating an intention to attend the appeal hearing or otherwise.

(6) The Comptroller may attend the appeal hearing and oppose the appeal –

(a) in any case where notice has been given under paragraph (5) of the intention to attend; and
(b) in any other case (including, in particular, a case where the respondent withdraws his opposition to the appeal during the hearing) if the Court of Appeal so directs or permits.

Appeal from Proscribed Organisations Appeal Commission

15.1 The appellant's notice must be filed at the Court of Appeal within 14 days after the date when the Proscribed Organisations Appeal Commission –

(a) granted; or
(b) where section 6(2)(b) of the Terrorism Act 2000 applies, refused permission to appeal.

Appeals in relation to serious crime prevention orders

16.1 (1) This paragraph applies to an appeal under section 23(1) of the Serious Crime Act 2007 or section 16 of the Senior Courts Act 1981 in relation to a serious crime prevention order and is made.

(2) The appellant must serve the appellant's notice on any person who made representations in the proceedings by virtue of section 9(1), (2) or (3) of the Serious Crime Act 2007 in addition to the persons to be served under rule 52.4(3) and in accordance with that rule.

Appeal from Special Immigration Appeals Commission

17.1 (1) An application for permission to appeal to the Court of Appeal must first be made to the Special Immigration Appeals Commission pursuant section 7(2) of the Special Immigration Appeals Commission Act 1997 and paragraph 27 of the SIAC (Procedure) Rules 2003 (as amended).

(2) The appellant's notice must be filed at the Court of Appeal within 21 days of the date on which the Special Immigration Appeals Commission's decision granting or refusing permission to appeal to the Court of Appeal is given.

Appeals to the High Court

Reference of question of law by Agricultural Land Tribunal

18.1 (1) A question of law referred to the High Court by an Agricultural Land Tribunal under section 6 of the Agriculture (Miscellaneous Provisions) Act 1954 shall be referred by way of case stated by the Tribunal.

(2) Where the proceedings before the tribunal arose on an application under section 11 of the Agricultural Holdings Act 1986, an –

(a)   application notice for an order under section 6 that the tribunal refers a question of law to the court; and

(b)   appellant's notice by which an appellant seeks the court's determination on a question of law,

must be served on the authority having power to enforce the statutory requirement specified in the notice in addition to every other party to those proceedings and on the secretary of the tribunal.

(3) Where, in accordance with sub-paragraph (2), a notice is served on the authority mentioned in that paragraph, that authority may attend the appeal hearing and make representations to the court.

Appeals against decisions affecting the registration of architects and health care professionals

19.1 (1) This paragraph applies to an appeal to the High Court under –

(a)   section 22 of the Architects Act 1997;

(b)   section 31 of the Chiropractors Act 1994;

(c)   section 29 or section 44 of the Dentists Act 1984;

(d)   article 38 of the Health Professions Order 2001;

(e)   section 40 of the Medical Act 1983;

(f)   section 82(3) and 83(2) of the Medicines Act 1968;

(g)   section 12 of the Nurses, Midwives and Health Visitors Act 1997;

(h)   article 38 of the Nursing and Midwifery Order 2001;

(i)   section 23 of the Opticians Act 1989;

(j)   section 31 of the Osteopaths Act 1993;

(k)   section 10 of the Pharmacy Act 1954;

(l)   article 58 of the Pharmacy Order 2010.

(2) Every appeal to which this paragraph applies must be supported by written evidence and, if the court so orders, oral evidence and will be by way of re-hearing.

(3) The appellant must file the appellant's notice within 28 days after the decision that the appellant wishes to appeal.

(4) In the case of an appeal under an enactment specified in column 1 of the following table, the persons to be made respondents are the persons specified in relation to that enactment in column 2 of the table and the person to be served with the appellant's notice is the Registrar of the relevant Council.

1 Enactment	2 Respondent
Architects Act 1997, s 22	The Architects' Registration Council of the United Kingdom
Chiropractors Act 1994, s 31	The General Chiropractic Council

1 Enactment	2 Respondent
Dentists Act 1984, ss 29 and 44	The General Dental Council
Health Professions Order 2001, art 38	The Health Professions Council
Medical Act 1983, s 40	The General Medical Council
Medicines Act 1968, ss 82(3) and 83(2)	The Pharmaceutical Society of Great Britain
Nurses, Midwives and Health Visitors Act 1997, s 12; Nursing and Midwifery Order 2001, art 38	The Nursing and Midwifery Council
Opticians Act 1989, s 23	The General Optical Council
Osteopaths Act 1993, s 31	The General Osteopathic Council
Pharmacy Act 1954, s 10	The Royal Pharmaceutical Society of Great Britain
Pharmacy Order 2010, art 58	The General Pharmaceutical Council

Appeals under regulation 74 of the European Public Limited-Liability Company Regulations 2004

20.1 (1) In this paragraph –

    (a) "the 2004 Regulations" means the European Public Limited-Liability Company Regulations 2004;

    (b) "the EC Regulation" means Council Regulation (EC) No 2157/2001 of 8 October 2001 on the Statute for a European company (SE);

    (c) "SE" means a European public limited-liability company (Societas Europaea) within the meaning of Article 1 of the EC Regulation.

(2) This paragraph applies to appeals under regulation 74 of the 2004 Regulations against the opposition –

    (a) of the Secretary of State or national financial supervisory authority to the transfer of the registered office of an SE under Article 8(14) of the EC Regulation; and

    (b) of the Secretary of State to the participation by a company in the formation of an SE by merger under Article 19 of the EC Regulation.

(3) Where an SE seeks to appeal against the opposition of the national financial supervisory authority to the transfer of its registered office under Article 8(14) of the EC Regulation, it must serve the appellant's notice on both the national financial supervisory authority and the Secretary of State.

(4) The appellant's notice must contain an application for permission to appeal.

(5) The appeal will be a review of the decision of the Secretary of State and not a re-hearing. The grounds of review are set out in regulation 74(2) of the 2004 Regulations.

(6) The appeal will be heard by a High Court judge.

Appeals under the Extradition Act 2003

21.1 (1) In this paragraph, "the Act" means the Extradition Act 2003.

(2) Appeals to the High Court under the Act must be started in the Administrative Court of the Queen's Bench Division at the Royal Courts of Justice in London.

(3) Where an appeal is brought under section 26 or 28 of the Act –

    (a)   the appellant's notice must be filed and served before the expiry of 7 days, starting with the day on which the order is made;

    (b)   the appellant must endorse the appellant's notice with the date of the person's arrest;

    (c)   the High Court must begin to hear the substantive appeal within 40 days of the person's arrest; and

    (d)   the appellant must serve a copy of the appellant's notice on the Crown Prosecution Service, if they are not a party to the appeal, in addition to the persons to be served under rule 52.4(3) and in accordance with that rule.

(4) The High Court may extend the period of 40 days under sub-paragraph (3)(c) if it believes it to be in the interests of justice to do so.

(5) Where an appeal is brought under section 103 of the Act, the appellant's notice must be filed and served before the expiry of 14 days, starting with the day on which the Secretary of State informs the person under section 100(1) or (4) of the Act that an order has made in respect of the person.

(6) Where an appeal is brought under section 105 of the Act, the appellant's notice must be filed and served before the expiry of 14 days, starting with the day on which the order for discharge is made.

(7) Where an appeal is brought under section 108 of the Act the appellant's notice must be filed and served before the expiry of 14 days, starting with the day on which the Secretary of State informs the person that an order for extradition has been made.

(8) Where an appeal is brought under section 110 of the Act the appellant's notice must be filed and served before the expiry of 14 days, starting with the day on which the Secretary of State informs the person acting on behalf of a category 2 territory, as defined in section 69 of the Act, of the order for discharge. (Section 69 of the Act provides that a category 2 territory is that designated for the purposes of Part 2 of the Act.)

(9) Subject to sub-paragraph (10), where an appeal is brought under section 103, 105, 108 or 110 of the Act, the High Court must begin to hear the substantive appeal within 76 days of the appellant's notice being filed.

(10) Where an appeal is brought under section 103 of the Act before the Secretary of State has decided whether the person is to be extradited –

    (a)   the period of 76 days does not start until the day on which the Secretary of State informs the person of the decision; and

    (b)   the Secretary of State must, as soon as practicable after the person has been informed of the decision, inform the High Court –

        (i)   of the decision; and

        (ii) of the date on which the person was informed of the decision.

(11) The High Court may extend the period of 76 days if it believes it to be in the interests of justice to do so.

(12) Where an appeal is brought under section 103, 105, 108 or 110 of the Act, the appellant must serve a copy of the appellant's notice on –

    (a)   the Crown Prosecution Service; and

    (b)   the Home Office,

if they are not a party to the appeal, in addition to the persons to be served under rule 52.4(3) and in accordance with that rule.

Appeals affecting industrial and provident societies etc.

22.1 (1) This paragraph applies to all appeals under –

    (a)   the Friendly Societies Act 1974;

    (b)   the Friendly Societies Act 1992 and;

    (c)   the Industrial and Provident Societies Act 1965.

(2) At any stage on an appeal, the court may –

    (a)   direct that the appellant's notice be served on any person;

    (b)   direct that notice be given by advertisement or otherwise of –

        (i)   the bringing of the appeal;

        (ii)   the nature of the appeal; and

        (iii)   the time when the appeal will or is likely to be heard; or

    (c)   give such other directions as it thinks proper to enable any person interested in –

        (i)   the society, trade union, alleged trade union or industrial assurance company; or

        (ii)   the subject matter of the appeal, to appear and be heard at the appeal hearing.

Appeals under section 222 of the Inheritance Tax Act 1984 and regulation 8(3) of the Stamp Duty Reserve Tax Regulations 1986

23.1 (1) This paragraph applies to appeals to the High Court under section 222(3) of the Inheritance Tax Act 1984 (the "1984 Act") and regulation 8(3) of the Stamp Duty Reserve Tax Regulations 1986 (the "1986 Regulations").

(2) The appellant's notice must –

    (a)   state the date on which the Commissioners for Her Majesty's Revenue and Customs (the "Board") gave notice to the appellant under section 221 of the 1984 Act or regulation 6 of the 1986 Regulations of the determination that is the subject of the appeal;

    (b)   state the date on which the appellant gave to the Board notice of appeal under section 222(1) of the 1984 Act or regulation 8(1) of the 1986 Regulations and, if notice was not given within the time permitted, whether Her Majesty's Revenue and Customs (HMRC) have given their consent or the tribunal has given permission for notice to be given after the time permitted, and where applicable, the date of such consent or permission; and

    (c)   either state that the appellant and the Board have agreed that the appeal may be to the High Court or contain an application for permission to appeal to the High Court.

(3) The appellant must file the following documents with the appellant's notice –

    (a)   2 copies of the notice referred to in sub-paragraph 2(a);

    (b)   2 copies of the notice of appeal (under section 222(1) of the 1984 Act or regulation 8(1) of the 1986 Regulations) referred to in paragraph 2(b); and

    (c)   where the appellant's notice contains an application for permission to appeal, written evidence setting out the grounds on which it is alleged that the matters to be decided on the appeal are likely to be substantially confined to questions of law.

(4) The appellant must –

    (a)   file the appellant's notice at the court; and

    (b)   serve the appellant's notice on the Board, within 30 days of the date on which the appellant gave to the Board notice of appeal under section 222(1) of the

PART III

1984 Act or regulation 8(1) of the 1986 Regulations or, if HMRC have given consent or the tribunal has given permission for notice to be given after the time permitted, within 30 days of the date on which such consent or permission was given.

(5) The court will set a date for the hearing of not less than 40 days from the date that the appellant's notice was filed.

(6) Where the appellant's notice contains an application for permission to appeal –

    (a)   a copy of the written evidence filed in accordance with sub-paragraph (3)(c) must be served on the Board with the appellant's notice; and

    (b)   the Board –
        (i)   may file written evidence; and
        (ii) if it does so, must serve a copy of that evidence on the appellant, within 30 days after service of the written evidence under subparagraph (6)(a).

(7) The appellant may not rely on any grounds of appeal not specified in the notice referred to in sub-paragraph (2)(b) on the hearing of the appeal without the permission of the court.

Appeal against a decision of the adjudicator under section 111 of the Land Registration Act 2002

24.1 (1) A person who is aggrieved by a decision of the adjudicator and who wishes to appeal that decision must obtain permission to appeal.

(2) The appellant must serve on the adjudicator a copy of the appeal court's decision on a request for permission to appeal as soon as reasonably practicable and in any event within 14 days of receipt by the appellant of the decision on permission.

(3) The appellant must serve on the adjudicator and the Chief Land Registrar a copy of any order by the appeal court to stay a decision of the adjudicator pending the outcome of the appeal as soon as reasonably practicable and in any event within 14 days of receipt by the appellant of the appeal court's order to stay.

(4) The appellant must serve on the adjudicator and the Chief Land Registrar a copy of the appeal court's decision on the appeal as soon as reasonably practicable and in any event within 14 days of receipt by the appellant of the appeal court's decision.

Appeals under the Merchant Shipping Act 1995

25.1 (1) This paragraph applies to appeals under the Merchant Shipping Act 1995 and for this purpose a re-hearing and an application under section 61 of the Merchant Shipping Act 1995 are treated as appeals.

(2) The appellant must file any report to the Secretary of State containing the decision from which the appeal is brought with the appellant's notice.

(3) Where a re-hearing by the High Court is ordered under sections 64 or 269 of the Merchant Shipping Act 1995, the Secretary of State must give reasonable notice to the parties whom he considers to be affected by the re-hearing.

Appeals under s 289(6) of the Town and Country Planning Act 1990 and s 65(5) of the Planning (Listed Buildings and Conservation Areas) Act 1990

26.1 (1) An application for permission to appeal to the High Court under section 289 of the Town and Country Planning Act 1990 ("the TCP Act") or section 65 of the Planning

(Listed Buildings and Conservation Areas) Act 1990 ("the PLBCA Act") must be made within 28 days after notice of the decision is given to the applicant.

(2) The application –

    (a)   must be in writing and must set out the reasons why permission should be granted; and

    (b)   if the time for applying has expired, must include an application to extend the time for applying, and must set out the reasons why the application was not made within that time.

(3) The applicant must, before filing the application, serve a copy of it on the persons referred to in sub-paragraph (12) with the draft appellant's notice and a copy of the witness statement or affidavit to be filed with the application.

(4) The applicant must file the application in the Administrative Court Office with –

    (a)   a copy of the decision being appealed;

    (b)   a draft appellant's notice;

    (c)   a witness statement or affidavit verifying any facts relied on; and

    (d)   a witness statement or affidavit giving the name and address of, and the place and date of service on, each person who has been served with the application. If any person who ought to be served has not been served, the witness statement or affidavit must state that fact and the reason why the person was not served.

(5) An application will be heard –

    (a)   by a single judge; and

    (b)   unless the court otherwise orders, not less than 21 days after it was filed at the Administrative Court Office.

(6) Practice direction 54D applies to applications and appeals under this paragraph.

(7) Any person served with the application is entitled to appear and be heard.

(8) Any respondent who intends to use a witness statement or affidavit at the hearing –

    (a)   must file it in the Administrative Court Office; and

    (b)   must serve a copy on the applicant as soon as is practicable and in any event, unless the court otherwise allows, at least 2 days before the hearing.

(9) The court may allow the applicant to use a further witness statement or affidavit.

(10) Where on the hearing of an application the court is of the opinion that a person who ought to have been served has not been served, the court may adjourn the hearing, on such terms as it directs, in order that the application may be served on that person.

(11) Where the court grants permission –

    (a)   it may impose terms as to costs and as to giving security;

    (b)   it may give directions; and

    (c)   the relevant appellant's notice must be served and filed within 7 days of the grant.

(12) The persons to be served with the appellant's notice are –

    (a)   the Secretary of State;

    (b)   the local planning authority who served the notice or gave the decision, as the case may be, or, where the appeal is brought by that authority, the appellant or applicant in the proceedings in which the decision appealed against was given;

    (c)   in the case of an appeal brought by virtue of section 289(1) of the TCP Act or section 65(1) of the PLBCA Act, any other person having an interest in the land to which the notice relates; and

PART III

(d) in the case of an appeal brought by virtue of section 289(2) of the TCP Act, any other person on whom the notice to which those proceedings related was served.

(13) The appeal will be heard and determined by a single judge unless the court directs that the matter be heard and determined by a Divisional Court.

(14) The court may remit the matter to the Secretary of State to the extent necessary to enable the Secretary of State to provide the court with such further information in connection with the matter as the court may direct.

(15) Where the court is of the opinion that the decision appealed against was erroneous in point of law, it will not set aside or vary that decision but will remit the matter to the Secretary of State for re-hearing and determination in accordance with the opinion of the court.

(16) The court may give directions as to the exercise, until an appeal brought by virtue of section 289(1) of the TCP Act is finally concluded and any re-hearing and determination by the Secretary of State has taken place, of the power to serve, and institute proceedings (including criminal proceedings) concerning –

(a) a stop notice under section 183 of that Act; and

(b) a breach of condition notice under section 187A of that Act.

Appeals from decisions of the Law Society or the Solicitors Disciplinary Tribunal to the High Court

27.1 (1) This paragraph applies to appeals from the Law Society or the Solicitors Disciplinary Tribunal ("the Tribunal") to the High Court under the Solicitors Act 1974, Administration of Justice Act 1985, the Courts and Legal Services Act 1990, the European Communities (Lawyer's Practice) Regulations 2000 or the European Communities (Recognition of Professional Qualifications) Regulations 2007.

(2) The appellant must file the appellant's notice in the Administrative Court.

(3) Unless the court otherwise orders the appellant must serve the appellant's notice on –

(a) every party to the proceedings before the Tribunal; and

(b) the Law Society.

Appeals to the County Court

Appeals under sections 204 and 204A of the Housing Act 1996

28.1 (1) An appellant should include appeals under section 204 and section 204A of the Housing Act 1996 in one appellant's notice.

(2) If it is not possible to do so (for example because an urgent application under section 204A is required) the appeals may be included in separate appellant's notices.

(3) An appeal under section 204A may include an application for an order under section 204A(4)(a) requiring the authority to secure that accommodation is available for the applicant's occupation.

(4) If, exceptionally, the court makes an order under section 204A(4)(a) without notice, the appellant's notice must be served on the authority together with the order. Such an order will normally require the authority to secure that accommodation is available until a hearing date when the authority can make representations as to whether the order under section 204A(4)(a) should be continued.

(5) Unless the court orders otherwise –

(a) the appellant shall file and serve its proposed case management directions for the appeal together with the appellant's notice;

(b) the respondent shall within 14 days thereafter either agree those directions or file and serve alternative proposed directions;

(c) within 14 days after service of the appellant's notice the respondent must disclose any documents relevant to the decision under appeal, in so far as not previously disclosed;

(d) within 14 days after receipt of any documents disclosed under subparagraph (c) the appellant may make any amendments to its grounds of appeal which arise out of those documents.

Appeal under Part II of the Immigration and Asylum Act 1999 (carriers' liability)

29.1 (1) A person appealing to a county court under section 35A or section 40B of the Immigration and Asylum Act 1999 ("the Act") against a decision by the Secretary of State to impose a penalty under section 32 or a charge under section 40 of the Act must, subject to sub-paragraph (2), file the appellant's notice within 28 days after receiving the penalty notice or charge notice.

(2) Where the appellant has given notice of objection to the Secretary of State under section 35(4) or section 40A(3) of the Act within the time prescribed for doing so, the appellant must file the appellant's notice within 28 days after receiving notice of the Secretary of State's decision in response to the notice of objection.

(3) Sections 35A and 40B of the Act provide that any appeal under those sections shall be a re-hearing of the Secretary of State's decision to impose a penalty or charge, and therefore rule 52.11(1) does not apply.

Local Government (Miscellaneous Provisions) Act 1976

30.1 Where one of the grounds upon which an appeal against a notice under sections 21, 23 or 35 of the Local Government (Miscellaneous Provisions) Act 1976 is brought is that –

(a) it would have been fairer to serve the notice on another person; or

(b) that it would be reasonable for the whole or part of the expenses to which the appeal relates to be paid by some other person,

that person must be made a respondent to the appeal, unless the court, on application of the appellant made without notice, otherwise directs.

Representation of the People Act 1983 – appeals against decisions of registration officers

31.1 (1) This paragraph applies in relation to an appeal against a decision of a registration officer, being a decision referred to in section 56(1) of the Representation of the People Act 1983 ("the Act").

(2) Where a person ("the appellant") has given notice of such an appeal in accordance with the relevant requirements of section 56, and of the regulations made under section 53 ("the Regulations"), of the Act, the registration officer must, within 7 days after the appellant receives the notice, forward –

(a) the notice; and

(b) the statement required by the Regulations, by post to the county court.

(3) The respondents to the appeal will be –

(a) the registration officer; and

(b)   if the decision of the registration officer was given in favour of any other person than the appellant, that other person.

(4) On the hearing of the appeal –

(a)   the statement forwarded to the court by the registration officer, and any document containing information submitted to the court by the registration officer pursuant to the Regulations, are admissible as evidence of the facts stated in them; and

(b)   the court –

(i)   may draw any inference of fact that the registration officer might have drawn; and

(ii)   may give any decision and make any order that the registration officer ought to have given or made.

(5) A respondent to an appeal (other than the registration officer) is not liable for nor entitled to costs, unless he appears before the court in support of the registration officer's decision.

(6) Rule 52.4 (appellant's notice) does not apply to an appeal to which this paragraph applies.

Representation of the People Act 1983 – special provision in relation to anonymous entries in the register

31.2 (1) In this paragraph –

(a)   "anonymous entry" has the meaning given by section 9B(4) of the Representation of the People Act 1983;

(b)   "appeal notice" means the notice required by regulation 32 of the Representation of the People (England and Wales) Regulations 2001.

(2) This paragraph applies to an appeal to a county court to which paragraph 31.1 (Representation of the People Act 1983 – appeals against decisions of registration officers) applies if a party to the appeal is a person –

(a)   whose entry in the register is an anonymous entry; or

(b)   who has applied for such an entry.

(3) This paragraph also applies to an appeal to the Court of Appeal from a decision of a county court in an appeal to which paragraph 31.1 applies.

(4) The appellant may indicate in the appeal notice that an application for an anonymous entry has been applied for, or that the entry in the register is an anonymous entry.

(5) The respondent or any other person who applies to become a party to the proceedings may indicate in a respondent's notice or an application to join the proceedings that the entry in the register is an anonymous entry, or that an application has been made for an anonymous entry.

(6) Where the appellant gives such an indication in the appeal notice, the court will refer the matter to a district judge for directions about the further conduct of the proceedings, and, in particular, directions about how the matter should be listed in the court list.

(7) Where the court otherwise becomes aware that a party to the appeal is a person referred to in sub-paragraph (2), the court will give notice to the parties that no further step is to be taken until the court has given any necessary directions for the further conduct of the matter.

Representation of the People Act 1983 – appeals selected as test cases

31.3 (1) Where two or more appeals to which paragraph 31.1 (Representation of the People Act 1983 – appeals against decisions of registration officers) applies involve the same point of law, the court may direct that one appeal ("the test-case appeal") is to be heard first as a test case.

(2) The court will send a notice of the direction to each party to all of those appeals.

(3) Where a notice under sub-paragraph (2) is served on any party to an appeal (other than the test-case appeal), that party may (within 7 days after the notice is served on that party) give notice to the court requesting the appeal to be heard and –

(a)   the court will hear that appeal after the test-case appeal is disposed of;

(b)   the court will give the parties to that appeal notice of the day on which it will be heard; and

(c)   the party who gave the notice is not entitled to receive any costs of the separate hearing of that appeal unless the judge otherwise orders.

(4) Where no notice is given under sub-paragraph (3) within the period limited by that paragraph –

(a)   the decision on the test-case appeal binds the parties to each of the other appeals;

(b)   without further hearing, the court will make, in each other appeal, an order similar to the order in the test-case appeal; and

(c)   the party to each other appeal who is in the same interest as the unsuccessful party to the selected appeal is liable for the costs of the test-case appeal in the same manner and to the same extent as the unsuccessful party to that appeal and an order directing the party to pay such costs may be made and enforced accordingly.

(5) Sub-paragraph (4)(a) does not affect the right to appeal to the Court of Appeal of any party to an appeal other than the test-case appeal.

Appeals under section 11 of the UK Borders Act 2007

32.1 (1) A person appealing to a county court under section 11 of the UK Borders Act 2007 ("the Act") against a decision by the Secretary of State to impose a penalty under section 9(1) of the Act, must, subject to sub-paragraph (2), file the appellant's notice within 28 days after receiving the penalty notice.

(2) Where the appellant has given notice of objection to the Secretary of State under section 10 of the Act within the time prescribed for doing so, the appellant's notice must be filed within 28 days after receiving notice of the Secretary of State's decision in response to the notice of objection.

Practice Direction 52E –
Appeals by way of Case Stated

This Practice Direction supplements CPR Part 52

Contents of this Practice Direction

This Practice Direction is divided into the following sections:

1   Introduction: Appeals by way of case stated

2   Case stated by Crown Court or Magistrates' Court
3   Case stated by Minister, Government department, tribunal or other person

SECTION 1: INTRODUCTION: APPEALS BY WAY OF CASE STATED

1.1 An appeal by case stated is an appeal to a superior court on the basis of a set of facts specified by the inferior court for the superior court to make a decision on the application of the law to those facts.

1.2 (1) This section applies where, under any enactment –

(a)   an appeal lies to the court by way of case stated; or
(b)   a question of law may be referred to the court by way of case stated.

(2) This section is subject to any provision governing a specific category of appeal in any enactment or Practice Direction 52A, 52B or 52D.

SECTION 2: CASE STATED BY CROWN COURT OR MAGISTRATES' COURT

Application to state a case

2.1 The procedure for applying to the Crown Court or a Magistrates' Court to have a case stated for the opinion of the High Court is set out in the Criminal Procedure Rules.

Filing of appellant's notice

2.2 An appellant must file the appellant's notice at the appeal court within 10 days of the date of the case stated by the court.

Documents to be lodged

2.3 The appellant must lodge the following documents with the appellant's notice –

(a)   the stated case;
(b)   a copy of the judgment, order or decision in respect of which the case has been stated; and
(c)   where the judgment, order or decision in respect of which the case has been stated was itself given or made on appeal, a copy of the judgment, order or decision appealed from.

Service of appellant's notice

2.4 The appellant must serve the appellant's notice and accompanying documents on all respondents within 4 days after they are filed or lodged at the appeal court.

SECTION 3: CASE STATED BY MINISTER, GOVERNMENT DEPARTMENT, TRIBUNAL OR OTHER PERSON

Application to state a case

3.1 The procedure for applying to a Minister, Government department, tribunal or other person ("Minister or tribunal etc.") to have a case stated for the opinion of the court may be set out in –

    (a)   the enactment which provides for the right of appeal; or

    (b)   any rules of procedure relating to the Minister or tribunal etc.

Signing of stated case by Minister or tribunal etc.

3.2 (1) A case stated by a tribunal must be signed by –

    (a)   the chairman or president (where there is one); or

    (b)   in any other instance, by the member or members, of the tribunal.

(2) A case stated by any other person must be signed by that person or by a person authorised to do so.

Service of stated case by Minister or tribunal etc.

3.3 The Minister or tribunal etc. must serve the stated case on –

    (a)   the party who requested it; or

    (b)   the party as a result of whose application to the court the case was stated.

3.4 Where an enactment provides that a Minister or tribunal etc. may state a case or refer a question of law to the court by way of case stated without a request being made, the Minister or tribunal etc. must –

    (a)   serve the stated case on those parties that the Minister or tribunal etc. considers appropriate and on any other party who may be affected by the decision of the court; and

    (b)   give notice to every other party to the proceedings that the stated case has been served on the party named and on the date specified in the notice.

Filing and service of appellant's notice

3.5 The party on whom the stated case was served must file the appellant's notice and the stated case at the appeal court and serve copies of the notice and stated case on –

    (a)   the Minister or tribunal etc. who stated the case; and

    (b)   every party to the proceedings to which the stated case relates, within 4 days after the stated case was served on that party.

3.6 Where paragraph 3.4 applies the Minister or tribunal etc. must –

    (a)   file an appellant's notice and the stated case at the appeal court; and

    (b)   serve copies of those documents on the persons served under paragraph 3.4 within 14 days after stating the case.

3.7 Where –

    (a)   a stated case has been served by the Minister or tribunal etc. in accordance with paragraph 3.3; and

    (b)   the party on whom the stated case was served does not file an appellant's notice in accordance with paragraph 3.5,

any other party may file an appellant's notice with the stated case at the appeal court and serve a copy of the notice and the case on the persons listed in paragraph 3.5 within the period of time set out in paragraph 3.8.

3.8 The period of time referred to in paragraph 3.7 is 14 days from the last day on which the party on whom the stated case was served may file an appellant's notice in accordance with paragraph 3.5.

PART III

Amendment of stated case

3.9 The court may amend the stated case or order it to be returned to the Minister or tribunal etc. for amendment and may draw inferences of fact from the facts stated in the case.

Right of Minister or Government department to be heard on the appeal

3.10 Where the case is stated by a Minister or government department, that Minister or department, as the case may be, is entitled to appear on the appeal and to make representations to the court.

Application for order to state a case

3.11 An application to the court for an order requiring a minister or tribunal etc. to state a case for the decision of the court, or to refer a question of law to the court by way of case stated must be made to the court, which would be the appeal court if the case were stated.

3.12 An application to the court for an order directing a Minister or tribunal etc. to –

  (a)   state a case for determination by the court; or
  (b)   refer a question of law to the court by way of case stated, must be made in accordance with Part 23.

3.13 The application notice must contain –

  (a)   the grounds of the application;
  (b)   the question of law on which it is sought to have the case stated; and
  (c)   any reasons given by the Minister or tribunal etc. for the refusal to state a case.

3.14 The application notice must be filed at the appeal court and served on –

  (a)   the Minister, department, secretary of the tribunal or other person as the case may be; and
  (b)   every party to the proceedings to which the application relates, within 14 days after the appellant receives notice of the refusal of his request to state a case.

****

PART 54
JUDICIAL REVIEW AND STATUTORY REVIEW

CONTENTS OF THIS PART

Section I
Judicial Review

PART III

Section I
Judicial Review

54.1 Scope and interpretation

(1) This Section of this Part contains rules about judicial review.

(2) In this Section –

   (a) a "claim for judicial review" means a claim to review the lawfulness of –
     (i)   an enactment; or
     (ii) a decision, action or failure to act in relation to the exercise of a public function.

   (b)–(d) (*revoked*)

   (e) "the judicial review procedure" means the Part 8 procedure as modified by this Section;

   (f) "interested party" means any person (other than the claimant and defendant) who is directly affected by the claim; and

   (g) "court" means the High Court, unless otherwise stated.

   (Rule 8.1(6)(b) provides that a rule or practice direction may, in relation to a specified type of proceedings, disapply or modify any of the rules set out in Part 8 as they apply to those proceedings)

Amendments—Inserted by SI 2000/2092; amended by SI 2003/364; SI 2003/3361.

Scope—This rule provides the procedure for an application to the Administrative Court for judicial review. A claim for judicial review means a claim to review the lawfulness of an enactment or a decision, action or failure to act in relation to the exercise of a public function. The procedure must be used where the claimant is seeking a mandatory order (formerly known as an order of mandamus), a prohibiting order (formerly known as an order of prohibition) and a quashing order (formerly known as an order of certiorari) (see r 52.2). The procedure may also be used to obtain a declaration, injunction, order for damages, restitution or the recovery of a sum due (see r 52.3 and SCA 1981, s 31). Note the provisions of the CPR Pre-action Protocol for Judicial Review.

The Administrative Court—All applications for judicial review in England must be made to the Administrative Court, either at The Royal Courts of Justice, The Strand, London WC2A 2LL or at one of the regional centres: Cardiff Civil Justice Centre, 2 Park Street, Cardiff CF10 1ET; Birmingham Civil Justice Centre Priory Courts, 5th Floor, 33 Bull Street, Birmingham B4 6DS; Leeds Combined Court, 1 Oxford Row, Leeds, West Yorkshire LS1 3BG; or Manchester Civil Justice Centre, 12th Floor, 1 Bridge

Street West, Manchester M3 3FX. Where a judicial review application is proceeding in Wales (because there is a devolution issue arising out of the Government of Wales Act 1998 or an issue concerning the National Assembly of Wales, the Welsh executive, or any Welsh public body) an application may be lodged at the Royal Courts of Justice in London or at the Cardiff Civil Justice Centre (see also PD54A, para 3.1).

54.1A Who may exercise the powers of the High Court

(1) A court officer assigned to the Administrative Court office who is –

    (a)   a barrister; or

    (b)   a solicitor,

may exercise the jurisdiction of the High Court with regard to the matters set out in paragraph (2) with the consent of the President of the Queen's Bench Division.

(2) The matters referred to in paragraph (1) are –

    (a)   any matter incidental to any proceedings in the High Court;

    (b)   any other matter where there is no substantial dispute between the parties; and

    (c)   the dismissal of an appeal or application where a party has failed to comply with any order, rule or practice direction.

(3) A court officer may not decide an application for –

    (a)   permission to bring judicial review proceedings;

    (b)   an injunction;

    (c)   a stay of any proceedings, other than a temporary stay of any order or decision of the lower court over a period when the High Court is not sitting or cannot conveniently be convened, unless the parties seek a stay by consent.

(4) Decisions of a court officer may be made without a hearing.

(5) A party may request any decision of a court officer to be reviewed by a judge of the High Court.

(6) At the request of a party, a hearing will be held to reconsider a decision of a court officer, made without a hearing.

(7) A request under paragraph (5) or (6) must be filed within 7 days after the party is served with notice of the decision.

Amendments—Inserted by SI 2012/2208.

54.2 When this Section must be used

The judicial review procedure must be used in a claim for judicial review where the claimant is seeking –

    (a)   a mandatory order;

    (b)   a prohibiting order;

    (c)   a quashing order; or

    (d)   an injunction under section 30 of the Senior Courts Act 1981 (restraining a person from acting in any office in which he is not entitled to act).

Amendments—Inserted by SI 2000/2092; amended by SI 2003/364; CRA 2005, Sch 11, para 1(2).

Scope—Pt 54 provides the only method of seeking the orders set out (see also SCA 1981, ss 29–31; CCA 1984, s 38).

54.3 When this Section may be used

(1) The judicial review procedure may be used in a claim for judicial review where the claimant is seeking –

(a)   a declaration; or

(b)   an injunction^(GL).

> (Section 31(2) of the Senior Courts Act 1981 sets out the circumstances in which the court may grant a declaration or injunction in a claim for judicial review)

> (Where the claimant is seeking a declaration or injunction in addition to one of the remedies listed in rule 54.2, the judicial review procedure must be used)

(2) A claim for judicial review may include a claim for damages, restitution or the recovery of a sum due but may not seek such a remedy alone.

> (Section 31(4) of the Senior Courts Act sets out the circumstances in which the court may award damages, restitution or the recovery of a sum due on a claim for judicial review)

Amendments—Inserted by SI 2000/2092; amended by SI 2003/364; SI 2003/3361; CRA 2005, Sch 11, para 1(2).

Scope—Pt 54 provides the method of seeking the orders set out (see also SCA 1981, ss 29–31). A declaration or injunction may also be obtained in other proceedings (under the inherent jurisdiction of the High Court; see SCA 1981, s 37 and CCA 1984, s 38 for injunctions). Guidance is given by the Court of Appeal on the approach to damages in judicial review cases where a breach of human rights is alleged: see *Anufrijeva v Southwark LBC* [2004] 1 FLR 8; *Re C (Breach of Human Rights: Damages)* [2007] 1 FLR 1957.

Appeals—Although the Court of Appeal had no original jurisdiction in judicial review cases, it had jurisdiction to consider a new decision within an appeal against an old decision by virtue of SCA 1981, s 9 and of the right to admit fresh evidence as part of an appeal. There could be no latitude on appeal to taking such a pragmatic approach to consider the new decision if that would cause prejudice to either party or because the court would be deprived of any other material required for its decision: *R (O) v London Borough of Hammersmith and Fulham* [2012] 2 FLR 290.

54.4 Permission required

The court's permission to proceed is required in a claim for judicial review whether started under this Section or transferred to the Administrative Court.

Amendments—Inserted by SI 2000/2092; amended by SI 2003/364.

Scope—There is a filter process for all applications for judicial review. Permission to apply must be obtained. This is usually considered, in the first instance without a hearing (see PD54A, para 8.4). The decision of the judge (Form JRJ) will be served upon the claimant, the defendant and any other person named on the claim form. If permission is granted, the claimant must lodge the application fee (£135 with the Administrative Office within 7 days of service of the judge's decision upon him. If permission is refused or granted subject to conditions or on certain grounds, the claimant may request an oral hearing. Such a request must be filed within 7 days after service of the notification of the decision (see r 54.12 and PD54A, para 8.5). At the oral hearing the claimant is allocated 20 minutes of court time. If this is considered insufficient, the claimant must file a written estimate and request a special fixture. It is not necessary for the defendant or any interested party to attend, but they may do so (see PD54A, para 8.5). An appeal may be made to the Court of Appeal in respect of the judge's decision, following an oral hearing (see r 52.15).

Documents—The claimant must file a claim form in accordance with CPR 1998, Pt 8 as modified by this rule. The standard form N461 should be used, which may be obtained from the Administrative Office or on the Court Service website (*www.justice.gov.uk/forms*). The following documents must be filed with the claim form (PD54A, para 5.6). The claimant must lodge two copies of a paginated and indexed bundle containing the claim form, which must include or be accompanied by:

(1)   a detailed statement of the claimant's grounds for bringing the claim for judicial review;

(2)   a statement of the facts relied on;

(3)   any application to extend the time limit for filing the claim form;

(4)   any application for directions; and

(5)   a time estimate for the hearing.

In addition, the claim form must be accompanied by:

(i)   any written evidence in support of the claim or application to extend time;

(ii) a copy of any order that the claimant seeks to have quashed;
(iii) where the claim for judicial review relates to a decision of a court or tribunal, an approved copy of the reasons for reaching that decision;
(iv) copies of any documents on which the claimant proposes to rely;
(v)   copies of any relevant statutory material;
(vi) a list of essential documents for advance reading by the court (with page references to the passages relied on).

Where it is not possible to file all the above documents, the claimant must indicate which documents have not been filed and the reasons why they are not currently available (see PD54A, para 5.6).

Human rights issues—Where the claimant is seeking to raise any human rights issue the claim form must include the information specified in PD16, para 15.1, namely:

(a) give details of the alleged convention right infringed;
(b) specify the relief sought;
(c) state if the relief sought includes a declaration of incompatibility or damages in respect of a judicial act;
(d) where there is a claim for a declaration of incompatibility, give details of the legislative provision;
(e) where the claim relates to unlawfulness by another court or tribunal, give details of the finding;
(f) where the claim relates to a judicial act, provide details of the act complained of and the court or tribunal concerned.

54.5 Time limit for filing claim form

(1) The claim form must be filed –

(a) promptly; and
(b) in any event not later than 3 months after the grounds to make the claim first arose.

(2) The time limit in this rule may not be extended by agreement between the parties.

(3) This rule does not apply when any other enactment specifies a shorter time limit for making the claim for judicial review.

Amendments—Inserted by SI 2000/2092.

54.6 Claim form

(1) In addition to the matters set out in rule 8.2 (contents of the claim form) the claimant must also state –

(a) the name and address of any person he considers to be an interested party;
(b) that he is requesting permission to proceed with a claim for judicial review;
(c) any remedy (including any interim remedy) he is claiming; and
(d) where appropriate, the grounds on which it is contended that the claim is an Aarhus Convention claim.

(Rules 45.41 to 45.44 make provision about costs in Aarhus Convention claims)

(Part 25 sets out how to apply for an interim remedy)

(2) The claim form must be accompanied by the documents required by Practice Direction 54A.

Amendments—Inserted by SI 2000/2092; amended by SI 2009/3390; SI 2013/262.

Scope—See notes to r 54.4 (above).

54.7 Service of claim form

The claim form must be served on –

(a) the defendant; and
(b) unless the court otherwise directs, any person the claimant considers to be an interested party,

within 7 days after the date of issue.

Amendments—Inserted by SI 2000/2092.

Scope—Once permission to apply for judicial review has been granted, the application will be issued by the Administrative Court. Within 7 days of the date of issue, the claimant must serve the defendant and any interested party with the claim form and accompanying documents. Once service has been effected, the claimant must lodge a certificate of service in the Administrative Court Office within 7 days of service. The Administrative Court will not effect service (see PD54A, para 6.1).

54.7A Judicial review of decisions of the Upper Tribunal

(1) This rule applies where an application is made, following refusal by the Upper Tribunal of permission to appeal against a decision of the First Tier Tribunal, for judicial review –

    (a) of the decision of the Upper Tribunal refusing permission to appeal; or

    (b) which relates to the decision of the First Tier Tribunal which was the subject of the application for permission to appeal.

(2) Where this rule applies –

    (a) the application may not include any other claim, whether against the Upper Tribunal or not; and

    (b) any such other claim must be the subject of a separate application.

(3) The claim form and the supporting documents required by paragraph (4) must be filed no later than 16 days after the date on which notice of the Upper Tribunal's decision was sent to the applicant.

(4) The supporting documents are –

    (a) the decision of the Upper Tribunal to which the application relates, and any document giving reasons for the decision;

    (b) the grounds of appeal to the Upper Tribunal and any documents which were sent with them;

    (c) the decision of the First Tier Tribunal, the application to that Tribunal for permission to appeal and its reasons for refusing permission; and

    (d) any other documents essential to the claim.

(5) The claim form and supporting documents must be served on the Upper Tribunal and any other interested party no later than 7 days after the date of issue.

(6) The Upper Tribunal and any person served with the claim form who wishes to take part in the proceedings for judicial review must, no later than 21 days after service of the claim form, file and serve on the applicant and any other party an acknowledgment of service in the relevant practice form.

(7) The court will give permission to proceed only if it considers –

    (a) that there is an arguable case, which has a reasonable prospect of success, that both the decision of the Upper Tribunal refusing permission to appeal and the decision of the First Tier Tribunal against which permission to appeal was sought are wrong in law; and

    (b) that either –

        (i) the claim raises an important point of principle or practice; or

        (ii) there is some other compelling reason to hear it.

(8) If the application for permission is refused on paper without an oral hearing, rule 54.12(3) (request for reconsideration at a hearing) does not apply.

(9) If permission to apply for judicial review is granted –

    (a) if the Upper Tribunal or any interested party wishes there to be a hearing of the

PART III

substantive application, it must make its request for such a hearing no later than 14 days after service of the order granting permission; and

(b)   if no request for a hearing is made within that period, the court will make a final order quashing the refusal of permission without a further hearing.

(10) The power to make a final order under paragraph (9)(b) may be exercised by the Master of the Crown Office or a Master of the Administrative Court.

Amendments—Inserted by SI 2012/2208.

Note—Rule 54.7A gives effect to the decision of the Supreme Court in *Cart v The Upper Tribunal* [2012] 1 FLR 997.

54.8 Acknowledgment of service

(1) Any person served with the claim form who wishes to take part in the judicial review must file an acknowledgment of service in the relevant practice form in accordance with the following provisions of this rule.

(2) Any acknowledgment of service must be –

(a)   filed not more than 21 days after service of the claim form; and

(b)   served on –

(i)   the claimant; and

(ii)   subject to any direction under rule 54.7(b), any other person named in the claim form,

as soon as practicable and, in any event, not later than 7 days after it is filed.

(3) The time limits under this rule may not be extended by agreement between the parties.

(4) The acknowledgment of service –

(a)   must –

(i)   where the person filing it intends to contest the claim, set out a summary of his grounds for doing so; and

(ii)   state the name and address of any person the person filing it considers to be an interested party; and

(b)   may include or be accompanied by an application for directions.

(5) Rule 10.3(2) does not apply.

Amendments—Inserted by SI 2000/2092.

Scope—Any person served with a claim form who wishes to take part in the proceedings must file in the Administrative Court Office an acknowledgment of service on Form N462 (available from the Office or the Court Service website on *www.justice.gov.uk/forms*) within 21 days of service. The acknowledgment of service must state whether the defendant intends to contest the claim and whether he seeks a different remedy (CPR 1998, r 8.3(2)). The acknowledgment must be served upon the claimant within 7 days of it being filed. The court, if requested, will serve this (the defendant must provide the copies for service). The acknowledgment of service may only be amended or withdrawn with permission of the court (see PD10, para 5.4).

54.9 Failure to file acknowledgment of service

(1) Where a person served with the claim form has failed to file an acknowledgment of service in accordance with rule 54.8, he –

(a)   may not take part in a hearing to decide whether permission should be given unless the court allows him to do so; but

(b)   provided he complies with rule 54.14 or any other direction of the court regarding the filing and service of –

> (i) detailed grounds for contesting the claim or supporting it on additional grounds; and
>
> (ii) any written evidence,
>
> may take part in the hearing of the judicial review.

(2) Where that person takes part in the hearing of the judicial review, the court may take his failure to file an acknowledgment of service into account when deciding what order to make about costs.

(3) Rule 8.4 does not apply.

Amendments—Inserted by SI 2000/2092.

54.10 Permission given

(1) Where permission to proceed is given the court may also give directions.

(2) Directions under paragraph (1) may include –

    (a)   a stay$^{(GL)}$ of proceedings to which the claim relates;

    (b)   directions requiring the proceedings to be heard by a Divisional Court.

> (Rule 3.7 provides a sanction for the non-payment of the fee payable when permission to proceed has been given)

Amendments—Inserted by SI 2000/2092; amended by SI 2010/2577.

Scope—Upon the granting of permission to proceed, directions may be made about serving the claim form/evidence on any other person and the need for expedition.

Human Rights issues—Where a claim relates to a human rights issue, a direction may be made for giving notice to the Crown or joining it as a party to the proceedings. By virtue of CPR 1998, r 19.4A the court is not entitled to make a declaration of incompatibility in accordance with HRA 1998, s 4 unless 21 days' notice (or such other period as the court may direct) has been given to the Crown. Where notice has been given to the Crown, a Minister or other person permitted by the Act must be joined as a party. There is a similar provision where the claim under HRA 1998, s 9 seeks damages and notice must be given to the Crown. The notice given under r 19.4A must be served on the person named in the list published under Crown Proceedings Act 1947, s 17. The list is annexed to PD66 (see PD19A, para 6.4(1)).

54.11 Service of order giving or refusing permission

The court will serve –

    (a)   the order giving or refusing permission; and

    (b)   any directions,

    on –

    (i)   the claimant;

    (ii)   the defendant; and

    (iii)   any other person who filed an acknowledgment of service.

Amendments—Inserted by SI 2000/2092.

54.12 Permission decision without a hearing

(1) This rule applies where the court, without a hearing –

    (a)   refuses permission to proceed; or

    (b)   gives permission to proceed –

    (i)   subject to conditions; or

    (ii)   on certain grounds only.

(2) The court will serve its reasons for making the decision when it serves the order giving or refusing permission in accordance with rule 54.11.

PART III

(3) The claimant may not appeal but may request the decision to be reconsidered at a hearing.

(4) A request under paragraph (3) must be filed within 7 days after service of the reasons under paragraph (2).

(5) The claimant, defendant and any other person who has filed an acknowledgment of service will be given at least 2 days' notice of the hearing date.

(6) The court may give directions requiring the proceedings to be heard by a Divisional Court.

Amendments—Inserted by SI 2000/2092; amended by SI 2010/2577.

Scope—The court will generally, in the first instance, consider the question of permission without a hearing (PD54A, para 8.4). Where permission has been refused or granted with conditions or on a limited basis, the claimant may seek an oral hearing for reconsideration of the decision (see notes to r 54.4).

54.13 Defendant etc may not apply to set aside^(GL)

Neither the defendant nor any other person served with the claim form may apply to set aside^(GL) an order giving permission to proceed.

Amendments—Inserted by SI 2000/2092.

54.14 Response

(1) A defendant and any other person served with the claim form who wishes to contest the claim or support it on additional grounds must file and serve –

    (a) detailed grounds for contesting the claim or supporting it on additional grounds; and

    (b) any written evidence,

within 35 days after service of the order giving permission.

(2) The following rules do not apply –

    (a) rule 8.5(3) and 8.5(4) (defendant to file and serve written evidence at the same time as acknowledgment of service); and

    (b) rule 8.5(5) and 8.5(6) (claimant to file and serve any reply within 14 days).

Amendments—Inserted by SI 2000/2092.

Scope—A party who has been served with a claim form may contest the claim. To do so they must, within 35 days of service of the order granting permission, file and serve their grounds and written evidence in a paginated bundle (PD54A, para 10.1).

54.15 Where claimant seeks to rely on additional grounds

The court's permission is required if a claimant seeks to rely on grounds other than those for which he has been given permission to proceed.

Amendments—Inserted by SI 2000/2092.

54.16 Evidence

(1) Rule 8.6(1) does not apply.

(2) No written evidence may be relied on unless –

    (a) it has been served in accordance with any –

        (i) rule under this Section; or

        (ii) direction of the court; or

    (b) the court gives permission.

Amendments—Inserted by SI 2000/2092; amended by SI 2002/2058; SI 2003/364.

Scope—The provisions for filing evidence in judicial review proceedings are contained within this rule, as Pt 8 is disapplied. When the claim form is lodged, it should be accompanied by written evidence (see notes to r 54.4). If the claimant seeks to rely on further evidence permission must be obtained to do so.

Skeleton arguments—The claimant must file and serve a skeleton argument not less than 21 days before the hearing (or the warned date) (PD54A, para 15.1; for documents to be filed see notes to r 54.4). The skeleton argument must contain:

(1) a time estimate for the complete hearing, including delivery of judgment;
(2) a list of issues;
(3) a list of the legal points to be taken (together with any relevant authorities with page references to the passages relied on);
(4) a chronology of events, with page references to the bundle of documents (see para 16.1);
(5) a list of essential documents for the advance reading of the court, with page references to the passages relied on (if different from that filed with the claim form) and a time estimate for that reading; and
(6) a list of persons referred to.

Any defendant or interested party must file a skeleton argument not less than 14 days before the hearing.

Documents—The claimant must file a paginated and indexed bundle of all relevant documents required for the hearing of the judicial review when he files his skeleton argument. The bundle must also include those documents required by the defendant and any other party who is to make representations at the hearing (PD54A, para 16).

54.17 Court's powers to hear any person

(1) Any person may apply for permission –

    (a)   to file evidence; or
    (b)   make representations at the hearing of the judicial review.

(2) An application under paragraph (1) should be made promptly.

Amendments—Inserted by SI 2000/2092.

Scope—Where the parties consent, the court may deal with an application to file evidence without a hearing. Permission to file evidence may be given on conditions or with directions (PD54A, para 13).

54.18 Judicial review may be decided without a hearing

The court may decide the claim for judicial review without a hearing where all the parties agree.

Amendments—Inserted by SI 2000/2092.

54.19 Court's powers in respect of quashing orders

(1) This rule applies where the court makes a quashing order in respect of the decision to which the claim relates.

(2) The court may –

    (a)
        (i)   remit the matter to the decision-maker; and
        (ii) direct it to reconsider the matter and reach a decision in accordance with the judgment of the court; or
    (b)   in so far as any enactment permits, substitute its own decision for the decision to which the claim relates.

        (Section 31 of the Senior Courts Act 1981 enables the High Court, subject to certain conditions, to substitute its own decision for the decision in question.)

Amendments—Inserted by SI 2000/2092; amended by SI 2007/3543; CRA 2005, Sch 11, para 1(2).

Scope—The court is entitled to quash a decision and direct there be a further consideration, or make the decision itself.

54.20 Transfer

The court may –

    (a)   order a claim to continue as if it had not been started under this Section; and

    (b)   where it does so, give directions about the future management of the claim.

        (Part 30 (transfer) applies to transfers to and from the Administrative Court)

Amendments—Inserted by SI 2000/2092; amended by SI 2003/364.

Scope—Under CPR 1998, r 30.5 the High Court may transfer proceedings from one Division to another. Any application to transfer should be made to the Judge of the Administrative Court for a matter to proceed in that court. In deciding whether to transfer to the Administrative Court, the court will consider whether the case contains issues of public law (PD54A, para 14.2).

Practice Direction 54A – Judicial Review

This Practice Direction supplements CPR Part 54

SECTION I: GENERAL PROVISIONS RELATING TO JUDICIAL REVIEW

1.1 In addition to Part 54 and this practice direction attention is drawn to –

- section 31 of the Senior Courts Act 1981; and
- the Human Rights Act 1998.

The court

2.1 Part 54 claims for judicial review are dealt with in the Administrative Court.

    (Practice Direction 54D contains provisions about where a claim for judicial review may be started, administered and heard.)

Rule 54.5 – Time limit for filing claim form

4.1 Where the claim is for a quashing order in respect of a judgment, order or conviction, the date when the grounds to make the claim first arose, for the purposes of rule 54.5(1)(b), is the date of that judgment, order or conviction.

Rule 54.6 – Claim form

Interested parties

5.1 Where the claim for judicial review relates to proceedings in a court or tribunal, any other parties to those proceedings must be named in the claim form as interested parties under rule 54.6(1)(a) (and therefore served with the claim form under rule 54.7(b)).

5.2 For example, in a claim by a defendant in a criminal case in the Magistrates' or Crown Court for judicial review of a decision in that case, the prosecution must always be named as an interested party.

Human rights

5.3 Where the claimant is seeking to raise any issue under the Human Rights Act 1998, or seeks a remedy available under that Act, the claim form must include the information required by paragraph 15 of Practice Direction 16.

Devolution issues

5.4 Where the claimant intends to raise a devolution issue, the claim form must –

    (1) specify that the applicant wishes to raise a devolution issue and identify the relevant provisions of the Government of Wales Act 2006, the Northern Ireland Act 1998 or the Scotland Act 1998; and

    (2) contain a summary of the facts, circumstances and points of law on the basis of which it is alleged that a devolution issue arises.

5.5 In this practice direction 'devolution issue' has the same meaning as in paragraph 1, Schedule 9 to the Government of Wales Act 2006, paragraph 1, Schedule 10 to the Northern Ireland Act 1998; and paragraph 1, Schedule 6 to the Scotland Act 1998.

Claim form

5.6 The claim form must include or be accompanied by –

    (1) a detailed statement of the claimant's grounds for bringing the claim for judicial review;

    (2) a statement of the facts relied on;

    (3) any application to extend the time limit for filing the claim form;

    (4) any application for directions.

5.7 In addition, the claim form must be accompanied by –

    (1) any written evidence in support of the claim or application to extend time;

    (2) a copy of any order that the claimant seeks to have quashed;

    (3) where the claim for judicial review relates to a decision of a court or tribunal, an approved copy of the reasons for reaching that decision;

    (4) copies of any documents on which the claimant proposes to rely;

    (5) copies of any relevant statutory material;

    (6) a list of essential documents for advance reading by the court (with page references to the passages relied on); and

5.8 Where it is not possible to file all the above documents, the claimant must indicate which documents have not been filed and the reasons why they are not currently available.

Bundle of documents

5.9 The claimant must file two copies of a paginated and indexed bundle containing all the documents referred to in paragraphs 5.6 and 5.7.

5.10 Attention is drawn to rules 8.5(1) and 8.5(7).

Rule 54.7 – Service of claim form

6.1 Except as required by rules 54.11 or 54.12(2), the Administrative Court will not serve documents and service must be effected by the parties.

6.2 Where the defendant or interested party to the claim for judicial review is –

    (a) the Immigration and Asylum Chamber of the First-tier Tribunal, the address for service of the claim form is Official Correspondence Unit, PO Box 6987, Leicester, LE1 6ZX or fax number 0116 249 4240;

(b)   the Crown, service of the claim form must be effected on the solicitor acting for the relevant government department as if the proceedings were civil proceedings as defined in the Crown Proceedings Act 1947.

(Practice Direction 66 gives the list published under section 17 of the Crown Proceedings Act 1947 of the solicitors acting in civil proceedings (as defined in that Act) for the different government departments on whom service is to be effected, and of their addresses.)

(Part 6 contains provisions about the service of claim forms.)

Rule 54.8 – Acknowledgment of service

7.1 Attention is drawn to rule 8.3(2) and the relevant practice direction and to rule 10.5.

Rule 54.10 – Permission given

Directions

8.1 Case management directions under rule 54.10(1) may include directions about serving the claim form and any evidence on other persons.

8.2 Where a claim is made under the Human Rights Act 1998, a direction may be made for giving notice to the Crown or joining the Crown as a party. Attention is drawn to rule 19.4A and paragraph 6 of Practice Direction 19A.

Permission without a hearing

8.4 The court will generally, in the first instance, consider the question of permission without a hearing.

Permission hearing

8.5 Neither the defendant nor any other interested party need attend a hearing on the question of permission unless the court directs otherwise.

8.6 Where the defendant or any party does attend a hearing, the court will not generally make an order for costs against the claimant.

Rule 54.11 – Service of order giving or refusing permission

9.1 An order refusing permission or giving it subject to conditions or on certain grounds only must set out or be accompanied by the court's reasons for coming to that decision.

Rule 54.14 – Response

10.1 Where the party filing the detailed grounds intends to rely on documents not already filed, he must file a paginated bundle of those documents when he files the detailed grounds.

Rule 54.15 – Where claimant seeks to rely on additional grounds

11.1 Where the claimant intends to apply to rely on additional grounds at the hearing of the claim for judicial review, he must give notice to the court and to any other person served with the claim form no later than 7 clear days before the hearing (or the warned date where appropriate).

Rule 54.16 – Evidence

12.1 Disclosure is not required unless the court orders otherwise.

Rule 54.17 – Court's powers to hear any person

13.1 Where all the parties consent, the court may deal with an application under rule 54.17 without a hearing.

13.2 Where the court gives permission for a person to file evidence or make representations at the hearing of the claim for judicial review, it may do so on conditions and may give case management directions.

13.3 An application for permission should be made by letter to the Administrative Court office, identifying the claim, explaining who the applicant is and indicating why and in what form the applicant wants to participate in the hearing.

13.4 If the applicant is seeking a prospective order as to costs, the letter should say what kind of order and on what grounds.

13.5 Applications to intervene must be made at the earliest reasonable opportunity, since it will usually be essential not to delay the hearing.

Rule 54.20 – Transfer

14.1 Attention is drawn to rule 30.5.

14.2 In deciding whether a claim is suitable for transfer to the Administrative Court, the court will consider whether it raises issues of public law to which Part 54 should apply.

Skeleton arguments

15.1 The claimant must file and serve a skeleton argument not less than 21 working days before the date of the hearing of the judicial review (or the warned date).

15.2 The defendant and any other party wishing to make representations at the hearing of the judicial review must file and serve a skeleton argument not less than 14 working days before the date of the hearing of the judicial review (or the warned date).

15.3 Skeleton arguments must contain –

    (1)   a time estimate for the complete hearing, including delivery of judgment;

    (2)   a list of issues;

    (3)   a list of the legal points to be taken (together with any relevant authorities with page references to the passages relied on);

    (4)   a chronology of events (with page references to the bundle of documents (see paragraph 16.1);

    (5)   a list of essential documents for the advance reading of the court (with page references to the passages relied on) (if different from that filed with the claim form) and a time estimate for that reading; and

    (6)   a list of persons referred to.

Bundle of documents to be filed

16.1 The claimant must file a paginated and indexed bundle of all relevant documents required for the hearing of the judicial review when he files his skeleton argument.

16.2 The bundle must also include those documents required by the defendant and any other party who is to make representations at the hearing.

Agreed final order

17.1 If the parties agree about the final order to be made in a claim for judicial review, the claimant must file at the court a document (with 2 copies) signed by all the parties setting out the terms of the proposed agreed order together with a short statement of the matters relied on as justifying the proposed agreed order and copies of any authorities or statutory provisions relied on.

17.2 The court will consider the documents referred to in paragraph 17.1 and will make the order if satisfied that the order should be made.

17.3 If the court is not satisfied that the order should be made, a hearing date will be set.

17.4 Where the agreement relates to an order for costs only, the parties need only file a document signed by all the parties setting out the terms of the proposed order.

SECTION II: APPLICATIONS FOR PERMISSION TO APPLY FOR JUDICIAL REVIEW IN IMMIGRATION AND ASYLUM CASES – CHALLENGING REMOVAL

18.1

  (1)   This Section applies where –
       (a)   a person has been served with a copy of directions for his removal from the United Kingdom by the UK Border Agency of the Home Office and notified that this Section applies; and
       (b)   that person makes an application for permission to apply for judicial review before his removal takes effect.
  (2)   This Section does not prevent a person from applying for judicial review after he has been removed.
  (3)   The requirements contained in this Section of this Practice Direction are additional to those contained elsewhere in the Practice Direction.

18.2

  (1)   A person who makes an application for permission to apply for judicial review must file a claim form and a copy at court, and the claim form must –
       (a)   indicate on its face that this Section of the Practice Direction applies; and
       (b)   be accompanied by –
            (i)   a copy of the removal directions and the decision to which the application relates; and
            (ii) any document served with the removal directions including any document which contains the UK Border Agency's factual summary of the case; and
       (c)   contain or be accompanied by the detailed statement of the claimant's grounds for bringing the claim for judicial review; or
       (d)   if the claimant is unable to comply with paragraph (b) or (c), contain or be accompanied by a statement of the reasons why.
  (2)   The claimant must, immediately upon issue of the claim, send copies of the issued claim form and accompanying documents to the address specified by the UK Border Agency.

(Rule 54.7 also requires the defendant to be served with the claim form within 7 days of the date of issue. Rule 6.10 provides that service on a Government Department must be effected on the solicitor acting for that Department, which in the case of the UK Border Agency is the Treasury Solicitor. The address for the Treasury Solicitor may be found in the Annex to Part 66 of these Rules.)

18.3 Where the claimant has not complied with paragraph 18.2(1)(b) or (c) and has provided reasons why he is unable to comply, and the court has issued the claim form, the Administrative Court –

(a)   will refer the matter to a Judge for consideration as soon as practicable; and
(b)   will notify the parties that it has done so.

18.4 If, upon a refusal to grant permission to apply for judicial review, the Court indicates that the application is clearly without merit, that indication will be included in the order refusing permission.

SECTION III – APPLICATIONS FOR PERMISSION TO APPLY FOR JUDICIAL REVIEW OF DECISIONS OF THE UPPER TRIBUNAL

19.1 A person who makes an application for permission to apply for judicial review of the decision of the Upper Tribunal refusing permission to appeal must file a claim form which must –

(a)   state on its face that the application is made under Rule 54.7A;
(b)   set out succinctly the grounds on which it is argued that the criteria in Rule 54.7A(7) are met; and
(c)   be accompanied by the supporting documents required under Rule 54.7A(4).

19.2 If the Upper Tribunal or any interested party wishes there to be a hearing of the substantive application under Rule 54.7A(9), it must make its request in writing (by letter copied to the claimant) for such a hearing no later than 14 days after service of the order granting permission.

Practice Direction 54C –
References by the Legal Services Commission

This Practice Direction supplements CPR Part 54

Note—The Legal Aid Agency replaced the Legal Services Commission on 1 April 2013.

1.1 This Practice Direction applies where the Legal Services Commission ('the Commission') refers to the High Court a question that arises on a review of a decision about an individual's financial eligibility for a representation order in criminal proceedings under the Criminal Defence Service (Financial Eligibility) Regulations 2006.

1.2 A reference of a question by the Legal Services Commission must be made to the Administrative Court.

1.3 Part 52 does not apply to a review under this paragraph.

1.4 The Commission must –

(a)   file at the court –
(i)   the individual's applications for a representation order and for a review, and any supporting documents;

PART III

    (ii) a copy of the question on which the court's decision is sought; and

    (iii) a statement of the Commission's observations on the question; and

  (b) serve a copy of the question and the statement on the individual.

1.5 The individual may file representations on the question at the court within 7 days after service on him of the copy of the question and the statement.

1.6 The question will be decided without a hearing unless the court directs otherwise.

Practice Direction 54D – Administrative Court (Venue)

This Practice Direction supplements CPR Part 54

Scope and purpose

1.1 This Practice Direction concerns the place in which a claim before the Administrative Court should be started and administered and the venue at which it will be determined.

1.2 This Practice Direction is intended to facilitate access to justice by enabling cases to be administered and determined in the most appropriate location. To achieve this purpose it provides flexibility in relation to where claims are to be administered and enables claims to be transferred to different venues.

Venue – General provisions

2.1 The claim form in proceedings in the Administrative Court may be issued at the Administrative Court Office of the High Court at –

  (1) the Royal Courts of Justice in London; or

  (2) at the District Registry of the High Court at Birmingham, Cardiff, Leeds, or Manchester unless the claim is one of the excepted classes of claim set out in paragraph 3 of this Practice Direction which may only be started and determined at the Royal Courts of Justice in London.

2.2 Any claim started in Birmingham will normally be determined at a court in the Midland region (geographically covering the area of the Midland Circuit); in Cardiff in Wales; in Leeds in the North-Eastern Region (geographically covering the area of the North Eastern Circuit); in London at the Royal Courts of Justice; and in Manchester, in the North-Western Region (geographically covering the Northern Circuit).

Excepted classes of claim

3.1 The excepted classes of claim referred to in paragraph 2.1(2) are –

  (1) proceedings to which Part 76 or Part 79 applies, and for the avoidance of doubt –

    (a) proceedings relating to control orders (within the meaning of Part 76);

    (b) financial restrictions proceedings (within the meaning of Part 79);

    (c) proceedings relating to terrorism or alleged terrorists (where that is a relevant feature of the claim); and

    (d) proceedings in which a special advocate is or is to be instructed;

  (2) proceedings to which RSC Order 115 applies;

(3) proceedings under the Proceeds of Crime Act 2002;

(4) appeals to the Administrative Court under the Extradition Act 2003;

(5) proceedings which must be heard by a Divisional Court; and

(6) proceedings relating to the discipline of solicitors.

3.2 If a claim form is issued at an Administrative Court office other than in London and includes one of the excepted classes of claim, the proceedings will be transferred to London.

Urgent applications

4.1 During the hours when the court is open, where an urgent application needs to be made to the Administrative Court outside London, the application must be made to the judge designated to deal with such applications in the relevant District Registry.

4.2 Any urgent application to the Administrative Court during the hours when the court is closed, must be made to the duty out of hours High Court judge by telephoning 020 7947 6000.

Assignment to another venue

5.1 The proceedings may be transferred from the office at which the claim form was issued to another office. Such transfer is a judicial act.

5.2 The general expectation is that proceedings will be administered and determined in the region with which the claimant has the closest connection, subject to the following considerations as applicable –

(1) any reason expressed by any party for preferring a particular venue;

(2) the region in which the defendant, or any relevant office or department of the defendant, is based;

(3) the region in which the claimant's legal representatives are based;

(4) the ease and cost of travel to a hearing;

(5) the availability and suitability of alternative means of attending a hearing (for example, by videolink);

(6) the extent and nature of media interest in the proceedings in any particular locality;

(7) the time within which it is appropriate for the proceedings to be determined;

(8) whether it is desirable to administer or determine the claim in another region in the light of the volume of claims issued at, and the capacity, resources and workload of, the court at which it is issued;

(9) whether the claim raises issues sufficiently similar to those in another outstanding claim to make it desirable that it should be determined together with, or immediately following, that other claim; and

(10) whether the claim raises devolution issues and for that reason whether it should more appropriately be determined in London or Cardiff.

5.3

(1) When an urgent application is made under paragraph 4.1 or 4.2, this will not by itself decide the venue for the further administration or determination of the claim.

(2) The court dealing with the urgent application may direct that the case be assigned to a particular venue.

(3) When an urgent application is made under paragraph 4.2, and the court does not make a direction under sub-paragraph (2), the claim will be assigned in the first place to London but may be reassigned to another venue at a later date.

5.4 The court may on an application by a party or of its own initiative direct that the claim be determined in a region other than that of the venue in which the claim is currently assigned. The considerations in paragraph 5.2 apply.

5.5 Once assigned to a venue, the proceedings will be both administered from that venue and determined by a judge of the Administrative Court at a suitable court within that region, or, if the venue is in London, at the Royal Courts of Justice. The choice of which court (of those within the region which are identified by the Presiding Judge of the circuit suitable for such hearing) will be decided, subject to availability, by the considerations in paragraph 5.2.

5.6 When giving directions under rule 54.10, the court may direct that proceedings be reassigned to another region for hearing (applying the considerations in paragraph 5.2). If no such direction is given, the claim will be heard in the same region as that in which the permission application was determined (whether on paper or at a hearing).

****

PART 57
PROBATE AND INHERITANCE

CONTENTS OF THIS PART

57.1 Scope of this Part and definitions

(1) This Part contains rules about –

    (a)   probate claims;

    (b)   claims for the rectification of wills;

    (c)   claims and applications to –

        (i)   substitute another person for a personal representative; or

        (ii)   remove a personal representative; and

    (d)   claims under the Inheritance (Provision for Family and Dependants) Act 1975.

(2) In this Part:

    (a)   "probate claim" means a claim for –

        (i)   the grant of probate of the will, or letters of administration of the estate, of a deceased person;

        (ii)   the revocation of such a grant; or

       (iii) a decree pronouncing for or against the validity of an alleged will;

        not being a claim which is non-contentious (or common form) probate business;

        (Section 128 of the Senior Courts Act 1981 defines non-contentious (or common form) probate business.)

(b) "relevant office" means –
    (i) in the case of High Court proceedings in a Chancery district registry, that registry;
    (ii) in the case of any other High Court proceedings, Chancery Chambers at the Royal Courts of Justice, Strand, London, WC2A 2LL; and
    (iii) in the case of county court proceedings, the office of the county court in question;
(c) "testamentary document" means a will, a draft of a will, written instructions for a will made by or at the request of, or under the instructions of, the testator, and any document purporting to be evidence of the contents, or to be a copy, of a will which is alleged to have been lost or destroyed;
(d) "will" includes a codicil.

Amendments—Inserted by SI 2001/1388; amended by SI 2002/2058; CRA 2005, Sch 11, para 1(2).

****

Section IV
Claims under the Inheritance (Provision for Family and Dependants) Act 1975

57.14 Scope of this Section

This Section contains rules about claims under the Inheritance (Provision for Family and Dependants) Act 1975 ("the Act").

Amendments—Inserted by SI 2002/2058.

57.15 Proceedings in the High Court

(1) Proceedings in the High Court under the Act shall be issued in either –
    (a) the Chancery Division; or
    (b) the Family Division.

(2) The Civil Procedure Rules apply to proceedings under the Act which are brought in the Family Division, except that the provisions of the Family Procedure Rules 2010 relating to the drawing up and service of orders apply instead of the provisions in Part 40 and Practice Direction 40B.

Amendments—Inserted by SI 2002/2058; amended by SI 2009/3390; SI 2011/1045.

Jurisdiction—See **"court"** under I(PFD)A 1975, s 1. The county court has unlimited jurisdiction to hear claims under the Act: CCA 1984, s 25. For transfer of proceedings to a county court and from a county court, see CPR 1998, Pt 30.

Transfer of proceedings—The criteria to which the court must have regard include those set out in CPR 1998, r 30.3(2). Where there are existing related proceedings, these may make transfer appropriate. Where the application involves the taking of complicated accounts, a transfer to the Chancery Division may be considered appropriate as it is better equipped to deal with such issues.

57.16 Procedure for claims under section 1 of the Act

(1) A claim under section 1 of the Act must be made by issuing a claim form in accordance with Part 8.

(2) Rule 8.3 (acknowledgment of service) and rule 8.5 (filing and serving written evidence) apply as modified by paragraphs (3) to (5) of this rule.

(3) The written evidence filed and served by the claimant with the claim form must have exhibited to it an official copy of –

(a) the grant of probate or letters of administration in respect of the deceased's estate; and

(b) every testamentary document in respect of which probate or letters of administration were granted.

(4) Subject to paragraph (4A), the time within which a defendant must file and serve –

(a) an acknowledgment of service; and

(b) any written evidence,

is not more than 21 days after service of the claim form on him.

(4A) If the claim form is served out of the jurisdiction under rule 6.32 or 6.33, the period for filing an acknowledgment of service and any written evidence is 7 days longer than the relevant period specified in rule 6.35 or Practice Direction 6B.

(5) A defendant who is a personal representative of the deceased must file and serve written evidence, which must include the information required by Practice Direction 57.

Amendments—Inserted by SI 2002/2058; amended by SI 2004/1306; SI 2008/2178; SI 2009/3390.

Time for application—Save with the leave of the court, an application under the I(PFD)A 1975 may not be made after the end of the period of 6 months from the date on which representation with respect to the estate is first taken out (I(PFD)A 1975, s 4). Where an extension of time is sought this must be applied for specifically in the claim form.

Procedure on application—The claim is issued in the case of High Court proceedings either in London (in Chancery Chambers at the Royal Courts of Justice, Strand, London WC2A 2LL or the Principal Registry of the Family Division) or in any district registry of the High Court. In the case of county court proceedings, the office of the county court in question. The claimant must file any written statement or an affidavit in support of the claim when he files the claim form and serve a copy on the defendant with the claim form. It should be intituled "In the matter of [the estate in which the claim arises] and in the matter of the Inheritance (Provision for Family and Dependants) Act 1975". It must set out concisely the relief or remedy which is claimed in the proceedings. The CPR 1998 apply to service. For service outside the jurisdiction and the court's discretion to grant retrospective permission for service and the application of the overriding objectives, see *Nesheim v Kosa* [2006] EWHC 2710 (Ch).

"claim under section 1" (r 57.16(1))—This is an application for financial provision from a deceased's estate. The relief claimed will generally be that available under ss 2, 5, 10–13, 16 and 17 of the Act.

Subsequent application—Where an order has been made under s 1 of the Act any subsequent applications, eg, under ss 6 and 7 of the Act for variation, discharge or suspension of an order under s 2(1) for periodical payments and a lump sum by instalment, whether by a party to the proceedings or by any other person, should be made by issuing on notice an "application notice" form in accordance with Pt 23, supported by a witness statement/affidavit. It is submitted that since the application is akin to an application for a variation of an order in matrimonial proceedings the procedure laid down under FPR 2010, Pt 8 should be followed.

Claimants—See PD57, para 17. Where it is discovered that there may be conflicting interests between two or more claimants, eg between mother and a child, the court, on an application for directions, may direct that the claimants be separately represented or that some of the claimants be made defendants, direct that separate applications be issued and then make an order consolidating all the applications.

Witness statement/affidavit in support—This rule and r 8.5 refer to written evidence being filed without referring to the form in which that evidence should be given. It is suggested that the evidence should either take the form of a written statement with the appropriate declaration or an affidavit. This rule does not prescribe the contents of the applicant's witness statement/affidavit but clearly the statement/affidavit must set out facts which establish the right to apply and exhibit to it an official copy of the grant of probate or letters of administration in respect of the deceased's estate and any other testamentary document in respect of which probate or letters of administration was granted. In the case of a spouse the marriage certificate should be exhibited or where a certificate is not available (eg in the case of a customary or religious ceremony) the facts to establish that a ceremony of marriage was performed (see *MA v JA* [2012] EWHC 2219 (Fam)); where there has been a divorce, or a decree of nullity or judicial separation a certified copy of the decree should be exhibited. A certified copy of the death certificate should always be exhibited. The applicant should also set out the basis upon which the claim is made. Where a transfer of proceedings is sought between county courts, within the High Court or between the High Court and a county court, it is important to set out particulars of any known proceedings relevant to the application and any other matter referred to in CPR 1998, r 30.3. Such proceedings will often be material to the question whether the application ought to be transferred from the Family Division to the Chancery Division or vice versa. Where the application seeks an order for the avoidance of a disposition, the witness statement/affidavit must show that the conditions set out in ss 10 and 11 are satisfied. In a case where the application seeks the variation of a maintenance agreement, the provisions of FPR 2010, rr 8.6–8.11 should be used as a guide.

Defendants—The personal representatives and the beneficiaries under the will or on intestacy are the defendants to an application under I(PFD)A 1975. Where the defendant is a child or under disability, the usual procedure for the appointment of a litigation friend should be followed. CPR 1998, Sch 1, RSC Ord 99, r 4 provided that the court could direct any person to be added to the proceedings or that notice of the proceedings be served on any person. It also provided that CPR, r 19.7 should apply to proceedings under the Act. CPR, Pt 57 is silent on this issue. However it is submitted that CPR, r 19.7 continues to apply because that rule provides that it applies to "claims about the estate of a deceased person". Thus, where there are possible claimants under the deceased's will or intestacy who cannot be ascertained or found, or it appears to the court expedient for the purpose of saving costs, the Official Solicitor can be appointed under this rule to represent the missing beneficiaries or possible claimants. Where the proceedings raise issues of disputed facts, it is not appropriate to order a third party, such as the Official Solicitor, to represent the missing defendant/s (*Cotton v Official Solicitor* [1989] 6 CL 385). This rule is not however confined to cases of missing claimants or defendants. The court may use its power to join a person, for example a person lacking capacity who may have a possible claim against the estate. In such an instance the person may be joined by his litigation friend and the usual procedure for the appointment of a litigation friend should be followed. If there is a possibility of conflict arising and it is difficult to appoint a suitable person to act for the person lacking capacity it may be more appropriate to invite the Official Solicitor to act.

Acknowledgement of service by personal representative—See PD57, para 15. Where the personal representatives wish to remain neutral, Section A of the acknowledgement of service should be completed with a statement to that effect and agreeing to abide by any decision of the court.

Personal representative's statement/affidavit—For contents of the statement/affidavit see PD57, para 16. It is mandatory for the personal representative to file a statement/affidavit in answer within 21 days of service (including the day of service). The information required to be particularised in the statement/affidavit is that contained in r 5(2). With reference to r 5(2)(d), the facts which might be relevant to the exercise of the court's powers depend on the circumstances of each case. I(PFD)A 1975, s 3(1)(g) requires the court to have regard to "any other matter … which in the circumstances of the case the court may consider relevant". This provision is wide enough to include, for example, the deceased's reasons for making or not making any provision in his will for the applicant. The deceased's reasons may have been given orally, in writing or otherwise, and may be very relevant. For cases where the deceased's reasons were found to be relevant, see the commentary under I(PFD)A 1975, s 3. The personal representatives must produce the original grant of representation on the hearing of the claim, because if an order is made the court is required to send the original grant together with the order made to the Principal Registry for a memorandum of the order to be endorsed on or permanently annexed to the grant.

Practice Direction 57 – Probate

This Practice Direction supplements CPR Part 57

****

IV CLAIMS UNDER THE INHERITANCE (PROVISION FOR FAMILY AND DEPENDANTS) ACT 1975

Acknowledgment of service by personal representative – Rule 57.16(4)

15 Where a defendant who is a personal representative wishes to remain neutral in relation to the claim, and agrees to abide by any decision which the court may make, he should state this in Section A of the acknowledgment of service form.

Written evidence of personal representative – Rule 57.16(5)

16 The written evidence filed by a defendant who is a personal representative must state to the best of that person's ability –

    (1)   full details of the value of the deceased's net estate, as defined in section 25(1) of the Act;

    (2)   the person or classes of persons beneficially interested in the estate, and –

        (a)   the names and (unless they are parties to the claim) addresses of all living beneficiaries; and

        (b)   the value of their interests in the estate so far as they are known.

    (3)   whether any living beneficiary (and if so, naming him) is a child or a person who lacks capacity (within the meaning of the Mental Capacity Act 2005); and

    (4)   any facts which might affect the exercise of the court's powers under the Act.

Separate representation of claimants

17 If a claim is made jointly by two or more claimants, and it later appears that any of the claimants have a conflict of interests –

    (1)   any claimant may choose to be represented at any hearing by separate solicitors or counsel, or may appear in person; and

    (2)   if the court considers that claimants who are represented by the same solicitors or counsel ought to be separately represented, it may adjourn the application until they are.

Production of the grant

18.1 On the hearing of a claim the personal representative must produce to the court the original grant of representation to the deceased's estate.

18.2 If the court makes an order under the Act, the original grant (together with a sealed copy of the order) must be sent to the Principal Registry of the Family Division for a memorandum of the order to be endorsed on or permanently annexed to the grant in accordance with section 19(3) of the Act.

****

PART 65

PROCEEDINGS RELATING TO ANTI-SOCIAL BEHAVIOUR AND
HARASSMENT

CONTENTS OF THIS PART

Section V
Proceedings under the Protection from Harassment Act 1997

Practice Direction—*PD (Anti-Social Behaviour and Harassment)*, which supplements this Part generally, is set out in *Civil Court Service* (Jordan Publishing Ltd).

****

Section V
Proceedings under the Protection from Harassment Act 1997

65.27 Scope of this Section

This Section applies to proceedings under section 3 of the Protection from Harassment Act 1997 ("the 1997 Act").

Amendments—Inserted by SI 2004/1306.

65.28 Claims under section 3 of the 1997 Act

A claim under section 3 of the 1997 Act –

    (a)   shall be subject to the Part 8 procedure; and

    (b)   must be commenced –

        (i)   if in the High Court, in the Queen's Bench Division;

        (ii)   if in the county court, in the court for the district in which the defendant resides or carries on business or the court for the district in which the claimant resides or carries on business.

Amendments—Inserted by SI 2004/1306.

65.29 Applications for issue of a warrant of arrest under section 3(3) of the 1997 Act

(1) An application for a warrant of arrest under section 3(3) of the 1997 Act –

    (a)   must be made in accordance with Part 23; and

    (b)   may be made without notice.

(2) The application notice must be supported by affidavit evidence which must –

    (a)   set out the grounds for the application;

    (b)   state whether the claimant has informed the police of the conduct of the defendant as described in the affidavit; and

    (c) state whether, to the claimant's knowledge, criminal proceedings are being pursued.

Amendments—Inserted by SI 2004/1306.

65.30 Proceedings following arrest

(1) The judge before whom a person is brought following his arrest may –

    (a) deal with the matter; or

    (b) adjourn the proceedings.

(2) Where the proceedings are adjourned and the arrested person is released –

    (a) the matter must be dealt with (whether by the same or another judge) within 28 days of the date on which the arrested person appears in court; and

    (b) the arrested person must be given not less than 2 days' notice of the hearing.

Amendments—Inserted by SI 2004/1306.

****

PART 69
COURT'S POWER TO APPOINT A RECEIVER

****

Note—Pt 69 of the CPR finally replaces CCR Ord 32 and RSC 51 in relation to family proceedings. The appointment of a receiver is a remedy that is occasionally useful (it may enable a judgment creditor to reach interests of the debtor that cannot be taken in execution by other means) but the expense means that it is seldom appropriate. See *Civil Court Service* (Jordan Publishing Ltd).

PART 70
GENERAL RULES ABOUT ENFORCEMENT OF JUDGMENTS AND ORDERS

CONTENTS OF THIS PART

General note—This Part is reproduced as modified for family proceedings by FPR 2010, r 33.2.

70.1 Scope of this Part and interpretation

(1) This Part contains general rules about enforcement of judgments and orders.

    (Rules about specific methods of enforcement are contained in Parts 71 to 73, Schedule 1 RSC Orders 45 to 47 and 52 and Schedule 2 CCR Orders 25 to 29)

(2) In this Part and in Parts 71 to 73 –

    (a) 'judgment creditor' means a person who has obtained or is entitled to enforce a judgment or order;

    (b) 'judgment debtor' means a person against whom a judgment or order was given or made;

(c)   'judgment or order' includes an award which the court has –
  (i)   registered for enforcement;
  (ii)   ordered to be enforced; or
  (iii) given permission to enforce
  as if it were a judgment or order of the court, and in relation to such an award, 'the court which made the judgment or order' means the court which registered the award or made such an order; and

(d)   'judgment or order for the payment of money' includes a judgment or order for the payment of costs.

Amendments—Inserted by SI 2001/2792; amended by SI 2002/2058.

70.2 Methods of enforcing judgments or orders

(1) Practice Direction 70 sets out methods of enforcing judgments or orders for the payment of money.

(2) A judgment creditor may, except where an enactment, rule or practice direction provides otherwise –

  (a)   use any method of enforcement which is available; and
  (b)   use more than one method of enforcement, either at the same time or one after another.

Amendments—Inserted by SI 2001/2792; amended by SI 2009/3390.

"at the same time" (r 70.2(2)(b))—Although concurrent enforcement by different methods is normally permitted, judgment creditors are obliged by PD70, paras 7.1 and 7.2 to notify in writing either the court or the enforcement officer in the case of a High Court writ of execution, if any payment is made by the judgment debtor in the period between issue and hearing or execution.

70.3 Transfer of proceedings for enforcement

(1) A judgment creditor wishing to enforce a High Court judgment or order in a county court must apply to the High Court for an order transferring the proceedings to that county court.

(2) A practice direction may make provisions about the transfer of proceedings for enforcement.

  (CCR Order 25 rule 13 contains provisions about the transfer of county court proceedings to the High Court for enforcement)

Amendments—Inserted by SI 2001/2792.

70.4 Enforcement of judgment or order by or against non-party

If a judgment or order is given or made in favour of or against a person who is not a party to proceedings, it may be enforced by or against that person by the same methods as if he were a party.

Amendments—Inserted by SI 2001/2792.

****

70.6 Effect of setting aside judgment or order

If a judgment or order is set aside, any enforcement of the judgment or order shall cease to have effect unless the court otherwise orders.

Amendments—Inserted by SI 2001/2792.

"unless the court otherwise orders"—This provision enables the court to preserve the security and priority of a charging order obtained by the judgment creditor as a condition of setting aside a judgment.

Practice Direction 70 – Enforcement of Judgments and Orders

This Practice Direction supplements CPR Part 70

Methods of Enforcing Money Judgments – Rule 70.2

1.1 A judgment creditor may enforce a judgment or order for the payment of money by any of the following methods:

    (1)   a writ of fieri facias or warrant of execution (see RSC Orders 46 and 47 and CCR Order 26);

    (2)   a third party debt order (see Part 72);

    (3)   a charging order, stop order or stop notice (see Part 73);

    (4)   in a county court, an attachment of earnings order (see CCR Order 27);

    (5)   the appointment of a receiver (see Part 69);

1.2 In addition the court may make the following orders against a judgment debtor –

    (1)   an order of committal, but only if permitted by –

        (a) a rule; and

        (b) the Debtors Acts 1869 and 1878

        (See Part 81 – Applications and proceedings in relation to contempt of court, in particular Sections 2 and 8 and the Practice Direction supplementing Part 81, and CCR Order 28); and

    (2)   in the High Court, a writ of sequestration, but only if permitted by rule 81.20.

"permitted by a rule" (para 1.2(1)(a))—Family proceedings are one of the few situations in which the judgment summons procedure, memorably described by Hedley J as "a peculiarity of the London County Courts that is not used anywhere else in the world as far as I know" (see *Corbett v Corbett* [2003] 2 FLR 385) remains available. The procedure is governed by CPR 1998, Sch 2, CCR Ord 28.

"See Part 81 – Applications and proceedings in relation to contempt of court" (para 1.2)—Note that in relation to family proceedings, RSC Ord 52 and CCR Ord 29 continue to apply as they were on 30 September 2012.

1.3 The enforcement of a judgment or order may be affected by –

    (1)   the enactments relating to insolvency; and

    (2)   county court administration orders.

Transfer of County Court Proceedings to another Court for Enforcement – Rule 70.3

2.1 If a judgment creditor is required by a rule or practice direction to enforce a judgment or order of one county court in a different county court, he must first make a request in writing to the court in which the case is proceeding to transfer the proceedings to that other court.

2.2 On receipt of such a request, a court officer will transfer the proceedings to the other court unless a judge orders otherwise.

2.3 The court will give notice of the transfer to all the parties.

2.4 When the proceedings have been transferred, the parties must take any further steps in the proceedings in the court to which they have been transferred, unless a rule or practice direction provides otherwise.

> (Part 52 and Practice Directions 52A and 52B provide to which court or judge an appeal against the judgment or order, or an application for permission to appeal, must be made)

Enforcement of High Court Judgment or Order in a County Court – Rule 70.3

3.1 If a judgment creditor wishes to enforce a High Court judgment or order in a county court, he must file the following documents in the county court with his application notice or request for enforcement –

(1)   a copy of the judgment or order;

(2)   a certificate verifying the amount due under the judgment or order;

(3)   if a writ of execution has previously been issued in the High Court to enforce the judgment or order, a copy of the relevant enforcement officer's return to the writ; and

(4)   a copy of the order transferring the proceedings to the county court.

3.2 In this paragraph and paragraph 7 –

(1)   'enforcement officer' means an individual who is authorised to act as an enforcement officer under the Courts Act 2003; and

(2)   'relevant enforcement officer' means –

(a)   in relation to a writ of execution which is directed to a single enforcement officer, that officer;

(b)   in relation to a writ of execution which is directed to two or more enforcement officers, the officer to whom the writ is allocated.

****

Registration of decisions in the High Court for enforcement – rule 70.5(8)

5.1 An application to the High Court under an enactment to register a decision for enforcement must be made in writing to the head clerk of the Action Department at the Royal Courts of Justice, Strand, London WC2A 2LL.

5.2 The application must –

(1)   specify the statutory provision under which the application is made;

(2)   state the name and address of the person against whom it is sought to enforce the decision;

(3)   if the decision requires that person to pay a sum of money, state the amount which remains unpaid.

Interest on Judgment Debts

6 If a judgment creditor is claiming interest on a judgment debt, he must include in his application or request to issue enforcement proceedings in relation to that judgment details of –

(1)   the amount of interest claimed and the sum on which it is claimed;

(2)   the dates from and to which interest has accrued; and

(3)   the rate of interest which has been applied and, where more than one rate of interest has been applied, the relevant dates and rates.

PART III

(Interest may be claimed on High Court judgment debts under section 17 of the Judgments Act 1838. The County Courts (Interest on Judgment Debts) Order 1991 specifies when interest may be claimed on county court judgment debts)

"Interest may be claimed"—In the county court, interest may be claimed on relevant "judgments", see County Courts (Interest on Judgment Debts) Order 1991. The terms of the order are not without difficulty but broadly interest runs at the rate prescribed for the High Court from the date when payment is due under a judgment or order for at least £5000. The judgment rate is currently 8% per annum (Judgment Debts (Rate of Interest) Order 1993). If a lump sum financial provision order is made for less than £5000, any interest ordered to be paid under MCA 1973, s 23(6) will not bring the judgment debt under this rule even though the total due may exceed £5000. Interest will remain payable where a payment on account reduces the balance to less than £5000. Interest ceases to accrue as soon as any enforcement step is taken, including an application for oral examination but excluding an application for a charging order, if the step produces any payment at all from the debtor. No more than 6 years' interest may be recovered (*Lowsley and another v Forbes* [1998] 1 AC 329, HL).

Enforcing a judgment or order against a partnership

6A.1 A judgment or order made against a partnership may be enforced against any property of the partnership within the jurisdiction.

6A.2 Subject to paragraph 6A.3, a judgment or order made against a partnership may be enforced against any person who is not a limited partner and who –

(1)   acknowledged service of the claim form as a partner;

(2)   having been served as a partner with the claim form, failed to acknowledge service of it;

(3)   admitted in his statement of case that he is or was a partner at a material time; or

(4)   was found by the court to have been a partner at a material time.

6A.3 A judgment or order made against a partnership may not be enforced against a limited partner or a member of the partnership who was ordinarily resident outside the jurisdiction when the claim form was issued unless that partner or member –

(1)   acknowledged service of the claim form as a partner;

(2)   was served within the jurisdiction with the claim form as a partner; or

(3)   was served out of the jurisdiction with the claim form, as a partner, with the permission of the court given under Section IV of Part 6.

6A.4 A judgment creditor wishing to enforce a judgment or order against a person in circumstances not set out in paragraphs 6A.2 or 6A.3 must apply to the court for permission to enforce the judgment or order.

Payment of Debt after Issue of Enforcement Proceedings

7.1 If a judgment debt or part of it is paid –

(1)   after the judgment creditor has issued any application or request to enforce it; but

(2)   before –
    (a)   any writ or warrant has been executed; or
    (b)   in any other case, the date fixed for the hearing of the application;
    the judgment creditor must, unless paragraph 7.2 applies, immediately notify the court in writing.

7.2 If a judgment debt or part of it is paid after the judgment creditor has applied to the High Court for a writ of execution, paragraph 7.1 does not apply, and the judgment creditor must instead immediately notify the relevant enforcement officer in writing.

PART 71
ORDERS TO OBTAIN INFORMATION FROM JUDGMENT DEBTORS

CONTENTS OF THIS PART

PART III

71.1 Scope of this Part

This Part contains rules which provide for a judgment debtor to be required to attend court to provide information, for the purpose of enabling a judgment creditor to enforce a judgment or order against him.

Amendments—Inserted by SI 2001/2792.

Procedural guide—See Procedural Guide C12.

71.2 Order to attend court

(1) A judgment creditor may apply for an order requiring –

    (a)   a judgment debtor; or

    (b)   if a judgment debtor is a company or other corporation, an officer of that body;

to attend court to provide information about –

        (i)   the judgment debtor's means; or

        (ii)   any other matter about which information is needed to enforce a judgment or order.

(2) An application under paragraph (1) –

    (a)   may be made without notice; and

    (b)   must be issued in the court which made the judgment or order which it is sought to enforce, except that –

        (i)   if the proceedings have since been transferred to a different court, it must be issued in that court; or

        (ii)   subject to subparagraph (b)(i), if it is to enforce a judgment made in Northampton County Court in respect of a designated money claim, it must be issued in accordance with section 2 of Practice Direction 70.

(3) The application notice must –

    (a)   be in the form; and

    (b)   contain the information

required by Practice Direction 71.

(4) An application under paragraph (1) may be dealt with by a court officer without a hearing.

(5) If the application notice complies with paragraph (3), an order to attend court will be issued in the terms of paragraph (6).

(6) A person served with an order issued under this rule must –

(a) attend court at the time and place specified in the order;

(b) when he does so, produce at court documents in his control which are described in the order; and

(c) answer on oath such questions as the court may require.

(7) An order under this rule will contain a notice in the following terms, or in terms to substantially the same effect –

"If you the within-named [ ] do not comply with this order you may be held to be in contempt of court and imprisoned or fined, or your assets may be seized."

Amendments—Inserted by SI 2001/2792; amended by SI 2009/3390; SI 2012/505; SI 2012/2208.

Practice Direction—See PD71, para 1.2 (r 71.2(3)).

"to provide information" (r 71.2(1))—The purpose of the rule is to enable the judgment creditor to obtain information as to the best means of satisfying his judgment debt. The judgment debtor is under a duty to make full and frank disclosure of his means.

"will be issued" (r 71.2(5))—The judgment creditor will be entitled to an order as of right if any part of a judgment debt remains outstanding. Paragraph (4) merely permits the order to be issued by a court officer rather than a judge but does not confer any discretion on the court.

"answer on oath such questions" (r 71.2(6)(c))—The judgment creditor may cross-examine the debtor vigorously as to his assets (*Republic of Costa Rica v Strousberg* (1880) 16 Ch D 8), including those overseas (*Interpool Ltd v Galani* [1988] QB 738) and as to any means by which the judgment debt may be satisfied, but not for some other purpose (*Watkins v Ross* (1893) 68 LT 423).

The fact that the judgment debtor has obtained a stay of execution does not prevent a judgment creditor from proceeding under this rule, *Sucden Financial v Fluxo-Cane Overseas Ltd* [2009] EWHC 3555.

71.3 Service of order

(1) An order to attend court must, unless the court otherwise orders, be served personally on the person ordered to attend court not less than 14 days before the hearing.

(2) If the order is to be served by the judgment creditor, he must inform the court not less than 7 days before the date of the hearing if he has been unable to serve it.

Amendments—Inserted by SI 2001/2792.

71.4 Travelling expenses

(1) A person ordered to attend court may, within 7 days of being served with the order, ask the judgment creditor to pay him a sum reasonably sufficient to cover his travelling expenses to and from court.

(2) The judgment creditor must pay such a sum if requested.

Amendments—Inserted by SI 2001/2792.

71.5 Judgment creditor's affidavit

(1) The judgment creditor must file an affidavit$^{(GL)}$ or affidavits –

(a) by the person who served the order (unless it was served by the court) giving details of how and when it was served;

(b) stating either that –

(i) the person ordered to attend court has not requested payment of his travelling expenses; or

(ii)   the judgment creditor has paid a sum in accordance with such a request; and

(c)   stating how much of the judgment debt remains unpaid.

(2) The judgment creditor must either –

(a)   file the affidavit$^{(GL)}$ or affidavits not less than 2 days before the hearing; or

(b)   produce it or them at the hearing.

Amendments—Inserted by SI 2001/2792.

"unless it was served by the court" (r 71.5(1)(a))—In which case service will be proved by a certificate under CCA 1984, s 133. Such certificate is not conclusive but merely evidence of service (*Maher v Gower (formerly Kubilius)* (1982) 3 FLR 287).

71.6 Conduct of the hearing

(1) The person ordered to attend court will be questioned on oath.

(2) The questioning will be carried out by a court officer unless the court has ordered that the hearing shall be before a judge.

(3) The judgment creditor or his representative –

(a)   may attend and ask questions where the questioning takes place before a court officer; and

(b)   must attend and conduct the questioning if the hearing is before a judge.

Amendments—Inserted by SI 2001/2792.

"hearing is before a judge" (r 71.6(3)(b))—The hearing will only take place before a judge if there are compelling reasons to make such an order (PD71, para 2.2).

71.7 Adjournment of the hearing

If the hearing is adjourned, the court will give directions as to the manner in which notice of the new hearing is to be served on the judgment debtor.

Amendments—Inserted by SI 2001/2792.

"notice of service of adjourned hearing"—Where the judgment debtor is present and can be given personal notice then and there of the date and time of the new hearing, the court will normally dispense with personal service of notice of the new hearing in accordance with r 1.1(2)(c).

71.8 Failure to comply with order

(1) If a person against whom an order has been made under rule 71.2 –

(a)   fails to attend court;

(b)   refuses at the hearing to take the oath or to answer any question; or

(c)   otherwise fails to comply with the order;

the court will refer the matter to a High Court judge or circuit judge.

(2) That judge may, subject to paragraphs (3) and (4), make a committal order against the person.

(3) A committal order for failing to attend court may not be made unless the judgment creditor has complied with rules 71.4 and 71.5.

(4) If a committal order is made, the judge will direct that –

(a)   the order shall be suspended provided that the person –

(i)   attends court at a time and place specified in the order; and

(ii)   complies with all the terms of that order and the original order; and

(b) if the person fails to comply with any term on which the committal order is suspended, he shall be brought before a judge to consider whether the committal order should be discharged.

(Part 81 contains provisions in relation to committal.)

Amendments—Inserted by SI 2001/2792; amended by SI 2001/4015; SI 2012/2208.

"High Court or circuit judge" (r 71.8(1))—Although suspended committal orders can only be made by judges at this level, the hearing at which the decision is made as to whether the committal order should be discharged may take place before a master or district judge (PD71, para 8.4).

"may ... make a committal order" (r 71.8(2))—The Court of Appeal in *Broomleigh Housing Association Ltd v Okonkwo* [2010] EWCA Civ 1113 was critical of the routine use of suspended committal orders under r 71.8 whenever a judgment debtor had failed to comply with an order to attend court to be questioned about his or her means under CPR, r 71.2. It appeared that a suspended order of committal was being used as little more than a vehicle for fixing a date for an effective adjourned hearing. An order for committal was, it was said, too serious a matter to be used in that way and the Court of Appeal gave guidance to judges on how to exercise their discretion when considering whether to make such an order.

"shall be suspended" (r 71.8(4)(a))—See PD71, para 7.1 for the detailed provisions as to the suspended order.

"he shall be brought before a judge" (r 71.8(4)(b))—The procedure for dealing with a judgment debtor who fails to comply with a suspended committal order raises serious issues under HRA 1998, Sch 1, Pt I, Art 6. See PD71, para 8 and the notes thereto for details of the problems that may arise. On the arrest of the judgment debtor, the judgment creditor is likely to have to be prepared to attend court at very short notice to conduct the hearing to decide whether the committal order should be discharged or the hearing will have to be adjourned. It will be for the judgment creditor to prove to the criminal standard that the judgment debtor has been served both with the original order to attend court and the suspended committal order, and that he has failed to comply with the terms of the suspended committal order (PD71, para 8.5).

Practice Direction 71 – Orders to Obtain Information from Judgment Debtors

This Practice Direction supplements CPR Part 71

Application Notice – Rule 71.2

1.1 An application by a judgment creditor under rule 71.2(1) must be made by filing an application notice in Practice Form N316 if the application is to question an individual judgment debtor, or N316A if the application is to question an officer of a company or other corporation.

1.2 The application notice must –

(1) state the name and address of the judgment debtor;
(2) identify the judgment or order which the judgment creditor is seeking to enforce;
(3) if the application is to enforce a judgment or order for the payment of money, state the amount presently owed by the judgment debtor under the judgment or order;
(4) if the judgment debtor is a company or other corporation, state –
    (a) the name and address of the officer of that body whom the judgment creditor wishes to be ordered to attend court; and
    (b) his position in the company;

(5)   if the judgment creditor wishes the questioning to be conducted before a judge, state this and give his reasons;

(6)   if the judgment creditor wishes the judgment debtor (or other person to be questioned) to be ordered to produce specific documents at court, identify those documents; and

(7)   if the application is to enforce a judgment or order which is not for the payment of money, identify the matters about which the judgment creditor wishes the judgment debtor (or officer of the judgment debtor) to be questioned.

1.3   The court officer considering the application notice –

(1)   may, in any appropriate case, refer it to a judge (rule 3.2); and

(2)   will refer it to a judge for consideration, if the judgment creditor requests the judgment debtor (or officer of the judgment debtor) to be questioned before a judge.

"amount presently owed" (para 1.2(3))—If part of the judgment debt has been paid, the judgment creditor should state the date and amount of the last payment that has been taken into account in arriving at the balance due.

"before a judge" (para 1.2(5))—Note that if the questioning is to take place before a judge, the judgment creditor or his representative must attend the hearing to conduct the questioning (para 5.1).

"give his reasons" (para 1.2(5))—The judgment creditor must show compelling reasons for a hearing before a judge (see para 2.2, below).

Order to Attend Court – Rule 71.2

2.1   The order will provide for the judgment debtor (or other person to be questioned) to attend the county court for the district in which he resides or carries on business, unless a judge decides otherwise.

2.2   The order will provide for questioning to take place before a judge only if the judge considering the request decides that there are compelling reasons to make such an order.

Service of Order to Attend Court – Rule 71.3

3   Service of an order to attend court for questioning may be carried out by –

(a)   the judgment creditor (or someone acting on the judgment creditor's behalf);

(b)   a High Court enforcement officer; or

(c)   a county court bailiff.

"service of an order"—The judgment creditor has four options to effect personal service: (a) he can serve the order himself; (b) he can employ a process server; (c) he can employ a High Court enforcement officer; or (d) he may request a county court bailiff to serve, paying the appropriate fee (£105). If personal service cannot be effected he may then apply for permission to serve by another method under rr 6.15 and 6.27.

Attendance at Court: Normal Procedure – Rule 71.6

4.1   The court officer will ask a standard series of questions, as set out in the forms in Appendixes A and B to this practice direction. The form in Appendix A will be used if the person being questioned is the judgment debtor, and the form in Appendix B will be used if the person is an officer of a company or other corporation.

4.2   The judgment creditor or his representative may either –

(1)   attend court and ask questions himself; or

(2)   request the court officer to ask additional questions, by attaching a list of proposed additional questions to his application notice.

PART III

4.3 The court officer will –

(1) make a written record of the evidence given, unless the proceedings are tape recorded;

(2) at the end of the questioning, read the record of evidence to the person being questioned and ask him to sign it; and

(3) if the person refuses to sign it, note that refusal on the record of evidence.

"list of proposed additional questions" (para 4.2(2))—The list should allow sufficient space for the answer to each question to be recorded immediately after the question.

"make a written record" (para 4.3(1))—Although both Pt 71 and the PD are silent, the court will send a copy of the record to the judgment creditor.

"unless the proceedings are tape recorded" (para 4.3(1))—Presumably tape-recording is envisaged when the judgment creditor is present or represented and elects to make his own written note of the evidence. Subpara (2) cannot apply when the proceedings have been recorded. It is difficult to see what benefit a recording will be to the judgment creditor until the court is in a position to e-mail the digital recording to the judgment creditor as a file, except as a record in case of subsequent dispute about what was said.

"refuses to sign" (para 4.3(3))—The debtor signs to confirm that his replies have been accurately recorded. There is no sanction for a refusal to sign.

Attendance at Court: Procedure Where the Order is to Attend Before a Judge – Rule 71.6

5.1 Where the hearing takes places before a judge, the questioning will be conducted by the judgment creditor or his representative, and the standard questions in the forms in Appendixes A and B will not be used.

5.2 The proceedings will be tape recorded and the court will not make a written record of the evidence.

"will not be used" (para 5.1)—Some questions in the standard forms may still be relevant and can be asked.

"will be tape recorded" (para 5.2)—The judgment creditor must take a note of the answers given or request a transcript at his (considerable) expense.

Failure to Comply with Order: Reference to Judge – Rule 71.8(1)

6 If a judge or court officer refers to a High Court judge or circuit judge the failure of a judgment debtor to comply with an order under rule 71.2, he shall certify in writing the respect in which the judgment debtor failed to comply with the order.

"certify in writing"—Surprisingly, the PD makes no provision for a copy of the certificate to be sent to either the judgment creditor or judgment debtor. The failure to provide for the judgment debtor to receive a copy of the certificate at any stage of the proceedings may give rise to challenge to this procedure under HRA 1998, Sch 1, Pt I, Art 6 (*Newman (t/a Mantella Publishing) v Modern Bookbinders Ltd* [2000] 1 WLR 2559). The usual form of suspended committal order (Form N79A) does, however, recite the breach found by the judge in reliance on the certificate and will be served on the debtor.

Suspended Committal Order – Rule 71.8(2) and (4)(a)

7.1 A committal order will be suspended provided that the person attends court at a time and place specified in the order (rule 71.8(4)(a)(i)). The appointment specified will be –

(1) before a judge, if –
    (a) the original order under rule 71.2 was to attend before a judge; or
    (b) the judge making the suspended committal order so directs; and

(2) otherwise, before a court officer.

7.2 Rule 71.3 and paragraph 3 of this practice direction (service of order), and rule 71.5(1)(a) and (2) (affidavit of service), apply with the necessary changes to a suspended committal order as they do to an order to attend court.

"service of order" (para 7.2)—Judgment creditors may wish to serve a copy of the certificate under para 6 with the suspended committal order to reduce the risk of the particular HRA challenge mentioned in the note to para 6, above.

Breach of Terms on which Committal Order is Suspended – Rule 71.8(4)(b)

8.1 If –

    (1)   the judgment debtor fails to attend court at the time and place specified in the suspended committal order; and

    (2)   it appears to the judge or court officer that the judgment debtor has been duly served with the order,

the judge or court officer will certify in writing the debtor's failure to attend.

8.2 If the judgment debtor fails to comply with any other term on which the committal order was suspended, the judge or court officer will certify in writing the non-compliance and set out details of it.

8.3 A warrant to bring the judgment debtor before a judge may be issued on the basis of a certificate under paragraph 8.1 or 8.2.

8.4 The hearing under rule 71.8(4)(b) may take place before a master or district judge.

8.5 At the hearing the judge will discharge the committal order unless he is satisfied beyond reasonable doubt that –

    (1)   the judgment debtor has failed to comply with –

        (a)   the original order to attend court; and

        (b)   the terms on which the committal order was suspended; and

    (2)   both orders have been duly served on the judgment debtor.

8.6 If the judge decides that the committal order should not be discharged, a warrant of committal shall be issued immediately.

"certify in writing" (para 8.2)—See **"certify in writing"** under para 6.

"certificate" (para 8.3)—See **"certify in writing"** under para 6.

"A warrant" (para 8.3)—In a county court, the warrant (Form N40A) authorises the court bailiff to arrest the judgment debtor (and, to be effective, impliedly in so doing to use such force as is necessary) and bring him before a judge.

"At the hearing" (para 8.5)—On its face, this provision bristles with potential HRA pitfalls. First, there is no specific requirement that the judgment debtor must have received a copy of the certificates under paras 6 and 8.1 or para 8.2. This was held to be a mandatory requirement in *Newman v Modern Bookbinders* (see **"certify in writing"** under para 6). Second, the judgment debtor is likely to be unrepresented. Since he is alleged to be in breach of a suspended committal order he may be sent to prison (*Hammerton v Hammerton* [2007] 2 FLR 1133). He must, therefore, be offered an adjournment and the opportunity to apply for legal aid or to take legal advice. Third, if the judgment debtor wishes to challenge the evidence of service or the contents of either certificate he must be given an opportunity for cross-examination of witnesses. Fourth, even if the judgment debtor is found to be in contempt of court he must be given a chance to address the court in mitigation before sentence is passed (*Goldsmith v Goldsmith* [2006] EWCA Civ 1670). In practice, however, if the judgment debtor submits to the original order for questioning, the committal order will be discharged.

"shall be issued immediately" (para 8.6)—Again, if read literally with para 8.5, there are serious HRA problems with this provision. First, the original committal order will have specified a term of imprisonment that appeared appropriate to the contempt on the information available to the judge at the time. There appears to be no power to vary the term (in clear breach of HRA 1998, Sch 1, Art 6) to take account of proper mitigation advanced by the judgment debtor. Even more serious breaches of Art 6 may arise if the original committal was for non-attendance and the judgment debtor subsequently attends and commits a breach of a different term of the original order, e g by neglecting to produce a document. The sentence that was passed for failure to attend could, at least in theory, then be put into effect as a result of a less serious breach.

The court will in practice do everything possible to obtain the information required without sending the judgment debtor to prison. Thus, a judge before whom a judgment debtor is brought may use the general powers contained in r 3.1(2) and (3) to adjourn the hearing for a short time to allow the judgment debtor a final opportunity to purge his apparent contempt. Paragraph 8.5 should not be interpreted as limiting the judge's power to discharge the order to the matters specified in that paragraph and if the judgment debtor complies the committal order will be discharged. If a full hearing has to take place, the judge will first consider the matters set out in **"At the hearing"** above, if necessary adjourning the hearing on terms as to the judgment debtor's attendance. The judge will further make sure that the judgment debtor is aware of the adjourned hearing before leaving the court building, so that service of the notice of the adjourned hearing can be dispensed with, and warn him that if he fails to attend the court will proceed in his absence. Ultimately, the court retains a discretion whether or not to activate the terms of a suspended committal order (*Re W (B)* [1969] 1 All ER 594).

Appendices—Appendices A and B to this PD contain Records of Examination EX140 and EX141. These can be accessed on the *Civil Court Service* CD-ROM (Jordan Publishing Ltd).

****

PART 72
THIRD PARTY DEBT ORDERS

CONTENTS OF THIS PART

General note—This Part is reproduced as modified for family proceedings by FPR 2010, r 33.24.

Procedural Guide—See Procedural Guide C9.

72.1 Scope of this Part and interpretation

(1) This Part contains rules which provide for a judgment creditor to obtain an order for the payment to him of money which a third party who is within the jurisdiction owes to the judgment debtor.

(2) In this Part, 'bank or building society' includes any person carrying on a business in the course of which he lawfully accepts deposits in the United Kingdom.

Amendments—Inserted by SI 2001/2792; amended by SI 2001/4015.

72.2 Third party debt order

(1) Upon the application of a judgment creditor, the court may make an order (a 'final third party debt order') requiring a third party to pay to the judgment creditor –

(a) the amount of any debt due or accruing due to the judgment debtor from the third party; or

(b) so much of that debt as is sufficient to satisfy the judgment debt and the judgment creditor's costs of the application.

(2) The court will not make an order under paragraph 1 without first making an order (an 'interim third party debt order') as provided by rule 72.4(2).

(3) In deciding whether money standing to the credit of the judgment debtor in an account to which section 40 of the Senior Courts Act 1981 or section 108 of the County Courts Act 1984 relates may be made the subject of a third party debt order, any condition applying to the account that a receipt for money deposited in the account must be produced before any money is withdrawn will be disregarded.

> (Section 40(3) of the Senior Courts Act 1981 and section 108(3) of the County Courts Act 1984 contain a list of other conditions applying to accounts that will also be disregarded)

Amendments—Inserted by SI 2001/2792; amended by CRA 2005, Sch 11, para 1(2).

"any debt" (r 72.2(1)(a))—There must be in existence something recognised in law as a debt, notwithstanding that it may be payable on a future date (*O'Driscoll v Manchester Insurance Committee* [1915] 3 KB 499). Thus, a cause of action in damages is not attachable (*Johnson v Diamond* (1855) 11 Exch 73) until judgment is pronounced (*Holtby v Hodgson* (1889) 24 QBD 103). Once an order is made, a subsequent cross-claim by the third party against the judgment debtor does not reduce the third party's liability under the order (*Wolfe v Marshall and Harding (Garnishee)* [1997] EWCA Civ 1329). In the case of a foreign debt, the court has no jurisdiction to make a third party debt order unless compliance with the order will be recognised as discharging the debt owed by the third party to the judgment debtor under the law that governs that debt (*Société Eram Shipping Co Ltd v Compagnie Internationale de Navigation* [2004] 1 AC 260). If necessary, the court will be prepared to pierce the corporate veil to ascertain the real identity of the person to whom the debt is due. However, this rule is not intended to deal with debts other than those actually owed in the name of the judgment debtor (*Continental Transfert Technique Ltd v Federal Government of Nigeria & ors* [2009] EWHC 2898).

"any condition applying to the account" (r 72.2(3))—If a liability is conditional, there may be no debt if the condition is not satisfied. In the case of balances held for the debtor by banks, building societies and the like, this difficulty is removed by SCA 1981, s 40, and CCA 1984, s 108, which provide that requirements for notice, personal application and production of a passbook are to be disregarded.

The Crown—This procedure is not available against the Crown as third party (CPR 1998, r 66.7(1)(a)). An equivalent procedure is provided by Crown Proceedings Act 1947, s 27. This restriction includes the National Savings Bank and, although SCA 1981, s 139(2) enables the Lord Chancellor to make an order removing the restriction, no such order has been made.

72.3 Application for third party debt order

(1) An application for a third party debt order –

(a) may be made without notice; and

(b) must be issued in the court which made the judgment or order which it is sought to enforce, except that –

    (i) if the proceedings have since been transferred to a different court, it must be issued in that court; or

    (ii) subject to subparagraph (b)(i), if it is to enforce a judgment made in Northampton County Court in respect of a designated money claim, it must be issued in accordance with section 2 of Practice Direction 70.

(2) The application notice must –

(a) (i) be in the form; and
    (ii) contain the information
    required by Practice Direction 72; and

(b)   be verified by a statement of truth.

Amendments—Inserted by SI 2001/2792; amended by SI 2009/3390; SI 2012/505.

72.4 Interim third party debt order

(1) An application for a third party debt order will initially be dealt with by the court without a hearing.

(2) The court may make an interim third party debt order –

    (a)   fixing a hearing to consider whether to make a final third party debt order; and

    (b)   directing that until that hearing the third party must not make any payment which reduces the amount he owes the judgment debtor to less than the amount specified in the order.

(3) An interim third party debt order will specify the amount of money which the third party must retain, which will be the total of –

    (a)   the amount of money remaining due to the judgment creditor under the judgment or order; and

    (b)   an amount for the judgment creditor's fixed costs of the application, as specified in Practice Direction 72.

(4) An interim third party debt order becomes binding on a third party when it is served on him.

(5) The date of the hearing to consider the application shall be not less than 28 days after the interim third party debt order is made.

Amendments—Inserted by SI 2001/2792; amended by SI 2009/3390.

Time for making interim order—If the order requires payment by a stated date, then the interim third party debt order will not be made before that date. An interim order is analogous to execution against goods and will not be made where such execution would not issue (*White, Son & Pill v Stennings* [1911] 2 KB 418).

"the judge court may make" (r 72.4(2))—The court has a discretion as to whether to make the interim order and may decline to do so where, for example, the judgment debt is so small that the costs would be disproportionately burdensome.

72.5 Service of interim order

(1) Copies of an interim third party debt order, the application notice and any documents filed in support of it must be served –

    (a)   on the third party, not less than 21 days before the date fixed for the hearing; and

    (b)   on the judgment debtor not less than –

        (i)   7 days after a copy has been served on the third party; and

        (ii) 7 days before the date fixed for the hearing.

(2) If the judgment creditor serves the order, he must either –

    (a)   file a certificate of service not less than 2 days before the hearing; or

    (b)   produce a certificate of service at the hearing.

Amendments—Inserted by SI 2001/2792.

Documents to be served—Note that the rule requires the third party to be served not only with the order, but also with the application notice and any documents filed in support.

"must be served" (r 72.5(1))—The general rules as to service set out in Pt 6 apply. Where the third party is a deposit-taking institution, the best practice will be to effect service at the branch where the judgment debtor's account is believed to be held as being a place of business that has a real connection with the claim under r 6.9, as well as at the head office.

72.6 Obligations of third parties served with interim order

(1) A bank or building society served with an interim third party debt order must carry out a search to identify all accounts held with it by the judgment debtor.

(2) The bank or building society must disclose to the court and the creditor within 7 days of being served with the order, in respect of each account held by the judgment debtor –

    (a) the number of the account;

    (b) whether the account is in credit; and

    (c) if the account is in credit –

        (i)   whether the balance of the account is sufficient to cover the amount specified in the order;

        (ii)   the amount of the balance at the date it was served with the order, if it is less than the amount specified in the order; and

        (iii) whether the bank or building society asserts any right to the money in the account, whether pursuant to a right of set-off or otherwise, and if so giving details of the grounds for that assertion.

(3) If –

    (a) the judgment debtor does not hold an account with the bank or building society; or

    (b) the bank or building society is unable to comply with the order for any other reason (for example, because it has more than one account holder whose details match the information contained in the order, and cannot identify which account the order applies to),

the bank or building society must inform the court and the judgment creditor of that fact within 7 days of being served with the order.

(4) Any third party other than a bank or building society served with an interim third party debt order must notify the court and the judgment creditor in writing within 7 days of being served with the order, if he claims –

    (a) not to owe any money to the judgment debtor; or

    (b) to owe less than the amount specified in the order.

Amendments—Inserted by SI 2001/2792; amended by SI 2001/4015.

"must disclose to the court and the creditor" (r 72.6(2))—Note that unlike other third parties, banks and building societies are not required to make disclosure in writing, presumably opening the way to allow fax or e-mail communication with the court and judgment creditor.

Effect of interim third party debt order—There seems to be no reason why the relevant law that applied to garnishee orders should not continue to apply to third party debt orders. Thus, the third party's debt to the debtor is not transferred to the judgment creditor, but an equitable charge is created (to the extent stated in the interim order) so that, if a third party who has been served with the interim order makes payment otherwise than to the judgment creditor, he risks having to pay twice (*Galbraith v Grimshaw & Baxter* [1910] AC 508). The judgment creditor can be in no better position against the third party than was the judgment debtor (*Levene v Maton* (1907) 51 SJ 532). If, for example, the judgment debtor assigned the debt to a fourth party before the interim order was served, then there will be no debt due to him for the interim order to attach, even though it was served before the third party had notice of the assignment (*Holt v Heatherfield Trust* [1942] 2 KB 1). If the third party is aware that a fourth party claims the debt, he must so inform the court, or the fact that he paid the judgment creditor under a third party debt order will not provide a defence to the fourth party's claim (*The Leader* (1868) LR 2 A&E 314). The third party is not protected if he pays the judgment creditor upon receipt of the interim order but before it is made final (*Re Webster* [1907] 1 KB 623).

72.7 Arrangements for debtors in hardship

(1) If –

- (a) a judgment debtor is an individual;
- (b) he is prevented from withdrawing money from his account with a bank or building society as a result of an interim third party debt order; and
- (c) he or his family is suffering hardship in meeting ordinary living expenses as a result,

the court may, on an application by the judgment debtor, make an order permitting the bank or building society to make a payment or payments out of the account ('a hardship payment order').

(2) An application for a hardship payment order may be made –

- (a) in High Court proceedings, at the Royal Courts of Justice, or the principal registry or to any district registry; and
- (b) in county court proceedings, to any county court.

(3) A judgment debtor may only apply to one court for a hardship payment order.

(4) An application notice seeking a hardship payment order must –

- (a) include detailed evidence explaining why the judgment debtor needs a payment of the amount requested; and
- (b) be verified by a statement of truth.

(5) Unless the court orders otherwise, the application notice –

- (a) must be served on the judgment creditor at least 2 days before the hearing; but
- (b) does not need to be served on the third party.

(6) A hardship payment order may –

- (a) permit the third party to make one or more payments out of the account; and
- (b) specify to whom the payments may be made.

Amendments—Inserted by SI 2001/2792.

Scope—This rule, which had no counterpart in the previous rules, was introduced to meet possible challenges to the third party debt order either under HRA 1998, Sch 1, Pt I, Art 8 or Art 1 of the First Protocol. It requires a high degree of communication and co-operation between the court in which the interim order is made and any court that deals with an application for a hardship payment order. Its use is most appropriate when the credit balance that has been frozen by the interim order is one that the judgment debtor reasonably expected would be available to fund essential payments for living expenditure, such as rent or mortgage instalments.

"suffering hardship" (r 72.7(1)(c))—The test is ordinary and not exceptional hardship. A judgment debtor is likely to establish hardship if the interim order prevents him from having sufficient money to cover his rent or mortgage, the cost of travel to work and at least the weekly basic DWP entitlement for himself and his family.

Venue—Although the application is made in the proceedings, it does not have to be made to the court that made the interim order and will not be transferred to that court for hearing (see PD72, para 5.2).

"must be served" (r 72.7(5)(a))—See PD72, paras 5.4 and 5.5 for the procedure where the application is dealt with without the required notice to the judgment creditor.

72.8 Further consideration of the application

(1) If the judgment debtor or the third party objects to the court making a final third party debt order, he must file and serve written evidence stating the grounds for his objections.

(2) If the judgment debtor or the third party knows or believes that a person other than the judgment debtor has any claim to the money specified in the interim order, he must file and serve written evidence stating his knowledge of that matter.

(3) If –

    (a)   the third party has given notice under rule 72.6 that he does not owe any money to the judgment debtor, or that the amount which he owes is less than the amount specified in the interim order; and

    (b)   the judgment creditor wishes to dispute this,

the judgment creditor must file and serve written evidence setting out the grounds on which he disputes the third party's case.

(4) Written evidence under paragraphs (1), (2) or (3) must be filed and served on each other party as soon as possible, and in any event not less than 3 days before the hearing.

(5) If the court is notified that some person other than the judgment debtor may have a claim to the money specified in the interim order, it will serve on that person notice of the application and the hearing.

(6) At the hearing the court may –

    (a)   make a final third party debt order;

    (b)   discharge the interim third party debt order and dismiss the application;

    (c)   decide any issues in dispute between the parties, or between any of the parties and any other person who has a claim to the money specified in the interim order; or

    (d)   direct a trial of any such issues, and if necessary give directions.

Amendments—Inserted by SI 2001/2792.

"[may] make a final ... order" (r 72.8(6)(a))—There is a general discretion as to whether to make an order. Relevant considerations will include the size of the judgment debt, the existence of an instalment order in respect of that debt, the amount of the debt due from the third party, the existence of an instalment order or agreement in respect of the debt attached and the burden of costs resulting from an order. The interests of any other creditors of the judgment debtor are also material (*Roberts Petroleum Ltd v Bernard Kenny Ltd* [1983] 2 AC 192). However, there is no principle that where a living debtor is insolvent or may be insolvent in the sense of having insufficient assets to pay his judgment creditors, all such creditors should benefit pari passu from the assets found by one such creditor. In *FG Hemisphere Associates LLC v The Republic of Congo* [2005] EWHC 3103, Cooke J applied the dictum of Lord Goddard CJ in *James Bibby Ltd v Woods* [1949] 2 KB 449: "the person who gets in first gets the fruits of his diligence". All of the cases where courts have refused to make orders final have concerned statutory insolvency schemes, whether company liquidation or the administration of insolvent estates. The same principles apply to charging orders.

    The court will be reluctant to attach the debtor's normal source of the proper living expenses of himself and his family – e g earnings that happened to be passing through the target bank account when the order nisi was served. If there is doubt as to whether the judgment debtor is solvent, the court may order the third party to pay the money into court pending its decision (*George Lee & Sons (Builders) Ltd v Olink* [1972] 1 WLR 214, a case of a questionably solvent estate). If the proceedings concern a "qualifying periodical maintenance order" within the meaning of MEA 1991, s 1 then the court may of its own motion make a "means of payment order" under s 1(4)(a) of that Act or an attachment of earnings order by virtue of s 1(4)(b).

"any issues in dispute" (r 72.8(6)(c))—Primarily, the issue is between the judgment creditor and the third party; the judgment debtor is not a party to it. However, if there is a question as to whether another party is interested in or entitled to the fund, that other party may be joined to the proceedings under r 72.8(5). If the judgment creditor prefers not to contest the issue raised, he may abandon his application, but he may be liable in costs (*Wintle v Williams* (1858) 3 H&N 288).

72.9 Effect of final third party order

(1) A final third party debt order shall be enforceable as an order to pay money.

(2) If –

    (a)   the third party pays money to the judgment creditor in compliance with a third party debt order; or

    (b)   the order is enforced against him,

the third party shall, to the extent of the amount paid by him or realised by enforcement against him, be discharged from his debt to the judgment debtor.

(3) Paragraph (2) applies even if the third party debt order, or the original judgment or order against the judgment debtor, is later set aside.

Amendments—Inserted by SI 2001/2792.

****

72.11 Costs

If the judgment creditor is awarded costs on an application for an order under rule 72.2 or 72.10 –

- (a) he shall, unless the court otherwise directs, retain those costs out of the money recovered by him under the order; and
- (b) the costs shall be deemed to be paid first out of the money he recovers, in priority to the judgment debt.

Amendments—Inserted by SI 2001/2792.

Practice Direction 72 – Third Party Debt Orders

This Practice Direction supplements CPR Part 72

Application Notice – Rule 72.3

1.1 An application for a third party debt order must be made by filing an application notice in Practice Form N349.

1.2 The application notice must contain the following information –

- (1) the name and address of the judgment debtor;
- (2) details of the judgment or order sought to be enforced;
- (3) the amount of money remaining due under the judgment or order;
- (4) if the judgment debt is payable by instalments, the amount of any instalments which have fallen due and remain unpaid;
- (5) the name and address of the third party;
- (6) if the third party is a bank or building society –
  - (a) its name and the address of the branch at which the judgment debtor's account is believed to be held; and
  - (b) the account number;
  or, if the judgment creditor does not know all or part of this information, that fact;
- (7) confirmation that to the best of the judgment creditor's knowledge or belief the third party –
  - (a) is within the jurisdiction; and
  - (b) owes money to or holds money to the credit of the judgment debtor;
- (8) if the judgment creditor knows or believes that any person other than the judgment debtor has any claim to the money owed by the third party –
  - (a) his name and (if known) his address; and
  - (b) such information as is known to the judgment creditor about his claim;

(9) details of any other applications for third party debt orders issued by the judgment creditor in respect of the same judgment debt; and

(10) the sources or grounds of the judgment creditor's knowledge or belief of the matters referred to in (7), (8) and (9).

"the amount of money remaining due under the judgment or order" (para 1.2(3))—While the Practice Direction does not explicitly require this, it is good practice to set out how the amount is arrived at, by analogy with FPR 20.0, r 33.3(1)(a).

1.3 The court will not grant speculative applications for third party debt orders, and will only make an interim third party debt order against a bank or building society if the judgment creditor's application notice contains evidence to substantiate his belief that the judgment debtor has an account with the bank or building society in question.

Interim Third Party Debt Order – Rule 72.4

2 An interim third party debt order will specify the amount of money which the third party must retain (rule 72.4(3)). This will include, in respect of the judgment creditor's fixed costs of the application, the amount which would be allowed to the judgment creditor under rule 45.8 if the whole balance of the judgment debt were recovered.

Interim Orders Relating to Bank or Building Society Accounts – Rule 72.6(1)–(3)

3.1 A bank or building society served with an interim third party debt order is only required by rule 72.6, unless the order states otherwise –

(1) to retain money in accounts held solely by the judgment debtor (or, if there are joint judgment debtors, accounts held jointly by them or solely by either or any of them); and

(2) to search for and disclose information about such accounts.

3.2 The bank or building society is not required, for example, to retain money in, or disclose information about –

(1) accounts in the joint names of the judgment debtor and another person; or

(2) if the interim order has been made against a firm, accounts in the names of individual members of that firm.

Attachment of debts owed by a partnership

3A.1 This paragraph relates to debts due or accruing due to a judgment creditor from a partnership.

3A.2 An interim third party debt order under rule 72.4(2) relating to such debts must be served on –

(1) a member of the partnership within the jurisdiction;

(2) a person authorised by a partner; or

(3) some other person having the control or management of the partnership business.

3A.3 Where an order made under rule 72.4(2) requires a partnership to appear before the court, it will be sufficient for a partner to appear before the court.

Transfer

4 The court may, on an application by a judgment debtor who wishes to oppose an application for a third party debt order, transfer it to the court for the district where the judgment debtor resides or carries on business, or to another court.

PART III

Applications for Hardship Payment Orders – Rule 72.7

5.1 The court will treat an application for a hardship payment order as being made –

    (1)   in the proceedings in which the interim third party debt order was made; and

    (2)   under the same claim number,

regardless of where the judgment debtor makes the application.

5.2 An application for a hardship payment order will be dealt with by the court to which it is made.

        (Rule 72.7(2) provides that an application may be made –

- in High Court proceedings, in the Royal Courts of Justice or to any district registry; and
- in county court proceedings, to any county court.)

5.3 If the application is made to a different court from that dealing with the application for a third party debt order –

    (1)   the application for a third party debt order will not be transferred; but

    (2)   the court dealing with that application will send copies of –

        (a)   the application notice; and

        (b)   the interim third party debt order

    to the court hearing the application for a hardship payment order.

5.4 Rule 72.7(3) requires an application for a hardship payment order to be served on the judgment creditor at least 2 days before the court is to deal with the application, unless the court orders otherwise. In cases of exceptional urgency the judgment debtor may apply for a hardship payment order without notice to the judgment creditor and a judge will decide whether to –

    (1)   deal with the application without it being served on the judgment creditor; or

    (2)   direct it to be served.

5.5 If the judge decides to deal with the application without it being served on the judgment creditor, where possible he will normally –

    (1)   direct that the judgment creditor be informed of the application; and

    (2)   give him the opportunity to make representations,

by telephone, fax or other appropriate method of communication.

5.6 The evidence filed by a judgment debtor in support of an application for a hardship payment order should include documentary evidence, for example (if appropriate) bank statements, wage slips and mortgage statements, to prove his financial position and need for the payment.

Final Orders Relating to Building Society Accounts

6 A final third party debt order will not require a payment which would reduce to less than £1 the amount in a judgment debtor's account with a building society or credit union.

PART 73
CHARGING ORDERS, STOP ORDERS AND STOP NOTICES

CONTENTS OF THIS PART

General note—This Part is reproduced as modified for family proceedings by FPR 2010, r 33.25.

Procedural Guide—See Procedural Guide C6.

73.1 Scope of this Part and interpretation

(1) This Part contains rules which provide for a judgment creditor to enforce a judgment by obtaining –

(a) a charging order (Section I);
(b) a stop order (Section II); or
(c) a stop notice (Section III),

over or against the judgment debtor's interest in an asset.

(2) In this Part –

(a) 'the 1979 Act' means the Charging Orders Act 1979;
...

(d) 'securities' means securities of any of the kinds specified in section 2(2)(b) of the 1979 Act.

Amendments—Inserted by SI 2001/2792.

Section 1
Charging Orders

73.2 Scope of this Section

This Section applies to an application by a judgment creditor for a charging order under section 1 of the 1979 Act.

Amendments—Inserted by SI 2001/2792.

73.3 Application for charging order

(1) An application for a charging order may be made without notice.

(2) An application for a charging order must be issued in the court which made the judgment or order which it is sought to enforce, unless –

  (a) the proceedings have since been transferred to a different court, in which case the application must be issued in that court;

       …

  (d) the application is to enforce a judgment or order of the High Court and it is required by section 1(2) of the 1979 Act to be made to a county court;

  (e) the application is to enforce a judgment made in Northampton County Court in respect of a designated money claim, in which event the application must be issued in accordance with section 2 of Practice Direction 70.

(3) Subject to paragraph (2), a judgment creditor may apply for a single charging order in respect of more than one judgment or order against the same debtor.

(4) The application notice must –

  (a) (i)   be in the form; and
       (ii) contain the information,
       required by Practice Direction 73; and

  (b) be verified by a statement of truth.

Amendments—Inserted by SI 2001/2792; amended by SI 2009/3390; SI 2012/505.

"a single charging order in respect of more than one judgment or order" (r 73.3(3))—Issuing separate applications in respect of each of several judgments is likely to be oppressive and the creditor is unlikely to recover more than one set of costs.

73.4 Interim charging order

(1) An application for a charging order will initially be dealt with by the court without a hearing.

(2) The court may make an order (an 'interim charging order') –

  (a) imposing a charge over the judgment debtor's interest in the asset to which the application relates; and

  (b) fixing a hearing to consider whether to make a final charging order as provided by rule 73.8(2)(a).

Amendments—Inserted by SI 2001/2792.

"may make an order" (r 73.4(2))—An interim order is not granted automatically. It may be refused not only if the application notice fails to comply with PD73, para 1.2 but also if the debt is too small to justify the remedy or the application appears otherwise oppressive. From 1 October 2012, the fact that an instalment order is being complied with is a matter the court must consider in deciding whether to make a charging order, rather than being a bar to making an order: Tribunals, Courts and Enforcement Act 2007, s 93.

"an interim charging order" (r 73.4(2))—A charging order is made initially in the form of an interim order, to be confirmed by a final charging order or discharged on the hearing. Any Land Registry notice or caution or Land Charges Registry entry is properly effected pursuant to COA 1979, s 3(2) or (3) on the making of the interim order and should not be repeated when a final charging order is made. Any such entry should be removed promptly if the interim order is discharged.

"asset to which the application relates" (r 73.4(2)(a))—More than one asset belonging to the judgment debtor may be included in a single application but a separate interim order will be drawn in respect of each asset (PD73, para 1.3).

73.5 Service of interim order

(1) Copies of the interim charging order, the application notice and any documents filed in support of it must, not less than 21 days before the hearing, be served on the following persons –

    (a)   the judgment debtor;

    (b)   such other creditors as the court directs;

    (c)   if the order relates to an interest under a trust, on such of the trustees as the court directs;

    (d)   if the interest charged is in securities other than securities held in court, then –

        (i)   in the case of stock for which the Bank of England keeps the register, the Bank of England;

        (ii)   in the case of government stock to which (i) does not apply, the keeper of the register;

        (iii)   in the case of stock of any body incorporated within England and Wales, that body;

        (iv)   in the case of stock of any body incorporated outside England and Wales or of any state or territory outside the United Kingdom, which is registered in a register kept in England and Wales, the keeper of that register;

        (v)   in the case of units of any unit trust in respect of which a register of the unit holders is kept in England and Wales, the keeper of that register; and

    (e)   if the interest charged is in funds in court, the Accountant General at the Court Funds Office.

(2) If the judgment creditor serves the order, he must either –

    (a)   file a certificate of service not less than 2 days before the hearing; or

    (b)   produce a certificate of service at the hearing.

Amendments—Inserted by SI 2001/2792.

"Service of interim order"—The normal procedure is for the interim order to be served by the court by first-class post. Judgment creditors should take care to supply the court with the names and addresses of all persons required to be served under r 73.5(1), together with sufficient copies of the application for service.

"other creditors" (r 73.5(1)(b))—The general rules as to service in Pt 6 will apply. The court will usually direct service on all known creditors (see COA 1979, s 1(5)(b)), although service on prior chargees appears not to be necessary for their protection on the basis that they cannot be prejudiced by the making of the order. The former rule, requiring persons interested in the asset sought to be charged to be served at this stage of the proceedings, has not been reproduced. The expression "creditor" may be given a purposive interpretation to include spouses or former spouses, where the asset sought to be charged is or was a matrimonial home, particularly where rights of occupation have been registered under Family Law Act 1996, s 30 or where an application for ancillary relief has been registered as a pending action against the property. The form of application notice, Form N379 (or N380), requires all persons interested to be identified. A direction is likely to be given that any such person identified be served (*Harman v Glencross* [1986] 2 FLR 241). Alternatively, such persons may apply after the event under r 73.9 for the final charging order to be varied or discharged.

73.6 Effect of interim order in relation to securities

(1) If a judgment debtor disposes of his interest in any securities, while they are subject to an interim charging order which has been served on him, that disposition shall not, so long as that order remains in force, be valid as against the judgment creditor.

(2) A person served under rule 73.5(1)(d) with an interim charging order relating to securities must not, unless the court gives permission –

(a)   permit any transfer of any of the securities; or

(b)   pay any dividend, interest or redemption payment relating to them.

(3) If a person acts in breach of paragraph (2), he will be liable to pay to the judgment creditor –

(a)   the value of the securities transferred or the amount of the payment made (as the case may be); or

(b)   if less, the amount necessary to satisfy the debt in relation to which the interim charging order was made.

Amendments—Inserted by SI 2001/2792.

73.7 Effect of interim order in relation to funds in court

If a judgment debtor disposes of his interest in funds in court while they are subject to an interim charging order which has been served on him and on the Accountant General in accordance with rule 73.5(1), that disposition shall not, so long as that order remains in force, be valid as against the judgment creditor.

Amendments—Inserted by SI 2001/2792.

73.8 Further consideration of the application

(1) If any person objects to the court making a final charging order, he must –

(a)   file; and

(b)   serve on the applicant,

written evidence stating the grounds of his objections, not less than 7 days before the hearing.

(2) At the hearing the court may –

(a)   make a final charging order confirming that the charge imposed by the interim charging order shall continue, with or without modification;

(b)   discharge the interim charging order and dismiss the application;

(c)   decide any issues in dispute between the parties, or between any of the parties and any other person who objects to the court making a final charging order; or

(d)   direct a trial of any such issues, and if necessary give directions.

(3) If the court makes a final charging order which charges securities other than securities held in court, the order will include a stop notice unless the court otherwise orders.

(Section III of this Part contains provisions about stop notices)

(4) Any order made at the hearing must be served on all the persons on whom the interim charging order was required to be served.

Amendments—Inserted by SI 2001/2792.

"the court may" (r 73.8(2))—For the principles on which the court will exercise its discretion, see *Roberts Petroleum Ltd v Bernard Kenny Ltd* [1983] 2 AC 192, CA at [690] and *British Arab Commercial Bank Plc & Ors v Algosaibi & Ors* [2011] EWHC 2444 (Comm). See **"[may] make a final ... order"** under r 72.8.

"final charging order" (r 73.8(2)(a))—The charge is effective from the day that the interim order was made (*Haley v Barry* (1868) 3 Ch App 452).

"with or without modification" (r 73.8(2)(a))—As there remains only one charging order, it cannot be modified to extend to property that was not included in the interim order. Modifications may include the imposition of conditions on enforcement under COA 1979, s 3(1) (see **Conditions**, below).

"discharge the interim charging order" (r 73.8(2)(b))—All of the factors that are relevant in the exercise of the court's discretion as to whether to grant an interim order under r 73.4(2) apply also in considering whether to make a final charging order or discharge the interim order and dismiss the application. The interim order should be discharged if the debtor had no interest in the property when the interim order was made or if the debtor has since parted with it and passed it on to someone who would not be affected by a mere equitable charge, such as a bona fide purchaser for value without notice (*Howell v Montey* (1990) *The Times*, 17 March).

It is necessary to strike a balance between the normal expectation of a judgment creditor that an order will be made to enforce his judgment and the hardship that such an order may entail to the spouse and children of the debtor: *Harman v Glencross* [1986] 2 FLR 241. There can never be automatic predominance for any claim; each case depends upon striking a fair balance: *Austin-Fell v Austin-Fell and Midland Bank* [1989] 2 FLR 497. In some cases, the balance will be achieved by an order postponing any sale of the property and in a more extreme case it will be achieved by withholding a charging order altogether and transferring the debtor's interest to the spouse free of any encumbrance, as in *Kremen v Agrest & Chesnokov* [2013] EWCA Civ 41.

Adjournment—The court does have power to adjourn a hearing to another date under r 3.1(2)(b). Any adjournment should either be to a fixed date or to a particular event, e g the hearing of an application for ancillary relief. It is usual when adjourning to direct specifically that the interim order remain in force.

Conditions—COA 1979, s 3(1) enables the order to be made subject to conditions. Where the order is against the judgment debtor's interest in a family home, conditions delaying execution may now be more frequently used to comply with HRA 1998, Sch 1, Pt I, Art 8.

Costs—Fixed costs of £110 are specified in r 45.6. Courts may also (and normally will) allow Land Registry fees as disbursements.

73.9 Discharge or variation of order

(1) Any application to discharge or vary a charging order must be made to the court which made the charging order.

> (Section 3(5) of the 1979 Act provides that the court may at any time, on the application of the debtor, or of any person interested in any property to which the order relates make an order discharging or varying the charging order)

(2) The court may direct that –

    (a) any interested person should be joined as a party to such an application; or

    (b) the application should be served on any such person.

(3) An order discharging or varying a charging order must be served on all the persons on whom the charging order was required to be served.

Amendments—Inserted by SI 2001/2792.

"any interested person" (r 73.9(2)(a))—In particular, interested persons who did not receive notice of the making of an interim order may apply under this rule to be joined as parties to the application and for the order to be discharged or varied. Such applications may become inextricably linked with ancillary relief applications under MCA 1973 to the extent that they must be heard together. The competing interests of judgment creditor, judgment debtor and former spouse can then all be decided on a single occasion.

73.10 Enforcement of charging order by sale

(1) Subject to the provisions of any enactment, the court may, upon an application by a person who has obtained a charging order over an interest in property, order the sale of the property to enforce the charging order.

(2) An application for an order for sale under this rule should be made to the court which made the charging order, unless that court does not have jurisdiction to make an order for sale.

> (An application under this rule is a proceeding for the enforcement of a charge, and section 23(c) of the County Courts Act 1984 provides the extent of the county court's jurisdiction to hear and determine such proceedings)

(3) The applicant must use the Part 8 procedure.

(4) A copy of the charging order must be filed with the application.

(5) The applicant's written evidence must include the information required by Practice Direction 73.

Amendments—Inserted by SI 2001/2792; amended by SI 2009/3390.

"the court may" (r 73.10(1))—It sometimes seems to be assumed that a creditor is entitled to an order for sale under this provision as a matter of right, but this is not the case. In the common case where the property concerned is the debtor's home, the debtor's right to respect for his home under ECHR Art 8 must be balanced against the creditor's right to secure payment of his debt, as was emphasised in the ECtHR case of *Zehentner v Austria* [2009] ECHR 1119. The claimant's written evidence should address this issue.

In the case of the debtor's home, it is a draconian step to require a sale to satisfy a simple debt. It is rarely done, except in response to the debtor's contumelious neglect or refusal to pay; even then, the order will often be suspended on terms as to payment. It may be otherwise in the case of investment property. Where the order to be enforced is a maintenance order, the debtor's resources will have been taken into account when it was made and his neglect or refusal may thus be easier to demonstrate.

The fact that the value of the property charged significantly exceeds the judgment debt is not a reason for refusing a sale; it is "just one of the considerations to be taken into account and not an overriding one"; *Packman Lucas Ltd v (1) Mentmore Towers Ltd (2) Charles Street Holdings Ltd* [2010] EWHC 1037.

"interest in property" (r 73.10(1))—Application under this rule is likely to be useful only where the legal estate of the judgment debtor has been charged. Where the charge has been imposed on the judgment debtor's beneficial interest, sale of that interest alone may be difficult or impossible to achieve and in that case the judgment creditor should take fresh proceedings under TLATA 1996, s 14 using the Pt 8 procedure.

"jurisdiction to make an order for sale" (r 73.10(2))—A county court has jurisdiction to make orders for sale where the amount of the charge at the date of commencement of the proceedings does not exceed £30,000 (CCA 1984, s 23(c)) or where the amount exceeds £30,000 and both parties consent under CCA 1984, s 24. The High Court can, however, transfer an application to the county court (*National Westminster Bank Plc v King* [2008] Ch 385).

"Part 8 procedure"—That is, the procedure under Pt 8 of the CPR, as to which see *Civil Court Service* (Jordan Publishing Ltd).

Section II
Stop Orders

73.11 Interpretation

In this Section, 'stop order' means an order of the High Court not to take, in relation to securities specified in the order, any of the steps listed in section 5(5) of the 1979 Act.

Amendments—Inserted by SI 2001/2792.

73.12 Application for stop order

(1) The High Court may make –

    (a) ...

    (b) a stop order relating to securities, on the application of any person claiming to be beneficially entitled to an interest in the securities.

(2) An application for a stop order must be made –

    (a) by application notice in existing proceedings; or

    (b) by Part 8 application notice if there are no existing proceedings in the High Court.

(3) The application notice must be served on –

    (a) every person whose interest may be affected by the order applied for; and

    (b) the person specified in rule 73.5(1)(d).

Amendments—Inserted by SI 2001/2792.

****

73.14 Stop order relating to securities

(1) A stop order relating to securities may prohibit all or any of the following steps –

    (a) the registration of any transfer of the securities;

    (b) the making of any payment by way of dividend, interest or otherwise in respect of the securities; and

    (c) in the case of units of a unit trust, any acquisition of or other dealing with the units by any person or body exercising functions under the trust.

(2) The order shall specify –

    (a) the securities to which it relates;

    (b) the name in which the securities stand;

    (c) the steps which may not be taken; and

    (d) whether the prohibition applies to the securities only or to the dividends or interest as well.

Amendments—Inserted by SI 2001/2792.

73.15 Variation or discharge of order

(1) The court may, on the application of any person claiming to have a beneficial interest in the funds or securities to which a stop order relates, make an order discharging or varying the order.

(2) An application notice seeking the variation or discharge of a stop order must be served on the person who obtained the order.

Amendments—Inserted by SI 2001/2792.

Section III
Stop Notices

73.16 General

In this Section –

    (a) 'stop notice' means a notice issued by the court which requires a person or body not to take, in relation to securities specified in the notice, any of the steps listed in section 5(5) of the 1979 Act, without first giving notice to the person who obtained the notice.

(b)   ...

Amendments—Inserted by SI 2001/2792.

73.17 Request for stop notice

(1) The High Court may, on the request of any person claiming to be beneficially entitled to an interest in securities, issue a stop notice.

> (A stop notice may also be included in a final charging order, by either the High Court or a county court, under rule 73.8(3))

(2) A request for a stop notice must be made by filing –

    (a)   a draft stop notice; and

    (b)   written evidence which –

        (i)   identifies the securities in question;

        (ii)   describes the applicant's interest in the securities; and

        (iii) gives an address for service for the applicant.

> (A sample form of stop notice is annexed to Practice Direction 73)

(3) If a court officer considers that the request complies with paragraph (2), he will issue a stop notice.

(4) The applicant must serve copies of the stop notice and his written evidence on the person to whom the stop notice is addressed.

Amendments—Inserted by SI 2001/2792; amended by SI 2009/3390.

73.18 Effect of stop notice

(1) A stop notice –

    (a)   takes effect when it is served in accordance with rule 73.17(4); and

    (b)   remains in force unless it is withdrawn or discharged in accordance with rule 73.20 or 73.21.

(2) While a stop notice is in force, the person on whom it is served –

    (a)   must not –

        (i)   register a transfer of the securities described in the notice; or

        (ii)   take any other step restrained by the notice,

without first giving 14 days' notice to the person who obtained the stop notice; but

    (b)   must not, by reason only of the notice, refuse to register a transfer or to take any other step, after he has given 14 days' notice under paragraph (2)(a) and that period has expired.

Amendments—Inserted by SI 2001/2792.

73.19 Amendment of stop notice

(1) If any securities are incorrectly described in a stop notice which has been obtained and served in accordance with rule 73.17, the applicant may request an amended stop notice in accordance with that rule.

(2) The amended stop notice takes effect when it is served.

Amendments—Inserted by SI 2001/2792.

73.20 Withdrawal of stop notice

(1) A person who has obtained a stop notice may withdraw it by serving a request for its withdrawal on –

    (a)   the person or body on whom the stop notice was served; and

    (b)   the court which issued the stop notice.

(2) The request must be signed by the person who obtained the stop notice, and his signature must be witnessed by a practising solicitor.

Amendments—Inserted by SI 2001/2792.

73.21 Discharge or variation of stop notice

(1) The court may, on the application of any person claiming to be beneficially entitled to an interest in the securities to which a stop notice relates, make an order discharging or varying the notice.

(2) An application to discharge or vary a stop notice must be made to the court which issued the notice.

(3) The application notice must be served on the person who obtained the stop notice.

Amendments—Inserted by SI 2001/2792.

73.22 Practice Direction 73 makes provision for the procedure to be followed when applying for an order under section 23 of the Partnership Act 1890.

Amendments—Inserted by SI 2006/1689; amended by SI 2009/3390.

Practice Direction 73 –
Charging Orders, Stop Orders and Stop Notices

This Practice Direction supplements CPR Part 73

SECTION I: CHARGING ORDERS

Application Notice – Rule 73.3

1.1 An application for a charging order must be made by filing an application notice in Practice Form N379 if the application relates to land, or N380 if the application relates to securities.

1.2 The application notice must contain the following information –

    (1)   the name and address of the judgment debtor;

    (2)   details of the judgment or order sought to be enforced;

    (3)   the amount of money remaining due under the judgment or order;

    (4)   if the judgment debt is payable by instalments, the amount of any instalments which have fallen due and remain unpaid;

    (5)   if the judgment creditor knows of the existence of any other creditors of the judgment debtor, their names and (if known) their addresses;

    (6)   identification of the asset or assets which it is intended to charge;

    (7)   details of the judgment debtor's interest in the asset; and

    (8)   the names and addresses of the persons on whom an interim charging order must be served under rule 73.5(1).

PART III

"the amount of money remaining due under the judgment or order" (para 1.2(3))—While the Practice Direction does not explicitly require this, it is good practice to set out how the amount is arrived at, by analogy with FPR 2010, r 33.3(1)(a).

1.3 A judgment creditor may apply in a single application notice for charging orders over more than one asset, but if the court makes interim charging orders over more than one asset, it will draw up a separate order relating to each asset.

High Court and County Court Jurisdiction

2 The jurisdiction of the High Court and the county court to make charging orders is set out in section 1(2) of the 1979 Act.

Transfer

3 The court may, on an application by a judgment debtor who wishes to oppose an application for a charging order, transfer it to the court for the district where the judgment debtor resides or carries on business, or to another court.

Enforcement of Charging Orders by Sale – Rule 73.10

4.1 A county court has jurisdiction to determine a claim under rule 73.10 for the enforcement of a charging order if the amount owing under the charge does not exceed the county court limit.

4.2 A claim in the High Court for an order for sale of land to enforce a charging order must be started in Chancery Chambers at the Royal Courts of Justice, or a Chancery district registry.

> (There are Chancery district registries at Birmingham, Bristol, Caernarfon, Cardiff, Leeds, Liverpool, Manchester, Mold, Newcastle upon Tyne and Preston)

4.3 The written evidence in support of a claim under rule 73.10 must –
  (1)   identify the charging order and the property sought to be sold;
  (2)   state the amount in respect of which the charge was imposed and the amount due at the date of issue of the claim;
  (3)   verify, so far as known, the debtor's title to the property charged;
  (4)   state, so far as the claimant is able to identify –
      (a)   the names and addresses of any other creditors who have a prior charge or other security over the property; and
      (b)   the amount owed to each such creditor; and
  (5)   give an estimate of the price which would be obtained on sale of the property.
  (6)   if the claim relates to land, give details of every person who to the best of the claimant's knowledge is in possession of the property; and
  (7)   if the claim relates to residential property –
      (a)   state whether –
          (i)   a land charge of Class F; or
          (ii)   a notice under section 31(10) of the Family Law Act 1996, or under any provision of an Act which preceded that section,
      has been registered; and
      (b)   if so, state –
          (i)   on whose behalf the land charge or notice has been registered; and
          (ii)   that the claimant will serve notice of the claim on that person.

4.4 The claimant must take all reasonable steps to obtain the information required by paragraph 4.3(4) before issuing the claim.

4.5 Sample forms of orders for sale are set out in Appendix A to this practice direction for guidance. These are not prescribed forms of order and they may be adapted or varied by the court to meet the requirements of individual cases.

4A.1 A charging order or interim charging order may be made against any property, within the jurisdiction, belonging to a judgment debtor that is a partnership.

4A.2 For the purposes of rule 73.5(1)(a) (service of the interim order), the specified documents must be served on –

(1)   a member of the partnership within the jurisdiction;
(2)   a person authorised by a partner; or
(3)   some other person having the control or management of the partnership business.

4A.3 Where an order requires a partnership to appear before the court, it will be sufficient for a partner to appear before the court.

SECTION II: STOP NOTICES

5 A sample form of stop notice is set out in Appendix B to this practice direction.

SECTION III: APPLICATIONS FOR ORDERS MADE UNDER SECTION 23 OF THE PARTNERSHIP ACT 1890

6.1 This paragraph relates to orders made under section 23 of the Partnership Act 1890 ('Section 23').

6.2 The following applications must be made in accordance with Part 23 –

(1)   an application for an order under Section 23 of the 1890 Act made by a judgment creditor of a partner;
(2)   an application for any order by a partner of the judgment debtor in consequence of any application made by the judgment creditor under Section 23.

6.3 The powers conferred on a judge by Section 23 may be exercised by –

(1)   a Master;
(2)   the Admiralty Registrar; or
(3)   a district judge.

6.4 Every application notice filed under this paragraph by a judgment creditor, and every order made following such an application, must be served on the judgment debtor and on any of the other partners that are within the jurisdiction.

6.5 Every application notice filed under this paragraph by a partner of a judgment debtor, and every order made following such an application, must be served –

(1)   on the judgment creditor and the judgment debtor; and
(2)   on the other partners of the judgment debtor who are not joined in the application and who are within the jurisdiction.

6.6 An application notice or order served under this paragraph on one or more, but not all, of the partners of a partnership shall be deemed to have been served on all the partners of that partnership.

APPENDIX A – ORDER OF SALE FOLLOWING A CHARGING ORDER

ORDER FOR SALE	**In the**	**Claim No**
following a charging order		**Appn No**

(property solely owned by
judgment debtor)

Claimant

Defendant

On the   20 ,   sitting at

heard

The claimant is entitled to an equitable charge upon the defendant's interest in the property

[registered at HM Land Registry under Title No   ]

('the property')

under a charging order made on the

in the   in Claim No

and the court orders that

1 The remainder of this order will not take effect if the defendant by 4.00 pm on
the   20   pays to the claimant the judgment debt of £   secured by the charge
and his costs to date of this application assessed at £   , making together
£   [together with interest at the rate of £   per day from the date of this order until
payment is received by the claimant].

2 The property shall be sold without further reference to the court at a price not less than
£   , unless that figure is changed by a further order of the court.

3 The [claimant] [claimant's solicitor] will have conduct of the sale.

4 To enable the claimant to carry out the sale, there be created and vested in the claimant
pursuant to section 90 of the Law of Property Act 1925 a legal term in the property of [3000
years] [one day less than the remaining period of the term created by the lease under which
the defendant holds the property].

5 The defendant must deliver possession of the property to the claimant [on or before
the   20   ] [within [   ] days of this order being served on him].

6 The claimant shall first apply the proceeds of sale of the property –

(i) to pay the costs and expenses of effecting the sale; and

(ii) to discharge any charges or other securities over the property which have priority over
the charging order.

7 Out of the remaining proceeds of sale the claimant shall –

(i) retain the amount due to him as stated in paragraph 1; and

(ii) pay the balance (if any) [to the Defendant] [to   ] [into court].

8 Either party may apply to the court to vary any of the terms of this order, or for further
directions about the sale or the application of the proceeds of sale, or otherwise.

[ORDER FOR SALE	**In the**
following a charging order	**Claim No**

**(property owned by
judgment debtor and
another person)**

Claimant

Defendants

On the   20 ,   sitting at

heard

The claimant is entitled to an equitable charge upon the first defendant's interest in the property

[registered at HM Land Registry under Title No   ]

('the property')

under a charging order made on the

in the   in Claim No

and the court orders that

1 The remainder of this order will not take effect if the defendant by 4.00 pm on the   20   pays to the claimant the judgment debt of £   secured by the charge and his costs to date of this application assessed at £   , making together £   [together with interest at the rate of £   per day from the date of this order until payment is received by the claimant].

2 The property shall be sold without further reference to the court at a price not less than £   , unless that figure is changed by a further order of the court.

3 The [claimant] [claimant's solicitor] will have conduct of the sale.

4 The court pursuant to section 50 of the Trustee Act 1925 appoints the [claimant] [claimant's solicitor] to convey the property.

5 The defendant must deliver possession of the property to the claimant [on or before the   20   ] [within [   ] days of this order being served on him].

6 The claimant shall first apply the proceeds of sale of the property –

(i) to pay the costs and expenses of effecting the sale; and

(ii) to discharge any charges or other securities over the property which have priority over the charging order.

7 The claimant shall then divide the remaining proceeds of sale into two equal shares and –

(i) pay one equal share to the second defendant; and

(ii) out of the other equal share, retain the amount due to him stated in paragraph 1, and pay the balance (if any) [to the first defendant] [to   ] [into court].

8 Any party may apply to the court to vary any of the terms of this order, or for further directions about the sale or the application of the proceeds of sale, or otherwise.

APPENDIX B – STOP NOTICE

CPR rule 73.17

To [*insert name of person or body to whom the notice is addressed*]

TAKE NOTICE that

[*insert name and address*]

claims to be beneficially entitled to an interest in the following securities –

[*specify the securities, giving the name(s) in which they stand*]

This Notice requires you to refrain from –

(1) registering a transfer of the securities specified above; or

(2) paying any dividend or interest in respect of the securities [delete if inappropriate];

without first giving 14 days' notice in writing to the said [insert name] of the above address.

PART 74
ENFORCEMENT OF JUDGMENTS IN DIFFERENT JURISDICTIONS
****

Scope—Pt 74 and its accompanying PD set out the procedural rules relating to a number of pieces of legislation allowing foreign judgments to be directly enforced in England and Wales, and English judgments to be directly enforced in foreign courts. The text of Pt 74 with detailed annotation and the PDs are set out in *Civil Court Service* (Jordan Publishing Ltd). The following note is intended as a brief introduction.

General note—A money judgment of a foreign court cannot be directly enforced in England and Wales. However, it can be made the basis of an action in the English courts, in which summary judgment will be granted (see *Colt Industries Inc v Sarlie* (No 2) [1966] 1 WLR 1287) unless the defendant can establish one of a limited number of defences.

Four pieces of legislation, which will be briefly discussed, allow foreign judgments to be registered in the High Court for enforcement, without the claimant needing to bring a fresh action. A fifth, the European Enforcement Order, allows certain judgments from EU countries to be enforced in the High Court or the county court. It is important to realise that unless the case falls within the scope of one of them, there is no power to register a foreign money judgment for enforcement.

Arrears under foreign maintenance orders can generally not be the subject of an action in England (*Harrop v Harrop* [1920] 3 KB 386) but arrangements have been made for their reciprocal enforcement, for details of which see Procedural Guides C3(1)–C3(16). In *O'Farrell v O'Farrell* [2013] 1 FLR 77, a European judgment for arrears of maintenance was registered for enforcement in the High Court, but the Court suggested that registration would have been discharged had the payor appealed and references to judgments in Pt 74 should be construed as references to judgments other than maintenance orders.

The Administration of Justice Act 1920 ("the 1920 Act")—This Act provides for reciprocal enforcement of judgments of the superior courts in countries to which the Act had been applied by Order in Council before the 1933 Act came into force. The consolidated list is as follows:

Anguilla, Antigua and Barbuda, Bahamas, Barbados, Belize, Bermuda, Botswana, British Indian Ocean Territory, British Virgin Islands, Cayman Islands, Christmas Island, Cocos (Keeling) Islands, Republic of Cyprus, Dominica, Falkland Islands, Fiji, The Gambia, Ghana, Grenada, Guyana, Jamaica, Kenya, Kiribati, Lesotho, Malawi, Malaysia, Malta, Mauritius, Montserrat, New Zealand, Nigeria, Territory of Norfolk Island, Papua New Guinea, St Christopher and Nevis, St Helena, St Lucia, St Vincent and the Grenadines, Seychelles, Sierra Leone, Singapore, Solomon Islands, Sovereign Base Area of Akrotiri and Dhekelia in Cyprus, Sri Lanka, Swaziland, Tanzania, Tasmania, Trinidad and Tobago, Turks and Caicos Islands, Tuvalu, Uganda, Zambia, Zimbabwe.

The 1920 Act no longer applies to Hong Kong or Gibraltar; Gibraltar is now subject to the Brussels Convention.

See s 9(2) for limitations on the judgments which may be registered.

The Foreign Judgments (Reciprocal Enforcement) Act 1933 ("the 1933 Act")—This Act made further provision for reciprocal enforcement of judgments with a number of countries. The only non-Commonwealth countries to which the 1933 Act is still relevant are Israel, Surinam and Tonga. All of the other countries formerly covered by the Act are now parties to the Brussels or Lugano conventions or to the various European regulations and applications should be made under the 1982 Act, the Judgments Regulation or the European Enforcement Order procedure as appropriate. The list of Commonwealth countries to which the Act has been applied is as follows:

Australia including the Australian Capital Territory, the Federal Court of Canada and courts of all provinces except Quebec, Island of Guernsey, Isle of Man, Bailiwick of Jersey, certain territories of the Republic of India named in the Schedule to the Reciprocal Enforcement of Judgments (India) Order 1958 and Pakistan.

A judgment which is capable of being registered under the 1933 Act cannot be made the subject of an action (see s 6 and *Yukon Consolidated Gold Corporation Ltd v Clark* [1938] 2 KB 241).

The Civil Jurisdiction and Judgments Act 1982 ("the 1982 Act")—This Act gives effect to the Brussels Convention (to which the EEC countries were parties) and the similar Lugano Conventions of 1988 and 2007 signed by the Member States of EFTA. As with the 1933 Act, a registrable judgment cannot be made the subject of an action. The grounds on which registration may be set aside are very limited.

Council Regulation (EC) No 44/2001 ("the Judgments Regulation")—Council Regulation (EC) No 44/2001 (see *The Family Court Practice 2011*), on jurisdiction and the recognition and enforcement of judgments in civil and commercial matters, applies a uniform regime, similar although not identical to that under the Brussels Convention, to the Member States of the European Union.

The European Enforcement Order (EEO)—Council Regulation (EC) No 805/2004 created an alternative enforcement regime for uncontested claims. It applies to all Member States of the EU other than Denmark. The intention is that a judgment which is certified as an EEO shall be recognised and enforced in the other Member States without the need for a declaration of enforceability and without any possibility of opposing its recognition. Specifically, an application to stay or limit enforcement proceedings under an EEO, must be made to the courts of the Member State of origin. Only then may the courts of the Member State of enforcement stay enforcement to await the outcome of that application. Apart from that, the only power the enforcing court has to refuse to enforce an EEO is that under Art 21 of the Regulation, where the EEO is irreconcilable with an earlier judgment and the irreconcilability was not and could not have been raised as an objection in the court proceedings in the court of origin. Under no circumstances may the judgment, or its certification as an EEO, be reviewed as to their substance in the Member State of enforcement.

It should be noted that a claim may be regarded as "uncontested" if the debtor has not appeared or been represented at a court hearing regarding it, provided the debtor has been satisfactorily served. The EEO regime applies to any judgment given by a court or tribunal of a Member State, whatever the judgment may be called, and also applies to "court settlements and authentic instruments". However, since the coming into force of the Maintenance Regulation (EC) Reg No 4/2009, the EEO procedure no longer applies to maintenance claims.

A judgment creditor is not obliged to use the EEO.

The details of the EEO procedure are to be found in Pt V of Pt 74 comprising rr 74.27–74.33, PD74B and the Regulation itself, which is annexed to the PD.

****

PART 81
APPLICATIONS AND PROCEEDINGS IN RELATION TO CONTEMPT OF COURT

Scope—CPR 1998, Pt 81 came into force on 1 October 2012. It applies only to civil proceedings (such as an application to commit for breach of an order under the Protection from Harassment Act 1997) but does not apply to family proceedings governed by FPR 2010. Regrettably, FPR 2010 have not been updated and a new r 2.3(4) (SI 2012/2046) provides that "Where these Rules apply RSC Order 52 and CCR Order 29, they apply those rules as they appear in Schedule 1 and Schedule 2 to the CPR on 30 September 2012". Thus, bizarrely, committal in family proceedings still relies on rules some of which are more than 50 years old, whereas there is a clear modern code for civil cases.

The law on contempt is a complicated mixture of common law and statute and the jurisdictions of the High Court and county courts are substantially different. Pt 81 is divided into Sections, each being structured to deal with a specific type of contempt. This has the disadvantage that the Part is long and repetitive but that is outweighed by the advantage that each of its nine Sections is self-contained and clear. After the necessary "Scope and interpretation" in Section 1, the most common type of committal, "Committal for breach of a judgment, order or undertaking to do or abstain from doing an act" is found in Section 2. "General rules about committal applications, orders for committal and writs of sequestration" are set out in Section 8. These three Sections will need to be referred to more frequently than the others. Pt 81 is supplemented by CPR PD81.

Pt 81 largely replicates the former practice and procedure but does so in a much clearer and more logical fashion. Nowhere is the need for clarity greater than when dealing with the liberty of the subject and it is hoped that FPR 2010 will be modernised during the currency of this edition. One significant change in Pt 81 is in Section 3, "Committal for interference with the due administration of justice", where a permission stage is introduced.

Section 1
Scope and interpretation

81.1 Scope

(1) This Part sets out the procedure in respect of –

    (a)   contempt of court; and

    (b)   the penal, contempt and disciplinary provisions of the County Courts Act 1984.

(2) So far as applicable, and with the necessary modifications, this Part applies in relation to an order requiring a person –

(a) guilty of contempt of court; or

(b) punishable by virtue of any enactment as if that person had been guilty of contempt of the High Court,

to pay a fine or to give security for good behaviour, as it applies in relation to an order of committal.

(3) Unless otherwise stated, this Part applies to procedure in the Court of Appeal, the High Court and county courts.

81.2 Saving for other powers

(1) This Part is concerned only with procedure and does not itself confer upon the court the power to make an order for –

(a) committal;

(b) sequestration; or

(c) the imposition of a fine in respect of contempt of court.

(2) Nothing in this Part affects the power of the court to make an order requiring a person –

(a) guilty of contempt of court; or

(b) punishable by virtue of any enactment as if that person had been guilty of contempt of the High Court,

to pay a fine or to give security for good behaviour.

(3) Nothing in this Part affects any statutory or inherent power of the court to make a committal order of its own initiative against a person guilty of contempt of court.

81.3 Interpretation

In this Part –

"applicant" means a person making –

(i) an application for permission to make a committal application;

(ii) a committal application; or

(iii) an application for a writ of sequestration;

"committal application" means any application for an order committing a person to prison;

"respondent" means a person –

(i) against whom a committal application is made or is intended to be made; or

(ii) against whose property it is sought to issue a writ of sequestration; and

"undertaking" means an undertaking to the court.

Section 2
Committal for breach of a judgment, order or undertaking to do or abstain from doing an act

81.4 Enforcement of judgment, order or undertaking to do or abstain from doing an act

(1) If a person –

(a) required by a judgment or order to do an act does not do it within the time fixed by the judgment or order; or

(b) disobeys a judgment or order not to do an act,

then, subject to the Debtors Acts 1869 and 1878 and to the provisions of these Rules, the judgment or order may be enforced by an order for committal.

(2) If the time fixed by the judgment or order for doing an act has been varied by a subsequent order or agreement of the parties under rule 2.11, then references in paragraph (1)(a) to the time fixed are references to the time fixed by that subsequent order or agreement.

(3) If the person referred to in paragraph (1) is a company or other corporation, the committal order may be made against any director or other officer of that company or corporation.

(4) So far as applicable, and with the necessary modifications, this Section applies to undertakings given by a party as it applies to judgments or orders.

> (Rules 81.17(3) and (4) make provision for cases in which both this Section and Section 6 (Committal for making a false statement of truth or disclosure statement) may be relevant.)

(5) If a judgment or order requires a person to deliver goods or pay their value –

- (a) the judgment or order may not be enforced by a committal order under paragraph (1);
- (b) the person entitled to enforce the judgment or order may apply to the court for an order requiring that the goods be delivered within a specified time; and
- (c) where the court grants such an order, that order may be enforced under paragraph (1).

81.5 Requirement for service of a copy of the judgment or order and time for service

(1) Unless the court dispenses with service under rule 81.8, a judgment or order may not be enforced under rule 81.4 unless a copy of it has been served on the person required to do or not do the act in question, and in the case of a judgment or order requiring a person to do an act –

- (a) the copy has been served before the end of the time fixed for doing the act, together with a copy of any order fixing that time;
- (b) where the time for doing the act has been varied by a subsequent order or agreement under rule 2.11, a copy of that subsequent order or agreement has also been served; and
- (c) where the judgment or order was made under rule 81.4(5), or was made pursuant to an earlier judgment or order requiring the act to be done, a copy of the earlier judgment or order has also been served.

(2) Where the person referred to in paragraph (1) is a company or other corporation, a copy of the judgment or order must also be served on the respondent before the end of the time fixed for doing the act.

(3) Copies of the judgment or order and any orders or agreements fixing or varying the time for doing an act must be served in accordance with rule 81.6 or 81.7, or in accordance with an order for alternative service made under rule 81.8(2)(b).

81.6 Method of service – copies of judgments or orders

Subject to rules 81.7 and 81.8, copies of judgments or orders and any orders or agreements fixing or varying the time for doing an act must be served personally.

81.7 Method of service – copies of undertakings

(1) Subject to paragraph (2) and rule 81.8, a copy of any document recording an undertaking will be delivered by the court to the person who gave the undertaking –

   (a) by handing to that person a copy of the document before that person leaves the court building;
   (b) by posting a copy to that person at the residence or place of business of that person where this is known; or
   (c) by posting a copy to that person's solicitor.

(2) If delivery cannot be effected in accordance with paragraph (1), the court officer will deliver a copy of the document to the party for whose benefit the undertaking was given and that party must serve it personally on the person who gave the undertaking as soon as practicable.

(3) Where the person referred to in paragraph (1) is a company or other corporation, a copy of the judgment or order must also be served on the respondent.

81.8 Dispensation with personal service

(1) In the case of a judgment or order requiring a person not to do an act, the court may dispense with service of a copy of the judgment or order in accordance with rules 81.5 to 81.7 if it is satisfied that the person has had notice of it –

   (a) by being present when the judgment or order was given or made; or
   (b) by being notified of its terms by telephone, email or otherwise.

(2) In the case of any judgment or order the court may –

   (a) dispense with service under rules 81.5 to 81.7 if the court thinks it just to do so; or
   (b) make an order in respect of service by an alternative method or at an alternative place.

81.9 Requirement for a penal notice on judgments and orders

(1) Subject to paragraph (2), a judgment or order to do or not do an act may not be enforced under rule 81.4 unless there is prominently displayed, on the front of the copy of the judgment or order served in accordance with this Section, a warning to the person required to do or not do the act in question that disobedience to the order would be a contempt of court punishable by imprisonment, a fine or sequestration of assets.

(2) An undertaking to do or not do an act which is contained in a judgment or order may be enforced under rule 81.4 notwithstanding that the judgment or order does not contain the warning described in paragraph (1).

> (Paragraphs 2.1 to 2.4 of the Practice Direction supplementing this Part and form N117 contain provisions about penal notices and warnings in relation to undertakings.)

81.10 How to make the committal application

(1) A committal application is made by an application notice under Part 23 in the proceedings in which the judgment or order was made or the undertaking was given.

(2) Where the committal application is made against a person who is not an existing party to the proceedings, it is made against that person by an application notice under Part 23.

(3) The application notice must –

   (a) set out in full the grounds on which the committal application is made and must identify, separately and numerically, each alleged act of contempt including, if known, the date of each of the alleged acts; and

(b)   be supported by one or more affidavits containing all the evidence relied upon.

(4)   Subject to paragraph (5), the application notice and the evidence in support must be served personally on the respondent.

(5)   The court may –

(a)   dispense with service under paragraph (4) if it considers it just to do so; or
(b)   make an order in respect of service by an alternative method or at an alternative place.

81.11 Committal for breach of a solicitor's undertaking

(1) The applicant must obtain permission from the court before making a committal application under this rule.

(2) The application for permission must be made by filing an application notice under Part 23.

(3) The application for permission must be supported by an affidavit setting out –

(a)   the name, description and address of the respondent; and
(b)   the grounds on which the committal order is sought.

(4) The application for permission may be made without notice.

(5) Rules 23.9 and 23.10 do not apply.

(6) Unless the applicant makes the committal application within 14 days after permission has been granted under this rule, the permission will lapse.

Section 3
Committal for interference with the due administration of justice

81.12 Scope

(1) This Section regulates committal applications in relation to interference with the due administration of justice in connection with proceedings –

(a)   in the High Court;
(b)   in a Divisional Court;
(c)   in the Court of Appeal;
(d)   in an inferior court (which includes a county court); or
(e)   which are criminal proceedings,

except where the contempt is committed in the face of the court or consists of disobedience to an order of the court or a breach of an undertaking to the court.

(2) This Section also regulates committal applications otherwise than in connection with any proceedings.

(3) A committal application under this Section may not be made without the permission of the court.

(The procedure for applying for permission to make a committal application is set out in rule 81.14.)

(Rules 81.17(5) and (6) make provision for cases in which both this Section and Section 6 (Committal for making a false statement of truth or disclosure statement) may be relevant.)

81.13 Court to which application for permission under this Section is to be made

(1) Where contempt of court is committed in connection with any proceedings –

  (a)   in the High Court (other than proceedings in a Divisional Court), the application for permission may be made only to a single judge of the Division of the High Court in which the proceedings were commenced or to which they have subsequently been transferred;

  (b)   in a Divisional Court, the application for permission may be made only to a single judge of the Queen's Bench Division;

  (c)   in the Court of Appeal, the application for permission may be made only to a Divisional Court of the Queen's Bench Division;

  (d)   in an inferior court, the application for permission may be made only to a single judge of the Queen's Bench Division; and

  (e)   which are criminal proceedings, the application for permission may be made only to a Divisional Court of the Queen's Bench Division.

(2) Where contempt of court is committed otherwise than in connection with any proceedings, the application for permission may be made only to the Administrative Court.

81.14 Application for permission (High Court, Divisional Court or Administrative Court)

(1) The application for permission to make a committal application must be made by a Part 8 claim form which must include or be accompanied by –

  (a)   a detailed statement of the applicant's grounds for bringing the committal application; and

  (b)   an affidavit setting out the facts and exhibiting all documents relied upon.

(2) The claim form and the documents referred to in paragraph (1) must be served personally on the respondent unless the court otherwise directs.

(3) Within 14 days of service on the respondent of the claim form, the respondent –

  (a)   must file and serve an acknowledgment of service; and

  (b)   may file and serve evidence.

(4) The court will consider the application for permission at an oral hearing, unless it considers that such a hearing is not appropriate.

(5) If the respondent intends to appear at the permission hearing referred to in paragraph (4), the respondent must give 7 days' notice in writing of such intention to the court and any other party and at the same time provide a written summary of the submissions which the respondent proposes to make.

(6) Where permission to proceed is given, the court may give such directions as it thinks fit, and may –

  (a)   transfer the proceedings to another court; or

  (b)   direct that the application be listed for hearing before a single judge or a Divisional Court.

Section 4
(1) Certifications by any court, tribunal etc to the High Court under any enactment; and (2) Applications to the High Court under section 336 of the Charities Act 2011

81.15 Certifications of conduct, and applications under section 336 of the Charities Act 2011, to the High Court under this Section

(1) This Section applies where, by virtue of any enactment, the High Court has power to punish or take steps for the punishment of any person charged with having done or omitted to do anything in relation to a court, tribunal or person which, if it had been an act or omission in relation to the High Court, would have been a contempt of that court.

(2) Subject to paragraph (3), an order under this Section may be made by a single judge of the Administrative Court.

(3) An order made on an application under section 336 of the Charities Act 2011 ("a section 336 application") may be made only by a single judge of the Chancery Division.

(4) The certification or section 336 application, as appropriate, must be in the form annexed to Practice Direction 81 at Annex A, and include or be accompanied by –

    (a)   a detailed statement of the grounds for the certification or section 336 application;

    (b)   any written evidence relied upon; and

    (c)   any other documents required for the disposal of the certification or section 336 application.

(5) Subject to paragraph (6), the certification or section 336 application, accompanied by the other documents referred to in paragraph (4), must be served personally on the respondent.

(6) The court may –

    (a)   dispense with service under paragraph (5) if it thinks it just to do so; or

    (b)   make an order in respect of service by an alternative method or at an alternative place.

(7) Within 14 days of service on the respondent of the certification or section 336 application, the respondent –

    (a)   must file and serve an acknowledgment of service in the form annexed to Practice Direction 81 at Annex B; and

    (b)   may file and serve evidence.

Section 5
Contempt in the face of the court

81.16 Committal for contempt in the face of the court

(1) Where –

    (a)   contempt has occurred in the face of the court; and

    (b)   that court has power to commit for contempt,

the court may deal with the matter of its own initiative and give such directions as it thinks fit for the disposal of the matter.

Section 6
Committal for making a false statement of truth (rule 32.14) or disclosure
statement (rule 31.23)

81.17 Scope and interaction with other Sections of this Part

(1) This Section contains rules about committal applications in relation to making, or causing to be made –

(a)   a false statement in a document verified by a statement of truth; or

(b)   a false disclosure statement,

without an honest belief in its truth.

(2) Where the committal application relates only to a false statement of truth or disclosure statement, this Section applies.

(3) Where the committal application relates to both –

(a)   a false statement of truth or disclosure statement; and

(b)   breach of a judgment, order or undertaking to do or abstain from doing an act,

Section 2 (Committal for breach of a judgment, order or undertaking to do or abstain from doing an act) applies, but subject to paragraph (4).

(4) To the extent that a committal application referred to in paragraph (3) relates to a false statement of truth or disclosure statement –

(a)   the applicant must obtain the permission of the court in accordance with rule 81.18; or

(b)   the court may direct that the matter be referred to the Attorney General with a request that the Attorney General consider whether to bring proceedings for contempt of court.

(5) Where the committal application relates to both –

(a)   a false statement of truth or disclosure statement; and

(b)   other interference with the due administration of justice,

Section 3 (Committal for interference with the due administration of justice) applies, but subject to paragraph (6).

(6) To the extent that a committal application referred to in paragraph (5) relates to a false statement of truth or disclosure statement, the court may direct that the matter be referred to the Attorney General with a request that the Attorney General consider whether to bring proceedings for contempt of court.

81.18 Committal application in relation to a false statement of truth or disclosure statement

(1) A committal application in relation to a false statement of truth or disclosure statement in connection with proceedings in the High Court, a Divisional Court or the Court of Appeal, may be made only –

(a)   with the permission of the court dealing with the proceedings in which the false statement or disclosure statement was made; or

(b)   by the Attorney General.

(2) Where permission is required under paragraph (1)(a), rule 81.14 applies as if the reference in that rule to a Part 8 claim form were a reference to a Part 23 application notice and the references to the claim form were references to the Part 23 application notice.

(3) A committal application in relation to a false statement of truth or disclosure statement in connection with proceedings in a county court may be made only –

    (a)   with the permission of a single judge of the Queen's Bench Division; or

    (b)   by the Attorney General.

(4) Where permission is required under paragraph (3)(a) rule 81.14 applies without the modifications referred to in paragraph (2).

        (Under rule 81.14(6)(b), the court granting permission may direct that the application be listed for hearing before a single judge or a Divisional Court.)

(5) The court may direct that the matter be referred to the Attorney General with a request that the Attorney General consider whether to bring proceedings for contempt of court.

(6) Where the committal application is made by the Attorney General, the application may be made to a single judge or a Divisional Court of the Queen's Bench Division.

Section 7
Writ of sequestration to enforce a judgment, order or undertaking

81.19 Scope

This Section contains rules about applications to the High Court for a writ of sequestration to enforce a judgment, order or undertaking.

81.20 Writ of sequestration to enforce a judgment, order or undertaking

(1) If –

    (a)   a person required by a judgment or order to do an act does not do it within the time fixed by the judgment or order; or

    (b)   a person disobeys a judgment or order not to do an act,

then, subject to the provisions of these Rules and if the court permits, the judgment or order may be enforced by a writ of sequestration against the property of that person.

(2) If the time fixed by the judgment or order for doing an act has been varied by a subsequent order or agreement of the parties under rule 2.11, references in paragraph (1)(a) to the time fixed are references to the time fixed by that subsequent order or agreement.

(3) If the person referred to in paragraph (1) is a company or other corporation, the writ of sequestration may in addition be issued against the property of any director or other officer of that company or corporation.

(4) So far as applicable, and with the necessary modifications, this Section applies to undertakings given by a party as it applies to judgments or orders.

81.21 Requirement for service of a copy of the judgment or order and time for service

(1) Unless the court dispenses with service under rule 81.24, a judgment or order may not be enforced by writ of sequestration unless a copy of it has been served on the person required to do or not do the act in question, and in the case of a judgment or order requiring a person to do an act –

    (a)   the copy has been served before the end of the time fixed for doing the act, together with a copy of any order fixing that time;

(b) where the time for doing the act has been varied by a subsequent order or agreement under rule 2.11, a copy of that subsequent order or agreement has also been served; and

(c) where the judgment or order was made under rule 81.4(5), or was made pursuant to an earlier judgment or order requiring the act to be done, a copy of the earlier judgment or order has also been served.

(2) Where the person referred to in paragraph (1) is a company or other corporation, a copy of the judgment or order must also be served on the respondent before the end of the time fixed for doing the act.

(3) Copies of the judgment or order and any orders or agreements fixing or varying the time for doing an act must be served in accordance with rule 81.22 or 81.23, or in accordance with an order for alternative service made under rule 81.24(2)(b).

81.22 Method of service – copies of judgments or orders

Subject to rules 81.23 and 81.24, copies of judgments or orders and any orders or agreements fixing or varying the time for doing an act must be served personally.

81.23 Method of service – copies of undertakings

(1) Subject to paragraph (2) and rule 81.24, a copy of any document recording an undertaking will be delivered by the court to the person who gave the undertaking –

(a) by handing to that person a copy of the document before that person leaves the court building;

(b) by posting a copy to that person at the residence or place of business of that person where this is known; or

(c) by posting a copy to that person's solicitor.

(2) If delivery cannot be effected in accordance with paragraph (1), the court officer will deliver a copy of the document to the party for whose benefit the undertaking was given and that party must serve it personally on the person who gave the undertaking as soon as practicable.

(3) Where the person referred to in paragraph (1) is a company or other corporation, a copy of the judgment or order must also be served on the respondent.

81.24 Dispensation with personal service

(1) In the case of a judgment or order requiring a person not to do an act, the court may dispense with service of a copy of the judgment or order in accordance with rules 81.21 to 81.23 if it is satisfied that the person has had notice of it –

(a) by being present when the judgment or order was given or made; or

(b) by being notified of its terms by telephone, email or otherwise.

(2) In the case of any judgment or order the court may –

(a) dispense with service under rules 81.21 to 81.23 if the court thinks it just to do so; or

(b) make an order in respect of service by an alternative method or at an alternative place.

81.25 Requirement for a penal notice on judgments and orders

(1) Subject to paragraph (2), a judgment or order to do or not do an act may not be enforced by a writ of sequestration unless there is prominently displayed, on the front of the copy of the judgment or order served in accordance with this Section, a warning to

the person required to do or not do the act in question that disobedience to the order would be a contempt of court punishable by imprisonment, a fine or sequestration of assets.

(2) An undertaking to do or not do an act which is contained in a judgment or order may be enforced by a writ of sequestration notwithstanding that the judgment or order does not contain the warning described in paragraph (1).

> (Paragraphs 2.1 to 2.4 of the Practice Direction supplementing this Part and form N117 contain provisions about penal notices and warnings in relation to undertakings.)

81.26 How to make an application for permission to issue a writ of sequestration

(1) An application for permission to issue a writ of sequestration must be made –

    (a)   to a single judge of the Division of the High Court in which the proceedings were commenced or to which they have subsequently been transferred; or

    (b)   in any other case, to a single judge of the Queen's Bench Division.

(2) An application for permission to issue a writ of sequestration must be made by filing an application notice under Part 23.

(3) The application notice must –

    (a)   set out in full the grounds on which the application is made and must identify, separately and numerically, each alleged act of contempt including, if known, the date of each of the alleged acts; and

    (b)   be supported by one or more affidavits containing all the evidence relied upon.

(4) Subject to paragraph (5), the application notice must be served personally on the respondent.

(5) The court may –

    (a)   dispense with service under paragraph (4) if the court thinks it just to do so; or

    (b)   make an order in respect of service by an alternative method or at an alternative place.

81.27 Form of writ of sequestration

A writ of sequestration must be in Form No 67 as set out in Practice Direction 4.

Section 8
General rules about committal applications, orders for committal and writs of sequestration

81.28 The hearing

(1) Unless the court hearing the committal application or application for sequestration otherwise permits, the applicant may not rely on –

    (a)   any grounds other than –

        (i)   those set out in the claim form or application notice; or

        (ii)   in relation to a committal application under Section 3 or 4, the statement of grounds required by rule 81.14(1)(a) (where not included in the claim form) or 81.15(4)(a); or

    (b)   any evidence unless it has been served in accordance with the relevant Section of this Part or the Practice Direction supplementing this Part.

(2) At the hearing, the respondent is entitled –

    (a)   to give oral evidence, whether or not the respondent has filed or served written evidence, and, if doing so, may be cross-examined; and

    (b)   with the permission of the court, to call a witness to give oral evidence whether or not the witness has made an affidavit or witness statement.

(3) The court may require or permit any party or other person (other than the respondent) to give oral evidence at the hearing.

(4) The court may give directions requiring the attendance for cross-examination of a witness who has given written evidence.

(5) If the court hearing an application in private decides to make a committal order against the respondent, it will in public state –

    (a)   the name of the respondent;

    (b)   in general terms, the nature of the contempt of court in respect of which the committal order is being made; and

    (c)   the length of the period of the committal order.

       (Rule 39.2 contains provisions about hearings in private.)

(6) Where a committal order is made in the absence of the respondent, the court may on its own initiative fix a date and time when the respondent is to be brought before the court.

81.29 Power to suspend execution of a committal order

(1) The court making the committal order may also order that its execution will be suspended for such period or on such terms or conditions as it may specify.

(2) Unless the court otherwise directs, the applicant must serve on the respondent a copy of any order made under paragraph (1).

81.30 Warrant of committal

(1) If a committal order is made, the order will be for the issue of a warrant of committal.

(2) Unless the court orders otherwise –

    (a)   a copy of the committal order must be served on the respondent either before or at the time of the execution of the warrant of committal; or

    (b)   where the warrant of committal has been signed by the judge, the committal order may be served on the respondent at any time within 36 hours after the execution of the warrant.

(3) Without further order of the court, a warrant of committal must not be enforced more than 2 years after the date on which the warrant is issued.

81.31 Discharge of a person in custody

(1) A person committed to prison for contempt of court may apply to the court to be discharged.

(2) The application must –

    (a)   be in writing and attested by the governor of the prison (or any other officer of the prison not below the rank of principal officer);

    (b)   show that the person committed to prison for contempt has purged, or wishes to purge, the contempt; and

(c) be served on the person (if any) at whose instance the warrant of committal was issued at least one day before the application is made.

(3) Paragraph (2) does not apply to –

(a) a warrant of committal to which CCR Order 27 rule 8, or CCR Order 28 rule 4 or 14 relates; or

(b) an application made by the Official Solicitor acting with official authority for the discharge of a person in custody.

(4) If the committal order is made in a county court and –

(a) does not direct that any application for discharge must be made to a judge; or

(b) was made by a district judge under section 118 of the County Courts Act 1984,

the application for discharge may be made to a district judge.

(5) If the committal order is made in the High Court, the application for discharge may be made to a single judge of the Division in which the committal order was made.

81.32 Discharge of a person in custody where a writ of sequestration has been issued

(1) Where –

(a) a writ of sequestration has been issued to enforce a judgment or order;

(b) the property is in the custody or power of the respondent;

(c) the respondent has been committed for failing to deliver up any property or deposit it in court or elsewhere; and

(d) the commissioners appointed by the writ of sequestration take possession of the property as if it belonged to the respondent,

then, without prejudice to rule 81.31(1), the court may discharge the respondent and give such directions for dealing with the property taken by the commissioners as it thinks fit.

Section 9
Penal, contempt and disciplinary provisions under the County Courts Act 1984

81.33 Scope

(1) This Section applies to county courts only and contains rules in relation to the penal, contempt and disciplinary provisions of the County Courts Act 1984.

(2) In this Section, "the Act" means the County Courts Act 1984.

81.34 Offences under sections 14, 92 or 118 of the Act

(1) This rule applies where it is alleged that any person has committed an offence–

(a) under section 14 of the Act, by assaulting an officer of the court acting in the execution of the officer's duties;

(b) under section 92 of the Act, by rescuing or attempting to rescue any goods seized in execution; or

(c) under section 118 of the Act, by wilfully insulting a judge, juror, witness or any officer of the court or by wilfully interrupting the proceedings of a county court or otherwise misbehaving in court,

and the alleged offender has not been taken into custody and brought before the court.

(2) The court will issue a summons, which must be served on the alleged offender personally not less than 7 days before the day of the hearing stated in the summons.

(3) Rule 81.30 applies, with the necessary modifications, where an order is made under section 14, 92 or 118 of the Act committing a person to prison.

81.35 Offences under section 124 of the Act

Where a complaint is made against an officer of the court under section 124 of the Act for having lost the opportunity of levying execution, the court will issue a summons, which must be served on the alleged offender personally not less than 7 days before the day of the hearing stated in the summons.

81.36 Notice to give evidence before or after a fine is imposed under section 55 of the Act

(1) Before or after imposing a fine on any person under section 55 of the Act for disobeying a witness summons or refusing to be sworn or give evidence, the court may direct that notice be given to that person in accordance with paragraph (2).

(2) The notice must state that if the recipient of the notice can demonstrate any reason why a fine should not be or should not have been imposed, that person may give evidence –

    (a)   by witness statement, affidavit or otherwise; and

    (b)   on a day named in the notice.

81.37 Non-payment of fine

(1) If a fine is not paid in accordance with the order imposing it, the court officer will, as soon as reasonably possible, report the matter to a judge.

(2) Where by an order imposing a fine –

    (a)   the amount of the fine is directed to be paid by instalments; and

    (b)   default is made in the payment of any instalment,

the same proceedings may be taken as if default had been made in payment of the whole of the fine.

(3) If the court makes an order for payment of a fine to be enforced by warrant of execution, the order will be treated as an application to the court for the issue of the warrant at the time when the order was made.

81.38 Repayment of fine

If a person pays a fine and later gives evidence to satisfy the court that, if the evidence had been given earlier, no fine or a smaller fine would have been imposed, the court may order the whole or part of the fine to be repaid.

Amendments—Inserted by SI 2012/2208, subject to transitional provisions and savings.

Practice Direction 81 –
Applications and Proceedings in relation to Contempt of Court

This Practice Direction supplements CPR Part 81

SECTION 2 OF PART 81 – COMMITTAL FOR BREACH OF A JUDGMENT, ORDER OR UNDERTAKING TO DO OR ABSTAIN FROM DOING AN ACT

1 Requirement for a penal notice on judgments and orders – form of penal notice – Rule 81.9

A judgment or order which restrains a party from doing an act or requires an act to be done must, if disobedience is to be dealt with by proceedings for contempt of court, have a penal notice endorsed on it as follows (or in words to substantially the same effect) –

> "If you the within-named [ ] do not comply with this order you may be held to be in contempt of court and imprisoned or fined, or your assets may be seized.".

Requirement for a penal notice on judgments and orders – undertakings – Rule 81.9

2.1 The provisions of paragraph 8.1 of Practice Direction 40B – Judgments and orders that supplements Part 40 apply to an order which contains an undertaking by a party to do or not do an act, subject to paragraph 2.2 below.

> (Paragraph 8.1 of Practice Direction 40B contains provisions about specifying the time within which acts must be done.)

2.2 The court may decline to –

(1) accept an undertaking; and
(2) deal with disobedience in respect of an undertaking by contempt of court proceedings,

unless the party giving the undertaking has made a signed statement to the effect that that party understands the terms of the undertaking and the consequences of failure to comply with it.

2.3 The statement may be endorsed on the order containing the undertaking or may be filed in a separate document such as a letter.

2.4 Where the order containing an undertaking is made in a county court, form N117 may be used.

SECTION 4 OF PART 81 – (1) CERTIFICATIONS BY ANY COURT, TRIBUNAL ETC TO THE HIGH COURT UNDER ANY ENACTMENT; (2) APPLICATIONS TO THE HIGH COURT UNDER SECTION 336 OF THE CHARITIES ACT 2011

3 Scope of Section 4 of Part 81

Section 4 of Part 81 contains rules in relation to statutory powers of the High Court to commit any person for contempt in respect of anything done or not done in relation to a court, tribunal or person. The statutory powers include –

(1) section 336 of the Charities Act 2011;
(2) sections 436 and 453C of the Companies Act 1985;

PART III

(3)   paragraph 8 of Schedule 6 to the Data Protection Act 1998; and

(4)   sections 18, 161 and 232 of the Financial Services and Markets Act 2000.

SECTION 5 OF PART 81 – CONTEMPT IN THE FACE OF THE COURT

Committal for contempt in the face of the court – Rule 81.16

4.1 Where the committal proceedings relate to a contempt in the face of the court the matters referred to in paragraph 4.3 should be given particular attention. Normally, it will be appropriate to defer consideration of the respondent's actions and behaviour to allow the respondent time to reflect on what has occurred. The time needed for the following procedures should allow such a period of reflection.

4.2 A Part 8 claim form and an application notice are not required for contempt falling under Section 5 of Part 81, but other provisions of this Practice Direction should be applied, as necessary, or adapted to the circumstances.

4.3 The judge should –

(1)   tell the respondent of the possible penalty that the respondent faces;

(2)   inform the respondent in detail, and preferably in writing, of the actions and behaviour of the respondent which have given rise to the committal application;

(3)   if the judge considers that an apology would remove the need for the committal application, tell the respondent;

(4)   have regard to the need for the respondent to be –

(a)   allowed a reasonable time for responding to the committal application, including, if necessary, preparing a defence;

(b)   made aware of the availability of assistance from the Community Legal Service and how to contact the Service;

(c)   given the opportunity, if unrepresented, to obtain legal advice;

(d)   if unable to understand English, allowed to make arrangements, seeking the court's assistance if necessary, for an interpreter to attend the hearing; and

(e)   brought back before the court for the committal application to be heard within a reasonable time;

(5)   allow the respondent an opportunity to –

(a)   apologise to the court;

(b)   explain the respondent's actions and behaviour; and

(c)   if the contempt is proved, to address the court on the penalty to be imposed on the respondent; and

(6)   where appropriate, nominate a suitable person to give the respondent the information. (It is likely to be appropriate to nominate a person where the effective communication of information by the judge to the respondent was not possible when the incident occurred.)

4.4 If there is a risk of the appearance of bias, the judge should ask another judge to hear the committal application.

4.5 Where the committal application is to be heard by another judge, a written statement by the judge before whom the actions and behaviour of the respondent which have given rise to the committal application took place may be admitted as evidence of those actions and behaviour.

SECTION 6 OF PART 81 – COMMITTAL FOR MAKING A FALSE STATEMENT OF TRUTH OR DISCLOSURE STATEMENT

Committal application in relation to a false statement of truth or disclosure statement – Rule 81.18

5.1 Rules 81.18(1)(b) and 81.18(3)(b) provide that a committal application may be made by the Attorney General. However, the Attorney General prefers a request that comes from the court to one made direct by a party to the proceedings in which the alleged contempt occurred without prior consideration by the court. A request to the Attorney General is not a way of appealing against, or reviewing, the decision of the judge.

5.2 Where the permission of the court is sought under rule 81.18(1)(a) or 81.18(3)(a) so that rule 81.14 is applied by rule 81.18(2) or 81.18(4), the affidavit evidence in support of the application must –

(1) identify the statement said to be false;
(2) explain –
    (a) why it is false; and
    (b) why the maker knew the statement to be false at the time it was made; and
(3) explain why contempt proceedings would be appropriate in the light of the overriding objective in Part 1.

5.3 The court may –

(1) exercise any of its powers under the rules (including the power to give directions under rule 81.14(6));
(2) initiate steps to consider if there is a contempt of court and, where there is, to punish it; or
(3) as provided by rule 81.18(5), direct that the matter be referred to the Attorney General with a request to consider whether to bring proceedings for contempt of court.

5.4 A request to the Attorney General to consider whether to bring proceedings for contempt of court must be made in writing and sent to the Attorney General's Office at 20 Victoria Street, London, SW1H 0NF.

5.5 A request to the Attorney General must be accompanied by a copy of any order directing that the matter be referred to the Attorney General and must –

(1) identify the statement said to be false;
(2) explain –
    (a) why it is false; and
    (b) why the maker knew the statement to be false at the time it was made; and
(3) explain why contempt proceedings would be appropriate in the light of the overriding objective in Part 1.

5.6 Once the applicant receives the result of the request to the Attorney General, the applicant must send a copy of it to the court that will deal with the committal application, and the court will give such directions as it sees fit.

5.7 The rules do not change the law of contempt or introduce new categories of contempt. A person applying to commence such proceedings should consider whether the incident complained of does amount to contempt of court and whether such proceedings would further the overriding objective in Part 1.

SECTION 7 OF PART 81 – WRIT OF SEQUESTRATION TO ENFORCE A JUDGMENT, ORDER OR UNDERTAKING

6   Requirement for a penal notice on judgments and orders – form of penal notice – Rule 81.25

Paragraphs 1 and 2.1 to 2.4 apply to judgments and orders to be enforced by a writ of sequestration.

Levying execution on certain days

7.1 Unless the court orders otherwise, a writ of sequestration to enforce a judgment, order or undertaking must not be executed on a Sunday, Good Friday or Christmas Day.

7.2 Paragraph 7.1 does not apply to an Admiralty claim in rem.

SECTION 8 OF PART 81 – GENERAL RULES ABOUT COMMITTAL APPLICATIONS, ORDERS FOR COMMITTAL AND WRITS OF SEQUESTRATION

General rules

8.1 Subject to paragraph 8.2, this Section of the Practice Direction applies in relation to all matters covered by Part 81.

8.2 Where there is a conflict between the provisions in this Section of the Practice Direction and specific provisions elsewhere in this Practice Direction or in Part 81, the specific provisions prevail.

9   Human rights

In all cases the Convention rights of those involved should particularly be borne in mind. It should be noted that the standard of proof, having regard to the possibility that a person may be sent to prison, is that the allegation be proved beyond reasonable doubt.

> (Section 1 of the Human Rights Act 1998 defines 'the Convention rights'.)

Court to which applications should be made and levels of judiciary

10.1 A committal application or an application for permission to make a committal application –

    (1) may be made in a county court if the alleged contempt is a contempt which a county court has power to punish; and

    (2) must otherwise be made in the High Court.

10.2 Except where under an enactment a Master or district judge has power to make a committal order, a committal order can only be made –

    (1) in High Court proceedings, by a High Court Judge or a person authorised to act as such; or

    (2) in county court proceedings, by a Circuit Judge or a person authorised to act as such.

10.3 Paragraph 10.4 applies in relation to proceedings in any court (the first court) where the judge or judges exercising the jurisdiction of the first court are deemed to constitute a court of the High Court by virtue of an enactment.

10.4 The reference in paragraph 10.2(1) to a High Court Judge will be construed as a reference to a judge of the first court.

11 General rules about applications: applications which cannot be made without permission

If the committal application is one which cannot be made without permission –

(1) the permission may only be granted by a judge who would have power to hear the committal application if permission were granted;

(2) the date on which and the name of the judge by whom the requisite permission was granted must be stated on the claim form or application notice by which the committal application is commenced;

(3) the claim form or application notice may not be issued or filed until the requisite permission has been granted; and

(4) Rules 23.9 and 23.10 do not apply.

12 General rules about applications: applications by claim form

If the application for permission to make a committal application or the committal application is commenced by the issue of a claim form –

(1) Part 8 will apply –

  (a) subject to the provisions of Part 81 and this Practice Direction, in particular sub-paragraphs (2) to (4);

  (b) as though references to "claimant" were references to the applicant; and

  (c) as though references to "defendant" were references to the respondent;

(2) an amendment to the claim form may be made with the permission of the court but not otherwise;

(3) rule 8.4 does not apply; and

(4) the claim form must contain a prominent notice stating the possible consequences of the court making a committal order and of the respondent not attending the hearing. A form of notice which may be used is annexed to this Practice Direction at Annex 3.

General rules about applications: applications by application notice

13.1 Where the application is made by application notice, the application notice must state that the application is made in the proceedings in question, and its title and reference number must correspond with the title and reference number of those proceedings.

13.2 If the application for permission to make a committal application or the committal application is commenced by the filing of an application notice –

(1) Part 23 will apply subject to the provisions of Part 81 and this Practice Direction, in particular sub-paragraphs (2) to (4);

(2) an amendment to the application notice may be made with the permission of the court but not otherwise;

(3) the court may not dispose of the application without a hearing; and

(4) the application notice must contain a prominent notice stating the possible consequences of the court making a committal order and of the respondent not attending the hearing. A form of notice which may be used is annexed to this Practice Direction at Annex 3.

Evidence and information

14.1 Written evidence in support of or in opposition to a committal application must be given by affidavit.

14.2 Written evidence served in support of or in opposition to a committal application must, unless the court otherwise directs, be filed.

14.3 The following rules do not apply to committal applications –

    (1)   rule 35.7 (Court's power to direct that evidence is to be given by a single joint expert);

    (2)   rule 35.8 (Instructions to single joint expert); and

    (3)   rule 35.9 (Power of court to direct a party to provide information).

14.4 An order under rule 18.1 (Obtaining further information) may not be made against a respondent to a committal application.

The hearing – Rule 81.28

15.1 When issuing or filing the claim form or application notice for a committal application, the applicant must obtain from the court a date for the hearing of the committal application.

15.2 Unless the court otherwise directs, the hearing date of a committal application must not be less than 14 days after service of the claim form or application notice on the respondent. The hearing date must be specified in the claim form or application notice or in a Notice of Hearing attached to and served with the claim form or application notice.

15.3 Paragraphs 15.1 and 15.2 apply to certifications of conduct and applications under section 336 of the Charities Act 2011 ("section 336 application") referred to in Section 4 of Part 81 as if references to the claim form or application notice were references to the certification or section 336 application.

> (The definition of "applicant" in rule 81.3 includes a person who makes a committal application by way of certification or section 336 application.)

15.4 The court may on the hearing date –

    (1)   give case management directions with a view to a hearing of the committal application on a future date; or

    (2)   if the committal application is ready to be heard, proceed to hear it.

15.5 In dealing with any committal application, the court will have regard to the need for the respondent to have details of the alleged acts of contempt and the opportunity to respond to the committal application.

15.6 The court will also have regard to the need for the respondent to be –

    (1)   allowed a reasonable time for responding to the committal application including, if necessary, preparing a defence;

    (2)   made aware of the availability of assistance from the Community Legal Service and how to contact the Service;

    (3)   given the opportunity, if unrepresented, to obtain legal advice; and

    (4)   if unable to understand English, allowed to make arrangements, seeking the assistance of the court if necessary, for an interpreter to attend the hearing.

Striking out, procedural defects and discontinuance

16.1 On application by the respondent or on its own initiative, the court may strike out a committal application if it appears to the court –

    (1)   that the application and the evidence served in support of it disclose no reasonable ground for alleging that the respondent is guilty of a contempt of court;

(2) that the application is an abuse of the court's process or, if made in existing proceedings, is otherwise likely to obstruct the just disposal of those proceedings; or

(3) that there has been a failure to comply with a rule, practice direction or court order.

16.2 The court may waive any procedural defect in the commencement or conduct of a committal application if satisfied that no injustice has been caused to the respondent by the defect.

16.3 A committal application may not be discontinued without the permission of the court.

****

SCHEDULE 1

****

RSC ORDER 45
ENFORCEMENT OF JUDGMENTS AND ORDERS: GENERAL

1A Interpretation (RSC Ord 45, r 1A)

In this Order, and in RSC Orders 46 and 47 –

(a) 'enforcement officer' means an individual who is authorised to act as an enforcement officer under the Courts Act 2003; and

(b) 'relevant enforcement officer' means –

(i) in relation to a writ of execution which is directed to an single enforcement officer, that officer;

(ii) in relation to a writ of execution which is directed to two or more enforcement officers, the officer to whom the writ is allocated.

Amendments—Inserted by SI 2003/3361.

1 Enforcement of judgment, etc, for payment of money (RSC Ord 45, r 1)

(1)–(3) ...

(4) In this Order references to any writ shall be construed as including references to any further writ in aid of the first mentioned writ.

Amendments—SI 2001/2792.

2 Notice of seizure (RSC Ord 45, r 2)

When first executing a writ of fieri facias, the Sheriff or his officer or the relevant enforcement officer shall deliver to the debtor or leave at each place where execution is levied a notice in Form No 55 in Practice Direction 4 informing the debtor of the execution.

Amendments—SI 2003/3361; SI 2009/3390.

3 Enforcement of judgment for possession of land (RSC Ord 45, r 3)

(1) Subject to the provisions of these rules, a judgment or order for the giving of possession of land may be enforced by one or more of the following means, that is to say –

(a) writ of possession;
(b) in a case in which rule 81.4 applies, an order of committal;
(c) in a case in which rule 81.20 applies, writ of sequestration.

(2) A writ of possession to enforce a judgment or order for the giving of possession of any land shall not be issued without the permission of the court except where the judgment or order was given or made in proceedings by a mortgagee or mortgagor or by any person having the right to foreclose or redeem any mortgage, being proceedings in which there is a claim for –

(a) payment of moneys secured by the mortgage;
(b) sale of the mortgaged property;
(c) foreclosure;
(d) delivery of possession (whether before or after foreclosure or without foreclosure) to the mortgagee by the mortgagor or by any other person who is alleged to be in possession of the property;
(e) redemption;
(f) reconveyance of the land or its release from the security; or
(g) delivery of possession by the mortgagee.

(2A) In paragraph (2) 'mortgage' includes a legal or equitable mortgage and a legal or equitable charge, and reference to a mortgagor, a mortgagee and mortgaged land is to be interpreted accordingly.

(3) Such permission as is referred to in paragraph (2) shall not be granted unless it is shown –

(a) that every person in actual possession of the whole or any part of the land has received such notice of the proceedings as appears to the court sufficient to enable him to apply to the court for any relief to which he may be entitled; and
(b) if the operation of the judgment or order is suspended by subsection (2) of section 16 of the Landlord and Tenant Act 1954, that the applicant has not received notice in writing from the tenant that he desires that the provisions of paragraphs (a) and (b) of that subsection shall have effect.

(4) A writ of possession may include provision for enforcing the payment of any money adjudged or ordered to be paid by the judgment or order which is to be enforced by the writ.

Amendments—SI 2001/256; SI 2012/2208.

"permission of the court" (r 3(2))—See Ord 46, r 4 for the procedure to be followed where permission is required. The court will expect notice of the judgment or order to have been given to the defendant and (if different) the occupier, and possession to have been demanded. The affidavit must deal with these matters and give details of the tenancy of any other occupier than the person against whom the order was made. Where the order was suspended subject to a condition that is said to have been broken, notice must be given to the defendant (*Fleet Mortgage and Investment Co Ltd v Lower Maisonette, 46 Eaton Place Ltd* [1972] 1 WLR 765).

Restitution—If, after a writ of possession has been executed, possession is unlawfully regained, the plaintiff may obtain a writ of restitution to have the occupants again evicted. Such a writ is in aid of the original writ (see Ord 46, rr 3 and 4).

4 Enforcement of judgment for delivery of goods (RSC Ord 45, r 4)

(1) Subject to the provisions of these rules, a judgment or order for the delivery of any goods which does not give a person against whom the judgment is given or order made the alternative of paying the assessed value of the goods may be enforced by one or more of the following means, that is to say –

(a)   writ of delivery to recover the goods without alternative provision for recovery of the assessed value thereof (hereafter in this rule referred to as a 'writ of specific delivery');

(b)   in a case in which rule 81.4 applies, an order of committal;

(c)   in a case in which rule 81.20 applies, writ of sequestration.

(2) Subject to the provisions of these rules, a judgment or order for the delivery of any goods or payment of their assessed value may be enforced by one or more of the following means, that is to say –

(a)   writ of delivery to recover the goods or their assessed value;

(b)   by order of the court, writ of specific delivery;

(c)   in a case in which rule 81.20 applies, writ of sequestration.

An application for an order under sub-paragraph (b) shall be made in accordance with CPR Part 23, which must be served on the defendant against whom the judgment or order sought to be enforced was given or made.

(3) A writ of specific delivery, and a writ of delivery to recover any goods or their assessed value, may include provision for enforcing the payment of any money adjudged or ordered to be paid by the judgment or order which is to be enforced by the writ.

(4) A judgment or order for the payment of the assessed value of any goods may be enforced by the same means as any other judgment or order for the payment of money.

Amendments—SI 2012/2208.

5–7 (*revoked*)

8 Court may order act to be done at expense of disobedient party (RSC Ord 45, r 8)

If a mandatory order, an injunction or a judgment or order for the specific performance of a contract is not complied with, then, without prejudice to its powers under section 39 of the Act and its powers to punish the disobedient party for contempt, the court may direct that the act required to be done may, so far as practicable, be done by the party by whom the order or judgment was obtained or some other person appointed by the court, at the cost of the disobedient party, and upon the act being done the expenses incurred may be ascertained in such manner as the court may direct and execution may issue against the disobedient party for the amount so ascertained and for costs.

Amendments—SI 2003/3361.

Scope—Rather than coerce a person into doing the required act himself, the court may, if it is practicable to do so, authorise it to be done by someone else at his expense. If the act is not one that requires personal attention and a fund is available from which the expense can be met, it will be preferable to proceed under this rule. Although the rule gives powers additional to, not in substitution for, those of committal and sequestration, if the object of the order can be achieved under this rule the court will be reluctant also to commit, save in the case of blatant, contumelious contempt. In cases where large sums are at stake, the rule may be used as an adjunct to sequestration.

Undertakings—This rule does not apply in the case of a breach of an undertaking, but the court may be prepared to exercise its inherent powers to similar effect (*Mortimer v Wilson* (1885) 33 WR 927). It may be prudent to apply in the alternative for an order in the terms of the undertaking, which order could be enforced subsequently under this rule if it is not complied with.

Execution of documents—A similar but specific remedy is available, where a person has been ordered to execute a document but neglects or refuses to do so or cannot be found, under SCA 1981, s 39.

****

PART III

11 Matters occurring after judgment: stay of execution, etc (RSC Ord 45, r 11)

Without prejudice to Order 47, rule 1, a party against whom a judgment has been given or an order made may apply to the court for a stay of execution of the judgment or order or other relief on the ground of matters which have occurred since the date of the judgment or order, and the court may by order grant such relief, and on such terms, as it thinks just.

Scope—This rule gives the court extremely wide powers to control the execution of a judgment or order if some occurrence since it was given or made makes that appropriate. The rule is not confined to cases of inability to pay, or indeed to money judgments.

"Order 47, rule 1"—This rule enables the court to stay execution of a money judgment against the debtor's goods by reason of inability to pay (whenever arising) or in other special circumstances.

12 Forms of writs (RSC Ord 45, r 12)

(1) A writ of fieri facias must be in such of the Forms Nos 53 to 63 in Practice Direction 4 as is appropriate in the particular case.

(2) A writ of delivery must be in Form No 64 or 65 in Practice Direction 4, whichever is appropriate.

(3) A writ of possession must be in Form No 66 or 66A in Practice Direction 4, whichever is appropriate.#

(4) (*revoked*)

Amendments—SI 2009/3390; SI 2012/2208.

Practice Direction 4—That is, CPR PD4.

RSC ORDER 46
WRITS OF EXECUTION: GENERAL

1 Definition (RSC Ord 46, r 1)

In this Order, unless the context otherwise requires, 'writ of execution' includes a writ of fieri facias, a writ of possession, a writ of delivery, a writ of sequestration and any further writ in aid of any of the aforementioned writs.

2 When permission to issue any writ of execution is necessary (RSC Ord 46, r 2)

(1) A writ of execution to enforce a judgment or order may not issue without the permission of the court in the following cases, that is to say –

    (a) where 6 years or more have elapsed since the date of the judgment or order;

    (b) where any change has taken place, whether by death or otherwise, in the parties entitled or liable to execution under the judgment or order;

    (c) where the judgment or order is against the assets of a deceased person coming to the hands of his executors or administrators after the date of the judgment or order, and it is sought to issue execution against such assets;

    (d) where under the judgment or order any person is entitled to a remedy subject to the fulfilment of any condition which it is alleged has been fulfilled;

    (e) where any goods sought to be seized under a writ of execution are in the hands of a receiver appointed by the court or a sequestrator.

(2) Paragraph (1) is without prejudice to section 2 of the Reserve and Auxiliary Forces (Protection of Civil Interests) Act 1951, or any other enactment or rule by virtue of

which a person is required to obtain the permission of the court for the issue of a writ of execution or to proceed to execution on or otherwise to the enforcement of a judgment or order.

(3) Where the court grants permission, whether under this rule or otherwise, for the issue of a writ of execution and the writ is not issued within one year after the date of the order granting such permission, the order shall cease to have effect, without prejudice, however, to the making of a fresh order.

Insolvency of debtor—Where the debt to be enforced is arrears of periodical payments, leave is not needed merely because a bankruptcy order has been made against the debtor.

"6 years or more have elapsed" (r 2(1)(a))—The delay should be explained in the witness statement or affidavit (see r 4(2)). The court may be reluctant to allow execution on a stale judgment or order and will not do so if the debtor is prejudiced by the delay.

"any change ... in the parties" (r 2(1)(b))—The alternative is to apply to change the party under CPR 1998, Pt 19. It is not thought that, following an order under that rule, permission would also be required under this rule. An order under Pt 19 would still be needed before other enforcement proceedings were taken following a (presumably abortive) writ of execution issued with permission under this rule.

"within one year" (r 2(3))—The limitation on the time within which the writ of execution must be issued does not apply only to cases where permission is required by virtue of this rule but to all cases where permission is required.

3 Permission required for issue of writ in aid of other writ (RSC Ord 46, r 3)

A writ of execution in aid of any other writ of execution shall not issue without the permission of the court.

4 Application for permission to issue writ (RSC Ord 46, r 4)

(1) An application for permission to issue a writ of execution may be made in accordance with CPR Part 23 but the application notice need not be served on the respondent unless the court directs.

(2) Such an application must be supported by a witness statement or affidavit –

  (a) identifying the judgment or order to which the application relates and, if the judgment or order is for the payment of money, stating the amount originally due thereunder and the amount due thereunder at the date the application notice is filed;

  (b) stating, where the case falls within rule 2(1)(a), the reasons for the delay in enforcing the judgment or order;

  (c) stating where the case falls within rule 2(1)(b), the change which has taken place in the parties entitled or liable to execution since the date of the judgment or order;

  (d) stating, where the case falls within rule 2(1)(c) or (d), that a demand to satisfy the judgment or order was made on the person liable to satisfy it and that he has refused or failed to do so;

  (e) giving such other information as is necessary to satisfy the court that the applicant is entitled to proceed to execution on the judgment or order in question and that the person against whom it is sought to issue execution is liable to execution on it.

(3) The court hearing such application may grant permission in accordance with the application or may order that any issue or question, a decision on which is necessary to determine the rights of the parties, be tried in any manner in which any question of fact or law arising in proceedings may be tried and, in either case, may impose such terms as to costs or otherwise as it thinks just.

5 Application for permission to issue writ of sequestration (RSC Ord 46, r 5)

Notwithstanding anything in rules 2 and 4, an application for permission to issue a writ of sequestration must be made in accordance with Part 81 and in particular Section 7 of that Part.

Amendments—SI 2012/2208.

Sequestration—Sequestration is a process corresponding to contempt of court. In general terms, all of the considerations that apply to committal apply to sequestration, save that the restrictions imposed on the court's power to commit for non-compliance with a money judgment by Debtors Acts 1869 and 1878 do not apply. Confusingly, the provisions of CPR 1998, Pt 81 relating to sequestration do appear now to apply in family proceedings even though at the present time those relating to committal do not. It is an expensive process and by application of the overriding objective permission is unlikely to be granted unless the contemnor's assets are considerable; permission is also unlikely to be given if the contempt can appropriately be met by a fine, or if the judgment or order can readily be enforced by execution against goods, a third party debt order or the like.

Sequestration is available to enforce a restraining order or an order requiring an act to be done ("a positive order"), provided, in the latter case, that the time for doing the act is stated and has passed (see Ord 45, r 5(1)). An order to pay money (including a periodical payments order) is a positive order and, in family proceedings, will often state the time for payment. If it does not, a further order may be sought under Ord 45, r 6. However, an application for such a further order may be refused if its sole object is to found an application under this rule, unless it is shown that the debtor is wilfully neglecting or refusing to pay.

Subject to the court's power to dispense with service, which is rarely exercised, particularly in the case of a positive order, the order (bearing an appropriate "penal" notice) must have been personally served on the contemnor before the date specified so that he has had the opportunity to comply with it (see Ord 45, r 7).

Dispensing with service (r 5(3))—In view of the draconian nature of the remedy, the court exercises this power only in cases of extreme urgency (i e where it appears that the assets to be sequestrated are about to be removed from the reach of the proposed sequestrators or are being dissipated). If personal service is impracticable, the court prefers to order service by an alternative method under r 6.8. If service is dispensed with, i e if the order giving leave/permission is made without notice, the order may be made subject to terms that provide some protection for the defendant (e g an undertaking as to damages) and the contemnor is entitled to have the matter reconsidered.

Effect of writ of sequestration—The writ requires the four sequestrators named to take possession of the contemnor's land and collect in his other property and hold them until further order. It does not itself automatically vest the property in them but gives them authority to demand and receive it (*Bucknell v Bucknell* [1969] 1 WLR 1204). A mortgagee under a mortgage given after issue of the writ is not affected by it unless he had notice of the sequestration when the mortgage was given (*Ward v Booth* (1872) LR 14 Eq 195). The writ should be registered as a land charge (Land Charges Act 1972, s 6).

Application of property—The court may authorise the sale of sequestered property and payment out of the proceeds of sale (as well as out of any ready money received) of the costs and expenses of the sequestration and the judgment debt and costs due to the claimant/judgment creditor.

Discharge—The contemnor may, on purging his contempt, apply for the sequestration to be discharged. The order, if made, will require the sequestrators to pass their final accounts, authorise payment of their outstanding costs and expenses and discharge them from liability on their paying the balance in their hands to the contemnor.

6 Issue of writ of execution (RSC Ord 46, r 6)

(1) Issue of a writ of execution takes place on its being sealed by a court officer of the appropriate office.

(2) Before such a writ is issued, a praecipe for its issue must be filed.

(3) The praecipe must be signed by or on behalf of the solicitor of the person entitled to execution or, if that person is acting in person, by him.

(4) No such writ shall be sealed unless at the time of the tender thereof for sealing –

   (a)   the person tendering it produces –

       (i)   the judgment or order on which the writ is to issue, or an office copy thereof;

      (ii)   where the writ may not issue without the permission of the court, the order granting such permission or evidence of the granting of it;

     (iii)   where judgment on failure to acknowledge service has been entered against a State, as defined in section 14 of the State Immunity Act 1978, evidence that the State has been served in accordance with CPR rule 40.10 and that the judgment has taken effect; and

   (b)   the court officer authorised to seal it is satisfied that the period, if any, specified in the judgment or order for the payment of any money or the doing of any other act thereunder has expired.

(5) Every writ of execution shall bear the date of the day on which it is issued.

(6) In this rule 'the appropriate office' means –

   (a)   where the proceedings in which execution is to issue are in a district registry, that registry;

   (b)   where the proceedings are in the Principal Registry of the Family Division, that registry;

   (c)   where the proceedings are Admiralty proceedings or commercial proceedings which are not in a district registry, the Admiralty and Commercial Registry;

  (ca)   where the proceedings are in the Chancery Division, Chancery Chambers;

   (d)   in any other case, the Central Office of the Senior Courts.

Amendments—Inserted by SI 2009/2092.

Modifications—RSC Ord 46, r 6 is modified for certain purposes by SI 2011/2866, Art 8(1), Sch 2.

8 Duration and renewal of writ of execution (RSC Ord 46, r 8)

(1) For the purpose of execution, a writ of execution is valid in the first instance for 12 months beginning with the date of its issue.

(2) Where a writ has not been wholly executed the court may by order extend the validity of the writ from time to time for a period of 12 months at any one time beginning with the day on which the order is made, if an application for extension is made to the court before the day next following that on which the writ would otherwise expire or such later day, if any, as the court may allow.

(3) Before a writ the validity of which had been extended under paragraph (2) is executed either the writ must be sealed with the seal of the office out of which it was issued showing the date on which the order extending its validity was made or the applicant for the order must serve a notice (in Form No 71 in Practice Direction 4) sealed as aforesaid, on the sheriff to whom the writ is directed or the relevant enforcement officer informing him of the making of the order and the date thereof.

(4) The priority of a writ, the validity of which has been extended under this rule, shall be determined by reference to the date on which it was originally delivered to the sheriff or relevant enforcement officer.

(5) The production of a writ of execution, or of such a notice as is mentioned in paragraph (3) purporting in either case to be sealed as mentioned in that paragraph, shall be evidence that the validity of that writ, or, as the case may be, of the writ referred to in that notice, has been extended under paragraph (2).

(6) If, during the validity of a writ of execution, an interpleader summons is issued in relation to an execution under that writ, the validity of the writ shall be extended until the expiry of 12 months from the conclusion of the interpleader proceedings.

Amendments—SI 2003/3361; SI 2009/3390.

Order to extend validity (r 8(2))—The extension is for a period of 12 months and commences with the date of the order so that, strangely, there may be a gap in the writ's validity if the order is made after the original date of expiry.

Priority—Once extended, the writ retains its original priority date. If necessary, the court will direct that an application notice be served on other execution creditors whose position may be prejudiced if the writ is extended. Preservation of priority will be important if there are protracted interpleader proceedings.

Procedure on application for extension—The application is initially made by application notice without a hearing under r 23.8(c). The application must be supported by a witness statement or affidavit, which should specify the reason for preferring not to proceed by issuing a fresh writ, give the reason why (if applicable) the application is made beyond the writ's expiry and indicate the steps taken to ascertain the views of any other execution creditors, exhibiting their responses.

9 Return to writ of execution (RSC Ord 46, r 9)

(1) Any party at whose instance or against whom a writ of execution was issued may serve a notice on the sheriff to whom the writ was directed or the relevant enforcement officer requiring him, within such time as may be specified in the notice, to indorse on the writ a statement of the manner in which he has executed it and to send to that party a copy of the statement.

(2) If a sheriff or enforcement officer on whom such a notice is served fails to comply with it the party by whom it was served may apply to the court for an order directing the sheriff or enforcement officer to comply with the notice.

Amendments—SI 2003/3361.

Practice Direction RSC 46 and CCR 26 – Execution

This Practice Direction supplements RSC Order 46 (Schedule 1 to the CPR) and CCR Order 26 (Schedule 2 to the CPR)

Levying Execution on Certain Days

1.1 Unless the court orders otherwise, a writ of execution or a warrant of execution to enforce a judgment or order must not be executed on a Sunday, Good Friday or Christmas Day.

1.2 Paragraph 1.1 does not apply to an Admiralty claim in rem.

RSC ORDER 47
WRITS OF FIERI FACIAS

1 Power to stay execution by writ of fieri facias (RSC Ord 47, r 1)

(1) Where a judgment is given or an order made for the payment by any person of money, and the court is satisfied, on an application made at the time of the judgment or order, or at any time thereafter, by the judgment debtor or other party liable to execution –

  (a) that there are special circumstances which render it inexpedient to enforce the judgment or order; or

(b) that the applicant is unable from any cause to pay the money,

then, notwithstanding anything in rule 2 or 3, the court may by order stay the execution of the judgment or order by writ of fieri facias either absolutely or for such period and subject to such conditions as the court thinks fit.

(2) An application under this rule, if not made at the time the judgment is given or order made, must be made in accordance with CPR Part 23 and may be so made notwithstanding that the party liable to execution did not acknowledge service of the claim form or serve a defence or take any previous part in the proceedings.

(3) The grounds on which an application under this rule is made must be set out in the application notice and be supported by a witness statement or affidavit made by or on behalf of the applicant substantiating the said grounds and, in particular, where such application is made on the grounds of the applicant's inability to pay, disclosing his income, the nature and value of any property of his and the amount of any other liabilities of his.

(4) The application notice and a copy of the supporting witness statement or affidavit must, not less than 4 clear days before the hearing, be served on the party entitled to enforce the judgment or order.

(5) An order staying execution under this rule may be varied or revoked by a subsequent order.

...

Procedure on application for stay—The application may be made at any hearing at which the judgment or order is given or made. It may also be made subsequently by application notice under CPR 1998, Pt 23, which must be supported by a witness statement or affidavit containing the information described in r 1(3). The court has a wide discretion that must be exercised from the starting point that there must be good reason to deny the creditor the fruits of his judgment (*Winchester Cigarette Machinery Ltd v Payne* (No 2) (1993) *The Times*, December 15, CA). If the debtor has other assets, such as property, that may provide security for the judgment debt the court may grant a stay conditional upon the debtor agreeing to an immediate charging order over that property without going through the formalities required by CPR 1998, Pt 73.

"special circumstances" (r 1(1)(a))—Special circumstances do not include the fact of a pending appeal, as an application for a stay in those circumstances would be made under the rule governing the appeal. It may include a pending application to set aside the judgment or order. For the factors to be considered in an application under this paragraph, see *Burnet v Francis Industries plc* [1987] 2 All ER 323.

Effect of order—The order stays execution against goods only. Whereas it may make an instalment order on giving judgment in default (CPR 1998, Pt 12) or on admission (CPR 1998, Pt 14), the High Court does not, after judgment, except on a judgment summons under DA 1869, s 5, make an order staying the judgment or order generally on terms of instalment payments. However, other enforcement remedies are available only in the court's discretion and it seems likely that this discretion would be influenced by the same factors that justify stay of execution under this rule.

3 Separate writs to enforce payment of costs, etc (RSC Ord 47, r 3)

(1) Where only the payment of money, together with costs to be assessed in accordance with CPR Part 47 (detailed costs assessment), is adjudged or ordered, then, if when the money becomes payable under the judgment or order the costs have not been assessed, the party entitled to enforce that judgment or order may issue a writ of fieri facias to enforce payment of the sum (other than for costs) adjudged or ordered and, not less than 8 days after the issue of that writ, he may issue a second writ to enforce payment of the assessed costs.

(2) A party entitled to enforce a judgment or order for the delivery of possession of any property (other than money) may, if he so elects, issue a separate writ of fieri facias to enforce payment of any damages or costs awarded to him by that judgment or order.

4 No expenses of execution in certain cases (RSC Ord 47, r 4)

Where a judgment or order is for less than £600 and does not entitle the claimant to costs against the person against whom the writ of fieri facias to enforce the judgment or order is issued, the writ may not authorise the sheriff or enforcement officer to whom it is directed to levy any fees, poundage or other costs of execution.

Amendments—SI 2003/3361.

5 Writ of fieri facias de bonis ecclesiasticis, etc (RSC Ord 47, r 5)

(1) Where it appears upon the return of any writ of fieri facias that the person against whom the writ was issued has no goods or chattels in the county of the sheriffs to whom the writ was directed or the district of the relevant enforcement officer but that he is the incumbent of a benefice named in the return, then, after the writ and return have been filed, the party by whom the writ of fieri facias was issued may issue a writ of fieri facias de bonis ecclesiasticis or a writ of sequestrari de bonis ecclesiasticis directed to the bishop of the diocese within which that benefice is.

(2) Any such writ must be delivered to the bishop to be executed by him.

(3) Only such fees for the execution of any such writ shall be taken by or allowed to the bishop or any diocesan officer as are for the time being authorised by or under any enactment, including any measure of the General Synod.

Amendments—SI 2003/3361.

6 Order for sale otherwise than by auction (RSC Ord 47, r 6)

(1) An order of the court under paragraph 10 of Schedule 7 to the Courts Act 2003 that a sale of goods seized under an execution may be made otherwise than by public auction may be made on the application of –

    (a)   the person at whose instance the writ of execution under which the sale is to be made was issued;

    (b)   the person against whom that writ was issued (in this rule referred to as 'the judgment debtor');

    (c)   if the writ was directed to a sheriff, that sheriff; and

    (d)   if the writ was directed to one or more enforcement officers, the relevant enforcement officer.

(2) Such an application must be made in accordance with CPR Part 23 and the application notice must contain a short statement of the grounds of the application.

(3) Where the applicant for an order under this rule is not the sheriff or enforcement officer, the sheriff or enforcement officer must, on the demand of the applicant, send to the applicant a list stating –

    (a)   whether he has notice of the issue of another writ or writs of execution against the goods of the judgment debtor; and

    (b)   so far as is known to him, the name and address of every creditor who has obtained the issue of another such writ of execution,

and where the sheriff or enforcement officer is the applicant, he must prepare such a list.

(4) Not less than 4 clear days before the hearing the applicant must serve the application notice on each of the other persons by whom the application might have been made and on every person named in the list under paragraph (3).

(5) Service of the application notice on a person named in the list under paragraph (3) is notice to him for the purpose of paragraph 10(3) of Schedule 7 to the Courts Act 2003.

(Paragraph 10(3) provides that if the person who seized the goods has notice of another execution or other executions, the court must not consider an application for leave to sell privately until the notice prescribed by Civil Procedure Rules has been given to the other execution creditor or creditors)

(6) The applicant must produce the list under paragraph (3) to the court on the hearing of the application.

(7) Every person on whom the application notice was served may attend and be heard on the hearing of the application.

Amendments—SI 2003/3361.

Applicant (r 6(1))—The application may be made by either party or by the sheriff or enforcement officer.

Procedure on application—The application is by application notice under Pt 23, which must be served on any party who is not the applicant, on the sheriff or enforcement officer if he is not the applicant and on any other known execution creditor.

Private sale—The advantage of seeking a private sale is that a better price may be obtained than at auction, to the benefit of both debtor and creditors. It is preferable for the order to authorise a particular sale and the application should be specific as to the actual sale proposed. The purchaser may be the execution creditor (*Ex parte Villars* (1874) LR 9 Ch 432). If the point is contentious, the applicant must be prepared to compare the proposed sale price with what is likely to be achieved at auction. The procedure may be particularly useful where the creditor has an intimate knowledge of the debtor's leviable assets and, therefore, some idea of the best market for them, or where the goods are of a specialised nature for which there is no ready market.

****

RSC ORDER 52
COMMITTAL

1 Committal for contempt of court (RSC Ord 52, r 1)

Note—By virtue of the Civil Procedure (Amendment No 2) Rules 2012, SI 2012/2208, CPR 1998, Sch 1, RSC Ord 52 is revoked as of 1 October 2012. However, where FPR 2010 apply RSC Ord 52, they apply those rules as they appeared in Sch 1 to the CPR on 30 September 2012 (FPR 2010, r 2.3(4)).

(1) The power of the High Court or Court of Appeal to punish for contempt of court may be exercised by an order of committal.

(2) Where contempt of court –

    (a)   is committed in connection with –
        (i)   any proceedings before a Divisional Court of the Queen's Bench Division; or
        (ii) criminal proceedings, except where the contempt is committed in the face of the court or consists of disobedience to an order of the court or a breach of an undertaking to the court; or
        (iii) proceedings in an inferior court; or
    (b)   is committed otherwise than in connection with any proceedings,

then, subject to paragraph (4), an order of committal may be made only by a Divisional Court of the Queen's Bench Division.

This paragraph shall not apply in relation to contempt of the Court of Appeal.

(3) Where contempt of court is committed in connection with any proceedings in the High Court, then, subject to paragraph (2), an order of committal may be made by a single judge of the Queen's Bench Division except where the proceedings were assigned or subsequently transferred to some other Division, in which case the order may be made only by a single judge of that other Division.

PART III

The reference in this paragraph to a single judge of the Queen's Bench Division shall, in relation to proceedings in any court the judge or judges of which are, when exercising the jurisdiction of that court, deemed by virtue of any enactment to constitute a court of the High Court, be construed as a reference to a judge of that court.

(4) Where by virtue of any enactment the High Court has power to punish or take steps for the punishment of any person charged with having done anything in relation to a court, tribunal or person which would, if it had been done in relation to the High Court, have been a contempt of that Court, an order of committal may be made –

(a) on an application under section 88 of the Charities Act 1993, by a single judge of the Chancery Division; and

(b) in any other case, by a single judge of the Queen's Bench Division.

Amendments—SI 2002/2058; SI 2012/2208.

Scope—Rule 1(1) and (3) applies in connection with the enforcement of orders made in family proceedings.

Procedure—*PD (Committal Applications)* regulates the mode of application for committals in family proceedings, including the requirement that each allegation be identified, separately and numerically in the form of application, the period of 14 days for service in such proceedings, the form of evidence, case management and conduct of the hearing. Although CPR 1998, r 81.10(3) does not apply to family proceedings, if it is followed the procedure in a family case will be correct.

"order of committal" (r 1(1))—Under an order of committal the contemnor's person is seized by the tipstaff, or by a police officer as his assistant, and taken to prison. A fixed term of imprisonment must be imposed, which may not exceed 2 years (CCA 1981, s 14(1)). Consecutive terms may be imposed if more than one contempt is proved (*Lee v Walker* [1985] FLR 701), although not totalling more than 2 years on any one occasion (s 14(1); *Villiers v Villiers* [1994] 1 FLR 647). The sentence may be suspended (see *Hale v Tanner* [2000] 2 FLR 879). The terms of the suspension must be clearly set out. See also commentary to CCA 1981, s 14.

Other remedies—On hearing the application, the court may fine the contemnor instead of (or as well as) committing him, or may require him to give security for his future good behaviour (see r 9). There is no limit to the amount of the fine that may be imposed. For a case where, in family proceedings, a fine was imposed in lieu of committal even though the contemnor was in breach of an earlier suspended committal order, see *Banton v Banton* [1990] 2 FLR 465.

Contempt may be met by sequestration (see RSC Ord 46, r 5), which is likely to be appropriate in family proceedings only where the assets are substantial, but in such a case sequestration may be a preferable and more effective remedy. In a suitable case the court may authorise the breach of an order to be remedied by the applicant at the contemnor's expense under RSC Ord 45, r 8.

Contempt proceedings should not be brought to enforce an order which may be adequately enforced by writ of execution (e g writ of possession or writ of delivery) or other means (e g appointment of a person to execute a document under SCA 1981, s 39 or a vesting order under the Trustee Act 1925) (*Clements v Erlanger* (1877) 46 LJ Ch 382; *Danchevsky v Danchevsky* [1975] Fam 17).

Maximum sentence—Generally, the maximum sentence is 2 years (see further commentary on the CCA 1981). But where the sentence is under DA 1869, it is only 6 weeks (*Bhura v Bhura* [2012] EWHC 3633 (Fam); *Zuk v Zuk* [2012] EWCA Civ 1871).

Orders which may be enforced by committal—As to the types of orders, and undertakings, which may be enforced by committal, see RSC Ord 45, rr 5–7.

Form—Order of committal: RSC, App A, Form No 85. The Court of Appeal has repeatedly stressed the need for detail and accuracy in drawing the order. Although in family proceedings it will be drawn up by the court, the applicant's solicitor should seek the opportunity of checking it before it is perfected as any significant defect may result in its being quashed. The order breached and the breaches of it must be clearly stated so that the contemnor knows the reason for the committal from the face of the order (*Parra v Rones* [1986] Fam Law 262; *Linkleter v Linkleter* [1988] 1 FLR 360; *Langley v Langley* [1994] 1 FLR 383). Allegations of which the contemnor was not given notice must not be referred to (*Tabone v Seguna* [1986] 1 FLR 591). The order must accord with the oral judgment given (*Re C (Contempt: Committal Order)* [1989] 1 FLR 288, CA), but a minor irregularity will not be fatal and can be corrected under the "slip rule" (*Nicholls v Nicholls* [1997] 1 FLR 649; see **The importance of abiding by correct procedure** in commentary under CPR 1998, Sch 2, CCR Ord 29, r 1). The procedure and resulting order must be fair but that includes fair to the victim as well as the contemnor (see *Nicholls v Nicholls*, above and contrast *Amberley Construction Ltd v Beamish* [2003] EWCA Civ 1267).

2 Application to Divisional Court (RSC Ord 52, r 2)

(1) No application to a Divisional Court for an order of committal against any person may be made unless permission to make such an application has been granted in accordance with this rule.

(2) An application for such permission must be made without notice to a Divisional Court, except in vacation when it may be made to a judge in chambers and must be supported by a statement setting out the name and description of the applicant, the name, description and address of the person sought to be committed and the grounds on which his committal is sought, and by an affidavit, to be filed before the application is made, verifying the facts relied on.

(3) The applicant must give notice of the application for permission not later than the preceding day to the Crown Office and must at the same time lodge in that office copies of the statement and affidavit.

(4) Where an application for permission under this rule is refused by a judge in chambers, the applicant may make a fresh application for such permission to a Divisional Court.

(5) An application made to a Divisional Court by virtue of paragraph (4) must be made within 8 days after the judge's refusal to give permission or, if a Divisional Court does not sit within that period, on the first day on which it sits thereafter.

3 Application for order after leave to apply granted (RSC Ord 52, r 3)

(1) When permission has been granted under rule 2 to apply for an order of committal, the application for the order must be made to a Divisional Court and, unless the court or judge granting permission has otherwise directed, there must be at least 14 clear days between the service of the claim form and the day named therein for the hearing.

(2) Unless within 14 days after such permission was granted, the claim form is issued the permission shall lapse.

(3) Subject to paragraph 4, the claim form, accompanied by a copy of the statement and affidavit in support of the application for permission, must be served personally on the person sought to be committed.

(4) Without prejudice to the powers of the court or judge under Part 6 of the CPR, the court or judge may dispense with service under this rule if it or he thinks it just to do so.

4 Application to Court other than Divisional Court (RSC Ord 52, r 4)

(1) Where an application for an order of committal may be made to a court other than a Divisional Court, the application must be made by claim form or application notice and be supported by an affidavit.

(2) Subject to paragraph (3) the claim form or application notice, stating the grounds of the application and accompanied by a copy of the affidavit in support of the application, must be served personally on the person sought to be committed.

(3) Without prejudice to its powers under Part 6 of the CPR, the court may dispense with service under this rule if it thinks it just to do so.

(4) This rule does not apply to committal applications which under rules 1(2) and 3(1) should be made to a Divisional Court but which, in vacation, have been properly made to a single judge in accordance with RSC Order 64, rule 4.

Scope—Derived from the former RSC Ord 44, r 2(3), this rule gives the procedure by which an application to commit is made. Reference should be made to Ord 45, rr 5–7 as to the steps which must have been taken before this stage is reached.

Manner of application (r 4(1),(2))—In High Court family proceedings the application is made either by claim form or application notice. The affidavit in support should identify the terms of the order said to have been breached and set out the facts relied on as constituting the breach. It may be an affidavit of information and belief (*Savings & Investment Bank Ltd v Gasco Investments (Netherlands) BV (No 2)* [1988] Ch 422).

"the grounds of the application" (r 4(2))—It is not enough merely to refer to the affidavit (*Harmsworth v Harmsworth* [1988] 1 FLR 349). The grounds for the application (which constitute the charge faced by the respondent) must be set out in the summons itself or at least in a schedule annexed to it and forming part of it. The grounds must be sufficiently particularised to enable the respondent to meet the charge (*Chiltern District Council v Keane* [1985] 1 WLR 619).

"must be served personally" (r 4(2))—At least 2 clear days' notice must be given (Ord 32, r 3). The court may abridge the time for service or may order substituted service, but it will be slow to do so when the respondent's liberty is at stake. Even when an order for substituted service has been complied with, a committal order may be set aside and a new trial ordered if the contemnor did not have actual notice of the hearing (*Duo v Osborne (formerly Duo)* [1992] 2 FLR 425, CA). If the application is adjourned, notice of the adjourned hearing must be similarly served (*Chiltern District Council v Keane* (above)).

Dispensing with service (r 4(3))—To dispense with service of the summons (ie to hear an application to commit ex parte) "is a wholly exceptional course to take and one which can only be justified if no other course is open either to uphold the authority of the court or to protect the applicant" (*Wright v Jess* [1987] 2 FLR 373). An order made ex parte is provisional (*R v R (Contempt of Court)* [1988] Fam Law 388). The contemnor is entitled to apply for its discharge (*Wright v Jess* (above)), which will in effect mean a complete rehearing (*Aslam v Singh* [1987] 1 FLR 122), though no greater sentence can then be imposed than was originally imposed (*Lamb v Lamb* [1984] FLR 278).

Standard of proof—The appropriate standard of proof in committal proceedings is the criminal standard (*Dean v Dean* [1987] 1 FLR 517).

5 Saving for power to commit without application for purpose (RSC Ord 52, r 5)

Nothing in the foregoing provisions of this Order shall be taken as affecting the power of the High Court or Court of Appeal to make an order of committal of its own initiative against a person guilty of contempt of court.

Scope—The court retains the power to commit a contemnor of its own motion. This power is exercised to deal with contempt in the face of the court (see *Wilkinson v S* [2003] 1 WLR 1254). Very rarely it has been used to punish blatant disregard of an order, for example in wardship cases (see *Warwick Corporation v Russell* [1964] 1 WLR 613).

6 Provisions as to hearing (RSC Ord 52, r 6)

(1) Subject to paragraph (2), the court hearing an application for an order of committal may sit in private in the following cases, that is to say –

   (a)   where the application arises out of proceedings relating to the wardship or adoption of an infant or wholly or mainly to the guardianship, custody, maintenance or upbringing of an infant, or rights of access to an infant;

   (b)   where the application arises out of proceedings relating to a person suffering or appearing to be suffering from mental disorder within the meaning of the Mental Health Act 1983;

   (c)   where the application arises out of proceedings in which a secret process, discovery or invention was in issue;

   (d)   where it appears to the court that in the interests of the administration of justice or for reasons of national security the application should be heard in private;

but, except as aforesaid, the application shall be heard in public.

(2) If the court hearing an application in private by virtue of paragraph (1) decides to make an order of committal against the person sought to be committed, it shall in public state –

    (a)   the name of that person;

    (b)   in general terms the nature of the contempt of court in respect of which the order of committal is being made; and

    (c)   the length of the period for which he is being committed.

(3) Except with the permission of the court hearing an application for an order of committal, no grounds shall be relied upon at the hearing except the grounds set out in the statement under rule 2 or, as the case may be, in the claim form or application notice under rule 4.

(4) If on the hearing of the application the person sought to be committed expresses a wish to give oral evidence on his own behalf, he shall be entitled to do so.

Amendments—SI 1999/1008.

Remedying irregularity—If, in wardship proceedings, the name of the person committed, the nature of the contempt and the length of sentence are not stated in open court, in breach of r 6(2), the court may remedy the situation by making a subsequent statement in open court of the particulars required. However, the Court of Appeal has a discretion to set aside the order (*Re C (A Minor)* (1988) *The Times*, 16 November). As to irregularities in orders, see *Nicholls v Nicholls* [1997] 1 FLR 649.

7 Power to suspend execution of committal order (RSC Ord 52, r 7)

(1) The Court by whom an order of committal is made may by order direct that the execution of the order of committal shall be suspended for such period or on such terms or conditions as it may specify.

(2) Where execution of an order of committal is suspended by an order under paragraph (1), the applicant for the order of committal must, unless the Court otherwise directs, serve on the person against whom it was made a notice informing him of the making and terms of the order under that paragraph.

"for such period or on such terms ..." (r 7(1))—The court has an unfettered discretion as to the period of the suspension and the terms or conditions of the suspension. The power is commonly exercised in the case of a matrimonial injunction; in such a case, the conditions of the suspension will normally be that there be no further breach and that the committal order cease to have effect at the end of the suspension period. The order may be, and usually is, suspended for a definite period. However, in *Griffin v Griffin* [2000] 2 FLR 44, the Court of Appeal (Simon Brown and Hale LJJ) upheld the validity of a committal order suspended so long as the contemnor complied with the terms of an order expressed to last "until further order" (see **Duration** in commentary under FLA 1996, s 42), even though the effect was to suspend the sentence of imprisonment indefinitely.

"the applicant ... must ... serve ... a notice" (r 7(2))—There is no requirement for personal service but, if there should be an application to activate the sentence for breach of the terms, the court will require to be satisfied that the contemnor had notice of them.

"unless the court otherwise directs" (r 7(2))—For example, if the terms are straightforward and the contemnor is present to hear the order made.

7A Warrant for arrest (RSC Ord 52, r 7A)

A warrant for the arrest of a person against whom an order of committal has been made shall not, without further order of the court, be enforced more than 2 years after the date on which the warrant is issued.

Amendments—Inserted by SI 2003/3361.

8 Discharge of person committed (RSC Ord 52, r 8)

(1) The Court may, on the application of any person committed to prison for any contempt of Court, discharge him.

(2) Where a person has been committed for failing to comply with a judgment or order requiring him to deliver any thing to some other person or to deposit it in Court or elsewhere, and a writ of sequestration has also been issued to enforce that judgment or order, then, if the thing is in the custody or power of the person committed, the commissioners appointed by the writ of sequestration may take possession of it as if it were the property of that person and, without prejudice to the generality of paragraph (1), the Court may discharge the person committed and may give such directions for dealing with the thing taken by the commissioners as it thinks fit.

(RSC Order 46, rule 5 contains rules relating to writs of sequestration)

Scope—This rule enables the court to discharge a contemnor before the end of the term for which he was imprisoned. On an application to purge, the court must grant or refuse the application: it cannot suspend the remainder of the sentence (*Harris v Harris* [2002] 1 FLR 248, CA).

Procedure on application—The application is made by notice of application (although in practice, a letter from the contemnor will be treated as the application). Generally, an application to purge is best made to the judge who passed the sentence. However, where that judge is not conveniently available to hear the application, it may be made to any judge (but as to the circumstances in which the application can be heard by a district judge see CPR 1998, Sch 2, CCR Ord 29, r 3).

Attendance on hearing—In family proceedings the contemnor should be present to hear the outcome of his application unless, in his solicitor's view, his mental condition makes that undesirable.

Court's discretion—Discharge is subject to the discretion of the court. Even if the order has not been fully complied with, the contemnor may be released where it is clear that further imprisonment will not secure compliance, provided he has been sufficiently punished for his disobedience (*Re Barrell Enterprises* [1973] 1 WLR 19).

9 Saving for other powers (RSC Ord 52, r 9)

Nothing in the foregoing provisions of this Order shall be taken as affecting the power of the Court to make an order requiring a person guilty of contempt of court, or a person punishable by virtue of any enactment in like manner as if he had been guilty of contempt of the High Court, to pay a fine or to give security for his good behaviour, and those provisions, so far as applicable, and with the necessary modifications, shall apply in relation to an application for such an order as they apply in relation to an application for an order of committal.

Scope—This rule has the effect of confirming the retention of the court's power to require payment of a fine or the giving of security for good behaviour (see **Other remedies** under r 1).

Practice Direction RSC 52 and CCR 29
Committal Applications

This Practice Direction is supplemental to RSC Order 52 (Schedule 1 to the CPR) and CCR Order 29 (Schedule 2 to the CPR)

Note—By virtue of the Civil Procedure (Amendment No 2) Rules 2012, SI 2012/2208, CPR 1998, Sch 1, RSC Ord 52 and CPR 1998, Sch 2, CCR Ord 29 are revoked as of 1 October 2012. However, note that where FPR 2010 apply those rules, they apply those rules as they appeared in Sch 1 to the CPR on 30 September 2012 (FPR 2010, r 2.3(4)).

General

1.1 Part I of this practice direction applies to any application for an order for committal of a person to prison for contempt of court (a 'committal application'). Part II makes additional provision where the committal application relates to a contempt in the face of the court.

1.2 Where the alleged contempt of court consists of or is based upon disobedience to an order made in a county court or breach of an undertaking given to a county court or consists of an act done in the course of proceedings in a county court, or where in any other way the alleged contempt is a contempt which the county court has power to punish, the committal application may be made in the county court in question.

1.3 In every other case (other than one within Part II of this practice direction), a committal application must be made in the High Court.

1.4 In all cases the Convention rights of those involved should particularly be borne in mind. It should be noted that the burden of proof, having regard to the possibility that a person may be sent to prison, is that the allegation be proved beyond reasonable doubt.

(Section 1 of the Human Rights Act defines 'the Convention rights')

PART I

Commencement of Committal Proceedings

2.1 A committal application must, subject to paragraph 2.2, be commenced by the issue of a Part 8 claim form. The Part 8 claim form must be used (see paragraph 2.5).

2.2

(1) If the committal application is made in existing proceedings it must be commenced by the filing of an application notice in those proceedings.

(2) An application to commit for breach of an undertaking or order must be commenced by the filing of an application notice in the proceedings in which the undertaking was given or the order was made.

(3) The application notice must state that the application is made in the proceedings in question and its title and reference number must correspond with the title and reference number of those proceedings.

2.3 If the committal application is one which cannot be made without permission, the claim form or application notice, as the case may be, may not be issued or filed until the requisite permission has been granted.

2.4 If the permission of the court is needed in order to make a committal application –

(1) the permission must be applied for by filing an application notice (see CPR rule 23.2(4));

(2) the application notice need not be served on the respondent;

(3) the date on which and the name of the judge by whom the requisite permission was granted must be stated on the claim form or application notice by which the committal application is commenced;

(4) the permission may only be granted by a judge who, under paragraph 11, would have power to hear the committal application if permission were granted; and

(5) CPR rules 23.9 and 23.10 do not apply.

2.5 If the committal application is commenced by the issue of a claim form, CPR Part 8 shall, subject to the provisions of this practice direction, apply as though references to 'claimant' were references to the person making the committal application and references to 'defendant' were references to the person against whom the committal application is made (in this practice direction referred to as 'the respondent') but:

(1) the claim form together with copies of all written evidence in support must, unless the court otherwise directs, be served personally on the respondent,

(2) the claim form must set out in full the grounds on which the committal application is made and must identify, separately and numerically, each alleged act of contempt including, if know, the date of each alleged act,

(3) an amendment to the claim form can be made with the permission of the court but not otherwise,

(4) CPR rule 8.4 does not apply, and

(5) the claim form must contain a prominent notice stating the possible consequences of the court making a committal order and of the respondent not attending the hearing. A form of notice, which may be used is annexed to this practice direction.

2.6 If a committal application is commenced by the filing of an application notice, CPR Part 23 shall, subject to the provisions of this practice direction, apply, but:

(1) the application notice together with copies of all written evidence in support must, unless the court otherwise directs, be served personally on the respondent,

(2) the application notice must set out in full the grounds on which the committal application is made and must identify, separately and numerically, each alleged act of contempt including, if known, the date of each of the alleged acts,

(3) an amendment to the application notice can be made with the permission of the court but not otherwise, and

(4) the court may not dispose of the committal application without a hearing.

(5) the application notice must contain a prominent notice stating the possible consequences of the court making a committal order and of the respondent not attending the hearing. A form of notice, which may be used, is annexed to this practice direction.

Written Evidence

3.1 Written evidence in support of or in opposition to a committal application must be given by affidavit.

3.2 Written evidence served in support of or in opposition to a committal application must, unless the court otherwise directs, be filed.

3.3 A respondent may give oral evidence at the hearing, whether or not he has filed or served any written evidence. If he does so, he may be cross-examined.

3.4 A respondent may, with the permission of the court, call a witness to give oral evidence at the hearing whether or not the witness has sworn an affidavit.

Case Management and Date of Hearing

4.1 The applicant for the committal order must, when lodging the claim form or application notice with the court for issuing or filing, as the case may be, obtain from the court a date for the hearing of the committal application.

4.2 Unless the court otherwise directs, the hearing date of a committal application shall be not less than 14 clear days after service of the claim form or of the application notice, as the case may be, on the respondent. The hearing date must be specified in the claim form or application notice or in a Notice of Hearing or Application attached to and served with the claim form or application notice.

4.3 The court may, however, at any time give case management directions, including directions for the service of written evidence by the respondent and written evidence in reply by the applicant, or may convene and hold a directions hearing.

4.4 The court may on the hearing date –

(1)   give case management directions with a view to a hearing of the committal application on a future date, or

(2)   if the committal application is ready to be heard, proceed forthwith to hear it.

4.5 In dealing with any committal application, the court will have regard to the need for the respondent to have details of the alleged acts of contempt and the opportunity to respond to the committal application.

4.6 The court should also have regard to the need for the respondent to be –

(1)   allowed a reasonable time for responding to the committal application including, if necessary, preparing a defence;

(2)   made aware of the availability of assistance from the Community Legal Service and how to contact the Service;

(3)   given the opportunity, if unrepresented, to obtain legal advice; and

(4)   if unable to understand English, allowed to make arrangements, seeking the assistance of the court if necessary, for an interpreter to attend the hearing.

Striking Out

5 The court may, on application by the respondent or on its own initiative, strike out a committal application if it appears to the court:

(1)   that the committal application and the evidence served in support of it disclose no reasonable ground for alleging that the respondent is guilty of a contempt of court,

(2)   that the committal application is an abuse of the court's process or, if made in existing proceedings, is otherwise likely to obstruct the just disposal of those proceedings, or

(3)   that there has been a failure to comply with a rule, practice direction or court order.

(CPR Part 3 contains general powers for the management by the court.)

Miscellaneous

6 CPR Rules 35.7 (Court's power to direct that evidence is to be given by a single joint expert), 35.8 (Instructions to single joint expert) and 35.9 (Power of court to direct a party to provide information) do not apply to committal applications.

7 An order under CPR rule 18.1 (Order for a party to give additional information) may not be made against a respondent to a committal application.

8 A committal application may not be discontinued without the permission of the court.

9 A committal application should normally be heard in public (see CPR rule 39.2), but if it is heard in private and the court finds the respondent guilty of contempt of court, the judge shall, when next sitting in public, state:

(1)   the name of the respondent,

(2)   in general terms the nature of the contempt or contempts found proved, and,

(3)   the penalty (if any) imposed.

10 The court may waive any procedural defect in the commencement or conduct of a committal application if satisfied that no injustice has been caused to the respondent by the defect.

11 Except where under an enactment a master or district judge has power to make a committal order[1], a committal order can only be made:

    (1)   in High Court proceedings, by a High Court judge or a person authorised to act as such[2],

    (2)   in county court proceedings by a circuit judge or a person authorised to act or capable by virtue of his office of acting as such[3].

1   Eg ss 14 and 118, County Courts Act 1984.
2   See s 9(1), Senior Courts Act 1981.
3   See s 5(3), County Courts Act 1984.

PART II

12 Where the committal application relates to a contempt in the face of the court the following matters should be given particular attention. Normally, it will be appropriate to defer consideration of the behaviour to allow the respondent time to reflect on what has occurred. The time needed for the following procedures should allow such a period of reflection.

13 A Part 8 claim form and an application notice are not required for Part II, but other provisions of this practice direction should be applied, as necessary, or adapted to the circumstances. In addition the judge should:

    (1)   tell the respondent of the possible penalty he faces;

    (2)   inform the respondent in detail, and preferably in writing, of the actions and behaviour of the respondent which have given rise to the committal application;

    (3)   if he considers that an apology would remove the need for the committal application, tell the respondent;

    (4)   have regard to the need for the respondent to be –

        (a)   allowed a reasonable time for responding to the committal application, including, if necessary, preparing a defence;

        (b)   made aware of the availability of assistance from the Community Legal Service and how to contact the Service;

        (c)   given the opportunity, if unrepresented, to obtain legal advice;

        (d)   if unable to understand English, allowed to make arrangements, seeking the court's assistance if necessary, for an interpreter to attend the hearing; and

        (e)   brought back before the court for the committal application to be heard within a reasonable time.

    (5)   allow the respondent an opportunity to –

        (a)   apologise to the court;

        (b)   explain his actions and behaviour; and,

        (c)   if the contempt is proved, to address the court on the penalty to be imposed on him;

    (6)   if there is a risk of the appearance of bias, ask another judge to hear the committal application.

    (7)   where appropriate, nominate a suitable person to give the respondent the information.

        (It is likely to be appropriate to nominate a person where the effective communication of information by the judge to the respondent was not possible when the incident occurred)

14 Where the committal application is to be heard by another judge, a written statement by the judge before whom the actions and behaviour of the respondent which have given rise to the committal application took place may be submitted as evidence of those actions and behaviour.

ANNEX – IMPORTANT NOTICE

The court has power to send you to prison and to fine you if it finds that any of the allegations made against you are true and amount to a contempt of court.

You must attend court on the date shown on the front of this form. It is in your own interest to do so. You should bring with you any witnesses and documents which you think will help you put your side of the case.

If you consider the allegations are not true you must tell the court why. If it is established that they are true, you must tell the court of any good reason why they do not amount to a contempt of court, or, if they do, why you should not be punished.

If you need advice you should show this document at once to your solicitor or go to a Citizens' Advice Bureau.

Amendments—SI 2012/2208.

****

SCHEDULE 2

****

CCR ORDER 25
ENFORCEMENT OF JUDGMENTS AND ORDERS: GENERAL

1 Judgment creditor and debtor (CCR Ord 25, r 1)

In this Order and Orders 26 to 29 'judgment creditor' means the person who has obtained or is entitled to enforce a judgment or order and 'debtor' means the person against whom it was given or made.

****

6 Description of parties (CCR Ord 25, r 6)

Where the name or address of the judgment creditor or the debtor as given in the request for the issue of a warrant of execution or delivery, judgment summons or warrant of committal differs from his name or address in the judgment or order sought to be enforced and the judgment creditor satisfies the court officer that the name or address as given in the request is applicable to the person concerned, the judgment creditor or the debtor, as the case may be, shall be described in the warrant or judgment summons as 'CD of [name and address as given in the request] suing [or sued] as AD of [name and address in the judgment or order]'.

7 Recording and giving information as to warrants and orders (CCR Ord 25, r 7)

(1) Subject to paragraph (1A), every district judge by whom a warrant or order is issued or received for execution shall from time to time state in the records of his court what has been done in the execution of the warrant or order.

(1A) Where a warrant of execution issued by a court ('the home court') is sent to another court for execution ('the foreign court'), paragraph (1) shall not apply to the district judge of the home court, but when such a warrant is returned to the home court under paragraph (7), the court officer of the home court shall state in the records of his court what has been done in the execution of the warrant or order.

(2) If the warrant or order has not been executed within one month from the date of its issue or receipt by him, the court officer of the court responsible for its execution shall, at the end of that month and every subsequent month during which the warrant remains outstanding, send notice of the reason for non-execution to the judgment creditor and, if the warrant or order was received from another court, to that court.

(3) The district judge responsible for executing a warrant or order shall give such information respecting it as may reasonably be required by the judgment creditor and, if the warrant or order was received by him from another court, by the district judge of that court.

(4) Where money is received in pursuance of a warrant of execution or committal sent by one court to another court, the foreign court shall, subject to paragraph (5) and to section 346 of Insolvency Act 1986 and section 326 of the Companies Act 1948, send the money to the judgment creditor in the manner prescribed by the Court Funds Rules 1987 and, where the money is received in pursuance of a warrant of committal, make a return to the home court.

(5) Where interpleader proceedings are pending, the court shall not proceed in accordance with paragraph (4) until the interpleader proceedings are determined and the district judge shall then make a return showing how the money is to be disposed of and, if any money is payable to the judgment creditor, the court shall proceed in accordance with paragraph (4).

(6) Where a warrant of committal has been received from another court, the foreign court shall, on the execution of the warrant, send notice thereof to the home court.

(7) Where a warrant of execution has been received from another court, either –

    (a)   on the execution of the warrant; or

    (b)   if the warrant is not executed –

        (i)   on the making of a final return to the warrant; or

        (ii) on suspension of the warrant under rule 8 (suspension of judgment or execution) or Order 26, rule 10 (withdrawal and suspension of warrant at creditor's request),

the foreign court shall return the warrant to the home court.

"such information … as may reasonably be required" (r 7(3))—Resources expended on dealing with enquiries are necessarily diverted from dealing with the process itself. Rule 7(3) has to be construed in the light of the overriding objective.

8 Suspension of judgment or execution (CCR Ord 25, r 8)

(1) The power of the court to suspend or stay a judgment or order or to stay execution of any warrant may be exercised by the district judge or, in the case of the power to stay execution of a warrant of execution and in accordance with the provisions of this rule, by the court officer.

(2) An application by the debtor to stay execution of a warrant of execution shall be in the appropriate form stating the proposed terms, the grounds on which it is made and including a signed statement of the debtor's means.

(3) Where the debtor makes an application under paragraph (2), the court shall –

    (a)   send the judgment creditor a copy of the debtor's application (and statement of means); and

    (b)   require the creditor to notify the court in writing, within 14 days of service of notification upon him, giving his reasons for any objection he may have to the granting of the application.

(4) If the judgment creditor does not notify the court of any objection within the time stated, the court officer may make an order suspending the warrant on terms of payment.

(5) Upon receipt of a notice by the judgment creditor under paragraph (3)(b), the court officer may, if the judgment creditor objects only to the terms offered, determine the date and rate of payment and make an order suspending the warrant on terms of payment.

(6) Any party affected by an order made under paragraph (5) may, within 14 days of service of the order on him and giving his reasons, apply on notice for the order to be reconsidered and the court shall fix a day for the hearing of the application before the district judge and give to the judgment creditor and the debtor not less than 8 days' notice of the day so fixed.

(7) On hearing an application under paragraph (6), the district judge may confirm the order or set it aside and make such new order as he thinks fit and the order so made shall be entered in the records of the court.

(8) Where the judgment creditor states in his notice under paragraph (3)(b) that he wishes the bailiff to proceed to execute the warrant, the court shall fix a day for a hearing before the district judge of the debtor's application and give to the judgment creditor and to the debtor not less than 2 days' notice of the day so fixed.

(9) Subject to any directions given by the district judge, where a warrant of execution has been suspended, it may be re-issued on the judgment creditor's filing a request showing that any condition subject to which the warrant was suspended has not been complied with.

(10) Where an order is made by the district judge suspending a warrant of execution, the debtor may be ordered to pay the costs of the warrant and any fees or expenses incurred before its suspension and the order may authorise the sale of a sufficient portion of any goods seized to cover such costs, fees and expenses and the expenses of sale.

Amendments—SI 2001/2792.

Scope—This rule covers applications to suspend or stay judgments or orders or to stay execution. In the case of warrants of execution where the only question is the terms of payment of the stay, the order is made in the first instance by the proper officer or an officer of the court on his behalf, subject to review on application to the district judge.

"power of the court to suspend or stay" (r 8(1))—Power to stay a judgment on terms is given by CCA 1984, s 71(2) and that to stay execution by s 88. In each case the ground is the debtor's inability to pay. The proper officer's authority does not extend to applications to stay on any other ground because he can make an order suspending the warrant only on terms as to payment.

"may make an order" (r 8(4))—The proper officer is not obliged to exercise his powers under this rule. If he declines to do so, the application will be listed before a district judge in the same way as an application where the creditor opposes any suspension.

Costs (r 8(10))—The proper officer has no power to deal with the question of costs. Where it seems that an order for costs may be appropriate, the application will be listed for hearing before a district judge.

****

13 Transfer to High Court for enforcement (CCR Ord 25, r 13)

(1) Where the judgment creditor makes a request for a certificate of judgment under Order 22, rule 8(1) for the purpose of enforcing the judgment or order in the High Court –

    (a)   by execution against goods; or

    (b)   where the judgment or order to be enforced is an order for possession of land made in a possession claim against trespassers, the grant of a certificate by the court shall take effect as an order to transfer the proceedings to the High Court and the transfer shall have effect on the grant of that certificate.

(2) On the transfer of proceedings in accordance with paragraph (1), the court shall give notice to the debtor or the person against whom the possession order was made that the proceedings have been transferred and shall make an entry of that fact in the records of his court.

(3) In a case where a request for a certificate of judgment is made under Order 22, rule 8(1) for the purpose of enforcing a judgment or order in the High Court and –

(a)   an application for a variation in the date or rate of payment of money due under a judgment or order;

(b)   an application under either CPR rule 39.3(3) or CPR rule 13.4;

(c)   a request for an administration order; or

(d)   an application for a stay of execution under section 88 of the Act,

is pending, the request for the certificate shall not be dealt with until those proceedings are determined.

Amendments—SI 2001/2792.

Jurisdiction—This is governed by HCCCJO 1991, art 8. A practice direction relating to the enforcement of county court judgments in the High Court issued by the Senior Master is set out at [1998] 4 All ER 63.

"a possession claim against trespassers" (r 13(1)(b))—This purely administrative procedure is only available to enforce possession orders against trespassers. If it is desired to enforce other possession orders in the High Court, an application must be made to a judge for transfer of the proceedings to the High Court. Simply filing a (false) certificate in such circumstances, which has been known to occur, is quite improper and will usually involve professional misconduct.

CCR ORDER 26
WARRANTS OF EXECUTION, DELIVERY AND POSSESSION

1 Application for warrant of execution (CCR Ord 26, r 1)

(1) A judgment creditor desiring a warrant of execution to be issued shall file a request in that behalf certifying –

(a)   the amount remaining due under the judgment or order; and

(b)   where the order made is for payment of a sum of money by instalments –

(i)   that the whole or part of any instalment due remains unpaid; and

(ii)   the amount for which the warrant is to be issued.

(1A) The court officer shall discharge the functions –

(a)   under section 85(2) of the Act of issuing a warrant of execution;

(b)   under section 85(3) of the Act of entering in the record mentioned in that subsection and on the warrant the precise time of the making of the application to issue the warrant; and

(c)   under section 103(1) of the Act of sending the warrant of execution to another county court.

(2) Where the court has made an order for payment of a sum of money by instalments and default has been made in payment of such an instalment, a warrant of execution may be issued for the whole of the said sum of money and costs then remaining unpaid or, subject to paragraph (3), for such part as the judgment creditor may request, not being in the latter case less than £50 or the amount of one monthly instalment or, as the case may be, 4 weekly instalments, whichever is the greater.

(3) In any case to which paragraph (2) applies no warrant shall be issued unless at the time when it is issued –

(a) the whole or part of an instalment which has already become due remains unpaid; and

(b) any warrant previously issued for part of the said sum of money and costs has expired or has been satisfied or abandoned.

(4) Where a warrant is issued for the whole or part of the said sum of money and costs, the court officer shall, unless the district judge responsible for execution of the warrant directs otherwise, send a warning notice to the person against whom the warrant is issued and, where such a notice is sent, the warrant shall not be levied until 7 days thereafter.

(5) Where judgment is given or an order made for payment otherwise than by instalments of a sum of money and costs to be assessed in accordance with CPR Part 47 (detailed assessment procedure) and default is made in payment of the sum of money before the costs have been assessed, a warrant of execution may issue for recovery of the sum of money and a separate warrant may issue subsequently for the recovery of the costs if default is made in payment of them.

Considerations affecting issue of warrant—The power to enforce judgments by execution against goods and to issue a warrant of execution to the like effect as a writ of fieri facias is given by CCA 1984, s 85 and controlled by ss 86–104. Practical considerations include:

(a) *Priority* The court records the time that the warrant is applied for (s 85(3)) and the warrant "binds the property in the goods" (and therefore has priority over later executions) from that time (s 99(1)), unless it is used to levy on goods in another county court district, in which case the time of its receipt by that county court is recorded and governs its priority as regards those goods (s 103(2)).

(b) *Instalment judgments* Execution may not be issued unless the debtor is in arrears (s 86).

(c) *Suspension* The court may suspend or stay the execution (on terms if it thinks fit) if the debtor is unable to pay (s 88 – see also Ord 25, r 8). Where the warrant has been sent to another court, both courts have this power (s 103(5)).

(d) *Goods* Section 89 exempts certain goods from execution. Cash and valuable securities may be taken in the execution of the warrant.

(e) *Rescue* The rescue by any person of goods seized in execution is punishable by up to 1 month's imprisonment or a fine of up to £1000 (s 92).

(f) *Sale* Goods seized must be sold by public auction unless the court otherwise orders (s 97 – see also r 15).

Availability of warrant of execution—HCCCJO 1991, art 8 prohibits enforcement by execution of county court judgments for £5000 or more in the county court or less than £2000 in the High Court.

It is no longer possible to enforce a High Court judgment or order immediately by execution in the county court following the repeal of CCA 1984, s 105. The action must first be transferred to the county court under CCA 1984, s 40.

Insolvency of debtor—Note Insolvency Act 1986, s 285(3), which prevents enforcement of provable debts against a bankrupt.

"file a request" (r 1(1))—Form N323 should be used as it contains space for recording of information by the court staff.

Warning notice (r 1(4))—The usual form of warning notice is set out in Practice Form N326, which informs the debtor that extra costs may be incurred if goods are seized and sold and that further interest will accrue (if the judgment is for more than £5000) unless the warrant and any balance of the judgment debt are paid off. Courts' practices on sending this notice vary. If there is any particular reason to fear that the debtor may hide goods if warned, the court should be advised of this at the time of issue and requested not to use the notice.

2 Execution of High Court judgment (CCR Ord 26, r 2)

(1) Where it is desired to enforce by warrant of execution a judgment or order of the High Court, or a judgment, order, decree or award which is or has become enforceable as if it were a judgment of the High Court, the request referred to in rule 1(1) may be filed in any court in the district of which execution is to be levied.

PART III

(2) Subject to Order 25, rule 9(5), any restriction imposed by these rules on the issue of execution shall apply as if the judgment, order, decree or award were a judgment or order of the county court, but permission to issue execution shall not be required if permission has already been given by the High Court.

(3) Notice of the issue of the warrant shall be sent by the county court to the High Court.

3 Execution against farmer (CCR Ord 26, r 3)

If after the issue of a warrant of execution the district judge for the district in which the warrant is to be executed has reason to believe that the debtor is a farmer, the execution creditor shall, if so required by the district judge, furnish him with an official certificate, dated not more than 3 days beforehand, of the result of a search at the Land Registry as to the existence of any charge registered against the debtor under the Agricultural Credits Act 1928.

4 Concurrent warrants (CCR Ord 26, r 4)

Two or more warrants of execution may be issued concurrently for execution in different districts, but –

(a) no more shall be levied under all the warrants together than is authorised to be levied under one of them; and

(b) the costs of more than one such warrant shall not be allowed against the debtor except by order of the court.

5 Permission to issue certain warrants (CCR Ord 26, r 5)

(1) A warrant of execution shall not issue without the permission of the court where –

(a) six years or more have elapsed since the date of the judgment or order;

(b) any change has taken place, whether by death or otherwise in the parties entitled to enforce the judgment or order or liable to have it enforced against them;

(c) the judgment or order is against the assets of a deceased person coming into the hands of his executors or administrators after the date of the judgment or order and it is sought to issue execution against such assets; or

(d) any goods to be seized under a warrant of execution are in the hands of a receiver appointed by a court.

(2) An application for permission shall be supported by a witness statement or affidavit establishing the applicant's right to relief and may be made without notice being served on any other party in the first instance but the court may direct the application notice to be served on such persons as it thinks fit.

(3) Where, by reason of one and the same event, a person seeks permission under paragraph (1)(b) to enforce more judgments or orders than one, he may make one application only, specifying in a schedule all the judgments or orders in respect of which it is made, and if the application notice is directed to be served on any person, it need set out only such part of the application as affects him.

(4) Paragraph (1) is without prejudice to any enactment, rule or direction by virtue of which a person is required to obtain the permission of the court for the issue of a warrant or to proceed to execution or otherwise to the enforcement of a judgment or order.

6 Duration and renewal of warrant (CCR Ord 26, r 6)

(1) A warrant of execution shall, for the purpose of execution, be valid in the first instance for 12 months beginning with the date of its issue, but if not wholly executed, it

may be renewed from time to time, by order of the court, for a period of 12 months at any one time, beginning with the day next following that on which it would otherwise expire, if an application for renewal is made before that day or such later day (if any) as the court may allow.

(2) A note of any such renewal shall be indorsed on the warrant and it shall be entitled to priority according to the time of its original issue or, where appropriate, its receipt by the district judge responsible for its execution.

Extension—The extension covers the 12 months immediately following the original period of validity (or previous extension). Only one extension may be granted at a time. An extension may be granted after a warrant has expired, but the period of 12 months will run from the expiry date, not from the date of the order (the converse of the position in the High Court: see CPR 1998, Sch 1, RSC Ord 46, r 8(2)). Thus an extension given more than 12 months after expiry would be ineffective and will not be granted (cf *Rolph v Zolan* [1993] 1 WLR 1305, CA).

Priority—Rule 6(2) preserves the existing priority of the warrant (see note **Considerations affecting issue of warrant**: (a) *Priority* under r 1). Extension therefore prejudices any other execution creditors who would have achieved a higher priority on the expiry of the applicant's warrant.

Procedure for application for renewal—Note that the rule does not specify the use of the application notice procedure under Pt 23. In practice, courts often allow the application to be made by letter. The grounds of the application, including any reason for allowing the warrant to expire, should be given. The High Court practice is to extend only if priority is important (as fresh execution can be issued if it is not) and accordingly to require the applicant to identify any other execution creditors and give them the opportunity to make representations. In the county court, the delay will usually have occurred because the warrant has been suspended (with consequent loss of priority) and, in such a case, the court will be the more ready to extend. Nevertheless, if it appears to the proper officer that other execution creditors would be significantly prejudiced, he may require the application to be made on notice to them, by analogy with the High Court practice under CPR 1998, Sch 1, RSC Ord 46, r 8.

7 Notice on levy (CCR Ord 26, r 7)

Any bailiff upon levying execution shall deliver to the debtor or leave at the place where execution is levied a notice of the warrant.

8 Bankruptcy or winding up of debtor (CCR Ord 26, r 8)

(1) Where the district judge responsible for the execution of a warrant is required by any provision of the Insolvency Act 1986 or any other enactment relating to insolvency to retain the proceeds of sale of goods sold under the warrant or money paid in order to avoid a sale, the court shall, as soon as practicable after the sale or the receipt of the money, send notice to the execution creditor and, if the warrant issued out of another court, to that court.

(2) Where the district judge responsible for the execution of a warrant –

    (a)   receives notice that a bankruptcy order has been made against the debtor or, if the debtor is a company, that a provisional liquidator has been appointed or that an order has been made or a resolution passed for the winding up of the company; and

    (b)   withdraws from possession of goods seized or pays over to the official receiver or trustee in bankruptcy or, if the debtor is a company, to the liquidator the proceeds of sale of goods sold under the warrant or money paid in order to avoid a sale or seized or received in part satisfaction of the warrant,

the court shall send notice to the execution creditor and, if the warrant issued out of another court, to that court.

(3) Where the court officer of a court to which a warrant issued out of another court has been sent for execution receives any such notice as is referred to in paragraph (2)(a) after

he has sent to the home court any money seized or received in part satisfaction of the warrant, he shall forward the notice to that court.

10 Withdrawal and suspension of warrant at creditor's request (CCR Ord 26, r 10)

(1) Where an execution creditor requests the district judge responsible for executing a warrant to withdraw from possession, he shall, subject to the following paragraphs of this rule, be treated as having abandoned the execution, and the court shall mark the warrant as withdrawn by request of the execution creditor.

(2) Where the request is made in consequence of a claim having been made under Order 33, rule 1, to goods seized under the warrant, the execution shall be treated as being abandoned in respect only of the goods claimed.

(3) If the district judge responsible for executing a warrant is requested by the execution creditor to suspend it in pursuance of an arrangement between him and the debtor, the court shall mark the warrant as suspended by request of the execution creditor and the execution creditor may subsequently apply to the district judge holding the warrant for it to be re-issued and, if he does so, the application shall be deemed for the purpose of section 85(3) of the Act to be an application to issue the warrant.

(4) Nothing in this rule shall prejudice any right of the execution creditor to apply for the issue of a fresh warrant or shall authorise the re-issue of a warrant which has been withdrawn or has expired or has been superseded by the issue of a fresh warrant.

Scope—A distinction must be made between withdrawal or abandonment of a warrant by the creditor on the one hand and its suspension by him on the other. This rule deals with the consequences of both.

Suspension by court—This rule does not apply to suspension by the court; Ord 25, r 8 applies in such circumstances.

Priority—The effect of r 10(3) is that on suspension the priority of the warrant is lost and on re-issue it is accorded priority as if issued on the re-issue date, or presumably its re-delivery to the foreign court (see note **Considerations affecting issue of warrant**: (a) *Priority* under r 1). It is otherwise if the bailiff maintains the levy, by taking "walking possession", for example so as to allow the debtor time to raise money to pay. However, the creditor is not entitled to require the bailiff to proceed thus and in view of the heavy burden that it places on the court he may well decline to maintain "walking possession" for any great length of time.

11 Suspension of part warrant (CCR Ord 26, r 11)

Where a warrant issued for part of a sum of money and costs payable under a judgment or order is suspended on payment of instalments, the judgment or order shall, unless the court otherwise directs, be treated as suspended on those terms as respects the whole of the sum of money and costs then remaining unpaid.

12 Inventory and notice where goods removed (CCR Ord 26, r 12)

(1) Where goods seized in execution are removed, the court shall forthwith deliver or send to the debtor a sufficient inventory of the goods removed and shall, not less than 4 days before the time fixed for the sale, give him notice of the time and place at which the goods will be sold.

(2) The inventory and notice shall be given to the debtor by delivering them to him personally or by sending them to him by post at his place of residence or, if his place of residence is not known, by leaving them for him, or sending them to him by post, at the place from which the goods were removed.

13 Account of sale (CCR Ord 26, r 13)

Where goods are sold under an execution, the court shall furnish the debtor with a detailed account in writing of the sale and of the application of the proceeds.

14 Notification to foreign court of payment made (CCR Ord 26, r 14)

Where, after a warrant has been sent to a foreign court for execution but before a final return has been made to the warrant, the home court is notified of a payment made in respect of the sum for which the warrant is issued, the home court shall send notice of the payment to the foreign court.

15 Order for private sale (CCR Ord 26, r 15)

(1) Subject to paragraph (6), an order of the court under section 97 of the Act that a sale under an execution may be made otherwise than by public auction may be made on the application of the execution creditor or the debtor or the district judge responsible for the execution of the warrant.

(2) Where he is not the applicant for an order under this rule, the district judge responsible for the execution of the warrant shall, on the demand of the applicant, furnish him with a list containing the name and address of every execution creditor under any other warrant or writ of execution against the goods of the debtor of which the district judge has notice, and where the district judge is the applicant, he shall prepare such a list.

(3) Not less than 4 days before the day fixed for the hearing of the application, the applicant shall give notice of the application to each of the other persons by whom the application might have been made and to every person named in the list referred to in paragraph (2).

(4) The applicant shall produce the list to the court on the hearing of the application.

(5) Every person to whom notice of the application was given may attend and be heard on the hearing of the application.

(6) Where the district judge responsible for the execution of the warrant is the district judge by whom it was issued and he has no notice of any other warrant or writ of execution against the goods of the debtor, an order under this rule may be made by the court of its own motion with the consent of the execution creditor and the debtor or after giving them an opportunity of being heard.

16 Warrant of delivery (CCR Ord 26, r 16)

(1) Except where an Act or rule provides otherwise, a judgment or order for the delivery of any goods shall be enforceable by warrant of delivery in accordance with this rule.

(2) If the judgment or order does not give the person against whom it was given or made the alternative of paying the value of the goods, it may be enforced by a warrant of specific delivery, that is to say, a warrant to recover the goods without alternative provision for recovery of their value.

(3) If the judgment or order is for the delivery of the goods or payment of their value, it may be enforced by a warrant of delivery to recover the goods or their value.

(4) Where a warrant of delivery is issued, the judgment creditor shall be entitled, by the same or a separate warrant, to execution against the debtor's goods for any money payable under the judgment or order which is to be enforced by the warrant of delivery.

PART III

(4A) Where a judgment or order is given or made for the delivery of goods or payment of their value and a warrant is issued to recover the goods or their value, money paid into court under the warrant shall be appropriated first to any sum of money and costs awarded.

(5) The foregoing provisions of this Order, so far as applicable, shall have effect, with the necessary modifications, in relation to warrants of delivery as they have effect in relation to warrants of execution.

17 Warrant of possession (CCR Ord 26, r 17)

(1) A judgment or order for the recovery of land shall be enforceable by warrant of possession.

(2) Without prejudice to paragraph (3A), the person applying for a warrant of possession must file a certificate that the land which is subject of the judgment or order has not been vacated.

(2A) When applying for a warrant of possession of a dwelling-house subject to a mortgage, the claimant must certify that notice has been given in accordance with the Dwelling Houses (Execution of Possession Orders by Mortgagees) Regulations 2010(7).

(3) Where a warrant of possession is issued, the judgment creditor shall be entitled, by the same or a separate warrant, to execution against the debtor's goods for any money payable under the judgment or order which is to be enforced by the warrant of possession.

(3A) In a case to which paragraph (3) applies or where an order for possession has been suspended on terms as to payment of a sum of money by instalments, the judgment creditor shall in his request certify –

(a)   the amount of money remaining due under the judgment or order; and

(b)   that the whole or part of any instalment due remains unpaid.

(4) A warrant of restitution may be issued, with the permission of the court, in aid of any warrant of possession.

(5) An application for permission under paragraph (4) may be made without notice being served on any other party and shall be supported by evidence of wrongful re-entry into possession following the execution of the warrant of possession and of such further facts as would, in the High Court, enable the judgment creditor to have a writ of restitution issued.

(6) Rules 5 and 6 shall apply, with the necessary modifications, in relation to a warrant of possession and any further warrant in aid of such a warrant as they apply in relation to a warrant of execution.

Amendments—SI 2008/3327; SI 2010/1953.

Issue—The warrant cannot be issued until the date for possession in the order has passed. However, where the order requires possession "forthwith", the warrant can be issued immediately. Normal administrative processes mean that several days or weeks may elapse before the eviction takes place. Fixing the actual date is a matter of administrative process, which may be controlled by the court in appropriate cases (*Air Ministry v Harris* [1951] 2 All ER 862, CA). If it is thought necessary, a direction to this effect should be sought from the judge either when the order is made or subsequently.

Effect—When enforcing a warrant of possession, the bailiff need not remove chattels (CCA 1984, s 111(1)) but may evict any person on the premises even though not a party (*R v Wandsworth County Court ex parte London Borough of Wandsworth* [1975] 1 WLR 1314). An occupier who claims the right to stay may apply to be added as a defendant (r 19.3) in order to apply for the judgment to be set aside.

Warrant of restitution (r 17(4),(5))—If after possession has been recovered the land or premises are re-occupied, application may be made ex parte for a warrant of restitution to eject the occupier. There must be a sufficient connection between the original eviction and the re-occupation, but it may be that restitution is effective against someone other than those originally evicted (*Wiltshire County Council v Frazer* [1986] 1 WLR 109, where, however, there had been a summary order for possession against trespassers). See also notes to CPR 1998, Sch 1, RSC Ord 46, r 3.

Application of other rules to warrants of possession (r 17(6))—Only rr 5 (leave to issue certain warrants) and 6 (duration and renewal of warrant) apply to possession warrants.

18 Saving for enforcement by committal (CCR Ord 26, r 18)

Nothing in rule 16 or 17 shall prejudice any power to enforce a judgment or order for the delivery of goods or the recovery of land by an order of committal.

Committal generally—The court will be reluctant to commit where the order could have been satisfactorily enforced by the less draconian (and much less expensive) option of a warrant (*Danchevsky v Danchevsky* [1975] Fam 17, CA). The applicant for committal should therefore be prepared to show that a warrant has been issued but has proved ineffective or that that method of enforcement is for some reason inappropriate.

CCR ORDER 27
ATTACHMENT OF EARNINGS

Part I
General

1 Interpretation (CCR Ord 27, r 1)

(1) In this Order –

'the Act of 1971' means the Attachment of Earnings Act 1971 and, unless the context otherwise requires, expressions used in that Act have the same meanings as in that Act.

Scope—This rule and Ord 27 generally provide a code, largely delegated to court staff, for attachment of earnings applications to enforce judgment debts, while reserving to the district judge attachment of earnings applications to enforce maintenance orders. Where the paying party is a member of the armed forces, an application should normally be made instead to the relevant service authorities for a deduction to be made from pay under the Armed Forces (Forfeitures and Deductions) Regulations 2009.

"expressions used" (r 1(1))—AEA 1971, ss 2, 24, 25 define the expressions used therein. Note in particular the extended meaning of "maintenance order" given in s 2(a) (i e order specified in Sch 1 to the Act). As well as orders for periodical maintenance payments, such orders include orders for lump sums and other capital amounts that therefore do not create "judgment debts" for the purposes of this order. Costs awarded on the making of "maintenance orders" are treated as part of the maintenance orders (s 25(2)). Orders for costs made, for example, on pronouncement of a decree would not be within Sch 1 and would be "judgment debts".

2 Index of orders (CCR Ord 27, r 2)

(1) The court officer of every court shall keep a nominal index of the debtors residing within the district of his court in respect of whom there are in force attachment of earnings orders which have been made by that court or of which the court officer has received notice from another court.

(2) Where a debtor in respect of whom a court has made an attachment of earnings order resides within the district of another court, the court officer of the first-mentioned court shall send a copy of the order to the court officer of the other court for entry in his index.

(3) The court officer shall, on the request of any person having a judgment or order against a person believed to be residing within the district of the court, cause a search to be made in the index of the court and issue a certificate of the result of the search.

3 Appropriate court (CCR Ord 27, r 3)

(1) Subject to paragraphs (2), (3) and (4), an application for an attachment of earnings order may be made to the court for the district in which the debtor resides.

(2) Subject to paragraph 4, if the debtor does not reside within England or Wales, or the creditor does not know where the debtor resides, the application may be made to the court in which, or for the district in which, the judgment or order sought to be enforced was obtained.

(3) Subject to paragraph 4, where the creditor applies for attachment of earnings orders in respect of two or more debtors jointly liable under a judgment or order, the application may be made to the court for the district in which any of the debtors resides, so however that if the judgment or order was given or made by any such court, the application shall be made to that court.

(4) Where the judgment was made in Northampton County Court in respect of a designated money claim and the proceedings have not since been transferred to a different court, the application must be made in accordance with section 2 of Practice Direction 70.

Amendments—SI 2012/505.

4 Mode of applying (CCR Ord 27, r 4)

(1) A judgment creditor who desires to apply for an attachment of earnings order shall file his application certifying the amount of money remaining due under the judgment or order and that the whole or part of any instalment due remains unpaid and, where it is sought to enforce an order of a magistrates' court –

(a) a certified copy of the order; and

(b) a witness statement or affidavit verifying the amount due under the order or, if payments under the order are required to be made to the justices' chief executive for the magistrates' court, a certificate by that chief executive to the same effect.

(2) On the filing of the documents mentioned in paragraph (1) the court officer shall, where the order to be enforced is a maintenance order, fix a day for the hearing of the application.

Amendments—SI 2001/256.

Form of application (r 4(1))—Form N337 should be used which, in family proceedings, must be accompanied by a statement, verified by a statement of truth, stating the amount due under the order and showing how that amount is arrived at (FPR 2010, r 33.3). If the cause or matter is not proceeding in the county court to which the attachment of earnings application is being made, a copy of the judgment or order should be exhibited.

"fix a day for the hearing" (r 4(2))—A hearing date is fixed only if the judgment or order is a maintenance order.

5 Service and reply (CCR Ord 27, r 5)

(1) Notice of the application together with a form of reply in the appropriate form, shall be served on the debtor in the manner set out in CPR rule 6.20.

(2) The debtor shall, within 8 days after service on him of the documents mentioned in paragraph (1), file a reply in the form provided, and the instruction to that effect in the notice to the debtor shall constitute a requirement imposed by virtue of section 14(4) of the Act of 1971:

Provided that no proceedings shall be taken for an offence alleged to have been committed under section 23(2)(c) or (f) of the Act of 1971 in relation to the requirement unless the said documents have been served on the debtor personally or the court is satisfied that they came to his knowledge in sufficient time for him to comply with the requirement.

(2A) Nothing in paragraph (2) shall require a defendant to file a reply if, within the period of time mentioned in that paragraph, he pays to the judgment creditor the money remaining due under the judgment or order and, where such payment is made, the judgment creditor shall so inform the court officer.

(3) On receipt of a reply the court officer shall send a copy to the applicant.

Amendments—SI 2000/221; SI 2001/2792; SI 2008/2178.

"the form provided" (r 5(2))—The debtor replies on Form N56.

"an offence" (r 5(2))—The combined effect of this rule and r 15 is that the debtor does not actually commit an offence until he has been served either personally or by another method with an order in Form N61 endorsed with a penal notice.

"served on the debtor personally" (r 5(2))—If personal service is impractical, the court may order service by another method (r 6.15).

"the money remaining due" (r 5(2A))—Rule 5(2A) does not apply in the case of maintenance orders (r 17(3A)). The hearing fixed in the case of a maintenance order is not vacated by payment of the arrears and the district judge may still proceed to make an attachment of earnings order if appropriate and to deal with the costs of the application. In other cases, the payment will have included the issue fee, which is added into the "amount due" on the Form N55, and in most cases no further action will be taken.

Debtor's application—This rule does not apply when the debtor applies for an attachment of earnings order on the making or variation of a maintenance order (r 17(4)).

Failure to reply—If the debtor does not return the Form N56, the court will automatically issue a Form N61 endorsed with a penal notice for personal service on the debtor, see r 7A.

6 Notice to employer (CCR Ord 27, r 6)

Without prejudice to the powers conferred by section 14(1) of the Act of 1971, the court officer may, at any stage of the proceedings, send to any person appearing to have the debtor in his employment a notice requesting him to give to the court, within such period as may be specified in the notice, a statement of the debtor's earnings and anticipated earnings with such particulars as may be so specified.

Statement of earnings—The form is N338. A creditor who knows the name of the debtor's employer should always request the issue of Form N338 when applying for attachment of earnings. If the debtor then fails to return Form N56, the court may proceed to make an order without further delay, on the basis of the information given by the employer. The debtor retains the right to apply for reconsideration of the order under r 7(2) below.

"notice requesting"—There is no compulsion on the employer to comply with the request but, if he does not do so, the court may decide to make an order under AEA 1971, s 14(1); failure to comply with such an order would be an offence (s 23(2)(c)).

7 Attachment of earnings order (CCR Ord 27, r 7)

(1) On receipt of the debtor's reply, the court officer may, if he has sufficient information to do so, make an attachment of earnings order and a copy of the order shall be sent to the parties and to the debtor's employer.

(2) Where an order is made under paragraph (1), the judgment creditor or the debtor may, within 14 days of service of the order on him and giving his reasons, apply on notice for the order to be re-considered and the court officer shall fix a day for the hearing of the application and give to the judgment creditor and the debtor not less than 2 days' notice of the day so fixed.

(3) On hearing an application under paragraph (2), the district judge may confirm the order or set it aside and make such new order as he thinks fit and the order so made shall be entered in the records of the court.

(4) Where an order is not made under paragraph (1), the court officer shall refer the application to the district judge who shall, if he considers that he has sufficient information to do so without the attendance of the parties, determine the application.

(5) Where the district judge does not determine the application under paragraph (4), he shall direct that a day be fixed for the hearing of the application whereupon the court officer shall fix such a day and give to the judgment creditor and the debtor not less than 8 days' notice of the day so fixed.

(6) Where an order is made under paragraph (4), the judgment creditor or the debtor may, within 14 days of service of the order on him and giving his reasons, apply on notice for the order to be re-considered; and the court officer shall fix a day for the hearing of the application and give to the judgment creditor and the debtor not less than 2 days' notice of the day so fixed.

(7) On hearing an application under paragraph (6), the district judge may confirm the order or set it aside and make such new order as he thinks fit and the order so made shall be entered in the records of the court.

(8) If the creditor does not appear at the hearing of the application under paragraph (5) but –

    (a)   the court has received a witness statement or affidavit of evidence from him; or

    (b)   the creditor requests the court in writing to proceed in his absence,

the court may proceed to hear the application and to make an order thereon.

(9) An attachment of earnings order may be made to secure the payment of a judgment debt if the debt is –

    (a)   of not less than £50; or

    (b)   for the amount remaining payable under a judgment for a sum of not less than £50.

Scope—This rule gives the procedure when the application is to enforce a judgment debt (usually, in family proceedings, an order for costs). It does not apply in the case of a maintenance order, including a lump sum order (see "expressions used" under r 1), as r 7(1)–(8) is replaced by a straightforward provision that the application may be heard by the district judge in chambers (r 17(5) and r 7(9) have no application).

Procedure—If the debtor files a reply under r 5(2), a senior member of the court staff may (though he need not) make an attachment of earnings order on the information before him without a hearing. Otherwise, the application is referred to the district judge, who similarly may make an attachment of earnings order on the information before him without a hearing. Either the debtor or the creditor may apply on notice to the other for any order so made to be reconsidered by the district judge. On the hearing he may confirm the order or make a different one.

If neither of those procedures is followed, the application itself is listed for hearing before the district judge. In that event, the creditor need not attend if he either files an affidavit of evidence or writes asking the court to proceed in his absence.

7A Failure by debtor (CCR Ord 27, r 7A)

(1) If the debtor has failed to comply with rule 5(2) or to make payment to the judgment creditor, the court officer may issue an order under section 14(1) of the Act of 1971 which shall –

    (a)   be indorsed with or incorporate a notice warning the debtor of the consequences of disobedience to the order;

    (b)   be served on the debtor personally; and

(c) direct that any payments made thereafter shall be paid into the court and not direct to the judgment creditor.

(2) Without prejudice to rule 16, if the person served with an order made pursuant to paragraph (1) fails to obey it or to file a statement of his means or to make payment, the court officer shall issue a notice calling on that person to show good reason why he should not be imprisoned and any such notice shall be served on the debtor personally not less than 5 days before the hearing.

(3) (*revoked*)

(4) In this rule 'statement of means' means a statement given under section 14(1) of the Act of 1971.

Amendments—SI 2013/262.

Maintenance orders—This rule does apply where the application relates to a maintenance order, but it is perhaps unlikely to be used because a hearing will have been fixed at which the district judge will have wider powers available, in particular the power to order the debtor to attend an adjourned hearing under AEA 1971, s 23(1) and, if he still fails to respond, either to have him arrested and brought to court or to make a suspended or outright committal order (see rr 7B and 8). If Form N61 or N63 is used in the case of a maintenance order, it will need some adaptation to fit the case.

7B Suspended committal order (CCR Ord 27, r 7B)

(1) If the debtor fails to attend at an adjourned hearing of an application for an attachment of earnings order and a committal order is made, the judge or district judge may direct that the committal order shall be suspended so long as the debtor attends at the time and place specified in the committal order and paragraphs (2), (4) and (5) of Order 28, rule 7 shall apply, with the necessary modifications, where such a direction is given as they apply where a direction is given under paragraph (1) of that rule.

(2) Where a committal order is suspended under paragraph (1) and the debtor fails to attend at the time and place specified under paragraph (1), a certificate to that effect given by the court officer shall be sufficient authority for the issue of a warrant of committal.

8 Failure by debtor – maintenance orders (CCR Ord 27, r 8)

(1) An order made under section 23(1) of the Act of 1971 for the attendance of the debtor at an adjourned hearing of an application for an attachment of earnings order to secure payments under a maintenance order shall –

(a) be served on the debtor personally not less than 5 days before the day fixed for the adjourned hearing; and

(b) direct that any payments made thereafter shall be paid into the court and not direct to the judgment creditor.

(2) An application by a debtor for the revocation of an order committing him to prison and, if he is already in custody, for his discharge under subsection (7) of the said section 23 shall be made to the judge or district judge in writing without notice to any other party showing the reasons for the debtor's failure to attend the court or his refusal to be sworn or to give evidence, as the case may be, and containing an undertaking by the debtor to attend the court or to be sworn or to give evidence when next ordered or required to do so.

(3) The application shall, if the debtor has already been lodged in prison, be attested by the governor of the prison (or any other officer of the prison not below the rank of principal officer) and in any other case be made on witness statement or affidavit.

(4) Before dealing with the application the judge or district judge may, if he thinks fit, cause notice to be given to the judgment creditor that the application has been made and of a day and hour when he may attend and be heard.

9 Costs (CCR Ord 27, r 9)

(1) Where costs are allowed to the judgment creditor on an application for an attachment of earnings order, there may be allowed –

    (a)   a charge of a solicitor for attending the hearing and, if the court so directs, for serving the application;

    (b)   if the court certifies that the case is fit for counsel, a fee to counsel; and

    (c)   the court fee on the issue of the application.

(2) For the purpose of paragraph (1)(a) a solicitor who has prepared on behalf of the judgment creditor a witness statement or affidavit or request under rule 7(8) shall be treated as having attended the hearing.

(3) The costs may be fixed and allowed without detailed assessment under CPR Part 47.

Modifications—CCR Ord 27, r 9 is modified for certain purposes by SI 2011/2866, Art 8(1), Sch 2.

Costs—The power to order detailed assessment is likely to be reserved for those rare cases that involve some substantial issue, e g under s 16 of the Act. Where fixed costs are allowed under CPR 1998, r 45.8, the sum allowed is the princely £8.50 for each attendance at the hearing.

10 Contents and service of order (CCR Ord 27, r 10)

(1) An attachment of earnings order shall contain such of the following particulars relating to the debtor as are known to the court, namely –

    (a)   his full name and address;

    (b)   his place of work; and

    (c)   the nature of his work and his works number, if any,

and those particulars shall be the prescribed particulars for the purposes of section 6(3) of the Act of 1971.

(2) An attachment of earnings order and any order varying or discharging such an order shall be served on the debtor and on the person to whom the order is directed, and CPR Part 6 and CPR rules 40.4 and 40.5 shall apply with the further modification that where the order is directed to a corporation which has requested the court that any communication relating to the debtor or to the class of persons to whom he belongs shall be directed to the corporation at a particular address, service may, if the district judge thinks fit, be effected on the corporation at that address.

(3) Where an attachment of earnings order is made to enforce a judgment or order of the High Court or a magistrates' court, a copy of the attachment of earnings order and of any order discharging it shall be sent by the court officer of the county court to the court officer of the High Court, or, as the case may be, the justices' chief executive for the magistrates' court.

Amendments—SI 2001/256.

11 Application to determine whether particular payments are earnings (CCR Ord 27, r 11)

An application to the court under section 16 of the Act of 1971 to determine whether payments to the debtor of a particular class or description are earnings for the purpose of an attachment of earnings order may be made to the district judge in writing and the court officer shall thereupon fix a date and time for the hearing of the application by the court and give notice thereof to the persons mentioned in the said section 16(2)(a), (b) and (c).

12 Notice of cesser (CCR Ord 27, r 12)

Where an attachment of earnings order ceases to have effect under section 8(4) of the Act of 1971, the court officer of the court in which the matter is proceeding shall give notice of the cesser to the person to whom the order was directed.

13 Variation and discharge by court of own motion (CCR Ord 27, r 13)

(1) Subject to paragraph (9), the powers conferred by section 9(1) of the Act of 1971 may be exercised by the court of its own motion in the circumstances mentioned in the following paragraphs.

(2) Where it appears to the court that a person served with an attachment of earnings order directed to him has not the debtor in his employment, the court may discharge the order.

(3) Where an attachment of earnings order which has lapsed under section 9(4) of the Act of 1971 is again directed to a person who appears to the court to have the debtor in his employment, the court may make such consequential variations in the order as it thinks fit.

(4) Where, after making an attachment of earnings order, the court makes or is notified of the making of another such order in respect of the same debtor which is not to secure the payment of a judgment debt or payments under an administration order, the court may discharge or vary the first-mentioned order having regard to the priority accorded to the other order by paragraph 8 of Schedule 3 to the Act of 1971.

(5) Where, after making an attachment of earnings order, the court makes an order under section 4(1)(b) of the Act of 1971 or makes an administration order, the court may discharge the attachment of earnings order or, if it exercises the power conferred by section 5(3) of the said Act, may vary the order in such manner as it thinks fit.

(6) On making a consolidated attachment of earnings order the court may discharge any earlier attachment of earnings order made to secure the payment of a judgment debt by the same debtor.

(7) Where it appears to the court that a bankruptcy order has been made against a person in respect of whom an attachment of earnings order is in force to secure the payment of a judgment debt, the court may discharge the attachment of earnings order.

(8) Where an attachment of earnings order has been made to secure the payment of a judgment debt and the court grants permission to issue execution for the recovery of the debt, the court may discharge the order.

(9) Before varying or discharging an attachment of earnings order of its own motion under any of the foregoing paragraphs of this rule, the court shall, unless it thinks it unnecessary in the circumstances to do so, give the debtor and the person on whose application the order was made an opportunity of being heard on the question whether the order should be varied or discharged, and for that purpose the court officer may give them notice of a date, time and place at which the question will be considered.

14 Transfer of attachment order (CCR Ord 27, r 14)

(1) Where the court by which the question of making a consolidated attachment order falls to be considered is not the court by which any attachment of earnings order has been made to secure the payment of a judgment debt by the debtor, the district judge of

the last-mentioned court shall, at the request of the district judge of the first-mentioned court, transfer to that court the matter in which the attachment of earnings order was made.

(2) Without prejudice to paragraph (1), if in the opinion of the judge or district judge of any court by which an attachment of earnings order has been made, the matter could more conveniently proceed in some other court, whether by reason of the debtor having become resident in the district of that court or otherwise, he may order the matter to be transferred to that court.

(3) The court to which proceedings arising out of an attachment of earnings are transferred under this rule shall have the same jurisdiction in relation to the order as if it has been made by that court.

Family proceedings—Whereas r 14(1) refers to "the matter in which" the attachment of earnings order was made, it is in practice often applied to the attachment of earnings matter itself so that the cause or matter remains untransferred: see "the court for the district in which the debtor resides" under r 3. If there is a question of transferring the cause or matter then it will not in practice be transferred to a county court that is not a divorce county court or a civil partnership proceedings county court, as the case may be.

15 Exercise of power to obtain statement of earnings etc (CCR Ord 27, r 15)

(1) An order under section 14(1) of the Act of 1971 shall be indorsed with or incorporate a notice warning the person to whom it is directed of the consequences of disobedience to the order and shall be served on him personally.

(2) Order 34, rule 2, shall apply, with the necessary modifications, in relation to any penalty for failure to comply with an order under the said section 14(1) or, subject to the proviso to rule 5(2), any penalty for failure to comply with a requirement mentioned in that rule, as it applies in relation to a fine under section 55 of the County Courts Act 1984.

16 Offences (CCR Ord 27, r 16)

(1) Where it is alleged that a person has committed any offence mentioned in section 23(2)(a), (b), (d), (e) or (f) of the Act of 1971 in relation to proceedings in, or to an attachment of earnings order made by, a county court, the district judge shall, unless it is decided to proceed against the alleged offender summarily, issue a summons calling upon him to show cause why he should not be punished for the alleged offence.

The summons shall be served on the alleged offender personally not less than 14 days before the return day.

(2) Order 34, rules 3 and 4, shall apply, with the necessary modifications, to proceedings for an offence under section 23(2) of the Act of 1971 as they apply to proceedings for offences under the County Courts Act 1984.

"any offence" (r 16(1))—AEA 1971, s 23(2) gives the exact definitions but the offences may be summarised as follows: employer failing to comply with an attachment of earnings order or variation order (s 23(2)(a)); employer failing to tell the court that the debtor is not in, or has left, his employment (s 23(2)(b)); debtor failing to tell the court of a change in his employment or new employer, who is aware of the order, failing to report the new employment to the court (s 23(2)(c)); and giving false information to the court (s 23(2)(e),(f)).

17 Maintenance orders (CCR Ord 27, r 17)

(1) The foregoing rules of this Order shall apply in relation to maintenance payments as they apply in relation to a judgment debt, subject to the following paragraphs.

(2) An application for an attachment of earnings order to secure payments under a maintenance order made by a county court shall be made to that county court.

(3) Any application under section 32 of the Matrimonial Causes Act 1973 for permission to enforce the payment of arrears which became due more than 12 months before the application for an attachment of earnings order shall be made in that application.

(3A) Notice of the application together with a form of reply in the appropriate form, shall be served on the debtor in the manner set out in CPR rule 6.20.

(3B) Service of the notice shall be effected not less than 21 days before the hearing, but service may be effected at any time before the hearing on the applicant satisfying the court by witness statement or affidavit that the respondent is about to remove from his address for service.

(3C) Rule 5(2A) shall not apply.

(4) An application by the debtor for an attachment of earnings order to secure payments under a maintenance order may be made on the making of the maintenance order or an order varying the maintenance order, and rules 4 and 5 shall not apply.

(5) Rule 7 shall have effect as if for paragraphs (1) to (8) there were substituted the following paragraph –

"(1) An application for an attachment of earnings order may be heard and determined by the district judge, who shall hear the application in private.".

(6) Rule 9 shall apply as if for the reference to the amount payable under the relevant adjudication there were substituted a reference to the arrears due under the related maintenance order.

(7) Where an attachment of earnings order made by the High Court designates the court officer of a county court as the collecting officer, that officer shall, on receipt of a certified copy of the order from the court officer of the High Court, send to the person to whom the order is directed a notice as to the mode of payment.

(8) Where an attachment of earnings order made by a county court to secure payments under a maintenance order ceases to have effect and –

    (a)   the related maintenance order was made by that court; or

    (b)   the related maintenance order was an order of the High Court and –

        (i)   the court officer of the county court has received notice of the cessation from the court officer of the High Court; or

        (ii)   a committal order has been made in the county court for the enforcement of the related maintenance order,

the court officer of the county court shall give notice of the cessation to the person to whom the attachment of earnings order was directed.

(9) Where an attachment of earnings order has been made by a county court to secure payments under a maintenance order, notice under section 10(2) of the Act of 1971 to the debtor and to the person to whom the district judge is required to pay sums received under the order shall be in the form provided for that purpose, and if the debtor wishes to request the court to discharge the attachment of earnings order or to vary it otherwise than by making the appropriate variation, he shall apply to the court, within 14 days after the date of the notice, for the remedy desired.

(10) Rule 13 shall have effect as if for paragraphs (4) to (7) there were substituted the following paragraph –

"(4) Where it appears to the court by which an attachment of earnings order has been made that the related maintenance order has ceased to have effect, whether by

PART III

virtue of the terms of the maintenance order or under section 28 of the Matrimonial Causes Act 1973 or otherwise, the court may discharge or vary the attachment of earnings order.".

Amendments—SI 1999/1008; SI 2000/221; SI 2001/2792; SI 2008/2178.

"heard and determined" (r 17(5))—Rule 7(8), which enables the court to proceed in the absence of the applicant, does not apply in the case of a maintenance order. It is necessary to attend and prove the exact and up-to-date amount of the arrears. If the proceedings concern a "qualifying periodical maintenance order" within the meaning of MEA 1991, s 1, the court may make a "means of payment order" under s 1(4)(a) of that Act. This might occur where it appears that the debtor is self-employed.

"the related maintenance order has ceased to have effect" (r 17(10))—Normally an attachment of earnings order does not record the details of the maintenance order that it enforces and vigilance is needed to avoid overpayment, as in the Irish case of *McGrath v District Court Clerk* [2008] I EHC 116, where it appears that the payor did not have a copy of the original order and only realised that it had ceased to have effect after an overpayment of £31,520 had occurred.

Part II
Consolidated Attachment of Earnings Orders

18 Cases in which consolidated order may be made (CCR Ord 27, r 18)

Subject to the provisions of rules 19 to 21, the court may make a consolidated attachment order where –

(a)   two or more attachment of earnings orders are in force to secure the payment of judgment debts by the same debtor; or

(b)   on an application for an attachment of earnings order to secure the payment of a judgment debt, or for a consolidated attachment order to secure the payment of two or more judgment debts, it appears to the court that an attachment of earnings order is already in force to secure the payment of a judgment debt by the same debtor.

General note—Maintenance orders (widely defined) cannot be the subject of consolidated attachment of earnings orders. Accordingly they are not considered further in this work – readers are referred to *Civil Court Service* (Jordan Publishing Ltd).

****

CCR ORDER 28
JUDGMENT SUMMONSES

Note—Reproduced as modified for family proceedings by FPR 2010, r 33.18.

1 Application for judgment summons (CCR Ord 28, r 1)

(1) An application for the issue of a judgment summons may be made to the court for the district in which the debtor resides or carries on business or, if the summons is to issue against two or more persons jointly liable under the judgment or order sought to be enforced, in the court for the district in which any of the debtors resides or carries on business.

(2) The judgment creditor shall make his application by filing a request in that behalf certifying the amount of money remaining due under the judgment or order, the amount in respect of which the judgment summons is to issue and that the whole or part of any instalment due remains unpaid.

(3) The judgment creditor must file with the request all written evidence on which he intends to rely.

Amendments—SI 2001/4015.

2 Mode of service (CCR Ord 28, r 2)

(1) Subject to paragraph (2), a judgment summons shall be served personally on every debtor against whom it is issued.

(2) Where the judgment creditor or the judgment creditor's solicitor gives a certificate for postal service in respect of a debtor residing or carrying on business within the district of the court, the judgment summons will, unless the district judge otherwise directs, be served on that debtor by the court sending it to the debtor by first-class post at the address stated in the request for the judgment summons and, unless the contrary is shown, the date of service is deemed to be the seventh day after the date on which the judgment summons was sent to the debtor.

(3) Where a judgment summons has been served on a debtor in accordance with paragraph (2), no order of commitment shall be made against him unless –

   (a) he appears at the hearing; or

   (b) it is made under section 110(2) of the Act.

(4) The written evidence on which the judgment creditor intends to rely must be served with the judgment summons.

Amendments—SI 2001/4015; SI 2008/2178.

Modifications—CCR Ord 28, r 2 is modified for certain purposes by SI 2011/2866, Art 8(1), Sch 2.

3 Time for service (CCR Ord 28, r 3)

(1) The judgment summons and written evidence must be served not less than 14 days before the day fixed for the hearing.

(2) A notice of non-service will be sent pursuant to CPR rule 6.18 in respect of a judgment summons which has been sent by post under rule 2(2) and has been returned to the court undelivered.

(3) CPR rules 7.5 and 7.6 apply, with the necessary modifications, to a judgment summons as they apply to a claim form.

Amendments—SI 2001/4015; SI 2008/2178.

4 Enforcement of debtor's attendance (CCR Ord 28, r 4)

(1) Order 27, rules 7B and 8, shall apply, with the necessary modifications, to an order made under section 110(1) of the Act for the attendance of the debtor at an adjourned hearing of a judgment summons as they apply to an order made under section 23(1) of the Attachment of Earnings Act 1971 for the attendance of the debtor at an adjourned hearing of an application for an attachment of earnings order.

(1A) An order made under section 110(1) of the Act must be served personally on the judgment debtor.

(1B) Copies of –

   (a) the judgment summons; and

   (b) the written evidence,

must be served with the order.

PART III

(2) At the time of service of the order there shall be paid or tendered to the debtor a sum reasonably sufficient to cover his expenses in travelling to and from the court, unless such a sum was paid to him at the time of service of the judgment summons.

Amendments—SI 2001/4015.

Order for attendance (r 4(1))—The consequence of failure to attend on the original hearing is not that the court may commit the debtor but that, pursuant to CCA 1984, s 110(1), it may order his attendance at an adjourned hearing. Failure to comply with that order is punishable by committal for up to 14 days (s 110(2)). There is also a power to order the debtor to be arrested and brought before the court (s 110(3)). Conduct money must have been paid or tendered (s 110(4)) and there is power to revoke or discharge the committal (s 110(5)). There is a close parallel with the procedure on failure to attend an attachment of earnings application, but in the case of a judgment summons the court's powers are not exercisable by the district judge. In family proceedings, both the judgment summons (FPR 2010, r 33.11(2)) and the order to attend (FPR 2010, r 33.13) must be served personally. It has been held (in *Mubarak v Mubarak* [2001] 1 FLR 698, CA) that the debtor cannot be compelled to give evidence, so there may be cases where the creditor sees little value in seeking an order compelling his attendance.

"paid or tendered" (r 4(2))—In family proceedings, the sum will have been paid or tendered when the judgment summons was served (FPR 2010, r 33.11(3)).

5 Evidence (CCR Ord 28, r 5)

(1) No person may be committed on an application for a judgment summons unless –

    (a)   the order is made under section 110(2) of the Act; or

    (b)   the judgment creditor proves that the debtor –

        (i)   has or has had since the date of the judgment or order the means to pay the sum in respect of which he has made default; and

        (ii)   has refused or neglected or refuses or neglects to pay that sum.

(2) The debtor may not be compelled to give evidence.

Amendments—Substituted by SI 2001/4015.

7 Suspension of committal order (CCR Ord 28, r 7)

(1) If on the hearing of a judgment summons a committal order is made, the judge may direct execution of the order to be suspended to enable the debtor to pay the amount due.

(2) A note of any direction given under paragraph (1) shall be entered in the records of the court and notice of the suspended committal order shall be sent to the debtor.

(3) Where a judgment summons is issued in respect of one or more but not all of the instalments payable under a judgment or order for payment by instalments and a committal order is made and suspended under paragraph (1), the judgment or order shall, unless the judge otherwise orders, be suspended for so long as the execution of the committal order is suspended.

(4) Where execution of a committal order is suspended under paragraph (1) and the debtor subsequently desires to apply for a further suspension, the debtor shall attend at or write to the court office and apply for the suspension he desires, stating the reasons for his inability to comply with the terms of the original suspension, and the court shall fix a day for the hearing of the application by the judge and give at least 3 days' notice thereof to the judgment creditor and the debtor.

(5) The district judge may suspend execution of the committal order pending the hearing of an application under paragraph (4).

"to enable the debtor to pay" (r 7(1))—This provision is in effect superseded by FPR 2010, r 33.16, at least in the case of arrears under a periodical payments order, because FPR 2010, r 33.16(2) expressly authorises terms requiring the debtor to pay the amount due, the costs of the judgment summons and "any sums accruing due under the original order". Payments are then attributed first to sums accruing due second to the amount in respect of which the judgment summons was issued and the costs (FPR 2010, r 33.16(4)(a)).

8 New order on judgment summons (CCR Ord 28, r 8)

(1) Where on the hearing of a judgment summons, the judge makes a new order for payment of the amount of the judgment debt remaining unpaid, there shall be included in the amount payable under the order for the purpose of any enforcement proceedings, otherwise than by judgment summons, any amount in respect of which a committal order has already been made and the debtor imprisoned.

(2) No judgment summons under the new order shall include any amount in respect of which the debtor was imprisoned before the new order was made, and any amount subsequently paid shall be appropriated in the first instance to the amount due under the new order.

No judgment summons under the new order—Debtors Act 1869, s 5 permits a term of imprisonment in respect of any debt or instalment under any judgment or order, and this means one term only (*Evans v Wills* (1876) 1 CPD 229). This rule prohibits a second judgment summons for the same debt or instalment, notwithstanding that it has become due under a different order, namely the new order.

9 Notification of order on judgment of High Court (CCR Ord 28, r 9)

(1) Notice of the result of the hearing of a judgment summons on a judgment or order of any other court shall be sent by the county court to that other court.

If a committal order or a new order for payment is made on the hearing, the office copy of the judgment or order filed in the county court shall be deemed to be a judgment or order of the court in which the judgment summons is heard.

Amendments—SI 2001/2792.

10 Costs on judgment summons (CCR Ord 28, r 10)

(1) No costs shall be allowed to the judgment creditor on the hearing of a judgment summons unless –

- (a) a committal order is made; or
- (b) the sum in respect of which the judgment summons was issued is paid before the hearing.

(2) Where costs are allowed to the judgment creditor,

- (a) there may be allowed –
  - (i) a charge of the judgment creditor's solicitor for attending the hearing and, if the judge so directs, for serving the judgment summons;
  - (ii) a fee to counsel if the court certifies that the case is fit for counsel;
  - (iii) any travelling expenses paid to the debtor; and
  - (iv) the court fee on the issue of the judgment summons;
- (b) the costs may be fixed and allowed without detailed assessment under CPR Part 47.

Amendments—SI 2001/4015.

Modifications—CCR Ord 28, r 10 is modified for certain purposes by SI 2011/2866, Art 8(1), Sch 2.

"No costs shall be allowed ... unless" (r 10(1))—Not only is the creditor deprived of costs if the debt is not paid and no committal order is made, he is also at risk as to the debtor's costs if he fails to prove means and refusal or neglect. The request for the judgment summons (Form M16) includes an acknowledgement of this risk.

PART III

11 Issue of warrant of committal (CCR Ord 28, r 11)

(1) A judgment creditor desiring a warrant to be issued pursuant to a committal order shall file a request in that behalf.

(2) Where two or more debtors are to be committed in respect of the same judgment or order, a separate warrant of committal shall be issued for each of them.

(3) Where a warrant of committal is sent to a foreign court for execution, that court shall indorse on it a notice as to the effect of section 122(3) of the Act addressed to the governor of the prison of that court.

Affidavit of default—In the case of a suspended committal order, a statement of default (which must, of course, be verified by a statement of truth, must be filed by the creditor before the suspended order is executed (FPR 2010, r 33.16(4)(b)).

12 Notification to foreign court of part payment before debtor lodged in prison (CCR Ord 28, r 12)

Where, after a warrant of committal has been sent to a foreign court for execution but before the debtor is lodged in prison, the home court is notified that an amount which is less than the sum on payment of which the debtor is to be discharged has been paid, the home court shall send notice of the payment to the foreign court.

13 Payment after debtor lodged in prison (CCR Ord 28, r 13)

(1) Where, after the debtor has been lodged in prison under a warrant of committal, payment is made of the sum on payment of which the debtor is to be discharged, then –

(a) if the payment is made to the court responsible for the execution of the warrant, the court officer shall make and sign a certificate of payment and send it by post or otherwise to the gaoler;

(b) if the payment is made to the court which issued the warrant of committal after the warrant has been sent to a foreign court for execution, the home court shall send notice of the payment to the foreign court, and the court officer at the foreign court shall make and sign a certificate of payment and send it by post or otherwise to the gaoler;

(c) if the payment is made to the gaoler, he shall sign a certificate of payment and send the amount to the court which made the committal order.

(2) Where, after the debtor has been lodged in prison under a warrant of committal, payment is made of an amount less than the sum on payment of which the debtor is to be discharged, then subject to paragraph (3), paragraph (1)(a) and (b) shall apply with the substitution of references to a notice of payment for the references to a certificate of payment and paragraph (1)(c) shall apply with the omission of the requirement to make and sign a certificate of payment.

(3) Where, after the making of a payment to which paragraph (2) relates, the balance of the sum on payment of which the debtor is to be discharged is paid, paragraph (1) shall apply without the modifications mentioned in paragraph (2).

Amendments—SI 1999/1008.

14 Discharge of debtor otherwise than on payment (CCR Ord 28, r 14)

(1) Where the judgment creditor lodges with the district judge a request that a debtor lodged in prison under a warrant of committal may be discharged from custody, the district judge shall make an order for the discharge of the debtor in respect of the warrant of committal and the court shall send the gaoler a certificate of discharge.

(2) Where a debtor whc has been lodged in prison under a warrant of committal desires to apply for his discharge under section 121 of the Act, the application shall be made to the judge in writing and without notice showing the reasons why the debtor alleges that he is unable to pay the sum in respect of which he has been committed and ought to be discharged and stating any offer which he desires to make as to the terms on which his discharge is to be ordered, and Order 27, rule 8(3) and (4), shall apply, with the necessary modifications, as it applies to an application by a debtor for his discharge from custody under section 23(7) of the Attachment of Earnings Act 1971.

(3) If in a case to which paragraph (2) relates the debtor is ordered to be discharged from custody on terms which include liability to re-arrest if the terms are not complied with, the judge may, on the application of the judgment creditor if the terms are not complied with, order the debtor to be re-arrested and imprisoned for such part of the term of imprisonment as remained unserved at the time of discharge.

(4) Where an order is made under paragraph (3), a duplicate warrant of committal shall be issued, indorsed with a certificate signed by the court officer as to the order of the judge.

CCR ORDER 29
COMMITTAL FOR BREACH OF ORDER OR UNDERTAKING

Note—By virtue of the Civil Procedure (Amendment No 2) Rules 2012, SI 2012/2208, CPR 1998, Sch 2, CCR Ord 29 is revoked as of 1 October 2012. However, where FPR 2010 apply CCR Ord 29, they apply those rules as they appeared in Sch 2 to the CPR on 30 September 2012 (FPR 2010, r 2.3(4)).

1 Enforcement of judgment to do or abstain from doing any act (CCR Ord 29, r 1)

(1) Where a person required by a judgment or order to do an act refuses or neglects to do it within the time fixed by the judgment or order or any subsequent order, or where a person disobeys a judgment or order requiring him to abstain from doing an act, then, subject to the Debtors Acts 1869 and 1878 and to the provisions of these rules, the judgment or order may be enforced, by order of the judge, by a committal order against that person or, if that person is a body corporate, against any director or other officer of the body.

(2) Subject to paragraphs (6) and (7), a judgment or order shall not be enforced under paragraph (1) unless –

    (a) a copy of the judgment or order has been served personally on the person required to do cr abstain from doing the act in question and also, where that person is a body corporate, on the director or other officer of the body against whom a committal order is sought; and

    (b) in the case of a judgment or order requiring a person to do an act, the copy has been so served before the expiration of the time within which he was required to do the act and was accompanied by a copy of any order, made between the date of the judgment or order and the date of service, fixing that time.

(3) Where a judgment or order enforceable by committal order under paragraph (1) has been given or made, the court officer shall, if the judgment or order is in the nature of an injunction, at the time when the judgment or order is drawn up, and in any other case on the request of the judgment creditor, issue a copy of the judgment or order, indorsed with or incorporating a notice as to the consequences of disobedience, for service in accordance with paragraph (2).

(4) If the person served with the judgment or order fails to obey it, the judgment creditor may issue a claim form or, as the case may be, an application notice seeking the

committal for contempt of court of that person and subject to paragraph (7), the claim form or application notice shall be served on him personally.

(4A) The claim form or application notice (as the case may be) shall –

(a)   identify the provisions of the injunction or undertaking which it is alleged have been disobeyed or broken;

(b)   list the ways in which it is alleged that the injunction has been disobeyed or the undertaking has been broken;

(c)   be supported by an affidavit stating the grounds on which the application is made,

and unless service is dispensed with under paragraph (7), a copy of the affidavit shall be served with the claim form or application notice.

(5) If a committal order is made, the order shall be for the issue of a warrant of committal and, unless the judge otherwise orders –

(a)   a copy of the order shall be served on the person to be committed either before or at the time of the execution of the warrant; or

(b)   where the warrant has been signed by the judge, the order for issue of the warrant may be served on the person to be committed at any time within 36 hours after the execution of the warrant.

(5A) A warrant of committal shall not, without further order of the court, be enforced more than 2 years after the date on which the warrant is issued.

(6) A judgment or order requiring a person to abstain from doing an act may be enforced under paragraph (1) notwithstanding that service of a copy of the judgment or order has not been effected in accordance with paragraph (2) if the judge is satisfied that, pending such service, the person against whom it is sought to enforce the judgment or order has had notice of the judgment or order either –

(a)   by being present when the judgment or order was given or made; or

(b)   by being notified of the terms of the judgment or order whether by telephone, fax, e-mail or otherwise.

(7) Without prejudice to its powers under Part 6 of the CPR, the court may dispense with service of a copy of a judgment or order under paragraph (2) or a claim form or application notice under paragraph (4) if the court thinks it just to do so.

(8) Where service of the claim form or application notice has been dispensed with under paragraph (7) and a committal order is made in the absence of the respondent, the judge may on his own initiative fix a date and time when the person to be committed is to be brought before him or before the court.

Amendments—SI 2003/3361; SI 2008/2178.

Modifications—CCR Ord 29, r 1(3) is set out above as it appears in the CPR, but various versions of this rule appear in the FPR for different purposes: for applications under FLA 1996, Pt IV (domestic violence), see FPR 2010, r 10.12; for applications under FLA 1996, Pt 4A (forced marriage) see r 11.15(2); and for CA 1989, s 8 orders (except those referred to in r 33.7(2)(a)) and orders under ss 14A, 14B(2)(b), 14C(3)(b) and 14D, see r 33.7(1). Paragraph (3) is omitted for purposes listed under FPR 2010, r 33.7(2). This is an unsatisfactory form of drafting.

Forms—As committal proceedings are expressly governed by the CCR, the better view is that CCR forms must be used. Therefore, Form N78 should be used. This is considered to be so notwithstanding FPR PD5A, para 2.1 and the reference to Form FP2. However, any doubt in such an important area is unfortunate. The FPR are due to be amended in 2013 now that CPR 1998, Pt 81 has replaced CCR Order 29 in civil proceedings, but not yet in family proceedings.

Disobedience of an order as a contempt of court – "refuses ... neglects ... disobeys" (r 1(1))—This rule regulates an enforcement procedure in respect of an order directing a person, or an undertaking promising, to do an act at or within a specified time (such as an occupation order for a person to leave the family home), or to abstain from doing an act (such as a non-molestation order). Disobedience of a directive order capable of enforcement by committal, or an undertaking to like effect, is a civil contempt of court. Refusal, neglect and disobedience are all forms of contempt. The purpose of the powers available on proof of such contempt is enforcement – to compel obedience (*Lightfoot v Lightfoot* [1989] 1 FLR 414), to punish (*Martin v Bannister* (1899) 4 QBD 491) and to deter disobedience by others (*James v Cliffe* (1987) *The Times*, 16 June). Contempt consists of "actus reus" and "mens rea". This means a deliberate act, or neglect to act, by the respondent who knew what the order was (*Re the Supply of Ready Mixed Concrete (No 2)* [1995] 1 AC 456). It is not necessary to prove that the respondent's purpose was to breach the order or undertaking. See further commentary to CCA 1981, s 14.

Power to enforce injunctive orders and undertakings—The power to commit, and the other forms of enforcement available in the High Court for disobedience of an injunctive order or breach of an undertaking, are also available in the county court by virtue of CCA 1984, s 38(1).

Approach of court when selecting disposal—See *Hale v Tanner* [2000] 2 FLR 879 and annotations under CCA 1981, s 14.

Immediate committal—See annotations to CCA 1981, s 14; CPR 1998, Sch 1, RSC Ord 46, rr 1, 7.

Adjournment of consideration of penalty—The court may, where disobedience of an injunctive order or breach of an undertaking has been proved, adjourn consideration of the penalty. If this is done, the terms which are required to be obeyed and breach of which may result in imposition of a penalty, and the period during which such conduct may so result, must be specified in the order (CC Form N79 and see *Pidduck v Molloy* [1992] 2 FLR 202).

Fines—Although fines are not mentioned in this rule, the House of Lords held in *Heatons Transport (St Helens) Ltd v TGWU* [1973] AC 15 at [109] that the High Court may impose a fine in lieu of, or in addition to, committal; county courts also have this power (*Rose v Laskington* [1990] 1 QB 562 at [567]). For an example of this provision, see *Banton v Banton* [1990] 2 FLR 465; there is no statutory limit to such a fine.

Sequestration—Despite the absence of a county court rule referring to sequestration, it was held in *Rose v Laskington* [1990] 1 QB 562 that sequestration is available in county courts. However, under CPR 1998, applications for sequestration are confined to the High Court (see PD70, para 1.2(2)). In practice the expense of sequestration confines it to the larger cases. A case not already in the High Court may be transferred pursuant to FPR 2010, r 33.4.

Other remedies—In *Danchevsky v Danchevsky* [1975] Fam 17 at [22], Lord Denning MR said "Whenever there is a reasonable alternative available instead of committal to prison, that alternative must be taken". The power to authorise an act to be done at the respondent's expense under CPR 1998, Sch 1, RSC Ord 45, r 8 is available in a county court by virtue of CCA 1984, ss 38 and 76. Similarly, the High Court's power to nominate a person to execute a document when the respondent having been so ordered neglects or refuses to do so or cannot be found is available (see SCA 1981, s 39).

Residence or contact orders under CA 1989, s 8 which contain orders to "give up" a child may be enforceable, in an appropriate case, by an application under FLA 1986, s 34.

Undertaking (r 1(4A))—See under r 1A.

Enforcement of orders or undertakings to pay money—See FPR PD33A. An order to pay money, or an undertaking to do so, cannot be enforced by committal proceedings, except in the very limited circumstances permitted under Debtors Act 1869, s 5, as limited by AJA 1970, s 11 and Sch 8 (*Symmons v Symmons* [1993] 1 FLR 317). An application to commit for non-payment requires not merely proof of non-payment but proof (beyond reasonable doubt) that the non-payer had the means to pay but refused or neglected to pay. By Debtors Act 1869, s 5, "...any court may commit to prison for a term not exceeding six weeks, or until payment of the sum due...". Although the Act does not say "earlier payment", that is what it means, because the main purpose of the Act was to abolish indefinite imprisonment until payment (which was possible, without proof of means, before the Act). Imprisonment does not satisfy or extinguish the debt. (See also (c) *Judgment summonses* below.)

"subject to ... these rules" (r 1(1))—The principal special cases are:

(a) *Attachment of earnings* Specific powers to deal with disobedience of orders in such proceedings are contained in AEA 1971, s 23, and are governed by CPR 1998, Sch 2, Ord 27.

(b) *Orders to obtain information from judgment debtors* (formerly known as "oral examination") See CPR 1998, Pt 71.

(c) *Judgment summonses* Specific powers and a procedure similar to that which applies in attachment of earnings cases are created by CCA 1984, s 112 and CPR 1998, Sch 2, Ord 28. Criticism of the procedure in *Mubarak v Mubarak* [2001] 1 FLR 698 has been addressed. See FPR 2010, Pt 33, Ch 2.

PART III

"notice as to the consequences of disobedience" (r 1(3))—An injunctive order capable of enforcement by committal may be thus enforced, subject to the requirements as to service, if it has on it a penal notice warning the respondent of the consequences of breach. Prescribed Form FL404 and county court injunction Form N78 have a penal notice incorporated in the text. See also the form of words used in FPR PD33A. The person who has the benefit of a directive occupation order, or an injunction order against torts, is entitled to have the order issued with a penal notice incorporated or endorsed on it. A warning notice cannot be added to an order under CA 1989, s 8 without the leave of a judge (FPR 2010, rr 12.33, 33.7). Such leave should be sought on notice. The form of notice on FL404a (non-molestation order) differs in that it also warns the respondent that breach of a non-molestation order is a criminal offence with a maximum sentence of 5 years' imprisonment.

"served personally", "pending such service", and "dispense with service" (r 1(2)(a),(6) and (7))—An order which is capable of enforcement by committal must, in general, be served personally on the respondent to make it enforceable. See the Family Justice Council *Protocol for Process Servers: Non-Molestation Orders*, November 2011 in Part V.

Issue of the "Notice to show good reason" and evidence in support—Penal enforcement under Ord 29, r 1 is initiated on request by the applicant for the issue of Form N78, entitled "Notice to show good reason why you should not be committed to prison" (r 1(4)), supported by an affidavit stating the grounds relied upon (r 1(4A)(c)). There is no separate form for the request for issue. County court practice is that the applicant drafts and submits Form N78, which is treated as the request for issue, and the court revises it only if it appears to be defective.

Drafting the "Notice to show good reason" and the affidavit or statement in support—The precise requirements for the request for issue are prescribed in r 1(4A). The specific allegations relied on as amounting to the breaches must be listed sufficiently clearly to enable the respondent to know the case that he has to answer (*Harmsworth v Harmsworth* [1988] 1 FLR 349 and see *PD (Committal Applications)*, para 2.5(2)). The affidavit or statement in support is to narrate the events, not to specify the allegations. If the particulars of the alleged breaches have not been included in Form N78, but are adequately particularised in the evidence in support, the court should be asked for leave to amend the Notice before the hearing begins. The court must not act on allegations of which notice has not been given, unless exceptional circumstances justify an application being made ex parte (*Tabone v Seguna* [1986] 1 FLR 591; *Wright v Jess* [1987] 2 FLR 373).

Service of Notice in Form N78 and affidavit in support (r 1(4))—The Notice instructs the respondent to attend the hearing of the application for an order of committal and, together with the affidavit in support, must be served personally on the respondent (r 1(4),(4A)) unless service is dispensed with under r 1(7), or an order has been made for service by an alternative method. Enforcement is governed by FPR 2010, Pt 33. This Part applies CPR 1998, Pt 50 and Schs 1 and 2. *PDCommittal* supplements both Sch 1, RSC Ord 52 and CCR Ord 29. Paragraph 4.2 provides that the hearing date for a committal application shall be not less than 14 days after service unless the court otherwise directs.

Procedural requirements—*PD (Committal Applications)* regulates the mode of application for committals in family cases, including the requirement that each allegation be identified, separately and numerically in the form of application, the period of 14 days for service in such proceedings, the form of evidence, case management and conduct of the hearing.

Service of notice of adjourned hearing in "Notice to show good reason"—The respondent must be personally served with notice of an adjourned hearing, unless he was present when the adjournment was granted and was given the new date (*Chiltern District Council v Keane* [1985] 1 WLR 619).

Dispensing with service of "Notice to show good reason" and ex parte committal (r 1(7),(8))—Proceeding ex parte by dispensation with service of the Notice is exceptional, but may be allowed by the court where the respondent is shown to be evading service (*Wright v Jess* [1987] 2 FLR 373). If this course is taken and an order of committal is made, the court should provide for the respondent to be brought before it at the earliest opportunity after he has been arrested (r 1(8); *Lamb v Lamb* [1984] FLR 278). The respondent is entitled to a complete rehearing (*Aslam v Singh* [1987] 1 FLR 122) and the court cannot impose a sentence greater than was ordered at the ex parte hearing (*Lamb v Lamb* above). An order made ex parte is provisional (*R v R (Contempt of Court)* [1988] Fam Law 388), and the contemnor is entitled to apply for it to be discharged (*Wright v Jess* above).

Production in court of person arrested under FLA 1996, s 47 and attendance of the victim—A person arrested by virtue of a power of arrest under s 47(6) must be brought before the court within 24 hours of the arrest (s 47(7)(a)). A warrant of arrest authorises the immediate arrest of the respondent for failing to comply with the provisions of a non-molestation or occupation order but, unlike the requirement in s 47(7)(a), there is no provision that a person arrested on a warrant must be brought before the court within 24 hours of the arrest. In practice, a person arrested under a warrant will be produced before the court as soon as reasonably practicable, regard being given to enabling the applicant to attend, unless the respondent is arrested some distance from the court which issued the warrant. When an arrested respondent is brought before the court, the attendance of the applicant will almost always be needed to enable the court to deal with the alleged breach, and if she is not available within a reasonable time the court may have to adjourn the matter, and consider whether to remand the respondent.

Procedural powers of court when person arrested under FLA 1996, s 47 is brought before the court—When a respondent is brought before the court following arrest, whether under a power of arrest or a warrant, the court may hear and deal with the alleged breach, or adjourn the hearing. The court may adjourn without having determined whether a breach has been proved, or after finding a breach proved. If the hearing is adjourned, the arrested person may be (i) released without remand, in which case additional injunctive directions may be appropriate; (ii) remanded in custody under s 47(7)(b) or s 47(10), and s 47(11) and Sch 5, para 2(1)(a); (iii) remanded on bail under s 47(7)(b) or s 47(10), and s 47(11) and (12) and Sch 5, para 2(1)(b); or (iv) remanded for the purpose of enabling a medical examination to be made under s 48(1) or for a report on his mental condition under s 48(4). See further commentary to FPR 2010, Pt 10 and to CCA 1981.

Remand under FLA 1996, s 47(7)(b),(10),(11) or s 48—A person arrested and brought before the court can be remanded under s 47(7)(b) or s 47(10), and s 47(11), (12) and Sch 5, in custody or on bail, or remanded for a medical report under s 48, in custody or on bail (s 47(11),(12) and Sch 5).

Bail under FLA 1996, Sch 5—FPR 2010, r 10.17 provides for an application for bail by an arrested person, which may be with or without a surety. The following prescribed forms should be referred to for the requirements of bail: recognizance of the person making an application (FL411); recognizance of a surety (FL411); and bail notice (FL412).

Warrant of arrest for breach of an injunction under the Protection from Harassment Act 1997—Enforcement of orders under PHA 1997 is now governed by CPR 1998, Pt 81 and not by CCR Ord 29. PHA 1997, s 3(3) provides for issue of a warrant for the arrest of a defendant. A warrant of arrest may be issued by a judge or a district judge upon an application substantiated on oath, if the court concludes that the defendant has done anything which he is prohibited from doing by the injunction. PHA 1997 makes no provision for remand of a defendant. Therefore, it appears that the court before which the defendant is brought must either deal with him for the alleged breach, or adjourn and release the defendant. Consequently, the defendant should usually be brought before the court at the earliest reasonable time at which the claimant can attend and give evidence. Although a district judge has power to issue a warrant, neither the PHA nor any rule gives power to deal with the committal itself which must therefore be before a circuit judge.

Further arrest where the respondent fails to appear at an adjourned hearing after being released following arrest by virtue of a power of arrest under FLA 1996, s 47—Where a person has been arrested by virtue of a power of arrest under s 47, and the case has been adjourned but the respondent fails to appear for the adjourned hearing following his remand or release, the court cannot grant a warrant of arrest under s 47(8) (unless the power of arrest was only attached to some of the terms of the occupation order). However, it is arguable that the respondent can be re-arrested under the original power of arrest, provided that he is again brought before a judge within 24 hours of the second arrest. In *Wheeldon v Wheeldon* [1998] 1 FLR 463 the Court of Appeal held that, where a person had been arrested for a criminal offence of assault and released on bail, he was validly re-arrested under a power of arrest for domestic violence, and brought before a judge within 24 hours of the second arrest, although the "spirit (of the statutory power of arrest) requires that he be brought before the judge within 24 hours of the initial arrest where the circumstances clearly indicate two reasons for the arrest prevail" (at [468G]); thus a power of arrest is a procedural device which can be used for detaining the respondent and bringing him before the court even though the breach of the injunction is not continuing. In practice, re-arrest is rare. As with any civil case, provided that the court is satisfied that the absent party has been served, and is aware of the trial date, the court can simply proceed in his absence.

Warrant of arrest where the respondent fails to appear at an adjourned hearing, having appeared at the first hearing of a "Notice to show good reason" for breach of an order under FLA 1996, Pt IV—Where a person appears in answer to a "Notice to show good reason", and the case is adjourned, if he subsequently fails to appear at the adjourned hearing, and no power of arrest has been attached to the occupation order, a warrant for arrest under FLA 1996 can be granted in respect of the order (s 47(8),(9)). If a power of arrest was attached to all of the terms of the order, and a warrant of arrest cannot be granted because there are no terms of the original injunction to which the power of arrest was not attached, it is arguable that the respondent can be arrested under the original power of arrest. Alternatively, as with any civil case, provided that the court is satisfied that the absent party has been served, and is aware of the trial date, the court can simply proceed in his absence.

PART III

Hearing where respondent fails to attend despite having been given due "Notice to show good reason"—If the contemnor fails to attend, having been given due Notice, the committal hearing can proceed in his absence and committal or a penalty can be imposed.

Committal hearing while criminal proceedings pending—Breach of an injunction can lead to concurrent civil proceedings to commit and criminal proceedings for an offence. The first court to sentence must not anticipate or allow for a likely further sentence; it is for the second court to reflect the prior sentence in its judgment (see *Lomas v Parle* [2004] 1 FLR 812). There is never any need for the civil court to adjourn to await the outcome of criminal proceedings (which are not in any event under the control of the victim). Sentencing courts have different objectives and different powers. An important objective of contempt proceedings is to uphold the authority of the court by demonstrating that its orders should not be flouted with impunity (see further, per Thorpe LJ in *Lomas v Parle* (above)). Concurrent civil and criminal proceedings are less likely now that breach of a non-molestation order is itself a crime and, in any event, it is not possible for the same breach to be dealt with in both civil and criminal courts; see FLA 1996, s 42A(3) and 42A(4). If a civil judge regards the punishment given by a criminal court as too lenient it is not permitted to "top up" the punishment. The civil judge must sentence only for such conduct which was not the subject of criminal proceedings: *Slade v Slade* [2010] 1 FLR 160.

Unrepresented contemnors—It is generally desirable that a person alleged to be in contempt of court be legally represented but, as with any other litigant, a contemnor is entitled to act in person (with or without a McKenzie friend). The court has no power to compel representation nor to grant legal aid. However, persons in danger of losing their liberty are, subject to means, eligible for legal aid under LASPOA 2012. Accordingly, the court should always consider adjourning (and, in FLA cases, remanding) to enable the alleged contemnor to seek legal representation. If a hearing proceeds without the contemnor being represented, the judge should ensure that he understands his right to cross-examine, give evidence and call witnesses (*Shoreditch County Court Bailiffs v Madeiros* (1988) *The Times*, 24 February).

The importance of abiding by correct procedure—The Court of Appeal has stressed in several cases that, because committal for contempt of court is concerned with offences of a quasi-criminal nature and the liberty of the subject is at stake, the relevant rules of court must be complied with and the prescribed forms must be used. However, *PD (Committal Applications)*, para 10 provides that "Any procedural defect in the commencement or conduct by the applicant of a committal application may be waived by the court if satisfied that no injustice has been caused to the respondent by the defect". In *Nicholls v Nicholls* [1997] 1 FLR 649, Lord Woolf MR, giving the judgment of the Court of Appeal, stated (at [655D]) that "While the ... requirements of Ord 29, r 1 are there to be observed, in the absence of authority to the contrary, even though the liberty of the subject is involved, we would not expect the requirements to be mandatory, in the sense that any non-compliance with the rule means that a committal for contempt is irredeemably invalid." Lord Woolf gave the following guidance (at [661E]):

"(1) As committal orders involve the liberty of the subject it is particularly important that the relevant rules are duly complied with. It remains the responsibility of the judge when signing the committal order to ensure that it is properly drawn and that it adequately particularises the breaches which have been proved and for which the sentence has been imposed.

(2) As long as the contemnor has had a fair trial and the order has been made on valid grounds the existence of a defect either in the application to commit or in the committal order served will not result in the order being set aside except insofar as the interests of justice require this to be done.

(3) Interests of justice will not require an order to be set aside where there is no prejudice caused as the result or errors in the application to commit or in the order to commit. When necessary the order can be amended.

(4) When considering whether to set aside the order, the court should have regard to the interests of any other party and the need to uphold the reputation of the justice system.

(5) If there has been a procedural irregularity or some other defect in the conduct of the proceedings which has occasioned injustice, the court will consider exercising its powers to order a new trial unless there are circumstances which indicate that it would not be just to do so."

In *Devjee v Patel* [2006] EWCA Civ 1211 the fact that the exact process for bringing committal proceedings for breach of a non-molestation order had not been followed did not render the proceedings unfair as no injustice was caused to the contemnor: 6 months' imprisonment was upheld. But see *Re S-C (Contempt)* [2010] 1 FLR 1478, where omission of a penal notice was fatal to the committal application.

Committal hearing procedure—In general terms, hearings of committal proceedings are in many respects similar to hearings of criminal charges. The burden of proof rests on the person making the allegation of contempt. The standard of proof is the criminal standard (*Re C (A Minor) (Contempt)* [1986] 1 FLR 578 at [588]). The respondent must be allowed to cross-examine witnesses and to call evidence. The respondent is entitled to submit that there is no case to answer (*Savings and Investment Bank v Gasco Investments (Netherlands)* (1986) 136 NLJ 657). If a contempt is found proved, the contemnor must be allowed to address the court by way of mitigation or seeking to purge his contempt (*Stilwell v Williamson* (1986) *The Times*, 1 September). Autrefois acquit and autrefois convict apply.

Evidence and witnesses at hearing—An alleged contemnor is not a compellable witness (*Comet Products UK Ltd v Hawkex Plastics Ltd* [1971] 2 QB 67). The court can issue a witness summons to a person who witnessed an alleged contempt to attend committal proceedings although no application has been made by a party (*Yianni v Yianni* [1966] 1 WLR 120). Hearsay evidence is admissible but caution should be exercised (*Savings and Investment Bank v Gasco Investments (Netherlands) BV (No 2)* [1988] Ch 422). Respondents to a motion to commit can be required by the court to swear, file and serve affidavits, or produce statements of witnesses of fact upon which they might wish to rely before the hearing, in order to enable proper preparation of the evidence in reply (*Re B (Contempt: Evidence)* [1996] 1 FLR 239). However, the applicant must prove his case on the evidence filed in support of the application, supplemented by any admissions made by the alleged contemnor upon which the applicant was entitled to rely, and the applicant can make no use of the respondent's evidence until it has been deployed by the respondent. A respondent who complies with a direction from the court in the foregoing terms is not in peril of cross-examination until such time as he deploys the evidence in his own case (*Re B (Contempt: Evidence)*, above).

Form N79 committal order and Form N80 committal warrant (r 1(5))—Form N79, the prescribed form for a committal order in county courts, can be relied on as a checklist for committal procedures, and incorporates most of the usual orders which can be made on proof of disobedience of an injunctive order or breach of an undertaking. The court should complete the relevant parts of Form N79 and delete the parts not required. The most important requirements are that the contempt(s) found proved must have been alleged in the "Notice to show good reason" (*Tabone v Seguna* [1986] 1 FLR 591), must accord with the evidence accepted by the judge (*Re C (Contempt: Committal Order)* [1989] 1 FLR 288), and must be clearly and precisely recited (*Parra v Rones* [1986] Fam Law 262; *Linkleter v Linkleter* [1988] 1 FLR 360; *C v Hackney London Borough Council* [1995] 2 FLR 681). The precise details of the orders made must be entered. The committal warrant is in Form N80.

1A Undertaking given by party (CCR Ord 29, r 1A)

Rule 1 (except paragraph (6)) shall apply to undertakings as it applies to orders with the necessary modifications and as if –

    (a)   for paragraph (2) of that rule there were substituted the following –

"(2) A copy of the document recording the undertaking shall be delivered by the court officer to the party giving the undertaking –

        (a)   by handing a copy of the document to him before he leaves the court building; or

        (b)   where his place of residence is known, by posting a copy to him at his place of residence; or

        (c)   through his solicitor,

and, where delivery cannot be effected in this way, the court officer shall deliver a copy of the document to the party for whose benefit the undertaking is given and that party shall cause it to be served personally as soon as is practicable.".

    (b)   in paragraph (7), the words from 'a copy of' to 'paragraph (2) or' were omitted.

Undertaking to pay money—An order to pay money in general is not enforceable as a civil contempt under Ord 29, r 1, but may be enforced by judgment summons under Debtors Act 1869, s 5, if it is a maintenance order (AJA 1970, s 11). An undertaking to pay money may not be enforced by committal, except as permitted under Debtors Act 1869, s 5 (*Buckley v Crawford* [1893] 1 QB 105). An undertaking can be enforced as if it were an order (*Gandolfo v Gandolfo (Standard Bank, Garnishee)* [1981] QB 359). Paragraph 2.1 of FPR PD33A provides that "any undertaking for the payment of money that has effect as if it was an order made under Part 2 of the Matrimonial Causes Act 1973 may be enforced as if it was an order of the court and Part 33 applies accordingly". See the requirements of para 2 of PD33A as to the appropriate wording of the penal notice.

Form N117 general form of undertaking—Following *Hussain v Hussain* [1986] 2 FLR 271, r 1A was introduced, in addition to Form N117, to provide for delivery, usually by the court, of a copy of the form of undertaking to the giver. This was to redress the problem identified in *Hussain v Hussain* (above) that if, upon answering to a "Notice to show good reason", the giver of an undertaking asserts that he did not

PART III

adequately understand the promises given to the court, or the consequences of breach, it is difficult for the court to be sure what occurred when the undertaking was given. It is good practice for the judge to require the giver to sign the acknowledgement of giving the undertaking, in the box provided on the back of Form N117. The court can require the giver of an undertaking to sign a statement that he understands the terms of his undertaking and the consequences of failure to comply with it (*PD (Judgments and Orders)* (PD40B), para 9.3).

Personal attendance of giver of the undertaking generally essential—Form N117 provides for the court to accept the undertaking, having explained its meaning and the consequences of failing to keep the promises. The giver should normally be required to sign the acknowledgement on the back of Form N117. The court may accept an undertaking in the absence of the giver (see *PD (Judgments and Orders)* (PD40B), para 9.4), provided that it is satisfied that he understands the promises and the consequences of a breach. This should happen only where an appropriately worded document is given to the judge, or where the advocate satisfies the court that he is adequately instructed to give the undertaking on behalf of his absent client.

"shall be delivered by the proper officer to the party giving the undertaking" (r 1A(a))—An undertaking duly given to the court (recorded in county court Form N117), in promised terms which are within its powers, by a person who has been told what the consequences of breach may be, is enforceable as soon as it has been given (*D v A & Co* [1900] 1 Ch 484; *Hussain v Hussain* [1986] 2 FLR 271). The rules specify that the form shall be "delivered", not served, because delivery is an administrative act, and it is the giving of the undertaking which makes it enforceable, not delivery of the copy. Where the court accepts an undertaking from the giver who is absent, the proper officer must ensure that the document recording the undertaking, which should be in the form of an order or a suitably amended N117, is posted to the giver at his place of residence, or delivered through the giver's solicitor.

"where delivery cannot be effected in this way ... served personally as soon as is practicable"—This provision should only apply very rarely, for example where a giver of the undertaking is not represented by a solicitor and, with his address unknown, leaves the court before receiving a copy of the undertaking.

2 Solicitor's undertaking (CCR Ord 29, r 2)

(1) An undertaking given by a solicitor in relation to any proceeding in a county court may be enforced, by order of the judge of that court, by committal order against the solicitor.

(2) Where it appears to the judge that a solicitor has failed to carry out any such undertaking, he may of his own initiative direct the court officer to issue a notice calling on the solicitor to show cause why he should not be committed to prison.

(3) Where any party to the proceedings desires to have the undertaking enforced by committal order, the court officer shall, on the application of the party supported by an affidavit setting out the facts on which the application is based, issue such a notice as is referred to in paragraph (2).

Enforceability of undertakings (r 2(1))—To be enforceable against the solicitor, the undertaking must have been given in his capacity as solicitor (*United Mining and Finance Corporation Ltd v Becher* [1910] 2 KB 276), and personally, not merely as agent for his client (*Burnett v Proois* (1870) 22 LT 543). If the solicitor is not accepting personal responsibility, it is for him to make this clear (*Re Marchant* [1908] 1 KB 998). For civil cases, see CPR 1998, r 81.11.

Forms—The form of notice to show cause is Form N81; the form of committal order is Form N82.

3 Discharge of person in custody (CCR Ord 29, r 3)

(1) Where a person in custody under a warrant or order, other than a warrant of committal to which Order 27, rule 8, or Order 28, rule 4 or 14, relates, desires to apply to the court for his discharge, he shall make his application in writing attested by the governor of the prison (or any other officer of the prison not below the rank of principal officer) showing that he has purged or is desirous of purging his contempt and shall, not less than one day before the application is made, serve notice of it on the party, if any, at whose instance the warrant or order was issued.

(2) If the committal order –

    (a)   does not direct that any application for discharge shall be made to a judge; or

    (b)   was made by the district judge under section 118 of the Act,

any application for discharge may be made to the district judge.

(3) Nothing in paragraph (1) shall apply to an application made by the Official Solicitor in his official capacity for the discharge of a person in custody.

Amendments—SI 2012/2208.

Scope—A person committed to prison for contempt is entitled to apply to purge his contempt and to be discharged from prison (r 3(1); Form N79). This rule provides a simple procedure for the prisoner to apply for his discharge, whether committed under the preceding rules of this order or, where there is no separate procedure, otherwise. It should be noted that CCA 1981, s 14(1) expressly saves the court's power to order a prisoner's early discharge (see further commentary to this Act). In *Enfield London Borough Council v Mahoney* [1983] 1 WLR 749, it was held that a contemnor may be released, even though he has not purged his contempt, where he has been sufficiently punished by the term already served and further imprisonment will have no coercive effect. On an application to purge the court can say "yes", "no" or "not yet"; it does not have power to suspend the remainder of the sentence (*Harris v Harris* [2002] 1 FLR 248).

"Order 27, rule 8, or Order 28, rule 4 or 14" (r 3(1))—As in the case of the committal proceedings themselves, separate procedures exist for debtors committed in oral examination, attachment of earnings and judgment summons proceedings to seek their discharge.

Attendance on hearing—The contemnor should be present to hear the outcome of his application unless, in his solicitor's view, his mental condition makes that undesirable.

Forms—No form of application is prescribed but Form N244 may be used; the form of order for discharge is Form N83.

****

Magistrates' Courts (Enforcement or Variation of Orders Made in Family Proceedings and Miscellaneous Provisions) Rules 2011, SI 2011/1329

Note—These Rules primarily make provision for procedure in "non family" proceedings as defined by MCA 1980, s 65(2) and in respect of which proceedings under FPR 2010 do not apply. This is achieved by consolidating a number of separate provisions in former Rules dealing with enforcement of maintenance orders in magistrates' courts (e g enforcement under MOA 1950 and MOA 1958), applying FPR 2010 with modifications to various proceedings in magistrates' courts (e g in relation to variation of maintenance orders and enforcement of contact orders) and making separate provision in respect of certain other applications in magistrates' courts (e g enforcement of residence orders). These Rules also amend MCR 1981 to reflect the application of Council Regulation (EC) No 4/2009 (the Maintenance Regulation) on jurisdiction, recognition and enforcement of decisions and cooperation in matters relating to maintenance obligations from 18 June 2011.

PART III

PART 1
INTRODUCTORY

CONTENTS OF THIS PART

1 Citation and commencement

These Rules may be cited as the Magistrates' Courts (Enforcement or Variation of Orders Made in Family Proceedings and Miscellaneous Provisions) Rules 2011 and shall come into force on 18 June 2011.

2 Interpretation

In these Rules –

"the 1950 Act" means the Maintenance Orders Act 1950;

"the 1958 Act" means the Maintenance Orders Act 1958;

"the 1972 Act" means the Maintenance Orders (Reciprocal Enforcement) Act 1972;

"the 1980 Act" means the Magistrates' Courts Act 1980;

"the 1986 Act" means the Family Law Act 1986;

"the 1989 Act" means the Children Act 1989;

"the 1996 Act" means the Family Law Act 1996;

"the FPR" means the Family Procedure Rules 2010;

"designated officer" has the meaning given in section 37(1) of the Courts Act 2003;

"justices' clerk" has the meaning given in section 27(1) of the Courts Act 2003;

"legal representative" means a –

    (a)   barrister;

    (b)   solicitor;

    (c)   solicitor's employee;

    (d)   manager of a body recognised under section 9 of the Administration of Justice Act 1985; or

    (e)   a person who, for the purposes of the Legal Services Act 2007 is an authorised person in relation to an activity which constitutes the conduct of litigation (within the meaning of that Act),

    who has been instructed to act for a party in relation to proceedings;

"the Forms Practice Direction" means the practice direction issued by the Lord Chief Justice listing the forms to be used in relation to the matters to which provisions in these Rules relate;

"the register" means the register kept in accordance with rule 66 of the Magistrates' Courts Rules 1981; and

"statement of truth" means a statement as follows "[I believe] [the applicant believes] that the facts stated in this document are true.".

3 Application of these Rules

(1) These Rules apply to the proceedings referred to in rules 4 to 81 in a magistrates' court.

(2) Nothing in these Rules is to be construed as conferring upon a magistrate a function which a magistrate is not permitted by statute to perform.

PART 2
GENERAL PROVISION

CONTENTS OF THIS PART

Chapter 1
Proceedings where the FPR are Not Applied

4 Application of this Chapter

This Chapter applies in respect of Parts 3 and 4, rule 54, Chapter 2 of Part 5 and rules 73, 77 and 79.

5 The overriding objective

(1) The provisions to which this Part applies have the overriding objective of enabling the court to deal with cases justly, having regard to any welfare issues involved.

(2) Dealing with a case justly includes, so far as is practicable –

(a) ensuring that it is dealt with expeditiously and fairly;
(b) dealing with the case in ways which are proportionate to the nature, importance and complexity of the issues;
(c) ensuring that the parties are on an equal footing;
(d) saving expense; and
(e) allotting to it an appropriate share of the court's resources, while taking into account the need to allot resources to other cases.

6 Application by the court of the overriding objective

The court must seek to give effect to the overriding objective when it –

(a)   exercises any power given to it by the provisions to which this Part applies; or

(b)   interprets any such provision.

7 Duty of the parties

The parties are required to help the court to further the overriding objective.

8 Court's duty to manage cases

(1) The court must further the overriding objective by actively managing cases.

(2) Active case management includes –

(a)   encouraging the parties to co-operate with each other in the conduct of the proceedings;

(b)   identifying at an early stage –
   (i)   the issues; and
   (ii)   who should be a party to the proceedings;

(c)   deciding promptly –
   (i)   which issues need full investigation and hearing and which do not; and
   (ii)   the procedure to be followed in the case;

(d)   deciding the order in which issues are to be resolved;

(e)   encouraging the parties to use an alternative dispute resolution procedure if the court considers that appropriate and facilitating the use of such procedure;

(f)   helping the parties to settle the whole or part of the case;

(g)   fixing timetables or otherwise controlling the progress of the case;

(h)   considering whether the likely benefits of taking a particular step justify the cost of taking it;

(i)   dealing with as many aspects of the case as it can on the same occasion;

(j)   dealing with the case without the parties needing to attend at court;

(k)   making use of technology; and

(l)   giving directions to ensure that the case proceeds quickly and efficiently.

9 The court's general powers of management

(1) In this rule –

"disclosure" means stating that a document exists or has existed;

"hearing" includes a directions appointment;

"inspection" of a document occurs when a party is permitted to inspect a document disclosed by another person.

(2) For the purposes of the references to disclosure and inspection in this rule –

"document" means anything in which information of any description is recorded; and

"copy" in relation to a document, means anything onto which information recorded in the document has been copied, by whatever means and whether directly or indirectly.

(3) The list of powers in this rule is in addition to any powers given to the court by any other rule or practice direction or by any other enactment or any powers it may otherwise have.

(4) Except where any provision to which this rule applies provides otherwise, the court may –

(a)   extend or shorten the time for compliance with any rule, practice direction or court order (even if an application for extension is made after the time for compliance has expired);

(b)   make such order for disclosure and inspection, including specific disclosure of documents, as it thinks fit;

(c)   adjourn or bring forward a hearing;

(d)   require a party or a party's legal representative to attend the court;

(e)   hold a hearing and receive evidence by telephone or by using any other method of direct oral communication;

(f)   direct that part of any proceedings be dealt with as separate proceedings;

(g)   consolidate proceedings;

(h)   hear two or more applications on the same occasion;

(i)   direct a separate hearing of any issue;

(j)   decide the order in which issues are to be heard;

(k)   exclude an issue from consideration;

(l)   dismiss or give a decision on an application after a decision on a preliminary issue;

(m)   direct any party to file and serve an estimate of costs; and

(n)   take any other step or make any other order for the purpose of managing the case and furthering the overriding objective.

(5) When the court makes an order, it may –

(a)   make it subject to conditions, including a condition to pay a sum of money into court; and

(b)   specify the consequences of failure to comply with the order or a condition.

(6) Where the court gives directions, it will take into account whether or not a party has complied with any relevant pre-action protocol (being a statement of best practice about pre-action conduct which has been approved by the Lord Chief Justice and which is annexed to a practice direction).

(7) A power of the court under the provisions to which this Part applies to make an order includes a power to vary or revoke the order.

(8) Any provision to which this Part applies –

(a)   requiring or permitting directions to be given by the court is to be taken as including provision for such directions to be varied or revoked; and

(b)   requiring or permitting a date to be set is to be taken as including provision for that date to be changed or cancelled.

10 Designated officer's power to refer to the court

Where in any provision to which this Part applies a step is to be taken by a designated officer the designated officer may consult the court before taking that step.

11 General power of the court to rectify matters where there has been an error of procedure

Where there has been an error of procedure such as a failure to comply with a rule or a practice direction –

(a)   the error does not invalidate any step taken in the proceedings unless the court so orders; and

(b)   the court may make an order to remedy the error.

12 Forms

(1) The forms referred to in the provisions to which this Chapter applies and in the Forms Practice Direction must be used in the cases to which they apply.

(2) A form may be varied by the court or a party if the variation is required by the circumstances of a particular case.

(3) A form must not be varied so as to leave out any information or guidance which the form gives to the recipient.

(4) Where the provisions to which this Part applies require a form to be sent by the court or by a party for another party to use, it must be sent without variation except such as is required by the circumstances of the particular case.

13 Documents to be attached to a form

Subject to any provision to which this Part applies, unless the court directs otherwise, a form must have attached to it any documents which, in the form, are –

  (a) stated to be required; or
  (b) referred to.

14 Power of the single justice to perform functions conferred on the court by rules 4 to 13

Where –

  (a) by virtue of section 65 of the 1980 Act the proceedings are treated by the court as family proceedings; and
  (b) rules 4 to 13 provide for a court to perform any function,

that function may be performed by a single justice of the peace except that such a justice cannot perform the functions referred to in rule 9(4)(k) and (l), 9(5)(a) and 9(6).

15 Power of a justices' clerk to perform functions conferred on the court by rules 4 to 13

Where rules 4 to 13 provide for a court to perform any function, that function may be performed by a justices' clerk except that such a justices' clerk cannot perform the functions referred to in rule 9(4)(k) and (l).

> (Provision in respect of the enforcement of a magistrates' court maintenance order, or an order enforceable as a magistrates' court maintenance order is made in the Magistrates' Courts Rules 1981.)

Chapter 2
Proceedings where the FPR are Applied

16 Application of this Chapter

This Chapter applies in respect of rules 50 to 53, 69, 71, 74 to 76, 78 and 80.

17 Power of the single justice where the FPR are applied

Where proceedings are not treated by the court as family proceedings by virtue of section 65 of the 1980 Act, rule 2.5 of the FPR will not apply in respect of the powers of the single justice.

18 Power of a justices' clerk where the FPR are applied

(1) Subject to the Justices' Clerks Rules 2005, a justices' clerk may perform all the functions which a single justice may perform in accordance with rule 2.5(1)(c)(ii) of the FPR.

(2) Where a justices' clerk –

    (a) is performing the function of a single justice in accordance with paragraph (1); and

    (b) considers, for whatever reason, that it is inappropriate to perform the function,

the justices' clerk must refer the matter to the magistrates' court which may perform the function.

(3) Paragraph (1) applies irrespective of whether proceedings are treated by the court as family proceedings by virtue of section 65 of the 1980 Act.

Chapter 3
All Proceedings to which these Rules Apply

19 Delegation by justices' clerk

(1) Anything authorised to be done by, to or before a justices' clerk under these Rules may be done instead by, to or before an assistant clerk where the assistant clerk has been specifically authorised in writing by the justices' clerk for that purpose.

(2) In this rule "assistant clerk" has the meaning assigned to it by section 27 of the Courts Act 2003.

PART 3
PROCEEDINGS UNDER THE 1950 ACT

CONTENTS OF THIS PART

Chapter 1
Interpretation of this Part

20 Interpretation

(1) In this Part –

"appropriate officer of the High Court" means the District Judge of the Principal
Registry of the Family Division of the High Court or the district judge of the
relevant district registry;

"certified copy" means a copy order certified by the designated officer of the court to
be a true copy of the order or of the official record of the order; and

"maintenance order" has the meaning assigned in section 16(2) of the 1950 Act.

(2) References in Chapter 3 of this Part to the clerk of the court by which the order was
made are to be construed, in relation to a maintenance order made by a county court in
Northern Ireland, as references to the Chief Clerk for the appropriate county in Northern
Ireland.

Chapter 2
Maintenance Orders Made by a Magistrates' Court in England and Wales

21 Procedure under Part 2 of the 1950 Act in relation to a maintenance order made by a magistrates' court in England and Wales

(1) An application under Part 2 of the 1950 Act for the registration in a court in Scotland
or Northern Ireland of a maintenance order made by a magistrates' court in England and
Wales –

(a) may be made either orally or in writing; and

(b) must be made to a justice or justices acting in the same place as the court which
     made the order.

(2) Unless the applicant appears in person, the applicant must file with the court a
document verified by a statement of truth signed by the applicant or the applicant's legal
representative which states –

(a) the address of the person liable to make payments under the order;

(b) the reason why it is convenient that the order should be enforced in Scotland or
     Northern Ireland, as the case may be;

(c) unless a certificate of arrears is lodged under section 20 of the 1950 Act, the
     amount of any arrears due under the order;

(d) that the order is not already registered under Part 2 of the 1950 Act.

(3) If it appears to the justice that the person liable to make payments under the order resides in Scotland or Northern Ireland and that it is convenient that the order should be enforceable there, the designated officer for the court which made the order will send to the sheriff-clerk of the sheriff court in Scotland or to the clerk of the court of summary jurisdiction in Northern Ireland (as the case may be) having jurisdiction in the place in which the person liable to make payments under the order appears to be –

    (a) a certified copy of the order;

    (b) the certificate of arrears or the document referred to in paragraph (2) (if there is any such document);

    (c) if no document referred to in paragraph (2) has been lodged, written notice of the address of the person liable to make payments under the order.

(4) A memorandum of any proceedings taken under paragraph (1) must be entered in the register.

(5) The designated officer for the court which made the order must, on receipt of notice under section 17(4) of the 1950 Act of the registration of the order, enter a memorandum of that notice in the register.

(6) The designated officer for the court which made the order is the prescribed officer for the purposes of section 17(4) of the 1950 Act.

"sheriff-clerk" (r 21(3))—See Home Office Circular 241/1950 and *www.scotcourts.gov.uk* for addresses of sheriff clerks.

22 Application under section 22 of the 1950 Act to adduce evidence: maintenance order made by a magistrates' court in England and Wales

(1) An application to a magistrates' court in England and Wales under section 22(5) of the 1950 Act to adduce evidence in connection with a maintenance order made by that court and registered in a court in Scotland or Northern Ireland may be made orally.

(2) The application may be made, and the proceedings heard, without notice to the respondent.

(3) The court in which the application is made must ensure that a transcript or summary of any evidence taken is sent to the clerk of the court in which the order is registered.

(4) The designated officer for the court in England and Wales which made the maintenance order will be the prescribed officer to whom any transcript or summary of evidence adduced in the court in Scotland or Northern Ireland under section 22(5) of the 1950 Act must be sent.

23 Variation of a maintenance order made by a magistrates' court in England and Wales: section 22(1) of the 1950 Act

(1) Where a maintenance order made by a magistrates' court in England and Wales and registered in a court in Scotland or Northern Ireland is varied under section 22(1) of the 1950 Act by the court in which it is registered –

    (a) the designated officer for the court which made the order will be the prescribed officer to whom, under section 23(1) of the 1950 Act, notice of the variation must be given;

    (b) on receipt of a notice under section 23(1) of the 1950 Act, the designated officer must enter a memorandum of that notice in the register.

(2) Where a maintenance order made by a magistrates' court in England and Wales and registered in a court in Scotland or Northern Ireland is discharged or varied by the court which made it, the designated officer for the court which made the order must give notice

PART III

of the discharge or variation to the clerk of the court in which the order is registered by sending a certified copy of the order discharging or varying the maintenance order.

24 Cancellation of registration of a maintenance order made by a magistrates' court in England and Wales: section 24 of the 1950 Act

(1) An application under section 24(2) of the 1950 Act for the cancellation of the registration of a maintenance order made by a magistrates' court in England and Wales and registered in a court in Scotland or in Northern Ireland –

(a) may be made orally or in writing by the person liable to make the payments under the order; and

(b) must be made to a justice acting in the same place as the court which made the order.

(2) Unless the applicant appears in person, the applicant must file with the court a document verified by a statement of truth signed by the applicant or the applicant's legal representative stating the facts relied upon in support of the application.

(3) If it appears to the justice dealing with the application that the person liable to make payments under the order has ceased to reside in Scotland or Northern Ireland (as the case may be), the designated officer for the court which made the order must send notice to that effect to the clerk of the court in which the order is registered.

(4) On the cancellation of the registration of an order, the designated officer for the court in England and Wales which made the order is the prescribed officer to whom, under section 24(3)(a) of the 1950 Act, notice of the cancellation must be given.

(5) On receipt of notice of the cancellation of the registration of an order, the designated officer must enter a memorandum of that notice in the register.

Chapter 3
Maintenance Orders Registered in a Magistrates' Court in England and Wales

25 Procedure under Part 2 of the 1950 Act in relation to a maintenance order made by a court in Scotland or Northern Ireland

(1) The designated officer for the magistrates' court specified in section 17(3)(b) of the 1950 Act will be the prescribed officer for the purpose of section 17(2) of the 1950 Act.

(2) On receipt, further to section 17 of the 1950 Act, of a certified copy of a maintenance order made by a court in Scotland or Northern Ireland, the designated officer must –

(a) enter a memorandum of that order in the register; and

(b) send written notice that the order has been so registered to the clerk of the court by which the order was made.

26 Payments in respect of a maintenance order registered in a magistrates' court in England and Wales

(1) This rule applies where in exercise of –

(a) the duty imposed by section 19(2) of the 1950 Act; or

(b) the powers conferred by section 18(2ZA) or 22(1A) or (1E) of the 1950 Act,

a magistrates' court in England and Wales orders that payments under a maintenance order registered in that court are to be made by a particular means.

(2) The justices' clerk must record on a copy of the order the means of payment which the court has ordered.

(3) As soon as practicable, the designated officer must notify in writing the person liable to make payments under the order of how payments are to be made.

(4) Where the court orders payment to the designated officer for the court, or to the designated officer for any other magistrates' court, by a method of payment falling within section 59(6) of the 1980 Act (standing order etc), the designated officer to whom payments are to be made must notify the person liable to make the payments under the order of sufficient details of the account into which the payments should be made to enable payments to be made into that account.

(5) Where, under section 60(4) of the 1980 Act as modified by section 22(1E) of the 1950 Act, the court receives an application from an interested party for the method of payment to be varied –

    (a)   the designated officer must, as soon as practicable, notify in writing that interested party and, where practicable, any other interested party, of the result of the application, including any decision to refer the matter to the court; and

    (b)   where the justices' clerk grants the application, the justices' clerk must record the variation on a copy of the order.

27 Application under section 21(2) of the 1950 Act to adduce evidence: maintenance order made by the Court of Session and registered in a magistrates' court in England and Wales

(1) An application to a magistrates' court under section 21(2) of the 1950 Act to adduce evidence in connection with a maintenance order made by the Court of Session and registered in the magistrates' court under Part 1 of the 1958 Act by virtue of section 1(2) of that Act may be made orally.

(2) The complaint may be made, and the proceedings heard, without notice to the respondent.

(3) The court in which the application is made must ensure that a transcript or summary of any evidence taken is sent to the Deputy Principal Clerk of Session.

28 Variation of a maintenance order registered in a magistrates' court in England and Wales: section 22(1) of the 1950 Act

(1) An application under section 22(1) of the 1950 Act for the variation of the rate of the payments under a maintenance order registered under Part 2 of the 1950 Act in a magistrates' court in England and Wales must be made by way of complaint in accordance with the 1980 Act.

(2) When the complaint is made, a summons may be issued directed to any person to whom the justice to whom the complaint is made may consider proper to answer it.

(3) Where the maintenance order is varied, the designated officer must –

    (a)   give notice of the variation to the clerk of the court in Scotland or Northern Ireland by which the order was made; and

    (b)   if the order is registered in the High Court under Part 1 of the 1958 Act by virtue of section 1(2) of that Act, give notice of the variation to the appropriate officer of the High Court,

by sending to the clerk of the court and, where necessary, the appropriate officer of the High Court, a certified copy of the order of variation.

(4) Where a maintenance order registered under Part 2 of the 1950 Act in a magistrates' court is discharged or varied by any other court, the designated officer for the court in which it is registered will be the prescribed officer to whom, under section 23(1)(a) of the 1950 Act, notice of the discharge or variation must be given.

PART III

(5) On receipt of a certified copy of an order discharging or varying the registered order, the designated officer must enter a memorandum of that order in the register.

29 Application under section 22(5) of the 1950 Act to adduce evidence: maintenance order registered in England and Wales

(1) An application to a magistrates' court in England and Wales under section 22(5) of the 1950 Act to adduce evidence in connection with a maintenance order registered in that court may be made orally.

(2) The application may be made, and the proceedings heard, without notice to the respondent.

(3) The court in which the application is made must ensure that a transcript or summary of any evidence taken is sent to the clerk of the court in Scotland or Northern Ireland by which the order was made.

(4) The designated officer for the court in England and Wales in which the maintenance order is registered will be the prescribed officer under section 22(5) of the 1950 Act to whom any transcript or summary of evidence adduced in the court in Scotland or Northern Ireland by which the order was made must be sent.

30 Cancellation of registration of a maintenance order registered in a magistrates' court in England and Wales: section 24 of the 1950 Act

(1) An application under section 24(1) of the 1950 Act for the cancellation of the registration of a maintenance order registered under Part 2 of the 1950 Act in a magistrates' court in England and Wales must –

  (a) be made to the designated officer for the court in which the maintenance order is registered;
  (b) be made in writing and state the date of the registration of the order; and
  (c) have attached to it a copy of the order the registration of which it is sought to cancel.

(2) Where the designated officer cancels the registration of the maintenance order, the designated officer must send written notice of the cancellation –

  (a) to the clerk of the court by which the order was made; and
  (b) where the order is registered in the High Court under Part 1 of the 1958 Act by virtue of section 1(2) of that Act, to the appropriate officer of the High Court.

(3) Where a maintenance order is registered under Part 2 of the 1950 Act in a magistrates' court in England and Wales, the designated officer for the court in which the order is registered will be the prescribed officer to whom notice must be sent under section 24(2) of the 1950 Act that the person liable to make the payments under the order has ceased to reside in England and Wales.

(4) On receipt of a notice referred to in paragraph (3), the designated officer must –

  (a) cancel the registration of the order; and
  (b) send written notice of the cancellation to –
     (i)   the clerk of the court by which the order was made; and
     (ii) where the order is registered in the High Court under Part 1 of the 1958 Act by virtue of section 1(2) of that Act, to the appropriate officer of the High Court.

(5) Where the designated officer for a magistrates' court in which a maintenance order is registered under Part 1 of the 1958 Act receives a notice of cancellation under section 24(3) of the 1950 Act from the appropriate officer of the High Court, the designated officer must –

(a) ensure that the particulars of the notice are entered in the register;

(b) cancel the registration under Part 1 of the 1958 Act; and

(c) give notice of the cancellation to, the appropriate officer of the court in Scotland or Northern Ireland which made the order, being –

    (i) the Deputy Principal Clerk of Session, in the case of the Court of Session; or

    (ii) the Chief Registrar of the Queen's Bench Division (Matrimonial), in the case of the High Court of Justice in Northern Ireland.

Chapter 4
Forms

31 Notices under section 19(4) of the 1950 Act

(1) A notice under section 19(4) of the 1950 Act that the payments under a maintenance order made by a sheriff court in Scotland or a court of summary jurisdiction in Northern Ireland have become payable through or to any officer or person will be in the form number 1 in Schedule 1.

(2) The notice referred to in paragraph (1) must be sent by recorded delivery by the designated officer to the person liable to make the payments under the order at that person's last known address.

(3) A notice under section 19(4) of the 1950 Act that the payments under a maintenance order made by a magistrates' court in England and Wales have, on its registration under Part 2 of the 1950 Act in a court in Scotland or Northern Ireland, ceased to be payable through or to any officer or person will be in the form number 2 in Schedule 1.

(4) The notice referred to in paragraph (3) must be sent by recorded delivery by the designated officer for the court in England and Wales to the person liable to make payments under the order at that person's last known address.

32 Certificates under section 20(1) of the 1950 Act

A certificate lodged under section 20(1) of the 1950 Act as to the amount of any arrears due under a maintenance order made by a magistrates' court in England and Wales will be in the form number 3 in Schedule 1.

33 Notices under section 24 of the 1950 Act

(1) A notice under section 24(5) or (5A) of the 1950 Act of the cancellation of the registration under Part 2 of the 1950 Act of a maintenance order in a magistrates' court in England and Wales will be in the form number 4 in Schedule 1.

(2) The notice referred to in paragraph (1) must be sent by recorded delivery by the designated officer for the court which cancelled the registration to the person liable to make the payments under the order at that person's last known address.

PART III

PART 4
PROCEEDINGS UNDER THE 1958 ACT

CONTENTS OF THIS PART

Chapter 1
Interpretation of this Part

Chapter 1
Interpretation of this Part

34 Interpretation

(1) Section 1(3) of the 1958 Act applies to the interpretation of Chapter 2 of this Part as it applies to the interpretation of Part 1 of the 1958 Act.

(2) Section 21 of the 1958 Act applies to the interpretation of this Part as it applies to the interpretation of the 1958 Act.

(3) In this Part, "appropriate officer of the original court" means –

    (a)   the Sheriff-clerk, in the case of a sheriff court in Scotland;

    (b)   the clerk of petty sessions, in the case of a magistrates' court in Northern Ireland;

    (c)   the Deputy Principal Clerk of Session, in the case of the Court of Session;

    (d)   the Chief Registrar of the Queen's Bench Division (Matrimonial), in the case of the High Court of Justice in Northern Ireland.

(4) In this Part any reference to "the administering court" in relation to a maintenance order is a reference to the magistrates' court –

    (a)   which made the maintenance order;

(b)   in which the maintenance order is registered under the 1958 Act, under Part 2 of the 1950 Act or under the Maintenance Orders (Facilities for Enforcement) Act 1920; or

(c)   by which the maintenance order was confirmed under the Maintenance Orders (Facilities for Enforcement) Act 1920.

Chapter 2
Procedure Under Part 1 of the 1958 Act

35 Applications for registration under section 2(3) of the 1958 Act

An application under section 2(3) of the 1958 Act for the registration in the High Court of a magistrates' courts order need not be in writing or on oath.

36 Manner in which a magistrates' court is to be satisfied as to various matters

(1) An applicant wishing to show, in accordance with section 2A(1) of the 1958 Act, that –

(a)   the order to which the application relates, though deemed to have been made by a magistrates' court in England and Wales, was in fact made in another part of the United Kingdom or a country or territory outside the United Kingdom; and

(b)   by the law of that part or of that country or territory, interest is recoverable under the order,

may do so by producing the original court order or an authenticated copy of that order showing the date or time from which, and the rate at which, interest is so recoverable.

(2) For the purposes of paragraph (1), a copy is deemed to be authenticated if it purports to be certified by a judge or official of the court which made the original order to be a true copy of the original order, but it is not necessary to prove the signature or official position of the person appearing to have given such a certificate.

(3) Where an application for the registration in the High Court of a magistrates' court order is granted, the court must be satisfied in the manner provided by paragraph (5) that no process for the enforcement of the order issued before the grant of the application remains in force.

(4) Where the court receives notice under section 5 of the 1958 Act, the court must be satisfied in the manner provided by paragraph (5) that no process for the enforcement of the order issued before the giving of the notice remains in force and that no proceedings for the variation of the order are pending in a magistrates' court.

(5) For the purpose of satisfying the court as to the matters referred to in paragraphs (3) and (4) –

(a)   if the person through or to whom payments are ordered to be made is the designated officer for a magistrates' court, a certificate signed by the designated officer must be produced;

(b)   in any other case, a document verified by a statement of truth from a Justice of the Peace must be produced.

37 Receipt by a magistrates' court of a notice of registration in the High Court of an order previously registered in a magistrates' court

Where a magistrates' court receives from the High Court notice of the registration in the High Court of an order made by a sheriff court in Scotland or a court of summary jurisdiction in Northern Ireland and previously registered in the magistrates' court in accordance with section 17(4) of the 1950 Act, the designated officer for the court will enter the particulars of such a notice in the register.

38 Copy of a magistrates' court order sent to the High Court for registration

(1) Where –

    (a)   an application for the registration of a magistrates' court order is granted; and

    (b)   the court is satisfied that no process issued for the enforcement of the order before the grant of the application remains in force,

the court will, in accordance with section 2(4)(c) of the 1958 Act, direct the designated officer to send a copy of the order, which is certified to be a true copy, to the appropriate officer of the High Court.

(2) Where the court is satisfied in accordance with rule 36 that interest is recoverable under the order in respect of which the application has been granted, the court will, in accordance with section 2A(1) of the 1958 Act, direct the designated officer to send, together with the certified copy of the order mentioned in paragraph (1), a certificate in respect of the interest so recoverable in the form numbered 1 in Schedule 2 to the appropriate officer of the High Court.

39 Registration of a High Court or county court order in a magistrates' court

Where a designated officer for a magistrates' court, in accordance with section 2(2)(b) of the 1958 Act, receives from a court officer of the High Court or the county court a certified copy of a High Court or county court order, the designated officer will –

    (a)   register the order in the designated officer's court by means of a memorandum in the register; and

    (b)   send written notice to the court officer of the High Court or the county court (as the case may be) that the order has been registered.

40 Registration in a magistrates' court of an order made in the Court of Session or in the High Court in Northern Ireland

Where a designated officer for a magistrates' court, in accordance with section 2(2)(b) of the 1958 Act, receives from the appropriate officer of the original court in Scotland or Northern Ireland a certified copy of an order made by the Court of Session or by the High Court in Northern Ireland, the designated officer will –

    (a)   register the order in the designated officer's court by means of a memorandum in the register; and

    (b)   send written notice to the appropriate officer of the High Court and to the appropriate officer of the original court that the order has been registered.

41 Notices: payments made through a designated officer

(1) A notice under section 2(6ZC) of the 1958 Act that the payments under a High Court or county court order or an order made by the Court of Session or by the High Court in Northern Ireland have, on its registration in a magistrates' court, become payable through the designated officer for a magistrates' court will be given by the designated officer for the court of registration in the form numbered 2 in Schedule 2.

(2) Paragraphs (3) and (4) apply in relation to a notice under section 2(6ZC) of the 1958 Act that payments under –

(a) a magistrates' court order; or
(b) an order which is registered in a magistrates' court under Part 2 of the 1950 Act
and which was made by –
(i) a sheriff court in Scotland; or
(ii) a court cf summary jurisdiction in Northern Ireland,

have, on the registration of the order in the High Court, ceased to be payable to a designated officer for a magistrates' court.

(3) The notice must be –

(a) given by the designated officer for the administering court; and
(b) in form numbered 3 in Schedule 2.

(4) Where payments have been made through a designated officer other than the designated officer for the administering court, the designated officer for the administering court must send a copy of the notice to the designated officer through whom payments have been made.

(5) Paragraphs (6) and (7) apply in relation to a notice under section 5(5)(b) of the 1958 Act that the registration in a magistrates' court of an order of the High Court, a county court, the Court of Session or the High Court in Northern Ireland has been cancelled and that payments under the order have ceased to be payable through a designated officer for a magistrates' court.

(6) The notice must be –

(a) given by the designated officer for the court of registration; and
(b) be in the form numbered 4 in Schedule 2.

(7) Where payments have been payable through a designated officer other than the designated officer for the court of registration, the designated officer for the court of registration must send a copy of the notice to the designated officer through whom payments have been payable.

(8) A notice given in accordance with this rule must be served personally on to the person liable to make payments under the order to which the notice relates or sent by post to that person at that person's last known address.

42 Method of payment

(1) This rule applies where the court exercises its duties or powers under section 2(6ZA), 3(2A) or (2B) or 4(2A), (5A) or (5B) of the 1958 Act.

(2) Where the court orders that payments under a registered order are to be made by a particular means –

(a) the justices' clerk will record on a copy of the order the means of payment which the court has ordered; and
(b) as soon as practicable, the designated officer will notify in writing the person liable to make payments under the order, how payments are to be made.

(3) Paragraph (4) applies where the court orders that payments be made –

(a) by the debtor to the creditor;
(b) by the debtor to the designated officer for the court; or
(c) to the designated officer for any other court,

by a method of payment falling within section 59(6) of the 1980 Act.

(4) The designated officer to whom payments are to be made must notify the person liable to make payments under the order of sufficient details of the account into which the payments should be made to enable payments to be made into that account.

43 Variation of method of payment

(1) This rule applies where, under section 60(4) of the 1980 Act as applied by section 4(5A) of the 1958 Act or as modified by section 4(5B) of the 1958 Act, the designated officer receives an application from an interested party for the method of payment to be varied.

(2) The designated officer must as soon as practicable notify in writing the interested party who made the application and, where practicable, any other interested party, of the result of the application including any decision to refer the matter to the court.

(3) Where the justices' clerk grants the application, the justices' clerk must record the variation on a copy of the order.

44 Notice of variation, remission, discharge or cancellation of registration by a magistrates' court of a registered order

(1) Where, under section 4(2) of the 1958 Act, a High Court or county court order registered in a magistrates' court is varied by a magistrates' court, the designated officer for the magistrates' court making the variation must give notice of the variation to the High Court or county court, as the case may be.

(2) Where, under section 4(4) of the 1958 Act, an application for the variation of a High Court or county court order registered in a magistrates' court is remitted to the original court by a magistrates' court, the designated officer for the remitting court must give notice of the remission to the High Court or county court, as the case may be.

(3) Where, under section 5(4) of the 1958 Act, the registration of a High Court or county court order in a magistrates' court is cancelled by the court of registration, the designated officer for the court of registration must give notice of cancellation to the High Court or county court, as the case may be, stating (if applicable) that the cancellation is in consequence of a notice given under section 5(1) of the 1958 Act.

(4) Where under section 5(4) of the 1958 Act the registration in a magistrates' court of an order made in the Court of Session or the High Court in Northern Ireland is cancelled by that magistrates' court, the designated officer for that magistrates' court must give notice of the cancellation to –

    (a)   the appropriate officer of the original court; and

    (b)   where the order is registered by virtue of Part 2 of the 1950 Act, to the appropriate officer of the High Court.

(5) Where under section 5(4) of the 1958 Act the registration in a magistrates' court of an order under Part 2 of the 1950 Act is cancelled by that magistrates' court, the designated officer for that magistrates' court must give notice of the cancellation to –

    (a)   the appropriate officer of the original court; and

    (b)   where the order is registered under Part 1 of the 1958 Act, to the appropriate officer of the High Court.

(6) Where a magistrates' court order registered in the High Court is varied or discharged by a magistrates' court, the designated officer for the magistrates' court which varies or discharges the order must give notice of the variation or discharge to the High Court.

(7) Notice under this rule will be given by sending to the appropriate officer of the High Court or the registrar of the county court (as the case may be) a copy of the order in question, certified to be a true copy by the designated officer for the magistrates' court.

(8) For the purposes of this rule, the appropriate officer of the High Court will be –

    (a)   in relation to a High Court order registered in a magistrates' court, the officer to whom notice of registration was given under rule 39; or

(b)   in relation to a magistrates' court order registered in the High Court, the officer to whom a copy of the order was sent under rule 38.

(9) In the case of a High Court maintenance order, the notice referred to in paragraph (6) must be marked with the title and case number, if any.

(10) In the case of a county court maintenance order, any notice referred to in this rule must be marked with the complaint or application number.

(11) Where a magistrates' court order registered in the High Court is discharged by a magistrates' court and it appears to the magistrates' court ordering the discharge that no arrears remain to be recovered, notice under section 5(3) of the 1958 Act must be given by an endorsement on the certified copy of the order of discharge referred to in paragraph (7).

45 Notices received from the High Court or a county court or from a person entitled to payments

(1) Subject to paragraph (4), this rule applies where any notice is received –

(a)   of the registration in the High Court of a magistrates' court order;

(b)   of the discharge or variation by the High Court or a county court of a High Court or county court order registered in a magistrates' court;

(c)   of the discharge or variation by the Court of Session or High Court in Northern Ireland of an order made by such a court and registered in a magistrates' court;

(d)   under section 5(1) or (2) of the 1958 Act.

(2) The designated officer for the magistrates' court must register the notice in that officer's court by means of a memorandum in the register.

(3) In the case of a notice under section 5(1) or (2) of the 1958 Act, the designated officer for the magistrates' court must ensure that the person in possession of any warrant of commitment, issued but not executed, for the enforcement of the order is informed of the giving of that notice.

(4) Where any notice is received by a court that the registration of an order in the High Court has been cancelled under section 5(4) of the 1958 Act, the designated officer must enter the particulars of the notice in the register.

46 Complaints for variation of High Court maintenance orders: jurisdiction

Rule 41 of the Magistrates' Courts Rules 1981 applies to a complaint for the variation of a High Court or county court order registered in a magistrates' court as if –

(a)   the order were a magistrates' court maintenance order made by the court of registration; and

(b)   in paragraph (4) of that rule, for the words "shall cause" there were substituted "may cause".

Chapter 3
Miscellaneous

47 Administering court to be informed of proceedings in a foreign court

(1) This rule applies where any decision is reached, or warrant of distress or commitment is issued, in pursuance of a complaint or application relating to a maintenance order or the enforcement of a maintenance order, being a complaint or application heard by a magistrates' court other than the administering court.

PART III

(2) The designated officer for the magistrates' court referred to in paragraph (1) must immediately send to the designated officer for the administering court an extract from the register containing a minute or memorandum of the decision, or the issue of the warrant, as the case may be.

(3) On receipt of the extract, the designated officer for the administering court must enter the minute or memorandum in the register for that officer's court.

48 Review of committals, etc

(1) Paragraph (2) applies where, for the purposes of enforcing a maintenance order, a magistrates' court has exercised its power to postpone the issue of a warrant of commitment under –

    (a)   section 77(2) of the 1980 Act; or

    (b)   section 18(3) or (5) of the 1958 Act,

and, under the terms of the postponement, the warrant falls to be issued.

(2) The designated officer must –

    (a)   give notice to the defendant; and

    (b)   attach to that notice a copy of the form referred to in the Forms Practice Direction.

(3) An application under section 18(1) of the 1958 Act requesting that a warrant not be issued must be in the form referred to in the Forms Practice Direction and must be sent to the designated officer.

(4) For the purposes of section 18(2) of the 1958 Act, the period for the receipt by the designated officer of an application under section 18(1) of the 1958 Act is eight days beginning with the day on which the designated officer sends to the defendant the notice referred to in paragraph (2).

(5) Where the period of eight days referred to in paragraph (4) ends on a day when the court office is closed, an application received by the designated officer on the next day on which the court office is open will be made within time.

(6) An application under section 18(4) of the 1958 Act (requesting cancellation of a warrant of commitment which has been executed) must be in the form referred to in the Forms Practice Direction.

(7) Where an application by a defendant under section 18(1) or (4) of the 1958 Act is considered by the court, the designated officer must give notice of the decision of the court, if the person in question is not present –

    (a)   to the person in whose favour the maintenance order in question was made; and

    (b)   except where an application under section 18(1) of the 1958 Act is dismissed, to the defendant.

(8) Where, on considering an application by a defendant under section 18(4) of the 1958 Act, the court –

    (a)   makes an order under section 18(5)(b) of the 1958 Act for the cancellation of the warrant of commitment; or

    (b)   remits under section 18(6) of the 1958 Act the whole or any part of the sum in respect of which the warrant was issued,

the designated officer must immediately give written notice of the decision to the person in charge of the prison or other place in which the defendant is detained.

PART 5
PROCEEDINGS UNDER THE 1972 ACT

CONTENTS OF THIS PART

Chapter 1
Proceedings Under Part 1 of the 1972 Act

Chapter 2
Proceedings under Part 2 of the 1972 Act

Chapter 1
Proceedings Under Part 1 of the 1972 Act

49 Interpretation

(1) In this Chapter –

"Hague Convention Country" means a country listed in Schedule 1 to the Reciprocal Enforcement of Maintenance Orders (Hague Convention Countries) Order 1993;

"payee", in relation to a maintenance order, means the person eligible to receive the payments for which the order provides;

"payer", in relation to a maintenance order, means the person liable to make the payments for which the order provides; and

"reciprocating country" means a country to which Part 1 of the 1972 Act extends.

(2) In this Chapter, an expression defined in the 1972 Act has the meaning given to it in that Act.

50 Confirmation of a provisional order made in a reciprocating country

(1) The FPR as modified by paragraph (2) shall apply to proceedings in a magistrates' court for the confirmation of a provisional order made in a reciprocating country varying a maintenance order to which section 5(5) or 9(6) of the 1972 Act applies.

(2) The modification is that in rule 34.16, paragraph (6) is omitted.

51 Consideration of variation of a maintenance order made by a magistrates' court: Hague Convention Countries

(1) The FPR as modified by paragraph (2) shall apply where –

  (a)   an application has been made to a magistrates' court by a payee for the variation of an order to which section 5 of the 1972 Act applies; and
  (b)   the payer resides in a Hague Convention Country.

(2) The modifications are, in rule 34.17 as substituted by rule 34.27(5) –

  (a)   in the heading, after "Consideration of" insert "variation or"; and
  (b)   in paragraph (1)(a), after "for the" insert "variation or".

52 Consideration of variation of a maintenance order made by a magistrates' court: United States of America

(1) The FPR as modified by paragraph (2) shall apply where –

  (a)   an application has been made to a magistrates' court by a payee for the variation of an order to which section 5 of the 1972 Act applies; and
  (b)   the payer resides in the United States of America.

(2) The modifications are, in rule 34.17 as substituted by rule 34.28(5) –

  (a)   in the heading, after "Consideration of" insert "variation or"; and
  (b)   in paragraph (1)(a), after "for the" insert "variation or".

53 Notification of variation of a maintenance order by a magistrates' court

(1) The FPR as modified by paragraph (2) shall apply where a magistrates' court makes an order –

  (a)   not being a provisional order, varying a maintenance order to which section 5 of the 1972 Act applies;
  (b)   under section 9 of the 1972 Act, varying a registered order.

(2) The modifications are, in rule 34.19 –

  (a)   in the heading, after "confirmation" insert ", variation";
  (b)   in paragraph (1)(a) and (b), before "revoking" insert "varying or";
  (c)   in paragraph (2), after "making," insert "variation,"; and
  (d)   omit paragraph (3).

54 Notification of proceedings in a Hague Convention Country or in the United States of America

(1) This rule applies where the designated officer receives from the Lord Chancellor notice of the institution of proceedings, including notice of the substance of the claim, in a Hague Convention Country or in the United States of America in relation to the making, variation or revocation of a maintenance order.

(2) If it appears to the designated officer that the person against whom the proceedings were instituted is residing within the local justice area for which the court acts, the

designated officer must serve the notice on that person by sending it by recorded delivery addressed to that person at that person's last known or usual address.

(3) If it appears to the designated officer that the person concerned is not residing within the area, the court officer must inform the Lord Chancellor and return the notice.

Chapter 2
Proceedings under Part 2 of the 1972 Act

55 Interpretation

In this Chapter –

    (a) "convention country" means a country or territory specified in an Order in Council made under section 25 of the 1972 Act; and

    (b) an expression defined in the 1972 Act has the meaning given to it in that Act.

56 Dismissal of an application under section 27A of the 1972 Act or application for variation

(1) Where a magistrates' court dismisses an application under –

    (a) section 27A of the 1972 Act (application for recovery of maintenance); or

    (b) an application by a person in a convention country for the variation of a registered order, the designated officer must send a written notice of the court's decision to the Lord Chancellor.

(2) The notice referred to in paragraph (1) must include a statement of the justices' reasons for their decision.

57 Application for recovery of maintenance in England and Wales: section 27B of the 1972 Act

(1) Where a designated officer receives an application for the recovery of maintenance in England and Wales sent from the Lord Chancellor to a magistrates' court under section 27B of the 1972 Act –

    (a) the justices' clerk must fix the date, time and place for a hearing or a directions appointment, allowing sufficient time for service under this rule to be effected at least 21 days before the date so fixed; and

    (b) the designated officer must serve copies of the application and any accompanying documents, together with a notice stating the date, time and place so fixed, on the respondent.

(2) Within 14 days of service under this rule, the respondent must file an answer to the application in the form referred to in the Forms Practice Direction.

58 Application under section 26(1) or (2) of the 1972 Act and certificate under section 26(3A) of the 1972 Act: registration

Where –

    (a) an application under section 26(1) or (2) of the 1972 Act; or

    (b) a certificate under section 26(3A) of the 1972 Act,

is required to be registered in a magistrates' court in pursuance of the Recovery of Maintenance (United States of America) Order 2007, the designated officer must enter a minute or memorandum of the application or certificate in the register.

PART III

59 Registration of an order: sections 27C(7) and 32(2), (3) and (6) of the 1972 Act

(1) Where a magistrates' court makes an order which is required under section 27C(7) of the 1972 Act to be registered, the justices' clerk must enter a minute or memorandum of the order in the register.

(2) Where a designated officer in pursuance of section 32(2) or (3) of the 1972 Act receives a certified copy of an order, the officer must register the order in the officer's court by means of a minute or memorandum in the register.

(3) Every minute or memorandum entered in pursuance of paragraph (1) or (2) must specify the section and subsection of the 1972 Act under which the order in question is registered.

(4) Where a designated officer registers an order in pursuance of section 27C(7) or 32(2) or (3) of the 1972 Act, the designated officer must send written notice to the Lord Chancellor that the order has been duly registered.

(5) Where a designated officer is required by section 32(6) of the 1972 Act to give notice of the registration of an order, the designated officer will do so by sending written notice to the officer specified in that subsection that the order has been duly registered.

60 Payments made to a designated officer

(1) A designated officer to whom payments are made by virtue of section 27C, section 33(3A) or section 34A of the 1972 Act must send those payments by post to such person or authority as the Lord Chancellor may from time to time direct.

(2) Subject to paragraph (3), where it appears to a designated officer to whom payments under a registered order are made that any sums payable under the order are in arrear, the designated officer may proceed in the designated officer's own name for the recovery of those sums.

(3) Where it appears to the designated officer referred to in paragraph (2) that sums payable under the order are in arrear to an amount equal –

    (a)   in the case of payments to be made monthly or less frequently, to twice the sum payable periodically; or

    (b)   in any other case, to four times the sum payable periodically,

the designated officer must proceed in the designated officer's own name for the recovery of those sums, unless it appears to the designated officer that it is unreasonable in the circumstances to do so.

61 Method of payment

(1) This rule applies where the court exercises its duties or powers under section 27C, 33(3A) or 34A of the 1972 Act.

(2) Where the court orders that payments under the order are to be made by a particular means –

    (a)   the justices' clerk will record on the copy of the order the means of payment which the court has ordered; and

    (b)   the designated officer will notify in writing, as soon as practicable, the person liable to make the payments under the order, how payments are to be made.

(3) Paragraph (4) applies where the court orders that payments be made to the designated officer for the court, or to the designated officer for any other magistrates' court, by a method of payment falling within section 59(6) of the 1980 Act.

(4) The designated officer for the court to whom the payments are to be made must notify the person liable to make the payments under the order of sufficient details of the account into which the payments should be made to enable payments to be made into that account.

62 Variation of method of payment

(1) This rule applies where, under section 34A(4) of the 1972 Act, the designated officer receives an application from an interested party for the method of payment to be varied.

(2) As soon as practicable, the designated officer must notify in writing the interested party who made the application and, where practicable, any other interested party, of the result of the application, including any decision to refer the matter to the court.

(3) Where the justices' clerk grants the application, the justices' clerk must record the variation on the copy of the order.

63 Application under section 34 of the 1972 Act: variation or revocation

(1) This rule applies in relation to an application under section 34 of the 1972 Act for the variation or revocation of a registered order.

(2) An application which is made directly to the registering court must be filed in the form referred to in the Forms Practice Direction.

(3) Where the designated officer receives an application, either filed in accordance with paragraph (2) or sent from the Lord Chancellor under section 34(3) of the 1972 Act –

(a) the justices' clerk must set the date, time and place for a hearing or a directions appointment; and

(b) the designated officer must notify the applicant of that date, time and place.

64 Application under section 35 of the 1972 Act: variation or revocation

(1) This rule applies in relation to an application under section 35 of the 1972 Act for the variation or revocation of a registered order.

(2) Notice under section 35(3)(b) of the 1972 Act of the time and place appointed for the hearing of the application must be in the form specified in Schedule 3.

(3) The notice referred to in paragraph (2) must be sent by post by the designated officer to the Lord Chancellor for onward transmission to the appropriate authority in the convention country in which the respondent is residing.

(4) The time appointed for the hearing of the application must not be less than six weeks later than the date on which the notice referred to in paragraph (2) is sent to the Lord Chancellor.

65 Request under section 38(1) of the 1972 Act to a magistrates' court

(1) This rule applies where a magistrates' court receives from the Lord Chancellor a request under section 38(1) of the 1972 Act (taking evidence at the request of a court in a convention country) to take the evidence of any person.

(2) Subject to paragraph (3) –

(a) the evidence must be taken in the same manner as if the person concerned were a witness in proceedings on a complaint;

(b) any oral evidence so taken must be put into writing and read to the person who gave it, who must be required to sign the document; and

(c) the justices by whom the evidence of any person is so taken must certify at the foot of any document setting out the evidence of, or produced in evidence by, that person that such evidence was taken, or document received in evidence, as the case may be, by them.

(3) Where the request referred to in section 38(1) of the 1972 Act includes a request that the evidence be taken in a particular manner, the court by which the evidence is taken must, so far as circumstances permit, comply with that request.

66 Request under section 38(1) of the 1972 Act to a designated officer

(1) This rule applies where a designated officer receives from the Lord Chancellor a request under section 38(1) of the 1972 Act to take the evidence of any person.

(2) Subject to paragraph (3) –

(a) the person whose evidence is to be taken must be examined on oath by or before a justices' clerk;

(b) any oral evidence must be put into writing and read to the person who gave it, who must be required to sign the document; and

(c) the justices' clerk must certify at the foot of any document setting out the evidence of, or produced by, that person, that such evidence was taken, or document received in evidence, as the case may be, by that justices' clerk.

(3) Where the request referred to in section 38(1) of the 1972 Act includes a request that the evidence be taken in a particular manner, the justices' clerk by whom the evidence is taken must, so far as circumstances permit, comply with that request.

(4) For the purposes of this rule, a justices' clerk has the same power to administer oaths as a single justice of the peace.

67 Onward transmission of documents

Any document mentioned in paragraph (2)(c) of rule 65 or 66 must be sent to the Lord Chancellor for onward transmission to the appropriate authority in the convention country in which the request referred to in section 38(1) of the 1972 Act originated.

68 Procedural rules: proceedings pursuant to rules 57 and 63

(1) Schedule 4 applies to proceedings pursuant to rules 57 and 63.

(2) In Schedule 4 as it applies to rule 57, "the resident party" and "the non-resident party" are to be taken mean the respondent and the applicant respectively.

(3) In Schedule 4 as it applies to rule 63, "the resident party" and "the non-resident party" are to be taken to mean the payer and the payee under the order in question respectively.

PART 6
THE DOMESTIC PROCEEDINGS AND MAGISTRATES' COURTS ACT 1978 AND THE CIVIL PARTNERSHIP ACT 2004

CONTENTS OF THIS PART

69 Applications for variation under section 20 of the Domestic Proceedings and Magistrates' Courts Act 1978 or Schedule 6 to the Civil Partnership Act 2004

(1) The FPR shall apply to an application in a magistrates' court –

    (a)   under section 20 of the Domestic Proceedings and Magistrates' Courts Act 1978 for the variation of an order; or

    (b)   paragraphs 30 to 34 of Schedule 6 to the Civil Partnership Act 2004 for the variation of an order, with the modifications in paragraph (2).

(2) The modifications are –

    (a)   in rule 9.10 –

        (i)   in paragraph (1), for "The" substitute "Subject to paragraph (1A), the"; and

        (ii)   after paragraph (1), insert –

"(1A) Where the application is –

    (a)   for the variation of an order under section 2(1)(c), 6 or 7 of the 1978 Act or paragraph 2(1)(c) of or Part 2 or 3 of Schedule 6 to the 2004 Act for periodical payments in respect of a child;

    (b)   the application is made by the child in question; and

    (c)   the child in question is aged 16 or over,

the child does not require permission to make the application."; and

    (b)   in the table in rule 9.21 ", except an application" is omitted in both of the places where those words occur.

PART 7

THE CIVIL JURISDICTION AND JUDGMENTS ACT 1982, THE LUGANO CONVENTION, THE 1988 CONVENTION AND THE MAINTENANCE REGULATION: APPLICATIONS FOR VARIATION OF MAINTENANCE ORDERS

CONTENTS OF THIS PART

70 Interpretation

In this Part –

    "the 1982 Act" means the Civil Jurisdiction and Judgments Act 1982;

    "the 1988 Convention" means the Convention on jurisdiction and the enforcement of judgments in civil and commercial matters done at Lugano on 16 September 1988;

    "the Lugano Convention" means the Convention on jurisdiction and the recognition and enforcement of judgments in civil and commercial matters, between the European Community and the Republic of Iceland, the Kingdom of Norway, the Swiss Confederation and the Kingdom of Denmark signed on behalf of the European Community on 30 October 2007; and

PART III

"the Maintenance Regulation" means Council Regulation (EC) No 4/2009 of 18 December 2008 on jurisdiction, applicable law, recognition and enforcement of decisions and co-operation in matters relating to maintenance obligations, including as applied in relation to Denmark by virtue of the Agreement made on 19 October 2005 between the European Community and the Kingdom of Denmark.

71 Application for the variation of a maintenance order to which the 1982 Act, the Lugano Convention, the 1988 Convention or the Maintenance Regulation applies

(1) The FPR shall apply to an application for the variation of a maintenance order in relation to which the court has jurisdiction by virtue of the 1982 Act, the Lugano Convention, the 1988 Convention or the Maintenance Regulation, and the respondent is outside the United Kingdom, with the modification in paragraph (2).

(2) The modification is that that in rule 9.22(1), after "or for" insert "the variation or".

PART 8
THE 1986 ACT

CONTENTS OF THIS PART

72 Interpretation of this Part

In this Part –
"appropriate court" means, in relation to –
  (a)   Scotland, the Court of Session;
  (b)   Northern Ireland, the High Court in Northern Ireland; and
  (c)   a specified dependent territory, the corresponding court in that territory;
"Part 1 Order" means an order under Part 1 of the 1986 Act; and
"specified dependent territory" means a dependent territory specified in column 1 of Schedule 1 to the Family Law Act 1986 (Specified Dependent Territories) Order 1991.

73 Section 5 of the 1986 Act: staying of proceedings

(1) Where under section 5(2) of the 1986 Act a magistrates' court stays proceedings on an application for a Part 1 order, notice of the stay must be given to the parties to the proceedings.

(2) Where under section 5(3) of the 1986 Act a magistrates' court removes a stay granted in accordance with section 5(2) of the 1986 Act –

  (a)   notice of the removal of the stay must be given to the parties to the proceedings; and
  (b)   the court must proceed to deal with the application accordingly.

74 Chapter 5 of the 1986 Act: registration and enforcement

(1) The FPR shall apply to an application under section 27 of the 1986 Act for the registration and enforcement of a custody order made in a magistrates' court, with the modifications in paragraph (2).

(2) The modifications are –

    (a) in rule 32.25 –
        (i) in the heading, omit "made by the High Court or a county court";
        (ii) in paragraph (1), omit "made in the High Court or a county court";
        (iii) in paragraph (5)(b), after "district judge,", insert "or, in a magistrates' court, to the court"; and
        (iv) after paragraph (5), insert –

"(6) A memorandum of the granting by a magistrates' court of an application referred to in paragraph (1) must be entered in the register of the court to which the application was made.

(7) Where the court officer for a magistrates' court which granted an application referred to in paragraph (1) receives notice of the registration of the order in the appropriate court, the court officer must enter particulars of the notice in the register of that court officer's court."; and

    (b) in rule 32.32, in paragraphs (b) and (c), after "judge" insert ", or in a magistrates' court, the court".

(3) The FPR shall apply where an order under Part 1 of the 1986 Act registered in an appropriate court is varied or revoked, with the modifications in paragraph (4).

(4) The modification are that in rule 32.27 –

    (a) in the heading, omit "in the High Court or a county court"; and
    (b) after paragraph (2), insert –

"(3) Where the court officer referred to in paragraph (1) or (2) is a court officer of a magistrates' court, the court officer will record the fact referred to in paragraph (1) or (2)(a) or (b) by entering a notice in the register.".

75 Orders under section 33 or 34 of the 1986 Act

The FPR shall apply to an application in a magistrates' court for an order –

    (a) for the disclosure of information of the whereabouts of a child under section 33 of the 1986 Act; and
    (b) authorising the taking charge and delivery of a child under section 34 of the 1986 Act.

PART 9
THE 1989 ACT

CONTENTS OF THIS PART

76 Applications under the 1989 Act in respect of enforcement of contact orders

(1) The FPR shall apply to –

   (a)   an application in the magistrates' court under any of the following provisions of the 1989 Act –
      (i)   section 11J (enforcement orders);
      (ii)   section 11O (compensation for financial loss);
      (iii) paragraph 4 of Schedule A1 (enforcement orders: power to revoke);
      (iv)   paragraph 5, 6 or 7 of Schedule A1 (enforcement orders: amendment);
      (v)   paragraph 9 of Schedule A1 (breach of an enforcement order); or
   (b)   an application in the magistrates' court under section 8(2)(a) of the Children and Adoption Act 2006, with the modifications in paragraph (2).

(2) The modifications are –

   (a)   where the proceedings referred to in paragraph (1)(a) are treated as family proceedings by virtue of section 65 of the 1980 Act, in rule 2.6 –
      (i)   in paragraph (1) –
             (aa) in sub-paragraph (f), delete "or";
             (bb) in sub-paragraph (g), for ";" substitute "; or";
             (cc) after sub-paragraph (g), insert –
      "(h)   under paragraph 5 of Schedule A1."; and
      (ii)   in paragraph (3), for "paragraphs (a), (c) and (d)" substitute "paragraphs (a), (b), (d) and (h)";
   (b)   in rule 12.33(1), omit "to the High Court or a county court"; and
   (c)   in rule 12.35(1), for "the High Court or a county court" substitute "the court".

(3) The FPR shall apply in a case where a magistrates' court is considering exercising, or has exercised, a power under either of the following provisions of the 1989 Act –
      (i)   section 11L(5) (enforcement orders: provision of information); or
      (ii)   section 11M(1) (enforcement orders: monitoring).

77 Enforcement of a residence order or a special guardianship order under the 1989 Act

(1) Where a person in whose favour a residence order or a special guardianship order is in force wishes to enforce that order, that person must file with the court a written statement describing the alleged breach of the order.

(2) When a statement referred to in paragraph (1) is received by the court –

   (a)   the justices' clerk must fix a date, time and place for a hearing of the proceedings;
   (b)   the designated officer must give notice of the hearing as soon as practicable to –
      (i)   the person wishing to enforce the order; and
      (ii)   any person who is alleged to be in breach of the order.

(3) In this rule –

   "residence order" has the meaning given in section 8(1) of the 1989 Act; and
   "special guardianship order" has the meaning assigned to it by section 14A(1) of the 1989 Act.

78 Application to vary a contribution order under the 1989 Act

(1) The FPR shall apply to an application under paragraph 23(8) of Schedule 2 to the 1989 Act to vary a contribution order, with the modifications in paragraph (2).

(2) The modifications are –

    (a)   in rule 12.2, in the definition of "public law proceedings", in paragraph (p), after "a contribution order," insert "variation"; and

    (b)   in the table in rule 12.3(1), in the column 1 entry relating to proceedings for an order revoking a contribution order, after "order" insert "varying or".

(Paragraph 6A of Schedule 1 to the 1989 Act sets out the procedure for an application for the variation of an order made by a magistrates' court under Schedule 1 to the 1989 Act for periodical payments or for the payment of a lump sum by instalments.)

PART 10
THE EDUCATION ACT 1996

CONTENTS OF THIS PART

79 Direction to a local authority under section 447(2) and (3) of the Education Act 1996

(1) For the purposes of section 447(2) and (3) of the Education Act 1996, a direction by a magistrates' court to a local authority to apply for an education supervision order must be made in writing.

(2) Where following such a direction, a local authority informs the court that they have decided not to apply for an education supervision order, they must do so in writing.

(3) In this rule, "education supervision order" has the meaning assigned to it by section 36(2) of the 1989 Act.

PART 11
THE 1996 ACT

CONTENTS OF THIS PART

80 Applications under Part 4 of the 1996 Act: enforcement and bail

(1) In respect of –

    (a)   an application for enforcement of an order made on an application under Part 4 of the 1996 Act in the magistrates' court; and

    (b)   an application for bail made to a magistrates' court by a person arrested under a power of arrest attached to an occupation order made under section 47 of the 1996 Act,

the FPR shall apply, with the modifications in paragraph (2).

(2) The modifications are that after rule 10.17 there is inserted –

"10.18 Enforcement of orders made in a magistrates' court

(1) Where a power of arrest is attached to one or more of the provisions ("the relevant provisions") of an occupation order, the relevant provisions must be set out in a separate form, which must not include any provisions of the order to which the power of arrest was not attached.

(2) Where the court makes a non-molestation order or paragraph (1) applies, the following documents must be delivered to the officer for the time being in charge of any police station for the applicant's address or of such other police station as the court may specify –

    (a)   a copy of the non-molestation order or the form referred to in paragraph (1); and

    (b)   a statement showing that the respondent has been served with the order or informed of its terms (whether by being present when the order was made or by telephone or otherwise).

(3) The documents referred to in paragraphs (2)(a) and (b) must be delivered by –

    (a)   the applicant, if the applicant is responsible for serving the order on the respondent in accordance with rule 10.6(1); or

    (b)   the court officer, if the court is responsible for serving the order on the respondent in accordance with rule 10.6(2).

(4) Where an order is made varying or discharging the relevant provisions of the occupation order or, as the case may be, any provisions of the non-molestation order, the court officer must –

    (a)   immediately inform the officer who received a copy of any order or form under paragraph (2) and, if the applicant's address has changed, the officer for the time being in charge of the police station for the new address; and

    (b)   deliver a copy of the order to any officer so informed.

(5) Any warrant for the arrest of the respondent issued on an application under section 47(8) of the 1996 Act must be delivered by the court officer to the officer for the time being in charge of any police station for the respondent's address or of such other police station as the court may specify.

(6) The court before which a person is brought following that person's arrest may –

    (a)   determine whether the facts, and the circumstances which led to the arrest, amounted to disobedience of the order; or

    (b)   adjourn the proceedings and, where such an order is made, the arrested person may be released and –

        (i)   unless the court directs otherwise, be dealt with within 14 days of the day on which the arrested person was arrested; and

        (ii) be given not less than 2 business days' notice of the adjourned hearing.

Nothing in this paragraph prevents the issue of a notice under paragraph (10) if the arrested person is not dealt with within the period mentioned in sub-paragraph (b)(i) above.

(7) Paragraphs (8) to (15) apply for the enforcement of orders made on applications under Part 4 of the 1996 Act by committal order.

(8) Subject to paragraphs (13) and (14), an order must not be enforced by committal order unless –

    (a)   a copy of the occupation order or non-molestation order has been served personally on the respondent; and

    (b)   where the order requires the respondent to do an act, the copy has been so served before the expiration of the time within which the respondent was required to do the act and was accompanied by a copy of any order, made between the date of the order and the date of service, fixing that time.

(9) At the time when the order is drawn up, the court officer must –

    (a)   where the order made is (or includes) a non-molestation order; and

    (b)   where the order made is an occupation order and the court so directs,

issue a copy of the order, indorsed with or incorporating a notice as to the consequences of disobedience, for service in accordance with paragraph (8).

(10) If the respondent fails to obey the order, the court officer must, at the request of the applicant, issue a notice warning the respondent that an application will be made for the respondent to be committed and, subject to paragraph (14), the notice must be served on the respondent personally.

(11) The request for issue of the notice under paragraph (10) must be treated as a complaint and must –

    (a)   identify the provisions of the order or undertaking which it is alleged have been disobeyed or broken;

    (b)   list the ways in which it is alleged that the order or undertaking has been disobeyed or broken; and

    (c)   be supported by a statement which is signed and is declared to be true and which states the grounds on which the application is made,

and, unless service is dispensed with under paragraph (14), a copy of the statement must be served with the notice.

(12) If a committal order is made, it must include provision for the issue of a warrant of committal and, unless the court otherwise orders –

    (a)   a copy of the order must be served personally on the person to be committed either before or at the time of the execution of the warrant; or

    (b)   the order for the issue of the warrant may be served on the person to be committed at any time within 36 hours after the execution of the warrant.

(13) An order requiring a person to abstain from doing an act may be enforced by committal order notwithstanding that a copy of the order has not been served personally if the court is satisfied that, pending such service, the respondent had notice thereof either by being –

    (a)   present when the order was made;

    (b)   notified of the terms of the order whether by telephone or otherwise.

(14) The court may dispense with service of a copy of the order under paragraph (8) or a notice under paragraph (10) if the court thinks it just to do so.

(15) Where service of a notice to show cause is dispensed with under paragraph (14) and a committal order is made, the court may of its own motion fix a date and time when the person to be committed is to be brought before the court.

(16) Paragraphs (8) to (12), (14) and (15) apply to the enforcement of undertakings with the necessary modifications and as if –

    (a)   for paragraph (8) there were substituted the following –

"(8) A copy of a form recording the undertaking must be delivered by the court officer to the party giving the undertaking –

    (a)   by handing a copy of the document to that person before that person leaves the court building; or

    (b)   where that person's place of residence is known, by posting a copy to that person's place of residence; or

    (c)   through that person's solicitor,

and, where delivery cannot be effected in this way, the court officer must deliver a copy of the document to the party for whose benefit the undertaking is given and that party must serve it personally as soon as is practicable.";

(b)   in paragraph (14), the words from "a copy" to "paragraph (8) or" were omitted.

(17) Where a person in custody under a warrant or order desires to apply to the court for discharge, that person must make an application in writing attested by the governor of the prison showing that that person has purged or is desirous of purging his or her contempt and the court officer must, not less than one day before the application is heard, serve notice of it on the party (if any) at whose instance the warrant or order was issued.

(18) The court by which an order of committal is made may by order direct that the execution of the order of committal be suspended for such period or on such terms or conditions as it may specify.

(19) Where execution of an order of committal is suspended by an order under paragraph (18), the applicant for the order of committal must, unless the court otherwise directs, serve on the person against whom it was made a notice informing that person of the making and terms of the order under that paragraph.

(20) The court may adjourn consideration of the penalty to be imposed for contempts found proved and such consideration may be restored if the respondent does not comply with any conditions specified by the court.

(21) Where the court makes a hospital order or a guardianship order under the Mental Health Act 1983, the court officer must –

(a)   send to the hospital any information which will be of assistance in dealing with the patient; and

(b)   inform the applicant when the respondent is being transferred to hospital.

(22) Where a transfer direction given by the Secretary of State under section 48 of the Mental Health Act 1983 is in force in respect of a person remanded in custody by the court, the court officer must notify –

(a)   the governor of the prison to which that person was remanded; and

(b)   the hospital where he is detained,

of any committal hearing which that person is required to attend and the court officer must give notice in writing to the hospital where that person is detained of any further remand.

(23) In paragraph (6) "arrest" means arrest under a power of arrest attached to an occupation order under section 47(2) or (3) of the 1996 Act or under a warrant of arrest issued on an application under section 47(8) of the 1996 Act.

10.19 Applications under Part 4 of the 1996 Act: bail

(1) An application for bail made by a person arrested under a power of arrest attached to an occupation order or a warrant of arrest issued on an application under section 47(8) of the 1996 Act may be made either orally or in writing.

(2) Where an application is made in writing, it must contain –

(a)   the full name of the person making the application;

(b)   the address of the place where the person making the application is detained at the time when the application is made;

(c)   the address where the person making the application would reside if that person were to be granted bail;

(d) the amount of the recognizance in which that person would agree to be bound; and

(e) the grounds on which the application is made and, where a previous application has been refused, full particulars of any change in circumstances which has occurred since that refusal.

(3) An application made in writing must be signed by the person making the application or by a person duly authorised by that person or, where the person making the application is a minor or is for any reason incapable of acting, by a litigation friend or children's guardian acting on that person's behalf, and a copy must be served by the person making the application on the applicant for the order under Part 4 of the 1996 Act.

(4) A bail notice must be given to the respondent where the respondent is remanded on bail.

10.20 Powers of a single justice

Where the proceedings are treated by the court as family proceedings by virtue of section 65 of the 1980 Act, a single justice of the peace cannot perform the functions conferred on the court by rule 10.18(9)(b), (12) to (15) and (18) to (20).

10.21 Powers of a justices' clerk

A justices' clerk cannot perform the functions conferred on the court by rules 10.18(6), 10.18(9)(b), (12) to (15) and (18) to (20).".

****

Magistrates' Courts Rules 1981, SI 1981/552

ARRANGEMENT OF RULES

General

Modifications—MCR 1981 (except rr 4, 7, 25, 107) are modified for certain purposes by SI 2011/2866, Art 8(1), Sch 2.

General

1 Citation, operation and revocations

(1) These Rules may be cited as the Magistrates' Courts Rules 1981 and shall come into operation on 6 July 1981.

(2) The Rules mentioned in the Schedule to these Rules are hereby revoked; but where proceedings were commenced before 6 July 1981 and the old enactments within the meaning of paragraphs 1 and 2(2) of Schedule 8 to the Magistrates' Courts Act 1980 continue to apply by virtue of paragraph 2(1) of the said Schedule 8, the provisions of the Rules so mentioned continue to apply and nothing in these Rules affects those provisions.

2 Interpretation

(1) In these Rules –

"the Act of 1978" means the Domestic Proceedings and Magistrates' Courts Act 1978;

"the Act of 1980" means the Magistrates' Courts Act 1980;

"the Act of 1989" means the Children Act 1989;

"the Act of 2000" means the Powers of Criminal Courts (Sentencing) Act 2000;

"the Act of 1998" means the Crime and Disorder Act 1998;

"child" means a person who has not attained the age of 18;

"court computer system" means a computer or computer system which is used to assist to discharge and record the business of the court;

"electronic signature" is as much of anything in electronic form as –

(a) is incorporated into or otherwise logically associated with any electronic communication or electronic data; and

(b) purports to be so incorporated or associated for the purpose of being used in establishing the authenticity of the communication or data, the integrity of the communication or data, or both.

"judgment summons" has the meaning assigned to it by rule 58.

(2) In these Rules "representation order" has the meaning assigned to it by section 14 of the Access to Justice Act 1999.

(3) In these Rules a reference to the person with whom a child has his home shall be construed in accordance with the Act of 1989, except that, in the case of any child in the

care of a local authority, the local authority shall be treated for the purposes of these Rules as the person with whom the child has his home.

(4) In these Rules a reference to "the authorised persons for the area in which they are employed" is a reference to the persons employed by an authority which performs its functions within that area who are authorised to execute warrants within that area in pursuance of rule 3 of the Magistrates' Courts (Civilian Fine Enforcement Officers) (No 2) Rules 1990.

(5) Any requirement in these Rules that a document shall be in the prescribed form shall be construed as a requirement that the document shall be in the form prescribed in that behalf by rules made under section 144 of the Act of 1980, or a form to like effect.

(6) In these Rules any reference to a rule shall be construed as a reference to a rule contained in these Rules; and any reference in a rule to a paragraph shall be construed as a reference to a paragraph of that rule.

(7) Subject to rules 15 and 99, where these Rules require a document to be given or sent, or a notice to be communicated in writing, it may, with the consent of the addressee, be sent by electronic communication.

(8) Electronic communication means a communication transmitted (whether from one person to another, from one device to another or from a person to a device or vice versa) –

    (a)   by means of a telecommunication system (within the meaning of the Telecommunications Act 1984); or

    (b)   by other means but while in an electronic form.

Amendments—SI 1990/1190; SI 1990/2260; SI 1991/1991; SI 2000/3361; SI 2003/1236.

"prescribed in that behalf by rules" (r 2(5))—Prescribed by the Magistrates' Courts (Forms) Rules 1981.

3 Provisions to which these Rules are subject

The provisions of these Rules shall have effect subject to the provisions of the Family Proceedings Courts (Children Act 1989) Rules 1991, the Family Proceedings Courts (Matrimonial Proceedings etc) Rules 1991, the Family Procedure Rules 2010 and the Magistrates' Courts (Enforcement or Variation of Orders Made in Family Proceedings and Miscellaneous Provisions) Rules 2011.

Amendments—SI 1991/1991; SI 2011/1045; SI 2011/1329.

"the Family Proceedings Courts (Children Act 1989) Rules 1991, the Family Proceedings Courts (Matrimonial Proceedings etc) Rules 1991"—Both sets of rules were revoked by MC(EVOFP & MR)R 2011 to the extent that they remained in force following the implementation of the FPR 2010.

3A Case management

(1) The court must actively manage the case. That includes –

    (a)   the early identification of the real issues;

    (b)   the early identification of the needs of witnesses;

    (c)   achieving certainty as to what must be done, by whom and when, in particular by the early setting of a timetable for the progress of the case;

    (d)   monitoring the progress of the case and compliance with directions;

    (e)   ensuring that evidence, whether disputed or not, is presented in the shortest and clearest way;

    (f)   discouraging delay, dealing with as many aspects of the case as possible on the same occasion and avoiding unnecessary hearings;

(g)   encouraging the participants to co-operate in the progression of the case; and

(h)   making use of technology.

(2) The court must actively manage the case by giving any direction appropriate to the needs of that case as early as possible.

(3) Each party must –

(a)   actively assist the court in managing the case without, or if necessary with, a direction; and

(b)   apply for a direction if needed to assist with the management of the case.

(4) At the beginning of the case each party must, unless the court otherwise directs –

(a)   nominate an individual responsible for progressing that case; and

(b)   tell other parties and the court who he is and how to contact him.

(5) In fulfilling its duty under paragraphs (1) and (2), the court must where appropriate –

(a)   nominate a court officer responsible for progressing the case; and

(b)   make sure the parties know who he is and how to contact him.

(6) In this rule a person nominated under paragraphs (4) and (5) is called a case progression officer. A case progression officer must –

(a)   monitor compliance with directions;

(b)   make sure that the court is kept informed of events that may affect the progress of that case;

(c)   make sure that he can be contacted promptly about the case during ordinary business hours;

(d)   act promptly and reasonably in response to communications about the case; and

(e)   if he will be unavailable, appoint a substitute to fulfil his duties and inform the other case progression officers.

(7) In fulfilling its duty under paragraph (2) actively to manage the case the court may give any direction and take any step unless that direction or step would be inconsistent with legislation, including these Rules. In particular, the court may –

(a)   nominate a magistrate, justices' clerk or assistant to a justices' clerk to manage the case;

(b)   give a direction on its own initiative or on application by a party;

(c)   ask or allow a party to propose a direction;

(d)   for the purpose of giving directions, receive applications and representations by letter, by telephone or by any other means of electronic communication, and conduct a hearing by such means;

(e)   give a direction without a hearing;

(f)   fix, postpone, bring forward, extend or cancel a hearing;

(g)   shorten or extend (even after it has expired) a time limit fixed by a direction;

(h)   require that issues in the case should be determined separately, and decide in what order they will be determined; and

(i)   specify the consequences of failing to comply with a direction.

(8) Any power to give a direction under this rule includes a power to vary or revoke that direction.

(9) A party may apply to vary a direction if –

(a)   the court gave it without a hearing;

(b)   the court gave it at a hearing in that party's absence; or

(c)   circumstances have changed.

(10) A party who applies to vary a direction must –

(a)   apply as soon as practicable after becoming aware of the grounds for doing so; and

(b) give as much notice to the other parties as the nature and urgency of the application permits.

(11) The parties may agree to vary a time limit fixed by a direction, but only if –

   (a) the variation will not –
     (i) affect the date of any hearing that has been fixed, or
     (ii) significantly affect the progress of the case in any other way; and
   (b) the court has not prohibited variation by agreement.

(12) The court's case progression officer must refer any agreement by the parties to vary a time limit under paragraph (11) to the court if he doubts the condition in paragraph (11) is satisfied.

(13) At every hearing, if a case cannot be concluded there and then the court must give directions so that it can be concluded at the next hearing or as soon as possible after that.

(14) At every hearing the court must, where relevant –

   (a) if a party is absent, decide whether to proceed nonetheless;
   (b) set, follow or revise a timetable for the progress of the case, which may include a timetable for any hearing;
   (c) in giving directions, ensure continuity in relation to the court and to the parties' representatives where that is appropriate and practicable; and
   (d) where a direction has not been complied with, find out why, identify who was responsible, and take appropriate action.

(15) In fulfilling his duty under paragraph (3) actively to assist the court in managing the case, each party must –

   (a) comply with directions given by the court;
   (b) take every reasonable step to make sure that that party's witnesses will attend when they are needed;
   (c) make appropriate arrangements to present any written or other material; and
   (d) promptly inform the court and the other parties of anything that may –
     (i) affect the date or duration of any hearing, or
     (ii) significantly affect the progress of the case in any other way.

(16) The court may require a party to give a certificate of readiness.

(17) In order to manage the case –

   (a) the court must establish, with the active assistance of the parties, what disputed issues they intend to explore; and
   (b) the court may require a party to identify –
     (i) which witnesses will give oral evidence,
     (ii) the order in which those witnesses will give their evidence;
     (iii) whether that party requires an order compelling the attendance of a witness;
     (iv) what arrangements are desirable to facilitate the giving of evidence by a witness;
     (v) what arrangements are desirable to facilitate the participation of any other person;
     (vi) what written evidence that party intends to introduce;
     (vii) what other material, if any, that party intends to make available to the court in the presentation of the case;
     (viii) whether that party intends to raise any point of law that could affect the conduct of the case; and
     (ix) what timetable that party proposes and expects to follow.

(18) The court must make available to the parties a record of directions given.

Amendments—Inserted by SI 2009/3362.

Scope—This rule provides magistrates' courts with specific case management powers when dealing with civil cases but it does not apply in family proceedings that are subject to the case management powers set out in FPR 2010 or in those proceedings to which provisions in FPR 2010 are applied by virtue of MC(EVOFP & MP)R 2011. It will enable the court to make directions, if required, in enforcement proceedings under CSA 1991.

Information and complaint

4 Information and complaint

(1) An information may be laid or complaint made by the prosecutor or complainant in person or by his counsel or solicitor or other person authorised in that behalf.

(2) Subject to any provision of the Act of 1980 and any other enactment, an information or complaint need not be in writing or on oath.

(3) It shall not be necessary in an information or complaint to specify or negative an exception, exemption, proviso, excuse or qualification, whether or not it accompanies the description of the offence or matter of complaint contained in the enactment creating the offence or on which the complaint is founded.

****

Summary trial of information and hearing of complaint

****

14 Order of evidence and speeches: complaint

(1) On the hearing of a complaint, except where the court determines under section 53(3) of the Act of 1980 to make the order with the consent of the defendant without hearing evidence, the complainant shall call his evidence, and before doing so may address the court.

(2) At the conclusion of the evidence for the complainant the defendant may address the court, whether or not he afterwards calls evidence.

(3) At the conclusion of the evidence, if any, for the defence, the complainant may call evidence to rebut that evidence.

(4) At the conclusion of the evidence for the defence and the evidence, if any, in rebuttal, the defendant may address the court if he has not already done so.

(5) Either party may, with the leave of the court, address the court a second time, but where the court grants leave to one party it shall not refuse leave to the other.

(6) Where the defendant obtains leave to address the court for a second time his second address shall be made before the second address, if any, of the complainant.

Scope—It should be noted that separate procedures are specified for the hearing of applications; see, for example, FPR 2010, r 12.21.

"the defendant may address the court" (r 14(2))—The right to address the court is retained even after a submission of no case to answer (*Disher v Disher* [1965] P 31). Dismissal on the grounds of no case to answer may be of the court's own motion or on the defendant's submission. The complainant is entitled to address the court before dismissal (*Mayes v Mayes* [1971] 1 WLR 679).

"the complainant may call evidence to rebut" (r 14(3))—Although r 14(3) does not restrict the right to call evidence in rebuttal, the cases show that the right is restricted to matters which have arisen unexpectedly in the course of the defence case. If the matters could have been foreseen the right to call evidence in rebuttal does not exist (see, for example, *Price v Humphries* [1958] 2 QB 353).

Evidence—There is no general power to receive unsworn statements in civil proceedings except by agreement (*Aggas v Aggas* [1971] 1 WLR 1409).

Addressing the court—The defendant may restrict the right of the complainant to have the last word by reserving his address to the conclusion of the evidence for the defence.

****

16 Record of adjudication

(1) A record of summary conviction or order made on complaint required for an appeal or other legal purpose may be in the form of certified extract from the court register.

(2) (*revoked*)

Amendments—SI 2003/1236.

****

Remand

23 Remand on bail for more than 8 days where sureties have not entered into recognizances

Where the court, with a view to a person's being remanded on bail under paragraph (a) of section 128(6) of the Act of 1980 for a period exceeding 8 days, has fixed the amount of the recognizances to be taken for that purpose but commits that person to custody because the recognizances of the sureties have not yet been taken, the warrant of commitment shall direct the governor or keeper of the prison or place to which he is committed to bring him before the court at the end of 8 clear days or at such earlier time as may be specified in the warrant, unless in the meantime the sureties have entered into their recognizances.

****

Domestic proceedings
****

38 Certification of records

For the purposes of section 84(2) of the Act of 1978 (which provides that a copy of any record made by virtue of section 84 of the reasons for a decision of a magistrates' court shall, if certified by such officer of the court as may be prescribed, be admissible as evidence of those reasons) the certifying officer shall be the designated officer for the magistrates' court concerned.

Amendments—SI 2001/610; SI 2005/617.

"certified"—No form of certification is prescribed; the words "certified true copy", signed by the designated officer, would appear to be sufficient.

Orders for periodical payments

39 Method of making periodical payments

(1) Where a magistrates' court makes a means of payment order, the clerk of the court shall record on the order for periodical payments to which the means of payment order relates, the means of payment which the court has ordered and the designated officer shall notify in writing, as soon as practicable, the person liable to make payments under the order of how payments are to be made.

(2) Where the court orders that payments by the debtor to the creditor are to be made to the designated officer for the court or to the designated officer for any other magistrates' court under section 59(3)(b) of the Act of 1980, the designated officer to whom the payments are ordered to be made shall notify the person liable to make the payments of the hours during which, and the place at which, payments are to be made.

(3) The clerk to the court to whom any periodical payments are made shall send them by post to –

(a) the person entitled to them; or
(b) if the person entitled to them is a child, to the child or to the person with whom the child has his home:

Provided that the designated officer may –

(a) at the request of the person entitled to the payments; or
(b) if the person entitled to them is a child, at the request of the child or the person with whom the child has his home,

make other arrangements for making the payments.

(4) If a person makes any periodical payments to the designated officer for a magistrates' court otherwise than in person at the office of the designated officer, he shall do so at his own risk and expense.

(5) Where the court orders the payments by the debtor to the creditor be made by a method of payment falling within section 59(6) of the Act of 1980 (standing order, etc), the designated officer for the court shall notify the person liable to make payments under the order of the number and location of the account into which the payments should be made.

(6) Where the designated officer for a magistrates' court receives an application from an interested party under section 20ZA(2) of the Act of 1978, paragraph 36(1) of Schedule 6 to the Civil Partnership Act 2004, section 60(4) of the Act of 1980 or paragraph 6A(2) of Schedule 1 to the Children Act 1989 for the method of payment to be varied, the designated officer shall notify in writing, as soon as practicable, that party and, where practicable, any other interested party, of the result of the application, including any decision to refer the matter to the court; where the clerk of the court grants the application, he shall record the variation on the order for periodical payments to which the variation relates.

(7) In this rule "means of payment order" means an order of a magistrates' court under paragraphs (a) to (d) of section 59(3) of the Act of 1980.

Amendments—SI 1992/457; SI 2001/610; SI 2005/2930.

Sending periodical payments by post (r 39(3))—The cost of sending payments by post should be borne by the court and not the creditor (see Home Office Circular 214/1971).

****

41 Revocation, variation etc of orders for periodical payments

(1) This rule shall apply to a complaint for the revocation, discharge, revival, alteration or variation of a magistrates' court maintenance order or order enforceable as a magistrates' court maintenance order, but shall not apply –

(a) where jurisdiction is confined by paragraph (a) of subsection (2) of section 88 of the Children and Young Persons Act 1933 to courts acting in the local justice area where the person liable is residing;
(b) where an order has been made under the proviso to subsection (4) of that section;
(c) to a contribution order;

    (d) to a complaint for an order under section 26(4) of the Children Act 1948;

    (e) to a complaint for an order under section 22(1) of the Maintenance Orders Act 1950.

(2) A complaint to which this rule applies may be made to a justice of the peace acting in the same local justice area as the responsible court or to a justice of the peace acting in the local justice area where the complainant is for the time being.

(3) A justice of the peace shall not take action on a complaint to which this rule applies unless either the complainant has furnished him with written particulars –

    (a) of the nature of the evidence that the complainant proposes to adduce at the hearing of the complaint and the names and addresses and, if known to him, the occupations of his witnesses; and

    (b) of the occupations of the complainant and defendant and the address of the complainant and last address of the defendant known to the complainant

or the justice is acting in the same local justice area as the responsible court and it appears to him that the last address of the defendant known to the complainant is within that area.

(4) Where a complaint to which this rule applies is made to a justice of the peace acting in the same local justice area as the responsible court, and it appears to him that either of the places stated in the said particulars as being the addresses of the complainant and defendant is within another local justice area, then, if the justice determines that the complaint could more conveniently be dealt with by a magistrates' court acting in that other local justice area, he shall cause the designated officer for the responsible court to send by post to the designated officer for that other court the complaint, the said particulars and a copy of any relevant record of reasons for a decision kept in pursuance of rule 36.

(5) Where the places stated in the said particulars as being the addresses of the complainant and the defendant appear to the justice to be outside the local justice area in which the justice is acting and in other and different local justice areas, the reference in the last preceding paragraph to another local justice area shall be construed as a reference to such one of those other areas aforesaid as appears to the justice convenient.

(6) On receipt by the designated officer for a magistrates' court of a complaint, the particulars and a copy of any relevant record of reasons under paragraph (4), he shall bring the complaint before the court, and the court shall issue a summons requiring the defendant to appear before it, and shall hear and determine the complaint.

(7) Where a complaint to which this rule applies is made to a justice of the peace acting in a local justice area other than that in which the responsible court acts, the justice shall cause the designated officer for the magistrates' court acting in that other local justice area to send the complaint, the said particulars and the said copy of any relevant record of reasons by post to the designated officer for the responsible court; and the designated officer for the responsible court shall bring the complaint before the court; and thereupon paragraphs (4) to (6) shall have effect as if the complaint had been made and the particulars and the copy of any relevant record of reasons furnished to a justice of the peace acting in the same local justice area as the responsible court.

(8) Notwithstanding the foregoing provisions of this rule, a justice to whom a complaint is made may refer the complaint to the responsible court which may, in such case or when the complaint is brought before the court in accordance with paragraph (6), cause the complaint, the particulars and the copy of any relevant record of reasons to be sent by post to the designated officer for the court which made the original order and that designated officer and that court shall proceed in accordance with the provisions of paragraph (6).

(9) Where a magistrates' court makes an order on a complaint to which this rule applies affecting an order made by another magistrates' court or affecting an order under which payments are made to the designated officer for another magistrates' court, the designated officer for the first-mentioned court shall cause a copy of the order to be sent to the designated officer for that other court.

(10) In this rule "responsible court" means –

    (a)   where payments under the order are made to the designated officer for a magistrates' court, that court;

    (b)   where payments are not so made, the court which made the order.

Amendments—SI 2001/610; SI 2005/617.

Defined terms—"responsible court": r 41(10).

"section 22(1) of the Maintenance Orders Act 1950" (r 41(1)(e))—Section 22(1) relates to discharge and variation of maintenance orders between England, Scotland and Northern Ireland.

"if the justice determines that the complaint could more conveniently be dealt with" (r 41(4))—If the complaint is not made on oath, the complaint and determination as to venue may also be made by the justices' clerk (JCR 2005, Sch, para 44). In determining convenience, representations should be allowed where necessary in the interests of fairness (*R v Wareham Magistrates' Court ex parte Seldon* [1988] 2 FLR 269).

"send by post ... the complaint, the said particulars and a copy of any relevant record of reasons" (r 41(4))—For information to be sent with the complaint see Home Office Circular 278/1947 and *John v John (Practice Note)* [1959] 1 WLR 60. The designated officer should send any information which would be helpful to the other court in dealing with the complaint, e g on enforcement of the order, details of the payment history; on variation, details of the defendant's circumstances when the order was made.

****

43 Service of copy of order

Where a magistrates' court makes, revokes, discharges, suspends, revives, alters or varies a magistrates' court maintenance order or order enforceable as a magistrates' court maintenance order or allows time or further time for payment of a lump sum under any such order or orders payment of a lump sum under any such order to be paid by instalments or various any such order for payment by instalments the court shall cause a copy of its order to be served on the defendant by delivering it to him or by sending it by post in a letter addressed to him at his last known or usual place of abode.

Amendments—SI 1989/384.

"sending it by post"—Service is deemed to be effected by properly addressing, prepaying and posting a letter containing the document. Unless the contrary is proved, it is deemed to have been effected, in the case of first class mail, on the second working day after posting and, in the case of second class mail, on the fourth working day after posting. Working days are Mondays to Fridays, excluding bank holidays (Interpretation Act 1978, s 7).

44 Remission of sums due under order

(1) Before remitting the whole or any part of a sum due under a magistrates' court maintenance order or an order enforceable as a magistrates' court maintenance order under section 95 of the Act of 1980, the court shall, except save where it appears to it to be unnecessary or impracticable to do so, cause the person in whose favour the order is made or, if that person is a child, the child or the person with whom the child has his home to be notified of its intention and shall afford to such person a reasonable opportunity to make representations to the court, either orally at an adjourned hearing of the complaint for enforcement or in writing and such representations shall be considered by the court.

PART III

(2) Any written representations may be considered by the court if they purport to be signed by or on behalf of the person in whose favour the order is made or, if that person is a child, by or on behalf of the child or the person with whom the child has his home.

Amendments—SI 1989/384.

Requirement to notify person in whose favour the order is made (r 44(1))—Rule 44(1) is mandatory, and the normal remedy where such notice is not given is by way of appeal to a county court under MCA 1980, s 111A. Judicial review will only be granted in exceptional circumstances (*R v Bristol Magistrates' Court ex parte Hodge* [1997] 1 FLR 88).

45 Duty of designated officer to notify subsequent marriage or formation of civil partnership of person entitled to payments under a maintenance order

(1) Where the designated officer for a magistrates' court to whom any payments under an order to which this rule applies are required to be made is notified in writing by or on behalf of the person entitled to payments under such an order, the person liable to make payments under such an order or the personal representatives of either of those persons that the person so entitled has subsequently married or formed a civil partnership, the designated officer shall forthwith in writing so notify the designated officer for or other appropriate officer of each of the courts mentioned in paragraph (2) for which he is not the designated officer.

(2) The courts referred to in paragraph (1) are –

    (a)   any court which has made a relevant order or, in the case of a provisional order made under section 3 of the Maintenance Orders (Facilities for Enforcement) Act 1920 or section 3 of the Maintenance Orders (Reciprocal Enforcement) Act 1972, the court which confirmed the order;

    (b)   if a relevant order has been transmitted abroad for registration under section 2 of the said Act of 1920 or section 2 of the said Act of 1972, the court in which the order is registered; and

    (c)   if a complaint for the enforcement of a relevant order has been sent to a court under rule 59(2), that court.

(3) This rule applies to an order of a kind mentioned in paragraph (4) and an attachment of earnings order made to secure payments under an order of that kind, and in paragraph (2) "relevant order" means any such order to which the payments referred to in paragraph (1) relate.

Amendments—SI 2001/610; SI 2005/2930.

Satisfaction, enforcement and application of payments
****

48 To whom payments are to be made

(1) A person adjudged by the conviction of a magistrates' court to pay any sum shall, unless the court otherwise directs, pay that sum, or any instalment of that sum, to the designated officer for the court.

(2) Where payment of any sum or instalment of any sum adjudged to be paid by the conviction or order of a magistrates court is made to any person other than the designated officer for the court, that person, unless he is the person to whom the court has directed payment to be made or, in the case of a child, is the person with whom the child has his home, shall, as soon as may be, account for and, if the designated officer so requires, pay over the sum or instalment to the designated officer for the court.

(3) Where payment of any sum adjudged to be paid by the conviction or order of a magistrates' court, or any instalment of such a sum, if directed to be made to the designated officer for some other magistrates' court, the designated officer for the court that adjudged the sum to be paid shall pay over any sums received by him on account of the said sum or instalment to the designated officer for that other court.

Amendments—SI 1992/457; SI 2001/610.

49 Duty of designated officer to give receipt

The designated officer for a magistrates' court shall give or send a receipt to any person who makes a payment to him in pursuance of a conviction or order of a magistrates' court and who asks for a receipt.

Amendments—SI 2001/610.

50 (*revoked*)

51 Application for further time

An application under section 75(2) of the Act of 1980, section 22 of the Act of 1978, or paragraph 41 of Schedule 6 to the Civil Partnership Act 2004 may, unless the court requires the applicant to attend, be made in writing.

Amendments—SI 1989/384; SI 1991/1991; SI 2005/2930.

52 Notice of date of hearing of means inquiry etc

Where a magistrates' court, under subsection (1) of section 86 of the Act of 1980 (power of magistrates' court to fix day for appearance of offender at means inquiry etc), has fixed a day on which an offender must appear in person before the court and, under subsection (3) of that section, fixes a later day in substitution for the day previously fixed, service of the notice of the substituted day may be effected in any manner in which service of a summons may be effected under rule 99(1).

52A Review of terms of postponement of warrant of commitment

An application under section 77(5) of the Magistrates' Courts Act 1980 may be made in writing or in person and where under that subsection a justice of the peace refers such an application to the court, notice of the time and place fixed under section 77(6) for the hearing of the application may be deemed to have been given if it is sent by registered post or the recorded delivery service addressed to the applicant at his last known address, notwithstanding that the notice is returned as undelivered or is for any other reason not received by the applicant.

"application under section 77(5) of the Magistrates' Courts Act 1980"—This is an application to vary the time or conditions of postponement of a warrant of commitment for non-payment.

53 Notice to defendant before enforcing order

(1) A warrant of distress shall not be issued for failure to pay a sum enforceable as a civil debt unless the defendant has been previously served with a copy of the minute of the order, or the order was made in his presence and the warrant is issued on that occasion.

(2) A warrant of commitment shall not be issued for disobedience to an order of a magistrates' court unless the defendant has been previously served with a copy of the minute of the order, or the order was made in his presence and the warrant is issued on that occasion:

Provided that this paragraph shall not apply to –

    (a)   an order to pay money; or

    (b)   an expedited order under section 16(2) and (6) of the Act of 1978.

(3) A copy of the minute of the order shall be served under this rule by delivering it to the defendant or by sending it to him by post in a letter addressed to him at his last known or usual place of abode.

(4) In relation to an order under section 16 of the Act of 1978 (other than an expedited order under subsections (2) and (6) of that section) paragraphs (2) and (3) shall have effect as if for the references to a copy of a minute of the order there were substituted references to a copy of the order.

Scope—This rule limits the circumstances in which a warrant of distress or committal may be issued for enforcement of a civil debt. It does not apply to the enforcement of a magistrates' court maintenance order.

"order of a magistrates' court" (r 53(2))—See MCA 1980, s 63.

"sending it to him by post" (r 53(3))—See Interpretation Act 1978, s 7 for the presumption of due delivery.

54 Execution of distress warrant

(1) A warrant of distress issued for the purpose of levying a sum adjudged to be paid by a summary conviction or order –

    (a)   shall name or otherwise describe the person against whom the distress is to be levied;

    (b)   shall be directed to the constables of the police area in which the warrant is issued or to the civilian enforcement officers for the area in which they are employed, or to a person named in the warrant and shall, subject to, and in accordance with, the provisions of this rule, require them to levy the said sum by distress and sale of the goods belonging to the said person;

    (c)   may where it is directed to the constables of a police area, instead of being executed by any of those constables, be executed by any person under the direction of a constable.

(2) The warrant shall authorise the person charged with the execution of it to take as well any money as any goods of the person against whom the distress is levied; and any money so taken shall be treated as if it were the proceeds of the sale of goods taken under the warrant.

(3) The warrant shall require the person charged with the execution to pay the sum to be levied to the designated officer for the court that issued the warrant.

(3A) A warrant to which this rule applies may be executed by the persons to whom it was directed or by any of the following persons, whether or not the warrant was directed to them –

    (a)   a constable for any police area in England and Wales, acting in his own police area;

    (b)   where the warrant is one to which section 125A of the Act of 1980 applies, a civilian enforcement officer within the meaning of section 125A of the Act of 1980;

    (c)   where the warrant is one to which section 125A of the Act of 1980 applies, any of the individuals described in section 125B(1) of the Act of 1980;

and in this rule any reference to the person charged with the execution of a warrant includes any of the above persons who is for the time being authorised to execute the warrant, whether or not they have the warrant in their possession at the time.

(3B) A person executing a warrant of distress shall –

    (a)   either –
           (i)   if he has the warrant with him, show it to the person against whom the distress is levied, or
           (ii)   otherwise, state where the warrant is and what arrangements may be made to allow the person against whom distress is levied to inspect it;
    (b)   explain, in ordinary language, the sum for which distress is levied and the reason for the distress;
    (c)   where the person executing the warrant is one of the persons referred to in paragraph (3A)(b) or (c) above, show the person against whom distress is levied a written statement under section 125A(4) or 125B(4) as appropriate; and
    (d)   in any case, show documentary proof of his identity.

(4) There shall not be taken under the warrant the clothing or bedding of any person or his family or the tools, books, vehicles or other equipment which he personally needs to use in his employment, business or vocation, provided that in this paragraph the word "person" shall not include a corporation.

(5) The distress levied under any such warrant as aforesaid shall be sold within such period beginning not earlier than the 6th day after the making of the distress as may be specified in the warrant, or if no period is specified in the warrant, within a period beginning on the 6th day and ending on the 14th day after the making of the distress: Provided that with the consent in writing of the person against whom the distress is levied the distress may be sold before the beginning of the said period.

(5A) The clerk of the court which issued the warrant may, on the application of the person charged with the execution of it, extend the period within which the distress must be sold by any number of days not exceeding 60; but following the grant of such an application there shall be no further variation or extension of that period.

(6) The said distress shall be sold by public auction or in such other manner as the person against whom the distress is levied may in writing allow.

(7) Notwithstanding anything in the preceding provisions of this rule, the said distress shall not be sold if the sum for which the warrant was issued and the charges of taking and keeping the distress have been paid.

(8) Subject to any direction to the contrary in the warrant, where the distress is levied on household goods, the goods shall not, without the consent in writing of the person against whom the distress is levied, be removed from the house until the day of sale; and so much of the goods shall be impounded as is in the opinion of the person executing the warrant sufficient to satisfy the distress, by affixing to the articles impounded a conspicuous mark.

(9) The person charged with the execution of any such warrant as aforesaid shall cause the distress to be sold, and may deduct out of the amount realised by the sale all costs and charges incurred in effecting the sale; and he shall return to the owner the balance, if any, after retaining the amount of the sum for which the warrant was issued and the proper costs and charges of the execution of the warrant.

(10) The person charged with the execution of any such warrant as aforesaid shall as soon as practicable send to the designated officer for the court that issued it a written account of the costs and charges incurred in executing it; and the designated officer shall allow the person against whom the distress was levied to inspect the account within one month after the levy of the distress at any reasonable time to be appointed by the court.

PART III

(11) If any person pays or tenders to the person charged with the execution of any such warrant as aforesaid the sum mentioned in the warrant, or produces a receipt for that sum given by the designated officer for the court that issued the warrant, and also pays the amount of the costs and charges of the distress up to the time of the payment or tender or the production of the receipt, the person as aforesaid shall not execute the warrant, or shall cease to execute it, as the case may be.

Amendments—SI 1983/523; SI 1990/1190; SI 1992/729; SI 1999/2765; SI 2001/167; SI 2001/610.

"conspicuous mark" (r 54(8))—It is an offence under MCA 1980, s 78(4) to remove marked goods or to deface or remove the mark.

"costs and charges" (r 54(10))—It is an offence to exact excessive costs and charges (MCA 1980, s 78(5)).

55 Payment after imprisonment imposed

(1) The persons authorised for the purposes of section 79(2) of the Act of 1980 to receive a part payment are –

  (a) unless there has been issued a warrant of distress or commitment, the designated officer for the court enforcing payment of the sum, or any person appointed under section 88 of that Act to supervise the offender;

  (b) where the issue of a warrant of commitment has been suspended on conditions which provide for payment to be made to the designated officer for some other magistrates' court, that designated officer;

  (c) any constable holding a warrant of distress or commitment or, where the warrant is directed to some other person, that person;

  (d) the governor or keeper of the prison or place in which the defaulter is detained, or other person having lawful custody of the defaulter:

Provided that –

  (i)   the said governor or keeper shall not be required to accept any sum tendered in part payment under the said subsection (2) except on a week-day between 9 o'clock in the morning and 5 o'clock in the afternoon; and

  (ii) no person shall be required to receive in part payment under the said subsection (2) an amount which, or so much of an amount as, will not procure a reduction of the period for which the defaulter is committed or ordered to be detained.

(2) Where a person having custody of a defaulter received payment of any sum he shall note receipt of the sum on the warrant of commitment.

(3) Where the designated officer for a court other than the court enforcing payment of the sums receives payment of any sum he shall inform the designated officer for the other court.

(4) Where a person appointed under section 88 of the Act of 1980 to supervise an offender receives payment of any sum, he shall send it forthwith to the designated officer for the court which appointed him.

(5) (*ceased to have effect*)

Amendments—SI 2001/610; SI 2005/617.

"unless there has been issued a warrant of distress or commitment" (r 55(1)(a))—A warrant of commitment has not been issued where the issue of the warrant has been suspended on conditions.

****

58 Civil debt: judgment summons

(1) A summons issued on a complaint made for the purposes of section 96 of the Act of 1980 (in these rules referred to as a "judgment summons") shall be served on the judgment debtor personally:

Provided that if a justice of the peace is satisfied by evidence on oath that prompt personal service of the summons is impracticable, he may allow the summons to be served in such a way as he may think just.

(2) Unless the judgment debtor appears and consents to an immediate hearing, the court shall not hear the complaint unless the summons was served at least 3 clear days before the hearing.

(3) Service of a judgment summons outside the local justice area in which the justice issuing the summons acted may, without prejudice to any other provision of these rules enabling service of a summons to be proved, be proved by affidavit.

Amendments—SI 2005/617.

Scope—This rule makes provision for the service or substituted service of a judgment summons. It should be noted that, although there is some overlap of terminology, a judgment summons in the magistrates' court is substantially different from that in the county court.

"section 96 of the Act of 1980" (r 58(1))—The obligations under this rule are imposed in respect of civil debt enforcement under MCA 1980, s 96. The rule is not applicable to enforcement of a magistrates' court maintenance order as a separate procedure is defined under MCA 1980, s 93.

"if a justice of the peace is satisfied ... he may allow the summons to be served in such a way as he may think just" (r 58(1))—The summons should be endorsed by the justice with the points under the rule with which he is satisfied. If alternative service is authorised ("substituted service"), the method of service should also be endorsed on the summons. The method of substituted service is entirely within the justices' discretion.

"3 clear days" (r 58(2))—A longer period of notice may be appropriate where substituted service is allowed.

"without prejudice to any other provision" (r 58(3))—For example under r 67.

59 Enforcement of magistrates' court maintenance orders etc

(1) Subject to the following provisions of this rule, a complaint for the enforcement of a magistrates' court maintenance order, or an order enforceable as a magistrates' court maintenance order, shall be heard by the court that made the order:

Provided that –

    (a)   where –
        (i)   the complainant is the person in whose favour the order was made or, if that person is a child, is the child or the person with whom the child has his home; and
        (ii)   the complainant resides in a local justice area other than that in which the court acts; and
        (iii)   payment is directed to be made either to the complainant or the designated officer for a magistrates' court acting in that local justice area,
        the complaint may be heard by the last-mentioned court;
    (b)   where the complainant is the designated officer for a magistrates' court, the complaint may be heard by that court.

(2) Where a complaint is made to a justice of the peace for the enforcement of such an order as aforesaid and it appears to him that the defendant is for the time being in some local justice area other than that in which the justice is acting and that the order may be more conveniently enforced by a magistrates' court acting in that area, the justice shall cause the designated officer for the court to send the complaint by post to the designated

officer for a magistrates' court acting in that other local justice area, and for that purpose shall write down the complaint if this has not already been done.

(3) On receipt by the designated officer for a magistrates' court of a complaint sent under the last preceding paragraph, he shall bring it before the court; and the court shall issue a summons or warrant for procuring the appearance of the defendant before it, and shall hear and determine the complaint.

(4) If, after a complaint has been sent to the designated officer for a magistrates' court under this rule, the designated officer for the court to which the complaint was made receives any payment under the order, he shall forthwith send by post to the designated officer to whom the complaint was sent a certificate of the amount of the payments and of the date when it was made.

(5) If, after a complaint has been sent as aforesaid, payment under the order is made, not to the designated officer for the court to which the complaint was originally made, but to the person specified in the order or, in the case of a child, to the person with whom the child has his home, that person shall forthwith inform the designated officer for the amount and date as aforesaid and the designated officer shall forthwith send a certificate of the amount and date as required by the last preceding paragraph.

(6) A certificate under this rule purporting to be signed by the designated officer for the court to which the complaint was originally made shall be admissible as evidence on the hearing of the complaint that the amount specified in the certificate was paid on the date so specified.

(7) This rule shall not apply –

    (a)   where jurisdiction is confined by section 88(2)(a) of the Children and Young Persons Act 1933, to courts having jurisdiction in the place where the person liable is residing;

    (b)   to a contribution order.

Amendments—SI 1989/384; SI 2001/610; SI 2005/617.

"magistrates' court maintenance order" (r 59(1))—This term is defined in MCA 1980, s 150(1). For a list of orders see note under MCA 1980, s 92.

"Where a complaint is made to a justice of the peace" (r 59(2))—Where the complaint is not made on oath, this function may be exercised by the justices' clerk (JCR 2005, Sch 2, para 6).

"shall write down the complaint" (r 59(2))—By virtue of r 4(2), a complaint need not be in writing. An oral complaint must be written down if it is to be sent to another magistrates' court.

Warrants (r 59(3))—Before a warrant is issued, the court must be sure that the complaint was made on oath.

"forthwith send ... a certificate of the amount of the payment" (r 59(4))—It is of vital importance that this requirement is complied with. A failure to send details of payments may result in the receiving court issuing process wrongly, or delays in the enforcement of remaining arrears while proceedings are adjourned for the investigation of the defendant's claim that payments have been made (see Home Office Circular 278/1947).

59A Court to which complaint for the enforcement of a maintenance decision to which Section 1 of Chapter IV of the Maintenance Regulation applies must be made

(1) In this rule and in rule 59B –

    "the Maintenance Regulation" means Council Regulation (EC) No 4/2009 of 18 December 2009 on jurisdiction, applicable law, recognition and enforcement of decisions and cooperation in matters relating to maintenance obligations including as applied in relation to Denmark by virtue of the Agreement made on 19 October 2005 between the European Community and the Kingdom of Denmark;

"decision" has the meaning given in Article 2 of that Regulation.

(2) A complaint for the enforcement of a decision to which Section 1 of Chapter IV of the Maintenance Regulation applies (that is, a decision made in any other Member State of the European Union except Denmark) shall be heard by the court for the local justice area in which –

(a) the person against whom enforcement is sought is resident,

(b) that person has assets to which the Maintenance Orders Act 1958 applies, or

(c) any other matter relating to enforcement arises.

(3) Where –

(a) the complainant is the person in whose favour the order was made or, if that person is a child, is the child or the person with whom the child has his or her home,

(b) the complainant resides in a local justice area other than that in which the court acts, and

(c) payment is directed to be made to the complainant, the complaint may be heard by the court for that local justice area.

(4) Where an application for enforcement is made under Article 56 of the Maintenance Regulation on the form at Annex VI to that Regulation, the complaint may be made using that form.

Amendments—Inserted by SI 2011/1329.

Scope—This rule makes specific provision in respect of the appropriate magistrates' court with jurisdiction to deal with enforcement of a maintenance order from a European Member State except Denmark (the provisions in MCR 1981, r 59 being applicable to Danish orders registered for enforcement in the magistrates' court).

59B Complaint by debtor under Article 21 of the Maintenance Regulation for refusal or suspension of enforcement

A complaint by a debtor under Article 21 of the Maintenance Regulation for the refusal or suspension of enforcement of a decision shall be heard by –

(a) the court to which a complaint for enforcement of that decision has been made in accordance with rule 59A, or

(b) where no such complaint has been made at the date at which the debtor makes a complaint under this rule, the court to which a complaint for enforcement would be required to be made under rule 59A.

Amendments—Inserted by SI 2011/1329.

60 Enforcement where periodical payments made under more than one order

(1) Where periodical payments are required to be made to any person by another person under more than one periodical payments order, proceedings for the recovery of the payments may be brought by way of one complaint. Any such complaint shall indicate the payments due under each order referred to in the complaint.

(2) Any sum paid to the designated officer for a magistrates' court on any date by a person liable to make payments under 2 or more periodical payments orders which is less than the total sum required to be paid on that date to that designated officer by that person in respect of those orders (being orders one of which requires payments to be

made for the benefit of a child to the person with whom the child has his home and one or more of which requires payments to be made to that person either for his own benefit or for the benefits of another child who has his home with him) shall be apportioned between the orders in proportion to the amounts respectively due under each order over a period of one year and if, as a result of the apportionment, the payments under any such order are no longer in arrears the residue shall be applied to the amount due under the other order or (if there is more than one other order) shall be apportioned as aforesaid between the other orders.

(3) For the purposes of calculating the apportionment of any sum under paragraph (2) –

    (a)   a month shall be treated as consisting of 4 weeks; and

    (b)   a year shall be treated as consisting of 52 weeks.

Amendments—SI 1983/523; SI 2001/610; SI 2005/617.

61 Notice of adjudication on complaint for enforcement of a magistrates' court maintenance order etc

A magistrates' court shall give notice in writing to the complainant of its adjudication on a complaint for the enforcement of a magistrates' court maintenance order, or order enforceable as a magistrates' court maintenance order, unless the complainant is present or is the designated officer for the court.

Amendments—SI 1989/384; SI 2001/610.

62 Particulars relating to payment of lump sum under a magistrates' court maintenance order etc to be entered in register

Where a magistrates' court allows time for payment of a lump sum required to be paid under a magistrates' court maintenance order, or order enforceable as a magistrates' court maintenance order, or orders that any such lump sum shall be paid by instalments or varies the number of instalments payable, the amount of any instalment payable or the date on which any instalment becomes payable, particulars thereof shall be entered in the register or in any separate record kept for the purpose of recording particulars of lump sum payments.

Amendments—SI 1989/384.

63 Notice of date of reception in custody and discharge

(1) Where in proceedings to enforce a magistrates' court maintenance order, or an order enforceable as a magistrates' court maintenance order, the defendant is committed to custody, then on his discharge the governor or keeper of the prison or place of detention shall send to the designated officer for the court that committed the defendant a certificate showing the dates of the defendant's reception and discharge; and that designated officer shall, if the payments under the order are required to be made to the designated officer for any other court, send the certificate to the last-mentioned designated officer.

(2) …

Amendments—SI 1989/384; SI 2001/610; SI 2005/617.

"magistrates' court maintenance order"—See the list of orders under MCA 1980, s 92.

64 Direction that money found on defaulter shall not be applied in satisfaction of debt

Where the defaulter is committed to, or ordered to be detained in, a prison or other place of detention, any direction given under section 80(2) of the Act of 1980 shall be endorsed on the warrant of commitment.

Scope—If no direction is given or no indorsement made, any monies found will be applied to the debt.

"section 80(2) of the Act of 1980"—This subsection makes provision for the application of any money found on a person committed to prison for non-payment of a magistrates' court maintenance order.

****

Register

66 Register of convictions etc

(1) The designated officer for every magistrates' court shall keep a register in which there shall be entered –

  (a) a minute or memorandum of every adjudication of the court;
  (b) a minute or memorandum of every other proceeding or thing required by these rules or any other enactment to be so entered.

(2) The register may be stored in electronic form on the court computer system and entries in the register shall include, where relevant, the following particulars –

  (a) the name of the informant, complainant or applicant;
  (b) the name and date of birth (if known) of the defendant or respondent;
  (c) the nature of offence, matter of complaint or details of the application;
  (d) the date of offence or matter of complaint;
  (e) the plea or consent to order; and
  (f) the minute of adjudication.

(3) Particulars of any entry relating to a decision about bail or the reasons for any such decisions or the particulars of any certificate granted under section 5(6A) of the Bail Act 1976 may be made in a book separate from that in which the entry recording the decision itself is made, but any such separate book shall be regarded as forming part of the register.

(3A)–(11A) ...

(12) Every register shall be open to inspection during reasonable hours by any justice of the peace, or any person authorised in that behalf by a justice of the peace or the Lord Chancellor.

Amendments—SI 1992/709; SI 1993/1183; SI 2001/610; SI 2003/1236.

Adoption register—See FPR 2010, r 14.28 for special provisions relating to the adoption register.

"minute or memorandum" (r 66(1))—A certified extract from the register is admissible evidence under r 68.

"adjudication" (r 66(1))—This includes the dismissal of a complaint (*Baker v Baker (Practice Note)* [1961] 1 WLR 1016). The register is an official record of the justices' decision but the decision exists independently of the record. The justices' clerk is acting within the scope of his duty if he corrects a verbal error in an entry in the register (*R v Manchester Justices ex parte Lever* [1937] 2 KB 96 and *R v Huntingdon Justices ex parte Simpkin and Coombes* (1959) 123 JP 166).

****

Evidence – General

67 Proof of service, handwriting etc

(1) The service on any person of a summons, process, notice or document required or authorised to be served in any proceedings before a magistrates' court, and the handwriting or seal of a justice of the peace or other person on any warrant, summons, notice, process or documents issued or made in any such proceedings, may be proved in any legal proceedings by a document purporting to be a solemn declaration in the prescribed form made before a justice of the peace, commissioner for oaths, clerk of a magistrates' court or registrar of a county court or a sheriff or sheriff clerk (in Scotland) or a clerk of petty sessions (in Northern Ireland).

(2) The service of any process or other document required or authorised to be served may be proved in any proceedings before a magistrates' court by a document purporting to be a certificate signed by the person by whom the service was effected.

(3) References in paragraph (2) to the service of any process shall, in their application to a witness summons, be construed as including references to the payment or tender to the witness of his costs and expenses.

(4) Any process or other document produced by the court computer system on a given day shall be sufficient evidence that the process or other document was sent to the person to whom it is addressed within 2 days of it being produced, unless the contrary is proved.

Amendments—SI 2003/1236.

"The service of any process ... may be proved" (r 67(2))—A certificate of service is not conclusive proof of service (see *Maher v Gower (formerly Kubilius)* (1982) 3 FLR 287).

68 Proof of proceedings

The register of a magistrates' court, or an extract from the register certified by the designated officer as a true extract, shall be admissible in any legal proceedings as evidence of the proceedings of the court entered in the register.

Amendments—SI 2001/610; SI 2003/1236.

69 Proof that magistrates' court maintenance orders, maintenance orders etc have not been revoked etc

A certificate purporting to be signed by the designated officer for a magistrates' court, and stating that no minute or memorandum of an order revoking, discharging, suspending, reviving, altering or varying a magistrates' court maintenance order, or order enforceable as a magistrates' court maintenance order or an order made under Part I of the Act of 1978 or under Schedule 6 to the Civil Partnership Act 2004 enforceable otherwise than as a magistrates' court maintenance order made by the court is entered in the register of the court shall, in any proceedings relating to the enforcement of the order or the revocation, discharge, suspension, revival, alteration or variation of the order, be evidence that the order has not been revoked, discharged, suspended, revived, altered or varied.

Amendments—SI 1989/384; SI 2001/610; SI 2005/2930.

****

Recognizances and bail

****

83 Application to vary order for sureties or dispense with them

Where a person has been committed to custody in default of finding sureties and the order to find sureties was made at the instance of another person, an application under section 118 of the Act of 1980 shall be made by complaint against that other person.

84 Notice of enlargement of recognizances

(1) If a magistrates' court before which any person is bound by a recognizance to appear enlarges the recognizance to a later time under section 129 of the Act in his absence, it shall give him and his sureties, if any, notice thereof.

(2) If a magistrates' court, under section 129(4) of the Act of 1980, enlarges the recognizance of a surety for a person committed for trial on bail, it shall give the surety notice thereof.

****

86 Requirements to be complied with before release

(1) Where a magistrates' court has fixed the amount in which a person (including any surety) is to be bound by a recognizance, the recognizance may be entered into –

- (a) in the case of a surety in connection with bail in criminal proceedings where the accused is in a prison or other place of detention, before the governor or keeper of the prison or place as well as before the persons mentioned in section 8(4)(a) of the Bail Act 1976;
- (b) in any other case, before a justice of the peace, a justices' clerk, the designated officer for a magistrates' court, a police officer who either is of the rank of inspector or above or is in charge of a police station or, if the person to be bound is in a prison or other place of detention, before the governor or keeper of the prison or place; or
- (c) where a person other than a police officer is authorised under section 125A or 125B of the Act of 1980 to execute a warrant of arrest providing for a recognizance to be entered into by the person arrested (but not by any other person), before the person executing the warrant.

(2) The designated officer for a magistrates' court which has fixed the amount in which a person (including any surety) is to be bound by a recognizance or, under section 3(5), (6) or (6A) of the Bail Act 1976, imposed any requirement to be complied with before a person's release on bail or any condition of bail shall issue a certificate showing the amount and conditions, if any, of the recognizance or, as the case may be, containing a statement of the requirement or condition of bail; and a person authorised to take the recognizance or do anything in relation to the compliance with such requirement or condition of bail shall not be required to take or do it without production of the certificate as aforesaid.

(3) If any person proposed as a surety for a person committed to custody by a magistrates' court produces to the governor or keeper of the prison or other place of detention in which the person so committed is detained a certificate to the effect that he is acceptable as a surety, signed by any of the justices composing the court or the clerk of the court and signed in the margin by the person proposed as surety, the governor or keeper shall take the recognizance of the person so proposed.

(4) Where the recognizance of any person committed to custody by a magistrates' court or of any surety of such a person is taken by any person other than the court which committed the first-mentioned person to custody, the person taking the recognizance shall send it to the designated officer for that court:

Provided that, in the case of a surety, if the person committed has been committed to the Crown Court for trial or under any of the enactments mentioned in rule 17(1), the person taking the recognizance shall send it to the appropriate officer of the Crown Court.

Amendments—SI 2001/167; SI 2001/610; SI 2003/1236; SI 2005/617.

87 Notice to governor of prison etc where release from custody is ordered

Where a magistrates' court has, with a view to the release on bail of a person in custody, fixed the amount in which he or any surety of such a person shall be bound or, under section 3(5), (6) or (6A) of the Bail Act 1976, imposed any requirement to be complied with before his release or any condition of bail –

   (a)   the designated officer for the court shall give notice thereof to the governor or keeper of the prison or place where that person is detained by sending him such a certificate as is mentioned in rule 86(2);

   (b)   any person authorised to take the recognizance of a surety or do anything in relation to the compliance with such requirement shall, on taking or doing it, send notice thereof by post to the said governor or keeper and, in the case of a recognizance of a surety, shall give a copy of the notice to the surety.

Amendments—SI 2001/610; SI 2003/1236.

88 Release when recognizances have been taken or requirements complied with

Where a magistrates' court has, with a view to the release on bail of a person in custody, fixed the amount in which he or any surety of such a person shall be bound or, under section 3(5) or (6) of the Bail Act 1976, imposed any requirement to be complied with before his release and given notice thereof in accordance with these Rules to the governor or keeper of the prison or place where that person is detained, the governor or keeper shall, when satisfied that the recognizances of all sureties required have been taken and that all such requirements have been complied with –

   (a)   in the case of bail in criminal proceedings, unless he is in custody for some other cause, release him;

   (b)   in the case of bail otherwise than in criminal proceedings, take the recognizances of that person if this has not already been done and, unless he is in custody for some other cause, release him.

****

Warrant

94 Committal to custody to be by warrant

A justice of the peace shall not commit any person to a prison, young offender institution or a remand centre, or to a police station under section 128(7) of the Act of 1980, or to customs detention under section 152 of the Criminal Justice Act 1988 except by a warrant of commitment.

Amendments—Substituted by SI 1988/2132.

95 Warrant to be signed

Except where signature by the clerk of a magistrates' court is permitted by rule 109 or by the Magistrates' Courts (Forms) Rules 1981, every warrant under the Act of 1980 shall be signed by the justice issuing it.

95A Warrant issued out of hours

Where a warrant is issued by a justice of the peace for any local justice area at a time when the office of the designated officer for that area is closed, the applicant for the warrant shall within 72 hours serve upon the designated officer any information on which the warrant was issued.

Amendments—Inserted by SI 1993/1183; amended by SI 2001/610; SI 2005/617.

96 Warrant of arrest

(1) A warrant issued by a justice of the peace for the arrest of any person shall require the persons to whom it is directed, that is to say, the constables of the police area in which the warrant is issued, or the civilian enforcement officers for the police area specified in the warrant, or any persons named in that behalf in the warrant, to arrest the person against whom the warrant is issued.

(2) The warrant shall name or otherwise describe the person for whose arrest it is issued, and shall contain a statement of the offence charged in the information or, as the case may be, the ground on which the warrant is issued.

(3) A warrant to which this rule applies may be executed by the persons to whom it was directed or by any of the following persons, whether or not the warrant was directed to them –

    (a) a constable for any police area in England and Wales, acting in his own police area;

    (b) where the warrant is one to which section 125A of the Act of 1980 applies, a civilian enforcement officer within the meaning of section 125A of the Act of 1980;

    (c) where the warrant is one to which section 125A of the Act of 1980 applies, any of the individuals described in section 125B(1) of the Act of 1980;

and in this rule any reference to the person charged with the execution of a warrant includes any of the above persons who is for the time being authorised to execute the warrant, whether or not they have the warrant in their possession at the time.

(4) A person executing a warrant of arrest shall, upon arresting the person against whom the warrant is issued –

    (a) either

        (i) if he has the warrant with him, show it to the person against whom the warrant is issued, or

        (ii) otherwise, state where the warrant is and what arrangements may be made to allow the person arrested to inspect it;

    (b) explain, in ordinary language, the offence or default with which the person is charged and the reason for the arrest;

    (c) where the person executing the warrant is one of the persons referred to in paragraph (3)(b) or (c) above, show the person arrested a written statement under section 125A(4) or 125B(4) as appropriate; and

    (d) in any case, show documentary proof of his identity.

(5) A warrant of arrest issued under any of the provisions in paragraph (6) shall cease to have effect when –

PART III

   (a)   the sum in respect of which the warrant is issued is paid to the person charged with the execution of the warrant;

   (b)   that sum is tendered to and refused by the person charged with the execution of the warrant; or

   (c)   a receipt for that sum given by –

      (i)   the designated officer for the court which issued the warrant; or

      (ii)   the charging or billing authority,

      is produced to the person charged with the execution of the warrant.

(6) Those provisions are –

   (a)   sections 83(1), 83(2), 86(4) and 93(5) of the Act of 1980;

   (b)   (*revoked*)

   (c)   regulation 17(5)(b) of the Non-Domestic Rating (Collection and Enforcement) (Local Lists) Regulations 1989; and

   (d)   regulation 48(5)(b) of the Council Tax (Administration and Enforcement) Regulations 1992.

Amendments—SI 2001/167; SI 2003/1236.

Defined terms—"the authorised persons for the police area": r 2(4).

97 Warrant of commitment

(1) A warrant of commitment or detention, other than a warrant committing a person to customs detention under section 152 of the Criminal Justice Act 1988, issued by a justice of the peace –

   (a)   shall name or otherwise describe the person committed or detained;

   (b)   shall contain a statement of the offence with which the person committed or detained is charged, or of which he has been convicted, or of any other ground on which he is committed;

   (c)   shall be directed to a person named in the warrant or to the constables of the police area in which the warrant is issued or to the civilian enforcement officers for the area in which they are employed and to the governor or keeper of the prison or place of detention specified in the warrant, and shall require –

      (i)   the named person or the constables or civilian enforcement officers to arrest the person committed or detained, if he is at large, and convey him to that prison or place and deliver him with the warrant to the governor or keeper;

      (ii)   the governor or keeper to keep in his custody the person committed or detained until that person be delivered in due course of law, or until the happening of an event specified in the warrant, or for the period specified in the warrant, as the case may be.

(1A) A warrant issued by a justice of the peace committing a person to customs detention under section 152 of the Criminal Justice Act 1988 –

   (a)   shall name or otherwise describe the person committed;

   (b)   shall contain a statement of the offence with which the person committed is charged;

   (c)   shall be directed to the officers of Her Majesty's Customs and Excise and shall require those officers to keep the person committed in their custody, unless in the meantime he be otherwise delivered in due course of law, for a period (not exceeding 192 hours) specified in the warrant.

(1B) A warrant of commitment or detention other than a warrant committing a person to customs detention under section 152 of the Criminal Justice Act 1988 may be executed by the persons to whom it was directed or by any of the following persons, whether or not the warrant was directed to them –

(a) a constable for any police area in England and Wales, acting in his own police area;

(b) where the warrant is one to which section 125A of the Act of 1980 applies, a civilian enforcement officer within the meaning of section 125A of the Act of 1980;

(c) where the warrant is one to which section 125A of the Act of 1980 applies, any of the individuals described in section 125B(1) of the Act of 1980;

and in this rule any reference to the person charged with the execution of a warrant includes any of the above persons who is for the time being authorised to execute the warrant, whether or not they have the warrant in their possession at the time.

(1C) A person executing a warrant of commitment or detention shall, upon arresting the person against whom the warrant is issued –

(a) either

    (i) if he has the warrant with him, show it to the person against whom the warrant is issued, or

    (ii) otherwise, state where the warrant is and what arrangements may be made to allow the person against whom the warrant was issued to inspect it;

(b) explain, in ordinary language, the offence or default with which the person is charged and the reason for the commitment or detention;

(c) where the person executing the warrant is one of the persons referred to in paragraph (1B)(b) or (c) above, show the person against whom the warrant was issued a written statement under section 125A(4) or 125B(4) as appropriate; and

(d) in any case, show documentary proof of his identity.

(2) A warrant of commitment or detention, other than a warrant committing a person to customs detention under section 152 of the Criminal Justice Act 1988, may be executed by conveying the person committed or detained to any prison or place of detention in which he may lawfully be detained and delivering him there together with the warrant; and, so long as any person is detained in any such prison or place other than that specified in the warrant, the warrant shall have effect as if the other prison or place were the prison or place specified in it.

(3) Notwithstanding the preceding provisions of this rule, a warrant of commitment or detention issued in pursuance of a valid conviction, or of a valid order requiring the person committed or detained to do or abstain from doing anything, shall not, if it alleges that the person committed or detained has been convicted, or ordered to do or abstain from doing that thing, be held void by reason of any defect in the warrant.

(4) The governor or keeper of the prison or place of detention at which any person is delivered in pursuance of a warrant of commitment or detention shall give to the constable or other person making the delivery a receipt for that person.

(5) Notwithstanding the preceding provisions of this rule, a warrant of a justice of the peace to commit to custody any person who to the justice's knowledge is already detained in a prison or other place of detention shall be delivered to the governor or keeper of the prison or place of detention in which that person is detained.

(6) A warrant of commitment or detention issued under any of the provisions in paragraph (7) shall cease to have effect if, at any time before the person for whose commitment or detention the warrant was issued is placed in custody –

    (a)   the sum in respect of which the warrant is issued, together with the costs and charges, if any, of the commitment, is paid to the person charged with the execution of the warrant;

    (b)   that sum is tendered to and refused by the person charged with the execution of the warrant; or

    (c)   a receipt for that sum given by –

        (i)   the designated officer for the court which issued the warrant; or

        (ii) the charging or billing authority,

        is produced to the person charged with the execution of the warrant.

(7) Those provisions are –

    (a)   sections 76 and 136 of the Act of 1980;

    (b)   section 40 of the Child Support Act 1991;

    (c)   (*revoked*)

    (d)   regulation 16(3)(a) of the Non-Domestic Rating (Collection and Enforcement) (Local Lists) Regulations 1989; and

    (e)   regulation 47(3)(a) of the Council Tax (Administration and Enforcement) Regulations 1992.

(8) A warrant of commitment issued for the enforcement of a maintenance order to which Part I of the Maintenance Orders Act 1958 applies shall cease to have effect if, at any time when the defendant is not already detained in pursuance of the warrant, the person charged with the execution of the warrant is informed –

    (a)   that an application for registration of the order has been granted under section 2 of the Maintenance Orders Act 1958; or

    (b)   that notice seeking the cancellation of such registration has been given under section 5 of that Act.

Amendments—SI 1988/2132; SI 1990/1190; SI 2001/167; SI 2003/1236.

Defined terms—"the authorised persons for the police area": r 2(4).

Procedure—For the form of a warrant of commitment see MC(MOA 1958)R 1959.

Circumstances in which warrant may be held void (r 97(3))—Despite the general rule that a warrant "shall not … be held void by virtue of a defect", it may be avoided in the case of a fundamental error. In *R v Doherty ex parte Isaacs* (1910) 74 JP 304, a warrant was issued in error on the grounds of non-payment of an order although payment had been made; the warrant was quashed by certiorari.

Summons

98 Form of summons

(1) A summons shall be signed by the justice issuing it or state his name and be authenticated by the signature of the clerk of a magistrates' court.

(2) A summons requiring a person to appear before a magistrates' court to answer to an information or complaint shall state shortly the matter of the information or complaint and shall state the time and place at which the defendant is required by the summons to appear.

(3) A single summons may be issued against a person in respect of several informations or complaints; but the summons shall state the matter of each information or complaint separately and shall have effect as several summonses, each issued in respect of one information or complaint.

(4) In this rule where a signature is required, an electronic signature incorporated into the document shall satisfy this requirement.

Amendments—SI 2003/1236.

"**signed by the justice**" (r 98(1))—The signature may be in the form of a rubber stamp and may be applied by the justice or a person acting with his general or specific authority (*R v Brentford Justices ex parte Catlin*) [1975] QB 455). For power to authorise the signature of summonses in batches, see *R v Gateshead Justices ex parte Tesco Stores* [1981] QB 470. Summonses may be signed by a justices' clerk (r 109 and JCR 2005).

99 Service of summons etc

(1) Service of a summons issued by a justice of the peace on a person other than a corporation may be effected –

   (a)   by delivering it to the person to whom it is directed; or
   (b)   by leaving it for him with some person at his last known or usual place of abode; or
   (c)   by sending it by post in a letter addressed to him at his last known or usual place of abode.

(2) (*revoked*)

(3) Service for the purposes of the Act of 1980 of a summons issued by a justice of the peace on a corporation may be effected by delivering it at, or sending it by post to, the registered office of the corporation, if that office is the United Kingdom, or, if there is no registered office in the United Kingdom, any place in the United Kingdom where the corporation trades or conducts its business.

(4) Paragraph (3) shall have effect in relation to a document (other than a summons) issued by a justice of the peace as it has effect in relation to a summons so issued, but with the substitution of references to England and Wales for the references to the United Kingdom.

(5) Any summons or other document served in manner authorised by the preceding provisions of this rule shall, for the purposes of any enactment other than the Act of 1980 or these Rules requiring a summons or other document to be served in any particular manner, be deemed to have been as effectively served as if it had been served in that manner; and nothing in this rule shall render invalid the service of a summons or other document in that manner.

(6) Sub-paragraph (c) of paragraph (1) shall not authorise the service by post of –

   (a)   a summons requiring the attendance of any person to give evidence or produce a document or thing; or
   (b)   a summons issued under any enactment relating to the liability of members of the naval, military or air forces of the Crown for the maintenance of their husbands, wives or civil partners, as the case may be, and children, whether legitimate or illegitimate.

(7) In the case of a summons issued on an application for an order under section 16 or 17(1) of the Act of 1978 (powers of court to make orders for the protection of a party to a marriage or a child of the family) service of the summons shall not be effected in manner authorised by sub-paragraph (b) or (c) of paragraph (1) unless a justice of the peace is satisfied by evidence on oath that prompt personal service of the summons is impracticable and allows service to be effected in such manner.

(8) Where this rule or any other of these Rules provides that a summons or other document may be sent by post to a person's last known or usual place of abode that rule shall have effect as if it provided also for the summons or other document to be sent in the manner specified in the rule to an address given by that person for that purpose.

(9) This rule shall not apply to a judgment summons.

Amendments—SI 1983/523; SI 1993/1183; SI 2005/2930.

Service of summons—Service may be proved in accordance with r 67.

Service in Scotland and Northern Ireland—See also Summary Jurisdiction (Process) Act 1881, s 4 and MOA 1950, s 15 for service in Scotland and Northern Ireland.

"place of abode" (r 99(1))—Service under r 99(1)(b) or (c) is not permitted other than at the person's place of abode, although postal service at a person's business premises is permissible if that address has been nominated under r 99(8).

Proof of service (r 99(1))—The same degree of proof of service is required in the case of an adjournment notice in family proceedings (*Unitt v Unitt* (1981) 2 FLR 89).

Service by post—Although postal service is normally effective, a witness summons may not be served by post (r 99(6)).

Judgment summons (r 99(9))—For service of a judgment summons see r 58.

****

Miscellaneous
****

105 Application for alteration of maintenance agreement under s 35 of Matrimonial Causes Act 1973 or under paragraph 69 of Schedule 5 to the Civil Partnership Act 2004 or under s 15 of the Family Law Reform Act 1987

An application to a magistrates' court under section 35 of the Matrimonial Causes Act 1973, under paragraph 69 of Schedule 5 to the Civil Partnership Act 2004 for the alteration of a maintenance agreement shall be by complaint.

Amendments—SI 1989/384; SI 1991/1991; SI 2005/2930.

106 Proceedings against person outside the United Kingdom on application for variation etc of certain maintenance orders

(1) The period referred to in section 41(2A) of the Maintenance Orders (Reciprocal Enforcement) Act 1972 (which provide that, subject to certain conditions, a magistrates' court may, if it is satisfied that the respondent has been outside the United Kingdom during such period as may be prescribed by rules, proceed on an application made under sections 11B or 11C of the Guardianship of Minors Act 1971 notwithstanding that the respondent has not been served with the summons) shall be the whole of the period beginning one month before the making of the application and ending with the date of the hearing.

(2) Before proceeding in any such case as is referred to in the said section 41(2A), the court shall be satisfied that, in addition to the matter referred to in those subsections, the applicant has taken steps to notify the respondent of the making of the application and of the time and place appointed for the hearing by –

  (a) causing a notice in writing to that effect to be delivered to the respondent; or
  (b) causing a notice in writing to that effect to be sent by post addressed to the respondent at his last known or usual place of abode or at his place of business or at such other address at which there is ground for believing that it will reach the respondent, in accordance with directions given for the purpose by a justice of the peace acting in the same local justice area as that of the court; or
  (c) causing a notice to that effect to be inserted in one or more newspapers, in accordance with directions given as aforesaid;

and that it is reasonable in all the circumstances to proceed in the absence of the respondent.

(3) In any such case as is referred to in the said section 41(2A), the court shall not make the order for which the application is made unless it is satisfied that during the period of 6 months immediately preceding the making of the application the respondent was continuously outside the United Kingdom or was not in the United Kingdom on more than 30 days and that, having regard to any communication to the court in writing purporting to be from the respondent, it is reasonable in all the circumstances so to do.

(4) Paragraph (1) of rule 67 of these Rules shall apply for the purpose of proving the delivery of a written notice in pursuance of paragraph (2)(a) as it applies for the purpose of proving the service of a summons.

In relation to a solemn declaration made outside the United Kingdom, paragraph (1) of the said rule 67 as applied by this paragraph, shall have effect as if for the reference to the authorities mentioned in the said paragraph (1) there were substituted a reference to a consular officer of Her Majesty's Government in the United Kingdom or any person for the time being authorised by law, in the place where the declarant is, to administer an oath for any judicial or other legal purpose.

(5) Paragraph (2) of the said rule 67 shall apply for the purpose of proving the sending of a written notice in pursuance of paragraph (2)(b) or the insertion of a notice in a newspaper in pursuance of paragraph (2)(c) as it applies for the purpose of proving the service of any process, provided, as respects the insertion of a notice in a newspaper, that a copy of the newspaper containing the notice is annexed to the certificate.

Amendments—SI 1989/384; SI 2005/617.

107 Application for summons to witness or warrant for his arrest

(1) An application for the issue of a summons or warrant under section 97 or 97A of the Act of 1980 or paragraph 4 of Schedule 3 to the Act of 1998 may be made by the applicant in person or by his counsel or solicitor.

(2) An application for the issue of such a summons may be made by delivering or sending the application in writing to the designated officer for the magistrates' court.

Amendments—SI 1983/523; SI 1997/706; SI 2000/3361; SI 2001/610.

****

109 Signature of forms prescribed by rules made under the Act of 1980

(1) Subject to paragraph (2), where any form prescribed by Rules made or having effect as if made under section 144 of the Act of 1980 contains provision for signature by a justice of the peace only, the form shall have effect as if it contained provision in the alternative for signature by the clerk of a magistrates' court.

(2) This rule shall not apply to any form of warrant, other than a warrant of commitment or of distress, or to any form prescribed in the Magistrates' Courts (Forms) Rules 1981.

(3) In this rule where a signature is required on a form or warrant other than an arrest, remand or commitment warrant, an electronic signature incorporated into the document will satisfy this requirement.

Amendments—SI 2003/1236.

****

Supreme Court Rules 2009, SI 2009/1603

PART 1
INTERPRETATION AND SCOPE

CONTENTS OF THIS PART

1 Citation and commencement

These Rules may be cited as the Supreme Court Rules 2009 and shall come into force on 1 October 2009.

2 Scope and objective

(1) These Rules apply to civil and criminal appeals to the Court and to appeals and references under the Court's devolution jurisdiction.

(2) The overriding objective of these Rules is to secure that the Court is accessible, fair and efficient.

(3) The Court must interpret and apply these Rules with a view to securing that the Court is accessible, fair and efficient and that unnecessary disputes over procedural matters are discouraged.

The overriding objective (r 2(2))—The SCR follow the example of the CPR in declaring at the outset the "overriding objective" of the rules. It will be noted that the overriding objective of the SCR is very different from that in Pt 1 of the CPR. There is no statement comparable to the declaration in CPR 1998, r 1.1(1) that these Rules are "a new procedural code", presumably out of a desire to avoid stating the obvious.

"unnecessary disputes over procedural matters are discouraged" (r 2(3))—Compare CPR 1998, r 1.3.

3 Interpretation

(1) In these Rules –

"the Act" means the Constitutional Reform Act 2005;
"the Court" means the Supreme Court of the United Kingdom;
"Justice" means a judge of the Court and includes its President and Deputy President;
"the Registrar" means the Registrar of the Court;
"the Registry" means the Registry of the Court.

(2) In these Rules except where the context otherwise requires –

"appellant" means a person who files an application for permission to appeal or who files a notice of appeal;

"business day" means any day other than a Saturday, Sunday, Christmas Day, Good Friday or a bank holiday under the Banking and Financial Dealings Act 1971, in England and Wales;

"certificate of service" means a certificate given under rule 6;

"counsel" includes any person with the right to be heard as an advocate at a full hearing before the Court;

"court below" means the court from which an appeal (or application for permission to appeal) is made to the Court;

"court officer" means the Registrar or a member of the court staff;

"devolution jurisdiction" means the jurisdiction transferred to the Court by section 40 of, and Schedule 9 to, the Act;

"electronic means" means CD ROMs, memory sticks, email, fax or other means of electronic communication of the contents of documents;

"filing" means filing in the Registry in accordance with rule 7 and related expressions have corresponding meanings;

"form" and the "appropriate form" have the meanings given by rule 4;

"panel of Justices" means a panel of at least three Justices;

"party" means an appellant, a respondent and a person who has been given permission to intervene under rule 26;

"the relevant officer" means –

(a) in relation to proceedings in England and Wales, the Attorney General and, in relation to proceedings that particularly affect Wales, the Counsel General to the Welsh Assembly Government,

(b) in relation to proceedings in Scotland, the Advocate General for Scotland and the Lord Advocate; and

(c) in relation to proceedings in Northern Ireland, the Advocate General for Northern Ireland and (when section 22 of the Justice (Northern Ireland) Act 2002 comes into force) the Attorney General for Northern Ireland;

"requisite number of copies" means the number of copies which are to be provided under the relevant practice direction or as directed by the Court;

"respondent" includes a respondent to an application for permission to appeal and means –

(a) a person other than the appellant who was a party to the proceedings in the court below and who is affected by the appeal; and

(b) a person who is permitted by the Court to be a party to the appeal;

"service" and related expressions have the meanings given by rule 6;

"solicitor" includes any person authorised to provide legal services other than as counsel in connection with proceedings before the Court.

(3) References in these Rules to a practice direction means a practice direction issued by the President of the Court.

(4) References in these Rules or in any form to a party's signing, filing or serving any document or taking any other procedural step include the signature, filing or service of that document or the taking of such other procedural step by the party's solicitor.

(5) Where any of these Rules or any practice direction requires a document to be signed, that requirement shall be satisfied if the signature is printed by computer or other mechanical means.

(6) Where these Rules require or permit the Court to perform an act of a formal or administrative character, that act may be performed by a court officer.

"a practice direction" (r 3(3))—The *Supreme Court Practice Direction*s (referred to below as SCPD) may be found at *www.supremecourt.gov.uk/procedures/practice-directions.html* and are clearly expressed in up-to-date language.

PART III

"signature ... printed by computer or other mechanical means" (r 3(5))—Compare para 10.1 of *PD 5C – Electronic Working Pilot Schemes*, which supplements CPR 1998, r 5.5.

4 Forms

(1) In these Rules, a form means a form set out in a practice direction and a reference to the "appropriate form" means the form provided by the relevant practice direction for any particular case.

(2) The forms shall be used in the cases to which they apply, and in the circumstances for which they are provided by the relevant practice direction, but a form may be varied by the Court or a party if the variation is required by the circumstances of a particular case.

5 Time limits

(1) The Court may extend or shorten any time limit set by these Rules or any relevant practice direction (unless to do so would be contrary to any enactment).

(2) The Court may exercise these powers either on an application by one or more parties or without an application being made.

(3) The Registrar must notify the parties when a time limit is varied under this rule.

(4) An application for an extension of time may be granted after the time limit has expired.

(5) Where a party to a proposed appeal has applied for public funding and the Registrar is informed of the application, the time limits in rules 11 and 19 shall be extended until 28 days after the final determination of the application for public funding.

(6) When the period specified –

    (a) by these Rules or a practice direction, or

    (b) by any judgment or court order,

for doing any act at the Registry ends on a day on which the Registry is closed, that act shall be in time if done on the next day on which the Registry is open.

6 Service

(1) A document may be served by any of the following methods –

    (a) personal service;

    (b) first class post (or an alternative service which provides for delivery on the next working day);

    (c) (with the consent of the party to be served) through a document exchange;

    (d) (with the consent of the party to be served or at the direction of the Registrar) by electronic means in accordance with the relevant practice direction.

(2) Where the address of the person on whom a document is to be served is unknown, the Registrar may direct that service is effected by an alternative method of service.

(3) A document served by first-class post or through a document exchange will be taken to have been served on the second day after it was posted or left at the document exchange, as the case may be (not including days which are not business days).

(4) A certificate of service must give details of the persons served, the method of service used and must state the date on which the document was served personally, posted, delivered to the document exchange or sent electronically, as the case may be.

"the address of the person on whom a document is to be served is unknown" (r 6(2))—Note that this is much more restrictive than the provisions in CPR 1998, r 6.15 for service "by an alternative method".

7 Filing

(1) A document may be filed by any of the following methods –

(a)   personal delivery;

(b)   first class post (or an alternative service which provides for delivery on the next working day);

(c)   through a document exchange;

(d)   (with the consent of the Registrar) by electronic means in accordance with the relevant practice direction.

(2) A document filed by first-class post or through a document exchange will be taken to have been filed on the second day after it was posted or left at the document exchange, as the case may be (not including days which are not business days).

(3) Except with the consent of the Registrar, the contents of documents –

(a)   filed in hard copy must also be provided to the Registry by electronic means, and

(b)   filed by electronic means must also be provided to the Registry in hard copy,

in accordance with the relevant practice direction.

(4) A court officer must seal the following documents when they are filed –

(a)   an application for permission to appeal,

(b)   a notice of objection or acknowledgement by the respondent,

(c)   a notice of appeal,

(d)   an application form,

and may place the seal on the document by hand or by printing a facsimile of the seal on the document whether electronically or otherwise.

(5) A document purporting to bear the Court's seal shall be admissible in evidence without further proof.

"the contents of documents ... filed by electronic means must also be provided to the Registry in hard copy" (r 7(3))—Note particularly that the Supreme Court's requirements are diametrically opposite to those meant to prevail in the courts below under para 8.1 of *PD 5B – Electronic Communication and Filing of Documents* (which supplements CPR 1998, r 5.5): "Where a party files a document electronically, he *must not* send a hard copy of that document to the court".

8 Non-compliance with these Rules

(1) Any failure by a party to comply with these Rules or any relevant practice direction shall not have the effect of making the proceedings invalid.

(2) Where any provision in these Rules or any relevant practice direction is not complied with, the Court may give whatever directions appear appropriate, having regard to the seriousness of the non-compliance and generally to the circumstances of the case.

(3) In particular, the Registrar may refuse to accept any document which does not comply with any provision in these Rules or any relevant practice direction and may give whatever directions appear appropriate.

(4) Directions given under this rule may include the summary dismissal of an appeal or debarring a respondent from resisting an appeal.

9 Procedural decisions

(1) Subject to paragraph (2), the powers of the Court under the following rules may be exercised by a single Justice or the Registrar without an oral hearing –

(a)   rule 5 (time limits),

(b)   rule 8 (non-compliance with Rules),

    (c)   rule 33 (change of interest),

    (d)   rule 34 (withdrawal of appeal),

    (e)   rule 35 (advocate to the Court and assessors),

    (f)   rule 36 (security for costs),

    (g)   rule 37 (stay of execution) and

    (h)   rule 41 (devolution jurisdiction).

(2) Any contested application –

    (a)   alleging contempt of the Court; or

    (b)   for a direction under rule 8 dismissing an appeal or debarring a respondent from resisting an appeal; or

    (c)   for security for costs,

shall be referred to a panel of Justices who shall, in a case of alleged contempt, and may, in any other case, hold an oral hearing.

(3) Where under these Rules any matter falls to be decided by a single Justice, that Justice may, where it appears appropriate, direct an oral hearing or may refer the matter to a panel of Justices to be decided with or without an oral hearing.

(4) Where under these Rules any matter falls to be decided by the Registrar, the Registrar may –

    (a)   direct an oral hearing;

    (b)   refer the matter to a single Justice (and paragraphs (1) and (3) shall then apply);

    (c)   refer the matter to a panel of Justices to be decided with or without an oral hearing.

(5) A party may apply for a decision of the Registrar to be reviewed by a single Justice (in which case paragraphs (1) and (3) shall apply) and any application under this rule must be made in the appropriate form and be filed within 14 days of the Registrar's decision.

(6) Subject to rule 27, oral hearings on procedural matters must be heard in open court or in a place to which the public are admitted.

(7) If any procedural question arises which is not dealt with by these Rules, the Court or the Registrar may adopt any procedure that is consistent with the overriding objective, the Act and these Rules.

PART 2
APPLICATION FOR PERMISSION TO APPEAL

CONTENTS OF THIS PART

10 Form of application

(1) Every application to the Court for permission to appeal shall be made in the appropriate form.

(2) An application for permission to appeal must be made first to the court below, and an application may be made to the Supreme Court only after the court below has refused to grant permission to appeal.

"the appropriate form" (r 10(1))—This is Form 1 (see SCPD 3 para 3.1.2 and SCPD 7 Annex 1).

11 Filing of application

(1) Subject to any enactment which makes special provision with regard to any particular category of appeal, an application for permission to appeal must be filed within 28 days from the date of the order or decision of the court below.

(2) The Registrar may refuse to accept any application on the ground that –

    (a)   the Court does not have jurisdiction under section 40 of the Act to issue it;

    (b)   it contains no reasonable grounds; or

    (c)   it is an abuse of process,

and may give whatever directions appear appropriate.

> (Section 2 of the Administration of Justice Act 1960 provides that an application for permission to appeal to the Supreme Court in a case involving civil contempt of court must be filed within 14 days, beginning with the date on which the application for permission is refused by the court below.)

> (Section 13 of the Administration of Justice Act 1969 provides that an application for permission to appeal to the Supreme Court in a "leapfrog appeal" from the High Court must be filed within one month from the date on which the High Court judge grants a certificate under section 12.)

12 Service of application

Before the application is filed, a copy must be served –

    (a)   on every respondent, and

    (b)   on any person who was an intervener in the court below,

and, when the application is filed, the appellant must file a certificate of service.

13 Notice of objection by respondent

(1) Each respondent who wishes to object to the application must, within 14 days after service, file notice of objection in the appropriate form together with a certificate of service.

(2) Before the notice is filed, a copy must be served on –

    (a)   he appellant,

    (b)   any other respondent, and

    (c)   any person who was an intervener in the court below.

(3) A respondent who does not file notice under this rule will not be permitted to participate in the application and will not be given notice of its progress.

"the appropriate form" (r 13(1))—This is Form 3 (SCPD 3, para 3.1.8 and SCPD 7, Annex 1).

14 Documents in support of application

(1) The requisite number of copies of the application must be filed together with –

PART III

(a)   a copy of the order appealed from, and

(b)   (if separate) a copy of any order refusing permission to appeal

and, if the order appealed from is not immediately available, the application should be filed without delay and the order filed as soon as it is available.

(2) The appellant must file the further documents required for the use of the Court within 7 days after filing the application.

"requisite number of copies" (r 14(1))—There is a helpful table at SCPD 7, para 7.2.3, setting out the number of copies of various documents required at various stages of the Court's procedures.

"the further documents required" (r 14(2))—See SCPD 3 para 3.2.1.

15 Interventions in applications

(1) Any person and in particular –

(a)   any official body or non-governmental organization seeking to make submissions in the public interest or

(b)   any person with an interest in proceedings by way of judicial review,

may make written submissions to the Court in support of an application for permission to appeal and request that the Court takes them into account.

(2) Before the submissions are filed, a copy must be served on –

(a)   the appellant,

(b)   every respondent, and

(c)   any person who was an intervener in the court below

and the requisite number of copies of the submissions must be filed together with a certificate of service.

(3) Any submissions which are made shall be referred to the panel of Justices which considers the application for permission to appeal.

(4) If permission to appeal is granted –

(a)   a person whose submissions were taken into account by the panel will be notified but, if that person wishes to intervene in the appeal, an application must be made under rule 26;

(b)   the appellant must notify any person who was an intervener in the court below whether or not that person made submissions under this rule.

16 Consideration on paper

(1) Every admissible application for permission to appeal (together with any submissions made under rule 15 and any respondent's notice of objection) shall be considered on paper without a hearing by a panel of Justices.

(2) The panel may –

(a)   grant or refuse permission to advance all or any of the grounds of appeal;

(b)   invite the parties to file written submissions within 14 days as to the grant of permission on terms (whether as to costs or otherwise); or

(c)   direct an oral hearing.

(3) Where the panel has invited the parties' submissions as to terms, it shall reconsider the application on paper without a hearing and may refuse permission or grant permission (either unconditionally or on terms) to advance all or any of the grounds of appeal.

(4) Where the panel grants permission to advance limited grounds of appeal it shall (unless it directs otherwise) be taken to have refused permission to advance the other grounds.

(5) An order of the Court shall be prepared and sealed by the Registrar to record any decision made under this rule.

17 Oral hearing of application

(1) Where the panel has directed an oral hearing, the appellant and every respondent who has given notice under rule 13 will be informed of the date of the oral hearing.

(2) An order of the Court shall be prepared and sealed by the Registrar to record any decision made under this rule.

PART 3
COMMENCEMENT AND PREPARATION OF APPEAL

CONTENTS OF THIS PART

18 Form and filing of notice where permission granted by the Court

(1) Where the Court grants permission to appeal, rules 19 and 20 shall not apply and

    (a) the application for permission to appeal shall stand as the notice of appeal;

    (b) the grounds of appeal shall be limited to those on which permission has been granted;

    (c) the appellant must, within 14 days of the grant by the Court of permission to appeal, file notice under this rule of an intention to proceed with the appeal.

(2) When notice is filed under rule 18(1)(c), the application for permission to appeal will be resealed and the appellant must then –

    (a) serve a copy on each respondent and on any person who was an intervener in the court below or whose submissions were taken into account under rule 15; and

    (b) file the requisite number of copies and a certificate of service.

(3) In any other case an appellant must file a notice of appeal under rule 19.

19 Form and filing of notice where permission not required

(1) Every notice of appeal shall be made in the appropriate form.

(2) The notice of appeal together with the requisite number of copies must be filed within 42 days of the date of the order or decision of the court below.

(3) The appellant must also file –

    (a)   a copy of the order appealed from and

    (b)   (if separate) a copy of the order granting permission to appeal

and, if the order appealed from is not immediately available, the notice of appeal must be filed without delay and the order filed as soon as it is available.

20 Service of notice

(1) Before the notice of appeal is filed, a copy must be served on each respondent and on any person who was an intervener in the court below.

(2) When the notice of appeal is filed, the appellant must file a certificate of service.

21 Acknowledgement by respondent

(1) Each respondent who intends to participate in the appeal must, within 14 days after service under rule 18(2)(a) or 20, file notice in the appropriate form together with a certificate of service.

(2) Before the notice is filed, a copy must be served on –

    (a)   the appellant,

    (b)   any other respondent, and

    (c)   any person who was an intervener in the court below or whose submissions were taken into account under rule 15.

(3) A respondent who does not file notice under this rule will not be permitted to participate in the appeal and will not be given notice of its progress.

22 Documents for appeal hearing

(1) Within 112 days after the filing of the notice under rule 18(1)(c) or the filing of the notice of appeal, the appellant must file –

    (a)   a statement of the relevant facts and issues; and

    (b)   an appendix (prepared in accordance with the relevant practice direction) of the essential documents which were in evidence before, or which record the proceedings in, the courts below.

(2) Both the statement and the appendix must be submitted to, and agreed with, every respondent before being filed.

(3) Within 7 days after the filing of the statement and the appendix, every party must –

    (a)   notify the Registrar that the appeal is ready for listing, and

    (b)   specify the number of hours that their respective counsel estimate to be necessary for their oral submissions

and the Registrar will subsequently inform the parties of the date fixed for the hearing.

(4) The appellant and every respondent (and any intervener and advocate to the Court) must then sequentially exchange their respective written cases and file them, and every respondent (and any intervener and advocate to the Court) must for the purposes of rule 23 provide copies of their respective written cases, in compliance with the relevant practice direction.

23 The core volumes

As soon as the parties' cases have been exchanged and in any event not later than 14 days before the date fixed for the hearing the appellant must file the requisite number of core volumes and, if necessary, additional volumes containing further parts of the appendix, in compliance with the relevant practice direction.

"must file the requisite number of core volumes"—Note that as one would expect from r 7(3), the contents of the core volumes must also be filed electronically. The SCPD set out detailed provisions as to the preferred format of the electronic copy. It should be noted that if core volumes or other documents exceed 10 megabytes they must be submitted on a memory stick – another respect in which the Supreme Court is breaking new ground.

24 Authorities

The volumes of authorities that may be referred to during the hearing must be prepared in accordance with the relevant practice direction and the requisite number of copies of the volumes of authorities must be filed by the appellant at the same time as the core volumes.

25 Cross-appeals

(1) A respondent who wishes to argue that the order appealed from should be upheld on grounds different from those relied on by the court below, must state that clearly in the respondent's written case (but need not cross-appeal).

(2) Except where –

    (a)   leave is required from the Court of Session for an appeal from that court, or

    (b)   an appeal lies to the Court as of right, a respondent who wishes to argue that the order appealed from should be varied must obtain permission to cross-appeal from the Court.

(3) Part 2 of these Rules shall apply (with appropriate modifications) to an application to the Court for permission to cross-appeal and (if practicable) applications for permission to appeal and to cross-appeal shall be considered together by the same panel of Justices.

(4) Where there is a cross-appeal, this Part of these Rules shall apply with appropriate modifications and in particular –

    (a)   either the application for permission to cross-appeal to the Court shall stand as a notice of cross-appeal, or such a notice (in the appropriate form) shall be filed and served within 42 days of the grant by the Court of permission to appeal or of the filing of the notice of appeal;

    (b)   there shall be a single statement of facts and issues, a single appendix of essential documents (divided if necessary into parts) and a single case for each party in respect of the appeal and the cross-appeal (and each case should state clearly that it is in respect of both the appeal and the cross-appeal); and

    (c)   the appellant shall remain primarily responsible for the preparation of all the papers for the appeal and for notifying the Registrar under rule 22(3).

26 Intervention

(1) After permission to appeal has been granted by the Court or a notice of appeal has been filed, any person and in particular –

    (a)   any official body or non-governmental organization seeking to make submissions in the public interest,

    (b)   any person with an interest in proceedings by way of judicial review,

    (c)   any person who was an intervener in the court below or whose submissions were taken into account under rule 15,

may apply to the Court for permission to intervene in the appeal.

PART III

(2) An application under this rule must be made in the appropriate form and shall be considered on paper by a panel of Justices who may refuse permission to intervene or may permit intervention –

    (a) by written submissions only; or

    (b) by written submissions and oral submissions

and any oral submissions may be limited to a specified duration.

(3) No permission is required –

    (a) for an intervention by the Crown under section 5 of the Human Rights Act 1998, or

    (b) for an intervention by the relevant officer in a case where the Court is exercising its devolution jurisdiction.

       (For rules relating to Human Rights Act issues and the Court's devolution jurisdiction see rules 40 and 41.)

PART 4
HEARING AND DECISION OF APPEAL

CONTENTS OF THIS PART

27 Hearing in open court

(1) Every contested appeal shall be heard in open court except where it is necessary in the interests of justice or in the public interest to sit in private for part of an appeal hearing.

(2) Where the Court considers it necessary for a party and that party's representative to be excluded from a hearing or part of a hearing in order to secure that information is not disclosed contrary to the public interest, the Court must conduct the hearing, or that part of it from which the party and the representative are excluded, in private but the Court may exclude a party and any representative only if a person who has been appointed as a special advocate to represent the interests of that party is present when the party and the representative are excluded.

(3) Where the Court decides it is necessary for the Court to sit in private, it shall announce its reasons for so doing publicly before the hearing begins.

(4) Hearings shall be conducted in accordance with –

    (a) the relevant practice direction, and

    (b) any directions given by the Court

and directions given by the Court may limit oral submissions to a specified duration.

"directions given by the Court may limit oral submissions to a specified duration" (r 27(4))—Note that SCPD 6, para 6.2.2, indicates that not more than 2 days will "normally" be allowed for hearing an appeal. Of the 57 cases reported from 2010, only 10 were allowed 3 days of hearing and just 2 (including *Manchester CC v Pinnock* [2011] 2 AC 104, where a nine-judge court effectively overruled three decisions of the House of Lords) managed 4 days.

28 Judgment

A judgment may be –

- (a) delivered in open court; or
- (b) if the Court so directs, promulgated by the Registrar.

29 Orders

(1) In relation to an appeal or a reference, the Supreme Court has all the powers of the court below and may –

- (a) affirm, set aside or vary any order or judgment made or given by that court;
- (b) remit any issue for determination by that court;
- (c) order a new trial or hearing;
- (d) make orders for the payment of interest;
- (e) make a costs order.

(2) An order of the Supreme Court may be enforced in the same manner as an order of the court below or of the appropriate superior court.

(3) For the purposes of paragraph (2) "the appropriate superior court" means –

- (a) in the case of an appeal or reference from a court in England and Wales, the High Court;
- (b) in the case of an appeal or reference from a court in Scotland –
  - (i) where the appeal or reference is in civil proceedings, the Court of Session; and
  - (ii) where the appeal or reference is in criminal proceedings, the High Court of Justiciary;
- (c) in the case of an appeal or reference from a court in Northern Ireland, the High Court in Northern Ireland.

(4) In the case of references other than those mentioned in paragraph (3) "the appropriate superior court" in paragraph (2) means –

- (a) where the reference is under the Scotland Act 1998, the Court of Session;
- (b) where the reference is under the Northern Ireland Act 1998, the High Court in Northern Ireland; and
- (c) where the reference is under the Government of Wales Act 2006, the High Court.

(5) Every order of the Court shall be prepared and sealed by the Registrar who may invite written submissions as to the form of the order.

"An order of the Supreme Court may be enforced" (r 29(2))—This provision appears to render redundant para 13.1 of *PD40B – Judgments and Orders* (which supplements CPR 1998, Pt 40), under which an order of the Supreme Court may be made an order of the High Court.

PART 5
FURTHER GENERAL PROVISIONS

CONTENTS OF THIS PART

30 Procedural applications

(1) Every procedural application to the Court must be made in the appropriate form for general procedural applications unless a particular form is provided for a specific case.

(2) An application must be made in the appropriate form and must –

  (a)   set out the reasons for making the application, and
  (b)   where necessary, be supported by written evidence.

(3) A copy of the application must be served on every other party before it is filed and, when the application is filed, the applicant must file a certificate of service.

(4) A party who wishes to oppose an application must, within 7 days after service, file notice of objection in the appropriate form and must (before filing) serve a copy on the applicant and any other parties.

(5) An application for permission to appeal, a notice of appeal or any other document filed under these Rules may be amended on application under this rule or with the permission of the Registrar on such terms as appear appropriate, and the Registrar may invite the parties' written submissions on any application to amend.

31 Requests for expedition

(1) Any request for urgent consideration of an application for permission to appeal or for an expedited hearing must be made to the Registrar.

(2) Wherever possible the views of all parties should be obtained before such a request is made.

32 Grouping appeals

The Registrar may direct that appeals raising the same or similar issues shall be heard either together or consecutively by the Court constituted by the same Justices and may give any consequential directions that appear appropriate.

33 Change of interest

The Court must be informed promptly of –

  (a)   he death or bankruptcy of any individual party;
  (b)   the winding up or dissolution of any corporate party;
  (c)   any compromise of the subject matter of an appeal;
  (d)   any event which does or may deprive an appeal of practical significance to the parties, and the Court may give any consequential directions that appear appropriate.

34 Withdrawal etc of application for permission to appeal or of appeal

(1) An application for permission to appeal or a notice of appeal may be withdrawn with the written consent of all parties or with the permission of the Court on such terms as appear appropriate.

(2) The Court may set aside or vary the order appealed from by consent and without an oral hearing if satisfied that it is appropriate so to do.

(3) In this rule "a notice of appeal" includes an application for permission to appeal or cross-appeal which (under rule 18 or rule 25) stands as a notice of appeal or cross-appeal.

35 Advocate to the Court and assessors

(1) The Court may request the relevant officer to appoint, or may itself appoint, an advocate to the Court to assist the Court with legal submissions.

(2) In accordance with section 44 of the Act the Court may, at the request of the parties or of its own initiative, appoint one or more independent specially qualified advisers to assist the Court as assessors on any technical matter.

(3) The fees and expenses of any advocate to the Court or assessor shall be costs in the appeal.

36 Security for costs

(1) The Court may on the application of a respondent order an appellant to give security for the costs of the appeal and any order for security shall determine –

    (a)   the amount of that security, and
    (b)   the manner in which, and the time within which, security must be given.

(2) An order made under this rule may require payment of the judgment debt (and costs) in the court below instead of, or in addition to, the amount ordered by way of security for costs.

37 Stay of execution

Any appellant who wishes to obtain a stay of execution of the order appealed from must seek it from the court below and only in wholly exceptional circumstances will the Court grant a stay.

38 Change of solicitor and London agents

(1) If a party for whom a solicitor is acting wishes to change solicitors, that party or the new solicitor must give the Registrar and the former solicitor written notice of the change.

(2) Until such notices are given the former solicitor shall continue to be treated as the party's solicitor.

(3) Solicitors practising outside London may appoint London agents and additional costs incurred by not appointing London agents may be disallowed.

39 Disposal of documents

(1) All documents filed become the property of the Court and original documents must be retained in the records of the Registry.

(2) Other documents shall be destroyed unless the Registrar (on a written application made within 21 days of the end of the proceedings) directs otherwise.

(3) All documents held by the Court may be inspected by the press or members of the public on application to the Registrar but the Registrar may refuse an application for reasons of commercial confidentiality, national security or in the public interest.

(4) Before allowing an application for inspection under this rule, the Registrar may impose terms or conditions such as the redaction of certain material where such a condition is necessary in the interests of justice or in the public interest.

PART 6
PARTICULAR APPEALS AND REFERENCES

CONTENTS OF THIS PART

40 Human Rights Act issues

(1) Where an appeal raises a question of incompatibility under section 4 of the Human Rights Act 1998 and the Crown is not already a party to the appeal, the Registrar shall give 21 days' notice of the question to the Crown.

(2) If notice is given that the Crown wishes to be joined, the appropriate Minister or other person shall be joined accordingly.

(3) If such a question arises for the first time during the course of an appeal hearing the Court will if necessary adjourn the proceedings to enable the Registrar to give notice under paragraph (1).

41 Devolution jurisdiction

(1) Appeals or references under the Court's devolution jurisdiction shall in general be dealt with in accordance with these Rules but the Court shall give special directions as and when necessary, and in particular as to –

(a) any question referred under section 33 of the Scotland Act 1998, section 11 of the Northern Ireland Act 1998 or section 96, 99 or 112 of the Government of Wales Act 2006,

(b) any reference of a devolution issue,

(c) any direct references under paragraph 33 or 34 of Schedule 6 to the Scotland Act 1998, paragraph 33 or 34 of Schedule 10 to the Northern Ireland Act 1998 or paragraph 29 or 30 of Schedule 9 to the Government of Wales Act 2006.

(2) A reference made by the relevant officer is made by filing the reference and by serving a copy on any other relevant officer who is not already a party and who has a potential interest in the proceedings.

(3) A reference must state the question or issue to be decided by the Court.

(4) The Registrar shall give notice of the question or issue to the appropriate relevant officer where that officer is not already a party to any proceedings.

42 Court of Justice of the European Communities

(1) Where it is contended on an application for permission to appeal that it raises a question of Community law which should be the subject of a reference under Article 267 of the Treaty on the Functioning of the European Union and permission to appeal is refused, the panel of Justices will give brief reasons for its decision.

(2) Where on an application for permission to appeal a panel of Justices decides to make a reference under Article 267 before determining the application, it will give consequential directions as to the form of the reference and the staying of the application (but it may if it thinks fit dispose of other parts of the application at once).

(3) Where at the hearing of an appeal the Court decides to make a reference under Article 267 it will give consequential directions as to the form of the reference and the staying of the appeal (but it may if it thinks fit dispose of other parts of the appeal at once).

(4) An order of the Court shall be prepared and sealed by the Registrar to record any decision made under this rule.

Amendments—SI 2012/1809.

43 Revocation of patents

(1) On any appeal under sections 12 and 13 of the Administration of Justice Act 1969 from an order for revocation of a patent the appellant must serve notice of the appeal on the Comptroller-General of Patents ("the Comptroller") as well as on every respondent.

(2) A respondent who decides not to oppose the appeal must serve notice of that decision on the Comptroller together with the relevant statements of case.

(3) The Comptroller shall within 14 days serve on the appellant and file a notice stating whether or not the Comptroller intends to appear on the appeal.

(4) Where notice is given under paragraph (3), the Comptroller may appear on the appeal.

44 Criminal appeals

The Court must apply in accordance with the relevant practice direction the code of practice for victims issued under section 32 of the Domestic Violence, Crime and Victims Act 2004.

PART 7
FEES AND COSTS

CONTENTS OF THIS PART

45 Fees

Where a fee is prescribed by any order made under section 52 of the Act, the Registrar may refuse to accept a document or refuse to allow a party to take any step unless the relevant fee is paid.

46 Orders for costs

(1) The Court may make such orders as it considers just in respect of the costs of any appeal, application for permission to appeal, or other application to or proceeding before the Court.

(2) The Court's powers to make orders for costs may be exercised either at the final determination of an appeal or application for permission to appeal or in the course of the proceedings.

(3) Orders for costs will not normally be made either in favour of or against interveners but such orders may be made if the Court considers it just to do so (in particular if an intervener has in substance acted as the sole or principal appellant or respondent).

47 Submissions as to costs

(1) If a party wishes to defer making submissions as to costs until after judgment, the Court must be informed of this not later than at the close of the oral argument.

(2) If the Court accedes to the request it will give such directions as appear appropriate and it may, in particular, give directions –

    (a)   for the hearing of oral submissions as to costs immediately after judgment;

    (b)   for the simultaneous or sequential filing of written submissions as to costs within a specified period after judgment;

    (c)   for the hearing of oral submissions after the filing of written submissions.

48 Claim for costs

(1) Where the Court has made an order for costs, the claim for costs must be submitted to the Registrar within three months beginning with the date on which the costs order was made.

(2) The form and contents of a claim for costs must comply with the relevant practice direction and the receiving party must supply such further particulars, information and documents as the Registrar may direct.

(3) The receiving party must serve a copy of a claim for costs on the paying party.

(4) Within 21 days beginning with the day on which a claim for costs is served, the paying party may (or, in the circumstances specified in the relevant practice direction, must) file points of dispute and, if so, must serve a copy on the receiving party.

(5) Within 14 days beginning with the day on which points of dispute are served, the receiving party may file a response and, if so, must serve a copy on the paying party.

49 Assessment of costs

(1) Every detailed assessment of costs shall be carried out by two costs officers appointed by the President and –

    (a)   one costs officer must be a Costs Judge (a Taxing Master of the Senior Courts), and

    (b)   the second may be the Registrar.

(2) A disputed assessment shall be dealt with at an oral hearing.

(3) An assessment may provide for the costs of the assessment procedure.

(4) The Registrar will give the receiving party and the paying party written notice of the date of the assessment.

(5) Where one of the parties so requests or in the circumstances specified in the relevant practice direction, the Registrar may make a provisional assessment of costs without the attendance of the parties.

(6) The Registrar must inform the parties in writing of the outcome of a provisional assessment and, if a party is dissatisfied with the outcome, or if points of disagreement cannot be resolved in correspondence, the Registrar shall appoint a date for an oral hearing.

(7) Any request for an oral hearing following a provisional assessment of costs must be made within 14 days of the receipt of the Registrar's decision on the assessment.

50 Basis of assessment

(1) Where the Court is to assess the amount of costs it will assess those costs –

  (a) on the standard basis, or
  (b) on the indemnity basis,

in the manner specified by rule 51 or (where appropriate) on the relevant bases that apply in Scotland or Northern Ireland.

(2) Where –

  (a) the Court makes an order about costs without indicating the basis on which the costs are to be assessed, or
  (b) the Court makes an order for costs to be assessed on a basis other than one specified in paragraph (1),

the costs will be assessed on the standard basis.

(3) This rule applies subject to any order or direction to the contrary.

51 The standard basis and the indemnity basis

(1) Costs assessed on the standard basis are allowed only if they are proportionate to the matters in issue and are reasonably incurred and reasonable in amount.

(2) Any doubt as to whether costs assessed on the standard basis are reasonably incurred and are reasonable and proportionate in amount will be resolved in favour of the paying party.

(3) Costs assessed on the indemnity basis are allowed only if they are reasonably incurred and reasonable in amount.

(4) Any doubt as to whether costs assessed on the indemnity basis are reasonably incurred and are reasonable in amount will be resolved in favour of the receiving party.

52 Amount of assessed costs to be specified

The amount of any assessed costs will be inserted in the order made under rule 29 but, if that order is drawn up before the assessment has been completed, the amount assessed will be certified by the Registrar.

53 Appeal from assessment

(1) A party who is dissatisfied with the assessment of costs made at an oral hearing may apply for that decision to be reviewed by a single Justice and any application under this rule must be made in the appropriate form and be filed within 14 days of the decision.

(2) The single Justice may (without an oral hearing) affirm the decision made on the assessment or may, where it appears appropriate, refer the matter to a panel of Justices to be decided with or without an oral hearing.

PART III

(3) An application may be made under this rule only on a question of principle and not in respect of the amount allowed on any item in the claim for costs.

54 Payment out of security for costs

Any security for costs lodged by an appellant will be dealt with by the Registrar in accordance with the directions of the Court.

PART 8
TRANSITIONAL ARRANGEMENTS

55 Transitional arrangements

(1) Unless the Court or the Registrar directs otherwise, these Rules shall apply, with any necessary modifications, to appeals which were proceeding, and petitions for leave which were lodged, in the House of Lords before 1 October 2009.

(2) The Court or the Registrar may give special directions, as and when necessary, in relation to appeals which were proceeding, and petitions for leave which were lodged, in the House of Lords.

PART IV

Statutory Instruments

PART IV: Statutory Instruments

Contents

All relevant procedural provisions in the following legislation, as amended and fully annotated:

PART IV

Access to Justice Act 1999 (Destination of Appeals) (Family Proceedings) Order 2011, SI 2011/1044

1 Citation, commencement, interpretation and application

(1) This Order may be cited as the Access to Justice Act 1999 (Destination of Appeals) (Family Proceedings) Order 2011 and shall come into force on 6 April 2011.

(2) In this Order –

"costs judge" means a Taxing Master of the Senior Courts;
"decision" means a judgment, order or direction of the High Court or a county court;
"family proceedings" has the meaning assigned to it by section 32 of the Matrimonial and Family Proceedings Act 1984.

(3) This Order applies to a decision made in family proceedings in the High Court or a county court and has effect subject to –

    (a) any enactment that provides a different route of appeal (other than section 16(1) of the Senior Courts Act 1981 or section 77(1) of the County Courts Act 1984); and

    (b) any requirement to obtain permission to appeal.

2 Appeals to a judge of the High Court

(1) An appeal shall lie to a judge of the High Court from a decision in family proceedings made by –

    (a) a district judge of the High Court;

    (b) a district judge of the principal registry of the Family Division;

    (c) a costs judge; or

    (d) a person appointed to act as a deputy for any person holding an office referred to in subparagraphs (a) to (c) or to act as a temporary additional officer in any such office.

(2) Paragraph (1) applies irrespective of whether the family proceedings in which the decision was made are in the High Court or whether they are in the principal registry of the Family Division of the High Court when it is treated as if it were –

    (a) a divorce county court;

    (b) a civil partnership proceedings county court;

    (c) a family hearing centre;

    (d) a care centre;

    (e) an adoption centre;

    (f) an intercountry adoption centre;

    (g) a forced marriage county court; or

    (h) a county court for the purposes of appeals from decisions of a magistrates' court under –

        (i) section 94 of the Children Act 1989; and

        (ii) section 61 of the Family Law Act 1996.

3 Appeals to a judge of a county court

An appeal shall lie to a judge of a county court from a decision in family proceedings made by a district judge or deputy district judge of a county court (and for this purpose "judge of a county court" does not include a district judge or a deputy district judge).

PART IV

4 Revocation

The Access to Justice Act 1999 (Destination of Appeals) (Family Proceedings) Order 2005 is revoked.

Adoptions with a Foreign Element Regulations 2005, SI 2005/392

PART I
GENERAL

1 Citation, commencement and application

(1) These Regulations may be cited as the Adoptions with a Foreign Element Regulations 2005 and shall come into force on 30 December 2005.

(2) These Regulations apply to England and Wales.

2 Interpretation

In these Regulations –

"the Act" means the Adoption and Children Act 2002;

"adoption support services" has the meaning given in section 2(6)(a) of the Act and any regulations made under section 2(6)(b) of the Act;

"adoptive family" has the same meaning as in regulation 31(2)(a) of the Agencies Regulations or corresponding Welsh provision;

"adoption panel" means a panel established in accordance with regulation 3 of the Agencies Regulations or corresponding Welsh provision;

"the Agencies Regulations" means the Adoption Agencies Regulations 2005;

"child's case record" has the same meaning as in regulation 12 of the Agencies Regulations or corresponding Welsh provision;

"CA of the receiving State" means, in relation to a Convention country other than the United Kingdom, the Central Authority of the receiving State;

"CA of the State of origin" means, in relation to a Convention country other than the United Kingdom, the Central Authority of the State of origin;

"Convention adoption" is given a meaning by virtue of section 66(1)(c) of the Act;

"Convention country" has the same meaning as in section 144(1) of the Act;

"Convention list" means –

    (a)   in relation to a relevant Central Authority, a list of children notified to that Authority in accordance with regulation 40; or

    (b)   in relation to any other Central Authority within the British Islands, a list of children notified to that Authority in accordance with provisions, which correspond to regulation 40.

"corresponding Welsh provision" in relation to a Part or a regulation of the Agencies Regulations means the provision of regulations made by the Assembly under section 9 of the Act which corresponds to that Part or regulation;

"prospective adopter's case record" has the same meaning as in regulation 22(1) of the Agencies Regulations or corresponding Welsh provision;

"prospective adopter's report" has the same meaning as in regulation 25(5) of the Agencies Regulations or corresponding Welsh provisions;

"receiving State" has the same meaning as in Article 2 of the Convention;

"relevant Central Authority" means –

(a) in Chapter 1 of Part 3, in relation to a prospective adopter who is habitually resident in –
    (i) England, the Secretary of State; and
    (ii) Wales, the National Assembly for Wales; and
(b) in Chapter 2 of Part 3 in relation to a local authority in –
    (i) England, the Secretary of State; and
    (ii) Wales, the National Assembly for Wales;

"relevant local authority" means in relation to a prospective adopter –
(a) the local authority within whose area he has his home; or
(b) in the case where he no longer has a home in England or Wales, the local authority for the area in which he last had his home;

"relevant foreign authority" means a person, outside the British Islands performing functions in the country in which the child is, or in which the prospective adopter is, habitually resident which correspond to the functions of an adoption agency or to the functions of the Secretary of State in respect of adoptions with a foreign element;

"State of origin" has the same meaning as in Article 2 of the Convention.

PART 2
BRINGING CHILDREN INTO AND OUT OF THE UNITED KINGDOM

Chapter 1
Bringing Children into the United Kingdom

3 Requirements applicable in respect of bringing or causing a child to be brought into the United Kingdom

A person intending to bring, or to cause another to bring, a child into the United Kingdom in circumstances where section 83(1) of the Act applies must –

(a) apply in writing to an adoption agency for an assessment of his suitability to adopt a child; and
(b) give the adoption agency any information it may require for the purpose of the assessment.

4 Conditions applicable in respect of a child brought into the United Kingdom

(1) This regulation prescribes the conditions for the purposes of section 83(5) of the Act in respect of a child brought into the United Kingdom in circumstances where section 83 applies.

(2) Prior to the child's entry into the United Kingdom, the prospective adopter must –

(a) receive in writing, notification from the Secretary of State that she has issued a certificate confirming to the relevant foreign authority –
    (i) that the person has been assessed and approved as eligible and suitable to be an adoptive parent in accordance with Part 4 of the Agencies Regulations or corresponding Welsh provision; and
    (ii) that if entry clearance and leave to enter and remain, as may be necessary, is granted and not revoked or curtailed, and an adoption order is made or an overseas adoption is effected, the child will be authorised to enter and reside permanently in the United Kingdom;
(b) before visiting the child in the State of origin –
    (i) notify the adoption agency of the details of the child to be adopted;

PART IV

      (ii) provide the adoption agency with any information and reports received from the relevant foreign authority; and

      (iii) meet with the adoption agency to discuss the proposed adoption and information received from the relevant foreign authority;

  (c) visit the child in the State of origin (and where the prospective adopters are a couple each of them); and

  (d) after that visit –

      (i) confirm in writing to the adoption agency that he has done so and wishes to proceed with the adoption;

      (ii) provide the adoption agency with any additional reports and information received on or after that visit; and

      (iii) notify the adoption agency of his expected date of entry into the United Kingdom with the child.

(3) The prospective adopter must accompany the child on entering the United Kingdom unless, in the case of a couple, the adoption agency and the relevant foreign authority have agreed that it is necessary for only one of them to do so.

(4) Except where an overseas adoption is or is to be effected, the prospective adopter must within the period of 14 days beginning with the date on which the child is brought into the United Kingdom give notice to the relevant local authority –

  (a) of the child's arrival in the United Kingdom; and

  (b) of his intention –

      (i) to apply for an adoption order in accordance with section 44(2) of the Act; or

      (ii) not to give the child a home.

(5) In a case where a prospective adopter has given notice in accordance with paragraph (4) and subsequently moves his home into the area of another local authority, he must within 14 days of that move confirm in writing to that authority, the child's entry into the United Kingdom and that notice of his intention –

  (a) to apply for an adoption order in accordance with section 44(2) of the Act has been given to another local authority; or

  (b) not to give the child a home,

has been given.

5 Functions imposed on the local authority

(1) Where notice of intention to adopt has been given to the local authority, that authority must –

  (a) if it has not already done so, set up a case record in respect of the child and place on it any information received from the –

      (i) relevant foreign authority;

      (ii) adoption agency, if it is not the local authority;

      (iii) prospective adopter;

      (iv) entry clearance officer; and

      (v) Secretary of State, or as the case may be, the Assembly;

  (b) send the prospective adopter's general practitioner written notification of the arrival in England or Wales of the child and send with that notification a written report of the child's health history and current state of health, so far as is known;

  (c) send to the clinical commissioning group or Local Health Board (Wales), in whose area the prospective adopter has his home, and to the National Health Service Commissioning Board if the prospective adopter's home is in England, written notification of the arrival in England or Wales of the child;

(d) (*revoked*)

(e) ensure that the child and the prospective adopter are visited within one week of receipt of the notice of intention to adopt and thereafter not less than once a week until the review referred to in sub-paragraph (f) and thereafter at such frequency as the authority may decide;

(f) carry out a review of the child's case not more than 4 weeks after receipt of the notice of intention to adopt and –

    (i) visit and, if necessary, review not more than 3 months after that initial review; and

    (ii) thereafter not more than 6 months after the date of the previous visit,

unless the child no longer has his home with the prospective adopter or an adoption order is made;

(g) when carrying out a review consider –

    (i) the child's needs, welfare and development, and whether any changes need to be made to meet his needs or assist his development;

    (ii) the arrangements for the provision of adoption support services and whether there should be any re-assessment of the need for those services; and

    (iii) the need for further visits and reviews; and

(h) ensure that –

    (i) advice is given as to the child's needs, welfare and development;

    (ii) written reports are made of all visits and reviews of the case and placed on the child's case record; and

    (iii) on such visits, where appropriate, advice is given as to the availability of adoption support services.

(2) Part 7 of the Agencies Regulations or corresponding Welsh provision (case records) shall apply to the case record set up in respect of the child as a consequence of this regulation as if that record had been set up under the Agencies Regulations or corresponding Welsh provision.

(3) In a case where the prospective adopter fails to make an application under section 50 or 51 of the Act within two years of the receipt by a local authority of the notice of intention to adopt the local authority must review the case.

(4) For the purposes of the review referred to in paragraph (3), the local authority must consider –

(a) the child's needs, welfare and development, and whether any changes need to be made to meet his needs or assist his development;

(b) the arrangements, if any, in relation to the exercise of parental responsibility for the child;

(c) the terms upon which leave to enter the United Kingdom is granted and the immigration status of the child;

(d) the arrangements for the provision of adoption support services for the adoptive family and whether there should be any re-assessment of the need for those services; and

(e) in conjunction with the appropriate agencies, the arrangements for meeting the child's health care and educational needs.

(5) In a case where the local authority to which notice of intention to adopt is given ("the original authority") is notified by the prospective adopter that he intends to move or has moved his home into the area of another local authority, the original authority must notify the local authority into whose area the prospective adopter intends to move or has moved, within 14 days of receiving information in respect of that move, of –

(a) the name, sex, date and place of birth of child;

(b) the prospective adopter's name, sex and date of birth;

PART IV

(c)   the date on which the child entered the United Kingdom;

(d)   where the original authority received notification of intention to adopt, the date of receipt of such notification whether an application for an adoption order has been made and the stage of those proceedings; and

(e)   any other relevant information.

Amendments—SI 2010/1172; SI 2013/235.

6 Application of Chapter 3 of the Act

In the case of a child brought into the United Kingdom for adoption in circumstances where section 83 of the Act applies –

(a)   the modifications in regulations 7 to 9 apply;

(b)   section 36(2) and (5) (restrictions on removal) and section 39(3)(a) (partners of parents) of the Act shall not apply.

7 Change of name and removal from the United Kingdom

Section 28(2) of the Act (further consequences of placement) shall apply as if from the words "is placed" to "then", there is substituted "enters the United Kingdom in the circumstances where section 83(1)(a) of this Act applies".

8 Return of the child

(1) Section 35 of the Act (return of child) shall apply with the following modifications.

(2) Subsections (1), (2) and (3) shall apply as if in each place where –

(a)   the words "is placed for adoption by an adoption agency" occur there were substituted "enters the United Kingdom in circumstances where section 83(1) applies";

(b)   the words "the agency" occur there were substituted the words "the local authority"; and

(c)   the words "any parent or guardian of the child" occur there were substituted "the Secretary of State or, as the case may be, the Assembly".

(3) Subsection (5) shall apply as if for the words "an adoption agency" or "the agency" there were substituted the words "the local authority".

9 Child to live with adopters before application

(1) In a case where the requirements imposed by section 83(4) of the Act have been complied with and the conditions required by section 83(5) of the Act have been met, section 42 shall apply as if –

(a)   subsection (3) is omitted; and

(b)   in subsection (5) the words from "three years" to "preceding" there were substituted "six months".

(2) In a case where the requirements imposed by section 83(4) of the Act have not been complied with or the conditions required by section 83(5) have not been met, section 42 shall apply as if –

(a)   subsection (3) is omitted; and

(b)   in subsection (5) the words from "three years" to "preceding" there were substituted "twelve months".

Chapter 2
Taking Children out of the United Kingdom

10 Requirements applicable in respect of giving parental responsibility prior to adoption abroad

The prescribed requirements for the purposes of section 84(3) of the Act (requirements to be satisfied prior to the making of an order) are that –

(a) in the case of a child placed by an adoption agency, that agency has –
  (i) confirmed to the court that it has complied with the requirements imposed in accordance with Part 3 of the Agencies Regulations or corresponding Welsh provision;
  (ii) submitted to the court –
    (aa) the reports and information referred to in regulation 17(2D) and (3), as appropriate of the Agencies Regulations or corresponding Welsh provision;
    (bb) the recommendations made by the adoption panel in accordance with regulations 18 (placing child for adoption), where applicable, and 33 (proposed placement) of the Agencies Regulations or corresponding Welsh provision;
    (cc) the adoption placement report prepared in accordance with regulation 31(2)(d) of the Agencies Regulations or corresponding Welsh provision;
    (dd) the reports of and information obtained in respect of the visits and reviews referred to in regulation 36 of the Agencies Regulations or corresponding Welsh provision; and
    (ee) the report referred to in section 43 of the Act as modified by regulation 11;
(b) in the case of a child placed by an adoption agency the relevant foreign authority has –
  (i) confirmed in writing to that agency that the prospective adopter has been counselled and the legal implications of adoption have been explained to him;
  (ii) prepared a report on the suitability of the prospective adopter to be an adoptive parent;
  (iii) determined and confirmed in writing to that agency that he is eligible and suitable to adopt in the country or territory in which the adoption is to be effected; and
  (iv) confirmed in writing to that agency that the child is or will be authorised to enter and reside permanently in that foreign country or territory; and
(c) in the case of a child placed by an adoption agency the prospective adopter has confirmed in writing to the adoption agency that he will accompany the child on taking him out of the United Kingdom and entering the country or territory where the adoption is to be effected, or in the case of a couple, the agency and relevant foreign authority have confirmed that it is necessary for only one of them to do so.

Amendments—SI 2012/1410.

11 Application of the Act in respect of orders under section 84

(1) The following provisions of the Act which refer to adoption orders shall apply to orders under section 84 as if in each place where the words "adoption order" appear there were substituted "order under section 84" –

(a) section 1(7)(a) (coming to a decision relating to adoption of a child);

PART IV

(b)   section 18(4) (placement for adoption by agencies);
(c)   section 21(4)(b) (placement orders);
(d)   section 22(5)(a) and (b) (application for placement orders);
(e)   section 24(4) (revoking placement orders);
(f)   section 28(1) (further consequences of placement);
(g)   section 29(4)(a) and (5)(a) (further consequences of placement orders);
(h)   section 32(5) (recovery by parent etc where child placed and consent withdrawn);
(i)   section 42(7) (sufficient opportunity for adoption agency to see the child);
(j)   section 43 (reports where child placed by agency);
(k)   section 44(2) (notice of intention to adopt);
(l)   section 47(1) to (5), (8) and (9) (conditions for making orders);
(m)   section 48(1) (restrictions on making applications);
(n)   section 50(1) and (2) (adoption by a couple);
(o)   section 51(1) to (4) (adoption by one person);
(p)   section 52(1) to (4) (parental etc consent);
(q)   section 53(5) (contribution towards maintenance); and
(r)   section 141(3) and (4)(c) (rules of procedure).

(2) Section 35(5) of the Act (return of child in other cases) shall apply to orders under section 84 of that Act as if in paragraph (b) of that subsection –

(a)   for the first reference to "adoption order" there were substituted "order under section 84(1)"; and
(b)   the words in brackets were omitted.

PART 3
ADOPTIONS UNDER THE CONVENTION

Chapter 1
Requirements, Procedure, Recognition and Effect of Adoptions where the United Kingdom is the Receiving State

12 Application of Chapter 1
The provisions in this Chapter shall apply where a couple or a person, habitually resident in the British Islands, wishes to adopt a child who is habitually resident in a Convention country outside the British Islands in accordance with the Convention.

13 Requirements applicable in respect of eligibility and suitability
(1) A couple or a person who wishes to adopt a child habitually resident in a Convention country outside the British Islands shall –

(a)   apply in writing to an adoption agency for a determination of eligibility, and an assessment of his suitability, to adopt; and
(b)   give the agency any information it may require for the purposes of the assessment.

(2) An adoption agency may not consider an application under paragraph (1) unless at the date of that application –

(a)   in the case of an application by a couple, they have both –
    (i)   attained the age of 21 years; and
    (ii)   been habitually resident in a part of the British Islands for a period of not less than one year ending with the date of application; and
(b)   in the case of an application by one person, he has –

    (i)   attained the age of 21 years; and

    (ii) been habitually resident in a part of the British Islands for a period of not less than one year ending with the date of application.

14 Counselling and information

(1) An adoption agency must provide a counselling service in accordance with regulation 21(1)(a) of the Agencies Regulations or corresponding Welsh provision and must –

    (a)   explain to the prospective adopter the procedure in relation to, and the legal implications of, adopting a child from the State of origin from which the prospective adopter wishes to adopt in accordance with the Convention; and

    (b)   provide him with written information about the matters referred to in sub-paragraph (a).

(2) Paragraph (1) does not apply if the adoption agency is satisfied that the requirements set out in that paragraph have been carried out in respect of the prospective adopter by another agency.

15 Procedure in respect of carrying out an assessment

(1) Regulation 22 of the Agencies Regulations (requirement to consider application for an assessment of suitability) or corresponding Welsh provision shall apply as if the reference to an application in those Regulations or corresponding Welsh provision was to an application made in accordance with regulation 13.

(2) Where the adoption agency is satisfied that the requirements in –

    (a)   regulation 14; and

    (b)   regulations 23 (police checks) and 24 (preparation for adoption) of the Agencies Regulations or corresponding Welsh provision,

have been meet, regulations 25 (prospective adopter's report) and 26 (adoption panel) of the Agencies Regulations or corresponding Welsh provisions shall apply.

(3) The adoption agency must place on the prospective adopter's case record any information obtained as a consequence of this Chapter.

(4) The adoption agency must include in the prospective adopter's report –

    (a)   the State of origin from which the prospective adopter wishes to adopt a child;

    (b)   confirmation that the prospective adopter is eligible to adopt a child under the law of that State;

    (c)   any additional information obtained as a consequence of the requirements of that State; and

    (d)   the agency's assessment of the prospective adopter's suitability to adopt a child who is habitually resident in that State.

(5) The references to information in regulations 25(5) and 26(2) of the Agencies Regulations or corresponding Welsh provisions shall include information obtained by the adoption agency or adoption panel as a consequence of this regulation.

16 Adoption agency decision and notification

The adoption agency must make a decision about whether the prospective adopter is suitable to adopt a child in accordance with regulation 27 of the Agencies Regulations and regulations made under section 45 of the Act, or corresponding Welsh provisions.

PART IV

17 Review and termination of approval

The adoption agency must review the approval of each prospective adopter in accordance with regulation 29 of the Agencies Regulations or corresponding Welsh provision unless the agency has received written notification from the relevant Central Authority that the agreement under Article 17(c) of the Convention has been made.

18 Procedure following decision as to suitability to adopt

(1) Where an adoption agency has made a decision that the prospective adopter is suitable to adopt a child in accordance with regulation 16, it must send to the relevant Central Authority –

- (a) written confirmation of the decision and any recommendation the agency may make in relation to the number of children the prospective adopter may be suitable to adopt, their age range, sex, likely needs and background;
- (b) the enhanced criminal record certificate obtained under regulation 23 of the Agencies Regulations or corresponding Welsh provision;
- (c) all the documents and information which were passed to the adoption panel in accordance with regulation 25(9) of the Agencies Regulations or corresponding Welsh provision;
- (d) the record of the proceedings of the adoption panel, its recommendation and the reasons for its recommendation; and
- (e) any other information relating to the case as the relevant Central Authority or the CA of the State of origin may require.

(2) If the relevant Central Authority is satisfied that the adoption agency has complied with the duties and procedures imposed by the Agencies Regulations or corresponding Welsh provision, and that all the relevant information has been supplied by that agency, the Authority must send to the CA of the State of origin –

- (a) the prospective adopter's report prepared in accordance with regulation 25 of the Agencies Regulations or corresponding Welsh provision;
- (b) (revoked)
- (c) a copy of the adoption agency's decision and the adoption panel's recommendation;
- (d) any other information that the CA of the State of origin may require;
- (da) if the prospective adopter applied to the appropriate Minister for a review under section 12 of the Adoption and Children Act 2002, the record of the proceedings of the panel, its recommendation and the reasons for its recommendation; and
- (e) a certificate in the form set out in Schedule 1 confirming that the –
  - (i) prospective adopter is eligible to adopt;
  - (ii) prospective adopter has been assessed in accordance with this Chapter;
  - (iii) prospective adopter has been approved as suitable to adopt a child; and
  - (iv) child will be authorised to enter and reside permanently in the United Kingdom if entry clearance, and leave to enter or remain as may be necessary, is granted and not revoked or curtailed and a Convention adoption order or Convention adoption is made.

(3) The relevant Central Authority must notify the adoption agency and the prospective adopter in writing that the certificate and the documents referred to in paragraph (2) have been sent to the CA of the State of origin.

Amendments—SI 2005/3482.

19 Procedure following receipt of the Article 16 Information from the CA of the State of origin

(1) Where the relevant Central Authority receives from the CA of the State of origin, the Article 16 Information relating to the child whom the CA of the State of origin considers should be placed for adoption with the prospective adopter, the relevant Central Authority must send that Information to the adoption agency.

(2) The adoption agency must consider the Article 16 Information and –

    (a)   send that Information to the prospective adopter;

    (b)   meet with him to discuss –

        (i)   that Information;

        (ii)   the proposed placement;

        (iii) the availability of adoption support services; and

    (c)   if appropriate, offer a counselling service and further information as required.

(3) Where –

    (a)   the procedure in paragraph (2) has been followed; and

    (b)   the prospective adopter has confirmed in writing to the adoption agency that he wishes to proceed to adopt the child,

the agency must notify the relevant Central Authority in writing that the requirements specified in sub-paragraphs (a) and (b) have been satisfied and at the same time it must confirm that it is content for the adoption to proceed.

(4) Where the relevant Central Authority has received notification from the adoption agency under paragraph (3), the relevant Central Authority shall –

    (a)   notify the CA of the State of origin that –

        (i)   the prospective adopter wishes to proceed to adopt the child;

        (ii)   it is prepared to agree with the CA of the State of origin that the adoption may proceed; and

    (b)   confirm to the CA of the State of origin that –

        (i)   in the case where the requirements specified in section 1(5A) of the British Nationality Act 1981 are met that the child will be authorised to enter and reside permanently in the United Kingdom; or

        (ii)   in any other case, if entry clearance and leave to enter and remain, as may be necessary, is granted and not revoked or curtailed and a Convention adoption order or a Convention adoption is made, the child will be authorised to enter and reside permanently in the United Kingdom.

(5) The relevant Central Authority must inform the adoption agency and the prospective adopter when the agreement under Article 17(c) of the Convention has been made.

(6) For the purposes of this regulation and regulation 20 "the Article 16 Information" means –

    (a)   the report referred to in Article 16(1) of the Convention including information about the child's identity, adoptability, background, social environment, family history, medical history including that of the child's family and any special needs of the child;

    (b)   proof of confirmation that the consents of the persons, institutions and authorities whose consents are necessary for adoption have been obtained in accordance with Article 4 of the Convention; and

    (c)   the reasons for the CA of the State of origin's determination on the placement.

Amendments—SI 2009/2563.

PART IV

20 Procedure where proposed adoption is not to proceed

(1) If, at any stage before the agreement under Article 17(c) of the Convention is made, the CA of the State of origin notifies the relevant Central Authority that it has decided the proposed placement should not proceed –

  (a) the relevant Central Authority must inform the adoption agency of the CA of the State of origin's decision;

  (b) the agency must then inform the prospective adopter and return the Article 16 Information to the relevant Central Authority; and

  (c) the relevant Central Authority must then return those documents to the CA of the State of origin.

(2) Where at any stage before the adoption agency receives notification of the agreement under Article 17(c) of the Convention the approval of the prospective adopter is reviewed under regulation 29 of the Agencies Regulations or corresponding Welsh provision, and as a consequence, the agency determines that the prospective adopter is no longer suitable to adopt a child –

  (a) the agency must inform the relevant Central Authority and return the documents referred to in regulation 19(1);

  (b) the relevant Central Authority must notify the CA of the State of origin and return those documents.

(3) If, at any stage before any Convention adoption is made and before the child's entry into the United Kingdom, the prospective adopter notifies the adoption agency that he does not wish to proceed with the adoption of the child –

  (a) that agency must inform the relevant Central Authority and return the documents to that Authority; and

  (b) the relevant Central Authority must notify the CA of the State of origin of the prospective adopter's decision and return the documents to the CA of the State of origin.

Amendments—SI 2009/2563.

21 Applicable requirements in respect of prospective adopter entering the United Kingdom with a child

Following any agreement under Article 17(c) of the Convention, the prospective adopter must –

  (a) notify the adoption agency of his expected date of entry into the United Kingdom with the child;

  (b) confirm to the adoption agency when the child is placed with him by the competent authority in the State of origin; and

  (c) accompany the child on entering the United Kingdom unless, in the case of a couple, the adoption agency and the CA of the State of origin have agreed that it is necessary for only one of them to do so.

22 Applicable requirements in respect of an adoption agency before the child enters the United Kingdom

Where the adoption agency is informed by the relevant Central Authority that the agreement under Article 17(c) of the Convention has been made and the adoption may proceed, before the child enters the United Kingdom that agency must –

  (a) send the prospective adopter's general practitioner written notification of the proposed placement and send with that notification a written report of the child's health history and current state of health, so far as it is known; and

(b) send the local authority (if that authority is not the adoption agency) and the clinical commissioning group or Local Health Board (Wales), in whose area the prospective adopter has his home, and to the National Health Service Commissioning Board if the prospective adopter's home is in England, written notification of the proposed arrival of the child into England or Wales; and, where the child is of compulsory school age, include in the notification to the local authority information about the child's educational history and whether the child has been or is likely to be assessed for special educational needs under the Education Act 1996.

(c) (*revoked*)

Amendments—SI 2010/1172; SI 2013/235.

23 Applicable provisions following the child's entry into the United Kingdom where no Convention adoption is made

Regulations 24 to 27 apply where –

(a) following the agreement between the relevant Central Authority and the CA of the State of origin under Article 17(c) of the Convention that the adoption may proceed, no Convention adoption is made, or applied for, in the State of origin; and

(b) the child is placed with the prospective adopter in the State of origin who then returns to England or Wales with that child.

24 Applicable requirements in respect of prospective adopter following child's entry into the United Kingdom

(1) A prospective adopter must within the period of 14 days beginning with the date on which the child enters the United Kingdom give notice to the relevant local authority –

(a) of the child's arrival in the United Kingdom; and

(b) of his intention –

(i) to apply for an adoption order in accordance with section 44(2) of the Act; or

(ii) not to give the child a home.

(2) In a case where a prospective adopter has given notice in accordance with paragraph (1) and he subsequently moves his home into the area of another local authority, he must within 14 days of that move confirm to that authority in writing the child's entry into the United Kingdom and that notice of his intention –

(a) to apply for an adoption order in accordance with section 44(2) of the Act has been given to another local authority; or

(b) not to give the child a home,

has been given.

25 Functions imposed on the local authority following the child's entry into the United Kingdom

(1) Where notice is given to a local authority in accordance with regulation 24, the functions imposed on the local authority by virtue of regulation 5 shall apply subject to the modifications in paragraph (2).

(2) Paragraph (1) of regulation 5 shall apply as if –

(a) in sub-paragraph (a) –

(i) in head (i) for the words "relevant foreign authority" there is substituted "CA of the State of origin and competent foreign authority";

PART IV

(ii) in head (v) there is substituted "the relevant Central Authority"; and
(b) sub-paragraphs (b) to (d) were omitted.

26 Prospective adopter unable to proceed with adoption

(1) Where the prospective adopter gives notice to the relevant local authority that he does not wish to proceed with the adoption and no longer wishes to give the child a home, he must return the child to that authority not later than the end of the period of seven days beginning with the date on which notice was given.

(2) Where a relevant local authority have received a notice in accordance with paragraph (1), that authority must give notice to the relevant Central Authority of the decision of the prospective adopter not to proceed with the adoption.

Amendments—SI 2005/3482.

27 Withdrawal of child from prospective adopter

(1) Where the relevant local authority are of the opinion that the continued placement of the child is not in the child's best interests –

(a) that authority must give notice to the prospective adopter of their opinion and request the return of the child to them; and
(b) subject to paragraph (3), the prospective adopter must, not later than the end of the period of seven days beginning with the date on which notice was given, return the child to that authority.

(2) Where the relevant local authority has given notice under paragraph (1), that authority must at the same time notify the relevant Central Authority that they have requested the return of the child.

(3) Where notice is given under paragraph (1) but –

(a) an application for a Convention adoption order was made prior to the giving of that notice; and
(b) the application has not been disposed of,

the prospective adopter is not required by virtue of paragraph (1) to return the child unless the court so orders.

(4) This regulation does not affect the exercise by any local authority or other person of any power conferred by any enactment or the exercise of any power of arrest.

28 Breakdown of placement

(1) This regulation applies where –

(a) notification is given by the prospective adopter under regulation 26 (unable to proceed with adoption);
(b) the child is withdrawn from the prospective adopter under regulation 27 (withdrawal of child from prospective adopter);
(c) an application for a Convention adoption order is refused;
(d) a Convention adoption which is subject to a probationary period cannot be made; or
(e) a Convention adoption order or a Convention adoption is annulled pursuant to section 89(1) of the Act.

(2) Where the relevant local authority are satisfied that it would be in the child's best interests to be placed for adoption with another prospective adopter habitually resident in the United Kingdom they must take the necessary measures to identify a suitable adoptive parent for that child.

(3) Where the relevant local authority have identified and approved another prospective adopter who is eligible, and has been assessed as suitable, to adopt in accordance with these Regulations –

    (a)   that authority must notify the relevant Central Authority in writing that –
        (i)   another prospective adopter has been identified; and
        (ii)   the provisions in regulations 14, 15 and 16 have been complied with; and
    (b)   the requirements specified in regulations 18 and 19 have been complied with.

(4) Where the relevant Central Authority has been notified in accordance with paragraph (3)(a) –

    (a)   it shall inform the CA of the State of origin of the proposed placement; and
    (b)   it shall agree the placement with the CA of the State of origin in accordance with the provisions in this Chapter.

(5) Subject to paragraph (2), where the relevant local authority is not satisfied it would be in the child's best interests to be placed for adoption with another prospective adopter in England or Wales, it must liaise with the relevant Central Authority to arrange for the return of the child to his State of origin.

(6) Before coming to any decision under this regulation, the relevant local authority must have regard to the wishes and feelings of the child, having regard to his age and understanding, and where appropriate, obtain his consent in relation to measures to be taken under this regulation.

29 Convention adoptions subject to a probationary period

(1) This regulation applies where –

    (a)   the child has been placed with the prospective adopters by the competent authority in the State of origin and a Convention adoption has been applied for by the prospective adopters in the State of origin but the child's placement with the prospective adopter is subject to a probationary period before the Convention adoption is made; and
    (b)   the prospective adopter returns to England or Wales with the child before that probationary period is completed and the Convention adoption is made in the State of origin.

(2) The relevant local authority must, if requested by the competent authority of the State of origin, submit a report about the placement to that authority and such a report must be prepared within such timescales and contain such information as the competent authority may reasonably require.

30 Report of local authority investigation

The report of the investigation which a local authority must submit to the court in accordance with section 44(5) of the Act must include –

    (a)   confirmation that the Certificate of eligibility and approval has been sent to the CA of the State of origin in accordance with regulation 18;
    (b)   the date on which the agreement under Article 17(c) of the Convention was made; and
    (c)   details of the reports of the visits and reviews made in accordance with regulation 5 as modified by regulation 25.

31 Convention adoption order

An adoption order shall not be made as a Convention adoption order unless –

   (a) in the case of –
      (i)   an application by a couple, both members of the couple have been habitually resident in any part of the British Islands for a period of not less than one year ending with the date of the application; or
      (ii) an application by one person, the applicant has been habitually resident in any part of the British Islands for a period of not less than one year ending with the date of the application;
   (b) the child to be adopted was, on the date on which the agreement under Article 17(c) of the Convention was made, habitually resident in a Convention country outside the British Islands; and
   (c) in a case where one member of a couple (in the case of an application by a couple) or the applicant (in the case of an application by one person) is not a British citizen, the Home Office has confirmed that the child is authorised to enter and reside permanently in the United Kingdom.

32 Requirements following a Convention adoption order or Convention adoption

(1) Where the relevant Central Authority receives a copy of a Convention adoption order made by a court in England or Wales that Authority must issue a certificate in the form set out in Schedule 2 certifying that the adoption has been made in accordance with the Convention.

(2) A copy of the certificate issued under paragraph (1) must be sent to the –

   (a) CA of the State of origin;
   (b) adoptive parent; and
   (c) adoption agency and, if different, the relevant local authority.

(3) Where a Convention adoption is made and the relevant Central Authority receives a certificate under Article 23 of the Convention in respect of that Convention adoption, the relevant Central Authority must send a copy of that certificate to the –

   (a) adoptive parent; and
   (b) adoption agency and, if different, the relevant local authority.

33 Refusal of a court in England or Wales to make a Convention adoption order

Where an application for a Convention adoption order is refused by the court or is withdrawn, the prospective adopter must return the child to the relevant local authority within the period determined by the court.

34 Annulment of a Convention adoption order or a Convention adoption

Where a Convention adoption order or a Convention adoption is annulled under section 89(1) of the Act and the relevant Central Authority receives a copy of the order from the court, it must forward a copy of that order to the CA of the State of origin.

Chapter 2
Requirements, Procedure, Recognition and Effect of Adoptions in England and Wales where the United Kingdom is the State of Origin

35 Application of Chapter 2

The provisions in this Chapter shall apply where a couple or a person habitually resident in a Convention country outside the British Islands, wishes to adopt a child who is habitually resident in the British Islands in accordance with the Convention.

36 Counselling and information for the child

(1) Where an adoption agency is considering whether a child is suitable for an adoption in accordance with the Convention, it must provide a counselling service for and information to that child in accordance with regulation 13 of the Agencies Regulations or corresponding Welsh provision and it must –

(a) explain to the child in an appropriate manner the procedure in relation to, and the legal implications of, adoption under the Convention for that child by a prospective adopter habitually resident in the receiving State; and

(b) provide him with written information about the matters referred to in sub-paragraph (a).

(2) Paragraph (1) does not apply if the adoption agency is satisfied that the requirements set out in that paragraph have been carried out in respect of the prospective adopter by another agency.

37 Counselling and information for the parent or guardian of the child etc

(1) An adoption agency must provide a counselling service and information in accordance with regulation 14 of the Agencies Regulations or corresponding Welsh provision for the parent or guardian of the child and, where regulation 14(4) of the Agencies Regulations or corresponding Welsh provision applies, for the father.

(2) The adoption agency must also –

(a) explain to the parent or guardian, and, where regulation 14(4) of the Agencies Regulations or corresponding Welsh provision applies, the father the procedure in relation to, and the legal implications of, adoption under the Convention by a prospective adopter in a receiving State; and

(b) provide him with written information about the matters referred to in sub-paragraph (a).

(3) Paragraphs (1) and (2) do not apply if the adoption agency is satisfied that the requirements set out in that paragraph have been carried out in respect of the prospective adopter by another agency.

38 Requirements in respect of the child's permanence report and information for the adoption panel

(1) The child's permanence report which the adoption agency is required to prepare in accordance with regulation 17 of the Agencies Regulations or corresponding Welsh provision must include –

(a) a summary of the possibilities for placement of the child within the United Kingdom; and

(b) an assessment of whether an adoption by a person in a particular receiving State is in the child's best interests.

PART IV

(2) In a case falling within regulation 17(2C) of the Agencies Regulations or the corresponding Welsh provision, the adoption agency must send –

    (a)   if received, the Article 15 Report; and

    (b)   their observations on that Report,

together with the reports and information referred to in regulation 17(2D) of the Agencies Regulations or corresponding Welsh provision to the adoption panel.

(3) In a case falling within regulation 17(2) of the Agencies Regulations or the corresponding Welsh provision, the adoption agency must consider –

    (a)   if received, the Article 15 Report; and

    (b)   their observations on that Report together with the reports and information referred to in regulation 17(2D) of the Agencies Regulations or the corresponding Welsh provision

in deciding whether the child should be placed for adoption in accordance with the Convention.

Amendments—SI 2012/1410.

39 Recommendation of adoption panel

Where an adoption panel make a recommendation in accordance with regulation 18(1) of the Agencies Regulations or corresponding Welsh provision it must consider and take into account the Article 15 Report, if available, and the observations thereon together with the information passed to it as a consequence of regulation 38.

40 Adoption agency decision and notification

Where the adoption agency decides in accordance with regulation 19 of the Agencies Regulations or corresponding Welsh provision that the child should be placed for an adoption in accordance with the Convention it must notify the relevant Central Authority of –

    (a)   the name, sex and age of the child;

    (b)   the reasons why they consider that the child may be suitable for such an adoption;

    (c)   whether a prospective adopter has been identified and, if so, provide any relevant information; and

    (d)   any other information that Authority may require.

41 Convention list

(1) The relevant Central Authority is to maintain a Convention list of children who are notified to that Authority under regulation 40 and shall make the contents of that list available for consultation by other Authorities within the British Islands.

(2) Where an adoption agency –

    (a)   places for adoption a child whose details have been notified to the relevant Central Authority under regulation 40; or

    (b)   determines that an adoption in accordance with the Convention is no longer in the best interests of the child,

it must notify the relevant Central Authority accordingly and that Authority must remove the details relating to that child from the Convention list.

42 Receipt of the Article 15 Report from the CA of the receiving State

(1) This regulation applies where –

    (a) the relevant Central Authority receives a report from the CA of the receiving State which has been prepared for the purposes of Article 15 of the Convention ("the Article 15 Report");

    (b) the Article 15 Report relates to a prospective adopter who is habitually resident in that receiving State; and

    (c) the prospective adopter named in the Article 15 Report wishes to adopt a child who is habitually resident in the British Islands.

(2) Subject to paragraph (3), if the relevant Central Authority is satisfied the prospective adopter meets the following requirements –

    (a) the age requirements as specified in section 50 of the Act in the case of adoption by a couple, or section 51 of the Act in the case of adoption by one person; and

    (b) in the case of a couple, both are, or in the case of adoption by one person, that person is habitually resident in a Convention country outside the British Islands,

that Authority must consult the Convention list and may, if the Authority considers it appropriate, consult any Convention list maintained by another Central Authority within the British Islands.

(3) Where a prospective adopter has already been identified in relation to a proposed adoption of a particular child and the relevant Central Authority is satisfied that prospective adopter meets the requirements referred to in paragraph (2)(a) and (b), that Authority –

    (a) need not consult the Convention list; and

    (b) must send the Article 15 Report to the local authority which referred the child's details to the Authority.

(4) The relevant Central Authority may pass a copy of the Article 15 Report to any other Central Authority within the British Islands for the purposes of enabling that Authority to consult its Convention list.

(5) Where the relevant Central Authority identifies a child on the Convention list who may be suitable for adoption by the prospective adopter, that Authority must send the Article 15 Report to the local authority which referred the child's details to that Authority.

43 Proposed placement and referral to adoption panel

(1) Where the adoption agency is considering whether a proposed placement should proceed in accordance with the procedure provided for in regulation 31 of the Agencies Regulations or corresponding Welsh provision it must take into account the Article 15 Report.

(2) Where the adoption agency refers the proposal to place the child with the particular prospective adopter to the adoption panel in accordance with regulation 31 of the Agencies Regulations or corresponding Welsh provision, it must also send the Article 15 Report to the panel.

44 Consideration by adoption panel

The adoption panel must take into account when considering what recommendation to make in accordance with regulation 32(1) of the Agencies Regulations or corresponding

PART IV

Welsh provision the Article 15 Report and any other information passed to it as a consequence of the provisions in this Chapter.

45 Adoption agency's decision in relation to the proposed placement

(1) Regulation 33 of the Agencies Regulations or corresponding Welsh provision shall apply as if paragraph (3) of that regulation or corresponding Welsh provision was omitted.

(2) As soon as possible after the agency makes its decision, it must notify the relevant Central Authority of its decision.

(3) If the proposed placement is not to proceed –

    (a)   the adoption agency must return the Article 15 Report and any other documents or information sent to it by the relevant Central Authority to that Authority; and

    (b)   the relevant Central Authority must then send that Report, any such documents or such information to the CA of the receiving State.

46 Preparation of the Article 16 Information

(1) If the adoption agency decides that the proposed placement should proceed, it must prepare a report for the purposes of Article 16(1) of the Convention which must include –

    (a)   the information about the child which is specified in Schedule 1 to the Agencies Regulations or corresponding Welsh provision; and

    (b)   the reasons for their decision.

(2) The adoption agency must send the following to the relevant Central Authority –

    (a)   the report referred to in paragraph (1);

    (b)   details of any placement order or other orders, if any, made by the courts; and

    (c)   confirmation that the parent or guardian consents to the proposed adoption.

(3) The relevant Central Authority must then send the documents referred to in paragraph (2) to the CA of the receiving State.

47 Requirements to be met before the child is placed for adoption with prospective adopter

(1) The relevant Central Authority may notify the CA of the receiving State that it is prepared to agree that the adoption may proceed provided that CA has confirmed that –

    (a)   the prospective adopter has agreed to adopt the child and has received such counselling as may be necessary;

    (b)   the prospective adopter has confirmed that he will accompany the child to the receiving State, unless in the case of a couple, the adoption agency and the CA of the receiving State have agreed that it is only necessary for one of them to do so;

    (c)   it is content for the adoption to proceed;

    (d)   in the case where a Convention adoption is to be effected, it has explained to the prospective adopter the need to make an application under section 84(1) of the Act; and

    (e)   the child is or will be authorised to enter and reside permanently in the Convention country if a Convention adoption is effected or a Convention adoption order is made.

(2) The relevant Central Authority may not make an agreement under Article 17(c) of the Convention with the CA of the receiving State unless –

(a)   confirmation has been received in respect of the matters referred to in paragraph (1); and

(b)   the adoption agency has confirmed to the relevant Central Authority that –

    (i)   it has met the prospective adopter and explained the requirement to make an application for an order under section 84 of the Act before the child can be removed from the United Kingdom;

    (ii)   the prospective adopter has visited the child; and

    (iii)   the prospective adopter is content for the adoption to proceed.

(3) An adoption agency may not place a child for adoption unless the agreement under Article 17(c) of the Convention has been made and the relevant Central Authority must advise that agency when that agreement has been made.

(4) In this regulation, the reference to "prospective adopter" means in the case of a couple, both of them.

48 Requirements in respect of giving parental responsibility prior to a proposed Convention adoption

In the case of a proposed Convention adoption, the prescribed requirements for the purposes of section 84(3) of the Act (requirements to be satisfied prior to making an order) are –

(a)   the competent authorities of the receiving State have –

    (i)   prepared a report for the purposes of Article 15 of the Convention;

    (ii)   determined and confirmed in writing that the prospective adoptive parent is eligible and suitable to adopt;

    (iii)   ensured and confirmed in writing that the prospective adoptive parent has been counselled as may be necessary; and

    (iv)   determined and confirmed in writing that the child is or will be authorised to enter and reside permanently in that State;

(b)   the report required for the purposes of Article 16(1) of the Convention has been prepared by the adoption agency;

(c)   the adoption agency confirms in writing that it has complied with the requirements imposed upon it under Part 3 of the Agencies Regulations or corresponding Welsh provision and this Chapter;

(d)   the adoption agency has obtained and made available to the court –

    (i)   the reports and information referred to in regulation 17(2D) of the Agencies Regulations or corresponding Welsh provision;

    (ii)   the recommendation made by the adoption panel in accordance with regulations 18, where applicable, and 33 of the Agencies Regulations or corresponding Welsh provisions; and

    (iii)   the adoption placement report prepared in accordance with regulation 31(2) of the Agencies Regulations or corresponding Welsh provision;

(e)   the adoption agency includes in their report submitted to the court in accordance with section 43(a) or 44(5) of the Act as modified respectively by regulation 11, details of any reviews and visits carried out as consequence of Part 6 of the Agencies Regulations or corresponding Welsh provision; and

(f)   the prospective adopter has confirmed in writing that he will accompany the child on taking the child out of the United Kingdom to travel to the receiving State or in the case of a couple the agency and competent foreign authority have confirmed that it is necessary for only one of them to do so.

Amendments—SI 2012/1410.

PART IV

49 Local authority report

In the case of a proposed application for a Convention adoption order, the report which a local authority must submit to the court in accordance with section 43(a) or 44(5) of the Act must include a copy of the –

    (a)   Article 15 Report;

    (b)   report prepared for the purposes of Article 16(1); and

    (c)   written confirmation of the agreement under Article 17(c) of the Convention.

50 Convention adoption order

An adoption order shall not be made as a Convention adoption order unless –

    (a)   in the case of –

        (i)   an application by a couple, both members of the couple have been habitually resident in a Convention country outside the British Islands for a period of not less than one year ending with the date of the application; or

    (aa) an application by one person, the applicant has been habitually resident in a Convention country outside the British Islands for a period of not less than one year ending with the date of the application;

    (b)   the child to be adopted was, on the date on which the agreement under Article 17(c) of the Convention was made, habitually resident in any part of the British Islands; and

    (c)   the competent authority has confirmed that the child is authorised to enter and remain permanently in the Convention country in which the applicant is habitually resident.

51 Requirements following a Convention adoption order or Convention adoption

(1) Where the relevant Central Authority receives a copy of a Convention adoption order made by a court in England or Wales, that Authority must issue a certificate in the form set out in Schedule 2 certifying that the adoption has been made in accordance with the Convention.

(2) A copy of the certificate must be sent to the –

    (a)   CA of the receiving State; and

    (b)   the relevant local authority.

(3) Where a Convention adoption is made and the Central Authority receives a certificate under Article 23 in respect of that Convention adoption, the relevant Central Authority must send a copy of that certificate to the relevant local authority.

Chapter 3
Miscellaneous Provisions

52 Application, with or without modifications, of the Act

(1) Subject to the modifications provided for in this Chapter, the provisions of the Act shall apply to adoptions within the scope of the Convention so far as the nature of the provision permits and unless the contrary intention is shown.

53 Change of name and removal from the United Kingdom

In a case falling within Chapter 1 of this Part, section 28(2) of the Act shall apply as if –

(a) at the end of paragraph (a), "or" was omitted;

(b) at the end of paragraph (b) there were inserted "or (c) a child is placed by a competent foreign authority for the purposes of an adoption under the Convention,"; and

(c) at the end of subsection (2) there were inserted "or the competent foreign authority consents to a change of surname.".

54 Removal of children

(1) In a case falling within Chapter 1 of this Part, sections 36 to 40 of the Act shall not apply.

(2) In a case falling within Chapter 2 of this Part –

(a) section 36 of the Act shall apply, as if –
   (i) for the words "an adoption order" in paragraphs (a) and (c) in subsection (1) there were substituted "a Convention adoption order"; and
   (ii) subsection (2) was omitted; and

(b) section 39 of the Act shall apply as if subsection (3)(a) was omitted.

55 Modifications of the Act in respect of orders under section 84 where child is to be adopted under the Convention

The modifications set out in regulation 11 shall apply in the case where a couple or person habitually resident in a Convention country outside the British Islands intend to adopt a child who is habitually resident in England or Wales in accordance with the Convention.

56 Child to live with adopters before application for a Convention adoption order

Section 42 of the Act shall apply as if –

(a) subsections (1)(b) and (3) to (6) were omitted; and

(b) in subsection (2) from the word "If" to the end of paragraph (b) there were substituted "In the case of an adoption under the Convention,".

57 Notice of intention to adopt

Section 44 of the Act shall apply as if subsection (3) was omitted.

58 Application for Convention adoption order

Section 49 of the Act shall apply as if –

(a) in subsection (1), the words from "but only" to the end were omitted;

(b) subsections (2) and (3) were omitted.

59 Offences

Any person who contravenes or fails to comply with –

(a) regulation 24 (requirements in respect of prospective adopter following child's entry into the United Kingdom);

(b) regulation 26(1) (return of child to relevant local authority where prospective adopter does not wish to proceed);

(c) regulation 27(1)(b) (return of child to relevant local authority on request of local authority or by order of court); or

PART IV

(d) regulation 33 (refusal of a court in England or Wales to make a Convention adoption order)

is guilty of an offence and liable on summary conviction to imprisonment for a term not exceeding three months, or a fine not exceeding level 5 on the standard scale, or both.

Amendments—SI 2005/3482.

SCHEDULE 1
CERTIFICATE OF ELIGIBILITY AND APPROVAL

To the Central Authority of the State of origin

Re . . . [*name of applicant*]

In accordance with Article 5 of the Convention, I hereby certify on behalf of the Central Authority for [*England*] [*Wales*] that .... [*name of applicant*] has been counselled, is eligible to adopt and has been assessed and approved as suitable to adopt a child from .... [*State of origin*] by .... [*public authority or accredited body for the purposes of the Convention*].

The attached report has been prepared in accordance with Article 15 of the Convention for presentation to the competent authority in .... [*State of origin*].

This certificate of eligibility and approval and the report under Article 15 of the Convention are provided on the condition that a Convention adoption or Convention adoption order will not be made until the agreement under Article 17(c) of the Convention has been made.

I confirm on behalf of the Central Authority that if following the agreement under Article 17(c) of the Convention that –

[in the case, where the requirements specified in section 1(5A) of the British Nationality Act 1981 are met that the child .... [*name*] will be authorised to enter and reside permanently in the United Kingdom]; or

[in any other case, if entry clearance and leave to enter and remain, as may be necessary, is granted and not revoked, or curtailed and a Convention adoption order or Convention adoption is made, the child .... [*name*] will be authorised to enter and reside permanently in the United Kingdom.]

Name

[*On behalf of the Secretary of State, the Central Authority for England*]

Date

[*the National Assembly for Wales, the Central Authority for Wales*]

SCHEDULE 2
CERTIFICATE THAT THE CONVENTION ADOPTION ORDER HAS BEEN MADE IN ACCORDANCE WITH THE CONVENTION

1 The Central Authority as the competent authority for [*England*] [*Wales*] being the country in which the Convention adoption order was made hereby certifies, in accordance with Article 23(1) of the Convention, that the child:

(a) name .... [name on birth certificate, also known as/now known as ....]
sex: ....
date and place of birth: ....
habitual residence at the time of the adoption: ....

State of origin: ....
(b)   was adopted on: ....
by order made by: .... court in [*England*] [*Wales*]
(c)   by the following person(s):
    (i)   family name and first name(s): ....
          sex: ....
          date and place of birth: ....
          Habitual residence at the time adoption order was made: ....
    (ii)   family name and first name(s): ....
          sex: ....
          date and place of birth: ....
          habitual residence at the time adoption order made: ....

2 The competent authority for [*England*] [*Wales*] in pursuance of Article 23(1) of the Convention hereby certifies that the adoption was made in accordance with the Convention and that the agreement under Article 17(c) was given by:

(a)   name and address of the Central Authority in State of origin: ....
     date of the agreement: ....
(b)   name and address of the Central Authority of receiving State: ....
     date of the agreement: ....

Signed

Date

Allocation and Transfer of Proceedings Order 2008, SI 2008/2836

ARRANGEMENT OF ARTICLES

PART 1
PRELIMINARY

PART 2
STARTING PROCEEDINGS

Section 1
Starting Proceedings in Specified Level of Court

Section 2
Starting Proceedings in Specified Class of County Court

PART IV

PART 3
TRANSFER OF PROCEEDINGS

Section 1
General

Section 2
Transfer of Proceedings to Specified Level of Court

Section 3
Transfer of Proceedings to a Specified Class of County Court

Section 4
Transfer of Proceedings to Particular Court

PART 4
APPLICATION FOLLOWING REFUSAL TO TRANSFER FROM MAGISTRATES' COURT TO COUNTY COURT AND APPEAL AGAINST TRANSFER TO MAGISTRATES' COURT BY COUNTY COURT

PART 5
REVOCATIONS, CONSEQUENTIAL AMENDMENTS AND TRANSITIONAL PROVISIONS

Note—*PD: Allocation and Transfer of Proceedings* (25 November 2008) is set out in Part V.

PART 1
PRELIMINARY

1 Citation, commencement, interpretation and application

(1) This Order may be cited as the Allocation and Transfer of Proceedings Order 2008 and, subject to paragraph (2), shall come into force on 25 November 2008.

(2) Articles 6(a)(i), 9(1) and 20(1), in so far as they apply to section 11J(6) or 11O(7) of, and paragraphs 4 to 7 and 9 of Schedule A1 to, the 1989 Act, shall come into force on the same day as sections 4 and 5 of the Children and Adoption Act 2006 come into force.

(3) In this Order –

"the 1989 Act" means the Children Act 1989;

"the 1996 Act" means the Family Law Act 1996;

"the 2002 Act" means the Adoption and Children Act 2002;

"Convention adoption order" means an adoption order under the 2002 Act which, by virtue of regulations under section 1 of the Adoption (Intercountry Aspects) Act 1999 (regulations giving effect to the Convention), is made as a Convention adoption order;

"proceedings" means, unless the context otherwise requires, proceedings under –

    (a)   section 55A of the Family Law Act 1986 (declarations of parentage);

    (b)   the 1989 Act;

    (c)   section 20 of the Child Support Act 1991 (appeals);

    (d)   section 54 of the Human Fertilisation and Embryology Act 2008 (parental orders);

    (e)   Part 4 of the 1996 Act; and

    (f)   the 2002 Act.

(4) The provisions in this Order apply unless any enactment or rule provides otherwise.

Amendments—SI 2010/986.

Objective—The practical objective of this order, in combination with the PD, is to ensure that the work of the family courts is pushed downwards. Thus the majority of private law family cases should be dealt with in the family proceedings court. The magistracy has benefitted from further training and therefore the previous guidance that cases exceeding 3 days should be transferred to the county court no longer applies without further extenuating circumstances. Cases may only be transferred (ordinarily) to the High Court after the trial judge has consulted with the Family Division Liaison Judge. The aim is to keep many cases which would have previously been transferred to the High Court in the county court. It is suggested that contested cases of inflicted injury, especially head or eye injury, where there is an issue on the medical evidence, ought to continue to be heard by a judge of the Division.

2 Classes of county court

For the purposes of this Order there are the following classes of county court –

    (a)   family hearing centres, being those courts against which the word yes appears in column 2 of the table in Schedule 1;

    (b)   care centres, being those courts against which the word yes appears in column 3 of that table;

    (c)   adoption centres, being those courts against which the word yes appears in column 4 of that table;

    (d)   intercountry adoption centres, being those courts against which the word yes appears in column 5 of that table; and

    (e)   forced marriage county courts, being those courts against which the word yes appears in column 6 of that table.

Classes of county courts—The family hearing centres may hear private law applications relating to children (art 9(1) below). The care centres may deal with public law applications under Pts 3, 4 and 5 of CA 1989 (art 9(2) below). The adoption centres deal with all applications concerning the adoption of a

PART IV

child, save for those applications concerning a Convention adoption order or an adoption order to which ACA 2002, s 83 applies, which must be commenced in an intercountry adoption centre (art 11 below). All applications under FLA 1996, Pt 4A must be commenced in a forced marriage county court (art 10 below).

3 Principal Registry of the Family Division

(1) The principal registry of the Family Division of the High Court is treated, for the purposes of this Order, as if it were –

    (a)   a family hearing centre;
    (b)   a care centre;
    (c)   an adoption centre;
    (d)   an intercountry adoption centre; and
    (e)   a forced marriage county court.

(2) The principal registry of the Family Division of the High Court is treated as if it were a county court for the purposes of appeals from decisions of a magistrates' court under –

    (a)   section 94 of the 1989 Act; and
    (b)   section 61 of the 1996 Act.

Amendments—SI 2009/871.

The Principal Registry—May deal with all applications under CA 1989, ACA 2002 and FLA 1996, Pt 4A. The Principal Registry may also hear appeals from magistrates' courts concerning CA 1989 or FLA 1996, Pts IV and 4A.

4 Contravention of a provision of this Order

Where proceedings are started or transferred in contravention of a provision of this Order, the contravention does not have the effect of making the proceedings invalid.

PART 2
STARTING PROCEEDINGS

Section 1
Starting Proceedings in Specified Level of Court

5 Proceedings which must be started in a magistrates' court

(1) Proceedings under the following provisions must be started in a magistrates' court –

    (a)   section 79K of the 1989 Act (protection of children in an emergency);
    (b)   paragraph 23 of Schedule 2 to the 1989 Act (contribution order);
    (c)   paragraph 8 of Schedule 8 to the 1989 Act (certain appeals);
    (d)   section 23 of the 2002 Act (varying placement order);
    (e)   section 50 or 51 of the 2002 Act (adoption order), unless any local authority will be a party to the proceedings or article 6(c) or (d) applies;
    (f)   section 20 of the Child Support Act 1991 (appeals) where the proceedings are to be dealt with in accordance with the Child Support Appeals (Jurisdiction of Courts) Order 2002; and
    (g)   section 54 of the Human Fertilisation and Embryology Act 2008 (parental orders).

(2) Subject to paragraphs (3) and (4), proceedings under the following provisions must be started in a magistrates' court –

    (a)   section 4 of the 1989 Act (acquisition of parental responsibility by father);

(b)   section 4A of the 1989 Act (acquisition of parental responsibility by step-parent);

(c)   section 25 of the 1989 Act (use of accommodation for restricting liberty);

(d)   section 31 of the 1989 Act (care and supervision orders);

(e)   section 33(7) of the 1989 Act (leave to change surname of, or remove from United Kingdom, child in care);

(f)   section 34 of the 1989 Act (parental contact etc. with children in care);

(g)   section 36 of the 1989 Act (education supervision orders);

(h)   section 43 of the 1989 Act (child assessment orders);

(i)   section 44 of the 1989 Act (emergency protection orders);

(j)   section 45 of the 1989 Act (extension, variation or discharge of emergency protection order);

(k)   section 46(7) of the 1989 Act (emergency protection order by police officer);

(l)   section 48 of the 1989 Act (powers to assist in discovery of children etc.);

(m)   section 50 of the 1989 Act (recovery orders);

(n)   section 102 of the 1989 Act (warrant authorising a constable to assist in exercise of certain powers to search for children etc.); and

(o)   paragraph 19 of Schedule 2 to the 1989 Act (approval of arrangements to assist child to live abroad).

(3) Proceedings to which paragraph (2) applies which –

(a)   concern a child who is the subject of proceedings which are pending in a county court or the High Court; and

(b)   arise out of the same circumstances as gave rise to those proceedings

may be started in the court in which those proceedings are pending.

(4) Proceedings under section 4 or 4A of the 1989 Act which are started at the same time as proceedings in a county court or the High Court for an order under section 8 of the 1989 Act (residence, contact and other applications in relation to children) in relation to the same child must be started in the court in which proceedings under section 8 are started.

Amendments—SI 2010/986.

Restriction of commencement—Where this article applies, it restricts the choice of forum which would otherwise exist by reason of the fact that CA 1989 confers jurisdiction in each of the relevant types of proceedings on "the court", which is defined by s 92(7) to mean the High Court, a county court or a magistrates' court.

Leave to change name etc (art 5(2)(e))—Although under this article an application for leave pursuant to s 33(7) should be commenced in the family proceedings court, an application properly made ex parte by a local authority without notice to the child's parents for a change of the child's name should be transferred for consideration by a higher court (*Re J (A Minor) (Change of Name)* [1993] 1 FLR 699).

Pending proceedings—The phrase "arise out of the same circumstances" is not a precise term. If the basis of the new application is factually connected or related to the underlying facts of the pending application, it may be commenced in the court in which proceedings are pending and does not have to be commenced in a magistrates' court.

Parental responsibility—Applications by a father or step father for parental responsibility pursuant to CA 1989, s 4 or s 4A must be commenced in a magistrates' court, save where there are pending proceedings in the High Court or a county court when the application must be commenced in that court (art 5(2) and (4)).

Procedure—The making of applications under CA 1989 in magistrates' courts is governed by FPR 2010, Pt 12.

6 Proceedings which must be started in a county court

Subject to article 7, proceedings –

    (a)   brought by an applicant who is under the age of eighteen under –
        (i)   section 10(2)(b), 11J(6) or 11O(7) of, or paragraph 9(6) of Schedule A1
             to, the 1989 Act (leave of the court to make an application); or
        (ii) Part 4 of the 1996 Act;
    (b)   under section 43 of the 1996 Act (leave of the court for applications by children under sixteen);
    (c)   for a Convention adoption order; or
    (d)   for an adoption order under the 2002 Act where section 83 of that Act (restriction on bringing children in) applies,

must be started in a county court.

7 Proceedings which may be started in the High Court

Subject to articles 5(3) and (4) and 8, proceedings may be started in the High Court only if –

    (a)   the proceedings are exceptionally complex;
    (b)   the outcome of the proceedings is important to the public in general; or
    (c)   there is another substantial reason for the proceedings to be started in the High Court.

Factors to consider—Para 5.1 of the PD issued 3 November 2008 (see Part V) sets out the factors to be taken into account when considering whether the criteria in arts 7 or 18 apply (e g the death of another child in the family, a parent or material person may have committed a grave crime such as murder, manslaughter or rape, an adoption order is sought where the foreign adoption order is not recognised in this jurisdiction or a child has been brought into the UK in breach of the regulations made under ACA 2002, s 83). Para 5.2 sets out the types of proceedings which are likely to fall within the criteria (e g contested issues of domicile, an application is opposed for want of jurisdiction, those in which there is a complex foreign element or removal of a child temporarily or permanently to a non-Hague Convention country). Para 5.3 sets out the factors which will *not* normally render proceedings suitable to be dealt with in the High Court (e g sexual abuse, intractable contact disputes, routine neglect – even if it spans many years and the documentation is copious, length of hearing, number of experts, possible speedier hearing, standard human rights issues or the celebrity of the parties).

8 Proceedings which must be started in the court where proceedings under the 2002 Act are pending

(1) Where proceedings under section 50 or 51 of the 2002 Act (adoption order) are pending, proceedings concerning the same child under –

    (a)   section 29(4)(b) of the 2002 Act (leave to apply for a residence order);
    (b)   section 29(5)(b) of the 2002 Act (leave to apply for a special guardianship order);
    (c)   section 8 of the 1989 Act where section 28(1)(a) or 29(4)(b) of the 2002 Act applies (leave obtained to make application for a residence order);
    (d)   section 14A of the 1989 Act where section 28(1)(b) or 29(5)(b) of the 2002 Act applies (leave obtained to make application for a special guardianship order);
    (e)   section 37(a) of the 2002 Act (leave to remove the child); or
    (f)   section 47(3) or (5) of the 2002 Act (leave to oppose the making of an adoption order),

must be started in the court in which the proceedings under section 50 or 51 are pending.

(2) Where proceedings under section 22 of the 2002 Act (placement order) are pending, proceedings under section 30(2)(b) of that Act (leave to remove a child from accommodation provided by the local authority) must be started in the court in which the proceedings under section 22 are pending.

(3) Where proceedings under section 42(6) of the 2002 Act (leave to apply for an adoption order) are pending, proceedings under section 38(3)(a) or 40(2)(a) of that Act (leave to remove a child) must be started in the court in which the proceedings under section 42(6) are pending.

General—Where proceedings are pending for an adoption order or a placement order, or for leave to apply for an adoption order, all applications specified in the paragraph for orders relating to the subject child must be made to the court in which the former proceedings are pending.

Section 2
Starting Proceedings in Specified Class of County Court

9 Starting proceedings under the 1989 Act

(1) Subject to article 8(1)(c) and (d), proceedings under Part 1 or 2 of, or Schedule 1 or paragraphs 4 to 7 or 9 of Schedule A1 to, the 1989 Act which are to be started in a county court must be started in a family hearing centre.

(2) Proceedings under Part 3, 4 or 5 of the 1989 Act which are to be started in a county court must be started in a care centre.

General—Save for residence and special guardianship applications made where a placement order is in force, all applications for parental responsibility or s 8 orders, contact activity orders, contact enforcement orders or child financial provision orders that are issued out of a county court must be started in a family hearing centre. All applications for public law orders in respect of a child must be issued out of a care centre.

10 Starting proceedings under Part 4A of the 1996 Act

(1) Proceedings under Part 4A of the 1996 Act which are to be started in a county court must be started in a forced marriage county court.

(2) Article 7 applies to proceedings under Part 4A of the 1996 Act as it applies to other proceedings.

11 Starting proceedings under the 2002 Act

(1) Subject to paragraph (2), proceedings under the 2002 Act which are to be started in a county court must be started in an adoption centre.

(2) Proceedings for –

    (a)   a Convention adoption order; or
    (b)   an adoption order under the 2002 Act where section 83 of that Act applies

which are to be started in a county court must be started in an intercountry adoption centre.

PART 3
TRANSFER OF PROCEEDINGS

Section 1
General

12 Disapplication of enactments about transfer

The proceedings to which this Order applies are excluded from the operation of sections 38 and 39 of the Matrimonial and Family Proceedings Act 1984 (transfer of family proceedings).

PART IV

MFPA 1984 (ss 38, 39)—Section 38 allows the High Court to transfer to a county court any family proceedings which are within that county court's jurisdiction. Section 39 allows a county court to transfer family proceedings to the High Court. The effect of their disapplication is that the order contains the only provisions enabling proceedings under CA 1989 or ACA 2002 to be transferred between the High Court and county courts. The general transfer provisions of CCA 1984, ss 40–42 do not apply to family proceedings within the meaning of MFPA 1984, Pt V.

13 General rules about transfer of proceedings

(1) When making any decision about the transfer of proceedings under articles 14, 15, 17 and 18 the court must have regard to the need to avoid delay in the proceedings.

(2) Articles 16 and 19 do not apply if the transfer of proceedings would cause the determination of the proceedings to be delayed.

(3) The transfer of proceedings under this Part may be made at any stage of the proceedings and whether or not the proceedings have already been transferred.

Transfer—Paragraphs 3.1–4.4 of the PD issued 3 November 2008 set out additional factors to be taken into account when making a decision about the transfer of proceedings. Where a decision to transfer is finely balanced the proceedings should *not* be transferred if the transfer would lead to delay (para 4.2). While there is no express reference in the Order to the length of the hearing or to judicial continuity, such issues may be relevant (para 4.4).

Section 2
Transfer of Proceedings to Specified Level of Court

14 Transfer of proceedings from one magistrates' court to another

A magistrates' court (the "transferring court") may transfer proceedings to another magistrates' court (the "receiving court") only if the transferring court considers that –

    (a)   the transfer will significantly accelerate the determination of the proceedings;

    (b)   it is more convenient for the parties or for the child who is the subject of the proceedings for the proceedings to be dealt with by the receiving court; or

    (c)   there is another good reason for the proceedings to be transferred.

Defined terms—"child": art 1(2); "family proceedings": CA 1989, s 8(3).

"magistrates' court"—The jurisdiction of a magistrates' court to transfer proceedings to which this article applies may be exercised by a justices' clerk (JCR 2005, para 37) or, where the proceedings are under CA 1989, by court clerks authorised under FPR 2010, r 2.5.

15 Transfer of proceedings from magistrates' court to county court

(1) Subject to paragraphs (2) and (3), a magistrates' court may transfer the whole or any part of proceedings to a county court only if the magistrates' court considers that –

    (a)   the transfer will significantly accelerate the determination of the proceedings;

    (b)   there is a real possibility of difficulty in resolving conflicts in the evidence of witnesses;

    (c)   there is a real possibility of a conflict in the evidence of two or more experts;

    (d)   there is a novel or difficult point of law;

    (e)   there are proceedings concerning the child in another jurisdiction or there are international law issues;

    (f)   there is a real possibility that enforcement proceedings may be necessary and the method of enforcement or the likely penalty is beyond the powers of a magistrates' court;

    (g)   there is a real possibility that a guardian ad litem will be appointed under rule 9.5 of the Family Proceedings Rules 1991;

(h) *(revoked)*

(i) there is another good reason for the proceedings to be transferred.

(2) Proceedings under any of the provisions mentioned in articles 5(1)(a) to (c) or 5(2)(i) to (l) may not be transferred from a magistrates' court.

(3) Proceedings under section 25 of the 1989 Act (use of accommodation for restricting liberty) may not be transferred from a magistrates' court which is not a family proceedings court within the meaning of section 67 of the Magistrates' Courts Act 1980.

Amendments—SI 2011/1045.

Defined terms—"child": art 1(2); "family proceedings": CA 1989, s 8(3).

Proceedings within scope of art 15—The following are, in principle, transferable under the article: proceedings under CA 1989, s 25 (use of accommodation for restricting liberty), s 31 (care and supervision orders), s 33(7) (leave to change name or remove from United Kingdom), s 34 (parental contact), s 36 (education supervision order), s 43 (child assessment order), s 50 (recovery orders), s 102 (powers of constable to assist etc), Sch 2, para 19 (approval of arrangements to assist child to live abroad) and AA 1976, s 21 (substitution of one adoption agency for another).

Grounds for transfer (art 15(1))—The test of "grave, important or complex" in the old Order is gone. The most common grounds for transfer are likely to be a real possibility of difficulty in resolving the evidence of witnesses, a real possibility of conflict in the evidence of two or more experts and/or there is a novel or difficult point of law. The test of "a real possibility" sets the threshold fairly low.

Reducing delay (arts 13 and 15(1)(a))—Delay is only one of the factors relevant to the assessment of whether a case is suitable for upwards transfer.

No transfer from a magistrates' court which is not a family proceedings court (art 15(3))—Article 15(3) affects proceedings to authorise the use of secure accommodation under CA 1989, s 25. Such proceedings are referred to in MCA 1980, s 65(1)(n) and are thus family proceedings which, by virtue of s 67 of that Act, are to be heard by a family proceedings court. However, this is subject to an exception made by the Criminal Justice Act 1991, s 60(3), which provides for applications under CA 1989, s 25 to be made to a youth court or a magistrates' court (ie an adult court convened to deal with criminal business) in certain circumstances. Article 15(3) restricts the scope of the article to proceedings under s 25 which are family proceedings; proceedings arising in the general magistrates' court or the youth court will not be so transferred.

Timing of application—In many cases, an application for transfer will be made soon after the proceedings are commenced Where this does not happen (or where an initial transfer application is rejected) and it later becomes apparent that the case is more complex than had originally been anticipated, it is essential that action is taken swiftly to transfer it to the appropriate level of court (PD, para 3.1).

Procedure—In relation to proceedings under CA 1989, the procedure as to transfer is contained in FPR 2010, rr 2.7, 12.12.

16 Transfer of proceedings from county court to magistrates' court

(1) A county court must transfer to a magistrates' court proceedings which were transferred under article 15(1) if the county court considers that none of the criteria in article 15(1) applies.

(2) Subject to articles 5(3) and (4), 6 and 8, a county court must transfer to a magistrates' court proceedings which were started in the county court if the county court considers that none of the criteria in article 15(1)(b) to (i) applies.

Procedure—If the county court considers none of the art 15(1) criteria apply, the requirement to transfer to a magistrates' court is mandatory – the county court has no discretion to retain the matter.

17 Transfer of proceedings from one county court to another

Subject to articles 16, 20, 21 and 22 a county court (the "transferring court") may transfer proceedings to another county court (the "receiving court") only if the transferring court considers that –

(a) the transfer will significantly accelerate the determination of the proceedings;

(b) it is more convenient for the parties or for the child who is the subject of the proceedings for the proceedings to be dealt with by the receiving court;

(c) the proceedings involve the determination of a question of a kind mentioned in section 59(1) of the 1996 Act and the property in question is situated in the district of the receiving court; or

(d) there is another good reason for the proceedings to be transferred.

18 Transfer of proceedings from county court to High Court

A county court may transfer proceedings to the High Court only if the county court considers that –

(a) the proceedings are exceptionally complex;

(b) the outcome of the proceedings is important to the public in general; or

(c) there is another substantial reason for the proceedings to be transferred.

Factors to consider—See the note to art 7 above.

19 Transfer of proceedings from High Court

The High Court must transfer to a county court or a magistrates' court proceedings which were started in, or transferred to, the High Court if the High Court considers that none of the criteria in article 18 applies.

Procedure—The High Court is not restricted to transferring down to a county court but may transfer directly to a magistrates' court. Article 19 is silent on the factors to be taken into account when deciding whether to transfer proceedings from the High Court to a magistrates' court but it is suggested, having regard to the provisions of art 16, that the High Court should only take this course if satisfied that none of the criteria in art 15 apply. The power to transfer from the High Court to the magistrates' court is disapplied in all proceedings under FLA 1996, Pt 4A (art 22).

Section 3
Transfer of Proceedings to a Specified Class of County Court

20 Transfer of proceedings under the 1989 Act

(1) Where proceedings under Part 1 or 2 of, or Schedule 1 or paragraphs 4 to 7 or 9 of Schedule A1 to, the 1989 Act are to be transferred to a county court, they must be transferred to a family hearing centre.

(2) Where proceedings under Part 3, 4 or 5 of the 1989 Act are to be transferred to a county court, they must be transferred to a care centre.

21 Transfer of proceedings under the 2002 Act

(1) Subject to paragraph (2), where proceedings under the 2002 Act are to be transferred to a county court, they must be transferred to an adoption centre.

(2) Where proceedings for –

(a) a Convention Adoption Order; or

(b) an adoption order under the 2002 Act where section 83 of that Act applies,

are to be transferred to a county court, they must be transferred to an intercountry adoption centre.

22 Transfer of proceedings under Part 4A of the 1996 Act

(1) Where proceedings under Part 4A of the 1996 Act are to be transferred to a county court, they must be transferred to a forced marriage county court.

(2) Articles 17 to 19 apply to the transfer of proceedings under Part 4A of the 1996 Act as they apply to the transfer of other proceedings but as if the modification in paragraph (3) were made.

(3) Article 19 is to be read as if "or a magistrates' court" were omitted.

Section 4
Transfer of Proceedings to Particular Court

23 Transfer of proceedings when arrested for breach of order under Part 4 of the 1996 Act

Where a person is brought before –

    (a)   the relevant judicial authority in accordance with section 47(7)(a) of the 1996 Act (arrest for breach of order); or

    (b)   a court by virtue of a warrant issued under section 47(9) of the 1996 Act,

and the matter is not then disposed of immediately, the relevant judicial authority or the court may transfer the matter to the relevant judicial authority or court which attached the power of arrest under section 47(2) or (3) of the 1996 Act or which issued the warrant.

24 Transfer of proceedings when arrested for breach of order under Part 4A of the 1996 Act

Where a person is brought before –

    (a)   the relevant judge in accordance with section 63I(3) of the 1996 Act (arrest for breach of order); or

    (b)   a court by virtue of a warrant issued under section 63J(3) of the 1996 Act,

and the matter is not then disposed of immediately, the relevant judge or the court may transfer the matter to the relevant judge or court which attached the power of arrest under section 63H(2) or (4) of the 1996 Act or which issued the warrant.

PART 4
APPLICATION FOLLOWING REFUSAL TO TRANSFER FROM MAGISTRATES' COURT TO COUNTY COURT AND APPEAL AGAINST TRANSFER TO MAGISTRATES' COURT BY COUNTY COURT

25 Application following refusal to order transfer of proceedings from magistrates' court to county court

(1) Where a magistrates' court refuses to order the transfer of proceedings to a county court under article 15(1), an application may be made for an order transferring proceedings to a county court.

(2) An application under paragraph (1) must be made –

    (a)   in relation to proceedings under the 2002 Act, to an adoption centre;

    (b)   in relation to proceedings under Parts 3, 4 and 5, to a care centre; and

    (c)   in any other case, to a family hearing centre.

PART IV

(3) In this article, "proceedings" means the proceedings under the 1989 Act or the 2002 Act and proceedings under section 55A of the Family Law Act 1986 (declarations of parentage).

Procedure—There is no need to appeal a refusal to transfer to the county court. An application is made to the county court to transfer the proceedings which applications are usually dealt with by a district judge.

26 Appeal against transfer of proceedings to magistrates' court by county court

Where a county court orders the transfer of proceedings to a magistrates' court under article 16, an appeal may be made against that decision –

    (a)   where the decision was made by a district judge or deputy district judge of a county court, to a circuit judge; or

    (b)   where the decision was made by a district judge or deputy district judge of the principal registry of the Family Division, to a judge of the Family Division of the High Court.

PART 5
REVOCATIONS, CONSEQUENTIAL AMENDMENTS AND TRANSITIONAL PROVISIONS

27 Revocations

Subject to article 29(2) and (3), the instruments listed in column 1 of the table in Schedule 2 (which have the references listed in column 2) are revoked to the extent indicated in column 3.

****

29 Transitional provisions

(1) This Order applies, so far as practicable, to proceedings started before but not concluded by 25 November 2008.

(2) Where, by reason of paragraph (1), this Order does not apply to particular proceedings which have been started but not concluded before the 25 November 2008, the Children (Allocation of Proceedings) Order 1991 or the Family Law Act 1996 (Part IV) (Allocation of Proceedings) Order 1997, as the case may be, continue to apply to those proceedings.

(3) The Children (Allocation of Proceedings) (Appeals) Order 1991 continues to apply to –

    (a)   an appeal started before 25 November 2008; and

    (b)   an appeal in proceedings to which the Children (Allocation of Proceedings) Order 1991 still applies by virtue of paragraph (2).

(4) The amendments in article 28 do not apply in relation to proceedings to which the Children (Allocation of Proceedings) Order 1991 or the Family Law Act 1996 (Part IV) (Allocation of Proceedings) Order 1997 still apply by virtue of paragraph (2).

(5) In relation to an appeal in respect of a type of case before the commencement of section 10 of the Child Support, Pensions and Social Security Act 2000 for the purposes of that type of case, the reference to the Child Support Appeals (Jurisdiction of Courts) Order 2002 in article 5(1)(f) is to be read as a reference to the Child Support Appeals (Jurisdiction of Courts) Order 1993.

SCHEDULE 1
CLASSES OF COUNTY COURT

Column 1 County court	Column 2 Family Hearing Centre	Column 3 Care Centre	Column 4 Adoption Centre	Column 5 Inter-country Adoption Centre	Column 6 Forced Marriage county court
Aberystwyth County Court	Yes		Yes		
Accrington County Court	Yes				
Aldershot County Court	Yes				
Altrincham County Court	Yes				
Barnet County Court	Yes				
Barnsley County Court	Yes				
Barnstaple County Court	Yes				
Barrow in Furness County Court	Yes				
Basingstoke County Court	Yes				
Bath County Court	Yes				
Bedford County Court	Yes				
Birkenhead County Court	Yes				
Birmingham County Court	Yes	Yes	Yes	Yes	Yes
Blackburn County Court	Yes	Yes	Yes		Yes
Blackpool County Court	Yes				
Blackwood County Court	Yes				
Bodmin County Court	Yes				
Bolton County Court	Yes		Yes		
Boston County Court	Yes				
Bournemouth County Court	Yes	Yes	Yes	Yes	
Bow County Court	Yes		Yes		
Bradford County Court	Yes		Yes		Yes
Brecon County Court	Yes				
Brentford County Court	Yes		Yes		

Column 1 County court	Column 2 Family Hearing Centre	Column 3 Care Centre	Column 4 Adoption Centre	Column 5 Inter- country Adoption Centre	Column 6 Forced Marriage county court
Bridgend County Court	Yes				
Brighton County Court	Yes	Yes	Yes		
Bristol County Court	Yes	Yes	Yes	Yes	Yes
Bromley County Court	Yes		Yes		
Burnley County Court	Yes				
Burton-on-Trent County Court	Yes				
Bury County Court	Yes				
Bury St. Edmunds County Court	Yes				
Caernarfon County Court	Yes	Yes			
Cambridge County Court	Yes	Yes	Yes		
Canterbury County Court	Yes	Yes	Yes		
Cardiff County Court	Yes	Yes	Yes	Yes	Yes
Carlisle County Court	Yes	Yes	Yes		
Carmarthen County Court	Yes				
Chelmsford County Court	Yes	Yes	Yes		
Chester County Court	Yes	Yes	Yes	Yes	
Chesterfield County Court	Yes				
Chichester County Court	Yes				
Chippenham and Trowbridge County Court	Yes				
Clerkenwell & Shoreditch County Court	Yes				
Colchester and Clacton County Court	Yes				
Coventry County Court	Yes	Yes	Yes		
Crewe County Court	Yes				
Croydon County Court	Yes		Yes		

Column 1 *County court*	Column 2 *Family Hearing Centre*	Column 3 *Care Centre*	Column 4 *Adoption Centre*	Column 5 *Inter-country Adoption Centre*	Column 6 *Forced Marriage county court*
Darlington County Court	Yes				
Dartford County Court	Yes				
Derby County Court	Yes	Yes	Yes		Yes
Doncaster County Court	Yes				
Dudley County Court	Yes				
Durham County Court	Yes				
Eastbourne County Court	Yes				
Edmonton County Court	Yes				
Exeter County Court	Yes	Yes	Yes	Yes	
Gateshead County Court	Yes				
Gloucester County Court	Yes				
Grimsby County Court	Yes				
Guildford County Court	Yes	Yes	Yes		
Halifax County Court	Yes				
Harrogate County Court	Yes				
Hartlepool County Court	Yes				
Hastings County Court	Yes				
Haverfordwest County Court	Yes				
Hereford County Court	Yes				
Hertford County Court	Yes				
Horsham County Court	Yes				
Huddersfield County Court	Yes				
Ipswich County Court	Yes	Yes	Yes		
Kendal County Court	Yes				
King's Lynn County Court	Yes				

Column 1 County court	Column 2 Family Hearing Centre	Column 3 Care Centre	Column 4 Adoption Centre	Column 5 Inter- country Adoption Centre	Column 6 Forced Marriage county court
Kingston-upon-Hull County Court	Yes	Yes	Yes		
Kingston-upon-Thames County Court	Yes				
Lambeth County Court	Yes				
Lancaster County Court	Yes	Yes	Yes		
Leeds County Court	Yes	Yes	Yes	Yes	Yes
Leicester County Court	Yes	Yes	Yes		Yes
Lincoln County Court	Yes	Yes	Yes		
Liverpool County Court	Yes	Yes	Yes	Yes	
Llanelli County Court	Yes				
Llangefni County Court	Yes		Yes		
Luton County Court	Yes	Yes	Yes		Yes
Macclesfield County Court	Yes		Yes		
Maidstone County Court	Yes				
Manchester County Court	Yes	Yes	Yes	Yes	Yes
Mansfield County Court	Yes				
Medway County Court	Yes	Yes	Yes		
Merthyr Tydfil County Court	Yes				
Middlesbrough County Court at Teesside Combined Court	Yes	Yes	Yes		Yes
Milton Keynes County Court	Yes	Yes	Yes		
Morpeth County Court	Yes				
Neath County Court	Yes				
Newcastle-upon-Tyne County Court	Yes	Yes	Yes	Yes	Yes
Newport (Gwent) County Court	Yes	Yes	Yes		

Column 1 *County court*	Column 2 *Family Hearing Centre*	Column 3 *Care Centre*	Column 4 *Adoption Centre*	Column 5 *Inter-country Adoption Centre*	Column 6 *Forced Marriage county court*
Newport (Isle of Wight) County Court	Yes				
Northampton County Court	Yes	Yes	Yes		
North Shields County Court	Yes				
Norwich County Court	Yes	Yes	Yes		
Nottingham County Court	Yes	Yes	Yes	Yes	
Oldham County Court	Yes				
Oxford County Court	Yes	Yes	Yes		
Peterborough County Court	Yes	Yes	Yes		
Plymouth County Court	Yes	Yes	Yes		
Pontypridd County Court	Yes	Yes	Yes		
Portsmouth County Court	Yes	Yes	Yes	Yes	
Preston County Court	Yes				
Reading County Court	Yes	Yes	Yes		
Reigate County Court	Yes				
Rhyl County Court	Yes	Yes	Yes		
Romford County Court	Yes		Yes		Yes
Rotherham County Court	Yes				
St. Helens County Court	Yes				
Salisbury County Court	Yes				
Scarborough County Court	Yes				
Scunthorpe County Court	Yes				
Sheffield County Court	Yes	Yes	Yes		
Skipton County Court	Yes				
Slough County Court	Yes				
Southampton County Court	Yes		Yes		

Column 1 County court	Column 2 Family Hearing Centre	Column 3 Care Centre	Column 4 Adoption Centre	Column 5 Inter-country Adoption Centre	Column 6 Forced Marriage county court
Southend County Court	Yes				
South Shields County Court	Yes				
Stafford County Court	Yes				
Staines County Court	Yes				
Stockport County Court	Yes		Yes		
Stoke-on-Trent County Court	Yes	Yes	Yes		
Sunderland County Court	Yes	Yes	Yes		
Swansea County Court	Yes	Yes	Yes		
Swindon County Court	Yes	Yes	Yes		
Tameside County Court	Yes				
Taunton County Court	Yes	Yes	Yes		
Telford County Court	Yes	Yes	Yes		
Thanet County Court	Yes				
Torquay County Court	Yes				
Truro County Court	Yes	Yes	Yes		
Tunbridge Wells County Court	Yes				
Uxbridge County Court	Yes				
Wakefield County Court	Yes				
Walsall County Court	Yes				
Wandsworth County Court	Yes				
Warrington County Court	Yes	Yes	Yes		
Watford County Court	Yes	Yes	Yes		
Welshpool and Newtown County Court	Yes				
Weston Super Mare County Court	Yes				
Weymouth County Court	Yes				
Wigan County Court	Yes				

Column 1 *County court*	Column 2 *Family Hearing Centre*	Column 3 *Care Centre*	Column 4 *Adoption Centre*	Column 5 *Inter-country Adoption Centre*	Column 6 *Forced Marriage county court*
Willesden County Court	Yes				Yes
Winchester County Court	Yes				
Wolverhampton County Court	Yes	Yes	Yes		
Woolwich County Court	Yes				
Worcester County Court	Yes	Yes	Yes		
Worthing County Court	Yes				
Wrexham County Court	Yes	Yes	Yes	Yes	
Yeovil County Court	Yes				
York County Court	Yes	Yes	Yes		

Amendments—SI 2009/3319; SI 2011/1460; SI 2011/2064; SI 2012/642; SI 2012/1955; SI 2013/421.

****

Care Planning, Placement and Case Review (England) Regulations 2010, SI 2010/959

ARRANGEMENT OF REGULATIONS

PART 1
GENERAL

PART 2
ARRANGEMENTS FOR LOOKING AFTER A CHILD

PART 3
PLACEMENTS – GENERAL PROVISIONS

PART 7

ARRANGEMENTS MADE BY THE RESPONSIBLE AUTHORITY FOR CEASING TO LOOK AFTER A CHILD

PART 8

INDEPENDENT REVIEWING OFFICERS AND INDEPENDENT VISITORS

PART 8A

APPLICATION OF THESE REGULATIONS WITH MODIFICATIONS TO CHILDREN ON REMAND

PART 9

MISCELLANEOUS

PART IV

PART 1
GENERAL

1 Citation and commencement

(1) These Regulations may be cited as the Care Planning, Placement and Case Review (England) Regulations 2010 and come into force on 1 April 2011.

(2) These Regulations apply in relation to England only.

2 Interpretation

(1) In these Regulations –

"the 1989 Act" means the Children Act 1989;

"the 2012 Act" means the Legal Aid, Sentencing and Punishment of Offenders Act 2012;

"the Fostering Services Regulations" means the Fostering Services (England) Regulations 2011;

"appropriate person" means –

    (a) P, where C is to live, or lives, with P;

    (b) F, where C is to be placed, or is placed, with F;

    (c) where C is to be placed, or is placed, in a children's home, the person who is registered under Part 2 of the Care Standards Act 2000 in respect of that home; or

    (d) where C is to be placed, or is placed, in accordance with other arrangements under section 22C(6)(d), the person who will be responsible for C at the accommodation;

"area authority" means the local authority for the area in which C is placed, or is to be placed, where this is different from the responsible authority;

"C" means a child who is looked after by the responsible authority;

"care plan" means the plan for the future care of C prepared in accordance with Part 2;

"case record" has the meaning given in regulation 49;

"connected person" has the meaning given in regulation 24;

"detention placement plan" has the meaning given in regulation 47C;

"director" means the person in charge of a secure training centre;

"director of children's services" means the officer of the responsible authority appointed for the purposes of section 18 of the Children Act 2004;

"F" means a person who is approved as a local authority foster parent and with whom it is proposed to place C or, as the case may be, with whom C is placed;

"fostering service provider" has the meaning given in regulation 2(1) of the Fostering Services Regulations;

"full assessment process" has the meaning given in regulation 24(2)(c);

"governor" means the person in charge of a young offender institution;

"health plan" has the meaning given in regulation 5(b)(i);

"independent visitor" means the independent person appointed to be C's visitor under section 23ZB;

"IRO" means the independent reviewing officer appointed for C's case under section 25A(1);

"nominated officer" means a senior officer of the responsible authority nominated in writing by the director of children's services for the purposes of these Regulations;

"P" means –

    (a) a person who is C's parent;

(b)   a person who is not C's parent but who has parental responsibility for C; or

(c)   where C is in the care of the responsible authority and there was a residence order in force with respect to C immediately before the care order was made, a person in whose favour the residence order was made;

"pathway plan" has the meaning given in section 23E(1)(a);

"personal adviser" means the personal adviser arranged for C under paragraph 19C of Schedule 2 to the 1989 Act;

"personal education plan" has the meaning given in regulation 5(b)(ii);

"placement" means –

(i)   arrangements made by the responsible authority for C to live with P in accordance with section 22C(2), where C is in the care of the responsible authority, or

(ii)   arrangements made by the responsible authority to provide for C's accommodation and maintenance by any of the means specified in section 22C(6);

"placement plan" has the meaning given in regulation 9(1)(a);

"R" means the representative of the responsible authority who is appointed to visit C in accordance with arrangements made by them under section 23ZA;

"registered manager" means the person who is registered under Part 2 of the Care Standards Act 2000 as a manager of a secure children's home;

"remand to local authority accommodation" has the meaning given in section 91(3) of the 2012 Act;

"remand to youth detention accommodation" has the meaning given in section 91(4) of the 2012 Act;

"responsible authority" means the local authority that looks after C;

"secure children's home" has the meaning given in section 102(11) of the 2012 Act;

"secure training centre" has the meaning given in section 43(1)(d) of the Prison Act 1952;

"special educational needs" and "special educational provision" have the meanings given in section 312 of the Education Act 1996;

"temporary approval" has the meaning given in regulation 24(1); and

"working day" means any day other than –

(a)   a Saturday or a Sunday,

(b)   Christmas day or Good Friday, or

(c)   a bank holiday in England and Wales under the Banking and Financial Dealings Act 1971.

"young offender institution" has the meaning given in section 43(1)(aa) of the Prison Act 1952.

(2) In these Regulations any reference to any document or other record includes any such document or record that is kept or provided in a readily accessible form and includes copies of original documents and electronic methods of recording information.

(3) Save as otherwise appears –

(a)   any reference in these Regulations to a numbered section is a reference to that section in the 1989 Act; and

(b)   any reference in these Regulations to a numbered regulation, Part or Schedule is a reference to that regulation, Part or Schedule in these Regulations.

Amendments—SI 2011/581; SI 2013/706.

PART IV

3 These Regulations do not apply in relation to any child who is looked after by a local authority and who has been placed for adoption under the Adoption and Children Act 2002 unless the child falls within regulation 47A.

Amendments—SI 2013/706.

PART 2
ARRANGEMENTS FOR LOOKING AFTER A CHILD

4 Care planning

(1) Where C is not in the care of the responsible authority and a care plan for C has not already been prepared, the responsible authority must assess C's needs for services to achieve or maintain a reasonable standard of health or development, and prepare such a plan.

(2) Except in the case of a child to whom section 31A (care orders: care plans) applies, or where paragraph (6) applies, the care plan must be prepared before C is first placed by the responsible authority or, if it is not practicable to do so, within ten working days of the start of the first placement.

(3) When assessing C's needs under paragraph (1), the responsible authority must consider whether C's placement meets the requirements of Part 3 of the 1989 Act.

(4) Unless paragraph (5) applies, the care plan should, so far as is reasonably practicable, be agreed by the responsible authority with –

    (a) any parent of C's and any person who is not C's parent but who has parental responsibility for C, or

    (b) if there is no such person, the person who was caring for C immediately before the responsible authority arranged a placement for C.

(5) Where C is aged 16 or over and agrees to be provided with accommodation under section 20, the care plan should be agreed with C by the responsible authority.

(6) Where C was first placed by the responsible authority before 1 April 2011, the care plan must be prepared as soon as reasonably practicable.

5 Preparation and content of the care plan

The care plan must include a record of the following information –

    (a) the long term plan for C's upbringing ("the plan for permanence"),

    (b) the arrangements made by the responsible authority to meet C's needs in relation to –

        (i) health, including the information set out in paragraph 1 of Schedule 1 ("the health plan"),

        (ii) education and training, including, so far as reasonably practicable, the information set out in paragraph 2 of Schedule 1 ("the personal education plan"),

        (iii) emotional and behavioural development,

        (iv) identity, with particular regard to C's religious persuasion, racial origin and cultural and linguistic background,

        (v) family and social relationships and in particular the information set out in paragraph 3 of Schedule 1,

        (vi) social presentation, and

        (vii) self-care skills,

   (c)   except in a case where C is in the care of the responsible authority but is not provided with accommodation by them by any of the means specified in section 22C, the placement plan,

   (d)   the name of the IRO, and

   (e)   details of the wishes and feelings of the persons listed in section 22(4) about the arrangements referred to in sub-paragraph (b) and the placement plan that have been ascertained and considered in accordance with section 22(4) and (5) and the wishes and feelings of those persons in relation to any change, or proposed change, to the care plan.

6 (1) The responsible authority must keep C's care plan under review in accordance with Part 6 and, if they are of the opinion some change is required, they must revise the care plan or prepare a new care plan accordingly.

(2) Save as otherwise provided in these Regulations, the responsible authority must not make any significant change to the care plan unless the proposed change has first been considered at a review of C's case.

(3) Subject to paragraph (4), the responsible authority must give a copy of the care plan –

   (a)   to C, unless it would not be appropriate to do so having regard to C's age and understanding,

   (b)   to P,

   (c)   to the IRO,

   (d)   where C is to be placed, or is placed, with F, to the fostering service provider that approved F in accordance with the Fostering Services Regulations,

   (e)   where C is to be placed, or is placed, in a children's home, to the person who is registered under Part 2 of the Care Standards Act 2000 in respect of that home, and

   (f)   where C is to be placed, or is placed, in accordance with other arrangements under section 22C(6)(d), to the person who will be responsible for C at the accommodation.

(4) The responsible authority may decide not to give a copy of the care plan, or a full copy of the care plan, to P if to do so would put C at risk of significant harm.

Amendments—SI 2011/581.

7 Health care

(1) Before C is first placed by them or, if that is not reasonably practicable, before the first review of C's case, the responsible authority must make arrangements for a registered medical practitioner to –

   (a)   carry out an assessment of C's state of health, and

   (b)   provide a written report of the assessment, addressing the matters specified in paragraph 1 of Schedule 1,

as soon as reasonably practicable.

(2) Paragraph (1) does not apply if, within a period of three months immediately preceding the placement, an assessment of C's state of health has been carried out and the responsible authority has obtained a written report that meets the requirements of that paragraph.

(3) The responsible authority must make arrangements for a registered medical practitioner or a registered nurse or registered midwife acting under the supervision of a registered medical practitioner to review C's state of health and provide a written report of each review, addressing the matters specified in paragraph 1 of Schedule 1 –

PART IV

    (a)   at least once in every period of six months before C's fifth birthday, and

    (b)   at least once in every period of 12 months after C's fifth birthday.

(4) Paragraphs (1) and (3) do not apply if C refuses consent to the assessment, being of sufficient age and understanding to do so.

(5) The responsible authority must take all reasonable steps to ensure that C is provided with appropriate health care services, in accordance with the health plan, including –

    (a)   medical and dental care and treatment, and

    (b)   advice and guidance on health, personal care and health promotion issues.

8 Contact with a child in care

(1) This regulation applies if C is in the care of the responsible authority and they have decided under section 34(6) (refusal of contact as a matter of urgency) to refuse to allow contact that would otherwise be required by virtue of section 34(1) or an order under section 34 (parental contact etc. with children in care).

(2) The responsible authority must immediately give written notification to the following persons of the information specified in paragraph (3) ("the specified information") –

    (a)   C, unless it would not be appropriate to do so having regard to C's age and understanding,

    (b)   P,

    (c)   where, immediately before the care order was made, a person had care of C by virtue of an order made in exercise of the High Court's inherent jurisdiction with respect to children, that person,

    (d)   any other person whose wishes and feelings the responsible authority consider to be relevant, and

    (e)   the IRO.

(3) The specified information is –

    (a)   the responsible authority's decision,

    (b)   the date of the decision,

    (c)   the reasons for the decision,

    (d)   the duration of the decision (if applicable), and

    (e)   remedies available in case of dissatisfaction.

(4) The responsible authority may depart from the terms of any order made under section 34 by agreement with the person in relation to whom the order is made, provided that –

    (a)   C, being of sufficient age and understanding, also agrees, and

    (b)   written notification of the specified information is given within five working days to the persons listed in paragraph (2).

(5) Where the responsible authority has decided to vary or suspend any arrangements made (otherwise than under an order under section 34) with a view to affording any person contact with C, the responsible authority must immediately give written notification containing the specified information to the persons listed in paragraph (2).

(6) The responsible authority must record any decision made under this regulation in C's care plan.

PART 3
PLACEMENTS – GENERAL PROVISIONS

9 Placement plan

(1) Subject to paragraphs (2) and (4), before making arrangements in accordance with section 22C for C's placement, the responsible authority must –

    (a)   prepare a plan for the placement ("the placement plan") which –
          (i)   sets out how the placement will contribute to meeting C's needs, and
          (ii) includes all the matters specified in Schedule 2 as are applicable, having regard to the type of the placement, and
    (b)   ensure that –
          (i)   C's wishes and feelings have been ascertained and given due consideration, and
          (ii) the IRO has been informed.

(2) If it is not reasonably practicable to prepare the placement plan before making the placement, the placement plan must be prepared within five working days of the start of the placement.

(3) The placement plan must be agreed with, and signed by, the appropriate person.

(4) Where the arrangements for C's placement were made before 1 April 2011, the responsible authority must prepare the placement plan as soon as reasonably practicable.

10 Avoidance of disruption in education

(1) Subject to paragraphs (2) and (3), if C is a registered pupil at a school in the fourth key stage, a decision to make any change to C's placement that would have the effect of disrupting the arrangements made for C's education must not be put into effect until it has been approved by a nominated officer.

(2) Before approving a decision under paragraph (1), the nominated officer must be satisfied that –

    (a)   the requirements of regulation 9(1)(b)(i) have been complied with,
    (b)   the educational provision made for C at the placement will promote C's educational achievement and is consistent with C's personal education plan,
    (c)   the designated teacher at the school has been consulted, and
    (d)   the IRO has been consulted.

(3) Paragraph (1) does not apply in any case where –

    (a)   the responsible authority terminates C's placement in accordance with regulation 14(3), or
    (b)   it is necessary for any other reason to change C's placement in an emergency,

and in such a case the responsible authority must make appropriate arrangements to promote C's educational achievement as soon as reasonably practicable.

(4) In any case not falling within paragraph (1), but where the responsible authority propose making any change to C's placement that would have the effect of disrupting the arrangements made for C's education or training, the responsible authority must ensure that other arrangements are made for C's education or training that meet C's needs and are consistent with C's personal education plan.

(5) In this regulation –

    (a)   "registered pupil" has the meaning given in section 20(7) of the Children and Young Persons Act 2008, and
    (b)   "school" has the meaning given in section 4 of the Education Act 1996.

PART IV

Placement out of area

11 Placement decision

(1) Subject to paragraphs (3) and (4), a decision to place C outside the area of the responsible authority (including a placement outside England) must not be put into effect until it has been approved by a nominated officer.

(2) Before approving a decision under paragraph (1), the nominated officer must be satisfied that –

    (a)   the requirements of regulation 9(1)(b)(i) have been complied with,

    (b)   the placement is the most appropriate placement available for C and consistent with C's care plan,

    (c)   C's relatives have been consulted, where appropriate,

    (d)   the area authority have been notified, and

    (e)   the IRO has been consulted.

(3) In the case of a placement made in an emergency, paragraph (2) does not apply and before approving a decision under paragraph (1) the nominated officer must –

    (a)   be satisfied that regulation 9(1)(b)(i) and the requirements of sub-paragraph (2)(b) have been complied with, and

    (b)   take steps to ensure that regulation 9(1)(b)(ii) and the requirements set out in sub-paragraphs (2)(c) and (d) are complied with by the responsible authority within five working days of approval of the decision under paragraph (1).

(4) Paragraphs (1) and (2) do not apply to a decision to place C outside the area of the responsible authority with –

    (a)   F who is a connected person, or

    (b)   F who is approved as a local authority foster parent by the responsible authority.

12 Placements outside England and Wales

(1) This regulation applies if –

    (a)   C is in the care of the responsible authority, and

    (b)   the responsible authority make arrangements to place C outside England and Wales in accordance with the provisions of paragraph 19 of Schedule 2 to the 1989 Act (placement of a child in care outside England and Wales).

(2) The responsible authority must take steps to ensure that, so far as is reasonably practicable, requirements corresponding with the requirements which would have applied under these Regulations had C been placed in England, are complied with.

(3) The responsible authority must include in the care plan details of the arrangements made by the responsible authority to supervise C's placement.

13 Notification of placement

(1) Subject to paragraph (3), the responsible authority must give written notification to the persons listed in paragraph (2) of the arrangements for C's placement before the placement is made or, if the placement is made in an emergency, within five working days of the start of the placement, unless it is not reasonably practicable to do so.

(2) The persons referred to in paragraph (1) are –

    (a)   C, unless it would not be appropriate to do so having regard to C's age and understanding,

    (b)   P,

    (c)   if C is in the care of the responsible authority, any person who is allowed contact with C under section 34(1) and any person who has contact with C by virtue of an order under section 34,

    (d)   if C is looked after but is not in the care of the responsible authority, any person who has contact with C pursuant to an order made under section 8 (residence, contact and other orders with respect to children),

    (e)   any person who was caring for C immediately before the arrangements were made,

    (f)   the National Health Service Commissioning Board and the clinical commissioning group (or in the case of a child living or to be placed in Wales, the local health board) for the area in which C is living and, if different, for the area in which C is to be placed,

    (g)   C's registered medical practitioner and, where applicable, the registered medical practitioner with whom C is to be registered during the placement,

    (h)   any educational institution attended by, or person providing education or training for, C, and

    (i)   the IRO.

(3) The responsible authority may decide not to give notification to any of the persons listed in sub-paragraphs (b) to (e) if to do so would put C at risk of significant harm.

Amendments—SI 2013/235.

14 Termination of placement by the responsible authority

(1) Subject to paragraphs (3) and (5), the responsible authority may only terminate C's placement following a review of C's case in accordance with Part 6.

(2) Subject to paragraphs (3) and (4), before terminating C's placement, the responsible authority must –

    (a)   make other arrangements for C's accommodation, in accordance with section 22C,

    (b)   inform the IRO,

    (c)   so far as is reasonably practicable, give written notification of their intention to terminate the placement to –

        (i)   all the persons to whom notification of the placement was given under regulation 13,

        (ii)   the person with whom C is placed,

        (iii)   where C is placed in the area of another local authority, that authority.

(3) Where there is an immediate risk of significant harm to C, or to protect others from serious injury, the responsible authority must terminate C's placement, and in those circumstances –

    (a)   paragraph (1) does not apply, and

    (b)   they must comply with paragraph (2)(a) and (b) as soon as reasonably practicable.

(4) If it is not reasonably practicable to notify any person in accordance with paragraph (2)(c), then the responsible authority must give written notification to that person, within ten working days of the date on which the placement is terminated, of the fact that the placement has been terminated.

(5) This regulation does not apply where C's placement is terminated under regulation 19(c), regulation 23(2) or regulation 25(6), nor where section 22D (review of child's case before making alternative arrangements for accommodation) applies.

PART IV

PART 4
PROVISION FOR DIFFERENT TYPES OF PLACEMENT

Chapter 1
Placement of a child in care with P

15 Application

(1) This Chapter applies if C is in the care of the responsible authority and they, acting in accordance with section 22C(2), propose to place C with P.

(2) Nothing in this Chapter requires the responsible authority to remove C from P's care if C is living with P before a placement decision is made about C.

16 Effect of contact order

The responsible authority must not place C with P if to do so would be incompatible with any order made by the court under section 34.

17 Assessment of P's suitability to care for a child

Before deciding to place C with P, the responsible authority must –

(a)   assess the suitability of P to care for C, including the suitability of –
   (i)   the proposed accommodation, and
   (ii) all other persons aged 18 and over who are members of the household in which it is proposed that C will live,
(b)   take into account all the matters set out in Schedule 3 in making their assessment,
(c)   consider whether, in all the circumstances and taking into account the services to be provided by the responsible authority, the placement will safeguard and promote C's welfare and meet C's needs set out in the care plan, and
(d)   review C's case in accordance with Part 6.

18 Decision to place a child with P

(1) The decision to place C with P must not be put into effect until it has been approved by a nominated officer, and the responsible authority have prepared a placement plan for C.

(2) Before approving a decision under paragraph (1), the nominated officer must be satisfied that –

(a)   the requirements of regulation 9(1)(b)(i) have been complied with,
(b)   the requirements of regulation 17 have been complied with,
(c)   the placement will safeguard and promote C's welfare, and
(d)   the IRO has been consulted.

19 Circumstances in which a child may be placed with P before assessment completed

Where the nominated officer considers it to be necessary and consistent with C's welfare, the responsible authority may place C with P before their assessment under regulation 17 ("the assessment") is completed provided that they –

(a)   arrange for P to be interviewed in order to obtain as much of the information specified in Schedule 3 about P and the other persons living in P's household who are aged 18 and over as can be readily ascertained at that interview,

    (b)   ensure that the assessment and the review of C's case are completed in accordance with regulation 17 within ten working days of C being placed with P, and

    (c)   ensure that a decision in accordance with regulation 18 is made and approved within ten working days after the assessment is completed, and –

        (i)   if the decision is to confirm the placement, review the placement plan and, if appropriate amend it, and

        (ii)   if the decision is not to confirm the placement, terminate the placement.

20 Support for P

Where C is placed, or is to be placed, with P, the responsible authority must provide such services and support to P as appear to them to be necessary to safeguard and promote C's welfare and must record details of such services and support in C's care plan.

Chapter 2
Placement with local authority foster parents

21 Interpretation

(1) In this Chapter "registered person" has the same meaning as in the Fostering Services Regulations.

(2) Where C is placed jointly with two persons each of whom is approved as a local authority foster parent, any reference in these Regulations to a local authority foster parent is to be interpreted as referring equally to both such persons and any requirement to be satisfied by or relating to a particular local authority foster parent must be satisfied by, or treated as relating to, both of them.

Amendments—SI 2011/581.

22 Conditions to be complied with before placing a child with a local authority foster parent

(1) This regulation applies where the responsible authority propose to place C with F.

(2) The responsible authority may only place C with F if –

    (a)   F is approved by –

        (i)   the responsible authority, or

        (ii)   provided that the conditions specified in paragraph (3) are also satisfied, another fostering service provider,

    (b)   the terms of F's approval are consistent with the proposed placement, and

    (c)   F has entered into a foster care agreement either with the responsible authority or with another fostering service provider in accordance with regulation 27(5)(b) of the Fostering Services Regulations.

(3) The conditions referred to in paragraph (2)(a)(ii) are that –

    (a)   the fostering service provider by whom F is approved consents to the proposed placement, and

    (b)   where any other local authority currently have a child placed with F, that local authority consents to the proposed placement.

Amendments—SI 2011/581.

23 Emergency placement with a local authority foster parent

(1) Where it is necessary to place C in an emergency, the responsible authority may place C with any local authority foster parent who has been approved in accordance with the Fostering Services Regulations, even if the terms of that approval are not consistent with the placement, provided that the placement is for no longer than six working days.

(2) When the period of six working days referred to in paragraph (1) expires, the responsible authority must terminate the placement unless the terms of that person's approval have been amended to be consistent with the placement.

Amendments—SI 2011/581.

24 Temporary approval of relative, friend or other person connected with C

(1) Where the responsible authority is satisfied that –

(a) the most appropriate placement for C is with a connected person, notwithstanding that the connected person is not approved as a local authority foster parent, and

(b) it is necessary for C to be placed with the connected person before the connected person's suitability to be a local authority foster parent has been assessed in accordance with the Fostering Services Regulations,

they may approve that person as a local authority foster parent for a temporary period not exceeding 16 weeks ("temporary approval") provided that they first comply with the requirements of paragraph (2).

(2) Before making a placement under paragraph (1), the responsible authority must –

(a) assess the suitability of the connected person to care for C, including the suitability of –
(i)   the proposed accommodation, and
(ii) all other persons aged 18 and over who are members of the household in which it is proposed that C will live,
taking into account all the matters set out in Schedule 4,

(b) consider whether, in all the circumstances and taking into account the services to be provided by the responsible authority, the proposed arrangements will safeguard and promote C's welfare and meet C's needs set out in the care plan, and

(c) make immediate arrangements for the suitability of the connected person to be a local authority foster parent to be assessed in accordance with the Fostering Services Regulations ("the full assessment process") before the temporary approval expires.

(3) In this regulation "connected person" means a relative, friend or other person connected with C.

Amendments—SI 2011/581.

25 Expiry of temporary approval

(1) Subject to paragraph (4), the responsible authority may extend the temporary approval of a connected person if –

(a) it is likely to expire before the full assessment process is completed, or

(b) the connected person, having undergone the full assessment process, is not approved and seeks a review of the decision in accordance with Regulations made under paragraph 12F(1)(b) of Schedule 2 to the 1989 Act.

(2) In a case falling within paragraph (1)(a), the responsible authority may extend the temporary approval once for a further period of up to eight weeks.

(3) In a case falling within paragraph (1)(b), the responsible authority may extend the temporary approval until the outcome of the review is known.

(4) Before deciding whether to extend the temporary approval in the circumstances set out in paragraph (1), the responsible authority must first –

(a) consider whether placement with the connected person is still the most appropriate placement available,

(b) seek the views of the fostering panel established by the fostering service provider in accordance with the Fostering Services Regulations, and

(c) inform the IRO.

(5) A decision to extend temporary approval must be approved by a nominated officer.

(6) If the period of temporary approval and of any extension to that period expires and the connected person has not been approved as a local authority foster parent in accordance with the Fostering Services Regulations, the responsible authority must terminate the placement after first making other arrangements for C's accommodation.

Amendments—SI 2011/581.

26 Independent fostering agencies – discharge of responsible authority functions

(1) A responsible authority may make arrangements in accordance with this regulation for the duties imposed on it as responsible authority by regulation 14(3) and regulation 22 to be discharged on their behalf by a registered person.

(2) No arrangements may be made under this regulation unless the responsible authority has entered into a written agreement with the registered person which includes the information set out in paragraph 1 of Schedule 5, and where the responsible authority proposes to make an arrangement under this regulation in relation to a particular child, the written agreement must also include the matters set out in paragraph 2 of Schedule 5.

(3) The responsible authority must report to the Chief Inspector of Education, Children's Services and Skills any concerns they may have about the services provided by a registered person.

Chapter 3
Other arrangements

27 General duties of the responsible authority when placing a child in other arrangements

Before placing C in accommodation in an unregulated setting under section 22C(6)(d), the responsible authority must –

(a) be satisfied that the accommodation is suitable for C, having regard to the matters set out in Schedule 6,

(b) unless it is not reasonably practicable, arrange for C to visit the accommodation, and

(c) inform the IRO.

PART IV

PART 5
VISITS BY THE RESPONSIBLE AUTHORITY'S REPRESENTATIVE ETC.

28 Frequency of visits

(1) As part of their arrangements for supervising C's welfare, the responsible authority must ensure that their representative ("R") visits C in accordance with this regulation, wherever C is living.

(2) Subject to paragraphs (3) to (6), the responsible authority must ensure that R visits C –

    (a)   within one week of the start of any placement,

    (b)   at intervals of not more than six weeks for the first year of any placement, and

    (c)   thereafter –

        (i)   where the placement is intended to last until C is aged 18, at intervals of not more than three months,

        (ii)   and in any other case, at intervals of not more than six weeks.

(3) Where regulation 19 applies, the responsible authority must ensure that R visits C –

    (a)   at least once a week until the first review carried out in accordance with Part 6, and

    (b)   thereafter at intervals of not more than six weeks.

(4) Where regulation 24 applies, or where an interim care order has been made in relation to C under section 38 (interim orders) and C is living with P, the responsible authority must ensure that R visits C –

    (a)   at least once a week until the first review carried out in accordance with Part 6, and

    (b)   thereafter at intervals of not more than four weeks.

(5) Where a care order has been made in relation to C under section 31 (care and supervision orders) and C is living with P, the responsible authority must ensure that R visits C –

    (a)   within one week of the making of the care order, and

    (b)   thereafter at intervals of not more than six weeks.

(6) Where C is in the care of the responsible authority but another person is responsible for the arrangements under which C is living for the time being ("C's living arrangements"), the responsible authority must ensure that R visits C –

    (a)   within one week of the start of C's living arrangements and within one week of any change to C's living arrangements,

    (b)   at intervals of not more than six weeks for the first year thereafter, and

    (c)   at intervals of not more than three months in any subsequent year.

(7) In addition to visits in accordance with paragraphs (2) to (6), the responsible authority must ensure that R visits C –

    (a)   whenever reasonably requested to do so by –

        (i)   C,

        (ii)   where paragraphs (2), (3) or (4) apply, the appropriate person, or

        (iii)   where paragraph (5) applies, the person responsible for C's living arrangements,

    (b)   within one week of first receiving notification under section 30A of the Care Standards Act 2000 (notification of matters relating to persons carrying on or managing certain establishments or agencies), where the children's home in which C is placed for the time being is referred to in that notification.

29 Conduct of visits

On each visit, R must speak to C in private unless –

    (a)   C, being of sufficient age and understanding to do so, refuses,

    (b)   R considers it inappropriate to do so, having regard to C's age and understanding, or

    (c)   R is unable to do so.

30 Consequences of visits

Where, as the result of a visit carried out in accordance with this Part, R's assessment is that C's welfare is not adequately safeguarded and promoted by the placement, the responsible authority must review C's case in accordance with Part 6.

31 Advice, support and assistance for the child

When making arrangements in accordance with section 23ZA(2)(b) for advice, support and assistance to be available to C between R's visits, the responsible authority must ensure that –

    (a)   the arrangements –

        (i)   are appropriate having regard to C's age and understanding, and

        (ii)   give due consideration to C's religious persuasion, racial origin, cultural and linguistic background and to any disability C may have, and

    (b)   so far as is reasonably practicable having regard to C's age and understanding, C knows how to seek appropriate advice, support and assistance from them.

PART 6
REVIEWS OF THE CHILD'S CASE

32 General duty of the responsible authority to review the child's case

(1) The responsible authority must review C's case in accordance with this Part.

(2) The responsible authority must not make any significant change to C's care plan unless the proposed change has first been considered at a review of C's case, unless this is not reasonably practicable.

(3) Nothing in this Part prevents any review of C's case being carried out at the same time as any other review assessment or consideration of C's case under any other provision.

33 Timing of reviews

(1) The responsible authority must first review C's case within 20 working days of the date on which C becomes looked after.

(2) The second review must be carried out not more than three months after the first, and subsequent reviews must be carried out at intervals of not more than six months.

(3) The responsible authority must carry out a review before the time specified in paragraph (1) or (2) if –

    (a)   the IRO so requests,

    (b)   regulation 30 applies,

    (c)   C is provided with accommodation under section 21(2)(b) or (c) and a review would not otherwise occur before C ceases to be so provided with accommodation,

PART IV

(d)   C is in the care of the responsible authority and is detained in a secure training centre or a young offenders institution, and a review would not otherwise occur before C ceases to be so detained, or

(e)   C is looked after but is not in the care of the responsible authority and

(i)   the responsible authority propose to cease to provide accommodation for C, and

(ii)   accommodation will not subsequently be provided for C by C's parents (or one of them) or any person who is not C's parent but who has parental responsibility for C.

34 Conduct of reviews

Local authority's policy on reviews

(1) The responsible authority must prepare and implement a written policy regarding the manner in which they will review cases in accordance with this Part.

(2) The responsible authority must provide a copy of their policy to –

(a)   C, unless it would not be appropriate to do so having regard to C's age and understanding,

(b)   C's parents, or any person who is not C's parent but who has parental responsibility for C, and

(c)   any other person whose views the responsible authority consider to be relevant.

35 Considerations to which the responsible authority must have regard

The considerations to which the responsible authority must have regard in reviewing each case are set out in Schedule 7.

36 The role of the IRO

(1) The IRO must –

(a)   so far as reasonably practicable, attend any meeting held as part of the review ("the review meeting") and, if attending the review meeting, chair it,

(b)   speak to C in private about the matters to be considered at the review unless C, being of sufficient understanding to do so, refuses or the IRO considers it inappropriate having regard to C's age and understanding,

(c)   ensure that, so far as reasonably practicable, the wishes and feelings of C's parents, or any person who is not C's parent but who has parental responsibility for C, have been ascertained and taken into account, and

(d)   ensure that the review is conducted in accordance with this Part and in particular –

(i)   that the persons responsible for implementing any decision taken in consequence of the review are identified, and

(ii)   that any failure to review the case in accordance with this Part or to take proper steps to implement decisions taken in consequence of the review are brought to the attention of an officer at an appropriate level of seniority within the responsible authority.

(2) The IRO may, if not satisfied that sufficient information has been provided by the responsible authority to enable proper consideration of any of the matters in Schedule 7, adjourn the review meeting once for not more than 20 working days, and no proposal considered in the course of the review may be implemented until the review has been completed.

37 Arrangements for implementing decisions arising out of reviews

The responsible authority must –

(a) make arrangements to implement decisions made in the course, or as a result, of the review, and

(b) inform the IRO of any significant failure to make such arrangements, or any significant change of circumstances occurring after the review that affects those arrangements.

38 Records of reviews

The responsible authority must ensure that a written record of the review is prepared, and that the information obtained in the course of the review, details of proceedings at the review meeting, and any decisions made in the course, or as a result, of the review are included in C's case record.

PART 7
ARRANGEMENTS MADE BY THE RESPONSIBLE AUTHORITY FOR CEASING TO LOOK AFTER A CHILD

39 Arrangements for ceasing to look after a child who is not an eligible child

In any case where C is not in the care of the responsible authority and is not likely to be an eligible child when the local authority cease to look after him, the care plan (or where regulation 47B(4) applies, the detention placement plan) must include details of the advice, assistance and support that the responsible authority intend to provide for C when C ceases to be looked after by them.

Amendments—Substituted by SI 2013/706.

40 Eligible children

Meaning of eligible child

(1) For the purposes of paragraph 19B(2)(b) of Schedule 2 to the 1989 Act (meaning of eligible child), the prescribed period is 13 weeks and the prescribed age is 14.

(2) For the purposes of paragraph 19B(3)(b) of that Schedule, if C is a child to whom regulation 48 applies, C is not an eligible child despite falling within paragraph 19B(2) of that Schedule.

41 General duties

If C is an eligible child, the responsible authority must –

(a) assess C's needs in accordance with regulation 42, and

(b) prepare C's pathway plan, in accordance with regulation 43.

42 Assessment of needs

(1) The responsible authority must complete the assessment of C's needs in accordance with paragraph 19B(4) of Schedule 2 to the 1989 Act not more than three months after the date on which C reaches the age of 16 or becomes an eligible child after that age.

(2) In carrying out their assessment of C's likely needs when C ceases to be looked after, the responsible authority must take account of the following considerations –

PART IV

(a) C's state of health (including physical, emotional and mental health) and development,
(b) C's continuing need for education, training or employment,
(c) the support that will be available to C from C's parents and other connected persons,
(d) C's actual and anticipated financial resources and capacity to manage personal finances independently,
(e) the extent to which C possesses the practical and other skills necessary for independent living,
(f) C's need for continuing care, support and accommodation,
(g) the wishes and feelings of –
  (i)   C,
  (ii) any parent of C's and any person who is not C's parent but who has parental responsibility for C,
  (iii) the appropriate person,
(h) the views of –
  (i)   any person or educational institution that provides C with education or training and, if C has a statement of special educational needs, the local authority who maintain the statement (if different),
  (ii) the IRO,
  (iii) any person providing health (whether physical, emotional or mental health) or dental care or treatment to C,
  (iv) the personal adviser appointed for C, and
  (v)   any other person whose views the responsible authority, or C, consider may be relevant.

43 The pathway plan

(1) The pathway plan must be prepared as soon as possible after the assessment of C's needs and must include, in particular –

(a) C's care plan, and
(b) the information referred to in Schedule 8.

(2) The pathway plan must, in relation to each of the matters referred to in paragraphs 2 to 10 of Schedule 8, set out –

(a) the manner in which the responsible authority propose to meet C's needs, and
(b) the date by which, and by whom, any action required to implement any aspect of the plan will be carried out.

44 Functions of the personal adviser

The personal adviser's functions in relation to C are to –

(a) provide advice (including practical advice) and support,
(b) participate in reviews of C's case carried out under Part 6,
(c) liaise with the responsible authority in the implementation of the pathway plan,
(d) co-ordinate the provision of services and take reasonable steps to ensure C makes use of such services,
(e) remain informed about C's progress and wellbeing, and
(f) maintain a written record of their contacts with C.

PART 8
INDEPENDENT REVIEWING OFFICERS AND INDEPENDENT VISITORS

45 Additional functions of independent reviewing officers

(1) The IRO must ensure that, having regard to C's age and understanding, C has been informed by the responsible authority of the steps C may take under the 1989 Act and in particular, where appropriate, of –

(a) C's rights to apply, with leave, for a section 8 order (residence, contact and other orders with respect to children) and, where C is in the care of the responsible authority, to apply for the discharge of the care order, and

(b) the availability of the procedure established by them under section 26(3) for considering any representations (including complaints) C may wish to make about the discharge by the responsible authority of their functions, including the availability of assistance to make such representations under section 26A (advocacy services).

(2) If C wishes to take legal proceedings under the 1989 Act, the IRO must –

(a) establish whether an appropriate adult is able and willing to assist C to obtain legal advice or bring proceedings on C's behalf, and

(b) if there is no such person, assist C to obtain such advice.

(3) In the following circumstances the IRO must consider whether it would be appropriate to refer C's case to an officer of the Children and Family Court Advisory and Support Service –

(a) in the opinion of the IRO, the responsible authority have failed in any significant respect to –
   (i) prepare C's care plan in accordance with these Regulations,
   (ii) review C's case in accordance with these Regulations, or effectively implement any decision taken in consequence of a review,
   or are otherwise in breach of their duties to C in any material respect, and

(b) having drawn the failure or breach to the attention of persons at an appropriate level of seniority within the responsible authority, it has not been addressed to the satisfaction of the IRO within a reasonable period of time.

(4) When consulted by the responsible authority about any matter concerning C, or when informed of any matter relating to C in accordance with these Regulations, the IRO must –

(a) ensure that the responsible authority have ascertained and, subject to C's age and understanding, given due consideration to, C's wishes and feelings concerning the matter in question, and

(b) consider whether to request a review of C's case.

46 Qualifications and experience of independent reviewing officers

(1) The IRO must be registered as a social worker in Part 16 of the register maintained by the Health and Care Professions Council under article 5 of the Health and Social Work Professions Order 2001, in the register maintained by the Care Council for Wales under section 56 of the Care Standards Act 2000, or in a corresponding register maintained under the law of Scotland or Northern Ireland.

(2) The IRO must have sufficient relevant social work experience with children and families to perform the functions of an independent reviewing officer set out in section 25B(1) and under these Regulations in an independent manner and having regard to C's best interests.

(3) The responsible authority must not appoint any of the following as the IRO –

PART IV

(a)   a person involved in preparing C's care plan or the management of C's case,

(b)   R,

(c)   C's personal adviser,

(d)   a person with management responsibilities in relation to a person mentioned in sub-paragraphs (a) to (c), or

(e)   a person with control over the resources allocated to the case.

Amendments—SI 2012/1479.

47 Independent visitors

A person appointed by the responsible authority as an independent visitor under section 23ZB(1) is to be regarded as independent of that authority where the person appointed is not connected with the responsible authority by virtue of being –

(a)   a member of the responsible authority or any of their committees or sub-committees, whether elected or co-opted,

(b)   an officer of the responsible authority employed in relation to the exercise of the functions referred to in section 18(2) of the Children Act 2004, or

(c)   a spouse, civil partner or other person (whether of different sex or the same sex) living in the same household as the partner of a person falling within sub-paragraph (a) or (b).

PART 8A

APPLICATION OF THESE REGULATIONS WITH MODIFICATIONS TO CHILDREN ON REMAND

47A Application of these Regulations with modifications to children on remand

(1) These Regulations apply with the modifications set out in this Part while C is –

(a)   remanded to local authority accommodation, or

(b)   remanded to youth detention accommodation ("YDA").

(2) In these Regulations –

(a)   where C is remanded to local authority accommodation, or to YDA, references to "the responsible authority" are to be read as if they were references to the local authority designated by the court under section 92(2) or section 102(6), as the case may be, of the 2012 Act,

(b)   where C is remanded to YDA, references to C being "placed" are to be read as if they were references to C being so remanded,

(c)   where C is remanded to YDA, references to the "placement plan" (and where C is a looked after child only by reason of being so remanded, references to the "care plan") are to be read as if they were references to the "detention placement plan".

Amendments—Inserted by SI 2013/706.

47B (1) Part 2 (arrangements for looking after a child) applies with the following modifications.

(2) Where C is a looked after child only by reason of being remanded to local authority accommodation –

(a) in regulation 4(2), the care plan must be prepared within five working days of C being so remanded, and

(b) regulation 5(ε) does not apply.

(3) Where C is remanded to YDA and was a looked after child immediately before being so remanded –

(a) regulation 5(ε) does not apply, and instead the care plan must include a detention placement plan,

(b) in regulation 6(3), the responsible authority must also give a copy of the care plan to the director, governor or registered manager (as the case may be) of the YDA,

(c) regulation 7(1) to (4) does not apply.

(4) Where C is a looked after child only by reason of being remanded to YDA –

(a) regulation 5 does not apply, and instead the responsible authority must prepare a detention placement plan, which also includes details of the wishes and feelings of the persons listed in section 22(4) about the detention placement plan that have been ascertained and considered in accordance with section 22(4) and (5), and the wishes and feelings of those persons in relation to any change, or proposed change, to the detention placement plan,

(b) regulation 7(1) to (4) does not apply, and regulation 7(5) applies with the modification that for "health plan" there is substituted "detention placement plan".

Amendments—Inserted by SI 2013/706.

47C (1) Part 3 (placements) applies with the following modifications.

(2) Where C is remanded to YDA, regulations 9, 10, 11 and 14 do not apply, and instead –

(a) the responsible authority must prepare a plan for the remand ("the detention placement plan") within ten working days of C's remand to YDA which –

(i) sets out how the YDA will meet C's needs, and

(ii) includes the address of the YDA and all the matters specified in Schedule 2A,

(b) the responsible authority must ensure –

(i) that C's wishes and feelings have been ascertained and given due consideration,

(ii) where C was looked after immediately before being so remanded, that the IRO has been informed of the remand,

(c) the detention placement plan must be agreed with, and signed by, the director, governor or registered manager (as the case may be) of the YDA.

(3) Where C is remanded to local authority accommodation, regulation 9(1) applies with the modification that the placement plan must be prepared within five working days of C being so remanded.

47D Part 4 (provision for different types of placement) does not apply where C is remanded to YDA.

Amendments—Inserted by SI 2013/706.

47E Part 5 (visits by the responsible authority's representative etc.) applies with the modification that in regulation 28(7)(a), the responsible authority must also ensure that R visits C, where C is remanded to YDA, whenever reasonably requested to do so by the director, governor or registered manager (as the case may be) of the YDA.

Amendments—Inserted by SI 2013/706.

47F Part 6 (reviews) applies with the modification that in regulation 35, the considerations to which the responsible authority must have regard in reviewing C's case where C is remanded to YDA, are set out in paragraphs 1, 4, and 6 to 13, of Schedule 7 (considerations to which the responsible authority must have regard when reviewing C's case)."

Amendments—Inserted by SI 2013/706.

PART 9
MISCELLANEOUS

48 Application of these Regulations with modifications to short breaks

(1) In the circumstances set out in paragraph (2) these Regulations apply with the modifications set out in paragraph (3).

(2) The circumstances are that –

    (a) C is not in the care of the responsible authority,

    (b) the responsible authority have arranged to place C in a series of short-term placements with the same person or in the same accommodation ("short breaks"), and

    (c) the arrangement is such that –

        (i)   no single placement is intended to last for longer than 17 days,

        (ii) at the end of each such placement, C returns to the care of C's parent or a person who is not C's parent but who has parental responsibility for C, and

        (iii) the short breaks do not exceed 75 days in total in any period of 12 months.

(3) The modifications are that –

    (a) regulations 5 and 9 do not apply, but instead the care plan must set out the arrangements made to meet C's needs with particular regard to –

        (i)   C's health and emotional and behavioural development, in particular in relation to any disability C may have,

        (ii) promoting contact between C and C's parents and any other person who is not C's parent but who has parental responsibility for C, during any period when C is placed,

        (iii) C's leisure interests, and

        (iv) promoting C's educational achievement,

    and must include the name and address of C's registered medical practitioner, and the information set out in paragraph 3 of Schedule 2, where appropriate,

    (b) regulations 7, 13 and 49(2)(b) do not apply,

    (c) regulation 28(2) does not apply, but instead the responsible authority must ensure that R visits C on days when C is in fact placed, at regular intervals to be agreed with the IRO and C's parents (or any person who is not C's parent but who has parental responsibility for C) and recorded in the care plan before the start of the first placement, and in any event –

        (i)   the first visit must take place within three months of the start of the first placement, or as soon as practicable thereafter, and

        (ii) subsequent visits must take place at intervals of not more than six months, for as long as the short breaks continue,

(d) regulation 33 does not apply, but instead –

    (i) the responsible authority must first review C's case within three months of the start of the first placement, and

    (ii) the second and subsequent reviews must be carried out at intervals of not more than six months.

49 Records

Establishment of records

(1) The responsible authority must establish and maintain a written case record for C ("C's case record"), if one is not already in existence.

(2) The case record must include –

    (a) C's care plan, including any changes made to the care plan and any subsequent plans,

    (b) reports obtained under regulation 7,

    (c) any other document created or considered as part of any assessment of C's needs, or of any review of C's case,

    (d) any court order relating to C,

    (e) details of any arrangements that have been made by the responsible authority with any other local authority or with an independent fostering agency under regulation 26 and Schedule 5, or with a provider of social work services, under which any of the responsible authority's functions in relation to C are discharged by that local authority or independent fostering agency or provider of social work services.

50 Retention and confidentiality of records

(1) The responsible authority must retain C's case record either –

    (a) until the seventy-fifth anniversary of C's birth, or

    (b) if C dies before attaining the age of 18, for fifteen years beginning with the date of C's death.

(2) The responsible authority must secure the safe keeping of C's case record and take any necessary steps to ensure that information contained in it is treated as confidential subject only to –

    (a) any provision of, or made under or by virtue of, a statute under which access to such a record or information may be obtained or given,

    (b) any court order under which access to such a record or information may be obtained or given.

****

SCHEDULE 1

CARE PLANS

1 Information to be included in the health plan

(1) C's state of health including C's physical, emotional and mental health.

(2) C's health history including, so far as practicable, C's family's health history.

(3) The effect of C's health and health history on C's development.

(4) Existing arrangements for C's medical and dental care including –

    (a) routine checks of C's general state of health, including dental health,

PART IV

(b)   treatment for, and monitoring of, identified health (including physical, emotional and mental health) or dental care needs,

(c)   preventive measures such as vaccination and immunisation,

(d)   screening for defects of vision or hearing, and

(e)   advice and guidance on promoting health and effective personal care.

(5) Any planned changes to existing arrangements.

(6) The role of the appropriate person, and of any other person who cares for C, in promoting C's health.

2 Information to be included in the personal education plan

(1) C's educational and training history, including information about educational institutions attended and C's attendance and conduct record, C's academic and other achievements, and C's special educational needs, if any.

(2) Existing arrangements for C's education and training, including details of any special educational provision and any other provision made to meet C's particular educational or training needs, and to promote C's educational achievement, and including the name and contact details of the person responsible for discharging the responsible authority's duty under section 22(3A) (duty to promote the educational achievement of children looked after by the authority).

(3) Any planned changes to existing arrangements for C's education or training and, where any changes to the arrangements are necessary, provision made to minimise disruption to that education or training.

(4) C's leisure interests.

(5) The role of the appropriate person, and of any other person who cares for C, in promoting C's educational achievements and leisure interests.

Amendments—SI 2013/706.

3 Family and social relationships

(1) If C has a sibling for whom the responsible authority or another authority are providing accommodation, and the children have not been placed together, the arrangements made to promote contact between them, so far as is consistent with C's welfare.

(2) If C is looked after by, but is not in the care of, the responsible authority, details of any order relating to C made under section 8.

(3) If C is in the care of the responsible authority, details of any order relating to C made under section 34 (parental contact etc with children in care).

(4) Any other arrangements made to promote and maintain contact in accordance with paragraph 15 of Schedule 2 of the 1989 Act, so far as is reasonably practicable and consistent with C's welfare, between C and –

(a)   any parent of C's and any person who is not C's parent but who has parental responsibility for C, and

(b)   any other connected person.

(5) Where section 23ZB(1) applies, the arrangements made to appoint an independent visitor for C or, if section 23ZB(6) applies (appointment of independent visitor not made where child objects), that fact.

SCHEDULE 2

MATTERS TO BE DEALT WITH IN THE PLACEMENT PLAN

1 Information to be included in C's placement plan

(1) How on a day to day basis C will be cared for and C's welfare will be safeguarded and promoted by the appropriate person.

(2) Any arrangements made for contact between C and any parent of C's and any person who is not C's parent but who has parental responsibility for C, and between C and any other connected person including, if appropriate –

    (a)   the reasons why contact with any such person would not be reasonably practicable or would not be consistent with C's welfare,

    (b)   if C is not in the care of the responsible authority, details of any order made under section 8,

    (c)   if C is in the care of the responsible authority, details of any order relating to C made under section 34,

    (d)   the arrangements for notifying any changes in the arrangements for contact.

(3) The arrangements made for C's health (including physical, emotional and mental health) and dental care including –

    (a)   the name and address of C's registered medical and dental practitioners and, where applicable, any registered medical or dental practitioner with whom C is to be registered following the placement,

    (b)   any arrangements for the giving or withholding of consent to medical or dental examination or treatment for C.

(4) The arrangements made for C's education and training including –

    (a)   the name and address of any school at which C is a registered pupil,

    (b)   the name of the designated teacher at the school (if applicable),

    (c)   the name and address of any other educational institution that C attends, or of any other person who provides C with education or training,

    (d)   where C has a statement of special educational needs, details of the local authority that maintains the statement.

(5) The arrangements made for R to visit C in accordance with Part 5, the frequency of visits and the arrangements made for advice, support and assistance to be available to C between visits in accordance with regulation 31.

(6) If an independent visitor is appointed, the arrangements made for them to visit C.

(7) The circumstances in which the placement may be terminated and C removed from the appropriate person's care in accordance with regulation 14.

(8) The name and contact details of –

    (a)   the IRO,

    (b)   C's independent visitor (if one is appointed),

    (c)   R, and

    (d)   if C is an eligible child, the personal adviser appointed for C.

2 Additional information to be included where C is placed with P

(1) Details of support and services to be provided to P during the placement.

(2) The obligation on P to notify the responsible authority of any relevant change in circumstances, including any intention to change address, any changes in the household in which C lives, and of any serious incident involving C.

PART IV

(3) The obligation on P to ensure that any information relating to C or C's family or any other person given in confidence to P in connection with the placement is kept confidential, and that such information is not disclosed to any person without the consent of the responsible authority.

(4) The circumstances in which it is necessary to obtain the prior approval of the responsible authority for C to live in a household other than P's household.

(5) The arrangements for requesting a change to the placement plan.

(6) The circumstances in which the placement will be terminated in accordance with regulation 19(c)(ii).

3 Additional information to be included where C is placed with F, in a children's home or in other arrangements

(1) The type of accommodation to be provided, the address and, where C is placed under section 22C(6)(d), the name of the person who will be responsible for C at that accommodation on behalf of the responsible authority (if any).

(2) C's personal history, religious persuasion, cultural and linguistic background, and racial origin.

(3) Where C is not in the care of the responsible authority –

  (a) the respective responsibilities of the responsible authority and C's parents, or any person who is not C's parent but who has parental responsibility for C,

  (b) any delegation of responsibility to the responsible authority for C's day to day care there has been by C's parents, or any person who is not C's parent but who has parental responsibility for C,

  (c) the expected duration of the arrangements and the steps which should be taken to bring the arrangements to an end, including arrangements for C to return to live with C's parents, or any person who is not C's parent but who has parental responsibility for C, and

  (d) where C is aged 16 or over and agrees to being provided with accommodation under section 20, that fact.

(4) Any circumstances in which F must obtain the prior approval of either the responsible authority or P before making decisions in relation to C or C's care.

(5) The responsible authority's arrangements for the financial support of C during the placement.

(6) Where C is placed with F, the obligation on F to comply with the terms of the foster care agreement made under regulation 27(5)(b) of the Fostering Services Regulations.

Amendments—SI 2011/581.

SCHEDULE 2A

MATTERS TO BE DEALT WITH IN THE DETENTION PLACEMENT PLAN

1 How on a day to day basis C will be cared for and C's welfare will be safeguarded and promoted by the staff of the YDA.

2 Any arrangements made for contact between C and any parent of C's and any person who is not C's parent but who has parental responsibility for C, and between C and any other connected person including, if appropriate –

  (a) the reasons why contact with any such person would not be reasonably practicable or would not be consistent with C's welfare,

(b) if C is not in the care of the responsible authority, details of any order made under section 8,

(c) if C is in the care of the responsible authority, details of any order relating to C made under section 34,

(d) the arrangements for notifying any changes in the arrangements for contact.

3 The arrangements made for R to visit C in accordance with Part 5, the frequency of visits and the arrangements made for advice, support and assistance to be available to C between visits in accordance with regulation 31.

4 If an independent visitor is appointed, the arrangements made for them to visit C.

5 The arrangements made by the staff of the YDA for C's health (including physical, emotional and mental health) and dental care.

6 The arrangements made by staff of the YDA for C's education and training including –

(a) the name and address of any educational or training institution C was attending, or any other person providing C with education or training, immediately before his detention,

(b) where C has a statement of special educational needs, details of the local authority that maintains the statement.

7 C's personal history, religious persuasion, cultural and linguistic background, and racial origin, and the arrangement put in place by the staff of the YDA for meeting C's religious, cultural or linguistic needs.

8 The arrangements put in place by the staff of the YDA for supporting C to develop self-care skills.

9 The name and contact details of –

(a) the IRO,

(b) C's independent visitor (if one is appointed),

(c) R,

(d) if C is an eligible child, the personal adviser appointed for C,

(e) the person responsible for discharging the responsible authority's duty under section 22(3A) (duty to promote the educational achievement of children looked after by the authority).

10 Details of how C's welfare should be adequately safeguarded and promoted when C ceases to be remanded to YDA, in particular –

(a) whether C will be provided with accommodation by the responsible authority or another local authority, and

(b) whether any other services should be provided by the responsible authority or another local authority in the exercise of their duties under the 1989 Act.

Amendments—Inserted by SI 2013/706.

PART IV

SCHEDULE 3

MATTERS TO BE TAKEN INTO ACCOUNT WHEN ASSESSING THE
SUITABILITY OF P TO CARE FOR C

1 In respect of P –

   (a) P's capacity to care for children and in particular in relation to C to –

      (i)   provide for C's physical needs and appropriate medical and dental care,

      (ii) protect C adequately from harm or danger, including from any person who presents a risk of harm to C,

      (iii) ensure that the home environment is safe for C,

      (iv) ensure that C's emotional needs are met and C is provided with a positive sense of self, including any particular needs arising from C's religious persuasion, racial origin and cultural and linguistic background, and any disability C may have,

      (v)   promote C's learning and intellectual development through encouragement, cognitive stimulation and the promotion of educational success and social opportunities,

      (vi) enable C to regulate C's emotions and behaviour, including by modelling appropriate behaviour and interactions with others, and

      (vii) provide a stable family environment to enable C to develop and maintain secure attachments to P and other persons who provide care for C,

   (b) P's state of health including P's physical, emotional and mental health and medical history including any current or past issues of domestic violence, substance misuse or mental health problems,

   (c) P's family relationships and the composition of P's household, including particulars of –

      (i)   the identity of all other members of the household, including their age and the nature of their relationship with P and with each other, including any sexual relationship,

      (ii) any relationship with any person who is a parent of C,

      (iii) other adults not being members of the household who are likely to have regular contact with C, and

      (iv) any current or previous domestic violence between members of the household, including P,

   (d) P's family history, including –

      (i)   particulars of P's childhood and upbringing including the strengths and difficulties of P's parents or other persons who cared for P,

      (ii) P's relationships with P's parents and siblings, and their relationships with each other,

      (iii) P's educational achievement and any specific learning difficulty or disability,

      (iv) a chronology of significant life events, and

      (v)   particulars of other relatives and their relationships with C and P,

   (e) particulars of any criminal offences of which P has been convicted or in respect of which P has been cautioned,

   (f) P's past and present employment and other sources of income, and

   (g) the nature of the neighbourhood in which P's home is situated and resources available in the community to support C and P.

2 In respect of members of P's household aged 18 and over, so far as is practicable, all the particulars specified in paragraph 1 except sub-paragraphs (d), (f) and (g).

SCHEDULE 4

MATTERS TO BE TAKEN INTO ACCOUNT WHEN ASSESSING THE SUITABILITY OF A CONNECTED PERSON TO CARE FOR C

1 In respect of the connected person –

    (a)   the nature and quality of any existing relationship with C,

    (b)   their capacity to care for children and in particular in relation to C to –

        (i)   provide for C's physical needs and appropriate medical and dental care,

        (ii)   protect C adequately from harm or danger including from any person who presents a risk of harm to C,

        (iii)   ensure that the accommodation and home environment is suitable with regard to the age and developmental stage of C,

        (iv)   promote C's learning and development, and

        (v)   provide a stable family environment which will promote secure attachments for C, including promoting positive contact with P and other connected persons, unless to do this is not consistent with the duty to safeguard and promote C's welfare,

    (c)   their state of health including their physical, emotional and mental health and medical history including any current or past issues of domestic violence, substance misuse or mental health problems,

    (d)   their family relationships and the composition of their household, including particulars of –

        (i)   the identity of all other members of the household, including their age and the nature of their relationship with the connected person and with each other, including any sexual relationship,

        (ii)   any relationship with any person who is a parent of C,

        (iii)   any relationship between C and other members of the household

        (iv)   other adults not being members of the household who are likely to have regular contact with C, and

        (v)   any current or previous domestic violence between members of the household, including the connected person,

    (e)   their family history, including –

        (i)   particulars of their childhood and upbringing including the strengths and difficulties of their parents or other persons who cared for them,

        (ii)   their relationships with their parents and siblings, and their relationships with each other,

        (iii)   their educational achievement and any specific learning difficulty or disability,

        (iv)   a chronology of significant life events, and

        (v)   particulars of other relatives and their relationships with C and the connected person,

    (f)   particulars of any criminal offences of which they have been convicted or in respect of which they have been cautioned,

    (g)   their past and present employment and other sources of income, and

    (h)   the nature of the neighbourhood in which their home is situated and resources available in the community to support C and the connected person.

SCHEDULE 5

AGREEMENT WITH AN INDEPENDENT FOSTERING AGENCY RELATING TO THE DISCHARGE OF THE RESPONSIBLE AUTHORITY'S FUNCTIONS

1 The agreement must contain the following information –

PART IV

(1)   the services to be provided to the responsible authority by the registered person,
(2)   the arrangements for the selection by the responsible authority of F from those approved by the registered person,
(3)   a requirement for the registered person to submit reports to the responsible authority on any placements as may be required by the responsible authority, and
(4)   the arrangements for the termination of the agreement.

2 Where the agreement relates to a particular child, it must also contain the following information –

(1)   F's details,
(2)   details of any services that C is to receive and whether the services are to be provided by the responsible authority or by the registered person,
(3)   the terms (including as to payment) of the proposed placement agreement,
(4)   the arrangements for record keeping about C and for the return of records at the end of the placement,
(5)   a requirement for the registered person to notify the responsible authority immediately in the event of any concerns about the placement, and
(6)   whether, and on what basis, other children may be placed with F.

SCHEDULE 6
MATTERS TO BE CONSIDERED BEFORE PLACING C IN ACCOMMODATION IN AN UNREGULATED SETTING UNDER SECTION 22(6)(D)

1 In respect of the accommodation, the –

(a)   facilities and services provided,
(b)   state of repair,
(c)   safety,
(d)   location,
(e)   support,
(f)   tenancy status, and
(g)   the financial commitments involved for C and their affordability.

2 In respect of C, C's –

(a)   views about the accommodation,
(b)   understanding of their rights and responsibilities in relation to the accommodation, and
(c)   understanding of funding arrangements.

SCHEDULE 7
CONSIDERATIONS TO WHICH THE RESPONSIBLE AUTHORITY MUST HAVE REGARD WHEN REVIEWING C'S CASE

1 The effect of any change in C's circumstances since the last review, in particular of any change made by the responsible authority to C's care plan, whether decisions taken at the last review have been successfully implemented, and if not, the reasons for that.

2 Whether the responsible authority should seek any change in C's legal status.

3 Whether there is a plan for permanence for C.

4 The arrangements for contact and whether there is any need for changes to the arrangements in order to promote contact between C and P, or between C and other connected persons.

5 Whether C's placement continues to be the most appropriate available, and whether any change to the placement plan or any other aspects of the arrangements made to provide C with accommodation is, or is likely to become, necessary or desirable before the next review of C's case.

6 C's educational needs, progress and development and whether any change to the arrangements for C's education or training is, or is likely to become, necessary or desirable to meet C's particular needs and to promote C's educational achievement before the next review of C's case, having regard to the advice of any person who provides C with education or training, in particular the designated teacher of any school at which C is a registered pupil.

7 C's leisure interests.

8 The report of the most recent assessment of C's state of health obtained in accordance with regulation 8 and whether any change to the arrangements for C's health care is, or is likely to become, necessary or desirable before the next review of C's case, having regard to the advice of any health care professional received since the date of that report, in particular C's registered medical practitioner.

9 Whether C's needs related to C's identity are being met and whether any particular change is required, having regard to C's religious persuasion, racial origin and cultural background.

10 Whether the arrangements made in accordance with regulation 31 continue to be appropriate and understood by C.

11 Whether any arrangements need to be made for the time when C will no longer be looked after by the responsible authority.

12 C's wishes and feelings, and the views of the IRO, about any aspect of the case and in particular about any changes the responsible authority has made since the last review or proposes to make to the C's care plan.

13 Where regulation 28(3) applies, the frequency of R's visits.

Amendments—SI 2011/581.

PART IV

SCHEDULE 8

MATTERS TO BE DEALT WITH IN THE PATHWAY PLAN

1 The name of C's personal adviser.

2 The nature and level of contact and personal support to be provided to C, and by whom.

3 Details of the accommodation C is to occupy when C ceases to be looked after.

4 The plan for C's continuing education or training when C ceases to be looked after.

5 How the responsible authority will assist C in obtaining employment or other purposeful activity or occupation.

6 The support to be provided to enable C to develop and sustain appropriate family and social relationships.

7 A programme to develop the practical and other skills C needs to live independently.

8 The financial support to be provided to enable C to meet accommodation and maintenance costs.

9 C's health care needs, including any physical, emotional or mental health needs and how they are to be met when C ceases to be looked after.

10 The responsible authority's contingency plans for action to be taken in the event that the pathway plan ceases to be effective for any reason.

SCHEDULE 9

REVOCATIONS

The Regulations set out in the table are revoked –

Regulations Revoked	Series number
Contact with Children Regulations 1991	SI 1991/891
Definition of Independent Visitors (Children) Regulations 1991	SI 1991/892
Placement of Children with Parents etc Regulations 1991	SI 1991/893

Child Abduction and Custody (Parties to Conventions) Order 1986, SI 1986/1159

1 This Order may be cited as the Child Abduction and Custody (Parties to Conventions) Order 1986, and shall come into operation on 1 August 1986.

2 (1) In this Article of, and in Schedule 1 to, this Order "the Convention" means the Convention on the Civil Aspects of International Child Abduction which was signed at The Hague on 25 October 1980.

(2)

    (a)   The Contracting States to the Convention shall be as specified in the first column of Schedule 1 to this Order.

    (b)   Where the Convention applies, or applies only, to a particular territory or particular territories specified in a declaration made by a Contracting State under Article 39 or 40 of the Convention, the territory or territories in question shall be as specified in the second column of Schedule 1 to this Order.

(c) The date of the coming into force of the Convention as between the United Kingdom and any State or territory so specified shall be as specified in the third column of Schedule 1 to this Order.

3 (1) In this Article of, and in Schedule 2 to, this Order "the Convention" means the European Convention on Recognition and Enforcement of Decisions concerning Custody of Children and on the Restoration of Custody of Children which was signed in Luxembourg on 20 May 1980.

(2)

(a) The Contracting States to the Convention shall be as specified in the first column of Schedule 2 to this Order.

(b) Where the Convention applies, or applies only, to a particular territory or particular territories specified by a Contracting State under Article 24 or 25 of the Convention, the territory or territories in question shall be as specified in the second column of Schedule 2 to this Order.

(c) The date of the coming into force of the Convention as between the United Kingdom and any State or territory so specified shall be as specified in the third column of Schedule 2 to this Order.

SCHEDULE 1

CONVENTION ON THE CIVIL ASPECTS OF INTERNATIONAL CHILD ABDUCTION, THE HAGUE, 25 OCTOBER 1980

Contracting States to the Convention	*Territories specified in Declarations under Article 39 or 40 of the Convention*	*Date of Coming into Force of Convention as between the United Kingdom and the State or Territory*
Argentina	—	1 June 1991
Australia	Australian States and mainland Territories	1 January 1987
Austria	—	1 October 1988
The Bahamas	—	1 January 1994
Belarus	—	1 October 2003
Belgium	—	1 May 1999
Belize	—	1 October 1989
Bosnia and Herzegovina	—	1 December 1991
Brazil	—	1 March 2005
Bulgaria	—	1 May 2009
Burkina Faso	—	1 November 1992
Canada	Ontario	1 August 1986
	New Brunswick	1 August 1986
	British Columbia	1 August 1986
	Manitoba	1 August 1986
	Nova Scotia	1 August 1986
	Newfoundland and Labrador	1 August 1986
	Prince Edward Island	1 August 1986
	Quebec	1 August 1986
	Yukon Territory	1 August 1986

PART IV

Contracting States to the Convention	Territories specified in Declarations under Article 39 or 40 of the Convention	Date of Coming into Force of Convention as between the United Kingdom and the State or Territory
	Saskatchewan	1 November 1986
	Alberta	1 February 1987
	Northwest Territories	1 April 1988
	Nunavut	1 January 2001
Chile	—	1 May 1994
China	Hong Kong Special Administrative Region	1 September 1997
	Macau Special Administrative Region	1 March 1999
Columbia	—	1 March 1996
Costa Rica	—	1 May 2009
Croatia	—	1 December 1991
Cyprus	—	1 February 1995
Czech Republic	—	1 March 1998
Denmark	—	1 July 1991
Ecuador	—	1 June 1992
El Salvador	—	1 May 2009
Estonia	—	1 October 2003
Fiji	—	1 October 2003
Finland	—	1 August 1994
France	—	1 August 1986
Georgia	—	1 October 1997
Germany	—	1 December 1990
Greece	—	1 June 1993
Honduras	—	1 March 1994
Hungary	—	1 September 1986
Iceland	—	1 November 1996
Ireland	—	1 October 1991
Israel	—	1 December 1991
Italy	—	1 May 1995
Latvia	—	1 October 2003
Lithuania	—	1 March 2005
Luxembourg	—	1 January 1987
Macedonia	—	1 December 1991
Malta	—	1 March 2002
Mauritius	—	1 June 1993
Mexico	—	1 October 1991
Monaco	—	1 February 1993
Montenegro	—	1 December 1991
Netherlands	—	1 September 1990
New Zealand	—	1 October 1991
Norway	—	1 April 1989

Contracting States to the Convention	Territories specified in Declarations under Article 39 or 40 of the Convention	Date of Coming into Force of Convention as between the United Kingdom and the State or Territory
Panama	—	1 May 1994
Peru	—	1 October 2003
Poland	—	1 November 1992
Portugal	—	1 August 1986
Romania	—	1 February 1993
St Kitts and Nevis	—	1 August 1994
San Marino	—	1 June 2011
Serbia	—	1 December 1991
Slovakia	—	1 February 2001
Slovenia	—	1 June 1994
South Africa	—	1 October 1997
Spain	—	1 September 1987
Sweden	—	1 June 1989
Switzerland	—	1 August 1986
Turkey	—	1 August 2000
Turkmenistan	—	1 March 1998
Ukraine	—	1 June 2011
United States of America	—	1 July 1988
Uruguay	—	1 October 2003
Uzbekistan	—	1 October 2003
Venezuela	—	1 January 1997
Zimbabwe	—	1 July 1995

Amendments—Schedule last substituted by SI 2011/1081.

SCHEDULE 2

EUROPEAN CONVENTION ON RECOGNITION AND ENFORCEMENT OF DECISIONS CONCERNING CUSTODY OF CHILDREN AND ON THE RESTORATION OF CUSTODY OF CHILDREN, LUXEMBOURG, 20TH MAY 1980

Contracting States to the Convention	Territories specified in Declarations under Article 24 or 25 of the Convention	Date of Coming into Force of Convention as between the United Kingdom and the State or Territory
Austria	—	1 August 1986
Belgium	—	1 August 1986
Bulgaria	—	1 October 2003
Cyprus	—	1 October 1986
Czech Republic	—	1 July 2000
Denmark	—	1 August 1991
Estonia	—	1 September 2001
Finland	—	1 August 1994

PART IV

Contracting States to the Convention	Territories specified in Declarations under Article 24 or 25 of the Convention	Date of Coming into Force of Convention as between the United Kingdom and the State or Territory
France	—	1 August 1986
Germany	—	1 February 1991
Greece	—	1 July 1993
Hungary	—	1 June 2004
Iceland	—	1 November 1996
Ireland	—	1 October 1991
Italy	—	1 June 1995
Latvia	—	1 August 2002
Liechtenstein	—	1 August 1997
Lithuania	—	1 May 2003
Luxembourg	—	1 August 1986
Macedonia	—	1 March 2003
Malta	—	1 February 2000
Moldova	—	1 May 2004
Montenegro	—	6 June 2006
Netherlands	—	1 September 1990
Norway	—	1 May 1989
Poland	—	1 March 1996
Portugal	—	1 August 1986
Romania	—	1 September 2004
Serbia	—	1 May 2002
Slovakia	—	1 September 2001
Spain	—	1 August 1986
Sweden	—	1 July 1989
Switzerland	—	1 August 1986
Turkey	—	1 June 2000

Amendments—Schedule last substituted by SI 2009/702.

Child Support (Maintenance Arrangements and Jurisdiction) Regulations 1992, SI 1992/2645

1 Citation, commencement and interpretation

(1) These Regulations may be cited as the Child Support (Maintenance Arrangements and Jurisdiction) Regulations 1992 and shall come into force on 5 April 1993.

(2) In these Regulations –

"the Act" means the Child Support Act 1991;

...

"effective date" means the date on which a maintenance calculation takes effect for the purposes of the Act;

"maintenance order" has the meaning given in section 8(11) of the Act.

(3) In these Regulations, unless the context otherwise requires, a reference –

    (a)   to a numbered regulation is to the regulation in these Regulations bearing that number;

    (b)   in a regulation to a numbered paragraph is to the paragraph in that regulation bearing that number;

    (c)   in a paragraph to a lettered or numbered sub-paragraph is to the sub-paragraph in that paragraph bearing that letter or number.

Amendments—SI 1995/1045; SI 2001/161; SI 2012/2785.

****

3 Relationship between maintenance calculations and certain court orders

(1) Orders made under the following enactments are of a kind prescribed for the purposes of section 10(1) of the Act –

    (a)–(n)   ...

    (o)   Part II of the Matrimonial Causes Act 1973;

    (p), (q)   ...

    (r)   the Domestic Proceedings and Magistrates' Courts Act 1978;

    (s)   Part III of the Matrimonial and Family Proceedings Act 1984;

    (t)   ...

    (u)   the Social Security Act 1986;

    (v)   Schedule 1 to the Children Act 1989;

    (w)   the Social Security Administration Act 1992;

    (x)   Schedule 5, 6 or 7 to the Civil Partnership Act 2004.

(2) Subject to paragraphs (3) and (4), where a maintenance calculation is made with respect to –

    (a)   all of the children with respect to whom an order falling within paragraph (1) is in force; or

    (b)   one or more but not all of the children with respect to whom an order falling within paragraph (1) is in force and where the amount payable under the order to or for the benefit of each child is separately specified,

that order shall, so far as it relates to the making or securing of periodical payments to or for the benefit of the children with respect to whom the maintenance calculation has been made, cease to have effect on the effective date of the maintenance calculation.

(3) The provisions of paragraph (2) shall not apply where a maintenance order has been made in accordance with section 8(7) or (8) of the Act.

(4)–(8) ...

Amendments—SI 1995/123; SI 1995/1045; SI 1995/3261; SI 1999/1510; SI 2001/161; SI 2005/2877.

Defined terms—"the Act", "effective date": reg 1(2); "maintenance calculation": s 54; "maintenance order": reg 1(2) and s 8(11).

Scope—CSA 1991, s 10 deals with the relationship between maintenance calculations and continuing court orders. This regulation deals with the effect of a calculation on such orders, namely that any child maintenance order ceases to have effect except to the extent that s 8(7) and (8) apply (top-up orders and for education and disability expenses).

Effective date—The effective date of a calculation is the date from which payments are due under CSA 1991 payable by the non-resident parent in respect of qualifying children. The date is defined by Child Support (Maintenance Calculation Procedure) Regulations 2001, Pt VII (for example for a new calculation this will normally be when the non-resident parent is told that application has been made: reg 25(3)).

Effective date of new calculation which replaces a child maintenance order—CSA 1991, s 10(1)(a) provides powers to the Secretary of State to deal with the "ceasing to have effect" of a child maintenance

PART IV

order where a child support maintenance calculation is made under the 1991 Act. The powers are exercised by reference to regs 3 and 4 in Child Support (Maintenance Calculation Procedure) Regulations 2000, regs 26 and 28 (court orders) and 29 (maintenance agreements). A child maintenance court order (other than under s 8(7) and (8)) ceases to have effect on the effective date of the new maintenance calculation (Child Support (Maintenance Arrangements and Jurisdiction) Regulations 1992, reg 3(2). The "effective date of the maintenance calculation" is defined by Child Support (Maintenance Calculation Procedure) Regulations 2000, regs 26 and 28, which provide for court orders to cease to have effect, as follows:

(a) Where there is an existing order made since 3 March 2003 (orders made before this date cannot be varied save in the case of an application originally made under s 6) the effective date is 2 months and 2 days after the date of the making of the new calculation (Child Support (Maintenance Calculation Procedure) Regulations 2000, reg 26(2)).

(b) Where there is an order that ends on the making of an application for a calculation (other than in the circumstances of reg 26), the effective date is the day after that application being made (Child Support (Maintenance Calculation Procedure) Regulations 2000, reg 28).

Court orders "cease to have effect" (reg 3(2))—CSA 1991, s 10(1) and this regulation use the term "cease to have effect", which can be taken to mean that the order is discharged and that it cannot be revived (*Askew Page v Page* [2001] Fam Law 794), although this is not to prevent a parent with care making an application for a top-up order (CSA 1991, s 8(7),(8).

"section 8(7) or (8) of the Act" (reg 3(3))—Reg 3(3) emphasises that the provisions of reg 3(2) have no effect on the ability of the courts to make effective orders under s 8(6),(7) and that orders made under these provisions remain effective despite the coming to an end of any child maintenance order under s 10(1) and reg 3.

4 Relationship between maintenance calculations and certain agreements

(1) Maintenance agreements within the meaning of section 9(1) of the Act are agreements of a kind prescribed for the purposes of section 10(2) of the Act.

(2) Where a maintenance calculation is made with respect to –

(a) all of the children with respect to whom an agreement falling within paragraph (1) is in force; or

(b) one or more but not all of the children with respect to whom an agreement falling within paragraph (1) is in force and where the amount payable under the agreement to or for the benefit of each child is separately specified,

that agreement shall, so far as it relates to the making or securing of periodical payments to or for the benefit of the children with respect to whom the maintenance calculation has been made, become unenforceable from the effective date of the calculation.

(3) Where an agreement becomes unenforceable under the provisions of paragraph (2) to the extent specified in that paragraph, it shall remain unenforceable in relation to a particular child until such date as the Secretary of State no longer has jurisdiction to make a maintenance calculation with respect to that child.

Amendments—SI 1999/1510; SI 2001/161.

Defined terms—"the Act", "effective date": reg 1(2); "maintenance agreement": s 8(11); "maintenance calculation": s 54.

Scope—CSA 1991, s 10(2) enables the Secretary of State to provide for termination of agreements for payment of child maintenance on the making of a calculation under CSA 1991, and reg 4 gives effect to that power. The agreement becomes unenforceable from the effective date of the calculation, which in this case is the date of notification of the application to the non-resident parent (Child Support (Maintenance Calculation Procedure) Regulations 2000, reg 25(3): see further under reg 3, above).

5 Notifications by the Secretary of State

(1) Where the Secretary of State is aware that an order of a kind prescribed in paragraph (2) is in force and considers that the making of a maintenance calculation has affected, or is likely to affect, that order, he shall notify the persons prescribed in

paragraph (3) in respect of whom that maintenance calculation is in force, and the persons prescribed in paragraph (4) holding office in the court where the order in question was made or subsequently registered, of the calculation and its effective date.

(2) The prescribed orders are those made under an enactment mentioned in regulation 3(1).

(3) The prescribed persons in respect of whom the maintenance calculation is in force are –

    (a)   a person with care;

    (b)   a non-resident parent;

    (c)   a person who is treated as a non-resident parent under regulation 50 of the Child Support Maintenance Calculation Regulations 2012;

    (d)   a child who has made an application for a maintenance calculation under section 7 of the Act.

(4) The prescribed person holding office in the court where the order in question was made or subsequently registered is –

    (a)   in England and Wales –

        (i)   in relation to the High Court, the senior district judge of the principal registry of the Family Division or, where proceedings were instituted in a district registry, the district judge;

        (ii)   in relation to a county court, the proper officer of that court within the meaning of Order 1, Rule 3 of the County Court Rules 1981;

        (iii)   in relation to a magistrates' court, the designated officer for that court;

    (b)   ...

Amendments—SI 1999/1510; SI 2001/161; SI 2005/617; SI 2012/2785.

Defined terms—"the Act". "effective date": reg 1(2); "maintenance calculation": s 54.

6 Notification by the court

(1) Where a court is aware that a maintenance calculation is in force and makes an order mentioned in regulation 3(1) which it considers has affected, or is likely to affect, that calculation, the person prescribed in paragraph (2) shall notify the Secretary of State to that effect.

(2) The prescribed person is the person holding the office specified below in the court where the order in question was made or subsequently registered –

    (a)   in England and Wales –

        (i)   in relation to the High Court, the senior district judge of the principal registry of the Family Division or, where proceedings were instituted in a district registry, the district judge;

        (ii)   in relation to a county court, the proper officer of that court within the meaning of Order 1, Rule 3 of the County Court Rules 1981;

        (iii)   in relation to a magistrates' court, the designated officer for that court;

    (b)   ...

Amendments—*SI 2001/161*; SI 2005/617.

Defined terms—"maintenance calculation": s 54.

****

8 Maintenance calculations and maintenance orders made in error

(1) Where –

PART IV

(a)   at the time that a maintenance calculation with respect to a qualifying child was made a maintenance order was in force with respect to that child;

(aa) the maintenance order has ceased to have effect by virtue of the provisions of regulation 3;

(b)   the non-resident parent has made payments of child support maintenance due under that calculation; and

(c)   the Secretary of State revises the decision as to the maintenance calculation under section 16 of the Act and decides that no child support maintenance was payable on the ground that the previous decision was made in error,

the payments of child support maintenance shall be treated as payments under the maintenance order and that order shall be treated as having continued in force.

(2) Where –

(a)   at the time that a maintenance order with respect to a qualifying child was made a maintenance calculation was in force with respect to that child;

(aa) the maintenance calculation ceases to have effect;

(b)   the non-resident parent has made payments of maintenance due under that order; and

(c)   the maintenance order is revoked by the court on the grounds that it was made in error,

the payments under the maintenance order shall be treated as payments of child support maintenance and the maintenance calculation shall be treated as not having ceased to have effect.

Amendments—SI 1993/913; SI 1999/1510; SI 2001/161.

Defined terms—"non-resident parent": CSA 1991, s 3(2); "child support maintenance": s 3(6); "maintenance calculation": s 54; "maintenance order": reg 1(2); "qualifying child": s 3(1).

8A Maintenance calculations and maintenance orders – payments

Where –

(a)   a maintenance calculation has been made with respect to a qualifying child in response to an application made under section 4 or 7 of the Act;

(b)   at the time that maintenance calculation was made a maintenance order was in force with respect to that child;

(c)   the maintenance order has ceased to have effect by virtue of the provisions of regulation 3; and

(d)   the non-resident parent has made payments of maintenance due under that order after the date on which the maintenance calculation took effect,

the payments made under the maintenance order shall be treated as payments of child support maintenance.

Amendments—Inserted by SI 2005/785; amended by SI 2012/2785.

9 Cases in which application may be made under section 4 or 7 of the Act

The provisions of section 4(10) or 7(10) of the Act shall not apply to prevent an application being made under those sections after 22 January 1996 where a decision has been made by the relevant court either that it has no power to vary or that it has no power to enforce a maintenance order in a particular case.

Amendments—Inserted by SI 1995/3261.

Scope—CSA 1991, s 4(10) prevents an application being made for a calculation where there is in force a written maintenance agreement (made before 5 April 1993) or a maintenance order. Thus, if application has been made unsuccessfully to vary the order, or a court has decided that it has no power to enforce an order, application can be made under CSA 1991, s 4 for a calculation.

"relevant court"—This term is not defined in these regulations, so may be taken to apply to the courts with power to vary periodical payments orders for children, namely the High Court, county courts and magistrates' courts.

Children (Admissibility of Hearsay Evidence) Order 1993, SI 1993/621

1 Citation and commencement

This Order may be cited as the Children (Admissibility of Hearsay Evidence) Order 1993 and shall come into force on 5 April 1993.

2 Admissibility of hearsay evidence

In –
  (a)   civil proceedings before the High Court or a county court; and
  (b)   (i)   family proceedings, and
       (ii) civil proceedings under the Child Support Act 1991 in a magistrates' court,

evidence given in connection with the upbringing, maintenance or welfare of a child shall be admissible notwithstanding any rule of law relating to hearsay.

Defined terms—"child": CA 1989, s 105(1).

"civil proceedings"—This term is not defined for the purposes of the Order but will not usually cause any difficulty. The Civil Evidence Act 1968 contains a definition of civil proceedings but only for the purpose of clarifying the position of proceedings before tribunals and arbitrations, which do not arise in relation to the scope of this Order, and excluding certain proceedings from the strict rules of evidence, which is immaterial for the purposes of this Order as it imposes no preconditions for admissibility.

"family proceedings ... in a magistrates' court"—This concept is not defined by the Order. CA 1989, s 8(3) defines "family proceedings" for the purposes of the Act, but s 92(2) provides that "proceedings under this Act shall be treated as family proceedings in relation to magistrates' courts". The term family proceedings is defined in: Courts Act 2003, s 75; MFPA 1984, s 32; and MCA 1980, s 65.

"civil proceedings under the Child Support Act 1991"—The relevant proceedings in a magistrates' court are under s 20 (appeals from a child support officer where made in accordance with the Child Support Appeals (Jurisdiction of Courts) Order 2002, i e on an issue of parentage), s 26 (reference to court for declaration of parentage), and certain proceedings on enforcement under ss 33–40.

"in connection with the upbringing, maintenance or welfare of a child"—This is a flexible form of words which will need to be applied in relation to each individual case. The concept of a question with respect to the upbringing of a child is also one of the triggers for activating the principle that the court should treat the child's welfare as its paramount consideration (CA 1989, s 1(1)). "In connection with" leaves some uncertainty about what it is that should relate to the "upbringing etc". It is submitted that if the proceedings are about the child's upbringing, maintenance or welfare, e g s 8 proceedings, it is not necessary to determine whether particular things that are sought to be proved in those proceedings so relate; if the proceedings so relate, every piece of evidence allowed to be adduced will necessarily be relevant to the outcome and thus within the scope of the Order, even though the evidence itself may not directly relate to any of the three things specified in the Order. For example, in proceedings for child maintenance the respondent's income is clearly relevant and, although his wage slips do not relate directly to the maintenance of the child, they are relevant to the issue of how much child maintenance should be ordered and are therefore admissible under the Order. Where proceedings consist of more than one aspect not all of which relate to any of the three issues, it will be necessary to analyse whether the fact sought to be admitted by virtue of the Order relates to any of those issues.

  The Order clearly applies to contempt proceedings which take place as part of "family proceedings". For hearsay evidence to be admissible under the Order, the onus lies on the applicant seeking to rely on the hearsay evidence to show that the evidence has a "substantial connection with the upbringing, maintenance or welfare of a child". If the injunctive relief is being granted to protect a child, evidence from the child of any breach of the injunction is likely to have a "substantial connection" with his welfare. However, if the injunction was granted in a parental dispute to protect one parent, the evidence of a child as to a breach of that injunction, where he himself was not directly affected by it, would be unlikely to show a "substantial connection" with his welfare (*C v C (Contempt: Evidence)* [1993] 1 FLR 220). The decision as to admissibility will be for the judge to consider on the particular facts of each case. Where this Order does not apply, hearsay evidence may nevertheless be admissible following the ruling in *Savings and Investment Bank Ltd v Gasco Investments (Netherlands) BV (No 2)* [1988] 1 All ER 975.

"**shall be admissible**"—The effect of this Order is to render hearsay evidence admissible. Thus, a local authority is entitled to adduce in evidence the written and videotaped record of a child's interview in which allegations of sexual abuse are made, and can decline to call her to give oral evidence. In *Re P (Witness Summons)* [1997] 2 FLR 447 it was observed that the only way in which another party could secure the child's attendance to give evidence was to issue a witness summons against the child under CCR Ord 20, r 12 (now FPR 2010, r 24.2), and that the judge had a discretion whether to issue such a summons. In *Re P* it was held that the question of whether to issue a witness summons against a child was not a question with respect to upbringing and therefore CA 1989, s 1(1) did not apply (though the case provides useful guidance on the factors to be considered in the exercise of the discretion).

As to the right approach to hearsay evidence in care proceedings see *Re H (Care: Change in Care Plan)* [1998] 1 FLR 193 where the Court of Appeal accepted that even an unsworn allegation was capable of constituting a very serious cause for concern which a court could accept provided it was evaluated against testimony on oath. What weight should be attached to the particular piece of hearsay evidence is a question for the court to decide (*F v Child Support Agency* [1999] 2 FLR 244).

"**rule of law relating to hearsay**"—Hearsay evidence is, at common law, inadmissible save in certain circumstances. The number of exceptions to the rule against hearsay has been increased by or under statute over the years. This Order may be relied on in preference to other exceptions which may also apply and which are less attractive because they have preconditions; for example, if evidence is admissible under the Order, no notice need be served in accordance with the exception created by the Civil Evidence Act 1995.

****

Children (Secure Accommodation) Regulations 1991, SI 1991/1505

****

3 Approval by Secretary of State of secure accommodation in a children's home

Accommodation in a children's home shall not be used as secure accommodation unless it has been approved by the Secretary of State for such use and approval shall be subject to such terms and conditions as he sees fit.

Amendments—SI 1995/1398.

4 Placement of a child aged under 13 in secure accommodation in a children's home

A child under the age of 13 years shall not be placed in secure accommodation in a children's home without the prior approval of the Secretary of State to the placement of that child and such approval shall be subject to such terms and conditions as he sees fit.

Amendments—SI 1992/2117; SI 1995/1398.

5 Children to whom section 25 of the Act shall not apply

(1) Section 25 of the Act shall not apply to a child who is detained under any provision of the Mental Health Act 1983 or in respect of whom an order has been made under section 90 or 91 of the Powers of the Criminal Courts (Sentencing) Act 2000 (detention at Her Majesty's pleasure or for specified period).

(2) Section 25 of the Act shall not apply to a child –

    (a) to whom section 20(5) of the Act (accommodation of persons over 16 but under 21) applies and who is being accommodated under that section,

    (b) in respect of whom an order has been made under section 43 of the Act (child assessment order) and who is kept away from home pursuant to that order.

Amendments—SI 2002/546.

5A Section 25 of the Act shall not apply to a child who is remanded to youth detention accommodation and who is to be treated as looked after by virtue of section 104(1) of the Legal Aid, Sentencing and Punishment of Offenders Act 2012.

Amendments—Inserted by SI 2012/2813.

6 Detained and remanded children to whom section 25 of the Act shall have effect subject to modifications

(1) Subject to regulation 5, section 25 of the Act shall have effect subject to the modification specified in paragraph (2) in relation to children who are being looked after by a local authority and are of the following descriptions –

    (a) children aged 12 or over but under the age of 17 detained under section 38(6) of the Police and Criminal Evidence Act 1984 (detained children),

    (b) *(revoked)*

(2) The modification referred to in paragraph (1) is that, for the words "unless it appears" to the end of subsection (1), there shall be substituted the following words –

"unless it appears that any accommodation other than that provided for the purpose of restricting liberty is inappropriate because –

    (a) the child is likely to abscond from such other accommodation, or

    (b) the child is likely to injure himself or other people if he is kept in any such other accommodation".

Amendments—SI 1992/2117; SI 2012/3134.

Regulation 5A—By virtue of LASPOA 2012, s 104, any child who is remanded to youth detention accommodation is to be treated as "looked after" by the designated authority.

Regulation 6(1)(b)—Where a child is detained under Police and Criminal Evidence Act 1984, s 38(6), the Youth Court has power to make a secure accommodation order even if the s 25 criteria are not met, provided that the criteria in reg 6(2) are met. Where the conditions in reg 6(1)(b) are not met, the Youth Court can nonetheless make a secure accommodation order if the s 25(1) criteria are met (*Re G (Secure Accommodation Order)* [2001] 1 FLR 884).

7 Children to whom section 25 of the Act shall apply and have effect subject to modifications

(1) Subject to regulation 5 and paragraphs (2) and (3) of this regulation section 25 of the Act shall apply (in addition to children looked after by a local authority) –

    (a) to children, other than those looked after by a local authority, who are accommodated by health authorities, National Health Service trusts established under section 5 of the National Health Service and Community Care Act 1990,

PART IV

NHS foundation trusts or local authorities in the exercise of education functions or who are accommodated pursuant to arrangements made by the Secretary of State, the National Health Service Commissioning Board or a clinical commissioning group under the National Health Service Act 2006, and

(b)   to children, other than those looked after by a local authority, who are accommodated in care homes or independent hospitals.

(2) In relation to the children of a description specified in paragraph (1)(a) section 25 of the Act shall have effect subject to the following modifications –

(a)   for the words "who is being looked after by a local authority" in subsection (1) there shall be substituted the words "who is being provided with accommodation by a health authority, a National Health Service trust established under section 5 of the National Health Service and Community Care Act 1990, an NHS foundation trust or a local authority in the exercise of education functions or who is being provided with accommodation pursuant to arrangements made by the Secretary of State, the National Health Service Commissioning Board or a clinical commissioning group under the National Health Service Act 2006".

(b)   for the words "local authorities" in subsection (2)(c) there shall be substituted the words "health authorities, National Health Service trusts, NHS foundation trusts, local authorities, the Secretary of State, the National Health Service Commissioning Board or clinical commissioning groups".

(3) In relation to the children of a description specified in paragraph (1)(b), section 25 of the Act shall have effect subject to the following modifications –

(a)   for the words "who is being looked after by a local authority" in subsection (1) there shall be substituted the words "who is being provided with accommodation in a care home or an independent hospital"; and

(b)   for the words "local authorities" in subsection (2)(c) there shall be substituted the words "persons carrying on care homes or independent hospitals".

Amendments—SI 2000/694; SI 2002/546; SI 2004/696; SI 2010/1172; SI 2013/235.

8 Applications to court

Subject to section 101 of the Local Government Act 1972 or to provisions in or under sections 14 to 20 of the Local Government Act 2000, applications to a court under section 25 of the Act in respect of a child shall be made only by the local authority which are looking after that child.

Amendments—SI 2001/2237.

"local authority which are looking after that child"—See CA 1989, s 22(1) and, as to a child who is bailed with a condition of residence to the local authority, see *Re C (Secure Accommodation: Bail)* [1994] 2 FLR 922.

****

10 Maximum period in secure accommodation without court authority

(1) Subject to paragraphs (2) and (3), the maximum period beyond which a child to whom section 25 of the Act applies may not be kept in secure accommodation without the authority of a court is an aggregate of 72 hours (whether or not consecutive) in any period of 28 consecutive days.

(2) Where authority of a court to keep a child in secure accommodation has been given, any period during which the child has been kept in such accommodation before the giving of that authority shall be disregarded for the purposes of calculating the maximum

period in relation to any subsequent occasion on which the child is placed in such accommodation after the period authorised by court has expired.

(3) Where a child is in secure accommodation at any time between 12 midday on the day before and 12 midday on the day after a public holiday or a Sunday, and

(a) during that period the maximum period specified in paragraph (1) expires, and
(b) the child had, in the 27 days before the day on which he was placed in secure accommodation, been placed and kept in such accommodation for an aggregate of more than 48 hours,

the maximum period does not expire until 12 midday on the first day, which is not itself a public holiday or a Sunday, after the public holiday or Sunday.

Period—A freestanding application for an interim secure accommodation order cannot be made. Where the court was satisfied it had all the information needed to determine the issues raised by the application and that it would be procedurally fair to proceed, it is unlikely there would be grounds upon which the court could properly adjourn the application. Prolonging secure accommodation proceedings simply in order to keep a children's guardian involved for the purposes of assisting the child or overseeing the performance of the local authority's statutory duties, was not a proper use of the court's power (*Birmingham City Council v M* [2008] 2 FLR 542).

11 Maximum initial period of authorisation by a court

Subject to regulations 12 and 13 the maximum period for which a court may authorise a child to whom section 25 of the Act applies to be kept in secure accommodation is three months.

12 Further periods of authorisation by a court

Subject to regulation 13 a court may from time to time authorise a child to whom section 25 of the Act applies to be kept in secure accommodation for a further period not exceeding six months at any one time.

****

14 Duty to inform parents and others in relation to children in secure accommodation in a children's home

Where a child to whom section 25 of the Act applies is kept in secure accommodation in a children's home and it is intended that an application will be made to a court to keep the child in that accommodation, the local authority which are looking after the child shall if practicable inform of that intention as soon as possible –

(a) his parents,
(b) any person who is not a parent of his but who has parental responsibility for him,
(c) the child's independent visitor, if one has been appointed, and
(d) any other person who that local authority consider should be informed.

Amendments—SI 1995/1398.

****

PART IV

Children (Secure Accommodation) (No 2) Regulations 1991, SI 1991/2034

1 Citation and commencement

(1) These Regulations may be cited as the Children (Secure Accommodation) (No 2) Regulations 1991 and shall come into force on 14 October 1991 immediately after the Children (Secure Accommodation) Regulations 1991.

2 Applications to court – special cases

(1) Applications to a court under section 25 of the Children Act 1989 in respect of a child provided with accommodation by a health authority, a National Health Service trust established under section 5 of the National Health Service and Community Care Act 1990, an NHS foundation trust or a local authority in the exercise of education functions or provided with accommodation pursuant to arrangements made by the Secretary of State, the National Health Service Commissioning Board or a clinical commissioning group under the National Health Service Act 2006 shall, unless the child is looked after by a local authority, be made only by the health authority, National Health Service trust, NHS foundation trust or local authority providing accommodation for the child or by the person (namely, the Secretary of State, the National Health Service Commissioning Board or a clinical commissioning group) who has made arrangements for the provision of accommodation for the child.

(2) Applications to a court under section 25 of the Children Act 1989 in respect of a child provided with accommodation in a care home or independent hospital shall, unless the child is looked after by a local authority, be made only by the person carrying on the home in which accommodation is provided for the child.

Amendments—SI 2000/694; SI 2002/546; SI 2004/696; SI 2010/1172; SI 2013/235.

"looked after by a local authority"—See CA 1989, s 22(1) and, as to a child who is bailed with a condition of residence to the local authority, see *Re C (Secure Accommodation: Bail)* [1994] 2 FLR 922.

Civil Jurisdiction and Judgments (Maintenance) Regulations 2011, SI 2011/1484

Scope—These Regulations facilitate the application of Council Regulation (EC) No 4/2009 ("the Maintenance Regulation") in the UK from 18 June 2011. Reference should be made to the annotations to the Maintenance Regulation. The Family Procedure (Amendment) Rules 2011 amended FPR 2010 to take account of the application of the Maintenance Regulation. FPR PD34C, which came into force on 31 October 2011, also makes provision for the application of the Maintenance Regulations. Reference should also be made to MC(EVOFP & MP)R 2011 (and, in particular, Pt 12, which contains amendments to MCR 1981 to reflect the application of the Maintenance Regulation).

The Regulations are structured by division into schedules:

Reg 3 and Sch 1	Provisions relating to the recognition and enforcement in the UK jurisdictions of maintenance decisions from other Member States
Reg 4 and Sch 2	Provisions regarding the sharing of information between the designated central authorities of the UK and certain designated public bodies under Arts 61–62 of the Maintenance Regulation

Reg 5 and Sch 3	Provisions relating to the recognition and enforcement in the UK jurisdictions of authentic instruments and court settlements from other Member States as required by Art 48 of the Maintenance Regulation
Reg 6 and Sch 4	Amendments to CJJA 1982 arising from the application of the Maintenance Regulation
Reg 7 and Sch 5	Amendments to the Civil Jurisdiction and Judgments Order 2001 arising from the application of the Maintenance Regulation
Reg 8 and Sch 6	Provisions relating to the allocation of jurisdiction to hear maintenance matters as between the courts of the different parts of the UK (England and Wales, Scotland and Northern Ireland) adapting the jurisdictional rules of the Maintenance Regulation
Reg 9 and Sch 7	Consequential amendments

1 Citation, commencement and extent

(1) These Regulations may be cited as the Civil Jurisdiction and Judgments (Maintenance) Regulations 2011, and shall come into force on 18 June 2011.

(2) These Regulations extend to England and Wales, Scotland and Northern Ireland.

(3) An amendment, repeal or revocation made by these Regulations has the same extent as the enactment amended, repealed or revoked.

2 Interpretation

In these Regulations –

"the Act" means the Civil Jurisdiction and Judgments Act 1982;
"the Order" means the Civil Jurisdiction and Judgments Order 2001;
"the Maintenance Regulation" means Council Regulation (EC) No 4/2009 including as applied in relation to Denmark by virtue of the Agreement made on 19 October 2005 between the European Community and the Kingdom of Denmark;
"Maintenance Regulation State" in any provision, in the application of that provision in relation to the Maintenance Regulation, refers to any of the Member States.

3 The Maintenance Regulation

Schedule 1 (which contains provisions relating to the enforcement of maintenance decisions pursuant to the Maintenance Regulation) has effect.

4 Provisions relating to information

Schedule 2 (which contains provisions relating to access to, and the transmission and use of, information) has effect.

5 Provisions relating to authentic instruments and court settlements

Schedule 3 (which contains provisions relating to authentic instruments and court settlements) has effect.

****

8 Allocation of jurisdiction within the United Kingdom

Schedule 6 (which contains rules for the allocation of jurisdiction within the United Kingdom in relation to maintenance) has effect.

****

10 Review

(1) Before the end of each review period, the Secretary of State must –

(a)   carry out a review of the provisions of these Regulations,
(b)   set out the conclusions of the review in a report, and
(c)   publish the report.

(2) The review shall relate to the operation of these Regulations as they affect England and Wales only.

(3) In carrying out the review the Secretary of State must, so far as is reasonable, have regard to how the Maintenance Regulation has been given effect in other Member States.

(4) The report must in particular –

(a)   set out the objectives intended to be achieved by the provisions of these Regulations,
(b)   assess the extent to which those objectives are achieved, and
(c)   assess whether those objectives remain appropriate, and, if so, the extent to which they could be achieved in a manner that imposes less regulation.

(5) "Review period" means –

(a)   the period of five years beginning with the day on which these Regulations come into force, and
(b)   subject to paragraph (6), each successive period of five years.

(6) If a report under this regulation is published before the last day of the review period to which it relates, the following review period is to begin with the day on which that report is published.

SCHEDULE 1

THE MAINTENANCE REGULATION

Scope—Sch 1 is divided into four parts: Pts 1 and 4 being a general application, Pt 2 applying to decisions made by courts in Member States other than Denmark (to which the procedures in Ch 4, S 1 of the Maintenance Regulation apply) and Pt 3 applying to decisions made by courts in Denmark, and in transitional cases (Art 75) (to which Ch 4, S 2 of the Maintenance Regulation applies).

PART 1
INTRODUCTORY

1 Interpretation

(1) In this Schedule –

"court" includes a tribunal, and any administrative authority which is a court for the purposes of the Maintenance Regulation by virtue of Article 2(2) of that Regulation;

"debtor", in relation to a maintenance decision, means the person liable, or alleged to be liable, to make the payments for which that decision provides;

"maintenance decision" has the meaning given to "decision" by Article 2 of the Maintenance Regulation.

(2) In this Schedule –

- (a) any reference to a numbered Article is a reference to the Article so numbered in the Maintenance Regulation and any reference to a sub-division of a numbered Article shall be construed accordingly;
- (b) references to a registered decision include, to the extent of its registration, references to a decision so registered to a limited extent only.

(3) Anything authorised or required by the Maintenance Regulation or by this Schedule to be done by, to or before a particular magistrates' court may be done by, to or before any magistrates' court acting for the same local justice area (or, in Northern Ireland, the same petty sessions district) as that court.

2 Central authorities

(1) The following are designated as Central Authorities under Article 49 of the Maintenance Regulation –

- (a) in relation to England and Wales, the Lord Chancellor;
- (b) in relation to Scotland, the Scottish Ministers;
- (c) in relation to Northern Ireland, the Department of Justice.

(2) If a person outside the United Kingdom does not know to which Central Authority in the United Kingdom a communication should be addressed, the person may address it to the Lord Chancellor.

PART 2

Recognition and enforcement of maintenance decisions made by courts in Maintenance Regulation States other than Denmark

3 Application of Part 2

This Part shall apply to maintenance decisions made by courts in Maintenance Regulation States other than Denmark.

4 Enforcement of maintenance decisions

(1) Subject to sub-paragraph (2), where a maintenance decision falls to be enforced in the United Kingdom under Section 1 of Chapter IV of the Maintenance Regulation, the court to which an application for enforcement is to be made is –

- (a) in England and Wales, a magistrates' court,
- (b) in Scotland, a sheriff court, and
- (c) in Northern Ireland, a magistrates' court.

(2) An application for enforcement is to be transmitted to the magistrates' court or sheriff court designated for these purposes by rules of court ("the enforcing court") –

- (a) in England and Wales, by the Lord Chancellor,
- (b) in Scotland, by the Scottish Ministers, and
- (c) in Northern Ireland, by the Department of Justice.

(3) Jurisdiction in relation to applications for enforcement of such maintenance decisions lies with the courts for the part of the United Kingdom in which –

- (a) the person against whom enforcement is sought is resident,
- (b) assets belonging to that person and which are susceptible to enforcement are situated or held.

(4) For the purposes of the enforcement of a maintenance decision –

  (a)   the decision shall be of the same force and effect,

  (b)   the enforcing court shall have in relation to its enforcement the same powers, and

  (c)   proceedings for or with respect to its enforcement may be taken, as if the decision had originally been made by the enforcing court.

(5) Sub-paragraph (4) is subject to sub-paragraphs (6) and (7).

(6)

  (a)   A maintenance decision which is enforceable in England and Wales by virtue of Section 1 of Chapter IV of the Maintenance Regulation and these Regulations shall be enforceable in a magistrates' court in England and Wales in the same manner as a maintenance order made by that court, save that sections 76 and 93 of the Magistrates' Courts Act 1980 have effect as modified by section 5(5B) and (5C) of the Act.

  (b)   In this sub-paragraph "maintenance order" has the meaning given by section 150(1) of the Magistrates' Courts Act 1980.

(7) A maintenance decision which is enforceable in Northern Ireland by virtue of Section 1 of Chapter IV of the Maintenance Regulation and these Regulations shall be enforceable in a magistrates' court in Northern Ireland in the same manner as an order made by that court, save that Article 98 of the Magistrates' Courts (Northern Ireland) Order 1981 has effect as modified by section 5(6A) of the Act.

(8) Sub-paragraph (4) is also subject to –

  (a)   Article 21 (application by debtor for refusal or suspension of enforcement);

  (b)   paragraph 8 below;

  (c)   any provision made by rules of court as to the procedure for the enforcement of maintenance decisions given in another Maintenance Regulation State.

(9)

  (a)   The debtor under a maintenance decision which is or has been the subject of enforcement proceedings in England and Wales or Northern Ireland by virtue of Section 1 of Chapter IV of the Maintenance Regulation and these Regulations must give notice of any change of address to the designated officer, or in Northern Ireland, the clerk, of the court in which enforcement proceedings have been, or are being, taken.

  (b)   A person who without reasonable excuse fails to comply with this sub-paragraph shall be guilty of an offence and liable on summary conviction to a fine not exceeding level 2 on the standard scale.

(10) An application for refusal or suspension of enforcement under Article 21(2) or (3) of the Maintenance Regulation shall be made –

  (a)   in England and Wales and Northern Ireland, to a magistrates' court by way of complaint, and

  (b)   in Scotland, to a sheriff court by way of summary application.

Amendments—SI 2012/2814.

PART 3
RECOGNITION AND ENFORCEMENT OF MAINTENANCE DECISIONS
MADE BY COURTS IN DENMARK ETC

5 Application of Part 3

This Part applies in relation to –

    (a) maintenance decisions made by courts in Denmark, and

    (b) maintenance decisions to which Sections 2 and 3 of Chapter IV of the Maintenance Regulation apply by virtue of Article 75(2)(a) or (b).

6 Recognition and enforcement of maintenance orders

(1) Subject to sub-paragraph (2), the court to which an application for registration of a maintenance decision under Section 2 of Chapter IV of the Maintenance Regulation is to be made is –

    (a) in England and Wales, a magistrates' court,

    (b) in Scotland, a sheriff court, and

    (c) in Northern Ireland, a magistrates' court.

(2) An application for registration is to be transmitted to the magistrates' court or sheriff court designated for these purposes by rules of court ("the registering court") –

    (a) in England and Wales, by the Lord Chancellor,

    (b) in Scotland, by the Scottish Ministers, and

    (c) in Northern Ireland, by the Department of Justice.

(3) Where an application for registration of a maintenance decision is transmitted to a court –

    (a) the decision may be registered for enforcement by the court, and

    (b) if so registered, the decision shall be treated as having been declared enforceable for the purposes of Section 2 of Chapter IV of the Maintenance Regulation.

(4)

    (a) An application for registration shall be determined in the first instance by the prescribed officer of the registering court.

    (b) In this sub-paragraph, "prescribed" means prescribed by rules of court.

(5) For the purposes of the enforcement of a registered maintenance decision –

    (a) the decision shall be of the same force and effect,

    (b) the registering court shall have in relation to its enforcement the same powers, and

    (c) proceedings for or with respect to its enforcement may be taken, as if the decision had originally been made by the registering court.

(6) Sub-paragraph (5) is subject to sub-paragraphs (7) and (8).

(7)

    (a) A maintenance decision which is enforceable in England and Wales by virtue of Section 2 of Chapter IV of the Maintenance Regulation and these Regulations shall be enforceable in a magistrates' court in England and Wales in the same manner as a maintenance order made by that court, save that sections 76 and 93 of the Magistrates' Courts Act 1980 have effect as modified by section 5(5B) and (5C) of the Act.

    (b) In this sub-paragraph "maintenance order" has the meaning given by section 150(1) of the Magistrates' Courts Act 1980.

(8) A maintenance decision which is enforceable in Northern Ireland by virtue of Section 2 of Chapter IV of the Maintenance Regulation and these Regulations shall be enforceable in a magistrates' court in Northern Ireland in the same manner as an order made by that court, save that Article 98 of the Magistrates' Courts (Northern Ireland) Order 1981 has effect as modified by section 5(6A) of the Act.

(9) Sub-paragraph (5) is also subject to –

    (a)   Article 36(3) (restriction on enforcement where appeal pending or time for appeal unexpired);

    (b)   paragraph 8 below;

    (c)   any provision made by rules of court as to the procedure for the enforcement of maintenance decisions registered under the Maintenance Regulation and these Regulations.

(10)

    (a)   The debtor under a maintenance decision registered in accordance with this paragraph in a magistrates' court in England and Wales or Northern Ireland must give notice of any change of address to the designated officer, or in Northern Ireland, the clerk of that court.

    (b)   A person who without reasonable excuse fails to comply with this sub-paragraph shall be guilty of an offence and liable on summary conviction to a fine not exceeding level 2 on the standard scale.

7 Proceedings to contest decisions given on appeal in connection with applications for registration

An appeal under Article 33 may only be on a point of law and lies –

    (a)   in England and Wales, to a county court in accordance with section 111A of the Magistrates' Courts Act 1980;

    (b)   in Scotland, to the Inner House of the Court of Session;

    (c)   in Northern Ireland, to the Court of Appeal.

PART 4
RECOGNITION AND ENFORCEMENT OF MAINTENANCE DECISIONS – GENERAL

8 Interest on judgments

(1) Subject to sub-paragraphs (2) and (3) and rules of court as to the payment of interest under this paragraph, where a person applying for registration or enforcement of a maintenance decision shows that –

    (a)   the decision provides for the payment of a sum of money, and

    (b)   in accordance with the law of the Maintenance Regulation State in which the maintenance decision was given and the terms of the decision, interest on that sum is recoverable at a particular rate and from a particular date or time, the debt resulting from registration or enforcement of the decision is to carry interest at that rate and from that date or time.

(2) In the case of an application for registration of a maintenance decision, interest is not recoverable unless the rate of interest and the date or time referred to in sub-paragraph (1)(b) are registered with the decision.

(3)

    (a)   Interest on arrears of sums payable under a maintenance decision which falls to be enforced in a magistrates' court in England and Wales or Northern Ireland by virtue of the Maintenance Regulation and these Regulations shall not be recoverable in that court.

(b)   But this sub-paragraph does not affect the operation in relation to any such maintenance decision of section 2A of the Maintenance Orders Act 1958 or section 11A of the Maintenance and Affiliation Orders Act (Northern Ireland) 1966 (which enables interest to be recovered if the decision is registered for enforcement in the High Court).

(4) Except as mentioned in sub-paragraph (3), debts under maintenance decisions enforceable in the United Kingdom by virtue of the Maintenance Regulation shall carry interest only as provided by this paragraph.

9 Currency of payments under maintenance decisions

(1) Sums payable under a maintenance decision enforceable in the United Kingdom by virtue of the Maintenance Regulation, including any arrears so payable, shall be paid in sterling where an order is made on an application for enforcement in England and Wales, Scotland or Northern Ireland.

(2) Where the maintenance decision is expressed in any other currency, the amount shall be converted on the basis of the exchange rate prevailing on the date on which the application for enforcement or registration of the decision was received by a Central Authority in the United Kingdom for transmission to a court.

(3) For the purposes of this paragraph, a written certificate purporting to be signed by an officer of any bank in the United Kingdom and stating the exchange rate prevailing on a specified date shall be evidence of the facts stated (and in Scotland, sufficient evidence of those facts).

10 Proof and admissibility of certain maintenance decisions and related documents

(1) For the purposes of proceedings relating to the Maintenance Regulation –

(a)   a document, duly authenticated, which purports to be a copy of a maintenance decision given by a court in a Maintenance Regulation State shall without further proof be deemed to be a true copy, unless the contrary is shown; and

(b)   an extract from a maintenance decision issued by a court in a Maintenance Regulation State in accordance with Article 20 or Article 28 (as the case may be) shall be evidence that that decision is enforceable there.

(2) A document purporting to be a copy of a maintenance decision given by a court mentioned in sub-paragraph (1)(a) is duly authenticated for the purposes of this paragraph if it purports –

(a)   to bear the seal of that court; or

(b)   to be certified by any person in his capacity as a judge or officer of that court to be a true copy of a maintenance decision given by that court.

(3) Nothing in this paragraph shall prejudice the admission in evidence of any document which is admissible apart from this paragraph.

PART IV

PART 5
ESTABLISHMENT AND MODIFICATION OF MAINTENANCE UNDER THE MAINTENANCE REGULATION

11 (1) This paragraph applies to an application submitted under Article 56 for establishment or modification of a decision to the Lord Chancellor, in relation to England and Wales, or to the Department of Justice in relation to Northern Ireland.

(2) Upon receipt of an application submitted under Article 56 for establishment or modification of a decision in England and Wales, the Lord Chancellor shall send that application to the designated officer for the magistrates' court in the local justice area in which the respondent is residing.

(3) Upon receipt of the application under sub-paragraph (2), the designated officer of that court shall decide –

  (a) whether the courts of England and Wales have jurisdiction to determine the application by virtue of the Maintenance Regulation and Schedule 6 to these Regulations; and
  (b) if so, whether the magistrates' court has power to make the decision or modification sought under –
      (i)   the Domestic Proceedings and Magistrates' Courts Act 1978, or
      (ii) section 15 of and Schedule 1 to the Children Act 1989.

(4) Where the designated officer decides under sub-paragraph (3)(a) that the courts of England and Wales do not have jurisdiction to determine the application, the designated officer shall return the application to the Lord Chancellor with a written explanation of the reasons for that decision.

(5) Where the designated officer decides under sub-paragraph (3)(b) that the magistrates' court does not have power to make the decision or modification sought, the designated officer shall send the application to –

  (a) the High Court, or
  (b) a county court

as appears to the designated officer to be appropriate.

(6) Subject to sub-paragraph (7), if the designated officer decides under sub-paragraph (3)(b) that the magistrates' court has power to make the decision or modification sought, the designated officer shall issue the application and serve it on the respondent.

(7) If the respondent does not reside in the local justice area for which the magistrates' court acts, the designated officer shall –

  (a) if satisfied that the respondent is residing within another local justice area, send the application to the designated officer of a magistrates' court acting in that other area and inform the Lord Chancellor that it has been so sent; or
  (b) if unable to establish where the respondent is residing, return the application to the Lord Chancellor.

(8) A designated officer who receives an application by virtue of sub-paragraph (7)(a) shall proceed under sub-paragraph (6) as if that designated officer had decided that the magistrates' court has power to make the decision or modification sought.

(9) Where the designated officer has determined in accordance with sub-paragraph (3)(b) that the magistrates' court has power to make the decision or modification sought, the application shall be treated for the purpose of establishment or modification of a decision under the Maintenance Regulation as an application under the Domestic Proceedings and Magistrates' Courts Act 1978, or under section 15 of and Schedule 1 to the Children Act 1989, as appropriate.

(10) Sub-paragraphs (2) to (9) apply to an application submitted under Article 56 for establishment or modification of a decision in Northern Ireland to the Department of Justice in relation to Northern Ireland as if –

    (a)   references to England and Wales were references to Northern Ireland;

    (b)   references to the Lord Chancellor were references to the Department of Justice;

    (c)   for "designated officer" were substituted "clerk of petty sessions";

    (d)   for "local justice area" were substituted "petty sessions district";

    (e)   references to the courts of England and Wales were references to the courts of Northern Ireland;

    (f)   references to the Domestic Proceedings and Magistrates' Courts Act 1978, and to section 15 of and Schedule 1 to the Children Act 1989 were references to the Domestic Proceedings (Northern Ireland) Order 1980 and Article 15 of and Schedule 1 to the Children (Northern Ireland) Order 1995 respectively.

(11) In this paragraph –

    "respondent" means the person who is alleged in an application for establishment of a decision under Article 56 to owe maintenance, or where the application is for modification of a decision, the person against whom the modification is sought;

and a reference to an application is a reference to an application together with any documents which accompany it.

Amendments—Inserted by SI 2012/2814.

SCHEDULE 2
PROVISIONS RELATING TO INFORMATION

Scope—Sch 2 makes necessary provision for the sharing of information between public bodies designated for the task and designated central authorities. Para 1 lists the public bodies designated by the UK to share the information identified in Art 61(2) of the Maintenance Regulation with the three UK central authorities (Sch 1, para 2). The giving of access to specific information held by public bodies is intended to facilitate the collection of maintenance. Information may only be withheld for national security or public safety reasons (Maintenance Regulation, Art 61). The information must be information already held by the relevant public body. There is no requirement to seek out, compile and maintain additional information not already held on databases in the public domain. The information sought must be adequate, relevant and not excessive and must relate to (a) the address of the debtor or of the creditor; (b) the debtor's income; (c) the identification of the debtor's employer and/or of the debtor's bank account(s); (d) the debtor's assets (Maintenance Regulation, Art 61.2). Information may only be used for recovery of maintenance claims (Maintenance Regulation, Arts 62.1 and 62.2).

1 (1) The following are designated for the purposes of Article 61(1) of the Maintenance Regulation to provide the information referred to in Article 61(2) to the Central Authorities designated under paragraph 2 of Schedule 1 –

    (a)   the Secretary of State;

    (b)   (*revoked*)

    (c)   the Revenue and Customs officers;

    (d)   the Department for Employment and Learning in Northern Ireland;

    (e)   the Department of the Environment in Northern Ireland;

    (f)   the Department of Finance and Personnel in Northern Ireland;

    (g)   the Department for Social Development in Northern Ireland.

(2) The information to be supplied by the Secretary of State is limited to information held for functions relating to social security, child support or employment or training.

PART IV

(3) In sub-paragraph (2), "functions relating to social security" includes functions relating to statutory payments as defined in section 4C(11) of the Social Security Contributions and Benefits Act 1992 and maternity allowance under section 35 of that Act.

(4) In this Schedule, references to the Secretary of State include a person providing services to the Secretary of State in connection with the functions mentioned in sub-paragraph (2).

Amendments—SI 2012/2814.

"the Child Maintenance and Enforcement Commission" (para 1(1)(b))—By virtue of SI 2012/2007, art 5(3), this should be read as "the Secretary of State".

2 Subject to the provisions of Chapter VII of the Maintenance Regulation, the persons and authorities to whom the Central Authorities transmit information in accordance with Article 62(1) of that Regulation may process that information in any manner necessary to facilitate the adjudication and recovery of maintenance claims.

3 (1) Information referred to in Article 61(2) of the Maintenance Regulation which is received by a Central Authority, or by a person supplying services to a Central Authority, from a body or person designated under paragraph 1 cannot be disclosed to another person unless the disclosure is in connection with a function of the Central Authority under, and is in accordance with, Chapter VII of the Maintenance Regulation.

(2) Sub-paragraph (1) does not apply to –

  (a)   the disclosure of information which is in the form of a summary or collection of information so framed as not to enable identification of any person from the information;

  (b)   disclosure which is made in pursuance of an order of a court;

  (c)   disclosure which is required by any other enactment.

4 (1) Subject to sub-paragraph (3), a person who –

  (a)   is or has been employed by a Central Authority designated under paragraph 2 of Schedule 1; or

  (b)   provides or has provided services to such a Central Authority,

is guilty of an offence if he or she discloses, otherwise than in accordance with paragraph 3, information referred to in Article 61(2) of the Maintenance Regulation which has been obtained from a person or body designated under paragraph 1 and which relates to a person whose identity is specified in the information disclosed or can be deduced from it.

(2) It is a defence to prove that, at the time of the alleged offence, the person believed that he or she was making the disclosure lawfully in accordance with this Schedule and the Maintenance Regulation, and had no reasonable cause to believe otherwise.

(3) Sub-paragraph (1) does not apply to disclosure of information received by such a person –

  (a)   from the Department for Employment and Learning in Northern Ireland, the Department of the Environment in Northern Ireland, or the Department of Finance and Personnel in Northern Ireland;

  (b)   from the Secretary of State where the information so disclosed is held by the Secretary of State for the purposes of employment and training only.

5 A person found guilty of an offence under this Schedule shall be liable –

(a) on conviction on indictment, to imprisonment for a term not exceeding two years, to a fine or to both;

(b) on summary conviction, to imprisonment for a term not exceeding 3 months or to a fine not exceeding the statutory maximum or to both.

SCHEDULE 3
PROVISIONS RELATING TO AUTHENTIC INSTRUMENTS AND COURT SETTLEMENTS

Scope—Sch 3 makes provision relating to authentic instruments and court settlements that are sent to the UK for enforcement from other Member States. The purpose of the Schedule is to modify the application of Sch 1 to these instruments, as appropriate, so as to respect the obligation in Art 48 of the Maintenance Regulation to recognise and enforce such instruments in the same way as decisions.

1 References in this Schedule to authentic instruments and court settlements are references to those authentic instruments and court settlements (as defined in Article 2 of the Maintenance Regulation) which are to be recognised and enforceable in the same way as maintenance decisions by virtue of Article 48 of that Regulation.

2 (1) In relation to an authentic instrument or court settlement which is enforceable in the Maintenance Regulation State of origin, Schedule 1 applies, subject to the modifications in subparagraphs (2), (3) and (4), as if that authentic instrument or court settlement was a maintenance decision given by a court in that Maintenance Regulation State.

(2) Paragraphs 4(4) and 6(5) of Schedule 1 apply in relation to authentic instruments and court settlements as if, for the words "as if the decision had been originally made" there were substituted "as if it was a decision which had originally been made".

(3) Paragraph 10 of Schedule 1 applies to authentic instruments as if –

(a) in sub-paragraph (1)(a), for the words "given by a court" there were substituted "drawn up by, registered by, authenticated by or concluded before a competent authority";

(b) for sub-paragraph (1)(b) there were substituted –
"(b) an extract from an authentic instrument issued by a competent authority in a Maintenance Regulation State in accordance with Article 48 shall be evidence that that instrument is enforceable there.";

(c) for sub-paragraph (2) there were substituted –

"(2) A document purporting to be a copy of an authentic instrument drawn up by, registered by, authenticated by or concluded before a competent authority in a Maintenance Regulation State is duly authenticated for the purposes of this paragraph if it purports to be certified to be a true copy of such an instrument by a person duly authorised in that State to do so."

(4) Paragraph 10(1)(b) of Schedule 1 applies to court settlements as if, for the words "Article 20 or Article 28 (as the case may be)" there were substituted "Article 48".

3 Section 18(7) of the Act (disapplication of section 18) has effect to disapply section 18 in relation to an authentic instrument or court settlement to which Article 48 applies.

****

PART IV

SCHEDULE 6

ALLOCATION WITHIN THE UNITED KINGDOM OF JURISDICTION RELATING TO MAINTENANCE MATTERS

Scope—"Maintenance" has been excluded by Sch 4 from the regime contained in CJJA 1982 ("the 1982 Act"), s 16 and Sch 4 and s 20 and Sch 8 (Scotland) regarding the allocation of jurisdiction as between the different parts of the UK. Sch 6 establishes a replacement regime relating to maintenance within the UK previously contained in Sch 4 of the 1982 Act based on the Maintenance Regulation. Sch 6, para 16 lists the matters and proceedings in which the rules in the Schedule do not apply, in particular, the jurisdiction of the CSA on behalf of the Department for Work and Pensions following the abolition of CMEC to make child support calculations in the UK is not subject to the Schedule.

1 The provisions of this Schedule have effect for determining, as between the parts of the United Kingdom, whether the courts of a particular part of the United Kingdom, or any particular court in that part, have or has jurisdiction in proceedings where the subject-matter of the proceedings is within the scope of the Maintenance Regulation as determined by Article 1 of that Regulation.

2 In this Schedule, a reference to an Article by number alone is a reference to the Article so numbered in the Maintenance Regulation.

3 The provisions of Chapter II of the Maintenance Regulation apply to the determination of jurisdiction in the circumstances mentioned in paragraph 1, subject to the modifications specified in the following provisions of this Schedule.

4 Article 3 applies as if –

    (a)   the references in Article 3(a) and (b) to the court for the place where the defendant or the creditor is habitually resident were references to the court for the part of the United Kingdom in which the defendant, or the creditor, as the case may be, is habitually resident;

    (b)   the references to a person's nationality were references to a person's domicile.

5 Article 4(1) to (3) applies as if –

    (a)   for "Member State", wherever it occurs, there were substituted "part of the United Kingdom";

    (b)   the reference to a person's nationality was a reference to a person's domicile.

6 Article 5 applies as if –

    (a)   after "this Regulation" there were inserted "as modified by Schedule 6 to the Civil Jurisdiction and Judgments (Maintenance) Regulations 2011";

    (b)   for "Member State" there were substituted "part of the United Kingdom".

7 Where Article 6, as read with the second paragraph of Article 2(3), indicates that the courts of the United Kingdom have jurisdiction under the Maintenance Regulation, and the parties are domiciled in different parts of the United Kingdom, the courts of either part may exercise jurisdiction (subject to Article 12 as it has effect by virtue of this Schedule).

8 Article 7 applies as if for the second sentence there were substituted –

"The dispute must have a sufficient connection with the part of the United Kingdom in which the court seised is located.".

9 (1) Sub-paragraphs (2) and (3) have effect in addition to Article 8.

(2) Where a decision is given in a part of the United Kingdom where the creditor is habitually resident, proceedings to modify the decision or to have a new decision given cannot be brought by the debtor in any other part of the United Kingdom as long as the creditor remains habitually resident in the part of the United Kingdom in which the decision was given.

(3) Sub-paragraph (2) does not apply where –

   (a)   the parties have agreed that the courts of that other part of the United Kingdom are to have jurisdiction in accordance with Article 4 as applied by paragraph 5 of this Schedule, or

   (b)   the creditor submits to the jurisdiction of the courts of that other part of the United Kingdom pursuant to Article 5 as applied by paragraph 6 of this Schedule.

10 Article 9 does not apply.

11 (1) Sub-paragraphs (2) and (3) have effect instead of Articles 10 and 11.

(2) Where a defendant habitually resident in one part of the United Kingdom is sued in a court of another part of the United Kingdom and does not enter an appearance, the court will declare of its own initiative that it has no jurisdiction unless its jurisdiction is derived from the provisions of this Schedule.

(3) The court will stay the proceedings so long as it is not shown that the defendant has been able to receive the document instituting the proceedings or an equivalent document in sufficient time to enable him to arrange for his defence, or that all necessary steps have been taken to this end.

12 Article 12 applies as if after "different Member States" there were inserted "or different parts of the United Kingdom".

13 Article 13 applies as if after "different Member States" there were inserted "or different parts of the United Kingdom".

14 Article 14 applies as if –

   (a)   for "a Member State" there were substituted "a part of the United Kingdom";

   (b)   after "another Member State" there were inserted "or another part of the United Kingdom".

15 Notwithstanding the preceding provisions of this Schedule, the exercise of jurisdiction in any proceedings in a court in the United Kingdom is subject to –

   (a)   the Maintenance Regulation;

   (b)   the Convention on jurisdiction and the recognition and enforcement of judgments in civil and commercial matters, between the European Community and the Republic of Iceland, the Kingdom of Norway, the Swiss Confederation and the Kingdom of Denmark signed on behalf of the European Community on 30 October 2007;

   (c)   the Convention on jurisdiction and the enforcement of judgments in civil and commercial matters signed at Brussels on the 27 September 1968; and

   (d)   the Convention on jurisdiction and the enforcement of judgments in civil and commercial matters concluded at Lugano on the 16 September 1988.

PART IV

16 This Schedule does not apply to –

    (a)   matters in relation to which –

        (i)   the Secretary of State has jurisdiction to make a maintenance calculation by virtue of section 44 of the Child Support Act 1991;

        (ii)   the Department for Social Development in Northern Ireland has jurisdiction to make a maintenance calculation by virtue of Article 41 of the Child Support (Northern Ireland) Order 1991;

    (b)   proceedings for, or otherwise relating to, an order under any of the following Provisions –

        (i)   paragraph 23 of Schedule 2 to the Children Act 1989 (contribution orders);

        (ii)   section 106 of the Social Security Administration Act 1992 (recovery of expenditure on benefit from person liable for maintenance);

        (iii)   section 80 of the Social Work (Scotland) Act 1968 (enforcement of duty to make contributions);

        (iv)   section 81 of the Social Work (Scotland) Act 1968 (provisions as to decrees for aliment);

        (v)   Article 101 of the Health and Personal Social Services (Northern Ireland) Order 1972 (recovery of cost of accommodation for persons in need);

        (vi)   section 101 of the Social Security Administration (Northern Ireland) Act 1992 (recovery of expenditure on benefit from person liable for maintenance);

        (vii)   Article 41 of the Children (Northern Ireland) Order 1995 (contribution orders).

Amendments—SI 2012/2814.

"the Child Maintenance and Enforcement Commission" (para 16(a)(i))—By virtue of SI 2012/2007, art 5(3), this should be read as "the Secretary of State".

****

Community Legal Service (Funding) Order 2007,
SI 2007/2441
****

SCHEDULE 6

EXPERTS' FEES AND RATES

Section 1

Table

Expert	Non-London Hourly Rate or fixed fee	London Hourly Rate or fixed fee	Comments
A&E consultant	£126	£135	
Accident reconstruction	£90	£68	

Expert	Non-London Hourly Rate or fixed fee	London Hourly Rate or fixed fee	Comments
Accountant	£50–£135	£50–£144	Partner £144, Manager £108, Accountant £80, General staff £50
Anaesthetist	£135	£135	
Architect	£99	£90	
Cardiologist	£144	£144	
Cell telephone site analysis	£90	£90	
Child psychiatrist	£135	£90	
Child psychologist	£126	£90	
Computer expert	£90	£90	
Consultant engineer	£90	£68	
Dentist	£117	£117	
Dermatologist	£108	£108	
Disability consultant	£68	£68	
DNA (per person) – testing of sample	£315 per test	£315 per test	
DNA (per person) – preparation of report	£90	£90	
Doctor (GP)	£99	£90	
Employment consultant	£68	£68	
Enquiry agent	£32	£23	
ENT surgeon	£126	£126	
General surgeon	£135	£90	
Geneticist	£108	£108	
GP (records report)	£63 fixed fee	£90 fixed fee	
Gynaecologist	£135	£90	
Haematologist	£122	£90	
Handwriting expert	£90	£90	
Interpreter	£32	£25	
Lip reader/Signer	£72	£41	
Mediator	£126	£126	
Medical consultant	£135	£90	
Medical microbiologist	£135	£135	
Meteorologist	£126	£180 fixed fee	
Midwife	£90	£90	
Neonatologist	£135	£135	
Neurologist	£153	£90	
Neuropsychiatrist	£158	£90	
Neuroradiologist	£171	£171	
Neurosurgeon	£171	£90	

PART IV

Expert	Non-London Hourly Rate or fixed fee	London Hourly Rate or fixed fee	Comments
Nursing expert	£81	£81	
Obstetrician	£135	£135	
Occupational therapist	£68	£68	
Oncologist	£140	£140	
Orthopaedic surgeon	£144	£144	
Paediatrician	£135	£90	
Pathologist	£153	£540 fixed fee	
Pharmacologist	£122	£122	
Photographer	£32	£23	
Physiotherapist	£81	£81	
Plastic surgeon	£135	£135	
Process server	£32	£23	
Psychiatrist	£135	£90	
Psychologist	£117	£90	
Radiologist	£135	£135	
Rheumatologist	£135	£135	
Risk assessment expert	£63	£63	
Speech therapist	£99	£99	
Surveyor	£50	£50	
Telecoms expert	£90	£90	
Toxicologist	£135	£135	
Urologist	£135	£135	
Vet	£90	£90	
Voice recognition	£117	£90	

****

Amendments—Inserted by SI 2011/2066.

Note—The following guidance has been provided by the Legal Services Commission (which was replaced by the Legal Aid Agency on 1 April 2013) to accompany the insertion of Sch 6 into the Community Legal Service (Funding) Order 2007, SI 2007/2441:
   "**LEGAL AID REFORM – EXPERT RATES**
   FOR THE PURPOSES OF IMPLEMENTING THE MINISTRY OF JUSTICE'S 'PROPOSALS FOR THE REFORM OF LEGAL AID IN ENGLAND AND WALES'
   To be implemented on 3 October 2011
   Following the consultations on the Community Legal Service (Funding) (Amendment No 2) Order 2011 and the Criminal Defence Service (Funding) (Amendment) Order 2011 maximum rates have been introduced for certain types of expert.
   These rates will apply to all work undertaken by experts in all civil, family and crime work with a case start date or representation order date of on or after the 3 October 2011
   The rates were consulted on as part of the Ministry of Justice consultation 'Proposals for the Reform of Legal Aid in England and Wales'. They are set out in the Payment Annex of the Unified Contract 2007 (Civil), 2010 Standard Civil Contract and Schedule 6 of the Criminal Defence Service (Funding) (Amendment) Order 2011), and a list is also enclosed herewith.
   The Commission may increase the fixed fees or rates if it considers it reasonable to do so due to exceptional circumstances. These are:
      where the expert's evidence is key to the client's case and either –
   (a) the complexity of the material is such that an expert with a high level of seniority is required; or

(b) the material is of such a specialised and unusual nature that only very few experts are available to provide the necessary evidence

Payments on account for experts' fees will be rejected if they exceed the codified rate unless a prior authority has been granted demonstrating that the case is exceptional.

Where an expert is not listed in the Payment Annex to either the 2010 Standard Civil Contract or the 2007 Unified Contract or in Schedule 6 of the Criminal Defence Service (Funding) (Amendment) Order 2011), then the LSC or the Court will assess these costs on an individual basis.

In these cases, when considering the rate at which to fund the expert service, the Commission:

(a) must have regard to the rates set out in Part 14 of the Payment annex; and

(b) may require a number of quotes for provision of the relevant service to be submitted to the Commission.

Prior authority is not mandatory. The contract provisions provide that prior authority may be submitted whenever the proposed incurred costs are either unusual in nature or unusually large. If prior authority is not sought and costs exceed the expert rates and fees contained in the Funding Order then they will be subject to assessment and may be reduced

You are reminded that changes to expert funding have already been introduced to expert witness funding through the introduction of the Standard Contracts (Crime and Civil) in 2010 and the amendment of the Unified Contract in family matters through the Community Legal Service (Funding) (Amendment) Order 2011, which came into force on 9 May 2011.

These changes:

- Remove experts' cancellation fees from the scope of funding other than in exceptional circumstances;
- Remove experts' administration costs from the scope of public funding;
- Cap the remuneration rates for travel time to £40 per hour; and
- Cap the mileage rates to the current guidance for solicitor travel, currently 45p per mile.
- Cap the fees paid by the LSC for Independent Social Work at the same level as those paid by the Children and Family Court Advisory Support Service (Cafcass)."

The following guidance is taken from the Legal Services Commission's (which was replaced the Legal Aid Agency on 1 April 2013) document containing frequently asked questions on the Legal Aid Reform Implementation Programme:

"**What cases do these expert rates apply to?**

Civil

Experts instructed in cases where the date of application (for licensed work) or case start date (for all other cases) is on or after 3 October 2011 are subject to the new codified rates.

The new rates apply, regardless of the type of contract held by the solicitor.

In licensed work:

- **The new rates for experts** will apply to all applications signed on or after 3 October 2011, as well as those applications which have been signed before 3 October 2011 but not received by the LSC by 10 October 2011.
- **The old rates/expert provisions** will apply to certificates where the application for funding was made before 3 October 2011 (i.e. it will need to have been signed before 3 October 2011) and received by the LSC on or before 10 October 2011.

What determines whether the London or non-London rate will apply?

The location of the expert will be the determining factor as to whether London or non-London rates or fees apply.

Where applicable the location of the expert's registered office will be used to determine which rate will apply.

Providers must have regard to the purpose and importance of the expert witness service to the case, and the extent to which there is a choice of alternative expert. For instance, if the expert is based some distance from the client's home and the client is required to attend a meeting with the expert (or vice versa), justification should be provided as to why a local expert should not or could not be instructed.

The expert type I wish to instruct does not appear in the codified rates. What rate will be acceptable?

Caseworkers will have regard to the codified rates where a comparison with a codified expert type is appropriate.

Where the expert type is not listed in the codified rates and comparison with the codified rates is not appropriate the LSC may require a provider to submit multiple quotes from different experts of that type to demonstrate that the rates being charged are in line with market rates.

Do the codified rates also apply to overseas experts?

The codified rates apply to all experts undertaking legally aided work, whether they are located within the UK or overseas.

Under the Practice Direction *Experts in Family Proceedings Relating to Children* (1 April 2008) in public law proceedings under the Children Act 1989 the proposal to instruct an expert should be considered "by or at the Case Management Conference".

As prior authority is necessary to instruct an expert who exceeds the codified rate in 'exceptional circumstances' should an application for prior authority be submitted to the LSC before or after the Case Management Conference?

The LSC can approve a prior authority without the court having previously approved the expert; however this would be rendered ineffectual if the court subsequently decided that the expert was not necessary or appropriate. Providers will need to submit the Court Order alongside the prior authority approval when submitting their application for a Payment on Account for the expert.

If there is uncertainty as to the need for an expert or the type of expert required then it will be advisable for court to make a determination of that issue before prior authority is sought.

If time is at issue a provider may apply to the LSC for prior authority in parallel with making an application to Court, however:

- The LSC cannot bind the Court on the use of an expert in court.
- The Court cannot bind the LSC to pay a particular hourly rate for an expert."

County Court Remedies Regulations 1991,
SI 1991/1222

General note—These Regulations were made to clarify the power of a county court to grant the orders known as "search orders" and "freezing injunctions". In their amended form the general rule is that a county court may not grant a search order and can grant a freezing injunction only in the limited defined circumstances. See in particular reg 3(3)(a), which does empower a county court to grant a freezing injunction in family proceedings.

1 These Regulations may be cited as the County Court Remedies Regulations 1991 and shall come into force on 1 July 1991.

2 In these Regulations, "prescribed relief" means relief of any of the following kinds –

    (a)   an order requiring a party to admit any other party to premises for the purpose of inspecting or removing documents or articles which may provide evidence in any proceedings, whether or not the proceedings have been commenced;

    (b)   an interlocutory injunction –

        (i)   restraining a party from removing from the jurisdiction of the High Court assets located within that jurisdiction; or

        (ii) restraining a party from dealing with assets whether located within the jurisdiction of the High Court or not.

3 (1) Subject to the following provisions of this regulation, a county court shall not grant prescribed relief or vary or revoke an order made by the High Court granting such relief.

(2) Paragraph (1) shall not apply to –

    (a)   any county court held by a judge of the Court of Appeal or judge of the High Court sitting as a judge for any county court district;

    (b)   a patents county court held by a person nominated under section 291 of the Copyright, Designs and Patents Act 1988 to sit as a judge of that court.

(3) A county court may grant relief of a kind referred to in regulation 2(b) –

    (a)   when exercising jurisdiction in family proceedings within the meaning of Part V of the Matrimonial and Family Proceedings Act 1984;

    (b)   for the purpose of making an order for the preservation, custody or detention of property which forms or may form the subject matter of proceedings,

  (c) in aid of execution of a judgment or order made in proceedings in a county court to preserve assets until execution can be levied upon them, or

  (d) where the proceedings are to be or are included in the Central London County Court Mercantile List and the application is made to a Circuit judge nominated by the Senior Presiding Judge.

(3A) In paragraph (3)(d) –

 "the Central London County Court Mercantile List" means the Mercantile Court established at the Central London County Court pursuant to Part 59 of the Civil Procedure Rules 1998; and

 "the Senior Presiding Judge" means the judge appointed as such under section 72(2) of the Courts and Legal Services Act 1990.

(4) Paragraph (1) shall not –

  (a) affect or modify powers expressly conferred on a county court by or under any enactment other than section 38 of the County Courts Act 1984; or

  (b) prevent a county court from varying an order granting prescribed relief where all the parties are agreed on the terms of the variation.

Amendments—SI 1995/206; SI 2002/439.

Freezing injunctions—Although county courts generally have no power to grant such injunctions, the power is expressly preserved in family proceedings by reg 3(3)(a). Similarly, such injunctions can be obtained in aid of a judgment or order made to preserve assets until execution can be levied (reg 3(3)(c)). For the procedure see FPR 2010, Pt 20 and PD20A.

4 An application to the High Court for relief of a kind referred to in regulation 2(a) in county court proceedings shall be deemed to include an application for transfer of the proceedings to the High Court.

5 (1) After an application for prescribed relief has been disposed of by the High Court, the proceedings shall, unless the High Court orders otherwise, be transferred to a county court if –

  (a) they were transferred to the High Court; or

  (b) apart from these Regulations, they should have been commenced in a county court.

(2) Where an order is made on an ex parte application, the application shall not be treated as disposed of for the purposes of paragraph (1) until any application to set aside or vary the order has been heard, or until the expiry of 28 days (or such other period as the Court may specify) during which no such application has been made.

Divorce etc (Pensions) Regulations 2000, SI 2000/1123

ARRANGEMENT OF REGULATIONS

PART IV

General note—These regulations relate in the main to pension attachment (regs 4–8). However, reg 3 sets out the valuation methodology for the purposes of both pension sharing and attachment and reg 9 makes provision as to when a pension sharing order takes effect. These regulations apply only to pension arrangements (MCA 1973, ss 21A(2)(a) and 25D(3)). The corresponding regulations in relation to PPF compensation are the Divorce and Dissolution etc (Pension Protection Fund) Regulations 2011, which came into effect on 6 April 2011. The 2011 Regulations follow the scheme of the 2000 Regulations as to valuation, change in circumstances, service and the date when a pension compensation sharing order takes effect.

1   Citation, commencement and transitional provisions

(1) These Regulations may be cited as the Divorce etc (Pensions) Regulations 2000 and shall come into force on 1 December 2000.

(2) These Regulations shall apply to any proceedings for divorce, judicial separation or nullity of marriage commenced on or after 1 December 2000, and any such proceedings commenced before that date shall be treated as if these Regulations had not come into force.

2   Interpretation

In these Regulations –

    (a)   a reference to a section by number alone means the section so numbered in the Matrimonial Causes Act 1973;

    (b)   "the 1984 Act" means the Matrimonial and Family Proceedings Act 1984;

    (c)   expressions defined in sections 21A and 25D(3) have the meanings assigned by those sections;

    (d)   every reference to a rule by number alone means the rule so numbered in the Family Procedure Rules 2010.

Amendments—SI 2011/1045.

3   Valuation

(1) For the purposes of the court's functions in connection with the exercise of any of its powers under Part II of the Matrimonial Causes Act 1973, benefits under a pension arrangement shall be calculated and verified in the manner set out in regulation 3 of the Pensions on Divorce etc (Provision of Information) Regulations 2000, and –

    (a)   the benefits shall be valued as at a date to be specified by the court (being not earlier than one year before the date of the petition and not later than the date on which the court is exercising its power);

    (b)   in determining that value the court may have regard to information furnished by the person responsible for the pension arrangement pursuant to any of the provisions set out in paragraph (2); and

    (c)   in specifying a date under sub-paragraph (a) above the court may have regard to the date specified in any information furnished as mentioned in sub-paragraph (b) above.

(2) The relevant provisions for the purposes of paragraph (1)(b) above are –

    (a)   the Pensions on Divorce etc (Provision of Information) Regulations 2000;

    (b)   regulation 5 of and Schedule 2 to the Occupational Pension Schemes (Disclosure of Information) Regulations 1996 and regulation 11 of and Schedule 1 to the Occupational Pension Schemes (Transfer Value) Regulations 1996;

(c)   section 93A or 94(1)(a) or (aa) of the Pension Schemes Act 1993;

(d)   section 94(1)(b) of the Pension Schemes Act 1993 or paragraph 2(a) (or, where applicable, 2(b)) of Schedule 2 to the Personal Pension Schemes (Disclosure of Information) Regulations 1987.

Scope—This regulation provides the valuation methodology for pension sharing and attachment by cross-referencing to the Pensions on Divorce etc (Provision of Information) Regulations 2000, reg 3, (ie the Cash Equivalent (CE)); reference should be made to the annotations to this regulation. The date of valuation referred to in this regulation is the date of the CE put before the court as valuation evidence. The CE used for this purpose may range from not earlier than 1 year before the date of the petition up to the date on which the court makes an order. The valuation may be furnished specifically for the purpose of family proceedings under the Pensions on Divorce etc (Provision of Information) Regulations 2000 or may be one supplied in the ordinary course of events under the provisions referred to in reg 3(2)(b)–(d).

"a date to be specified by the court" (reg 3(1)(a))—This date was included in the original version of Form P1 (pension sharing annex), but was omitted in the form prescribed by the Family Proceedings (Amendment) (No 5) Rules 2005 because of the confusion caused by reason of the fact that the date specified was not the date adopted by the pension arrangement to whom the order was directed for implementation purposes under WRPA 1999, s 29(7); reference should be made to the annotations to this subsection for a discussion of "moving target syndrome".

4 Pension attachment: notices

(1) This regulation applies in the circumstances set out in section 25D(1)(a) (transfers of pension rights).

(2) Where this regulation applies, the person responsible for the first arrangement shall give notice in accordance with the following paragraphs of this regulation to –

(a)   the person responsible for the new arrangement, and

(b)   the other party.

(3) The notice to the person responsible for the new arrangement shall include copies of the following documents –

(a)   every order made under section 23 imposing any requirement on the person responsible for the first arrangement in relation to the rights transferred;

(b)   any order varying such an order;

(c)   all information or particulars which the other party has been required to supply under any provision of rule 9.33 or 9.34 for the purpose of enabling the person responsible for the first arrangement –

(i)   to provide information, documents or representations to the court to enable it to decide what if any requirement should be imposed on that person; or

(ii)   to comply with any order imposing such a requirement;

(d)   any notice given by the other party to the person responsible for the first arrangement under regulation 6;

(e)   where the pension rights under the first arrangement were derived wholly or partly from rights held under a previous pension arrangement, any notice given to the person responsible for the previous arrangement under paragraph (2) of this regulation on the occasion of that acquisition of rights.

(4) The notice to the other party shall contain the following particulars –

(a)   the fact that the pension rights have been transferred;

(b)   the date on which the transfer takes effect;

(c)   the name and address of the person responsible for the new arrangement;

(d)   the fact that the order made under section 23 is to have effect as if it had been made in respect of the person responsible for the new arrangement.

(5) Both notices shall be given –

PART IV

    (a)   within the period provided by section 99 of the Pension Schemes Act 1993 for the person responsible for the first arrangement to carry out what the member requires; and

    (b)   before the expiry of 21 days after the person responsible for the first arrangement has made all required payments to the person responsible for the new arrangement.

Amendments—SI 2011/1045.

Scope—This regulation provides for the situation where a scheme member transfers the whole of his pension rights which are the subject of a pension attachment order into another pension arrangement, for example, on a change of employment. Providing the notices referred to in this regulation have been given, the pension attachment order will have effect as if it had been made in respect of the new pension arrangement (MCA 1973, s 25D(1)).

5 Pension attachment: reduction in benefits

(1) This regulation applies where –

    (a)   an order under section 23 or under section 17 of the 1984 Act has been made by virtue of section 25B or 25C imposing any requirement on the person responsible for a pension arrangement;

    (b)   an event has occurred which is likely to result in a significant reduction in the benefits payable under the arrangement, other than:

        (i)   the transfer from the arrangement off all the rights of the party with pension rights in the circumstances set out in section 25D(1)(a), or

        (ii)   a reduction in the value of assets held for the purposes of the arrangement by reason of a change in interest rates or other market conditions.

(2) Where this regulation applies, the person responsible for the arrangement shall, within 14 days of the occurrence of the event mentioned in paragraph (1)(b), give notice to the other party of –

    (a)   that event;

    (b)   the likely extent of the reduction in the benefits payable under the arrangement.

(3) Where the event mentioned in paragraph (1)(b) consists of a transfer of some but not all of the rights of the party with pension rights from the arrangement, the person responsible for the first arrangement shall, within 14 days of the transfer, give notice to the other party of the name and address of the person responsible for any pension arrangement under which the party with pension rights has acquired rights as a result of that event.

Scope—This regulation applies where the scheme member transfers some, but not all, of his accrued rights in a pension arrangement against which a pension attachment order has been made into a new arrangement, or some other event occurs which is likely to result in a significant reduction in the benefits payable (apart from a transfer of all of the accrued rights or a reduction in the value of the assets of the arrangement by reason of a change in interest rates or other market condition). In these circumstances, the pension arrangement against which the pension attachment order was made must give notice under this regulation to the party with the benefit of the pension attachment order enabling that party to apply for a variation of the pension attachment order.

6 Pension attachment: change of circumstances

(1) This regulation applies where –

    (a)   an order under section 23 or under section 17 of the 1984 Act has been made by virtue of section 25B or 25C imposing any requirement on the person responsible for a pension arrangement; and

    (b)   any of the events set out in paragraph (2) has occurred.

(2) Those events are –

(a)   any of the particulars supplied by the other party under rule 9.33 or 9.34 for any purpose mentioned in regulation 4(3)(c) has ceased to be accurate; or

(b)   by reason of the remarriage of the other party, or his having formed a subsequent civil partnership, or otherwise, the order has ceased to have effect.

(3)   Where this regulation applies, the other party shall, within 14 days of the event, give notice of it to the person responsible for the pension arrangement.

(4)   Where, because of the inaccuracy of the particulars supplied by the other party under rule 9.33 or 9.34 or because the other party has failed to give notice of their having ceased to be accurate, it is not reasonably practicable for the person responsible for the pension arrangement to make a payment to the other party as required by the order:

(a)   it may instead make that payment to the party with pension rights, and

(b)   it shall then be discharged of liability to the other party to the extent of that payment.

(5)   Where an event set out in paragraph (2)(b) has occurred and, because the other party has failed to give notice in accordance with paragraph (3), the person responsible for the pension arrangement makes a payment to the other party as required by the order –

(a)   its liability to the party with pension rights shall be discharged to the extent of that payment, and

(b)   the other party shall, within 14 days of the payment being made, make a payment to the party with pension rights to the extent of that payment.

Amendments—SI 2005/2114, art 2(1)· Sch 1, para 8; SI 2011/1045.

Scope—This regulation provides for the person with the benefit of a pension attachment order to give notice to the pension arrangement against which the order has been made of a specified change of circumstances (e g of address, remarriage or formation of a subsequent civil partnership). Where, because of the inaccuracy of the information held by the pension arrangement, it is not reasonably practicable for the pension arrangement to make payment to the party with the benefit of the pension attachment order, it may discharge its liability by making payment to the party with pension rights.

7 Pension attachment: transfer of rights

(1)   This regulation applies where –

(a)   a transfer of rights has taken place in the circumstances set out in section 25D(1)(a);

(b)   notice has been given in accordance with regulation 4(2)(a) and (b);

(c)   any of the events set out in regulation 6(2) has occurred; and

(d)   the other party has not, before receiving notice under regulation 4(2)(b), given notice of that event to the person responsible for the first arrangement under regulation 6(3).

(2)   Where this regulation applies, the other party shall, within 14 days of the event, give notice of it to the person responsible for the new arrangement.

(3)   Where, because of the inaccuracy of the particulars supplied by the other party under rule 9.33 or 9.34 for any purpose mentioned in regulation 4(3)(c) or because the other party has failed to give notice of their having ceased to be accurate, it is not reasonably practicable for the person responsible for the new arrangement to make a payment to the other party as required by the order –

(a)   it may instead make that payment to the party with pension rights, and

(b)   it shall then be discharged of liability to the other party to the extent of that payment.

(4)   Subject to paragraph (5), where this regulation applies and the other party, within one year from the transfer, gives to the person responsible for the first arrangement

PART IV

notice of the event set out in regulation 6(2) in purported compliance with regulation 7(2), the person responsible for the first arrangement shall –

(a)   send that notice to the person responsible for the new arrangement, and

(b)   give the other party a second notice under regulation 4(2)(b);

and the other party shall be deemed to have given notice under regulation 7(2) to the person responsible for the new arrangement.

(5) Upon complying with paragraph (4) above, the person responsible for the first arrangement shall be discharged from any further obligation under regulation 4 or 7(4), whether in relation to the event in question or any further event set out in regulation 6(2) which may be notified to it by the other party.

Amendments—SI 2011/1045.

Scope—This regulation deals with the situation which arises where there has been a transfer of all of the accrued pension rights subject to a pension attachment order and a change of circumstances as provided for by reg 6(2) occurs.

7A Pension attachment: discharge of liability of the Board

(1) This regulation applies where –

(a)   the Board has assumed responsibility for a pension arrangement as mentioned in section 25E(2)(a); and

(b)   the Board has given notice that it has so assumed responsibility to members and beneficiaries of the pension arrangement in compliance with regulation 3(6) of the Pension Protection Fund (Provision of Information) Regulations 2005.

(2) Where –

(a)   any of the events set out in regulation 6(2) have occurred; and

(b)   the other party has not, before receiving the notice referred to in (1)(b) above, given notice of that event to the person responsible for the pension arrangement in accordance with regulation 6(3),

the other party shall, within 14 days of the event, give notice of it to the Board.

(3) Paragraph (4) applies where it is not reasonably practicable for the Board to make a payment to the other party as required by the order because –

(a)   of the inaccuracy of the particulars supplied by the other party under rule 9.33 or 9.34 for any purpose mentioned in regulation 4(3)(c); or

(b)   the other party has failed to give notice that the particulars have ceased to be accurate.

(4) Where this paragraph applies, the Board –

(a)   may instead make the payment due to the other party to the party entitled to PPF compensation; and

(b)   shall then be discharged of liability to the other party to the extent of that payment.

(5) Where an event set out in regulation 6(2)(b) has occurred and, because the other party has failed to give notice in accordance with paragraph (2), the Board makes a payment to the other party as required by the order –

(a)   its liability to the party entitled to PPF compensation shall be discharged to the extent of that payment; and

(b)   the other party shall, within 14 days of the payment being made, make a payment to the party entitled to PPF compensation to the extent of that payment.

(6) In this regulation "the Board" and "PPF compensation" have the meanings given in section 25E(9).

Amendments—SI 2011/1045.

Modification—By virtue of SI 2006/1932, in relation to modified pension attachment orders, the Divorce etc (Pensions) Regulations 2000 are modified with effect from 8 August 2006 so as to apply as if the above reg 7A were inserted.

Scope—This regulation deals with the situation which arises where the Pension Protection Fund (PPF) has assumed responsibility for a pension arrangement. It provides for the person with the benefit of a pension attachment order ("the other party") to give notice to the PPF, rather than to the pension arrangement against which the order has been made, of specified changes in circumstances, enabling the PPF to discharge its liability by making payment to the party entitled to PPF compensation where it is not practicable to make a payment to the other party. Alternatively, where the PPF makes a payment in error to the other party because of a failure by that party to notify the PPF of the change of circumstances, the liability of the PPF is discharged to the extent of the payment and the other party is required, within 14 days of the payment being made, to make a payment to the party entitled to the PPF compensation.

As to the PPF generally, reference should be made to the annotations to MCA 1973, ss 21B and 25E and FPR 2010, r 9.37.

8 Service

A notice under regulation 4, 5, 6 *or 7* [, 7 or 7A] may be sent by fax or by ordinary first class post to the last known address of the intended recipient and shall be deemed to have been received on the seventh day after the day on which it was sent.

Modification—By virtue of SI 2006/1932, in relation to modified pension attachment orders, the Divorce etc (Pensions) Regulations 2000 are modified with effect from 8 August 2006 so that they apply as if in reg 8 for the words in italics "or 7" there were substituted the words ", 7 or 7A" in brackets.

9 Pension sharing order not to take effect pending appeal

(1) No pension sharing order under section 24B or variation of a pension sharing order under section 31 shall take effect earlier than 7 days after the end of the period for filing notice of appeal against the order.

(2) The filing of a notice of appeal within the time allowed for doing so prevents the order taking effect before the appeal has been dealt with.

Notice of appeal—Time for filing notice of appeal is 21 days (FPR 2010, r 30.4). See also MCA 1973, s 24C.

****

Family Law Act 1986 (Dependent Territories) Order 1991, SI 1991/1723

1 This Order may be cited as the Family Law Act 1986 (Dependent Territories) Order 1991 and shall come into force on 14 October 1991.

2 In this Order –

"the Act" means the Family Law Act 1986;
"specified dependent territory" means a dependent territory specified in column 1 of Schedule 1 to this Order;
"Part I order" has the meaning given by section 1(1) of the Act;
"part of the United Kingdom" has the meaning given by section 42(1) of the Act.

PART IV

3 (1) This Order applies in relation to a specified dependent territory from the date specified opposite the name of that territory in column 2 of Schedule 1 to this Order.

(2) Part I of the Act shall apply, for the purpose of regulating, as between any specified dependent territory and any part of the United Kingdom, the jurisdiction of courts to make Part I orders, and the recognition and enforcement of orders corresponding to such orders, with the modifications specified in Schedule 2 to this Order.

(3) Each Part of Schedule 3 to this Order shall have effect for the construction of Part I of the Act as modified by this Order in relation to the specified dependent territory named in the heading to that Part of that Schedule.

4 This Order does not extend to any territory outside the United Kingdom.

SCHEDULE 1
SPECIFIED DEPENDENT TERRITORIES

Dependent Territory	Date from which this Order applies
The Isle of Man	14 October 1991
Jersey	10 July 2006

Amendments—SI 2006/1456.

****

SCHEDULE 3
INTERPRETATION OF CERTAIN EXPRESSIONS IN PART I OF THE FAMILY LAW ACT 1986 AS MODIFIED BY SCHEDULE 2 TO THIS ORDER

PART I
THE ISLE OF MAN

1 In section 1(1)(f) "an order made by the court in a specified dependent territory corresponding to an order within paragraphs (a) to (e) above" means –

(a)   an order under section 9 of the Family Law Act 1991 (an Act of Tynwald) or any of the following enactments (being enactments repealed by that Act) –
   (i)   section 3(5) of the Guardianship of Infants Act 1953 (an Act of Tynwald), so far as it relates to the custody of infants;
   (ii)   section 4(1) of that Act, except so far as it relates to costs, but including that section as applied by section 3(1) of the Legitimacy Act 1962 (an Act of Tynwald);
   (iii) section 42(1) or (2) of the Judicature (Matrimonial Causes) Act 1976 (an Act of Tynwald);
   (iv)   section 8(2) or 18(1)(ii) of the Domestic Proceedings Act 1983 (an Act of Tynwald);
   (v)   section 34(1) of that Act;
   (vi)   section 49(1) of that Act, so far as it relates to the custody of or access to a child;

    (b)   an order made by the High Court of Justice of the Isle of Man in the exercise of its jurisdiction relating to wardship or its inherent jurisdiction with respect to children –
        (i)   so far as it gives care of a child to any person or provides for contact with or access to, or the education of, a child but
        (ii) excluding an order varying or revoking such an order, or an order relating to a child of whom care or control is (immediately after the making of the order) vested in a public authority in the Isle of Man.

2 In each of sections 2A(3), 3(3), 6(4), 11(2), 13(5), 20(3), 21(4) and 23(4) –

    (a)   in paragraph (a) "corresponding dependent territory order" means an order under section 3(3) of the Child Custody Act 1987 (an Act of Tynwald);
    (b)   in paragraph (b) "corresponding dependent territory order" means an order under section 4(2) of that Act.

3 In section 13(6)(a)(ii), "corresponding dependent territory provision" means section 2(2) or 5(3) of the Child Custody Act 1987 (an Act of Tynwald).

4 (1) In section 27(1) "corresponding provision" means section 7 of the Child Custody Act 1987 (an Act of Tynwald).

(2) In section 27(4) "corresponding dependent territory provision" means section 12(3) of that Act.

5 (1) In section 32(1) "the corresponding court" means the High Court of Justice of the Isle of Man.

(2) In section 32(1) and (3)(a) "the corresponding dependent territory provisions" means Part I of the Child Custody Act 1987 (an Act of Tynwald).

6 In section 42(6)(e) "corresponding dependent territory provision" means –

    (a)   section 42(6) or (7) of the Judicature (Matrimonial Causes) Act 1976 (an Act of Tynwald);
    (b)   section 18(6) of the Domestic Proceedings Act 1983 (an Act of Tynwald).

PART II
JERSEY

7 In section 1(1)(f), "an order made by the court in a specified dependent territory corresponding to an order within paragraphs (a) to (e) above" means –

    (a)   an order under Article 10 of the Children (Jersey) Law 2002;
    (b)   an order referred to in paragraph 2(1) of Schedule 5 to the Children (Jersey) Law 2002;
    (c)   an order made by the Royal Court in the exercise of its inherent jurisdiction with respect to children –
        (i)   so far as it gives care of the child to any person or provides for contact with or access to, or the education of, a child; but
        (ii) excluding an order varying or revoking such an order, or an order relating to a child of whom care or control is (immediately after the making of the order) vested in a public authority in Jersey.

8 In each of sections 2A(3), 3(3), 6(4), 11(2), 13(5), 20(3), 21(4) and 23(4) –

PART IV

(a) in paragraph (a), "corresponding dependent territory order" means an order under Article 7(3) of the Child Custody (Jurisdiction) (Jersey) Law 2005;

(b) in paragraph (b), "corresponding dependent territory order" means an order under Article 8(2) of that Law.

9 In section 13(6)(a)(ii), "corresponding dependent territory provision" means Article 6(2) or 9(3) of the Child Custody (Jurisdiction) (Jersey) Law 2005.

10 (1) In section 27(1), "corresponding provision" means Article 11 of the Child Custody (Jurisdiction) (Jersey) Law 2005.

(2) In section 27(4), "corresponding dependent territory provision" means Article 16(3) of that Law.

11 (1) In section 32(1), "the corresponding court" means the Royal Court of Jersey.

(2) In section 32(1) and (3)(a), "the corresponding dependent territory provisions" means the Child Custody (Jurisdiction) (Jersey) Law 2005.

Amendments—SI 2006/1456.

Family Proceedings Fees Order 2008, SI 2008/1054

1 Citation and commencement

(1) This Order may be cited as the Family Proceedings Fees Order 2008 and shall come into force on 1 May 2008.

(2) In this Order –

(a) "LSC" means the Legal Services Commission established under section 1 of the Access to Justice Act 1999;

(b) "the FPR 2010" means the Family Procedure Rules 2010; and

(c) expressions also used in the FPR 2010 have the same meaning as in the FPR 2010.

Amendments—SI 2011/1045.

2 Fees payable

The fees set out in column 2 of Schedule 1 are payable in family proceedings in the High Court and in county courts in respect of the items described in column 1 in accordance with and subject to the directions specified in that column.

3 Where by any convention entered into by Her Majesty with any foreign power it is provided that no fee is required to be paid in respect of any proceedings, the fees specified in this Order are not payable in respect of those proceedings.

4 Remissions and part remissions

Schedule 2 applies for the purpose of ascertaining whether a party is entitled to a remission or part remission of a fee prescribed by this Order.

5 Revocations

The instruments listed in column 1 of the table in Schedule 3 (which have the references listed in column 2) are revoked.

6 Transitional provision

Fees 2.2(b) and (c) are not payable in respect of an issues resolution hearing, pre-hearing review or final hearing which has been listed on any day between 1 May 2008 and 14 May 2008 inclusive.

SCHEDULE 1

FEES TO BE TAKEN

Column 1 *Number and description of fee*	Column 2 *Amount of fee*
Section 1: Fees to be taken in the High Court and in county courts	
Commencement 1 of proceedings	
1.1 On filing an application to start proceedings, where no other fee is specified.	£230
1.2 On presenting any application for –	
(a) a matrimonial or civil partnership order, other than an application to which rule 7.7(1)(b) of the FPR 2010 applies;	
(b) a declaration to which Chapter 5 of Part 8 of the FPR 2010 applies.	£340
1.3 On applying for a non-molestation order, an occupation order or a forced marriage protection order under Part 4 or Part 4A of the Family Law Act 1996 (or on applying for two or more of those orders).	£70
1.4 On amending an application for a matrimonial or civil partnership order, amending an application for a declaration to which Chapter 5 of Part 8 of the FPR 2010 applies, or making an application to which rule 7.7(1)(b) of the FPR 2010 applies.	£90
1.5 On filing an answer to an application for a matrimonial or civil partnership order.	£230
1.6 On applying for an order under Part 3 of the Solicitors Act 1974 for the assessment of costs payable to a solicitor by a client; or on the commencement of costs-only proceedings.	£40
2 *Proceedings under the Children Act 1989*	
2.1 On an application for an order in form C1 or form C100 (free standing application), form C79 (application related to enforcement of a contact order), form C2 (application in existing proceedings) or a request for permission to apply for an order in form C2 under the following provisions of the Children Act 1989 –	
(a) section 4(1)(c) or (3), 4A(1)(b) or (3) (parental responsibility);	£200
(b) section 4ZA (1)(c) or (6) (parental responsibility);	£200
(c) section 5(1) or 6(7) (guardians);	£200

Column 1 Number and description of fee	Column 2 Amount of fee
(d) section 10(1) or (2) (section 8 orders);	£200
(e) section 11J(2) (enforcement orders);	£200
(f) section 11O(2) (compensation for financial loss);	£200
(g) section 13(1) (change of child's surname or removal from jurisdiction while residence order in force);	£200
(h) section 14A(3) or (6)(a), 14C(3) or 14D(1) (special guardianship orders);	£160
(i) section 25 (secure accommodation order);	£170
(j) section 33(7) (change of child's surname or removal from jurisdiction while care order in force);	£170
(k) section 34(2), (3), (4) or (9) (contact with child in care);	£170
(l) section 36(1) (education supervision order);	£170
(m) section 39 (variation or discharge etc of care and supervision orders);	£170
(n) section 43(1) (child assessment order);	£170
(o) sections 44, 45 and 46 (emergency protection orders);	£170
(p) section 48 (warrant to assist person exercising powers under emergency protection order);	£170
(q) section 50 (recovery order);	£170
(r) section 102 (warrant to assist person exercising powers to search for children or inspect premises);	£170
(s) paragraph 4(2), 6(2), 7(2) or 9(2) of Schedule A1 (applications in respect of enforcement orders);	£90
(t) paragraph 5(2) of Schedule A1 (amendment of enforcement order by reason of change of address);	£45
(u) paragraph 1(1) or (4), 2(1) or (5), 5(6), 6(5), (7) or (8), 8(2), 10(2), 11 or 14(1) of Schedule 1 (financial provision for children);	£200
(v) paragraph 19(1) of Schedule 2 (approval of court for child in care of local authority to live abroad);	£170
(w) paragraph 6 of Schedule 3 (extension of supervision order);	£170
(x) paragraph 15(2) or 17(1) of Schedule 3 (extension or discharge of education supervision order).	£170
2.2 In relation to proceedings under section 31 of the Children Act 1989 (care and supervision orders) –	
(a) on an application;	£2,225
(b) where an issues resolution hearing or pre-hearing review has been listed;	£700
(c) where a final hearing has been listed.	£1,900

Notes to fees 2.1 and 2.2

Where an application requires the permission of the court, the relevant fee is payable when permission is sought but no further fee will be charged if permission is granted and the application is made.

Column 1 *Number and description of fee*	Column 2 *Amount of fee*
Where an application is made, permission is sought or an appeal is commenced under or relating to provisions of the Children Act 1989 which are listed in two or more different numbered fees, or require two or more different numbered forms, only one fee is payable, and if those fees are different, only the highest fee is payable.	
Where an application is made, permission is sought or an appeal is commenced under or relating to two or more provisions of the Children Act 1989 which are listed in the same numbered fee, that fee is payable only once.	
Where the same application is made, permission is sought or an appeal is commenced in respect of two or more children, who are siblings or children of the family, at the same time, only one fee is payable in respect of each numbered fee.	
Notes to fee 2.2 only	
Where a final order is made at a case management conference, £500 of the amount paid under fee 2.2(a) will be refunded.	
Where the court lists more than one issues resolution hearing or prehearing review, the fee is payable only once.	
Where proceedings are consolidated with other proceedings, any fee which falls to be paid after the date on which the proceedings are consolidated is payable only once.	
Where a fee is paid under fee 2.2(b) or (c) in relation to a hearing that is cancelled, for example, because a final order is made at earlier hearing, the application is withdrawn, or the hearing is no longer needed, the fee will be refunded. A refund will not be given if the hearing is adjourned to a later date or to a date to be fixed.	
The fee in 2.2(b) and (c) is payable 14 days before the hearing or review.	
2.3 On commencing an appeal under section 94 of the Children Act 1989 relating to proceedings to which the following fees apply –	
(a) 2.1(a) to (g) and (u);	£200
(b) 2.1(h);	£160
(c) 2.1(i) to (r), (v) to (x) and 2.2.	£170
2.4 On commencing an appeal under paragraph 23(11) of Schedule 2 to the Children Act 1989 (appeal against contribution order).	£170
3 *Adoption and wardship applications*	
3.1 On applying or requesting permission to apply under any provision in Part 1 of the Adoption and Children Act 2002, other than an application under section 22 of that Act.	£160
3.2 On applying under section 22 of the Adoption and Children Act 2002 (placement order).	£400
3.3 On applying for the exercise by the High Court of its inherent jurisdiction with respect to children.	£160

PART IV

Column 1 *Number and description of fee*	Column 2 *Amount of fee*
When an application requires the permission of the court, the relevant fee is payable when permission is sought but no further fee will be charged if permission is granted and the application is made.	
Where an application is made or permission is sought under or relating to two or more provisions of the Adoption and Children Act 2002 only one fee is payable.	
Where the same application is made or permission is sought in respect of two or more children, who are siblings or children of the same family, at the same time, only one fee is payable.	
4 *Applications in proceedings*	
4.1 On an application without notice or by consent (including an application to make a decree nisi absolute or a conditional order final) except where separately listed in this Schedule.	£45
Note: Fee 4.1 is not payable in relation to an application by consent for an adjournment of a hearing where the application is received by the court at least 14 days before the date set for that hearing.	
4.2 On an application under rule 7.19 of the FPR 2010 for the court to consider the making of a decree nisi, a conditional order, a decree of judicial separation or a separation order (other than in an undefended case where no fee is payable).	£45
4.3 On an application on notice except where separately listed in the schedule.	£90
4.4 On the filing of –	
(a) a notice of intention to proceed with an application for a financial order to which rule 9.4(a) of the FPR 2010 applies; or	
(b) an application for a financial order to which rule 9.4(b) of the FPR 2010 applies,	
other than an application for a consent order.	£240
5 *Appeal from a district judge*	
5.1 On filing an appeal notice from a district judge to a judge.	£115
6 *Searches*	
6.1 On making a search in the central index of decrees absolute or of final orders kept at the Principal Registry of the Family Division for any specified period of ten calendar years or, if no such period is specified, for the ten most recent years, and, if appropriate, providing a certificate of decree absolute or of final order, as the case may be.	£60
6.2 On making a search in the central index of parental responsibility agreements kept at the Principal Registry of the Family Division in accordance with regulations made under section 4(2) of the Children Act 1989 and, if appropriate, providing a copy of the agreement.	£40

Column 1 *Number and description of fee*	Column 2 *Amount of fee*
6.3 On making a search in the index of decrees absolute or of final orders kept at any designated county court or district registry for any specified period of ten calendar years or, if no period is specified, for the ten most recent years, and if appropriate, providing a certificate of decree absolute or of final order, as the case may be.	£40
7 *Copy documents*	
7.1 On a request for a copy document (other than where fee 7.2 applies) –	
(a) for ten pages or less; and	£5
(b) for each subsequent page.	50p
Note: The fee payable under fee 7.1 includes –	
• where the court allows a party to fax to the court for the use of that party a document that has not been requested by the court and is not intended to be placed on the court file.	
• where a party requests that the court fax a copy of a document from the court file.	
• where the court provides a subsequent copy of a document which it has previously provided.	
7.2 On a request for a copy of a document on a computer disk or in other electronic form, for each such copy.	£5
8 *Determination of costs*	
8.1 On filing a request for detailed assessment where the party filing the request is legally aided, is funded by the LSC or is a person for whom civil legal services have been made available under arrangements made by the Lord Chancellor under Part 1 of the Legal Aid, Sentencing and Punishment of Offenders Act 2012 and no other party is ordered to pay the costs of the proceedings.	£145
8.2 On filing a request for detailed assessment in any case where fee 8.1 does not apply; or on filing a request for a hearing date for the assessment of costs payable to a solicitor by a client pursuant to an order under Part 3 of the Solicitors Act 1974 where the amount of the costs claimed –	
(a) does not exceed £15,000;	£325
(b) exceeds £15,000 but does not exceed £50,000;	£655
(c) exceeds £50,000 but does not exceed £100,000;	£980
(d) exceeds £100,000 but does not exceed £150,000;	£1,310
(e) exceeds £150,000 but does not exceed £200,000;	£1,635
(f) exceeds £200,000 but does not exceed £300,000;	£2,455
(g) exceeds £300,000 but does not exceed £500,000;	£4,090
(h) exceeds £500,000.	£5,455
Where there is a combined standard basis and legal aid, or a combined standard basis and LSC, or a combined standard basis and Lord Chancellor, or a combined standard basis, and one or more of legal aid, LSC or Lord Chancellor determination of costs, fee 8.2 will be attributed proportionately to the standard basis, legal aid, LSC or Lord Chancellor (as the case may be) portions of the bill on the basis of the amount allowed.	

PART IV

Column 1 *Number and description of fee*	Column 2 *Amount of fee*
8.3 On a request for the issue of a default costs certificate.	£60
8.4 On commencing an appeal against a decision made in detailed assessment proceedings.	£205
8.5 On applying for the court's approval of a certificate of costs payable from the Community Legal Service Fund or by the Lord Chancellor under Part 1 of the Legal Aid, Sentencing and Punishment of Offenders Act 2012.	£50
Fee 8.5 is payable at the time of applying for approval and is recoverable only against the Community Legal Service Fund or against the Lord Chancellor under Part 1 of the Legal Aid, Sentencing and Punishment of Offenders Act 2012.	
8.6 On an application to set aside a default costs certificate.	£105
9 *Registration of maintenance orders*	
9.1 On an application for a maintenance order to be registered under the Maintenance Orders Act 1950 or the Maintenance Orders Act 1958.	£40
9.2 On an application for a Maintenance order to be sent abroad for enforcement under the Maintenance Orders (Reciprocal Enforcement) Act 1972.	£40
10 *Enforcement*	
10.1 On an application to question a judgment debtor or other person on oath in connection with enforcement of a judgment, or on an application to which rule 33.3(2)(b) of the FPR 2010 applies.	£50
10.2 On an application for a third party debt order or the appointment of a receiver by way of equitable execution.	£100
Note: Fee 10.2 is payable in respect of each third party against whom the order is sought.	
10.3 On an application for a charging order.	£100
Note: Fee 10.3 is payable in respect of each charging order applied for.	
10.4 On an application for a judgment summons.	£100
Section 2: Fees to be taken in a county court only	
11 *Service*	
11.1 On a request for service by bailiff of any document except –	£105
(a) an order for a debtor to attend the adjourned hearing of a judgment summons;	
(b) an interpleader summons under an execution;	
(c) an order made under section 23 of the Attachment of Earnings Act 1971 (enforcement provisions); or	
(d) an order for a debtor to attend an adjourned oral examination of means.	

Column 1 — Number and description of fee	Column 2 — Amount of fee
12 Enforcement in the County Courts	
12.1 On an application for or in relation to enforcement of a judgment or order of a county court or through a county court, by the issue of a warrant of execution against goods except a warrant to enforce payment of a fine.	£100
12.2 On a request for further attempt at execution of a warrant at a new address where the warrant has been returned to the court not executed (except where the warrant has been returned after it has been suspended by the court).	£30
12.3 On the issue of a warrant of possession or a warrant of delivery. Where the recovery of a sum of money is sought in addition, no further fee is payable.	£110
12.4 On an application for an attachment of earnings order to secure money due under an order made in family proceedings.	£100
Fee 12.4 is payable in respect of each defendant against whom an order is sought.	
Fee 12.4 is not payable where the attachment of earnings order is made on the hearing of a judgment summons.	
13 Sale	
13.1 For removing or taking steps to remove goods to a place of deposit.	The reasonable expenses incurred.
Fee 13.1 is to include the reasonable expenses of feeding and caring for animals.	
13.2 For advertising a sale by public auction pursuant to section 97 of the County Courts Act 1984.	The reasonable expenses incurred.
13.3 For the appraisement of goods.	5p in the £1 or part of a £1 of the appraised value.
13.4 For the sale of goods (including advertisements, catalogues, sale and commission and delivery of goods).	15p in the £1 or part of a £1 on the amount realised by the sale or such other sum as the district judge may consider to be justified in the circumstances.
13.5 Where no sale takes place by reason of an execution being withdrawn, satisfied or stopped.	(a) 10p in the £1 or part of a £1 on the value of the goods seized, the value to be the appraised value where the goods have been appraised or such other sum as the district judge may consider to be justified in the circumstances; and in addition (b) any sum payable under fee 13.1, 13.2 or 13.3.

PART IV

Column 1 *Number and description of fee*	Column 2 *Amount of fee*
Section 3: Fees to be taken in the High Court only	
14 *Enforcement in the High Court*	
14.1 On sealing a writ of execution/possession/delivery.	£60
Where the recovery of a sum of money is sought in addition to a writ of possession and delivery, no further fee is payable.	
14.2 On a request or application to register a judgment or order; or for permission to enforce an arbitration award; or for a certified copy of a judgment or order for use abroad.	£60
15 *Affidavits*	
15.1 On taking an affidavit or an affirmation or attestation upon honour in lieu of an affidavit or a declaration.	£10
15.2 For each exhibit referred to and required to be marked.	£2

Amendments—SI 2008/2856; SI 2008/3106; SI 2009/1499; SI 2010/1916; SI 2011/587; SI 2011/1045; SI 2013/534, subject to savings.

SCHEDULE 2
REMISSIONS AND PART REMISSIONS

1 Interpretation

(1) In this Schedule –

"child" means a child or young person in respect of whom a party is entitled to receive child benefit in accordance with section 141, and regulations made under section 142, of the Social Security Contributions and Benefits Act 1992;

"child care costs" has the meaning given in Part 3 of the Criminal Legal Aid (Financial Resources) Regulations 2013;

"couple" has the meaning given in section 3(5A) of the Tax Credits Act 2002;

"disposable monthly income" has the meaning given in paragraph 5;

"excluded benefits" means –

    (a)   any of the following benefits payable under the Social Security Contributions and Benefits Act 1992 –

        (i)   attendance allowance paid under section 64;

        (ii)   severe disablement allowance;

        (iii)   carer's allowance;

        (iv)   disability living allowance;

        (v)   constant attendance allowance paid under section 104 or paragraph 4 or 7(2) of Schedule 8 as an increase to a disablement pension;

        (vi)   council tax benefit;

        (vii)   any payment made out of the social fund;

        (viii)   housing benefit;

    (b)   any direct payment made under the Community Care, Services for Carers and Children's Services (Direct Payments) (England) Regulations 2003 or the Community Care, Services for Carers and Children's Services (Direct Payments) (Wales) Regulations 2004;

    (c)   a back to work bonus payable under section 26 of the Jobseekers Act 1995;

    (d)   any exceptionally severe disablement allowance paid under the Personal Injuries (Civilians) Scheme 1983;

(e) any pension paid under the Naval, Military and Air Forces etc (Disablement and Death) Service Pension Order 2006;

(f) any payment made from the Independent Living Funds;

(g) any financial support paid under an agreement for the care of a foster child;

(h) personal independence payment under Part 4 of the Welfare Reform Act 2012, and

(i) armed forces independence payment under the Armed Forces and Reserve Forces (Compensation Scheme) Order 2011;

...

"gross annual income" means total annual income, for the 12 months preceding the application for remission or part remission, from all sources other than receipt of any of the excluded benefits;

"gross monthly income" means total monthly income, for the month in which the application for remission or part remission is made, from all sources other than receipt of any of the excluded benefits;

"the Independent Living Funds" means any payment made from the funds listed at regulation 20(2)(b) of the Criminal Legal Aid (Financial Resources) Regulations 2013;

"partner" means a person with whom the party lives as a couple and includes a person with whom the party is not currently living but from whom the party is not living separate and apart;

"party" means the individual who would, but for this Schedule, be liable to pay the fee required under this Order;

"restraint order" means –

(a) an order under section 42(1A) of the Senior Courts Act 1981;

(b) a civil restraint order under rule 3.11 of the Civil Procedure Rules 1998 or a practice direction made under that rule; or

(c) a civil restraint order under rule 4.8 of the FPR 2010 or the practice direction referred to in that rule.

(2) Paragraphs 2, 3 and 4 –

(a) do not apply to a party for whom civil legal services, for which a certificate has been issued under the Civil Legal Aid (Procedure) Regulations 2012, have been made available under arrangements made for the purposes of Part 1 of that Act for the purposes of the proceedings; and

(b) are subject to the provisions of paragraph 10 (vexatious litigants).

Amendments—SI 2013/388; SI 2013/534, subject to savings; SI 2013/591.

Couple—Tax Credits Act 2002, s 3(5A) provides as follows:
"(5A) In this Part "couple" means –
(a) a man and woman who are married to each other and are neither –
  (i) separated under a court order, nor
  (ii) separated in circumstances in which the separation is likely to be permanent,
(b) a man and woman who are not married to each other but are living together as husband and wife,
(c) two people of the same sex who are civil partners of each other and are neither –
  (i) separated under a court order, nor
  (ii) separated in circumstances in which the separation is likely to be permanent, or
(d) two people of the same sex who are not civil partners of each other but are living together as if they were civil partners."

2 Full remission of fees – qualifying benefits

(1) No fee is payable under this Order if, at the time when a fee would otherwise be payable, the party –

(a) is in receipt of a qualifying benefit; or

   (b) is not a beneficiary of a trust fund in court of a value of more than £50,000 and is –
      (i) under the age of eighteen; or
      (ii) a person for whose financial relief an order under paragraph 2 of Schedule 1 to the Children Act 1989 is in force or being applied for.

(2) The following are qualifying benefits for the purposes of sub-paragraph (1)(a) –

   (a) income support under the Social Security Contributions and Benefits Act 1992;
   (b) working tax credit, provided that no child tax credit is being paid to the party;
   (c) income-based jobseeker's allowance under the Jobseekers Act 1995;
   (d) guarantee credit under the State Pension Credit Act 2002; and
   (e) income-related employment and support allowance under the Welfare Reform Act 2007.

3 Full remission of fees – gross annual income

(1) No fee is payable under this Order if, at the time when the fee would otherwise be payable, the party has the number of children specified in column 1 of the following table and –

   (a) if the party is single, the gross annual income of the party does not exceed the amount set out in the appropriate row of column 2; or
   (b) if the party is one of a couple, the gross annual income of the couple does not exceed the amount set out in the appropriate row of column 3.

Column 1 Number of children of party paying fee	Column 2 Single	Column 3 Couple
no children	£13,000	£18,000
1 child	£15,930	£20,930
2 children	£18,860	£23,860
3 children	£21,790	£26,790
4 children	£24,720	£29,720

(2) If the party paying the fee has more than 4 children then the relevant amount of gross annual income is the amount specified in the table for 4 children plus the sum of £2,930 for each additional child.

4 Full and part remission of fees – disposable monthly income

(1) No fee is payable under this Order if, at the time when the fee would otherwise be payable, the disposable monthly income of the party is £50 or less.

(2) The maximum amount of fee payable is –

   (a) if the disposable monthly income of the party is more than £50 but does not exceed £210, an amount equal to one-quarter of every £10 of the party's disposable monthly income up to a maximum of £50; and
   (b) if the disposable monthly income is more than £210, an amount equal to £50 plus one-half of every £10 over £200 of the party's disposable monthly income.

(3) Where the fee that would otherwise be payable under this Order is greater than the maximum fee which a party is required to pay as calculated in sub-paragraph (2), the fee will be remitted to the amount payable under that sub-paragraph.

5 Disposable monthly income

(1) A party's disposable monthly income is the gross monthly income of the party for the month in which the fee becomes payable ("the period") less the deductions referred to in sub-paragraphs (2) and (3).

(2) There are to be deducted from the gross monthly income –

    (a) income tax paid or payable in respect of the period;

    (b) any contributions estimated to have been paid under Part 1 of the Social Security Contributions and Benefits Act 1992 in respect of the period;

    (c) either –

        (i) monthly rent or monthly payment in respect of a mortgage debt or hereditable security, payable in respect of the only or main dwelling of the party, less any housing benefit paid under the Social Security Contributions and Benefits Act 1992; or

        (ii) the monthly cost of the living accommodation of the party;

    (d) any child care costs paid or payable in respect of the period;

    (e) if the party is making bona fide payments for the maintenance of a child who is not a member of the household of the party, the amount of such payments paid or payable in respect of the period; and

    (f) any amount paid or payable by the party, in respect of the period, in pursuance of a court order.

(3) There will be deducted from the gross monthly income an amount representing the cost of living expenses in respect of the period being –

    (a) £315; plus

    (b) £244 for each child of the party; plus

    (c) £159, if the party has a partner.

6 Resources of partners

(1) For the purpose of determining whether a party is entitled to the remission or part remission of a fee in accordance with this Schedule, the income of a partner, if any, is to be included as income of the party.

(2) The receipt by a partner of a qualifying benefit does not entitle a party to remission of a fee.

7 Application for remission or part remission of fees

(1) An application for remission or part remission of a fee must be made to the court officer at the time when the fee would otherwise be payable.

(2) Where a claim for full remission of fees is made, the party must provide documentary evidence of, as the case may be –

    (a) entitlement to a qualifying benefit; or

    (b) gross annual income and, if applicable, the children included for the purposes of paragraph 3.

(3) Where a claim for full or part remission of fees under paragraph 4 is made, the party must provide documentary evidence of –

    (a) such of the party's gross monthly income as is derived from –

        (i) employment;

        (ii) rental or other income received from persons living with the party by reason of their residence in the party's home;

        (iii) a pension; or

        (iv) a state benefit, not being an excluded benefit; and

PART IV

(b) any expenditure being deducted from the gross monthly income in accordance with paragraph 5(2).

8 Remission in exceptional circumstances

Where it appears to the Lord Chancellor that the payment of any fee prescribed by this Order would, owing to the exceptional circumstances of the particular case, involve undue financial hardship, the Lord Chancellor may reduce or remit the fee in that case.

9 Refunds

(1) Subject to sub-paragraph (3), where a party has not provided the documentary evidence required by paragraph 7 and a fee has been paid at a time when, under paragraphs 2, 3 or 4, it was not payable, the fee will be refunded if documentary evidence relating to the time when the fee became payable is provided at a later date.

(2) Subject to sub-paragraph (3), where a fee has been paid at a time where the Lord Chancellor, if all the circumstances had been known, would have reduced or remitted the fee under paragraph 8, the fee or the amount by which the fee would have been reduced, as the case may be, will be refunded.

(3) No refund will be made under this paragraph unless the party who paid the fee applies within 6 months of paying the fee.

(4) The Lord Chancellor may extend the period of 6 months mentioned in sub-paragraph (3) if the Lord Chancellor considers that there is a good reason for an application being made after the end of the period of 6 months.

10 Vexatious litigants

(1) This paragraph applies where –

(a) a restraint order is in force against a party; and
(b) the party makes an application for permission to –
    (i) issue proceedings or take a step in proceedings as required by the restraint order;
    (ii) apply for amendment or discharge of the order; or
    (iii) appeal the order.

(2) The fee prescribed for the application by Schedule 1 is payable in full.

(3) If the court grants the permission requested the applicant will be refunded the difference between –

(a) the fee paid; and
(b) the fee that would have been payable if this Schedule had been applied without reference to this paragraph.

Amendments—CRA 2005, Sch 11, para 1(2); SI 2008/2856; SI 2009/1499; SI 2011/1045.

****

High Court (Distribution of Business) Order 1993, SI 1993/622

1 This order may be cited as the High Court (Distribution of Business) Order 1993 and shall come into force on 5 April 1993.

2 There shall be assigned to the Family Division all proceedings in the High Court under the Child Support Act 1991.

****

"all proceedings"—Such proceedings will be rare (e g declarations of parentage under CSA 1991, s 27 and transferred upwards) and may include judicial review applications brought as a result of the Act.

International Recovery of Maintenance (Hague Convention 2007 etc) Regulations 2012, SI 2012/2814

Scope—These Regulations support the application of the Convention on the International Recovery of Child Support and other forms of Family Maintenance of 23 November 2007 ("the 2007 Convention"; see Part VI) in England and Wales primarily. However, certain statutes with UK application have been amended by these Regulations, which have been made under the European Communities Act 1972, of which Act s 2(2) permits the amendment to primary legislation to remove inconsistencies with the 2007 Convention.

Reg 4 designates the Lord Chancellor as the Central Authority for England and Wales, as required by the 2007 Convention, Art 4.

Reg 5 and Sch 1 make provision for the enforcement of maintenance decisions and maintenance arrangements made in Contracting States to the 2007 Convention by the courts of England and Wales.

Reg 6 and Sch 2 enable courts to which an application is made to enforce a maintenance decision under certain international instruments by way of a driving disqualification order. These provisions apply to England, Wales and Scotland.

Reg 7 and Sch 3 make provision for the sharing of information by certain government departments to facilitate the establishment and enforcement of maintenance decisions to which the 2007 Convention applies. These provisions apply to England, Wales, Scotland and Northern Ireland.

Reg 8 and Sch 4 provide for consequential statutory amendments.

Reg 9 and Sch 5 make provision for consequential statutory amendments relating to the Maintenance Regulation.

1 Citation, commencement and extent

(1) In this Schedule –

"Contracting State" means a State bound by the Convention other than an EU Member State;

"court", in relation to a maintenance decision given in a Contracting State, includes a tribunal, and any administrative authority (within the meaning of Article 19(3)) with competence to make a decision in respect of a maintenance obligation;

"maintenance decision" means a decision, or part of a decision, made by a court in a Contracting State, to which Chapter V of the Convention applies by virtue of Article 19(1).

(2) In this Schedule, any reference to a numbered Article is a reference to the Article so numbered in the Convention and any reference to a sub-division of a numbered Article shall be construed accordingly.

(3) Anything authorised or required by the Convention or by this Schedule to be done by, to or before a particular magistrates' court may be done by, to or before any magistrates' court acting for the same local justice area as that court.

2 Recognition and enforcement of maintenance decisions made by courts in Contracting States

(1) Subject to sub-paragraph (2), the court in England and Wales to which an application for registration of a maintenance decision under the Convention is to be made is a magistrates' court.

(2) An application for registration is to be transmitted by the Lord Chancellor to the magistrates' court designated for these purposes by rules of court ("the registering court").

(3) Jurisdiction in relation to applications for registration of maintenance decisions lies with the courts of England and Wales if –

(a) the person against whom enforcement is sought is resident in England and Wales, or

(b) assets belonging to that person and which are susceptible to enforcement are situated or held in England and Wales.

(4) An application for registration shall be determined in the first instance by the prescribed officer of the registering court. In this sub-paragraph and in sub-paragraph (5), "prescribed" means prescribed by rules of court.

(5) The decision of the prescribed officer may be appealed to the registering court in accordance with rules of court.

(6) For the purposes of the enforcement of a maintenance decision registered under the Convention in the registering court –

(a) the decision shall be of the same force and effect,

(b) the registering court shall have in relation to its enforcement the same powers, and

(c) proceedings for or with respect to its enforcement may be taken, as if the decision had originally been made by the registering court.

(7) Sub-paragraph (6) is subject to sub-paragraph (8).

(8) A maintenance decision which is so registered shall be enforceable in a magistrates' court in England and Wales in the same manner as a maintenance order made by that court, save that sections 76 and 93 of the Magistrates' Courts Act 1980 have effect as modified by section 5(5B) and (5C) of the Civil Jurisdiction and Judgments Act 1982.

In this sub-paragraph "maintenance order" has the meaning given by section 150(1) of the Magistrates' Courts Act 1980.

(9) Sub-paragraph (6) is also subject to –

(a) paragraph 3;

(b) any provision made by rules of court as to the procedure for the enforcement of maintenance decisions registered in accordance with this paragraph.

(10) The debtor under a maintenance decision registered in accordance with this paragraph in a magistrates' court in England and Wales must give notice of any change of address to the designated officer for that court.

In this sub-paragraph, "debtor" has the meaning given by Article 3.

(11) A person who without reasonable excuse fails to comply with sub-paragraph (10) shall be guilty of an offence and liable on summary conviction to a fine not exceeding level 2 on the standard scale.

3 Interest on judgments

(1) Subject to sub-paragraphs (2) and (3) and rules of court as to the payment of interest under this paragraph, where a person applying for registration of a maintenance decision shows that –

(a) the decision provides for the payment of money, and

(b) in accordance with the law of the Contracting State in which the maintenance decision was given and the terms of the decision, interest on that sum is recoverable at a particular rate and from a particular date or time, the debt resulting from registration of the decision is to carry interest at that rate and from that date or time.

(2) Interest is not recoverable under sub-paragraph (1) unless the rate of interest and the date or time referred to in sub-paragraph (1)(b) are registered with the decision.

(3) Interest on arrears of sums payable under a maintenance decision registered under the Convention in a magistrates' court in England and Wales shall not be recoverable in that court.

But this sub-paragraph does not affect the operation in relation to any such maintenance decision of section 2A of the Maintenance Orders Act 1958 (which enables interest to be recovered if the decision is registered for enforcement in the High Court).

(4) Except as mentioned in sub-paragraph (3), debts under maintenance decisions registered in England and Wales under the Convention shall carry interest only as provided by this paragraph.

4 Currency of payments under a maintenance decision

(1) Sums payable under a maintenance decision registered in England and Wales under the Convention, including any arrears so payable, shall be paid in sterling.

(2) Where the maintenance decision is expressed in any other currency, the amounts shall be converted on the basis of the exchange rate prevailing on the date on which the application for registration was received by the Lord Chancellor for transmission to a court.

(3) For the purposes of this paragraph, a written certificate purporting to be signed by an officer of any bank in England and Wales and stating the exchange rate prevailing on a specified date shall be evidence of the facts stated.

5 Proof and admissibility of certain maintenance decisions and related documents

(1) For the purposes of proceedings relating to the Convention a document, duly authenticated, which purports to be a copy of a maintenance decision given by a court in a Contracting State shall without further proof be deemed to be a true copy, unless the contrary is shown.

(2) A document purporting to be a copy of a maintenance decision given by a court in a Contracting State is duly authenticated for the purposes of this paragraph if it purports –

(a)   to bear the seal of that court; or
(b)   to be certified by any person in that person's capacity as a judge or officer of that court to be a true copy of a maintenance decision given by that court.

(3) Nothing in this paragraph shall prejudice the admission in evidence of any document which is admissible apart from this paragraph.

6 Maintenance arrangements

(1) References in this paragraph to maintenance arrangements are to those maintenance arrangements (as defined in Article 3(e)) which are to be recognised and enforceable in the same way as maintenance decisions by virtue of Article 30.

(2) In relation to a maintenance arrangement which is enforceable as a maintenance decision in the Contracting State of origin, this Schedule applies, subject to the modifications in subparagraphs (3), (4) and (5), as if that maintenance arrangement was a maintenance decision given by a court of that State.

(3) Paragraph 2 applies to maintenance arrangements as if –

(a) in sub-paragraph (6), for "as if the decision had originally" there were substituted "as if it were a decision which had originally";

(b) after sub-paragraph (9)(b) there were inserted –

"(c) Article 30(6) (restriction on enforcement where there is a challenge to a maintenance arrangement in the Contracting State of origin).".

(4) Paragraph 3 applies to maintenance arrangements as if in sub-paragraph (1)(b), for the word "given" there were substituted "concluded".

(5) Paragraph 5 applies to maintenance arrangements as if –

(a) in sub-paragraph (1), for "given by a court" there were substituted "formally drawn up or registered as an authentic instrument by, or authenticated by, or concluded, registered or filed with a competent authority";

(b) for sub-paragraph (2) there were substituted –

"(2) A document purporting to be a copy of a maintenance arrangement drawn up or registered as an authentic instrument by, or authenticated by, or concluded, registered or filed with a competent authority in a Contracting State is duly authenticated for the purposes of this paragraph if it purports to be certified to be a true copy of such an arrangement by a person duly authorised in that State to do so.".

(6) Section 18 of the Civil Jurisdiction and Judgments Act 1982 does not apply to maintenance arrangements.

7 Applications for establishment or modification of maintenance in England and Wales

(1) Upon receipt of an application submitted under Article 10 for establishment or modification of a decision, the Lord Chancellor shall send that application to the designated officer for the magistrates' court in the local justice area in which the respondent is residing.

(2) Upon receipt of the application under sub-paragraph (1), the designated officer of that court shall decide –

(a) whether the courts of England and Wales have jurisdiction to determine the application by virtue of the Maintenance Regulation and Schedule 6 to the Civil Jurisdiction and Judgments (Maintenance) Regulations 2011; and

(b) if so, whether the magistrates' court has power to make the decision or modification sought under –

(i)   the Domestic Proceedings and Magistrates' Courts Act 1978, or

(ii) section 15 of and Schedule 1 to the Children Act 1989.

(3) Where the designated officer decides under sub-paragraph (2)(a) that the courts of England and Wales do not have jurisdiction to determine the application, the designated officer shall return the application to the Lord Chancellor with a written explanation of the reasons for that decision.

(4) Where the designated officer decides under sub-paragraph (2)(b) that the magistrates' court does not have power to make the decision or modification sought, the designated officer shall send the application to –

(a) the High Court, or

(b) a county court

as appears to the designated officer be appropriate.

(5) Subject to sub-paragraph (6), if the designated officer decides under sub-paragraph (2)(b) that the magistrates' court has power to make the decision or modification sought, the designated officer shall issue the application and serve it on the respondent.

(6) If the respondent does not reside in the local justice area for which the magistrates' court acts, the designated officer shall –

    (a)   if satisfied that the respondent is residing within another local justice area, send the application to the designated officer of a magistrates' court acting in that other area and inform the Lord Chancellor that it has been so sent; or

    (b)   if unable to establish where the respondent is residing, return the application to the Lord Chancellor.

(7) A designated officer who receives an application by virtue of sub-paragraph (6)(a) shall proceed under sub-paragraph (5) as if that designated officer had decided that the magistrates' court has power to make the decision or modification sought.

(8) Where the designated officer has determined in accordance with sub-paragraph (2)(b) that the magistrates' court has power to make the decision or modification sought, the application shall be treated for the purpose of establishment or modification of a decision under the Convention as an application under the Domestic Proceedings and Magistrates' Courts Act 1978, or under section 15 of and Schedule 1 to the Children Act 1989, as appropriate.

(9) In this paragraph –

    "respondent" means the person who is alleged in an application for establishment of a decision under Article 10 to owe maintenance, or where the application is for modification of a decision, the applicant for the original decision; and

    a reference to an application is a reference to an application together with any documents which accompany it.

SCHEDULE 2

ENFORCEMENT OF INTERNATIONAL MAINTENANCE ORDERS DRIVING DISQUALIFICATION ORDERS

Scope—Sch 2 applies to child maintenance decisions enforceable under the instruments, including the 2007 Convention, listed in para 1. The 2007 Convention, Art 33 requires that the same range of enforcement methods is made available to cases under the 2007 Convention as is available in domestic cases. Although driving disqualification orders are not available for cases of spousal maintenance or in relation to child maintenance orders made by a court, they are available under CSA 1991 for domestic cases and, therefore, an equivalent enforcement method is required for cases under the 2007 Convention. Under domestic law, driving disqualification orders may be made under CSA 1991, ss 39A and 40B and CS(CE)R 1992, Pt IV. A driving disqualification order may be used to enforce a "maintenance decision" as defined by Sch 2, para 2. The definition requires that the maintenance obligation being enforced has to be both an obligation to which an international agreement listed in Sch 2, para 1 applies and the magistrates' court maintenance order within the meaning of MCA 1980, s 150. Section 150 of that Act defines "magistrates' court maintenance order" as being a maintenance order enforceable by a magistrates' court, and a "maintenance order" as being any order, decision, settlement or instrument specified in AJA 1970, Sch 8, which includes the international instruments listed in Sch 2, para 1. Para 3 sets out the preconditions for an application for a driving disqualification order in England and Wales, making it clear that it is viewed as an enforcement measure of last resort.

1 Application

The provisions of this Schedule apply in relation to the enforcement of a maintenance decision relating to a child where that maintenance decision is registered for enforcement, or enforceable, by virtue of –

    (a)   the Council Regulation;

    (b)   the Lugano Convention;

    (c)   the Maintenance Regulation; or

    (d)   the Convention.

PART IV

2 Interpretation

(1) In this Schedule –

"the 1980 Act" means the Magistrates' Courts Act 1980;

"the Council Regulation" means Council Regulation (EC) No 44/2001 on jurisdiction and the recognition and enforcement of judgments in civil and commercial matters;

"the Lugano Convention" means the Convention on jurisdiction and the recognition and enforcement of judgments in civil and commercial matters signed on behalf of the European Community on 30 October 2007;

"arrears" means a sum or sums payable to the creditor from the debtor which have fallen due under the terms of a maintenance decision and which the debtor has not paid;

"the court" means –

in England and Wales, a magistrates' court;

in Scotland, the sheriff court;

"the creditor" means a person to whom a sum or sums of maintenance are owed by the debtor under the terms of a maintenance decision in relation to which an application under this Schedule is made, and includes –

a public body acting in place of an individual to whom maintenance is owed or to which reimbursement is owed for benefits provided in place of maintenance, to the extent that such a body may seek enforcement of a maintenance decision under the terms of an international agreement referred to in paragraph 1; and

where there is in force an order that the sum or sums of maintenance be paid to the designated officer of a magistrates' court, that officer.

"the debtor" means the person who is liable to pay a sum or sums to the creditor under the terms of the maintenance decision in relation to which a complaint referred to in paragraph 3(2) or an application referred to in paragraph 4(1) of this Schedule is made;

"driving disqualification order" means an order under paragraph 5(1)(a) of this Schedule;

"maintenance decision" means a maintenance obligation to which an international agreement mentioned in paragraph 1 applies and which is –

in England and Wales, a magistrates' court maintenance order within the meaning of section 150(1) of the 1980 Act;

in Scotland, a maintenance order within the meaning of section 106 of the Debtors (Scotland) Act 1987.

(2) In this Schedule –

(a)   "child" means a person who –

(i)   either –

(aa) has not attained the age of 16, or

(bb) has not attained the age of 20, and is receiving full time education or vocational training; and

(ii) is not or has not been party to a marriage, to a civil partnership or to an overseas relationship treated as a civil partnership under section 215 of the Civil Partnership Act 2004,

and for the purposes of sub-paragraph (ii) "marriage" and "civil partnership" include a void marriage and a void civil partnership respectively;

(b)   (i)   "driving licence" means a licence to drive a motor vehicle granted under Part III of the Road Traffic Act 1988;

(ii) references to "driving licence" in paragraphs 7, 10(1) and 11 include a reference to its counterpart within the meaning of section 108(1) of the Road Traffic Act 1988, pending repeal of that definition by the Road Safety Act 2006;

(c)   references to sections 76 and 93 of the 1980 Act are to those provisions as modified by section 5(5B) and (5C) of the Civil Jurisdiction and Judgments Act 1982.

3   Application for a driving disqualification order – England and Wales

(1) This paragraph applies to England and Wales only.

(2) Where a creditor makes a complaint under section 93 of the 1980 Act for enforcement under section 76 of that Act of a maintenance decision, the court may make a driving disqualification order.

(3) The court shall not make a driving disqualification order –

(a)   in the absence of the debtor;
(b)   if it considers that, in a case in which it has power to do so, it is appropriate to –
    (i)   make an attachment of earnings order;
    (ii) make an order under section 76(5) of the 1980 Act; or
    (iii) issue a warrant of control for the purpose of recovering the arrears under section 76(1) of that Act;
(c)   unless either –
    (i)   the creditor has sought to obtain a charging order or a third party debt order in respect of the arrears and the arrears or any portion of them remain unpaid; or
    (ii) the debtor has no assets in England and Wales which are susceptible to such methods of enforcement.

(4) Pending the entry into force of section 62 of, and Schedule 12 to, the Tribunals, Courts and Enforcement Act 2007, the reference in sub-paragraph (b)(iii) to obtaining a warrant of control is to be read as a reference to obtaining a warrant of distress.

4   Application for a driving disqualification order – Scotland

(1) In Scotland, the creditor may, by summary application, apply to the court for a driving disqualification order where the conditions mentioned in sub-paragraphs (2), (3) and (4) are met.

(2) The first condition is that arrears have arisen under the maintenance decision.

(3) The second condition is that –

(a)   a diligence against earnings listed in section 46(1) of the Debtors (Scotland) Act 1987 has been executed or made under Part 3 of that Act to secure the payment of sums due under the maintenance decision and it has proved ineffective as a means of securing that payments are made in accordance with the maintenance decision; or
(b)   such diligence against earnings is inappropriate because the debtor is unemployed or otherwise has no earnings which could be the subject of a diligence against earnings.

(4) The third condition is that the creditor has sought to recover the arrears by –

(a)   an attachment;
(b)   an arrestment; or
(c)   an inhibition,

and the arrears or any portion of them remain unpaid or the debtor has no assets in Scotland which are susceptible to the methods of enforcement mentioned in this sub-paragraph.

PART IV

5 Making of a driving disqualification order

(1) If, but only if, the court is of the opinion that the failure to pay the arrears is due to wilful refusal or culpable neglect on the part of the debtor, it may –

    (a)   make an order (a driving disqualification order) disqualifying the debtor from holding or obtaining a driving licence for such period specified in the order, not exceeding two years, as it thinks fit; or

    (b)   make a driving disqualification order but suspend its operation until such time and on such conditions (if any) as it thinks just.

(2) The court shall not make a driving disqualification order unless it has enquired, in the presence of the debtor, as to –

    (a)   the debtor's means;

    (b)   whether the debtor needs a driving licence to earn his or her living; and

    (c)   whether the failure to pay the arrears is due to wilful refusal or culpable neglect on the part of the debtor.

6 A driving disqualification order must state the amount of arrears in respect of which it is made and the period to which they relate and the amount may not exceed the arrears owing under the maintenance decision at the date on which the complaint referred to in paragraph 3 or the application under paragraph 4 was made.

7 A court which makes a driving disqualification order shall require the person to whom it relates to produce any driving licence held by that person.

8 (1) The court shall not, in relation to arrears –

    (a)   make a driving disqualification order during the currency of a warrant committing the debtor to prison in respect of the same arrears;

    (b)   issue a warrant committing the debtor to prison where a driving disqualification order has been made in respect of the same arrears but the period of disqualification specified in the driving disqualification order has not expired.

(2) In sub-paragraph (1) –

    (a)   references to a warrant committing the debtor to prison include such a warrant which has been postponed;

    (b)   references to a driving disqualification order include such an order which has been suspended in accordance with paragraph 5(1)(b); and

    (c)   references to the currency of a warrant, or to the period of disqualification specified in a driving disqualification order, are to be read as including references to the period of postponement of a warrant or suspension of disqualification respectively.

9 Variation, revocation and expiry of driving disqualification order

(1) On application by the creditor or the debtor, the court –

    (a)   may, if part of the amount in respect of which the order is made is paid to any person authorised to receive it, make an order substituting a shorter period of disqualification, or revoking the driving disqualification order; and

    (b)   must, if the whole of the amount is so paid, make an order revoking the driving disqualification order.

(2) An application under sub-paragraph (1) shall be made –

    (a)   in England and Wales, by complaint;

    (b)   in Scotland, by summary application.

10 Upon the making of a further complaint under section 93 of the 1980 Act or application under paragraph 4 of this Schedule, the court may make a further driving disqualification order if the arrears in respect of which the driving disqualification order was made have not been paid in full when the period of disqualification specified in that order expires.

11 Notification to the Secretary of State

Where a court –

 (a)   makes a driving disqualification order; or
 (b)   makes an order varying or revoking a driving disqualification order,

it shall send notice of that fact and any driving licence produced to the court to the Secretary of State.

12 Production of driving licence in England and Wales

In England and Wales, a justice of the peace may issue a summons to the debtor to produce to a magistrates' court any driving licence held by the debtor, and issue a warrant for the debtor's arrest if the debtor does not comply.

13 Procedure on an application for a driving disqualification order in Scotland

In Scotland, the power of the Court of Session by Act of Sederunt to regulate the procedure and practice in civil proceedings in the sheriff court includes the power to make, in relation to driving disqualification orders made under this Schedule, provision –

 (a)   as to the form of any order issued under this Schedule;
 (b)   allowing an application under this Schedule to be renewed where no order is issued;
 (c)   that a statement in writing to the effect that wages of any amount have been paid to the debtor during any period, purported to be signed by or on behalf of the debtor's employer, is sufficient evidence of the facts stated;
 (d)   that, for the purposes of enabling an inquiry to be made as to the debtor's conduct and means, the sheriff may issue a citation to the debtor to appear before the sheriff and (if the debtor does not obey) may issue a warrant for the debtor's arrest:
 (e)   that, for the purposes of enabling such an inquiry, the sheriff may issue a warrant for the debtor's arrest without issuing a citation;
 (f)   as to the execution of a warrant of arrest.

PART IV

SCHEDULE 3
PROVISIONS RELATING TO INFORMATION

Scope—To help the Central Authority fulfil its obligations under Arts 6 and 7 of 2007 Convention as to the location of the creditor or the debtor, and obtaining financial information on the debtor to assist in enforcement applications, Sch 3 provides a regime for data-sharing to the Central Authority from the Department for Work and Pensions and HMRC. There are restrictions on the circumstances in which information can be shared. The information is not available, unless the application is made under Art 10 of the 2007 Convention, through a Central Authority, and must be relevant to the recovery of maintenance in the 2007 Convention. Although information may be sought in relation to the debtor's financial circumstances, such information is available only in enforcement cases; information on the creditor's financial circumstances is not available under Sch 3 (para 3(2)). A request for information may be made by the Central Authority in relation to a specific measures request under Art 7 of the 2007 Convention, where no application under the 2007 Convention, Art 10 is pending. However, the details of the debtor's financial circumstances are not available at this stage, but only an indication that the debtor does or does not have an income or assets in this country (para 6).

1 (1) Subject to the provisions of this Schedule, the Secretary of State, and Revenue and Customs officials, shall provide to the Central Authority such information mentioned at paragraph 3 as they hold in the course of their ordinary activities and which is necessary to facilitate establishment, modification, recognition, registration or enforcement of a maintenance obligation to which the Convention applies, except that provision of information may be refused where it would pose a threat to public safety or national security.

(2) The information to be supplied by the Secretary of State is limited to information held for functions relating to social security, child support, employment or training.

(3) In this Schedule, references to the Secretary of State include a person providing services to the Secretary of State in connection with the functions mentioned at sub-paragraph (2).

2 (1) The information shall be provided to the Central Authority upon its request.

(2) The Central Authority may not request the information unless the following conditions are met –

    (a)   the application to which the request relates has been made under Chapter III of the Convention (applications through Central Authorities) or is an application for a specific measure under Article 7 relating to the location of the debtor or creditor, or to obtaining the information in Article 6(2)(c) (relevant financial circumstances);

    (b)   the request is limited to information which is relevant for the establishment, modification, recognition, registration or enforcement (as the case may be) of the maintenance obligation in question.

3 (1) Subject to sub-paragraphs (2) to (4), the information to be supplied under paragraph 1 is –

    (a)   the address of the debtor or of the creditor;

    (b)   details of the debtor's income;

    (c)   the identity and contact details of the debtor's employer;

    (d)   details of any deposit account or withdrawable share account that the debtor holds with a deposit-taker;

    (e)   details of the debtor's assets.

(2) Where the application to which the request relates is for establishment or modification of a maintenance obligation, the Central Authority may only request the address of the debtor or of the creditor.

(3) The information at sub-paragraph (1)(e) may not be requested unless the information at subparagraphs (1)(b) to (d) is insufficient to enable enforcement of the maintenance obligation.

(4) Where the application to which the request relates is for a specific measure in accordance with paragraph 2(2)(a), the information in sub-paragraph (1)(b), (d) and (e) –

    (a)   shall consist only of an indication as to whether the debtor has income or assets in England and Wales, Scotland or Northern Ireland (as the case may be); and

    (b)   shall be supplied only if the creditor produces to the Central Authority a copy of the maintenance obligation or an abstract from it together with the document required by Article 25(1)(b) or Article 30(3)(b), as appropriate, stating that it is enforceable in the Contracting State in which it was made, and no information may be supplied in relation to the identity and contact details of the debtor's employer.

4 (1) The Central Authority shall transmit the information received in accordance with this Schedule to

(a) the relevant court in England and Wales, or Scotland or Northern Ireland (as the case may be) seised of the application referred to in paragraph 2(2)(a);

(b) where necessary, the requesting Central Authority,

as appropriate.

5 Subject to the provisions of the Convention and of this Schedule, the persons and authorities to whom the Central Authority transmits information in accordance with this Schedule and the requirements of Articles 6 and 7 may process that information in any manner necessary to facilitate the adjudication and recovery of the maintenance obligation to which the request relates.

6 The Central Authority, any court to which it transmits information in accordance with paragraph 4, and any person or authority within the United Kingdom to whom that information is transmitted (whether by a court or by the Central Authority) –

(a) may use information provided under this Schedule only for the purpose of facilitating recovery of maintenance in accordance with this Schedule and the Convention;

(b) may not disclose to the applicant the information so provided, except that –

(i) the existence, or not as the case may be, of an address, income or assets in England and Wales, or Scotland or Northern Ireland (as relevant) may be so disclosed;

(ii) the information may be disclosed if required by rules of court;

(c) may not store the information beyond the period necessary for the purpose it was provided to it.

7 (1) Subject to paragraph 6(b), information referred to in paragraph 3(1) which is received by a Central Authority from a person or an authority listed in paragraph 1 cannot be disclosed to another person unless the disclosure is in connection with a function of the Central Authority under Articles 6 and 7, and Chapter III.

(2) Sub-paragraph (1) does not apply to –

(a) the disclosure of information which is in the form of a summary or collection of information so framed as not to enable identification of any person from the information;

(b) disclosure which is made in pursuance of an order of a court;

(c) disclosure which is required by any other enactment.

8 (1) Subject to sub-paragraph (3), a person who –

(a) is or has been employed by the Central Authority; or

(b) provides or has provided services to the Central Authority,

is guilty of an offence if that person makes disclosure, otherwise than in accordance with this Schedule, of information referred to in paragraph 3 which has been obtained from a person or authority listed in paragraph 1 and which relates to a person whose identity is specified in the information disclosed or can be deduced from it.

PART IV

(2) It is a defence to prove that, at the time of the alleged offence, the person making the disclosure believed that the person was making the disclosure lawfully in accordance with this Schedule and the Convention, and had no reasonable cause to believe otherwise.

(3) Sub-paragraph (1) does not apply to disclosure of information received by such a person from the Secretary of State where the information so disclosed is held by the Secretary of State for the purposes of employment or training only.

9 A person found guilty of an offence under this Schedule shall be liable –

    (a)   on conviction on indictment, to imprisonment for a term not exceeding 2 years, to a fine or to both;

    (b)   on summary conviction, to imprisonment for a term not exceeding 3 months or to a fine not exceeding the statutory maximum or to both.

10 (1) In this Schedule –

"Central Authority" means –

    (a)   in relation to England and Wales, the Lord Chancellor;

    (b)   in relation to Scotland, the Scottish Ministers; and

    (c)   in relation to Northern Ireland, the Department of Justice,

    and references to "Central Authority" include persons employed by or supplying services to that Central Authority;

"deposit-taker" means any person who may, in the course of their business, lawfully accept deposits in the United Kingdom;

"maintenance obligation" means any maintenance obligation to which the Convention (as applied by the United Kingdom) applies, and includes maintenance arrangements as defined in Article 3(e);

"requesting Central Authority" means the Central Authority of another Contracting State to the Convention which has made the request for information or sent the application under Article 10, or the specific measures request under Article 7;

"Revenue and Customs officials" has the meaning given by section 18 of the Commissioners for Revenue and Customs Act 2005;

"functions relating to social security" includes functions relating to statutory payments as defined in section 4C(11) of the Social Security Contributions and Benefits Act 1992 and maternity allowance under section 35 of that Act.

(2) In this Schedule any reference to a numbered Article or Chapter is to the Article or Chapter so numbered in the Convention and any reference to a sub-division of a numbered Article shall be construed accordingly.

****

Justices' Clerks Rules 2005, SI 2005/545

****

2 The things specified in Schedules 1 and 2 to these Rules, being authorised to be done by, to or before a single justice of the peace, may be done by, to or before a justices' clerk.

Amendments—SI 2011/633.

3 (1) The things specified in paragraphs 1 to 36 of Schedule 1 and paragraphs 1 to 7 of Schedule 2 to these Rules, being authorised to be done by, to or before a justices' clerk, may be done by, to or before an assistant clerk, provided that that person has been specifically authorised by the justices' clerk for that purpose, and any reference in these Rules to a justices' clerk shall be taken to include such a person.

(2) The powers authorised to be exercised by a justices' clerk at an early administrative hearing under section 50 of the Crime and Disorder Act 1998 may be exercised instead by an assistant clerk who has been specifically authorised by the justices' clerk for that purpose.

(3) Any authorisation by the justices' clerk under paragraph (1) or (2) above shall be recorded in writing at the time the authority is given or as soon as practicable thereafter.

Amendments—SI 2005/2796; SI 2011/633.

3A Where a justices' clerk –

(a) is performing the function of a single justice in accordance with paragraphs 1 to 7 of Schedule 2 to these Rules; and
(b) considers, for whatever reason, that it is inappropriate to perform the function,

the justices' clerk must refer the matter to the magistrates' court which may perform the function.

Amendments—Inserted by SI 2011/633.

****

SCHEDULE 1

1 The laying of an information or the making of a complaint, other than an information or complaint substantiated on oath.

2 The issue of any summons, including a witness summons.

****

7 The adjournment of the hearing of a complaint if the parties to the complaint consent to the complaint being adjourned.

****

Amendments—SI 2005/2796; SI 2011/633.

SCHEDULE 2
FAMILY ETC.

1 The transfer of proceedings in accordance with any order made by the Lord Chancellor under Part 1 of Schedule 11 to the Children Act 1989.

2 The appointment of a children's guardian or solicitor for a child under section 41 of the Children Act 1989.

3 The making of an order under section 11(3) or 38(1) of the Children Act 1989 where –

(a) a previous such order has been made in the same proceedings;
(b) the terms of the order sought are the same as those of the last such order made; and
(c) a written request for such an order has been made and –

   (i)   the other parties and any children's guardian consent to the request and they or their legal representatives have signed the request; or

   (ii) at least one of the other parties and any children's guardian consent to the request and they or their legal representatives have signed the request, and the remaining parties have not indicated that they either consent to or oppose the making of the order.

4 The issuing of a witness summons under section 97 of the Magistrates' Courts Act 1980 in family proceedings as defined in section 65 of that Act.

5 The request for a welfare report under section 7 of the Children Act 1989.

6 The determination that a complaint for the revocation, discharge, revival, alteration, variation or enforcement of a magistrates' court maintenance order be dealt with by a magistrates' court acting for another local justice area in accordance with the provisions of rule 41 or 59 of the Magistrates' Courts Rules 1981.

7 All the functions of a magistrates' court which a single justice may perform in accordance with rule 2.5 of the Family Procedure Rules 2010 and Practice Directions supplementing those rules except the functions listed in column 2 of the Table in accordance with the rules listed in column 1.

Table

8.20(4)	A direction that any person (who is not a child) should be made a respondent to the application for a declaration of parentage under section 55A of the Family Law Act 1986, except where the parties consent to that person (who is not a child) being made a respondent.
12.3(2)	Direction that a person with parental responsibility be made a party except where the parties consent to the person with parental responsibility (who is not a child) being made a party.
12.3(3)	Direction that any person or body be made a party to proceedings or a party be removed except where the parties consent to a person (who is not a child) or body being made a party or to a party (who is not a child) being removed
12.3(4)	Consequential directions following the addition or removal of a party except where a justices' clerk is able to make such a direction under rule 12.3(2) and (3).
12.14(7)	In relation to a hearing, other than a hearing for directions, if one or more respondents attend the hearing but the applicant does not, refuse the application or if sufficient evidence has previously been received proceed in the absence of the applicant.
12.14(8)	In relation to a hearing, other than a hearing for directions, if neither party attends a hearing, refuse the application.
12.17(2)	Adjournment of proceedings following a direction under section 37(1) of the Children Act 1989.
12.17(4)(b)	Direction for evidence to be served on appropriate authority.
12.17(6)	Direction that a copy of a report under section 37 of the Children Act 1989 need not be served on a party.

12.33(3) (insofar as it relates to r 12.33(1)(a))	Power to deal with an application for warning notices without a hearing.
12.34(2)	Consider whether it is necessary for information to be deleted from a copy of a risk assessment before that copy is served on a party or service of a copy of the risk assessment on a party to be delayed for a specified period and give directions accordingly.
13.3(3)	Direction that person with parental responsibility be made a party, except where parties consent to person with parental responsibility (who is not a child) being made a party.
13.3(4)	Direction that any person or body be made a party to proceedings or a party be removed, except where parties consent to a person (who is not a child) or body being made a party or to a party (who is not a child) being removed.
13.3(5)	Consequential directions following the addition or removal of a party, except where a justices' clerk is able to make such a direction under rule 13.3(3) and (4).
13.21(3)	Permission for the copy of any final order to be sent to any other person.
14.3(3)	Direction that any person or body be made a party to proceedings or a party be removed, except where parties consent to a person (who is not a child) or a body being a party or to a party (who is not a child) being removed.
14.3(4)	Consequential directions following the addition or removal of a party, except where a justices' clerk is able to make such a direction under rule 14.3(3).
14.6(3)(a)	Direction that the local authority prepare a report giving their reasons for placing the child for adoption.
14.26(3)	Permission for the copy of any final order to be sent to any other person.
16.19	Termination of appointment of children's guardian.
16.25(1)	Direction that a person may not act as a children's guardian, termination of an appointment, appointment of a children's guardian in substitution for an existing one.
16.29(9)	Giving reasons for the termination of an appointment of a solicitor for a child (the justices' clerk may make a note of such reasons).
18.3(1)(c)	In addition to a direction that a child be made a respondent to an application, a direction that any other person be a respondent to an application under Part 18 except where the parties consent to the person (other than a child) being made a respondent.
27.4(4)	Power of court to refuse the application, other than one for directions, where one or more respondents appear but the applicant does not.
27.4(5)	Power of court to refuse the application, other than one for directions, where neither the applicant nor any respondent appears.

PART IV

27.10(1)(b)	Direction that the proceedings to which the Rules apply will not be held in private, except that a justices' clerk may give such a direction in relation to a hearing which that justices' clerk is conducting.
27.11(2)(g)	Power to permit any other person to be present during any hearing, except that a justices' clerk may give such permission in relation to a hearing which that justices' clerk is conducting.
29.15	Specifying alternative date for an order, to take effect except an order which the justices' clerk has made.
29.16	Correcting an accidental slip or omission in an order except where that order was made by a justices' clerk.

8 In this Schedule, "hearing" and "order" have the meanings assigned to them by rule 2.3 of the Family Procedure Rules 2010.

Amendments—Inserted by SI 2011/633.

Magistrates' Courts (Attachment of Earnings) Rules 1971, SI 1971/809

ARRANGEMENT OF RULES

****

2 Interpretation

(1) Sections 2 and 25(1) of the Act shall apply to the interpretation of these Rules as they apply to the interpretation of the Act.

(2) The Interpretation Act 1978 shall apply to the interpretation of these Rules as it applies to the interpretation of an Act of Parliament.

(3) Any reference in these rules to "the Act" is a reference to the Attachment of Earnings Act 1971.

(4) Any reference in these Rules to any enactment or rule is a reference to that enactment or rule as amended by any enactment or rule.

(5) (*revoked*)

(6) Any reference in these Rules to an attachment of earnings order shall be construed subject to the provisions of Rule 23.

Amendments—SI 2003/1236.

****

4 Jurisdiction as respects complaints for an attachment of earnings order

A magistrates' court shall have the jurisdiction to hear a complaint for an attachment of earnings order if it would have jurisdiction to enforce payment of any arrears under the related maintenance order.

Defined terms—"maintenance order": r 2(1), AEA 1971, s 2(a), Sch 1.

Scope—An attachment of earnings order may be made on the making, variation, registration or confirmation of a range of orders; these additional powers are noted against the relevant statutory provisions.

****

6 Service of orders and notices

(1) Where a magistrates' court makes an attachment of earnings order or an order varying or discharging such an order, the designated officer for the court shall cause a copy of the order to be served on the employer and shall send a copy of the order to the debtor.

(2) Where an attachment of earnings order made by a magistrates' court ceases to have effect as provided in section 8 or 11 of the Act, notice of cessation shall be given to the employer.

(3) The notice required by the preceding paragraph shall be given by the designated officer for the magistrates' court –

(a) which made or confirmed the maintenance order (in a case to which section 11(1)(c) of the Act applies);

(b) in which the maintenance order is registered under any enactment (in a case to which section 11(1)(a), (b) or (d) of the Act applies); or

(c) which issued the warrant of commitment or exercised the power conferred by section 77(2) of the Magistrates' Courts Act 1980 (in a case to which section 8 of the Act applies).

Amendments—SI 2001/615; SI 2005/617.

Defined terms—"the employer": AEA 1971, s 25(1); "maintenance order": r 2(1), AEA 1971, s 2(a), Sch 1.

7 Particulars of debtor

The particulars of the debtor for the purpose of enabling him to be identified which, so far as they are known, are to be included in an attachment of earnings order under section 6(3) of the Act shall be –

(a) full name and address;

(b) place of work;

(c)   nature of work and works number, if any.

8 Notice of application for appropriate variation order

The designated officer for a magistrates' court, by which an application under section 10 of the Act for the appropriate variation of an attachment of earnings order is to be heard, shall give notice in writing of the time and place appointed for the hearing of the application to the person entitled to receive payment under the related maintenance order (whether directly or through the officer of any court).

Amendments—SI 2001/615; SI 2005/617.

Defined terms—"maintenance order": r 2(1), AEA 1971, s 2(a), Sch 1.

9 Jurisdiction as respects complaints for the discharge and variation of attachment of earnings order

(1) This Rule shall apply to a complaint for the discharge or variation of an attachment of earnings order except where the related maintenance order –

(a)   is an affiliation order to which section 88(2)(a) of the Children and Young Persons Act 1933 applies;

(b)   is an order made under section 87 of that Act;

(c)   is an order made under section 43 of the National Assistance Act 1948;

(d)   is an order made under section 30 of the Children and Young Persons Act 1963.

(2) Where a complaint is made to a justice of the peace acting in the same local justice area as the court which made the attachment of earnings order and it appears to him that –

(a)   the person in whose favour the attachment of earnings order was made, or

(b)   the debtor,

is for the time being in some local justice area other than that in which the justice is acting, or that the complainant is the designated officer for a magistrates' court acting in such other area, then, if it appears to the justice that the complaint may be more conveniently dealt with by a magistrates' court acting in that other area, he may cause the designated officer for the court to send the complaint by post to the designated officer for the other court and for that purpose shall write down the complaint, if this has not already been done.

(3) On receipt by the designated officer for a magistrates' court of a complaint under the preceding paragraph, he shall bring the complaint before the court and the court shall issue a summons requiring the person appropriate under section 19(4) of the Act to appear before it, and shall hear and determine the complaint.

Amendments—SI 2001/615; SI 2005/617.

Defined terms—"maintenance order": r 2(1), AEA 1971, s 2(a), Sch 1.

"justice of the peace" (r 9(2))—The same power applies where complaint is made to a justices' clerk (see r 22(2)(b)).

10 Complaints for variation or discharge of attachment of earnings orders against persons outside the United Kingdom

(1) Where a complaint for the variation or discharge of an attachment of earnings order is made against a person who resides outside the United Kingdom and that person does not appear at the time and place appointed for the hearing of the complaint, then, subject to paragraph (2) of this Rule, the court may, if it thinks it reasonable in all the circumstances to do so, proceed to hear and determine the complaint in accordance with

section 20(3) of the Act if it is proved to the satisfaction of the court that the complainant has taken any of the following steps to give the person against whom the complaint is made notice of the complaint and of the time and place appointed for the hearing thereof, that is to say–

(a) has caused written notice of the matters aforesaid to be delivered to the said person;

(b) has caused wr.tten notice of the matters aforesaid to be sent by post addressed to the said person at his last known or usual place of abode or at his place of business or at some other address at which there is ground for believing that it will reach him; or

(c) has caused notice of the matters aforesaid to be inserted in one or more newspapers or one or more occasions.

(2) Where it is proposed to take any such steps as are mentioned in subparagraph (b) or (c) of the preceding paragraph, the complainant shall apply for directions to a justice of the peace acting in the same local justice area as the court by which the complaint is to be heard, and the taking of such steps shall be effective for the purposes of this Rule only if they were taken in accordance with the directions given by the said justice.

(3) Paragraph (1) of Rule 67 of the Magistrates' Courts Rules 1981 shall apply for the purposes of proving the delivery of a written notice in pursuance of sub-paragraph (a) of paragraph (1) of this Rule as it applies for the purpose of proving the service of a summons.

In relation to a solemn declaration made outside the United Kingdom, paragraph (1) of the said Rule 67, as applied by this paragraph, shall have effect as if for the reference to the authorities mentioned in the said paragraph (1) there were substituted a reference to a consular officer of Her Majesty's Government in the United Kingdom or any person for the time being authorised by law, in the place where the declarant is, to administer an oath for any judicial or other legal purpose.

(4) Paragraph (2) of the said Rule 67 shall apply for the purpose of proving the sending of a written notice in pursuance of sub-paragraph (b) of paragraph (1) of this Rule, or the insertion of a notice in a newspaper in pursuance of sub-paragraph (c) thereof, as it applies for the purpose of proving the service of any process, provided, as respects the insertion of a notice in a newspaper, that a copy of the newspaper containing the notice is annexed to the certificate.

"justice of the peace" (r 10(2))—Directions may also be given by a justices' clerk see (r 22(2)(c)).

11 Complaints by debtors for variation or discharge of attachment of earnings orders against persons who cannot be found

(1) Where a complaint by the debtor for the variation or discharge of an attachment of earnings order is made against a person and that person does not appear at the time or place appointed for the hearing of the complaint, then, subject to paragraph (2) of this Rule, the court may, if it thinks it reasonable in all the circumstances to do so, proceed to hear and determine the complaint, notwithstanding the absence of proof that that person had knowledge of the summons as required by Rule 99 of the Magistrates' Court Rules 1981, if it is proved to the satisfaction of the court that the summons in respect of the complaint was served in accordance with the provisions of Rule 99 of those Rules and the complainant has caused notice of the complaint and of the time and place appointed for the hearing thereof to be inserted in one or more newspapers on one or more occasions.

(2) Where it is proposed to rely upon the provisions of the preceding paragraph of this Rule, the complainant shall apply for directions to a justice of the peace acting in the same local justice area as the court by which the complaint is to be heard, and the giving

PART IV

of notice in a newspaper shall be effective for the purposes of this Rule only if the notice was given in accordance with the directions given by the said justice.

(3) Paragraph (2) of Rule 67 of the Magistrates' Courts Rules 1981 shall apply for the purpose of proving the insertion of a notice in a newspaper in pursuance of paragraph (1) of this rule as it applies for the purpose of proving the service of any process, provided that a copy of the newspaper containing the notice is annexed to the certificate.

"justice of the peace" (r 11(2))—Directions may also be given by a justices' clerk (r 22(2)(c)).

12 Variation of attachment of earnings order on change of employment

Where an attachment of earnings order has lapsed under section 9(4) of the Act on the debtor's ceasing to be in the employment of the person to whom the order was directed and it appears to a magistrates' court, acting in the same local justice area as the court which made the order, that the debtor has subsequently entered the employment of a person (whether the same as before or another), the court may, of its own motion, vary the order by directing it to that person and may make any consequential amendment to the order made necessary by this variation.

"magistrates' court"—These powers may also be exercised by a justices' clerk (r 22(2)(d)).

13 Discharge of attachment of earnings order by court of its own motion

(1) Where it appears to a magistrates' court acting in the same local justice area as the magistrates' court which made the attachment of earnings order that the debtor is not in the employment of the person to whom the order is directed and that the likelihood of the debtor's entering the employment of any person is not such as to justify preserving the order, the court may, of its own motion, discharge the order.

(2) Where a magistrates' court has made an attachment of earnings order and, by virtue of section 7, 21 or 30 of the Matrimonial Proceedings and Property Act 1970, the related maintenance order ceases to have effect because of the remarriage of the person entitled to receive payments under it, a magistrates' court acting in the same local justice area as that court may, of its own motion, discharge the attachment of earnings order, if there are no arrears to be recovered.

"magistrates' court" (r 13(1))—This power of discharge may also be exercised by a justices' clerk (r 22(2)(d)).

14 Temporary variation of protected earnings rate

(1) A justice of the peace acting in the same local justice area as the magistrates' court which made the attachment of earnings order may, on a written application made by the debtor on the ground of a material change in the debtor's resources and needs since the order was made or last varied, by order (hereinafter referred to as a temporary variation order) vary the attachment of earnings order for a period of not more than four weeks by an increase of the protected earnings rate.

(2) *(revoked)*

(3) The designated officer for the magistrates' court which made the attachment of earnings order shall cause a copy of any temporary order to be served on the employer and shall give him notice if the temporary variation order is discharged and the designated officer shall also send a copy to the person entitled to receive payments under the related maintenance order (whether directly or through an officer of any court).

(4) Where an application for the variation or discharge of an attachment of earnings order is made to a magistrates' court and there is in existence a temporary variation order in respect of the attachment of earnings order, the court may, of its own motion, discharge the temporary variation order.

Amendments—SI 2001/615; SI 2003/1236; SI 2005/617.

"justice of the peace" (r 14(1))—This power to vary may also be exercised by a justices' clerk (r 22(2)(e)).

****

18 Method of making payment under attachment of earnings order

(1) A designated officer for a magistrates' court to whom any payment under an attachment of earnings order is to be made shall notify the employer and the person entitled to receive payments under the related maintenance order of the hours during which, and the place at which, payments are, subject to the provisions of this Rule, to be made and received.

(2) If an employer sends by post any payments under an attachment of earnings order to a designated officer for a magistrates' court, he shall do so at his own risk and expense.

(3) A designated officer for a magistrates' court may send by post any payment under an attachment of earnings order to the person entitled to receive payments under the related maintenance order at the request and at the risk of that person.

Amendments—SI 2001/615; SI 2005/617.

Defined terms—"the employer": AEA 1971, s 25(1).

19 Payments under attachment of earnings order after imprisonment imposed

(1) Where imprisonment or other detention has been imposed for the purpose of enforcing a maintenance order, the designated officer for a magistrates' court to whom any payment under a related attachment of earnings order is to be made –

  (a) in relation to such a payment shall be a person authorised to receive the said payment for the purposes of section 79(2) of the Magistrates' Courts Act 1980 (which relates to release from custody and reduction of detention on payment);

  (b) on receiving such a payment shall notify the person authorised for the said purposes by Rule 55 of the Magistrates' Courts Rules 1981 of the sum received.

(2) Where a person receives notice of the receipt of a sum under the preceding paragraph of this Rule, he shall note the receipt of that sum on the warrant of commitment, if any, held by him.

Amendments—SI 2001/615; SI 2005/617.

20 Service of orders and notices

Where under section 14 of the Act (which relates to statements of earnings etc) an order is directed to the debtor or to a person appearing to be an employer of the debtor or where under these Rules a copy of an order is to be served or a notice is to given to any person –

  (a) service may be effected on, or notice may be given to a person, other than a corporation, by delivering it to the person to whom it is directed or by sending it by post in a letter addressed to him at his last known or usual place of abode, or, in the case of an employer or a person appearing to be an employer of the debtor, at his place of business;

PART IV

(b)   service may be effected on, or notice given to, a corporation by delivering the document at, or sending it to –

  (i)   such office or place as the corporation may, for the purpose of this Rule, have specified in writing to the court in relation to the debtor or to a class or description of person to which he belongs, or

  (ii)   the registered office of the corporation if that office is in England and Wales or, if there is no registered office in England and Wales, any place therein where the corporation trades or conducts its business.

Defined terms—"the debtor": AEA 1971, s 2(e); "the employer": AEA 1971, s 25(1).

21 County court records

(1) Where a designated officer for a magistrates' court causes a copy of an order or notice to be given to any person under Rule 6 of these Rules, he shall cause a copy of the order or notice to be given also to the proper officer of the county court for the district in which the debtor resides.

(2) Where the designated officer for a magistrates' court which has made an attachment of earnings order is informed of a debtor's change of address, he shall notify the new address to the proper officer of the county court for the district in which the debtor resided before the change of address.

Amendments—SI 2001/615; SI 2005/617.

22 Justices' clerks

(1) The things specified in paragraph (2) of this Rule, being things authorised to be done by, to or before a single justice of the peace for a local justice area, may be done by, to or before the justices' clerk for that area.

(2) The things referred to in paragraph (1) above are –

(a)   the power to make an order under section 14(1) or (2) of the Act (power of court to obtain statements of earnings, etc) before the hearing of an application to a magistrates' court for an attachment of earnings order, or for the variation or discharge of such an order;

(b)   the determination that a complaint for the discharge or variation of an attachment of earnings order dealt with by a magistrates' court acting in another local justice area in accordance with Rule 9 of these Rules;

(c)   the giving of directions under Rule 10 or 11 of these Rules;

(d)   the discharge or variation by the court of its own motion of an attachment of earnings order in accordance with Rule 12 or 13 of these Rules;

(e)   the temporary variation of an attachment of earnings order by an increase of the protected earnings rate in accordance with Rule 14 of these Rules;

(f)   the making of an order under Rule 16 of these Rules (transfer of fines etc with view to making consolidated attachment order).

Defined terms—"single justice": AEA 1971, s 25(1); SI 2005/617.

****

Magistrates' Courts Fees Order 2008, SI 2008/1052

1 Citation and commencement

This Order may be cited as the Magistrates' Courts Fees Order 2008 and shall come into force on 1 May 2008.

2 Fees payable

The fees set out in column 2 of Schedule 1 are payable in magistrates' courts in respect of the items described in column 1 in accordance with and subject to the directions specified in that column.

3 (1) No fee is payable in respect of –

   (a)   criminal proceedings (except for documents that were used in, or result from, criminal proceedings that are subsequently required for civil or family proceedings);
   (b)   any summons, warrant, notice or order issued, given or made under sections 83(1) or (2), 88, 89 or 136 of the Magistrates' Courts Act 1980, or under any rule made for the purpose of those provisions; or
   (c)   binding over proceedings.

(2) In this article, "binding over proceedings" means any proceedings instituted (whether by way of complaint under section 115 of the Magistrates' Courts Act 1980 or otherwise) with a view to obtaining from a magistrates' court an order requiring a person to enter into a recognizance to keep the peace or to be of good behaviour.

Amendments—SI 2010/731.

4 Where by any convention entered into by Her Majesty with any foreign power it is provided that no fee is required to be paid in respect of any proceedings, the fees specified in this Order are not payable in respect of those proceedings.

5 Remissions and part remissions

Schedule 2 applies for the purpose of ascertaining whether a party is entitled to a remission or part remission of a fee prescribed by this Order.

6 Revocations

The instruments listed in column 1 of the table in Schedule 3 (which have the references listed in column 2) are revoked.

7 Transitional provision

Fees 10.2(b) and (c) are not payable in respect of an issues resolution hearing, pre-hearing review or final hearing which has been listed on any day between 1 May 2008 and 14 May 2008 inclusive.

PART IV

SCHEDULE 1
FEES TO BE TAKEN

Column 1 *Number and description of fee*	Column 2 *Amount of fee*
1 *Attendance*	
1.1 On an application which requires a justice of the peace to perform a function away from the court premises.	£50
Note: Fee 1.1 is payable in addition to other payable fees.	
2 *Appeals*	
2.1 On an application to state a case for the opinion of the High Court under section 111(1) of the Magistrates Court Act 1980.	£500
Note: where fee 2.1 is payable, no further fee is payable in respect of the preparation of a draft case by the justices' clerk, providing copies, taking recognizance as required by section 114 of that Act and enlargement and renewal of such recognizance.	
2.2 Proceedings under the Child Support Act 1991 –	
(a) On commencing an appeal under section 20;	£150
(b) On commencing an appeal against a deduction from earnings order.	£90
2.3 Proceedings under Schedule 5 to the Licensing Act 2003 –	
on commencing an appeal under paragraph 1, 2(2), 3(2)(a), 4(2), 7(2), 8(2)(b), 8A(2)(b), 10, 11(2), 12(2), 13(2)(b), 14, 16(2), 17(1), and (4) or 18(2)(a) of Schedule 5 to the Licensing Act 2003.	£400
2.4 On commencing an appeal where no other fee is specified.	£200
3 *Certificates and Certified Documents*	
3.1 On a request for a certificate of refusal to state a case.	£100
3.2 Register of judgments, orders and fines kept under section 98 of the Courts Act 2003 on a request for a certificate of satisfaction.	£15
3.3 On a request for a certified copy of a memorandum of conviction.	£60
3.4 On a request for a certificate or certified document where no other fee is specified.	£60
Note: Fee 3.4 includes any copy of a document certified by the court as a genuine copy of the original document.	
4 *Liability Orders*	
4.1 Proceedings under the Council Tax (Administration and Enforcement) Regulations 1992 or the Non-Domestic Rating (Collection and Enforcement) (Local Lists) Regulations 1989 on an application for a liability order.	£3
Note: Fee 4.1 is payable in respect of each defendant against whom the liability order is sought.	
4.2 Proceedings under the Child Support Act 1991 on an application for a liability order.	£40
Note: Fee 4.2 is payable in respect of each liability order applied for.	
5 *Copy Documents*	
5.1 On a request for a copy document (other than where fee 5.2 applies) –	
(a) of ten pages or less; and	£5
(b) for each subsequent page.	50p
Note: The fee payable under fee 5.1 includes –	

Column 1 *Number and description of fee*	Column 2 *Amount of fee*
• where the court allows a party to fax to the court for the use of that party a document that has not been requested by the court and is not intended to be placed on the court file;	
• where a party requests that the court fax a copy of a document from the court file; and	
• where the court provides a subsequent copy of a document which it has previously provided.	
5.2 On a request for a copy of a document on a computer disk or in other electronic form, for each such copy.	£5
6 *Financial Provision*	
6.1 Proceedings under the Domestic Proceedings and Magistrates' Courts Act 1978 or Schedule 6 to the Civil Partnership Act 2004 on an application for an order for financial provision (other than an application to vary or revoke such an order, or an application for an order for financial provision made for the benefit of, or against, a person residing outside the United Kingdom).	£200
7 *Proceedings under the Family Law Act 1986*	
7.1 On an application for a declaration of parentage (each child).	£150
8 *Proceedings under the Children Act 1989*	
8.1 On an application for an order in form C1 or form C100 (free-standing application), form C79 (application related to enforcement of a contact order), form C2 (application in existing proceedings) or a request for permission to apply for an order in form C2 under the following provisions of the Children Act 1989 –	
(a) section 4(1)(c) or (3) or 4A(1)(b) or (3) (parental responsibility);	£200
(b) section 4ZA(1)(c) or (6) (parental responsibility);	£200
(c) section 5(1) or 6(7) (guardians);	£200
(d) section 10(1) or (2) (section 8 orders);	£200
(e) section 11J(2) (enforcement orders);	£200
(f) section 11O(2) (compensation for financial loss);	£200
(g) section 13(1) (change of child's surname or removal from jurisdiction while residence order in force);	£200
(h) section 14A(3) or (6)(a), 14C(3) or 14D(1) (special guardianship orders);	£160
(i) section 25 (secure accommodation order);	£170
(j) section 33(7) (change of child's surname or removal from jurisdiction while care order in force);	£170
(k) section 34(2), (3), (4) or (9) (contact with child in care);	£170
(l) section 36(1) (education supervision order);	£170
(m) section 39 (variation or discharge etc of care and supervision orders);	£170
(n) section 43(1) (child assessment order);	£170
(o) sections 44, 45 and 46 (emergency protection order);	£170
(p) section 48 (warrant to assist person exercising powers under emergency protection order);	£170
(q) section 50 (recovery order);	£170

PART IV

Column 1 *Number and description of fee*	Column 2 *Amount of fee*
(r) section 79K (cancellation, variation or removal or imposition of condition of registration of child minder or day carer);	£170
(s) paragraph 4(2), 6(2), 7(2) or 9(2) of Schedule A1 (applications in respect of enforcement orders);	£90
(t) paragraph 5(2) of Schedule A1 (amendment of enforcement order by reason of change of address);	£45
(u) section 102 (warrant to assist person exercising powers to search for children or inspect premises);	£170
(v) paragraph 1(1) or (4), 2(1) or (5), 5(6), 6(5), (7) or (8), 8(2), 10(2), 11 or 14(1) of Schedule 1 (financial provision for children);	£200
(w) paragraph 19(1) of Schedule 2 (approval of court for child in care of local authority to live abroad);	£170
(x) paragraph 6 of Schedule 3 (extension of supervision order);	£170
(y) paragraph 15(2) or 17(1) of Schedule 3 (extension or discharge of education supervision order);	£170
(z) paragraph 8(1) of Schedule 8 (appeals concerning foster parenting).	£170
8.2 In relation to proceedings under section 31 of the Children Act 1989 (care and supervision orders) –	
(a) on an application;	£2,225
(b) where an issues resolution hearing or a pre-hearing review has been listed.	£700
(c) where a final hearing has been listed.	£1,900

Notes to fees 8.1 and 8.2:

Where an application requires the permission of the court, the relevant fee is payable when the permission is sought but no further fee will be charged if permission is granted and the application is made.

Where an application is made or permission is sought under or relating to provisions of the Children Act 1989 which are listed in two or more different numbered fees, or require two or more different numbered forms, only one fee is payable, and if those fees are different, only the highest fee is payable.

Where an application is made or permission is sought under or relating to two or more provisions of the Children Act 1989 which are listed in the same numbered fee, the fee is payable only once.

Where the application is made or permission is sought in respect of two or more children at the same time, and these children are siblings or children of the family, only one fee is payable in respect of each numbered fee.

Notes to fee 8.2 only:

Where a final order is made at a case management conference, £500 of the amount paid under fee 8.2(a) will be refunded.

Where the court lists more than one issues resolution hearing or prehearing review, the fee is payable only once.

Where proceedings are consolidated with other proceedings, any fee which falls to be paid after the date on which the proceedings are consolidated is payable only once.

Column 1 Number and description of fee	Column 2 Amount of fee
Where a fee is paid under fee 8.2(b) or (c) in relation to a hearing that is cancelled, for example, because a final order is made at earlier hearing, the application is withdrawn, or the hearing is no longer needed, the fee will be refunded. A refund will not be given if the hearing is adjourned to a later date or to a date to be fixed.	
The fee in 8.2(b) and (c) is payable 14 days before the hearing or review.	
9 *Proceedings under the Human Fertilisation and Embryology Act 2008*	
9.1 On an application under section 54 (parental order).	£200
10 *Proceedings under the Adoption and Children Act 2002*	
10.1 On an application or a request for permission to apply under any provision in Part 1 of the Adoption and Children Act 2002, other than an application under section 22 of that Act.	£160
10.2 On an application under section 22 of the Adoption and Children Act 2002 (placement order).	£400
Notes: Where an application requires the permission of the court, the relevant fee is payable when permission is sought but no further fee will be charged if permission is granted and the application is made.	
Where an application is made or permission is sought under or relating to two or more provisions of the Adoption and Children Act 2002 only one fee is payable.	
Where the same application is made or permission is sought in respect of two or more children at the same time, and these children are siblings or children of the family, only one fee is payable.	
11 *Proceedings under the Children and Adoption Act 2006*	
11.1 On an application for a warning notice to be attached to a contact order.	£45
Notes: Where an application is made or permission is sought under or relating to provisions of the Children Act 1989 and the Children and Adoption Act 2006 which are listed in two or more different numbered fees, only one fee is payable.	
Where the same application is made or permission is sought in respect of two or more children at the same time, and these children are siblings or children of the family, only one fee is payable in respect of each numbered fee.	
12 *Proceedings to vary, extend or revoke an order made in family proceedings*	
12.1 On an application to vary, extend or revoke an order made in family proceedings where no other fee is specified.	£20
13 *Licences*	
13.1 On a request for a licence, consent or authority where no other fee is specified.	£25
13.2 On an application for the renewal or variation of an existing licence.	£25
13.3 On an application for the revocation of a licence where no other fee is specified.	£25
14 *Oaths*	
14.1 On taking the attestation of a constable or special constable under the Police Act 1996.	£10

PART IV

Column 1 *Number and description of fee*	Column 2 *Amount of fee*
Note: Fee 14.1 is payable for every attestation made by every constable or special constable at or away from court premises.	
14.2 For every oath, affirmation, solemn declaration or statutory declaration where no other fee is specified.	£25
Note: No fee is payable for the swearing in of witnesses or in any case where an enactment directs that no fee will be taken.	
15 *Other civil proceedings*	
15.1 On commencing proceedings where no other fee is specified and where leave or permission is not required.	£200
15.2 On commencing proceedings where leave or permission is required –	
(a) on an application for leave or permission to commence proceedings where no other fee is specified; and	£100
(b) on commencing proceedings where leave or permission has been granted following payment of fee 15.2(a).	£100
Note: Fees 15.1 and 15.2 do not apply to family proceedings.	
15.3 Contested hearing –	
For a hearing at which the proceedings are contested.	£500
Note: Fee 15.3 –	
• applies only to hearings in proceedings to which fee 15.1 or 15.2 apply;	
• is payable by the party who commenced the proceedings;	
• is payable on the day that the hearing commences;	
• is payable only once in the same proceedings.	
16 *Warrants*	
16.1 On an application for a warrant of entry.	£18
16.2 On an application for any other warrant where no other fee is specified.	£75
Note: Fee 16.2 includes an application for a warrant made during a hearing. No fee is payable if the court issues a warrant of its own initiative.	
17 *Commitment*	
17.1 Proceedings under the Council Tax (Administration and Enforcement) Regulations 1992 or the Non-Domestic Rating (Collection and Enforcement) (Local Lists) Regulations 1989 on an application for a warrant for commitment.	£240
17.2 Proceedings under the Child Support Act 1991 on an application for a warrant for commitment.	£240
Note: Fees 17.1 and 17.2 do not include a warrant of arrest which is provided for under fee 16.2	
Note to all fees: Where proceedings are brought against the individual members of a partnership, any relevant fee is payable only once.	

Amendments—SI 2008/2855; substituted by SI 2009/1496; amended by SI 2010/731; SI 2010/1917.

SCHEDULE 2

REMISSIONS AND PART-REMISSIONS

1 Interpretation

(1) In this Schedule –

"child" means a child or young person in respect of whom a party is entitled to receive child benefit in accordance with section 141, and regulations made under section 142, of the Social Security Contributions and Benefits Act 1992;

"child care costs" has the meaning given in Part 3 of the Criminal Legal Aid (Financial Resources) Regulations 2013;

"couple" has the meaning given in section 3(5A) of the Tax Credits Act 2002;

"disposable monthly income" has the meaning given in paragraph 5;

"excluded benefits" means –

(a) any of the following benefits payable under the Social Security Contributions and Benefits Act 1992 –
  (i) attendance allowance paid under section 64;
  (ii) severe disablement allowance;
  (iii) carer's allowance;
  (iv) disability living allowance;
  (v) constant attendance allowance paid under section 104 or paragraph 4 or 7(2) of Schedule 8 as an increase to a disablement pension;
  (vi) council tax benefit;
  (vii) any payment made out of the social fund;
  (viii) housing benefit;

(b) any direct payment made under the Community Care, Services for Carers and Children's Services (Direct Payments) (England) Regulations 2003 or the Community Care, Services for Carers and Children's Services (Direct Payments) (Wales) Regulations 2004;

(c) a back to work bonus payable under section 26 of the Jobseekers Act 1995;

(d) any exceptionally severe disablement allowance paid under the Personal Injuries (Civilians) Scheme 1983;

(e) any pension paid under the Naval, Military and Air Forces etc (Disablement and Death) Service Pension Order 2006;

(f) any payment made from the Independent Living Funds;

(g) any financial support paid under an agreement for the care of a foster child;

(h) personal independence payment under Part 4 of the Welfare Reform Act 2012; and

(i) armed forces independence payment under the Armed Forces and Reserve Forces (Compensation Scheme) Order 2011;

...

"gross annual income" means total annual income, for the 12 months preceding the application for remission or part remission, from all sources other than receipt of any of the excluded benefits;

"gross monthly income" means total monthly income, for the month in which the application for remission or part remission is made, from all sources other than receipt of any of the excluded benefits;

"the Independent Living Funds" means any payment made from the funds listed at regulation 20(2)(b) of the Criminal Legal Aid (Financial Resources) Regulations 2013;

...

PART IV

"partner" means a person with whom the party lives as a couple and includes a person with whom the party is not currently living but from whom the party is not living separate and apart;

"party" means the individual who would, but for this Schedule, be liable to pay the fee required under this Order;

"restraint order" means –

    (a)   an order under section 42(1A) of the Senior Courts Act 1981; or

    (b)   a civil restraint order under rule 3.11 of the Civil Procedure Rules 1998 or a practice direction made under that rule.

(2) Paragraphs 2, 3 and 4 –

    (a)   do not apply to a party for whom civil legal services, for which a certificate has been issued under the Civil Legal Aid (Procedure) Regulations 2012, have been made available under arrangements made for the purposes of Part 1 of that Act for the purposes of the proceedings; and

    (b)   are subject to the provisions of paragraph 10 (vexatious litigants).

Amendments—SI 2008/2855; SI 2013/388; SI 2013/534, subject to savings; SI 2013/591.

Couple—See under FPFO 2008, Sch 2.

2 Full remission of fees – qualifying benefits

(1) No fee is payable under this Order if, at the time when a fee would otherwise be payable, the party –

    (a)   is in receipt of a qualifying benefit; or

    (b)   is not a beneficiary of a trust fund in court of a value of more than £50,000 and is –

        (i)   under the age of eighteen; or

        (ii) a person for whose financial relief an order under paragraph 2 of Schedule 1 to the Children Act 1989 is in force or being applied for.

(2) The following are qualifying benefits for the purposes of sub-paragraph (1)(a) –

    (a)   income support under the Social Security Contributions and Benefits Act 1992;

    (b)   working tax credit, provided that no child tax credit is being paid to the party;

    (c)   income-based jobseeker's allowance under the Jobseekers Act 1995;

    (d)   guarantee credit under the State Pension Credit Act 2002; and

    (e)   income-related employment and support allowance under the Welfare Reform Act 2007.

(3) Sub-paragraph (1)(b) applies to –

    (a)   an application to which fee 8, 9, 10, 11, 12, 13, 14 or 15 applies;

    (b)   an application or request to which fee 2, 3, 6 or 7 applies where the application or request is made in relation to proceedings to which fee 8, 9, 10, 11, 12, 13, 14 or 15 applies.

Amendments—SI 2008/2855.

3 Full remission of fees – gross annual income

(1) No fee is payable under this Order if, at the time when the fee would otherwise be payable, the party has the number of children specified in column 1 of the following table and –

    (a)   if the party is single, the gross annual income of the party does not exceed the amount set out in the appropriate row of column 2; or

    (b)   if the party is one of a couple, the gross annual income of the couple does not exceed the amount set out in the appropriate row of column 3.

Column 1 *Number of children of party paying fee*	Column 2 *Single*	Column 3 *Couple*
no children	£13,000	£18,000
1 child	£15,930	£20,930
2 children	£18,860	£23,860
3 children	£21,790	£26,790
4 children	£24,720	£29,720

(2) If the party paying the fee has more than 4 children then the relevant amount of gross annual income is the amount specified in the table for 4 children plus the sum of £2,930 for each additional child.

4 Full and part remission of fees – disposable monthly income

(1) No fee is payable under this Order if, at the time when the fee would otherwise be payable, the disposable monthly income of the party is £50 or less.

(2) The maximum amount of fee payable is –

    (a) if the disposable monthly income of the party is more than £50 but does not exceed £210, an amount equal to one-quarter of every £10 of the party's disposable monthly income up to a maximum of £50; and

    (b) if the disposable monthly income is more than £210, an amount equal to £50 plus one-half of every £10 over £200 of the party's disposable monthly income.

(3) Where the fee that would otherwise be payable under this Order is greater than the maximum fee which a party is required to pay as calculated in sub-paragraph (2), the fee will be remitted to the amount payable under that sub-paragraph.

5 Disposable monthly income

(1) A party's disposable monthly income is the gross monthly income of the party for the month in which the fee becomes payable ("the period") less the deductions referred to in sub-paragraphs (2) and (3).

(2) There are to be deducted from the gross monthly income –

    (a) income tax paid or payable in respect of the period;

    (b) any contributions estimated to have been paid under Part 1 of the Social Security Contributions and Benefits Act 1992 in respect of the period;

    (c) either –

        (i) monthly rent or monthly payment in respect of a mortgage debt or hereditable security, payable in respect of the only or main dwelling of the party, less any housing benefit paid under the Social Security Contributions and Benefits Act 1992; or

        (ii) the monthly cost of the living accommodation of the party;

    (d) any child care costs paid or payable in respect of the period;

    (e) if the party is making bona fide payments for the maintenance of a child who is not a member of the household of the party, the amount of such payments paid or payable in respect of the period; and

    (f) any amount paid or payable by the party, in respect of the period, in pursuance of a court order.

(3) There will be deducted from the gross monthly income an amount representing the cost of living expenses in respect of the period being –

    (a) £315; plus

PART IV

(b)   £244 for each child of the party; plus

(c)   £159, if the party has a partner.

6 Resources of partners

(1) For the purpose of determining whether a party is entitled to the remission or part remission of a fee in accordance with this Schedule, the income of a partner, if any, is to be included as income of the party.

(2) The receipt by a partner of a qualifying benefit does not entitle a party to remission of a fee.

7 Application for remission or part remission of fees

(1) An application for remission or part remission of a fee must be made to the court officer at the time when the fee would otherwise be payable.

(2) Where a claim for full remission of fees is made, the party must provide documentary evidence of, as the case may be –

(a)   entitlement to a qualifying benefit; or

(b)   gross annual income and, if applicable, the children included for the purposes of paragraph 3.

(3) Where a claim for full or part remission of fees under paragraph 4 is made, the party must provide documentary evidence of –

(a)   such of the party's gross monthly income as is derived from –
  (i)   employment;
  (ii)   rental or other income received from persons living with the party by reason of their residence in the party's home;
  (iii) a pension; or
  (iv)   a state benefit, not being an excluded benefit; and

(b)   any expenditure being deducted from the gross monthly income in accordance with paragraph 5(2).

8 Remission in exceptional circumstances

Where it appears to the Lord Chancellor that the payment of any fee prescribed by this Order would, owing to the exceptional circumstances of the particular case, involve undue financial hardship, the Lord Chancellor may reduce or remit the fee in that case.

9 Refunds

(1) Subject to sub-paragraph (3), where a party has not provided the documentary evidence required by paragraph 7 and a fee has been paid at a time when, under paragraphs 2, 3 or 4, it was not payable, the fee will be refunded if documentary evidence relating to the time when the fee became payable is provided at a later date.

(2) Subject to sub-paragraph (3), where a fee has been paid at a time where the Lord Chancellor, if all the circumstances had been known, would have reduced or remitted the fee under paragraph 8, the fee or the amount by which the fee would have been reduced, as the case may be, will be refunded.

(3) No refund will be made under this paragraph unless the party who paid the fee applies within 6 months of paying the fee.

(4) The Lord Chancellor may extend the period of 6 months mentioned in sub-paragraph (3) if the Lord Chancellor considers that there is a good reason for an application being made after the end of the period of 6 months.

10 Vexatious Litigants

(1) This paragraph applies where –

  (a) a restraint order is in force against a party; and
  (b) the party makes an application for permission to –
      (i)   issue proceedings or take a step in proceedings as required by the restraint order;
      (ii) apply for amendment or discharge of the order; or
      (iii) appeal the order.

(2) The fee prescribed for the application by Schedule 1 is payable in full.

(3) If the court grants the permission requested the applicant will be refunded the difference between –

  (a) the fee paid; and
  (b) the fee that would have been payable if this Schedule had been applied without reference to this paragraph.

Amendments—CRA 2005, Sch 11, para 1(2); SI 2009/1496.

****

Parental Responsibility Agreement Regulations 1991, SI 1991/1478

1 Citation, commencement and interpretation

(1) These regulations may be cited as the Parental Responsibility Agreement Regulations 1991 and shall come into force on 14 October 1991.

(2) In these Regulations, "the Principal Registry" means the principal registry of the Family Division of the High Court.

2 Form of parental responsibility agreement

A parental responsibility agreement –

  (a) under section 4(1)(b) of the Children Act 1989 (acquisition of parental responsibility by father), shall be made in form C(PRA1) set out in the Schedule to these Regulations;
  (b) under section 4A(1)(a) of that Act (acquisition of parental responsibility by step-parent), shall be made in form C(PRA2) set out in that Schedule; and
  (c) under section 4ZA(1)(b) of that Act (acquisition of parental responsibility by second female parent) shall be made in Form C(PRA3) set out in that Schedule.

Amendments—SI 2005/2808; SI 2009/2026.

Form of agreement—The prescribed form for the acquisition of parental responsibility by a father is C(PRA1), by a step-parent is C(PRA2) and by a second female parent is C(PRA3); they come with explanatory notes. As to evidence of identity, see further *Court Business* (June 1995), referred to at [1995] Fam Law 385, which also points out that, while the person who witnesses the signatures on Forms C(PRA1), C(PRA2) and C(PRA3) (who must be a justice of the peace, a justices' clerk or a court official who is authorised by the judge to administer oaths) need not be attached to a court *with family jurisdiction*, solicitors cannot witness the signatures because they are not officers of either the magistrates' courts or the county courts.

3 Recording of parental responsibility agreement

(1) A parental responsibility agreement shall be recorded by the filing of the agreement, together with sufficient copies for each person with parental responsibility for the child, in the Principal Registry.

(2) Upon the filing of documents under paragraph (1), an officer of the Principal Registry shall seal the copies and send one to each person with parental responsibility for the child.

(3) The record of an agreement under paragraph (1) shall be made available, during office hours, for inspection by any person upon –

(a) written request to an officer of the Principal Registry, and
(b) payment of such fee as may be prescribed in an Order under section 92 of the Courts Act 2003 (Fees).

Amendments—SI 2004/3123; SI 2005/2808.

Defined terms—"parental responsibility agreement": CA 1989, s 4(1)(b).

Scope—This regulation prescribes the method by which a parental responsibility agreement must be recorded. CA 1989, s 4(2) provides that, unless the regulations are complied with, the agreement is not valid for the purposes of CA 1989.

"payment of such fee as may be prescribed" (reg 3(3)(b))—The fee is prescribed by FPFO 2008, Sch 1, fee 6.2 and includes the cost of providing a copy of the agreement, if appropriate.

****

Parental Responsibility and Measures for the Protection of Children (International Obligations) (England and Wales and Northern Ireland) Regulations 2010, SI 2010/1898

1 Citation, commencement and extent

(1) These Regulations may be cited as the Parental Responsibility and Measures for the Protection of Children (International Obligations) (England and Wales and Northern Ireland) Regulations 2010.

(2) These Regulations come into force on the day on which the Convention enters into force for the United Kingdom, which date will be notified in the London, Edinburgh and Belfast Gazettes.

(3) These Regulations extend to England and Wales and Northern Ireland.

2 Interpretation

In these Regulations –

"Central Authority" has the meaning given by regulation 9(1);
"Contracting State" means a state party to the Convention;
"the Convention" means the Convention on Jurisdiction, Applicable Law, Recognition, Enforcement and Co-Operation in respect of Parental Responsibility and Measures for the Protection of Children that was signed at The Hague on 19 October 1996;

"the Council Regulation" means Council Regulation (EC) No 2201/2003 concerning jurisdiction and the recognition and enforcement of judgments in matrimonial matters and the matters of parental responsibility;

"Department of Justice" means the Department of Justice in Northern Ireland;

"local authority" means –

    (a)   in relation to England, the council of a county, a metropolitan district, the Council of the Isles of Scilly, a London borough or the Common Council of the City of London, and

    (b)   in relation to Wales, the council of a county or a county borough;

"member State" means a member State of the European Union which is bound by the Council Regulation;

"Northern Ireland authority' means an authority within the meaning given by Article 2(2) of the Children (Northern Ireland) Order 1995;

"public authority" means a body whose functions are wholly or mainly of a public nature;

"Welsh family proceedings officer" has the meaning given by section 35 of the Children Act 2004.

3 Power of court to remove stay under Article 8

(1) This regulation applies where –

    (a)   a court has exercised its power under Article 8 of the Convention to request an authority of another Contracting State to assume jurisdiction in relation to an application,

    (b)   the court has stayed proceedings on the application, and.

    (c)   Part 1 of the Family Law Act 1986 does not apply in relation to the application.

(2) The court may remove a stay granted in order for it to exercise its powers under Article 8 of the Convention, and withdraw any request made by it under that Article to an authority in another Contracting State to assume jurisdiction, if –

    (a)   the authority in the other Contracting State does not assume jurisdiction within the period for which the court granted the stay, or

    (b)   the parties do not, within the period specified by the court, request the authority in the other Contracting State to assume jurisdiction.

4 Local authorities and Northern Ireland authorities: application to court to make request under Article 9

(1) This regulation applies where –

    (a)   either –

        (i)   a local authority in England and Wales wishes to make an application in respect of a child under section 31 of the Children Act 1989 (care and supervision orders), or

        (ii)   a Northern Ireland authority wishes to make an application in respect of a child under Article 50 of the Children (Northern Ireland) Order 1995 (care and supervision orders), and

    (b)   the authorities of another Contracting State have jurisdiction in respect of the child under the Convention.

(2) The local authority or Northern Ireland authority must make an application to the High Court, requesting the court to exercise its power under Article 9 of the Convention (request to competent authority of the Contracting State of the habitual residence of the child for authorisation to exercise jurisdiction).

PART IV

5 Local authorities: application for interim care order or supervision order

(1) This regulation applies where –

   (a) a local authority in England and Wales thinks that the conditions in section 31(2)(a) and (b) of the Children Act 1989 (threshold for care and supervision orders) apply in relation to a child, and.

   (b) one of the following applies in relation to the child –

      (i) Article 11 of the Convention (measures of protection in cases of urgency),

      (ii) Article 12 of the Convention (measures of a provisional character), or

      (iii) Article 20 of the Council Regulation (provisional and protective measures).

(2) Where this regulation applies, section 38 of the Children Act 1989 (interim orders) has effect as if –

   (a) for subsection (1)(a) and (b) there were substituted –

     "(a) a local authority makes an application for an interim care order or interim supervision order in relation to a child, and.

     (b) one of the following applies in relation to the child –

      (i) Article 11 of the Convention on Jurisdiction, Applicable Law, Recognition, Enforcement and Co-Operation in respect of Parental Responsibility and Measures for the Protection of Children that was signed at The Hague on 19 October 1996 (measures of protection in cases of urgency) ('the Convention'),

      (ii) Article 12 of the Convention (measures of a provisional character), or

      (iii) Article 20 of Council Regulation (EC) No 2201/2003 concerning jurisdiction and the recognition and enforcement of judgments in matrimonial matters and the matters of parental responsibility (provisional and protective measures) ('the Council Regulation'),",

   (b) subsection (3) were omitted,

   (c) in subsection (4)(b) the words "in the same proceedings" were omitted, and

   (d) for subsection (4)(c) to (e) there were substituted –

     "(c) in a case which falls within subsection (1)(b)(i) or (ii), when –

      (i) the authorities in another Contracting State with jurisdiction under the Convention have taken the measures required by the situation, or

      (ii) measures taken by the authorities of another State are recognised in England and Wales;

     (d) in a case which falls within subsection (1)(b)(iii), when the court of the member State with jurisdiction under the Council Regulation has taken the measures it considers appropriate.".

(3) Where this regulation applies –

   (a) section 31 of the Children Act 1989 (care and supervision orders) has effect as if, in section 31(3A), after "care order" there were inserted the words ", other than an interim care order,"

   (b) section 31A of that Act (care plans) has effect as if subsection (5) were omitted, and

   (c) section 41 of that Act (representation of child's interests) has effect as if in subsection (6) there were included a reference to an application for an interim care order or interim supervision order by virtue of this regulation.

6 Northern Ireland authorities: application for interim care order or supervision order

(1) This regulation applies where –

(a) a Northern Ireland authority thinks that the conditions in Article 50(2)(a) and (b) of the Children (Northern Ireland) Order 1995 (threshold for care and supervision orders) are met, and

(b) one of the following applies in relation to the child –

    (i) Article 11 of the Convention (measures of protection in cases of urgency),

    (ii) Article 12 of the Convention (measures of a provisional character), or

    (iii) Article 20 of the Council Regulation (provisional and protective measures).

(2) Where this regulation applies, Article 57 of the Children (Northern Ireland) Order 1995 has effect as if –

(a) for paragraph (1)(a) and (b) there were substituted –

"(a) an authority makes an application for an interim care order or interim supervision order in relation to a child, and

(b) one of the following applies in relation to the child –

    (i) Article 11 of the Convention on Jurisdiction, Applicable Law, Recognition, Enforcement and Co-Operation in respect of Parental Responsibility and Measures for the Protection of Children that was signed at The Hague on 19 October 1996 (measures of protection in cases of urgency) ('the Convention'),

    (ii) Article 12 of the Convention (measures of a provisional character), or

    (iii) Article 20 of Council Regulation (EC) No. 2201/2003 concerning jurisdiction and the recognition and enforcement of judgments in matrimonial matters and the matters of parental responsibility (provisional and protective measures) ('the Council Regulation'),",

(b) paragraph (3) were omitted,

(c) in paragraph (4)(b) the words "in the same proceedings" were omitted, and

(d) for paragraph (4)(c) to (e) there were substituted –

"(c) in a case which falls within subsection (1)(b)(i) or (ii), when –

    (i) the authorities in another Contracting State with jurisdiction under the Convention have taken the measures required by the situation, or

    (ii) measures taken by the authorities of another State are recognised in Northern Ireland;

(d) in a case which falls within subsection (1)(b)(iii), when the court of the member State with jurisdiction under the Council Regulation has taken the measures it considers appropriate.".

(3) Where this regulation applies, Article 60 of the Children (Northern Ireland) Order 1995 (representation of child's interests) has effect as if in paragraph (6) there were included a reference to an application for an interim care order or interim supervision order by virtue of this regulation.

7 Application of Article 15

The reference to Chapter II of the Convention in Article 15(1) of the Convention is to be read as including a reference to Chapter II of the Council Regulation.

8 Judicial authorities

(1) The High Court has jurisdiction to entertain an application under Article 24 of the Convention for recognition, or non-recognition, of a measure taken in another Contracting State.

(2) But where the recognition or non-recognition of a measure is raised as an incidental question in another court, that court may determine the issue.

(3) The High Court is also to have jurisdiction –

PART IV

(a) to register a measure taken in another Contracting State for enforcement under Article 26 of the Convention, and

(b) to entertain an application for a declaration –

    (i)   that a person has, or does not have, parental responsibility for a child by virtue of Article 16 of the Convention, or

    (ii) as to the extent of a person's parental responsibility for a child by virtue of that Article.

9 Central authorities

(1) The functions under the Convention of a Central Authority are to be discharged –

(a) in England, by the Lord Chancellor,

(b) in Wales, by the Welsh Ministers, and

(c) in Northern Ireland, by the Department of Justice,

and a reference in these Regulations to a "Central Authority" means any of the Lord Chancellor, the Welsh Ministers or the Department of Justice in so far as they have functions under this regulation.

(2) If a person outside the United Kingdom does not know to which Central Authority in the United Kingdom a communication should be addressed, the person may address it to the Lord Chancellor.

10 Requests for information by Central Authority where request received under Article 31(c)

(1) Paragraphs (2), (3) and (4) apply if a Central Authority receives a request for assistance under Article 31(c) of the Convention (either directly or via another Central Authority in the United Kingdom).

(2) The Lord Chancellor may request information about the whereabouts of a child from –

(a) a local authority in England, or

(b) the Secretary of State.

(3) The Welsh Ministers may request information about the whereabouts of a child from –

(a) a local authority in Wales,

(b) a Local Health Board (within the meaning given by section 11 of the National Health Service (Wales) Act 2006), or

(c) an NHS Trust (within the meaning given by section 18 of that Act).

(4) The Department of Justice may request information about the whereabouts of a child from a public authority in Northern Ireland, but may do so only in circumstances where a requirement to provide information could be imposed on the public authority by an Act of the Northern Ireland Assembly without the consent of the Secretary of State (see sections 6 to 8 of the Northern Ireland Act 1998).

(5) A person (other than a court in Northern Ireland) who receives a request for information under this regulation must comply with the request as soon as reasonably practicable (but this is subject to paragraph (6)).

(6) Nothing in this regulation requires a person to disclose information if –

(a) Article 37 of the Convention applies, or

(b) the disclosure would constitute contempt of court or a criminal offence.

Parental Responsibility and Measures for the Protection of Children
(International Obligations) (England and Wales and Northern Ireland)
Regulations 2010 **reg 12**

(7) If a person who receives a request under this regulation thinks that it is desirable, in responding to the request, to refer to information the disclosure of which would constitute contempt of court, the person must notify the court.

(8) If a person who receives a request under this regulation thinks that it is desirable, in responding to the request, to refer to information the disclosure of which would constitute a criminal offence unless the disclosure were authorised by a court, the person must notify the court.

11 Requests for information under Council Regulation

(1) This regulation applies if the designated Central Authority in England and Wales under Article 53 of the Council Regulation receives a request for information from another member State under Article 55(a)(i) of the Council Regulation.

(2) The designated Central Authority in England and Wales may request information about the whereabouts of a child from –

    (a)   a local authority in England,
    (b)   a local authority in Wales,
    (c)   the Secretary of State,
    (d)   an officer of the Children and Family Court Advisory and Support Service,
    (e)   a Welsh family proceedings officer,
    (f)   a Local Health Board (within the meaning given by section 11 of the National Health Service (Wales) Act 2006), or
    (g)   an NHS Trust (within the meaning given by section 18 of that Act).

(3) The designated Central Authority in England and Wales may request a report on the situation of a child from –

    (a)   a local authority in England,
    (b)   a local authority in Wales,
    (c)   an officer of the Children and Family Court Advisory and Support Service, or
    (d)   a Welsh family proceedings officer.

(4) A person who receives a request for information under this regulation must comply with the request as soon as reasonably practicable (but this is subject to paragraph (5)).

(5) Nothing in this regulation requires a person to disclose information if the disclosure would constitute contempt of court or a criminal offence.

(6) If a person who receives a request under this regulation thinks that it is desirable, in responding to the request, to refer to information the disclosure of which would constitute contempt of court, the person must notify the court.

(7) If a person who receives a request under this regulation thinks that it is desirable, in responding to the request, to refer to information the disclosure of which would constitute a criminal offence unless the disclosure were authorised by a court, the person must notify the court.

12 Power to request report on child's situation

(1) This regulation applies where a Central Authority thinks it appropriate to provide a report on the situation of a child under Article 32(a) of the Convention.

(2) The Lord Chancellor may request a written report on the situation of the child from –

    (a)   a local authority in England, or
    (b)   an officer of the Children and Family Court Advisory and Support Service.

(3) The Welsh Ministers may request a written report on the situation of the child from –

    (a)   a local authority in Wales, or

PART IV

(b) a Welsh family proceedings officer.

(4) The Department of Justice may request a written report on the situation of the child from a public authority or other person in Northern Ireland, but may do so only in circumstances where a requirement to provide information could be imposed on the public authority or other person by an Act of the Northern Ireland Assembly without the consent of the Secretary of State (see sections 6 to 8 of the Northern Ireland Act 1998).

(5) A person in England and Wales or any public authority, other than a court, in Northern Ireland who receives a request for a report under this regulation must comply with the request as soon as reasonably practicable (but this is subject to paragraph (6)).

(6) Nothing in this regulation requires a person to disclose information if –

  (a) Article 37 of the Convention applies, or
  (b) the disclosure would constitute contempt of court or a criminal offence.

(7) If a person who receives a request under this regulation thinks that it is desirable, in responding to the request, to refer to information the disclosure of which would constitute contempt of court, the person must notify the court.

(8) If a person who receives a request under this regulation thinks that it is desirable, in responding to the request, to refer to information the disclosure of which would constitute a criminal offence unless the disclosure were authorised by a court, the person must notify the court.

13 Local authorities and Northern Ireland authorities: requirement to provide a report

(1) This regulation applies if a local authority in England and Wales or a Northern Ireland authority is contemplating –

  (a) placing a child in another Contracting State, within the meaning given by Article 33 of the Convention, or
  (b) placing a child in another member State, within the meaning given by Article 56 of the Council Regulation.

(2) Either the court or the local authority or Northern Ireland authority, whichever has jurisdiction under Articles 5 to 10 of the Convention or Articles 8 to 14 of the Council Regulation, as the case may be ("the authority") –

  (a) must provide a report to the Central Authority, or other competent authority, of the other Contracting State in accordance with Article 33(1) of the Convention, if the authority is exercising jurisdiction under the Convention, or
  (b) must consult the Central Authority, or other competent authority, of the other member State in accordance with Article 56 of the Council Regulation, if the authority is exercising jurisdiction under the Council Regulation.

14 Power to respond to a request under Article 34

A public authority in England and Wales or Northern Ireland may provide information in response to a request communicated to it by the Central Authority under Article 34 of the Convention.

15 Northern Ireland: power of court to authorise disclosure

If a court in Northern Ireland is satisfied that a disclosure of information relating to proceedings before a court sitting in private is for the purpose of enabling the Central Authority in Northern Ireland to exercise a function under the Convention –

  (a) the court may authorise the disclosure of the information, and.

(b) a disclosure authorised under paragraph (a) is not punishable as contempt of court.

16 Services under Article 35

(1) The Secretary of State may charge a reasonable fee in respect of the provision of a service under Article 35 (1) or (2) of the Convention.

(2) The Welsh Ministers may charge a reasonable fee in respect of the provision of a service under Article 35(1) or (2) of the Convention.

(3) The Department of Justice may charge a reasonable fee in respect of the provision of a service under Article 35(1) or (2) of the Convention.

(4) A request under Article 35(2) of the Convention is to be made –

(a) if the parent making the request resides in England and Wales, to the local authority in whose area the parent resides, and.

(b) if the parent making the request resides in Northern Ireland, to the Department of Justice.

(5) A local authority in England may charge a reasonable fee in respect of the provision of a service under Article 35(1) or (2) of the Convention.

(6) A local authority in Wales may charge a reasonable fee in respect of the provision of a service under Article 35(1) or (2) of the Convention.

(7) A fee is 'reasonable' for the purposes of this regulation if the income from fees of that kind equates as nearly as possible to the costs of providing the service to which the fees relate (including a reasonable share of expenditure which is referable only partly or only indirectly to the provision of that service).

17 Amendments to other enactments

The Schedule contains amendments to other enactments consequential on the entry into force of the Convention for the United Kingdom.

****

Pensions on Divorce etc (Provision of Information) Regulations 2000, SI 2000/1048

ARRANGEMENT OF REGULATIONS

PART IV

General Note—These regulations provide for the information that the pension arrangement must disclose (reg 2), specify the methodology for the valuation of pension benefits (reg 3), specify the information that the pension arrangement must provide once given notice that a pension sharing order may be made (reg 4), specify the information that both parties must give to a pension arrangement after a pension sharing order has been made before the four month implementation period can begin (reg 5) and the information that the pension arrangement must give after notice of a pension sharing or attachment order and after it has implemented the order (regs 7, 8 and 10).

When the Pension Protection Fund assumes responsibility for a pension scheme, reference should be made to the Pension Protection Fund (Provision of Information) Regulations 2005. See, further, annotations to MCA 1973, s 25E.

Where a pension compensation sharing order or a pension compensation attachment order is to be made against a pension arrangement for which the Pension Protection Fund has already assumed responsibility, the relevant corresponding regulations are the Pension Protection Fund (Pension Compensation Sharing and Attachment on Divorce etc) Regulations 2011.

Provision of information and valuation of shareable state scheme rights are dealt with in the Sharing of State Scheme Rights (Provision of Information and Valuation) (No 2) Regulations 2000 below.

1 Citation, commencement and interpretation

(1) These Regulations may be cited as the Pensions on Divorce etc (Provision of Information) Regulations 2000 and shall come into force on 1 December 2000.

(2) In these Regulations –

"the 1993 Act" means the Pension Schemes Act 1993;

"the 1995 Act" means the Pensions Act 1995;

"the 1999 Act" means the Welfare Reform and Pensions Act 1999;

"the Charging Regulations" means the Pensions on Divorce etc (Charging) Regulations 2000;

"the Implementation and Discharge of Liability Regulations" means the Pension Sharing (Implementation and Discharge of Liability) Regulations 2000;

"the Valuation Regulations" means the Pension Sharing (Valuation) Regulations 2000;

"active member" has the meaning given by section 124(1) of the 1995 Act;

"day" means any day other than –

    (a) Christmas Day or Good Friday; or

    (b) a bank holiday, that is to say, a day which is, or is to be observed as, a bank holiday or a holiday under Schedule 1 to the Banking and Financial Dealings Act 1971;

"deferred member" has the meaning given by section 124(1) of the 1995 Act;

"implementation period" has the meaning given by section 34(1) of the 1999 Act;

"member" means a person who has rights to future benefits, or has rights to benefits payable, under a pension arrangement;

"money purchase benefits" has the meaning given by section 181(1) of the 1993 Act;

"normal benefit age" has the meaning given by section 101B of the 1993 Act;

"normal pension age" has the meaning given in section 180 of the 1993 Act (normal pension age);

"notice of discharge of liability" means a notice issued to the member and his former spouse or former civil partner by the person responsible for a pension arrangement when that person has discharged his liability in respect of a pension credit in accordance with Schedule 5 to the 1999 Act;

"notice of implementation" means a notice issued by the person responsible for a pension arrangement to the member and his former spouse or former civil partner at the beginning of the implementation period notifying them of the day on which the implementation period for the pension credit begins;

"occupational pension scheme" has the meaning given by section 1 of the 1993 Act;

"the party with pension rights" and "the other party" have the meanings given by section 25D(3) of the Matrimonial Causes Act 1997;

"pension arrangement" has the meaning given in section 46(1) of the 1999 Act;

"pension credit" means a credit under section 29(1)(b) of the 1999 Act;

"pension credit benefit" means the benefits payable under a pension arrangement or a qualifying arrangement to or in respect of a person by virtue of rights under the arrangement in question which are attributable (directly or indirectly) to a pension credit;

"pension credit rights" means rights to future benefits under a pension arrangement or a qualifying arrangement which are attributable (directly or indirectly) to a pension credit;

"pension sharing order or provision" means an order or provision which is mentioned in section 28(1) of the 1999 Act;

"pensionable service" has the meaning given by section 124(1) of the 1995 Act;

"person responsible for a pension arrangement" has the meaning given by section 46(2) of the 1999 Act;

"personal pension scheme" has the meaning given by section 1 of the 1993 Act;

"qualifying arrangement" has the meaning given by paragraph 6 of Schedule 5 to the 1999 Act;

"retirement annuity contract" means a contract or scheme approved under Chapter III of Part XIV of the Income and Corporation Taxes Act 1988;

"salary related occupational pension scheme" has the meaning given by regulation 1A of the Transfer Values Regulations;

"transfer day" has the meaning given by section 29(8) of the 1999 Act;

"the Transfer Values Regulations" means the Occupational Pension Schemes (Transfer Values) Regulations 1996;

"transferee" has the meaning given by section 29(8) of the 1999 Act;

"transferor" has the meaning given by section 29(8) of the 1999 Act.

"trustees or managers" has the meaning given by section 46(1) of the 1999 Act.

Amendments—SI 2000/269 ; SI 2005/2877; SI 2007/60; SI 2008/1050; SI 2009/615.

2 Basic information about pensions and divorce or dissolution of a civil partnership

(1) The requirements imposed on a person responsible for a pension arrangement for the purposes of section 23(1)(a) of the 1999 Act (supply of pension information in connection with divorce etc) are that he shall furnish –

(a) on request from a member, the information referred to in paragraphs (2) and (3)(b) to (f);

(b) on request from the spouse or civil partner of a member, the information referred to in paragraph (3); or

(c) pursuant to an order of the court, the information referred to in paragraph (2), (3) or (4),

to the member, the spouse or civil partner of the member, or, as the case may be, to the court.

(2) The information in this paragraph is a valuation of pension rights or benefits accrued under that member's pension arrangement.

(3) The information in this paragraph is –

(a) a statement that on request from the member, or pursuant to an order of the court, a valuation of pension rights or benefits accrued under that member's pension arrangement, will be provided to the member, or, as the case may be, to the court;

(b)   a statement summarising the way in which the valuation referred to in paragraph (2) and sub-paragraph (a) is calculated;

(c)   the pension benefits which are included in a valuation referred to in paragraph (2) and sub-paragraph (a);

(d)   whether the person responsible for the pension arrangement offers membership to a person entitled to a pension credit, and if so, the types of benefits available to pension credit members under that arrangement;

(e)   whether the person responsible for the pension arrangements intends to discharge his liability for a pension credit other than by offering membership to a person entitled to a pension credit; and

(f)   the schedule of charges which the person responsible for the pension arrangement will levy in accordance with regulation 2(2) of the Charging Regulations (general requirements as to charges).

(4) The information in this paragraph is any other information relevant to any power with respect to the matters specified in section 23(1)(a) of the 1999 Act and which is not specified in Schedule 1 or 2 to the Occupational Pension Schemes (Disclosure of Information) Regulations 1996 (basic information about the scheme and information to be made available to individuals), or in Schedule 1 or 2 to the Personal Pension Schemes (Disclosure of Information) Regulations 1987 (basic information about the scheme and information to be made available to individuals), in a case where either of those Regulations applies.

(5) Where the member's request for, or the court order for the provision of, information includes a request for, or an order for the provision of, a valuation under paragraph (2), the person responsible for the pension arrangement shall furnish all the information requested, or ordered, to the member –

(a)   within 3 months beginning with the date the person responsible for the pension arrangement receives that request or order for the provision of the information;

(b)   within 6 weeks beginning with the date the person responsible for the pension arrangement receives the request, or order, for the provision of the information, if the member has notified that person on the date of the request or order that the information is needed in connection with proceedings commenced under any of the provisions referred to in section 23(1)(a) of the 1999 Act; or

(c)   within such shorter period specified by the court in an order requiring the person responsible for the pension arrangement to provide a valuation in accordance with paragraph (2).

(6) Where –

(a)   the member's request for, or the court order for the provision of, information does not include a request or an order for a valuation under paragraph (2); or

(b)   the member's spouse or civil partner requests the information specified in paragraph (3),

the person responsible for the pension arrangement shall furnish that information to the member, his spouse, civil partner, or the court, as the case may be, within one month beginning with the date that person responsible for the pension arrangement receives the request for, or the court order for the provision of, the information.

(7) At the same time as furnishing the information referred to in paragraph (1), the person responsible for a pension arrangement may furnish the information specified in regulation 4(2) (provision of information in response to a notification that a pension sharing order or provision may be made).

Amendments—SI 2005/2877.

Scope—This regulation specifies the information to be furnished by a pension arrangement on request from a member or the spouse/civil partner of a member or pursuant to a court order. All requests for information as to valuation must be made by the member, but the court may intervene to order the provision of a valuation to the non-member spouse/civil partner and may order a pension arrangement to supply "any other information relevant to any power with respect to the matters specified in WRPA 1999, s 23(1)(a) [financial relief under MCA 1973, Pt II]" (reg 2(4)). Regulation 2(5) and (6) sets out the time limits for provision of the requested or ordered information.

A charge may be made for the basic information requested or ordered under reg 2 (Pensions on Divorce etc (Charging) Regulations 2000, reg 3(1)). However, a charge will not be made for basic information under reg 2(2) and (3), including a valuation where there has been no valuation supplied within the previous 12 months (unless the information is required in less than 3 months of the date of request/order or the member has reached normal retirement age on or before the date of the request or the court order for the provision of the information or is due to reach normal retirement age within 12 months of such date) (Pensions on Divorce etc (Charging) Regulations 2000, reg 3(2)). A pension arrangement is not able to recover charges when a pension sharing order is made, unless a schedule of charges is provided as part of the basic information under reg 2 (Pensions on Divorce etc (Charging) Regulations 2000, reg 2). It is permissible for a pension arrangement to postpone implementation until its charges have been paid (WRPA 1999, s 41(2)(a); Pensions on Divorce etc (Charging) Regulations 2000, reg 7). In certain circumstances, a pension arrangement is allowed to deduct the costs directly from the pension credit (or, on an internal transfer, from the transferee's pension credit benefits), from the accrued rights of the member, from the calculation of a transfer value or, if the pension is in payment, from the member's pension benefits (WRPA 1999, s 38(2)(c); Pensions on Divorce etc (Charging) Regulations 2000, reg 9). Alternatively, the parties may pay in cash if they prefer. Pension arrangements are permitted to insist on payment before providing certain information for which a charge may be made, unless the information is sought pursuant to a court order (Pensions on Divorce etc (Charging) Regulations 2000, reg 4(1)(b)).

3 Information about pensions and divorce and dissolution of a civil partnership: valuation of pension benefits

(1) Where an application for financial relief under any of the provisions referred to in section 23(a)(i),(ia),(iii) or (iv) of the 1999 Act (supply of pension information in connection with domestic and overseas divorce etc in England and Wales and corresponding Northern Ireland powers) has been made or is in contemplation, the valuation of benefits under a pension arrangement shall be calculated and verified for the purposes of regulation 2 of these Regulations in accordance with –

    (a)   paragraph (3), if the person with pension rights is a deferred member of an occupational pension scheme;

    (b)   paragraph (4), if the person with pension rights is an active member of an occupational pension scheme;

    (c)   paragraphs (5) and (6), if –

        (i)   the person with pension rights is a member of a personal pension scheme; or

        (ii)   those pension rights are contained in a retirement annuity contract; or

    (d)   paragraphs (7) and (8) if –

        (i)   the pension of the person with pension rights is in payment;

        (ii)   the rights of the person with pension rights are contained in an annuity contract other than a retirement annuity contract; or

        (iii)   the rights of the person with pension rights are contained in a deferred annuity contract other than a retirement annuity contract; or

        (iv)   the pension of the person with pension rights is not in payment and the person has attained normal pension age.

(2) Where an application for financial provision under any of the provisions referred to in section 23(1)(a)(ii) of the 1999 Act (corresponding Scottish powers) has been made, or is in contemplation, the valuation of benefits under a pension arrangement shall be

PART IV

calculated and verified for the purposes of regulation 2 of these Regulations in accordance with regulation 3 of the Divorce etc (Pensions) (Scotland) Regulations 2000 (valuation).

(3) Where the person with pension rights is a deferred member of an occupational pension scheme, the value of the benefits which he has under that scheme shall be taken to be –

    (a)   in the case of an occupational pension scheme other than a salary related scheme, the cash equivalent to which he acquired a right under section 94(1)(a) of the 1993 Act (right to cash equivalent) on the termination of his pensionable service, calculated on the assumption that he has made an application under section 95 of that Act (ways of taking right to cash equivalent) on the date on which the request for the valuation was received; or

    (b)   in the case of a salary related occupational pension scheme, the guaranteed cash equivalent to which he would have acquired a right under section 94(1)(aa) of the 1993 Act if he had made an application under section 95(1) of that Act, calculated on the assumption that he has made such an application on the date on which the request for the valuation was received.

(4) Where the person with pension rights is an active member of an occupational pension scheme, the valuation of the benefits which he has accrued under that scheme shall be calculated and verified –

    (a)   on the assumption that the member had made a request for an estimate of the cash equivalent that would be available to him were his pensionable service to terminate on the date on which the request for the valuation was received; and

    (b)   in accordance with regulation 11 of, and Schedule 1 to, the Transfer Values Regulations (disclosure).

(5) Where the person with pension rights is a member of a personal pension scheme, or those rights are contained in a retirement annuity contract, the value of the benefits which he has under that scheme or contract shall be taken to be the cash equivalent to which he would have acquired a right under section 94(1)(b) of the 1993 Act, if he had made an application under section 95(1) of that Act on the date on which the request for the valuation was received.

(6) In relation to a personal pension scheme which is comprised in a retirement annuity contract made before 4 January 1988, paragraph (5) shall apply as if such a scheme were not excluded from the scope of Chapter IV of Part IV of the 1993 Act by section 93(1)(b) of that Act (scope of Chapter IV).

(7) Cash equivalents are to be calculated and verified in accordance with regulations 7 to 7C and 7E(1) to (3) of the Transfer Values Regulations as appropriate.

(8) But when calculating and verifying a cash equivalent in accordance with those regulations –

    (a)   references to "trustees" must be read as references to "person responsible for the pension arrangement";

    (b)   where the person with pension rights is a pensioner member on the date on which the request for the valuation is received, the value of his pension must be calculated and verified in accordance with regulations 7 to 7E of the Transfer Values Regulations as appropriate;

    (c)   where the person is over normal pension age but not in receipt of a pension –

        (i)   the value of his pension must be calculated and verified in accordance with regulations 7 to 7E of the Transfer Values Regulations as appropriate; and

       (ii)   the person responsible for the pension arrangement must assume that the pension came into payment on the date on which the request for the valuation was received; and

   (d)   the date by reference to which the cash equivalent is to be calculated and verified is to be the date on which the request for the valuation was received.

(9) (*revoked*)

(10) Where paragraph (3), (4) or (7) has effect by reference to provisions of Chapter IV of Part IV of the 1993 Act, section 93(1)(a)(i) of that Act (scope of Chapter IV) shall apply to those provisions as if the words "at least one year" had been omitted from section 93(1)(a)(i).

Amendments—SI 2005/2877; SI 2007/60; SI 2008/1050.

Scope—By a combination of this regulation and the Divorce (Pensions) Regulations 2000, reg 3, the valuation methodology prescribed is the Cash Equivalent (CE) in all cases (except pension schemes administered overseas), adopting the highly technical formulae of this regulation. All these technical formulae have in common the fact that they are founded on taking the value of the pension rights in today's terms on the basis that the member left service at the time of the valuation. Thus, no account is taken of future service. This regulation was significantly amended by the Occupational Pension Schemes (Transfer Values) (Amendment) Regulations 2008 ("the Amendment Regulations"). These amendments came into effect on 1 October 2008. As a result, the term Cash Equivalent Transfer Value (CETV) has been abandoned and there is no longer a separate valuation methodology for pensions in payment (formerly the Cash Equivalent of Benefits (CEB) as discussed in *Martin-Dye v Martin-Dye* [2006] 2 FLR 901, CA). Further, the Amendment Regulations introduced a new valuation category, namely, the pension rights not in payment of a person who has attained normal pension age, whose rights are to be calculated on the assumption that the pension came into payment on the date on which the valuation request was received and the Cash Equivalent is to be calculated also by reference to that date (reg 3(1)(d)(iv) and (8)(c) and (d)).

    Under the Amendment Regulations, the responsibility for the calculation of transfer values passed from scheme actuaries to scheme trustees. The mandatory Guidance Note (GN11) (referred to in reg 3(8) as originally drafted), formerly used by the actuarial profession to calculate transfer values, ceased to have effect on 1 October 2008 and the framework for transfer value calculations, adopting a scheme specific approach, is set out in the Amendment Regulations. The scheme specific approach is based on the anticipated cost to the scheme of providing alternative deferred benefits had the member remained in the scheme rather than transferring out. It enables scheme trustees to use assumptions in values that reflect the funding position of the specific scheme. The Pensions Regulator has published guidance for trustees on the operation of the Amendment Regulations (*www.thepensionsregulator.gov.uk/guidance/guidance-transfer-values.aspx*).

    The effect of the Amendment Regulations in a family law context is, broadly, as follows:

(i)   reference should be made to the Cash Equivalent (CE) rather than to the Cash Equivalent Transfer Value (CETV);

(ii)   there is no longer a separate valuation methodology for pensions in payment, formerly referred to as the Cash Equivalent of Benefits (CEB);

(iii)   regulation 3(1)(d)(iv) introduced a new valuation category: persons with pension rights not in payment where the person has attained normal pension age;

(iv)   trustees are responsible on a scheme specific basis for the calculation, which should use "best estimate" (or more cautious) assumptions based upon actuarial advice;

(v)   it is still possible to reduce transfer values if the scheme does not have sufficient assets to pay all transfer values in full, provided an insufficiency report has been prepared by the scheme actuary;

(vi)   there is no longer any equivalence in the valuation methodology used for the valuation of pension benefits contained in this regulation and in the methodology used to calculate the value of a pension credit for implementation purposes under the Pension Sharing (Implementation and Discharge of Liability) Regulations 2000, reg 10 which has itself been amended by the Amendment Regulations. Whereas formerly (before the Amendment Regulations) schemes were required to use the same basis for calculating the value of the former spouse's pension credit as they used for valuing the member's pension debit, there is no longer equivalence of treatment between pension credits and pension debits because the substituted reg 10 requires schemes to value pension credits "in a manner which is consistent with the methods adopted and assumptions made when transfers of other pension rights are received by the person responsible for the pension arrangement", ie using a transfer in methodology;

The satellite regulations to pension sharing are silent as to whether other evidence can be led as to the true value of the CE in such cases. It is submitted that it is nevertheless permissible (subject to proportionality) to lead expert evidence (subject to FPR, Pt 25) on the issue of what any given sharing or attachment would provide for each of the parties or where it is argued that the CE is an inadequate or inappropriate valuation methodology (*Martin-Dye v Martin-Dye* (above)). It was held in *BJ v MJ (Financial Order: Overseas Trust)* [2012] 1 FLR 667 at [75] that such projections should not be based upon the purchase of an annuity.

The CE is a calculation of the transfer value at the current time of the total of the following elements in a pension scheme:

(i) the member's pension at retirement;
(ii) the lump sum benefit payable on death after leaving active membership of the scheme, but before retirement;
(iii) the lump sum payable on retirement;
(iv) the lump sum payable on death after retirement; and
(v) the spouse's pension payable either on the member's death after leaving active membership of the scheme but before retirement or after the member's retirement.

The CE therefore does *not* include:

(i) any lump sum payable if the member died in service (which in many public service and company pension schemes is substantial);
(ii) the spouse's pension payable if the member died in service; and
(iii) future expectations based upon future salary increases and future pensionable service.

The CE may or may not include discretionary benefits, which usually relate to generous early retirement terms or increases in pensions in payment.

It is necessary to have regard when valuing a pension to the special characteristics of pension funds: present capital should not be confused with financial benefits on retirement, only part of which can be taken as a tax-free lump sum (*Cowan v Cowan* [2001] 2 FLR 192, CA; *Maskell v Maskell* [2003] 1 FLR 1138, CA; *F v F (Clean Break: Balance of Fairness)* [2003] 1 FLR 847; *Martin-Dye v Martin-Dye* (above); *Vaughan v Vaughan* [2008] 1 FLR 1108, CA). Attempts to discount the CE have so far failed (*Norris v Norris* [2003] 1 FLR 1142: fund not yet vested; *GW v RW (Financial Provision: Departure From Equality)* [2003] 2 FLR 108: discount for taxation declined).

A number of factors may lead to a cash equivalent not providing an adequate indication of value. These include scheme under-funding, the impact of market value adjusters and guaranteed annuity rates, the member's health and the fact that the member is close to retirement. Furthermore, there are particular valuation issues affecting several public sector pension schemes. All of these issues point to the need to obtain expert actuarial advice, where it is proportionate to do so. An adequate indication of value in a cash equivalent is to be distinguished from an actuarial or computer error in its calculation (*Clark v Cabinet Office and Paymaster* (1836) Limited (2007) 19 November, ref R00408, Pensions Ombudsman; *Brown v British Airways Pension Trustees Limited* (2012), 13 January, ref 83320/1, Deputy Pensions Ombudsman).

It is a convenient practice to include in a spreadsheet, underneath the total value of other capital, the capital value of pension rights, then arriving at a grand total (*Vaughan v Vaughan* (above) at [25]).

For a consideration of the effect of early retirement on the calculation of a CE, see *Slattery v Cabinet Office (Civil Service Pensions) and another* [2009] 1 FLR 1365.

4 Provision of information in response to a notification that a pension sharing order or provision may be made

(1) A person responsible for a pension arrangement shall furnish the information specified in paragraph (2) to the member or to the court, as the case may be –

(a) within 21 days beginning with the date that the person responsible for the pension arrangement received the notification that a pension sharing order or provision may be made; or

(b) if the court has specified a date which is outside the 21 days referred to in sub-paragraph (a), by that date.

(2) The information referred to in paragraph (1) is –

(a) the full name of the pension arrangement and address to which any order or provision referred to in section 28(1) of the 1999 Act (activation of pension sharing) should be sent;

(b)   in the case of an occupational pension scheme, whether the scheme is winding up, and, if so, –
    (i)   the date on which the winding up commenced; and
    (ii)   the name and address of the trustees who are dealing with the winding up;

(c)   in the case of an occupational pension scheme, whether a cash equivalent of the member's pension rights, if calculated on the date the notification referred to in paragraph (1)(a) was received by the trustees or managers of that scheme, would be reduced in accordance with the provisions of paragraphs 2,3 and 12 of Schedule 1A to the Transfer Values Regulations (reductions in initial cash equivalents);

(d)   whether the person responsible for the pension arrangement is aware that the member's rights under the pension arrangement are subject to any, and if so, to specify which, of the following –
    (i)   any order or provision specified in section 28(1) of the 1999 Act;
    (ii)   an order under section 23 of the Matrimonial Causes Act 1973 (financial provision orders in connection with divorce etc.), so far as it includes provision made by virtue of section 25B or 25C of that Act (powers to include provisions about pensions);
    (iii)   an order under section 12A(2) or (3) of the Family Law (Scotland) Act 1985 (powers in relation to pensions lump sums when making a capital sum order) which relates to benefits or future benefits to which the member is entitled under the pension arrangement;
    (iv)   an order under Article 25 of the Matrimonial Causes (Northern Ireland) Order 1978, so far as it includes provision made by virtue of Article 27B or 27C of that Order (Northern Ireland powers corresponding to those mentioned in paragraph (2)(d)(ii));
    (v)   a forfeiture order;
    (vi)   a bankruptcy order;
    (vii)   an award of sequestration on a member's estate or the making of the appointment on his estate of a judicial factor under section 41 of the Solicitors (Scotland) Act 1980 (appointment of judicial factor);

(e)   whether the member's rights under the pension arrangement include rights specified in regulation 2 of the Valuation Regulations (rights under a pension arrangement which are not shareable);

(f)   if the person responsible for the pension arrangement has not at an earlier stage provided the following information, whether that person requires the charges specified in regulation 3 (charges recoverable in respect of the provision of basic information), 5 (charges in respect of pension sharing activity), or 6 (additional amounts recoverable in respect of pension sharing activity) of the Charging Regulations to be paid before the commencement of the implementation period, and if so –
    (i)   whether that person requires those charges to be paid in full; or
    (ii)   the proportion of those charges which he requires to be paid;

(g)   whether the person responsible for the pension arrangement may levy additional charges specified in regulation 6 of the Charging Regulations, and if so, the scale of the additional charges which are likely to be made;

(h)   whether the member is a trustee of the pension arrangement;

(i)   whether the person responsible for the pension arrangement may request information about the member's state of health from the member if a pension sharing order or provision were to be made;

(j)   ...

(k)   whether the person responsible for the pension arrangement requires information additional to that specified in regulation 5 (information required by

the person responsible for the pension arrangement before the implementation
period may begin) in order to implement the pension sharing order or provision.

Amendments—SI 2000/2691; SI 2003/1727; SI 2008/1050.

Scope—This regulation sets out the information which a pension arrangement must furnish following
notification that a pension sharing order may be made, which will indicate whether the pension
arrangement is one in relation to which a pension sharing order may be made. It should be noted that the
pension sharing annex (Form P1) Pt E incorporates a certificate that the parties have received this
information attached to Form P (Pension Inquiry Form) and that it appears from that information that
there is power to make a pension sharing order (FPR 2010, r 9.35).

"notification that a pension sharing order ... may be made" (reg 4(1)(a))—It is submitted that
'notification' includes either formal service of Form A or prior informal notification by letter. In many
instances, Form A will not specify the terms of the order requested because the requisite information will
not be available at the time of issue. In such circumstances, this information will need to be added to
Form A at the First Appointment as suggested by FPR 2010, r 9.31, when a direction may be made for the
completion of Form P, Pt C of which seeks the information required by this regulation.

5 Information required by the person responsible for the pension arrangement before the implementation period may begin

The information prescribed for the purposes of section 34(1)(b) of the 1999 Act
(information relating to the transferor and the transferee which the person responsible for
the pension arrangement must receive) is –

(a) in relation to the transferor –
   (i) all names by which the transferor has been known;
   (ii) date of birth;
   (iii) address;
   (iv) National Insurance number;
   (v) the name of the pension arrangement to which the pension sharing order or provision relates; and
   (vi) the transferor's membership or policy number in that pension arrangement;
(b) in relation to the transferee –
   (i) all names by which the transferee has been known;
   (ii) date of birth;
   (iii) address;
   (iv) National Insurance number; and
   (v) if the transferee is a member of the pension arrangement from which the pension credit is derived, his membership or policy number in that pension arrangement;
(c) where the transferee has given his consent in accordance with paragraph 1(3)(c), 3(3)(c) or 4(2)(c) of Schedule 5 to the 1999 Act (mode of discharge of liability for a pension credit) to the payment of the pension credit to the person responsible for a qualifying arrangement –
   (i) the full name of that qualifying arrangement;
   (ii) its address;
   (iii) if known, the transferee's membership number or policy number in that arrangement; and
   (iv) the name or title, business address, business telephone number, and, where available, the business facsimile number and electronic mail address of a person who may be contacted in respect of the discharge of liability for the pension credit;
(d) where the rights from which the pension credit is derived are held in an occupational pension scheme which is being wound up, whether the transferee has given an indication whether he wishes to transfer his pension credit rights

which may have been reduced in accordance with the provisions of regulation 16(1) of the Implementation and Discharge of Liability Regulations (adjustments to the amount of the pension credit – occupational pension schemes which are underfunded on the valuation day) to a qualifying arrangement; and

(e) any information requested by the person responsible for the pension arrangement in accordance with regulation 4(2)(i) or (k).

Scope—This regulation sets out the specific information required by a pension arrangement in order to implement a pension sharing order about the parties and the destination arrangement for the pension credit. The 4-month implementation period will only begin on the later of the day on which the pension sharing order takes effect (MCA 1973, ss 24B(2), 24C(1)) and the day on which the pension arrangement receives the pension sharing order and decree absolute as well as the information under this regulation (WRPA 1999, s 34(1)). The 4-month implementation period is a maximum period; unnecessary delays within that period by a pension arrangement may give rise to an award of compensation by the Pensions Ombudsman (*Boughton v Punter Southall* (2009) 22 September, ref 74851/1, Pensions Ombudsman).

6 Provision of information after the death of the person entitled to the pension credit before liability in respect of the pension credit has been discharged

(1) Where the person entitled to the pension credit dies before the person responsible for the pension arrangement has discharged his liability in respect of the pension credit, the person responsible for the pension arrangement shall, within 21 days of the date of receipt of the notification of the death of the person entitled to the pension credit, notify in writing any person whom the person responsible for the pension arrangement considers should be notified of the matters specified in paragraph (2).

(2) The matters specified in this paragraph are –

(a) how the person responsible for the pension arrangement intends to discharge his liability in respect of the pension credit;

(b) whether the person responsible for the pension arrangement intends to recover charges from the person nominated to receive pension credit benefits, in accordance with regulations 2 to 9 of the Charging Regulations, and if so, a copy of the schedule of charges issued to the parties to pension sharing in accordance with regulation 2(2)(b) of the Charging Regulations (general requirements as to charges); and

(c) a list of any further information which the person responsible for the pension arrangement requires in order to discharge his liability in respect of the pension credit.

Amendments—SI 2000/269.

Scope—A pension sharing order is not affected by the death of either party, although an application for leave to appeal out of time might be made. If an application for leave is successful, one course might be an appeal under MCA 1973, s 40A or 40B. This assumes that the original pension sharing order has been implemented in full. If, however, it has not and the person entitled to the pension credit dies before the liability for the pension credit has been discharged, WRPA 1999, s 35(2) and the Pension Sharing (Implementation and Discharge of Liability) Regulations 2000, reg 6 prescribes how the liability is to be discharged. The Finance Act 2006, Sch 23, para 2 provides that, if a person dies having become entitled to pension credits but without having rights attributable to them, the person is to be treated as having acquired, immediately before the death, the rights by virtue of which the liability in respect of the pension credits is subsequently discharged. In this rare situation, the pension arrangement has full discretion to discharge its liability in accordance with appropriately drafted scheme rules subject to HMRC limits in favour of "one or more persons". Arguably, this expression could include the pension scheme member. In some cases, the discharge of liability will be effected by a lump sum payment; in others by payment of a pension or both a pension and a lump sum. Pension arrangements may discharge their liability by entering into an annuity contract and/or an insurance contract to provide benefits for survivors. If the scheme rules do not make provision for payments of the type mentioned, the pension credit will be retained by the pension arrangement from which it was derived (Pension Sharing (Implementation and Discharge of Liability) Regulations 2000, reg 6(4)). If the transferee would have become entitled to a personal pension, the amount of the pension credit may be paid into the deceased transferee's estate. For all of these reasons, the pension sharing order could be expressed only to take effect in the event of the transferee not predeceasing the transferor, where this is considered appropriate.

7 Provision of information after receiving a pension sharing order or provision

(1) A person responsible for a pension arrangement who is in receipt of a pension sharing order or provision relating to that arrangement shall provide in writing to the transferor and transferee, or, where regulation 6(1) applies, to the person other than the person entitled to the pension credit referred to in regulation 6 of the Implementation and Discharge of Liability Regulations (discharge of liability in respect of a pension credit following the death of the person entitled to the pension credit), as the case may be –

  (a)   a notice in accordance with the provisions of regulation 7(1) of the Charging Regulations (charges in respect of pension sharing activity – postponement of implementation period);
  (b)   a list of information relating to the transferor or the transferee, or, where regulation 6(1) applies, the person other than the person entitled to the pension credit referred to in regulation 6 of the Implementation and Discharge of Liability Regulations, as the case may be, which –
    (i)   has been requested in accordance with regulation 4(2)(i) and (k), or, where appropriate, 6(2)(c), or should have been provided in accordance with regulation 5;
    (ii)   the person responsible for the pension arrangement considers he needs in order to begin to implement the pension sharing order or provision; and
    (iii) remains outstanding;
  (c)   a notice of implementation; or
  (d)   a statement by the person responsible for the pension arrangement explaining why he is unable to implement the pension sharing order or agreement.

(2) The information specified in paragraph (1) shall be furnished in accordance with that paragraph within 21 days beginning with –

  (a)   in the case of sub-paragraph (a), (b) or (d) of that paragraph, the day on which the person responsible for the pension arrangement receives the pension sharing order or provision; or
  (b)   in the case of sub-paragraph (c) of that paragraph, the later of the days specified in section 34(1)(a) and (b) of the 1999 Act (implementation period).

Scope—This regulation sets out the information which the pension arrangement must provide to the parties after a pension sharing order has been made, but before implementation commences.

8 Provision of information after the implementation of a pension sharing order or provision

(1) The person responsible for the pension arrangement shall issue a notice of discharge of liability to the transferor and the transferee, or, as the case may be, the person entitled to the pension credit by virtue of regulation 6 of the Implementation and Discharge of Liability Regulations no later than the end of the period of 21 days beginning with the day on which the discharge of liability in respect of the pension credit is completed.

(2) In the case of a transferor whose pension is not in payment, the notice of discharge of liability shall include the following details –

  (a)   the value of the transferor's accrued rights as determined by reference to the cash equivalent value of those rights calculated and verified in accordance with regulation 3 of the Valuation Regulations (calculation and verification of cash equivalents for the purposes of the creation of pension debits and credits);

(b)   the value of the pension debit;

(c)   any amount deducted from the value of the pension rights in accordance with regulation 9(2)(c) of the Charging Regulations (charges in respect of pension sharing activity – method of recovery);

(d)   the value of the transferor's rights after the amounts referred to in sub-paragraphs (b) and (c) have been deducted; and

(e)   the transfer day.

(3) In the case of a transferor whose pension is in payment, the notice of discharge of liability shall include the following details –

(a)   the value of the transferor's benefits under the pension arrangement as determined by reference to the cash equivalent value of those rights calculated and verified in accordance with regulation 3 of the Valuation Regulations;

(b)   the value of the pension debit;

(c)   the amount of the pension which was in payment before liability in respect of the pension credit was discharged;

(d)   the amount of pension which is payable following the deduction of the pension debit from the transferor's pension benefits;

(e)   the transfer day;

(f)   if the person responsible for the pension arrangement intends to recover charges, the amount of any unpaid charges –

(i)   not prohibited by regulation 2 of the Charging Regulations (general requirements as to charges); and

(ii)   specified in regulations 3 and 6 of those Regulations;

(g)   how the person responsible for the pension arrangement will recover the charges referred to in sub-paragraph (f), including –

(i)   whether the method of recovery specified in regulation 9(2)(d) of the Charging Regulations will be used;

(ii)   the date when payment of those charges in whole or in part is required; and

(iii)   the sum which will be payable by the transferor, or which will be deducted from his pension benefits, on that date.

(4) In the case of a transferee –

(a)   whose pension is not in payment; and

(b)   who will become a member of the pension arrangement from which the pension credit rights were derived,

the notice of discharge of liability to the transferee shall include the following details –

(i)   the value of the pension credit;

(ii)   any amount deducted from the value of the pension credit in accordance with regulation 9(2)(b) of the Charging Regulations;

(iii)   the value of the pension credit after the amount referred to in sub-paragraph (b)(ii) has been deducted;

(iv)   the transfer day;

(v)   any periodical charges the person responsible for the pension arrangement intends to make, including how and when those charges will be recovered from the transferee; and

(vi)   information concerning membership of the pension arrangement which is relevant to the transferee as a pension credit member.

PART IV

(5) In the case of a transferee who is transferring his pension credit rights out of the pension arrangement from which those rights were derived, the notice of discharge of liability to the transferee shall include the following details –

(a) the value of the pension credit;

(b) any amount deducted from the value of the pension credit in accordance with regulation 9(2)(b) of the Charging Regulations;

(c) the value of the pension credit after the amount referred to in sub-paragraph (b) has been deducted;

(d) the transfer day; and

(e) details of the pension arrangement, including its name, address, reference number, telephone number, and, where available, the business facsimile number and electronic mail address, to which the pension credit has been transferred.

(6) In the case of a transferee, who has reached normal benefit age on the transfer day, and in respect of whose pension credit liability has been discharged in accordance with paragraph 1(2), 2(2), 3(2) or 4(4) of Schedule 5 to the 1999 Act (pension credits: mode of discharge – funded pension schemes, unfunded public service pension schemes, other unfunded pension schemes, or other pension arrangements), the notice of discharge of liability to the transferee shall include the following details –

(a) the amount of pension credit benefit which is to be paid to the transferee;

(b) the date when the pension credit benefit is to be paid to the transferee;

(c) the transfer day;

(d) if the person responsible for the pension arrangement intends to recover charges, the amount of any unpaid charges –

(i) not prohibited by regulation 2 of the Charging Regulations; and

(ii) specified in regulations 3 and 6 of those Regulations; and

(e) how the person responsible for the pension arrangement will recover the charges referred to in sub-paragraph (d), including –

(i) whether the method of recovery specified in regulation 9(2)(e) of the Charging Regulations will be used;

(ii) the date when payment of those charges in whole or in part is required; and

(iii) the sum which will be payable by the transferee, or which will be deducted from his pension credit benefits, on that date.

(7) In the case of a person entitled to the pension credit by virtue of regulation 6 of the Implementation and Discharge of Liability Regulations, the notice of discharge of liability shall include the following details –

(a) the value of the pension credit rights as determined in accordance with regulation 10 of the Implementation and Discharge of Liability Regulations (calculation of the value of appropriate rights);

(b) any amount deducted from the value of the pension credit in accordance with regulation 9(2)(b) of the Charging Regulations;

(c) the value of the pension credit;

(d) the transfer day; and

(e) any periodical charges the person responsible for the pension arrangement intends to make, including how and when those charges will be recovered from the payments made to the person entitled to the pension credit by virtue of regulation 6 of the Implementation and Discharge of Liability Regulations.

Scope—After the pension sharing order has been implemented, the pension arrangement must issue a *notice of discharge of liability* to the parties within 21 days of completing discharge of the liability in respect of the pension credit. The information required in the notice differs depending on whether, for example, the pension is in payment.

9 Penalties

Where any trustee or manager of an occupational pension scheme fails, without reasonable excuse, to comply with any requirement imposed under regulation 6, 7 or 8, the Regulatory Authority may by notice in writing require that trustee or manager to pay within 28 days from the date of its imposition, a penalty which shall not exceed –

    (a) £200 in the case of an individual, and

    (b) £1,000 in any other case.

Amendments—SI 2009/615.

10 Provision of information after receipt of an earmarking order

(1) The person responsible for the pension arrangement shall, within 21 days beginning with the day that he receives –

    (a) an order under section 23 of the Matrimonial Causes Act 1973, so far as it includes provision made by virtue of section 25B or 25C of that Act (powers to include provision about pensions);

    (b) an order under section 12A(2) or (3) of the Family Law (Scotland) Act 1985; or

    (c) an order under Article 25 of the Matrimonial Causes (Northern Ireland) Order 1978, so far as it includes provision made by virtue of Article 27B or 27C of that Order (Northern Ireland powers corresponding to those mentioned in sub-paragraph (a)),

issue to the party with pension rights and the other party a notice which includes the information specified in paragraphs (2) and (5), or (3), (4) and (5), as the case may be.

(2) Where an order referred to in paragraph (1)(a), (b) or (c) is made in respect of the pension rights or benefits of a party with pension rights whose pension is not in payment, the notice issued by the person responsible for a pension arrangement to the party with pension rights and the other party shall include a list of the circumstances in respect of any changes of which the party with pension rights or the other party must notify the person responsible for the pension arrangement.

(3) Where an order referred to in paragraph (1)(a) or (c) is made in respect of the pension rights or benefits of a party with pension rights whose pension is in payment, the notice issued by the person responsible for a pension arrangement to the party with pension rights and the other party shall include –

    (a) the value of the pension rights or benefits of the party with pension rights;

    (b) the amount of the pension of the party with pension rights after the order has been implemented;

    (c) the first date when a payment pursuant to the order is to be made; and

    (d) a list of the circumstances, in respect of any changes of which the party with pension rights or the other party must notify the person responsible for the pension arrangement.

(4) Where an order referred to in paragraph (1)(a) or (c) is made in respect of the pension rights of a party with pension rights whose pension is in payment, the notice issued by the person responsible for a pension arrangement to the party with pension rights shall, in addition to the items specified in paragraph (3), include –

    (a) the amount of the pension of the party with pension rights which is currently in payment; and

    (b) the amount of pension which will be payable to the party with pension rights after the order has been implemented.

PART IV

(5) Where an order referred to in paragraph (1)(a), (b) or (c) is made the notice issued by the person responsible for a pension arrangement to the party with pension rights and the other party shall include –

(a) the amount of any charges which remain unpaid by –
   (i)   the party with pension rights; or
   (ii) the other party,
   in respect of the provision by the person responsible for the pension arrangement of information about pensions and divorce or dissolution of a civil partnership pursuant to regulation 3 of the Charging Regulations, and in respect of complying with an order referred to in paragraph (1)(a), (b) or (c); and
(b) information as to the manner in which the person responsible for the pension arrangement will recover the charges referred to in sub-paragraph (a), including –
   (i)   the date when payment of those charges in whole or in part is required;
   (ii) the sum which will be payable by the party with pension rights or the other party, as the case may be; and
   (iii) whether the sum will be deducted from payments of pension to the party with pension rights, or, as the case may be, from payments to be made to the other party pursuant to an order referred to in paragraph (1)(a), (b) or (c).

Amendments—SI 2005/2877.

Scope—This regulation provides for the information to be provided to or by a pension arrangement where a pension attachment (earmarking) order has been made.

Reciprocal Enforcement of Maintenance Orders (Hague Convention Countries) Order 1993,
SI 1993/593

****

Note—The provisions of the Maintenance Orders (Reciprocal Enforcement) Act 1972 no longer apply to EU Member States following the coming into force of the Maintenance Regulation (EC) No 4/2009). They are modified in relation to the other Hague Convention countries (Australia, Norway, Switzerland and Turkey). The modifications are set out in FPR PD34A.

Reciprocal Enforcement of Maintenance Orders (United States of America) Order 2007, SI 2007/2005

Note—Maintenance Orders (Reciprocal Enforcement) Act 1972 are modified in relation to the USA. The modifications are set out in FPR PD34A.

Recovery of Maintenance (United States of America) Order 2007, SI 2007/2006

1 Citation and commencement

(1) This Order may be cited as the Recovery of Maintenance (United States of America) Order 2007.

(2) This Order shall come into force on 1 October 2007.

2 Interpretation

In this Order –

"the Act" means the Maintenance Orders (Reciprocal Enforcement) Act 1972;

"the applicant" means the applicant under section 26 of the Act;

"child" has the meaning it bears in the Child Support Act 1991;

"the United States of America" means the fifty States, the District of Columbia, Guam, Puerto Rico, the United States Virgin Islands, and any other jurisdiction of the United States participating in Title IV-D of the Social Security Act (Title 42, United States Code, Chapter 7, subchapter IV, Part D).

3 Application and modification of Part II of the Act in relation to the United States of America

(1) The provisions of Part II of the Act shall apply to the United States of America as they apply in relation to a convention country, subject to the modification set out in paragraph (2) below.

(2) After section 26(3) of the Act there shall be inserted –

"(3A) An application under subsection (1) or (2) above, for the purpose of recovering maintenance from a person in the United States of America within the meaning of the Recovery of Maintenance (United States of America) Order 2007, and a certificate signed by a justice of the peace or, where the applicant is residing in Northern Ireland, a resident magistrate or, where the applicant is residing in Scotland, by the sheriff, to the effect that the application sets forth facts from which it may be determined that the respondent owes a duty to maintain the applicant and any other person named in the application and that a court in the United States of America may obtain jurisdiction of the respondent or his property, shall be registered in the court in the prescribed manner by the appropriate officer or, in Scotland, by the sheriff clerk in the Maintenance Orders (Reciprocal Enforcement) Act 1972 Register."

4 Application to Scotland

This Order applies to Scotland only in respect of a claim for the recovery of maintenance where the Secretary of State would have had jurisdiction to make a maintenance calculation (within the meaning of the Child Support Act 1991) as regards that maintenance with respect to a child –

(a) who is the applicant claiming the maintenance; or

(b) where the applicant claiming the maintenance is another person in relation to whom the Secretary of State has arranged for the collection of payments for that child's benefit.

5 Transitional provisions

(1) This Order applies to –

(a) any application made on or after 1 October 2007 to the Lord Chancellor or to the Scottish Ministers under section 26(1) of the Act for a claim for the recovery of maintenance from a person in the United States of America to be transmitted to the United States of America;

(b) any application made on or after 1 October 2007 to the Lord Chancellor or to the Scottish Ministers under section 26(2) of the Act for the variation of provision made in the United States of America for the payment by another person of maintenance to the applicant, and for the application to be transmitted to the United States of America;

(c)   any application received on or after 1 October 2007 from the appropriate authority in the United States of America by the Lord Chancellor under section 27A(1) of the Act for the recovery of maintenance from a person who is for the time being residing in England and Wales, or under section 28C of the Act for the recovery of maintenance from a person who is for the time being resident in Northern Ireland, or by the Scottish Ministers under section 31(1) of the Act for the recovery of maintenance from a person who is for the time being resident in Scotland; or

(d)   any application made under Part II of the Act in respect of an application falling within paragraph (a), (b) or (c).

(2) Subject to paragraph (1), the Recovery of Maintenance (United States of America) Order 1993 shall continue in full force and effect.

Sharing of State Scheme Rights (Provision of Information and Valuation) (No 2) Regulations 2000, SI 2000/2914

General note—These Regulations set out the information which must be given by the Secretary of State and the method of valuation of the additional state pension element of the state retirement benefit scheme, which element can be subject to a pension sharing or attachment order. The Additional State Pension (ASP) is the collective term for the State Earnings Related Pension Scheme (SERPS) and the State Second Pension (S2P). S2P came into effect on 6 April 2002 replacing SERPS. Pension sharing is not available in relation to the basic state retirement pension (where the substitution rules apply). Pension sharing is, however, available in relation to ASP, including ASP in payment or rights derived from a pension share relating to ASP in previous family proceedings (a "shared additional pension"). No charge is made for the implementation of a pension sharing order in relation to ASP. As to the desirability of giving consideration to ASP valuation in a financial remedy application, see *B v B (Assessment of Assets: Pre-Marital Property)* [2012] 2 FLR 22 at [50].

A lump sum valuation of ASP entitlement may be obtained by submitting Form BR20 (original not photocopy) to the Future Pension Centre, The Pension Service, Tyneview Park, Whitley Road, Newcastle upon Tyne NE98 1BA.

The legislative background to the Regulations is found in WRPA 1999, ss 47–51 and Social Security Contributions and Benefits Act 1992, ss 55A–55C. Consequential amendments were made on the introduction of civil partnership by the Civil Partnership (Pensions, Social Security and Child Support) (Consequential, etc Provisions) Order 2005.

1 Citation, commencement and interpretation

(1) These Regulations may be cited as the Sharing of State Scheme Rights (Provision of Information and Valuation) (No 2) Regulations 2000 and shall come into force on 1 December 2000.

(2) In these Regulations –

"the 1992 Act" means the Social Security Contributions and Benefits Act 1992;

"the 1999 Act" means the Welfare Reform and Pensions Act 1999;

"shareable state scheme rights" has the meaning given by section 47(2) of the 1999 Act.

2 Basic information about the sharing of state scheme rights and divorce or the dissolution of a civil partnership

(1) The requirements imposed on the Secretary of State for the purposes of section 23(1)(a) of the 1999 Act (supply of pension information in connection with divorce etc) are that he shall furnish –

    (a)   the information specified in paragraphs (2) and (3) –
        (i)   to a person who has shareable state scheme rights on request from that person; or
        (ii) to the court, pursuant to an order of the court; or
    (b)   the information specified in paragraph (3) to the spouse or civil partner of a person who has shareable state scheme rights, on request from that spouse or civil partner.

(2) The information specified in this paragraph is a valuation of the person's shareable state scheme rights.

(3) The information in this paragraph is an explanation of –

    (a)   the state scheme rights which are shareable;
    (b)   how a pension sharing order or provision will affect a person's shareable state scheme rights; and
    (c)   how a pension sharing order or provision in respect of a person's shareable state scheme rights will result in the spouse or civil partner of the person who has shareable state scheme rights becoming entitled to a shared additional pension.

(4) The Secretary of State shall furnish the information specified in paragraphs (2) and (3) to the court or, as the case may be, to the person who has shareable state scheme rights within –

    (a)   3 months beginning with the date the Secretary of State receives the request or, as the case may be, the order for the provision of that information;
    (b)   6 weeks beginning with the date the Secretary of State receives the request or, as the case may be, the order for the provision of the information, if the person who has shareable state scheme rights has notified the Secretary of State on the date of the request or order that the information is needed in connection with proceedings commenced under any of the provisions referred to in section 23(1)(a) of the 1999 Act; or
    (c)   such shorter period specified by the court in an order requiring the Secretary of State to provide a valuation in accordance with paragraph (2).

(5) Where –

    (a)   the request made by the person with shareable state scheme rights for, or the court order requiring, the provision of information does not include a request or, as the case may be, an order for a valuation under paragraph (2); or
    (b)   the spouse or civil partner of the person with shareable state scheme rights requests the information specified in paragraph (3),

the Secretary of State shall furnish that information to the person who has shareable state scheme rights, his spouse, civil partner, or the court, as the case may be, within one month beginning with the date the Secretary of State receives the request or the court order for the provision of that information.

Amendments—SI 2005/2877.

Scope—This regulation specifies the information which the Secretary of State must supply to the parties to a marriage/civil partnership or the court in relation to the sharing of state scheme rights as well as the time limits within which that information must be furnished.

PART IV

3 Information about the sharing of state scheme rights and divorce or dissolution of a civil partnership: valuation of shareable state scheme rights

Where an application for financial relief or financial provision under any of the provisions referred to in section 23(1)(a) of the 1999 Act has been made or is in contemplation, the valuation of shareable state scheme rights shall be calculated and verified for the purposes of regulation 2(2) of these Regulations in such manner as may be approved by or on behalf of the Government Actuary.

Amendments—SI 2005/2877.

Scope—This regulation sets out how the value of the state scheme rights must be calculated and verified when a valuation of those rights is requested in connection with pension sharing.

4 Calculation and verification of cash equivalents for the purposes of the creation of state scheme pension debits and credits

For the purposes of –

    (a)   section 49 of the 1999 Act (creation of state scheme pension debits and credits);

    (b)   section 45B of the 1992 Act (reduction of additional pension in Category A retirement pension: pension sharing);

    (c)   section 55A of the 1992 Act (shared additional pension); and

    (d)   section 55B of the 1992 Act (reduction of shared additional pension: pension sharing),

cash equivalents shall be calculated and verified in such manner as may be approved by or on behalf of the Government Actuary.

Scope—This regulation provides for how cash equivalents are to be calculated and verified for the purposes of the creation of state scheme pension debits and credits, the reduction of the additional pension, the creation of the shared additional pension and the reduction of the shared additional pension as a result of pension sharing.

5 Revocation

The Sharing of State Scheme Rights (Provision of Information and Valuation) Regulations 2000 are revoked.

Supreme Court Fees Order 2009, SI 2009/2131

1 Citation, commencement and interpretation

(1) This Order may be cited as the Supreme Court Fees Order 2009 and comes into force on 1 October 2009.

(2) In this Order –

    "the 2009 Rules" means the Supreme Court Rules 2009;

    "devolution jurisdiction" means proceedings under the Scotland Act 1998, the Government of Wales Act 2006 or the Northern Ireland Act 1998.

(3) Subject to paragraph (2), expressions used in this Order which are also used in the 2009 Rules have the same meaning as in those Rules.

2 Fees payable

(1) Subject to the following paragraphs, the fees set out in column (2) of the table in Schedule 1 are payable in the Supreme Court in respect of the items described in column (1) of that table.

(2) No fee in column (2) is payable in respect of criminal proceedings, other than the fee payable on submitting a claim for costs.

(3) In relation to its devolution jurisdiction the fees set out in column (3) of that table are payable in the Supreme Court in respect of the items described in column (1) of that table.

3 Remissions and part remissions

Schedule 2 applies for the purpose of ascertaining whether a party is entitled to a remission or part remission of a fee prescribed by this Order.

SCHEDULE 1
FEES PAYABLE IN THE SUPREME COURT

(1) *Number and description of fee*	(2) *Amount of fee*	(3) *Amount of fee*
1 *Application for permission to appeal*		
1.1 On filing an application for permission to appeal.	£1000	£400
1.2 On filing notice of objection to an application for permission to appeal.	£160	£160
2 *Appeals etc*		
2.1 On filing notice under rule 18(1)(c) of the 2009 Rules of an intention to proceed with an appeal.	£800	£400
2.2 On filing a notice of appeal.	£1600	£400
2.3 On filing a reference under the Supreme Court's devolution jurisdiction. No fee is payable where the reference is made by a court.	n/a	£200
2.4 On filing notice under rule 21(1) of the 2009 Rules (acknowledgement by respondent).	£320	£160
2.5 On filing a statement of relevant facts and issues and an appendix of essential documents.	£4820	£800
3 *Procedural applications*		
3.1 On filing an application for a decision of the Registrar to be reviewed.	£1500	£200
3.2 On filing an application for permission to intervene in an appeal.	£800	£200
3.3 On filing any other procedural application.	£350	£200
3.4 On filing notice of objection to a procedural application.	£150	£150
4 *Costs*		
4.1 On submitting a claim for costs.	2.5% of the sum claimed	2.5% of the sum claimed

(1) *Number and description of fee*	*(2)* *Amount of fee*	*(3)* *Amount of fee*
4.2 On certification by the Registrar under rule 52 of the 2009 Rules of the amount of assessed costs, or on receipt of an order showing the amount.	2.5% of the sum allowed	2.5% of the sum allowed
5 *Copying*		
5.1 On a request for a copy of a document (other than where fee 5.2 or 5.3 applies) –		
(a) for ten pages or less;	£5	£5
(b) for each subsequent page	50p	50p
5.2 On a request for a copy of a document to be provided on a computer disk or in other electronic form, for each such copy.	£5	£5
5.3 On a request for a certified copy of a document.	£20	£20

Amendments—SI 2011/1737.

SCHEDULE 2

REMISSIONS AND PART REMISSIONS

1 Interpretation

(1) In this Schedule –

"couple" has the meaning given in section 3(5A) of the Tax Credits Act 2002;

"disposable monthly income" has the meaning given in paragraph 5;

"excluded benefits" means –

    (a) any of the following benefits payable under the Social Security Contributions and Benefits Act 1992 or the corresponding provisions of the Social Security Contributions and Benefits (Northern Ireland) Act 1992 –

        (i) attendance allowance;

        (ii) severe disablement allowance;

        (iii) carer's allowance;

        (iv) disability living allowance;

        (v) constant attendance allowance paid under section 104 or paragraph 4 or 7(2) of Schedule 8 as an increase to a disablement pension;

        (vi) council tax benefit;

        (vii) any payment made out of the social fund;

        (viii) housing benefit;

    (b) any direct payment made under the Community Care, Services for Carers and Children's Services (Direct Payments) (England) Regulations 2003, the Community Care, Services for Carers and Children's Services (Direct Payments) (Wales) Regulations 2004, the Carers and Direct Payments Act (Northern Ireland) 2002, the Children (Northern Ireland) Order 1995, or the Social Work (Scotland) Act 1968;

    (c) a back to work bonus payable under section 26 of the Jobseekers Act 1995 or the corresponding provision of the Jobseekers (Northern Ireland) Order 1995;

    (d) any exceptionally severe disablement allowance paid under the Personal Injuries (Civilians) Scheme 1983;

(e) any pension paid under the Naval, Military and Air Forces etc (Disablement and Death) Service Pension Order 2006;

(f) any payment made from the Independent Living Fund, the Independent Living (Extension) Fund, the Independent Living (1993) Fund and the Independent Living Fund 2006;

(g) any financial support paid under an agreement for the care of a foster child;

(h) personal independence payment under Part 4 of the Welfare Reform Act 2012; and

(i) armed forces independence payment under the Armed Forces and Reserve Forces (Compensation Scheme) Order 2011;

"gross annual income" means total annual income, for the 12 months preceding the application for remission or part remission, from all sources other than receipt of any of the excluded benefits;

"gross monthly income" means total monthly income, for the month in which the application for remission or part remission is made, from all sources other than receipt of any of the excluded benefits;

"the Independent Living Fund" means the charitable trust established out of funds provided by the Secretary of State for the purpose of providing financial assistance to those persons incapacitated by or otherwise suffering from very severe disablement who are in need of such assistance to enable them to live independently;

"the Independent Living (Extension) Fund" means the Trust of that name established by a deed dated 25 February 1993 and made between the Secretary of State for Social Security of the one part and Robin Glover Wendt and John Fletcher Shepherd of the other part;

"the Independent Living (1993) Fund" means the Trust of that name established by a deed dated 25 February 1993 and made between the Secretary of State for Social Security of the one part and Robin Glover Wendt and John Fletcher Shepherd of the other part;

"the Independent Living Fund (2006)" means the Trust of that name established by a deed dated 10 April 2006 and made between the Secretary of State for Work and Pensions of the one part and Margaret Rosemary Cooper, Michael Beresford Boyall and Marie Theresa Martin of the other part;

"partner" means a person with whom the party lives as a couple and includes a person with whom the party is not currently living but from whom the party is not living separate and apart;

"party" means the person who would, but for this Schedule, be liable to pay the fee required under this Order;

"qualifying benefit" means –

(a) income support under the Social Security Contributions and Benefits Act 1992 or the Social Security Contributions and Benefits (Northern Ireland) Act 1992;

(b) working tax credit, provided that no child tax credit is being paid to the party;

(c) income-based jobseeker's allowance under the Jobseekers Act 1995 or the Jobseekers (Northern Ireland) Order 1995;

(d) guarantee credit under the State Pension Credit Act 2002 or the State Pension Credit Act (Northern Ireland) 2002; and

(e) income-related employment and support allowance under the Welfare Reform Act 2007 or the Welfare Reform Act (Northern Ireland) 2007.

(2) Paragraphs 2, 3 and 4 do not apply to a party –

(a) for whom civil legal services, for which a certificate has been issued under the

Civil Legal Aid (Procedure) Regulations 2012, have been made available under arrangements made for the purposes of Part 1 of that Act for the purposes of the proceedings;

(b)   who is in receipt of legal aid under Part 2 of the Legal Aid, Advice and Assistance (Northern Ireland) Order 1981 for the purposes of the proceedings; or

(c)   who, if they are is living in Scotland, is in receipt of legal aid.

Amendments—SI 2013/388; SI 2013/534, subject to savings; SI 2013/591.

Couple—See under FPFO 2008, Sch 2.

2 Full remission of fees – qualifying benefits

No fee is payable under this Order if, at the time when a fee would otherwise be payable, the party is in receipt of a qualifying benefit.

3 Full remission of fees – gross annual income

(1) No fee is payable under this Order if, at the time when the fee would otherwise be payable, the party has the number of children specified in column (1) of the following table and –

(a)   if the party is single, the gross annual income of the party does not exceed the amount set out in the appropriate row of column (2); or

(b)   if the party is one of a couple, the gross annual income of the couple does not exceed the amount set out in the appropriate row of column (3).

(1) *Number of children of party paying fee*	*(2)* *Single*	*(3)* *Couple*
no children	£13,000	£18,000
1 child	£15,930	£20,930
2 children	£18,860	£23,860
3 children	£21,790	£26,790
4 children	£24,720	£29,720

(2) If the party paying the fee has more than 4 children then the relevant amount of gross annual income is the amount specified in the table for 4 children plus the sum of £2,930 for each additional child.

4 Full and part remission of fees – disposable monthly income

(1) No fee is payable under this Order if, at the time when the fee would otherwise be payable, the disposable monthly income of the party is £50 or less.

(2) The maximum amount of fee payable is –

(a)   if the disposable monthly income of the party is more than £50 but does not exceed £210, an amount equal to one-quarter of every £10 of the party's disposable monthly income, up to a maximum of £50; and

(b)   if the disposable monthly income is more than £210, an amount equal to £50 plus one-half of every £10 over £200 of the party's disposable monthly income.

(3) Where the fee that would otherwise be payable under this Order is greater than the maximum fee which a party is required to pay as calculated in sub-paragraph (2), the fee will be remitted to the amount payable under that sub-paragraph.

5 Disposable monthly income

(1) A party's disposable monthly income is the gross monthly income of the party for the month in which the fee becomes payable ("the period") less the deductions referred to in sub-paragraphs (2) and (3).

(2) There are to be deducted from the gross monthly income –

    (a) income tax paid or payable in respect of the period;

    (b) any contributions estimated to have been paid under Part 1 of the Social Security Contributions and Benefits Act 1992, or the corresponding provisions of the Social Security Contributions and Benefits (Northern Ireland) Act 1992, in respect of the period;

    (c) either –

        (i) monthly rent or monthly payment in respect of a mortgage debt or hereditable security, payable in respect of the only or main dwelling of the party, less any housing benefit paid under the Social Security Contributions and Benefits Act 1992 or the Social Security Contributions and Benefits (Northern Ireland) Act 1992; or

        (ii) the monthly cost of the living accommodation of the party;

    (d) any child care costs paid or payable in respect of the period;

    (e) if the party is making bona fide payments for the maintenance of a child who is not a member of the household of the party, the amount of such payments paid or payable in respect of the period; and

    (f) any amount paid or payable by the party, in respect of the period, in pursuance of a court order.

(3) There is to be deducted from the gross monthly income an amount representing the cost of living expenses in respect of the period being –

    (a) £315; plus

    (b) £244 for each child of the party; plus

    (c) £159, if the party has a partner.

(4) In this paragraph –

"child" means a child or young person in respect of whom a party is entitled to receive child benefit in accordance with section 141, and regulations made under section 142, of the Social Security Contributions and Benefits Act 1992, or the corresponding provisions of, or corresponding regulations made under, the Social Security Contributions and Benefits (Northern Ireland) Act 1992, and references to "children" in this Schedule should be construed accordingly;

"child care costs" means the costs of care which is provided by one of more of the following care providers –

    (a) a school on school premises, out of school hours;

    (b) a local authority, out of school hours –

        (i) for children who are not disabled, in respect of the period beginning on their eighth birthday and ending on the day preceding the first Monday in September following their fifteenth birthday;

        (ii) for children who are disabled, in respect of the period beginning on their eighth birthday and ending on the day preceding the first Monday in September following their sixteenth birthday;

    (c) a child care provider approved in accordance with the Tax Credit (New Category of Child Care Provider) Regulations 1999;

    (d) persons registered under Part XA of the Children Act 1989 or the corresponding provision of the Children (Northern Ireland) Order 1995;

    (e) persons in schools or establishments referred to in paragraph 1 or 2 of Schedule 9A to the Children Act 1989 or in the corresponding provision of the Children (Northern Ireland) Order 1995;

PART IV

(f)   persons prescribed in regulations made pursuant to section 12(4) of the Tax Credits Act 2002.

6 Resources of partners

(1) For the purpose of determining whether a party is entitled to the remission or part remission of a fee in accordance with this Schedule, the income of a partner, if any, is to be included as income of the party.

(2) The receipt by a partner of a qualifying benefit does not entitle a party to remission of a fee.

7 Application for remission or part remission of fees

(1) An application for remission or part remission of a fee must be made to the court officer at the time when the fee would otherwise be payable.

(2) Where a claim for full remission of fees is made, the party must provide documentary evidence of, as the case may be –

(a)   entitlement to a qualifying benefit; or
(b)   gross annual income and, if applicable, the children included for the purposes of paragraph 3.

(3) Where a claim for full or part remission of fees under paragraph 4 is made, the party must provide documentary evidence of –

(a)   such of the party's gross monthly income as is derived from –
  (i)   employment;
  (ii)   rental or other income received from persons living with the party by reason of their residence in the party's home;
  (iii)   a pension; or
  (iv)   a state benefit, not being an excluded benefit; and
(b)   any expenditure being deducted from the gross monthly income in accordance with paragraph 5(2).

8 Remission in exceptional circumstances

Where it appears to the Chief Executive of the Supreme Court that the payment of any fee prescribed by this Order would, owing to the exceptional circumstances of the particular case, involve undue financial hardship, the Chief Executive may reduce or remit the fee in that case.

9 Remission for charitable or not-for-profit organisations

Where an application for permission to intervene in an appeal is filed by a charitable or not-for-profit organisation which seeks to make submissions in the public interest, the Chief Executive of the Supreme Court may reduce or remit the fee in that case.

10 Refunds

(1) Subject to sub-paragraph (3), where a party has not provided the documentary evidence required by paragraph 7 and a fee has been paid at a time when, under paragraphs 2, 3 or 4, it was not payable, the fee will be refunded if documentary evidence relating to the time when the fee became payable is provided at a later date.

(2) Subject to sub-paragraph (3), where a fee has been paid at a time where the Chief Executive, if all the circumstances had been known, would have reduced or remitted the

fee under paragraph 8 or 9, the fee or the amount by which the fee would have been reduced, as the case may be, will be refunded.

(3) No refund will be made under this paragraph unless the party who paid the fee applies within 6 months of paying the fee.

(4) The Chief Executive may extend the period of 6 months mentioned in sub-paragraph (3) if the Chief Executive considers that there is a good reason for an application being made after the end of the period of 6 months.

PART IV

PART V

Practice Guidance

PART V: Practice Guidance

Contents

Since 6 April 2011, a number of practice directions supplement the Family Procedure Rules 2010 and are set out in Part III of this work, following their respective FPR 2010 Parts. These replace, in many cases, the previous judicial practice directions. The remaining judicial practice directions set out in Part V of this work are still in force. For any other of the previous practice directions, reference should be made to the 2010 edition of The Family Court Practice.

The Practice Directions in Part V are arranged in date order.

PART V

Practice Direction
19 August 1991

Citations: [1991] 1 WLR 955; [1991] 2 FLR 384; [1991] 3 All ER 896

Statutory Charge: Form of the Order of the Court

Regulation 90(3) of the Civil Legal Aid (General) Regulations 1989, SI 1989/339, directs that where, in proceedings under the Married Women's Property Act 1882, the Matrimonial Causes Act 1973 or the Inheritance (Provision for Family and Dependants) Act 1975 [or Sch 1 to the Children Act 1989], property is recovered or preserved for an assisted person, which by order of the court is to be used as a home or a sum of money is to be used to purchase a home for the assisted person or his dependants, the assisted person's solicitor shall inform the Area Director.

In such a case, by virtue of regs 96 and 97, the Legal Aid Board may, subject to conditions, agree to defer enforcing the statutory charge on the property recovered or preserved imposed by s 16(6) of the Legal Aid Act 1988.

To avoid any doubt whether the order of the court must expressly state that the property is to be used as a home or to purchase a home, the Legal Aid Board has agreed that a certificate incorporated in the body of the order in the following form will be regarded as a sufficient compliance with the Regulations:

> "And it is certified for the purpose of the Civil Legal Aid (General) Regulations 1989 [that the lump sum of £x has been ordered to be paid to enable the petitioner/respondent to purchase a home for himself/herself (or his/her dependants)] [that the property (*address*) has been preserved/recovered for the petitioner/respondent for use as a home for himself/herself (or his/her dependants)]."

Issued [in its original form] with the concurrence of the Lord Chancellor.

G. Angel
Senior District Judge

LASPOA 2012, s 25—This provides that where civil legal aid services are made available to an individual, such amounts are to be recovered as the first charge upon (a) property recovered or preserved in proceedings in connection with which services are provided and (b) any costs payable to an individual by another person in connection with the proceedings.

PART V

Practice Direction
26 September 1991

Citations: [1991] 1 WLR 1069; [1991] 2 FLR 462

Grants of Representation: Children Act 1989

The Non Contentious Probate (Amendment) Rules 1991, SI 1991/1876, in force from 14 October 1991, amend r 32 of the Non Contentious Probate Rules 1987, SI 1987/2024 which relates to grants on behalf of minors. The amendments are consequential upon the coming into effect of the Children Act 1989 (herein referred to as "the Act").

The evidence required in support of an application for such a grant in specified circumstances is as follows.

1 Where the applicant is the mother of the child she must state in the oath that she is the mother of the minor.

2 Where the applicant is the father of the child having parental responsibility under s 2(1) of the Act the oath must state that the applicant is the father of the minor and has parental responsibility under that provision.

3 Where the applicant is the father of the child, and has acquired parental responsibility as provided by s 4 of the Act the oath must state that he is the father of the minor and has parental responsibility "under an order" or "under a duly recorded parental responsibility agreement".

A copy of the order or sealed copy of the agreement recorded in the Principal Registry of the Family Division under the Parental Responsibility Agreement Regulations 1991, SI 1991/1478, must be produced.

4 Where the applicant is the father of the child and was not married to the mother at the time of the child's birth, but has parental responsibility in accordance with paras 4 or 6 of Sch 14 to the Act either:

    (a)   by virtue of an order under s 4(1) of the Family Law Reform Act 1987 or;

    (b)   by virtue of an order giving him custody or care and control of the child;

in force immediately before the commencement of Parts I and II of the Act the oath must state that he is the father of the minor and a parent having parental responsibility by virtue of such an order which was in force immediately before the commencement of the Children Act 1989.

A copy of the order must be produced in each instance.

5 Where the applicant has parental responsibility by virtue of an adoption order the oath must state that he or she is the adopter or one of the adopters of the minor by an order made within the meaning of s 12 of the Adoption Act 1976.

A copy of the order must be produced.

6 Where the applicant is a guardian who has been appointed in accordance with s 5 of the Act the oath must state that he or she is a guardian of the minor having parental responsibility by virtue of:

    (a)   an order made under s 5 of the Children Act 1989; or

    (b)   an appointment made by "AB, a parent having parental responsibility for the minor by will" (or "by deed" as appropriate); or

    (c)   an appointment made by "CD, a duly appointed guardian having parental responsibility for the minor by will" (or "by deed" as appropriate).

The order, will or deed must be produced (or in the case of a proved will, an official copy), together with such further evidence as a district judge or registrar may require in the circumstances of a case. The date of death of the person making the appointment must be included in the oath as must the date of death or any other person upon whose death the appointment takes effect.

7 An applicant who is a guardian of the child having parental responsibility by virtue of an appointment under the Guardianship of Minors Act 1971, the Sexual Offences Act 1956 or the High Court's inherent jurisdiction with respect to children which is deemed to be an appointment made and having effect under s 5 of the Children Act 1989 (by paras 12 and 13 of Sch 14 to the Act) must include such information in the oath.

A copy of the order must be produced.

G. Angel
Senior District Judge

Best Practice Guidance
June 1997

Note—The following material is taken from the *Children Act Advisory Committee Handbook of Best Practice in Children Act Cases*, and is reproduced with the kind permission of the President of the Family Division.

Public Law Outline (PLO)—The PLO is contained in FPR PD12A. It applies to all courts hearing applications issued by local authorities under CA 1989, Pt IV (care and supervision orders). See further **First appointment**, **Case management conference**, **Issues resolution hearing** under FPR 2010, r 12.25 and notes on the timetable for proceedings under FPR 2010, r 12.12.

Private Law Programme—The *Revised Private Law Programme* is contained in FPR PD12B. It applies in all courts hearing family proceedings. See further under FPR 2010, rr 12.31, 12.32. It is respectfully submitted that where the *Best Practice Guidance* below conflicts with the *Private Law Programme*, the latter is to be preferred.

Form C100—In CA 1989, s 8 applications for residence, contact, specific issue and prohibited steps orders, Form C100 must be used in place of Form C1. Any references in the *Best Practice Guidance* below to Form C1 should therefore be read with this in mind. The forms to be used for applications in family proceedings are set out in FPR 2010, PD5A.

Handbook of Best Practice in Children Act Cases

Introduction

When writing its final report, the Committee thought it might be helpful to gather together in a separate document the guidance available on best practice in Children Act proceedings with a view to providing a useful tool for the conscientious but busy practitioner. Some of this material is newly written and some is a compendium of guidance from our earlier reports updated both by experience and authoritative reported decisions. It follows that some of this guidance is firmly authoritative (deriving from binding decisions or practice directions) whilst much remains advisory, but based on accumulated experience of what works best.

The basic message of this Handbook is that the earlier matters are considered and acted upon by the parties and their advisers, and the more that can be done jointly with other parties, the better the court process can serve the interests of children. Work done in preparation, and in liaison with other parties, is rarely wasted and indeed is almost always productive in terms of avoiding, or at least reducing, the trial process which is after all both the most costly and certainly the most stressful part of the whole proceedings.

We hope that all practitioners (and not just the lawyers) will find this Handbook useful as we try to translate into practice in each case the obligation to promote the welfare of the children with whom we are dealing. We have set out this Handbook with a view primarily to ease of reference in the hope that it will find widespread use in practice.

Section 1 – Preparation for court in care proceedings

Local authority solicitors

1 At the earliest stage, when first consulted, focus on:

    (a)   the issues;
    (b)   the legal framework;
    (c)   the evidence needed to support an application;
    (d)   the proposed care plan;
    (e)   the appropriate level of court; and
    (f)   the likely time scale for concluding the court case in the light of:

PART V

> (i)   the complexities involved, and
> (ii) the ages and needs of the children.

2 If counsel is to be instructed, do so at an early stage. Consider together the preparation for trial and whether transfer to the care centre is appropriate.

All parties and their legal advisers

3 By the first directions hearing, consider whether the issues of fact are stark enough to justify a split hearing, with an early resolution of factual disputes to enable a definitive care plan to be formulated and to enable the guardian ad litem to make recommended actions as to outcome. For example, this is likely to arise in cases of alleged non-accidental injury where different persons are in the frame as possible perpetrators and/or accomplices, and in cases of sexual abuse.

4 Use directions hearings imaginatively. Anticipate problems and address them in advance.

> (a) Ensure strict compliance with timetables for filing evidence and documents.
> (b) Inform the court, as a matter of urgency, if the timetable cannot be met for any reason.
> (c) Be prepared in advance with dates and availability of witnesses and time needed to adduce evidence.
> (d) Liaise with other parties to ensure that all issues are addressed at an early stage, for example:
>> (i)   whether transfer to the care centre would be appropriate;
>> (ii)   which other persons are seeking party status;
>> (iii) issues of disclosure and confidentiality; or
>> (iv) any assessments or experts' reports sought by any party.
> (e) Fix the final hearing, even if only provisionally.

5 All parties, and in particular the guardian ad litem, have a duty to:

> (a) advise the court on the timetable appropriate to the issues and timescale of the child concerned;
> (b) keep the timetable under constant review throughout the preparation for the hearing; and
> (c) bring to the attention of the court promptly any significant developments and seek further directions.

Instruction of experts

6 See **Section 5** below.

The care plan

7 Ensure that the issues raised by the local authority are clearly set out with a fully researched care plan, to enable the parties to know what case they have to meet.

8 If permanent placement in an alternative family is the plan, prepare the ground as far as possible without pre-empting the court's decision.

9 If the plan is for an adoptive placement, the court will be handicapped in assessing the plan and the timescale, unless the child concerned has already been considered and approved by the adoption and fostering panel, and potential suitable adoptive families have been identified. It is not good practice to await the making of a care order before

obtaining such information, because the court is deprived of important background information and significant delay can occur in placing the child in the event of the court approving the plan.

10 If the plan involves a specialist placement with therapy and/or further assessment, identify the placement and any professionals involved, together with the timescale and the availability of appropriate funding.

11 If the plan depends upon the finding of facts or determination of particular issues by the court, state why and set out clear alternative proposals.

12 If no firm proposal can be made, that should be made clear and explained.

****

Note—Paragraphs 13–20: "Preparing the Evidence"; paragraph 21: "The Court"; paragraphs 22–32: "Section 2 – Renewal of Interim Care Orders"; and paragraphs 33–35: "Section 3 – First Appointments in Public Law Cases in the County Courts: The Role of the Court" have been removed on the basis that their substance has in part been superseded by FPR PD12A.

Section 4 – Private law cases

Note—See annotations **Private Law Programme** and **Form C100** at the start of this *Guidance*.

Introduction

36 The following is a brief guide to best practice in applications made under section 8 of the Children Act. This guidance may need to be tailored to deal with cases involving unrepresented litigants.

37 Specific good practice for cases involving allegations of sexual abuse is set out in the Annex to this section.

Before proceedings

38 Consider whether the dispute between the parties could be resolved in any way other than litigation. Most areas have a mediation service which would be able to attempt to deal with disputes by way of negotiation and agreement. There is rarely anything to be lost, and normally much to be gained, by mediation.

39 At the earliest stage, if it becomes clear that negotiated or mediated settlement will not be possible, focus on:

    (a) the issues, including the question of how crucial facts are to be proved;

    (b) the legal framework; and

    (c) the evidence needed to support the case to be put forward.

Issue of proceedings

40 Ensure that form C1 contains all relevant information, including a brief outline of the case (but not a detailed statement by the applicant).

41 To prevent unnecessary delay at the first directions appointment, prepare at least draft statements by:

    (a) the applicant, and

    (b) any witnesses who it is known will have to give evidence.

PART V

The first directions appointment

THE ROLE OF THE COURT

42 The court will fix a first directions appointment when an application is issued. The task of the court at the first appointment is to:

(a) investigate the issues;
(b) inquire into the possibility of settlement; and
(c) give directions in any case which has to proceed.

43 When giving directions, the court will normally:

(a) consider the appropriate tier of court;
(b) order the filing of witness statements;
(c) consider whether there are circumstances justifying sequential rather than simultaneous exchange;
(d) express times for filing (for example, of witness statements or the court welfare officer's report) by fixing a date, eg "by 28 April 1997" and not "within 14 days"; and
(e) include in the order the date for the next appointment and, even if only provisionally, the final hearing.

44 An order should not provide for an application to be adjourned generally unless the parties consider that it will not be necessary to return to court. In that event the order should also provide for the application to stand dismissed if not restored by a certain date.

45 The order should provide that any letter of instructions to experts (to be joint instructions wherever possible) is to be filed at court.

46 A paginated bundle of documents and chronology should be normal practice except in the simplest case.

THE ROLE OF THE PARTIES

47 Parties and their legal representatives must attend directions appointments unless specifically excused.

48 A party's legal representative must have both sufficient knowledge and authority to take any necessary decisions.

49 Use the first appointment imaginatively, anticipating problems and addressing them in advance, and dealing with questions of expert evidence. (See **Section 5**)

50 When it is to be suggested that there should be contact at a contact centre or supervised contact by an individual, make enquiries to ensure that the centre or individual will be available to provide the service.

Welfare reports

51 Parties should have access to a court welfare officer, or other person qualified to assist them, at or before the first appointment. Some courts achieve this by requiring a court welfare officer to attend the first appointment, others by referring the parties to the welfare officer before the date of the first appointment. Ask about the practice of the local court if you are in any doubt.

52 If a welfare officer has attempted to mediate between the parties, he should not be involved in the case in any other way.

53 When ordering a welfare report, the guidance as to best practice under "Welfare Reports" at *Best Practice Note of January 1995* should be followed. In particular:

(a) the request for a report should state the issue giving rise to the request;

(b) addendum reports should not normally be ordered, and should not be necessary for the hearing if timetabling has been effective;

(c) any request for the court welfare officer to attend the final hearing should be examined carefully, and not granted as a matter of course;

(d) when a court requires the court welfare officer to attend a hearing, enquiry should be made to ensure that he is available; and

(e) the court hearing the case should allow the officer to give evidence first and then to be released.

Final directions appointments or pre-trial reviews

54 The final directions appointment, or pre-trial review, should be timetabled to take place when any welfare report and all evidence has been filed.

55 The applicant's solicitor must prepare an agreed and paginated bundle of documents, containing an index and a chronology, not less than 24 hours before the hearing.

56 The court will expect the parties' advisers to have addressed the question of what evidence can be agreed and what is in dispute. An order will be made accordingly.

57 The counsel or solicitor who will attend the final hearing should attend the pre-trial review. If this is not possible, the person attending must be thoroughly conversant with the case and competent to make any necessary concessions or admissions and to advise the lay client in respect of settlement.

The final hearing

58 Except by direction of the court, children should not attend a hearing.

59 Consider how the decision of the court is to be communicated to the children. In some cases, particularly where the court's decision is contrary to the reported wishes of the child, it may be appropriate for the court welfare officer to see the child to explain what has happened.

PART V

ANNEX – FLAWED SEXUAL ABUSE INVESTIGATION

Despite the guidance in *B v B (Sexual Abuse: Procedural Delay)* [1994] 1 FLR 323 and *Re A and B (Minors) (No 2)* [1995] 1 FLR 351, problems continue to occur in private law cases where allegations of sexual abuse of a child are investigated by the police and/or social services. Frequently the cases involve an application for contact with a child, where the primary carer has refused contact on the ground that the child has been sexually abused by the applicant. Such cases cause particular difficulties where the applicant denies the allegation, and alleges that the other parent has either invented the sexual abuse or has brainwashed the child into believing that sexual abuse has occurred. The parent opposing contact may be obstructive and use delaying tactics in order to prevent contact taking place, even under supervision. If such cases are not strictly timetabled, resulting delays can achieve the object of frustrating resumption of contact, even if the court finds that sexual abuse is not proved. Good practice requires as follows:

(a) The legal representatives have a duty, irrespective of whether or not delay might be tactically of advantage to their client, to ensure that a case does not drift and is resolved with the minimum of delay.

(b) The timetable must be strictly controlled by the court and must never be left to the parties. As in public law cases, the court must monitor the procedural steps ordered, building in reviews of progress and setting stringent time limits and return dates.

(c) When the local authority is involved with a concurrent, but independent investigation, the principal co-ordinating agency for the determination of issues is the court, using section 7 of the Children Act 1989 which enables the court to require the local authority to report to the court on the nature, progress and outcome of the child protection investigation. Section 7 should be used to keep the parties informed of progress and material available.

(d) The local authority should make available a social worker to give evidence on the report and to be cross examined if so required.

(e) Any joint child abuse interview conducted by police and social services must follow the memorandum of good practice. Otherwise not only is the resulting interview of no forensic value, but it may impede or contaminate any further assessment of the child ordered by the court.

(f) The court has power to compel discovery of documents held by local authorities or the police, e g videos of interview with the child. If any arguments arise as to confidentiality, or public interest immunity, they should be determined at an early stage at a directions hearing.

(g) Although the court cannot compel a prosecuting authority to reach decisions speedily, the court can and should bring to the attention of the authority the need for a timely decision on criminal prosecution.

(h) Even when there is a police investigation, there is no good legal or social work reason why the social worker should not make contact with the parent under investigation, so that information can be given and exchanged which is relevant to the welfare of the child. The social worker should make it clear that until the police investigation is complete, the specific allegation cannot be discussed. Many parents under police investigation suffer a sense of grievance when no reason is given for denial of contact, with the result that the parent perceives the local authority as pursuing investigations with a closed mind and a presumption of guilt.

(i) The issue whether or not a child has been sexually abused is for decision by the court and it is essential that other agencies await that decision before introducing management, counselling or therapy that pre-judges the issue. Therefore, the welfare of the child demands speedy resolution of issues.

(j) If leave is sought to instruct an expert, it is essential to define the issues, to establish the area of expertise required and the proposed timetable, to consider joint instruction and to follow the guidance in **Section 5**. In deciding whether to grant leave for a child to be assessed the court should consider carefully the issues, and whether the court is likely to be assisted in determining whether sexual abuse has been established, as opposed to outcome, by the contribution from an expert in the field of psychological medicine.

(k) There is often a tension between a positive clinical finding of sexual abuse, and judicial findings that abuse has not occurred. In contested cases clinical methods will inevitably be subjected to scrutiny. Any investigation which focuses attention on the statements of the child runs the risk of producing a false result if what the child says is unreliable or if the child's primary caretaker is unreliable, particularly where the allegation emerges in bitterly contested section 8 proceedings. The dangers of a false conclusion are enhanced if the alleged perpetrator is excluded from clinical investigation. It is vital to approach a child abuse investigation with an open mind.

(l) Where possible directions appointments should be heard by the judge who is likely to determine the substantive issues.

(m) In cases in which there is a stark factual issue to be determined the court will need to consider carefully whether it is appropriate to obtain a section 7 report clarifying the issues before ordering a welfare report, whether factual issues need to be determined by the court before a welfare report is ordered as to outcome, or whether a report should be ordered at an early stage in the proceedings. Each case needs to be considered on its merits, and the court welfare service should be invited to make representations.

Section 5 – Experts and the courts

PLO – instructing and calling experts—In all public law proceedings under CA 1989, Pt IV, the PLO must be followed. It is contained FPR PD12A and is designed to streamline care proceedings by emphasising good case preparation by the parties and their legal representatives and promoting active case management by the court. The PLO must be read in conjunction with FPR PD25A–PD25F. See further **First appointment, Case management conference** and **Issues resolution hearing** under FPR 2010, r 12.25.

****

86 Further information about the Expert Witness Group and the Expert Witness Pack may be obtained from: Dr Eileen Vizard, Consultant Child and Adolescent Psychiatrist, Camden and Islington Community Health Services NHS Trust, Simmons House Adolescent Unit, St. Luke's-Woodside Hospital, Woodside Avenue, London N10 3HU (Telephone: 0181 219 1883).

Section 6 – Appeals from the Family Proceedings Courts under Section 94 of the Children Act 1989

****

Note—Section 6 has been overtaken by new procedural rules. All appeals from the Family Proceedings Court under CA 1989, s 94 are now governed by FPR 2010, Pt 30. The routes of appeal are set out in FPR PD30A, para 2.1, which provides that from the magistrates it is to a county court. See Procedural Guide E2.

Section 7 – Disclosure of local authority documents

Early consideration

93 Crown Prosecution Service and defence solicitors should give early consideration whether disclosure of records held in the possession of a local authority may be required. The appropriate time for such consideration will be at the commencement of the 4 weeks period (custody cases) or 6 weeks period (bail cases) between committal or transfer and the plea and directions hearing.

94 The parties should inform the judge of the steps that have been taken so that, if necessary, directions may be given and noted on the questionnaire.

95 Requests by the Crown Prosecution Service or the defence solicitor for disclosure should:

   (a) be made in writing to the legal services department of the local authority who will nominate a lawyer to deal with the matter;

   (b) provide specific details of the information required and an explanation as to why it is relevant to the proceedings, identifying as precisely as possible the category and nature of the documents for which disclosure is sought and

   (c) be accompanied by a copy of the indictment or of the schedule of charges upon committal.

96 If the defence solicitors request information, they should notify the Crown Prosecution Service of the request and vice versa.

97 Case records will be examined by legal services and the appropriate officer to identify whether they contain the information which is sought.

PART V

98 Information which is disclosed to the defence solicitors will also be disclosed to the Crown Prosecution Service and vice versa.

99 If the case records do *not* contain the requested information, the requester will be so informed by legal services which, subject to relevance and the principle of confidentiality, may be able (but is not bound) to provide a summary of the type of information which is on file.

100 If the requester is not satisfied with the response, legal services, after appropriate consultation, will provide the name of a person to be witness summonsed to attend court with the records.

101 Where the case records do contain the information requested, legal services will disclose it so long as it is not protected by public interest immunity, legal privilege or statutory confidentiality.

102 If the local authority wishes to assert protection from disclosure for the records requested or any of them, legal services, after appropriate consultation, will provide the name of a person to be witness summonsed to attend court with the records.

103 If the local authority wishes to make representations as to why the records requested should not be disclosed, it will inform:

    (a)   the requester;
    (b)   the opposing party's representative and
    (c)   the court listing officer,

and a convenient date for listing, before a judge will be set.

104 The local authority should provide a skeleton argument and serve it on the parties and the court.

105 At the hearing:

    (a)   the witness must produce the records to the judge;
    (b)   files must be flagged to identify the documents for which immunity from disclosure is sought;
    (c)   representations will be made on behalf of the parties; and
    (d)   the judge will give appropriate directions.

106 Whenever possible, the hearing will be before the judge who will be conducting the trial. If the trial judge has not been nominated, then the hearing judge may determine the issue of disclosure.

107 The judge will give his decision in court or chambers, in the presence of the parties' representatives.

108 The judge may also give direction as to the custody of the records pending trial and as to any copies to be obtained on behalf of the parties.

109 The hearing referred to above should take place not less than 4 weeks before trial.

110 Where the requester has reasonable grounds to believe that a witness or a defendant has been involved with social services, information may be obtained by writing to the relevant department stating the witness's or defendant's name, date of birth and address.

Confidentiality of records

111 The court will normally conduct the hearing at which public interest immunity is claimed in chambers, where the local authority may be represented by a solicitor.

112 When records are disclosed to the parties by order of the court, it is on the undertaking that:

(a) they will only be used for the purpose of the criminal proceedings before the court; and

(b) their contents are revealed only to the parties and their legal representatives. (Leave of the court must be obtained for wider disclosure, eg to an expert witness.)

Costs

113 An officer of the local authority who necessarily attends court for the purpose of the proceedings otherwise than as a witness may be allowed expenses (Regulation 18(2) within Costs in Criminal Cases (General) Regulations 1986).

114 The court has no power to order payment from central funds of the cost of a search or legal costs.

115 If the court rules that the application for disclosure is frivolous or by way of a fishing expedition, it may order that costs be paid by the applicant or his legal advisers.

APPENDIX A

GUIDANCE, BEST PRACTICE NOTES AND PRO FORMAS FROM THE COMMITTEE'S PREVIOUS ANNUAL REPORTS

I Best Practice Guidance on section 37(1) directions

Set out in the notes to CA 1989, s 37(1).

II Urgent hearings on Circuit before Family Division judges: standby procedure

[*see following page for Questionnaire on guardian ad litem performance*]

Note—See FPR PD12E.

PART V

III Questionnaire on guardian ad litem performance
Name of Guardian

Name of case: No:

Part one *(To be completed by the staff)*

1. Did the GAL appoint a solicitor for the first hearing?   Yes/No
2. Did the GAL attend all directions and interim hearings as appropriate?   Yes/No
3. Did the GAL adhere to the court timetable?   Yes/No
4. Did the GAL respond to telephone calls and letters satisfactorily?   Yes/No

Part two *(To be completed by the Judge/Magistrates)*

5.Did you consider the report to be *(Tick as appropriate)*   Good
                                                                                 Adequate
                                                                                 ˉPoor

6. Did the GAL give oral evidence *(Tick as appropriate)*   Well
                                                                                 Adequately
                                                                                 Inadequately

7. Did the GAL's argument / evidence justify the recommendation
made? *(Tick as appropriate)*   Well
                                                                                 Adequately
                                                                                 Inadequately

8. If you have any further comments as to any aspects of the GAL's work please
state them:

Name of court:

Date:

Signed:

Name:

Please return to:

IV Local authority assessments

Special considerations arise where the local authority wish to carry out an assessment eg a Section 37 assessment or family assessment.

In such cases the court should:

(i) Identify the purpose of the assessment.

(ii) Specify the time in which the assessment is to be carried out and direct that evidence of the outcome of the assessment be filed by a given date.

(iii) Fix a directions hearing for a date immediately after the date fixed for the completion of the assessment.

(iv) At the directions hearing the court should consider what evidence is needed to bring the case speedily and fairly to final or substantive hearing.

(v) Where the court exercises its discretion to grant leave for the papers to be shown to a particular expert, the court should go on to give directions.

These should:

– State the timescale in which the evidence in question should be produced.

– Provide for the disclosure of any written expert report both to all parties and to the other experts in the case. When a report is disclosed it should include a copy of the letter of instruction.

– Provide for discussion between experts following mutual disclosure of reports and for the filing of further evidence by the experts stating the areas of agreement and disagreement between the experts. Parties should only instruct experts who are willing to meet in advance of the hearing. When granting leave, the court must make this a condition of the appointment.

Where it proves impracticable to give such directions at the time when leave to disclose the report is granted, the court must set a date for a further directions hearing at which such directions can be given.

V Bundles of documents

Note—See FPR PD27A and r 12.12.

VI Best practice note for the judiciary and family proceedings courts when ordering a court welfare officer's report

Note—See FPR PD12B, which governs the procedure in private law cases.

VII Best practice note to court staff when welfare reports have been ordered

Note—See FPR PD12B, which governs the procedure in private law cases.

VIII Welfare report referral form

[*see following page for Receipt and undertaking for video recordings*]

Note—See FPR PD12B, which governs the procedure in private law cases.

PART V

IX Receipt and undertaking for video recordings

Name of solicitor _____ Name of firm _____

Address

Telephone _____ Solicitor's reference _____

I, the above named solicitor, hereby confirm that I am acting for (insert name of client):

_____

who is a party to the proceedings currently before the court concerning (insert name of child or children):

_____

I acknowledge receipt of the recording marked "Evidence of _____"

I acknowledge that this recording is and will remain the property of the Chief Constable of .... Police notwithstanding the fact that I agree to pay the reasonable expenses incurred by .... Police in providing me with this recording on loan.

I undertake that whilst the recording is in my possession I shall:
(a) not make or permit any other person to make a copy of the recording;
(b) not make or permit any disclosure of the recording or its contents to any person except when in my opinion it is strictly necessary in the interests of the child and / or the interests of justice;
(c) not part with possession of the recording to anyone other than to counsel instructed by me or to an expert witness authorised by the court, and in particular
(d) NOT PART WITH POSSESSION OF THE RECORDING TO *(insert name of client)*

_____

(e) at all times (except whilst being played) keep the recording in a locked, secure container and not leave it unattended in vehicles or otherwise unprotected;
(f) record details of the name of any person allowed access to the recording and produce such record to an officer of .... Police upon request;
(g) ensure that any person who takes possession of the recording under paragraph (c) above is supplied with a copy of this undertaking and agrees to be bound by its terms;
(h) return the recording to .... Police immediately upon the conclusion of the proceedings or when I am no longer professionally instructed in the matter whichever is sooner;
(i) give notice to .... Police of any application to the court which may result in the variation of the terms set out in this undertaking.

Signed:
Dated:

X Guidance as to preparation of the justices' written findings and reasons – The Honourable Mr Justice Cazalet

GENERAL

1 The obligations placed upon justices and their clerks are set out succinctly in Rules 21(5) and (6) of the Family Proceedings Courts (Children Act 1989) Rules 1991. Stated summarily these require that before the court makes an order or refuses an application or request, the justices' clerk shall record in writing, in consultation with the justices, the reason for the court's decision and any finding of fact. Furthermore, when justices make an order or refuse an application, the court, or one of the justices constituting the court by which the decision is made, shall state any finding of fact or reasons for the court's decision. These provisions are straightforward and are expressed in terminology which is unequivocal. They must be interpreted literally and strictly.

2 The justices and their clerks must ensure that the reasons and findings of fact are stated at the time the order is made. They cannot be added to subsequently. The written reasons and findings of fact must accord with what is stated in court. Justices cannot make an order and then reserve judgment (a luxury which the Court of Appeal is permitted). Justices must give their reasons, and any findings made, each time they make an order or decline to make an order.

3 There can be no "back door" process. That is to say that if, on appeal, a point is taken which the justices did consider in their deliberations but omitted to put in their reasons, they cannot formally make a subsequent addendum to those reasons and supply them to the appeal court.

4 Even when the parties are agreed, there is, none the less, an overriding duty in the court to investigate the proposals advanced by the parties. However, the extent of the investigation must reflect reality and so, when an agreed order is sought, the investigation of the evidence need not and should not be dealt with in full detail unless there are concerns as to the propriety of the order. Nevertheless, it is particularly important that in cases where a care order is made by consent the basis upon which the care order is made is clearly stated, for example because of a failure to protect from an abusive spouse or an agreed non-accidental injury as set out in some statement identified in the proceedings. If this step is taken it will avoid a long and perhaps inconclusive later trawl through the evidence in the earlier case in an attempt to establish what the actual finding then was and its relevance to a different child or new family situation. Also, justices must bear in mind that it will always be important for the child's wishes (given that the child is of sufficient age and maturity for those wishes to be relevant) to be taken into consideration. A consent order sought by the parents may not always properly reflect this.

5 The Children Act has brought two fundamental changes in the way that justices conduct hearings. First they must read all the papers before coming to court (that is to say they must come into court "hot"); second they must give their reasons and findings of fact in writing. It is essential that justices are fully conversant with the written documents before the case starts. This will have one advantage in particular. The justices will know when to intervene to stop evidence being led which simply repeats what has already been stated, usually in a statement of evidence in chief. This unnecessary repetition can be extremely time wasting.

6 It is vital to remember that the findings of fact and reasons will form the basis of any appeal accordingly they must be clearly stated. In order to avoid pressure of time when reasons are being prepared it may be appropriate to release the parties for a period or to require them to come back the next day. In this event only one of the justices concerned need attend and read out the written reasons and findings.

PART V

7 Clarity in findings and reasons is important not only so that the appeal court knows the basis on which the decision has been made but also so that the losing party knows why the decision has gone against him. It is worth remembering that decisions in family cases, unlike most other decisions in the courts, concern the future. If the losing party leaves court without understanding properly why the order has been made against him because the court has not clearly explained the reason for its decision then this will not augur well for later hearings and may well give rise to a sense of grievance which impedes the working of the order.

8 Do not be afraid to raise points with advocates during their speeches. This should help to clarify difficult points.

9 When justices make an order which differs from the advice or conclusion reached in the report of the court welfare officer or guardian ad litem it is imperative for them to set out in clear terms why they have done so. This need not be stated at great length but it must be possible for the parties (and if there is an appeal, for the appellate court) to follow the process whereby the different conclusion was reached.

10 When the arguments of the losing party are being dealt with in the findings state these first before the arguments of the party in whose favour the decision is to be made.

11 When you intervene because an advocate is being too long winded, repetitious or adversarial you will carry much more authority if you have read and fully understood the papers in the case. When you do intervene be firm, courteous and controlled.

12 When you are dealing with a care case it is usually helpful to require the advocate when opening the case for the local authority to state specifically the facts upon which he relies as establishing that the threshold criteria apply. This will enable the court to direct its mind to the material evidence as it emerges and should help to clarify at an early stage the findings which will have to be made to support a care order.

MORE SPECIFIC GUIDELINES IN SETTING OUT REASONS AND FINDINGS OF FACT

There are a number of different proformas used by different justices for the purposes of setting out their reasons and findings of fact. Once a particular system which works satisfactorily has evolved then it would be a mistake to interfere with it in any fundamental way. I accordingly set out below some guidelines which may be of assistance in formulating reasons and findings.

1 At the start state brief details about the child, parents and any other party (this includes dealing with family, siblings and where the child makes his/her home etc).

2 State, in concise form, the competing applications (ie the orders which each party is seeking).

3 State the relevant facts not in dispute, including appropriate background details (this will include stating physical injuries, emotional or educational problems from which the child may have suffered and which are not in dispute. This will *not* deal with the cause of such injuries unless that also is not in dispute). Keep this short.

4 Set out in general form the facts in dispute (for example the cause of a non-accidental injury). This will normally involve a short statement of the competing assertions by the parties concerned.

5 State your findings of fact including in particular, where appropriate, whose evidence was preferred. In general terms you should state the reasons for preferring one witness to another (for example because he or she was more convincing, because there was corroboration, or because one witness clearly had a better recollection than another and so forth). Be careful before you call a witness a liar. We are not infallible!

6 An appellate court cannot write into justices' reasons inference and findings working backwards from their conclusions. The material findings of fact must be stated so be as firm as you feel you can be when stating your findings.

7 State concisely any relevant law, and refer to the threshold criteria. Refer to any *relevant* passage of legal authority cited.

8 State your conclusions from the facts found. In particular, if you are dealing with a care case you should state why you consider the threshold criteria to apply.

9 State your decision and reasons for it, making clear that you have taken into account the welfare checklist by going through the relevant provisions.

CONCLUSION

The sequence stated above is the one that I usually follow. It matters not if you vary it somewhat or if your proforma follows a somewhat different sequence. The importance is that you should deal with all those particular headings.

The clerk is under a legal duty to record your findings and reasons in consultation with you. Once you have completed your deliberations you should call in the clerk and go through the record of your findings of fact and reasons. On the back of the proforma your clerk will enter the details of all the documentary evidence which was considered by the court.

Provided you follow these various heads you should cover all essential matters. The important thing is to get a system a sequence of headings under which you deal with the evidence and any submissions made by the advocates which lead on to your decision. Once you have learned to work within a particular framework, the preparation of the written findings and reasons will come much more easily.

PART V

APPENDIX B
THE OFFICIAL SOLICITOR: APPOINTMENT IN FAMILY PROCEEDINGS
(PRACTICE NOTE)

Appointment as guardian ad litem of child subject of proceedings
Note—See FPR PD16A.

APPENDIX C
PRACTICE DIRECTIONS BY THE PRESIDENT OF THE FAMILY DIVISION

I Applications by children

Note—See ATPO 2008 and *PD: Allocation and Transfer of Proceedings* (25 November 2008) which revokes *PD 22 February 1993: Children Act: Applications by Children* [1993] 1 FLR 668, except that it will continue to apply to any proceedings to which it is not practicable to apply the 2008 PD.

II Case management

Note—See FPR PD12A, which applies to all courts hearing applications issued by local authorities under CA 1989, Pt IV (care and supervision orders). See further **First appointment, Case management conference** and **Issues resolution hearing** under FPR 2010, r 12.25 and notes on the timetable for proceedings under FPR 2010, r 12.12.

Practice Statement
22 April 1998

Citations: [1998] 1 WLR 825; [1998] 1 FLR 1102; [1998] 2 All ER 667

Supreme Court: Judgments

New arrangements for the delivery of judgments in all divisions of the High Court and in the Court of Appeal would be introduced to facilitate the availability and speedy publication of the approved text of judgments and to prevent the dissemination of unapproved texts.

The arrangements, made in agreement with Lord Woolf MR, Sir Richard Scott V-C, and Sir Stephen Brown, President of the Family Division, were to be regarded as experimental and would apply forthwith.

Lord Bingham of Cornhill CJ: Unless the court otherwise ordered, for example, if a judgment contained price-sensitive information, copies of the written judgment would be made available to the parties' legal advisers at about 4pm on the second working day before judgment was due to be pronounced on condition that the contents were not communicated to the parties themselves until one hour before the listed time for pronouncement of judgment.

Delivery to legal advisers was made primarily to enable them to consider the judgment and decide what consequential orders they should seek. The condition was imposed to prevent the outcome of the case being publicly reported before judgment was given, since the judgment was confidential until then.

Some judges might decide to allow the parties' legal advisers to communicate the contents of the judgment to their clients 2 hours before the listed time, in order that they might be able to submit minutes of the proposed order, agreed by their clients, to the judge before the judge came into court, and it would be open to judges to permit more information about the result of a case to be communicated on a confidential basis to the client at an earlier stage if good reason were shown for making such a direction.

If, for any reason, a party's legal advisers had special grounds for seeking a relaxation of the usual condition restricting disclosure to the party itself, a request for relaxation of the condition might be made informally through the judge's clerk, or through the associate, if the judge had no clerk.

A copy of the written judgment would be made available to any party who was not legally represented at the same time as to legal advisers. It had to be treated as confidential until judgment was given.

Every page of every judgment which was made available in that way would be marked "Unapproved judgment: No permission is granted to copy or use in court". These words would carry the authority of the judge and would mean what they said.

The time at which copies of the judgment were being made available to the parties' legal advisers was being brought forward 24 hours in order to enable them to submit any written suggestions to the judge about typing errors, wrong references and other minor corrections of that kind in good time, so that, if the judge thought fit, the judgment could be corrected before it was handed down formally in court.

The parties' legal advisers were therefore requested to submit a written list of corrections of that kind to the judge's clerk, or to the associate, if the judge had no clerk, by 3pm on the day before judgment was handed down.

In divisions of the court which had two or more judges, the list should be submitted in each case to the judge who was to deliver the judgment in question.

Lawyers were not being asked to carry out proofreading for the judiciary, but a significant cause of the present delays was the fact that minor corrections of that type were being mentioned to the judge for the first time in court, when there was no time to make any necessary corrections to the text.

Availability of approved versions of handed-down judgments: new arrangements

That course would make it very much easier for the judge to make any necessary corrections and to hand down the judgment formally as the approved judgment of the court without any need for the delay involved in requiring the court shorthand writer, in courts which had an official shorthand writer, to resubmit the judgment to the judge for approval.

It would always be open to the judge to direct the shorthand writer at the time of the hearing in court to include in the text of the judgment any last-minute corrections which were mentioned for the first time in court, or which it had proved impractical to incorporate in the judgments handed down.

In such an event the judge would make it clear whether the shorthand writer could publish the judgment, as corrected, as the approved judgment of the court without any further reference to the judge, or whether it should be resubmitted to the judge for approval.

It would be open to judges, if they wished, to decline to approve their judgments at the time they were delivered, in which case the existing practice of submitting the judgment for their approval would continue.

Handing down judgment in court: availability of uncorrected copies

When the court handed down its written judgment, it would pronounce judgment in open court. Copies of the written judgment would then be made available to accredited representatives of the media, and to accredited law reporters who were willing to comply with restrictions on copying, who identified themselves as such.

In cases of particular interest to the media, it would be helpful if requests for copies could be intimated to the judge's clerk, or the presiding Lord Justice's clerk, in advance of judgment, so that the likely demand for copies could be accurately estimated.

Because there would usually be insufficient time for the judge's clerk to prepare the necessary number of copies of the corrected judgment in advance, in most cases these uncorrected copies would similarly bear the warning "Unapproved Judgment: No permission is granted to copy or use in court".

The purpose of those arrangements was to place no barrier in the way of accredited representatives of the media who wished to report the judgments of the court immediately in the usual way, or to accredited law reporters who wished to prepare a summary or digest of the judgment or to read it for the purpose of deciding whether to obtain an approved version for reporting purposes.

Its purpose was to put a stop to the dissemination of unapproved, uncorrected, judgments for other purposes, while seeking to ensure that everyone who was interested in the judgment, other than the immediate parties, might be able to buy a copy of the approved judgment in most cases much more quickly than was possible at present.

If any member of the public, other than a party to the case, or any law reporter who was not willing to comply with the restrictions on copying, wished to read the written judgment of the court on the occasion when it was handed down, a copy would be made available for him or her to read and note in court on request made to the associate or to the clerk to the judge or the presiding Lord Justice.

PART V

The copy could not be removed from the court and had to be handed back after reading. The object was to ensure that such a person was in no worse a position than if the judgment had been read aloud in full.

Availability of approved judgments

In courts without an official shorthand writer, the approved judgment should contain on its frontispiece the rubric: "This is the official judgment of the court and I direct that no further note or transcript be made".

That would cover the requirements of Ord 68, r 1 of the Rules of the Supreme Court, in the cases to which that rule applied, and would provide for certainty in all other cases.

In future, all judgments delivered at the Royal Courts of Justice would be published in a common format.

For cases decided in the two divisions of the Court of Appeal and in the Crown Office List, copies of the approved judgment could be ordered from the official shorthand writers, on payment of the appropriate fee.

In the other courts in the Royal Courts of Justice, copies of the approved judgment could be ordered from the Mechanical Recording Department, on payment of the fee prescribed for copy documents. Disks containing the judgment would also be available from the official shorthand writers, and the Mechanical Recording Department, where relevant, on payment of an appropriate charge.

It was hoped that in most cases copies of the approved judgment would be available from these sources on the same day as the judgment was handed down: they should no longer be sought from judges' clerks.

Restrictions on disclosure or reporting

Anyone who was supplied with a copy of the handed-down judgment, or who read it in court, would be bound by any direction which the court might have given in a child case under s 39 of the Children and Young Persons Act 1933, or any other form of restriction on disclosure, or reporting of information in the judgment.

Availability of approved versions of ex tempore judgments

Delays had also been experienced in the publication of approved versions of ex tempore judgments, whether they were produced by the official shorthand writers or by contractors transcribing the tapes which had been mechanically recorded.

Sometimes the delay was caused in courts without an official shorthand writer because a transcript was bespoken by one of the parties a long time after the judgment was delivered. If a transcribed copy of such a judgment was to be required, in connection with an appeal, for example, it should be ordered as soon as practicable after judgment was delivered.

Delays were also sometimes caused in those cases because judgments were delivered to a judge for approval without supplying the judge with copies of the material quoted in the judgment.

In future no judge should be invited to approve any such transcript unless the transcriber had been provided by the party ordering the transcript with copies of all the material from which the judge had quoted.

If the transcript was ordered by a person who was not a party to the case, such as a law reporter, that person should make arrangements with one of the parties to ensure that the transcriber, and the judge, would have access to all the material quoted in the judgment.

From time to time delays were also caused because judges had been slow in returning approved transcripts to the transcribers. His Lordship and the other heads of division had recently asked judges, as a general rule, that they should endeavour to return approved transcripts to the transcribers within 2 weeks of their being delivered to them for approval. If anyone encountered serious delay on that account, the relevant head of division should be informed.

Citation of authorities in court

(*revoked*)

Note—See PD of 24 March 2012: *Citation of Authorities.*

Conclusion

The purpose of these changes, which were being made on an experimental basis after full consultation with the Court Service, was to improve the quality of service rendered by the judges to those who used the courts.

Any comments on those changes, or suggestions about further improvements in relation to the matters set out in the statement, should be addressed to Brooke LJ at the Royal Courts of Justice.

They would be taken fully into account when the time came to decide whether these arrangements should be formalised, with or without amendment, in a Practice Direction.

Bingham of Cornhill LCJ

Practice Statement
25 November 1998

Citations: [1999] 1 WLR 1; [1999] 1 FLR 314; [1999] 1 All ER 125

Supreme Court: Judgments (No 2)

I am making this further statement with the agreement of Lord Woolf MR, Sir Richard Scott V-C, and Sir Stephen Brown P. Like the earlier statement I made on 22 April 1998 *(Practice Statement (Supreme Court: Judgments)* [1998] 1 FLR 1102), this statement applies to judgments delivered in all Divisions of the High Court and the Court of Appeal.

In my earlier statement I said that the arrangements I was announcing should be regarded as experimental, and that they would be kept under review. Experience since that time has shown that in general the new arrangements are working well, but that there is scope for some fine tuning. In particular, for a number of reasons it has not proved possible for the official shorthand writers to publish the official transcripts of approved, handed down, judgments quite as quickly as we had hoped, and there has been some uncertainty as to the status of the judgment given by the court to the shorthand writers.

We have decided to retain the embargo on copying the draft judgment which is sent to the parties 2 days before a judgment is handed down. An approved judgment, when handed down in court, will now be entitled "Judgment: Approved by the court for handing down (subject to editorial corrections)", and every page of a judgment which is handed down in this form will be marked in a similar manner. There will be no embargo on copying a judgment handed down in this form, so long as its status is made clear, and at present no charge will be made for permission to copy it.

In order to make it possible for approved judgments to be handed down in this way, the parties' legal advisers will be requested to submit their written list of suggested corrections by 12 noon, not 3pm, on the day before judgment is handed down. If it is not possible to comply with this deadline, any later corrections approved by the judge will be included in the final text which the official shorthand writer (or the judge's clerk, in courts which lack an official shorthand writer) will incorporate into the approved official text of the judgment as soon as practicable.

Where a reserved written judgment has not been reported, reference must still be made in court to the approved official transcript (if this is available) and not to the approved transcript which is handed down, since this may have been subject to late revision after the text was prepared for handing down.

We will continue to keep these experimental arrangements under review. Comments or suggestions about any aspect of the arrangements should, once again, be addressed to Brooke LJ.

Bingham of Cornhill LCJ

Practice Direction
12 January 1999

Citations: [1999] 1 FLR 503

Names of Deceased: Death Certificates

In order to facilitate the operation of standing searches and caveats and to ensure the accuracy of probate records, it is directed that in all instances where the deceased died in the UK and the death has been recorded in the Register of Deaths:

(a) the name and dates of birth and death of the deceased as recorded in the Register shall be included in the oath lodged in support of an application made through a solicitor or probate practitioner for a grant of representation;

(b) the name and date of death of the deceased as recorded in the Register shall be included in the notice lodged for a standing search or caveat; and

(c) in any case where the name of the deceased or by which the deceased was known differs from that recorded in the Register, that name shall also be included in the oath or the notice, as the case may be.

Gerald Angel
Senior District Judge

President's Direction
24 July 2000

Citations: [2000] 1 WLR 1782; [2000] 2 FLR 429; [2000] 4 All ER 288

Human Rights Act 1998

1 It is directed that the following practice shall apply as from 2 October 2000 in all family proceedings:

Citation of authorities

2 When an authority referred to in s 2 of the Human Rights Act 1998 ("the Act") is to be cited at a hearing:

    (a) the authority to be cited shall be an authoritative and complete report;

    (b) the court must be provided with a list of authorities it is intended to cite and copies of the reports:

        (i)   in cases to which *Practice Direction (Family Proceedings: Court Bundles)* (10 March 2000) [2000] 1 FLR 536 applies, as part of the bundle;

        (ii) otherwise, not less than 2 clear days before the hearing; and

    (c) copies of the complete original texts issued by the European Court and Commission, either paper based or from the Court's judgment database (HUDOC) which is available on the internet, may be used.

Note—*PD Family Proceedings: Court Bundles* of 10 March 2000, [2000] 1 FLR 536, has been replaced by *PD Family Proceedings: Court Bundles (Universal Practice to be Applied in all Courts other than the Family Proceedings Court)* of 27 July 2006, and any reference in any other PD to *PD Family Proceedings: Court Bundles* shall be read as if substituted by a reference to *PD Family Proceedings: Court Bundles (Universal Practice to be Applied in all Courts other than the Family Proceedings Court)* (see paras 13, 14)

Allocation to judges

3 (1) The hearing and determination of the following will be confined to a High Court judge:

    (a) a claim for a declaration of incompatibility under s 4 of the Act; or

    (b) an issue which may lead to the court considering making such a declaration.

(2) The hearing and determination of a claim made under the Act in respect of a judicial act shall be confined in the High Court to a High Court judge and in county courts to a circuit judge.

Issued with the concurrence and approval of the Lord Chancellor.

Dame Elizabeth Butler-Sloss
President

PART V

Practice Direction
2 October 2000

Citations: [2000] 1 WLR 1886; [2000] 4 All ER 895; [2000] 1 Cr App R 147

Justices: Clerk to Court

1 A justices' clerk is responsible for:

  (a) the legal advice tendered to the justices within the area;
  (b) the performance of any of the functions set out below by any member of his/her staff acting as legal adviser;
  (c) ensuring that competent advice is available to justices when the justices' clerk is not personally present in court;
  (d) the effective delivery of case management and the reduction of unnecessary delay.

2 Where a person other than the justices' clerk, a legal adviser who is authorised to do so, performs any of the functions referred to in this direction s/he will have the same responsibilities as the justices' clerk.

The legal adviser can consult the justices' clerk or other person authorised by the justices' clerk for that purpose before tendering advice to the bench. If the justices' clerk or that person gives any advice directly to the bench, s/he shall give the parties or their advocates an opportunity of repeating any relevant submissions prior to the advice being given.

3 It will be the responsibility of the legal adviser to provide the justices with any advice they require to properly perform their functions, whether or not the justices have requested that advice, on:

  (i)   questions of law, including European Court of Human Rights jurisprudence and those matters set out in section 2(1) of the Human Rights Act 1998;
  (ii)   questions of mixed law and fact;
  (iii) matters of practice and procedure;
  (iv)   the range of penalties available;
  (v)   any relevant decisions of the superior courts or other guidelines;
  (vi)   other issues relevant to the matter before the court;
  (vii) the appropriate decision-making structure to be applied in any given case.

In addition to advising the justices it will be the legal adviser's responsibility to assist the court, where appropriate, as to the formulation of reasons and the recording of those reasons.

4 A justices' clerk or legal adviser must not play any part in making findings of fact but can assist the bench by reminding them of the evidence, using any notes of the proceedings for that purpose.

5 A justices' clerk or legal adviser can ask questions of witnesses and the parties in order to clarify the evidence and any issues in the case.

6 A legal adviser has a duty to ensure that every case is conducted fairly.

7 When advising the justices the justices' clerk or legal adviser, whether or not previously in court, shall:

  (i)   ensure that s/he is aware of the relevant facts;
  (ii) provide the parties with the information necessary to enable the parties to make any representations they wish as to the advice before it is given.

8 At any time, justices are entitled to receive advice to assist them in discharging their responsibilities.

If they are in any doubt as to the evidence which has been given, they should seek the aid of their legal adviser, referring to his/her notes as appropriate. That should ordinarily be done in open court. Where the justices request their adviser to join them in the retiring room, that request should be made in the presence of the parties in court.

Any legal advice given to the justices other than in open court should be clearly stated to be provisional and the adviser should subsequently repeat the substance of the advice in open court and give the parties an opportunity to make any representations they wish on that provisional advice.

The legal adviser should then state in open court whether the provisional advice is confirmed or, if it is varied, the nature of the variation.

9 The performance of a legal adviser can be appraised by a person authorised by the magistrates' courts committee to do so.

For that purpose the appraiser can be present in the justices' retiring room. The content of the appraisal is confidential, but the fact that an appraisal has taken place, and the presence of the appraiser in the retiring room, should be briefly explained in open court.

10 The legal adviser is under a duty to assist unrepresented parties to present their case, but must do so without appearing to become an advocate for the party concerned.

11 The role of legal advisers in fine default proceedings or any other proceedings for the enforcement of financial orders, obligations or penalties is to assist the court. They must not act in an adversarial or partisan manner.

With the agreement of the justices a legal adviser can ask questions of the defaulter to elicit information which the justices will require to make an adjudication, for example to facilitate his or her explanation for the default.

A legal adviser can also advise the justices in the normal way as to the options open to them in dealing with the case. It will be inappropriate for the legal adviser to set out to establish wilful refusal or neglect or any other type of culpable behaviour, to offer an opinion on the facts, or to urge a particular course of action upon the justices.

The duty of impartiality is the paramount consideration for the legal adviser at all times, and that takes precedence over any role s/he may have as a collecting officer.

The appointment of other staff to "prosecute" the case for the collecting officer is not essential to ensure compliance with the law, including the Human Rights Act 1998. Whether to make such appointments is a matter for the justices' chief executive.

12 *Practice Direction (Justices: Clerk to Court)* ([1981] 1 WLR 1163) is revoked. *Practice Note (Justices' Clerks)* ([1954] 1 WLR 213) remains in force.

Lord Woolf
Lord Chief Justice

PART V

Practice Direction
11 January 2001

Citations: [2001] 1 WLR 194; [2001] 1 All ER 193; [2001] 1 Cr App R 426

Judgments: Form and Citation

Lord Woolf CJ: gave the following direction at the sitting of the court.

This practice direction is made with the concurrence of the Master of the Rolls, the Vice-Chancellor and the President of the Family Division. It represents the next stage in the process of modernising the arrangements for the preparation, distribution and citation of judgments given in every division of the High Court, whether in London or in courts outside London.

Form of judgments

1.1 With effect from 11 January 2001, all judgments in every division of the High Court and the Court of Appeal will be prepared for delivery, or issued as approved judgments, with single spacing, paragraph numbering (in the margins) but no page numbers. In courts with more than one judge, the paragraph numbering will continue sequentially through each judgment, and will not start again at the beginning of the second judgment. Indented paragraphs will not be given a number.

1.2 The main reason of these changes is to facilitate the publication of judgments on the World Wide Web and their subsequent use by the increasing numbers of those who had access to the Web. The changes should also assist those who used and wish to search judgments stored on electronic databases.

1.3 It is desirable in the interests of consistency that all judgments prepared for delivery (or issued as approved judgments) in county courts, should also contain paragraph numbering (in the margins).

Neutral citation of judgments

2.1 With effect from 11 January 2001 a form of neutral citation will be introduced in both divisions of the Court of Appeal and in the Administrative Court. A unique number will be given by the official shorthand writers to each approved judgment issued out of these courts. The judgments will be numbered in the following way:

> Court of Appeal (Civil Division) [2000] EWCA Civ 1, 2, 3 etc
> Court of Appeal (Criminal Division) [2000] EWCA Crim 1, 2, 3 etc
> High Court (Administrative Court) [2000] EWHC Admin 1, 2, 3 etc

2.2 Under these new arrangements, paragraph 59 in *Smith v Jones*, the tenth numbered judgment of the year in the Civil Division of the Court of Appeal, would be cited: *Smith v Jones* [2001] EWCA Civ 10 at [59].

2.3 The neutral citation will be the official number attributed to the judgment by the court and must always be used on at least one occasion when the judgment was cited in a later judgment. Once the judgment is reported, the neutral citation will appear in front of the familiar citation from the law report series: thus *Smith v Jones* [2001] EWCA Civ 10 at [30], [2001] QB 124, [2001] 2 All ER 364, etc. The paragraph number must be the number allotted by the court in all future versions of the judgment.

2.4 If a judgment is cited on more than one occasion in a later judgment, it will be of the greatest assistance if only one abbreviation, if desired, is used. Thus *Smith v Jones*

[2001] EWCA Civ 10 could be abbreviated on subsequent occasions to *Smith v Jones*, or *Smith's* case, but preferably not both in the same judgment.

2.5 If it is desired to cite more than one paragraph of a judgment each numbered paragraph should be enclosed with a square bracket: thus *Smith v Jones* [2001] EWCA Civ 10 at [30]–[35], or *Smith v Jones* [2001] EWCA Civ 10 at [30], [35], and [40]–[43].

2.6 The neutral citation arrangements will be extended to include other parts of the High Court as soon as the necessary administrative arrangements can be made.

2.7 The Administrative Court citation will be given to all judgments in the Administrative Court, whether they are delivered by a Divisional court or by a single judge.

Citation of judgments in court

(*revoked*)

Note—See PD of 24 March 2012: *Citation of Authorities*.

Concluding comments

4.1 The changes described in this practice direction follow what is becoming accepted international practice. They are intended to make it easier to distribute, store and search judgments, and less expensive and time-consuming to reproduce them for use in court. Lord Justice Brooke is still responsible for advising the Judges' Council on these matters, and any comments on these new arrangements, or suggestions about ways in which they could be improved still further, should be addressed to him at the Royal Courts of Justice, WC2A 2LL.

Lord Woolf
Lord Chief Justice

PART V

Practice Direction
9 April 2001

Citations: [2001] 1 WLR 1001; [2001] 2 All ER 510; [2001] Fam Law 794

Citation of Authorities

Introduction

1 In recent years, there has been a substantial growth in the number of readily available reports of judgments in this and other jurisdictions, such reports being available either in published reports or in transcript form. Widespread knowledge of the work and decisions of the courts is to be welcomed. At the same time, however, the current weight of available material causes problems both for advocates and for courts in properly limiting the nature and amount of material that is used in the preparation and argument of subsequent cases.

2 The latter issue is a matter of rapidly increasing importance. Recent and continuing efforts to increase the efficiency, and thus reduce the costs, of litigation, whilst maintaining the interests of justice, will be threatened if courts are burdened with a

weight of inappropriate and unnecessary authority, and if advocates are uncertain as to the extent to which it is necessary to deploy authorities in the argument of any given case.

3 With a view to limiting the citation of previous authority to cases that are relevant and useful to the court, this Practice Direction lays down a number of rules as to what material may be cited, and the manner in which that cited material should be handled by advocates. These rules are in large part such as many courts already follow in pursuit of their general discretion in the management of litigation. However, it is now desirable to promote uniformity of practice by the same rules being followed by all courts.

4 It will remain the duty of advocates to draw the attention of the court to any authority not cited by an opponent which is adverse to the case being advanced.

5 This Direction applies to all courts apart from criminal courts, including within that latter category the Court of Appeal (Criminal Division).

Categories of judgments that may only be cited if they fulfil specified requirements

6.1 A judgment falling into one of the categories referred to in paragraph 6.2 below may not in future be cited before any court unless it clearly indicates that it purports to establish a new principle or to extend the present law. In respect of judgments delivered after the date of this Direction, that indication must take the form of an express statement to that effect. In respect of judgments delivered before the date of this Direction that indication must be present in or clearly deducible from the language used in the judgment.

6.2 Paragraph 6.1 applies to the following categories of judgment:

> Applications attended by one party only;
> Applications for permission to appeal;
> Decisions on applications that only decide that the application is arguable;
> county court cases, unless:
> (a) cited in order to illustrate the conventional measure of damages in a personal injury case; or
> (b) cited in a county court in order to demonstrate current authority at that level on an issue in respect of which no decision at a higher level of authority is available.

6.3 These categories will be kept under review, such review to include consideration of adding to the categories.

Citation of other categories of judgment

7.1 Courts will in future pay particular attention, when it is sought to cite other categories of judgment, to any indication given by the court delivering the judgment that it was seen by that court as only applying decided law to the facts of the particular case; or otherwise as not extending or adding to the existing law.

7.2 Advocates who seek to cite a judgment that contains indications of the type referred to in paragraph 7.1 will be required to justify their decision to cite the case.

Methods of citation

8.1 Advocates will in future be required to state, in respect of each authority that they wish to cite, the proposition of law that the authority demonstrates, and the parts of the judgment that support that proposition. If it is sought to cite more than one authority in support of a given proposition, advocates must state the reason for taking that course.

8.2 The demonstration referred to in paragraph 8.1 will be required to be contained in any skeleton argument and in any appellant's or respondent's notice in respect of each authority referred to in that skeleton or notice.

8.3 Any bundle or list of authorities prepared for the use of any court must in future bear a certification by the advocate responsible for arguing the case that the requirements of this paragraph have been complied with in respect of each authority included.

8.4 The statements referred to in paragraph 8.1 should not materially add to the length of submissions or of skeleton arguments, but should be sufficient to demonstrate, in the context of the advocate's argument, the relevance of the authority or authorities to that argument and that the citation is necessary for a proper presentation of that argument.

Authorities decided in other jurisdictions

9.1 Cases decided in other jurisdictions can, if properly used, be a valuable source of law in this jurisdiction. At the same time, however, such authority should not be cited without proper consideration of whether it does indeed add to the existing body of law.

9.2 In future, therefore, any advocate who seeks to cite an authority from another jurisdiction must:

    (i)   comply in respect of that authority, with the rules set out in paragraph 8 above;

    (ii) indicate in respect of each authority what that authority adds that is not to be found in authority in this jurisdiction; or, if there is said to be justification for adding to domestic authority, what that justification is; and

    (iii) certify that there is no authority in this jurisdiction that precludes the acceptance by the court of the proposition that the foreign authority is said to establish.

9.3 For the avoidance of doubt, paragraphs 9.1 and 9.2 do not apply to cases decided in either the European Court of Justice or the organs of the European Convention of Human Rights. Because of the status in English law of such authority, as provided by, respectively, section 3 of the European Communities Act 1972 and section 2(1) of the Human Rights Act 1998, such cases are covered by the earlier paragraphs of this Direction.

Note—See also PD of 24 March 2012: *Citation of Authorities.*

Lord Woolf
Lord Chief Justice

Attorney-General's Memorandum
19 December 2001

Citations: [2002] Fam Law 229

Requests for the Appointment of an Advocate to the Court

1 The memorandum has been agreed between the Attorney-General and the Lord Chief Justice. It gives guidance about making a request for the appointment of an advocate to the court (formerly called an amicus curiae).

2 In most cases, an advocate to the court is appointed by the Attorney-General, following a request by the court. In some cases, an advocate to the court will be appointed by the Official Solicitor or the Children and Family Court Advisory and Support Service (CAFCASS) (see paras 11 and 12 below).

The role of an advocate to the court

3 A court may properly seek the assistance of an advocate to the court when there is a danger of an important and difficult point of law being decided without the court hearing relevant argument. In those circumstances the Attorney-General may decided to appoint an advocate to the court.

4 It is important to bear in mind that an advocate to the court represents no one. His or her function is to give to the court such assistance as he or she is able on the relevant law and its application to the facts of the case. An advocate to the court will not normally be instructed to lead evidence, cross-examine witnesses, or investigate the facts. In particular, it is not appropriate for the court to seek assistance from an advocate to the court simply because a defendant in criminal proceedings refuses representation.

5 The following circumstances are to be distinguished from those where it will be appropriate for the court to seek the assistance of an advocate to the court:

- (i)   where a point of law which affects a government department is being argued in a case where the department is not represented and where the court believes that the department may wish to be represented;
- (ii) where the Attorney believes it is necessary for him to intervene as a party in his capacity as guardian of the public interest;
- (iii) where the court believes it is appropriate for a litigant in person to seek free (pro bono) assistance;
- (iv) where, in a criminal trial, the defendant is unrepresented and the advocate to the court would be duplicating the prosecutor's duty as a minister of justice "to assist the court on all matters of law applicable to the case";
- (v)   where in a criminal case in relation to sentencing appeals there are issues of fact which are likely to arise and the prosecution ought to be represented, or it would be reasonable to ask the prosecutor to be present and address the court as to the relevant law.

6 In the first of these five cases, the court may invite the Attorney to make arrangements for the advocate to be instructed on behalf of the department. In the second, the court may grant the Attorney permission to intervene, in which case the advocate instructed represents the Attorney. In neither case is the advocate an advocate to the court.

7 In the third case the court may grant a litigant in person an adjournment to enable him or her to seek free (pro bono) assistance. In doing so, the court should bear in mind that it is likely to take longer to obtain free (pro bono) representation than funded representation. In contrast to an advocate to the court, a free (pro bono) legal representative will obtain his or her instructions from the litigant and will represent the interests of that party. His or her role before the court and duty to the court will be identical to that of any other representative of the parties. Accordingly it will not be appropriate for the court to take such a course where the type of assistance required is that provided by an advocate to the court.

8 In the fourth case the prosecutor's special duty is akin to an advocate to the court. In the fifth case, in relation to appeals against sentence where the defendant is represented, it may be preferable to request the attendance of the prosecutor, who will be able to address the court on issues of fact and law. It would not be proper for an advocate to the

court to take instructions from the prosecuting authority in relation to factual matters relating to the prosecution. An advocate to the court should only be asked to address the court as to the relevant law.

Making a request to the Attorney-General

9 A request for an advocate to the court should be made by the court as soon as convenient after it is made aware of the point of law which requires the assistance of an advocate to the court. The request should set out the circumstances which have occurred, identifying the point of law upon which assistance is sought and the nature of the assistance required. The court should consider whether it would be sufficient for such assistance to be in writing in the form of submissions as to the law, or whether the assistance should include oral submissions at the hearing. The request should ordinarily be made in writing and be accompanied by the papers necessary to enable the Attorney to reach a decision on the basis of a proper understanding of the case.

10 The Attorney will decide whether it is appropriate to provide such assistance and, if so, the form such assistance should take. Before reaching a decision he may seek further information or assistance from the court. The Attorney will also ask the court to keep under review the need for such assistance. Where the circumstances which gave rise to the original request have changed, such that the court may now anticipate hearing all relevant argument on the point of law without the presence of an advocate to the court, either the court or the Attorney may ask the advocate to the court to withdraw.

Requests to the Official Solicitor or CAFCASS

11 A request for an advocate to the court may be made to the Official Solicitor or CAFCASS (Legal Services and Special Casework) where the issue is one in which their experience of representing children and adults under disability gives rise to special experience. The division of responsibility between them is outlined in Practice Notes reported at [2001] 2 FLR 151 and [2001] 2 FLR 155.

12 The procedure and circumstances for requesting an advocate to the court to be appointed by the Official Solicitor or CAFCASS are the same as those applying to requests to the Attorney-General. In cases of extreme urgency, telephone requests may be made. In some cases, the Official Solicitor himself will be appointed as advocate to the court. He may be given directions by the court authorising him to obtain documents, conduct investigations and enquiries and to advise the court. He may appear by counsel or an in-house advocate.

Lord Goldsmith QC
Attorney-General

Lord Woolf
Lord Chief Justice

Requests for an advocate to the court should be addressed as follows:

> The Legal Secretary,
> The Legal Secretariat to the Law Officers,
> Attorney-General's Chambers,
> 9 Buckingham Gate,
> London SW1E 6JP,
> tel 020 7271 2417 (criminal), 020 7271 2413 (civil),
> fax 020 7271 2434.

PART V

Official Solicitor to the Supreme Court,
81 Chancery Lane,
London WC2A 1DD,
tel 020 7911 7127, fax 020 7911 7105.

CAFCASS (Legal Services and Special Casework),
Newspaper House,
8–16 Great New Street,
London EC4A 3BN,
tel 020 7904 0867, fax 020 7904 0868/9.

For information about free (pro bono) services: Bar Pro Bono Unit, 7 Gray's Inn Square, London WC1R 5AZ, tel 020 7831 9711, fax 020 7831 9733, email enquiries@barprobonounit.f9.co.uk.

Protocol
January 2003

Citations: [2003] Fam Law 199

Child Abduction Cases between the UK and Pakistan

The President of the Family Division and the Hon Chief Justice of Pakistan in consultation with senior members of the family judiciary of the United Kingdom ("the UK") and the Islamic Republic of Pakistan ("Pakistan"), having met on 15–17 January 2003 in the Royal Courts of Justice in London, reach the following consensus:

WHEREAS:

(a) Desiring to protect the children of the UK and Pakistan from the harmful effects of wrongful removal or retention from one country to the other;

(b) Mindful that the UK and Pakistan share a common heritage of law and a commitment to the welfare of children;

(c) Desirous of promoting judicial cooperation, enhanced relations and the free flow of information between the judiciaries of the UK and Pakistan; and

(d) Recognising the importance of negotiation, mediation and conciliation in the resolution of family disputes;

IT IS AGREED THAT:

1 In normal circumstances the welfare of a child is best determined by the courts of the country of the child's habitual/ordinary residence.

2 If a child is removed from the UK to Pakistan, or from Pakistan to the UK, without the consent of the parent with a custody/residence order or a restraint/interdict order from the court of the child's habitual/ordinary residence, the judge of the court of the country to which the child has been removed shall not ordinarily exercise jurisdiction over the child, save in so far as it is necessary for the court to order the return of the child to the country of the child's habitual/ordinary residence.

3 If a child is taken from the UK to Pakistan, or from Pakistan to the UK, by a parent with visitation/access/contact rights with the consent of the parent with a custody/residence order or a restraint/interdict order from the court of the child's habitual/ordinary residence or in consequence of an order from that court permitting the visit, and the child is retained in that country after the end of the visit without consent or

in breach of the court order, the judge of the court of the country in which the child has been retained shall not ordinarily exercise jurisdiction over the child, save in so far as it is necessary for the court to order the return of the child to the country of the child's habitual/ordinary residence.

4 The above principles shall apply without regard to the nationality, culture or religion of the parents or either parent and shall apply to children of mixed marriages.

5 In cases where the habitual/ordinary residence of the child is in dispute the court to which an application is made should decide the issue of habitual/ordinary residence before making any decision on the return or on the general welfare of the child, and upon determination of the preliminary issue as to habitual/ordinary residence should then apply the general principles set out above.

6 These applications should be lodged by the applicant, listed by the court and decided expeditiously.

7 It is recommended that the respective governments of the UK and Pakistan give urgent consideration to identifying or establishing an administrative service to facilitate or oversee the resolution of child abduction cases (not covered by the 1980 Hague Convention on the Civil Aspects of International Child Abduction).

8 It is further recommended that the judiciaries, the legal practitioners and the non-governmental organisations in the UK and Pakistan use their best endeavours to advance the objects of this protocol.

9 It is agreed that the UK and Pakistan shall each nominate a judge of the superior court to work in liaison with each other to advance the objects of this protocol.

SIGNED BY: Dame Elizabeth Butler-Sloss, DBE, President of the Family Division of the High Court of England and Wales and The Hon Mr Justice Sh Riaz Ahmad, Chief Justice of the Supreme Court of Pakistan

Dame Elizabeth Butler-Sloss
President

President's Guidance
21 January 2004

Citations: [2004] 1 FLR 746

UK Passport Applications on Behalf of Children in the Absence of the Signature of a Person with Parental Responsibility

1 This guidance deals with situations in which the court has decided that it is in a child's best interests that s/he be issued with a passport, but the adult/s with parental responsibility have refused to sign the passport application form.

2 This kind of situation might arise where a child is voluntarily accommodated by a local authority and, for example, wishes to go on holiday independently or with his/her carers.

3 The UK Passport Application form is in a standard form which will not be entirely suitable in these kinds of circumstances.

4 The UK Passport Service has therefore agreed that it will be acceptable to complete the form in the following manner:

Sections 1–6

5 These sections must be completed.

Section 7 (Relevant only re: Children aged 16 or 17)

6 If no person with parental responsibility is prepared to sign section 7, and the court has decided that it is in the best interests of the child that a passport be issued to the child, then the section may be left blank provided that the application is accompanied by an order of the court that:

(a)   the parent/s (as appropriate) should not use their parental responsibility to veto the application; and

(b)   that the court considers it to be in the best interests of the child that a passport be issued.

Section 8

7 This question should be completed if relevant to the application.

Section 9

8 *Where a child is aged 16 or 17*: the child may personally sign this section.

9 *Where a child is aged under 16*: it is imperative that an adult sign this section. In the absence of a person holding parental responsibility, there will presumably be another adult in a position to sign the form (eg the adult with whom the child is going on holiday). It would not be necessary or proper for the judge to sign the form personally.

10 If the adult signing the form is not a parent or guardian with parental responsibility for the child, the section can be manually altered as follows:

(a)   Clauses 2, 3, 4 and 6 may be deleted, if any of them causes any concern or difficulty for the adult signing the form.

(b)   Clauses 1, 5, 7 and 8 must not be deleted: they are mandatory declarations without which the application will not be processed.

11 If any clauses are deleted in accordance with para 10 above, then the application form must be accompanied by:

(a)   An order of the court that:
   (i)   the parent/s (as appropriate) should not use their parental responsibility to veto the application; and
   (ii)   that the court considers it to be in the best interests of the child that a passport be issued; plus

(b)   A statement from the adult signing s 9 setting out a written explanation as to why they are making the application on the child's behalf, what their relationship is to the child, and in the case of a child being accommodated by a local authority an explanation from that authority.

12 Additionally, if cl 3 is deleted, then the adult signing the form must instead enter at s 8 a statement in the following terms: "The person named at s 2 is, to the best of my knowledge and belief, a British national and has not lost or renounced his/her national status".

Ananda Hall
Family Division Lawyer

Cairo Declaration
17 January 2005

Resulting from Anglo-Egyptian Meetings on Judicial Co-operation in International Child Abduction Matters between Egypt and the UK

British and Egyptian judges commenced discussions in London on 19 and 20 January 2004 to effect judicial co-operation on international child abduction matters between the Arab Republic of Egypt and the UK. The British delegation was led by The Rt Hon Dame Elizabeth Butler-Sloss, President of the Family Division of the High Court of England and Wales, and included The Rt Hon Lord Justice Mathew Thorpe, of the Court of Appeal of England and Wales, The Hon Mr Justice John Gillen, of the High Court of Northern Ireland, and The Hon Lady Anne Smith, of the Supreme Court of Scotland. The Egyptian judicial delegation was let by The Hon Chief Justice Mamdouh Maruc and included The Hon Deputy Chief Justice Adel Omar Sherif, both of the Supreme Constitutional Court of Egypt.

On 20 January 2004, the participating judges agreed to recommend to their respective governments that they should institute proper procedures to adopt the following agreed principles (the Agreement):

(1) The principles of the UN Convention on the Rights of the Child 1989 are affirmed. Accordingly:
    (a) the child's best interests are the primary consideration;
    (b) the child's personal relations and direct contact with both parents, even if the parents live in different countries, are to be maintained;
    (c) the child is entitled to know and appreciate the culture and traditions of both his parents; and
    (d) States are obliged to take measures to combat the illicit transfer of children to, and non-return from, abroad.
(2) It is important to maintain the continuity of the religious upbringing of the child.
(3) The courts of the State where the child has his home should take decisions about the welfare of the child.
(4) Such decisions, as well as decisions as to the place of his home, should be respected by the courts of other States.
(5) It is important to ensure the proper implementation of court orders relating to children.
(6) Judges should be trained in international aspects of child and family disputes.
(7) Provision should be made for regular judicial exchanges between Egypt and the UK, enhancing opportunities for joint training.
(8) The practical benefits of closer judicial collaboration should be secured by the appointment of liaison judges and by facilitating other forms of direct judicial communication.
(9) In all family disputes early consideration should be given to resolution by all forms of alternative dispute resolution.

Further to these efforts, the British judicial delegation visited Cairo to continue the discussions on this topic, where they met with the Egyptian judicial delegation for a second time. During this round of discussions, an expanded Egyptian judicial delegation included The Hon Justice Elham Nawar, The Hon Justice Mohamad A El-Shenawy, The Hon Justice Mahor S Youseef and The Hon Justice Mahmoud M Guname, all of them judges of the Supreme Constitutional Court of Egypt. These discussions took place at the premises of the Supreme Constitutional Court of Egypt from 15 to 17 January 2005.

PART V

Following an official opening ceremony attended by His Excellency the Egyptian Minister of Justice Mahmoud Abou El Leil, who praised and gave his complete support to the Anglo-Egyptian judicial efforts, and following intensive discussions that took place over 3 days, the participating judges agreed to supplement the following principles to the ones agreed upon in London

(1) The Agreement shall apply only to children up to the age of 16.
(2) Reciprocal rights of access to the courts shall be available to parents of any child the subject of proceedings in either jurisdiction.
(3A) Emergency or provisional orders shall be made by the jurisdiction in which the child is currently present.
(3B) For the avoidance of doubt, in para 3 of the Agreement, the reference to the 'home' of the child is to the child's home immediately preceding the child's removal.
(4) Each State shall ensure reciprocal enforcement of orders relating to child proceedings to the full extent of its own laws and procedures and in a manner not contrary to public order or public policy in its own jurisdiction.
(5) The Family Court in Egypt and the Family Division of the High Court of England and Wales shall establish and maintain a register of child the subject of proceedings in Egypt and the UK respectively. The register shall record the nationality of each parent, the age of the child, copies of any order made in relation to the child and reports on the child's health, education and social circumstances. The data recorded in either register shall be made available to the other expeditiously upon request.
(6) The parties welcome the nomination made by The Hon Mamdouh Marie, Chief Justice of the Supreme Constitutional Court of Egypt, in agreement with His Excellency Minister of Justice Mahmoud Abou El Leil, of The Rt Hon Lord Justice Mathew Thorpe, Head of International Family Law for England and Wales, as Liaison Judge for UK with regard to this agreement.

The heads of the two judicial delegations have signed this agreement in two Arabic and two English originals at the premises of the Supreme Constitutional Court in Egypt on Monday 17 January 2005. Each delegation is in possession of the originals in Arabic and English and shall present them to its government and recommend their adoption or implementation as required.

The Hon Chief Justice Mamdouh Marie
Chief Justice of the Supreme Constitutional Court of Egypt

The Rt Hon Dame Elizabeth Butler-Sloss
President of the Family Division of the High Court of England and Wales

CAFCASS Practice Note
18 March 2005

Citations: [2005] 2 FLR 111

Applications for Reporting Restriction Orders

1 Introduction

This Note sets out recommended practice in relation to any application in the Family Division founded on Convention rights for an order which restricts freedom of expression. It is issued in conjunction with the *President's Practice Direction*

Applications For Reporting Restriction Orders dated 18 March 2005 and is subject to decisions of the courts. It applies directly to any proceedings in which CAFCASS or the Official Solicitor represent a child or incapacitated adult, and follows discussions between the Official Solicitor, the Deputy Director of Legal Services CAFCASS, and representatives of media interests.

2 Statutory provisions

An application founded on Convention rights need only be made where statutory provisions cannot provide adequate protection. Relevant provisions are Administration of Justice Act 1960, s 12(1); Children and Young Persons Act 1933, s 39; Contempt of Court Act 1981, s 11; Children Act 1989, s 8 (prohibited steps order preventing disclosure of information by parental figure) and s 97(2). While the President's Practice Direction is not aimed at applications under these provisions, s 12(2) of the Human Rights Act 1998 applies to any application for relief which might affect the exercise of the Convention right to freedom of expression and the procedures set out in this Note, including the arrangements for advance notification, can be used to secure compliance with this section in relation to any such application under these provisions.

An order founded on Convention rights may be required, for example, because:

– the need for protection is not linked to particular court proceedings
– the statutory provisions do not prevent publication of all kinds of information
– an injunction is needed to prevent approaches to family, doctors or carers.

3 Application and evidence

The application may be a freestanding claim brought under the Part 8 procedure in the Civil Procedure Rules 1998 or it may be made within existing proceedings to which either the CPR or Family Proceedings Rules 1991 apply. It may be appropriate to seek a direction under CPR 39.2(4), where it applies, that the identity of a party or witness should not be disclosed, and for documents to be drafted identifying individuals by initials.

The applicant should prepare (a) the application/claim form (b) a witness statement justifying the need for an order (c) any legal submissions (d) a draft order and (e) an explanatory note.

Model Forms of Order and an example of an explanatory note are attached to this Practice Note and can be downloaded from the websites of either the Official Solicitor (*www.offsol.demon.co.uk*) or CAFCASS (*www.cafcass.gov.uk*).

In the rare event that it is not possible to draft such documentation in the time available before the hearing, the court is likely to require the applicant to file a statement at the earliest opportunity, setting out the information placed orally before the Court.

Subject to any contrary direction of the court, this material should be made available on request to any person who is affected by the order. See *W v H (Family Division: Without Notice Orders)* [2001] 2 WLR 253; [2001] 2 FLR 927.

Note—The new website for the Official Solicitor is at *www.justice.gov.uk/about/ospt.*

4 Service of application

As required by the Practice Direction, advance notice should normally be given to the national media via the Press Association's CopyDirect service. Applicants should first telephone CopyDirect (tel. no 0870 837 6429). Documentation should be sent either by fax (fax no 0870 837 6429) or to the e-mail address provided by CopyDirect. CopyDirect

PART V

will be responsible for notifying the individual media organisations. In the case of an application against the world at large this is sufficient service for the purposes of advance notice. The website: *http://www.medialawyer.press.net/courtapplications* gives details of the organisations represented and instructions for service of the application. Unless there is a particular reason not to do so, copies of all the documents referred to above should be served. If there is a reason for not serving some or all of the documents (or parts of them), the applicant should ensure sufficient detail is given to enable the media to make an informed decision as to whether it wishes to attend or be legally represented.

The CopyDirect service does not extend to local or regional media or magazines. If service of the application on any specific organisation or person not covered is required it should be effected directly. The Official Solicitor and CAFCASS Legal hold lists of contact details for many national and some regional news organisations, and these are posted on their websites.

5 *The hearing*

Any application invoking Convention rights will involve a balancing of rights under Article 8 (right to respect for private and family life) and Article 10 (freedom of expression). There is no automatic precedence as between these Articles, and both are subject to qualification where (among other considerations) the rights of others are engaged. Section 12(4) of the Act requires the court to have particular regard to the importance of freedom of expression. It must also have regard to the extent to which material has or is about to become available to the public, the extent of the public interest in such material being published and the terms of any relevant privacy code (such as those of the Press Complaints Commission).

The court's approach is laid down in *Re S (a child) (identification: restriction on publication)* [2003] EWCA Civ 963, (CA) and [2004] UKHL 47, (HL) and *Campbell-v-Mirror Group Newspapers Ltd.* [2004] UKHL 22. Guidance on the application of s 12(3) is now also provided in *Cream Holdings Ltd v Bannerjee* [2004] UKHL 44.

6 *Scope of order*

Persons protected

The aim should be to protect the child or incapacitated adult, rather than to confer anonymity on other individuals or organisations. However, the order may include restrictions on identifying or approaching specified family members, carers, doctors or organisations in cases where the absence of such restriction is likely to prejudice their ability to care for the child or patient, or where identification of such persons might lead to identification of the child or patient and defeat the purpose of the order. In cases where the court receives expert evidence the identity of the experts (as opposed to treating clinicians) is not normally subject to restriction.

Identifying persons protected

Once an order has been made, the details of those protected by the order should normally be contained in the Schedule. In exceptional cases (for example *Leeds NHS Trust-v-A & B* [2003] 1 FLR 1091) where it is not appropriate for details to be given, a description by reference to the facts of the case should be contained in the Schedule to enable those reading the order to identify whether a person is likely to be the subject of the order.

Information already in the public domain

Orders will not usually prohibit publication of material which is already in the public domain, other than in exceptional cases such as *Venables and Thompson-v-News Group Newspapers Ltd* [2001] Fam 430.

Duration of order

Orders should last for no longer than is necessary to achieve the purpose for which they are made. The maximum extent of an order in a child case will usually be the child's 18th birthday. In the case of an incapacitated adult the order will normally end on death. In some cases a later date may be necessary, to protect safety or welfare, or the anonymity of other children who are named in the order and who are still under age, or to maintain the anonymity of doctors or carers after the death of a patient. See for example:

Re C (Adult Patient: Publicity [1996] 2 FLR 251; *Venables and Thompson-v-News Group Newspapers Ltd* [2001] Fam 430; *X (formerly known as Mary Bell)-v-Y and others* [2003] EWHC QB 1101.

7 Service of orders

Service of orders should be effected in the usual way, ie by fax or by post. Contact details for the national press and broadcasters can be found at *http://www.medialawyer.press.net/courtapplications.*

8 Undertakings in damages

The court will consider whether it is appropriate to require an applicant to give such an undertaking in an individual case, particularly when an order is made without notice, and will bear in mind the applicant's capacity to fulfil any such undertaking.

9 Explanatory notes

It is helpful if applications and orders are accompanied by an explanatory note, from which persons served can readily understand the nature of the case. In any case where notice of an application has not been given, the explanatory note should explain why.

10 Advice and assistance

Applicants or respondents are welcome to consult:

Deputy Director
CAFCASS Legal Services and Special Casework
8th floor, Wyndham House,
South Quay Plaza, London E14 9SH
DX: 42691 Isle of Dogs
Telephone: 020 7510 7080
Fax: 020 7510 7104
Email: legal@cafcass.gov.uk
Website: *www.cafcass.gov.uk*

PART V

Official Solicitor
81 Chancery Lane
London WC2A 1D
Telephone: 020 7911 7127
Fax: 020 7911 7105
Email: enquiries@offsol.gsi.gov.uk
Website: *www.offsol.demon.co.uk*

Mike Hinchliffe
Deputy Director of Legal Services, CAFCASS

Laurence Oates
Official Solicitor

Note—The new website for the Official Solicitor is at *www.justice.gov.uk/about/ospt*.

IN THE HIGH COURT OF JUSTICE   **Case Number:**
FAMILY DIVISION
[PRINCIPAL REGISTRY]

BEFORE [*JUDGE*] IN PRIVATE

IN THE MATTER OF THE COURT'S INHERENT JURISDICTION

BETWEEN

[   ]

and

[   ]

REPORTING RESTRICTION ORDER

IMPORTANT

If you disobey this order you may be found guilty of contempt of court and may be sent to prison or be fined or have your assets seized. You should read the order carefully and are advised to consult a solicitor as soon as possible. You have the right to ask the Court to vary or discharge the order.

EXPLANATION

A   On [*date*] the Court considered an application for a reporting restriction order.

B   The following persons and/or organisations were represented before the Court:
[*describe parties and their advocates*]

C   The Court read the following documents: [*list the documents*]
and/or
The Court directed the [Applicant/Claimant] to file a statement no later than [*date*] setting out the information presented to the court at the hearing.
and/or
The Court directed that copies of the attached Explanatory Note and [*list any other documents*] be made available by the [Applicant/Claimant] to any person affected by this Order.

[D   *In a case where an undertaking in damages is required by the Court:*
The Applicant gave an undertaking that if the Court later finds that this Order was obtained as a result of any deliberate or careless misrepresentation by the Applicant, and that this has caused loss to any person served with the Order, and that that person should be compensated, the Applicant will comply with any order the Court may make.]

E   *In the case of an order made without notice:*
This order was made without notice to those affected by it, the Court having considered section 12(2) Human Rights Act 1998 and being satisfied (i) that the [Applicant/Claimant] has taken all practicable steps to notify persons affected and/or (ii) that there are compelling reasons for notice not being given, namely: [*set out the Court's reasons for making the order without notice*]

[F   *In the case of an application by a local authority:*
The Court granted permission to the Applicant to apply for the exercise of the Court's inherent jurisdiction]

ORDER

1.   Duration
      Subject to any different order made in the meantime, this order shall have effect
      [*in the case of an adult*] during the lifetime of the [Defendant], whose details are set out in
      Schedule 1 to this order.
      [*in the case of a child*] until [date], the 18th birthday of the child whose details are set out in
      Schedule 1 to this order ("the Child").

2.   Who is bound
      This order binds all persons and all companies (whether acting by their directors, employees or
      agents or in any other way) who know that the order has been made.

3.   Publishing restrictions
      This order prohibits the publishing or broadcasting in any newspaper, magazine, public
      computer network, internet website, sound or television broadcast or cable or satellite
      programme service of:

      (a)   the name and address of

             (i)   the [Defendant/Child];

             (ii)   [*in the case of a child*] the Child's parents ("the parents"), whose details are set out
                     in Schedule 2 to this order;

             (iii)   any individual having day-to-day care of or medical responsibility for the
                     [Defendant/Child] ("a carer"), whose details are set out in Schedule 3 to this Order;

             (iv)   any residential home or hospital, or other establishment in which the
                     [Defendant/Child] is residing or being treated ("an establishment");

      (b)   any picture being or including a picture of either the [Defendant/Child], a carer or an
             establishment;

      (c)   any other particulars or information relating to the [Defendant/Child];

      IF, BUT ONLY IF, such publication is likely to lead to the identification of the [Defendant/ Child]
      as being [*set out the feature of the situation which has led to the granting of the order*].

4.   No publication of the text or a summary of this order (except for service of the order under
      paragraph 7 below) shall include any of the matters referred to in paragraph 3 above.

[5.   Restriction on seeking information
      This Order prohibits any person from seeking any information relating to the [Defendant/Child]
      [or the parents] or a carer from any of the following:
      (a)   the [Defendant/Child];
      [(b)   the parents];
      (c)   a carer;
      (d)   the staff or residents of an establishment.]

6.   What is not restricted by this Order
      Nothing in this Order shall prevent any person from:

      (a)   publishing information relating to any part of a hearing in a court in England and Wales
             (including a coroner's court) in which the court was sitting in public and did not itself make
             any order restricting publication.

      (b)   seeking or publishing information which is not restricted by Paragraph 3 above.

(c)   inquiring whether a person or place falls within paragraph 3(a) above.

(d)   seeking information relating to the [Defendant/Child] while acting in a manner authorised by statute or by any court in England and Wales.

(e)   seeking information from the responsible solicitor acting for any of the parties or any appointed press officer, whose details are set out in Schedule 4 to this order.

(f)   seeking or receiving information from anyone who before the making of this order had previously approached that person with the purpose of volunteering information (but this paragraph will not make lawful the provision or receipt of private information which would otherwise be unlawful).

(g)   publishing information which before the service on that person of this order was already in the public domain in England and Wales as a result of publication by another person in any newspaper, magazine, sound or television broadcast or cable or satellite programme service, or on the internet website of a media organisation operating within England and Wales.

7.   <u>Service</u>
Copies of this Order endorsed with a notice warning of the consequences of disobedience shall be served by the [Applicant/Claimant] (and may be served by any other party to the proceedings)

(a)   by service on such newspaper and sound or television broadcasting or cable or satellite or programme services as they think fit, by fax or first class post addressed to the editor (in the case of a newspaper) or senior news editor (in the case of a broadcasting or cable or satellite programme service) or website administrator (in the case of an internet website) and/or to their respective legal departments; and/or

(b)   on such other persons as the parties may think fit, by personal service.

8.   <u>Further applications about this Order</u>
The parties and any person affected by any of the restrictions in paragraphs 3-5 above may make application to vary or discharge it to a Judge of the High Court on not less than [*48 hours*] notice to the parties.

SCHEDULE 1
[*The [Defendant/Child]'s Full Name:*
Born:
Address:]
or
[*Information enabling those affected by order to identify the Defendant/Child*]

SCHEDULE 2
[*Similar details of parents*]

SCHEDULE 3
[*Similar details of carers or other persons protected*]

SCHEDULE 4
[*Contact details of responsible solicitor and/or press officer*]

Date of Order:[   ]

PART V

NHS TRUST X v AB

Application for a Reporting Restriction Order

EXPLANATORY NOTE

1   AB is in a permanent vegetative state. An application has been made by the NHS Hospital Trust responsible for his care for the Court's approval of the withdrawal of artificial nutrition and hydration. This course is supported by AB's family.

2   On [date] the application will be heard by the President of the Family Division, who will give judgment in open court.

3   A Reporting Restriction Order has been [made/applied for] to protect AB's right to confidentiality in respect of his medical treatment. This does not restrict publication of information or discussion about the treatment of patients in a permanent vegetative state, provided that such publication is not likely to lead to the identification of AB, those caring for him, the NHS Trust concerned or the establishment at which he is being cared for.

Protocol
December 2005

Protocol between the National Youth Advocacy Service and the Children and Family Court Advisory and Support Service

This protocol aims to clarify the roles of both agencies representing children in private law proceedings in order to meet, in the best possible way, the needs of all children and families.

General note—The purpose of the Protocol is to facilitate the exchange of information between Cafcass and NYAS when a case passes from one organisation to the other after a judge decides on an appointment.

Shared commitments
–   Compliance with article 12 of the United Nations Convention on the Rights of the Child
–   Improved Services for Children in family proceedings
–   A co-ordinated response to changing practice and regional needs

National Youth Advocacy Service

1 NYAS is a UK charity offering socio-legal information, advice and legal representation to children and young people up to the age of 25. NYAS has developed a strong identity as a leading Children's Rights organisation with provision of advocacy services. NYAS has advocates across England and Wales, supported by a Legal Team and a free phone helpline and advice service for children and young people. NYAS also provides separate representation for children and young people where the court considers that such representation is necessary under Rule 9.5 of the Family Proceedings Rules and in line with the Practice Direction of The President of the Family Division of April 2004.[1]

1   [2004] 1 FLR 1188

2 NYAS is committed to Article 12 of the UN Convention of the Rights of the Child. The object of NYAS representing young people is, wherever possible, to protect the young person from the damaging effects of being caught up in legal proceedings. It is a common misconception that children as parties to the proceedings would always give instructions, although they may do so with leave of the court or if they if they are competent to instruct a solicitor directly. A child who is capable of forming his or her own views has the right to express those views in the proceedings with the views being given due weight in accordance with the age and maturity of the child. The child's true wishes and feelings should be put before the court as part of an holistic approach in terms of assessing the whole background and dynamics of the situation. The child should have the opportunity to have their situation represented separately from that of any of the adults.

3 The suitability of NYAS to act as guardian in appropriate cases was approved by Dame Elizabeth Butler-Sloss in the case of *Re A (Separate Representation)*[2]. There are a number of accepted situations in which separate representation of children in private law proceedings is either appropriate or acceptable and NYAS has also been involved in the recent cases *A v A (Shared Residence)*[3] and *Re S (Unco-operative Mother)*[4].

2   [2001] 1 FLR 715; 3 [2004] EWHC 142 Fam; 4 [2004] EWCA Civ 597

4 It is the policy of NYAS to appoint a caseworker who is an independent social worker and usually a children's guardian in the public law sense. The lawyer and caseworker work in tandem to provide representation for children and young people.

PART V

Children and Family Court Advisory and Support Service (CAFCASS)

5 CAFCASS is a Non-Departmental Public Body. The service was established to combine the functions previously carried out by the Family Court Welfare Service provided by the Probation Service, the Children's Branch of the Official Solicitor's Department and the GALRO Service provided by local authorities. Its function is to safeguard the interests of children who are the subject of family proceedings. Social workers employed by CAFCASS are appointed as Family Court Advisers (FCAs) and carry out a number of roles according to the nature of the proceedings in which the child is involved.

CAFCASS duties are to:

- Safeguard and promote the welfare of the child
- Give advice to the court about any application made to it in such proceedings
- Make provision for children to be represented in such proceedings
- Provide information, advice and support for children and their families[5]

5   Criminal Justice and Court Services Act 2000, section 12

Safeguarding and promoting the interests of children

6 CAFCASS' responsibility is to safeguard and promote the interests of individual children who are the subject of family proceedings by providing independent social work advice to the court. In addition to its general duties it meets these responsibilities in some private law Children Act cases where an officer of CAFCASS accepts appointment as guardian under r 9.5 of the Family Proceedings Rules 1991. In these cases the child will always have the benefit of legal representation and the FCA acting as guardian will instruct the solicitor.

7 Certain specialist High Court appointments for children are handled by the CAFCASS High Court Team based at National Office in London. They are responsible for medical treatment cases and cases with particularly complex features.

Children made a party in private law proceedings

8 Rule 9.5 of the Family Proceedings Rules 1991 states:

"(1) ...if in any family proceedings it appears to the court that it is in the best interests of any child to be made a party to the proceedings, the court may appoint –

    (a)   an officer of the service
    (b)   (if he consents) the Official Solicitor[6]; or
    (c)   (if he consents) some other proper person,

to be the guardian ad litem of the child with authority to take part in the proceedings on the child's behalf."

6   For the Official Solicitor's functions in family cases see Practice Note dated 2 April 2001 [2001] 2 FLR 155. He acts as guardian ad litem of minors who are not subject of the proceedings such as respondent minor parents and child applicants.

Note—Practice Note of 2 April 2001 has been replaced by Practice Note of March 2013 (*The Official Solicitor to the Senior Courts: Appointment in Family Proceedings and Proceedings under the Inherent Jurisdiction in Relation to Adults*).

9 The President's Practice Direction makes it clear that the child should only be made a party in a minority of cases featuring issues of significant difficulty. Such decisions are only made by a Circuit Judge, High Court Judge or District Judge in the Principal Registry of the Family Division (unless there are exceptional circumstances when a District Judge can make an order).

10 CAFCASS should be approached first to provide a guardian. The provision of a guardian when requested by the court is a significant and core task for CAFCASS and CAFCASS has a duty to appoint a guardian and cannot refuse appointment. Guidance has been issued to clarify that where a judge has decided that an appointment under Rule 9.5 is necessary that Service Managers must prioritise the allocation of the case.

National Youth Advocacy Service and CAFCASS working together

11 The National Youth Advocacy Service often provided a guardian in private law proceedings before the inception of CAFCASS when there was limited provision for guardians to be appointed. NYAS has continued to provide such a service particularly where judges have previous experience of their effective work in this area. This is part of NYAS' broader commitment to provide information and advice to children and young people.

12 Since 2001 when CAFCASS was created to provide a service in both public and private law proceedings there has been a considerable growth in rule 9.5 appointments undertaken by CAFCASS. As clarified in the President's Direction it is recognised that in many cases the child will benefit from representation by a guardian who has already met them in their capacity as children and family reporter in the case.

When NYAS may be appointed guardian:

13 The Practice Direction of April 2004 states;

> "5 When a child is made a party and a guardian is to be appointed:
>
> 5.1 Consideration should first be given to appointing an officer of CAFCASS as guardian …
>
> 5.2 If CAFCASS is unable to provide a guardian without delay, or if for some other reason the appointment of a CAFCASS officer is not appropriate, FPR rule 9.5(1) makes further provision for the appointment of a guardian"

14 CAFCASS should be approached first and will usually provide a guardian. However, NYAS may, for example, be asked by the court to provide a guardian in any matter (likely to be long standing) where, despite the best efforts of CAFCASS staff, one or more members of the family can no longer work with the organisation.

General principles

15 Both agencies are committed to effective communication in the best interests of the child in accordance with the law. The normal points of contact should be the CAFCASS service manager and the nominated NYAS lawyer. If any case moves between the two agencies, it is particularly important to pass on information which may assist the work with the child and family, e g aspects of risk management, conflict of interest issues and any particular needs of the child. If NYAS is invited to provide r 9.5 representation where CAFCASS has not been approached, NYAS will discuss the matter with CAFCASS and will be responsible for notifying the court in the first instance.

16 CAFCASS and NYAS will work together to advise the court whenever there appears to be good reason for a guardian not to be appointed e g when there is an alternative preferable route such as a section 37 report from the local authority.

PART V

This Protocol will be reviewed in twelve months' time.

Elena Fowler
Chief Executive, NYAS

Anthony Douglas
Chief Executive, CAFCASS

Practice Note
3 January 2006

Citations: [2006] 1 FLR 480

Ancillary Relief Orders: Conveyancing for Mentally Incapacitated Adults

General note—This needs updating and should be read in the light of the changes made by MCA 2005.

1 This Practice Note is issued by the Official Solicitor to the Supreme Court. It gives his understanding of the law and practice applying to the implementation of property adjustment orders and orders for sale in ancillary relief proceedings under Part II of the Matrimonial Causes Act 1973 (MCA 1973) or Section 72 and Schedule 5 of the Civil Partnership Act 2004 (CPA 2004) where one of the parties is under mental incapacity. It has been seen in draft and approved by the Master of the Court of Protection and the Senior District Judge at the Principal Registry of the Family Division of the High Court.

2 A petitioner or respondent who lacks capacity to conduct matrimonial proceedings or civil partnership proceedings for himself or herself will require to be represented through a next friend or guardian ad litem. If he or she lacks capacity to conduct the proceedings, he or she is likely also to lack capacity to sign a contract for sale of a property, a transfer or conveyance arising from an order made in those proceedings. Capacity is issue specific, so medial evidence establishing incapacity to conduct the litigation may have to be supplemented by specific evidence as to capacity to execute the conveyancing documents.

Powers of the family court

3 On or after granting a decree of divorce, nullity or judicial separation in matrimonial proceedings or, in civil partnership proceedings, making a dissolution, nullity or separation order, the court may make an order for the transfer of the family home or other property from one party to the other, or other orders for property adjustment, under MCA 1973, s 24 or CPA 2004, Sch 5, para 7 (as the case may be). Further, where the court makes such an order or makes an order for secured periodical payments or for the payment of a lump sum under MCA 1973, s 23 or CPA 2004, Sch 5, para 2, it may make an order for the sale of any property in which, or in the proceeds of which, either party has an interest. However, for any such order to be put into effect where one of the parties is under mental incapacity, it will be necessary to obtain either an authority of the Court of Protection or, where that party is a trustee of a jointly owned property, an order providing for a substitute trustee to be made (see s 22 Law of Property Act 1925 which is explained in paragraph 8 below).

4 Only the persons listed in s 94 Mental Health Act 1983 may give any approval or make any order required for the management of property and affairs of a patient under Part VII

of that Act. These persons are the nominated judges of the Court of Protection (High Court judiciary of the Chancery and Family divisions), the Master of the Court of Protection and his nominated officers.

5 Section 39 of the Supreme Court Act 1981 (applied in County Courts by s 38 of the County Courts Act 1984) authorises the (High or County) Court to order that a person (usually the District Judge) may sign the conveyance on behalf of a litigant, where that litigant *"neglects or refuses"* to comply with an order. In the opinion of the Official Solicitor, a mentally incapacitated person who lacks capacity to sign a conveyance has neither neglected nor refused to comply with an order, hence this provision may not be used to avoid the need to obtain an authority of the Court of Protection or appoint a substitute trustee.

Where the patient is sole owner of the property

6 Where a receiver has been appointed, it is generally for the receiver to liaise with the Court of Protection and to obtain the necessary authority of that court to the sale (or any purchase). See Court of Protection Practice Note 4.

7 Where no receiver has been appointed, it is necessary to apply to the Court of Protection for a person to be authorised to carry the terms of the family court order into effect on behalf of the patient. The authority can be drafted to extend to ancillary documentation, such as surrender of an endowment policy. Where the Official Solicitor is acting as next friend or guardian ad litem, he can apply for authority and, once granted, will be able to sign the documentation on behalf of the patient to enable the transaction to proceed. The costs of this application should be provided for in the family court order as these will not be paid by any CLS funding that is available to the patient. The application to the Court of Protection must be supported by medical evidence in form CP3.

Patient as joint owner of the property

8 If a patient is a co-owner of property with another then s 22(2) of the Law of Property Act 1925 prevents the disposition of the legal estate in land so long as one trustee is a patient. It will therefore be necessary to replace the patient as trustee before a sale can proceed (unless there is a registered Enduring Power of Attorney).

9 The appointment of a new trustee can be made by the family court under ss 41 and 44 of the Trustee Act 1925. Where the Official Solicitor is acting as next friend or guardian ad litem, his family litigation division can provide precedent documentation for the appointment of the Official Solicitor as new trustee in the patient's place.

10 The county court has jurisdiction under section 41 where the trust or estate or fund to be dealt with in the court does not exceed the county court limit, currently £30,000 (see s 63A Trustee Act 1925). This jurisdictional limit may be exceeded by agreement of the parties (s 24 County Courts Act 1984).

11 Once the order appointing a substitute trustee has been made, the sale can proceed, the sellers being the co-owner and the new trustee (usually the Official Solicitor). No mention of the patient should appear on the contract nor on the transfer. A copy of the order providing for the new trustee will need to be produced to HM Land Registry with the transfer documentation. The costs of the new trustee should be provided for in the family court order and should generally be met from the gross proceeds of sale.

PART V

Property jointly owned to be jointly transferred to one party

12 If the family court orders the patient's share of jointly owned property to be transferred to the other joint owner it will usually be necessary for an application to be made to the Court of Protection for authority for the Official Solicitor (or some other party) to take all necessary steps in the name and on behalf of the patient to secure the transfer of all his/her legal and beneficial interest in the property. Similarly, where the share of the spouse with capacity is to be transferred to the patient, authority of the Court of Protection will be needed for any covenants to be executed on behalf of the patient as transferee. In either case, while awaiting the authority, the wording of the transfer should be agreed. The Official Solicitor has a form of transfer which may be used in such circumstances. Once the authority is received, the documentation can be completed. Provision will need to be made in the matrimonial court order for the costs of any application to the Court of Protection.

Laurence Oates
Official Solicitor

Note—Form EX660 was modified in April 2013 and can be found at *www.justice.gov.uk/forms*.

Practice Note
28 July 2006

Citations: [2006] 2 FLR 373

Official Solicitor: Declaratory Proceedings: Medical and Welfare Decisions for Adults who Lack Capacity

****

Explanatory note—This *Practice Note* related to the inherent jurisdiction of the High Court (Family Division) which has been replaced by the jurisdiction of the Court of Protection under MCA 2005. There remains uncertainty as to whether the inherent jurisdiction can still be exercised for vulnerable adults who do not lack capacity.

Practice Note
28 July 2006

Citations: [2006] 2 FLR 354

Official Solicitor, CAFCASS and the National Assembly for Wales: Urgent and Out of Hours Cases in the Family Division of the High Court

1 This Practice Note is issued jointly by the Official Solicitor, the Chief Executive of CAFCASS, and the Chief Executive of CAFCASS Cymru on behalf of the National Assembly for Wales. It describes the procedure to be followed in respect of urgent and out of hours cases in which a decision is sought by a judge of the Family Division of the High Court. It is issued with the approval of the President of the Family Division.

2 In some cases, urgent or out of hours applications become necessary because applications to the court have not been pursued sufficiently promptly. This is undesirable, in particular because urgent applications may be founded on incomplete evidence, inquiries and under-prepared advocacy, and should be avoided where possible. A judge who has concerns that the urgent or out of hours facilities may have been abused may require a representative of the claimant to attend at a subsequent directions hearing to provide an explanation.

3 Whenever possible, urgent applications should be made within court hours. The earliest possible liaison is required with the Clerk of the Rules. It will usually be possible to accommodate a genuinely urgent application (at least for initial directions) in the Family Division applications court, from which the matter may, if necessary and possible, be referred to another judge.

4 When it is not possible to apply within court hours, contact should be made with the security office at the Royal Courts of Justice (020 7947 6000) who will refer the matter to the urgent business officer. The urgent business officer can contact the duty judge. The judge may agree to hold a hearing, either convened at court or elsewhere, or by telephone. When the hearing is to take place by telephone it should be by tape-recorded conference call arranged (and paid for in the first instance) by the claimant's solicitors. Solicitors acting for NHS Trusts or other potential claimants should have standing arrangements with their telephone service providers under which such conference calls can be arranged. All parties (especially the judge) should be informed that the call is being recorded by the service provider. The claimant should order a transcript of the hearing from the service provider.

Adult medical treatment and welfare cases

5 The Official Solicitor will act in urgent cases under the inherent jurisdiction concerning medical treatment to, or the welfare of, an adult who lacks capacity to make decisions for himself or herself. His office should be contacted at the earliest possible opportunity if an urgent application is envisaged. Where cases arise out of hours the urgent business officer will be able to contact him or his representative. As with cases dealt with on a less urgent basis, evidence is required of incapacity and as to best interests. When written evidence is not available, oral evidence of incapacity must be available. When there is a telephone hearing, oral evidence must be given as part of the conference call.

6 When final evidence either as to capacity or best interests is not available, the court may be willing to grant an interim declaration (r 25.1(1)(b) of the Civil Procedure Rules 1998 (CPR) – *NHS Trust v T (Adult Patient: Refusal of Medical Treatment)* [2004] EWHC 1279 (Fam), [2005] 1 All ER 387). Evidence establishing on the balance of probability that the patient is under incapacity and that the treatment proposed is in his or her best interest must be adduced. An interim injunction to restrain treatment may be granted *Re C (Adult) (Refusal of Treatment)* [1994] 1 WLR 290, [1994] 1 FLR 31.

7 An adult patient must be a party and must be represented through a litigation friend (r 21.3 of the CPR). Notice of an application must be given to the patient (or his or her litigation friend). The claimant may be an NHS Trust, local authority, relative, carer, or the patient. The Official Solicitor stands ready to accept appointment as litigation friend (usually for the patient as defendant) if the conditions for his appointment are shown (either on an interim or final basis) to exist. Should a declaration be made without notice, it is of no effect and may be set aside – *St George's Healthcare NHS Trust v S; R (S) v Collins and Others* [1999] Fam 26, [1998] 2 FLR 728.

PART V

Children medical treatment and welfare cases

8 It may be desirable for a child who is the subject of such proceedings to be made a party and represented through a guardian ad litem (usually an officer of CAFCASS or a Welsh Family Proceedings Officer). CAFCASS and CAFCASS Cymru stand ready to arrange for an officer to accept appointment as guardian ad litem. They should be contacted at the earliest opportunity where an urgent application is envisaged. For urgent out of hours applications, the urgent business officer is able to contact a representative of CAFCASS. CAFCASS Cymru is not able to deal with cases that arise out of office hours and those cases should be referred to CAFCASS who will deal with the matter on behalf of CAFCASS Cymru until the next working day. A child of sufficient understanding to instruct his or her own solicitor should be made a party and given notice of any application.

9 Interim declarations/orders under the wardship jurisdiction (or the Children Act 1989) may be made on application either by an NHS trust, a local authority, an interested adult (where necessary with the leave of the court) or by the child if he or she has sufficient understanding to make the application.

General issues

10 Parents, carers or other necessary respondents should be given the opportunity to have independent legal advice or at least to have access to support or counselling.

11 In suitable cases, application may be made for direction providing for anonymity of the parties and others involved in the matter in any order or subsequent listing of the case. Exceptionally, a reporting restriction order may be sought – see the *President's Practice Direction (Applications for Reporting Restriction Orders)* [2005] 2 FLR 120 issued on 18 March 2005.

12 Either the Official Solicitor or CAFCASS, as the case may be, may be appointed by the court as advocate to the court – see Memorandum from the Lord Chief Justice and the Attorney-General reproduced in *The White Book Service 2006, Civil Procedure* (Sweet & Maxwell, 2006) at 39.8.2, especially at 39.8.5.

13 Draft standard form orders for use in urgent and out of hours medical treatment cases are annexed to this note. They should be adapted to suit the individual circumstances of each case.

Consultation with CAFCASS, CAFCASS CYMRU and Official Solicitor

14 Members of the Official Solicitor's legal staff, CAFCASS, and CAFCASS Cymru are prepared to discuss medical cases before proceedings are issued. In all cases in which the urgent and out of hours procedures are to be used it would be helpful if the Official Solicitor, CAFCASS or CAFCASS Cymru have had some advance notice of the application and its circumstances. Inquiries about adult medical and welfare cases should be addressed to a family and medical litigation lawyer at the office of the Official Solicitor, 81 Chancery Lane, London, WC2A, telephone 0207 911 7127, fax number: 0207 911 7105, email: inquiries@offsol.gsi.gov.uk. Inquiries about children medical cases should be directed to the duty lawyer at CAFCASS, 8th Floor, South Quay Plaza 3, 189 Marsh Wall, London, E14 9SH, telephone: 0207 510 7000, fax number: 0207 510 7104. Inquiries about children medical cases in Wales should be directed to the Social Care Team, Legal Services, National Assembly for Wales, Cathays Park, Cardiff, CF10 3NQ, telephone: 02920 826813, fax no: 02920 823834.

Laurence Oates
Official Solicitor

Anthony Douglas
Chief Executive
CAFCASS

Dafydd Ifans
Chief Executive
CAFCASS CYMRU
National Assembly for Wales

ANNEX
OUT OF HOURS ADULT INTERIM DECLARATION AND DIRECTIONS

****

The Law Society Legal Policy
April 2007

(© The Law Society 2007)

Appointing a Solicitor for the Child in Specified Proceedings: Guidelines for Courts

The following guidelines have been produced by the Law Society with the approval of the President of the Family Division and HM Court Service, having taken into account the views of Resolution, the Association of Lawyers for Children and CAFCASS.

These guidelines are intended for use nationally by courts throughout England and Wales from April 2007. They replace the 2003 Statement of Good Practice on appointing a solicitor for the child where it falls to the court to do so in specified proceedings under the Children Act 1989 and are an integral part of applying the Protocol for Judicial Case Management in Public Law Children Act Cases.

Introduction

1 The court and CAFCASS should always seek to achieve the timely appointment of a Guardian for the child in specified proceedings under the Children Act 1989 (CA 1989) in cases where a Guardian is needed. This guidance is intended to deal with cases where that has not happened. In such cases it is the responsibility of the court to consider the exercise of its powers to appoint a solicitor to represent the child pursuant to section 41(3) – (5) CA 1989 and paragraph 1.4 of the Protocol for Judicial Case Management in Public Law Children Act Cases. A solicitor for the child should be appointed in time to represent the child at the first hearing.

2 The choice of an individual solicitor to represent a child in such circumstances is a matter for the court and the court must use its own discretion on the information available to it.

3 In exercising its discretion the court should appoint a solicitor who is most appropriately qualified, taking all the facts and circumstances of the child and the case into account, and should seek to promote the best interests of the child. The court should, above all else, appoint a solicitor who is going to provide effective representation for the child.

PART V

4 The court should be aware of the benefits for children which can come from using a wide range of solicitors.

Purpose

5 This guidance describes the factors to be taken into account by a court when appointing a solicitor for the child. In exceptional cases, in order to discharge its duty under the CA 1989, the court may need to appoint a solicitor otherwise than in accordance with this guidance. This guidance also reminds solicitors and Guardians of some of their duties.

Objectives

6 The objectives of this guidance are to:

- assist the court in appointing the most appropriate solicitor for the child;
- provide guidance as to the criteria which should be taken into account in making an appointment.

Selection criteria

7 It is expected that the court will appoint a solicitor for the child who is accredited as a children representative member of the Law Society's Children Panel. There may be highly exceptional circumstances when a non-accredited solicitor is considered more suitable to be appointed. All Law Society Children Panel members as identified earlier in this paragraph are eligible for appointment by the court. The court must be satisfied on the suitability of the appointment of the solicitor for the child, considering all the circumstances of the case.

8 Where a solicitor has previously acted for a child or another child of the same family then they should usually be appointed in any further specified proceedings.

9 When appointing a solicitor the court should seek to promote the best interests of the child. The court should consider the papers filed and whether, on the face of those papers, there are any special features of the particular case and/or child that require that a solicitor with specific knowledge, particular skills or characteristics be appointed. These special features include:

- the ability to speak with the child in his/her first language;
- sign language skills;
- where there is a good specific reason to appoint a solicitor of particular gender for the child, for example, for a child who may have been sexually abused and shows signs of being afraid of persons of that gender; or for an older child who has expressed a strong preference for a solicitor of a particular gender;
- where there is a good specific reason to appoint or not to appoint a solicitor of the same ethnic background or culture as the child.

10 The court should have regard to and seek to balance other factors in choosing the solicitor for appointment as follows:

- knowledge of the local authority that initiated the proceedings and the court;
- the location of the child and whether it would be more appropriate to appoint a solicitor local to the particular child rather than the court.

11 It is expected that the court will generally seek to achieve a 'spread' in their selection of solicitors for children in order to assist in maintaining an adequate supply of accredited solicitors competent to represent children.

Practical guidance

12 The Selection Criteria above may be applied by the use of a local list of accredited solicitors within reasonable distance of the court. The next solicitor on the list should usually be invited to be appointed, (unless a solicitor who has previously acted for the child or another child of the same family is available) subject to their suitability to meet the special features of the particular case and/or the child that require that a solicitor with specific knowledge, particular skills or characteristics be appointed to act for the child. If the appointment would be unsuitable then the list should be gone down until a suitable appointment is found. Any overlooked solicitor should keep his/her place as the next solicitor on the list.

13 The court may exercise its discretion to divert from its local list, for example, if the exceptional circumstances of the case or child require it; where the older child who may be competent to give instructions lives some distance from the court and/or is placed away from the applicant local authority in which case the court should consider liaising with colleagues in the areas in which children are placed; if there is an insufficient number of accredited solicitors with sufficient capacity to deal with the volume of cases or multi-party cases at any given time.

14 The Solicitors Regulation Authority will regularly make available the full list of solicitors accredited to represent children, containing details of their title, name, date of admission, date of accreditation, address and telephone numbers. The Solicitors Regulation Authority will notify Family Proceedings Courts and Care Centres immediately of those solicitors who are no longer accredited. Solicitors will provide information on their language and sign language skills and ethnic background.

15 Courts should answer reasonable enquiries from solicitors on their appointments procedures. Courts should produce information to their Local Family Justice Council not less than once a year about the number of solicitor appointments by the court and the number of solicitors appointed, including on any departure from the use of the local list and on the appointment by the court of non-accredited solicitors, and on the number of applications to terminate the appointments of solicitors appointed by the court.

16 A solicitor should not agree to be appointed by a court to represent a child unless he/she believes on the basis of the information available that he/she will be able to act promptly, personally and effectively in the matter. Solicitors should have knowledge of the Law Society Good Practice Note on acting in the absence of a children's guardian December 2006 (or any update of this) including the need to comply with the Law Society Children Panel Undertaking (or any update of this).

17 Solicitors should continue to self-assess their suitability after accepting an appointment from the court to act for a child. It is a requirement of Law Society accreditation membership that practitioners do not continue with cases which are outside their expertise. Solicitors must be alert and sensitive to whether there is in fact a good specific reason for the particular child to:

- be represented by a solicitor of the other gender;
- be represented by a solicitor of the same ethnic background or culture as the child;
- not be represented by a solicitor with the particular ethnic background or culture of the appointed solicitor;
- be represented by someone with different specific knowledge and skills or experience relevant to the particular case or the particular child.

PART V

Subsequent allocation of the guardian

18 Where a solicitor for the child is appointed by the court, that solicitor should continue to act for the child after the subsequent allocation of a Guardian unless there are exceptional reasons to the contrary.

19 Where the appointment, or the solicitor's conduct gives rise to concern, the Guardian should seek to resolve those concerns by discussion and working together where possible, with the solicitor. In those exceptional cases where the Guardian considers that there is good reason to seek a change in the appointment of the solicitor for the child in the best interests of the child, the Guardian should make an application to terminate the appointment of the current solicitor pursuant to rule 12(4) FPC (CA 1989) R 1991 or rule 4.12(4) FPR 1991. The court should be satisfied that there are good reasons for such a change. If an application to terminate is made (including by the child) every effort should be made by the court, solicitors and the Guardian to ensure that it does not cause delay or interfere with the determination of the central issues in the case, and that it is dealt with as amicably as possible.

Note—For the *Law Society Practice Note of 25 August 2009 (Acting in the Absence of a Children's Guardian)* see *The Family Court Practice 2010.*

Protocol (Generic Template) July 2007

ACPO Pilots: Disclosure of Information in Family Proceedings

Police/Family Disclosure Protocol (generic template)

Note—An information-sharing pilot between the police and family courts was implemented as a protocol from April 2006.
    The London and Northern Circuit templates are only used as a starting point for areas planning to implement the protocol. There is one version for the Metropolitan Police Service (*www.dca.gov.uk/family/metpol-protocol.pdf*) and another for out of London areas based on the Northern Circuit version (*www.dca.gov.uk/family/metpol-northerncircuit.pdf*). Further information on the pilot is available in the explanatory memorandum (*www.dca.gov.uk/family/metpol-expmem.pdf*). There are local variations of the protocol implemented in police force areas across the country. With this in mind, the MoJ has created a generic template that can be distributed to force areas; the generic template is reproduced below.

Standard forms
The standard request form for practitioners to request information from the police (Annex B of the protocol) is available in word format. You can download it, fill it in and send it to your police information officer/chief officer. The standard police reply form for police to respond to practitioners is also available in word format to download.
Standard request form – Annex B *www.dca.gov.uk/family/stdreq-form-annexb.doc*
Standard request form – Annex C *www.dca.gov.uk/family/stdpol-replyform-annexc.doc*

Objective

The objective of this Protocol, which has been agreed between the Chief of Police for the [.............] and the Designated Family Judge for [.............], is to set out the mechanisms for the appropriate disclosure of police information in family proceedings in courts in the [.............] Area to provide the court with early information to enable it to properly determine any necessary direction(s) which need to be made in relation to documents, records or other evidential material held by the police in relevant criminal proceedings or investigations which may inform the Family Court (and the parties) in the determination of any factual or welfare issue within family proceedings, and:

- To provide timely advance notice to the Chief Officer of the existence of the family proceedings and the nature and detail of the information sought from the police
- To enable the police through the Chief Officer to indicate in advance what documents, records or other evidential material (including both used and unused material) is or may be available to be disclosed to the family court and whether there is any objection to or difficulty in the immediate disclosure of the same
- To assist the court (and the parties) in the framing of standard directions directed to the Chief Officer which will act (if necessary) as the conduit to process and deal with all such directions for disclosure affecting any division/borough of the [ ] Force Area without any undue delay
- To encourage early disclosure of full and frank information between the police, the parties and the Court subject only to the avoidance of prejudice to the proper conduct of ongoing police enquiries at the time of the request.

Understanding on confidentiality

Police Information will not be disclosed unless there are important considerations of public interest to depart from the general rule of confidentiality. The protection of children is one of the areas where exceptions may be made.

Information supplied by the police in pursuance to this protocol is subject to the following implicit undertakings on the part of the parties and their legal representatives unless otherwise specifically directed by the court: –

- Any material disclosed will only be used for the purposes of, and preparation for, the current proceedings unless the permission of the Court is obtained;
- It will only be disclosed to professionals in the proceedings (and the parties) unless the permission of the court is obtained;
- The material will otherwise be kept confidential and copying should be kept to the minimum necessary to avoid the proliferation of copies of sensitive material.
- Where there is a Best Evidence or other video recorded interview one copy will normally be made available on request as soon as police investigations allow **either** by providing one copy to the Local Authority (if a party to the proceedings) or via the solicitors acting for either party in private law proceedings. Copies of Video recorded interviews will not be provided to unrepresented parties. Copying of video evidence should be kept to a minimum and consideration should be given to the parties attending the appropriate police station or local authority premises in order to view the copy video evidence at a mutually convenient time. Where this is not possible and the evidence has to be further copied, the party(ies) will meet the police reasonable costs of copying unless alternative arrangements have been agreed between the police and the parties legal representatives for making copies;
- In relation to any Best Evidence or other interview, parties' representatives will sign and abide by the terms of the police Standard Form of Undertaking in order to prevent the unauthorised dissemination/copying/use of the evidence. See Annex A – Form of Undertaking – this form can be suitably "adapted" to cover other evidence if necessary. Note, where the party is able to say that it is or is not necessary for the purpose of the proceedings for the video to be copied or available for viewing, the party should state so;
- That the police will not transcribe or make arrangements to transcribe any video

PART V

interviews or tape-recorded interviews unless this has already been done in connection with a criminal prosecution/investigation.

Proportionality

All parties should use the protocol proportionately having regard to what is reasonable, directly relevant and necessary when seeking disclosure from any third party.

This protocol may be departed from in exceptional circumstances and does not apply to genuine emergency situations.

Action	Party	Timing
1. Written Requests for Disclosure		
It is incumbent on parties to give very early consideration to what material held by the police may be relevant to the care or family proceedings. Whenever possible an early request for documents should be made to police prior to any hearing or application being made to the court.	Party requesting disclosure	Prior to any proceedings
The request should be made in writing and state precisely what evidence and information is sought and why in accordance with the Standard Request Form at Annex B. The police will normally respond to that request within 5 working days in accordance with the Standard Reply Form at Annex C. The Request Form should be sent to the nominated police disclosure officer or police representative identified in the Schedule below as the person to whom any request is to be sent or upon whom any order is to be served for the relevant Police Force Area.		
In the event the police are unable or unwilling to disclose the evidence or information requested without a court order it will be incumbent on the requesting party to make the appropriate application to court in accordance with the following procedure.		
2. Preparation for Request for Disclosure		
2.1 Preliminary Enquiries of Police		
Not later than 10 working days before the relevant hearing the solicitors for any party who proposes to ask the Court for a direction requiring the Chief Officer of any Police Force to disclose within family proceedings any document, record or other evidential material or information shall send by way of written Standard Request Form (Annex B) to the nominated police disclosure officer or police representative identified in the Schedule below as the person to whom any request is to be sent or upon whom any order is to be served for the relevant Police Force Area. This may renew or reiterate an earlier request made under 1 above. The Request Form should set out the following information:	The party proposing direction for disclosure of police evidence	10 working days before relevant hearing

Action	Party	Timing
– The names and dates of birth of the parties including any relevant children and where possible, brief details of the circumstances of the incident(s) in respect of which the request is made		
– Any relevant addresses		
– The date and place of the specific incident or incidents upon which information is sought		
– The crime reference number (if known)		
– The name and "collar" number (if known) of the Officer(s) in the case (s)		
– The nature and relevance of the documents, records or other evidential material sought.		
– The date of the hearing at which the formal direction is to be sought		
– A draft of the proposed direction including the date by which the documents, records or other evidential material is likely to be directed to be disclosed (to be prepared in accordance with the wording of the public law Standard Variable Directions appended at Annex D wherever possible)		
– The likely timetable of legal and social work steps		
– Whether and if so what date has been fixed by the court for any final hearing or fact finding hearing and whether the officer in the case is likely to be required at that hearing to give evidence.		
2.2 Police Response Not later than 5 working days before the relevant hearing the solicitors for the party proposing the direction be made for disclosure of documents, records or other evidential material or information shall obtain by way of written reply on the Standard Reply Form (see Annex C) from the nominated police disclosure officer or police representative identified in the Schedule below as the person to whom any request is to be sent or upon whom any order is to be served for the relevant Police Force Area (or on his/her behalf) the following information: – A list of what documents, records or other evidential material or information which have been requested are available. – If the police are not willing to disclose the evidence sought, the reason(s) why and when it is anticipated that the information can be provided. – Whether the documents, records or other evidential material or information can be provided within the timescale proposed by the draft direction provided – If the documents, records or other evidential material or information cannot be provided within the timescale proposed by the draft direction, the reason why they can not be so provided and the timescale requested by the police for their disclosure	The party proposing direction for disclosure of police evidence	5 working days before relevant hearing

PART V

Action	Party	Timing
– Whether the police require the direction in relation to disclosure to be amended as to its terms from the draft provided, and if so in what terms do the police propose that the direction should be framed – Where it is indicated that a police officer may be required to give evidence at any hearing, when that police officer is available to give evidence, and the dates and/or times to avoid. – The police Standard Reply Form or other letter in reply will always be filed with the court in advance of the hearing by both the police and the requesting party. – The police and/or a representative of the CPS shall be permitted to attend the hearing at which any request for disclosure from the police is to be made to make oral representations on the issue of disclosure, with or without Counsel.		

3. Hearing

Action	Party	Timing
At the hearing where the request is made for disclosure the court shall consider: – The necessity and relevance to the issues required to be determined by the court, of the information sought to be disclosed – The wording of the proposed direction for disclosure, with reference to Standard Variable Directions wherever possible – The timing of any direction for disclosure with specific reference to any written representations by the police under 2.2 above. All disclosure directions should allow sufficient time for compliance which should in normal circumstances be 14 days – The making of a request to the Family Section Manager that the court order be expedited in its preparation in accordance with the process described in the Schedule hereto and served within 24 hours by the court upon the nominated police disclosure officer or police representative identified in the Schedule below as the person to whom any request is to be sent or upon whom any order is to be served for the relevant Police Force Area. Any necessary direction to the party making the request for disclosure, as to notice and service of the court order in accordance with this Protocol.		

Action	Party	Timing
4. Post-Hearing Action		
4.1 The solicitor securing the direction in respect of disclosure shall forthwith comply with the process described in the Schedule hereto and thereafter ensure that within 24 hours of the hearing the nominated police disclosure officer or police representative identified in the Schedule below as the person to whom any request is to be sent or upon whom any order is to be served for the relevant Police Force Area is aware of the terms of the direction made for disclosure.	The Party securing direction for disclosure	Within 24 hours of directions hearing
4.2 The solicitor securing the direction in respect of disclosure shall forthwith upon receipt of the court order (or in the Magistrates Court on drawing up the order for the Court) and in any event within 2 days of the hearing serve the court order upon the nominated police disclosure officer or police representative identified in the Schedule below as the person to whom any request is to be sent or upon whom any order is to be served for the relevant Force Area.	The Party securing direction for disclosure	Within 2 days of directions hearing

---

SCHEDULE TO PROTOCOL FOR DISCLOSURE OF POLICE EVIDENCE SERVICE OF REQUESTS & ORDERS

Following the relevant directions hearing the solicitors securing the direction for disclosure shall forthwith either:

a) Obtain immediately from the court clerk a sealed copy of the order in the terms approved; or

b) Attend at the court office with the approved order in the terms agreed (or, if attendance at the court office is not immediately practical send a copy by Fax) and arrange with the Family Section Manager (or such other representative of the court service as the Family Section Manager shall nominate) for the order to be drawn up and sealed immediately;

c) In any event the order shall be made available to the party securing it to enable compliance with Protocol steps 4.1 and 4.2.

The address for service of any order is – (see Force Areas separately attached)

PART V

Additional information

Where the information or documents sought do not relate to child abuse investigations and material is held by another unit, the Child Abuse Investigation Unit will pass the request form to the unit or units holding, or likely to hold, the information or documents requested and will supply the contact details of this unit to the requesting party. It is then for that unit and the requesting party to liaise co-operatively over disclosure of the material sought and all further correspondence or contact should pass between them.

Witness summons if necessary

Any requesting party may, if necessary, use the witness summons procedure to seek disclosure of specific files or documents outside the remit of the local borough Child Abuse Investigation Unit. This is of particular relevance to historic allegations or investigations into serious crime (e.g. murder, neglect, drugs offences, firearms offences). In such cases the requesting party may look to the head of the Child Abuse Investigation Unit to identify the appropriate police unit likely to have the material. It is then for the requesting party to liaise with that unit and only if necessary to obtain a witness summons directed to an officer of that unit to bring the relevant file to court where disclosure of it or any of its contents can be ruled upon by the judge. Parties should avoid witness summonsing the Chief Officer since they will have no personal knowledge of the documents sought.

Proportionality

It is to be understood by all parties that the protocol should be used proportionately and is designed to facilitate only requests for items of evidence which the requesting party cannot, or cannot easily, obtain for itself, which only the police have and which are of central and not peripheral importance to the issues and incidents under consideration by the Family Court.

Updating contact

A designated Policy Officer will liaise with the DCA and Office of the Senior District Judge for [..........] to update once a year the schedule of Child Abuse Investigation Unit contact details which forms Schedule A of this Protocol.

ANNEX A – VIDEO TAPED EVIDENCE OF A CHILD WITNESS
CONFIDENTIALITY UNDERTAKING

UPON { Solicitor } .... undertaking

1 To pay the reasonable costs incurred by the police in providing copies of the tapes referred to in the order ("tapes")

2 Not to cause or permit any further copies to be made of the tapes

3 To keep the tapes in a locked, secure container when not in use or in transit

4 To use his/her best endeavours to ensure that the tapes are kept within the personal custody of a single adult when in transit and not to deliver the tape to the Post Office or any commercial carrier

5 To release the tapes only to:

    (1)   Counsel instructed in the case

    (2)   any expert authorised by the court to prepare a report for use by the court

    (3)   any other person only with the leave of the court

6 To require any person to whom the tape is released to sign a form of undertaking in the same terms as this undertaking.

7 To use his/her best endeavours to obtain the return of the tapes to his/her personal possession within 28 days of its release to any person

8 To permit his/her client to view the tapes only at his/her professional premises and in his/her presence

9 To return the tapes to the police forthwith upon his/her ceasing to be instructed in this matter and in any event within 7 days of the final hearing of this matter

10 To keep a written record of the name of any person allowed access to the tapes and the date of such access

ANNEX B– STANDARD REQUEST FORM FOR DISCLOSURE OF POLICE INFORMATION

[This form should be completed in accordance with the agreed protocol]

Police information will not be disclosed unless there are important considerations of public interest to justify departure from the general rule of confidentiality. These considerations include the protection of vulnerable members of society. The information below is provided on the strict understanding that such information is only for the use of the courts. It will be treated as confidential and will not be used for any other purpose.

ADVANCE NOTICE OF REQUEST FOR INFORMATION

Person Requesting Information

....

Job Title

....

[e.g., solicitor/social worker/Local Authority Disclosure Officer/CAFCASS Officer

Contact Telephone Number

....

Date of Request

....

Case proceeding at (if underway)

....

High Court/ County / Family Proceedings Court *(delete as appropriate)*

CASE NO...

The next hearing date in this case is listed for

....

Advance notice of family proceedings and any request for [to indicate availability of] information should be made as soon as possible and at least 10 *working* **days in advance of the relevant directions hearing date**

Information is Required by [DATE] ....

Information should be received no later than 5 working days in advance of the hearing date

Purpose of the Information *(delete as appropriate)***:**

Enquiries connected with Care Proceedings / Other Family Proceedings/ Prospective Family Proceedings (please specify)

Request for Disclosure of Material held by ....
Constabulary/FSU/CPU

Information Requested about the following person(s):

NAME (ALLEGED PERPETRATOR (S)):	NAME OF OTHER PARTY/PARENT [if applicable]:
DoB:	**DoB:**
ADDRESS:	**ADDRESS:**

PART V

NAME(S) OF RELEVANT CHILD(REN) / (ALLEGED VICTIM(S)):	DoB	RELATIONSHIP TO ALLEGED PERPETRATOR

BRIEF DETAILS (INCLUDING DATE AND PLACE) OF THE CIRCUMSTANCES OF THE INCIDENT(S) IN RESPECT OF WHICH FAMILY PROCEEDINGS ARE BEING TAKEN /CONTEMPLATED

CRIME REFERENCE NUMBER (IF KNOWN):	NAME & COLLAR NUMBER OF OFFICER(S) (IF KNOWN):

BRIEF DETAILS (INCLUDING DATE AND PLACE) OF THE SPECIFIC INCIDENT(S) UPON WHICH INFORMATION IS SOUGHT.

PLEASE SET OUT THE NATURE OF THE DOCUMENTS, RECORDS OR OTHER EVIDENTIAL MATERIAL REQUESTED AND ITS RELEVANCE TO THE CIVIL/FAMILY PROCEEDINGS NOTED ABOVE: (List documents with as much particularity as possible e g father's interview, mother's statement, sister's video interview, medical report of Dr Jones etc)

DOCUMENT   RELEVANCE

1.

2.

3. etc

AN INDICATION OF THE PROPOSED DIRECTIONS FOR DISCLOSURE LIKELY TO BE MADE (INCLUDING THE DATE BY WHICH ACTUAL DOCUMENTS WILL BE REQUIRED)

(list directions or attach draft order for directions)

THE LIKELY TIMETABLE OF LEGAL AND SOCIAL WORK STEPS:	

WHETHER AND IF SO WHAT DATE HAS BE FIXED FOR ANY FINAL HEARING/FINDING OF FACT HEARING AND WHETHER THE OFFICER(S) INVOLVED IS LIKELY TO BE REQUIRED TO GIVE EVIDENCE

NO DATE FIXED / DATE FIXED FOR ....

FINAL / FINDING OF FACT HEARING

OFFICER(S) NOT REQUIRED / REQUIRED TO GIVE EVIDENCE {*DELETE AS APPROPRIATE*}

Signature of Person Making Request

....

PRINT NAME..

ON BEHALF OF (NAME OF PARTY/ORGANIZATION ETC)

....

ANNEX C – STANDARD POLICE REPLY FORM

REQUEST RECEIVED [DATE]

Information Found From Records held at

....

CONSTABULARY / FSU / CPU

Court Case Number (if applicable)

....

No Information Found (*delete if not applicable*)

NAME (ALLEGED PERPETRATOR):	NAME OF OTHER PARTY/PARENT [if applicable]:	
DoB:	DoB:	
ADDRESS:	ADDRESS:	
NAME(S) OF RELEVANT CHILD(REN) / (ALLEGED VICTIM(S)):	DoB	RELATIONSHIP TO ALLEGED PERPETRATOR

CRIME REFERENCE NUMBER (IF KNOWN):	NAME AND COLLAR NUMBER OF OFFICER/S (IF KNOWN):

THE NATURE OF THE DOCUMENTS, RECORDS OR OTHER EVIDENTIAL MATERIAL REQUESTED WHICH IS AVAILABLE FOR DISCLOSURE NOW: (*LIST DOCUMENTS etc*)

POLICE DOCUMENTS REQUESTED WHICH CANNOT CURRENTLY BE DISCLOSED

DOCUMENT *[delete as appropriate]*	WHEN Disclosure Could Be Made	COMMENT / REASON FOR NOT DISCLOSING
STATEMENTS – list of prosecution statements		
INTERVIEWS – with suspect under Police & Criminal Evidence Act 1984 (list & date) (where applicable)		

PART V

ABE Video Interviews (list &date) (where applicable)		
MEDICAL REPORTS (where applicable)		
MISCELLANEOUS / OTHER documents – eg CRIS/CRIME reports etc (where applicable)		

POLICE Contact / Officer completing form

....(signature)   **Tel. No**...

Disclosure Approved By ....**POLICE Supervisor** (signature)

Print Name................................**Rank/Number** ....

UNIT...

ANNEX D
STANDARD VARIABLE DIRECTIONS RELATING TO POLICE DISCLOSURE

	DD: Disclosure of Court Documents and by Other Agencies
DD1	*Criminal proceedings concluded against a party* The solicitors for the (*identify party*) shall file and serve by (time/date) copies of the (identify documents e.g. *indictments/ witness statements/ any written basis of plea placed before the court/ pre-sentence report(s) prepared by the National Probation Service/and other reports before the court/transcript of the judge's sentencing remarks*) in relation to the proceedings in the Crown Court (*include Calendar Number*) in respect of which he/she was sentenced on the (*insert date*) (together with any record of previous convictions).
DD2	*Criminal proceedings against a non party* The Chief Constable of (*identify police force*) is requested to disclose forthwith (or *state time limit*) to (*identify local authority*):- (a) Copies of witness statements/records of interview/charge sheet/other relating to the prosecution of (*identify relevant person*) pursuant to the complaint made by the (*identify relevant person/party*) arising out of the incident (*specify incident and date(s)*); and (b) Copies of records of all/any-recorded complaints of incidents of domestic violence between (*identify persons or parties concerned*).
DD3	*Liberty to apply* Liberty to apply on not less than 48 hours notice is given to the Chief Constable in the event of any objection being raised to disclosure of the information required by paragraph (*insert paragraph number*).

	DD: Disclosure of Court Documents and by Other Agencies
DD4	*Ongoing criminal investigation*
	The Chief Constable of (*identify police force*) is requested to disclose to the local authority by (time/date) all statements/ entries in pocket notebooks/ transcripts of interviews/ photographs/ and other material (*specify*) in the possession of the police relating to the investigation concerning the injuries sustained by (*identity of child*) with liberty to the Chief Constable to apply to vary this order on not less than 48 hours notice (*or specify*).
DD5	*Disclosure of court documents to the police*
	Permission is given to the local authority to disclose forthwith copies of the statements/reports of the (*Identify parties/persons*) to (*identify police force*).
DD6	*Service of order on the police*
	The local authority/children's solicitor/other shall serve a copy of this order on the Chief Constable of (*identify police force*) forthwith
DD7	*Service of disclosed police records – domestic violence*
	The local authority shall file and serve by (*time/date*) copies of documents and records relating to complaints to the police of incidents of domestic violence (*identify persons/parties*) upon receipt of the same from the Chief Constable
DD8	*Domestic violence incident records*
	The Chief Constable of (*name force*) is requested to disclose to the (*Party*) by 4pm on *(Date)* all records, FWINs or other relevant information in the possession of the police relating to all attendances made in respect of complaints relating to incidents of domestic violence at the addresses occupied by *(Name persons)* namely *(Addresses)* between *(Date)* and *(Date)*. Permission is granted to the Chief Constable to apply to vary this order on application to *(Case Management Judge)* on not less than 48 hours notice.

PART V

Guidance
December 2007

JSB's Equal Treatment Advisory Committee (ETAC) Guidance on Religious Dress

General note—See FPR 2010, r 12.21, **Wearing of veils in court**.

A person's religion or belief can influence the way they dress and present themselves in public. In most instances, such clothing will present few, if any, issues for judges. In practice, there are very few real clashes between the court process and different cultural practices within the UK. There is room for diversity, and there should be willingness to accommodate different practices and approaches to religious and cultural observance.

While there are other examples of religious items of clothing (the Jewish skullcap – the kippahor yarmulke- is one; the Sikh turban another), the issue of religious dress is one that is most likely to arise in relation to the niqab, or full veil, sometimes worn by Muslim women. As the niqab involves the full covering of the face, the judge may have to consider if any steps are required to ensure effective participation and a fair hearing, both for the woman wearing the niqab and other participants in the proceedings. Some useful guidance on the background to and religious significance of the wearing of different styles of Muslim headscarf can be found at *http://news.bbc.co.uk/1/hi/world/middle_east/5411320.stm.*

The following general guidance is designed to assist judges in relation to the matters that should be borne in mind if presented with this issue in courts and tribunals. While there are a range of different possible approaches, depending on the circumstances of the particular case and the individual concerned, the interests of justice remain paramount. In essence, it is for the judge, in any set of circumstances, to consider what difference, if any, would be made to those interests by the niqab being worn. It may well be, that after consideration, there is no necessity to take any steps at all.

A number of judges have provided helpful accounts as to how they have dealt with such situations themselves, and to which we have had regard in formulating the following guidance. It is not possible to give advice here on any specific situation. It is possible, however, to give some indication of the factors to be taken into account in different types of case, and where the woman concerned is fulfilling different roles in the proceedings. It is worth re-emphasising that on this issue, as in so many areas of courtroom practice, there are rarely 'model answers' in terms of a response to a given set of circumstances. Judges may find it helpful to contact Circuit Community Liaison Judges or the judicial members of ETAC if they wish to discuss further any of the issues raised.

It is important to acknowledge from the outset that for Muslim women who do choose to wear the niqab, it is an important element of their religious and cultural identity. To force a choice between that identity (or cultural acceptability), and the woman's involvement in the criminal, civil justice, or tribunal system (as a witness, party, member of court staff or legal office-holder) may well have a significant impact on that woman's sense of dignity and would likely serve to exclude and marginalise further women with limited visibility in courts and tribunals. This is of particular concern for a system of justice that must be, and must be seen to be, inclusive and representative of the whole community. While there may be a diversity of opinions and debates between Muslims about the nature of dress required, for the judicial system the starting point should be respect for the choice made, and for each woman to decide on the extent and nature of the dress she adopts.

Different roles

As in all walks of life, the justice system should encourage practices which will enable as many people as possible to participate and engage with judicial processes as effectively as possible in whatever position, whether as witnesses, complainants, jurors, judicial office-holders, advocates or court staff. Each situation should be considered individually in order to find the best solution in each case.

Essentially, any consideration concerning the wearing of the niqab should be functional; that is, on the basis that the niqab prevents a person from seeing a woman's face. The primary question that needs to be asked by any judicial office holder before coming to a decision is: What is the significance of seeing this woman's face to the judicial task that I have to fulfil? How does being capable of observing her facial expressions impact on the court's decision-making, given her particular role in the proceedings? A distinction can be made, therefore, between situations where this may be useful or important (for example, when assessing the evidence of a witness, particularly whose evidence is in dispute), situations where it is essential (for example, for purposes of identification), and other situations where it may not be of any relevance (for example, arguably, for court clerks or ushers).

As a judge. It is where the woman concerned is providing the 'face' of justice – as a judge, magistrate or tribunal member – that the question of the 'transparency of justice' might be said most obviously to come into play. Is the constituency which is served by the courts entitled to see the person dispensing justice? In reality, it will be rare for a set of circumstances to arise in which another judicial office-holder is called upon to make a decision on this point. Questions relating to the appointment of judges and the terms under which they hold office are matters for the Lord Chief Justice or other appropriate members of the senior judiciary, to whom the matter should be referred if the question arises.

As a juror. There may be circumstances where a judge has to hear a challenge for cause on the inclusion of a woman wearing the full veil as a member of a jury. The judge may feel the challenge justified and excuse her from serving on that jury, with the proviso that she may serve on another where no such challenge is made. Here, the decision must depend to a degree on the view of the parties to the particular case. But caution needs to be exercised, as in all such challenges, that there is a genuine and legitimate basis for such a challenge, based on the particular circumstances of the case. There may well be situations in which such a juror would be welcomed by the parties, or one party at least, as having some insight which may be relevant to the task of the jury in the case.

Steps are under way to enable the JSB to give guidance on what judges should say in summing up to a jury, where one of the witnesses or the defendant is wearing a niqab.

As a victim or complainant. The primary aim is, as stated before, to ensure a fair hearing. What needs to be considered, therefore, is: What is required to enable a woman wearing a niqab to participate in the legal process, to facilitate her ability to give her best evidence and to ensure, so far as practicable, a fair hearing for both sides? It should not automatically be assumed that any difficulty is created by a woman in court, in whatever capacity, who chooses to wear a niqab. Nor should it ever be assumed without good reason that it is inappropriate for a woman to give evidence in court wearing the full veil. Where, for example, the case involves domestic abuse or the possible abuse of her children, the judge may consider it contrary to the interests of justice to make her choose between giving evidence to secure a conviction and wearing the full veil.

Generally speaking, a woman who wears a niqab would do so because it enables her to participate in a public space, such as a court. In situations where a fair hearing may require a woman to remove her niqab, or where she feels she may be able to participate more effectively without her niqab, however, there are a whole variety of special measures available to the court (e.g. live link, screens, clearing the public gallery) that may be considered. The most appropriate course will depend on the issues in the case. As with any consideration of the permitted special measures in a criminal or family case, this is a point on which a decision should ideally be reached after discussion at a preparatory or preliminary hearing, rather than at a final hearing in open court.

As with all practices, the response must be thoughtful and sensitive. If having considered the nature of the case, the nature of the evidence and the prevailing circumstances, it is the view of the judicial office holder that he or she cannot properly ensure fairness or record the evidence fully in a way that will do justice to the case, then careful consideration will need to be given to asking the woman concerned whether she would remove simply that part of the veil that covers the main part of her face. It should be fully explained what the difficulty is, and why the judge considers that he or she will be in difficulty in properly fulfilling the judicial decision-making task and in ensuring fairness to all sides. Having given that explanation, one option might be to allow a short adjournment to enable the woman concerned to seek guidance or advice or possibly to enable her to attend court differently attired, or perhaps for the court to be cleared of anyone other than those directly involved with the case.

As a witness or defendant. For a witness or defendant, similarly, a sensitive request to remove a veil, with no sense of obligation or pressure, maybe appropriate, but careful thought must be given to such a request. The very fact of appearing in a court or tribunal

PART V

will be quite traumatic for many, and additional pressure may well have an adverse impact on the quality of evidence given. Any request to remove a veil should be accompanied by an explanation by the judge of their concern that, where there are crucial issues of credit, the woman might be at a disadvantage if the judge or jury is not able to assess her demeanour or facial expressions when responding to questions. The witness or party may wish to discuss the matter with her legal representative or witness support worker.

It is worth emphasising that while it may be more difficult in some cases to assess the evidence of a woman wearing a niqab, the experiences of judges in other cases have shown that it is often possible to do so, depending on all the circumstances – hence the need to give careful thought to whether the veil presents a true obstacle to the judicial task. Responses, behaviour and manner in which a person delivers evidence can be affected anyway by a range of matters, including social and cultural background and ethnicity or the effects of injury or disability. It will always be necessary to have regard to these factors in assessing the extent to which a person's demeanour or the way in which they give evidence otherwise assists in weighing or evaluating their evidence. Can it be said, in the circumstances of the particular case, that any assessment will be different where the judge is able to see the witness's face? In a criminal case, the position should be explained in the absence of the jury and the possibility considered of offering the use of permitted special measures, for example a TV link.

Where identification is an issue, then it must be dealt with appropriately, and may require the witness to make a choice between giving evidence in the case whilst showing her face, and not being able to be a witness.

Whilst not exact analogies, there are, of course, other circumstances in which a judge will take evidence without being able to see the face of the witness – for example, where evidence is taken on the phone, or where the judge is visually-impaired.

Sitting as a magistrate, or on other judicial tribunals of more than one member. Sitting as a magistrate, and therefore as one of a panel of three, can raise its own issues. The aim is, of course, the same – that is, to weigh and accurately evaluate the evidence of every witness appearing in the magistrates' court. As in the Crown Court, that assessment is based upon a number of different factors, and the degree to which it is relevant or necessary to that assessment to see a woman's face may depend on the type of case, and the nature of the evidence that the witness gives.

Taking all this into account (and the effect that a range of matters may have on the manner in which a person delivers their evidence, as acknowledged above), there may still be a concern about hearing and weighing the evidence from a woman whose face is veiled and whose expression is invisible.

It is possible that not all the panel will agree on the best way of proceeding. If any one of the magistrates is of the view that he or she may be disadvantaged in assessing the witness, then the magistrates should retire and discuss the most appropriate course of action. This is not to be decided on a majority decision because each magistrate must be faithful to his or her oath. If, following discussion, the question of a veil remains a matter for concern, such a course of action may well include asking the defendant or witness to remove that part of the veil which covers her face and to consider what might be done to facilitate a resolution to the difficulty.

If the court does decide to ask a defendant or witness to remove that part of the veil which covers the face, it should be fully explained that the reason for the request is that the role of the magistrates is to weigh and evaluate the evidence presented in court and that, in order to make that evaluation, magistrates draw on the full range of information available to them. This includes the oral evidence of witnesses whether called by the prosecution or the defence. In relation to witnesses (and the defendant generally), that evaluation also involves, to some extent, an assessment of the way in which the person gives that evidence, how each responds or reacts to questions to even to other people in court. In every case, magistrates will always try their best to do justice in the case before them and while the way in which evidence is given may only be part of the assessment, in certain cases they may feel that they cannot be assured that they can provide a fair and just assessment of all the evidence without seeing the defendant/witness's face during the course of the hearing, thereby potentially creating disadvantage. This is because the magistrate will not have had the benefit of what they consider to be the best evidence and as a result they may feel that their ability to ensure fairness to all sides is affected. It would need to be made clear that, whilst demeanour and facial expressions will not be allowed to over-influence the consideration given to any case, these features may be able to assist magistrates when weighing up the evidence. As an advocate. In the case of those who wish to practise as an advocate different considerations should be borne in mind. A general policy enabling the judiciary to decide whether the wearing of the niqab should be permitted or refused on a case by case basis would place Muslim women advocates, and their clients, at a disadvantage where the woman concerned felt unable to appear in a court or tribunal without her veil. This is because she would be unable to say in advance of any hearing whether the judge would allow her to appear in her niqab. The starting point should therefore be that she is entitled to appear as an advocate when wearing it.

Once again the interests of justice will be paramount and the judge may need to consider whether, in any particular circumstances which arise, the interests of justice are being impeded by the fact that the advocate's face cannot be seen. In reality, in the absence of any question relating to identification, there are few instances where an advocate or representative appearing in a niqab would be likely to present any real issue. Such concerns would be likely to centre round the fact that the woman could not be heard, rather than seen. So long as the advocate can be heard reasonably clearly it is unlikely that the interests of justice will be impeded. Just as in any case where a judge might have difficulty in hearing any party, witness or advocate, sensitively enquiring whether they can speak any louder or providing other means of amplification should suffice and such measures should be considered with the advocate before asking her to remove her veil.

Judge craft

As with so much guidance in this bench book, the best way of proceeding comes down to basic good judge craft. There is room for diversity in our system of justice, and there should be willingness to accommodate different practices and approaches to religious and cultural observance. A good understanding of the special measures that may be of use in the particular case, and of the need to identify the need for such adaptations at a preliminary hearing, are key.

When an issue relating to the wearing of the niqab does arise, the judicial office-holder must reach a decision on how to proceed having regard to the interests of justice in the particular case. This will include combining sensitivity to any expressed wish not to remove the niqab with a clear explanation, where appropriate, of the reasons for any request for its removal, and the disadvantages for the judge of not removing it. In many cases, there will be no need for a woman to remove her niqab, provided that the judge is of the view that justice can be properly served.

PART V

President's Guidance
3 October 2008

Citations: [2008] All ER (D) 134 (Oct)

Listing Final Hearings in Adoption Cases

1 This Guidance is issued with the purpose of clarifying the legal requirements and practical arrangements for final hearings in adoption applications.

2 This Guidance does not apply to any case where the child has been freed for adoption under the provisions of the Adoption Act 1976 or where the parent or guardian of the child cannot be found.

3 In this Guidance:

    (a) "the 2002 Act" means the Adoption and Children Act 2002;

    (b) any reference to a rule by number is a reference to the rule so numbered in the Family Procedure (Adoption) Rules 2005.

4 Section 141(3) of the 2002 Act and rule 31 place an obligation on the court officer to give to the persons listed in rule 31, including birth parent(s) with parental responsibility, notice of the date and place of the final hearing of an adoption application.

5 The requirement to give notice is mandatory. Notice of the final hearing must be given to any person listed in rule 31 who can be found and there is no discretion to dispense with such notice. The provisions of rule 39 (power of court to dispense with service) do not apply to notice of the final hearing. By rule 32(1) any person who has been given notice under rule 31 has the right to attend the final hearing and, except where rule 32(2) applies, to be heard on the question of whether an adoption order should be made.

6 In some cases the welfare of the child will require arrangements to be made to ensure that the birth parent(s) and the applicant(s) or the child do not meet at or in the vicinity of the court. This will apply particularly to proceedings in which a serial number has been assigned to the applicant under rule 20(2); rule 20(4)(b) provides that, in such a case, the proceedings will be conducted with a view to securing that the applicant is not seen by or made known to any party who is not already aware of his identity except with his consent.

7 Rule 32(6) provides that the court cannot make an adoption order unless the applicant and the child personally attend the final hearing. However, rule 32(6) is subject to rule 32(7), which gives the court a discretion to direct that the applicant or the child need not attend the final hearing; this provision permits the court, where appropriate, to direct that the attendance of the applicant or the child or both of them at the final hearing is not required.

8 When giving directions for the conduct of the final hearing of an adoption application, the court should consider in particular:

    (1) A person whose application for the permission of the court to oppose the making of an adoption order under section 47(3) or (5) of the 2002 Act has been refused is not entitled to be heard on the question of whether an order should be made.

    (2) (a) whether to give a direction under rule 32(7) that the applicant or the child need not attend the hearing;

           (b) whether to give a direction under rule 32(4) that any person must attend the hearing;

           (c) whether arrangements need to be made to ensure that the birth parent(s) and the applicant or the child do not meet at or in the vicinity of the court;

(d)   the arrangements for ensuring that the ascertainable wishes and feelings of the child regarding the adoption decision are placed before the court;

(e)   the facilities at the place where the final hearing is to take place, including the availability of suitable accommodation;

(f)   the use of any electronic information exchange and video or telephone conferencing links.

9 In proceedings in which a serial number has been assigned to the applicant under rule 20(2), it will generally be appropriate to excuse the attendance of the child at the final hearing. It may also be appropriate to excuse the attendance of the applicant, if necessary to ensure that confidentiality is preserved. Where in such a case the attendance of the applicant is required, arrangements must be made to ensure that the applicant is not seen by or made known to any party who is not already aware of his identity.

10 In any case in which a direction is given that the applicant or the child need not attend the final hearing, the order and any notice of hearing issued by the court must state clearly that the applicant or the child, as the case may be, should not attend.

11 Each Adoption Centre and each magistrates' court which hears family proceedings must have arrangements in place to provide information to the relevant parties about any special arrangements made for their attendance at and the conduct of the final hearing.

12 The application for an adoption order should be determined at the hearing of which notice has been given under rule 31. If the application is not determined at that hearing, notice of the adjourned final hearing should be given under rule 31 and this Guidance shall apply equally to the adjourned hearing.

13 Where an adoption order is made in the absence of the applicant or the child, the court should consider making facilities available for a celebratory event. The event should not normally be held before the expiry of the appeal period (generally 14 days). Except in exceptional circumstances, the judge or, in the magistrates' court at least one of the magistrates, who made the adoption order should host the celebratory event. Arrangements for the celebratory event should be made with the applicant(s) by the court.

PART V

Practice Direction
3 November 2008

Citation: [2009] 1 FLR 365

Allocation and Transfer of Proceedings

1.1 This Practice Direction is given by the President of the Family Division under the powers delegated to him by the Lord Chief Justice under paragraph 2(2) of part 1 of Schedule 2 to the Constitutional Reform Act 2005 and is agreed by the Lord Chancellor.

1.2 The objective of this Practice Direction is to ensure that the criteria for the transfer of proceedings are applied in such a way that proceedings are heard at the appropriate level of court, that the capacity of magistrates' courts is properly utilised and that proceedings are only dealt with in the High Court if the relevant criteria are met.

1.3 This Practice Direction will come into effect on 25 November 2008. Where practicable, it applies to proceedings started before but not concluded by 25 November. The Practice Directions of 5 June 1992 (distribution of business) and 22 February 1993 (applications under the Children Act 1989 by children) are revoked except that they will continue to apply to any proceedings to which it is not practicable to apply this Practice Direction.

1.4 A reference to an article is a reference to the article so numbered in the Allocation and Transfer of Proceedings Order 2008.

Note—ATPO 2008 is set out in Part IV.

PART 1

2 This Part of this Practice Direction applies to all family proceedings (whether or not the Allocation and Transfer of Proceedings Order 2008 applies to such proceedings).

Timing and continuing review of decision on appropriate venue

3.1 The issue as to which court is the most appropriate hearing venue must be addressed by the court speedily as soon as there is sufficient information to determine whether the case meets the criteria for hearing in that court. This information may come to light before, during or after the first hearing. It must then be kept under effective review at all times; it should not be assumed that proceedings will necessarily remain in the court in which they were started or to which they have been transferred. For example proceedings that have been transferred to a county court because one or more of the criteria in article 15 applies should be transferred back to the magistrates' court if the reason for transfer falls away. Conversely, an unforeseen late complication may require a transfer from a magistrates' court to a county court.

3.2 Where a court is determining where the proceedings ought to be heard it will consider all relevant information including that given by the applicant either in the application form or otherwise, for example in any request for proceedings to be transferred to another magistrates' court or to a county court under rule 6 of the Family Proceedings Courts (Children Act 1989) Rules 1991.

Timeliness

4.1 Article 13 and paragraph 12.1 require the court to have regard to delay. Therefore the listing availability of the court in which the proceedings have been started and in neighbouring magistrates' courts and county courts must always be ascertained before deciding where proceedings should be heard.

4.2 If a magistrates' court is considering transferring proceedings to a county court or a county court is considering transferring proceedings to the High Court but that decision is finely balanced, the proceedings should not be transferred if the transfer would lead to delay. Conversely, if the High Court is considering transferring proceedings to a county court or a county court is considering transferring proceedings to a magistrates' court but that decision is finely balanced, the proceedings should be transferred if retaining them would lead to delay.

4.3 Transferring proceedings may mean that there will be a short delay in the proceedings being heard since the papers may need to be sent to the court to which they are being transferred. The court will determine whether the delay is significant, taking into account the circumstances of the case and with reference to the interests of the child.

4.4 While there is no express reference in the Allocation and Transfer of Proceedings Order 2008 or in Part 3 of this Practice Direction to the length of the hearing or to judicial continuity such issues may be relevant.

Transfer of proceedings to or from the High Court

5.1 A court will take into account the following factors (which are not exhaustive) when considering whether the criteria in articles 7 or 18 or paragraph 11.2 or 12.3 apply, such that the proceedings ought to be heard in the High Court –

    (1) there is alleged to be a risk that a child concerned in the proceedings will suffer serious physical or emotional harm in the light of –

        (a) the death of another child in the family, a parent or any other material person; or

        (b) the fact that a parent or other material person may have committed a grave crime, for example, murder, manslaughter or rape,

in particular where the essential factual framework is in dispute or there are issues over the causation of injuries or a material conflict of expert evidence;

    (2) the application concerns medical treatment for a child which involves a risk to the child's physical or emotional health which goes beyond the normal risks of routine medical treatment;

    (3) an adoption order is sought in relation to a child who has been adopted abroad in a country whose adoption orders are not recognised in England and Wales;

    (4) an adoption order is sought in relation to a child who has been brought into the United Kingdom in circumstances where section 83 of the Adoption and Children Act 2002 applies and

        (a) the person bringing the child, or causing the child to be brought –

            (i) has not complied with any requirement imposed by regulations made under section 83(4); or

            (ii) has not met any condition required to be met by regulations made under section 83(5) within the required time; or

        (b) there are complicating features in relation to the application;

    (5) it is likely that the proceedings will set a significant new precedent or alter existing principles of common law;

    (6) where periodical payments, a lump sum or transfer of property are an issue –

        (a) the capital value of the assets involved and the extent to which they are available for, or susceptible to, distribution or adjustment;

        (b) any substantial allegations of fraud or deception or non-disclosure;

        (c) any substantial contested allegations of conduct.

5.2 The following proceedings are likely to fall within the criteria for hearing in the High Court unless the nature of the issues of fact or law raised in the proceedings may make them more suitable to be dealt with in a county court –

    (1) proceedings involving a contested issue of domicile;

    (2) applications to restrain a respondent from taking or continuing with foreign proceedings;

    (3) suits in which the Queen's Proctor intervenes or shows cause and elects trial in the High Court;

    (4) proceedings in which an application is opposed on the grounds of want of jurisdiction;

    (5) proceedings in which there is a complex foreign element or where the court has invited submissions to be made under Article 11(7) of Council Regulation (EC) No 2201/2003 of 27 November 2003 concerning jurisdiction and the recognition and enforcement of judgments in matrimonial matters and the matters of parental responsibility;

    (6) proceedings in which there is an application to remove a child permanently or temporarily from the jurisdiction to a non-Hague Convention country.

    (7) interlocutory applications involving –

        (a) search orders; or

PART V

(b)   directions as to dealing with assets out of the jurisdiction.

5.3 Proceedings will not normally be suitable to be dealt with in the High Court merely because of any of the following –

(1)   intractable problems with regard to contact;
(2)   sexual abuse;
(3)   injury to a child which is neither life-threatening nor permanently disabling;
(4)   routine neglect, even if it spans many years and there is copious documentation;
(5)   temporary or permanent removal to a Hague Convention country;
(6)   standard human rights issues;
(7)   uncertainty as to immigration status;
(8)   the celebrity of the parties;
(9)   the anticipated length of the hearing;
(10) the quantity of evidence;
(11) the number of experts;
(12) the possible availability of a speedier hearing.

5.4 A substantial reason for starting proceedings in the High Court will only exist where the nature of the proceedings or the issues raised are such that they ought to be heard in the High Court. Where proceedings have been started in the High Court under article 7(c) or paragraph 11.2(4) and the High Court considers that there is no substantial reason for them to have been started there, the High Court will transfer the proceedings to a county court or a magistrates' court and may make any orders about costs which it considers appropriate.

PART 2

6 This Part of this Practice Direction applies to family proceedings to which the Allocation and Transfer of Proceedings Order 2008 applies.

Transfer of proceedings from one magistrates' court to another or from one county court to another

7.1 Where a magistrates' court is considering transferring proceedings to another magistrates' court or a county court is considering transferring proceedings to another county court, the court will take into account the following factors (which are not exhaustive) when considering whether it would be more convenient for the parties for the proceedings to be dealt with by the other court –

(1)   the fact that a party is ill or suffers a disability which could make it inconvenient to attend at a particular court;
(2)   the fact that the child lives in the area of the other court;
(3)   the need to avoid delay.

Transfer of proceedings from a magistrates' court to a county court

8.1 Where a magistrates' court is considering whether one or more of the criteria in article 15(1) (except article 15(1)(g) and (h)) apply such that the proceedings ought to be heard in the county court, the magistrates' court will first consider whether another magistrates' court would have suitable experience to deal with the issues which have given rise to consideration of article 15. If so, the magistrates' court will then consider whether the proceedings could be dealt with more quickly or within the same time if they were transferred to the other magistrates' court rather than a county court. If so, the magistrates' court will transfer the proceedings to the other magistrates' court rather than a county court.

8.2 A magistrates' court may only transfer proceedings to a county court under article 15(1)(a) if it considers that the transfer will significantly accelerate the determination of the proceedings. Before considering a transfer on this ground, the magistrates' court must obtain information about the hearing dates available in other magistrates' courts and in the relevant county court. The fact that a hearing could be arranged in a county court at an earlier date than in any appropriate magistrates' court does not by itself justify the transfer of proceedings under article 15(1)(a); the question of whether the determination of the proceedings would be significantly accelerated must be considered in the light of all the circumstances.

Transfer of proceedings from a county court to a magistrates' court

9.1 A county court must transfer to a magistrates' court under article 16(1) proceedings that have previously been transferred under article 15(1) where the county court considers that none of the criteria in article 15(1) apply. In particular, proceedings transferred to a county court by a magistrates' court for resolution of a single issue, for example, use of the inherent powers of the High Court in respect of medical testing of a child or disclosure of information by HM Revenue and Customs, should be transferred back to the magistrates' court once the issue has been resolved.

9.2 Subject to articles 5(3), 6, 8 and 13 and paragraphs 4 and 12.1, straightforward proceedings for –

(1) a residence order;
(2) a contact order;
(3) a prohibited steps order;
(4) a specific issue order;
(5) a special guardianship order; or
(6) an order under Part 4 of the Family Law Act 1996

which are started in a county court should be transferred to a magistrates' court if the county court considers that none of the criteria in article 15(1)(b) to (i) apply to those proceedings.

PART 3

10 This Part of this Practice Direction applies to any family proceedings to which the Allocation and Transfer of Proceedings Order 2008 does not apply.

Starting proceedings

11.1 Subject to paragraph 11.2, family proceedings must be started in a county court.

11.2 Family proceedings may be started in the High Court only if –

(1) the proceedings are exceptionally complex;
(2) the outcome of the proceedings is important to the public in general;
(3) an enactment or rule requires the proceedings to be started in the High Court; or
(4) there is another substantial reason for starting the proceedings in the High Court.

Transferring proceedings

12.1 When making any decision about the transfer of proceedings the court must have regard to the need to avoid delay in the proceedings.

PART V

12.2 A county court will take into account the following factors (which are not exhaustive) when considering whether to transfer proceedings to another county court –

(1)   whether the transfer will significantly accelerate the determination of the proceedings;

(2)   whether it is more convenient for the parties for the proceedings to be dealt with by another county court; and

(3)   whether there is another good reason for the proceedings to be transferred.

12.3 A county court will take into account the following factors (which are not exhaustive) when considering whether to transfer proceedings to the High Court –

(1)   whether the proceedings are exceptionally complex;

(2)   whether the outcome of the proceedings is important to the public in general;

(3)   whether an enactment or rule requires the proceedings to be dealt with in the High Court; and

(4)   whether there is another substantial reason for the proceedings to be transferred.

12.4 The High Court will also take into account the factors in paragraph 12.3 when considering whether to transfer proceedings to a county court.

The Right Honourable
Sir Mark Potter
The President of the Family Division

The Right Honourable
Jack Straw MP
The Lord Chancellor

Practice Direction
6 November 2008

Citation: [2009] 1 FLR 373

Enforcement of Children Act 1989 Contact Orders: Disclosure of Information to Officers of the National Probation Service (High Court and County Court)

This Practice Direction is issued by the President of the Family Division with the agreement of the Lord Chancellor.

1 This Practice Direction applies to proceedings in the High Court or a county court where:

(a)   the court is considering an application for an enforcement order[1] or for an order following an alleged breach of an enforcement order[2] and asks an officer of the Service or a Welsh family proceedings officer to provide information to the court in accordance with section 11L(5) of the Children Act 1989; or

1   Under section 11J of the Children Act 1989.
2   Under paragraph 9 of Schedule A1 to the Children Act 1989.

(b)   the court makes an enforcement order or an order following an alleged breach of an enforcement order and asks an officer of the Service or a Welsh family proceedings officer to monitor compliance with that order and to report to the court in accordance with section 11M of the Children Act 1989.

2 In all cases in which paragraph 1 applies, the officer of the Service or Welsh family proceedings officer will need to discuss aspects of the court case with an officer of the National Probation Service.

3 In order to ensure that the officer of the Service or Welsh family proceedings officer will not potentially be in contempt of court by virtue of such discussions, the court should, when making a request under section 11L(5) or section 11M of the Children Act 1989, give leave to that officer to disclose to the National Probation Service such information (whether or not contained in a document filed with the court) in relation to the proceedings as is necessary.

4 This Practice Direction comes into force on 8 December 2008.

The Right Honourable Sir Mark Potter
President of the Family Division and Head of Family Justice

Practice Direction
6 November 2008

Citations: [2008] All ER (D) 74 (Nov)

Enforcement of Children Act 1989 Contact Orders: Disclosure of Information to Officers of the National Probation Service (Magistrates' Court)

This Practice Direction is issued by the Lord Chief Justice with the agreement of the Lord Chancellor.

1 This Practice Direction applies to proceedings in the magistrates' court where:

    (a)   the court is considering an application for an enforcement order[1] or for an order following an alleged breach of an enforcement order[2] and asks an officer of the Service or a Welsh family proceedings officer to provide information to the court in accordance with section 11L(5) of the Children Act 1989; or

1   Under section 11J of the Children Act 1989.
2   Under paragraph 9 of Schedule A1 to the Children Act 1989.

    (b)   the court makes an enforcement order or an order following an alleged breach of an enforcement order and asks an officer of the Service or a Welsh family proceedings officer to monitor compliance with that order and to report to the court in accordance with section 11M of the Children Act 1989.

2 In all cases in which paragraph 1 applies, the officer of the Service or Welsh family proceedings officer will need to discuss aspects of the court case with an officer of the National Probation Service.

3 In order to ensure that the officer of the Service or Welsh family proceedings officer will not potentially be in contempt of court by virtue of such discussions, the court should, when making a request under section 11L(5) or section 11M of the Children Act 1989, give leave to that officer to disclose to the National Probation Service such information (whether or not contained in a document filed with the court) in relation to the proceedings as is necessary.

4 This Practice Direction comes into force on 8 December 2008.

Lord Chief Justice

"officer of the service"—See CJCSA 2000, s 11(3).

President's Guidance
24 November 2008

Adoption Proceedings: Intercountry Adoption Centres

Introduction

1 In January 2008, the President of the Family Division issued revised intercountry adoption guidance entitled "Adoption Proceedings Intercountry Adoption Centres" (A20(1)). It set out the courts in which intercountry adoption proceedings must be commenced and which judges are approved to hear these proceedings. The revised guidance reflected the Family Procedure (Adoption) Rules 2005 which came into force on 30 December 2005 giving effect to the Adoption and Children Act 2002 (the Act).

2 On 25 November 2008 the Allocation and Transfer of Proceedings Order 2008 came into effect. The new Order provides for the allocation and transfer of certain proceedings concerning children, including intercountry adoption proceedings.

3 This guidance, issued by the President of the Family Division, updates the guidance issued in January 2008 to reflect the provisions in the new Order. This guidance shall apply whenever an application for, or in connection with, an intercountry adoption order is made from 25 November 2008. It shall also apply, so far as is practicable, to proceedings started before but not concluded by 25 November 2008 (Article 29(1)).

Commencement of proceedings

4 The Allocation and Transfer of Proceedings Order 2008 states that proceedings for a Convention adoption order (meaning an order which is made by virtue of regulations under section 1 of the Adoption (Intercountry Aspects) Act 1999) or for an adoption order where section 83 of the Act) (restriction on bringing children in) applies must be commenced in a county court (Article 6(c) and (d)). In view of the more specialised nature of intercountry adoption proceedings certain county court adoption centres have been designated as 'intercountry adoption centres'.

5 Therefore, proceedings for a Convention adoption order or for an adoption order under s 83 of the Act may only be commenced in one of the intercountry adoption centres (Article 11(2)) listed in Annex A.

6 Any other form of intercountry adoption application must be issued at one of the designated 'adoption centres' listed at Annex B. Where an application for intercountry adoption is listed at a general adoption centre, the adoption centre may transfer the proceedings to a convenient intercountry adoption centre only if the adoption centre considers that the transfer will significantly accelerate the determination of the proceedings, or if it is more convenient for the parties or for the child for the proceedings to be dealt with by an intercountry adoption centre or there is another good reason for the proceedings to be transferred.

Transfer of proceedings to the High Court

7 Proceedings may be started in the High Court only if the proceedings are exceptionally complex, the outcome of the proceedings is important to the public in general or there is another substantial reason for the proceedings to be started in the High Court. The President of the Family Division has given a practice direction requiring a court to take into account the following factors when considering whether intercountry adoption proceedings ought to be heard in the High Court:

- An adoption order is sought in relation to a child who has been adopted abroad in a country whose adoption orders are not recognised in England and Wales.

- An adoption order is sought in relation to a child who has been brought into the United Kingdom in circumstances where s 83 of the Act applies and:

    (a)   the person bringing the child, or causing the child to be brought –

        (i)   has not complied with any requirement imposed by regulations made under s 83(4); or

        (ii) has not met any condition required to be met by regulations made under s 83(5) within the required time: or

    (b)   there are complicating features in relation to the application.

Judges approved to hear Intercountry Adoption Proceedings

8 All intercountry adoption proceedings must be listed before, and may only be heard by a High Court Judge, a district judge of the Principal Registry of the Family Division, a Circuit Judge, a Deputy Circuit Judge or a Recorder who is nominated for adoption proceedings and who is authorised by the Family Division Liaison Judge to hear intercountry adoption proceedings. Directions hearings may be listed before a District Judge or a deputy district judge at an intercountry adoption centre under arrangements made by the local Circuit Judge in charge of adoption, in liaison with the Family Division Liaison Judge.

ANNEX A – DESIGNATED INTERCOUNTRY ADOPTION CENTRES

The following courts have been designated as Intercountry Adoption Centres:

Midland Region

Birmingham County Court

Nottingham County Court

North West Region

Chester County Court

Liverpool County Court

Manchester County Court

North East Region

Leeds County Court

Newcastle County Court

South East Region

Principal Registry of the Family Division

HMCS Wales

Cardiff County Court

Wrexham County Court

South West Region

Bournemouth County Court

Bristol County Court

Exeter County Court

PART V

Portsmouth County Court

London Region
Principal Registry of the Family Division

ANNEX B – ADOPTION CENTRES

The following courts have been designated as Adoption Centres:

Midlands Region
Birmingham County Court
Coventry County Court
Derby County Court
Leicester County Court
Lincoln County Court
Northampton County Court
Nottingham County Court
Stoke On Trent County Court
Telford County Court
Wolverhampton County Court
Worcester County Court

North West Region
Blackburn County Court
Bolton County Court
Carlisle County Court
Chester County Court
Lancaster County Court
Liverpool County Court
Macclesfield County Court
Manchester County Court
Stockport County Court
Warrington County Court

North East Region
Bradford County Court
Kingston Upon Hull County Court
Leeds County Court
Middlesbrough County Court at Teesside Combined Court
Newcastle County Court
Sheffield County Court
Sunderland County Court
York County Court

South East Region
Brighton County Court
Cambridge County Court
Canterbury County Court

Chelmsford County Court
Guildford County Court
Ipswich County Court
Luton County Court
Medway County Court
Milton Keynes County Court
Norwich County Court
Oxford County Court
Peterborough County Court
Reading County Court
Watford County Court

HMCS Wales
Aberystwyth County Court
Cardiff County Court
Llangefni County Court
Newport (Gwent) County Court
Pontypridd County Court
Rhyl County Court
Swansea County Court
Wrexham County Court

South West Region
Bournemouth County Court
Bristol County Court
Exeter County Court
Plymouth County Court
Portsmouth County Court
Southampton County Court
Swindon County Court
Taunton County Court
Truro County Court

London Region
Principal Registry of the Family Division
Bow County Court
Brentford County Court
Bromley County Court
Croydon County Court
Romford County Court
****

PART V

Family Proceedings Directions
16 February 2009

Citation: [2009] 2 FLR 51

Note—These Directions came into force on 16 February 2009. They apply not only to proceedings issued on or after 16 February 2009 but also "so far as is practicable" to proceedings started before, but not concluded by, that date. The Directions are based on the modern system of "nominated" judges (often colloquially referred to as "ticketed"). All nominated judges have received appropriate specialist training.

Allocation to Judiciary

The President of the Family Division, in exercise of the powers conferred on him by section 9 of the Courts and Legal Services Act 1990 and having consulted the Lord Chancellor, gives the following Directions:

Section 9 of the Courts and Legal Services Act 1990—Section 9(2) provides that these Directions have effect "regardless of any rules of court" and they therefore prevail over any inconsistent rule or provision. The Directions do not confer jurisdiction but narrow the class of judge who would otherwise have been capable of hearing the proceedings in question. Although the Directions are, of course, to be obeyed, disobedience does not vitiate jurisdiction in the legal sense since CLSA 1990, s 9(3) provides that "where any directions have been given under this section allocating any proceedings to specified judges, the validity of anything done by a judge in, or in relation to, the proceedings shall not be called into question by reason only of the fact that he was not a specified judge".

1 These Directions shall come into force on 16 February 2009.

2 In these Directions, in the absence of a contrary implication –

"adoption centre" means a court designated as an adoption centre by the Allocation and Transfer of Proceedings Order 2008;

"family proceedings" and "judge" have the meanings assigned to them in section 9 of the Courts and Legal Services Act 1990;

"nominated" in relation to a judge means a judge who has been approved as one to whom family proceedings may be allocated by the President of the Family Division;

"Schedule" means the Schedule to these Directions.

"family proceedings"—Section 9(5) of CLSA 1990 provides that "family proceedings" has the same meaning as in MFPA 1984, s 32, and also includes any other proceedings which are family proceedings for the purposes of CA 1989. FPR 2010, r 2.3 provides that "proceedings" means, unless the context requires otherwise, family proceedings as defined in Courts Act 2003, s 75(3).

"judge"—Section 9(5) of CLSA 1990 defines "judge" to mean any person who:

(a) is capable of sitting as a judge for a county court district;
(b) is a district judge, an assistant district judge or a deputy district judge; or
(c) is a district judge of the Principal Registry of the Family Division at the High Court.

   Section 5 of CCA 1984 states that the following may sit as a judge for a county court district: every circuit judge, every judge of the Court of Appeal, every judge of the High Court and every recorder.

"nominated"—Copies of the lists of judges nominated to sit in the various classes of family proceedings may be obtained from The Family Business Branch, Ministry of Justice, 4th Floor, 102 Petty France, London SW1H 9AJ.

3 Any reference in these Directions to the Allocation and Transfer of Proceedings Order 2008 ("the 2008 Order") is to be read as a reference to the Children (Allocation of Proceedings) Order 1991, the Children (Allocation of Proceedings) (Appeals) Order 1991 or the Family Law Act 1996 (Part IV) (Allocation of Proceedings) Order 1997, as appropriate, where any of those Orders applies as a result of Article 29 of the 2008 Order (transitional provisions).

4 These Directions apply to any family proceedings (except proceedings on appeal from an order or decision made by a magistrates' court) which are pending in a county court or which, by virtue of section 42 of the Matrimonial and Family Proceedings Act 1984 or of a provision of the Allocation and Transfer of Proceedings Order 2008, are treated as pending in a county court in the Principal Registry of the Family Division of the High Court.

"section 42 of the Matrimonial and Family Proceedings Act 1984"—Enables family proceedings to be dealt with in the Principal Registry as if it were a county court. A similar provision is contained in ATPO 2008.

5 (1) These Directions apply, so far as practicable, to proceedings started before but not concluded by 16 February 2009.

(2) Where, by reason of paragraph (1), these Directions do not apply to particular proceedings which have been started but not concluded before 16 February 2009, the Family Proceedings (Allocation to Judiciary) Directions 1999 continue to apply to those proceedings.

6 Subject to the following paragraphs of these Directions, the proceedings described in the Schedule shall be allocated to a judge or to a specified description of judge in accordance with the following Table, by reference to the categories shown in column (b) of the Table and described in the Schedule and subject to the limitations specified in column (c) of the Table.

(a) Judge or specified description of judge	(b) Categories of proceedings by reference to the Schedule	(c) Categories of proceedings by reference to the Schedule
A circuit judge, deputy circuit judge or recorder nominated for public family law proceedings	All categories of proceedings	
A circuit judge, deputy circuit judge or recorder nominated for private family law proceedings	B, D, E	
A district judge of the Principal Registry[1]	A, B, C, D	D Interlocutory matters only
A district judge nominated for public family law proceedings	A, B, C, D	D Interlocutory matters only
A district judge nominated for private family law proceedings	B, D	D Interlocutory matters only
A judge not referred to in any of the preceding entries in this table.	B(i), B(iii), B(vii)	B(i) Only: (1) proceedings in which an order under section 8 of the Children Act 1989 is sought at a without notice hearing where (a) no nominated judge is available to hear the proceedings; and (b) any order is limited in time until a hearing before a nominated judge; and (2) proceedings under section 15 of and Schedule 1 to the Children Act 1989. B(iii) In the case of a deputy district judge, all proceedings except enforcement

PART V

1   Including a deputy district judge of the Principal Registry.

Circuit judges—The categories of proceedings that can be allocated to circuit judges and recorders are clearly stated but note that the judge must be nominated for public or private family law proceedings. Not all circuit judges and recorders are so nominated.

District judges—The categories of proceedings that can be allocated to district judges are clearly stated but note the severe limitation on allocation to a district judge, and deputy judge, who has not been nominated for either public or private family law proceedings. The effect of the limitation is that district judges and deputy district judges who have not been nominated cannot give directions in applications under CA 1989, s 8.

"Own motion" powers to grant a section 8 order in family proceedings—Under CA 1989, s 10(1)(b), "In any family proceedings in which a question arises with respect to the welfare of any child", the court can, of its own motion, grant a s 8 order where "the court considers that the order should be made even though no ... application (for section 8 order) has been made". The 2009 Directions do not restrict to any specified judge the power of the court, of its own motion, to grant a s 8 order. Therefore, any judge can exercise the power conferred by s 10. Nonetheless, it is a power always to be exercised with extreme caution and should not be used to evade the policy of the Directions that these orders should be made by nominated judges.

7 Without prejudice to the provisions of paragraph 6, any proceedings to which these Directions apply, including any appeal referred to in paragraph 10, may be allocated to–

(a)   a judge of the Family Division of the High Court;

(b)   a person acting as a judge of the Family Division of the High Court in pursuance of a request made under section 9(1) of the Senior Courts Act 1981 other than a former judge of the Court of Appeal or a former puisne judge of the High Court; but proceedings in categories A and C of the Schedule shall be allocated only to a judge who has been nominated for them;

(c)   a person sitting as a recorder who has been authorised to act as a judge of the Family Division of the High Court under section 9(4) of the Senior Courts Act 1981;

(d)   a person sitting as a recorder who is a District Judge (Magistrates' Courts) and is nominated for public family law proceedings in the County Court;

(e)   a person sitting as a Recorder who is a District Judge of the Principal Registry of the Family Division.

Amendments—CRA 2005, Sch 11, para 1(2).

8 When a person sitting as a recorder is also a district judge nominated for public family law proceedings, any proceedings may be allocated to him which, under these Directions, may be allocated to a district judge nominated for public family law proceedings.

9 A circuit judge or district judge nominated for private family law proceedings who is sitting at an adoption centre may, with the agreement of the Family Division Liaison Judge for the relevant region, hear proceedings in category C of the Schedule, limited in the case of a district judge to interlocutory matters only.

10 Where in any proceedings to which these Directions apply an appeal may be heard by a circuit judge, deputy circuit judge or recorder, it may be heard by any judge of that description who under these Directions would have been able to hear the proceedings at first instance.

The Right Honourable Sir Mark Potter

President of the Family Division and Head of Family Justice

SCHEDULE

Category	Description of proceedings
A	(i) Proceedings under section 25 of the Children Act 1989; (ii) Proceedings under Parts IV and V of the Children Act 1989; (iii) Proceedings under Schedules 2 and 3 to the Children Act 1989; (iv) Applications for leave under section 91(14), (15) or (17) of the Children Act 1989; (v) Proceedings under section 102 of the 1989 Act or section 79 of the Childcare Act 2006; (vi) Proceedings for a residence order under section 8 of the Children Act 1989 or for a special guardianship order under section 14A of the Children Act 1989 with respect to a child who is the subject of a care order.
B	(i) Proceedings under Parts I and II of the Children Act 1989, except where the proceedings come within Category A(vi), C(iii) or C(iv) of this Schedule; (ii) Proceedings under sections 33, 34 and 37 of the Family Law Act 1986; (iii) Proceedings under Part 4 of the Family Law Act 1996; (iv) Proceedings under Part 4A of the Family Law Act 1996; (v) Proceedings under section 20 of the Child Support Act 1990; (vi) Proceedings under section 30 of the Human Fertilisation and Embryology Act 1990; (vii) Family proceedings for which no express provision is made in this Schedule.
C	(i) Proceedings under section 21 of the Adoption Act 1976; (ii) Proceedings under the Adoption and Children Act 2002; (iii) Proceedings for a residence order under section 8 of the Children Act 1989 where either section 28(1) (child placed for adoption) or 29(4) (placement order in force) of the Adoption and Children Act 2002 applies; (iv) Proceedings for a special guardianship order under section 14A of the Children Act 1989 where either section 28(1) (child placed for adoption) or section 29(5) (placement order in force) of the Adoption and Children Act 2002 applies.
D	Proceedings under sections 55, 55A, 56 and 57 of the Family Law Act 1986
E	The hearing of contested proceedings for (i) a decree of divorce, nullity or judicial separation; or (ii) an order for dissolution or nullity of civil partnership or a separation order.

PART V

President's Guidance
22 April 2009

Citation: [2009] 2 FLR 167

Applications Consequent upon the Attendance of the Media in Family Proceedings

1 The Government's announcement about the attendance of the media at hearings in family proceedings (see *Family Justice in View* Cm 7502, December 2008) has been implemented by a change to the Family Proceedings Rules made by *The Family Proceedings (Amendment) (No 2) Rules 2009* SI 2009 No 857 (county court and High Court) and *The Family Proceedings Courts (Miscellaneous Amendments) Rules 2009* SI 2009 No 858 (magistrates' courts) and two Practice Directions *Attendance of Media Representatives at Hearings in Family Proceedings* dated 20th April 2009 made by the President to support the rule changes in the respective courts.

2 In the county court and High Court media attendance is implemented by the change to FPR Rule 10.28. (to which the Practice Direction applies). Change regarding media attendance in the family proceedings courts is introduced through amendment to the Family Proceedings Courts (Children Act 1989) Rules 1991, with the insertion of rule 16A.

3 In broad terms the changes for the county court and the High Court relating to media attendance permit duly accredited representatives of news gathering and reporting organisations, and any other unaccredited person whom the court permits, to be present at hearings of all family proceedings (defined by s 32 Matrimonial and Family Proceedings Act 1984) except hearings conducted for the purposes of judicially assisted conciliation or negotiation. They also provide that the court can exclude media representatives

4 For the county court and the High Court, the change relates to most of the proceedings which are for the time being heard in private. It therefore covers a wide range of proceedings including for example public and private law proceedings under the Children Act 1989 and claims for ancillary relief under the Matrimonial Causes Act 1973.

5 Representatives of newspapers or news agencies are admitted to the family proceedings courts under section 69 (2) Magistrates' Courts Act 1980. Media attendance will now be regulated by the insertion of rule "16A Restrictions on presence of persons at directions appointment and hearing". Duly accredited representatives of news gathering and reporting organisations are not entitled to be present at hearings conducted for the purposes of judicially assisted conciliation or negotiation. They may also be excluded for reasons set out in rule 16A(3).

6 In respect of the county court and the High Court the new Part 11 of the FPR, and in respect of the family proceedings court the new Part 11C of the Family Proceedings Courts (Children Act 1989) Rules 1991 as amended, regarding communication of information only apply to proceedings concerning children. In particular, they do not apply to proceedings for ancillary relief. Nor do they expressly cover communication of information to representatives of the media.

7 As appears from the Practice Direction governing the county court and High Court, it is a premise of the change for these courts that the proceedings remain proceedings held in private and that therefore the existing position relating to the publication of matters relating to proceedings which are so heard continues to apply, both whilst the proceedings continue and when they have ended (see the Practice Direction paras 2.4 and 2.5)

8 Useful summaries of the position relating to the publication of matters relating to proceedings heard in private can be found in: *Clayton v Clayton* [2006] EWCA Civ 878 [2007] 1 FLR 11 (in particular at paragraphs 23 to 60, 82 to 85, 92 to 104 and 118 to 136 and *Re B (A Child) (Disclosure)* [2004] EWHC 411 (Fam), [2004] 2 FLR 142 (in particular at paragraphs 62 to 82 (on s 12 AJA 1960) and 83 to 107 (on the jurisdiction to relax or increase the statutory restrictions on publication). Other useful cases are listed in the footnote to this paragraph.[1]

1   *Re S (A Child) (Identification: Restrictions on Publication)* [2004] UKHL 47, [2005] 1 AC 593; *Pelling v Bruce-Williams (Secretary of State for Constitutional Affairs Intervening)* [2004] EWCA Civ 845, [2004] Fam 155, [2004] 2 FLR 823; *Re Webster; Norfolk County Council v Webster and Others (No 1)* [2006] EWHC 2733 (Fam), [2007] 1 FLR 1146; *Re Webster; Norfolk County Council v Webster and Others (No 2)* [2006] EWHC 2898 (Fam), [2007] 2 FLR 415; *Re B; X Council v B* [2007] EWHC 1622 (Fam), [2008] 1 FLR 482; *Re B; X Council v B (No 2)* [2008] EWHC 270 (Fam), [2008] 1 FLR 1460; *BBC v Cafcass* [2007] EWHC 616 (Fam), [2007] 2 FLR 765; *Oldham Metropolitan Borough Council v GW & PW* [2007] EWHC 136 (Fam), [2007] 2 FLR 597.

9 It is to be noted that the above decisions all concern the interests and welfare of children and that the approach in ancillary relief proceedings (which are also likely to be productive of media applications) has not been the subject of similar judicial consideration and guidance.

10 The new Rules and the Practice Directions include provisions relating to the exclusion of media representatives but are silent on the approach to be taken by the courts to the exercise of their discretion in respect of other issues which may well arise as a consequence of the attendance of media representatives at hearings in family proceedings. In this respect the Government declined to adopt the recommendation of the High Court judges to address the detail of such issues when introducing the change. It is therefore left to the courts to determine how such issues are to be approached and decided. It is clear that a principled approach to such issues should be applied by the courts and that this can only properly be developed by the courts with the benefit of full argument from the interested parties.

Note—The reference to a "discretion" to exclude the media is a misnomer: see *Re Child X (Residence and Contact: Rights of Media Attendance – FPR r 10.28(4)* [2009] 2 FLR 1467.

11 The change to admit media representatives to hearings in family proceedings in county courts and the High Court is likely to give rise to a number of issues relating to the exercise of discretion by all levels of court. In particular it is likely that courts will quickly be faced with applications for the provision of documents to media representatives present in court to enable them the better to follow the substance of the proceedings. If minded to grant such application, the court will need to consider the terms of any restriction relating to the use (and in particular the publication) of information contained in any such documents provided to media representatives as a condition of their being so provided.

12 In cases involving children, applications, whether by the media or the parties, are also likely to raise issues as to

(i) The proper application of the existing statutory provisions restricting the publication of the identity of children and information relating to proceedings heard in private;

(ii) the adequacy of the protection afforded in children cases by Section 12 of the Administration of Justice Act 1960 ('AJA 1960') which, inter alia, does not extend to the identity of the parties or witnesses;

(iii) the effect of the publication of any anonymised judgment;

and whether or not injunctive relief may be required upon a wider basis.

13 In relation to the need for injunctive relief in cases affecting children, particularly in local courts, it may be necessary to consider how far it is appropriate to protect from identification not only the children and the parties, but also witnesses and others whose identities will be known locally as associated with the child or his family.

14 Finally, there will be issues over the need on child welfare grounds for protection to extend beyond the end of the hearing (see paragraph 2.5 of the respective Practice Directions).

15 No doubt the basic opposing arguments in relation to the question of access to documents will be, on the one hand, that the Government has sought to retain the basic structure and rationale of the long standing policy of privacy in relation to children proceedings, while at the same time admitting the press, to avoid charges of "secret justice" and to promote better understanding of the working of the family courts. For these purposes, however, access to court documents is not generally necessary or desirable having regard to their confidential nature.

16 On the other hand, the media may argue that, particularly in those cases where there is not a formal oral opening, they should be enabled to see statements and documents filed in order fully to understand the nature and progress of the proceedings, and so as to be able to publish articles, within appropriate reporting constraints, about the cases which they attend. In this connection, it is likely, if not inevitable, that in individual cases of high interest to the media, courts at all levels and all over the country will be faced

PART V

with detailed legal argument relating to rival Convention Rights, public and private interests, the welfare of children, and the construction and application of the primary and secondary legislation.

17 Inconsistency of approach in children cases as to the principles to be applied to the determination of such issues on the part of the courts, parties, witnesses, other persons involved in the relevant events (e g social workers and doctors) and the media could well give rise to justified criticism on grounds of uncertainty. It would not promote the public interest in the proper administration of justice and could be damaging to children.

18 So far as ancillary relief proceedings are concerned, policy, privacy and Convention issues may also arise for decision, albeit the interests of children may not be engaged.

19 The purpose of this guidance is therefore to try to avoid, or at least to minimise, inconsistency by providing that decisions are made by the High Court (and the Appellate Courts) as soon as possible as to the principled approach to be taken. Its purpose is also to provide that, until that is done, delay in decision making in individual cases, (particularly those concerning children) should be avoided. It is to be hoped that the media will co-operate in these aims.

20 Pending the availability of formal judicial guidance from the High Court or Court of Appeal as to the principled approach to be adopted, all County Courts and Magistrates' Courts hearing family proceedings should carefully consider adopting the following course:

(i)   The court should deal in accordance with the Rules and Practice Directions with any application made for exclusion of the media from the proceedings or any part of them on any of the grounds set out in the Practice Directions.

(ii)   Where a representative of the media in attendance at the proceedings applies to be shown court documents, the court should seek the consent of the parties to such representative being permitted (subject to appropriate conditions as to anonymity and restrictions upon onward disclosure) to see such summaries, position statements and other documents as appear reasonably necessary to a broad understanding of the issues in the case.

(iii) If the objection of any of the parties is maintained, then in any case where the objecting party demonstrates reasonably arguable grounds for resisting disclosure of the document or documents sought, no order for disclosure should be made, but the following course of action should be considered.

(iv)   If considered necessary or appropriate the court should transfer (or, in the case of a family proceedings court, take the first step to bring about an urgent transfer of) the proceedings to the High Court for the determination of any disclosure and/or reporting issues.

(v)   Alternatively, in order to avoid delay in decision making on the substantive issues in the case, the court should adjourn determination of any disclosure and/or reporting issues pending a decision by the High Court (or the Appellate Courts) on the principled approach to be taken to them and should make any necessary interim orders in accordance with the argument mentioned in paragraph 15 above in order to secure the position meanwhile.

(vi)   Similarly, if a representative of the media applies for reporting restrictions to be lifted during the currency of a case, in the absence of agreement between the parties the court should consider following one or the other of the alternative steps set out in sub-paragraphs (iv)–(v) above.

(vii) If injunctive relief is sought restraining publication based on Convention rights rather than statutory provisions, the matter should in any event be transferred to the High Court to be dealt with under the *President's Practice Direction (Applications for Reporting Restriction Orders)* 18 March 2005 and the *Practice Note (Official Solicitor: Deputy Director of Legal Services CAFCASS: Applications for Reporting Restriction Orders* [2005] 2 FLR 111 and, if interim injunctive relief appears necessary under threat of publication before such application can be dealt with by a High Court judge, the county court should comply with s 12(2) of Human Rights Act 1998.

Note—The President has given guidance on the approach to be adopted when considering whether to exclude the media from hearings in *Re Child X* (above).

21 The underlying aim of this guidance is to seek to ensure that the principled approach to be taken is determined by the High Court (and the Appellate Courts) as soon as possible and that in the interim changes of practice do not take place which may not accord with that principled approach. Though this may result in delayed rulings on some early contested applications involving arguments such as those mentioned in paragraphs 15 and 16 above, it may be considered desirable, in the absence of legislative guidance, that such rulings should only be made on the basis of authoritative judicial guidance following proper determination, with the benefit of full argument, of the relevant principled approach for the longer term.

22 To assist in the early determination of the principled approach:

(i) Arrangements will be made in the High Court to identify appropriate test cases and for their early determination, and

(ii) Arrangements will be made to seek to ensure that directions are given as soon as is practicable in any proceedings that are transferred to the High Court because they raise substantial issues arising from the attendance of media representatives

(iii) Proceedings which are transferred to the High Court other than in the PRFD should be put before a family High Court Judge on circuit or, failing the presence on circuit of a High Court Judge, before the Family Division Liaison Judge as an urgent application for directions.

Sir Mark Potter
President of the Family Division

Best Practice Guide
August 2009

Note—FPR 2010, PD12A sets out the Public Law Outline that governs the procedure for all applications for care and supervision orders under CA 1989, Pt IV.

Preparing for Care and Supervision Proceedings

A best practice guide for use by all professionals involved with children and families pre-proceedings and in preparation for applications made under section 31 of the Children Act 1989.

Produced by the Care Proceedings Programme, Ministry of Justice, August 2009.

Foreword

This comprehensive best practice guide is based on the findings of inter agency workshops and has been extensively peer reviewed. It sets out examples and puts forward suggestions as to how we can all work together, valuing and understanding the work and roles of colleagues, and puts the needs of the child firmly back at the heart of care proceedings.

The guide will complement the Statutory Guidance and Public Law Outline but it is not intended to be prescriptive. However, it describes the processes involved; the respective roles of those involved; tackles some of the most difficult and frequently raised areas of uncertainty; and provides examples of good practice. It also acts as a sign post towards the regulations and Statutory Guidance on specific issues and is one of a range of measures aimed at developing a consistent and practical approach to care proceedings.

The publication of this guide is particularly timely in view of the recommendations in Lord Laming's report "The Protection of Children in England: A progress report", published in March 2009. The UK Government has accepted all 58 of Lord Laming's recommendations, and published an action plan on 6 May 2009, setting out the detailed response to the recommendations. The action plan is available at: *www.everychildmatters.gov.uk/laming*.

Note—The action plan can be found at *www.education.gov.uk/publications/eOrderingDownload/DCSF-Laming.pdf*.

The Welsh Assembly Government has put in place a programme of measures to strengthen arrangements to safeguard children. These include new arrangements to establish teams to provide intensive support to families whose children may be subject of a care order.

The guide has the full support of the National Family Justice Board. We would like to express our thanks to all those practitioners who have co-operated and contributed to this publication and in particular to the Family Law Bar Association and the Law Society for their endorsement.

Contents

Abbreviations

Chapter 3 – Making a section 31 Children Act 1989 application

Annexes

PART V

cg   Children's Guardians
j   Judiciary

Abbreviations

ACA 2002	Adoption and Children Act 2002
ALDT/CLDT	Adults with Learning Difficulties Team/Community Learning Disability Team or LA equivalent
CA 1989	Children Act 1989
CA 2004	Children Act 2004
Cafcass	Child and Family Court Advisory Service
CAFCASS CYMRU	The Welsh Assembly Government Service in Wales
CMC	Case Management Conference
Experts PD	Practice Direction: Experts in Family Proceedings Relating to Children (President of the Family Division, April 2008)
FA	First Appointment
FGC	Family Group Conference
FH	Final Hearing
Framework	Framework for the Assessment of Children in Need and their Families, 2000, Department of Health. Framework for the Assessment of Children in Need and their Families, 2001, Welsh Assembly Government
HMCS	Her Majesty's Court Service
IRH	Issues Resolution Hearing
IRO	Independent Reviewing Officer
LA	Local Authority
LbP	Letter before Proceedings
LSCB	Local Safeguarding Children's Board
LSC	Legal Services Commission
Parent	The term "parent" is used throughout but should be read to include "parent(s) or other person(s) with PR"
PD	Practice Direction: Guide to Case Management in Public Law Cases (Judiciary of England & Wales and Ministry of Justice, April 2008)
PLO	Public Law Outline (this is contained in the PD and replaces the previous 2003 protocol)
PPM	Pre-Proceedings Meeting
PR	Parental responsibility, defined in section 3 of the Children Act 1989
SG	Statutory Guidance The Children Act 1989 Guidance and Regulations, Volume 1: Court Orders (Department for Children, Schools and Families, April 2008) and the Welsh equivalent, The Children Act 1989 Guidance and Regulations, Volume 1: Court Orders (Wales)
Working Together	Working Together under the Children Act 2004 to Safeguard Children: Every Child matters. A guide to inter-agency working to safeguard and promote the welfare of children, 2006, HM Government Wales – Safeguarding Children – Working Together under the Children Act 2004

Chapter 1 – Introduction

1.1 Background to the reforms

Following the *Review of the Child Care Proceedings System in England and Wales*[1], reforms to s 31 CA 1989 proceedings were brought into effect in April 2008 by two key documents:

1   The Practice Direction: Guide to Case Management in Public Law Cases[2]; and
2   The Children Act 1989 Guidance and Regulations, Volume 1: Court Orders[3] in England, and The Children Act 1989 Guidance and Regulations, Volume 1: Court Orders (Wales)[4] in Wales.

The aim of the reforms can be broadly stated as an intention to make the system for s 31 CA 1989 proceedings more efficient by reducing delay and to improve the outcomes for children and families who may become the subject of court proceedings. The Statutory Guidance focuses on social work undertaken pre-proceedings for two principal reasons. In many cases there will still be an opportunity for the social worker to work with the child and family with a view to avoiding the need for court proceedings. Secondly, work done at these stages can impact on the proceedings (if proceedings are later initiated) and the ability for the proceedings to be conducted as smoothly and expeditiously as possible providing the best possible outcome for the child and his/her family.

1   Review of the Child Care Proceedings System in England and Wales, Department of Constitutional Affairs, Department for Education and Skills and Welsh Assembly Government (May 2006). Accessible at: http://www.dca.gov.uk/publications/reports_reviews/childcare_ps.pdf
2   The Practice Direction: Guide to Case Management in Public Law Cases, Judiciary of England & Wales and Ministry of Justice (April 2008). Accessible at: http://www.judiciary.gov.uk/docs/public_law_outline.pdf
3   The Children Act 1989 Guidance and Regulations, Volume 1: Court Orders, Department for Children, Schools and Families (April 2008). Accessible at: http://www.dcsf.gov.uk/localauthorities/_documents/content/chi.drensactguidance.pdf
4   The Children Act 1989 Guidance and Regulations, Volume 1: Court Orders, Welsh Assembly Government and NHS Wales (March 2008). Accessible at: http://new.wales.gov.uk/dhss/publications/children/guidance/actguidance/courtorderse.pdf?lang=en

Note—For the *Guide to Case Management in Public Law Cases*, see FPR PD12A; for the Children Act 1989 Guidance and Regulations, Volume 1: Court Orders, Department for Children, Schools and Families, see *www.education.gov.uk/publications/standard/publicationDetail/Page1/DCSF-10500-2008.*

1.2   The status of this best practice guide

Ten initiative areas[1] tested elements of the PLO prior to it being finalised. Professionals from those areas were well placed to share information about how their areas were dealing with the reforms "on the ground". The Ministry of Justice's Care Proceedings Programme Office[2] held two workshops in July 2008 (Reading and Liverpool). The "Moving Forward Workshops" brought together professionals from all fields of expertise (HMCS, legal, social work and Cafcass/CAFCASS CYMRU) from the initiative areas. A wealth of information came out of the workshops. We learned about the many examples of good practice, which some areas had already implemented and were working to; many of those ideas have been incorporated into this guide. We also learned of challenges, which some professionals were experiencing. We have sought to bring all that information into this one comprehensive guide to both share the ideas of good practice already operating but also to address and assist with some of the perceived problems.

The guide is not Statutory Guidance: it has no legal status. We have taken careful steps to ensure that various experts in their respective fields reviewed this guide before it was finalised. We hope practitioners may find it a useful additional source of information and explanation but it is no substitute for acting within the statutory framework set out in the Children Act 1989 and the regulations made under Part 3 of the Act and the Statutory Guidance on it.

1   Birmingham, London, Liverpool, Warrington/Chester, Newcastle/Sunderland, Exeter/Plymouth, Leicester, Milton Keynes/Oxford, Swansea, Portsmouth.
2   An inter-agency group set up to deliver the recommendations arising from the 2006 Care Review at: *http://www.justice.gov.uk/guidance/careproceedings.htm*

PART V

1.3 Who should read this guide

This guide is written for all professionals who work with or for children and families where s 31 CA 1989 care proceedings are being considered or applied for. In the main those who we hope will find the guide of most use to their work are: LA social workers, LA managers, lawyers for the LA and for parents, Children's Guardians, lawyers for children, HMCS court staff and legal advisers, the judiciary and expert assessors who may be instructed pre-proceedings and within proceedings.

1.4 How to use this guide

This guide is separated into two parts. Chapter 2 covers the pre-proceedings stages up to the point that a s 31 CA 1989 application is issued at court. Chapter 3 looks at the stages from the point that the LA issues a s 31 CA 1989 application through to disposal of the application and conclusion of the proceedings.

Some of the aspects discussed in this guide will be connected or relate to other aspects. We have used cross-referencing where this is the case. The intention of the guide is that it should act as a quick-reference tool to good practice. As the guide has been written to cater for all parties involved in care proceedings readers should gain a better understanding of the roles and responsibilities of other professionals involved. To make the guide as user-friendly as possible the contents identify the paragraphs which are recommended reading for the various professionals involved in s 31 CA 1989 proceedings.

Chapter 2 – Pre-proceedings stages

2.1 Introduction

In this document the term pre-proceedings is used to indicate the several stages of interaction between the child, family and the LA which occur prior to a court application being issued for a s 31 CA 1989 order. It is straightforward to ascertain the "end" of pre-proceedings because this will be the date that the application to court is issued. Where the pre-proceedings stages "begin" however, is less well defined. On the one hand all stages of involvement prior to an application being made could be termed "pre-proceedings" but for the purposes of the recent reforms the use of the term pre-proceedings is rather precise. It denotes the stages from the point that the LA is considering making an application to court to protect the child but the risk of harm to the child is manageable if an application is not made immediately. Effectively, the LA's approach will be to further attempt to engage with the parent in order to put an agreement in place which reduces the risk of significant harm to the child to a manageable level at that stage.

The point at which pre-proceedings stages nominally commence in view of the recent reforms is where the legal gateway/planning meeting (section 2.3) has been held and the LA makes the decision to send a Letter before Proceedings (LbP) (section 2.4).

2.2 Social work

Volume 1 of the Children Act Guidance and Regulations is issued under section 7 of the Local Authority Social Services Act 1970. Local Authorities must, in exercising their social services functions, act under this guidance.

The Children Act 1989, the Adoption and Children Act 2002, and the Children Act 2004 combined with Regulations made under those statutes and the Statutory Guidance set out the statutory framework within which social workers should perform functions on behalf of the LA. The Statutory Guidance seeks to provide advice to the LA on relevant matters. In relation to care proceedings the Guidance stipulates the "matters to be considered by the LA before making an application for a care or supervision order"[1]. The LA has many duties and obligations with which it must comply. The most relevant (at this stage) is the general duty to safeguard and promote the welfare of children in need and "so far as is consistent with that duty, to promote the upbringing of such children by their families by providing a range and level of services appropriate to those children's needs" (s 17(1) CA 1989).

The original version of Volume 1 was published in 1991. The revised Guidance gives updated advice to LAs on how they should meet their duties. Some key points from the Guidance are:

- That voluntary arrangements for the provision of services should be fully explored together with consideration of potential alternative carers
- That prior to proceedings, work should be undertaken to explore alternative care solutions for the child, assess the suitability of those arrangements and consider the legal status of those arrangements.

1   Statutory Guidance, paras 3.22–3.33.

2.3   The legal gateway/planning meeting

The purpose of a legal gateway or planning meeting is for the LA to seek legal advice about a particular case. These meetings should be attended by the child's social worker and managers together with the lawyer advising the LA. The social work team will usually set out the facts of the case, their concerns and explain what has been done to work with the child and family. The ultimate question will be "is the threshold criteria met and are court proceedings necessary at this stage?"

In those cases where it is agreed that it will be necessary to initiate Care Proceedings the LA will consider if it is appropriate to write to the parent to inform him or her that an application to court will be made shortly and to explain that he or she should seek legal advice. A template letter can be found at Annex A. There are two important points to note about sending such a letter to the parent:

- This letter is not intended to be a "LbP" and therefore may not act as the trigger letter for Family Help Lower (level 2) publicly funded advice and assistance (section 2.6.3). However, the parent may still be eligible for means-tested advice under Legal Help (level 1) from a solicitor. Parents should be advised to seek further guidance from a solicitor on this point; and
- It will not be appropriate to send this letter in all cases where immediate issue of proceedings is decided. Whether or not to send the letter requires very careful assessment by the LA. For example, there may be concerns that if a parent knows that the LA is going to apply to court for an order allowing it to remove the child from his or her care, the parent and their children may leave the area.

2.4   The Letter before Proceedings (LbP)

If following a legal gateway/planning meeting it is decided that there is time to work with the family to avoid proceedings, and the short term safety and welfare of the child permits, a LbP should be issued. The LbP allows social workers to structure their work with the child and family and to consider alternative options and services which could be provided to the family. Once the LbP inviting a parent to a Pre Proceedings Meeting (PPM) is sent out, the LA has an opportunity to work with the family and to explore all options prior to making an application to court. Some LAs have indicated that the use of

PART V

the LbP has helped to stop the drift in more long-standing cases. We found that many LAs have given lots of time and effort to adjusting the template LbP contained in the Statutory Guidance to their particular areas and we have been informed that generally parents have found the LbP useful as it sets out in one place the LA's concerns.

2.4.1 OWNERSHIP

As the LbP is a new stage in the process introduced by the revised Statutory Guidance (SG) we are aware that LAs have varying experiences of its use. The template LbP which is annexed to the SG envisages that the signature carried on the LbP will be that of the social worker's team manager.

The LA should request that their legal department check the contents of this letter to ensure that it includes all information relevant to the grounds for proceedings.

2.4.2 TIMING

In deciding the timing about when best to send the LbP, the LA will have first considered and sought legal advice about whether it should make an application to the court (section 2.3). If it makes an "in principle" decision that it would be appropriate to apply for an order but also concludes that the risk can be managed without an immediate application, the LA is effectively concluding that it can see a window of opportunity to try to continue to work with the family to maintain their children safely with their parents. The LbP should be sent at this point.

Once the LbP is sent the LA should utilise this opportunity to secure a plan or agreement to protect the child safely at home and work towards reducing the risk of significant harm to the child.

Where a local authority judges that there is not a window of opportunity to work with the family to continue to maintain the child at home, given its assessment of the safeguarding concerns in the case, the LA will need to apply immediately to court even on short notice for a s 31 CA 1989 order. Where this is the case LAs should consider using the immediate issue template letter at Annex A.

2.4.3 CONTENTS

The Letter before Proceedings (LbP) is an important letter and should be carefully drafted. It is the trigger for non-means, non-merits tested publicly funded legal advice and assistance under "Family Help Lower" (also referred to as Level 2 advice) (sections 2.6.2 & 2.6.3). It will be filed with the court, and it needs to be concise, clear and focused. For this reason the template LbP in the Statutory Guidance should be used as the basis for the letter.

It is important that the LbP is understood by the recipient. The template LbP in the Statutory Guidance uses very simple English and is jargon free so that it can be understood by recipients. If applicable it should be translated into the language used by the parent or carer. It is important that there should be no surprises in the LbP. Although the parent should already have had notice or knowledge of the LA's concerns, the purpose of the LbP is to be clear (in one place) about the concerns and what the LA needs to change or improve in order to reduce those concerns. Finally, it acts as formal notification that the parent should seek legal advice, together with a final warning that court proceedings may follow if the situation fails to improve.

The LbP also invites the parent to a Pre Proceedings Meeting (PPM) to discuss matters and hopefully finalise a plan or agreement. There needs to be sufficient time balanced against risk to the child to allow the recipient of the LbP to actually receive the letter, consider it and to seek advice from a lawyer in advance. Social workers will need to consider these factors when proposing the date and time of the PPM in the LbP.

2.4.4 PLANS AND AGREEMENTS

The Letter before Proceedings will state what concerns need to be addressed by the parent and what support will be provided by the LA to help. These issues will be reflected in the existing child in need/child protection or care plan. The plan may be one of the following formats:

(a) a care plan because the child is looked-after by the LA pursuant to a s 20 CA 1989 agreement; a looked after child's plan can only be amended at a Statutory review at which the parents will (hopefully) be present;

(b) a child protection plan if the child is already the subject of child protection measures;

(c) a Child in Need plan if the child is not looked-after but is deemed to be "in need" of services pursuant to s 17 CA 1989.

It follows that the LA should update the plan and send it to the parent as a draft plan (ideally with the LbP) which he or she will be asked to agree at the PPM.

The Pre Proceedings Meeting (PPM) will work best where both the LA and the parent have had a good opportunity to prepare. For the parent this will mean considering the LbP and understanding the plan which he or she is being asked to agree to. The LbP must actively encourage the parent to see a solicitor for advice; ideally he or she will have given instructions and at least sought some brief advice before coming to the PPM with the solicitor. Parents should understand the details of the concerns about the child's developmental needs, including the need for safeguarding and the plan to meet them in order to know what is required of them and how they can fulfil the requirements or discuss the issues if they feel unable to make a meaningful change. Alternatively, they will be in a position to suggest factual corrections or amendments to the proposed plan through the negotiation that will take place during the PPM.

2.4.5 COMMUNICATING MESSAGES

It is important to be sensitive and careful in communicating messages from the LbP. Nothing in the proposed plan should be new or a surprise to the parent. The concerns will have continuously been referred to during meetings, case conferences, documents or correspondence between the LA and the parent.

- The LA should consider hand delivering the LbP (taking into account if it is safe to do so) so that the social worker can be sure that the LbP was actually delivered.

- The social worker may wish to ask the parent to sign a "receipt" to evidence delivery of the LbP. Feedback informs us that parents are more likely to attend the PPM where the LA has met the parent to deliver the LbP to reinforce its meaning and purpose.

- If communication is difficult it will be even more important to record on the LA file the methods attempted by the social worker to deliver the letter.

- Where the LbP is being posted then use recorded delivery.

The expectation is that the parents will seek legal advice and take the LbP to their solicitor.

The Ministry of Justice's Care Proceedings Programme Office will be issuing in 2009 a written pack for parents to encourage better engagement during the pre-proceedings stages. The material's target audience will be parents who are involved with the LA at the pre-proceedings stages. It is hoped that social workers and lawyers for parents will be

PART V

able to refer parents to the material to aid their understanding of the pre-proceedings stages. It is intended that the material will be made more widely available within voluntary sector agencies/organisations whose service-user groups include parents involved with the LA in relation to their children.

2.5   The Pre Proceedings Meeting (PPM)

2.5.1   TIMING

The Letter before Proceedings will have stated a date, time and venue for the PPM. Consideration should be given to re-scheduling when requested by the parents so long as this not does affect the child's safety and welfare.

2.5.2   ORGANISATION AND CO-ORDINATION

Ethos: The aim of the PPM is to reach an agreement on the proposed plan between the family and the LA. Although agreement may not be able to be reached in all cases or about all areas of the plan, a conciliatory approach is encouraged of the participants and their lawyers. It should be noted that the PPM is not intended to be adversarial in nature and therefore it would be unhelpful for any participant to take such an approach. It must be borne in mind that the PPM is a social work led meeting and not a court or tribunal where a judge or arbiter listens to evidence, argument and makes decisions. Neither is the PPM a forum for disputed facts to be determined, such as in a fact finding hearing. If there are disputed facts or issues, the participants can through negotiation agree facts or narrow issues down voluntarily. The PPM will not however, decide on anything which fundamentally remains contested or disputed. No participant should feel pressured to agree to anything that he or she does not want to. Legal advice during the meeting will assist the parent with this. It is vital for the parent to understand that the proposed plan being put forward by the LA warrants careful thought so that the parent is aware of what is likely to happen in the event that an agreement to the plan or amended plan cannot be secured.

Venue of the PPM: We know that in certain familial situations the issue of where the PPM takes place can be "make or break" in terms of whether the parent will attend and engage in the PPM. The decision regarding venue will be taken by the social worker in conjunction with his or her manager and the person who will chair the PPM. The social worker will be key in influencing this decision – having the most detailed knowledge of the circumstances of the family.

Agenda for the PPM: Many LAs have formulated an outline agenda for use at the PPM. They have found that this is helpful as it formalises the meeting, ensures that everything is covered and demonstrates to the participants that the PPM is of a more serious nature than perhaps other routine meetings between a parent and the LA. Annex C is a list of points/agenda items which may be considered for inclusion in any agenda for such meetings. It remains, of course, for each LA to decide how it wishes to conduct the meetings and whether it chooses to create its own agenda using some or all of the suggestions contained in Annex C.

Engaging the parent: There may be times when a parent will either refuse to attend the PPM or disagree with the proposed plan. This can be a difficult process but there may still be an opportunity to narrow some of the issues. A brief case example is given at the bottom of Annex C.

Minutes of the PPM: It is good practice for minutes to be taken of the PPM and then for those to be approved by the LA and circulated to the parent as quickly as possible. The parent will then have the opportunity to suggest corrections or additions which the LA can then consider. We suggest that the LA adopt a similar practice regarding minutes of the PPM as they will have in place for child protection case/review conferences. Minutes are important for any formal meeting and it is preferable that they are provided in relation to all PPMs.

Communicating plans: The plan and any agreement which has been reached during the meeting will be a material document and it is important that it is accurate, and comprehensive.

2.5.3 PARTICIPANTS

Legal: If parents attend with their lawyer the LA lawyer should also attend.

Wider family members: Should a parent wish to bring a person in a supportive role it is in the discretion of the LA to allow this.

One possible tool that the LA might re-consider at this point is the use of a Family Group Conference/Family meeting which might assist identification of wider family support. However, it must be remembered that the child's welfare is paramount and also that the parents should be central to this process and their agreement obtained at the outset and throughout the process.

Other agencies/organisations: The PPM is not a multi-disciplinary meeting or forum and it is not appropriate for other agencies to attend.

Chairing the PPM: Some LAs have stated that they have not found it helpful for the child's social worker or manager to chair the PPM. Some suggestions on people who might be better suited to chair the PPM are:

- A senior manager from the LA; or
- A contracted person who is suitably qualified akin to an Independent Reviewing Officer.

In either case, it is preferable that the person who does chair should be someone with no prior direct involvement with the child and family and where practicable that this person should chair all the PPMs in that LA. LAs who are operating a system of one nominated person as chair for all meetings are finding this is beneficial to the outcome.

If this person has no prior involvement the chances of a productive meeting increase as the parent will hopefully look to the chair as someone who is fresh to the case, less likely to have preconceived ideas about the child or family, perhaps be more impartial than the child's social worker, and is sufficiently distanced to have a wider perspective on the issues. If the chair is able to gain the trust of the participants in the meeting, the meeting will proceed more effectively.

2.5.4 ATTENDEES WITH PARTICULAR NEEDS

Given the nature, sensitivity and seriousness of the issues which fall to be discussed at the PPM it is crucial that the participants understand and are able to follow the discussions.

Some of the issues which come within the remit of the pre-proceedings stages are just as important as some of those that arise within proceedings. Where a person lacks the capacity to follow the litigation within proceedings, it is likely that he or she would also find it difficult to understand everything that is being said and asked of him or her pre-proceedings. Where an informal assessment suggests a parent may struggle to follow the pre-proceedings discussions or otherwise may have a learning disability or mental health problems which affect the parent's ability to follow the issues, then an immediate and urgent referral must be made to the Adults with Learning Disability

Team/Community Learning Disability Team (ALDT/CLDT) or LA equivalent. Lord Justice Wall's comments in a recent case have clarified the Court's expectations in this instance:

> "It is, I think, inevitable that in its pre-proceedings work with a child's family, the local authority will gain information about the capacity of the child's parents. The critical question is what it does with that information, particularly in a case where the social workers form the view that the parent in question may have learning difficulties." (para 175).

> "At this point, in many cases, the local authority will be working with the child's parents in an attempt to keep the family together. In my judgment, the practical answer in these circumstances is likely to be that the parent in question should be referred to the local authority's adult learning disability team (or its equivalent) for help and advice. If that team thinks that further investigations are required, it can undertake them: it should, moreover, have the necessary contacts and resources to commission a report so that as soon as the pre-proceedings letter is written, and proceedings are issued, the legal advisers for the parent can be in a position, with public funding, to address the question of a litigation friend. It is, I think, important that judgments on capacity are not made by the social workers from the child protection team." (para 176).

> "In the pre-proceedings phase local authorities should feel free to do whatever is necessary in social work terms to assist parents who may become protected parties. My view, however, is that this is best achieved by members of the adult learning disabilities team who do not have responsibility for the children concerned." (para 181).

P v. Nottingham City Council and the Official Solicitor [2008] EWCA Civ 462.

On a practical level ALDT/CLDT must be asked to assess the parent and to make recommendations as to capacity to understand the information being discussed and shared at the pre-proceedings meetings. It may be that the parent can properly engage during pre-proceedings if supported by a social worker from the ALDT/CLDT. Alternatively, a voluntary sector organisation may be able to provide an advocate who is experienced in working with those with learning disability. If those options fail then the LA may wish to consider inviting a close family member or friend to support the parent during the PPM. That however is not ideal. Ultimately, if the social worker or the lawyer for the parent believes that the parent is unable to understand and follow the subject matter properly in order to then give considered instructions to the solicitor, it may be the case that the LA will have to issue an application to court so that the Official Solicitor can be invited to act for the parent within the proceedings.

Language barriers must also be considered where a parent's capacity to understand is clearly limited and the LA should make arrangements for a suitable independent interpreter and not rely on a family member or friend.

2.5.5   REVIEWING PLANS

The objective of the PPM is to:

- Agree a plan; and
- Track and monitor progress to implementing the plan.

The plan for the child might be that the child will be accommodated by the local authority. This is a key option for the child even if only as a temporary measure (section 2.8). If it is agreed that the child should be looked-after under s 20 1989 the LA must comply with all statutory duties in relation to looked after children.

Where the child is not a looked-after child because he or she will remain in the care of the family or be subject to a private fostering arrangement between the parent and a third person (such as a family friend or more distant relative) it is likely that the child will remain a child in need for the requisite period. The LA will however be responsible for checking and supervising any private fostering arrangements. If the arrangements are brokered by the LA then the child becomes a looked-after child under a s 23 placement.

2.5.6 CHILDREN'S PARTICIPATION AND THE PARTICIPATION OF THE CHILD

So far as it is reasonably practicable and consistent with the child's welfare, every child should be notified in age appropriate language by the LA that a PPM is to be held, with an explanation that the purpose is to help parents to keep them safe. The child should then be given the chance to make written representations to the PPM. The social worker has an ongoing duty to ascertain the wishes and feelings of the child[1]. The social worker should be in a position to feed those wishes and feelings into the PPM. Acting in the best interests of the child will be the responsibility which pervades everything the social worker does in a particular case. The social worker is therefore in a position to make clear the child's views at the PPM.

Additionally, the LA must decide in each individual case whether to invite the child to the PPM. In considering the matter, there will be a variety of factors which will be taken into account including:

- The child's age;
- The child's level of understanding as to what is involved;
- The child's coping skills; and
- Whether it is appropriate for the child to be present for all or for part of the PPM.

If the child is invited and attends the meeting, the LA should review agenda items, as there may be information that could be difficult for a child to manage within this forum. The social worker should also inform the chair of the PPM that the child will be attending.

If it is felt inappropriate to invite the child to attend the PPM or the child rejects the invitation, the social worker must consider how the child's wishes and feelings could be heard at the PPM.

The LA should ascertain the parent's views towards the child's attendance at the meeting. If the parents oppose the child's attendance at the meeting it must be remembered that the LA does not have parental responsibility at this stage.

If parents do not wish the child to attend, the child should be informed about the LAs complaints procedure. In these circumstances the LA should consider other methods of ensuring that the child's voice is heard, such as:

- the child making written representations for the meeting;
- the social worker having a meeting with the child;
- the child being referred to a local advocacy service able to support the child.

A template letter to the child can be found at Annex B. This should be tailored and adapted where the LA decide to notify a child about the PPM in writing. If the child does not attend the meeting the social worker will explain the plan to the child and take account of their wishes and feelings. As in all issues pre, during and after proceedings there must be a child focused timetable.

1   Amendments were made by s 53 CA 2004 to the following sections of CA 1989: s 17(4A), s 47(5A) and s 20(6) (all of which relate to ascertaining wishes and feelings of the child).

PART V

2.5.7   THE ROLE OF LAWYERS

The role of lawyers in PPMs is to provide impartial legal advice in private to a client if appropriate.

If the lawyer is able to familiarise himself or herself with the relevant papers at the outset this will aid his or her ability to properly advise the client when needed. Lawyers for LAs are likely to first hear about a particular case during the legal gateway/planning meeting. It may however, be some time later when the LA come back to the lawyer for further advice or to ask that the lawyer be present at the PPM. Reading updated social work documents is useful at this point. In relation to lawyers for parents, in some circumstances the lawyer will have been instructed even prior to the LbP being sent (section 2.6.1). Where this is the case, the lawyer may have already seen documents or will have sought disclosure from the LA. Otherwise the first involvement for the lawyer for the parent will be where the parent brings in the LbP to the first attendance with the solicitor. There may be very little time between instruction of lawyers and the PPM taking place.

2.5.8   LAWYER FOR THE PARENT

If the PPM is to have the best possible chance of resolving issues or identifying an alternative care solution it is vital that both the LA and the parent have appropriate advice from their qualified legal advisors.

2.6   Public funding (Legal Help and Legal Aid)

2.6.1   LEGAL HELP – PUBLIC LAW

Some parents may have had a lawyer during other stages of their involvement with the LA. In those cases the lawyer will have assessed the client's eligibility for Legal Help (referred to as "Level 1 Advice"). Unlike Family Help Lower this level of service is means-tested and therefore not all parents will be financially eligible. There is also a merits-test which has a low threshold ("the sufficient benefit test"). This is payable by way of a fixed fee.

2.6.2   IMPORTANCE OF THE LbP

Each local authority will have sent the parent a Letter before Proceedings (LbP) inviting the recipient of the letter to a meeting to discuss concerns and plans for the child and family. From the moment that the letter is received, the person to whom it is addressed automatically becomes eligible for advice and assistance. It is vital that the LA ensure that the parent receives the LbP (section 2.4). Only then will he or she be able to secure non-means, non-merits tested advice and assistance from a solicitor on this basis; the LbP acting as the trigger for eligibility. The LA are encouraged to enclose with the LbP a list of firms/organisations who do such work and in particular those that have staff who are members of the Solicitors Regulation Authority's (formerly the Law Society) Children Panel.

2.6.3   FAMILY HELP LOWER

Advice and assistance is provided by the legal advisor under a scheme called Family Help Lower (also referred to as "Level 2 Advice"). This is a form of Controlled Work and therefore it is for the lawyer to assess whether the person seeking assistance is eligible for this level of service. Any parent or person with Parental Responsibility (PR) who receives a LbP is entitled to this level of service; it is non-means and non-merits tested. The parent is free to instruct any firm or organisation which does public funded family work.

The level of service (Family Help Lower) is remunerated as a standard fee. The LSC has calculated this fee based upon Controlled Legal Representation rates, which are higher than Legal Help and are similarly used in mental health and immigration cases involving priority clients. The LSC has increased the fee so that it currently represents over 7 hours of work.

2.6.4   EXCEPTIONAL CASES

There may be cases where the issues are very complex or great in numbers. For example there may be several persons with PR or the LA has had long-standing involvement and so there are many historic but relevant issues and documents or the assisted person (client) has significant learning difficulties or mental health problems. Those circumstances may make taking instructions, advising the client or negotiation on behalf of the client difficult and complicated. Work done under either Legal Help, Family Help Lower (or both levels of service) when compared to hourly rates may exceed the fixed fee. Where the work was justified and the time spent (based on applicable hourly rates) amounts to three times or over the fixed fee the firm/organisation will be able to claim their costs on a full hourly rates basis rather than being restricted to the fixed fee.

2.6.5   FURTHER INFORMATION

Further information about publicly funded family services can be found on the Legal Service Commission's website: *www.legalservices.gov.uk*[1]. A list of LSC family regional contacts can be found at: *http//www.legalservices.gov.uk/civil/ civil_justice_system_initiatives.asp*.

1   A Q&A document is also helpful reading and is accessible at: *http://www.legalservices.gov.uk/docs/ cls_main/QandAPublicLawCareProceedings050308.pdf*

2.7   Assessments

2.7.1   ADAPTING TO CHANGE

The assessment of children and their families is a key task for social work professionals. What the reforms do is to focus on purposeful, analytical and evidence based assessments and their importance. The child's allocated social worker is responsible for coordinating the work on that child's case with support from team/service managers and possibly other agencies. The assessment process is discussed in the Statutory Guidance[1] and in Working Together[2]. Assessments, both Initial and Core should be undertaken in accordance with these documents and the detailed guidance set out in the Framework for the Assessment of Children in Need and their Families (DH et al (2000)). The LA must not work in isolation and it is imperative that the appropriate sharing of information between the professional network continues to take place to ensure that the child's safety and welfare is kept central to the process.

Where cases rely on specialist assessments to inform the assessment which may not be completed within the target time frame, the core assessment should still be completed and should note any timescales agreed with partners who may be undertaking specialist assessments documented[3]. Planning, intervention and urgent work to safeguard the child's welfare will need to continue not withstanding an incomplete or outstanding core assessment.

PART V

The core assessment is the means by which LAs gather and analyse information about the child and family as it undertakes its s 47 CA 1989 enquires[4]. It is the process by which evidence is gathered which is important to the LA's case when it applies to court[5]; the LA will file the core assessment record with the court as its primary piece of evidence to support its application. As it is a live document it will continue to be updated during the LA's involvement with the child and it may well evolve as circumstances change and new information about the family is obtained. Assessment is a continuing process and not a single event.

1   Statutory Guidance, paras 3.12–3.18.
2   *Working Together*, paras 5.60–5.67.
3   Statutory Guidance, para 3.16.
4   Statutory Guidance, para 3.15.
5   Statutory Guidance, para 3.16.

2.7.2   CHANGE OF CIRCUMSTANCES

It is essential that the extent to which a child is suffering, or is likely to suffer, harm is kept under constant review and that if necessary the matter proceeds immediately to court irrespective of whether or not the LA has completed its preparation or documentation.

Where the LA decides (usually having taken legal advice) that it needs to take steps to protect a child who it considers to be suffering or likely to suffer significant harm, the LA may take immediate protective measures which could include requesting police protection or an application at court for an order. This may be for an emergency protection order (EPO)[1] because the LA believes the child is in imminent danger, or for an interim care or supervision order[2] in order to safeguard the child. It is recognised that in some cases a core assessment will not have been completed or even started at the point that an application is made to the court. Where however, the LA has been involved with a family for some time and/or has already commenced enquiries pursuant to s 47 CA 1989 it should be conducting the enquiries via a core assessment and documenting findings from the assessment process in a core assessment record. Where the core assessment is not available or completed at the time of issue, the LA will inform the court of the reason why it has not been filed and of the expected date of filing. That information should be given at column (d) of Part 1 ("Pre-proceedings checklist") of the Supplementary PLO1 form. See the Practice Direction 10.2 and 10.3 for guidance on compliance with the pre-proceedings checklist.

1   Statutory Guidance, paras 4.25–4.63.
2   Statutory Guidance, paras 3.44–3.47.

2.7.3   SPECIALIST ASSESSMENTS (PRE-PROCEEDINGS)

The key question for the LA to ask itself is "is there an element or aspect of the core assessment process which cannot be completed because specialist expertise is required".

Specialist assessments are those assessments which the LA believe are required when for example there is a particular aspect of the child's or family's circumstances which require a specialist assessment from a professional other than a social worker such as an adult mental health assessment. The specialist assessment will only address that specific aspect and it will feed into the core assessment.

Where a specialist assessment is thought to be required, the decision to commission such an assessment must be made as soon as possible to avoid introducing unnecessary delay into resolution of the proceedings. Consideration should also be given to the joint instruction of experts. The PPM can be used for this purpose.

Any specialist assessments commissioned pre proceedings should be presented by the LA in any proceedings, and for that reason it is suggested that the LA consider the requirements of the Experts PD[1], particularly those that relate to pre-proceedings assessments.

1   *http://www.hmcourts-service.gov.uk/cms/files/Experts-PD-flagB-final-version-14-01-08.pdf*

2.8   Alternative care for children

SECTION 20 CHILDREN ACT 1989 AND THE FUNCTION OF THE INDEPENDENT REVIEWING OFFICER (IRO)

There will be some circumstances where it will be appropriate for children to be looked after by the local authority following agreement with those who have parental responsibility that this arrangement would be the best way to meet the child's needs. Where the authority provides accommodation for a child under a voluntary agreement, then the LA does not share parental responsibility for the child and the parents may remove the child from the arrangement at any time. The parents' wishes regarding the care of their child must be respected, unless they are putting the child at risk of significant harm, and the parents and the child must be consulted before any decisions are taking that affect their child. Providing services to children in this way will not be appropriate where there are continuing concerns about significant harm to the child.

Children accommodated under s 20. like every other looked after child, must have a care plan based on a comprehensive assessment of their needs, setting out how the authority intends to meet those needs in partnership with the child's parents. This will include detail about how the authority intends to establish legally secure care arrangements for the child (e.g. permanency options might include making arrangements to reunite the child with their birth family or planning for the child to be placed in a permanent substitute family or long term foster care). The care plan must be regularly reviewed. Review meetings must be held at minimum statutory intervals – within 28 days of placement, then within 3 months and six monthly thereafter. Reviews must involve the child, their carers and representatives of the local authority responsible for their care, most reviews will also involve other appropriate professionals. The LA must appoint an Independent Reviewing Officer (IRO) to chair reviews.

The IRO's functions are to

(a)   Participate in the review of the case of each looked after child
(b)   Monitor the authority's functions in respect of the review
(c)   Refer a case to Cafcass/CAFCASS CYMRU if the failure to implement the care plan might be considered to breach the child's human rights

Regulations require IROs to fulfil the following responsibilities

(a)   To ensure that the views of children and young people are understood and taken into account (in care planning);
(b)   that the person's responsible for implementing any decision taken in consequence of the review are identified; and
(c)   that any failure to review the case or to take proper steps (to implement review recommendations) is brought to the attention of person's at an appropriate level of seniority within the responsible authority.

The review meeting is one of the key components within the core processes of working with children and families. The purpose of the review meeting is to consider the plan for the welfare of the child and then to monitor the progress of the plan and make decisions to amend the plan as necessary in light of changed knowledge and circumstances. The appropriate legal status for the child's care must be considered at every review meeting and the review should make recommendations to senior managers in children's services

PART V

if the child's legal status no longer seems appropriate to the child's needs. For example, where the circumstances of a child accommodated under s 20 have changed such that it may be necessary for the authority to consider making application for a care order to make legally secure plans to meet the child's future needs.

DCSF are currently re-writing all the Children Act 1989 regulations and guidance and the NMS for fostering and adoption services. In addition DCSF will be issuing Strategic Guidance for consultation in October 2009 on a new framework for family and friends care which will contain a model for assessing relative carers.

2.9 Safeguarding and child protection

2.9.1 THRESHOLD

S 31 (2) Children Act 1989 sets out the threshold criteria. A court has no power to make a care or supervision order in favour of a local authority unless, as a matter of fact, it is satisfied that:

(a)   the child concerned is suffering, or is likely to suffer, significant harm, and

(b)   that the harm or likelihood of harm is attributable to either (i) the care given to a child or likely to be given to him if the order were not made not being what it would be reasonable to expect a parent to give him or (ii) the child is beyond parental control.

Harm includes impairment from seeing or hearing the ill treatment of another.

The court will only act on evidence and will make findings of fact about whether the child is suffering significant harm. If the LA have reasonable cause to suspect that a child is suffering significant harm they will make, or cause to be made, such enquiries as they consider necessary to enable them to decide whether they should take any action to safeguard or promote a child's welfare. The court has to establish that it is more probable that the fact(s) in question occurred than they did not. Mere suspicions are not sufficient. It has to be shown that the child is or is likely to suffer significant harm, with significant being the key word. The harm has to be due to unreasonable parenting i.e. parents not giving the care it would be reasonable for a parent to give that child.

The threshold is established as a matter of fact on the evidence at the point when protective measures are implemented.

Only once the court is satisfied that this threshold has been established does the court have the power to make a care or supervision order.

Finding that threshold is proven does not mean that the court must automatically make a care order. Once threshold is established, the court will then go on to hear argument and evidence to determine what order is in the best interests of the child having regard to the welfare checklist set out in section 1 of the Children Act 1989. This might be a care or supervision order or, for example where a suitable kinship carer has been identified, it might be a residence order. The final outcome may also be an order of "No Order" where the court believes that the interests of the child would be best served by no order being made.

The Public Law Outline usually needs to be considered in the context of whether or not there is a need for an order at that stage and the focus should be upon whether the risk is manageable without an order.

2.9.2 MANAGING SIGNIFICANT HARM

Managing possible harm to the child whilst working with families is a delicate task which demands careful social work judgement in discussion with line managers. The

Statutory Guidance emphasises the importance of taking pre-proceedings steps such as the Pre Proceedings Meeting which follows the Letter before Proceedings (LbP) and investigating alternative care solutions, it also recognises that there will be some cases where an immediate application to court will be required. The LA may consider that a case may fit into this category and that certain pre-proceedings steps e.g. dispatch of the LbP cannot be complied with because it might place the child at increased risk of harm or fail to stop the child suffering harm. A typical example might be where the social worker considers there is a real risk of a parent absconding with the child if he or she were to become aware that that the LA is considering applying to court. This is entirely a decision for the LA, making a judgement based on its professional experience of child protection and its knowledge of the child and the family.

When the court application is prepared there may be some information or documentation which cannot be submitted with the application such as the LbP or kinship assessments which may not yet be completed. It is again essential to emphasise that if the child is suffering or likely to suffer significant harm and s 31 threshold has been established following legal advice, the matter must proceed to court. The supplementary form PLO1 lists the documentation, which should accompany the application form itself. Column (d) on that form allows the Applicant Authority to state any reason why it has not filed any document. In an emergency LAs are not required to provide pre-proceedings documentation on issue but will be required to file it later.

2.10   Working with partner organisations and agencies

2.10.1   SHARING INFORMATION

Sharing information arising from the PPM is subject to the usual guidance and practice which governs the LA sharing of information. The general position is that "the consent of children, young people and their parents or caregivers should be obtained when sharing information, unless to do so would place the child at risk of significant harm. Decisions should also be made with their agreement, whenever possible, unless to do so would place the child at risk of significant harm"[1].

Where consent to sharing information cannot be secured it will generally be safe to share information where this is justified in the public interest. For example, where there is a clear risk of significant harm to a child or adult it will usually be justified to share information so long as sharing that information is in the best interest of the child's safety and welfare. Detailed guidance can be found in "Information sharing: Practitioners' guide"[2].

1   *Working Together* p 101.
2   "Information sharing: Practitioners' guide", HM Government 920020. Accessible at: *http://www.everychildmatters.gov.uk_files/ACB1BA35C20D4C42A1FE6F9133A7C614.pdf*

Chapter 3 – Making a section 31 CA 1989 application

3.1   Preparing an application for court

3.1.1   THE FORMS

Set out below is a list of some of the forms available at the present time with advice on their completion:

- **PLO1 – Application for a care order or supervision order: Supplementary form:** To be filed by the LA with its application. Part 1 is a checklist of the necessary documents. Part 2 is the Record of Case Management Documents filed and to record which case management documents are filed as the case progresses.

- **PLO2 – Local Authority Case Summary**: This standard form should be filed by the LA setting out its position, before the First Appointment (FA), Case Management Conference (CMC) and Issues Resolution Hearing (IRH) and will include details of: proceedings relating to the child, living arrangements, summary of incidents/concerns, key issues in the case and directions for the court to consider.
- **PLO3 – Case Management Order:** This contains standard provisions designed to help the parties, their legal representatives and the court, and has three sections: 1) Preliminary, 2) Order and 3) Recitals. The LA should prepare an initial draft in advance of each advocates' discussion/meeting and share this with all advocates involved in the case, as this document forms the basis of discussions at the advocates' meeting. Following each advocates' discussion/meeting, it is the responsibility of the local authority advocate to file the draft order with the court at least one working day before either the CMC or IRH.
- **PLO4 – Allocation Record and Timetable for the Child**: To be filed by the LA with its application. It sets out an allocation proposal regarding the appropriate tier of court. It will also be used to record the court's allocation decision and reasons. The LA also uses it to provide important dates in the child's life to assist the court set a suitable Timetable for the Child.
- **PLO5 – Standard Directions and allocation on issue of proceedings**
- **PLO6 – Standard Directions and allocation at First Appointment**: Forms PLO 5 and 6 are completed by a judge or legal adviser once an application is lodged at court and at the First Appointment. The court will consider giving standard directions appropriate to each case at Issue and First Appointment stages using these forms.

3.1.2   THE DOCUMENTATION

All pre-proceedings checklist documents should be filed with the application where available.

The documents which the LA are called upon to create specifically for filing with the application are:

1   The Schedule of Proposed Findings;
2   Initial Social Work Statement;
3   Care Plan for each child;
4   The Allocation Record; and
5   Timetable for the Child.

The Public Law Outline is explicit about the required documents that should be filed and issued by the court.

LAs should file and serve under the category of the "Other relevant reports and records" (see item 7 on form PLO1, Part 1) the child's full birth certificate or relevant ID as this is likely to be required by the court at some stage and therefore would be useful to be filed at the outset.

3.2   Parties with particular needs

In s 31 CA 1989 proceedings where the social worker or any party believes that a parent may not have capacity to conduct the litigation the court can be asked to make a direction inviting the Official Solicitor to act on that person's behalf. It must be considered that appropriate social work expertise within the local authority disability team can be used pre or post proceedings to inform a decision on their client's capacity. The Official Solicitor is a "litigation friend of last resort" and will only accept that invitation if there is no one else who is willing and suitable to conduct the litigation on the parent's behalf. Invariably in family proceedings it will be difficult to say with any certainty that another family member is suitable because he or she may have a view which is in conflict with the parent or otherwise because he or she is very close to the subject of the litigation so will not be able to present the parent's views properly. It is important that the Official Solicitor is approached as soon as possible if required to assist:

> "if all the professionals involved with the proceedings and with the parents, including the judges, solicitors, barristers, advocates, and court staff, are aware of the need from the start of the proceedings to take time to consider the parent and whether the proceedings are proving too much for the parent to fully understand. If at any time there is a genuine concern about the parent's capacity to understand the proceedings and to instruct their solicitor, the parent should be able to ask for, and to receive assistance without being made to feel stigmatised by their disability."

http://www.officialsolicitor.gov.uk/docs/parentsnetworkarticle.doc

3.3   Advocates' meetings

3.3.1   ATTENDEES

A Children's Guardian (CG) is a social work professional appointed by a court to independently represent a child subject a care or adoption procedures. They are officers of Cafcass/CAFCASS CYMRU. Children's Guardians and social workers must not attend Advocates' Meetings but they should be notified of the time and date of the meeting and they should be contactable throughout so that counsel may take instructions as necessary.

The Advocates' Meeting should not take place on the morning of the hearing but in accordance with the requirements of the PLO. It is advisable to book the meeting promptly following any previous meeting. When advocates are considering timetabling a meeting, due consideration should be given to utilising telephone or video conferencing where attendance in person is impractical.

It is recognised that it is sometimes unhelpful to a party to have a different advocates representing him or her at various hearings. At times, this can have a bearing on the smooth running of the proceedings. Any client should be free of constraints to choose who he or she wishes to instruct as his or her representative and therefore the Practice Direction (PD) cannot be prescriptive on the issue. Nevertheless the PD does acknowledge the concern and provides a reminder to advocates (for all parties) that the advocate who represents at the final hearing should be the same advocate representing the client at the CMC and IRH. Where this is not possible the PD suggests that an advocate who is familiar with the issues in the case should attend[1].

1   PD, para 16.

3.3.2   PREPARATION

The aim of the Advocates' Meeting is to facilitate agreement between the parties and narrow the issues in dispute[1]. In order to save valuable court time the Advocates' Meeting also acts as a forum where the draft Case Management Order is discussed and prepared[2]. Meetings will only be productive if all the advocates have prepared what is the background to and the issues in the case, what their respective client seeks to achieve from the proceedings, and up to date instructions from their clients in advance but as close to the Advocates' Meeting as possible.

PART V

To aid the smooth running of the Advocates' Meeting the draft Case Management Order should be prepared as an initial draft by the LA in advance of the Advocates' Meeting itself. If this is circulated to the other parties even a day before the Advocates' Meeting is scheduled to take place, it will act as a working document which all can come to the meeting armed with comments on. It will also act as the agenda for the meeting which would be helpful.

If proceedings are to run smoothly and with as little delay as possible, it will be important that all parties comply with the filing of evidence and in time. Where compliance with a particular direction is not looking possible, the relevant party's representative must seek agreement from all the parties for an extension of time or draw the non compliance to the attention of the court.

1   PD, para 3.11.
2   PD, paras 13.1–13.7.

3.3.3 DRAFTING THE CASE MANAGEMENT ORDER

During the Advocates' Meeting there will be a discussion about the Case Management Order and the Applicant's advocate (usually the LA) will take the lead in preparing or drafting that document together with the other advocates. Ideally matters can be agreed and the Case Management Order can be filed as a single agreed case management tool to assist the judge at the hearing. Where that is not possible the advocates will specify on the Case Management Order (or on a separate document if necessary) the provisions which they agree and disagree1. There must be a clear narrative detailing what the LA is asking the court to do, with the CMO fully completed. Detailed standard variable directions are available from the HMCS website to provide assistance on the full and appropriate wording to be used when considering the required directions for the draft case management order.

1   PD, para 13.5.

3.4 Care planning

The plan for the care of the child should be based on findings from the initial and core assessments. It should set out the aims of the plan and intended outcomes for the child, informed by the findings from the assessments ie. The identified developmental needs of the child and the capacity of the parents to respond to the child's needs in the context of their wide family and environmental factors. It will set out clearly what the plan for the child if the Court makes a care order.

In those relatively few cases where the identified permanence option, at the point of the commencement of proceedings, is for the adoption of the child, and where the decision that the child should be placed for adoption has been taken in accordance with the Adoption Agencies Regulations 2005 (SI 2005/389), the local authority must apply for a placement order issued simultaneously with, or as soon as possible after, the issue of the care proceedings.

3.5 Role of the Children's Guardian and the Independent Reviewing Officer

Where possible the Children's Guardian (CG) should meet with the child, where age appropriate, and with other parties in advance of the First Appointment (FA). The Guardian must have read the court papers and provided the required analysis.

The Practice Direction defines Case Analysis & Recommendation (A&R) as being a "written or oral outline of the case from the child's perspective prepared by the Children's Guardian or other officer…"[1]. A list follows that paragraph of the PD setting out the particular points that the Case A&R should address. It is anticipated that the CG may not always be in a position to file a written Case A&R and this is why the definition allows for an oral outline to be provided by the CG at the FA. Where an oral report is given it is suggested that the child's solicitor takes a note of the oral report and then files it as an agreed note. However, in Wales practice guidance requires that the CG provides an initial analysis in written form at the earliest stage and if feasible by the FA.

In subsequent hearings, the CG should be up to speed and in a position to provide written Case A&R that will be filed by the child's solicitor as per the court's directions.

The child's care plan must be maintained by the local authority and kept under review at the statutory intervals and whenever significant changes are proposed to the plan throughout proceedings. It will be good practice for the Children's Guardian and the IRO to maintain a constructive working relationship throughout proceedings. Both the Children's Guardian and the IRO should be properly informed about the local authority's plans for the child so they are able to scrutinise these plans to make sure that they are based on good quality assessment so that the plan demonstrates how the child's needs will be met, with the child being provided with the opportunity to be meaningfully involved in planning for their care. The local authority will need to take the views of the IRO on the quality of planning into account in formulating the final care plan to be put to the Court[2].

Where a child is accommodated by the LA upon issue of proceedings e.g. under s 20 of the CA 1989, it is good practice for the LA to serve a copy of the LA Case Summary (form PLO2) together with a copy of the Initial Social Work Statement, Schedule of Proposed Findings, Care Plan and Allocation Record and timetable for the child on the IRO. Additionally the LA should provide the parties and the Children's Guardian with the name and contact details of the IRO together with the dates of any statutory reviews which have been arranged.

At the conclusion of proceedings IROs may well have an important role in ensuring that the implications of the agreed care plan are understood by all professionals, cares and family members, as there will no longer be any oversight by the Court of the care planning process. In particular, the IRO will have a role in enabling the child to understand their plan and to participate in future care planning.

1   PD, para 25(8).
2   The Children and Young Person Act includes provision which significantly strengthens the IRO function. In future each looked after child must have their own personal named IRO; the IRO will be responsible for monitoring the quality of the local authority's care planning function; and ensure that in every care plan due consideration has been given to the child's wishes and feelings.

3.6   Issues Resolution Hearings and Final Hearings

The purpose of the Issues Resolution Hearing (IRH) is to narrow the issues in so far as to conclude proceedings if possible.

There is some concern amongst professionals that a final hearing is only listed by the court at the IRH. This seems to have given rise to some anxiety about the List Office's ability to secure a date in the court diary for a final hearing soon after the IRH. Where the court is able to do this, some are worried that there will not be an opportunity to give adequate notice to experts and that this may also cause difficulty for the consistency of advocates.

PART V

The Practice Direction itself does not require final hearings to only be listed at the IRH. The PD states that at the Case Management Conference (CMC) the court will set a date for the IRH and "if necessary, specify a period within which the Final Hearing of the application is to take place unless a date has already been set"[1]. Rather than taking a prescriptive approach the PD is flexible about the listing of final hearings leaving it for the court to decide when it lists the final hearing and in accordance with its case management functions. The Timetable for the Child will greatly influence how the court manages its case especially in regard to the listing of hearings.

1   PD, para 14.5(2).

3.7   Collective participation and co-operation

All professionals involved in public law proceedings will work together with the court to assist achievement of the overriding objective. The parties have a duty to do this, which is enshrined in the PD[1].

It is also emphasised[2] that the parties and their representatives should co-operate with the court in case management. Furthermore, the parties and representatives should monitor compliance (generally) with the Court's directions and inform the court or court officer about any failure to comply with a direction of the court or any other delay within the proceedings[3]. A number of courts have a case progression officer (CPO) who should be the first point of contact with regard to Public Law cases.

1   PD, para 2.3.
2   PD, para 5.4.
3   PD, para 5.5.

3.8   The nature of the Public Law Outline

The purpose of the PLO is to reduce delay in these important proceedings concerning the short and long-term placement future of children. It has had to be robust in order to achieve its objectives and to secure outcomes for children and families involved within the target timeframe set by the Timetable for the Child (which is one of the case management tools)[1]. It should be borne in mind that the PD does acknowledge that the court has flexible powers. At any stage in the proceedings the court may exercise those powers[2].

The expectations[3] are that the proceedings should be conducted using the Case Management Tools and Documentation and determined in accordance with the stages in the Timetable for the Child (together with the timeframes indicated for the various stages within the PLO). It is however, acknowledged that the child's welfare in some cases may require a more tailored approach; possibly one that does not fall firmly within the stages and expectations of the PLO. In those cases it will be for the court to determine the appropriate case management directions and timetable[4] but the court must record on the face of any order its reasons for departing from the PLO's general approach. This aids the parties' understanding of why the court is managing its case in the way it is and it also protects the court itself from any potential criticism for departing from the PLO's expectations.

1   PD, paras 3.2–3.4.
2   PD, paras 17.1–17.3.
3   PD, para 4.1.
4   PD, para 4.2.

ANNEX A – IMMEDIATE ISSUE LETTER (TEMPLATE)

SENT BY [RECORDED DELIVERY/BY HAND]

Office Address

Contact

Direct line

My ref

Fax

E-mail

Date

Dear [parent and/or full name(s) of all people with parental responsibility]

Re: [insert name of Local Authority] CONCERNS ABOUT [insert name(s) of child]

I am writing as you were told I would, when you spoke to [name of social worker] on [insert date of last interaction]. As you are aware [name of Local Authority] is extremely worried about your care of [name(s) of child/ren]. We told you about these main concerns in [reference to the Letter before Proceedings/PPM/child protection case conference/any social work meetings].

We have tried to work with you to help you improve your care of [name(s) of child/ren] but unfortunately things have not changed. We are writing to tell you again that we will be going to court to try and make sure [name of child] is safe. You will soon receive a copy of our application to the court and other important documents, which set out the key issues.

We would urge you, if you have not done so already, to get advice from a solicitor. We have sent with this letter a list of local solicitors who specialise in work with children and families. They are not part of Children's Services (Social Services).

Yours sincerely

[name]

Team Manager

Local office/service

cc. Social Worker [name]

Local Authority in house Legal Team

Enc. List of Law Society Children Panel Solicitors

ANNEX B – LETTER NOTIFYING A CHILD ABOUT A PRE-PROCEEDINGS MEETING (TEMPLATE)

Delivered by Hand

Office Address

Contact

Direct line

My ref

Fax

E-mail

Dear [name]

As you know, there have been some concerns about how your parents/carers [delete as appropriate and/or name] have been looking after you.

PART V

Although we have been trying hard to sort out these problems, unfortunately, at the moment, we are still worried that you may be at risk of harm.

Our next step therefore is to hold a "pre-proceedings meeting". At that meeting we will try to agree a plan with your parents/carers about what needs to be done to deal with our worries about you.

If we cannot sort things with your parents/carers at this meeting, it may mean that our only option is to go to court. Hopefully this will not happen but if it does, you will be given plenty of information about what happens and your role in it all.

I am now writing to invite you to attend the pre-proceedings meeting which is being held on [date] at [time] at [venue]. This will give you the chance to tell the meeting about your thoughts, wishes and feelings. If you would rather not attend the meeting, that is fine. You can always put your thoughts in writing if that is easier.

I shall be present at the meeting, with my manager, [name] and our legal advisor. Your parents have of course been invited and may have their lawyer with them.

I shall call you soon to check if you would like to attend all or part of the meeting. It may be that you would like an adult (who should be unconnected to the family) to support you during the meeting.

Alternatively, I may be able to arrange for an advocate to attend the meeting with you. An advocate's job is to make sure that a young person's views are heard, either through speaking for a young person or helping a young person speak for him or herself. Please let me know if you would like any more information on this and you can telephone me on [...........].

If you have any questions or worries please contact me on the above number.

Yours sincerely

Social Worker [name]
Local office/service

ANNEX C – LIST OF POTENTIAL AGENDA ITEMS FOR A PRE-PROCEEDINGS MEETING

- Introductions
- Setting out any special requirements (interpreter, sign language interpreter, presence of an advocate)
- Outline the purpose of the meeting and establish ground rules and specify roles
- Outline duty of the LA to protect children, duty (where possible) to promote the child living with the family, balance of that against need to protect and promote welfare of the child. Explaining why it may be that a court application is necessary but that the LA hopes that the meeting may avoid the need for that
- Explain the concerns of the LA and referencing the LbP
- Initial views and opinions of the parent and specifying or clarifying any areas of agreement and disagreement
- Discuss what can be done to help improve the child's situation on the part of the parent including any assessment outcomes and gaps identified
- Discuss what services have been be provided to the family by the LA and can be provided to help i.e. promoting the idea of collaborative working between family and the LA in the best interests of the child
- Discuss the outcome of the Family Group Conference/Family meeting
- Identification of alternative carers (this will be a revisit to the concept as it will have been discussed previously within the assessment process)

- Lead into a discussion of the proposed plan for the child including the need for any further assessments (the auspices of that plan i.e. Child in Need plan or Child Protection Plan)
- Break away for both parent and the LA to take advice from their respective lawyers
- Initial views from parent as to their thoughts on the plan/agreement
- Reconvene for focused discussion on the plan. Can an agreement be reached on the plan/agreement as it stands in draft or can revisions/amendments be agreed now to avoid proceedings
- If no agreement can be reached such that the LA believes it will have to issue an application with the court consider scope for discussion as to any issues which may be resolved now.

  Brief case example: mother abuses alcohol and her partner is abusive to her. Both elements raise safeguarding concerns. At the PPM the plan is that mother should (1) agree to cease excessive drinking and agree to attend a community drugs and alcohol programme; and (2) agree to her partner moving out of the family home and to seek assistance from domestic abuse support group/project to support mother with skills/knowledge to leave a violent relationship and to avoid entering into similar relationships in the future. Mother agrees to do (1) but not to do (2). Mother provides details for the first time of alternative carers but refuses to agree to information being disclosed to those persons. The LA decides that it will need to seek an interim care order to safeguard the child. Although proceedings have not been avoided, one crucial issue has (potentially) been resolved and the LA will now be able to press ahead with consideration of alternative carers whilst not disclosing information which the mother has not consented to.

PART V

Practice Note
April 2010

Citation: [2010] 2 FLR 1872

Guidelines for Judges Meeting Children who are Subject to Family Proceedings

Produced by the Family Justice Council and approved by the President of the Family Division. April 2010

In these Guidelines –

- All references to 'child or 'children' are intended to include a young person or young people the subject of proceedings under the Children Act 1989.
- 'Family proceedings' includes both public and private law cases.
- 'Judge' includes magistrates.
- Cafcass includes CAFCASS CYMRU.

Purpose

The purpose of these Guidelines is to encourage Judges to enable children to feel more involved and connected with proceedings in which important decisions are made in their lives and to give them an opportunity to satisfy themselves that the Judge has understood their wishes and feelings and to understand the nature of the Judge's task.

Preamble

– In England and Wales in most cases a child's needs, wishes and feelings are brought to the court in written form by a Cafcass officer. Nothing in this guidance document is intended to replace or undermine that responsibility.

– It is Cafcass practice to discuss with a child in a manner appropriate to their developmental understanding whether their participation in the process includes a wish to meet the Judge. If the child does not wish to meet the Judge discussions can centre on other ways of enabling the child to feel a part of the process. If the child wishes to meet the Judge, that wish should be conveyed to the Judge where appropriate.

– The primary purpose of the meeting is to benefit the child. However, it may also benefit the Judge and other family members.

Guidelines

1 The Judge is entitled to expect the lawyer for the child and/or the Cafcass officer:

 (i)   to advise whether the child wishes to meet the Judge;
 (ii)   if so, to explain from the child's perspective, the purpose of the meeting;
 (iii) to advise whether it accords with the welfare interests of the child for such a meeting take place; and
 (iv)   to identify the purpose of the proposed meeting as perceived by the child's professional representative/s.

2 The other parties shall be entitled to make representations as to any proposed meeting with the Judge before the Judge decides whether or not it shall take place.

3 In deciding whether or not a meeting shall take place and, if so, in what circumstances, the child's chronological age is relevant but not determinative. Some children of 7 or even younger have a clear understanding of their circumstances and very clear views which they may wish to express.

4 If the child wishes to meet the Judge but the Judge decides that a meeting would be inappropriate, the Judge should consider providing a brief explanation in writing for the child.

5 If a Judge decides to meet a child, it is a matter for the discretion of the Judge, having considered representations from the parties –

 (i)   the purpose and proposed content of the meeting;
 (ii)   at what stage during the proceedings, or after they have concluded, the meeting should take place;
 (iii) where the meeting will take place;
 (iv)   who will bring the child to the meeting;
 (v)   who will prepare the child for the meeting (this should usually be the Cafcass officer);
 (vi)   who shall attend during the meeting – although a Judge should never see a child alone;
 (vii) by whom a minute of the meeting shall be taken, how that minute is to be approved by the Judge, and how it is to be communicated to the other parties.

It cannot be stressed too often that the child's meeting with the judge is not for the purpose of gathering evidence. That is the responsibility of the Cafcass officer. The purpose is to enable the child to gain some understanding of what is going on, and to be reassured that the judge has understood him/her.

6 If the meeting takes place prior to the conclusion of the proceedings –

 (i)   The Judge should explain to the child at an early stage that a Judge cannot hold secrets. What is said by the child will, other than in exceptional circumstances, be communicated to his/her parents and other parties.

(ii) The Judge should also explain that decisions in the case are the responsibility of the Judge, who will have to weigh a number of factors, and that the outcome is never the responsibility of the child.

(iii) The Judge should discuss with the child how his or her decisions will be communicated to the child.

(iv) The parties or their representatives shall have the opportunity to respond to the content of the meeting, whether by way of oral evidence or submissions.

Sir Nicholas Wall
President of the Family Division and Head of Family Justice

President's Guidance
May 2010

Citations: [2010] 2 FLR 1897

From time to time issues will arise with which magistrates and judges at every level will have to grapple and which will cause difficulties. Against this background I intend from time to time to issue what I propose to call "Guidance" designed to help colleagues make difficult decisions. Self-evidently such Guidance is not designed to tell courts <u>what</u> to decide: the objective is to assist them in the process of going about the decision making progress. Plainly, it will be appropriate not to follow the Guidance in some circumstances: what I hope is that in a sufficiently large number of instances the Guidance will be of use and will help magistrates and judges in the decision making process.

Split Hearings (Bulletin Number 1)

Introduction

1 Over recent months and years it has become apparent to me that split hearings are: (1) taking place when they need not do so; and (2) are taking up a disproportionate amount of the court's time and resources.

2 I have therefore decided to issue the following Guidance in an attempt to assist judges and magistrates who are invited to direct split hearings.

3 Like all Guidance, what follows is not binding on the judiciary at any level. It is an attempt to identify good practice. Moreover, it is designed to apply in both private and public law proceedings.

4 In this Guidance, I propose to use the following terminology –

A "split hearing" is a hearing divided into two parts, during the first of which the court makes findings of fact on issues either identified by the parties or the court, and during the second part of which the court, based on the findings which it has made, decides the case.

A "fact finding hearing" is the first limb of a split hearing.

Guidance

5 Judges and magistrates should always remember that the decision to direct a split hearing or to conduct a fact finding hearing is a *judicial* decision. It is not a decision for

Cafcass or for the parties. It is a decision to be taken by the court. Thus the court should not direct a fact finding hearing simply because the parties agree that one is necessary or because *Cafcass* says that it cannot report without one. Such considerations are, of course, to be taken into account, but they are not conclusive. In any event, the focus of any report is a matter for the court.

6 Judges and magistrates should always remember that a fact finding hearing is a working tool designed to assist them to decide the case. Thus a fact finding hearing should only be ordered if the court takes the view that the case cannot properly be decided without such a hearing.

7 Even when the court comes to the conclusion that a fact finding hearing is necessary, it by no means follows that such a hearing needs to be separate from the substantive hearing. In nearly every case, the court's findings of fact inform its conclusions. In my judgment it will be a rare case in which a separate fact finding hearing is necessary.

8 Thus, for example, the fact that domestic abuse is put forward by the residential parent of a child as a reason for denying the non-residential parent contact with the child is not automatically as reason for a split hearing with a preliminary fact finding hearing. As the President's *Practice Direction: Residence and Contact order: Domestic Violence and Harm* of 14 January 2009 [2009] 2 FLR 1400 makes clear, the court must consider the nature of any allegations, and the extent to which those allegations, if admitted or proved *"would be relevant in deciding whether to make an order about residence or contact and, if so, in what terms"* – see para [3] (emphasis supplied). In para [11] the court is again instructed to *"consider the likely impact of that issue (domestic abuse) on the outcome of the proceedings"* (emphasis supplied) and whether or not the decision of the court is likely to be affected by findings of domestic abuse. Plainly, if the allegations are unlikely to have any impact on the court's order, there is no need for a separate fact finding hearing.

9 In addition, in cases in which the court concludes that a fact-finding hearing is necessary, the *Practice Direction* requires the court to give directions designed to ensure that *"the matters in issue are determined expeditiously and fairly"* (emphasis supplied).

10 None of the foregoing is designed to minimise or trivialise domestic abuse or its effects on children and upon its other victims, or to discourage victims from coming forward with abuse allegations. I repeat that the aim of the Guidance is to enable magistrates and judges fully to address their minds to the need for a separate fact finding hearing.

11 The rationale for split hearings in care proceedings was enunciated by Bracewell J in *Re S (Care Proceedings: Split Hearing)* [1996] 2 FLR 773 when, voicing the views of the Children Act Advisory Committee, she stated that consideration could usefully be given to whether or not there were questions of fact within a case which needed to be determined at an early stage. The advantages of doing so, she said were that early resolution of such facts "would enable the substantive hearing to proceed more speedily" and would enable the court to "focus on the child's welfare with greater clarity". Cases suitable for split hearings, she commented "would be likely to be cases in which there is a clear and stark issue, such as sexual abuse or physical abuse". Once again, the object was "to prevent delay and the ill-focused use of scarce expert resources". These factors should be borne in mind by the court when deciding whether or not to order a split hearing.

12 Magistrates and judges are reminded of the decision of the Court of Appeal in *Re C* [2009] EWCA Civ 994. They might also care to look at paragraphs 27 to 35 of my recent judgment in the case of *W (Children)* [2009] EWCA Civ 644, now also reported at [2009] 3 FCR 1.

13 Courts are also reminded of the provisions of the *Practice Direction: The Revised Private Law Programme* which came into effect from 1 April 2010.

Nicholas Wall

Practice Guidance
June 2010

Citations: [2011] 1 FLR 319

Re S (Wardship) Guidance in Cases of Stranded Spouses

Having given Judgment in respect of the fact-finding hearing and as there have been a number of similar cases, some of which have been reported, and counsel and solicitor for the mother are aware of other current cases where it is alleged that a parent has been left stranded abroad by the other parent, it was suggested that it would be helpful to practitioners and other Judges if I could provide some guidance and assistance with the issues that such cases raise, and which may need to be considered by the Court at an early stage in proceedings.

The suggestions I make are designed inter alia to ensure that the 'stranded spouse's' and indeed the other parties' Article 6 and 8 ECHR rights are upheld; to ensure that there is a fair trial of the factual allegations and to enable the child/children to have contact with both parents pending a final welfare based determination on issues of residence and contact.

1 Given the international element and the experience of the Judges of the Family Division in dealing with cases of this type, child abduction and other international cases, the best vehicle for these types of cases is wardship. Such proceedings should be managed, if possible, and heard by a Judge of the Family Division.

2 At the first hearing (on an ex parte basis) the making of a Tipstaff Passport order should be considered (amended where necessary) to include that the tipstaff shall search for and seize the mother's passport where it is alleged that the father has taken it. Location Orders are also suitable in these cases but Collections orders should only be employed in the most exceptional of cases.

3 There should be a Court request for disclosure from the Home Office in form EX660 at the ex parte stage to ascertain the spouses' immigration status so that s/he can immediately make arrangements to obtain an expedited visa/transfer of an existing valid visa to a new passport. This information may also assist the stranded parent in knowing which immigration application should be made. That parent's solicitor may also wish to consider whether expert immigration advice might assist, and if so seek the appropriate direction at an early date.

4 At an early stage the Court should consider whether there should be an urgent fact-finding hearing to investigate and ascertain the circumstances in which the parent and child/children came to be stranded internationally. Consideration should be given to any disputed allegations made by the stranded parent, as to the gravity of such allegation and if proved, the impact it may have upon the Court's determining the welfare issues and future upbringing of the child/children concerned. If a fact-finding hearing is thought to be appropriate, directions should be given for an early hearing, and thereafter the judgment to be disclosed to CAFCASS, and such other agencies including the Local Authority and local police as may be deemed appropriate.

PART V

5 If the Court considers that the stranded parent's presence in this jurisdiction is necessary to the Court's determination of the child's/children's welfare appropriate recitals in directions orders may assist with that parent's application for a visa to enter/re-enter the jurisdiction. Such directions could include:

    (a)   the mother must attend the hearing at .... on ....

    (b)   the Court indicating that the mother needs to be here to determine issues as to ....;

    (c)   the court expressing the view that the mother's evidence be best given in person in this jurisdiction.6 The Court could consider allowing semi-anonymised publicity in the media to highlight the stranded parent's circumstances, particularly if other efforts to secure that parent's return to participate in the proceedings have been unsuccessful. It would be appropriate to canvass the views of any CAFCASS officer/Guardian ad Litem in relation to publicity as CAFCASS would be concerned about publishing any information that would lead to identification of the child or potentially put the child at risk of harm.

7 The Court should consider whether to invite/order any members of the family to assist with funding flight costs to enable the stranded parent to return to participate in the proceedings. If they refuse such invitation or disobey an order the Court could consider making an order for costs at the conclusion of the fact-finding hearing/welfare hearing.

8 The Court should consider whether to request the relevant British High Commission/Embassy and/or FCO to assist by provision of information or otherwise as may be appropriate.

9 The Court should consider whether the Local Authority in which the child is living should be directed to investigate the child's/children's circumstances and report pursuant to S37 of the Children Act 1989. Such a direction will be dependent on whether the evidence filed indicates that the child/children may be suffering, or at risk of suffering significant harm.

10 In such cases, it would be appropriate to consider whether the child should be joined as a party and a Guardian ad Litem appointed. Given the expertise of the CAFCASS High Court Team the Court should consider referring the case to the manager of the team to consider the papers and the Courts invitation to appoint a Guardian. Until the stranded parent is able to return to the jurisdiction the Guardian's role may be limited and it may not be appropriate to expect the Guardian and lawyer to attend frequent review hearings during the fact-finding process. However, their assistance will be of importance when the Court deals with the issues of interim care and control, and interim contact issues that might arise particularly on the stranded parent's return to the jurisdiction and with safeguarding checks.

11 The Court may, and the stranded parent's solicitor should, consider that assistance may be provided by the various agencies to the stranded spouse upon the return to the jurisdiction, and what monetary or other applications should be made against the other parent.

12 Upon the return of the stranded parent there should be an urgent interlocutory hearing to consider further directions and the interim welfare arrangements for the child/children and the Court's managed reunification of the stranded parent and his/her child, which will probably require the input of the CAFCASS High Court Team Guardian.

Justice Hogg
Family Division

Revised Protocol
2 July 2010

Referrals of Families to Supported Child Contact Centres by Judges and Magistrates

The protocol for referrals of families to Child Contact Centres, designed to assist judges and magistrates who are proposing to make orders for contact involving the use of a Child Contact Centre, was originally introduced in 2000 following widespread consultation and had the endorsement of the President of the Family Division, Dame Elizabeth Butler-Sloss, and subsequently that of the former President, Sir Mark Potter.

Following recent changes in arrangements regarding referrals to supervised contact centres this protocol now governs only referrals to Supported Child Contact Centres. Consultation on practical matters affecting Supported Child Contact centres has shown the need to address some matters in more detail and has led to this revised Protocol, which has the support of Sir Nicholas Wall, President of the Family Division and Patron of The National Association of Child Contact Centres (NACCC) who said:

"Supported Child Contact Centres are integral to the better working of the wider family justice system, offering a most valuable resource to courts dealing with difficult and often acrimonious family disputes over contact. They also provide safe, comfortable and pleasant surroundings for children meeting the non-resident parents.

It is crucial that Supported Child Contact Centres are used appropriately. This means that the safety of the children being referred, the other families using the centre as well as the staff and volunteers must be considered before an order is made. Supported Child Contact Centres offer a voluntary service and must be able to decide whether to accept or refuse a referral.

Furthermore, Courts recognise that Supported Contact Centres are charities and nearly all the staff are volunteers. They can only undertake their work if free of any risk of being drawn into individual cases or disputes. Accordingly, courts and parties will not require or seek their involvement in resolving disputes, writing reports, noting events or attending, in any capacity, any family court hearing.

This admirable protocol will be of the greatest help to judges and magistrates to ensure that Supported Child Contact Centres are used to their best advantage for children needing this valuable and scarce resource."

Sir Nicholas Wall
President of the Family Division

Referrals to supported contact centres

Supported Child Contact Centres do not offer Supervised Contact. The provision offered by Supported Child Contact Centres is described in the Manual of Guidance produced by the National Association of Child Contact Centres as follows:

"Supported contact takes place in a variety of neutral community venues where there are safe facilities to enable children to develop and maintain positive relationships with non-resident parents and other family members. Supported Child Contact Centres are suitable for families when no risk to the child or those around the child, unmanageable by the centre, has been identified during an intake procedure."

It is a requirement that the parents and children attend a pre-contact meeting or equivalent (for example a telephone discussion). Parents are seen or spoken to separately

PART V

so that the Centres can follow their own risk assessment procedure. A number of children's story books about visiting a Child Contact Centre are available via the NACCC website www.naccc.org.uk.

The basic elements of supported contact are as follows:

- Impartiality.
- Staff and volunteers are available for practical assistance (for example calming a tearful child) and keeping a watchful eye. They do not monitor or evaluate individual contact/conversations.
- Several families are usually together in one or a number of rooms.
- Families are encouraged to develop mutual trust and consider more satisfactory family venues.
- Apart from confirmation of attendance dates and times, no report will be made to a referrer, CAFCASS, a party's solicitor or court.
- Supported Child Contact Centre staff and volunteers are not available to be called as witnesses unless it is a criminal matter.
- It is acknowledged that the Supported Child Contact Centre is a temporary arrangement, to be reviewed after an agreed period of time.

THINGS TO CHECK

Before making an Order for Contact at a Supported Child Contact Centre (whether interim or final) please check that the matters set out below have been addressed.

1   If you are considering making an Order for contact at a Supported Child Contact Centre, please ensure that you have addressed whether referral to a Supported as opposed to a Supervised Contact Centre is appropriate where any one or a combination of the following are present
    (a) Domestic Violence
    (b) Drug or substance misuse
    (c) Alcohol misuse
    (d) Mental illness.

2   That the Child Contact Centre Co-ordinator has been contacted and has confirmed that:
    (a) The centre is an accredited member of NACCC.
    (b) The referral appears to be suitable for that particular Centre, subject to a satisfactory pre-visit or equivalent. (In line with its Safeguarding Policy a Supported Child Contact Centre can refuse to accept families if the circumstances appear to them to be inappropriate for the Centre.)
    (c) The intended day and times are available at the particular Centre concerned.
    (d) A vacancy is available or a place on a waiting list has been allocated.

3   That you have directed that a copy of the Order is provided to the Centre by one or other of the parties within a specified time together with any other injunctive or relevant Orders on the court file.

4   That it has been agreed who will have responsibility for completing and returning the Centre's referral form. Solicitors for both parties should agree the contents and it should be forwarded to the Child Contact Centre within 24 hours of the court hearing.

5   That the parties understand that the Child Contact Centre offers supported contact only; and that parties and their solicitors are aware that apart from attendance dates and times, no report will be made to a referrer, CAFCASS, a party's solicitor or court; and that the parties understand that the centre staff and volunteers are not available to be called as witnesses unless it is a criminal matter.

6   That if contact is to be observed at the Child Contact Centre by a CAFCASS officer or other third party that this is a facility offered by that Centre and that the Centre has agreed to this course of action. Many do not permit such attendance.

7   That where there may be a communication problem related to language, arrangements have been made for the provision of an independent interpreter. This is not the responsibility of the Supported Child Contact Centre.

8   That the Order clearly defines whether or not any other family members are to be a part of the Contact visit.

9   That it is agreed who is going to tell the children where and when they will see their non-Resident parent.

10   That it has been agreed who will be responsible for informing the Centre when the place is no longer required.

11   That a date has been set for a review of contact, including the use of the Supported Child Contact Centre and of any other steps parties have been ordered or undertaken to take which are relevant to contact and for further directions if necessary. Only in exceptional circumstances should an order be made allowing for the open-ended use of a Supported Child Contact Centre.

PLEASE ALSO NOTE

1 The order should be worded "Subject to the parties attendance at a pre-contact meeting or equivalent, the availability of a place and the parties abiding by the rules of the centre................"

2 The Centre or Centres at which you direct contact should take place will very much welcome a visit from you and your colleagues. Volunteer staff greatly appreciate the Judiciary taking a positive interest in their local Centres. Such visits will also help you to understand the facilities available locally and thus the type of case that is most suited to contact at the Supported Child Contact Centre.

National Association of Child Contact Centres (NACCC) Minerva House, Spaniel Row, Nottingham, NG1 6EP; Tel: 0845 4500 280; Fax: 0845 4500 420; email: contact@naccc.org.uk; web site: www.naccc.org.uk

Practice Guidance
12 July 2010

Citation: [2010] 2 FLR 962

McKenzie Friends (Civil and Family Courts)

1 This Guidance applies to civil and family proceedings in the Court of Appeal (Civil Division), the High Court of Justice, the County Courts and the Family Proceedings Court in the Magistrates' Courts.[1] It is issued as guidance (**not** as a Practice Direction) by the Master of the Rolls, as Head of Civil Justice, and the President of the Family Division, as Head of Family Justice. It is intended to remind courts and litigants of the principles set out in the authorities and supersedes the guidance contained in *Practice Note (Family Courts: McKenzie Friends) (No 2)* [2008] 1 WLR 2757, which is now withdrawn.[2] It is issued in light of the increase in litigants-in-person (litigants) in all levels of the civil and family courts.

PART V

1   References to the judge or court should be read consistently with the provisions of FPR 2010, rr 2.5–2.7 and FPR PD2A.

2   *R v Leicester City Justices, ex parte Barrow* [1991] 260, *Chauhan v Chauhan* [1997] FCR 206, *R v Bow County Court, ex parte Pelling* [1999] 1 WLR 1807, *Attorney-General v Purvis* [2003] EWHC 3190 (Admin), *Clarkson v Gilbert* [2000] CP Rep 58, *United Building and Plumbing Contractors v Kajla* [2002] EWCA Civ 628, *Re O (Children) (Hearing in Private: Assistance)* [2005] 3 WLR 1191, *Westland Helicopters Ltd v Sheikh Salah Al-Hejailan (No 2)* [2004] 2 Lloyd's Rep 535. *Agassi v Robinson (Inspector of Taxes) (No 2)* [2006] 1 WLR 2126, *Re N (A Child) (McKenzie Friend: Rights of Audience) Practice Note* [2008] 1 WLR 2743.

The Right to Reasonable Assistance

2 Litigants have the right to have reasonable assistance from a layperson, sometimes called a McKenzie Friend (MF). Litigants assisted by MFs remain litigants-in-person. MFs have no independent right to provide assistance. They have no right to act as advocates or to carry out the conduct of litigation.

What McKenzie Friends may do

3 MFs may: i) provide moral support for litigants; ii) take notes; iii) help with case papers; iv) quietly give advice on any aspect of the conduct of the case.

What McKenzie Friends may not do

4 MFs may not: i) act as the litigants' agent in relation to the proceedings; ii) manage litigants' cases outside court, for example by signing court documents; or iii) address the court, make oral submissions or examine witnesses.

Exercising the Right to Reasonable Assistance

5 While litigants ordinarily have a right to receive reasonable assistance from MFs the court retains the power to refuse to permit such assistance. The court may do so where it is satisfied that, in that case, the interests of justice and fairness do not require the litigant to receive such assistance.

6 A litigant who wishes to exercise this right should inform the judge as soon as possible indicating who the MF will be. The proposed MF should produce a short curriculum vitae or other statement setting out relevant experience, confirming that he or she has no interest in the case and understands the MF's role and the duty of confidentiality.

7 If the court considers that there might be grounds for circumscribing the right to receive such assistance, or a party objects to the presence of, or assistance given by a MF, it is not for the litigant to justify the exercise of the right. It is for the court or the objecting party to provide sufficient reasons why the litigant should not receive such assistance.

8 When considering whether to circumscribe the right to assistance or refuse a MF permission to attend the right to a fair trial is engaged. The matter should be considered carefully. The litigant should be given a reasonable opportunity to argue the point. The proposed MF should not be excluded from that hearing and should normally be allowed to help the litigant.

9 Where proceedings are in *closed court*, i.e. the hearing is in chambers, is in private, or the proceedings relate to a child, the litigant is required to justify the MF's presence in court. The presumption in favour of permitting a MF to attend such hearings, and thereby enable litigants to exercise the right to assistance, is a strong one.

10 The court may refuse to allow a litigant to exercise the right to receive assistance at the start of a hearing. The court can also circumscribe the right during the course of a hearing. It may be refused at the start of a hearing or later circumscribed where the court forms the view that a MF may give, has given, or is giving, assistance which impedes the efficient administration of justice. However, the court should also consider whether a firm and unequivocal warning to the litigant and/or MF might suffice in the first instance.

11 A decision by the court not to curtail assistance from a MF should be regarded as final, save on the ground of subsequent misconduct by the MF or on the ground that the MF's continuing presence will impede the efficient administration of justice. In such event the court should give a short judgment setting out the reasons why it has curtailed the right to assistance. Litigants may appeal such decisions. MFs have no standing to do so.

12 The following factors should not be taken to justify the court refusing to permit a litigant receiving such assistance:

(i) The case or application is simple or straightforward, or is, for instance, a directions or case management hearing;

(ii) The litigant appears capable of conducting the case without assistance;

(iii) The litigant is unrepresented through choice;

(iv) The other party is not represented;

(v) The proposed MF belongs to an organisation that promotes a particular cause;

(vi) The proceedings are confidential and the court papers contain sensitive information relating to a family's affairs.

13 A litigant may be denied the assistance of a MF because its provision might undermine or has undermined the efficient administration of justice. Examples of circumstances where this might arise are: i) the assistance is being provided for an improper purpose; ii) the assistance is unreasonable in nature or degree; iii) the MF is subject to a civil proceedings order or a civil restraint order; iv) the MF is using the litigant as a puppet; v) the MF is directly or indirectly conducting the litigation; vi) the court is not satisfied that the MF fully understands the duty of confidentiality.

14 Where a litigant is receiving assistance from a MF in care proceedings, the court should consider the MF's attendance at any advocates' meetings directed by the court, and, with regard to cases commenced after 1.4.08, consider directions in accordance with paragraph 13.2 of the Practice Direction Guide to Case Management in Public Law Proceedings.

15 Litigants are permitted to communicate any information, including filed evidence, relating to the proceedings to MFs for the purpose of obtaining advice or assistance in relation to the proceedings.

16 Legal representatives should ensure that documents are served on litigants in good time to enable them to seek assistance regarding their content from MFs in advance of any hearing or advocates' meeting.

17 The High Court can, under its inherent jurisdiction, impose a civil restraint order on MFs who repeatedly act in ways that undermine the efficient administration of justice.

Rights of audience and rights to conduct litigation

18 MFs do **not** have a right of audience or a right to conduct litigation. It is a criminal offence to exercise rights of audience or to conduct litigation unless properly qualified and authorised to do so by an appropriate regulatory body or, in the case of an otherwise unqualified or unauthorised individual (i.e., a lay individual including a MF), the court grants such rights on a case-by-case basis.[3]

3 Legal Services Act 2007 s 12–19 and Schedule 3.

PART V

19 Courts should be slow to grant any application from a litigant for a right of audience or a right to conduct litigation to any lay person, including a MF. This is because a person exercising such rights must ordinarily be properly trained, be under professional discipline (including an obligation to insure against liability for negligence) and be subject to an overriding duty to the court. These requirements are necessary for the protection of all parties to litigation and are essential to the proper administration of justice.

20 Any application for a right of audience or a right to conduct litigation to be granted to any lay person should therefore be considered very carefully. The court should only be prepared to grant such rights where there is good reason to do so taking into account all the circumstances of the case, which are likely to vary greatly. Such grants should not be extended to lay persons automatically or without due consideration. They should not be granted for mere convenience.

21 Examples of the type of special circumstances which have been held to justify the grant of a right of audience to a lay person, including a MF, are: i) that person is a close relative of the litigant; ii) health problems preclude the litigant from addressing the court, or conducting litigation, and the litigant cannot afford to pay for a qualified legal representative; iii) the litigant is relatively inarticulate and prompting by that person may unnecessarily prolong the proceedings.

22 It is for the litigant to persuade the court that the circumstances of the case are such that it is in the interests of justice for the court to grant a lay person a right of audience or a right to conduct litigation.

23 The grant of a right of audience or a right to conduct litigation to lay persons who hold themselves out as professional advocates or professional MFs or who seek to exercise such rights on a regular basis, whether for reward or not, will however only be granted in exceptional circumstances. To do otherwise would tend to subvert the will of Parliament.

24 If a litigant wants a lay person to be granted a right of audience, an application must be made at the start of the hearing. If a right to conduct litigation is sought such an application must be made at the earliest possible time and must be made, in any event, before the lay person does anything which amounts to the conduct of litigation. It is for litigants to persuade the court, on a case-by-case basis, that the grant of such rights is justified.

25 Rights of audience and the right to conduct litigation are separate rights. The grant of one right to a lay person does not mean that a grant of the other right has been made. If both rights are sought their grant must be applied for individually and justified separately.

26 Having granted either a right of audience or a right to conduct litigation, the court has the power to remove either right. The grant of such rights in one set of proceedings cannot be relied on as a precedent supporting their grant in future proceedings.

Remuneration

27 Litigants can enter into lawful agreements to pay fees to MFs for the provision of reasonable assistance in court or out of court by, for instance, carrying out clerical or mechanical activities, such as photocopying documents, preparing bundles, delivering documents to opposing parties or the court, or the provision of legal advice in connection with court proceedings. Such fees cannot be lawfully recovered from the opposing party.

28 Fees said to be incurred by MFs for carrying out the conduct of litigation, where the court has not granted such a right, cannot lawfully be recovered from either the litigant for whom they carry out such work or the opposing party.

29 Fees said to be incurred by MFs for carrying out the conduct of litigation after the court has granted such a right are in principle recoverable from the litigant for whom the work is carried out. Such fees cannot be lawfully recovered from the opposing party.

30 Fees said to be incurred by MFs for exercising a right of audience following the grant of such a right by the court are in principle recoverable from the litigant on whose behalf the right is exercised. Such fees are also recoverable, in principle, from the opposing party as a recoverable disbursement: CPR 48.6(2) and 48(6)(3)(ii).

Note—For CPR 1998, r 48.6, see now CPR 1998, r 46.5.

Personal Support Unit & Citizen's Advice Bureau

31 Litigants should also be aware of the services provided by local Personal Support Units and Citizens' Advice Bureaux. The PSU at the Royal Courts of Justice in London can be contacted on 020 7947 7701, by email at cbps@bello.co.uk or at the enquiry desk. The CAB at the Royal Courts of Justice in London can be contacted on 020 7947 6564 or at the enquiry desk.

Lord Neuberger of Abbotsbury
Master of the Rolls

Sir Nicholas Wall
President of the Family Division

President's Guidance
18 November 2010

Citations: [2011] 1 FLR 303

Out of Hours Hearings

1 It is perhaps not sufficiently appreciated by the general public that there is always a High Court judge of the Family Division on duty "out of hours" – that is to say every day of the year including all holiday periods either: (1) between 16.15 on day one and 10.30 am on day two of a normal court sitting; or (2) between 16.15 on any given Friday and 10.30 the following Monday. In vacations, when the court is not sitting, a similar service is provided at any time of the day or night.

2 It is of the utmost importance that this service is used for its intended purposes and is not abused. It is designed for urgent cases. In this context "urgent" has a specific meaning. It means cases in which an order of the court is required to regulate the position between the moment the order is made and the next available sitting of the court in conventional court hours – that is, usually, 10.30 on the following morning.

3 Judges of the Family Division have no complaint, for example, if, in the middle of the night, they are asked to sanction life saving medical treatment, or if they have to visit a hospital at such a time in order to decide whether a given individual should undergo urgent and specific treatment.

4 Any application that is "urgent" within the definition set out in paragraph 2 above must be capable of being reduced to a faxed sheet of A4 (or its email equivalent), or a short telephone conversation. Whether or not a case is "urgent" will always be a matter for the judge.

PART V

5 What is unacceptable is an application which can plainly wait until the normal sitting of the court and/or which involves a substantial amount of documentation. A judge cannot and should not be expected either to receive or to assimilate a substantial volume of documentation in an urgent, out of hours application unless both are absolutely essential to a proper understanding of the order which the judge is being asked to make. Equally, judges who are on duty out of hours should not be expected to make arrangements to sit in court unless such a sitting is strictly necessary to enable an order to be made. The profession should also remember that the judge on duty, whilst always available on the telephone, will be at home, and that "home" may not be in London.

6 Lawyers who abuse the system, particularly those who seek to take advantage of an order not made on notice and out of hours with a speedy return date in hours may not only be the subject of orders for wasted costs, but may find themselves reported to their professional bodies for serious professional misconduct. The profession is thus reminded of the definition of "urgent" set out in paragraph 2 of this note.

7 Nothing in this note supersedes any previous Guidance or Practice Note relating to out of hours applications.

Sir Nicholas Wall
President of the Family Division

President's Joint Guidance December 2010

Citations: [2011] 1 FLR 943

Cases Involving Protected Parties in which the Official Solicitor is being invited to Act as Guardian Ad Litem or Litigation Friend

Public and private law children's cases

1 Many practitioners and judges will know of the Official Solicitor's recent difficulties in accepting requests to act as guardian ad litem/litigation friend for protected parties in proceedings relating to children. Although, currently, there are unallocated cases, the backlog has reduced significantly in recent months.

2 The Official Solicitor is subject to severe budgetary constraints – a situation which is unlikely to ameliorate in the medium term.

3 In all cases, the Official Solicitor will need to be satisfied of the following criteria before accepting a case, and parties may need reminding of the need to provide confirmation of these matters immediately on approaching the Official Solicitor's office:

- satisfactory evidence or a finding by the court that the party lacks capacity to conduct the proceedings and is therefore a protected party;
- confirmation that there is security for the costs of legal representation;
- there is no other person who is suitable and willing to act as guardian ad litem/litigation friend.

4 In order to assist the Official Solicitor in the decisions he makes about allocating case workers, in certain cases, judges should consider whether it may be appropriate to indicate with as much particularity as possible the relative urgency of the proceedings and the likely effect upon the child (and family) of delay. The Official Solicitor will very carefully consider giving priority to such cases.

5 It is and remains the judge's duty in children's cases, so far as he is able, to eradicate delay.

Court of Protection welfare cases (including medical cases)

6 The number of welfare cases brought under the provisions of the Mental Capacity Act 2005 is rising exponentially with concomitant resource implications for the Official Solicitor.

7 Judges should be alert to the problems the Official Solicitor may have in attending at each and every preliminary hearing. Consideration should be given, in appropriate cases, to dispensing with the requirement that he should be present at a time when he is unable to contribute meaningfully to the process. In circumstances where his position has been/will be communicated in writing it may be particularly appropriate for the judge to indicate that the Official Solicitor's attendance at the next directions' hearing is unnecessary.

8 The Court of Protection Rules make clear that the judge is under a duty to restrict expert evidence to that which is reasonably required to resolve the proceedings. The explanatory note to r 121 states that the court will consider what 'added value' expert evidence will give to the case. Unnecessary expert assessments must be avoided. It will be rare indeed for the court to sanction the instruction of more than one expert to advise in relation to the same issue.

9 The Practice Direction – *Experts in Family Proceedings Relating to Children*, 1 April 2008 specifies that the expert should assist by "providing objective, unbiased opinion on matters within his expertise, and should not assume the role of advocate". The form and content of the expert's report are prescribed, in detail, by paragraph 9 of the Practice Direction. It is no part of the expert's function to analyse or summarise the evidence. Focused brevity in report writing is to be preferred over discussion.

Note—PD of 1 April 2008: *Experts in Family Proceedings Relating to Children* was superseded by FPR PD25A (now FPR PDs 25A-25F) as of 6 April 2011.

Mrs Justice Pauffley

President's Guidance December 2010

Citations: [2011] Fam Law 189

Case Management Decisions and Appeals Therefrom (Bulletin Number 2)

Introduction

If my first "Guidance" (regarding split-hearings, issued in May 2010 and published in the July issue of *Family Law* at [2010] Fam Law 752) began with a note of a health warning, such a health warning applies even more strongly to what follows. I hope, however, that it will, nonetheless, be of assistance.

As I have gone around the country, a number of judges and magistrates have told me that they feel unsupported by appellate jurisdictions. They thus feel, for example, that they must order an expert's report or an additional assessment by an independent social worker for fear that if they do not they will be appealed and criticised on appeal for not having done so.

I cannot, of course, speak for the Court of Appeal, which will deal with any given appeal, or application for permission to appeal, on its merits. Equally, in my view, no court should ever deal with a case on the basis that one discretionary outcome rather than another may find greater favour with an appellate tribunal. I can, however, offer the following by way of guidance.

It seems to me that there are two particular types of case management decisions in which this dilemma principally arises. The first relates to additional reports or assessments of children and their parents in care proceedings. The second is applications under section 38(6) of the Children Act 1989. I propose to deal with each in turn. Before doing so, however, it will, I think, do no harm to repeat a few obvious messages: –

1 As a general proposition, and as a matter of policy, appellate courts recognise that decisions at first instance are often taken quickly and under pressure both of time and other work. It follows that the instinct of the appellate court is to support the decision made below, unless that decision is – as both Asquith LJ and Lord Fraser emphasise "plainly wrong"- see paragraph 3 below.

2 Judicial decisions under the Act are mostly discretionary. A judicial discretion must, of course, be exercised judicially. That said, the discretion is, usually, a wide one, particularly in relation to case management decisions.

3 It is worth remembering always what Atkin LJ said in *Bellenden* (formerly *Sattersthwaite v Sattersthwaite* [1948] 1 All ER 343T 345 (and cited by Lord Fraser in the Family case of *G v G* [1985] 1 WLR 647 at 651-2, [1985] FLR 894 at 898 namely: –

> "It is, of course, not enough … to establish that this court might, or would, have made a different order. We are here concerned with a judicial discretion, and it is of the essence of such a discretion that on the same evidence two minds may reach different conclusions in relation to the same subject matter without either being wrong: or, to put it another way, an appellate court cannot reverse a court of first instance unless the decision at first instance is plainly wrong."

4 When exercising a first instance discretion, it is essential for the tribunal to take all relevant matters into account and to exclude all irrelevant matters. The pros and cons should then be weighed and a decision reached. The decision itself must be reasoned and clearly articulated. Provided it follows these rules, the decision should be fireproof.

5 Decisions can, of course, be plainly wrong if judges or magistrates make an error or errors of law. However, such errors in this category of case are unusual. The argument is more likely to centre on the manner in which the discretion has been exercised, and this in turn will depend upon the performance of the balancing exercise.

6 So when you are performing such an exercise, even if you are entirely clear about what you intend to do, I suggest that you take a few moments in your room to jot down or underline the relevant points to ensure that you have taken everything relevant into account and discarded the irrelevant. Itemise the considerations for and against the application and explain why you have decided as you have. Don't labour the fact that you are exercising your discretion, but say so, and remind yourself that it has to be – and is being – exercised judicially.

7 Quite what the factual matrix will be in a given case will, self-evidently, depend upon the facts of that case. However, always bear in mind that assessments or additional reports take time. It is thus always important to take delay and the timing of the application in question into account. There will be cases in which an assessment will not cause additional delay: there will be other cases in which the delay caused by an

additional assessment may be a critical factor which tips the balance against it. Either way, ensure that you have dealt with the point in your judgment.

8 Any hearing you conduct must, of course, be ECHR Article 6 and 8 compliant.

9 Any appeal against a case management decision must be mounted swiftly – see the decisions of the Court of Appeal in *Re A (Residence Order)* [2007] EWCA Civ 899 [2007] Fam Law 1061, *Re S (Child Proceedings: Urgent Appeals)* [2007] EWCA Civ 958, [2007] 2 FLR 1044 and *Re P and P (Care Proceedings: Appointment of Experts)* [2009] EWCA Civ 610, [2009] 2 FLR 1370 (also discussed below).

Guidance

APPLICATIONS FOR ADDITIONAL ASSESSMENTS OR FOR EXPERT REPORTS

10 Re-read the experts' practice direction at [2009] 2 FLR 1383. Remember always that it is your case and your decision. An "expert" can only be instructed if you agree, and the function of the expert is "to provide an opinion about a question that is not within the skill and experience of the court" (PD paragraph 1.3). So always ask yourself: do I need this additional report to enable me to make a fair and proper decision? What can this expert add or contribute to the case? If the answer to the first question is "no" and to the second "nothing," you are unlikely to order a report.

11 Process is important in family law, and every hearing you conduct must be ECHR Articles 6 and 8 compliant. This does not, of course, mean that you must accede to every parent's application for a second opinion: each decision is a matter of judgment. What is important is that your conduct of the proceedings is transparent and your conclusion is fair. This will inevitably involve balancing different factors in the manner I have already described before reaching a reasoned conclusion.

12 Always bear in mind the effect which any order you are being asked to make has on the time-table for the child and the case overall.

13 Always remember that issues of fact and credibility (who is believed and who is not) are matters for you, and not for the expert.

14 In public law care proceedings, judges and magistrates cannot make care orders under the Act unless they are satisfied both that the threshold criteria under section 31 of the Act are satisfied and that it is in the best interests of the child for a care order to be made. If the material available to you does not enable you to fulfil your statutory obligations to the child, say so, specifying the gap that needs filling, and – if you make an order for an expert opinion – list that as a principal reason for doing so.

15 Note that by virtue of paragraph 4.3(8) of the Practice Direction the party seeking permission to instruct an expert must explain why the expert evidence proposed cannot be given by social services undertaking a core assessment or by the children's guardian in accordance with their respective statutory duties.

APPLICATIONS UNDER SECTION 38(6) OF THE ACT

16 There are additional factors which should be taken into account when dealing with applications under sections 38(6) and (7).

17 It is, I think, worthwhile remembering that section 38 of the Act deals with interim care orders and interim supervision orders. So the court cannot make an order under section 38 (6) unless such an order is or will be in place. Section 38(6) is thus an

PART V

exception to the general rule that where a care order is made, the local authority is in the driving seat and can effectively dictate how parental responsibility is to be exercised under section 33.

18 The two leading cases are the decisions in the House of Lords in *Re C (A Minor) (Interim Care Order: Residential Assessment)* [1997] AC 489, [1997] 1 FLR 1 (*Re C*) and *Re G (A Minor) (Interim Care Order: Residential Assessment)* [2005] UKHL 68, [2006] 1 AC 576, [2006] 1 FLR 601 (*Re G*). They should be re-read.

19 Two points of law were decided by *Re C*. They are: (1) that sections 38(6) and (7) of the Act are to be broadly construed and "confer jurisdiction on the court to order or prohibit any assessment which involves the participation of the child and is directed to providing the court with the material which, in the view of the court, is required to enable it to reach a proper decision at the final hearing of the application for a full care order" (per Lord Browne-Wilkinson); and (2) that the phrase "the medical or psychiatric examination or other assessment of the child" in section 38(6) is not to be interpreted so as to restrict assessments to the medical or psychiatric.

20 In addition, *Re C* makes it clear that it is impossible to assess a young child divorced from his or her environment and thus the assessment includes the relationship between the parents and the child or children concerned.

21 *Re G*, whilst adopting the broad approach set out in *Re C* decides that an assessment under section 38(6) does not include therapy or treatment, particularly for a parent. Inpatient treatment was thus beyond section 38(6) and the court had no power to order it under the sub-section.

22 Lord Scott, who conducts a helpful review of the authorities, specifically agreed with a statement by Holman J in *Re M (Residential Assessment Directions)* [1998] 2 FLR 371 at 381 which I think it useful to follow. Holman J said: –

"… The court's powers … are limited to a process that can properly be described as 'assessment' rather than 'treatment' although no doubt all treatment is accompanied by a continuing process of assessment. And they are limited to a process which bona fide involves the participation of the child as an integral part of what is being assessed."

23 Section 38(6) should thus be seen as part of the essential evidence gathering process. Plainly, if the proposed assessment is in fact a therapeutic intervention for the benefit of the parents, you will refuse the application. If, on the other hand, the assessment falls within Holman J's statement in *Re M*, that will be a factor which opens the door to the exercise of your discretion.

I propose to illustrate this guidance by reference to examples of decisions of the Court of Appeal in which I gave the leading judgment.

In the first, we supported the decision of the judge not to allow a further assessment.

The second is a reversal of the judge's decision, but is largely concerned with an error in law.

The third is an example of further expert evidence being required to assist the court.

The fourth concerns the question of a second opinion, but was wholly exceptional on its facts.

Example 1

24 *Re S* [2008] EWCA Civ 1078, [2008] Fam Law 1267 (not otherwise reported). In this case, the Court of Appeal (Mummery LJ and myself) refused an application for permission to appeal the decision not to allow a section 38(6) assessment. We did so because: –

(a)   the judge was exercising a discretion, and had done so judicially;

(b)   the judge had conducted a careful balancing exercise: he had identified all the factors in favour of an assessment and had balanced them against the factors which militated against it;

(c)   he cited from and followed the relevant authorities;

(d)   he expressly weighed the question of delay;

(e)   he also considered carefully the likely disruption to the child caused by the assessment;

(f)   the judge was concerned about the information the mother had made available to those proposing the assessment, and took into account what he found to be the mother's lack of frankness in this respect;

(g)   the judge asked himself the question: would the report give him any important additional information? In this case, although it might not be necessary in all cases, there had been a previous, unsuccessful attempt at a residential assessment;

(h)   the judge found that, as an exercise of discretion, the "antis" outweighed the "pros" by a significant margin and he refused the application.

25 Such a decision is plainly incapable of being appealed, even if the appellate court would be inclined to disagree with it.

Example 2

26 *Re L and H (Residential Assessment)* [2007] EWCA Civ 213. [2007] 1 FLR 1370, a decision of Thorpe LJ and myself.

27 What is important to note about this decision is that it is a rare example of where we took the view that the judge had made an error of law. The two factors which predominated in the case were: (1) that the judge had refused the assessment on the grounds that it involved a therapeutic element and was thus outside section 38(6); and (2) he gave no weight to the fact that a previous psychological assessment had strongly recommended a residential parenting assessment both to give the professionals involved in the case important information about the mother's practical parenting, and also to provide important, even vital information about how the parents' relationship bore up under stress.

28 In our view, the judge had been plainly wrong to characterise the recommended assessment as outside section 38(6). The psychologist had suggested a concurrent therapeutic intervention by others, not a therapeutic intervention as part of the residential assessment.

29 The judge had also been wrong in saying, as he did, that the assessment would "of necessity give rise to considerable and in my judgement unacceptable delay…". Had he ordered an assessment it would have been completed well in advance of the fixed date for the final hearing.

30 Our decision in *Re L and H*, therefore, was not primarily concerned with the reversal of the judge's discretionary judgment.

31 It is, of course, the case, that I go on to discuss the principles underlying the 1989 Act and describe fairness and a full and proper investigation as points which go to the "root of family justice". I do not, however, think that I am saying more than the following: -

(1)   that care proceedings are important;

(2)   that the court has a duty to act in conformity with ECHR Articles 6 and 8;

(3)   that before making a care order the court has to be satisfied about the threshold criteria and that a care order is in the best interests of the child concerned; and

PART V

(4)   that given the importance of the issues to the child concerned and his or her family every case needs to be fully and properly investigated.

32 In my view, there is nothing in *Re L and H* to lead anyone to the view that they cannot take difficult decisions about disadvantaged children with impunity. This is, after all, what judges and magistrates are doing day in and day out.

Example 3

33 A rare example of a case management decision being reversed is *Re P and P (Care Proceedings: Appointment of Experts)* [2009] EWCA Civ 610, [2009] 2 FLR 1370 in which Smith LJ and I felt compelled to reverse a decision by Coleridge J who had refused permission to a local authority to instruct an paediatric pathologist to investigate an earlier child death which had manifested symptoms similar to those shown by one of the children who were the subject of the care proceedings before the judge.

Coleridge J refused the application on the ground that it would lead to an extensive investigation and that the resulting delay could not be justified. We took the view that his decision was premature: the judge should have ordered the report and then decided upon the direction of the case. He had deprived himself of information which would have enabled him to make an informed decision. The appeal was supported by the guardian, and the enquiries were plainly material.

Example 4

34 *W v Oldham MBC* [2005] EWCA Civ 1247; [2006] 1 FLR 543. A decision of Thorp LJ, Black J (as she then was) and myself.

35 This case, although required reading, was wholly exceptional on its facts. It is an example of circumstances when it is necessary in the interests of fairness and justice to allow a parent a second opinion. The judge thought she was dealing with a medical consensus. In reality, it turned out to be nothing of the sort. All the doctors in the case at first instance simply deferred to the one doctor who had the specialism lacked by the others. When a second specialist was instructed, he took a different view (which proved to be that adopted by the judge). The parents were initially deprived of the opportunity to challenge the medical evidence.

Summary

36 As we stated in *Re P and P* (see 33 above):

> [17] Case management decisions are not to be challenged on a whim, or because one party simply happens to disagree with them. They are discretionary decisions in which the allocated judge enjoys a very wide discretion to deal with the case within the confines of the overriding objective and taking into account the best interests of the child. There must be a point of substance which requires an urgent challenge and speedy resolution. In the overwhelming majority of cases, no such point will arise. Where it does, however, speed is of the essence. Delay, as the 1989 Act makes clear, is usually contrary to the interests of children, as well as being the enemy of justice in most child cases.

Conclusion

37 Having sat in the county court, and having listened to everything which is said to me, I know how difficult and stressful these cases are. But the message of this guidance, I hope, is that provided it is followed, your work will be respected and supported, even if it may look to you as though the case being heard in the Court of Appeal bears little or no resemblance to the case you heard.

Nicholas Wall

President's Guidance
April 2011

Citations: [2011] Fam Law 647

Listing and Hearing Care Cases (Bulletin Number 3)

Issued by the President of the Family Division following consultation with the Senior Presiding Judge and the Chief Executive of Her Majesty's Courts and Tribunals Service, and with the approval of the Lord Chief Justice.

Background

1 On 1 October 2010 the President's Agreements with CAFCASS and with CAFCASS CYMRU (the Children and Families Court Advisory and support services for England and for Wales) came into effect.

2 The Agreements were circulated with a message from the President entitled "What case management means in practice", which (inter alia) emphasised the importance of the Public Law Outline [2010] 2 FCR 477, (the PLO) a copy of which accompanied the message.

3 3.1 of the PLO sets out the main principles governing court case management. Judicial continuity is one of the main principles and the PLO provides guidance on how to achieve such continuity.

4 It is understood that most legal advisers, magistrates and judges of all levels do not sit exclusively in the family jurisdiction, and there is a need for arrangements to be made to allow care cases to be heard in accordance with these principles.

5 In the December issue of *Family Law* the President emphasised the need to give priority to cases involving children [2010] Fam Law 1251.

6 In subsequent correspondence with the Chief Executive of Her Majesty's Courts (and now Tribunals) Service, Peter Handcock, the President (1) made it clear that both he and the Senior Presiding Judge are committed to ensuring that all cases receive appropriate judicial attention and proceed as expeditiously as possible; (2) re-emphasised the need for care cases to be heard within the timetable for the child; and (3) proposed issuing guidance the purpose of which was –

(1) to re-emphasise the need for avoiding unnecessary delay;
(2) to repeat the need for judicial continuity and efficient case management; and
(3) to encourage local discussions between the relevant parties, notably the case managers, case management judges and listing officers designed to underscore the PLO and ensure that final hearings of care proceedings in particular are timeously allocated.

7 The President is conscious of the fact that the Family Justice System has now received the interim report of the Family Justice Review headed by David Norgrove with its emphases on judicial continuity and on proactive judicial case management.

8 The President and the Senior Presiding Judge encourage discussions between the Family Division Liaison Judges and the Presiding Judges to clarify any support they may give to the Designated Family Judges, Resident Judges and Justices' Clerks so that the Designated Family Judges are able to work with HMCTS and secure listing arrangements to support this Guidance.

The Guidance

9 In the FPC, the case manager is the Justices' Clerk or assistant Justices' Clerk who manages the case. Continuity of case manager in the FPC is as essential as continuity of case management judge in the county court or the High Court.

10 In accordance with the PLO, on issue of a care case in the Family Proceedings Court (FPC) the court must nominate case manager(s) to be responsible for the management of the case throughout its hearings in the FPC. The name of the case manager(s) must be clearly noted on the outside of the court file.

11 Discussions on how to achieve continuity of magistrates and DJ(MC)s in their decisions in the Family Proceedings Courts will be held separately. Guidance on this will be issued when it has been prepared.

12 In accordance with the PLO, as soon as a care case is transferred to the county court from the FPC it must be allocated to one or not more than two case management judges who will be responsible for every case management stage in the proceedings through to the final hearing. One of the two judges may be a district judge with a care ticket. The arrangements for allocation will be determined by the Designated Family Judge for the care centre to which the case is transferred. It may be sensible to write the name(s) of the case management judge(s) on the outside of the court file.

13 In accordance with the PLO, as soon as a case is transferred to the High Court from the county court it must be allocated to a Judge of the High Court as set out in the scheme for the Royal Courts of Justice.

14 The PLO is not written in stone. It is a working tool designed to ensure that care cases are heard swiftly and efficiently. The case managers and case management judges will require and should expect the cooperation of the other parties. Statements and reports must be filed on time. But the key person is the case manager. He or she must be available to hear the case when it requires to be heard and what he or she says must go.

15 The PLO envisages four stages in each case. These are (1) the First Appointment; (2) the Case Management Conference; (3) the Issues Resolution Hearing; and (4) the Final Hearing. In some instances, these stages can be telescoped: in complex cases, it may be necessary for them to be extended. What is important at all levels of court is that (a) no hearing at any stage of the case should conclude without a date for the next hearing having been fixed for the earliest possible date; and (b) that the date fixed for the next hearing is a date on which one of the two case managers or management judges can sit to hear the case

16 It is not good practice for the case to have to wait until the case manager is available to hear it. Discussions must have taken place as at 8 above to ensure that one of the two case managers or case management judges is available to take the case on the date fixed for the next appointment. In other words, the legal advisers and judges must fit their availability around the case, not the other way around. Continuity of representation is also important, and the lawyers will be expected to play their part in ensuring cases are heard without delay.

17 Under the PLO the final hearing is not usually fixed until the Issue Resolutions Hearing (the IRH). This makes sense in the majority of cases, since it is only at the IRH that the time needed for the final hearing can be realistically assessed. It is of vital importance that the final hearing should not be delayed by waiting for the allocated judge to become available. This will mean close liaison between the allocated judge and the listing officer in accordance with the arrangements made at 8 above. It is recognised that the judge will have other important commitments (including trying civil actions) but a balance must be struck and the judge's other commitments can and must as far as possible be fitted round the need swiftly to hear care cases.

Nicholas Wall

Guidance Note
16 June 2011

In-Court Family Mediation Services

Introduction

The pre-application protocol for family Mediation Information and Assessment Meetings (MIAM) came into effect on 6 April 2011. This aims to help the public become aware of mediation and understand how it could support them going through separation and divorce. Those individuals wishing to make an application to court, whether publicly funded or otherwise, will have to first consider, as appropriate, alternative means of resolving their disputes

From April 2011, all potential applicants for a court order in relevant family proceedings are expected, before making their application, to have followed the steps set out in the Protocol. This requires a potential applicant, except in certain specified circumstances, to consider with a mediator whether the dispute may be capable of being resolved through mediation. The court will expect all applicants to have complied with the Protocol before commencing proceedings and (except where exceptional circumstances apply) will expect any respondent to have attended a MIAM, if invited to do so.

If court proceedings are taken, the court will wish to know at the first hearing whether mediation has been considered by the parties. In considering the conduct of any relevant family proceedings, the court will take into account any failure to comply with the Protocol and may refer the parties to a meeting with a mediator before the proceedings continue further.

New guidance for in-court mediation

There will be instances where self-funding individuals will attend court and be unaware of the need to have MIAM. Or they may be referred to a MIAM at the first hearing. It has been agreed by the Justice Minister Jonathan Djanogly MP that mediators ought to be able to charge those that are self-funded for the MIAM or Mediation Sessions within the court precinct.

This is comes into effect immediately and will help to provide improve access to mediation services and prevent delays.

PART V

What you need to do

The majority of courts already know their local family mediation services and will have mediators who come into court on a regular basis. However, with this new guidance, courts may be approached by new mediation services. You should make sure:

- the mediation service is recognised by the Family Mediation Council, who ensure that mediators are trained to an appropriate standard
- consider whether you have suitable accommodation for a consulting room
- advise your judges of the arrangements you have made with the local mediation services

If you have any questions regarding this guidance, please contact:

Atul Sharda (Head of Family ADR Branch) Ministry of Justice;

Tel: 0203 334 4273; e-mail: atul.sharda@justice.gsi.gov.uk

President's Guidance
July 2011

Citations: [2011] Fam Law 1021

Allocation and Continuity of Case Managers in the Family Proceedings Courts (Bulletin Number 4)

Issued by the President of the Family Division following consultation with the Senior Presiding Judge, HMCTS and with the endorsement of the Justices' Clerks Society.

Background

1 In April 2011 the President issued his Guidance Bulletin Number 3, *Listing and Hearing Care Cases*. That Guidance emphasised the principles of judicial continuity and efficient case management and, in the Family Proceedings Court (FPC), the importance of the role of the Justices' Clerk/Assistant Justices' Clerk as case manager. The purpose of this Guidance is to set out the expectations on FPCs in relation to the allocation and continuity of case managers and to provide some practical guidance.

2 Practice Direction 12A "Public Law Proceedings Guide to Case Management: April 2010" (PLO) applies to care and supervision proceedings. It also applies, in so far as practicable to all other Public Law Proceedings.

3 Part 4 Family Procedure Rules 2010 set out the courts' general case management powers.

4 Paragraph 2 of the PLO sets out the main principles underlying case management and the means of the court furthering the overriding objective. These principles are set out in Part 1 of the Family Procedure Rules 2010.

5 A key element of these principles is the requirement under paragraph 3.1(2) of the PLO for judicial continuity. That requires that each case be allocated to one or not more than two ... in the case of magistrates courts ... case managers who will be responsible for every case management stage in the proceedings through to the Final Hearing.

6 Those stages are First Appointment, Case Management Conference, Issues Resolution Hearing together with any other hearing at which case management directions are being given.

Allocation

7 In the Family Proceedings Court the case manager is the Justices' Clerk or the Assistant Justices' Clerk. Continuity of case manager in the FPC is as essential as continuity of case management judge in the County or High Court.

8 In accordance with the PLO, case managers must be nominated to be responsible for the management of the case throughout its hearings in the FPC.

9 The requirement to allocate case managers in the FPC applies equally to cases transferred from the County Court.

10 The name of the case managers must be clearly noted on the front of the court file together with the target date by which the case should be completed. Where possible, the target date for completion should be determined at the First Appointment and certainly no later than the Case Management Conference. In determining the target date, the court should have regard to the timetable for the child.

11 The name of the case managers and the target date by which the case should be completed should appear on the face of any order or case management documents.

12 It is a matter for Justices' Clerks to determine how legal advisers are deployed, however, my attention has been drawn to a number of ways in which FPCs have acted to ensure the appropriate allocation of cases. These include –

(a) determining the number of legal advisers authorised to make case management decisions in family work so as to ensure regular exposure to public law cases, that supports the principles of and ensures robust case management
(b) allocation to case managers who work consistently together as a pair
(c) legal advisers dealing with family work on a set day each week and are allocated as case manager(s) from the First Appointment onwards
(d) cases are allocated to case managers on a rota basis to ensure an even spread
(e) cases are allocated to a legal manager as the primary case manager with a member of the legal team as case manager 2
(f) the legal adviser dealing with the First Appointment is the case manager and any legal adviser who deals with a subsequent hearing is the second case manager.

13 All of these systems have resulted in the early allocation and continuity of case manager and are to be commended.

14 Justices' Clerks should determine the arrangements to be applied locally in order to achieve allocation on issue, and certainly no later than by First Appointment.

15 This Guidance recognises that Justices' Clerks and those who line manage legal advisers will also have arrangements in place to ensure there is oversight of the allocation of cases to case managers, but more importantly, that cases are being managed in accordance with the practice directions and rules at points 2, 3 and 4 of this Guidance.

Continuity

16 Listing arrangements should be in place to support continuity of case managers. Discussions must have taken place to ensure that one of the two case managers is available to take the case for the date fixed for the next appointment. In other words, legal advisers must fit their availability around the case, not the other way round. Continuity of representation is also important and lawyers are expected to play their part in ensuring that continuity, and that cases are heard without delay.

17 In order to help facilitate this, once a date is fixed, court hearing diaries should be noted with the name/initials of the case managers concerned.

PART V

18 Any case management decisions required to be taken between hearings, such as a variance of the timetable or any failure to comply with directions should be dealt with by a case manager. There must therefore be close liaison between the case managers and those members of the administration having case progression responsibilities.

19 It is acknowledged that in some circumstances it may be appropriate for the reallocation of a case manager. It expected that this will be the exception rather than the norm. Circumstances where it might be appropriate are where –

    (a)   it is necessary to achieve ongoing continuity e g absence of a case manager

    (b)   a legal adviser other than one of the case managers has been present at an interim contested hearing

    (c)   the circumstances of a case are such that there is a need for increased attention to case management. In such cases the Justices' Clerk or the nominated legal manager, should determine whether they should be one of the designated case managers. Increased attention to case management may be appropriate where –

        (i)   any case where it appears that the timetable for the child or completion is at risk

        (ii)   where the local authority care plan is unclear (the court may have had difficulty in identifying a timetable for completion)

        (iii)   where there is an application in writing to adjourn the IRH or final hearing

        (iv)   where a final hearing is adjourned

        (v)   in any case where one of the two case managers has concerns about the substantial non-compliance of any party with directions

    (d)   where a District Judge (MC) has assumed one of the case manager roles.

Case management

20 Case managers should ensure that cases are actively case managed and that the principles of the PLO and Family Procedure Rules are applied.

21 The President is aware of and commends various case management tools which have assisted case managers in FPCs. These include –

    (a)   the use of recitals in orders and directions setting out the stage that the case has reached, including reference to whether the threshold is conceded, matters agreed, and the expectations about how the case is to progress

    (b)   electronic case histories, updated by and accessed by the case managers(s)/case progression officers

    (c)   for case management hearings, which includes the IRH, filing of bundles by local authorities as agreed locally, parties position statements (which are not evidential statements nor the Guardians analysis), case summaries and a schedule of issues.

22 Where there has been a failure to comply with case management directions, case managers should consider full use of Part 4 of the Family Procedure Rules 2010, in particular, the ability to make orders of their own motion without requiring attendance at court giving the parties the opportunity to make representations.

23 In some cases, however the current practice of listing a non-compliance hearing, may continue to be appropriate. Where judicial continuity is maintained through a bench of magistrates or by a District Judge (MC), the case managers' responsibilities will include close liaison with them. This will apply when the District Judge (MC) is a nominated case manager or where the District Judge (MC)/Magistrates are required to maintain judicial continuity following the hearing of evidence or determination of a point at an interim hearing.

Transfer

24 Where continuity of case manager cannot otherwise be achieved, consideration should be given to transferring laterally or to the County Court, depending on the issues involved in the case.

Justices' Clerks' Society's Guidance Note July 2011

Citations: [2012] 1 FLR 432, [2011] Fam Law 1024

Note—The Family Procedure Rules 2010 have introduced into the family proceedings courts the following powers: to appoint a litigation friend or the official solicitor for a protected party and to hear such cases; to make a child a party to non-specified proceedings and to appoint a children's guardian in those proceedings; and to stay the whole or part of any proceedings or order. This guidance sets out the considerations that lay magistrates should apply when deciding whether to exercise any of these powers. It also includes a reminder of the need to bear in mind that other factors in the case may indicate that the case should be transferred in accordance with the criteria in ATPO 2008.

Guidance Note to Family Proceedings Courts

Issued by the Justices' Clerks Society, with the approval of the President of the Family Division and the Family Procedure Rules Committee.

Introduction

The Family Procedure Rules 2010 have consolidated the pre-existing rules applicable to family courts and with particular reference to the Family Proceedings Courts have brought about a number of changes of substance. Of these changes guidance has been sought in relation to three matters –

- **making a child party to proceedings under Rules 16.2 of the new rules and the appointment of a guardian under Rule 16.4.**
- **the ability to appoint a litigation friend or the official solicitor in protected party cases and the option to retain jurisdiction in such cases.**
- **when to exercise the power to stay proceedings under Rule 4.1(3)(g) of the new rules**

The following guidance notes are intended to assist Magistrates and Legal Advisers in the Family Proceedings courts when considering these matters in the Family Proceedings Courts. It is accepted that different considerations may apply when a District Judge (Magistrates' Courts) is adjudicating in these courts.

Making a child a party to proceedings under Rule 16.2 of the new rules and the appointment of a guardian under Rule 16.4

Whenever consideration is given to the exercise of this power the first point of reference should be Practice Direction 16A Representation of Children.

Section 1 of Part 4 of the Practice Direction reads as follows:

7.1 Making the child a party to the proceedings is a step that will be taken only in cases which involve an issue of significant difficulty and consequently will occur in only a minority of cases. Before taking the decision to make the child a party, consideration should be given to whether an alternative route might be preferable,

PART V

such as asking an officer of the Service or a Welsh family proceedings officer to carry out further work or by making a referral to social services or, possibly, by obtaining expert evidence.

7.2 The decision to make the child a party will always be exclusively that of the court, made in the light of the facts and circumstances of the particular case. The following are offered, solely by way of guidance, as circumstances which may justify the making of such an order –

- (a) where an officer of the Service or Welsh family proceedings officer has notified the court that in the opinion of that officer the child should be made a party;
- (b) where the child has a standpoint or interest which is inconsistent with or incapable of being represented by any of the adult parties;
- (c) where there is an intractable dispute over residence or contact, including where all contact has ceased, or where there is irrational but implacable hostility to contact or where the child may be suffering harm associated with the contact dispute;
- (d) where the views and wishes of the child cannot be adequately met by a report to the court;
- (e) where an older child is opposing a proposed course of action;
- (f) where there are complex medical or mental health issues to be determined or there are other unusually complex issues that necessitate separate representation of the child;
- (g) where there are international complications outside child abduction, in particular where it may be necessary for there to be discussions with overseas authorities or a foreign court;
- (h) where there are serious allegations of physical, sexual or other abuse in relation to the child or there are allegations of domestic violence not capable of being resolved with the help of an officer of the Service or Welsh family proceedings officer;
- (i) where the proceedings concern more than one child and the welfare of the children is in conflict or one child is in a particularly disadvantaged position;
- (j) where there is a contested issue about scientific testing.

7.3 It must be recognised that separate representation of the child may result in a delay in the resolution of the proceedings. When deciding whether to direct that a child be made a party, the court will take into account the risk of delay or other facts adverse to the welfare of the child. The court's primary consideration will be the best interests of the child.

7.4 When a child is made a party and a children's guardian is to be appointed –

- (a) consideration should first be given to appointing an officer of the Service or Welsh family proceedings officer. Before appointing an officer, the court will cause preliminary enquiries to be made of Cafcass or CAFCASS CYMRU. For the relevant procedure, reference should be made to the practice note issued by Cafcass in June 2006 and any modifications of that practice note.
- (b) If Cafcass or CAFCASS CYMRU is unable to provide a children's guardian without delay, or if for some other reason the appointment of an officer of the Service of Welsh family proceedings officer is not appropriate, rule 16.24 makes further provision for the appointment of a children's guardian.

7.5 The court may, at the same time as deciding whether to join a child as a party, consider whether the proceedings should be transferred to another court taking into account Part 3 of the Allocation and Transfer of Proceedings Order 2008.

The content of the Practice Direction points to the conclusion that it will be unusual if not rare for Magistrates sitting in the Family Proceedings Courts to retain jurisdiction where there is a proposal to make a child party to the proceedings under Rule 16.2. Bearing in mind the sentence highlighted above such an order will only be appropriate in cases where there is an issue of significant difficulty and this in itself should trigger consideration of transfer to a Judge (including a District Judge (Magistrates' Courts)) irrespective of the additional complication of the appointment of a children's guardian. Unless there is a pressing need to do otherwise and depending on the timetabling of the case it may also be preferable to leave the decision whether to make a child a party to the Judge when a case is being transferred.

The ability to appoint a litigation friend or the official solicitor in protected party cases and the option to retain jurisdiction in such cases

For the first time the FPC has jurisdiction to appoint litigation friends and where necessary invite the Official Solicitor to act for a party who lacks capacity – see Part 15 of the Family Procedure Rules 2010 and amendment to the Allocation and Transfer of Proceedings Order 2008, art 15. As a consequence of this change there will be a number of cases where the Family Proceedings Court is the appropriate venue for hearing e.g. where lack of capacity is not in dispute and other factors in the case do not prompt a transfer.

However, there will also be cases where the issues are not suitable for retention by the Family Proceedings Courts and a transfer is appropriate under Article 15(1)(i) of the Allocation Order – examples are:

1   Where the court has to make a finding as to capacity because the party either disputes the expert opinion or refuses to be assessed or where experts disagree about capacity.
2   The party is a litigant in person who is likely to dispute any assessment as to capacity or is unlikely to attend for assessment
3   The consequence of being a protected party will cause complications within the proceedings which may prolong the proceedings, impact on the number of assessments required or cause difficulties in terms of the manner in which proceedings are conducted (e.g. where there is a necessary finding of fact and issues as to how evidence will be given if at all by the protected person).

It is also suggested that a case would be suitable for transfer if the court is asked to dispense with consent to placement for adoption on grounds of lack of capacity but it seems unlikely that the FPC would rely on that ground when there is the alternative and more commonly used ground that the welfare of the child requires the consent to be dispensed with (see Adoption and Children Act 2002, s 52(1)).

Finally, do not forget that whatever the issues relating to capacity, if there are other issues that would merit transfer then the court should give them due consideration before retaining jurisdiction.

When to exercise the power to stay proceedings under Rule 4.1(3)(g) of the new rules

It is anticipated that applications to stay will be made most often in the Family Proceedings Courts when a decision has been made and there is an indication that an appeal is to be lodged against the decision.

PART V

When deciding whether to agree to stay the implementation of the decision the court should balance the factors in the case and in particular consider the risk of harm to children either as a result of postponing implementation of the decision or conversely implementing the decision when an appeal can be heard in a short time. In making such decisions it is important firstly that an appeal notice is lodged or an assurance is given that a notice will be lodged within a period specified by the court, secondly that an indication of the timescale for any appeal is given and thirdly that consideration is given to limiting the length of the stay until the case can be listed before the Judge who will be hearing the appeal. If for example a listing can be arranged before a Judge in two days then a stay for that period may be appropriate and the Judge can then, if necessary, consider whether to extend the stay until the appeal can be heard.

President's Joint Message
29 July 2011

Joint Message from Sir Nicholas Wall, President of the Family Division and Anthony Douglas CBE, the Chief Executive of Cafcass

Note—The Agreement between the President of the Family Division and the Chief Executive of Cafcass dated 1 October 2010 expired on 30 September 2011. It was felt that the good practice generated by it is now so well established that it would continue without the need for any formal agreement. The expired Agreement is set out in *The Family Court Practice 2011*. It was to be read alongside the Public Law Outline (FPR PD12A) and set out guidelines that aimed to improve inter-agency working, reduce the backlog in the allocation of public law guardians, assist guardians to make the best use of their time and minimise the use of Cafcass "duty advisers".

On 1 October 2009 and again on 1 April 2010 Sir Mark Potter P and the Chief Executives of HMCS (as it then was) and Cafcass entered into agreements for what were described as "short-term measures" and which became known as his "Interim Guidance" (PIG1 and PIG2). Each was designed initially to last six months.

On the Expiry of PIG2 on 1 October 2010, we came to an Agreement to assist Cafcass to manage constantly increasing demand for its services pending implementation of the Family Justice Review.

The Agreement was to last until 30 September 2011 and contained provision for the Ministry of Justice, HMC(T)S, and the Department for Education to monitor its effect. The Ministry of Justice and the Department for Education have sent the Local Performance Improvement Groups the results of their 'Review of local arrangements between Cafcass and Designated Family Judges.' This review document concludes that the Agreement, "has been successful in achieving its aims, which is demonstrably clear from the statistical evidence, supported by concurring opinion from frontline practitioners collected through an online survey."

The success of the Agreement has been as a result of two main factors –

1   Cooperative working between the courts, Cafcass and other agencies with strong information-sharing across the system being used to identify ways of improving the system locally.
2   Improved good practice in observing the detailed case management provisions of the Public Law Outline Practice Direction.

While we accept the recommendation in the review document that, "with the continued high levels of s 31 applications being forecast and the consequent continuation of high demand for Cafcass services, there is strong evidence that the successful working practices adopted by local areas to manage current workloads should be maintained", we are confident that the arrangements for good communication and working relations which were already in existence in some areas, but which were formalised by the Designated Family Judges and Cafcass Heads of Service under the PIGs and restated at paragraph 4 of the Agreement will be maintained.

In these circumstances, we have come to the conclusion, after consulting the Designated Family Judges and local Cafcass managers, that it would not be right formally to renew the Agreement and that in any event it is unnecessary to do so.

We are both of the view that the good practice generated by the PIGs and by the Agreement is now well established and should continue without the need for any formal agreement between us. Thus the spirit of the Agreement will continue to operate: local discussions and initiatives will continue and local agreements or protocols will remain in place or new ones be drawn up as the need arises. We are confident that Judges and magistrates hearing cases under the Children Act will continue to manage according to the Public Law Outline and the Private Law Programme and will continue to assist guardians in the manner envisaged in paragraphs 9 to 11 of the Agreement and set out in the final paragraph of the joint message which we sent with the Agreement on 1 October 2010.

Sir Nicholas Wall
President of the Family Division

Anthony Douglas, CBE
Chief Executive, Cafcass

Domestic Abuse Committee of the Family Justice Council Protocol November 2011

PART V

Citations: [2012] 1 FLR 1226, [2012] Fam Law 338

Process Servers: Non-Molestation Orders

Introduction

This is to set out clearly an agreed protocol for the service of non-molestation orders and injunctions made by the courts to protect people from violence and harassment.

Without these orders being correctly served on the person against whom they are made, and proper proof of that service, the courts cannot enforce the orders or punish any breach or the breaking of any term of the order.

All process servers must ensure that the rules of service are followed carefully or the order served will not be enforceable; **orders that are not enforceable do not protect.**

Steps to take

These are the steps which should be taken with orders from both the Family Proceedings Courts (Magistrates' Court) and the County Court to put them in force.

1 Service on the respondent against whom the order was made. When the court makes a non-molestation order and/or any other order/s to which a power of arrest is attached the orders are to be set out in Form FL406 or Form FL404a. That form (and any other order of the court made at the same time) must be served directly and personally on the respondent (or he must have been present when the order was made or be told by telephone or told directly in some other way).The respondent does not need to take the form or orders in his hand but some attempt must be made to hand them to him and tell him of their contents.

2 Statement or proof of service. As soon as the respondent has been handed the forms or orders (or told of the details of the order/s and power of arrest by telephone or otherwise) the process server (or person who has told him of the details of the order) must prepare a statement of service which will be served on the relevant police station. This statement will be used as proof that the respondent knew that there were orders made by the court that he had to obey. This statement should be made under oath or affirmation so that it can be relied on in the civil and the criminal courts.

3 Statement requirement for the Criminal Courts. In addition, so as to comply with legal requirements in the Criminal Courts, all statements must include the following words at the beginning –

> "Criminal Justice Act 1967, s 9; Magistrates' Courts Act 1980, ss 5A(3)(a) & 5B; Magistrates' Courts Rules 1981, Rule 70.
>
> This statement consisting of __ pages each signed by me, is true to the best of my knowledge and belief and I make it knowing that if it is tendered in evidence I shall be liable to prosecution if I have wilfully stated anything which I know to be false or do not believe to be true.
>
> Signed ......"

This should avoid the need for attendance at the criminal courts as statements in this form can be accepted as evidence: without these words they cannot. Therefore, **all statements should start with these words. Proof of service means that orders can be enforced.**

4 Identification. The statement must include details of how the respondent was identified as the person to be served. Identification is important and how it took place must be clearly set out in the sworn statement. Ideally, identification should be from a photograph given to the process server but it can be from a description given to the process server by someone who knows the respondent well. The respondent admitting his identity is not enough on its own, but can be part of the identification. Identification can also be because he was identified by someone else. The statement must contain a description of the respondent, as seen by the process server and a detailed description of service or the attempt at service on him.

5 Service on the Police. Without delay, the Form FL404a or FL406, and a copy of the statement showing that the respondent has been served with a copy of the order and/or informed of its terms, must be delivered to the officer in charge at that time at the police station for the applicant's address or the police station which has been named (or specified) by the court.

Proper service means proper protection.

Working Party of the Family Justice Council Guidelines December 2011

Citations: [2012] Fam Law 79

These guidelines on the issue of children giving evidence in family proceedings, have been produced by the Family Justice Council Working Party on Children Giving Evidence, chaired by the Rt Hon. Lord Justice Thorpe. They have been approved by the Council and I wish to add my endorsement.

The working party was set up following a referral from the Court of Appeal in *Re W* [2010] EWCA Civ 57. The Supreme Court in *Re W* [2010] UKSC 12 subsequently held that there was no longer a presumption or even a starting point against children giving evidence in such cases.

I am sure that these guidelines will be of benefit to members of the judiciary, lawyers and professionals, who have to deal with applications for children to give evidence in family proceedings.

May I take this opportunity to express my gratitude to all the members of the working party, and in particular to Alex Verdan QC, for the final version of these guidelines.

Sir Nicholas Wall
President of the Family Division

Children Giving Evidence in Family Proceedings

1 These Guidelines have been produced by Lord Justice Thorpe's Working Party.

2 This Working Party was set up following a request to the President of the Family Division by the Court of Appeal in *Re W* [2010] EWCA Civ 57, a case which considered the issue of children giving evidence in family proceedings.

3 That same case then went to the Supreme Court and is reported as *Re W* [2010] UKSC 12. It is now the leading authority on this issue. The Supreme Court held that there was no longer a presumption or even a starting point against children giving evidence in such cases.

4 Enquiries by this Working Party suggests that the number of applications for children giving evidence since this decision may be increasing.

5 The aim of these Guidelines is to provide those involved in family proceedings with advice as to what matters should be taken into account in such situations.

6 Hearsay evidence is of course admissible in family proceedings: Children (Admissibility of Hearsay Evidence) Order 1993, SI 1993/621.

7 The issue of whether a child should be further questioned or give evidence in family proceedings should be considered at the earliest possible opportunity by the court and all the parties and not left to the party intending to so apply.

Legal considerations

8 In light of *Re W*, in deciding whether a child should give evidence, the court's principal objective should be achieving a fair trial.

9 With that objective the court should carry out a balancing exercise between the following primary considerations:

PART V

(i)   the possible advantages that the child being called will bring to the determination of truth balanced against;

(ii) the possible damage to the child's welfare from giving evidence i.e. the risk of harm to the child from giving evidence;

having regard to:

(a)   the child's wishes and feelings, in particular their willingness to give evidence, as an unwilling child should rarely if ever be obliged to give evidence;

(b)   the child's particular needs and abilities;

(c)   the issues that need to be determined;

(d)   the nature and gravity of the allegations;

(e)   the source of the allegations;

(f)   whether the case depends on the child's allegations alone;

(g)   corroborative evidence;

(h)   the quality and reliability of the existing evidence;

(i)   the quality and reliability of any ABE interview;

(j)   whether the child has retracted allegations;

(k)   the nature of any challenge a party wishes to make;

(l)   the age of the child; generally the older the child the better;

(m)   the maturity, vulnerability and understanding, capacity and competence of the child; this may be apparent from the ABE or from professionals' discussions with the child;

(n)   the length of time since the events in question;

(o)   the support or lack of support the child has;

(p)   the quality and importance of the child's evidence;

(q)   the right to challenge evidence;

(r)   whether justice can be done without further questioning;

(s)   the risk of further delay;

(t)   the views of the guardian who is expected to have discussed the issue with the child concerned if appropriate and those with parental responsibility;

(u)   specific risks arising from the possibility of the child giving evidence twice in criminal or other and family proceedings taking into account that normally the family proceedings will be heard before the criminal; and

(v)   the serious consequences of the allegations i.e. whether the findings impact upon care and contact decisions.

10 The Court must always take into account the risk of harm which giving evidence may do to children and how to minimise that harm, although that may vary from case to case but the Court does not necessarily need expert evidence in order to assess the risk.

11 Where there are concurrent or linked criminal proceedings there should be close liaison between the respective parties and the allocated judges and ideally linked directions hearings. The Police/CPS should be informed of any proposal that a child give evidence in family proceedings and their views obtained before any such decision is made.

Alternatives to child giving live evidence at a hearing

12 The Court needs to consider seriously the possibility of further questions being put to the child on an occasion distinct from the substantive hearing so as to avoid oral examination. This option would have significant advantages to the child and should be considered at the earliest opportunity and in any event before that substantive hearing. Such further questioning should be carried out as soon as possible after the incident in question.

The Court will need to take into account practical and procedural issues including:

(a)   giving the child the opportunity to refresh his memory;

(b)   the appropriate identity of the questioner;

(c)   matching the skills of the questioner to the communication needs of the child;

(d)   where the questioning should take place;

(e)   the type and nature of the questions;

(f)   advance judicial approval of any questions proposed to be put to the child;

(g)   the need for ground rules to be discussed ahead of time by the judge, lawyers (and intermediary, if applicable) about the examination; and

(h)   how the interview should be recorded.

Practical considerations pre-hearing

13   Once a decision has been made that a child should give evidence at a hearing and be questioned at court, the Court must factor in steps to improve the quality of the child's evidence and minimise the risk of harm to the child.

14   At the earliest opportunity and in any event before the hearing at which the child's evidence is taken, the following matters need to be considered:

(a)   if "live" cross examination is appropriate, the need for and use of a registered intermediary (subject to their availability) or other communication specialist to facilitate the communication of others with the child or relay questions directly, if indicated by the needs of the child;

(b)   the use of other "special measures" in particular live video link and screens;

(c)   the full range of special measures in light of the child's wishes and needs;

(d)   advance judicial approval of any questions proposed to be put to the child;

(e)   the need for ground rules to be discussed ahead of time by the judge, lawyers (and intermediary, if applicable) about the examination;

(f)   information about the child's communication skills, length of concentration span and level of understanding e.g. from an expert or an intermediary or other communication specialist;

(g)   the need for breaks;

(h)   the involvement and identity of a supporter for the child;

(i)   the timetable for children's evidence to minimise time at court and give them a fresh clear start in the morning;

(j)   the child's dates to avoid attending court;

(k)   the length of any ABE recording, the best time for the child and the Court to view it (the best time for the child may not be when the recording is viewed by the court);

(l)   admissions of as much of the child's evidence as possible in advance; including locations, times, and lay-outs;

(m)   save in exceptional circumstances, agreement as to (i) the proper form and limit of questioning and (ii) the identity of the questioner.

15   If a child is to give oral evidence at the hearing the following should occur:

(a)   a familiarisation visit by the child to the court before the hearing with a demonstration of special measures, so that the child can make an informed view about their use;

(b)   the child should be accompanied and have a known neutral supporter, not directly involved in the case, present during their evidence;

(c)   the child should see their ABE interview and/or their existing evidence before giving evidence for the purpose of memory refreshing;

(d)   consideration of the child's secure access to the building and suitability of waiting/eating areas so as to ensure there is no possibility of any confrontation

PART V

with anyone which might cause distress to the child (where facilities are inadequate, use of a remote link from another court or non-court location);

(e)   identification of where the child will be located at court and the need for privacy.

16 Where possible the children's solicitor/Cafcass should be deputed to organise these matters.

17 A child should never be questioned directly by a litigant in person who is an alleged perpetrator.

Practical considerations at hearing

18 If the decision has been made that the child should give oral evidence at the hearing the following should occur:

(a)   advocates should introduce themselves to the child;

(b)   judges and magistrates should ask if the child would like to meet them, to help to establish rapport and reinforce advice;

(c)   children should be encouraged to let the court know if they have a problem or want a break but cannot be relied upon to do so;

(d)   professionals should be vigilant to identify potential miscommunication;

(e)   the child should be told how the live video link works and who can see who;

(f)   a check should be made (before the child is seated in the TV link room) to ensure that the equipment is working, recordings can be played and that camera angles will not permit the witness to see the Respondents;

(g)   the parties should agree which documents the child will be referred to and ensure they are in the room where the child is situated for ease of access.

Examination of children

19 If the Court decides a child should give oral evidence, the Court and all parties should take into account the Good Practice Guidance in managing young witness cases and questioning children (part of the NSPCC/Nuffield Foundation research "Measuring Up" July 2009 by Joyce Plotnikoff and Richard Woolfson) and the subsequent Progress Report which Guidance has been endorsed by the Judicial Studies Board, the Director of Public Prosecutions, the Criminal Bar Association and the Law Society: http://www.nspcc.org.uk/Inform/research/findings/measuring_up_guidance_wdf66581.pdf.

20 Examination of the child should take into account the Court of Appeal judgment in *R v Barker* [2010] EWCA Crim 4, para [42], which called for the advocacy to be adapted "to enable the child to give the best evidence of which he or she is capable" and which questioning should:

(a)   be at the child's pace and consistent with their understanding;

(b)   use simple common words and phrases;

(c)   repeat names and places frequently;

(d)   ask one short question (one idea) at a time;

(e)   let the child know the subject of the question;

(f)   follow a structured approach, signposting the subject;

(g)   avoid negatives;

(h)   avoid repetition;

(i)   avoid suggestion or leading, including "tag" questions;

(j)   avoid a criminal or "Old Bailey" style cross examination;

(k)   avoid "do you remember" questions;

(l)   avoid restricted choice questions;

(m)   be slow and allow enough time to answer;
(n)   check child's understanding;
(o)   test the evidence not trick the witness;
(p)   take into account and check the child's level of understanding;
(q)   not assume the child understands;
(r)   be alert to literal interpretation;
(s)   take care with times, numbers and frequency;
(t)   avoid asking the child to demonstrate intimate touching on his or her own body (if such a question is essential, an alternative method, such as pointing to a body outline, should be agreed beforehand).

Court's overriding duty

21 All advocates have a responsibility to manage the questioning of a child witness fairly. However, the ultimate responsibility for ensuring that the child gives the best possible evidence in order to inform the court's decision rests with the tribunal. It should set out its expectations of the advocates and make it clear to the child witness that they can indicate to the court if they feel they are not saying what they want to say or do not understand what is being said to them.

The court must be scrupulous in the attention it gives to the case management and control of the questioning process and should be prepared to intervene if the questioning is inappropriate or unnecessary.

22 These Guidelines will be reviewed periodically. Those involved in family proceedings are invited to contact the Family Justice Council with any relevant comments.

Working Party of the Family Justice Council

PART V

Working Party of the Family Justice Council Guidance December 2011

Citations: [2012] 1 FLR 980, [2012] Fam Law 202

MARACs and Disclosure into Court Proceedings

1 Multi-agency risk assessment conferences (MARACs) are a recent development in addressing the highest risk cases of domestic abuse. There are regular MARAC meetings held in most local authority areas in England and Wales that collate information about high risk cases of domestic abuse with a view to creating a co-ordinated safety plan for the victim and children (if any). The work is case specific and all relevant agencies (both statutory and voluntary) will attend at or contribute to the conference. MARACs can therefore appear a valuable source of information in court proceedings where domestic abuse may be an issue.

2 Normally, if it is a matter of public record that domestic abuse has occurred (e.g. through Police involvement), the victim is aware that a MARAC is taking place and should be offered support through an Independent Domestic Violence Advisor (IDVA). However, the alleged perpetrator will not have been so informed but may sometimes be aware of it e.g. through the victim.

3 The essential purposes of a MARAC are:

   (a)   To share information about risk;
   (b)   To devise a co-ordinated safety plan for the adult victim;
   (c)   To liaise with appropriate agencies to address safety of children and include as needed safety actions in the plan;
   (d)   To address the behaviour of the alleged perpetrator;
   (e)   To address the safety of staff working with the family.

Clearly it is of importance that generally the details of the MARAC safety plan are kept confidential if it is to be effective for to do otherwise would be to increase risk. Hence the tension between the potential existence of relevant information and the need for confidentiality.

4 MARAC staff members are neither lawyers nor paralegals. Thus they will have no inherent appreciation of what may be 'disclosable material'. Moreover, minute-taking may not be seen as a primary skill and thus minutes may be neither full nor entirely reliable.

5 Accordingly it is thought helpful to offer some guidance both to legal practitioners and to MARACs where consideration is being given to seeking disclosure of documents or other information. Such a request is most likely to come from the one whose conduct is under scrutiny at the MARAC.

6 Three key principles underpin this guidance –

   (a)   A MARAC is not a legal entity and therefore the owner of information shared at a MARAC is the original supplying agency;
   (b)   MARACs should only be required to disclose information by an order of the court;
   (c)   Any request for information must be an informed request setting out the nature of the information sought i.e. there must be no 'fishing expedition'.

7 The question of disclosure should always be considered well in advance of a contested hearing and be dealt with by an order for directions. Notice should ordinarily be given to the Chair of the MARAC; if that is not practicable, the order should allow a MARAC representative to appear and object before compliance is required. Any order should be addressed to the Chair of the MARAC.

8 When any such order for disclosure is made and served on a MARAC, the Chair of the MARAC is under a duty to raise formal objection if any disclosure will interfere significantly with a safety plan or may cause harm to any relevant child. If, however, a decision is made not to make a formal objection –

   (a)   The MARAC Chair should identify the documents currently held (which in practice will usually only be the minutes);
   (b)   If the minutes refer to information supplied and held by another organisation, the court should be invited to make an order directed to that organisation (if necessary) unless the Chair has that organisation's consent to disclose;
   (c)   This approach should apply both to statutory and voluntary organisations;
   (d)   If any document ordered to be disclosed is believed by the Chair to be potentially unreliable (e.g. the minutes), the court should be so informed;
   (e)   If a MARAC is in doubt whether to disclose they may make disclosure to the court setting out their concerns and reservations (e.g. any potential impact on safety) but, in so doing, they accept that the court may nevertheless order disclosure;
   (f)   The MARAC Chair may also draw to the attention of the court, the parties or the relevant organisation (as the case may be) that the significance of any information held depends upon other information held by a participating organisation and identify that organisation.

9 It will sometimes happen that MARACs hold information that they believe would be useful to a court but which they do not want to disclose to all parties. In those circumstances they should disclose the information to the relevant statutory body (local authority, Police, Cafcass) for them to use as appropriate in court proceedings.

10 As with supported contact centres, MARAC workers and IDVAs (as opposed to professional representatives of organisations attending a MARAC) should not ordinarily be called as a witness in court proceedings.

Working Party of the Family Justice Council

ANNEX – WHAT IS A MARAC?

More detailed information is available from the CAADA website[1]. In brief:

A MARAC is a meeting where information is shared on the highest risk domestic abuse cases between representatives of local police, health, child protection, housing practitioners, Independent Domestic Violence Advisors (IDVAs) and other specialists from the statutory and voluntary sectors. After sharing all relevant information they have about a victim, the representatives discuss options for increasing the safety of the victim and turn these into a co-ordinated action plan. The primary focus of the MARAC is to safeguard the adult victim. The MARAC will also make links with other fora to safeguard children and manage the behaviour of the perpetrator.

1   http://www.caada.org.uk/News/FAQs.htm#whatismarac

At the heart of a MARAC is the working assumption that no single agency or individual can see the complete picture of the life of a victim, but all may have insights that are crucial to their safety. The victim does not attend the meeting but is represented by an IDVA who speaks on their behalf and whose work has been found to make a significant positive difference for the non-abusive adult and children[2].

2   Safety in Numbers research 2009: http://www.caada.org.uk/research/research.html

Any frontline agency representative that undertakes a risk assessment with a victim, and thereby determines that their case meets the high risk threshold, can refer a victim's case to a local MARAC. IDVAs, police and health professionals commonly refer high risk victims to MARAC. This represents about 10% of the most serious domestic violence cases, including honour-based violence.

MARACs operate at a local level and are now in almost every area of England and Wales with 250 operational. The meeting takes place either fortnightly or monthly. All agencies contribute what is known about a family, and the agreed actions are noted for the follow-up safety plan. In the 12 months to June 2011, MARACs considered over 47,000 cases, which involved almost 64,000 children.

The membership of MARACs is taken from statutory and voluntary agencies. They have become the broadest multi-agency fora for considering the safety of adults and children affected by domestic abuse. The role of a dedicated caseworker or IDVA and the contribution of agencies that have been traditionally harder to engage – e.g. women's refuges, health professionals, housing – are important reasons for their perceived success.

Note—A summary of the 2009 Safety in Numbers research is available at *www.caada.org.uk/policy/Safety%20In%20Numbers%202pp%20October%202010.pdf.*

PART V

Experts Committee of the Family Justice Council Guidelines December 2011

Citations: [2012] 1 FLR 889, [2012] Fam Law 335

Instruction of Medical Experts from Overseas in Family Cases

Foreword by the President of the Family Division

These guidelines for the instruction of medical experts from overseas in family cases have been produced by the Experts Committee of the Family Justice Council. They have been approved by the Council and I wish to add my endorsement.

We live in an age where people and ideas are much more mobile than hitherto and it is, perhaps, not surprising that the use of experts from overseas has grown in recent years. The welfare of the child demands that the best quality evidence should be available to the court, and specific expertise unavailable in the UK may be found elsewhere. In addition, given the problems that family courts experience with the supply of appropriately qualified experts, any enlargement of the pool of expertise is to be welcomed.

However, there are a number of issues relating to the regulation of overseas experts and to the need to have a clear understanding of their qualifications and credentials, as well as the applicability of their expertise to the UK context, which are addressed in this guidance.

Ultimately, it is for the court to be satisfied that it is appropriate for a suitably qualified overseas expert to be instructed to provide evidence on the issues identified by the court. I believe that this guidance will be of benefit to the judges, barristers, solicitors and experts dealing with family proceedings where expert evidence is required.

The Rt Hon. Sir Nicholas Wall

Background

Cases that come before the family courts involving issues of potential physical or psychological abuse and/or neglect and where there is a requirement for expert evidence are, by their very nature, complex.

The cases and the expert opinion which may be required cover the entire spectrum of child maltreatment and neglect. For the efficient delivery of justice in the Family Division, the courts require timely access to expert evidence and need to have confidence in the quality and validity of the expert advice and opinion given.

Whilst the initial draft discussion document was initially produced by a number of doctors who sit on the Expert Committee of the Family Justice Council, it is acknowledged that the principles discussed apply equally to non-medical experts working in the Family Justice system and indeed all experts in the jurisdiction. We are extremely grateful for the very helpful comments on earlier drafts of this document by the General Medical Council (GMC) and, particularly, by the Safeguarding Committee of the FJC and the Family Subcommittee of the Council of Circuit Judges.

Availability of experts

Many different aspects of medical expert evidence may be called for by the courts but in cases of child maltreatment there are usually relatively small numbers of individuals who are willing to act as experts, a problem which is acknowledged to have been exacerbated by the publicity that a small number of high profile cases has attracted over recent years.

Although in the main these high-profile cases have related to cases before the criminal courts, the implications for expert evidence as a whole have been all too apparent in the courts of the Family Division.

Advantages and disadvantages of the use of experts from overseas

Experts from overseas represent a valuable resource for the family justice system but it is recognised that there are potential advantages and disadvantages to their use.

(I) POTENTIAL ADVANTAGES

(a)   May create a greater pool of expertise available to the courts.

(b)   May make available to the courts expertise from very small super specialist areas where similar expertise is simply not available in the UK (but the number of cases where this is likely to be an issue would be very small).

(c)   Allows the availability of a further opinion from outwith the jurisdiction which may occasionally be of use to the court in arbitrating between opposing views.

(d)   Use of an expert with genuinely new evidence and opinion can help promote discussion and dissemination of information.

(II) POTENTIAL DISADVANTAGES

(a)   UK medical experts are almost invariably involved in active clinical practice appropriate to their expertise and are usually current NHS employees. The clinical practice of overseas experts may be organised in an entirely different way and the reason they may become known to advocates is as a result of "headline" publications. There may be difficulties for the courts in obtaining appropriate information about an overseas expert's practice and/or experience.

(b)   Experts chosen because they are known to hold opinions which are acknowledged to be consistently outwith the range of mainstream or reasonable range of opinion runs the risk of returning to a "hired gun" mentality that the reforms of expert evidence over the past few years have sought to prevent.

(c)   Need for the courts to ensure that overseas experts are familiar with UK court process.

(d)   Cost.

(e)   Possible need to ensure a regulatory system in place which is (i) applicable to all experts and (ii) has ability to impose sanctions on overseas experts who fail in their duties to UK courts.

Recommendations regarding the instruction of experts from overseas

We believe that there are sufficient safeguards currently available regarding the instruction of experts provided those safeguards are rigorously and consistently applied by the courts.

It is critical that all experts are properly instructed in accordance with the 2008 Practice Direction "Experts in Family Proceedings Relating to Children" and any subsequent relevant Practice Direction issued by the President. It is for the court and not the parties to determine whether a particular expert is instructed and, if so, on what terms. Strict compliance with the terms of the Practice Direction by both advocates and Judges should obviate the potential disadvantages of the use of overseas experts addressed above. The

PART V

court will no doubt wish to consider whether the instruction of an expert from overseas is justified according to the welfare needs of the child or children concerned and/or the Article 6 rights of any of the parties.

An application to instruct an expert from overseas should set out in writing:

(a)   Why a UK-based expert is not to be used;

(b)   What efforts have been made to identify a suitable UK expert;

(c)   The financial implications of the instruction of the overseas expert and

(d)   What consideration has been given as to the practical arrangements required to allow the foreign expert to contribute fully to experts meetings and for giving evidence to the court?

Prior to the instruction of an expert from outside the jurisdiction that expert should provide information that fulfils the recommendations outlined in Baroness Kennedy's report into *Sudden Unexpected Death in Infancy*[1]. This details the characteristics of the expert which are of equal importance to all experts instructed by the courts in England and Wales and is a position recently endorsed in a decision of the Court of Appeal (Criminal Division)[2].

1   *Sudden Unexpected Death in Infancy: The Report of a Working Group by the Royal College of Pathologists and the Royal College of Paediatrics and Child Health* (2004). Royal College of Pathologists and the Royal College of Paediatrics and Child Health.

2   *Henderson v R* [2010] EWCA Crim 1269.

Therefore, before an expert is instructed, the trial judge should in all cases establish:

- What is the expert's area of practice in terms of the relevance to the issues upon which the court requires guidance? Does the expert have something genuinely exceptional to offer in terms of his/her expertise?

This should be detailed in the curriculum vitae.

- Whether the expert is still in active clinical practice?

This has been modified by the CMO's report (Bearing Good Witness) to accept clinicians who are recently retired, within two years of active NHS equivalent practice.

- To what extent is the prospective witness an expert in the subject in which he or she will be required to give an opinion in written or oral evidence?

This should be apparent from the CV.

- When did he/she last see a case relevant to the instant case in their own clinical practice?

This is important and should differentiate those experts who offer an opinion in a clinical area in which they do not practise.

- Whether the prospective witness is in good standing with their Medical Royal College or overseas equivalent? Is he/she up-to-date with Continuing Professional Development? Is their current practice regulated by a Statutory Body? If so what is that body?

This should be apparent from the CV which should list membership of the appropriate professional organisation and make comment upon maintaining CPD.

- Has he/she received training in the role of the Expert Witness within the last five years? What experience does the expert have in providing reports for and giving evidence to the Courts in this and other jurisdictions over a similar period of time?

Expert Witness training is discussed in Baroness Kennedy's report, but is aspirational in the CMO's report.

- To what extent is his/her view widely held in terms of accepted mainstream views and the spectrum of opinion overall?

This information may be more readily available for UK based experts but should be sought as assiduously for experts from overseas.

- That the expert has confirmed his/her familiarity with the Practice Direction, is willing to comply with all its requirements and acknowledges the potential consequences cf failure to so comply. These consequences would include:
  - that any judgment arising from the case is likely to be made available to the GMC (or any other equivalent regulatory body) should a complaint be made about the experts conduct within the proceedings and
  - that judgments in which criticisms are made of experts who are judged to be partial are likely to be made in the public domain.
- The Judge should also direct the means by which feedback regarding the outcome of the case should be provided to all of the experts instructed.

This should in most cases be by means of provision of a copy of the Judgment or those aspects of it of direct relevance to the Court's assessment of the relevant expert's evidence.

Conclusions

We believe that the above principles regarding the instruction of all experts, whether UK-based or from overseas, should be considered a Guide to Best Practice and that their universal and consistent application will go as far as is reasonably possible to ensure that appropriate expert evidence is available to the courts of the Family Division and that, when required, such evidence is given by individuals with the appropriate expertise and experience.

Experts Committee of the Family Justice Council

PART V

Practice Direction
24 March 2012

Citation of Authorities

Preamble

1 This Practice Direction is issued in order to clarify the practice and procedure governing the citation of authorities and applies throughout the Senior Courts of England and Wales, including the Crown Court, in county courts and in magistrates' courts.

Repeal

2 Practice Direction (Court of Appeal: Citation of Authority) [1995] 1 WLR 1096 of 22 June 1995, Practice Statement (Court of Appeal: Authorities) [1996] 1 WLR 854 of 15 May 1996, paragraph 8 of Practice Statement (Supreme Court: Judgments) [1998] 1 WLR 825 of 22 April 1998, paragraph 3 of Practice Direction (Judgments: Form and Citation) [2001] 1 WLR 194 of 11 January 2001, and, in so far as they remain in force, paragraphs 10.1 and 10.2 of Practice Direction ((Court of Appeal (Civil Division)) [1999] 1 WLR 1027 of 19 April 1999 are hereby revoked.

Variation

3 Practice Direction (Criminal Proceedings: Consolidation) [2002] 1 WLR 2870 of 8 July 2002 (as amended) is varied so that all references to paragraph 10.1 of Practice Direction (Court of Appeal (Civil Division)) [1999] 1 WLR 1027; [1999] 2 All ER 490 are to read as references to paragraphs 5–13 of this Practice Direction.

4 Practice Direction 52 supplementing CPR Pt 52 is varied so that paragraph 15.11(2) reads as follows:

"(2) The bundle of authorities should comply with the requirements of Practice Direction: Citation of Authorities (2012) and in general –

(a)   have the relevant passages of the authorities marked;
(b)   not include authorities for propositions not in dispute; and
(c)   not contain more than 10 authorities unless the scale of the appeal warrants more extensive citation."

Citation of Authority

5 When authority is cited, whether in written or oral submissions, the following practice should be followed.

6 Where a judgment is reported in the Official Law Reports (AC, QB, Ch, Fam) published by the Incorporated Council of Law Reporting for England and Wales, that report must be cited. These are the most authoritative reports; they contain a summary of the argument. Other series of reports and official transcripts of judgment may only be used when a case is not reported in the Official Law Reports.

7 If a judgment is not (or not yet) reported in the Official Law Reports but it is reported in the Weekly Law Reports (WLR) or the All England Law Reports (All ER) that report should be cited. If the case is reported in both the WLR and the All ER either report may properly be cited.

8 If a judgment is not reported in the Official Law Reports, the WLR, or the All ER, but it is reported in any of the authoritative specialist series of reports which contain a headnote and are made by individuals holding a Senior Courts qualification (for the purposes of section 115 of the Courts and Legal Services Act 1990), the specialist report should be cited.

9 Where a judgment is not reported in any of the reports referred to in paragraphs [6] to [8] above, but is reported in other reports, they may be cited.

10 Where a judgment has not been reported, reference may be made to the official transcript if that is available, not the handed-down text of the judgment, as this may have been subject to late revision after the text was handed down. Official transcripts may be obtained from, for instance, BAILLI (http://www.bailii.org/). An unreported case should not usually be cited unless it contains a relevant statement of legal principle not found in reported authority.

11 Occasions arise when one report is fuller than another, or when there are discrepancies between reports. On such occasions, the practice outlined above need not be followed, but the court should be given a brief explanation why this course is being taken, and the alternative references should be given.

12 If a judgment under appeal has been reported before the hearing but after skeleton arguments have been filed with the court, and counsel wish to argue from the published report rather than from the official transcript, the court should be provided with photocopies of the report for the use of the court.

13 Judgments reported in any series of reports, including those of the Incorporated Council of Law Reporting, should be provided either by way of a photocopy of the

published report or by way of a copy of a reproduction of the judgment in electronic form that has been authorised by the publisher of the relevant series, but in any event (1) the report must be presented to the court in an easily legible form (a 12-point font is preferred but a 10- or 11-point font is acceptable) and (2) the advocate presenting the report is satisfied that it has not been reproduced in a garbled form from the data source. In any case of doubt the court will rely on the printed text of the report (unless the editor of the report has certified that an electronic version is more accurate because it corrects an error contained in an earlier printed text of the report).

14 This Direction is made by the Lord Chief Justice with the agreement of the Master of the Rolls and the President of the Family Division. It is issued in accordance with the procedure laid down in Part 1 of Schedule 2 to the Constitutional Reform Act 2005.

The Right Honourable
The Lord Judge
The Lord Chief Justice of England and Wales

President's Guidance
May 2012

Prior Authority for Experts

Background

On 11 October 2011, as part of the legal aid reform programme, the Ministry of Justice (MoJ) enacted a new Funding Order that set maximum hourly rates and prescribed fees for certain types of experts. The Order does not prescribe the amount of time that may be spent by an expert on a case. The Order does allow for higher rates to be paid if specific exceptional criteria are met. The LSC is required to make funding decisions in accordance with the Order.

Solicitors may make an application to the LSC for prior authority for expert costs in certain circumstances.

VOLUMES OF APPLICATIONS FOR PRIOR AUTHORITIES RECEIVED BY THE LSC

Monthly applications	Nov	Dec	Jan	Feb	Mar	April
Applications for Prior Authority	216	492	784	1140	1840	1855

The number of prior authority applications received overall in this period is significantly higher than the same period the previous year. It is difficult to predict whether the numbers of applications will continue to increase.

The LSC contract states that prior authority should only be sought where the request is for exceptional rates or where the costs sought are unusual or unusually high. The LSC agreed that as a transitional arrangement it would grant requests for standard expenditure for 3 months after the enactment of the Order to provide certainty for solicitors. The LSC is now working with the Law Society to discourage applications where no unusual costs are sought.

PART V

TIME TAKEN TO PROCESS APPLICATIONS

The time taken to process applications as at March 2012 is set out below. The LSC is monitoring the volumes of applications and the time taken to process them.

Time taken to process	
Standard applications	8 days
Urgent applications	3 days

There are no specific criteria for urgent applications other than that the solicitor has stated that it is urgent, for example a Court hearing is imminent.

The time taken to process the applications is calculated from the date that all of the necessary information has been received from the solicitor and would exclude time taken waiting for additional information if this had been requested.

May 2012

The above analysis does not include applications for experts in very high cost cases which are dealt with under individual high cost case contracts. In these cases it may take longer to authorise expert costs as the total costs of the cases need to be agreed. The number of these cases is small (around 1,950 of care certificates which represent 5% of the total number of care certificates granted). However, these cases cost around £60 million taking up 20% of the public law spend.

The LSC is looking at how the system for approving costs in these cases can be made simpler for all parties and is currently piloting a new "events model" with some solicitor firms.

DECISIONS MADE

The LSC may grant, refuse or reject an application. The meanings of these decisions are:

(i)   Where applications are granted the prior authority for hourly rates and/or hours is approved as requested;

(ii) Where the prior authority was refused it may be for a number of reasons e.g. the hours are excessive (following the introduction of the Order there has been a significant increase in the number of hours requested in some cases) or there are issues with apportionment of costs;

(iii) Where applications are rejected the solicitor has provided insufficient information to enable the LSC to make a determination e.g. requesting a global sum without a breakdown of the work to be done, the number of hours and the requested hourly rate. In these cases the solicitor is asked to re-submit the application with the relevant information.

There was previously a right of appeal against a funding decision by the LSC on a prior authority. Following the introduction of the new family contracts in 2012 there is no longer this right. Solicitors are able to re-submit their application where they have additional information that they wish to have considered.

A refusal of prior authority does not necessarily mean the cost of the expert will not be met. Refusals may take the form of telling the solicitor to "Justify on taxation" i.e. as part of their usual application for payment at the end of the case. This applies in particular to cases where the assessor decides the case does not justify an exceptional rate.

Future data

The LSC is committed, as a member of the Family Justice System, to improve the management information that it collects. One of the areas where more data is being collected is on prior authority requests. This data will be shared once a representative sample has been analysed and should be available by October 2012. It will look at things such as the:

- Types of experts for whom prior authority is sought
- The nature of the authority i.e. in relation to rates or hours
- The number of applications that are refused or rejected.

May 2012

Guidance from the Legal Services Commission—In January 2013, the Legal Services Commission (which was replaced by the Legal Aid Agency on 1 April 2013) published guidance entitled *Applications for Prior Authorities for Experts in Family Cases* (below). The guidance includes information on the timing of the application for prior authority and what constitutes exceptional circumstances for the purpose of approving higher rates than those set out in the regulations.

Legal Services Commission Guidance January 2013

Applications for Prior Authorities for Experts in Family Cases

1 When should you apply for prior authority to incur costs of an expert service?

You <u>must</u> always apply for prior authority where you seek to incur costs of an expert service at higher rates than are set out in the Remuneration Regulations for that service.

Where a rate set out in the Remuneration Regulations has been exceeded and no authority to exceed the maximum rates has previously been granted the LSC will disallow any fees exceeding the maximum rates.

You <u>may</u> apply for prior authority in the following circumstances:

- The item of costs (which may consist of an expert fee or other disbursement) is either unusual in nature or is unusually large (paragraph 5.25 of the Standard Civil Contract specification); or
- There are no codified rates set out in the Remuneration Regulations for a particular expert service.

2 What are exceptional circumstances where the LSC would approve higher rates than are set out in the Remuneration Regulations?

Exceptional circumstances are where the expert service or evidence is key to the client's case and either:

- the complexity of the material is such that an expert with a high level of seniority is required; or
- the material is of such a specialised and unusual nature that only very few experts are available to provide the necessary service or evidence.

Some examples of where higher rates have been granted are set out below:

- Paediatricians where the children who were subject to care proceedings had an unusual genetic disorder;

PART V

- Interpreters where there was a scarcity of interpreters due to an unusual language or dialect.

3 When is an item of costs considered unusual or unusually large?

An item of costs is considered unusually large where it is greater than £5,000 per funded client or where the hours requested are in excess of those set out in Table 1 below.

The figures set out in Table 1 below are intended to provide a benchmark of an "unusual" number of hours. This does not mean that hours in excess of these will be refused, only that prior authority may be sought where an expert's time is expected to exceed these benchmarks.

Prior authority should not be sought where the expert is to be paid at the hourly rates set out in the Remuneration Regulations and the hours quoted by the expert are less than the hours set out in Table 1 below.

Table 1 – Number of hours above which prior authority should be applied for

Expert Type	One party to be assessed	Two parties to be assessed
Psychologist (inc Child Psychologist)	20	30
Psychiatrist (inc Child Psychiatrist)	15	25
Independent Social Workers	30	40
Paediatrician	15	25
Radiologist	10	–

These benchmarks include all aspects of expert service provision and not just the assessment of parties

An item of costs is unusual in nature where, for example, more than 2 parties are to be assessed.

The number of hours allowed on prior authority is not a cap on the work that may be done, it is authority for an amount of work based on the known relevant facts of a case at a particular time. Providers are always able to seek to justify on assessment/taxation why a greater number of hours were required.

4 What happens where there are no rates set out in the Remuneration Regulations for a particular expert service?

Where there are no rates set out in the Remuneration Regulations prior authority may be sought and 3 alternative quotes (if possible) should be provided to the LSC. The quotes will need to include details of both the hourly rate and total number of hours quoted. You must also include a copy of the Court Order and the expert's CV.

In agreeing an hourly rate the LSC will have regard to the rates set out in the Remuneration Regulations and as a starting point will look at the most comparable expert type rate if applicable. The LSC will take into account all the circumstances of the case and any evidence supplied by the provider to decide on the appropriate rate for each case.

One of the most frequent types of application for prior authority in relation to non-codified rates is for drug and alcohol tests. It is not necessary to apply for prior authority in these cases provided that the tests carried out reflect what has been directed in the Court Order.

The main reason for refusing requested costs for drug and alcohol tests are:

- The length of time the testing should cover. The standard period of testing is 3 months and a longer period will only be allowed if specified in the Court Order.
- The type of analysis/testing required e.g. is it an **Overview/Standard testing** basis or on a Month-by-month/Segmented testing basis. **Month-by-month/ Segmented testing** is a more costly method of testing and funding on this basis will be refused unless specified in the Court Order.
- If the Court Order specifies the types of drugs that should be tested then funding will only be agreed to test these specific drugs.
- When the Court Order orders alcohol testing it should state whether this is for hair, blood or liver function tests. Funding will only be provided for the tests specified in the Court Order.

5 What happens where I do not have prior authority?

The amounts claimed for the provision of expert services <u>must</u> be justified on detailed assessment by the Court or assessment by the LSC in the normal way. Details of the work must include:

- A breakdown of the hours spent on the case with a justification of why the hours are necessary;
- A breakdown of the work done on the different aspects of the case e.g. assessment of clients, writing report, interviewing other relevant parties;
- Details of the expert/s and evidence of their qualifications, skills and expertise e.g. a CV; and
- Copy of the Court Order

The figures set out in Table 2 below are intended to be a guide for providers and experts on the number of hours within which **prior authority** applications have previously typically been granted for psychologists and psychiatrists (these are the most commonly instructed expert types). If the hours requested are within these hours then generally they would be allowed on assessment subject to the necessary information set out above being provided in full.

Table 2 – Hours granted (the modal figure is the figure most commonly granted)

Expert Type	**One party (modal)**	**Two parties (modal)**
Psychologist	19	32
Child psychologist	20	30
Psychiatrist	10	23

However we would still expect to see a range of hours claimed i.e. we would not expect to see the hours in every case falling just below the "unusually large" threshold.

Providers are reminded that whilst the LSC is the paying authority it does not contract directly with expert witnesses; this is the responsibility of Legal Aid service providers

PART V

who are required to ensure that any amounts claimed are fully justified. Terms of instruction should be agreed between the two parties in advance of the expert undertaking any work.

President's Guidance May 2012—Reference should also be made to the President's Guidance of May 2012: *Prior Authority for Experts* (above), which deals with the time in which, and the basis upon which, the LSC will determine applications for prior authority.

Practice Guidance
March 2013

Terminology for Litigants in Person

1 In its Report of November 2011 the Civil Justice Council (CJC) recommended that in future individuals who conduct legal proceedings on their own behalf, and have traditionally been referred to as Litigants in Person (LiPs), should in future be referred to as self-represented litigants (SRLs). Subsequently the term SRL has gained some currency. LiP has however also continued to be used. The use of two terms to refer to the same thing is less than ideal. It is confusing both for individual litigants and the courts.

2 The Judges' Council (including the Lord Chief Justice and President of the Family Division) has consequently considered the CJC's recommendation, and authorised me as Master of the Rolls and Head of Civil Justice, to issue Guidance, to promote clarity, certainty and simplicity, on the term to be used in future.

3 I have considered all the circumstances, including the fact that the term LiP: is used in statute (eg, The Litigants in Person (Costs and Expenses) Act 1975); is and will continue to be used by Government; is commonly understood and well-known both by the legal profession and individuals generally; the term SRL is unclear in its scope, as it can variously be understood to suggest that individuals are conducting the entirety of legal proceedings on their own behalf, that they are only conducting court advocacy on their own behalf or, that they have themselves obtained representation i.e., secured the service of an advocate.

4 In the light of these factors I have therefore determined, with the unanimous agreement of the Judges' Council, that the term SRL should not be adopted or used in future.

5 The term "Litigant in Person" (LiP) should continue to be the sole term used to describe individuals who exercise their right to conduct legal proceedings on their own behalf.

6 This Guidance applies to all proceedings in all criminal, civil and family courts.

Lord Dyson MR
March 2013

Practice Note
March 2013

The Official Solicitor to the Senior Courts: Appointment in Family Proceedings and Proceedings under the Inherent Jurisdiction in Relation to Adults

Introduction

1 This Practice Note replaces the Practice Note dated 2 April 2001 issued by the Official Solicitor.

2 It concerns:

    (a) the appointment of the Official Solicitor as "litigation friend" of a "protected party" or child in family proceedings or where the Family Division of the High Court is being invited to exercise its inherent jurisdiction in relation to a vulnerable adult[1];

    (b) requests by the court to the Official Solicitor to conduct *Harbin v Masterman*[2] enquiries; and

    (c) requests by the court to the Official Solicitor to act as, or appoint counsel to act as, an advocate to the court[3].

The Note is intended to be helpful guidance, but is always subject to legislation including the Rules of Court, to Practice Directions, and to case law.

---

1   In this context a "vulnerable adult" is a person who has mental capacity in respect of the decisions in question but who lacks litigation capacity.

2   [1896] 1 Ch 351.

3   Pursuant to the Memorandum "Requests for the appointment of an advocate to the court" of the Attorney General and the Lord Chief Justice of 19 December 2001.

3 For the avoidance of doubt, the Children and Family Court Advisory and Support Service (Cafcass) has responsibilities in relation to a child in family proceedings in which their welfare is or may be in question (Criminal Justice and Court Services Act 2000, section 12). Since 1 April 2001 the Official Solicitor has not represented a child who is the subject of family proceedings (other than in very exceptional circumstances or where a transfer to the Court of Protection is being considered see paragraph 7 below). In cases of doubt or difficulty, staff of the Official Solicitor's office will liaise with staff of Cafcass Legal Services to avoid duplication and ensure the most suitable arrangements are made.

Children and Protected Parties who require a litigation friend in proceedings

4 Adults: a "protected party" requires a litigation friend. In family proceedings this requirement appears in Part 15 of the Family Procedure Rules 2010 ("FPR 2010") and in proceedings in the Family Division of the High Court of Justice under the court's inherent jurisdiction it appears in Part 21 of the Civil Procedure Rules 1998 ("CPR 1998"). In family proceedings, a "protected party" means a party, or an intended party, who lacks capacity (within the meaning of the Mental Capacity Act 2005) to conduct the proceedings: FPR 2010, rule 2.3; and in proceedings under the inherent jurisdiction the expression has the same meaning: CPR 1998, rule 21.2. The following should be noted:

    (a) there must be undisputed evidence that the party, or intended party, lacks capacity to conduct the proceedings;

PART V

(b) that evidence, and what flows from the party, or intended party, being a protected party, should have been disclosed to, and carefully explained to, the party or intended party;

(c) the party, or intended party, is entitled to dispute an opinion that they lack litigation capacity and there may be cases where the party's, or intended party's, capacity to conduct the proceedings is the subject of dispute between competent experts. In either case a formal finding by the court under FPR 2010, rule 2.3, or CPR 1998, rule 21.2 is required.

5 Non-subject child: a child whose own welfare is not the subject of family proceedings may nevertheless be a party. The most common examples are:

(a) a child who is also the parent of a child, and who is a respondent to a Children Act 1989 or Adoption and Children Act 2002 application;

(b) a child who wishes to make an application for a Children Act 1989 order naming another child (typically a contact order naming a sibling);

(c) a child witness to some disputed factual issue in a children case and who may require intervenor status;

(d) a child party to an application for a declaration of status under Part III of the Family Law Act 1986;

(e) a child intervenor in financial remedy proceedings ;

(f) a child applicant for, or respondent to, an application for an order under Part IV (Family Homes and Domestic Violence) or Part 4A (Forced Marriage) of the Family Law Act 1996.

6 FPR 2010 Part 16 makes provision for the representation of children. Rule 16.6 sets out the circumstances in which a child does not need a children's guardian or litigation friend. Any child party to proceedings under the Children Act 1989, Part 4A Family Law Act 1996, applications in adoption, placement and related proceedings, or proceedings relating to the exercise of the court's inherent jurisdiction with respect to children may rely on the provisions of rule 16.6.

7 Children aged 16–17 years: the Mental Capacity Act 2005 (Transfer of Proceedings) Order 2007 (SI 2007/1899) makes provision for the transfer of proceedings from the Court of Protection to a court having jurisdiction under the Children Act 1989. The Order also makes provision for the transfer of the whole or part of the proceedings from a court having jurisdiction under the Children Act 1989 to the Court of Protection where it considers that in all circumstances, it is just and convenient to transfer the proceedings. Article 3(3) of the Order lists those factors to which the court must have regard when making a determination about transfer either on an application or of its own initiative. Court of Protection proceedings are not family proceedings and therefore transfer of proceedings into the Court of Protection will mean that any involvement by Cafcass in those proceedings will end.

8 The Court of Protection Rules 2007 apply to proceedings in the Court of Protection. Rule 141(4)–(6) of those Rules make provision for a child to be permitted to conduct proceedings in the Court of Protection without a litigation friend. However if the child is 'P' within the meaning of rule 6 of the Court of Protection Rules 2007 reference should be made to rule 141(1) and rule 147 of those Rules in relation to the appointment of a litigation friend.

The role of a litigation friend

9 The case law and the Rules provide that a litigation friend must fairly and competently conduct the proceedings in the protected party's or child's best interests, and must have no interest in the proceedings adverse to that of the protected party or child. The procedure and basis for the appointment of a litigation friend and the duty of a litigation

friend are contained in Part 15 (Representation of Protected Parties) FPR 2010 and Part 16 (Representation of Children and Reports in Proceedings Involving Children) FPR 2010 and the associated Practice Directions.

The Official Solicitor's criteria for consenting to act as litigation friend

10 The Official Solicitor is the litigation friend of last resort. No person, including the Official Solicitor, can be appointed to act as litigation friend without their consent. The Official Solicitor will not accept appointment where there is another person who is suitable and willing to act as litigation friend. The Official Solicitor's criteria for consenting to act as litigation friend are:

(a) in the case of an adult that the party or intended party is a protected party[4];

(b) there is security for the costs of legal representation of the protected party which the Official Solicitor considers satisfactory. Sources of security may be

(i) the Legal Aid Agency where the protected party or child is eligible for public funding;

(ii) the protected party's or child's own funds where they have financial capacity or where they do not where the Court of Protection has given him authority to recover the costs from the adult's or child's funds;

(iii) an undertaking from another party to pay his costs;

(c) the case is a last resort case.

4   The Official Solicitor is able to provide a pro forma certificate of capacity to conduct proceedings and notes for guidance.

Invitations to the Official Solicitor: new cases

11 Solicitors who have been consulted by a child or a protected party (or by someone acting on their behalf, or concerned about their interests) should write to the Official Solicitor setting out the background to the proposed case and explaining the basis on which the Official Solicitor's criteria for acting are met.

Invitations to the Official Solicitor: pending proceedings

12 Where a case is already before the court, an order inviting the Official Solicitor to act should be expressed as being made subject to his consent. The Official Solicitor aims to provide an initial response to any invitation within 10 working days. But he cannot consent to act unless and until he is satisfied both that his criteria are met and that he has a member of his staff to whom the case can be allocated as the case's case manager. So from time to time there will be a waiting list of cases which meet the Official Solicitor's acceptance criteria but in respect of which, because he has no case manager available to take the case, he cannot accept appointment as litigation friend. Save in exceptional circumstances, cases will be accepted in strict chronological order starting with the earliest placed on the waiting list of cases which have met the criteria for acceptance. What constitutes exceptional circumstances will be fact specific; the decision to expedite acceptance of a case is one for the Official Solicitor.

13 To enable the Official Solicitor to consider the invitation to him to act, he should be provided with the following as soon as possible:

(a) the sealed court order inviting him to act as litigation friend (with a note of the reasons approved by the Judge if appropriate);

(b) a copy of the letter of instruction to the expert by which an opinion was sought as to the party's capacity to conduct the proceedings whether in the form of the Official Solicitor's certificate of capacity to conduct the proceedings or otherwise;

(c)   (adult party) the opinion on capacity (the Official Solicitor's pro forma certificate of capacity to conduct proceedings may be requested from his office for the purpose of obtaining an opinion);

(d)   confirmation that there is satisfactory security for the costs of legal representation (including any relevant supporting documents); it is a matter for the Official Solicitor whether the proposed security for costs is satisfactory;

(e)   confirmation that there is no other person suitable and willing to act as litigation friend (including the enquiries made to this end);

(f)   the court file (provision of the court file may not be necessary if the court directs a party to provide a full indexed copy of the bundle to the Official Solicitor on a timely basis).

Litigants in person

14 If one or more parties is or are litigants in person, and there is reason to believe that any litigant in person may lack capacity to conduct the proceedings, the court will need to consider, and if necessary give directions as to:

(a)   who is to arrange for the assessment of capacity to conduct the proceedings;

(b)   how the cost of that assessment is to be funded;

(c)   how any invitation to act as litigation friend is to be made to either any suitable and willing person or the Official Solicitor so as to provide him with the documents and information (including information to enable him to make the enquiries necessary to establish whether or not there is funding available;

(d)   any resulting timetabling and, where the Official Solicitor is being invited to be litigation friend, having regard to the Official Solicitor's need to investigate whether his acceptance criteria are met, the need for him to have a case manager available to deal with the case and the possibility that an application to the Court of Protection (for authority to pay the costs out of the protected party's or child's funds) may be necessary.

15 The Official Solicitor will notify the court in the event he expects a delay in accepting appointment either because it is not evident that his criteria are met or for any other reason. The court may wish to consider:

(a)   making enquiries of the parties as to the steps being taken by them to establish that the Official Solicitor's criteria for acting are met in the particular case;

(b)   whether directions should be made to ensure that such enquiries are progressed on a timely basis;

(c)   fixing a further directions appointment.

16 If, at any time, another litigation friend is appointed before the Official Solicitor is in a position to accept the invitation to him to act, the Official Solicitor should be notified without delay.

Where the Official Solicitor has accepted appointment as litigation friend

17 Once the Official Solicitor is able to accept appointment as litigation friend he will need time to prepare the case on behalf of the protected party or child and may wish to make submissions about any substantive hearing date.

18 To avoid unnecessary delay in progression of the case, he will require from the solicitors he appoints for the protected party or child:

(a)   a reading list identifying the material which the solicitors considers will assist by way of introduction to the case in obtaining an overview of the issues from the perspective of the protected party or child;

(b)   a summary of the background to the proceedings, of any major steps that have occurred within the proceedings, and identification of the issues in the proceedings;

(c)   advice as to the steps the Official Solicitor should now take in the proceedings on behalf of the protected party or child;

(d)   copies of all notes of attendance on the protected party or child so that the Official Solicitor is properly informed as to the views and wishes expressed by the protected party or child to date;

(e)   confirmation of the protected party's or child's present ascertainable views and wishes in relation to the proceedings.

Advising the court: *Harbin v Masterman* enquiries and Advocate to the Court

19 Where the Official Solicitor is invited, with his consent, to conduct enquiries under *Harbin v Masterman* and it appears to the Official Solicitor that any public body wishes to seek the assistance of the court but is unwilling to carry out the enquiries itself, the Official Solicitor may seek an undertaking from that public body to indemnify him in respect of his costs of carrying out those enquiries.

20 As noted at paragraph 2(c) above, the Official Solicitor may be invited, with his consent, to act or instruct counsel as a friend of the court (advocate to the court) if it appears to the court that such an invitation is more appropriately addressed to him rather than (or in addition to) Cafcass Legal Services or to the Attorney-General.

Contacting the Official Solicitor

21 It may be helpful to discuss the question of appointment with the Official Solicitor or one of his staff by telephoning 020 7911 7127 (family litigation) or 020 7911 7233 (divorce litigation), in particular:

(a)   if in doubt about whether his criteria for acting are met, or

(b)   to request a copy of the Official Solicitor's pro forma certificate of capacity to conduct proceedings and notes for guidance.

The Official Solicitor's certificate of capacity to conduct proceedings, a sample letter of instruction, other precedent documents and further guidance in relation to the appointment of the Official Solicitor are also available at www.justice.gov.uk (follow the links to the Official Solicitor).

22 Enquiries about the appointment of the Official Solicitor as litigation friend should be addressed:

(a)   (in divorce and financial remedy proceedings) to the Divisional Manager, Divorce Litigation;

(b)   (in children proceedings or proceedings under Part IV Family Law Act 1996) to the Divisional Manager, Family Litigation;.

All other enquiries should be addressed to a family lawyer.

The contact details are:

81 Chancery Lane,
London WC2A 1DD.
DX 0012 London Chancery Lane
Fax: 020 7911 7105
E-mail address: enquiries@offsol.gsi.gov.uk

Alastair Pitblado

Official Solicitor

PART V

President's Guidance
April 2013

Communicating with the Home Office in Family Proceedings

1 The 'Communicating with the Home Office in Family Proceedings' protocol enables the family courts to communicate with the Home Office (UK Borders Agency and Identity and Passport Service) to obtain immigration, visa and passport information for family court proceedings.

2 This guidance has been reissued to replace & amalgamate previous guidance issued in 2002, 2004, 2006 & 2010 (including the Communicating with the Passport Service 2004) to reflect the new contact details for the Home Office Liaison Officer who has responsibility for administering requests made under the Protocol. It does not alter the nature or purpose of the Protocol.

3 Where an order is made against the Home Office in Family Proceedings, the court shall draw up the relevant order. The HMCTS form EX660 should be fully completed (including specifying the details of the relevant family members and their relationship to the child). Parties should provide details of both mother and father if known, whether or not they are involved in the proceedings.

4 The sealed order and the completed EX660 should be sent immediately to:

> Home Office Liaison Team
> Her Majesty's Courts and Tribunal Service
> Arnhem House
> PO Box 6987
> Leicester
> LE1 6ZX
> Email: homeofficeliaison@hmcts.gsi.gov.uk
> Telephone: 0116 249 4309
> Fax: 0116 249 4302

5 Please note that all information provided in the EX660 will be forwarded to the Home Office. Parties should ensure that any additional information, such as a case synopsis, which it wishes the Home Office to view, has the required leave of the court, set out in the order, to be disclosed to the Home Office. (Note that it is a contempt of court to disclose this information otherwise).

6 Where the query relates to the proposed adoption of a foreign national minor, the Home Office Liaison Officer can advise as to the additional information which will be required.

7 The order and EX660 should clearly state the time by which the information is required. In order to comply with the agreed four (4) week period in for the Home Office to provide a response to the court, parties and court staff should ensure that the Home Office Liaison Officer receives the court order on the day the order is made.

8 Where it will not be possible for court to send the sealed order to the Home Office Liaison Officer on the day it is made, the court when stating the required date of receipt by the court of the information should allow any additional time necessary for the preparation and sending of the order. This is in order to ensure that Home Office has 4 weeks to provide a response from the time it receives the order from the Home Office Liaison Officer. Any reduction in this period may result in a request by the Home Office for further time in which to reply.

9 The request or order should identify the questions it wishes to be answered by the Home Office.

10 Parties should provide the name and contact details of someone who has agreed and is able to provide further information should it be needed.

11 The order and EX660 should be forwarded to the Home Office Liaison Officer together with such information as is sufficient to enable the Home Office to understand the nature of the case, to identify whether the case involves an adoption, and to identify whether the immigration issues raised might relate to an asylum or non-asylum application.

12 The Home Office Liaison Officer will then send to an appropriate officer in the Home Office the enquiry, together with a copy of any order made. The Home Office official will be personally responsible for either:

  (a) answering the query themselves, by retrieving the file and preparing a statement for the court; or
  (b) forwarding the request to a caseworker or relevant official with carriage of that particular file.

13 The Home Office Liaison Officer will follow up as required in order to ensure that the information is received by the court in time, and will receive the information before forwarding it on as instructed by the judge or court making the request.

14 Attached is a sample court order and completed EX660 which should provide further useful guidance. **Please note the change in contact details in the form EX660.**

****

Originally issued December 2002

Re-issued April 2013

The Rt Hon Sir James Munby
President of the Family Division

Note—The contact details in Form EX660 are the same as in para 4.

PART V

PART VI

European Material

PART VI: European Material

Contents

PART VI

PART VI: Ethics and Politics

Contents

Convention on Jurisdiction, Applicable Law, Recognition, Enforcement and Co-Operation in Respect of Parental Responsibility and Measures for the Protection of Children

Scope—The Convention on Jurisdiction, Applicable Law, Recognition, Enforcement and Co-Operation in Respect of Parental Responsibility and Measures for the Protection of Children is also referred to as the 1996 Hague Convention on the Protection of Children, the 1996 Hague Child Protection Convention, the Hague Convention 1996 or the 1996 Convention. It was signed on 19 October 1996, but pursuant to Art 61 it could only come into force on the first day of the month following the expiration of 3 months after three States had ratified the Convention. The first three States to ratify it were Monaco in May 1997, the Czech Republic in March 2000 and Slovakia in 2001 and thus it came into force in January 2002. It was ratified by the UK on 27 July 2012 and came into force on 1 November 2012.

The aim of the Convention is to provide a uniform system to improve cross-border protection of children, to avoid conflict between the legal systems in respect of jurisdiction, applicable law, recognition and enforcement of measures and to provide co-operation and collaboration between States, with the best interests of the child as the primary consideration.

The Convention is divided into seven Chapters:

Chapter 1 (Arts 1–4) deals with the scope of the Convention. It sets out the objectives of the Convention, affirms that it applies to children from the moment of birth until they reach the age of 18 years and sets out a non-exhaustive list of measures that may be covered by the Convention and a list of those matters that are excluded and to which the Convention does not apply.

Chapter 2 (Arts 5–14) deals with jurisdiction and makes the child's habitual residence the basis on which a State has jurisdiction to take measures to protect the child and his property. It makes provisions for jurisdiction in respect of refugee children and those children who are internationally displaced to be based on presence. It deals with jurisdiction in respect of abducted children and the transfer by agreement of jurisdiction between States when it is considered that another Contracting State would be better placed in the particular case to assess the best interest of the child. It provides for a Contracting State dealing with the parents' divorce, legal separation or nullity to deal also with matters in relation to the child, notwithstanding the fact the child is habitually resident in another Contracting State, providing that certain conditions set out in Art 10 are met. It also makes provisions in all cases of urgency for a Contracting State in whose territory the child or the property of the child is present to have jurisdiction to take any necessary measures for the protection of the child and his property. Provision is also made for provisional protective (not urgent) measures to be taken by the State in whose territory the child or his property is, provided it is not incompatible with measures already taken by authorities that have jurisdiction.

Chapter 3 (Arts 15–22) deals with the applicable law and laying down the principle that in exercising jurisdiction the authorities of the Contracting States should apply their own domestic law save in exceptional circumstances. It also specifically deals with issues of attribution and extinction of parental responsibility

Chapter 4 (Arts 23–28) deals with recognition, non-recognition, registration and enforcement of measures taken across all Contracting States. It sets out the principle that measures taken by the authorities of a Contracting State shall be recognised by operation of law in all other Contracting States without the need to take proceedings for registration. Where there is non-compliance or opposition, recognition may only be refused on the specified grounds only.

Chapter 5 (Arts 29–39) deals with co-operation and collaboration through the Central Authorities, with specific and obligatory provisions for the sharing and exchange of information and cross-border placement of children.

Chapter 6 (Arts 40–56) sets out general provisions, such as the issuing of certificates of parental responsibility, confidentiality and the interplay between various international instruments, specifically the 1980 Hague Convention and Brussels IIA.

Chapter 7 (Arts 57–63) contain the final provisions, which deal with the process of ratification and accession to the Convention.

The Explanatory Report prepared by Professor Paul Lagarde ("the *Lagarde Report*") provides useful material for interpreting the Convention. The *Draft Revised Practical Handbook* ("the *Handbook*") is also a useful guide on the operation of the Convention and provides many examples. Both are available on the Hague Conference website (*www.hcch.net*). A final version of the *Handbook* is currently being prepared and is expected to be available in 2013. Practitioners may also find the Ministry of Justice *1996 Hague Convention Practice Guide* (published on 8 February 2013) useful as a quick guide. It is available on the MOJ website.

PART VI

Table of 1996 Convention Contracting States

Country	Ratified date	Entry into force
Albania A*	18 May 2006	1 April 2007
Australia	29 April 2003	1 August 2003
Austria	22 December 2010	1 April 2011
Armenia A*	1 March 2007	1 May 2008
Bulgaria	8 March 2006	1 February 2007
Croatia	4 September 2009	1 January 2010
Cyprus	21 July 2010	1 November 2010
Czech Republic	13 March 2000	1 January 2002
Denmark	30 June 2011	1 October 2011
Dominican Republic A*	14 December 2009	1 October 2010
Ecuador A*	5 November 2002	1 September 2003
Estonia	6 August 2002	1 June 2003
Finland	19 November 2010	1 March 2011
France	15 October 2010	1 February 2011
Germany	17 September 2010	1 January 2011
Greece	7 February 2012	1 June 2012
Hungary	13 January 2006	1 May 2006
Ireland	30 September 2010	1 January 2011
Latvia	12 December 2002	1 April 2003
Lesotho A	18 June 2012	1 June 2013
Lithuania	29 October 2003	1 September 2004
Luxembourg	5 August 2010	1 December 2010
Malta A	24 February 2011	1 January 2012
Monaco	14 May 1997	1 January 2002
Montenegro A	14 February 2012	1 January 2013
Morocco	22 August 2002	1 December 2002
Netherlands	31 January 2011	1 May 2011
Poland	27 July 2010	1 November 2010
Portugal	14 April 2011	1 August 2011

Country	Ratified date	Entry into force
Romania	8 September 2010	1 January 2011
Russian Federation A	20 August 2012	1 June 2013
Slovakia	21 September 2001	1 January 2002
Slovenia	11 October 2004	1 February 2005
Spain	6 September 2010	1 January 2011
Sweden	26 September 2012	1 January 2013
Switzerland	27 March 2009	1 July 2009
Ukraine A*	3 April 2007	1 February 2008
United Kingdom of Great Britain and Northern Ireland	27 July 2012	1 November 2012
Uruguay	17 November 2009	1 March 2010

A—Accession: see Arts 58(1) and 61(1).

A*—Accession giving rise to an acceptance procedure. Denmark has raised objections against these countries. Therefore, the Convention will not enter into force between these countries and Denmark (see Art 58(3)).

Contracting States—The above table sets out the full list of contracting States to the 1996 Convention on Jurisdiction, Applicable Law, Recognition, Enforcement and Co-operation in Respect of Parental Responsibility and Measures for the Protection of Children. The Hague Conference on Private International Law (HccH) may publish, from time to time, updates on States' accession to the Convention on the relevant part of its website (*www.hcch.net*), which also contains information on any declarations/reservations that particular States may have recorded (e g under Arts 29, 54, 55 or 59).

(Concluded 19 October 1996)

The States signatory to the present Convention,

Considering the need to improve the protection of children in international situations,

Wishing to avoid conflicts between their legal systems in respect of jurisdiction, applicable law, recognition and enforcement of measures for the protection of children,

Recalling the importance of international co-operation for the protection of children,

Confirming that the best interests of the child are to be a primary consideration,

Noting that the Convention of 5 October 1961 concerning the powers of authorities and the law applicable in respect of the protection of minors is in need of revision,

Desiring to establish common provisions to this effect, taking into account the United Nations Convention on the Rights of the Child of 20 November 1989,

Have agreed on the following provisions –

CHAPTER I
SCOPE OF THE CONVENTION

Article 1

(1) The objects of the present Convention are –

(a)   to determine the State whose authorities have jurisdiction to take measures directed to the protection of the person or property of the child;

(b)   to determine which law is to be applied by such authorities in exercising their jurisdiction;

(c)   to determine the law applicable to parental responsibility;

(d)   to provide for the recognition and enforcement of such measures of protection in all Contracting States;

(e)   to establish such co-operation between the authorities of the Contracting States as may be necessary in order to achieve the purposes of this Convention.

(2) For the purposes of this Convention, the term 'parental responsibility' includes parental authority, or any analogous relationship of authority determining the rights, powers and responsibilities of parents, guardians or other legal representatives in relation to the person or the property of the child.

Contracting States—This means States that are party to the Convention. For an up-to-date list of Contracting States, see *www.hcch.net*.

"parental responsibility" (Art 1(2))—The definition is intended to have an autonomous wide international meaning (see the *Lagarde Report*, para 14), so it does not follow that it will necessarily have the same meaning as that which applies under CA 1989.

Article 2

The Convention applies to children from the moment of their birth until they reach the age of 18 years.

Age—Note that unlike the Hague Convention 1980, the 1996 Convention defines the term "child" as continuing to apply "from the moment of birth" until the child attains the age of 18, irrespective of the age of majority under the law of a Contracting State. Thus it may in appropriate cases be relied on to obtain relief when the 1980 Convention does not apply. For other instances where the Convention may be useful, see the *Revised Draft Practical Handbook on the Operation of the Convention*. The Convention will continue to apply even to a person who is married but under the age of 18. For those children beyond the age of 18 and whose capacity is impaired and who are not in a position to protect their interests, the Hague Convention of 13 January 2000 on the International Protection of Adults will apply if the relevant States are Contracting States to that Convention (see further the *Handbook*, para 3.10–3.13 and the examples therein)

"from the moment of their birth"—The Convention thus does not apply to an unborn child.

Article 3

The measures referred to in Article 1 may deal in particular with –

(a)   the attribution, exercise, termination or restriction of parental responsibility, as well as its delegation;

(b)   rights of custody, including rights relating to the care of the person of the child and, in particular, the right to determine the child's place of residence, as well as rights of access including the right to take a child for a limited period of time to a place other than the child's habitual residence;

(c)   guardianship, curatorship and analogous institutions;

(d)   the designation and functions of any person or body having charge of the child's person or property, representing or assisting the child;

(e)   the placement of the child in a foster family or in institutional care, or the provision of care by kafala or an analogous institution;

(f)   the supervision by a public authority of the care of a child by any person having charge of the child;

(g)   the administration, conservation or disposal of the child's property.

The issues listed in (a) to (f)—This list is not exhaustive but is set out to identify some of the issues that may be covered by the Convention. See further the *Lagarde Report*, paras 18–36.

Measures—No definition is provided but since it refers to Art 1 it must be confined to decisions made and actions taken by the judicial or administrative authorities of the Contracting States and that can be enforced.

The issues listed in (a)–(f)—This list is not exhaustive list but identifies some of the issues that may be covered by the Convention. See further the *Lagarde Report*, paras 18–36.

"rights of custody" (Art 3(b))—Note that the definition is similar to that in Art 5 of the Hague Convention 1980. See also para 3.22 of the *Handbook* for situations that may be covered under this definition.

Guardianship etc—This will cover situations such as a guardianship order under CA 1989 or guardianship that may arise on the death of a parent where parental responsibility for a child is exercised by a person other than a parent.

"designation and functions of any person or body" (Art 3(d))—This could include any person who has the care and responsibility for a child temporarily or for a defined period, for example when a child is on a school or holiday outing.

Supervision by a public authority—See further, the *Handbook*, para 3.28 and generally paras 3.15–3.30.

"the administration, conservation or disposal of the child's property" (Art 3(g))—This would include the authority of a person to represent the child in order to authorise or approve a sale or purchase of property, but it does not seek to interfere with substantive rules of property or trusts law (see the *Lagarde Report*, paras 25 and 32). See also Art 55, which permits Contracting States to reserve jurisdiction to its authorities to take measures directed to the protection of a child's property that is situated on its territory and the right not to recognise any parental responsibility or measures insofar as they are incompatible with any measures taken by its authorities in relation to that property.

Article 4

The Convention does not apply to –

- (a) the establishment or contesting of a parent-child relationship;
- (b) decisions on adoption, measures preparatory to adoption, or the annulment or revocation of adoption;
- (c) the name and forenames of the child;
- (d) emancipation;
- (e) maintenance obligations;
- (f) trusts or succession;
- (g) social security;
- (h) public measures of a general nature in matters of education or health;
- (i) measures taken as a result of penal offences committed by children;
- (j) decisions on the right of asylum and on immigration.

Matters not covered by the Convention—This list is exhaustive and it is apparent that some of the matters set out are not concerned with the protection of a child and others (such as maintenance obligations) will be covered by other international instruments. (For further information on why and how far the above matters are excluded, see the *Handbook*, paras 3.31–3.51.)

CHAPTER II
JURISDICTION

Article 5

(1) The judicial or administrative authorities of the Contracting State of the habitual residence of the child have jurisdiction to take measures directed to the protection of the child's person or property.

(2) Subject to Article 7, in case of a change of the child's habitual residence to another Contracting State, the authorities of the State of the new habitual residence have jurisdiction.

Jurisdiction—The Convention determines only the Contracting States whose authorities have jurisdiction to take measures directed at the protection of the child's person or property, but not the authority within the Contracting State that is competent to do so, which question is left to the national procedural law. The Convention rules apply where a child is habitually resident in a Contracting State that is not a Brussels IIA State (see Council Regulation (EC) No 2201/2003, Art 61(a)). Thus, in what will be the vast majority of cases, where the child is habitually resident in the European Union, in respect of matters falling within its scope Brussels IIA must be applied. Where, however, the child is habitually resident in a Contracting State that is not subject to Brussels IIA, the Convention will apply.

Judicial or administrative authorities—The use of the words "judicial or administrative authorities" means that the Convention is intended to cover decisions made not only by the courts but also by other public bodies who have responsibility for child protection and are authorised to take measures to protect a child. Thus, in England and Wales the Convention will apply both to child protection measures within the scope of the Convention taken by the courts and to those taken by the local authority that do not require court intervention.

Habitual residence—Whereas the term "habitual residence" is not defined, it is the key connecting factor in the Convention and central to the determination of which State has jurisdiction to take measures directed to the protection of the child's person or property. The *Convention Handbook* stipulates that habitual residence is a factual concept to be determined by the relevant authorities on the basis of factual elements. The large number of cases under the Hague Convention 1980 and Brussels IIA may be of some relevance when dealing with the determination of habitual residence under the Convention (see **Habitual residence** under CACA 1985, Sch 1, Art 4 and under Council Regulation (EC) No 2201/2003, Art 3), but since habitual residence is a factual concept it is important to remember that there may be different considerations to be taken into account when determining the habitual residence of the child for the purposes of the Convention. In particular, it is important to note that whereas under the Hague Convention 1980 and Brussels IIA the determination of habitual residence is a prerequisite for remedies to apply and is part of the wider enquiry as to whether there has been a wrongful retention of the child, the role of habitual residence under the Convention is generally to assess which Contracting State's authorities have jurisdiction to take measures of protection and whether their decisions should be recognised and enforced in other Contracting States. Accordingly, under the Convention, habitual residence is an autonomous concept and should be interpreted in light of the objectives of the Convention rather than according to the constraints of domestic law. This would appear to suggest that the European cases concerned with the question of jurisdiction, and the concept of a degree of integration in a societal and family environment, will be central in determining whether, as a matter of fact, a child is habitually resident in a particular Contracting State for the purposes of the Convention (*Re A (Area of Freedom, Security and Justice)* (C-532/01) [2009] 2 FLR 1, ECJ; *Mercredi v Chaffe* [2011] 1 FLR 1293). Note that where a child is habitually resident in the European Union, jurisdiction must be exercised under Brussels IIA in respect of matters falling within its scope rather than Art 5 of the Convention (see Council Regulation (EC) No 2201/2003, Art 61(a)).

A change of the child's habitual residence—Jurisdiction moves with the child. Accordingly, where a child's habitual residence changes to another Contracting State, that State will have jurisdiction. Note, however, that in some cases the principal of perpetuation fori may apply under Brussels IIA (see Council Regulation (EC) No 2201/2003, Art 12 and *Re A; HA v MB (Brussels II Revised: Article 11(7) Application)* [2008] 1 FLR 289). For the situation where there has been a wrongful removal or retention, see the commentary under Art 7 below. The change of habitual residence does not act to terminate any measures already taken (see Art 14). Authorities of a Contracting State must abstain from exercising jurisdiction (other than under the emergency and temporary jurisdiction provisions of Arts 11 and 12) if, at the time of commencement of proceedings, corresponding measures have been requested from the authorities of another Contracting State having jurisdiction under Art 5 and those proceedings are still pending, save where the authority first seised declines jurisdiction (see Art 13(2)). Where a child's habitual residence changes from a Contracting State to a non-Contracting State, Art 5 will cease to apply from the time of the change of the child's habitual residence, although the Contracting State of the child's former habitual residence may still be able to take measures of protection under the Convention if Arts 11 or 12 apply.

Article 6

(1) For refugee children and children who, due to disturbances occurring in their country, are internationally displaced, the authorities of the Contracting State on the territory of which these children are present as a result of their displacement have the jurisdiction provided for in paragraph 1 of Article 5.

(2) The provisions of the preceding paragraph also apply to children whose habitual residence cannot be established.

Internationally displaced children—This term is intended to be sufficiently broad to surmount the limits that individual States may place on the definition of "refugee" (see the *Handbook*, para 4.13). The *Lagarde Report* (para 44) suggests that these are likely to be "limited to those who have left their countries because of conditions which were arising there, and who often are not accompanied and, in any case, are temporarily or definitively deprived of their parents".

Jurisdiction—The jurisdiction in cases of refugee children or children internationally displaced due to disturbances occurring in their country is based on the presence of those children in a Contracting State. The concept of "presence" denotes mere physical presence in the territory of the Contracting State concerned. Note that where a child is a refugee or internationally displaced, both Brussels IIA and the Convention will apply.

Children whose habitual residence cannot be established—Where the habitual residence of a child cannot be established, jurisdiction is based on the presence of the child in the territory of the Contracting State. Where the habitual residence of the child becomes established, the jurisdiction under Art 6(2) will cease and the jurisdiction of the Contracting State will become limited to taking necessary urgent or provisional protective measures under Arts 11 and 12. It should not be lightly concluded that a child's habitual residence cannot be established. Note that where a child has no habitual residence, both Brussels IIA and the Convention will apply.

Article 7

(1) In case of wrongful removal or retention of the child, the authorities of the Contracting State in which the child was habitually resident immediately before the removal or retention keep their jurisdiction until the child has acquired a habitual residence in another State, and

  (a) each person, institution or other body having rights of custody has acquiesced in the removal or retention; or

  (b) the child has resided in that other State for a period of at least one year after the person, institution or other body having rights of custody has or should have had knowledge of the whereabouts of the child, no request for return lodged within that period is still pending, and the child is settled in his or her new environment.

(2) The removal or the retention of a child is to be considered wrongful where –

  (a) it is in breach of rights of custody attributed to a person, an institution or any other body, either jointly or alone, under the law of the State in which the child was habitually resident immediately before the removal or retention; and

  (b) at the time of removal or retention those rights were actually exercised, either jointly or alone, or would have been so exercised but for the removal or retention.

The rights of custody mentioned in sub-paragraph a above, may arise in particular by operation of law or by reason of a judicial or administrative decision, or by reason of an agreement having legal effect under the law of that State.

(3) So long as the authorities first mentioned in paragraph 1 keep their jurisdiction, the authorities of the Contracting State to which the child has been removed or in which he or she has been retained can take only such urgent measures under Article 11 as are necessary for the protection of the person or property of the child.

Scope—Art 7 deals with an important jurisdictional ground in cases concerning international child abduction. The State of the child's habitual residence immediately before the wrongful removal or retention will retain its jurisdiction until the child acquires habitual residence in another State provided that either there has been acquiescence or the child has resided in the new Contracting State for at least 1 year after those having rights of custody have or should have had knowledge of the whereabouts of the child and no request for return lodged within that period is pending and the child is settled in his/her new environment (ie the child has become settled). This Article is bound to have an impact on the Hague Convention 1980.

Habitual residence—This is not defined but, as with the Hague Convention 1980 and Brussels IIA, it is central to the determination of which State has jurisdiction. Issues of whether this should be determined on the basis of the traditional English approach (set out in *Re J (A Minor) (Abduction: Custody Rights)* [1990] 2 FLR 442 and *Re P-J (Abduction: Habitual Residence: Consent)* [2009] 2 FLR 1051) or the European approach of the "centre of interests" test will undoubtedly arise (see the 1980 Hague Convention under CACA 1985, Sch 1, where this is discussed in detail). Some insight on how those drafting the Convention intended it be determined may be obtained from the *Handbook*, where at para 4.5 it is stated that habitual residence is fact-specific and has to determined on the basis of "factual elements" and that it is an autonomous concept and should be interpreted in the light of the objective of the Convention rather than under domestic law constraints. This appears to suggest that the approach adopted by the UK courts in cases under the 1980 Hague Convention would not be the appropriate test but that the European approach will be the preferred option, as the Convention is concerned with determining which State has jurisdiction and is better placed to deal with the case and to ensure that judgments and orders of the Contracting States should be recognised and enforced.

"acquiesced" (Art 1(a))—This is not defined. Consent or acquiescence is one of the grounds of opposing a return order under the 1980 Hague Convention so the case-law that has developed under that Convention may provide some guidance (see the 1980 Hague Convention under CACA 1985, Sch 1).

"the child has resided in that other State" (Art 1(b))—Contrast this provision with that under Art 12 of the 1980 Convention, where the period of 1 year begins from the date of the wrongful removal or retention. Under the 1996 Convention, it will be necessary first to establish that the child has acquired a habitual residence in the new State (State B) and then to establish that the child has lived in State B for at least 1 year after the person, institution or other body having "rights of custody" has or should have had knowledge of the child's whereabouts. It must also be shown that no request for return lodged within that period is still pending and that the child is settled in his or her new environment. However, where there is a need to take urgent measures to protect a child, the State where the child or his property is present may exercise jurisdiction under Art 12, notwithstanding that it does not have jurisdiction under Art 7, but such measures will lapse as soon as a Contracting State that has jurisdiction under Arts 5-10 has taken appropriate protective measures. (See further under Art 11.)

Article 8

(1) By way of exception, the authority of a Contracting State having jurisdiction under Article 5 or 6, if it considers that the authority of another Contracting State would be better placed in the particular case to assess the best interests of the child, may either

- request that other authority, directly or with the assistance of the Central Authority of its State, to assume jurisdiction to take such measures of protection as it considers to be necessary, or
- suspend consideration of the case and invite the parties to introduce such a request before the authority of that other State.

(2) The Contracting States whose authorities may be addressed as provided in the preceding paragraph are

(a) a State of which the child is a national,
(b) a State in which property of the child is located,
(c) a State whose authorities are seised of an application for divorce or legal separation of the child's parents, or for annulment of their marriage,
(d) a State with which the child has a substantial connection.

(3) The authorities concerned may proceed to an exchange of views.

(4) The authority addressed as provided in paragraph 1 may assume jurisdiction, in place of the authority having jurisdiction under Article 5 or 6, if it considers that this is in the child's best interests.

Scope—This Article (along with Art 9) applies to cases where a State does not have jurisdiction but is better placed to assess the best interests of the child and the Contracting State that does have jurisdiction may transfer jurisdiction for the purposes of protective measures being taken (provided that a connection between that State and the child is established on the basis of the criteria set out in Art 8(2)). Both the requesting State and the requested State must be satisfied that the transfer would allow a better assessment of the child's best interests (ie both States must agree to the transfer). The assumption of jurisdiction on such a transfer would not be permanent. The transfer may involve a transfer of a specific issue. The *Handbook* provides further guidance on this. See also Brussels IIA, Art 15 and *VC v GC (Jurisdiction: Brussels II Revised Art 12)* [2013] 1 FLR 244, where a transfer was refused in the child's best interest, and *Mercredi v Chaffe* [2011] 1 FLR 1293.

"request that other authority" (Art 8(1))—The request may be made directly or with the assistance of the Central Authority or it may stay proceedings to enable the parties to make the request before the authority of the other State. Parental Responsibility and Measures for the Protection of Children (International Obligations) (England and Wales and Northern Ireland) Regulations 2010, reg 3(2) enables the court in England and Wales to remove a stay granted for these purposes if jurisdiction is not assumed within the period for which the stay was granted or the parties do not within the time limit specified by the court make a request to the authority in the other Contracting State to assume jurisdiction.

"The authorities concerned may proceed to an exchange of views" (Art 8(3))—This provision implies that there will be liaison between the liaison judges and Central Authorities of the respective States as there is in international child abduction and under the Hague Convention 1980.

Central Authority—In England, this is the Lord Chancellor but the functions will be discharged by the International Child Abduction Unit; in Wales, by the Welsh Ministers; in Scotland, by the Scottish Ministers; and in Northern Ireland, by the Department of Justice.

Article 9

(1) If the authorities of a Contracting State referred to in Article 8, paragraph 2, consider that they are better placed in the particular case to assess the child's best interests, they may either

– request the competent authority of the Contracting State of the habitual residence of the child, directly or with the assistance of the Central Authority of that State, that they be authorised to exercise jurisdiction to take the measures of protection which they consider to be necessary, or

– invite the parties to introduce such a request before the authority of the Contracting State of the habitual residence of the child.

(2) The authorities concerned may proceed to an exchange of views.

(3) The authority initiating the request may exercise jurisdiction in place of the authority of the Contracting State of the habitual residence of the child only if the latter authority has accepted the request.

Scope—This Article should be read alongside Art 8, which permits transfers to be made from authorities with jurisdiction under Arts 5 and 6. Art 9 permits requests to be made to the competent authority of the child's habitual residence (ie having jurisdiction under Art 5). Thus, under Art 9 the request may only be made to the Contracting State of the child's habitual residence and it is thus narrower than the provisions under Art 8. Note also that the jurisdiction may only be exercised by the State that does not have jurisdiction if the Contracting State of the child's habitual residence agrees and accepts the request. The procedure for a transfer of jurisdiction is the same as that provided for Brussels IIA, Art 15. FPR 2010, rr 12.60–12.66 apply to such applications.

Article 10

(1) Without prejudice to Articles 5 to 9, the authorities of a Contracting State exercising jurisdiction to decide upon an application for divorce or legal separation of the parents of a child habitually resident in another Contracting State, or for annulment of their marriage, may, if the law of their State so provides, take measures directed to the protection of the person or property of such child if

(a)   at the time of commencement of the proceedings, one of his or her parents habitually resides in that State and one of them has parental responsibility in relation to the child, and

(b)   the jurisdiction of these authorities to take such measures has been accepted by the parents, as well as by any other person who has parental responsibility in relation to the child, and is in the best interests of the child.

(2) The jurisdiction provided for by paragraph 1 to take measures for the protection of the child ceases as soon as the decision allowing or refusing the application for divorce, legal separation or annulment of the marriage has become final, or the proceedings have come to an end for another reason.

Scope—Art 10 is one of the exceptions to the general rule that measures of protection in relation to children should be taken by the judicial/administrative authorities of the Contracting State (CS) in which the child is habitually resident. It is possible for the authorities of a CS exercising jurisdiction in an application for divorce, legal separation or annulment of the marriage of the parents of a child habitually resident in another Contracting State to take measures relating to the person and property of the child if the cumulative conditions set out in Art 10(1)(a),(b) are met. Such a situation may occur, for example, where a parent lawfully relocates with a child from one CS to another following the breakdown of the marriage and the other parent remains in the first CS and issues proceedings for divorce there. It would, of course, be a matter for the law of the CS where the proceedings were issued to determine whether it had jurisdiction to hear them and to determine whether its law permits it to take such measures relating to the person and/or property of the child in such circumstances (see the *Handbook*, para 4.26, note 131). This jurisdiction ceases when the divorce proceedings come to an end. This might be when the proceedings have resulted in a decision that has become final, granting or refusing the request for divorce, or for another reason such as the withdrawal or lapsing of the request or the death of a party (*Handbook*, para 4.27). The date on which the divorce proceedings come to an end is a matter for determination by the law of the Contracting State in which they take place (*Handbook*, para 4.28). See also the example at 4(e) of the *Handbook*.

Article 11

(1) In all cases of urgency, the authorities of any Contracting State in whose territory the child or property belonging to the child is present have jurisdiction to take any necessary measures of protection.

(2) The measures taken under the preceding paragraph with regard to a child habitually resident in a Contracting State shall lapse as soon as the authorities which have jurisdiction under Article 5 to 10 have taken the measures required by the situation.

(3) The measures taken under paragraph 1 with regard to a child who is habitually resident in a non-Contracting State shall lapse in each Contracting State as soon as measures required by the situation and taken by the authorities of another State are recognised in the Contracting State in question.

Jurisdiction—The jurisdiction to take necessary measures of protection in cases of urgency is based on the child being present in the territory of the relevant Contracting State. The concept of "presence" denotes mere physical presence in the territory of the Contracting State concerned. The jurisdiction of a Contracting State based on urgency is a jurisdiction concurrent with the general jurisdiction under Arts 5–10 and subordinate to the latter jurisdiction. Art 11(2),(3) provides that necessary measures taken under Art 11(1) will lapse either once the authorities of the Contracting State that has general jurisdiction under Arts 5–10 has taken measures required by the situation or, where the child is habitually resident in a non-Contracting State, once the measures required by the situation and taken by the authorities of another State are recognised by the Contracting State in question. Note that Art 13 of the Convention does not apply where necessary measures of protection are taken under Art 11. Art 11 may be relied on for necessary protective measures in cases of wrongful removal (see Art 7(3)). The Parental Responsibility and Measures for the Protection of Children (International Obligations) (England and Wales and Northern Ireland) Regulations 2010, r 5 amends CA 1989, s 38 where Art 11 applies to permit an interim care or interim supervision order to be made in respect of the child to provide temporary protection, notwithstanding that the court has no international jurisdiction to make a final care or supervision order.

Urgency—The Convention does not define "urgency" and it will be for the judicial or administrative authorities of the Contracting State in question to determine whether a particular situation is one of urgency. The *Handbook* to the Convention suggests that a useful approach to establishing whether a given situation is one of urgency is to ask "whether the child is likely to suffer irreparable harm or to have his or her protection or interests compromised if a measure is not taken to protect him/her in the period that is likely to elapse before the authorities with general jurisdiction under Arts 5 to 10 can take the necessary measures of protection" (*Handbook*, para 6.2 and the examples in para 6.4).

Necessary measures of protection—The measures of protection available under Art 11 will be materially the same as those that can be taken under Arts 5–10 in accordance with the provisions of Arts 3 and 4. However, the Convention does not define "necessary" and it will be a matter for the judicial or administrative authorities in each Contracting State to determine, based upon the facts of the particular case, what measures within the scope of the Convention are necessary to deal with a situation of urgency (*Handbook*, para 6.5).

Recognition and enforcement of measures taken under Art 11—Measures of protection taken in cases of urgency under Art 11 are entitled to recognition and enforcement in accordance with Ch IV of the Convention (see Art 23 et seq). The grounds of non-recognition are limited in cases of urgency (see Art 23(2)(b) and (c)).

Article 12

(1) Subject to Article 7, the authorities of a Contracting State in whose territory the child or property belonging to the child is present have jurisdiction to take measures of a provisional character for the protection of the person or property of the child which have a territorial effect limited to the State in question, in so far as such measures are not incompatible with measures already taken by authorities which have jurisdiction under Articles 5 to 10.

(2) The measures taken under the preceding paragraph with regard to a child habitually resident in a Contracting State shall lapse as soon as the authorities which have jurisdiction under Articles 5 to 10 have taken a decision in respect of the measures of protection which may be required by the situation.

(3) The measures taken under paragraph 1 with regard to a child who is habitually resident in a non-Contracting State shall lapse in the Contracting State where the measures were taken as soon as measures required by the situation and taken by the authorities of another State are recognised in the Contracting State in question.

Scope—This Article relates to States that are Contracting States and situations where one State is a Contracting State and the State of habitual residence is not. It authorises a Contracting State to exercise jurisdiction to take "provisional measures" in non-urgent situations to protect the child or his property, provided the child or his property is present within that State (although it does not have jurisdiction under the provisions of Arts 5–10). However, the measures taken will only have effect within the territory of the State in question and provided that the measures taken are not incompatible with any measures already taken by a State with jurisdiction under Arts 5–10. Any measure taken will also lapse as soon as the Contracting State with jurisdiction takes protective measures. Where the child is habitually resident in a non-Contracting State, any provisional measures taken in the Contracting State in relation to the child or his property will lapse on measures being taken by the authorities of another State being recognised in the Contracting State. The provisions in this Article are aimed at dealing with situations that could arise when a child is on holiday or attending an educational establishment. Although there may appear to be similarities between this Article and Art 11, there are subtle differences. The effects of Art 12 orders are limited in that they will only have effect within the territory of the State in question. Art 12 does not apply to a child who has been abducted (see Art 7(3)) and it specifically provides that the measures taken must not be incompatible with measures taken by an authority of competent jurisdiction. However, subject to them not being incompatible, the measures can be taken even if there is no urgency. There is no equivalent provision within Brussels IIA, which only provides for measures to be taken if the situation is urgent.

Provisional measures—This is not defined but the *Handbook*, by way of example of when this Article may be invoked, refers to a situation where there is a need for a child to be placed in alternative care under state supervision or where the child's placement has broken down and an alternative placement is needed in the best interests of the child. Where provisional measures are taken under this Article by a Contracting State, that State should inform the authorities of the State in which the child is habitually resident of the measures taken. (See the *Handbook* para 7.49 and generally Ch 7.)

PART VI

Article 13

(1) The authorities of a Contracting State which have jurisdiction under Articles 5 to 10 to take measures for the protection of the person or property of the child must abstain from exercising this jurisdiction if, at the time of the commencement of the proceedings, corresponding measures have been requested from the authorities of another Contracting State having jurisdiction under Articles 5 to 10 at the time of the request and are still under consideration.

(2) The provisions of the preceding paragraph shall not apply if the authorities before whom the request for measures was initially introduced have declined jurisdiction.

Scope—Art 13 provides for the resolution of possible conflicts of jurisdiction in cases where the authorities of more than one Contracting State (CS) have jurisdiction to take measures of protection in respect of a child. The authorities of a CS that has jurisdiction under Arts 5–10 must abstain from exercising it if, at the time of the commencement of the proceedings, "corresponding measures" have been requested from the authorities of another CS having jurisdiction under Arts 5–10 at the time of the request and those measures are still under consideration. "Corresponding measures" is not defined in the Convention but it appears that, for Art 13 to apply, the requests before both the CSs must be the same or similar in substance (*Handbook*, para 4.31, and *Lagarde Report*, para 79). For example, if one CS is seised of custody proceedings in respect of a child and another CS is requested to take measures of protection in relation to his property, the latter CS may decide that "corresponding measures" have not been requested from the first CS and it can, therefore, hear the request regarding the child's property. Art 13 applies for as long as the proceedings in respect of the "corresponding measures" in the other CS are still under consideration. However, it does not apply if the authorities of the CS initially seised have declined jurisdiction (Art 13(2)). The *Lagarde Report* states that the ability of the authorities of the first CS to decline or renounce their jurisdiction enables that CS to give precedence to the CS second seised, despite Art 13(1), if it is considered a more appropriate forum. However, to ensure the protection of the child where a CS is considering declining jurisdiction it will usually be good practice for communication to take place between the two CSs involved (through Central Authorities or direct judicial communications) to ensure that no gap in the protection of the child results. See the examples at 4(f) and (g) in the *Handbook*.

Article 14

The measures taken in application of Articles 5 to 10 remain in force according to their terms, even if a change of circumstances has eliminated the basis upon which jurisdiction was founded, so long as the authorities which have jurisdiction under the Convention have not modified, replaced or terminated such measures.

The measures taken remain in force—The provisions of Art 14 ensure that measures taken by an authority having jurisdiction under Arts 5–10 to protect a child continue, where for instance the child subsequently moves and establishes habitual residence in another Contracting State, until the authorities in the new State modify, replace or terminate those measures. The measures taken will, however, continue only for the duration of the term specified. If the term refers to the occurrence of an event, the measures will lapse when the event occurs. For examples of instances to which Art 14 applies, see the *Handbook*, Ch 8. When provisional measures are taken, the order should specify either the period for which such measures are to remain in force or the occurrence or termination of an event.

"change of circumstances"—This will depend on the basis on which jurisdiction was based within Arts 5–10. If the jurisdiction was based on Arts 8 and 9, the change will be the conclusion of the proceedings.

CHAPTER III
APPLICABLE LAW

Article 15

(1) In exercising their jurisdiction under the provisions of Chapter II, the authorities of the Contracting States shall apply their own law.

(2) However, in so far as the protection of the person or the property of the child requires, they may exceptionally apply or take into consideration the law of another State with which the situation has a substantial connection.

(3) If the child's habitual residence changes to another Contracting State, the law of that other State governs, from the time of the change, the conditions of application of the measures taken in the State of the former habitual residence.

Modifications—Art 15(1) modified for certain purposes by SI 2010/1898, reg 7.

Scope—Art 15(1) applies the basic principle that the Contracting State should apply its own law when exercising jurisdiction, but Art 15(2) makes it clear that this principle may be departed from in exceptional circumstances and the law of another State with which the situation has a substantial connection may be applied or taken into consideration. It should be noted that Art 15(2) refers to the "the law of another State", and not a Contracting State, and thus the law applied in such circumstances may be that of a non-Contracting State. The Handbook suggests that the authorities should be satisfied that the application of the foreign law under this provision is in the best interests of the child. (See the *Handbook* for examples of instances where the law of another State may be applied and see also the *Lagarde Report*, para 89.)

"In exercising ... jurisdiction under the provision of Chapter II" (Art 15(1)—This provision should be read with the provisions set out in Parental Responsibility and Measures for the Protection of Children (International Obligations) (England and Wales and Northern Ireland) Regulations 2010, reg 6, which provides that the reference to Ch II of the Convention in Art 15(1) is to be read as including a reference to Ch II of the Council Regulations (ie Brussels IIA).

"If the child's habitual residence changes to another Contracting State" (Art 15(3))—The provisions of Art 15(3) thus do not apply to non-Contracting States. In such a case, the *Handbook* (para 9.8) suggests that the international private law rules of the non-Contracting State would apply to determine if the measures of protection could be recognised in that State and the conditions under which it could be applied. Where there is a change in the child's habitual residence, the law of that State will govern from the time of the change. If measures to protect the child have been taken to provide continuity pursuant to Art 14, those measures will remain in force until they have been modified, replaced or terminated.

"the conditions of application of the measures" (Art 15(3))—This is not defined. The *Handbook* suggests that the term relates to the way the measure is to be exercised in the "other State" (State B) but it also makes reference to the difficulty in distinguishing between the subsistence of a measure taken under Art 14 by State A that is to continue and applying "the conditions of application of that measure" (ie the manner of its application) under the law of State B. (See the *Handbook* for further guidance.) When considering this Article, reference should also be made to Art 22, which allows the application of the measure to be refused if this would be manifestly contrary to the public policy, taking into account the best interests of the child.

Article 16

(1) The attribution or extinction of parental responsibility by operation of law, without the intervention of a judicial or administrative authority, is governed by the law of the State of the habitual residence of the child.

(2) The attribution or extinction of parental responsibility by an agreement or a unilateral act, without intervention of a judicial or administrative authority, is governed by the law of the State of the child's habitual residence at the time when the agreement or unilateral act takes effect.

(3) Parental responsibility which exists under the law of the State of the child's habitual residence subsists after a change of that habitual residence to another State.

(4) If the child's habitual residence changes, the attribution of parental responsibility by operation of law to a person who does not already have such responsibility is governed by the law of the State of the new habitual residence.

Scope—Art 16 stipulates the law applicable to the attribution or extinction of parental responsibility without intervention by judicial or administrative authority (Art 16(1),(2)) and what happens to the attribution (but not extinction) of parental responsibility when the habitual residence of a child changes (Art 16(3)). Note that Art 22 of the Convention provides a general release from applying these provisions

PART VI

where to do so would be manifestly contrary to the public policy of the State, taking into account the child's best interests. Specific provision is made by FPR 2010, r 12.4 for notice of proceedings to be given to a person with parental responsibility conferred by the law of another State. Pursuant to FPR 2010, r 12.71(1)(b), an application may be made for declaration as to the extent, or existence, of parental responsibility in relation to a child under Art 16.

Parental responsibility—Art 1(2) of the Convention defines the term "parental responsibility" as including "parental authority, or any analogous relationship of authority determining the rights, powers and responsibilities of parents, guardians or other legal representatives in relation to the person or the property of the child".

Agreement—Under the law of England and Wales, the "agreement" will be a parental responsibility agreement under CA 1989, s 4(1)(b).

Article 17

The exercise of parental responsibility is governed by the law of the State of the child's habitual residence. If the child's habitual residence changes, it is governed by the law of the State of the new habitual residence.

Scope—Art 17 stipulates the law governing the exercise of parental responsibility, namely its exercise is always governed by the law of the State of the child's current habitual residence.

Article 18

The parental responsibility referred to in Article 16 may be terminated, or the conditions of its exercise modified, by measures taken under this Convention.

Scope—Art 18 provides for measures of protection to be taken under the Convention, which have the effect of terminating or modifying parental responsibility subject to the Convention rules on jurisdiction and applicable law.

Article 19

(1) The validity of a transaction entered into between a third party and another person who would be entitled to act as the child's legal representative under the law of the State where the transaction was concluded cannot be contested, and the third party cannot be held liable, on the sole ground that the other person was not entitled to act as the child's legal representative under the law designated by the provisions of this Chapter, unless the third party knew or should have known that the parental responsibility was governed by the latter law.

(2) The preceding paragraph applies only if the transaction was entered into between persons present on the territory of the same State.

Scope—Art 19 stipulates the circumstances in which a third party will be held liable if they enter into a contract with a person whom they believe to be the holder of parental responsibility but who in fact is not. Such a third party may not be held liable on the ground that the other person was not entitled to act as the child's legal representative under the law designated by the rules of the Convention unless that third party knew, or should have known, that the parental responsibility was governed by that law (see also Art 40). The protection is not entirely absolute because the requirement "should have known" suggests that the third party has a duty to exercise due diligence. The protection thus will only apply if the third party acted in good faith. Note also that this protection is only available "if the transaction was entered into between persons present on the territory of the same State" (Art 19(2)).

Article 20

The provisions of this Chapter apply even if the law designated by them is the law of a non-Contracting State.

Article 21

(1) In this Chapter the term "law" means the law in force in a State other than its choice of law rules.

(2) However, if the law applicable according to Article 16 is that of a non-Contracting State and if the choice of law rules of that State designate the law of another non-Contracting State which would apply its own law, the law of the latter State applies. If that other non-Contracting State would not apply its own law, the applicable law is that designated by Article 16.

Scope—This Article excludes the choice of law rules save for the exceptions in Arts 15(2) and 21(2). Art 21(2) is designed so as not to interfere with the private international law rules that apply between non-Contracting States (*Handbook*, para 9.24).

Article 22

The application of the law designated by the provisions of this Chapter can be refused only if this application would be manifestly contrary to public policy, taking into account the best interests of the child.

Taking account of the best interests of the child—In applying this exception, one must not lose sight of what is in the best interests of the child and Art 22 clearly indicates that the best interests of the child remains the focal point of any decision. The *Handbook* (para 9.26) suggests that the "use of public policy" to refuse the application of the designated law can only occur when the best interests of child are taken into account. Therefore, the emphasis is more on what is in the best interests of the child.

CHAPTER IV
RECOGNITION AND ENFORCEMENT

Article 23

(1) The measures taken by the authorities of a Contracting State shall be recognised by operation of law in all other Contracting States.

(2) Recognition may however be refused –

    (a) if the measure was taken by an authority whose jurisdiction was not based on one of the grounds provided for in Chapter II;

    (b) if the measure was taken, except in a case of urgency, in the context of a judicial or administrative proceeding, without the child having been provided the opportunity to be heard, in violation of fundamental principles of procedure of the requested State;

    (c) on the request of any person claiming that the measure infringes his or her parental responsibility, if such measure was taken, except in a case of urgency, without such person having been given an opportunity to be heard;

    (d) if such recognition is manifestly contrary to public policy of the requested State, taking into account the best interests of the child;

    (e) if the measure is incompatible with a later measure taken in the non-Contracting State of the habitual residence of the child, where this later measure fulfils the requirements for recognition in the requested State;

    (f) if the procedure provided in Article 33 has not been complied with.

Scope—The aim of the Convention is to create a unified approach to the recognition of measures taken in a Contracting State (CS) in all other CSs so as to reduce the need to issue fresh proceedings in relation to cases that have already been adjudicated upon by another CS. Art 23(1) confirms this position, save for the exceptions set out in Art 23(2). The *Handbook* also suggests that recognition of the measure by operation of law will be sufficient where the measure is voluntarily complied with or where there is no opposition (*Handbook*, para 10.3 and see also the examples given). The Convention does not set out any formal procedure but it would be good practice for written confirmation to be provided and in an emergency a telephone call may suffice (see the *Handbook*, para 10.2). Where there is no compliance or where there is opposition to the measures, it may be necessary to commence enforcement proceedings under Art 26.

"Recognition may however be refused" (Art 23(2))—Recognition may only be refused on the limited grounds set out in Art 23(2). This is an exhaustive list of circumstances where recognition of a measure taken by a Contracting State may be refused. The power to refuse is not mandatory and, therefore, there is a discretion to recognise the measures taken even if the conditions are met.

"manifestly contrary to public policy" (Art 23(2)(d))—See *Re L (Brussels II Revised: Appeal)* [2013] 1 FLR 430.

Jurisdiction not based on the grounds under the Convention—This may occur where State A has taken measures under its own domestic law of jurisdiction that does not accord with the jurisdictional grounds under the Convention (e g where jurisdiction was based on nationality or presence, State B may verify what the ground of jurisdiction was, but pursuant to Art 25 it is bound by the findings of fact on which the authority of State A based its jurisdiction).

Article 24

Without prejudice to Article 23, paragraph 1, any interested person may request from the competent authorities of a Contracting State that they decide on the recognition or non-recognition of a measure taken in another Contracting State. The procedure is governed by the law of the requested State.

Scope—This Article permits any interested party to seek a declaration from the authorities of a Contracting State (CS) whether or not an order in their favour (e g for contact) will be recognised in another CS (i e an advanced recognition of the order). There is no time limit within which a decision must be given, neither is there any requirement as under Art 26 for a simple and rapid procedure.

The procedure is governed by the law of the requested State—The procedure to be followed in England and Wales is set out in FPR 2010, Pt 31 and PD31A.

Article 25

The authority of the requested State is bound by the findings of fact on which the authority of the State where the measure was taken based its jurisdiction.

Article 26

(1) If measures taken in one Contracting State and enforceable there require enforcement in another Contracting State, they shall, upon request by an interested party, be declared enforceable or registered for the purpose of enforcement in that other State according to the procedure provided in the law of the latter State.

(2) Each Contracting State shall apply to the declaration of enforceability or registration a simple and rapid procedure.

(3) The declaration of enforceability or registration may be refused only for one of the reasons set out in Article 23, paragraph 2.

"procedure provided in the law of the latter State" (Art 26(1))—The procedure for applying for enforcement will be that provided by the domestic law of the requested State. This recognises that the internal laws of enforcement of Contracting States may differ. It will be of interest to see how contact orders made in a Contracting State (CS) that are not drafted in an injunctive form will be enforced in the UK or how the matter will be dealt with if a *Gillick*-competent child refuses to attend for contact, particularly when this Article clearly envisages that if the measures taken in the CS of origin are enforceable there and require enforcement in another CS, that measure "shall be declared enforceable in that other State". Also note that the application may be refused only on the grounds set out in Art 23(2) and it is expected that this will be applied strictly, as occurs in cases under the Hague Convention 1980. These grounds mirror those in Brussels IIA. As regards the effect of a declaration of enforcement, see Art 28. The procedure for making an application is set out in FPR 2010, Pt 31 and PD31A.

"an interested party" (Art 26(1))—Any interested party may request that the measure be declared enforceable or registered for enforcement in the requested State and require enforcement. Contrast this with Art 24 in relation to recognition or non-recognition, under which any interested party has merely a right to apply.

"simple and rapid procedure" (Art 26(2))—Unlike the Hague Convention 1980 and Brussels IIA (although the Article provides for a rapid disposal) there is no time limit set within which such proceedings should be completed. The *Handbook* does not provide any guidance. As an analogy, applying the decisions under the Hague Convention 1980 it could be argued that failure to provide an effective speedy procedure and to enforce the measures is a breach of the rights of the person in whose favour the order was made and that of the child under Art 8 of the European Convention on Human Rights.

Article 27

Without prejudice to such review as is necessary in the application of the preceding Articles, there shall be no review of the merits of the measure taken.

There shall be no review of the merits of the measure taken—This is a mandatory provision. As with an application under the Hague Convention 1980, in determining an application for a declaration of recognition, non-recognition registration and enforcement, the authorities of the Contracting State to whom the application is made must not review the merits of the measures taken and thus reopen the case. (See also Art 25.)

Article 28

Measures taken in one Contracting State and declared enforceable, or registered for the purpose of enforcement, in another Contracting State shall be enforced in the latter State as if they had been taken by the authorities of that State. Enforcement takes place in accordance with the law of the requested State to the extent provided by such law, taking into consideration the best interests of the child.

"taking into consideration the best interests of the child"—The reference to "the best interests of the child" in Art 28 should not be interpreted as an invitation to a further enquiry on the merits (see *Handbook*, para 10.17). In any event, any review of the merits is prohibited under the mandatory provisions of Art 27.

CHAPTER V
CO-OPERATION

Article 29

(1) A Contracting State shall designate a Central Authority to discharge the duties which are imposed by the Convention on such authorities.

(2) Federal States, States with more than one system of law or States having autonomous territorial units shall be free to appoint more than one Central Authority and to specify the territorial or personal extent of their functions. Where a State has appointed more than one Central Authority, it shall designate the Central Authority to which any communication may be addressed for transmission to the appropriate Central Authority within that State.

Central Authority—See under Art 8 and note that the Central Authority for Wales under this Convention is not the same as under the Hague Convention 1980 and Brussels IIR and, therefore, it will be necessary to ensure that there is an effective and efficient level of communication and collaboration between them where there is an interplay between these three international instruments.

Article 30

(1) Central Authorities shall co-operate with each other and promote co-operation amongst the competent authorities in their States to achieve the purposes of the Convention.

(2) They shall, in connection with the application of the Convention, take appropriate steps to provide information as to the laws of, and services available in, their States relating to the protection of children.

Scope—There are two situations in which there is an obligation to cooperate, consult and share information, namely when an authority with jurisdiction under Arts 5–10 is contemplating the placement of a child in another Contracting State (see Art 33) and in any case where a child is exposed to serious danger and the competent authorities of the Contracting State where measures for the protection of the child have been taken or are under consideration are informed that the child's residence has changed to, or that the child is present in, another State (see Arts 36).

Article 31

The Central Authority of a Contracting State, either directly or through public authorities or other bodies, shall take all appropriate steps to –

(a)   facilitate the communications and offer the assistance provided for in Articles 8 and 9 and in this Chapter;

(b)   facilitate, by mediation, conciliation or similar means, agreed solutions for the protection of the person or property of the child in situations to which the Convention applies;

(c)   provide, on the request of a competent authority of another Contracting State, assistance in discovering the whereabouts of a child where it appears that the child may be present and in need of protection within the territory of the requested State.

Regulations—The Parental Responsibility and Measures for the Protection of Children (International Obligations) (England and Wales and Northern Ireland) Regulations 2010, reg 10 prescribes the domestic rules that apply and identifies the "public bodies and other bodies" to whom request for assistance and information may be made where a Central Authority receives a request for assistance under Art 31(c) of the Convention, either directly or via another Central Authority in the United Kingdom.

Article 32

On a request made with supporting reasons by the Central Authority or other competent authority of any Contracting State with which the child has a substantial connection, the Central Authority of the Contracting State in which the child is habitually resident and present may, directly or through public authorities or other bodies,

(a)   provide a report on the situation of the child;

(b)   request the competent authority of its State to consider the need to take measures for the protection of the person or property of the child.

Scope—The provision of a report on the situation of the child and/or a request that a Contracting State consider the need to take protective measures for the child is not mandatory. The request must be accompanied by "supporting reasons". For what is meant by "substantial connection", see the *Handbook*, para 13.82.

Regulations—The Parental Responsibility and Measures for the Protection of Children (International Obligations) (England and Wales and Northern Ireland) Regulations 2010, reg 12 prescribes the domestic rules that apply and identifies the bodies to whom a request for a written report may be made where a Central Authority thinks it appropriate to provide a report on the situation of the child under Art 32(a) of the Convention.

Article 33

(1) If an authority having jurisdiction under Articles 5 to 10 contemplates the placement of the child in a foster family or institutional care, or the provision of care by kafala or an analogous institution, and if such placement or such provision of care is to take place in another Contracting State, it shall first consult with the Central Authority or other

competent authority of the latter State. To that effect it shall transmit a report on the child together with the reasons for the proposed placement or provision of care.

(2) The decision on the placement or provision of care may be made in the requesting State only if the Central Authority or other competent authority of the requested State has consented to the placement or provision of care, taking into account the child's best interests.

Failure to comply with consultation and consent provisions—Where the procedure under Art 33(1) is not followed, the measure can be refused recognition under the Convention (see Art 23(2)(f)). See *Re AB (BIIR: Care Proceedings)* [2013] 1 FLR 168, dealing with the similar provisions of Council Regulation (EC) No 2201/2003, Art 56(1),(2). See also *HSE Ireland v SF (A Minor)* [2012] 2 FLR 1131.

Regulations—The Parental Responsibility and Measures for the Protection of Children (International Obligations) (England and Wales and Northern Ireland) Regulations 2010, reg 13 prescribes the domestic rules that apply to the transmission of a report on the child under Art 33(1) where a local authority is contemplating placing a child in another Contracting State within the meaning of Art 33.

Article 34

(1) Where a measure of protection is contemplated, the competent authorities under the Convention, if the situation of the child so requires, may request any authority of another Contracting State which has information relevant to the protection of the child to communicate such information.

(2) A Contracting State may declare that requests under paragraph 1 shall be communicated to its authorities only through its Central Authority.

Grounds for request—The request for information may only be made where the competent authority is contemplating taking a measure of protection in respect of the child and the situation of the child requires a request to be made.

Regulations—The Parental Responsibility and Measures for the Protection of Children (International Obligations) (England and Wales and Northern Ireland) Regulations 2010, reg 14 permits a public authority in England and Wales to provide information in response to a request communicated to it by the Central Authority under Art 34 of the Convention.

"Contracting State may declare" (Art 34(2))—Art 34(1) provides for the request for information to be made to "any authority" of another Contracting State unless a declaration has been made that such requests may only be made through its Central Authority. Art 63(d) requires the declaration under this Article to be made to the Government of the Kingdom of Netherlands in its capacity as the depository of the Convention (to establish whether a Contracting State has made such a declaration, see the Status table for the Convention at *www.hcch.net*). Therefore, if a request is to be made by a competent authority in England to another Contracting State, it will be necessary to ascertain whether that State has opted to have all communication (including under Art 34) to be made through its Central Authority. The UK has made such a declaration, hence the provision contained in reg 14 above.

Article 35

(1) The competent authorities of a Contracting State may request the authorities of another Contracting State to assist in the implementation of measures of protection taken under this Convention, especially in securing the effective exercise of rights of access as well as of the right to maintain direct contacts on a regular basis.

(2) The authorities of a Contracting State in which the child does not habitually reside may, on the request of a parent residing in that State who is seeking to obtain or to maintain access to the child, gather information or evidence and may make a finding on the suitability of that parent to exercise access and on the conditions under which access is to be exercised. An authority exercising jurisdiction under Articles 5 to 10 to determine an application concerning access to the child, shall admit and consider such information, evidence and finding before reaching its decision.

(3) An authority having jurisdiction under Articles 5 to 10 to decide on access may adjourn a proceeding pending the outcome of a request made under paragraph 2, in particular, when it is considering an application to restrict or terminate access rights granted in the State of the child's former habitual residence.

(4) Nothing in this Article shall prevent an authority having jurisdiction under Articles 5 to 10 from taking provisional measures pending the outcome of the request made under paragraph 2.

Scope—The provisions of Art 35 are clearly aimed on the one hand at providing child protection measures and on the other at safeguarding rights of access to a child as well as the right to maintain direct contact on a regular basis in another Contracting State.

Regulations—The Parental Responsibility and Measures for the Protection of Children (International Obligations) (England and Wales and Northern Ireland) Regulations 2010, reg 16 prescribes the domestic rules that will apply in respect of Art 35 of the Convention.

Securing the effective exercise of rights of access—Art 35 specifically seeks to secure effective rights of access, as well as the right to maintain direct contact on a regular basis. See also Art 10 of the United Nations Convention on the Rights of the Child.

Duty to consider information—Art 35(2) permits the authorities of a Contracting State in which the child is not habitually resident but in which a parent resides to gather information or evidence and make a finding on the suitability of that parent to exercise access and on the conditions under which that access is to be exercised. Where the authorities of a Contracting State in which the child does not habitually reside have gathered such information or made a finding, an authority exercising jurisdiction under Arts 5–10 must admit and consider that information, evidence and finding before reaching a decision.

Adjournment—Where an authority having jurisdiction under Arts 5–10 is waiting for the receipt of the information, evidence and finding requested pursuant to Art 35(2), it may adjourn proceedings, in particular if the proceedings concern an application to restrict or terminate rights of access granted in the State of the child's former habitual residence.

Article 36

In any case where the child is exposed to a serious danger, the competent authorities of the Contracting State where measures for the protection of the child have been taken or are under consideration, if they are informed that the child's residence has changed to, or that the child is present in another State, shall inform the authorities of that other State about the danger involved and the measures taken or under consideration.

Scope—Art 36 compels the competent authorities of a Contracting State where measures of protection have been taken or are under consideration in respect of a child who is exposed to serious danger to inform the authorities of the State to which the child's residence has changed or in which the child is present about the danger involved and the measures taken or under consideration. The information, however, should not be requested or transmitted if the conditions in Art 37 apply (see below). For examples on how this Article operates, see the *Handbook*, examples 11(c)–11(f).

Non-Contracting States—The words "another State" in Art 36 mean that the obligation to provide information about the danger to the child and the measures taken or under consideration by the Contracting State extends to children who have become resident in or are present in a non-Contracting State.

Location of a child exposed to serious danger—Where the competent authorities suspect that a child may have become resident in or is present in another Contracting State, those authorities may use Art 31(c) to ascertain the whereabouts of the child so that information can be provided pursuant to Art 36.

Article 37

An authority shall not request or transmit any information under this Chapter if to do so would, in its opinion, be likely to place the child's person or property in danger, or constitute a serious threat to the liberty or life of a member of the child's family.

Scope—The restrictions imposed by this Article apply to all authorities, which includes courts local authorities and other public bodies. It may be desirable to undertake a risk assessment regarding those who are directly connected with the child and his or her family before information is transmitted. See also the provisions of Arts 41 and 42 regarding the restriction on personal data and the need to ensure confidentiality.

Article 38

(1) Without prejudice to the possibility of imposing reasonable charges for the provision of services, Central Authorities and other public authorities of Contracting States shall bear their own costs in applying the provisions of this Chapter.

(2) Any Contracting State may enter into agreements with one or more other Contracting States concerning the allocation of charges.

"Without prejudice to the possibility of imposing reasonable charges for the provision of services" (Art 38(1))—The Parental Responsibility and Measures for the Protection of Children (International Obligations) (England and Wales and Northern Ireland) Regulations 2010, reg 16 authorises a reasonable fee to be charged for services provided under Art 35.

"public authorities"—This term in Art 38 refers to the administrative authorities of the Contracting States and not to the courts. Court costs and the cost of proceedings and lawyers do not fall within the ambit of Art 38.

Article 39

Any Contracting State may enter into agreements with one or more other Contracting States with a view to improving the application of this Chapter in their mutual relations. The States which have concluded such an agreement shall transmit a copy to the depositary of the Convention.

"The States which have concluded such an agreement"—To establish which Contracting States have concluded agreements, see the table in the notes at the beginning of this Convention.

CHAPTER VI
GENERAL PROVISIONS

Article 40

(1) The authorities of the Contracting State of the child's habitual residence, or of the Contracting State where a measure of protection has been taken, may deliver to the person having parental responsibility or to the person entrusted with protection of the child's person or property, at his or her request, a certificate indicating the capacity in which that person is entitled to act and the powers conferred upon him or her.

(2) The capacity and powers indicated in the certificate are presumed to be vested in that person, in the absence of proof to the contrary.

(3) Each Contracting State shall designate the authorities competent to draw up the certificate.

"a certificate indicating the capacity in which that person is entitled to act" (Art 40(1)—Note that this provision is not mandatory.

"shall designate the authorities competent to draw up the certificate" (Art 40(3))—This is a mandatory provision. The Contracting State competent to deliver a certificate is the Contracting State of the child's habitual residence or the Contracting State of origin of the measure. The designated authorities can be found at: *www.hcch.net*.

Content of the certificate—The certificate should usually indicate:
* Who is the holder of parental responsibility;
* Whether this results by operation of law (from the law that is applicable under Art 16) or from a measure of protection taken by a competent authority according to Ch II of the Convention;
* The powers of the person having parental responsibility; and

PART VI

- Where appropriate, the powers that the person does not have.

The capacity and powers indicated in the certificate are presumed to be vested in that person in the absence of proof to the contrary. It will, therefore, be possible for any interested party to contest the correctness of the indications appearing on the certificate, but in the absence of a contest, a third party may act on a certificate provided it is within the limits of the powers mentioned in the certificate.

Article 41

Personal data gathered or transmitted under the Convention shall be used only for the purposes for which they were gathered or transmitted.

Scope—The information gathered under the Convention must be treated confidentially and the authorities to whom the information is given must ensure its confidentiality in accordance with the law of their State (see Art 42).

Article 42

The authorities to whom information is transmitted shall ensure its confidentiality, in accordance with the law of their State.

Article 43

All documents forwarded or delivered under this Convention shall be exempt from legalisation or any analogous formality.

Article 44

Each Contracting State may designate the authorities to which requests under Articles 8, 9 and 33 are to be addressed.

Designated authorities—See under Art 8.

Article 45

(1) The designations referred to in Articles 29 and 44 shall be communicated to the Permanent Bureau of the Hague Conference on Private International Law.

(2) The declaration referred to in Article 34, paragraph 2, shall be made to the depositary of the Convention.

Article 46

A Contracting State in which different systems of law or sets of rules of law apply to the protection of the child and his or her property shall not be bound to apply the rules of the Convention to conflicts solely between such different systems or sets of rules of law.

Article 47

In relation to a State in which two or more systems of law or sets of rules of law with regard to any matter dealt with in this Convention apply in different territorial units –

(1) any reference to habitual residence in that State shall be construed as referring to habitual residence in a territorial unit;

(2) any reference to the presence of the child in that State shall be construed as referring to presence in a territorial unit;

(3) any reference to the location of property of the child in that State shall be construed as referring to location of property of the child in a territorial unit;

(4) any reference to the State of which the child is a national shall be construed as

referring to the territorial unit designated by the law of that State or, in the absence of relevant rules, to the territorial unit with which the child has the closest connection;

(5) any reference to the State whose authorities are seised of an application for divorce or legal separation of the child's parents, or for annulment of their marriage, shall be construed as referring to the territorial unit whose authorities are seised of such application;

(6) any reference to the State with which the child has a substantial connection shall be construed as referring to the territorial unit with which the child has such connection;

(7) any reference to the State to which the child has been removed or in which he or she has been retained shall be construed as referring to the relevant territorial unit to which the child has been removed or in which he or she has been retained;

(8) any reference to bodies or authorities of that State, other than Central Authorities, shall be construed as referring to those authorised to act in the relevant territorial unit;

(9) any reference to the law or procedure or authority of the State in which a measure has been taken shall be construed as referring to the law or procedure or authority of the territorial unit in which such measure was taken;

(10) any reference to the law or procedure or authority of the requested State shall be construed as referring to the law or procedure or authority of the territorial unit in which recognition or enforcement is sought.

Article 48

For the purpose of identifying the applicable law under Chapter III, in relation to a State which comprises two or more territorial units each of which has its own system of law or set of rules of law in respect of matters covered by this Convention, the following rules apply –

(a) if there are rules in force in such a State identifying which territorial unit's law is applicable, the law of that unit applies;

(b) in the absence of such rules, the law of the relevant territorial unit as defined in Article 47 applies.

Article 49

For the purpose of identifying the applicable law under Chapter III, in relation to a State which has two or more systems of law or sets of rules of law applicable to different categories of persons in respect of matters covered by this Convention, the following rules apply –

(a) if there are rules in force in such a State identifying which among such laws applies, that law applies;

(b) in the absence of such rules, the law of the system or the set of rules of law with which the child has the closest connection applies.

Article 50

This Convention shall not affect the application of the Convention of 25 October 1980 on the Civil Aspects of International Child Abduction, as between Parties to both Conventions. Nothing, however, precludes provisions of this Convention from being invoked for the purposes of obtaining the return of a child who has been wrongfully removed or retained or of organising access rights.

PART VI

The impact of the Convention on child abduction cases—Art 50 acknowledges the primacy of the 1980 Convention but, by also stating that nothing precludes its provisions "from being invoked for the purposes of obtaining the return of a child who has been wrongfully removed or retained or of organising access rights" and providing for the recognition and enforcement of custody and access orders, it provides an alternative means of dealing with child abduction, especially in situations where neither the 1980 Convention nor Brussels IIA applies.

The 1996 Convention will apply where a State is a Contracting State under the 1996 Convention but not under the 1980 Convention or where a State has acceded to the Convention but that accession is not recognised by the other State (see *www.hcch.net* for a list of ratifying States and acceding States). There may also be instances, for example, where the child is over 16 years of age where although the relevant States are parties to the 1980 Convention, the remedies available under that Convention cannot be pursued or where the lapse of time or delay may prove to be a hurdle. In such instances, consideration should be given to whether the matter can be pursued under the 1996 Convention.

Even where the 1980 Convention applies, consideration would have to be given to the provisions set out in Arts 5–14 on the issue of jurisdiction and in Arts 15–22, which deal with the applicable law that would be particularly relevant on the issue of attribution and extinction of parental responsibility and more specially in relation to an unmarried father. The power given to the courts to take necessary measures in an emergency for the protection of the child under the 1996 Convention (see Art 7(3) or in the best interest of the child (Arts 5–10) may also prove useful in a case under the 1980 Convention.

Art 7(2) of the 1996 Hague Convention provides an identical basis for determining whether removal or retention is wrongful to that set out in Art 3 of the 1980 Convention. It also provides that rights of custody may arise in three different ways: (a) by operation of law; (b) by reason of a judicial or administrative decision (e g when a court makes a residence order or grants parental responsibility); or (c) by reason of an agreement (i e without intervention by the court) having legal effect under the law of that State. Art 7(1) confirms that where there has been a wrongful removal or retention of the child, the authorities of the Contracting State in which the child was habitually resident immediately before the removal or retention keep their jurisdiction until the child has acquired a habitual residence in another State and each person, institution or other body having rights of custody has acquiesced in the removal or retention or the child has resided in that other State for a period of 1 year after that person, institution or other body has or should have had knowledge of the whereabouts of the child and no request for the return of the child has been lodged and the child is settled in his or her new environment. This provision is clearly aimed at indicating that abductors cannot assume that they will achieve an advantage by their wrongful action. The exception of acquiescence echoes the position that applies under Art 13(a) of the 1980 Convention and the second exception is similar to the provision of Art 12 of the 1980 Convention but with the difference that the period of 1 year starts after "knowledge of the whereabouts of the child", whereas under the 1980 Convention it starts with the wrongful removal or retention. Since the Convention is intended to provide protection of children, provision is also made that in the case of urgency the State to which the child has been removed or in which the child is retained may take such urgent measures under Art 11 as are necessary for the protection of the child or property of the child (Art 7(3)), for example by way of an injunction or, in an extreme case, the placement of a child in the care of a local authority.

The provision in Art 7(1) of the 1996 Convention that the State in which the child was habitually resident before the wrongful removal or retention retains jurisdiction also reasserts the provisions of Brussels IIA, Arts 10 and 17 that where there has been a wrongful detention, the court must of its own motion decline to entertain an application that offends the primary responsibility of another European Court. It also echoes the provision that the abductor is prevented from asserting a change of residence in such a case, bar the two exceptions. *Re AJ (Brussels II Revised)* [2012] 2 FLR 689 and *Re H (Child Abduction)* [2012] EWCA Civ 913 are examples of how the provisions in Brussels IIA and the 1996 Convention (which are identical) operate, so that despite a non-return order (in the former case) or delay (in the latter case) the State of origin retains jurisdiction unless the conditions set out in Art 10 of Brussels IIA and Art 7 of the 1996 Convention are met. See also *JRG v EB (Abduction: Brussels II Revised)* [2013] 1 FLR 203, where the court declined to adjudicate on the application under the 1980 Hague Convention because there was in existence a French residence and contact order and, therefore, Brussels IIA had precedence over the Hague Convention. In such cases, application should be made for recognition and enforcement of the order of the State of origin. This is the correct route both in respect of cases that fall under Brussels IIA and from 1 November 2012 under the 1996 Convention. However, Brussels IIA applies only to Member States within the European Union and makes its own provisions of how matters should be dealt with following a decision under the 1980 Convention, especially if a non-return order is made. It also has its own regulations for recognition and enforcement of the order of the State of origin. The 1996 Convention has its own provision for the recognition and enforcement of orders. Recognition may only be refused under the 1996 Convention on any one of the six grounds set out in Art 23.

The applicable law provision in the 1996 Convention will also be relevant on the issue of "rights of custody and access" and parental responsibility, especially in relation to unmarried fathers who do not acquire parental responsibility unless they are registered on the child's birth certificate or are granted parental responsibility by a court order or acquire it by agreement. Under the 1996 Convention:

- the attribution and extinction of parental responsibility by operation of law without the intervention of a judicial or administrative authority is governed by the law of the State of the child's habitual residence;
- the attribution and extinction of parental responsibility by agreement or a unilateral act without intervention of a judicial or administrative authority is governed by the law of the State of the child's habitual residence at the time when the agreement or unilateral act takes effect;
- parental responsibility that exists under the law of the State of the child's habitual residence subsists after a change of the habitual residence to another State (Art 16);
- The above provisions will apply even if the law designated by them is the law of a non-contracting State (Art 21).

The application of these provisions may be refused only if it would be manifestly contrary to public policy of the State to which the family has moved, taking into account the best interests of the child (Art 22). The *Handbook* gives an example of a same-sex female couple where both have parental responsibility under the law of the original State but under the law of Contracting State B, where the family has become habitually resident, that is considered to be contrary to public policy. It suggests that State B should give careful consideration as to whether it would be in the best interests of the children to refuse to do so. Morocco is a good example of a Contracting State where such a situation might occur.

Article 51

In relations between the Contracting States this Convention replaces the Convention of 5 October 1961 concerning the powers of authorities and the law applicable in respect of the protection of minors, and the Convention governing the guardianship of minors, signed at The Hague 12 June 1902, without prejudice to the recognition of measures taken under the Convention of 5 October 1961 mentioned above.

Article 52

(1) This Convention does not affect any international instrument to which Contracting States are Parties and which contains provisions on matters governed by the Convention, unless a contrary declaration is made by the States Parties to such instrument.

(2) This Convention does not affect the possibility for one or more Contracting States to conclude agreements which contain, in respect of children habitually resident in any of the States Parties to such agreements, provisions on matters governed by this Convention.

(3) Agreements to be concluded by one or more Contracting States on matters within the scope of this Convention do not affect, in the relationship of such States with other Contracting States, the application of the provisions of this Convention.

(4) The preceding paragraphs also apply to uniform laws based on special ties of a regional or other nature between the States concerned.

Article 53

(1) The Convention shall apply to measures only if they are taken in a State after the Convention has entered into force for that State.

(2) The Convention shall apply to the recognition and enforcement of measures taken after its entry into force as between the State where the measures have been taken and the requested State.

Scope—Note that the Convention is not retrospective. This ensures reciprocity. It will, therefore, be necessary to ascertain whether the Convention has come into force in a State and on what date it did so. As between States, it will be necessary to establish if the Convention has come into force between the two States and if so on what date.

PART VI

Article 54

(1) Any communication sent to the Central Authority or to another authority of a Contracting State shall be in the original language, and shall be accompanied by a translation into the official language or one of the official languages of the other State or, where that is not feasible, a translation into French or English.

(2) However, a Contracting State may, by making a reservation in accordance with Article 60, object to the use of either French or English, but not both.

Article 55

(1) A Contracting State may, in accordance with Article 60,

  (a) reserve the jurisdiction of its authorities to take measures directed to the protection of property of a child situated on its territory;
  (b) reserve the right not to recognise any parental responsibility or measure in so far as it is incompatible with any measure taken by its authorities in relation to that property.

(2) The reservation may be restricted to certain categories of property.

Article 56

The Secretary General of the Hague Conference on Private International Law shall at regular intervals convoke a Special Commission in order to review the practical operation of the Convention.

CHAPTER VII
FINAL CLAUSES

Scope—The Articles under this Chapter provide for the process that must be used for ratification of the Convention and any reservations that a Contracting State wishes to make. For example, where the State consists of several territorial units that apply their own laws, the Contracting State may identify to which territorial units within its State the Convention is to apply (see Art 59).

Article 57

(1) The Convention shall be open for signature by the States which were Members of the Hague Conference on Private International Law at the time of its Eighteenth Session.

(2) It shall be ratified, accepted or approved and the instruments of ratification, acceptance or approval shall be deposited with the Ministry of Foreign Affairs of the Kingdom of the Netherlands, depositary of the Convention.

Scope—The rules regarding whether the Convention has come into force in a State differ depending on whether the State has ratified or acceded to the Convention. Ratification is only open to those States that were already members of the 18th Session of the Hague Conference on Private International Law (19 October 1996). All other States may only accede to the Convention (see Art 58).

Article 58

(1) Any other State may accede to the Convention after it has entered into force in accordance with Article 61, paragraph 1.

(2) The instrument of accession shall be deposited with the depositary.

(3) Such accession shall have effect only as regards the relations between the acceding State and those Contracting States which have not raised an objection to its accession in the six months after the receipt of the notification referred to in sub-paragraph b of

Article 63. Such an objection may also be raised by States at the time when they ratify, accept or approve the Convention after an accession. Any such objection shall be notified to the depositary.

Scope—For those States that can only accede to the Convention, it takes 9 months for the process of accession to be completed. During the first 6 months, Contracting States have the opportunity to raise objections and then it will take another 3 months for the accession to be completed. Accession will take effect only between those States that have not raised any objections in the 6-month period. Where a State ratifies the Convention after another State has already acceded to it, it can raise objections at the time of ratification.

Article 59

(1) If a State has two or more territorial units in which different systems of law are applicable in relation to matters dealt with in this Convention, it may at the time of signature, ratification, acceptance, approval or accession declare that the Convention shall extend to all its territorial units or only to one or more of them and may modify this declaration by submitting another declaration at any time.

(2) Any such declaration shall be notified to the depositary and shall state expressly the territorial units to which the Convention applies.

(3) If a State makes no declaration under this Article, the Convention is to extend to all territorial units of that State.

Article 60

(1) Any State may, not later than the time of ratification, acceptance, approval or accession, or at the time of making a declaration in terms of Article 59, make one or both of the reservations provided for in Articles 54, paragraph 2, and 55. No other reservation shall be permitted.

(2) Any State may at any time withdraw a reservation it has made. The withdrawal shall be notified to the depositary.

(3) The reservation shall cease to have effect on the first day of the third calendar month after the notification referred to in the preceding paragraph.

Scope—This Article sets the time limit within which any reservations under the preceding Articles must be made.

Article 61

(1) The Convention shall enter into force on the first day of the month following the expiration of three months after the deposit of the third instrument of ratification, acceptance or approval referred to in Article 57.

(2) Thereafter the Convention shall enter into force –

   (a)   for each State ratifying, accepting or approving it subsequently, on the first day of the month following the expiration of three months after the deposit of its instrument of ratification, acceptance, approval or accession;

   (b)   for each State acceding, on the first day of the month following the expiration of three months after the expiration of the period of six months provided in Article 58, paragraph 3;

   (c)   for a territorial unit to which the Convention has been extended in conformity with Article 59, on the first day of the month following the expiration of three months after the notification referred to in that Article.

Scope—See notes under Arts 57 and 58.

PART VI

Article 62

(1) A State Party to the Convention may denounce it by a notification in writing addressed to the depositary. The denunciation may be limited to certain territorial units to which the Convention applies.

(2) The denunciation takes effect on the first day of the month following the expiration of twelve months after the notification is received by the depositary. Where a longer period for the denunciation to take effect is specified in the notification, the denunciation takes effect upon the expiration of such longer period.

Article 63

The depositary shall notify the States Members of the Hague Conference on Private International Law and the States which have acceded in accordance with Article 58 of the following –

(a)   the signatures, ratifications, acceptances and approvals referred to in Article 57;
(b)   the accessions and objections raised to accessions referred to in Article 58;
(c)   the date on which the Convention enters into force in accordance with Article 61;
(d)   the declarations referred to in Articles 34, paragraph 2, and 59;
(e)   the agreements referred to in Article 39;
(f)   the reservations referred to in Articles 54, paragraph 2, and 55 and the withdrawals referred to in Article 60, paragraph 2;
(g)   the denunciations referred to in Article 62.

Council Regulation (EC) No 2201/2003

of 27 November 2003

concerning jurisdiction and the recognition and enforcement of judgments in matrimonial matters and the matters of parental responsibility, repealing Regulation (EC) No 1347/2000

Scope—Brussels IIA (variously otherwise referred to as Brussels II bis, Brussels IIA or the Council Regulation) came into force on 1 March 2005 in all 26 Member States of the European Union (EU) other than Denmark including the 10 Accession States which joined the EU on 1 May 2004. Brussels IIA replaced Brussels II (Council Regulation (EC) No 1347/1000) concerning jurisdiction and the recognition and enforcement of judgments and matrimonial matters and in matters of parental responsibility for children of both spouses, which came into force on 1 March 2001. Brussels IIA is an EU Regulation (and not a Directive) and is therefore directly applicable in Member States. It does not need implementation through UK legislation and prevails over domestic law. For the purposes of Brussels IIA, the UK includes Gibraltar (Treaty on the Functioning of the European Union, Art 349), but not the Isle of Man nor the Channel Islands. Although a member of the EU, Denmark has opted out of Brussels IIA. Forum disputes involving Denmark must therefore be treated in the same way as forum disputes involving non-EU countries in Europe and the rest of the world.

Chapter I (Arts 1 and 2) deals with scope and definitions. Chapter II (Arts 3–20) deals with jurisdiction. Section 1 of Chapter II (Arts 3–7) deals with jurisdiction in relation to divorce, legal separation and marriage annulment. The provisions of Brussels II in this context remain unchanged (subject to changes to Article numbering). Cases decided under Brussels II retain their force. It establishes the principle of lis pendens or "the first to issue secures jurisdiction". Section 2 of Chapter I (Arts 8–15) relates to jurisdiction in the context of parental responsibility and brings about changes to Brussels II, creating a scheme for jurisdiction in matters of parental responsibility which is much closer to the scheme for jurisdiction for divorce etc in Section 1 than was the case under Brussels II. Section 3 of Chapter II (Arts 16–20) contains provisions which are common to both divorce etc and parental responsibility.

Chapter III (Arts 21–52) deals with recognition and enforcement. Section 1 of Chapter III (Arts 21–27) provides for recognition of judgments covered by Brussels IIA without any special procedure subject to specific grounds for non-recognition. Section 2 of Chapter III (Arts 28–36) deals with an application for a declaration of enforceability. Section 3 of Chapter III (Arts 37–39) contains provisions common to recognition and enforcement. Many of the provisions are common to divorce etc and questions of parental responsibility, and are derived from Brussels I. Section 4 of Chapter III (Arts 40–45) deals with the enforceability of judgments concerning rights of access and the return of a child. Section 5 of Chapter III (Art 46) provides for authentic instruments and agreements enforceable in one Member State to be recognised and enforceable in the same way as judgments. Section 6 of Chapter III (Arts 47–52) contains other provisions dealing with practical enforcement arrangements, the exercise of the rights of access, costs and legal aid.

Chapter IV (Arts 53–58) deals with the cooperation between Central Authorities in matters of parental responsibility.

Chapter V (Arts 59–63) deals with the relationship of Brussels IIA with other instruments (e g the Hague Conventions).

Chapter VI (Art 64) contains transitional provisions and Chapter VII (Arts 65–72) final provisions which provide (Art 65) for a review of Brussels IIA on 1 January 2012 and every 5 years thereafter, and for Member States (e g the UK) with two or more legal systems (Art 66).

The recitals to Brussels IIA set out areas that are not intended to be covered including the grounds for divorce, property consequences of the marriage and other ancillary measures (recital 8) and maintenance obligations (recital 11).

THE COUNCIL OF THE EUROPEAN UNION,

Having regard to the Treaty establishing the European Community, and in particular Article 61(c) and Article 67(1) thereof,

Having regard to the proposal from the Commission,

Having regard to the opinion of the European Parliament,

Having regard to the opinion of the European Economic and Social Committee,

Whereas:

(1) The European Community has set the objective of creating an area of freedom, security and justice, in which the free movement of persons is ensured. To this end, the Community is to adopt, among others, measures in the field of judicial cooperation in civil matters that are necessary for the proper functioning of the internal market.

(2) The Tampere European Council endorsed the principle of mutual recognition of judicial decisions as the cornerstone for the creation of a genuine judicial area, and identified visiting rights as a priority.

(3) Council Regulation (EC) No 1347/2000 sets out rules on jurisdiction, recognition and enforcement of judgments in matrimonial matters and matters of parental responsibility for the children of both spouses rendered on the occasion of the matrimonial proceedings. The content of this Regulation was substantially taken over from the Convention of 28 May 1998 on the same subject matter.

(4) On 3 July 2000 France presented an initiative for a Council Regulation on the mutual enforcement of judgments on rights of access to children.

(5) In order to ensure equality for all children, this Regulation covers all decisions on parental responsibility, including measures for the protection of the child, independently of any link with a matrimonial proceeding.

(6) Since the application of the rules on parental responsibility often arises in the context of matrimonial proceedings, it is more appropriate to have a single instrument for matters of divorce and parental responsibility.

(7) The scope of this Regulation covers civil matters, whatever the nature of the court or tribunal.

PART VI

(8) As regards judgments on divorce, legal separation or marriage annulment, this Regulation should apply only to the dissolution of matrimonial ties and should not deal with issues such as the grounds for divorce, property consequences of the marriage or any other ancillary measures.

(9) As regards the property of the child, this Regulation should apply only to measures for the protection of the child, i.e. (i) the designation and functions of a person or body having charge of the child's property, representing or assisting the child, and (ii) the administration, conservation or disposal of the child's property. In this context, this Regulation should, for instance, apply in cases where the parents are in dispute as regards the administration of the child's property. Measures relating to the child's property which do not concern the protection of the child should continue to be governed by Council Regulation (EC) No 44/2001 of 22 December 2000 on jurisdiction and the recognition and enforcement of judgments in civil and commercial matters.

(10) This Regulation is not intended to apply to matters relating to social security, public measures of a general nature in matters of education or health or to decisions on the right of asylum and on immigration. In addition it does not apply to the establishment of parenthood, since this is a different matter from the attribution of parental responsibility, nor to other questions linked to the status of persons. Moreover, it does not apply to measures taken as a result of criminal offences committed by children.

(11) Maintenance obligations are excluded from the scope of this Regulation as these are already covered by Council Regulation No 44/2001. The courts having jurisdiction under this Regulation will generally have jurisdiction to rule on maintenance obligations by application of Article 5(2) of Council Regulation No 44/2001.

(12) The grounds of jurisdiction in matters of parental responsibility established in the present Regulation are shaped in the light of the best interests of the child, in particular on the criterion of proximity. This means that jurisdiction should lie in the first place with the Member State of the child's habitual residence, except for certain cases of a change in the child's residence or pursuant to an agreement between the holders of parental responsibility.

(13) In the interest of the child, this Regulation allows, by way of exception and under certain conditions, that the court having jurisdiction may transfer a case to a court of another Member State if this court is better placed to hear the case. However, in this case the second court should not be allowed to transfer the case to a third court.

(14) This Regulation should have effect without prejudice to the application of public international law concerning diplomatic immunities. Where jurisdiction under this Regulation cannot be exercised by reason of the existence of diplomatic immunity in accordance with international law, jurisdiction should be exercised in accordance with national law in a Member State in which the person concerned does not enjoy such immunity.

(15) Council Regulation (EC) No 1348/2000 of 29 May 2000 on the service in the Member States of judicial and extrajudicial documents in civil or commercial matters should apply to the service of documents in proceedings instituted pursuant to this Regulation.

(16) This Regulation should not prevent the courts of a Member State from taking provisional, including protective measures, in urgent cases, with regard to persons or property situated in that State.

(17) In cases of wrongful removal or retention of a child, the return of the child should be obtained without delay, and to this end the Hague Convention of 25 October 1980 would continue to apply as complemented by the provisions of this Regulation, in particular Article 11. The courts of the Member State to or in which the child has been wrongfully removed or retained should be able to oppose his or her return in specific,

duly justified cases. However, such a decision could be replaced by a subsequent decision by the court of the Member State of habitual residence of the child prior to the wrongful removal or retention. Should that judgment entail the return of the child, the return should take place without any special procedure being required for recognition and enforcement of that judgment in the Member State to or in which the child has been removed or retained.

(18) Where a court has decided not to return a child on the basis of Article 13 of the 1980 Hague Convention, it should inform the court having jurisdiction or central authority in the Member State where the child was habitually resident prior to the wrongful removal or retention. Unless the court in the latter Member State has been seised, this court or the central authority should notify the parties. This obligation should not prevent the central authority from also notifying the relevant public authorities in accordance with national law.

(19) The hearing of the child plays an important role in the application of this Regulation, although this instrument is not intended to modify national procedures applicable.

(20) The hearing of a child in another Member State may take place under the arrangements laid down in Council Regulation (EC) No 1206/2001 of 28 May 2001 on cooperation between the courts of the Member States in the taking of evidence in civil or commercial matters.

(21) The recognition and enforcement of judgments given in a Member State should be based on the principle of mutual trust and the grounds for non-recognition should be kept to the minimum required.

(22) Authentic instruments and agreements between parties that are enforceable in one Member State should be treated as equivalent to "judgments" for the purpose of the application of the rules on recognition and enforcement.

(23) The Tampere European Council considered in its conclusions (point 34) that judgments in the field of family litigation should be "automatically recognised throughout the Union without any intermediate proceedings or grounds for refusal of enforcement". This is why judgments on rights of access and judgments on return that have been certified in the Member State of origin in accordance with the provisions of this Regulation should be recognised and enforceable in all other Member States without any further procedure being required. Arrangements for the enforcement of such judgments continue to be governed by national law.

(24) The certificate issued to facilitate enforcement of the judgment should not be subject to appeal. It should be rectified only where there is a material error, i.e. where it does not correctly reflect the judgment.

(25) Central authorities should cooperate both in general matter and in specific cases, including for purposes of promoting the amicable resolution of family disputes, in matters of parental responsibility. To this end central authorities shall participate in the European Judicial Network in civil and commercial matters created by Council Decision 2001/470/EC of 28 May 2001 establishing a European Judicial Network in civil and commercial matters.

(26) The Commission should make publicly available and update the lists of courts and redress procedures communicated by the Member States.

(27) The measures necessary for the implementation of this Regulation should be adopted in accordance with Council Decision 1999/468/EC of 28 June 1999 laying down the procedures for the exercise of implementing powers conferred on the Commission.

(28) This Regulation replaces Regulation (EC) No 1347/2000 which is consequently repealed.

PART VI

(29) For the proper functioning of this Regulation, the Commission should review its application and propose such amendments as may appear necessary.

(30) The United Kingdom and Ireland, in accordance with Article 3 of the Protocol on the position of the United Kingdom and Ireland annexed to the Treaty on European Union and the Treaty establishing the European Community, have given notice of their wish to take part in the adoption and application of this Regulation.

(31) Denmark, in accordance with Articles 1 and 2 of the Protocol on the position of Denmark annexed to the Treaty on European Union and the Treaty establishing the European Community, is not participating in the adoption of this Regulation and is therefore not bound by it nor subject to its application.

(32) Since the objectives of this Regulation cannot be sufficiently achieved by the Member States and can therefore be better achieved at Community level, the Community may adopt measures, in accordance with the principle of subsidiarity as set out in Article 5 of the Treaty. In accordance with the principle of proportionality, as set out in that Article, this Regulation does not go beyond what is necessary in order to achieve those objectives.

(33) This Regulation recognises the fundamental rights and observes the principles of the Charter of Fundamental Rights of the European Union. In particular, it seeks to ensure respect for the fundamental rights of the child as set out in Article 24 of the Charter of Fundamental Rights of the European Union,

HAS ADOPTED THE PRESENT REGULATION:

Note—The EC Treaty has become the Treaty on the Functioning of the European Union (TFEU) and the Articles have been re-numbered: Art 5 is replaced, in substance, by Art 5 of the Treaty on the European Union; Art 61 is Art 67 TFEU; and Art 67 is repealed.

CHAPTER I
SCOPE AND DEFINITIONS

Article 1

Scope

1 This Regulation shall apply, whatever the nature of the court or tribunal, in civil matters relating to:

    (a)   divorce, legal separation or marriage annulment;
    (b)   the attribution, exercise, delegation, restriction or termination of parental responsibility.

2 The matters referred to in paragraph 1(b) may, in particular, deal with:

    (a)   rights of custody and rights of access;
    (b)   guardianship, curatorship and similar institutions;
    (c)   the designation and functions of any person or body having charge of the child's person or property, representing or assisting the child;
    (d)   the placement of the child in a foster family or in institutional care;
    (e)   measures for the protection of the child relating to the administration, conservation or disposal of the child's property.

3 This Regulation shall not apply to:

    (a)   the establishment or contesting of a parent-child relationship;
    (b)   decisions on adoption, measures preparatory to adoption, or the annulment or revocation of adoption;
    (c)   the name and forenames of the child;
    (d)   emancipation;

(e)   maintenance obligations;

(f)   trusts or succession;

(g)   measures taken as a result of criminal offences committed by children.

"Civil matters" (Art 1.1)—This term encompasses public law care proceedings (*Re C* (Case C–435/06) [2008] 1 FLR 490, ECJ; *Re A (Area of Freedom, Security and Justice)* (C-523/07) [2009] 2 FLR 1, ECJ).

Article 2

Definitions

For the purposes of this Regulation:

1 the term "court" shall cover all the authorities in the Member States with jurisdiction in the matters falling within the scope of this Regulation pursuant to Article 1;

2 the term "judge" shall mean the judge or an official having powers equivalent to those of a judge in the matters falling within the scope of the Regulation;

3 the term "Member State" shall mean all Member States with the exception of Denmark;

4 the term "judgment" shall mean a divorce, legal separation or marriage annulment, as well as a judgment relating to parental responsibility, pronounced by a court of a Member State, whatever the judgment may be called, including a decree, order or decision;

5 the term "Member State of origin" shall mean the Member State where the judgment to be enforced was issued;

6 the term "Member State of enforcement" shall mean the Member State where enforcement of the judgment is sought;

7 the term "parental responsibility" shall mean all rights and duties relating to the person or the property of a child which are given to a natural or legal person by judgment, by operation of law or by an agreement having legal effect. The term shall include rights of custody and rights of access;

8 the term "holder of parental responsibility" shall mean any person having parental responsibility over a child;

9 the term "rights of custody" shall include rights and duties relating to the care of the person of a child, and in particular the right to determine the child's place of residence;

10 the term "rights of access" shall include in particular the right to take a child to a place other than his or her habitual residence for a limited period of time;

11 the term "wrongful removal or retention" shall mean a child's removal or retention where:

(a)   it is in breach of rights of custody acquired by judgment or by operation of law or by an agreement having legal effect under the law of the Member State where the child was habitually resident immediately before the removal or retention; and

(b)   provided that, at the time of removal or retention, the rights of custody were actually exercised, either jointly or alone, or would have been so exercised but for the removal or retention. Custody shall be considered to be exercised jointly when, pursuant to a judgment or by operation of law, one holder of parental responsibility cannot decide on the child's place of residence without the consent of another holder of parental responsibility.

"Rights of custody" (Arts 2.9, 2.11)—"Rights of custody" is an autonomous concept independent of the law of Member States. It is a separate matter from the identity of the person who has rights of custody and it is for the Member State to determine who has rights of custody at the relevant time (*JMcB v Le* C-400/10 [2011] 1 FLR 518).

CHAPTER II
JURISDICTION

Section 1
Divorce, legal separation and marriage annulment

Article 3

General jurisdiction

1 In matters relating to divorce, legal separation or marriage annulment, jurisdiction shall lie with the courts of the Member State

(a)   in whose territory:
– the spouses are habitually resident, or
– the spouses were last habitually resident, insofar as one of them still resides there, or
– the respondent is habitually resident, or
– in the event of a joint application, either of the spouses is habitually resident, or
– the applicant is habitually resident if he or she resided there for at least a year immediately before the application was made, or
– the applicant is habitually resident if he or she resided there for at least six months immediately before the application was made and is either a national of the Member State in question or, in the case of the United Kingdom and Ireland, has his or her "domicile" there;

(b)   of the nationality of both spouses or, in the case of the United Kingdom and Ireland, of the "domicile" of both spouses.

2 For the purpose of this Regulation, "domicile" shall have the same meaning as it has under the legal systems of the United Kingdom and Ireland.

Defined terms—"court": Art 2.1; "Member State": Art 2.3.

Scope—In respect of proceedings for divorce or judicial separation commenced on or after 1 March 2005, the court has jurisdiction to entertain proceedings only if the court has jurisdiction under Art 3 or no court of a Contracting State has jurisdiction under Art 3 and either of the parties to the marriage is domiciled in England and Wales on the date when the proceedings are begun (DMPA 1973, s 5(2)). In respect of proceedings for nullity commenced on or after 1 March 2005, the position is the same save that, where no court of a Contracting State has jurisdiction under Art 3, jurisdiction may alternatively be established where either of the parties to the marriage died before the date when proceedings are begun and either was at death domiciled in England and Wales or had been habitually resident in England and Wales throughout the period of 1 year ending with the date of death (DMPA 1973, s 5(3)). Parallel provision is made in relation to proceedings for a decree of presumption of death and dissolution (DMPA 1973, s 5(4)). Jurisdiction under Art 3.1(a) is founded on habitual residence and applies whether or not the parties are nationals of another EU Member State (*Sulaiman v Juffali* [2002] 1 FLR 479). A person's presence in England for the purpose of receiving medical treatment, which prevented him from leaving the jurisdiction, did not enable a divorce petition to be based upon habitual residence in England (*Breuning v Breuning* [2002] 1 FLR 888). Jurisdiction may only be based on the domicile of *either* party in England and Wales on the date when proceedings are begun if no Member State has jurisdiction under Arts 3, 4 or 5 (Art 7 and DMPA 1973, s 5(2)(b)).

Where a court has jurisdiction under Art 3, it will also have jurisdiction to examine a counterclaim (e g an application for divorce by a respondent) (Art 4). Where a court has given a judgment on a legal separation, it will also have jurisdiction to convert that judgment into a divorce (Art 5). Articles 3, 4 and 5 provide an exclusive jurisdictional code (Art 6).

The court's jurisdiction under Art 3 should not be exercised by analogy with the decision in *Owusu v Jackson* [2005] QB 801, ECJ under Brussels I. Where a state has jurisdiction under Brussels IIA, there remains a jurisdiction to grant a stay of English proceedings under DMPA 1973, Sch 1, para 9 on the ground of forum non conveniens (*JKN v JCN (Divorce: Forum)* [2011] 1 FLR 826).

The court may permit amendment to the pleaded grounds for jurisdiction in a petition that is first in time, even though the original grounds were open to serious challenge and proceedings had been issued in a second Member State which would become first seised in the event of the first in time petition being dismissed unamended (*Rogers-Headicar v Headicar* [2005] 2 FCR 1 (CA); *R v R (Divorce: Jurisdiction: Domicile)* [2006] 1 FLR 389 (FD)). Despite the court's obligation to conduct an examination as to jurisdiction (Art 17), it is advisable to plead jurisdiction under as many cases as possible under Art 3.1.

In the UK and Ireland, joint domicile provides jurisdictional basis under Art 3.1(b); in all other Member States, joint nationality must be shown to establish jurisdiction under Art 3.1(b). It is not necessary in the UK and Ireland to demonstrate joint domicile as well as joint nationality (*Re N (Jurisdiction)* [2007] 2 FLR 1196).

Habitual residence—Habitual residence is "the place where the person had established, on a fixed basis, his permanent or habitual centre of interests, with all the relevant facts being taken into account for the purpose of determining such residence" (*L-K v K (No 2)* [2007] 2 FLR 729). This approach evolved in the European Court of Justice rather than under English domestic law is the applicable test (*L-K v K (No 2)* [2007] 2 FLR 729; *Marinos v Marinos* [2007] 2 FLR 1018; *Z v Z (Divorce: Jurisdiction)* [2010] 1 FLR 694). Habitual residence is interpreted differently in the context of Art 8 (parental responsibility). There is no requirement that the centre of interests must be permanent; it need only be habitual. However, it must have a stable character. A person can only have one habitual residence at a given date (*Z v Z (Divorce: Jurisdiction)*. Although the test for habitual residence is objective, when considering a party's centre of interests, the party's intention forms part of the court's overall assessment. This enables the court objectively to assess the mental element in concepts such as "permanent", "habitual", "residence" and "home". Intention in this context means the reasons for the parties' actions and is not synonymous with the subjective capricious wish-fulfilment of one party (*V v V (Divorce: Jurisdiction)* [2011] 2 FLR 778).

As to whether there is any distinction between "habitual residence" and "residence" for the purposes of cases 2, 5 and 6 of Art 3(1)(a), Munby J held in *Marinos v Marinos* [2007] 2 FLR 1018 that mere residence would suffice, whereas Bennett J took an opposing view in *Munro v Munro* [2008] 1 FLR 1613. See, also, *Olafisoye v Olafisoye* [2011] 2 FLR 553. *Marinos* was followed in preference to *Munro* in *V v V* (above). It is possible to be habitually resident in one country and resident (but not habitually) in another. It is also possible to be resident in more than one country (*V v V* (above) applying *Marinos*).

"Domicile" (Art 3.1(b))—In deciding a person's domicile for the purposes of jurisdiction, the applicable law is the lex fori, namely, the law of England and Wales (*Chandler v Chandler* [2011] EWCA Civ 143).

Article 4

Counterclaim

The court in which proceedings are pending on the basis of Article 3 shall also have jurisdiction to examine a counterclaim, insofar as the latter comes within the scope of this Regulation.

Defined terms—"court": Art 2.1.

Article 5

Conversion of legal separation into divorce

Without prejudice to Article 3, a court of a Member State that has given a judgment on a legal separation shall also have jurisdiction for converting that judgment into a divorce, if the law of that Member State so provides.

Defined terms—"court": Art 2.1; "Member State": Art 2.3; "judgment": Art 2.4.

Article 6

Exclusive nature of jurisdiction under Articles 3, 4 and 5

A spouse who:

(a)   is habitually resident in the territory of a Member State; or

(b)   is a national of a Member State, or, in the case of the United Kingdom and Ireland, has his or her "domicile" in the territory of one of the latter Member States,

may be sued in another Member State only in accordance with Articles 3, 4 and 5.

PART VI

Defined terms—"Member State": Art 2.3.

Scope—This Article sets out the exclusive nature of jurisdiction under Arts 3, 4 and 5. As to the interrelationship between this exclusive jurisdiction and the residual jurisdiction under Art 7, see *Sundelind Lopez v Lopez Lizazo* [2008] 1 FLR 582.

Article 7

Residual jurisdiction

1 Where no court of a Member State has jurisdiction pursuant to Articles 3, 4 and 5, jurisdiction shall be determined, in each Member State, by the laws of that State.

2 As against a respondent who is not habitually resident and is not either a national of a Member State or, in the case of the United Kingdom and Ireland, does not have his "domicile" within the territory of one of the latter Member States, any national of a Member State who is habitually resident within the territory of another Member State may, like the nationals of that State, avail himself of the rules of jurisdiction applicable in that State.

Defined terms—"court": Art 2.1; "Member State": Art 2.3.

Scope—This Article provides for a residual jurisdiction where no court of a Member State has jurisdiction under the exclusive jurisdictional code of Arts 3–5 to be determined by domestic law, ie on the sole domicile of one party under DMPA 1973, s 5(2)(b) (eg *F v F (Divorce: Jurisdiction)* [2009] 2 FLR 1496). This does not enable a spouse who is neither a national of nor habitually resident in a Member State to be sued under Art 7, even if another Member State has jurisdiction under Art 3 (*Sundelind Lopez v Lopez Lizazo* [2008] 1 FLR 582).

Section 2
Parental responsibility

Article 8

General jurisdiction

1 The courts of a Member State shall have jurisdiction in matters of parental responsibility over a child who is habitually resident in that Member State at the time the court is seised.

2 Paragraph 1 shall be subject to the provisions of Articles 9, 10 and 12.

Defined terms—"court": Art 2.1; "Member State": Art 2.3; "parental responsibility": Art 2.7; "seised": Art 16.

Scope—The scope of matters covered by Brussels IIA in relation to parental responsibility are set out in Art 1.2. However, Brussels IIA does not apply to those matters of parental responsibility set out in Art 1.3. Article 8 sets out the general rule as to jurisdiction that jurisdiction lies with the courts of the Member State in which the child is habitually resident at the time the court is seised. Articles 9–15 set out the exceptions to this general rule.

"Habitually resident"—"Habitual residence" under Brussels IIA, Arts 8 and 10 must be given an independent and uniform interpretation throughout the EU, having regard to the context in Brussels IIA. Brussels IIA, Arts 8 and 10 do not make express reference to the law of the Member States for the purpose of determining the meaning and scope of "habitual residence", which is to be interpreted for the purposes of Arts 8 and 10 as corresponding to the place that reflected some degree of integration by a child in a social and family environment (*Mercredi v Chaffe* [2011] 1 FLR 1293, ECJ at [56]; see also *Re A (Area of Freedom, Security and Justice)* (C-532/01) [2009] 2 FLR 1, ECJ; *Re S (Habitual Residence)* [2010] 1 FLR 1146; *Re P-J (Abduction: Habitual Residence: Consent)* [2009] 2 FLR 1051, CA; *FVS v MGS (Habitual Residence)* [2012] 1 FLR 1184; *A v P (Habitual Residence)* [2012] 1 FLR 125). Habitual residence is an issue of fact depending upon the particular facts before the court (*Re P-J (Abduction: Habitual Residence: Consent)* (above), CA; *A v P (Habitual Residence)*, above). The acquisition of habitual residence in any country requires the adult or child in question to be physically present there. Thus, it would be artificial to say that a child was habitually resident at birth in a country to which he/she had never been. Where the parent or parents had established a place of habitual residence in a particular country, it would usually require no more than a moment's presence in that jurisdiction for a newborn child to acquire the same status. The position of a newborn child is, therefore, completely different from that of an adult or a child who already has a place of habitual residence in one country that he/she left to establish a life elsewhere. In such a case, an appreciable period of time might have to pass before the process of transition to a new place of habitual residence was complete. Thus, a newborn child is not presumed to take on birth the habitual residence of his/her parents or custodial parent (*ZA v NA* [2012] EWCA Civ 1396, applying *Re J (A Minor) (Abduction: Custody Rights)* [1990] 2 FLR 442; *Re M (Abduction: Habitual Residence)* [1996] 1 FLR 887; *Al Habtoor v Fotheringham* [2001] 1 FLR 951, CA). One parent is unable unilaterally to terminate the habitual residence of a child (*FVS v MGS (Habitual Residence)*, above; *ZA v NA*, above). Habitual residence is interpreted differently in the context of Art 3 (divorce, legal separation and annulment).

Liaison judge—In [2008] Fam Law 105 Thorpe LJ offered the following information as to his role: "In trans-national cases there is a high chance of contemporaneous proceedings in both the involved jurisdictions. Unless the two responsible judges communicate, there is an obvious risk of conflict, legal complexity, delay and wasted costs. Each jurisdiction needs a co-ordinator, a liaison judge available to facilitate the essential communication. In this jurisdiction I am responsible for that service. My office is well equipped to initiate the process that results in judge communicating with judge."
The preferred route for contact is via Edward Bennett, lawyer to Thorpe LJ, International Family Justice Office. His office is in room C101 at the Royal Courts of Justice; tel: 0207 947 7906; email: edward.bennett@judiciary.gsi.gov.uk. He is supported by Karen Wheller.

Article 9

Continuing jurisdiction of the child's former habitual residence

1 Where a child moves lawfully from one Member State to another and acquires a new habitual residence there, the courts of the Member State of the child's former habitual residence shall, by way of exception to Article 8, retain jurisdiction during a three-month period following the move for the purpose of modifying a judgment on access rights issued in that Member State before the child moved, where the holder of access rights pursuant to the judgment on access rights continues to have his or her habitual residence in the Member State of the child's former habitual residence.

2 Paragraph 1 shall not apply if the holder of access rights referred to in paragraph 1 has accepted the jurisdiction of the courts of the Member State of the child's new habitual residence by participating in proceedings before those courts without contesting their jurisdiction.

Defined terms—"Member State": Art 2.3; "judgment": Art 2.4.

Scope—Article 9 provides by way of exception to the general rule in Art 8, that where a child has moved lawfully from one Member State to another and becomes habitually resident there, the courts of the original Member State continue in specified circumstances to have jurisdiction for 3 months after the move for limited purposes in relation to access (contact).

"Date of service"—Issues as to the timing and regularity of service are determined by reference to the Second Service Regulation and not the law of the Member State addressed (*Tavoulareas v Tsavliris* [2004] 2 All ER (Comm) 221, CA).

Article 10

Jurisdiction in cases of child abduction

In case of wrongful removal or retention of the child, the courts of the Member State where the child was habitually resident immediately before the wrongful removal or retention shall retain their jurisdiction until the child has acquired a habitual residence in another Member State and:

(a) each person, institution or other body having rights of custody has acquiesced in the removal or retention; or

(b) the child has resided in that other Member State for a period of at least one year after the person, institution or other body having rights of custody has had or should have had knowledge of the whereabouts of the child and the child is settled in his or her new environment and at least one of the following conditions is met:

(i) within one year after the holder of rights of custody has had or should have had knowledge of the whereabouts of the child, no request for return has been lodged before the competent authorities of the Member State where the child has been removed or is being retained;

(ii) a request for return lodged by the holder of rights of custody has been withdrawn and no new request has been lodged within the time limit set in paragraph (i);

(iii) a case before the court in the Member State where the child was habitually resident immediately before the wrongful removal or retention has been closed pursuant to Article 11(7);

(iv) a judgment on custody that does not entail the return of the child has been issued by the courts of the Member State where the child was habitually resident immediately before the wrongful removal or retention.

Defined terms—"court": Art 2.1; "Member State": Art 2.3; "rights of custody": Art 2.9; "judgment": Art 2.4; "wrongful removal or retention": Art 2.11.

Scope—Article 10 provides that, in cases of child abduction, again by way of exception to the general rule in Art 8, the courts of the Member State from which the child was wrongfully removed/retained retain jurisdiction subject to certain conditions (*Re A; HA v MB (Brussels II Revised: Article 11(7) Application)* [2008] 1 FLR 289). Art 10 ensures that an abductor is prevented from successfully asserting a change of habitual residence as a consequence of wrongful retention (*Re H (Child Abduction)* [2012] EWCA Civ 913). Where there is a wrongful removal or retention, an application may either be made for an order under the Hague Convention 1980 (see Art 11) in the Member State where the child is resident or an application may be made under this Article in the Member State from which the child has been removed/retained, in which event such an order will be automatically enforceable in the Member State in which the child is now resident. Where two remedies are available in different courts in different jurisdictions, Hague Convention proceedings do not take automatic precedence (*B v D (Abduction: Inherent Jurisdiction)* [2009] 1 FLR 1015). A child can be habitually resident in only one country at a time (*Re A; HA v MB (Brussels II Revised: Article 11(7) Application)* (above)). Where two children had been abducted from Poland and accommodated by the local authority, the English court had jurisdiction to make care orders under Art 10 either by acquiescence or because the children had been in the jurisdiction with the knowledge of all concerned for over a year, were settled and no request for a return had been made (*Tower Hamlets London Borough Council v MK and Others* [2012] 2 FLR 762). See also **Liaison judge** under Art 8.

Habitual residence—See annotations to Art 8.

"Knowledge of whereabouts" (Art 10(b)–(c))—*M v M (Abduction: Settlement)* [2008] 2 FLR 1884.

"Judgment on custody that does not entail the return of the child" (Art 10(b)(iv))—A provisional measure does not constitute a "judgment on custody that does not entail the return of the child" and cannot be the basis of a transfer of jurisdiction to the courts of the country to which a child has been unlawfully removed (*Povse v Alpago* [2010] 2 FLR 1343, ECJ). See also *Re AJ (Brussels II Revised)* [2012] 2 FLR 689 and *Re AJ (Contact: Brussels II Revised)* [2012] 2 FLR 1065.

Article 11

Return of the child

1 Where a person, institution or other body having rights of custody applies to the competent authorities in a Member State to deliver a judgment on the basis of the Hague Convention of 25 October 1980 on the Civil Aspects of International Child Abduction (hereinafter "the 1980 Hague Convention"), in order to obtain the return of a child that has been wrongfully removed or retained in a Member State other than the Member State where the child was habitually resident immediately before the wrongful removal or retention, paragraphs 2 to 8 shall apply.

2 When applying Articles 12 and 13 of the 1980 Hague Convention, it shall be ensured that the child is given the opportunity to be heard during the proceedings unless this appears inappropriate having regard to his or her age or degree of maturity.

3 A court to which an application for return of a child is made as mentioned in paragraph 1 shall act expeditiously in proceedings on the application, using the most expeditious procedures available in national law.

Without prejudice to the first subparagraph, the court shall, except where exceptional circumstances make this impossible, issue its judgment no later than six weeks after the application is lodged.

4 A court cannot refuse to return a child on the basis of Article 13b of the 1980 Hague Convention if it is established that adequate arrangements have been made to secure the protection of the child after his or her return.

5 A court cannot refuse to return a child unless the person who requested the return of the child has been given an opportunity to be heard.

6 If a court has issued an order on non-return pursuant to Article 13 of the 1980 Hague Convention, the court must immediately either directly or through its central authority, transmit a copy of the court order on non-return and of the relevant documents, in particular a transcript of the hearings before the court, to the court with jurisdiction or central authority in the Member State where the child was habitually resident immediately before the wrongful removal or retention, as determined by national law. The court shall receive all the mentioned documents within one month of the date of the non-return order.

7 Unless the courts in the Member State where the child was habitually resident immediately before the wrongful removal or retention have already been seised by one of the parties, the court or central authority that receives the information mentioned in paragraph 6 must notify it to the parties and invite them to make submissions to the court, in accordance with national law, within three months of the date of notification so that the court can examine the question of custody of the child.

Without prejudice to the rules on jurisdiction contained in this Regulation, the court shall close the case if no submissions have been received by the court within the time limit.

8 Notwithstanding a judgment of non-return pursuant to Article 13 of the 1980 Hague Convention, any subsequent judgment which requires the return of the child issued by a court having jurisdiction under this Regulation shall be enforceable in accordance with Section 4 of Chapter III below in order to secure the return of the child.

Defined terms—"rights of custody": Art 2.9; "Member State": Art 2.3; "wrongful removal or retention": Art 2.11; "court": Art 2.1.

Scope—The Hague Convention 1980 continues to apply but is supplemented by Brussels IIA, which complements the Convention (recital 17). However, Brussels IIA takes precedence over the Hague Convention 1980 (Art 60; *JRG v EB (Abduction: Brussels II Revised)* [2013] 1 FLR 203). Art 11 only applies to return applications in cases of wrongful removal/retention (as defined by Art 2.11) made under the Hague Convention 1980 by one Member State (excluding Denmark: Art 2.3) to another. Reference should also be made to the annotations to Arts 10, 40 and 42. Where a parent has failed to obtain a summary return order under the Hague Convention 1980, Art 12, it may be wiser to pursue the procedure provided by Art 11 to obtain an order that would be automatically enforced in the requested state rather than to pursue the appellate process in the requested state (*Re F (Abduction: Refusal to Return)* [2009] 2 FLR 1023). Only if a child's non-return is pursuant to the Hague Convention 1980, Art 13, is the court or Central Authority of the home state competent to examine the question of the custody of a child under Art 11.7 (*Re RC and BC (Child Abduction) (Brussels II Revised: Article 11(7))* [2009] 1 FLR 574; *Re RD (Child Abduction) (Brussels II Revised: Arts 11(7) and 19)* [2009] 1 FLR 586).

"Opportunity to be heard" (Art 11.2)—Ensuring that a child is given the opportunity to be heard will normally be through a Cafcass report (*Re D (Abduction: Rights of Custody)* [2007] 1 FLR 961, HL; *Re F (Abduction: Child's Wishes)* [2007] 2 FLR 697, CA; *K v K* [2007] 1 FCR 355), although it may lead to

PART VI

the child being given separate party status (*Re D* (above); *Re F (Abduction: Joinder of Child as Party)* [2007] 2 FLR 313, CA; *Re M (Abduction: Zimbabwe)* [2008] 1 FLR 251, HL; *Re C (Abduction: Separate Representation of Children)* [2008] 2 FLR 6; *M v T (Abduction: Brussels II Revised, Art 11(7))* [2010] 2 FLR 1685). It may be appropriate to take into account the objections of younger children, although the objections of an older child will deserve greater weight (*Re R (Child Abduction: Acquiescence)* [1995] 1 FLR 716; *Re D* (above); *Re W (Abduction: Child's Objections)* [2010] 2 FLR 1165). There must be a clear distinction between a child's objections and a child's wishes and feelings (*Re K (Abduction: Case Management)* [2011] 1 FLR 1268, CA).

"Expeditiously" (Art 11.3)—Guidance has been given by the Court of Appeal in *Vigreux v Michel* [2006] 2 FLR 1180, at [33].

"Adequate arrangements ... to secure the protection of the child" (Art 11.4)—See *F v M (Abduction: Grave Risk of Harm)* [2008] 2 FLR 1263; *WF v FJ, BF and RF (Abduction: Child's Objections)* [2011] 1 FLR 1153; *Re K (Abduction: Case Management)*, above. The focus of Art 11.4 is to design arrangements to protect a child from being exposed on return to a grave risk of harm or placed in an intolerable situation so as to give rise to a defence under Art 13b of the Hague Convention 1980 (*WF v FJ, BF and RF (Abduction: Child's Objections)* [2011] 1 FLR 1153).

"Examine the question of custody of the child" (Art 11.7)—In exercising jurisdiction under Art 11.7, the court is neither carrying out an appeal process in respect of a decision by a foreign court nor applying Hague Convention 1980, Art 13. Rather, it is exercising its jurisdiction under Art 10 (which is a welfare jurisdiction). In exercising its welfare jurisdiction, the court has the power to make a summary order under Art 11.7 in an appropriate case. This will not involve a full welfare enquiry, even though a welfare approach is to be applied (*M v T (Abduction: Brussels II Revised, Art 11(7))* [2010] 2 FLR 1685). The foundation for this welfare jurisdiction is based on Art 11.7 and need not be categorised as deriving from the inherent jurisdiction (*D v N and D (by her Guardian Ad Litem)* [2011] 2 FLR 464). See, also, *AF v T and another (Brussels II Revised: Art II(7) Application)* [2011] 2 FLR 891, *Re H (Jurisdiction)* [2010] 1 FLR 598 and *WF v FJ, BF and RF*, above. The decision of the European Court of Human Rights in *Neulinger and Shuruk v Switzerland* [2011] 1 FLR 122 (where it was held that to enforce an order under the Hague Convention 1980 to return a child to Israel would be in breach of the right to respect for the private and family lives of mother and child under ECHR, Art 8, the mother's defence under Art 13b of the Hague Convention having been rejected) does not require a departure from the normal summary process, provided that the decision is not arbitrary or mechanical (*Re E (Children)* [2011] UKSC 84).

"Judgment which requires the return of the child" (Art 11.8)—Neither a contact order nor a shared residence order amounts to such a judgment (*Re A; HA v MB (Brussels II Revised: Article 11(7) Application)* [2008] 1 FLR 289). A judgment of the court with jurisdiction ordering the return of a child fell within the scope of Art 11.8, even if not preceded by a final judgment of that court relating to rights of custody concerning the child (*Povse v Alpago* [2010] 2 FLR 1343, ECJ).

"Shall be enforceable" (Art 11.8)—See *WF v FJ, BF and RF (Abduction: Child's Objections)* [2011] 1 FLR 1153.

Article 12

Prorogation of jurisdiction

1 The courts of a Member State exercising jurisdiction by virtue of Article 3 on an application for divorce, legal separation or marriage annulment shall have jurisdiction in any matter relating to parental responsibility connected with that application where:

 (a) at least one of the spouses has parental responsibility in relation to the child; and

 (b) the jurisdiction of the courts has been accepted expressly or otherwise in an unequivocal manner by the spouses and by the holders of parental responsibility, at the time the court is seised, and is in the superior interests of the child.

2 The jurisdiction conferred in paragraph 1 shall cease as soon as:

 (a) the judgment allowing or refusing the application for divorce, legal separation or marriage annulment has become final;

(b) in those cases where proceedings in relation to parental responsibility are still pending on the date referred to in (a), a judgment in these proceedings has become final;

(c) the proceedings referred to in (a) and (b) have come to an end for another reason.

3 The courts of a Member State shall also have jurisdiction in relation to parental responsibility in proceedings other than those referred to in paragraph 1 where:

(a) the child has a substantial connection with that Member State, in particular by virtue of the fact that one of the holders of parental responsibility is habitually resident in that Member State or that the child is a national of that Member State; and

(b) the jurisdiction of the courts has been accepted expressly or otherwise in an unequivocal manner by all the parties to the proceedings at the time the court is seised and is in the best interests of the child.

4 Where the child has his or her habitual residence in the territory of a third State which is not a contracting party to the Hague Convention of 19 October 1996 on jurisdiction, applicable law, recognition, enforcement and cooperation in respect of parental responsibility and measures for the protection of children, jurisdiction under this Article shall be deemed to be in the child's interest, in particular if it is found impossible to hold proceedings in the third State in question.

Defined terms—"court": Art 2.1; "Member State": Art 2.3; "parental responsibility": Art 2.7; "holder of parental responsibility": Art 2.8; "seised": Art 16.

Scope—The combined effect of Arts 3 and 8 is that the courts of one Member State may be seised with jurisdiction for divorce etc and the courts of another Member State seised with jurisdiction in relation to parental responsibility. Article 12 permits parties in certain circumstances to confer a time-limited parental responsibility jurisdiction on the court dealing with the divorce etc. The filing of a statement of arrangements in answer in relation to children in English divorce proceedings does not amount to unequivocal acceptance of the parental responsibility jurisdiction of the English court (*Bush v Bush* [2008] 2 FLR 1437, CA). The fact that the question of the residence of children was in issue would prevent there being "unequivocal" acceptance of jurisdiction (*Re A (Removal Outside Jurisdiction: Habitual Residence)* [2011] 1 FLR 2025). The acceptance of jurisdiction does not have to be in writing and subsequent acts and contact can illuminate the quality of the acceptance at the time the court was seised (*VC v GC (Jurisdiction: Brussels II Revised Art 12)* [2013] 1 FLR 244, applying *Re I* [2010] 1 FLR 361, SC). Where Member State 1 acquires jurisdiction under Art 12 for issues of parental responsibility concerning a child who subsequently becomes habitually resident in Member State 2, the retention of jurisdiction by Member State 1 is not conditional upon the courts of Member State 2 finding that that was in the superior interests of the child, nor could the jurisdiction of the courts of Member State 1 be terminated by a decision of the courts of Member State 2 (*Re S-R (Jurisdiction: Contact)* [2008] 2 FLR 1741; *AP v TD (Relocation: Retention of Jurisdiction)* [2011] 1 FLR 1851).

Where there are no matrimonial proceedings, Art 12.3 additionally provides that the courts of a Member State will have jurisdiction in relation to parental responsibility in specified circumstances including a substantial connection between the child and the Member State (*B v B (Brussels II Revised: Jurisdiction)* [2011] 1 FLR 54). See also, *H v H (Jurisdiction to Grant Wardship)* [2012] 1 FLR 23 and *Re A*, above.

"Superior interests of the child" (Art 12.1(b))—This is to be determined on forum conveniens principles as between competing Member States (on the balance of fairness including convenience): *Bush v Bush* [2008] 2 FLR 1437 (CA).

"Final" (Arts 12.2(a) and (b))—See *Re A (Foreign Contact Order: Jurisdiction)* [2004] 1 FLR 641; *A v L (Jurisdiction: Brussels II)* [2002] 1 FLR 1042 (judgment has not become final where there is an outstanding appeal).

"Best interests of the child" (Art 12.3(b))—See *Butt v Butt* [2011] 1 FLR 54 (jurisdiction not established despite a substantial connection and acceptance of jurisdiction where acceptance of jurisdiction is not in the best interests of the child).

"Third State" (Art 12.4)—Art 12 could apply to a child who is lawfully resident outside the EU (*Re I* [2010] 1 FLR 361).

Article 13

Jurisdiction based on the child's presence

1 Where a child's habitual residence cannot be established and jurisdiction cannot be determined on the basis of Article 12, the courts of the Member State where the child is present shall have jurisdiction.

2 Paragraph 1 shall also apply to refugee children or children internationally displaced because of disturbances occurring in their country.

Defined terms—"court": Art 2.1; "Member State": Art 2.3.

Scope—Where Arts 8–12 are not engaged because a child's habitual residence cannot be established and jurisdiction cannot be established by prorogation of jurisdiction under Art 12, the courts of the Member State where the child is present will have jurisdiction. See *Mercredi v Chaffe* [2011] 1 FLR 1293, CJEU at [57].

Article 14

Residual jurisdiction

Where no court of a Member State has jurisdiction pursuant to Articles 8 to 13, jurisdiction shall be determined, in each Member State, by the laws of that State.

Defined terms—"court": Art 2.1; "Member State": Art 2.3.

Scope—Article 14 provides for residual jurisdiction where no courts of a Member State have jurisdiction under Arts 8–13, which jurisdiction is to be determined in each Member State according to its own domestic law.

Article 15

Transfer to a court better placed to hear the case

1 By way of exception, the courts of a Member State having jurisdiction as to the substance of the matter may, if they consider that a court of another Member State, with which the child has a particular connection, would be better placed to hear the case, or a specific part thereof, and where this is in the best interests of the child:

    (a)   stay the case or the part thereof in question and invite the parties to introduce a request before the court of that other Member State in accordance with paragraph 4; or

    (b)   request a court of another Member State to assume jurisdiction in accordance with paragraph 5.

2 Paragraph 1 shall apply:

    (a)   upon application from a party; or

    (b)   of the court's own motion; or

    (c)   upon application from a court of another Member State with which the child has a particular connection, in accordance with paragraph 3.

A transfer made of the court's own motion or by application of a court of another Member State must be accepted by at least one of the parties.

3 The child shall be considered to have a particular connection to a Member State as mentioned in paragraph 1, if that Member State:

    (a)   has become the habitual residence of the child after the court referred to in paragraph 1 was seised; or

    (b)   is the former habitual residence of the child; or

    (c)   is the place of the child's nationality; or

    (d)   is the habitual residence of a holder of parental responsibility; or

    (e)   is the place where property of the child is located and the case concerns measures for the protection of the child relating to the administration, conservation or disposal of this property.

4 The court of the Member State having jurisdiction as to the substance of the matter shall set a time limit by which the courts of that other Member State shall be seised in accordance with paragraph 1.

If the courts are not seised by that time, the court which has been seised shall continue to exercise jurisdiction in accordance with Articles 8 to 14.

5 The courts of that other Member State may, where due to the specific circumstances of the case, this is in the best interests of the child, accept jurisdiction within six weeks of their seisure in accordance with paragraph 1(a) or 1(b). In this case, the court first seised shall decline jurisdiction. Otherwise, the court first seised shall continue to exercise jurisdiction in accordance with Articles 8 to 14.

6 The courts shall cooperate for the purposes of this Article, either directly or through the central authorities designated pursuant to Article 53.

Defined terms—"court": Art 2.1; "Member State": Art 2.3; "parental responsibility": Art 2.7; "holder of parental responsibility": Art 2.8; "particular connection": Art 15.3.

Scope—Article 15 provides an exceptional mechanism to transfer a (specific part of a) case to another Member State with which the child has a particular connection if that court is better placed to hear the case and it is in the best interests of the child. As to the exceptional nature of this mechanism, see *Re EC (Child Abduction: Stayed Proceedings)* [2007] 1 FLR 57, CA; *Mercredi v Chaffe* [2011] 2 FLR 515, CA; *A v B (Jurisdiction)* [2012] 1 FLR 768; and *J v J (Relinquishment of Jurisdiction)* [2012] 1 FLR 1259. The only court able to make the substantive decision under Art 15.1 is the court having jurisdiction as to the substance of the matter, although a court not having such jurisdiction could make an application to the court with jurisdiction seeking a transfer under Art 15.2(c) (see, eg *Re H (Abduction)* [2009] 2 FLR 1513). More than one such application could be made, but to justify a request for a reconsideration of an earlier decision it is not enough to demonstrate changed circumstances. It has to be shown that it is highly probable that the court seised would now come to a different decision because of a decisive change in circumstances (*AB v JLB (Brussels II Revised: Article 15)* [2009] 1 FLR 517). It is unnecessary for the English court to request a foreign court to transfer jurisdiction under art 15 in relation to family proceedings involving a child, where it could properly assume jurisdiction under art 8 where the child is habitually resident in England and where the foreign court's jurisdiction under art 12.3 (prorogation of jurisdiction) has ceased (*Re S (A Child); sub nom PB v SE* [2013] EWHC 647 (Fam)).

For an example of an application by a court of another Member State (Art 15.2(c)), see *Re S-R (Jurisdiction: Contact)* [2008] 2 FLR 1741; *LAB v KB (Abduction: Brussels II Revised)* [2010] 2 FLR 1664; *Re LM (A Child)* [2013] EWHC 646 (Fam) (High Court in England agreed to a request from the Irish High Court under art 15.1(b) to accept jurisdiction over care proceedings begun in Ireland in respect of a baby who had been born in Ireland, but whose mother was English and had returned to England).

The procedure for transfer of proceedings under Art 15 is set out in FPR 2010, rr 12.61–12.66.

Section 3
Common provisions

Article 16

Seising of a Court

1 A court shall be deemed to be seised:

(a) at the time when the document instituting the proceedings or an equivalent document is lodged with the court, provided that the applicant has not subsequently failed to take the steps he was required to take to have service effected on the respondent; or

(b) if the document has to be served before being lodged with the court, at the time when it is received by the authority responsible for service, provided that the applicant has not subsequently failed to take the steps he was required to take to have the document lodged with the court.

Defined terms—"court": Art 2.1.

Scope—A court is deemed to be seised only where a document instituting proceedings or its equivalent is lodged with the court subject to taking steps to effect service (see below). A court will not, therefore, be seised by the making of a telephone application (*Mercredi v Chaffe* [2011] 1 FLR 1293, CJEU). To ensure that a court is seised, proceedings must not simply be issued but the process of service must be started. However, there is no time limit for service of divorce proceedings in England and Wales. Furthermore, irregular service (eg on a Sunday) will not necessarily nullify the proceedings (*W v W (Divorce Proceedings)* [2011] 1 FLR 372). Issuing proceedings as a precautionary measure, but not then effecting service, will not gain priority under Brussels IIA (*R v R (Divorce: Stay of Proceedings)* [1994] 2 FLR 1036). See, also, *C v S (Divorce: Jurisdiction)* [2011] 2 FLR 19. Actual service need not be effected to establish jurisdiction. The International Committee of Resolution (*International Aspects of Family Law* (3rd edn 2009), p 359) expressed the view that the required steps to effect service will have been taken when documents have been sent to the transmitting agency, eg the Foreign Process Section of the RCJ.

Service is available through formal channels: see the EU Service Regulation 1393/2007 of 13 November 2007 (set out below) on the service in the Member States of judicial and extra-judicial documents in civil or commercial matters, which applies from 13 November 2008. It provides a procedure for the service of documents through designated "transmitting agencies" and "receiving agencies" in Member States without recourse to consular and diplomatic channels. The Regulation applies to all EU Member States including Denmark.

"Lodged"—Lodged means that a document is filed with the court in a manner which is accepted by the court and which leads to the institution of proceedings by the court. There is no sanction for failing to file a marriage certificate as required by FPR PD7A, para 3 (*L-K v K (No 3)* [2007] 2 FLR 741). Such a failure is a minor procedural irregularity and not fatal to England being seised with jurisdiction. The requirement is administrative rather than substantive and the court may dispense with the requirement retrospectively (*L-K v K (Brussels II Revised: Maintenance Pending Suit)* [2006] 2 FLR 1113). Article 16.1 does not say that a court is seised when a document has been lodged and the applicant has effected (or taken the required step to effect) service, but that the court is seised when the document is lodged, subject to the proviso that there has not been a subsequent failure to take required steps (*W v W (Divorce Proceedings)* [2011] 1 FLR 372).

Article 17

Examination as to jurisdiction

Where a court of a Member State is seised of a case over which it has no jurisdiction under this Regulation and over which a court of another Member State has jurisdiction by virtue of this Regulation, it shall declare of its own motion that it has no jurisdiction.

Defined terms—"court": Art 2.1; "Member State": Art 2.3.

Scope—Article 17 places a duty upon the courts of Member States to conduct an examination as to jurisdiction. See also FPR 2010, r 7.27(4); *Re H (Child Abduction)* [2012] EWCA Civ 913.

Article 18

Examination as to admissibility

1 Where a respondent habitually resident in a State other than the Member State where the action was brought does not enter an appearance, the court with jurisdiction shall stay the proceedings so long as it is not shown that the respondent has been able to receive the document instituting the proceedings or an equivalent document in sufficient time to enable him to arrange for his defence, or that all necessary steps have been taken to this end.

2 Article 19 of Regulation (EC) No 1348/2000 shall apply instead of the provisions of paragraph 1 of this Article if the document instituting the proceedings or an equivalent document had to be transmitted from one Member State to another pursuant to that Regulation.

3 Where the provisions of Regulation (EC) No 1348/2000 are not applicable, Article 15 of the Hague Convention of 15 November 1965 on the service abroad of judicial and

extrajudicial documents in civil or commercial matters shall apply if the document instituting the proceedings or an equivalent document had to be transmitted abroad pursuant to that Convention.

Defined terms—"Member State": Art 2.3; "court": Art 2.1.

Scope—Comparable with the duty imposed by Art 17 to conduct an examination as to the court's jurisdiction is the duty imposed by this Article to stay proceedings until it can be shown that a respondent, habitually resident in a Member State other than that in which the proceedings are taking place and who has not entered an appearance (e g an acknowledgment of service), has been able to receive the relevant documents in sufficient time to enable him to arrange for his defence, or that all necessary steps have been taken to this end. This duty does not apply if service was in accordance with the EU Service Regulation (EC) 1393/2007 of 13 November 2007 (set out below): see annotations to Art 16.

Article 19

Lis pendens and dependent actions

1 Where proceedings relating to divorce, legal separation or marriage annulment between the same parties are brought before courts of different Member States, the court second seised shall of its own motion stay its proceedings until such time as the jurisdiction of the court first seised is established.

2 Where proceedings relating to parental responsibility relating to the same child and involving the same cause of action are brought before courts of different Member States, the court second seised shall of its own motion stay its proceedings until such time as the jurisdiction of the court first seised is established.

3 Where the jurisdiction of the court first seised is established, the court second seised shall decline jurisdiction in favour of that court.

In that case, the party who brought the relevant action before the court second seised may bring that action before the court first seised.

Defined terms—"court": Art 2.1; "Member State": Art 2.3; "seised": Art 16; "parental responsibility": Art 2.7.

Scope—Where there are concurrent proceedings relating to either divorce, legal separation or marriage annulment or parental responsibility between the same parties before courts of different Member States, the court second seised must, of its own motion, stay its proceedings until such time as the jurisdiction of the court first seised is established (e g *Re RD (Child Abduction) (Brussels II Revised: Arts 11(7) and (19))* [2009] 1 FLR 586; *A v B (Jurisdiction)* [2012] 1 FLR 768). There is no provision to decline jurisdiction on the basis that another jurisdiction is the forum conveniens (*Wermuth v Wermuth (No 1)* [2003] 1 FLR 1022; *Wermuth v Wermuth (No 2)* [2003] 1 FLR 1029, CA). However, determination of which of the competing jurisdictions is first seised may be left to the court of another Member State in an appropriate case (*Chorley v Chorley* [2005] 2 FLR 38 (CA)). Where proceedings in the court first seised have been brought to an end, that court will no longer be seised for the purposes of Art 19, unless and until an application for revival was made, and accordingly a court second seised could correctly assume jurisdiction (*C v S (Divorce: Jurisdiction)* [2011] 2 FLR 19). Art 19.2 is not applicable where a court of a Member State first seised for the purposes of obtaining measures in matters of parental responsibility is seised only for the purposes of it granting provisional measures under Art 20 (*Purrucker v Vallés Pérez (No 2)* Case C-296/10 [2012] 1 FLR 925, CJEU).

For the procedure for an application for a stay under Art 19, see FPR 2010, r 7.27.

Article 20

Provisional, including protective, measures

1 In urgent cases, the provisions of this Regulation shall not prevent the courts of a Member State from taking such provisional, including protective, measures in respect of persons or assets in that State as may be available under the law of that State, even if, under this Regulation, the court of another Member State has jurisdiction as to the substance of the matter.

PART VI

2 The measures referred to in paragraph 1 shall cease to apply when the court of the Member State having jurisdiction under this Regulation as to the substance of the matter has taken the measures it considers appropriate.

Defined terms—"court": Art 2.1; "Member State": Art 2.3.

Scope—In urgent cases, Art 20 enables the courts of a Member State to take such provisional, including protective, measures even if the courts of another Member State have jurisdiction as to the substance of the matter. Art 20.1 entitles the courts of a Member State to take provisional or other protective measures only if three cumulative conditions are satisfied: the measures concerned must be urgent, must be taken in respect of persons or assets in the Member State and must be provisional (*Detiček v Sgueglia* [2010] 1 FLR 1381, ECJ). A measure under Art 20 may prevail over an earlier judgment adopted by the court of another Member State that has substantive jurisdiction. However, the system of recognition and enforcement provided for by Brussels IIA is not applicable to measures that fall within Art 20 (*Purrucker v Vallés Pérez (No 1)* Case C-256/09 [2012] 1 FLR 903, CJEU). Measures under Art 20 include the power to make interim orders, including care orders in public law proceedings in respect of a child who is habitually resident in another Member State where the child is currently living in the Member State making the interim order (*Re A (Area of Freedom, Security and Justice)* (C-523/07) [2009] 2 FLR 1, ECJ; *Re S (Care: Jurisdiction)* [2009] 2 FLR 550). Article 20 refers to measures intended to preserve the factual or legal situation so as to safeguard rights, the recognition of which is being sought elsewhere in litigation in the court which has jurisdiction as to the substance of the matter. Maintenance pending suit does not fall within Art 20 (*Wermuth v Wermuth (No 2)* [2003] 1 FLR 1029 (CA)). However, where there are concurrent proceedings and the other Member State has declined jurisdiction at first instance on the basis that it was not first seised, but its appeal process is not completed, there is jurisdiction to make an order for maintenance pending suit so long as the decision of the court at first instance in the other Member State remains in force (*L-K v K (Brussels II Revised: Maintenance Pending Suit)* [2006] 2 FLR 1113). It was held in *Moses-Taiga v Taiga* [2006] 1 FLR 1074 that an order for maintenance pending suit could be made even when the divorce jurisdiction was subject to challenge. See also the notes to Art 56.

CHAPTER III
RECOGNITION AND ENFORCEMENT

Section 1
Recognition

Article 21

Recognition of a judgment

1 A judgment given in a Member State shall be recognised in the other Member States without any special procedure being required.

2 In particular, and without prejudice to paragraph 3, no special procedure shall be required for updating the civil-status records of a Member State on the basis of a judgment relating to divorce, legal separation or marriage annulment given in another Member State, and against which no further appeal lies under the law of that Member State.

3 Without prejudice to Section 4 of this Chapter, any interested party may, in accordance with the procedures provided for in Section 2 of this Chapter, apply for a decision that the judgment be or not be recognised.

The local jurisdiction of the court appearing in the list notified by each Member State to the Commission pursuant to Article 68 shall be determined by the internal law of the Member State in which proceedings for recognition or non-recognition are brought.

4 Where the recognition of a judgment is raised as an incidental question in a court of a Member State, that court may determine that issue.

Defined terms—"judgment": Art 2.4; "Member State": Art 2.3; "court": Art 2.1.

Scope—Article 21 establishes the principle of automatic recognition in all Member States of orders covered by Brussels IIA made in one Member State without any special procedure, although some Member States insist on the filing of a certificate under Art 34. The general rule established in Art 21 is subject to the exceptions contained in Arts 22 (divorce, legal separation and marriage annulment) and 23 (parental responsibility) as well as the stay provisions of Art 27.

For a discussion of the relationship between ss 1 (recognition) and 2 (enforceability) of Chapter III, see annotations to Art 28. Registration of a judgment under FPR 2010, r 31.1 serves for the purposes of Art 21.3 as a decision that the judgment is recognised (FPR 2010, r 31.12).

Article 22

Grounds of non-recognition for judgments relating to divorce, legal separation or marriage annulment

A judgment relating to a divorce, legal separation or marriage annulment shall not be recognised:

(a) if such recognition is manifestly contrary to the public policy of the Member State in which recognition is sought;

(b) where it was given in default of appearance, if the respondent was not served with the document which instituted the proceedings or with an equivalent document in sufficient time and in such a way as to enable the respondent to arrange for his or her defence unless it is determined that the respondent has accepted the judgment unequivocally;

(c) if it is irreconcilable with a judgment given in proceedings between the same parties in the Member State in which recognition is sought; or

(d) if it is irreconcilable with an earlier judgment given in another Member State or in a non-Member State between the same parties, provided that the earlier judgment fulfils the conditions necessary for its recognition in the Member State in which recognition is sought.

Defined terms—"judgment": Art 2.4; "Member State": Art 2.3.

"Public policy"—See annotations to Art 23.

Article 23

Grounds of non-recognition for judgments relating to parental responsibility

A judgment relating to parental responsibility shall not be recognised:

(a) if such recognition is manifestly contrary to the public policy of the Member State in which recognition is sought taking into account the best interests of the child;

(b) if it was given, except in case of urgency, without the child having been given an opportunity to be heard, in violation of fundamental principles of procedure of the Member State in which recognition is sought;

(c) where it was given in default of appearance if the person in default was not served with the document which instituted the proceedings or with an equivalent document in sufficient time and in such a way as to enable that person to arrange for his or her defence unless it is determined that such person has accepted the judgment unequivocally;

(d) on the request of any person claiming that the judgment infringes his or her parental responsibility, if it was given without such person having been given an opportunity to be heard;

(e) if it is irreconcilable with a later judgment relating to parental responsibility given in the Member State in which recognition is sought;

(f) if it is irreconcilable with a later judgment relating to parental responsibility given in another Member State or in the non-Member State of the habitual residence of the child provided that the later judgment fulfils the conditions necessary for its recognition in the Member State in which recognition is sought; or

(g) if the procedure laid down in Article 56 has not been complied with.

Defined terms—"judgment": Art 2.4; "parental responsibility": Art 2.7; "Member State": Art 2.3.

Scope—Art 23 sets out the grounds on which a judgment relating to parental responsibility will not be recognised. Only in the most exceptional circumstances would the policy of Brussels IIA be allowed to be subverted by non-recognition and/or non-enforcement (*Re S (Brussels II: Recognition: Best Interests of the Child) (No 1)* [2004] 1 FLR 571; *W v W (Residence: Enforcement of Order)* [2005] EWHC 1811 (Fam); *Re D (Brussels II Revised: Contact)* [2008] 1 FLR 516; *LAB v KB (Abduction: Brussels II Revised)* [2010] 2 FLR 1664). The passage of time is not, without substantially more, sufficient to avoid recognition (*LAB v KB (Abduction: Brussels II Revised)*).

"Public policy"—There is no definition of "public policy" in Brussels IIA. A refusal to recognise a judgment based on public policy should operate only in exceptional circumstances (*Hoffman v Krieg* (No 145/86) [1988] ECR 645, (1988) *The Times*, March 26 ECJ) in relation to Brussels I; *Re S (Brussels II: Recognition: Best interests of the child) (No 1)* [2004] 1 FLR 571; *LAB v KB (Abduction: Brussels II Revised)* [2010] 2 FLR 1664; *Re L (Brussels II Revised: Appeal)* [2013] 1 FLR 430; *JRG v EB (Abduction: Brussels II Revised)* [2013] 1 FLR 203). However, there might be extremely rare cases in which the order of a foreign court was so contrary to the welfare of the child that its recognition was manifestly contrary to English public policy (*LAB v KB (Abduction: Brussels II Revised)*).

Article 24

Prohibition of review of jurisdiction of the court of origin

The jurisdiction of the court of the Member State of origin may not be reviewed. The test of public policy referred to in Articles 22(a) and 23(a) may not be applied to the rules relating to jurisdiction set out in Articles 3 to 14.

Defined terms—"court": Art 2.1; "Member State": Art 2.3.

"Public policy"—See annotations to Art 23.

Article 25

Differences in applicable law

The recognition of a judgment may not be refused because the law of the Member State in which such recognition is sought would not allow divorce, legal separation or marriage annulment on the same facts.

Defined terms—"judgment": Art 2.4; "Member State": Art 2.3.

Article 26

Non-review as to substance

Under no circumstances may a judgment be reviewed as to its substance.

Defined terms—"judgment": Art 2.4.

Article 27

Stay of proceedings

1 A court of a Member State in which recognition is sought of a judgment given in another Member State may stay the proceedings if an ordinary appeal against the judgment has been lodged.

2 A court of a Member State in which recognition is sought of a judgment given in Ireland or the United Kingdom may stay the proceedings if enforcement is suspended in the Member State of origin by reason of an appeal.

Defined terms—"court": Art 2.1; "Member State": Art 2.3; "judgment": Art 2.4.

Scope—Recognition proceedings of an order made in another Member State may be stayed if the order is under appeal or, in the case of an order given in Ireland or the UK, if enforcement is suspended by reason of an appeal.

Section 2
Application for a declaration of enforceability

Article 28
Enforceable judgments

1 A judgment on the exercise of parental responsibility in respect of a child given in a Member State which is enforceable in that Member State and has been served shall be enforced in another Member State when, on the application of any interested party, it has been declared enforceable there.

2 However, in the United Kingdom, such a judgment shall be enforced in England and Wales, in Scotland or in Northern Ireland only when, on the application of any interested party, it has been registered for enforcement in that part of the United Kingdom.

Defined terms—"judgment": Art 2.4; "parental responsibility": Art 2.7; "Member State": Art 2.3.

Scope—Section 2 of Chapter III (Arts 28–36) provides for an application for a declaration of enforceability in the Member State where it is sought to enforce the judgment. Recognition (Section 1 of Chapter III) is dealt with separately from enforceability (Section 2 of Chapter III) in Brussels IIA. Nonetheless, an application for a declaration of enforceability (in the rest of Europe) or for registration (in the UK) and applying for a judgment to be recognised are one and the same thing. Similarly, an appeal against the registration of a judgment is the means by which an application is made for a judgment not to be recognised (*Re D (Brussels II Revised: Contact)* [2008] 1 FLR 516).

Article 28.2 provides that in the UK a judgment on parental responsibility given in another Member State is only enforceable when, on the application of any interested party, it has been registered for enforcement in the relevant part of the UK. References to a "declaration of enforceability" in the UK are references to a notice of registration of the judgment under FPR 2010, r 31.11 (*Re D (Brussels II Revised: Contact)* [2008] 1 FLR 516).

The procedure for registration of incoming orders from another Member State under Brussels IIA is to be found in FPR 2010, Pt 31 and PD31A.

Article 29
Jurisdiction of local courts

1 An application for a declaration of enforceability shall be submitted to the court appearing in the list notified by each Member State to the Commission pursuant to Article 68.

2 The local jurisdiction shall be determined by reference to the place of habitual residence of the person against whom enforcement is sought or by reference to the habitual residence of any child to whom the application relates.

Where neither of the places referred to in the first subparagraph can be found in the Member State of enforcement, the local jurisdiction shall be determined by reference to the place of enforcement.

Defined terms—"Member State": Art 2.3: "Member State of enforcement": Art 2.6.

Scope—An application for permission under Art 29 should be submitted to the Principal Registry of the Family Division and is essentially administrative, falling within the province of a district judge (*Re S (Foreign Contact Order)* [2010] 1 FLR 982).

PART VI

Article 30

Procedure

1 The procedure for making the application shall be governed by the law of the Member State of enforcement.

2 The applicant must give an address for service within the area of jurisdiction of the court applied to. However, if the law of the Member State of enforcement does not provide for the furnishing of such an address, the applicant shall appoint a representative ad litem.

3 The documents referred to in Articles 37 and 39 shall be attached to the application.

Defined terms—"Member State of enforcement": Art 2.3; "court": Art 2.1.

Article 31

Decision of the court

1 The court applied to shall give its decision without delay. Neither the person against whom enforcement is sought, nor the child shall, at this stage of the proceedings, be entitled to make any submissions on the application.

2 The application may be refused only for one of the reasons specified in Articles 22, 23 and 24.

3 Under no circumstances may a judgment be reviewed as to its substance.

Defined terms—"court": Art 2.1; "judgment": Art 2.4.

"Submissions" (Art 31.1)—Art 31.1 does not apply to proceedings for non-recognition of a judicial decision (*Re Rinau (Case C-195/08 PPU)* [2008] 2 FLR 1495, ECJ).

Article 32

Notice of the decision

The appropriate officer of the court shall without delay bring to the notice of the applicant the decision given on the application in accordance with the procedure laid down by the law of the Member State of enforcement.

Defined terms—"court": Art 21; "Member State of enforcement": Art 2.6.

Article 33

Appeal against the decision

1 The decision on the application for a declaration of enforceability may be appealed against by either party.

2 The appeal shall be lodged with the court appearing in the list notified by each Member State to the Commission pursuant to Article 68.

3 The appeal shall be dealt with in accordance with the rules governing procedure in contradictory matters.

4 If the appeal is brought by the applicant for a declaration of enforceability, the party against whom enforcement is sought shall be summoned to appear before the appellate court. If such person fails to appear, the provisions of Article 18 shall apply.

5 An appeal against a declaration of enforceability must be lodged within one month of service thereof. If the party against whom enforcement is sought is habitually resident in a Member State other than that in which the declaration of enforceability was given, the time for appealing shall be two months and shall run from the date of service, either on him or at his residence. No extension of time may be granted on account of distance.

Defined terms—"court": Art 2.1; "Member State": Art 2.3.

Scope—An appeal under Art 33 against registration is directed to the Principal Registry of the Family Division of the High Court to be heard by a Family Division judge. No permission to appeal is required. A second appeal lies under Art 34 to the Court of Appeal and permission to appeal is required (*Re S (Foreign Contact Order)* [2010] 1 FLR 982).

Article 34

Courts of appeal and means of contest

The judgment given on appeal may be contested only by the proceedings referred to in the list notified by each Member State to the Commission pursuant to Article 68.

Defined terms—"judgment": Art 2.4; "Member State": Art 2.3.

Article 35

Stay of proceedings

1 The court with which the appeal is lodged under Articles 33 or 34 may, on the application of the party against whom enforcement is sought, stay the proceedings if an ordinary appeal has been lodged in the Member State of origin, or if the time for such appeal has not yet expired. In the latter case, the court may specify the time within which an appeal is to be lodged.

2 Where the judgment was given in Ireland or the United Kingdom, any form of appeal available in the Member State of origin shall be treated as an ordinary appeal for the purposes of paragraph 1.

Defined terms—"court": Art 2.1; "Member State of origin": Art 2.5; "judgment": Art 2.4.

Article 36

Partial enforcement

1 Where a judgment has been given in respect of several matters and enforcement cannot be authorised for all of them, the court shall authorise enforcement for one or more of them.

2 An applicant may request partial enforcement of a judgment.

Defined terms—"judgment": Art 2.4; "court": Art 2.1.

Section 3
Provisions common to Sections 1 and 2

Article 37

Documents

1 A party seeking or contesting recognition or applying for a declaration of enforceability shall produce:

    (a) a copy of the judgment which satisfies the conditions necessary to establish its authenticity; and

    (b) the certificate referred to in Article 39.

2 In addition, in the case of a judgment given in default, the party seeking recognition or applying for a declaration of enforceability shall produce:

PART VI

  (a) the original or certified true copy of the document which establishes that the
       defaulting party was served with the document instituting the proceedings or
       with an equivalent document; or
  (b) any document indicating that the defendant has accepted the judgment
       unequivocally.

Defined terms—"judgment": Art 2.4.

Article 38

Absence of documents

1 If the documents specified in Article 37(1)(b) or (2) are not produced, the court may
specify a time for their production, accept equivalent documents or, if it considers that it
has sufficient information before it, dispense with their production.

2 If the court so requires, a translation of such documents shall be furnished. The
translation shall be certified by a person qualified to do so in one of the Member States.

Defined terms—"court": Art 2.1; "Member State": Art 2.3.

Article 39

Certificate concerning judgments in matrimonial matters and certificate concerning judgments on parental responsibility

The competent court or authority of a Member State of origin shall, at the request of any
interested party, issue a certificate using the standard form set out in Annex I (judgments
in matrimonial matters) or in Annex II (judgments on parental responsibility).

Defined terms—"court": Art 2.1; "Member State of origin": Art 2.5.

"Certificate"—See *MA v DB (Inherent Jurisdiction)* [2011] 1 FLR 724.

Section 4
Enforceability of certain judgments concerning rights of access and of certain judgments which require the return of the child

Article 40

Scope

1 This Section shall apply to:

  (a) rights of access; and
  (b) the return of a child entailed by a judgment given pursuant to Article 11(8).

2 The provisions of this Section shall not prevent a holder of parental responsibility
from seeking recognition and enforcement of a judgment in accordance with the
provisions in Sections 1 and 2 of this Chapter.

Defined terms—"right of access": Art 2.10; "judgment": Art 2.4; "holder of parental responsibility":
Art 2.8.

Scope—Section 4 of Chapter 3 makes special provision for the enforceability of judgments relating to
rights of access (Art 41) and the return of a child (Art 42). In these two categories the requirement to
obtain the declaration of enforceability is substituted by a certificate granted by the court in the Member
State where the order was made.

Article 41

Rights of access

1 The rights of access referred to in Article 40(1)(a) granted in an enforceable judgment given in a Member State shall be recognised and enforceable in another Member State without the need for a declaration of enforceability and without any possibility of opposing its recognition if the judgment has been certified in the Member State of origin in accordance with paragraph 2.

Even if national law does not provide for enforceability by operation of law of a judgment granting access rights, the court of origin may declare that the judgment shall be enforceable, notwithstanding any appeal.

2 The judge of origin shall issue the certificate referred to in paragraph 1 using the standard form in Annex III (certificate concerning rights of access) only if:

(a) where the judgment was given in default, the person defaulting was served with the document which instituted the proceedings or with an equivalent document in sufficient time and in such a way as to enable that person to arrange for his or her defense, or, the person has been served with the document but not in compliance with these conditions, it is nevertheless established that he or she accepted the decision unequivocally;

(b) all parties concerned were given an opportunity to be heard; and

(c) the child was given an opportunity to be heard, unless a hearing was considered inappropriate having regard to his or her age or degree of maturity.

The certificate shall be completed in the language of the judgment.

3 Where the rights of access involve a cross-border situation at the time of the delivery of the judgment, the certificate shall be issued ex officio when the judgment becomes enforceable, even if only provisionally. If the situation subsequently acquires a cross-border character, the certificate shall be issued at the request of one of the parties.

Defined terms—"rights of access": Art 2.10; "judgment": Art 2.4; "Member State": Art 2.3; "Member State of origin": Art 2.5.

"Certificate"—See *Re C (Costs: Enforcement of Foreign Contact Order)* [2008] 1 FLR 619; *AD v CD and AD* [2008] 1 FLR 1003; *Re S (Brussels II Revised: Enforcement of Contact Order)* [2008] 2 FLR 1358; *MA v DB (Inherent Jurisdiction)* [2011] 1 FLR 724.

Article 42

Return of the child

1 The return of a child referred to in Article 40(1)(b) entailed by an enforceable judgment given in a Member State shall be recognised and enforceable in another Member State without the need for a declaration of enforceability and without any possibility of opposing its recognition if the judgment has been certified in the Member State of origin in accordance with paragraph 2.

Even if national law does not provide for enforceability by operation of law, notwithstanding any appeal, of a judgment requiring the return of the child mentioned in Article 11(b)(8), the court of origin may declare the judgment enforceable.

2 The judge of origin who delivered the judgment referred to in Article 40(1)(b) shall issue the certificate referred to in paragraph 1 only if:

(a) the child was given an opportunity to be heard, unless a hearing was considered inappropriate having regard to his or her age or degree of maturity;

(b) the parties were given an opportunity to be heard; and

PART VI

(c)   the court has taken into account in issuing its judgment the reasons for and
        evidence underlying the order issued pursuant to Article 13 of the 1980 Hague
        Convention.

In the event that the court or any other authority takes measures to ensure the protection
of the child after its return to the State of habitual residence, the certificate shall contain
details of such measures.

The judge of origin shall of his or her own motion issue that certificate using the standard
form in Annex IV (certificate concerning return of the child(ren)).

The certificate shall be completed in the language of the judgment.

Defined terms—"judgment": Art 2.4; "Member State": Art 2.3; "Member State of origin": Art 2.5;
"court": Art 2.1; "judge": Art 2.2.

Certificate—See *Re Rinau* [2008] 2 FLR 1495, ECJ (a certificate under Art 42 cannot be issued unless a
judgment of non-return has been issued beforehand, even if that decision has been challenged).
Enforcement of a certified judgment could not be refused in the enforcement state because of welfare
concerns, which must be pleaded in the Member State of origin and which should also hear any
application to suspend enforcement of its judgment.

"Opportunity to be heard"—The requirement to give the child and the parties an opportunity to be
heard does not impose an obligation to do nothing until the child and/or the parents have been heard (*Re A
(Custody Decision after Maltese Non-Return Order)* [2007] 1 FLR 1923).

Article 43

Rectification of the certificate

1 The law of the Member State of origin shall be applicable to any rectification of the
certificate.

2 No appeal shall lie against the issuing of a certificate pursuant to Articles 41(1) or
42(1).

Defined terms—"Member State of origin": Art 2.5.

Article 44

Effects of the certificate

The certificate shall take effect only within the limits of the enforceability of the
judgment.

Defined terms—"judgment": Art 2.4.

Article 45

Documents

1 A party seeking enforcement of a judgment shall produce:

(a)   a copy of the judgment which satisfies the conditions necessary to establish its
        authenticity; and

(b)   the certificate referred to in Article 41(1) or Article 42(1).

2 For the purposes of this Article,

–   the certificate referred to in Article 41(1) shall be accompanied by a translation
     of point 12 relating to the arrangements for exercising right of access,

–   the certificate referred to in Article 42(1) shall be accompanied by a translation
     of its point 14 relating to the arrangements for implementing the measures
     taken to ensure the child's return.

The translation shall be into the official language or one of the official languages of the Member State of enforcement or any other language that the Member State of enforcement expressly accepts. The translation shall be certified by a person qualified to do so in one of the Member States.

Defined terms—"judgment": Art 2.4; rights of access": Art 2.10; "Member State of enforcement": Art 2.6; "Member State": Art 2.3.

Section 5
Authentic instruments and agreements

Article 46

Documents which have been formally drawn up or registered as authentic instruments and are enforceable in one Member State and also agreements between the parties that are enforceable in the Member State in which they were concluded shall be recognised and declared enforceable under the same conditions as judgments.

Defined terms—"Member State": Art 2.3; "judgment": Art 2.4.

Section 6
Other provisions

Article 47

Enforcement procedure

1 The enforcement procedure is governed by the law of the Member State of enforcement.

2 Any judgment delivered by a court of another Member State and declared to be enforceable in accordance with Section 2 or certified in accordance with Article 41(1) or Article 42(1) shall be enforced in the Member State of enforcement in the same conditions as if it had been delivered in that Member State.

In particular, a judgment which has been certified according to Article 41(1) or Article 42(1) cannot be enforced if it is irreconcilable with a subsequent enforceable judgment.

Defined terms—"Member State": Art 2.3; "judgment": Art 2.4; "Member State of enforcement": Art 2.6.

"Subsequent enforceable judgment" (Art 47.2)—Art 47.2 is to be interpreted as meaning that a judgment delivered subsequently by a court in the enforcement state, awarding provisional custody rights, and deemed to be enforceable under the law of that state, could not preclude enforcement of a certified judgment delivered previously by the court with jurisdiction in the Member State of origin, ordering the return of the child (*Povse v Alpago* [2010] 2 FLR 1343, ECJ).

Article 48

Practical arrangements for the exercise of rights of access

1 The courts of the Member State of enforcement may make practical arrangements for organising the exercise of rights of access, if the necessary arrangements have not or have not sufficiently been made in the judgment delivered by the courts of the Member State having jurisdiction as to the substance of the matter and provided the essential elements of this judgment are respected.

PART VI

2 The practical arrangements made pursuant to paragraph 1 shall cease to apply pursuant to a later judgment by the courts of the Member State having jurisdiction as to the substance of the matter.

Defined terms—"court": Art 2.1; "Member State of enforcement": Art 2.6; "Member State": Art 2.3; "rights of access": Art 2.10; "judgment": Art 2.4.

Scope—Article 48 provides that the courts of a Member State where access is to be enforced may make practical arrangements for organising access if not set out sufficiently or at all in the original order. Any arrangements made under Art 48 cease to apply if the courts of the Member State having jurisdiction as to the substance of the matter make a further order.

Article 49

Costs

The provisions of this Chapter, with the exception of Section 4, shall also apply to the determination of the amount of costs and expenses of proceedings under this Regulation and to the enforcement of any order concerning such costs and expenses.

Article 50

Legal aid

An applicant who, in the Member State of origin, has benefited from complete or partial legal aid or exemption from costs or expenses shall be entitled, in the procedures provided for in Articles 21, 28, 41, 42 and 48 to benefit from the most favourable legal aid or the most extensive exemption from costs and expenses provided for by the law of the Member State of enforcement.

Defined terms—"Member State of origin": Art 2.5; "Member State of enforcement": Art 2.6.

Article 51

Security, bond or deposit

No security, bond or deposit, however described, shall be required of a party who in one Member State applies for enforcement of a judgment given in another Member State on the following grounds:

  (a) that he or she is not habitually resident in the Member State in which enforcement is sought; or
  (b) that he or she is either a foreign national or, where enforcement is sought in either the United Kingdom or Ireland, does not have his or her "domicile" in either of those Member States.

Defined terms—"Member State": Art 2.3; "judgment": Art 2.4.

Article 52

Legalisation or other similar formality

No legalisation or other similar formality shall be required in respect of the documents referred to in Articles 37, 38 and 45 or in respect of a document appointing a representative ad litem.

CHAPTER IV
COOPERATION BETWEEN CENTRAL AUTHORITIES IN MATTERS OF
PARENTAL RESPONSIBILITY

Article 53

Designation

Each Member State shall designate one or more central authorities to assist with the
application of this Regulation and shall specify the geographical or functional
jurisdiction of each. Where a Member State has designated more than one central
authority, communications shall normally be sent direct to the relevant central authority
with jurisdiction. Where a communication is sent to a central authority without
jurisdiction, the latter shall be responsible for forwarding it to the central authority with
jurisdiction and informing the sender accordingly.

Defined terms—"Member State": Art 2.3.

Scope—Chapter IV (Arts 53–58) places the responsibility on Central Authorities in Member States to
communicate requests for assistance by holders of parental responsibility and to facilitate international
cooperation under Brussels IIA in the context of comity, information, child welfare and child protection.

Article 54

General functions

The central authorities shall communicate information on national laws and procedures
and take measures to improve the application of this Regulation and strengthening their
cooperation. For this purpose the European Judicial Network in civil and commercial
matters created by Decision No 2001/470/EC shall be used.

Article 55

Cooperation on cases specific to parental responsibility

The central authorities shall, upon request from a central authority of another Member
State or from a holder of parental responsibility, cooperate on specific cases to achieve
the purposes of this Regulation. To this end, they shall, acting directly or through public
authorities or other bodies, take all appropriate steps in accordance with the law of that
Member State in matters of personal data protection to:

  (a)   collect and exchange information:
        (i)   on the situation of the child;
        (ii)   on any procedures under way; or
        (iii) on decisions taken concerning the child;
  (b)   provide information and assistance to holders of parental responsibility seeking
        the recognition and enforcement of decisions on their territory, in particular
        concerning rights of access and the return of the child;
  (c)   facilitate communications between courts, in particular for the application of
        Article 11(6) and (7) and Article 15;
  (d)   provide such information and assistance as is needed by courts to apply
        Article 56; and
  (e)   facilitate agreement between holders of parental responsibility through
        mediation or other means, and facilitate cross-border cooperation to this end.

Defined terms—"Member State": Art 2.3; "holder of parental responsibility": Art 2.8.

PART VI

Article 56

Placement of a child in another Member State

1 Where a court having jurisdiction under Articles 8 to 15 contemplates the placement of a child in institutional care or with a foster family and where such placement is to take place in another Member State, it shall first consult the central authority or other authority having jurisdiction in the latter State where public authority intervention in that Member State is required for domestic cases of child placement.

2 The judgment on placement referred to in paragraph 1 may be made in the requesting State only if the competent authority of the requested State has consented to the placement.

3 The procedures for consultation or consent referred to in paragraphs 1 and 2 shall be governed by the national law of the requested State.

4 Where the authority having jurisdiction under Articles 8 to 15 decides to place the child in a foster family, and where such placement is to take place in another Member State and where no public authority intervention is required in the latter Member State for domestic cases of child placement, it shall so inform the central authority or other authority having jurisdiction in the latter State.

Defined terms—"court": Art 2.1; "Member State": Art 2.3; "judgment": Art 2.4.

Scope—This article permits the placement of a child in institutional care or with a foster family in another Member State following consultation with, and the consent of, the competent authority in the requested state. FPR 2010, r 31.17 has been amended by the Family Procedure (Amendment) (No 2) Rules 2012 with effect from 1 July 2012 so that the court has a discretion to permit urgent enforcement where necessary to secure a child's welfare, notwithstanding the general position that enforcement is suspended pending expiry of the relevant appeal period. The amendment ensures compliance with the judgment of the CJEU in *Health Service Executive v SC and AC* (Case C-92/12) [2012] 2 FLR 1040, CJEU, which determined that the possibility of appeals against a decision on registration of an order from another Member State under Brussels IIA should not result in automatic suspension of enforcement of a registered order during the time limit for appealing where the best interests of the child require enforcement as a matter of urgency. The amendment obviates the need to resort to Art 20 (provisional, including protective, measures). See, also, *HSE Ireland v SF (A Minor)* [2012] 2 FLR 1131.

"Placement of a child in institutional care or with a foster family" (Art 56.1)—The purpose of Art 56 is to require a court that is considering placing a child in institutional or foster care in another Member State to consult any authority responsible for child placements in that Member State and not to decide on any such placement without that authority's consent. Art 56 does not give a Member State an entitlement to call for the placement of a child within its jurisdiction (*Re AB (BIIR: Care Proceedings)* [2013] 1 FLR 168).

"Institutional care" (Art 56.1)—Institutional care includes a placement in a secure care institution (*Health Service Executive v SC and AC* (Case C-92/12) [2012] 2 FLR 1040, CJEU).

"Consented to the placement" (Art 56.2)—The consent must be given before the making of the judgment on the placement of the child by the competent authority and not merely by the institution where the child is to be placed (*Health Service Executive v SC and AC* (Case C-92/12) [2012] 2 FLR 1040, CJEU). Where consent to the placement is given for a specified period of time, that consent does not apply to orders that are intended to extend the duration of the placement. In such circumstances, an application for a new consent must be made, together with a new declaration of enforceability under Art 28 (*Health Service Executive v SC and AC*, above).

Article 57

Working method

1 Any holder of parental responsibility may submit, to the central authority of the Member State of his or her habitual residence or to the central authority of the Member State where the child is habitually resident or present, a request for assistance as mentioned in Article 55. In general, the request shall include all available information of relevance to its enforcement. Where the request for assistance concerns the recognition

or enforcement of a judgment on parental responsibility that falls within the scope of this Regulation, the holder of parental responsibility shall attach the relevant certificates provided for in Articles 39, 41(1) or 42(1).

2 Member States shall communicate to the Commission the official language or languages of the Community institutions other than their own in which communications to the central authorities can be accepted.

3 The assistance provided by the central authorities pursuant to Article 55 shall be free of charge.

4 Each central authority shall bear its own costs.

Defined terms—"holder of parental responsibility": Art 2.8; "Member State": Art 2.3.

Article 58

Meetings

1 In order to facilitate the application of this Regulation, central authorities shall meet regularly.

2 These meetings shall be convened in compliance with Decision No 2001/470/EC establishing a European Judicial Network in civil and commercial matters.

CHAPTER V
RELATIONS WITH OTHER INSTRUMENTS

Article 59

Relation with other instruments

1 Subject to the provisions of Articles 60, 63, 64 and paragraph 2 of this Article, this Regulation shall, for the Member States, supersede conventions existing at the time of entry into force of this Regulation which have been concluded between two or more Member States and relate to matters governed by this Regulation.

2

(a) Finland and Sweden shall have the option of declaring that the Convention of 6 February 1931 between Denmark, Finland, Iceland, Norway and Sweden comprising international private law provisions on marriage, adoption and guardianship, together with the Final Protocol thereto, will apply, in whole or in part, in their mutual relations, in place of the rules of this Regulation. Such declarations shall be annexed to this Regulation and published in the Official Journal of the European Union. They may be withdrawn, in whole or in part, at any moment by the said Member States.

(b) The principle of non-discrimination on the grounds of nationality between citizens of the Union shall be respected.

(c) The rules of jurisdiction in any future agreement to be concluded between the Member States referred to in subparagraph (a) which relate to matters governed by this Regulation shall be in line with those laid down in this Regulation.

(d) Judgments handed down in any of the Nordic States which have made the declaration provided for in subparagraph (a) under a forum of jurisdiction corresponding to one of those laid down in Chapter II of this Regulation, shall be recognised and enforced in the other Member States under the rules laid down in Chapter III of this Regulation.

3 Member States shall send to the Commission:

PART VI

    (a)   a copy of the agreements and uniform laws implementing these agreements referred to in paragraph 2(a) and (c);

    (b)   any denunciations of, or amendments to, those agreements or uniform laws.

Defined terms—"Member State": Art 2.3; "judgment": Art 2.4.

Article 60

Relations with certain multilateral conventions

In relations between Member States, this Regulation shall take precedence over the following Conventions in so far as they concern matters governed by this Regulation:

    (a)   the Hague Convention of 5 October 1961 concerning the Powers of Authorities and the Law Applicable in respect of the Protection of Minors;

    (b)   the Luxembourg Convention of 8 September 1967 on the Recognition of Decisions Relating to the Validity of Marriages;

    (c)   the Hague Convention of 1 June 1970 on the Recognition of Divorces and Legal Separations;

    (d)   the European Convention of 20 May 1980 on Recognition and Enforcement of Decisions concerning Custody of Children and on Restoration of Custody of Children; and

    (e)   the Hague Convention of 25 October 1980 on the Civil Aspects of International Child Abduction.

Defined terms—"Member State": Art 2.3.

Article 61

Relation with the Hague Convention of 19 October 1996 on Jurisdiction, Applicable law, Recognition, Enforcement and Cooperation in Respect of Parental Responsibility and Measures for the Protection of Children

As concerns the relation with the Hague Convention of 19 October 1996 on Jurisdiction, Applicable law, Recognition, Enforcement and Cooperation in Respect of Parental Responsibility and Measures for the Protection of Children, this Regulation shall apply:

    (a)   where the child concerned has his or her habitual residence on the territory of a Member State;

    (b)   as concerns the recognition and enforcement of a judgment given in a court of a Member State on the territory of another Member State, even if the child concerned has his or her habitual residence on the territory of a third State which is a contracting Party to the said Convention.

Defined terms—"Member State": Art 2.3.

Article 62

Scope of effects

1 The agreements and conventions referred to in Articles 59(1), 60 and 61 shall continue to have effect in relation to matters not governed by this Regulation.

2 The conventions mentioned in Article 60, in particular the 1980 Hague Convention, continue to produce effects between the Member States which are party thereto, in compliance with Article 60.

Defined terms—"Member State": Art 2.3.

Article 63

Treaties with the Holy See

1 This Regulation shall apply without prejudice to the International Treaty (Concordat) between the Holy See and Portugal, signed at the Vatican City on 7 May 1940.

2 Any decision as to the invalidity of a marriage taken under the Treaty referred to in paragraph 1 shall be recognised in the Member States on the conditions laid down in Chapter III, Section 1.

3 The provisions laid down in paragraphs 1 and 2 shall also apply to the following international treaties (Concordats) with the Holy See:

(a) "Concordato lateranense" of 11 February 1929 between Italy and the Holy See, modified by the agreement, with additional Protocol signed in Rome on 18 February 1984;

(b) Agreement between the Holy See and Spain on legal affairs of 3 January 1979.

(c) Agreement between the Holy See and Malta on the recognition of civil effects to canonical marriages and to decisions of ecclesiastical authorities and tribunals on those marriages of 3 February 1993, including the Protocol of application of the same date, with the second Additional Protocol of 6 January 1995.

4 Recognition of the decisions provided for in paragraph 2 may, in Spain, Italy or Malta, be subject to the same procedures and the same checks as are applicable to decisions of the ecclesiastical courts handed down in accordance with the international treaties concluded with the Holy See referred to in paragraph 3.

5 Member States shall send to the Commission:

(a) a copy of the Treaties referred to in paragraphs 1 and 3;

(b) any denunciations of or amendments to those Treaties.

Defined terms—"Member State": Art 2.3.

CHAPTER VI
TRANSITIONAL PROVISIONS

Article 64

1 The provisions of this Regulation shall apply only to legal proceedings instituted, to documents formally drawn up or registered as authentic instruments and to agreements concluded between the parties after its date of application in accordance with Article 72.

2 Judgments given after the date of application of this Regulation in proceedings instituted before that date but after the date of entry into force of Regulation (EC) No 1347/2000 shall be recognised and enforced in accordance with the provisions of Chapter III of this Regulation if jurisdiction was founded on rules which accorded with those provided for either in Chapter II or in Regulation (EC) No 1347/2000 or in a convention concluded between the Member State of origin and the Member State addressed which was in force when the proceedings were instituted.

3 Judgments given before the date of application of this Regulation in proceedings instituted after the entry into force of Regulation (EC) No 1347/2000 shall be recognised and enforced in accordance with the provisions of Chapter III of this Regulation provided they relate to divorce, legal separation or marriage annulment or parental responsibility for the children of both spouses on the occasion of these matrimonial proceedings.

PART VI

4 Judgments given before the date of application of this Regulation but after the date of entry into force of Regulation (EC) No 1347/2000 in proceedings instituted before the date of entry into force of Regulation (EC) No 1347/2000 shall be recognised and enforced in accordance with the provisions of Chapter III of this Regulation provided they relate to divorce, legal separation or marriage annulment or parental responsibility for the children of both spouses on the occasion of these matrimonial proceedings and that jurisdiction was founded on rules which accorded with those provided for either in Chapter II of this Regulation or in Regulation (EC) No 1347/2000 or in a convention concluded between the Member State of origin and the Member State addressed which was in force when the proceedings were instituted.

Defined terms—"judgment": Art 2.4; "Member State of origin": Art 2.5; "Member State": Art 2.3; "parental responsibility": Art 2.7.

CHAPTER VII
FINAL PROVISIONS

Article 65
Review

No later than 1 January 2012, and every five years thereafter, the Commission shall present to the European Parliament, to the Council and to the European Economic and Social Committee a report on the application of this Regulation on the basis of information supplied by the Member States. The report shall be accompanied if need be by proposals for adaptations.

Defined terms—"Member State": Art 2.3.

Article 66
Member States with two or more legal systems

With regard to a Member State in which two or more systems of law or sets of rules concerning matters governed by this Regulation apply in different territorial units:

  (a) any reference to habitual residence in that Member State shall refer to habitual residence in a territorial unit;
  (b) any reference to nationality, or in the case of the United Kingdom "domicile", shall refer to the territorial unit designated by the law of that State;
  (c) any reference to the authority of a Member State shall refer to the authority of a territorial unit within that State which is concerned;
  (d) any reference to the rules of the requested Member State shall refer to the rules of the territorial unit in which jurisdiction, recognition or enforcement is invoked.

Defined terms—"Member State": Art 2.3.

Article 67
Information on central authorities and languages accepted

The Member States shall communicate to the Commission within three months following the entry into force of this Regulation:

  (a) the names, addresses and means of communication for the central authorities designated pursuant to Article 53;
  (b) the languages accepted for communications to central authorities pursuant to Article 57(2); and

(c)   the languages accepted for the certificate concerning rights of access pursuant to Article 45(2).

The Member States shall communicate to the Commission any changes to this information.

The Commission shall make this information publicly available.

Defined terms—"Member State": Art 2.3.

Article 68

Information relating to courts and redress procedures

The Member States shall notify to the Commission the lists of courts and redress procedures referred to in Articles 21, 29, 33 and 34 and any amendments thereto.

The Commission shall update this information and make it publicly available through the publication in the Official Journal of the European Union and any other appropriate means.

Defined terms—"Member State": Art 2.3.

"Lists of courts"—It is not open to an English court to depart from the court designations incorporated within the lists attached to Art 68 (*Re S (Foreign Contact Order)* [2010] 1 FLR 982).

Article 69

Amendments to the Annexes

Any amendments to the standard forms in Annexes I to IV shall be adopted in accordance with the consultative procedure set out in Article 70(2).

Article 70

Committee

1   The Commission shall be assisted by a committee (committee).

2   Where reference is made to this paragraph, Articles 3 and 7 of Decision 1999/468/EC shall apply.

3   The committee shall adopt its rules of procedure.

Article 71

Repeal of Regulation (EC) No 1347/2000

1   Regulation (EC) No 1347/2000 shall be repealed as from the date of application of this Regulation.

2   Any reference to Regulation (EC) No 1347/2000 shall be construed as a reference to this Regulation according to the comparative table in Annex V.

Article 72

Entry into force

This Regulation shall enter into force on 1 August 2004.

The Regulation shall apply from 1 March 2005, with the exception of Articles 67, 68, 69 and 70, which shall apply from 1 August 2004.

This Regulation shall be binding in its entirety and directly applicable in the Member States in accordance with the Treaty establishing the European Community.

PART VI

Done at Brussels, 27 November 2003.

For the Council

The President

R. CASTELLI

ANNEX I
CERTIFICATE REFERRED TO IN ARTICLE 39 CONCERNING JUDGMENTS IN MATRIMONIAL MATTERS[1]

1 Member State of origin

2 Court or authority issuing the certificate

    2.1   Name

    2.2   Address

    2.3   Tel./fax/e-mail

3 Marriage

    3.1   Wife

        3.1.1   Full name

        3.1.2   Address

        3.1.3   Country and place of birth

        3.1.4   Date of birth

    3.2   Husband

        3.2.1   Full name

        3.2.2   Address

        3.2.3   Country and place of birth

        3.2.4   Date of birth

    3.3   Country, place (where available) and date of marriage

        3.3.1   Country of marriage

        3.3.2   Place of marriage (where available)

        3.3.3   Date of marriage

4 Court which delivered the judgment

    4.1   Name of Court

    4.2   Place of Court

5 Judgment

    5.1   Date

    5.2   Reference number

    5.3   Type of judgment

        5.3.1   Divorce

        5.3.2   Marriage annulment

        5.3.3   Legal separation

    5.4   Was the judgment given in default of appearance?

        5.4.1   No

        5.4.2   Yes[2]

6 Names of parties to whom legal aid has been granted

7 Is the judgment subject to further appeal under the law of the Member State of origin?

    7.1   No

    7.2   Yes

8 Date of legal effect in the Member State where the judgment was given

    8.1   Divorce

8.2   Legal separation

Done at . . ., date . . .

Signature and/or stamp

1   Council Regulation (EC) No 2201/2003 of 27 November 2003 concerning jurisdiction and the recognition and enforcement of judgments in matrimonial matters and the matters of parental responsibility, repealing Regulation (EC) No 1347/2000.
2   Documents referred to in Article 37(2) must be attached.

ANNEX II
CERTIFICATE REFERRED TO IN ARTICLE 39 CONCERNING JUDGMENTS ON PARENTAL RESPONSIBILITY[1]

1   Member State of origin

2   Court or authority issuing the certificate

    2.1   Name
    2.2   Address
    2.3   Tel./Fax/e-mail

3   Person(s) with rights of access

    3.1   Full name
    3.2   Address
    3.3   Date and place of birth (where available)

4   Holders of parental responsibility other than those mentioned under 3[2]

    4.1   4.1.1   Full name
           4.1.2   Address
           4.1.3   Date and place of birth (where available)
    4.2   4.2.1   Full Name
           4.2.2   Address
           4.2.3   Date and place of birth (where available)
    4.3   4.3.1   Full name
           4.3.2   Address
           4.3.3   Date and place of birth (where available)

5   Court which delivered the judgment

    5.1   Name of Court
    5.2   Place of Court

6   Judgment

    6.1   Date
    6.2   Reference number
    6.3   Was the judgment given in default of appearance?
           6.3.1   No
           6.3.2   Yes[3]

7   Children who are covered by the judgment[4]

    7.1   Full name and date of birth
    7.2   Full name and date of birth
    7.3   Full name and date of birth
    7.4   Full name and date of birth

8   Names of parties to whom legal aid has been granted

9 Attestation of enforceability and service

   9.1 Is the judgment enforceable according to the law of the Member State of
        origin?
        9.1.1 Yes
        9.1.2 No
   9.2 Has the judgment been served on the party against whom enforcement is
        sought?
        9.2.1 Yes
               9.2.1.1   Full name of the party
               9.2.1.2   Address
               9.2.1.3   Date of service
        9.2.2 No

10 Specific information on judgments on rights of access where "exequatur" is
requested under Article 28. This possibility is foreseen in Article 40(2).

   10.1 Practical arrangements for exercise of rights of access (to the extent stated in
         the judgment)
         10.1.1 Date and time
                 10.1.1.1   Start
                 10.1.1.2   End
         10.1.2 Place
         10.1.3 Specific obligations on holders of parental responsibility
         10.1.4 Specific obligations on the person with right of access
         10.1.5 Any restrictions attached to the exercise of rights of access

11 Specific information for judgments on the return of the child in cases where the
"exequatur" procedure is requested under Article 28. This possibility is foreseen under
Article 40(2).

   11.1 The judgment entails the return of the child
   11.2 Person to whom the child is to be returned (to the extent stated in the
         judgment)
         11.2.1 Full name
         11.2.2 Address

Done at . . ., date . . ..

Signature and/or stamp

1   Council Regulation (EC) No 2201/2003 of 27 November 2003 concerning jurisdiction and the
    recognition and enforcement of judgments in matrimonial matters and the matters of parental
    responsibility, repealing Regulation (EC) No 1347/2000.
2   In cases of joint custody, a person already mentioned under item 3 may also be mentioned under
    item 4.
3   Documents referred to in Article 37(2) must be attached.
4   If more than four children are covered, use a second form.

ANNEX III
CERTIFICATE REFERRED TO IN ARTICLE 41(1) CONCERNING JUDGMENTS
ON RIGHTS OF ACCESS[1]

1 Member State of origin

2 Court or authority issuing the certificate

   2.1 Name
   2.2 Address
   2.3 Tel./fax/e-mail

3 Person(s) with rights of access

   3.1 Full name
   3.2 Address
   3.3 Date and place of birth (where available)

4 Holders of parental responsibility other than those mentioned under 3[2,3]

   4.1 4.1.1 Full name
          4.1.2 Address
          4.1.3 Date and place of birth (where available)
   4.2 4.2.1 Full name
          4.2.2 Address
          4.2.3 Date and place of birth (where available)
   4.3 Other
          4.3.1 Full name
          4.3.2 Address
          4.3.3 Date and place of birth (where available)

5 Court which delivered the judgment

   5.1 Name of Court
   5.2 Place of Court

6 Judgment

   6.1 Date
   6.2 Reference number

7 Children who are covered by the judgment[4]

   7.1 Full name and date of birth
   7.2 Full name and date of birth
   7.3 Full name and date of birth
   7.4 Full name and date of birth

8 Is the judgment enforceable in the Member State of origin?

   8.1 Yes
   8.2 No

9 Where the judgment was given in default of appearance, the person defaulting was served with the document which instituted the proceedings or with an equivalent document in sufficient time and in such a way as to enable that person to arrange for his or her defence, or the person has been served with the document but not in compliance with these conditions, it is nevertheless established that he or she accepted the decision unequivocally

10 All parties concerned were given an opportunity to be heard

11 The children were given an opportunity to be heard, unless a hearing was considered inappropriate having regard to their age or degree of maturity

12 Practical arrangements for exercise of rights of access (to the extent stated in the judgment)

   12.1 Date and time
          12.1.1 Start
          12.1.2 End
   12.2 Place
   12.3 Specific obligations on holders of parental responsibility
   12.4 Specific obligations on the person with right of access
   12.5 Any restrictions attached to the exercise of rights of access

13 Names of parties to whom legal aid has been granted

PART VI

Done at . . ., date . . ..

Signature and/or stamp

1   Council Regulation (EC) No 2201/2003 of 27 November 2003 concerning jurisdiction and the recognition and enforcement of judgments in matrimonial matters and the matters of parental responsibility, repealing Regulation (EC) No 1347/2000.
2   In cases of joint custody, a person already mentioned under item 3 may also be mentioned in item 4.
3   Please put a cross in the box corresponding to the person against whom the judgment should be enforced.
4   If more than four children are concerned, use a second form.

ANNEX IV
CERTIFICATE REFERRED TO IN ARTICLE 42(1) CONCERNING THE RETURN OF THE CHILD[1]

1 Member State of origin

2 Court or authority issuing the certificate

    2.1   Name
    2.2   Address
    2.3   Tel./fax/e-mail

3 Person to whom the child has to be returned (to the extent stated in the judgment)

    3.1   Full name
    3.2   Address
    3.3   Date and place of birth (where available)

4 Holders of parental responsibility[2]

    4.1   Mother
        4.1.1   Full name
        4.1.2   Address (where available)
        4.1.3   Date and place of birth (where available)
    4.2   Father
        4.2.1   Full name
        4.2.2   Address (where available)
        4.2.3   Date and place of birth (where available)
    4.3   Other
        4.3.1   Full name
        4.3.2   Address (where available)
        4.3.3   Date and place of birth (where available)

5 Respondent (where available)

    5.1   Full name
    5.2   Address (where available)

6 Court which delivered the judgment

    6.1   Name of Court
    6.2   Place of Court

7 Judgment

    7.1   Date
    7.2   Reference number

8 Children who are covered by the judgment[3]

    8.1   Full name and date of birth
    8.2   Full name and date of birth
    8.3   Full name and date of birth

    8.4 Full name and date of birth

9 The judgment entails the return of the child

10 Is the judgment enforceable in the Member State of origin?

    10.1 Yes
    10.2 No

11 The children were given an opportunity to be heard, unless a hearing was considered inappropriate having regard to their age or degree of maturity

12 The parties were given an opportunity to be heard

13 The judgment entails the return of the children and the court has taken into account in issuing its judgment the reasons for and evidence underlying the decision issued pursuant to Article 13 of the Hague Convention of 25 October 1980 on the Civil Aspects of International Child Abduction

14 Where applicable, details of measures taken by courts or authorities to ensure the protection of the child after its return to the Member State of habitual residence

15 Names of parties to whom legal aid has been granted

Done at . . ., date . . ..

Signature and/or stamp

1   Council Regulation (EC) No 2201 of 27 November 2003 concerning jurisdiction and the recognition and enforcement of judgments in matrimonial matters and the matters of parental responsibility, repealing Regulation (EC) No 1347/2000.

2   This item is optional.

3   If more than four children are covered, use a second form.

ANNEX V
COMPARATIVE TABLE WITH REGULATION (EC) NO 1347/2000

Articles repealed	Corresponding Articles of new text	Articles repealed	Corresponding Articles of new text
1	1, 2	27	34
2	3	28	35
3	12	29	36
4		30	50
5	4	31	51
6	5	32	37
7	6	33	39
8	7	34	38
9	17	35	52
10	18	36	59
11	16, 19	37	60, 61
12	20	38	62
13	2, 49, 46	39	
14	21	40	63
15	22, 23	41	66
16		42	64
17	24	43	65
18	25	44	68, 69
19	26	45	70
20	27	46	72
21	28	Annex I	68
22	21, 29	Annex II	68
23	30	Annex III	68
24	31	Annex IV	Annex I
25	32	Annex V	Annex II
26	33		

ANNEX VI
DECLARATIONS BY SWEDEN AND FINLAND PURSUANT TO
ARTICLE 59(2)(A) OF THE COUNCIL REGULATION CONCERNING
JURISDICTION AND THE RECOGNITION AND ENFORCEMENT OF
JUDGMENTS IN MATRIMONIAL MATTERS AND MATTERS OF PARENTAL
RESPONSIBILITY, REPEALING REGULATION (EC) NO 1347/2000.

Declaration by Sweden:

Pursuant to Article 59(2)(a) of the Council Regulation concerning jurisdiction and the recognition and enforcement of judgments in matrimonial matters and matters of parental responsibility, repealing Regulation (EC) No 1347/2000, Sweden hereby declares that the Convention of 6 February 1931 between Denmark, Finland, Iceland, Norway and Sweden comprising international private law provisions on marriage, adoption and guardianship, together with the Final Protocol thereto, will apply in full in relations between Sweden and Finland, in place of the rules of the Regulation.

Declaration by Finland:

Pursuant to Article 59(2)(a) of the Council Regulation concerning jurisdiction and the recognition and enforcement of judgments in matrimonial matters and matters of parental responsibility, repealing Regulation (EC) No 1347/2000, Finland hereby declares that the Convention of 6 February 1931 between Finland, Denmark, Iceland, Norway and Sweden comprising international private law provisions on marriage, adoption and guardianship, together with the Final Protocol thereto, will apply in full in relations between Finland and Sweden, in place of the rules of the Regulation.

Date:

Signature and/or stamp:

Council Regulation (EC) No 805/2004

of 21 April 2004

creating a European Enforcement Order for uncontested claims

Scope—The European Enforcement Order (EEO) came into force on 21 October 2005 and applies to uncontested judgments, court settlements and authentic instruments made after 21 January 2005. The EEO is not concerned exclusively with family law obligations. The EEO has now been replaced by the Maintenance Regulation, except where the maintenance obligations arise in a Member State not bound by the 2007 Hague Protocol (ie the UK and Denmark) (Maintenance Regulation, Art 68.2). (See, further, the annotations to the Maintenance Regulation, Art 68.2.) However, the EEO does not apply to Denmark (Recital 25 and Art 2.3). Subject to these limitations, the EEO provides a simpler method of reciprocal enforcement than the Maintenance Regulation for English outgoing orders, which require registration to become enforceable under the simplified exequatur procedure for Member States not bound by the 2007 Hague Protocol.

The recipient of an uncontested maintenance obligation in the Member State of origin may apply for an EEO certificate from their domestic court, which allows the judgment to be transferred to another Member State for enforcement. It is unnecessary to obtain a declaration of enforceability under the exequatur procedure (Art 5). Art 6 sets out the conditions required for certification. Disputes regarding the EEO certificate are dealt with in the court of origin and not the enforcing jurisdiction (Art 10). However, the maintenance creditor is limited to the methods of enforcement available in the enforcing jurisdiction (Art 20.1). The definition of "uncontested" is found in Art 3. Where the maintenance claim is contested, the Maintenance Regulation applies as between Member States. A "claim" is defined by Art 4.2 as a claim for payment of a specific sum of money that has fallen due or for which the due date is indicated in the judgment. A claim therefore could encompass not only a maintenance order but also lump sum orders or property adjustment orders by way of capitalised maintenance (see annotations to the Maintenance Regulation). The EEO does not apply to rights in property arising out of a matrimonial relationship

(Art 2.2(a)). It does apply to orders for costs (Art 7), claims under CA 1989, Sch 1 and child maintenance calculations by the CSA. Owing to different procedural requirements between Member States (particularly in relation to service), Chapter III of the EEO lays down minimum standards for uncontested claims procedure.

The Annexes to the EEO, which contain a series of standard forms, were replaced by the Commission Regulation (EC) No 1869/2005 of 16 November 2005.

Chapter I (Arts 1–4) deals with subject matter, scope and definitions.

Chapter II (Arts 5–11) sets out the requirements for an EEO.

Chapter III (Arts 12–19) deals with the minimum standards for uncontested claims procedures.

Chapter IV (Arts 20–23) deals with enforcement.

Chapter V (Arts 24–25) deals with court settlements and authentic instruments.

Chapter VI (Art 26) deals with transitional provision.

Chapter VII (Arts 27–28) deals with the relationship with other community instruments.

Chapter VIII (Arts 29–33) contains general and final provisions.

The procedural requirements are regulated by CPR 1998, rr 74.27–74.33 and PD74B.

THE EUROPEAN PARLIAMENT AND THE COUNCIL OF THE EUROPEAN UNION,

Having regard to the Treaty establishing the European Community, and in particular Articles 61(c) and the second indent of Article 67(5) thereof,

Having regard to the proposal from the Commission,

Having regard to the Opinion of the European Economic and Social Committee,

Acting in accordance with the procedure laid down in Article 251 of the Treaty,

Whereas:

(1) The Community has set itself the objective of maintaining and developing an area of freedom, security and justice, in which the free movement of persons is ensured. To this end, the Community is to adopt, inter alia, measures in the field of judicial cooperation in civil matters that are necessary for the proper functioning of the internal market.

(2) On 3 December 1998, the Council adopted an Action Plan of the Council and the Commission on how best to implement the provisions of the Treaty of Amsterdam on an area of freedom, security and justice (the Vienna Action Plan).

(3) The European Council meeting in Tampere on 15 and 16 October 1999 endorsed the principle of mutual recognition of judicial decisions as the cornerstone for the creation of a genuine judicial area.

(4) On 30 November 2000, the Council adopted a programme of measures for implementation of the principle of mutual recognition of decisions in civil and commercial matters. This programme includes in its first stage the abolition of exequatur, that is to say, the creation of a European Enforcement Order for uncontested claims.

(5) The concept of "uncontested claims" should cover all situations in which a creditor, given the verified absence of any dispute by the debtor as to the nature or extent of a pecuniary claim, has obtained either a court decision against that debtor or an enforceable document that requires the debtor's express consent, be it a court settlement or an authentic instrument.

(6) The absence of objections from the debtor as stipulated in Article 3(1)(b) can take the shape of default of appearance at a court hearing or of failure to comply with an invitation by the court to give written notice of an intention to defend the case.

(7) This Regulation should apply to judgments, court settlements and authentic instruments on uncontested claims and to decisions delivered following challenges to judgments, court settlements and authentic instruments certified as European Enforcement Orders.

(8) In its Tampere conclusions, the European Council considered that access to enforcement in a Member State other than that in which the judgment has been given

should be accelerated and simplified by dispensing with any intermediate measures to be taken prior to enforcement in the Member State in which enforcement is sought. A judgment that has been certified as a European Enforcement Order by the court of origin should, for enforcement purposes, be treated as if it had been delivered in the Member State in which enforcement is sought. In the United Kingdom, for example, the registration of a certified foreign judgment will therefore follow the same rules as the registration of a judgment from another part of the United Kingdom and is not to imply a review as to the substance of the foreign judgment. Arrangements for the enforcement of judgments should continue to be governed by national law.

(9) Such a procedure should offer significant advantages as compared with the exequatur procedure provided for in Council Regulation (EC) No 44/2001 of 22 December 2000 on jurisdiction and the recognition and enforcement of judgments in civil and commercial matters, in that there is no need for approval by the judiciary in a second Member State with the delays and expenses that this entails.

(10) Where a court in a Member State has given judgment on an uncontested claim in the absence of participation of the debtor in the proceedings, the abolition of any checks in the Member State of enforcement is inextricably linked to and dependent upon the existence of a sufficient guarantee of observance of the rights of the defence.

(11) This Regulation seeks to promote the fundamental rights and takes into account the principles recognised in particular by the Charter of Fundamental Rights of the European Union. In particular, it seeks to ensure full respect for the right to a fair trial as recognised in Article 47 of the Charter.

(12) Minimum standards should be established for the proceedings leading to the judgment in order to ensure that the debtor is informed about the court action against him, the requirements for his active participation in the proceedings to contest the claim and the consequences of his non-participation in sufficient time and in such a way as to enable him to arrange for his defence.

(13) Due to differences between the Member States as regards the rules of civil procedure and especially those governing the service of documents, it is necessary to lay down a specific and detailed definition of those minimum standards. In particular, any method of service that is based on a legal fiction as regards the fulfilment of those minimum standards cannot be considered sufficient for the certification of a judgment as a European Enforcement Order.

(14) All the methods of service listed in Articles 13 and 14 are characterised by either full certainty (Article 13) or a very high degree of likelihood (Article 14) that the document served has reached its addressee. In the second category, a judgment should only be certified as a European Enforcement Order if the Member State of origin has an appropriate mechanism in place enabling the debtor to apply for a full review of the judgment under the conditions set out in Article 19 in those exceptional cases where, in spite of compliance with Article 14, the document has not reached the addressee.

(15) Personal service on certain persons other than the debtor himself pursuant to Article 14(1)(a) and (b) should be understood to meet the requirements of those provisions only if those persons actually accepted/received the document in question.

(16) Article 15 should apply to situations where the debtor cannot represent himself in court, as in the case of a legal person, and where a person to represent him is determined by law as well as situations where the debtor has authorised another person, in particular a lawyer, to represent him in the specific court proceedings at issue.

(17) The courts competent for scrutinising full compliance with the minimum procedural standards should, if satisfied, issue a standardised European Enforcement Order certificate that makes that scrutiny and its result transparent.

PART VI

(18) Mutual trust in the administration of justice in the Member States justifies the assessment by the court of one Member State that all conditions for certification as a European Enforcement Order are fulfilled to enable a judgment to be enforced in all other Member States without judicial review of the proper application of the minimum procedural standards in the Member State where the judgment is to be enforced.

(19) This Regulation does not imply an obligation for the Member States to adapt their national legislation to the minimum procedural standards set out herein. It provides an incentive to that end by making available a more efficient and rapid enforceability of judgments in other Member States only if those minimum standards are met.

(20) Application for certification as a European Enforcement Order for uncontested claims should be optional for the creditor, who may instead choose the system of recognition and enforcement under Regulation (EC) No 44/2001 or other Community instruments.

(21) When a document has to be sent from one Member State to another for service there, this Regulation and in particular the rules on service set out herein should apply together with Council Regulation (EC) No 1348/2000 of 29 May 2000 on the service in the Member States of judicial and extrajudicial documents in civil or commercial matters, and in particular Article 14 thereof in conjunction with Member States declarations made under Article 23 thereof.

(22) Since the objectives of the proposed action cannot be sufficiently achieved by the Member States and can therefore, by reason of the scale or effects of the action, be better achieved at Community level, the Community may adopt measures, in accordance with the principle of subsidiarity as set out in Article 5 of the Treaty. In accordance with the principle of proportionality, as set out in that Article, this Regulation does not go beyond what is necessary in order to achieve those objectives.

(23) The measures necessary for the implementation of this Regulation should be adopted in accordance with Council Decision 1999/468/EC of 28 June 1999 laying down the procedures for the exercise of implementing powers conferred on the Commission.

(24) In accordance with Article 3 of the Protocol on the position of the United Kingdom and Ireland annexed to the Treaty on European Union and the Treaty establishing the European Community, the United Kingdom and Ireland have notified their wish to take part in the adoption and application of this Regulation.

(25) In accordance with Articles 1 and 2 of the Protocol on the position of Denmark annexed to the Treaty on European Union and the Treaty establishing the European Community, Denmark does not take part in the adoption of this Regulation, and is therefore not bound by it or subject to its application.

(26) Pursuant to the second indent of Article 67(5) of the Treaty, the codecision procedure is applicable from 1 February 2003 for the measures laid down in this Regulation,

HAVE ADOPTED THIS REGULATION:

Note—The EC Treaty has become the Treaty on the Functioning of the European Union (TFEU) and the Articles have been re-numbered: Art 251 is now Art 294 TFEU.

CHAPTER I
SUBJECT MATTER, SCOPE AND DEFINITIONS

Article 1

Subject matter

The purpose of this Regulation is to create a European Enforcement Order for uncontested claims to permit, by laying down minimum standards, the free circulation of judgments, court settlements and authentic instruments throughout all Member States without any intermediate proceedings needing to be brought in the Member State of enforcement prior to recognition and enforcement.

Article 2

Scope

1 This Regulation shall apply in civil and commercial matters, whatever the nature of the court or tribunal. It shall not extend, in particular, to revenue, customs or administrative matters or the liability of the State for acts and omissions in the exercise of State authority ("acta iure imperii").

2 This Regulation shall not apply to:

    (a)   the status or legal capacity of natural persons, rights in property arising out of a matrimonial relationship, wills and succession;

    (b)   bankruptcy, proceedings relating to the winding-up of insolvent companies or other legal persons, judicial arrangements, compositions and analogous proceedings;

    (c)   social security;

    (d)   arbitration.

3 In this Regulation, the term "Member State" shall mean Member States with the exception of Denmark.

Article 3

Enforcement titles to be certified as a European Enforcement Order

1 This Regulation shall apply to judgments, court settlements and authentic instruments on uncontested claims.

A claim shall be regarded as uncontested if:

    (a)   the debtor has expressly agreed to it by admission or by means of a settlement which has been approved by a court or concluded before a court in the course of proceedings; or

    (b)   the debtor has never objected to it, in compliance with the relevant procedural requirements under the law of the Member State of origin, in the course of the court proceedings; or

    (c)   the debtor has not appeared or been represented at a court hearing regarding that claim after having initially objected to the claim in the course of the court proceedings, provided that such conduct amounts to a tacit admission of the claim or of the facts alleged by the creditor under the law of the Member State of origin; or

    (d)   the debtor has expressly agreed to it in an authentic instrument.

2 This Regulation shall also apply to decisions delivered following challenges to judgments, court settlements or authentic instruments certified as European Enforcement Orders.

Article 4

Definitions

For the purposes of this Regulation, the following definitions shall apply:

1 "judgment": any judgment given by a court or tribunal of a Member State, whatever the judgment may be called, including a decree, order, decision or writ of execution, as well as the determination of costs or expenses by an officer of the court;

2 "claim": a claim for payment of a specific sum of money that has fallen due or for which the due date is indicated in the judgment, court settlement or authentic instrument;

3 "authentic instrument":

    (a) a document which has been formally drawn up or registered as an authentic instrument, and the authenticity of which:

        (i) relates to the signature and the content of the instrument; and

        (ii) has been established by a public authority or other authority empowered for that purpose by the Member State in which it originates;

    or

    (b) an arrangement relating to maintenance obligations concluded with administrative authorities or authenticated by them;

4 "Member State of origin": the Member State in which the judgment has been given, the court settlement has been approved or concluded or the authentic instrument has been drawn up or registered, and is to be certified as a European Enforcement Order;

5 "Member State of enforcement": the Member State in which enforcement of the judgment, court settlement or authentic instrument certified as a European Enforcement Order is sought;

6 "court of origin": the court or tribunal seised of the proceedings at the time of fulfilment of the conditions set out in Article 3(1)(a), (b) or (c);

7 in Sweden, in summary proceedings concerning orders to pay (*betalningsföreläggande*), the expression "court" includes the Swedish enforcement service (*kronofogdemyndighet*).

CHAPTER II
EUROPEAN ENFORCEMENT ORDER

Article 5

Abolition of exequatur

A judgment which has been certified as a European Enforcement Order in the Member State of origin shall be recognised and enforced in the other Member States without the need for a declaration of enforceability and without any possibility of opposing its recognition.

Article 6

Requirements for certification as a European Enforcement Order

1 A judgment on an uncontested claim delivered in a Member State shall, upon application at any time to the court of origin, be certified as a European Enforcement Order if:

    (a) the judgment is enforceable in the Member State of origin; and

    (b) the judgment does not conflict with the rules on jurisdiction as laid down in sections 3 and 6 of Chapter II of Regulation (EC) No 44/2001; and

(c) the court proceedings in the Member State of origin met the requirements as set out in Chapter III where a claim is uncontested within the meaning of Article 3(_)(b) or (c); and

(d) the judgment was given in the Member State of the debtor's domicile within the meaning cf Article 59 of Regulation (EC) No 44/2001, in cases where
- a claim is uncontested within the meaning of Article 3(1)(b) or (c); and
- it relates to a contract concluded by a person, the consumer, for a purpose which can be regarded as being outside his trade or profession; and
- the debtor is the consumer.

2 Where a judgment certified as a European Enforcement Order has ceased to be enforceable or its enforceability has been suspended or limited, a certificate indicating the lack or limitation of enforceability shall, upon application at any time to the court of origin, be issued, using the standard form in Annex IV.

3 Without prejudice to Article 12(2), where a decision has been delivered following a challenge to a judgment certified as a European Enforcement Order in accordance with paragraph 1 of this Article, a replacement certificate shall, upon application at any time, be issued, using the standard form in Annex V, if that decision on the challenge is enforceable in the Member State of origin.

Article 7

Costs related to court proceedings

Where a judgment includes an enforceable decision on the amount of costs related to the court proceedings, including the interest rates, it shall be certified as a European Enforcement Order also with regard to the costs unless the debtor has specifically objected to his obligation to bear such costs in the course of the court proceedings, in accordance with the law of the Member State of origin.

Article 8

Partial European Enforcement Order certificate

If only parts of the judgment meet the requirements of this Regulation, a partial European Enforcement Order certificate shall be issued for those parts.

Article 9

Issue of the European Enforcement Order certificate

1 The European Enforcement Order certificate shall be issued using the standard form in Annex I.

2 The European Enforcement Order certificate shall be issued in the language of the judgment.

Article 10

Rectification or withdrawal of the European Enforcement Order certificate

1 The European Enforcement Order certificate shall, upon application to the court of origin, be

(a) rectified where, due to a material error, there is a discrepancy between the judgment and the certificate;

(b) withdrawn where it was clearly wrongly granted, having regard to the requirements laid down in this Regulation.

PART VI

2 The law of the Member State of origin shall apply to the rectification or withdrawal of the European Enforcement Order certificate.

3 An application for the rectification or withdrawal of a European Enforcement Order certificate may be made using the standard form in Annex VI.

4 No appeal shall lie against the issuing of a European Enforcement Order certificate.

Note—A miscalculation of arrears was corrected under Art 10 in a European Enforcement Order certificate based on an authentic instrument (*Vogel v Lothschütz* [2012] EWHC 3411 (QB)).

Article 11

Effect of the European Enforcement Order certificate

The European Enforcement Order certificate shall take effect only within the limits of the enforceability of the judgment.

CHAPTER III
MINIMUM STANDARDS FOR UNCONTESTED CLAIMS PROCEDURES

Article 12

Scope of application of minimum standards

1 A judgment on a claim that is uncontested within the meaning of Article 3(1)(b) or (c) can be certified as a European Enforcement Order only if the court proceedings in the Member State of origin met the procedural requirements as set out in this Chapter.

2 The same requirements shall apply to the issuing of a European Enforcement Order certificate or a replacement certificate within the meaning of Article 6(3) for a decision following a challenge to a judgment where, at the time of that decision, the conditions of Article 3(1)(b) or (c) are fulfilled.

Article 13

Service with proof of receipt by the debtor

1 The document instituting the proceedings or an equivalent document may have been served on the debtor by one of the following methods:

(a) personal service attested by an acknowledgement of receipt, including the date of receipt, which is signed by the debtor;

(b) personal service attested by a document signed by the competent person who effected the service stating that the debtor has received the document or refused to receive it without any legal justification, and the date of the service;

(c) postal service attested by an acknowledgement of receipt including the date of receipt, which is signed and returned by the debtor;

(d) service by electronic means such as fax or e-mail, attested by an acknowledgement of receipt including the date of receipt, which is signed and returned by the debtor.

2 Any summons to a court hearing may have been served on the debtor in compliance with paragraph 1 or orally in a previous court hearing on the same claim and stated in the minutes of that previous court hearing.

Article 14

Service without proof of receipt by the debtor

1 Service of the document instituting the proceedings or an equivalent document and any summons to a court hearing on the debtor may also have been effected by one of the following methods:

(a) personal service at the debtor's personal address on persons who are living in the same household as the debtor or are employed there;

(b) in the case of a self-employed debtor or a legal person, personal service at the debtor's business premises on persons who are employed by the debtor;

(c) deposit of the document in the debtor's mailbox;

(d) deposit of the document at a post office or with competent public authorities and the placing in the debtor's mailbox of written notification of that deposit, provided that the written notification clearly states the character of the document as a court document or the legal effect of the notification as effecting service and setting in motion the running of time for the purposes of time limits;

(e) postal service without proof pursuant to paragraph 3 where the debtor has his address in the Member State of origin;

(f) electronic means attested by an automatic confirmation of delivery, provided that the debtor has expressly accepted this method of service in advance.

2 For the purposes of this Regulation, service under paragraph 1 is not admissible if the debtor's address is not known with certainty.

3 Service pursuant to paragraph 1, (a) to (d), shall be attested by:

(a) a document signed by the competent person who effected the service, indicating:

  (i) the method of service used; and

  (ii) the date of service; and

  (iii) where the document has been served on a person other than the debtor, the name of that person and his relation to the debtor,

  or

(b) an acknowledgement of receipt by the person served, for the purposes of paragraphs 1(a) and (b).

Article 15

Service on the debtor's representatives

Service pursuant to Articles 13 or 14 may also have been effected on a debtor's representative.

Article 16

Provision to the debtor of due information about the claim

In order to ensure that the debtor was provided with due information about the claim, the document instituting the proceedings or the equivalent document must have contained the following:

(a) the names and the addresses of the parties;

(b) the amount of the claim;

(c) if interest on the claim is sought, the interest rate and the period for which interest is sought unless statutory interest is automatically added to the principal under the law of the Member State of origin;

(d) a statement of the reason for the claim.

PART VI

Article 17

Provision to the debtor of due information about the procedural steps necessary to contest the claim

The following must have been clearly stated in or together with the document instituting the proceedings, the equivalent document or any summons to a court hearing:

   (a)   the procedural requirements for contesting the claim, including the time limit for contesting the claim in writing or the time for the court hearing, as applicable, the name and the address of the institution to which to respond or before which to appear, as applicable, and whether it is mandatory to be represented by a lawyer;

   (b)   the consequences of an absence of objection or default of appearance, in particular, where applicable, the possibility that a judgment may be given or enforced against the debtor and the liability for costs related to the court proceedings.

Article 18

Cure of non-compliance with minimum standards

1 If the proceedings in the Member State of origin did not meet the procedural requirements as set out in Articles 13 to 17, such non-compliance shall be cured and a judgment may be certified as a European Enforcement Order if:

   (a)   the judgment has been served on the debtor in compliance with the requirements pursuant to Article 13 or Article 14; and

   (b)   it was possible for the debtor to challenge the judgment by means of a full review and the debtor has been duly informed in or together with the judgment about the procedural requirements for such a challenge, including the name and address of the institution with which it must be lodged and, where applicable, the time limit for so doing; and

   (c)   the debtor has failed to challenge the judgment in compliance with the relevant procedural requirements.

2 If the proceedings in the Member State of origin did not comply with the procedural requirements as set out in Article 13 or Article 14, such non-compliance shall be cured if it is proved by the conduct of the debtor in the court proceedings that he has personally received the document to be served in sufficient time to arrange for his defence.

Article 19

Minimum standards for review in exceptional cases

1 Further to Articles 13 to 18, a judgment can only be certified as a European Enforcement Order if the debtor is entitled, under the law of the Member State of origin, to apply for a review of the judgment where:

   (a)   (i)   the document instituting the proceedings or an equivalent document or, where applicable, the summons to a court hearing, was served by one of the methods provided for in Article 14; and

         (ii) service was not effected in sufficient time to enable him to arrange for his defence, without any fault on his part;

         or

   (b)   the debtor was prevented from objecting to the claim by reason of force majeure, or due to extraordinary circumstances without any fault on his part,

provided in either case that he acts promptly.

2 This Article is without prejudice to the possibility for Member States to grant access to a review of the judgment under more generous conditions than those mentioned in paragraph 1.

CHAPTER IV
ENFORCEMENT

Article 20

Enforcement procedure

1 Without prejudice to the provisions of this Chapter, the enforcement procedures shall be governed by the law of the Member State of enforcement.

A judgment certified as a European Enforcement Order shall be enforced under the same conditions as a judgment handed down in the Member State of enforcement.

2 The creditor shall be required to provide the competent enforcement authorities of the Member State of enforcement with:

- (a) a copy of the judgment which satisfies the conditions necessary to establish its authenticity; and
- (b) a copy of the European Enforcement Order certificate which satisfies the conditions necessary to establish its authenticity; and
- (c) where necessary, a transcription of the European Enforcement Order certificate or a translation thereof into the official language of the Member State of enforcement or, if there are several official languages in that Member State, the official language or one of the official languages of court proceedings of the place where enforcement is sought, in conformity with the law of that Member State, or into another language that the Member State of enforcement has indicated it can accept. Each Member State may indicate the official language or languages of the institutions of the European Community other than its own which it can accept for the completion of the certificate. The translation shall be certified by a person qualified to do so in one of the Member States.

3 No security, bond or deposit, however described, shall be required of a party who in one Member State applies for enforcement of a judgment certified as a European Enforcement Order in another Member State on the ground that he is a foreign national or that he is not domiciled or resident in the Member State of enforcement.

Article 21

Refusal of enforcement

1 Enforcement shall, upon application by the debtor, be refused by the competent court in the Member State of enforcement if the judgment certified as a European Enforcement Order is irreconcilable with an earlier judgment given in any Member State or in a third country, provided that:

- (a) the earlier judgment involved the same cause of action and was between the same parties; and
- (b) the earlier judgment was given in the Member State of enforcement or fulfils the conditions necessary for its recognition in the Member State of enforcement; and
- (c) the irreconcilability was not and could not have been raised as an objection in the court proceedings in the Member State of origin.

PART VI

2 Under no circumstances may the judgment or its certification as a European Enforcement Order be reviewed as to their substance in the Member State of enforcement.

Article 22

Agreements with third countries

This Regulation shall not affect agreements by which Member States undertook, prior to the entry into force of Regulation (EC) No 44/2001, pursuant to Article 59 of the Brussels Convention on jurisdiction and the enforcement of judgments in civil and commercial matters, not to recognise judgments given, in particular in other Contracting States to that Convention, against defendants domiciled or habitually resident in a third country where, in cases provided for in Article 4 of that Convention, the judgment could only be founded on a ground of jurisdiction specified in the second paragraph of Article 3 of that Convention.

Article 23

Stay or limitation of enforcement

Where the debtor has

- challenged a judgment certified as a European Enforcement Order, including an application for review within the meaning of Article 19, or
- applied for the rectification or withdrawal of a European Enforcement Order certificate in accordance with Article 10,

the competent court or authority in the Member State of enforcement may, upon application by the debtor:

(a)   limit the enforcement proceedings to protective measures; or
(b)   make enforcement conditional on the provision of such security as it shall determine; or
(c)   under exceptional circumstances, stay the enforcement proceedings.

CHAPTER V
COURT SETTLEMENTS AND AUTHENTIC INSTRUMENTS

Article 24

Court settlements

1 A settlement concerning a claim within the meaning of Article 4(2) which has been approved by a court or concluded before a court in the course of proceedings and is enforceable in the Member State in which it was approved or concluded shall, upon application to the court that approved it or before which it was concluded, be certified as a European Enforcement Order using the standard form in Annex II.

2 A settlement which has been certified as a European Enforcement Order in the Member State of origin shall be enforced in the other Member States without the need for a declaration of enforceability and without any possibility of opposing its enforceability.

3 The provisions of Chapter II, with the exception of Articles 5, 6(1) and 9(1), and of Chapter IV, with the exception of Articles 21(1) and 22, shall apply as appropriate.

Article 25

Authentic instruments

1 An authentic instrument concerning a claim within the meaning of Article 4(2) which is enforceable in one Member State shall, upon application to the authority designated by the Member State of origin, be certified as a European Enforcement Order, using the standard form in Annex III.

2 An authentic instrument which has been certified as a European Enforcement Order in the Member State of origin shall be enforced in the other Member States without the need for a declaration of enforceability and without any possibility of opposing its enforceability.

3 The provisions of Chapter II, with the exception of Articles 5, 6(1) and 9(1), and of Chapter IV, with the exception of Articles 21(1) and 22, shall apply as appropriate.

CHAPTER VI
TRANSITIONAL PROVISION

Article 26

Transitional provision

This Regulation shall apply only to judgments given, to court settlements approved or concluded and to documents formally drawn up or registered as authentic instruments after the entry into force of this Regulation.

CHAPTER VII
RELATIONSHIP WITH OTHER COMMUNITY INSTRUMENTS

Article 27

Relationship with Regulation (EC) No 44/2001

This Regulation shall not affect the possibility of seeking recognition and enforcement, in accordance with Regulation (EC) No 44/2001, of a judgment, a court settlement or an authentic instrument on an uncontested claim.

Article 28

Relationship with Regulation (EC) No 1348/2000

This Regulation shall not affect the application of Regulation (EC) No 1348/2000.

CHAPTER VIII
GENERAL AND FINAL PROVISIONS

Article 29

Information on enforcement procedures and authorities

The Member States shall cooperate to provide the general public and professional circles with information on:

(a) the methods and procedures of enforcement in the Member States; and
(b) the competent authorities for enforcement in the Member States,

in particular via the European Judicial Network in civil and commercial matters established in accordance with Decision 2001/470/EC.

Article 30

Information relating to redress procedures, languages and authorities

1 The Member States shall notify the Commission of:

(a) the procedures for rectification and withdrawal referred to in Article 10(2) and for review referred to in Article 19(1);

(b) the languages accepted pursuant to Article 20(2)(c);

(c) the lists of the authorities referred to in Article 25;

and any subsequent changes thereof.

2 The Commission shall make the information notified in accordance with paragraph 1 publicly available through publication in the *Official Journal of the European Union* and through any other appropriate means.

Article 31

Amendments to the Annexes

The Commission shall amend the standard forms set out in the Annexes. Those measures, designed to amend nonessential elements of this Regulation, shall be adopted in accordance with the regulatory procedure with scrutiny referred to in Article 32(2).

Article 32

Committee

1 The Commission shall be assisted by the committee provided for by Article 75 of Regulation (EC) No 44/2001.

2 Where reference is made to this paragraph, Articles 3 and 7 of Decision 1999/468/EC shall apply, having regard to the provisions of Article 8 thereof.

Article 33

Entry into force

This Regulation shall enter into force on 21 January 2005.

It shall apply from 21 October 2005, with the exception of Articles 30, 31 and 32, which shall apply from 21 January 2005.

This Regulation shall be binding in its entirety and directly applicable in the Member States in accordance with the Treaty establishing the European Community.

Done at Strasbourg, 21 April 2004.

For the European Parliament

The President

P. COX

For the Council

The President

D. ROCHE

****

Council Regulation (EC) No 1393/2007

of 13 November 2007

on the service in the Member States of judicial and extrajudicial documents in civil or commercial matters (service of documents), and repealing Council Regulation (EC) No 1348/2000

Scope—This Regulation (the Second Service Regulation) repeals Council Regulation (EC) No 1348/2000 of 29 May 2000 (the First Service Regulation). The Second Service Regulation came into effect on 13 November 2008. However, the First Service Regulation is still applicable in relation to issues of service before 13 November 2008. The Second Service Regulation applies to all EU Member States including Denmark, to which the provisions of the First Service Regulation were extended from 1 July 2007.

The Second Service Regulation provides an official system of service within the EU (Arts 4–11). Its scope extends beyond family proceedings (Art 1). It is not mandatory – other means of service are permitted: transmission by consular or diplomatic channels (Art 12); service by diplomatic or consular agents (Art 13); service by post (Art 14); and direct service (Art 15). See, however, restrictions on other methods of service discussed below under Ch 11. The Second Service Regulation does not establish any hierarchy between the methods of service referred to in it (*Plumex v Young Sports NV* (2006) The Times, 22 February). See, further, annotations to Art 7. The official system of service provided by the Second Service Regulation may be more persuasive in some EU jurisdictions than other methods of service, which is an important factor to be taken into account when establishing which EU member is first seised for the purposes of Brussels IIA.

The Regulations must be read in conjunction with the information that Member States must communicate in accordance with Art 23, which may be found at *http://ec.europa.eu/justice_home/ judicialatlascivil/html/pdf/vers_consolide_en_1348.pdf*.

The structure of the Second Service Regulation is broadly similar to that of the First.

Chapter I (Arts 1–3) contains general provisions. Art 2 provides for the designation of "transmitting agencies" and "receiving agencies" for each Member State, which for England and Wales is the Senior Master, Queen's Bench Division, Foreign Process Section, Room E16, Royal Courts of Justice, Strand, London WC2A 2LL, DX 44450 Strand (tel 0207 947 6691/6327/6488/7786; fax 0870 324 0025; email: foreignprocess.rcj@hmcts.gsi.gov.uk).

Chapter II (Arts 4–15) deals with judicial documents. Section 1 (Arts 4–11) provides for the transmission and service of judicial documents. Art 4 governs the means by which documents requiring to be served are transmitted between Member States (ie between transmitting and receiving agencies). Art 5 sets out the requirement for translations and Art 6 the obligations upon the receiving agency upon receipt of documents for service. Art 7 provides for the service of documents by the receiving agency as soon as possible and in any event within 1 month of receipt. Art 8 contains provisions as to circumstances in which a respondent may refuse to accept service. Art 9 provides that the date of service is the date on which the documents are served in accordance with the law of the receiving Member State. Art 10 provides for certificates of service and Art 11 for the costs of service. Section 2 (Arts 12–16) provides for means of transmission and service of judicial documents other than through transmitting and receiving agencies. Arts 12 and 13 deal with transmission and service by diplomatic or consular channels or agents. Art 14 provides for postal service by Member States on persons residing in another Member State by registered letter with acknowledgment of receipt or equivalent. Art 15 provides for direct service by any person through judicial offices or other competent persons of the Member State addressed, where such direct service is permitted under the law of the Member State. The Second Service Regulation envisages methods of service other than through transmitting and receiving agencies (Chapter II, section 2). However, such service must be effected by the transmitting Member State rather than by the applicant attempting to serve an addressee in another Member State by direct postal service, unless the provisions of Art 15 apply.

Chapter III (Art 16) provides for the transmission of extra-judicial documents for service in the same way as judicial documents.

Chapter IV (Arts 17–26) contains final provisions.

The procedure for service out of England and Wales is governed by FPR 2010, Pt 6, Ch 4. For those proceedings to which the FPR do not apply (e g I(PFD)A 1975, TLATA 1996 and PHA 1997), reference should be made to CPR 1998, rr 6.17–6.31.

As to the service in England and Wales of foreign proceedings, where the Second Service Regulation applies, the transmitting agency of the other Member State should be used.

When an application is served out of the jurisdiction, the time limit for serving an acknowledgment of service or answer to the application is longer (FPR 2010, r 6.42 and PD6B). The procedure for service in accordance with the Second Service Regulation is contained in FPR 2010, r 6.44 and PD6B, para 2.

To ensure that a court is seised, proceedings must simply not be issued but the process of service must be started (Brussels IIA, Art 16). Issuing proceedings as a precautionary measure but not then effecting service will not gain priority under Brussels IIA (*R v R (Divorce: Stay of Proceedings)* [1994] 2 FLR 1036). Actual service does not need to have been effected to establish jurisdiction: see annotations to Brussels IIA, Art 16.

The Annexes to the Second Service Regulation contain the standard forms that should be used: Annex I – request for service of documents; Annex II – information to the addressee about the right to refuse to accept a document; Annex III – correlation table [as between the First Service Regulation and the Second Service Regulation].

THE EUROPEAN PARLIAMENT AND THE COUNCIL OF THE EUROPEAN UNION,

Having regard to the Treaty establishing the European Community, and in particular Article 61(c) and Article 67(5), second indent, thereof,

Having regard to the proposal from the Commission,

Having regard to the opinion of the European Economic and Social Committee,

Acting in accordance with the procedure laid down in Article 251 of the Treaty,

Whereas:

(1) The Union has set itself the objective of maintaining and developing the Union as an area of freedom, security and justice, in which the free movement of persons is assured. To establish such an area, the Community is to adopt, among others, the measures relating to judicial cooperation in civil matters needed for the proper functioning of the internal market.

(2) The proper functioning of the internal market entails the need to improve and expedite the transmission of judicial and extrajudicial documents in civil or commercial matters for service between the Member States.

(3) The Council, by an Act dated 26 May 1997, drew up a Convention on the service in the Member States of the European Union of judicial and extrajudicial documents in civil or commercial matters and recommended it for adoption by the Member States in accordance with their respective constitutional rules. That Convention has not entered into force. Continuity in the results of the negotiations for conclusion of the Convention should be ensured.

(4) On 29 May 2000 the Council adopted Regulation (EC) No 1348/2000 on the service in the Member States of judicial and extrajudicial documents in civil or commercial matters. The main content of that Regulation is based on the Convention.

(5) On 1 October 2004 the Commission adopted a report on the application of Regulation (EC) No 1348/2000. The report concludes that the application of Regulation (EC) No 1348/2000 has generally improved and expedited the transmission and the service of documents between Member States since its entry into force in 2001, but that nevertheless the application of certain provisions is not fully satisfactory.

(6) Efficiency and speed in judicial procedures in civil matters require that judicial and extrajudicial documents be transmitted directly and by rapid means between local bodies designated by the Member States. Member States may indicate their intention to designate only one transmitting or receiving agency or one agency to perform both functions, for a period of five years. This designation may, however, be renewed every five years.

(7) Speed in transmission warrants the use of all appropriate means, provided that certain conditions as to the legibility and reliability of the document received are observed. Security in transmission requires that the document to be transmitted be

accompanied by a standard form, to be completed in the official language or one of the official languages of the place where service is to be effected, or in another language accepted by the Member State in question.

(8) This Regulation should not apply to service of a document on the party's authorised representative in the Member State where the proceedings are taking place regardless of the place of residence of that party.

(9) The service of a document should be effected as soon as possible, and in any event within one month of receipt by the receiving agency.

(10) To secure the effectiveness of this Regulation, the possibility of refusing service of documents should be confined to exceptional situations.

(11) In order to facilitate the transmission and service of documents between Member States, the standard forms set out in the Annexes to this Regulation should be used.

(12) The receiving agency should inform the addressee in writing using the standard from that he may refuse to accept the document to be served at the time of service or by returning the document to the receiving agency within one week if it is not either in a language which he understands or in the official language or one of the official languages of the place of service. This rule should also apply to the subsequent service once the addressee has exercised his right of refusal. These rules on refusal should also apply to service by diplomatic or consular agents, service by postal services and direct service. It should be established that the service of the refused document can be remedied through the service on the addressee of a translation of the document.

(13) Speed in transmission warrants documents being served within days of receipt of the document. However, if service has not been effected after one month has elapsed, the receiving agency should inform the transmitting agency. The expiry of this period should not imply that the request be returned to the transmitting agency where it is clear that service is feasible within a reasonable period.

(14) The receiving agency should continue to take all necessary steps to effect the service of the documents also in cases where it has not been possible to effect service within the month, for example, because the defendant has been away from his home on holiday or away from his office on business. However, in order to avoid an open-ended obligation for the receiving agency to take steps to effect the service of a document, the transmitting agency should be able to specify a time limit in the standard form after which service is no longer required.

(15) Given the differences between the Member States as regards their rules of procedure, the material date for the purposes of service varies from one Member State to another. Having regard to such situations and the possible difficulties that may arise, this Regulation should provide for a system where it is the law of the Member State addressed which determines the date of service. However, where according to the law of a Member State a document has to be served within a particular period, the date to be taken into account with respect to the applicant should be that determined by the law of that Member State. This double date system exists only in a limited number of Member States. Those Member States which apply this system should communicate this to the Commission, which should publish the information in the *Official Journal of the European Union* and make it available through the European Judicial Network in Civil and Commercial Matters established by Council Decision 2001/470/EC.

(16) In order to facilitate access to justice, costs occasioned by recourse to a judicial officer or a person competent under the law of the Member State addressed should correspond to a single fixed fee laid down by that Member State in advance which respects the principles of proportionality and non-discrimination. The requirement of a single fixed fee should not preclude the possibility for Member States to set different fees for different types of service as long as they respect these principles.

PART VI

(17) Each Member State should be free to effect service of documents directly by postal services on persons residing in another Member State by registered letter with acknowledgement of receipt or equivalent.

(18) It should be possible for any person interested in a judicial proceeding to effect service of documents directly through the judicial officers, officials or other competent persons of the Member State addressed, where such direct service is permitted under the law of that Member State.

(19) The Commission should draw up a manual containing information relevant for the proper application of this Regulation, which should be made available through the European Judicial Network in Civil and Commercial Matters. The Commission and the Member States should do their utmost to ensure that this information is up to date and complete especially as regards contact details of receiving and transmitting agencies.

(20) In calculating the periods and time limits provided for in this Regulation, Regulation (EEC, Euratom) No 1182/71 of the Council of 3 June 1971 determining the rules applicable to periods, dates and time limits should apply.

(21) The measures necessary for the implementation of this Regulation should be adopted in accordance with Council Decision 1999/468/EC of 28 June 1999 laying down the procedures for the exercise of implementing powers conferred on the Commission.

(22) In particular, power should be conferred on the Commission to update or make technical amendments to the standard forms set out in the Annexes. Since those measures are of general scope and are designed to amend/delete non-essential elements of this Regulation, they must be adopted in accordance with the regulatory procedure with scrutiny provided for in Article 5a of Decision 1999/468/EC.

(23) This Regulation prevails over the provisions contained in bilateral or multilateral agreements or arrangements having the same scope, concluded by the Member States, and in particular the Protocol annexed to the Brussels Convention of 27 September 1968 and the Hague Convention of 15 November 1965 in relations between the Member States party thereto. This Regulation does not preclude Member States from maintaining or concluding agreements or arrangements to expedite or simplify the transmission of documents, provided that they are compatible with this Regulation.

(24) The information transmitted pursuant to this Regulation should enjoy suitable protection. This matter falls within the scope of Directive 95/46/EC of the European Parliament and of the Council of 24 October 1995 on the protection of individuals with regard to the processing of personal data and on the free movement of such data, and of Directive 2002/58/EC of the European Parliament and of the Council of 12 July 2002 concerning the processing of personal data and the protection of privacy in the electronic communications sector (Directive on privacy and electronic communications).

(25) No later than 1 June 2011 and every five years thereafter, the Commission should review the application of this Regulation and propose such amendments as may appear necessary.

(26) Since the objectives of this Regulation cannot be sufficiently achieved by the Member States and can therefore, by reason of the scale or effects of the action, be better achieved at Community level, the Community may adopt measures, in accordance with the principle of subsidiarity as set out in Article 5 of the Treaty. In accordance with the principle of proportionality, as set out in that Article, this Regulation does not go beyond what is necessary in order to achieve those objectives.

(27) In order to make the provisions more easily accessible and readable, Regulation (EC) No 1348/2000 should be repealed and replaced by this Regulation.

(28) In accordance with Article 3 of the Protocol on the position of the United Kingdom and Ireland, annexed to the Treaty on European Union and to the Treaty establishing the European Community, the United Kingdom and Ireland are taking part in the adoption and application of this Regulation.

(29) In accordance with Articles 1 and 2 of the Protocol on the position of Denmark, annexed to the Treaty on European Union and to the Treaty establishing the European Community, Denmark does not take part in the adoption of this Regulation and is not bound by it or subject to its application,

HAVE ADOPTED THIS REGULATION:

Note—The EC Treaty has become the Treaty on the Functioning of the European Union (TFEU) and the Articles have been re-numbered: Art 5 is replaced, in substance, by Art 5 of the Treaty on the European Union; Art 61 is now Art 67 TFEU; Art 67 is repealed; and Art 251 is now Art 294 TFEU.

CHAPTER I
GENERAL PROVISIONS

Article 1

Scope

1 This Regulation shall apply in civil and commercial matters where a judicial or extrajudicial document has to be transmitted from one Member State to another for service there. It shall not extend in particular to revenue, customs or administrative matters or to liability of the State for actions or omissions in the exercise of state authority (*acta iure imperii*).

2 This Regulation shall not apply where the address of the person to be served with the document is not known.

3 In this Regulation, the term 'Member State' shall mean the Member States with the exception of Denmark.

Article 2

Transmitting and receiving agencies

1 Each Member State shall designate the public officers, authorities or other persons, hereinafter referred to as 'transmitting agencies', competent for the transmission of judicial or extra-judicial documents to be served in another Member State.

2 Each Member State shall designate the public officers, authorities or other persons, hereinafter referred to as 'receiving agencies', competent for the receipt of judicial or extrajudicial documents from another Member State.

3 A Member State may designate one transmitting agency and one receiving agency, or one agency to perform both functions. A federal State, a State in which several legal systems apply or a State with autonomous territorial units shall be free to designate more than one such agency. The designation shall have effect for a period of five years and may be renewed at five-year intervals.

4 Each Member State shall provide the Commission with the following information:

  (a) the names and addresses of the receiving agencies referred to in paragraphs 2 and 3;
  (b) the geographical areas in which they have jurisdiction;
  (c) the means of receipt of documents available to them; and
  (d) the languages that may be used for the completion of the standard form set out in Annex I.

PART VI

Member States shall notify the Commission of any subsequent modification of such information.

Article 3

Central body

Each Member State shall designate a central body responsible for:

    (a)   supplying information to the transmitting agencies;

    (b)   seeking solutions to any difficulties which may arise during transmission of documents for service;

    (c)   forwarding, in exceptional cases, at the request of a transmitting agency, a request for service to the competent receiving agency.

A federal State, a State in which several legal systems apply or a State with autonomous territorial units shall be free to designate more than one central body.

CHAPTER II
JUDICIAL DOCUMENTS

Section 1
Transmission and service of judicial documents

Article 4

Transmission of documents

1 Judicial documents shall be transmitted directly and as soon as possible between the agencies designated pursuant to Article 2.

2 The transmission of documents, requests, confirmations, receipts, certificates and any other papers between transmitting agencies and receiving agencies may be carried out by any appropriate means, provided that the content of the document received is true and faithful to that of the document forwarded and that all information in it is easily legible.

3 The document to be transmitted shall be accompanied by a request drawn up using the standard form set out in Annex I. The form shall be completed in the official language of the Member State addressed or, if there are several official languages in that Member State, the official language or one of the official languages of the place where service is to be effected, or in another language which that Member State has indicated it can accept. Each Member State shall indicate the official language or languages of the institutions of the European Union other than its own which is or are acceptable to it for completion of the form.

4 The documents and all papers that are transmitted shall be exempted from legalisation or any equivalent formality.

5 When the transmitting agency wishes a copy of the document to be returned together with the certificate referred to in Article 10, it shall send the document in duplicate.

Scope—Art 4 governs the means by which documents requiring to be served are transmitted between Member States. Documents are to be transmitted directly and as soon as possible between the designated agencies by "any appropriate means", provided that the content of the document received is "true and faithful" and all information is "easily legible", encompassing the possible use of fax or email. The document(s) to be transmitted must be accompanied by a request drawn up using the form set out in Annex I (not reproduced here) completed in the official language (or one of them) of the Member State addressed. Translations of the documents to be served are required (Arts 5 and 8).

Article 5

Translation of documents

1 The applicant shall be advised by the transmitting agency to which he forwards the document for transmission that the addressee may refuse to accept it if it is not in one of the languages provided for in Article 8.

2 The applicant shall bear any costs of translation prior to the transmission of the document, without prejudice to any possible subsequent decision by the court or competent authority on liability for such costs.

Article 6

Receipt of documents by receiving agency

1 On receipt of a document, a receiving agency shall, as soon as possible and in any event within seven days of receipt, send a receipt to the transmitting agency by the swiftest possible means of transmission using the standard form set out in Annex I.

2 Where the request for service cannot be fulfilled on the basis of the information or documents transmitted, the receiving agency shall contact the transmitting agency by the swiftest possible means in order to secure the missing information or documents.

3 If the request for service is manifestly outside the scope of this Regulation or if non-compliance with the formal conditions required makes service impossible, the request and the documents transmitted shall be returned, on receipt, to the transmitting agency, together with the notice of return using the standard form set out in Annex I.

4 A receiving agency receiving a document for service but not having territorial jurisdiction to serve it shall forward it, as well as the request, to the receiving agency having territorial jurisdiction in the same Member State if the request complies with the conditions laid down in Article 4(3) and shall inform the transmitting agency accordingly using the standard form set out in Annex I. That receiving agency shall inform the transmitting agency when it receives the document, in the manner provided for in paragraph 1.

Article 7

Service of documents

1 The receiving agency shall itself serve the document or have it served, either in accordance with the law of the Member State addressed or by a particular method requested by the transmitting agency, unless that method is incompatible with the law of that Member State.

2 The receiving agency shall take all necessary steps to effect the service of the document as soon as possible, and in any event within one month of receipt. If it has not been possible to effect service within one month of receipt, the receiving agency shall:

   (a) immediately inform the transmitting agency by means of the certificate in the standard form set out in Annex I, which shall be drawn up under the conditions referred to in Article 10(2); and

   (b) continue to take all necessary steps to effect the service of the document, unless indicated otherwise by the transmitting agency, where service seems to be possible within a reasonable period of time.

Scope—The receiving agency must serve the documents or have them served either in accordance with the receiving Member State's internal law or by any particular method requested by the transmitting agency (unless the method requested is incompatible with the law of the receiving Member State). All necessary steps must be taken to effect service as soon as possible and in any event within 1 month of receipt. If that is not possible, the receiving agency must inform the transmitting agency of the delay and

PART VI

must continue to take all necessary steps to effect service. Issues as to the timing and validity of service are to be determined by reference to the Second Service Regulation and not the law of the receiving Member State (*Tavoulareas v Tsavliris* [2004] 2 All ER 221, CA). The methods of service stipulated in the Second Service Regulation are not hierarchical. It is therefore possible to attempt service by two or more methods simultaneously so that time will begin to run from the date on which service was first validly effected in compliance with the Second Service Regulation (*Plumex v Young Sports NV* (2006) *The Times*, 22 February). Being aware of proceedings does not amount to service within the meaning of the Second Service Regulation (*Tavoulareas v Tsavliris (The Atlas Pride)* [2007] 2 All ER (Comm) 356, CA).

Article 8

Refusal to accept a document

1 The receiving agency shall inform the addressee, using the standard form set out in Annex II, that he may refuse to accept the document to be served at the time of service or by returning the document to the receiving agency within one week if it is not written in, or accompanied by a translation into, either of the following languages:

    (a)   a language which the addressee understands; or

    (b)   the official language of the Member State addressed or, if there are several official languages in that Member State, the official language or one of the official languages of the place where service is to be effected.

2 Where the receiving agency is informed that the addressee refuses to accept the document in accordance with paragraph 1, it shall immediately inform the transmitting agency by means of the certificate provided for in Article 10 and return the request and the documents of which a translation is requested.

3 If the addressee has refused to accept the document pursuant to paragraph 1, the service of the document can be remedied through the service on the addressee in accordance with the provisions of this Regulation of the document accompanied by a translation into a language provided for in paragraph 1. In that case, the date of service of the document shall be the date on which the document accompanied by the translation is served in accordance with the law of the Member State addressed. However, where according to the law of a Member State, a document has to be served within a particular period, the date to be taken into account with respect to the applicant shall be the date of the service of the initial document determined pursuant to Article 9(2).

4 Paragraphs 1, 2 and 3 shall also apply to the means of transmission and service of judicial documents provided for in Section 2.

5 For the purposes of paragraph 1, the diplomatic or consular agents, where service is effected in accordance with Article 13, or the authority or person, where service is effected in accordance with Article 14, shall inform the addressee that he may refuse to accept the document and that any document refused must be sent to those agents or to that authority or person respectively.

Scope—An addressee may refuse to accept service of documents that are not in a language that the addressee understands or that are not in the official language of the Member State addressed. An initial invalid attempt to serve without a translation may be rectified by commissioning a translation and then re-serving (Art 8.3; *Leffler v Berlin Chemie AG* [2006] ILPr 6).

Article 9

Date of service

1 Without prejudice to Article 8, the date of service of a document pursuant to Article 7 shall be the date on which it is served in accordance with the law of the Member State addressed.

2 However, where according to the law of a Member State a document has to be served within a particular period, the date to be taken into account with respect to the applicant shall be that determined by the law of that Member State.

3 Paragraphs 1 and 2 shall also apply to the means of transmission and service of judicial documents provided for in Section 2.

Article 10

Certificate of service and copy of the document served

1 When the formalities concerning the service of the document have been completed, a certificate of completion of those formalities shall be drawn up in the standard form set out in Annex I and addressed to the transmitting agency, together with, where Article 4(5) applies, a copy of the document served.

2 The certificate shall be completed in the official language or one of the official languages of the Member State of origin or in another language which the Member State of origin has indicated that it can accept. Each Member State shall indicate the official language or languages of the institutions of the European Union other than its own which is or are acceptable to it for completion of the form.

Article 11

Costs of service

1 The service of judicial documents coming from a Member State shall not give rise to any payment or reimbursement of taxes or costs for services rendered by the Member State addressed.

2 However, the applicant shall pay or reimburse the costs occasioned by:

(a) recourse to a judicial officer or to a person competent under the law of the Member State addressed;

(b) the use of a particular method of service.

Costs occasioned by recourse to a judicial officer or to a person competent under the law of the Member State addressed shall correspond to a single fixed fee laid down by that Member State in advance which respects the principles of proportionality and non-discrimination. Member States shall communicate such fixed fees to the Commission.

Section 2
Other means of transmission and service of judicial documents

Article 12

Transmission by consular or diplomatic channels

Each Member State shall be free, in exceptional circumstances, to use consular or diplomatic channels to forward judicial documents, for the purpose of service, to those agencies of another Member State which are designated pursuant to Articles 2 or 3.

Article 13

Service by diplomatic or consular agents

1 Each Member State shall be free to effect service of judicial documents on persons residing in another Member State, without application of any compulsion, directly through its diplomatic or consular agents.

PART VI

2 Any Member State may make it known, in accordance with Article 23(1), that it is opposed to such service within its territory, unless the documents are to be served on nationals of the Member State in which the documents originate.

Article 14

Service by postal services

Each Member State shall be free to effect service of judicial documents directly by postal services on persons residing in another Member State by registered letter with acknowledgement of receipt or equivalent.

Article 15

Direct service

Any person interested in a judicial proceeding may effect service of judicial documents directly through the judicial officers, officials or other competent persons of the Member State addressed, where such direct service is permitted under the law of that Member State.

CHAPTER III
EXTRAJUDICIAL DOCUMENTS

Article 16

Transmission

Extrajudicial documents may be transmitted for service in another Member State in accordance with the provisions of this Regulation.

CHAPTER IV
FINAL PROVISIONS

Article 17

Implementing rules

Measures designed to amend non-essential elements of this Regulation relating to the updating or to the making of technical amendments to the standard forms set out in Annexes I and II shall be adopted in accordance with the regulatory procedure with scrutiny referred to in Article 18(2).

Article 18

Committee

1 The Commission shall be assisted by a committee.

2 Where reference is made to this paragraph, Article 5a(1) to (4), and Article 7 of Decision 1999/468/EC shall apply, having regard to the provisions of Article 8 thereof.

Article 19

Defendant not entering an appearance

1 Where a writ of summons or an equivalent document has had to be transmitted to another Member State for the purpose of service under the provisions of this Regulation and the defendant has not appeared, judgment shall not be given until it is established that:

   (a) the document was served by a method prescribed by the internal law of the Member State addressed for the service of documents in domestic actions upon persons who are within its territory; or

   (b) the document was actually delivered to the defendant or to his residence by another method provided for by this Regulation; and that in either of these cases the service or the delivery was effected in sufficient time to enable the defendant to defend.

2 Each Member State may make it known, in accordance with Article 23(1), that the judge, notwithstanding the provisions of paragraph 1, may give judgment even if no certificate of service or delivery has been received, if all the following conditions are fulfilled:

   (a) the document was transmitted by one of the methods provided for in this Regulation;

   (b) a period of time of not less than six months, considered adequate by the judge in the particular case, has elapsed since the date of the transmission of the document;

   (c) no certificate of any kind has been received, even though every reasonable effort has been made to obtain it through the competent authorities or bodies of the Member State addressed.

3 Notwithstanding paragraphs 1 and 2, the judge may order, in case of urgency, any provisional or protective measures.

4 When a writ of summons or an equivalent document has had to be transmitted to another Member State for the purpose of service under the provisions of this Regulation and a judgment has been entered against a defendant who has not appeared, the judge shall have the power to relieve the defendant from the effects of the expiry of the time for appeal from the judgment if the following conditions are fulfilled:

   (a) the defendant, without any fault on his part, did not have knowledge of the document in sufficient time to defend, or knowledge of the judgment in sufficient time to appeal; and

   (b) the defendant has disclosed a *prima facie* defence to the action on the merits.

An application for relief may be filed only within a reasonable time after the defendant has knowledge of the judgment.

Each Member State may make it known, in accordance with Article 23(1), that such application will not be entertained if it is filed after the expiry of a time to be stated by it in that communication, but which shall in no case be less than one year following the date of the judgment.

5 Paragraph 4 shall not apply to judgments concerning the status or capacity of persons.

"Defendant not entering an appearance"—This will include, in the context of an English divorce petition, not completing an acknowledgment of service.

PART VI

Article 20

Relationship with agreements or arrangements to which Member States are party

1 This Regulation shall, in relation to matters to which it applies, prevail over other provisions contained in bilateral or multilateral agreements or arrangements concluded by the Member States, and in particular Article IV of the Protocol to the Brussels Convention of 1968 and the Hague Convention of 15 November 1965.

2 This Regulation shall not preclude individual Member States from maintaining or concluding agreements or arrangements to expedite further or simplify the transmission of documents, provided that they are compatible with this Regulation.

3 Member States shall send to the Commission:

(a)   a copy of the agreements or arrangements referred to in paragraph 2 concluded between the Member States as well as drafts of such agreements or arrangements which they intend to adopt; and

(b)   any denunciation of, or amendments to, these agreements or arrangements.

Article 21

Legal aid

This Regulation shall not affect the application of Article 23 of the Convention on civil procedure of 17 July 1905, Article 24 of the Convention on civil procedure of 1 March 1954 or Article 13 of the Convention on international access to justice of 25 October 1980 between the Member States party to those Conventions.

Article 22

Protection of information transmitted

1 Information, including in particular personal data, transmitted under this Regulation shall be used by the receiving agency only for the purpose for which it was transmitted.

2 Receiving agencies shall ensure the confidentiality of such information, in accordance with their national law.

3 Paragraphs 1 and 2 shall not affect national laws enabling data subjects to be informed of the use made of information transmitted under this Regulation.

4 This Regulation shall be without prejudice to Directives 95/46/EC and 2002/58/EC.

Article 23

Communication and publication

1 Member States shall communicate to the Commission the information referred to in Articles 2, 3, 4, 10, 11, 13, 15 and 19. Member States shall communicate to the Commission if, according to their law, a document has to be served within a particular period as referred to in Articles 8(3) and 9(2).

2 The Commission shall publish the information communicated in accordance with paragraph 1 in the *Official Journal of the European Union* with the exception of the addresses and other contact details of the agencies and of the central bodies and the geographical areas in which they have jurisdiction.

3 The Commission shall draw up and update regularly a manual containing the information referred to in paragraph 1, which shall be available electronically, in particular through the European Judicial Network in Civil and Commercial Matters.

Article 24

Review

No later than 1 June 2011, and every five years thereafter, the Commission shall present to the European Parliament, the Council and the European Economic and Social Committee a report on the application of this Regulation, paying special attention to the effectiveness of the agencies designated pursuant to Article 2 and to the practical application of Article 3(c) and Article 9. The report shall be accompanied if need be by proposals for adaptations of this Regulation in line with the evolution of notification systems.

Article 25

Repeal

1 Regulation (EC) No 1348/2000 shall be repealed as from the date of application of this Regulation.

2 References made to the repealed Regulation shall be construed as being made to this Regulation and should be read in accordance with the correlation table in Annex III.

Article 26

Entry into force

This Regulation shall enter into force on the 20th day following its publication in the *Official Journal of the European Union*.

It shall apply from 13 November 2008 with the exception of Article 23 which shall apply from 13 August 2008.

This Regulation shall be binding in its entirety and directly applicable in the Member States in accordance with the Treaty establishing the European Community.

Done at Strasbourg, 13 November 2007.

For the European Parliament

The President

H.-G. PÖTTERING

For the Council

The President

M. LOBO ANTUNES

Convention on the International Recovery of Child Support and Other Forms of Family Maintenance

Scope—The Hague Convention on the International Recovery of Child Support and other forms of Family Maintenance of 23 November 2007 (the 2007 Convention) was negotiated by the Hague Conference on Private International Law at the same time as the Maintenance Regulation was under negotiation by EU Member States. The EU is a party to the 2007 Convention, thus binding all EU Member States. All EU Member States were asked to be ready for the conclusion of the Convention by the EU (the EU equivalent of ratification) by 10 December 2012 in accordance with the EU Council Decision of 9 June 2011 (2011/432/EU). Note that at the time of *The Family Court Practice 2013* going to press, the EU had not yet ratified the 2007 Convention.

The 2007 Convention is intended to provide a simpler, quicker and more efficient global system for the reciprocal enforcement of family maintenance. EU Member States will use the 2007 Convention with non-EU Contracting States only; the Maintenance Regulation will be used as between Member States.

Most of the 2007 Convention is directly applicable in European law and, therefore, under the law of England and Wales. Although no specific legislation is required in England and Wales to implement the 2007 Convention, it is supported by the International Recovery of Maintenance (Hague Convention 2007 etc) Regulation 2012 (set out in Part V), the International Recovery of Maintenance (Hague Convention 2007) (Rules of Court) Regulations 2012, SI 2012/1770, which amends MCA 1980 and CJJA 1982, and the Family Procedure (Amendment No 4) Rules 2012, which amend principally FPR 2010, Pts 9 and 34 and insert a new PD34A: Reciprocal Enforcement of Maintenance Orders.

Administrative cooperation is carried out by the designated Central Authority for each Contracting State (Art 4). The Central Authority for England and Wales is the Lord Chancellor, whose functions are carried out by the Reciprocal Enforcement of Maintenance Unit (REMO) in the Office of the Official Solicitor and Public Trustee, 81 Chancery Lane, London WC2A 1DD; tel: 0845 345 5303; fax: 020 7911 7030; email: remo@offsol.gsi.gov.uk. Sch 3 makes provision on date-sharing to facilitate the performance of Central Authority functions.

The 2007 Convention replaces the Convention of 2 October 1973 on the Recognition and Enforcement of Decisions relating to Maintenance Obligations (the 1973 Convention) (Art 48) and the EU Convention on the Recovery Abroad of Maintenance 1956 (the New York Convention) (Art 49) as between Contracting States to each except where there is a difference in the scope applied by one or both states.

Chapter I provides for the object (Art 1), scope (Art 2) and definitions (Art 3).

Chapters II and III contain administrative cooperation provisions. Chapter II (Arts 4–8) deals with the designation and functions of Central Authorities. Chapter III (Arts 9–17) deals with the process of applying through Central Authorities.

Chapter IV (Art 18) provides for restrictions on bringing proceedings in jurisdictional terms.

Chapter V (Arts 19–31) deals with recognition and enforcement.

Chapter VI (Arts 32-35) makes provision as to how a decision, once recognised and declared enforceable, is enforced in the requested Contracting State.

Chapter VII (Art 36) provides for the position of public bodies as applicants.

Chapter VIII (Arts 37–57) contains general provisions.

Chapter IX (Arts 58–65) contains final provisions.

Forms are contained in the Annexes:

Annex 1: Transmittal form under Art 12(2).

Annex 2: Acknowledgment form under Art 12(3).

(Concluded 23 November 2007)

The States signatory to the present Convention,

Desiring to improve co-operation among States for the international recovery of child support and other forms of family maintenance,

Aware of the need for procedures which produce results and are accessible, prompt, efficient, cost-effective, responsive and fair,

Wishing to build upon the best features of existing Hague Conventions and other international instruments, in particular the United Nations Convention on the Recovery Abroad of Maintenance of 20 June 1956,

Seeking to take advantage of advances in technologies and to create a flexible system which can continue to evolve as needs change and further advances in technology create new opportunities,

Recalling that, in accordance with Articles 3 and 27 of the United Nations Convention on the Rights of the Child of 20 November 1989,

–   in all actions concerning children the best interests of the child shall be a primary consideration,

–   every child has a right to a standard of living adequate for the child's physical, mental, spiritual, moral and social development,

–   the parent(s) or others responsible for the child have the primary responsibility to secure, within their abilities and financial capacities, the conditions of living necessary for the child's development, and

–   States Parties should take all appropriate measures, including the conclusion of international agreements, to secure the recovery of maintenance for the child from the parent(s) or other responsible persons, in particular where such persons live in a State different from that of the child,

Have resolved to conclude this Convention and have agreed upon the following provisions –

CHAPTER I
OBJECT, SCOPE AND DEFINITIONS

Article 1

Object

The object of the present Convention is to ensure the effective international recovery of child support and other forms of family maintenance, in particular by –

(a) establishing a comprehensive system of co-operation between the authorities of the Contracting States;
(b) making available applications for the establishment of maintenance decisions;
(c) providing for the recognition and enforcement of maintenance decisions; and
(d) requiring effective measures for the prompt enforcement of maintenance decisions.

Article 2

Scope

(1) This Convention shall apply –

(a) to maintenance obligations arising from a parent-child relationship towards a person under the age of 21 years;
(b) to recognition and enforcement or enforcement of a decision for spousal support when the application is made with a claim within the scope of sub-paragraph (a); and
(c) with the exception of Chapters II and III, to spousal support.

(2) Any Contracting State may reserve, in accordance with Article 62, the right to limit the application of the Convention under sub-paragraph (1)(a), to persons who have not attained the age of 18 years. A Contracting State which makes this reservation shall not be entitled to claim the application of the Convention to persons of the age excluded by its reservation.

(3) Any Contracting State may declare in accordance with Article 63 that it will extend the application of the whole or any part of the Convention to any maintenance obligation arising from a family relationship, parentage, marriage or affinity, including in particular obligations in respect of vulnerable persons. Any such declaration shall give rise to obligations between two Contracting States only in so far as their declarations cover the same maintenance obligations and parts of the Convention.

(4) The provisions of this Convention shall apply to children regardless of the marital status of the parents.

Scope—Art 2(1) provides for the core scope of the 2007 Convention. The core scope is: maintenance owed by a parent to a child under the age of 21 (regardless of the marital status of the parents); recognition and enforcement of spousal maintenance where the claim is made together with a child maintenance claim; and spousal support where no child claim is made, but in such cases Chs II and III (the administration cooperation provisions) do not apply. It is possible to limit or extend the core scope. By Art 2(1), a Contracting State may reserve the right to limit the scope of child maintenance to persons under 18 years, but will not then be able to use the 2007 Convention for its own children between the ages of 18 and 21. By Art 2(3), a Contracting State may declare that it will extend the provisions of the 2007

PART VI

Convention to wider forms of family maintenance (e g affinity cases, such as support by a person to his/her parent). The effect of such a declaration is that the relevant Contracting State will give, and receive, such extended assistance only to and from other Contracting States whose declarations as to scope match. By the Council Decision of 9 June 2011 (2011/432/EU), the EU has extended the scope of the 2007 Convention by applying Chs II and III on administrative cooperation to all cases of spousal support, regardless of whether or not they accompany a child maintenance claim.

Article 3

Definitions

For the purposes of this Convention –

   (a)   "creditor" means an individual to whom maintenance is owed or is alleged to be owed;

   (b)   "debtor" means an individual who owes or who is alleged to owe maintenance;

   (c)   "legal assistance" means the assistance necessary to enable applicants to know and assert their rights and to ensure that applications are fully and effectively dealt with in the requested State. The means of providing such assistance may include as necessary legal advice, assistance in bringing a case before an authority, legal representation and exemption from costs of proceedings;

   (d)   "agreement in writing" means an agreement recorded in any medium, the information contained in which is accessible so as to be usable for subsequent reference;

   (e)   "maintenance arrangement" means an agreement in writing relating to the payment of maintenance which –

      (i)   has been formally drawn up or registered as an authentic instrument by a competent authority; or

      (ii)   has been authenticated by, or concluded, registered or filed with a competent authority, and may be the subject of review and modification by a competent authority;

   (f)   "vulnerable person" means a person who, by reason of an impairment or insufficiency of his or her personal faculties, is not able to support him or herself.

CHAPTER II
ADMINISTRATIVE CO-OPERATION

Article 4

Designation of Central Authorities

(1) A Contracting State shall designate a Central Authority to discharge the duties that are imposed by the Convention on such an authority.

(2) Federal States, States with more than one system of law or States having autonomous territorial units shall be free to appoint more than one Central Authority and shall specify the territorial or personal extent of their functions. Where a State has appointed more than one Central Authority, it shall designate the Central Authority to which any communication may be addressed for transmission to the appropriate Central Authority within that State.

(3) The designation of the Central Authority or Central Authorities, their contact details, and where appropriate the extent of their functions as specified in paragraph 2, shall be communicated by a Contracting State to the Permanent Bureau of the Hague Conference on Private International Law at the time when the instrument of ratification or accession is deposited or when a declaration is submitted in accordance with Article 61. Contracting States shall promptly inform the Permanent Bureau of any changes.

"Federal states"—Because the UK has more than one system of law, there are separate Central Authorities for England and Wales, Scotland and Northern Ireland. The Central Authority for England and Wales acts as the "lead" Central Authority under Art 4(2).

Article 5

General functions of Central Authorities

Central Authorities shall –

(a) co-operate with each other and promote co-operation amongst the competent authorities in their States to achieve the purposes of the Convention;

(b) seek as far as possible solutions to difficulties which arise in the application of the Convention.

Article 6

Specific functions of Central Authorities

(1) Central Authorities shall provide assistance in relation to applications under Chapter III. In particular they shall –

(a) transmit and receive such applications;

(b) initiate or facilitate the institution of proceedings in respect of such applications.

(2) In relation to such applications they shall take all appropriate measures –

(a) where the circumstances require, to provide or facilitate the provision of legal assistance;

(b) to help locate the debtor or the creditor;

(c) to help obtain relevant information concerning the income and, if necessary, other financial circumstances of the debtor or creditor, including the location of assets;

(d) to encourage amicable solutions with a view to obtaining voluntary payment of maintenance, where suitable by use of mediation, conciliation or similar processes;

(e) to facilitate the ongoing enforcement of maintenance decisions, including any arrears;

(f) to facilitate the collection and expeditious transfer of maintenance payments;

(g) to facilitate the obtaining of documentary or other evidence;

(h) to provide assistance in establishing parentage where necessary for the recovery of maintenance;

(i) to initiate or facilitate the institution of proceedings to obtain any necessary provisional measures that are territorial in nature and the purpose of which is to secure the outcome of a pending maintenance application;

(j) to facilitate service of documents.

(3) The functions of the Central Authority under this Article may, to the extent permitted under the law of its State, be performed by public bodies, or other bodies subject to the supervision of the competent authorities of that State. The designation of any such public bodies or other bodies, as well as their contact details and the extent of their functions, shall be communicated by a Contracting State to the Permanent Bureau of the Hague Conference on Private International Law. Contracting States shall promptly inform the Permanent Bureau of any changes.

(4) Nothing in this Article or Article 7 shall be interpreted as imposing an obligation on a Central Authority to exercise powers that can be exercised only by judicial authorities under the law of the requested State.

PART VI

Article 7

Requests for specific measures

(1) A Central Authority may make a request, supported by reasons, to another Central Authority to take appropriate specific measures under Article 6(2)(b), (c), (g), (h), (i) and (j) when no application under Article 10 is pending. The requested Central Authority shall take such measures as are appropriate if satisfied that they are necessary to assist a potential applicant in making an application under Article 10 or in determining whether such an application should be initiated.

(2) A Central Authority may also take specific measures on the request of another Central Authority in relation to a case having an international element concerning the recovery of maintenance pending in the requesting State.

Scope—Art 7(1) permits pre-application investigation and imposes a duty on the receiving Central Authority to take the requested specific measure if it is satisfied that it is necessary to assist a potential applicant in making an application or in determining whether such an application should be initiated. Art 7(2) also gives a discretion to a receiving Central Authority to take a specific measure in a case pending in the requesting Contracting State having an international element (e g where it would be relevant to have information on the debtor's assets).

Article 8

Central Authority costs

(1) Each Central Authority shall bear its own costs in applying this Convention.

(2) Central Authorities may not impose any charge on an applicant for the provision of their services under the Convention save for exceptional costs arising from a request for a specific measure under Article 7.

(3) The requested Central Authority may not recover the costs of the services referred to in paragraph 2 without the prior consent of the applicant to the provision of those services at such cost.

CHAPTER III
APPLICATIONS THROUGH CENTRAL AUTHORITIES

Scope—Chapter III deals with applications that may be made to a Central Authority and the processes involved. Art 10 permits applications for the establishment of a maintenance decision in the territory of the requested Contracting State, recognition and enforcement in maintenance decisions from another Contracting State and modification of decisions. The law to be applied is that of the requesting Contracting State and establishment decisions are subject to the relevant jurisdictional provisions of that Contracting State, which in the case of the UK is the Maintenance Regulation (Art 10). Art 11 provides for the minimum contents of an application and Art 12 makes provisions for the methods by which Central Authorities must process applications. Arts 14–17 make provision for legal aid. The general principle is that entitlement to legal aid should not be less than in equivalent domestic cases (Art 14(4)). The general rule for child support cases is free legal aid for all applications concerning a child (Art 15). The EU has decided not to make a declaration for use of the child-centred means test in Art 16 and, therefore, Art 15 is the applicable system for the UK. However, for any application except for recognition and enforcement, a Contracting State may refuse legal aid if the application crosses the high threshold of being manifestly unfounded (Art 15(2)). In consequence, the vast majority of child cases will be dealt with on the basis of free legal aid under Chs II and III. For non-child cases, Art 17 provides the basic rule that, for all applications, provision of legal aid may be subject to means and merit testing in accordance with national law. For recognition and enforcement cases, there is a special rule so that, where the applicant received legal aid in the proceedings in the Contracting State of origin, he/she will receive legal aid to at least the same extent in the recognition and enforcement proceedings.

Article 9

Application through Central Authorities

An application under this Chapter shall be made through the Central Authority of the Contracting State in which the applicant resides to the Central Authority of the requested State. For the purpose of this provision, residence excludes mere presence.

Article 10

Available applications

(1) The following categories of application shall be available to a creditor in a requesting State seeking to recover maintenance under this Convention –

    (a)   recognition or recognition and enforcement of a decision;

    (b)   enforcement of a decision made or recognised in the requested State;

    (c)   establishment of a decision in the requested State where there is no existing decision, including where necessary the establishment of parentage;

    (d)   establishment of a decision in the requested State where recognition and enforcement of a decision is not possible, or is refused, because of the lack of a basis for recognition and enforcement under Article 20, or on the grounds specified in Article 22(b) or (e);

    (e)   modification of a decision made in the requested State;

    (f)   modification of a decision made in a State other than the requested State.

(2) The following categories of application shall be available to a debtor in a requesting State against whom there is an existing maintenance decision –

    (a)   recognition of a decision, or an equivalent procedure leading to the suspension, or limiting the enforcement, of a previous decision in the requested State;

    (b)   modification of a decision made in the requested State;

    (c)   modification of a decision made in a State other than the requested State.

(3) Save as otherwise provided in this Convention, the applications in paragraphs 1 and 2 shall be determined under the law of the requested State, and applications in paragraphs 1(c) to (f) and 2(b) and (c) shall be subject to the jurisdictional rules applicable in the requested State.

Article 11

Application contents

(1) All applications under Article 10 shall as a minimum include –

    (a)   a statement of the nature of the application or applications;

    (b)   the name and contact details, including the address and date of birth of the applicant;

    (c)   the name and, if known, address and date of birth of the respondent;

    (d)   the name and date of birth of any person for whom maintenance is sought;

    (e)   the grounds upon which the application is based;

    (f)   in an application by a creditor, information concerning where the maintenance payment should be sent or electronically transmitted;

    (g)   save in an application under Article 10(1)(a) and (2)(a), any information or document specified by declaration in accordance with Article 63 by the requested State;

    (h)   the name and contact details of the person or unit from the Central Authority of the requesting State responsible for processing the application.

(2) As appropriate, and to the extent known, the application shall in addition in particular include –

(a) the financial circumstances of the creditor;
(b) the financial circumstances of the debtor, including the name and address of the employer of the debtor and the nature and location of the assets of the debtor;
(c) any other information that may assist with the location of the respondent.

(3) The application shall be accompanied by any necessary supporting information or documentation including documentation concerning the entitlement of the applicant to free legal assistance. In the case of applications under Article 10(1)(a) and (2)(a), the application shall be accompanied only by the documents listed in Article 25.

(4) An application under Article 10 may be made in the form recommended and published by the Hague Conference on Private International Law.

Article 12

Transmission, receipt and processing of applications and cases through Central Authorities

(1) The Central Authority of the requesting State shall assist the applicant in ensuring that the application is accompanied by all the information and documents known by it to be necessary for consideration of the application.

(2) The Central Authority of the requesting State shall, when satisfied that the application complies with the requirements of the Convention, transmit the application on behalf of and with the consent of the applicant to the Central Authority of the requested State. The application shall be accompanied by the transmittal form set out in Annex 1. The Central Authority of the requesting State shall, when requested by the Central Authority of the requested State, provide a complete copy certified by the competent authority in the State of origin of any document specified under Articles 16(3), 25(1)(a), (b) and (d) and (3)(b) and 30(3).

(3) The requested Central Authority shall, within six weeks from the date of receipt of the application, acknowledge receipt in the form set out in Annex 2, and inform the Central Authority of the requesting State what initial steps have been or will be taken to deal with the application, and may request any further necessary documents and information. Within the same six-week period, the requested Central Authority shall provide to the requesting Central Authority the name and contact details of the person or unit responsible for responding to inquiries regarding the progress of the application.

(4) Within three months after the acknowledgement, the requested Central Authority shall inform the requesting Central Authority of the status of the application.

(5) Requesting and requested Central Authorities shall keep each other informed of –

(a) the person or unit responsible for a particular case;
(b) the progress of the case, and shall provide timely responses to enquiries.

(6) Central Authorities shall process a case as quickly as a proper consideration of the issues will allow.

(7) Central Authorities shall employ the most rapid and efficient means of communication at their disposal.

(8) A requested Central Authority may refuse to process an application only if it is manifest that the requirements of the Convention are not fulfilled. In such case, that Central Authority shall promptly inform the requesting Central Authority of its reasons for refusal.

(9) The requested Central Authority may not reject an application solely on the basis that additional documents or information are needed. However, the requested Central Authority may ask the requesting Central Authority to provide these additional documents or information. If the requesting Central Authority does not do so within

three months or a longer period specified by the requested Central Authority, the requested Central Authority may decide that it will no longer process the application. In this case, it shall inform the requesting Central Authority of this decision.

Article 13

Means of communication

Any application made through Central Authorities of the Contracting States in accordance with this Chapter, and any document or information appended thereto or provided by a Central Authority, may not be challenged by the respondent by reason only of the medium or means of communication employed between the Central Authorities concerned.

Article 14

Effective access to procedures

(1) The requested State shall provide applicants with effective access to procedures, including enforcement and appeal procedures, arising from applications under this Chapter.

(2) To provide such effective access, the requested State shall provide free legal assistance in accordance with Articles 14 to 17 unless paragraph 3 applies.

(3) The requested State shall not be obliged to provide such free legal assistance if and to the extent that the procedures of that State enable the applicant to make the case without the need for such assistance, and the Central Authority provides such services as are necessary free of charge.

(4) Entitlements to free legal assistance shall not be less than those available in equivalent domestic cases.

(5) No security, bond or deposit, however described, shall be required to guarantee the payment of costs and expenses in proceedings under the Convention.

Article 15

Free legal assistance for child support applications

(1) The requested State shall provide free legal assistance in respect of all applications by a creditor under this Chapter concerning maintenance obligations arising from a parent-child relationship towards a person under the age of 21 years.

(2) Notwithstanding paragraph 1, the requested State may, in relation to applications other than those under Article 10(1)(a) and (b) and the cases covered by Article 20(4), refuse free legal assistance if it considers that, on the merits, the application or any appeal is manifestly unfounded.

Article 16

Declaration to permit use of child-centred means test

(1) Notwithstanding Article 15(1), a State may declare, in accordance with Article 63, that it will provide free legal assistance in respect of applications other than under Article 10(1)(a) and (b) and the cases covered by Article 20(4), subject to a test based on an assessment of the means of the child.

(2) A State shall, at the time of making such a declaration, provide information to the Permanent Bureau of the Hague Conference on Private International Law concerning the

PART VI

manner in which the assessment of the child's means will be carried out, including the financial criteria which would need to be met to satisfy the test.

(3) An application referred to in paragraph 1, addressed to a State which has made the declaration referred to in that paragraph, shall include a formal attestation by the applicant stating that the child's means meet the criteria referred to in paragraph 2. The requested State may only request further evidence of the child's means if it has reasonable grounds to believe that the information provided by the applicant is inaccurate.

(4) If the most favourable legal assistance provided for by the law of the requested State in respect of applications under this Chapter concerning maintenance obligations arising from a parent-child relationship towards a child is more favourable than that provided for under paragraphs 1 to 3, the most favourable legal assistance shall be provided.

Article 17

Applications not qualifying under Article 15 or Article 16

In the case of all applications under this Convention other than those under Article 15 or Article 16 –

(a) the provision of free legal assistance may be made subject to a means or a merits test;

(b) an applicant, who in the State of origin has benefited from free legal assistance, shall be entitled, in any proceedings for recognition or enforcement, to benefit, at least to the same extent, from free legal assistance as provided for by the law of the State addressed under the same circumstances.

CHAPTER IV
RESTRICTIONS ON BRINGING PROCEEDINGS

Article 18

Limit on proceedings

(1) Where a decision is made in a Contracting State where the creditor is habitually resident, proceedings to modify the decision or to make a new decision cannot be brought by the debtor in any other Contracting State as long as the creditor remains habitually resident in the State where the decision was made.

(2) Paragraph 1 shall not apply –

(a) where, except in disputes relating to maintenance obligations in respect of children, there is agreement in writing between the parties to the jurisdiction of that other Contracting State;

(b) where the creditor submits to the jurisdiction of that other Contracting State either expressly or by defending on the merits of the case without objecting to the jurisdiction at the first available opportunity;

(c) where the competent authority in the State of origin cannot, or refuses to, exercise jurisdiction to modify the decision or make a new decision; or

(d) where the decision made in the State of origin cannot be recognised or declared enforceable in the Contracting State where proceedings to modify the decision or make a new decision are contemplated.

Scope—Art 18 contains the only direct rule of jurisdiction in the 2007 Convention, in contrast to the Maintenance Regulation, which contains a comprehensive jurisdictional code. This rule of jurisdiction was incorporated in the Maintenance Regulation and is, therefore, already part of UK law. It reflects a deliberate policy choice in the 2007 Convention to favour the creditor.

CHAPTER V
RECOGNITION AND ENFORCEMENT

Article 19

Scope of the Chapter

(1) This Chapter shall apply to a decision rendered by a judicial or administrative authority in respect of a maintenance obligation. The term "decision" also includes a settlement or agreement concluded before or approved by such an authority. A decision may include automatic adjustment by indexation and a requirement to pay arrears, retroactive maintenance or interest and a determination of costs or expenses.

(2) If a decision does not relate solely to a maintenance obligation, the effect of this Chapter is limited to the parts of the decision which concern maintenance obligations.

(3) For the purpose of paragraph 1, "administrative authority" means a public body whose decisions, under the law of the State where it is established –

(a) may be made the subject of an appeal to or review by a judicial authority; and
(b) have a similar force and effect to a decision of a judicial authority on the same matter.

(4) This Chapter also applies to maintenance arrangements in accordance with Article 30.

(5) The provisions of this Chapter shall apply to a request for recognition and enforcement made directly to a competent authority of the State addressed in accordance with Article 37.

Scope—The scope of the recognition and enforcement provisions is defined in wide terms to include decisions of administrative authorities (e g the CSA; Art 19(1),(3)) and maintenance arrangements (Arts 3 and 30). Partial enforcement of a decision is possible where the decision is not enforceable as a whole (Arts 19(2) and 21).

Defined term—"maintenance arrangement": Art 3(e).

Article 20

Bases for recognition and enforcement

(1) A decision made in one Contracting State ("the State of origin") shall be recognised and enforced in other Contracting States if –

(a) the respondent was habitually resident in the State of origin at the time proceedings were instituted;
(b) the respondent has submitted to the jurisdiction either expressly or by defending on the merits of the case without objecting to the jurisdiction at the first available opportunity;
(c) the creditor was habitually resident in the State of origin at the time proceedings were instituted;
(d) the child for whom maintenance was ordered was habitually resident in the State of origin at the time proceedings were instituted, provided that the respondent has lived with the child in that State or has resided in that State and provided support for the child there;
(e) except in disputes relating to maintenance obligations in respect of children, there has been agreement to the jurisdiction in writing by the parties; or
(f) the decision was made by an authority exercising jurisdiction on a matter of personal status or parental responsibility, unless that jurisdiction was based solely on the nationality of one of the parties.

PART VI

(2) A Contracting State may make a reservation, in accordance with Article 62, in respect of paragraph 1(c), (e) or (f).

(3) A Contracting State making a reservation under paragraph 2 shall recognise and enforce a decision if its law would in similar factual circumstances confer or would have conferred jurisdiction on its authorities to make such a decision.

(4) A Contracting State shall, if recognition of a decision is not possible as a result of a reservation under paragraph 2, and if the debtor is habitually resident in that State, take all appropriate measures to establish a decision for the benefit of the creditor. The preceding sentence shall not apply to direct requests for recognition and enforcement under Article 19(5) or to claims for support referred to in Article 2(1)(b).

(5) A decision in favour of a child under the age of 18 years which cannot be recognised by virtue only of a reservation in respect of paragraph 1(c), (e) or (f) shall be accepted as establishing the eligibility of that child for maintenance in the State addressed.

(6) A decision shall be recognised only if it has effect in the State of origin, and shall be enforced only if it is enforceable in the State of origin.

Scope—Because the 2007 Convention contains no rules as to jurisdiction (apart from Art 18), a mechanism is provided by Art 20, which stipulates that recognition and enforcement occurs in another Contracting State where the decision in the State of origin (as defined in Art 20(1)) complies with one of the jurisdictional bases in Art 20(1). The authorities of the Contracting State addressed are bound by any findings of fact on which the requesting Contracting State based jurisdiction (Art 27). A decision must first be enforceable in the State of origin to qualify for recognition and enforcement in another Contracting State (Art 20(6)).

"Reservation"—Whereas reservations under Art 62 are possible as the basis of providing alternative means of obtaining maintenance, no such reservations have been made by the EU.

Article 21

Severability and partial recognition and enforcement

(1) If the State addressed is unable to recognise or enforce the whole of the decision, it shall recognise or enforce any severable part of the decision which can be so recognised or enforced.

(2) Partial recognition or enforcement of a decision can always be applied for.

Article 22

Grounds for refusing recognition and enforcement

Recognition and enforcement of a decision may be refused if –

- (a) recognition and enforcement of the decision is manifestly incompatible with the public policy ("*ordre public*") of the State addressed;
- (b) the decision was obtained by fraud in connection with a matter of procedure;
- (c) proceedings between the same parties and having the same purpose are pending before an authority of the State addressed and those proceedings were the first to be instituted;
- (d) the decision is incompatible with a decision rendered between the same parties and having the same purpose, either in the State addressed or in another State, provided that this latter decision fulfils the conditions necessary for its recognition and enforcement in the State addressed;
- (e) in a case where the respondent has neither appeared nor was represented in proceedings in the State of origin –

- (i) when the law of the State of origin provides for notice of proceedings, the respondent did not have proper notice of the proceedings and an opportunity to be heard; or
- (ii) when the law of the State of origin does not provide for notice of the proceedings, the respondent did not have proper notice of the decision and an opportunity to challenge or appeal it on fact and law; or

(f) the decision was made in violation of Article 18.

Scope—Art 22 provides for the discretionary grounds for refusal of recognition and enforcement. Art 22(c) is a necessary accommodation of the fact that there are no direct rules of jurisdiction in the 2007 Convention.

Article 23

Procedure on an application for recognition and enforcement

(1) Subject to the provisions of the Convention, the procedures for recognition and enforcement shall be governed by the law of the State addressed.

(2) Where an application for recognition and enforcement of a decision has been made through Central Authorities in accordance with Chapter III, the requested Central Authority shall promptly either –

- (a) refer the application to the competent authority which shall without delay declare the decision enforceable or register the decision for enforcement; or
- (b) if it is the competent authority take such steps itself.

(3) Where the request is made directly to a competent authority in the State addressed in accordance with Article 19(5), that authority shall without delay declare the decision enforceable or register the decision for enforcement.

(4) A declaration or registration may be refused only on the ground set out in Article 22(a). At this stage neither the applicant nor the respondent is entitled to make any submissions.

(5) The applicant and the respondent shall be promptly notified of the declaration or registration, made under paragraphs 2 and 3, or the refusal thereof in accordance with paragraph 4, and may bring a challenge or appeal on fact and on a point of law.

(6) A challenge or an appeal is to be lodged within 30 days of notification under paragraph 5. If the contesting party is not resident in the Contracting State in which the declaration or registration was made or refused, the challenge or appeal shall be lodged within 60 days of notification.

(7) A challenge or appeal may be founded only on the following –

- (a) the grounds for refusing recognition and enforcement set out in Article 22;
- (b) the bases for recognition and enforcement under Article 20;
- (c) the authenticity or integrity of any document transmitted in accordance with Article 25(1)(a), (b) or (d) or (3)(b).

(8) A challenge or an appeal by a respondent may also be founded on the fulfilment of the debt to the extent that the recognition and enforcement relates to payments that fell due in the past.

(9) The applicant and the respondent shall be promptly notified of the decision following the challenge or the appeal.

(10) A further appeal, if permitted by the law of the State addressed, shall not have the effect of staying the enforcement of the decision unless there are exceptional circumstances.

(11) In taking any decision on recognition and enforcement, including any appeal, the competent authority shall act expeditiously.

PART VI

Scope—Art 23 describes the procedure on an application for recognition and enforcement, which applies both to applications made through Central Authorities (Art 23(2)) and those made directly (Art 23(3)). The procedure is in two stages, with the possibility of an appeal against the second stage. First, the application is considered without submissions from either party and will be recognised unless Art 22(a) (recognition manifestly incompatible with the public policy of the Contracting State addressed) applies. At the second stage, the parties are notified of the decision and either may appeal (Art 23(5)). The bases of appeal are limited to the grounds set out in Art 23(7),(8).

"Further appeal" (Art 23(10))—A further appeal from the second stage of the procedure is provided for in England and Wales by MCA 1980, s 111A.

Article 24

Alternative procedure on an application for recognition and enforcement

(1) Notwithstanding Article 23(2) to (11), a State may declare, in accordance with Article 63, that it will apply the procedure for recognition and enforcement set out in this Article.

(2) Where an application for recognition and enforcement of a decision has been made through Central Authorities in accordance with Chapter III, the requested Central Authority shall promptly either –

    (a)   refer the application to the competent authority which shall decide on the application for recognition and enforcement; or

    (b)   if it is the competent authority, take such a decision itself.

(3) A decision on recognition and enforcement shall be given by the competent authority after the respondent has been duly and promptly notified of the proceedings and both parties have been given an adequate opportunity to be heard.

(4) The competent authority may review the grounds for refusing recognition and enforcement set out in Article 22(a), (c) and (d) of its own motion. It may review any grounds listed in Articles 20, 22 and 23(7)(c) if raised by the respondent or if concerns relating to those grounds arise from the face of the documents submitted in accordance with Article 25.

(5) A refusal of recognition and enforcement may also be founded on the fulfilment of the debt to the extent that the recognition and enforcement relates to payments that fell due in the past.

(6) Any appeal, if permitted by the law of the State addressed, shall not have the effect of staying the enforcement of the decision unless there are exceptional circumstances.

(7) In taking any decision on recognition and enforcement, including any appeal, the competent authority shall act expeditiously.

Article 25

Documents

(1) An application for recognition and enforcement under Article 23 or Article 24 shall be accompanied by the following –

    (a)   a complete text of the decision;

    (b)   a document stating that the decision is enforceable in the State of origin and, in the case of a decision by an administrative authority, a document stating that the requirements of Article 19(3) are met unless that State has specified in accordance with Article 57 that decisions of its administrative authorities always meet those requirements;

    (c)   if the respondent did not appear and was not represented in the proceedings in the State of origin, a document or documents attesting, as appropriate, either that the respondent had proper notice of the proceedings and an opportunity to be heard, or that the respondent had proper notice of the decision and the opportunity to challenge or appeal it on fact and law;

(d)   where necessary, a document showing the amount of any arrears and the date such amount was calculated;

(e)   where necessary, in the case of a decision providing for automatic adjustment by indexation, a document providing the information necessary to make the appropriate calculations;

(f)   where necessary, documentation showing the extent to which the applicant received free legal assistance in the State of origin.

(2) Upon a challenge or appeal under Article 23(7)(c) or upon request by the competent authority in the State addressed, a complete copy of the document concerned, certified by the competent authority in the State of origin, shall be provided promptly –

(a)   by the Central Authority of the requesting State, where the application has been made in accordance with Chapter III;

(b)   by the applicant, where the request has been made directly to a competent authority of the State addressed.

(3) A Contracting State may specify in accordance with Article 57 –

(a)   that a complete copy of the decision certified by the competent authority in the State of origin must accompany the application;

(b)   circumstances in which it will accept, in lieu of a complete text of the decision, an abstract or extract of the decision drawn up by the competent authority of the State of origin, which may be made in the form recommended and published by the Hague Conference on Private International Law; or

(c)   that it does not require a document stating that the requirements of Article 19(3) are met.

Article 26

Procedure on an application for recognition

This Chapter shall apply mutatis mutandis to an application for recognition of a decision, save that the requirement of enforceability is replaced by the requirement that the decision has effect in the State of origin.

Article 27

Findings of fact

Any competent authority of the State addressed shall be bound by the findings of fact on which the authority of the State of origin based its jurisdiction.

Article 28

No review of the merits

There shall be no review by any competent authority of the State addressed of the merits of a decision.

Article 29

Physical presence of the child or the applicant not required

The physical presence of the child or the applicant shall not be required in any proceedings in the State addressed under this Chapter.

PART VI

Article 30

Maintenance arrangements

(1) A maintenance arrangement made in a Contracting State shall be entitled to recognition and enforcement as a decision under this Chapter provided that it is enforceable as a decision in the State of origin.

(2) For the purpose of Article 10(1)(a) and (b) and (2)(a), the term "decision" includes a maintenance arrangement.

(3) An application for recognition and enforcement of a maintenance arrangement shall be accompanied by the following –

    (a)   a complete text of the maintenance arrangement; and

    (b)   a document stating that the particular maintenance arrangement is enforceable as a decision in the State of origin.

(4) Recognition and enforcement of a maintenance arrangement may be refused if –

    (a)   the recognition and enforcement is manifestly incompatible with the public policy of the State addressed;

    (b)   the maintenance arrangement was obtained by fraud or falsification;

    (c)   the maintenance arrangement is incompatible with a decision rendered between the same parties and having the same purpose, either in the State addressed or in another State, provided that this latter decision fulfils the conditions necessary for its recognition and enforcement in the State addressed.

(5) The provisions of this Chapter, with the exception of Articles 20, 22, 23(7) and 25(1) and (3), shall apply mutatis mutandis to the recognition and enforcement of a maintenance arrangement save that –

    (a)   a declaration or registration in accordance with Article 23(2) and (3) may be refused only on the ground set out in paragraph 4(a);

    (b)   a challenge or appeal as referred to in Article 23(6) may be founded only on the following –

        (i)   the grounds for refusing recognition and enforcement set out in paragraph 4;

        (ii)   the authenticity or integrity of any document transmitted in accordance with paragraph 3;

    (c)   as regards the procedure under Article 24(4), the competent authority may review of its own motion the ground for refusing recognition and enforcement set out in paragraph 4(a) of this Article. It may review all grounds listed in paragraph 4 of this Article and the authenticity or integrity of any document transmitted in accordance with paragraph 3 if raised by the respondent or if concerns relating to those grounds arise from the face of those documents.

(6) Proceedings for recognition and enforcement of a maintenance arrangement shall be suspended if a challenge concerning the arrangement is pending before a competent authority of a Contracting State.

(7) A State may declare, in accordance with Article 63, that applications for recognition and enforcement of a maintenance arrangement shall only be made through Central Authorities.

(8) A Contracting State may, in accordance with Article 62, reserve the right not to recognise and enforce a maintenance arrangement.

Scope—Art 30 sets out the circumstances in which a maintenance arrangement may be recognised and enforced under the 2007 Convention. Recognition and enforcement of a maintenance arrangement may be sought through a Central Authority under the administrative cooperation procedures because it will be treated as a "decision" under Art 10(1)(a),(b) and (2)(a) (Art 30(2)). The accompanying documentation required for an application for recognition and enforcement of a maintenance arrangement differs from other decisions (Art 30(3)) and the grounds for refusal of recognition and enforcement are more restricted, owing to the nature of maintenance arrangements (Art 30(4)). Art 30(5) makes necessary modifications to the Ch IV procedure. The EU has not chosen to reserve a right not to recognise and enforce maintenance arrangements in accordance with Art 62 (Art 30(8)).

Defined term—"maintenance arrangement": Art 3(e).

Article 31

Decisions produced by the combined effect of provisional and confirmation orders

Where a decision is produced by the combined effect of a provisional order made in one State and an order by an authority in another State ("the confirming State") confirming the provisional order –

(a)   each of those States shall be deemed for the purposes of this Chapter to be a State of origin;

(b)   the requirements of Article 22(e) shall be met if the respondent had proper notice of the proceedings in the confirming State and an opportunity to oppose the confirmation of the provisional order;

(c)   the requirement of Article 20(6) that a decision be enforceable in the State of origin shall be met if the decision is enforceable in the confirming State; and

(d)   Article 18 shall not prevent proceedings for the modification of the decision being commenced in either State.

Scope—Art 31 refers to the process of provisional and confirmation orders, which, as far as the UK is concerned, is in use primarily for Commonwealth jurisdictions, the relevant domestic legislation being MO(RE)A 1972, Pt I and MO(FE)A 1920. Art 31 provides for the application of the 2007 Convention to such procedures.

CHAPTER VI
ENFORCEMENT BY THE STATE ADDRESSED

Article 32

Enforcement under internal law

(1)   Subject to the provisions of this Chapter, enforcement shall take place in accordance with the law of the State addressed.

(2)   Enforcement shall be prompt.

(3)   In the case of applications through Central Authorities, where a decision has been declared enforceable or registered for enforcement under Chapter V, enforcement shall proceed without the need for further action by the applicant.

(4)   Effect shall be given to any rules applicable in the State of origin of the decision relating to the duration of the maintenance obligation.

(5)   Any limitation on the period for which arrears may be enforced shall be determined either by the law of the State of origin of the decision or by the law of the State addressed, whichever provides for the longer limitation period.

Scope—Enforcement is, under domestic law, subject to the provisions of the 2007 Convention.

Article 33

Non-discrimination

The State addressed shall provide at least the same range of enforcement methods for cases under the Convention as are available in domestic cases.

Note—See annotations to the International Recovery of Maintenance (Hague Convention 2007 etc) Regulations 2012, Sch 2.

Article 34

Enforcement measures

(1) Contracting States shall make available in internal law effective measures to enforce decisions under this Convention.

(2) Such measures may include –

    (a)   wage withholding;

    (b)   garnishment from bank accounts and other sources;

    (c)   deductions from social security payments;

    (d)   lien on or forced sale of property;

    (e)   tax refund withholding;

    (f)   withholding or attachment of pension benefits;

    (g)   credit bureau reporting;

    (h)   denial, suspension or revocation of various licenses (for example, driving licenses);

    (i)   the use of mediation, conciliation or similar processes to bring about voluntary compliance.

Scope—Art 34 requires the provision of effective enforcement measures. However, the list in Art 34(2) is illustrative and not exhaustive.

Article 35

Transfer of funds

(1) Contracting States are encouraged to promote, including by means of international agreements, the use of the most cost-effective and efficient methods available to transfer funds payable as maintenance.

(2) A Contracting State, under whose law the transfer of funds is restricted, shall accord the highest priority to the transfer of funds payable under this Convention.

CHAPTER VII
PUBLIC BODIES

Article 36

Public bodies as applicants

(1) For the purposes of applications for recognition and enforcement under Article 10(1)(a) and (b) and cases covered by Article 20(4), "creditor" includes a public body acting in place of an individual to whom maintenance is owed or one to which reimbursement is owed for benefits provided in place of maintenance.

(2) The right of a public body to act in place of an individual to whom maintenance is owed or to seek reimbursement of benefits provided to the creditor in place of maintenance shall be governed by the law to which the body is subject.

(3) A public body may seek recognition or claim enforcement of –

    (a)   a decision rendered against a debtor on the application of a public body which claims payment of benefits provided in place of maintenance;

    (b)   a decision rendered between a creditor and debtor to the extent of the benefits provided to the creditor in place of maintenance.

(4) The public body seeking recognition or claiming enforcement of a decision shall upon request furnish any document necessary to establish its right under paragraph 2 and that benefits have been provided to the creditor.

Scope—Art 36 provides for the position of public bodies as applicants and permits a public body to obtain recognition or enforcement of a decision against a debtor where the public body seeks reimbursement of benefits paid to the creditor in lieu of maintenance.

CHAPTER VIII
GENERAL PROVISIONS

Article 37

Direct requests to competent authorities

(1) The Convention shall not exclude the possibility of recourse to such procedures as may be available under the internal law of a Contracting State allowing a person (an applicant) to seise directly a competent authority of that State in a matter governed by the Convention including, subject to Article 18, for the purpose of having a maintenance decision established or modified.

(2) Articles 14(5) and 17(b) and the provisions of Chapters V, VI, VII and this Chapter, with the exception of Articles 40(2), 42, 43(3), 44(3), 45 and 55, shall apply in relation to a request for recognition and enforcement made directly to a competent authority in a Contracting State.

(3) For the purpose of paragraph 2, Article 2(1)(a) shall apply to a decision granting maintenance to a vulnerable person over the age specified in that sub-paragraph where such decision was rendered before the person reached that age and provided for maintenance beyond that age by reason of the impairment.

Scope—The 2007 Convention does not exclude the possibility of a direct request to competent authorities (in the UK, the court), even though an application through the Central Authority would be available. However, in relation to applications for registration and enforcement, all such applications must be made through the Lord Chancellor as the Central Authority for England and Wales (International Recovery of Maintenance (Hague Convention 2007 etc) Regulations 2012).

Article 38

Protection of personal data

Personal data gathered or transmitted under the Convention shall be used only for the purposes for which they were gathered or transmitted.

Article 39

Confidentiality

Any authority processing information shall ensure its confidentiality in accordance with the law of its State.

PART VI

Article 40

Non-disclosure of information

(1) An authority shall not disclose or confirm information gathered or transmitted in application of this Convention if it determines that to do so could jeopardise the health, safety or liberty of a person.

(2) A determination to this effect made by one Central Authority shall be taken into account by another Central Authority, in particular in cases of family violence.

(3) Nothing in this Article shall impede the gathering and transmitting of information by and between authorities in so far as necessary to carry out the obligations under the Convention.

Article 41

No legalisation

No legalisation or similar formality may be required in the context of this Convention.

"Under the same conditions" (Art 41.1)—In consequence of this provision, driving disqualification orders have been extended to the Maintenance Regulation by the International Recovery of Maintenance (Hague Convention 2007 etc) Regulations 2012, Sch 2.

Article 42

Power of attorney

The Central Authority of the requested State may require a power of attorney from the applicant only if it acts on his or her behalf in judicial proceedings or before other authorities, or in order to designate a representative so to act.

Article 43

Recovery of costs

(1) Recovery of any costs incurred in the application of this Convention shall not take precedence over the recovery of maintenance.

(2) A State may recover costs from an unsuccessful party.

(3) For the purposes of an application under Article 10(1)(b) to recover costs from an unsuccessful party in accordance with paragraph 2, the term "creditor" in Article 10(1) shall include a State.

(4) This Article shall be without prejudice to Article 8.

Article 44

Language requirements

(1) Any application and related documents shall be in the original language, and shall be accompanied by a translation into an official language of the requested State or another language which the requested State has indicated, by way of declaration in accordance with Article 63, it will accept, unless the competent authority of that State dispenses with translation.

(2) A Contracting State which has more than one official language and cannot, for reasons of internal law, accept for the whole of its territory documents in one of those languages shall, by declaration in accordance with Article 63, specify the language in which such documents or translations thereof shall be drawn up for submission in the specified parts of its territory.

(3) Unless otherwise agreed by the Central Authorities, any other communications between such Authorities shall be in an official language of the requested State or in either English or French. However, a Contracting State may, by making a reservation in accordance with Article 62, object to the use of either English or French.

Article 45

Means and costs of translation

(1) In the case of applications under Chapter III, the Central Authorities may agree in an individual case or generally that the translation into an official language of the requested State may be made in the requested State from the original language or from any other agreed language. If there is no agreement and it is not possible for the requesting Central Authority to comply with the requirements of Article 44(1) and (2), then the application and related documents may be transmitted with translation into English or French for further translation into an official language of the requested State.

(2) The cost of translation arising from the application of paragraph 1 shall be borne by the requesting State unless otherwise agreed by Central Authorities of the States concerned.

(3) Notwithstanding Article 8, the requesting Central Authority may charge an applicant for the costs of translation of an application and related documents, except in so far as those costs may be covered by its system of legal assistance.

Article 46

Non-unified legal systems – interpretation

(1) In relation to a State in which two or more systems of law or sets of rules of law with regard to any matter dealt with in this Convention apply in different territorial units –

(a) any reference to the law or procedure of a State shall be construed as referring, where appropriate, to the law or procedure in force in the relevant territorial unit;

(b) any reference to a decision established, recognised, recognised and enforced, enforced or modified in that State shall be construed as referring, where appropriate, to a decision established, recognised, recognised and enforced, enforced or modified in the relevant territorial unit;

(c) any reference to a judicial or administrative authority in that State shall be construed as referring, where appropriate, to a judicial or administrative authority in the relevant territorial unit;

(d) any reference to competent authorities, public bodies, and other bodies of that State, other than Central Authorities, shall be construed as referring, where appropriate, to those authorised to act in the relevant territorial unit;

(e) any reference to residence or habitual residence in that State shall be construed as referring, where appropriate, to residence or habitual residence in the relevant territorial unit;

(f) any reference to location of assets in that State shall be construed as referring, where appropriate, to the location of assets in the relevant territorial unit;

(g) any reference to a reciprocity arrangement in force in a State shall be construed as referring, where appropriate, to a reciprocity arrangement in force in the relevant territorial unit;

(h) any reference to free legal assistance in that State shall be construed as referring, where appropriate, to free legal assistance in the relevant territorial unit;

PART VI

> (i)   any reference to a maintenance arrangement made in a State shall be construed as referring, where appropriate, to a maintenance arrangement made in the relevant territorial unit;
>
> (j)   any reference to recovery of costs by a State shall be construed as referring, where appropriate, to the recovery of costs by the relevant territorial unit.

(2)   This Article shall not apply to a Regional Economic Integration Organisation.

Article 47

Non-unified legal systems – substantive rules

(1)   A Contracting State with two or more territorial units in which different systems of law apply shall not be bound to apply this Convention to situations which involve solely such different territorial units.

(2)   A competent authority in a territorial unit of a Contracting State with two or more territorial units in which different systems of law apply shall not be bound to recognise or enforce a decision from another Contracting State solely because the decision has been recognised or enforced in another territorial unit of the same Contracting State under this Convention.

(3)   This Article shall not apply to a Regional Economic Integration Organisation.

Article 48

Co-ordination with prior Hague Maintenance Conventions

In relations between the Contracting States, this Convention replaces, subject to Article 56(2), the Hague Convention of 2 October 1973 on the Recognition and Enforcement of Decisions Relating to Maintenance Obligations and the Hague Convention of 15 April 1958 concerning the recognition and enforcement of decisions relating to maintenance obligations towards children in so far as their scope of application as between such States coincides with the scope of application of this Convention.

Article 49

Co-ordination with the 1956 New York Convention

In relations between the Contracting States, this Convention replaces the United Nations Convention on the Recovery Abroad of Maintenance of 20 June 1956, in so far as its scope of application as between such States coincides with the scope of application of this Convention.

Article 50

Relationship with prior Hague Conventions on service of documents and taking of evidence

This Convention does not affect the Hague Convention of 1 March 1954 on civil procedure, the Hague Convention of 15 November 1965 on the Service Abroad of Judicial and Extrajudicial Documents in Civil or Commercial Matters and the Hague Convention of 18 March 1970 on the Taking of Evidence Abroad in Civil or Commercial Matters.

Article 51

Co-ordination of instruments and supplementary agreements

(1) This Convention does not affect any international instrument concluded before this Convention to which Contracting States are Parties and which contains provisions on matters governed by this Convention.

(2) Any Contracting State may conclude with one or more Contracting States agreements, which contain provisions on matters governed by the Convention, with a view to improving the application of the Convention between or among themselves, provided that such agreements are consistent with the objects and purpose of the Convention and do not affect, in the relationship of such States with other Contracting States, the application of the provisions of the Convention. The States which have concluded such an agreement shall transmit a copy to the depositary of the Convention.

(3) Paragraphs 1 and 2 shall also apply to reciprocity arrangements and to uniform laws based on special ties between the States concerned.

(4) This Convention shall not affect the application of instruments of a Regional Economic Integration Organisation that is a Party to this Convention, adopted after the conclusion of the Convention, on matters governed by the Convention provided that such instruments do not affect, in the relationship of Member States of the Regional Economic Integration Organisation with other Contracting States, the application of the provisions of the Convention. As concerns the recognition or enforcement of decisions as between Member States of the Regional Economic Integration Organisation, the Convention shall not affect the rules of the Regional Economic Integration Organisation, whether adopted before or after the conclusion of the Convention.

Scope—Art 51 enables EU Member States to continue to operate the Maintenance Regulation, giving it precedence over the 2007 Convention as between EU Member States, whereas EU Member States will have to apply the 2007 Convention in their relations with non-EU Contracting States that are Contracting States to the 2007 Convention.

Article 52

Most effective rule

(1) This Convention shall not prevent the application of an agreement, arrangement or international instrument in force between the requesting State and the requested State, or a reciprocity arrangement in force in the requested State that provides for –

  (a) broader bases for recognition of maintenance decisions, without prejudice to Article 22(f) of the Convention;
  (b) simplified, more expeditious procedures on an application for recognition or recognition and enforcement of maintenance decisions;
  (c) more beneficial legal assistance than that provided for under Articles 14 to 17; or
  (d) procedures permitting an applicant from a requesting State to make a request directly to the Central Authority of the requested State.

(2) This Convention shall not prevent the application of a law in force in the requested State that provides for more effective rules as referred to in paragraph 1(a) to (c). However, as regards simplified, more expeditious procedures referred to in paragraph 1(b), they must be compatible with the protection offered to the parties under Articles 23 and 24, in particular as regards the rights of the parties to be duly notified of the proceedings and be given adequate opportunity to be heard and as regards the effects of any challenge or appeal.

PART VI

Article 53

Uniform interpretation

In the interpretation of this Convention, regard shall be had to its international character and to the need to promote uniformity in its application.

Article 54

Review of practical operation of the Convention

(1) The Secretary General of the Hague Conference on Private International Law shall at regular intervals convene a Special Commission in order to review the practical operation of the Convention and to encourage the development of good practices under the Convention.

(2) For the purpose of such review, Contracting States shall co-operate with the Permanent Bureau of the Hague Conference on Private International Law in the gathering of information, including statistics and case law, concerning the practical operation of the Convention.

Article 55

Amendment of forms

(1) The forms annexed to this Convention may be amended by a decision of a Special Commission convened by the Secretary General of the Hague Conference on Private International Law to which all Contracting States and all Members shall be invited. Notice of the proposal to amend the forms shall be included in the agenda for the meeting.

(2) Amendments adopted by the Contracting States present at the Special Commission shall come into force for all Contracting States on the first day of the seventh calendar month after the date of their communication by the depositary to all Contracting States.

(3) During the period provided for in paragraph 2 any Contracting State may by notification in writing to the depositary make a reservation, in accordance with Article 62, with respect to the amendment. The State making such reservation shall, until the reservation is withdrawn, be treated as a State not Party to the present Convention with respect to that amendment.

Article 56

Transitional provisions

(1) The Convention shall apply in every case where –

  (a) a request pursuant to Article 7 or an application pursuant to Chapter III has been received by the Central Authority of the requested State after the Convention has entered into force between the requesting State and the requested State;

  (b) a direct request for recognition and enforcement has been received by the competent authority of the State addressed after the Convention has entered into force between the State of origin and the State addressed.

(2) With regard to the recognition and enforcement of decisions between Contracting States to this Convention that are also Parties to either of the Hague Maintenance Conventions mentioned in Article 48, if the conditions for the recognition and enforcement under this Convention prevent the recognition and enforcement of a decision given in the State of origin before the entry into force of this Convention for that

State, that would otherwise have been recognised and enforced under the terms of the Convention that was in effect at the time the decision was rendered, the conditions of that Convention shall apply.

(3) The State addressed shall not be bound under this Convention to enforce a decision or a maintenance arrangement, in respect of payments falling due prior to the entry into force of the Convention between the State of origin and the State addressed, except for maintenance obligations arising from a parent-child relationship towards a person under the age of 21 years.

Article 57

Provision of information concerning laws, procedures and services

(1) A Contracting State, by the time its instrument of ratification or accession is deposited or a declaration is submitted in accordance with Article 61 of the Convention, shall provide the Permanent Bureau of the Hague Conference on Private International Law with –

  (a) a description of its laws and procedures concerning maintenance obligations;
  (b) a description of the measures it will take to meet the obligations under Article 6;
  (c) a description of how it will provide applicants with effective access to procedures, as required under Article 14;
  (d) a description of its enforcement rules and procedures, including any limitations on enforcement, in particular debtor protection rules and limitation periods;
  (e) any specification referred to in Article 25(1)(b) and (3).

(2) Contracting States may, in fulfilling their obligations under paragraph 1, utilise a country profile form recommended and published by the Hague Conference on Private International Law.

(3) Information shall be kept up to date by the Contracting States.

CHAPTER IX
FINAL PROVISIONS

Article 58

Signature, ratification and accession

(1) The Convention shall be open for signature by the States which were Members of the Hague Conference on Private International Law at the time of its Twenty-First Session and by the other States which participated in that Session.

(2) It shall be ratified, accepted or approved and the instruments of ratification, acceptance or approval shall be deposited with the Ministry of Foreign Affairs of the Kingdom of the Netherlands, depositary of the Convention.

(3) Any other State or Regional Economic Integration Organisation may accede to the Convention after it has entered into force in accordance with Article 60(1).

(4) The instrument of accession shall be deposited with the depositary.

(5) Such accession shall have effect only as regards the relations between the acceding State and those Contracting States which have not raised an objection to its accession in the 12 months after the date of the notification referred to in Article 65. Such an objection may also be raised by States at the time when they ratify, accept or approve the Convention after an accession. Any such objection shall be notified to the depositary.

PART VI

Article 59

Regional Economic Integration Organisations

(1) A Regional Economic Integration Organisation which is constituted solely by sovereign States and has competence over some or all of the matters governed by this Convention may similarly sign, accept, approve or accede to this Convention. The Regional Economic Integration Organisation shall in that case have the rights and obligations of a Contracting State, to the extent that the Organisation has competence over matters governed by the Convention.

(2) The Regional Economic Integration Organisation shall, at the time of signature, acceptance, approval or accession, notify the depositary in writing of the matters governed by this Convention in respect of which competence has been transferred to that Organisation by its Member States. The Organisation shall promptly notify the depositary in writing of any changes to its competence as specified in the most recent notice given under this paragraph.

(3) At the time of signature, acceptance, approval or accession, a Regional Economic Integration Organisation may declare in accordance with Article 63 that it exercises competence over all the matters governed by this Convention and that the Member States which have transferred competence to the Regional Economic Integration Organisation in respect of the matter in question shall be bound by this Convention by virtue of the signature, acceptance, approval or accession of the Organisation.

(4) For the purposes of the entry into force of this Convention, any instrument deposited by a Regional Economic Integration Organisation shall not be counted unless the Regional Economic Integration Organisation makes a declaration in accordance with paragraph 3.

(5) Any reference to a "Contracting State" or "State" in this Convention shall apply equally to a Regional Economic Integration Organisation that is a Party to it, where appropriate. In the event that a declaration is made by a Regional Economic Integration Organisation in accordance with paragraph 3, any reference to a "Contracting State" or "State" in this Convention shall apply equally to the relevant Member States of the Organisation, where appropriate.

Article 60

Entry into force

(1) The Convention shall enter into force on the first day of the month following the expiration of three months after the deposit of the second instrument of ratification, acceptance or approval referred to in Article 58.

(2) Thereafter the Convention shall enter into force –

(a) for each State or Regional Economic Integration Organisation referred to in Article 59(1) subsequently ratifying, accepting or approving it, on the first day of the month following the expiration of three months after the deposit of its instrument of ratification, acceptance or approval;

(b) for each State or Regional Economic Integration Organisation referred to in Article 58(3) on the day after the end of the period during which objections may be raised in accordance with Article 58(5);

(c) for a territorial unit to which the Convention has been extended in accordance with Article 61, on the first day of the month following the expiration of three months after the notification referred to in that Article.

Article 61

Declarations with respect to non-unified legal systems

(1) If a State has two or more territorial units in which different systems of law are applicable in relation to matters dealt with in the Convention, it may at the time of signature, ratification, acceptance, approval or accession declare in accordance with Article 63 that this Convention shall extend to all its territorial units or only to one or more of them and may modify this declaration by submitting another declaration at any time.

(2) Any such declaration shall be notified to the depositary and shall state expressly the territorial units to which the Convention applies.

(3) If a State makes no declaration under this Article, the Convention shall extend to all territorial units of that State.

(4) This Article shall not apply to a Regional Economic Integration Organisation.

Article 62

Reservations

(1) Any Contracting State may, not later than the time of ratification, acceptance, approval or accession, or at the time of making a declaration in terms of Article 61, make one or more of the reservations provided for in Articles 2(2), 20(2), 30(8), 44(3) and 55(3). No other reservation shall be permitted.

(2) Any State may at any time withdraw a reservation it has made. The withdrawal shall be notified to the depositary.

(3) The reservation shall cease to have effect on the first day of the third calendar month after the notification referred to in paragraph 2.

(4) Reservations under this Article shall have no reciprocal effect with the exception of the reservation provided for in Article 2(2).

Article 63

Declarations

(1) Declarations referred to in Articles 2(3), 11(1)(g), 16(1), 24(1), 30(7), 44(1) and (2), 59(3) and 61(1), may be made upon signature, ratification, acceptance, approval or accession or at any time thereafter, and may be modified or withdrawn at any time.

(2) Declarations, modifications and withdrawals shall be notified to the depositary.

(3) A declaration made at the time of signature, ratification, acceptance, approval or accession shall take effect simultaneously with the entry into force of this Convention for the State concerned.

(4) A declaration made at a subsequent time, and any modification or withdrawal of a declaration, shall take effect on the first day of the month following the expiration of three months after the date on which the notification is received by the depositary.

Article 64

Denunciation

(1) A Contracting State to the Convention may denounce it by a notification in writing addressed to the depositary. The denunciation may be limited to certain territorial units of a multi-unit State to which the Convention applies.

(2) The denunciation shall take effect on the first day of the month following the expiration of 12 months after the date on which the notification is received by the depositary. Where a longer period for the denunciation to take effect is specified in the notification, the denunciation shall take effect upon the expiration of such longer period after the date on which the notification is received by the depositary.

Article 65

Notification

The depositary shall notify the Members of the Hague Conference on Private International Law, and other States and Regional Economic Integration Organisations which have signed, ratified, accepted, approved or acceded in accordance with Articles 58 and 59 of the following –

   (a) the signatures, ratifications, acceptances and approvals referred to in Articles 58 and 59;
   (b) the accessions and objections raised to accessions referred to in Articles 58(3) and (5) and 59;
   (c) the date on which the Convention enters into force in accordance with Article 60;
   (d) the declarations referred to in Articles 2(3), 11(1)(g), 16(1), 24(1), 30(7), 44(1) and (2), 59(3) and 61(1);
   (e) the agreements referred to in Article 51(2);
   (f) the reservations referred to in Articles 2(2), 20(2), 30(8), 44(3) and 55(3), and the withdrawals referred to in Article 62(2);
   (g) the denunciations referred to in Article 64.

In witness whereof the undersigned, being duly authorised thereto, have signed this Convention.

Done at The Hague, on the 23rd day of November 2007, in the English and French languages, both texts being equally authentic, in a single copy which shall be deposited in the archives of the Government of the Kingdom of the Netherlands, and of which a certified copy shall be sent, through diplomatic channels, to each of the Members of the Hague Conference on Private International Law at the date of its Twenty-First Session and to each of the other States which have participated in that Session.

****

Council Regulation (EC) No 4/2009

of 18 December 2008
on jurisdiction, applicable law, recognition and enforcement of decisions and cooperation in matters relating to maintenance obligations

Scope—The Regulation (known as the Maintenance Regulation) came into force in the UK on 18 June 2011. It replaced Brussels I (Council Regulation (EC) No 44/2001 of 22 December 2000 on Jurisdiction and Recognition and Enforcement of Judgments in Civil and Commercial Matters) in relation to maintenance obligations except in relation to procedures underway on 18 June 2011 (Art 75). As to Brussels I, see *The Family Court Practice 2011*. The Regulation does not as such provide for rules of applicable law, but instead refers (Art 15) to the Hague Protocol on the Law Applicable to Maintenance Obligations of 23 November 2007 (the Hague Protocol). Denmark (see, however, below) and the UK are not bound by the Hague Protocol (see annotations to Art 15).
    The Regulation is designed to offer greater certainty and predictability to creditors and debtors of maintenance obligations and establishes common procedural rules in relation to cross-border disputes by

permitting maintenance decisions, court settlements and authentic instruments (Art 2) made in one Member State to be recognised and enforced in another Member State without further formality (Recital 9). However, because cf the position of the UK and Denmark, the Maintenance Regulation establishes two parallel recognition and enforcement regimes, described below.

"Maintenance obligation" is not defined. However, the Regulation applies to maintenance obligations arising from a family relationship, parentage, marriage or affinity and is to be interpreted autonomously (Recital (11)). See also, *Van den Boogaard v Laumen* [1997] 2 FLR 399; *Moore v Moore* [2007] 2 FLR 339; *T v T (Occupation Orders)* [2013] 1 FLR 364; *Traversa v Freddi* [2011] 2 FLR 272.

The Maintenance Regulation is used between Member States. Where non-EU Contracting States are concerned, Member States must use the Hague Convention 2007 on the International Recovery of Child Support and other forms of Family Maintenance.

To enable a maintenance creditor to obtain a decision easily in a Member State that will be automatically enforceable in another Member State without further formalities, the Regulation brings together provisions on jurisdiction, conflict of laws, recognition and enforceability, enforcement, legal aid and co-operation between Central Authorities. The available applications that can be made pursuant to the Regulation are set out at Art 56.

A decision given in a Member State bound by the Hague Protocol is recognised in another Member State without any special procedure being required and without any possibility of its recognition being opposed. Further, a decision that is enforceable in the originating Member State is enforceable in another Member State without the need for a declaration of enforceability (Art 17). Thus, the Regulation abolishes the exequatur procedure for decisions given by a Member State bound by the Hague Protocol.

For those Member States not bound by the Hague Protocol (the UK and Denmark), a decision will still be recognised without any special procedure being required. However, if the recognition of a decision is contested, it will be necessary for any interested party to apply for a decision that the decision be recognised (Art 23). Art 24 provides for when a decision is not to be recognised. Further, for a decision in a Member State not bound by the Hague Protocol to be enforceable in another Member State, it is necessary for it first to be declared enforceable in that Member State (Art 26). Art 28 deals with the procedure to follow for such a declaration of enforceability. The decision on the application for a declaration of enforceability may be appealed by either party (Art 32).

For Member States, whether or not bound by the Hague Protocol, the procedure for the enforcement of decisions given in another Member State is governed by the law of the Member State of enforcement (Art 41).

The Regulation does not in any way imply recognition of the family relationship, parentage, marriage or affinity underlying the maintenance obligation (Art 22).

As to procedure under the Regulation, see CJJ(M)R 2011 (in Part IV of this work), the Family Procedure (Amendment) Rules 2011 (amending FPR 2010 (principally Pt 34) so as to take account of the Regulation) and FPR PD34C.

Denmark is in a special position so far as the Maintenance Regulation is concerned. Recital 48 records Denmark's non-participation in the Regulation. However, Denmark subsequently entered into a side agreement with the European Community to apply the Regulation in part by notification under Art 3.2 of the Agreement of 19 October 2005 between the European Community and the Kingdom of Denmark on jurisdiction and the recognition and enforcement of judgments in civil and commercial matters (Council Decision 2006/325/EC). On 14 January 2009, Denmark gave notice of its intention to implement the Maintenance Regulation to the extent to which it modified Brussels I. The Maintenance Regulation applies to Denmark to this extent:

- Ch III (applicable law) and Ch VII (cooperation between Central Authorities) do not apply;
- Art 2 (definitions) and Ch IX (final provisions) apply only to the extent relevant to Denmark's participation.
- Ch II (jurisdiction) applies, as does Ch IV, S 2 (recognition and enforcement as a non-Hague Protocol Member State) and the provisions relating to legal aid (limited by Denmark's non-participation in Ch VII) and as to public bodies as creditors, authentic instruments and court settlements.

The Forms prescribed by the Maintenance Regulation are contained in its Annexes (not reproduced in this work), updates to which may be accessed at http://ec.europa.eu/justice_home/judicialatlascivil/html/mo_information_en.htm.

THE COUNCIL OF THE EUROPEAN UNION,

Having regard to the Treaty establishing the European Community,

and in particular Article 61(c) and Article 67(2) thereof,

Having regard to the proposal from the Commission,

PART VI

Having regard to the opinion of the European Parliament,

Having regard to the opinion of the European Economic and

Social Committee,

Whereas:

(1) The Community has set itself the objective of maintaining and developing an area of freedom, security and justice, in which the free movement of persons is ensured. For the gradual establishment of such an area, the Community is to adopt, among others, measures relating to judicial cooperation in civil matters having cross-border implications, in so far as necessary for the proper functioning of the internal market.

(2) In accordance with Article 65(b) of the Treaty, these measures must aim, inter alia, to promote the compatibility of the rules applicable in the Member States concerning the conflict of laws and of jurisdiction.

(3) In this respect, the Community has among other measures already adopted Council Regulation (EC) No 44/2001 of 22 December 2000 on jurisdiction and the recognition and enforcement of judgments in civil and commercial matters, Council Decision 2001/470/EC of 28 May 2001 establishing a European Judicial Network in civil and commercial matters, Council Regulation (EC) No 1206/2001 of 28 May 2001 on cooperation between the courts of the Member States in the taking of evidence in civil or commercial matters, Council Directive 2003/8/EC of 27 January 2003 to improve access to justice in cross-border disputes by establishing minimum common rules relating to legal aid for such disputes, Council Regulation (EC) No 2201/2003 of 27 November 2003 on jurisdiction and the recognition and enforcement of judgments in matrimonial matters and in matters of parental responsibility, Regulation (EC) No 805/2004 of the European Parliament and of the Council of 21 April 2004 creating a European Enforcement Order for uncontested claims, and Regulation (EC) No 1393/2007 of the European Parliament and of the Council of 13 November 2007 on the service in the Member States of judicial and extrajudicial documents in civil or commercial matters (service of documents).

(4) The European Council in Tampere on 15 and 16 October 1999 invited the Council and the Commission to establish special common procedural rules to simplify and accelerate the settlement of cross-border disputes concerning, inter alia, maintenance claims. It also called for the abolition of intermediate measures required for the recognition and enforcement in the requested State of a decision given in another Member State, particularly a decision relating to a maintenance claim.

(5) A programme of measures for the enforcement of the principle of mutual recognition of decisions in civil and commercial matters, common to the Commission and to the Council, was adopted on 30 November 2000. That programme provides for the abolition of the exequatur procedure for maintenance claims in order to boost the effectiveness of the means by which maintenance creditors safeguard their rights.

(6) The European Council meeting in Brussels on 4 and 5 November 2004 adopted a new programme called 'The Hague Programme: strengthening freedom, security and justice in the European Union' (hereinafter referred to as The Hague Programme).

(7) At its meeting on 2 and 3 June 2005, the Council adopted a Council and Commission Action Plan which implements The Hague Programme in concrete actions and which mentions the necessity of adopting proposals on maintenance obligations.

(8) In the framework of The Hague Conference on Private International Law, the Community and its Member States took part in negotiations which led to the adoption on 23 November 2007 of the Convention on the International Recovery of Child Support and other Forms of Family Maintenance (hereinafter referred to as the 2007 Hague Convention) and the Protocol on the Law Applicable to Maintenance Obligations

(hereinafter referred to as the 2007 Hague Protocol). Both those instruments should therefore be taken into account in this Regulation.

(9) A maintenance creditor should be able to obtain easily, in a Member State, a decision which will be automatically enforceable in another Member State without further formalities.

(10) In order to achieve this goal, it is advisable to create a Community instrument in matters relating to maintenance obligations bringing together provisions on jurisdiction, conflict of laws, recognition and enforceability, enforcement, legal aid and cooperation between Central Authorities.

(11) The scope of this Regulation should cover all maintenance obligations arising from a family relationship, parentage, marriage or affinity, in order to guarantee equal treatment of all maintenance creditors. For the purposes of this Regulation, the term 'maintenance obligation' should be interpreted autonomously.

(12) In order to take account of the various ways of resolving maintenance obligation issues in the Member States, this Regulation should apply both to court decisions and to decisions given by administrative authorities, provided that the latter offer guarantees with regard to, in particular, their impartiality and the right of all parties to be heard. Those authorities should therefore apply all the rules of this Regulation.

(13) For the reasons set out above, this Regulation should also ensure the recognition and enforcement of court settlements and authentic instruments without affecting the right of either party to such a settlement or instrument to challenge the settlement or instrument before the courts of the Member State of origin.

(14) It should be provided in this Regulation that for the purposes of an application for the recognition and enforcement of a decision relating to maintenance obligations the term 'creditor' includes public bodies which are entitled to act in place of a person to whom maintenance is owed or to claim reimbursement of benefits provided to the creditor in place of maintenance. Where a public body acts in this capacity, it should be entitled to the same services and the same legal aid as a creditor.

(15) In order to preserve the interests of maintenance creditors and to promote the proper administration of justice within the European Union, the rules on jurisdiction as they result from Regulation (EC) No 44/2001 should be adapted. The circumstance that the defendant is habitually resident in a third State should no longer entail the non-application of Community rules on jurisdiction, and there should no longer be any referral to national law. This Regulation should therefore determine the cases in which a court in a Member State may exercise subsidiary jurisdiction.

(16) In order to remedy, in particular, situations of denial of justice this Regulation should provide a forum necessitates allowing a court of a Member State, on an exceptional basis, to hear a case which is closely connected with a third State. Such an exceptional basis may be deemed to exist when proceedings prove impossible in the third State in question, for example because of civil war, or when an applicant cannot reasonably be expected to initiate or conduct proceedings in that State. Jurisdiction based on the forum necessitatis should, however, be exercised only if the dispute has a sufficient connection with the Member State of the court seised, for instance the nationality of one of the parties.

(17) An additional rule of jurisdiction should provide that, except under specific conditions, proceedings to modify an existing maintenance decision or to have a new decision given can be brought by the debtor only in the State in which the creditor was habitually resident at the time the decision was given and in which he remains habitually resident. To ensure proper symmetry between the 2007 Hague Convention and this Regulation, this rule should also apply as regards decisions given in a third State which is

party to the said Convention in so far as that Convention is in force between that State and the Community and covers the same maintenance obligations in that State and in the Community.

(18) For the purposes of this Regulation, it should be provided that in Ireland the concept of 'domicile' replaces the concept of 'nationality' which is also the case in the United Kingdom, subject to this Regulation being applicable in the latter Member State in accordance with Article 4 of the Protocol on the position of the United Kingdom and Ireland annexed to the Treaty on European Union and the Treaty establishing the European Community.

(19) In order to increase legal certainty, predictability and the autonomy of the parties, this Regulation should enable the parties to choose the competent court by agreement on the basis of specific connecting factors. To protect the weaker party, such a choice of court should not be allowed in the case of maintenance obligations towards a child under the age of 18.

(20) It should be provided in this Regulation that, for Member States bound by the 2007 Hague Protocol, the rules on conflict of laws in respect of maintenance obligations will be those set out in that Protocol. To that end, a provision referring to the said Protocol should be inserted. The 2007 Hague Protocol will be concluded by the Community in time to enable this Regulation to apply. To take account of a scenario in which the 2007 Hague Protocol does not apply to all the Member States a distinction for the purposes of recognition, enforceability and enforcement of decisions needs to be made in this Regulation between the Member States bound by the 2007 Hague Protocol and those not bound by it.

(21) It needs to be made clear in this Regulation that these rules on conflict of laws determine only the law applicable to maintenance obligations and do not determine the law applicable to the establishment of the family relationships on which the maintenance obligations are based. The establishment of family relationships continues to be covered by the national law of the Member States, including their rules of private international law.

(22) In order to ensure swift and efficient recovery of a maintenance obligation and to prevent delaying actions, decisions in matters relating to maintenance obligations given in a Member State should in principle be provisionally enforceable. This Regulation should therefore provide that the court of origin should be able to declare the decision provisionally enforceable even if the national law does not provide for enforceability by operation of law and even if an appeal has been or could still be lodged against the decision under national law.

(23) To limit the costs of proceedings subject to this Regulation, the greatest possible use of modern communications technologies, particularly for hearing parties, would be helpful.

(24) The guarantees provided by the application of rules on conflict of laws should provide the justification for having decisions relating to maintenance obligations given in a Member State bound by the 2007 Hague Protocol recognised and regarded as enforceable in all the other Member States without any procedure being necessary and without any form of control on the substance in the Member State of enforcement.

(25) Recognition in a Member State of a decision relating to maintenance obligations has as its only object to allow the recovery of the maintenance claim determined in the decision. It does not imply the recognition by that Member State of the family relationship, parentage, marriage or affinity underlying the maintenance obligations which gave rise to the decision.

(26) For decisions on maintenance obligations given in a Member State not bound by the 2007 Hague Protocol, there should be provision in this Regulation for a procedure for

recognition and declaration of enforceability. That procedure should be modelled on the procedure and the grounds for refusing recognition set out in Regulation (EC) No 44/2001. To accelerate proceedings and enable the creditor to recover his claim quickly, the court seised should be required to give its decision within a set time, unless there are exceptional circumstances.

(27) It would also be appropriate to limit as far as possible the formal enforcement requirements likely to increase the costs to be borne by the maintenance creditor. To that end, this Regulation should provide that a maintenance creditor ought not to be required to have a postal address or an authorised representative in the Member State of enforcement, without this otherwise affecting the internal organisation of the Member States in matters relating to enforcement proceedings.

(28) In order to limit the costs of enforcement proceedings, no translation should be required unless enforcement is contested, and without prejudice to the rules applicable to service of documents.

(29) In order to guarantee compliance with the requirements of a fair trial, this Regulation should provide for the right of a defendant who did not enter an appearance in the court of origin of a Member State bound by the 2007 Hague Protocol to apply for a review of the decision given against him at the stage of enforcement. However, the defendant must apply for this review within a set period which should start no later than the day on which, in the enforcement proceedings, his property was first made non-disposable in whole or in part. That right to apply for a review should be an extraordinary remedy granted to the defendant in default and not affecting the application of any extraordinary remedies laid down in the law of the Member State of origin provided that those remedies are not incompatible with the right to a review under this Regulation.

(30) In order to speed up the enforcement in another Member State of a decision given in a Member State bound by the 2007 Hague Protocol it is necessary to limit the grounds of refusal or of suspension of enforcement which may be invoked by the debtor on account of the cross-border nature of the maintenance claim. This limitation should not affect the grounds of refusal or of suspension laid down in national law which are not incompatible with those listed in this Regulation, such as the debtor's discharge of his debt at the time of enforcement or the unattachable nature of certain assets.

(31) To facilitate cross-border recovery of maintenance claims, provision should be made for a system of cooperation between Central Authorities designated by the Member States. These Authorities should assist maintenance creditors and debtors in asserting their rights in another Member State by submitting applications for recognition, enforceability and enforcement of existing decisions, for the modification of such decisions or for the establishment of a decision. They should also exchange information in order to locate debtors and creditors, and identify their income and assets, as necessary. Lastly, they should cooperate with each other by exchanging general information and promoting cooperation amongst the competent authorities in their Member States.

(32) A Central Authority designated under this Regulation should bear its own costs, except in specifically determined cases, and should provide assistance for all applicants residing in its Member State. The criterion for determining a person's right to request assistance from a Central Authority should be less strict than the connecting factor of 'habitual residence' used elsewhere in this Regulation. However, the 'residence' criterion should exclude mere presence.

(33) In order to provide full assistance to maintenance creditors and debtors and to facilitate as much as possible crossborder recovery of maintenance, the Central Authorities should be able to obtain a certain amount of personal information. This Regulation should therefore oblige the Member States to ensure that their Central

PART VI

Authorities have access to such information through the public authorities or administrations which hold the information concerned in the course of their ordinary activities. It should however be left to each Member State to decide on the arrangements for such access. Accordingly, a Member State should be able to designate the public authorities or administrations which will be required to supply the information to the Central Authority in accordance with this Regulation, including, if appropriate, public authorities or administrations already designated in the context of other systems for access to information. Where a Member State designates public authorities or administrations, it should ensure that its Central Authority is able to access the requisite information held by those bodies as provided for in this Regulation. A Member State should also be able to allow its Central Authority to access requisite information from any other legal person which holds it and controls its processing.

(34) In the context of access to personal data and the use and transmission thereof, the requirements of Directive 95/46/EC of the European Parliament and of the Council of 24 October 1995 on the protection of individuals with regard to the processing of personal data and on the free movement of such data, as transposed into the national law of the Member States, should be complied with.

(35) For the purposes of the application of this Regulation it is however necessary to define the specific conditions of access to personal data and of the use and transmission of such data. In this context, the opinion of the European Data Protection Supervisor has been taken into consideration. Notification of the data subject should take place in accordance with national law. It should however be possible to defer the notification to prevent the debtor from transferring his assets and thus jeopardising the recovery of the maintenance claim.

(36) On account of the costs of proceedings it is appropriate to provide for a very favourable legal aid scheme, that is, full coverage of the costs relating to proceedings concerning maintenance obligations in respect of children under the age of 21 initiated via the Central Authorities. Specific rules should therefore be added to the current rules on legal aid in the European Union which exist by virtue of Directive 2003/8/EC thus setting up a special legal aid scheme for maintenance obligations. In this context, the competent authority of the requested Member State should be able, exceptionally, to recover costs from an applicant having received free legal aid and lost the case, provided that the person's financial situation so permits. This would apply, in particular, where someone well-off had acted in bad faith.

(37) In addition, for maintenance obligations other than those referred to in the preceding recital, all parties should be guaranteed the same treatment in terms of legal aid at the time of enforcement of a decision in another Member State. Accordingly, the provisions of this Regulation on continuity of legal aid should be understood as also granting such aid to a party who, while not having received legal aid in the proceedings to obtain or amend a decision in the Member State of origin, did then benefit from such aid in that State in the context of an application for enforcement of the decision. Similarly, a party who benefited from free proceedings before an administrative authority listed in Annex X should, in the Member State of enforcement, benefit from the most favourable legal aid or the most extensive exemption from costs or expenses, provided that he shows that he would have so benefited in the Member State of origin.

(38) In order to minimise the costs of translating supporting documents the court seised should only require a translation of such documents when this is necessary, without prejudice to the rights of the defence and the rules applicable concerning service of documents.

(39) To facilitate the application of this Regulation, Member States should be obliged to provide the Commission with the names and contact details of their Central Authorities and with other information. That information should be made available to practitioners

and to the public through publication in the Official Journal of the European Union or through electronic access to the European Judicial Network in civil and commercial matters established by Decision 2001/470/EC. Furthermore, the use of forms provided for in this Regulation should facilitate and speed up communication between the Central Authorities and make it possible to submit applications electronically.

(40) The relationship between this Regulation and the bilateral or multilateral conventions and agreements on maintenance obligations to which the Member States are party should be specified. In this context it should be stipulated that Member States which are party to the Convention of 23 March 1962 between Sweden, Denmark, Finland, Iceland and Norway on the recovery of maintenance by the Member States may continue to apply that Convention since it contains more favourable rules on recognition and enforcement than those in this Regulation. As regards the conclusion of future bilateral agreements on maintenance obligations with third States, the procedures and conditions under which Member States would be authorised to negotiate and conclude such agreements on their own behalf should be determined in the course of discussions relating to a Commission proposal on the subject.

(41) In calculating the periods and time limits provided for in this Regulation, Regulation (EEC, Euratom) No 1182/71 of the Council of 3 June 1971 determining the rules applicable to periods, dates and time limits should apply.

(42) The measures necessary for the implementation of this Regulation should be adopted in accordance with Council Decision 1999/468/EC of 28 June 1999 laying down the procedures for the exercise of implementing powers conferred on the Commission.

(43) In particular, the Commission should be empowered to adopt any amendments to the forms provided for in this Regulation in accordance with the advisory procedure provided for in Article 3 of Decision 1999/468/EC. For the establishment of the list of the administrative authorities falling within the scope of this Regulation, and the list of authorities competent to certify the right to legal aid, the Commission should be empowered to act in accordance with the management procedure provided for in Article 4 of that Decision.

(44) This Regulation should amend Regulation (EC) No 44/2001 by replacing the provisions of that Regulation applicable to maintenance obligations. Subject to the transitional provisions of this Regulation, Member States should, in matters relating to maintenance obligations, apply the provisions of this Regulation on jurisdiction, recognition, enforceability and enforcement of decisions and on legal aid instead of those of Regulation (EC) No 44/2001 as from the date on which this Regulation becomes applicable.

(45) Since the objectives of this Regulation, namely the introduction of a series of measures to ensure the effective recovery of maintenance claims in cross-border situations and thus to facilitate the free movement of persons within the European Union, cannot be sufficiently achieved by the Member States and can therefore, by reason of the scale and effects of this Regulation, be better achieved at Community level, the Community may adopt measures in accordance with the principle of subsidiarity as set out in Article 5 of the Treaty. In accordance with the principle of proportionality as set out in that Article this Regulation does not go beyond what is necessary to achieve those objectives.

(46) In accordance with Article 3 of the Protocol on the position of the United Kingdom and Ireland, annexed to the Treaty on European Union and to the Treaty establishing the European Community, Ireland has given notice of its wish to take part in the adoption and application of this Regulation.

(47) In accordance with Articles 1 and 2 of the Protocol on the position of the United Kingdom and Ireland, annexed to the Treaty on European Union and to the Treaty

PART VI

establishing the European Community, the United Kingdom is not taking part in the adoption of this Regulation and is not bound by it or subject to its application. This is, however, without prejudice to the possibility for the United Kingdom of notifying its intention of accepting this Regulation after its adoption in accordance with Article 4 of the said Protocol.

(48) In accordance with Articles 1 and 2 of the Protocol on the position of Denmark annexed to the Treaty on European Union and the Treaty establishing the European Community, Denmark is not taking part in the adoption of this Regulation and is not bound by it or subject to its application, without prejudice to the possibility for Denmark of applying the amendments made here to Regulation (EC) No 44/2001 pursuant to Article 3 of the Agreement of 19 October 2005 between the European Community and the Kingdom of Denmark on jurisdiction and the recognition and enforcement of judgments in civil and commercial matters,

HAS ADOPTED THIS REGULATION:

CHAPTER I
SCOPE AND DEFINITIONS

Article 1

Scope of application

1 This Regulation shall apply to maintenance obligations arising from a family relationship, parentage, marriage or affinity.

2 In this Regulation, the term 'Member State' shall mean Member States to which this Regulation applies.

Scope—The scope of the Regulation is wide and could cover, for example, maintenance obligations arising from overseas relationships entitled to be treated as civil partnerships.

Article 2

Definitions

1 For the purposes of this Regulation:

1   the term 'decision' shall mean a decision in matters relating to maintenance obligations given by a court of a Member State, whatever the decision may be called, including a decree, order, judgment or writ of execution, as well as a decision by an officer of the court determining the costs or expenses. For the purposes of Chapters VII and VIII, the term 'decision' shall also mean a decision in matters relating to maintenance obligations given in a third State;

2   the term 'court settlement' shall mean a settlement in matters relating to maintenance obligations which has been approved by a court or concluded before a court in the course of proceedings;

3   the term 'authentic instrument' shall mean:

    (a) a document in matters relating to maintenance obligations which has been formally drawn up or registered as an authentic instrument in the Member State of origin and the authenticity of which:

        (i)   relates to the signature and the content of the instrument, and

        (ii) has been established by a public authority or other authority empowered for that purpose; or,

    (b) an arrangement relating to maintenance obligations concluded with administrative authorities of the Member State of origin or authenticated by them;

4   the term 'Member State of origin' shall mean the Member State in which, as the

case may be, the decision has been given, the court settlement has been approved or concluded, or the authentic instrument has been established;

5   the term 'Member State of enforcement' shall mean the Member State in which the enforcement of the decision, the court settlement or the authentic instrument is sought;

6   the term 'requesting Member State' shall mean the Member State whose Central Authority transmits an application pursuant to Chapter VII;

7   the term 'requested Member State' shall mean the Member State whose Central Authority receives an application pursuant to Chapter VII;

8   the term '2007 Hague Convention Contracting State' shall mean a State which is a contracting party to the Hague Convention of 23 November 2007 on the International Recovery of Child Support and other Forms of Family Maintenance (hereinafter referred to as the 2007 Hague Convention) to the extent that the said Convention applies between the Community and that State;

9   the term 'court of origin' shall mean the court which has given the decision to be enforced;

10   the term 'creditor' shall mean any individual to whom maintenance is owed or is alleged to be owed;

11   the term 'debtor' shall mean any individual who owes or who is alleged to owe maintenance.

2 For the purposes of this Regulation, the term 'court' shall include administrative authorities of the Member States with competence in matters relating to maintenance obligations provided that such authorities offer guarantees with regard to impartiality and the right of all parties to be heard and provided that their decisions under the law of the Member State where they are established:

(i)   may be made the subject of an appeal to or review by a judicial authority; and

(ii)   have a similar force and effect as a decision of a judicial authority on the same matter.

These administrative authorities shall be listed in Annex X. That Annex shall be established and amended in accordance with the management procedure referred to in Article 73(2) at the request of the Member State in which the administrative authority concerned is established.

3 For the purposes of Articles 3, 4 and 6, the concept of 'domicile' shall replace that of 'nationality' in those Member States which use this concept as a connecting factor in family matters.

For the purposes of Article 6, parties which have their 'domicile' in different territorial units of the same Member State shall be deemed to have their common 'domicile' in that Member State.

"court settlement"—This term would cover a consent order made by a court in England or Wales: see further, Art 48.

"authentic instrument"—This is not a concept explicitly recognised by English law, but is a form of agreement between the parties formally notarised or converted into a deed in those Member States whose law provides for it: see Art 48.

CHAPTER II
JURISDICTION

Scope—Chapter 2 sets out an exhaustive code as to the international jurisdiction of Member States with regard to maintenance obligations.

PART VI

Article 3

General provisions

In matters relating to maintenance obligations in Member States, jurisdiction shall lie with:

    (a)   the court for the place where the defendant is habitually resident, or

    (b)   the court for the place where the creditor is habitually resident, or

    (c)   the court which, according to its own law, has jurisdiction to entertain proceedings concerning the status of a person if the matter relating to maintenance is ancillary to those proceedings, unless that jurisdiction is based solely on the nationality of one of the parties, or

    (d)   the court which, according to its own law, has jurisdiction to entertain proceedings concerning parental responsibility if the matter relating to maintenance is ancillary to those proceedings, unless that jurisdiction is based solely on the nationality of one of the parties.

Scope—This Article provides the basic rules or default position as to jurisdiction. The Maintenance Regulation contains a comprehensive system of jurisdictional rules that governs all maintenance applications in EU Member States, regardless of whether or not the other jurisdiction involved is an EU Member State. Art 3(c) in conjunction with Art 2.3 confers jurisdiction where the maintenance matter is ancillary to divorce proceedings unless the jurisdictional basis of the divorce is the sole domicile of one party. Therefore, in the case of a divorce petition issued after 18 June 2011 on the basis of the sole domicile of one party, the English court will not have jurisdiction to hear a claim for spousal maintenance, unless Art 3(a) or (b) can be relied on. Article 3(d) was not found in Brussels I and allows the court to take jurisdiction on the basis that the maintenance matter is ancillary to parental responsibility proceedings where it has jurisdiction under its own law, unless the jurisdictional basis for the proceedings is the sole domicile of one party. In the case of the UK and Ireland, "domicile" should be substituted for "nationality" (Art 2.3).

Article 4

Choice of court

1 The parties may agree that the following court or courts of a Member State shall have jurisdiction to settle any disputes in matters relating to a maintenance obligation which have arisen or may arise between them:

    (a)   a court or the courts of a Member State in which one of the parties is habitually resident;

    (b)   a court or the courts of a Member State of which one of the parties has the nationality;

    (c)   in the case of maintenance obligations between spouses or former spouses:

        (i)   the court which has jurisdiction to settle their dispute in matrimonial matters; or

        (ii)   a court or the courts of the Member State which was the Member State of the spouses' last common habitual residence for a period of at least one year.

    The conditions referred to in points (a), (b) or (c) have to be met at the time the choice of court agreement is concluded or at the time the court is seised.

    The jurisdiction conferred by agreement shall be exclusive unless the parties have agreed otherwise.

2 A choice of court agreement shall be in writing. Any communication by electronic means which provides a durable record of the agreement shall be equivalent to 'writing'.

3 This Article shall not apply to a dispute relating to a maintenance obligation towards a child under the age of 18.

4 If the parties have agreed to attribute exclusive jurisdiction to a court or courts of a State party to the Convention on jurisdiction and the recognition and enforcement of

judgments in civil and commercial matters, signed on 30 October 2007 in Lugano (hereinafter referred to as the Lugano Convention), where that State is not a Member State, the said Convention shall apply except in the case of the disputes referred to in paragraph 3.

Scope—Article 4 (derived from Brussels I, Art 23) permits the parties a certain degree of autonomy to designate a court to have jurisdiction to settle a maintenance dispute. Such a court will have exclusive jurisdiction, unless otherwise agreed, precluding recourse to alternative grounds for jurisdiction under the Regulation, even if another Member State is validly seised of jurisdiction for divorce under Brussels IIA. Such a choice may be made in advance of proceedings or at the time that the court is seised. Such an agreement may be informal (as Art 4.2 indicates), for example in solicitors' correspondence. Most commonly, such an agreement will be found in a premarital agreement. An agreement as to choice of court may not be applied to maintenance for a child under 18 (Art 4.3) (see also, Recital 19). Article 4 applies to agreements entered into before 18 June 2011, providing that the proceedings are instituted after that date (Art 75). A choice of court agreement is treated as waived if an unconditional appearance is entered to the proceedings (Art 5). There is no requirement in Art 4 that the parties should obtain independent legal advice or formal disclosure before making such an agreement. In the case of the UK and Ireland, "domicile" should be substituted for "nationality" (Art 2.3).

Article 5

Jurisdiction based on the appearance of the defendant

Apart from jurisdiction derived from other provisions of this Regulation, a court of a Member State before which a defendant enters an appearance shall have jurisdiction. This rule shall not apply where appearance was entered to contest the jurisdiction.

Scope—Article 5 bases jurisdiction on submission, ie the rule that, if a defendant appears before the court that does not have jurisdiction under the Regulation, that court will have jurisdiction, unless the defendant did so simply to contest jurisdiction (as under Brussels I, Art 24).

Article 6

Subsidiary jurisdiction

Where no court of a Member State has jurisdiction pursuant to Articles 3, 4 and 5 and no court of a State party to the Lugano Convention which is not a Member State has jurisdiction pursuant to the provisions of that Convention, the courts of the Member State of the common nationality of the parties shall have jurisdiction.

Scope—Article 6 provides a new subsidiary jurisdiction, providing common nationality as a basis for jurisdiction where no court of a Member State has jurisdiction under Arts 3, 4 or 5. It is, therefore, no longer left to national law to determine jurisdiction, as was the case under Brussels I, Art 4. In the case of the UK and Ireland, "domicile" should be substituted for "nationality" (Art 2.3).

Article 7

Forum necessitatis

Where no court of a Member State has jurisdiction pursuant to Articles 3, 4, 5 and 6, the courts of a Member State may, on an exceptional basis, hear the case if proceedings cannot reasonably be brought or conducted or would be impossible in a third State with which the dispute is closely connected. The dispute must have a sufficient connection with the Member State of the court seised.

Scope—Article 7 is another novel concept introducing a forum necessitatis, which provides jurisdiction for the courts of a Member State on an exceptional basis so that it may hear the case if proceedings cannot reasonably be brought or conducted, or would be impossible, in a third State with which the dispute is closely connected. Recital 16 suggests that this might be, for example, where there is civil war in that third State. The dispute must still have a sufficient connection with the forum necessitatis.

PART VI

Article 8

Limit on proceedings

1 Where a decision is given in a Member State or a 2007 Hague Convention Contracting State where the creditor is habitually resident, proceedings to modify the decision or to have a new decision given cannot be brought by the debtor in any other Member State as long as the creditor remains habitually resident in the State in which the decision was given.

2 Paragraph 1 shall not apply:

  (a) where the parties have agreed in accordance with Article 4 to the jurisdiction of the courts of that other Member State;

  (b) where the creditor submits to the jurisdiction of the courts of that other Member State pursuant to Article 5;

  (c) where the competent authority in the 2007 Hague Convention Contracting State of origin cannot, or refuses to, exercise jurisdiction to modify the decision or give a new decision; or

  (d) where the decision given in the 2007 Hague Convention Contracting State of origin cannot be recognised or declared enforceable in the Member State where proceedings to modify the decision or to have a new decision given are contemplated.

Scope—Article 8 provides a restrictive jurisdiction for applications to vary, reflecting the philosophy of protection of the creditor. If an order has been made in the Member State where the creditor is habitually resident, the debtor cannot apply to vary that order or apply for a new order in any other Member State so long as the debtor remains resident in the State where the order was made.

Article 9

Seising of a court

For the purposes of this Chapter, a court shall be deemed to be seised:

  (a) at the time when the document instituting the proceedings or an equivalent document is lodged with the court, provided that the claimant has not subsequently failed to take the steps he was required to take to have service effected on the defendant; or

  (b) if the document has to be served before being lodged with the court, at the time when it is received by the authority responsible for service, provided that the claimant has not subsequently failed to take the steps he was required to take to have the document lodged with the court.

Scope—Articles 9–13 make provision for determining when a court is seised, when a court may accept jurisdiction and/or when it must stay proceedings. The aim is to ensure that there are not parallel proceedings in Member States. Where there is more than one basis upon which jurisdiction may be accepted under the Regulation, it is necessary to make provision to ensure that only one court is able to proceed.

Article 10

Examination as to jurisdiction

Where a court of a Member State is seised of a case over which it has no jurisdiction under this Regulation it shall declare of its own motion that it has no jurisdiction.

Article 11

Examination as to admissibility

1 Where a defendant habitually resident in a State other than the Member State where the action was brought does not enter an appearance, the court with jurisdiction shall stay the proceedings so long as it is not shown that the defendant has been able to receive the document instituting the proceedings or an equivalent document in sufficient time to enable him to arrange for his defence, or that all necessary steps have been taken to this end.

2 Article 19 of Regulation (EC) No 1393/2007 shall apply instead of the provisions of paragraph 1 of this Article if the document instituting the proceedings or an equivalent document had to be transmitted from one Member State to another pursuant to that Regulation.

3 Where the provisions of Regulation (EC) No 1393/2007 are not applicable, Article 15 of the Hague Convention of 15 November 1965 on the service abroad of judicial and extrajudicial documents in civil or commercial matters shall apply if the document instituting the proceedings or an equivalent document had to be transmitted abroad pursuant to that Convention

Scope—Article 11 protects the rights of defendants by ensuring that proceedings cannot proceed against them in a Member State other than that of their habitual residence, unless they have properly been made aware of the proceedings.

Article 12

Lis pendens

1 Where proceedings involving the same cause of action and between the same parties are brought in the courts of different Member States, any court other than the court first seised shall of its own motion stay its proceedings until such time as the jurisdiction of the court first seised is established.

2 Where the jurisdiction of the court first seised is established, any court other than the court first seised shall decline jurisdiction in favour of that court.

Scope—Article 12 (cf Brussels I, Art 27) provides that, for proceedings with the same cause of action (lis pendens), the court of any Member State other than that first seised must stay the proceedings of its own initiative, until the jurisdiction of the Member State first seised is established. If it is so established, the other court(s) must decline jurisdiction. It should be noted that Art 12 deals with the same cause of action and imposes an obligatory stay, whereas Art 13 deals with connected but different issues and imposes only a discretionary stay. For a discussion of the interrelation between the counterpart provisions of Brussels I (Arts 27 and 28), see *Re PJ (Adoption: Practice on Appeal)* [1998] 2 FLR 252, CA; *J v P* [2007] EWHC 704 (Fam); *B v R* [2010] 1 FLR 563; *T v T (Occupation Orders)* [2013] 1 FLR 364; *Traversa v Freddi* [2011] 2 FLR 272.

Article 13

Related actions

1 Where related actions are pending in the courts of different Member States, any court other than the court first seised may stay its proceedings.

2 Where these actions are pending at first instance, any court other than the court first seised may also, on the application of one of the parties, decline jurisdiction if the court first seised has jurisdiction over the actions in question and its law permits the consolidation thereof.

3 For the purposes of this Article, actions are deemed to be related where they are so closely connected that it is expedient to hear and determine them together to avoid the risk of irreconcilable judgments resulting from separate proceedings.

PART VI

Scope—Article 13 (cf Brussels I, Art 28) makes provision for related actions, under which the court of the Member State other than that first seised may stay proceedings and may, on the application of one of the parties, decline jurisdiction if the court first seised has jurisdiction over the related action and can consolidate those actions.

"Irreconcilable judgments" (Art 13.3) See *Prazic v Prazic* [2006] 2 FLR 1128, CA (in relation to Brussels I, Art 28, in which English proceedings under TLATA 1996 were struck out where there were prior French divorce proceedings).

"related actions"—See Art 13.3.

Article 14

Provisional, including protective, measures

Application may be made to the courts of a Member State for such provisional, including protective, measures as may be available under the law of that State, even if, under this Regulation, the courts of another Member State have jurisdiction as to the substance of the matter.

Scope—Article 14 ensures that, notwithstanding that a court does not have jurisdiction under the Regulation, it can still make interim protective orders in relation to the matter, provided that the national law permits this (ie the Regulation does not provide jurisdiction as such, but will not prevent such jurisdiction being accepted on the limited basis provided for by Art 14).

CHAPTER III
APPLICABLE LAW

Article 15

Determination of the applicable law

The law applicable to maintenance obligations shall be determined in accordance with the Hague Protocol of 23 November 2007 on the law applicable to maintenance obligations (hereinafter referred to as the 2007 Hague Protocol) in the Member States bound by that instrument.

Scope—Chapter III, Art 15 of the Regulation deals with the law applicable to maintenance obligations, stating that the applicable law is to be determined in accordance with the Hague Protocol of 23 November 2007 in those Member States bound by the Protocol. The UK and Denmark (see introductory annotations) have not ratified the Protocol and, therefore, the law applied to maintenance obligations in England is English law. The applicable law provisions apply in other Member States with the result that they must apply English law in appropriate circumstances, for example where the parties have so agreed (Art 8 of the Protocol). The general rule under the Protocol is that the law governing the dispute is that of the State of the creditor's habitual residence, save where the Protocol provides otherwise (Art 3 of the Protocol). This gives rise to the two different systems for enforcement under Ch IV. Where a Member State applies the Hague Protocol, the decisions of its court are not subject to the exequatur system requiring a declaration of enforceability (or in the UK and Ireland, registration) of that decision before the decision being enforceable in another Member State.

CHAPTER IV
RECOGNITION, ENFORCEABILITY AND ENFORCEMENT OF DECISIONS

Scope—Under Brussels I, a declaration of enforceability (exequatur) was required. The aim of the Regulation is automatic enforcement in one Member State of a decision relating to maintenance made in another. Accordingly, the process of exequatur (or "registration" for the UK: Art 38.2 of Brussels I) has been abolished in relation to decisions made in those Member States bound by the Hague Protocol (all Member States except the UK and Denmark). Where a decision by a Member State bound by the Protocol is enforceable in that State, it is enforceable in another Member State (including England) without the need for registration (Art 17). For non-Hague Protocol Member States (the UK and Denmark: see introductory annotations), Ch IV, S 2 applies.

Article 16

Scope of application of this Chapter

1 This Chapter shall govern the recognition, enforceability and enforcement of decisions falling within the scope of this Regulation.

2 Section 1 shall apply to decisions given in a Member State bound by the 2007 Hague Protocol.

3 Section 2 shall apply to decisions given in a Member State not bound by the 2007 Hague Protocol.

4 Section 3 shall apply to all decisions.

Section 1
Decisions given in a Member State bound by the 2007 Hague Protocol

Article 17

Abolition of exequatur

1 A decision given in a Member State bound by the 2007 Hague Protocol shall be recognised in another Member State without any special procedure being required and without any possibility of opposing its recognition.

2 A decision given in a Member State bound by the 2007 Hague Protocol which is enforceable in that State shall be enforceable in another Member State without the need for a declaration of enforceability.

Scope—Article 17 allows the Hague Protocol Member State decision to be immediately enforceable in another Member State without more. The procedure is governed by the Maintenance Regulation, Ch IV, SS 1 and 3 and CJJ(M)R 2011, reg 3 and Sch 1, Pt 2.

"exequatur"—This Latin term approximates to "let it be executed" and is the "declaration of enforceability" referred to in Art 17(2). Compare Art 38(1) of Council Regulation (EC) No 44/2001 (Brussels I) (see *The Family Court Practice 2011*).

"a Member State bound by the 2007 Hague Protocol"—At present this includes all Member States other than Denmark and the UK.

Article 18

Protective measures

An enforceable decision shall carry with it by operation of law the power to proceed to any protective measures which exist under the law of the Member State of enforcement.

Scope—Article 18 allows automatic access to any protective measures available under the requested Member State's law.

Article 19

Right to apply for a review

1 A defendant who did not enter an appearance in the Member State of origin shall have the right to apply for a review of the decision before the competent court of that Member State where:

    (a) he was not served with the document instituting the proceedings or an equivalent document in sufficient time and in such a way as to enable him to arrange for his defence; or

    (b) he was prevented from contesting the maintenance claim by reason of force majeure or due to extraordinary circumstances without any fault on his part;

unless he failed to challenge the decision when it was possible for him to do so.

2 The time limit for applying for a review shall run from the day the defendant was effectively acquainted with the contents of the decision and was able to react, at the latest from the date of the first enforcement measure having the effect of making his property non-disposable in whole or in part. The defendant shall react promptly, in any event within 45 days. No extension may be granted on account of distance.

3 If the court rejects the application for a review referred to in paragraph 1 on the basis that none of the grounds for a review set out in that paragraph apply, the decision shall remain in force.

If the court decides that a review is justified for one of the reasons laid down in paragraph 1, the decision shall be null and void. However, the creditor shall not lose the benefits of the interruption of prescription or limitation periods, or the right to claim retroactive maintenance acquired in the initial proceedings.

Scope—Article 19 gives a defendant who did not enter an appearance (in the circumstances set out in Art 19.1) to the original decision the right to obtain a review in the Member State of origin with appropriate protection for the creditor relating to limitation periods. The right to a review is subject to strict time limits (Art 19.2) and should be considered an extraordinary remedy (Recital 29). The right to apply for a review under Art 19 is a limited exception to the general principle contained in Art 42.

Article 20

Documents for the purposes of enforcement

1 For the purposes of enforcement of a decision in another Member State, the claimant shall provide the competent enforcement authorities with:

   (a)   a copy of the decision which satisfies the conditions necessary to establish its authenticity;
   (b)   the extract from the decision issued by the court of origin using the form set out in Annex I;
   (c)   where appropriate, a document showing the amount of any arrears and the date such amount was calculated;
   (d)   where necessary, a transliteration or a translation of the content of the form referred to in point (b) into the official language of the Member State of enforcement or, where there are several official languages in that Member State, into the official language or one of the official languages of court proceedings of the place where the application is made, in accordance with the law of that Member State, or into another language that the Member State concerned has indicated it can accept. Each Member State may indicate the official language or languages of the institutions of the European Union other than its own which it can accept for the completion of the form.

2 The competent authorities of the Member State of enforcement may not require the claimant to provide a translation of the decision. However, a translation may be required if the enforcement of the decision is challenged.

3 Any translation under this Article must be done by a person qualified to do translations in one of the Member States.

Scope—Article 20 explains that documents must be provided for the purposes of enforcement in the requested Member State. See also, the Family Procedure (Amendment) Rules 2011.

"may not require the claimant to provide a translation of the decision" (Art 20(2))—Compare Art 55(2) of Brussels I (see *The Family Court Practice 2011*). If, exceptionally, a translation is called for, see Article 45(f).

Article 21

Refusal or suspension of enforcement

1 The grounds of refusal or suspension of enforcement under the law of the Member State of enforcement shall apply in so far as they are not incompatible with the application of paragraphs 2 and 3.

2 The competent authority in the Member State of enforcement shall, on application by the debtor, refuse, either wholly or in part, the enforcement of the decision of the court of origin if the right to enforce the decision of the court of origin is extinguished by the effect of prescription or the limitation of action, either under the law of the Member State of origin or under the law of the Member State of enforcement, whichever provides for the longer limitation period.

Furthermore, the competent authority in the Member State of enforcement may, on application by the debtor, refuse, either wholly or in part, the enforcement of the decision of the court of origin if it is irreconcilable with a decision given in the Member State of enforcement or with a decision given in another Member State or in a third State which fulfils the conditions necessary for its recognition in the Member State of enforcement.

A decision which has the effect of modifying an earlier decision on maintenance on the basis of changed circumstances shall not be considered an irreconcilable decision within the meaning of the second subparagraph.

3 The competent authority in the Member State of enforcement may, on application by the debtor, suspend, either wholly or in part, the enforcement of the decision of the court of origin if the competent court of the Member State of origin has been seised of an application for a review of the decision of the court of origin pursuant to Article 19.

Furthermore, the competent authority of the Member State of enforcement shall, on application by the debtor, suspend the enforcement of the decision of the court of origin where the enforceability of that decision is suspended in the Member State of origin.

Scope—Whereas there are no grounds for refusing to recognise a decision on maintenance to which Ch IV, S 1 applies, Art 21 provides a basis for refusing or suspending enforcement in the requested Member State in restricted circumstances (based on limitation, or irreconcilability with another decision enforceable in that requested Member State).

Article 22

No effect on the existence of family relationships

The recognition and enforcement of a decision on maintenance under this Regulation shall not in any way imply the recognition of the family relationship, parentage, marriage or affinity underlying the maintenance obligation which gave rise to the decision.

Section 2
Decisions given in a Member State not bound by the 2007 Hague Protocol

Scope—Section 2 makes provision for the enforcement of decisions in non-Hague Protocol Member States (the UK and Denmark (see introductory annotations)) and follows the model of registration before enforcement. Following recognition, a maintenance decision of a non-Hague Protocol Member State requires a declaration of enforceability (Art 26). In effect, S 2 contains a simplified exequatur procedure.

Article 23

Recognition

1 A decision given in a Member State not bound by the 2007 Hague Protocol shall be recognised in the other Member States without any special procedure being required.

2 Any interested party who raises the recognition of a decision as the principal issue in a dispute may, in accordance with the procedures provided for in this Section, apply for a decision that the decision be recognised.

3 If the outcome of proceedings in a court of a Member State depends on the determination of an incidental question of recognition, that court shall have jurisdiction over that question.

Scope—Article 23 provides that recognition of the maintenance decision is automatic, but an interested party can apply for a specific decision on the point. Article 23.3 enables a court of a Member State to deal with the question of recognition where it arises incidentally in other proceedings.

"a Member State not bound by the 2007 Hague Protocol"—Currently, this refers to Denmark (see introductory annotations) and the UK.

Article 24

Grounds of refusal of recognition

A decision shall not be recognised:

   (a)   if such recognition is manifestly contrary to public policy in the Member State in which recognition is sought. The test of public policy may not be applied to the rules relating to jurisdiction;

   (b)   where it was given in default of appearance, if the defendant was not served with the document which instituted the proceedings or with an equivalent document in sufficient time and in such a way as to enable him to arrange for his defence, unless the defendant failed to commence proceedings to challenge the decision when it was possible for him to do so;

   (c)   if it is irreconcilable with a decision given in a dispute between the same parties in the Member State in which recognition is sought;

   (d)   if it is irreconcilable with an earlier decision given in another Member State or in a third State in a dispute involving the same cause of action and between the same parties, provided that the earlier decision fulfils the conditions necessary for its recognition in the Member State in which recognition is sought.

A decision which has the effect of modifying an earlier decision on maintenance on the basis of changed circumstances shall not be considered an irreconcilable decision within the meaning of points (c) or (d).

Scope—Article 24 contains grounds for non-recognition, including public policy (Art 24(a)), rights of the defendant (Art 24(b)) and irreconcilability with other maintenance decisions of the Member State in which enforcement is sought, or which are susceptible to recognition in that State (Art 24(c) and (d)).

Article 25

Staying of recognition proceedings

A court of a Member State in which recognition is sought of a decision given in a Member State not bound by the 2007 Hague Protocol shall stay the proceedings if the enforceability of the decision is suspended in the Member State of origin by reason of an appeal.

Article 26

Enforceability

A decision given in a Member State not bound by the 2007 Hague Protocol and enforceable in that State shall be enforceable in another Member State when, on the application of any interested party, it has been declared enforceable there.

"Declared enforceable"—See Art 30.

Article 27

Jurisdiction of local courts

1 The application for a declaration of enforceability shall be submitted to the court or competent authority of the Member State of enforcement notified by that Member State to the Commission in accordance with Article 71.

2 The local jurisdiction shall be determined by reference to the place of habitual residence of the party against whom enforcement is sought, or to the place of enforcement.

Article 28

Procedure

1 The application for a declaration of enforceability shall be accompanied by the following documents:

    (a) a copy of the decision which satisfies the conditions necessary to establish its authenticity;

    (b) an extract from the decision issued by the court of origin using the form set out in Annex II, without prejudice to Article 29;

    (c) where necessary, a transliteration or a translation of the content of the form referred to in point (b) into the official language of the Member State of enforcement or, where there are several official languages in that Member State, into the official language or one of the official languages of court proceedings of the place where the application is made, in accordance with the law of that Member State, or into another language that the Member State concerned has indicated it can accept. Each Member State may indicate the official language or languages of the institutions of the European Union other than its own which it can accept for the completion of the form.

2 The court or competent authority seised of the application may not require the claimant to provide a translation of the decision. However, a translation may be required in connection with an appeal under Articles 32 or 33.

3 Any translation under this Article must be done by a person qualified to do translations in one of the Member States.

Procedure—See FPR 2010, rr 34.39, 34.40.

Article 29

Non-production of the extract

1 If the extract referred to in Article 28(1)(b) is not produced, the competent court or authority may specify a time for its production or accept an equivalent document or, if it considers that it has sufficient information before it, dispense with its production.

2 In the situation referred to in paragraph 1, if the competent court or authority so requires, a translation of the documents shall be produced. The translation shall be done by a person qualified to do translations in one of the Member States.

Article 30

Declaration of enforceability

The decision shall be declared enforceable without any review under Article 24 immediately on completion of the formalities in Article 28 and at the latest within 30 days of the completion of those formalities, except where exceptional circumstances

PART VI

make this impossible. The party against whom enforcement is sought shall not at this stage of the proceedings be entitled to make any submissions on the application.

Procedure—A declaration of enforceability is obtained by means of registration of the order in the magistrates' court (CJJ(M)R 2011, reg 3 and Sch 1, Pt 3 and FPR 2010, Pt 34 and PD34A, paras 1.1–2.3.

Article 31

Notice of the decision on the application for a declaration

1 The decision on the application for a declaration of enforceability shall forthwith be brought to the notice of the applicant in accordance with the procedure laid down by the law of the Member State of enforcement.

2 The declaration of enforceability shall be served on the party against whom enforcement is sought, accompanied by the decision, if not already served on that party.

Article 32

Appeal against the decision on the application for a declaration

1 The decision on the application for a declaration of enforceability may be appealed against by either party.

2 The appeal shall be lodged with the court notified by the Member State concerned to the Commission in accordance with Article 71.

3 The appeal shall be dealt with in accordance with the rules governing procedure in contradictory matters.

4 If the party against whom enforcement is sought fails to appear before the appellate court in proceedings concerning an appeal brought by the applicant, Article 11 shall apply even where the party against whom enforcement is sought is not habitually resident in any of the Member States.

5 An appeal against the declaration of enforceability shall be lodged within 30 days of service thereof. If the party against whom enforcement is sought has his habitual residence in a Member State other than that in which the declaration of enforceability was given, the time for appealing shall be 45 days and shall run from the date of service, either on him in person or at his residence. No extension may be granted on account of distance.

Article 33

Proceedings to contest the decision given on appeal

The decision given on appeal may be contested only by the procedure notified by the Member State concerned to the Commission in accordance with Article 71.

Article 34

Refusal or revocation of a declaration of enforceability

1 The court with which an appeal is lodged under Articles 32 or 33 shall refuse or revoke a declaration of enforceability only on one of the grounds specified in Article 24.

2 Subject to Article 32(4), the court seised of an appeal under Article 32 shall give its decision within 90 days from the date it was seised, except where exceptional circumstances make this impossible.

3 The court seised of an appeal under Article 33 shall give its decision without delay.

Article 35

Staying of proceedings

The court with which an appeal is lodged under Articles 32 or 33 shall, on the application of the party against whom enforcement is sought, stay the proceedings if the enforceability of the decision is suspended in the Member State of origin by reason of an appeal.

Article 36

Provisional, including protective measures

1 When a decision must be recognised in accordance with this Section, nothing shall prevent the applicant from availing himself of provisional, including protective, measures in accordance with the law of the Member State of enforcement without a declaration of enforceability under Article 30 being required.

2 The declaration of enforceability shall carry with it by operation of law the power to proceed to any protective measures.

3 During the time specified for an appeal pursuant to Article 32(5) against the declaration of enforceability and until any such appeal has been determined, no measures of enforcement may be taken other than protective measures against the property of the party against whom enforcement is sought.

Article 37

Partial enforceability

1 Where a decision has been given in respect of several matters and the declaration of enforceability cannot be given for all of them, the competent court or authority shall give it for one or more of them.

2 An applicant may request a declaration of enforceability limited to parts of a decision.

Article 38

No charge, duty or fee

In proceedings for the issue of a declaration of enforceability, no charge, duty or fee calculated by reference to the value of the matter at issue may be levied in the Member State of enforcement.

Section 3
Common provisions

Scope—Section 3 sets out common provisions for recognition and enforcement whether or not the decision was given in a Member State bound by the 2007 Hague Protocol. The procedure for enforcement is governed by the law of the Member State of enforcement (Art 41).

Article 39

Provisional enforceability

The court of origin may declare the decision provisionally enforceable, notwithstanding any appeal, even if national law does not provide for enforceability by operation of law.

"provisionally enforceable, notwithstanding any appeal"—Compare FPR 2010, r 30.8.

PART VI

Article 40

Invoking a recognised decision

1 A party who wishes to invoke in another Member State a decision recognised within the meaning of Article 17(1) or recognised pursuant to Section 2 shall produce a copy of the decision which satisfies the conditions necessary to establish its authenticity.

2 If necessary, the court before which the recognised decision is invoked may ask the party invoking the recognised decision to produce an extract issued by the court of origin using the form set out in Annex I or in Annex II, as the case may be.

The court of origin shall also issue such an extract at the request of any interested party.

3 Where necessary, the party invoking the recognised decision shall provide a transliteration or a translation of the content of the form referred to in paragraph 2 into the official language of the Member State concerned or, where there are several official languages in that Member State, into the official language or one of the official languages of court proceedings of the place where the recognised decision is invoked, in accordance with the law of that Member State, or into another language that the Member State concerned has indicated it can accept. Each Member State may indicate the official language or languages of the institutions of the European Union other than its own which it can accept for the completion of the form.

4 Any translation under this Article must be done by a person qualified to do translations in one of the Member States.

Procedure—See FPR 2010, rr 34.39, 34.40.

Article 41

Proceedings and conditions for enforcement

1 Subject to the provisions of this Regulation, the procedure for the enforcement of decisions given in another Member State shall be governed by the law of the Member State of enforcement. A decision given in a Member State which is enforceable in the Member State of enforcement shall be enforced there under the same conditions as a decision given in that Member State of enforcement.

2 The party seeking the enforcement of a decision given in another Member State shall not be required to have a postal address or an authorised representative in the Member State of enforcement, without prejudice to persons with competence in matters relating to enforcement proceedings.

Article 42

No review as to substance

Under no circumstances may a decision given in a Member State be reviewed as to its substance in the Member State in which recognition, enforceability or enforcement is sought.

Article 43

No precedence for the recovery of costs

Recovery of any costs incurred in the application of this Regulation shall not take precedence over the recovery of maintenance.

CHAPTER V
ACCESS TO JUSTICE

Article 44

Right to legal aid

1 Parties who are involved in a dispute covered by this Regulation shall have effective access to justice in another Member State, including enforcement and appeal or review procedures, in accordance with the conditions laid down in this Chapter. In cases covered by Chapter VII, effective access to justice shall be provided by the requested Member State to any applicant who is resident in the requesting Member State.

2 To ensure such effective access, Member States shall provide legal aid in accordance with this Chapter, unless paragraph 3 applies.

3 In cases covered by Chapter VII, a Member State shall not be obliged to provide legal aid if and to the extent that the procedures of that Member State enable the parties to make the case without the need for legal aid, and the Central Authority provides such services as are necessary free of charge.

4 Entitlements to legal aid shall not be less than those available in equivalent domestic cases.

5 No security, bond or deposit, however described, shall be required to guarantee the payment of costs and expenses in proceedings concerning maintenance obligations.

"Member States shall provide legal aid" (Art 44.2)—Save in respect of child maintenance, such legal aid may be means-tested or subject to a merits test (Art 47.1), but the entitlements to it "shall not be less than those available in equivalent domestic proceedings" (Art 44.4). Legal aid is envisaged as enabling parties to *assert* their rights and to *bring a case before* the court; as Art 56.2 specifically refers to applications by the paying party, the principle of equality of arms ought to allow legal aid to a paying party in an appropriate case.

Article 45

Content of legal aid

Legal aid granted under this Chapter shall mean the assistance necessary to enable parties to know and assert their rights and to ensure that their applications, lodged through the Central Authorities or directly with the competent authorities, are fully and effectively dealt with. It shall cover as necessary the following:

(a) pre-litigation advice with a view to reaching a settlement prior to bringing judicial proceedings;

(b) legal assistance in bringing a case before an authority or a court and representation in court;

(c) exemption from or assistance with the costs of proceedings and the fees to persons mandated to perform acts during the proceedings;

(d) in Member States in which an unsuccessful party is liable for the costs of the opposing party, if the recipient of legal aid loses the case, the costs incurred by the opposing party, if such costs would have been covered had the recipient been habitually resident in the Member State of the court seised;

(e) interpretation;

(f) translation of the documents required by the court or by the competent authority and presented by the recipient of legal aid which are necessary for the resolution of the case;

(g) travel costs to be borne by the recipient of legal aid where the physical presence of the persons concerned with the presentation of the recipient's case is required

PART VI

in court by the law or by the court of the Member State concerned and the court decides that the persons concerned cannot be heard to the satisfaction of the court by any other means.

Article 46

Free legal aid for applications through central authorities concerning maintenance to children

1 The requested Member State shall provide free legal aid in respect of all applications by a creditor under Article 56 concerning maintenance obligations arising from a parent-child relationship towards a person under the age of 21.

2 Notwithstanding paragraph 1, the competent authority of the requested Member State may, in relation to applications other than those under Article 56(1)(a) and (b), refuse free legal aid if it considers that, on the merits, the application or any appeal or review is manifestly unfounded.

"The requested Member State shall provide free legal aid" (Art 46(1))—In relation to child maintenance, free legal aid must be provided in respect of all applications by the receiving party unless (save in the case of recognition or enforcement of an existing decision) the application, or any appeal or review, is "manifestly unfounded". This requirement does not extend to applications by the paying party.

Article 47

Cases not covered by Article 46

1 Subject to Articles 44 and 45, in cases not covered by Article 46, legal aid may be granted in accordance with national law, particularly as regards the conditions for the means test or the merits test.

2 Notwithstanding paragraph 1, a party who, in the Member State of origin, has benefited from complete or partial legal aid or exemption from costs or expenses, shall be entitled, in any proceedings for recognition, enforceability or enforcement, to benefit from the most favourable legal aid or the most extensive exemption from costs or expenses provided for by the law of the Member State of enforcement.

3 Notwithstanding paragraph 1, a party who, in the Member State of origin, has benefited from free proceedings before an administrative authority listed in Annex X, shall be entitled, in any proceedings for recognition, enforceability or enforcement, to benefit from legal aid in accordance with paragraph 2. To that end, he shall present a statement from the competent authority in the Member State of origin to the effect that he fulfils the financial requirements to qualify for the grant of complete or partial legal aid or exemption from costs or expenses. Competent authorities for the purposes of this paragraph shall be listed in Annex XI. That Annex shall be established and amended in accordance with the management procedure referred to in Article 73(2).

CHAPTER VI
COURT SETTLEMENTS AND AUTHENTIC INSTRUMENTS

Article 48

Application of this Regulation to court settlements and authentic instruments

1 Court settlements and authentic instruments which are enforceable in the Member State of origin shall be recognised in another Member State and be enforceable there in the same way as decisions, in accordance with Chapter IV.

2 The provisions of this Regulation shall apply as necessary to court settlements and authentic instruments.

3 The competent authority of the Member State of origin shall issue, at the request of any interested party, an extract from the court settlement or the authentic instrument using the forms set out in Annexes I and II or in Annexes III and IV as the case may be.

CHAPTER VII
COOPERATION BETWEEN CENTRAL AUTHORITIES

Scope—Chapter 7 provides for cooperation between and assistance from Central Authorities, both in relation to making applications (transmission and processing) and obtaining information about a creditor or debtor and their respective financial circumstances.

"Central Authority"—The Lord Chancellor has been designated as the Central Authority in relation to England and Wales (CJJ(M)R 2011, reg 2(1)(a)). The Lord Chancellor's powers are exercised by the Reciprocal Enforcement of Maintenance Unit (REMO), Office of the Official Solicitor and Public Trustee, 81 Chancery Lane, London WC2A 1DD, DX 0012 London/Chancery Lane; tel: 020 7911 7127; fax: 020 7911 7105.

Article 49
Designation of Central Authorities

1 Each Member State shall designate a Central Authority to discharge the duties which are imposed by this Regulation on such an authority.

2 Federal Member States, Member States with more than one system of law or Member States having autonomous territorial units shall be free to appoint more than one Central Authority and shall specify the territorial or personal extent of their functions. Where a Member State has appointed more than one Central Authority, it shall designate the Central Authority to which any communication may be addressed for transmission to the appropriate Central Authority within that Member State. If a communication is sent to a Central Authority which is not competent, the latter shall be responsible for forwarding it to the competent Central Authority and for informing the sender accordingly.

3 The designation of the Central Authority or Central Authorities, their contact details, and where appropriate the extent of their functions as specified in paragraph 2, shall be communicated by each Member State to the Commission in accordance with Article 71.

Scope—Article 49 creates the obligation to establish a Central Authority. It also provides that Member States with more than one system of law or having autonomous territorial units must establish more than one Central Authority. Accordingly, there are three Central Authorities within the UK, one for each of England and Wales, Scotland and Northern Ireland.

"Central Authority"—See annotations to Art 48.

Article 50
General functions of Central Authorities

1 Central Authorities shall:
  (a) cooperate with each other, including by exchanging information, and promote cooperation amongst the competent authorities in their Member States to achieve the purposes of this Regulation;
  (b) seek as far as possible solutions to difficulties which arise in the application of this Regulation.

2 Central Authorities shall take measures to facilitate the application of this Regulation and to strengthen their cooperation. For this purpose the European Judicial Network in civil and commercial matters established by Decision 2001/470/EC shall be used.

"Central Authority"—See annotations to Art 48.

Article 51

Specific functions of Central Authorities

1 Central Authorities shall provide assistance in relation to applications under Article 56 and shall in particular:

    (a)   transmit and receive such applications;

    (b)   initiate or facilitate the institution of proceedings in respect of such applications.

2 In relation to such applications Central Authorities shall take all appropriate measures:

    (a)   where the circumstances require, to provide or facilitate the provision of legal aid;

    (b)   to help locate the debtor or the creditor, in particular pursuant to Articles 61, 62 and 63;

    (c)   to help obtain relevant information concerning the income and, if necessary, other financial circumstances of the debtor or creditor, including the location of assets, in particular pursuant to Articles 61, 62 and 63;

    (d)   to encourage amicable solutions with a view to obtaining voluntary payment of maintenance, where suitable by use of mediation, conciliation or similar processes;

    (e)   to facilitate the ongoing enforcement of maintenance decisions, including any arrears;

    (f)   to facilitate the collection and expeditious transfer of maintenance payments;

    (g)   to facilitate the obtaining of documentary or other evidence, without prejudice to Regulation (EC) No 1206/2001;

    (h)   to provide assistance in establishing parentage where necessary for the recovery of maintenance;

    (i)   to initiate or facilitate the institution of proceedings to obtain any necessary provisional measures which are territorial in nature and the purpose of which is to secure the outcome of a pending maintenance application;

    (j)   to facilitate the service of documents, without prejudice to Regulation (EC) No 1393/2007.

3 The functions of the Central Authority under this Article may, to the extent permitted under the law of the Member State concerned, be performed by public bodies, or other bodies subject to the supervision of the competent authorities of that Member State. The designation of any such public bodies or other bodies, as well as their contact details and the extent of their functions, shall be communicated by each Member State to the Commission in accordance with Article 71.

4 Nothing in this Article or in Article 53 shall impose an obligation on a Central Authority to exercise powers that can be exercised only by judicial authorities under the law of the requested Member State.

"Central Authority"—See annotations to Art 48.

Article 52

Power of attorney

The Central Authority of the requested Member State may require a power of attorney from the applicant only if it acts on his behalf in judicial proceedings or before other authorities, or in order to designate a representative so to act.

"Central Authority"—See annotations to Art 48.

Article 53

Requests for specific measures

1 A Central Authority may make a request, supported by reasons, to another Central Authority to take appropriate specific measures under points (b), (c), (g), (h), (i) and (j) of Article 51(2) when no application under Article 56 is pending. The requested Central Authority shall take such measures as are appropriate if satisfied that they are necessary to assist a potential applicant in making an application under Article 56 or in determining whether such an application should be initiated.

2 Where a request for measures under Article 51(2)(b) and (c) is made, the requested Central Authority shall seek the information requested, if necessary pursuant to Article 61. However, the information referred to in points (b), (c) and (d) of Article 61(2) may be sought only when the creditor produces a copy of the decision, court settlement or authentic instrument to be enforced, accompanied by the extract provided for in Articles 20, 28 or 48, as appropriate.

The requested Central Authority shall communicate the information obtained to the requesting Central Authority. Where that information was obtained pursuant to Article 61, this communication shall specify only the address of the potential defendant in the requested Member State. In the case of a request with a view to recognition, declaration of enforceability or enforcement, the communication shall, in addition, specify merely whether the debtor has income or assets in that State.

If the requested Central Authority is not able to provide the information requested it shall inform the requesting Central Authority without delay and specify the grounds for this impossibility.

3 A Central Authority may also take specific measures at the request of another Central Authority in relation to a case having an international element concerning the recovery of maintenance pending in the requesting Member State.

4 For requests under this Article, the Central Authorities shall use the form set out in Annex V.

Scope—The purpose of "specific measures" under Art 53 may be, for example, to establish before making an application whether the intended defendant is in the requested Member State or, in enforcement proceedings whether the defendant is in receipt of an income in that Member State.

"Central Authority"—See annotations to Art 48.

Article 54

Central Authority costs

1 Each Central Authority shall bear its own costs in applying this Regulation.

2 Central Authorities may not impose any charge on an applicant for the provision of their services under this Regulation save for exceptional costs arising from a request for a specific measure under Article 53.

For the purposes of this paragraph, costs relating to locating the debtor shall not be regarded as exceptional.

3 The requested Central Authority may not recover the costs of the services referred to in paragraph 2 without the prior consent of the applicant to the provision of those services at such cost.

"Central Authority"—See annotations to Art 48.

PART VI

Article 55

Application through Central Authorities

An application under this Chapter shall be made through the Central Authority of the Member State in which the applicant resides to the Central Authority of the requested Member State.

"Central Authority"—See annotations to Art 48.

Article 56

Available applications

1 A creditor seeking to recover maintenance under this Regulation may make applications for the following:

    (a)   recognition or recognition and declaration of enforceability of a decision;

    (b)   enforcement of a decision given or recognised in the requested Member State;

    (c)   establishment of a decision in the requested Member State where there is no existing decision, including where necessary the establishment of parentage;

    (d)   establishment of a decision in the requested Member State where the recognition and declaration of enforceability of a decision given in a State other than the requested Member State is not possible;

    (e)   modification of a decision given in the requested Member State;

    (f)   modification of a decision given in a State other than the requested Member State.

2 A debtor against whom there is an existing maintenance decision may make applications for the following:

    (a)   recognition of a decision leading to the suspension, or limiting the enforcement, of a previous decision in the requested Member State;

    (b)   modification of a decision given in the requested Member State;

    (c)   modification of a decision given in a State other than the requested Member State.

3 For applications under this Article, the assistance and representation referred to in Article 45(b) shall be provided by the Central Authority of the requested Member State directly or through public authorities or other bodies or persons.

4 Save as otherwise provided in this Regulation, the applications referred to in paragraphs 1 and 2 shall be determined under the law of the requested Member State and shall be subject to the rules of jurisdiction applicable in that Member State.

"establishment of a decision in the requested Member State where there is no existing decision, including where necessary the establishment of parentage" (Art 56.1(c))—The ability of a court in England and Wales to make such a decision (for example, to establish paternity) will depend on whether it otherwise has jurisdiction under the Maintenance Regulation. Article 56 does not of itself confer jurisdiction.

Article 57

Application contents

1 An application under Article 56 shall be made using the form set out in Annex VI or in Annex VII.

2 An application under Article 56 shall as a minimum include:

    (a)   a statement of the nature of the application or applications;

    (b)   the name and contact details, including the address, and date of birth of the applicant;

(c)   the name and, if known, address and date of birth of the defendant;

(d)   the name and the date of birth of any person for whom maintenance is sought;

(e)   the grounds upon which the application is based;

(f)   in an application by a creditor, information concerning where the maintenance payment should be sent or electronically transmitted;

(g)   the name and contact details of the person or unit from the Central Authority of the requesting Member State responsible for processing the application.

3 For the purposes of paragraph 2(b), the applicant's personal address may be replaced by another address in cases of family violence, if the national law of the requested Member State does not require the applicant to supply his or her personal address for the purposes of proceedings to be brought.

4 As appropriate, and to the extent known, the application shall in addition in particular include:

(a)   the financial circumstances of the creditor;

(b)   the financial circumstances of the debtor, including the name and address of the employer of the debtor and the nature and location of the assets of the debtor;

(c)   any other information that may assist with the location of the defendant.

5 The application shall be accompanied by any necessary supporting information or documentation including, where appropriate, documentation concerning the entitlement of the applicant to legal aid. Applications under Article 56(1)(a) and (b) and under Article 56(2)(a) shall be accompanied, as appropriate, only by the documents listed in Articles 20, 28 and 48, or in Article 25 of the 2007 Hague Convention.

"Central Authority"—See annotations to Art 48.

Article 58

Transmission, receipt and processing of applications and cases through Central Authorities

1 The Central Authority of the requesting Member State shall assist the applicant in ensuring that the application is accompanied by all the information and documents known by it to be necessary for consideration of the application.

2 The Central Authority of the requesting Member State shall, when satisfied that the application complies with the requirements of this Regulation, transmit the application to the Central Authority of the requested Member State.

3 The requested Central Authority shall, within 30 days from the date of receipt of the application, acknowledge receipt using the form set out in Annex VIII, and inform the Central Authority of the requesting Member State what initial steps have been or will be taken to deal with the application, and may request any further necessary documents and information. Within the same 30-day period, the requested Central Authority shall provide to the requesting Central Authority the name and contact details of the person or unit responsible for responding to inquiries regarding the progress of the application.

4 Within 60 days from the date of acknowledgement, the requested Central Authority shall inform the requesting Central Authority of the status of the application.

5 Requesting and requested Central Authorities shall keep each other informed of:

(a)   the person or unit responsible for a particular case;

(b)   the progress of the case;

and shall provide timely responses to enquiries.

6 Central Authorities shall process a case as quickly as a proper consideration of the issues will allow.

PART VI

7 Central Authorities shall employ the most rapid and efficient means of communication at their disposal.

8 A requested Central Authority may refuse to process an application only if it is manifest that the requirements of this Regulation are not fulfilled. In such a case, that Central Authority shall promptly inform the requesting Central Authority of its reasons for refusal using the form set out in Annex IX.

9 The requested Central Authority may not reject an application solely on the basis that additional documents or information are needed. However, the requested Central Authority may ask the requesting Central Authority to provide these additional documents or this information. If the requesting Central Authority does not do so within 90 days or a longer period specified by the requested Central Authority, the requested Central Authority may decide that it will no longer process the application. In this case, it shall promptly notify the requesting Central Authority using the form set out in Annex IX.

"Central Authority"—See annotations to Art 48.

Article 59

Languages

1 The request or application form shall be completed in the official language of the requested Member State or, if there are several official languages in that Member State, in the official language or one of the official languages of the place of the Central Authority concerned, or in any other official language of the institutions of the European Union which that Member State has indicated it can accept, unless the Central Authority of that Member State dispenses with translation.

2 The documents accompanying the request or application form shall not be translated into the language determined in accordance with paragraph 1 unless a translation is necessary in order to provide the assistance requested, without prejudice to Articles 20, 28, 40 and 66.

3 Any other communication between Central Authorities shall be in the language determined in accordance with paragraph 1 unless the Central Authorities agree otherwise.

"Central Authority"—See annotations to Art 48.

Article 60

Meetings

1 In order to facilitate the application of this Regulation, Central Authorities shall meet regularly.

2 These meetings shall be convened in compliance with Decision 2001/470/EC.

"Central Authority"—See annotations to Art 48.

Article 61

Access to information for Central Authorities

1 Under the conditions laid down in this Chapter and by way of exception to Article 51(4), the requested Central Authority shall use all appropriate and reasonable means to obtain the information referred to in paragraph 2 necessary to facilitate, in a given case, the establishment, the modification, the recognition, the declaration of enforceability or the enforcement of a decision.

The public authorities or administrations which, in the course of their ordinary activities, hold, within the requested State, the information referred to in paragraph 2 and which control the processing thereof within the meaning of Directive 95/46/EC shall, subject to limitations justified on grounds of national security or public safety, provide the information to the requested Central Authority at its request in cases where the requested Central Authority does not have direct access to it.

Member States may designate the public authorities or administrations able to provide the requested Central Authority with the information referred to in paragraph 2. Where a Member State makes such a designation, it shall ensure that its choice of authorities and administrations permits its Central Authority to have access, in accordance with this Article, to the information requested.

Any other legal person which holds within the requested Member State the information referred to in paragraph 2 and controls the processing thereof within the meaning of Directive 95/46/EC shall provide the information to the requested Central Authority at the latter's request if it is authorised to do so by the law of the requested Member State.

The requested Central Authority shall, as necessary, transmit the information thus obtained to the requesting Central Authority.

2 The information referred to in this Article shall be the information already held by the authorities, administrations or persons referred to in paragraph 1. It shall be adequate, relevant and not excessive and shall relate to:

(a) the address of the debtor or of the creditor;
(b) the debtor's income;
(c) the identification of the debtor's employer and/or of the debtor's bank account(s);
(d) the debtor's assets.

For the purpose of obtaining or modifying a decision, only the information listed in point (a) may be requested by the requested Central Authority.

For the purpose of having a decision recognised, declared enforceable or enforced, all the information listed in the first subparagraph may be requested by the requested Central Authority. However, the information listed in point (d) may be requested only if the information listed in points (b) and (c) is insufficient to allow enforcement of the decision.

"**Central Authority**"—See annotations to Art 48.

Article 62
Transmission and use of information

1 The Central Authorities shall, within their Member State, transmit the information referred to in Article 61(2) to the competent courts, the competent authorities responsible for service of documents and the competent authorities responsible for enforcement of a decision, as the case may be.

2 Any authority or court to which information has been transmitted pursuant to Article 61 may use this only to facilitate the recovery of maintenance claims.

Except for information merely indicating the existence of an address, income or assets in the requested Member State, the information referred to in Article 61(2) may not be disclosed to the person having applied to the requesting Central Authority, subject to the application of procedural rules before a court.

3 Any authority processing information transmitted to it pursuant to Article 61 may not store such information beyond the period necessary for the purposes for which it was transmitted.

PART VI

4 Any authority processing information communicated to it pursuant to Article 61 shall ensure the confidentiality of such information, in accordance with its national law.

"Central Authority"—See annotations to Art 48.

Article 63

Notification of the data subject

1 Notification of the data subject of the communication of all or part of the information collected on him shall take place in accordance with the national law of the requested Member State.

2 Where there is a risk that it may prejudice the effective recovery of the maintenance claim, such notification may be deferred for a period which shall not exceed 90 days from the date on which the information was provided to the requested Central Authority.

"Central Authority"—See annotations to Art 48.

CHAPTER VIII
PUBLIC BODIES

Scope—Chapter VIII makes provision for recovery of maintenance by public bodies that have been obliged to pay benefits to the maintenance creditor due to the debtor's failure to pay what is owed. Article 64 enables such a public body effectively to recover maintenance in lieu of benefits paid by it under the recognition and enforcement provisions of the Maintenance Regulation, subject to certain conditions.

Article 64

Public bodies as applicants

1 For the purposes of an application for recognition and declaration of enforceability of decisions or for the purposes of enforcement of decisions, the term 'creditor' shall include a public body acting in place of an individual to whom maintenance is owed or one to which reimbursement is owed for benefits provided in place of maintenance.

2 The right of a public body to act in place of an individual to whom maintenance is owed or to seek reimbursement of benefits provided to the creditor in place of maintenance shall be governed by the law to which the body is subject.

3 A public body may seek recognition and a declaration of enforceability or claim enforcement of:

   (a)   a decision given against a debtor on the application of a public body which claims payment of benefits provided in place of maintenance;
   (b)   a decision given between a creditor and a debtor to the extent of the benefits provided to the creditor in place of maintenance.

4 The public body seeking recognition and a declaration of enforceability or claiming enforcement of a decision shall upon request provide any document necessary to establish its right under paragraph 2 and to establish that benefits have been provided to the creditor.

CHAPTER IX
GENERAL AND FINAL PROVISIONS

Article 65

Legalisation or other similar formality

No legalisation or other similar formality shall be required in the context of this Regulation.

Article 66

Translation of supporting documents

Without prejudice to Articles 20, 28 and 40, the court seised may require the parties to provide a translation of supporting documents which are not in the language of proceedings only if it deems a translation necessary in order to give a decision or to respect the rights of the defence.

Article 67

Recovery of costs

Without prejudice to Article 54, the competent authority of the requested Member State may recover costs from an unsuccessful party having received free legal aid pursuant to Article 46, on an exceptional basis and if his financial circumstances so allow.

Article 68

Relations with other Community instruments

1 Subject to Article 75(2), this Regulation shall modify Regulation (EC) No 44/2001 by replacing the provisions of that Regulation applicable to matters relating to maintenance obligations.

2 This Regulation shall replace, in matters relating to maintenance obligations, Regulation (EC) No 805/2004, except with regard to European Enforcement Orders on maintenance obligations issued in a Member State not bound by the 2007 Hague Protocol.

3 In matters relating to maintenance obligations, this Regulation shall be without prejudice to the application of Directive 2003/8/EC, subject to Chapter V.

4 This Regulation shall be without prejudice to the application of Directive 95/46/EC.

"Regulation (EC) No 805/2004"—This is the European Enforcement Order (EEO) for uncontested claims (see above). Under Art 68.2, the Maintenance Regulation replaces the EEO in matters relating to maintenance obligations except with regard to EEOs on maintenance obligations issued in Member States not bound by the 2007 Hague Protocol, i e the UK and Denmark. The rationale behind this provision is that the EEO provided a speedy means of enforcing an uncontested claim in another Member State because it did not require the exequatur procedure of Brussels I. Where a Member State is bound by the Hague Protocol, the Maintenance Regulation itself provides for such a speedy enforcement procedure without the former exequatur procedure. In consequence of this, uncontested claims from such Member States no longer need to apply the EEO. However, S 2 of Ch IV still maintains a simplified exequatur procedure for Member States not bound by the 2007 Hague Protocol, which States do therefore still require a EEO for uncontested claims.

Article 69

Relations with existing international conventions and agreements

1 This Regulation shall not affect the application of bilateral or multilateral conventions and agreements to which one or more Member States are party at the time of adoption of

PART VI

this Regulation and which concern matters governed by this Regulation, without prejudice to the obligations of Member States under Article 307 of the Treaty.

2 Notwithstanding paragraph 1, and without prejudice to paragraph 3, this Regulation shall, in relations between Member States, take precedence over the conventions and agreements which concern matters governed by this Regulation and to which Member States are party.

3 This Regulation shall not preclude the application of the Convention of 23 March 1962 between Sweden, Denmark, Finland, Iceland and Norway on the recovery of maintenance by the Member States which are party thereto, since, with regard to the recognition, enforceability and enforcement of decisions, that Convention provides for:

(a)   simplified and more expeditious procedures for the enforcement of decisions relating to maintenance obligations, and

(b)   legal aid which is more favourable than that provided for in Chapter V of this Regulation.

However, the application of the said Convention may not have the effect of depriving the defendant of his protection under Articles 19 and 21 of this Regulation.

Scope—The Maintenance Regulation takes precedence over all instruments concerning matters governed by it. Because of the comprehensive coverage contained in the Maintenance Regulation, there will be no scope for the application of other instruments (for example, the 2007 Lugano Convention) as between Member States. However, Member States will continue to apply other international instruments as they relate to other States. The rules as to jurisdiction contained in Ch II will bind Member States regardless of whether the issue relates to a third State or a Member State.

Article 70

Information made available to the public

The Member States shall provide within the framework of the European Judicial Network in civil and commercial matters established by Decision 2001/470/EC the following information with a view to making it available to the public:

(a)   a description of the national laws and procedures concerning maintenance obligations;

(b)   a description of the measures taken to meet the obligations under Article 51;

(c)   a description of how effective access to justice is guaranteed, as required under Article 44, and

(d)   a description of national enforcement rules and procedures, including information on any limitations on enforcement, in particular debtor protection rules and limitation or prescription periods.

Member States shall keep this information permanently updated.

Article 71

Information on contact details and languages

1 By 18 September 2010, the Member States shall communicate to the Commission:

(a)   the names and contact details of the courts or authorities with competence to deal with applications for a declaration of enforceability in accordance with Article 27(1) and with appeals against decisions on such applications in accordance with Article 32(2);

(b)   the redress procedures referred to in Article 33;

(c)   the review procedure for the purposes of Article 19 and the names and contact details of the courts having jurisdiction;

(d)   the names and contact details of their Central Authorities and, where appropriate, the extent of their functions, in accordance with Article 49(3);

(e) the names and contact details of the public bodies or other bodies and, where appropriate, the extent of their functions, in accordance with Article 51(3);

(f) the names and contact details of the authorities with competence in matters of enforcement for the purposes of Article 21;

(g) the languages accepted for translations of the documents referred to in Articles 20, 28 and 40;

(h) the languages accepted by their Central Authorities for communication with other Central Authorities referred to in Article 59.

The Member States shall apprise the Commission of any subsequent changes to this information.

2 The Commission shall publish the information communicated in accordance with paragraph 1 in the Official Journal of the European Union, with the exception of the addresses and other contact details of the courts and authorities referred to in points (a), (c) and (f).

3 The Commission shall make all information communicated in accordance with paragraph 1 publicly available through any other appropriate means, in particular through the European Judicial Network in civil and commercial matters established by Decision 2001/470/EC.

Article 72

Amendments to the forms

Any amendment to the forms provided for in this Regulation shall be adopted in accordance with the advisory procedure referred to in Article 73(3).

Article 73

Committee

1 The Commission shall be assisted by the committee established by Article 70 of Regulation (EC) No 2201/2003.

2 Where reference is made to this paragraph, Articles 4 and 7 of Decision 1999/468/EC shall apply.

The period laid down in Article 4(3) of Decision 1999/468/EC shall be set at three months.

3 Where reference is made to this paragraph, Articles 3 and 7 of Decision 1999/468/EC shall apply.

Article 74

Review clause

By five years from the date of application determined in the third subparagraph of Article 76 at the latest, the Commission shall submit to the European Parliament, the Council and the European Economic and Social Committee a report on the application of this Regulation, including an evaluation of the practical experiences relating to the cooperation between Central Authorities, in particular regarding those Authorities' access to the information held by public authorities and administrations, and an evaluation of the functioning of the procedure for recognition, declaration of enforceability and enforcement applicable to decisions given in a Member State not bound by the 2007 Hague Protocol. If necessary the report shall be accompanied by proposals for adaptation.

PART VI

Article 75

Transitional provisions

1 This Regulation shall apply only to proceedings instituted, to court settlements approved or concluded, and to authentic instruments established as from its date of application, subject to paragraphs 2 and 3.

2 Sections 2 and 3 of Chapter IV shall apply:

    (a)   to decisions given in the Member States before the date of application of this Regulation for which recognition and the declaration of enforceability are requested as from that date;

    (b)   to decisions given as from the date of application of this Regulation following proceedings begun before that date,

in so far as those decisions fall with the scope of Regulation (EC) No 44/2001 for the purposes of recognition and enforcement.

Regulation (EC) No 44/2001 shall continue to apply to procedures for recognition and enforcement under way on the date of application of this Regulation.

The first and second subparagraphs shall apply mutatis mutandis to court settlements approved or concluded and to authentic instruments established in the Member States.

3 Chapter VII on cooperation between Central Authorities shall apply to requests and applications received by the Central Authority as from the date of application of this Regulation.

Scope—Sections 2 and 3 of Ch IV apply to decisions given in Member States before 18 June 2011, where the request for recognition or enforceability is made after that date, as well as to decisions given in Member States after 18 June 2011 where the application was made before that date, provided that the decision is within the scope of Brussels I. Therefore, where the decision or application pre-dates 18 June 2011, it can be recognised and enforced under the regime applying to non-Hague Protocol Member States contained in Sections 2 and 3 of Ch IV, regardless of whether it comes from a Hague Protocol Member State. However, Brussels I will continue to apply where the recognition and enforcement procedure was in train at 18 June 2011. The provisions as to the cooperation between Central Authorities contained in Ch VII only apply as from 18 June 2011.

"as from" (Arts 75.1 and 75.2)—"after" was used in the original version of Art 75 rather than "as from", meaning that it was arguable that the transitional provisions only applied from 19 June 2011.

Article 76

Entry into force

This Regulation shall enter into force on the 20th day following its publication in the Official Journal of the European Union.

Articles 2(2), 47(3), 71, 72 and 73 shall apply from 18 September 2010.

Except for the provisions referred to in the second paragraph, this Regulation shall apply from 18 June 2011, subject to the 2007 Hague Protocol being applicable in the Community by that date. Failing that, this Regulation shall apply from the date of application of that Protocol in the Community.

This Regulation shall be binding in its entirety and directly applicable in the Member States in accordance with the Treaty establishing the European Community.

Done at Brussels, 18 December 2008.

For the Council

The President

M. BARNIER

Index

References are to page numbers.

Abduction *see also* Removal of child from England and Wales
Anglo-Egyptian co-operation (Cairo Declaration)   2921
application in respect of abducted child *see also* Custody (of child); Hague Convention   212, 215, 955
child in care, police protection etc, of   644
international, Practice Direction   1808
liaison judge   430, 3101
non-Convention cases   215, 1814
parental responsibility judgment, recognition and enforcement of   3100
recovery order *see* Recovery order
tracing   1549
UK/Pakistan Protocol   1819, 2918
Abroad *see also* England and Wales; Removal of child from UK
assistance to child to live   735
enforcement
  custody etc order, of *see* Custody (of child)
  maintenance order *see* Maintenance order enforcement; Maintenance order registration
  recovery of maintenance *see* Maintenance order enforcement
  registration of order *see* Registration of orders
Abuse
prevention of   729
Access
order, recognition   452, 954
Accommodation, provision of
adoption agency, by, inspection   670
alternative, for person living with child   729
boarding school/college, by, meaning   677
care home or hospital, child in   676
ceasing to provide   2743
child between 16 and 21, for   555
child ceasing to be looked after, for   568
child in care   561
  Wales   561
child in need, for   555
  wishes and feelings of child   555
family centre, at   730
information on change of authority   734
inspection   670
local authority duty   555
  accommodated children   730
  child in police protection etc   558
local authority power   555, 556

Accommodation, provision of—*continued*
looked after child   562
  general duty   564
  review before change   564
notification requirements   675, 676
  visits to child after   676
police protection, etc, during   558
private fostering *see* Private fostering
removal from   556
  exceptions   556
secure *see* Secure accommodation
services for accommodated child   730
voluntary organisation, by   651
welfare of child, and   555
Accounts
order for preparation and filing   2291
Acknowledgment of service   2248
appeal, for   2668
filing
  failure, consequences   2249
  period for   1565
  period for, service out of jurisdiction   1527
service deemed on   1519
Supreme Court   2668
Part 8 claim   2248, 2249
Acting in person *see* Litigant in person
Address
child, of, information on   734
  education supervision order, under   748
  supervision order, under   745
disclosure
  attachment of earnings order   130
  charging order   133
  committal by way of judgment summons   144
  execution of goods, for   137
  Government Department, by   1549
  judgment debtor   147
  means of payment order   146
  non-disclosure application   2080
notification of change, magistrates' maintenance order   726
proper   705
reporting of, in family proceedings   1186
service, for   705
  matrimonial/civil partnership order application   1516
  not matrimonial etc application   1522
Adjournment
magistrates' court complaint, of   1170
Administration order
attachment of earnings *see* County court, attachment of earnings order in
county court powers   397

SUMMARY OF FEES

This non-exhaustive list sets out the fees relating to applications most frequently made by family law practitioners.

FAMILY PROCEEDINGS

A *High Court and county courts* £

1 Issue of application to start proceedings not mentioned below   230

2 Matrimonial causes
   (*a*) Any application for a declaration of parentage, divorce or dissolution of a civil partnership   340
   (*b*) Amending an application for a matrimonial or civil partnership order   90
   (*c*) Filing an answer to an application for a matrimonial or civil partnership order   230
   (*d*) Application to make decree nisi absolute (without notice)   45
   (*e*) Application for financial relief (except consent application)   240
   (*f*) Application for consent order for financial relief   45
   (*g*) Application for directions for trial in defended cause   45
   (*h*) Any other application on notice   90

3 Children Act 1989 proceedings
   (*a*) Commencement application or requesting permission for:
      (i) parental responsibility order (ss 4–4ZA)   200
      (ii) section 8 order (s 10)   200
      (iii) leave to take child out of jurisdiction or change surname (s 13)   200
      (iv) financial provision for children (Sch 1)   200
      (v) variation, revocation or discharge of financial provision order (Sch 1)   200
      (vi) care or supervision order (s 31)   2225/700/1900
      (vii) discharge or variation of care or supervision order (s 39)   170
      (viii) contact with child in care (s 34)   170
      (ix) child assessment order (s 43)   170
      (x) emergency protection order (s 44)   170
      (xi) recovery order (s 50)   170
      (xii) secure accommodation order (s 25)   170
      (xiii) special guardianship order (ss 14A–14F)   160
   (*b*) Appeals from magistrates' court to High Court (s 94)   160/170/200

4 Application under Family Law Act 1996, Pt IV or 4A   70

5 Application under Adoption and Children Act 2002, Pt I (except s 22)   160

6 Originating application (eg in wardship/inherent jurisdiction)   160

7 Appeal from district judge to judge   115

8 Enforcement
   (*a*) Application for third party debt order, each charging order or appointment of receiver   100
   (*b*) Application for judgment summons   100

County courts only

9 Enforcement
   – Attachment of earnings order   100